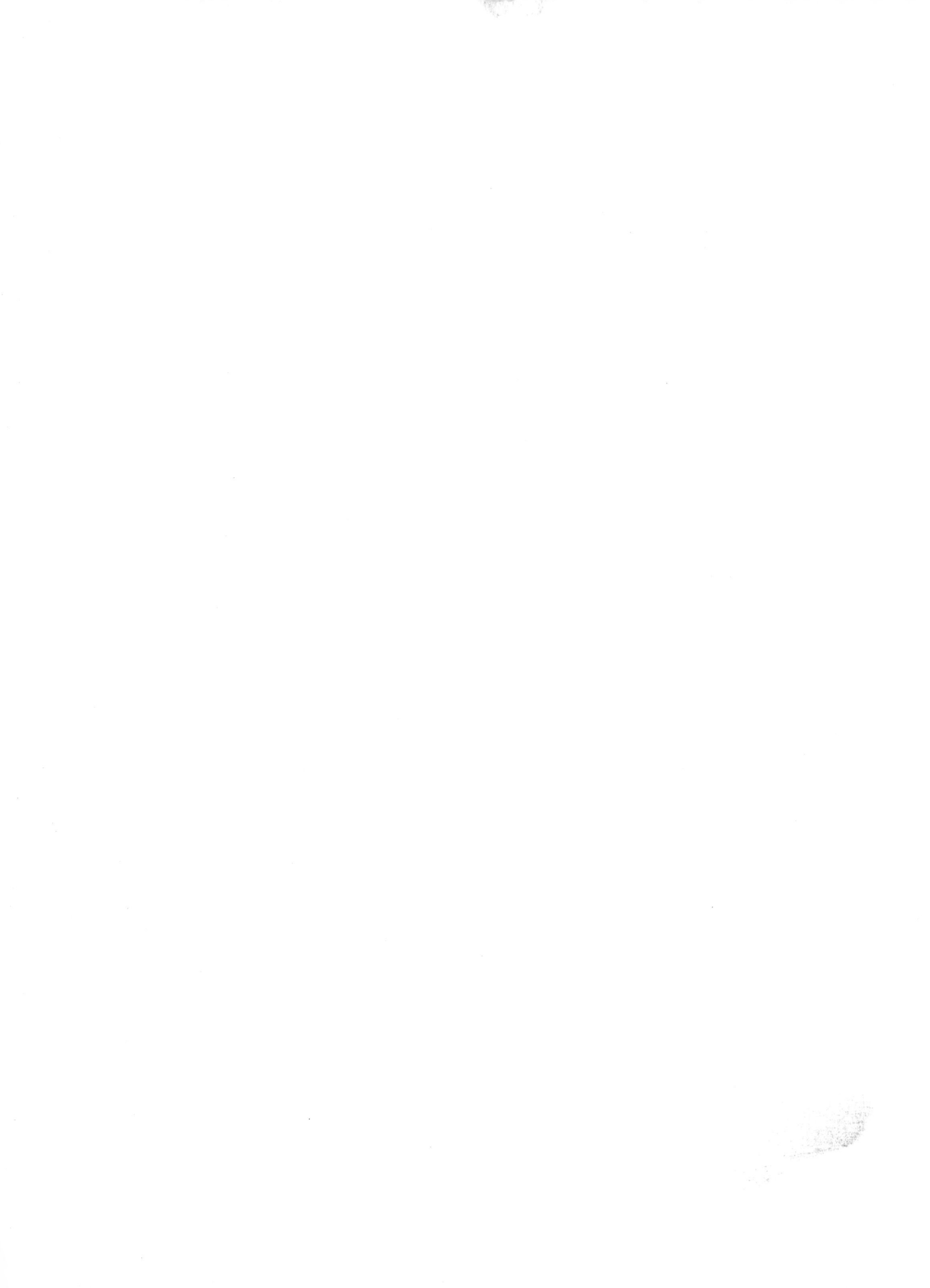

Acronyms, Initialisms & Abbreviations Dictionary

Acronyms, Initialisms
& Abbreviations
Dictionary
was named an
***"Outstanding
Reference Source,"***
*the highest honor
given by the
American Library
Association Reference
and User Services
Association.*

ISSN 0270-4404

Acronyms, Initialisms & Abbreviations Dictionary

A Guide to Acronyms, Abbreviations, Contractons, Alphabetic Symbols, and Similar Condensed Appelations

Covering: Aerospace, Associatons, Banking, Biochemistry, Business, Data Processing, Domestic and International Affairs, Economics, Education, Electronics, Genetics, Government, Information Technology, Internet, Investment, Labor, Language, Law, Medicine, Military Affairs, Pharmacy, Physiology, Politics, Religion, Science, Societies, Sports, Technical Drawings and Specifications, Telecommunications, Trade, Transportation, and Other Fields

35th Edition

Volume 1

Part 3

J-P

Michael Reade and Bohdan Romaniuk,
Project Editors

THOMSON
GALE

Detroit • New York • San Francisco • San Diego • New Haven, Conn. • Waterville, Maine • London • Munich

THOMSON
GALE

Acronyms, Initialisms & Abbreviations Dictionary, 35th Edition, Volume 1

Project Editor
Michael Reade and Bohdan Romaniuk

Editorial
Ken Karges

Editorial Support Services
Charlene Lewis

Composition and Electronic Prepress
Gary Leach

Manufacturing
Rita Wimberley

For more information, contact
Thomson Gale
27500 Drake Rd.
Farmington Hills, MI 48331-3535
Or you can visit our Internet site at
http://www.gale.com

LIBRARY OF CONGRESS CATALOG CARD NUMBER 84-643188

ISBN 0-7876-7811-2 (Volume 1 Complete)
ISBN 0-7876-7812-0 (Part 1: A-C only)
ISBN 0-7876-7813-9 (Part 2: D-I only)
ISBN 0-7876-7814-7 (Part 3: J-P only)
ISBN 0-7876-7815-5 (Part 4: Q-Z only)

ISSN 0270-4404

This title is also available as an e-book.
ISBN 1-4144-1457-3

Printed in the United States of America
10 9 8 7 6 5 4 3 2 1

Contents

Gale Publications in the Acronyms and Abbreviations Field

Acronyms, Initialisms & Abbreviations Dictionary series:

***Acronyms, Initialisms & Abbreviations Dictionary* (Volume 1).** A guide to acronyms, initialisms, abbreviations, and similar contractions, arranged alphabetically by abbreviation.

***Reverse Acronyms, Initialisms & Abbreviations Dictionary* (Volume 3).** A companion to Volume 1 in which terms are arranged alphabetically by meaning of the acronym, initialism, or abbreviation.

Acronyms, Initialisms & Abbreviations Dictionary Subject Guide series:

***Computer & Telecommunications Acronyms* (Volume 1).** A guide to acronyms, initialisms, abbreviations, and similar contractions used in the field of computers and telecommunications in which terms are arranged alphabetically both by abbreviation and meaning.

***Business Acronyms* (Volume 2).** A guide to business-oriented acronyms, initialisms, abbreviations, and similar contractions in which terms are arranged alphabetically both by abbreviation and by meaning.

International Acronyms, Initialisms & Abbreviations Dictionary series:

***International Acronyms, Initialisms & Abbreviations Dictionary* (Volume 1).** A guide to foreign and international acronyms, initialisms, abbreviations, and similar contractions, arranged alphabetically by abbreviation.

***Reverse International Acronyms, Initialisms & Abbreviations Dictionary* (Volume 2).** A companion to Volume 1, in which terms are arranged alphabetically by meaning of the acronym, initialism, or abbreviation.

Periodical Title Abbreviations series:

***Periodical Title Abbreviations: By Abbreviation* (Volume 1).** A guide to abbreviations commonly used for periodical titles, arranged alphabetically by abbreviation.

***Periodical Title Abbreviations: By Title* (Volume 2).** A guide to abbreviations commonly used for periodical titles, arranged alphabetically by title.

Users Guide

The following examples illustrate possible elements of entries in *AIAD*:

Sample Entry A

FATAC .... Force Aerienne Tactique [Tactical Air Force] [French] (NATG)

▮1▮ FATAC
▮2▮ Force Aerienne Tactique
▮3▮ [Tactical Air Force]
▮4▮ [French]
▮5▮ (NATG)

Description of Numbered Elements

▮1▮ Acronym, Initialism, or Abbreviation

▮2▮ Meaning or Phrase

▮3▮ English Translation

▮4▮ Language (for non-English entries)

▮5▮ Source code (Allows users to verify entries or find additional information. Decoded in the List of Selected Sources section.)

Sample Entry B

MMT .... Multiple-Mirror Telescope [Mount Hopkins, AZ] [Jointly operated by Smithsonian Institution and the University of Arizona] [Astronomy]

▮6▮ MMT
▮7▮ Multiple-Mirror Telescope
▮8▮ [Mount Hopkins, AZ]
▮9▮ [Jointly operated by Smithsonian Institution and the University of Arizona]
▮10▮ [Astronomy]

Description of Numbered Elements

▮6▮ Acronym, Initialism, or Abbreviation

▮7▮ Meaning or Phrase

▮8▮ Location or Country of origin (Provides geographic identifiers for airports, colleges and universities, libraries, military bases, political parties, radio and television stations, and others)

▮9▮ Sponsoring organizations

▮10▮ Subject category (Clarifies entries by providing appropriate context)

The completeness of a listing is dependent on both the nature of the term and the amount of information provided by the source. If additional information becomes available during future research, an entry is revised.

Arrangement of Entries

Acronyms, initialisms, and abbreviations are arranged alphabetically in a letter-by-letter sequence. Spacing, punctuation, and capitalization are not considered. If the same term has more than one meaning, the various meanings are also subarranged in a letter-by-letter sequence.

Should you wish to eliminate the guesswork from acronym formation and usage, a companion volume could help. *Reverse Acronyms, Initialisms & Abbreviations Dictionary* contains essentially the same entries as *AIAD,* but arranges them alphabetically by meaning, rather than by acronym or initialism.

List of Selected Sources

Each of the sources included in the following list contributed at least fifty terms. It would be impossible to cite a source for every entry because the majority of terms are sent by outside contributors, are uncovered through independent research by the editorial staff, or surface as miscellaneous broadcast or print media references. For sources used on an ongoing basis, only the latest edition is listed. For most of the remaining sources, the edition that was used is cited. The editors will provide further information about these sources upon request.

(AABC) *Catalog of Abbreviations and Brevity Codes.* Washington, DC: U.S. Department of the Army, 1981.

(AAEL) "Common Abbreviations and Acronyms in Electronics." Gunham Kaytaz. http://www.seas.smu.edu/~kaytaz/menu.html (accessed April 27, 1999).

(AAG) *Aerospace Abbreviations Glossary. Report Number AG60-0014.* General Dynamics/Astronautics. San Diego, CA: 1962.

(AAGC) *Acronyms and Abbreviations in Government Contracting.* 2d ed. Patricia A. Tobin and Joan Nelson Phillips. Washington, DC: George Washington University, 1997.

(AAMN) *Abbreviations and Acronyms in Medicine and Nursing.* Solomon Garb, Eleanor Krakauer, and Carson Justice. New York: Springer Publishing Co., 1976.

(ABAC) "Abbreviations, Acronyms, and Initialisms." http://www.pnl.gov/ag/usage/acroel.html (accessed January 27, 2000).

(ABAR) "Abbreviations." *American Journal of Archaeology.* http://www.ajaonline.org (accessed May 4, 2002).

(ABBR) *Abbreviations: The Comprehensive Dictionary of Abbreviations and Letter Symbols.* Vol. 1C. Edward Wall. Ann Arbor, MI: Pierian Press, 1984.

(AC) *Associations Canada: 1995/96.* Ward McBurney, Ed. Toronto: Canadian Almanac & Directory Publishing Co. Ltd., 1995.

(ACAE) *Aerospace and Defense Acronyms.* 2d ed. Fernando B. Morinigo, Comp. Washington, DC: American Institute of Aeronautics and Astronautics, 1992.

(ACII) "Acronym and Initials Index." http://www.ioi.ie/~readout/cl.html (accessed November 7, 1996).

(AD) *Abbreviations Dictionary.* 8th ed. Ralph De Sola. Boca Raton, FL: CRC Press, 1992.

(ADA) *The Australian Dictionary of Acronyms and Abbreviations.* 2d ed. David J. Jones, Comp. Leura, NSW, Australia: Second Back Row Press Pty. Ltd., 1981.

(ADDR) *Army Dictionary and Desk Reference.* Tim Zurick. Harrisburg, PA: Stackpole Books, 1992.

(ADWA) *Abbreviations Dictionary: A Practical Compilation of Todays Acronyms and Abbreviations.* Robert S. Wachal. Boston: Houghton Mifflin Co., 1999.

(AEBE) *Acronyms in Electronics Business and Eng- ineering.* Ken Westover. Boulder, CO: Cliff Canyon Publishing Co., 1998.

(AEBS) *Acronyms in Education and the Behavioral Sciences.* Toyo S. Kawakami. Chicago, IL: American Library Association, 1971.

(AEE) *American Educators Encyclopedia.* Edward L. Dejnozka and David E. Kapel. Westport, CT: Greenwood Press, 1991.

(AEPA) *ACCESS EPA.* 1995/96 ed. U.S. Environmental Protection Agency. Washington, DC: Office of Information Resources Management, 1996.

(AF) *Reference Aid: Abbreviations in the African Press.* Arlington, VA: Joint Publications Research Service, 1979.

(AFIT) *Compendium of Authenticated Systems and Logistics.* Washington, DC: Air Force Institute of Technology, 1984.

(AFM) *Air Force Manual of Abbreviations.* Washington, DC: U.S. Department of the Air Force, 1975.

(AG) "Acronym Glossary." http://www.disa.org/apps/acrolook.cfm?acronym= (accessed October 23, 2002).

(AGLO) *Abbreviations, Acronyms, Glossary for American Readers.* 13th ed. San Jose, CA: American Readers Publishing Co., 2001.

(AIA) *Aviation Insurance Abbreviations, Organizations and Institutions.* M. J. Spurway. London, UK: Witherby & Co. Ltd., 1983.

(AIE) *Acronyms and Initialisms in Education.* 6th ed. John Hutchins, Comp. Norwich, UK: Librarians of Institutes and Schools of Education, 1995.

(AL) "Acronyms & Abbreviations." American Library Association. http://www.ala.org/ (accessed December 2, 1997).

(ALAC) "Alaska Acronyms Glossary." Washington, DC: USDA Forest Service, 1993. http://www.fs.fed.us/r10/ro/epb/otherpdf/acronym.pdf (accessed May 29, 2003).

(ALHF) "Alaska Housing Finance Corporation Glossary." http://www.ahfc.state.ak.us.index.htm (accessed October 18, 1999).

(AMHC) *Glossary of Managed Care Medical Terms, Abbreviations and Acronyms.* Margaret D. Bischel, M.D. Santa Barbara, CA: Apollo Managed Care Consultants, 1998.

(ANA) *Abbreviations—U.S. Navy Dictionary.* 3rd rev. Washington, DC: DCP, 1989.

(ANEX) *American Novel Explication 1969-1980.* Catherine Glitsch, Comp. New Haven, CT: Archon Books, 2000.

(APTA) *Australian Periodical Title Abbreviations.* David J. Jones, Comp. Leura, NSW, Australia: Second Back Row Press Pty. Ltd., 1985.

(ARC) *Agricultural Research Centres: A World Directory of Organizations and Programmes.* 2 vols. Nigel Harvey, Ed. Harlow, Essex, UK: Longman Group, 1983.

(ARCH) *Dictionary of Architecture and Construction.* Cyril M. Harris, Ed. New York: McGraw-Hill, Inc., 1975.

(ARMP) "Global Change Acronyms and Abbreviations." http://www.arm.gov/docs/index/html (accessed February 8, 2000).

(ASC) *Associations Canada 1995/96.* Ward McBurney, Ed. Toronto: Canadian Almanac & Directory Publishing Co Ltd., 1995.

(ASF) *Guide to Names and Acronyms of Organizations, Activities, and Projects. Reference Series.* Number 10. n.p. By Food and Agriculture Organization of the United Nations, Fishery Information, Data, and Statistics Service, U.S. National Oceanic and Atmospheric Administration, Aquatic Sciences and Fisheries Information System, 1982.

(AUEG) "Acronyms Used by Environmental Groups and Agencies." http://www.etd.ameslab.gov/etd/library/acronyms/acronym.html (accessed 2000).

(AUER) "Abbreviations Used for Navy Enlisted Ratings." http://www.history.navy.mil/faq78.2html (accessed October 19, 2000).

(AVGL) "Aircraft Owners and Pilots Association Aviation Glossary." http://www.aopa.ch/xgloss.htm (accessed October 20, 1999).

(BABM) *Bailliere's Abbreviations in Medicine.* 5th ed. Edwin B. Steen. London, UK: Bailliere Tindall, 1984.

(BARN) *The Barnhart Abbreviations Dictionary.* Robert K. Barnhart, Ed. New York: John Wiley & Sons, Inc., 1995.

(BB) "Acronyms Finder: Acronyms for Training, Business and Communication." http://www.businessballs.com/acronyms.htm (accessed October 23, 2002).

(BCP) "BCP Guidebook." http://www.dtic.dla.mil/environdod/ (accessed Fall 1995).

(BCRPG) *Barcena's Clinical Reference Pocket Guide to Abbreviations and Symbols Used in Hospitals.* Theresa L. Barcena. Claremont, CA: Barcena & Company, 1995.

(BEE) "The Beeline." http://www.bton.com/tb17/abbr/a.html (accessed November 17, 1999).

(BI) *British Initials and Abbreviations.* 3rd ed. Ian H. Wilkes. London, UK: Leonard Hill Books, 1971.

(BIB) *Bibliotech.* Ottawa: National Library of Canada, 1988-89.

(BIBA) "North American 4 Letter Codes to Identify Birds." http://www.birding.about/library/weekly/aa0011601b.htm (accessed October 23, 2001).

(BJA) *Biblical and Judaic Acronyms.* Lawrence Marwick. New York: Ktav Publishing House, Inc., 1979.

(BRI) *Book Review Index.* 1997 Cumulation. Beverly Baer, Ed. Detroit: Gale Research, 1998.

(BROA) *Broadcasting & Cable Yearbook 2002-2003.* New York: Reed Elsevier Inc., 2002.

(BTTJ) *Breaking Through Technical Jargon: A Dictionary of Computer and Automation Acronyms.* Mark S. Merkow. New York: Van Nostrand Reinhold, 1990.

(BUAC) *Buttress's World Guide to Abbreviations of Organizations.* 11th Revised ed. L. M. Pitman. London, UK: Blackie Academic and Professional, 1997.

(BUR) *Computer Acronyms and Abbreviations Handbook.* Tokyo, Japan: Burroughs Co. Ltd., 1978.

(BYTE) *Byte: The Small Systems Journal.* Peterborough, NH: McGraw-Hill Information Systems, Inc., 1987-89.

(CAAL) *CAAL COMOPTEVFOR Acronym and Abbreviation List.* Norfolk, VA: (CAAL-U) Operational Test and Evaluation Force, 1981.

(CABS) "Serials Source List for Computer and Information Systems Abstracts." Internet Database Service. http://www.csa.com/htbin/sjldisp.cgi?filename=/wais/data/srcjnl/comp001 (accessed March 12, 2002).

(CARB) "Carbon Dioxide Information Analysis Center—Acronyms and Abbreviations." http://www.cdiac.esd.oorni.gov/cdiac/pns/acronyms.html (accessed July 18, 1996).

(CARL) *The International Dictionary of Intelligence*. Leo D. Carl. McLean, VA: International Defense Consultant Services, Inc., 1990.

(CB) *Centres & Bureaux: A Directory of Concentrations of Effort, Information and Expertise*. Lindsay Sellar, Ed. Beckenham, Kent, UK: CBD Research Ltd., 1987.

(CCCA) *ABC Pocket Guide for the Field on C3 Acronyms: An Anthology of Command, Control, and Communications Acronyms and Abbreviations*. 2d ed. Charles R. Wolfson, Ed. Geneva, IL: ABC TeleTraining, Inc., 1986.

(CDAI) *Concise Dictionary of Acronyms and Initialisms*. Stuart W. Miller. New York: Facts on File, Inc., 1988.

(CDE) *The Computer Desktop Encyclopedia*. Alan Freedman. New York: AMACOM, 1996.

(CDI) *The Cancer Dictionary*. Roberta Altman and Michael Sarg, M.D. New York: Facts on File, Inc., 1992.

(CED) *Current European Directories*. 2d ed. G. P. Henderson, Ed. Beckenham, Kent, UK: CBD Research, 1981.

(CET) "Communications-Electronics Terminology." *AFM 11-1*. Vol. 3. U.S. Department of the Air Force, 1973.

(CGWS) *The Comprehensive Guide to Wireless Resources; Definitions and Acronyms, and National Trade Shows, Association and Publication Listings*. Lawrence Harte and Steven Kellogg. Fuquay-Varina, NC: APDG Publishing, 1998.

(CINC) *A CINCPAC Glossary of Commonly Used Abbreviations and Short Titles*. Ltc. J. R. Johnson. Washington, DC: 1968.

(CIST) *Computer & Information Science & Technology Abbreviations & Acronyms Dictionary*. David W. South, Ed. Boca Raton, FL: CRC Press, Inc., 1994.

(CMD) *Complete Multilingual Dictionary of Computer Terminology*. Georges Nania, Comp. Chicago, IL: National Textbook Co., 1984.

(CNC) *American National Standard Codes for the Representation of Names of Countries, Dependencies, and Areas of Special Sovereignty for Information Interchange*. U.S. National Bureau of Standards. Washington, DC: Government Printing Office, 1986.

(COBU) "Common Business and Professional Abbreviations and Acronyms." http://www.instantaccess.co.uk/infozone/abbreviations.html (accessed January 27, 2000).

(COE) *Cooper's Comprehensive Environmental Desk Reference*. Andre R. Cooper, Ed. New York: John Wiley & Sons, 1990.

(COMM) *Common Stock Newspaper Abbreviations and Trading Symbols*. Howard R. Jarrell. Metuchen, NJ: Scarecrow Press, 1989.

(CPGU) *Canadian Parliamentary Guide, Parlementaire Canadien, 1998-1999*. Kathryn OHandley, Ed. Farmington Hills, MI: Gale Group, Inc., 1999.

(CPH) *The Charles Press Handbook of Current Medical Abbreviations*. 3rd ed. Philadelphia, PA: Charles Press Publishers, Inc., 1991.

(CRD) *Computer-Readable Databases: A Directory and Data Sourcebook*. 6th ed. Kathleen Young Marcaccio, Ed. Detroit, MI: Gale Research, 1990.

(CROSS) *Cross-Border Links: A Directory of Organizations in Canada, Mexico, and the United States*. Ricardo Hernandez and Edith Sanchez, Eds. Albuquerque, NM: Inter-Hemispheric Education Resource Center, 1992.

(CSR) *Computer Science Resources: A Guide to Professional Literature*. Darlene Myers, Ed. White Plains, NY: Knowledge Industry Publications, Inc., 1981.

(CTAA) *Common Terminology, Abbreviations and Symbols for Therapeutic Recreation and Other Activity Therapies*. David L. Jewell. Springfield, IL: Charles C. Thomas Publisher, Ltd., 2002.

(CTAS) "CTAS Acronym Dictionary." http://www.ctas.arc.nase.gov/acronyms (accessed October 10, 2000).

(CTT) *Corporate TrendTrac*. A. Dale Timpe, Ed. Detroit, MI: Gale Research, 1988-89.

(CWA) "Civil War Acronyms." http://www.antiqueresources.com/articles/cwacronyms.html (accessed 1998).

(DA) *Dictionary of Aviation*. R. J. Hall and R. D. Campbell. Chicago, IL: St. James Press, 1991.

(DAS) *Dictionary of Abbreviations and Symbols*. Edward Frank Allen. London, UK: Cassell and Co. Ltd., 1949.

(DAVI) *Medical Abbreviations: 14,000 Conveniences at the Expense of Communications and Safety*. 9th ed. Neil M. Davis. Huntingdon Valley, PA: Neil M. Davis Associates, 1999.

(DB) *Dictionary of Biomedical Acronyms and Abbreviations.* 2d ed. Jacques Dupayrat. New York: John Wiley & Sons, 1990.

(DBA) *Directory of British Associations.* G. P. Henderson and S. P. A. Henderson, Eds. Beckenham, Kent, UK: CBD Research, Ltd., 1990.

(DBQ) *A Dictionary of British Qualifications.* London, UK: Kogan Page Ltd., 1985.

(DCDG) *The Dictionary of Computing & Digital Media; Terms & Acronyms.* Brad Hansen, Ed. Wilsonville, OR: Franklin, Beedle & Associates, Inc., 1999.

(DCOM) *The Dictionary of Computing & Digital Media; Terms and Acronyms.* Brad Hansen. Wilsonville, OR: ABF Content, 1999.

(DCT) *Dictionary of Communications Technology.* 3rd ed. Gilbert Held. New York: John Wiley & Sons Ltd., 1998.

(DCTA) *Dictionary of Commercial Terms and Abbreviations.* Alan E. Branch. London, UK: Witherby & Co. Ltd., 1984.

(DD) *The Financial Post Directory of Directors 1997.* Toronto: Financial Post, 1996.

(DDC) *The International Dictionary of Data Communications.* Robert A. Saigh. Chicago, IL: Glenlake Publishing Company, Ltd., 1998.

(DDSO) *D & D Standard Oil Abbreviator.* 4th ed. Association of Desk and Derrick Clubs. Tulsa, OK: PennWell Books, 1994.

(DEEM) "Acronyms List." Office of Environmental Management, U.S. Department of Energy, 2003. http://www.em.doe.gov/acronym (accessed May 8, 2003).

(DEMM) "Department of Emergency Management Master List of Acronyms." http://bcem.co.bay.fl.us/dem/htm (accessed January 27, 2000).

(DEN) *Dictionary of Electronics and Nucleonics.* L. E. C. Hughes, R. W. B. Stephens, and L. D. Brown. New York: Barnes & Noble, 1969.

(DET) *Dictionary of Educational Terms.* David Blake and Vincent Hanley, Eds. Brookfield, VT: Ashgate Publishing Co., 1995.

(DFIT) *Dictionary of Finance and Investment Terms.* 4th ed. John Downes and Jordan Elliot Goodman, Eds. Hauppauge, NY: Barrons Educational Series, 1995.

(DGA) *Dictionary of Graphic Arts Abbreviations.* L. W. Wallis. Rockport, MA: Rockport Publishers, Inc., 1986.

(DHP) *Dictionary of Abbreviations and Acronyms in Helping Professions.* John W. Hollis. Muncie, IN: Accelerated Development, Inc., 1987.

(DHSM) *Dictionary of Health Services Management.* 2d ed. Thomas C. Timmreck. Owings Mills, MD: Rynd Communications, 1987.

(DI) *The Dictionary of Initials: What They Mean.* Harriette Lewis, Comp. and Ed. Kingswood, Surrey, UK: Paper Fronts Elliot Right Way Books, 1983.

(DIAR) *The Dictionary of Art.* Jane Turner, Ed. London, UK: MacMillan Publishers Limited, 1996.

(DICI) *The Dictionary of Initials.* Betsy M. Parks. Secaucus, NJ: Citadel Press, 1981.

(DINT) *Dictionary of Internetworking Terms and Acronyms.* San Jose, CA: Cisco Press for Cisco Systems, 2001.

(DIPS) *The Dictionary of Psychology.* Raymond J. Corsini. Philadelphia, PA: Taylor and Francis, 1999.

(DIT) *Dictionary of Informatics Terms in Russian and English.* G. S. Zhdanov et al. Moscow: Nauka, 1971.

(DLA) *Bieber's Dictionary of Legal Abbreviations.* 3rd ed. Mary Miles Prince. Buffalo, NY: William S. Hein & Co., 1988.

(DMA) *Dictionary of Military Abbreviations: British, Empire, Commonwealth.* B. K. C. Scott. Hastings, East Sussex, UK: Tamarisk Books, 1982.

(DMAA) *Dictionary of Medical Acronyms and Abbreviations.* 3rd ed. Stanley Jablonski, Ed. Philadelphia, PA: Hanley & Belfus, Inc., 1998.

(DMC) *Websters New World Dictionary of Media and Communications.* Revised ed. Richard Weiner. New York: Macmillan, 1996.

(DNAB) *Dictionary of Naval Abbreviations.* 3rd ed. Bill Wedertz, Comp. and Ed. Annapolis, MD: Naval Institute Press, 1984.

(DOAD) *The Dictionary of Advertising.* Laurence Urdang, Ed. Lincolnwood, IL: NTC Business Books, 1986.

(DOG) *A Dictionary of Genetics.* 5th ed. Robert C. King and William D. Stansfield. New York: Oxford University Press, 1997.

(DOGT) "List of Acronyms." http://www.em.doe.gov/rtc1994/loa.html (accessed March 5, 1997).

(DOM) *The Dictionary of Multimedia: Terms & Acronyms.* Brad Hansen. Wilsonville, OR: Franklin, Beedle & Associates, Inc., 1997.

(DOMA) *Dictionary of Military Abbreviations.* Norman Polmar, Mark Warren, and Eric Wertheim. Annapolis, MD: Naval Institute Press, 1994.

(DS) *Dictionary of Shipping International Trade Terms and Abbreviations.* 3rd ed. Alan E. Branch. London, UK: Witherby & Co. Ltd., 1986.

(DSA) *Dictionary of Sigla and Abbreviations to and in Law Books before 1607*. William Hamilton Bryson. Charlottesville: University Press of Virginia, 1975.

(DSUE) *A Dictionary of Slang and Unconventional English*. 8th ed. Eric Partridge. New York: Macmillan Publishing Co., 1984.

(DUND) *Directory of United Nations Databases and Information Services*. 4th ed. Advisory Committee for the Coordination of Information Systems. New York: United Nations, 1990.

(DWSG) *Defense Weapon Systems Glossary*. David Trotz. Piscataway, NJ: Target Marketing, 1992.

(EA) *Encyclopedia of Associations: National Organizations of the U.S.* 41st ed., Vol. 1. Farmington Hills, MI: Thomson Gale, 2004.

(EAAP) *Encyclopedia of Associations: Association Periodicals*. Denise M. Allard and Robert C. Thomas, Eds. Detroit, MI: Gale Research, 1987.

(EAGT) "Environmental Acronyms, Abbreviations, and Glossary of Terms." *United States Environmental Protection Agency Information Resources Directory*. OPA 003-89. Washington, DC: Environmental Protection Agency, Spring 1989.

(EAIO) *Encyclopedia of Associations: International Organizations*. 41st ed. Farmington Hills, MI: Thomson Gale, 2004.

(EARSL) *Encyclopedia of Associations: Regional, State and Local Organizations*. 15th ed. Farmington Hills, MI: Thomson Gale, 2004.

(EBF) *Encyclopedia of Banking and Finance*. 10th ed. Charles J. Woelfel, Ed. Chicago, IL: Probus Publishing Co., 1994.

(ECED) *The European Communities Encyclopedia and Directory 1992*. London, UK: Europa Publications Ltd., 1991. Distributed in the United States by Gale Research (Detroit).

(ECII) *Electronics, Computers and Industrial Instrumentation Abbreviations and Acronyms*. Sergio Sobredo, Ed. Miami, FL: Sergio Sobredo Technical Services, 1986.

(ECON) *The Economist*. London, UK: The Economist Newspaper Ltd., 2001.

(EDAA) *Elsevier's Dictionary of Abbreviations, Acronyms, Synonyms and Symbols Used in Medicine*. Dr. Samuel A. Tsur (Mansoor), Comp. New York: Elsevier Science, 1999.

(EDAC) *Dictionary of Educational Acronyms, Abbreviations, and Initialisms*. 2d ed. James C. Palmer and Anita Y. Colby, Eds. Phoenix, AZ: Oryx Press, 1985.

(EDCT) *Encyclopedic Dictionary of Chemical Technology*. Dorit Noether and Herman Noether. New York: VCH Publishers, Inc., 1993.

(EE) *Eastern Europe and the Commonwealth of Independent States 1992*. London, UK: Europa Publications Ltd., 1992. Distributed in the United States by Gale Research (Detroit).

(EECA) *Dictionary of Electrical, Electronics, and Computer Abbreviations*. Phil Brown. London, UK: Buttersworth, 1985.

(EES) *A Dictionary of Ecology, Evolution and Systematics*. 2d ed. Roger Lincoln, Geoff Boxshall, and Paul Clark, Eds. New York: Cambridge University Press, 1998.

(EEVL) *Environmental Engineering Dictionary*. 3rd ed. C. C. Lee, Ed. Rockville, MD: Government Institutes, 1998.

(EFIS) *Corporate Acronym Resource Guide, 1800s-1995*. Seattle, WA: Environmental Financial Information Services, Inc., 1996.

(EG) *Environmental Glossary*. 4th ed. G. William Frick and Thomas F. P. Sullivan, Ed. Rockville, MD: Government Institutes, Inc., 1986.

(EGA) "Acronyms Used by Environment Groups and Agencies." http://www.epsci.aimeslab.gov/etd/library/acronyms/acronym.html (accessed October 23, 2002).

(EGAO) *Encyclopedia of Governmental Advisory Organizations*. 9th ed. Donna Batten, Ed. Detroit: Gale Research, 1994-95 (and supplement, 1995).

(ELAL) *Computer Acronyms & Abbreviations: Over 4,000 Entries and What They Stand For*. Elie Albala, Comp. Quebec, Canada: Alpel Publishing, 1992.

(EMA) *Emergency Management Acronyms*. Vol. 1. Walter G. Green III. Universal Publishers/uPublish.com, 2001.

(EMRF) *The St. James Encyclopedia of Mortgage & Real Estate Finance*. James Newell, Albert Santi, and Chip Mitchell. Chicago, IL: St. James Press, 1991.

(EOSA) "Earth Observing System (EOS) Acronyms and Abbreviations." http://eospso.gsfc.nasa/eos_homepage/misc (accessed October 5, 1999).

(EPA) *Glossary of EPA Acronyms*. Washington, DC: Environmental Protection Agency, 1987.

(EPAT) "Terms of Environment." http://www.epa.gov/OCEPAterms/aaad.html (accessed November 3, 1999).

(EPT) "The Extended Periodic Table." Wolfram Klehr. http://www.apsidium.com (accessed March 1, 2005).

(ERG) *Environmental Regulatory Glossary*. 5th ed. G. William Frick and Thomas F. P. Sullivan, Eds. Rockville, MD: Government Institutes, Inc., 1990.

(ETLW) *The Ethnologue: Languages of the World.* 10th ed. Barbara Grimes. Dallas, TX: Wycliffe Bible Translators, 1984.

(EURO) *Eurojargon: A Dictionary of European Union Acronyms, Abbreviations, and Sobriquets.* 6th ed. Anne Ramsay, Ed.. Chicago, IL: Fitzroy Dearborn Publishers, 2000.

(EY) *The Europa World Year Book 1992.* London, UK: Europa Publications Ltd., 1992. Distributed in the United States by Gale Research (Detroit).

(FAAC) *Contractions Handbook.* Changes. U.S. Department of Transportation, Federal Aviation Administration, 1993.

(FAAL) *Location Identifiers.* U.S. Department of Transportation, Federal Aviation Administration, Air Traffic Service, 1982.

(FEA) *The Far East and Australasia 1987.* 18th ed. London, UK: Europa Publications Ltd., 1986. Distributed in the United States by Gale Research (Detroit).

(FFDE) *The Facts on File Dictionary of Environmental Science.* L. Harold Stevenson and Bruce Wyman. New York: Facts on File, Inc., 1991.

(FOTI) *Acrobuster: Dictionary of Canadian English Acronyms, Initialisms, and Abbreviations.* Vadim Fotinov and Svetlana Fotinov, Ed. Ottawa, Canada: Fotinov and Fotinov, 2000.

(FUCW) "Frequently Used Contractions in National Weather Service Products." http://www.awc-kc.noaa.gov/info/domestic_contractions.html

(GA) *Countries of the World and Their Leaders 2003.* Farmington Hills, MI: Gale, 2002.

(GAAI) "Glossary of Abbreviations, Acronyms, and Initialisms." http://www.em.doe.gov/idb97/acropdf.html (accessed February 17, 1998).

(GART) *The Gartner Glossary of Information Technology Acronyms and Terms.* 4th ed. Stamford, CT: Gartner Group, Inc., 2000.

(GAVI) "Glossary of Aviation Acronyms and Abbreviations." http://olias.arc.nasa.gov/AFO_Acronyms_ html (accessed March 5, 1997).

(GDD) *Gale Directory of Databases.* 2005 ed. Farmington Hills, MI: Thomson Gale, 2005.

(GDPB) *Gale Directory of Publications and Broadcast Media.* 139th ed. Kristen B. Malleg, Ed. Farmington Hills, MI: Thomson Gale, 2004.

(GEA) *Government Economic Agencies of the World: An International Directory of Governmental Organisations Concerned with Economic Development and Planning.* A Keesings Reference Publication. Alan J. Day, Ed. Harlow, Essex, UK: Longman Group Ltd., 1985.

(GEAB) "Genealogy Abbreviations." http://www.genweb.net/~samcasey/abbre.html (accessed November 17, 1999).

(GEOI) "Dictionary of Abbreviations and Acronyms in Geographic Information Systems, Cartography, and Remote Sensing." Philip Hoehn and Mary Lynette Larsgaard. http://www.lib.berkeley.edu/EART/ abbrev.html (accessed June 1999).

(GFGA) *Guide to Federal Government Acronyms.* William R. Evinger, Ed. Phoenix, AZ: The Oryx Press, 1989.

(GNE) *The Green Encyclopedia.* Irene Franck and David Brownstone. New York: Prentice Hall General Reference, 1992.

(GOBB) *The Gobbledygook Book: Dictionary of Acronyms, Abbreviations, Initializations & Esoteric Terminology.* Franklin W. Fox, III, Comp. Troy, MI: Momentum Books, Ltd., 1996.

(GPO) *Style Manual.* Washington, DC: Government Printing Office, 1984.

(GRD) *Government Research Directory.* 8th ed. Joseph M. Palmisano, Ed. Detroit: Gale Research, 1994 (and supplement, 1994).

(GROV) "Abbreviation List." http://www.grovemusic.com/grovemusic/az/general00.html (accessed January 16, 2001).

(GRST) "Glossary of Remote Sensing Terms." http://ceo1409.ceo.sai.jrc.it:8080...2/tutorials/glossary (accessed October 5, 1999).

(GVA) "Glossary of Veterinary Acronyms." http://www/spvs.org.uk/glossary.htm (accessed October 1999).

(HAWK) "Hawkman's Automotive Abbreviations." http://www3.sympatico.ca/dhaughey/index2.htm (accessed October 19, 2000).

(HCT) *Health Care Terms.* 2d ed. Vergil N. Slee and Debora A. Slee. St. Paul, MN: Tringa Press, 1991.

(HEAS) "Acronyms and Abbreviations Used in Health and Safety Executive Information Services." http://www.healthandsafety.co.uk/acronyms.html (accessed September 26, 2000).

(HGAA) *The Handy Guide to Abbreviations and Acronyms for the Automated Office.* Mark W. Greenia. Seattle: Self-Counsel Press, Inc., 1986.

(HGEN) "Human Genome Acronym List." http://www.ornl.gov/hgmis/acronym.html (accessed December 2, 1998).

(HLLA) "Honeywell Abbreviation and Acronym Dictionary." http://www.cas.honeywell.com/ats/acronym.html (accessed January 27, 2000).

(HODG) *Computers: Systems, Terms and Acronyms.* 12th ed. M. Susan Hodges. Winter Park, FL: SemCo Enterprises, Inc., 2000.

(HRG) *The Human Resources Glossary: The Complete Desk Reference for HR Executives, Managers, and Practitioners.* 2d ed. William R. Tracey. Boca Raton, FL: St. Lucie Press, 1998.

(HRNC) *How to Read a Nautical Chart: A Complete Guide to the Symbols, Abbreviations, and Data Displayed on Nautical Charts.* Nigel Calder. Camden, ME: International Marine/McGraw-Hill, 2003.

(HVTR) "HIV Vaccine Trials Network, Abbreviations & Acronyms: Medical Abbreviations." http://www.scharp.org/hvtn/resources/abbrev.other.html (accessed March 12, 2002).

(IAA) *Index of Acronyms and Abbreviations in Electrical and Electronic Engineering.* Compiled by Buro Scientia. New York: VCH Publishers, 1989.

(IAS) "International Arctic Science Committee." http://www.iasc.no/acronyms.htm (October 20, 1999).

(IBMDP) *IBM Data Processing Glossary.* 6th ed. White Plains, NY: IBM Corp., 1977.

(ICAO) *Aircraft Type Designators.* 13th ed. International Civil Aviation Organization. August, 1981.

(ICDA) *Designators for Aircraft Operating Agencies, Aeronautical Authorities and Services.* 49th ed. International Civil Aviation Organization. June, 1982.

(ICLI) *Location Indicators.* 51st ed. International Civil Aviation Organization. February, 1987.

(IDAI) *The International Dictionary of Artificial Intelligence.* William Raynor. Chicago, IL: Glenlake Publishing Co., Ltd., 1999.

(IDOE) *The Illustrated Dictionary of Electronics.* 6th ed. Stan Gibilisco. New York: TAB Books, 1994.

(IDYL) *Medical Abbreviations for the Health Professions.* Thomas K. Skalko, Ed. Ravensdale, WA: Idyll Arbor, Inc., 1998.

(IEEE) *IEEE Standard Dictionary of Electrical and Electronics Terms.* Frank Jay, Ed. New York: Institute of Electrical and Electronics Engineers, Inc., 1977, 1984.

(IEL) *International Encyclopedia of Linguistics.* 2d ed. William J. Frawley, Ed. New York: Oxford University Press, 2003.

(IGQR) *The Internet Glossary & Quick Reference Guide.* Alan Freedman, Alfred Glossbrenner, and Emily Glossbrenner. New York: AMACOM, 1998.

(IGSL) *International Reference Guide to Space Launch Systems.* 3rd ed. Steven J. Isakowitz, Joseph P. Hopkins, Jr., and Joshua B. Hopkins, Eds. Reston, VA: American Institute of Aeronautics and Astronautics, 1999.

(IIA) *Index of Initials and Acronyms.* Richard Kleiner, Comp. New York: Auerbach Publishers, 1971.

(IID) *Information Industry Directory.* 27th ed. Farmington Hills, MI: Thomson Gale, 2004.

(ILCA) *Index to Legal Citations and Abbreviations.* Donald Raistrick. Abingdon, Oxfordshire, UK: Professional Books Ltd., 1981.

(IMH) *International Marketing Handbook.* 2d ed. Frank Bair, Ed. Detroit, MI: Gale Research, 1985.

(INF) *Infantry.* Fort Benning, GA: U.S. Army Infantry Training School, 1996.

(IOWA) "Iowa Department of Natural Resources Quick Facts." http://www.state.ia.us/government/dnr/part1.htm (accessed October 19, 1999).

(IRC) *International Research Centers Directory 1992-93.* 6th ed. Annette Piccirelli, Ed. Detroit, MI: Gale Research, 1991.

(IRUK) *Industrial Research in the UK.* 12th ed. Harlow, Essex, UK: Longman Group UK Ltd., 1987.

(ISAK) *International Reference Guide to Space Launch Systems.* 3rd ed. Steven J. Isakowitz, Joseph P. Hopkins, Jr., and Joshua B. Hopkins, Eds. Reston, VA: American Institute of Aeronautics and Astronautics, 1999.

(IT) *Information Today: The Newspaper for Users and Producers of Electronic Information Services.* Medford, NJ: Learned Information, Inc., 1988-89.

(ITCA) *Internet Terms and Computer Acronyms, A Useful Guide.* Mary Brookhart. Charlotte, NC: Southeast Consulting, Inc., 1998.

(ITD) *International Tradeshow Directory.* 5th ed. Frankfurt, Germany: M + A Publishers for Fairs, Exhibitions and Conventions Ltd., 1989.

(IUSS) "IUSS Acronyms." http://206.239.241.41/Acronym/1.html (accessed October 12, 1999).

(IYR) *The 1989-92 International Yacht Racing Rules.* London, UK: International Yacht Racing Union, 1989.

(JAGO) *Export Terms and Acronyms: Glossary of the Export Sales and Marketing Manual.* John R. Jagoe. Minneapolis, MN: Export Institute, 2000.

(JLIT) "Journal of Economic Literature, Journal Abbreviation List." http://www.aeaweb.org/journal/abbrev.html (accessed March 12, 2002).

(KSC) *A Selective List of Acronyms and Abbreviations.* Documents Department. Kennedy Space Center Library, 1971, 1973.

(LAIN) *Latest Intelligence: An International Directory of Codes Used by Government, Law Enforcement,*

Military, and Surveillance Agencies. James E. Tunnell. Blue Ridge Summit, PA: TAB BOOKS, 1990.

(LCCP) *MARC Formats for Bibliographic Data: Appendix II.* Washington, DC: Library of Congress, 1982.

(LCLS) *Symbols of American Libraries.* 14th ed. Enhanced Cataloging Division, Eds. Washington, DC: Library of Congress, 1992.

(LDOE) *Lewis' Dictionary of Occupational and Environmental Safety and Health.* Jeffrey W. Vinvoli. Boca Raton, FL: Lewis Publishers, 2000.

(LPT) "Learning, Performance, and Training Acronyms." http://www.nwlink.com/~donclark/hrd/acron.html (accessed October 23, 2002).

(LWAP) *Legal Words and Phrases: Speed Abbreviations.* Joel Larus. Boston, MA: Aurico Publishing, 1965.

(MAE) *Medical Abbreviations and Eponyms.* Sheila B. Sloane. Philadelphia, PA: W. B. Saunders Co., 1985.

(MAH) *Medical Abbreviations Handbook.* 2d ed. Oradell, NJ: Medical Economics Co., Inc., 1983.

(MARI) "Glossary of Marine Abbreviations." http://www.royalsunalliance.ca/rsa.arine/glossabbrevdisp.html (accessed September 26, 2000).

(MCD) *Acronyms, Abbreviations, and Initialisms.* Carl Lauer, Comp. St. Louis, MO: McDonnell Douglas Corp., 1989.

(MDG) *Microcomputer Dictionary and Guide.* Charles J. Sippl. Champaign, IL: Matrix Publishers, Inc., 1975.

(ME) *The Marine Encyclopaedic Dictionary.* 5th ed. Eric Sullivan. London, UK: LLP Ltd., 1996.

(MEC) *Macmillan Encyclopedia of Chemistry.* Vol. 1. Joseph J. Lagowski, Ed. New York: Macmillan Reference USA, 1997.

(MED) *McGraw-Hill Electronic Dictionary.* 5th ed. John Markus and Neil Sclater, Eds. New York: McGraw-Hill, Inc., 1994.

(MEDA) *Medical Acronyms.* 2d ed. Marilyn Fuller Delong. Oradell, NJ: Medical Economic Books, 1989.

(MELL) *Melloni's Illustrated Dictionary of Medical Abbreviations.* John Melloni and Ida G. Dox. Pearl River, NY: Parthenon Publishing Group, Inc., 1998.

(MENA) *The Middle East and North Africa 1987.* 33rd ed. London, UK: Europa Publications Ltd., 1986. Distributed in the United States by Gale Research (Detroit).

(MGMA) "Medical Group Management Associations Book of Acronyms for Medical Practice Executives." http://www.mgma.com/library/acronyms.html (accessed October 19, 1999).

(MHCS) *Managed Health Care Simplified: A Glossary of Terms.* Michael S. Austrin. Albany, NY: Delmar, 1999.

(MHDB) *McGraw-Hill Dictionary of Business Acronyms, Initials, and Abbreviations.* Jerry M. Rosenberg. New York: McGraw-Hill, Inc., 1992.

(MHDI) *McGraw-Hill Dictionary of Information Technology and Computer Acronyms, Initials, and Abbreviations.* Jerry M. Rosenberg. New York: McGraw-Hill, Inc., 1992.

(MHDW) *McGraw-Hill Dictionary of Wall Street Acronyms, Initials, and Abbreviations.* Jerry M. Rosenberg. New York: McGraw-Hill, Inc., 1992.

(MHID) *Medical and Health Information Directory.* 17th ed. Sonya D. Hill, Ed. Detroit, MI: Thomson Gale, 2005.

(MILB) *The Military Balance 1998/99.* London, UK: Oxford University Press for the International Institute for Strategic Studies, 1998.

(MIST) *Means Illustrated Construction Dictionary.* 3rd ed. Kingston, MA: R. S. Means Co., 2000.

(MLOA) "Marconi—List of Acronyms." http://www.fore.com/atm-edu/acronyms.html (accessed 1999).

(MSA) "Military Standard Abbreviations for Use on Drawings, and in Specifications, Standards, and Technical Documents." *MIL-STD-12D.* U.S. Department of Defense, 1981.

(MSC) *Annotated Acronyms and Abbreviations of Marine Science Related Activities.* 3rd Revised ed. Charlotte M. Ashby and Alan R. Flesh. Washington, DC: U.S. Department of Commerce, National Oceanographic and Atmospheric Administration, Environmental Data Service, National Oceanographic Data Center, 1976, 1981.

(MTAA) *Medical Terms & Abbreviations.* 2d ed. Juliet McCleery, Ed. Springhouse, PA: Lippincott Williams & Wilkins, 2002.

(MUGU) *The Mugu Book of Acronyms and Abbreviations.* Missile Range, CA: Management Engineering Office, 1963, 1964.

(MUSM) *Dictionary of Modern United States Military.* S. F. Tomajczyk. Jefferson, NC: McFarland and Co., Inc., 1996.

(MVRD) *The MVR Decoder Digest.* Michael L. Sankey, Ed. Tempe, AZ: BRB Publications, 2001.

(MWOL) "Commonly Used Acronyms." http://www.microsoft.com/hwdev/acronym.htm (accessed November 20, 2001).

(NADA) *The New American Dictionary of Abbreviations.* Mary A. De Vries. New York: Signet, 1991.

JNP .... Joint Nuclear Plot (CINC)
JNP .... Jump if No Parity (SAUO)
JNP .... Newport Beach, CA [*Location identifier*] [*FAA*] (FAAL)
J NPA .... Journal. Nepal Pharmaceutical Association (journ.) (SAUS)
JNPC .... Joint Nuclear Power Committee (SAUO)
JNPE .... Joint Nuclear Planning Element (MCD)
JNPGC ...... Japan Nuclear Power Generation Corp. (SAUS)
JNPGC ...... Japan Nuclear Power Generation Corporation (SAUO)
JNPI .... Jetevator Null Position Indicator
JNPR .... Juniper (ABBR)
JNPR .... Juniper Networks [*NASDAQ symbol*] (SG)
JNPRD ...... Journal of Natural Products (journ.) (SAUS)
JNPT .... Johnson Noise Power Thermometer (SAUS)
JNR .... Hamilton Aeroservices (SAUS)
JNR .... Jammer-to-Noise Ratio (CCCA)
JNR .... Japanesae National Railways (BARN)
JNR .... Japan National Railways (SAUO)
JNR .... Joiner (ABBR)
JNR .... June Resources, Inc. [*Vancouver Stock Exchange symbol*]
JNR .... Junior (EY)
JNR .... Unalakleet, AK [*Location identifier*] [*FAA*] (FAAL)
JNRC .... Joint Nuclear Research Center [*EURATOM*]
JNRI .... Joint Nuclear Research Institute [*Former USSR*]
JNRM .... Journal of Natural Resources Management and Interdisciplinary Studies (journ.) (SAUS)
JNRM .... Journal of Nursing Risk Management (SAUO)
JNROTC ..... Junior Naval Reserve Officer Training Corps
JNRREQ ..... Journal of Natural Rubber Research (journ.) (SAUS)
Jnr Tech ..... Junior Technician (SAUS)
JNS .... Chic by HIS, Inc. [*NYSE symbol*] (SPSG)
JNS .... International Graduate School, St. Louis, MO [*OCLC symbol*] (OCLC)
JNS .... Janus Capital Group [*NYSE symbol*]
JNS .... Jaunsari [*Language symbol*] (ETLW)
JNS .... Jet Noise Survey
JNS .... Joins [*Telegraphy*] (PCTE)
JNS .... Jugoslovenska Nacionalna Stranka [*Yugoslav National Party*] [*Political party*] (PPE)
JNS .... Jump if No Sign (VLIE)
JNS .... Justification for New Start (SAUS)
JNS .... Just Noticeable Shift (PDAA)
JNS .... Minneapolis, MN [*Location identifier*] [*FAA*] (FAAL)
JNSC .... Japanese Nuclear Ship Corp. (SAUS)
JNSC .... Japan Nuclear Safety Commission (BUAC)
JNSC .... Joint Navigation Satellite Committee
JNSCA ...... Journal of the Neurological Sciences (journ.) (SAUS)
JNSD .... Journal of Nurses in Staff Development (SAUO)
JNSD .... Journal of Nursing Staff Development (journ.) (SAUS)
JNSI .... Journal. Numismatic Society of India (journ.) (SAUS)
JNSMP ...... Journal Numismatic Society of Madhya Pradesh (journ.) (SAUS)
JNSNA ...... Journal of Neurosurgical Nursing (journ.) (SAUS)
JNSP .... Joint WHO/UNICEF Nutrition Support Programme (SAUO)
Jn Spectros Co Appl Notes... Japan Spectroscopic Company. Application Notes (SAUO)
Jn Spectros Co Appl Notes... Japan Spectroscopic Company. Application Notes (journ.) (SAUS)
JNSRDA ..... Japan Nuclear Ship Research and Development Agency (BUAC)
JNSSB ...... Journal of Neurosurgical Sciences (journ.) (SAUS)
JNSTN ...... Johnstown, PA [*American Association of Railroads railroad junction routing code*]
JNSV .... Jones &. Vining, Inc. (SAUO)
J NSW Council for Mentally Handicapped... Journal. New Soulh Wales Council for the Mentally Handicapped (journ.) (SAUS)
JNT .... Jaunt (ABBR)
JNT .... Java Network Technology (SAUS)
jnt .... Joint [*Construction term*] (MIST)
JNT .... Joint
JNT .... Joint Network Scheme [*British*]
JNT .... Joint Network Team [*British*] (NITA)
JNT .... Jonathan [*Italy*] [*FAA designator*] (FAAC)
JNT .... Journal of Narrative Technique [*A publication*] (ANEX)
JNT .... Journal of Narrative Technique (journ.) (SAUS)
JNT .... Junction (ABBR)
JNT .... Juncture (ABBR)
JNT .... New York, NY [*Location identifier*] [*FAA*] (FAAL)
JNTA .... Japan National Tourist Association (BUAC)
JNTAD ...... Journal. National Technical Association (journ.) (SAUS)
JNTD .... Jointed (ABBR)
JNTG .... Jensen Trucking Service [*Common carrier symbol*]
JNTINS ...... Jauntiness (ABBR)
JNTIR .... Jauntier (ABBR)
JNTLY .... Jauntily (ABBR)
JNTLY .... Jointly (ABBR)
JNTO .... Japan National Tourist Office (SAUO)
JNTO .... Japan National Tourist Organization (EA)
JNTR .... Janitor (ABBR)
JNTR .... Jointer (ABBR)
JNTST .... Jauntiest (ABBR)
JNT STK CO... Joint Stock Co. (DLA)
JNT STK CO... Joint Stock Company (SAUO)
JNTUR .... Jointure (ABBR)
JNTURD ..... Jointured (ABBR)
JNTURG ..... Jointuring (ABBR)
JNT VEN .... Joint Venture [*Legal term*] (DLA)
JNTY .... Jaunty (ABBR)
JNTY .... Jointly (ABBR)
JNU .... Jiangnan University [*China*] (BUAC)
JNU .... Jiangxi Normal University [*China*] (BUAC)
JNU .... Juneau [*Alaska*] [*Airport symbol*] (OAG)
JNU .... Juneau, AK [*Location identifier*] [*FAA*] (FAAL)
JNU .... Universal Jet Navigation Charts [*Air Force*]
JNU .... Universal Set Navigation Charts (SAUS)
JNUCA .... Journal of Nuclear Energy (journ.) (SAUS)
J Nucl Agric Biol... Journal of Nuclear Agriculture and Biology (journ.) (SAUS)
J Nucl Energy Part A... Journal of Nuclear Energy. Part A. Reactor Science (journ.) (SAUS)
J Nucl Energy Part B... Journal of Nuclear Energy. Part B. Reactor Technology (journ.) (SAUS)
J Nucl Energy Part C... Journal of Nuclear Energy. Part C. Plasma Physics, Accelerators, Thermonuclear Research (journ.) (SAUS)
J Nucl Energy Parts A/B... Journal of Nuclear Energy. Parts A/B. Reactor Science and Technology (journ.) (SAUS)
J Nucl Mater... Journal of Nuclear Materials [*A publication*] (CABS)
J Nucl Mater Manage... Journal of Nuclear Materials Management (journ.) (SAUS)
J Nucl Med Allied Sci... Journal of Nuclear Medicine and Allied Sciences (journ.) (SAUS)
J Nucl Med Pam... Journal of Nuclear Medicine. Pamphlet (journ.) (SAUS)
J Nucl Med Suppl... Journal of Nuclear Medicine. Supplement (journ.) (SAUS)
J Nucl Med Technol... Journal of Nuclear Medicine Technology (journ.) (SAUS)
J Nucl Sci Technol... Journal of Nuclear Science and Technology [*A publication*] (CABS)
JNUL .... Jewish National and University Library
J Number Theory... Journal of Number Theory (journ.) (SAUS)
J Nurs Care... Journal of Nursing Care (journ.) (SAUS)
J Nurs Care Qual... Journal of Nursing Care Quality (journ.) (SAUS)
J Nurs Ed... Journal of Nursery Education (journ.) (SAUS)
J Nurse Midwifery... Journal of Nurse-Midwifery (journ.) (SAUS)
J Nurs Ethics... Journal of Nursing Ethics (journ.) (SAUS)
J Nurs Hist... Journal of Nursing History (journ.) (SAUS)
J Nurs Manag... Journal of Nursing Management (journ.) (SAUS)
J Nurs Meas... Journal of Nursing Measurement (journ.) (SAUS)
J Nurs Staff Dev... Journal of Nursing Staff Development (journ.) (SAUS)
J Nutr .... Journal of Nutrition (journ.) (SAUS)
J Nutr Ass... Journal of Nutritional Assessment (journ.) (SAUS)
J Nutr Biochem... Journal of Nutritional Biochemistry (journ.) (SAUS)
J Nutr Diet... Journal of Nutrition and Dietetics (journ.) (SAUS)
J Nutr Educ... Journal of Nutrition Education (journ.) (SAUS)
J Nutr Elderly... Journal of Nutrition for the Elderly (journ.) (SAUS)
J Nutr Growth Cancer... Journal of Nutrition, Growth and Cancer (journ.) (SAUS)
J Nutr Sci... Journal of Nutritional Sciences (journ.) (SAUS)
J Nutr Supl... Journal of Nutrition. Supplement (journ.) (SAUS)
JNuveen .... Nuveen [*John*] Co. [*Associated Press*] (SAG)
JNVBDV ..... Journal of Nonverbal Behavior (journ.) (SAUS)
JNVOA ...... Jewish Nazi Victims Organization of America (EA)
JNW .... Joint Committee on New Weapons and Equipment
JNW .... Joint Nuclear Research Institute (SAUS)
JNW .... Newport, OR [*Location identifier*] [*FAA*] (FAAL)
JNWEB ...... Joint New Weapons and Equipment Board (ACAE)
JNWOC ...... Joint Warfare Operations Center
JNWP .... Joint Numerical Weather Prediction (SAUS)
JNWP .... Joint Numerical Weather Prediction Unit (IAA)
JNWPS ...... Joint Nuclear Weapons Publication Systems (MCD)
JNWPU ...... Joint Numerical Weather Prediction Unit
JNW Semi .. Journal of the Northwest Semitic Languages (journ.) (SAUS)
J Nw SL ...... Journal of the Northwest Semitic Languages (journ.) (SAUS)
JNX .... Jackson [*Michigan*] [*Airport symbol*] (AD)
JNY .... January (ABBR)
JNY .... Jenney Beechcraft, Inc. [*ICAO designator*] (FAAC)
JNY .... Jones Apparel Group [*NYSE symbol*] (SPSG)
JNY .... Journey [*Telegraphy*] (PCTE)
JNY State Nurses Ass... Journal. New York State Nurses Association (journ.) (SAUS)
JNY State Sch Nurse Teach Assoc... Journal. New York State School Nurse Teachers Association (journ.) (SAUS)
JNZ .... Jennings, LA [*Location identifier*] [*FAA*] (FAAL)
JNZ .... Jewelers of New Zealand (SAUO)
JNZ .... Jump if Not Zero (VLIE)
JNZ .... Jump on Not Zero [*Computer science*] (PCM)
JNZ Ass Bacteriol... Journal. New Zealand Association of Bacteriologists (journ.) (SAUS)
JNZ Fed Hist S... Journal. New Zealand Federation of Historical Societies (journ.) (SAUS)
JNZ Inst Chem... Journal. New Zealand Institute of Chemistry (journ.) (SAUS)
JNZ Inst Med Lab Technol... Journal. New Zealand Institute of Medical Laboratory Technology (journ.) (SAUS)
JNZ Soc Periodontol... Journal. New Zealand Society of Periodontology (journ.) (SAUS)
JO .... Holiday Airlines [*ICAO designator*] (AD)
JO .... Jewish Orphanage (SAUO)
JO .... Job Order
Jo .... Joel [*Old Testament book*] (BJA)
JO .... Jogging Operation (SAUS)
Jo .... Johannes Faventinus [*Deceased circa 1187*] [*Authority cited in pre-1607 legal work*] (DSA)
JO .... Joint Organization
JO .... Joint Ownership [*Business term*]
Jo .... Jones' Irish Exchequer Reports [*A publication*] (DLA)
JO .... Jordan [*ANSI two-letter standard code*] (CNC)

jo — Jordan [*MARC country of publication code*] [*Library of Congress*] (LCCP)
Jo — Joseph (BJA)
JO — Joseph Orville [*Shelby*] [*Civil War term*]
JO — Journalist [*Navy rating*]
JO — Journal Officiel des Communautes Europeennes [*Official Journal of the European Communities*] [*A publication*] (ILCA)
JO — Judicial Officer [*Department of Agriculture*] (GFGA)
JO — Jump Order (SAUS)
JO — Junction Office [*Telecommunications*] (OA)
JO — Junior Officer
JO — Jupiter Orbiter [*NASA*]
JO — Juvenile Offenders
JO — Senior Chief Journalist (SAUS)
JO1 — Journalist, First Class [*Navy rating*]
JO2 — Journalist, Second Class [*Navy rating*]
JO3 — Journalist, Third Class [*Navy rating*]
JOA — Joint Objective Agreement (SAUS)
JOA — Joint Objective Area (NVT)
JOA — Joint Oceanographic Assembly [*Marine science*] (MSC)
JOA — Joint Operating Agency (SAUO)
JOA — Joint Operating Agreement
JOA — Joint Operations Area (COE)
JOABAW — Journal of Applied Behavior Analysis (journ.) (SAUS)
Joa Bologne — Johannes Bolognetus [*Deceased, 1575*] [*Authority cited in pre-1607 legal work*] (DSA)
JOAC — Joachim Bancorp [*NASDAQ symbol*] (TTSB)
JOAC — Joachim Bancorp, Inc. [*NASDAQ symbol*] (SAG)
JOAC — Junior Officers Advisory Council (SAUO)
Joachim — Joachim Bancorp, Inc. [*Associated Press*] (SAG)
JOAD — Journal. American Dietetic Association (journ.) (SAUS)
JOAD — Junior Olympic Archery Development
JOADEB — Journal of Adolescence (journ.) (SAUS)
JOAEEB — Journal of Applied Entomology (journ.) (SAUS)
JOAG — Juvenile Open Angle Glaucoma [*Ophthalmology*]
JO AI — Jahreshefte des Oesterreichischen Archaeologischen Instituts in Wien [*A publication*] (OCD)
Joa Imo — Johannes de Imola [*Deceased, 1436*] [*Authority cited in pre-1607 legal work*] (DSA)
JOALAS — Journal of Allergy (journ.) (SAUS)
JOAN — Journal of Applied Nutrition (journ.) (SAUS)
Joan Andr — Johannes Andreae [*Deceased, 1348*] [*Authority cited in pre-1607 legal work*] (DSA)
JOANAY — Journal of Anatomy (journ.) (SAUS)
Joan Bapt Villalob — Johannes Baptista Villalobos [*Authority cited in pre-1607 legal work*] (DSA)
Joan Bologne — Johannes Bolognetus [*Deceased, 1575*] [*Authority cited in pre-1607 legal work*] (DSA)
Joan Borcholt — Johannes Borcholten [*Deceased, 1593*] [*Authority cited in pre-1607 legal work*] (DSA)
Jo & Car — Jones and Cary's Irish Exchequer Reports [*1838-39*] [*A publication*] (DLA)
Joan de Ces — Johannes de Cesena [*Flourished, 13th century*] [*Authority cited in pre-1607 legal work*] (DSA)
Joan de Lign — Johannes de Lignano [*Deceased, 1383*] [*Authority cited in pre-1607 legal work*] (DSA)
Jo & La T — Jones and La Touche's Irish Chancery Reports [*A publication*] (DLA)
JOANDR — Journal of Andrology (journ.) (SAUS)
Joan Fan — Johannes Faventinus [*Deceased circa 1187*] [*Authority cited in pre-1607 legal work*] (DSA)
Joan Mon — Johannes Monachus [*Deceased, 1313*] [*Authority cited in pre-1607 legal work*] (DSA)
Joann — Johannes Teutonicus [*Deceased circa 1246*] [*Authority cited in pre-1607 legal work*] (DSA)
Joannes — Johannes Franciscus Pavinus [*Flourished, 1448-82*] [*Authority cited in pre-1607 legal work*] (DSA)
Joann Teut — Johannes Teutonicus [*Deceased, 1246*] [*Authority cited in pre-1607 legal work*] (DSA)
Joan Vaud — Johannes Vaudus [*Flourished, 16th century*] [*Authority cited in pre-1607 legal work*] (DSA)
JOAP — Joint Oil Analysis Program [*Military*] (NVT)
JOAP — Journal of Applied Psychology (journ.) (SAUS)
JOAP-CG — Joint Oil Analysis Program Coordinating Group (MCD)
JOAP-TSC — Joint Oil Analysis Program Technical Support Center (MCD)
JOAT — Jack Of All Trades (SAUS)
JOB — Aerojobeni SA de CV [*Mexico*] [*ICAO designator*] (FAAC)
JOB — General Employment Enterprises, Inc. [*AMEX symbol*] (SPSG)
JOB — Genl Employ Enterpr [*AMEX symbol*] (TTSB)
JOB — Jobber
Jo B — Johannes Bassianus [*Flourished, 12th century*] [*Authority cited in pre-1607 legal work*] (DSA)
JOB — Journal of Business Administration (journ.) (SAUS)
JOB — Journal of Occupational Behaviour (journ.) (SAUS)
JOB — Judicial Officers Bulletin [*A publication*]
JOB — Just One Break (EA)
JOB — Talware Networx [*Toronto Stock Exchange symbol*] [*Canada*]
JOBAPT — John the Baptist
JOBCAT — Job Catalog (HGAA)
JOBD — Jobbed (ABBR)
JOBDOC — Job Documentation (SAUS)
J Obes Weight Regul — Journal of Obesity and Weight Regulation (journ.) (SAUS)
JOBG — Jobbing (ABBR)
JOBHLDR — Jobholder (ABBR)
JOBLIB — Job Library [*Computer science*]
JOBM — Journal of Behavioral Medicine (journ.) (SAUS)
JOBMAN — Job Management (SAUS)
JOBNO — Job Number (SAUS)
Johns Hopkins Ser in Math Sci — Johns Hopkins Series in the Mathematical Sciences (journ.) (SAUS)
Johns Hopkins Univ Stud — Johns Hopkins University. Studies in Historical and Political Science (journ.) (SAUS)
Johns HU Stud — Johns Hopkins University. Studies in Historical and Political Science (journ.) (SAUS)
JOBOL — Job Organization Language (SAUS)
Job Outlk — Job Outlook for College Graduates through 1990 (journ.) (SAUS)
JOBR — Jobber (ABBR)
JOBRESA — Joint Board of Remote Sensing Activities (SAUS)
JOBS — Job Opportunities for Better Skills (SAUS)
JOBS — Job Opportunities in the Business Sector (WDAA)
JOBS — Job Oriented Basic Skills [*Program*] [*Military*]
JOBS — Job Site Trailer [*NCIC trailer make code*]
JOBS — Josephson Broadband Spectrometer (SAUS)
Job Safe & H — Job Safety and Health (journ.) (SAUS)
Jobsons Min Yearb — Jobsons Mining Yearbook (journ.) (SAUS)
J Obstet Gynaecol Br Commonw — Journal of Obstetrics and Gynaecology of the British Commonwealth (SAUO)
J Obstet Gynaecol Br Emp — Journal of Obstetrics and Gynaecology of the British Empire (journ.) (SAUS)
J Obstet Gynecol Neonatal Nurs — Journal of Obstetric, Gynecologic and Neonatal Nursing (journ.) (SAUS)
JOBTAP — Job Training Assessment Program [*Vocational guidance test*]
JOBTICS — Job and Time Control System (SAUS)
JOC — Cambria County Library System, Johnstown, PA [*OCLC symbol*] (OCLC)
JOC — Chief Journalist [*Navy rating*]
JOC — Japan Olympic Committee (SAUO)
JOC — Jewett Owners Club (EA)
JOC — Jewish Occupational Council [*Later, NAJVS*] (EA)
JOC — Job Order Contract (SAUO)
JOC — Job Order Contracting
JOC — Job Order Costing (MHDI)
JOC — Job Ordering Contract
JOC — Jocose [*or Jocular*]
JOC — Jocular (ABBR)
JOC — John Coutts Library Services [*ACCORD*] [*UTLAS symbol*]
JOC — Joint Operational Community (SAUO)
JOC — Joint Operation Center (SAUS)
JOC — Joint Operations Center
JOC — Joint Operations Committee (SAUO)
JOC — Joint Opposition Council (SAUO)
JOC — Joint Organizing Committee [*Global Atmospheric Research Program*]
JOC — Journal of Communication Management (journ.) (SAUS)
JOC — Journal of Organic Chemistry [*A publication*]
JOC — Judgments on Copyright (SAFN)
JOC — Junior Officer Council [*Army*]
JOC — Junior Optimist Clubs (EA)
JOC — New York, NY [*Location identifier*] [*FAA*] (FAAL)
JOCAR — Joint Communications Allocation Requirement (SAUO)
JOCARG — Joint Wideband Circuit Allocation and Requirement Group (SAUO)
JOCARG — Joint Wideband Circuit Allocation and Requirement Group, Thailand [*Military*] (CINC)
JOCAS — Job Order Cost Accounting System (MCD)
JOCC — Jeunesse Ouvriere Catholique Canadienne [*Young Canadian Catholic Workers*] [*Established 1930*]
JOCC — Joint Operations Command Centre (SAUO)
JOCC — Joint Operations Control Center
J OCCA — Journal of the Oil and Colour Chemists Association (journ.) (SAUS)
J OCCA — Journal Oil and Colour Chemists Association (journ.) (SAUS)
J Occ Health Safety Aust — Journal of Occupational Health and Safety in Australia [*A publication*]
J Occup Accid — Journal of Occupational Accidents (journ.) (SAUS)
J Occup Behav — Journal of Occupational Behaviour (journ.) (SAUS)
J Occup Environ Med — Journal of Occupational and Environmental Medicine (journ.) (SAUS)
J Occup Health Safety — Journal of Occupational Health and Safety-Australia and New Zealand (journ.) (SAUS)
J Occup Med — Journal of Occupational Medicine (journ.) (SAUS)
J Oceanogr — Journal of Oceanography [*A publication*] (PABS)
J Oceanogr Soc Jpn — Journal. Oceanographical Society of Japan (journ.) (SAUS)
J Oceanol Soc Kor — Journal. Oceanological Society of Korea (journ.) (SAUS)
J Ocean Technol — Journal of Ocean Technology (journ.) (SAUS)
JOCF — Joint Operations Capability File (SAUO)
JOCG — Joint Ordnance Commanders Group
Jo Ch — Johnson's New York Chancery Reports [*A publication*] (DLA)
JOCH — Journal of Community Health (journ.) (SAUS)
JOCI — Jeunesse Ouvriere Chretienne Internationale [*International Young Christian Workers - IYCW*] (EAIO)
JOCK — Jockey (ABBR)
JOCK — Jockstrap (ABBR)
JockeyC — Jockey Club, Inc. [*Associated Press*] (SAG)
JOCM — Master Chief Journalist [*Navy rating*]
JOCMA — Journal of Occupational Medicine (journ.) (SAUS)
JOCNEE — Journal of Child Neurology (journ.) (SAUS)
JOCO — Jointly-Owned Contractor-Operated Facility (MCD)
JOCOMEX — Joint Communication Exercise (SAUS)
Jo Comm Eur — Journal Officiel des Communautes Europeennes [*Official Journal of the European Communities*] [*A publication*] (ILCA)
JOCOTAS — Joint Committee on Tactical Shelters (MCD)
JOCR — Joint Observation for Cometary Research (MCD)

(NAKS) "NASA/KSC Acronym List." http://www.ksc.nasa.gov/facts/acronyms.html (accessed May 27, 1999).

(NASA) *Space Transportation System and Associated Payloads: Glossary, Acronyms, and Abbreviations.* Washington, DC: U.S. National Aeronautics and Space Administration, 1985.

(NASQ) *1999 Nasdaq-AMEX Fact Book and Company Directory.* Washington, DC: Nasdaq-MAEX Market Group, 2000.

(NATG) *Glossary of Abbreviations Used in NATO Documents.* AAP 15 (B). n.p., 1979.

(NAU) "The Nautical Institute: Acronyms & Abbreviations." http://www.nautinst.org/Acronyms.htm (accessed October 20, 1999).

(NAV) "Navoceano Acronym List." http://www.navo.hpc.mil (accessed November 12, 1993).

(NCC) *NCC The National Centre for Information Technology. Guide to Computer Aided Engineering, Manufacturing and Construction Software.* Manchester, UK: NCC Publications, National Computing Centre Ltd., 1985.

(NDBD) *The New Dickson Baseball Dictionary.* Paul Dickson. San Diego, CA: Harcourt, Brace, and Co., 1999.

(NETL) *NetLingo: The Internet Dictionary.* Erin Jansen and Vincent James. Ojai, CA: NetLingo, Inc., 2003.

(NFD) *The NSFRE Fund-Raising Dictionary.* Barbara R. Levy, Ed. New York: John Wiley & Sons, Inc., 1996.

(NFLA) "National Football League Abbreviations and Team Histories." http://maxwell.uhh.hawaii.edu/football/archive/nflAbbreviations.html (accessed 1998).

(NFPA) *Standard for Fire Safety Symbols.* NFPA170. Quincy, MA: National Fire Protection Association, 1994.

(NG) *NAVAIR Glossary of Unclassified Common-Use Abbreviated Titles and Phrases.* NAVAIRNOTE 5216 AIR-6031. n.p. July, 1969.

(NGC) *Catalogue of the National Gallery of Canada.* National Gallery of Canada. Ottawa, Canada: National Gallery of Canada, 1998.

(NHD) *The New Hacker's Dictionary.* Eric Raymond, Ed. Cambridge, MA: MIT Press, 1991.

(NITA) *Dictionary of New Information Technology Acronyms.* 2d ed. Michael Gordon, Alan Singleton, and Clarence Rickards. London, UK: Kogan Page, Ltd., 1986.

(NLC) *Symbols of Canadian Libraries.* 12th ed. National Library of Canada. Canada: Minister of Supply and Services, 1987.

(NOAA) *NOAA Directives Manual.* 66-13 Acronyms. 1977.

(NQ) *NASDAQ Company Directory.* New York: National Association of Securities Dealers, Inc., 1990.

(NRCH) *A Handbook of Acronyms and Initialisms.* Washington, DC: U.S. Nuclear Regulatory Commission. Division of Technical Information and Document Control, 1985.

(NRGU) *NORD Resource Guide.* 4th ed. New Fairfield, CT: National Organization for Rare Disorders, Inc., 2000.

(NTA) *The Boat Book's Nautical Terms and Abbreviations: The Language of Boats and Boating.* Helene Gaillet de Neergaard, Comp. and Ed. Roslyn Harbor, NY: Near Field Press, 1994.

(NTCM) *NTCs Mass Media Dictionary.* R. Terry Ellmore. Lincolnwood, IL: National Textbook Co., 1991.

(NTIO) *NTC's Dictionary of Acronyms and Abbreviations.* Steven R. Kleinedler, Comp.; Richard A. Spears, Ed. Lincolnwood, IL: NTC Publishing Group, 1996.

(NTPA) *NTPA '97: National Trade and Professional Associations of the United States.* 32d ed. John J. Russell, Ed. Washington, DC: Columbia Books, Inc., 1997.

(NUCP) *A Dictionary of Nuclear Power and Waste Management with Abbreviations and Acronyms.* Foo-Sun Lau. Letchworth, UK: Research Studies Press Ltd., 1987.

(NUJO) "Initials, Credentials, Abbreviations Found on Medical Resumes." http://www.nursesearch.net/initials.html (accessed February 1, 2000).

(NUMA) "The Numa Dictionary of Derivatives Acronyms." http://www.numa.com/ref/acronym.html (accessed February 24, 1999).

(NVT) *Naval Terminology.* NWP3. Rev ed. U.S. Department of the Navy, Office of the Chief of Naval Operations, 1980.

(OA) *Ocran's Acronyms: A Dictionary of Abbreviations and Acronyms Used in Scientific and Technical Writing.* Emanuel Benjamin Ocran. London, UK: Routledge & Kegan Paul Ltd., 1978.

(OAG) *Official Airline Guide Worldwide Edition.* Oak Brook, IL: Official Airlines Guide, Inc., 1984.

(OCD) *Oxford Classical Dictionary.* 2d ed. N. G. Hammond and H. H. Scullard, Eds. London, UK: Oxford University Press, 1970.

(OCLC) *OCLC Participating Institutions Arranged by OCLC Symbol.* Dublin, OH: OCLC, 1981.

(ODA) *The Oxford Dictionary of Abbreviations.* Fran Alexander, et al, Eds. New York: Oxford University Press, 1998.

(ODAA) *The OSI Dictionary of Acronyms & Related Abbreviations.* Wendy E. Brown and Colin Macleod Simpson, Eds. New York: McGraw-Hill, Inc, 1993.

(ODBW) *The Oxford Dictionary for the Business World.* New York: Oxford University Press, Inc., 1993.

(ODCC) *The Oxford Dictionary of the Christian Church.* F. L. Cross and E. A. Livingstone, Eds. New York: Oxford University Press, 1997.

(OHS) *Occupational Health and Safety: Terms, Definitions, and Abbreviations.* 2d ed. Robert G. Confer and Thomas R. Confer. Boca Raton, FL: Lewis Publishers, 1999.

(OICC) *Abbreviations and Acronyms.* Des Moines: Iowa State Occupational Information Coordinating Committee, 1986.

(OLDSS) *Online Database Search Services Directory.* 2d ed. Doris Morris Maxfield, Ed. Detroit, MI: Gale Research, 1988.

(OPSA) "Official Postal Service Abbreviations." http://www.usps.gov/ncsc/lookups/abbr_suffix.txt (accessed December 17, 1996).

(OSI) *OSI Standards and Acronyms.* 3rd ed. Adrian V. Stokes, Comp. UK: Stokes, 1991.

(OTD) *Official Telecommunications Dictionary.* Thomas F. P. Sullivan, Ed. Rockville, MD: Government Institutes, Inc., 1997.

(PA) "Planning Acronyms." http://www.planning.org/info/acronyms/html (accessed February 24, 1999).

(PABS) "Serials Source List for Pollution Abstracts." Internet Database Service. http://www.csa.com/htbin/sjldisp.cgi?filename=/wais/data/srcjnl/polu001 (accessed March 12, 2002).

(PACS) "Pacronyms: A List of Acronyms, Abbreviations, Initials and Common Names of Federal Political Action Committees (PACs)." *Federal Election Commission.* http://www.fec.gov/pages/pacronym.htm (accessed August 2004).

(PALA) *Stedman's Pathology & Lab Medicine Words.* 2d ed. Christa Scott, Ed. Baltimore, MD: Lippincott Williams and Wilkins, 1993.

(PAZ) *Parenting A to Z.* Irene M. Franck and David M. Brownstone. New York: HarperCollins Publishers, Inc., 1996.

(PCM) *PC Magazine.* New York: Ziff-Davis Publishing Co., 1997.

(PCTE) *The Phillips Code.* Walter P. Phillips. New York: New York Telegraph and Telephone Age, 1925.

(PD) *Political Dissent: An International Guide to Dissident, Extra-Parliamentary, Guerrilla and Illegal Political Movements.* Henry W. Degenhardt, Comp.; Alan J. Day, Ed. Harlow, Essex, UK: Longman Group, 1983.

(PDAA) *Pugh's Dictionary of Acronyms and Abbreviations: Abbreviations in Management, Technology and Information Science.* 5th ed. Eric Pugh. Chicago, IL: American Library Association, 1987.

(PGP) *Peterson's Graduate Programs in the Humanities, Arts & Social Sciences.* 31st ed. Princeton, NJ: Petersons, 1997.

(PHSD) *1998/1999 Public Human Services Directory.* Vol. 59. Washington, DC: American Public Human Services Association, 1998.

(PIAV) "Pilot's Magazine's A to Z Aviation Jargon." James Allan and Mike Jerran, Comps. http://web1.hiway.co.uk/aviation/pterms.html (accessed October 10, 2000).

(PIPO) *Pilot's Pocket Handbook.* 4th ed. n.p. Flight Time Publishing, 1999.

(POLM) *Dictionary of Military Abbreviations.* Norman Polmar, Mark Warren, and Eric Wertheim. Anapolis, MD: Naval Institute Press, 1994.

(PPE) *Political Parties of Europe.* 2 vols. Vincent E. McHale, Ed. Greenwood Historical Encyclopedia of the Worlds Political Parties. Westport, CT: Greenwood Press, 1983.

(PPW) *Political Parties of the World.* 2d ed. A Keesings Reference Publication. Alan J. Day and Henry W. Degenhardt, Comps. and Eds. Harlow, Essex, UK: Longman Group, 1980, 1984.

(PROS) *Prospector's Choice: Users Guide.* Detroit, MI: Taft Group, 1997.

(PS) *Popular Science.* New York: Times-Mirror Magazines, Inc., 2001.

(PSAP) *World Encyclopedia of Political Systems and Parties.* 3rd ed. George E. Delury and Deborah A. Kaple, Eds. New York: Facts on File, Inc., 1999.

(PSS) *Peterson's Sports Scholarships & College Athletic Programs.* 3rd ed. Ron Walker, Ed. Princeton, NJ: Petersons, 1998.

(QSUL) *Quantities, Symbols, Units, & Abbreviations in the Life Sciences.* Arnost Kotyk. Totowa, NJ: Humana Press, 1999.

(QUAC) "Dictionary of Quaternary Acronyms." http://www.ualberta.ca/abeaudoi/cap/diction/atoc.html (accessed October 12, 1999).

(QUAN) "Gateway to Investor Info Online." http://www.quantumonline.com/NSCList.htm (accessed May 29, 2003).

(RALS) *Encyclopedia of Computer Science.* 4th ed. Anthony Ralston, Edwin E. Reilly, and David

Hemmendinger, Eds. London, UK: Nature Publishing Group, 2000.

(RAWO) *Stedmans Radiology Words.* 3rd ed. Kathryn Mason, Ed. Baltimore, MD: Lippincott Williams and Wilkins, 2000.

(RCD) *Research Centers Directory,* 33rd ed. Farmington Hills, MI: Thomson Gale, 2004.

(RDA) *Army RD and A Magazine.* Alexandria, VA: Development, Engineering, and Acquisition Directorate, Army Materiel Command, 1997.

(REAL) "Abbreviations." http://www.reboc.on.ca/abbreviations.html (accessed February 24, 1999).

(RIMS) "Rimship AS Forkortelser." http://www.rimship.no/sider/liste.html (accessed September 26, 2000).

(RION) *Religion Index One: Periodicals. A Subject Index to Periodical Literature Including an Author/Editor Index and a Scripture Index.* Semiannual ed. Carolyn K. Coates, Ed. Evanston, IL: American Theological Library Association, 1999.

(ROAS) "Acronym and Abbreviation Server Results." http://www.ucc.ie/cgi-bin/acronym (accessed September 20, 1999).

(ROG) *Dictionary of Abbreviations.* Walter T. Rogers. London, UK: George Allen & Co. Ltd., 1913; reprinted by Gale Research, 1969.

(SAA) *Space-Age Acronyms, Abbreviations and Designations.* 2d ed. Reta C. Moser. New York: IFI/Plenum, 1969.

(SAFN) *South African Legal Abbreviations.* Nico M. Ferreira and Karen E. Breckon. Buffalo, NY: William S. Hein and Co., 1999.

(SAG) *Stock Abbreviation Guide.* New York: Associated Press.

(SARE) "Safety and Related Acronyms." http://www.labsafety.org/acro.htm (accessed 1999).

(SAUO) *International Encyclopedia of Abbreviations and Acronyms of Organizations.* 3rd ed. Paul Spillner and Peter Wennrich, Comps. Munich, Germany: K. G. Saur, 1990.

(SAUS) *International Encyclopedia of Abbreviations and Acronyms in Science and Technology.* Michael Peschke, Comp. Munich, Germany: K. G. Saur, 1996.

(SDI) *Report to the Congress on the Strategic Defense Initiative.* U.S. Department of Defense. Strategic Defense Initiative Organization, April 1987.

(SEAT) "Dictionary of Initials, Acronyms, and Abbreviations Used by Counselors and Social Workers." http://www.counselingseattle.com/initials.htm (accessed March 12, 2002).

(SEIS) "Seismograph Station Codes and Characteristics." *U. S. Geological Survey.* Circular 791. Barbara B. Poppe, Debbi A. Naab, and John S. Derr. Washington, DC: U.S. Department of the Interior, 1978.

(SEWL) "Space and Electronic Warfare Lexicon." http://www.sew-lexicon.com (accessed October 10, 2000).

(SG) *Standard & Poor's Stock Guide.* New York: Standard & Poor's, 2001.

(SHCU) *Short Cuts: The Dictionary of Useful Abbreviations.* Steven Kleinedler, Ed. Lincolnwood, IL: NTC Publishing Group, 1997.

(SLS) *World Guide to Scientific Associations and Learned Societies/Internationales Verzeichnis Wissenschaftlicher Verbande und Gesellschaften.* 4th ed. Barbara Verrel, Ed. New York: K. G. Saur, 1984.

(SPSG) *Security Owner's Stock Guide.* New York: Standard & Poor's Corp., 1994.

(SPST) "Space Station Acronyms." http://www.spacefllight.nasa.gov/cgi-bi (accessed 1999).

(SPVS) "SPVS: Glossary of Veterinary Clinical Abbreviations and Acronyms." http://www.spvs.org.uk/clinglos.htm (accessed October 23, 2002).

(SRA) *State and Regional Associations of the United States.* 9th ed. Tracey E. Chirico, Buck J. Downs, and John J. Russell, Eds. Washington, DC: Columbia Books, Inc., 1997.

(SSD) *Space Station Directory and Program Guide.* Melinda Gipson, Jane Glass, and Mary Linden, Eds. and Comps. Arlington, VA: Pasha Publications, Inc., 1988.

(STAH) *Abbreviations Dictionary.* 10th ed. Dean Stahl and Karen Kerchelich, Eds.; originated by Ralph DeSola. Boca Raton, FL: CRC Press, 2001.

(STED) *Stedman's Abbreviations, Acronyms and Symbols.* William R. Hensyl, Ed. Baltimore, MD: Williams & Wilkins, 1992.

(TAD) *The AIDS Dictionary.* Sarah Barbara Watstein and Karen Chandler. New York: Facts on File, Inc., 1998.

(TAG) *Transportation Acronym Guide 1996.* U.S. Department of Transportation. Washington, DC: Bureau of Transportation Statistics, 1996.

(TBD) *Thomson Bank Directory.* Skokie, IL: Thomson Financial Publishing, 1991.

(TDOB) *The Dictionary of Banking.* Charles J. Woelfel. Chicago, IL: Probus Publishing Company, 1994.

(TED) *The Equine Dictionary: An Ultimate Reference Book for the Horse Owner.* Maria Ann Belknap. North Pomfret, VT: Trafalgar Square Publishing, 1997.

(TEL) *Telephony's Dictionary.* 2d ed. Graham Langley. Chicago, IL: Telephony Publishing Corp., 1986.

(TELE) "List of Libraries Abbreviations Encountered in the Context of EU R&D." http://www2.echo.lu/libraries/en/acronym.html (accessed February 24, 1999).

(TES) *Tests: A Comprehensive Reference for Assessments in Psychology, Education, and Business.* 3rd ed. Austin, TX: PRO-ED, Inc., 1991.

(TIMI) "Texas Instruments Military Acronym List." http://www.ti.com/sc/docs/military/millprdov/acroindx.htm (accessed September 28, 2000).

(TIR) "Indian Railways FAQ: Acronyms and Abbreviations." http://www.irfca.org/faq/faq-acronym.html (accessed October 23, 2002).

(TMMY) *The Thirteenth Mental Measurements Yearbook.* James C. Impara and Barbara S. Plake, Eds. Lincoln, NE: Buros Institute of Mental Measurements of the University of Nebraska-Lincoln, 1998.

(TNIG) *Telecommunications, Networking and Internet Glossary.* George S. Machovec. Chicago, IL: American Library Association, 1993.

(TOCD) *The Official Catholic Directory 1997.* New Providence, NJ: P. J. Kennedy & Sons, 1997.

(TRID) "Travel Industry Dictionary." http://www.hometravelagency.com/dictionary/itra/html (accessed August 15, 2000).

(TSPED) *Trade Shows and Professional Exhibits Directory.* 2d ed. Robert J. Elster, Ed. Detroit, MI: Gale Research, 1987.

(TSSD) *Telecommunications Systems and Services Directory.* 4th ed. (and supplement). John Krol, Ed. Detroit, MI: Gale Research, 1989.

(TVEL) *The Travel Dictionary.* Claudine Dervaes. Tampa, FL: Solitaire Publishing, 1998.

(TVRC) "Truck, Vessel, and Rail SCAC Codes." U.S. Census Bureau. http://www.aesdirect.gov/support/tables/scar.txt (accessed March 1, 2005).

(USCA) "U.S. Census Bureau Abbreviations and Acronyms." http://www.census.gov/cgi-bin/main/alla cro.pl (accessed October 20, 1999).

(USDC) "Glossary of Acronyms." U.S. Department of Commerce. http://www.pmel.noaa.gov/pubs/acronym.html (accessed March 5, 1997).

(USGC) "U.S. Government Commonly Used Abbreviations and Acronyms." http://www.fed.gov/hptext/infohwy/gov_acro.html (accessed March 5, 1997).

(USMO) *The Military Online: A Directory for Internet Access to the Development of Defense.* William M. Arkin, Ed. Washington, DC: Brasseys, 1997.

(UWER) *Scientific and Technical Acronyms, Symbols, and Abbreviations.* Uwe Erb and Harald Keller. New York: John Wiley & Sons, Inc., 2001.

(VERA) "VERA-Virtual Entity of Relevant Acronyms." http://www/thphy.uni~duesseldorf.de/~gnu/info/VERA/vera_2.html#SEC3 (accessed December 1, 1998).

(VLIE) *Dictionary of Acronyms and Technical Abbreviations: For Information and Communication Technologies and Related Areas.* 2d ed. Jakob Vliestra. London, UK: Springer, 2001.

(VNW) *Words of the Vietnam War.* Gregory R. Clark. Jefferson, NC: McFarland and Co., Inc., 1990.

(VRA) *VRA Special Bulletin: Standard Abbreviations for Image Descriptions for Use in Fine Arts Visual Resources Collections.* No. 2. Nancy S.

Schuller, Comp. Austin, TX: Visual Resources Association, 1987.

(WA) *Whitakers Almanack 1998.* London, UK: Stationery Office, Ltd., 1997.

(WDAA) *Webster's New World Dictionary of Acronyms and Abbreviations.* Auriel Douglas and Michael Strumpf. New York: Webster's New World, 1989.

(WDMC) *Webster's New World Dictionary of Media and Communications.* Revised and updated ed. Richard Weiner. New York: Webster's New World, 1996.

(WEAT) "Weather Abbreviations." http://www.ukweather.freeserve.co.uk/abbrev.html (accessed November 16, 1999).

(WGA) *Webster's Guide to Abbreviations.* Springfield, MA: Merriam-Webster, Inc., 1985.

(WORL) *World Guide to Libraries.* 14th ed. Willemina van der Meer, Ed. Munich, Germany: Saur, 1999.

(WPI) "Selected Acronyms and Abbreviations for Wood Products, Forest Industry and Governmental Affairs." http://www.ari.net/awpi/acronyms.html (accessed March 3, 1999).

(WYGK) *HR Words You Gotta Know!* William R. Tracey. New York: AMACOM, 1994.

J
By Acronym

J.............. Action Variable [*Physics*] (BARN)
J.............. Advance Ratio [*Engineering*] (ODA)
J.............. Air Force Training Category [*Officer training program*]
J.............. Angular Momentum [*Physics*] (BARN)
J.............. Australian Journalist [*A publication*]
J.............. Business Class [*Also, C*] [*Airline fare code*]
J.............. By Which [*Telegraphy*] (PCTE)
J.............. Cable Jointing [*Section of the British Royal Navy*]
J.............. Chain [*Symbol*] [*A part of the immunoglobulin molecular structure*] (DAVI)
J.............. Clubs [*Public-performance tariff class*] [*British*]
J.............. Current Density [*Physics*] (ODA)
j.............. Dissenting Opinion Citation in Dissenting Opinion [*Used in Shepard's Citations*] [*Legal term*] (DLA)
J.............. Durham (SAUS)
J.............. Dynamic Movement of Inertia (STED)
J.............. Electric Current Density [*Symbol*] [*IUPAC*] (DEN)
J.............. Electromechanical [*JETDS nomenclature*]
J.............. Field Testing Division (SAUO)
J.............. Flux [*Symbol*] [*IUPAC*]
J.............. Flux Density [*Medicine*] (EDAA)
J.............. Institutes of Justinian [*Roman law*] [*A publication*] (DLA)
J.............. Irradiation Correction
J.............. Jack [*In card game*]
J.............. Jack [*Technical drawings*]
J.............. Jackpot Enterprises [*NYSE symbol*] (TTSB)
J.............. Jackpot Enterprises, Inc. [*NYSE symbol*] (CTT)
J.............. Jacobeian Determinant (ROG)
J.............. Jacobus de Porta Ravennate [*Deceased, 1178*] [*Authority cited in pre-1607 legal work*] (DSA)
J.............. Jaeger point (SAUS)
J.............. Jail [*Motor vehicle term used in state of Washington*] (MVRD)
J.............. Jammer (CCCA)
J.............. Jamming (ACAE)
J.............. January
J.............. Japan [*IYRU nationality code*]
J.............. Japonica (SAUO)
J.............. Jargon [*Used in correcting manuscripts, etc.*]
j.............. Jaundice [*Medicine*] (DMAA)
J.............. Jena [*German license plate city code*]
J.............. Jenkins Fine Arts Center (SAUS)
J.............. Jerusalem Talmud (BJA)
J.............. Jesus (ROG)
J.............. Jet [*Aircraft*]
J.............. Jet Fuel
J.............. Jet Route [*Followed by identification*]
J.............. Jewels Horology (BARN)
J.............. Jewish
J.............. Jewish Chaplain [*Territorial Force*] [*Military*] [*British*] (ROG)
J.............. Jewish School [*British*]
J.............. Jig [*Phonetic alphabet*] [*World War II*] (DSUE)
J.............. Job (IEEE)
J.............. Jobber [*Merchant middleman*]
J.............. Johannes Galensis [*Flourished, 13th century*] [*Authority cited in pre-1607 legal work*] (DSA)
J.............. Johnnie [*Phonetic alphabet*] [*Royal Navy*] [*World War I*] (DSUE)
J.............. Johnny [*Phonetic alphabet*] [*Pre-World War II*] (DSUE)
J.............. Johnson's New York Reports [*A publication*] (DLA)
J.............. Join
J.............. Joinable Containers [*Shipping*] (DCTA)
J.............. Joiner [*Machinery*]
J.............. Joining [*Also, JNG*] [*Genetics*]
J.............. Joining Region [*of an Immunoglobulin Chain*] [*Immunology*] (ODA)
J.............. Joint
J.............. Joint Matriculation Board [*British*]
J.............. Joist [*Technical drawings*]
J.............. Jonckheere Test [*Fisheries*]
J.............. Joshua [*Old Testament book*] [*Freemasonry*]
J.............. Joule [*Symbol*] [*SI unit of energy*] (GPO)
j.............. Jour [*Day*] [*French*]
j.............. Journal (RION)
J.............. Journal
J.............. Journalism
J.............. Judaeo-Persian
J.............. Judean or Yahwistic [*Used in biblical criticism to designate Yahwistic material*]
J.............. Judex [*Judge*] [*Latin*]
J.............. Judge
J.............. Judgment
J.............. Judiciary (journ.) (SAUS)
J.............. Juice
J.............. Juliett [*Phonetic alphabet*] [*International*] (DSUE)
J.............. July
J.............. Jump (PIPO)
J.............. Junction
J.............. Junction Devices [*JETDS nomenclature*] [*Military*] (CET)
J.............. Junction Services (SAUS)
J.............. June
J.............. Jungle
J.............. Junior
J.............. Jupiter
J.............. Jurassic [*Paleontology*] (QSUL)
J.............. Juris [*Of Law*] [*Latin*] (ADA)
J.............. Jus [*Law*] [*Latin*]
J.............. Justice [*i.e., a judge; plural is JJ*]
J.............. Justiciary Cases [*Scotland*] [*A publication*] (DLA)
J.............. Justification (WDMC)
J.............. Justinian's Institutes (SAFN)
J.............. Juta's South African Reports [*A publication*] (DLA)
J.............. Jute-Asphalted [*Nonmetallic armor*] (AAG)
J.............. Juvenile
J.............. Juvenile (Amaurotic Idiocy) [*Medicine*] (DAVI)
J.............. Kansas City [*Branch in the Federal Reserve regional banking system*] (BARN)
J.............. Lower Canada Jurist, Quebec [*1848-91*] [*A publication*] (DLA)
J.............. Magnetic Poparization [*Physics*] (BARN)
J.............. Massieu Function [*Symbol*] [*IUPAC*]
J.............. Mechanical Equivalent of Heat [*Symbol*]
J.............. Nuclear Spin Quantum Number [*Physics*] (ODA)
J.............. Polypeptide Chain in Polymeric Immunoglobulins (STED)
J.............. Radiant Intensity [*Symbol*]
J.............. Rotational Quantum Number [*Chemistry*] (ODA)
J.............. Scottish Jurist [*1829-73*] [*A publication*] (DLA)
J.............. Sound Intensity (STED)
J.............. Special Test, Temporary [*Aircraft classification letter*]
j.............. Total Angular Momentum Quantum Number of a Single Particle [*Symbol*] [*Spectroscopy*]
J.............. Total Angular Momentum Quantum Number of a System [*Symbol*] [*Spectroscopy*]
J.............. VEB Fahlberg-List [*East Germany*] [*Research code symbol*]
J.............. Work Boat [*Army ship designation*] (POLM)
J.............. Yahwist Source [*Biblical scholarship*]
j.............. Yellow [*Symbol*] (DAVI)
J .... Coupling Constant [*Physics*] (ODA)
j .... Unit Coordinate Vector (ODA)
J-1.......... Jaeger Test Type One [*Ophthalmology*]
J-1.......... Personnel Section [*of a joint military staff; also, the officer in charge of this section*]
J2.......... Djibouti [*Aircraft nationality and registration mark*] (FAAC)
J-2.......... Intelligence Section [*of a joint military staff; also, the officer in charge of this section*]
J2.......... JTwo Communications [*Associated Press*] (SAG)
J2 Com...... JTwo Communications [*Associated Press*] (SAG)
J2EE......... Java 2 Enterprise Edition (SAUS)
J2ME......... Java 2 Micro Edition (SAUS)
J2SE......... Java 2 Standard Edition (SAUS)
J3.......... Grenada [*Aircraft nationality and registration mark*] (FAAC)
J-3.......... Operations and Training Section [*of a joint military staff; also, the officer in charge of this section*]
J-4.......... fuel jet-engine fuel (SAUS)
J-4.......... Logistics Section [*of a joint military staff; also, the officer in charge of this section*]
J-4/JCS...... Medical Readiness Division, Office of the Joint Chiefs of Staff (SAUO)
J-5.......... General Administration Section [*of a joint military staff; also the officer in charge of this section*]
J5.......... Guinea-Bissau [*International civil aircraft marking*] (ODBW)
J-6.......... Command, Control and Communications Systems Directorate (SAUO)
J-6.......... Communications-Electronics Section [*of a joint military staff; also, the officer in charge of this section*]
J6.......... Director for Command, Control, Communications and Computer Systems, Joint Staff (SAUO)
J6.......... St. Lucia [*Aircraft nationality and registration mark*] (FAAC)
J7.......... Dominica [*Aircraft nationality and registration mark*] (FAAC)
J-7.......... Joint Interoperability (SAUO)

J8 .... St. Vincent and the Grenadines [*Aircraft nationality and registration mark*] (FAAC)
J-14/CA ..... Jet 14 Class Association (EA)
J17 .... Just Seventeen (journ.) (SAUS)
J31 .... British Aerospace Jetstream 31 [*Airplane code*]
J-54 .... MAC Aeromedical Evacuation System (SAUO)
JA .... Bankair [*ICAO designator*] (AD)
JA .... FRY Armed Forces (SAUO)
JA .... Jack Adapter
Ja .... Jacobus Balduini [*Deceased, 1235*] [*Authority cited in pre-1607 legal work*] (DSA)
Ja .... Jacobus de Albenga [*Flourished, 13th century*] [*Authority cited in pre-1607 legal work*] (DSA)
Ja .... Jacobus de Ravanis [*Deceased, 1296*] [*Authority cited in pre-1607 legal work*] (DSA)
ja .... Jade (VRA)
JA .... Jama'at Ahmadiyyah [*Ahmadiyya Muslim Association*] (EAIO)
Ja .... Jamaica (MILB)
JA .... Jamaica
JA .... January
ja .... Japan [*ry (Ryukyu Islands, Southern) used in records cataloged before January 1978*] [*MARC country of publication code*] [*Library of Congress*] (LCCP)
JA .... Japan Academy (SAUS)
JA .... Japan Architect (journ.) (SAUS)
JA .... Japan Association (SAUO)
JA .... Jetevator Assembly
JA .... Jewelers of America (EA)
JA .... Jewish Advocate (journ.) (SAUS)
JA .... Jewish Agency (SAUS)
JA .... Jewish Agency for Palestine (SAUO)
JA .... Jewish Art, An Illustrated History [*A publication*] (BJA)
JA .... Job Accounting (SAUS)
JA .... Job Aid
JA .... Job Analysis
JA .... Job Authorization (TIMI)
JA .... Jockey's Association [*Defunct*] (EA)
JA .... John Adams [*US president, 1735-1826*]
JA .... John Alden Financial [*NYSE symbol*] (SPSG)
J/A .... Joint Account (SHCU)
JA .... Joint Agency (SAUO)
JA .... Joint Agent
JA .... Joint Air Defense Operation Center (SAUS)
JA .... Journal Announcement [*Dialog*] [*Searchable field*] [*Information service or system*] (NITA)
JA .... Journal A Presses Academiques Europeenes (journ.) (SAUS)
JA .... Journal Article (SAUS)
JA .... Journal of Aesthetics (SAUO)
JA .... Journal of Andrology (journ.) (SAUS)
JA .... Journal of Apocrypha (journ.) (SAUS)
JA .... Judge Advocate
JA .... Judge of Appeal
JA .... Judgment Analysis [*Medicine*] (EDAA)
JA .... Judicature Act (ROG)
JA .... Judicial Authority [*British*]
JA .... Jump Address
JA .... Jump If Above [*Computer science*] (PCM)
JA .... Jump of Above (SAUS)
JA .... Junior Achievement [*Stamford, CT*] (EA)
JA .... Junior Ambassadors [*Defunct*] (EA)
JA .... Justice of Appeal [*Legal term*] (DLA)
JA .... Juvenile Arthritis (MELL)
JA .... Juvenile Atrophy [*Medicine*] (DAVI)
JA .... Juxta-Articular [*Orthopedics*] (DAVI)
JAA .... American Dental Association, Chicago, IL [*OCLC symbol*] (OCLC)
JAA .... Jamiat Adduwal Alarabia [*League of Arab States - LAS*] (EAIO)
JAA .... Japan Asia Airways
JAA .... Japan Asia Airways Co. Ltd. [*ICAO designator*] (FAAC)
JAA .... Japanese Archaeologists Association (SAUO)
JAA .... Japanese Association of Anatomists (SAUO)
JAA .... Jewish Athletic Association (SAUO)
JAA .... Joint Airways Association (SAUO)
JAA .... Joint Airworthiness Authorities (or Authority) (SAUO)
JAA .... Joint Airworthiness Authority [*Aviation*]
JAA .... Joint Aviation Authorities (BUAC)
JAA .... Journal. British Archaeological Association (journ.) (SAUS)
JAA .... Journal of Accounting Auditing and Finance (journ.) (SAUS)
JAA .... Journal of African Administration (journ.) (SAUS)
JAA .... Journal of Anthropological Archaeology (journ.) (SAUS)
JAA .... Journal of Astrophysics and Astronomy (journ.) (SAUS)
JAA .... Judge Advocates Association (EA)
JAA .... Japan Aeronautic Association (ODA)
JAAA .... Jabara Award for Airmanship [*Military decoration*]
JAAA .... Japan Amateur Athletic Association (SAUO)
JAAA .... Journal of the American Academy of Audiology (journ.) (SAUS)
JAAB .... Joint Airlift Allocations Board
JAAC .... Joint Airlift Allocations Committee
JAAC .... Journal of Aesthetics and Art Criticism [*A publication*] (BRI)
JAAC .... Journal of the Association of Analytical Chemists [*Medicine*] (EDAA)
JAACP .... Journal. American Chamber of Commerce of the Philippines (journ.) (SAUS)
JAACS .... John A. Andrew Clinical Society (EA)
JA(ACT) ..... Jobless Action (Australian Capital Territory) [*An association*]
JAAD .... Journal of the American Academy of Dermatology (SAUO)
JAAD .... Justification, Approval and Acquisition Documentation (SAUO)
JAADDB ..... Journal. American Academy of Dermatology (journ.) (SAUS)
JAAF .... Japanese Army Air Force
JAAF .... Joint Action Armed Forces
JAAF .... Joint Army-Air Force
JAAFAR ..... Joint Army-Air Force Adjustment Regulations
JAAFCTB .... Joint Army-Air Force Commercial Traffic Bulletin
JAAFPC ..... Joint Army-Air Force Procurement Circular
JAAFU .... Joint Anglo-American Foul Up [*World War II slang*] [*Bowdlerized version*]
JAAG .... Judge Advocate General Legal Service Office (ACAE)
JAAGL .... Journal of the American Association of Gynecologic Laparoscopists (SAUO)
JAAGL .... Journal of the American Association of Gynecologic Laparoscopists (journ.) (SAUS)
JAAHA .... Journal of the American Animal Hospital Association (SAUO)
JAAHBL ..... Journal. American Animal Hospital Association (journ.) (SAUS)
JAAL .... Jewish Anti-Abortion League (EA)
JAAL .... Journal of Adolescent & Adult Literacy [*A publication*] (BRI)
JAAL .... Junior Auxiliary of the American Legion (SAUO)
JAALD .... Japanese Association of Agricultural Librarians and Documentalists (SAUS)
JAAM .... Japanese Association for Acute Medicine (SAUO)
JAAMI .... Journal of the Association for the Advancement of Medical Instrumentation [*Now MIJ*] [*Medicine*] (EDAA)
JAAMI J Assoc Adv Med Instrum... JAAMI Journal. Association for the Advancement of Medical Instrumentation (journ.) (SAUS)
JAAML .... Journal. American Academy of Matrimonial Lawyers [*A publication*] (DLA)
JAAMPAC ... National Japanese American PAC [*Washington, DC*] (PACS)
JAAMRS .... Joint Air-to-Air Missile Requirement (SAUS)
JAAMRS .... Joint Air-to-Air Missile Requirement Study (MCD)
JA & FC ..... Jonrnal of Agricultural and Food Chemistry (journ.) (SAUS)
Ja Ann Int Law... Japanese Annual of International Law (journ.) (SAUS)
J AANNT .... Journal. American Association of Nephrology Nurses and Technicians (journ.) (SAUS)
JAAOC .... Joint Antiaircraft Operation Center [*NATO*] (NATG)
JAAOS .... Journal of the American Academy of Orthopaedic Surgeons (SAUO)
JAAOS .... Journal of the American Academy of Orthopaedic Surgeons (journ.) (SAUS)
JAAP .... Joint Airborne Advance Party [*Military*] (AFM)
JAAP .... Joliet Army Ammunition Plant (AABC)
JAAP .... Journal of the Amecian Academy of Psychoanalysis (journ.) (SAUS)
JAAPA .... Journal of the American Academy of Physician Assistants (SAUO)
JAAPA .... Journal of the American Academy of Physician Assistants (journ.) (SAUS)
JAAPOS ..... Journal of American Association for Pediatric Ophthalmology and Strabismus [*Database*] (GDD)
JAAR .... Job Area Acceptance Range (AAGC)
JAAR .... Journal. American Academy of Religion (journ.) (SAUS)
JAAR .... Journal of the American Academy of Religion [*A publication*] (BRI)
Jaarb Inst Biol Scheih Onden Landb Gewss... Jaarboek. Instituut voor Biologisch en Scheikundig Ondenoek van Landbouwgewassen (journ.) (SAUS)
Ja Are .... Jacobus de Arena [*Deceased, 1297*] [*Authority cited in pre-1607 legal work*] (DSA)
JAARS .... Joint After-Action Reporting System (COE)
JAARS .... Jungle Aviation & Radio Service, Inc. [*Mission plane service*]
JAART .... Joint Attack of Artillery (SAUS)
JAAR Thematic St... Journal. American Academy of Religion. Thematic Studies (journ.) (SAUS)
JAAS .... Jewish Academy of Arts and Sciences (EA)
JAAS .... Journal. Aberystwyth Agriculture Society (journ.) (SAUS)
JAAS .... Journal of Analytical Atomic Spectrometry [*Formerly, ARAAS*] [*A publication*]
JAASAJ .... Journal. Alabama Academy of Science (journ.) (SAUS)
JAASD .... Journal. American Audiology Society (journ.) (SAUS)
JAASPO ..... Joint Army-Air Force Special Project Office (ACAE)
JAAT .... Joint Air Attack Team [*Military*] (INF)
JAATT .... Joint Air Attack Team Tactics (MCD)
JA/ATT .... Joint Airborne/Air Transportability Training
JAAW .... Juvenile Arthritis Awareness Week [*Arthritis Foundation*]
JAAWSC ..... Joint Anti-Air Warfare Shore Co-ordination Network (SAUO)
JAB .... American Library Association, Booklist, Chicago, IL [*OCLC symbol*] (OCLC)
JAB .... Jackson Air Base (SAUS)
JAB .... January Assumption Budget [*Budget based on economic forecasts available as of January*]
JAB .... Japan Accreditation Board for Conformity Assessment (SAUO)
JAB .... Jet Business Airlines [*Belgium*] [*ICAO designator*] (FAAC)
JAB .... Job Analysis and Billing (SAUS)
JAB .... Join Amphibious Board (SAUS)
JAB .... Joint Activity Briefing [*Military*] (AFM)
JAB .... Joint Amphibious Board [*Military*]
JAB .... Joint Audit Board (SAUO)
JAB .... Journal of Applied Bacteriology [*Medicine*] (EDAA)
JAB .... Journal of Applied Biomechanics (journ.) (SAUS)
JAB .... Junior Advisory Board (SAUO)
JAB .... Juvenile Aid Bureau (SAUO)
JABA .... Jefferson Area Board for Aging (SAUO)
JABA .... Journal of Applied Behavior Analysis (journ.) (SAUS)
JABAA4 ..... Journal of Applied Bacteriology (journ.) (SAUS)
JABC .... Japan Audit Bureau of Circulations (SAUO)
JABCAA ..... Journal of Abnormal Child Psychology (journ.) (SAUS)
J Abdom Surg... Journal of Abdominal Surgery (journ.) (SAUS)
JABE .... John A. Blume and Associates, Engineers (SAUO)

JABES .... Journal of Agricultural, Biological, and Environmental Statistics [*Database*] (GDD)
JABES .... Just Another Break-Even Situation [*Slang*]
JABGDP ..... Journal. Adelaide Botanic Gardens (journ.) (SAUS)
Jabil .... Jabil Circuit, Inc. [*Associated Press*] (SAG)
JABM .... J and B Murphy Trucking [*Common carrier symbol*]
J Abnorm Child Psychol... Journal of Abnormal Child Psychology (journ.) (SAUS)
J Abnorm Psychol Monogr... Journal of Abnormal Psychology. Monographs (journ.) (SAUS)
J Abnorm S Psychol... Journal of Abnormal and Social Psychology (journ.) (SAUS)
JABOWA .... Janak-Botkin-Wallis [*Data processing program regarding forest growth; named for three men involved in program*]
JabP .... Journal of Abnormal Psychology (journ.) (SAUS)
JABPAF ...... Journal of Abnormal Psychology. Monographs (journ.) (SAUS)
JABPPC ..... Joint Animal By Products Parliamentary and Advisory Committee [*British*] (DBA)
JABQC .... Job Assembly Breakdown and Quality Control Section [*Social Security Administration*]
JABREG ..... Journal of Animal Breeding and Genetics (journ.) (SAUS)
JABRO .... James Broadwell [*Custom-built racing car*]
JABS .... Joint Automated Booking Station [*Communications term*] (DCT)
JABS .... Justice, Awareness & Basic Support (WDAA)
JABSBP ..... Journal of Abdominal Surgery (journ.) (SAUS)
J Abstr Br Ship... Journal of Abstracts. British Ship Research Association (journ.) (SAUS)
J Abstr Int Educ... Journal of Abstracts in International Education (journ.) (SAUS)
JABUP .... Joint Air Base Utilization Plan (MCD)
Jac .... Book of Jacob (SAUS)
JAC .... CEGEP [*College d'Enseignement General et Professionnel*] John Abbott College Library [*UTLAS symbol*]
JAC .... Eastern Jacalteco [*Language symbol*] (ETLW)
JAC .... Jackson [*Wyoming*] [*Airport symbol*] (OAG)
JAC .... Jackson Trailer [*NCIC trailer make code*]
JAC .... Jacksonville [*Florida*] [*Seismograph station code, US Geological Survey*] [*Closed*] (SEIS)
Jac .... Jacksonville Jaguars [*National Football League*] [*1995-present*] (NFLA)
JAC .... Jackson, WY [*Location identifier*] [*FAA*] (FAAL)
JAC .... Jacobean (WDAA)
Jac .... Jacob's English Chancery Reports [*1821-22*] [*A publication*] (DLA)
Jac .... Jacob's Law Dictionary [*A publication*] (DLA)
Jac .... Jacobus [*James*] [*King of England*] (DLA)
Jac .... Jacobus Balduini [*Deceased, 1235*] [*Authority cited in pre-1607 legal work*] (DSA)
JAC .... Japan Advisory Committee (SAUO)
JAC .... Japan Air Commuter Co. Ltd. [*ICAO designator*] (FAAC)
JAC .... Jet Age Conference
JAC .... Jet Aircraft Coating
JAC .... Jeunesse Anarchiste Communiste [*French student group*]
JAC .... Jewellery Advisory Centre (BUAC)
JAC .... Job Assistance Center (DOMA)
JAC .... Johnstown American Co. (MHDW)
JAC .... Joint Accrediation Committee [*Amer Hosp Assn*] [*Medicine*] (EDAA)
JAC .... Joint Action Co. [*Marine Corps*]
JAC .... Joint Advisory Airworthiness Committee (SAUS)
JAC .... Joint Advisory Committee [*Military*]
JAC .... Joint Aircraft Committee [*World War II*]
JAC .... Joint Airworthiness Committee (SAUO)
JAC .... Joint Analysis Center (SAUO)
JAC .... Joint Apprenticeship Committee
JAC .... Joint Apprenticeship Council (SAUO)
JAC .... Joint Arms Control
JAC .... Joint Automatic Control (SAUS)
JAC .... Journal of Ancient Civilizations (journ.) (SAUS)
JAC .... Journal of Antimicrobial Chemotherapy [*Database*] [*United Kingdom*] (GDD)
JAC .... Journal of Applied Chemistry [*A publication*]
JAC .... Junior American Citizens [*An association*] (EA)
JAC .... Junior Association of Commerce (BARN)
JAC .... Juvenile Advisory Council (SAUO)
JACA .... Journal of the American Chiropractic Association (SAUO)
JACA .... Journal of the American Chiropractic Association (journ.) (SAUS)
J Acad Gen Dent... Journal. Academy of General Dentistry (journ.) (SAUS)
J Acad Libr... Journal of Academic Librarianship (journ.) (SAUS)
J Acad Nat Sci Phila... Journal. Academy of Natural Sciences of Philadelhia (journ.) (SAUS)
JACADS ..... Johnston Atoll Chemical Agent Disposal System (SAUO)
JACADS ..... Johnston Atoll Chemical Agents Disposal System
Jac & W .... Jacob and Walker's English Chancery Reports [*37 English Reprint*] [*A publication*] (DLA)
Jac & Walk... Jacob and Walker's English Chancery Reports [*37 English Reprint*] [*A publication*] (DLA)
Jac & Walk... Jacob and Walkers English Chancery Reports (journ.) (SAUS)
Jac & W (Eng)... Jacob and Walker's English Chancery Reports [*37 English Reprint*] [*A publication*] (DLA)
JACAPHO ... Joint Commission on Allied Health in Ophthalmology (ADWA)
JACARI ..... Joint Action Committee Against Racial Interference (BUAC)
JACBB .... Journal of Applied Chemistry and Biotechnology (journ.) (SAUS)
JACB-E ...... Joint Acquisition Coordinating Board-Europe (AAGC)
Jacbn .... Jacobean (VRA)
Jacbsn ...... Jacobson Stores, Inc. [*Associated Press*] (SAG)
JACC .... Jackson Cartage Company [*Common carrier symbol*]
JACC .... Jayhawk Acceptance [*NASDAQ symbol*] (TTSB)
JACC .... Jayhawk Acceptance Corp. [*NASDAQ symbol*] (SAG)
JACC .... Joint Admissions Centre for Colleges (SAUO)
JACC .... Joint Airborne Command Center (SAUO)
JACC .... Joint Airborne Communications Center (MCD)
JACC .... Joint Air Command Center [*Army*] (DOMA)
JACC .... Joint Alternate Command Center [*Military*] (CINC)
JACC .... Joint Area Collection Center (SAUS)
JACC .... Joint Area Collection Centre (SAUO)
JACC .... Joint Automatic Control Conference [*IEEE*]
JACC .... Journalism Association of Community Colleges (EA)
JACC .... Journal of the American College of Cardiology [*A publication*] (ROAS)
J Acc Aud Finance... Journal of Accounting, Auditing and Finance [*A publication*] (JLIT)
JACCC .... Japanese-American Cultural and Community Center (SAUO)
JACCC .... Joint Air Control and Coordination Center [*Air Force*] (AFM)
JACC/CP .... Joint Airborne Command Center/Command Post (SAUO)
JACC/CP .... Joint Airborne Communications Center/Command Post (AFM)
JACCDI ...... Journal. American College of Cardiology (journ.) (SAUS)
J Acc Econ... Journal of Accounting and Economics [*A publication*] (JLIT)
J Accel Sci Technol... Journal of Accelerator Science and Technology (journ.) (SAUS)
JACCI .... Joint Allocation Committee Civil Intelligence [*of US and Great Britain*] [*World War II*]
J Accid Emerg Med... Journal of Accident and Emergency Medicine (journ.) (SAUS)
J Account... Journal of Accountancy [*A publication*] (BRI)
J Account Audit Finance... Journal of Accounting Auditing and Finance (journ.) (SAUS)
J Account EDP... Journal of Accounting and EDP (journ.) (SAUS)
JACCP .... Joint Airborne Communication and Command Post (IAA)
J Acc Res... Journal of Accounting Research [*A publication*] (JLIT)
JACCS .... Japanese Cloud and Climate Study (SAUO)
J Acct .... Journal of Accountancy [*A publication*] (DLA)
J Acct Res... Journal of Accounting Research (journ.) (SAUS)
J Accy .... Journal of Accountancy (journ.) (SAUS)
JACD .... Joint Architectural Control Document (SAUS)
JACD .... Journal of the American College of Dentists (SAUO)
JACDA .... Journal. American College of Dentists (journ.) (SAUS)
Jac Dict ..... Jacob's Law Dictionary [*A publication*] (DLA)
JACE .... Joint Allied Communications Element (AFM)
JACE .... Joint Alternate Command Element
JACE .... Judge Advocate Civil Law, Environmental (SAUO)
JACE .... Just Another Confused Elephant
JACEB .... JACEP Journal of the American College of Emergency Physicians (journ.) (SAUS)
JACEE .... Japanese-American Cooperative Emulsion Experiment (SAUO)
JACEP .... Journal. American College of Emergency Physicians and the University Association for Emergency Medical Services (journ.) (SAUS)
JACEPUAEMS... Journal of the American College of Emergency Physicians and the University Association for Emergency Medical Services [*Medicine*] (EDAA)
JACERS ..... Japan Research Committee of Environmental Remote Sensing (SAUO)
JACES .... Joint Advisory Committee for Engineering Services (BUAC)
Jac Fish Dig... Jacob's American Edition of Fisher's English Digest [*A publication*] (DLA)
JACFU .... Joint American-Chinese Foul Up [*World War II slang*] [*Bowdlerized version*]
JACG .... Joint Aeronautical Commanders Group (ACAE)
JACGUAR ... Johns and Call Girls United Against Repression (EA)
J A Che J... Journal. Agricultural Chemical Society of Japan (journ.) (SAUS)
Ja Christ Q... Japan Christian Quarterly (journ.) (SAUS)
JACHS .... Australian Catholic Historical Society. Journal (journ.) (SAUS)
JACIBY ...... Journal of Allergy and Clinical Immunology (journ.) (SAUS)
Jac Int .... Jacob's Introduction to the Common, Civil, and Canon Law [*A publication*] (DLA)
JACK .... Golden Bear Golf, Inc. [*NASDAQ symbol*] (SAG)
JACK .... Jackpot Enterprises Inc. (SAUO)
JACK .... Jack's Trailer Manufacturing [*NCIC trailer make code*]
JACK .... Junior American Coin Klub (EA)
JACK .... Junior Assistant Cook [*British military*] (DMA)
Jack & G Landl & Ten... Jackson and Gross' Treatise on the Law of Landlord and Tenant in Pennsylvania [*A publication*] (DLA)
Jack & G Landl & Ten... Jackson and Gross Treatise on the Law of Landlord and Tenant in Pennsylvania (journ.) (SAUS)
Jack & L .... Jackson and Lumpkin's Reports [*59-64 Georgia*] [*A publication*] (DLA)
Jack Geo Ind... Jackson's Index to the Georgia Reports [*A publication*] (DLA)
JackHwt ..... Jackson Hewitt [*Associated Press*] (SAG)
Jack Journal... Jackson Journal of Business (journ.) (SAUS)
JACKPHY ... Japanese, Arabic, Chinese, Korean, Persian, Hebrew, Yiddish [*Non-roman languages*] [*Library of Congress*]
Jack Pl ...... Jackson on Pleadings [*1933*] [*A publication*] (DLA)
Jack Pl ...... Jackson on Pleadings (journ.) (SAUS)
Jackpot ...... Jackpot Enterprises, Inc. [*Associated Press*] (SAG)
JACKPOT .... Joint Airborne Communications Center and Command Post
Jackpt .... Jackpot Enterprises [*Associated Press*] (SAG)
JACKS .... Jackson, OH [*American Association of Railroads railroad junction routing code*]
Jackson ..... Jackson's Reports [*46-58 Georgia*] [*A publication*] (DLA)
Jackson ..... Jackson's Reports [*1-29 Texas Court of Appeals*] [*A publication*] (DLA)
Jackson & Lumpkin... Jackson and Lumpkin's Reports [*59-64 Georgia*] [*A publication*] (DLA)
Jackson St U... Jackson State University (GAGS)

Jacksonville St U... Jacksonville State University (GAGS)
Jacksonville U... Jacksonville University (GAGS)
Jack Tex App... Jackson's Reports [*A publication*] (DLA)
JACL......... Jaclen Manufacturing Company [*NCIC trailer make code*]
JACL......... Japanese American Citizens League (EA)
JACLAP..... Joint Advisory Committee on Local Authority Purchasing (SAUO)
Jac Law Dict... Jacob's Law Dictionary [*A publication*] (DLA)
Jac Law Dict... Jacobs Law Dictionary (journ.) (SAUS)
Jac LD...... Jacob's Law Dictionary [*A publication*] (DLA)
Jac L Dict... Jacob's Law Dictionary [*A publication*] (DLA)
Jac Lex Mer... Jacob's Lex Mercatoria [*A publication*] (DLA)
Jac LG...... Jacob's Law Grammar [*A publication*] (DLA)
Jaclyn........ Jaclyn, Inc. [*Associated Press*] (SAG)
JACM........ Journal. Association for Computing Machinery (journ.) (SAUS)
JACM........ Journal of Alternative and Complementary Medicine (journ.) (SAUS)
JACM........ Journal of the Association for Computing Machinery [*A publication*]
JACMAS..... Joint Approach Central Meteorological Advisory Service (SAUO)
JACNE....... Joint Advisory Committee on Nutrition Education [*British*]
JACO........ Jaco Electronics [*NASDAQ symbol*] (TTSB)
JACO........ Jaco Electronics, Inc. [*NASDAQ symbol*] (NQ)
JACO........ Joint Actions Control Office (AABC)
Jacob........ Jacob's English Chancery Reports [*1821-22*] [*A publication*] (DLA)
Jacob........ Jacob's Law Dictionary [*A publication*] (DLA)
JACOB....... Junior Achievement Corporation of Business (SAUO)
Jacob Ardiz... Jacobus de Ardizone [*Flourished, 1213-50*] [*Authority cited in pre-1607 legal work*] (DSA)
Jacobs...... Jacobs Engineering Group, Inc. [*Associated Press*] (SAG)
JACODEC... Japan Agricultural Chemicals Overseas Development Commission (SAUO)
JACODK..... Journal of Altered States of Consciousness (journ.) (SAUS)
JacoEl....... Jaco Electronics, Inc. [*Associated Press*] (SAG)
JacoElec.... Jaco Electronics, Inc. [*Associated Press*] (SAG)
JACOLA..... Joint Airports Committee of Local Authorities (SAUS)
JACOPIS.... Joint Advisory Committee on Pets in Society [*British*] (DI)
JACOPIS.... Joint Advisory Committee on Poets in Society (SAUO)
JacorC....... Jacor Communications, Inc. [*Associated Press*] (SAG)
JacorCm.... Jacor Communications, Inc. [*Associated Press*] (SAG)
J Acoust Soc Am Spl... Journal. Acoustical Society of America. Supplement (journ.) (SAUS)
J Acoust Soc India... Journal. Acoustical Society of India (journ.) (SAUS)
J Acoust Soc India... Journal of the Acoustical Society of India (journ.) (SAUS)
J Acoust Soc Jpn... Journal. Acoustical Society of Japan (journ.) (SAUS)
J Acoust Soc Jpn... Journal of the Acoustical Society of Japan (journ.) (SAUS)
JACP......... Japanese American Curriculum Project (EA)
JACPA....... Journal. American Academy of Child Psychiatry (journ.) (SAUS)
J Acquir Immune Defic Syndr Hum Retrovirol... Journal of Acquired Immune Deficiency Syndromes and Human Retrovirology (journ.) (SAUS)
JACR........ Joint Advisory Committee Report (HEAS)
JACRAQ..... Journal of Apicultural Research (journ.) (SAUS)
JacrCm...... Jacor Communications, Inc. [*Associated Press*] (SAG)
JACRD....... Joint Committee for Agricultural Research and Development (BUAC)
JACS......... Jacobsen Mobile Homes [*NCIC trailer make code*]
JACS......... Japan-American Cultural Society (EAIO)
JACS......... Jet Attitude Control System (KSC)
JACS......... Jewish Alcoholics, Chemically Dependent Persons, and Significant Others
JACS......... Joint Action in Community Service (EA)
JACS......... Journal of American Chemical Society (SAUO)
JACS......... Journal of Applied Communication Series (journ.) (SAUS)
JACS......... Journal of the Acoustical Society of America (journ.) (SAUS)
JACS......... Journal of the American Ceramic Society (journ.) (SAUS)
JACS......... Journal of the American Chemical Society (journ.) (SAUS)
Jac Sea laws... Jacobsens Law of the Sea (journ.) (SAUS)
Jac Sea Laws... Jacobsen's Law of the Sea [*A publication*] (DLA)
JACSPAC.... Joint Air Communications of the Pacific
JACT......... Jack's Trailer Manufacturing of Florida [*NCIC trailer make code*]
JACT......... [*The*] Joint Association of Classical Teachers [*British*]
JACTA....... Journal. American Ceramic Society (journ.) (SAUS)
JACTA....... Journal. Australasian Commercial Teachers Association (journ.) (SAUS)
JACTRU..... Joint Air Traffic Control RADAR Unit (IAA)
JACult....... Journal of American Culture [*A publication*] (ANEX)
JACVL....... Jacksonville, FL [*American Association of Railroads railroad junction routing code*]
JACWA...... Joint Allied Command Western Approaches [*NATO*] (LAIN)
JACX......... Johnstown America [*Federal Railroad Administration identification code*]
JAD.......... Jamaican Dollar (SAUS)
JAD.......... Joint Analyses Directorate (SAUO)
JAD.......... Joint Analysis and Design (ABAC)
JAD.......... Joint Analysis Directorate (ACAE)
JAD.......... Joint Application Design [*Computer science*] (HODG)
JAD.......... Joint Application Development [*Computer science*] (CIST)
JAD.......... Joint Application Point (SAUS)
JAD.......... Joint Assembly Demonstration (SAUS)
JAD.......... Joint Resource Assessment Database
JAD.......... Julian Astronomical Day (SAUS)
JAD.......... Wheaton Public Library, Wheaton, IL [*OCLC symbol*] (OCLC)
JADA........ Japan Automobile Dealers Association (SAUO)
JADA........ Joint Agency Data Agreement (SAUO)
JADA........ Journal of American Dental Association [*A publication*] (DHP)
JADA........ Journal of the American Dental Association (journ.) (SAUS)
JADARA..... Journal for Professionals Networking for Excellence in Service Delivery with Individuals who are Deaf and Hard of Hearing (SAUO)
Jadav J Comp Lit... Jadavpur Journal of Comparative Literature (journ.) (SAUS)
JADB........ Joint Air Defense Board
JADC........ Joint Administrative Committee [*Military*]
JADC........ Joint Air Defence Centre (SAUO)
JADD........ Joint Air Defense Division (SAA)
J Addict Dis... Journal of Addictive Diseases (journ.) (SAUS)
J Addict Res Found... Journal. Addiction Research Foundation (journ.) (SAUS)
JADDIN...... Joint Air Defence Digital Information System (SAUO)
JADE......... Japan Area Defense Environment
JADE......... Japan Asian Dance Event
JADE......... Japanese Air Defence (or Defense) Environment (SAUS)
JADE......... Japanese Air Defense Environment
JADE......... Jasmine Application Development Environment (SAUS)
JADE......... Joint Allied Defense Experiment (ACAE)
JADE......... Journal Abstracts Delivered Electronically (SAUO)
JADE......... Journal of Alcohol and Drug Education (journ.) (SAUS)
JADE......... Junior Administrator Development Examination (AFM)
JADE......... LJ International [*NASDAQ symbol*]
JADE......... LJ International, Inc. [*NASDAQ symbol*] (NASQ)
J Adelaide Bot Gard... Journal. Adelaide Botanic Gardens (journ.) (SAUS)
JADF......... Japan Air Defense Force
JADF......... Joint Air Defense Force (AAG)
JADF......... Jordan Airports Duty Free
J Adhes Sci Technol... Journal of Adhesion Science and Technology (journ.) (SAUS)
J Adhes Sealant Counc... Journal. Adhesive and Sealant Council (journ.) (SAUS)
J Adhes Soc Jpn... Journal. Adhesion Society of Japan (journ.) (SAUS)
JADI......... Japan Association of Defence Industries (SAUO)
JADID7...... Journal of Affective Disorders (journ.) (SAUS)
JADIS........ Joint Air Defense Interoperability Study
JADITBHKNYC... Just a Drop in the Basket Helps Keep New York Clean [*Antilitter campaign*]
JADITBHKYCC... Just a Drop in the Basket Helps Keep Your City Clean (SAUS)
JADMAG.... Joint Aeronautics Depot Maintenance Action Group (ACAE)
JADO......... Joint Air Defense Operations [*Marine Corps*] (DOMA)
JADO......... Journal of Administration Overseas (journ.) (SAUS)
JADOC....... Joint Air Defense Operation Center
J Adolesc Health... Journal of Adolescent Health (journ.) (SAUS)
J Adolesc Health Care... Journal of Adolescent Health Care (journ.) (SAUS)
JADOR...... Joint Advertising Directors of Recruiting [*Navy*] (NVT)
JADP........ Jordanian Arab Democratic Party [*Political party*] (PSAP)
JADPDS..... Journal of Applied Developmental Psychology (journ.) (SAUS)
JADPU....... Joint Automatic Data Processing Unit
JAD/RAD.... Joint Application Design/Rapid Application Design [*Computer science*]
JADREP..... Joint Resource Assessment Damage Report (SAUO)
JADREP..... Joint Resource Assessment Data Base Report [*Military*] (AABC)
JADS........ Joint Advanced Distributed Simulation [*Military*]
JADS........ Journal Article Delivery Service [*Carnegie Mellon University*]
jadt.......... Jadeite (VRA)
J Adult Ed... Journal of Adult Fducation (journ.) (SAUS)
J Adv........ Judge Advocate [*Legal term*] (DLA)
J Adv Ed.... Journal of Advanced Education [*A publication*]
J ADV GEN. Judge Advocate General [*Military*] (WDAA)
J Adv Nurs... Journal of Advanced Nursing (journ.) (SAUS)
J Adv Z...... Journal of Advanced Zoology (journ.) (SAUS)
JADW........ Joint Air Defense Wing (SAA)
JAE.......... Illinois Agricultural Association & Affiliated Co., Bloomington, IL [*OCLC symbol*] (OCLC)
JAE.......... Jacksonville [*Illinois*] [*Airport symbol*] (AD)
JAE.......... Jaeger Machine Company (SAUO)
JAE.......... Japan Aviation Electronics Industry Ltd.
JAE.......... Java Application Environment (SAUS)
JAE.......... Joint Atomic Exercise [*NATO*] (NATG)
JAE.......... Journal of Accounting and Economics (journ.) (SAUS)
JAE.......... Journal of Advanced Education [*A publication*] (ADA)
JAE.......... Journal of Agricultural Economics [*A publication*]
JAE.......... Jump If Above or Equal [*Computer science*] (PCM)
JAEB......... Jason Express [*Common carrier symbol*]
JAEC......... Japan Atomic Energy Commission
JAEC......... Joint Atomic Energy Commission
JAEC......... Joint Atomic Energy Committee (SAUO)
JAED......... Journal of Agricultural Economics and Development (SAUO)
JAEG......... Jaegdtiger [*Tank-destroyer*] [*German military - World War II*]
Jaeger Labor Law... Jaeger's Cases and Statutes on Labor Law [*A publication*] (DLA)
Jaeger Labor Law... Jaegers Cases and Statutes on Labor Law (journ.) (SAUS)
JAEH......... Journal of Aquatic Ecosystem Health [*A publication*]
JAEIA........ Japan Atomic Energy Industrial Association (SAUO)
JAEIC........ Joint Atomic Energy Intelligence Center [*Military*]
JAEIC........ Joint Atomic Energy Intelligence Committee (KSC)
JAEIP........ Japan Atomic Energy Insurance Pool
JAEL......... JSC Avionics Engineering Laboratory (SAUO)
JAEMA...... Journal. Albert Einstein Medical Center (journ.) (SAUS)
JAENFS..... Journal of Agricultural Entomology (journ.) (SAUS)
JAERES..... Journal of Agricultural Engineering Research (journ.) (SAUS)
JAERI........ Japan Atomic Energy Research Institute [*Tokyo*]
JAERI........ Japanese Atomic Energy Research Institute (SAUS)
J Aeronaut Mater... Journal of Aeronautical Materials (journ.) (SAUS)
J Aeronaut Soc India... Journal of the Aeronautical Society of India (journ.) (SAUS)

J Aeronaut Soc S Afr... Journal. Aeronautical Society of South Africa (journ.) (SAUS)
J Aero Sci... Journal of the Aeronautical Sciences (journ.) (SAUS)
J Aerosol Sci... Journal of Aerosol Science (journ.) (SAUS)
J Aero/Space Sci... Journal of the Aero/Space Sciences (journ.) (SAUS)
J Aerosp Eng... Journal of Aerospace Engineering [*A publication*] (CABS)
J Aerosp Trans Div Am Soc Civ Eng... Journal. Aerospace Transpon Division. American Society of Civil Engineering (journ.) (SAUS)
JAERT....... Journal. Association for Education by Radio-Television (journ.) (SAUS)
JAERT....... Journal of the Association for Education by Radio-Television (SAUO)
JAERT....... Journal of the Association for Education by Radio-Television (journ.) (SAUS)
JAES......... Japan Atomic Energy Society (BUAC)
JAES......... Journal of African Earth Sciences (journ.) (SAUS)
J Aes Art Crit... Journal of Aesthetic and Art Criticism (journ.) (SAUS)
J Aes Ed.... Journal of Aesthetic Education [*A publication*] (BRI)
J Aesthetics Art Criticism... Journal of Aesthetics and Art Criticism. American Society of Aesthetics. Johns Hopkins University. Baltimore (SAUO)
JAEU......... Journal of Asia Electronics Union (SAUO)
JAEU......... Journal of Asia Electronics Union (journ.) (SAUS)
JAEW........ Japanese Airborne Early Warning
JAF.......... Corn Belt Library System, Normal, IL [*OCLC symbol*] (OCLC)
JAF.......... Jaffna [*Ceylon*] [*Airport symbol*] (AD)
JAF.......... James A. Fitzpatrick [*Nuclear power plant*] (NRCH)
JAF.......... Jamestown Area Furniture Haulers Association, Inc., Buffalo NY [*STAC*]
JAF.......... Jamestown Area Furniture Haulets Association, Inc (SAUS)
JAF.......... Japan-Australia Foundation
JAF.......... Japan Automobile Federation
JAF.......... Job Accounting Facility
JAF.......... John Augustus Foundation (EA)
JAF.......... Joint Armed Forces (SAUO)
JAF.......... Joint Attack Fighter [*Air Force*] [*Navy*] [*DoD*] (DOMA)
JAF.......... Jordanian Air Force
JAF.......... Journal of American Folklore [*A publication*] (BRI)
JAF.......... Judge Advocate of the Fleet
JAF.......... Judge-Advocate of the Fleet (SAUO)
JAFA......... Japan Auto-Focus Association (SAUO)
JAFA......... Japanese Art Festival Association (SAUO)
JAFAE....... Japan Auto-Focus Association in Europe (SAUO)
JAFB......... Johnson Air Force Base (SAUS)
JAFC......... James Allen Fan Club (EA)
JAFC......... Jammie Ann Fan Club (EA)
JAFC......... Japan Atomic Fuel Corp.
JAFC......... Japan Atomic Fuel Corporation (SAUO)
JAFC......... Japanese Atomic Fuel Corp. (SAUS)
JAFC......... John Anderson Fan Club [*Defunct*] (EA)
JAFC......... Junior Acting Field Captain [*Military*] [*British*] (ROG)
JAFE......... Joint Advanced Fighter Engine
JAFE......... Joint Advance Fighter Engine (SAUS)
JAFF......... Electronic and Chaff Jamming (IEEE)
JAFHRO..... Joint Armed Forces Housing Referral Office (MCD)
JAFNA....... Joint Air Force (SAUS)
JAFNA....... Joint Air Force NASA Facility (SAUS)
JAFNC....... Joint Air Force-Navy Committee
JAFO......... Junior Acting Field Officer [*Military*] [*British*] (ROG)
JAFP......... Jewish Agency for Palestine
JAFPUB..... Joint Armed Forces Publication
JAFPUB..... Joint Army-Air Force Publication (SAUO)
JAFRC....... Joint Anti-Fascists Refugee Committee (SAUO)
J Afr Earth Sci... Journal of African Earth Sciences (journ.) (SAUS)
J Afr Earth Sci Middle East... Journal of African Earth Sciences and the Middle East (journ.) (SAUS)
J African Economies... Journal of African Economies [*A publication*] (JLIT)
J African Finance Econ Devel... Journal of African Finance and Economic Development [*A publication*] (JLIT)
J African L... Journal of African Law [*A publication*] (DLA)
JAfrS........ Journal of the African Society (SAUO)
JAfrS........ Journal of the African Society (journ.) (SAUS)
J Afr Soc.... Journal. African Society (journ.) (SAUS)
JAFS......... Japan Asian Association and Asian Friendship Society (BUAC)
JAFS......... Journal. Audio Engineering Society (journ.) (SAUS)
JAFSA....... Japan Foundation For Shipbuilding Advancement (SAUS)
JaG.......... Book of Jarom (SAUS)
JAG.......... Indian Trails Public Library District, Wheeling, IL [*OCLC symbol*] (OCLC)
JAG.......... Jaguar [*Automobile*]
JAG.......... James Abram Garfield [*US president, 1831-1881*]
jag.......... jargonish (SAUS)
JAG.......... Jetag AB [*Switzerland*] [*ICAO designator*] (FAAC)
JAG.......... Jobs for America's Graduates [*An association*] (EA)
JAG.......... Joint Action Group (SAUO)
JAG.......... Joint Analyses Group (SAUO)
JAG.......... Journal. Alaska Geological Society (journ.) (SAUS)
JAG.......... Judge Advocate General [*Air Force, Army, Navy*]
JAG-A....... Judge Advocate General-Army (SAUO)
JAGA........ Judge Advocate General, United States Army (SAUS)
JAGA........ Military Affairs Division, Office of Judge Advocate General, United States Army (DLA)
JAGAR...... Judge Advocate General Area Representatives (SAUO)
JAGAR...... Judge Advocate General's Area Representatives
JAGB........ Jockeys' Association [*British*] (DBA)
JAGB........ Jockeys Association of Great Britain (BUAC)
JAG Bull.... Judge Advocate General Bulletin [*Air Force*] [*A publication*] (DLA)
JAGC........ Judge Advocate General's Corps
JAG CMR (AF)... Judge Advocate General Court-Martial Reports [*Air Force*] [*A publication*] (DLA)
JAG Comp CMO (Navy)... Judge Advocate General Compilation of Court-Martial Orders [*Navy*] [*A publication*] (DLA)
JAGD........ Judge Advocate General's Department [*Air Force, Army*]
JAG Dig Op... Judge Advocate General Digest of Opinions [*A publication*] (DLA)
JAGDR...... Judge Advocate General's Department Reserve
JAGET....... Judge Advocates General Network
Jagg Torts... Jaggard on Torts [*A publication*] (DLA)
JAGINST.... Office of the Judge Advocate General Instructions [*Navy*]
JAGIS........ Journalism and GIS Interest Group (SAUO)
JAGIT........ Joint Air-Ground Instruction (SAUS)
JAGIT........ Joint Air-Ground Instruction Team
JAG Journal... Judge Advocate General of the Navy. Journal (journ.) (SAUS)
JAG L Rev... Judge Advocate General. Law Review (journ.) (SAUS)
JAG L Rev... United States. Air Force Judge Advocate General. Law Review [*A publication*] (DLA)
JAG Man.... Judge Advocate General Manual (journ.) (SAUS)
JAG Man.... Judge Advocate General Manual (Navy) [*A publication*] (DLA)
JAG-N........ Judge Advocate General-Navy (SAUS)
JAGN........ Judge Advocate General of the Navy
J Ag New Zlnd... New Zealand Journal of Agriculture (SAUS)
JAGO........ Judge Advocate General's Office
JAGOS....... Joint Air-Ground Operations System [*Military*]
JAGOS....... Joint Air-Ground Operations Systems (SAUO)
JAGRA....... Journal of Agricultural Research (journ.) (SAUS)
J Agr Appl Econ... Journal of Agricultural and Applied Economics [*A publication*] (JLIT)
J Agr Econ... Journal of Agricultural Economics [*A publication*] (JLIT)
J Agr Econ Res... Journal of Agricultural Economics Research [*A publication*] (JLIT)
J Agr Eng Soc Jap... Journal. Agricultural Engineering Society of Japan (journ.) (SAUS)
J Agric...... Journal of Agriculture (journ.) (SAUS)
J Agric Chem Soc Jpn... Journal. Agricultural Chemical Society of Japan (journ.) (SAUS)
J Agric Eng... Journal of Agricultural Engineering (journ.) (SAUS)
J Agric Entomol... Journal of Agricultural Entomology (journ.) (SAUS)
J Agric Food Chem... Journal of Agriculturul and Food Chemistry (journ.) (SAUS)
J Agric For... Journal of Agriculture and Forestry (journ.) (SAUS)
J Agric Meteorol... Journal of Agricultural Meteorology [*A publication*] (PABS)
J Agric Res China... Journal of Agricultural Research of China (journ.) (SAUS)
J Agric Res Icel... Journal of Agricultural Research in Iceland (journ.) (SAUS)
J Agric Sci... Journal of Agricultural Science [*A publication*] (PABS)
J Agric Sci Finl... Journal of Agricultural Science in Finland (journ.) (SAUS)
J Agric Sci Res... Journal of Agricultural and Scientific Research (journ.) (SAUS)
J Agric Soc Jpn... Journal. Agricultural Society of Japan (journ.) (SAUS)
J Agric Soc Trin & Tobago... Journal. Agricultural Society of Trinidad and Tobago (journ.) (SAUS)
J Agric Soc Univ Coll Wales... Journal. Agricultural Society. University College of Wales (journ.) (SAUS)
J Agric Vict Dep Agric... Journal of Agriculture. Victoria Department of Agriculture (journ.) (SAUS)
J Agric W A... Journal of Agriculture of Western Australia [*A publication*] (PABS)
J Agric Water Resour Res... Journal of Agriculture and Water Resources Research (journ.) (SAUS)
J Agric W Aust... Journal of Agriculture of Western Australia [*A publication*]
J Agr Ind SA... Journal of Agricultural Industry, South Australia [*A publication*]
J Agr Ind SA... Journal of Agricultural Industry, South Australia (journ.) (SAUS)
J Agromed... Journal of Agromedicine [*A publication*] (PABS)
J Agron Crop Sci... Journal of Agronomy and Crop Science (journ.) (SAUS)
J Agr Resource Econ... Journal of Agricultural and Resource Economics [*A publication*] (JLIT)
J Agr Res Tokai-Kinki Reg... Journal of the Agricultural Research in the Tokai-Kinki Region (journ.) (SAUS)
J Agr Soc Wales... Journal. Agricultural Society. University College of Wales (journ.) (SAUS)
J Agr Tax'n & L... Journal of Agricultural Taxation and Law [*A publication*] (DLA)
J Agr Taxn & L... Journal of Agricultural Taxation and Law (journ.) (SAUS)
JAGRY....... Jaguar PLC (MHDW)
JAGS........ Joint Army-Air Force Air-Ground Study
JAGS........ Journal of the American Geriatrics Society (journ.) (SAUS)
JAGS........ Judge Advocate General's School (DLA)
JAGSA....... Journal. American Geriatrics Society (journ.) (SAUS)
JAGSAF..... Journal. American Geriatrics Society (journ.) (SAUS)
JAGT......... Judge Advocate General, United States Army (SAUS)
JAGT......... Procurement Division, Judge Advocate General, United States Army (DLA)
J Ag T and L... Journal of Agricultural Taxation and Law (journ.) (SAUS)
JAGU........ Jaguar [*NCIC car make code*]
JAGU........ Jean Abile Gal [*Intermodal shipping container symbol*] (TVRC)
Ja Guara.... Jacobus Guaraguilia [*Authority cited in pre-1607 legal work*] (DSA)
JAGUAR-V... Jamming Guarded Radio - VHF [*Very High Frequency*] (PDAA)
JAGUAR-V... Jamming Guarded Radio. VHF frequency hopping radio system (SAUS)
JAGX........ JA Garfield [*Private rail car owner code*]
JAH.......... Glencoe Public Library, Glencoe, IL [*OCLC symbol*] (OCLC)
JAH.......... John Adams House (SAUO)
JAH.......... Journal of African History [*A publication*]
JAH.......... Journal of American History [*A publication*] (BRI)
JAHCD9..... Journal of Adolescent Health Care (journ.) (SAUS)
JAHEDF..... Journal of Allied Health (journ.) (SAUS)

JAHI .... Jordan Amer Hldgs [*NASDAQ symbol*] (TTSB)
JAHI .... Jordan American Holdings, Inc. [*NASDAQ symbol*] (SAG)
JAHIW .... Jordan Amer Hldgs Wrrt [*NASDAQ symbol*] (TTSB)
JAHL .... Jahn Transfer [*Common carrier symbol*]
JAHN .... Jahn Flatbed Trailer [*NCIC trailer make code*]
Jahrb f Cl Phil Suppl ... Jahrbucher fuer Classische Philologie. Supplementband [*A publication*] (OCD)
Jahresb ..... Jahresberichte ueber die Fortschritte der Altertumswissenschaft [*1873-*] [*A publication*] (OCD)
JAHRS .... Journal. Andhra Historical Research Society (journ.) (SAUS)
JAHWGS .... Joint Ad Hoc Working Group on Shipping [*ASEAN*]
JAI .... JAI Press [*Division of Johnson Associates, Inc.*]
JAI .... Jaipur [*India*] [*Airport symbol*] (OAG)
JAI .... Jaipur [*India*] [*Geomagnetic observatory code*]
JAI .... Jami'at Al Islan [*Defunct*] (EA)
JAI .... Japan-America Institute [*Defunct*] (EA)
JAI .... Jewish Agency for Israel [*United Israel Appeal*] [*Absorbed by*] (EA)
JAI .... Job Accounting Interface
JAI .... Johnson Associates Inc. (GAAI)
Jai .... Johnson Associates Incorporated (SAUO)
Jai .... Johnson Associates, Incorporated, Greenwich, CT [*Library symbol*] [*Library of Congress*] (LCLS)
JAI .... Joint Administrative Instruction
JAI .... Joint Airdrop Inspection (SAUO)
JAI .... Joint Staff Administrative Instruction [*Military*]
JAI .... Journal of American Insurance (journ.) (SAUS)
JAI .... Journal of Anthropological Institute of Great Britain (SAUO)
JAI .... Journal of Artificial Intelligence [*A publication*]
JAI .... Journal of the Anthropological Institute (journ.) (SAUS)
JAI .... Journal of the Anthropological Institute of America (SAUO)
JAI .... Journal of the Royal Anthropological Institute (SAUO)
JAI .... Journal. Royal Archaeological Institute (journ.) (SAUS)
JAI .... Juvenile Amaurotic Idiocy [*Medicine*]
JAI .... Lake Forest Library, Lake Forest, IL [*OCLC symbol*] (OCLC)
JAI .... M/S Jet Airways Ltd. [*India*] [*FAA designator*] (FAAC)
JAIA .... Japan Automobile Importers Association
JAIA .... Journal. Archaeological Institute of America (journ.) (SAUS)
JAIA .... Journal. Australian Indonesian Association [*A publication*]
JAIA .... Journal. Australian Indonesian Association (journ.) (SAUS)
JAIA .... Journal of the Archaeological Institute of America (journ.) (SAUS)
JAIAS .... Journal. Australian Institute of Agricultural Science (journ.) (SAUS)
JAIB .... Journal of the Royal Anthropological Institute (SAUO)
JAIC .... Joint Air Intelligence Center (DOMA)
J Aic Ass China New Ser ... Journal. Agricultural Association of China. New Series (journ.) (SAUS)
JAICC .... Joint Arab-Irish Chamber of Commerce (BUAC)
J Aichi Med Univ Assoc ... Journal. Aichi Medical University Association (journ.) (SAUS)
JAICI .... Japanese Association for International Chemical Information [*Tokyo*]
JAIEA .... Joint Atomic Information Exchange Agency (SAA)
JAIEE .... Journal American Institute Electrical Engineer (SAUO)
JAIEG .... Joint Atomic Information Exchange Group [*DoD*]
JAIF .... Japan Atomic Industrial Forum
JAIH .... Journal of Ancient Indian History (journ.) (SAUS)
JAII .... Johnstown America Indus [*NASDAQ symbol*] (TTSB)
JAII .... Johnstown America Industries, Inc. [*NASDAQ symbol*] (SAG)
JAIL .... Adtec, Inc. (SAUO)
JAIL .... Japanese Annual of International Law (journ.) (SAUS)
JAIL .... Justice Against Identification Laws (SAUS)
JAIM .... Job Analysis and Interest Measurement
JAIMS .... Japan-American Institute of Management Science
JAIMS .... Jobber Automatic Inventory Management System (TIMI)
JAIN .... Japan Academic Inter-University Network
JAINAA ...... Journal. Anatomical Society of India (journ.) (SAUS)
Jaina Antiq ... Jaina Antiquary (journ.) (SAUS)
Jain J .... Jain Journal (journ.) (SAUS)
Ja Interp .... Japan Interpreter (journ.) (SAUS)
JAIO .... Joint Assessment and Initiatives Office [*Military*]
Jaipur LJ ... Jaipur Law Journal [*India*] [*A publication*] (DLA)
J Aircr .... Journal of Aircraft [*A publication*] (CABS)
J Air Pollut Contr A ... Air Pollution Control Association. Journal (journ.) (SAUS)
J Air Pollut Control Assoc ... Journal of the Air Pollution Control Association (journ.) (SAUS)
J Air Transp Div Am Soc Civ Eng ... Journal. Air Transport Division. American Society of Civil Engineers (journ.) (SAUS)
J Air Waste Manag Assoc ... Journal of the Air and Waste Management Association (SAUO)
JAIS .... Japan Aircraft Industry Society (BUAC)
JAIS .... Japan Air Intelligence System (SAUO)
JAISDS ..... Journal. All India Institute of Medical Sciences (journ.) (SAUS)
JAISPAC .... Joint Area Information System Pacific (SAUO)
JAIX .... JAIX Leasing [*Private rail car owner code*]
JAJ .... J. A. Jones Construction Services Co. (SAUO)
JAJ .... Judge Advocate Journal (journ.) (SAUS)
JAJ .... Waubonsee Community College, Sugar Grove, IL [*OCLC symbol*] (OCLC)
JAJC .... Journalism Association of Junior Colleges [*Later, JACC*]
JAJO .... January, April, July, and October [*Denotes quarterly payments of interest or dividends in these months*] [*Business term*]
Ja J Rel Stud ... Japanese Journal of Religious Studies (journ.) (SAUS)
Jak .... Jakowlew (SAUS)
JAK .... Janus Kinase [*Biochemistry*] (QSUL)
JAK .... Just Another Kinase [*Biochemistry*] (QSUL)
Jakarta ..... Jakarta Growth Fund [*Associated Press*] (SAG)
JAKE .... Jakes Pizza International [*NASDAQ symbol*] (SAG)
JAKE .... Jakes Pizza Intl [*NASDAQ symbol*] (TTSB)
jake .... Jointly Administered Knowledge Environment
JakePza ..... Jakes Pizza International [*Associated Press*] (SAG)
JAKFORCE ... Jammu and Kashmir Force [*British military*] (DMA)
JAKIS .... Japanese Keyword Indexing Simulation (or Simulator) (SAUS)
JAKIS .... Japanese Keyword Indexing Simulator
JAKIS System ... Japanese Keyword Indexing Simulation (or Simulator) System (SAUS)
JAKK .... JAKKS Pacific [*NASDAQ symbol*] (TTSB)
JAKK .... Jakks Pacific, Inc. [*NASDAQ symbol*] (SAG)
JAL .... Jalpa [*NCIC car model code*]
JAL .... Japan Air Lines
JAL .... Japan Air Lines Co. Ltd. (SAUO)
JAL .... Japan Air Lines Ltd. [*ICAO designator*] (FAAC)
JAL .... Jet Approach and Landing (SAUS)
JAL .... Jet Approach Landing Charts (FAAC)
JAL .... Jewish Apocryphal Literature [*A publication*] (BJA)
JAL .... Job Account Log (SAUS)
JAL .... Journal of Academic Librarianship [*A publication*] (BRI)
JAL .... Journal of African Law (journ.) (SAUS)
JAL .... Journal of Applied Law [*A publication*] (SAFN)
JAL .... Judge Advocate Library, Department of the Navy, Alexandria, VA [*OCLC symbol*] (OCLC)
J Ala Acad Sci ... Journal. Alabama Academy of Science (journ.) (SAUS)
J Alab Acd Sci ... Journal. Alabama Academy of Science (journ.) (SAUS)
Ja Labor B ... Japan Labor Bulletin (journ.) (SAUS)
JALAM ...... Japanese Association for Laboratory Animal Medicine (GVA)
JALAP .... Jalapae [*Jalap*] [*Pharmacology*] (ROG)
Jalate .... Jalate, Inc. [*Associated Press*] (SAG)
JALB .... Joint Administration and Logistics Board (SAUO)
JALB .... Journal. American Physical Therapy Association (journ.) (SAUS)
J Alberta Soc Pet Geol ... Journal. Alberta Society of Petroleum Geologists (journ.) (SAUS)
J Albert Einstein Med Cent ... Journal. Albert Einstein Medical Center (journ.) (SAUS)
JAlbert Einstein MedCent ... Journal of the Albert Einstein Medical Center (SAUO)
J Albert Einstein Med Cent ... Journal of the Albert Einstein Medical Center (journ.) (SAUS)
JALC .... Japan American Lumber Conference (BUAC)
JALC .... Jet Approach and Landing Chart (AFM)
JALC .... John Adams Life (EFIS)
JALC .... John Adams Life Corporation (SAUO)
JALC .... Journal of Air Law and Commerce (journ.) (SAUS)
JALCBR ..... Journal of Alcoholism (journ.) (SAUS)
J Alc Drug ... Journal of Alcohol and Drug Education (journ.) (SAUS)
J Alcohol ... Journal of Alcoholism (journ.) (SAUS)
J Alcohol & Drug Educ ... Journal of Alcohol and Drug Education (journ.) (SAUS)
JAlden .... Alden [*John*] Financial Corp. [*Associated Press*] (SAG)
J Al Dent Assoc ... Journal. Alabama Dental Association (journ.) (SAUS)
J Algebra ... Journal of Algebra (journ.) (SAUS)
J Algorithms ... Journal of Algorithms (journ.) (SAUS)
JALL .... Jalldee [*NCIC trailer make code*]
JALL .... Journal of African Languages and Linguistics (journ.) (SAUS)
J Allied Dent Soc ... Journal. Allied Dental Societies (journ.) (SAUS)
J Allied Health ... Journal of Allied Health (journ.) (SAUS)
J All India Dent Assoc ... Journal. All India Dental Association (journ.) (SAUS)
J All India Inst Med Sci ... Journal. All India Institute of Medical Sciences (journ.) (SAUS)
J All India Inst Ment Health ... Journal. All India Institute of Mental Health (journ.) (SAUS)
J All India Ophthalmol S ... Journal. All-India Ophthalmological Society (journ.) (SAUS)
J All Ind Ophth Soc ... Journal. All-India Ophthalmological Society (journ.) (SAUS)
J Alloy Phase Diagrams ... Journal of Alloy Phase Diagrams (journ.) (SAUS)
J Alloys Compd ... Journal of Alloys and Compounds [*A publication*] (CABS)
JALMA ...... Japan Leprosy Mission for Asia (BUAC)
JALP .... Japan Annual of Law and Politics (journ.) (SAUS)
JALPAS ..... Japan Airlines Passenger Autoprocessing System (SAUS)
JALPG .... Joint Automatic Language Processing Group
J ALS .... Journal. American Liszt Society (journ.) (SAUS)
JALT .... Japan Association for/of Language Teachers (SAUO)
JALT .... Journal. Association of Law Teachers [*A publication*] (DLA)
J Altered States Conscious ... Journal of Altered States of Consciousness (journ.) (SAUS)
JALTOS ...... Japan Air Lines Computerized Air Cargo Terminal System (SAUS)
JALX .... JAIX Leasing [*Private rail car owner code*]
JAM .... Jail Accounting Microcomputer System
JAM .... Jamaica [*ANSI three-letter standard code*] (CNC)
Jam .... Jamaica (SHCU)
JAM .... Jamaica Exports. Complimentary Guide to Trade and Investment Opportunities (journ.) (SAUS)
Jam .... Jamaican (DIAR)
JAM .... James [*New Testament Book*] (WDAA)
JaM .... J A Micropublishing, Inc., Eastchester, NY [*Library symbol*] [*Library of Congress*] (LCLS)
JAM .... Jamieson Scotch Dictionary [*A publication*] (ROG)
Jam .... Jamieson Scotch Dictionary (journ.) (SAUS)
JAM .... Jammed (SAUS)
JAM .... Jamming [*Military*] (NVT)
JAM .... Jet Age Malfunction (IAA)
JAM .... Job Administration Management
JAM .... Job Analysis Memorandum
JAM .... Job Assignment Memo (SAUS)

JAM.......... Job Assignment Memorandum
JAM.......... Joint Action for Mission (SAUO)
JAM.......... Joint Analysed Make-up [*Computer-controlled attachment*] (PDAA)
JAM.......... Joslyn Art Museum (SAUO)
JAM.......... Journal of American Musicology (journ.) (SAUS)
JAM.......... Journal of Applied Mechanics (journ.). (SAUS)
JAM.......... Journal of Audiological Medicine (journ.) (SAUS)
JAM.......... JUMPS [*Joint Uniform Military Pay System*] Action Memorandum (NVT)
JAM.......... Junction Adhesion Molecule
JAM.......... Just a Minute [*Computer hacker terminology*] (NHD)
JAM.......... Just a Moment (SAUS)
JAM.......... Justified Ancients of Mummus (SAUO)
JAM.......... Jyacc Application Manager (SAUO)
JAM.......... Moraine Valley Community College, Palos Hills, IL [*OCLC symbol*] (OCLC)
Jama........ Jamaica (VRA)
JAMA........ Ja-Mar Manufacturing [*NCIC trailer make code*]
JAMA........ Japan Air Materiel Area (SAUO)
JAMA........ Japan Automobile Manufacturers Association (SAUO)
JAMA........ Japan Automobile Manufacturers Association, Washington Office (EA)
JAMA........ Journal of the American Medical Association [*A publication*]
JAMA........ Moslem People's Revolutionary Movement [*Iran*] [*Political party*] (PPW)
JAMAC...... Job Analysis Memorandum Activity Chart
JAMAC...... Joint Aeronautical Materials Activity [*Military*] (AABC)
JAMAC...... Joint Aeronautical Materials Agency (SAUO)
J Am Acad Appl Nutr... Journal. American Academy of Applied Nutrititin (journ.) (SAUS)
J Am Acad Audiol... Journal of the American Academy of Audiology (SAUO)
J Am Acad Audiol... Journal of the American Academy of Audiology (journ.) (SAUS)
J Am Acad Cbild Psychiatry... Journal. American Academy of Child Psychiatry (journ.) (SAUS)
J Am Acad Child Adolesc Psychiatry... Journal. American Academy of Child and Adolescent Psychiatry (journ.) (SAUS)
J Am Acad Child Adolesc Psychiatry... Journal of the American Academy of Child and Adolescent Psychiatry (SAUO)
J Am Acad Child Adolesc Psychiatry... Journal of the American Academy of Child and Adolescent Psychiatry (journ.) (SAUS)
J Am Acad Child Psych... Journal. American Academy of Child Psychiatry (journ.) (SAUS)
J Am Acad Dermatol... Journal. American Academy of Dermatology (journ.) (SAUS)
J Am Acad Dermatol... Journal of the American Academy of Dermatology (SAUO)
J Am Acad Dermatol... Journal of the American Academy of Dermatology (journ.) (SAUS)
J Am Acad Gnathol Orthop... Journal. American Academy of Gnathologic Orthopedics (journ.) (SAUS)
J Am Acad Gold Foil Oper... Journal. American Academy of Gold Foil Operators (journ.) (SAUS)
J Am Acad Psychoanal... Journal of the American Academy of Psychoanalysis (SAUO)
J Am Acad Psychoanal... Journal of the American Academy of Psychoanalysis (journ.) (SAUS)
J Am Ac Chil... Journal. American Academy of Child Psychiatry (journ.) (SAUS)
JAMAET...... Journal. American Mosquito Control Association (journ.) (SAUS)
JAMAG...... Joint American Military Advisory Group
Jamaica..... English-speaking West Indian island nation (SAUS)
Jamaica Agr Soc J... Jamaica Agricultural Society. Journal (journ.) (SAUS)
Jamaica Archt... Jamaica Architect (journ.) (SAUS)
Jamaica Geol Survey Dept Ann Rept... Jamaica. Geological Survey Department. Annual Report (journ.) (SAUS)
Jamaica Geol Survey Dept Bull... Jamaica. Geological Survey Department. Bulletin (journ.) (SAUS)
Jamaica Geol Survey Dept Occ Pap... Jamaica. Geological Survey Department. Occasional Paper (journ.) (SAUS)
Jamaica Geol Survey Dept Short Pap... Jamaica. Geological Survey Department. Short Paper (journ.) (SAUS)
JAMAL...... Jamaican Movement for the Advancement of Literacy (BUAC)
J Am Analg Soc... Journal. American Analgesia Society (journ.) (SAUS)
J Am Anim Hosp Assoc... Journal. American Animal Hospital Association (journ.) (SAUS)
J Am Anim Hosp Assoc... Journal of the American Animal Hospital Association (SAUO)
J Am Anim Hosp Assoc... Journal of the American Animal Hospital Association (journ.) (SAUS)
JAMASS..... Japanese Medical Abstract Scanning System [*International Medical Information Center*] [*Japan*] (NITA)
J Am Ass Med Rec Libr... Journal. American Association of Medical Record Librarians (journ.) (SAUS)
J Am Assoc... Journal. American Association for Hygiene and Baths (journ.) (SAUS)
J Am Assoc Cereal Chem... Journal American Association of Cereal Chemists (journ.) (SAUS)
J Am Assoc Nephrol Nurses Tech... Journal. American Association of Nephrology Nurses and Technicians (journ.) (SAUS)
J Am Assoc Nurse Anesth... Journal. American Association of Nurse Anesthetists (journ.) (SAUS)
J Am Assoc Promot Hyg Public Baths... Journal. American Association for Promoting Hygiene and Public Baths (journ.) (SAUS)
J Am Assoc Var Star Obs... Journal of the American Association of Variable Star Observers (journ.) (SAUS)
J Am Ass Teach Educ Agric... Journal. American Association of Teacher Educators in Agriculture (journ.). (SAUS)
J Am Audiol Soc... Journal. American Audiology Society (journ.) (SAUS)
J Am Aud Soc... Journal. American Auditory Society (journ.) (SAUS)
JAMB........ Jamboree (trucks) [*NCIC truck make code*]
JAMB........ Joint Air Movements Board [*Military*]
JAMBA...... Japan-Australia Migratory Birds Agreement (SAUO)
J Am Bankers' Assn... Journal. American Bankers Association [*A publication*] (DLA)
J Am Bankers Assoc... Journal. American Bankers Association (journ.) (SAUS)
J Am Board Fam Pract... Journal of the American Board of Family Practice (SAUO)
J Am Board Fam Pract... Journal of the American Board of Family Practice (journ.) (SAUS)
JAMC........ Japan Aircraft Manufacturers Corporation (SAUO)
JAMC........ Japan Aircraft Manufacturing Corporation (SAUO)
JAMC........ Joint Amphibious Mines Countermeasures [*Military*]
Jamcaia Geol Survey Pub... Jamaica. Geological Survey Department. Publication (journ.) (SAUS)
JAMCAT..... Jammer Communications Attachment (SAUS)
J Am Ceram... Journal. American Ceramic Society (journ.) (SAUS)
J Am Ceram Soc... Journal of American Ceramic Society (journ.) (SAUS)
J Am Ceram Soc... Journal of the American Ceramic Society (SAUO)
J Am Chem Soc... Journal of American Chemical Society (MEC)
J Am Chem Soc... Journal of the American Chemical Society (SAUO)
JAMCO...... Japan Aircraft Maintenance Company Ltd. (SAUO)
JAMColl..... Journal of the American Medical College (SAUO)
J Am Coll Cardiol... Journal. American College of Cardiology (journ.) (SAUS)
J Am Coll Cardiol... Journal of the American College of Cardiology (SAUO)
J Am Coll Cardiol... Journal of the American College of Cardiology (journ.) (SAUS)
J Am Coll Dent... Journal of the American College of Dentists (SAUO)
J Am Coll Dent... Journal of the American College of Dentists (journ.) (SAUS)
J Am Coll H... Journal. American College Health Association (journ.) (SAUS)
J Am Coll Health... Journal of American College Health (journ.) (SAUS)
J Am Coll Health... Journal of the American College of Health (journ.) (SAUS)
J Am Coll Nutr... Journal. American College of Nutrition (journ.) (SAUS)
J Am Coll Nutr... Journal of the American College of Nutrition (SAUO)
J Am Coll Nutr... Journal of the American College of Nutrition (journ.) (SAUS)
J Am Coll Surg... Journal of the American College of Surgeons (SAUO)
J Am Coll Surg... Journal of the American College of Surgeons (journ.) (SAUS)
J Am Coll Toxicol... Journal. American College of Toxicology (journ.) (SAUS)
J Am Coll Toxicol... Journal of the American College of Toxicology (journ.) (SAUS)
J Am Concr Inst... Journal. American Concrete Institute (journ.) (SAUS)
Jam Cre..... Jamaican Creole (SAUS)
J Am Cult... Journal of American Culture [*A publication*] (BRI)
J Am Cult... Journal of American Culture (journ.) (SAUS)
JAMDA....... Journal of the American Medical Directors Association (SAUO)
JAMDAY...... Journal. American Medical Technologists (journ.) (SAUS)
J Am Dent Assoc... Journal of the American Dental Association (SAUO)
J Am Dent Assoc... Journal of the American Dental Association (journ.) (SAUS)
J Am Dent Assoc Dent Cosmos... Journal. American Dental Association and the Dental Cosmos (journ.) (SAUS)
J Am Dent Hyg Assoc... Journal. American Dental Hygienists Association (journ.) (SAUS)
J Am Dent Soc Anesthesiol... Journal. American Dental Society of Anesthesiology (journ.) (SAUS)
J Am Diet Assoc... Journal of the American Dietetic Association (SAUO)
JAME........ Jamesbury Corp. (SAUO)
Jam Eng.... Jamaican English (SAUS)
J Amer Ceram Soc... Journal of the American Ceramic Society (SAUO)
J Amer Chem Soc... Journal of the American Chemical Society (SAUO)
J Amer Dent Assoc... Journal of the American Dental Association (SAUO)
J Amer Diet Assoc... Journal of the American Dietetic Association (SAUO)
J Amer Geriat Soc... Journal of the American Geriatrics Society (SAUO)
J Amer Geriat Soc... Journal of the American Geriatrics Society (journ.) (SAUS)
J Amer Inst Planners... Journal of the American Institute of Planners (SAUO)
J Amer Inst Planners... Journal of the American Institute of Planners (journ.) (SAUS)
J Amer Med Assoc... Journal of the American Medical Association (journ.) (SAUS)
J Amer Oil Chem Soc... Journal of the American Oil Chemists Society (SAUO)
J Amer Osteopath Assoc... Journal of the American Osteopathic Association (SAUO)
J Amer Pharm Assoc... Journal of the American Pharmaceutical Association (SAUO)
J Amer Pharm Assoc... Journal of the American Pharmaceutical Association (journ.) (SAUS)
J Amer Podiatry Assoc... Journal of the American Podiatry Association (SAUO)
J Amer Podiatry Assoc... Journal of the American Podiatry Association (journ.) (SAUS)
J Amer S Farm Manage Rural Appraisers... Journal. American Society of Farm Managers and Rural Appraisers (journ.) (SAUS)
J Amer Soc Hort Sci... Journal of the American Society for Horticultural Science (SAUO)
J Amer Soc Safety Eng... Journal of the American Society of Safety Engineers (SAUO)
J Amer Soc Safety Eng... Journal of the American Society of Safety Engineers (journ.) (SAUS)
J Amer Soc Sugar Beet Techn... Journal of the American Society of Sugar Beet Technologists (journ.) (SAUS)
J Amer Statist Assoc... Journal of the American Statistical Association (SAUO)
J Amer Statist Assoc... Journal of the American Statistical Association (journ.) (SAUS)
J Amer Stud... Journal of American Studies (journ.) (SAUS)
J Amer Vet Med Assoc... Journal of the American Veterinary Medical Association (SAUO)
J Amer Vet Radiol Soc... Journal of the American Veterinary Radiology Society (SAUO)

JAmerWater Works Assoc... Journal of the American Water Works Association (SAUO)
J Amer Water Works Assoc... Journal of the American Water Works Association (journ.) (SAUS)
James....... James' Reports [*2 Nova Scotia*] [*A publication*] (DLA)
JAMES...... Java Architecture for Mobile Extended Service [*Computer science*]
JAMES...... Joint Automated Message Editing Software (SAUO)
James & Mont... Jameson and Montagu's English Bankruptcy Reports [*Vol. 2 of Glyn and Jameson*] [*1821-28*] [*A publication*] (DLA)
James Arthur Lect Evol Hum Brain... James Arthur Lecture on the Evolution of the Human Brain (journ.) (SAUS)
James Bk L... James Bankrupt Law (journ.) (SAUS)
James Bk L... James' Bankrupt Law PB (DLA)
James Const Con... Jameson's Constitutional Convention [*A publication*] (DLA)
James Ct Mar... James on Courts-Martial [*A publication*] (DLA)
James Fr Soc... James' Guide to Friendly Societies [*A publication*] (DLA)
James JS... James' Law of Joint Stock Companies [*A publication*] (DLA)
James JS... James Law of Joint Stock Companies (journ.) (SAUS)
James Madison U... James Madison University (GAGS)
JamesnIn... Jameson Inns, Inc. [*Associated Press*] (SAG)
James (N Sc)... James' Reports [*2 Nova Scotia*] [*A publication*] (DLA)
James Op... James' Opinions, Charges, Etc. [*A publication*] (DLA)
James Salv... James on Salvage [*1867*] [*A publication*] (DLA)
James Sel Cas... James' Select Cases [*1835-55*] [*Nova Scotia*] [*A publication*] (DLA)
James Sel Cases... James' Select Cases [*1835-55*] [*Nova Scotia*] [*A publication*] (DLA)
James Sh... James' Merchant Shipping [*1866*] [*A publication*] (DLA)
James Sprunt Hist Publ... James Sprunt Histoncal Publications (journ.) (SAUS)
James Sprunt Hist Stud... James Sprunt Historical Studies (journ.) (SAUS)
JAMEX...... Jamming Exercise [*Military*] (NVT)
J Am Folk... Journal of American Folklore. American Folklore Society. Washington (SAUO)
JAMG........ Jamming
JAMG........ Juvenile Autoimmune Myasthenia Gravis [*Medicine*] (DAVI)
Jam Geol Surv Dep Econ Geol Rep... Jamaica. Geological Survey Department. Economic Geology Report (journ.) (SAUS)
JAMGIS..... Jamaica GIS (SAUO)
J Am Health Care As... Journal. American Health Care Association (journ.) (SAUS)
J Am Helicopter Soc... Journal. American Helicopter Society (journ.) (SAUS)
J Am Helicopter Soc... Journal of the American Helicopter Society (journ.) (SAUS)
JAMHEP..... Joint Aircraft Hurricane Plan
J Am Hist... Journal of the American History (journ.) (SAUS)
Jam Hist Rev... Jamaican Historical Review (journ.) (SAUS)
Jam Hist Soc... Jamaican Historical Society Bulletin. Jamaican Historical Society. Kingston (SAUO)
Jam Hist Soc... Jamaican Historical Society Bulletin. Jamaican Historical Society. Kingston (journ.) (SAUS)
JAMI........ Japan Association for Medical Informatics (SAUO)
JAMIA....... Journal of the American Medical Informatics Association [*A publication*] (DMAA)
JAMIE....... Joint Analogue Microelectronics Initiative of Europe (SAUS)
J Am Ind Hyg Assoc... Journal. American Industrial Hygiene Association (journ.) (SAUS)
J Am Indian Ed... Journal of American Indian Education (journ.) (SAUS)
J Am Inst Archit... Journal of the American Institute of Architects. Washington (journ.) (SAUS)
J Am Inst Electr Eng... Journal. American Institute of Electrical Engineers (journ.) (SAUS)
J Am Inst Electr Eng... Journal of the American Institute of Electrical Engineers (journ.) (SAUS)
JAMINTEL... Jamaica International Telecommunications Ltd. [*Kingston*] [*Telecommunications service*]
J Am Intraocul Implant Soc... Journal. American Intraocular Implant Society (journ.) (SAUS)
JAMIP....... Journal of the Alliance of Medical Internet Professionals (SAUO)
Ja Mission B... Japan Missionary Bulletin (journ.) (SAUS)
JAMIT....... Japanese Society of Medical Imaging Technology (SAUO)
Jam J....... Jamaica Journal. Institute of Jamaica. Kingston (journ.) (SAUS)
J Am Jud Soc... Journal. American Judicature Society (journ.) (SAUS)
JamKI-L..... Institute of Jamaica, National Library of Jamaica, Kingston, Jamaica [*Library symbol*] [*Library of Congress*] (LCLS)
JamKLS..... Jamaica Library Service, Kingston, Jamaica [*Library symbol*] [*Library of Congress*] (LCLS)
JamKU...... University of the West Indies, Mona, Kingston, Jamaica [*Library symbol*] [*Library of Congress*] (LCLS)
JAML........ Journal of Arts Management, Law & Society [*A publication*] (BRI)
J Am Leather Chem Assoc... Journal of the American Leather Chemists Association (journ.) (SAUS)
Jam LJ...... Jamaica Law Journal [*A publication*] (DLA)
Jam Lt...... Jamaica Law Journal (journ.) (SAUS)
JAMLW...... Journal of Applied Metalworking (journ.) (SAUS)
JAMM....... Journal for Australian Music and Musicians (journ.) (SAUS)
JAMMAT.... Joint American Military Mission for Aid to Turkey (MUGU)
JAMMAT.... Joint Military Mission for Aid to Turkey (SAUS)
J Am Math Soc... Journal of the American Mathematical Society (journ.) (SAUS)
JAMMD..... Journal. Australian Mathematical Society. Series B. Applied Mathematics (journ.) (SAUS)
J Am Med Inform Assoc... Journal of the American Medical Informatics Association (SAUO)
J Am Med Inform Assoc... Journal of the American Medical Informatics Association (journ.) (SAUS)
J Am Med Rec Assoc... Journal. American Medical Record Association (journ.) (SAUS)
Jam Med Rev... Jamaica Medical Review (journ.) (SAUS)
J Am Med Technol... Journal. American Medical Technologists (journ.) (SAUS)
J Am Med Wom Assoc... Journal of the American Medical Womens Association (SAUO)
J Am Med Wom Assoc... Journal of the American Medical Womens Association (journ.) (SAUS)
Jam Mines Geol Div Spec Publ... Jamaica. Mines and Geology Division. Special Publication (journ.) (SAUS)
Jam Minist Agric Bull... Jamaica. Ministry of Agriculture. Bulletin (journ.) (SAUS)
Jam Minist Agric Fish Bull... Jamaica. Ministry of Agriculture and Fisheries. Bulletin (journ.) (SAUS)
Jam Minist Agric Lands Annu Rep... Jamaica. Ministry of Agriculture and Lands. Annual Report (journ.) (SAUS)
Jam Minist Agric Lands Bull... Jamaica. Ministry of Agriculture and Lands. Bulletin (journ.) (SAUS)
J Am Mosq Control Assoc... Journal. American Mosquito Control Association (journ.) (SAUS)
J Am Mosq Control Assoc... Journal of the American Mosquito Control Association (SAUO)
J Am Mosq Control Assoc... Journal of the American Mosquito Control Association (journ.) (SAUS)
J Am Mosq Control Assoc Suppl... Journal of the American Mosquito Control Association. Supplement (journ.) (SAUS)
J Am Mus In... Journal. American Musical Instrument Society (journ.) (SAUS)
J Am Optom Assoc... Journal. American Optometric Association (journ.) (SAUS)
J Am Optom Assoc... Journal of the American Optometric Association (SAUO)
J Am Optom Assoc... Journal of the American Optometric Association (journ.) (SAUS)
J Am Or Soc... Journal of the American Oriental Society (SAUO)
J Am Osteopath Assoc... Journal of the American Osteopathic Association (SAUO)
JAMOT...... Julie/Jesebel Airborne Maintenance Operator Training (SAUS)
JAMOT...... Julie/Jezebel [*Sonobuoy Systems*] Airborne Maintenance Operator Trainee [*Navy*] (MCD)
JAMP........ JINTACCS [*Joint Interoperability of Tactical Command and Control System*] Army Management Plan (MCD)
JAMP........ Joint Automated Mapping Project (SAUO)
JAMPA2..... Journal of Animal Morphology and Physiology (journ.) (SAUS)
JAMPAC..... Jamming Package [*Air Force*]
JAMPACK... Jamming Package [*Air Force*] (MCD)
J Am Paraplegia Soc... Journal of the American Paraplegia Society (journ.) (SAUS)
J Am Paraplegics Soc... Journal. American Paraplegics Society (journ.) (SAUS)
J Am Peat S... Journal. American Peat Society (journ.) (SAUS)
J Am Penut Res Educ Ass... Journal. American Peanut Research and Education Association (journ.) (SAUS)
JAMPO...... Joint Allied Military Petroleum Office [*NATO*]
J Am Podiatr Med Assoc... Journal. American Podiatric Medical Association (journ.) (SAUS)
J Am Podiatr Med Assoc... Journal of the American Podiatric Medical Association (SAUO)
J Am Podiatr Med Assoc... Journal of the American Podiatric Medical Association (journ.) (SAUS)
J Am Podiatry Assoc... Journal. American Podiatry Association (journ.) (SAUS)
JAMPRE..... Journal. American Peanut Research and Education Association (journ.) (SAUS)
JAMPRESS... Jamaican Government News Agency (BUAC)
JAMPS...... Japan Medical Programming System (SAUS)
JAMPS...... JINTACCS Automated Message Preparation System (SAUO)
J Am Psychoanal Assoc... Journal of the American Psychoanalytic Association (SAUO)
J Am Psychoanal Assoc... Journal of the American Psychoanalytic Association (journ.) (SAUS)
J Am Real Estate Urban Econ Assoc... Journal. American Real Estale and Urban Economics Association (journ.) (SAUS)
JAMREP..... Jamming Report
J Am Rocket S... Journal. American Rocket Society (journ.) (SAUS)
JAMS........ Jameson Inns [*NASDAQ symbol*] (TTSB)
JAMS........ Jameson Inns, Inc. [*NASDAQ symbol*] (SAG)
JAMS........ Jamming Analysis Measurement System
JAMS........ Japan Association for Mathematical Sciences (SAUO)
JAMS........ Job Activities Management System (SAUS)
JAMS........ Joint Agency for Municipal Securities Dealers
JAMS........ Journal. Academy of Marketing Science [*A publication*]
JAMS........ Journal. Academy of Marketing Science (journ.) (SAUS)
JAmS........ Journal of American Studies [*A publication*] (ANEX)
JAmS........ Journal of American Studies (journ.) (SAUS)
JAMS........ Journal of the American Musicological Society [*A publication*] (WDAA)
JAMS........ Judicial Arbitration and Mediation Services (SAUS)
JAMSA....... Journal. Arkansas Medical Society (journ.) (SAUS)
JAMSAT..... Japanese Satellite for Amateur Radio (SAUS)
Jamsat...... Japan radio Amateur Satellite (SAUS)
JAMSAT..... Japan Radio Amateur Satellite Corp. (BUAC)
J Am Soc Brew Chem... Journal. American Society of Brewing Chemists (journ.) (SAUS)
J Am Soc Brew Chem... Journal of the American Society of Brewing Chemists (journ.) (SAUS)
J Am Soc Echocardiogr... Journal of the American Society of Echocardiography (SAUO)
J Am Soc Echocardiogr... Journal of the American Society of Echocardiography (journ.) (SAUS)
J Am Soc Geriatr Dent... Journal. American Society for Geriatric Dentistry (journ.) (SAUS)

J Am Soc Heat Vent Eng... Journal. American Society of Heating and Ventilating Engineers (journ.) (SAUS)
J Am Soc Inf Sci... Journal of the American Society for Information Science (journ.) (SAUS)
J Am Soc Inf Sci... Journal of the American Society of Information Science (SAUO)
J Am Soc Inf Sci... Journal of the American Society of Information Science (journ.) (SAUS)
J Am Soc Mech Eng... Journal. American Society of Mechanical Engineers (journ.) (SAUS)
J Am Soc Nav Eng... Journal. American Society of Naval Engineers (journ.) (SAUS)
J Am Soc Nephrol... Journal of the American Society of Nephrology (SAUO)
J Am Soc Nephrol... Journal of the American Society of Nephrology (journ.) (SAUS)
J Am Soc Prev Dent... Journal. American Society for Preventive Dentistry (journ.) (SAUS)
J Am Soc Study Orthod... Journal. American Society for the Study of Orthodontics (journ.) (SAUS)
JAMSS ...... Japan Manned Space Systems Corporation (SAUO)
Jam St ...... Jamaica Statutes [*A publication*] (DLA)
J Am St ..... Journal of American Studies [*A publication*] (BRI)
J Am Stat Assoc... Journal of the American Statistical Association (SAUO)
JAMSTEC ... Japanese Marine Science and Technology Center (SAUS)
JAMSTEC ... Japan Marine Science and Technology Center (or Centre) (SAUS)
JAMTD ...... Journal. Canadian Association for Music Therapy (journ.) (SAUS)
JAMTO ...... Joint Airlines Military Traffic Office
JAMTRAC... Jammers Tracked by Azimuth Crossings [*RADAR*]
JAMTS ...... Japan Association of Motor Trade and Service (BUAC)
JAMU........ Locatainers [*Intermodal shipping container symbol*] (TVRC)
J Am Vener Dis Assoc... Journal. American Venereal Disease Association (journ.) (SAUS)
J Am Vet Med Assoc... Journal of the American Veterinary Medical Association (SAUO)
JAMWA...... Journal of the American Medical Women's Association [*A Publication*] (MHID)
JAMWA...... Journal of the American Medical Womens Association (journ.) (SAUS)
J Am Water Works Assoc... Journal of the American Water Works Association (journ.) (SAUS)
Jamwich .... Jam Sandwich (SAUS)
J Am Zinc Inst... Journal. American Zinc Institute (journ.) (SAUS)
JAN .... Emerald Airways Ltd. [*British*] [*FAA designator*] (FAAC)
JAN .... Jackson [*Mississippi*] [*Airport symbol*] (OAG)
JAN .... Jackson, MS [*Location identifier*] [*FAA*] (FAAL)
JAN .... Janes Aviation 748 Ltd. [*British*] [*ICAO designator*] (FAAC)
JAN .... Janina [*Greece*] [*Seismograph station code, US Geological Survey*] (SEIS)
JAN .... Janitor
JAN .... Jantar Resources Corp. [*Vancouver Stock Exchange symbol*]
Jan........... January (ASC)
JAN .... January (EY)
jan .... Janvier [*January*] [*French*] (ASC)
JAN .... Japanese Accepted Name (DMAA)
JAN .... Japanese Animation Network (EA)
JAN .... Japan. The Economic and Trade Picture (journ.) (SAUS)
JAN .... Jet Aircraft Noise
JAN .... Job Accommodation Network [*President's Committee on Employment of the Handicapped*] [*Information service or system*] (IID)
JAN .... Job Action Network (SAUS)
JAN .... Joint Army and Navy
JAN .... Judgment Analysis [*Psychology*]
JAN .... Justification for Authority to Negotiate [*Military*]
JAN .... Lincoln Christian College, Lincoln, IL [*OCLC symbol*] (OCLC)
JANA .... Jamahiriyah News Agency [*Libya*]
JANA .... Junior Achievement of Northern Alabama (EARSL)
JANAC....... Joint Army-Navy Assessment Committee [*World War II*]
JANAC....... Journal of the Association of Nurses in AIDS Care (journ.) (SAUS)
JANAF....... Joint Army-Navy-Air Force
JANAFPAC... Joint Army-Navy-Air Force, Pacific General Message [*Serially numbered*] (CINC)
JANAF Panel... Joint Army-Navy-Air Force Panel (SAUO)
JANAIA...... Joint Army-Navy Aircraft Instrument Action (MCD)
JANAIC ...... Joint Army-Navy Air Intentions-of-the-Enemy Council (SAUO)
JANAIR...... Joint Army-Navy Aircraft Instrumentation (ACAE)
JANAIR...... Joint Army-Navy Aircraft Instrument Research
J Anal Appl Pyrolysis... Journal of Analytical and Applied Pyrolysis (journ.) (SAUS)
J Anal Chem USSR... Journal of the Analytical Chemistry of the USSR (journ.) (SAUS)
JANALP ..... Joint Army-Navy-Air Force Logistics Policy
JANALP ..... Joint Army-Navy-Air Force Logistics Publication
J Anal Toxicol... Journal of Analytical Toxicology [*A publication*] (PABS)
J Anal Toxicol... Journal of Analytical Toxicology (journ.) (SAUS)
Jan Angl .... Jani Anglorum Facies Nova [*1680*] [*A publication*] (DLA)
JANAP....... Joint Army-Navy Acceptance Procedures (SAUS)
JANAP....... Joint Army-Navy-Air Force Procedure [*NATO*] (NATG)
JANAP....... Joint Army, Navy, Air Force Publication (SAUO)
JANAP....... Joint Army-Navy-Air Force Publication
JANAP....... United States Joint Services Side Word GPO Index (SAUS)
JANARS ..... Joint Army-Navy-Air Force Radiotelephone System (IAA)
JANAST ..... Joint Army-Navy-Air Force Sea Transport (SAUO)
JANAST ..... Joint Army-Navy-Air Force Sea Transportation Message
JANAST Message... Joint Army-Navy-Air-Force Sea Transportation Message (SAUS)
J Anat .... Journal of Anatomy (SAUO)
J Anat .... Journal of Anatomy (journ.) (SAUS)
J Anat Phys... Journal of Anatomy and Physiology (journ.) (SAUS)
JanBell...... Jan Bell Marketing, Inc. [*Associated Press*] (SAG)
JANBEMI.... Jan Bell Marketing, Inc. (SAUO)
JANBMC .... Joint Army-Navy Ballistic Missile Committee
JANC .... Junior Army and Navy Club [*British*] (DSUE)
J Anc Ind Hist... Journal of Ancient Indian History (journ.) (SAUS)
JANCOM .... Joint Army-Navy Communications
JANCPEC.... Japan National Committee for Pacific Economic Cooperation
JANCWR .... Joint Army and Navy Committee on Welfare and Recreation
J&A.......... Justification and Analysis (SAUS)
J & A........ Justification and Approval [*Army*]
J & B........ Justerini and Brooks [*Scotch*]
J & C........ Jones and Cary's Irish Exchequer Reports [*1838-39*] [*A publication*] (DLA)
J & D........ June and December [*Denotes semiannual payments of interest or dividends in these months*] [*Business term*]
J & E........ Jehovistic and Elohistic [*Theology*]
J&F.......... Job & Function (SAUS)
J & F........ Job and Function [*Air Force*] (AAG)
J & H........ Johnson and Hemming's English Vice-Chancellors' Reports [*A publication*] (DLA)
J & H Hind L... Johnson and Houghton's Institutes of Hindoo Law [*A publication*] (DLA)
J Andhra Hist Res Soc... Journal. Andhra Historical Research Society (journ.) (SAUS)
J & J... January and July [*Denotes semiannual payments of interest or dividends in these months*] [*Business term*]
J & J........ Johnson and Johnson [*Commercial firm*] (DAVI)
J & J Sn.... J & J Snack Foods Corp. [*Associated Press*] (SAG)
J & K........ All India Reporter, Jammu and Kashmir [*A publication*] (DLA)
J&K.......... Jammu and Kashmir (SAUO)
J&K.......... University of Jamu and Kashmir (SAUO)
J & L........ Jones and La Touche's Irish Chancery Reports [*A publication*] (DLA)
J & La T.... Jones and La Touche's Irish Chancery Reports [*A publication*] (DLA)
J & L SpSt... J & L Specialty Steel [*Associated Press*] (SAG)
J & P........ Joannou & Paraskevaides [*Construction company*] [*British*]
J & P........ Joists and Planks [*Technical drawings*]
J & P........ Journal and Proceedings [*Australia*] [*A publication*]
J & P........ Justice and Peace [*An association*] [*Scotland*] (EAIO)
J & Proc Aust Chem Inst... Journal and Proceedings. Australian Chemical Institute. [*A publication*]
J & Proc Aust Chem Inst... Journal and Proceedings. Australian Chemical Institute. (journ.) (SAUS)
J & Proc Roy Soc WA... Journal and Proceedings. Royal Society of Western Australia [*A publication*]
J Androl..... Journal of Andrology (journ.) (SAUS)
J & S........ Jebb and Symes' Irish Queen's Bench Reports [*A publication*] (DLA)
J & S........ Jones and Spencer's Superior Court Reports [*33-61 New York*] [*A publication*] (DLA)
J & S........ Judah and Swan's Jamaica Reports [*1839*] [*A publication*] (DLA)
J & S Jam... Judah and Swan's Jamaica Reports [*1839*] [*A publication*] (DLA)
J & V........ Jones and Varick's Laws of New York [*A publication*] (DLA)
J&V.......... Jones and Varicks Laws of New York (journ.) (SAUS)
J & W........ Jacob and Walker's English Chancery Reports [*A publication*] (DLA)
J&W.......... Jacob and Walkers English Chancery Reports (journ.) (SAUS)
J & WO ..... Jettison and Washing Overboard
JANE......... Joint Air Force-Navy Experiment (MUGU)
JANE......... Journalists Against Nuclear Extermination [*British*] (DI)
JANER....... Journal of Ancient Near Eastern Religions [*A publication*] (ABAR)
JANES....... Journal. Ancient Near Eastern Society. Columbia University (journ.) (SAUS)
J Anesth .... Journal of Anesthesia (journ.) (SAUS)
JANET....... Computing Joint Academic Network (SAUS)
JANET....... Joint Academic Network [*Proposed supercomputer network*]
JANET....... Joint Army-Navy Experimental and Testing Board
JANET....... Joint Army-Navy Expetimental and Testing Board (SAUS)
JANET....... Just Another Network [*University of Waterloo*] [*Canada*]
Janex........ Janex International, Inc. [*Associated Press*] (SAG)
JANF......... Joint Army-Navy Facility (SAUO)
Jan-Feb ..... January and February (SAUS)
JANFU....... Joint Army-Navy Foul Up [*Military slang*] [*Bowdlerized version*]
J Anglo-Mongol Soc... Journal. Anglo-Mongolian Society (journ.) (SAUS)
JANGO ...... Junior Army-Navy Guild Organization [*Organization of teenage daughters of military officers, who helped out in war work*] [*World War II*]
JAN grid .... Joint Army-Navy Grid
JANGRID.... Joint Army-Navy Grid System [*NATO*]
JANIC........ Japanese NGO Center for International Cooperation (SAUO)
JANIC........ Joint Army-Navy Information Center
J Anim Breed Genet... Journal of Animal Breeding and Genetics (journ.) (SAUS)
J Anim Physiol Anim Nutr... Journal of Animal Physiology and Animal Nutrition (journ.) (SAUS)
J Anim Prod Res... Journal of Animal Production Research (journ.) (SAUS)
JANIS........ Joint ANZECC/MCFFA NFPS Implementation Sub-Committee (SAUO)
JANIS........ Joint Army-Navy Intelligence Studies
JANIS........ Joint Army-Navy Intelligence Surveys (SAUS)
JANMA ...... Japanese Nuclear Medicine (journ.) (SAUS)
JANMAT..... Joint Army-Navy Machine Tools Committee (AAG)
JANMAT..... Joint Army-Navy Material
JANMB ...... Joint Army and Navy Munitions Board [*Terminated, 1947*]
JANN .... Jannock, Ltd. [*NASDAQ symbol*] (NASQ)

JANNAF..... Joint-Army-Navy-NASA-Air Force Interagency Propulsion Committee (MCD)
JANNAF-IPC... Joint Army-Navy-NASA-Air Force Interagency Propulsion Committee (SAUO)
J Annamalai Univ... Journal. Annamalai University (journ.) (SAUS)
J Annamalai Univ... Journal of the Annamalai University (SAUO)
J Annamalai Univ Part B... Journal. Annamalai University. Part B (journ.) (SAUS)
J Annamalai Univ Part B... Journal of the Annamalai University, Part B (journ.) (SAUS)
JANNF....... Jannock Ltd. [*NASDAQ symbol*] (SAG)
Jannock..... Jannock Ltd. [*Associated Press*] (SAG)
JANNVSA... Joint Army-Navy War Shipping Administration (SAUS)
JANOT....... Joint Army-Navy Ocean Terminal
JANP........ Joint Army-Navy Procedure
JANP........ Joint Army-Navy Publication
JANPA7..... Journal of Analytical Psychology (journ.) (SAUS)
JANPPA..... Joint Army-Navy Petroleum Purchase Agency
JANS........ Jet Aircraft Noise Survey
JANS........ Joint Army-Navy Specification (IAA)
JANSA....... Janatorial Supplies Association (BUAC)
Jans Def Wkly... Janes Defence Weekly (journ.) (SAUS)
JANSE....... Jansen, CO [*American Association of Railroads railroad junction routing code*]
JANSPEC.... Joint Army-Navy Specification
JANSRP..... Jet Aircraft Noise Survey Research Program
JANSTD..... Joint Army-Navy Standard [*NATO*] (NATG)
JANSX....... Janus Fund [*Mutual fund ticker symbol*] (SG)
JANT......... Jantz Manufacturing [*NCIC trailer make code*]
JANTA....... Journal of the Australian Natural Therapists Association [*A publication*]
JANTAB..... Joint Army and Navy Technical Aeronautical Board
JANTB....... Joint Army-Navy Technical Board (SAUO)
JAnthArch... Journal of Anthropological Archaeology [*A publication*] (ABAR)
JAnthrl...... Journal. Royal Anthropological Institute of Great Britain and Ireland (journ.) (SAUS)
J Anthrol Soc Oxford... Journal. Anthropological Society of Oxford (journ.) (SAUS)
J Anthropol Archaeol... Journal of Anthropological Archaeology (journ.) (SAUS)
J Anthrop Soc Bomby... Journal. Anthropological Society of Bombay (journ.) (SAUS)
J Antibiot... Journal of Antibiotics (journ.) (SAUS)
J Antimicrob Chemother... Journal of Antimicrobial Chemotherapy (journ.) (SAUS)
J Ant Ire.... Journal. Royal Society of Antiquaries of Ireland (journ.) (SAUS)
JANTRL..... Janitorial
JANTX....... Joint Army-Navy Tested Extra
JANU........ Jumbo Navigation [*Intermodal shipping container symbol*] (TVRC)
JANUS....... Force Model (SAUS)
JANUS....... Joint Academic Network Using Satellite for European Distance Education and Training (SAUO)
JANUS....... Joint Analog Numeric Understanding System
JANUS....... Joint Army-Navy Uniform Simulation (SAUS)
JANV........ Janvier [*January*] [*French*]
JANVL....... Janesville, WI [*American Association of Railroads railroad junction routing code*]
JANWSA.... Joint Army-Navy War Shipping Administration
JANX........ JAN [*Private rail car owner code*]
JANX........ Janex International, Inc. [*NASDAQ symbol*] (SAG)
JANX........ Janex Intl. [*NASDAQ symbol*] (TTSB)
JANXW...... Janex Intl. Wrrt [*NASDAQ symbol*] (TTSB)
JANY........ January (ROG)
JAO.......... Joint Area of Operations (DOMA)
JAO.......... Prospect Heights Public Library District, Prospect Heights, IL [*OCLC symbol*] (OCLC)
JAO.......... Yanyuwa [*Language symbol*] (ETLW)
JAOA........ Journal of the American Osteopathic Association (SAUO)
JAOA........ Journal of the American Osteopathic Association (journ.) (SAUS)
JAOAC....... Journal. Association of Official Analytical Chemists (journ.) (SAUS)
JAOAC....... Journal of the Association of Official Agricultural Chemists (SAUO)
J AOAC Int... Journal of AOAC International (SAUS)
JAOC........ Joint Air Operations Center [*Air Force*]
JAOCS....... Journal. American Oil Chemists Society (journ.) (SAUS)
JAOLX....... Janus Olympus
JAOS........ Journal. American Oriental Society (journ.) (SAUS)
JAOS........ Journal of American Oriental Society (journ.) (SAUS)
JAOS........ Journal of the American Oriental Society (journ.) (SAUS)
J Aoyama Gakuin Womans Jr Coll... Journal. Aoyama Gakuin Womans Junior College (journ.) (SAUS)
JAp.......... Against Apion [*Josephus*] (BJA)
JAP.......... G. D. Searle & Co., Inc., Skokie, IL [*OCLC symbol*] (OCLC)
JAP.......... Jamaica American Party [*Political party*] (BUAC)
JAP.......... Japan (KSC)
Jap.......... Japan (NTIO)
Jap.......... Japanese (ODBW)
JAP.......... Japanese (ROG)
jap.......... Japanned [*Finished with a hard, glossy varnish*] (BARN)
JAP.......... Japan Photo [*Norway*] [*FAA designator*] (FAAC)
JAP.......... J. A. Prestwick [*British auto and motorcycle engine maker*]
JAP.......... Jerusalem Academic Press (BJA)
JAP.......... Jewish Agency for Palestine
JAP.......... Jewish-American Princess [*Slang*]
JAP.......... Joint Acceptance Plan (AAG)
JAP.......... Joint Apprenticeship Program [*Department of Labor*]
JAP.......... Journal of American Photography (journ.) (SAUS)
JAP.......... Journal of Applied Physics (journ.) (SAUS)
JAP.......... Journal of Applied Physiology (SAUO)
JAP.......... Judicial Appointments Project (EA)
JAP.......... Juntas de Accao Patriotica [*Patriotic Action Boards*] [*Portuguese*] [*Political party*] (PPE)
JAP.......... Jupiter Atmospheric Probe
JAP.......... Juventudes de Accion Popular [*Spanish*] (PPE)
JAP.......... O. D. Searle & Co., Inc. (SAUO)
JAP.......... Prestwich and Co. (SAUO)
JAPA......... Jane Addams Peace Association (EA)
JAPA......... Japan Aircraft Pilots Association (BUAC)
JAPA......... Japan Area
JAPA......... Journal. American Planning Association (journ.) (SAUS)
JAPA......... Journal of the American Pharmaceutical Association (SAUO)
JAPA......... Journal of the American Psychoanalytic Association (journ.) (SAUS)
JAPAC....... Japan Atomic Power Company (SAUO)
JAPAC....... Jewelers of America PAC [*New York, NY*] (PACS)
JAPAC....... Joint Air Photo Center (SAUO)
Jap Acad Proc... Japan Academy. Proceedings (journ.) (SAUS)
JAPACS..... Japanese Pacific Climate Studies (or Study) (SAUO)
JAPACS..... Japanese Pacific Climate Study [*Marine science*] (OSRA)
JAPACS..... Japanese Pacific Ocean Climate Studies (USDC)
JAPAEA...... Journal. American Podiatric Medical Association (journ.) (SAUS)
Japan Ann L & Pol... Japan Annual of Law and Politics [*A publication*] (DLA)
Japan Annu Int Law... Japanese Annual of International Law (journ.) (SAUS)
Japan A Soc Psychol... Japanese Annals of Social Psychology (journ.) (SAUS)
Japan Chem... Japan Chemical Week (journ.) (SAUS)
Japanese An Internat Law... Japanese Annual of International Law (journ.) (SAUS)
Japanese Fin and Industry... Japanese Finance and Industry (journ.) (SAUS)
Japanese MT... Japanese Military Technology. Procedures for Transfers to the United States (journ.) (SAUS)
Japan Gensuikyo... Japan Council against A and H Bombs (SAUO)
Japan J Math... Japanese Journal of Mathematics (journ.) (SAUS)
Japan J Math NS... Japanese Journal of Mathematics. New Series (journ.) (SAUS)
Japan J Med Sc Pt 4 Pharmacol... Japanese Journal of Medical Sciences. Part 4. Pharmacology (journ.) (SAUS)
Japan Lbr Bul... Japan Labor Bulletin (journ.) (SAUS)
JAPANMEC... Japan International Measuring and Control Industry Show
Japan Med Gaz... Japan Medical Gazette (journ.) (SAUS)
Japan Med World... Japan Medical World (journ.) (SAUS)
Japan Soc B... Japan Society Bulletin (journ.) (SAUS)
Japan Stat... Japan Statistical Yearbook (journ.) (SAUS)
Japan Stud... Japanese Studies (journ.) (SAUS)
Japan TAPPI... Japan Technical Association of the Tulp and Paper Industry (SAUO)
JapARE...... Japanese Antarctic Research Expedition [*1956-*]
Jap Assoc Mineral Petrol Econ Geol J... Japanese Association of Mineralogists Petrologists and Economic Geologists. Journal (journ.) (SAUS)
Jap Assoc Pet Technol J... Japanese Association of Petroleum Technologists. Journal (journ.) (SAUS)
JAPATIC..... Japan Patient Information Center [*Information service or system*] (IID)
JAPBP....... Jordanian Arab Progressive Ba'th Party [*Political party*] (PSAP)
JAPC......... Japan Air Proto Center (SAUS)
JAPC......... Joint Air Photo Center [*NATO*] (NATG)
JAPCA....... Journal. Air Pollution Control Association (journ.) (SAUS)
JAPCA....... Journal of Air Pollution Control Association [*A publication*] (EPAT)
Jap Chem Week... Japan Chemical Week (journ.) (SAUS)
Jap Circ J... Japanese Circulation Journal (journ.) (SAUS)
JAPCO....... Jamestown Paint & Varnish Co.
JAPCO....... Japan Atomic Power Co.
JAPCo....... Japan Atomic Power Company (BUAC)
JAPCO....... Japan Power Demonstration Reactor Company (SAUO)
Jap Cur..... Japan Current (SAUS)
JapDic....... Japanese Dictionary (SAUS)
JAPE......... Journal of Australian Political Economy (journ.) (SAUS)
JAPEAI....... Journal of Applied Ecology (journ.) (SAUS)
Jap Econ St... Japanese Economic Studies (journ.) (SAUS)
JAPEX....... Japan Express (SAUS)
JAPEX....... Japan Petroleum Exploitation Co. (SAUS)
JAPEX....... Japan Petroleum Exploration Co. (BUAC)
Jap Geol Surv Bull... Japan Geological Survey. Bulletin (journ.) (SAUS)
Jap Geol Surv Rep... Japan Geological Survey. Report (journ.) (SAUS)
Jap Geotherm Energy Ass J... Japan Geothermal Energy Association. Journal (journ.) (SAUS)
JAPGWC.... Jewish Association for the Protection of Girls, Women and Children (SAUO)
JAPH........ Just Another PERL Hacker (SAUS)
JAPhA....... Journal of the American Pharmaceutical Association (SAUO)
JAPHA....... Journal of the American Public Health Association [*Publication*] [*Association*] [*Medicine*] (MTAA)
Jap Heart J... Japanese Heart Journal (journ.) (SAUS)
JAPI......... Journal of the Association of Physicians of India (journ.) (SAUS)
JAPIA........ Japan Auto Parts Industries Association
JAPIB........ Joint Air Photographic Intelligence Board (SAUO)
JAPIC........ Japanese Project Industry Council (SAUO)
JAPIC........ Japan Pharmaceutical Information Center [*Tokyo*] [*Information service or system*] (IID)
JAPIC........ Joint Air Photographic Intelligence Center (SAUS)
JAPIC........ Joint Air Photographic Intelligence Centre (SAUO)
JAPIC........ Joint Air Photo Interpretation Center (SAUO)
JAPINFO.... Japanese Information on Scientific and Technical Information (MHID)
Jap Inst Nav J... Japan. Institute of Navigation. Journal (journ.) (SAUS)
JAPIO........ Japan Patent Information Organization [*Database producer*]
JAPIsA...... Japan Auto Parts Industries Association (SAUO)
JAPIT........ Japanese Association for the Promotion of International Trade (EY)

JAPIU........ Joint Air Photo Interpretation Unit (SAUO)
Jap J Allergy... Japanese Journal of Allergy (journ.) (SAUS)
Jap J A Phy... Japanese Journal of Applied Physics (journ.) (SAUS)
Jap J Appl Phys... Japanese Journal of Applied Physics (journ.) (SAUS)
Jap J Appl Phys Suppl... Japanese Journal of Applied Physics. Supplement (journ.) (SAUS)
Jap J Appl Zool... Japanese Journal of Applied Zoology (journ.) (SAUS)
Jap J Astr... Japanese Journal of Astronomy (journ.) (SAUS)
Jap J Astr Geophys... Japanese Journal of Astronomy and Geophysics (journ.) (SAUS)
Jap J Breed... Japanese Journal of Breeding (journ.) (SAUS)
Jap J Canc Res... Japanese Journal of Cancer Research (journ.) (SAUS)
Jap J Child... Japanese Journal of Child Psychiatry (journ.) (SAUS)
Jap J Clin Med... Japanese Journal of Clinical Medicine (journ.) (SAUS)
Jap J Clin Path... Japanese Journal of Clinical Pathology (journ.) (SAUS)
Jap J Ecol... Japanese Journal of Ecology (journ.) (SAUS)
Jap J Edu P... Japanese Journal of Educational Psychology (journ.) (SAUS)
Jap J Geophys... Japanese Journal of Geophysics (journ.) (SAUS)
Jap J Limnol... Japanese Journal of Limnology (journ.) (SAUS)
Jap J Med... Japanese Journal of Medicine (journ.) (SAUS)
Jap J Nurs... Japanese Journal of Nursing (journ.) (SAUS)
Jap J Nurs Educ... Japan Journal of Nurses Education (journ.) (SAUS)
Jap J Nurs Res... Japanese Journal of Nursing Research (journ.) (SAUS)
Jap J Nutr... Japanese Journal of Nutrition (journ.) (SAUS)
Jap J Ophthal... Japanese Journal of Ophthalmology (journ.) (SAUS)
Jap J Palynol... Japanese Journal of Palynology (journ.) (SAUS)
Jap J Parasit... Japanese Journal of Parasitology (journ.) (SAUS)
Jap J Pharmacogn... Japanese Journal of Pharmacognosy (journ.) (SAUS)
Jap J Sanit Zool... Japanese Journal of Sanitary Zoology (journ.) (SAUS)
Jap J Trop Agr... Sapanese Journal of Tropical Agriculture (SAUS)
Jap J Zool... Japanese Journal of Zoology (journ.) (SAUS)
Jap J Zootech Sci... Japanese Journal of Zootechnical Science (journ.) (SAUS)
JAPLA....... Journal. Atlantic Provinces Linguistic Association/Revue. Association de Linguistique des Provinces Atlantiques (journ.) (SAUS)
JAPLD....... Japanese Journal of Applied Physics. Part 2. Letters (journ.) (SAUS)
Japlish...... Japanese & English (SAUS)
JAPMAB..... Journal. American Pharmaceutical Association. Scientific Edition (journ.) (SAUS)
Jap Meteorol Agency Volcanol Bull... Japan Meteorological Agency. Volcanological Bulletin (journ.) (SAUS)
JAPN........ Japan Air Lines Co. Ltd. [*NASDAQ symbol*] (NQ)
JapnAr...... Japan Airlines [*Associated Press*] (SAG)
JapnAr...... Japan Airlines Co. Ltd. [*Associated Press*] (SAG)
Jap Nat Ry Ry Tech Res... Japanese National Railways. Railway Technical Research (journ.) (SAUS)
JAPND....... Japanese Journal of Applied Physics. Part 1. Regular Papers and Short Notes (journ.) (SAUS)
JAPNEF..... Journal of Animal Physiology and Animal Nutrition (journ.) (SAUS)
JapnEq...... [*The*] Japan Equity Fund, Inc. [*Associated Press*] (SAG)
JAPNMS.... JTIDS Air Platform Network Management System (SAUS)
J Ap Nutrition... Journal of Applied Nutrition (journ.) (SAUS)
JAPNY....... Japan Airlines Co. Ltd ADR [*NASDAQ symbol*] (TTSB)
JAPO........ Joint Area Petroleum Office
JAP Online... Journal of Applied Physiology Online [*Database*] (GDD)
JAPOS....... JAPOS Study Group [*Defunct*] (EA)
JAPOS....... Journalists, Authors and Poets on Stamps Study Group (SAUO)
JAPOS....... Journalists, Authors and Poets on Stamps Study Unit (EA)
JAPP......... Japanese Patent (IAA)
Jap P........ [*The*] Pharmacopoeia of Japan [*A publication*]
Jap Per Ind... Japanese Periodicals Index.(journ.) (SAUS)
J Appl Aquacult... Journal of Applied Aquaculture [*A publication*] (PABS)
J Appl Biochem... Journal of Applied Biochemistry (journ.) (SAUS)
J Appl Biol... Journal of Applied Biology (journ.) (SAUS)
J Appl Biomater... Journal of Applied Biomaterials (journ.) (SAUS)
J Appl Botany... Journal of Applied Botany (journ.) (SAUS)
J Appl Bus Res... Journal of Applied Business Research [*A publication*] (JLIT)
J Appl Chem... Journal of Applied Chemistry (journ.) (SAUS)
J Appl Chem Abstr... Journal of Applied Chemistry. Abstracts (journ.) (SAUS)
J Appl Chem Biotechnol Abstr... Journal of Applied Chemistry and Biotechnology. Abstracts (journ.) (SAUS)
J Appl Cosmetol... Journal of Applied Cosmetology (journ.) (SAUS)
J Appl Crystallogr... Journal of Applied Crystallography [*A publication*] (CABS)
J Appl Dev Psychol... Journal of Applied Developmental Psychology (journ.) (SAUS)
J Appl Ecol... Journal of Applied Ecology [*A publication*] (PABS)
J Appl Econ... Journal of Applied Economics [*A publication*] (JLIT)
J Appl Econometrics... Journal of Applied Econometrics [*A publication*] (JLIT)
J Appl Electrochem... Journal of Applied Electrochemistry [*A publication*] (PABS)
J Appl Entomol... Journal of Applied Entomology (journ.) (SAUS)
J Appl Geophys... Journal of Applied Geophysics [*A publication*] (PABS)
J Appl Gerontol... Journal of Applied Gerontology (journ.) (SAUS)
J Appl Ichthyol... Journal of Applied Ichthyology (journ.) (SAUS)
J Appl Manage... Journal of Applied Management (journ.) (SAUS)
J Appl Med... Journal of Applied Medicine (journ.) (SAUS)
J Appl Metalwork... Journal of Applied Metalworking (journ.) (SAUS)
J Appl Meteorol... Journal of Applied Meteorolgy [*A publication*] (PABS)
J Appl Microbiol... Journal of Applied Microbiology [*A publication*] (PABS)
J Appl Microbiol Biotech... Journal of Applied Microbiology and Biotechnology (journ.) (SAUS)
J Appl Ntr... Journal of Applied Nutrition (journ.) (SAUS)
J Appl Phycol... Journal of Applied Phycology [*A publication*] (PABS)
J Appl Pneum... Journal of Applied Pneumatics (journ.) (SAUS)
J Appl Polym Sci... Journal of Applied Polymer Science [*A publication*] (CABS)
J Appl Polym Sci Appl Polym Symp... Journal of Applied Polymer Science. Applied Polymer Symposium (journ.) (SAUS)
J Appl Spectrosc... Journal of Applied Spectroscopy (journ.) (SAUS)
J Appl Statist... Journal of Applied Statistics [*A publication*] (JLIT)
J Appl Toxicol... Journal of Applied Toxicology (journ.) (SAUS)
J App Nutr... Journal of Applied Nutrition (journ.) (SAUS)
Jap Prog Climatol... Japanese Progress on Climatology (journ.) (SAUS)
Jap Psy Res... Japanese Psychological Research (journ.) (SAUS)
JAPRCP..... Journal of Anthropological Research (journ.) (SAUS)
JAPRDQ..... Journal of Animal Production Research (journ.) (SAUS)
JAPRRCC... Japan Authors' and Publishers' Reprographic Rights Clearance Centre (BUAC)
JAPRW...... Japanese Association of Photosynthesis Research Workers (BUAC)
JAPS......... Japanese American Philatelic Society [*Later, JASP*]
JAP S........ Japan Sea (SAUS)
JAPS......... Joint Administration Planning Staff (SAUO)
JAPS......... Joint Administrative Planning Section [*Joint Planning Staff*] [*World War II*]
JAPS......... Joint Administrative Planning Staff (SAUO)
JAPsAs...... Journal of the American Psychoanalytic Association (SAUO)
Jap Semicond Tech N... Japanese Semiconductor Technology News (journ.) (SAUS)
Jap Shipbldg Mar Eng... Japan Shipbuilding and Marine Engineering (journ.) (SAUS)
Jap Shipbuild & Mar Engng... Japan Shipbuilding and Marine Engineering (journ.) (SAUS)
Jap Soc..... Japan Society (SAUO)
J Ap Sociol... Journal of Applied Sociology (journ.) (SAUS)
Jap Soc Promot Sci Sub-Comm Phys Chem Stlmaking Spec Rep... Japan Society for the Promotion of Science. Sub-Committee for Physical Chemistry of Steelmaking. Special Report (journ.) (SAUS)
JAPSS....... Joint Automated Planning Support System [*of JOPS*] [*Military*]
JAPT......... Journal for Approximation Theory (journ.) (SAUS)
JAPT......... Journal of Approximation Theory (journ.) (SAUS)
Jap Telecom... Japan Telecommunications Review (journ.) (SAUS)
Jap Weld Soc Trans... Japan Welding Society. Transactions (journ.) (SAUS)
JAQ.......... Jacquinot Bay [*Papua New Guinea*] [*Airport symbol*] (OAG)
JAQ.......... Job Activities Questionnaire
JAQ.......... Journal of Buyouts and Acquisitions (journ.) (SAUS)
JAQ.......... Passionist Academic Institute, Chicago, IL [*OCLC symbol*] (OCLC)
J Aqiaric & Aquat Sci... Journal of Aquariculture and Aquatic Sciences (journ.) (SAUS)
J Aquacult Trop... Journal of Aquaculture in the Tropics [*A publication*] (PABS)
J Aquaric... Journal of Aquariculture (journ.) (SAUS)
JA Quart J Automat Control... Journal. A Quarterly Journal of Automatic Control (journ.) (SAUS)
J Aquat Anim Health... Journal of Aquatic Animal Health (journ.) (SAUS)
J Aquat Plant Manage... Journal of Aquatic Plant Management [*A publication*] (PABS)
J Aquat Sci... Journal of Aquatic Sciences [*A publication*] (PABS)
JAR.......... Airlink Luftverkehrsgesellschaft GmbH [*Austria*] [*ICAO designator*] (FAAC)
JAR.......... Jamming Avoidance Response
JAR.......... Jargon (WDAA)
JAR.......... Jarma [*NCIC car model code*]
JAR.......... J. Arthur Rank [*Motion picture company in England*]
JAR.......... Java Archive [*Computer science*] (IGQR)
JAR.......... Java Archive File (SAUS)
JAR.......... JavaSoft Java Archive [*Computer science*]
JAr........... Jewish Aramaic (BJA)
JAR.......... Jewish Autonomous Region [*Eastern Siberia*]
JAR.......... Jews for Animal Rights (EA)
JAR.......... Job Appraisal Review (PDAA)
JAR.......... Joint Airworthiness Requirements (MCD)
JAR.......... Joint Aviation Requirement [*FAA*] (TAG)
JAR.......... Journal of Accounting Research (journ.) (SAUS)
JAR.......... Journal of Advertising Research [*Advertising Research Foundation*] [*A publication*]
JAR.......... Journal of Anthropological Research (journ.) (SAUS)
JAR.......... Jump Address Register
JAR.......... Junior Admitting Resident [*Medicine*] (DAVI)
JAR.......... Just Ain't Right (SPVS)
JAR.......... Justice Acquisition Regulation [*A publication*] (AAGC)
JAR.......... Zion-Benton Library District, Zion, IL [*OCLC symbol*] (OCLC)
JAR-145..... Joint Aviation Requirement on Approved Maintenance Organisations (SAUO)
JARA........ Japan Antibiotics Research Association (BUAC)
J Ar Aad Sci... Journal. Arizona Academy of Science (journ.) (SAUS)
J Arab Affairs... Journal of Arab Affairs (journ.) (SAUS)
J Arachnol... Journal of Arachnology (journ.) (SAUS)
Jar & By Conv... Jannan and Bythewoods Conveyancing (journ.) (SAUS)
Jar & By Conv... Jarman and Bythewood's Conveyancing [*A publication*] (DLA)
JARB........ Joint Acquisition Review Board [*Army*]
J Arboric.... Journal of Arboriculture (journ.) (SAUS)
J Arb Vet Med As... Journal. Arab Veterinary Medical Association (journ.) (SAUS)
JARC........ Jarco [*NCIC trailer make code*]
JARC........ Jewish Association for Retarded Citizens (EA)
JARC........ Joint Air Reconnaissance Center [*NATO*] (NATG)
JARC........ Joint Air Reconnaissance Centre (SAUO)
JARC........ Joint Avionics Research Committee (SAUS)
JARCA....... Journal of Aesthetic and Art Criticism (journ.) (SAUS)
JARCC....... Joint Air Reconnaissance Coordination Center [*Military*] (MCD)
JARCE....... Journal. American Research Center in Egypt (journ.) (SAUS)
JARCE....... Journal of the American Research Center in Egypt (SAUO)
JARCE....... Journal of the American Research Center in Egypt (journ.) (SAUS)

J Archaeol Chem... Journal of Archaeological Chemistry (journ.) (SAUS)
J Archaeol Res... Journal of Archaeological Research (journ.) (SAUS)
Jar Chancery Pr... Jarmans Chancery Practics (journ.) (SAUS)
J Archit Plan Res... Journal of Architectural and Planning Research (journ.) (SAUS)
Jar Chy Pr... Jarman's Chancery Practice [*A publication*] (DLA)
Jar Cr Tr.... Jardine's Criminal Trials [*A publication*] (DLA)
Jar Cr Tr.... Jardines Criminal Trials (journ.) (SAUS)
JARD........ Jardines
JARDB....... Joint Advisory Rehabilitation and Disability Board (SAUS)
JardFICh.... Jardine Fleming China Region [*Associated Press*] (SAG)
Jard Ind.... Jardine's Index to Howell's State Trials [*A publication*] (DLA)
JARE......... Japanese Antarctic Research Expedition [*1956-*]
JAREB....... Japanese Railway Engineering (journ.) (SAUS)
JARECT..... Japan Annual Reviews in Electronics, Computers and Telecommunications (journ.) (SAUS)
JARE Scientific Reports... Japanese Antarctic Research Expedition Scientific Reports (journ.) (SAUS)
JARF......... Journal. Addiction Research Foundation (journ.) (SAUS)
JAR-FCL.... JAR on Flight Crew Licensing (SAUS)
JAR file..... Java Archive File [*Commission*] (NETL)
jarg.......... jargonese (SAUS)
jarg.......... jargonize (SAUS)
Jarg Soc.... Jargon Society (SAUO)
J Ar Hist.... Journal of Arizona History (journ.) (SAUS)
JARI......... Japan Association of Railway Industries (SAUO)
JARI......... Japan Automobile Research Institute
JARI......... Japan Automotive Research Institute
JARI......... Japanese Association of Railway Industries (BUAC)
JARI......... Journal of Agricultural Research in Iceland (journ.) (SAUS)
JARI......... Journal of Applied Radiation and Isotopes (journ.) (SAUS)
JARI......... Jute Agricultural Research Institute [*India*] (BUAC)
JARIB........ Joint Air Reconnaissance Intelligence Board [*Australia*]
JARIC........ Joint Aerial Reconnaissance Interpretation Center (MCD)
JARIC........ Joint Air Reconnaissance Centre (SAUO)
JARIC........ Joint Air Reconnaissance Intelligence Center (or Centre) (SAUS)
JARIC........ Joint Air Reconnaissance Intelligence Centre [*British*]
J Arid Environ... Journal of Arid Environments (journ.) (SAUS)
JARIV........ Joint Air Reconnaissance Intelligence Centre (SAUO)
J Ariz Ner Ad Sci... Journal. Arizona-Nevada Academy of Science(journ.) (SAUS)
J Arkan Med Soc... Journal. Arkansas Medical Society (journ.) (SAUS)
JARL......... Japan Amateur Radio League (BUAC)
JARM........ Jammer, Artillery, Radar Missile (ACAE)
JAR-MED... JAR on Medical (SAUS)
J Arms Armour Soc... Journal. Arms and Armour Society (journ.) (SAUS)
J Arn Arbor... Journal. Arnold Arboretum (journ.) (SAUS)
J Arnold Arbor... Journal. Arnold Arboretum. Harvard University (journ.) (SAUS)
JARO........ Johore Area Rehabilitation Organization (SAUO)
JARO........ Journal of the Association for Research in Otolaryngology [*Database*] (GDD)
JAR-OPS.... JAR on Flight Operations (SAUS)
JAROS........ Japanese Resources Observation System Organization (SAUS)
JARP......... Japanese Association of Radiological Physicists [*Medicine*] (EDAA)
JARPA....... Jam-Resistant Phased Array (ACAE)
Jar Pow Dev... Jarman's Edition of Powell on Devises [*A publication*] (DLA)
Jar Pow Dev... Jarmans Edition of Powell on Devises (journ.) (SAUS)
JARQ Jap Agric Res Q... JARQ Japan Agricultural Research Quarterly (journ.) (SAUS)
JARQ Jpn Agric Res Q... JARQ Japan Agricultural Research Quarterly (journ.) (SAUS)
JARR........ Journal of Architectural Research (journ.) (SAUS)
JARRA....... Jarratt, VA [*American Association of Railroads railroad junction routing code*]
JARRP....... Japan Association for Radiation Research on Polymers
JARS........ Alltrista Corp. [*NASDAQ symbol*] (SAG)
JARS........ Jamming Aircraft and Radar Simulation (ACAE)
JARS........ Java Applet Rating Service (SAUO)
JARS........ Job Accounting Report System (MHDI)
JARS........ Joliet Amateur Radio Society (SAUO)
JARS........ Journal. Assam Research Society (journ.) (SAUS)
JARS........ Journalization and Recovery System (PDAA)
JARS........ Journalization and Recovery System (journ.) (SAUS)
J Arthroplasty... Journal of Arthroplasty (journ.) (SAUS)
J Art Mgmt L... Journal of Arts Management and Law (journ.) (SAUS)
JARTRAN... James A. Ryder Transportation [*Acronym is trade name of truck-rental firm*]
JARTS....... Japan Railway Technical Service (BUAC)
JARTS....... Japan Railway Technical Services (SAUO)
J Arts Mgt and L... Journal of Arts Management and Law (journ.) (SAUS)
JAR-TSO.... Joint Aviation Requirement on Technical Standard Orders (SAUO)
JARU........ Industrielle de Sucrerie [*Intermodal shipping container symbol*] (TVRC)
JARVI........ Jarvis, ON [*American Association of Railroads railroad junction routing code*]
Jar Wills.... Jarman on Wills [*8 eds.*] [*1841-51*] [*A publication*] (DLA)
JAS.......... Jamaica Agricultural Society (BUAC)
JAS.......... Jamaica Air Service (SAUO)
JAS.......... James [*Telegraphy*] (PCTE)
Jas........... James [*New Testament book*]
JAS.......... Jamestown [*California*] [*Seismograph station code, US Geological Survey*] (SEIS)
JAS.......... Jane Austen Society [*Basingstoke, Hampshire, England*] (EAIO)
JAS.......... Japan Air System
JAS.......... Japan Air System Co. Ltd. [*ICAO designator*] (FAAC)
JAS.......... Japan Association of Shipbuilders (BUAC)
JAS.......... Japan Astronautical Society (SAUO)
J-A S........ Japan-Australia Society (SAUO)
JAS.......... Jasper, TX [*Location identifier*] [*FAA*] (FAAL)
JAS.......... Jazz Arts Society (EA)
JAS.......... Jenkins Activity Survey [*Personality development test*] [*Psychology*]
JAS.......... Jewish Agricultural Society (EA)
JAS.......... Jo Ann Stores [*NYSE symbol*]
JAS.......... Job Accounting System
JAS.......... Job Action Sheet [*Emergency Management*] (EMA)
JAS.......... Job Activity Survey
JAS.......... Job Analysis Schedule [*Department of Labor*]
JAS.......... Job Analysis System [*Computer program*]
JAS.......... Job Attitude Scale [*Employment test*]
JAS.......... Johnny Alfalfa Sprout [*Defunct*] (EA)
JAS.......... Joint Administration Services
JAS.......... Joint Airmiss Section [*Aviation*] (DA)
JAS.......... Joint Anti-Submarine School (SAUO)
JAS.......... Joint Association Survey [*American Petroleum Institute, Independent Petroleum Association of America, and Mid-Continent Oil and Gas Association*]
JAS.......... Joint Automated Planning Support System (SAUS)
JAS.......... Jordanian Agricultural Society (SAUO)
JAS.......... Journal Abbreviation Sources (SAUO)
JAS.......... Journal Access Service [*Center for Research Libraries*]
JAS.......... Journal. Acoustical Society of America (journ.) (SAUS)
JAS.......... Journal. Asiatic Society of Great Britain and Ireland (journ.) (SAUS)
JAS.......... Journal of Abdominal Surgery [*Medicine*] (EDAA)
JAS.......... Journal of Aerospace Science [*A publication*] (NAKS)
JAS.......... Journal of Aerospace Science (journ.) (SAUS)
JAS.......... Journal of Agricultural/Animal Science [*Medicine*] (EDAA)
JAS.......... Journal of Archaeological Science (journ.) (SAUS)
JAS.......... Journal of Asian Studies [*A publication*] (BRI)
JAS.......... Journal of Asiatic Society (journ.) (SAUS)
JAS.......... Journal of Atmospheric Sciences [*A publication*] (SSD)
JAS.......... Journal of Australian Studies (journ.) (SAUS)
JAS.......... Journal of Austronesian Studies (journ.) (SAUS)
JAS.......... Journal of the Acoustical Society (journ.) (SAUS)
JAS.......... Journals Access Service [*Center for Research Libraries*]
J As......... Judicial Assessor [*Ghana*] [*A publication*] (DLA)
J As......... Judicial Assessor (journ.) (SAUS)
JAS.......... Junior Astronomical Society (EAIO)
JAS.......... Just a Second (SAUS)
JAS.......... Juvenile Ankylosing Spondylitis [*Medicine*] (DMAA)
JAS.......... Lake Villa District Library, Lake Villa, IL [*OCLC symbol*] (OCLC)
JAS-1........ Japan Amateur Satellite-1
JASA......... Japan Amateur Sports Association (SAUO)
JASA......... Jewish Association for Services for the Aged (EA)
JASA......... Jewish Association for the Services of the Aged, New York (SAUO)
JASA......... Jo-Ann Stores [*NYSE symbol*]
JASA......... Jo-Ann Stores "A" [*Formerly, Fabri-Centers Amer. "B"*] [*NYSE symbol*]
JASA......... Joint Airworthiness Steering Committee (SAUS)
JASA......... Joint Antisubmarine Action
JASA......... Journal. Acoustical Safety of America (journ.) (SAUS)
JASA......... Journal. American Scientific Affiliation (journ.) (SAUS)
JASA......... Journal. American Statistical Association (journ.) (SAUS)
JASA......... Journal of the Acoustical Society of America (journ.) (SAUS)
JASA......... Journal of the American Society of Acoustics (journ.) (SAUS)
JASA......... Journal of the American Statistical Association (SAUO)
JASA......... Journal of the American Statistical Association (journ.) (SAUS)
JASA......... Junior Assistant Stores Accountant [*British military*] (DMA)
J As Aff..... Journal of Asian Affairs (journ.) (SAUS)
JASAP....... Julie [*Sonobuoy System*] Automatic Search and Attack Plotter [*Navy*] (MCD)
JASAR....... Jittered and Swept Active RADAR
JASASA..... Joint Air-Surface Antisubmarine Action
JASAT....... Journal. American Studies Association of Texas (journ.) (SAUS)
JASB......... Jo-Ann Stores "B" [*Formerly, Fabri-Centers Amer. "A"*] [*NYSE symbol*]
JASB......... Joint Advisory Survey Board [*British*]
JASB......... Journal. Asiatic Society of Bengal (journ.) (SAUS)
JAS B........ Journal. Asiatic Society of Bombay (journ.) (SAUS)
JASB......... Journal of the Anthropological Society of Bombay (journ.) (SAUS)
JASB......... Journal of the Asiatic Society of Bengal (SAUO)
JASB......... Journal of the Asiatic Society of Bombay (journ.) (SAUS)
JASBP....... Jordanian Arab Socialist Ba'th Party [*Political party*] (PSAP)
JASC......... Japan Academic Societies Center (SAUS)
JASC......... Japan-America Society of Southern California (SAUO)
JASC......... Japan-America Student Conference (EA)
JASC......... Japan Asia Sea Cable
JASC......... Japan-Asia Sea Cable (SAUS)
JASC......... Japan Sea Cable (SAUS)
JASC......... Joint Actions Steering Committee (SAUO)
JASC......... Journal. Asiatic Society of Calcutta (journ.) (SAUS)
JASC......... JPL [*Jet Propulsion Laboratory*] Astronautical Star Catalog (KSC)
JASC......... Junior Achievement of Southern California (EARSL)
JAS Calcutta... Journal. Asiatic Society of Calcutta (journ.) (SAUS)
JASCEV..... Journal of Agronomy and Crop Science (journ.) (SAUS)
J A Science... Journal of Archaeological Science (journ.) (SAUS)
JASCO....... Joint American Study Commission (SAUO)
JASCO....... Joint Assault Signal Co. [*Small unit in Pacific amphibious warfare*] [*World War II*]

JASCO Appl Notes... Japan Spectroscopic Company. Application Notes (journ.) (SAUS)
J As Cult.... Journal of Asian Culture (journ.) (SAUS)
JASDA....... Julie [*Sonobuoy System*] Automatic Sonic Data Analyzer [*Navy*]
JASDF....... Japan Air Self-Defense Force (SAUS)
JASDF....... Japanese Air Self-Defense Force
JASE......... Just Another System Error (SAUS)
JASFA....... Japan Sea-Farming Association (SAUO)
JASFE6...... Journal of Agricultural Science in Finland (journ.) (SAUS)
JASG........ Joint Advanced Study Group
JASGP....... Joint Advanced Study Group
JASH........ Jason, Inc. (SAUO)
J As Ht...... Journal of Asian History (journ.) (SAUS)
JASI......... Joint Asian Surgical Industries (SAUO)
J Asian & Afric Stud... Journal of Asian and African Studies (journ.) (SAUS)
J Asian Econ... Journal of Asian Economics [*A publication*] (JLIT)
J Asian Stud... Journal of Asian Studies [*A publication*] (JLIT)
J Asian Stud... Journal of Asian Studies (journ.) (SAUS)
J Asia-Pacific Bus... Journal of Asia-Pacific Business [*A publication*] (JLIT)
J Asiat Soc Bangla... Journal. Asiatic Society of Bangladesh (journ.) (SAUS)
J Asiat Soc Bangladesh Sci... Journal. Asiatic Society of Bangladesh. Science (journ.) (SAUS)
J Asiat Soc Bengal Lett... Journal. Asiatic Society of Bengal. Letters (journ.) (SAUS)
J Asiat Soc Bengal Sci... Journal. Asiatic Society of Bengal. Science (journ.) (SAUS)
J Asiat Soc Bombay... Journal. Asiatic Society of Bombay (journ.) (SAUS)
J Asiat Soc Sci... Journal Asiatic Society. Science (journ.) (SAUS)
J Asiat Stud... Journal of Asiatic Studies (journ.) (SAUS)
JASIN........ Joint Air Sea Interaction [*National Science Foundation/United Kingdom*]
JASIN........ Joint Air-Sea Interaction Experiment (SAUO)
JASIN........ Joint Air-Sea Interaction Program [*Global Atmospheric Research Program*] (USDC)
JASIN........ Joint Air-Sea Interaction Project (SAUO)
JASIS........ Journal of the American Society for Information Science (SAUO)
JASIS........ Journal of the American Society for Information Science (journ.) (SAUS)
J Asist Soc... Journal. Asiatic Society (journ.) (SAUS)
JASL......... Joint Archive for Sea Level (SAUO)
JASL......... Journal. Asiatic Society. Letters (journ.) (SAUS)
JASL......... Journal of the Asiatic Society, Letters (SAUO)
JASL......... Journal of the Asiatic Society, Letters (journ.) (SAUS)
JASLS........ Japanese American Society for Legal Studies (EA)
JASMMM... Joint Aviation Supply and Maintenance Material Management (DNAB)
JASMU...... Journal pour l'Avancement des Soins Medicaux d'Urgence [*A publication*]
JASN........ Jason, Inc. [*NASDAQ symbol*] (NQ)
JASN........ Journal of the American Society of Nephrology (SAUO)
JASNA....... Jane Austen Society of North America (EA)
JASO........ Japan Standards Organization (SAUS)
JASO........ Jason Manufacturing [*NCIC trailer make code*]
Ja Soc Lond B... Japan Society of London. Bulletin (journ.) (SAUS)
JASON....... Group of physicists at Stanford that study various projects and are funded by government defense money (SAUO)
Jason........ Jason, Inc. [*Associated Press*] (SAG)
JASON....... Journal Articles Sent On Demand (SAUO)
JASON....... Scientific panel MITRE Corporation (SAUO)
JASORS..... Joint Advanced Special Operations Radio System [*Military*] (RDA)
JASP......... Japan-America Society of Arizona (EARSL)
JASP......... Japanese American Society for Philately (EA)
JASP......... Journal. Asiatic Society of Pakistan (journ.) (SAUS)
JASp......... Journal of Applied Social Psychology (journ.) (SAUS)
JASPA....... Jesuit Association of Student Personnel Administrators (EA)
JASPA....... Jobs and Skills Programme for Africa (BUAC)
J As Pac World... Journal of Asian-Pacific and World Perspectives (journ.) (SAUS)
JASPE....... Jasper, AL [*American Association of Railroads railroad junction routing code*]
JASPER..... Joint Academic Services Providers to Education and Research (AIE)
JASPR....... Jasper [*Gem*] (ROG)
JASPR....... Journal. American Society for Psychical Research Technologists (journ.) (SAUS)
JASR........ JTPA [*Job Training and Partnership Act*] Annual Status Report (OICC)
JASRAC..... Japanese Society of Rights of Authors and Composers (SAUO)
JASRES..... Journal of Agricultural and Scientific Research (journ.) (SAUS)
JASS......... Javascript-Accessable Style Sheets (SAUS)
JASS......... Joint Antisatellite Study
JASS......... Joint Anti-Submarine School [*British military*] (DMA)
JASS......... JUMPS [*Joint Uniform Military Pay System*] Automated Support System [*or Supplemental*] [*Military*]
JASSA....... JASSA. Journal of the Australian Society of Security Analysts (journ.) (SAUS)
JASSA....... Journal of Applied Science in Southern Africa (SAUO)
JASS-AC.... JUMPS [*Joint Uniform Military Pay System*] Automated Supplemental System-Active Component [*Military*]
J Assa Hosp Med Educ... Journal. Association for Hospital Medical Education (journ.) (SAUS)
J Assam Res Soc... Journal. Assam Research Society (journ.) (SAUS)
J Assam Sci Soc... Journal. Assam Science Society (journ.) (SAUS)
JASSC....... Japan-America Society of Southern California
JASSCC..... Japan Academic Society System for Copyright Clearance (BUAC)
J Ass Comput Mach... Journal of the Association of Computing Machinery (SAUO)
J Ass Comput Mach... Journal of the Association of Computing Machinery (journ.) (SAUS)
JASSM...... Joint Acoustic Surveillance System Model [*Military*] (CAAL)
JASSM...... Joint Air-to-Surface Standoff Missile [*Military*]
J Assn Law Teachers... Journal. Association of Law Teachers (journ.) (SAUS)
J Ass'n L Teachers... Journal. Association of Law Teachers [*A publication*] (DLA)
J Assoc Acad Minor Phys... Journal of the Association for Academic Minority Physicians (SAUO)
J Assoc Acad Minor Phys... Journal of the Association for Academic Minority Physicians (journ.) (SAUS)
J Assoc Am Med Coll... Journal. Association of American Medical Colleges (journ.) (SAUS)
J Assoc Care Child Health... Journal. Association for the Care of Childrens Health (journ.) (SAUS)
J Assoc Care Child Hos... Journal. Association for the Care of Children in Hospitals (journ.) (SAUS)
J Assoc Comput Mach... Journal of the Association for Computing Machinery (journ.) (SAUS)
J Assoc Eng Archit Isr... Journal. Association of Engineers and Architects in Israel (journ.) (SAUS)
J Assoc Eng Archit Palest... Journal. Association of Engineers and Architects in Palestine (journ.) (SAUS)
J Assoc Eng Soc... Journal. Association of Engineering Societies (journ.) (SAUS)
J Assoc Law Teachers... Journal. Association of Law Teachers (journ.) (SAUS)
J Assoc L Teachers... Journal. Association of Law Teachers [*A publication*] (DLA)
J Assoc Lunar and Planet Obs Strolling Astron... Journal. Association of Lunar and Planetary Observers. Strolling Astronomer (journ.) (SAUS)
J Assoc Lunar Planet Obs Strolling Astron... Journal of the Association of Lunar and Planetary Observers, Strolling Astronomer (journ.) (SAUS)
J Assoc Med Illus... Journal. Association of Medical Illus- trators (journ.) (SAUS)
J Assoc Nurses AIDS Care... Journal of the Association of Nurses in Aids Care (SAUO)
J Assoc Nurses AIDS Care... Journal of the Association of Nurses in AIDS Care (journ.) (SAUS)
J Assoc Off Anal Chem... Journal of the Association of Official Analytical Chemists (SAUO)
J Assoc Off Anal Chem... Journal of the Association of Official Analytical Chemists (journ.) (SAUS)
J Assoc Pediatr Oncol Nurses... Journal. Association of Pediatric Oncology Nurses (journ.) (SAUS)
J Assoc Physicians India... Journal of the Association of Physicians of India (SAUO)
J Assoc Physicians India... Journal of the Association of Physicians of India (journ.) (SAUS)
J Assoc Phys Ment Rehabil... Journal. Association for Physical and Mental Rehabilitation (journ.) (SAUS)
J Ass Off Agric Chem... Journal. Asciation of Official Agricultural Chemists (journ.) (SAUS)
J Asso Teach Ja... Journal. Association of Teachers of Japanese (journ.) (SAUS)
J Assot Pers Comput Chem... Journal. Association of Personal Computers for Chemists (journ.) (SAUS)
J Ass Physicians India... Journal. Association of Physicians of India (journ.) (SAUS)
JASS-RC.... JUMPS [*Joint Uniform Military Pay System*] Automated Support System - Reserve Corps
JAST......... Jamaican Association of Sugar Technologists (BUAC)
JAST......... Japan Association of Sugar Technologists (SAUO)
JAST......... Jazz Action Society of Tasmania
JAST......... Joint Advanced Strike Technology [*Program*] [*Air Force*] [*Navy*] (DOMA)
JAST......... Joint Air Support Tactics [*Military*]
JASTAA...... Journal. Agricultural Society of Trinidad and Tobago (journ.) (SAUS)
JASTD....... Junior Assistant Steward [*British military*] (DMA)
JASTIS...... Japan Science and Technology Information System (SAUS)
JASTOP..... Jet-Assisted Stop (SAUS)
JASTOP..... Jet Assist Stop
JASTP....... Joint Advanced Srike Technology Program (SAUS)
JASTPRO... Japanese Trade Facilitation Organization (AG)
J Astronomical Soc Vic... Journal. Astronomical Society of Victoria (journ.) (SAUS)
J Astron Soc Egypt... Journal of the Astronomical Society of Egypt (journ.) (SAUS)
JAStud...... Journal of American Studies (journ.) (SAUS)
JASU........ Jackson Shipping [*Common carrier symbol*]
JASU........ Jet Aircraft Starting Unit (AFM)
JASW........ Japan-America Society of Washington (EA)
JASWG...... Joint Safety Assurance Working Group [*NASA*] (SPST)
JAT........... Jabat [*Marshall Islands*] [*Airport symbol*] (OAG)
JAT........... Jam Angle Tracking
JAT........... Job Accounting Table
JAT........... Joint Agency Training
JAT........... Journal of Accounting and Public Policy (journ.) (SAUS)
JAT........... Journal of Analytical Toxicology (SAUO)
JAT........... Journal of Applied Toxicology (journ.) (SAUS)
JAT........... Jugoslovenski Aerotransport [*Yugoslav Air Transport*] [*ICAO designator*]
JAT........... Junior Aptitude Tests [*Educational test*]
JAT........... Mennonite Hospital, Health Sciences Library, Bloomington, IL [*OCLC symbol*] (OCLC)
JAT........... Yugoslav Airlines (SAUS)
JATAAQ...... Journal. Animal Technicians Association (journ.) (SAUS)
JATAN....... Japan Tropical Rainforest Action Network
JATC......... Japan Association for Tissue Culture (BUAC)
JATC......... Joint Apprenticeship and Training Committee [*Bureau of Apprenticeship and Training*] [*Department of Labor*]
JATC......... Joint Apprenticeship Training Committee (SAUS)

JATC........ Journal of Air Traffic Control (journ.) (SAUS)
JATCA....... Joinery and Timber Construction Association (SAUO)
JATCC....... Joint Air Traffic Control Center [*Military*]
JATCC....... Joint Aviation Telecommunications Co- ordination Committee (SAUS)
JATCC....... Joint Aviation Telecommunications Coordination Committee (BUAC)
JATCCCP.... Joint Advanced Tactical Command, Control, and Communications Program [*Military*]
JATCCCS.... Joint Advanced Tactical Command, Control, and Communications System [*Military*] (MCD)
JATCCS...... Joint Advanced Tactical Command and Control System [*Military*] (SAA)
JATCO....... Japan Automatic Transmission Co.
JATCRU..... Joint Air Traffic Control Radar Unit (SAUO)
JATE......... Japan Techno-Economics Society (SAUO)
JATE......... Joint Air Transport Establishment [*Military*] [*British*]
JATEC....... Japan Technical Committee to Aid US Anti-War Deserter (BUAC)
J At Energy Soc Jpn... Journal. Atomic Energy Society of Japan (journ.) (SAUS)
J At Energy Soc Jpn... Journal of the Atomic Energy Society of Japan (journ.) (SAUS)
JATES....... Japan Techno-Economics Society (EA)
JATF......... Joint Amphibious Task Force (NVT)
JATFC....... JATF Commander (SAUO)
JATFOR..... Joint Amphibious Task Force (SAUO)
JATFS....... Japan Technno-Economics Society (SAUO)
JATI......... Journal. Association of Teachers of Italian (journ.) (SAUS)
JATIS....... Japan Technical Information Service (SAUS)
JATJ......... Journal-Newsletter. Association of Teachers of Japanese (journ.) (SAUS)
JATLA....... Journal. American Trial Lawyers Association [*A publication*] (DLA)
JATM........ Joint Antitactical Missile System (Provisional) [*Army*] (RDA)
JATMA....... Japan Automobile Tire Manufacturers Association
J Atmos Chem... Journal of Atmospheric Chemistry (journ.) (SAUS)
J Atmos Sci... Journal of Atmospheric Science (MEC)
J Atmos Sci... Journal of Atmospheric Sciences (journ.) (SAUS)
JATO......... Jet-Assisted Take-Off. More correct: Rocket-Assisted Take-Off (SAUO)
JATOD3..... Journal of Analytical Toxicology (journ.) (SAUS)
JATOP....... Army Topographic Service (SAUO)
JATO unit... Jet-Assisted Takeoff Unit
JATP......... Jazz at the Philharmonic
JATP......... Joint Air Training Plan
JATP......... Joint Air Transportation Plan (AABC)
JATR......... Japan Advanced Thermal Reactor (SAUS)
JATS......... Jamming Analysis & Transmission Selection (SAUS)
JATS......... Job Application Tracking System (SAUO)
JATS......... Joint Air Transportation Service
JATT......... Joint Air Attack Team (SAUO)
JAU.......... American Hospital Supply Corp., Evanston, IL [*OCLC symbol*] (OCLC)
JAU.......... Jacksboro, TN [*Location identifier*] [*FAA*] (FAAL)
JAU.......... Jiangxi Agricultural University (SAUO)
JAUA......... Just Another Useless Answer (SAUS)
JAUCB....... Journal of Autism and Childhood Schizophrenia (journ.) (SAUS)
J Audio Eng Soc... Journal of the Audio Engineering Society (SAUO)
J Audio Eng Soc... Journal of the Audio Engineering Society (journ.) (SAUS)
J Audiov Media Med... Journal of Audiovisual Media in Medicine (journ.) (SAUS)
J Aud Res... Journal of Auditory Research (journ.) (SAUS)
JAUEA......... Journal of Automotive Engineering (journ.) (SAUS)
JAUMA...... Journal. Australasian Universities Modern Language Association (journ.) (SAUS)
JAUMLA..... Journal of the Australasian Universities Modern Language Association (SAUO)
JAUMLA..... Journal of the Australasian Universities Modern Language Association (journ.) (SAUS)
JAUMS...... Journal. Australian Mathematical Society (journ.) (SAUS)
JAUN........ Jaundice [*Medicine*]
JAUND...... Jaundice [*Medicine*]
JAUNT...... Jefferson Area United Transportation (SAUO)
JAURA....... Journal of Auditory Research (journ.) (SAUS)
J Aus Mat B... Journal. Australian Mathematical Society. Series B. Applied Mathematics (journ.) (SAUS)
J Aus Math A... Journal. Australian Mathematical Society. Series A. Pure Mathematics and Statistics (journ.) (SAUS)
J Aust Cath Hist S... Journal. Australian Catholic Historical Society (journ.) (SAUS)
J Aust Ceram Soc... Journal of the Australian Ceramic Society (SAUO)
J Aust Ceram Soc... Journal of the Australian Ceramics Society (journ.) (SAUS)
J Aust Coll Speech Ther... Journal. Australian College of Speech Therapists (journ.) (SAUS)
J Aust Entomol Soc... Journal of the Australian Entomological Society (SAUO)
J Aust Entomol Soc... Journal of the Australian Entomological Society (journ.) (SAUS)
J Aust Inst Agric Sci... Journal of the Australian Institute of Agricultural Science (SAUO)
J Aust Inst Agric Sci... Journal of the Australian Institute of Agricultural Science (journ.) (SAUS)
J Aust Inst Metals... Journal of the Australian Institute of Metals (SAUO)
J Aust Inst Metals... Journal of the Australian Institute of Metals (journ.) (SAUS)
J Aust Inst Surg Dent Tech... Journal. Australian Institute of Surgical and Dental Technicians (journ.) (SAUS)
J Aust Math Soc... Journal. Australian Mathematical Society (journ.) (SAUS)
J Aust Planning Inst... Journal. Australian Planning Institute (journ.) (SAUS)
J Aust Polit Econ... Journal of Australian Political Economy (journ.) (SAUS)
J Austral Math Soc Ser A... Journal. Australian Mathematical Society. Series A. Pure Mathematics and Statistics (journ.) (SAUS)
J Austral Math Soc Ser B... Journal. Australian Mathematical Society. Series B. Applied Mathematics (journ.) (SAUS)
J Austronesian Stud... Journal of Austronesian Studies (journ.) (SAUS)
J Aust Stud... Journal of Australian Studies [*A publication*]
J Aust Stud... Journal of Australian Studies (journ.) (SAUS)
J Aus War M... Journal. Australian War Memorial [*A publication*]
J Aus War M... Journal. Australian War Memorial (journ.) (SAUS)
J Autoimmun... Journal of Autoimmunity (journ.) (SAUS)
J Autom Chem... Journal of Automatic Chemistry (journ.) (SAUS)
J Automot Eng... Journal of Automotive Engineering (journ.) (SAUS)
J Autom Reasoning... Journal of Automated Reasoning (journ.) (SAUS)
J Auton Nerv Syst... Journal of the Autonomic Nervous System (journ.) (SAUS)
J Auton Pharmacol... Journal of Autonomic Pharmacology (journ.) (SAUS)
JAUW........ Japanese Association of Unversity Women (BUAC)
JAV.......... Chicago, IL [*Location identifier*] [*FAA*] (FAAL)
JAV.......... Dr. William M. Scholl College of Podiatric Medicine, Chicago, IL [*OCLC symbol*] (OCLC)
JAV.......... Janes Aviation Ltd. [*British*] [*ICAO designator*] (FAAC)
JAV.......... Java
Jav........... Javanese (DIAR)
jav........... Javanese [*MARC language code*] [*Library of Congress*] (LCCP)
JAV.......... Javelin [*NCIC car model code*]
Jav........... Javolenus Priscus [*Flourished, 60-120*] [*Authority cited in pre-1607 legal work*] (DSA)
JAV.......... Job Analysis Vocabulary (OICC)
JAVA......... Jamaica Association of Villas and Apartments [*Later, JRJ*]
JAVA......... Jamming Amplitude Versus Azimuth (NVT)
JAVA......... Jandel Video Analysis System
JAV/A........ Journal. South African Veterinary Association (journ.) (SAUS)
JAVAC........ Java Compiler (VLIE)
JavaCt....... Java Centrale, Inc. [*Associated Press*] (SAG)
JavaCtrl..... Java Centrale, Inc. [*Associated Press*] (SAG)
JAVADS..... Journal. American Venereal Disease Association (journ.) (SAUS)
JAVAOS..... Java Operating System (SAUS)
JAVC......... Java Centrale [*NASDAQ symbol*] (TTSB)
JAVC......... Java Centrale, Inc. [*NASDAQ symbol*] (SAG)
JAVCF....... Japan Australia Venture Capital Fund
JAVEA....... Japan Audio-Visual Education Association (SAUO)
Javelin...... Javelin Systems, Inc. [*Associated Press*] (SAG)
JAVHS....... Jane Addams Vocational High School (SAUO)
JAVI......... Javelin International Ltd. (SAUO)
J Avian Biol... Journal of Avian Biology (SAUO)
J Aviat Hist S Aust... Aviation Historical Society of Australia. Journal (journ.) (SAUS)
J Aviation Med... Journal of Aviation Medicine (journ.) (SAUS)
JAVIC........ Japan Audio-Visual Information Centre (BUAC)
JAVLX....... Janus Twenty Fund [*Mutual fund ticker symbol*] (SG)
JAVMA...... Journal of American Veterinary Medical Association [*A publication*] (GVA)
Javole....... Javolenus Priscus [*Flourished, 60-120*] [*Authority cited in pre-1607 legal work*] (DSA)
JAVR......... Jewish Audio-Visual Review (journ.) (SAUS)
JAVRAJ...... Journal. American Veterinary Radiology Society (journ.) (SAUS)
JAVS......... Josephson Array Voltage Standards (VLIE)
JAVS......... JOVIAL Automated Verification System (MCD)
JAVTX........ Janus Venture Fund [*Mutual fund ticker symbol*] (SG)
JAW.......... Jamahiriya Airways [*Libya*] [*ICAO designator*] (FAAC)
JAW.......... Japan Automobile Workers' Unions
JAW.......... Standard Oil Co. (Indiana), Central Research Library, Naperville, IL [*OCLC symbol*] (OCLC)
JAWA......... Janes All the World Aircraft (SAUS)
JAWAA7..... Journal of Agriculture of Western Australia (journ.) (SAUS)
JAWC........ Joint Animal Welfare Council (BUAC)
JAWF......... Jet Augmented Wing Flap
JAWF......... Joint Agriculture Weather Facility [*Marine science*] (OSRA)
JAWG........ Joint Airmiss Working Group (BUAC)
JAWG........ Joint Atomic Demolition Munitions Working Group (SAUO)
JAWNY...... Junior Achievement of Western New York (EARSL)
JAWOP...... Joint Automated Weather Observation Program (ACAE)
JAWOP...... Joint Automated Weather Observing (or Observation) Program (SAUO)
JAWPB...... Joint Atomic Weapons Publications Board (AABC)
JAWPM...... Joint Atomic Weapons Planning Manual (AFM)
JAWPS...... Joint Atomic Weapons Publication System
JAWRFS..... Journal of Agriculture and Water Resources Research (journ.) (SAUS)
JAWS......... Jamming and Warning System (MCD)
JAWS......... Japan Animal Welfare Society [*London, England*]
JAWS......... Jet Advance Warning System (PDAA)
JAWS......... Job Access with Speech [*A voice-synthesizer software*]
JAWS......... Joint AAR Warfighting System (SAUS)
JAWS......... Joint Action for Water Services (BUAC)
JAWS......... Joint Air Force Systems Command War Game System (SAUO)
JAWS......... Joint Airport Weather Studies [*National Center for Atmospheric Research*]
JAWS......... Joint All Weather Seeker (ACAE)
JAWS......... Joint Arctic Weather Stations [*Canada-US*]
JAWS......... Joint Attack Weapon System [*Military*] (MCD)
JAWS......... Josephson AttoWeber Switch [*Data processor circuitry*]
JAWS......... Junk Acronyms When Speaking [*Program*]
JAWS......... Just Another Windows Shell (SAUS)
JAWS......... Just Another Work Station [*Jargon*] (NITA)
JAWSAT..... Joint Air Force-Weber State College Satellite (SAUO)
JAWTR....... Junior Assistant Writer [*British military*] (DMA)
JAWWA...... Journal. American Water Works Association (journ.) (SAUS)

JAWWAS.... American Water Works Association (SAUO)
JAWYS...... Join Airways (FAAC)
JAX......... Chicago School of Professional Psychology, Chicago, IL [*OCLC symbol*] (OCLC)
JAX......... Jacksonville [*Florida*] [*Airport symbol*] (OAG)
JAX......... J. Alexander's Corp. [*NYSE symbol*] (SG)
JAX......... JanAir, Inc. [*ICAO designator*] (FAAC)
JAX......... Mister Jax Fashions, Inc. [*Toronto Stock Exchange symbol*]
JAXVL....... Jacksonville, IL [*American Association of Railroads railroad junction routing code*]
JAY......... J & J Air Charters Ltd. [*British*] [*ICAO designator*] (FAAC)
JAY......... Jayapura [*Indonesia*] [*Seismograph station code, US Geological Survey*] (SEIS)
JAY......... Jayco [*NCIC truck make code*]
JAY......... Jayco [*NCIC trailer make code*]
JAY......... Journal of Applied Psychology (journ.) (SAUS)
Jay......... Marijuana Cigarette [*Joint*] [*Medicine*] (EDAA)
JAy......... Travenol Laboratories, Monon Grove (SAUS)
JAY......... Travenol Laboratories, Morton Grove, IL [*OCLC symbol*] (OCLC)
JAYA........ Jayark Corp. [*NASDAQ symbol*] (NQ)
Jayark....... Jayark Corp. [*Associated Press*] (SAG)
JAYCEES.... Junior Chamber of Commerce (ADWA)
JAYD........ Jay Dee Industries [*NCIC trailer make code*]
JAYF........ Jersey Association of Youth and Friendship (SAUO)
Jayhwk...... Jayhawk Acceptance Corp. [*Associated Press*] (SAG)
JAYJ........ Jay Jacobs [*NASDAQ symbol*] (TTSB)
JAYJ........ Jay Jacobs, Inc. [*NASDAQ symbol*] (NQ)
JAYK........ Jay-Kee Manufacturing [*NCIC trailer make code*]
JAYM........ Jay-Mar Leasing [*Common carrier symbol*]
JAYT........ Jacobs [*Jay*], Inc. (MHDW)
JAYU........ Jay Container Services [*Intermodal shipping container symbol*] (TVRC)
JAYW........ Jay Wren Trailer [*NCIC trailer make code*]
JAZ......... Japan Air Charter Co. Ltd. [*ICAO designator*] (FAAC)
JAZ......... JCC Holding 'A' [*AMEX symbol*] (SG)
JAZODX..... Journal of Advanced Zoology (journ.) (SAUS)
JB.......... Bachelor of Laws (SAUS)
JB.......... British Caledonian Airways Ltd. (SAUO)
J-B......... Fr. Jean-Baptiste (SAUS)
JB.......... IML Air Services Ltd. [*British*] [*ICAO designator*] (ICDA)
Jb.......... Jaarboek [*Yearbook*] [*Netherlands*] (BJA)
JB.......... Jahrbuch [*Yearbook*] [*German*]
JB.......... James Boswell [*Initials used as pseudonym*]
JB.......... James Buchanan [*US president, 1791-1868*]
JB.......... Jerusalem Bible
JB.......... Jervis Bay (SAUS)
J-B......... Jet Barrier
JB.......... Jet Black [*Derogatory nickname for a black person*]
JB.......... Jet Bomb
JB.......... Jet powered Bomb (SAUS)
JB.......... Jiffy Bag
JB.......... Job (MCD)
Jb.......... Job [*Old Testament book*]
JB.......... Job Bank (OICC)
JB.......... Job Blank (SAUS)
JB.......... Job Book
JB.......... Jodrell Bank (SAUS)
JB.......... Joggle Blocks (MCD)
JB.......... Johannes Baptista [*John the Baptist*] [*Authority cited in pre-1607 legal work*] (DSA)
JB.......... John Bull [*The typical Englishman*]
JB.......... Johore Bahru [*Refers to Europeans named after Malaysian towns*] (DSUE)
JB.......... Joint Army-Navy Board
JB.......... Joint Bond
JB.......... Journal of Bacteriology (SAUO)
JB.......... Journal of Biochemistry (SAUO)
JB.......... Jubilee [*Telegraphy*] (PCTE)
JB.......... Juggle Box
JB.......... Jukeboxes [*Public-performance tariff class*] [*British*]
JB.......... Jump If Below [*Computer science*] (PCM)
JB.......... Jump of Below (SAUS)
JB.......... Junction Block [*Automotive engineering*]
JB.......... Junction Box [*Technical drawings*]
JB.......... Junior Beadle [*Ancient Order of Foresters*]
JB.......... Junior Birdman [*Slang*]
JB.......... Junior Bookshelf [*A publication*] (BRI)
JB.......... Juris Baccalaureus [*Bachelor of Laws*]
JB.......... Lakeside Laboratories, Inc. [*Research code symbol*]
JB.......... Pioneer Airways [*ICAO designator*] (AD)
JB.......... Stetson Hat [*After John Batterson Stetson, 19th-century American hat manufacturer*] [*Slang*]
JB 251...... Protokylol Hydrochloride [*Medicine*] (EDAA)
JB 336...... Methyl-Piperidyl-Benzitate Hydrochloride [*Medicine*] (EDAA)
JB 516...... Pheniprazine Hydrochloride [*Medicine*] (EDAA)
JB 8181..... Desipramine Hydrochloride [*Medicine*] (EDAA)
JBA......... Helijet Airways [*Canada*] [*ICAO designator*] (FAAC)
JBA......... Japan Bankers Association (BUAC)
JBA......... Japan Binoculars Association (SAUO)
JBA......... Japanese Bioindustry Association (BUAC)
JBA......... JBA International Ltd. (HODG)
JBA......... Jewel Bearing Assembly
JBA......... Jewish Book Annnal (journ.) (SAUS)
JBA......... Job Buffer A (SAUS)
JBA......... John Burroughs Association (EA)
JBA......... Journal. Board of Agriculture (journ.) (SAUS)
JBA......... Journal of Belizean Affairs. Belize City (journ.) (SAUS)
JBA......... Journal of Business Administration (journ.) (SAUS)
JBA......... Junction Box Assembly
JBA......... Junior Bluejackets of America (EA)
JBAA........ Journal. British Archaeological Association (journ.) (SAUS)
JBAA........ Journal of the British Archaeological Association [*A publication*] (WDAA)
JBAA........ Journal of the British Astronomical Association (SAUO)
J BAC........ Journal. International Union of Bricklayers and Allied Craftsmen (journ.) (SAUS)
J Bacteriol... Journal of Bacteriology (SAUO)
JBADC....... Journal of the Bar Association of the District of Columbia (SAUO)
JBAFC....... Jan Berry and the Alohas Fan Club (EA)
JBAK........ Baker [*J.*], Inc. [*NASDAQ symbol*] (NQ)
JBAKC....... John Brown Anti-Klan Committee (EA)
J Ballist..... Journal of Ballistics (journ.) (SAUS)
J Baltimore Coll Dent Surg... Journal. Baltimore College of Dental Surgery (journ.) (SAUS)
JBANC....... Joint Baltic American National Committee (EA)
JB&C........ John Brown and Company (SAUO)
JB&Co....... John Brown and Company (SAUO)
J Band Res... Journal of Band Research (journ.) (SAUS)
J Bangladesh Ad Sci... Journal. Bangladesh Academy of Sciences (journ.) (SAUS)
J Bangladesh Acad Sci... Journal of the Bangladesh Academy of Sciences (journ.) (SAUS)
J Bank Financ... Journal of Banking and Finance (journ.) (SAUS)
J Bank Res... Journal of Bank Research [*A publication*] (JLIT)
J-Bar........ Jet Runway Barrier [*Aviation*] (FAAC)
J Barbados Mus Hist Soc... Journal of the Barbados Museum and Historical Society. Bridgetown (SAUO)
J Barbados Mus Hist Soc... Journal of the Barbados Museum and Historical Society (journ.) (SAUS)
JBAS........ Jussi Bjorling Appreciation Society [*British*] (DBA)
J Basic Clin Physiol Pharmacol... Journal of Basic and Clinical Physiology and Pharmacology (journ.) (SAUS)
J Basic Microbiol... Journal of Basic Microbiology (journ.) (SAUS)
J Basic Sci Hanyng Inst Basic Sci... Journal of Basic Sciences. Hanyang Institute of Basic Science (journ.) (SAUS)
J Bas S...... Journal of Basque Studies (journ.) (SAUS)
JBAU........ Distillerie de l'Ouest [*Intermodal shipping container symbol*] (TVRC)
JBB......... John Birch Society (SAUO)
JBBB........ JB's Restaurants, Inc. [*NASDAQ symbol*] (COMM)
JBBF........ Judo Black Belt Federation [*Later, USJE*]
JBBFC....... James Bond British Fan Club (EAIO)
JBBL........ Jamming of Beacons and Blind Landing [*Aviation*] (IAA)
JBBMD....... Journal of Biochemical and Biophysical Methods (journ.) (SAUS)
JBC......... Jamaica Broadcasting Corp.
JBC......... Jamaica Broadcasting Corporation (SAUO)
JBC......... Japan Broadcasting Corp. (SAUS)
JBC......... Japan Broadcasting Corporation (SAUO)
JBC......... Japanese Broadcasting Corporation (BUAC)
JBC......... [*The*] Jerome Biblical Commentary [*Englewood Cliffs, NJ*] [*A publication*] (BJA)
JBC......... Jesness Behavior Checklist [*Psychology*] (DAVI)
JBC......... Jewelers' Book Club (EA)
JBC......... Jewish Book Council [*of the National Jewish Welfare Board*] [*Later, JWBJBC*] (EA)
JBC......... Johnson Bible College [*Tennessee*]
JBC......... Joint Blood Council [*Defunct*] (EA)
JBC......... Joint Broadcasting Committee [*British*] (CARL)
JBC......... Joint Budget Committee (OICC)
JBC......... Journal of Biological Chemistry (journ.) (SAUS)
JBC......... Journal of Business Communication (journ.) (SAUS)
JBC......... Journal. State Bar of California [*A publication*] (DLA)
JBCA........ Jewish Book Council of America (SAUO)
JBck & L..... Jackson and Lumpkins Reports (journ.) (SAUS)
JBc L Dict... Jacobs Law Dictionary (journ.) (SAUS)
JBc Lex Mer... Jacobs Lex Mercatoria (journ.) (SAUS)
JBCNS....... Joint Board of Clinical Nursing Studies (SAUS)
JBCNTRL..... Job Control (SAUS)
JBCOUNT.... Job Account (SAUS)
JBC PAC.... JBC International Trade Development PAC [*Washington, DC*] (PACS)
JBCPS....... Journeyman Bakers' and Confectioners Pension Society [*British*] (BI)
JBCS........ James Branch Cabell Society (EA)
JBCSA....... Joint British Committee for Stress Analysis (BUAC)
JBCSA....... Journal. British Ceramic Society (journ.) (SAUS)
JBCZ........ Jack Bean [*Federal Railroad Administration identification code*]
JBD......... Becton, Dickinson & Co., Paramus, NJ [*OCLC symbol*] (OCLC)
JBD......... James Brake [*Aviation*] (DA)
JBD......... James Brake Decelerometer (SAUS)
JBD......... Jet Blast Deflector
JBD......... Jet Blast Detector (SAUS)
JBD......... Jewish Board of Deputies [*Australia*]
JBD......... Joint Battlefield Digitization (SAUS)
JBDAAFES... Joint Board of Directors, Army-Air Force Exchange Service (AABC)
JBDFC....... James Bond 007 Fan Club [*Defunct*] (EA)
JBDK........ Java Beans Development Kit (HODG)
JBE......... Japanese B Encephalitis [*Medicine*]
JBE......... Journal of Behavioral Economics (journ.) (SAUS)
JBE......... Journal of Business Education (journ.) (SAUS)
JBE......... Judeo-Berber [*Language symbol*] (ETLW)
JBE......... Jump If Below or Equal [*Computer science*] (PCM)

J Behavioral Econ... Journal of Behavioral Economics [*A publication*] (JLIT)
J Behav Sci... Journal of Behavioral Science (journ.) (SAUS)
J Behav Ther Exp Psychiatry... Journal of Behavior Therapy and Experimental Psychiatry (journ.) (SAUS)
J Beijing Univ Iron Steel Technol... Journal of Beijing University of Iron and Steel Technology (journ.) (SAUS)
JBEN......... JB Enterprises [*NCIC trailer make code*]
Jber......... annual report (SAUS)
Jber......... Jahresbericht [*Journal, Annual Report*] [*German*] (BJA)
J Bergen Cty Dent S... Journal. Betgen County Dental Safety (journ.) (SAUS)
JBES......... Jodrell Bank Experimental Station [*British*]
JBES......... Journal of Business & Economic Statistics [*Database*] (GDD)
J Bethune Univ Med Sci... Journal. Bethune Umversity of Medical Sciences (journ.) (SAUS)
JBF......... James Beard Foundation (EA)
JBF......... James Buchanan Foundation (EA)
JBF......... Japan Booksellers' Federation (BUAC)
JBF......... Jeune Ballet de France
JBFC......... James Bond 007 Fan Club [*British*] (EAIO)
JBFC......... Jennifer Bassey Fan Club (EA)
JBFC......... Jennifer Burnett Fan Club (EA)
JBFC......... Johnny Bernard Fan Club (EA)
JBFCI......... Jon Beryl Fan Club International (EA)
JBFL&P..... Journal of Banking and Finance Law and Practice [*A publication*]
JBFLP......... Journal of Banking and Finance Law and Practice [*A publication*]
JBFSAW..... Joint Board on Future Storage of Atomic Weapons
JBG......... Jewish Board of Guardians (EA)
JBG......... Jewish Brigade Group (SAUO)
JBG......... Johannesburg, South Africa Scientology organization (SAUO)
JBHCPIUA... Journeymen Barbers, Hairdressers, Cosmetologists and Proprietors' International Union of America (EA)
JBHS......... John Bartram High School (SAUO)
JBHS&R...... Journal of Behavioral Health Services & Research (SAUO)
JBHT......... Hunt(JB)Transport [*NASDAQ symbol*] (TTSB)
JBHT......... Hunt [*J. B.*] Transport Services, Inc. [*NASDAQ symbol*] (NQ)
JBHU......... JB Hunt Transport [*Intermodal shipping container symbol*] (TVRC)
JBHX......... John Brown Harris [*Federal Railroad Administration identification code*]
JBHZ......... JB Hunt Transport [*Intermodal trailer symbol*]
JBI......... Jacob Blaustein Institute for the Ad- vancement of Human Rights (SAUS)
JBI......... Jacob Blaustein Institute for the Advancement of Human Rights (EA)
JBI......... Jamaica Bauxite Institute (BUAC)
JBI......... James Brake Index (SAUS)
JBI......... J. Baker, Inc. (EFIS)
JBI......... Jewish Braille Institute of America (EA)
JBIA......... Jewish Braille Institute of America (EA)
JBIC......... Journal of Biological Inorganic Chemistry [*A publication*]
JBIG......... Joint Bi-level Group (SAUO)
JBIG......... Joint Bi-Level Image Experts Group (RALS)
JBIG......... Joint Bi-Level Imaging Group (VLIE)
JBIG......... Joint Binary Image Group (VLIE)
JBIG......... Joint Bitonal Image Group (GART)
J Bihar Agric Coll... Journal. Bihar Agricultural College (journ.) (SAUS)
J Bihar RS... Journal. Bihar Research Society (journ.) (SAUS)
JBIL......... Bildner & Sons Inc. (SAUO)
JBIL......... Jabil Circuit [*NASDAQ symbol*] (TTSB)
JBIL......... Jabil Circuit, Inc. [*NASDAQ symbol*] (SAG)
Jb Int R..... Jahrbuch fuer Internationales und Auslaendisches Oeffentliches Recht [*1948-*] [*A publication*] [*German*] (ILCA)
J Biochem Toxicol... Journal of Biochemical Toxicology (journ.) (SAUS)
J Biocommun... Journal of Biocommunication (journ.) (SAUS)
J Bioecon... Journal of Bioeconomics [*A publication*] (JLIT)
J Bioelectr... Journal of Bioelectricity (journ.) (SAUS)
J Bioenerg... Journal of Bioenergetics (journ.) (SAUS)
J Bioenerg Biomembr... Journal of Bioenergetics and Biomembranes (journ.) (SAUS)
J Bioeth..... Journal of Bioethics (journ.) (SAUS)
J Biol Board Cn... Journal. Biological Board of Canada (journ.) (SAUS)
J Biol Inorg Chem Soc... Journal of the Biological Inorganic Chemistry Society (SAUO)
J Biol Inorg Chem Soc... Journal of the Biological Inorganic Chemistry Society (journ.) (SAUS)
J Biologicl Ed... Journal of Biological Education (journ.) (SAUS)
J Biol Osaka City Univ... Journal of Biology. Osaka City University (journ.) (SAUS)
J Biol Photogr... Journal of Biological Photography (journ.) (SAUS)
J Biol Photogr Assoc... Journal of the Biological Photographic Association (SAUO)
J Biol Photogr Assoc... Journal of the Biological Photographic Association (journ.) (SAUS)
J Biol Phys... Journal of Biological Physics (journ.) (SAUS)
J Biol Psychol... Journal of Biological Psychology (journ.) (SAUS)
J Biol Regul Homeost Agents... Journal of Biological Regulators and Homeostatic Agents (journ.) (SAUS)
J Biol Sci... Journal of Biological Sciences (journ.) (SAUS)
J Biol Sci Res Publ... Journal of Biological Sciences Research Publication (journ.) (SAUS)
J Biol Syst... Journal of Biological Systems [*A publication*] (PABS)
J Biolumin Chemilumin... Journal of Bioluminescence and Chemiluminescence (journ.) (SAUS)
J Biomater Appl... Journal of Biomaterials Applications (journ.) (SAUS)
J Biomater Sci Polym Ed... Journal of Biomaterials Science, Polymer Edition (journ.) (SAUS)
J Biomech... Journal of Biomechanics [*A publication*] (CABS)
J Biomech Eng... Journal of Biomechanical Engineering (journ.) (SAUS)
J Biomed Eng... Journal of Biomedical Engineering (journ.) (SAUS)
J Biomed Mater Res... Journal of Biomedical Materials Research (SAUO)
J Biomed Mater Res Biomed Mater Symp... Journal of Biomedical Materials Research. Biomedical Materials Symposium (journ.) (SAUS)
J Biomed Syst... Journal of Biomedical Systems (journ.) (SAUS)
J Biomol NMR... Journal of Biomolecular NMR (journ.) (SAUS)
J Biopharm Stat... Journal of Biopharmaceutical Statistics (journ.) (SAUS)
J Biophys Biochem Cytol... Journal of Biophysical and Biochemical Cytology. (journ.) (SAUS)
J Biophys S Jpn... Journal. Biophysical Society of Japan (journ.) (SAUS)
J Biosci Bioeng... Journal of Bioscience and Bioengineering [*A publication*] (PABS)
J Biosoc Sci... Journal of Biosocial Science (journ.) (SAUS)
J Biosoc Sci Suppl... Journal of Biosocial Science. Supplement (journ.) (SAUS)
J Birla Inst Technol Sci... Journal of the Birla Institute of Technology and Science (journ.) (SAUS)
J Birmingham Metall Soc... Journal. Birmingham Metallurgical Society (journ.) (SAUS)
JBIS......... Journal. British Interplanetary Society (journ.) (SAUS)
JBIS......... Journal of Baltic Studies (journ.) (SAUS)
JBIS......... Journal of the British Interplanetary Society (SAUO)
JBIS......... Journal of the British Interplanetary Society (journ.) (SAUS)
JBITD4...... Journal of Biotechnology (journ.) (SAUS)
JBJ......... Bellum Judaicum [*Josephus*] [*Classical studies*] (BJA)
JBJ......... James Bond Journalism [*Term coined by leader Sinnathamby Bajaratman of Singapore and referring to Western journalism*]
JBJS......... Journal of Bone and Joint Surgery (SAUO)
JBJS......... Journal of Bone and Joint Surgery (journ.) (SAUS)
JBK......... Berkeley, CA [*Location identifier*] [*FAA*] (FAAL)
JBK......... Journal of Banking and Finance (journ.) (SAUS)
JBL......... Jabil Circuit [*NYSE symbol*] (SG)
JBL......... James B. Lansing Sound, Inc.
JBL......... Jonesboro, LA [*Location identifier*] [*FAA*] (FAAL)
JBL......... Journal of Biblical Literature [*A publication*] (BRI)
JBL......... Journal of Business Law [*A publication*]
JBL......... Jubilee
JBL......... Junior Bird League [*British*] (BI)
JBL......... Juta's Business Law (SAFN)
JB Lit Today... Japanese Literature Today (journ.) (SAUS)
J/BLK......... Junction Block [*Automotive engineering*]
JBLMS...... Journal of Biblical Literature. Monog- raph Series (journ.) (SAUS)
J Bl St....... Journal of Black Studies [*A publication*] (BRI)
JBLU......... JetBlue Airways [*NASDAQ National Market symbol*]
JBM......... Jan Bell Marketing [*AMEX symbol*] (TTSB)
JBM......... Jan Bell Marketing, Inc. [*AMEX symbol*] (SPSG)
JBM......... Just Beat Maiden [*Equine term*] (TED)
JBMA......... John Burroughs Memorial Association (EA)
JBMBB...... Journal of Biochemistry, Molecular Biology and Biophysics (SAUO)
JBMBB...... Journal of Biochemistry, Molecular Biology and Biophysics (journ.) (SAUS)
JBMI......... Journalist Biographies Master Index [*A publication*]
JBMMA...... Japan Business Machine Makers Association (SAUS)
JBMMA...... Japanese Business Machine Makers Association (SAUS)
JB MoU..... Joint Ballistic MoU (SAUS)
JBMR......... Journal of Biomedical Materials Research [*Medicine*] (EDAA)
JBMTO...... Joint Bus Military Traffic Office (AABC)
JBMZ......... Jacobs Branch Mine [*Federal Railroad Administration identification code*]
JBN......... Jubilation [*Telegraphy*] (PCTE)
JBN......... Judaica Book News (journ.) (SAUS)
JBNC......... Jefferson Bancorp (FL) [*NASDAQ symbol*] (TTSB)
JBNC......... Jefferson Bancorp, Inc. [*NASDAQ symbol*] (NQ)
JBNK......... Jefferson Bankshares, Inc. [*NASDAQ symbol*] (NQ)
JBNQA...... James Bay and Northern Quebec Agreement (SAUS)
JBNSA...... Journal. British Nuclear Energy Society (journ.) (SAUS)
JBO......... Journal of Behavioral Optometry (SAUO)
JBO......... Journal of Economic Behavior and Organization (journ.) (SAUS)
jbo......... Jumbo
J Board Dir Am S Civ Eng... Journal. Board of Direction. American Society of Civil Engineers (journ.) (SAUS)
J Board Greenkeeping Res... Journal. Board of Greenkeeping Research (journ.) (SAUS)
JBOD......... Just a Bunch of Disks [*Computer science*]
JBOH......... Oxford [*J. B.*] Oxford Holdings [*NASDAQ symbol*] (SAG)
J-bolt......... Capital-J-shaped bolt (SAUS)
J Bombay Nat Hist Soc... Journal. Bombay Natural History Society (journ.) (SAUS)
J Bone-Am V... Journal of Bone and Joint Surgery. American Volume (journ.) (SAUS)
J Bone-Br V... Journal of Bone and Joint Surgery. British Volume (journ.) (SAUS)
J Bone Joint Surg... Journal of Bone and Joint Surgery (journ.) (SAUS)
J Bone Miner Res... Journal of Bone and Mineral Research (journ.) (SAUS)
JBOR......... Job Bank Operations Review [*Employment and Training Administration*] [*Department of Labor*]
J Borderl Stud... Journal of Borderlands Studies (journ.) (SAUS)
JBORS....... Journal. Bihar and Orissa Research Society (journ.) (SAUS)
JBORS....... Journal of the Bihar and Orissa Research Society (SAUO)
JBORS....... Journal of the Bihar and Orissa Research Society (journ.) (SAUS)
JBOS......... Job Banks Opening Summary [*Department of Labor*]
J Boston S Civ Eng Sect ASCE... Journal. Boston Society of Civil Engineers Section. American Society of Civil Engineers (journ.) (SAUS)
J Boston Soc Civ Eng... Journal. Boston Society of Civil Engineers (journ.) (SAUS)
J Bot Br Foreign... Journal of Botany. British and Foreign (journ.) (SAUS)

J Bot Soc S Afr... Journal. Botanical Society of South Africa (journ.) (SAUS)
J Bot UAR... Journal of Botany. United Arab Republic (journ.) (SAUS)
J Bowman Grsy Scb Med Wake For Coll... Journal. Bowman Gray School of Medicine. Wake Forest College (journ.) (SAUS)
J-box........ J-shaped bleaching box (SAUS)
JB Oxfrd.... JB Oxford Holdings [*Associated Press*] (SAG)
JBP.......... Jettison Booster Package [*NASA*]
JBP.......... Jewel Bearing Program (SAUS)
JBP.......... John B. Piera Foundation Laboratory (SAUO)
JBP.......... John B. Pierce Foundation Laboratory [*New Haven, CT*]
JBP.......... Joint Blood Program (COE)
JBP.......... Junior Bowhunter Program (EA)
JBPA......... Japan Book Publishers (SAUS)
JBPA......... Japan Book Publishers Association (BUAC)
JBPAA....... Journal. Biological Photographic Association (journ.) (SAUS)
JBPI......... Japanese Bicycle Promotion Institute (SAUO)
JBPI......... Journal of Biological Physics (journ.) (SAUS)
JBPO........ Joint Blood Program Office (DOMA)
JBPS......... Jamaica Banana Producers Steamship (SAUO)
JBPU........ Jamaica Banana Producers Steamship [*Intermodal shipping container symbol*] (TVRC)
JBPVE....... Joint Board for Pre-Vocational Education (BUAC)
JBR.......... Job Air Ltd. [*Czechoslovakia*] [*FAA designator*] (FAAC)
JBR.......... Jonesboro [*Arkansas*] [*Airport symbol*] (OAG)
JBR.......... Jonesboro, AR [*Location identifier*] [*FAA*] (FAAL)
JBR.......... Journal of Bible and Religion (journ.) (SAUS)
JBR.......... Journal of Biological Rhythms (SAUS)
J BRAN-NAM Just Brand Names [*Division of F. W. Woolworth Co.*]
JBRAS........ Journal of Bombay Branch of the Royal Asiatic Society (journ.) (SAUS)
J Br Astron Assoc... Journal. British Astronomical Association (journ.) (SAUS)
J Br Astron Assoc... Journal of the British Astronomical Association (journ.) (SAUS)
J Br Boot Shoe Instn... Journal. British Boot and Shoe Institution (journ.) (SAUS)
J Br Dent Assoc... Journal. British Dental Association (journ.) (SAUS)
J Br Endod Soc... Journal. British Endodontic Society (journ.) (SAUS)
J Brew Soc Jpn... Journal. Brewing Society of Japan (journ.) (SAUS)
J Br Fire Serv Ass... Journal. British Fire Services Association (journ.) (SAUS)
J Br Grassl Soc... Journal of the British Grassland Society (SAUO)
J Br Inst Radio Eng... Journal. British Institution of Radio Engineers (journ.) (SAUS)
J Brit Archaeol Ass 3 Ser... Journal. British Archaeological Association. Series 3 (journ.) (SAUS)
J Brit Ceram Soc... Journal. British Ceramic Society (journ.) (SAUS)
J Brit Interplanet S... Journal. British Interplanetary Society (journ.) (SAUS)
JBrit IRE.... Journal of the British Institute of Radio Engineers (SAUO)
J Brit Ship Res Ass... Journal. British Ship Research Association (journ.) (SAUS)
J Brit Soc Phenomenol... Journal. British Society for Phenomenology (journ.) (SAUS)
JBRM......... Journal of Biological Response Modifiers (journ.) (SAUS)
J Br Nucl Energy Soc... Journal of the British Nuclear Energy Society (SAUO)
J Br Nucl Energy Soc... Journal of the British Nuclear Energy Society (journ.) (SAUS)
J Broadcst... Journal of Broadcasting and Electronic Media [*A publication*] (BRI)
J Bromeliad Soc... Journal. Bromeliad Society (journ.) (SAUS)
JBRS........ Journal. Burma Research Society (journ.) (SAUS)
JBRS........ Journal of the Burma Research Society (SAUO)
JBRS........ Journal of the Burma Research Society (journ.) (SAUS)
J Br S Ph... Journal. British Society for Phenomenology (journ.) (SAUS)
JBRU........ Johann Brucken [*Intermodal shipping container symbol*] (TVRC)
J Br Waterworks As... Journal. British Waterworks Association (journ.) (SAUS)
J Br Waterworks Assoc... Journal of the British Waterworks Association (SAUO)
J Br Wood Preserv Ass... Journal. British Wood Preserving Association (journ.) (SAUS)
J Bryol...... Journal of Bryology (journ.) (SAUS)
JBS.......... Jagdbomberfliegerstaffel (SAUO)
JBS.......... Jamaican Bureau of Standards (SAUS)
JBS.......... Jane Badler Society (EA)
JBS.......... Japan British Society (SAUO)
JBS.......... Japan Broadcasting System (SAUO)
JBS.......... Japanese Biochemical Society (BUAC)
JBS.......... Japanese Broadcast Satellite (SAUS)
JBS.......... Jewish Burial Society [*Australia*]
JBS.......... Job Search [*Job Training and Partnership Act*] (OICC)
JBS.......... Johanson-Bizzard Syndrome [*Medicine*] (EDAA)
JBS.......... John Birch Society (EA)
JBS.......... Joly Black Screen
JBS.......... Josephine Butler Society (EAIO)
JBS.......... Journal of Biomedical Systems [*Medicine*] (EDAA)
JBS.......... Journal of Biopharmaceutical Statistics (SAUO)
JBS.......... Journal of Black Studies [*A publication*] (ANEX)
JBS.......... Journal of British Studies (journ.) (SAUS)
JBS.......... Journal of Business Research (journ.) (SAUS)
JBS.......... Journal of Byelorussian Studies (journ.) (SAUS)
JBSDD6...... Journal of Biomolecular Structure and Dynamics (journ.) (SAUS)
JBSG........ Joyce Brothers Storage and Van Company [*Common carrier symbol*]
JBSRES..... Journal of Biological Sciences Research (journ.) (SAUS)
JBSS......... Sanfilippo [*John B.*] & Son [*NASDAQ symbol*] (SPSG)
JBSTD....... Journal of Biological Standardization (journ.) (SAUS)
JB St Univ... John B. Stetson University (SAUO)
JBSW........ Joseph Bulova School of Watchmaking (SAUO)
JBT.......... Bethel, AK [*Location identifier*] [*FAA*] (FAAL)
JBT.......... Jewelers Board of Trade (EA)
JBT.......... Jubilant [*Telegraphy*] (PCTE)
JBTE......... Bert E. Jessup [*Common carrier symbol*]
JBTEP....... Journal of Behavior Therapy and Experimental Psychiatry [*Medicine*] (EDAA)
JBTS......... Journal of the Buddhist Text Society (SAUO)
JBTS......... Journal of the Buddhist Text Society (journ.) (SAUS)
JBTU......... Jumbotainers Barendrecht [*Intermodal shipping container symbol*] (TVRC)
JBU.......... John Brown University [*Siloam Springs, AR*]
JBUA......... Journal. Bombay University. Arts (journ.) (SAUS)
JB Univ..... John Brown University (SAUO)
J Bus........ Journal of Business [*A publication*] (JLIT)
J Bus........ Journal of Business. University of Chicago (SAUO)
J Busan Med Coll... Journal. Busan Medical College (journ.) (SAUS)
JBUSDC..... Joint Brazil-United States Defense Commission [*Terminated, 1977*]
J Bus Econ Statist... Journal of Business and Economic Statistics [*A publication*] (JLIT)
J Bus Ethics... Journal of Business Ethics (journ.) (SAUS)
JBUSMC.... Joint Brazil-United States Military Commission
JBUSMC.... Joint Brazil-US Military Commission (SAUS)
J Bus Res... Journal of Business Research [*A publication*] (JLIT)
J Bus Strategy... Journal of Business Strategy (journ.) (SAUS)
JBV.......... Jolt Beverage Co. Ltd. [*Vancouver Stock Exchange symbol*]
JBW.......... J Brian Naylor and Fred Wilkinson [*Motorsports*]
JBX.......... Jack in the Box [*NYSE symbol*]
JBXR........ JBS Express [*Common carrier symbol*]
JBYC......... Jamaica Bay Yacht Club (SAUO)
JC............ All Seasons Aviation Ltd. (SAUO)
JC............ Community Colleges [*Educational Resources Information Center (ERIC) Clearinghouse*] [*University of California at Los Angeles (UCLA)*] (PAZ)
JC............ Jack Connection [*Electronics*] (IAA)
JC............ Jack Cover
JC............ Jacket Crown (MELL)
JC............ Jackson College (SAUO)
JC............ Jacksonville College (SAUO)
JC............ Jaguar [*Society of Automotive Engineers auto manufacturer code for service information interchange*]
JC............ Jakob-Creutzfeldt [*Disease or syndrome*] [*Neurology*] (DAVI)
JC............ Jam Contact (SAUS)
JC............ James Crean plc (EFIS)
JC............ Jamestown College (SAUO)
JC............ Janitor Closet (MSA)
JC............ Java Computer (GART)
JC............ Jayhawk Conference (PSS)
JC............ J. C. Smith Marketing Corp. [*Vancouver Stock Exchange symbol*]
JC............ Jeanswear Communication (EA)
JC............ Jefferson City [*Diocesan abbreviation*] [*Missouri*] (TOCD)
JC............ Jefferson College (SAUS)
JC............ Jenny Craig [*NYSE symbol*] (SPSG)
JC............ Jersey Central Railroad
JC............ Jersey City (SAUO)
JC............ Jesus Christ
JC............ Jesus College [*Oxford or Cambridge*] [*England*] (DAS)
JC............ Jet Club (SAUO)
JC............ Jewelcor, Inc. (SAUO)
JC............ Jewish Care [*British*] (EAIO)
JC............ Jewish Chronicle (ODA)
JC............ [*The*] Jewish Community: Its History and Structure to the American Revolution [*A publication*] (BJA)
JC............ Jimmy Carter [*James Earl Carter, Jr.*] [*US president, 1924-*]
JC............ Job Card (SAUS)
JC............ Job Center
JC............ Job Club
JC............ Job Control (VLIE)
JC............ Job Corps [*Department of Labor*]
JC............ Jockey Club [*Later, TJC*] (EA)
JC............ Johannesburg Consolidated (SAUS)
JC............ Johnson Controls, Inc. (SAUO)
JC............ Johnson Counter (SAUS)
JC............ Johnson's New York Cases [*or Reports*] [*A publication*] (DLA)
JC............ Johnstown College (SAUO)
JC............ Joint Commission (SAUS)
JC............ Joint Committee (SAUO)
JC............ Joint Communications (ELAL)
JC............ Joint Compound [*Plumbing*]
JC............ Joint Conference (SAUS)
JC............ Joint Contracture [*Medicine*] (MELL)
JC............ Joist Chair (SAUS)
JC............ Joliet College (SAUO)
JC-.......... Jones Criteria Negative [*Medicine*] (EDAA)
JC+.......... Jones Criteria Positive [*Medicine*] (EDAA)
JC............ Joule Cycle [*Physics*]
J/C........... Joule per Coulomb [*Physics*] (DAVI)
JC............ Journal Citation (NITA)
JC............ Journal Code [*Online database field identifier*]
JC............ Journal Coden [*Searchable fields*] (NITA)
JC............ Journalists' Club [*Australia*]
JC............ Journal of Chemotherapy [*Medicine*] (EDAA)
JC............ Journal of Chromatography [*A publication*]
JC............ Journal of Communication [*A publication*] (BRI)
JC............ JOVIAL Compiler [*Computer science*]
JC............ Judicial Council (SAUO)
JC............ Judson College (SAUO)

Jc .... Juglans cinerea [*Butternut tree*]
JC .... Juice
jc .... Juice
JC .... Julius Caesar [*Shakespearean work*]
JC .... Jump Command (SAUS)
JC .... Jump Condition (VLIE)
JC .... Jump if Carry set (SAUO)
JC .... Jump on Carry (SAUS)
JC .... Jump on Condition [*Computer science*] (BUR)
JC .... Jump-to-Contact [*Physics*]
JC .... Junction (ADA)
JC .... Junction Center [*Civil engineering*] (IAA)
JC .... Junction Connector [*Automotive engineering*]
JC .... Juniata College (SAUO)
JC .... Junior Chamber (SAUO)
JC .... Junior Chamber of Commerce (WDAA)
JC .... Junior Clinicians [*Medical students*] (DAVI)
JC .... Junior College
JC .... Jurisconsult
JC .... Just Compensation [*Business term*] (MHDB)
JC .... Justice Clerk
JC .... Justiciary Case (SAUS)
JC .... Justiciary Cases [*Scotland*] [*A publication*] (DLA)
JC .... Juvenile Cataract (MELL)
JC .... Juvenile Corps (SAUO)
JC .... Juvenile Coupled Radioactivity (SAUS)
JC .... Juvenile Court
JC .... Rocky Mountain Airways [*ICAO designator*] (AD)
JC2WC ...... Joint Command and Control Warfare Center (SAUS)
JC3CM ...... Joint Command, Control and Communications Countermeasures (SAUO)
JC3SOC ..... Joint C3 Staff And Operations Course (SAUO)
JCA .... Jamming Control Authority (NATG)
JCA .... Japan Container Association (BUAC)
JCA .... Javelin Class Association (EA)
JCA .... Jetcom SA [*Switzerland*] [*ICAO designator*] (FAAC)
JCA .... Jewelry Crafts Association [*Later, JMA*]
JCA .... Jewish Ceremonial Art [*A publication*] (BJA)
JCA .... Jewish Colonization Association [*British*]
JCA .... Job Communication Area (TIMI)
JCA .... Job Control Administrator (SAUS)
JCA .... Job Control Area (TIMI)
JCA .... Johnston(e) Clan in America (EA)
JCA .... Johore Consumers Association (SAUO)
JCA .... Joint Center for Astrophysics [*University of Maryland*] (RCD)
JCA .... Joint Church Aid [*Biafra relief program in late 1960's*] [*Defunct*]
JCA .... Joint Commission on Accreditation (SAUS)
JCA .... Joint Commission on Accreditation of Universities [*Military*]
JCA .... Joint Communication Activity
JCA .... Joint Communications Agency [*Military*]
JCA .... Joint Construction Agency
JCA .... Joint Cooperative Agreement (SAUO)
JCA .... Joint Countermine Application [*Military*]
JCA .... Joint Cultural Appeal (EA)
JCA .... Joint Custody Association (EA)
JCA .... Journal of Clinical Anesthesia (SAUO)
JCA .... Journal of Color and Appearance (journ.) (SAUS)
JCA .... Junior Catering Accountant [*British military*] (DMA)
JCA .... Junior College of Albany (SAUO)
JCA .... Juvenile Chronic Arthritis [*Medicine*] (DAVI)
JCAA .... Japanese Civil Aviation Authority (SAUO)
JCAAD .... Joint Counter Air/Air Defense (SAUO)
JCAAI .... Joint Council of Allergy, Asthma, and Immunology (NTPA)
JCAB .... Japan Civil Aviation Bureau (MCD)
JCAB .... Japanese Civil Aviation Bureau (SAUS)
JCAC .... Joint Civil Affairs Committee
JCACC .... Joint Combat Airspace Command and Control Course (DOMA)
JCACDM ..... Journal of Carbohydrate Chemistry (journ.) (SAUS)
JCAD .... Joint Committee on Agricultural Research and Development (SAUO)
JCADIS ...... Joint Continental Aerospace Defense Integration Staff [*Military*] (AABC)
JCADM ...... Joint Committee on Antarctic Data Management (SAUO)
JCADR .... Japan Centre for Area Development (BUAC)
JCAE .... Joint Committee on Atomic Energy [*of the US Congress*] [*Terminated*]
JCAEC .... Joint Congressional Atomic Energy Commission (MUGU)
JCAEC .... Joint Congressional Atomic Energy Committee (SAUO)
JCAED .... Joint Committee on Audiology and Education of the Deaf [*Medicine*] (EDAA)
JCAESSL .... Joint Council of the Associated Engineering Societies of St. Louis (SAUO)
JCAFB .... James Connally Air Force Base (SAUO)
JCAH .... Joint Commission for/on Accreditation of Hospitals (SAUO)
JCAH .... Joint Commission on Accreditation of Hospitals [*Later, JCAHO*] (EA)
JCAH .... Joint Committee on Accreditation of Hospitals (SAUS)
JCAHCA ..... Joint Commission on Accreditation of Health Care Organizations
JCAHO ...... Joint Commission on Accreditation of Healthcare Organizations [*An association*]
JCAHPO ..... Joint Commission on Allied Health in Ophthalmology (SAUS)
JCAHPO ..... Joint Commission on Allied Health Personnel in Ophthalmology (EA)
JCAHPO ..... Joint Committee on Allied Health Personnel in Ophthalmology (SAUO)
JCAI .... Joint Council of Allergy and Immunology (EA)
J Calif Dent Assoc... Journal. California Dental Association (journ.) (SAUS)
J Calif Hortic Soc... Journal. California Horticultural Society (journ.) (SAUS)
J CalifState Dent Ass... Journal. California State Dental Association (journ.) (SAUS)
J Calif State Dent Assoc... Journal of the California State Dental Association (SAUO)
J Calif State Dent Assoc... Journal of the California State Dental Association (journ.) (SAUS)
JCALM ...... Joint Committee on Aboriginal Lands and Mining [*Australia*]
JCALS .... Joint Computer-Aided Acquisition and Logistic Support [*DoD*]
JCALS .... Joint Computer Aided Acquisition and Logistic Support System (SAUO)
JCALS .... Joint Computer-Aided Acquisition Logistics System [*Army*] (RDA)
JCALS .... Joint Computer-Aided Logistics System (SAUS)
JCALS .... Joint Continuous Acquisition and Life-Cycle Support (GART)
JCAM .... Joint Commission on Atomic Masses
J Camborne Sch Mines... Journal. Cambome School of Mines (journ.) (SAUS)
JCAN .... Jewish Children's Adoption Network (EA)
J Can Art Hist... Journal of Canadian Art History (journ.) (SAUS)
J Can Assoc Radiol... Journal. Canadian Association of Radiologists (journ.) (SAUS)
J Can Ath Ther Assoc... Journal. Canadian Athletic Therapists Association (journ.) (SAUS)
J Can B ..... Juris Canna Baccalaureus [*Bachelor of Canon Law*]
J Can Ceram Soc... Journal. Canadian Ceramic Society (journ.) (SAUS)
J Can Ceram Soc... Journal of the Canadian Ceramic Society (SAUO)
J Can Ceram Soc... Journal of the Canadian Ceramic Society (journ.) (SAUS)
J Cancer Educ... Journal of Cancer Education (journ.) (SAUS)
J Cancer Res... Journal of Cancer Research (journ.) (SAUS)
J Cancer Res Clin Oncol... Journal of Cancer Research and Clinical Oncology (journ.) (SAUS)
J Cancer Res Comm... Journal. Cancer Research Committee. University of Sydney [*A publication*]
J Can Ch H... Journal Canadian Church Historical Society (journ.) (SAUS)
J Can Chiro Ass... Journal. Canadian Chiropractic Associa- tion (journ.) (SAUS)
J Can D ..... Juris Canna Doctor [*Doctor of Canon Law*]
JC & ED ..... Journal of Chemical and Engineering Data (journ.) (SAUS)
J Can Dent Assoc... Journal of the Canadian Dental Association (SAUO)
J Can Dent Assoc... Journal of the Canadian Dental Association (journ.) (SAUS)
J Can Inst Food Sci Technol... Journal. Canadian Institute of Food Science and Technology (journ.) (SAUS)
J Can M ..... Juris Canna Magister [*Master of Canon Law*]
J Can Min Inst... Journal. Canadian Mining Institute (journ.) (SAUS)
J Can S Forensic Sci... Journal. Canadian Society of Forensic Science (journ.) (SAUS)
J Cant Bot Soc... Journal. Canterbury Botanical Society (journ.) (SAUS)
JCAP .... Japan, Canada, Austral Asia/Pacific (EFIS)
JCAP .... Joint Committee on Aviation Pathology (BUAC)
JCAP .... Joint Conventional Ammunition Panel (SAUO)
JCAP .... Joint Conventional Ammunition Program [*Army*]
JCAP .... Joint Coordinated Ammunition Production (MCD)
JCAP .... Journal of Child and Adolescent Psychopharmacology (SAUO)
JCAP .... Journal of Child and Adolescent Psychotherapy (SAUO)
JCAP-CG .... Joint Conventional Ammunition Program Coordinating Group [*Army*]
J Cap Inst Med... Journal Capital Institute of Medicine (journ.) (SAUS)
J Cap Mgmt... Journal of Capacity Management (journ.) (SAUS)
JCAPN ...... Journal of Child and Adolescent Psychiatric Nursing (SAUO)
JCAPN ...... Journal of Child and Adolescent Psychiatric Nursing (journ.) (SAUS)
JCAR .... Joint Commission on Applied Radioactivity
JCARA .... Journal. Canadian Association of Radiologists (journ.) (SAUS)
J card .... Jacket Card [*A printed card inside the box holding a cassette tape or compact disc*] (WDMC)
JCARD .... Joint Committee on Agricultural Research and Development [*Agency for International Development*]
J Cardciogr... Journal of Cardiography (journ.) (SAUS)
J Cardiol .... Journal of Cardiology (journ.) (SAUS)
J Cardiol Suppl... Journal of Cardiology. Supplement (journ.) (SAUS)
J Cardiothorac Vasc Anesth... Journal of Cardiothoracic and Vascular Anesthesics (journ.) (SAUS)
J Cardiovasc Electrophysiol... Journal of Cardiovascular Electrophysiology (journ.) (SAUS)
J Cardiovasc Med... Journal of Cardiovascular Medicine (journ.) (SAUS)
J Cardiovasc Nurs... Journal of Cardiovascular Nursing (journ.) (SAUS)
J Cardiovasc Pharmacol... Journal of Cardiovascular Pharmacology (journ.) (SAUS)
J Cardiovasc Risk... Journal of Cardiovascular Risk (journ.) (SAUS)
J Cardiovasc Ultrason... Journal of Cardiovascular Ultrasonography (journ.) (SAUS)
J Cardpulm Rehabil... Journal of Cardiopulmonary Rehabilitation (journ.) (SAUS)
J Card Surg... Journal of Cardiac Surgery (journ.) (SAUS)
J Car Ed .... Journal of Career Education (journ.) (SAUS)
J Caribb Hist... Journal of Caribbean History. St. Lawrence (journ.) (SAUS)
J Caribb Stud... Journal of Caribbean Studies (journ.) (SAUS)
JCarlFut ..... Jack Carl/312 Futures, Inc. [*Associated Press*] (SAG)
J Car P & E... Journal of Career Planning and Employment [*A publication*] (BRI)
J Cars .... Designation for certain General Motors frontwheel-drive cars (SAUS)
JCASR .... Joint Committee on Avionic Systems Research (SAUS)
JCAT .... Joint Crisis Action Team [*Environmental science*] (COE)
JCAT .... Journal of Computer Assisted Tomography (SAUO)
J Catal ...... Journal of Catalysis (MEC)
J Cat & Class... Journal of Cataloging and Classification (journ.) (SAUS)
J Cataract Refract Surg... Journal of Cataract and Refractive Surgery (journ.) (SAUS)
J-CATCH .... Joint Countering Attack Helicopter Exercises (RDA)
JCATD .... Journal of Computer Assisted Tomography (journ.) (SAUS)
J Cathol Med Coll... Journal. Catholic Medical College (journ.) (SAUS)

J Cathol Nurses Guild Engl Wales... Journal. Catholic Nurses Guild of England and Wales (journ.) (SAUS)
JCATS .... Journal of the Centre of Advanced Television Studies (journ.) (SAUS)
JCAUDB ..... Journal of Cardiovascular Ultrasonography (journ.) (SAUS)
JCA-USA .... Joint Church Aid - United States of America [*See also JCA*] [*Defunct*] (EA)
JCB .... Bachelor of Canon Law (SAUS)
JCB .... Bachelor of Civil Law (SAUS)
JCB .... Japan California Bank (SAUO)
JCB .... Japan Convention Bureau (EA)
JCB .... Japan Credit Bank (SAUO)
JCB .... J. C. Bamford Excavators [*British*]
JCB .... Joacaba [*Brazil*] [*Airport symbol*] (AD)
JCB .... Job Control Block [*Computer science*] (BUR)
JCB .... Joint Coal Board (BUAC)
JCB .... Joint Communications Board
JCB .... Joint Computer Bureau [*Office of Population Census and Surveys*] [*British*]
JCB .... Joint Consultative Board [*NATO*] (NATG)
JCB .... Joint Coordinating Board (SAUO)
JCB .... Joseph Cyril Bamford [*Off-Highway equipment*]
JCB .... Journal of Cell Biology (journ.) (SAUS)
JCB .... Journal of Cellular Biochemistry (journ.) (SAUS)
JCB .... Journal of Creative Behavior (journ.) (SAUS)
JCB .... Junior College of Business (ACAE)
JCB .... Juris Canonici Baccalaureus [*Bachelor of Canon Law*]
JCB .... Juris Civilis Baccalaureus [*Bachelor of Civil Law*]
JCB .... Justification Control Bit (SAUS)
JCBA......... Jewish Conciliation Board of America (EA)
JCBADL ..... Biomedical Applications (journ.) (SAUS)
J Cbangchun Univ Earth Sci... Journal. Changchun University of Earth Science (journ.) (SAUS)
JCBAS .... Journal of the Ceylon Branch of the Royal Asiatic Society (SAUO)
JCBC......... Joint Committee on Building Codes [*Later, Model Code Standardization Council*] (EA)
JCBC......... Junior College of Broward County (SAUO)
JCBC......... Jute Carpet Backing Council (EA)
J Cbem Soc Jpn... Journal of the Chemical Society of Japan (journ.) (SAUS)
JCBF......... Journal of Cerebral Blood Flow and Metabolism (journ.) (SAUS)
JCBL......... John Carter Brown Library (SAUO)
JCBMDN .... Journal of Cerebral Blood Flow and Metabolism (journ.) (SAUS)
JCBMI .... Joint Committee for the British Memorial Industry (DBA)
JCBMI .... Joint Committee for the British Monumental Industry (SAUO)
JCBR .... Jefferson & Cypress Bayou Railroad [*Federal Railroad Administration identification code*]
JCBR .... Jefferson Center for Biomedical Research [*Thomas Jefferson University*] (RCD)
JCBS......... Jacobson Stores, Inc. [*NASDAQ symbol*] (COMM)
JCBSD7 ..... Journal of Cellular Biochemistry. Supplement (journ.) (SAUS)
JCBSF....... Joint Commission for Black Sea Fisheries
JCBSSA ..... Jersey Cattle Breeders Society of South Africa (BUAC)
JCBU .... JC Bentzen Industries [*Intermodal shipping container symbol*] (TVRC)
JCC .... Jamestown Community College [*New York*]
JCC .... Janney Cylinder Co.
JCC .... Japan Cotton Center (SAUO)
JCC .... Japanese Chamber of Commerce of New York [*Later, JCCINY*] (EA)
JCC .... Jarvis Christian College [*Hawkins, TX*]
JCC .... Jarvis Christian College, Hawkins, TX [*OCLC symbol*] (OCLC)
JCC .... Java Competence Center (SAUO)
JCC .... Jefferson Community College (SAUO)
JCC .... Jesus College, Cambridge [*England*] (ROG)
JCC .... Jet Circulation Control
JCC .... Jewish Chaplains Council (EA)
JCC .... Jewish Community Center
JCC .... Jharkhand Coordination Committee [*Jharkhand Samanvaya Samiti*] [*India*] [*Political party*]
JCC .... Jilin Chemical Inc ADS [*NYSE symbol*] (TTSB)
JCC .... Jilin Chemical Industrial Co. Ltd. [*NYSE symbol*] (SAG)
JCC .... Job Control Card [*Computer science*] (ELAL)
JCC .... Job Control Command (SAUS)
JCC .... Job Corps Camp [*Department of Labor*]
JCC .... Job Corps Center (SAUO)
JCC .... Joint Committee on Contraception (DMAA)
JCC .... Joint Communications Center (MCD)
JCC .... Joint Communications Committee (SAUO)
JCC .... Joint Computer Committee (SAUO)
JCC .... Joint Computer Conference
JCC .... Joint Conciliation Committee (SAUO)
JCC .... Joint Conference Committee (SAUS)
JCC .... Joint Consultative Committee [*of the National Joint Advisory Council*] [*British*] [*World War II*]
JCC .... Joint Consultative Council of the Fresh Fruit and Vegetable Industry (BUAC)
JCC .... Joint Contracting Center
JCC .... Joint Control Center (MCD)
JCC .... Joint Coordinating Committee (SAUO)
JCC .... Joint Coordination Center (NVT)
JCC .... Joint Cryptographic Centre (SAUO)
JCC .... JORN Co-ordination Centre (SAUO)
JCC .... Journal of Carbohydrate Chemistry (journ.) (SAUS)
JCC .... Journal of Clinical Chiropratic (SAUO)
JCC .... Journal of Computational Chemistry (journ.) (SAUS)
JCC .... Jowett Car Club (EA)
JCC .... Junior Carlton Club (SAUO)
JCC .... Junior Chamber of Commerce
JCC .... Junior Command Course [*British military*] (DMA)
JCC .... San Francisco [*California*] China Bas [*Airport symbol*] (OAG)
JCC(1)....... Joint Consultants Committee (SAUO)
JCC(2)....... Joint Consultative Committee (SAUO)
JCCA......... Japanese Canadian Citizens' Association
JCCA......... Japanese Chin Club of America (EA)
JCCA......... Jewish Community Centers Association of North America (NTPA)
JCCA......... Joint CONEX [*Container Express*] Control Agency
JCCA......... Journal of Canadian Chiropractic Association (SAUO)
JCCAE .... Joint Congressional Committee on Atomic Energy (SAUO)
JCCANA ..... Jewish Community Centers Association of North America (EA)
JCCB......... Joint Configuration Control Board [*DoD*]
JCCBD....... Journal of Clinical Chemistry and Clinical Biochemistry (journ.) (SAUS)
JCCBI........ Joint Committee for the Conservation of British Insects (BUAC)
JCCBI........ Joint Committee for the Conservation of British Invertebrates (BUAC)
JCCC......... Japanese Canadian Citizens' Council
JCCC......... Joint Committee on Contemporary China (EA)
JCCC......... Joint Communications Control Center (COE)
JCCC......... Joint COMSEC Coordination Center (MCD)
JCCC......... Joint Configuration Control Committee [*DoD*]
JCCC......... Jonsson Comprehensive Cancer Center [*University of California, Los Angeles*] (RCD)
JCCD .... Japanese Canadian Committee for Democracy
JCCD .... Journal of Childhood Communications Disorders (journ.) (SAUS)
JCCDC....... Jackson County Civil Defense Council [*Emergency Management*] (EMA)
JCCDG....... Joint Command and Control Development Group [*DoD*]
JCCDS....... Joint Committee on Cartographic Data Standardization (SAUO)
JCCE......... Joint Committee on Communications and Electronics (SAUS)
JCCEA .... Joint Committee of Customs and Excise Associations (SAUO)
JCCEM ...... Joint Committee of Cultural and Education Ministers [*Australia*]
JCCEM ...... Joint Coordinating Committee for Environmental Restoration and Waste Management (SAUO)
JCCEP .... Joint Crisis Communications Exercise Program (MCD)
JCCF......... Jamaica Combined Cadet Force (BUAC)
JCCFC .... June Carter Cash Fan Club (EA)
JCCFE .... Joint Coordination Center, Far East [*Military*] (CINC)
JCCFEP...... Joint Commission on Cooperation in the Field of Environmental Protection [*US-USSR*] [*Marine science*] (OSRA)
JCC-FPM.... Joint Coordinating Committee on Fundamental Properties of Matter [*US Department of Energy and USSR State Committee on Peaceful Uses of Atomic Energy*]
JCCG .... Joint/Combined Coordinating Group (SAUO)
JCCI .... Japan Chamber of Commerce and Industry (BUAC)
JCCINY...... Japanese Chamber of Commerce and Industry of New York (EA)
JCCIS........ Japan Chamber of Commerce and Industry, Sydney [*Australia*]
JCCIUK...... Japanese Chamber of Commerce and Industry in the United Kingdom (DS)
JCCJ......... Jeune Chambre du Canada - Jaycees [*Association*] [*Canada*] (EAIO)
JCCL......... Japanese Canadian Citizens' League
JCCLE .... Joint Committee on Continuing Legal Education [*Later, ALI-ABA Committee on Con tinuing Professional Education*] (EA)
JCCMB ...... Journal of Coordination Chemistry (journ.) (SAUS)
JCCMI .... Joint Committee for the Church Music in Ireland (BUAC)
JCCN .... Journal of Critical Care Nutrition (SAUO)
JCCN .... Journal of Critical Care Nutrition (journ.) (SAUS)
JCCO .... Joint Container Control Office (MCD)
JCCom ...... Japan Computers and Communication
JCCOMNET... Joint Coordination Center Communications Network
JCCP......... Joint Casualty Collection Point [*Environmental science*] (COE)
JCCP......... Journal of Cross-Cultural Psychology (journ.) (SAUS)
JCCR .... Joint Command and Control Requirements [*Military*] (GFGA)
JCCR .... Joint Committee on Cellular Roaming (SAUO)
JCCRG....... Joint Command and Control Requirements Group [*Joint Chiefs of Staff*] [*DoD*]
JCCRS....... Joint Contingency Construction Requirements System (SAUO)
JCCS......... Jewish Cultural Clubs and Societies (EA)
JCCSA....... Joint Communication Contingency Station Assets (SAUO)
JCCSA....... Joint Communications Contingency Station Activity (MCD)
JCCSC....... Joint Command and Control Standards Committee (AFM)
JCCSMAS... Joint Commission on Competitive Safeguards and the Medical Aspects of Sports [*Later, JCSMS*] (EA)
JCCSO....... Jewish Community Center Symphony Orchestra (SAUO)
JCCSO....... Jewish Community Center Symphony Orchestra America (SAUS)
JCCSWO .... Joint Committee on Cooperation in Studies of the World Ocean [*US-USSR*] [*Marine science*] (OSRA)
JCCSWO .... Joint Committee on Cooperation on Studies of the World Ocean [*US-USSR*] (USDC)
JCCTC .... Joint Customs Consultative Technical Committee [*British*] (DCTA)
JCCX......... Jefferson Chemical [*Federal Railroad Administration identification code*]
JCD .... Doctor of Canon Law (SAUS)
JCD .... Doctor of Civil Law (SAUS)
JCD .... John Chard Decoration [*British military*] (DMA)
JCD .... Journal of Community Development [*A publication*]
JCD .... Journal of Counseling and Development [*A publication*] (DHP)
JCD .... Journal of Crime and Delinquency (SAUS)
JCD .... Junior College District
JCD .... Juris Canonici Doctor [*Doctor of Canon Law*] [*Latin*]
JCD .... Juris Civilis Doctor [*Doctor of Civil Law*] [*Latin*]
JCDA .... Journal of Clinical Data and Analysis [*Medicine*] (EDAA)
JCDA .... Journal of the Canadian Dental Association (SAUO)
JCDA .... Junior Catholic Daughters of America (SAUO)

JCDA .... Junior Catholic Daughters of the Americas [*Defunct*] (EA)
JCDAA .... Journal. Canadian Dental Association (journ.) (SAUS)
JCDalT ...... Journal. Chemical Society. Dalton Transactions (journ.) (SAUS)
JCDEA .... Journal. California State Dental Association (journ.) (SAUS)
JCDIA .... Journal of Communication Disorders (journ.) (SAUS)
JCDSC .... Joint Communication Decision Support Center
JCDSG .... Joint Civil Defense Support Group
JCDSI .... Joint Continental Defense Systems Integration (ACAE)
JCDSIPS .... Joint Continental Defense Systems Integration Planning Staff [*Air Force*]
JCDT .... Jamaica Conservation and Development Trust (BUAC)
JCDTA .... Joint Commission on Dance and Theatre Accreditation (EA)
JCDVA .... Journal of Child Development (journ.) (SAUS)
JCE .... Java Cryptographic Extension (SAUS)
JCE .... Jet Control Electronics (ACAE)
JCE .... Jockey Club of Egypt, Alexandria (SAUO)
JCE .... Joint Cadet Executive [*British military*] (DMA)
JCE .... Joint Committee on Education (SAUO)
JCE .... Journal of Chemical Education [*A publication*] (WDAA)
JCE .... Journal of Christian Education (journ.) (SAUS)
JCE .... Journal of Clinical Epidemiology (SAUS)
JCE .... Junior Certificate Examination (SAUS)
JCEA .... Jesuit Conference of East Asia (BUAC)
JCEA .... Joint Committee for European Affairs [*Defunct*] (EA)
JCEADF ..... Joint Central Air Defense Force (SAA)
JCEAG .... Joint Civilian Employee Advisory Group [*Military*] (CINC)
JCEB .... Joint Council on Educational Broadcasting [*Later, JCET*] (EA)
JCEBD .... Journal of Cellular Biochemistry (journ.) (SAUS)
JCEC .... Joint Chapters - Educational Council
JCEC .... Joint Chiefs Electronic Committee (ACAE)
JCEC .... Joint Communications-Electronics Committee [*Military*]
JCECPAC .... Joint Communications-Electronics Committee, Pacific [*Military*] (CINC)
JCED... Japan Committee for Economic Development (SAUO)
JCEE .... Joint Council on Economic Education (EA)
JCEG .... Joint Communications-Electronics Group [*Military*]
JCEG .... Joint Concepts and Evaluation Group [*Military*] (CINC)
JCEGP .... Joint Communications-Electronics Group [*Military*]
JCEHP .... Journal of Continuing Education in the Health Professions (SAUO)
JCEHP .... Journal of Continuing Education in the Health Professions (journ.) (SAUS)
JCEI .... Joint Council of Engineering Institutions (SAUO)
J Cell Biochem... Journal of Cellular Biochemistry (journ.) (SAUS)
J Cell Biochem Suppl... Journal of Cellular Biochemistry. Supplement (journ.) (SAUS)
J Cell Biol... Journal of Cell Biology (journ.) (SAUS)
J Cell Comp Physiol... Journal of Cellular and Comparative Physiology (journ.) (SAUS)
J Cell Physiol Suppl... Journal of Cellular Physiology. Supplement (journ.) (SAUS)
J Cell Sci... Journal of Cell Science (journ.) (SAUS)
J Cell Sci Suppl... Journal of Cell Science. Supplement (journ.) (SAUS)
JCEM .... Joint Center for Energy Management [*Research center*] (RCD)
JCEM .... Journal of Clinical Endocrinology and Metabolism (journ.) (SAUS)
JCEM .... Junior Control Electrical Mechanic [*British military*] (DMA)
JCEN .... Journal of Continuing Education in Nursing (journ.) (SAUS)
JCEND .... Journal of Clinical Engineering (journ.) (SAUS)
JCENS .... Joint Communications-Electronics Nomenclature System [*Military*]
J Cent Bur Anim Husb Dairy India... Journal. Central Bureau for Animal Husbandry and Dairying in India (journ.) (SAUS)
J Cent China Norm Univ Nat Sci... Journal. Central China Normal University. Natural Sciences (journ.) (SAUS)
J Cent Eur Aff... Journal of Central European Affairs (journ.) (SAUS)
J Cent S Inst Min Metall... Journal of Central-South Institute of Mining and Metallurgy (journ.) (SAUS)
JCEOI .... Joint Communications-Electronics Operating Instructions [*Military*] (CET)
JCEPC .... Joint United States/Canada Civil Emergency Planning Committee
JCEPF .... Federation of Junior Economic Chambers in Francophone Countries (SAUO)
JCER .... Japan Center for Economic Research (SAUS)
J Ceram Assoc Jpn... Journal. Ceramic Association of Japan (journ.) (SAUS)
J Ceram Soc Jpn... Journal. Ceramic Society of Japan (journ.) (SAUS)
J Ceram Soc Jpn... Journal of the Ceramic Society of Japan (journ.) (SAUS)
J Cereb Blood Flow Metab... Journal of Cerebral Blood Flow and Metabolism (journ.) (SAUS)
J Cerebral Sci... Journal of Cerebral Science (journ.) (SAUS)
J Cer Soc Jap... Journal. Ceramic Society of Japan (journ.) (SAUS)
JCESR .... Job Control Engineering Service Request (SAUO)
JCESS .... Joint Centre for Earth System Science (SAUO)
JCET .... Joint Center for Earth Systems Technology (RCD)
JCET .... Joint Committee on Educational Telecommunications (SAUS)
JCET .... Joint Committee on Educational Television (SAUO)
JCET .... Joint Council on Educational Telecommunications [*Defunct*] (EA)
JCET .... Joint Council on Educational Television (SAUO)
JCEU .... Consafe JCE [*Intermodal shipping container symbol*] (TVRC)
JCEW .... Joint Communications Electronic Warfare Simulation
JCEWG .... Joint Communications and Electronics Working Group [*NATO*] (NATG)
JCEWS .... Joint Command, Control, and Electronic Warfare School
JCEWS .... Joint Commanders Electronic Warfare Staff (SAUO)
JCEWS .... Joint Force Commander's Electronic Warfare Staff [*Military*]
J Ceylon Br Brit Med Ass... Journal. Ceylon Branch. British Medical Association (journ.) (SAUS)
J Ceylon Law... Journal of Ceylon Law [*A publication*] (ILCA)
JCF .... Jamaican Constabulary Force (BUAC)
JCF .... Jaycees Community Foundation [*Australia*]
JCF .... JESSI Common Framework (SAUS)
JCF .... Jet Center Flight Training SA [*Spain*] [*ICAO designator*] (FAAC)
JCF .... Job Control File (SAUS)
JCF .... Joint Communications Facility (SAUO)
JCF .... Joint Coordinating Forum (SAUS)
JCF .... Joseph Campbell Foundation [*Association*] (EA)
JCF .... Journal of Canadian Fiction (journ.) (SAUS)
JCF .... Juvenile Calcaneal Fracture [*Medicine*] (DMAA)
JCFA .... Japan Chemical Fibres Association (BUAC)
JCFAS .... Joint Council on Food and Agricultural Sciences (SAUO)
JCF AWE.... Joint Contingency Force Advanced Warfighting Experiment [*Army*]
JCFBC .... Joint Committee on Fire Brigade Communications (WDAA)
JCFBO .... Joint Committee on Fire Brigade Operations (WDAA)
JCFBS .... Joint Commission on the Fisheries in the Black Sea (BUAC)
JCFC .... Jeff Carson Fan Club [*Association*] (EA)
JCFC .... Jesse Couch Fan Club (EA)
JCFC .... John Conlee Fan Club (EA)
JCFC .... Judaica Captioned Film Center (EA)
JCFI .... Job Control File Internal (IAA)
JCFR .... Junior College of Flat River [*Missouri*]
JCFRB .... Journal of Coffee Research (journ.) (SAUS)
JCFS .... Job Control File Source (IAA)
JCFS .... Journal of Comparative Family Studies (journ.) (SAUS)
JCFSBFC.... Jerry Campbell and Five Star Band Fan Club (EA)
JCFSO .... Joint Council of Fire Service Organizations [*Defunct*] (EA)
JCG .... Jacobi Conjugate Gradient (SAUS)
JCG .... Joint Commanders Group (ACAE)
JCG .... Joint Conservation Group
JCG .... Joint Consultative Group (SAUO)
JCG .... Joint Coordinating Group [*Military*] (AFIT)
JCG .... Joint Coordination Group (SAUO)
JCG .... Journal of Crystal Growth (journ.) (SAUS)
JCGP .... Joint Consultative Group on Policy (SAUO)
JCGRO .... Joint Central Graves Registration Office [*Military*] (CINC)
JCGS .... Joint Center for Graduate Study [*Research center*] (RCD)
JCGS .... Journal of Computational and Graphical Statistics [*Database*] (GDD)
JCGU .... Jeuro Container Transport [*Intermodal shipping container symbol*] (TVRC)
J Ch .... Johnson's New York Chancery Reports [*A publication*] (DLA)
JCHA .... Joint Commission on Hospital Accreditation
J Changcbun Coll Geol... Journal. Changchun College of Geology (journ.) (SAUS)
J Changchun Geol Inst... Journal. Changchun Geological Institute (journ.) (SAUS)
JCHARS ..... Joint Commission of High Altitude Research Stations (SAUS)
J Chart Inst Transp... Journal. Chartered Institute of Transport (journ.) (SAUS)
JCHAS .... Journal. Cork Historical and Archaeological Society (journ.) (SAUS)
JCHC .... Journal of Compliance in Health Care (SAUO)
JCHC .... Journal of Compliance in Health Care (journ.) (SAUS)
JCHC .... Journal of Correctional Health Care (SAUO)
JCHC .... Journal of Correctional Health Care (journ.) (SAUS)
JCHE .... Joint Center for Higher Education (SAUO)
J Chekiang Univ... Journal. Chekiang University (journ.) (SAUS)
J Chem An... Japan Chemical Annual (journ.) (SAUS)
J Chem Ecol... Journal of Chemical Ecology (journ.) (SAUS)
J Chem Ed... Journal of Chemical Education [*A publication*] (BRI)
J Chem Ed... Journal of Chemical Education. American Chemical Society. Division of Chemical Education. Easton (SAUO)
J Chem Educ Softwe... Journal of Chemical Education. Software (journ.) (SAUS)
J Chem Eng Educ... Journal of Chemical Engineering Education (journ.) (SAUS)
J Chem Eng Jap... Journal of Chemical Engineering of Japan (journ.) (SAUS)
J Chem Eng Jpn... Journal of Chemical Engineering of Japan (journ.) (SAUS)
J Chem Metall Min Soc S Afr... Journal. Chemical, Metallurgical and Mining Society of South Africa (journ.) (SAUS)
J Chem Neuroanat... Journal of Chemical Neuroanatomy (journ.) (SAUS)
J Chemom... Journal of Chemometrics (journ.) (SAUS)
J Chemother... Journal of Chemotherapy (journ.) (SAUS)
J Chemother Adv Ther... Journal of Chemotherapy and Advanced Therapeutics (journ.) (SAUS)
J Chem Phys... Journal of Chemical Physics (journ.) (SAUS)
J Chem Phys... Journal of Physical Chemistry (MEC)
J Chem Res... Journal of Chemical Research (journ.) (SAUS)
J Chem Res M... Journal of Chemical Research. Part M (journ.) (SAUS)
J Chem Res Miniprint... Journal of Chemical Research. Miniprint (journ.) (SAUS)
J Chem Res S... Journal of Chemical Research. Part S (journ.) (SAUS)
J Chem Res Synop... Journal of Chemical Research. Synopses (journ.) (SAUS)
J Chem Rev... Japan Chemical Review. Japan Chemical Week Supplement (journ.) (SAUS)
J Chem S... Japan Chemical Week. Supplement (journ.) (SAUS)
J Chem S Dalton Trans... Journal. Chemical Society. Dalton Trans- actions (SAUS)
J Chem S Dalton Trans... Journal. Chemical Society. Dalton Transactions (SAUO)
J Chem S D Chem Commun... Journal. Chemical Society. D. Chemical Communications (journ.) (SAUS)
J Chem SF I... Journal. Chemical Society. Faraday Transactions I (journ.) (SAUS)
J Chem SF II... Journal. Chemical Society. Faraday Transactions. II (journ.) (SAUS)
J Chem Soc... Journal of the Chemical Society (MEC)
J Chem Soc A... Journal. Chemical Society. A. Inorganic, Physical, Theoretical (journ.) (SAUS)
J Chem Soc A... Journal of the Chemical Society, A. Inorganic Physical Theoretical (SAUS)
J Chem Soc A... Journal of the Chemical Society A (journ.) (SAUS)
J Chem Soc Abstr... Journal. Chemical Society. Abstracts (journ.) (SAUS)

J Chem Soc B... Journal. Chemical Society. B. Physical, Organic (journ.) (SAUS)
J Chem Soc B... Journal of the Chemical Society, B. Physical Organic (SAUS)
J Chem Soc C... Journal of the Chemical Society, C. Organic (SAUS)
J Chem Soc Chem Commum... Journal of the Chemical Society, Chemical Communications (journ.) (SAUS)
J Chem Soc Da... Journal. Chemical Society. Dalton Transactions (journ.) (SAUS)
J Chem Soc Jap Ind Chem Sect... Journal. Chemical Society of Japan. Industrial Chemistry Section (journ.) (SAUS)
J Chem Soc Jpn Chem Ind Chem... Journal. Chemical Society of Japan. Chemistry and Industrial Chemistry (journ.) (SAUS)
J Chem Soc Jpn Pure Chem Sect... Journal. Chemical Society of Japan. Pure Chemistry Section (journ.) (SAUS)
J Chem Tech and Biotech... Journal of Chemical Technology and Biotechnology (MEC)
J Chem Technol Biotechnol A Chem Technol... Journal of Chemical Technology and Biotechnology. A. Chemical Technology (journ.) (SAUS)
J Chem Technol Biotechnol B Biotechnology... Journal of Chemical Technology and Biotechnology. B. Biotechnology (journ.) (SAUS)
J Chem UAR... Journal of Chemistry. United Arab Republic (journ.) (SAUS)
J Cheng Kung Univ Sci Eng... Journal. Cheng Kung University. Science and Engineering (journ.) (SAUS)
J Chiba Med S... Journal. Chiba Medical Society (journ.) (SAUS)
J Child Contemp Soc... Journal of Children in Contemporary Society (journ.) (SAUS)
J Child Neurol... Journal of Child Neurology (journ.) (SAUS)
J Child Psychol Psychtry Book Suppl... Journal of Child Psychology and Psychiatry. Book Supplement (journ.) (SAUS)
J Child Psychotherapy... Journal of Child Psychotherapy (journ.) (SAUS)
J Chin Agri Chem Soc... Journal. Chinese Agricultural Chemical Society (journ.) (SAUS)
J China Pharm Univ... Journal. China Pharmaceutical University (journ.) (SAUS)
J China Soc Chem Ind... Journal. China Society of Chemical Industry (journ.) (SAUS)
J Chin Assoc Refrig... Journal. Chinese Association of Refrigeration (journ.) (SAUS)
J China Univ Sci Technol... Journal. China University of Science and Technology (journ.) (SAUS)
J Chin Biothem Soc... Journal Chinese Biochemical Society (journ.) (SAUS)
J Chin Ceram Soc... Journal. Chinese Ceramic Society (journ.) (SAUS)
J Chin Ceram Soc... Journal of the Chinese Ceramic Society (journ.) (SAUS)
J Chin Chem Soc... Journal of the Chinese Chemical Society (journ.) (SAUS)
J Chin Colloid Interface Soc... Journal. Chinese Colloid and Interface Society (journ.) (SAUS)
J Chin Electron Microsc Soc... Journal of Chinese Electron Microscopy Society (journ.) (SAUS)
J Chinese Inst Chem Engrs... Journal. Chinese Institute of Chemical Engineers (journ.) (SAUS)
J Chin Foundmens Assoc... Journal of Chinese Foundrymens Association (journ.) (SAUS)
J Ching Hua Univ... Journal. Ching Hua University (journ.) (SAUS)
J Chin Inst Chem Eng... Journal of the Chinese Institute of Chemical Engineers (journ.) (SAUS)
J Chin Inst Eng... Journal of Chinese Institute of Engineers (journ.) (SAUS)
J Chin Lang Teach Asso... Journal. Chinese Language Teachers Association (journ.) (SAUS)
J Chin Rare Earth Soc... Journal. Chinese Rare Earth Society (journ.) (SAUS)
J Chin Rare Earth Soc... Journal of the Chinese Rare Earth Society (journ.) (SAUS)
J Chin Silic Soc... Journal of the Chinese Silicate Society (journ.) (SAUS)
J Chins Inst Commun... Journal of the China Institute of Communications (journ.) (SAUS)
J Chin Soc Mech Eng... Journal of the Chinese Society of Mechanical Engineers (journ.) (SAUS)
J Chin Soc Vet Sci... Journal. Chinese Society of Veterinary Science (journ.) (SAUS)
J Chiro...... Journal of Chiropractic (journ.) (SAUS)
J Ch L....... Journal of Child Language (journ.) (SAUS)
JChLaw..... Journal of Child Law [*A publication*] (SAFN)
JCHMT...... Joint Committee for Higher Medical Training (CMD)
JCHO........ Joint Commission on Healthcare Organizations (SAUS)
JCHOD...... Journal of Clinical Hematology and Oncology (journ.) (SAUS)
J Chongqing Unir... Journal. Chongqing University (journ.) (SAUS)
J Chosen Med Assoc... Journal. Chosen Medical Association (journ.) (SAUS)
JCHPME..... Joint Commission on Higher Professional Medical Education (SAUS)
JCHPME..... Joint Committee on the Higher Professional Medical Education [*Nigeria*] (BUAC)
JCHPME..... WAPMC-WACP/WACS Joint Committee on Higher Professional Medical Education (SAUO)
JCHQA....... Japan Chemical Quarterly (journ.) (SAUS)
JChr.......... Jewish Chronicle (SAUO)
J Christ Med Assoc India... Journal. Christian Medical Association of India (journ.) (SAUS)
J Chromat Chromat Rev... Journal of Chromatography. Chromatographic Reviews (journ.) (SAUS)
J Chromatogr... Journal of Chromatography [*A publication*] (PABS)
J Chromatogr B Biomed Appl... Journal of Chromatography. B, Biomedical Applications (SAUS)
J Chromatogr Libr... Journal of Chromatography Library (journ.) (SAUS)
J Chromatogr Sci... Journal of Chromatographic Science [*A publication*] (PABS)
J Chr Philos... Journal of Christian Philosophy (journ.) (SAUS)
JCHST....... Joint Committee for Higher Surgical Training (SAUO)
JCHST....... Joint Committe on Higher Surgical Training [*Royal College of Surgeons*] (PDAA)
J Ch St...... Journal of Church and State [*A publication*] (BRI)
JCHU........ Chevallier [*Intermodal shipping container symbol*] (TVRC)
J Church S... Journal of Church and State [*A publication*] (DLA)
JCI.......... Jaycees International (EA)
JCI.......... Job Characteristics Inventory
JCI.......... Job Control Information (VLIE)
JCI.......... Johnson Controls [*NYSE symbol*] (TTSB)
JCI.......... Johnson Controls, Inc. [*NYSE symbol*] (SPSG)
JCI.......... Joint Communications Instruction
JCI.......... Journal Communications (IID)
JCI.......... Journal of Clinical Investigation (SAUO)
JCI.......... Junior Chamber International (EAIO)
JCI.......... Jute Corp. of India
JCI.......... Olathe [*Kansas*] [*Airport symbol*] (OAG)
JCIA......... Japan Camera Industry Association (SAUO)
JCIA......... Japan Communication Industrial Association (SAUO)
JCIAMR..... Joint Commission on the International Aspects of Mental Retardation (BUAC)
JCIC......... Japan Center for Intercultural Communications (SAUS)
JCIC......... Japan Consumer Information Center (SAUO)
JCIC......... Jewish Community Information Center [*Australia*]
JCIC......... Johannesburg Consolidated Investment Co. (SAUS)
JCIC......... Johannesburg Consolidated Investment Company (SAUO)
JCIC......... Joint Committee for Intersociety Coordination (SAUO)
JCIC......... Joint Committee on Intersociety Coordination [*Defunct*] (EA)
JCIC......... Joint Compliance & Inspection Commission (SAUO)
JCIC......... Joint Compliance & Inspection Committee (SAUO)
JCICS........ Journal of Chemical Information and Computer Sciences (journ.) (SAUS)
JCIDO....... Joint Combat Identification Office [*Military*]
JCIE.......... Joint Center for International Exchange (SAUS)
JCIEABJ..... Joint Commission for the Investigation of the Effects of the Atomic Bomb in Japan (SAUO)
JCIE/USA.... Japan Center for International Exchange (EA)
JCIF.......... Japan Center for International Finance (SAUO)
JCIFC........ Johnny Comfort International Fan Club [*Defunct*] (EA)
JCIHCA...... Joint Council to Improve Health Care of the Aged [*Defunct*] (EA)
JCII.......... Japan Camera and Optical Instruments Inspection and Testing Institute (BUAC)
JCII.......... Japan Camera Inspection Institute (SAUO)
JCIM......... Joint Council of Immunohistochemical Manufacturers
JCIMD....... Journal of Clinical Immunology (journ.) (SAUS)
J Cin BA.... Journal. Cincinnati Bar Association [*A publication*] (DLA)
JCIOC........ Joint Counterintelligence Operations Center (SAUO)
JCIOMATIC... Job Control Language Automatic Generator (SAUS)
JCIPP........ Jewish Committee for Israeli-Palestinian Peace (EA)
J Cir Eng Des... Journal of Civil Engineering Design (journ.) (SAUS)
JCIS......... Joint Command Information Systems (SAUO)
JCIS......... Joint Counterintelligence Section (SAUO)
JCIS......... Journal of Colloid and Interface Science [*Medicine*] (EDAA)
JCISE........ Journal of Computing and Information Science in Engineering [*Database*] (GDD)
JCIT.......... Jerusalem Conference on Information Technology (ELAL)
JCIT.......... Joint Combat Information Terminal [*Military*]
J City Plan Dir Am Soc Civ Eng... Journal. City Planning Division. American Society of Civil Engineers (journ.) (SAUS)
J Civ D...... Journal of Civil Defense (journ.) (SAUS)
JCIWG....... Joint Cutover Integrated Working Group [*Military*] (RDA)
JCIX.......... Jones Chemicals [*Private rail car owner code*]
JCJ........... Journalist Committee of Japan (BUAC)
JCJC......... Jasper County Junior College (SAUO)
JCJC......... Jefferson City Junior College [*Discontinued operation, 1958*] [*Missouri*]
JCJC......... Jefferson County Junior College (SAUO)
JCJC......... Jones County Junior College [*Ellisville, MS*]
JCJCCIFC... Johnny Cash and June Carter Cash International Fan Club (EA)
JCJDMU..... Jewel Case & Jewellery Display Makers' Union (WDAA)
JCJU......... Daclim Engineering [*Intermodal shipping container symbol*] (TVRC)
JCK.......... Jackson Air Services Ltd. [*Canada*] [*ICAO designator*] (FAAC)
JCK.......... Joint Commission on Korea
JCK.......... Julia Creek [*Australia*] [*Airport symbol*] (OAG)
JCKO........ Jackson Trucking Company [*Common carrier symbol*]
JCL.......... Jackson County Library System, Medford, OR [*OCLC symbol*] (OCLC)
JCL.......... Jet Cargo-Liberia [*ICAO designator*] (FAAC)
JCL.......... Job Command Language (NITA)
JCL.......... Job Control Language [*High-level programming language*] [*1979*] [*Computer science*]
JCL.......... John Crerar Library [*National Translation Center*]
JCL.......... Johnny Come Lately [*Slang*]
JCL.......... Joint Logistics Commanders (SAUO)
JCL.......... Journal of Child Law [*A publication*] (SAFN)
JCL.......... Journal of Commonwealth Literature [*A publication*] (ANEX)
JCL.......... Journal of Commonwealth Literature (journ.) (SAUS)
JCL.......... Journal of Contract Law [*Australia*] [*A publication*]
JCL.......... Journal of Corporation Law (journ.) (SAUS)
JCL.......... Journal of Criminal Law [*A publication*] (SAFN)
JCL.......... Junior Classical League (EA)
JCL.......... Juris Canonici Lector [*Reader in Canon Law*]
JCL.......... Juris Canonici Licentiatus [*Licentiate in Canon Law*]
JCL.......... Juris Civilis Licentiatus [*Licentiate of Civil Law*]
JCLA......... Joint Council of Language Associations [*British*]
JCLA......... Journal. Canadian Linguistic Association (journ.) (SAUS)
JCLa......... Journal of Child Language (journ.) (SAUS)
JCLA......... Journal of Comparative Literature and Aesthetics (journ.) (SAUS)
JCLA......... Journal of the Canadian Language Association (SAUO)
JCLA......... Journal of the Canadian Linguistic Association (SAUO)
JCL&Crim... Journal of Criminal Law and Criminology [*A publication*] (SAFN)

J Classif.... Journal of Classification (journ.) (SAUS)
J Clay Prod Inst Am... Journal. Clay Products Institute of America (journ.) (SAUS)
J Clay Res Group Jpn... Journal. Clay Research Group of Japan (journ.) (SAUS)
J Clay Sci Soc Jpn... Journal. Clay Science Society of Japan (journ.) (SAUS)
JCIC......... Joint Committee on Intersociety Coordination (SAUO)
JCLC......... Joint Committee [*of Congress*] on the Library of Congress
JCLE......... Joint Committee on Library Education
JCIE/USA.... Japan Center for Intertiational Exchange (SAUS)
J Cleveland Eng Soc... Journal. Cleveland Engineering Society (journ.) (SAUS)
JCLGEN..... Job Control Language Generation [*Computer science*] (MHDB)
JCLI......... Joint Council for Landscape Industries (BUAC)
JCLIC......... Joint Center for Low-Intensity Conflict (SAUO)
JCLIL........ Journal of Comparative Legislation and International Law [*A publication*]
J Climatol... Journal of Climatology (journ.) (SAUS)
J Clin Anesth... Journal of Clinical Anesthesia (journ.) (SAUS)
J Clin Apheresis... Journal of Clinical Apheresis (journ.) (SAUS)
J Clin Biochem Nu... Journal of Clinical Biochemistry and Nutrition (journ.) (SAUS)
J Clin Chem Clin Biochem... Journal of Clinical Chemistry and Clinical Biochemistry (journ.) (SAUS)
J Clin Child... Journal of Clinical Child Psychology (journ.) (SAUS)
J Clin Comput... Journal of Clinical Computing (journ.) (SAUS)
J Clin Dent... Journal of Clinical Dentistry (journ.) (SAUS)
J Clin Dermatol... Journal of Clinical Dermatology (journ.) (SAUS)
J Clin Dysmorphol... Journal of Clinical Dysmorphology (journ.) (SAUS)
J Clin Elecn Microsc... Journal of Clinical Electron Microscopy (journ.) (SAUS)
J Clin Electron Mic Soc Jpn... Journal. Clinical Electron Microscopy Society of Japan (journ.) (SAUS)
J Clin Endocrinol Metab... Journal of Clinical Endocrinology and Metabolism (journ.) (SAUS)
J Clin Eng... Journal of Clinical Engineering (journ.) (SAUS)
J Clin Ethics... Journal of Clinical Ethics (journ.) (SAUS)
J Clin Exp Gerontol... Journal of Clinical and Experimental Gerontology (journ.) (SAUS)
J Clin Exp Hypn... Journal of Clinical and Experimental Hypnosis (journ.) (SAUS)
J Clin Exp Neuropsychol... Journal of Clinical and Experimental Neuropsychology (journ.) (SAUS)
J Clin Exp Psychopathol... Journal of Clinical and Experimental Psychopathology (journ.) (SAUS)
J Clin Exp Psychopathol Q Rev Psychiahy Neurol... Journal of Clinical and Experimental Psychopathology and Quarterly Review of Psychiatry and Neurology (journ.) (SAUS)
J Clin Gastroenterol... Journal of Clinical Gastroenterology (journ.) (SAUS)
J Clin Hematol Oncol... Journal of Clinical Hematology and Oncology (journ.) (SAUS)
J Clin Hosp Pharm... Journal of Clinical and Hospital Pharmacy (journ.) (SAUS)
J Clin Immunoassay... Journal of Clinical Immunoassay (journ.) (SAUS)
J Clin Immunol... Journal of Clinical Immunology (journ.) (SAUS)
J Clin Lab Anal... Journal of Clinical Laboratory Analysis (journ.) (SAUS)
J Clin Lab Autom... Journal of Clinical Laboratory Automatiton (journ.) (SAUS)
J Clin Lab Immunol... Journal of Clinical and Laboratory Immunology (journ.) (SAUS)
J Clin Med... Journal of Clinical Medicine (journ.) (SAUS)
J Clin Microbiol... Journal of Clinical Microbiology [*A publication*] (PABS)
J Clin Monit... Journal of Clinical Monitoring (journ.) (SAUS)
J Clin Neuro-Ophthalmol... Journal of Clinical Neuro-Ophthalmology (journ.) (SAUS)
J Clin Neurophysiol... Journal of Clinical Neurophysiology (journ.) (SAUS)
J Clin Neuropsychol... Journal of Clinical Neuropsychology (journ.) (SAUS)
J Clin Nurs... Journal of Clinical Nursing (journ.) (SAUS)
J Clin Oncol... Journal of Clinical Oncology (journ.) (SAUS)
J Clin Orthod... Journal of Clinical Orthodontics (journ.) (SAUS)
J Clin Pathol... Journal of Clinical Pathology (journ.) (SAUS)
J Clin Periodontol... Journal of Clinical Periodontology (journ.) (SAUS)
J Clin Pharm... Journal of Clinical Pharmacy (journ.) (SAUS)
J Clin Pharmacol J New Drugs... Journal of Clinical Pharmacology and the Journal of New Drugs (journ.) (SAUS)
J Clin Pharmacol New Drugs... Journal of Clinical Pharmacology and New Drugs (journ.) (SAUS)
J Clin Pharm Ther... Journal of Clinical Pharmacy and Therapeutics (journ.) (SAUS)
J ClinPsyc... Journal of Clinical Psychiatry [*A publication*] (BRI)
J Clin Psychiatry... Journal of Clinical Psychiatry (journ.) (SAUS)
J Clin Psychopharmacol... Journal of Clinical Psychopharmacology (journ.) (SAUS)
J Clin Stomatol Conf... Journal of Clinical Stomatology Conferences (journ.) (SAUS)
J Clin Surg... Journal of Clinical Surgery (journ.) (SAUS)
J Clin Ultrasound... Journal of Clinical Ultrasound (journ.) (SAUS)
J Clin Virol... Journal of Clinical Virology (journ.) (SAUS)
JCLL......... Joint Center for Lessons Learned (DOMA)
JCLMS...... Journal of Clinical Laser Medicine and Surgery (SAUO)
JCLMS...... Journal of Clinical Laser Medicine and Surgery (journ.) (SAUS)
JCL-OMATIC... Job Control Language Automatic Generator [*Computer science*]
JCLOT....... Joint Closed Loop Operations Test (SAA)
JCLPB....... Journal of Consulting and Clinical Psychology (journ.) (SAUS)
JCLPREP.... Job Control Language Preprocessor [*Computer science*] (MHDB)
JCLS......... Junior College Libraries Section [*Association of College and Research Libraries*]
JCLTA........ Journal. Chinese Language Teachers Association (journ.) (SAUS)
J Cluster Sci... Journal of Cluster Science (journ.) (SAUS)
JCLWC....... Joint Committee on Library Work as a Career (SAUO)
JCM.......... Jacobina [*Brazil*] [*Airport symbol*] (OAG)
JCM.......... Japanese Collection of Microorganisms [*Medicine*] (EDAA)
JCM.......... Jettison Control Module
JCM.......... Jeunesse Canada Monde (AC)
JCM.......... Jeunesse Chretienne Malgache [*Malagasy Christian Youth*]
JCM.......... Job Cylinder Map [*Computer science*] (IBMDP)
JCM.......... Joint Committee on Microcards (SAUO)
JCM.......... Joint Conflict Model [*Military*]
JCM.......... Joint Countermeasures [*Military*]
JCM.......... Joule Ceramic Melter (PDAA)
JCM.......... Journal of Clinical Microbiology (SAUO)
JCM.......... Juris Civilis Magister [*Master of Civil Law*]
JCM.......... Malagasy Christian Youth (SAUO)
JCM.......... Standing Conference of Jews, Christians and Muslims in Europe (SAUO)
JCMA........ Junior Clergy Missionary Association [*British*]
JCMB........ Joint Committee on Medicine and Biology (SAUS)
JCMBS...... Journeymen Curriers' Mutual Benefit Society [*A union*] [*British*]
JCMC....... Joint Conference on Medical Conventions (BUAC)
JCMC....... Joint Crisis Management Capability [*DoD*]
JCMC....... Junta Civico-Militar Cubana [*An association*] (EA)
JCMD........ Joint Committee on Mobility for the Disabled [*British*]
JCMD........ Juvenile Chronic Myelogenous Leukemia [*Therapy term*] (CTAA)
JCMEB...... Joint Civil-Military Engineering Board (COE)
JCMEC...... Joint Captured Materiel Exploitation Center (SAUO)
JCMEDK..... Journal of Cardiovascular Medicine (journ.) (SAUS)
JCMHC...... Joint Commission on Mental Health of Children
JCMIH....... Joint Commission on Mental Illness and Health [*Defunct*] (EA)
JCMJC....... Joint Committee of Master and Journeyman Cloggers (SAUO)
JCML........ Juvenile Chronic Myelogenous [*or Myelocytic*] Leukemia [*Medicine*] (DMAA)
JCMOS...... Joint Complementary Metal Oxide Semiconductor (SAUS)
JCMP........ Joint Cruise Missile Project (ACAE)
JCMPO...... Joint Cruise Missile Program (SAUS)
JCMPO...... Joint Cruise Missile Program [*or Project*] Office (MCD)
JCMPO...... Joint Cruise Missile Project Office (SAUO)
JCMR........ Japan Congress on Materials Research (SAUS)
JCMRFA..... Joseph Cox and Mary Rue Family Association (EA)
JCMS........ Jackson Country Medical Society (SAUO)
JCMS........ Journal of Crystal and Molecular Structure (journ.) (SAUS)
JCMSPO.... Joint Cruise Missile System Program Office (ACAE)
JCMST...... Journal of Computers in Math and Science Teaching (NITA)
JCMT........ James Clerk Maxwell Telescope [*Mauna Kea, HI*] [*Operated by the Royal Observatory in Edinburgh, Scotland*]
JCMT........ Joint Collection Management Tools [*Army*] (RDA)
JCMT........ Journal of Cranio-Maxillofacial Trauma (SAUO)
JCMVASA... Journal of the Central Mississippi Valley American Studies Association (SAUO)
JCMVASA... Journal of the Central Mississippi Valley American Studies Association (journ.) (SAUS)
JCMWA...... Joint Christian Ministry in West Africa (BUAC)
JCN.......... Jewish Communication Network (SAUS)
JCN.......... Job Change Notice [*Form*] (AAG)
JCN.......... Job Control Number
JCN.......... Joint Communications Network (COE)
JCN.......... Joint Control Number
JCN.......... Journal of Cardiovascular Nursing (SAUO)
JCN.......... Journal of Child Neurology (SAUO)
JCN.......... Journal of Christian Nursing (SAUO)
JCN.......... Journal of Clinical Nutrition [*Medicine*] (EDAA)
JCN.......... Journal of Comparative Neurology [*WIAB*] [*Medicine*] (EDAA)
JCN.......... Jump Conditionally (SAUS)
JCN.......... Jump on Condition [*Computer science*]
JCN.......... Junction (NITA)
JCNA........ Jaguar Clubs of North America (EA)
JCNAFF..... Joint Canadian Navy-Army-Air Force (SAUO)
JCNEA....... Journal of Comparative Neurology (journ.) (SAUS)
JCNFC....... Jimmy C. Newman Fan CLub (EA)
JCNM........ Jewel Cave National Monument (SAUO)
JCNMT...... Joint Committee of Nordic Marine Technology [*See also NSTM*] (EAIO)
JCNMT...... Joint Committee of Nordic Master Tailors (EA)
JCNNM...... Johnson Controls Northern New Mexico (SAUO)
JCNNSRC... Joint Committee of the Nordic Natural Science Research Councils (EA)
JCNOD...... Journal of Clinical Neuro-Ophthalmology (journ.) (SAUS)
JCNP........ Joint Committee on Nuclear Power (SAUS)
JCNPS...... Joint Committee on Nuclear Power Standards (SAUS)
JCNRD...... Journal of Cyclic Nucleotide Research (journ.) (SAUS)
JCNSW...... Judicial Commission of New South Wales [*Australia*]
JCO.......... Jesus College, Oxford [*England*] (ROG)
JCO.......... Joint Consultative Organization for Research and Development in Agriculture and Food (SAUO)
JCO.......... Joint Contracting Offices [*Army*]
JCO.......... Jordan Cooperative Organization (SAUO)
JCO.......... Journal of Clinical Oncology (journ.) (SAUS)
JCO.......... Journal of Clinical Orthodontics (journ.) (SAUS)
JCO.......... Justification for Conditional Operation (SAUO)
JCO.......... Justification for Continued Operation [*Nuclear energy*] (NRCH)
JCOA........ Japanese Clinical Orthopaedic Association (SAUO)
JCOA........ Jazz Composers Orchestra Association (EA)
J Coal Min Eng Assoc Kyushu... Journal. Coal Mining Engineers Association of Kyushu (journ.) (SAUS)
J-COARE.... Japanese COARE [*Coupled Ocean-Atmosphere Response Experiment*] (USDC)
JCOARE..... Japanese Coupled Ocean-Atmosphere Response Experiment [*Marine science*] (OSRA)

J Coastal Res... Journal of Coastal Research (journ.) (SAUS)
J Coast Res... Journal of Coastal Research (SAUO)
J Coated Fibrous Mater... Journal of Coated Fibrous Materials (journ.) (SAUS)
J Coatings Technol... Journal of Coatings Technology [*A publication*] (PABS)
JCOC........ Joint Civilian Orientation Conference [*DoD*]
JCOC........ Joint Combat Operations Center [*Navy*] (NVT)
JCOC........ Joint Combined Operations Center (SAUO)
JCOC........ Joint Command Operations Center [*NATO*] (NATG)
JCOCG....... Joinl Cadre Operation Control Group (SAUS)
JCOCG....... Joint Cadre Operation Control Group [*Military*]
J Coconut Ind... Journal of Coconut Industries (journ.) (SAUS)
J-code....... Japan Code [*Software slang*] (NETL)
J-CODE...... Justification Code (LAIN)
J codes..... Joint Staff Positions (SAUS)
JC of C...... Junior Chamber of Commerce
J Cogn Rehab... Journal of Cognitive Rehabilitation (SAUS)
JCOI......... Journal. Cama Oriental Institute (journ.) (SAUS)
J Co Kildare Archaeol Soc... Journal. County Kildare Archaeological Society (journ.) (SAUS)
J Colfee Res... Journal of Coffee Research (journ.) (SAUS)
J Coll Agric Hokkaido Imp Univ... Journal. College of Agriculture. Hokkaido Imperial University (journ.) (SAUS)
J Coll Agric Tokyo... Journal. College of Agriculture. Tokyo Imperial University (journ.) (SAUS)
J Coll & Univ L... Journal of College and University Law (journ.) (SAUS)
J Coll & Univ Personnel Assn... Journal. College and University Personnel Association (journ.) (SAUS)
J Coll Arts Sci Chiba Unir... Journal College of Arts and Sciences. Chiba University (journ.) (SAUS)
J Coll Ceram Technol Univ Calcutta... Journal College of Ceramic Technology. University of Calcutta (journ.) (SAUS)
J Collect Negotiations Public Sect... Journal of Collective Negotiations in the Public Sector (journ.) (SAUS)
J College Place... Journal of College Placement (journ.) (SAUS)
J Coll Eng Technol Jadrapur Univ... Journal. College of Engineering and Technology Jadrapur University (journ.) (SAUS)
J Coll Eng Tokyo Imp Univ... Journal. College of Engineering. Tokyo Imperial University (journ.) (SAUS)
J Coll Gen Pract... Journal. College of General Practitioners (journ.) (SAUS)
J Coll Ind Technol Nihon Univ... Journal. College of Industnal Technology. Nihon University (journ.) (SAUS)
J Coll Ind Technol Nihon Univ A... Journal. College of Industrial Technology. Nihon University. Series A (journ.) (SAUS)
J Coll Ind Technol Nihon Univ B... Journal. College of Industrial Technology. Nihon University. Series B (journ.) (SAUS)
J Coll I Sc... Journal of Colloid and Interface Science (journ.) (SAUS)
J Coll Msr Sci Technol Tokai Univ... Journal. College of Marine Science and Technology. Tokai University (journ.) (SAUS)
J Coll Radiol Aust... Journal. College of Radiologists of Australia (journ.) (SAUS)
J Coll Sci Eng Natl Chung Hsing Univ... Journal. College of Science and Engineering. National Chung Hsing University (journ.) (SAUS)
J Coll Sci Imp Univ Tokyo... Journal. College of Science. Imperial University of Tokyo (journ.) (SAUS)
J Coll Sci King Saud Univ... Journal. College of Science. King Saud University (journ.) (SAUS)
J Coll Sci Teach... Journal of College Science Teaching (journ.) (SAUS)
J Coll Univ... Journal. College and University Personnel Association (journ.) (SAUS)
J Colo Dent Assoc... Journal. Colorado Dental Association (journ.) (SAUS)
J Colo-Wyo Acad Sci... Journal. Colorado-Wyoming Academy of Science (journ.) (SAUS)
JCOM........ Journal of Clinical Outcomes Management (SAUO)
JCOM........ Journal of Clinical Outcomes Management (journ.) (SAUS)
J Comb Theory... Journal of Combinatorial Theory (journ.) (SAUS)
JCOMCEN... Joint Communications Center
JCOME...... Jewish Committee on the Middle East (EA)
JCOMM...... Joint Commission for Ocean and Marine Measurements (SAUO)
J Com Mkt S... Journal of Common Market Studies (journ.) (SAUS)
J Comm Mt Stud... Journal of Common Market Studies [*A publication*] (DLA)
J Common Market Stud... Journal of Common Market Studies (journ.) (SAUS)
J Commun Dis... Journal of Communicable Diseases (journ.) (SAUS)
J Communist Stud... Journal of Communist Studies. London (journ.) (SAUS)
J Community Health Nurs... Journal of Community Health Nursing (journ.) (SAUS)
J Community Psychol... Journal of Community Psychology (journ.) (SAUS)
J Commun Res Lab... Journal of the Communications Research Laboratory (journ.) (SAUS)
J Compar Econ... Journal of Comparative Economics [*A publication*] (JLIT)
J Comp Corp L... Journal of Comparative Corporate Law and Securities Regulation [*A publication*] (ILCA)
J Comp Ethol... Journal of Comparative Ethology (journ.) (SAUS)
J Com Physl... Journal of Comparative and Physiological Psychology (journ.) (SAUS)
J Comp Leg... Journal of the Society of Comparative Legislation (SAUO)
J Comp Leg... Journal. Society of Comparative Legislation [*A publication*] (DLA)
J Complex... Journal of Complexity (journ.) (SAUS)
J Comp Lg... Journal. Society of Comparative Legislation (journ.) (SAUS)
J Compliance Health Care... Journal of Compliance in Health Care (journ.) (SAUS)
J Comp Med and Vet Arch... Journal of Comparative Medicine and Veterinary Archives (journ.) (SAUS)
J Compos Mater... Journal of Composite Materials [*A publication*] (CABS)
J Compos Technol Res... Journal of Composites Technology and Research (journ.) (SAUS)
J Comp Pathol Ther... Journal of Comparative Pathology and Therapeutics (journ.) (SAUS)
J Comp Physiol A... Journal of Comparative Physiology. A. Sensory, Neural and Behavioral Physiology (journ.) (SAUS)
J Comp Physiol B... Journal of Comparative Physiology. B. Biochemical, Systemic and Environmental Physiology (journ.) (SAUS)
J Comp Physiol B Metab Transp Funct... Journal of Comparative Physiology. B. Metabolic and Transport Functions (journ.) (SAUS)
J Comp Psychol... Journal of Comparative Psychology (journ.) (SAUS)
J Comput Aided Mol Des... Journal of Computer-Aided Molecular Design (journ.) (SAUS)
J Comput Appl Math... Journal of Computational and Applied Mathematics (journ.) (SAUS)
J Comput Assist Microsc... Journal of ComputerAssisted Microscopy (journ.) (SAUS)
J Comput Based Instr... Journal of Computer-Based Instruction (journ.) (SAUS)
J Comput Biol... Journal of Computational Biology (journ.) (SAUS)
J Comput Chem... Journal of Computational Chemistry (journ.) (SAUS)
J Comput Graph Stat... Journal of Computational and Graphical Statistics (SAUS)
J Comput Math... Journal of Computational Mathematics (journ.) (SAUS)
J Comput Math and Sci Teach... Journal of Computers in Mathematics and Science Teaching (journ.) (SAUS)
J Comput Neurosci... Journal of Computational Neuroscience (journ.) (SAUS)
J Comput Soc India... Journal. Computer Society of India (journ.) (SAUS)
J Comput Syst Sci... Journal of Computer System Sciences (journ.) (SAUS)
J Comput Tomogr... Journal of Computed Tomography (journ.) (SAUS)
J Con A..... Journal of Consumer Affairs [*A publication*] (BRI)
J Conat Law... Journal of Conational Law [*A publication*] (DLA)
J Conchol... Journal of Conchology (journ.) (SAUS)
J Cond Monit... Journal of Condition Monitoring (journ.) (SAUS)
J Conf Chem Inst Can Am Chem Soc Abstr Pap... Joint Conference. Chemical Institute of Canada/American Chemical Society. Abstracts of Papers (journ.) (SAUS)
J Conflict Resolution... Journal of Conflict Resolution [*A publication*] (JLIT)
J Conn State Dent Assoc... Journal. Connecticul State Dental Association (journ.) (SAUS)
J Conn State Med Soc... Journal. Connecticut State Medical Society (journ.) (SAUS)
J Cons Aff... Journal of Consumer Affairs [*A publication*] (JLIT)
J Cons ASCE... Journal. Construction Division. Proceedings of the American Society of Civil Engineers (journ.) (SAUS)
J Cons Policy... Journal of Consumer Policy [*A publication*] (JLIT)
J Cons Res... Journal of Consumer Research [*A publication*] (JLIT)
J Constr Steel Res... Journal of Constructional Steel Research (journ.) (SAUS)
J Consumer Res... Journal of Consumer Research (journ.) (SAUS)
J Consumer Studies and Home Econ... Journal of Consumer Studies and Home Economics (journ.) (SAUS)
J Contam Hydrol... Journal of Contaminant Hydrology (SAUS)
J Cont Bus... Journal of Contemporary Business (journ.) (SAUS)
J Contemp Afr Stud... Journal of Contemporary African Studies (journ.) (SAUS)
J Contemp Health Law Policy... Journal of Contemporary Health Law and Policy (journ.) (SAUS)
J Contemp Hist... Journal of Contemorary History (journ.) (SAUS)
J Contemp RDL... Journal of Contemporary Roman-Dutch Law [*A publication*] (DLA)
J Contin Educ Obstet Gynecol... Journal of Continuing Education in Obstetrics and Gynecology (journ.) (SAUS)
J Cont Psychoth... Journal of Contempotary Psychotherapy (journ.) (SAUS)
J Contracept... Journal of Contraception (journ.) (SAUS)
J Cooling Tower Inst... Journal. Cooling Tower Institute (journ.) (SAUS)
J Coop Educ... Journal of Cooperative Education (journ.) (SAUS)
JCOP........ JCS Concept and Objectives Paper (SAUO)
J Copr Soc'y... Journal. Copyright Society of the USA [*A publication*] (DLA)
J Copyright Ent & Sports L... Journal of Copyright, Entertainment, and Sports Law [*A publication*] (DLA)
J Copyright Entertainment Sports L... Journal of Copyright, Entertainment, and Sports Law [*A publication*] (DLA)
JCOR........ Jacor Communications [*NASDAQ symbol*] (TTSB)
JCOR........ Jacor Communications, Inc. [*NASDAQ symbol*] (NQ)
J Cork Hist Archaeol Soc... Journal. Cork Historical and Archaeological Society (journ.) (SAUS)
J Corp Finan Contracting Governance Organ... Journal of Corporate Finance: Contracting, Governance and Organization [*A publication*] (JLIT)
J Corp Tax'n... Journal of Corporate Taxation [*A publication*] (DLA)
J Corros Sci Soc Korea... Journal. Corrosion Science Society of Korea (journ.) (SAUS)
JCORW...... Jacor Communications Wrrt [*NASDAQ symbol*] (TTSB)
JCOS........ Job Corps Opportunity Specialist [*Department of Labor*]
JCOS........ Joint Chiefs of Staff [*Military*]
JCOS........ Joint Countermine Operational Simulation [*Military*]
J Cost Manage Manuf Ind... Journal of Cost Management for the Manufacturing Industry (journ.) (SAUS)
JCOT......... Joint Committee on College Teaching
J Coun Psyc... Journal of Counseling Psychology (journ.) (SAUS)
J Counsel & Devt... Journal of Counseling and Development (journ.) (SAUS)
JCOX........ Jordan [*Private rail car owner code*]
JCP.......... Clinical Pharmacology [*Medicine*] [*Formerly Journal of New Drugs*] (EDAA)
JCP.......... Jamaican Communist Party [*Political party*] (BUAC)
JCP.......... Janna Contact Personal [*Janna Systems*] [*Computer interface*] (PCM)
JCP.......... Japan Communist Party [*Nikon Kyosanto*] [*Political party*] (PPW)
JCP.......... Java Community Process (GART)
JCP.......... JC Penney Co. [*NYSE symbol*]
JCP.......... J. C. Penney Co. Inc. (SAUO)
JCP.......... J.C.Penney Company (SAUO)

JCP .... Jetcopter [*Denmark*] [*ICAO designator*] (FAAC)
JCP .... Jettison Control Panel
JCP .... Jewish Communist Party [*Political party*] (BJA)
JCP .... Job Content Protection [*UAW*]
JCP .... Job Control Parameter (SAUS)
JCP .... Job Control Processor (SAUS)
JCP .... Job Control Program (CMD)
JCP .... Job Creation Programme [*Manpower Services Commission*] (AIE)
JCP .... John Crowe Productions, Inc. [*Houston, TX*] [*Telecommunications*] (TSSD)
JCP .... Joint Chiefs of Staff Publications [*Military*]
JCP .... Joint Committee for Palestine (BUAC)
JCP .... Joint [*Congressional*] Committee on Printing
JCP .... Joint Contact Point Division [*Desert Test Center*] [*Fort Douglas, UT*]
JCP .... Joint Power Conditions [*NASA*] (LAIN)
JCP .... Jordanian Communist Party [*Political party*] (PSAP)
JCP .... Journal of Cellular Physiology [*Formerly JCCP*] [*Medicine*] (EDAA)
JCP .... Journal of Chemical Physics [*Database*] (GDD)
JCP .... Journal of Clinical Pathology (SAUS)
JCP .... Journal of Clinical Pathology (journ.) (SAUS)
JCP .... Journal of Clinical Psychiatry (journ.) (SAUS)
JCP .... Journal of Communication Pathology (journ.) (SAUS)
JCP .... Journal of Comparative Psychology (journ.) (SAUS)
JCP .... Journal of Counseling Psychology (journ.) (SAUS)
JCP .... JOVIAL [*Joule's Own Version of the International Algorithmic Language*] Control Program [*Computer science*]
JCP .... Junction Call Processing (SAUS)
JCP .... Jungle Canopy Penetration
JCP .... Junior Capital Pool (FOTI)
JCP .... Junior Collegiate Players [*Later, Associate Collegiate Players*] (EA)
JCP .... Justice of the Common Pleas [*Legal term*] (DLA)
JCP .... Juvenile Chronic Polyarthritis [*Medicine*] (DB)
JCP .... Penney [*J. C.*] Co., Inc. [*NYSE symbol*] (SPSG)
JCP .... Penney (J.C.) [*NYSE symbol*] (TTSB)
JCPC .... J. C. Penney Communications, Inc. [*J. C. Penney Co., Inc.*] [*Telecommunications service*] (TSSD)
JCPC .... Judicial Committee of the Privy Council (SAUO)
JCPCap ...... JCP & L Capital LP [*Associated Press*] (SAG)
JCPCI .... Junior College of Packer Collegiate Institute (SAUO)
JCPCUS ..... Joint Committee on Printing of the Congress of the United States (SAUO)
JCPDS .... Joint Committee on Powder Diffraction Standards (MCD)
JCPDS .... Joint Committee on Powder Diffraction Studies (SAUS)
JCPDS .... Joint Committee on Power Diffraction Standards (BUAC)
JCPDS-ICDD ... Joint Committee on Powder Diffraction Standards-International Center for Diffraction Data (SAUS)
JCPE .... Jersey City Port of Embarkation (SAUS)
JCPES .... Joint Center for Political and Economic Studies (EA)
JCPES .... Joint Contingency Planning and Execution Support (SAUO)
JCPHA .... Journal of Consulting and Clinical Psychology (journ.) (SAUS)
JCPHLD ..... Journal of the Conference of Public Health Laboratory Directors [*Medicine*] (EDAA)
JCPI .... Japan Cotton Promotion Institute (BUAC)
JCPN .... Journal of Child and Adolescent Psychiatric and Mental Health Nursing (SAUO)
JCPOA .... Joint Council of Post Office Associations [*South Africa*]
JCPP .... Journal of Comparative and Physiological Psychology [*Medicine*] (EDAA)
JCP/PO ...... Joint Climate Program/Projects Office (SAUO)
JCPPRFNA ... Joint Commission on Political Prisoners and Refugees in French North Africa [*World War II*]
JCPS .... Joint Center for Political Studies [*Later, JCPES*] (EA)
JCPS .... Journal of Constitutional and Parliamentary Studies (journ.) (SAUS)
JCPS .... Junction Call Processing Subsystem (SAUS)
JCPSB .... Journal of Cellular Physiology. Supplement (journ.) (SAUS)
JCPSD .... Journal of Community Psychology (journ.) (SAUS)
JCPT .... Journal of Canadian Petroleum Technology (journ.) (SAUS)
JCPT .... Journal of Cardiovascular and Pulmonary Technology [*Medicine*] (EDAA)
JCPT .... Journal of Comparative Pathology and Therapeutics [*Medicine*] (EDAA)
JCPT .... Journal of Comparative Pathology and Therapeutics (journ.) (SAUS)
JCPTGP ..... Joint Committee on Postgraduate Training for General Practice (SAUO)
JCPT J Can Pet Technol ... JCPT. Journal of Canadian Petroleum Technology (journ.) (SAUS)
JCPWG .... Joint Certification Procedures Working Group (SAUO)
JCPX .... Joint Command Post Exercise [*Military*] (AABC)
JCPYA .... Journal of Clinical Psychology (journ.) (SAUS)
JCPZ .... JC Penney [*Federal Railroad Administration identification code*]
JCQ .... Jacqueline Gold [*Vancouver Stock Exchange symbol*]
JCQ .... Jefferson City, MO [*Location identifier*] [*FAA*] (FAAL)
JCQA .... Joint Committee on Quality Assurance [*Medicine*] (EDAA)
JCQD .... Jersey City Quartermaster Depot (SAUO)
JCQE .... Joint Council on Quantum Electronics (MCD)
JCR .... Jack Criswell Resources [*Vancouver Stock Exchange symbol*]
JCR .... Jesus Cares Refuge Incorporated [*Australia*] [*An association*]
JCR .... Johnson's New York Chancery Reports [*A publication*] (DLA)
JCR .... Johnsoris New York Chancery Reports (journ.) (SAUS)
JCR .... Joint Casualty Resolution (SAUS)
JCR .... Joint Council for Repatriation (EA)
JCR .... Journal Citation Reports [*A publication*]
JCR .... Journal of Cardiopulmonary Rehabilitation (journ.) (SAUS)
JCR .... Journal of Christian Reconstruction (journ.) (SAUS)
JCR .... Journal of Clinical Rheumatology (journ.) (SAUS)
JCR .... Journal of Coastal Research (journ.) (SAUS)
JCR .... Journal of Conflict Resolution (journ.) (SAUS)
JCR .... Journal of Consumer Research (journ.) (SAUS)
JCR .... Journal of Court Reporting [*A publication*]
JCR .... Judicial Conduct Reporter [*Database*] (GDD)
JCR .... Judicial Council Reports [*A publication*] (DLA)
JCR .... Junction Current Recovery [*in silicon devices*]
JCR .... Junior Common Room [*in British colleges and public schools*]
JCR .... Junta for Revolutionary Coordination [*Argentina*] [*Political party*] (BUAC)
JCRA .... Jewish Committee for Relief Abroad
J Craniofac Genet Dev Biol Suppl ... Journal of Craniofacial Genetics and Developmental Biology Supplement (journ.) (SAUS)
J Craniomandibular Pract ... Journal of Cranio-Mandibular Practice (journ.) (SAUS)
J Craniomaxillofac Surg ... Journal of Cranio-Maxillo-Facial Surgery (journ.) (SAUS)
JCRAS .... Journal. Ceylon Branch. Royal Asiatic Society (journ.) (SAUS)
JCRAS .... Journal of the Ceylon Branch of the Royal Asiatic Society (SAUO)
JCRAS .... Journal of the Ceylon Branch of the Royal Asiatic Society (journ.) (SAUS)
JCRC .... Jewish Community Relations Council (BARN)
JCRC .... Joint Casualty Resolution Center (MCD)
JCRC .... Joint Concept Review Committee (AAGC)
JCRDD ...... Journal of Clinical Research and Drug Development (SAUO)
JCRDD ...... Journal of Clinical Research and Drug Development (journ.) (SAUS)
JCRe .... Judentum im Christlichen Religionsunterricht (BJA)
JC Rettie .... Rettie, Crawford, and Melville's Session Cases, Fourth Series [*1873-98*] [*Scotland*] [*A publication*] (DLA)
JCRF .... Joint Climate Research Fund (SAUO)
JCRFC .... Jeannie C. Riley Fan Club (EA)
JCRFD .... Joint Commission for Regulation of Fishing on the Danube (SAUO)
J Criminal Law and Criminology ... Journal of Criminal Law and Criminology (journ.) (SAUS)
J Crim L & Crim ... Journal of Criminal Law and Criminology [*A publication*] (DLA)
J Crim Sci ... Journal of Criminal Science [*A publication*] (DLA)
J Crit Anal ... Journal of Critical Analysis (journ.) (SAUS)
J Crit Care ... Journal of Critical Care (journ.) (SAUS)
JCRLCMP ... Joint Computer Resource Life Cycle Management Program (SAUO)
JCRMOD .... Joint Center for Research in the Management of Ocean Data (SAUO)
JCRNFE ..... Joint Committee on Reduction of Nonessential Federal Expenditures (SAUO)
J Croatian Studies ... Journal of Croatian Studies (journ.) (SAUS)
J Crop Prod ... Journal of Crop Production [*A publication*] (PABS)
JCRPCC ..... Joint Council on Research in Pastoral Care and Counseling [*Later, COMISS*] (EA)
JCRS .... Joint Casualty Resolution Center [*Established in 1973 to coordinate U.S. military activities regarding American MIA/POWs*] (VNW)
JCRT .... Joint Center for Radiation Therapy (SAUS)
JCRWD ...... Jersey Committee of Resistance Workers and Deportees (EAIO)
J Cryptol ... Journal of Cryptology (journ.) (SAUS)
J Crysllogr Soc Jap ... Journal. Crystalioaphic Society of Japan (journ.) (SAUS)
J Crystallogr Soc Jpn ... Journal of Crystallographic Society of Japan (journ.) (SAUS)
J Cryst Growth ... Journal of Crystal Growth [*A publication*] (CABS)
J Cryurg .... Journal of Cryosurgery (journ.) (SAUS)
JCS .... Communications Systems [*AMEX symbol*]
JCS .... Jaicos [*Brazil*] [*Airport symbol*] (AD)
JCS .... James Connolly Society (BUAC)
JCS .... JANET Connection Service (SAUO)
JCS .... Japan Club of Sydney [*Australia*]
JCS .... Jazz Centre Society [*British*]
JCS .... Jersey Cattle Society [*British*] (DBA)
JCS .... Jersey Cattle Society of the United Kingdom (BUAC)
JCS .... Jewish Chautauqua Society (EA)
JCS .... Jewish Community Center (SAUO)
JCS .... Job Control Statement [*Computer science*]
JCS .... Job Control System (IAA)
JCs .... Job Corpsmen (SAUS)
JCS .... Job Cost Sheet (DGA)
JCS .... Job Creation Scheme [*Department of Employment*] [*British*]
JCS .... Job Creation Subsidy (SAUS)
JCS .... Joint Chiefs of Staff [*United States*] [*Military*]
JCS .... Joint Commission for Spectroscopy (SAUO)
JCS .... Joint Commonwealth Societies (BUAC)
JCS .... Joint Coordinate System (SAUS)
JCS .... Journal. Chemical Society (journ.) (SAUS)
JCS .... Journal of Cardiac Surgery (journ.) (SAUS)
JCS .... Journal of Cell Science (journ.) (SAUS)
JCS .... Journal of Chromatographic Science [*A publication*]
JCS .... Journal of Croatian Studies (journ.) (SAUS)
JCS .... Journal of Curriculum Studies (journ.) (SAUS)
JCS .... Journal of Management Consulting (journ.) (SAUS)
JCS .... Journal of the Chemical Society (SAUO)
JCS .... JTWG Joint Test Working Group (SAUO)
JCS .... Justices' Clerks' Society [*British*] (DBA)
JCSA .... Jewish Communal Service Association of North America (EA)
JCSA .... Joint Committee for Soviet Aid (SAUO)
JCSA .... Joseph Conrad Society of America (EA)
JCSA .... Journal. Chemical Society. Abstracts (journ.) (SAUS)
JCS-ACA .... JCS Automatic Conference Arranger (SAUS)
JCS-ACA .... Joint Chiefs of Staff Automatic Conference Arranger [*Military*] (CET)
JCSAN .... Joint Chiefs of Staff Alerting Network [*Military*]
JCSAS .... Joint Chiefs of Staff Alerting System (MCD)

JCSat........ Japan Communications Satellite (SAUS)
JCSC......... Joint Communications Satellite Center (COE)
JCSCA....... Journal of Colloid and Interface Science (journ.) (SAUS)
JC/SCAMEP... Joint Commonwealth/States Committee on the Adult Migration Education Program [*Australia*]
JCSCCF..... Joint Commission of the Socialist Countries on Cooperation in the Field of Fisheries (PDAA)
JCS Chem Comm... Journal. Chemical Society. Chemical Communications (journ.) (SAUS)
JCS Chem Commun... Journal of the Chemical Society, Chemical Communications (journ.) (SAUS)
JCS Dalton... Journal. Chemical Society. Dalton Transactions. Inorganic Chemistry (journ.) (SAUS)
JCS Dalton... Journal of the Chemical Society, Dalton Transactions (journ.) (SAUS)
JCSE......... Joint Communications Support Element [*DoD*]
JCSE......... Joint Communications Systems Elements (MCD)
JCSEA....... JCS Emergency Actions (SAUS)
JCSEA....... Joint Chiefs of Staff Emergency Actions (SAUO)
JCS Faraday I... Journal. Chemical Society. Faraday Transactions. I Physical Chemistry (journ.) (SAUS)
JCS Faraday I... Journal of the Chemical Society, Faraday Transactions I (journ.) (SAUS)
JCS Faraday II... Journal. Chemical Society. Faraday Transactions. II Chemical Physics (journ.) (SAUS)
JCS Faraday II... Journal of the Chemical Society, Faraday Transactions II (journ.) (SAUS)
JCSFJ....... Jesuit Centre for Social Faith and Justice [*Canada*] (EAIO)
JCSHR....... Joint Centre for Scottish Housing Research [*United Kingdom*] (RCD)
JCSI......... Joint Combat Systems Integrating
JCSI......... Joint Command Systems Initiative (SAUO)
JCSIDBAD... Joint Chiefs of Staff Identification Badge [*Military decoration*] (GFGA)
JCSIdentBad... Joint Chiefs of Staff Identification Badge [*Military decoration*] (AABC)
JCSIDTN.... Joint Chiefs of Staff Interim Data Transmission Network [*Military*] (CET)
JCS-IDTN... Joint Chiefs of Staff-Interim Data Transmission Network (SAUO)
JCSLHG..... Joint Center for the Study of Law and Human Genetics
JCSM........ JCS Memorandum (SAUS)
JCSM........ Joint Chiefs of Staff Memorandum [*Military*]
J/CSM....... Junior Company Sergeant-Major [*British military*] (DMA)
JCSMC...... JCS Message Center (SAUS)
JCSMC...... Joint Chiefs of Staff Message Center (SAUO)
JCSMR...... John Cultin School of Medical Research (SAUS)
JCSMS...... Joint Commission on Sports Medicine and Science (EA)
JCS NICA... Joint Chiefs of Staff NICA Support (SAUO)
JCSNMCC... Joint Chiefs of Staff National Military Command Center (DNAB)
JCSO........ Joint Chiefs of Staff Organization [*Military*] (MCD)
JCSOS....... Joint and Combined Staff Officer School
JCSP......... Joint Chiefs of Staff Plans
JCSP......... Joint Chiefs of Staff Publication (SAUO)
JCSP......... Journal of College Student Personnel [*A publication*] (DHP)
JCS Perkin I... Journal. Chemical Society. Perkin Trans- actions. I Organic and Bioorganic Chemistry (journ.) (SAUS)
JCS Perkin II... Journal. Chemical Society. Perkin Transactions. II Physical Oiganic Chemistry (journ.) (SAUS)
JCSPUB..... Joint Chiefs of Staff Publications [*Military*]
JCSR........ Journal of Crystallographic and Spectroscopic Research (journ.) (SAUS)
JCSRE....... Joint Chiefs of Staff Representative, Europe [*NATO*] (NATG)
JCSRG....... Joint Chiefs of Staff Requirements Group (SAUO)
JCSS......... Jaffee Center for Strategic Studies [*Israel*] (BUAC)
JCSS......... Japan Calibration Service System (SAUO)
JCSS......... Jesuit Center for Social Studies [*Defunct*] (EA)
JCSS......... Jesus Christ Superstar [*Rock opera*]
JCSS......... Joint Committee on Slavic Studies (SAUO)
JCSS......... Joint Communications Support Squadron
JCSS......... Journal of Computer and System Sciences (journ.) (SAUS)
JCSSA....... Journal of the Cactus and Succulent Society of America (SAUO)
JCSSAB..... Joint Committee of the States to Study Alcoholic Beverage Laws (EA)
JCS(SASM)... Joint Chiefs of Staff (Special Assistant for Strategic Mobility) (DNAB)
JCST......... Joint Combined System Test (KSC)
JC St........ Journal of Caribbean Studies (journ.) (SAUS)
JCST......... Journal of Chemical Society Transactions (journ.) (SAUS)
JCSTA....... Junction Station, CA [*American Association of Railroads railroad junction routing code*]
JCSTC....... Joint Council for Scientific and Technical Communication [*British*]
JCSTD....... Journal of Contemporary Studies (journ.) (SAUS)
JCSTELECON... Joint Chiefs of Staff Teletypwriter Conference Network [*Military*] (MCD)
JCSTI........ Joint Council for Scientific and Technical Information (SAUO)
JCSTR....... Joint Commission on Solar and Terrestrial Relationships (BUAC)
JCSU........ Indu Containers [*Intermodal shipping container symbol*] (TVRC)
JCSUCR..... Joint Commission on Standards, Units and Constants of Radioactivity (SAUO)
JCSUK....... Jersey Cattle Society of the United Kingdom (SAUO)
JCT.......... Jacket (ROG)
JCT.......... James Cook University of North Queensland Herbarium (SAUO)
JCT.......... James Cook University of North Queensland Herbarium International Acronym (SAUS)
JCT.......... Jerusalem College of Technology (SAUS)
JCT.......... Jewett-Cameron [*Vancouver Stock Exchange symbol*]
JCT.......... Jewish Cemetery Trust [*Australia*]
JCT.......... Job Control Table (CMD)
JCT.......... Job-Control-Tecknique (SAUS)
JCT.......... Johnstown/Consolidated Realty Trust (MHDW)
JCT.......... Joint Central Team (SAUS)
JCT.......... Joint Committee on Taxation [*US Congress*]
JCT.......... Joint Contracts Tribunal for the Standard Form of Building Contract (BUAC)
JCT.......... Joint Tribunal on the Standard Form of Building Contract (SAUS)
JCT.......... Jordan Cosmological Theory
JCT.......... Journal Control Table (IAA)
JCT.......... Journal of Corporate Taxation (journ.) (SAUS)
JCT.......... Junction [*Texas*] [*Seismograph station code, US Geological Survey*] (SEIS)
jct........... Junction (SHCU)
Jct........... Junction (TBD)
JCT.......... Junction, TX [*Location identifier*] [*FAA*] (FAAL)
JCT.......... Jurisconsult (ROG)
JCT.......... Juxtaglomerular Cell Tumor [*Medicine*] (PALA)
JCT & M.... Jordan, Case, Taylor & McGrath [*Advertising agency*]
JCTC......... Japanese Cultural and Trade Center (or Centre) (SAUS)
JCTC......... Jewett-Cameron Trading Co. Ltd. [*NASDAQ symbol*] (SAG)
JCTC......... Juneau County Teachers College (SAUO)
JCTCF....... Jewett-Cameron Trading [*NASDAQ symbol*] (TTSB)
JCTCF....... Jewett Cameron Trading Company Ltd. [*NASDAQ symbol*]
JCTCY....... Junction City, KY [*American Association of Railroads railroad junction routing code*]
JCTFI........ Joint Committee for Training in Foundry Industry (SAUO)
JCTFI........ Joint Committee for Training in the Foundry Industry (SAUS)
JCTG......... Joint Contingency Task Group [*Military*] (VNW)
JCTI.......... James Crowe Traders International [*Commercial firm*] [*British*]
JCTI.......... Jurisconsulti [*Counselors at Law*] [*Latin*] (ROG)
JCTION...... Junction [*Commonly used*] (OPSA)
JCTK......... JC Trucking [*Common carrier symbol*]
JCTN......... Joint Composite Tracking Net [*Military*]
JCTN......... Junction [*Commonly used*] (OPSA)
JCTNS....... Junctions [*Commonly used*] (OPSA)
JCTO......... Jesse Cervantes Trucking [*Common carrier symbol*]
JCTOD....... Journal of Combustion Toxicology (journ.) (SAUS)
JCTPT....... Junction Point (IAA)
JCTS......... Junctions [*Postal Service standard*] (OPSA)
JCTU......... Shandong Economitrade International Transportation [*Intermodal shipping container symbol*] (TVRC)
JCTUS....... Jurisconsultus [*Counselor at Law*] [*Latin*] (ROG)
JCTV......... Japan Cable Television Company Ltd. (SAUO)
JCTV......... Joint Committee on Tactical Vehicles (SAUO)
JCU.......... John Carroll University [*University Heights, OH*]
JCU.......... John Carroll University, Grasselli Library, University Heights, OH [*OCLC symbol*] (OCLC)
JCU.......... Joist Chair Upper (SAUS)
JCU.......... Journal of Clinical Ultrasound (journ.) (SAUS)
JCUD........ Joint Centre for Urban Design [*Oxford Brookes University*] [*United Kingdom*] (RCD)
JCUDI....... Japan Computer Usage Development Institute (BUAC)
JCUF......... Joint Communications Unit, Falkland Islands (SAUO)
JCUIS........ Joint Committee on the Union List of Serials (SAUO)
JCU J Clin Ultrasound... JCU, Journal of Clinical Ultrasound (journ.) (SAUS)
JCULS....... Joint Committee on the Union List of Serials
J Cult Econ... Journal of Cultural Economics [*A publication*] (JLIT)
J Cult Geogr... Journal of Cultural Geography (SAUS)
JC Univ..... John Carroll University (SAUO)
JCUNQ...... James Cook University of North Queensland (BUAC)
J Curric St... Journal of Curriculum Studies (journ.) (SAUS)
J Curr Laser Abstr... Journal of Current Laser Abstracls (journ.) (SAUS)
J Curr Stud... Journal of Curriculum Studies (journ.) (SAUS)
JCUS........ Joint Center for Urban Studies of MIT [*Massachusetts Institute of Technology*] and Harvard University [*Research center*] (RCD)
JCUS........ Judicial Conference of the United States (SAUO)
JCUSD....... Joint Committee on Urban Storm Drainage (BUAC)
JCV.......... Jamestown Canyon Virus [*Medicine*] (DMAA)
JCV.......... JC Virus (SAUS)
JCV.......... Jentech Ventures Corp. [*Vancouver Stock Exchange symbol*]
JCV.......... Joule-Clausius Velocity [*Physics*]
JCVI......... Joint Committee on Vaccination and Immunisation (BUAC)
JCVS......... JOVIAL Compiler Validation System [*Computer science*]
JCW.......... Japan Chemical Week (journ.) (SAUS)
JCW.......... JC Whitney [*Automotive parts and accessories*]
JCW.......... Jim Creek [*Washington*] [*Seismograph station code, US Geological Survey*] (SEIS)
JCW.......... Journal of Comparative Business and Capital Market Law (journ.) (SAUS)
JCWA........ Japan Child Welfare Association (SAUO)
JCWA........ Japan Clock and Watch Association (BUAC)
JCWE........ Joint Contingency Warfighting Experiment [*Military*]
JCWG........ Joint Checklist Working Group [*Military*] (AFIT)
JCWG........ Joint Configuration Working Group (SAUO)
JCWI......... Joint Council for the Welfare of Immigrants [*British*] (DI)
JCWP........ Joint Conservation Working Party [*Australia*] [*Political party*]
JCWTS...... Journal. Civil War Token Society (journ.) (SAUS)
JCXP........ JC Express Company [*Common carrier symbol*]
JCY.......... Johnson City, TX [*Location identifier*] [*FAA*] (FAAL)
J Cycle Res... Journal of Cycle Research (journ.) (SAUS)
J Cyclic Nucleotide Protein Phosphor Res... Journal of Cyclic Nucleotide and Protein Phosphorylation Research (journ.) (SAUS)
J Cytol Genet... Journal of Cytology and Genetics (journ.) (SAUS)
JD........... Diploma in Journalism (ADA)

JD........... Doctor of Jurisprudence (DD)
JD........... Doctor of Jurisprudence Laws (SAUS)
JD........... Doctor of Laws or Jurisprudence (SAUS)
JD........... Jack Daniels [*A brand name of whiskey*]
JD........... Jaundice [*Medicine*] (MELL)
JD........... J-Band Detector
JD........... Jejunal Diverticulitis [*Gastroenterology*] (DAVI)
JD........... Jet Driver (KSC)
JD........... Jewish Division [*New York Public Library*] (BJA)
JD........... Job Description [*Department of Labor*]
JD........... Job Development (OICC)
JD........... Joggle Die (MCD)
JD........... Joined (AABC)
JD........... Joint Dependency (SAUS)
JD........... Joint Determination (AFM)
JD........... Joint Dictionary [*Dictionary of US Military Terms for Joint Usage*] [*A publication*] (AFM)
JD........... Jordan Dinar (SAUS)
JD........... Jordanian Dinar [*Monetary unit*] (BJA)
Jd........... Jude [*New Testament book*] (BJA)
JD........... Jugulodigastric [*Node*] [*Gastroenterology*] (DAVI)
JD........... Julian Date [*or Day*]
JD........... Julian Day (SAUO)
JD........... Junction Diode (SAUS)
JD........... Junior Deacon [*Freemasonry*]
JD........... Junior Dean
jd........... Junior Debutante (SAUS)
JD........... Junior Division [*British military*] (DMA)
JD........... Junkyard Dog [*Automotive restoration*]
JD........... Junta Democratica [*Democratic Junta*] [*Spain*] [*Political party*] (PPE)
JD........... Jurisdiction [*Legal shorthand*] (LWAP)
JD........... Juris Doctor [*Doctor of Jurisprudence*] [*Latin*]
JD........... Jurum Doctor [*Doctor of Laws*] [*Latin*]
JD........... Jury Duty (WGA)
JD........... Justice Department
JD........... Juvenile Delinquency [*or Delinquent*]
JD........... Juvenile Delinquent (NTIO)
JD........... Juvenile Diabetes [*Medicine*] (DAVI)
JD........... People's Party (India) [*Political party*] (PSAP)
JD........... Toa Domestic Airlines [*ICAO designator*] (AD)
JDA.......... Japan Defence (or Defense) Agency (SAUS)
JDA.......... Japan Defense Agency-Japan Domestic Airline (SAUS)
JDA.......... Japan Domestic Airlines (PDAA)
JDA.......... Japanese Defense Agency (MCD)
JDA.......... Jefferson Davis Association (EA)
JDA.......... Jewelery Distributors Association [*British*] (DBA)
JDA.......... Jewellery Distributors Association of the United Kingdom (BUAC)
JDA.......... Jewish Direct Action (SAUS)
JDA.......... Joint Defense Appeal [*Defunct*] (EA)
JDA.......... Joint Deployment Agency [*DoD*]
JDA.......... Joint Development Agency [*DoD*]
JDA.......... Joint Development Agreement [*Business term*] (PCM)
JDA.......... Joint Duty Assignment (DOMA)
JDA.......... Journal of Developing Areas (journ.) (SAUS)
JDA.......... Juvenile Delinquency Act
J Dairy Res... Journal of Dairy Research (journ.) (SAUS)
J Dairy Sci... Journal of Dairy Science (journ.) (SAUS)
JDAL......... Joint Duty Assignment List (DOMA)
JDAL......... Jurisdictional [*Legal shorthand*] (LWAP)
J Dalian Eng Inst... Journal. Dalian Engineering Institute (journ.) (SAUS)
J Dalian Inst Technol... Journal. Dalian Institute of Technology (journ.) (SAUS)
J Dalian Univ Technol... Journal of Dalian University of Technology (journ.) (SAUS)
JDAM......... Joint Direct Attack Munition (DOMA)
JDAM......... Joint Direct Attack Munition programme (SAUS)
JDAM......... Joint Direct Attack Munitions [*DoD*]
JDAMIS....... Joint Duty Assignment Management Information System (DOMA)
JDAP......... Joint Direct Attack Program [*Air Force*] (DOMA)
JDAS......... JDA Software Group [*NASDAQ symbol*] (TTSB)
JDAS......... JDA Software Group, Inc. [*NASDAQ symbol*] (NASQ)
JDASoft...... JDA Software Group, Inc. [*Associated Press*] (SAG)
J Data Ed... Journal of Data Education (journ.) (SAUS)
J Data Manage... Journal of Data Management (journ.) (SAUS)
J Data Mgt... Journal of Data Management (journ.) (SAUS)
J-day........ Judas Day (SAUS)
JDB.......... Japan Development Bank (PDAA)
JDB.......... Java Debugger (SAUS)
JDBC......... Java Database Connect [*Computer science*]
JDBC......... Java Database Connection (SAUS)
JDBC......... Java Data Base Connectivity [*Computer science*] (IGQR)
JDBP......... Journal of Developmental and Behavioral Pediatrics (journ.) (SAUS)
JDC.......... American Jewish Joint Distribution Committee (EA)
JDC.......... Deere & Co. [*ICAO designator*] (FAAC)
JDC.......... Jackson Development Corporation
JDC.......... Japan Airlines Development Co.
JDC.......... Japan Digital Cellular (SAUO)
JDC.......... Japan Documentation Center [*Columbia University*]
JDC.......... Jet Deflection Control (AAG)
JDC.......... Jet Detection Control (SAUS)
JDC.......... Jeunesse Democratique Camerounaise [*Cameroonian Democratic Youth*]
JDC.......... Jewish Documentation Centre [*See also BJVN*] (EAIO)
JDC.......... Job Description Card
JDC.......... John Deere Company
JDC.......... Joint Deployment Community [*Military*] (INF)
JDC.......... Joint Development Community [*DoD*]
JDC.......... Joint Doctrine Center (COE)
JDC.......... Joslin Diabetes Center (EA)
JDC.......... Junction Diode Circuit
JDC.......... Junior Doctors Committee (SAUO)
JDC.......... Just Discriminable Change (IAA)
JDC.......... Juvenile Delinquency Control (SAUS)
JDC.......... Juvenile Detention Center
JDCA......... Japan Designer and Craftsman Association (BUAC)
JDCC......... Juneau-Douglas Community College (SAUO)
J DC DentS... Journal. District of Columbia Dental Society (journ.) (SAUS)
JDCE......... Jeunes Democrates Chretiens Europeens [*European Young Christian Democrats - EYCD*] (EA)
JDCHA........ Journal of Dentistry for Children (journ.) (SAUS)
JDCMC........ Joint Department of Defense Configuration Management Committee (MCD)
JDCS......... Joint Deputy Chiefs of Staff [*Military*]
JDCU......... Jamming Detection Control Unit (SAUS)
JDD.......... Joint Doctrine Division (COE)
JDDD......... Judicial Discipline and Disability Digest [*American Judicature Society*] [*Information service or system*] (CRD)
JDE.......... Air Med Jetoperations [*Austria*] [*ICAO designator*] (FAAC)
JDE.......... Journal of Dental Education (SAUO)
JDE.......... Journal of Development Economics (journ.) (SAUS)
J De Agric Un S Afr... Journal. Department of Agriculture. Union of South Africa (journ.) (SAUS)
JDEC......... J D Edwards [*NYSE symbol*] (SG)
JDEC......... Joint Documents Exploitation Center (SAUO)
J Decor Propag Arts... Journal of Decorative and Propaganda Arts. Wolfson Foundation of Decorative and Propaganda Arts. Miami (SAUO)
JDECU........ Journal. Department of English. Calcutta University (journ.) (SAUS)
J/deg........ Joule per degree (SAUS)
JDEG......... Joules per Degree [*Physics*] (IAA)
J Dendrol... Journal of Dendrology (journ.) (SAUS)
JDENL........ Joined by Enlistment [*Military*]
J Denning LS... Journal. Denning Law Society [*Tanzania*] [*A publication*] (DLA)
J Denning L Soc'y... Journal. Denning Law Society [*Tanzania*] [*A publication*] (DLA)
J Dent....... Journal of Dentistry (journ.) (SAUS)
J Dent Assoc S Afr... Journal. Dental Association of South Africa (journ.) (SAUS)
J Dent Assoc Thai... Journal. Dental Association of Thailand (journ.) (SAUS)
JDent Aux... Journal of the Dental Auxiliaries (journ.) (SAUS)
J Dent Educ... Journal of Dental Education (journ.) (SAUS)
J Dent Eng... Journal of Dental Engineering (journ.) (SAUS)
J Dent Guid Counc Handicap... Journal. Dental Guidance Council on the Handicapped (journ.) (SAUS)
JDent Handicap... Journal of Dentistry for the Handicapped (journ.) (SAUS)
J Dent Med... Journal of Dental Medicine (journ.) (SAUS)
J Dent Sch NU Univ Iran... Journal of the Dental School. National University of Iran (journ.) (SAUS)
J Dent Tech... Journal of Dental Technics (journ.) (SAUS)
JDEP......... Juvenile Delinquency Evaluation Project
J Dep Agric Fish Irl... Journal. Department of Agriculture and Fisheries. Republic of Ireland (journ.) (SAUS)
J Dep Agric Kyushu Imp Univ... Journal. Department of Agriculture. Kyushu Imperial University (journ.) (SAUS)
J Dep Geogr Natl Univ Malaysia... Journal. Department of Geography. National University of Malaysia (journ.) (SAUS)
J Dept Ag Ireland... Journal. Irish Free State Department of Agriculture (journ.) (SAUS)
J Dept Ag S Africa... Journal. Department of Agriculture. South Africa (journ.) (SAUS)
J Dermatol Sci... Journal of Dermatological Science (journ.) (SAUS)
J Dermatol Surg... Journal of Dermatologic Surgery (journ.) (SAUS)
J Dermatol Surg Oncol... Journal of Dermatologic Surgery and Oncology (journ.) (SAUS)
JDES......... Joint Density of Electronic State [*Semiconductor technology*] (OA)
J Des Autom Fault Tolerant Comput... Journal of Design Automation and Fault Tolerant Computing (journ.) (SAUS)
J Desert Res... Journal of Desert Research [*A publication*] (PABS)
J Deterg Collect Chem... Journal of Detergents and Collective Chemistry (journ.) (SAUS)
J Dev Behav Pediatr... Journal of Developmental and Behavioral Pediatrics (journ.) (SAUS)
J Dev Econ... Journal of Development Economics [*A publication*] (PABS)
J Devel Econ... Journal of Development Economics [*A publication*] (JLIT)
J Developing Areas... Journal of Developing Areas [*A publication*] (JLIT)
J Develop Read... Journal of Development Reading (journ.) (SAUS)
J Devel Stud... Journal of Development Studies [*A publication*] (JLIT)
J Devon Trust Nat Conserv... Journal. Devon Trust for Nature Conservation (journ.) (SAUS)
J Dev Studies... Journal of Development Studies (journ.) (SAUS)
JDEWN........ John Denver Early Warning Network (EA)
JDF.......... Jamaican Defense Forces
JDF.......... Jamming Direction Finder [*Military*] (CAAL)
JDF.......... Job Description Form (SAUO)
JDF.......... Juiz De Fora [*Brazil*] [*Airport symbol*] (OAG)
JDF.......... Juvenile Diabetes Foundation [*Later, JDFI*] (EA)
JDF.......... Juvenile Diabetes Foundation International (SAUO)
JDFA......... Juvenile Diabetes Foundation Australia (NRGU)
JDFAA........ Japanese Defense Facilities Administration Agency (SAUO)
JDFC......... James Darren Fan Club [*Defunct*] (EA)
JDFC......... Jimmie Dale Fan Club (EA)
JDFC......... Joanie Dale Fan Club (EA)

JDFC......... Joint Danube Fishery Commission [*See also ZKRVD*] [*Zilina, Czechoslovakia*] (EAIO)
JDFCG....... Jamaica Defence Force Coast Guard (SAUO)
JDFI......... Joslin Diabetes Foundation, Inc. [*Later, JDC*] (EA)
JDFI......... Juvenile Diabetes Foundation International (EA)
JDF International... Juvenile Diabetes Foundation International (SAUO)
JDFR........ Joined From [*Military*]
JdFR........ Juan de Fuca Ridge [*Marine science*] (OSRA)
JDFR........ Juan de Fuca Ridge (USDC)
JDG.......... Judge
JDH.......... Jodhpur [*India*] [*Airport symbol*] (OAG)
JDH.......... Journal of Dental Hygiene (SAUO)
JDHE........ Joint Directory of Higher Education [*A publication*]
JDHHFC..... John Denver Heart to Heart Fan Club (EA)
JDHQ-SV-W Joint Defense Headquarters Services Washington (ACAE)
JDHS........ Jefferson Davis High School (SAUO)
JDHT........ Jaguar-Daimler Heritage Trust [*Automotive history*]
JDHTC....... Jaguar-Daimler Heritage Trust Collection
JDI........... JDS Investments Ltd. [*Toronto Stock Exchange symbol*]
JDI........... Job Description Index
JDI........... Joint Declaration of Interest (DS)
JDI........... Juvenile Delinquency Index (SAUS)
J Diabetes Complications... Journal of Diabetes and Its Complica- tions (journ.) (SAUS)
J Diabetic Assoc India... Journal. Diabetic Association of India (journ.) (SAUS)
JDIAD....... Journal of Dialysis (journ.) (SAUS)
J Diarrhoeal Dis Res... Journal of Diarrhoeal Diseases Research (journ.) (SAUS)
JDIC........ Justice Data Interface Controller (SAUS)
J Digit Imaging... Journal of Digital Imaging (journ.) (SAUS)
JDIMP....... Joint Data and Information Management Panel (SAUO)
JDIND....... Joined by Induction [*Military*]
JDIND....... Joint by Induction (SAUS)
JDipMA..... Joint Diploma in Management Accounting Services [*British*]
JDIS......... Joint Defense/Deployable Intelligence Support (SAUS)
J Dispersion Sci Technol... Journal of Dispersion Science and Technology (journ.) (SAUS)
JDISS........ Joint Deployable Intelligence Support System (SAUO)
J Distrib.... Journal of Distribution (journ.) (SAUS)
JDIX......... Jim Dobbas [*Private rail car owner code*]
JDK.......... Java Developer's Kit (PCM)
JDK.......... Java Development Kit [*Computer science*] (FOTI)
JDK.......... Joodsch-Democratische Kiespartij [*Political party*] (BJA)
JDL.......... Japan Digital Laboratory (SAUS)
JDL.......... Jewish Defense League (EA)
JDL.......... Job Description Language [*Computer science*]
JDL.......... Job Description Library
JDL.......... Job Descriptor Language (NITA)
JDL.......... Job Drawing List (MCD)
JDL.......... Joint Directors of Laboratories [*Military*]
JDL.......... Judicial [*Telegraphy*] (PCTE)
JDL.......... Juneau, AK [*Location identifier*] [*FAA*] (FAAL)
JDL.......... Junior Drama League (SAUO)
JDL.......... Lynn-01, AK [*Location identifier*] [*FAA*] (FAAL)
JDM.......... Jarso Democratic Movement (SAUO)
JDM.......... Jersey Democratic Movement (SAUO)
JDM.......... Journal of Data Management (journ.) (SAUS)
JDM.......... Juvenile Diabetes Mellitus [*Medicine*]
JDMA........ Japan Diet Marketing Association (BUAC)
JDMAG...... Joint Depot Maintenance Analysis Group [*Military*]
JD/MBA..... Juris/Doctor/Master of Business Administration
JDMC........ James Dean Memory Club (EA)
JDMC........ Joint Depot Maintenance Command (SAUO)
JDMC........ JOPES Development Management Center (SAUO)
JDMP........ Joint Deployment Master Plan [*Military*] (MUSM)
JDMS........ John Deere Materials Specification
JDMS........ Journal of Diagnostic Medical Sonography (SAUO)
JDMS........ Juvenile Dermatomyositis [*Medicine*] (DAVI)
JDN.......... JDN Realty [*NYSE symbol*] (TTSB)
JDN.......... JDN Realty Corp. [*NYSE symbol*] (SAG)
JDN.......... Joint Data Network [*Army*]
JDN.......... Jordan (SAUS)
JDN.......... Jordan, MT [*Location identifier*] [*FAA*] (FAAL)
JDN.......... Jordan Petroleum Ltd. [*Toronto Stock Exchange symbol*]
JDN.......... Julian Day Number
JDNB........ Jewish Telegraphic Agency. Daily News Bulletin (journ.) (SAUS)
JDO.......... Jewish Defense Organization (EA)
JDO.......... Job Delivery Orders (MCD)
JDO.......... Junior Duty Officer (MCD)
J Doc Reprod... Journal of Documentary Reproduction (journ.) (SAUS)
JDOP........ Joint Development Objectives Plan (SAA)
JDOP........ Joint Doppler Operational Project [*For tornado warning*] [*Meteorology*]
JDOYM...... Jewish Defense Organization Youth Movement (EA)
JDP.......... Covington/Cincinnati, OH [*Location identifier*] [*FAA*] (FAAL)
JDP.......... Job Development Program
JDP.......... Joint Declaration of Principles
JDP.......... Joint Development Program
JDP.......... Joint Development Project (SAUS)
JDP.......... Paris-Moulineaux [*France*] [*Airport symbol*] (OAG)
JDPA......... Japan Dairy Products Association (SAUO)
JDPA......... Japan Directory of Professional Associations [*Japan Publications Guide Service*] [*Information service or system*] (CRD)
JDPA......... Journal of Dental Practice Administration (SAUO)
JDPA......... Juvenile Justice Planning Agency (OICC)
JDPC........ Joint Defense Production Committee [*Later, Joint War Production Committee*] [*World War II*]
JDPC........ Junior Daughters of Peter Claver (EA)
JDPUP....... Jordanian Democratic Popular Unity Party [*Political party*] (PSAP)
JDR.......... Jamnagar and Dwarka Railway [*Indian Railway*] (TIR)
JDR.......... Japanese Depository Receipts (SAUS)
JDR.......... Job Distribution Register (SAUS)
JDR.......... Journal of Dairy Research (journ.) (SAUS)
JDR.......... Journal of Defense Research (journ.) (SAUS)
JDR.......... Journal of Dental Research (SAUO)
JDR.......... Junior Dispatch Riders (SAUS)
JDR.......... Juta's Daily Reporter, Cape Provincial Division [*South Africa*] [*A publication*] (DLA)
JDR3........ John D. Rockefeller III [*American philanthropist, 1906-1978*]
JDREENL.... Joined by Reenlistment [*Military*]
JDREMC.... Joint Departmental Radio and Electronics Measurements Committee (BUAC)
JDRMA....... Japanese Digital Road Mapping Association
JDRP........ Joint Dissemination Review Panels
J Drug Dev... Journal of Drug Development (journ.) (SAUS)
J Drug Educ... Journal of Drug Education (journ.) (SAUS)
J Drugther Res... Journal for Drugtherapy and Research (journ.) (SAUS)
JDS.......... Doctor of Juridical Science
JDS.......... Jaguar Diagnostic System [*Automotive engineering*]
JDS.......... JDS Capital Ltd. [*Toronto Stock Exchange symbol*]
JDS.......... Job Data Sheet (IEEE)
JDS.......... Job Diagnosis Survey (PDAA)
JDS.......... John Dewey Society (EA)
JDS.......... Joint Defense Staff [*NATO*] (NATG)
JDS.......... Joint Deployment System
JDS.......... Joint Disciplinary Scheme [*British*]
JDS.......... Journal of Development Studies (journ.) (SAUS)
JDS.......... Judaean Desert Studies (SAUS)
JDS.......... Jugoslovenska Demokratska Stranka [*Yugoslav Democratic Party*] [*Political party*] (PPE)
JDS.......... Julian Day of Spring
JDS.......... Justice Data System (SAUS)
JDSC........ Junior Division Staff College (SAUO)
JDSCS....... Joint Defense Space Communications Station
JDSE......... JD's Equipment Rental [*Common carrier symbol*]
JDSFA....... Japan Self-Defense Forces Academy (SAUO)
JDSIP........ JDS Interface Processor (SAUS)
JDSIR........ JDS Incident Reporting (SAUO)
JDSQP....... JDS Query Processor (SAUS)
JDSRF....... Joint Defense Space Research Facility (CARL)
JDSSC....... Joint Data Systems Support Center [*Military*]
JDSU........ JDS Uniphase Corp. [*NASDAQ symbol*] (SG)
JDSUP....... JDS Update Processor (SAUS)
JDSWRL.... Jay Dow Sr. Wetlands Research Laboratory [*University of Nevada, Reno*] (RCD)
JDSX........ J and J Railcar Leasing [*Private rail car owner code*]
JDT.......... Joint Design Team [*Military*]
JDT.......... Joint Development Team (MCD)
JDT.......... Joint Development Testing
JDT.......... Journal of Dental Technology (SAUO)
Jdt........... Judith [*Old Testament book*] [*Roman Catholic canon*]
JDT.......... Judson Dance Theater
JDTK......... Dick Jones Trucking [*Common carrier symbol*]
JDTU........ Jan Dohmen [*Intermodal shipping container symbol*] (TVRC)
JDU.......... Journal. Durham University (journ.) (SAUS)
J Durham Sch Agr... Journal. Durham School of Agriculture (journ.) (SAUS)
JDW.......... Jacket Decladding Waste (PDAA)
JDW.......... Jacket Declatting Waste (SAUS)
JDWC........ Jazz Dance World Congress
JDW Solution... Jacket Declatting Waste Solution (SAUS)
JDX.......... Judicious [*Telegraphy*] (PCTE)
JDXY........ Judiciously [*Telegraphy*] (PCTE)
JDY.......... Downey (SAUS)
JDY.......... Downey, CA [*Location identifier*] [*FAA*] (FAAL)
JDY.......... Judiciary [*Telegraphy*] (PCTE)
JDYD........ Juvenile Delinquency and Youth Development Office [*Federal government*]
JDZ.......... Jingdezhen [*China*] [*Airport symbol*] (OAG)
JDZ.......... John Deere [*Federal Railroad Administration identification code*]
JE............ Eurojet SA (SAUS)
JE............ Jacksonian Epilepsy [*Medicine*] (MELL)
JE............ Jacobs Engineering Group Inc. (EFIS)
JE............ Jamin Effect [*Electronics*]
JE............ Jamming Effect (SAUS)
JE............ Jamming Equipment
JE............ Japanese Encephalitis [*Medicine*]
J/E........... Japan/Europe (SAUS)
Je............ Jeremiah [*Old Testament book*] (BJA)
JE............ Jerseyville & Eastern [*AAR code*]
JE............ Jet Engine
JE............ Jet Exhaust
JE............ Jewish Encyclopaedia [*A publication*] (BJA)
JE............ Job Enlargement (MHDB)
JE............ Job Enrichment (MHDB)
JE............ Job Entry (SAUS)
JE............ Job Estimate (AAG)
JE............ Johnson Engineering Corp. (SAUO)
JE............ Joint Engineers [*Army*] (RDA)

JE Joint Enterprise (SAUO)
JE Joppa & Eastern Railroad [*Federal Railroad Administration identification code*]
JE Joshi Effect [*Physics*]
JE Joule Effect [*Physics*]
JE Journal Entry (TIMI)
JE Journal of Education [*A publication*] (BRI)
JE Jump If Equal [*Computer science*] (PCM)
JE Junctional Escape [*Cardiology*] (DAVI)
JE Junction Exchange [*Telecommunications*] (OA)
Je June (RION)
JE June
JE Manx Airlines [*Airline flight code*] (ODBW)
JE Yosemite Airlines [*ICAO designator*] (AD)
JEA Jacksonville Electric Authority
JEA Jamaica Exporters Association (BUAC)
JEA Japan Electric Association (BUAC)
JEA Japan Environmental Agency (QUAC)
JEA Japan Export Association (SAUO)
JEA Jersey European Airways [*British*] [*ICAO designator*] (FAAC)
JEA Jesuit Educational Association [*Later split into AJCU and JSEA*] (EA)
JEA Jewish Education Association (SAUO)
JEA Jewish Educators Assembly (EA)
JEA Joint Endeavor Agreement
JEA Joint Engineering Agency
JEA Joint Export Agent
JEA Joint Export Association [*Department of Commerce*]
JEA Jordan Engineers Association (SAUO)
JEA Journalism Education Association (EA)
JEAB Journal of the Experimental Analysis of Behavior (journ.) (SAUS)
JEAC Journal of Electroanalytical Chemistry [*A publication*]
JEADF Joint Eastern Air Defense Force (MUGU)
JEADV Journal of the European Academy of Dermatology and Venereology (SAUO)
JEADV Journal of the European Academy of Dermatology and Venereology (journ.) (SAUS)
Jeaf Jeaffreson's Book about Lawyers [*A publication*] (DLA)
JEAH Jewish Endowment for the Arts and Humanities
JEAL Junction Emitting Avalanche Light
JEAN Jean Philippe Fragrances [*NASDAQ symbol*] (TTSB)
JEAN Jean Philippe Fragrances, Inc. [*NASDAQ symbol*] (NQ)
JEAN JOSS-Based Expression Analyser for the Nineteen Hundred (NITA)
Jean Charcot... French research vessel (SAUS)
JeanPhl Jean Philippe Fragrances, Inc. [*Associated Press*] (SAG)
JEARD Journal of Eastern African Research and Development [*A publication*]
J Earth Sci... Journal of Earth Sciences (journ.) (SAUS)
J Earth Sci Nagoya Unir... Journal of Earth Sciences. Nagoya University (journ.) (SAUS)
JEAS Journal of East Asiatic Studies (journ.) (SAUS)
JEASC Journal. East African Swahili Committee [*A publication*]
J East Afr Nat Hist Soc Natl Mus... Journal. East Africa Natural History Society and National Museum (journ.) (SAUS)
J East Afr Res Develop... Journal of Eastern African Research and Development (journ.) (SAUS)
J East Chin Inst Text Sci Technol... Journal. East China Institute of Textile Science Technology (journ.) (SAUS)
J East Chin Petrol Inst... Journal. East China Petroleum Institute (journ.) (SAUS)
J East-West Bus... Journal of East-West Business [*A publication*] (JLIT)
J East West Stud... Journal of East and West Studies (journ.) (SAUS)
JEAT Joint Emergency Airlift Traffic (SAUS)
JEAT Joint Emergency Airlift Traffic Management Plan [*DoD*]
JEB James Ewell Brown Stuart [*American Confederate general known as Jeb Stuart, 1833-1864*]
JEB Jansen Engineering Building (SAUS)
JEB Japan Evangelical Board (SAUO)
JEB Jewish Education Bureau [*British*] (CB)
JEB Joint Economy Board [*Abolished, 1947*] [*Army-Navy*]
JEB Joint Electronics Board
JEB Joint Emergency Board (SAUO)
JEB Journal of Economic Behavior (journ.) (SAUS)
JEB Journal of Economics and Business (journ.) (SAUS)
JEB Journal of Experimental Biology (journ.) (SAUS)
JEB Journal of Experimental Botany (journ.) (SAUS)
JEB Junctional Epidermolysis Bullosa [*Medicine*]
JEB Junctional Escape Beat [*Medicine*] (MELL)
Jebb Jebb's Irish Crown Cases [*1822-40*] [*A publication*] (DLA)
Jebb Jebbs Irish Crown Cases (journ.) (SAUS)
Jebb & B ... Jebb and Bourke's Irish Queen's Bench Reports [*1841-42*] [*A publication*] (DLA)
Jebb & B ... Jebb and Bourkes Irish Queens Bench Reports (journ.) (SAUS)
Jebb & B (Ir)... Jebb and Bourke's Irish Queen's Bench Reports [*1841-42*] [*A publication*] (DLA)
Jebb & S ... Jebb and Symes' Irish Queen's Bench Reports [*A publication*] (DLA)
Jebb & S (Ir)... Jebb and Symes' Irish Queen's Bench Reports [*A publication*] (DLA)
Jebb & Sym... Jebb and Symes' Irish Queen's Bench Reports [*A publication*] (DLA)
Jebb CC Jebb's Irish Crown Cases [*1822-40*] [*A publication*] (DLA)
Jebb CC (Ir)... Jebb's Irish Crown Cases [*1822-40*] [*A publication*] (DLA)
Jebb Cr & Pr Cas... Jebb's Irish Crown and Presentment Cases [*A publication*] (DLA)
JEBC Jefferson Bancorp, Inc. (Los Angeles) [*NASDAQ symbol*] (SAG)
JEBC Jefferson Bancorp(LA) [*NASDAQ symbol*] (TTSB)
JEBD Journal of Emotional and Behavioral Disorders (SAUO)
JEBG Japan Electronics Buyers Guide (journ.) (SAUS)
JEBH Journal of Economic and Business History (journ.) (SAUS)
JEBM Jet Engine Base Maintenance
JEBM-RR ... Jet Engine Base Maintenance - Return Rate (PDAA)
JEBPAC New Jersey Bankers Association Jersey Bankers PAC - Federal Fund [*Princeton, NJ*] (PACS)
JEC Jacobs Engineering Group, Inc. [*NYSE symbol*] (SPSG)
JEC Jacobs Engr Group [*NYSE symbol*] (TTSB)
JEC Japanese Electrotechnical Committee
JEC Jardine Engineering Corp. (SAUS)
JEC Jeisey Electric Co. (SAUS)
JEC Jersey Electric Co. [*British*]
JEC Jeunesse Etudiante Catholique Internationale [*International Young Catholic Students*] (EAIO)
JEC John E. Chance & Associates (SAUO)
JEC Joint Economic Committee (COE)
JEC Joint Economic Committee of Congress
JEC Joint Economic Congress (SAUO)
JEC Joint Economics Committee (ACAE)
JEC Joint Emergency Committee (SAUO)
JEC Joint European Committee of Paper Experts (SAUO)
JEC Joint European Committee of Paper Exporters (BUAC)
JEC Joint Evaluation Committee [*NSF-UCAR*]
JEC Joint Exchanges Committee [*British*] (NUMA)
JEC Journal Editorial Committee (ACII)
JECA Japan Electrical Construction Association (SAUS)
JECA Japan Electrical Construction Association, Inc. (SAUO)
JECA Jewel Cave National Monument
JECA John E. Chance & Associates (SAUO)
JECA Joint Engineers Council of Alabama (SAUO)
JECAB Journal of Electrocardiology (journ.) (SAUS)
JECB Jet Engine Control Bearing
JECC Japan Electric Computer Corporation [*Japan*] (NITA)
JECC Japan Electronic Computer Center (SAUO)
JECC Japan Electronic Computer Company, Ltd. (SAUO)
JECC Japan Electronic Computer Corporation (SAUO)
JECC Japanese Electronic Computer Co.
JECC Joint Economic Committee of Congress (MCD)
JECC Joint Egyptian Cotton Committee (BUAC)
JECC Joint Electronic Components Conference (SAUS)
JECC Joint Exercise Control Center (MCD)
JECCS Joint Enhanced Core Communications System [*Military*]
JECEJA Joint Emergency Committee for European Jewish Affairs (SAUO)
JECEWSI Joint Electronic Combat Electronic Warfare Simulator (SAUS)
JECFA Joint Expert Committee of/on Food Additives (SAUS)
JECFA Joint Expert Committee on Food Additives [*FDA/WHO*]
JECFA Joint FAO/WHO Expert Committee of/on Food Additives (SAUO)
JECFI Joint Expert Committee on Food Irradiation (BUAC)
JECG Joint Exercise Control Group (SAUO)
JECH Journal of Epidemiology & Community Health (SAUO)
JECH Journal of Epidemiology and Community Health (journ.) (SAUS)
J E China Inst Chem Technol... Journal of the East China Institute of Chemical Technology (journ.) (SAUS)
JECI Jeunesse Etudiante Catholique Internationale [*International Young Catholic Students*]
Je Ci Jewish Civilisation (journ.) (SAUS)
JECL JEC Lasers Inc. (SAUO)
JECL Job Entry Control Language
JECMA Japan Export Clothing Makers Association (BUAC)
JECMA Journal of Electronic Materials (journ.) (SAUS)
JECMB Joint Executive Committee on Medicine and Biology
JECMB Joint Experimental Committee on Medicine and Biology (SAUS)
JECMOS Joint Electronic Countermeasures Operation Section [*NATO*] (NATG)
JECNS Joint Electronic Communications Nomenclature System [*Military*] (IAA)
J Ecol Journal of Ecology (journ.) (SAUS)
J Ecom Dynamics Control... Journal of Economic Dynamics and Control (journ.) (SAUS)
J Econ Aff... Journal of Economic Affairs (journ.) (SAUS)
J Econ Behav Organ... Journal of Economic Behavior and Organization [*A publication*] (JLIT)
J Econ Biol... Journal of Economic Biology (journ.) (SAUS)
J Econ Bs... Journal of Economics and Business (journ.) (SAUS)
J Econ Bus Hist... Journal of Economic and Business History (journ.) (SAUS)
J Econ Cooperation Islamic Countries... Journal of Economic Cooperation among Islamic Countries [*A publication*] (JLIT)
J Econ Dev... Journal of Economic Development. Chung-Ang Univ., Economic Research Institute. Seoul (journ.) (SAUS)
J Econ Devel... Journal of Economic Development [*A publication*] (JLIT)
J Econ Dynam Control... Journal of Economic Dynamics and Control [*A publication*] (JLIT)
J Econ Dyn and Control... Journal of Economic Dynamics and Control (journ.) (SAUS)
J Econ Ed... Journal of Economic Education (journ.) (SAUS)
J Econ Educ... Journal of Economic Education [*A publication*] (JLIT)
J Econ Growth... Journal of Economic Growth [*A publication*] (JLIT)
J Econ Hist... Journal of Economic History [*A publication*] (JLIT)
J Econ Integration... Journal of Economic Integration [*A publication*] (JLIT)
J Econ Issues... Journal of Economic Issues [*A publication*] (JLIT)
J Econ Lit... Journal of Economic Literature [*A publication*] (JLIT)
J Econ Methodology... Journal of Economic Methodology [*A publication*] (JLIT)
J Econ of Bus... Journal of the Economics of Business [*A publication*] (JLIT)
J Econometrics... Journal of Econometrics [*A publication*] (JLIT)
J Econ Perspect... Journal of Economic Perspectives [*A publication*] (JLIT)
J Econ Psych... Journal of Economic Psychology [*A publication*] (JLIT)

J Econ Res... Journal of Economic Research [*A publication*] (JLIT)
J Econ S Hist Or... Journal of the Economic and Social History of the Orient (journ.) (SAUS)
J Econ Soc Meas... Journal of Economic and Social Measurement (journ.) (SAUS)
J Econ Stud... Journal of Economic Studies [*A publication*] (JLIT)
J Econ Studies... Journal of Economic Studies (journ.) (SAUS)
J Econ Surveys... Journal of Economic Surveys [*A publication*] (JLIT)
J Econ Taxon Bot... Journal of Economic and Taxonomic Botany (journ.) (SAUS)
J Econ Theory... Journal of Economic Theory [*A publication*] (JLIT)
J Econ Theory Econometrics... Journal of Economic Theory and Econometrics [*A publication*] (JLIT)
JECOR....... U.S.-Saudi Arabian Joint Commission of Economic Cooperation (SAUO)
JECPA....... Journal of Experimental Child Psychology (journ.) (SAUS)
JECR......... Jec Ro [*NCIC trailer make code*]
JECRA....... Jewish Committee for Relief Abroad (SAUO)
JECS......... Job Entry Central Services (MCD)
JECSS....... Japan and East China Seas Study [*Marine science*] (OSRA)
JECU......... Jeco Shipping [*Intermodal shipping container symbol*] (TVRC)
JECZ......... Johnson Elk Coal [*Federal Railroad Administration identification code*]
JED......... Japan Economic Daily [*Database*] [*Kyodo News International, Inc.*] [*Information service or system*] (CRD)
JED......... Japan Engineering Development (SAUO)
JED......... Jeddah [*Saudi Arabia*] [*Airport symbol*] (OAG)
Jed......... Jedediah (BJA)
JED......... Jet East, Inc. [*ICAO designator*] (FAAC)
JED......... Jet Engine Duct
J Ed......... Jewish Education (journ.) (SAUS)
JED......... Job Entry Definition (SAUS)
JED......... Joint Educational Development (EA)
JED......... Joint Exercise Division (SAUO)
JED......... Journal of Economic Dynamics and Control (journ.) (SAUS)
JED......... Journal of Electronic Defense (SAUO)
JED......... Journal of Esthetic Dentistry (SAUO)
JED......... Julian Ephemeris Data (MCD)
JEDA......... Joint Environmental Data Analysis Center [*Army*] [*Marine science*] (OSRA)
J Ed Admin... Journal of Educational Administration (journ.) (SAUS)
J Ed Data Process... Journal of Educational Data Processing (journ.) (SAUS)
JEDDS....... Joint Electronic Document Delivery Software (SAUS)
JEDEC....... Joint Electron Device Engineering Council (EA)
JEDI......... Jobs for Employable Dependent Individuals Program [*Federal government*]
JEDI......... Joint Electronic Data Interchange [*International trade*]
JEDI......... Justice, Economic Dignity and Independence for Women [*Association*] (EA)
JEDMICS.... Joint Engineering and Data Management Information and Control System [*Military*]
JEDPE....... Joint Emergency Defense Plan Europe [*NATO*] (NATG)
JEDS......... Japanese Expeditions to the Deep Sea
JEDS......... Jedburgh Teams [*Allied intelligence-gathering units in Europe*] [*World War II*]
J Ed Soc.... Journal of Educational Sociology. Payne Educational Sociology Foundation. New York (SAUO)
JEDTC....... Joint Electron Device Tube Council (SAUO)
J Educ Adm... Journal of Educational Administration (journ.) (SAUS)
J Educ Adm Hist... Journal of Educational Administration and History (journ.) (SAUS)
J Educ Comput Res... Journal of Educational Computing Research (journ.) (SAUS)
J Educ Data Proc... Journal of Educational Data Processing (journ.) (SAUS)
J Educ Dept Nugata Univ... Journal Education Department. Nugata University (journ.) (SAUS)
J Educ DP... Journal of Educational Data Processing (journ.) (SAUS)
J Educ for Teach... Journal of Education for Teaching (journ.) (SAUS)
J Educ Media Science... Journal of Educational Media Science (journ.) (SAUS)
J Educ Method... Journal of Educational Method (journ.) (SAUS)
J Educ Modules Mater Sci Eng... Journal of Educational Modules for Materials Science and Engineering (journ.) (SAUS)
J Educ Soc... Journal of Education for Social Work (journ.) (SAUS)
J EducTh... Journal of Educational Thought (journ.) (SAUS)
JEE........... Japan Electronic Engineering (journ.) (SAUS)
JEE........... Japan Environment Agency (SAUO)
JEE........... Japanese Equine Encephalitis [*Medicine*]
JEE........... Jet Engine Exhaust
JEE........... Journal of Economic Entomology [*ESA*] [*Medicine*] (EDAA)
JEE........... Journal of Electronic Engineering (journ.) (SAUS)
JEE........... Journal of Engineering Education (journ.) (SAUS)
JEE........... Journal of Experimental Education (journ.) (SAUS)
JEEC......... Joint ETSI/ECMA Committee (SAUO)
JEEC......... Kenneth E. Johnson Environmental and Energy Center [*University of Alabama in Huntsville*] [*Research center*] (RCD)
JEED......... Journal. Environmental Engineering Division. Proceedings of the American Society of Civil Engineers (journ.) (SAUS)
JEEGA....... Journal. Environmental Engineering Division. American Society of Civil Engineers (journ.) (SAUS)
JEEJ Electron Eng... JEE. Journal of Electronic Engineering (journ.) (SAUS)
JEEM......... Journal of Embryology and Experimental Morphology (SAUO)
JEEM......... Journal of Embryology and Experimental Morphology (journ.) (SAUS)
JEEP......... General Purpose Military Utility Vehicle (SAUS)
JEEP......... General-Purpose Quarter-Ton Military Utility Vehicle
Jeep......... Graduated Payment Mortgage (DFIT)
JEEP......... Joint Effort Evaluation Program [*Military*] (AFM)
JEEP......... Joint Emergency Evacuation Plan [*Military*] (AABC)
JEEP......... Joint Environmental Effects Program [*Military*] (AFM)
JEEP......... Joint Establishment Experimental Pile [*Nuclear reactor*] [*Norway*]
JEEP......... Joint Ethics Enforcement Plan (SAUO)
JEEP......... Joint Export Establishment Promotion [*Trade exhibition*] [*Department of Commerce*]
JEEPS....... GNMA Graduated Payment Mortgage Securities (EBF)
JEF........... Jacobi Elliptic Function [*Mathematics*]
JEF........... Jefferies Group [*NYSE symbol*] (TTSB)
JEF........... Jefferson City [*Missouri*] [*Airport symbol*] (OAG)
JEF........... Jefferson City, MO [*Location identifier*] [*FAA*] (FAAL)
JEF........... Jefferson Educational Foundation (EA)
JEF........... Jefjen Capital [*Vancouver Stock Exchange symbol*]
JEF........... JEM Exposure Facility (SAUS)
JEF........... Jet Engine Fuel
JEF........... Jetflite OY [*Finland*] [*ICAO designator*] (FAAC)
JEF........... Jeunesses Europeennes Federalistes
JEF........... Jewish Expeditionary Force (SAUO)
JEF........... Jugoslavia Esperanto-Federacio (SAUO)
JEFAD....... Joint ECA/FAO Agriculture Division (SAUO)
JefBsh....... Jefferson Bankshares, Inc. [*Associated Press*] (SAG)
JEFDSS..... Journal of the English Folk Dance and Song Society (SAUO)
JEFDSS..... Journal of the English Folk Dance and Song Society (journ.) (SAUS)
JEFF......... JeffBanks, Inc. [*NASDAQ symbol*] (SAG)
JEFF......... Jefferson National Corp. (SAUO)
JEFF......... Jefferson National Expansion Memorial National Historic Site
Jeff......... Jefferson's Virginia General Court Reports [*A publication*] (DLA)
JEFF......... Judiciously Efficient Fixed Frame [*Computer science*] (MCD)
JeffBanks... JeffBanks, Inc. [*Associated Press*] (SAG)
JeffBcLA.... Jefferson Bancorp, Inc. [*Los Angles*] [*Associated Press*] (SAG)
JeffBcp...... Jefferson Bancorp, Inc. [*Associated Press*] (SAG)
Jeff Man.... Jefferson's Manual of Parliamentary Law [*A publication*] (DLA)
JeffPilot..... Jefferson-Pilot Corp. [*Associated Press*] (SAG)
JeffPlt...... Jefferson Pilot [*Associated Press*] (SAG)
JeffPOO..... Jefferson Pilot [*Associated Press*] (SAG)
JeffrGp...... Jefferies Group, Inc. [*Associated Press*] (SAG)
JeffSvg...... Jefferson Savings Bancorp [*Associated Press*] (SAG)
Jeff (VA).... Jefferson's Virginia General Court Reports [*A publication*] (DLA)
JEFG......... Jefferies Group, Inc. [*NASDAQ symbol*] (NQ)
JEFM......... Jet Engine Field Maintenance
JEFP......... Jefferson Park Cartage [*Common carrier symbol*]
JefSmrf..... Jefferson Smurfit Corp. [*Associated Press*] (SAG)
JEFVL....... Jeffersonville, IN [*American Association of Railroads railroad junction routing code*]
JEFW........ Jefferson Warrior Railroad [*Federal Railroad Administration identification code*]
JEG.......... Joint Evaluation Group (SAUO)
JEG.......... Joint Exploratory Group [*NATO*] (NATG)
J Eg Or Soc... Journal Egyptian and Oriental Society (journ.) (SAUS)
JEGP......... Journal of English and Germanic Philology [*A publication*] (BRI)
JEGPA....... Journal. Egyptian Public Health Association (journ.) (SAUS)
JEGR......... Jegeroil Corp. (SAUO)
J Egypt Med Soc... Journal Egyptian Medical Society (journ.) (SAUS)
J Egypt Pharm... Journal of Egyptian Pharmacy (journ.) (SAUS)
J Egypt Public Health Assoc... Journal. Egyptian Public Health Association (journ.) (SAUS)
J Egypt Public Health Assoc... Journal of the Egyptian Public Health Association (SAUO)
J Egypt Public Health Assoc... Journal of the Egyptian Public Health Association (journ.) (SAUS)
J Egypt Soc Parasitol... Journal. Egyptian Society of Parasitology (journ.) (SAUS)
J Egypt Soc Parasitol... Journal of the Egyptian Society of Parasitology (journ.) (SAUS)
J Egypt Vet Med Ass... Journal. Egyptian Veterinary Medical Association (journ.) (SAUS)
JEH......... Journal of Ecclesiastical History [*A publication*] (ODCC)
JEH......... Journal of Economic History [*A publication*] (BRI)
JEHFC....... Jon-Erik Hexum Fan Club (EA)
JEHO........ Jehosaphat [*Biblical*] (ROG)
JEHU........ Joint Experimental Helicopter Unit [*British military*] (DMA)
JEI........... Jaeneung Education Co. (EFIS)
JEI........... Japana Esperanto-Instituto (SAUO)
JEI........... Japan Economic Institute of America (EA)
JEI........... Japan Electronics Industry (journ.) (SAUS)
JEI........... Jones Environmental, Inc. (EFIS)
JEI........... Journal. English Institute (journ.) (SAUS)
JEI........... Journal of Economic Issues (journ.) (SAUS)
JEI........... Journal of Electronic Imaging (SAUS)
JEI........... Yei [*Language symbol*] (ETLW)
JEIA......... Japanese Electronic Industries Association
JEIA......... Joint Electronics Information Agency
JEIA......... Joint Export-Import Agency [*Munich*] [*Allied German Occupation Forces*]
J El Ass J... Journal. Electrochemical Association of Japan (journ.) (SAUS)
JEIB......... Joint Export Import Board (SAUO)
JEIDA....... Japanese Electronic Industry Development Association (CDE)
JEIM......... Jet Engine Intermediate Maintenance
JEIND....... Journal of Endocrinological Investigation (journ.) (SAUS)
JEIOG....... Joint Emissions Inventory Oversight Group (SAUO)
JEIPAC...... Japan Electronic Information Processing Automatic Computer (SAUS)
JEIPAC...... JICST [*Japan Information Center of Science and Technology*] Electronic Information Processing Automatic Computer (NITA)
JEISSO...... Joint Expeditions in the Indian Ocean Sector of the Southern Ocean (SAUO)

JEIT.......... Joint Equipment Identification Team [*Military*] (CINC)
JEIZ.......... Jeffrey Energy Center Industries [*Federal Railroad Administration identification code*]
JEJ.......... Japan Economic Journal (journ.) (SAUS)
JEJ.......... Jejunum [*Medicine*]
JEJ.......... Jets Ejecutivos SA [*Mexico*] [*ICAO designator*] (FAAC)
JEJUN....... Jejunectomy (ABBR)
JEJUN....... Jejunitis (ABBR)
JEL.......... Aerojelk, SA de CV [*Mexico*] [*FAA designator*] (FAAC)
JEL.......... Jackson Estuarine Laboratory [*University of New Hampshire*] [*Research center*] (RCD)
JEL.......... Jeunesses Europeennes Liberales [*Liberal European Youth*]
JEL.......... Johnson Elastic Limit (SAUS)
JEL.......... Joint Electronic Library [*Military*]
JEL.......... Journal of Economic Literature [*A publication*] (BRI)
JEL.......... Young European Liberals (SAUS)
J Elastomers Plast... Journal of Elastomers and Plastics (journ.) (SAUS)
J Elastoplast... Journal of Elastoplastics (journ.) (SAUS)
JELC.......... Joint Effort Against Lefthanded Complications
JELCO....... Japan Elanco Company (EFIS)
JELCY....... Johnson Electric Holdings ADR [*NASDAQ symbol*] (QUAN)
J Elec....... Journal of Electricity (journ.) (SAUS)
J Elechochem Soc... Journal. Electrochemical Society (journ.) (SAUS)
J Electr Eng... Journal of Electrical Engineering (journ.) (SAUS)
J Electroanal Chem... Journal of Electroanalytical Chemistry (journ.) (SAUS)
J Electroanal Chem Abstract... Journal of Electroanalytical Chemistry. Abstract Section (journ.) (SAUS)
J Electroanal Chem Interfacial Elechochem... Journal of Electroanalytical Chemistry and Interfacial Electrochemistry (journ.) (SAUS)
J Electrocardiol... Journal of Electrocardiology (journ.) (SAUS)
J Electrochem Soc... Journal of the Electrochemical Society (MEC)
J Electrochem Soc India... Journal. Electrochemical Society of India (journ.) (SAUS)
J Electrochem Soc India... Journal of Electrochemical Society of India (journ.) (SAUS)
J Electrochem Soc Japan... Journal. Electrochemical Society of Japan (journ.) (SAUS)
J Electrodepositors Tech S... Journal. Electrodepositors Technical Society (journ.) (SAUS)
J Electromagn Waves Appl... Journal of Electromagnetic Waves and Applications (journ.) (SAUS)
J Electromyography Kinesiol... Journal of Electromyography and Kinesiology (SAUS)
J Electron... Journal of Electronics (journ.) (SAUS)
J Electron Comput Res... Journal of Electronics and Computers Research (journ.) (SAUS)
J Electron Control... Journal of Electronics and Control (journ.) (SAUS)
J Electron Microsc Tech... Journal of Electron Microscopy Technique (journ.) (SAUS)
J Electron Micry... Journal of Electron Microscopy (journ.) (SAUS)
J Electron Spectrosc... Journal of Electron Spectroscopy (journ.) (SAUS)
J Electrostatics... Journal of Electrostatics [*A publication*] (CABS)
J Electro Th... Journal of Electrophysiological Techniques (journ.) (SAUS)
J Electr West Ind... Journal of Electririty and Western Indus- try (journ.) (SAUS)
J Elisha Mitchell Scient Soc... Journal. Elisha Mitchell Scientific Society (journ.) (SAUS)
JEl J Electron Ind... JEL Journal of the Electronics Industry (journ.) (SAUS)
JELLI........ Jellico, TN [*American Association of Railroads railroad junction routing code*]
JELM........ Japanese Experiment Logistics Module (SAUO)
JELOS........ Jealous (ABBR)
JELOSY..... Jealousy (ABBR)
JEM.......... Jaish-e-Mohammed [*Government term*] (GA)
JEM.......... Japanese Experiment Module
JEM.......... Japanese Experiment Module [*for SSF*] [*Astronomy term*]
JEM.......... Japan Experiment Module (SAUS)
JEM.......... Jerusalem and the East Mission
JEM.......... Jet Engine Modulation (MCD)
JEM.......... Jewelmasters, Inc. (SAUS)
JEM.......... Joint Endeavor Manager
JEM.......... Joint Environmental Monitoring (SAUS)
JEM.......... Joint Exercise Manual (MCD)
JEM.......... Joint Experts Meeting (SAUO)
JEM.......... Jordon Electronic Manufacturing Co. (SAUO)
JEM.......... Journal of Enterprise Management (journ.) (SAUS)
JEM.......... Journal of Environmental Economics and Management (journ.) (SAUS)
JEM.......... Journal of Experimental Medicine (SAUO)
JEM.......... Journey's End Motel Corp. [*Toronto Stock Exchange symbol*]
JEMA........ Japan Electronic Messaging Association (DDC)
JEM(A)....... Junior Electrical Mechanic (Air) [*British military*] (DMA)
JEMAA...... Journal. Egyptian Medical Association (journ.) (SAUS)
JEM(AW).... Junior Electrical Mechanic (Air Weapon) [*British military*] (DMA)
JEMC........ Joint Engineering Management Conference
J Emerg Med... Journal of Emergency Medicine (journ.) (SAUS)
J Emerg Med Serv... Journal of Emergency Medical Services (journ.) (SAUS)
JEMI......... Joint Electromagnetic Interference [*Military*]
JEMI......... Joint Equipment Manufacturers Initiative (SAUS)
JEMIC....... Japan Electric Meters Inspection Corp. (BUAC)
JEMIMA..... [*The*] Japan Electrical Measurements Manufacturers' Association (ACII)
JEMP........ Joint Engineers Management Panel [*Army*] (RDA)
J Empl Coun... Journal of Employment Counseling (journ.) (SAUS)
JEMR........ Jem Records Inc. (SAUS)
JEMR........ Jem Reeords Inc. (SAUO)
JEMRB...... Joint European Medical Research Board (BUAC)
JEMS........ Journal of Emergency Medical Services (SAUO)
JEMS........ Journal of Emergency Medical Services (journ.) (SAUS)
JEMSA...... Journal. Elisha Mitchell Scientific Society (journ.) (SAUS)
JEN.......... Japan Economic Newswire [*Kyodo News International, Inc.*] [*Information service or system*] (CRD)
JEN.......... Jena [*German Democratic Republic*] [*Seismograph station code, US Geological Survey*] [*Closed*] (SEIS)
JEN.......... Jenair Ltd. [*Cyprus*] [*ICAO designator*] (FAAC)
JEN.......... Journal of Emergency Nursing (journ.) (SAUS)
J En.......... Journal of English (journ.) (SAUS)
JEN.......... Junta de Energia Nuclear [*Spanish nuclear agency*]
JEN.......... Junularo Esperantista de Nord-Ameriko (SAUO)
JEN.......... Nuclear Energy Authority (SAUS)
JENAKAT.... Jeunesse Nationale Katangaise [*Katangan National Youth*]
Jena Rev... Jena Review (journ.) (SAUS)
Jena Rev Suppl... Jena Review. Supplement (journ.) (SAUS)
JENC......... Joint Emergency National Committee for the Building Industry (SAUO)
Jenck Bills... Jencken's Bills of Exchange [*1880*] [*A publication*] (DLA)
Jenck Neg S... Jencken's Negotiable Securities [*1880*] [*A publication*] (DLA)
JenCrg...... Jenny Craig [*Associated Press*] (SAG)
JENDD....... Journal of Energy and Development (journ.) (SAUS)
J Endocrinol Invest... Journal of Endocrinological Investigation (journ.) (SAUS)
J Endotoxin Res... Journal of Endotoxin Research [*A publication*] (PABS)
J Endourol... Journal of Endourology (journ.) (SAUS)
JENDRPC.... Joint Euratom Nuclear Data and Reactor Physics Committee (BUAC)
JENE......... Jen Sell Corporation [*NCIC trailer make code*]
JENER........ Joint Establishment for Nuclear Energy Research
J Energy.... Journal of Energy (journ.) (SAUS)
J Energy & Devel... Journal of Energy and Development [*A publication*] (DLA)
J Energy Eng... Journal of Energy Engineering (journ.) (SAUS)
J Energy Lit... Journal of Energy Literature [*A publication*] (JLIT)
J Energy LP... Journal of Energy Law and Policy (journ.) (SAUS)
J Energy Resour Technol Trans ASME... Journal of Energy Resources Technology. Transactions of the American Society of Mechanical Engineers (journ.) (SAUS)
JENER Report... Joint Establishment for Nuclear Energy Research Report (journ.) (SAUS)
JENEX....... Japanese El Nino Experiment [*Marine science*] (OSRA)
JenfCv....... Jennifer Convertibles, Inc. [*Associated Press*] (SAG)
J Eng and Germ Philol... Journal of English and Germanic Philology (journ.) (SAUS)
J Eng Ind... Journal of Engineering for Industry (SAUS)
J Engl Agric Soc... Journal. English Agricultural Society (journ.) (SAUS)
J Eng Mat & Tech... Journal of Engineering Materials and Technology (journ.) (SAUS)
J Eng Mater Technol Trans ASME... Journal of Engineering Materials and Technology. Transactions of the American Society of Mechanical Engineers (journ.) (SAUS)
J Eng Mech... Journal of Engineering Mechanics (journ.) (SAUS)
J Eng Mech Div Amer Soc... Journal of the Engineering Mechanics Division, Proceedings of the American Society (journ.) (SAUS)
Jengo........ Junior Engineering Officer (SAUO)
J Eng Power... Journal of Engineering for Power (SAUS)
J Eng Power... Journal of Engineering for Power (journ.) (SAUS)
J Eng Psychol... Journal of Engineering Psychology (journ.) (SAUS)
J Engrg Math... Journal of Engineering Mathematics (journ.) (SAUS)
J Engrg Phys... Journal of Engineering Physics (journ.) (SAUS)
J Eng Sci King Saud Univ... Journal of Engineering King Saud University (journ.) (SAUS)
J Eng Technol Manage... Journal of Engineering and Technology Management (journ.) (SAUS)
Jenk......... Jenkins' Eight Centuries of Reports, English Exchequer [*145 English Reprint*] [*1220-1623*] [*A publication*] (DLA)
Jenk & Formoy... Jenkinson and Formoy's Select Cases in the Exchequer of Pleas [*Selden Society Publication, Vol. 48*] [*A publication*] (DLA)
Jenk Cent... Jenkins' Eight Centuries of Reports, English Exchequer [*145 English Reprint*] [*1220-1623*] [*A publication*] (DLA)
Jenk Cent... Jenkins Eight Centuries of Reports, Eng- lish Exchequer (journ.) (SAUS)
Jenkins (Eng)... Jenkins' Eight Centuries of Reports, English Exchequer [*145 English Reprint*] [*1220-1623*] [*A publication*] (DLA)
Jenks........ Jenks' Reports [*58 New Hampshire*] [*A publication*] (DLA)
JENN........ Jennifer Convertibles, Inc. (SAUO)
Jenn......... Jennison's Reports [*14-18 Michigan*] [*A publication*] (DLA)
Jenn Sug A... Jennett's Sugden Acts [*A publication*] (DLA)
J Enriron Econ Manage... Journal of Environmental Economics and Management (journ.) (SAUS)
JENS......... Jensen [*NCIC car make code*]
Jen-Soc J... Jen-Soc Journal (journ.) (SAUS)
J Ent......... Journal of Entomology (journ.) (SAUS)
JENTAC...... Jentaculum [*Breakfast*] [*Pharmacy*]
J Enterostom Ther... Journal of Enterostomal Therapy (journ.) (SAUS)
J Entomol A... Journal of Entomology. Series A. General Entomology (journ.) (SAUS)
J Entomol B... Journal of Entomology. Series B. Taxonomy (journ.) (SAUS)
J Entomol Sci... Journal of Entomological Science (journ.) (SAUS)
J Entomol Ser A Physiol Behav... Journal of Entomology. Series A. Physiology and Behaviour (journ.) (SAUS)
J Entomol Ser B Taxon Syst... Journal of Entomology. Series B. Taxonomy and Systematics (journ.) (SAUS)
J Entomol Soc BC... Journal. Entomological Society of British Columbia (journ.) (SAUS)
J Entomol Zool... Journal of Entomology and Zoology (journ.) (SAUS)

J Ent Soc Qd... Journal. Entomological Society of Queensland (journ.) (SAUS)
JENV......... Joint Environmental Department (SAUO)
JENV COLL LOND... Jewish College, London (SAUS)
J Envir Eng... Journal. Environmental Engineering Division. American Society of Civil Engineers (journ.) (SAUS)
J Envir Mgm... Journal of Environmental Management (journ.) (SAUS)
J Environ Biol... Journal of Environmental Biology (journ.) (SAUS)
J Environ Dev... Journal of Environment and Development [*A publication*] (PABS)
J Environ Devel... Journal of Environment and Development [*A publication*] (JLIT)
J Environ Econ Manage... Journal of Environmental Economics and Management [*A publication*] (JLIT)
J Environ Eng... Journal of Environmental Engineering (journ.) (SAUS)
J Environ Engng Dir Proc ASCE... Journal. Environmental Engineering Division. Proceedings of the American Society of Civil Engineering (journ.) (SAUS)
J Environ Health... Journal of Environmental Health (journ.) (SAUS)
J Environ Horticulture... Journal of Environmental Horticulture [*A publication*] (PABS)
J Environ Hydrol... Journal of Environmetnal Hydrology [*A publication*] (PABS)
J Environ Law Litigation... Journal of Environmental Law and Litigation [*A publication*] (PABS)
J Environ Law Policy... Journal of Environmental Law & Policy [*A publication*] (PABS)
J Environ Law Pract... Journal of Environmental Law & Practice [*A publication*] (PABS)
J Environ Manage... Journal of Environmental Management (SAUO)
J Environ Pathol Toxicol... Journal of Environmental Pathology and Toxicology (journ.) (SAUS)
J Environ Pathol Toxicol Oncol... Journal of Environmental Pathology, Toxicology and Oncology (journ.) (SAUS)
J Environ Planning Manage... Journal of Environmental Planning and Management [*A publication*] (JLIT)
J Environ Plan Pollut Control... Journal of Environmental Planning and Pollution Control (journ.) (SAUS)
J Environ Pollut... Journal of Environment and Pollution [*A publication*] (PABS)
J Environ Polym Degrad... Journal of Environmental Polymer Degradation (journ.) (SAUS)
J Environ Radioact... Journal of Environmental Radioactivity (journ.) (SAUS)
J Environ Syst... Journal of Environmental Systems [*A publication*] (PABS)
J Envir Sci Hlth... Journal of Environmental Science and Health (journ.) (SAUS)
J Enzym Inhib... Journal of Enzyme Inhibition (journ.) (SAUS)
JEOCN....... Joint European Operations Communications Network
JEOF......... Joint Exercise Observation File (SAUO)
JEOL......... Japan Electron Optics Co., Limited (SAUO)
JEOL......... Japan Electron Optics Laboratory Co. (BUAC)
JEOL......... Japan Electro-Optics Laboratories (or Laboratory) (SAUS)
JEOLCO..... Japan Electron Optics Laboratory Co. (SAUS)
JEOLCO..... Japan Electron Optics Laboratory Company (SAUO)
JEOP......... Jeopardy (ABBR)
JEOPZ........ Jeopardize (ABBR)
JEOPZD..... Jeopardized (ABBR)
JEOPZG..... Jeopardizing (ABBR)
JEOS......... Janus Earth Observation Satellite (SAUS)
JEOS......... Japanese Earth Observation System (SAUS)
JEOS......... Japanese Earth Observing Satellite (EOSA)
JEOS......... Japanese Earth Observing System (CARB)
JEP.......... Jeep [*NCIC car model code*]
JEP.......... Jeep (trucks) [*NCIC truck make code*]
Jep........... Jeopardy (BARN)
JEP.......... Jepson Corp. (SAUO)
JEP.......... Jet Engine Processor
JEP.......... Jewish Elite Person
JEP.......... Job Entry Program [*Computer science*] (HODG)
JEP.......... Joint European Project (EURO)
JEP.......... Joint Experiments Program (ACAE)
JEP.......... Journal of Economic Psychology (journ.) (SAUS)
JEP.......... Journal of Educational Psychology (journ.) (SAUS)
JEP.......... Jupiter Entry Probe
JEPA......... Job Evaluation Policy Act (SAUS)
JEPA......... Job Evaluation Policy Act of 1970
JEPABP...... Journal of Experimental Psychology: Animal Behavior Processes (journ.) (SAUS)
JEPAP....... Joint Emergency Personnel Augmentation Plan [*Military*] (CINC)
JEPCE....... Joint Exercise Planning Committee (SAUO)
JEPDS....... Jet Exhaust Powered Decontamination System (ACAE)
JEPES....... Joint Engineering Planning Execution System (VLIE)
JEPES....... Joint Engineer Planning and Execution System [*Environmental science*] (COE)
JEPG......... Joint Exercise Planning Group [*Military*]
JEPI......... Joint Electronic Payment Intitiative [*Proposed*] [*Computer science*]
JEPI......... Joint Electronic Payments Initiative
JEPI......... Junior Eysenck Personality Inventory [*Psychology*]
JEPIA........ Japan Electronic Parts Industry Association
J Epidemiol Community Health... Journal of Epidemiology and Community Health (journ.) (SAUS)
J Epilepsy... Journal of Epilepsy (journ.) (SAUS)
JEPLA....... Journal of Elastomers and Plastics (journ.) (SAUS)
JEPO......... Jet Engine Project Office (SAUO)
JEPO......... Joint Engine Project Office (MCD)
JEPOSS..... Javelin Experimental and Theoretical Physics Protection Oil Sands System (SAUS)
JEPOSS..... Javelin Experimental Protection Oil Sands System (SAUS)
JEPP......... Japan English Publications in Print [*Japan Publications Guide Service*] [*Japan*] [*Information service or system*] (CRD)
JEPP......... Japanese Earthquake Prediction Plan
JEPP......... Joint Emergency Planning Program (SAUS)
JEPS......... Job Effectiveness Prediction System [*Test for insurance company employees*]
JEPS......... Job Entry Peripheral Services [*IBM Corp.*] (MCD)
JEPS......... Joint Exercise Planning Staff [*NATO*] (NATG)
JEPSBL...... European Journal of Steroids (journ.) (SAUS)
JEPTO....... Journal of Environmental Pathology, Toxicology and Oncology (journ.) (SAUS)
JEPX......... PSI Energy [*Private rail car owner code*]
JEQ.......... Japan Equity Fund [*NYSE symbol*] (SPSG)
JEQ.......... Jequie [*Brazil*] [*Airport symbol*] (OAG)
JEQ.......... Jump Equal (SAUS)
J Equine Med Surg... Journal of Equine Medicine and Surgery (journ.) (SAUS)
JER.......... Japan Economic Review [*A publication*] (WDAA)
JER.......... Japanese Erection Ring [*Medicine*] (BABM)
Jer........... Jeremiah [*Old Testament book*]
Jer........... Jeremiah, The Book of the Prophet (SAUS)
Jer........... Jeremias (BJA)
Jer........... Jericho (BJA)
JER.......... Jersey [*Channel Islands*] [*Airport symbol*] (OAG)
JER.......... Jerusalem [*Israel*] [*Seismograph station code, US Geological Survey*] (SEIS)
Jer........... Jerusalem Talmud (BJA)
Jer........... Jerushalmi (BJA)
JER.......... Journal of Educational Research (journ.) (SAUS)
JER.......... Junctional Escape Rhythm (STED)
JERA......... James E. Rush Associates, Inc. [*Also, an information service or system*] (IID)
JERA......... Jeraco Enterprises [*NCIC trailer make code*]
JERAC....... Jerramungup Extension and Research Advisory Committee (SAUO)
JERC......... Japan Economic Research Centre (BUAC)
JERC......... Japan-Europe Economic Research Center (SAUS)
JerC.......... Jersey Central Power & Light [*Associated Press*] (SAG)
JERC......... Joint Electsonic Research Committee (SAUS)
Jerc.......... Junior Executive Research Consultant [*Fictitious position in Commerce Bank of Beverly Hills created for Jethro Bodine on the television show "The Beverly Hillbillies"*]
Jer Car...... Jeremy on Carriers [*A publication*] (DLA)
Jer Dig...... Jeremy's Digest [*1817-49*] [*A publication*] (DLA)
Jeremy Eq.. Jeremy's Equity Jurisdiction [*A publication*] (DLA)
Jeremy Eq Jur... Jeremy's Equity Jurisdiction [*A publication*] (DLA)
Jer Eq Jur... Jeremy's Equity Jurisdiction [*A publication*] (DLA)
JERI......... Japan Economics Research Institute (BUAC)
JERI......... Joint Economic Research Institute (SAUO)
JERK......... Journalists Easy Road to Knowledge (journ.) (SAUS)
JERL......... Journal of Energy and Natural Resources Law [*A publication*] (SAFN)
JerM......... Jersey Microfilming, Clifton, NJ [*Library symbol*] [*Library of Congress*] (LCLS)
JEROB....... Jeroboam (WDAA)
jeroboam... Five-liter resealable container for ethanol-water solutions (SAUS)
JerPes....... Jerusalem Talmud. Pesahim (BJA)
JERR........ Jerrytime Camper [*NCIC trailer make code*]
Jerr Copyr... Jerrold on Copyright [*A publication*] (DLA)
JERS......... Japan Earth Remote Sensing Satellite
JERS......... Japan Ergonomics Research Society (BUAC)
JERS......... Japanese Earth Resource Remote-Sensing Satellite (SAUS)
JERS......... Japanese Earth Resources Satellite
JERS......... Japanese Ergonomics Research Society (SAUO)
JERS......... Jersey Trailer [*NCIC trailer make code*]
JERS......... Joint Emergency Relocation Site
JERS-1...... Japanese Earth Remote-Sensing Satellite-1 (EOSA)
Jersey City St C... Jersey City State College (GAGS)
JERS-I....... Japan Earth Resources Satellite [*Marine science*] (OSRA)
JERS-OPS.. Japanese Earth Resources Satellite-OPS Sensor (SAUO)
JERT......... Journal of Energy Resources Technology [*Database*] (GDD)
JERTD....... Journal of Energy Resources Technology (journ.) (SAUS)
JERU......... Joint Environmental Research Unit (MCD)
Jerus........ Jerusalem (BJA)
Jerus Symp Quantum Chem Biochem... Jerusalem Symposia on Quantum Chemistry and Biochemistry (journ.) (SAUS)
Jerv Cor..... Jervis. Coroners [*9th ed.*] [*1957*] [*A publication*] (DLA)
Jerv NR..... Jervis' New Rules [*A publication*] (DLA)
JERW........ Jerry's Welding Service [*NCIC trailer make code*]
JerW......... Jerusalemer Warte (BJA)
JerYeb....... Jerusalem Talmud. Yebamoth (BJA)
Jes........... Analysis and Digest of the Decisions of Sir George Jessel, by A. P Peter [*England*] [*A publication*] (DLA)
JES.......... James Ewing Society (SAUO)
JES.......... Japan/East Sea (SAUS)
JES.......... Japan Electronics Show
JES.......... Japan Engineering Standards (SAUS)
JES.......... Japan Environmental Systems
JES.......... Japanese Economic Studies. A Journal of Translations (journ.) (SAUS)
JES.......... Japanese Electroplating Society (BUAC)
JES.......... Japanese Export Standard
JES.......... Jes Air [*Bulgaria*] [*ICAO designator*] (FAAC)
JES.......... Jesuit (DSUE)
JES.......... Jesup, GA [*Location identifier*] [*FAA*] (FAAL)
JES.......... Jesus
Jes........... Jesus College, Cambridge (SAUO)
JES.......... Jet Ejector System
JES.......... Job Entry Subsystem (SAUS)
JES.......... Job Entry System [*or Subsystem*] [*IBM Corp.*] [*Computer science*]

JES .... John Ericsson Society (EA)
JES .... Joint Efficiency Study (AIE)
JES .... Joint Environmental Service (SAUS)
JES .... Joint Environmental Simulator (SAUS)
JES .... Joint Environment Simulator (SAUS)
JES .... Journal of Economics and Siology (journ.) (SAUS)
JES .... Journal of Economic Studies (journ.) (SAUS)
JES .... Journal of Ecumenical Studies (journ.) (SAUS)
JES .... Journal of European Studies (journ.) (SAUS)
JES .... Journal of the Electrochemical Society [*Database*] (GDD)
JESA......... Japanese Engineering Standards Association (BUAC)
JESAC .... Joint Engineering Student Activity Committee (SAUS)
JESAP .... Jet Engine Smoke Abatement Program
JESAUG ..... Journal of the Environmental Satellite Amateur Users Group (journ.) (SAUS)
JESC......... Japanese Engineering Standards Committee (BUAC)
JESC......... Joint Electronics Standardisation Committee (BUAC)
JESC......... Joint Equipment Standardization Committee (SAUO)
JES COLL... Jesus College [*Oxford or Cambridge*] [*England*] (ROG)
Jes Coll..... Jesus College, Cambridge (SAUS)
JESCOM..... Jesuits in Communication in the US (EA)
JESHO....... Journal of Economic and Social History of the Orient (journ.) (SAUS)
JESHO....... Journal of the Economic and Social History of the Orient (journ.) (SAUS)
JESIA........ Journal. Electrochemical Society of India (journ.) (SAUS)
JESNA....... Jewish Education Service of North America (EA)
JES/NJE..... Job Entry System/Network Job Entry (SAUS)
JESOA....... Journal. Electrochemical Society (journ.) (SAUS)
JES/RES..... Job Entry System/Remote Entry Subsystem (SAUS)
JESS......... Joint Exercise Simulation System [*DoD*]
JESS......... Joint Exercise Support System [*Military*]
J Essent Oil Res... Journal of Essential Oil Research (journ.) (SAUS)
JESSI........ Joint European Semiconductor Consortium (SAUO)
JESSI........ Joint European Semiconductor Silicon Initiative
JESSI........ Joint European Submicron Silicon [*Project*]
JESSI........ Joint European Submicron Silicon Initiative (BUAC)
JESSI........ Junior Engineers' and Scientists' Summer Institute
JESS-TACSIM... Joint Exercise Simulation System (SAUS)
JESS-TACSIM... Joint Exercise Simulation System-Tactical Simulation (SAUO)
JESSU....... Jesup, GA [*American Association of Railroads railroad junction routing code*]
JEST......... Journal of Extraneous Scientific Topics (journ.) (SAUS)
JEST......... Jungle Environmental Survival Training [*Military*]
JEST......... Jungle Environmental Survival Training School (SAUO)
JEST School... Jungle Environmental Survival Training School (SAUS)
Jesus........ Jesus College Oxford (SAUS)
JESUS....... Job Entry System of the University of Saskatuan (SAUO)
JET........... European Jet Ltd. [*British*] [*ICAO designator*] (FAAC)
JET........... Frankfort (SAUS)
JET........... Frankfort, KY [*Location identifier*] [*FAA*] (FAAL)
JET........... Jam Exceeds Threshold
JET........... Japanese Exchange and Teaching Programme (SAUO)
JET........... Japan-Europa-Trade Co., Ltd. (SAUO)
JET........... Java Enabled Type (SAUS)
JET........... JDS Evaluation Team (SAUO)
JET........... Jet [*NCIC car model code*]
JET........... Jetronic Industries, Inc. [*AMEX symbol*] (SPSG)
JET........... Jetsam (ABBR)
JET........... Jetta [*NCIC car model code*]
JET........... Jettison
JET........... Jitter Equivalent Target (CCCA)
JET........... Job Element Text (AFM)
JET........... Job English Training
JET........... Job Express Transportation (SAUS)
JET........... Jobs Evaluation and Training
JET........... Joint Economic Team
JET........... Joint Effort for Talent [*Navy*] (NG)
JET........... Joint Engine Technology (SAUS)
JET........... Joint Enroute Terminal (SAUS)
JET........... Joint European TOKAMAK [*Toroidal Kamera Magnetic*] [*or Torus*] [*Nuclear reactor*]
JET........... Joint European Transport (SAUS)
JET........... Jointly Endorsed Training [*Union-management*]
JET........... Journal Entries Transfer [*Computer science*] (MHDI)
JET........... Journal of Economic Theory (journ.) (SAUS)
JET........... Journal of Real Estate Taxation (journ.) (SAUS)
JET........... Judicial Education Teleseminar System [*Defunct*] (TSSD)
JET........... Junior Enlisted Travel [*Entitlement*] (MCD)
JET........... Junior Executives Training (SAUO)
JETA......... Jet America Inc. (SAUO)
JET A........ Kerosene-Freeze Point -40 Deg. F [*Aviation*] (PIPO)
JET-A1....... Jet Fuel type A1 (SAUS)
JET A1 ...... Kerosene with Additive Freeze Point -58 Deg. [*Aviation*] (PIPO)
JETAA .... Journal. Faculty of Engineering. University of Tokyo. Series A. Annual Report (journ.) (SAUS)
JETAI .... Journal of Experimental and Theoretical Artificial Intelligence (journ.) (SAUS)
JETAM....... Jet Engine Thrust Augmentation Mix (SAA)
JETAV........ Jet Aviation (SAA)
JETBA .... Journal. Faculty of Engineering. University of Tokyo. Series B (journ.) (SAUS)
JETCA .... Journal of Ethnic Studies (journ.) (SAUS)
JETCO .... Jamaican Export Trading Co. (SAUS)
JETCO .... Jamaican Export Trading Company (SAUO)
JETCO .... Japan Export Trading Co. (SAUS)
JETCO .... Japan Export Trading Company (SAUO)
JETD......... Jetted (ABBR)
JETD......... Joint Electronics Type Designator [*Military*] (AABC)
JETDLAG.... Joint European Development of Tunable Diode Laser Absorption Spectometry for the Measurement of Atmospheric Gases (SAUO)
JETDS .... Joint Electronics Type Data System (ACAE)
JETDS .... Joint Electronics Type Designation System [*Military*] (AFM)
JETEC .... Joint Electron Tube Engineering Council [*Later, JEDEC*] (MCD)
JETEC .... Joint Expendable Turbine Engine Concept (SAUS)
JET FAG..... Jet Flight Fatigue (SAUS)
JetForm..... Jet Form Corp. [*Associated Press*] (SAG)
JETG......... Jetting (ABBR)
J Eth L ...... Journal of Ethiopian Law [*A publication*] (DLA)
J Eth L ...... Journal of Ethiopian Law (journ.) (SAUS)
J Ethnopharmacol... Journal of Ethnopharmacology (journ.) (SAUS)
JEthS .... Journal of Ethiopian Studies (journ.) (SAUS)
JETI.......... JETI. Japan Energy and Technology Intelligence (journ.) (SAUS)
JETLNR ..... Jetliner (ABBR)
JETM .... Jetmobile [*NCIC car make code*]
JETMA....... Jet Mechanic (SAUS)
JETN......... Jettison
JETOAS ..... European Journal of Toxicology (journ.) (SAUS)
JETOC .... Japan Chemical Industry Ecology-Toxicology & Information Center (SAUO)
JETP......... Jet-Propelled
JETP......... Journal of Experimental and Theoretical Physics (journ.) (SAUS)
JETP......... Journal of Experimental Purpose (journ.) (SAUS)
JETP......... Journal of Experimental Theoretical Physics (journ.) (SAUS)
JETPA .... Jet Propulsion (journ.) (SAUS)
Jet Propul... Jet Propulsion (journ.) (SAUS)
Jet Propul Lab Publ... Jet Propulsion Laboratory. Publication (journ.) (SAUS)
Jet Propul Lab Tech Memo... Jet Propulsion Laboratory. Technical Memorandum (journ.) (SAUS)
JETR......... Japan Engineering Test Reactor
JETR......... Jetevator
JETRO....... Japanese External Trade Recovery Organization (SAUO)
JETRO....... Japan Export and Trade Research Organization (SAUO)
JETRO....... Japan Exterior Trade Research Organization (SAUO)
JETRO....... Japan External Trade Organization [*New York, NY*] (EA)
JETRON..... Jetronic Industries, Inc. (SAUO)
Jetronic..... Jetronic Industries, Inc. [*Associated Press*] (SAG)
JETS......... Institute for Japanese-European Technology Studies [*University of Edinburgh*] [*United Kingdom*] (RCD)
JETS......... Jammer Technique Simulation (ACAE)
JETS......... Jetbome International, Inc. (SAUO)
JETS......... Jet Express Ticketing System
JETS......... Jet Stream Camping Trailer [*NCIC trailer make code*]
JETS......... Job Executive and Transport Satellite [*NCR Corp.*]
JETS......... Joint Electronics Type [*Designation*] System [*Military*] (NASA)
JETS......... Joint Enroute Terminal System [*Canada*] (MCD)
JETS......... Journal. Evangelical Theological Society (journ.) (SAUS)
JETS......... Junior Engineering Technical Society
JETS......... Junior Engineers Technical Society (SAUO)
JETS......... Junior Engineers, Technicians, Scientists Organization of Zambia (SAUO)
JETSB .... Joint European Torus Supervisory Board (BUAC)
JET Scheme... Jobs, Education & Training Scheme [*Australia*] (WDAA)
JETT......... Jettison (KSC)
JET-X........ Joint European Telescope for X-rays on Spectrum-X-Gamma (SAUO)
JETXA .... Journal of Existentialism (journ.) (SAUS)
JEU .... Journal of European Industrial Training (journ.) (SAUS)
J Eukaryot Microbiol... Journal of Eukaryotic Microbiology (journ.) (SAUS)
J Eur Ceram S... Journal. European Ceramic Society (journ.) (SAUS)
J Eur Ceram Soc... Journal of the European Ceramic Society (journ.) (SAUS)
J Eur Econ Hist... Journal of European Economic History (journ.) (SAUS)
J Eur Stud... Journal of European Studies (journ.) (SAUS)
JEV .... Japanese Encephalitis Virus [*Medicine*]
JEV .... Jesuit European Volunteers [*An association*] (BUAC)
JEV .... Joint European Venture (EURO)
JEVA......... Jammer Evaluation Versus Amplitude (ACAE)
JEVA......... Japan Electric Vehicle Association (SAUO)
JEVA......... Japan Electric Vehicle Birthday Association (SAUO)
J Eval Clin Pract... Journal of Evaluation in Clinical Practice (journ.) (SAUS)
J Evang Th S... Journal. Evangelical Theological Society (journ.) (SAUS)
JEVC......... Jevic Transportation [*Common carrier symbol*]
JEVC......... Jevic Transportation, Inc. [*NASDAQ symbol*] (NASQ)
Jev Cr Law... Jevons on Criminal Law [*A publication*] (DLA)
Jev Cr Lw... Jevons on Criminal Law (journ.) (SAUS)
JEVED .... Journal of Environmental Education (journ.) (SAUS)
J Evolutionary Econ... Journal of Evolutionary Economics [*A publication*] (JLIT)
JEVQA....... Journal of Environmental Quality (journ.) (SAUS)
JEVSB .... Journal of Environmental Systems (journ.) (SAUS)
JEW.......... Jewellery [*British*] (ROG)
Jew .... Jewelry (SAUS)
Jew .... Jewish (DIAR)
JEW.......... Jewish
JEWC......... Joint Electronic Warfare Center (MCD)
JEW COLL LOND... Jewish College, London [*England*] (ROG)
JEWE .... Jewel Trailer [*NCIC trailer make code*]
Jewel......... Jewellery (DIAR)
JEWEL....... Joint Endeavor for Welfare, Education, and Liberation [*Part of Grenadian political party, the New JEWEL Movement*]
JewettC ..... Jewett-Cameron Trading Co. Ltd. [*Associated Press*] (SAG)

Jew Hist Soc Engl Trans... Jewish Historical Society of England. Transactions (journ.) (SAUS)
Jewish Soc Stud... Jewish Social Studies (journ.) (SAUS)
JEWLF....... IWI Holding Ltd. [*NASDAQ symbol*] (SAG)
JEWOC...... Joint Electronic Warfare Orientation Course (SAUO)
JEWSOC.... Joint Electronic Warfare Staff Officer Course (DOMA)
JewSocSt... Jewish Social Studies (journ.) (SAUS)
Jew Soc Stud... Jewish Social Studies. Conference on Jewish Social Studies. New York (SAUS)
JEWT........ Jungle Exercise without Trees [*British military*] (DMA)
Jew YB Int'l L... Jewish Yearbook of International Law [*A publication*] (DLA)
Jew YB Intl L... Jewish Yearbook of International Law (journ.) (SAUS)
JEX.......... Jenks, OK [*Location identifier*] [*FAA*] (FAAL)
JEX.......... Jet Express, Inc. [*ICAO designator*] (FAAC)
JEX.......... Joint Exercise (NVT)
JEXAM...... Japanese Experiment on Asia Monsoon (SAUO)
J Ex An Beh... Journal of the Experimental Analysis of Behavior (journ.) (SAUS)
J Excep Child... Journal of Exceptional Children (journ.) (SAUS)
JEXI.......... Jones Express [*Common carrier symbol*]
J Existent... Journal of Existentialism (journ.) (SAUS)
JExP......... Journal of Experimental Psychology (journ.) (SAUS)
J Exp Anal Behav... Journal of Experimental Analysis of Behavior (SAUS)
J Exp Anim Sci... Journal of Experimental Animal Science (journ.) (SAUS)
J Exp Biol Med... Journal of Experimental Biology and Medicine (journ.) (SAUS)
J Exp Bot... Journal of Experimental Botany [*A publication*] (PABS)
J Exp Clin Cancer Res... Journal of Experimental and Clinical Cancer Research (journ.) (SAUS)
J Ex PHP.... Journal of Experimental Psychology Human Perception and Performance (journ.) (SAUS)
JEx PL....... Journal of Experimental Psychology Human Learning and Memory (journ.) (SAUS)
J Expl Eng... Journal of Explosives Engineering (journ.) (SAUS)
J Exp Mar Biol Ecol... Journal of Experimental Marine Biology and Ecology (journ.) (SAUS)
J Exp Marine Biol... Journal of Experimental Marine Biology (journ.) (SAUS)
J Exp Med Sci... Journal of Experimental Medical Sciences (journ.) (SAUS)
J Expo Anal Environ Epidemiol... Journal of Exposure Analysis and Environmental Epidemiology (journ.) (SAUS)
J Exp Pathol... Journal of Experimental Pathology (journ.) (SAUS)
J Exp Psychol... Journal of Experimental Psychology (journ.) (SAUS)
J Exp Psychol Hum Learn Mem... Journal of Experimental Psychology Human Learning and Memory (journ.) (SAUS)
J Exp Psychol Monogr... Journal of Experimental Psychology Monograph (journ.) (SAUS)
J Exp Psy H... Journal of Experimental Psychology Human Learning and Memory (journ.) (SAUS)
J Exp Psy P... Journal of Experimental Psychology Human Perception and Performance (journ.) (SAUS)
J Exp Res Pers... Journal of Experimental Research in Personality (journ.) (SAUS)
J Exp Ther... Journal of Experimental Therapeutics (journ.) (SAUS)
J Exp Zool... Journal of Experimental Zoology (journ.) (SAUS)
J Exp Zool Suppl... Journal of Experimental Zoology. Supplement (journ.) (SAUS)
J Ext......... Journal of Extension (journ.) (SAUS)
J Extra Corporeal Technol... Journal of Extra-Corporeal Technology (journ.) (SAUS)
JEY.......... Journal of Employment Counseling (journ.) (SAUS)
J Eye........ Journal of the Eye (journ.) (SAUS)
JEZ.......... Joice Elevator [*Federal Railroad Administration identification code*]
JEZ.......... Joint Engagement Zone [*Marine Corps*] (DOMA)
JEZEX....... Jezebel [*Sonobuoy*] Exercise [*Navy*] (NVT)
JF............ Crest Aviation (SAUS)
jf............ distant fog (SAUS)
JF............ Jack Field
JF............ Jackstone Froster Ltd. [*Commercial firm*] [*British*]
JF............ Jamestown Foundation (EA)
JF............ Japan Foundation [*Also, Kokusai Koryu*] (EA)
JF............ Japan Fund (SAUS)
JF............ Jefferson Foundation (EA)
JF............ Jet Fighter (SAUS)
JF............ Jet Flap
JF............ Jewish Federation (SAUO)
J/F........... Jigs and Fixtures (SAUS)
JF............ John Flanagan [*Designer's mark, when appearing on US coins*]
JF............ Joint Filler [*Technical drawings*]
JF............ Joint Fluid [*Orthopedics*] (DAVI)
JF............ Joint Force [*Military*]
JF............ Jordan Foundation (SAUO)
JF............ Journal Folio (ROG)
JF............ Jugular Forainen [*Anatomy*] (DAVI)
JF............ Jugular Foramen (STED)
JF............ Jump Function (SAUS)
JF............ Junctional Fold [*Anatomy*] (DAVI)
JF............ Junction Frequency [*Telecommunications*] (TEL)
JF............ Junctor Frame [*Telecommunications*] (TEL)
JF............ Jundt Growth Fund [*NYSE symbol*] (SPSG)
JF............ Junior Fiction [*Library science*] (TELE)
JF............ Justice Fellowship (EA)
JF............ Justify [*Telegraphy*] (PCTE)
JF............ LAB Flying Service [*ICAO designator*] (AD)
JF............ Trehaven Aviation Ltd. [*British*] [*ICAO designator*] (ICDA)
JFA.......... Aviones Ejecutivos, JFA [*Mexico*] [*FAA designator*] (FAAC)
JFA.......... Jaffa [*Israel*] [*Airport symbol*] (AD)
JFA.......... Japanese Food Agency (SAUO)
JFA.......... Japan Fisheries Agency (SAUO)
JFA.......... Japan Fishery Agency (BUAC)
JFA.......... Journal of Field Archaeology (journ.) (SAUS)
JFA.......... Joyner Family Association (EA)
JFA.......... Judkins Family Association (EA)
JFA.......... Justice for Animals (EARSL)
JFAAD....... Joint Forward-Area Air Defense (MCD)
JFAADS..... Joint Forward-Area Air Defense System
JFAC......... Joint Flight Acceptance Composite Test [*Gemini*] [*NASA*] (IAA)
J Fac Agric Hokkaido Univ... Journal. Faculty of Agriculture. Hokkaido University (journ.) (SAUS)
J Fac Agric Hokkaido Univ Ser Entomol... Journal. Faculty of Agriculture. Hokkaido University. Series Entomology (journ.) (SAUS)
J Fac Agric Iwate Univ... Journal. Faculty of Agriculture. Iwate University (journ.) (SAUS)
J Fac Agric Kyushu Univ... Journal. Faculty of Agriculture. Kyushu University (journ.) (SAUS)
J Fac Agric Shinshu Univ... Journal. Faculty of Agriculture. Shinshu University (journ.) (SAUS)
J Fac Agric Tottori Univ... Journal. Faculty of Agriculture. Tottori University (journ.) (SAUS)
J Fac Appl Biol Sci Hirosbima Univ... Journal. Faculty of Applied Biological Science. Hiroshima University (journ.) (SAUS)
JFACC....... Joint Force Air Component Commander (DOMA)
J Fac Ed Saga Univ... Journal. Faculty of Education. Saga University (journ.) (SAUS)
J Fac Ed Saga Univ Part 1... Journal. Faculty of Education. Saga University. Part 1 (journ.) (SAUS)
J Fac Educ Nat Sci Tottori Univ... Journal. Faculty of Education. Natural Sciences. Tottori University (journ.) (SAUS)
J Fac Engng Univ Tokyo... Journal. Faculty of Engineering. University of Tokyo (journ.) (SAUS)
J Fac Eng Shinshu Univ... Journal. Faculty of Engineering. Shinshu University (journ.) (SAUS)
J Fac Eng Univ Tokyo Ser A... Journal. Faculty of Engineering. University of Tokyo. Series A. Annual Report (journ.) (SAUS)
J Fac Fish Anim Husb Hiroshima Univ... Journal. Faculty of Fisheries and Animal Husbandry. Hiroshima University. (journ.) (SAUS)
J Fac Fish Prefect Univ Mie... Journal. Faculty of Fisheries. Prefectural University of Mie (journ.) (SAUS)
J Fac Lib Arts Shinshu Univ Part II Nat Sci... Journal. Faculty of Liberal Arts. Shinshu University. Part II Natural Sciences (journ.) (SAUS)
J Fac Liberal Arts Yamaguchi Univ... Journal. Faculty of Liberal Arts. Yamaguchi University (journ.) (SAUS)
J Fac Mar Sci King Abdulalaz Univ... Journal. Faculty of Marine Science. King Abdulaziz University (journ.) (SAUS)
J Fac Mar Sci Technol Tokai Univ... Journal. Faculty of Marine Science and Technology. Tokai University (journ.) (SAUS)
J Fac Med Shin Univ... Journal. Faculty of Medicine. Shinshu University (journ.) (SAUS)
J Fac Med Univ Ankara... Journal. Faculty of Medicine. University of Ankara (journ.) (SAUS)
J Fac Med Univ Ankara Suppl... Journal. Faculty of Medicine. University of Ankara. Supplement (journ.) (SAUS)
J Fac Oceanogr Tokai Univ... Journal. Faculty of Oceanography. Tokai University (journ.) (SAUS)
J Fac Pharm Istanbul Univ... Journal. Faculty of Pharmacy. Istanbul University (journ.) (SAUS)
J Fac Polit Sci Econ Tokai Univ... Journal. Faculty of Political Science and Economics. Tokai University (journ.) (SAUS)
J Fac Sci Ege Univ Ser A... Journal. Faculty of Science. Ege University. Series A (journ.) (SAUS)
J Fac Sci Hokkaido Imp Univ Ser 4... Journal. Faculty of Science. Hokkaido Imperial University. Series 4. Geology and Mineralogy (journ.) (SAUS)
J Fac Sci Hokkaido Imp Univ Ser 5... Journal. Faculty of Science. Hokkaido Imperial University. Series 5. Botany (journ.) (SAUS)
J Fac Sci Hokkaido Univ Ser I... Journal. Faculty of Science. Hokkaido University Series I Mathematics (journ.) (SAUS)
J Fac Sci Hokkaido Univ Ser IV... Journal. Faculty of Science. Hokkaido University. Series IV. Geology and Mineralogy (journ.) (SAUS)
J Fac Sci Hokkaido Univ Ser V Bot... Journal. Faculty of Science. Hokkaido University. Series V. Botany (journ.) (SAUS)
J Fac Sci Hokkaido Univ Ser VI... Journal. Faculty of Science. Hokkaido University. Series VI Zoology (journ.) (SAUS)
J Fac Sci Hokkaido Univ Ser VII... Journal. Faculty of Science. Hokkaido University. Series VII Geophysics (journ.) (SAUS)
J Fac Sci Hokkaido Univ Ser VIII Zool... Journal. Faculty of Science. Hokkaido University. Series VIII Zoology (journ.) (SAUS)
J Fac Sci Imp Univ Tokyo Sect II... Journal. Faculty of Science. Imperial University of Tokyo. Section II Geology, Mineralogy, Geography, Seismology (journ.) (SAUS)
J Fac Sci Ser A Ege Univ... Journal. Faculty of Science. Series A. Ege University (journ.) (SAUS)
J Fac Sci Ser B Ege Univ... Journal. Faculty of Science. Series B. Ege University (journ.) (SAUS)
J Fac Sci Shinshu Univ... Journal. Faculty of Science. Shinshu University (journ.) (SAUS)
J Fac Sci Tokyo Univ... Journal. Faculty of Science. Tokyo University (journ.) (SAUS)
J Fac Sci Univ Tokyo Sect IA... Journal. Faculty of Science. University of Tokyo. Section IA. Mathematics (journ.) (SAUS)
J Fac Sci Univ Tokyo Sect II General Mineral Geogr Geophys... Journal. Faculty of Science. University of Tokyo. Section II Geology, Mineralogy, Geography, Geophysics (journ.) (SAUS)
J Fac Sci Univ Tokyo Sect III Bot... Journal. Faculty of Science. University of Tokyo. Section III. Botany (journ.) (SAUS)

J Fac Sci Univ Tokyo Sect IV... Journal. Faculty of Science. University of Tokyo. Section IV. Zoology (journ.) (SAUS)
J Fac Sci Univ Tokyo Sect V... Journal. Faculty of Science. University of Tokyo. Section V. Anthropology (journ.) (SAUS)
JFACSU...... Joint Forward Air Controllers Training and Standards Unit (SAUS)
J-FACT...... Joint Flight Acceptance Composite Test [*Gemini*] [*NASA*]
J-FACT...... Joint Flight Acceptance Test (ACAE)
J Fac Text Sci Technol Sbinshu Univ Ser F... Journal. Faculty of Textile Science and Technology. Shinshu University. Series F. Physics and Mathematics (journ.) (SAUS)
J Fac Text Sci Technol Shinshu Univ Ser A... Journal. Faculty of Textile Science and Technology. Shinshu University. Se- ries A. Biology (journ.) (SAUS)
J Fac Text Sci Technol Shinshu Univ Ser B... Journal. Faculty of Textile Science and Technology. Shinshu University. Series B. Textile Engineering (journ.) (SAUS)
J Fac Text Sci Technol Shinshu Univ Ser C... Journal. Faculty of Textile Science and Technology. Shinshu University. Se- ries C. Chemistry (journ.) (SAUS)
J Fac Text Sci Technol Shinshu Univ Ser D... Journal. Faculty of Textile Science and Technology. Shinshu University. Series D. Arts (journ.) (SAUS)
J Fac Tok I... Journal. Faculty of Science. University of Tokyo. Section I. Mathematics, Astronomy, Physics, Chemistry (journ.) (SAUS)
JFACTSU.... Joint Forward Air Controllers Training and Standards Unit [*British*]
J Faculty Arts Roy Univ Malta... Journal. Faculty of Arts. Royal University of Malta (journ.) (SAUS)
J Fac Vet Med Univ Tokyo... Journal. Faculty of Veterinary Medicine. University of Anka (journ.) (SAUS)
JFAI.......... Joint Formal Acceptance Inspection [*NATO*] (NATG)
JFAKA........ Journal. Faculty of Agriculture. Kyushu University (journ.) (SAUS)
J Fam Hist... Journal of Family History (journ.) (SAUS)
J Family L... Journal of Family Law (journ.) (SAUS)
JFAP......... Joint Frequency Allocation Panel
J Far Eastern Bus... Journal of Far Eastern Business [*A publication*] (JLIT)
J Farm Econ... Journal of Farm Economics [*A publication*] (JLIT)
J Farnham Mus Soc... Journal. Farnham Museum Society (journ.) (SAUS)
JFAST....... Joint Flow and Analysis System for Transportation [*Model USA*]
JFAST....... Joint Flow and Analysis System Test [*Environmental science*] (COE)
JFAX......... JFAX.COM, Inc. [*NASDAQ symbol*] (SG)
JFB.......... Jet Flying Belt (PDAA)
JFB.......... John Freeman Building (SAUS)
JFBC......... Jeffersonville Bancorp [*NASDAQ symbol*]
JFC.......... Japan Film Center (SAUO)
JFC.......... Japan Food Co. (SAUS)
JFC.......... Jardine Fleming China Reg Fd [*NYSE symbol*] (TTSB)
JFC.......... Jardine Fleming China Regular Fund [*NYSE symbol*] (SPSG)
JFC.......... Java Foundation Classes [*Sun Microsystems, Inc.*] (IGQR)
JFC.......... Jewish Folk Center [*Australia*]
JFC.......... John Forsyth Co., Inc. [*Toronto Stock Exchange symbol*]
JFC.......... Joint Force Commander [*DoD*]
JFC.......... Joint Formulary Committee (SAUO)
JFC.......... Journal of Business Forecasting (journ.) (SAUS)
JFC.......... Jupiter-family Comets [*Astronomy*]
JFC.......... LTV Jet Fleet Corp. [*ICAO designator*] (FAAC)
JFCA......... Japan Fine Ceramics Association (SAUO)
JFCB......... Job File Control Block [*Computer science*] (BUR)
JFCC......... Japanese Federation of Culture Collections of Microorganisms (BUAC)
JFCC......... Japan Federation of Culture Collections (SAUS)
JFCC......... Joint Force Fires Coordinator (SAUO)
JFCC......... Joint Frequency Coordination Committee (SAUO)
JFCL......... Jump if Flag Set and Then Clear the Flag [*Computer science*] (NHD)
JFCS......... Jewish Family and Child Services (SAUO)
JFCZ......... Jackson Farmers Co-Operative [*Federal Railroad Administration identification code*]
JFD.......... Joint Frequency Distribution (SAUS)
JFD.......... Justified [*Telegraphy*] (PCTE)
JFDA......... Jewish Funeral Directors of America (EA)
J Fd Hyg Soc Jp... Journal. Food Hygienic Society of Japan (journ.) (SAUS)
JFDP......... Joint Force Development Process [*or Program*] [*Army*]
JFDP......... Junior Faculty Development Program (SAUS)
JFE.......... Joint Fighter Engine (DWSG)
JFE.......... Journal of Farm Economics (journ.) (SAUS)
JFE.......... Journal of Financial Economics (journ.) (SAUS)
JFE.......... Journal of Fluids Engineering (journ.) (SAUS)
JFE.......... Justified Field Entry (SAUS)
JFEA......... Japan Federation of Employers Association
JFEA......... Joint Foreign Exchange Agency [*Berlin*] [*Post-World War II, Germany*]
JFEA......... Juneau Federal Executive Association [*Alaska*] (ALAC)
JFEB......... Japan Fast Experimental Breeder (SAUS)
JFED......... Junction Field-Effect Device
J Feng Chi Univ... Journal. Feng Chia University (journ.) (SAUS)
JFEO......... Japanese Federation of Economic Organizations
JFER......... Junction Field-Effect Resistor (SAUS)
J Ferment Ass Jpn... Journal. Fermentation Association of Japan (journ.) (SAUS)
J Ferment Bioeng... Journal of Fermentation and Bioengineering [*A publication*] (PABS)
J Ferment Ind... Journal of Fermentation Industries (journ.) (SAUS)
J Ferment Techn... Journal of Fermentation Technology (journ.) (SAUS)
J Ferment Technol (1944-1976)... Journal of Fermentation Technology (1944-1976) [*Japan*] [*A publication*]
J Fert Issues... Journal of Fertilizer Issues (journ.) (SAUS)
JFES......... Japan Federation of Engineering Societies (SAUO)
JFET......... Junction Field-Effect Transistor
JFETT........ Junction Field-Effect Transistor Tetrode (SAUS)
JFEW........ Jewish Foundation for Education of Women (EA)
JFF.......... Aguadilla, PR [*Location identifier*] [*FAA*] (FAAL)
JFF.......... Jobs for the Future [*An association*]
JFF.......... Junior Fashion Fair International [*British*] (ITD)
JFf.......... Junior Firefighter (WDAA)
JFF.......... Just for Fun (SAUS)
JFFC......... Jewish Fighting Force Committee [*British*]
JFFC......... John Fricke Fan Club [*Defunct*] (EA)
JFFC......... Judy Fields Fan Club (EA)
JFFG......... Jaguar Fast Freight [*Common carrier symbol*]
JFFN......... Jefferson Bank (Pennsylvania) [*NASDAQ symbol*] (COMM)
JFFSC....... Joint Force Fire Support Coordinator (SAUO)
JFG.......... Jumbogroup Frequency Generator [*Bell System*]
JFG.......... Justifying [*Telegraphy*] (PCTE)
JFGP......... Jewish Federation of Greater Philadelphia (EARSL)
JFH.......... Jam Frequency Hopper
JFH.......... Joint Force Harrier (SAUO)
JFHQ......... Joint Force Headquarters [*Military*]
JFHS......... Journal. Flintshire Historical Society (journ.) (SAUS)
JFI.......... James Franck Institute [*University of Chicago*] [*Research center*] (RCD)
JFI.......... Japanese Fermentation Institute
JFI.......... Jardine Fleming India Fund [*NYSE symbol*] (SAG)
JFI.......... Jet Flight Information (AFM)
JFI.......... John La Farge Institute (EA)
JFI.......... Journal of the Franklin Institute (SAUO)
JFI.......... New Orleans, LA [*Location identifier*] [*FAA*] (FAAL)
JFIAP........ Joint Foreign Intelligence Assistance Program (AFM)
JFIC......... Juneau Family Investment Center (SAUO)
JFIDS........ J-5 Force Structure Information Display System (SAUO)
JFIF......... JPEG [*Joint Photographic Experts Group*] File Interchange Format [*Computer science*] (CDE)
J Film & Vid... Journal of Film & Video [*A publication*] (BRI)
J Finance... Journal of Finance [*A publication*] (JLIT)
J Financ Quant Anal... Journal of Financial and Quantitative Analysis (journ.) (SAUS)
J Finan Econ... Journal of Financial Economics [*A publication*] (JLIT)
J Finan Intermediation... Journal of Financial Intermediation [*A publication*] (JLIT)
J Finan Res... Journal of Financial Research [*A publication*] (JLIT)
J Finan Services Res... Journal of Financial Services Research [*A publication*] (JLIT)
JFIndia...... Jardine Fleming India Fund [*Associated Press*] (SAG)
J Fin Planning... Journal of Financial Planning (journ.) (SAUS)
JFINT........ Joint Field Interrogation Team (SAUO)
J Fire Flamm... Journal of Fire and Flammability (journ.) (SAUS)
J Fire Retardant Chem... Journal of Fire Retardant Chemistry (journ.) (SAUS)
J Fire Sci... Journal of Fire Sciences (journ.) (SAUS)
J Fish Biol... Journal of Fish Biology (journ.) (SAUS)
J Fisheries Res Board Can... Journal. Fisheries Research Board of Canada (journ.) (SAUS)
J Fish Res Board Can... Journal of the Fisheries Research Board of Canada (SAUO)
J Fish Res Board Can... Journal of the Fisheries Research Board of Canada (journ.) (SAUS)
JFIT......... Joint Framework for Information Technology [*British*]
JFJ.......... Jewish Fund for Justice (EA)
JFJ.......... Jews for Jesus (EA)
JFK.......... John Fitzgerald Kennedy [*US president, 1917-1963*]
JFK.......... John F. Kennedy International Airport (NTIO)
JFK.......... Kennedy International Airport [*New York*] [*Airport symbol*]
JFKC......... John Fitzgerald Kennedy Center for the Performing Arts
JFKC......... John F. Kennedy Center (SAUS)
JFKC......... John F. Kennedy Center for the Performing Arts (SAUO)
JFKCAS..... John F. Kennedy College of Arts and Sciences (SAUO)
JFKCPA..... John F. Kennedy Center for the Performing Arts (SAUO)
JFKCTRMA... John F. Kennedy Center for Military Assistance (MCD)
JFK FDC SU... John F. Kennedy First Day Cover Study Unit (EA)
JFK Fdn..... John F. Kennedy Foundation (SAUO)
JFKI......... John F. Kennedy Library (SAUS)
JFKL......... John F. Kennedy Library
JFKLF....... John F. Kennedy Library Foundation (EA)
JFKMF....... John F. Kennedy Memorial Forest (SAUO)
JFKMH....... John F. Kennedy Memorial Highway (SAUO)
JFKML....... John F. Kennedy Memorial Library (SAUO)
JFKMR....... John F. Kennedy Memorial Highway (SAUS)
JFKPS....... John F. Kennedy Philatelic Society (EA)
JFKSC....... John Fitzgerald Kennedy Spaceflight Center [*Also known as KSC*] [*NASA*]
JFKSC....... John F. Kennedy Spaceflight Center (SAUO)
JFKYCC..... John F. Kennedy Youth Correctional Center (SAUO)
JFL.......... Joint Frequency List
JFL.......... Judy Farquharson Ltd. [*British*]
JFL.......... Justifiable [*Telegraphy*] (PCTE)
JFLA......... Jewish Free Loan Association (EA)
J Fla Acad Gen Pract... Journal. Florida Academy of General Practice (journ.) (SAUS)
J Fla Med Ass... Journal. Florida Medical Association (journ.) (SAUS)
J Fla Med Assoc... Journal of the Florida Medical Association (SAUO)
J Fla Med Assoc... Journal of the Florida Medical Association (journ.) (SAUS)
J Fla State Dent Soc... Journal. Florida State Dental Society (journ.) (SAUS)
JFLC......... Joint Forces Land Component (DOMA)
JFLCC....... Joint Forces Land Component Commander (DOMA)

J Florida MA... Journal. Florida Medical Association (journ.) (SAUS)
JFLU......... Japan Federation of Labour Unions (SAUO)
J Fluid Control... Journal of Fluid Control (journ.) (SAUS)
J Fluid Eng Trans ASME... Journal of Fluids Engineering. Transactions of the American Society of Mechanical Engineers (journ.) (SAUS)
J Fluids Eng... Journal of Fluids Engineering (journ.) (SAUS)
J Fluids Struct... Journal of Fluids and Structures (journ.) (SAUS)
J Fluorescence... Journal of Fluorescence (journ.) (SAUS)
J Fluoresc Miner S... Journal. Fluorescent Mineral Society (journ.) (SAUS)
JFM.......... Jet Flap Model
JFM.......... Jews for Morality (EA)
JFM.......... Job Function Manual (AAG)
JFM.......... Joint Force Memorandum [*Military*]
JFM.......... Journal of Fluid Mechanics (journ.) (SAUS)
JFM.......... Journal of Forms Management (journ.) (SAUS)
JFM.......... Journal of Futures Markets (journ.) (SAUS)
JFM.......... June Fourth Movement (SAUO)
JFM.......... Jupiter Flyby Mission [*Aerospace*]
JFMA......... Journal. Florida Medical Association (journ.) (SAUS)
JFMAMJJASOND... January, February, March, April, May, June, July, August, September, October, November, December (SAUS)
JFMC......... Jewish Federation of Metropolitan Chicago (EARSL)
JFMCC....... Joint Force Maritime Component Commander (SAUO)
JFMCC....... Joint Forces Maritime Component Commander (SAUO)
JFMFO....... Johann Frederick Mouser Family Organization [*Association*] (EA)
JFMIP....... Joint Financial Management Improvement Program
JFMO........ Joint Financial Management Office (ACAE)
JFMO........ Joint Frequency Management Office (MCD)
JFMS........ Jeffery's Motor Service [*Common carrier symbol*]
JFMS........ Journal of Feline Medicine & Surgery [*Database*] (GDD)
JFMS........ Journal of Feline Medicine and Surgery [*A Publication*] (MHID)
JFMSES..... Joint Frequency Management and Spectrum Engineering System (SAUO)
JFMU........ Joint Force Meteorological and Oceanographic Forecast Unit (COE)
JFN.......... Jefferson, OH [*Location identifier*] [*FAA*] (FAAL)
JFN.......... Job File Number
JFN.......... Justification [*Telegraphy*] (PCTE)
JFNF......... Jewish Family Name File [*Association for the Study of Jewish Languages*] [*Information service or system*] (CRD)
JFNP......... John Forest National Park (SAUS)
JFNP......... Joseph M. Farley Nuclear Plant (NRCH)
JFNPP....... James A. FitzPatrick Nuclear Power Plant (NRCH)
JFO.......... Just for Openers [*An association*] (EA)
J Foetal Med... Journal of Foetal Medicine (journ.) (SAUS)
JF of L...... Japan National Federation of Labor (SAUO)
J Folk Res... Journal of Folklore Research (journ.) (SAUS)
J Food Biochem... Journal of Food Biochemistry (journ.) (SAUS)
J Food Compos Anal... Journal of Food Composition and Analysis (journ.) (SAUS)
J Food Eng... Journal of Food Engineering (journ.) (SAUS)
J Food Hygienic Soc Jap... Journal. Food Hygienic Society of Japan (journ.) (SAUS)
J Food Process Eng... Journal of Food Process Engineering (journ.) (SAUS)
J Food Process Eng... Journal of Food Processing Engineering (journ.) (SAUS)
J Food Process Preserv... Journal of Food Processing and Preservation (journ.) (SAUS)
J Food Prot... Journal of Food Protection [*A publication*] (PABS)
J Food Qual... Journal of Food Quality (journ.) (SAUS)
J Food Resour Dev... Journal of Food Resources Development (journ.) (SAUS)
J Food Saf... Journal of Food Safety (journ.) (SAUS)
J Food Serv Syst... Journal of Food Service Systems (journ.) (SAUS)
J Foot Ankle Surg... Journal of Foot and Ankle Surgery (journ.) (SAUS)
J Foot Surg... Journal of Foot Surgery (journ.) (SAUS)
J For......... Journal of Forestry [*A publication*] (PABS)
J For Comm... Journal. Forestry Commission (journ.) (SAUS)
J Forecasting... Journal of Forecasting (journ.) (SAUS)
J Forensic Econ... Journal of Forensic Economics [*A publication*] (JLIT)
J Forensic Odontostomatol... Journal of Forensic Odonto-Stomatology (journ.) (SAUS)
J Forensic Sci Soc... Journal-Forensic Science Society (SAUO)
J For Hist... Journal of Forest History (journ.) (SAUS)
J Formosan Med Ass... Journal. Formosan Medical Association (journ.) (SAUS)
J Formos Med Assoc... Journal of the Formosan Medical Association (SAUO)
J Formos Med Assoc... Journal of the Formosan Medical Association (journ.) (SAUS)
J For Prod Res Soc... Journal. Forest Products Research Society (journ.) (SAUS)
J For Sci Soc... Journal. Forensic Science Society [*A publication*] (DLA)
J Forth Appl Res... Journal of Forth Application and Research (journ.) (SAUS)
JFP.......... Jewish Family Purity (BJA)
JFP.......... Jobs For Progress (SAUS)
JFP.......... Joint Frequency Panel
JFP.......... Journal of Family Practice (SAUO)
JFP.......... Journal of Financial Planning Today (journ.) (SAUS)
JFPA......... Jamaica Family Planning Association (BUAC)
JFPC......... Joint Fire Prevention Committee (WDAA)
JFPCC....... Joint Fusion Power Coordination Committee (SAUS)
JFPH......... JUMPS [*Joint Uniform Military Pay System*] Field Procedures Handbook (NVT)
JFPRD....... Journal of Food Protection (journ.) (SAUS)
JFPS......... Japan Fire Prevention Service (SAUS)
JFPS......... Japan Fire Prevention Society (BUAC)
JFR.......... Jamie Frontier Resources, Inc. [*Toronto Stock Exchange symbol*]
JFR.......... Jet Flap Rotor
JFR.......... Jet Flog Rotor (SAUS)
JFR.......... Joint Fiction Reserve
JFR.......... Journal of Financial Research (journ.) (SAUS)
JFR.......... Journal of Folklore Research (journ.) (SAUS)
J Franklin Inst... Journal of the Franklin Institute [*A publication*] (CABS)
J Franklin Inst Mono... Journal. Franklin Institute. Monograph (journ.) (SAUS)
JFRC......... James Forrestal Research Center [*Princeton University*] (MCD)
JFRCA....... Japanese Fisheries Resources Conservation Association (BUAC)
JFRCD....... Journal of Fire Retardant Chemistry (journ.) (SAUS)
JFRDD....... Journal of Food Resources Development (journ.) (SAUS)
J Fresbwater... Journal of Freshwater (journ.) (SAUS)
J Freshwat Biol... Journal of Freshwater Biology [*A publication*] (PABS)
J Freshwat Ecol... Journal of Freshwater Ecology [*A publication*] (PABS)
JFRF......... Japan Frame Relay Forum (DDC)
JFRO......... Joint Fire Research Organisation (HEAS)
JFRO......... Joint Fire Research Organization (SAUO)
JFRO......... Joint Fisheries Research Organisation [*Malawi, Zambia*] (BUAC)
JFRSN....... Jefferson, TX [*American Association of Railroads railroad junction routing code*]
JFRY......... Jeffrey Manin, Inc. (SAUO)
JFS.......... Jamaica Freight and Shipping Co. Ltd. (EY)
JFS.......... Java File System (SAUS)
JFS.......... Jet Fuel Starter
JFS.......... Jewish Family Service (EA)
JFS.......... Jewish Friends Society (EA)
JFS.......... Job Findcar System (SAUS)
JFS.......... Job Finder System
JFS.......... Johnston & Frye [*Vancouver Stock Exchange symbol*]
JFS.......... Joint Foundation Support (EA)
JFS.......... Journaled File System (SAUO)
JFS.......... Journalized File System (VLIE)
JFS.......... Journal of Food Science (journ.) (SAUS)
JFS.......... Juanda Flying School [*Indonesia*] [*ICAO designator*] (FAAC)
JFS.......... Jugular Foramen Syndrome [*or Vernet's syndrome*] [*Medicine*] (DAVI)
JFS.......... Jumbogroup Frequency Supply [*Bell System*]
JFS.......... Justice for Scotland (SAUO)
JFS.......... Justifies [*Telegraphy*] (PCTE)
JFSC......... Joint Forces Staff College (SAUO)
JFSE......... Japan Federation of Small Enterprises (SAUO)
JFSEO....... Japan Federation of Smaller Enterprises (BUAC)
JFSG......... Joint Feasibility Study Group [*Air Force*] (MCD)
JFSNY....... Jewish Folk Schools of New York (EA)
JFSOC....... Junior Foreign Service Officers Club (SAUO)
JFSOCC..... Joint Force Special Operations Component Commander (SAUS)
JFSP......... Joint Forecast System Project [*Marine science*] (OSRA)
JFSR......... Jewish Fund for Soviet Russia (SAUO)
JFSS......... Joint Force Signals Staff [*Military*]
JFSS......... Journal of the Forensic Science Society [*UK*] [*Medicine*] (EDAA)
JFSSG....... Joint Food Safety and Standards Group [*British*] (GVA)
JFSUR....... Journal of Foot Surgery (journ.) (SAUS)
JFT.......... Jet Fret [*France*] [*ICAO designator*] (FAAC)
JFT.......... Job File Table (PCM)
JFT.......... Joint Field Trial (NATG)
JFTC......... Japan Foreign Trade Council (BUAC)
JFTC......... Joint For Trade Committee (SAUS)
JFTC......... Joint Fur Trade Committee (BUAC)
JFTCG....... Joint Flight Test Control Group (AAG)
JFTEC....... Journal of Fermentation Technology (journ.) (SAUS)
JFTG......... Joint Fuze Task Group [*Army*]
JFTOT....... Jet Fuel Thermal Oxidation Test [*or Tester*] [*Analytical chemistry*] [*Air Force*]
JFTR......... Joint Federal Travel Regulations (DOMA)
JFTS......... Jet Fuel Thermal Stability
JFTU......... Jordan Federation of Trade Unions
JFTX......... Joint Field Training Exercise [*Military*]
JFU.......... Jersey Farmers' Union [*British*] (DBA)
JFUB......... Joint Facilities Utilization Board [*Military*]
J Fudan Univ Nat Sci... Journal. Fudan University. Natural Science (journ.) (SAUS)
J Fuel Heat Technol... Journal of Fuel and Heating Technology (SAUS)
J Fuel Heat Technol... Journal of Fuel and Heat Technology (journ.) (SAUS)
J Fuel Soc Jap... Journal. Fuel Society of Japan (journ.) (SAUS)
J Fuel Soc Jpn... Journal of the Fuel Society of Japan (journ.) (SAUS)
J Fujian Agric Coll... Journal. Fujian Agricultural College (journ.) (SAUS)
J Fujian Teach Univ Nat Sci Ed... Journal. Fujian Teachers University. Natural Science Edition (journ.) (SAUS)
J Fur Higher Educ... Journal of Further and Higher Education (journ.) (SAUS)
JFUS......... Journal of Forestry (journ.) (SAUS)
J Fusion Energy... Journal of Fusion Energy [*A publication*] (CABS)
J Fusion Energy... Journal of Fusion Energy (journ.) (SAUS)
J Futures Markets... Journal of Futures Markets (journ.) (SAUS)
JFuU......... Fukui University, Fukui-shi, Japan [*Library symbol*] [*Library of Congress*] (LCLS)
JFV.......... Jersey Farmers Union (SAUS)
JFV.......... Jobs for Veterans (SAUO)
JFV.......... Jobs for Veterans National Committee [*Defunct*] (EA)
JFV.......... Jupiter Flyby Vehicle [*Aerospace*]
JFW.......... Jamaica Federation of Women (BUAC)
JFW.......... JFW Manufacturing [*NCIC trailer make code*]
JFW.......... Justice for Women (EA)
JFWX......... JF White Contracting [*Private rail car owner code*]
JFY.......... Foster Yeoman Ltd. [*British*] [*ICAO designator*] (FAAC)
JFY.......... Japanese Fiscal Year (CINC)
JFY.......... Jiffy (ABBR)
JFYI......... Just For Your Information (SAUS)
JG........... Bumthills Aviation Ltd. (SAUO)

JG.......... Jahrgang [*Year of Publication/Volume*] [*German*]
JG.......... Jerusalem und Seine Gelaende [*A publication*] (BJA)
JG.......... Jockeys' Guild (EA)
J/g.......... Joule per gram (SAUS)
JG.......... Joules Gram (SAUS)
JG.......... Joules per Gram [*Physics*] (IAA)
JG.......... Journal of Geography (journ.) (SAUS)
JG.......... Journal of Gerontology [*Medicine*] (EDAA)
JG.......... Judge [*Telegraphy*] (PCTE)
Jg.......... Judges [*Old Testament book*] (BJA)
JG.......... Judgment [*Legal shorthand*] (LWAP)
JG.......... Juedisches Gemeindeblatt fuer die Britische Zone [*A publication*] (BJA)
JG.......... Jumbogroup (SAUO)
JG.......... Jump if Greater (VLIE)
JG.......... Junction Grammar [*Computer science*]
JG.......... June Grass [*Test*] [*Medicine*] (DAVI)
JG.......... Junior Girls [*School department*] [*British*] (DI)
JG.......... Junior Grade
jg.......... Juxtaglomerular (STED)
JG.......... Juxtaglomerular [*Histology*]
JG.......... Swedair [*ICAO designator*] (AD)
JGA.......... Jamnagar [*India*] [*Airport symbol*] (OAG)
JGA.......... Japan Gas Association (BUAC)
JGA.......... Japan Golf Association (BUAC)
JGA.......... Jojoba Growers Association (EA)
JGA.......... Joseph Guzman & Associates, Inc. [*Palatine, IL*] [*Telecommunications*] [*Defunct*] (TSSD)
JGA.......... Jute Goods Association (SAUO)
JGA.......... Juxtaglomerular Apparatus [*Histology*]
JGAB.......... Joint Government Agencies Board (SSD)
J GA Dent Assoc... Journal. Georgia Dental Association (journ.) (SAUS)
J Gakugei Tokushima Univ Nat Sci... Journal. Gakugei Tokushima University. Natural Science (journ.) (SAUS)
J Galway Archaeol Hist S... Journal. Galway Archaeological and Historical Society (journ.) (SAUS)
JGAM.......... Junior Gas Association of Manchester (SAUO)
JG & C.......... Joint Guidance and Control (KSC)
JG-APP.......... Joint Group on Acquisition Pollution Prevention (BCP)
J Gas Chromatogr... Journal of Gas Chromatography (journ.) (SAUS)
J Gas Light Water Supply Sanit Improv... Journal of Gas Lighting, Water Supply and Sanitary Improvement (journ.) (SAUS)
J Gastroenterol... Journal of Gastroenterology (journ.) (SAUS)
J Gastroenterol Hepatol... Journal of Gastroenterology and Hepatology (journ.) (SAUS)
JGB.......... Japanese Government Bond (ECON)
JGB.......... Jewish Guild for the Blind (EA)
JGC.......... Grand Canyon [*Arizona*] [*Airport symbol*] (OAG)
JGC.......... Jacob Gold Corp. [*Vancouver Stock Exchange symbol*]
JGC.......... Japan Gas Chemical (SAUO)
JGC.......... Japan Gasoline Co. (SAUS)
JGC.......... JGC Corp. [*Formerly, Japan Gasoline Co. Ltd.*]
JGC.......... Journal of General Chemistry (journ.) (SAUS)
JGC.......... Juxtaglomerular Cells [*Histology*]
JGCC.......... Juxtaglomerular Cell Count [*Endocrinology*]
JGCEA.......... Journal of Geochemical Exploration (journ.) (SAUS)
JGCRA.......... Journal of Gas Chromatography (journ.) (SAUS)
JGCT.......... Juvenile Granulosa Cell Tumor [*Medicine*] (PALA)
JGCT.......... Juxtaglomerular Cell Tumor [*Histology*] (DAVI)
JGD.......... JOPES Global Dictionary (SAUO)
JGD.......... Judged [*Telegraphy*] (PCTE)
JG/D.......... Judgement for the Defendant [*Legal shorthand*] (LWAP)
JGD.......... Junior Grand Deacon [*Freemasonry*]
JGDI.......... Joggle Die (SAUS)
J/Gdsmn.......... Junior Guardsman [*British military*] (DMA)
JGDX.......... Jackson, Gordonville & Delta Railroad [*Federal Railroad Administration identification code*]
JGE.......... Jaguar Equity, Inc. [*Vancouver Stock Exchange symbol*]
JGE.......... Joint Group of Experts [*Marine science*] (MSC)
JGE.......... Journal of General Education (journ.) (SAUS)
JGE.......... Jump if Greater or Equal (VLIE)
J Gemmol.. Journal of Gemmology (journ.) (SAUS)
J Gen Chem... Journal of General Chemistry (journ.) (SAUS)
J Gen Chem USSR... Journal of General Chemistry of the USSR (journ.) (SAUS)
J Genet..... Journal of Genetics (journ.) (SAUS)
J Genet & Breed... Journal of Genetics and Breeding (journ.) (SAUS)
J Gen Intern Med... Journal of General Internal Medicine (journ.) (SAUS)
J Gen Manag... Journal of General Management (journ.) (SAUS)
J Gen Virol... Journal of General Virology (journ.) (SAUS)
J Geobot.... Journal of Geobotany (journ.) (SAUS)
J Geochem Soc India... Journal. Geochemical Society of India (journ.) (SAUS)
JGEOD.......... Journal of Geophysics (journ.) (SAUS)
J Geodesy... Journal of Geodesy [*A publication*] (PABS)
J Geodyn... Journal of Geodynamics (journ.) (SAUS)
J Geog...... Journal of Geography (journ.) (SAUS)
J Geograph Systems... Journal of Geographical Systems [*A publication*] (JLIT)
J Geo Higher Educ... Journal of Geography in Higher Education (journ.) (SAUS)
J Geolectr... Journal of Geoelectricity (journ.) (SAUS)
J Geol Educ... Journal of Geological Education (journ.) (SAUS)
J Geol Sci Appl Geophys... Journal of Geological Sciences. Applied Geophysics (journ.) (SAUS)
J Geol Sci Palaeontol... Journal of Geological Sciences. Palaeontology (journ.) (SAUS)
J Geol Soc... Journal of Geological Society (journ.) (SAUS)
J Geol Soc Aust... Journal of the Geological Society of Australia (SAUO)
J Geol Soc Aust... Journal of the Geological Society of Australia (journ.) (SAUS)
J Geol Soc In... Journal. Geological Society of India (journ.) (SAUS)
J Geol Soc India... Journal of the Geological Society of India (SAUO)
J Geol Soc India... Journal of the Geological Society of India (journ.) (SAUS)
J Geol Soc Iraq... Journal. Geological Society of Iraq (journ.) (SAUS)
J Geol Soc Jam... Journal. Geological Society of Jamaica (journ.) (SAUS)
J Geol Soc Jam... Journal of the Geological Society of Jamaica (journ.) (SAUS)
J Geol Soc Jpn... Journal. Geological Society of Japan (journ.) (SAUS)
J Geol Soc london... Journal. Geological Society of London (journ.) (SAUS)
J Geol Soc Philipp... Journal. Geological Society of the Philippines (journ.) (SAUS)
J Geol Soc Thailand... Journal. Geological Society of Thailand (journ.) (SAUS)
J Geol Soc Tokyo... Journal. Geological Society of Tokyo (journ.) (SAUS)
J Geol UAR... Journal of Geology. United Arab Republic (journ.) (SAUS)
J Geol Ukr Aad Sci Inst Geol... Journal of Geology. Ukrainian Academy of Sciences. Institute of Geology (journ.) (SAUS)
J Geom Phys... Journal of Geometry and Physics (journ.) (SAUS)
J Geophys.. Journal of Geophysics (journ.) (SAUS)
J Geophys Prospect... Journal of Geophysical Prospecting (journ.) (SAUS)
J Geophys Res D Atm... Journal of Geophysical Research. Series D. Atmospheres (journ.) (SAUS)
J Geo R-SP... Journal of Geophysical Research. Space Physics (journ.) (SAUS)
J Geosci Osska City Univ... Journal of Geosciences. Osaka City University (journ.) (SAUS)
J Geotech Eng... Journal of Geotechnical Engineering (journ.) (SAUS)
J Geotech Eng Div Amer Soc Civil Eng Proc... Journal. Geotechnical Engineering Division. Proceedings of the American Society of Civil Engineers (journ.) (SAUS)
J Geotech Engng Div ASCE... Journal Geotechnical Engineering Division. American Society of Civil Engineers (journ.) (SAUS)
J Geotech Engng Div Proc ASCE... Journal. Geotechnical Engineering Division. Proceedings of the American Society of Civil Engineers (journ.) (SAUS)
J Geotherm Energy Res Dev Co Ltd... Journal. Geothermal Energy Research and Development Company, Limited (journ.) (SAUS)
J Geriatr Psychiatry Neurol... Journal of Geriatric Psychiatry and Neurology (journ.) (SAUS)
J Gerontol A Biol Sci Med Sci... Journals of Gerontology. Series A, Biological Sciences and Medical Sciences (journ.) (SAUS)
J Gerontol B Psychol Sci Soc Sci... Journals of Gerontology. Series B, Psychological Sciences and Social Sciences (journ.) (SAUS)
J Gerontol Nurs... Journal of Gerontological Nursing (journ.) (SAUS)
J Gerontol Soc Work... Journal of Gerontological Social Work (journ.) (SAUS)
JGF.......... Jakarta Growth Fund [*NYSE symbol*] (SPSG)
JGF.......... Junctor Grouping Frame [*Telecommunications*] (TEL)
JGFC.......... Joe Gallison Fan Club (EA)
JGFC.......... John Gilbert Fan Club (EA)
JGFC.......... John Gill Fan Club (EA)
JGFET.......... Junction Gate Field-Effect Transistor [*Electronics*] (IAA)
JGFO.......... Jeremiah Greene Family Organization [*Association*] (EA)
JGG.......... Judging [*Telegraphy*] (PCTE)
JGGAS.......... Journal. Hongkong University. Geographical, Geological and Archaeological Society (journ.) (SAUS)
JGH.......... Jig Grinder Head
JGH.......... Journal of Garden History [*A publication*] (ABAR)
JGI.......... Jejunogastric Intussusception [*Gastroenterology*] (DAVI)
JGI.......... Joint Genome Institute (HGEN)
JGI.......... Juxtaglomerular Granulation Index [*Endocrinology*]
JGI.......... Juxtaglomerular Index [*Endocrinology*]
JGIFC.......... John Gary International Fan Club (EA)
JGIM.......... Journal of General Internal Medicine (SAUO)
JGIM.......... Journal of General Internal Medicine (journ.) (SAUS)
JGIN.......... JG Industries [*NASDAQ symbol*] (TTSB)
JGIN.......... JG Industries, Inc. [*NASDAQ symbol*] (NQ)
JG Ind.......... JG Industries, Inc. [*Associated Press*] (SAG)
JGL.......... Java Generic Library (VLIE)
J Glass Stud... Journal of Glass Studies (journ.) (SAUS)
JGLC.......... Joint Government Liaison Committee [*Composed of Association of Brass and Bronze Ingot Manufacturers and Brass and Bronze Ingot Institute*] (EA)
JGLMA.......... Journal of the Gay and Lesbian Medical Association (SAUO)
JGLMA.......... Journal of the Gay and Lesbian Medical Association (journ.) (SAUS)
JGLRD.......... Journal of Great Lakes Research (journ.) (SAUS)
JGLS.......... Journal of the Gypsy Lore Society (SAUO)
JGLU.......... Juglinija Lines [*Intermodal shipping container symbol*] (TVRC)
JGM.......... Jig Grinding Machine
JGM.......... Job Guide Manual (PDAA)
JGM.......... Journal of General Microbiology (journ.) (SAUS)
JGM.......... Judgment [*Telegraphy*] (PCTE)
JGMC.......... Judy Garland Memorial Club (EA)
J GMS OSU.......... Journal. Graduate Music Students. Ohio State University (journ.) (SAUS)
JGN.......... Junction Gate Number
J Gnathol... Journal of Gnathology (journ.) (SAUS)
Jgn J Aerosp Med Psychol... Japanese Journal of Aerospace Medicine and Psychology (journ.) (SAUS)
JGNP.......... Japanese Gross National Product (SAUS)
JGOFS.......... Joint Global Ocean Flux Study [*International experiment*]
JGOFS.......... Joint Global Ocean Flux Study Program of the IGBP (SAUO)
JGOFS GS... JGOFS Global Synthesis (SAUS)
JGOFS GS... Joint Global Ocean Flux Study Global Synthesis (SAUO)
JGOFS PM... JGOFS Photosynthetic Measurements (SAUS)
JGOFS-SSC... JGOFS Scientific Steering Committee (SAUS)

JGOFS-SSC... Joint Global Ocean Flux Study Scientific Steering Committee (SAUO)
J-GOOS ..... Joint Global Ocean Flux Study Scientific and Technical Committee (SAUO)
J-GOOS ..... Joint GOOS Scientific and Technical Committee (SAUS)
J-GOOS ..... Joint Scientific and Technical Committee for GOOS (SAUS)
JGOS .... Journal of the German Oriental Society (SAUO)
JGOS .... Journal of the German Oriental Society (journ.) (SAUS)
JGO-US ..... Job Guarantee Office of the United States (OICC)
J Gov Info... Journal of Government Information [*A publication*] (BRI)
JGP .... Houston [*Texas*] Greenway [*Airport symbol*] (OAG)
JGP .... Jem Group Products [*Vancouver Stock Exchange symbol*]
JGP .... Journal of General Physiology (journ.) (SAUS)
JG/P .... Judgement for the Plaintiff [*Legal shorthand*] (LWAP)
JGP .... Juvenile General Paralysis [*Medicine*] (DAVI)
JGP .... Juvenile General Paresis [*Medicine*] (DMAA)
JGPA......... Jobbing Grinders' Provident Association [*A union*] [*British*]
JGPAC .... Jenkens & Gilchrist, P.C. PAC [*Dallas, TX*] (PACS)
JGPN .... Journal of Geriatric Psychiatry and Neurology (journ.) (SAUS)
JGQ .... Houston [*Texas*] Guest Quarters [*Airport symbol*] (OAG)
JGQ .... Jean Gilbert Quilting (EFIS)
JGR .... Belize Trans Air [*ICAO designator*] (FAAC)
JGR .... Jaldapara Game Reserve (SAUO)
JGR .... Journal of Geophysical Research
J Grad Res Cent... Journal. Graduate Research Center (journ.) (SAUS)
J Grad Res Cent South Metbodist Univ... Journal. Graduate Research Center. Southern Methodist University (journ.) (SAUS)
J Graph Theory... Journal of Graph Theory (journ.) (SAUS)
J Grey Syst... Journal of Grey Systems (journ.) (SAUS)
JGRIP .... Japanese Government and Public Research in Progress [*International database*]
J Group Experts Sci Aspects Mr Pollut... Joint Group of Experts on the Scientific Aspects of Marine Pollution (SAUO)
J Group Experts Sci Aspects Mr Pollut... Joint Group of Experts on the Scientific Aspects of Marine Pollution (journ.) (SAUS)
J Growth.... Journal of Growth (journ.) (SAUS)
JGRP .... Jesup Group, Inc. (SAUO)
JGRU .... John G Russell Transport [*Intermodal shipping container symbol*] (TVRC)
JGS .... James Griffiths & Sons [*AAR code*]
JGS .... Jewish Genealogical Society (EA)
JGS .... Joint General Staff [*Military*] (NATG)
JGS .... Journal of Glass Studies (journ.) (SAUS)
JGS .... Judges [*Telegraphy*] (PCTE)
Jgs........... Judges [*Old Testament book*]
JGSA .... John G. Shedd Aquarium (SAUO)
JGSDF....... Japanese Ground Self-Defense Forces (AABC)
JGSI .... Jewish Genealogical Society of Illinois (EARSL)
JGSLA....... Journal. Geological Society of London (journ.) (SAUS)
JGSTD....... Journal. Gyeongsang National University. Science and Technology (journ.) (SAUS)
JGSW........ Jigsaw (ABBR)
JGSW........ Journal of Gerontological Social Work (journ.) (SAUS)
JGT .... Judgment [*Legal term*] (ROG)
JGT .... Junction Growth Technique
JGTC......... Junior Girls' Training Corps [*British*] [*World War II*]
JG-TE........ Jumbogroup-Translation Equipment (SAUO)
JGTL......... Job Grading System for Trades and Labor Occupations
JGTOI........ [*The*] Judge GTO International (EA)
JGU .... Japanese Geomorphological Union (SAUO)
JGUAG ...... Joint Government/UNICEF Advisory Group (SAUO)
J Guid Control and Dyn... Journal of Guidance, Control and Dynamics (journ.) (SAUS)
J Guid Control Dyn... Journal of Guidance, Control, and Dynamics [*A publication*] (CABS)
JGW .... Junior Grand Warden [*Freemasonry*]
JGWTC ...... Jungle and Guerrilla Warfare Training Center [*Army*]
J Gyeongsang Ntl Univ Nat Sci... Journal. Gyeongsang National University. Natural Sciences (journ.) (SAUS)
J Gyeongsang Ntl Univ Sci Technol... Journal. Gyeongsang National University. Science and Technology (journ.) (SAUS)
J Gynecol Pract... Journal of Gynecological Practice (journ.) (SAUS)
JH............ Echovirus 28 [*Virology*] (DAVI)
JH............ Harland [*John H.*] Co. [*NYSE symbol*] (SPSG)
JH............ Harland (John H.) [*NYSE symbol*] (TTSB)
JH............ Jacob's Horse [*British military*] (DMA)
J-H........... Jarisch-Herxheimer [*Reaction*] [*Medicine*] (EDAA)
JH............ Jogger's Heel (MELL)
JH............ John H Harland Co. [*NYSE symbol*]
JH............ Journal of History (journ.) (SAUS)
J H........... Journal of Hygiene (journ.) (SAUS)
JH............ Journal of the House of Representatives [*United States*] [*A publication*] (DLA)
JH............ Juvenile Hormone [*Entomology*]
JH............ Nordeste-Lineas Aereas Regionais [*ICAO designator*] (AD)
JHA .... Japan Hour Association [*Later, JHB*] (EA)
JHA .... Job Hazard Analysis (PDAA)
JHA .... John Howard Association (EA)
JHA .... Justice and Home Affairs (SAUO)
JHA .... Juvenile Hormone Analog [*Entomology*]
JHAH .... John Howard Association of Hawaii (SAUO)
JHAI .... John Herron Art Institute (SAUO)
J Hand Surg... Journal of Hand Surgery (journ.) (SAUS)
J Hand Ther... Journal of Hand Therapy (journ.) (SAUS)
JHAR .... Johns Hopkins Autopsy Resource (SAUO)
J Harbin Ind Coll... Journal. Harbin Industrial College (journ.) (SAUS)
J Harbin Inst Tecbnol... Journal. Harbin Institute of Technology (journ.) (SAUS)
J Harbin Inst Technol... Journal of the Harbin Institute of Technology (journ.) (SAUS)
JHAS .... John Herron Art School (SAUO)
JHAT......... Japan Helicopter Air Transport Company (SAUO)
J Hattori Bot Lab... Journal. Hattori Botanical Laboratory (journ.) (SAUS)
J Hattori Bot Lab... Journal of the Hattori Botanical Laboratory (SAUO)
J Hawaii Dent Ass... Journal. Hawaii Dental Association (journ.) (SAUS)
J Hawaii State Dent Assoc... Journal. Hawaii State Dental Association (journ.) (SAUS)
J Hazard Mater... Journal of Hazardous Materials (journ.) (SAUS)
J Hazard Waste Hazard Mater... Journal of Hazardous Waste and Hazardous Materials (journ.) (SAUS)
JHB .... Japan Hour Broadcasting (EA)
JHB .... Job Hazard Breakdown (SAUS)
JHB .... Johannesburg [*South Africa*] (ABBR)
JHB .... Johore Bahru [*Malaysia*] [*Airport symbol*] (OAG)
JHBLEN ..... Journal of Human Behavior and Learning (journ.) (SAUS)
JHBP .... Juvenile Hormone Binding Protein [*Entomology*]
JHBSA....... Journal of the History of the Behavioral Sciences (journ.) (SAUS)
JHC .... Garden City [*New York*] [*Airport symbol*] (OAG)
JHC .... John Hancock Center (SAUO)
JHC .... Johnson Canyon [*California*] [*Seismograph station code, US Geological Survey*] (SEIS)
JHC .... Joint Helicopter Control (SAUS)
JHC .... Joint High Command (DNAB)
JHC .... Joint Hulls Committee (MARI)
JHC .... Journal of Histochemistry and Cytochemistry [*Medicine*] (EDAA)
JHCC .... Joint Health Care Committee [*Medicine*] (EDAA)
JHCM........ Journal of Health Care Marketing (journ.) (SAUS)
JHCNHS..... John Henry Cardinal Newman Honorary Society [*Defunct*] (EA)
JHCU .... Spedition JUU Hammelmann [*Intermodal shipping container symbol*] (TVRC)
JHD .... Jehuda [*On Hebrew coins of the fourth century*]
JHD .... Joint Hypocenter Determination [*Earthquake study*]
JHD .... Journal of the Hellenic Diaspra (journ.) (SAUS)
JHDA .... Journal. Hawaii Dental Association (journ.) (SAUS)
JHDA .... Junior Hospital Doctors Association [*British*]
Jhdf.......... Japanese haakon-dahl feet (SAUS)
JHDP .... Journal of Hospital Dental Practice [*AAHD*] [*Medicine*] (EDAA)
JHe .... Jewish Heritage [*A publication*] (BJA)
JHE .... Johns Hopkins University, Baltimore, MD [*OCLC symbol*] (OCLC)
JHE .... Journal of Higher Education (journ.) (SAUS)
JHE .... Juvenile Hormone Esterase [*An enzyme*]
J Health Adm Educ... Journal of Health Administration Education (journ.) (SAUS)
J Health Care Finance... Journal of Health Care Finance (journ.) (SAUS)
J Health Care Poor Underserved... Journal of Health Care for the Poor and Underserved (journ.) (SAUS)
J Health Care Technol... Journal of Health Care Technology (journ.) (SAUS)
J Healthc Mater Manage... Journal of Healthcare Material Management (journ.) (SAUS)
J Healthc Prot Manage... Journal of Healthcare Protection Management (journ.) (SAUS)
J Health Econ... Journal of Health Economics (journ.) (SAUS)
J Health Hum Behav... Journal of Health and Human Behavior (journ.) (SAUS)
J Health Phys Radiat Prot... Journal of Health Physics and Radiation Protection (journ.) (SAUS)
J Health Politics Pol Law... Journal of Health Politics, Policy and Law [*A publication*] (JLIT)
J Health Sci... Journal of Health Science [*A publication*] (PABS)
J Heart Lung Transplant... Journal of Heart and Lung Transplantation (journ.) (SAUS)
J Heart Valve Dis... Journal of Heart Valve Disease (journ.) (SAUS)
J Heat Recovery Syst... Journal of Heat Recovery Systems (journ.) (SAUS)
J Heat Transfer... Journal of Heat Transfer (SAUS)
J Heat Treat... Journal of Heat Treating (journ.) (SAUS)
J Hebei Univ Nat Sci Ed... Journal. Hebei University. Natural Science Edition (journ.) (SAUS)
J Hebr St ... Journal of Hebraic Studies (journ.) (SAUS)
JHEL......... Journal of Hellenic Studies (journ.) (SAUS)
JHellSt ...... Journal of Hellenic Studies (journ.) (SAUS)
J Helth Phys Ed Rec... Journal of Health, Physical Education, Recreation (journ.) (SAUS)
J Hematother... Journal of Hematotherapy (journ.) (SAUS)
J Hepatol ... Journal of Hepatology (journ.) (SAUS)
J Herpetol... Journal of Herpetology (journ.) (SAUS)
J Herpetol Assoc Afr... Journal. Herpetological Association of Africa (journ.) (SAUS)
JHF .... Jackson, MS [*Location identifier*] [*FAA*] (FAAL)
JHF .... John Hancock Fin'l Svcs. [*NYSE symbol*] (SG)
JHFA......... Jacob Hochstetler Family Association (EA)
JHFC......... Jan Howard Friends Club (EA)
JHFC......... Jeff Healey Fan Club (EA)
JHFO .... James Happy Family Organization [*Association*] (EA)
JHG .... Joule Heat Gradient (IEEE)
JHGA .... Jewish Historical General Archives [*Jerusalem*] (BJA)
JHGSOWA... Joint Household Goods Shipping Office (SAUO)
JHGSOWA... Joint Household Goods Shipping Office, Washington Area [*Military*] (AABC)
JHGSW...... Journal. Heraldic and Genealogical Society of Wales (journ.) (SAUS)
JHH .... John Hopkins Hospital (SAUS)
JHH .... Johns Hopkins Hospital (SAUO)

JHH .... Journal of Health and Human Resources Administration (journ.) (SAUS)
JHHGSO ..... Joint Household Goods Shipping Office [*Military*]
JHI .... Hancock, John, Investors Trust [*NYSE symbol*] (SAG)
JHI .... Jacob Hiatt Institute (SAUO)
JHI .... Jeffreys Henry International (BUAC)
JHI .... Jesuit Historical Society (SAUO)
JHI .... Jewish Historical Society (SAUO)
JHI .... John Hancock Investors, Incorporated (SAUO)
JHI .... John Hancock Investors Trust [*NYSE symbol*] (SPSG)
JHI .... John Hancock Inv Tr [*NYSE symbol*] (TTSB)
JHI .... Journal of Hospital Infection (SAUO)
JHI .... Journal of the History of Ideas [*A publication*] (BRI)
J Hi E .... Journal of Higher Education [*A publication*] (BRI)
J High Resolut Chromatogr Chromatogr Commun... Journal of High Resolution Chromato- graphy and Chromatography Communications (journ.) (SAUS)
J High Temp Soc... Journal. High Temperature Society (journ.) (SAUS)
J High Temp Soc Jpn... Journal of High Temperature Society of Japan (journ.) (SAUS)
J Highw Dir Am Soc Civ Eng... Journal. Highway Division. American Society of Civil Engineers (journ.) (SAUS)
J Hillside Hosp... Journal. Hillside Hospital (journ.) (SAUS)
JHINDS ...... Journal of Hospital Infection (journ.) (SAUS)
J Hiroshim Univ Dent Soc... Journal. Hiroshima University. Dental Society (journ.) (SAUS)
J Hist Arabic Sci... Journal for the History of Arabic Science (journ.) (SAUS)
J Hist Astron... Journal of the History of Astronomy (journ.) (SAUS)
J Hist Biol... Journal of the History of Biology (journ.) (SAUS)
J Hist Econ Thought... Journal of the History of Economic Thought [*A publication*] (JLIT)
J Hist G ..... Journal of Historical Geography [*A publication*] (BRI)
J Hist Med Allied Sci... Journal of the History of Medicine and Allied Sciences, Department of the History of Medicine. Yale University. New Haven (SAUO)
J Histochem Biochem... Journal of Histochemistry and Biochemistry (journ.) (SAUS)
J Histotechnol... Journal of Histotechnology (journ.) (SAUS)
J Hist Res... Journal of Historical Research (journ.) (SAUS)
J Hist Soc Church Wales... Journal. Historical Society of the Church in Wales (journ.) (SAUS)
J Hist Sociol... Journal of the History of Sociology (journ.) (SAUS)
J Hist Soc Nigeria... Journal. Historical Society of Nigeria (journ.) (SAUS)
J Hist Soc QD... Historical Society of Queensland. Journal (journ.) (SAUS)
J Hist Soc SA... Journal. Historical Society of South Australia [*A publication*]
J Hist Stud... Journal of Historical Studies (journ.) (SAUS)
JHjelm ...... Hjelms [*Jim*] Private Collection [*Associated Press*] (SAG)
JHjelm ...... Jim Hjelms Private Collection [*Associated Press*] (SAG)
JHL .... Jet Heritage Ltd. [*British*] [*ICAO designator*] (FAAC)
JHL .... John Harvard Library (SAUO)
JHLB .... Journal of the Federal Home Loan Bank Board (SAUO)
JHLX .... JH Leftwich [*Private rail car owner code*]
JHM .... Dr. J. Howard Mueller (SAUS)
JHM .... Journal of Hazardous Materials [*Medicine*] (EDAA)
JHM .... Journal of the History of Medicine (journ.) (SAUS)
JHM .... Juvenile Hormone Mimic [*Entomology*]
JHMA .... Japan Heat Management Association (SAUO)
JHMC .... Jamaica Hospital Medical Center (MHID)
JHMCO ...... J. H. Morgan Consultants [*Morristown, NJ*] [*Information service or system*] [*Telecommunications*] (TSSD)
JHMCS ...... Joint Helmet-Mounted Cueing System [*Military*]
JHMEDL ..... Journal of Holistic Medicine (journ.) (SAUS)
JHMET ...... Joint Health-Care Management Engineering Team (ACAE)
JHMI .... Johns Hopkins Medical Institutions (SAUO)
JHMN .... JHM Leasing [*Common carrier symbol*]
JHMO .... Johnson's Motor Express [*Common carrier symbol*]
JHMO .... Junior Hospital Medical Officer
JHMSDT .... Journal of Human Movement Studies (journ.) (SAUS)
JHM Virus .. Dr. J. Howard Mueller Virus (SAUS)
JHN .... Japanese Helicopter Network (SAUS)
JHN .... John Henry Newman [*Initials used as pseudonym*]
JHN .... Johnson Air, Inc. [*ICAO designator*] (FAAC)
JHN .... Johnson, KS [*Location identifier*] [*FAA*] (FAAL)
JHNBX .... Hancock(J) Bond Cl.A [*Mutual fund ticker symbol*] (SG)
JHND .... Dale Johnson Trucking [*Common carrier symbol*]
JHNPD ...... Johnson Products Co., Inc. (SAUO)
JHNS .... Johns Corporation [*NCIC trailer make code*]
JHNU .... Journeyman Horseshoers National Union [*Equine term*] (TED)
JHO .... Jam Handy Organization (SAUO)
JHO .... Japan Hydrographic Office (SAUO)
JHO .... Junior House Officer [*Military*]
JHOGB ...... Jewish Health Organization of Great Britain (SAUO)
J Hokkaido Dent Assc... Journal. Hokkaido Dental Association (journ.) (SAUS)
J Hokkaido Fish Sci Inst... Journal. Hokkaido Fisheries Scientific Institution (journ.) (SAUS)
J Hokkaido Forest Prod Res Inst... Journal Hokkaido Forest Products Research Institute (journ.) (SAUS)
J Hokkaido Gakugei Univ... Journal. Hokkaido Gakugei University (journ.) (SAUS)
J Hokkaido Gakugei Univ Sect B... Journal. Hokkaido Gakugei University. Section B (journ.) (SAUS)
J Hokkaido Gynecol Obstet Soc... Journal. Hokkaido Gynecology and Obstetrical Society (journ.) (SAUS)
J Hokkaido Univ Ed Sect II-A... Journal. Hokkaido University of Education. Section II-A (journ.) (SAUS)
J Hokkaido Univ Educ... Journal. Hokkaido University of Education (journ.) (SAUS)
J Hokkaido Univ Educ II-B... Journal. Hokkaido University of Education. Section II-B (journ.) (SAUS)
J Hokkaido Univ Educ Sect II-C... Journal. Hokkaido University of Education. Section II-C (journ.) (SAUS)
J Holistic Med... Journal of Holistic Medicine (journ.) (SAUS)
J Holistic Nurs... Journal of Holistic Nursing (journ.) (SAUS)
J Homosex . Journal of Homosexuality [*A publication*] (BRI)
J Hopeh Univ Nat Sci... Journal. Hopeh University. Natural Science (journ.) (SAUS)
J Horol Inst Jpn... Journal. Horological Institute of Japan (journ.) (SAUS)
J Horol Inst Jpn... Journal of the Horological Institute of Japan (journ.) (SAUS)
J Hortic Assoc London... Journal. Horticulture Association of London (journ.) (SAUS)
J Hortic Sci... Journal of Horticultural Science [*A publication*] (PABS)
JHOS .... John Hopkins Oceanographic Studies (SAUS)
JHOS .... Johns Hopkins Oceanographic Studies (SAUO)
JHOS .... Johns Hopkins Oceanographic Studies (journ.) (SAUS)
J Hosp Dent Pract... Journal of Hospital Dental Practice (journ.) (SAUS)
J Hosp Infect... Journal of Hospital Infection (journ.) (SAUS)
J Hospitality Educ... Journal of Hospitality Education (journ.) (SAUS)
J Hosp Supply Process Distrib... Journal of Hospital Supply, Processing and Distribution (journ.) (SAUS)
J Housing Econ... Journal of Housing Economics [*A publication*] (JLIT)
J Housing Res... Journal of Housing Research [*A publication*] (JLIT)
JHP .... Jacketed Hollow-Point [*Ammunition*]
JHP .... Jackson Hole Preserve (EA)
JHP .... Johns Hopkins Press (SAUO)
JHP .... Journal of Hispanic Philology (journ.) (SAUS)
JHP .... Peabody Institute of Johns Hopkins University, Conservatory Library Baltimore (SAUO)
JHP .... Peabody Institute of Johns Hopkins University, Conservatory Library, Baltimore, MD [*OCLC symbol*] (OCLC)
JHPC .... Jim Hielms Private Coll'n [*NASDAQ symbol*] (TTSB)
JHPC .... Jim Hjelms Private Collection [*NASDAQ symbol*] (SPSG)
JHPC .... JLM Couture [*NYSE symbol*] (SG)
JHPN .... Journal of Hospice and Palliative Nursing (SAUO)
JHPPL .... Journal of Health Politics, Policy and Law (SAUO)
JHPS .... Japan Hydraulics and Pneumatics Society (SAUO)
JHPS .... Judaica Historical Philatelic Society (EA)
JHQ .... Job Hazards Questionnaire (SAUS)
JHQ .... Joint Headquarters [*British military*] (DMA)
JHQ .... Shute Harbour [*Australia*] [*Airport symbol*]
JHR .... Jarisch-Herxheimer Reaction [*Immunology*] (DAVI)
JHR .... Journal Holdings Report (AEPA)
JHR .... Journal of Human Resources (journ.) (SAUS)
JHRP .... Joint Highway Research Project [*Purdue University*] [*Research center*] (RCD)
JHS .... Hancock, John, Income Securities Trust [*NYSE symbol*] (SAG)
JHS .... Jesus Hominum Salvator [*Jesus, Savior of Men*] (ROG)
JHS .... Jewish History Series (journ.) (SAUS)
JHS .... Job History System [*Computer science*] (HODG)
JHS .... Job Hunter's Sourcebook [*A publication*]
JHS .... John Hampden Society (BUAC)
JHS .... John Hancock Income Securities Trust [*NYSE symbol*] (SPSG)
JHS .... John Hancock Inc. Sec [*NYSE symbol*] (TTSB)
JHS .... John Howard Society (SAUO)
JHS .... Journal of Hellenic Studies [*A publication*] (ABAR)
JHS .... Judaic Heritage Society (SAUO)
JHS .... Junior High School
JHS .... School of Advanced International Studies Johns Hopkins University (SAUO)
JHS .... School of Advanced International Studies, Johns Hopkins University, Washington, DC [*OCLC symbol*] (OCLC)
JHS-AR ...... Journal of Hellenic Studies. Archaeological Reports (journ.) (SAUS)
JHSCW ...... Journal Historical Society of the Church in Wales (journ.) (SAUS)
JHSE .... JCI Health, Safety & Environmental Department (SAUO)
JHSE .... Jewish Historical Society of England
JHSEM ...... Jewish Historical Society of England. Miscellanies (journ.) (SAUS)
JHSET ...... Jewish Historical Society of England. Transactions (journ.) (SAUS)
JHSF .... Japan Health Sciences Foundation (BUAC)
JHSL .... John Hanson Savings Bank FSB [*NASDAQ symbol*] (COMM)
JHSM .... Jewish Historical Society of Michigan (EARSL)
JHSN .... Johnson Electronics, Inc. (SAUO)
JHSN .... Journal. Historical Society of Nigeria [*A publication*]
JHSPCW .... Journal. Historical Society of the Presbyterian Church of Wales (journ.) (SAUS)
JHSRLL ..... Johns Hopkins Studies in Romans Language and Literature (journ.) (SAUS)
JHSS .... Journal of History for Senior Students (journ.) (SAUS)
JHSSA .... Journal. Historical Society of South Australia (journ.) (SAUS)
JHSU .... Joint Helicopter Support Unit (SAUO)
JHSUR ...... Journal of Hand Surgery (journ.) (SAUS)
JHTR .... Japan High Tech Review [*Database*] [*Kyodo News International, Inc.*] [*Information service or system*] (CRD)
JHU .... Johns Hopkins University [*Maryland*]
JHU .... Journeymen Horseshoers of the United States and Canada [*International Union*] [*Equine term*] (TED)
JHU/AJE ..... American Journal of Epidemiology. Johns Hopkins University, School of Hygiene. Baltimore (SAUS)
JHU/APL .... John Hopkins University/Applied Physics Laboratory (SAUS)
JHU/APL .... Johns Hopkins University Applied Physics Laboratory [*Laurel, MD*]
J Huazhong Inst Tech... Journal. Huazhong Institute of Technology. English Edition (journ.) (SAUS)

J Huazhong Inst Technol... Journal. Huazhong Institute of Technology (journ.) (SAUS)
J Huazhong Univ Sci Tech... Journal. Huazhong University of Science and Technology. English Edition (journ.) (SAUS)
JHUC........ Journal. Hebrew Union College (journ.) (SAUS)
JHUCCP..... Johns Hopkins University Center for Communications Programs (SAUO)
JHU-CRSC... Johns Hopkins University - Center for Research in Scientific Communication (PDAA)
JHU-CRSC... Johns Hopkins University-Center for Research in Scientific Communication (SAUO)
JHU-DDB.... Johns Hopkins University - Dyslexia and Dysgraphia Batteries
JHU-DDB.... Johns Hopkins University-Dyslexica and Dysgraphica Batteries (SAUO)
JHUL........ Johns Hopkins University Library (SAUO)
J Human Res... Journal of Human Resources [*A publication*] (JLIT)
J Hum Behav Lrn... Journal of Human Behavior and Learning (journ.) (SAUS)
J Hum Evol... Journal of Human Evolution (journ.) (SAUS)
J Hum Hypertens... Journal of Human Hypertension (journ.) (SAUS)
J Hum Nut... Journal of Human Nutrition (journ.) (SAUS)
J Hum Relat... Journal of Human Relations (journ.) (SAUS)
J Hum Sci Technol Univ... Journal. Human Science and Technology University (journ.) (SAUS)
J Hunan Sci Technol Univ... Journal of Hunan Science and Technology University (journ.) (SAUS)
J Hunan Univ... Journal. Hunan University (journ.) (SAUS)
J Hung Vet Surg... Journal. Hungarian Veterinary Surgeons (journ.) (SAUS)
J Hunter Valley Research Foundrtion... Journal. Hunter Valley Research Foundation (journ.) (SAUS)
JHUP........ Johns Hopkins University Press
JHUSM...... Johns Hopkins University School of Medicine (SAUO)
JHU Studies... Johns Hopkins University. Studies in Historical and Political Science (journ.) (SAUS)
JHVA......... Jehovah (ROG)
JHVH........ Jehovah (ABBR)
JHW......... Jamestown [*New York*] [*Airport symbol*] (OAG)
JHW......... Jamestown, NY [*Location identifier*] [*FAA*] (FAAL)
JHW......... Johns Hopkins University, Welch Medical Library, Baltimore, MD [*OCLC symbol*] (OCLC)
JHWC........ Joint Hurricane Warning Center (CINC)
JHWH....... Jehovah (ADWA)
JHWRP...... Joint Hawaii Warm Rain Project (SAUO)
J Hyderabad Geol Surv... Journal. Hyderabad Geological Survey (journ.) (SAUS)
J Hydraul Div Amer Soc Civil Eng Proc... Journal. Hydraulics Division. Proceedings of the American Society of Civil Engineers (journ.) (SAUS)
J Hydraul Div Am Soc Civ Eng... Journal. Hydrautics Division. American Society of Civil Engineers (journ.) (SAUS)
J Hydraul Div Pr ASCE... Journal. Hydraulics Division. Proceedings of the American Society of Civil Engineers (journ.) (SAUS)
J Hydraul Eng... Journal of Hydraulic Engineering [*A publication*] (CABS)
J Hydraul Res... Journal of Hydraulic Research [*A publication*] (CABS)
J Hydr-E..... Journal Hydraulics Division. American Society of Civil Engineers (journ.) (SAUS)
J Hydrogeol... Journal of Hydrogeology (journ.) (SAUS)
J Hydroinf... Journal of Hydroinformatics [*A publication*] (PABS)
J Hydrol..... Journal of Hydrology [*A publication*] (CABS)
J Hydrol Amst... Journal of Hydrology (Amsterdam) [*A publication*] (PABS)
J Hydrol Eng... Journal of Hydrologic Engineering [*A publication*] (PABS)
J Hydrol Sci... Journal of Hydrological Sciences (journ.) (SAUS)
J Hydrometeorol... Journal of Hydrometeorology [*A publication*] (PABS)
J Hydronaut... Journal of Hydronautics (journ.) (SAUS)
J Hydrosci Hydraul Eng... Journal of Hydroscience and Hydraulic Engineering (journ.) (SAUS)
J Hyg Chem... Journal of Hygiene Chemistry (journ.) (SAUS)
J Hyg Chem... Journal of Hygienic Chemistry (journ.) (SAUS)
J Hyg Chem Soc Jpn... Journal. Hygienic Chemical Society of Japan (journ.) (SAUS)
J Hyogo Coll Med... Journal. Hyogo College of Medicine (journ.) (SAUS)
J Hypertens... Journal of Hypertension (journ.) (SAUS)
J Hypertens Suppl... Journal of Hypertension. Supplement (journ.) (SAUS)
JI............ Air Balear [*ICAO designator*] (ICDA)
JI............ Gull Air [*ICAO designator*] (AD)
JI............ Islamic Assembly (Bangladesh) [*Political party*] (PSAP)
JI............ Jamaat-i-Islami [*Pakistan*] [*Political party*] (FEA)
JI............ Japan Institute [*Defunct*] (EA)
JI............ Japan Interpreter (journ.) (SAUS)
JI............ Jazz Interactions (EA)
JI............ Jazz International
JI............ Jejunal Intestinal [*Medicine*] (DB)
JI............ Jejunoileitis [*Gastroenterology*] (DAVI)
JI............ Jejunoileostomy [*Gastroenterology*] (DAVI)
JI............ Jemaah Islamivah [*Government term*]
JI............ Jemaah Islamiya [*Government term*] (GA)
JI............ Jersey Institute
JI............ Jesness Inventory [*Psychology*]
JI............ Jet Express [*ICAO designator*] (AD)
JI............ Jet Interaction (RDA)
JI............ Jigging Information
JI............ Job Information (SAUS)
JI............ Job Instruction
JI............ Job Insurance [*Job Service*] (OICC)
ji............ Johnston Atoll [*MARC country of publication code*] [*Library of Congress*] (LCCP)
JI............ Joint Identification (DNAB)
JI............ Joint Implementation
JI............ Josephson Interferometer [*Optics*] (IAA)
JI............ Journal. American Musical Instrument Society (journ.) (SAUS)
JI............ Journal of Immunology (journ.) (SAUS)
JI............ Jump Instruction (SAUS)
JI............ Junction Isolation [*Electronics*]
JI............ Jupiter Inlet [*NASA*] (KSC)
JI............ Justice, Inc. (SAUS)
JIA.......... Japanese Interchange Association (SAUO)
JIA.......... Jetstream International Airlines [*ICAO designator*] (FAAC)
JIA.......... Joint Industry Alliance [*Automotive manufacturing*]
JIA.......... Joint Interest Audiovisual Requirements (MCD)
JIA.......... Jordan International Airline
JIA.......... Journal of Industrial Archaeology (journ.) (SAUS)
JIA.......... Journal of International Affairs (journ.) (SAUS)
JIA.......... Jute Importers' Association [*British*] (DBA)
JIAA......... Joint Institute for Aeronautics and Acoustics [*Stanford University*] (PDAA)
JIAD......... Joint Integrated Avionics Directorate (DOMA)
JIAFS........ Joint Institute for Acoustics and Flight Sciences (MCD)
JIAFS........ Joint Institute for Advancement of Flight Science [*Research center*] (RCD)
Jiangsu Med J... Jiangsu Medical Journal (journ.) (SAUS)
JIAP......... Journal. Indian Academy of Philosophy (journ.) (SAUS)
JIAS......... Japan International Artists Society (SAUO)
JIAS......... Jewish Immigrant Aid Society (SAUO)
JIAS......... Jewish Immigration Aid Society (SAUO)
JIAS......... Journal. Indian Anthropological Society (journ.) (SAUS)
JIAS......... Journal of Inter-American Studies (SAUO)
JIAS......... Journal of Interamerican Studies and World Affairs (journ.) (SAUS)
JIASRA...... Journal. International Arthur Schnitzler Research Association (journ.) (SAUS)
JIAWG....... Joint Integrated Avionics Working Group [*DoD*]
JIB........... Djibouti [*Airport symbol*] (OAG)
JIB........... Foodmaker Inc. (SAUO)
JIB........... Jack-in-the-Box Dummy [*CIA*]
JIB........... Japan International Bank (SAUO)
JIB........... Jejunoileal Bypass [*Gastroenterology*] (DAVI)
JIB........... Jewish Information Bureau [*Defunct*] (EA)
JIB........... Job Information Block [*Computer science*] (BUR)
JIB........... Jobs Impact Bulletin [*National Committee for Full Employment*] [*A publication*]
JIB........... Joint Industry Board for the Electrical Contracting Industry (HEAS)
JIB........... Joint Information Bureau [*Military*] (MCD)
JIB........... Joint Intelligence Bureau [*British*] (MCD)
JIB........... Jordan Information Bureau (EA)
JIB........... Journal of International Business Studies [*A publication*] (BRI)
JIB........... Journal of the Institute of Bankers [*A publication*] (SAFN)
JIBA......... Japanese Institute of Business Administration (BUAC)
JIBA......... Japan Institute of Business Administration (SAUO)
JIBC......... Japan International Biological Program (SAUS)
JIBECI....... Joint Industry Board for the Electrical Contracting Industry (BUAC)
JIBEI........ Joint Industry Board of the Electrical Industry (EA)
JIBF......... Jerusalem International Book Fair (SAUO)
JIBG......... Jibing (ABBR)
JIBICO...... Japan International Bank and Investment (BUAC)
JIBICO...... Japan International Bank and Investment Co. (SAUS)
JIBL......... Journal of International Banking Law [*A publication*] (SAFN)
JIBP......... Japan International Biological Programme (SAUO)
JI Brewing... Journal. Institute of Brewing (journ.) (SAUS)
JIBS......... Journal of Indian and Buddhist Studies (journ.) (SAUS)
Jibuti........ Djibouti (SAUS)
JIC........... Japan Information Center (SAUS)
JIC........... Japan International Cooperation (SAUS)
JIC........... Jet Induced Circulation (SAUS)
JIC........... Jet-Induced Circulation [*Combustor*]
JIC........... Jet Induced Combustion (SAUS)
JIC........... Jet Interaction Control (MCD)
JIC........... Jewelry Industry Council (EA)
JIC........... Jewelry Information Center (NTPA)
JIC........... Job Information Card (SAUS)
JIC........... Job Information Centre [*Canada*]
JIC........... Job Instruction and Communication (PDAA)
JIC........... Joint Ice Center [*US Navy*] [*Marine science*] (OSRA)
JIC........... Joint Imperial Committee (SAUO)
JIC........... Joint Implementation Committee [*Military*] (SAA)
JIC........... Joint Industrial Company (SAUO)
JIC........... Joint Industrial Council [*Defunct*] (EA)
JIC........... Joint Industry Committee (SAUO)
JIC........... Joint Industry Conference (SAUS)
JIC........... Joint Industry Council (EAIO)
JIC........... Joint Information Center (SAUO)
JIC........... Joint Insurance Committee [*under the Trading with the Enemy Act*] [*World War II*]
JIC........... Joint Intelligence Center
JIC........... Joint Intelligence Committee
JIC........... Joint Intelligence Curriculum (SAUO)
JIC........... Joint Interrogation Center (MCD)
JIC........... Joint Iron Council (SAUO)
JIC........... Journal of Internet Cataloging [*Publication*]
JIC........... Junior International Club (EA)
JIC........... Just in Case (WDMC)
JIC........... Juventudes Inconformes de Colombia [*Political party*] (EY)
JIC........... Morgan Stanley Group, Inc. [*AMEX symbol*] (SAG)

JIC .... Tol [*Language symbol*] (ETLW)
JICA .... Japan International Cooperation Agency
JICA .... Jiangsu Provincial Institute of Culture and Art [*China*] (BUAC)
JICA .... Joint Intelligence Center, Africa
JICA .... Joint Intelligence Collecting Agency
JICACBI ..... Joint Intelligence Collecting Agency, China, Burma, India [*World War II*]
JICAME...... Joint Intelligence Collecting Agency, Middle East [*World War II*]
JICANA...... Joint Intelligence Collecting Agency, North Africa [*World War II*]
JICARC...... Joint Intelligence Collecting Agency, Reception Committee [*Navy*]
JICC .... Japanese ICC (SAUO)
JICC .... Japan Information and Cultural Centre (BUAC)
JICC .... Job Item Cost Code (MCD)
JICC .... Joint Interservice Coordinating Committee (SAUO)
JICCAR...... Joint Industry Committee for Cable Audience Research [*Television*] [*British*]
JICG .... Joint International Coordination Group (MSC)
JICGI .... Joint Industrial Council for the Gas Industry (SAUO)
JICHS......... Joint Industrial Conference on Hydraulic Standards
J Ichthyol... Journal of Ichthyology (journ.) (SAUS)
JICI .... Jeunesse Independante Chretienne Internationale [*International Independent Christian Youth - IICY*] (EA)
JICJ.......... Journal. International Commission of Jurists [*A publication*] (DLA)
Jick Est ..... Jickling. Legal and Equitable Estates [*1829*] [*A publication*] (DLA)
JICMARS.... Joint Industry Committee of Medical Advertisers for Readership Surveys (BUAC)
JICMB .... Joint Interface Configuration Management Board (SAUO)
JICNARS .... Joint Industry Committee for National Readership Surveys [*British*]
JICOA........ Japan Information and Communication Association [*Information service or system*] (IID)
JICPAC ...... Joint Intelligence Center Pacific (DOMA)
JICPAR ...... Joint Industry Committee for Postal Audience Research (BUAC)
JICPAS ...... Joint Industry Committee for Poster Audience Surveys [*British*]
JICPOA...... Joint Intelligence Center, Pacific Ocean Areas
JICP/PO ..... Joint International Climate Projects/Planning Office (SAUO)
JICRAR...... Joint Industry Committee for Radio Audience Reserach (BUAC)
JICRAR...... Joint Industry Committee for Radio Audience Research [*British*]
JICS .... Joint Intelligence Coordination Staff [*Central Intelligence Agency*] (AABC)
JICS .... Joint Interpreting and Conference Service (BUAC)
JICST........ Japan Information Center for Science and Technology
JICST........ Japan Information Center of Science and Technology [*Tokyo*] (IID)
JICST........ Japan International Center of Science and Technology (USGC)
JICT.......... Japan Information Center of Science and Technology (SAUO)
JICTAR ...... Joint Industry Committee for Television Advertising Research [*Database producer*]
JICUF........ Japan International Christian University Foundation (EA)
JID .... Air Condal SA [*Spain*] [*ICAO designator*] (FAAC)
JID .... Journal of Infectious Diseases (journ.) (SAUS)
JID .... Journal of Investigative Dermatology (journ.) (SAUS)
JIDA .... Japan Industrial Designers Association (BUAC)
JIDA .... Jewelry Industry Distributors Association (EA)
J Idaho Acad Sci... Journal. Idaho Academy of Science (journ.) (SAUS)
JIDC .... Jamaica Industrial Development Corp. (BUAC)
JIdeD........ Inter-American Defense Board (SAUO)
JIDS .... Job Information Delivery System [*US Employment Service*] [*Department of Labor*]
JIDSDP...... Journal. Idaho Academy of Science (journ.) (SAUS)
JIDXA........ Journal. Indiana State Medical Association (journ.) (SAUS)
JIE .... Japan Information Exchange [*Comtex Scientific Corp.*] [*Information service or system*] [*Defunct*] (CRD)
JIE .... Jobs in Energy (EA)
JIE .... Journal of Industrial Economics (journ.) (SAUS)
JIE .... Journal of International Economics (journ.) (SAUS)
JIE .... Junior Institute of Engineers
JIEA.......... Japan Industrial Explosives Association (BUAC)
JI/EC......... Joint Interrogation/Exploitation Center (SAUS)
JIECh .... Journal of Industrial and Engineering Chemistry (journ.) (SAUS)
JIEE.......... Japanese Institute of Electrical Engineers
JIEE.......... Japanese Institution of Electrical Engineers (SAUS)
JIEE.......... Joint Institute for Energy and Environment [*University of Tennessee, Knoxville*] (RCD)
JIEE.......... Journal of the Institution of Electrical Engineers (SAUO)
J IEE......... Journal of the Institution of Electrical Engineers (journ.) (SAUS)
JIEEJ......... Journal of the Institute of Electrical Engineers of Japan (SAUO)
JIEEJ .... Journal of the Institute of Electrical Engineers of Japan (journ.) (SAUS)
JIEO .... Joint Interoperability and Engineering Organization [*DoD*]
JIEO .... Joint Interoperability Engineering Organization (SAUS)
JIEP.......... Joint Intelligence Estimate for Planning (AFM)
JIES.......... Joint Interoperability Evaluation System (SAUO)
JIES.......... Journal of Indo-European Studies (journ.) (SAUS)
JIF .... French Lick, IN [*Location identifier*] [*FAA*] (FAAL)
JIF .... Janus Information Facility [*Later, J2CP Information Services*] (EA)
JIF .... Jet Interaction Fuel
JIF .... Job Information Form (SAUS)
JIF .... Joint Integrated Firepower [*Task force*] (MCD)
JIF .... Joint Interrogation Facility (DOMA)
JIF .... Journal of Information Systems Management (journ.) (SAUS)
JIF .... JPEG Interchange Format (SAUS)
JIFA.......... Japanese Institute for Foreign Affairs (BUAC)
JIFA.......... Japan Institute of Foreign Affairs (SAUS)
JIFC.......... Janis Ian Fan Club (EA)
JIFC.......... Julio Iglesias Fan Club [*Defunct*] (EA)
JIFDATS..... Joint In-Flight Data Acquisition and Transmission System (SAUS)
JIFDATS..... Joint In-Flight Data Transmission System [*Army*] (MCD)
JIFE.......... Junta Internacional de Fiscalizacion de Estupefacientes [*International Narcotics Control Board*]
JIFFQ........ Jiffy Foods Corp. (SAUO)
JIFS.......... Jerusalem Institute for Federal Studies (BUAC)
JIFSA........ Journal. Indian Academy of Forensic Sciences (journ.) (SAUS)
JIFSAN...... Joint Institute of Food Safety and Applied Nutrition
JIFTS........ Joint In-Flight Transmission System [*Army*] (IEEE)
JIFUA........ Journal. Institute of Fuel (journ.) (SAUS)
JIFY.......... Jiffy Industries (SAUS)
JIG........... Jigging (SAUS)
JIG........... Jinotega [*Nicaragua*] [*Seismograph station code, US Geological Survey*] (SEIS)
JIG........... Joint Implementation Committee (SAUO)
JIG........... Joint Industry Group [*An association*] (EA)
JIG........... Joint Intelligence Group [*Military*]
JIG........... Joule Impulse Generator [*Physics*]
JIG........... Journal of Irish Genealogy (journ.) (SAUS)
JIGC......... JIT Logistics [*Common carrier symbol*]
JIGFET...... Junction and Insulated Gate Field Effect Transistor (MCD)
JIGG......... Jet Interaction Gas Generator
JIGI.......... Java Interface for Geospatial Information (SAUO)
JIGL.......... Jiggle (ABBR)
JIGLD........ Jiggled (ABBR)
JIGLG........ Jiggling (ABBR)
JIGLY........ Jiggly (ABBR)
JIGR......... Jigger (ABBR)
JIGS......... Joule Impulse Generator System [*Physics*]
JIGTSC...... Joint Industry-Government Tall Structures Committee
JIH........... Joint Interval Histogram [*Histology*] (DAVI)
JIH........... Journal of Indian History (journ.) (SAUS)
JIH........... Journal of Interdisciplinary History [*A publication*] (BRI)
JIHI.......... John Innes Horticultural Institution (SAUO)
JIHIR........ Joint Institute for Heavy Ion Research (SAUO)
JIHTA........ Journal of Industrial Hygiene and Toxicology (journ.) (SAUS)
JIHVE........ Journal. Institution of Heating and Ventilating Engineers (journ.) (SAUS)
JII............ John Innes Institute [*British*] (ARC)
JII............ Johnston Industries [*NYSE symbol*] (TTSB)
JII............ Johnston Industries, Inc. [*NYSE symbol*] (COMM)
JIIA.......... Japan Institute of International Affairs (BUAC)
JIIB.......... Jewish Immigrants Information Bureau (BJA)
JIIG-CAL.... Job Ideas and Information Generator - Computer Assisted Learning (AIE)
JIII........... Japan Institute of Invention and Innovation (BUAC)
JIIKS......... Joint Imagery Interpretation Key Structure (MCD)
JIIM.......... Journal of Information and Image Management (journ.) (SAUS)
JIIP.......... Joint Interface Implementation Program [*Army*] (MCD)
JIISC......... Joing Industrial Investment Service Center (SAUS)
JIIST......... Japan Institute for International Studies and Training
Jikeitai Med J... Jikeikai Medical Journal (journ.) (SAUS)
JIL........... George Washinglon Journal of International Law and Economics (journ.) (SAUS)
JIL........... Jet-Induced Lift
JIL........... Journal of Irish Literature (journ.) (SAUS)
JIL........... Joy Industries Ltd. [*Vancouver Stock Exchange symbol*]
JILA.......... Japanese Institute of Landscape Architects (BUAC)
JILA.......... Joint Institute for Laboratory Astrophysics [*University of Colorado, National Bureau of Standards*] (EA)
JILA-IC...... Joint Institute for Laboratory Astrophysics-Information Center [*University of Colorado*] (PDAA)
JILA IniCent Rep... Joint Institute for Laboratory Astrophysics. Informatinn Center. Report (journ.) (SAUS)
JILE.......... Joint Intelligence Liaison Element (MCD)
JILEA........ Journal. Institution of Locomotive Engineers (journ.) (SAUS)
JILI.......... Journal. Indian Law Institute (journ.) (SAUS)
JilinCh....... Jilin Chemical Industrial Co. Ltd. [*Associated Press*] (SAG)
JILL.......... J Jill Group [*NASDAQ symbol*]
JILL.......... Jobs Illustrated [*CD-ROM*]
JillEnt....... Jillians Entertainment Corp. [*Associated Press*] (SAG)
J Illum Eng Inst Jap... Journal. Illuminating Engineering Institute of Japan (journ.) (SAUS)
J Illum Eng Inst Jpn... Journal of the Illuminating Engineering Institute of Japan (journ.) (SAUS)
J Illum Eng Soc... Journal of the Illuminating Engineering Society (journ.) (SAUS)
JILM......... Japan Institute of Light Metals (SAUS)
JILO......... Joint Information Liaison Office [*Military*]
JILSMT...... Joint Integrated Logistics Support Management Team (ACAE)
JILSP........ Joint Integrated Logistic Support Plan (ACAE)
JILTA........ Journal. Indian Law Teachers Association [*A publication*] (DLA)
JIM.......... Jakarta Informal Meetings (SAUS)
JIM.......... Japan Institute of Metals (SAUO)
JIM.......... Jevreiski Istoriski Muzej (BJA)
JIM.......... Jimma [*Ethiopia*] [*Airport symbol*] (OAG)
JIM.......... Job Information Memorandum (SAUS)
JIM.......... Job Instruction Manual
JIM.......... Journal of Information Management (journ.) (SAUS)
JIM.......... Journal of Investigative Medicine (SAUO)
JIM.......... Junctor Isolated Monolithic (SAUS)
JIM.......... Junior Index of Motivation (SAUS)
JIM.......... Memphis, TN [*Location identifier*] [*FAA*] (FAAL)
JIM.......... Sark International Airways Ltd. [*British*] [*ICAO designator*] (FAAC)
JIMA......... Japan Industrial Management Association (BUAC)
JIMA......... JDS Interface Method of Access (SAUS)
JIMA......... Jim Dandy [*NCIC trailer make code*]

JIMA......... John Innes Manufacturers Association (DBA)
J IMA........ Journal. Islamic Medical Association of the United States and Canada (journ.) (SAUS)
JIMA......... Journal of the Indian Medical Associations (journ.) (SAUS)
JIMA......... Journal of the Israel Medical Association (journ.) (SAUS)
J Imaging Sci... Journal of Imaging Science (journ.) (SAUS)
J Imaging Sci Technol... Journal of Imaging Science and Technology [*A publication*] (CABS)
J Imaging Technol... Journal of Imaging Technology (journ.) (SAUS)
JIMAR....... Joint Institute for Marine and Atmospheric Research [*Honolulu, HI*] [*National Oceanic and Atmospheric Administration*] (GRD)
JIMC......... Japan Immuno-Monitoring Centre (BUAC)
JIMD......... Jim & Dave's Trailer Manufacturing [*NCIC trailer make code*]
JIMEA....... Journal. Institute of Metals (journ.) (SAUS)
JIMG......... Jim Glo Trailers [*NCIC trailer make code*]
JIMGA....... Journal of Immunogenetics (journ.) (SAUS)
J Img Guided Surg... Journal of Image Guided Surgery (journ.) (SAUS)
JIMI.......... Jimi Hendrix Information Management Institute (EA)
JIMIS........ Japan Institute of Metals International Symposium (SAUS)
J Immunoassay... Journal of Immunoassay (journ.) (SAUS)
J Immunopharmacol... Journal of Immunopharmacology (journ.) (SAUS)
J Immunother... Journal of Immunotherapy (journ.) (SAUS)
J Immunother Emphasis Tumor Immunol... Journal of Immunotherapy with Emphasis on Tumor Immunology (journ.) (SAUS)
JIMO......... Joint Institute for Marine Observations [*University of California, San Diego*] (RCD)
JIMP......... Center for the Study of Japanese Industry and Management of Technology (SAUO)
JIMPACS.... Joint Improved Multimission Payload Aerial Surveillance Combat Survivable (ACAE)
J Imp Coll Chem Eng S... Journal. Imperial College. Chemical Engineering Society (journ.) (SAUS)
J Imp Coll Chem Soc... Journal. Imperial College. Chemical Society (journ.) (SAUS)
JIMPP....... Joint Industrial Mobilization Planning Process [*Environmental science*] (COE)
JIMR......... Journal of International Medical Research (SAUO)
JIMS......... Jim's Trailer Shop [*NCIC trailer make code*]
JIMS......... Job Information Matrix System
JIMS......... Joint Industrial Measurement Programme (ACII)
JIMS......... Journal. Indian Mathematical Society (journ.) (SAUS)
JIMS......... Journal of Indian Mathematical Society (journ.) (SAUS)
JIMS......... Jukebox Interface Management System (ACAE)
JIMSA....... Journal. Irish Medical Association (journ.) (SAUS)
JIMSDZ..... Journal of Interdisciplinary Modeling and Simulation (journ.) (SAUS)
JIMTOF...... Japan International Machine Tool Fair (SAUS)
JIMU......... Mitchell Leasing [*Intermodal shipping container symbol*] (TVRC)
JIN........... Japanese Institution of Navigation (BUAC)
JIN........... Japan Institute of Navigation (SAUS)
JIN........... Jindabyne [*Australia*] [*Seismograph station code, US Geological Survey*] [*Closed*] (SEIS)
JIN........... Jinja [*Uganda*] [*Airport symbol*] (AD)
JIN........... Joint Implementation Network (CARB)
JIN........... Jump Indirectly [*Computer science*]
JIN........... Justice Institute of British Columbia, Instructional Service [*UTLAS symbol*]
JINBA........ Journal. Institute of Brewing (journ.) (SAUS)
J Inc Aust Insurance Inst... Journal. Incorporated Australian Insurance Institute (journ.) (SAUS)
J Inc Brew Guild... Journal. Incorporated Brewers Guild (journ.) (SAUS)
J Inc Clerks Works Ass GB... Journal. Incorporated Clerks of Works Association of Great Britain (SAUO)
J Inc Clerks Works Ass GB... Journal. Incorporated Clerks of Works Association of Great Britain (journ.) (SAUS)
J Inclusion Phenom Mol Recognit Chem... Journal of Inclusion Phenomena and Molecular Recognition in Chemistry (journ.) (SAUS)
J Income Distribution... Journal of Income Distribution [*A publication*] (JLIT)
J Ind Arts Ed... Journal of Industrial Arts Education (journ.) (SAUS)
J Ind Ch S... Journal. Indian Chemical Society (journ.) (SAUS)
J Ind Ecol... Journal of Industrial Ecology [*A publication*] (PABS)
J Ind Econ... Journal of Industrial Economics (journ.) (SAUS)
J Ind Eng... Journal of Industrial Engineering (journ.) (SAUS)
J Ind Hyg... Journal of Industrial Hygiene (journ.) (SAUS)
J Indian Acad Dent... Journal. Indian Academy of Dentistry (journ.) (SAUS)
J Indian Acad Geosci... Journal. Indian Academy of Geoscience (journ.) (SAUS)
J Indian Acad Sci... Journal. Indian Academy of Sciences (journ.) (SAUS)
J Indian Acad Wood Sci... Journal. Indian Academy of Wood Science (journ.) (SAUS)
J Indian Acad Wood Sci... Journal of the Indian Academy of Wood Science (SAUO)
J Indian Acad Wood Sci... Journal of the Indian Academy of Wood Science (journ.) (SAUS)
J Indiana Dent Assoc... Journal. Indiana Dental Association (journ.) (SAUS)
J Indiana MA... Journal. Indiana State Medical Association (journ.) (SAUS)
J Indianap Dist Dent S... Journal. Indianapolis District Dental Society (journ.) (SAUS)
J Indian Assoc Commun Dis... Journal. Indian Association for Communicable Diseases (journ.) (SAUS)
JIndiana State MedAssoc... Journal of Indiana State Medical Association (SAUO)
J Indiana State Med Assoc... Journal of Indiana State Medical (journ.) (SAUS)
J Indian Bot Soc... Journal of the Indian Botanical Society (SAUO)
J Indian Bot Soc... Journal of the Indian Botanical Society (journ.) (SAUS)
J Indian Ceram Soc... Journal. Indian Ceramic Society (journ.) (SAUS)
J Indian Chem Soc... Journal. Indian Chemical Society (journ.) (SAUS)
J Indian Chem Soc... Journal of the Indian Chemical Society (SAUO)
J Indian Chem Soc... Journal of the Indian Chemical Society (journ.) (SAUS)
J Indian Chem Soc Ind News Ed... Journal. Indian Chemical Society. Industrial and News Edition (journ.) (SAUS)
J Indian Dent Assoc... Journal. Indian Dental Association (journ.) (SAUS)
JIndian Dent Assoc... Journal of the Indian Dental Association (SAUO)
J Indian Dent Assoc... Journal of the Indian Dental Association (journ.) (SAUS)
J Indian Geophys Union... Journal. Indian Geophysical Union (journ.) (SAUS)
J Indian Gesci Assoc... Journal. Indian Geoscience Association (journ.) (SAUS)
J Indian Ind Labour... Journal of Indian Industries and Labour (journ.) (SAUS)
J Indian Inst Sci... Journal of the Indian Institute of Science (journ.) (SAUS)
J Indian Inst Sci A... Journal of the Indian Institute of Science A (journ.) (SAUS)
J Indian Inst Sci B... Journal of the Indian Institute of Science B (journ.) (SAUS)
J Indian Inst Sci C... Journal of the Indian Institute of Science C (journ.) (SAUS)
J Indian Inst Sci Sect A... Journal. Indian Institute of Science. Section A (journ.) (SAUS)
J Indian Inst Sci Sect B... Journal. Indian Institute of Science. Section B (journ.) (SAUS)
J Indian Leather Technol Assoc... Journal. Indian Leather Technologists Association (journ.) (SAUS)
J Indian Math Soc... Journal. Indian Mathematical Society (journ.) (SAUS)
J Indian Med Assoc... Journal of the Indian Medical Association (SAUO)
J Indian Med Assoc... Journal of the Indian Medical Associations (journ.) (SAUS)
J Indian Med Prof... Journal of the Indian Medical Profession (journ.) (SAUS)
J Indian Nat Soc Soil Mech Found Eng... Journal. Indian National Society of Soil Mechanics and Foundation Engineering (journ.) (SAUS)
J Indian Pediatr Soc... Journal. Indian Pediatric Society (journ.) (SAUS)
J Indian Plywood Ind Res Inst... Journal. Indian Plywood Industries Research Institute (journ.) (SAUS)
J Indian Potato Assoc... Journal. Indian Potato Association (journ.) (SAUS)
J Indian Refract Makers Asc... Journal of Indian Refractory Makers Association (journ.) (SAUS)
J Indian Refract Makers Ass... Journal. Indian Refractory Makers Association (journ.) (SAUS)
J Indian Roads Congr... Journal. Indian Roads Congress (journ.) (SAUS)
J Indian Soc Pedod Prev Dent... Journal. Indian Society of Pedodontics and Preventive Dentistry (journ.) (SAUS)
J Indian Soc Soil Sci... Journal. Indian Society of Soil Science (journ.) (SAUS)
J Indian Soc Statist Oper Res... Journal. Indian Society of Statistics and Operations Research (journ.) (SAUS)
J Indian State Med Assoc... Journal. Indiana State Medical Association (journ.) (SAUS)
J Indian Statist Assoc... Journal. Indian Statistical Association (journ.) (SAUS)
J Indian Waterworks Assoc... Journal of the Indian Waterworks Association (journ.) (SAUS)
J India Soc Eng... Journal. India Society of Engineers (journ.) (SAUS)
J Indina State Dent Assoc... Journal. Indiana State Dental Association (journ.) (SAUS)
J Ind Irradiat Technol... Journal of Industrial Irradiation Technology (journ.) (SAUS)
J Ind L Inst... Journal. Indian Law Institute [*A publication*] (DLA)
J Indn Acad Math... Journal Indian Academy of Mathematics (SAUS)
J Indn St A... Journal. Indian Statistical Association (journ.) (SAUS)
J Ind Philo... Journal of Indian Philosophy (journ.) (SAUS)
J Ind Pollut Control... Journal of Industrial Pollution Control [*A publication*] (PABS)
J Ind Pollut Control... Journal of Industrial Pollution Control (journ.) (SAUS)
J Ind R...... Journal of Industrial Relations [*A publication*]
J Ind Technol... Journal of Industrial Technology (journ.) (SAUS)
J Ind Trade... Journal of Industry and Trade (journ.) (SAUS)
J Indush Econ... Journal of Industrial Economics (journ.) (SAUS)
J Indust Hyg... Journal of Industrial Hygiene (journ.) (SAUS)
J Indust Rel... Journal of Industrial Relations [*A publication*]
J Industry Stud... Journal of Industry Studies [*A publication*] (JLIT)
JINEA........ Journal. Indian Chemical Society. Industrial and News Edition (journ.) (SAUS)
J Infect...... Journal of Infection (journ.) (SAUS)
J Infect Dis... Journal of Infectious Diseases (journ.) (SAUS)
J Inferential Deductive Biol... Journal of Inferential and Deductive Biology (journ.) (SAUS)
J InfImage Manage... Journal of Information and Image Management (journ.) (SAUS)
J Inflamm... Journal of Inflammation (journ.) (SAUS)
J Inf Process Cybern... Journal of Information Processing and Cybernetics (journ.) (SAUS)
J Inf Process Soc Jap... Journal. Information Processing Society of Japan (journ.) (SAUS)
J Inf Sci..... Journal of Information Science (journ.) (SAUS)
J Inf Sci Princ Pract... Journal of Information Science, Principles and Practice (journ.) (SAUS)
J Inf Syst Manage... Journal of Information Systems Management (journ.) (SAUS)
J Inf Technol... Journal of Information Technology (journ.) (SAUS)
J Infus Chemother... Journal of Infusional Chemotherapy (journ.) (SAUS)
JINGLD...... Jingled (ABBR)
JINGLG...... Jingling (ABBR)
J Inherit Metab Dis... Journal of Inherited Metabolic Disease (journ.) (SAUS)
J Inl Fish Soc India... Journal. Inland Fisheries Society of India (journ.) (SAUS)
J Inorg Mat... Journal of Inorganic Materials (journ.) (SAUS)
J Inorg Organomet Polym... Journal of Inorganic and Organometallic Polymers (journ.) (SAUS)
J INOR NUCL CHEM... Journal of Inorganic and Nuclear Chemistry [*A publication*] (WDAA)
JINR......... Joint Institute of Nuclear Research [*Dubna, USSR*]
JINS......... Japan Institute of Nuclear Safety (SAUO)
J Ins......... Journal of Insurance (journ.) (SAUS)
JINS......... Journal of the International Neuropsychological Society (SAUO)

JINS .... Juveniles in Need of Supervision [*Classification for delinquent children*]
JINSA........ Jewish Institute for National Security Affairs (EA)
Jinsen Med J... Jinsen Medical Journal (journ.) (SAUS)
J Inst Agric Resour Utiliz Chinju Agric Coll... Journal. Institute for Agricultural Resources Utilization. Chinju Agricultural College (journ.) (SAUS)
J Inst Anim Tech... Journal. Institute of Animal Technicians (journ.) (SAUS)
J Inst Brew... Journal. Institute of Brewing (journ.) (SAUS)
J Inst Brew Suppl... Journal. Institute of Brewing. Supplement (journ.) (SAUS)
J Inst Chem Irel... Journal. Institute of Chemistry of Ireland (journ.) (SAUS)
J Inst Civ Eng... Journal. Institution of Civil Engineers (journ.) (SAUS)
J Inst Comput Sci... Journal. Institution of Computer Sciences (journ.) (SAUS)
J Inst Def Stud Anal... Journal. Institute for Defence Studies and Analyses (journ.) (SAUS)
JINSTE ...... Junior Institution of Engineers [*British*]
J Inst Elec Eng Jpn... Journal. Institution of Electrical Engineers of Japan (journ.) (SAUS)
J Inst Elec Eng Part 1... Journal. Institution of Electrical Engineers. Part 1. General (journ.) (SAUS)
J Inst Electr Commun Eng Jap... Journal. Institute of Electrical Communication Engineers of Japan (journ.) (SAUS)
J Inst Electr Eng... Journal. Institute of Electrical Engineers (journ.) (SAUS)
J Inst Electr Eng... Journal. Institution of Electrical Engineers (journ.) (SAUS)
J Inst Electr Eng (1949-63)... Journal. Institution of Electrical Engineers (1949-63) [*A publication*]
J Inst Electr Eng (1889-1940)... Journal. Institution of Electrical Engineers (1889-1940) [*A publication*]
J Inst Electr Eng Part 2... Journal. Institution of Electrical Engineers. Part 2. Power Engineering (journ.) (SAUS)
J Inst Electr Eng Part 3... Journal. Institution of Electrical Engi- neers. Part 3. Radio and Communica- tion Engineering (journ.) (SAUS)
J Inst Electron Commun EngJap... Journal. Institute of Electronics and Communication Engineers of Japan (journ.) (SAUS)
J Inst Electron Inf Commun Eng... Journal of the Institute of Electronics, Information and Communication Engineers (journ.) (SAUS)
J Inst Electron Radio Eng... Journal of the Institution of Electronic and Radio Engineers (journ.) (SAUS)
J Inst Electron Telecommun... Journal of the Institution of Electronics and Telecommunication Engineers (journ.) (SAUS)
J Inst Electron Telecommun Eng... Journal Institution of Electronics and Telecommunication Engineers (journ.) (SAUS)
J Inst Electron Telecommun Eng... Journal of the Institution of Electronics and Telecommunications Engineering [*A publication*] (CABS)
J Inst Energy... Journal. Institute of Energy (journ.) (SAUS)
J Inst Energy... Journal of the Institute of Energy (journ.) (SAUS)
J Inst Eng Aust... Journal of the Institution of Engineers, Australia (SAUS)
J Inst Fuel... Journal of the Institute of Fuel (SAUO)
J Inst Fuel... Journal of the Institute of Fuel (journ.) (SAUS)
J Inst Fuel Suppl... Journal. Institute of Fuel. Supplement (journ.) (SAUS)
J Inst Gas Eng... Journal. Institution of Gas Engineers (journ.) (SAUS)
J Inst Gas Engrs... Journal. Institution of Gas Engineers (journ.) (SAUS)
J Inst Geol Vikram Univ... Journal. Institute of Geology. Vikram University (journ.) (SAUS)
J Inst Highw Eng... Journal. Institute of Highway Engineers (journ.) (SAUS)
J Inst Math Appl... Journal of the Institute of Mathematics and its Applications (journ.) (SAUS)
J Inst Met... Journal of the Institute of Metals with Bulletin and Metallurgical Abstracts (SAUO)
J Inst Met... Journal of the Institute of Metals with Bulletin and Metallurgical Abstracts (journ.) (SAUS)
J Inst Meth Appl... Journal of the Institute of Mathematics and its Applications (SAUO)
J Inst Met Suppl... Journal. Institute of Metals. Supplement (journ.) (SAUS)
J Inst Nav... Journal of the Institute of Navigation (journ.) (SAUS)
J Inst Navig... Journal. Institute of Navigation (journ.) (SAUS)
J Instn Eng Aust... Journal. Institution of Engineers of Australia. [*A publication*]
J Instn Heat Vent Engrs... Journal. Institution of Heating and Ventilating Engineers (journ.) (SAUS)
J Instn Highw Engrs... Journal. Institution of Highway Engineers (journ.) (SAUS)
J Instn Loc Engrs... Journal. Institution of Locomotive Engineers (journ.) (SAUS)
J Inst Nucl Eng... Journal of the Institution of Nuclear Engineers (SAUO)
J Inst Nucl Eng... Journal of the Institution of Nuclear Engineers (journ.) (SAUS)
J Inst Nucl Mater Manage... Journal. Institute of Nuclear Materials Management (journ.) (SAUS)
J Inst Pet... Journal. Institute of Petroleum (journ.) (SAUS)
J Inst Pet Absh... Journal. Institute of Petroleum. Abstracts (journ.) (SAUS)
J Inst Pet Technol... Journal. Institution of Petroleum Technologists (journ.) (SAUS)
J Inst Polytech Osaka City Univ... Journal. Institute of Polytechnics. Osaka City University (journ.) (SAUS)
J Inst Polytech Osaka City Univ Ser C... Journal. Institute of Polytechnics. Osaka City University. Series C. Chemistry (journ.) (SAUS)
J Inst Polytech Osaka City Univ Ser D... Journal. Institute of Polytechnics. Osaka City University. Series D. Biology (journ.) (SAUS)
J Inst Polytech Osaka City Univ Ser E... Journal. Institute of Polytechnics. Osaka City University. Series E. Engineering (journ.) (SAUS)
J Inst Polytech Osaka City Univ Ser G... Journal. Institute of Polytechnics. Osaka City University. Series G. Geoscience (journ.) (SAUS)
J Inst Prod Eng... Journal. Institution of Production Engineers (journ.) (SAUS)
J Inst Public Health Eng... Journal. Institution of Public Health Engineers (journ.) (SAUS)
J Inst Refract Eng... Journal of the Institute of Refractories Engineers (journ.) (SAUS)
J Instr Psychol... Journal of Instructional Psychology (journ.) (SAUS)
J Instrum Soc Am... Journal. Instrument Society of America (journ.) (SAUS)
J Instrum Soc India... Journal. Instrument Society of India (journ.) (SAUS)
J Inst Saf High Pressure Gas Eng... Journal. Institute of Safety of High Pressure Gas Engineering (journ.) (SAUS)
J Inst Sanit Eng... Journal. Institution of Sanitary Engineers (journ.) (SAUS)
J Inst Sci Tech Inf Czech Acad Agric... Journal. Institute for Scientific and Technical Information. Czechoslovak Academy of Agriculture (journ.) (SAUS)
J Inst Sci Technol... Journal. Institute of Science Technology (journ.) (SAUS)
J Inst Sewgae Purif... Journal. Institute of Sewage Purification (journ.) (SAUS)
J Inst Socioecon Stud... Journal. Institute for Socioeconomic Studies (journ.) (SAUS)
J Inst Telecommun Eng... Journal. Institution of Telecommunication Engineers (journ.) (SAUS)
J Inst Telecommun Eng... Journal of the Institution of Telecommunication Engineers (SAUO)
J Inst Telecommun Eng... Journal of the Institution of Telecommunication Engineers (journ.) (SAUS)
J Inst Telev Eng Jpn... Journal. Institute of Television Engineers of Japan (journ.) (SAUS)
J Inst Telev Eng Jpn... Journal of the Institute of Television Engineers of Japan (journ.) (SAUS)
J Inst Theoretical Econ... Journal of Institutional and Theoretical Economics [*A publication*] (JLIT)
J Inst Water Eng Environ Manage... Journal of the Institution of Water Engineers and Environmental Management (journ.) (SAUS)
J Inst Wood Sci... Journal of the Institute of Wood Science (journ.) (SAUS)
JINTACCS... Joint Interoperability Command and Control System (SAUS)
JINTACCS... Joint Interoperability of Tactical Command and Control Systems (MCD)
J Int Ad Pre Med... Journal. International Academy of Preventive Medicine (journ.) (SAUS)
J Int Ass Dent Child... Journal International Association of Dentistry for Children (journ.) (SAUS)
J Int Ass Math Geol... Journal International Association for Mathematical Geology (journ.) (SAUS)
J Int Biomed Inf Data... Journal of International Biomedical Information and Data (journ.) (SAUS)
J Int Bus Stud... Journal of International Business Studies [*A publication*] (JLIT)
JINTCCS .... Joint Interoperability of Tactical Command and Control Systems (DOMA)
J Int Compar Econ... Journal of International and Comparative Economics [*A publication*] (JLIT)
JINTD........ Journal of Industrial Technology. Myong-Ji University (journ.) (SAUS)
J Int Devel... Journal of International Development [*A publication*] (JLIT)
J Int Econ... Journal of International Economics [*A publication*] (JLIT)
J Int Econ Law... Journal of International Economic Law [*A publication*] (JLIT)
J Integral Equations... Journal of Integral Equations (journ.) (SAUS)
J Intell Rob Syst... Journal of Intelligent and Robotic Systems [*A publication*] (CABS)
J Intell Syst... Journal of Intelligent Systems (journ.) (SAUS)
J Intensiv Care Med... Journal of Intensive Care Medicine (journ.) (SAUS)
J Interamer Stud World Aff... Journal of Interamerican Studies and World Affairs [*A publication*] (JLIT)
J Interam Stud World Aff... Journal of Interamerican Studies and World Affairs (journ.) (SAUS)
J Interferon Res... Journal of Interferon Research (journ.) (SAUS)
J Internat Affairs... Journal of International Affairs (journ.) (SAUS)
J Intern Med... Journal of Internal Medicine (journ.) (SAUS)
J Int Fed Gynael Obstet... Journal. International Federation of Gynaecology and Obstetrics (journ.) (SAUS)
J Int Finan Markets Inst Money... Journal of International Financial Markets, Institutions and Money [*A publication*] (JLIT)
J Int Inst Aerial Surv Earth Sci... Journal. International Institute for Aerial Survey and Earth Sciences (journ.) (SAUS)
J Int Inst Sugar Beet Res... Journal. International Institute for Sugar Beet Research (journ.) (SAUS)
J Int'l & Comp L... Journal of International and Comparative Law [*A publication*] (DLA)
J Int'l Comm Jur... Journal. International Commission of Jurists [*A publication*] (DLA)
J Int'l L & Dipl... Journal of International Law and Diplomacy [*A publication*] (DLA)
J Int'l L & Pol... Journal of International Law and Politics [*A publication*] (DLA)
J Intl L & Pol... Journal of International Law and Politics (journ.) (SAUS)
J Int Market Market Res... Journal of International Marketing and Marketing Research (journ.) (SAUS)
J Int Money Financ... Journal of International Money and Finance. Guildford (journ.) (SAUS)
J Int Phonetic As... Journal. International Phonetic Association (journ.) (SAUS)
J Int Relations... Journal of International Relations (journ.) (SAUS)
J Int Res Commun... Journal of International Research Communications (journ.) (SAUS)
J Int Soc Leather Trades Chem... Journal. International Society of Leather Trades Chemists (journ.) (SAUS)
J Int Trade Econ Devel... Journal of International Trade and Economic Development [*A publication*] (JLIT)
J Investig Allergol Clin Immunol... Journal of Investigational Allergology and Clinical Immunology (journ.) (SAUS)
J Investig Med... Journal of Investigative Medicine (journ.) (SAUS)
J Invest Surg... Journal of Investigative Surgery (journ.) (SAUS)
J In Vitro Fert Enbryo Transf... Journal of In Vitro Fertilization and Embryo Transfer (journ.) (SAUS)
JIO.......... Joint Information Office [*Military*]
JIO.......... Joint Integration Office [*Department of Energy*] [*Albuquerque, NM*] (GAAI)
JIO.......... Joint Intelligence Organization (BUAC)
JIO.......... Ontario, CA [*Location identifier*] [*FAA*] (FAAL)
JIOA......... Joint Intelligence Objectives Agency (MCD)

JIOC .... Jensen Interceptor Owners Club (EA)
JIOP .... Joint Interface Operational Procedures (COE)
JIOS .... Journal of Information and Optimization Sciences (journ.) (SAUS)
J Iowa Acad Sci... Journal of the Iowa Academy of Sciences (journ.) (SAUS)
J Iow Acad Sci... Journal. Iowa Academy of Science (journ.) (SAUS)
J Iowa Med S... Journal. Iowa Medical Society (journ.) (SAUS)
J Iowa State Med Soc... Journal. Iowa State Medical Society (journ.) (SAUS)
JIP .... Jipijapa [*Ecuador*] [*Airport symbol*] (AD)
JIP .... Job Improvement Plan
JIP .... Job the Impatient (BJA)
JIP .... Join in Progress [*Broadcasting*] (WDMC)
JIP .... Joint Identifier Program (SAUO)
JIP .... Joint Impact Protection
JIP .... Joint Implementation Plan [*Military*]
JIP .... Joint Input
JIP .... Joint Input Processing (IEEE)
JIP .... Joint Installation Plan (AAG)
JIP .... Joint Interface Plan (ACAE)
JIP .... Joint Interface Program (SAUS)
JIP .... Joint Investment Plan (SAUO)
JIP .... Journal of Indian Philosophy (journ.) (SAUS)
JIPA.......... Journal. Indian Potato Association (journ.) (SAUS)
JIPA.......... Journal. International Phonetic Association (journ.) (SAUS)
JIPA.......... Journal of International Phonetic Association, London (SAUO)
JIP/AMD .... JIP/Areal Marketing Database [*Toyo Keizai Shinposha Co. Ltd.*] [*Japan*] [*Information service or system*] (CRD)
JIPC .... Joint Imagery Processing Complex (SAUS)
JIPC .... Joint Imagery Production Complex (DOMA)
JIPC .... Jordan Is Palestine Committee (EA)
JIPD .... JINTACCS Interoperability Planning Document (SAUO)
JIPDC........ Japan Iraq Petroleum Development Corporation (SAUO)
Jipdec........ Japanese Informations Processing Development Center (SAUO)
JIPDEC....... Japan Information Processing Development Center (NITA)
JIPEA........ Journal. Institute of Petroleum (journ.) (SAUS)
JIPEX........ Johannesburg International Philatelic Exhibition (SAUO)
JIPG .... Joint Interoperability Planners Group (SAUO)
JIPHA........ Journal of Insect Physiology (journ.) (SAUS)
JIPID .... Japanese International Protein Information Database
JIPID .... Japanese International Protein Sequence Database (SAUO)
JIPMER ..... Jawahrlal Institute of Postgraduate Medical Education and Research [*India*]
JIPNET ...... Japan Information Processing Network (SAUS)
JIPO .... Jordan Investment Promotion Office (SAUO)
JIPS .... JANET Internet Protocol Service (SAUS)
JIPS .... JANET IP Service (SAUS)
JIPS .... Japanese Information Processing Service (SAUO)
JIPS .... Joint Internet Protocol Service (SAUS)
JIR........... Jewish Institute of Religion
JIR........... Jiri [*Nepal*] [*Airport symbol*] (OAG)
JIR........... Job Improvement Request
JIR........... Joint Intelligence Room (SAUS)
JIR........... JOPES Information Requirements (SAUO)
JIR........... Journal of Industrial Relations (journ.) (SAUS)
JIR........... Journal of Irreproducible Results (journ.) (SAUS)
JIRA .... Japanese Industrial Robot Association (CIST)
JIRA .... Japan Industrial Robot Association (BUAC)
J Iraqi Chem Soc... Journal. Iraqi Chemical Society (journ.) (SAUS)
JIRC .... Journal of Information Research Communications [*British*] (NITA)
JIRCAS ...... Japan International Research Center for Agricultural Sciences (SAUO)
J Ir Coll Physicians Surg... Journal. Irish Colleges of Physicians and Surgeons (journ.) (SAUS)
JIRCSM ..... Joint Industry Research Committee for Standardization of Miniature Precision Coaxial Connectors
J Ir Dent Ass... Journal. Irish Dental Association (journ.) (SAUS)
JIREDJ ...... Journal of Interferon Research (journ.) (SAUS)
JIRI .... Johnson Informal Reading Inventory (EDAC)
J Irish CP... Journal. Irish Colleges of Physicians and Surgeons (journ.) (SAUS)
J Irish Lit... Journal of Irish Literature (journ.) (SAUS)
J Irish MA... Journal. Irish Medical Association (journ.) (SAUS)
J Ir Med Assoc... Journal. Irish Medical Association (journ.) (SAUS)
J Iron & Steel Eng... Journal of Iron and Steel Engineering (journ.) (SAUS)
J Iron Steel Assoc... Journal. Iron and Steel Association (journ.) (SAUS)
J Iron Steel Inst Jpn... Journal. Iron and Steel Institute of Japan (journ.) (SAUS)
J Iron Steel Inst Jpn... Journal of the Iron and Steel Institute of Japan (journ.) (SAUS)
J Iron Steel Inst West Scotl... Journal. Iron and Steel Institute of West Scotland (journ.) (SAUS)
JIRP .... Juneau Icefield Research Project [*University of Idaho*] [*Research center*]
J Irrig Drain Div; Amer Soc... Journal of the Irrigation and Drainage Division, Proceedings of the American Society (journ.) (SAUS)
J Irrig Drain Div Am Soc Civ Eng... Journal. Irrigation and Drainage Division. Proceedings of the American Society of Civil Engineers (journ.) (SAUS)
JIRS .... Jewish Information and Referral Service Directory [*A publication*] (EAAP)
JIRS .... Joint Information and Retrieval System [*DoD*] (MCD)
JIRV .... Jet Interaction Reentry Vehicle (SAUS)
JIS .... Jail Inspection Service (SAUO)
JIS .... Jamaica Information Service (BUAC)
JIS .... Japanese Industrial Standards
JIS .... Japanese Institute for Standards (SAUS)
JIS .... Japanese Institute of Standards (SAUS)
JIS .... Japan Industry Standard
JIS .... Japan Investment Service [*Reuters Holdings Ltd.*] [*British*] [*Information service or system*] (CRD)
JIS .... Jet Inlet System
JIS .... Jet Interaction Steering
JIS .... Jewish Information Society (SAUS)
JIS .... Jewish Information Society of America (EA)
JIS .... Job Information Service [*Department of Labor*]
JIS .... Job Information Station [*Department of Labor*] (IAA)
JIS .... Job Information System (NITA)
JIS .... Job Input Station (SAUS)
JIS .... Job Input Stream (SAUS)
JIS .... Job Input System (NITA)
JIS .... Joint Information System (SAUO)
JIS .... Joint Integrated Simulation (NASA)
JIS .... Joint Intelligence Staff
JIS .... Joint Interoperability System (SAUO)
JIS .... Joint Operations Interim Software (MCD)
JIS .... JOPS Interim System (SAUO)
JIS .... Journal of Information Science [*A publication*] (NITA)
JIS .... Journal of Insect Science
JIS .... Just-In-Sequence [*Manufacturing operations*]
JIS .... Juvenile Idiopathic Scoliosis [*Medicine*] (DMAA)
JISA .... Japan Industrial Safety Association (SAUO)
JISA .... Japan Information Service Association (SAUO)
JISAO........ Joint Institute for Study of the Atmosphere and Ocean [*Seattle, WA*] [*University of Washington, NOAA*] (GRD)
JISAO........ Joint Institute for the Study of the Atmosphere and Ocean (SAUO)
JISC .... Japanese Industrial Standards Committee [*Agency of Industrial Science and Technology, Ministry of International Trade and Industry*]
JISC .... Joint Implementation Steering Committee (SAUO)
JISC .... Joint Information Services Committee (BUAC)
JISC .... Joint Information Systems Committee [*British*] (TELE)
JISCII........ Japanese Industrial Standard Code for Information Interchange (SAUS)
JISCR........ Judicial Information System Committee Rules (SAUO)
JISEA........ Japan Iron and Steel Exporters Association (BUAC)
JISETA....... Joint Investigation of the Southeastern Tropical Atlantic [*Angola, US*] (MSC)
JISF.......... Japan Iron and Steel Federation (BUAC)
JISHA........ Japan Industrial Safety and Health Association (BUAC)
JISHS........ Journal of the Illinois State Historical Society (SAUO)
JISHS........ Journal of the Illinois State Historical Society (journ.) (SAUS)
JI/SI .... Jet Interaction / Secondary Injection
JISI .... Journal of Iron and Steel Industry (journ.) (SAUS)
J Islam & Comp L... Journal of Islamic and Comparative Law [*Nigeria*] [*A publication*] (DLA)
JIS-Link..... Judicial Information System (SAUO)
JISM.......... Jordan Institution for Standards and Metrology (SAUO)
JISO .... Japanese International Satellite Organization [*Cable-television system*]
JISP .... Jack Island State Park (SAUO)
JISPB........ Joint Intelligence Studies Publishing Board
JISR .... Joint Information Search and Retrieval (SAUO)
JISR .... Joint Information Search Unit Retrieval System (MCD)
J Isr Med Assoc... Journal. Israel Medical Association (journ.) (SAUS)
JISS .... Japan Intelligence Support System (SAUO)
JISS .... Jet Impurity Survey Spectrometer [*Nuclear energy*] (NUCP)
JISS .... Journal. Indian Sociological Society (journ.) (SAUS)
JISTA........ Journal of the Indian Scientific Translators Association (SAUO)
JISTEC....... Japan International Science and Technology Exchange Center
JIS Technique... Junction Insulated Schottky Technique (SAUS)
JISTIC .... Japan Iron and Steel Technical Information Center (SAUS)
JIT .... Frozen Food Express Industries, Inc. (SAUO)
JIT .... Jamiat-i-Talaba [*Pakistan*] [*Political party*] (PD)
JIT .... Jita [*Language symbol*] (ETLW)
JIT .... Job Information Table (TIMI)
JIT .... Job Information Test [*Military*] (AFM)
JIT .... Job Instruction Training
JIT .... Joint Interest Test [*Navy*] (NG)
JIT .... Just in Time
jit .... Just-In-Time [*Industry*] (ODBW)
JIT .... Just-in-Time Inventory (TDOB)
JITA.......... Japanese Industrial Technology Association
JITA.......... Jet Interaction Test Apparatus (MCD)
J Ital Dairy Sci Assoc... Journal. Italian Dairy Science Association (journ.) (SAUS)
JITC.......... Jewelry Industry Tax Committee [*Defunct*] (EA)
JITC.......... Joint Interoperability Technology Center (SAUO)
JITC.......... Joint Interoperability Test Center [*Military*]
JITC.......... Juneau Intergovernmental Training Council [*An association*] [*Alaska*] (ALAC)
JIT compiler... Just-in-Time Compiler [*Computer science*] (IGQR)
JITE.......... Journal. Institution of Telecommunication Engineers (journ.) (SAUS)
JITE.......... Journal of Institutional and Theoretical Economics (SAUO)
JITEC .... Joint Information Technology Experts Committee [*Open Systems Interconnection*] (ODAA)
JITF.......... Japan International Trade Fair (SAUO)
JITF.......... Joint Interface Test Facility [*Army*] (RDA)
JITF.......... Joint Interface Test Force [*Military*] (RDA)
JITF.......... Joint Interservice Task Force (MCD)
JITH .... Journal of Indian Textile History (journ.) (SAUS)
JITHA........ Journal of Ichthyology (journ.) (SAUS)
JITOL........ Just in Time Open Learning (SAUO)
JITP.......... Japan Intermodal Transport [*Common carrier symbol*]

JITPA........ Japanese International Trade Promotion Association (BUAC)
JITR........ Jitter (ABBR)
JITRBG...... Jitterbug (ABBR)
JITRY........ Jittery (ABBR)
JITS.......... Joint Interface Test System (SAUO)
JITT.......... Just-In Time Training (AGLO)
JITT.......... Just-in-Time Training (GART)
JIT/TQC..... Just-In-Time/Total Quality Control (SAUS)
JITUD........ Journal of Industrial Technology. Daegu University (journ.) (SAUS)
JIU.......... Joint Inspection Unit [*United Nations*]
JIU.......... Jones International University
JIVA.......... Joint Intelligence Virtual Architecture [*Military*]
JIVE.......... Joint Institute for VLBI in Europe (SAUS)
JIVPAZ...... Journal of Invertebrate Pathology(journ.) (SAUS)
JIW.......... J. Inglis Wright [*Advertising agency*] [*New Zealand*]
JIW.......... Jiwani [*Pakistan*] [*Airport symbol*] (OAG)
J Iwate Med Assoc... Journal. Iwate Medical Association (journ.) (SAUS)
JIWC......... Joint Industrial Whitley Council (SAUO)
JIWE......... Journal of Indian Writing in English (journ.) (SAUS)
JIWP......... Joint Interim Working Party
JIWSA....... Journal. Institute of Wood Science (journ.) (SAUS)
JJ............ Coddair Air East [*ICAO designator*] (AD)
JJ............ J & J Flatbed Trailer [*NCIC trailer make code*]
JJ............ Janet Jackson
JJ............ Jaw Jerk [*Medicine*]
JJ............ Jeep Junior [*Automobile model designation*]
JJ............ Jejunojejunostomy [*Gastroenterology*] (DAVI)
JJ............ Jennifer Jo [*In TV series "The Governor and JJ'*]
JJ............ Jews for Jews [*Defunct*] (EA)
JJ............ Josephson Junction [*Cryogenics*] (IAA)
JJ............ Judges [*Old Testament book*]
JJ............ Judges, Justices (SAUS)
JJ............ Jungle Jeep (SAUS)
JJ............ Junior Judge [*Legal term*] (DLA)
JJ............ Justices
JJ............ Just Joking (SAUS)
JJA.......... Jack and Jill of America (EA)
JJA.......... Journal of Judicial Administration [*A publication*] (SAFN)
JJA.......... Judges of Appeal [*Legal term*]
JJA.......... June-July-August [*Marine science*] (OSRA)
JJA.......... Justices of Appeal [*Legal term*] (DLA)
JJAF......... Jack and Jill of America Foundation (EA)
JJAMD...... Jaw Joints and Allied Musculo-Skeletal Disorders Foundation (EA)
J Jan Acad Surg Metab Nutr... Journal. Japan Academy of Surgical Metabolism and Nutrition (journ.) (SAUS)
JJAP......... Japanese Journal of Applied Physics (journ.) (SAUS)
JJAP......... Japan Society of Applied Physics (SAUO)
J Japanese Trade and Industry... Journal of Japanese Trade and Industry (journ.) (SAUS)
J Jap Ass Philos Sci... Journal. Japan Association for Philosophy of Science (journ.) (SAUS)
J Jap Biochem S... Journal. Japanese Biochemical Society (journ.) (SAUS)
J Jap Chem... Journal of Japanese Chemistry (journ.) (SAUS)
J Jap Soc Air Pol... Journal. Japan Society of Air Pollution (journ.) (SAUS)
J Jap Soc Food Nutr... Journal. Japanese Society of Food and Nutrition (journ.) (SAUS)
J Jap Soc Grassland Sci... Journal. Japanese Society of Grassland Science (journ.) (SAUS)
J Jap Soc Technol Plast... Journal. Japan Society for Technology of Plasticity (journ.) (SAUS)
J Jap S Powder Met... Journal. Japan Society of Powder and Powder Metallurgy (journ.) (SAUS)
J Jap Stud... Journal of Japanese Studies (journ.) (SAUS)
JJATS........ Journal of the Japanese Association for Thoracic Surgery (SAUS)
JJC........... Jackson Junior College [*Florida; Michigan*]
JJC........... James Jones Company (SAUO)
JJC........... Japanese Joint Committee (SAUS)
JJC........... Jiffy Junction Connector
JJC........... Joliet Junior College [*Illinois*]
JJC........... Juvenile Justice Center (SAUO)
JJC........... Juvenile Justice Clearinghouse (SAUS)
JJCCJ........ John Jay College of Criminal Justice (SAUO)
JJCL.......... Jadavpur Journal of Comparative Literature (journ.) (SAUS)
JJCRA........ Japanese Journal of Clinical Radiology (journ.) (SAUS)
JJDP.......... Juvenile Justice and Delinquency Prevention
JJDPA........ Juvenile Justice and Delinquency Prevention Act
JJE........... Japanese Journal of Ethnology (journ.) (SAUS)
J Jew Lore Ph... Journal of Jewish Lore and Philosophy (journ.) (SAUS)
JJ FAD....... Just Jammin' Fresh and Def [*Rap recording group*]
JJFC......... Jana Jae Fan Club (EA)
JJFC......... Jim and Jesse Fan Club (EA)
JJFC......... Joan Jett Fan Club (EA)
JJFC......... Johnny and Jack Fan Club (EA)
J Jgn Pap Pulp Assoc... Journal. Japan Paper and Pulp Association (journ.) (SAUS)
JJHL......... John Jay Hopkins Laboratory (SAUS)
JJHL......... John Jay Hopkins Laboratory for Pure and Applied Science (SAUO)
JJHS......... John Jay High School (SAUO)
JJHS......... John Jay Hopkins School (SAUS)
JJI........... Juanjui [*Peru*] [*Airport symbol*] (OAG)
J Jinsen Med Sci... Journal of Jinsen Medical Sciences (journ.) (SAUS)
JJITC........ Jayco Jafari International Travel Club (EA)
JJJ........... JJJ [*NCIC trailer make code*]
JJKQ......... Jack Jones Trucking [*Common carrier symbol*]
JJL........... Josephson Junction Logic (ELAL)
JJLD......... JJL Distribution Systems [*Common carrier symbol*]
JJM.......... John Judkyn Memorial (EA)
JJ Marsh (KY)... Marshall's Reports [*Kentucky*] [*A publication*] (DLA)
JJMAS....... Jack Jones Music Appreciation Society [*Defunct*] (EAIO)
JJN........... Jinjiang [*China*] [*Airport symbol*] (OAG)
JJN........... J.J.Newberry Company (SAUO)
JJO........... Mountain City, TN [*Location identifier*] [*FAA*] (FAAL)
J Johannesburg Hist Found... Journal. Johannesburg Historical Foundation (journ.) (SAUS)
JJOPA7...... Japanese Journal of Ophthalmology (journ.) (SAUS)
JJP........... Jatiya Janata Party [*National People's Party*] [*Bangladesh*] [*Political party*] (PPW)
JJP........... Journal of Juristic Papyrology (journ.) (SAUS)
JJPHDP..... Japanese Journal of Phycology (journ.) (SAUS)
J Jpn Air Clean Asc... Journal of the Japan Air Cleaning Association (journ.) (SAUS)
J Jpn Assoc Infect Dis... Journal. Japanese Association for Infectious Diseases (journ.) (SAUS)
J Jpn Assoc Phys Med Bineol Climatol... Journal. Japanese Association of Physical Medicine, Balneology and Climatology (journ.) (SAUS)
J Jpn Assoc Thorac Surg... Journal. Japanese Association for Thoracic Surgery (journ.) (SAUS)
J Jpn Boiler Assoc... Journal. Japan Boiler Association (journ.) (SAUS)
J Jpn Bot... Journal of Japanese Botany (SAUO)
J Jpn Bot... Journal of Japanese Botany (journ.) (SAUS)
J Jpn Chem... Journal of Japanese Chemistry (journ.) (SAUS)
J Jpn Chem Suppl... Journal of Japanese Chemistry. Supplement (journ.) (SAUS)
J Jpn Compos Mater... Journal of Japan Composite Materials (journ.) (SAUS)
J Jpn Dent Assoc... Journal. Japan Dental Association (journ.) (SAUS)
J Jpn Diabetes Soc... Journal. Japan Diabetes Society (journ.) (SAUS)
J Jpn Electr Assoc... Journal. Japan Electric Association (journ.) (SAUS)
J Jpn Health Phys Soc... Journal. Japan Health Physics Society (journ.) (SAUS)
J Jpn Hydraul Pneum Soc... Journal of the Japan Hydraulics and Pneumatics Society (journ.) (SAUS)
J Jpn Inst Light Met... Journal of the Japan Institute of Light Metals (journ.) (SAUS)
J Jpn Inst Met... Journal of the Japan Institute of Metals (journ.) (SAUS)
J Jpn Inst Nevig... Journal of the Japan Institute of Navigation (journ.) (SAUS)
J Jpn Obstet Gynecol... Journal. Japanese Obstetrics and Gynecology (journ.) (SAUS)
J Jpn Psychosom S... Journal. Japanese Psychosomatic Society (journ.) (SAUS)
J Jpn Sewage Works Assoc... Journal of the Japan Sewage Works Association (journ.) (SAUS)
J Jpn Soc Aeronaut Space Sci... Journal of the Japan Society for Aeronautical and Space Sciences (journ.) (SAUS)
J Jpn Soc Air Pollut... Journal of the Japan Society of Air Pollution (journ.) (SAUS)
J Jpn Soc Artf Intell... Journal of the Japanese Society for Artificial Intelligence (journ.) (SAUS)
J Jpn Soc Civ Eng... Journal of the Japan Society of Civil Engineers (journ.) (SAUS)
J Jpn Soc Colour Mater... Journal of the Japan Society of Colour Material (journ.) (SAUS)
J Jpn Soc Compos Mater... Journal of the Japan Society for Composite Materials (journ.) (SAUS)
J Jpn Soc Heat Treat... Journal of the Japan Society of Heat Treatment (journ.) (SAUS)
J Jpn Soc Lubr Eng... Journal of the Japan Society of Lubrication Engineers (journ.) (SAUS)
J Jpn Soc Mech Eng... Journal. Japan Society of Mechanical Engineers (journ.) (SAUS)
J Jpn Soc Powder Powder Metall... Journal of the Japan Society of Powder and Powder Metallurgy (journ.) (SAUS)
J Jpn Soc Precis Eng... Journal of the Japan Society of Precision Engineering (journ.) (SAUS)
J Jpn Soc Simul Technol... Journal of the Japan Society for Simulation Technology (journ.) (SAUS)
J Jpn Soc Strength Fract Mater... Journal of the Japanese Society for Strength and Fracture of Materials (journ.) (SAUS)
J Jpn Soc Technol Plast... Journal of the Japan Society for Technology of Plasticity (journ.) (SAUS)
J Jpn Soc Tribol... Journal Japanese Society of Tribologists (journ.) (SAUS)
J Jpn Soc Tribol... Journal of the Japanese Society of Tribologists (journ.) (SAUS)
J Jpn Stud... Journal of Japanese Studies (journ.) (SAUS)
J Jpn Sur Soc... Journal. Japanese Surgical Society (journ.) (SAUS)
J Jpn Vet Med Asc... Journal. Japan Veterinary Medical Association (journ.) (SAUS)
J Jpn Water Works Asc... Journal of the Japan Water Works Association (journ.) (SAUS)
J Jpn Weld Soc... Journal of the Japan Welding Society (journ.) (SAUS)
J Jpn Wood Res Soc... Journal of the Japan Wood Research Society (journ.) (SAUS)
JJPTP....... Joint Jet-Pilot Training Programme (SAUS)
JJRD......... J & J Railroad [*Federal Railroad Administration identification code*]
JJRX......... Joliet Junction Railroad [*Federal Railroad Administration identification code*]
JJS........... James Joyce Society (EA)
JJS........... Journal of Japanese Studies (journ.) (SAUS)
JJS........... Journal of Juridical Science [*A publication*] (SAFN)
JJS........... Jumping-JacksShoes, Inc. (SAUO)
JJSAAG..... Japanese Journal of Studies on Alcohol (journ.) (SAUS)
JJSC......... Jefferson Smurfit [*NASDAQ symbol*] (TTSB)
JJSC......... Jefferson Smurfit Corp. [*NASDAQ symbol*] (SAG)
JJSC......... Justices of the Supreme Court [*Legal term*] (DLA)
JJSC......... Juvenile Justice Standards Committee (SAUO)

JJSF .... J&J Snack Foods [*NASDAQ symbol*] (TTSB)
JJSF .... J & J Snack Foods Corp. [*NASDAQ symbol*] (NQ)
J-J S-S .... Jean-Jacques Servan-Schreiber [*French publisher*]
JJSSPA ...... Jewish Social Service Professionals Association (NTPA)
JJSTR .... Jetstream [*Weather codes - aviation*] (PIPO)
JJSU .... JJ Sietas Schiffswerft [*Intermodal shipping container symbol*] (TVRC)
JJSWC ...... Jiffy Junction Single Wire Connector
JJT .... Jerry James Trailers [*NCIC trailer make code*]
JJT .... Josephson Junction Transistor [*Electronics*] (AAEL)
JJT .... Jumbo Jet Transport
JJTCAR ...... Japanese Journal of Tuberculosis and Chest Diseases (journ.) (SAUS)
JJU .... Julienhaab [*Greenland*] [*Airport symbol*] (AD)
J Jur .... Journal of Jurisprudence [*A publication*] (DLA)
JJurP .... Journal of Juristic Papyrology [*A publication*] (ABAR)
J Jur Papyrol... Journal of Juristic Papyrology [*A publication*] (DLA)
J Juvenile Res... Journal of Juvenile Research (journ.) (SAUS)
J Juv L .... Journal of Juvenile Law (journ.) (SAUS)
JJW .... Sternair, Inc. [*FAA designator*] (FAAC)
JJWC .... Jiffy Junction Wire Connector
JJWFC .... Jerry Jeff Walker Fan Club (EA)
JJZOAP ...... Japanese Journal of Zoology (journ.) (SAUS)
JK .... Central Caribbean Air Ltd. (SAUO)
JK .... Flip-Flop Circuit [*Computer science*]
JK .... Jack (MSA)
JK .... Jammu & Kashmir [*Indian Railway*] (TIR)
JK .... J and K input (SAUS)
JK .... Jishu Kanri [*Voluntary Management*] [*Japanese method for increasing productivity of industrial workers by involving them in planning*]
J/K .... Joule per Kelvin [*Physics*]
J/K .... Joules per Kelvin (SAUS)
JK .... Jumper's Knee (MELL)
JK .... Junk [*Ship's rigging*] (ROG)
JK .... Just Kidding [*Online dialog*]
JK .... Sun World [*ICAO designator*] (AD)
JK .... Trabajos Aereos y Enlaces SA [*Spain*] [*ICAO designator*] (ICDA)
JKA .... Jakarta [*Indonesia*] (ABBR)
Jk^a .... Kidd A [*Blood group*] (DAVI)
JKAA .... Japan Karate Association of Australia
J Kagawa Nutr Coll... Journal. Kagawa Nutrition College (journ.) (SAUS)
JKAHS .... Journal. Kerry Archaeological and Historical Society (journ.) (SAUS)
J Kanagawa Odontol S... Journal. Kanagawa Odontological Society (journ.) (SAUS)
J Kanagawa Prefect J Coll Nutr... Journal. Kanagawa Prefectural Junior College of Nutrition (journ.) (SAUS)
J Kanazawa Med Univ... Journal. Kanazawa Medical University (journ.) (SAUS)
J Kan B Ass'n... Journal. Kansas Bar Association [*A publication*] (DLA)
JK & A ...... John Krucek & Associates [*Telecommunications service*] (TSSD)
J Kansai Med Univ... Journal. Kansai Medical University (journ.) (SAUS)
J Kansas Geol Surv... Journal. Kansas Geological Survey (journ.) (SAUS)
J Kans Dent Assoc... Journal. Kansas Dental Association (journ.) (SAUS)
J Kans Med Soc... Journal of the Kansas Medical Society (SAUO)
J Kans Med Soc... Journal of the Kansas Medical Society (journ.) (SAUS)
J Kans State Dent Assoc... Journal. Kansas State Dental Association (journ.) (SAUS)
J Kanto-Tosan Agr Exp Sta... Journal. Kanto-Tosan Agricultural Experiment Station (journ.) (SAUS)
J Karnatak Univ... Journal. Karnatak University (journ.) (SAUS)
J Karnatak Univ Hum... Journal. Karnatak University. Humanities (journ.) (SAUS)
J Karnatak Univ Sci... Journal. Karnatak University. Science (journ.) (SAUS)
J Karntak Univ Soc Sci... Journal. Karnatak University. Social Sciences (journ.) (SAUS)
J Karyopathol Esp Tumor Tumorvirus... Journal of Karyopathology Especially Tumor and Tumorvirus (journ.) (SAUS)
JKAS .... Jackass (ABBR)
JKAS .... Jack Knight Airmail Society (EA)
JKAUA .... Journal. Karnatak University (journ.) (SAUS)
JKB .... Justice of the King's Bench (ROG)
Jk^b .... Kidd B [*Blood group*] (DAVI)
JKBIR .... Justice of the King's Bench, Ireland (ROG)
JKBT .... Jackboot (ABBR)
JKBX .... Jukebox (ABBR)
JKC .... Japan Kennel Club (SAUO)
JKC .... Jidosha Kiki Co. Ltd.
JKC .... Shreveport, LA [*Location identifier*] [*FAA*] (FAAL)
JKCL .... Jockey Club, Inc. [*NASDAQ symbol*] (SAG)
JKD .... Jacked (ABBR)
JKDU .... Container Management [*Intermodal shipping container symbol*] (TVRC)
JKE .... Journal of Post Keynesian Economics (journ.) (SAUS)
J Kerala Ad Biol... Journal. Kerala Academy of Biology (journ.) (SAUS)
J Kerry Archaeol Hist Soc... Journal. Kerry Archaeological and Historical Society (journ.) (SAUS)
JKET .... Jacket (ABBR)
JKETD .... Jacketted (ABBR)
JKFC .... Japan-Republic of Korea Joint Fisheries Commission [*Marine science*] (OSRA)
JKFCFC ...... Jimmy Kish "The Flying Cowboy" Fan Club (EA)
JKFF .... JK Flip-Flop (SAUS)
JKFSD .... Journal. Korean Forestry Society (journ.) (SAUS)
JKG .... Jacking (ABBR)
JKG .... Jonkoping [*Sweden*] [*Airport symbol*] (OAG)
J/kg .... Joule per Kilogram [*Physics*]
Jkg .... Joules per kilogram (SAUS)
J/(KG K) ..... Joules per Kilogram Kelvin
JKH .... Chios [*Greece*] [*Airport symbol*] (OAG)
JKHHA .... Journal. Korea Institute of Electronics Engineers (journ.) (SAUS)
JKHY .... Henry (Jack) & Assoc [*NASDAQ symbol*] (TTSB)
JKHY .... Henry, Jack Associates [*NASDAQ symbol*] (SAG)
JKHY .... Jack Henry & Associates, Inc. (SAUO)
JKIEA .... Journal. Korean Institute of Electrical Engineers (journ.) (SAUS)
J King Abdulaziz Univ Islamic Econ... Journal of King Abdulaziz University: Islamic Economics [*A publication*] (JLIT)
J Kirin Univ Nt Sci... Journal. Kirin University. Natural Science (journ.) (SAUS)
JKKB .... Jeunesse du Kwilu-Kwango-Bateke [*Kwilu-Kwango-Bateke Youth*]
JkksPac ..... Jakks Pacific, Inc. [*Associated Press*] (SAG)
JKL .... Jackal (ABBR)
JKL .... Jackson, KY [*Location identifier*] [*FAA*] (FAAL)
JKL .... JK Line [*Federal Railroad Administration identification code*]
JKLF .... Jammu and Kashmir Liberation Front [*India*] [*Political party*] (ECON)
JKMAD ...... Journal. Korea Military Academy (journ.) (SAUS)
JKMR .... Jackhammer (ABBR)
JKMS .... Jack Knight Air Mail Society (EA)
JKMS .... Joint Key Management System (SAUO)
JKMSA ...... Journal. Kansas Medical Society (journ.) (SAUS)
JKMSD ...... Journal. Korean Mathematical Society (journ.) (SAUS)
JKNC .... Jammu and Kashmir National Conference [*India*] [*Political party*] (PPW)
JKNC .... Jammu and Kashmir National Congress (BUAC)
JKNCD .... Journal. Kongju National Teachers College (journ.) (SAUS)
JKNIF .... Jackknife (ABBR)
J Kongju Natl Teach Coll... Journal. Kongju National Teachers College (journ.) (SAUS)
J Korea Electr Assoc... Journal. Korea Electric Association (journ.) (SAUS)
J Korea Inf Sci Soc... Journal of the Korea Information Science Society (journ.) (SAUS)
J Korea Inst Electron Eng... Journal. Korea Institute of Electronics Engineers (journ.) (SAUS)
J Korea Inst Electron Eng... Journal of the Korea Institute of Electronics Engineers (journ.) (SAUS)
J Korea Merch Mar Coll Nat Sci Ser... Journal. Korea Merchant Marine College. Natural Sciences Series (journ.) (SAUS)
J Korea Mil Acad... Journal. Korea Military Academy (journ.) (SAUS)
J Korean Acad Maxillofac Radiol... Journal. Korean Academy of Maxillofacial Radiology (journ.) (SAUS)
J Korean Acad Periodontol... Journal. Korean Academy of Periodontology (journ.) (SAUS)
J Korean Agric Chem Soc... Journal. Korean Agricultural Chemical Society (journ.) (SAUS)
J Korean Ass Radit Prot... Journal. Korean Association for Radiation Protection (journ.) (SAUS)
J Korean Astron Soc... Journal. Korean Astronomical Society (journ.) (SAUS)
J Korean Cancer Res Ass... Journal. Korean Cancer Research Association (journ.) (SAUS)
J Korean Ceram Soc... Journal. Korean Ceramic Society (journ.) (SAUS)
J Korean Ceram Soc... Journal of the Korean Ceramic Society (journ.) (SAUS)
J Korean Chem Soc... Journal. Korean Chemical Society (journ.) (SAUS)
J Korean Dent Assoc... Journal. Korean Dental Association (journ.) (SAUS)
J Korean Inst Chem Eng... Journal. Korean Institute of Chemical Engineers (journ.) (SAUS)
J Korean Inst Chem Eng... Journal of the Korean Institute of Chemieal Engineers (journ.) (SAUS)
J Korean Inst Electr Eng... Journal. Korean Institute of Electrical Engineers (journ.) (SAUS)
J Korean Inst Electron Eng... Journal. Korean Institute of Electronics Engineers (journ.) (SAUS)
J Korean Inst Met... Journal. Korean Institute of Metals (journ.) (SAUS)
J Korean Inst Met... Journal of the Korean Institute of Metals (journ.) (SAUS)
J Korean Inst Min... Journal. Korean Institute of Mining (journ.) (SAUS)
J Korean Inst Miner Min Eng... Journal of the Korean Institute of Mineral and Mining Engineers (journ.) (SAUS)
J Korean Inst Miner Mining Eng... Journal. Korean Institute of Mineral and Mining Engineers (journ.) (SAUS)
J Korean Inst Min Geol... Journal. Korean Institute of Mining Geology (journ.) (SAUS)
J Korean Inst Rubber Ind... Journal. Korean Institute of Rubber Industry (journ.) (SAUS)
J Korean Inst Telemet Electron... Journal of the Korean Institute of Telematics and Electronics (journ.) (SAUS)
J Korean Math Soc... Journal. Korean Mathematical Society (journ.) (SAUS)
J Korean Med Assoc... Journal. Korean Medical Association (journ.) (SAUS)
J Korean Med Sci... Journal of Korean Medical Science (journ.) (SAUS)
J Korean Meteorol Soc... Journal. Korean Meteorological Society (journ.) (SAUS)
J Korean Nucl Soc... Journal. Korean Nuclear Society (journ.) (SAUS)
J Korean Nucl Soc... Journal of the Korean Nuclear Society (journ.) (SAUS)
J Korean Ophthalmol Soc... Journal. Korean Ophthalmological Society (journ.) (SAUS)
J Korean Orient Med Soc... Journal. Korean Oriental Medical Society (journ.) (SAUS)
J Korean Pharm Sci... Journal of Korean Pharmaceutical Sciences (journ.) (SAUS)
J Korean Phys Soc... Journal. Korean Physical Society (journ.) (SAUS)
J Korean Phys Soc... Journal of the Korean Physical Society (journ.) (SAUS)
J Korean Radiol Soc... Journal. Korean Radiological Society (journ.) (SAUS)
J Korean Res Inst Better Living... Journal. Korean Research Institute for Better Living (journ.) (SAUS)
J Korean Res Soc Dent Hypn... Journal. Korean Research Society for Dental Hypnosis (journ.) (SAUS)
J Korean Res Soc Radiol Technol... Journal. Korean Research Society of Radiolocal Technology (journ.) (SAUS)

J Korean Soc Agric Eng... Journal. Korean Society of Agricultural Engineers (journ.) (SAUS)
J Korean Soc Agric Mach... Journal. Korean Society of Agricultural Machinery (journ.) (SAUS)
J Korean Soc Civ Eng... Journal. Korean Society of Civil Engineers (journ.) (SAUS)
J Korean Soc Crop Sci... Journal. Korean Society of Crop Science (journ.) (SAUS)
J Korean Soc Mech Eng... Journal. Korean Society of Mechanical Engineers (journ.) (SAUS)
J Korean Soc Microbiol... Journal. Korean Society for Microbiology (journ.) (SAUS)
J Korean Soc Soil Sci Fert... Journal. Korean Society of Soil Science and Fertilizer (journ.) (SAUS)
J Korean Soc Text Eng Chem... Journal. Korean Society of Textile Engineers and Chemists (journ.) (SAUS)
J Korean Statist Soc... Journal. Korean Statistical Society (journ.) (SAUS)
J Korean Surg Soc... Journal. Korean Surgical Society (journ.) (SAUS)
J Koren For Soc... Journal. Korean Forestry Society (journ.) (SAUS)
J Kores Inf Sci Soc... Journal. Korean Infomation Science Society (journ.) (SAUS)
JKORS....... Journal. Korean Operations Research Society (journ.) (SAUS)
J Koyasan Univ... Journal. Koyasan University (journ.) (SAUS)
JKP.......... James Knox Polk [*US president, 1795-1849*]
JKPC......... Junior Knights of Peter Claver (EA)
JKPMA........ James K. Polk Memorial Association (EA)
JKPT......... Jackpot (ABBR)
JKPT......... Jackpot Enterprises [*NASDAQ symbol*] (SAG)
JKPTW...... Jackpot Enterprises Wrrt [*NASDAQ symbol*] (TTSB)
JKR.......... Janakpur [*Nepal*] [*Airport symbol*] (OAG)
JKS.......... Jacks (ABBR)
JKS.......... Jacks Creek, TN [*Location identifier*] [*FAA*] (FAAL)
JKS.......... Jackson [*Diocesan abbreviation*] [*Mississippi*] (TOCD)
JKSCR....... Jackscrew [*Mechanical engineering*]
JKSNV....... Jacksonville, TX [*American Association of Railroads railroad junction routing code*]
Jksnvll...... Jacksonville Bancorp, Inc. [*Associated Press*] (SAG)
JksnvlSL.... Jacksonville Savings & Loan Association [*Texas*] [*Associated Press*] (SAG)
JksnvSB..... Jacksonville Savings Bank (Illinois) [*Associated Press*] (SAG)
JKSON....... Jackson, TN [*American Association of Railroads railroad junction routing code*]
JKST......... Johnson-Kenney Screening Test [*Psychology*] (DAVI)
JKT.......... Djakarta [*Java, Indonesia*] [*Airport symbol*] (AD)
JKT.......... Jacket (KSC)
jkt.......... Jacket
JKT.......... Jakarta [*Indonesia*] [*Airport symbol*] (OAG)
JKT.......... Job Knowledge Test [*Military*] (AFM)
JKTD......... Jacketed (ABBR)
JKTG......... Jacketing (ABBR)
JKU.......... Kyoto University, Kyoto, Japan [*Library symbol*] [*Library of Congress*] (LCLS)
J Kumamoto Med Soc... Journal. Kumamoto Medical Society (journ.) (SAUS)
J Kumamoto Womens Univ... Journal. Kumamoto Womens University (journ.) (SAUS)
J Kumasi Univ Sci Technol... Journal. Kumasi University of Science and Technology (journ.) (SAUS)
JKUR........ Jammu and Kashmir University Review (journ.) (SAUS)
J Kurume Med Assoc... Journal. Kurume Medical Association (journ.) (SAUS)
J Kuwait Med Ass... Journal. Kuwait Medical Association (journ.) (SAUS)
JKW......... Juvonen, K. W., Winnipeg, Manitoba CDA [*STAC*]
JKWI......... Johnsonburg, Kane, Warren & Irvine Railroad [*Federal Railroad Administration identification code*]
J KY Med Assoc... Journal. Kentucky Medical Association (journ.) (SAUS)
J Ky Med Assoc... Journal of the Kentucky Medical Association (SAUO)
J Ky Med Assoc... Journal of the Kentucky Medical Association (journ.) (SAUS)
JKYND....... Journal. Materials Science Research Institute. Dongguk University (journ.) (SAUS)
J Kyorin Med Soc... Journal. Kyorin Medical Society (journ.) (SAUS)
J Kyoto Med Assoc... Journal. Kyoto Medical Assocation (journ.) (SAUS)
J Kyoto Prefect Med Univ... Journal. Kyoto Prefectural Medical University (journ.) (SAUS)
J Kyoto Prefect Univ Med... Journal. Kyoto Prefectural University of Medicine (journ.) (SAUS)
J Ky State Med Assoc... Journal. Kentucky State Medical Association (journ.) (SAUS)
J Kyungpook Eng... Journal. Kyungpook Engineering (journ.) (SAUS)
J Kyungpook Eng Kyungpook Natl Univ... Journal. Kyungpook Engineering. Kyungpook National University (journ.) (SAUS)
J Kyushu Coal Min Tech Assoc... Journal. Kyushu Coal Mining Technicians Association (journ.) (SAUS)
J Kyushu Dent Soc... Journal. Kyushu Dental Society (journ.) (SAUS)
J Kyushu Hematol Soc... Journal. Kyushu Hematological Society (journ.) (SAUS)
JL........... Jadassohn-Lewandowsky [*Syndrome*] [*Thickening of the nails*] [*Medicine*] (DAVI)
JL........... Jaffe-Lichtenstein [*Syndrome*] [*or Fibrous dysplasia*] [*Orthopedics*] (DAVI)
JL........... Jail [*Telegraphy*] (PCTE)
JL........... Jaksch-Luzet [*Disease*] [*Medicine*] (DB)
JL........... Jamming Locator (SAUS)
JL........... J & L Specialty Steel [*NYSE symbol*] (SPSG)
JL........... Japan Air Lines [*ICAO designator*] (OAG)
JL........... Japan Line (SAUS)
JL........... Javan LASER
JL........... Jazz-Lift [*Provides jazz records to persons in Iron Curtain countries*] [*Defunct*] (EA)
JL........... Jefferson Lyons [*Commercial firm*] [*British*]
Jl........... Jejunoileal [*Medicine*] (MEDA)
JL........... Jerichower Land [*German license plate city code*]
JL........... Job Library [*Computer science*] (ELAL)
Jl........... Joel [*Old Testament book*]
JL........... John Laing plc (EFIS)
JL........... Johnny Lightnings [*Topper Toys*]
JL........... Johnson Line (SAUS)
Jl........... Joliotium [*Chemistry*] (MEC)
JL........... Jones & Laughlin Steel [*Federal Railroad Administration identification code*]
JL........... Joule's Law [*Physics*]
JL........... Journal [*Online database field identifier*]
JL........... Journal. American Liszt Society (journ.) (SAUS)
JL........... Journal of Linguistics (journ.) (SAUS)
Jl........... July (ADWA)
JL........... July
JL........... Jump if Less (VLIE)
JL........... Jump Last (SAUS)
JL........... Junior Leaders Regiment [*British military*] (DMA)
JL........... Jurin Law [*Electronics*]
JL........... JustLife [*Defunct*] (EA)
JL........... Just Looking [*A browser*] [*Retail slang*]
JL........... Lab. Jacques Logeais [*France*] [*Research code symbol*]
JLA.......... Cooper Landing, AK [*Location identifier*] [*FAA*] (FAAL)
JLA.......... Jack L. Ahr [*Designer's mark on US bicentennial quarter*]
JLA.......... Jalna Resources [*Vancouver Stock Exchange symbol*]
JLA.......... Jamaica Library Association (SAUO)
JLA.......... Japanese Library Association (BUAC)
JLA.......... Jet Lift Aircraft
JLA.......... Jewish Law Association (BUAC)
JLA.......... Jewish Librarians Association [*Later, AJL*] (EA)
JLA.......... Jordan Library Association (BUAC)
J Lab Econ... Journal of Labor Economics [*A publication*] (JLIT)
J Label Compound Radiopharm... Journal of Labelled Compounds and Radiopharmaceuticals (journ.) (SAUS)
J Labor Research... Journal of Labor Research (journ.) (SAUS)
J Labour Hyg Iron Steel Ind... Journal of Labour Hygiene in Iron and Steel Industry (journ.) (SAUS)
J Lab Res.. Journal of Labor Research [*A publication*] (JLIT)
J LA Dent Assoc... Journal. Louisiana Dental Association (journ.) (SAUS)
JLAEA....... Journal. Language Association of Eastern Africa (journ.) (SAUS)
Jl Aesthet... Journal of Aesthetic and Art Criticism (journ.) (SAUS)
JLAF......... Joint Lithuanian-American Fund (BUAC)
J Lake Sci... Journal of Lake Sciences [*A publication*] (PABS)
J Lanchow Univ Nat Sci... Journal. Lanchow University. Natural Sciences (journ.) (SAUS)
J L and Com... Journal of Law and Commerce (journ.) (SAUS)
JL & Com S... Journal. Law and Commerce Society (journ.) (SAUS)
JL & Com Soc... Journal. Law and Commerce Society [*Hong Kong*] [*A publication*] (DLA)
JL & Information Science... Journal of Law and Information Science [*A publication*]
J L & Information Science... Journal of Law and Information Science (journ.) (SAUS)
JL & Pol.... Journal of Law and Politics [*A publication*] (DLA)
JL & Pol.... Journal of Law and Politics (journ.) (SAUS)
JL & Religion... Journal of Law and Religion [*A publication*] (DLA)
JL & Religion... Journal of Law and Religion (journ.) (SAUS)
J Lang Teach... Journal for Language Teaching (journ.) (SAUS)
JLA:NWO... Justice League of America: New World Order (SAUS)
J Laparoendosc Surg... Journal of Laparoendoscopic Surgery (journ.) (SAUS)
J Laryngol Otol Suppl... Journal of Laryngology and Otology. Supplement (journ.) (SAUS)
J Laryng Otol... Journal of Laryngology and Otology (MEC)
JLAS......... Jordanian Laboratories Accreditation System (SAUO)
JLAS......... Journal. Linguistic Association of the Southwest (journ.) (SAUS)
JLAS......... Journal of Latin American Studies (journ.) (SAUS)
JLAS......... JUMPS [*Joint Uniform Military Pay System*] Leave Accounting System (DNAB)
J Laser Appl... Journal of Laser Applications [*A publication*] (CABS)
J La State Med Soc... Journal of the Louisiana State Medical Society (SAUO)
J La State Med Soc... Journal of the Louisiana State Medical Society (journ.) (SAUS)
J Lat Am Stud... Journal of Latin American Studies (journ.) (SAUS)
JLAU......... Japan Line [*Intermodal shipping container symbol*] (TVRC)
J Law & Ed... Journal of Law and Education [*A publication*] (DLA)
J Law Econ... Journal of Law and Economics [*A publication*] (JLIT)
J Law Econ Organ... Journal of Law, Economics, and Organization [*A publication*] (JLIT)
J Law Reform... Journal of Law Reform [*A publication*] (DLA)
J Law Soc... Journal of Law and Society (journ.) (SAUS)
J Law Soc'y Scotland... Law Society of Scotland. Journal [*A publication*] (DLA)
JLB.......... Jewish Labor Bund (EA)
JLB.......... Jewish Lads' Brigade [*British*] (DI)
JLB.......... Journal of Labor Economics (journ.) (SAUS)
JLBC......... JLB Transfer Company [*Common carrier symbol*]
JLBD......... Jailbird (ABBR)
JLBRK....... Jailbreak (ABBR)
J Lbr Res... Journal of Labor Research (journ.) (SAUS)
JLB Smith Inst Ichthyol Spec Publ... J. L. B. Smith Institute of Ichthyology. Special Publication (journ.) (SAUS)
JLBTS....... Japanese Land-Based Test Site (MCD)
Jl Bus Fin... Journal of Business Finance and Accounting (journ.) (SAUS)
Jl Bus Strat... Journal of Business Strategy (journ.) (SAUS)

JLC .... Houston [*Texas*] Allen Center [*Airport symbol*] (OAG)
JLC .... Jaeger LeCoultre
JLC .... Japanese Linear Collider [*High energy physics*]
JLC .... Japan Logistical Command (SAUO)
JLC .... Jewish Labor Committee (EA)
JLC .... Joint Logistic Commander (ACAE)
JLC .... Joint Logistics Command (SAUO)
JLC .... Joint Logistics Commanders [*Military*]
JLC .... Joint Logistics Committee [*Military*]
JLC .... Junction Latching Circulator
JLC .... Justification for Limited Competition (COE)
JLC & E ..... Jonesboro, Lake City & Eastern Railroad
JLCAT .... Joint Logistics Commanders' Action Team [*Military*]
JLCC .... Joint Logistics Co-ordination Centre (SAUS)
JLCD .... Joint Liaison Committee on Documents [*Used in the international carriage of goods*] (BUAC)
JLCM .... Journal of Laboratory and Clinical Medicine [*CSCR*] [*Medicine*] (EDAA)
J L-C Met... Journal of the Less-Common Metals (journ.) (SAUS)
Jl Commun... Journal of Communication (journ.) (SAUS)
Jl Consmr R... Journal of Consumer Research (journ.) (SAUS)
JLCPA .... Journal of Counseling Psychology (journ.) (SAUS)
J/L/Cpl ...... Junior Lance-Corporal [*British military*] (DMA)
JLCRD .... Journal of Labelled Compounds and Radiopharmaceuticals (journ.) (SAUS)
JLCST .... Joint Legislative Committee on Science and Technology (SAUO)
JLCU .... Johnson Line [*Intermodal shipping container symbol*] (TVRC)
JLCU .... Johnson Line Container Unit (SAUS)
JLD .... Jammer Locator Detector (CCCA)
J/Ldr .... Junior Leader [*British military*] (DMA)
JLDS .... Journal. Lancashire Dialect Society (journ.) (SAUS)
JLDU .... Japan Line [*Intermodal shipping container symbol*] (TVRC)
JLE .... Japanese Language Enveronment (SAUS)
JLE .... Jet Lift Engine
JLE .... Journal of Law and Economics (journ.) (SAUS)
JLE .... Jump if Less than or Equal To (VLIE)
Jl E Asiat Stud... Journal of East Asiatic Studies (journ.) (SAUS)
J Leather Ind Res Inst S Afr... Journal. Leather Industries Research Institute of South Africa (journ.) (SAUS)
J Leather Res... Journal of Leather Research (journ.) (SAUS)
J Leeds Univ Text Stud Assa... Journal. Leeds University Textile Students. Association (journ.) (SAUS)
J Legal Prof... Journal of the Legal Profession (journ.) (SAUS)
J Legal Econ... Journal of Legal Economics [*A publication*] (JLIT)
J Legal Stud... Journal of Legal Studies [*A publication*] (JLIT)
J Leg Hist... Journal of Legal History (journ.) (SAUS)
JLEI .... Lee Jennings Enterprises [*Common carrier symbol*]
J Leisure Res... Journal of Leisure Research [*A publication*] (PABS)
Jl Electrochem Soc... Journal of the Electrochemical Society (SAUO)
JLEM .... Jerusalem (ABBR)
JLEMA .... Journal of Engineering Mathematics (journ.) (SAUS)
JLEN .... Julienne (ABBR)
JLEP .... Julep (ABBR)
J Lepid Soc... Journal. Lepidopterists Society (journ.) (SAUS)
JLER .... Journal of Leisure Research (journ.) (SAUS)
J Less-Common Met... Journal of Less-Common Metals (journ.) (SAUS)
JLEU .... Japan Line [*Intermodal shipping container symbol*] (TVRC)
J Leukoc Biol Suppl... Journal of Leukocyte Biology. Supplement (journ.) (SAUS)
JLEZ .... Japan Line [*Intermodal trailer symbol*]
JLF .... Joint Landing Force
JLF .... Joint Live Fire [*Military*]
JLF .... Joint Live-Fire programme (SAUS)
JLFA .... John Libby Family Association (EA)
JLFB .... Joint Landing Force Board
JLFC .... Joan Lunden Fan Club [*Defunct*] (EA)
JLFC .... Johnny Len Fan Club (EA)
JLG .... Jewish Lawyers Guild (EA)
JLG .... JLG Industries, Inc. [*Associated Press*] (SAG)
JLG .... Joint Liaison Group (ECON)
JLGA .... James L. Grant and Associates (EFIS)
JLGI .... JLG Indus [*NASDAQ symbol*] (TTSB)
JLGI .... JLG Industries Inc. (SAUO)
JLH .... Arlington Heights, IL [*Location identifier*] [*FAA*] (FAAL)
JLH .... Journal of Legal History [*A publication*]
JLH .... Journal of Library History (journ.) (SAUS)
JLH .... Journal of Library History, Philosophy and Comparative Librarianship (journ.) (SAUS)
JLHC .... Just Like Home [*NASDAQ symbol*] (TTSB)
JLHC .... Just Like Home, Inc. [*NASDAQ symbol*] (SAG)
JLHU .... Japan Line [*Intermodal shipping container symbol*] (TVRC)
JLI .... Jiffy Lube International, Inc. (EFIS)
JLI .... Julian, CA [*Location identifier*] [*FAA*] (FAAL)
JLIA .... Japan Lumber Importers Association (BUAC)
J Lib Admin... Journal of Library Administration (journ.) (SAUS)
J Lib Arts Nat Sci Sapporo Med Coll... Journal of Liberal Arts and Natural Sciences. Sapporo Medical College (journ.) (SAUS)
J Lib Arts Sci Kitasato Unir... Journal of Liberal Arts and Sciences. Kitasato University (journ.) (SAUS)
J Lib Arts Sci Sapporo Med Coll... Journal of Liberal Arts and Sciences. Sapporo Medical College (journ.) (SAUS)
J Lib Automation... Journal of Library Automation (journ.) (SAUS)
JLIEA .... Journal of Industrial Engineering (journ.) (SAUS)
J Life Sci R Dublin Soc... Journal of Life Sciences. Royal Dublin Society (journ.) (SAUS)
J Light Met Weld Constr... Journal of Light Metal Welding and Construction (journ.) (SAUS)
J Light Vis Environ... Journal of Light and Visual Environment (journ.) (SAUS)
J Lightwave Technol... Journal of Lightwave Technology (journ.) (SAUS)
J Limnol Soc South Afr... Journal. Limnological Society of South Africa (journ.) (SAUS)
J Linguist Anthropol... Journal of Linguistic Anthropology (journ.) (SAUS)
J Linn Soc Lond Bot... Journal. Linnean Society of London. Botany (journ.) (SAUS)
J Linn Soc Lond Zool... Journal. Linnean Society of London. Zoology (journ.) (SAUS)
JLIOOF ...... Junior Lodge, Independent Order of Odd Fellows (EA)
JLIP .... Joint Level Interface Protocol (SAUS)
J Lipid Mediat Cell Signal... Journal of Lipid Mediators and Cell Signalling (journ.) (SAUS)
J Lipid Mediators... Journal of Lipid Mediators (journ.) (SAUS)
J Lipos Res... Journal of Liposome Research (journ.) (SAUS)
J Liq Chromatogr... Journal of Liquid Chromatography [*A publication*] (CABS)
JLIRI .... Jinan Light Industry Research Institute (BUAC)
JLIS .... Journal of Law and Information Science (journ.) (SAUS)
J-List .... Journalist (ADWA)
J Lit Sem... Journal of Literary Semantics (journ.) (SAUS)
JLK .... JLK Direct Distribution [*NYSE symbol*]
JLK .... JLK Direct Distribution'A' [*NYSE symbol*] (SG)
JLL .... Jones Lang LaSalle [*NYSE symbol*] (SG)
JLLU .... Japan Line [*Intermodal shipping container symbol*] (TVRC)
JLLX .... Laroche Industries [*Private rail car owner code*]
JLLZ .... Japan Line [*Intermodal trailer symbol*]
JLM .... JLM Industries [*NCIC trailer make code*]
JLM .... Journal of Law and Medicine (SAUS)
JLM .... Journal of Lipid Mediators (journ.) (SAUS)
JLM .... Junior Legacy Melbourne [*Australia*] [*An association*]
JLMA .... Japan Light Metal Association (SAUO)
JLMC .... Joint Labor Management Committee of the Retail Food Industry (EA)
JLMI .... JLM Industries, Inc. [*NASDAQ symbol*] (NASQ)
JLMIC .... Japan Light Machinery Information Center (EA)
JLMPA .... Journal of Microwave Power (journ.) (SAUS)
JLMS .... Journal. London Mathematical Society (journ.) (SAUS)
JLMS .... Journal of the London Mathematical Society (journ.) (SAUS)
JLMSA ...... Jewish Liturgical Music Society of America (EA)
JLMU .... Japan Line [*Intermodal shipping container symbol*] (TVRC)
Jl Musicology... Journal of Musicology (journ.) (SAUS)
JLN .... Jaclyn, Inc. [*AMEX symbol*] (SPSG)
JLN .... Joplin [*Missouri*] [*Airport symbol*] (OAG)
JLN .... Joplin, MO [*Location identifier*] [*FAA*] (FAAL)
JLNI .... J-Line [*Common carrier symbol*]
JLNY .... Jenna Lane, Inc. [*NASDAQ symbol*] (NASQ)
Jl NY Ent S... Journal. New York Entomological Society (journ.) (SAUS)
JLO .... Jesolo [*Italy*] [*Airport symbol*] (AD)
JLO .... Joint Liaison Organization (SAUO)
JLO .... Junction Light Output
Jl of Research... Journal of Research in Music Education (journ.) (SAUS)
J Logic Program... Journal of Logic Programming [*A publication*] (CABS)
J Log Program... Journal of Logic Programming (journ.) (SAUS)
JLOIC .... Joint Logistics, Operations, Intelligence Center [*NATO*] (NATG)
JLOIC .... Joint Logistics, Operations, Intelligence Centre (SAUO)
J London School Trop Med... Journal. London School of Tropical Medicine (journ.) (SAUS)
JLOTA .... Journal of Laryngology and Otology (journ.) (SAUS)
JLOTS .... Joint Logistics Over-the-Shore [*Military*] (RDA)
J Louis St Med Soc... Journal. Louisiana State Medical Society (journ.) (SAUS)
J Low Freq Noise Vib... Journal of Low Frequency Noise and Vibration (journ.) (SAUS)
JLP .... Jamaica Labour Party [*Political party*] (PPW)
JLP .... Jazz for Life Project [*Defunct*] (EA)
JLP .... Jig Leg Plate (SAUS)
JLP .... John Lewis Partnership [*British*] (ECON)
JLP .... Juan-les-Pins [*France*] [*Airport symbol*] (AD)
JLP .... Juvenile Laryngeal Papilloma [*Medicine*] (DAVI)
JLPB .... Joint Logistics Planning Board
JLPC .... Joint Logistics Planning Committee (SAUO)
JLPC .... Joint Logistics Plans Committee [*Military*]
JLPG .... Joint Logistics Plans Group [*Military*]
JLPPG .... Joint Logistics and Personnel Policy Guidance [*Military*] (AFM)
JLPU .... Japan Line [*Intermodal shipping container symbol*] (TVRC)
JLR .... Jabalpur [*India*] [*Airport symbol*] (OAG)
JLR .... Jailer (ABBR)
JLR .... Jamaica Law Reports [*1953-55*] [*A publication*] (DLA)
JLR .... Jeweler (ABBR)
JLR .... Jewish Language Review (journ.) (SAUS)
JLR .... Johore Law Reports [*India*] [*A publication*] (DLA)
JLR .... Journal of Labor Research (journ.) (SAUS)
JLR .... Journal of Linguistic Research (journ.) (SAUS)
JLR .... Junction Loudness Rating (SAUS)
JLR .... Junior Leaders Regiment [*British military*] (DMA)
Jl R Agric S... Journal. Royal Agricultural Society of England (journ.) (SAUS)
Jl R Anthrop Inst... Journal. Royal Anthropological Institute of Great Britain and Ireland (journ.) (SAUS)
Jl R Aust Hist S... Royal Australian Historical Society (SAUO)
JLRB .... Joint Labor Relations Board
JLRB .... Joint Logistics Review Board [*Military*]
JLRC .... Jack London Research Center (EA)
JLREID ...... Joint Long-Range Estimative Intelligence Document [*Military*]

Jl R Hist Soc Qd... Journal. Royal Historical Society of Queensland (journ.) (SAUS)
Jl R Hort Soc... Journal. Royal Horticulture Society (journ.) (SAUS)
JLRPG....... Joint Long-Range Proving Ground (KSC)
JLRRT....... Jordan Left-Right Reversal Test [*Educational test*]
JLRSA....... Joint Long-Range Strategic Appraisal [*Military*]
JLRSA....... Joint Long-Range Strategic Assessment (SAUO)
Jl RS Arts... Journal. Royal Society of Arts (journ.) (SAUS)
JLRSE....... Joint Long-Range Strategic Estimates [*Military*]
JLRSS....... Joint Long-Range Strategic Study [*Military*] (AFM)
JLRU........ Lauritzen Reefers [*Intermodal shipping container symbol*] (TVRC)
jlry........... Jewelry (VRA)
JLS.......... Jail Library Service (SAUO)
JLS.......... Jet Alsace [*France*] [*ICAO designator*] (FAAC)
JLS.......... Jet Lag Syndrome (MELL)
JLS.......... Jet Lift System
JLS.......... Jewels (ADA)
JLS.......... Joint Least Squares [*Statistics*]
JLS.......... Journal of Law and Society [*A publication*]
JLS.......... Journal of Literary Semantics (journ.) (SAUS)
JLS.......... Journal of the Law Society of Scotland [*A publication*] (SAFN)
JLS.......... Junior Literary Society (SAUO)
JLSC......... Joint Electronics Standardization Committee (SAUO)
JLSC......... Joint Logistics System Center (SAUO)
JLSC......... Joint Logistics System Command (DOMA)
Jl S-East Agric Coll... Journal. South-Eastern Agricultural College (journ.) (SAUS)
JLSGI........ Japanese Local Self Government Institute (SAUO)
J/L/Sgt...... Junior Lance-Sergeant [*British military*] (DMA)
JLSMA...... Journal. Louisiana State Medical Society (journ.) (SAUS)
Jl Small Bus... American Journal of Small Business (journ.) (SAUS)
JL Soc....... Journal. Law Society of Scotland [*A publication*] (DLA)
Jl Sol State Cir... Journal of Solid State Circuits (SAUS)
JLSP......... Joint Logistics Support Plan
JLSPAO...... Joint United States Public Affairs Office (SAUS)
JLST......... Joint Laser Safety Team (SAUO)
J L Studies... Journal of Legal Studies (journ.) (SAUS)
JLSU......... Japan Line [*Intermodal shipping container symbol*] (TVRC)
JLSX......... Jones and Laughlin Steel [*Private rail car owner code*]
JLSY......... Jealousy [*Telegraphy*] (PCTE)
JLSZ......... Japan Line [*Intermodal trailer symbol*]
J-LT.......... IEEE/OSA Journal of Lightwave Technology [*Database*] (GDD)
JLT........... Jalate, Inc. [*AMEX symbol*] (SAG)
JLT........... Jalate Ltd [*AMEX symbol*] (TTSB)
JLT........... Junior Leader Training [*Boy Scouts of America*]
JLT........... Junior Lord of the Treasury
Jl Test Eval... Journal of Testing and Evaluation (journ.) (SAUS)
JLTF......... Jewish Librarians Caucus (SAUO)
JLTF......... Jewish Librarians Task Force (EA)
JLTL......... J & L Tank [*NCIC trailer make code*]
JLTPB........ Joint Logistics Techniques and Procedures Board [*Military*]
JLTR......... Jilter (ABBR)
JLTU......... Japan Line [*Intermodal shipping container symbol*] (TVRC)
JLU.......... Jilin University (BUAC)
JLUAC....... Joint Land Use Advisory Committee
JLUB......... Jiffy Lube International, Inc. [*NASDAQ symbol*] (COMM)
JLUS......... Jealous (ABBR)
JLUSLY...... Jealously (ABBR)
JLUSNS..... Jealousness (ABBR)
JLUSY....... Jealousy (ABBR)
J LUU Chem Soc... Journal. Leeds University Union Chemical Society (journ.) (SAUS)
JLW.......... Jahrbuch fuer Liturgiewissenschaft [*A publication*] (ODCC)
JLW-155..... Joint Lightweight 155mm Howitzer (RDA)
JLWFO....... James Leonard Williams Family Organization [*Association*] (EA)
JLWU......... Jones Lane Watson [*Intermodal shipping container symbol*] (TVRC)
JLX........... Jealous [*Telegraphy*] (PCTE)
JLXY......... Jealously [*Telegraphy*] (PCTE)
JLY........... Jelly (ABBR)
JLY........... Jena, LA [*Location identifier*] [*FAA*] (FAAL)
JLY........... July [*Telegraphy*] (PCTE)
JLYBN....... Jellybean (ABBR)
JLYD......... Jellied (ABBR)
JLYFSH...... Jellyfish (ABBR)
JLYLK........ Jellylike (ABBR)
J Lymphol... Journal of Lymphology (journ.) (SAUS)
JM........... Air Jamaica Ltd. [*ICAO designator*] (OAG)
JM........... Jactitation of Marriage [*Legal*] [*British*] (ROG)
JM........... Jakarta Mandate on Coastal and Marine Biodiversity (SAUS)
JM........... Jakarta Mandate on Marine and Coastal Biodiversity (or Biological Diversity) (SAUO)
JM........... Jamaica [*ANSI two-letter standard code*] (CNC)
jm............ Jamaica [*MARC country of publication code*] [*Library of Congress*] (LCCP)
Jm........... James [*New Testament book*] (BJA)
JM........... James Madison [*US president, 1751-1836*]
JM........... James Monroe [*US president, 1758-1831*]
JM........... Japan Mail (SAUS)
JM........... Jesuit Missions (EA)
JM........... Jet Mixing (SAUS)
J/M.......... Jettison Motor (KSC)
JM........... Jewish Male [*Classified advertising*]
JM........... Jewish Museum (SAUS)
JM........... Jiyu-Minshuto [*Liberal-Democratic Party*] [*Japan*] [*Political party*]
JM........... Job Management (SAUS)
JM........... Job Memory [*Computer science*] (ELAL)
JM........... John Mercanti [*Designer's mark, when appearing on US coins*]
JM........... Johns Manville Corp. (MCD)
JM........... Joint Mission (SAUO)
JM........... Journal of Marketing [*A publication*] (BRI)
JM........... Journal of Micrographics (NITA)
JM........... Jugomaxillary [*Dentistry*] (DAVI)
JM........... Julia MacRae [*Publisher*] [*British*]
JM........... Julian Messner [*Publisher's imprint*]
JM........... Jump on Minus (SAUS)
JM........... Junction Module [*Deep Space Instrumentation Facility, NASA*]
JM........... Juris Magister [*Master of Laws*]
JM........... Juris Master (SAUS)
JM........... Justizminister [*Minister of Justice*] [*German*] (ILCA)
JM........... Justizministerium [*Ministry of Justice*] [*German*] (ILCA)
JM........... Juxtamembrane Domain
jM........... Mass Transfer Factor [*Physics*] (DAVI)
J/M^2........ Joules per Square Meter
J/m3......... Joule per Cubic Metre (SAUS)
J/M^3........ Joules per Cubic Meter [*Physics*]
JM3.......... Journal of Microlithography, Microfabrication, and Microsystems [*Database*] (GDD)
JMA.......... Houston [*Texas*] Astrodome [*Airport symbol*] (OAG)
JMA.......... Jamaica Manufacturers Association (BUAC)
JMA.......... Jamara Memorial Association (BUAC)
JMA.......... James Martin Associates [*Database consulting group*] [*British*]
JMA.......... Jamming Modulation Analysis
JMA.......... Japanese Medical Association [*Medicine*] (EDAA)
JMA.......... Japanese Meteorological Agency (SAUO)
JMA.......... Japanese Military Administration
JMA.......... Japan Management Association (BUAC)
JMA.......... Japan Medical Association (SAUO)
JMA.......... Japan Meteorological Agency
JMA.......... Japan Meteorological Association (SAUO)
JMA.......... Japan Microfilm Association (SAUO)
JMA.......... Japan Microphotography Association
JMA.......... Jewelry Manufacturers Association (EA)
JMA.......... Jewish Music Alliance (EA)
JMA.......... John More Association (EA)
JMA.......... Joinery Managers' Association [*British*] (BI)
JMA.......... Joint Mission Analysis
JMA.......... Joint Mission Application (SAUO)
JMA.......... Joint Mobilization Augmentation (SAUO)
JMA.......... Journal of Macronomics (journ.) (SAUS)
JMA.......... Journal of Mediterranean Archaeology [*A publication*] (ABAR)
JMA.......... Julia Morgan Association [*Defunct*] (EA)
JMA.......... Junior Management Assistant
JMA.......... Junior Medical Assistant [*British military*] (DMA)
JMA.......... Junior Military Aviator
JMA.......... Juvenile Missionary Association [*British*] (BI)
JMA.......... Juvenile Muscular Atrophy [*Medicine*] (EDAA)
JMAAD...... Joint Military Assistance Affairs Division (CINC)
JMAC........ Joint Munitions Allocation Committee
J Macomb Dent Soc... Journal. Macomb Dental Society (journ.) (SAUS)
J Macroecon... Journal of Macroeconomics [*A publication*] (JLIT)
J Macromol Chem... Journal of Macromolecular Chemistry (journ.) (SAUS)
J Macromol Sci... Journal of Macromolecular Science (SAUS)
J Macromol Sci A... Journal of Macromolecular Science. Part A (journ.) (SAUS)
J Macromol Sci C... Journal of Macromolecular Science. Part C (journ.) (SAUS)
J Macromol Sci Chem... Journal of Macromolecular Science. Chemistry (journ.) (SAUS)
J Macromol Sci Chem A... Journal of Macromolecular Science. Part A. Chemistry (journ.) (SAUS)
J Macromol Sci Part A... Journal of Macromolecular Science. Part A. Chemistry (journ.) (SAUS)
J Macromol Sci Part C... Journal of Macromolecular Science. Part C. Reviews in Macromolecular Chemistry (journ.) (SAUS)
J Macromol Sci Part D... Journal of Macromolecular Science. Part D. Reviews in Polymer Technology (journ.) (SAUS)
J Macromol Sci Phys... Journal of Macromolecular Science. Part B. Physics (journ.) (SAUS)
J Macromol Sci Phys... Journal of Macromolecular Science-Physics (journ.) (SAUS)
J Macromol Sci Rev Macromol Chem... Journal of Macromolecular Science. Part C. Reviews in Macromolecular Chemistry (journ.) (SAUS)
J Macromol Sci Rev Macromol Chem Phys... Journal of Macromolecular Science. Reviews in Macromolecular Chemistry and Physics (journ.) (SAUS)
J Macromol Sci Rev Polym Technol... Journal of Macromolecular Science. Part D. Reviews in Polymer Technology (journ.) (SAUS)
J Macr S Ch... Journal of Macromolecular Science. Part A. Chemistry (journ.) (SAUS)
J Macr S Ph... Journal of Macromolecular Science. Part B. Physics (journ.) (SAUS)
J Madras Agric Stud Union... Journal. Madras Agricultural Students. Union (journ.) (SAUS)
J Madras Inst Technol... Journal. Madras Institute of Technology (journ.) (SAUS)
J Madras Univ... Journal. Madras University (journ.) (SAUS)
JMADSN.... James Madison Ltd. (SAUO)
J Madurai Kamaraj Univ... Journal. Madurai Kamaraj University (journ.) (SAUS)
J Madurai Univ... Journal Madurai University (journ.) (SAUS)
JMAG........ Journal of Molecular and Applied Genetics (journ.) (SAUS)
J Magn Magn Mater... Journal of Magnetism and Magnetic Materials [*A publication*] (CABS)
J Magn Reson B... Journal of Magnetic Resonance. Series B (journ.) (SAUS)

J Magn Reson Imaging... Journal of Magnetic Resonance Imaging (journ.) (SAUS)
J Maharaja Sayayira Univ Baroda... Journal. Maharaja Sayayira University of Baroda (journ.) (SAUS)
J Maharasbtra Agric Univ... Journal. Maharasbtra Agricultural Universities (journ.) (SAUS)
JMAHEP..... Joint Military Aircraft Hurricane Evacuation Plan (AFM)
J Maine Dent Assoc... Journal. Maine Dental Association (journ.) (SAUS)
J Maine Med Assoc... Journal. Maine Medical Association (journ.) (SAUS)
J Malac Soc Aust... Journal. Malacological Society of Australia (journ.) (SAUS)
J Mal & Comp L... Journal of Malaysian and Comparative Law (journ.) (SAUS)
J Malar Inst India... Journal. Malaria Institute of India (journ.) (SAUS)
J Malaya Branch Br Med Asoc... Journal. Malaya Branch. British Medical Association (journ.) (SAUS)
J Malaya Branch Br Med Assoc... Journal. Malayan Branch. British Medical Association (journ.) (SAUS)
J Malay Branch Roy Asiatic Soc... Journal. Malaysian Branch. Royal Asiatic Society (journ.) (SAUS)
J Mal Br Brit Med Ass... Journal. Malayan Branch. British Medical Association (journ.) (SAUS)
J Mal Vasc... Journal des Maladies Vasculaires (journ.) (SAUS)
JMAM....... Journal of Mammalogy (journ.) (SAUS)
J Mammal... Journal of Mammalogy (journ.) (SAUS)
J Mammal Soc Jpn... Journal. Mammalogical Society of Japan (journ.) (SAUS)
J Manage... Journal of Management (journ.) (SAUS)
J Manage Acc Res... Journal of Management Accounting Research [*A publication*] (JLIT)
J Manage Governance... Journal of Management and Governance [*A publication*] (JLIT)
J Manage Inf Syst... Journal of Management Information Systems (journ.) (SAUS)
J Manage Stud... Journal of Management Studies (journ.) (SAUS)
J Manch Geogr Soc... Journal. Manchester Geographical Society (journ.) (SAUS)
J Manch Geol Ass... Journal. Manchester Geological Association (journ.) (SAUS)
J MAN GS... Journal of the Manchester Geographical Society [*A publication*] (ROG)
J MAN GS... Journal of the Manchester Geographical Society (journ.) (SAUS)
J Manuf Oper Manage... Journal of Manufacturing and Operations Management (journ.) (SAUS)
J Manuf Syst... Journal of Manufacturing Systems (journ.) (SAUS)
JMAP....... Joint Mutual Aid Program (SAUO)
JMAPI....... Java Management Application Program Interface [*Computer science*] (IGQR)
JMAR........ JMAR Industries [*NASDAQ symbol*] (SPSG)
JMAR........ JMAR Technologies [*NASDAQ symbol*] [*Formerly, JMAR Industries*]
J Mar Eng Soc Jpn... Journal. Marine Engineering Society in Japan (journ.) (SAUS)
J Mar J Prac & Proc... John Marshall Journal of Practice and Procedure (journ.) (SAUS)
J Mark... Journal ot Marketing (journ.) (SAUS)
J Marketing... Journal of Marketing [*A publication*] (JLIT)
J Marketing Res... Journal of Marketing Research [*A publication*] (JLIT)
J Market Research Society Vic... Journal. Market Research Society of Victoria (journ.) (SAUS)
J Market Res Soc... Journal. Market Research Society (journ.) (SAUS)
J Market Res Soc... Journal of the Market Research Society (SAUO)
J Market Res Soc... Journal of the Market Research Society (journ.) (SAUS)
J Markets Morality... Journal of Markets and Morality [*A publication*] (JLIT)
J Mark Prof... Journal of Marketing for Professions (journ.) (SAUS)
J Mar L Rev... John Marshall Law Review (journ.) (SAUS)
J Mar Res... Journal of Marine Research [*A publication*] (PABS)
J Mar Sci... Journal of Marine Science (journ.) (SAUS)
J Mar Syst... Journal of Marine Systems [*A publication*] (PABS)
JMARW..... JMAR Inds Wrrt [*NASDAQ symbol*] (TTSB)
JMAS........ James Mason Appreciation Society [*United Kingdom*] (EAIO)
JMAS........ Joint Manpower Automation System (COE)
JMAS........ Joint Mission Application Software (SAUO)
JMAS........ Journal of Modern African Studies (journ.) (SAUS)
J-Mass...... Joint-Modeling and Simulation System
J Mass Dent Soc... Journal Massachusetts Dental Society (journ.) (SAUS)
JMAT........ Joint Medium-calibre Automatic cannon Technology (SAUS)
J Mater...... Journal of Materials (journ.) (SAUS)
J Mater Energy Syst... Journal of Materials for Energy Systems (journ.) (SAUS)
J Mater Eng... Journal of Materials Engineering (journ.) (SAUS)
J Mater Process Technol... Journal of Materials Processing Technology (journ.) (SAUS)
J Mater Res... Journal of Materials Research (journ.) (SAUS)
J Mater Sci... Journal of Materials Science [*A publication*] (CABS)
J Mater Sci Lett... Journal of Materials Science Letters [*A publication*] (CABS)
J Mater Sci Res Inst Dongguk Univ... Journal. Malerials Science Research Institute. Dongguk University (journ.) (SAUS)
J Mater Sci Soc Jpn... Journal. Materials Science Society of Japan (journ.) (SAUS)
J Mater Sci Soc Jpn... Journal of the Materials Science Society of Japan (journ.) (SAUS)
J Mater Sci Technol... Journal of Materials Science and Technology [*A publication*] (CABS)
J Mater Shaping Technol... Journal of Materials Shaping Technology (journ.) (SAUS)
J Mater Technol... Journal of Materials Technology (journ.) (SAUS)
J Math Biol... Journal of Mathematical Biology (journ.) (SAUS)
J Math Chem... Journal of Mathematical Chemistry (journ.) (SAUS)
J Math Econ... Journal of Mathematical Economics [*A publication*] (JLIT)
J Math Econom... Journal of Mathematical Economics (journ.) (SAUS)
J Math Kyoto Univ... Journal of Mathematics. Kyoto University (journ.) (SAUS)
J Math Mech... Journal of Mathematics and Mechanics (journ.) (SAUS)
J Math Modelling Teach... Journal of Mathematical Modelling for Teachers (journ.) (SAUS)
J Math NS... Journal of Mathematics. New Series (journ.) (SAUS)
J Math Physics... Journal of Mathematical Physics (MEC)
J Math Res Exposition... Journal of Mathematical Research and Exposition (journ.) (SAUS)
J Math Soc Jpn... Journal. Mathematical Society of Japan (journ.) (SAUS)
J Math Soc Jpn... Journal of the Mathematical Society of Japan (journ.) (SAUS)
J Math Tokushima Univ... Journal of Mathematics. Tokushima University (journ.) (SAUS)
J Matsumoto Dent Coll Soc... Journal. Matsumoto Dental College Society (journ.) (SAUS)
J Maulana Acad College Tech... Journal. Maulana Acad College of Technology (journ.) (SAUS)
J Maxillofac Orthop... Journal of Maxillofacial Orthopedics (journ.) (SAUS)
J Maxillofac Surg... Journal of Maxillofacial Surgery (journ.) (SAUS)
J Mayan Linguist... Journal of Mayan Linguistics (journ.) (SAUS)
JMB.......... Jamb (ABBR)
JMB.......... Jewelers Memorandum Bureau (EA)
JMB.......... Johnson Matthey Bankers [*Commercial firm*] [*British*]
JMB.......... Joint Matriculation Board [*British*] (DCTA)
JMB.......... Joint Meteorological Board (AAG)
JMB.......... Joint Movements Branch [*NATO*] (NATG)
JMB.......... Journal of Molecular Biology (journ.) (SAUS)
JMBA........ Journal of the Marine Biological Association (SAUO)
JMBA........ Journal of the Marine Biological Association (journ.) (SAUS)
JMBL........ Jumble (ABBR)
JMBLD...... Jumbled (ABBR)
JMBLG...... Jumbling (ABBR)
JMBR........ JMB Reality Trust (SAUS)
JMBRE...... Jamboree (ABBR)
JMBU........ Panthers Container [*Intermodal shipping container symbol*] (TVRC)
JMBX........ Jumbo Transportation [*Private rail car owner code*]
JMC.......... James Mitchell & Co. (EFIS)
JMC.......... Japan Map Center (SAUO)
JMC.......... Japan Medical Congress (journ.) (SAUS)
JMC.......... Japan Metals and Chemicals (SAUO)
JMC.......... Japan Monopoly Corp. (BUAC)
JMC.......... JASC Media Center (SAUS)
JMC.......... Jefferson Medical College (SAUO)
JMC.......... Jerden Manufacturing Corporation (SAUO)
JMC.......... Jerusalem Music Centre (SAUO)
JMC.......... Jewish Marriage Council (BUAC)
JMC.......... Jiangxi Medical College [*China*] (BUAC)
JMC.......... J. Mori [*Federal Railroad Administration identification code*]
JMC.......... Joint Management Centers (SAUS)
JMC.......... Joint Management Committee (SAUO)
JMC.......... Joint Maritime Commission
JMC.......... Joint Maritime Congress [*Washington, DC*] (EA)
JMC.......... Joint Maritime Course (SAUO)
JMC.......... Joint Mathematical Council of the United Kingdom (BUAC)
JMC.......... Joint Message Center
JMC.......... Joint Meteorological Committee
JMC.......... Joint Military Commission [*US, North Vietnam, South Vietnam, Viet Cong*]
JMC.......... Joint Monitoring Commission (SAUO)
JMC.......... Joint Movement Center (COE)
JMC.......... Journal of Medicinal Chemistry (journ.) (SAUS)
JMC.......... Justice Mining Corp. [*Vancouver Stock Exchange symbol*]
JMC.......... Justi Mining Corp. (SAUS)
JMC.......... Sausalito, CA [*Location identifier*] [*FAA*] (FAAL)
Jmca.......... Jamaica (SAUS)
JMCA........ Jewish Ministers Cantors Association of America and Canada (EA)
JMCA........ John M. Cockerham and Associates (SAUO)
JMCA........ Joint Movement Coordination Agency
JMCA........ Judges, Marshals, and Constables Association
JMCAA...... Jewish Minister and Cantors Association of America [*Later, JMCA*] (EA)
JMCAAC..... Jewish Ministers Cantors Association of America and Canada (EA)
JMCAD...... Journal of Molecular Catalysis (journ.) (SAUS)
JMCC........ Joint Manoeuvre Control Command (SAUO)
JMCC........ Joint Maritime Communications Centre (SAUO)
JMCC........ Joint Message Co-ordinating Centre (SAUO)
JMCC........ Joint Message Coordinating Committee (SAUS)
JMCC........ Joint Mobile Command Capability (SAUS)
JMCC........ Joint Mobile Communications Center [*NATO*] (NATG)
JMCC........ Joint Mobile Communications Centre (SAUO)
JMCC........ Joint Movement Control Center (SAUO)
JMCC........ Joint Movements Coordinating Committee [*British*]
JM Cenet... Journal of Medical Genetics (journ.) (SAUS)
JMCG........ JMC Group [*NASDAQ symbol*] (TTSB)
JMCG........ JMC Group, Inc. [*NASDAQ symbol*] (SAG)
JMC Gp..... JMC Group, Inc. [*Associated Press*] (SAG)
JMCHP...... Jubilee. A Magazine of the Church and Her People (journ.) (SAUS)
JMCI......... Journal of Molecular and Cellular Immunology (journ.) (SAUS)
JMCI J Mol Cell Immunol... JMCI. Journal of Molecular and Cellular Immunology (journ.) (SAUS)
JMCIS........ Joint Maritime Command Information System (SAUO)
JMCM........ Journal of Managed Care Medicine (SAUO)
JMCOL...... JUMPS [*Joint Uniform Military Payment System*] Monthly Compute Output Listing [*Military*] (AABC)
JMCP........ Jefferson Medical College of Philadelphia
JMCP........ Journal of Managed Care Pharmacy (SAUO)
JMCQ........ Journalism & Mass Communication Quarterly [*A publication*] (BRI)

JMCS........ Junior Mountaineering Club of Scotland (SAUO)
JMCSSG.... Joint Management Control System Study Group (SAUO)
JMCY........ Jet [*NCIC motorcycle make code*]
JMCY........ Joseph Malins Crusade of Youth [*British*] (BI)
JMD......... Jamaican Dollar (SAUS)
JMD......... Japan Medical Depot (SAUO)
JMD......... Joint Managing Director (DCTA)
JMD......... Joint Monitor Display
JMD......... JOPES Management Division (SAUO)
JMD......... Journal of Management Development (journ.) (SAUS)
JMD......... Jungle Message Decoder (SAUS)
JMD......... Justice Management Division [*U.S. Department of Justice*] (BARN)
JMD......... Juvenile Macular Degeneration [*Medicine*] (MEDA)
J MD Acad Sci... Journal. Maryland Academy of Sciences (journ.) (SAUS)
JMDC........ Japan Machinery Design Center (or Centre) (SAUS)
JMDC........ Joint Manual Direction Center [*Air Force*]
JMDC........ Joint Message Distribution Centre (SAUO)
Jm Dep Agric Bull... Jamaica. Department of Agriculture. Bulletin (journ.) (SAUS)
JMDR........ Journal of Mental Defficiency Research (journ.) (SAUS)
JMDR........ Journal of Missile Defense Research (journ.) (SAUS)
JMDS........ Joint Manpower Data System (SAUO)
J MD State Dent Assoc... Journal. Maryland State Dental Association (journ.) (SAUS)
J Md State Dent Assoc... Journal of the Maryland State Dental Association (SAUO)
J Md State Dent Assoc... Journal of the Maryland State Dental Association (journ.) (SAUS)
JME.......... James Industries [*Vancouver Stock Exchange symbol*]
JME.......... Joint Maximum Effort
JME.......... Journal of Mathematical Economics (journ.) (SAUS)
JME.......... Journal of Medical Education [*AAMC*] [*Medicine*] (EDAA)
JME.......... Journal of Monetary Economics (journ.) (SAUS)
JME.......... Jungle Message Encoder (SAUS)
JME.......... Juvenile Myoclonic Epilepsy [*Medicine*]
JMEA........ Japan Machinery Exporters Association (BUAC)
JMEA........ Jewish Music Educators Association [*Defunct*] (EA)
JMEC........ Joint Materiel Exploitation Center (SAUO)
JMECFC...... Johnny Mathis East Coast Fan Club (EARSL)
J Mech...... Journal of Mechanisms (journ.) (SAUS)
J Mech Behav Mater... Journal of the Mechanical Behavior of Materials (journ.) (SAUS)
J Mech Eng Assoc Witwatersrand... Journal. Mechanical Engineers Association of Witwatersrand (journ.) (SAUS)
J Mech Eng Lab... Journal of Mechanical Engineering Laboratory (journ.) (SAUS)
J Mech Lab Jap... Journal. Mechanical Laboratory of Japan (journ.) (SAUS)
J Mech Phys Solids... Journal of the Mechanics and Physics of Solids [*A publication*] (CABS)
JMED........ Jones Medical Indus [*NASDAQ symbol*] (TTSB)
JMED........ Jones Medical Industries, Inc. [*NASDAQ symbol*] (NQ)
JMED........ Jones Pharma [*NASDAQ symbol*] [*Formerly, Jones Medical Indus.*]
J Med....... Journal of Medicine (journ.) (SAUS)
JMED........ Jungle Message Encoder-Decoder (MCD)
JMEDA...... Journal of Medical Education (journ.) (SAUS)
J Med Ass Form... Jonrnal. Medical Association of Formosa (journ.) (SAUS)
J Med Assoc Ga... Journal of the Medical Association of Georgia (SAUO)
J Med Assoc Ga... Journal of the Medical Association of Georgia (journ.) (SAUS)
J Med Assoc Isr... Journal. Medical Assiation of Israel (journ.) (SAUS)
J Med Assoc Iwate Prefect Hosp... Journal. Medical Association of Iwate Prefectural Hospital (journ.) (SAUS)
J Med Assoc Jam... Journal. Medical Assoriation of Jamaica (journ.) (SAUS)
J Med Assoc Thai... Journal of the Medical Association of Thailand (SAUO)
J Med Assoc Thai... Journal of the Medical Association of Thailand (journ.) (SAUS)
J Med Ass Ok... Journal. Medical Association of Okayama (journ.) (SAUS)
J Med Chem... Journal of Medicinal Chemistry (journ.) (SAUS)
J Med Chir... Journal Medico-Chirurgical (journ.) (SAUS)
J Med Coll Keijo... Journal. Medical College in Keijo (journ.) (SAUS)
J Med Dent Assoc Botswana... Journal. Medical and Dental Association of Botswana (journ.) (SAUS)
J Med Eng Technol... Journal of Medical Engineering & Technology [*A publication*] (CABS)
J Med Enzymol... Journal of Medical Enzymology (journ.) (SAUS)
J Med Exp Clin... Journal of Medicine. Experimental and Clinical (journ.) (SAUS)
J Med Genet... Journal of Medical Genetics (journ.) (SAUS)
J Medicinal Chem... Journal of Medicinal Chemistry (MEC)
J Mediev Hi... Journal of Medieval History (journ.) (SAUS)
J Mediterr Anthropol Archaeol... Journal of Mediterranean Anthropology and Archaeology (journ.) (SAUS)
J Med Lab Technol... Journal of Medical Laboratory Technology (journ.) (SAUS)
J Med Mie Prefect Univ... Journal of Medicine. Mie Prefectural University (journ.) (SAUS)
J Med Pharm Chem... Journal of Medicinal and Pharmaceutical Chemistry (journ.) (SAUS)
J Med Pharm Soc Wkan Yaku... Journal. Medical and Pharmaceutical Society for Wakan-Yaku (journ.) (SAUS)
J Med Prof Ass... Journal. Medical Professions Association (journ.) (SAUS)
J Med Sci... Journal of Medical Sciences (journ.) (SAUS)
J Med Sci Banaras Hindu Univ... Journal of Medical Sciences. Banaras Hindu University (journ.) (SAUS)
J Med Screen... Journal of Medical Screening (journ.) (SAUS)
J Med Soc NJ... Journal of the Medical Society of New Jersey (SAUO)
J Med Soc Toho Univ... Journal. Medical Society of Toho University (journ.) (SAUS)
J Med Syst... Journal of Medical Systems (journ.) (SAUS)
J Med Vet Mycol... Journal of Medical and Veterinary Mycology (journ.) (SAUS)
JMeH........ Journal of Medieval History (journ.) (SAUS)
J Mell Soc Jpn... Journal. Metallurgical Society of Japan (journ.) (SAUS)
JMEM....... Job Memory [*Computer science*] (MHDB)
JMEM....... Joint Munitions Effectiveness Manual [*Military*] (AFM)
JMEM....... Joint Munitions Effects Manual (SAUO)
JMEM....... Junior Marine Engineering Mechanic [*British military*] (DMA)
JMEM/AS... Joint Munitions Effectiveness Manuals, Air-to-Surface (SAUS)
J Membrane Sci... Journal of Membrane Science (MEC)
J Membr Sci... Journal of Membrane Science [*A publication*] (CABS)
JMEMS...... Joint Munition Effectiveness Manual [*Navy*] (DOMA)
JMEM-SO... Joint Munitions Effectiveness Manual-Special Operations (SAUO)
JMEMT...... John Morgan Evans of Merthyr Tydil [*An association*] (EA)
JMEMTF.... Joint Munitions Effectiveness Manual Task Force (MCD)
JMENS...... Joint Mission Element Need Statement (MCD)
J Ment Defic Res... Journal of Mental Defficiency Research (journ.) (SAUS)
J Ment Health... Journal of Mental Health (journ.) (SAUS)
J Ment Health Adm... Journal. Mental Health Administlation (journ.) (SAUS)
J Mercer Dent Soc... Journal. Mercer Dental Society (journ.) (SAUS)
JMES........ Journal. Middle East Society (journ.) (SAUS)
J Metab Res... Journal of Metabolic Research (journ.) (SAUS)
J Metall Club R Coll Sci Technol... Journal. Metallurgical Club. Royal College of Science and Technology (journ.) (SAUS)
J Metall Club Univ Strathclyde... Journal. Metallurgical Club. University of Strathclyde (journ.) (SAUS)
J Metamorph Geol... Journal of Metamorphic Geology (journ.) (SAUS)
J Meteorol Res... Journal of Meteorological Research (journ.) (SAUS)
J Meteorol Soc Jpn... Journal. Meteorological Society of Japan (journ.) (SAUS)
J Met Finish Soc Jp... Journal. Metal Finishing Society of Japan (journ.) (SAUS)
J Met Finish Soc Jpn... Journal of the Metal Finishing Society of Japan (journ.) (SAUS)
J Met Finish Soc Korea... Journal. Metal Finishing Society of Korea (journ.) (SAUS)
J Met Finish Soc Korea... Journal of the Metal Finishing Society of Korea (journ.) (SAUS)
JMETL....... Joint Mission Essential Task List (DOMA)
J Met Soc Jap... Journal. Meteorological Society of Japan (journ.) (SAUS)
J Mex Am Hist... Journal of Mexican American History (journ.) (SAUS)
JMF.......... James Madison Foundation (EA)
JMF.......... Java Media Framework [*Computer science*]
JMF.......... Jeffrey Modell Foundation [*Association*] (EA)
JMF.......... Jet Mixing Flow
JMF.......... Jewish Music Forum
JMF.......... John Marshall Foundation (EA)
JMF.......... Johnston Mutual Fund, Inc. (SAUO)
JMF.......... Joint Mission Force [*Army*]
JMF.......... Journal of Marriage and the Family [*A publication*] (BRI)
JMF.......... Juilliard Musical Foundation (SAUO)
JMFA........ Journal of the Museum of Fine Arts, Boston [*A publication*] (ABAR)
JMFC........ Jared Martin Fan Club [*Defunct*] (EA)
JMFC........ Jayne Mansfield Fan Club (EA)
JMFC........ Jimmy Murphy Fan Club (EA)
JMFR........ Johnson Motor Freight [*Common carrier symbol*]
JMFT........ Journal of Milk and Food Technology (journ.) (SAUS)
JMFU........ Joint force Meteorological and oceanographic Forecast Unit (SAUO)
JMFU........ Joint METOC Forecast Unit (SAUO)
JMG......... Jewelry Manufacturers Guild (EA)
JMG......... Joint Meteorological Group [*DoD*]
JMG......... Joint Monitoring Group (SAUO)
JMG......... Journal of Management Consulting (journ.) (SAUS)
JMG......... Journal of Medical Genetics (SAUO)
JMG......... Journal of Molecular Graphics (journ.) (SAUS)
JMGR........ JCI Site Management (SAUO)
JMGS........ Journal of Modern Greek Studies (journ.) (SAUS)
J Mgt........ Journal of Management (journ.) (SAUS)
JMH......... John Milton Hagen [*Antibody*] [*Immunology*] (DAVI)
JMH......... Joint Mission Hardware (SAUO)
JMH......... Journal of Mental Health [*Medicine*] (EDAA)
JMH......... Journal of Mississippi History (journ.) (SAUS)
JMH......... Journal of Modern History [*A publication*] (BRI)
JMH......... Journal of Modern History (journ.) (SAUS)
JMHC........ Joint Mission Hardware Contractor (SAUO)
JMHO........ Just My Honest Opinion (SAUS)
JMHO........ Just My Humble Opinion (SAUS)
JMHS........ James Madison High School (SAUO)
JMHS........ James Monroe High School (SAUO)
JMHS........ John Muir High School (SAUO)
JMHX........ JM Huber [*Private rail car owner code*]
JMI.......... Jackson & Moreland, Inc. (MCD)
JMI.......... Jackson & Moreland, Incorporated (SAUO)
JMI.......... Jan Mayen Island [*Seismograph station code, US Geological Survey*] (SEIS)
JMI.......... Japan Machinery and Metal Inspection (SAUS)
JMI.......... Japan Management Institute (BUAC)
JMI.......... Japan Metals Institute (SAUS)
JMI.......... John Muir Institute (SAUS)
JMI.......... John Muir Institute for Environmental Studies [*Defunct*] (EA)
JMI.......... Jones Medical Industries, Inc. (EFIS)
JmI.......... Jorm Microlab, Inc., Cedar Rapids, IA [*Library symbol*] [*Library of Congress*] (LCLS)
JMI.......... Journal of Medical Imaging (journ.) (SAUS)
JMI.......... Justice Management Institute
JMI.......... Justice Mortgage Investors (SAUO)
JMIA........ Japan Mining Industry Association (BUAC)
JMIA........ JCI Internal Auditor (SAUO)

JMIC .... Joint Maritime Intelligence Centre (SAUO)
J Mich Dent Assoc... Journal. Michigan Dental Association (journ.) (SAUS)
J Mich State Dent Assoc... Journal. Michigan State Dental Association (journ.) (SAUS)
J Mich State Dent Assoc... Journal of the Michigan State Dental Association (SAUO)
J Mich State Dent Assoc... Journal of the Michigan State Dental Association (journ.) (SAUS)
J Mich State Dent Soc... Journal. Michigan State Dental Society (journ.) (SAUS)
J Micr and Nat Sc... Journal of Microscopy and Natural Science (journ.) (SAUS)
J Microb Biotechnol... Journal of Microbical Biotechnology (journ.) (SAUS)
J Microbiol UAR... Journal of Microbiology of the United Arab Republic (journ.) (SAUS)
J Microcomput Appl... Journal of Microcomputer Applications (journ.) (SAUS)
J Microcomput Syst Manage... Journal of Microcomputer Systems Management (journ.) (SAUS)
J Micronutr Anal... Journal of Micronutrient Analysis (journ.) (SAUS)
J Microorg Ferment... Journal of Microorganisms and Fermentation (journ.) (SAUS)
J Microsurg... Journal of Microsurgery (journ.) (SAUS)
J Microw Power Electromagn Energy... Journal of Microwave Power and Electromagnetic Energy (journ.) (SAUS)
JMIE .... Joint Maritime Information Element [*Coast Guard*]
JMIE .... Joint Maritime Information Exchange
J Mie Med Coll... Journal. Mie Medical College (journ.) (SAUS)
JMIF .... Japan Motor Industrial Federation (BUAC)
JMIFC .... Jeanette MacDonald International Fan Club (EA)
JMIFC .... Johnny Mathis International Fan Club (EA)
JMiH .... Journal of Mississippi History (journ.) (SAUS)
J Mil H ...... Journal of Military History [*A publication*] (BRI)
J Mil Serv Inst... Journal of the Military Institution (journ.) (SAUS)
J Mil Soc... Journal of Political and Military Sociology. (journ.) (SAUS)
J Min Coll Akita Univ Ser A... Journal. Mining College. Akita Univer- sity. Series A. Mining Geology (journ.) (SAUS)
J Mineral Petrol Econ Geol... Journal of Mineralogy, Petrology and Economic Geology (journ.) (SAUS)
J Mineral Soc Jpn... Journal. Mineralogical Society of Japan (journ.) (SAUS)
J Mine Vent Soc S Afr... Journal. Mine Ventilation Society of South Africa (journ.) (SAUS)
J Mine Vent Soc S Afr... Journal of the Mine Ventilation Society of South Africa (journ.) (SAUS)
J Min Geol... Journal of Mining and Geology (journ.) (SAUS)
J Minist Health... Journal. Ministry of Health (journ.) (SAUS)
J Min Mater Process Inst Jpn... Journal of the Mining and Materials Processing Institute of Japan (journ.) (SAUS)
J Min Mat Process Inst Jpn... Journal. Mining and Materials Processing Institute of Japan (journ.) (SAUS)
J Min Metall Foundry... Journal of Mining and Metallurgy. Foundry (journ.) (SAUS)
J Min Metall Inst Jpn... Journal of the Mining and Metallurgical Institute of Japan (journ.) (SAUS)
J Min Metall Metall... Journal of Mining and Metallurgy. Metallurgy (journ.) (SAUS)
J Minn Acad Sci... Journal. Minnesota Academy of Science (journ.) (SAUS)
JMIR .... Journal of Medical Internet Research (SAUO)
J Miss Acad Sci... Journal. Mississippi Academy of Sciences (journ.) (SAUS)
J Miss Hist... Journal of Mississippi History. Mississippi Historical Society. Jackson (SAUO)
J Miss State Med Assoc... Journal of the Mississippi State Medical Association (SAUO)
J Miss State Med Assoc... Journal of the Mississippi State Medical Association (journ.) (SAUS)
JMithSt ...... Journal of Mithraic Studies [*A publication*] (ABAR)
JMIZ .... Joanna Mills [*Federal Railroad Administration identification code*]
JMJ .... James J. Johnston [*FAA designator*] (FAAC)
JMJ .... Jesus, Mary, and Joseph
JMJ .... JMJ Children's Fund of Canada (EAIO)
JMJ .... Johnston Airways (SAUO)
JMJZ .... JMJ Projects [*Intermodal trailer symbol*]
JMK .... Jamtska [*Language symbol*] (ETLW)
JMK .... Mikonos [*Greece*] [*Airport symbol*] (OAG)
J Mktg Res... Journal of Marketing Research (journ.) (SAUS)
JMKU .... Journal of Mathematics. Kyoto University (journ.) (SAUS)
JMKU .... Journal of Mathematics of Kyoto University (journ.) (SAUS)
JmKU .... University of the West Indies (SAUO)
JMKWA2 .... Annual Reports. Institute of Population Problems (journ.) (SAUS)
JML .... James Madison Ltd. (EFIS)
JML .... Job Method Learning (PDAA)
JML .... Journal of Modern Literature [*A publication*] (ANEX)
JML .... Journal of Modern Literature (journ.) (SAUS)
JML .... JW Martin Laboratory (SAUS)
JML .... Taxi Aereo de Jimulco SA de CV [*Mexico*] [*ICAO designator*] (FAAC)
JML&P ...... Journal of Media Law and Practice [*A publication*] (SAFN)
JMLC .... JCI Legal Counsel (SAUO)
JmLibS ...... Jamaica Library Service (SAUS)
JM Ling ..... Journal of Mayan Linguistics (journ.) (SAUS)
JMLR .... John Marshall Law Review (journ.) (SAUS)
JMLS .... John Marshall Law School [*Chicago, IL*] (DLA)
JMLS .... John Menzies Library Services [*Information service or system*] (IID)
J Ml Vet Med Ass... Journal. Malayan Veterinary Medical Association (journ.) (SAUS)
JMM .... Jacobi Matrix Method [*Mathematics*]
JMM .... Jamaica Merchant Marine (EY)
JMM .... Joint Man Machine (IAA)
JMM .... Journal of Macromarketing (journ.) (SAUS)
JMM .... Journal of Microbiological Methods (journ.) (SAUS)
JMM .... Journal of Molecular Medicine [*A publication*]
JMMA .... Japan Materials Management Association (BUAC)
JMMA .... Japan Microscope Manufacturers Association (BUAC)
JMMAA ...... Journal. Maine Medical Association (journ.) (SAUS)
JMMAT ...... Joint Military Mission for Aid to Turkey (SAUO)
JMMC .... James Madison Memorial Commission (SAUO)
JMMC .... Joint Military Medical Command (SAUO)
JMMF .... James Monroe Memorial Foundation (EA)
JMMII .... Japan Machinery and Metals Inspection Institute (BUAC)
JMMMD ..... Journal of Magnetism and Magnetic Materials (journ.) (SAUS)
JMMO .... Joint Medical Mobilization Office (SAUO)
JMMSD ..... Journal. Korea Merchant Marine College. Natural Sciences Series (journ.) (SAUS)
JMM System... Joint Man-Machine System (SAUS)
JMN .... Jeweled-Orifice Misting Nozzle
JMN .... Johan Mangku Negara [*Malaysian Honour*]
JMN .... Justification for Mission Need (SAUO)
JMNA .... Joint Military Net Assessment [*A publication*] (RDA)
JMNCL ...... Jeunesse du Mouvement National Congolaise - Lumumba [*Youth of the Lumumba Wing of the Congolese National Movement*]
J/Mne .... Junior Marine [*British military*] (DMA)
JMNR .... Journal of Military Nursing and Research (SAUO)
JMNR .... Journal of Military Nursing and Research (journ.) (SAUS)
JMO .... Jesuit Mission Office [*Australia*]
JMO .... Joint Force Meteorological and Oceanographic Officer (COE)
JMO .... Joint Maritime Operations (COE)
JMO .... Jomsom [*Nepal*] [*Airport symbol*] (OAG)
JMO .... Jugoslovenska Muslimanska Organizacija [*Yugoslav Moslem Organization*] [*Political party*] (PPE)
JMO .... Just My Opinion [*Online dialog*]
JMOA .... Joint Memorandum of Agreement (ACAE)
JMOB .... Joint Mobile Offshore Base [*Military*]
JMOC .... Joint METOC Operations Center (SAUO)
J Mo Dent Assoc... Journal. Missouri Dental Association (journ.) (SAUS)
JModH ...... Journal of Modern History (SAUS)
J Mod Lit... Journal of Modern Literature (journ.) (SAUS)
J Mod Opt... Journal of Modern Optics (journ.) (SAUS)
JMOF .... Joint Meteorological Observing Facility (SAUO)
J/MOL .... Joules per Mole [*Physics*]
J Molec Struct... Journal of Molecular Structure (MEC)
J Mol Electron... Journal of Molecular Electronics (journ.) (SAUS)
J Mol Endocrinol... Journal of Molecular Endocrinology (journ.) (SAUS)
J Mol Evol... Journal of Molecular Evolution (journ.) (SAUS)
J Mol Graph... Journal of Molecular Graphics (journ.) (SAUS)
J Mol Graphics... Journal of Molecular Graphics [*A publication*] (CABS)
J/(MOL K)... Joules per Mole Kelvin [*Physics*]
J Mol Liq... Journal of Molecular Liquids (journ.) (SAUS)
J Molluscan Stud... Journal of Molluscan Studies (journ.) (SAUS)
J Molluscan Stud Suppl... Journal of Molluscan Studies. Supplement (journ.) (SAUS)
J Mol Med... Journal of Molecular Medicine (MEC)
J Mol Med... Journal of Molecular Medicine (journ.) (SAUS)
J Mol Recognit... Journal of Molecular Recognition (journ.) (SAUS)
J Mol Sci... Journal of Molecular Science (journ.) (SAUS)
J Mol Struct... Journal of Molecular Structure (journ.) (SAUS)
J Monetary Econ... Journal of Monetary Economics (journ.) (SAUS)
J Monet Econ... Journal of Monetary Economics [*A publication*] (JLIT)
J Money Credit Bank... Journal of Money, Credit and Banking. Columbus (SAUS)
JMOOC ...... Just My Opinion of Course (SAUS)
JMOP .... Joint Memorandum of Policy [*Military*]
J Mormon Hist... Journal of Mormon History (journ.) (SAUS)
JMOS .... Job Management Operations System (PDAA)
JMOTS ...... Joint Maritime Operational Training Staffs (SAUO)
J Mo Water Sewerage Conf... Journal. Missouri Water and Sewerage Conference (journ.) (SAUS)
JMP .... Jack Morton Productions, Inc. [*New York, NY*] [*Telecommunications*] (TSSD)
JMP .... Jen Min Piao [*or Yuan*] [*Peoples money of China*] (BARN)
JMP .... J.M. Peters (EFIS)
JMP .... Job Monitor Protocol (SAUS)
JMP .... John M. Poindexter [*National Security Advisor during the Reagan Administration*]
JMP .... Johnson Matthey Public Ltd. Co. [*Toronto Stock Exchange symbol*]
JMP .... Joint Manpower Program [*Military*] (CINC)
JMP .... Joint Mission Processor (SAUO)
JMP .... Joint Monitoring Programme (SAUO)
JMP .... Journal of Public Policy and Marketing (journ.) (SAUS)
JMP .... Jump [*Computer science*]
JMPA .... Joint Military Passenger Equalization Agreement (SAUO)
JMPAB ...... Joint Materiel Priorities and Allocation Board [*Military*] (AABC)
JMPC .... Joint Mapping and Photography Committee (SAUO)
JMPC .... Joint Military Procurements Control [*World War II*]
JMPC .... Joint Session of the Manpower Committees (SAUO)
JMPD .... Jumped (ABBR)
JMPE .... Joint Mission Processing Environment (SAUO)
JMPE .... Joint Mission Processing Equipment (SAUO)
JMPG .... Jumping (ABBR)
JMPI .... Jumpmaster Personnel Inspection [*Army*] (ADDR)
J M Plant Res... Journal of Medicinal Plant Research. Planta Medica (journ.) (SAUS)
JMPLY ...... Johnson Matthey PLC [*OTCBB symbol*]
JMPMA ...... Journal of Medical Primatology (journ.) (SAUS)
JMPNS ...... Jumpiness (ABBR)

JMPO .... Joint MILSTAR Program Office (SAUO)
JMPO .... Journal of Microwave Power (journ.) (SAUS)
JMPOF ...... Jumpoff (ABBR)
JMPP .... Joint Munitions Production Panel (MCD)
JMPR .... Joint FAO/WHO Meeting and/on Pesticide Residues (SAUO)
JMPR .... Joint Meeting on Pesticide Residues [*Environmental Protection Agency*] (EPAT)
JMPR .... Jumper (MSA)
JMPS .... Journal of Medical and Pharmaceutical Marketing [*Medicine*] (EDAA)
JMPSB ...... Journal of Mathematical and Physical Sciences (journ.) (SAUS)
JMPT .... Joint Military Potential Test (MCD)
JMPT .... Journal of Manipulative and Physiological Therapeutics [*A Publication*] (MHID)
JMPT .... Journal of Manipulative and Physiological Therapeutics (journ.) (SAUS)
JMPTC ...... Joint Military Packaging Training Center
JMR .... Alexandair, Inc. [*Canada*] [*ICAO designator*] (FAAC)
JMR .... Jamair Inc. (SAUO)
JMR .... Job Manager Request (TIMI)
JMR .... Johannesburg Mounted Rifles [*British military*] (DMA)
JMR .... Journal of Magnetic Resonance (journ.) (SAUS)
JMR .... Journal of Marketing Research (journ.) (SAUS)
JMR .... Journal of Materials Research (journ.) (SAUS)
JMR .... Journal of Molecular Recognition (journ.) (SAUS)
JMRAS ...... Journal of the Malayan Branch of the Royal Asiatic Society (SAUO)
JMRAS ...... Journal of the Malayan Branch of the Royal Asiatic Society (journ.) (SAUS)
JMRC .... Joint Mobile Relay Center (MCD)
JMRC .... Joint Mobile Relay Center (or Centre) (SAUO)
JMRCM ..... Journal of Muscle Research and Cell Motility (journ.) (SAUS)
JMRE .... JM Resources, Inc. (SAUO)
JMRI .... Journal of Magnetic Resonance Imaging (journ.) (SAUS)
JMRMA ..... John and Mable Ringling Museum of Art (SAUO)
JMRNSC .... Joint Meteorological Rocket Network Steering Committee (SAUO)
JMRO .... Joint Medical Regulating Office (AABC)
JMRO .... Joint Military Regulating Office
JMRP .... Joint Meteorological Radio Propagation (SAUS)
JMRP .... Joint Meteorological Radio Propagation Committee [*British*] (MCD)
JMRP .... Joint Meteorological Radio Propagation Sub-Committee (BUAC)
JMRP Committee... Joint Meteorological Radio Propagation Committee (SAUS)
JMRPDC .... Japan Medical Research Foundation. Publication (journ.) (SAUS)
JMRPS ...... Joint Meteorological Radio Propagation Subcommittee (SAUS)
JMRS .... Journal of Medieval and Renaissance Studies (journ.) (SAUS)
JMRT .... Jomar Truck Line [*Common carrier symbol*]
JMRT .... Junior Members Round Table [*American Library Association*]
J Mr Technol Soc... Journal. Marine Technology Society (journ.) (SAUS)
JMRZ .... Jacobs Mine Ranch [*Federal Railroad Administration identification code*]
JMS .... Jacob More Society (EA)
JMS .... James Madison Society (SAUO)
JMS .... James (motorcycle) [*NCIC motorcycle make code*]
JMS .... Jamestown [*North Dakota*] [*Airport symbol*] (OAG)
JMS .... Jamestown, ND [*Location identifier*] [*FAA*] (FAAL)
JMS .... Japan Medical Society (SAUO)
JMS .... Java Message Service (SAUS)
JMS .... Java Messaging Service (VLIE)
JMS .... Jewish Media Service [*Defunct*] (EA)
JMS .... J.M. Smucker Company (EFIS)
JMS .... Job Management System (SAUS)
JMS .... Johannesburg Musical Society (SAUO)
JMS .... John Milton Society for the Blind [*Later, JMSB*] (EA)
JMS .... Joint Mission Software (SAUO)
JMS .... Joint Movements Staff [*British*]
J/MS .... Joules per Cubic Meter (SAUS)
J/Ms .... Joules per Square Meter (SAUS)
JMS .... Journal of Maltese Studies (journ.) (SAUS)
JMS .... Journal of Management Studies (journ.) (SAUS)
JMS .... Journal of Manufacturing Systems (journ.) (SAUS)
JMS .... Journal of Medical Science [*IRCS*] [*Mental Science*] [*Medicine*] (EDAA)
JMS .... Journal of Molecular Structure [*Medicine*] (EDAA)
JMS .... Jump to Subroutine Instruction [*Computer science*]
JMS .... Junior Medical Student (DAVI)
JMS .... Morgan Stanley Group, Inc. [*AMEX symbol*] (SAG)
JMSA .... Japanese Maritime Safety Association (SAUS)
JMSA .... Japan Marine Safety Agency [*Marine science*] (OSRA)
JMSAC ...... Joint Meteorological Satellite Advisory Committee
JMSB .... John Milton Society for the Blind (EA)
JMSBA ...... Journal of Mental Subnormality (journ.) (SAUS)
JMSC .... Japanese MIDI Standard Committee (SAUO)
JmSC .... Japan Microfilm Service Center Co. Ltd., Tokyo, Japan [*Library symbol*] [*Library of Congress*] (LCLS)
JMSC .... Japan MIDI Standard Committee (SAUS)
JMSC .... Joint Meteorological Satellite Communication (SAUO)
JMSCA ...... Journal of Mental Science (journ.) (SAUS)
JMSDC ...... Joint Merchant Shipping Defence Committee [*General Council of British Shipping*] (DS)
JMSDF ...... Japanese Maritime Self-Defense Force
JMSDF ...... Japan Maritime Self-Defense Force (SAUS)
JMSEP ...... Joint Modeling and Simulation Executive Panel [*DoD*]
JMSJ .... Journal. Mathematical Society of Japan (journ.) (SAUS)
JMSJ .... Journal of the Mathematical Society of Japan (journ.) (SAUS)
JMSLS ...... Joliet Three-Minute Speech and Language Screen [*Test*]
JMSMD ..... Journal of Materials for Energy Systems (journ.) (SAUS)
JMSNA ...... Journal. Medical Society of New Jersey (journ.) (SAUS)
JMSNS ...... Justification for Major System New Start (SAUO)
JMSNS ...... Justification of Major System New Start [*Military*]
JMSO .... Joint Meetings of Seafarers Organization (SAUS)
JMSPO ...... Joint Meteorological Satellite Program Office
JMSPO ...... Joint Meteorological System Project Office (ACAE)
JMSW .... Joint Mission Software Subsystem (SAUO)
JMSW .... Journal of Multicultural Social Work [*A publication*] (BRI)
JMSWG ..... Joint Message Standard Working Group (SAUO)
JMSWG ..... Joint Multi-TADIL Standards Working Group (SAUO)
JMSX .... Job Memory Switch Matrix
JMT .... Job Methods Training
JMT .... Johnson, Mirmiran and Thompson (SAUO)
JMT .... Jointly-Managed Trust (SAUS)
JMT .... Joint Management Team (MCD)
JMT .... Journal of Music Therapy (journ.) (SAUS)
JMT .... Judgment (DCTA)
JMTAA .... Journal. Institute of Mathematics and Its Applications (journ.) (SAUS)
JMTB .... Joint Military Transportation Board
JMTBA ...... Japan Machine Tool-Builders Association (BUAC)
JMTC .... Joint Military Transportation Committee
JMTE .... Journal. Michigan Teachers of English (journ.) (SAUS)
J M Technol.... Journal of Medical Technology (journ.) (SAUS)
JMTG .... Joint Military Task Group (MUGU)
JMTG .... Joint Military Terminology Group (AFM)
JMTG .... Joint Missile Task Group (SAUO)
JMTI .... Michael Joboian [*Common carrier symbol*]
JMTK .... Joint Mapping Tool Kit
JMTR .... Japan Materials Testing Reactor (SAUS)
JMTR .... Japan Material Testing Reactor (SAUS)
J Mt Sinai Hosp... Journal Mount Sinai Hospital (journ.) (SAUS)
JMTSS ...... Joint Multichannel Trunking and Switching System (MCD)
JMTT .... J-M Transports [*Common carrier symbol*]
JMTTA .... Japan Machine Tool Trade Association (SAUO)
JMU .... James Madison University [*Virginia*]
JMU .... James Millikin University (SAUO)
JMU .... Jamshedpur Mazdoor Union [*India*]
JMU .... Job Management Unit (SAUS)
JMU .... John Moores University [*British*]
JMUA .... Joint Meritorious Unit Award [*Military decoration*] (GFGA)
J Multinat Finan Manage... Journal of Multinational Financial Management [*A publication*] (JLIT)
JMUSA ...... Journal. American Musicological Society (journ.) (SAUS)
JMUSDC .... Joint Mexican-United States Defense Commission
JMUSDC .... Joint Mexico-United States Defense Commission (SAUO)
J Music Res... Journal of Musicological Research (journ.) (SAUS)
J Music Thr... Journal of Music Theory (journ.) (SAUS)
J/Musn ...... Junior Musician [*British military*] (DMA)
J Mus Therapy... Journal of Music Therapy (journ.) (SAUS)
JMV .... Justice for Murder Victims [*An association*]
JMVA .... Joint Meritorious Unit Award (SAUO)
JMVB .... Joint Merchant Vessels Board [*World War II*]
JMW .... James McNeill Whistler [*Nineteenth-century American painter and etcher*]
JMWH .... Journal Watch: Womens Health (SAUS)
JMWU .... Johannesburg Municipal Workers Union (SAUO)
JMX .... Jumbogroup Multiplex [*Bell System*]
JMY .... Jamesway Corp. (SAUO)
JMY .... Jimmy (ABBR)
JMY .... Jimmy [*NCIC car model code*]
J/my .... Joule per meter squared (SAUS)
JMYG .... Jimmying (ABBR)
J Mysore Agr Exp Union... Journal. Mysore Agricultural and Experimental Union (journ.) (SAUS)
J Mysore Med Assoc... Journal. Mysore Medical Association (journ.) (SAUS)
J Mysore U Arts... Journal. Mysore University. Section A. Arts (journ.) (SAUS)
JMYUAP .... Journal. Mysore University. Section B. Science (journ.) (SAUS)
JMZU .... Jansen Meijer [*Intermodal shipping container symbol*] (TVRC)
JN .... Jamaican Neuropathy [*Medicine*] (EDAA)
JN .... Jam Nut (SAUS)
jn .... Jan Mayen [*MARC country of publication code*] [*Library of Congress*] (LCCP)
JN .... Jannock Ltd. [*Toronto Stock Exchange symbol*]
jn .... January (RION)
J-N .... Jet Navigation (AAG)
JN .... Jet Navigation Chart
JN .... Jim's Neighbors (EA)
JN .... Job Number
Jn .... John [*New Testament book*]
JN .... Johnson Noise [*Thermal noise, that made by a resistor at a temperature above absolute zero*]
JN .... Join (MSA)
JN .... Journal Name [*Online database field identifier*]
JN .... Journal of Neurochemistry Neurophysiology/Neurosurgery [*AANS*] [*Medicine*] (EDAA)
JN .... Journal of Neurophysiology (SAUS)
JN .... Journal of Nutrition (SAUS)
Jn .... Juglans nigra [*Eastern black walnut*]
Jn .... Junction [*Indian Railway*] (TIR)
JN .... Junction
JN .... Junctional Nevus [*Medicine*] (MELL)
JN .... June (ROG)
JN .... Junior (ROG)
JN .... Junior Navigator [*Nautical term*] (NTA)
JN .... Justice Now [*An association*]

Jn.......... King John [*Shakespearean work*]
JNA.......... Januaria [*Brazil*] [*Airport symbol*] (AD)
JNA.......... Jena Nomina Anatomica [*Also, INA*] [*Anatomy*]
JNA.......... Jewish News Agency (BJA)
JNA.......... John Nurminen, OY [*Finland*] [*FAA designator*] (FAAC)
JNA.......... Joint Navy (IAA)
JNA.......... Jordanian News Agency
JNA.......... Jordan News Agency (SAUS)
JNA.......... Journal of Nursing Administration (SAUO)
JNA.......... Jump If Not Above [*Computer science*] (PCM)
JNA.......... Junior Naval Airman [*British military*] (DMA)
JNA.......... Northern Illinois University, De Kalb, IL [*OCLC symbol*] (OCLC)
JNA.......... Yugoslav People's Army
JNABD....... Journal of Nuclear Agriculture and Biology (journ.) (SAUS)
JNAC....... Japan-North American Commission on Cooperative Mission (EA)
JNACC....... Joint Nuclear Accident Coordinating Center
JNADPI...... Japan National Assembly of Disabled Peoples' International (EAIO)
JNAE......... Jump If Not Above or Equal [*Computer science*] (PCM)
JNAF......... Japanese Navy Air Force
JNAF......... Joint Navy-Air Force
J Nagasaki Earth Sci Ass... Journal. Nagasaki Earth Science Associa- tion (journ.) (SAUS)
J Nagasaki Public Health Soc... Journal. Nagasaki Public Health Society (journ.) (SAUS)
J Nagoya Med Assoc... Journal. Nagoya Medical Association (journ.) (SAUS)
J Nagoy City Univ Med Ass... Journal. Nagoya City University Medical Association (journ.) (SAUS)
J Nakanihon Automot Jr Coll... Journal. Nakanihon Automotive Junior College (journ.) (SAUS)
JNALA....... Journal of the New African Literature and the Arts (journ.) (SAUS)
JNAM........ Junior Naval Air Mechanic [*British military*] (DMA)
J Nanjing Agric Coll... Journal. Nanjing Agricultural College (journ.) (SAUS)
J Nanjing Coll Pharm... Journal. Nanjing College of Pharmacy (journ.) (SAUS)
J Nanjing Inst For... Journal. Nanjing Institute of Forestry (journ.) (SAUS)
J Nanjing Inst Technol... Journal. Nanjing Institute of Technology (journ.) (SAUS)
J Nanjing Technol Coll For Prod... Journal. Nanjing Technological College of Forest Produds (journ.) (SAUS)
J Nanjing Univ Nat Sci Ed... Journal. Nanjing University. Natural Science Edition (journ.) (SAUS)
J Nara Gakugei Univ... Journal. Nara Gakugei University (journ.) (SAUS)
J Nara Gakugei Univ Nat Sci... Journal. Nara Gakugei University. Natural Science (journ.) (SAUS)
JNA Referees Bank... Journal. National Association of Referees in Bankruptcy [*A publication*] (DLA)
J Narr Tech... Journal of Narrative Technique (journ.) (SAUS)
J Natal Zulu Hist... Journal of Natal and Zulu History (journ.) (SAUS)
J Nat Chiao Tung Univ... National Chiao Tung University (SAUO)
J Nating Inst Technol... Journal of Nating Institute of Technology (journ.) (SAUS)
J Nat Inst Hospitl Adm... Journal. National Institute of Hospital Administration (journ.) (SAUS)
J Nat Inst Soc Sci... Journal. National Institute of Social Sciences (journ.) (SAUS)
J Natl Acad Sci... Journal. National Academy of Sciences (journ.) (SAUS)
J Natl Analg Soc... Journal. National Analgesia Society (journ.) (SAUS)
J Natl Assoc Hosp Dev... Journal. National Association for Hospital Development (journ.) (SAUS)
J Natl Assoc Priv Psychiatr Hosp... Journal. National Association of Private Psychiatric Hospitals (journ.) (SAUS)
J Natl Cancer Inst... Journal of the National Cancer Institute (SAUO)
J Natl Cancer Inst... Journal of the National Cancer Institute (journ.) (SAUS)
J Natl Chem Lab Ind... Journal of the National Chemical Laboratory for Industry (journ.) (SAUS)
J Natl Chiao Tung Univ... Journal. National Chiao Tung University (journ.) (SAUS)
J Natl Def Med Coll... Journal. National Defense Medical College (journ.) (SAUS)
J Natl Inst Agric Bot... Journal. Nabonal Institute of Agricultural Botany (journ.) (SAUS)
J Natl Inst Pers Res S Afr CSIR... Journal. National Institute for Personnel Research. South African Council for Scientific and Industrial Research (journ.) (SAUS)
J Natl Med Ass... Journal. National Medical Association (journ.) (SAUS)
J Natl Med Assoc... Journal of the National Medical Association (SAUO)
J Natl Med Assoc... Journal of the National Medical Association (journ.) (SAUS)
J Natl Res Counc Thail... Journal of the National Research Council of Thailand (journ.) (SAUS)
J Natl Tech Assoc... Journal of the National Technical Asso- ciation (journ.) (SAUS)
J Natn Cancer Inst... Journal. National Cancer Institute (journ.) (SAUS)
J Natn Inst Agric Bot... Journal. National Institute of Agricultural Botany (journ.) (SAUS)
J Nat Prod... Journal of Natural Products (journ.) (SAUS)
J Nat Rubber Res... Journal of Natural Rubber Research (journ.) (SAUS)
J Nat Sci.... Jeju University Journal. Natural Sciences (journ.) (SAUS)
J Nat Sci and Math... Journal of National Science and Mathematics (journ.) (SAUS)
J Nat Sci Coll Gen Stud Seoul Natl Univ... Journal of Natural Sciences. College of General Studies. Seoul National University (journ.) (SAUS)
J Nat Sci Res Inst Yonsei Univ... Journal. Natural Science Research Institute. Yonsei University (journ.) (SAUS)
J Nat Sci Soc Ichimura Gakuen J Coll... Journal. Natural Scientific Society. Ichimura Gakuen Junior College (journ.) (SAUS)
J Nat Sci Yeungnam Univ... Journal of Natural Sciences. Yeungnam University (journ.) (SAUS)
JNAU........ Jawaharlal Nehru Agricultural University [*India*] (BUAC)
JNAU........ Jumbo America [*Intermodal shipping container symbol*] (TVRC)
J Naut Soc Jpn... Journal. Nautical Society of Japan (journ.) (SAUS)
J Navig...... Journal of Navigation (journ.) (SAUS)
JNB.......... Johannesburg [*South Africa*] [*Airport symbol*] (OAG)
JNB.......... Joinable (ABBR)
JNB.......... Jump If Not Below [*Computer science*] (PCM)
JNBE......... Jump If Not Below or Equal [*Computer science*] (PCM)
JNBIA........ Journal. Newark Beth Israel Hospital (journ.) (SAUS)
JNBK......... Jefferson National Bank (SAUO)
JNBMDW... Journal. New Brunswick Museum (journ.) (SAUS)
JNBNA....... Journal of National Black Nurses Association (SAUO)
JNBNA....... Journal of National Black Nurses Association (journ.) (SAUS)
JNC.......... Jet Navigation Chart
JNC.......... John Nuveen 'A' [*NYSE symbol*] (TTSB)
JNC.......... Joint National Council (AIE)
JNC.......... Joint Negotiating Committee (SAUO)
JNC.......... Joint Negotiating Council [*British*] (DCTA)
JNC.......... Journal. National Cancer Institute (journ.) (SAUS)
JNC.......... Journal of the National Cancer Institute (SAUO)
JNC.......... Jump If No Carry [*Computer science*] (PCM)
JNC.......... Jump on No Carry (SAUS)
JNC.......... Junction (ADA)
JNC.......... Nuveen [*John*] & Co. [*NYSE symbol*] (SPSG)
JNCA........ Junior Naval Cadets of America (SAUO)
JNCC........ Joint National Conciliation Committee (SAUO)
JNCC........ Joint Nature Conservation Committee (BUAC)
JNCC........ Joint Nuclear Control Commission (SAUO)
JNCC........ Junior Naval Command Course
JNCCY....... Junction City, WI [*American Association of Railroads railroad junction routing code*]
J NC Dent Soc... Journal. North Carolina Dental Society (journ.) (SAUS)
JNCG........ Japan Nuclear Codes Group
JNCH........ Jones Transport [*Common carrier symbol*]
JNChBAS.... Journal of the North China Branch of the Royal Asiatic Society (SAUO)
Jn Chem Q... Japan Chemical Quarterly (journ.) (SAUS)
J N Ch RAS... Journal. North China Branch. Royal Asiatic Society (journ.) (SAUS)
JNCI.......... Jounal of the National Cancer Institute (SAUO)
JNCIMC..... Japanese National Committee of the International Music Council (EAIO)
JNCL......... Joint National Committee for Languages (EA)
JNCLA....... Journal. National Chemical Laboratory for Industry (journ.) (SAUS)
JNCM........ Journal of New Chinese Medicine [*Medicine*] (EDAA)
JNCN........ Journal of Neuropsychiatry and Clinical Neurosciences (journ.) (SAUS)
JNCN........ Junction (ABBR)
JNCO........ Junior Non-Commissioned Officer [*British military*] (DMA)
JNCP........ Justification for Non-Competitive Procurement (GFGA)
JNCQ........ Journal of Nursing Care Quality (journ.) (SAUS)
JNC Referees Bank... Journal. National Conference of Referees in Bankruptcy [*A publication*] (DLA)
J NC Sect Am Water Works Assoc NC Water PollutConhol Assoc... Journal. North Carolina Section of the American Water Works Association and North Carolina Water Pollution Control Association (journ.) (SAUS)
JNCUD...... Journal of Natural Science. Chonnam Natianal University (journ.) (SAUS)
JNCUR...... Juncture (ABBR)
JNCYA....... Journal of Neurocytology (journ.) (SAUS)
JND.......... Air East Africa Ltd. [*Kenya*] [*FAA designator*] (FAAC)
JND.......... Joined (ABBR)
JND.......... Just Noticeable Difference [*Psychology*]
jnd.......... Just-Noticeable Difference (DIPS)
JND.......... Just-Noticeable Distortion (SAUS)
JND.......... Juvenile Narcotics Division (SAUO)
JNDC........ Jamaica National Dance Company (SAUO)
JNDI......... Java Naming and Directory Interface (VLIE)
J NDI........ Journal of Nondestructive Inspection (journ.) (SAUS)
JNDR........ Joinder (ABBR)
JNDRA...... Journal of New Drugs (journ.) (SAUS)
JNDSPI...... Java Naming and Directory Service Provider Interface (SAUS)
JNE.......... Ja Niin Edespain [*And So On*] [*Finnish*]
JNE.......... Journal of Negro Education [*A publication*] (BRI)
JNE.......... Journal of Nursing Education (journ.) (SAUS)
JNE.......... Jump Not Equal [*Computer science*] (OA)
JNE.......... June (ABBR)
JNE.......... National Board of Elections (Peru) [*Political party*] (PSAP)
J Nebr Dent Assoc... Journal. Nebraska Dental Association (journ.) (SAUS)
JNEC......... Jamaica National Export Corp. (BUAC)
JNEC......... Jamaican National Export Corp. (SAUS)
J Ne Exp Ne... Journal of Neuropathology and Experimental Neurology (journ.) (SAUS)
JNELDA..... Journal of Nutrition for the Elderly (journ.) (SAUS)
JNEMA...... Jefferson National Expansion Memorial Association (SAUO)
J Nematol.. Journal of Nematology (journ.) (SAUS)
J Ne Ne Psy... Journal of Neurology, Neurosurgery and Psychiatry (journ.) (SAUS)
J N Engl Water Pollut Control Assoc... Journal. New England Water Pollution Control Association (journ.) (SAUS)
J Nepal Chem Soc... Journal. Nepal Chemical Society (journ.) (SAUS)
J Nephrol Nurs... Journal of Nephrology Nursing (journ.) (SAUS)
J Nerv Ment Disord... Journal of Nervous and Mental Disorder (journ.) (SAUS)
JNES......... Journal of Near Eastern Studies (journ.) (SAUS)
JNET......... Japanese Network (SAUO)
J Network Syst Manage... Journal of Network and Systems Management [*A publication*] (CABS)
J Neumpsychiatr Suppl... Journal of Neuropsychiatry. Supplement (journ.) (SAUS)

J Neural Transm Gen Sect... Journal of Neural Transmission. General Section (journ.) (SAUS)
J Neural Transm Park Dis Dement Sect... Journal of Neural Transmission. Parkinsons Disease and Dementia Section (journ.) (SAUS)
J Neural Transm Suppl... Journal of Neural Transmission. Supplementum (journ.) (SAUS)
J Neural Transplant Plast... Journal of Neural Transplantation and Plasticity (journ.) (SAUS)
J Neurobiol... Journal of Neurobiology (journ.) (SAUS)
J Neurochem... Journal of Neurochemistry (journ.) (SAUS)
J Neuroendocrinol... Journal of Neuroendocrinology (journ.) (SAUS)
J Neuroimaging... Journal of Neuroimaging (journ.) (SAUS)
J Neurol Soc Indi... Journal. Neurological Society of India (journ.) (SAUS)
J Neuro-Oncol... Journal of Neuro-Oncology (journ.) (SAUS)
J Neuroophthalmol... Journal of Neuro-Ophthalmology (journ.) (SAUS)
J Neuropsychiatry Clin Neurosci... Journal of Neuropsychiatry and Clinical Neurosciences (journ.) (SAUS)
J Neuroradiol... Journal of Neuroradiology (journ.) (SAUS)
J Neurosci Methods... Journal of Neuroscience Methods (journ.) (SAUS)
J Neurosci Nurs... Journal of Neuroscience Nursing (journ.) (SAUS)
J Neurosci Res... Journal of Neuroscience Research (journ.) (SAUS)
J Neurosurg... Journal of Neurosurgery (journ.) (SAUS)
J Neurosurg Anesthesiol... Journal of Neurosurgical Anesthesiology (journ.) (SAUS)
J Neurosurg Nurs... Journal of Neurosurgical Nursing (journ.) (SAUS)
J Neurotrauma... Journal of Neurotrauma (journ.) (SAUS)
J Neurovirol... Journal of Neurovirology (journ.) (SAUS)
J Newark Beth Isr Med Cent... Journal. Newark Beth Israel Medical Center (journ.) (SAUS)
J Newcastle Sch Arts... Newcastle School of Arts (SAUS)
J New Drugs... Journal of New Drugs (journ.) (SAUS)
J New Gener Comput Syst... Journal of New Generation Computer Systems (journ.) (SAUS)
J New Rem Clin... Journal of New Remedies and Clinics (journ.) (SAUS)
J New World Archaeol... Journal of New World Archaeology (journ.) (SAUS)
JNF.......... Japan Nuclear Fuel Co. (BUAC)
JNF.......... Jewish National Fund (EA)
JNF.......... Junior Non-Fiction [*Library science*] (TELE)
JNFA.......... Jewish National Fund of Australia
JNFA.......... Journal of Numismatic Fine Arts (journ.) (SAUS)
JNFC.......... Joint National Frequency Committee (SAUO)
JNFC.......... Juice Newton Fan Club (EA)
JNFI.......... Japan's Nuclear Fuel Industries (BUAC)
JNG.......... [*The*] Jews in NAZI Germany; A Handbook of Facts Regarding Their Present Situation [*A publication*] (BJA)
JNG.......... Joining [*Also, J*]
JNG.......... Jump if Not Greater (VLIE)
JNGE.......... Jump if Not Greater or Equal (VLIE)
JNGL.......... Jonquil (ABBR)
JNGL.......... Jungle (ABBR)
JNH.......... Journal of Negro History [*A publication*] (GEAB)
JNHAC.......... Jewish National Home for Asthmatic Children
J NH Dent Soc... Journal. New Hampshire Dental Society (journ.) (SAUS)
JNI.......... Jacor Networks, Inc. (EFIS)
JNI.......... Java Native Interface [*Computer science*] (IGQR)
JNI.......... Journal of the Nautical Institute (journ.) (SAUS)
JNIB.......... Jamaica National Investment Bank (BUAC)
JNIC.......... JNI Corp. [*NASDAQ symbol*]
JNICT.......... National Board of Scientific and Technical Research Portugal (SAUO)
J Nigeria Assoc Dent Stud... Journal. Nigeria Association of Dental Students (journ.) (SAUS)
J Nigerian Inst Oil Palm Res... Journal. Nigerian Institute for Oil Palm Research (journ.) (SAUS)
J Nihon Univ Med Ass... Journal. Nihon University Medical Association (journ.) (SAUS)
J Nihon Univ Sch Dent... Journal. Nihon University School of Dentistry (journ.) (SAUS)
J Nihon Univ Sch Dent... Journal of Nihon University School of Dentistry (SAUO)
J Nihon Univ Sch Dent... Journal of Nihon University School of Dentistry (journ.) (SAUS)
J Niigata Agric Exp Shi... Journal. Niigata Agricultural Experiment Station (journ.) (SAUS)
JNIP.......... Jamaica National Investment Promotions (BUAC)
JNIP.......... Jamaican National Investment Promotion (SAUS)
J Nippon Dent Coll... Journal. Nippon Dental College (journ.) (SAUS)
J Nippon UnivSch Dent... Journal. Nippon University School of Dentistry (journ.) (SAUS)
JNIPRMSI.......... Japan. National Institute of Polar Research. Memoirs. Special Issue (journ.) (SAUS)
J Nissei Hosp... Journal Nissei Hospital (journ.) (SAUS)
JNJ.......... Johnson & Johnson [*NYSE symbol*] (SPSG)
JNJ.......... Journal of Nursing Jocularity (journ.) (SAUS)
J NJ Dent Assoc... Journal. New Jersey Dental Association (journ.) (SAUS)
J NJ Dent Hyg Assoc... Journal. New Jersey Dental Hygienists Association (journ.) (SAUS)
JNJQ.......... J and J Truck Line [*Common carrier symbol*]
J NJ State Dent Soc... Journal. New Jersey State Dental Society (journ.) (SAUS)
J NJ State Dent Soc... Journal of the New Jersey State Dental Society (SAUO)
J N J State Dent Soc... Journal of the New Jersey State Dental Society (journ.) (SAUS)
JNKD.......... Junked (ABBR)
JNKG.......... Junking (ABBR)
JNKI.......... Junkie (ABBR)
JNKMA.......... Junkman (ABBR)
JNKN.......... Jenkon International [*NASDAQ symbol*]
JNKT.......... Junket (ABBR)
JNKTD.......... Junketed (ABBR)
JNKTG.......... Junketing (ABBR)
JNKTR.......... Junketer (ABBR)
JNL.......... Atchison, KS [*Location identifier*] [*FAA*] (FAAL)
JNL.......... Japanese National Laboratory
JNL.......... Jefferson National Life Insurance Co. (EFIS)
JNL.......... Jenolan [*Australia*] [*Seismograph station code, US Geological Survey*] (SEIS)
JNL.......... Journal
JNL.......... Jump Not Last (SAUS)
JNLA.......... Japan National Laboratory Accreditation System (SAUO)
Jnl Asn Stud... Journal of Asian Studies (journ.) (SAUS)
Jnl Basque Stud... Journal of Basque Studies (journ.) (SAUS)
Jnl Constr Div Am Soc Civ Eng... Journal. Construction Division. American Society of Civil Engineers (journ.) (SAUS)
Jnl Consuel Psych... Journal of Counseling Psychology (journ.) (SAUS)
Jnl Diet Home Ec... Journal of Dietetics and Home Economics (journ.) (SAUS)
JNLE.......... Jump if Not Less or Equal (SAUO)
Jnl Engl Ger Philol... Journal of English and Germanic Philology (journ.) (SAUS)
Jnl Gen Ed... Journal of General Education (journ.) (SAUS)
Jnl Heptol... Journal of Hepatology (journ.) (SAUS)
Jnl Higher Ed... Journal of Higher Education (journ.) (SAUS)
Jnl Ital Ling... Journal of Italian Linguistics (journ.) (SAUS)
Jnl Lib Hist... Journal of Library History (journ.) (SAUS)
Jnl Marketing... Journal of Marketing (journ.) (SAUS)
Jnl Mol Appl Genet... Journal of Molecular and Applied Genetics (journ.) (SAUS)
Jnl Negro Ed... Journal of Negro Education (journ.) (SAUS)
Jnl Negro Hist... Journal of Negro History (journ.) (SAUS)
JNLNO.......... Journal Number (SAUS)
Jnl Ocular Ther Surg... Journal of Ocular Therapy and Surgery (journ.) (SAUS)
Jnl of Archtl Education... Journal of Architectural Education (journ.) (SAUS)
Jnl of Archtl Research... Journal of Architectural Research (journ.) (SAUS)
Jnl of Canadian Art History... Journal of Canadian Art History (journ.) (SAUS)
Jnl of Environmental Psychology... Journal of Environmental Psychology (journ.) (SAUS)
Jnl Orthomol Psych... Journal of Orthomolecular Psychiatry (journ.) (SAUS)
Jnl Polit Econ... Journal of Political Economy (journ.) (SAUS)
Jnl Politics... Journal of Politics (journ.) (SAUS)
JNLS.......... Journals (ADA)
JNLST.......... Journalist
JNLWP.......... Joint Non-Lethal Weapons Program [*Military*] (STAH)
JNM.......... JNM. Journal of Nuclear Medicine (journ.) (SAUS)
JNM.......... Journal of Nuclear Medicine (journ.) (SAUS)
JNMA.......... Journal of the National Medical Association (SAUO)
JNMA.......... Journal of the National Medical Association (journ.) (SAUS)
JNMA.......... Journal of the Nepal Medical Association (journ.) (SAUS)
JNMED.......... Journal of Neuroscience Methods (journ.) (SAUS)
JNMI.......... J and M Cartage [*Common carrier symbol*]
JNMM.......... Journal of Nuclear Materials Management (journ.) (SAUS)
JNMM.......... Journal of the Institute of Nuclear Materials Management (journ.) (SAUS)
JNMR.......... Joint National Media Research [*Database producer*]
JNMS.......... Journal of the Neuromusculoskeletal System (SAUO)
JNMS.......... Journal of the Neuromusculoskeletal System (journ.) (SAUS)
JNMSD.......... Journal of Nuclear Medicine and Allied Sciences (journ.) (SAUS)
JNMT.......... Journal of Nuclear Medicine Technology (SAUO)
JNMT.......... Journal of Nuclear Medicine Technology (journ.) (SAUS)
JNMTA.......... Journal of Nonmetals (journ.) (SAUS)
JNN.......... Japan News Network (SAUO)
JNN.......... Journal of Neonatal Nursing (journ.) (SAUS)
JNND.......... Just Not Noticeable Difference (MSA)
JNNP.......... Journal of Neurology, Neurosurgery, & Psychiatry (SAUS)
JNNPA.......... Journal of Neurology, Neurosurgery and Psychiatry (journ.) (SAUS)
JNNS.......... Japanese Neural Network Society (BUAC)
Jno.......... John [*Name*] [*Civil War term*]
JNO.......... Journal of Neuro-Oncology (journ.) (SAUS)
JNO.......... Jump if No Overflow (VLIE)
JNOC.......... Japan National Oil Corp. (BUAC)
JNODC.......... Japanese National Oceanographic Data Center (SAUO)
JNODC.......... Japanese National Oceanographic Data Center (or Centre) (SAUS)
J Non Cryst Solids... Journal of Non-Crystalline Solids [*A publication*] (CABS)
J Non-Desh Insp... Journal of Non-Destructive Inpesction (journ.) (SAUS)
J Nondestr Eval... Journal of Nondestructive Evaluation (journ.) (SAUS)
J Non-Equilib Thermodyn... Journal of Non-Equilibrium Thermodynamics (journ.) (SAUS)
J Nonlinear Sci... Journal of Nonlinear Science (journ.) (SAUS)
J Nonmet... Journal of Nonmetals (journ.) (SAUS)
J Non-Newtonian Fluid Mech... Journal of Non-Newtonian Fluid Mechanics (journ.) (SAUS)
J Nonverbal Behav... Journal of Nonverbal Behavior (journ.) (SAUS)
J Northampton Mus... Journal. Northampton Museum and Art Gallery (journ.) (SAUS)
J Northamptonshire Natur Hist Soc Field Club... Journal. Northamptonshire Natural History Society and Field Club (journ.) (SAUS)
J Northeast Asian Studies... Journal of Northeast Asian Studies (journ.) (SAUS)
J Northeast Univ Technol... Journal of Northeast University of Technology (journ.) (SAUS)
J Northwest Atl Fish Sci... Journal of Northwest Atlantic Fishery Science (journ.) (SAUS)
J Northwest Univ Nt Sci Ed... Journal. Northwest University. Natural Science Edition (journ.) (SAUS)
J Norw Med Ass... Journal. Norwegian Medical Association (journ.) (SAUS)
JNOV.......... Judgment Not Withstanding Verdict (HGAA)
JNP.......... Jasper National Park [*Alberta*] [*Airport symbol*] (AD)

Jo Cre .... Johannes Bassianus de Cremona [*Flourished, 12th century*] [*Authority cited in pre-1607 legal work*] (DSA)
JOCS .... Japan Overseas Christian Medical Cooperative Service (SAUO)
JOCS .... Joint Operational Climatological Support (SAUO)
JOCS .... Joint Operations Command System [*Military*]
JOCS .... Senior Chief Journalist [*Navy rating*]
JOCSG....... Joint Ordnance Commanders Supply Group [*DoD*]
J-OCT........ Joint Operational Compatibility Tests
JOCT......... Junior Officers Common Training
J Ocul Pharmacol... Journal of Ocular Pharmacology (journ.) (SAUS)
J Ocul Pharmacol Ther... Journal of Ocular Pharmacology and Therapeutics (journ.) (SAUS)
JOCV .... Japan Overseas Cooperation Volunteers (SAUO)
JOCZ......... Jones County [*Federal Railroad Administration identification code*]
JOD.......... Joint Occupancy Data (NAKS)
JOD.......... Joint Occupancy Date (MCD)
JOD.......... Joint Operations Division (SAUO)
JOD.......... Jordanian Dinar (SAUS)
JOD.......... Journal of Development (ELAL)
JOD.......... Journal of Development (journ.) (SAUS)
JOD.......... Juvenile Onset Diabetes [*Medicine*]
JODC .... Japanese Oceanographic Data Center (or Centre) (SAUS)
JODC .... Japanese Oceanographic Data Centre (SAUO)
JODC .... Japan Ocean Data Center (SAUO)
JODC .... Japan Oceanographic Data Center [*Information service or system*] (IID)
JODC .... Japan Overseas Development Corp. (SAUS)
JODC .... Journal of Dentistry for Children (journ.) (SAUS)
JODC .... Juvenile Osteochondritis Dissecans [*Medicine*]
JODCO ...... Japan Oil Development Co. (BUAC)
JODE .... Journal of Drug Education (journ.) (SAUS)
Jo de Ana... Johannes de Anania [*Deceased, 1457*] [*Authority cited in pre-1607 legal work*] (DSA)
Jo de Anna... Johannes de Anania [*Deceased, 1457*] [*Authority cited in pre-1607 legal work*] (DSA)
Jo de Bor... Johannes de Borbonio [*Flourished, 1317-30*] [*Authority cited in pre-1607 legal work*] (DSA)
Jo de Cre... Johannes Bassianus de Cremona [*Flourished, 12th century*] [*Authority cited in pre-1607 legal work*] (DSA)
Jo de F...... Johannes de Fintona [*Flourished, 13th century*] [*Authority cited in pre-1607 legal work*] (DSA)
Jo de Fi...... Johannes de Fintona [*Flourished, 13th century*] [*Authority cited in pre-1607 legal work*] (DSA)
Jo de Imol... Johannes de Imola [*Deceased, 1436*] [*Authority cited in pre-1607 legal work*] (DSA)
Jo de Mo ... Johannes de Monciaco [*Flourished, 1263-66*] [*Authority cited in pre-1607 legal work*] (DSA)
JODI......... Journal of Drug Issues (journ.) (SAUS)
JODIN........ Iodinium [*Iodine*] [*Symbol is I*] [*Chemical element*] [*Pharmacy*] (ROG)
JODIV .... John the Divine
JODM........ Juvenile Onset Diabetes Mellitus [*Medicine*]
JODS .... Jasmine Object Database Server (SAUS)
JODU .... Josef Dunstinger Transporte [*Intermodal shipping container symbol*] (TVRC)
JODV .... Journal of Divorce (journ.) (SAUS)
joe........... Java Objects Everywhere [*Computer science*] (IGQR)
Joe........... Java Objects Everywhere [*Computer science*]
JOE .... Joensuu [*Finland*] [*Airport symbol*] (OAG)
JOE .... Joensuu [*Finland*] [*Seismograph station code, US Geological Survey*] [*Closed*] (SEIS)
JOE .... Journal of Endodontics (journ.) (SAUS)
JOE .... Juvenile Opportunities Endeavor
JOE .... Juvenile Opportunities Extension (SAUO)
JOE .... St Joe Co. [*NYSE symbol*]
JOEEA .... Journal of Emotional Education (journ.) (SAUS)
JOEG .... Joint Operations Evaluation Group (AABC)
JOEG-V...... Joint Operations Evaluation Group, Vietnam [*Air Force*] (MCD)
JOEM........ Journal of Occupational and Environmental Medicine (SAUO)
JOEM........ Junior Ordnance Electrical Mechanic [*British military*] (DMA)
JOENA....... Journal of Endocrinology (journ.) (SAUS)
JOE-PAC .... Jobs, Opportunities, and Education PAC [*Elmhurst, NY*] (PACS)
JOERA....... Japan Optical Engineering Research Association (BUAC)
JOERA....... Journal of Educational Research (journ.) (SAUS)
JOERS....... Joint Opto-Electronics Research Scheme [*British*]
JOES......... Joe's Custom Boat Trailer [*NCIC trailer make code*]
JOET......... Journal of Education for Teaching (journ.) (SAUS)
JOEVANG ... John the Evangelist
JOEW........ Joe's Welding Service [*NCIC trailer make code*]
Jo Ex Ir ..... Jones' Irish Exchequer Reports [*A publication*] (DLA)
Jo Ex Pro W... Jones' Exchequer Proceedings Concerning Wales [*1939*] [*A publication*] (DLA)
JOF .... Japan OTC Equity Fund [*NYSE symbol*] (TTSB)
JOF .... Japan OTC Equity Fund, Inc. [*NYSE symbol*] (SPSG)
Jo F.......... Johannes de Fintona [*Flourished, 13th century*] [*Authority cited in pre-1607 legal work*] (DSA)
JOF .... Journal of Forecasting (journ.) (SAUS)
Jo Fa .... Johannes Faventinus [*Deceased circa 1187*] [*Authority cited in pre-1607 legal work*] (DSA)
J of Air L & Commerce... Journal of Air Law and Commerce (journ.) (SAUS)
Jo Fav....... Johannes Faventinus [*Deceased circa 1187*] [*Authority cited in pre-1607 legal work*] (DSA)
J of Ceylon L... Journal of Ceylon Law [*Colombo, Ceylon*] [*A publication*] (DLA)
J of E........ Journal of Education [*A publication*] (ROG)
J of EL ...... Journal of Electric Lighting [*A publication*] (ROG)
J of Ethiop L... Journal of Ethiopian Law [*Addis Ababa, Ethiopia*] [*A publication*] (DLA)
J of Home Econ Ed... Journal of Home Economics Education (journ.) (SAUS)
J of Human Rel... Journal of Human Relations (journ.) (SAUS)
J of Ins of Arbitrators... Journal. Institute of Arbitrators [*A publication*] (DLA)
J of Internat L and Econ... Journal of International Law and Economics (journ.) (SAUS)
JOFL......... Johnstown Flood National Memorial
JOFOC....... Justification for Other Than Full and Open Competition (SAUO)
J of Pract APP... Journal of Practical Approaches to Developmental Handicapped (journ.) (SAUS)
JOFRE....... Joffre, PQ [*American Association of Railroads railroad junction routing code*]
J of Relig Thought... Journal of Religious Thought (journ.) (SAUS)
JOFRO....... Joined Fisheries Research Organization of Northern Rhodesia and Nyassaland (SAUO)
J of the Assoc of Anal Chem... Journal of the Association of Analytical Chemists (SAUO)
J of the Assoc of Anal Chem... Journal of the Association of Analytical Chemists (journ.) (SAUS)
JOG.......... Joggle [*Engineering*]
JOG.......... Jogyakarta [*Indonesia*] [*Airport symbol*] (OAG)
JOG.......... Joint Operating Group [*SLA/ASIS*]
JOG.......... Joint Operations Graphics [*Military*]
JOG.......... Joint Operations Group [*DoD*]
JOG.......... Junior Ocean Group (SAUO)
JOG.......... Junior Offshore Group [*Racing*] [*British*]
JOG-A .... Joint Operations Graphics - Air [*Military*] (PDAA)
JOGD .... Jogged (ABBR)
JOGEA....... Journal of Gerontology (journ.) (SAUS)
JOGG .... Jogging (ABBR)
JOG-G .... Joint Operations Graphics - Ground (PDAA)
JOGG A ..... Journal of Geography (journ.) (SAUS)
JOGL .... Joggle (ABBR)
JOGLD....... Joggled (ABBR)
JOGLG....... Joggling (ABBR)
JOGNN ...... Journal of Obstetric, Gynecologic and Neonatal Nursing (journ.) (SAUS)
JOGR .... Jogger (ABBR)
JOG-R .... Joint Operations Graphic-Radar (SAUS)
JOGS .... Joint Operation Graphics System (COE)
JOH.......... Johannesburg [*South Africa*] [*Seismograph station code, US Geological Survey*] [*Closed*] (SEIS)
Joh........... Johannine (BJA)
Joh........... John [*New Testament book*] (BJA)
JOH.......... Johnstone Point, AK [*Location identifier*] [*FAA*] (FAAL)
JOH.......... Journal of Housing (journ.) (SAUS)
JOH.......... St. John's College [*Cambridge, England*] (DAS)
Joh Ch Rep... Johnson's New York Chancery Reports [*A publication*] (DLA)
JOHCY....... Johnson City, TN [*American Association of Railroads railroad junction routing code*]
JOHE .... Journal of Health Economics (journ.) (SAUS)
JOHEA....... Journal of Heredity (journ.). (SAUS)
JOHH .... Journal of Holistic Health (journ.) (SAUS)
J Ohio Herpetol Soc... Journal. Ohio Herpetological Society (journ.) (SAUS)
John .... Chase's United States Circuit Court Decisions, Edited by Johnson [*A publication*] (DLA)
JOHN........ Johnson Corporation [*NCIC trailer make code*]
John......... Johnson's English Vice-Chancellors' Reports [*A publication*] (DLA)
John......... Johnson's Maryland Chancery Reports [*A publication*] (DLA)
John......... Johnson's New York Reports [*A publication*] (DLA)
John......... Johnson's New York Supreme Court Reports [*A publication*] (DLA)
John Alexander Monogr Ser Var Phases Thorac Surg... John Alexander Monograph Series on Various Phases of Thoracic Surgery (journ.) (SAUS)
John Am Not... John's American Notaries [*A publication*] (DLA)
John & H ... Johnson and Hemming's English Chancery Reports [*70 English Reprint*] [*A publication*] (DLA)
JOHNB ...... Johnsonburg, PA [*American Association of Railroads railroad junction routing code*]
John Carroll U... John Carroll University (GAGS)
John Cas.... Johnson's New York Cases [*A publication*] (DLA)
John Chan.. Johnson's New York Chancery Reports [*A publication*] (DLA)
John Ch Rep... Johnson's New York Chancery Reports [*A publication*] (DLA)
JohnCn...... Johnson Controls, Inc. [*Associated Press*] (SAG)
John Dewey Soc Yrbk... John Dewey Society. Yearbook (journ.) (SAUS)
John Dict ... Johnson's English Dictionary [*A publication*] (DLA)
John Did.... Johnsons English Dictionary (journ.) (SAUS)
John Eng Ch... Johnson's English Vice-Chancellors' Reports [*A publication*] (DLA)
John Herron Art Inst Bul... John Herron Art Institute. Bulletin (journ.) (SAUS)
John Innes Horhc Inst Annu Rep... John Innes Horticultural Institution. Annual Report (journ.) (SAUS)
John Innes Sym... John Innes Symposium (journ.) (SAUS)
John Jay C (CUNY)... John Jay College of Criminal Justice of The City University of New York (GAGS)
JohnJn ...... Johnson & Johnson [*Associated Press*] (SAG)
John Lawrence Interdiscip Symp Phys Biomed Sci... John Lawrence Interdisciplinary Symposium on the Physical and Biomedical Sciences (journ.) (SAUS)
John Marshall Law Sch... John Marshall Law School (GAGS)
John Marshall LQ... John Marshall Law Quarterly [*A publication*] (DLA)
John Marsh LJ... John Marshall Law Journal [*A publication*] (DLA)
John Marsh LQ... John Marshall Law Quarterly [*A publication*] (DLA)
JOHNNIAC... John Neumann Integrator and Automatic Computer (SAUS)

JOHNNIAC... John's [*Von Neumann*] Integrator and Automatic Computer [*An early computer*]
John Oxley J... John Oxley Journal [*A publication*]
John Rylands Lib Bul... John Rylands Library. Bulletin (journ.) (SAUS)
Johns........ Chase's United States Circuit Court Decisions, Edited by Johnson [*A publication*] (DLA)
Johns........ Johnson's English Vice-Chancellors' Reports [*A publication*] (DLA)
Johns........ Johnson's Maryland Chancery Reports [*A publication*] (DLA)
Johns........ Johnson's New York Supreme Court Reports [*A publication*] (DLA)
Johns & H... Johnson and Hemming's English Chancery Reports [*70 English Reprint*] [*A publication*] (DLA)
Johns & Hem... Johnson and Hemming's English Chancery Reports [*70 English Reprint*] [*A publication*] (DLA)
Johns & H (Eng)... Johnson and Hemming's English Chancery Reports [*70 English Reprint*] [*A publication*] (DLA)
Johns Bills... Johnson's Bills of Exchange [*2nd ed.*] [*1839*] [*A publication*] (DLA)
Johns C..... Johnson's New York Cases [*A publication*] (DLA)
Johns Cas.. Johnson's New York Cases [*A publication*] (DLA)
Johns Cases... Johnson's New York Cases [*A publication*] (DLA)
Johns Cas (NY)... Johnson's New York Cases [*A publication*] (DLA)
Johns Ch.... Johnson's English Vice-Chancellors' Reports [*A publication*] (DLA)
Johns Ch.... Johnson's Maryland Chancery Decisions [*A publication*] (DLA)
Johns Ch.... Johnson's New York Chancery Reports [*A publication*] (DLA)
Johns Ch Cas... Johnson's New York Chancery Reports [*A publication*] (DLA)
Johns Ch (NY)... Johnson's New York Chancery Reports [*A publication*] (DLA)
Johns Civ L Sp... Johnson's Civil Law of Spain [*A publication*] (DLA)
Johns Civ L Sp... Johnsons Civil Law of Spain (journ.) (SAUS)
Johns Ct Err... Johnson's New York Court of Errors Reports [*A publication*] (DLA)
Johns Dec... Johnson's Maryland Chancery Decisions [*A publication*] (DLA)
Johns Eccl L... Johnson's Ecclesiastical Law [*A publication*] (DLA)
Johns Eccl L... Johnsons Ecclesiastical Law (journ.) (SAUS)
Johns Eng Ch... Johnson's English Chancery Reports [*A publication*] (DLA)
Johns H..... Johns Hopkins University (SAUO)
Johns Hopkins Hp Bull... Johns Hopkins Hospital. Bulletin (journ.) (SAUS)
Johns Hopkins Mag... Johns Hopkins Magazine. Johns Hopkins University. Baltimore (SAUO)
Johns Hopkins Med J Suppl... Johns Hopkins Medical Journal. Supplement (journ.) (SAUS)
Johns Hopkins Oceanogr Stud... Johns Hopkins Oceanographic Studies (journ.) (SAUS)
Johns Hopkins U... [*The*] Johns Hopkins University (GAGS)
Johns Hopkins Univ Appl Phys Lab Spec Rep... Johns Hopkins University. Applied Physics Laboratory. Sperial Report (journ.) (SAUS)
Johns Hopkins Univ Appl Phys Lab Tech Dig... Johns Hopkins University. Applied Physics Laboratory. Technical Digest (journ.) (SAUS)
Johns Hopkins Univ Chesapeake Bay Inst Tech Rept... Johns Hopkins University. Chesapeake Bay Institute. Technical Report (journ.) (SAUS)
Johns Hopkins Univ Cir... Johns Hopkins University. Circular (journ.) (SAUS)
Johns Hopkins Univ McCollum Pratt Inst Contrib... Johns Hopkins University. McCollum Pratt Institute. Contribution (journ.) (SAUS)
Johns Hopkins Univ Studies in Geology... Johns Hopkins University. Studies in Geology (journ.) (SAUS)
Johns HRV... Johnson's English Chancery Reports [*A publication*] (DLA)
Johns Mar R... Johnson on Maritime Rights [*A publication*] (DLA)
Johns (NY)... Johnson's New York Reports [*A publication*] (DLA)
Johns NZ... Johnson's New Zealand Reports [*A publication*] (DLA)
Johnson..... Johnson's English Vice-Chancellors' Reports [*A publication*] (DLA)
Johnson..... Johnson's Maryland Chancery Decisions [*A publication*] (DLA)
Johnson..... Johnson's New York Reports [*A publication*] (DLA)
Johnson NYR... Johnson's New York Reports [*A publication*] (DLA)
Johnson R... Johnson's New York Reports [*A publication*] (DLA)
Johnson's Quarto Dict... Johnson's Quarto Dictionary [*A publication*] (DLA)
Johnson's Rep... Johnson's New York Reports [*A publication*] (DLA)
Johns Pat Man... Johnson's Patent Manual [*A publication*] (DLA)
Johns Pat Man... Johnsons Patent Manual (journ.) (SAUS)
Johns R..... Johnson's New York Reports [*A publication*] (DLA)
Johns Rep.. Johnson's New York Supreme Court Reports [*A publication*] (DLA)
Johnst Inst... Johnston's Institutes of the Laws of Spain [*A publication*] (DLA)
Johnst Inst... Johnstons Institutes of the Laws of Spain (journ.) (SAUS)
JohnstnA.... Johnstown America Industries, Inc. [*Associated Press*] (SAG)
Johnst (NZ)... Johnston's New Zealand Reports [*A publication*] (DLA)
Johnston.... Johnston Industries, Inc. [*Associated Press*] (SAG)
Johns Tr..... Johnson's Impeachment Trial [*A publication*] (DLA)
Johns US... Johnson's Reports of Chase's United States Circuit Court Decisions [*A publication*] (DLA)
Johns VC... Johnson's English Vice-Chancellors' Reports [*A publication*] (DLA)
Johns VC (Eng)... Johnson's English Vice-Chancellors' Reports [*A publication*] (DLA)
JOHO........ Johnson Motors [*NCIC trailer make code*]
JOHPER..... Journal of Health, Physical Education, Recreation (journ.) (SAUS)
Johs........ Johannes Galensis [*Flourished, 13th century*] [*Authority cited in pre-1607 legal work*] (DSA)
JOHS........ Johnson's Trailer [*NCIC trailer make code*]
Joh Teut..... Johannes Teutonicus [*Deceased circa 1246*] [*Authority cited in pre-1607 legal work*] (DSA)
JOHX........ Johnson Flying Service [*Air carrier designation symbol*]
JOHX........ Journal of Homosexuality (journ.) (SAUS)
JOI........... Jewish Outreach Institute (SAUS)
JOI........... Joint Oceanographic Institution (USDC)
JOI........... Joint Oceanographic Institutions, Inc. [*Research center*] (RCD)
JOI........... Joinville [*Brazil*] [*Airport symbol*] (OAG)
JOIA........ Japan Ocean Industries Association (BUAC)
JOI-BOG..... JOI Board of Governors (SAUS)
JOICA........ Journal. Institution of Chemists (journ.) (SAUS)
JOICFP...... Japanese Organisation for International Cooperation in Family Planning (BUAC)
JOIDES...... JODC [*Japan Oceanographic Data Center*] On-Line Information and Data Exchange Service [*Marine science*] (OSRA)
JOIDES...... Joint Oceanographic Institutes for Deep Earth Sampling (SAUO)
JOIDES...... Joint Oceanographic Institutions for Deep Earth Sampling
JOIDESP.... Joint Oceanographic Institutions Deep Earth Sampling Program (SAUO)
J Oil Colour Chem Assoc... Journal of the Oil and Colour Chemists Association (journ.) (SAUS)
J Oilseeds Res... Journal of Oilseeds Research (journ.) (SAUS)
JOIN......... Job Opportunities in Neighbourhoods (SAUO)
JOIN......... Job Orientation in Neighborhoods (AEBS)
JOIN......... Job Orientation in the Neighbourhoods (SAUO)
JOIN......... Jobs or Income Now [*Students for a Democratic Society*] [*Defunct*]
JOIN......... Joinery (ADA)
JOIN......... Joint Optical Information Network [*Army*]
JOIN......... Jones Intercable [*NASDAQ symbol*] (TTSB)
JOIN......... Jones Intercable, Inc. [*NASDAQ symbol*] (NQ)
JOINA....... Jones Intercable Cl'A' [*NASDAQ symbol*] (TTSB)
Joining Mater... Joining and Materials (journ.) (SAUS)
JOINREP.... Joining Report (MCD)
Joint Automat Contr Conf PreprTech Pap... Joint Automatic Control Conference. Preprints of Technical Papers (journ.) (SAUS)
JOINTCINCEASTLANT... Commander-in-Chief Eastern Atlantic Area, Air Commander-in-Chief Eastern Atlantic Area (SAUO)
Joint Four... Joint Executive Committee of Associations of Head Masters, Head Mistresses, Assistant Masters and Assistant Mistresses (SAUO)
Joint STARS... Joint Surveillance Target Attack RADAR System [*Air Force*] (CARL)
JOIP......... Joint Operations Interface Procedure (NASA)
JOIS......... Japan Online Information System [*Database*]
JOISTS...... Joint Operational Interface Simulation Training System (SAUO)
JOIT......... Joiner Transportation Company [*Common carrier symbol*]
JOJA......... July, October, January, and April [*Denotes quarterly payments of interest or dividends in these months*] [*Business term*]
JOJAA....... Journal of Otolaryngology of Japan (journ.) (SAUS)
Jo Je S...... Journal of Jewish Studies (journ.) (SAUS)
JOJO......... Jojoba Horizons, Inc. (SAUO)
Jo Jur....... Journal of Jurisprudence [*A publication*] (DLA)
JOK......... Airtaxi Bedarfsluftverkehrsges GmbH [*Austria*] [*ICAO designator*] (FAAC)
J Okayama Dent Soc... Journal. Okayama Dental Society (journ.) (SAUS)
J Okayama Med Soc... Journal. Okayama Medical Society (journ.) (SAUS)
J Okayama Med Soc Suppl... Journal. Okayama Medical Society. Supplement (journ.) (SAUS)
JOKG........ Joking (ABBR)
JOKGLY..... Jokingly (ABBR)
JOKGY....... Jokingly (ABBR)
JOKI......... John Fitzgerald Kennedy National Historical Site
JOKING...... Joint Kinematics and Geometry (PDAA)
J Okla Dent Assoc... Journal. Oklahoma Dental Association (journ.) (SAUS)
J Okla State Dent Ass... Journal. Oklahoma State Dental Association (journ.) (SAUS)
J Okla State Med Assoc... Journal of the Oklahoma State Medical Association (journ.) (SAUS)
J Okla State Med Assoc... Journal-Oklahoma State Medical Association (SAUO)
JOKP........ Junior Order, Knights of Pythias (EA)
JOKSTR..... Jokester (ABBR)
JOL.......... Job Organization Language [*1979*] [*Computer science*] (CSR)
JOL.......... Job Orientation Language (SAUS)
JOL.......... Joilet in Illinois [*Diocesan abbreviation*] [*Illinois*] (TOCD)
JOL.......... Jolo [*Philippines*] [*Airport symbol*] (OAG)
JOL.......... Jolon [*California*] [*Seismograph station code, US Geological Survey*] (SEIS)
JOL.......... Joule, Inc. [*AMEX symbol*] (SPSG)
JOL.......... Journal of Online Law (SAUO)
JOL.......... Journal of Oriental Literature (journ.) (SAUS)
JOL.......... Judgements of Learning (SAUS)
JOLA......... Journal of Library Automation (journ.) (SAUS)
JOLD........ Jollied (ABBR)
Jo Le........ Johannis Lectura [*A publication*] (DSA)
JOLF......... Jolliff Transportation [*Common carrier symbol*]
JOLI......... Johnny Lightning [*NCIC motorcycle make code*]
JOLIE........ Joliet, IL [*American Association of Railroads railroad junction routing code*]
JOLIS........ Joint Library and Information System (SAUS)
JOLT......... Java Online Transactions (SAUS)
JOLT......... Java Open Language Toolkit [*Computer science*] (DCDG)
JOLT......... Juvenile Offenders Learn the Truth [*Program*]
JOLTGLY.... Joltingly (ABBR)
JOM......... Jeunesse Ouvriere Marocaine [*Moroccan Working Youth*]
JOM......... Job Operation Manual (AAG)
JOM......... Job-Oriented Manual (AAG)
JOM......... Johnson-O'Malley Act [*1934*]
JOM......... Joining of Materials (SAUS)
JOM......... Journal of Management (journ.) (SAUS)
JOM......... Journal of Metals (journ.) (SAUS)
JOM......... Journal of Orthomolecular Medicine (SAUS)
JOM......... Njombe [*Tanzania*] [*Airport symbol*] (AD)
JOMA........ Japan Oriental Music Association (BUAC)
JOMA........ Journal of Military Assistance (journ.) (SAUS)
JOMAC...... Judgement, Orientation, Memory, Abstraction, and Calculation [*Medicine*] (DAVI)

JOMACI ..... Judgment, Orientation, Memory, Abstraction, and Calculation Intact [*Medicine*] (DAVI)
JOMAR ...... John and Margaret Seidel [*Children of US importer after whom British sports car was named*]
JOMAR ...... Joint Office for Mapping and Research (SAUO)
JOMI .... International Journal of Oral & Maxillofacial Implants (SAUO)
JOM J Occup Med... JOM. Journal of Occupational Medicine (journ.) (SAUS)
JOML .... Journal of Organometallic Chemistry (journ.) (SAUS)
JOMMA ..... Journal of Mathematics and Mechanics (journ.) (SAUS)
JOMN .... Jeweled-Orifice Misting Nozzle
JOMO .... Job Mix Optimization [*Computer science*] (MHDB)
JOMO .... Junta of Militant Organizations (SAUO)
Jo Mon ...... Johannes Monachus [*Deceased, 1313*] [*Authority cited in pre-1607 legal work*] (DSA)
JOMU .... John Muir National Historic Site
JON .... Jeweled-Orifice Nozzle
JON .... Job Order Number (MCD)
JON .... Johnston Island [*Airport symbol*] (OAG)
Jon .... Jonah [*Old Testament book*]
JON .... Jonas [*Old Testament book*] [*Douay version*]
Jon .... Jones' Irish Exchequer Reports [*A publication*] (DLA)
JON .... Jonpol Explorations Ltd. [*Toronto Stock Exchange symbol*]
JONA .... Journal of Nursing Administration (SAUO)
JONAH ...... Jews Organised for a Nuclear Arms Halt [*An association*] (BUAC)
Jon & Car... Jones and Cary's Irish Exchequer Reports [*1838-39*] [*A publication*] (DLA)
Jon & L ..... Jones and La Touche's Irish Chancery Reports [*A publication*] (DLA)
Jon & La T... Jones and La Touche's Irish Chancery Reports [*A publication*] (DLA)
JONEA .... Journal of Neurophysiology (journ.) (SAUS)
JoneI .... Jones Intercable, Inc. [*Associated Press*] (SAG)
JoneInt ...... Jones Intercable Investors Ltd. [*Associated Press*] (SAG)
J Onenl Tianjin Med J Suppl... Journal of Oncology. Tianjin Medical Journal. Supplement (journ.) (SAUS)
JONES .... Jonesboro, AR [*American Association of Railroads railroad junction routing code*]
Jones .... Jones' Irish Exchequer Reports [*A publication*] (DLA)
Jones .... Jones' North Carolina Equity Reports [*54-59*] [*1853-63*] [*A publication*] (DLA)
Jones .... Jones' North Carolina Law Reports [*A publication*] (DLA)
Jones .... Jones' Reports [*43-48, 52-57, 61, 62 Alabama*] [*A publication*] (DLA)
Jones .... Jones' Reports [*22-30 Missouri*] [*A publication*] (DLA)
Jones .... Jones' Reports [*11, 12 Pennsylvania*] [*A publication*] (DLA)
Jones .... Jones' Upper Canada Common Pleas Reports [*A publication*] (DLA)
Jones & C... Jones and Cary's Irish Exchequer Reports [*1838-39*] [*A publication*] (DLA)
Jones & H Hind Law... Jones and Haughton's Hindoo Law [*A publication*] (DLA)
Jones & H Hind law... Jones and Hauglitons Hindoo Law (journ.) (SAUS)
Jones & L... Jones and La Touche's Irish Chancery Reports [*A publication*] (DLA)
Jones & La T... Jones and La Touche's Irish Chancery Reports [*A publication*] (DLA)
Jones & L (Ir)... Jones and La Touche's Irish Chancery Reports [*A publication*] (DLA)
Jones & McM... Jones and McMurtrie's Pennsylvania Supreme Court Reports [*A publication*] (DLA)
Jones & McM (PA)... Jones and McMurtrie's Pennsylvania Supreme Court Reports [*A publication*] (DLA)
Jones & S... Jones and Spencer's Superior Court Reports [*33-61 New York*] [*A publication*] (DLA)
Jones & Sp... Jones and Spencer's Superior Court Reports [*33-61 New York*] [*A publication*] (DLA)
Jones & Spen... Jones and Spencer's Superior Court Reports [*33-61 New York*] [*A publication*] (DLA)
Jones & V Laws... Jones and Varick's Laws of New York [*A publication*] (DLA)
JonesAp..... Jones Apparel Group, Inc. [*Associated Press*] (SAG)
Jones B ...... Jones' Law of Bailments [*A publication*] (DLA)
Jones Bailm... Jones' Law of Bailments [*A publication*] (DLA)
Jones B & W (MO)... Jones, Barclay, and Whittelsey's Reports [*31 Missouri*] [*A publication*] (DLA)
Jones Barclay & Whittelsey... Jones, Barclay, and Whittelsey's Reports [*31 Missouri*] [*A publication*] (DLA)
Jones Ch Mort... Jones on Chattel Mortgages [*A publication*] (DLA)
Jones curities... Jones on Railroad Securities (journ.) (SAUS)
Jones Easem... Jones' Treatise on Easements [*A publication*] (DLA)
Jones Eq.... Jones' North Carolina Equity Reports [*54-59*] [*1853-63*] [*A publication*] (DLA)
Jones Eq (NC)... Jones' North Carolina Equity Reports [*54-59*] [*1853-63*] [*A publication*] (DLA)
Jones Exch... Jones' Irish Exchequer Reports [*A publication*] (DLA)
Jones Fr Bar... Jones' History of the French Bar [*A publication*] (DLA)
Jones French Bar... Jones' History of the French Bar [*A publication*] (DLA)
Jones Inst... Jones' Institutes of Hindoo Law [*A publication*] (DLA)
Jones Intr... Jones' Introduction to Legal Science [*A publication*] (DLA)
Jones Intr... Jones Introduction to the Science (journ.) (SAUS)
Jones Ir ..... Jones' Irish Exchequer Reports [*A publication*] (DLA)
Jones L ..... Jones' Law Reports [*A publication*] (DLA)
Jones L ..... Jones Law Reports (journ.) (SAUS)
Jones Law... Jones' North Carolina Law Reports [*A publication*] (DLA)
Jones Lib... Jones on Libel [*1812*] [*A publication*] (DLA)
Jones L Of T... Jones on Land and Office Titles [*A publication*] (DLA)
JonesM ..... Jones Medical Industries, Inc. [*Associated Press*] (SAG)
Jones Mort... Jones on Mortgages [*A publication*] (DLA)
Jones NC ... Jones' North Carolina Law Reports [*A publication*] (DLA)
Jones NC ... Jones North Carolina Law Reports (journ.) (SAUS)
Jones PA.... Jones' Reports [*11, 12 Pennsylvania*] [*A publication*] (DLA)
JonesPl ..... Jones Plumbing Systems, Inc. [*Associated Press*] (SAG)
Jones Pledges... Jones on Pledges and Collateral Securities [*A publication*] (DLA)
Jones Ry Sec... Jones on Railway Securities [*A publication*] (DLA)
Jones Salv... Jones' Law of Salvage [*A publication*] (DLA)
Jones Securities... Jones on Railroad Securities [*A publication*] (DLA)
JonesSp..... Jones Spacelink Ltd. [*Associated Press*] (SAG)
Jones UC ... Jones' Upper Canada Common Pleas Reports [*A publication*] (DLA)
Jones Uses... Jones' Law of Uses [*A publication*] (DLA)
Jones Uses... Jones Law of Uses (journ.) (SAUS)
Jon Ex....... Jones' Irish Exchequer Reports [*A publication*] (DLA)
Jon Exch.... Jones' Irish Exchequer Reports [*A publication*] (DLA)
JONFSPL.... Jones Plumbing Systems, Inc. (SAUO)
JonIcbl ...... Jones Intercable, Inc. [*Associated Press*] (SAG)
Jon Ir Exch... Jones' Irish Exchequer Reports [*A publication*] (DLA)
JONR .... Joiner (ABBR)
JONS .... Jones Motor Company [*Common carrier symbol*]
JONS .... Journal of Northern Studies (journ.) (SAUS)
JONS .... Juntas de Ofensiva Nacional Sindicalista [*Syndicalist Juntas of the National Offensive*] [*Spain*] [*Political party*] (PPE)
JONSDAP ... Joint North Sea Data Acquisition Project [*An informal group of Belgian, German, British, Dutch, and Swedish scientific institutes*] (PDAA)
JONSIS...... Joint North Sea Information Systems (PDAA)
JONSWAP... Joint North Sea Wave Analysis Project (SAUS)
JONSWAP... Joint North Sea Wave Atmosphere Program [*Global Atmospheric Research Program*] (USDC)
JONSWAP... Joint North Sea Wave Project [*An informal group of Belgian, German, British, Dutch, and Swedish scientific institutes*] (PDAA)
JONT .... Journal of Ophthalmic Nursing and Technology (SAUO)
JONT .... Journal of Ophthalmic Nursing and Technology (journ.) (SAUS)
J Ont Dent Assoc... Journal. Ontario Dental Association (journ.) (SAUS)
JONU .... Jonker Veendam [*Intermodal shipping container symbol*] (TVRC)
JONUDL..... Journal. American College of Nutrition (journ.) (SAUS)
JONUS ...... Joint Nutrient Studies (SAUO)
JOO .... Jonesboro, GA [*Location identifier*] [*FAA*] (FAAL)
JOOD .... Junior Officer of the Day [*or Deck*] [*Navy*]
JOOD .... Junior Officer of the Deck (SAUO)
JOOI .... Junior Optimist Octagon International [*An association*] (EA)
JOOM........ Junior Observers of Meteorology (SAUO)
JOOMS ...... Junior Observers of Meteorology [*Trainees for government service to replace Weather Bureau men who had gone to war*] [*World War II*]
JOOP .... Journal of Object Orientated Programming (SAUS)
JOOS .... Job-Oriented Organizational Structure (AAG)
JOOTT....... Just One of Those Things [*Internet lingo*] (NETL)
JOOW .... Junior Officer of the Watch [*Navy*]
JOP .... Job Opportunity Program (OICC)
JOP .... Jobs Optional Program [*Combination job opportunities in the business sector and on the job training*] (OICC)
JOP .... Joint Observing Program [*NASA*]
JOP .... Joint Operating Plan
JOP .... Joint Operating Procedure (SAUO)
JOP .... Joint Operation Procedure (AAG)
JOP .... Joint Optoelectronics Project [*Japan*] [*Agreement for conducting cooperative global research*]
JOP .... Journal of Occupational Psychology (journ.) (SAUS)
JOP .... Junior Officer Pilot (SAUO)
JOp .... Jupiter Orbiter Probe [*Later, Project Galileo*] [*NASA*]
JOP .... Jupiter Orbiter with Probe (SAUS)
JOP .... Justice of the Peace [*Telegraphy*] (PCTE)
JOPA......... Junior Officers and Professional Association
JOPA......... Juventud Organizada del Pueblo en Armas [*Armed People's Organized Youth*] [*Guatemala*] (PD)
JOPA......... PA Johnson [*Common carrier symbol*]
JOPC .... Junior Olympic Pistol Championship [*National Rifle Association*]
JOPCN....... Job Order Program Control Number (SAUS)
JO/PCN...... Job Order/Program Control Number [*Army*]
JOPD .... Journal of Psychoactive Drugs (journ.) (SAUS)
JOPD .... Junior Officer Professional Development Program [*Army*] (RDA)
JOPDA....... Journal of Pediatrics (journ.) (SAUS)
J Open Educ Ass Qld... Journal. Open Education Association of Queensland (journ.) (SAUS)
J Operational Psychiatr... Journal of Operational Psychiatry (journ.) (SAUS)
J Operator Theory... Journal of Operator Theory (journ.) (SAUS)
J Oper Manage... Journal of Operations Management (journ.) (SAUS)
J Oper Res Soc... Journal of the Operational Research Society (SAUO)
J Oper Res Soc... Journal of the Operation and Research Society (journ.) (SAUS)
J Oper Res Soc Am... Journal. Operation Research Society of America (journ.) (SAUS)
JOPES....... Joint Operating Planning and Execution System (SAUS)
JOPES....... Joint Operation Planning and Execution System [*DoD*]
JOPES....... Joint Operations Planning and Execution System [*Military*]
JOPES ROLSTK... JOPES-Rolling Stock Summary Report (SAUO)
JOPh......... Journal of Physiology (journ.) (SAUS)
JOPHA....... Journal de Physiologie (journ.) (SAUS)
J Ophthalmic Nurs Technol... Journal of Ophthalmic Nursing and Technology (journ.) (SAUS)
JOPID .... Journal of Pipelines (journ.) (SAUS)
JOPL......... Joplin [*NCIC trailer make code*]
JOPL......... Journal of Paleolimnology (journ.) (SAUS)
JOPL......... Paul Johnson [*Common carrier symbol*]
JOPLI........ Joplin, MO [*American Association of Railroads railroad junction routing code*]

JOPM .... Joint Occupancy Plan Memorandum (AAG)
JOPM .... Joint Operation Procedure Memorandum (AAG)
JOPP .... Joint Operational Policies and Procedures (MCD)
JOPP .... Journal of Primary Prevention (journ.) (SAUS)
JOPR .... Joint Operation Procedure Report (AAG)
JOPREP ..... Joint Operational Report [*Military*] (AFM)
JOPREP ..... Joint Operational Reporting System (SAUO)
JOPS .... Joint Operating Study (SAUS)
JOPS .... Joint Operational Planning System [*Military*]
JOPS .... Joint Operations Planning System (SAUO)
JOPS .... Journal of the Patent Office Society (journ.) (SAUS)
JOPSA .... Journal of Psychology (journ.) (SAUS)
JOPS III ..... Joint Operations Planning Software Support System (SAUO)
JOPSREP ... Joint Operations Planning System Reporting System (SAUO)
JOPSREP ... JOPS Reporting System (SAUS)
JOPS ROLSTK... Joint Operations Planning System Rolling Stock Summary Report (SAUO)
JOPS ROLSTK... JOPS Rolling Stock Summary Report (SAUS)
JOPSRSS ... Joint Operations Planning System Rolling Stock Sum System (SAUO)
JOPSRSS ... JOPS Rolling Stock Sum System (SAUS)
J Opt Commun... Journal of Optical Communications (journ.) (SAUS)
J Opt Soc Am A... Journal of the Optical Society of America A. Optics and Image Science (SAUO)
J Opt Soc Am A... Journal. Optical Society of America. A. Optics and Image Science (journ.) (SAUS)
J Opt Soc Am B Opt Phys... Journal. Optical Society of America. B. Optical Physics (journ.) (SAUS)
J Opt Soc Am Rev Sci Instrum... Journal. Optical Society of America and Review of Scientific Instruments (journ.) (SAUS)
J Opt Soc Cum Ind... Journal. Optical Society of America. Cumulative Index (journ.) (SAUS)
JOQ .... Job Order Quantity [*Military*] (AFIT)
JOR .... Earle M. Jorgensen Co. [*NYSE symbol*] (COMM)
JOR .... Jet Operations Requirements
JOR .... Job Operations Report
JOR .... Job Order Request (AAG)
JOR .... Joint Occupancy Rate (ACAE)
JOR .... Joint Operational Requirement (SAUO)
JOR .... Joint Operations Requirements [*Military*] (AFM)
JOR .... Jordan [*ANSI three-letter standard code*] (CNC)
Jor .... Jordan (VRA)
JOR .... Journal of Oriental Research (journ.) (SAUS)
JOR .... Yorkshire European Airways Ltd. [*British*] [*ICAO designator*] (FAAC)
JORAC .... Joint Operations Radar Airspace Control (SAUO)
Jo Radio Law... Journal of Radio Law [*A publication*] (DLA)
J Oral Implantol... Journal of Oral Implantology (journ.) (SAUS)
J Oral Implant Transplant Surg... Journal of Oral Implant and Transplant Surgery (journ.) (SAUS)
J Oral Maxillofac Surg... Journal of Oral and Maxillofacial Surgery (journ.) (SAUS)
J Oral Med... Journal of Oral Medicine (journ.) (SAUS)
J Oral Pathol... Journal of Oral Pathology (journ.) (SAUS)
J Oral Pathol Med... Journal of Oral Pathology and Medicine (journ.) (SAUS)
J Oral Rehabil... Journal of Oral Rehabilitation (journ.) (SAUS)
J Oral Surg... Journal of Oral Surgery (journ.) (SAUS)
J Oral Surg Anesth Hp Dent Serv... Journal of Oral Surgery Anesthesia and Hospital Dental Service (journ.) (SAUS)
J Oral Therp Pharmacol... Journal of Oral Therapeutics and Pharmacology (journ.) (SAUS)
JORC .... Jeddah Oil Refinery Co. [*Saudi Arabia*] (BUAC)
JORC .... Junior Olympic Rifle Championship [*National Rifle Association*]
JORD .... Jordan (ABBR)
Jord .... Jordanian (DIAR)
Jordan .... Jordan American Holdings, Inc. [*Associated Press*] (SAG)
Jordan Dent J... Jordan Dental Journal (journ.) (SAUS)
Jordan Med J... Jordan Medical Journal (journ.) (SAUS)
Jord Jt St Comp... Jordan on Joint Stock Companies [*A publication*] (DLA)
Jord PJ ...... Jordan's Parliamentary Journal [*A publication*] (DLA)
JOREA .... Journal of Rehabilitation (journ.) (SAUS)
JOREDR ..... Journal of Orthopaedic Research (journ.) (SAUS)
JOREES ..... Journal of Oilseeds Research (journ.) (SAUS)
J Oreg Dent Assoc... Journal Oregon Dental Association (journ.) (SAUS)
JORG .... Ira Jorgenson [*NCIC trailer make code*]
JORG .... Joint Oceanographic Research Group
J Organ Change Manage... Journal of Organizational Change Management [*A publication*] (PABS)
J Organomet Chem Libr... Journal. Organometallic Chemistry Library (journ.) (SAUS)
J Org Chem... Journal of Organic Chemistry (MEC)
J Org Chem USSR... Journal of Organic Chemistry of the USSR (journ.) (SAUS)
J Orgl Behav Mgt... Journal of Organizational Behavior Management (journ.) (SAUS)
J Orgl Com... Journal of Organizational Communica- tion (journ.) (SAUS)
J Or Inst .... Journal. Oriental Institute (journ.) (SAUS)
J Orissa Bot Soc... Journal Orissa Botanical Society (journ.) (SAUS)
J Orissa Math Soc... Journal. Orissa Mathematical Society (journ.) (SAUS)
JORITDS .... Joint Optical Range Instrumentation Type Designation System
JORN .... Jindalee Perational/OTH Radar Network (SAUS)
Jor of Indian Art and Ind... Journal of Indian Art and Industry (journ.) (SAUS)
JORP .... Jet Operations Requirements Panel (SAUS)
JORRI .... Journal. Operating Room Research Institute (journ.) (SAUS)
JORS .... Journal. Operational Research Society (journ.) (SAUS)
JORSJ .... Journal of the Operations Research Society of Japan (SAUO)
JORSJ .... Journal of the Operations Research Society of Japan (journ.) (SAUS)
JORSJ .... Journal. Operations Research Society of Japan (journ.) (SAUS)
J Or Stud ... Journal of Oriental Studies (journ.) (SAUS)
J Orthomol Psychiatry... Journal of Orthomolecular Psychiatry (journ.) (SAUS)
J Orthop Res... Journal of Orthopaedic Research [*A publication*] (CABS)
J Orthop Sports Phys Ther... Journal of Orthopaedic and Sports Physical Therapy (journ.) (SAUS)
J Orthop Tech... Journal of Orthopaedic Techniques (journ.) (SAUS)
J Orthop Trauma... Journal of Orthopaedic Trauma (journ.) (SAUS)
JOS .... Java-based Operating System (SAUS)
JOS .... Jeunesse Ouvriere du Senegal [*Senegalese Working Youth*]
JOS .... Job Opportunity System (TIMI)
JOS .... Job Order Sheet (SAUS)
JOS .... Job Order Supplement (MCD)
JOS .... Joint Oil Staff (SAUO)
JOS .... Joint Operations Staff [*Military*]
JOS .... Jos [*Nigeria*] [*Airport symbol*] (OAG)
Jos .... Joseph (BJA)
Jos .... Joseph's Reports [*21 Nevada*] [*A publication*] (DLA)
Jos .... Josephus (BJA)
Jos .... Joshua [*Old Testament book*]
Jos .... Josiah (BJA)
JOS .... Joss Energy Ltd. [*Toronto Stock Exchange symbol*]
JOS .... Jostens, Inc. [*NYSE symbol*] (SPSG)
JOS .... Josvafo [*Hungary*] [*Seismograph station code, US Geological Survey*] (SEIS)
JOS .... Journal of Oman Studies [*A publication*] (ABAR)
JOS .... Journal of Oriental Studies (journ.) (SAUS)
JOS .... Journal of Quaternary Science [*A publication*] (QUAC)
JOS .... Junior Ordinary Seaman (SAUO)
JOSA .... Journal of the Optical Society of America (SAUO)
JOSA .... Seaman Apprentice, Journalist, Striker [*Navy rating*]
JOSAF .... Joint Operations Support Activity Frankfurt [*National Security Agency*]
J Osaka City Med Cent... Journal. Osaka City Medical Center (journ.) (SAUS)
J Osaka Dent Univ... Journal. Osaka Dental University (journ.) (SAUS)
J Osaka Ind Univ Nat Sci... Journal. Osaka Industrial University. Natural Sciences (journ.) (SAUS)
J Osaka Odontol Soc... Journal. Osaka Odontological Society (journ.) (SAUS)
J Osaka Univ Dent Soc... Journal. Osaka University Dental Society (journ.) (SAUS)
J Osakg Univ Dent Sch... Journal. Osaka University Dental School (journ.) (SAUS)
J Osak Inst Sci Technol Part 1... Journal. Osaka Institute of Science and Technology Part 1 (journ.) (SAUS)
J Osak Med Coll... Journal. Osaka Medical College (journ.) (SAUS)
Jos & Bev... Joseph and Beven's Digest of Decisions [*Ceylon*] [*A publication*] (DLA)
JosAnt .... Jewish Antiquities [*Josephus*] (BJA)
JosApion .... Against Apion [*Josephus*] (BJA)
JOSB .... Bank [*Joseph A.*] Clothiers, Inc. [*NASDAQ symbol*] (SAG)
JOSB .... Jos.A. Bank Clothiers [*NASDAQ symbol*] (TTSB)
JOSB .... Joseph A Bank Clothiers [*NASDAQ symbol*] (SAG)
JosBank ..... Bank [*Joseph A.*] Clothiers, Inc. [*Associated Press*] (SAG)
JosBank ..... Joseph A. Bank Clothers [*Associated Press*] (SAG)
JOSCO .... Joint Overseas Shipping Control Office
JOSDEPS ... Joint Strategic Defense Concept Plan (SAUO)
JOSE .... Joint Optics Structures Experiment (ACAE)
JOSEP .... Josephine, PA [*American Association of Railroads railroad junction routing code*]
Joseph ...... Josephus [*First century AD*] [*Classical studies*] (OCD)
JOSH .... Job Safety and Health [*Bureau of National Affairs*] [*Information service or system*] (CRD)
Josh .... Joshua [*Old Testament book*]
JOSH .... Joshua Trailer [*NCIC trailer make code*]
JOSH .... Journal of School Halth (journ.) (SAUS)
JOSHUA ..... Joint Sticking Hemoglobin Universal Assay [*Sickle cell anemia test*]
JOSIC .... Joint Ocean Surveillance Information Centre (SAUO)
JOSL .... Joslyn Corp. (SAUO)
JO/SL .... Jupiter Orbiter Satellite Lander [*NASA*]
JosLife ...... Life of Josephus (BJA)
J Oslo City Hosp... Journal Oslo City Hospital (journ.) (SAUS)
JOSM .... Jesuit Office of Social Ministry [*Later, NOJSM*] (EA)
J Osmania Univ... Journal. Osmania University (journ.) (SAUS)
JOSN .... Seaman, Journalist, Striker [*Navy rating*]
JOSO .... Joint Organization for Solar Observations
JOSP .... Junior Olympic Shooting Program [*National Rifle Association*]
JOSPRO ..... Joint Ocean [*or Overseas*] Shipping Procedure
JOSPT .... Journal of Orthopaedic and Sports Physical Therapy (journ.) (SAUS)
JOSS .... Job Sharing System (SAUS)
JOSS .... JOHNNIAC [*John's Integrator and Automatic Computer*] Open Shop System [*Time-sharing language*] [*Rand Corp.*] [*1962*] [*Computer science*]
JOSS .... Joint Object Services Submission (SAUO)
JOSS .... Joint Ocean Surface Study
JOSS .... Joint Office for Science Support (SAUO)
JOSS .... Joint Overseas Switchboard (SAUS)
JOSS .... Joint Overseas Switchboard Switch (SAUO)
JOSS .... Joint Overseas Switching System [*Military*] (AABC)
Jostens ...... Jostens, Inc. [*Associated Press*] (SAG)
JosWars ..... Wars [*Josephus*] (BJA)
JOT .... Jam on Target
JOT .... Job-Oriented Terminal (SAUS)

Jo T.......... John of Tynemouth [*Deceased, 1221*] [*Authority cited in pre-1607 legal work*] (DSA)
JOT.......... Joint Observer Team (SAUO)
JOT.......... Joint Operational Test
JOT.......... Joliet, IL [*Location identifier*] [*FAA*] (FAAL)
JOT.......... Journal of Orthopaedic Trauma (journ.) (SAUS)
JOT.......... Journal of Taxation (journ.) (SAUS)
JOT.......... Jump-Oriented Terminal (SAUS)
JOT.......... Junction Optimization Technique (SAUS)
JOT.......... Junior Officer Trainee (GOBB)
JOTA......... Jamboree on the Air [*Boy Scouts of America*]
JOT & E..... Joint Operational Test and Evaluation (MCD)
JOT&E....... Joint Operational Test and Evaluation (SAUS)
JOTB......... Jungle Operations Training Battalion [*Military*]
JOTC......... Joint Oil Targets Committee [*World War II*]
JOTC......... Jungle Operations Training Center [*Army*] (INF)
JOTD........ Jotted (ABBR)
Jo Te........ Johannes Teutonicus [*Deceased circa 1246*] [*Authority cited in pre-1607 legal work*] (DSA)
JOTFOC..... Justification for Other than Full and Open Competition (AAGC)
JOTG........ Jotting (ABBR)
J Otolaryngol... Journal of Otolaryngology (journ.) (SAUS)
J Otolaryngol Soc Aust... Journal. Oto-laryngological Society of Australia (journ.) (SAUS)
J Otolaryngol Suppl... Journal of Otolaryngology. Supplement (journ.) (SAUS)
J Oto-Rhino-Laryngol Soc Jpn... Journal. Oto-Rhino-Laryngological Society of Japan (journ.) (SAUS)
JOTPA....... Journal of Oral Therapeutics and Pharmacology (journ.) (SAUS)
JOTR........ Joint Operational and Technical Reviews [*Military*] (AFIT)
JOTR........ Joshua Tree National Monument
JOTS......... Job-Oriented Training Standards (AFM)
JOTS......... Joint Operational Tactical System [*Navy*] (DOMA)
JOTS......... Joint Operational Telephone System (SAUO)
JOTS II...... Joint Operational Tactical System Version II (SAUS)
JOTT......... Junior Officer Tactics Team (SAUO)
JOTU........ Japan Oil Transportation [*Intermodal shipping container symbol*] (TVRC)
JOU.......... Osaka University, Kita-ku (SAUO)
JOU.......... Osaka University, Kita-ku, Osaka, Japan [*Library symbol*] [*Library of Congress*] (LCLS)
JOU.......... Sioux Falls, SD [*Location identifier*] [*FAA*] (FAAL)
JOUAM...... Junior Order of United American Mechanics (SAUO)
JOULE....... Joint Opportunities for Unconventional or Long-Term Energy Supply (SAUO)
Joule........ Joules, Inc. [*Associated Press*] (SAG)
JOU-N....... Osaka University, Nakanishima Library (SAUO)
JOU-N....... Osaka University, Nakanishima Library, Osaka, Japan [*Library symbol*] [*Library of Congress*] (LCLS)
JOUR........ DIALOG Journal Name Finder [*Database*] (GDD)
JOUR........ Journal (ABBR)
Jour.......... Journal (EBF)
jour.......... Journal (SHCU)
JOUR........ Journalist (GOBB)
JOUR........ Journey (WGA)
jour.......... Journeyman (MIST)
JOUR........ Journeyman
JOUR........ Journey (trucks) [*NCIC truck make code*]
Jour Acoust Soc... Journal. Acoustical Society of America (journ.) (SAUS)
Jour Acoust Soc... Journal of the Acoustical Society of America (SAUO)
Jour Aesthetics and Art Crit... Journal of Aesthetic and Art Criticism (journ.) (SAUS)
Jour Amer Inst Arch... Journal of the American Institute of Architects. Washington (journ.) (SAUS)
Jour Am Inst Archit... Journal. American Institute of Architecture (journ.) (SAUS)
Jour Brit Hond agri soc... Journal of the British Honduras Agricultural Society. Belize (SAUO)
Jour Brit Hond Agri Soc... Journal of the British Honduras Agricultural Society (journ.) (SAUS)
Jour Brit Studies... Journal of British Studies (journ.) (SAUS)
Jour bus.... Journal of Business of the University of Chicago. Chicago (SAUO)
Jour Chem Physics... Journal of Chemical Physics (journ.) (SAUS)
Jour Church and State... Journal of Church and State (journ.) (SAUS)
Jour Comp Leg... Journal. Society of Comparative Legislation [*A publication*] (DLA)
Jour Conat Law... Journal of Conational Law [*A publication*] (DLA)
Jour Contemp Hist... Journal of Contemporary History (journ.) (SAUS)
Jour Crim L... Journal of Criminal Law and Criminology (journ.) (SAUS)
Jour D C bar assoc... Journal of the District of Columbia bar association. District of Columbia (SAUS)
Jour Devel Ares... Journal of Developmental Areas (journ.) (SAUS)
Jour Eccl Hist... Journal of Ecclesiastical History (journ.) (SAUS)
Jour ecol... Journal of Ecology. British Ecological Society. London (SAUO)
Jour Econ and Bus Hist... Journal of Economic and Business History (journ.) (SAUS)
Jour Econ Hist... Journal of Economic History (journ.) (SAUS)
Jour educ soc... Journal of Educational Sociology. Payne Educational Sociology Foundation, Inc. New York (SAUO)
Jour Farm Econ... Journal of Farm Economics (journ.) (SAUS)
Jour Farm Hist... Journal of Farm History (journ.) (SAUS)
Jour forestry... Journal of Forestry. Official Organ of the Society of American Foresters. Washington (SAUO)
Jour Geol Eductihon... Journal of Geological Education (journ.) (SAUS)
Jour Hist Ideas... Journal of the History of Ideas (journ.) (SAUS)
Jour Hist Med... Journal of the History of Medicine (journ.) (SAUS)
Jour Hist Phil... Journal of the History of Philosophy (journ.) (SAUS)
Jour Human Rel... Journal of Human Relations (journ.) (SAUS)
Jour Inst Petrol... Journal of the Institute of Petroleum (journ.) (SAUS)
Jour Interam Studies... Journal of Interamerican Studies and World Affairs (journ.) (SAUS)
Jour Jamaica agric soc... Journal of the Jamaica Agricultural Society. Kingston (SAUO)
Jour Jur..... Journal of Jurisprudence [*A publication*] (DLA)
Jour Juris... Hall's Journal of Jurisprudence [*A publication*] (DLA)
Jour Jur Sc... Journal of Jurisprudence and Scottish Law Magazine [*A publication*] (DLA)
Jour Land Public Uhlity Econ... Journal of Land and Public Utility Economics (journ.) (SAUS)
Jour land publ util econ... Journal of Land & Public Utility Economics. University of Wisconsin. Madison (SAUO)
Jour Law.... Journal of Law [*A publication*] (DLA)
Jour Law and Econ... Journal of Law and Economic Development (journ.) (SAUS)
Jour Legal Ed... Journal of Legal Education (journ.) (SAUS)
Jour Lib Hist... Journal of Library History (journ.) (SAUS)
Jour meteorology... Journal of Meteorology. American Meteorological Society. Lancaster (SAUO)
Jour Miss Hist... Journal of Mississippi History (journ.) (SAUS)
Jour Mod Hist... Journal of Modern History (journ.) (SAUS)
JOURN...... Journal
Journ........ Journalism (DD)
JOURN...... Journey (ABBR)
Journal Geomorph... Journal of Geomorphology (journ.) (SAUS)
Journal Greater India Soc... Journal. Greater India Society (journ.) (SAUS)
Journalism Educ... Journalism Educator (journ.) (SAUS)
Journal-Net... International Journalist Network (SAUS)
Journal of RPS... Journal. Royal Photographic Society (journ.) (SAUS)
Journal Q... Journalism Quarterly. Association for Education in Journalism; American Association of Schools and Departments of Journalism; Kappa Tau Alpha Society; University of Minnesota (SAUO)
Journal Q... Journalism Quarterly (journ.) (SAUS)
Journ Atm Terr Phys... Journal of Atmospheric and Terrestrial Physics (journ.) (SAUS)
Journ Bib Lit... Journal of Biblical Literature [*A publication*] (OCD)
Journ Bib Lit... Journal of Biblical Literature (journ.) (SAUS)
Journ Biophys Biochem Cytol... Journal of Biohysical and Biochemical Cytology (journ.) (SAUS)
Journ Bot Brit For... Journal of Botany. British and Foreign (journ.) (SAUS)
Journ Br Astr Ass... Journal. British Astronomical Association (journ.) (SAUS)
Journ Ceyl Obstet Gyn Ass... Journal. Ceylon Obstetric and Gynaecological Association (journ.) (SAUS)
Journ Chem Phys... Journal of Chemical Physics (journ.) (SAUS)
Journ Chim Phys Chim... Journal de Chimie Physique et de Physico-Chimie Biologique (journ.) (SAUS)
Journ Clin Ophthal... Journal of Clinical Ophthalmology (journ.) (SAUS)
Journ Clin Path... Journal of Clinical Pathology (journ.) (SAUS)
Journ Clin Psychol... Journal of Clinical Psychology (journ.) (SAUS)
Jour negro hist... Journal of Negro History. Association for the Study of Negro Life and History, Inc. (SAUO)
Jour New York Bot Garden... Journal of the New York Botanical Garden. New York (journ.) (SAUS)
Journ Hist Behavioral Sci... Journal of the History of the Behavioral Sciences (journ.) (SAUS)
Journ Jur... Journal of Jurisprudence [*A publication*] (DLA)
Journl Cork Hist S... Journal. Cork Historical and Archaeological Society (journ.) (SAUS)
Journ Phil... Journal of Philology [*A publication*] (OCD)
Journ Phil... Journal of Philology (journ.) (SAUS)
Journ Sav... Journal des Savants [*A publication*] (OCD)
Jour of ecology... Journal of ecology, British Ecological Society (SAUO)
Jour of Int Affairs... Journal of International Affairs (journ.) (SAUS)
Jour of Relig... Journal of Religion (journ.) (SAUS)
Jour of Soc Issues... Journal of Social Issues (journ.) (SAUS)
Jour Pac Hist... Journal of Pacifc History (journ.) (SAUS)
Jour Pol Econ... Journal of Political Economy (journ.) (SAUS)
Jour Polit... Journal of Politics (journ.) (SAUS)
Jour Presby Hist... Journal of Presbyterian History (journ.) (SAUS)
Jour Ps Med... Journal of Psychological Medicine and Medical Jurisprudence [*A publication*] (DLA)
Jour Ps Med... Journal of Psychological Medicine and Medical Jurisprudence (journ.) (SAUS)
Jour Relig Hist... Journal of Religious History (journ.) (SAUS)
Jour soc arch hist... Journal of the Society of Architectural Historians. Urbana (SAUO)
Jour Soc Civ... Journal des Societes Civiles et Commerciales [*A publication*] (DLA)
Jour Society Archit Historians... Journal. Society of Architecture and Historians (journ.) (SAUS)
Jour Speech Disorders... Journal of Speech Disorders (journ.) (SAUS)
Jour Trib Com... Journal des Tribunaux de Commerce [*A publication*] (DLA)
Jour Warburg Courtauld Inst... Journal of the Warburg and Courtauld Institutes (journ.) (SAUS)
JOUSD...... Journal of Science. Busan National University (journ.) (SAUS)
JOUT........ Johnson Outdoors [*NASDAQ symbol*]
Jov........... Hymnus in Jovem [*of Callimachus*] [*Classical studies*] (OCD)
JOV.......... Japanese Overseas Volunteers (SAUS)
JOV.......... Joint Venture (SAUO)
JOVE......... Job Placement on the Job Training Vocational Education Educational Assistance (SAUS)
JOVE......... Joint Operations Visualization Environment [*Military*]
JOVE......... Jonathans Own Version of Emacs (SAUS)
JOVE......... Jupiter Orbiting Vehicle for Exploration (MCD)

JOVIAL...... Joule's Own Version of the International Algebraic [*or Algorithmic*] Language [*1958*] [*Computer science*]
JOVIAL...... Joules Own Version of the International Algorithmic Language (SAUS)
JOVIAL...... Jules Own Version of the International Algebraic Language (SAUO)
Jow Dict.... Jowitt's Dictionary of English Law [*2nd ed.*] [*1977*] [*A publication*] (DLA)
JOWE........ Jowett [*NCIC car make code*]
JOWIP....... Joint Ocean Wave Investigation Project [*US and Canadian venture*]
JOWOG....... Joint Working Group
JOWRDN.... Journal of Obesity and Weight Regulation (journ.) (SAUS)
JOY.......... Job Opportunity for Youth [*NASA employment program*]
JOY.......... Joy [*Poland*] [*ICAO designator*] (FAAC)
JOY.......... Joy Technologies Inc. (SAUO)
JOYA......... Journal of Youth and Adolescence (journ.) (SAUS)
Joy Acc..... Joy's Evidence of Accomplices [*1836*] [*A publication*] (DLA)
JOYC........ Joy Manufacturing Company [*NCIC trailer make code*]
Joyce Ins... Joyce on Insurance [*A publication*] (DLA)
Joyce Ins... Joyce on Insurance (journ.) (SAUS)
Joyce Lim... Joyce on Limitations [*A publication*] (DLA)
Joyce Prac Inj... Joyce's Law and Practice of Injunctions [*1872*] [*A publication*] (DLA)
Joyce Prac Inj... Joyces Law and Practice of Injunctions (journ.) (SAUS)
Joyce Prin Inj... Joyce's Doctrines and Principles of Injunctions [*1877*] [*A publication*] (DLA)
Joy Chal.... Joy's Peremptory Challenge of Jurors [*1844*] [*A publication*] (DLA)
Joy Conf.... Joy. Admissibility of Confessions [*1842*] [*A publication*] (DLA)
Joy Ev....... Joy's Evidence of Accomplices [*1836*] [*A publication*] (DLA)
JOYG........ Joy Global [*Company symbol*]
Joy Leg Ed... Joy on Legal Education [*A publication*] (DLA)
Joyn Lim.... Joynes on Limitations [*A publication*] (DLA)
JOYO........ Japanese Breeder Reactor (SAUS)
JOY Program... Job Opportunity for Youth Program (SAUS)
JOYS........ Journal of Youth Services in Libraries [*American Library Association*]
JOZ.......... Jozini [*South Africa*] [*Seismograph station code, US Geological Survey*] (SEIS)
JOZU........ S and ZN Jongsma Holding [*Intermodal shipping container symbol*] (TVRC)
JP............ Adria Airways [*Airline flight code*] (ODBW)
JP............ Die Juedische Presse [*The Jewish Press*] [*German*] (BJA)
JP............ Fighter [*Russian aircraft symbol*]
JP............ Indo-Pacific International [*ICAO designator*] (AD)
JP............ Jack Panel
JP............ Jackson-Pratt [*Drain*] [*Surgery*] (DAVI)
JP............ Jacobi Polynomial [*Mathematics*]
JP............ Jacobi Polynominal (SAUS)
JP............ James M. Peed [*Designer's mark when appearing on US coins*]
JP............ Janata Party [*India*] [*Political party*] (PPW)
JP............ Japan [*ANSI two-letter standard code*] (CNC)
Jp............ Japanese (SAUS)
JP............ Japan Paper
JP............ Japan Press (SAUO)
JP............ Jarrow Press, Inc.
JP............ Jarvis [*Artificial heart*] [*Medicine*] (EDAA)
JP............ Jatiya Party [*Bangladesh*] [*Political party*]
JP............ Jean Pierre Cosmetiques, Inc. [*Vancouver Stock Exchange symbol*]
JP............ Jefferson Pilot [*NYSE symbol*] (SAG)
JP............ Jefferson-Pilot Corp. [*NYSE symbol*] (SPSG)
JP............ Jet Penetration
JP............ Jet Petroleum (AFM)
JP............ Jet Pilot
JP............ Jet Pipe
JP............ Jet Power
jp............ Jet Propellant (NAKS)
JP............ Jet Propellant [*or Propulsion*]
JP............ Jet-Propelled (SAUS)
jp............ Jet Propulsion (NAKS)
JP............ Jet Propulsion Fuel
JP............ Jet Publications [*DoD*]
JP............ Jet Pump [*Bioinstrumentation*]
JP............ Jewish Press [*Brooklyn, NY*] [*A publication*] (BJA)
JP............ Jig Pin (SAUS)
JP............ Jiji Press, Ltd. (SAUO)
JP............ Jobbing Printer [*A publication*] (DGA)
JP............ Job Placement [*Job Service*] (OICC)
JP............ Job Processing (SAUS)
JP............ Job Processor
JP............ Jobst Pump [*Medicine*]
JP............ Job the Patient (BJA)
JP............ Joining Peptide [*Medicine*] (DMAA)
JP............ Joint Pacific [*Military*] (CINC)
JP............ Joint Protection (STED)
JP............ Joint Publication [*Military*]
JP............ Jones Party [*Malta*] [*Political party*] (PPE)
JP............ Jones Plug [*Electricity*] (IAA)
JP............ Joseph Pennell [*Specification-made paper*]
JP............ Journal of Paleontology (journ.) (SAUS)
JP............ Journal of Parapsychology [*A publication*] (BRI)
JP............ Journal of Philology [*A publication*] (ABAR)
JP............ Judge of Probate [*British*] (ROG)
JP............ Judge President (SAFN)
JP............ Juice Packed (SAUS)
JP............ Jumper (IAA)
JP............ Jump on Positive (SAUS)
JP............ Junction Panel [*or Point*] [*Electronics*]
JP............ Junction Point (SAUS)
JP............ Junge Pioniero
JP............ Jungle Penetrator [*A helicopter rescue device*] [*Military*] (VNW)
JP............ Junior Partner [*i.e., a husband*] [*Slang*]
JP............ Junior Principal [*Freemasonry*] (ROG)
JP............ Junior Probationer [*British*] (ROG)
JP............ Justice of the Peace
JP............ Justice of the Peace and Local Government Review [*A publication*] (DLA)
JP............ Justice of the Peace. Weekly Notes of Cases [*England*] [*A publication*] (DLA)
JP............ Justice Party [*Turkey*] [*Political party*]
JP............ Jute-Protected (SAUS)
JP............ Jute Protection [*Telecommunications*] (TEL)
JP............ Juvenile Periodontist [*Dentistry*] (DAVI)
JP............ Juventud Peronista [*Peronist Youth*] [*Argentina*]
JP............ Kim Jong Pil [*South Korean politician*]
JPA.......... Jack Panel Assembly
JPA.......... Jacksonville Port Authority [*Federal Railroad Administration identification code*]
JPA.......... Jamaica Press Association (BUAC)
JPA.......... Japan Petroleum Association (BUAC)
JPA.......... Japan Procurement Agency
JPA.......... Jesuit Philosophical Association of the United States and Canada (EA)
JPA.......... Jet Pioneers Association of the United States of America (EA)
JPA.......... Jewish Palestinian Aramaic (BJA)
JPA.......... Joao Pessoa [*Brazil*] [*Airport symbol*] (OAG)
JPA.......... Job Application Aid (SAUS)
JPA.......... Job Pack Area [*Computer science*] (IBMDP)
JPA.......... Job Performance Aid
JPA.......... Job Performance Assistance (SPST)
JPA.......... Joint Palestine Appeal (SAUO)
JPA.......... Joint Passover Association (SAUS)
JPA.......... Joint Passover Association of the City of New York (EA)
JPA.......... Joint Permitting Agency (SAUO)
JPA.......... Joint Permitting Agreement (COE)
JPA.......... Joint Planning Activity [*DoD*]
JPA.......... Joint Powers Agreement (SAUO)
JPA.......... Junior Philatelists of America (EA)
JPA.......... Justices of the Peace Association [*Australia*]
JPA.......... Juvenile Pilocytic Astrocytoma [*Medicine*] (DMAA)
JPA.......... Juvenile Psoriatic Arthritis [*Medicine*] (MELL)
JPA.......... La Porte, TX [*Location identifier*] [*FAA*] (FAAL)
J PA Acad Sci... Journal. Pennsylvania Academy of Science (journ.) (SAUS)
J-PAAS...... Jubilation - Paul Anka Admiration Society [*Defunct*] (EA)
JPAC......... Joint Planning Advisory Committee (SAUO)
JPAC......... Joint Public Advisory Committee (SAUO)
J Pac H..... Journal of Pacific History [*A publication*]
J Packag Technol... Journal of Packaging Technology (journ.) (SAUS)
JPACO....... Job Pack Area Control Queue (VLIE)
JPACQ....... Job Pack Area Control Queue (SAUS)
J Paediatr Child Health... Journal of Paediatrics and Child Health (journ.) (SAUS)
J Paediatr Dent... Journal of Paediatric Dentistry (journ.) (SAUS)
J Pain Symptom Manage... Journal of Pain and Symptom Management (journ.) (SAUS)
J Paint Tec... Journal of Paint Technology (journ.) (SAUS)
J Pak Hist Soc... Journal. Pakistan Historical Society (journ.) (SAUS)
J Pal Ada Modul-2... Journal of Pascal, Ada and Modula 2 (journ.) (SAUS)
J Palaegr Soc... Journal. Palaeographical Society (journ.) (SAUS)
J Paleolimnol... Journal of Paleolimnology [*A publication*] (PABS)
J Palest Arab Med Ass... Journal. Palestine Arab Medical Association (journ.) (SAUS)
J Palliat Care... Journal of Palliative Care (journ.) (SAUS)
J Palynol Palynol Soc India... Journal of Palynology. Palynological Society of India (journ.) (SAUS)
JPAM........ Joint Program Assessment Memorandum (MCD)
JPANDA..... Journal of Psychoanalytic Anthropology (journ.) (SAUS)
J Pang Med S... Journal. Pangasinan Medical Society (journ.) (SAUS)
J Pang Med Soc... Journal. Pangasinan Medical Society (journ.) (SAUS)
JPAO......... Joint Public Affairs Office (DOMA)
J Pa Or Soc... Journal. Palestine Oriental Society (journ.) (SAUS)
JPAP......... Jet Penetration Approach
JPAPS....... Job Performance Aids Production System (SAUO)
J Papua NG Society... Journal. Papua and New Guinea Society (journ.) (SAUS)
J Parametrics... Journal of Parametrics (journ.) (SAUS)
J Parasitol... Journal of Parasitology [*A publication*] (PABS)
J Parenter Drug Ass... Journal. Parenteral Drug Association (journ.) (SAUS)
J Parenter Sci Technol... Journal of Parenteral Science and Technology (journ.) (SAUS)
J Park Rec Adm... Journal of Park and Recreation Administration (journ.) (SAUS)
J Parlia Info... Journal of Parliamentary Information (journ.) (SAUS)
JPAT......... Joint Process Action Team
J Pathol..... Journal of Pathology (journ.) (SAUS)
J Patient Acc Manage... Journal of Patient Account Management (journ.) (SAUS)
JPATS....... Joint Primary Aircraft Trainer System (SAUO)
JPATS....... Joint Primary Aircraft Training System [*Air Force*] [*Navy*] (DOMA)
JPAV......... Joint Personnel Asset Visibility [*Military*]
J PA Water Works Oper Assoc... Journal. Pennsylvania Water Works Operators Asiation (journ.) (SAUS)
JPB.......... Joint Planning Board
JPB.......... Joint Procurement Board [*Military*] (AABC)
JPB.......... Joint Production Board [*US and Great Britain*]

JPB .... Joint Purchasing Board
JPB .... Junctional Premature Beat [*Cardiology*]
JPBAEB ..... Journal of Psychopathology and Behavioral Assessment (journ.) (SAUS)
JPBHS........ Judah P. Benjamin High School (SAUO)
JPBPB........ Journal of Pharmacokinetics and Biopharmaceutics (journ.) (SAUS)
JPBS.......... Jettison Pushbutton Switch
JPC .... Jack Patch Cord
JpC .... Japanese Columbia [*Record label*]
JPC .... Japan Productivity Center (SAUO)
JPC .... Japan Productivity Centre (BUAC)
JPC .... Jet Propulsion Center (SAUO)
JPC .... Jeunesse pour Christ [*Youth for Christ International - YFCI*] (EA)
JPC .... Jeunesse Progressiste Casamancaise [*Casamance Progressive Youth*] [*Senegal*]
JPC .... Johnson Products (EFIS)
JPC .... Johnson Products Company, Inc. (SAUO)
JPC .... Joint Partnering Contracting
JPC .... Joint Pensions Committee (WDAA)
JPC .... Joint Planning Center
JPC .... Joint Planning Committee
JPC .... Joint Planning Conference (SAUO)
JPC .... Joint Planning Council (SAUO)
JPC .... Joint Power Condition [*Aerospace*] (NAKS)
JPC .... Joint Power Conditioner
JPC .... Joint Practice Committee (SAUO)
JPC .... Joint Production Committee [*British*] (DCTA)
JPC .... Joint Production Council (SAUO)
JPC .... Joint Project Committee (SAUO)
JPC .... Joint Publishers Committee (SAUO)
JPC .... Journal of Pharmaceutical Care (journ.) (SAUS)
JPC .... Journal of Planar Chromatography (journ.) (SAUS)
JPC .... Journal of Popular Culture [*A publication*] (BRI)
JPC .... Judgement Purchase Corp.
JPC .... Judge of the Prize Court (DLA)
JPC .... Judicial Planning Council (OICC)
JPC .... Junctional Premature Contraction [*Cardiology*]
JPC .... Justice of Peace Court [*Court type found in state of Virginia*] (MVRD)
JPC .... Justice of the Peace Clerk [*British*] (ROG)
JPC .... Just Prior Condition [*Computer science*]
JPC .... Polar Air Co. [*Russian Federation*] [*ICAO designator*] (FAAC)
JPCA......... Japan Petrochemical Industry Association (BUAC)
JPCA......... Jewish Penicillin Connoisseurs Association (EA)
JPCA......... Journal of Physical Chemistry A [*Database*] (GDD)
JPCAAC ..... Journal. Air Pollution Control Association (journ.) (SAUS)
JP Cable .... Jute-Protected Cable (SAUS)
JPCB......... Journal of Physical Chemistry B [*Database*] (GDD)
JPCC......... Joint Pacific Command Control Network (MCD)
JPCC......... Joint Petroleum Coordination Center (SAUO)
JPCC......... Joint Petroleum Coordination Center/Committee [*NATO*] (NATG)
JPCC......... Joint Petroleum Coordination Committee (SAUO)
JPCCA....... Journal of Physical and Colloid Chemistry (journ.) (SAUS)
JPCD .... Just Perceptible Color Difference [*Telecommunications*] (TEL)
J Pce Sci ... Journal of Peace Science (journ.) (SAUS)
JPCF......... JPC Freight Forwarding [*Common carrier symbol*]
JPCG .... Joint Policy Coordinated Group (SAUO)
JPCG-CRM... Joint Policy Coordinating Group on Computer Resources Management (MCD)
JPCG/DIMM... Joint Policy Coordinating Group on Defense Integrated Materiel Management (AFIT)
JPCG/DIMM... Joint Policy Coordinating Group on Defense Integrated Materiel Management (SAUS)
JPCG-DMI... Joint Policy Coordinating Group on Depot Maintenance Interservicing
J PCI .... Journal of the Prestressed Concrete Institute (journ.) (SAUS)
JPCMA ...... Journal of Photochemistry (journ.) (SAUS)
JP COMNET... Joint Pacific Command Teletype Network (SAUO)
JPCRM .... Joint Policy Coordinating Group on Computer Resources (SAUO)
JPCRSP..... John Pennekamp Coral Reef State Park (SAUO)
JPCS......... Journal of Physics and Chemistry of Solids. Supplement (journ.) (SAUS)
JP Ct .... Justice of the Peace's Court [*Legal term*] (DLA)
JPD .... Japan Publishers Directory [*Japan Publications Guide Service*] [*Japan*] [*Information service or system*] (CRD)
JPD .... Joint Planning Document (COE)
JPD .... Joint Potential Designator [*DoD*]
JPD .... Joint Product Development [*Automotive engineering*]
JPD .... Just Perceptible Difference (SAUS)
JPD .... Juvenile Plantar Dermatosis [*Medicine*] (DAVI)
JPDAAH..... Journal. American Podiatry Association (journ.) (SAUS)
JPDADK..... Journal. Parenteral Drug Association (journ.) (SAUS)
JPDC......... Japan Petroleum Development Co.
JPDC .... Japan Petroleum Development Corporation (SAUO)
JPDEN....... Journal of Prosthetic Dentistry (journ.) (SAUS)
JPDF......... Joint Probability Density Function (SAUS)
JPDMB ...... American Society of Psychosomatic Dentistry and Medicine. Journal (journ.) (SAUS)
JPDPA....... Journal of Periodontology-Periodontics (journ.) (SAUS)
JPDR .... Japan Power Demonstration Reactor
JPDRD ...... Joint Program Definition and Requirements Document (SAUS)
JPDS .... Joint Petroleum Data System (SAUO)
JPE .... Japanese [*Telegraphy*] (PCTE)
JPE .... Job Performance Evaluation (PDAA)
J PE .... Journal of Physical Education and Program (journ.) (SAUS)
JPE .... Journal of Political Economy [*A publication*] (BRI)
JPE .... JPE, Inc. [*Associated Press*] (SAG)
JPE .... Jump if Parity Even (VLIE)
JPE .... Jump in Parity Even (SAUS)
JPE .... Jump on Parity Even (SAUS)
J Peace Res... Journal of Peace Research [*A publication*] (JLIT)
J Peace Sci... Journal of Peace Science [*A publication*] (JLIT)
J Peas Stud... Journal of Peadant Studies (journ.) (SAUS)
JPEC......... Joint Planning and Execution Community (DOMA)
JPEC......... Joint Planning and Execution Course (SAUO)
JPEC......... JOPES Planning and Execution Community (SAUO)
JP ECON .... Journal of Political Economy [*A publication*] (ROG)
J PED......... Journal of Pedagogy [*New York*] [*A publication*] (ROG)
JPEDB....... Joint Planning and Execution Data Base (SAUO)
JPEDD....... Journal of Physics Education (journ.) (SAUS)
J Pediat..... Journal of Pediatrics (SAUS)
J Pediatr Endocrinol Metab... Journal of Pediatric Endocrinology and Metabolism (journ.) (SAUS)
J Pediatr Hematol Oncol... Journal of Pediatric Hematology/Oncology (journ.) (SAUS)
J Pediatr Nurs... Journal of Pediatric Nursing (journ.) (SAUS)
J Pediatr Nurs... Journal of Pediatric Nursing, Nursing Care of Children and Families (journ.) (SAUS)
J Pediatr Oncol Nurs... Journal of Pediatric Oncology Nursing (journ.) (SAUS)
J Pediatr Ophtbalmol... Journal of Pediatric Ophthalmology (journ.) (SAUS)
J Pediatr Ophthalmol Strabismus... Journal of Pediatric Ophthalmology and Strabismus (journ.) (SAUS)
J Pediatr Psychol... Journal of Pediatric Psychology [*A publication*] (PABS)
J Pedi Endocr... Journal of Pediatric Endocrinology (journ.) (SAUS)
J Pedod..... Journal of Pedodontics (journ.) (SAUS)
JPEG......... Joint Photographic Experts Group [*International video standard*] (PCM)
jpeg.......... Joint Photographic Experts Group [*Computer science*]
JPEG......... Joint Picture Experts Group (SAUO)
JPEG......... Joint Planning and Execution Graphics (SAUO)
JPEI.......... JPE, Inc. [*NASDAQ symbol*] (SAG)
JPEL......... Journal of Planning and Environment Law (journ.) (SAUS)
JPEN......... Journal of Parenteral & Enteral Nutrition (SAUO)
JPEN......... Journal of Parenteral and Enteral Nutrition (journ.) (SAUS)
JPEN J Parenter Enteral Nutr... JPEN. Journal of Parenteral and Enteral Nutrition (journ.) (SAUS)
J Penn Way Instn... Permanent Way Institution. Journal (SAUS)
JPEQ......... JP's Express [*Common carrier symbol*]
J Perinat Med... Journal of Perinatal Medicine (journ.) (SAUS)
J Periodontal Res Suppl... Journal of Periodontal Research. Supplement (journ.) (SAUS)
J Periodontol-Periodontics... Journal of Periodontology-Periodontics (journ.) (SAUS)
J Pers Assess... Journal of Personality Assessment (journ.) (SAUS)
JPERSTAT... Joint Personnel Status and Casualty Report (COE)
J Perth Hosp... Journal. Perth Hospital (journ.) (SAUS)
JPESC .... Joint Planning and Execution Steering Committee (SAUO)
JPESJ .... Jewish Palestine Exploration Society. Journal [*A publication*] (BJA)
J Pestic Sci... Journal of Pesticide Science (journ.) (SAUS)
JPET......... Job Placement and Employment Training
JPET......... Journal of Pharmacology and Experimental Therapeutics (SAUO)
J Petrol ..... Journal of Petrology (journ.) (SAUS)
J Petrol Geol... Journal of Petrology and Geology (journ.) (SAUS)
J Petrol Techn... Journal of Petroleum Technology (journ.) (SAUS)
JPF .... Jewish Peace Fellowship (EA)
JPF .... Jewish Philanthropic Fund (SAUO)
JPF .... Jewish Philanthropic Fund of 1933 (EA)
JPF .... Job Planning Form
JPF .... Justice of the Peace Fiscal [*British*] (ROG)
JPFAEV...... Journal of Psychotherapy and the Family (journ.) (SAUS)
JPFC......... Jane Powell Fan Club (EA)
JPFC......... Jeanne Pruett Fan Club (EA)
JPFC......... Judas Priest Fan Club (EA)
JPFFI .... Jiangsu Provincial Freshwater Fisheries Institute [*China*] (BUAC)
JPFI.......... Joslin Diabetes Foundation I (SAUO)
JPFMP ...... Journal of Physics. F Metal Physics (journ.) (SAUS)
JPFO......... Jews for the Preservation of Firearms Ownership (EA)
JP Food..... JP Foodservice, Inc. [*Associated Press*] (SAG)
JPFR......... Japan Prototype Fast Reactor (SAUS)
JPFS......... JP Foodservice [*NASDAQ symbol*] (TTSB)
JPFS......... JP Foodservice, Inc. [*NASDAQ symbol*] (SAG)
JPFT......... Joiner Pilaster Fumetight [*Technical drawings*]
J-P Fuel..... Jet-Propulsion Fuel (SAUS)
JPG .... Jefferson Proving Ground [*Madison, IN*] [*Army*] (AABC)
JPG .... Job Performance [*or Proficiency*] Guide (AFM)
JPG .... Job Proficiency Guide (SAUS)
JPG .... Joint Photographic experts Group (SAUO)
JPG .... Joint Planning Group [*NATO*] (NATG)
JPG .... Joint Presidents Group (SAUO)
JPG .... JOPES Project Group (SAUO)
JPG .... JPEG/JFIF compliant image format (SAUS)
JPG .... Jumping (SAUS)
JPGA .... Japan Professional Golf Association (SAUO)
JPGC .... Joint Power Generation Conference
JPGEN....... Journal of Experimental Psychology: General (SAUS)
JPGM........ Joint Planning Graphics Module (SAUO)
JPGM........ J Paul Getty Museum (SAUO)
JPGR .... Journal of Plant Growth Regulation (journ.) (SAUS)

JPGS .... Japan Publications Guide Service [*Information service or system*] (IID)
JPH .... Jones, Paul H., Romulus MI [*STAC*]
JPH .... Journal of Pacifc History (journ.) (SAUS)
JPH .... Journal of Policy History (SAUO)
JPH .... Journal of Presbyterian History (journ.) (SAUS)
JPHA .... John Pelham Historical Association (EA)
JPHAA .... Journal. American Pharmaceutical Association (journ.) (SAUS)
JPHAC .... Journal of Physics. A Mathematical and General (journ.) (SAUS)
J Phann Market Manage... Journal of Pharmaceutical Marketing and Management (journ.) (SAUS)
J Pharmacobiodyn... Journal of Pharmacobio-Dynamics (journ.) (SAUS)
J Pharmacol Methods... Journal of Pharmacological Methods (journ.) (SAUS)
J Pharmacol Toxicol Methods... Journal of Pharmacological Toxicol Methods (journ.) (SAUS)
J Pharmac Sci... Journal of the Pharmaceutical Sciences (journ.) (SAUS)
J Pharm Assoc Thailand... Journal. Pharmaceutical Association of Thailand (journ.) (SAUS)
J Pharm Med... Journal of Pharmaceutical Medicine (journ.) (SAUS)
J Pharm Pharmacol... Journal of Pharmacy and Pharacology [*A publication*] (PABS)
J Pharm Pharmacol Suppl... Journal of Pharmacy and Pharmacology. Supplement (journ.) (SAUS)
J Pharm Sci... Journal of Pharmaceutical Science (MEC)
J Pharm Sci UAR... Journal of Pharmaceutical Sciences of the United Arab Republic (journ.) (SAUS)
J Pharm Soc Jap... Journal. Pharmaceutical Society of Japan (journ.) (SAUS)
J Pharm Soc Jpn... Journal of the Pharmaceutical Society of Japan (journ.) (SAUS)
J Pharm Soc Jpn... Journal. Pharmaceutical Society of Japan (journ.) (SAUS)
J Pharm Soc Korea... Journal. Pharmaceutical Society of Korea (journ.) (SAUS)
J Pharm Technol... Journal of Pharmacy Technology (journ.) (SAUS)
J Pharm Univ Karachi... Journal of Pharmacy. University of Karachi (journ.) (SAUS)
J Ph Ch Ref Data... Journal of Physical and Chemical Reference Data (journ.) (SAUS)
JPHD .... Journal of Public Health Dentistry (journ.) (SAUS)
J Phenomen... Journal of Phenomenological Psychology (journ.) (SAUS)
JPHGB....... Journal of Physics. G Nuclear Physics (journ.) (SAUS)
J Phil........ Journal of Philosophy [*A publication*] (BRI)
J Phila Ass Psychoanal... Journal. Philadelphia Association for Psychoanalysis (journ.) (SAUS)
J Phila County Dent Soc... Journal. Philadelphia County Dental Society (journ.) (SAUS)
J Philadelphia Gen Hosp... Journal. Philadelphia General Hospital (journ.) (SAUS)
J Phildelphia Coll Pharm... Journal. Philadelphia College of Pharmacy (journ.) (SAUS)
J Phil Educ... Journal of Philosophy of Education (journ.) (SAUS)
J Philipp Dent Assoc... Journal. Philippine Dental Association (journ.) (SAUS)
J Philipp Fed Priv Med Pract... Journal. Philippine Federation of Private Medical Practitioners (journ.) (SAUS)
J Philippine MA... Journal. Philippine Medical Association (journ.) (SAUS)
J Philipp Isl Med Assoc... Journal. Philippine Islands Medical Association (journ.) (SAUS)
J Philipp Med Assoc... Journal. Philippine Medical Association (journ.) (SAUS)
J Philipp Pharm Assoc... Journal. Philippine Pharmaceutical Association (journ.) (SAUS)
J Philipp Vet Med Assoc... Journal. Philippine Veterinary Medical Association (journ.) (SAUS)
J Phil Stat... Journal of Philippine Statistics (journ.) (SAUS)
J Phil Stud... Journal of Philosophical Studies (journ.) (SAUS)
JPHMD...... Journal of Experimental Psychology Human Learning and Memory (journ.) (SAUS)
JPhon .... Journal of Phonetics (journ.) (SAUS)
J Photoacoust... Journal of Photoacoustics (journ.) (SAUS)
J Photochem... Journal of Photochemistry (journ.) (SAUS)
J Photochem Etching... Journal of Photochemical Etching (journ.) (SAUS)
J Photochem Photobiol B... Journal of Photochemistry and Photobiology. B, Biology (journ.) (SAUS)
J Photogr Soc Am... Journal. Photographic Society of America (journ.) (SAUS)
J Photomicrogr Soc... Journal. Photomicroaphic Society (journ.) (SAUS)
J Phot Soc Amer... Journal. Photographic Society of America (journ.) (SAUS)
JPHP .... Journal of Public Health Policy (journ.) (SAUS)
JPHPD....... Journal of Experimental Psychology Human Perception and Performance (journ.) (SAUS)
JPHS .... Journal of the Presbyterian Historical Society (SAUO)
JPHS .... Journal of the Presbyterian Historical Society (journ.) (SAUS)
JPHS .... Journal. Presbyterian Historical Society (journ.) (SAUS)
JPHS .... Pakistan Historical Society (SAUO)
JPHYA....... Journal of Physiology (journ.) (SAUS)
J Phys....... Journal of Physics (journ.) (SAUS)
J Phys A Gen Phys... Journal of Physics. A General Physics (journ.) (SAUS)
J Phys A Math Nucl Gen... Journal of Physics. A Mathematical, Nuclear and General (journ.) (SAUS)
J Phys B At Mol Opt Phys... Journal of Physics B, Atomic, Molecular and Optical Physics (journ.) (SAUS)
J Phys Chem... Journal of Physical Chemistry (MEC)
J Phys Chem Ref Data Suppl... Journal of Physical and Chemical Reference Data. Supplement (journ.) (SAUS)
J Phys Chem Solids Suppl... Journal of Physics and Chemistry of Solids. Supplement (journ.) (SAUS)
J Phys D Appl Phys... Journal of Physics. D Applied Physics (journ.) (SAUS)
J Phys Earth... Journal of Physics of the Earth (journ.) (SAUS)
J Phys Educ Rec & Dance... Journal of Physical Education, Recreation and Dance (journ.) (SAUS)
J Phys Educ Recr... Journal of Physical Educalion and Recreation (journ.) (SAUS)
J Physiol Soc Jpn... Journal. Physiological Society of Japan (journ.) (SAUS)
J Phys Jap... Journal. Physical Society of Japan (journ.) (SAUS)
J Phys Oceanogr... Journal of Physical Oceanography [*A publication*] (PABS)
J Phys Org Chem... Journal of Physical Organic Chemistry (journ.) (SAUS)
J Phys Soc... Journal of the Physical Society (journ.) (SAUS)
J Phys Soc Jp... Journal. Physical Society of Japan (journ.) (SAUS)
J Phys Soc Jpn... Journal of Physical Society of Japan (journ.) (SAUS)
J Phys Soc Jpn... Journal of the Physical Society of Japan (SAUO)
J Phys Soc Jpn... Journal of the Physical Society of Japan (journ.) (SAUS)
J Phys Soc Jpn Suppl... Journal. Physical Society of Japan. Supplement (journ.) (SAUS)
JPI .... Jackson Personality Inventory [*Personality development test*] [*Psychology*]
JPI .... Japanese Petroleum Institute [*Fuels and lubricants*]
JPI .... Japan Packaging Institute (BUAC)
JPI .... Jianghan Petroleum Institute [*China*] (BUAC)
JPI .... Job Performance Illustrations (MCD)
JPI .... Joint Packaging Instruction
JPI .... Joint Precision Interdiction [*NATO*] (DOMA)
JPI .... JP Industries, Inc. (SAUO)
JPI .... Jupiter Industries, Inc. (SAUO)
JPI .... Jupiter National, Inc. (SPSG)
JPI .... Sitka, AK [*Location identifier*] [*FAA*] (FAAL)
JPIA .... Japan Plastics Industry Association (BUAC)
JPIC .... Joint Program Integration Committee [*NASA*] (NASA)
JPIC .... Joint Public Information Center (COE)
JPIFA1....... Japan Pesticide Information (journ.) (SAUS)
JPIM......... Journal of Product Innovation Management [*Product Development and Management Association*] [*A publication*]
J Pineal Res... Journal of Pineal Rearch (journ.) (SAUS)
J Pipeline Div Am Soc Civ Eng... Journal. Pipeline Division. American Society of Civil Engineers (journ.) (SAUS)
J Pipelines... Journal of Pipelines (journ.) (SAUS)
JPJ.......... Justice of the Peace and Local Government Review [*A publication*] (DLA)
JPJ.......... Justice of the Peace Journal [*A publication*]
JPJ.......... Justice of the Peace. Weekly Notes of Cases [*England*] [*A publication*] (DLA)
JPJ.......... Paterson, NJ [*Location identifier*] [*FAA*] (FAAL)
JPJo .... Justice of the Peace. Weekly Notes of Cases [*England*] [*A publication*] (DLA)
JPJu .... Journal of Psychology and Judaism (journ.) (SAUS)
J Pkg Technol... Journal of Packaging Technology (journ.) (SAUS)
J PL .... Jack Plug (SAUS)
JPL .... Jacksonville Public Library System, Jacksonville, FL [*OCLC symbol*] (OCLC)
JPL .... JAM Programming Language (SAUS)
JPL .... Japan Planetarium Laboratory
JPL .... Java Pacific Line (SAUO)
JPL .... Java Perl Lingo (SAUS)
JPL .... Jet Propulsion Laboratory [*Renamed H. Allen Smith Jet Propulsion Laboratory, 1973, after a retiring congressman. However, JPL is used officially*] [*California Institute of Technology*] [*Pasadena, CA*] [*NASA*] [*Research center*]
JPL .... Jet Propulsion Laboratory of Caltech (SAUS)
JPL .... Jewish Peace Lobby (EA)
JPL .... Job Parts List (AAG)
JPL .... Job Plans List (SAUS)
JPL .... Joint Propulsion Laboratory (SAUO)
JPL .... Journal of Philosophical Logic (journ.) (SAUS)
JPL .... Journal of Planning and Environment Law [*A publication*] (SAFN)
JPL .... Journal of Products Liabilily (journ.) (SAUS)
JPL .... Journal of Psychiatry and Law [*Medicine*] (EDAA)
JPL .... Jyacc Procedural Language (SAUS)
JPL .... Journal of Planning Law (ODA)
J Plankton Res... Journal of Plankton Research (journ.) (SAUS)
J Plan Property Law... Journal of Planning and Property Law (journ.) (SAUS)
J Plant Breed... Journal of Plant Breeding (journ.) (SAUS)
J Plant Dis Prot... Journal of Plant Diseases and Protection (journ.) (SAUS)
J Plant Growth Regul... Journal of Plant Growth Regulation (journ.) (SAUS)
J Plant Growth Regul... Journal of Plant Orowth Regulation (journ.) (SAUS)
J Plant Nutr... Journal of Plant Nutrition [*A publication*] (PABS)
J Plant Nutr Soil Sci... Journal of Plant Nutrition and Soil Science (journ.) (SAUS)
J Plant Pathol... Journal of Plant Pathology [*A publication*] (PABS)
J Plant Physiol... Journal of Plant Physiology (journ.) (SAUS)
J Plant Prot... Journal of Plant Protection (journ.) (SAUS)
J Plant Res... Journal of Plant Research [*A publication*] (PABS)
J Plast An... Japan Plastics Industry Annual (journ.) (SAUS)
J Plast Film Sheet... Journal of Plastic Film and Sheeting (journ.) (SAUS)
J Plast Reconstr Surg Nurs... Journal of Plastic and Reconstructive Surgical Nursing (journ.) (SAUS)
JPLDIS ...... Jet Propulsion Laboratory Display Information System (SAUO)
JPLE......... Journal of Professional Legal Education [*Australia*] [*A publication*]
JPL/ETR..... Jet Propulsion Laboratory Field Station, Air Force Eastern Test Range (SAUS)
JPL/ETR..... Jet Propulsion Laboratory Field Station, Air Force Eastern Test Range
J Pln & Prop L... Journal of Planning and Property Law (journ.) (SAUS)
JPL/PODS... Jet Propulsion Laboratory/Pilot Ocean Data System (MCD)
JPL Publ 78... Jet Propulsion Laboratory. Publication 78 (journ.) (SAUS)
JPLRC....... Joint Port Labor Relations Committee (SAUO)
JPLSA....... Journal. Polarographic Society (journ.) (SAUS)
JPL Space Programs Summ... Jet Propulsion Laboratory. Space Programs Summary (journ.) (SAUS)

JPL-STAR... Jet Propulsion Laboratory Self Testing and Repairing Computer [*California Institute of Technology*] (PDAA)
JPL/STAR Computer... Jet Propulsion Laboratory/Self-Testing and Repair Computer (SAUS)
JPM.......... Jet-Piercing Machine
JPM.......... Job Performance Manual (MCD)
JPM.......... Job Performance Measure
JPM.......... Joint Program Manager (ACAE)
JPM.......... Joint Project Manager
JPM.......... Journal of Perinatal Medicine [*Medicine*] (EDAA)
JPM.......... Journal of Property Management (journ.) (SAUS)
JPM.......... Journal of Purchasing and Materials Management (journ.) (SAUS)
JPM.......... J. P. Morgan & Co., Inc. (SAUO)
JPM.......... JP Morgan Chase and Co. [*NYSE symbol*]
JPM.......... Morgan [*J. P.*] & Co., Inc. [*NYSE symbol*] (SPSG)
JPM.......... Morgan (J.P.) [*NYSE symbol*] (TTSB)
JPMA........ Japan Plywood Manufactures Association (BUAC)
JPMA........ Japan Powder Metallurgy Association (SAUO)
JPMA........ Juvenile Products Manufacturers Association (EA)
JPMA J Pak Med Assoc... JPMA. Journal of the Pakistan Medical Association (SAUO)
JPMA J Pak Med Assoc... JPMA. Journal of the Pakistan Medical Association (journ.) (SAUS)
JPMC........ JPM Co. [*NASDAQ symbol*] (TTSB)
JPMCo...... JPM Co. (The) [*Associated Press*] (SAG)
JPMEA....... Journal. Philippine Medical Association (journ.) (SAUS)
JPMI....... JPM Industries, Inc. (SAUO)
JPMO........ Jersey Potato Marketing Organisation (BUAC)
JPMO........ Joint Program Management Office (MCD)
JPMPrA..... Morgan(JP) Adj Rt A Pfd [*NYSE symbol*] (TTSB)
JPMPrH..... Morgan(JP)6.625% Dep'H'Pfd [*NYSE symbol*] (TTSB)
JPMR........ Joint Program Management Review (ACAE)
JPMR........ Joint Projected Manpower Requirements [*Military*] (AABC)
JPMS........ J. P. Morgan Securities
JPMSA....... Journal of Pharmaceutical Sciences (journ.) (SAUS)
JPMT....... Joint Patient Movement Team (SAUO)
JPMX........ JPM Co. [*OTCBB symbol*]
JPMX........ JPM Co. (The) [*NASDAQ symbol*] (SAG)
JPN.......... Japan [*ANSI three-letter standard code*] (CNC)
Jpn........... Japan (SHCU)
jpn........... Japanese [*MARC language code*] [*Library of Congress*] (LCCP)
JPN.......... Japan Fund, Inc. (SAUO)
JPN.......... Memrykord Ltd. [*British*] [*ICAO designator*] (FAAC)
JPN.......... Washington, DC [*Location identifier*] [*FAA*] (FAAL)
Jpn Agric Res Q... Japan Agricultural Research Quarterly (journ.) (SAUS)
Jpn Alum News... Japan Aluminum News (journ.) (SAUS)
Jpn Analyst... Japan Analyst (journ.) (SAUS)
Jpn Annu Rev Electron Comput Telecommun... Japan Annual Reviews in Electronics, Computers and Telecommunications (journ.) (SAUS)
Jpn Arch Histol... Japanese Archives of Histology (journ.) (SAUS)
Jpn Arch Intern Med... Japanese Archives of Internal Medicine (journ.) (SAUS)
Jpn Archit... Japan Architect (journ.) (SAUS)
Jpn At Energy Res Inst Annu Rep Acc... Japan. Atomic Energy Research Institute. Annual Report and Account (journ.) (SAUS)
Jpn At Energy Res Inst Rep Res Rep... Japan. Atomic Energy Research Institute. Report. Research Report (journ.) (SAUS)
Jpn Chem Ind... Japan Chemical Industry (journ.) (SAUS)
Jpn Chem Rev... Japan Chemical Review (journ.) (SAUS)
Jpn Chem Week... Japan Chemical Week (journ.) (SAUS)
Jpn Circ J... Japanese Circulation Journal (journ.) (SAUS)
Jpn Dent J... Japanese Dental Journal (journ.) (SAUS)
Jpn EA...... Japan Economic Almanac (SAUS)
Jpn Elec I... Japan Electronics Industry (journ.) (SAUS)
Jpn Electron Eng... Japan Electronic Engineering (journ.) (SAUS)
Jpn Energy Technol Intell... Japan Energy and Technology Intelligence (journ.) (SAUS)
Jpn Export... Export Statistical Schedule (journ.) (SAUS)
Jpn Gas Assoc J... Japan Gas Association. Journal (journ.) (SAUS)
Jpn-Ger Med Rep... Japan-Germany Medical Reports (journ.) (SAUS)
Jpn Heart J... Japanese Heart Journal (journ.) (SAUS)
Jpn Hosp... Japan Hospitals (journ.) (SAUS)
Jpn Import... Import Statistical Schedule (journ.) (SAUS)
Jpn Ind Technol Bull... Japan Industrial and Technological Bulletin (journ.) (SAUS)
Jpn J Alcohol Stud & Drug Degend... Japanese Journal of Alcohol Studies and Drug Dependence (journ.) (SAUS)
Jpn J Allergy... Japanese Journal of Allergy (journ.) (SAUS)
Jpn J Anim Reprod... Japanese Journal of Animal Reproduction (journ.) (SAUS)
Jpn J Antibiot... Japanese Journal of Antibiotics (journ.) (SAUS)
Jpn J Appl Entomol Zool... Japanese Journal of Applied Entomology and Zoology (journ.) (SAUS)
Jpn J Appl Phys... Japanese Journal of Applied Physics (journ.) (SAUS)
Jpn J Appl Phys... Japan Journal of Applied Physics (journ.) (SAUS)
Jpn J Appl Phys 2 Lett... Japanese Journal of Applied Physics. Part 2. Letters (journ.) (SAUS)
Jpn J Appl Phys Part 2... Japanese Journal of Applied Physics. Part 2. Letters (journ.) (SAUS)
Jpn J Appl Phys Suppl... Japanese Journal of Applied Physics. Supplement (journ.) (SAUS)
Jpn J Astron... Japanese Journal of Astronomy (journ.) (SAUS)
Jpn J Astron Geophys... Japanese Journal of Astronomy and Geophysics (journ.) (SAUS)
Jpn J Bacteriol... Japanese Journal of Bacteriology (journ.) (SAUS)
Jpn J Breed... Japanese Journal of Breeding (journ.) (SAUS)
Jpn J Cancer Clin... Japanese Journal of Cancer Clinics (journ.) (SAUS)
Jpn J Cancer Res... Japanese Journal of Cancer Research (journ.) (SAUS)
Jpn J Chem... Japanese Journal of Chemistry (journ.) (SAUS)
Jpn J Chest Dis... Japanese Journal of Chest Diseases (journ.) (SAUS)
Jpn J Child Adoles Psychiatry... Japanese Journal of Child and Adolescent Psychiatry (journ.) (SAUS)
Jpn J Clin Electron Microsc... Japanese Journal of Clinical Electron Microscopy (journ.) (SAUS)
Jpn J Clin Exp Med... Japanese Journal of Clinical and Experimental Medicine (journ.) (SAUS)
Jpn J Clin Hematol... Japanese Journal of Clinical Hematology (journ.) (SAUS)
Jpn J Clin Med... Japanese Journal of Clinical Medicine (journ.) (SAUS)
Jpn J Clin Oncol... Japanese Journal of Clinical Oncology (journ.) (SAUS)
Jpn J Clin Ophthalmol... Japanese Journal of Clinical Ophthalmology (journ.) (SAUS)
Jpn J Clin Pathol... Japanese Journal of Clinical Pathology (journ.) (SAUS)
Jpn J Clin Pathol Suppl... Japanese Journal of Clinical Pathology. Supplement (journ.) (SAUS)
Jpn J Clin Pharmacol... Japanese Journal of Clinical Pharmacology (journ.) (SAUS)
Jpn J Clin Radiol... Japanese Journal of Clinical Radiology (journ.) (SAUS)
Jpn J Clin Urol... Japanese Journal of Clinical Urology (journ.) (SAUS)
Jpn J Const Med... Japanese Journal of Constitutional Medi- cine (journ.) (SAUS)
Jpn J Crop Sci... Japanese Journal of Crop Science (journ.) (SAUS)
Jpn J Dairy Food Sci... Japanese Journal of Dairy and Food Science (journ.) (SAUS)
Jpn J Dairy Sci... Japanese Journal of Dairy Science (journ.) (SAUS)
Jpn J Dermatol... Japanese Journal of Dermatology (journ.) (SAUS)
Jpn J Ecol... Japanese Journal of Ecology (journ.) (SAUS)
Jpn J Eng Abstr... Japanese Journal of Engineering. Abstracts (journ.) (SAUS)
Jpn J Ethnol... Japanese Journal of Ethnology (journ.) (SAUS)
Jpn J Exp Med... Japanese Journal of Experimental Medicine (journ.) (SAUS)
Jpn J Exp Morphol... Japanese Journal of Experimenlal Morphology (journ.) (SAUS)
Jpn J Fertil Steril... Japanese Journal of Fertility and Sterility (journ.) (SAUS)
Jpn J Freezing Dying... Japanese Journal of Freezing and Dying (journ.) (SAUS)
Jpn J Gastroenterol... Japanese Journal of Gastroenterology (journ.) (SAUS)
Jpn J Genet... Japanese Journal of Genetics (journ.) (SAUS)
Jpn J Genet Suppl... Japanese Journal of Genetics. Supple- ment (journ.) (SAUS)
Jpn J Geol Geogr... Japanese Journal of Geology and Geography (journ.) (SAUS)
Jpn J Geriatr... Japanese Journal of Geriatrics (journ.) (SAUS)
Jpn J Herpetol... Japanese Journal of Herpetology (journ.) (SAUS)
Jpn J Hum Genet... Japanese Journal of Human Genetics (journ.) (SAUS)
Jpn J Hyg... Japanese Journal of Hygiene (journ.) (SAUS)
Jpn J Ind Health... Japanese Journal of Industrial Health (journ.) (SAUS)
Jpn J Lepr... Japanese Journal of Leprosy (journ.) (SAUS)
Jpn J Limnol... Japanese Journal of Limnology (journ.) (SAUS)
Jpn J Malacol... Japanese Journal of Malacology (journ.) (SAUS)
Jpn J Med.. Japanese Journal of Medicine (journ.) (SAUS)
Jpn J Med Sci 1... Japanese Journal of Medical Sciences. Part 1 (journ.) (SAUS)
Jpn J Med Sci 2... Japanese Journal of Medical Sciences. Part 2. Biochemistry (journ.) (SAUS)
Jpn J Med Sci 3... Japanese Journal of Medical Sciences. Part 3. Biophysics (journ.) (SAUS)
Jpn J Med Sci 5... Japanese Journal of Medical Sciences. Part 5. Pathology (journ.) (SAUS)
Jpn J Med Sci 6... Japanese Journal of Medical Sciences. Part 6. Bacteriology and Parasitology (journ.) (SAUS)
Jpn J Med Sci 7... Japanese Journal of Medical Sciences. Part 7. Social Medicine and Hygiene (journ.) (SAUS)
Jpn J Med Sci 8... Japanese Journal of Medical Sciences. Part 8. Internal Medicine, Pediatry and Psychiatry (journ.) (SAUS)
Jpn J Med Sci 9... Japanese Journal of Medical Sciences. Part 9. Surgery, Onhopedy and Odontology (journ.) (SAUS)
Jpn J Med Sci 10... Japanese Journal of Medical Sciences. Part 10. Ophthalmology (journ.) (SAUS)
Jpn J Med Sci 11... Japanese Journal of Medical Sciences. Part 11 (journ.) (SAUS)
Jpn J Med Sci 12... Japanese Journal of Medical Sciences. Part 12. Oto-Rhino-Laryngology (journ.) (SAUS)
Jpn J Med Sci 13... Japanese Journal of Medical Sciences. Part 13. Dermatology and Urology (journ.) (SAUS)
Jpn J Med Sci Biol... Japanese Journal of Medical Science and Biology (journ.) (SAUS)
Jpn J Michurin Biol... Japanese Journal of Michurin Biology (journ.) (SAUS)
Jpn J Microbiol... Japanese Journal of Microbiology (journ.) (SAUS)
Jpn J Nephrol... Japanese Journal of Nephrology (journ.) (SAUS)
Jpn J Neurol Psychiatry... Japanese Journal of Neurology and Psychiatry (journ.) (SAUS)
Jpn J Nucl Med... Japanese Journal of Nuclear Medicine (journ.) (SAUS)
Jpn J Nurs... Japanese Journal of Nursing (journ.) (SAUS)
Jpn J Nutr... Japanese Journal of Nutrition (journ.) (SAUS)
Jpn J Obstet Gynecol... Japanese Journal of Obstetrics and Gynecology (journ.) (SAUS)
Jpn J Ophthalmol... Japanese Journal of Ophthalmology (journ.) (SAUS)
Jpn J Oral Biol... Japanese Journal of Oral Biology (journ.) (SAUS)
Jpn J Palynol... Japanese Journal of Palynology (journ.) (SAUS)
Jpn J Parasitol... Japanese Journal of Parasitology (journ.) (SAUS)
Jpn J Pediat... Japanese Journal of Pediatrics (journ.) (SAUS)
Jpn J Pediat Surg Med... Japanese Journal of Pedatric Surgery and Medicine (journ.) (SAUS)
Jpn J Pharmacol... Japanese Journal of Pharmacology (journ.) (SAUS)
Jpn J Pharm Chem... Japanese Journal of Pharmacy and Chemistry (journ.) (SAUS)
Jpn J Phys... Japanese Journal of Physics (journ.) (SAUS)
Jpn J Phys Educ... Japanese Journal of Physical Education (journ.) (SAUS)

Jpn J Phys Fitess Sports Med... Japanese Journal of Physical Fitness and Sports Medicine (journ.) (SAUS)
Jpn J Physiol... Japanese Journal of Physiology (journ.) (SAUS)
Jpn J Plast Reconstr Surg... Japanese Journal of Plastic and Reconstructive Surgery (journ.) (SAUS)
Jpn J Psychiatry Neurol... Japanese Journal of Psychiatry and Neurology (journ.) (SAUS)
Jpn J Psychol... Japanese Journal of Psychology (journ.) (SAUS)
Jpn J Psychopharmacol... Japanese Journal of Psychopharmacology (journ.) (SAUS)
Jpn J Psychosom Med... Japanese Journal of Psychosomatic Medicine (journ.) (SAUS)
Jpn J Radiol Technol... Japanese Journal of Radiological Technology (journ.) (SAUS)
Jpn J Relig... Japanese Journal of Religious Studies (journ.) (SAUS)
Jpn J Sanit Zool... Japanese Journal of Sanitary Zoology (journ.) (SAUS)
Jpn J Smooth Muscle Res... Japanese Journal of Smooth Muscle Research (journ.) (SAUS)
Jpn J Stud Alcohol... Japanese Journal of Studies on Alcohol (journ.) (SAUS)
Jpn J Surg... Japanese Journal of Surgery (journ.) (SAUS)
Jpn J Tborac Dis... Japanese Journal of Thoracic Diseases (journ.) (SAUS)
Jpn J Trop Agric... Japanese Journal of Tropical Agriculture (journ.) (SAUS)
Jpn J Trop Med Hyg... Japanese Journal of Tropical Medicine and Hygiene (journ.) (SAUS)
Jpn J Tuberc Chest Dis... Japanese Journal of Tuberculosis and Chest Diseases (journ.) (SAUS)
Jpn J Urol... Japanese Journal of Urology (journ.) (SAUS)
Jpn J Vet Sci... Japanese Journal of Veterinary Science (journ.) (SAUS)
Jpn J Water Pollut Res... Japanese Journal of Water Pollution Research (journ.) (SAUS)
Jpn J Water Res... Japan Journal of Water Research (journ.) (SAUS)
Jpn J Zool... Japanese Journal of Zoology (journ.) (SAUS)
Jpn J Zootech Sci... Japanese Journal of Zootechnical Science (journ.) (SAUS)
JPNL......... Judged Perceived Noise Level (OA)
Jpn Light Met Weld... Japan Light Metal Welding (journ.) (SAUS)
Jpn Math ... Japanese Journal of Mathematics (journ.) (SAUS)
Jpn Med J.. Japanese Medical Journal (journ.) (SAUS)
Jpn Med Res Found Publ... Japan Medical Research Foundation. Publication (journ.) (SAUS)
Jpn Met Bull... Japan Metal Bulletin (journ.) (SAUS)
Jpn Msrket... Dentsu Japan Marketing/Advertising Yearbook (journ.) (SAUS)
JPNNB....... Journal of Psychiatric Nursing and Mental Health Services (journ.) (SAUS)
Jpn Nucl Med... Japanese Nuclear Medicine (journ.) (SAUS)
Jpn P Comp... Japanese Invasion of Americas Personal Computer Market (journ.) (SAUS)
Jpn Pestic Inf... Japan Pesticide Information (journ.) (SAUS)
Jpn Petrol... Japan Petroleum and Energy Weekly (journ.) (SAUS)
Jpn P Indx... Japan Price Indexes Annual (journ.) (SAUS)
Jpn Plast ... Japan Plastics (journ.) (SAUS)
Jpn Plast Age... Japan Plastics Age (journ.) (SAUS)
Jpn Plast Ind Ann... Japan Plastics Industry Annual (journ.) (SAUS)
Jpn Poult Sci... Japanese Poultry Science (journ.) (SAUS)
Jpn Printer... Japan Printer (journ.) (SAUS)
Jpn Psychol Res... Japanese Psychological Research (journ.) (SAUS)
Jpn Pulp Paper... Japan Pulp and Paper (journ.) (SAUS)
Jpn Railw Eng... Journal of Railway Engineering (journ.) (SAUS)
Jpn Rev Clin Ophthalmol... Japanese Review of Clinical Ophthalmology (journ.) (SAUS)
Jpn Rilw Eng... Japanese Railway Engineering (journ.) (SAUS)
JPNS .... Journal of the Peripheral Nervous System (journ.) (SAUS)
Jpn S Aeronaut Space Sci Trans... Japan Society for Aeronautical and Space Sciences. Transactions (journ.) (SAUS)
Jpn Sci Mon... Japanese Scientific Monthly (journ.) (SAUS)
Jpn Sci Rer Med Sci... Japan Science Review. Medical Sciences (journ.) (SAUS)
Jpn Sci Rev Min Metall... Japanese Science Review. Mining and Metallurgy (journ.) (SAUS)
Jpn Soc Tuberc Annu Rep... Japanese Society for Tuberculosis. Annual Report (journ.) (SAUS)
Jpn Steel Bull... Japan Steel Bulletin (journ.) (SAUS)
Jpn Steel Tube Tb Rev... Japan Steel and Tube Technical Review (journ.) (SAUS)
Jpn Steel Works... Japan Steel Works (journ.) (SAUS)
Jpn Steel Works Tech News... Japan Steel Works. Technical News (journ.) (SAUS)
Jpn Stud Hist Sci... Japanese Studies in the History of Science (journ.) (SAUS)
JPNT......... Joiner Pilaster Nontight [*Technical drawings*]
Jpn Telecomun Rev... Japan Telecommunications Review (journ.) (SAUS)
JPO .... Japanese Patent Office (TELE)
JPO .... Japan Patent Office (SAUS)
JPO .... Joint Personal Property Shipping Office (SAUS)
JPO .... Joint Petroleum Office
JPO .... Joint Planning Office (SAUO)
JPO .... Joint Program Office [*Military*] (SDI)
JPO .... Joint Project Office [*or Officer*]
JPO .... Journal of Portfolio Management (journ.) (SAUS)
JPO .... Journal of Prosthetics and Orthotics (journ.) (SAUS)
JPO .... J.P. Morgan Index Funding Company, LLC [*AMEX symbol*] (NASQ)
JPO .... Jump if Parity Odd (VLIE)
JPO .... Jump on Parity Odd (SAUS)
JPO .... Junior Police Officer (SAUO)
JPO .... Junior Professional Officer [*United Nations*]
JPO .... Juvenile Probation Officer (OICC)
JPO .... Pomona [*California*] [*Airport symbol*] (AD)
JPOAA....... Junior Panel Outdoor Advertising Association [*Later, ESOAA*]
JPO-BD....... Joint Program Office for Biological Defense [*Army*] (RDA)
JPOC .... Johnson Space Center Payload Operations Center (SAUO)
JPOC .... Joint Planning Orientation Course (SAUO)
JPOC .... JSC [*Johnson Space Center*] Payload Operations Center (MCD)
J Poditr Med Educ... Journal of Podiatric Medical Education (journ.) (SAUS)
JPOG .... Journal of Psychosomatic Obstetrics and Gynecology (SAUO)
JPOGDP..... Journal of Psychosomatic Obstetrics and Gynaecology (journ.) (SAUS)
J-Point ...... Junction Point (SAUS)
JPO J Prc Ortbod... JPO Journal of Practical Orthodontics (journ.) (SAUS)
J Pol......... Journal of Politics [*A publication*] (BRI)
J Polar Soc... Journal. Polarographic Society (journ.) (SAUS)
J Pol Econ... Journal of Political Economy. University of Chicago. Department of Political Economy. Chicago (SAUO)
J Policy Anal Mnage... Journal of Policy Analysis and Management (journ.) (SAUS)
J Policy Analysis and Mgt... Journal of Policy Analysis and Management (journ.) (SAUS)
J Policy Model... Journal of Policy Modeling (journ.) (SAUS)
J Polit Economy... Journal of Political Economy [*A publication*] (JLIT)
J Pol S...... Journal. Polynesian Society (journ.) (SAUS)
J Pol Sci & Admin... Journal of Police Science and Administration [*A publication*] (DLA)
J Pol Sc PC... Journal of Polymer Science. Polymer Chemistry Edition (journ.) (SAUS)
J Pol Sc PL... Journal of Polymer Science. Polymer Letters Edition (journ.) (SAUS)
J Pol Sc PP... Journal of Polymer Science. Polymer Physics Edition (journ.) (SAUS)
J Polym Eng... Journal of Polymer Engineering (journ.) (SAUS)
J Polym Environ... Journal of Polymers and the Environment [*A publication*] (PABS)
J Polym Mater... Journal of Polymer Materials (journ.) (SAUS)
J Polym Sci Lett... Journal of Polymer Science Letters (journ.) (SAUS)
J Polym Sci Macromol Rev... Journal of Polymer Science. Macromolecular Reviews (journ.) (SAUS)
J Polym Sci Polym Chem... Journal of Polymer Science. Polymer Chemistry Edition (journ.) (SAUS)
J Polym Sci Polym Chem Ed... Journal of Polymer Science. Polymer Chemistry Edition (journ.) (SAUS)
J Polym Sci Polym Lett... Journal of Polymer Science. Polymer Letters Edition (journ.) (SAUS)
J Polym Sci Polym Phys... Journal of Polymer Science. Polymer Physics Edition (journ.) (SAUS)
J Polym Sci Polym Phys Ed... Journal of Polymer Science. Polymer Physics Edition (journ.) (SAUS)
J Polym Sci Polym Symp... Journal of Polymer Science. Polymer Symposia Edition (journ.) (SAUS)
J Pomology... Journal of Pomology and Horticultural Science (journ.) (SAUS)
JPONED ..... Journal of Psychosonal Oncology (journ.) (SAUS)
JPOP .... Japanese Polar Orbiting Platform (EOSA)
J Pop F&TV... Journal of Popular Film and Television [*A publication*] (BRI)
J Pop Res .. Journal of Population Research (journ.) (SAUS)
J Popul...... Journal of Population (journ.) (SAUS)
J Population Econ... Journal of Population Economics [*A publication*] (JLIT)
J Popul Behar Soc Environ Issues... Journal of Population. Behavioral, Social and Environmental Issues (journ.) (SAUS)
J Portfol Manage... Journal of Portfolio Management [*A publication*] (JLIT)
JPOS .... Journal of Pediatric Ophthalmology and Strabismus (journ.) (SAUS)
JPOS .... Journal of the Palestine Oriental Society (SAUO)
JPOS .... Journal of the Patent Office Society (SAUO)
JPOS .... Journal of the Patent Office Society (journ.) (SAUS)
JPOS .... Journal. Palestine Oriental Society (journ.) (SAUS)
J POS .... Journal. Patent Office Society (journ.) (SAUS)
J Post Anesth Nurs... Journal of Post Anesthesia Nursing (journ.) (SAUS)
J Post Grd Sch Indian Agr Res Inst... Journal. Post Graduate School. Indian Agricultural Research Institute (journ.) (SAUS)
J Post Keynes Econ... Journal of Post Keynesian Economics (journ.) (SAUS)
JpOTC .... Japan OTC Equity Fund, Inc. [*Associated Press*] (SAG)
JPOTS .... Joint Panel on Oceanographic Tables and Standards [*Marine science*] [*United Nations*] (OSRA)
JPO-TT ...... Joint Program Office-Transition Team [*DoD*]
J Power Div; Amer Soc Civi... Journal of the Power Division; Proceedings of the American Society of Civil Engineering (SAUO)
J Power Div Am S Civ Eng... Journal. Power Division. American Society of Civil Engineers (journ.) (SAUS)
J Power Sources... Journal of Power Sources (journ.) (SAUS)
JPP .... Jalkeen Puolenpaiuan [*Afternoon*] [*Finland*]
JPP .... Japan Paper Proofs
JPP .... Joint Planning Process [*Military*] (NVT)
jpp .... Joint Program Plan (NAKS)
JPP .... Joint Program Plan (NASA)
JPP .... Journal of Pastoral Practice (journ.) (SAUS)
JPP .... Journal of Periodontology-Periodontics [*Now JP*] [*Medicine*] (EDAA)
JPPDA....... Journal of Child Psychology and Psychiatry and Allied Disciplines (journ.) (SAUS)
JPPL......... JAR-FCL Private Pilots License (SAUS)
JPPL......... Joint Personnel Priority List
JPPL......... Journal of Planning and Property Law (journ.) (SAUS)
JpPol .... Japanese Polydor-Deutsche Grammophon [*Record label*]
JPPP......... Jewish People, Past and Present [*Jewish Encyclopedic Handbooks*] [*A publication*] (BJA)
JPPR .... Journal of Psychotherapy Practice and Research (journ.) (SAUS)
JPPRI........ Jewish Planning Policy and Research Institute (BUAC)
JPPRI........ Jewish Policy Planning and Research Institute [*Synagogue Council of America*]

JPPS......... Jack Point Preservation Society (EA)
JPPS......... Japan Pearl Promoting Society (SAUO)
JPPS......... Joint Petroleum Products Subcommittee (SAUS)
JPPS......... Journal of Pharmacy and Pharmaceutical Sciences (journ.) (SAUS)
JPPSA....... Journal of Pharmacy and Pharmacology. Supplement (journ.) (SAUS)
JPPSO....... Joint Personal Property Shipping Office [*Military*] (DNAB)
JPPSOWA... Joint Personal Property Shipping Office, Washington, DC [*Military*] (AABC)
JPPSST..... Joseph Preschool and Primary Self-Concept Screening Test [*Child development test*] [*Psychology*]
JpPV......... Japanese Polydor Variable Microgroove [*Record label*]
JPPZ......... Jacksonville Port Authority [*Federal Railroad Administration identification code*]
JPQ......... Journal of Pediatric Ophthalmology [*Medicine*] (EDAA)
JPQ......... Jung Personality Questionnaire [*Personality development test*] [*Psychology*]
JPR......... Air International (Holdings) PLC [*British*] [*ICAO designator*] (FAAC)
JPR......... Institute for Jewish Policy Research [*United Kingdom*] (EAIO)
JPR......... Inversiones Ayacucho, SA, "Jet Privado" [*Peru*] [*FAA designator*] (FAAC)
JPR......... Joint Procurement Regulations [*of Army and Air Force*]
JPR......... Journal of Peace Research [*A publication*] (BRI)
JPR......... Journal of Pediatric Surgery/of Pharmaceutical Sciences [*APA*] [*Medicine*] (EDAA)
JPR......... Journal of Prehistoric Religion [*A publication*] (ABAR)
JPR......... Journal of Psychiatric/Psychosomatic Research [*Medicine*] (EDAA)
JPR......... Journal of Purchasing and Materials Management [*A publication*] (AAGC)
JPR......... JP Realty [*NYSE symbol*] (SPSG)
jpr......... Judaeo-Persian [*MARC language code*] [*Library of Congress*] (LCCP)
JPR......... Justice of the Peace and Local Government Review Reports [*A publication*] (DLA)
JPR......... Justice Procurement Regulation [*A publication*] (AAGC)
JPRA........ Japanese Phonograph Record Association [*An association*] (NITA)
JPRA........ Japan Phonographic Record Association (SAUS)
JPRA........ Joint Personnel Recovery Agency [*Military*]
J Pract Nurs... Journal of Practical Nursing (journ.) (SAUS)
J Prag....... Journal of Pragmatics (journ.) (SAUS)
JPRC........ Joint Personnel Recovery Center [*Military*]
J PR CT..... Judge Prerogative Court, Canterbury [*British*] (ROG)
JPRDY....... Jeopardy (ABBR)
JPRDZ....... Jeopardize (ABBR)
JPRDZG..... Jeopardizing (ABBR)
J Presby H... Journal of Presbyterian History (journ.) (SAUS)
J Presby Hist Soc... Journal. Presbyterian Historical Society (journ.) (SAUS)
J Pressure Vessel Technol... Journal of Pressure Vessel Technology (journ.) (SAUS)
J Prestressed Concrete Inst... Journal of the Prestressed Concrete Institute (journ.) (SAUS)
J Prestressed Concr Iost... Journal. Prestressed Concrete Institute (journ.) (SAUS)
J Prev Dent... Journal of Preventive Dentistry (journ.) (SAUS)
J Prev Psychiatry... Journal of Preventive Psychiatry (journ.) (SAUS)
JPRH........ Journal of Prison Health (journ.) (SAUS)
J Print Hist S... Journal Printing Historical Society (journ.) (SAUS)
J Private Enterprise... Journal of Private Enterprise [*A publication*] (JLIT)
JP Rlty...... JP Realty [*Associated Press*] (SAG)
JPRO........ Joint Photographic Reconnaissance Organization [*World War II*]
JPROB....... Judge of Probate [*British*] (ROG)
J Proc Am Hort S... Journal of Proceedings. American Horticultural Society (journ.) (SAUS)
J Proc Asiat Soc Bengal... Journal and Proceedings. Asiatic Society of Bengal (journ.) (SAUS)
J Proc Boken Hill Hist S... Broken Hill Historical Society. Journal and Proceedings (journ.) (SAUS)
J Proc Inst Rd Transp Engrs... Journal and Proceedings. Institute of Road Transport Engineers (journ.) (SAUS)
J Proc Inst Sewage Purif... Journal and Proceedings. Institute of Sewage Purification (journ.) (SAUS)
J Proc Newcastle Hunter Dist Hist Soc... Journal and Proceedings. Newcastle and Hunter District Historical Society (journ.) (SAUS)
J Proc Oil Technol Ass... Journal and Proceedings. Oil Technologists Association (journ.) (SAUS)
J Proc Parramatta Dist Hist S... Journal and Proceedings. Parramatta and District Historical Society (journ.) (SAUS)
J Proc R Aust Hist Soc... Journal and Proceedings. Royal Australian Historical Society (journ.) (SAUS)
J Proc Roy Soc NSW... Journal and Proceedings. Royal Society of New South Wales (journ.) (SAUS)
J Proc Roy Soc NWW... Journal and Proceedings of the Royal Society of New South Wales (SAUO)
J Proc Sydney Tech Coll Chem S... Journal and Proceedings. Sydney Technical College. Chemical Society (journ.) (SAUS)
J Proc W Aust Hist Soc... Journal and Proceedings. Western Australian Historical Society (journ.) (SAUS)
J Prod Agric... Journal of Production Agriculture (journ.) (SAUS)
J Prod Innov Manage... Journal of Product Innovation Management (journ.) (SAUS)
J Prod L.... Journal of Products Law (DLA)
J Prod L.... Journal of Products Law (journ.) (SAUS)
J Prod Liab... Journal of Products Liabilily (journ.) (SAUS)
J Productiv Anal... Journal of Productivity Analysis [*A publication*] (JLIT)
J Prof Legal Ed... Journal of Professional Legal Education (journ.) (SAUS)
J Prof Nurs... Journal of Professional Nursing (journ.) (SAUS)
J Proj Tech... Journal of Projective Techniques. Society for Projective Techniques and Rorschach Institute. Glendale (SAUO)
J Prop Power... Journal of Propulsion and Power (journ.) (SAUS)
J Propul P... Journal of Propulsion and Power (journ.) (SAUS)
J Propul Power... Journal of Propulsion and Power [*A publication*] (CABS)
J Prot Coatings Linings... Journal of Protective Coatings and Linings (journ.) (SAUS)
J Protein Chem... Journal of Protein Chemistry (journ.) (SAUS)
J Protozool... Journal of Protozoology (journ.) (SAUS)
JPRRI....... Japan Public Relations Research Institute (SAUS)
JPRS........ Joint Publications Research Service [*Department of Commerce*]
JPRSA....... Journal and Proceedings. Royal Society of New South Wales (journ.) (SAUS)
J Prsbyt Hist... Journal of Presbyterian History (journ.) (SAUS)
JPRS-GUO... Joint Publications Research Service Translations - Government Use Only [*Department of Commerce*]
JPRST-GUO... Joint Publications Research Service Translations-Government Use Only (SAUO)
JPS.......... Japan Physical Society (SAUO)
JPS.......... Japan Press Service
JPS.......... Javad Positioning Systems, Inc. (SAUO)
JPS.......... Jean Piaget Society [*Later, JPSSSKD*] (EA)
JPs.......... Jesuit Priests (SAUS)
JPS.......... Jet Plume Simulation
JPS.......... Jeunesse Populaire Senegalaise [*Senegalese People's Youth*]
JPS.......... Jewish Publication Society (EA)
JPS.......... JICST Photoduplication Service (SAUS)
JPS.......... Johannesburg Philharmonic Society (SAUO)
JPS.......... John Player Special [*Sponsor of British Lotus Formula I racing car*]
JPS.......... Joint Parliamentary Secretary (SAUS)
JPS.......... Joint Planning Staff [*US and Great Britain*] [*World War II*]
JPS.......... Joint Position Sense [*Medicine*]
JPS.......... Jones Plumbing Systems, Inc. [*AMEX symbol*] (SPSG)
JPS.......... Journal of Peadant Studies (journ.) (SAUS)
JPS.......... Journal of Plant Studies (journ.) (SAUS)
JPS.......... Journal of Polymer Science (journ.) (SAUS)
JPS.......... Journal. Polynesian Society (journ.) (SAUS)
JPS.......... Junior Philatelic Society [*British*] (BI)
JPS.......... Juvenile Polyposis Syndrome [*Medicine*]
JPS.......... Juvenile Probation Services (SAUO)
JPS.......... Jet-Propulsion System (ODA)
JPSA......... Jacob's Prevocational Skills Assessment
JPSA......... Japanese Plating Supplier's Association [*Environmetal science*]
JPSA......... Jewish Pharmaceutical Society of America (EA)
JPSA......... Jewish Publication Society of America (DGA)
JPSA......... Joint Program for the Study of Abortion
JPSA......... Journal of Police Science and Administation (journ.) (SAUS)
JPSA......... Journal. Photographic Society of America (journ.) (SAUS)
JPSA......... Junior Philatelic Society of America [*Later, JPA*] (EA)
JPSBA....... Journal of Psychology of the Blind (journ.) (SAUS)
JPSC........ Joint Production Survey Committee
JPSCD........ Journal of Polymer Science. Part C Polymer Symposia (journ.) (SAUS)
JPSDTF..... Joint Precision Strike Demonstration Task Force (SAUO)
JPSG........ Joint Planning and Scheduling Group
JPSJ........ Journal of the Physical Society of Japan (SAUO)
JPSO........ Jamaica Philharmonic Symphony Orchestra (SAUO)
JPSO........ Journal of Psychosocial Oncology (journ.) (SAUS)
JPSP........ Journal of Personality and Social Psychology [*A publication*] (DHP)
JPSP........ JPS Packaging Co. [*NASDAQ symbol*] (NASQ)
JPSRB....... Journal of Psychological Researches (journ.) (SAUS)
JPSS......... Journal of Personality and Social Systems (journ.) (SAUS)
JPSS......... Just, Participatory, and Sustainable Society [*World Council of Churches*]
JPSSSKD... Jean Piaget Society: Society for the Study of Knowledge and Development (EA)
JPST......... Journal of Parenteral Science and Technology [*A publication*] (EAAP)
JPST......... JPS Textile Group, Inc. [*NASDAQ symbol*] (NASQ)
JPSTH....... Joint Peristimulus Time Histograms [*For study of physiology*]
J Psychiatr Law... Journal of Psychiatry and Law (journ.) (SAUS)
J Psychiatr Mental Health Nurs... Journal of Psychiatric & Mental Health Nursing (journ.) (SAUS)
J Psychiatr Nurs... Journal of Psychiatric Nursing and Mental Health Services (journ.) (SAUS)
J Psychiatr Treat Eval... Journal of Psychiatric Treatment and Evaluation (journ.) (SAUS)
J Psychiatry Neurosci... Journal of Psychiatry and Neuroscience (journ.) (SAUS)
J Psychoanal Anthropol... Journal of Psychoanalytic Anthropology (journ.) (SAUS)
J Psycho Drugs... Journal of Psychoactive Drugs (MEC)
J Psychohist... Journal of Psychohistory (journ.) (SAUS)
J Psychol... Journal of Psychology (journ.) (SAUS)
J Psychological Medicine... Journal of Psychological Medicine and Medical Jurisprudence [*A publication*] (DLA)
J Psychologic Medicine... Journal of Psychological Medicine and Medical Jurisprudence (journ.) (SAUS)
J Psychol Res... Journal of Psychological Researches (journ.) (SAUS)
J Psychol T... Journal of Psychology and Theology (journ.) (SAUS)
J Psychopathol Behav Assess... Journal of Psychopathology and Behavioral Assessment (journ.) (SAUS)
J Psychosom Obstet Gynaecol... Journal of Psychosomatic Obstetrics and Gynaecology (journ.) (SAUS)
J Psychos Oncol... Journal of Psychosocial Oncology (journ.) (SAUS)
J Psychother & Fm... Journal of Psychotherapy and the Family (journ.) (SAUS)
J Psych Th... Journal of Psychology and Theology (journ.) (SAUS)
JPsyR....... Journal of Psycholinguistic Research (journ.) (SAUS)
JPT.......... Houston [*Texas*] Park-Ten [*Airport symbol*] (OAG)

JPT .... Japanese Proficiency Test [*Educational test*]
JPT .... Jet Pipe Temperature
JPT .... Job Process Ticket (SAUS)
JPT .... Job Progress Ticket
JPT .... Joint Planning Team (COE)
JPT .... Joint Project Team (SAUO)
JPT .... Journal of Paint Technology (journ.) (SAUS)
JPT .... Journal of Parenteral Therapy [*Medicine*] (EDAA)
JPT .... Journal of Psychology and Theology (journ.) (SAUS)
JPT .... Jupiter Resources Ltd. (SAUO)
JPT .... Jupitor Resources Ltd. [*Vancouver Stock Exchange symbol*]
JPTA .... J and P Transportation [*Common carrier symbol*]
JPTDS .... Joint Photographic Type Designation System [*Military*]
JPTDS .... Junior Participating Tactical Data System [*Also known as "Jeep"*] (MCD)
JPTEA .... Journal of Projective Techniques (journ.) (SAUS)
JPTF .... Joint Parachute Test Facility [*DoD*]
JPTL .... Jet Pipe Temperature Limiter (MCD)
JPTM .... Joint Procedures Training Manual (SAUO)
JPTO .... Jet-Propelled Takeoff
JPTR .... Jupiter [*NCIC motorcycle make code*]
JPTS .... Jet Petroleum, Thermally Stable (DOMA)
JPTS .... Juvenile Pancreatitis Tropical Syndrome [*Medicine*] (EDAA)
JPTU .... Daikin Industries [*Intermodal shipping container symbol*] (TVRC)
JPTUN .... Japanese Journal of Tuberculosis (journ.) (SAUS)
JPTY .... Jones Properties [*Federal Railroad Administration identification code*]
JPU .... Job Processing Unit
JPU .... Journal of Public Economics (journ.) (SAUS)
JPU .... Journal. Poona University (journ.) (SAUS)
JPU .... Just Publishable Unit
J Public and Internat Affairs... Journal of Public and International Affairs (journ.) (SAUS)
J Public Econ... Journal of Public Economics [*A publication*] (JLIT)
J Public Health... Journal of Public Health (journ.) (SAUS)
J Public Health Dent... Journal of Public Health Dentistry (journ.) (SAUS)
J Public Health Med... Journal of Public Health Medicine (journ.) (SAUS)
J Public Health Med Technol Korea Univ... Journal of Public Health and Medical Technology. Korea University (journ.) (SAUS)
J Public Health Policy... Journal of Public Health Policy (journ.) (SAUS)
J Public Health Pract... Journal of Public Health Practice (journ.) (SAUS)
J Public Policy... Journal of Public Policy (journ.) (SAUS)
J Pul and Pap Sci... Journal of Pulp and Paper Science (journ.) (SAUS)
J-Punkt ...... EKG: Junction Point (am Ende des QRS-Komplex, Beginn der ST Strecke) (SAUS)
J Purch Mater Manage... Journal of Purchasing and Materials Management (journ.) (SAUS)
J Pure Appl Algebra... Journal of Pure and Applied Algebra (journ.) (SAUS)
J Pure Appl Ultrason... Journal of Pure and Applied Ultrasonics (journ.) (SAUS)
J Pusan Med Coll... Journal. Pusan Medical College (journ.) (SAUS)
JpV .... Japanese Victor [*Record label*]
JPV .... Japan Peace Volunteers (SAUO)
JPV .... Joint Pacific Voice [*Military*] (CINC)
JPVDA .... Journal of Preventive Dentistry (journ.) (SAUS)
JPVL .... JP Van Lines [*Common carrier symbol*]
JP VOICE ... Joint Pacific Command Control Voice Network (SAUO)
JPVTA .... Journal of Pressure Vessel Technology (journ.) (SAUS)
JPW .... Job Processing Word
JPW .... J.P. Morgan Index Funding Company I [*AMEX symbol*] (NASQ)
JPW .... Just Plain Weird (SAUS)
JPWC .... Joint Postwar Committee
JPWC .... Joint Psychological Warfare Committee (LAIN)
JPWG .... Joint Projects Working Group (SAUO)
JPX .... Jeopardous [*Telegraphy*] (PCTE)
JP-X .... Jet-Propellant rocket fuel (SAUS)
JPXS .... JP Express Service [*Common carrier symbol*]
JPY .... Jeopardy [*Telegraphy*] (PCTE)
JPYBA .... Journal of Polymer Science. Polymer Letters Edition (journ.) (SAUS)
JPZ .... Jeopardize [*Telegraphy*] (PCTE)
JPz4-5 .... German tank-destroyer (SAUS)
JQ .... Job Questionnaire
JQ .... Job Queue (SAUS)
JQ .... Journalism Quarterly [*A publication*] (BRI)
JQ .... J-Q Resources, Inc. [*Toronto Stock Exchange symbol*]
JQ .... Trans-Jamaican Airlines [*ICAO designator*] (AD)
JQ .... Trans Jamaican Airlines Ltd. (SAUO)
JQA .... Japan Quality Assurance Organization (SAUO)
JQA .... John Quincy Adams [*US president, 1767-1848*]
JQA .... Trans Jamaican Airlines Ltd. [*ICAO designator*] (FAAC)
JQAH .... John Quincy Adams House (SAUO)
JQAP .... Joint Quality Assurance Department (SAUO)
JQB .... Justice of the Queen's Bench [*Legal term*] (DLA)
JQC .... Dayton, OH [*Location identifier*] [*FAA*] (FAAL)
JQD .... Jeffersonville Quartermaster Depot (SAUO)
JQE .... Jaque [*Panama*] [*Airport symbol*] (OAG)
JQG .... Joint Question Group (SAUO)
JQGX .... James Quinlan [*Private rail car owner code*]
JQH .... Hammons [*John Q.*] Hotels, Inc. [*NYSE symbol*] (SAG)
JQHamm .... Hammons [*John Q.*] Hotel, Inc. [*Associated Press*] (SAG)
J Qing Hua Univ... Journal Qing Hua University (journ.) (SAUS)
JQP .... Josephson Quasi Particle (AAEL)
JQR .... Hammons(John Q)Hotels'A' [*NYSE symbol*] (TTSB)
JQR .... Jewish Quarterly Review [*A publication*] (ODCC)
JQS .... Job Qualification Standard (SAUO)
JQS .... Journal of Quaternary Science (journ.) (SAUS)
JQSRT .... Journal of Quantitative Spectroscopy and Radiative Transfer (journ.) (SAUS)
JQT .... Journal of Quality Technology (journ.) (SAUS)
J Quant Econ... Journal of Quantitative Economics [*A publication*] (JLIT)
J Quant Trait Loci... Journal of Quantitative Trait Loci (journ.) (SAUS)
J Quat Sci... Journal of Quaternary Science (SAUS)
J Quekett Microsc Club... Journal. Quekett Microscopical Club (journ.) (SAUS)
JR .... Air Yugoslavia (SAUS)
JR .... Jacobus Rex [*King James*]
JR .... James River Corp. [*NYSE symbol*] (TTSB)
JR .... James River Corp. of Virginia [*NYSE symbol*] (SPSG)
JR .... Jam Resistant
JR .... Japan Railways (SAUS)
JR .... Jar (MCD)
jr .... Jarosite (SAUS)
Jr .... Jeremiah [*Old Testament book*] (BJA)
JR .... [*The*] Jewish Right (EA)
JR .... Jigger [*Ship's rigging*] (ROG)
jr .... jinx ratio (SAUS)
JR .... Job Request (SAUS)
JR .... Job Rotation [*Computer science*] (MHDB)
JR .... Job Routed [*Military*] (AFIT)
JR .... Jodhpur Railway [*Indian Railway*] (TIR)
JR .... John Ross Ewing, Jr. [*Character in TV series "Dallas"*]
JR .... Johnson's New York Reports [*A publication*] (DLA)
JR .... Joint Research (SAUS)
JR .... Joint Resolution [*Usually, of the US Senate and House of Representatives*]
JR .... Joint Return (MHDB)
JR .... Joint Review
JR .... Jolly Reaction (STED)
JR .... Jolly's Reaction [*Neurology*] (DAVI)
JR .... Jordan Register (EA)
JR .... Jour [*Day*] [*French*]
JR .... Journal (ADA)
JR .... Journal of Rehabilitation/Rheumatology [*Medicine*] (EDAA)
JR .... Journal of Religion [*A publication*] (BRI)
JR .... Judge's Remand (WDAA)
JR .... Judges' Rules [*A publication*] (DLA)
Jr .... Juglans regia [*Persian walnut*]
JR .... Junctional Rhythm [*Cardiology*]
JR .... Junction Rack (KSC)
Jr .... Junior (ASC)
jr .... Junior (SHCU)
JR .... Junior
JR .... Juridical Review (journ.) (SAUS)
JR .... Jurist Reports [*1873-78*] [*New Zealand*] [*A publication*] (DLA)
JR .... Juror
JR .... Juvenile Rheumatoid Arthritis [*Also, JRA*] [*Medicine*] (DAVI)
JRA .... Jam Resistant Aerial (or Antenna) (SAUS)
JRA .... Jam-Resistant Antenna
JRA .... Japanese Racing Association
JRA .... Japanese Red Army (SAUO)
JRA .... Japan Racing Association (ECON)
JRA .... Japan Ryokan Association (SAUO)
JRA .... Jewish Royalty Association (EA)
JRA .... Job Release Analysis
JRA .... Joint Rear Area (SAUO)
Jr A .... Journal of Arizona History (journ.) (SAUS)
JRA .... Journal of Radiation Research (journ.) (SAUS)
JRA .... Journal of Roman Archaeology (journ.) (SAUS)
JRA .... Journal. Royal African Society (journ.) (SAUS)
JRA .... Journal. Society of Research Administrators (journ.) (SAUS)
JRA .... Junior Rheumatoid Arthritis (SAUS)
JRA .... Juvenile Rheumatoid Arthritis [*Medicine*]
JRA .... New York, NY [*Location identifier*] [*FAA*] (FAAL)
J Race Dev... Journal of Race Development (journ.) (SAUS)
J Racial AFF... Journal of Racial Affairs (journ.) (SAUS)
JRAD .... Joint Resource Assessment Data
JRAD .... Judicial Recommendation against Deportation
JRADA .... Journal of Radiology (journ.) (SAUS)
J Radiat Res... Journal of Radiation Research (journ.) (SAUS)
J Radioanal Nucl Chem... Journal of Radioanalytical and Nuclear Chemistry (journ.) (SAUS)
J Radio L... Journal of Radio Law [*A publication*] (DLA)
J Radiol Phys Ther Univ Kanzawa... Journal of Radiology and Physical Therapy. University of Kanzawa (journ.) (SAUS)
J Radiol Prot... Journal of Radiological Protection (journ.) (SAUS)
J Radio Res Lab... Journal of the Radio Research Laboratories (journ.) (SAUS)
J Radit Curing... Journal of Radiation Curing (journ.) (SAUS)
J Radit Res Radiat Process... Journal of Radiation Research and Radiation Processing (journ.) (SAUS)
JRADS .... Joint Resource Assessment Data Base System (SAUO)
J R Afr Soc... Journal. Royal African Society (journ.) (SAUS)
JRAG .... Joint Registration Authority Group (AG)
J R Agric Soc Engl... Journal. Royal Agricultural Society of England (journ.) (SAUS)
JRAGSOC ... Journal. Royal Agricultural Society of England (journ.) (SAUS)
JRAHS .... Journal. Royal Australian Historical Society (journ.) (SAUS)
JRAI .... Journal. Royal Anthropological Institute of Great Britain and Ireland (journ.) (SAUS)
J R Aic Soc... Journal. Royal Agricultural Society (journ.) (SAUS)

J Rakuno Gakuen Univ Nt Sci... Journal. Rakuno Gakuen University. Natural Science (journ.) (SAUS)
JRAMA...... Journal. Royal Army Medical Corps (journ.) (SAUS)
J Raman Spectrosc... Journal of Raman Spectroscopy (journ.) (SAUS)
JRAN........ Junior Resident Admission Note (STED)
J Range Manage... Journal of Range Management (journ.) (SAUS)
J R Anthropol Inst GB Irel... Journal. Royal Anthropological Institute of Great Britain and Ireland (journ.) (SAUS)
J R Army Med Corps... Journal of the Royal Army Medical Corps (SAUO)
J R Army Med Corps... Journal. Royal Army Medical Corps (journ.) (SAUS)
J R Army Vet Corps... Journal. Royal Army Veterinary Corps (journ.) (SAUS)
JRAS........ Journal of the Royal Agricultural Society [*A publication*] (ROG)
JRAS........ Journal. Royal Asiatic Society of Great Britain and Ireland (journ.) (SAUS)
JRASA....... Journal. Royal Astronomical Society of Canada (journ.) (SAUS)
JRAS Bengl... Journal. Royal Asiatic Society of Bengal (journ.) (SAUS)
JRASCB..... Journal. Royal Asiatic Society. Ceylon Branch (journ.) (SAUS)
JRASHKB... Journal. Royal Asiatic Society. Hong Kong Branch (journ.) (SAUS)
JR Asiat Soc GB Irel... Journal. Royal Asiatic Society of Great Britain and Ireland (journ.) (SAUS)
J R Astron Soc Can... Journal of the Royal Astronomical Society of Canada (journ.) (SAUS)
JRATA....... Joint Research and Test Activities (or Activity) (SAUS)
JRATA....... Joint Research and Test Activity (MCD)
JRATA....... Joint Research and Test Agency [*Terminated, 1966*] [*Military*]
J R Aust Hist Soc... Journal. Royal Australian Historical Society (journ.) (SAUS)
JRB.......... Jig Rest Button (SAUS)
JRB.......... Joint Radio Board
JRB.......... Joint Reconnaissance Board [*Military*] (AABC)
JRB.......... Joint Rennaissance Board (SAUS)
JRB.......... Joint Review Board (MCD)
jrb........... Judaeo-Arabic [*MARC language code*] [*Library of Congress*] (LCCP)
JRB.......... New York, NY [*Location identifier*] [*FAA*] (FAAL)
JRBA-A...... Journal. Royal Institute of British Architects (journ.) (SAUS)
JRBEDZ..... Journal of Reproductive Biology and Comparative Endocrinology (journ.) (SAUS)
Jr BF........ Junior Baby Food (STED)
JRBK........ James River Bankshares [*NASDAQ symbol*] (TTSB)
JRBK........ James River Bankshares, Inc. [*NASDAQ symbol*] (SAG)
JRBM........ Journal of Renaissance and Baroque Music (journ.) (SAUS)
Jr Br AssocTeach Deaf... Journal. British Association of Teachers of the Deaf (journ.) (SAUS)
JRBSDA..... British Columbia Forest Service-Canadian Forestry Service (SAUS)
JRC.......... Jamaica Railway Corp. (SAUS)
JRC.......... Japan Red Cross (SAUO)
JRC.......... Japan Research Center (SAUS)
JRC.......... Japan Research Council (SAUO)
JRC.......... Jet Reaction Control
JRC.......... Jewish Refugees Committee (EAIO)
JRC.......... Johnson Reprint Corp. (SAUS)
JrC........... Johnson Reprint Corporation, New York, NY [*Library symbol*] [*Library of Congress*] (LCLS)
JRC.......... Joint Railroad Conference
JRC.......... Joint Reconnaissance Center [*Military*] (AFM)
JRC.......... Joint Recovery Center (MCD)
JRC.......... Joint Replacement Center [*Medicine*] (STED)
JRC.......... Joint Reporting Center (SAUO)
JRC.......... Joint Representation Committee [*British*] (DCTA)
JRC.......... Joint Research Center [*Commission of the European Communities*]
JRC.......... Joint Research Centre (HEAS)
JRC.......... Joint Rivers Commission (SAUO)
JRC.......... Journal Register [*NYSE symbol*] (SG)
JRC.......... Junior Red Cross
JRCA........ Junior Ruritan Clubs of America (SAUO)
JRCAS....... Journal. Royal Central Asian Society (journ.) (SAUS)
JRCAT....... Joint Research Center for Atom Technology [*Japan*]
JRCC........ Joint Radiation Control Center (SAUO)
JRCC........ Joint Radiological Control Center (SAUO)
JRCC........ Joint Reconnaissance Control Center (MCD)
JRCC........ Joint Regional Continuing Committee [*Later, RCEAC*] [*Civil Defense*]
JRCC........ Joint Rescue Coordination Center [*Military*] (AFM)
JRCC........ Joint Roland Control Committee (ACAE)
JRC-CVT.... Joint Review Committee on Education in Cardiovascular Technology (DAVI)
JRCD........ Journal of Research in Crime and Delinquency (journ.) (SAUS)
JRCDMS.... Joint Review Committee on Education in Diagnostic Medical Sonography (EA)
JRCE-A...... Journal. Irrigation and Drainage Division. Proceedings of the American Society of Civil Engineers (journ.) (SAUS)
JRC-EEG.... Joint Review Committee on Education in Electroencephalographic [*Technology*] (DAVI)
JRCEPPA.... Joint Review Committee on Educational Programs for Physician Assistants (EA)
JRCERT..... Joint Review Committee on Education in Radiologic Technology (EA)
JRCEST..... Joint Review Committee on Education for the Surgical Technologist (EA)
JRCEST..... Joint Review Committee on Education for the Surgical Technology (SAUS)
JRCI......... Jamming RADAR Coverage Indicator (MSA)
JRCI......... Journal of the Royal Colonial Institute (ROG)
JRCI......... Journal. Regional Cultural Institute (journ.) (SAUS)
JRC-ISPRA... Joint Research Center at Ispra (SAUS)
JRCN........ Japan Committee for Research Networks (SAUS)
JRC-NMT... Joint Review Committee on Educational Programs in Nuclear Medicine Technology (DAVI)
J R Coll Gen Pract... Journal. Royal College of General Practitioners (journ.) (SAUS)
J R Coll Gen Pract Ocs Pp... Journal. Royal College of General Prac- titioners. Occassional Paper (journ.) (SAUS)
J R Coll Physicians Lond... Journal of the Royal College of Physicians of London (SAUO)
J R Coll Physicians Lond... Journal of the Royal College of Physicians of London (journ.) (SAUS)
J R Coll Physicians Lond... Journal. Royal College of Physicians of London (journ.) (SAUS)
J R Coll Surg Edinb... Journal of the Royal College of Surgeons of Edinburgh (SAUO)
J R Coll Surg Edinb... Journal of the Royal College of Surgeons of Edinburgh (journ.) (SAUS)
J R Coll Surg Irel... Journal. Royal College of Surgeons in Ireland (journ.) (SAUS)
JRCOMA.... Joint Review Committee for the Ophthalmic Medical Assistant (EA)
JRCOMP.... Joint Review Committee for Ophthalmic Medical Personnel (EA)
JRCP........ Joint Reinforced Concrete Pavement
JRC-PA...... Joint Review Committee on Educational Programs for Physician Assistants (EA)
JRCPE....... Joint Review Committee for Perfusion Education (DAVI)
JRC Rev.... JRC Review (journ.) (SAUS)
JRCRTE..... Joint Review Committee for Respiratory Therapy Education (EA)
JRCS........ Jet Reaction Control System
JRCS........ John Reich Collectors Society (EA)
JRCSA....... Journal. Royal College of Surgeons of Edinburgh (journ.) (SAUS)
JRC-ST...... Joint Review Committee on Education for the Surgical Technologist (DAVI)
JRCX........ GLNX [*Private rail car owner code*]
JRCZ......... JR Chatham [*Federal Railroad Administration identification code*]
JRD.......... Japan Reconfiguration and Digitization (SAUO)
JRD.......... Jarred (ABBR)
JRD.......... Joint Research and Development (SAUS)
JRD.......... Jumbo Random Driver (SAUS)
JRD.......... Juneau Ranger District [*Alaska*] [*USDA Forest Service*] (ALAC)
JRD.......... Justification Review Document (AAGC)
JRD.......... Riverside, CA [*Location identifier*] [*FAA*] (FAAL)
JRD-3....... Japan Reconfiguration & Digitisation Program Phase III (SAUS)
JRDA........ Jeunesse du Rassemblement Democratique Africain [*Youth of the African Democratic Rally*]
JRDACI...... Jeunesse du Rassemblement Democratique Africain de Cote d'Ivoire [*Youth of the African Democratic Rally of the Ivory Coast*]
JRDB........ Joint Research and Development Board [*1946-1947*]
JRDC........ Japan Research and Development Corp. (SAUS)
JRDCA....... Journal of Radiation Curing (journ.) (SAUS)
JRDF........ Joint Rapid Deployment Force (SAUO)
JRDF........ Joint Rapid Development Force [*Military*] (WDAA)
JRDL........ Jam Resistant Data Link (ACAE)
JRDOD...... Joint Research and Development Objectives Document [*Military*] (AABC)
JRE.......... Java Runtime Environment (SAUS)
JRE.......... Joint Readiness Exercise (SAUS)
JRE.......... Journal of Real Estate Taxation (journ.) (SAUS)
JRE.......... Journal of Religious Ethics (journ.) (SAUS)
JRE.......... JR Energy Ltd. [*Vancouver Stock Exchange symbol*]
JRE.......... New York [*New York*] E. 60th Street [*Airport symbol*] (OAG)
JREA......... James Robison Evangelistic Association (EA)
JREA......... Japanese Railway Engineering Association (SAUS)
JREA......... Japan Railway Engineering Association (SAUS)
J Read...... Journal of Reading (journ.) (SAUS)
J Read Writ Learn Dissabil Int... Journal of Reading, Writing and Learning Disabilities International (journ.) (SAUS)
J Real Estate Finance Econ... Journal of Real Estate Finance and Economics [*A publication*] (JLIT)
J Real Estate Lit... Journal of Real Estate Literature [*A publication*] (JLIT)
J Real Estate Portfol Manage... Journal of Real Estate Portfolio Management [*A publication*] (JLIT)
J Real Estate Practice Educ... Journal of Real Estate Practice and Education [*A publication*] (JLIT)
J Real Estate Res... Journal of Real Estate Research [*A publication*] (JLIT)
J Real Est Tax... Journal of Real Estate Taxation (journ.) (SAUS)
JREB......... Jewish Religion Education Board (SAUO)
J receptor... Juxtapulmonary-Capillary Receptor [*Medicine*] (STED)
J Recept Res... Journal of Receptor Research (journ.) (SAUS)
J Recept Signal Transduct Res... Journal of Receptor and Signal Transduction Research (journ.) (SAUS)
J Reconstr Microsurg... Journal of Reconstructive Microsurgery (journ.) (SAUS)
J Recreational Math... Journal of Recreational Mathematics (journ.) (SAUS)
J Refrig..... Journal of Refrigeration (journ.) (SAUS)
J-Reg........ Junction Register (SAUS)
J Reg Anal Pol... Journal of Regional Analysis and Policy [*A publication*] (JLIT)
J Reg Sci... Journal of Regional Science [*A publication*] (JLIT)
J Regul Econ... Journal of Regulatory Economics [*A publication*] (JLIT)
J Rehabil Asia... Journal of Rehabilitalion in Asia (journ.) (SAUS)
J Rehabil D... Journal of Rehabilitation of the Deaf (journ.) (SAUS)
J Rehabil Res Dev... Journal of Rehabilitation Research and Development (journ.) (SAUS)
J Rehabil Res Dev Clin Suppl... Journal of Rehabilitation Research and Development Clinical Supplement (journ.) (SAUS)
J Rehab RD... Journal of Rehabilitation Research and Development [*A publication*] (BRI)
J Reinf Plast Compos... Journal of Reinforced Plastics and Composites [*A publication*] (CABS)

JRE/JRX..... Joint Readiness Exercise (SAUO)
JRel......... Journal of Religion [*A publication*] (ABAR)
J Rel Africa... Journal of Religion in Africa (journ.) (SAUS)
J R Electric Mech Eng... Journal of the Royal Electrical and Mechanical Engineers (journ.) (SAUS)
J Rel Eth.... Journal of Religious Ethics (journ.) (SAUS)
J Rel Hth... Journal of Religion and Health (journ.) (SAUS)
J Relig Afr... Journal of Religion in Africa (journ.) (SAUS)
J Relig Educ... Journal of Religious Education (journ.) (SAUS)
J Rel Psych Res... Journal of Religion and Psychical Research (journ.) (SAUS)
JREM........ Junior Radio Electrical Mechanic [*British military*] (DMA)
J Remote Smsing... Journal of Remote Sensing (journ.) (SAUS)
J Remount Vet Cors... Journal of the Remount and Veterinary Corps (journ.) (SAUS)
JR EN....... Junior Grade Enlisted Personnel [*Army*]
J Ren & Bar Mus... Journal of Renaissance and Baroque Music (journ.) (SAUS)
J Rep........ Johnson's Maryland Chancery Reports [*A publication*] (DLA)
J Rep........ Johnson's New York Reports [*A publication*] (DLA)
J Rep........ Johnson's Reports of Chase's United States Circuit Court Decisions [*A publication*] (DLA)
J Reprints Antitrust L & Econ... Journal of Reprints for Antitrust Law and Economics [*A publication*] (DLA)
J Reprints Antitrust L & Econ... Journal of Reprints for Antitrust Law and Economics (journ.) (SAUS)
J Reprod Biol Comp Endocrinol... Journal of Reproductive Biology and Comparative Endocrinology (journ.) (SAUS)
J Reprod Fertil... Journal of Reproduction and Fertility (journ.) (SAUS)
J Reprod Fertil Abstr Ser... Journal of Reproduction and Fertility. Abstract Series (journ.) (SAUS)
J Reprod Fertil Suppl... Journal of Reproduction and Fertility. Supplement (journ.) (SAUS)
J Reprod Immunol... Journal of Reproductive Immunology (journ.) (SAUS)
J Reprod Med... Journal of Reproductive Medicine (journ.) (SAUS)
J Reprod Med Lying-In... Journal of Reproductive Medicine. Lying-In (journ.) (SAUS)
JRERDM.... Journal of Receptor Research (journ.) (SAUS)
JRES-A...... Journal of Regional Science (journ.) (SAUS)
JRes Assam Agric Univ... Journal of Research. Assam Agricultural University (journ.) (SAUS)
J Res Comput Educ... Journal of Research on Computing in Education (journ.) (SAUS)
J Res Dev Lab Portland Cem Ass... Journal. Research and Development Laboratories. Portland Cement Association (journ.) (SAUS)
J Research M Eduation... Journal of Reascarch in Music Education (journ.) (SAUS)
J Res Haryana Agric Univ... Journal of Reascarch Haryana Agricultural University (journ.) (SAUS)
J Res Indian Med... Journal of Research in Indian Medicine (journ.) (SAUS)
J Res Indian Med Yog Homoeopathy... Journal of Research in Indian Medicine, Yoga and Homoeopathy (journ.) (SAUS)
JRes Inst Med Sci Kor... Journal. Research Institute of Medical Science of Korea (journ.) (SAUS)
J Res Islamic Econ... Journal of Research in Islamic Economics [*A publication*] (JLIT)
J Res Lepid... Journal of Research on the Lepidoptera (journ.) (SAUS)
J Res M & T... Journal of Resource Management and Technology (journ.) (SAUS)
J Res Math Educ... Journal for Research in Mathematics Education (journ.) (SAUS)
J Res Nat Bur Stand St A Phys Chem... Journal of Research. National Bureau of Standards. Section A. Physics and Chemistry (journ.) (SAUS)
J Res Nat Bur Stand St B Math Sci... Journal of Research. National Bureau of Standards. Section B. Mathematical Sciences (journ.) (SAUS)
J Res Nat Bur Stand St D Radio Sci... Journal of Research. National Bureau of Standards. Section D. Radio Science (journ.) (SAUS)
J Res Natl Bur Stand A... Journal of Research. National Bureau of Standards. Section A. Physics and Chemistry (journ.) (SAUS)
J Res Natl Bur Stand B... Journal of Research. National Bureau of Standards. Section B. Mathematics and Mathematical Physics (journ.) (SAUS)
J Res Natl Bur Stand C... Journal of Research. National Bureau of Standards. Section C. Engineering and Instrumentation (journ.) (SAUS)
J Res Natl Inst Stand Technol... Journal of Research of the National Institute of Standards and Technology (journ.) (SAUS)
J Res NBS.. Journal of Research. National Bureau of Standards (journ.) (SAUS)
J Res NBS A... Journal of Research. National Bureau of Standards. Section A. Physics and Chemistry (journ.) (SAUS)
J Res NBS B... Journal of Research. National Bureau of Standards. Section B. Mathematical Sciences (journ.) (SAUS)
J Res NIST... Journal of Research of the National Institute of Standards and Technology (journ.) (SAUS)
J Res Pers... Journal of Research in Personality (journ.) (SAUS)
J Res Pharmaceut Econ... Journal of Research in Pharmaceutical Economics [*A publication*] (JLIT)
J Res Read... Journal of Research in Reading (journ.) (SAUS)
J Res Sci Agra Univ... Journal of Research in Science. Agra University (journ.) (SAUS)
J Res Sci Teach... Journal of Research in Science Teaching (journ.) (SAUS)
J Res Soc Pak... Journal. Research Society of Pakistan (journ.) (SAUS)
J Res US GS... Journal of Research. United States Geological Survey (journ.) (SAUS)
JRF.......... Jackie Robinson Foundation (EA)
JRF.......... Jewish Reconstructionist Foundation (EA)
JRF.......... Job Request Form (SAUS)
JRF.......... Jog Request Form (SAUS)
JRF.......... John-Roger Foundation (EA)
JRF.......... Journal of Reproduction and Fertility (SAUO)
JRF.......... Judicial Research Foundation [*Defunct*]
JRF.......... Julius Rosenwald Fund (SAUO)
JRF.......... Junior Road Fellowship (SAUO)
JRFC......... Jerry Reed Fan Club [*Defunct*] (EA)
JRFC......... Johnny Rodriguez Fan Club (EA)
JRFL......... Jarful (ABBR)
JRFS......... Janssen Research Foundation Series (journ.) (SAUS)
JRFTNG..... Jet Refresher Training [*Navy*] (NVT)
JRG.......... Jarring (ABBR)
JRG.......... Joint Rapporteurs Group (SAUO)
JRG.......... Journal of Regional Science (journ.) (SAUS)
JRG.......... Junction Register (IAA)
JRGN........ Jargon (ABBR)
Jr Gr......... Junior Grade (SAUS)
JRGS........ Journal of the Royal Geographical Society (SAUO)
JRGS........ Journal of the Royal Geographical Society (journ.) (SAUS)
JRH.......... Jorhat [*India*] [*Airport symbol*] (OAG)
JRH.......... Journal of Religious History (journ.) (SAUS)
JRH.......... Journal of Rural Health (journ.) (SAUS)
JRH.......... Journal. Royal Historical Society of Queensland (journ.) (SAUS)
J Rheumatol... Journal of Rheumatology (journ.) (SAUS)
J Rheumatol Suppl... Journal of Rheumatology Supplement (journ.) (SAUS)
JRHS........ Julia Richman High School (SAUO)
JR HS........ Junior High School (WDAA)
JRHSQ...... Journal. Royal Historical Society of Queensland [*A publication*]
JRI........... Jail Release Information
JRI........... Japan Research Institute (SAUS)
JRI........... Jewel Resources [*Vancouver Stock Exchange symbol*]
JRI........... Journal of Risk and Insurance (journ.) (SAUS)
JRI........... Jules Richard Instruments (SAUS)
JRI........... Junction Route Indicator [*Indian Railway*] (TIR)
JRIA......... Japan Radio-Isotope Association (SAUO)
JRID......... Job Run Identification (SAUS)
JRIM......... Joint Requirements Integration Manager (SAUO)
JRIMD....... Journal of Reproductive Immunology (journ.) (SAUS)
JRINA....... Journal. Research Institute for Catalysis. Hokkaido University (journ.) (SAUS)
J R Inst Br Archit... Journal. Royal Institute of British Architects (journ.) (SAUS)
J R Inst Chem... Journal. Royal Institute of Chemistry (journ.) (SAUS)
J R Inst Hist Res... Journal. Rajasthan Institute of Historical Research (journ.) (SAUS)
J R Inst Public Health... Journal. Royal Institute of Public Health (journ.) (SAUS)
J R Inst Public Health Hyg... Journal. Royal Institute of Public Health and Hygiene (journ.) (SAUS)
J Rio Grande Val Hortic Soc... Journal. Rio Grande Valley Horticulture Society (journ.) (SAUS)
JRISDON.... Jurisdiction (ROG)
J Risk Ins... Journal of Risk and Insurance [*A publication*] (JLIT)
J Risk Uncertainty... Journal of Risk and Uncertainty [*A publication*] (JLIT)
J RI State Dent Soc... Journal. Rhode Island State Dental Society (journ.) (SAUS)
JRivBsh..... James River Bankshares, Inc. [*Associated Press*] (SAG)
JRiver....... James River Corp. of Virginia [*Associated Press*] (SAG)
JRJ.......... Jamaica Association of Villas and Apartments (EA)
JRJ.......... JAVA [*Jamaica Association of Villas and Apartments*] Reservations Jamaica (EA)
JRJ.......... Journal of Reform Judaism (journ.) (SAUS)
JRJR......... 800-JR Cigar, Inc. [*NASDAQ symbol*] (NASQ)
JRKD........ Jerked (ABBR)
JRKG........ Jerking (ABBR)
JRKIR....... Jerkier (ABBR)
JRKLY....... Jerkily (ABBR)
JRKN........ Jerkin (ABBR)
JRKNS....... Jerkiness (ABBR)
JRKR........ Jerker (ABBR)
JRKST....... Jerkiest (ABBR)
JRL.......... Cincinnati G&E8.28%JrSubDebs [*NYSE symbol*] (TTSB)
JRL.......... Cincinnati Gas & Electric [*NYSE symbol*] (SAG)
JRL.......... Jarvis Resources [*Vancouver Stock Exchange symbol*]
JRL.......... Jet Research Laboratory (MCD)
JRL.......... John Rylands Library (SAUO)
jrl........... Journal (DAVI)
JRL.......... Journal of Retailing (journ.) (SAUS)
Jrl Audit.... Journal of Accounting Auditing and Finance (journ.) (SAUS)
JRL/B........ Bulletin of the John Rylands Library. Manchester (journ.) (SAUS)
JRLB......... John Rylands Library. Bulletin (journ.) (SAUS)
Jrl Bldg S... Journal. Chartered Institution of Building Services (journ.) (SAUS)
Jrl Bus...... Journal of Business (journ.) (SAUS)
Jrl Comm.... Journal of Commerce (journ.) (SAUS)
Jrl Def& D... Journal of Defense and Diplomacy (journ.) (SAUS)
Jrl Elec I... Journal of the Electronics Industry (journ.) (SAUS)
Jrl Eng Pwr... Journal of Engineering for Power (journ.) (SAUS)
JRLI........ Life Outreach International (EA)
Jr Lib....... Junior Libraries (journ.) (SAUS)
Jrl Int B..... Journal of International Business Studies (journ.) (SAUS)
Jrl Irrep..... Journal of Irreproducible Results (journ.) (SAUS)
Jrl Market... Journal of Marketing (journ.) (SAUS)
Jrl Metals... Journal of Metals (journ.) (SAUS)
Jrl Mkt R... Journal of Marketing Research (journ.) (SAUS)
Jrl P......... Journal. Patent Office Society (journ.) (SAUS)
Jrl Petro.... Journal of Petroleum Technology (journ.) (SAUS)
Jrl Retail... Journal of Retailing (journ.) (SAUS)
Jrl RE Tax... Journal of Real Estate Taxation (journ.) (SAUS)
Jr LS........ Junior Life Saving [*Red Cross*]
Jrl Solar.... Journal of Solar Energy Engineering (journ.) (SAUS)

Jrl Sol Engr... Journal of Solar Energy Engineering (journ.) (SAUS)
JRLU........ Lauritzen Reefers [*Intermodal shipping container symbol*] (TVRC)
J Rly Div Inst Mech Engrs... Institution of Mechanical Engineers. Railway Division. Journal (journ.) (SAUS)
J Rly Div Inst Mech Engrs... Journal. Institution of Mechanical Engineers. Railway Division (journ.) (SAUS)
JRM......... Jettison Release Mechanism
JRM......... Joule-Rowland Method [*Physics*]
JRM......... Journal of Reproductive Medicine (SAUO)
JRM......... McDermott [*J. Ray*] SA [*NYSE symbol*] (SAG)
JRM......... Society of Combatant Clergy (Iran) [*Political party*] (PSAP)
JRMA........ Japan Hubber Manufacturers Association (SAUO)
JRMB........ Joint Requirements and Management Board [*Later, JROC*] [*Military*]
JRMB........ Joint Resources Management Board [*Military*]
JRMET...... Joint Reliability and Maintainability Evaluation Team (ACAE)
JRMF........ Joseph R. McCarthy Foundation (EA)
JRMFO...... James Redman Miller Family Organization [*Association*] (EA)
JRMIEZ...... Journal of Reconstructive Microsurgery (journ.) (SAUS)
JRMMRA.... Journal. Rocky Mountain Medieval and Renaissance Association (journ.) (SAUS)
JRMO........ Junior Resident Medical Office (SAUS)
JRMO........ Junior Resident Medical Officer (SAUO)
JRMP........ Java Remote Method Protocol (GART)
JRMPO...... Joint Regional Medical Planning Office (SAUO)
JRMS........ Journal. Royal Meteorological Society (journ.) (SAUS)
JRMTO...... Joint Rail Military Traffic Office (AABC)
JRMX........ JRM Holdings, Inc. (SAUO)
JRN.......... Japan Radio Network (SAUO)
JRN.......... Jet Rent SA [*Mexico*] [*ICAO designator*] (FAAC)
JRN.......... Junior Resident Note [*Medical records*] (DAVI)
JRN.......... Jurisdiction [*Telegraphy*] (PCTE)
JrNAD....... Junior National Association for the Deaf [*Defunct*] (EA)
J R Nav Med Serv... Journal of the Royal Naval Medical Service (SAUO)
J R Nav Med Serv... Journal of the Royal Naval Medical Service (journ.) (SAUS)
J R Nav Med Serv... Journal. Royal Naval Medical Service (journ.) (SAUS)
JRNBA....... Journal of Research (journ.) (SAUS)
JRNBA....... Journal of Research. National Bureau of Standards (journ.) (SAUS)
JRNCDM.... Journal of Radioanalytical and Nuclear Chemistry (journ.) (SAUS)
JR NCO..... Junior Grade Noncommissioned Officer [*Army*]
JRNDEX..... Journal Index
JRNIST...... Journalist
JRNL........ Journal
JRNL........ Jurisdictional [*Telegraphy*] (PCTE)
JRNLM...... Journalism (ABBR)
JRNLSM...... Journalism (ABBR)
JRNLST..... Journalist (ABBR)
JRNLSTC.... Journalistic (ABBR)
JRNLT....... Journalist (ABBR)
JRNLTC...... Journalistic (ABBR)
JRNLTCY.... Journalistically (ABBR)
JRNLZ....... Journalize (ABBR)
JRNLZD..... Journalized (ABBR)
JRNLZG..... Journalizing (ABBR)
JRNLZR..... Journalizer (ABBR)
JRNMA....... Journal. Royal Naval Medical Service (journ.) (SAUS)
JRNS........ Journal of the Russian Numismatic Society (SAUO)
JRNSCA..... Jurist Reports, New Series, Court of Appeal [*New Zealand*] [*A publication*] (DLA)
JRNSML.... Jurist Reports, New Series, Cases in Mining Law [*New Zealand*] [*A publication*] (DLA)
JRNSSC..... Jurist Reports, New Series, Supreme Court [*New Zealand*] [*A publication*] (DLA)
JRNY........ Journey (ABBR)
JRNYD...... Journeyed (ABBR)
JRNYG...... Journeying (ABBR)
JRNYMAN.. Journeyman (ABBR)
JRO.......... Jicamarca Radar Observatory [*Peru*]
JRO.......... J. Robert Oppenheimer
JRO.......... J. Robert Oppenheimer Fellowship (SAUO)
JRO.......... Junior Radio Operator [*British military*] (DMA)
JRO.......... Kilimanjaro [*Tanzania*] [*Airport symbol*] (OAG)
J Robot Syst... Journal of Robotic Systems (journ.) (SAUS)
J Rob Syst... Journal of Robotic Systems [*A publication*] (CABS)
JROC........ Joint Requirements Oversight Council [*Military*]
JROD........ J-Rod Trailer Company [*NCIC trailer make code*]
JROFC....... James "Rebel" O'Leary Fan Club (EA)
JROJATC.... James "Rebel" O'Leary and Jammie Ann Tape Club [*Defunct*] (EA)
J Root Crops... Journal of Root Crops (journ.) (SAUS)
JROSC....... J. Robert Oppenheimer Study Center (SAUO)
JROt......... Joint Requirements Oversight Council (SAUO)
JROTC....... Junior Reserve Officers' Training Corps (AABC)
J Roy Agr Soc... Journal. Royal Agricultural Society of England (journ.) (SAUS)
J Royal Aust Hist Soc... Journal. Royal Australian Historical Society (journ.) (SAUS)
J Royal Military College Aust... Journal. Royal Military College of Australia (journ.) (SAUS)
J Royal Soc New Zeal... Journal. Royal Society of New Zealand (journ.) (SAUS)
J Roy Artil... Journal of the Royal Artillery (journ.) (SAUS)
J Roy ASC.. Journal of the Royal Astronomical Society of Canada (SAUO)
JRoyASC.... Journal of the Royal Astronomical Society of Canada (journ.) (SAUS)
J Roy Astron Soc Can... Journal of the Royal Astronomical Society of Canada (SAUO)
J Roy At.... Journal. Royal Australian Historical Society (journ.) (SAUS)
J Roy Col P... Journal. Royal College of Physicians of London (journ.) (SAUS)
J Roy Inst Cornwall N Ser... Journal. Royal Institution of Cornwall. New Series (journ.) (SAUS)
J Roy Satist Soc Ser B... Journal. Royal Statistical Society. Series B. Methodological (journ.) (SAUS)
J Roy Soc Ant Ir... Journal. Royal Society of Antiquaries of Ireland (journ.) (SAUS)
J Roy Soc NSW... Journal. Royal Society of New South Wales (journ.) (SAUS)
J Roy Soc West Aust... Journal of the Royal Society of Western Australia (SAUO)
J Roy Soc West Aust... Journal of the Royal Society of Western Australia (journ.) (SAUS)
J Roy Sta A... Journal. Royal Statistical Society. Series A. General (journ.) (SAUS)
J Roy Statis Soc... Journal of the Royal Statistical Society (SAUO)
J Roy Statis Soc... Journal of the Royal Statistical Society (journ.) (SAUS)
J Roy Statist Soc Ser A... Journal. Royal Statistical Society. Series A. General (journ.) (SAUS)
J Roy Stats... Journal. Royal Statistical Society (journ.) (SAUS)
J Roy Stat Soc A J Verb Learn Verb Beh... Journal. Royal Statistical Society. A Journal of Verbal Learning and Verbal Behavior (journ.) (SAUS)
J Roy St B... Journal. Royal Statistical Society. Series B. Methodological (journ.) (SAUS)
J Roy St C... Journal. Royal Statistical Society. Series C. Applied Statistics (journ.) (SAUS)
JRP.......... Job Readiness Posture (OICC)
JRP.......... Joint Requirements Planning (CDE)
JRP.......... Jute Reinforced Plastics (SAUS)
JRPB........ Joint Radio Propagation Bureau (SAUO)
JRPB........ Joint Radio Propogation Bureau (SAUO)
JRPE......... Job-Relevant Professional Experience (SAUS)
JRPG........ Joint RADAR Planning Group [*Military*] (CET)
JRPM........ Joint Registered Publications Memorandum
JRPO........ Joint Research Projects Office [*Army and NASA joint operation*] (RDA)
JRPrK....... James River$3.375Cv Ex K Pfd [*NYSE symbol*] (TTSB)
JRPrL........ James River Dep Cv Ex Pfd [*NYSE symbol*] (TTSB)
JRPrO....... James River 8.25% Dep Pfd [*NYSE symbol*] (TTSB)
JRPrP....... James River 9% 'DECS' [*NYSE symbol*] (TTSB)
JRPS........ Japan Reinforced Plastics Society (SAUO)
JRPUA....... Journal of Research. Punjab Agricultural University (journ.) (SAUS)
JRR.......... Japanese Research Reactor
JRR.......... Joint Radio Reporting (SAUS)
JRR.......... Juror (ABBR)
JRRC........ Japanese Reprographic Rights Center (SAUO)
JRRC........ Joint Regional Reconnaissance Center [*NATO*] (NATG)
JRRI......... Journal of Rubber Research Institute of Malaya (journ.) (SAUS)
JRRI......... Juvenile Risk Reduction Initiative
JRRIAN...... Journal. Rubber Research Institute of Malaysia (journ.) (SAUS)
J RRI Malaysia... Journal. Rubber Research Institute of Malaysia (journ.) (SAUS)
J RRI Sri Lanka... Journal. Rubber Research Institute of Sri Lanka (journ.) (SAUS)
JRRLA....... Journal. Radio Research Laboratories (journ.) (SAUS)
JRRS........ Japan Hadiation Research Society (SAUO)
JRRT........ John Ronald Renel Tolkien [*British author, 1892-1973*]
JRS.......... Japanese Rocket Society
JRS.......... Jersey [*Channel Islands*] [*Seismograph station code, US Geological Survey*] [*Closed*] (SEIS)
JRS.......... Jerusalem [*Israel*] [*Airport symbol*] (OAG)
JRS.......... Jet Repair Service
JRS.......... Job Rehearsal Scheme (AIE)
JRS.......... Job Release Scheme (PDAA)
JRS.......... John R. Sinnock [*Designer's mark, when appearing on US coins*]
JRS.......... Joint Reconnaissance Schedule (CARL)
JRS.......... Joint Reconnaissance Structure (CCCA)
JRS.......... Joint Reporting Structure [*Military*] (AFM)
JRS.......... Journal of Refractive Surgery (SAUS)
JRS.......... Journal of Regional Science (journ.) (SAUS)
JRS.......... Journal of Roman Studies (journ.) (SAUS)
JRS.......... Journal. Roentgen Society [*A publication*] (ROG)
JRS.......... Judges and Judicial Retirement System (SAUO)
JRS.......... Junction Relay Set (IAA)
JRSA........ Japan Raw Silk Association (SAUO)
JRSA........ Justice Research and Statistics Association (NTPA)
JRSAA....... Journal. Royal Society of Arts (journ.) (SAUS)
JRSAI........ Journal. Royal Society of Antiquaries of Ireland (journ.) (SAUS)
JRSAnH...... Journal. Royal Society of Antiquaries of Ireland (journ.) (SAUS)
JRSC........ Jam-Resistant Secure Communications
JRSC........ Joint Rescue Sub-Center (COE)
JRSC........ Joint Resistant Secure Communications [*DoD*]
Jr Schol..... Junior Scholastic (journ.) (SAUS)
JRSDCNL... Jurisdictional (ABBR)
JRSH........ Journal. Royal Society of Health (journ.) (SAUS)
JRSI......... Journal of the Royal Sanitary Institute (journ.) (SAUS)
JR Sigls Inst... Journal. Royal Signals Institution (journ.) (SAUS)
J R Signals Inst... Journal of the Royal Signals Institution (journ.) (SAUS)
JRSM........ Journal of the Royal Society of Medicine (SAUO)
J/RSM....... Junior Regimental Sergeant-Major [*British military*] (DMA)
J RSNZ...... Journal. Royal Society of New Zealand (journ.) (SAUS)
JRSO........ Jewish Restitution Successor Organization (EA)
J R Soc Encour Art Manuf Commer... Journal. Royal Society for the Encouragement of Arts, Manufactures and Commerce (journ.) (SAUS)
J R Soc Health... Journal of the Royal Society of Health (SAUO)
J R Soc Health... Journal of the Royal Society of Health (journ.) (SAUS)
J R Soc Health... Journal. Royal Society of Health (journ.) (SAUS)
J R Soc Med... Journal of the Royal Society of Medicine (MEC)
J R Soc Med... Journal of the Royal Society of Medicine (journ.) (SAUS)

J R Soc Med... Journal. Royal Society of Medicine (journ.) (SAUS)
J R Soc NZ... Journal. Royal Society of New Zealand (journ.) (SAUS)
JRSOD ...... Journal. Reticuloendothelial Society (journ.) (SAUS)
JRSPDN..... Jurisprudent (ABBR)
JRSPDNC ... Jurisprudence (ABBR)
JRSPDTL.... Jurisprudential (ABBR)
JRSS .... Journal of the Royal Statistical Society (SAUO)
JRSS .... Journal of the Royal Statistical Society (journ.) (SAUS)
JRSS .... Journal. Royal Statistical Society (journ.) (SAUS)
JRST......... Jurist (ABBR)
J R Stat Soc... Journal of the Royal Statistical Society (SAUO)
J R Stat Soc... Journal. Royal Statistical Society (journ.) (SAUS)
JRSTE....... Junior Suite [*Travel industry*] (TRID)
JRS/USA.... Jesuit Refugee Service/USA (EA)
JRSVC....... Jam-Resistant Secure Voice Communications (MCD)
JRSWG....... Joint Reentry System Working Group
JRSX .... JR Simplot [*Private rail car owner code*]
JRSY .... Jersey (ABBR)
JRT .... Jaguar-Rover-Triumph
JRT .... Jaguar Rover Triumph Inc. (SAUO)
JRT .... Job Relations Training
JRT .... Joint Rapporteur Team (SAUO)
JRT .... Journal of Retailing (journ.) (SAUS)
JRT .... Jugoslovenska Radiotelevizija [*Association of Yugoslav Radio and Television Organizations*] (EY)
JRT .... Junctional Recovery Time [*Medicine*] (DMAA)
JRT .... Tampa, FL [*Location identifier*] [*FAA*] (FAAL)
JRTC......... Joint Readiness Training Center [*Fort Chaffee, AR*] (INF)
JRTCA....... Jack Russell Terrier Club of America (EA)
JRTC-IS ..... Joint Readiness Training Center Instrumentation System [*DoD*]
JRTC-OIS ... Joint Readiness Training Objective Instrumentation System (SAUS)
J R Telev Soc... Journal. Royal Televison Society (journ.) (SAUS)
JRTIG........ Joint Radiophone Technical Interfaces Group (SAUO)
JRTOC....... Joint Rear Tactical Operations Center (SAUO)
JRTP......... Jub Readiness Training Program (SAUS)
JRU........... Japreria [*Language symbol*] (ETLW)
J Rubber Res Inst Malays... Journal. Rubber Research Institute of Malaysia (journ.) (SAUS)
J Rubber Res Inst Sri Lanka... Journal. Rubber Research Institute of Sri Lanka (journ.) (SAUS)
JRUL .... Journal. Rutgers University Library (journ.) (SAUS)
J R United Serv Inst... Journal. Royal United Service Institution (journ.) (SAUS)
J Rurai Coop Int Res Cent Rural Coop Communities... Journal of Rural Cooperation. Inter- national Research Center on Rural Coopera-tive Communities (journ.) (SAUS)
J Rural Dev... Journal of Rural Development (journ.) (SAUS)
J Rural Econ and Derebpment... Journal of Rural Economics and Development (journ.) (SAUS)
J Rural Educ... Journal of Rural Education (journ.) (SAUS)
J Rural Eng Dev... Journal of Rural Engineering and Development (journ.) (SAUS)
J Rur Coop... Journal of Rural Cooperation (journ.) (SAUS)
JRUSI .... Journal of the Royal United Service Institution [*A publication*] (ROG)
J Russell Soc... Journal of the Russell Society (SAUO)
J Russell Soc... Journal. Russell Society (journ.) (SAUS)
J Rutgers Univ Libr... Journal. Rutgers University Library (journ.) (SAUS)
JRV .... Javelin Rocket Vehicle
JRV .... Polling Places (Nicaragua) [*Political party*] (PSAP)
JRV .... Vote Receiving Committees (Ecuador) [*Political party*] (PSAP)
JRvr .... James River Corp. of Virginia [*Associated Press*] (SAG)
JRVSB....... Jena Review. Supplement (journ.) (SAUS)
JRWG........ Job Redesign Working Group
JRX .... Joint Readiness Exercise (MCD)
JRY .... Jury (ABBR)
JRYBLD ..... Jerrybuild (ABBR)
JRYBLDG ... Jerrybuilding (ABBR)
JRYBLDR ... Jerrybuilder (ABBR)
JRYBLT...... Jerrybuilt (ABBR)
JryDeli ...... Jerrys Famous Deli, Inc. [*Associated Press*] (SAG)
JRYMA ...... Juryman (ABBR)
JRZ .... Jugoslovenska Radikalna Zajednica [*Yugoslav Radical Union*] [*Political party*] (PPE)
JS............ Jack Screw
JS............ Jamestowne Society (EA)
JS............ Jamestown Society (SAUO)
J/S .... Jammer-to-Signal Ratio (SAUO)
J/S .... Jamming to Signal
JS............ Jam Strobe (IEEE)
J/S .... Jam to Signal Ratio
JS............ Janus. Supplements (journ.) (SAUS)
JS............ Japan Society (EA)
JS............ Japan Society for the Study of Economic Policy (SAUO)
JS............ Jargon Society (EA)
JS............ JCS [*Joint Chiefs of Staff*] Support (MCD)
JS............ Jefferson Smurfit Group PLC [*NYSE symbol*] (SAG)
JS............ Jefferson Smurfit Grp ADS [*NYSE symbol*] (TTSB)
JS............ Jejunal Segment [*Gastroenterology*] (DAVI)
JS............ Jesus Saves [*Internet lingo*] (NETL)
JS............ Jetevator Sensor
JS............ Jet Stabilization
JS............ Jet Stream
JS............ Jet Study (AAG)
JS............ Jettison Signal
JS............ Jeumont-Schneider Trenformeteurs (EFIS)
JS............ Jewelry Show
J S........... Jewish Studies (journ.) (SAUS)
JS............ Job Scheduler (SAUS)
JS............ Job Search [*Job Training and Partnership Act*] (OICC)
JS............ Job Service (ELAL)
JS............ Job Set (ELAL)
JS............ Job Specification [*Department of Labor*]
JS............ Job Statement (ELAL)
JS............ Job Stream [*Computer science*]
JS............ John R. Sinnock [*Designer's mark, when appearing on US coins*]
JS............ Johnson Society (EA)
JS............ Joint Services [*British military*] (DMA)
JS............ Joint Spacing [*Mining technology*]
JS............ Joint Sparing (SAUS)
JS............ Joint Staff [*Military*] (CINC)
JS............ Joint Station (SAUS)
JS............ Joint Support [*Military*] (AFM)
JS............ Jones and Spencer's Superior Court Reports [*33-61 New York*] [*A publication*] (DLA)
JS............ Joshua [*Old Testament book*]
J/s .... Joules per Second (IDOE)
JS............ Jourdain Society [*British*]
JS............ Journal. Arnold Schoenberg Institute (journ.) (SAUS)
JS............ Judaic Studies (journ.) (SAUS)
JS............ Judaisme Sepharadi (BJA)
JS............ Judean Society (EA)
JS............ Judgment Summons [*British*] (ROG)
JS............ Judicial Separation [*British*] (ROG)
JS............ Jump if Sign (SAUO)
JS............ Junctional Slowing [*Cardiology*] (DAVI)
JS............ Junior Sailor (SAUS)
JS............ Junior Scholastic (journ.) (SAUS)
JS............ Junior Seaman [*British military*] (DMA)
JS............ Junkman-Shoeller Unit (MAE)
JS............ Jury Sittings (Faculty Cases) [*Scotland*] [*A publication*] (DLA)
JS............ Just [*Telegraphy*] (PCTE)
J/S .... Justified
JS............ Justifying Space [*Typography*] (DGA)
JS............ Just Scale
JS............ Korean Airways [*ICAO designator*] (AD)
JS............ Sea of Japan
JSA .... Jammer System Analysis
JSA .... Japanese Standards Association (NTCM)
JSA .... Japan Silk Association (EA)
JSA .... Jesuit Seismological Association (EA)
JSA .... Jet Show Assembly
JSA .... Jewelers Security Alliance (SAUS)
JSA .... Jewelers Security Alliance of the United States (SAUO)
JSA .... Jewelers Shipping Association (EA)
JSA .... Jewish Society of America
JSA .... Job Safety Analysis
JSA .... Job Search Allowance
JSA .... Job Seekers' Allowance (WDAA)
JSA .... Joint Security Area (MCD)
JSA .... Joint Security Area [*Film title*]
JSA .... Joint Steering Assembly (SAUO)
JSA .... Joint Supportability Assessment [*Army*]
JSA .... Journal of Substance Abuse (SAUO)
JSA .... Journeymen Stonecutters Association (SAUO)
JSA .... Journeymen Stone Cutters Association of North America [*Defunct*]
JSA .... Junior State of America (SAUS)
JSA .... Junior Statesmen of America (EA)
Js[a] .... Sutter Antigen [*Of Kell system blood group*] [*Hematology*] (DAVI)
JSAAE .... Japanese Society for Alternatives to Animal Experiments
JSAC......... Jet Strategic Airlift Capability [*of Military Air Command*] (AAG)
JSAC......... Joint State Area Command [*Emergency Management*] (EMA)
JSAC......... Joint Strategy and Action Committee [*Defunct*] (EA)
JSACA .... Journal. South African Chemical Institute (journ.) (SAUS)
J SA Chem I... Journal. South African Chemical Institute (journ.) (SAUS)
JSACT .... Jetstream Anti-Countermeasure Trainer (SAUS)
JSACT .... Joint Strategic Air Control Team (SAUO)
JSAE......... Japan Society of Automotive Engineers (SAUO)
JSAE......... Journal of the Society of Automotive Engineers (SAUO)
JSAE......... Journal of the Society of Automotive Engineers (journ.) (SAUS)
JSAE......... Journal Society of Automotive Engineers of Japan (journ.) (SAUS)
JSAED .... Journal of Strain Analysis for Engineering Design (journ.) (SAUS)
JSAFA4...... Journal. South African Forestry Association (journ.) (SAUS)
JSAFE .... Journal of South-East Asia and the Far Fast (journ.) (SAUS)
J S Afr Biol S... Journal. South African Biological Society (journ.) (SAUS)
J S Afr Bot Suppl Vol... Journal of South African Botany. Supplementary Volume (journ.) (SAUS)
J S Afr Inst Eng... Journal. South African Institution of Engineers (journ.) (SAUS)
J S Afr Speech Hear Assoc... Journal. South African Speech and Hearing Association (journ.) (SAUS)
J S Afr Vet Assoc... Journal of the South African Veterinary Association (SAUO)
J S Afr Vet Assoc... Journal of the South African Veterinary Association (journ.) (SAUS)
J S Afr Vet Med Assoc... Journal. South African Veterinary Medical Association (journ.) (SAUS)
JSAG .... Joint Service Advisory Group
JSAH .... Journal of Southeast Asian History (journ.) (SAUS)
JSAH .... Journal. Society of Architectural Historians (journ.) (SAUS)
JSAI .... Japanese Society for Artificial Intelligence (SAUS)
JSAI .... Japan Society fot Artificial Intelligence (SAUS)

J Sailama Univ Fac Ed Math Natur Sci... Journal. Sailama University. Faculty of Education. Mathematics and Natural Science (journ.) (SAUS)
J Sailama Univ Nt Sci... Journal. Sailama University. Natural Science (journ.) (SAUS)
J SA I Min... Journal. South African Institute of Mining and Metallurgy (journ.) (SAUS)
J Sains Nukl... Jernal Sains Nuklear (journ.) (SAUS)
J S Air-Cond Refrig Eng Korea... Journal Society of Air-Conditioning and Refrigerating Engineers of Korea (journ.) (SAUS)
JSAIS........ Junior South African Individual Scales [*Intelligence test*]
J-SAK........ Joint Attack of the Second Echelon (MCD)
JSAL......... Journal of South African Law [*A publication*] (ILCA)
JSAL......... Journal of South Asian Languages (journ.) (SAUS)
JSAL......... JSA Terminals [*Common carrier symbol*]
JSALO....... Journal of Studies on Alcohol (journ.) (SAUS)
JSAM........ Joint Security Assistance Memorandum [*Military*]
JSAM........ Joint Service Achievement Medal [*Military decoration*]
JSAMA...... Journal. South African Institute of Mining and Metallurgy (journ.) (SAUS)
JSAMSA..... Joint Security Assistance Memorandum Supporting Analysis (MCD)
JSAN........ Joint Staff Automation of the Nineties (SAUO)
J San Antonio Dent Soc... Journal. San Antonio District Dental Society (journ.) (SAUS)
JS&CS....... Jewish Family and Child Services (SAUO)
JS&TIC...... Joint Scientific and Technical Intelligence Committee (SAUO)
J Sanit Eng Div; Amer Soc... Journal of the Sanitary Engineering Division; Proceedings of American Society of Sanitary Engineering (SAUO)
J Sanit Eng Div Proc Am S Civ Eng... Journal. Sanitary Enneering Division. Proceedings. American Society of Civil Engineers (journ.) (SAUS)
JSAP......... Joint Security Assistance Planning (SAUO)
JSAP......... Joint Statement of Agreed Principles [*US-USSR*]
JSAP......... Journal of Small Animal Practice [*A publication*] (GVA)
JSAP......... JSA Rush Transportation Systems [*Common carrier symbol*]
JSAP......... Junior School of Applied Photography (SAUO)
J Sapporo Munic Gen Hp... Journal. Sapporo Municipal General Hospital (journ.) (SAUS)
JSAR......... Joint Search and Rescue [*Military*] (DNAB)
JSAR......... Joint Service Agreement Report [*Defense Supply Agency*]
JSARC....... Joint Search and Rescue Center [*Military*] (AABC)
J S Archit... Journal. Society of Architectural Historians (journ.) (SAUS)
JSAS......... Jammer System Analysis Simulator
JSAS......... Journal of Southeast Asian Studies (journ.) (SAUS)
JSAS......... Journal Supplement Abstract Service [*American Psychological Association*]
J S Asia L... Journal of South Asian Literature (journ.) (SAUS)
JSASS....... Japan Society for Aeronautical and Space Sciences (SAUO)
JSASWE..... Joint Services Anti-Submarine Warfare Establishment (SAUO)
JSAT......... Japan Satellite Systems [*Commercial firm*]
JSAT......... Joint System Acceptance Test (MCD)
JSAT......... Junior Scholastic Aptitude Test [*Education*] (AEBS)
JSATC....... Joint Service Air Trooping Centre (SAUO)
JSATG....... Joint Services Actions Task Group (MCD)
JSATP....... Joint Services Automatic Testing Panel (AAGC)
JSA-US...... Jewelers' Security Alliance of the United States (NTPA)
JSAVLA...... Joint Services Advanced Vertical Lift Aircraft (ACAE)
JSAWC....... Joint Services Amphibious Warfare Centre (SAUS)
JSB.......... Bachelor of Judicial Science
JSB.......... Japanese Society in Brisbane [*Australia*]
JSB.......... Jaswant Singh and Bhattacharji [*Staining method for blood cells, named for its discoverers*] [*Medicine*]
JSB.......... Jewish Society for the Blind (EA)
JSB.......... Jewish Statistical Bureau (EA)
JSB.......... Job Status Block (TIMI)
JSB.......... Joint Signal Board (SAUO)
JSB.......... Joint-Stock Bank [*Banking*]
JSB.......... JSB Financial [*NYSE symbol*] (SG)
JSB.......... Judicial Science Bachelor (SAUS)
JSBA........ Jacob Sheep Breeders Association (EA)
JSBA........ Jefferson Savings Bancorp [*NASDAQ symbol*] (SAG)
JSBCD3..... Journal. American Society of Brewing Chemists (journ.) (SAUS)
JSBF........ JSB Financial [*NASDAQ symbol*] (TTSB)
JSBF........ JSB Financial, Inc. [*NASDAQ symbol*] (SPSG)
JSB Fn...... JSB Financial, Inc. [*Associated Press*] (SAG)
JSBI......... JSB Trucking [*Common carrier symbol*]
JSBK........ Johnstown Savings Bank (SAUO)
JSBS........ Joint Strategic Bomber Study
JSC.......... ICSU/WMO Joint Scientific Committee for WCRP (SAUS)
JSC.......... Jackson State College [*Later, Jackson State University*] [*Mississippi*]
JSC.......... Janiaica Schools Certificate (SAUS)
JSC.......... Japanese Studies Center [*Monash University*] [*Australia*]
JSC.......... Jascan Resources, Inc. [*Toronto Stock Exchange symbol*]
JSC.......... Jenkinsville [*South Carolina*] [*Seismograph station code, US Geological Survey*] (SEIS)
JS-C......... Jesus College-Cambridge (SAUO)
JSC.......... Job-Site Component
JSC.......... Johnson Space Center (USDC)
JSC.......... Johnstown & Stony Creek Rail Road Co. [*AAR code*]
JSC.......... Joint Scientific Committee [*WMO/ICSU*]
JSC.......... Joint Scientific Committee, World Climate Research Program (SAUS)
JSC.......... Joint Sectoral Committee (SAUO)
JSC.......... Joint Security Control
JSC.......... Joint Selection Committee
JSC.......... Joint Service Committee [*Military*]
JSC.......... Joint Setup Cost
JSC.......... Joint Signal Committee (SAUO)
JSC.......... Joint Spectrum Center [*Illinois Institute of Technology*] [*IIT Research Institute*] (IID)
JSC.......... Joint Staff Council [*Japanese*] [*Military*] (CINC)
JSC.......... Joint Standing Committee (ADA)
JSC.......... Joint Steering Committee (SAUO)
JSC.......... Joint Steering Committee for Revision of Anglo-American Cataloging Rules (AL)
JSC.......... Joint Stock Co. (SAUS)
JSC.......... Joint Stock Company (SAUO)
JSC.......... Joint-Stock Company
JSC.......... Joint Strategic Capabilities [*Military*]
JSC.......... Joint Strategic Committee [*Military*]
JSC.......... Joint Support Command [*Navy*]
JSC.......... Joly Steam Calorimeter
J-SC......... Journal of Solid State Circuits (SAUS)
JSC.......... Journal of Structural Chemistry (journ.) (SAUS)
JSC.......... Judgments of the Supreme Court of Cyprus [*A publication*] (ILCA)
JSC.......... Judicial Service Commission (Sri Lanka) [*Political party*] (PSAP)
JSC.......... Junior Staff Course [*British*]
JSC.......... Justice [*Telegraphy*] (PCTE)
JSC.......... Justice of the Supreme Court
JSC.......... Justice of the Supreme Court (journ.) (SAUS)
JSC.......... Justice Statistics Clearinghouse (SAUS)
JSCA........ Japanese Spaniel Club of America [*Later, JCCA*] (EA)
JSCA........ Journeymen Stone Cutters Association of North America [*Defunct*] (EA)
JSCAACR... Joint Steering Committee for Revision of AACR [*Anglo-American Cataloging Rules*]
JSCAEN..... Joint Schools Committee for Academic Excellence Now (EA)
J S Calif State Dent Assoc... Journal of the Southern California State Dental Association (journ.) (SAUS)
JSCAMPS... Joint Service Common Airframe Multiple Purpose System [*Military*] (MCD)
JSCAS....... Japan Society for Computer Aided Surgery (SAUO)
JSCAS....... Johnson Space Center Astronomical Society
JSCAT....... Joint Staff Crisis Action Team [*Environmental science*] (COE)
JSCB........ Job Step Control Block [*Computer science*] (BUR)
JSCBIS...... Joint Service Chemical and Biological Information System
JSCC........ Japan Securities Clearing Corp. (SAUS)
JSCC........ Japan Society for Composite Materials (SAUO)
JSCC........ Joint Service Coordination Committee [*Military*] (DOMA)
JSCC........ Joint Staff Consultative Committee [*British*] (DI)
JSCC........ Joint Synod of the Convocation of Canterbury (SAUO)
JSCC........ Scott Cable Communications Inc. (SAUO)
JSCCB....... Joint Services Configuration Control Board [*Military*] (AFIT)
JSCCMP..... Joint Services Committee of Conservative Members of Parliament (SAUO)
J Sc D....... Doctor of Juridical Science
JScD........ Doctor of Juristic Science (SAUO)
JScD........ Doctor of Iuristic Science (SAUS)
JScE........ Eimac [*Division of Varian Associates*] Technical Library, San Carlos, CA [*Library symbol*] [*Library of Congress*] (LCLS)
JSCE........ Japanese Society of Civil Engineers (SAUS)
JSCE........ Japan Society of Civil Engineers (SAUS)
JSCE........ Japan Society of Corrosion Engineers (SAUO)
JSCE........ Joint Services Communications Element (CCCA)
JSCERDCG... Joint Service Civil Engineering Research and Development Coordination Group [*Military*] (RDA)
JSCFA....... Japan Steel Castings and Forgings Association (SAUO)
J Sc Food Agriculture... Journal of the Science of Food and Agriculture (journ.) (SAUS)
J Sch Health... Journal of School Halth (journ.) (SAUS)
J school..... Journalism School (WDMC)
J-School.... Journalism School (journ.) (SAUS)
J School Libr Ass Qd... Journal. School Library Association of Queensland [*A publication*]
J Sch Pharm Univ Tehran... Journal. School of Pharmacy. University of Tehran (journ.) (SAUS)
J Sci......... Journal of Science (journ.) (SAUS)
JSCI......... Journal of the Society of Chemical Industry (SAUO)
JSCI......... Journal of the Society of Chemical Industry (journ.) (SAUS)
J Sci Assoc Maharajahs Coll... Journal. Science Association. Maharajahs College (SAUS)
J Sci Busan Natl Univ... Journal of Science. Busan National University (journ.) (SAUS)
JSCIC........ Joint Space Command Intelligence Center [*Air Force*]
J Sci Club... Journal of the Science Club (journ.) (SAUS)
J Sci Coll Gen Educ Unir Tokushima... Journal of Science. College of General Education. University of Tokushima (journ.) (SAUS)
J Sci Comput... Journal of Scientific Computing (journ.) (SAUS)
J Sci Edc Chungbuk Natl Univ... Journal of Science Education. Chungbuk National University (journ.) (SAUS)
J Sci Educ Chonnam Natl Univ... Journal of Science Education. Chonnam National University (journ.) (SAUS)
J Sci Educ Sci Educ Res Inst Teach Coll Kyungpook Univ... Journal of Science Education. Science Education Research Institute Teachers College. Kyungpook University (journ.) (SAUS)
J Sci Educ Technol... Journal of Science Education and Technology (journ.) (SAUS)
J Scient Ind Res... Journal of Scientific and Industrial Research (journ.) (SAUS)
J Sci Food Agric Abstr... Journal of the Science of Food and Agriculture. Abstracts (journ.) (SAUS)

J Sci Hirosbima Univ Ser A Math Phys Chem... Journal of Science. Hiroshima University. Series A. Mathematics, Physics, Chemistry (journ.) (SAUS)
J Sci Hiroshima Univ... Journal of Hiroshima University (journ.) (SAUS)
J Sci Hiroshima Univ... Journal of Science. Hiroshima University (journ.) (SAUS)
J Sci Hiroshima Univ A... Journal of Hiroshima University, Series A (journ.) (SAUS)
J Sci Hiroshima Univ B... Journal of Hiroshima University, Series B (journ.) (SAUS)
J Sci Hiroshima Univ Ser A-II... Journal of Science. Hiroshima University. Series A-II (journ.) (SAUS)
J Sci Hiroshima Univ Ser B Div 2 Bot... Journal of Science. Hiroshima University. Series B. Division 2. Botany (journ.) (SAUS)
J Sci Ind Res Sect A... Journal of Scientific and Industrial Research. Section A. General (journ.) (SAUS)
J Sci Ind Res Sect B... Journal of Scientific and Industrial Research. Section B (journ.) (SAUS)
J Sci Ind Res Sect D... Journal of Scientific and Industrial Research. Section D Technolgy (journ.) (SAUS)
J Sci Instrum Phys Ind... Journal of Scientific Instruments and Physics in Industry (journ.) (SAUS)
J Sci Instrum Suppl... Journal of Scientific Instruments. Supplement (journ.) (SAUS)
J Sci Labor... Journal of Science of Labor (journ.) (SAUS)
J Sci Labour Prt 2... Journal of Science of Labour. Part 2 (journ.) (SAUS)
J Sci Res... Journal of Scientific Research (journ.) (SAUS)
J Sci Res Banaras Hindu Univ... Journal of Scientific Research. Banaras Hindu University (journ.) (SAUS)
J Sci Res Banaras Hindu Univ... Journal of Scientific Research of the Banaras Hindu University (journ.) (SAUS)
J Sci Res Counc Jam... Journal. Scientific Research Council of Jamaica (journ.) (SAUS)
J Sci Res Plants & Med... Journal of Scientific Research in Plants and Medicines (journ.) (SAUS)
J Sci Soc Thail... Journal of the Science Society of Thai- land (journ.) (SAUS)
J Sci Soc Thiland... Journal. Science Society of Thailand (journ.) (SAUS)
JSCLC....... Joint Standing Committee on Library Cooperation [*British*] (NITA)
JSCM........ Japanese Society for Contemporary Music (SAUO)
JSCM........ Japan Society for Composite Materials (SAUO)
JSCM........ Joint Service Commendation Medal [*Military decoration*] (AFM)
JSCM........ JSC [*Johnson Space Center*] Manual [*NASA*] (NASA)
JSCMA...... Journal. South Carolina Medical Association (journ.) (SAUS)
J S C Med Assoc... Journal of the South Carolina Medical Association (journ.) (SAUS)
J S C Med Assoc... Journal-South Carolina Medical Association (SAUO)
J SC Med Assoc... Journal. South Carolina Medical Association (journ.) (SAUS)
JSCMPO.... Joint Service Cruise Missile Program Office (MCD)
JSCNOET.... Joint Standing Committee on Nuclear and Other Energy Technologies (SAUO)
JSCO........ Joint Staff Communications Office [*Military*] (AABC)
JSCO........ Journal Status Central Operations Table (SAA)
JSCOM...... Joint Services Commendation Medal (RDA)
JS Com Ind L... Journal. Society of Commercial and Industrial Law [*A publication*] (ILCA)
J S Com Ind L... Journal. Society of Commercial and Industrial Law (journ.) (SAUS)
J S Cosm Ch... Journal. Society of Cosmetic Chemists (journ.) (SAUS)
J Scott...... Reporter, English Common Bench Reports [*A publication*] (DLA)
J Scott As Geogr Teach... Journal. Scottish Association of Geography Teachers (journ.) (SAUS)
JSCP........ Joint Strategic Capabilities Plan [*Military*]
JSCR........ Job Schedule Change Request
JSCR........ Joint Standing Committee Report (HEAS)
Jscript....... Java Script [*Microsoft Corp.*]
JSCS........ Job Shop Control System (MHDI)
JSCS........ Joint Strategic Connectivity Committee [*Joint Chiefs of Staff*]
JSCS........ Joint Strategic Connectivity Staff
JSCS........ Junior Slovak Catholic Sokol (EA)
JSCSA....... Journal of Statistical Computation and Simulation (journ.) (SAUS)
JSCSC....... Joint Service Command and Staff College (SAUO)
JSCU........ Joint Supply Council for Union of South Africa [*World War II*]
JSCU........ Sea Containers America [*Intermodal shipping container symbol*] (TVRC)
JSCUD....... Journal of Science Education. Chungbuk National University (journ.) (SAUS)
J Scunthorpe Mus Soc... Journal. Scunthorpe Museum Society (journ.) (SAUS)
JSC-WCRP... Joint Scientific Committee for the WCRP (SAUS)
JSC/WCRP... Joint Steering Committee of the World Climate Reseach Programme (SAUS)
JSCZ........ Flexi-Van Leasing [*Intermodal trailer symbol*]
JSD.......... Doctor of Judicial [*or Juridical*] Science [*or Doctor of the Science of Law*]
JSD.......... Doctor of Juristic Science (SAUS)
JSD.......... Doctor of the Science of Law (SAUS)
JSD.......... Jackson Structured Design (COE)
JSD.......... Jackson System Development [*Systems development methodology*] (NITA)
JSD.......... Jalousie Storm Door (SAUS)
JSD.......... Jatiya Samajtantrik Dal [*National Socialist Party*] [*Bangladesh*] [*Political party*] (PPW)
JSD.......... Jeunesse Social Democrate [*Social Democratic Youth*] [*Malagasy*]
JSD.......... Jewish Society for the Deaf [*Later, New York Society for the Deaf*] (EA)
JSD.......... JiJi Securities Data Service [*JiJi Press Ltd.*] [*Japan*] [*Information service or system*] (CRD)
JSD.......... Joint Standards Documents (SAUO)
JSD.......... Joint System Development (SAUS)
JSD.......... Judicial Science Doctor (SAUS)
JSD.......... Justification Service Digit [*Telecommunications*] (TEL)
JSD.......... Stratford, CT [*Location identifier*] [*FAA*] (FAAL)
JSDA........ Japanese Securities Dealers Association (ECON)
JSDA........ Japanese Self-Defense Agency
JSDA........ Japan Self-Defense Agency (SAUS)
JSDA........ Jones Soda Co. [*NASDAQ symbol*] (QUAN)
JSDC........ Joint Service Defence College (SAUO)
JSDC........ Joint System Development Corporated (SAUS)
JSDF......... Japanese Self-Defense Forces (SAUS)
JSDF......... Japan Self-Defense Force (CINC)
JSDF......... Jin Shin Do Foundation for Bodymind Acupressure (EA)
JSDFA....... Japan Self Defence Force Agency (SAUO)
JSDFA....... Japan Self-Defense Forces Academy (SAUO)
JSDFs....... Japan Self-Defense Forces (SAUO)
JSDIC........ Joint Services Detailed Interrogation Center (SAUO)
JSDK........ Java Servlet Development Kit (SAUS)
JSDM........ June, September, December, and March [*Denotes quarterly payments of interest or dividends in these months*] [*Business term*]
JSDN........ Juvenile Scleroderma Network [*Association*] (EA)
JSDOP........ Joint Strategic Defense Operations Plan (SAUO)
JSDP........ Jewish Social Democratic Party [*Political party*] (BJA)
JSDTI........ John S. Donaldson Technical Institute (SAUO)
JSDTI........ Sohn S Donaldson Technical Institute (SAUS)
JSE.......... Jakarta Stock Exchange (SAUO)
JSE.......... Jam Strobe Extractor
JSE.......... Johannesburg Stock Exchange
JSE.......... JOPES Support Element (SAUO)
JSEA......... Jesuit Secondary Education Association (EA)
JSEAC....... Joint Societies Employment Advisory Committee
J-SEAD...... Joint Suppression of Enemy Air Defenses [*Military*] (INF)
J Sea Res... Journal of Sea Research [*A publication*] (PABS)
J SE Asian Hist... Journal of Southeast Asian History (journ.) (SAUS)
J Seattle King Cty Dent Soc... Journal. Seattle-King County Dental Society (journ.) (SAUS)
JSEC......... Joint Services Electrical and Electronics Committee (SAUS)
J Sec Ed.... Journal of Secondary Education (journ.) (SAUS)
JSEDM...... Japan Society of Electrical-Discharge Machining (SAUO)
JSEE......... Japanese Society for Engineering Education (SAUO)
JSEE......... Japan Society for Engineering Education (SAUS)
JSEI......... Joint Second Echelon Interdiction
J Seismol Soc Jpn... Journal of the Seismological Society of Japan (journ.) (SAUS)
JSE/J........ Japanese Journal of Ethnology. Japanese Society of Ethnology. Tokyo (SAUO)
JSE/J........ Japanese Journal of Ethnology. Japanese Society of Ethnology. Tokyo (journ.) (SAUS)
J Semant... Journal of Semantics (journ.) (SAUS)
J Senticust ICs... Journal of Semicustom ICs (journ.) (SAUS)
JSEOD....... Joint Service Explosive Ordnance Disposal (SAUS)
JSEODOC... Joint Service Explosive Ordnance Disposal Operations Centre (SAUO)
J Seoul Womans Coll... Journal. Seoul Womans College (journ.) (SAUS)
JSEP......... Job Skills Education Program [*Military*]
JSEP......... Joint Services Electronics Program [*Military*]
J Serb Chem Soc... Journal of the Serbian Chemical Society (journ.) (SAUS)
J Serb Chem Soc... Journal. Serbian Chemical Society (journ.) (SAUS)
J Seric Sci Jpn... Journal of Sericultural Science of Japan (journ.) (SAUS)
JSESP....... Joint Surface Effect Ships Program (SAUS)
JSESPO..... Joint [*Maritime Administration - Navy*] Surface-Effects Ship Program Office
JSET......... Journal of Sex Education and Therapy (journ.) (SAUS)
JSeTU....... Tohoku University, Sendai, Japan [*Library symbol*] [*Library of Congress*] (LCLS)
J Severance Union Med Coll... Journal. Severance Union Medical College (journ.) (SAUS)
J Sex Marital Ther... Journal of Sex and Marital Therapy (journ.) (SAUS)
JSEXP....... Joint Services Explosives Program (MCD)
J Sex Res... Journal of Sex Research (journ.) (SAUS)
JSEY......... Jersey [*One of the Channel Islands*] (ROG)
JSF.......... Japan Scholarship Foundation (EA)
JSF.......... Jesse Stuart Foundation (EA)
JSF.......... Jewish Student Federation (SAUO)
JSF.......... Job Services File
JSF.......... Joint Security Force [*Army*] (INF)
JSF.......... Joint Stipulated Facts and Figures (AAGC)
JSF.......... Joint Strike Fighter
JSF.......... Junctor Switch Frame [*Telecommunications*] (TEL)
JSF.......... Junior Statesman Foundation (SAUO)
JSF.......... Junior Statesmen Foundation (EA)
JSFA......... Journal of Science of Food and Agriculture (SAUS)
JSFA......... Journal of the Science of Food and Agriculture (journ.) (SAUS)
JSFC......... Jack Scalia Fan Club (EA)
JSFC......... Japanese-Soviet Fisheries Commission (SAUS)
JSFC......... Japanese-Soviet Fisheries Commission for the Northwest Pacific
JSFC......... Joe Stampley Fan Club [*Defunct*] (EA)
JSFM......... Japan Society for Strength and Fracture of Materials (SAUO)
JSFP......... Joint Service Fuze Plan [*Army*]
JSFT......... Health and Safety Department (SAUO)
JSFU......... Joint Services Flail Unit (SAUS)
JSFZ......... Jefferson Smurfit [*Federal Railroad Administration identification code*]
JSG.......... Jamaica (BWI) Study Group [*Defunct*] (EA)

JSG .... Jamaica Study Group (SAUO)
JSG .... Jewish Socialists' Group [*United Kingdom*] (EAIO)
JSG .... Job Seekers Guide to Private and Public Companies [*A publication*]
JSG .... Joint Study Group (CARL)
JSG .... Jugoslavia Study Group (EA)
JSGCC .... Joint Service Guidance and Control Committee
JSGLL .... Japanese Studies in German Language and Literature (journ.) (SAUS)
JSGMF ...... John Simon Guggenheim Memorial Foundation (SAUO)
JSGMRAM... Joint Study Group for Material Resource Allocation Methodology (SAUO)
JSGMRAM... Joint Study Group on Military Resources Allocation Methodology (SAUO)
JSGOMRAM... Joint Study Group on Military Resources Allocation Methodology (MCD)
JSGPM ...... Joint Service General Purpose Mask [*Army*]
JSGQ .... JSG Trucking Company [*Common carrier symbol*]
J S Gr .... Greens Law Reports (journ.) (SAUS)
JSGRP .... Jewish Symbols in the Greco-Roman Period [*A publication*] (BJA)
JSG/TCCS... Joint Standardization Group for Tactical Communications and Control Systems (SAUO)
JSH .... Jetstream Ltd. [*Hungary*] [*ICAO designator*] (FAAC)
JSH .... Journal of Social History (journ.) (SAUS)
JSH .... Journal of Southern History [*A publication*] (BRI)
JSHA .... Johannes Schwalm Historical Association (EA)
JSHABP ..... Journal. South African Speech and Hearing Association (journ.) (SAUS)
J Shangbi Coll Text Tecbnol... Journal. Shanghai College of Textile Technology (journ.) (SAUS)
J Shanghai Jiaotong Univ... Journal of the Shanghai Jiaotong University (journ.) (SAUS)
J Shanghai Sci Inst Sect 1... Journal. Shanghai Science Institute. Section 1. Experimental Biology and Medicine (journ.) (SAUS)
J Shanghai Sci Inst Sect 1... Journal. Shanghai Science Institute. Section 1. Mathematics, Astronomy, Physics, Geophysics, Chemistry and Allied Sciences (journ.) (SAUS)
J Shanghai Sci Inst Sect 2... Journal. Shanghai Science Institute. Section 2. Geology Palaeontology, Mineralogy and Petrology (journ.) (SAUS)
J Shanghai Sci Inst Sect 3... Journal. Shanghai Science Institute. Section 3. Systematic and Morphological Biology (journ.) (SAUS)
J Shanghai Sci Inst Sect 5... Journal. Shanghai Science Institute. Section 5. General (journ.) (SAUS)
J Shanxi Univ Nat Sci Ed... Journal. Shanxi University. Natural Science Edition (journ.) (SAUS)
J SHASE .... Journal. Society of Heating, Air conditioning and Sanitary Engineers of Japan (SAUO)
J SHASE .... Journal. Society of Heating, Air conditioning and Sanitary Engineers of Japan (journ.) (SAUS)
J Shaw...... John Shaw's Justiciary Reports [*1848-52*] [*Scotland*] [*A publication*] (DLA)
J Shaw Just... John Shaw's Justiciary Reports [*1848-52*] [*Scotland*] [*A publication*] (DLA)
JSHDFC ..... Jean S. Harris Defense Fund Committee (EA)
JSHEA .... Journal of School Halth (journ.) (SAUS)
J Sheffield Univ Metall Soc... Journal of the Sheffield University Metallurgical Society (journ.) (SAUS)
J Sheffield Univ Met Soc... Journal. Sheffield University Metallurgical Society (journ.) (SAUS)
J Shellfish Res... Journal of Shellfish Research (journ.) (SAUS)
JSHG .... Hokkai Gakuen University, Sapporo, Japan [*Library symbol*] [*Library of Congress*] (LCLS)
JSHG/J ...... Japanese Journal of Human Genetics. Japan Society of Human Genetics. Tokyo (SAUO)
JSHG/J ...... Japanese Journal of Human Genetics. Japan Society of Human Genetics. Tokyo (journ.) (SAUS)
J Shimane Med Assoc... Journal. Shimane Medical Association (journ.) (SAUS)
J Shimonoseki Coll Fish... Journal. Shimonoseki College of Fisheries (journ.) (SAUS)
J Shimonoseki Univ Fish... Journal. Shimonoseki University of Fisheries (journ.) (SAUS)
J Ship Prod... Journal of Ship Production (journ.) (SAUS)
J Ship Res... Journal of Ship Research (journ.) (SAUS)
J Shivaji Univ... Journal. Shivaji University (journ.) (SAUS)
J Shnw Jt... John Shaws Justiciary Reports (journ.) (SAUS)
J Shoreline Manage... Journal of Shoreline Management (journ.) (SAUS)
J Shoulder Elbow Surg... Journal of Shoulder and Elbow Surgery (journ.) (SAUS)
JSHQ .... Job Safety & Health Quarterly (SAUO)
JSHR .... Journal of Speech and Hearing Research (journ.) (SAUS)
JSHS .... Jewish Society for Human Service [*British*]
JSHS .... Junior Science and Humanities Symposia [*Terminated, 1977*]
JSHS .... Junior Science and Humanities Symposium (SAUO)
J-S H Sch Clearing House... Junior-Senior High School Clearing House (journ.) (SAUS)
JSHT......... Japan Society of Heat Treatment (SAUO)
J S Ht .... Journal of Southern History (journ.) (SAUS)
JSI .... Jacobi Semi-Iterative (SAUS)
JSI .... Jansky Screening Index [*Psychology*] (DAVI)
JSI .... Japanese Studies Institute (SAUS)
JSI .... Java Script Index (SAUS)
JSI .... Job Satisfaction Inventory [*Guidance*]
JSI .... Job Schedule Items (MCD)
JSI .... Job Search Information
JSI .... Job Search Inventory [*Test*] (TMMY)
JSI .... Job Sensitivity Inventory [*Interpersonal skills and attitudes test*]
JSI .... Job Severity Index (LDOE)
JSI .... Job Step Index [*Computer science*] (IAA)
JSI .... Job Style Indicator [*Test*] (TMMY)
JSI .... John Snow Inc. (SAUO)
JSI .... Joint Support Item (DNAB)
JSI .... Journal. American Society for Information Science (journ.) (SAUS)
JSI .... Journal of Social Issues (journ.) (SAUS)
JSI .... JumboSports, Inc. [*NYSE symbol*] (SG)
JSI .... Skiathos [*Greece*] [*Airport symbol*] (OAG)
JSIA .... Japan Software Industry Association (CIST)
JSIA .... Joint Service Induction Area
JSIA .... Justice System Improvement Act [*1979*]
JSIAM .... Japan Society of Industrial and Applied Mathematics (SAUO)
J Siam Soc... Journal. Siam Society (journ.) (SAUS)
JSIC .... Joint Securities Industry Committee (SAUS)
JSIC .... Joint Space Command Intelligence Center (SAUO)
JSIC .... Joint Space Intelligence Center
J-SIDS....... Joint Service Intrusion Detection System [*Military*] (INF)
JSIF.......... Japan Shipbuilding Industry Foundation (SAUO)
JSIF.......... Japan Spinners Inspecting Officer Foundation (SAUS)
JSIID .... Joint Service Interior Intrusion Detection Devices [*Military*] (MCD)
JSIIDS....... Joint Service Interior Intrusion Detection System [*Military*]
JSIIDS....... Joint-Services Interior Intruder Detection System (SAUS)
JSIM......... Joint Service Intelligence Manual
JSIMS .... Joint Simulation System [*DoD*]
JSIN.......... Journal. Society for International Numismatics (journ.) (SAUS)
J Singap Natl Acad Sci... Journal of the Singapore National Academy of Science (journ.) (SAUS)
J Singapore Paediatr Soc... Journal of the Singapore Paediatric Society (SAUO)
J Singapore Paediatr Soc... Journal of the Singapore Paediatric Society (journ.) (SAUS)
J Singapore Pediatr Soc... Journal. Singapore Paediatric Society (journ.) (SAUS)
JSIP .... Job Service Improvement Program [*Department of Labor*]
JSIPS........ Joint Service Image Processing System (SAUS)
JSIPS........ Joint Services Imagery Processing System [*Military*]
JSIPS........ Joint Strategic Integrated Planning Staff (CCCA)
JSIPS........ Joint Strategic Integration Planning Staff (SAUO)
JSIPS........ Joint Systems Integration Planning Staff [*Air Force*]
JSIPS-N..... Joint Service Imagery Processing System-Navy (SAUS)
JSIS .... Japan Society of Iron and Steel (SAUO)
JSIS .... Jeumont-Schneider Industrial Systems (EFIS)
JSISD........ Journal of Current Social Issues (journ.) (SAUS)
JSIT.......... JDS Information Trace (SAUO)
JSIX.......... Jahncke Service [*Private rail car owner code*]
JSJ........... Journal for the Study of Judaism (journ.) (SAUS)
JSJHS .... Journal of the Southern Jewish Historical Society (SAUO)
JSJHS .... Journal of the Southern Jewish Historical Society (journ.) (SAUS)
JSK .... St. Cloud, MN [*Location identifier*] [*FAA*] (FAAL)
J Skt......... Jack Socket (SAUS)
JSL .... Japanese Studies in German Language and Literature (journ.) (SAUS)
JSL .... Jet Select Logic (MCD)
JSL .... Job Shop Labor (ACAE)
JSL .... Job Specification Language
JSL .... Johnson Society of London (EA)
JSL .... Joint Stock List [*Military*] (AFIT)
JSL .... Joint Support List [*Military*]
JSL .... Journal of Surgical Research (journ.) (SAUS)
JSL .... Journal of Symbolic Logic (journ.) (SAUS)
JSL .... Journal. School of Languages (journ.) (SAUS)
JSL .... Jurong Shipyard Limited (SAUO)
JSLAE .... Japanese Society for Laboratory Animal and Environment (GVA)
JSLB......... Japan Society of London. Bulletin (journ.) (SAUS)
JSLB......... Joint Services Liaison Staff (SAUS)
JSLB......... Joint Stock Land Banks [*New Deal*]
JSLC......... Jiuquan Satellite Launch Center (IGSL)
JSLE......... Japan Society of Lubrication Engineers (SAUO)
J Sleep Res... Journal of Sleep Research (journ.) (SAUS)
JSLGWCM.. Joint Services LASER-Guided Weapons Countermeasures (MCD)
JSLHR....... Journal of Speech, Language, and Hearing Research (SAUS)
JSLI.......... Johnson-Sea-Link I [*A submersible for deep sea studies*]
JSLIST ...... Joint Service Lightweight Integrated Suit Technology [*Military*] [*Chemical warfare*]
JSLO......... Joint Services Liaison Organization (SAUO)
JSLPA .... Journal of Speech-Language Pathology and Audiology (SAUS)
JSLPC .... Joint Service Local Planning Committee
JSLQ......... Journal of Symbolic Logic Quarterly (journ.) (SAUS)
JSLRMDO... Joint Service Large Rocket Motor Disposal Office [*Army*]
JSLS......... Japan Society of Library Science (NITA)
JSLS......... Joint Services Liaison Staff [*British*]
JSLWG ...... Joint Spacelab Working Group [*NASA*] (NASA)
JSM.......... Jesus Salvator Mundi [*Jesus the Savior of the World*] [*Latin*] (ROG)
JSM.......... Job Stream Manager [*Computer science*] (IAA)
JSM.......... Joint Staff Memorandum (MCD)
JSM.......... Joint Staff Mission [*British*] [*World War II*]
JSM.......... Jose de San Martin [*Argentina*] [*Airport symbol*] (OAG)
JSM.......... Journal of Synagogue Music (journ.) (SAUS)
JSM.......... Journal of Systems Management (journ.) (SAUS)
JSM.......... Judicial Science Master (SAUS)
JSM.......... Juilliard School of Music (SAUO)
JSM.......... Master of Judicial Science
JSMA........ Joint Sealer Manufacturers Association
J Smal Bus Mgt... Journal of Small Business Management (journ.) (SAUS)
JSMB........ Japan Society of Mechanical Engineers (SAUO)
JSMB........ Joint Sealift Movements Board [*Military*] (AFM)

JSMC........ Joint Staff Message Control (SAUS)
JSMDA...... Japan Ship Machinery Development Association (SAUO)
JSME........ Japan Society of Mechanical Engineers
JSME........ Joint Soil Moisture Experiment
JSMEBE..... Japan Society of Medical Electronics and Biological Engineering (SAUO)
JSMG........ Joint Service Materiel Group
JSMH........ JS Mobile Homes [*NCIC trailer make code*]
JSMIN....... Jasmine (ABBR)
JSMMART... Journal. Society for Mass Media and Resource Technology (journ.) ((SAUS)
J Smooth Muscle Res... Journal of Smooth Muscle Research (journ.) (SAUS)
JSMP........ JSIMS [*Joint Simulation (System)*] Master Plan [*DoD*]
JSMPE...... Journal of the Society of Motion Picture Engineers (SAUO)
JSMPE...... Journal of the Society of Motion Picture Engineers (journ.) (SAUS)
JSmrfG...... Jefferson Smurfit Group PLC [*Associated Press*] (SAG)
JSMRU...... Joint Service Medical Rehabilitation Unit (SAUS)
JSMS........ Japan Society of Materials Science (SAUO)
JSMS........ Job Service Matching Systems [*US Employment Service*] [*Department of Labor*]
JSMSM...... Joint Service Meritorious Service Medal [*Military decoration*]
JSMTC...... Joint Service Mountain Training Centre (SAUO)
JSMUG-K... Joint US Military Affairs Group, Korea (SAUO)
JSN.......... Job Sequence Number
JSN.......... Joint Space Narrowing [*Medicine*]
JSN.......... Junction Switch Number (SAUS)
JSNA........ Jaspers Society of North America (EA)
JSNM........ Japan Society of New Metals (AAEL)
JSNOOFC... Judson Scott Is Number 1 Official Fan Club (EA)
JSNP........ Japanese Single Nucleotide Polymorphisms (MHID)
JSNP........ Japan Satellite News Pool (SAUO)
JSNPE....... Joint Staff Nuclear Planning Element (MCD)
JSNPE....... Joint Strategic Nuclear Planning Element (SAUO)
JSNT......... Johnson Tower (SAUS)
JSNT......... Journal for the Study of the New Testament (journ.) (SAUS)
JSNUAA..... Jackson State University National Alumni Association (EA)
JSO.......... Jackson Symphony Orchestra (SAUO)
JSO.......... Jacksonville Symphony Orchestra (SAUO)
JSO.......... Jacksonville, TX [*Location identifier*] [*FAA*] (FAAL)
JSO.......... Job-Specific Orientation (SAUS)
JSO.......... Joint Service Office
JSO.......... Joint Services Organization (SAUO)
JSO.......... Joint Specialty Officer (DOMA)
JSOA........ Joint Special Operations Agency (SAUO)
JSOA........ Joint Special Operations Area [*Military*] (INF)
JSOACC..... Joint Special Operations Air Component Commander (SAUO)
J So AL...... Journal of South Asian Literature (journ.) (SAUS)
JSOC........ Joint Ship Operations Center
JSOC........ Joint Ship Operations Committee
JSOC........ Joint Special Operations Center (MCD)
JSOC........ Joint Special Operations Command [*Military*]
JSOC........ Joint Strategic Operations Command (MCD)
J Soc Arch... Journal. Society of Archivists (journ.) (SAUS)
J Soc Archit Hist... Journal of the Society of Architectural Historians (SAUO)
J Soc Archit Hist... Journal of the Society of Architectural Historians (journ.) (SAUS)
J Soc Army Hist Res... Journal. Society for Army Historical Research (journ.) (SAUS)
J Soc Arts... Journal of the Society of Arts (journ.) (SAUS)
J Soc Arts... Journal. Society of Arts (journ.) (SAUS)
J Soc Automot Eng... Journal. Society of Automotive Engineers (journ.) (SAUS)
J Soc Automot Eng Jpn Inc... Journal. Society of Automotive Engineers of Japan, Inc. (journ.) (SAUS)
J Soc Automot Engrs Australas... Journal. Society of Automotive Engineers of Australasia (SAUO)
J Soc Bibliogr Nat Hist... Journal. Society for the Bibliography of Natural History (journ.) (SAUS)
J Soc Chem Ind Vic... Journal. Society of Chemical Industry of Victoria (journ.) (SAUS)
J Soc Comp Leg... Journal. Society of Comparative Legislation (journ.) (SAUS)
J Soc Cosmet Chem... Journal of the Society of Cosmetic Chemists (SAUO)
J Soc Cosmet Chem... Journal of the Society of Cosmetic Chemists (journ.) (SAUS)
J Soc Cosmet Chem... Journal. Society of Cosmetic Chemists (journ.) (SAUS)
J Soc Dairy Technol... Journal. Society of Dairy Technology (journ.) (SAUS)
J Soc Dyers Color... Journal of the Society of Dyers and Colorists (journ.) (SAUS)
J Soc Econ Devel... Journal of Social and Economic Development [*A publication*] (JLIT)
J Soc Eng Miner Springs... Journal. Society of Engineers for Mineral Springs (journ.) (SAUS)
J Soc Environ Eng... Journal of the Society of Environmental Engineers (journ.) (SAUS)
J Soc Exp Agric... Journal. Society of Experimental Agriculturists (journ.) (SAUS)
J Soc Glass Technol... Journal. Society of Glass Technology (journ.) (SAUS)
J Soc H..... Journal of Social History [*A publication*] (BRI)
J Soc Health Syst... Journal of the Society for Health Systems (SAUO)
J Soc Health Syst... Journal of the Society for Health Systems (journ.) (SAUS)
J Social and Econ Studies... Journal of Social and Economic Studies (journ.) (SAUS)
J Social and Pol Studies... Journal of Social and Political Studies (journ.) (SAUS)
J Social Casework... Journal of Social Casework (journ.) (SAUS)
J Social Forces... Journal of Social Forces (journ.) (SAUS)
J Social Pol and Econ Studies... Journal of Social, Political and Economic Studies (journ.) (SAUS)
J Soc Inf Disp... Journal of the Society for Information Display [*A publication*] (CABS)
J Soc Instrum and Control... Journal. Society of Instrument and Control Engineers (journ.) (SAUS)
J Soc Instrum Control Eng... Journal of the Society of Instrument and Control Engineers (journ.) (SAUS)
J Soc Int Dev... Journal of the Society for International Development (journ.) (SAUS)
J Soc Int Dev... Journal of the Society for International Development. Society for International Development. Rome (SAUO)
J Socio-Econ... Journal of Socio-Economics [*A publication*] (JLIT)
J Soc Leath Technol Chem... Journal. Society of Leather Technologists and Chemists (journ.) (SAUS)
J Soc Leath Trades Chem... Journal. Society of Leather Trades Chemists (journ.) (SAUS)
J Soc Mater Sci Jpn... Journal of the Society of Materials Science, Japan (journ.) (SAUS)
J Soc Nav Archit Jpn... Journal. Society of Naval Architects of Japan (journ.) (SAUS)
J Soc Nav Arch Japan... Journal. Society of Naval Architects of Japan (journ.) (SAUS)
J Soc Non-Destr Test... Journal. Society for Non-Destructive Testing (journ.) (SAUS)
J Soc Occup Med... Journal of the Society of Occupational Medicine (journ.) (SAUS)
J Soc Pet Eng... Journal. Society of Petroleum Engineers (journ.) (SAUS)
J Soc Photogr Sci and Technol Jpn... Journal. Society of Photographic Science and Technology of Japan (journ.) (SAUS)
J Soc Photo Opt Instrum Eng... Journal. Society of Photo-Optical Instrumentation Engineers (journ.) (SAUS)
J Soc Photo Sci Technol Jpn... Journal of the Society of Photographic Science and Technology of Japan (journ.) (SAUS)
J Soc Psych Res... Journal. Society for Psychical Research (journ.) (SAUS)
J Soc Pub Teach Law N S... Journal. Society of Public Teachers of Law. New Series (journ.) (SAUS)
J Soc Radiol Prot... Journal. Society for Radiological Protection (journ.) (SAUS)
J Soc Res... Journal of Social Research (journ.) (SAUS)
J Soc Res Adm... Journal of the Society of Research Administrators (journ.) (SAUS)
J Soc Rheol... Journal of the Society of Rheology (journ.) (SAUS)
J Soc Rheol Jpn... Journal of the Society of Rheology of Japan (journ.) (SAUS)
J Soc Rubber Ind... Journal of the Society of Rubber Industry (journ.) (SAUS)
J Soc Sci... Journal of the Social Sciences [*A publication*] (JLIT)
J Soc Sci Hum... Journal of Social Sciences and Humanities (journ.) (SAUS)
J Soc Sci PhotogrJpn... Journal. Society of Scientific Photography of Japan (journ.) (SAUS)
J Soc Ther... Journal of Social Therapy (journ.) (SAUS)
J Soc Underwater Technol... Journal. Society for Undetwater Technology (journ.) (SAUS)
J Soc Welfare L... Journal of Social Welfare Law (journ.) (SAUS)
J Soc Work & Hum Sex... Journal of Social Work and Human Sexuality (journ.) (SAUS)
J Soc'y Comp Leg... Journal. Society of Comparative Legislation [*A publication*] (DLA)
J Soe Archit Hist... Journal of the Society of Architectural Historians. Louisville (SAUO)
JSOF......... Joint Special Operations Force (SAUO)
JSOFI........ Joint Special Operations Force Institute [*DoD*]
J Soil Biol & Etnl... Journal of Soil Biology and Ecology (journ.) (SAUS)
J Soil Mech Found Div; Ame... Journal of the Soil Mechanics and Foundations Division; Proceedings of the America (SAUO)
J Soil Mech Found Div Am Soc Civ Eng... Journal. Soil Mechanics and Foundations Division. American Society of Civil Engineers (journ.) (SAUS)
J Soil Sci... Journal of Soil Science (journ.) (SAUS)
J Soil Sci Soc Am... Journal. Soil Science Society of America (journ.) (SAUS)
J Soil Water Conserv India... Journal of Soil and Water Conservation in India (journ.) (SAUS)
J Sol Energy Eng... Journal of Solar Energy Engineering (journ.) (SAUS)
J Sol Energy Res... Journal of Solar Energy Research (journ.) (SAUS)
J Sol Energy S Korea... Journal. Solar Energy Society of Korea (journ.) (SAUS)
J Solid Lubr... Journal of Solid Lubrication (journ.) (SAUS)
J Solid-Phase Biochem... Journal of Solid-Phase Biochemistry (journ.) (SAUS)
J Solid State Chem... Journal of Solid State Chemistry (journ.) (SAUS)
J Solid Wastes... Journal of Solid Wastes (journ.) (SAUS)
J Solid Wastes Manage... Journal of Solid Wastes Management (journ.) (SAUS)
J Sol Sci Soc Philipp... Journal. Soil Science Society of the Philippines (journ.) (SAUS)
J Somerset Mines Res Group... Journal. Somerset Mines Research Group (journ.) (SAUS)
JSON........ Joint Services Operational Notice
JSON........ Josephson International Inc. (SAUO)
JSONOM.... Joint Specialty Officer Nominee (DOMA)
J Soonchunhyang Coll... Journal. Soonchunhyang College (journ.) (SAUS)
JSOP........ Dominican Oblates of Jesus (Spain) (TOCD)
JSOP........ Joint School of Photography (SAUO)
JSOP........ Joint Strategic Objectives Plan [*Military*]
JSOR........ Joint Services Operational Requirement [*Military*]
JSOR........ Joint Services Organizational Requirements (ACAE)
JSOR........ Joint Statements of Requirements (DOMA)
JSOR........ Joint Systems Operational Requirements (SAUO)
JSOR........ Journal. Society of Oriental Research (journ.) (SAUS)
JSORD...... Joint System Operational Requirements [*Document*] (DOMA)
JSORD...... Joint Systems Operational Requirements Document (SAUO)
JSORS....... Joint Service Operational Requirement Statement (MCD)
JSOSE....... Joint Special Operations Support Element [*DoD*]

JSOTF........ Joint Special Operations Task Force [*DoD*]
J Sound Vib... Journal of Sound and Vibration [*A publication*] (CABS)
J South Afr Chem Inst... Journal. South African Chemical Institute (journ.) (SAUS)
J South Afr Stud... Journal of Southern African Studies (journ.) (SAUS)
J South Afr Wildl Manage Ass... Journal. Southern African Wildlife Management Association (journ.) (SAUS)
J South Am Earth Sci... Journal of South American Earth Sciences (SAUS)
J South Calif Dent Assistants Assoc... Journal. Southern California Dental Assistants Association (journ.) (SAUS)
J South Calif Dent Assoc... Journal. Southern California Dental Association (journ.) (SAUS)
J South California Dent Ass... Journal. Southern California Dental Association (SAUS)
J South Calif State Dent Assoc... Journal. Southem California State Dental Association (journ.) (SAUS)
J Southeast Asian Stud... Journal of Southeast Asian Studies (journ.) (SAUS)
J Southeast Sect Am Water Works Ass... Journal. Southeastern Section. American Water Works Association (journ.) (SAUS)
J South Orthop Assoc... Journal of the Southern Orthopaedic Association (SAUO)
J South Orthop Assoc... Journal of the Southern Orthopaedic Association (journ.) (SAUS)
J South Res... Journal of Southern Research (journ.) (SAUS)
J Southwest... Journal of the Southwest (journ.) (SAUS)
J South West Afr Sc Soc... Journal. South West African Scientific Society (journ.) (SAUS)
J Sov Cardiovasc Res... Journal of Soviet Cardiovascular Research (journ.) (SAUS)
J Soviet Math... Journal of Soviet Mathematics (journ.) (SAUS)
J Sov Laser Res... Journal of Soviet Laser Research (journ.) (SAUS)
J Sov Oncol... Journal of Soviet Oncology (journ.) (SAUS)
JSOW........ Joint Service Stand-Off Weapon (SAUS)
JSOW........ Joint Standoff Weapons Program
JSOW........ Joint Statement of Work (ABAC)
JSP.......... Jacketed Soft-Point [*Ammunition*]
JSP.......... Jackson Structured Programming [*Program design tool*] (NITA)
JSP.......... Japanese Society of Periodontology (SAUO)
JSP.......... Japan Socialist Party [*Nikon Shakaito*] [*Political party*] (PPW)
jsp.......... Jasper (VRA)
JSP.......... Java Server Pages [*Computer science*] (FOTI)
JSP.......... Jesup, GA [*Amtrak rail station code*]
JSP.......... Job Support Program
JSP.......... Joint Services Development Program
JSP.......... Joint Services Publication
JSP.......... Joint Staff Planners [*Joint Chiefs of Staff*]
JSP.......... Joint Strategic Planning (SAUO)
JSP.......... Joint Support Plan (SAUO)
JSP.......... Journal of Sedimentary Petrology (journ.) (SAUS)
JSP.......... Journal of Statistical Planning and Inference (journ.) (SAUS)
JSP.......... Judicial Selection Project (EA)
JSP.......... Jupiter, Saturn, and Pluto Mission (MCD)
JSP.......... Jurisdictional Separation Process
JSPA........ Japan Screen Printing Association (SAUO)
J Space Astron Res... Journal of Space and Astronomy Research (journ.) (SAUS)
J Spacecr Rockets... Journal of Spacecraft and Rockets [*A publication*] (CABS)
J Space L... Journal of Space Law (AAGC)
J Spac Rock... Journal of Spacecraft and Rockets (journ.) (SAUS)
J Span Stud... Journal of Spanish Studies (journ.) (SAUS)
J Span Stud... Journal of Spanish Studies. Twentieth Century (journ.) (SAUS)
JSPB........ Joint Staff Pension Board [*United Nations*]
JSPC........ Japan Sports Prototype Championship [*Auto racing*]
JSPC........ Joint Service Parachute Centre (SAUO)
JSPC........ Joint Sobe Processing Center [*Okinawa*] [*Military*]
JSPC........ Joint Strategic Plans Committee [*Military*]
JSPC........ Joint Strobe Processing Center (SAUS)
JSPD........ Joint Strategic Planning Document (MCD)
JSPD........ Joint Subsidiary Plans Division [*Military*] (MUGU)
JSPDSA..... Joint Strategic Planning Document Supporting Analysis [*Military*] (AABC)
JSPE........ Japan Society of Precision Engineering (SAUO)
JSPEB....... Journal of Social Education (journ.) (SAUS)
J Spec Philos... Journal of Speculative Philosophy (journ.) (SAUS)
J Spec Philos... Journal of the Speculative Philosophy (journ.) (SAUS)
J Spectrosc Soc Jpn... Journal of the Spectroscopical Society of Japan (journ.) (SAUS)
J Spectros Soc Jpn... Journal. Spectroscopical Society of Japan (journ.) (SAUS)
J Sp Eduators... Journal for Special Educators (journ.) (SAUS)
J Speech D... Journal of Speech and Hearing Disorders (journ.) (SAUS)
JSPER....... Jasper, FL [*American Association of Railroads railroad junction routing code*]
JSPF........ Joint Staff Pension Fund [*United Nations*]
JSPFL....... Jointly Sponsored Program for Foreign Libraries [*Defunct*]
JSPG........ Joint Strategic Plans Group [*Military*]
JSPI........ Joint School of Photographic Interpretation (SAUO)
JSPIJ....... Journal of Social and Political Ideas in Japan (journ.) (SAUS)
J Spinal Disord... Journal of Spinal Disorders (journ.) (SAUS)
JSPMA...... Journal of Supramolecular Structure (journ.) (SAUS)
JSPMRC.... Joint Service Program Management Review Committee [*Military*]
JSPN........ Journal of the Society of Pediatric Nurses (SAUO)
JSPN........ Journal of the Society of Pediatric Nurses (journ.) (SAUS)
JSPO........ Joint System Program Office (ACAE)
JSPOG....... Joint Strategic Plans and Operations Group
J Sport Beh... Journal of Sport Behavior (journ.) (SAUS)
J Sport Hist... Journal of Sport History (journ.) (SAUS)
J Sport Med... Journal of Sports Medicine and Physical Fitness (journ.) (SAUS)
J Sports Med... Journal of Sports Medicine (journ.) (SAUS)
JSPP........ Japan Society of Plant Physiologists (SAUO)
JSPP........ Joint Service Program Plan [*Military*] (RDA)
JSPPM...... Japan Society of Powder and Powder Metallurgy (SAUO)
JSPR........ Journal. Society for Psychical Research (journ.) (SAUS)
JSPRS....... Japan Society of Photogrammetry and Remote Sensing (SAUO)
JSPS........ Japan Society for the Promotion of Science
JSPS........ Japan Sword Preservation Society (SAUO)
JSPS........ Jewish Student Press Service (EA)
JSPS........ Joint Strategic Planning System [*Military*]
JSPSE....... Journal. Society of Photographic Scientists and Engineers (journ.) (SAUS)
JSPTL....... Journal. Society of Public Teachers of Law (journ.) (SAUS)
JSPU........ Jadranska Slobodna Plovidba-Obala [*Intermodal shipping container symbol*] (TVRC)
JSQ.......... Jewish Studies Quarterly (journ.) (SAUS)
JSQC........ Japan Society for/of Quality Control (SAUO)
JSQC........ Japan Society of Quality Control (SAUS)
JSQL........ Java SQL (SAUS)
JSR.......... Jackson Resources Ltd. [*Vancouver Stock Exchange symbol*]
JSR.......... Jaipur State Railway [*Indian Railway*] (TIR)
JSR.......... Jammer Saturation Range (SAUS)
JSR.......... Jam to Signal Ratio (MCD)
JSR.......... Japanese Sociological Review (journ.) (SAUS)
JSR.......... Japan Science Review [*A publication*]
JSR.......... Japan Synthetic Rubber Co. Ltd.
JSR.......... Jessore [*Bangladesh*] [*Airport symbol*] (OAG)
JSR.......... Jewish Student Review (journ.) (SAUS)
JSR.......... Joint Staffing Review
JSR.......... Joint Status Review (ACAE)
JSR.......... Joint Strategic Review (DOMA)
JSR.......... Journal of Sex Research (SAUS)
JSR.......... Journal of Ship Research [*A publication*] (DNAB)
JSR.......... Journal of Social Research (journ.) (SAUS)
JSR.......... Journal of Spacecraft and Rockets [*A publication*] (AAGC)
JSR.......... Jump to Subroutine [*Computer science*] (BUR)
JSRA........ Job Search and Relocation Assistance Projects (OICC)
JSRA........ Joint Sponsored Research Agreement (GAVI)
JSRAAM..... Joint Short Range Air to Air Missile (ACAE)
J/S Ratio.... Jamming to Signal Ratio (SAUS)
JSRBA....... Journal of Scientific Research. Banaras Hindu University (journ.) (SAUS)
JSRC........ Jackson & Southern Railroad [*Federal Railroad Administration identification code*]
JSRC........ Joint Services Review Committee
JSRC........ Joint Ship Repair Committee
JSRCC....... Joint Search and Rescue Coordination Center (MCD)
JSRCSC..... Joint Services Radio Component Standardization Committee (SAUS)
JSRHS....... Japan Science Review. Humanistic Studies (journ.) (SAUS)
JSRJ........ Joint Services Recognition Journal (SAUS)
JSRK........ Jeunesse Socialiste Royale Khmere [*Royal Cambodian Socialist Youth*] [*Political party*]
JSRLPH..... Japan Science Review. Literature, Philosophy and History (journ.) (SAUS)
JSRP........ Joint Services Reading Panel [*Military*] [*British*]
JSRPO....... Justice System Reform Programme Office
JSRR........ Jamming To Signal Ratio Required (SAUS)
JSRR........ Jam/Signal Ratio Required (SAUS)
JSRS........ Jewish Social Research Series (journ.) (SAUS)
JSRS........ Jury System Reform Society [*British*]
JSRT........ Joint Short-Range Technology (MCD)
JSRU........ Joint Speech Research Unit [*British*] (NITA)
JSRW........ Jersey Southern Railway [*Federal Railroad Administration identification code*]
JSRWG...... JSIMS [*Joint Simulation (System)*] Requirements Working Group [*Military*]
JSRX........ Jim Smith Railroad [*Federal Railroad Administration identification code*]
JSS.......... Jacob Sheep Society [*British*] (DBA)
JSS.......... Japanese Society of Sydney [*Australia*]
JSS.......... Java-Script Style Sheet (SAUS)
JSS.......... Jet Steering System
JSS.......... Jet String System (SAUS)
JSS.......... Jet Strip System (PDAA)
JSS.......... Jewish Social Studies [*A publication*] (BRI)
JSS.......... Jim Smith Society (EA)
JSS.......... Job Schedule Status (SAA)
JSS.......... Job Segment Schedule (TIMI)
JSS.......... Job Shop Simulation (SAUS)
JSS.......... Job Shop Simulator
JSS.......... Johnson Scan Star (SAUO)
JSS.......... Joint Services Seeker (ACAE)
JSS.......... Joint Services Standard (SAUS)
JSS.......... Joint Signal Staff (SAUS)
JSS.......... Joint Surveillance System [*FAA*] [*Air Force*]
JSS.......... Joshua Slocum Society (EA)
JSS.......... Journal of Semitic Studies [*A publication*] (ABAR)
JSS.......... Journal of Social Sciences (journ.) (SAUS)
JSS.......... Journal of Sports Sciences (journ.) (SAUS)
JSS.......... Journal of Systems and Software (journ.) (SAUS)
JSS.......... Journal of the Siam Society (SAUO)
JSS.......... Junior Secondary School
JSSA........ Japan Science Student Awards (SAUS)
JSSA........ Japan Society for System Audits (SAUO)
JSSA........ John Steinbeck Society of America (EA)

JSSA......... Joint Services Survival, evasion, resistance & escape Agency (SAUO)
JSSA......... Joint Stealth Strike Aircraft [*DoD*] (DOMA)
JSSADC..... Joint Service Subaqua Diving Centre (SAUO)
JSSAM...... Joint Service Small Arms Management Committee (MCD)
JSSAP....... Joint Service Small Arms Panel (MCD)
JSSAP....... Joint Service Small Arms Program (RDA)
JSSAP....... Joint Service Small Arms Program Office [*Dover, NJ*] [*Military*]
JSSC......... Joint Services Staff College [*or Course*] [*Obsolete*] [*British*]
JSSC......... Joint Services Staff Course (SAUS)
JSSC......... Joint Services Standardization Committee (SAUS)
JSSC......... Joint Shop Stewards Committee [*British*]
JSSC......... Joint Space Surveillance Center (ACAE)
JSSC......... Joint Strategic Service Committee (SAUO)
JSSC......... Joint Strategic Survey Committee [*or Council*] [*DoD*]
JSSC......... Joint Strategic Survey Council (SAUO)
JSSC......... Journal of Solid State Circuits (SAUS)
JSSE......... Japanese Software Support Environment
JSSEA....... Journal. American Society of Safety Engineers (journ.) (SAUS)
JSSEE....... Joint Service Software Engineering Environment (SAUO)
JSSF......... Japanese Society of Scientific Fisheries (SAUO)
JSSFM...... Japan Society for Strength and Fracture of Materials (SAUO)
JSSG......... Jamming Signal Source Generator (ACAE)
JSSG......... Joint Signal Support Group (SAUO)
JSSI......... Japan Society of Snow and Ice (SAUO)
JSSIS........ Joint Staff Support Information System [*Military*] (GFGA)
JSSJ......... Jesse Jaca [*Common carrier symbol*]
JSSL......... Joint Services School of Linguists (SAUO)
JSSM......... Joint Services Staff Manual [*Military*] [*British*]
JSSMFE..... Japanese Society of Soil Mechanics and Foundation Engineering (SAUO)
JSSPA....... Jewish Social Services Professional Association (EA)
JSSPG....... Job Shop Simulation Program Generator (KSC)
JSSQ......... Jewish Social Service Quarterly (journ.) (SAUS)
JSSR......... Journal of Social Services Research (journ.) (SAUS)
JSSRel...... Journal for the Scientifc Study of Religion (journ.) (SAUS)
JSSS......... Job Seeking Skills Survey [*Test*] [*Donald S. Tackley*] (TES)
JSSST....... Japan Society for Software Science and Technology (SAUO)
JSST......... Job Seeking Skills Training (OICC)
JSSTD....... Joint SSTD (SAUS)
JSSU......... China Navigation [*Intermodal shipping container symbol*] (TVRC)
JSSU......... Joint Services Signals Unit (SAUS)
JSSUP....... Japanese Space Shuttle Utilization Program (MCD)
JSS/US...... Japanese Sword Society of the United States (EA)
JSSX......... Jersey Shore Steel [*Private rail car owner code*]
JST.......... Jamming Station (IAA)
JST.......... Japanese Society of Translators (SAUO)
JST.......... Japanese Standard Time
JST.......... Japan Society of Tribologists (SAUO)
JST.......... Japan Standard Time (SAUO)
JST.......... Japan Universal System Transport Co. Ltd. [*ICAO designator*] (FAAC)
JST.......... Javanese Standard Time (SAUS)
JST.......... Jet STOL [*Short Takeoff and Landing*] Transport [*Aircraft*]
JST.......... Jet Stream Turbulence (SAUS)
JST.......... Jinpan Intl. [*AMEX symbol*] (SG)
JST.......... Job Safety Training (SAUS)
JST.......... Job Skills Training
JST.......... Job Step Task (SAUS)
JST.......... Johnstown [*Pennsylvania*] [*Airport symbol*] (OAG)
JST.......... Johnstown, PA [*Location identifier*] [*FAA*] (FAAL)
JST.......... Joint Systems Test (KSC)
JST.......... Journal of Business Strategy (journ.) (SAUS)
JST.......... Journal of Science and Technology (journ.) (SAUS)
JSTA......... Justice System Training Association [*Defunct*] (EA)
JSTAA....... Journal. Royal Statistical Society. Series A. General (journ.) (SAUS)
J Starch Sweet Technol Res Soc Japan... Journal. Starch Sweetener Technological Research Society of Japan (journ.) (SAUS)
J Starch Technol Res Soc Jpn... Journal of Starch Technology. Research Society of Japan (journ.) (SAUS)
JSTARS..... Joint Strategic Airborne Reconnaissance System (MILB)
JSTARS..... Joint Surveillance and Target Attack RADAR System
JSTARS..... Joint Surveillance Target Acquisition and Reconnaissance System (ACAE)
JSTARS..... Joint Surveillance Target Attack Radar System
JSTARS-GSM... Joint Surveillance/Target Attack RADAR System Ground Station Module (RDA)
JSTASM..... Joint Surveillance/Target Attack Radar System Ground Station Module (SAUS)
J Stat Comput Simul... Journal of Statistical Computation and Simulation (SAUS)
J Statis Soc... Journal of the Statistical Society (SAUO)
J Statis Soc... Journal of the Statistical Society (journ.) (SAUS)
J Statis Soc... Journal. Statistical Society (journ.) (SAUS)
J Statist Res... Journal of Statistical Research (journ.) (SAUS)
J Stat Rsr... Journal of Statistical Research (journ.) (SAUS)
JSTB......... Jesuit School of Theology at Berkeley (SAUS)
J St Bar Calif... Journal. State Bar of California [*A publication*] (DLA)
J St Barnabas Med Cent... Journal. Saint Barnabas Medical Center (journ.) (SAUS)
JSTC......... Japan-Singapore Training Center (SAUO)
JSTC......... Job Skills Training Course
JSTC......... Joint Scientific and Technical Committee (SAUO)
JSTC......... Joint Services Test Command (ACAE)
JSTC......... Justice
JSTCB....... Job Step Task Control Block (SAUS)
JSTCC....... Joint Science and Technology Cooperation Committee (EURO)
JSTE......... Joint System Training Exercise [*Military*]
J Sterile Serv Manage... Journal of Sterile Services Management (journ.) (SAUS)
J Steroid Biochem Mol Biol... Journal of Steroid Biochemistry and Molecular Biology (journ.) (SAUS)
J Steward Anthropol Soc... Journal. Steward Anthropological Society (journ.) (SAUS)
JSTF......... Japan Science and Technology Foundation (SAUO)
JstFeet...... Just For Feet, Inc. [*Associated Press*] (SAG)
JSTG......... Jahressteuergesetz (SAUS)
JSTI.......... Jamaican Sugar Technologists Institution (SAUS)
J St Ju...... Journal for the Study of Judaism in the Persian, Hellenistic and Roman Periods (journ.) (SAUS)
J St Jud..... Journal for the Study of Judaism (journ.) (SAUS)
J St Med.... Journal of State Medicine (journ.) (SAUS)
JSTN......... Justin Indus [*NASDAQ symbol*] (TTSB)
JSTN......... Justin Industries, Inc. [*NASDAQ symbol*] (NQ)
J Stoch Process Appl... Journal of Stochastic Processes and their Applications (journ.) (SAUS)
JSTOR....... Journal Storage (journ.) (SAUS)
JSTOR....... Journal Storage Project
JSTP......... Japan Society for Technology of Plasticity (SAUO)
JSTP......... Job Search Training Program
JSTP......... Joint Services Test Plan (CCCA)
JSTP......... Joint Strike Technology Program (SAUS)
JSTP......... Joint System Test Plan [*Initial Defense Communications Satellite Program*] (DNAB)
JSTP......... Joint System Test Program (SAUO)
JSTPA....... Joint Strategic Target Planning Agency (NATG)
JSTPPC..... Joint Services Technical Publication Policy Committee [*Ministry of Defence*] (PDAA)
JSTPS....... Joint Strategic Target Planning Staff [*DoD*]
JSTR......... Job-Specific Training Required (SAUS)
JSTR......... Joint Systematic Troop Review [*Military*]
J Strain Mal... Journal of Strain Malysis (journ.) (SAUS)
JSTRC....... Joint Services Telecommunications Requirements Contract (SAUO)
J Struct Biol... Journal of Structural Biology (journ.) (SAUS)
J Struct Chem... Journal of Structural Chemistry (MEC)
J Struct Div; Amer Soc Ci... Journal of the Structural Division; Proceedings of the American Society of Civil Engineering (SAUO)
J Struct Div Proc ASCE... Journal. Structural Division. Proceedings of the American Society of Civil Engineers (journ.) (SAUS)
J Struct Eng... Journal of Structural Engineering (journ.) (SAUS)
J Struct Geol... Journal of Structural Geology (journ.) (SAUS)
jsts........... Joists [*Construction term*] (MIST)
JSTSSB..... Journal. Royal Statistical Society. Series B. Methodological (journ.) (SAUS)
J St Tax'n... Journal of State Taxation [*A publication*] (DLA)
J St Taxn.... Journal of State Taxation (journ.) (SAUS)
JSTU......... Joint Services Trials Unit (SAUO)
JSTU......... Tohoku University, Sendai, Japan [*Library symbol*] [*Library of Congress*] (LCLS)
J Stud Alcohol Suppl... Journal of Studies on Alcohol. Supplement (journ.) (SAUS)
J Stud Amer Med Ass... Journal. Student American Medical Association (journ.) (SAUS)
JSTX......... Joro Spider Toxin [*Biochemistry*]
JSU.......... Hokkaido University, Sapporo, Japan [*Library symbol*] [*Library of Congress*] (LCLS)
JSU.......... Jacksonville State University [*Jacksonville, AL*]
JSU.......... Jewish Student Union (SAUO)
JSU.......... Junta Socialista Unida [*United Socialist Party*] [*Spain*]
JSU.......... Sukkertoppen [*Greenland*] [*Airport symbol*] (AD)
J Submicrosc Cytol Pathol... Journal of Submicroscopic Cytology and Pathology (journ.) (SAUS)
J Subst Abuse... Journal of Substance Abuse (journ.) (SAUS)
J Subst Abuse Treat... Journal of Substance Abuse Treatment (journ.) (SAUS)
J Suffolk Acad L... Journal. Suffolk Academy of Law (journ.) (SAUS)
JSUM........ Japan Society of Ultrasonics in Medicine (SAUO)
JSUN........ Jupiter, Saturn, Uranus, and Neptune (PDAA)
JS Unit...... Junkmann-Schoeller Unit (SAUS)
J Supercomput... Journal of Supercomputing (journ.) (SAUS)
J Supercond... Journal of Superconductivity (journ.) (SAUS)
J Supramol Struct Cell Biochem... Journal of Supramolecular Structure and Cellular Biochemistry (journ.) (SAUS)
J Supra St... Journal of Supramolecular Structure (journ.) (SAUS)
J Surf Sci Soc Jpn... Journal of the Surface Science Society of Japan (journ.) (SAUS)
J Surg Oncol... Journal of Surgical Oncology (journ.) (SAUS)
J Surg Oncol Suppl... Journal of Surgical Oncology. Supplement (journ.) (SAUS)
J Surg Res... Journal of Surgical Research (journ.) (SAUS)
J Surv Eng... Journal of Surveying Engineering [*A publication*] (CABS)
JSV.......... Jerry-Slough Virus [*Medicine*] (DMAA)
JSVA......... Jewish Socialist Verband of America [*Defunct*] (EA)
JSVIA........ Journal of Sound and Vibration (journ.) (SAUS)
JSVS......... Japanese Society of Veterinary Science (GVA)
JSW.......... Junctor Switch (VLIE)
JSWA........ Japan Sewage Works Association (SAUO)
JSWAP...... Job Swapping (SAUS)
JSWAP...... Job Swapping Memory [*Computer science*] (MHDB)
J SWA Sci S... Journal. South West African Scientific Society (journ.) (SAUS)
JSWC........ Journal of Soil and Water Conservation (journ.) (SAUS)
JSWDL....... Joint Services Weapon Data Link (MCD)
JSWG........ Joint Science Working Group (ACAE)
JSWL........ Journal of Social Welfare Law (journ.) (SAUS)

JSWPB....... Joint Special Weapons Publications Board
JSWPR...... Japan Society on Water Pollution Research (SAUO)
JSWS........ Journal of Social Work and Human Sexuality (journ.) (SAUS)
JSY.......... Jersey Airlines (SAUS)
JSY.......... Justly [*Telegraphy*] (PCTE)
JSY.......... New Jersey Airways Inc. (SAUO)
JSYB......... Jewish Socialist Youth Bund [*Later, MJSG*] (EA)
J Syd Univ Eng Soc... Journal. Sydney University Engineering Society. [*A publication*]
J Syd Univ Eng Soc... Journal. Sydney Univetsity Engineering Society (journ.) (SAUS)
J Symb Anthropol... Journal of Symbolic Anthropology (journ.) (SAUS)
J Symb Comput... Journal of Symbolic Computation (journ.) (SAUS)
J Synth Lubr... Journal of Synthetic Lubrication (journ.) (SAUS)
J Systems Software... Journal of Systems and Software (journ.) (SAUS)
J Syst Software... Journal of Systems and Software [*A publication*] (CABS)
JSYX......... JS Young [*Private rail car owner code*]
JSZ.......... Yugoslav Welding Association (SAUO)
JSZT......... Japan Society of Zoological Science (SAUO)
JT........... Air Oregon (SAUS)
JT........... Iowa Airways [*ICAO designator*] (AD)
JT........... Jahn-Teller (AAEL)
JT........... Jamaica Air Service (SAUS)
JT........... James Taylor [*Singer*]
JT........... Japanese Tokamak (SAUS)
JT........... Japan Times [*A publication*] (BARN)
JT........... Japan Tobacco, Inc.
JT........... Jarno Taper (VLIE)
JT........... Java Time (SAUO)
JT........... Jejunostomy Tube [*Medicine*] (DMAA)
JT........... Jerusalem Talmud (BJA)
JT........... Jig Template (MSA)
JT........... Job Table [*Computer science*] (IAA)
JT........... Job Ticket (SAUS)
JT........... Job Time (SAUS)
JT........... Job Timing (SAUS)
JT........... John Tyler [*US president, 1790-1862*]
Jt........... Joint (EBF)
jt........... Joint (RION)
JT........... Joint
JT........... Joint Tenancy (MHDW)
J-T.......... Joule-Thompson (SAUS)
J-T.......... Joule-Thomson [*Physics*]
JT........... Journal Tape (SAUS)
JT........... Journal. Thailand Research Society (journ.) (SAUS)
JT........... Junction Transistor [*Electronics*] (IAA)
JT........... Juridisk Tidsskrift [*A publication*] (ILCA)
Jt........... Justiciary (SAUS)
JT........... Juvenile Templar [*Freemasonry*]
JT-60........ Japanese Torus (SAUS)
JTA.......... Azia Keizai Kenkyujo [*Institute for Developing Economies*], Tokyo, Japan [*Library symbol*] [*Library of Congress*] (LCLS)
JTA.......... Japanese Technical Abstracts [*A publication*]
JTA.......... Japan Tourist Association (SAUO)
JTA.......... Japan Transocean Air Co. Ltd. [*ICAO designator*] (FAAC)
JTA.......... Jewish Telegraphic Agency (EA)
JTA.......... Job Table Area (SAUS)
JTA.......... Job Task Analysis
JTA.......... Joint Table of Allowance
JTA.......... Joint Tactical Air (SAUO)
JTA.......... Joint Tariff Agreement (SAUS)
JTA.......... Joint Technical Architecture [*Office of the Secretary of Defense*]
JTA.......... Joint Tenancy Agreement [*Military*]
JTA.......... Joint Test Assembly (SAUO)
JTA.......... Journal of Thermal Analysis (journ.) (SAUS)
JTA-Army... Joint Technical Architecture-Army
JTAC......... Joint Technical Advisory Committee [*Electronics*]
JTAC......... Joint Technical Advisory Council (SAUO)
JTAC......... Joint Telecommunications Advisory Committee (SAUS)
JTACC....... Joint Tactical Air Control Center
JTACM....... Joint Tactical Missile (SAUS)
JTACMA...... Joint Tactical Missile System-Army (SAUS)
JTACMIS-A... Joint Tactical Missile System - Army
JTACMS...... Joint Tactical Cruise Missile System (ACAE)
JTACMS...... Joint Tactical Missile System
JTACMS-A.. Joint Tactical Missile System - Army
JTACS....... Japanese TACS System (SAUO)
JTACS....... Joint Tactical Area Communications System [*Army*] (RDA)
JTAD........ Joint Tactical Aids Detachment [*Military*]
JTAG........ Japan Trade Advisory Group [*British Overseas Trade Board*] (DS)
JTAG........ Joint Test Action Group [*European automotive industry*]
JTAGG....... Joint Turbine Advanced Gas Generator [*DoD*]
JTAGS....... Joint Tactical Ground Station [*Army*] (RDA)
JTAGS....... Joint Tactical Ground System (SAUS)
JTAGS....... Joint Target Acquistion Ground Station [*Military*]
JT AGT...... Joint Agent (WDAA)
J Taiwan Mus... Journal. Taiwan Museum (journ.) (SAUS)
JTA-M....... Jewish Teachers Association - Morim (EA)
JTAMD....... Joint Theater Air and Missile Defense [*Army*]
JT & E....... Joint Test and Evaluation [*DoD*]
JT & SEV... Joint and Several [*Legal shorthand*] (LWAP)
JTAO........ Joint Tactical Air Operations (SAUO)
JTAP........ JISC Technology Applications Programme (SAUS)
JTAP........ JTC1 TAG Application Portability Study Group (SAUO)
JTAPI....... JAVA Telephony API (SAUO)
JTAPI....... Java Telephony Application Program Interface (VLIE)
JTAPI....... Java Telephony Application Programming Interface (SAUS)
J TAPPIK.... Journal of the Technical Association of Pulp and Paper Industry of Korea (journ.) (SAUS)
JTARS....... Joint Tactical Aerial Reconnaissance/Surveillance [*Military*] (DNAB)
JTARS MISREP... Joint Tactical Aerial Reconnaissance/Surveillance Mission Report [*Military*] (DNAB)
JTASA....... Journal. Tennessee Academy of Science (journ.) (SAUS)
JTASB....... Joint Tactical Air Support Board
JTASC....... Joint Training and Analysis Simulation Center (SAUO)
jt asp....... Joint Aspiration [*Orthopedics*] (DAVI)
jt auth....... Joint Author
JTAV........ Joint Total Asset Visibility [*Military*]
JTAW........ Joint Tactical Autonomous Weapons (ACAE)
JTAWG...... Joint Targeting and Weapon Guidance (MCD)
JTAX........ Jackson Hewitt [*NASDAQ symbol*] (SAG)
JTAX........ Trinity Rail Management [*Private rail car owner code*]
J Taxation... Journal of Taxation [*A publication*] (JLIT)
JTB.......... Japanese Tourist Board
JTB.......... Joint Bar
JTB.......... Joint Targeting Board (SAUO)
JTB.......... Joint Training Board (SAUS)
JTB.......... Joint Transportation Board [*Military*]
JTB.......... Journal of Theoretical Biology (journ.) (SAUS)
JTB.......... Jump Trace Buffer (SAUS)
JTBBD7..... Journal of Chemical Technology and Biotechnology. B. Biotechnology (journ.) (SAUS)
JTBI......... Japan Travel Bureau International (TVEL)
JTBSMHS... Jacques Timothe Boucher Sieur de Montbrun Heritage Society (EA)
JTBX......... Baker Chemical [*Private rail car owner code*]
JTC.......... Houston [*Texas*] Town/Country [*Airport symbol*] (OAG)
JTC.......... Japan Tobacco Corporation (SAUO)
JTC.......... Jet Capital Corp. [*AMEX symbol*] (COMM)
JTC.......... Jets Corporativos SA de CV [*Mexico*] [*ICAO designator*] (FAAC)
JTC.......... Jewish Thought and Civilization (BJA)
JTC.......... Jewish Trust Corporation for Germany (SAUO)
JTC.......... JIRI Technical School (SAUS)
JTC.......... John Tracy Clinic [*Association*] (EA)
JTC.......... Joint Targeting Coordination (SAUO)
JTC.......... Joint Technical Committee (CDE)
JTC.......... Joint Technical Coordinating (SAUO)
JTC.......... Joint Technology Center (ACAE)
JTC.......... Joint Telecommunications Committee [*Military*] (AFM)
JTC.......... Joint Training Committee (WDAA)
JTC.......... Joint Transfer Correlation (SAUS)
JTC.......... Joint Transform Correlator [*Instrumentation*]
JTC.......... Joke to Come (WDMC)
JTC.......... Jordan Telecommunications Company (SAUO)
JTC.......... Joule-Thompson Coefficient (SAUS)
JTC.......... Joule-Thompson Cooler (SAUS)
JTC.......... Joule-Thomson Coefficient [*Physics*]
JTC.......... Joule-Thomson Cooler (SAUS)
JTC.......... Junior Training Corps [*British*]
JTC.......... Jurong Town Corp. [*Singapore*]
JTC1........ ISO standards Committee on IT (SAUO)
JTC1........ Joint Technical Committee 1 (SAUO)
JTC1 SGFS... JTC 1 Special Group on Functional Standardization (AG)
JTC2........ Joint Tactical Command and Control (SAUO)
JTC3A....... Joint Tactical Command, Control, and Communications Agency (USGC)
JTC3-CDBS... Joint Tactical Command, Control and Communications-Central (Data Base System (SAUO)
JTC^{3}S........ Joint Tactical Command and Control and Communications System [*Military*] (RDA)
JTCA........ Japanese Technical Communication Association (SAUO)
JTCB........ Joint Targeting Coordination Board (SAUO)
JTCC........ Joint Test Coordinating Committee (MCD)
JTCCCA..... Joint Tactical Command, Control, and Communications Agency (ACAE)
JTCCCS..... Joint Tactical Command, Control, and Communications System [*Military*] (MCD)
JTCCG....... Joint Technical Configuration Control Group [*Military*] (AABC)
JTCCS....... Joint Tactical Command and Control and Communications System (SAUS)
JTCE........ Journal of Transportation Engineering. Proceedings. American Society of Civil Engineers (journ.) (SAUS)
JTCG........ Joint Technical Coordinating Group [*Military*] (MCD)
JTCG/ALNNO... Joint Technical Coordinating Group for Air Launched Non-Nuclear Ordnance [*Military*] (AFM)
JTCG/AS.... Joint Technical Coordinating Group for Aircraft Survivability [*Military*]
JTCG-DLA... Joint Technical Coordinating Group for Data Link Acquisitions (MCD)
JTCG-DMI... Joint Technical Coordinating Group for Depot Maintenance Interservicing [*Military*] (AFIT)
JTCG-EER... Joint Technical Coordinating Group for Electronic Equipment Reliability (MCD)
JTCG-ESR... Joint Technical Coordinating Group for Electronics Systems Reliability (MCD)
JTCG-ESR... Joint Technical Coordinating Group for Electronic Systems Reliability (SAUS)
JTCG/EW.... Joint Technical Coordinating Group For Electronic Warfare (SAUO)
JTCGFSR.... Joint Technical Coordinating Group for Electronics Systems Reliability (SAUO)
JTCG/MD.... Joint Technical Coordinating Group for Munitions Development [*Military*]

JTCG/ME.... Joint Technical Coordinating Group for Munitions Effectiveness [*Military*] (AFM)
JTCG/MS.... Joint Technical Coordinating Group on Munitions Survivability [*Military*] (RDA)
JTCGP....... Joint Technical Coordinating Group [*Military*]
JTCGPaME... (Joint Technical Coordinating Group for Munitions Effectiveness ((SAUO)
JTCGP/ME... Joint Technical Coordinating Group for Munitions Effectiveness ([*Military*]
JTCGP-TACS... Joint Technical Coordinating Group for Tactical Air Control System [*Military*]
JTCG-STD... Joint Technical Coordinating Group on Simulators and Training Devi ces (MCD)
JTCGSTD.... Joint Technical Coordinating Group on Simulators and Training Devices (SAUS)
JTCHT....... Joshua's Tract Conservation and Historic Trust (EARSL)
JTC I......... Joint Technical Committee I (SAUO)
JTCIEDI..... Joint Technical Committee for EDI (SAUO)
JTCMD...... Journal of Tissue Culture Methods (journ.) (SAUS)
JTCMEC...... Journal of Traditional Chinese Medicine (journ.) (SAUS)
JTCMF....... Joint Technical Commission of the Marine Front (SAUO)
JTCMF....... Joint Technical Committee on Marine Front (SAUS)
JTCO......... Jacksonville Terminal Co. [*AAR code*]
JTCO......... Joint Tactical Communications Office (SAUO)
JTCO......... Junior Tactical Communications Operator (SAUS)
Jt Comm J Qual Improv... Joint Commission Journal on Quality Improvement (journ.) (SAUS)
JT COMP.... Joint Compiler (SAUS)
JTCP......... JOVIAL [*Joule's Own Version of the International Algorithmic Language*] Test Control Program [*Computer science*] (SAA)
JTCTS....... Joint Tactical Combat Training System [*Military*]
JTCY-P...... Jig Transit Central Y-Plane
JTD.......... Jahn-Teller Distortion (SAUS)
JTD.......... Jetronic Turbo Diesel [*Automotive engineering*]
JTD.......... Jet Turbo Diesel [*Automotive engineering*]
jtd........... Jointed [*Construction term*] (MIST)
JTD.......... Joint Table of Distribution [*Military*] (AFM)
JTD.......... Joint Technology Demonstration (SAUS)
JTD.......... Joint Test Director (SAUO)
JTD.......... Joint Test Directorate [*Military*] (CAAL)
JTDA......... Joint Track Data Storage
JTDAA....... Journal. Tennessee Dental Association (journ.) (SAUS)
JTDARMVAL... Joint Test Directorate Advanced Antiarmor Vehicle Evaluation [*Military*] (DNAB)
JTDE......... Joint Technology Demonstration Engine (SAUS)
JTDE......... Joint Technology Demonstrator Engine [*Air Force*] (MCD)
JTDP......... Joint Technical Development Plan
JTDS......... Joint Track Data Storage
JTDZ......... Joint Texas Division [*Federal Railroad Administration identification code*]
JTE........... Jahn-Teller Effect (SAUS)
JTE........... Jamming Tactics Evaluation
JTE........... Javelin Thrower's Elbow (MELL)
JTE........... Joint Technical Evaluation (MCD)
JTE........... Joint Test Element
JTE........... Joule-Thompson Effect (SAUS)
JTE........... Joule-Thomson Effect [*Physics*]
JTE........... Journal of Teacher Education (journ.) (SAUS)
JTE........... Junction Tandem Exchange [*Electronics*] (IAA)
JTE........... Junction Termination Extension (PDAA)
J Teach Ed... Journal of Teacher Education [*A publication*] (BRI)
J-teacher... Journalism teacher (SAUO)
J-teacher... Journalism teacher (journ.) (SAUS)
J Teach Learn... Journal of Teaching and Learning (journ.) (SAUS)
JTEC......... Japanese Technology Evaluation Center (SAUS)
JTEC......... Japan Telecommunications Engineering and Consultancy
JTEC......... Jeep-Truck Engine Controller
JTEC......... Joint Training Enhancement Committee [*Military*]
JTEC......... Joint Transmission-Engine Controller [*Automotive engineering*]
JTECH....... Japanese Technology Evaluation Database (SAUO)
J Tech Ass Fur Ind... Journal. Technical Association of the Fur Industry (journ.) (SAUS)
J Tech Bengal Engrg College... Journal of Technology. Bengal Engineering College (journ.) (SAUS)
J Tech Councils ASCE Proc ASCE... Journal. Technical Councils of ASCE. Proceedings of the American Society of Civil Engineers (journ.) (SAUS)
J Teching PE... Journal of Teaching in Physical Education (journ.) (SAUS)
J Techn Meth... Journal of Technical Methods and Bulletin (journ.) (SAUS)
J Technol Eng... Journal of Technology and Engineering (journ.) (SAUS)
J Tech Phys... Journal of Technical Physics (journ.) (SAUS)
J Tech Voct Educ S Afr... Journal for Technical and Vocational Education South Africa (journ.) (SAUS)
J Tech Writ Commun... Journal of Technical Writing and Communication (journ.) (SAUS)
JT ED........ Joint Editor
J Teflon..... Journal of Teflon (journ.) (SAUS)
J Tenn Acad Sci... Journal of the Tennessee Academy of Science (journ.) (SAUS)
J Tenn Acad Sci... Journal. Tennessee Academy of Science (journ.) (SAUS)
J Tenn Dent Assoc... Journal. Tennessee Dental Association (journ.) (SAUS)
J Tenn Med Assoc... Journal of the Tennessee Medical Association (SAUO)
J Tenn Med Assoc... Journal of the Tennessee Medical Association (journ.) (SAUS)
J Tenn State Dent Assoc... Journal. Tennessee State Dental Association (journ.) (SAUS)
J-TENS...... Joint Tactical Exploitation of National Systems [*Army*] (ADDR)
J Terramech... Journal of Terramechanics (SAUO)
J Terramech... Journal of Terramechanics (journ.) (SAUS)
J Tert Ed Admin... Journal of Tertiary Educational Administration [*A publication*]
JTES......... Japan Techno-Economics Society (SAUO)
J Test Eval... Journal of Testing & Evaluation [*A publication*] (CABS)
JTETF........ Joint Test and Evaluation Task Force [*Air Force*]
JTEV......... Joint Tactical Electric Vehicle [*Military*]
JTEVA........ Journal of Testing and Evaluation (journ.) (SAUS)
JTEX......... Jaytex Oil & Gas (SAUS)
JTEX......... Jemez Tomography Experiment (SAUO)
J Texas Dent Hyg Assoc... Journal. Texas Dental Hygienists Association (journ.) (SAUS)
J Text Inst... Journal of the Textile Institute (journ.) (SAUS)
J Text Inst Abstr... Journal. Textile Institute. Abstracts (journ.) (SAUS)
J Text Inst Proc... Journal. Textile Institute. Proceedings (journ.) (SAUS)
J Text Inst Proc Abstr... Journal. Textile Institute. Proceedings and Abstracts (journ.) (SAUS)
J Text Inst Trans... Journal. Textile Institute. Transactions (journ.) (SAUS)
J Text Mach Soc Jap... Journal. Textile Machinery Society of Japan (journ.) (SAUS)
JTF........... Japan Textile Federation
JTF........... Jejunostomy Tube Feeding [*Medicine*] (EDAA)
JTF........... Jetfire [*NCIC car model code*]
JTF........... Jet Tear-Down Facility (MCD)
JTF........... Joint Tactical Fusion [*Army*] (RDA)
JTF........... Joint Task Force [*Military*]
JTF........... Joint Test Force [*Military*]
JTF........... Joule-Thompson Flow (SAUS)
JTF........... Joule-Thomson Flow [*Physics*]
JTF........... Junior Tennis Foundation (EA)
JTF2......... Joint Task Force Two [*Sandia Base, NM*]
JTF-7......... Joint Task Force 7 Automation Support (SAUO)
JTF-A........ Joint Task Force-Alaska (SAUS)
JTFA......... Joint Time-Frequency Analysis [*Military*]
JTFAK....... Joint Task Force Alaska [*Military*]
JTF-AL....... Joint Task Force-Aleutians (SAUO)
JTF/ASAS... Joint Tactical Fusion/All Source Analysis System (AAGC)
JTF-CND.... Joint Task Force-Computer Network Defense [*Emergency Management*] (EMA)
JTFEX....... Joint Task Force Exercise (SAUO)
JTF-FA....... Joint Task Force-Full Accounting [*DoD*]
JTFHQ....... Joint Task Force Headquarters [*Military*] (MCD)
JTF/LOCE... Joint Tactical Division/Limited Operational Capability Europe (SAUO)
JTF-LOCE... Joint Task Force-Limited Operational Capability, Europe (SAUS)
JTFME....... Joint Task Force Middle East (DOMA)
JTFOA....... Joint Task Force Operating Area [*Military*] (NVT)
JTFP......... Joint Tactical Fusion Program [*Military*] (RDA)
JTFPMO..... Joint Tactical Fusion Program Management Office [*Army*] (RDA)
JTFREP..... Joint Task Force Report [*Military*]
JTFS......... Joint Tactical Fusion System [*Military*] (LAIN)
JTFS......... JTF [*Joint Task Force*] Simulation [*Model*] [*DoD*]
JTFS......... Juniata Terminal [*Federal Railroad Administration identification code*]
JTG.......... Joint Task Group [*Military*]
JTG.......... Joint Test Group [*Nuclear energy*] (NRCH)
JTG.......... Joint Training Group [*NASA*] (NASA)
JTG.......... Jordan Technology Group (ACAE)
JTGCD....... Joint Task Group Coordination Draft (SAUO)
JTGED....... Joint Task Group Evaluation Draft (SAUO)
JTGGAA..... Journal of Tropical Geography (journ.) (SAUS)
Jth........... Judith [*Old Testament book*] [*Roman Catholic canon*] (BJA)
J Thanatol... Journal of Thanatology (journ.) (SAUS)
J Themophys Heat Transfer... Journal of thermophysics and Heat Transfer [*A publication*] (CABS)
J Theol St... Journal of Theological Studies (journ.) (SAUS)
J Theol Sthn Afr... Journal of Theology for Southern Africa (journ.) (SAUS)
J Theor N... Journal of Theoretical Neurobiology (journ.) (SAUS)
J Thermal Biol... Journal of Themal Biology (SAUS)
J Therm Anal... Journal of Thermal Analysis [*A publication*] (CABS)
J Thermophys Heat Transf... Journal of Thermophysics and Heat Transfer (journ.) (SAUS)
J Therm Spray Technol... Journal of Thermal Spray Technology (journ.) (SAUS)
J Therm Stresses... Journal of Thermal Stresses (journ.) (SAUS)
JTHM........ Thomas M. Johnson [*Common carrier symbol*]
J Thought... Journal of Thought (journ.) (SAUS)
JTHP......... Joule-Thompson High Pressure (SAUS)
JTHP......... Joule-Thomson High Pressure [*Physics*]
JThS......... Journal of Theological Studies [*A publication*] (ABAR)
J Th So Africa... Journal of Theology for Southern Africa (journ.) (SAUS)
JTI........... Islamic Assembly (Student Wing) (Pakistan) [*Political party*] (PSAP)
JTI........... Jatai [*Brazil*] [*Airport symbol*] (AD)
JTI........... Journal of Taxation of Investments (journ.) (SAUS)
JTI........... Jydsk Teknologisk Institut [*Technological Institute of Jutland*] [*Denmark*]
JTIAP........ Joint Foreign Intelligence Assistance Program (SAUS)
JTIC.......... Japan Trade Information Center (SAUO)
JTIC.......... Joint Transportation Intelligence Center (COE)
JTIDS........ Joint Tactical Information Distribution System [*DoD*]
JTIDS........ Joint Tactical Integrated Display System (SAUO)
JTIDS........ Joint Tactical Interoperable Data System (ACAE)
J-TIES....... Japan Technology Information and Evaluation Service (IID)
JTIG......... Joint Target Intelligence Group [*Military*] (CINC)
JTII.......... Japan Telescopes Inspection Institute (SAUO)
JTIL.......... JT Industries [*NCIC trailer make code*]

J Timber Dev Assoc India... Journal. Timber Development Association of India (journ.) (SAUS)
J Time Ser Anal... Journal of Time Series Analysis (journ.) (SAUS)
Jt Inst Lab Astrophy Rep... Joint Institute for Laboratory Astrophysics. Report (journ.) (SAUS)
JTIP.......... Joint Technology Insertion Program (ACAE)
JTIR.......... Justice Court Traffic Infraction Rules (SAUO)
JTIRS.......... Japanese Technical Information Research Service (SAUO)
JTIS.......... Japanese Technical Information Service [*University Microfilms International*] [*Information service or system*] (IID)
JTIS.......... Japan Technical Information Service (SAUS)
J Tissue Cut Meth... Journal of Tissue Culture Methods (journ.) (SAUS)
JTJ.......... Japan Information Center of Science and Technology, Tokyo, Japan [*Library symbol*] [*Library of Congress*] (LCLS)
JTJ.......... Japan Information Center (or Centre) for/of Science and Technology (SAUS)
JTKG.......... Jetta Trucking [*Common carrier symbol*]
JTKU.......... Keio University, Tokyo, Japan [*Library symbol*] [*Library of Congress*] (LCLS)
JTL.......... Jetall Holdings, Corp. [*Canada*] [*ICAO designator*] (FAAC)
JTL.......... Joint Target List (SAUO)
JTL.......... Josephson Transmission Line [*Physics*]
JTL.......... Josephson Tunneling Logic (SAUS)
JTL.......... Joutel Resources Ltd. [*Toronto Stock Exchange symbol*]
Jtl.......... Joutel ResourcesLtd. (SAUO)
JTL ACTD... Joint Theater Logistics Advanced Concept Technology Demonstration Program [*Defense Advanced Research Projects Agency*] (RCD)
JTLAS.......... Jet Transport Landing Approach Simulator
JTLC.......... Joint Technical Language Service, London (SAUO)
J-TIES.......... Japan Technology Information and Evaluation Service (SAUS)
JTLR.......... Juta's Tax Law Reports (SAFN)
JTLS.......... Joint Theater Level Simulation [*Model*] [*DoD*]
JTLS.......... Joint Theater Level Simulator (SAUO)
JTLY.......... Jointly
JTM.......... Job Transfer and Management (ACRL)
JTM.......... Job Transfer and Manipulation [*Telecommunications*] (OSI)
JTM.......... Josephson Tunneling Memory (SAUS)
JTM.......... Josephson Tunnelling Memory (VLIE)
JTMA.......... Joint Traffic Management Agency (MCD)
JTMAE.......... Job Transfer and Manipulation Application Entity (SAUS)
JTM & H.... Journal of Tropical Medicine and Hygiene [*A publication*] (WDAA)
JTM&H.......... Journal of Tropical Medicine and Hygiene (journ.) (SAUS)
JTMB.......... Joint Transportation Movements Board [*Military*] (CINC)
JTMD.......... Joint Table of Mobilization Distribution (COE)
JTMD.......... Joint Theater Missile Defense [*DoD*]
JTMD.......... JTM Distributors [*Common carrier symbol*]
JTMFO.......... John Thomas Martin Family Organization [*Association*] (EA)
JTML.......... Junior Town Meeting League (EA)
JTMLS.......... Joint Tactical Microwave Landing System (MCD)
JTMMA.......... Journal. Tennesse Medical Assiation (journ.) (SAUS)
JTMMR.......... Joint Tactical Multi-Mode Radio (SAUS)
JTMP.......... Japan Technology Management Program [*University of Michigan*] (RCD)
JTMP.......... Job Transfer and Manipulation Protocol (NITA)
JTMP.......... Joint Technology Management Plan (EURO)
JTMPO.......... Joint Tactical Missile Project Office (ACAE)
JTMS.......... Jamb Template Machine Screw (SAUS)
JTMS.......... Joint Tactical Missiles Signature Program [*Military*]
JTMS.......... Justification based Truth Maintenance System (SAUS)
JTMSS.......... Joint Tactical Multichannel Switch System (MCD)
JTMTDE.......... Journal of Trace and Microprobe Techniques (journ.) (SAUS)
JTMX.......... JTM Industries [*Private rail car owner code*]
JTN.......... Jewish Television Network
JTN.......... Joint Targeting Network (SAUO)
JTNDL.......... Kokuritsu Kokkai Toshokan [*National Diet Library*], Tokyo, Japan [*Library symbol*] [*Library of Congress*] (LCLS)
JTNM.......... Joshua Tree National Monument (SAUO)
JTNS.......... Nihon Shinbun Kyokai [*Japanese Newspaper Association*], Tokyo, Japan [*Library symbol*] [*Library of Congress*] (LCLS)
JTO.......... Jeunesse Travailleuse Oubanguienne [*Ubangi Working Youth*]
JTO.......... Jewish Territorial Organization (SAUO)
JTO.......... Join Together [*Association*] (EA)
JTO.......... Joint Technical Operations (AAG)
JTO.......... Joint Test Organization [*Joint Tactical Communications Office*] [*Fort Huachuca, AZ*]
JTO.......... JOPES [*Joint Operations, Planning, and Execution System*] Training Org anization (DOMA)
JTO.......... Jordan Tourist Office (SAUO)
JTO.......... Jump Takeoff (WDAA)
JTO.......... Junction Temperature, Operating
JTOC.......... Joint Tactical Operations Center
J Tohoku Dent Univ... Journal. Tohoku Dental University (journ.) (SAUS)
J Tohoku Min Sa... Journal. Tohoku Mining Society (journ.) (SAUS)
J Tokyo Coll Fish... Journal. Tokyo College of Fisheries (journ.) (SAUS)
J Tokyo Dent Coll Soc... Journal. Tokyo Dental College Society (journ.) (SAUS)
J Tokyo Med Assoc... Journal. Tokyo Medical Association (journ.) (SAUS)
J Tokyo Med Coll... Journal. Tokyo Medical College (journ.) (SAUS)
J Tokyo Univ Fish... Journal. Tokyo University of Fishenes (journ.) (SAUS)
J Tokyo Womens Med Coll... Journal. Tokyo Womens Medical College (journ.) (SAUS)
J Tonghi Univ... Journal of Tonghi University (journ.) (SAUS)
J Tongi Med Univ... Journal. Tongi Medical University (journ.) (SAUS)
J Tongji Med Univ... Journal of Tongji Medical University (SAUO)
JTOR.......... Joint Terms of Reference (MCD)
J Tottori Daigaku Nogaku... Journal. Tottori Daigaku Nogaku-Buo (journ.) (SAUS)
J Town Pl I... Journal of Town Planning Institute (journ.) (SAUS)
J Town Reg Plann... Journal for Town and Regional Planning (journ.) (SAUS)
J Toxicol Clin Toxicol... Journal of Toxicology. Clinical Toxicol- ogy (journ.) (SAUS)
J Toxicol Cutaneous Ocul Toxicol... Journal of Toxicology. Cutaneous and Ocular Toxicology (journ.) (SAUS)
J Toxicol Environ Chem... Journal of Toxicological and Environmental Chemistry (journ.) (SAUS)
J Toxicol Environ Health... Journal of Toxicology and Environmental Health [*A publication*] (PABS)
J Toxicol Sci... Journal of Toxicological Sciences (journ.) (SAUS)
J Toxicol Toxin Rev... Journal of Toxicology. Toxin Reviews (journ.) (SAUS)
JTP.......... Job Ticket Processor (RALS)
JTP.......... Job Training Package
JTP.......... Job Training Program (OICC)
JTP.......... Joint Projection [*Medicine*] (EDAA)
JTP.......... Joint Technical Panel [*Aerospace*]
JTP.......... Joint Technology Program (CCCA)
JTP.......... Joint Training Package
JTP.......... Journal of Tropical Pediatrics [*Medicine*] (EDAA)
JTP.......... Journeyman Training Program
JTP.......... Juventud Trabajadora Peronista [*Working Peronist Youth*] [*Argentina*]
JTPA.......... Job Training Partnership Act [*Formerly, CETA*] [*1982*]
JTPA.......... Job Training Partnership Administration
JTPM.......... J and P Trucking Company [*Common carrier symbol*]
JTPS.......... Job and Tape Planning System
JTPS.......... Juvenile Tropical Pancreatitis Syndrome [*Medicine*] (DMAA)
JTPT.......... Job Task Performance Test
JTQ.......... Wrightstown, NJ [*Location identifier*] [*FAA*] (FAAL)
JTR.......... Jet-Air Bedarfsflugunternehmen [*Austria*] [*ICAO designator*] (FAAC)
JTR.......... Joint Rate (SAUS)
JTR.......... Joint Tactical Radio [*Army*]
JTR.......... Joint Termination Regulation
JTR.......... Joint Travel Regulations
JTR.......... Jordan Travel Research (SAUS)
JTR.......... Journal of European Industrial Training (journ.) (SAUS)
JTR.......... Journal of Travel Research (journ.) (SAUS)
JTR.......... Journal of Typographic Research (journ.) (SAUS)
JTR.......... Journal Tape Reader (SAUS)
JTR.......... Santorini [*Thira Islands*] [*Airport symbol*] (OAG)
JTR.......... Thira [*Greece*] [*Airport symbol*] (AD)
JTRA.......... Job Task Requirements Analysis (PDAA)
JTRAC.......... JPL [*Jet Propulsion Laboratory*] Transient Radiation Analysis by Computer Program [*NASA*]
J Trace Elem Exp Med... Journal of Trace Elements in Experimental Medicine (journ.) (SAUS)
J Trace Elem Med Biol... Journal of Trace Elements in Medicine and Biology (journ.) (SAUS)
J Trace Microprobe Tech... Journal of Trace and Microprobe Techniques (journ.) (SAUS)
J Tradit Chin Med... Journal of Traditional Chinese Medicine (journ.) (SAUS)
J Transnat Manage Devel... Journal of Transnational Management Development [*A publication*] (JLIT)
J Transp Econ Pol... Journal of Transport Economics and Policy [*A publication*] (JLIT)
J Transp Eng... Journal of Transportation Engineering [*A publication*] (CABS)
J Transp Eng Dir Amer Soc Civil Eng Proc... Journal. Transportation Engineering Division. American Society of Civil Engineers. Proceedings (journ.) (SAUS)
J Transp Geogr... Journal of Transport Geography [*A publication*] (PABS)
J Transp Hist... Journal of Transport History (journ.) (SAUS)
J Transp Med... Journal of Transportation Medicine (journ.) (SAUS)
J Transp Res Forum... Journal of the Transportation Research Forum (journ.) (SAUS)
J Trauma.... Journal of Trauma (journ.) (SAUS)
J Trauma Stress... Journal of Traumatic Stress (journ.) (SAUS)
J Travis County Med Soc... Journal. Travis County Medical Society (journ.) (SAUS)
JTRB.......... Joint Telecommunications Resource Board [*Office of Science and Technology Policy*] [*Washington, DC*] (EGAO)
JTRC.......... Joint Theater Reconnaissance Committee (SAUS)
JTRC.......... Joint Theatre Reconnaissance Committee [*NATO*] (NATG)
JTRCP.......... Joint Travel Regulations, Department of Defense Civilian Personnel
JTRE.......... JIMAP [*Joint Institute for Marine and Atmospheric Research*] Tsunami Research Effort [*Marine science*] (OSRA)
JTRE.......... JIMAR [*Joint Institute for Marine and Atmospheric Research*] Tsunami Research Effort (USDC)
JTRE.......... Joint Tsunami Research Effort
JTRL.......... Janitorial (ABBR)
J Trog Vet Sc... Journal of Tropical Veterinary Science (journ.) (SAUS)
J Trop For... Journal of Tropical Forestry (journ.) (SAUS)
J Trop Pediatr Afr Child Health... Journal of Tropical Pediatrics and African Child Health (journ.) (SAUS)
J Trop Pediatr Environ Child Health... Journal of Tropical Pediatrics and Environmental Child Health (journ.) (SAUS)
J Trop Pediatr Environ Child Health Monogr... Journal of Tropical Pediatrics and En- vironmental Child Health. Monograph (journ.) (SAUS)
JTRS.......... Joint Tactical Radio System [*Army*]
JTRS.......... Joint Tenant with Right of Survivorship [*Legal term*] (DLA)
JTRU.......... Joint-Services Tropical Research Unit (SAUO)
JTRU.......... Joint Tropical Research Unit [*Australia*]
JTRUS.......... Joint Travel Regulations
JTS.......... Arrendamiento de Aviones Jets, SA [*Mexico*] [*FAA designator*] (FAAC)

JTS .... Jahn-Teller Stripes [*Solid state physics*]
JTS .... Japan Troposcatter Systems
JTS .... Java Transaction Service (SAUO)
JTS .... Jetstar [*NCIC car model code*]
JTS .... Jewish Theological Seminary (SAUO)
JTS .... JICST Translation Service (SAUS)
JTS .... Job Tracking System (SAUS)
JTS .... Job Trainer Standard (SAUS)
JTS .... Job Training Scheme [*Government initiative*] [*British*]
JTS .... Job Training Standard
JTS .... Joint Test Subassembly (SAUO)
JTS .... Joint Training Scheme (AIE)
JTS .... Joint Training Squadron (SAUO)
JTS .... Joint Training Standards [*Military*] (KSC)
JTS .... Journal of Theological Studies [*A publication*] (ODCC)
JTS .... JTS Corp. [*AMEX symbol*] [*Formerly, Atari Corp.*] (SG)
JTS .... Justice Telecommunications Service [*Department of Justice*] (TSSD)
JTSA.......... Jewish Theological Seminary of America
JTSA.......... Joint Tactical Support Activity
JTSA.......... Joint Technical Support Activity
JTSB.......... Joint Target Selection Board (SAUO)
JTSC.......... Joint Technical Steering Committee (ACAE)
JTSCC....... Joint Telecommunications Standards Coordinating (SAUS)
JTSCC....... Joint Telecommunications Standards Coordinating Committee [*American National Standards Institute*] [*Telecommunications*]
JTS Corp.... JTS Corp. [*Associated Press*] (SAG)
JTSG.......... Joint Targeting Steering Group (SAUO)
JTSG.......... Joint Trials Subgroup [*NATO*] (NATG)
JTSH.......... Joint Threat Simulator Handbook (SAUO)
JTSIN......... Joint Transmission Services Information Network
J Tsinghua Univ... Journal of Tsinghua University (journ.) (SAUS)
J Tsing Hua Univ... Journal. Tsing Hua University (journ.) (SAUS)
JTSMA ...... Jennifer Trust for Spinal Muscular Atrophy [*Established in 1985*] (NRGU)
JTSN.......... Jettison (MSA)
JTSSG....... Joint Telecommunications Standards Steering Group (SAUO)
JTST.......... Jet Stream
JTSTR........ Jet Stream
J Tsuda College... Journal. Tsuda College (journ.) (SAUS)
JTSZ.......... Jontri Transportation [*Intermodal trailer symbol*]
JTT............ Executive Aircraft Leasing, Inc. (SAUO)
JTT/CIBSM... Joint Tactical Terminal/Common Integrated Broadcast System Module [*Military*] (RDA)
JTTCW ...... Jesus to the Communist World [*Later, CMCW*] (EA)
JT TEN ...... Joint Tenancy (SAUS)
JT TEN ...... Joint Tenant (SAUS)
JTTP.......... Joint Tactics, Techniques, and Procedures (DOMA)
JTTPRG..... Joint Tactics, Techniques, and Procedures Review Group
JTTQ.......... Jet Transit Company [*Common carrier symbol*]
JTTRD9 ..... Journal of Toxicology. Toxin Reviews (journ.) (SAUS)
JTTU.......... Jet Transitional Training Unit [*Navy*]
JTU .... Jackson Turbidity Unit [*Water pollution*]
JTU .... Jet Training Unit
JTUAC....... Joint Trade Union Advisory Committee
JTUAV....... Joint Tactical Unmanned Aerial Vehicle
J Tuberc Lepr... Journal of Tuberculosis and Leprosy (journ.) (SAUS)
JTUFA .... Journal. Tokyo University of Fishenes (journ.) (SAUS)
J Tung-Chi Univ... Journal. Tung-Chi University (journ.) (SAUS)
J Turk Phytopathol... Journal of Turkish Phytopathology (journ.) (SAUS)
JTV .... Jet Test Vehicle
JTV .... Jones Intercable Inv Cl'A' [*AMEX symbol*] (TTSB)
JTV .... Jones Intercable Investors Ltd. [*AMEX symbol*] (SPSG)
JTV .... Jones Intercable Investors Ltd. Class A (SAUO)
JT VENT.... Joint Venture (SAUS)
JTVI.......... Journal of Transactions. Victoria Institute (journ.) (SAUS)
J-T-W........ Journey to Work [*FHWA*] (TAG)
JTWC........ DD Jones Transfer and Warehouse Company [*Common carrier symbol*]
JTWC........ Joint Typhoon Warning Center
JTWO........ J2 Communications [*NASDAQ symbol*] (TTSB)
JTWO........ JTwo Communications [*NASDAQ symbol*] (SAG)
JTWOW ..... J2 Communications Wrrt'A' [*NASDAQ symbol*] (TTSB)
JTWROS .... Joint Tenants with Right of Survivorship [*Legal term*]
JTWS......... Journal of Third World Studies [*A publication*]
JTX .... Jet Aspen Air Lines, Inc. [*FAA designator*] (FAAC)
JTX .... Joint Test Exercises
JTX .... Joint Training Exercise [*Military*]
JTX .... Journal of Taxation (journ.) (SAUS)
JTXI.......... JTX [*Common carrier symbol*]
JTY .... Jointly [*Telegraphy*] (PCTE)
J-type .... Jungian judging type (SAUS)
J Typogr Res... Journal of Typographic Research (journ.) (SAUS)
JTYWTK..... Just Thought You Wanted To Know (SAUS)
JTZ........... Oklahoma City, OK [*Location identifier*] [*FAA*] (FAAL)
JTZ........... Zantop Airways, Inc. (SAUO)
JU............ Jacksonville University (SAUO)
JU............ Jack-Up (SAUS)
JU............ Jadavpore University (SAUO)
JU............ Jeunesse Universelle
JU............ Joint Use [*Military*] (AFIT)
JU............ Joint User [*Telecommunications*] (TEL)
JU............ Joygerms Unlimited (EA)
Ju............ Judges [*Old Testament book*] (BJA)
JU............ Juilliard Review. Annual (journ.) (SAUS)
JU............ Julep (ROG)
JU............ Jump Unit
JU............ June
JU............ Junker [*German aircraft type*] [*World War II*]
Ju............ Junkers (SAUS)
JU............ Jure Uxoris [*In Right of His Wife*] [*Latin*] (ROG)
JU............ Jury [*Telegraphy*] (PCTE)
JU............ Yugoslav Airlines [*ICAO designator*] (AD)
JU-52......... Gernan Junkers transport (SAUS)
JUA.......... Joint Underwriting Association [*Generic term*] (DHSM)
JUA.......... Joint Underwriting Authority [*Insurance*]
JUA.......... Joint Usage Agreement (SAUO)
JUARA....... Journal of Chemistry. United Arab Republic (journ.) (SAUS)
JUARE....... Cuidad Juarez, CI [*American Association of Railroads railroad junction routing code*]
JUB .... Job Unit Block [*Computer science*] (IAA)
JUB .... Journal. Bombay University (journ.) (SAUS)
JUB .... Juba [*Sudan*] [*Airport symbol*] (OAG)
Jub........... Jubilate (GROV)
JUB .... Jubilate
Jub........... Jubilees [*Pseudepigrapha*] (BJA)
JUB .... Justice of the Upper Bench [*Legal term*] (DLA)
JUBM........ Jubilee Materials [*Common carrier symbol*]
JUBU .... Journalistutbildningsutredningen [*Sweden*]
JUCG .... Joint Utilization Coordination Group [*DoD*]
JUCO .... Junior College (OICC)
JuCR......... Juvenile Court Rules (SAUO)
JUCSPA .... Joint University Council for Social and Public Administration (SAUO)
JUCUND..... Jucunde [*Pleasantly*] [*Latin*]
JUD .... Doctor of Canon and Civil Law (SAUS)
JuD .... Doctor of Law (SAUS)
JUD .... Duluth, MN [*Location identifier*] [*FAA*] (FAAL)
JUD .... Jam Until Destroyed (SAUS)
JUD .... Jeunesse d'Union Dahomeene [*Dahomean Youth Union*]
JUD .... Joliet Union Depot [*Federal Railroad Administration identification code*]
JUD .... Judah (WDAA)
Jud........... Judaic (BJA)
JUD .... Judea (WDAA)
Jud........... Judean (BJA)
JUD .... Judge (WDAA)
JUD .... Judges [*Old Testament book*] (ROG)
JUD .... Judgment
JUD .... Judicial
Jud........... Judith [*Old Testament book*] [*Roman Catholic canon*]
jud .... juditial (SAUS)
jud .... judo (SAUS)
JUD .... Jurisdiction (SAUS)
JUD .... Juris Utriusque Doctor [*Doctor of Both Laws; i.e., Canon and Civil Law*]
JUD .... US Department of Justice [*ICAO designator*] (FAAC)
Jud-Alg...... Judeo-Algerian (SAUS)
Jud-Amer ... Judeo-American (SAUS)
Jud & Sw... Judah and Swan's Jamaica Reports [*1839*] [*A publication*] (DLA)
Jud-Arg ..... Judeo-Argentinian (SAUS)
Jud-Ash ..... Judeo-Ashkenazic (SAUS)
Jud-Aus ..... Judeo-Austrian (SAUS)
Jud-Aust .... Judeo-Australian (SAUS)
Jud-Bel...... Judeo-Belgian (SAUS)
Jud-Bol...... Judeo-Bolivian (SAUS)
Jud-Bra ..... Judeo-Brazilian (SAUS)
Jud-Bul...... Judeo-Bulgarian (SAUS)
Jud-Can..... Judeo-Canadian (SAUS)
Jud-Chi...... Judeo-Chilean (SAUS)
Jud-Chr ..... Judeo-Christian (SAUS)
Jud Chr ..... Judicial Chronicle [*A publication*] (DLA)
Jud Chr ..... Judicial Chronicle (journ.) (SAUS)
Jud-Col...... Judeo-Colombian (SAUS)
Jud Com PC... Judicial Committee of the Privy Council [*A publication*] (DLA)
Jud Com PC... Judicial Committee of the Privy Council (journ.) (SAUS)
Jud Conduct Rep... Judicial Conduct Reporter [*A publication*] (DLA)
Jud Conduct Rep... Judicial Conduct Reporter (journ.) (SAUS)
Jud Coun (NY)... Judicial Council (New York). Annual Reports [*A publication*] (DLA)
Jud-CR...... Judeo-Costa Rican (SAUS)
Jud-Cub..... Judeo-Cuban (SAUS)
Jud-Czech .. Judeo-Czechoslovakian (SAUS)
Judd .... Judd's Reports [*4 Hawaii*] [*A publication*] (DLA)
Jud-Dan..... Judeo-Danish (SAUS)
Jud-Dut ..... Judeo-Dutch (SAUS)
JUDE .... Committee on Juvenile Delinquency (SAUO)
Jude .... General Epistle of Jude (SAUS)
JUDE .... Jude Tent Trailer [*NCIC trailer make code*]
JUDE .... Judicature (ROG)
Jud-Ecu ..... Judeo-Ecuadorean (SAUS)
Jud-Egy ..... Judeo-Egyptian (SAUS)
Jud-Eng..... Judeo-English (SAUS)
Jud-Eth...... Judeo-Ethiopian (SAUS)
Jud-Fin...... Judeo-Finnish (SAUS)
Jud-Fre...... Judeo-French (SAUS)
JUDG .... Judge
JUDG .... Judge Group, Inc. [*NASDAQ symbol*] (NASQ)
Judg .... Judges [*Old Testament book*]

JUDG .... Judgment [*Motor vehicle violation code used in state of Maryland*] (MVRD)
JUDG .... Judicate, Inc. [*NASDAQ symbol*] (NQ)
Jud GCC .... Judgments, Gold Coast Colony [*A publication*] (DLA)
Jud GCC .... Judgments, Gold Coast Colony (journ.) (SAUS)
JUDGE ..... Judged Utility Decision Generator
Judge Adv Gen... Judge Advocate General (SAUS)
Judge Advo J... Judge Advocate Journal (journ.) (SAUS)
Jud-Ger ..... Judeo-German (SAUS)
Jud-Gib ..... Judeo-Gibraltarian (SAUS)
Jud-Gre ..... Judeo-Grecian (SAUS)
JUDGT....... Judgment
Jud-Guat.... Judeo-Guatemalan (SAUS)
Judg UB..... Judgments of Upper Bench [*England*] [*A publication*] (DLA)
JUDGW...... Judicate, Inc. [*NASDAQ symbol*] (COMM)
Jud-His...... Judeo-Hispanic (SAUS)
Jud-HK ...... Judeo-Hong Kongese (SAUS)
Jud-Hung ... Judeo-Hungarian (SAUS)
Judic .... Judicature (journ.) (SAUS)
judic .... Judicial (GEAB)
JUDIC .... Judicial
Judicate..... Judicate, Inc. [*Associated Press*] (SAG)
Jud-Ind...... Judeo-Indian (SAUS)
Jud-Ire ...... Judeo-Irish (SAUS)
Jud-Irn ...... Judeo-Iranian (SAUS)
Jud-Isr ...... Judeo-Israeli (SAUS)
Jud-Itl .... Judeo-Italian (SAUS)
Juditure..... Journal. American Judicature Society (journ.) (SAUS)
Jud-Jam .... Judeo-Jamaican (SAUS)
Jud-Jap ..... Judeo-Japanese (SAUS)
Jud-Jor...... Judeo-Jordanian (SAUS)
JUDL .... Judicial (ROG)
Jud-Lad ..... Judeo-Ladino (SAUS)
Jud-Leb ..... Judeo-Lebanese (SAUS)
Jud-Mex .... Judeo-Mexican (SAUS)
Jud-Mor..... Judeo-Moresque (SAUS)
Jud-Mor..... Judeo-Moroccan (SAUS)
Jud-Nor ..... Judeo-Norwegian (SAUS)
Jud-NZ ...... Judeo-New Zealand (SAUS)
JUDO .... Judicial Officer Case Tracking System (SAUO)
JUDP .... Jordanian United Democratic Party [*Political party*] (PSAP)
Jud-Pan..... Judeo-Panamanian (SAUS)
Jud Pan Mult Lit... Rulings of the Judicial Panel on Multidistrict Litigation [*A publication*] (DLA)
Jud-Par ..... Judeo-Paraguayan (SAUS)
Jud-Per ..... Judeo-Peruvian (SAUS)
Jud-Pol...... Judeo-Polish (SAUS)
Jud-Port..... Judeo-Portuguese (SAUS)
Jud QR...... Judicature Quarterly Review [*1896*] [*A publication*] (DLA)
JUDr......... Juris Utriusque Doctor [*Doctor of Both Laws; i.e., Canon and Civil Law*]
JUDRE....... Judicature
Jud Rep..... New York Judicial Repository [*A publication*] (DLA)
Jud Repos... Judicial Repository [*New York*] [*A publication*] (DLA)
Jud-Rho..... Judeo-Rhodesian (SAUS)
Jud-Rom.... Judeo-Romanian (SAUS)
Jud-Rus..... Judeo-Russian (SAUS)
Jud-SAf .... Judeo-South African (SAUS)
Jud-Scot .... Judeo-Scottish (SAUS)
Jud-Sep..... Judeo-Sephardic (SAUS)
Jud-Sin...... Judeo-Singaporan (SAUS)
Jud-Slav .... Judeo-Slavic (SAUS)
Jud-Span ... Judeo-Spanish (SAUS)
Jud-Sur ..... Judeo-Surinamer (SAUS)
Jud-Swe .... Judeo-Swedish (SAUS)
Jud-Swiss... Judeo-Swiss (SAUS)
Jud-Syr...... Judeo-Syrian (SAUS)
Jud-Tun ..... Judeo-Tunisian (SAUS)
Jud-Tur...... Judeo-Turkish (SAUS)
Jud-Uru ..... Judeo-Uruguayan (SAUS)
Jud-Ven ..... Judeo-Venezuelan (SAUS)
JUDY .... Judy's, Inc. [*NASDAQ symbol*] (COMM)
JUDY .... Just a Useful Device for You (PDAA)
Jud-Yem .... Judeo-Yemenite (SAUS)
Jud-Yug ..... Judeo-Yugoslavian (SAUS)
JUE .... Journal of Urban Economics (journ.) (SAUS)
JUE .... Julich [*Federal Republic of Germany*] [*Seismograph station code, US Geological Survey*] (SEIS)
JUF .... Joint Users File (SAUO)
J U Film As... Journal. University Film Association (journ.) (SAUS)
JUG .... Java User Group (SAUO)
JUG .... Jet Upgrading (SAUS)
JUG .... Joint Users Group [*Computer science*]
JUG .... JOPES Users Group (SAUO)
JUG .... Jugenheim [*Federal Republic of Germany*] [*Seismograph station code, US Geological Survey*] [*Closed*] (SEIS)
JUG .... Jugoslav (DSUE)
Jug........... Jugoslavia (SAUS)
Jug........... Jugoton [*Former Yugoslavia*] [*Record label*]
jug .... Jugular [*Anatomy*] (DAVI)
JUG .... Jugulo [*To the Throat*] [*Pharmacy*]
JUG .... Junction Gate (IAA)
jug comp ... Jugular Compression [*Test*] [*Neurology*] (DAVI)
JUGD .... Java User Group Deutschland (SAUO)
JUGFET ..... Junction Gate Field-Effect Transistor (TEL)
Jughead..... Jonzy's Universal Gopher Hierachy Excavation and Display [*Internet*]
JUGHEAD ... Jonzys Universal Gopher Hierarchy Excavation and Display (SAUS)
JUGL .... JANET User Group for Libraries (SAUO)
JUGU .... Jogolinja [*Intermodal shipping container symbol*] (TVRC)
JUH-MTF.... Joint User Handbook for Message Text Formats (SAUO)
JUI .... Jamiatul Ulama-i-Islam [*Pakistan*] [*Political party*] (FEA)
JUI .... Juist [*Germany*] [*Airport symbol*] [*Obsolete*] (OAG)
JUIL .... Juili [*NCIC motorcycle make code*]
Juillard R... Juilliard Review (journ.) (SAUS)
Juilliard..... [*The*] Juilliard School (GAGS)
JUJ .... Jujuy [*Argentina*] [*Airport symbol*] (OAG)
JUJ .... Jujuy [*Argentina*] [*Seismograph station code, US Geological Survey*] (SEIS)
JUJAMCYN... Jujamcyn Theaters [*Established by William McKnight, and named for his three grandchildren, Judy, James, and Cynthia*]
JUKE......... Video Jukebox Network [*NASDAQ symbol*] (SAG)
JUKE......... Video Jukebox Network, Inc. (SAUO)
JUKGS....... Journal of Ukrainian Graduate Studies (journ.) (SAUS)
J Ukr Stud... Journal of Ukrainian Studies (journ.) (SAUS)
JUL .... Joint University Libraries
JUL .... Journal of Urban Law (journ.) (SAUS)
JUL .... Julepus [*Julep*] [*Pharmacy*] (ROG)
JUL .... Juliaca [*Peru*] [*Airport symbol*] (OAG)
JUL .... Julian [*Calendar*]
JUL .... Julianehab [*Denmark*] [*Later, NAQ*] [*Geomagnetic observatory code*]
JUL .... July (AFM)
Jul .... July (ODBW)
JUL .... Juris Utriusque Licentiatus [*Licentiate in Both Laws; i.e., Canon and Civil Law*]
JUL .... Yugoslav United Left [*Political party*] (PSAP)
Jul Caes .... Julius Caesar [*Shakespearean work*] (BARN)
Jul Frontin... Julius Frontinus [*Roman soldier and author, 40-103*] (DLA)
Julian .... Julianus Imperator [*332-363AD*] [*Classical studies*] (OCD)
Julians ...... Julian Alps (SAUS)
JULIE........ Joint Utility Locating Information for Excavators [*Telecommunications*] (TEL)
JULIE........ Joint Utilization of Laser Integrated Experiments (SAUS)
JULIEX ...... Julie [*Sonobuoy System*] Exercise [*Navy*] (NVT)
JULIEX ...... Julie Exercise (SAUS)
JULLS .... Joint Universal Lessons Learned System (DOMA)
JUL Res..... Journal of Ultrastructure Research (journ.) (SAUS)
J Ultrasound Med... Journal of Ultrasound in Medicine (journ.) (SAUS)
J Ultrastr Res... Journal of Ultrastructural Research (journ.) (SAUS)
J Ultrastruct Mol Struct Res... Journal of the Ultrastructure and Molecular Structure Research (journ.) (SAUS)
J Ultrastruct Mol Struct Res... Journal of Ultrastructure and Molecular Structure Research (journ.) (SAUS)
J Ultrastruct Res... Journal of Ultrastructure Research (journ.) (SAUS)
J Ultrastruct Res Suppl... Journal of Ultrastructure Research. Supplement (journ.) (SAUS)
Julust........ July and August (SAUS)
JUM .... Judaism (journ.) (SAUS)
JUM .... Jumla [*Nepal*] [*Airport symbol*] (OAG)
JUMAC....... Joint Union Management Advisory Committee (SAUO)
JUMBO ...... Java Universal Molecular Browser for Objects (SAUS)
JUMG........ Japanese Map/Top User Group [*Open Systems Interconnection*] (ODAA)
JUMIP .... Juror Utilization and Management Incentive Program (SAUS)
JUMO........ Junkers-Motor [*Junkers aircraft engine*] [*German military - World War II*]
JUMP........ Joint UHF Modernization Project (MCD)
JUMP........ Joint Urban Program (SAUS)
JUMPER .... Joint Unit for Minorities Policy & Research (WDAA)
JUMPS ...... Joint Uniform Military Pay Service [*or System*]
JUMPS ...... Joint Uniform Military Pay System (SAUO)
JUMPS/MMS... Joint Uniform Military Pay System/Manpower Management (System (DNAB)
JUMPS-RC... Joint Uniform Military Pay System - Reserve Components (MCD)
JUN .... Jump Unconditionally [*Computer science*]
JUN .... Jundah [*Queensland*] [*Airport symbol*] (AD)
JUN .... June (AFM)
Jun .... June (ODBW)
JUN .... Juneau [*Diocesan abbreviation*] [*Alaska*] (TOCD)
Jun........... Junior (EBF)
jun .... Junior (NTIO)
JUN .... Junior
JUN .... Junius (ROG)
JUN .... Jupiter, Uranus and Neptune (SAUS)
JUNAC....... Grupo Andino - Junta del Acuerdo de Cartagena [*Andean Group - Cartagena Agreement Board - ANCOM*] (EAIO)
JUNC .... Jeunesse d'Union Nationale Congolaise [*Congolese National Youth Union*]
Junc .... Junction (ADWA)
junc.......... Junction (NTIO)
JUNC .... Junction
Jun Col J ... Junior College Journal (journ.) (SAUS)
JUNCT....... Junction
JUNCTION... Junction [*Commonly used*] (OPSA)
JUNCTIONS... Junctions [*Commonly used*] (OPSA)
JUNCTN..... Junction [*Commonly used*] (OPSA)
JUNCTON ... Junction [*Commonly used*] (OPSA)

J Undergrad Res Phys... Journal of Undergraduate Research in Physics (journ.) (SAUS)
Jundt........ Jundt Growth Fund [*Associated Press*] (SAG)
JUNE........ Joint Utility Notification for Excavators (IEEE)
JUNET....... Japanese University Network (ACRL)
JUNET....... Japanese UNIX Network (SAUS)
JUNET....... Japan UNIX Network [*Japan*] [*Computer science*] (TNIG)
JunF......... Juniper Features Ltd. [*Associated Press*] (SAG)
JUNI......... Juniper Features Ltd. [*NASDAQ symbol*] (SAG)
JUNIC....... Joint United Nations Information Committee (SAUO)
Junior Coll J... Junior College Journal (journ.) (SAUS)
JUNIP....... Juniperus [*Juniper*] [*Pharmacy*] (ROG)
JuniprF...... Juniper Features Ltd. [*Associated Press*] (SAG)
J United Serv Inst India... Journal. United Service Institution of India (journ.) (SAUS)
J Univ Bombay NS... Journal. University of Bombay. New Series (journ.) (SAUS)
J Univ Bomby... Journal. University of Bombay (journ.) (SAUS)
J Univ Durban-Westville... Journal. University of Durban-Westville (journ.) (SAUS)
J Univ F Ass... Journal. University Film Association (journ.) (SAUS)
J Univ Gauhati... Journal. University of Gauhati (journ.) (SAUS)
J Univ Kuwait... Journal of the University of Kuwait (journ.) (SAUS)
J Univ Poona... Journal. Univetsity of Poona (journ.) (SAUS)
J Univ Poona Sci Technol... Journal. University of Poona. Science and Technology (journ.) (SAUS)
J Univ Saugar... Journal. University of Saugar (journ.) (SAUS)
J Univ Saugr Part 2 St A... Journal. University of Saugar. Part 2. Section A. Physical Sciences (journ.) (SAUS)
J Univ Sci Technol Bejing... Journal of the University of Science and Technology Bejing (journ.) (SAUS)
J Univ Sheffield Geol Soc... Journal. University of Sheffield. Geological Society (journ.) (SAUS)
J Univ S Med S... Journal. University of Sydney. Medical Society (journ.) (SAUS)
J Univ Stud... Journal of University Studies (journ.) (SAUS)
JUNIW....... Juniper Features Wrr'A' [*NASDAQ symbol*] (TTSB)
JUNIZ........ Juniper Features Wrrt'B' [*NASDAQ symbol*] (TTSB)
Junk......... Heroin [*Medicine*] (EDAA)
JUNKS....... Junction City, KS [*American Association of Railroads railroad junction routing code*]
JUNO........ Juno Lighting [*NASDAQ symbol*] (TTSB)
JUNO........ Juno Lighting, Inc. [*NASDAQ symbol*] (NQ)
JunoLt....... Juno Lighting, Inc. [*Associated Press*] (SAG)
Jun Part....... Junior Partner (SAUS)
junr......... Junior (GEAB)
JUNR........ Junior
JUNR........ Junior Camping Trailer [*NCIC trailer make code*]
JUNS........ Journal of Undergraduate Nursing Scholarship (SAUO)
JUNT........ Juntae (ROG)
Junta del Acuer... Grupo Andino - Junta del Acuerdo de Cartagena [*Andean Group - Cartagena Agreement Board - ANCOM*] (EA)
JUNU........ Maritima Juno [*Intermodal shipping container symbol*] (TVRC)
Junuly....... June and July (SAUS)
J Unv Peshawar... Journal. University of Peshawar (journ.) (SAUS)
JUO.......... Jiba [*Language symbol*] (ETLW)
JUO.......... Junior Under-Officer [*British military*] (DMA)
JUP.......... Jamiatul Ulama-i-Pakistan [*Political party*] (FEA)
JUP.......... Journal. University of Poona. Humanities Section (journ.) (SAUS)
JUP.......... Jupiter (KSC)
JUP.......... Juventud Universitaria Peronista [*University Peronist Youth*] [*Argentina*]
JUP.......... Juventud Uruguaya de Pie [*Upstanding Uruguayan Youth*] (PD)
JUP.......... Upland, CA [*Location identifier*] [*FAA*] (FAAL)
JUPD-A....... Journal. Urban Planning and Development Procedings. American Society of Civil Engineers (journ.) (SAUS)
JUPIND...... Jupiter Industries Inc. (SAUO)
JUPITER.... Judicial Precedent Information Trace by Electronic Retrieval [*Database*] [*Toyo Information Systems Co.*] [*Information service or system*] (CRD)
JUPITER.... JUGL Project for Information Transfer, Education and Research (SAUS)
JUPITER.... Juvenescent Pioneering Technology for Robots (SAUS)
JupNatl...... Jupiter National, Inc. [*Associated Press*] (SAG)
JUPOA....... Journal of Undergraduate Psychological Research (journ.) (SAUS)
JUPOA....... Journal. University of Poona. Science and Technology (journ.) (SAUS)
JUPPIE...... Japanese Urban Professional [*Lifestyle classification*]
JUPSA....... Journal. Physical Society of Japan (journ.) (SAUS)
JUR.......... Julia Resources [*Vancouver Stock Exchange symbol*]
JUR.......... Jurassic [*Period, era, or system*] [*Geology*]
JUR.......... Juridical (ROG)
JUR.......... Jurisprudence (ROG)
Jur.......... [*The*] Jurist [*Washington, DC*] [*A publication*] (DLA)
Jur.......... Jurist. Quarterly Journal of Jurisprudence (journ.) (SAUS)
Jur.......... Jurist Reports [*18 vols.*] [*England*] [*A publication*] (DLA)
Jur.......... London Jurist [*1854*] [*A publication*] (DLA)
JURA........ JPEG Utilities Registration Authority (SAUO)
J Urban Econ... Journal of Urban Economics [*A publication*] (JLIT)
J Urban H... Journal of Urban History [*A publication*] (BRI)
J Urban Plann Dev... Journal of Urban Planning and Development [*A publication*] (PABS)
Jur Com Brux... Jurisprudence Commerciale de Bruxelles (journ.) (SAUS)
JUR D........ Juris Doctor [*Doctor of Law*] [*Latin*] (ADA)
JUR DIG.... Jure Dignitatis [*By Right of Rank*] [*Latin*] (ROG)
JURE........ Junta Revolucionaria Cubana [*Exile action group*]
Jur Ex....... Hargrave's Francis-Jurisconsult Exercitations [*A publication*] (DLA)
Jur Ex....... Hargraves Francis-Jurisconsult Exercitations (journ.) (SAUS)
JURG........ Joint Users Requirements Group (NASA)
JURG........ Jurgensetis (SAUS)
Jurid Soc'y Pap... Juridical Society Papers [*England*] [*A publication*] (DLA)
JURIS....... Jurisdiction (AABC)
Juris........ Jurisdiction (DIAR)
JURIS....... Jurisprudence (ADA)
JURIS....... Juristisches Informationssystem [*Judicial Information System*] [*Federal Ministry of Justice*] [*Legal database*] [*Germany*] (IID)
JURIS....... Justice Retrieval and Inquiry System [*Department of Justice*] [*Legal databank*] [*Information service or system*] (IID)
JURIS....... Juvenile Referral Information System (SAUS)
JURISD...... Jurisdiction
JURISDN.... Jurisdiction (ROG)
JURISDON... Jurisdiction (ROG)
JURISP...... Jurisprudence
Jurispr...... Jurisprudence (DLA)
Jur M........ Master of Jurisprudence
Jur Mar..... Molloy's De Jure Maritimo [*A publication*] (DLA)
J Urn Affairs... Journal of Urban Affairs (journ.) (SAUS)
Jur NY....... Jurist, or Law and Equity Reporter [*New York*] [*A publication*] (DLA)
Jur Ouv..... Jurisprudence de Louage d Ouvrage (journ.) (SAUS)
Jur Ros..... Roscoe's Jurist [*London*] [*A publication*] (DLA)
Jur (Sc)..... [*The*] Scottish Jurist [*Edinburgh*] [*A publication*] (DLA)
Jur Sc D.... Doctor of Judicial Science [*or Doctor of the Science of Jurisprudence*]
Jur Sc D.... Doctor of the Science of Jurisprudence (SAUS)
JurScD...... Jurisprudence Science Doctor (SAUS)
Jur Soc P... Juridical Society Papers [*1858-74*] [*Scotland*] [*A publication*] (DLA)
Jur St........ Juridical Styles [*Scotland*] [*A publication*] (DLA)
JURUE....... Joint Unit for Research on the Urban Environment [*British*]
J Urusvati Himalayan Res Inst Roerich Mus... Journal. Urusvati Himalayan Research Institute of Roerich Museum (journ.) (SAUS)
Jur Utr Dr... Juris Utriusque Doctor [*Doctor of Both Laws; i.e., Canon and Civil Law*]
JUS.......... Active Aero Charter [*FAA designator*] (FAAC)
JUS.......... Department of Justice (SAUO)
JUS.......... Department of Justice Library [*UTLAS symbol*]
Jus.......... Jacobus de Porta Ravennate [*Deceased, 1178*] [*Authority cited in pre-1607 legal work*] (DSA)
JUS.......... Japan-U.S. Cable Network (SAUO)
JUS.......... Juries [*Telegraphy*] (PCTE)
JUS.......... Justice
JUS.......... Justice Court [*Court type found in state of Virginia*] (MVRD)
JUS.......... Justy [*NCIC car model code*]
JUS.......... Nenana, AK [*Location identifier*] [*FAA*] (FAAL)
J US Artillery... Journal. United States Artillery (journ.) (SAUS)
JUS AVEN... Jusculum Avenaceum [*Gruel*] [*Pharmacy*] (ROG)
JUSC........ Jusculum [*Broth*] [*Pharmacy*] (ROG)
JUSCADS... Joint United States Canadian Air Defense Study (CCCA)
JUSCADS... Joint US-Canada Air Defense Study (SAUS)
JUSCANZ... Japan, United States, Canada, Australia and New Zealand, Norway and Switzerland (SAUS)
JUSCANZ... Japan, United States of America, Canada, Australia and New Zealand (SAUO)
JUSCIMPC... Joint United States/Canada Industrial Mobilization Planning Committee [*NATO*] (NATG)
JUS/CIV..... Department of Justice, Civil Division
Jus Code.... Code of Justinian [*A publication*] (DLA)
Jus Code.... Code of Justinian (journ.) (SAUS)
Jus Code.... Justices' Code [*Oregon*] [*A publication*] (DLA)
Juscul....... Jusculum [*Broth*] [*Pharmacy*]
JUSE......... Japanese Union of Scientists and Engineers [*Databank originator*] (NITA)
JUSE......... Japan Union of Scientists and Engineers (BARN)
JUSE-AESOPP... Japanese Union of Scientists and Engineers-An Estimator of Physical Properties (SAUO)
JUSE-AESOPP... JUSE [*Japanese Union of Scientists and Engineers*] an Estimator of Phy sical Properties (NITA)
Jus Ecl...... Jus Eclesiasticum (journ.) (SAUS)
J-US FC..... Japan-United States Friendship Commission (SAUO)
JUSII........ Journal. United Service Institution of India (journ.) (SAUS)
Jus Inst..... Institutes of Justinian [*Roman law*] [*A publication*] (DLA)
Jus Inst..... Institutes of Justinian (journ.) (SAUS)
JUSMAAG... Joint United States Military Assistance Advisory Group
JUSMAG.... Joint United States Military Advisory Group
JUSMAG.... Joint United States Military Aid Group to Greece (SAUO)
JUSMAG.... Joint U.S. Military Assistance Group
JUSMAGG... Joint United States Military Aid Group, Greece
JUSMAG-K... Joint United States Military Advisor Group-Korea (DOMA)
JUSMAGPHIL... Joint United States Military Advisory Group to the Republic of the Philippines [*World War II*]
JUSMAGPHL... Joint United States Military Advisory Group to the Republic of the Philippines (SAUS)
JUSMAGTHAI... Joint United States Military Assistance Group, Thailand
JUSMAGTHAI... Joint United States Military Assistance Group Thailand (SAUS)
JUSMAP.... Joint United States Military Advisory and Planning Group
JUSMAT..... Joint United States Military Assistance, Turkey (SAUO)
JUSMG..... Joint United States Military Group
JUSMGP.... Joint United States Military Group
JUSMMAT... Joint United States Military Mission for Aid to Turkey
JUSMMAT... Joint U.S. Military Mission Aid Training (ACAE)
Jus Nav Rhod... Jus Navale Rhodiorum [*A publication*] (DLA)
Jus Nav Rhod... Jus Navale Rhodiorum (journ.) (SAUS)

JUSNC....... Journal of the United States National Committee (journ.) (SAUS)
JUSNC....... Journal. United States National Committee (journ.) (SAUS)
JUSO........ Jungsozialist [*Young Socialist*] [*Germany*]
JUSPAO..... Joint United States Public Affairs Office [*Vietnam*]
JUSS........ Jussien (ROG)
JUSS........ Jussive
JUSSC....... Joint United States Strategic Committee
JUSSIM..... Justice System Interactive Model (PDAA)
JUST......... Joint Users of Siemens Telecommunications (SAUO)
JUST......... Justice (ROG)
JUST......... Justice Sector Support (SAUO)
Just.......... Justices' Law Reporter [*Pennsylvania*] [*A publication*] (DLA)
Just.......... Justiciary [*Legal term*] (DLA)
JUST......... Justification (AABC)
Just.......... Justin (BJA)
JUST......... Justinian (ROG)
Just.......... Justinian's Institutes (SAFN)
Just.......... Justis Law Reporter (journ.) (SAUS)
JUST......... Just Toys [*NASDAQ symbol*] (TTSB)
JUST......... Just Toys, Inc. [*NASDAQ symbol*] (SAG)
JUST ANGL... Justiciarius Anglie [*Chief Justiciary of England*] [*Latin*] (ROG)
JUST CP..... Justice of the Common Pleas (ROG)
Just Dig..... Digest of Justinian [*A publication*] (DLA)
Just Econ... Just Economics (journ.) (SAUS)
Justice...... Department of Justice (SAUS)
JUSTICE..... Journeymen Under Specific Training in Construction Employment (PDAA)
Justices' LR (PA)... Justices' Law Reporter [*Pennsylvania*] [*A publication*] (DLA)
JUSTIFON... Justification (ROG)
Justin........ Justinian [*483-565, Byzantine emperor*] [*Authority cited in pre-1607 legal work*] (DSA)
Justin........ Justin Industries, Inc. [*Associated Press*] (SAG)
Just Inst.... Justinian's Institutes [*A publication*] (DLA)
JUSTINTAC... Joint User Supplier TIA ICEA NEMA Technical Advisory Committee (SAUO)
JUSTIS...... Japan-United States of America Textile Information (SAUS)
JUSTIS...... Japan-United States Textile Information Service (SAUO)
JUSTIS...... Joint Uniformed Services Technical Information System (AG)
JUSTIS...... Judicial State Information System (OICC)
JUST ITIN... Justice Itinerant [*Legal term*] (DLA)
JUST KB.... Justice of the King's Bench [*British*] (ROG)
JUST KB.... Justice of the Kings Bench (journ.) (SAUS)
JustLHo..... Just Like Home, Inc. [*Associated Press*] (SAG)
Just LR...... Justices' Law Reporter [*Pennsylvania*] [*A publication*] (DLA)
Justn........ Justinian [*Australia*] [*A publication*]
JUSTOS..... Japan-U.S. Tropical Ocean Study (SAUS)
Just P....... Justice of the Peace and Local Government Review [*A publication*] (DLA)
Just Peace... Justice of the Peace and Local Government Review [*A publication*] (DLA)
Just SL...... Justice's Sea Law [*A publication*] (DLA)
JustToys..... Just Toys, Inc. [*Associated Press*] (SAG)
JUST-US.... Joint Users of Siemens Technologies United States [*Association*] (EA)
JUT.......... Jamaica Union of Teachers (SAUO)
JUT.......... Jet Utility Transport
JUT.......... Jeunesse de l'Unite Togolaise [*Togolese Unity Youth*]
Juta.......... Juta's Daily Reporter [*South Africa*] [*A publication*] (DLA)
Juta.......... Juta's Prize Cases [*South Africa*] [*A publication*] (DLA)
Juta.......... Juta's Supreme Court Reports [*1880-1910*] [*Cape Of Good Hope, South Africa*] [*A publication*] (DLA)
JUTCPS..... Joint Uniform Telephone Communications Precedence System (DNAB)
Jute Bull.... Jute Bulletin (journ.) (SAUS)
Jute Jute Fabr Bangladesh Newsl... Jute and Jute Fabrics. Bangladesh Newsletter (journ.) (SAUS)
JUTEM...... Japan Ultrahigh Temperature Materials Research Center (SAUS)
Jutendo Med... Jutendo Medicine (journ.) (SAUS)
J Utiliz Agr Prod... Journal of Utilzation of Agricultural Products (journ.) (SAUS)
JUV.......... Juvenal [*Roman poet, 60-140AD*] [*Classical studies*] (ROG)
Juv........... Juvenile (AL)
juv........... Juvenile (SHCU)
JUV.......... Juvenile
JUV.......... Juvenile and Domestic Relations Court [*Court type found in state of Virginia*] (MVRD)
JUV.......... Juvenis [*Young*] [*Latin*]
Juv & Dom Rel Ct... Juvenile and Domestic Relations Court [*Legal term*] (DLA)
Juv Ct J..... Juvenile Court Journal [*A publication*] (DLA)
JUVE......... Juvenile
Juve Delinq... Juvenile Delinquent (SAUS)
juven........ juvenilization (SAUS)
juven........ juvenilized (SAUS)
juven........ juvenilizing (SAUS)
juvenile SMA... Spinal Muscular Atrophy [*Kugelberg-Welander disease*] (PAZ)
JUVF......... Juniata Valley Financial Corp. [*NASDAQ symbol*] (QUAN)
juvie......... Juvenile (ADWA)
JUV JUST... Juvenile Justice [*Legal term*] (DLA)
JUVL......... Juvenile Instruction Permit [*Vehicle license type used in state of Wisconsin*] (MVRD)
JUVOS....... Joint Unemployment, Vacancy, and Operating Statistics [*Department of Employment*] [*British*]
JUVP........ Juvenile, Probationary [*Vehicle license type used in state of Wisconsin*] (MVRD)
JUWAT...... Joint Unconventional Warfare Assessment Team [*Military*]
JUWC........ Joint Unconventional Warfare Command (MCD)
JUWTF...... Joint Unconventional Warfare Task Force
JUWTFA.... Joint Unconventional Warfare Task Force, Atlantic
jux........... juxtapose (SAUS)
JUX.......... Juxtaposition (WDAA)
JUXT......... Juxta [*Near*] [*Pharmacy*]
JUY.......... Andalusia, AL [*Location identifier*] [*FAA*] (FAAL)
JV............ Air Charters [*Senegal*] [*ICAO designator*] (ICDA)
JV............ Bearskin Lake [*ICAO designator*] (AD)
JV............ Jagdverband [*German aircraft fighter unit*] [*World War II*]
JV............ Jamahiriva Airways (SAUO)
JV............ Janesbury Valve [*Aerospace*] (KSC)
JV............ Japanese Vellum
Jv............ Java (SAUO)
JV............ Jersey European Airways [*ICAO designator*] (AD)
JV............ Jet Ventilation [*Medicine*]
JV............ Jewish Vegetarians of North America (EA)
JV............ Job Variable (SAUS)
JV............ Joint Venture [*Legal term*] [*Business term*]
JV............ Joint Venture [*Automotive industry*]
JV............ Journal. Violin Society of America (journ.) (SAUS)
JV............ Journal Voucher [*Accounting*]
JV............ Jugular Vein [*Anatomy*]
JV............ Jugular Venous [*Pressure and pulse*] [*Cardiology*] (DAVI)
JV............ Jugulovenous (SAUS)
JV............ Junin Virus [*Medicine*] (DMAA)
JV............ Junior Varsity
JVA.......... Ankavandra [*Madagascar*] [*Airport symbol*] (OAG)
JVA.......... Genavia SRL [*Italy*] [*ICAO designator*] (FAAC)
JVA.......... Jet Vane Actuators
JVA.......... Jewish Vacation Association [*Superseded by Association of Jewish Sponsored Camps*] (EA)
JVA.......... Joint Voluntary Agency (SAUS)
JVA.......... Jordan Valley Authority (SAUO)
JVA.......... Journal of Volunteer Administration (journ.) (SAUS)
JVA.......... Junior Victory Army [*World War II*]
JVAA......... Jewish Visual Artists Association [*Defunct*] (EA)
J Vac Soc Jpn... Journal of the Vacuum Society of Japan (journ.) (SAUS)
J Vac Soc Jpn... Journal. Vacuum Society of Japan (journ.) (SAUS)
J Value Eng... Journal of Value Engineering (journ.) (SAUS)
J Value Inq... Journal of Value Inquiry (journ.) (SAUS)
JVAN......... Journal of Vascular Access Nursing (SAUO)
Jv & Dom Rel Ct... Juvenile and Domestic Relations Court (SAUS)
JVAP......... Joint Vaccine Acquisition Program
JVAR......... Jordan Valley Applied Radiation Ltd. (SAUO)
JVAS......... Jandel Video Analysis System
J Vasc Interv Radiol... Journal of Vascular and Interventional Radiology (journ.) (SAUS)
J Vasc Res... Journal of Vascular Research (journ.) (SAUS)
J Vasc Surg... Journal of Vascular Surgery (journ.) (SAUS)
JVB.......... James V. Brown Library of Williamsport and Lycoming County, Williamsport, PA [*OCLC symbol*] (OCLC)
JVB.......... Joint Vulnerability Board
JVC.......... Japan Victor Co.
JVC.......... Japan Volunteer Center (SAUS)
JVC.......... Jesuit Volunteer Corps (SAUO)
JVC.......... Jesuit Volunteer Corps: Northwest (EA)
JVC.......... Jet Vane Control (MCD)
JVC.......... Jewelers Vigilance Committee (EA)
JVC.......... Jewelry Valuers' Council [*Australia*]
JVC.......... Joint Verification Committee (SAUS)
JVC.......... Jugular Venous Catheter [*Medicine*] (DMAA)
JVC.......... Jules Verne Circle (EA)
JVC.......... Junior Vice Commander
JVC.......... Victory Company of Japan (SAUO)
JVCC......... Joint Vocabulary Coordination Committee (SAUO)
JVD.......... Jet Vapor Deposition [*Coating technology*]
JVD.......... Journal of Venereal Diseases [*UK*] [*Medicine*] (EDAA)
JVD.......... Jugular Vein Distended [*Medicine*]
JVD.......... Jugular Venous Distention [*Medicine*]
JVD.......... Junction Varactor Doubler (SAUS)
JVD.......... Juris Utriusque Doctor [*Doctor of Both Laws; i.e., Canon and Civil Law*]
JVDHS....... Jahresverzeichnis der Deutschen Hochschulschriften [*A bibliographic publication*] [*Germany*]
JVDI......... Journal of Venereal Disease Information [*Medicine*] (EDAA)
JVE.......... Jeans Viscosity Equation [*Physics*]
JVE.......... Joint Verification (SAUS)
JVE.......... Joint Verification Experiment (SAUO)
J Veg Sci... Journal of Vegetation Science (SAUO)
J Vener Dis Inf... Journal of Venereal Disease Information (journ.) (SAUS)
JVER......... Journal of Vocational Education Research [*A publication*] (EAAP)
J Vertebr Paleontol... Journal of Vertebrate Paleontology (journ.) (SAUS)
J Vet Diagn Invest... Journal of Veterinary Diagnostic Investigation (journ.) (SAUS)
J Vet Fac Univ Tehran... Journal. Veterinary Faculty. University of Tehran (journ.) (SAUS)
J Vet Intern Med... Journal of Veterinary Internal Medicine (journ.) (SAUS)
J Vet Med Educ... Journal of Veterinary Medical Education (journ.) (SAUS)
J Vet Med Sci... Journal of Veterinary Medical Science (journ.) (SAUS)
J Vet Pharmacol TherJVPTD9... Journal of Veterinary Pharmacology and Therapeutics (SAUS)
J Vet Sci UAR... Journal of Veterinaiy Science of the United Arab Republic (journ.) (SAUS)
JVH.......... Bangor, ME [*Location identifier*] [*FAA*] (FAAL)

JVI .... Janesville, WI [*Amtrak rail station code*]
JVI .... Jet Vac, Inc. (EFIS)
JVI .... Journal of Virology (journ.) (SAUS)
JVI .... Jugular Venous Pulse Tracing (SAUS)
JVIB .... Journal of Visual Impairment & Blindness [*A publication*]
JVIBDM ..... Journal of Visual Impairment and Blindness (journ.) (SAUS)
J Vic Teachers Union... Journal of the Victorian Teachers Union (journ.) (SAUS)
JVIDS........ Joint Visually Integrated Display System (DOMA)
J Vinyl Technol... Journal of Vinyl Technology (journ.) (SAUS)
J Viola da Gamba Soc Amer... Journal. Viola da Gamba Society of America (journ.) (SAUS)
JVIR .... Journal of Vascular and Interventional Radiology (journ.) (SAUS)
J Virol Methods... Journal of Virological Methods (journ.) (SAUS)
JVIS .... Jackson Vocational Interest Survey [*Vocational guidance test*]
JVIS .... Joint Visual Information Services [*DoD*] (DOMA)
J Visual Impairment & Blind... Journal of Visual Impairment and Blindness (journ.) (SAUS)
JVita......... Life of Josephus (BJA)
J Vitaminol... Journal of Vitaminology (journ.) (SAUS)
JVL .... Beloit/Janesville [*Wisconsin*] [*Airport symbol*] (OAG)
JVL .... Janesville, WI [*Location identifier*] [*FAA*] (FAAL)
JVLN.......... Javelin Systems, Inc. [*NASDAQ symbol*] (SAG)
JVLVB .... Journal of Verbal Leaming and Verbal Behavior (journ.) (SAUS)
JVM.......... Java Virtual Machine [*Computer science*]
JVME .... Journal of Veterinary Medical Education (SAUO)
JVMED ...... Journal of Virological Methods (journ.) (SAUS)
JVMF .... Joint Variable Message Format
JVN .... Javelin [*Telegraphy*] (PCTE)
JVNC .... John von Neumann Center (SAUO)
JVNC .... John Von Neumann National Supercomputer Center [*Princeton, NJ*] (GRD)
JvNCnet..... John von Neumann Center Network
JvNCnet..... John Von Neumann Computer Center Network (ACRL)
JVNL.......... Juvenile
JVNTSC ..... John Volpe National Transportation Systems Center (SAUO)
J Voet Com ad Pand... Jan Voet's Commentarius ad Pandectas [*A publication*] (DLA)
J Voice...... Journal of Voice (journ.) (SAUS)
J Volanol Geotherm Res... Journal of Volcanology and Geothermal Research (journ.) (SAUS)
J Volcanol Geotherm Res... Journal of Volcanology and Geothermal Research [*A publication*] (PABS)
J Volc Geoth Res... Journal of Volcanology and Geothermal Research [*A publication*] (STAH)
J Volun Act... Journal of Voluntary Action Research (journ.) (SAUS)
J Volunteer Adm... Journal of Volunteer Administration (journ.) (SAUS)
JVP .... Janatha Vimukhti Peramuna [*People's Liberation Front*] [*Sri Lanka*] [*Political party*] (PPW)
JVP .... Janet-Viscount-Public libraries project (SAUS)
JVP .... Japanese Vellum Proofs
JVP .... Joint Venture Partners
JVP .... Juedische Volkspartei (BJA)
JVP .... Jugular Vein Pressure (WDAA)
JVP .... Jugular Vein [*or Venous*] Pulse [*Medicine*]
JVP .... Jugular Venous Pressure [*Cardiology*] (DAVI)
JVP .... Jugular Venous Pulse (SAUS)
JVP .... Junior Vice-President [*Freemasonry*] (ROG)
JVPT.......... Jugular Venous Pulse Tracing [*Medicine*]
JVR .... Jury Verdict Research, Inc. [*Information service or system*] (IID)
JVRR .... Juniata Valley Railroad [*Federal Railroad Administration identification code*]
JVRX .... Junction Valley Railroad [*Federal Railroad Administration identification code*]
JVS .... Jamaican Vomiting Sickness (MELL)
JVS .... Jewish Vegetarian Society - America [*Later, JVSNA*] (EA)
JVS .... Jewish Vocational Services
JVS .... Joint Venture Scheme
JVS .... Joint Vocational School
JVSNA....... Jewish Vegetarian Society-North America (EA)
JVSPLNMQNSC... Je Vous Salue par les Noms Maconniques que Nous Seul Connoissons [*I Salute You by the Masonic Names, Which We Only Know*] [*Freemasonry*] [*French*]
JVSR .... Journal of Vertebral Subluxation Research (SAUO)
JVSR .... Journal of Vertebral Subluxation Research (journ.) (SAUS)
JVST......... Journal of Vacuum Science and Technology (journ.) (SAUS)
JVSUES ..... Journal of Vascular Surgery (journ.) (SAUS)
JVT .... Current-density Voltage Temperature (SAUS)
JVVVA....... Justice for Veteran Victims of the Veterans Administration (EA)
JVX .... Joint Service Vertical-Lift Aircraft, Experimental [*Military*] (RDA)
JVX .... Joint Vertical Lift Airlift (SAUS)
JVY .... Jeffersonville, IN [*Location identifier*] [*FAA*] (FAAL)
JW .... Arrow Airways, Inc. (SAUO)
JW .... Jacket Water
JW .... Jamming War (SAUS)
JW.......... Jehovah's Witnesses (ADA)
JW .... [*The*] Jewish War [*A publication*] (BJA)
JW .... John Wiley [*& Sons*] [*Publisher*]
JW .... Joint Warfare
JW.......... Jordan Watch [*Database*] [*Jordan & Sons Ltd.*] [*Information service or system*] (CRD)
jw .... jugwell (SAUS)
JW .... Jump Walker [*Rehabilitation*] (DAVI)
JW .... Junction Wide [*Telecommunications*] (OA)
JW .... Junior Warden [*Freemasonry*]
JW .... Junior Wolf [*A young philanderer*] [*Slang*]
JW .... Junior Woodward [*Ancient Order of Foresters*]
JW .... Juvenile Water (SAUS)
JW .... Polar Avia [*ICAO designator*] (AD)
JW .... Royal American [*ICAO designator*] (AD)
JW .... Wiley [*John*] & Sons [*NYSE symbol*] (SAG)
JWA.......... Japan Whaling Association (SAUO)
JWA.......... Japati Whaling Association (SAUO)
JWA.......... Jetworld Airways Ltd. [*Antigua and Barbuda*] [*ICAO designator*] (FAAC)
JWA.......... Johnson Worldwide Associates, Inc. [*Associated Press*] (SAG)
JWa.......... John Wiley & Sons [*NYSE symbol*]
JWA.......... Journal of World Anthroplogy (journ.) (SAUS)
JWA.......... Jwalamukhi [*India*] [*Seismograph station code, US Geological Survey*] [*Closed*] (SEIS)
JWABAQ .... Journal for Water and Wastewater Research (journ.) (SAUS)
JWAC......... Jacket Water After Cooled (SAUS)
JWADF ...... Joint Western Air Defense Force (MUGU)
JWAI......... Johnson Worldwide Associates, Inc. [*NASDAQ symbol*] (NQ)
JWAIA .... Johnson Worldwide'A' [*NASDAQ symbol*] (TTSB)
J Wakyama Med Soc... Journal Wakayama Medical Society (journ.) (SAUS)
JWalt........ Journal of the Walters Art Gallery [*A publication*] (ABAR)
J Walter Roth Mus... Journal of the Walter Roth Museum of Archaeology and Anthropology (journ.) (SAUS)
JW & NW... Jamestown, Westfield & Northwestern Railroad (IIA)
J WA Nurses... Journal. Western Australian Nurses Association (journ.) (SAUS)
JWAR........ Jehovah's Witnesses for Animal Rights [*An association*] (EA)
JWarb .... Journal of the Warburg and Courtauld Institutes [*A publication*] (ABAR)
JWARS...... Joint Warfare System (SAUS)
J Wash Ac Sci... Journal of the Washington Academy of Sciences (journ.) (SAUS)
J Washington Acad Sci... Journal. Washington Academy of Sciences (journ.) (SAUS)
JWAT .... Jamaica Water Properties (SAUS)
J Water PC... Journal. Water Pollution Control Federation (journ.) (SAUS)
J Water Resour... Journal of Water Resources (journ.) (SAUS)
J Water Resour Plann Manage Div Am Soc Civ Eng... Journal. Water Resources Planning and Management Division. Proceedings of the American Society of Civil Engineers (journ.) (SAUS)
J Water Waste... Journal of Water and Waste (journ.) (SAUS)
J Water Wastewater Res... Journal for Water and Wastewater Research (journ.) (SAUS)
J Waterway... Journal. Waterways, Harbors and Coastal Engineering Division. American Society of Civil Engineers (journ.) (SAUS)
J Waterway Port Coastal & Ocean Div Proc ASCE... Journal. Waterways, Ports, Coastal and Ocean Division. American Society of Civil Engineers. Proceedings (journ.) (SAUS)
J Waterway Port Coastal Ocean Div Amer S Civil Eng Proc... Journal. Waterways, Ports, Coastal and Ocean Division. American Society of Civil Engineers. Proceedings (journ.) (SAUS)
J Waterw Harbors Div Am Soc Civ Eng... Journal. Waterways and Harbors Division. American Society of Civil Engineers (journ.) (SAUS)
J Water Works Assoc... Journal. Water Works Association (journ.) (SAUS)
J Waterw Port Coastal Ocean Div ASCE... Journal. Waterways, Ports, Coastal and Ocean Division. American Society of Civil Engineers (journ.) (SAUS)
JWB .... Jewish Welfare Board (SAUO)
JWb.......... John Wiley & Sons [*NYSE symbol*]
JWB .... Joint Wages Board (DAS)
JWB .... Joint Welfare Board (SAUO)
JWB .... National Jewish Welfare Board [*Later, JCCANA*] (EA)
JWBC........ Joint Whole Blood Center [*Military*]
JWBC........ JW Bill Christie [*NCIC trailer make code*]
JWBCA....... Joint Whole Blood Control Agency (MCD)
JWBJBC..... JWB [*Jewish Welfare Board*] Jewish Book Council (EA)
JWBJCC..... JWB Jewish Chaplains Council (NTPA)
JWBS........ Journal. Welsh Bibliographic Society (journ.) (SAUS)
JWC .... Jayhawk Western Conference (PSS)
JWC .... Joint Warfare Center [*DoD*]
JWC .... Joint Warfare Committee (SAUO)
JWC .... Joint Working Committee (SAUO)
JWC .... Junction Wire Connector
JWC .... Jungle Warfare Course [*Military*] (MCD)
JWCA........ Joint Warfighter Capability Assessment (SAUS)
JWD .... Journal of Wildlife Disease [*WDA*] [*Medicine*] (EDAA)
JWD .... Journal of Workforce Diversity [*A publication*]
JWD .... Juta's Weekly Digest [*1927-1949*] [*A publication*] (SAFN)
JWDSC ...... JOPES/WIS Data Standardization Committee (SAUO)
JWE.......... Joint Warfare Establishment [*British*]
J Weather Modif... Journal of Weather Modification (journ.) (SAUS)
JWEB........ Juno Online Svcs. [*NASDAQ symbol*] (SG)
JWEC........ Jefferson-Williams Energy Corp. (SAUS)
JWEC........ Jefferson-Williams Energy Corporation (SAUO)
JWEF .... Joinery and Woodwork Employers' Federation [*British*] (BI)
J West Afr Inst Oil Palm Res... Journal. West African Institute for Oil Palm Research (journ.) (SAUS)
J West Aust Nurses... Journal. West Australian Nurses (journ.) (SAUS)
J West Scot Iron Steel Inst... Journal. West of Scotland Iron and Steel Institute (journ.) (SAUS)
J West Soc Eng... Journal. Western Society of Engineers (journ.) (SAUS)
JWF.......... Job Work Folder (AABC)
JWFC........ Jacky Ward Fan Club [*Defunct*] (EA)
JWFC........ Jimmy Wakely Fan Club [*Defunct*] (EA)
JWFC........ Joe Waters Fan Club (EA)
JWFC........ Joint Warfighting Center [*DoD*]

JWFC........ June Wilkinson Fan Club [*Association*] (EA)
JWG......... GCOS/GOOS Joint Working Group (SAUS)
JWG......... Joint Working Group [*Military*]
JWG......... Jugendwohlfahrtsgesetz [*Youth Welfare Law*] [*German*] (ILCA)
JWG......... JWGenesis Financial [*AMEX symbol*] [*Formerly, Charles Financial Services*]
JWGA........ Joint War Games Agency [*JCS*] [*DoD*]
JWGA........ Joint Working Group ATMOS (SAUO)
JWGCG...... Joint War Games Control Group [*Military*] (CINC)
JWGFC...... John Wilson Gill Fan Club (EA)
JWGM........ Joint Working Group Meeting [*NASA*] (KSC)
JWH......... Journal of World History (journ.) (SAUS)
JWI.......... Jack Winter (SAUS)
JWI.......... Jehovahs Witnesses Information (SAUS)
JWI.......... Jewish Women International (EA)
JWI.......... Joint Worldwide Intelligence (SAUO)
JWIC......... Jewish Women International of Canada (EAIO)
JWICS....... Joint Worldwide Intelligence Communications System (COE)
JWID........ Joint Warrior Interoperability Demonstration (SAUS)
JWIDA....... Journal of Wildlife Diseases (journ.) (SAUS)
JWIDS....... Joint Worldwide Interoperability Demonstration System (SAUO)
J Wildl Dis... Journal of Wildlife Diseases (journ.) (SAUS)
J Wildlife Mgt... Journal of Wildlife Management (journ.) (SAUS)
J Wildl Manage... Journal of Wildlife Management (SAUO)
JWIM........ Journal of Wildlife Management (journ.) (SAUS)
J Wind Eng and Ind... Journal of Wind Engineering and Industrial Aerodynamics (journ.) (SAUS)
J Wind Engng & Ind Aerodyn... Journal of Wind Engineering and Industrial Aerodynamics (journ.) (SAUS)
J Wind Engng Ind Aerodyn... Journal of Wind Engineering and Industrial Aerodynamics (journ.) (SAUS)
JWIS......... Joint WWMCCS Information System (SAUO)
J Wis Dent Ass... Journal. Wiconsin Dental Association (journ.) (SAUS)
J Wis State Dent Soc... Journal. Wisconsin State Dental Society (journ.) (SAUS)
JWIT......... JustWebit.com, Inc. [*NASDAQ symbol*] (QUAN)
JwJ.......... Jobs with Justice [*Association*] (EA)
JWJL........ JW Jagger Library (SAUO)
JWKB........ Jordan-Wentzel-Kramers-Brillouin [*Physics*]
JWL.......... Jewel [*Telegraphy*] (PCTE)
JWL.......... Johnston Warren Lines (SAUO)
JWL.......... Whitehall Jewellers [*NYSE symbol*] (SG)
JWLMST.... Jewelmasters, Inc. (SAUO)
JWLO........ Joint Warfare Liaison Officer (SAUO)
jwlr.......... Jeweler (ADWA)
JWLR........ Jeweler
JWLR........ Jeweller [*British*] (ADA)
JWLRY...... Jewelry (WDAA)
JWM......... J.W. Mays, Inc. (EFIS)
JWMO........ Japan Waste Management Office (SAUO)
JWMPO..... Japan Waste Management Program Office (SAUO)
JWN......... Nordstrom [*Company symbol*]
JWNS........ Jewish News Service (BJA)
JWO......... Jardine Waugh Organization (SAUO)
jwo.......... Jettisoning and Washing Overboard [*Inventor*] (ODBW)
JWO......... Job Work Order
JWOC........ Joint Warrant Officer Course (SAUO)
JWOCN...... Journal of Wound, Ostomy and Continence Nursing (SAUO)
JWOCN...... Journal of Wound, Ostomy and Continence Nursing (journ.) (SAUS)
JWOD....... Javits-Wagner-O'Day Act
J Womens Hist... Journal of Womens History (journ.) (SAUS)
J Won Kwang Public Health JrColl... Journal. Won Kwang Public Health Junior College (journ.) (SAUS)
J Wood Chem Technol... Journal of Wood Chemistry and Technology (journ.) (SAUS)
J World Bus... Journal of World Business [*A publication*] (JLIT)
J World Hist... Journal of World History (journ.) (SAUS)
J World Prehist... Journal of World Prehistory (journ.) (SAUS)
J World Trade... Journal of World Trade [*A publication*] (JLIT)
J World Trade Law... Journal of World Trade Law [*A publication*] (JLIT)
JWP......... Jamaican Workers' Party [*Political party*] (PPW)
JWP......... Jamaica Water Properties (EFIS)
JWP......... Joint Working Paper
JWP......... Joint Working Party (ADA)
JWP......... JWP, Inc. [*NYSE symbol*] (COMM)
JWPAC...... Joint Waste Paper Advisory Council (SAUO)
JWPC........ Joint War Plans Committee
JWPC........ Joint War Production Committee
JWPCF...... Journal of the Water Pollution Control Federation (SAUO)
JWPNN...... Jobs with Peace National Network [*Later, NJWPC*] (EA)
JWPS........ Joint War Production Staff
JWPT........ Jersey Wildlife Preservation Trust (EAIO)
JWR......... Janes World Railways (SAUS)
JWR......... Jim Walters Resources [*Federal Railroad Administration identification code*]
JWR......... Joint War Room [*Military*]
JWR......... Juta's Weekly Reporter [*A publication*] (SAFN)
JWRA........ Joint War Room Annex [*Military*] (CINC)
JWRC........ Jewish Women's Resource Center (EA)
JWRC........ Joint Warfighter Range Complex [*Army*]
JWREEG.... Journal of Water Resources (journ.) (SAUS)
JWRI........ Japan Welding Research Institute (SAUS)
JWRS........ Japan Wood Research Society (SAUO)
JWRV........ Jewish War Relief Volunteers (SAUO)
JWS......... James W. Sewall Company, Inc. (SAUO)
JWS......... Japanese Weekend School
JWS......... Japan Welding Society (SAUO)
JWS......... Java Web Server (SAUS)
JWS......... Java Workshop (SAUO)
JWS......... Jazz World Society (EA)
JWS......... Jewish Welfare Society [*Australia*]
JWS......... John Wayne Syndrome [*Medicine*] (EDAA)
JwS.......... John Wiley & Sons, New York, NY [*Library symbol*] [*Library of Congress*] (LCLS)
JWS......... Joint Warfare Staff [*British*]
JWS......... Joint Work Statement (SAUO)
JWS......... Journal of Western Speech (journ.) (SAUS)
JWS......... Judson Welliver Society (EA)
JWSL........ Journal of Womens Studies in Literature (journ.) (SAUS)
JWSOL...... Joint Warfare Simulation Object Library [*DoD*]
JWSS........ James Willard Schultz Society (EA)
JWSS........ Johnson Welding & Steel Supply [*NCIC trailer make code*]
JWSS........ Joint Work Study School (SAUO)
JWST........ Jewish Studies (journ.) (SAUS)
JWS/TD..... Jungle Warfare School Trial and Development Wing [*Johore Bahru, Malaysia*]
JWSTP...... Joint Warfighting Science and Technology Plan [*Defense Technical Information Center*]
JWT.......... Journal of World Trade [*A publication*] (SAFN)
JWT.......... J. Walter Thompson (WDAA)
JWTC........ Jungle Warfare Training Center [*Army*]
JWTDC...... Joint Warfare Tactical Doctrine Committee (SAUO)
JWU......... International Jewelry Workers Union [*Later, Service Employees International Union*]
JWU......... Jewelry Workers Union (SAUO)
JWU......... Sumter, SC [*Location identifier*] [*FAA*] (FAAL)
JWV......... Jewish War Veterans (WDAA)
JWV......... Jewish War Veterans of the USA (EA)
JWVA........ Jewish War Veterans of the USA - National Ladies Auxiliary (EA)
JWVC........ Jewish War Veterans of Canada (EAIO)
JW Vir Phil Soc... Journal. West Virginia Philosophical Society (journ.) (SAUS)
JWV-NMI.... National Museum of American Jewish Military History (EA)
JWVUSANM... Jewish War Veterans USA National Memorial (EA)
JWWJA...... Journal. Japan Water Works Association (journ.) (SAUS)
JWY......... Jet Way, Inc. [*ICAO designator*] (FAAC)
JWY......... Jewelry [*Telegraphy*] (PCTE)
JWYCC...... Jamestown-Williamsburg-Yorktown Celebration Committee
JX............ Bougainville Air Service (SAUS)
JX............ Bougair [*ICAO designator*] (AD)
JX............ International Jet Air Ltd. (SAUO)
JX............ Jesus Christ (SAUS)
JX............ Jesus Christus [*Jesus Christ*] [*Latin*] (ROG)
JX............ Jorex Ltd. [*Toronto Stock Exchange symbol*]
JXCG........ Joint Exercise Control Group [*Military*] (AABC)
JXCU........ Jacksonville Caribbean Broker Services [*Intermodal shipping container symbol*] (TVRC)
JXG.......... Juvenile Xanthogranuloma [*Ophthalmology*]
J Xian Inst Metall Constr Eng... Journal of Xian Institute of Metallurgy and Construction Engineering (journ.) (SAUS)
JXN.......... Jackson [*Michigan*] [*Airport symbol*] (OAG)
Jxpan J Nurs Art... Japanese Journal of Nursing Art (journ.) (SAUS)
JXPT......... Jacksonville Port Terminal Railway [*Federal Railroad Administration identification code*]
JXSB......... Jacksonville Savings Bank (Illinois) [*NASDAQ symbol*] (SAG)
JXT.......... Morristown, TN [*Location identifier*] [*FAA*] (FAAL)
JXVL......... Jacksonville Bancorp, Inc. [*NASDAQ symbol*] (SAG)
JXVL......... Jacksonville Savings & Loan Association [*Texas*] [*NASDAQ symbol*] (SAG)
J XXII........ Extravagantes Johannes XXII [*A publication*] (DSA)
JY............ British United Channel Islands Airways (SAUS)
JY............ European Airways (SAUS)
Jy............ Jansky [*A unit of electromagnetic flux density*]
JY............ Japanese Yen [*Monetary unit*]
JY............ Jersey European [*ICAO designator*] (AD)
JY............ Jordan [*Civil aircraft markings - international*] (PIPO)
Jy............ July (ADWA)
JY............ July
JY............ Jury [*Ship's rigging*] (ROG)
JYA.......... Junior Year Abroad [*Collegiate term*]
JYADA6..... Journal of Youth and Adolescence (journ.) (SAUS)
J Yamashina Inst Ornithol... Journal. Yamashina Institute for Ornithology (journ.) (SAUS)
J Yamgata Agric For S... Journal. Yamagata Agriculture and Forestry Society (journ.) (SAUS)
JYC.......... Interstate Helicopters, Inc. (SAUO)
JYC.......... Jacques-Yves Cousteau [*French marine explorer*] [*Initialism pronounced "Jheek" when used as nickname*]
JYC.......... Judicial Youth Corps (SAUS)
JYCE-A...... Journal. Hydraulics Division. Proceedings of the American Society of Civil Engineers (journ.) (SAUS)
JYL.......... Jugolinja-Yugoslav Line (SAUO)
J Yokohama Munic Univ... Journal. Yokohama Municipal University (journ.) (SAUS)
J Yonago Med Assoc... Journal. Yonago Medical Association (journ.) (SAUS)
JYP.......... JCP & L Capital LP [*NYSE symbol*] (SAG)
JYP.......... Jersey Central Power & Light Co. [*NYSE symbol*] (SAG)
JYPPr........ Jersey Cent P&L 4%cmPfd [*NYSE symbol*] (TTSB)
JYPPrE...... Jersey Cent P&L7.88% Pfd [*NYSE symbol*] (TTSB)
JYPPrZ...... JCP&L Cap L.P.8.56%'MIPS' [*NYSE symbol*] (TTSB)
JYTP......... Joy Transport [*Common carrier symbol*]

JYV .... Houston, TX [*Location identifier*] [*FAA*] (FAAL)
JYV .... Jyvaskyla [*Finland*] [*Airport symbol*] (OAG)
JYY .... Jaya [*Language symbol*] (ETLW)
JZ .... Alamo Commuter Airlines [*ICAO designator*] (AD)
JZ .... Jazz [*A radio station format*] (WDMC)
JZ .... Juarez [*Telegraphy*] (PCTE)
JZ .... Juedische Zeremonialkunst [*A publication*] (BJA)
JZ .... Jump if Zero (VLIE)
JZ .... Jump on Zero [*Computer science*] (PCM)
JZ .... Zaire Aero Services (SAUS)
JZAM .... Journal of Zoo Animal Medicine [*Medicine*] (EDAA)
JZF .... Jannasch-Zafirion-Farrington [*Marine sediment trap*]
JZG .... Juedische Zeitschrift fuer Wissenschaft und Leben (A. Geiger) [*A publication*] (BJA)
JZGX .... James Quinlan [*Private rail car owner code*]
J Zhejiang Agric Univ... Journal of Zhejiang Agricultural University [*A publication*] (PABS)
J Zhejiang Med Univ... Journal. Zhejiang Medical University (journ.) (SAUS)
J Zhejiang Univ... Journal of Zhejiang University (journ.) (SAUS)
JZI .... Charleston, SC [*Location identifier*] [*FAA*] (FAAL)
JZM .... Jazzman Resources, Inc. [*Vancouver Stock Exchange symbol*]
J Zoo Anim Med... Journal of Zoo Animal Medicine (journ.) (SAUS)
J Zool Res... Journal of Zoological Research (journ.) (SAUS)
J Zool Ser A... Journal of Zoology. Series A (journ.) (SAUS)
J Zool Ser B... Journal of Zoology. Series B (journ.) (SAUS)
J Zool Soc Indi... Journal. Zoological Society of India (journ.) (SAUS)
J Zool Sys Evol Res... Journal of Zoological Systematics and Evolutionary Research (journ.) (SAUS)
JZP .... Jersey Zoological Park (SAUO)
JZQ .... Norfolk, VA [*Location identifier*] [*FAA*] (FAAL)
JZS .... Jersey Zoological Society (SAUO)
JZS .... Speleological Association of Slovenia (SAUO)
JZSAEU ..... Journal of Zoology. Series A (journ.) (SAUS)
JZSBEX ...... Journal of Zoology. Series B (journ.) (SAUS)
JZSU .... Zeleznicko Transportno Preduzece [*Intermodal shipping container symbol*] (TVRC)

K
By Acronym

K .... Absolute Zero [*Temperature*] (MAE)
K .... Absorption Index (SAUS)
K .... Amphibious [*JETDS*]
K .... Black (WDMC)
k .... Boltzmann Constant [*Symbol*] [*IUPAC*]
k .... Bulk Modulus of Elasticity [*Symbol*] (DEN)
K .... Calcium in the Solar Spectrum [*Astronomy*] (BARN)
K .... Calix [*Anatomy*] (MAE)
K .... Capacity (AAG)
K .... Capital [*Factor of production*]
K .... Capsular Antigen [*Immunology*] (MAE)
K .... Cara [*Dear One*] [*Latin*]
K .... Carat [*Unit of measure for precious stones or gold*]
K .... Care
K .... Carissimus [*Dearest*] [*Latin*]
K .... Carlo Erba [*Italy*] [*Research code symbol*]
K .... Carrying Capacity [*Genetics*] (DAVI)
K .... Carus
K .... Cathode [*Electron device*] (MSA)
K .... Cellophane (AAG)
K .... Certified Kosher [*Food labeling*]
K .... Chritiania Bank og Kreditkasse [*Bank*] [*Norway*]
K .... Circuses [*Public-performance tariff class*] [*British*]
k .... Coefficient of Alienation [*Psychology*]
K .... Coefficient of Scleral Rigidity [*Ophthalmology*] (DAVI)
k .... Cold Air Mass [*Meteorology*] (BARN)
K .... Computer [*JETDS nomenclature*]
K .... Consonantal [*Linguistics*]
K .... Constant
K .... Contiguous United States [*Aviation*] (PIPO)
K .... Contract [*Legal shorthand*] (LWAP)
K .... Cornea (SAUS)
K .... Cretaceous [*Period, era, or system*] [*Geology*]
K .... Cumulus [*Cloud*] [*Meteorology*]
K .... Dallas [*Branch in the Federal Reserve regional banking system*] (BARN)
K .... Danish National Museum (SAUO)
K .... Declared or Paid This Year on a Cumulative Issue with Dividends in Arrears [*Investment term*] (DFIT)
K .... Degrees Kelvin
K .... Dielectric Constant
K .... Electrostatic Capacity [*Symbol*] (AAMN)
K .... Equilibrium Constant [*Symbol*] [*Chemistry*]
K .... Exchangeable Body Potassium [*Medicine*] (EDAA)
K .... Incentive Motivation [*Psychology*] (QSUL)
K .... Ionization Constant [*Symbol*] [*Chemistry*]
K .... Kadenz [*Cadence*] [*Music*]
K .... Kaempferol [*Biochemistry*]
K .... Kainic Acid [*Biochemistry*]
K .... Kaiser [*In radio call signs west of the Mississippi River*] (ROG)
K .... Kaken Chemical Co. [*Japan*] [*Research code symbol*]
K .... Kalendas [*Calends*]
K .... Kalium [*Potassium*] [*Chemical element*]
K .... Kallikrein [*or Kininogenin*] Inhibiting Unit [*Hematology*]
K .... Kanamycin [*Antibacterial compound*]
K .... Kanone [*Gun*] [*German military - World War II*]
K .... Kansas State Library, Topeka, KS [*Library symbol*] [*Library of Congress*] (LCLS)
K .... Kappa [*Tenth letter of the Greek alaphabet*] (DAVI)
k .... Karat (SHCU)
K .... Karat [*A twenty-fourth part; unit of value for gold*]
K .... Karolus de Tocco [*Flourished, 13th century*] [*Authority cited in pre-1607 legal work*] (DSA)
K .... Karyotype [*Clinical chemistry*]
K .... Kathode [*Cathode*]
K .... Kayak
K .... Kayser
K .... K Capture [*A type of radioactive decay*]
K .... Keel
K .... Keg
K .... Kell [*Blood group*]
K .... Kell Factor (DMAA)
K .... Kellogg Co. [*NYSE symbol*] (SPSG)
K .... Keloid (MELL)
K .... Kelp [*Quality of the Bottom*] [*Nautical charts*]
K .... Kelvin [*Symbol*] [*SI unit of thermodynamic temperature*]
K .... Kennedy Space Center [*NASA*]
K .... Kensal Press [*Publisher*] [*British*]
K .... Kentish
K .... Kenyon's English King's Bench Reports [*A publication*] (DLA)
K .... Keratometry (MELL)
K .... Kerma (DMAA)
K .... Kern Wave [*Earthquakes*]
K .... Kerosene (AAG)
K .... Kerr Constant [*Optics*]
K .... Ketamine [*An anesthetic*]
K .... Ketch (ROG)
k .... Ketib (BJA)
K .... Ketotifen [*Pharmacology*]
K .... Key
k .... Keyboard
K .... Keyes' New York Court of Appeals Reports [*A publication*] (DLA)
K .... KGB [*Komitet Gossudarstvennoi Bezopasnosti*] Agent
K .... Kicker [*Football*]
K .... Kidney [*Anatomy*] (MAE)
K .... Kill [*Military*] (ACAE)
K .... Killed
K .... Killer [*Cells*] [*Cytology*] (DAVI)
K .... KILO [*Communications term*] (DCT)
k .... Kilo [*A prefix meaning multiplied by* 10^3] [*SI symbol*]
K .... Kilo [*Phonetic alphabet*] [*International*] (DSUE)
K .... Kilobyte [10^3 *bytes*] [*Computer science*]
K .... Kilocalorie (MELL)
K .... Kilocycle
K .... Kilodalton (MELL)
K .... Kilogram (SHCU)
k .... Kilogram [*Also, kg*] [*Symbol*] [*SI unit for mass*]
k .... Kilohm
K .... Kilometer (WDAA)
K .... Kilowatt (WDMC)
K .... Kindergarten
K .... Kinesthetic (AAG)
K .... Kinetic Energy [*Symbol*] [*IUPAC*]
K .... King [*Phonetic alphabet*] [*Royal Navy*] (DSUE)
K .... King [*Chess, card games*]
K .... King [*Monetary unit*][*Papua, New Guinea*] (BARN)
k .... King (GEAB)
K .... Kingdom (ROG)
K .... Kings [*Old Testament book*] (BJA)
K .... Kinross Gold Corp. [*Toronto Stock Exchange symbol*] [*Canada*]
K .... Kip [*1000 lbs.*]
K .... Kip [*Monetary unit*] [*Laos*]
K .... Kirk (ROG)
K .... Kirkpatrick [*Music*] (ODA)
K .... Kirschner [*Wire*] [*Orthopedics*] (DAVI)
K .... Kitchen
K .... Klebsiella [*Genus of microorganisms*] (DAVI)
K .... Klinge [*Germany*] [*Research code symbol*]
K .... Klystron
K .... Knee [*Anatomy*] (DAVI)
K .... Knight [*Chess, card games*]
K .... Knighthood
K .... Knit
K .... Knock [*Cardiology*]
k .... Knot (MIST)
K .... Knots [*Also, KT*] [*Nautical speed unit*]
K .... Knudsen Number
K .... Koechel [*Catalogue of Mozart's works*] (ODBW)
K .... Koechel Numeration [*Of Mozart's Works*] [*Music*] (WA)
K .... Koeln [*German license plate city code*]
K .... Kollaborateur [*Nickname given Alain Robbe-Grillet*] [*World War II*]
K .... Kontra [*Contra*] [*Music*]
K .... Kopeck [*Monetary unit*] [*Former USSR*]
k .... K-Orbital (MEC)
K .... Koruna [*Monetary unit*] [*Former Czechoslovakia*]
K .... Kosher
K .... Kosmos [*Publisher*] [*Holland*]
K .... Kotze's Transvaal High Court Reports [*South Africa*] [*A publication*] (DLA)
K .... Kouyunjik [*or Kuyounjik*] [*Collection of cuneiform tablets from Kuyounjik in the British Museum, London*] (BJA)
K .... Kraft [*Paper*] (DGA)
K .... Kraftfahrwesen [*Motor transport*] [*German military - World War II*]
K .... Kraftrad [*Motorcycle*] [*German military - World War II*]
K .... Krazy Kat [*Cartoon character by George Herriman*]
K .... Krona [*Monetary unit*] [*Iceland, Sweden*]

K Krone [*Crown*] [*Monetary unit*] [*Denmark, Norway*]
K Kroon [*Monetary unit*] [*Estonia*]
K Krupp Gun
K Kurus [*Monetary unit*] [*Turkey*]
K Kwacha [*Monetary unit*] [*Malawi, Zambia*]
K Kyat [*Monetary unit*] [*Myanmar*]
K Luminous Efficiency [*Physics*] (BARN)
K Lysine [*One-letter symbol; see Lys*]
k Magnetic Susceptibility (STED)
k Mass Transfer Coefficient [*Symbol*] [*IUPAC*]
K Motor Coordination [*Neurology and orthopedics*] (DAVI)
k Multiplication Factor [*or Constant*]
K NCO Logistics Program [*Army skill qualification identifier*] (INF)
K Okay (SAUS)
K One Thousand (NASA)
K Out of The [*Telegraphy*] (PCTE)
K Phylloquinone [*Vitamin K*] [*Also, PMQ*] [*Biochemistry*]
K Potassium [*Chemical element*]
K Promotional Fare [*Also, L, Q, V*] [*Airline fare code*]
K Radius of Curvature of Flattest Meridian of Apical Cornea [*Ophthalmology*] (DAVI)
k Rate (DAVI)
k Rate Constant [*Symbol*] [*Chemistry*]
k Reaction Rate Constant [*Chemistry*] (DAVI)
K Reactor Development Division (SAUO)
K Red Star of Maximum Intensity of Metal [*Astronomy*] (BARN)
K Relay (CET)
K Required Rate of Return [*Finance*]
K Smoke [*Weather charts*]
K Solar Absorption Index (CET)
K Solar Constant [*Astronomy*] (ODA)
K Strikeout [*Baseball symbol*]
K symbol for planetary wave number (SAUS)
K Tanker [*Designation for all US military aircraft*]
K Telemetering [*JETDS*]
k Thermal Conductivity [*Symbol*] [*IUPAC*]
K Thousand (ADA)
k Torsion Constant [*Physics*] (BARN)
K United Kingdom [*IYRU nationality code*] (IYR)
k Velocity [*Physics*] (DAVI)
K Wetboek van Koophandel [*Commercial Code*] [*Dutch*] (ILCA)
K Kaon [*Physics*] (ODA)
K1 Kayak, Single Person (ADA)
K2 Coefficient of Nondetermination (DIPS)
K2 Kayak, Two Person (ADA)
K2 Mount Godwin-Austen [*Initialism denotes that mountain is second highest (to Everest) in the Karakoram range in the Himalayas*] [*Initialism also used as brand name of skiing equipment*]
K-2 Taegu Air Base (SAUO)
K2Desgn K2 Design, Inc. [*Associated Press*] (SAG)
K2Dsgn K2 Design, Inc. [*Associated Press*] (SAG)
K-3 Krasnogorsk-3 [*A 16mm film camera*] (WDMC)
K-3 Kummer, Kneser, and Kodaira [*Surfaces*] [*Mathematics*]
K_3 Menadione [*Vitamin K_3*] (DAVI)
K4 Kayak, Four Person (ADA)
K-4 Kindergarten through 4th Grade [*Emergency Management*] (EMA)
K_4 Menadiol Sodium Diphosphate [*Vitamin K_4*] (DAVI)
K-5 Kindergarten-Fifth Grade (SAUO)
K9 Canine [*K9 Corps - Army Dogs*] [*World War II*]
K-10 Gastric Tube [*Medicine*] (STED)
K-12 Kindergarten through 12th Grade (WDAA)
K-12 Kindergarten-Twelfth Grade (SAUO)
K 17 Thalidomide [*Medicine*] (EDAA)
K24H Potassium, Urine 24 Hour [*Biochemistry*] (DAVI)
K-25 Oak Ridge Gaseous Diffusion Plant (SAUS)
K-25 Oak Ridge K-25 Site [*Department of Energy*] [*Oak Ridge, TN*] (GAAI)
K25 Oak Ridge Uranium Separation Plant [*Code designation*] (DEN)
K-25 Site Oak Ridge K-25 Site (SAUO)
K_a Acid Ionization Constant [*Physics*] (DAVI)
KA Alkair [*Denmark*] [*ICAO designator*] (ICDA)
KA Alkaline Phosphatase [*An enzyme*] (DAVI)
Ka Auroral Absorption Index (CET)
KA Australia [*IYRU nationality code*] (IYR)
Ka Cathode [*Electron device*] (AAMN)
KA Coastal Plains Commuter [*ICAO designator*] (AD)
KA Concrete Arch [*Bridges*]
KA Dragon Air Hong Kong (SAUS)
KA Eha-Kibbuts ha-Artsi (BJA)
KA HMS King Alfred [*British military*] (DMA)
KA Kainic Acid [*Biochemistry*]
KA Kaiser Engineering (SAUO)
Ka Kallikrein (MEDA)
KA Kamov [*Former USSR*] [*ICAO aircraft manufacturer identifier*] (ICAO)
Ka Kaolinite [*A mineral*]
KA Karlsruhe [*German license plate city code*]
Ka Karolus de Tocco [*Flourished, 13th century*] [*Authority cited in pre-1607 legal work*] (DSA)
KA Kathode [*Cathode*] (AAG)
KA Keratoacanthoma [*Dermatology*] (DAVI)
KA Keren Ami (BJA)
KA Keto Acid (DMAA)
KA Ketoacidosis [*Medicine*]
KA Ketoaciduria (MELL)
K/A Ketogenic to Anti-Ketogenic [*Ratio*] [*In diets*]
KA Keyed Address (IAA)
KA Keyed Alike [*Locks*] (ADA)
KA Kill Assessment [*Military*] (ACAE)
ka Killed in Action
KA Kilmarnock [*Postcode*] (ODBW)
kA Kiloampere
KA Kinetic Analyzer [*Medicine*] (EDAA)
KA King-Armstrong Unit [*Clinical chemistry*]
KA King of Arms
KA King Pin Angle [*Automotive engineering*]
KA Knight of St. Andrew [*Russia*] [*Obsolete*]
KA Knight of the Order of Australia (WDAA)
K/A Knights of the Altar (EA)
KA Knolls Atomic Power Laboratory (SAUO)
KA Knowledge Acquisition [*Training term*] (LPT)
KA Krama Andhap [*Linguistics*] (IEL)
K-A Kuhlmann-Anderson Intelligence Tests [*Education*]
KA Kuwait Airways Corp.
KA Kynurenic Acid [*Biochemistry*] (OA)
KA Kypriakes Aerogrammes [*Cyprus Airlines*]
KA Thousands of Amperes
ka thousands of year ago (SAUO)
ka thousands of years (SAUO)
KAA Asia Aero Survey & Consulting Engineers, Inc. [*Korea*] [*ICAO designator*] (FAAC)
Ka A Kansas Appeals Reports [*A publication*] (DLA)
kaa Karakalpak [*MARC language code*] [*Library of Congress*] (LCCP)
KAA Karratha [*Australia*] [*Seismograph station code, US Geological Survey*] [*Closed*] (SEIS)
KAA Kasama [*Zambia*] [*Airport symbol*] (OAG)
KAA Keep-Alive Anode
KAAA Kingman, AZ [*AM radio station call letters*]
KAAB Batesville, AR [*AM radio station call letters*]
KAAC Korean Association of Automatic Control (SAUO)
KAAD Kerosene, Alcohol, Acetic Acid, and Dioxane (DMAA)
KAAE Kansas Association of Agriculture Educators (EARSL)
KAAH Honolulu, HI [*Television station call letters*] (BROA)
KAAK Great Falls, MT [*FM radio station call letters*]
KAAL Austin, MN [*Television station call letters*]
KAAM Huntsville, MO [*FM radio station call letters*]
KAAM Plano, TX [*AM radio station call letters*] (RBYB)
KAAM-AM Garland, TX [*AM radio station call letters*] (BROA)
KAAN Bethany, MO [*AM radio station call letters*]
KAAN-FM Bethany, MO [*FM radio station call letters*]
KAAO Kabul [*Afghanistan*] [*Seismograph station code, US Geological Survey*] (SEIS)
KAAO Korean Air Area of Operations (SAUO)
KAAP Kansas Army Ammunition Plant (AABC)
KAAP Rock Island, WA [*FM radio station call letters*] (BROA)
KAAQ Alliance, NE [*FM radio station call letters*]
KAAR Butte, MT [*FM radio station call letters*]
KAAS Keele Assessment of Auditory Style (DMAA)
KAAS Salina, KS [*Television station call letters*]
KAAT Oakhurst, CA [*FM radio station call letters*]
KAAX Avenal, CA [*FM radio station call letters*]
KAAY Little Rock, AR [*AM radio station call letters*]
KAb Abilene Free Public Library, Abilene, KS [*Library symbol*] [*Library of Congress*] (LCLS)
KAB Kabansk [*Former USSR*] [*Seismograph station code, US Geological Survey*] (SEIS)
Kab Kabul (SAUO)
KAB Kaneb Services [*NYSE symbol*] (TTSB)
KAB Kaneb Services, Inc. [*NYSE symbol*] (SPSG)
KAB Kansas Association of Broadcasters (EARSL)
KAB Kariba Dam [*Zimbabwe*] [*Airport symbol*] (OAG)
KAB Katholieke Arbeidersbeweging [*Netherlands*]
KAB Keep America Beautiful (EA)
KAB Knowledge, Attitudes, and Behavior Survey [*Department of Health and Human Services*] (GFGA)
KAB Korean Accreditation Board (SAUO)
ka-band 0.8 cm wavelength radar (SAUS)
KABB San Antonio, TX [*Television station call letters*]
K-ABC Kaufman Assessment Battery for Children [*Diagnostic assessment test*] (PAZ)
KABC Los Angeles, CA [*AM radio station call letters*]
KABCC Korea Australia Business Cooperation Council
KABC-DT Los Angeles, CA [*Television station call letters*] (BROA)
KABC-TV Los Angeles, CA [*Television station call letters*]
KAbE Dwight D. Eisenhower Library, Abilene, KS [*Library symbol*] [*Library of Congress*] (LCLS)
KABF Little Rock, AR [*FM radio station call letters*]
KABG-FM Los Alamos, NM [*FM radio station call letters*] (BROA)
KABH Shawnee, OK [*FM radio station call letters*]
KABI Abilene, KS [*AM radio station call letters*]
KABI Abilene/Municipal [*Texas*] [*ICAO location identifier*] (ICLI)
KABINS Knowledge, Attitude, Behavior, and Improvement in Nutritional Status (STED)
KABIR Kapitalist Birokrat [*Capitalist Bureaucrat*] [*Term for foreigner*] [*Indonesia*]
KABK Augusta, AR [*FM radio station call letters*]
KABL Oakland, CA [*AM radio station call letters*]
KABLE Kennedy Space Center Atmospheric Boundary Layer Experiment (ACAE)
KABN Long Island, AK [*AM radio station call letters*]
KABO Lewiston, MT [*Television station call letters*] (BROA)

KABPrA...... Kaneb Svc Adj Rt A Pfd [*NYSE symbol*] (TTSB)
KABQ........ Albuquerque/International [*New Mexico*] [*ICAO location identifier*] (ICLI)
KABQ........ Albuquerque, NM [*AM radio station call letters*]
KABR........ Alamo Community, NM [*AM radio station call letters*] (BROA)
KABS........ Great Falls, MT [*FM radio station call letters*]
KABU-FM.... Fort Totten, ND [*FM radio station call letters*] (RBYB)
KABX........ Canadian Resource Distribution [*Private rail car owner code*]
KABX........ Merced, CA [*FM radio station call letters*]
KABY........ Aberdeen, SD [*Television station call letters*]
KABZ........ Little Rock, AR [*FM radio station call letters*] (BROA)
kac........... Kachin [*MARC language code*] [*Library of Congress*] (LCCP)
KAC.......... Kaman Aircraft Corporation (SAUO)
KAC.......... Kamishli [*Syria*] [*Airport symbol*] (AD)
KAC.......... Kanian Aircraft Corporation (SAUO)
KAC.......... Key Access Code (SAUO)
KAC.......... Kinetics and Catalysis
KAC.......... Knight Armament Co. (SAUO)
KAC.......... Komatsu America Corporation (SAUO)
KAC.......... Korean American Coalition (EA)
KAC.......... Kuwait Airways Corp. [*ICAO designator*] (FAAC)
KACB........ San Angelo, TX [*Television station call letters*]
KACC........ Alvin, TX [*FM radio station call letters*]
KACC........ Kaiser Aluminum & Chemical Corporation (SAUO)
KACC........ Kansas Association of Community Colleges (SAUO)
KACC........ Korean-American Chamber of Commerce [*Later, AAACC*]
KACD........ Kansas Association of Soil Conservation Districts (SRA)
KACD........ Santa Monica, CA [*FM radio station call letters*]
KACD-AM... Thousand Oaks, CA [*AM radio station call letters*] (BROA)
KACDC...... Kansas Association of Certified Development Companies (EARSL)
KACE........ Inglewood, CA [*FM radio station call letters*]
KACE........ Tremonton, UT [*AM radio station call letters*] (BROA)
KACEE....... Kansas Advisory Council on Environmental Education (EDAC)
KACF........ Korean-American Cultural Foundation (EA)
KACH........ Kaiser Chemical [*Federal Railroad Administration identification code*]
KACH........ Preston, ID [*AM radio station call letters*]
KACHA....... Kentuckiana Automated Clearing House (TBD)
KACHAPAG... Karlsruhe Charged Particle Group (NITA)
KACI......... The Dalles, OR [*AM radio station call letters*]
KACIA....... Korea-American Commerce and Industry Association [*Later, KS*]
KACI-FM.... The Dalles, OR [*FM radio station call letters*]
KACK........ Nantucket [*Massachusetts*] [*ICAO location identifier*] (ICLI)
KACL-FM.... Bismarck, ND [*FM radio station call letters*] (RBYB)
KACo........ Kentucky Association of Counties (EARSL)
KACO-FM... Ardmore, OK [*FM radio station call letters*] (RBYB)
KACP........ Custer, SD [*FM radio station call letters*]
KACP........ Kansas Association of Chiefs of Police (SRA)
KACQ........ Lometa, TX [*FM radio station call letters*] (RBYB)
KACS........ Chehalis, WA [*FM radio station call letters*]
KACT........ Andrews, TX [*AM radio station call letters*]
KACT........ Waco/Waco Municipal [*Texas*] [*ICAO location identifier*] (ICLI)
KACTE....... Kentucky Association for Career and Technical Education (EARSL)
KACT-FM.... Andrews, TX [*FM radio station call letters*]
KACTUS..... Modelling Knowledge About Complex Technical Systems for Multiple Use (SAUO)
KACU........ Abilene, TX [*FM radio station call letters*]
KACV........ Amarillo, TX [*FM radio station call letters*]
KACV-TV.... Amarillo, TX [*Television station call letters*]
KACW........ North Bend, OR [*FM radio station call letters*]
KACX........ Kaiser Aluminum and Chemical [*Private rail car owner code*]
KACY........ Atlantic City/Atlantic City [*New Jersey*] [*ICAO location identifier*] (ICLI)
KACY........ Lafayette, LA [*AM radio station call letters*]
KACZ........ Riley, KS [*FM radio station call letters*] (BROA)
KAD.......... Kadena Air Base, Ryuku Islands (NASA)
KAD.......... Kadette [*NCIC car model code*]
KAD.......... Kadrey Energy [*Vancouver Stock Exchange symbol*]
KAD.......... Kaduna [*Nigeria*] [*Airport symbol*] (OAG)
KAD.......... Karad [*India*] [*Seismograph station code, US Geological Survey*] (SEIS)
KAD.......... Kathmandu Association of Deaf (SAUO)
KAD.......... Keyboard and Display [*Computer science*]
KADA........ Ada, OK [*AM radio station call letters*]
KADA........ Kemubu Agricultural Development Authority (SAUO)
KADA........ Kemuta Agricultural Development Authority (SAUO)
KADA-FM... Ada, OK [*FM radio station call letters*]
KADD........ Laughlin, NV [*FM radio station call letters*]
KADE........ San Luis Obispo, CA [*Television station call letters*]
KaDeWe..... Kaufhaus des Westens [*Department Store of the West*] [*Germany*]
KADF........ Kuwait Air Defense Force (MCD)
KADI......... Republic, MO [*FM radio station call letters*]
KADM........ Ardmore [*Oklahoma*] [*ICAO location identifier*] (ICLI)
KADM........ Odessa, TX [*FM radio station call letters*]
KADN........ Lafayette, LA [*Television station call letters*]
KADOS...... Knowledge-Based Automated Design of Silencers [*Automotive engineering*]
KADP........ Kaduna State Agricultural Development Project [*Nigeria*] (ECON)
KADQ........ Rexburg, ID [*FM radio station call letters*]
KADR........ Elkader, IA [*AM radio station call letters*]
KADS........ Elk City, OK [*AM radio station call letters*]
KADS........ Kabul Amateur Dramatic Society (SAUO)
KADS........ Knowledge Acquisition and Documentation System (VLIE)
KADS........ Knowledge Acquisition Data System (SAUS)
KADS........ Korea Air Defense System (CINC)
KADS........ Korean Air Defense Sector (SAUO)
KADSE....... Knowledge Assisted Decision Support Environment
KADU........ Hibbing, MN [*FM radio station call letters*]
KADU........ Kenya African Democratic Union [*Political party*] (PPW)
KADV........ Modesto, CA [*FM radio station call letters*]
KADW....... Camp Springs/Andrews Air Force Base [*Maryland*] [*ICAO location identifier*] (ICLI)
KADX........ Houston, AK [*FM radio station call letters*]
KADY........ Oxnard, CA [*Television station call letters*]
KADZ........ Arvada, CO [*AM radio station call letters*] (BROA)
KAE.......... Kaena [*Hawaii*] [*Seismograph station code, US Geological Survey*] (SEIS)
KAE.......... Kake [*Alaska*] [*Airport symbol*] (OAG)
KAE.......... Keighley Association of Engineers (SAUO)
KAE.......... Kinesthetic Aftereffect (DIPS)
KAE.......... Knitting Arts Expo (TSPED)
KAE4-HA.... Kansas Association of Extension 4-H Agents (EARSL)
KAEA........ Korean Association of Electronics and Automation (SAUO)
KAEC........ Kentucky Association of Electric Cooperatives (SRA)
KAECT....... Kansas Association for Educational Communications & Technology
KAEDS....... Keystone Association for Educational Data Systems (HGAA)
KAEF......... Arcata, CA [*Television station call letters*]
KAEH........ Beaumont, CA [*FM radio station call letters*]
KAEH........ King Air Equivalent Hours (SAUS)
KAEP........ Spokane, WA [*FM radio station call letters*] (RBYB)
KAERI....... Korean Atomic Energy Research Institute (SAUO)
KAES........ Kaessbohrer [*NCIC truck make code*]
KAESP....... Kansas Association of Elementary School Principals (SAUO)
KAET........ Phoenix, AZ [*Television station call letters*]
KAEX........ Alexandria/England Air Force Base [*Louisiana*] [*ICAO location identifier*] (ICLI)
KAEZ......... Amarillo, TX [*FM radio station call letters*]
KAF.......... Conglutinogen Activating Factor [*Medicine*] (MELL)
KAF.......... Kafue International Air Services Ltd. [*Zambia*] [*FAA designator*] (FAAC)
KAF.......... Karato [*Papua New Guinea*] [*Airport symbol*] (OAG)
KAF.......... Kazakhstan Air Force (SAUO)
KAF.......... Kenya Air Force
KAF.......... Khmer [*Cambodia*] Air Force (VNW)
KAF.......... Killer-Assistng Factor (DAVI)
KAF.......... Kinase-Activating Factor [*Organic chemistry*] (DAVI)
KAF.......... Kuwaiti Air Force (DOMA)
KAFA......... Colorado Springs-Pueblo, CO [*FM radio station call letters*] (GDPB)
KAFAD....... Kuwait Air Force & Air Defence (SAUO)
KAFB........ Keesler Air Force Base [*Mississippi*]
KAFB........ Kirtland Air Force Base [*New Mexico*]
KAFC........ Kenny Antcliff Fan Club (EA)
KAFC-FM.... Anchorage, AK [*FM radio station call letters*] (BROA)
KAFE......... Bellingham, WA [*FM radio station call letters*]
KAFF......... Flagstaff, AZ [*AM radio station call letters*]
KAFF-FM.... Flagstaff, AZ [*FM radio station call letters*]
KAFFR....... Kaffaria [*South Africa*] (ROG)
Kaff R....... Kaffrarian Rifles (SAUO)
KAFH........ Ku-Band Antenna Feed Horn
KAFM........ Grand Junction, CO [*FM radio station call letters*] (BROA)
KAFN-FM... Gould, AR [*FM radio station call letters*] (BROA)
KAFO........ Knee-Ankle-Foot Orthosis [*Medicine*]
KAFP........ Kansas Academy of Family Physicians (SRA)
KAFP........ Kentucky Academy of Family Physicians (SRA)
KAFR........ Angel Fire, NM [*FM radio station call letters*]
KAFT......... Fayetteville, AR [*Television station call letters*]
KAFU........ Enid, OK [*Television station call letters*]
KAFW........ Wilson, AR [*FM radio station call letters*] (RBYB)
KAFX........ Lufkin, TX [*FM radio station call letters*] (GDPB)
KAFX-FM.... Diboll, TX [*FM radio station call letters*]
KAFY........ Bakersfield, CA [*AM radio station call letters*]
KAG.......... Cryptographic Aid, General Publication (CET)
KAG.......... Kagoshima [*Japan*] [*Seismograph station code, US Geological Survey*] (SEIS)
KAG.......... Kagoshima Space Center [*Japan*]
KAG.......... Kelvin Astatic Galvanometer [*Electronics*]
KAGA........ Santa Ynez, CA [*FM radio station call letters*]
KAGB........ Waimea, HI [*FM radio station call letters*] (BROA)
KAGC........ Bryan, TX [*AM radio station call letters*]
KAGE........ Winona, MN [*AM radio station call letters*]
KAGE-FM... Winona, MN [*FM radio station call letters*]
KAGG........ Madisonville, TX [*FM radio station call letters*]
KAGH........ Crossett, AR [*AM radio station call letters*]
KAGH-FM... Crossett, AR [*FM radio station call letters*]
KAGI......... Grants Pass, OR [*AM radio station call letters*]
KAGI......... Kesatuan Aksi Guru Indonesia [*Action Front of Indonesian Teachers*]
KAGJ........ Ephraim, UT [*FM radio station call letters*]
KAGL........ El Dorado, AR [*FM radio station call letters*] (RBYB)
KAGM........ Strasburg, CO [*FM radio station call letters*]
KAGO........ Klamath Falls, OR [*AM radio station call letters*]
KAGO-FM... Klamath Falls, OR [*FM radio station call letters*]
KAGP........ Grants, NM [*FM radio station call letters*]
KAGR........ Bemidji, MN [*Television station call letters*] (BROA)
KAGR........ Morro Bay, CA [*FM radio station call letters*] (RBYB)
KAGT........ Baird, TX [*FM radio station call letters*] (BROA)
KAGU........ Spokane, WA [*FM radio station call letters*]
KAGV........ Big Lake, AK [*AM radio station call letters*] (BROA)
KAGY........ Port Sulphur, LA [*AM radio station call letters*]
KAH.......... Keilschrifttexte aus Assur Historischen Inhalts [*A publication*] (BJA)

KAH Kent Aviation Ltd. [*Canada*] [*ICAO designator*] (FAAC)
KAH Kiloampere Hour (IAA)
KAH Knots an Hour [*Telegraphy*] (PCTE)
KAHA Honolulu, HI [*FM radio station call letters*] (BROA)
KAHA Kahala Corp. [*NASDAQ symbol*] (QUAN)
KAHC Kentucky Association of Highway Contractors (EARSL)
KAHF-FM Ortonville, MN [*FM radio station call letters*] (RBYB)
KAHI Auburn, CA [*AM radio station call letters*]
KAHI Keilschrifttexte aus Assur Historischen Inhalts [*A publication*] (BJA)
KAHK-FM Georgetown, TX [*FM radio station call letters*] (BROA)
Kahler Kahler Corp. [*Associated Press*] (SAG)
KAHM Prescott, AZ [*FM radio station call letters*]
KAHO Junction, TX [*FM radio station call letters*]
KAHP Kentucky Allied Health Project (EDAC)
KAHR Poplar Bluff, MO [*FM radio station call letters*]
KAHRP Knob-Associated Histidine-Rich Protein [*Cytology*]
KAHS El Dorado, KS [*AM radio station call letters*] (BROA)
KAHS Thousand Oaks, CA [*AM radio station call letters*] (RBYB)
KAHSLC Knoxville Area Health Science Consortium [*Library network*]
KAHTAFU Kenya African National Traders and Farmers Union (SAUO)
KAHU Hilo, HI [*AM radio station call letters*]
KAHX-FM Ingleside, TX [*FM radio station call letters*] (RBYB)
KAHY Myrtle Point, OR [*FM radio station call letters*]
KAHZ Fort Worth, TX [*AM radio station call letters*]
KAI Kaieteur [*Guyana*] [*Airport symbol*] (OAG)
KAI Kaimata [*New Zealand*] [*Seismograph station code, US Geological Survey*] (SEIS)
KAI Kanaanaeische und Aramaeische Inschriften [*A publication*] (BJA)
KAI Kansas Association of Inventors (EARSL)
KAI Kazan Aviation Institute
KAI Keep America Independent [*Defunct*] (EA)
KAI Key Asset Initiative [*Emergency Management*] (EMA)
KAI Knowledge Access, Inc.
KAI Korean Affairs Institute (EA)
KAI Kurzweil Applied Intelligence [*Computer science*]
KAIA Kansas Association of Insurance Agents (EARSL)
KAIC Komatsu America Industries Corporation (SAUO)
KAICA Korea Auto Industries Cooperation Association (SAUO)
KAID Boise, ID [*Television station call letters*]
KAIE Honolulu, HI [*Television station call letters*] (BROA)
KAIG Kearfott Acceleration Integrating Gyroscope
KAIGBZ Japanese Journal of Nuclear Medicine (journ.) (SAUS)
KAIH Jacksboro, TX [*FM radio station call letters*] (RBYB)
KAII Kiddie Academy International, Inc. [*NASDAQ symbol*] (SAG)
KAII Kiddie Academy Intl [*NASDAQ symbol*] (TTSB)
KAII Wailuku, HI [*Television station call letters*]
KAIIW Kiddie Academy Intl Wrrt [*NASDAQ symbol*] (TTSB)
KAIL Fresno, CA [*Television station call letters*]
KAIM Honolulu, HI [*AM radio station call letters*]
KAIM-FM Honolulu, HI [*FM radio station call letters*]
KAIMH Kansas Association for Infant Mental Health (SAUO)
KAIN Vidalia, LA [*AM radio station call letters*]
KAIO Rio Grande City, TX [*Television station call letters*] (BROA)
KAIQ Littlefield, TX [*FM radio station call letters*] (BROA)
KAIR Kansas City, MO (Lawrence, KS) [*FM radio station call letters*] (GDPB)
KAIR-AM Atchison, KS [*AM radio station call letters*] (RBYB)
KAIRE Ecumenical Group of Women (SAUO)
KAIR-FM Horton, KS [*FM radio station call letters*] (RBYB)
KAIS Kaiser [*NCIC car make code*]
KAIS Knowledge and Information Systems [*Database*] [*United Kingdom*] (GDD)
KAIS Korean Air Intelligence System (MCD)
KaisA Kaiser Aluminum & Chemical Corp. [*Associated Press*] (SAG)
KaisAl Kaiser Aluminum & Chemical Corp. [*Associated Press*] (SAG)
KAIST Korea Advanced Institute of Science and Technology [*Seoul*] [*Information service or system*] (IID)
KaisVent Kaiser Ventures, Inc. [*Associated Press*] (SAG)
KAIT Jonesboro, AR [*Television station call letters*]
KAIT Katzman Automatic Imaging Telescope [*University of California*]
KAIT Kaufman Adolescent and Adult Intelligence Test (DIPS)
KAIU-FM Grants, NM [*FM radio station call letters*] (BROA)
KAJ Kajaani [*Finland*] [*Airport symbol*] (OAG)
KAJ Kashiwara [*Japan*] [*Seismograph station code, US Geological Survey*] (SEIS)
KAJ Keilschrifttexte aus Assur Juridischen Inhalts [*A publication*] (BJA)
KAJA San Antonio, TX [*FM radio station call letters*]
KAJB Calipatria, CA [*Television station call letters*] (BROA)
KAJF Kids Against Junk Food [*An association*] (EA)
KAJI Keilschrifttexte aus Assur Juridischen Inhalts [*A publication*] (BJA)
KAJI Point Comfort, TX [*FM radio station call letters*] (RBYB)
KAJK Fortuna, CA [*AM radio station call letters*]
KAJK-FM Ferndale, CA [*FM radio station call letters*]
KAJL Winters, TX [*FM radio station call letters*] (RBYB)
KAJM Payson, AZ [*FM radio station call letters*] (BROA)
KAJN Crowley, LA [*FM radio station call letters*]
KAJO Grants Pass, OR [*AM radio station call letters*]
KAJP Firebaugh, CA [*FM radio station call letters*] (RBYB)
KAJQ Sibley, IA [*FM radio station call letters*] (RBYB)
KAJT K and J Trucking [*Common carrier symbol*]
KAJU Kajun [*NCIC truck make code*]
KAJW Tolleson, AZ [*Television station call letters*] (RBYB)
KAJX Aspen, CO [*FM radio station call letters*]
KAJZ El Paso, TX [*AM radio station call letters*] (BROA)
KAJZ-FM Killeen, TX [*FM radio station call letters*] (RBYB)
KAK Kakioka [*Japan*] [*Seismograph station code, US Geological Survey*] (SEIS)
KAK Kayapa Kallahan [*Language symbol*] (ETLW)
KAK Key-Auto-Key [*Computer science*]
KAK Kungliga Automobil Klubben
KAKA-FM Salina, KS [*FM radio station call letters*] (BROA)
KAKC Tulsa, OK [*AM radio station call letters*]
KAKD Eureka, CA [*FM radio station call letters*] (RBYB)
KAKE Wichita, KS [*Television station call letters*]
KAKI Kamp King [*NCIC truck make code*]
KAKI Kimes and Kimes [*Common carrier symbol*]
KAKJ Marianna, AR [*FM radio station call letters*]
KAKK Walker, MN [*AM radio station call letters*] (BROA)
KAKM Anchorage, AK [*Television station call letters*]
kakm Kakemono (VRA)
KAKN Naknek, AK [*FM radio station call letters*]
KAKO Gooding, ID [*FM radio station call letters*] (RBYB)
KAKP Bagdad, AZ [*FM radio station call letters*] (RBYB)
KAKP-FM Chino Valley, AZ [*FM radio station call letters*] (BROA)
KAKQ Fairbanks, AK [*FM radio station call letters*]
KAKQ-FM Fairbanks, AK [*FM radio station call letters*]
KAKR Akron [*Ohio*] [*ICAO location identifier*] (ICLI)
KAKR-FM Sterling City, TX [*FM radio station call letters*] (RBYB)
KAKT-FM Phoenix, OR [*FM radio station call letters*] (RBYB)
KAKU-FM Springfield, MO [*FM radio station call letters*] (RBYB)
KAKV-FM Lompoc, CA [*FM radio station call letters*] (RBYB)
KAKW Kileen, TX [*TV station call letters*] (RBYB)
KAKX Mendocino, CA [*FM radio station call letters*] (RBYB)
KAKZ Juneau, AK [*FM radio station call letters*] (RBYB)
KAL Caltech Data Ltd. [*Vancouver Stock Exchange symbol*]
KAL Kalamazoo [*Diocesan abbreviation*] [*Michigan*] (TOCD)
KAL Kalamein [*Trademark*]
KAL Kal-Custom Boat Trailer [*NCIC trailer make code*]
KAL Kalendae [*The Kalends*] [*First day of the ancient Roman month*]
Kal Kalium [*Potassium*] (STED)
KAL Kalium [*Potassium*] [*Pharmacy*]
Kal Kallah (BJA)
KAL Kallista [*NCIC car model code*]
KAL Kallmann [*Syndrome*] [*Medicine*] (DMAA)
KAL Kalocsa [*Hungary*] [*Seismograph station code, US Geological Survey*] [*Closed*] (SEIS)
KAL Kaltag [*Alaska*] [*Airport symbol*] (OAG)
KAL Kappa Application Language [*Artificial intelligence system*] [*Intelli-Corp*] (PCM)
KAL Key Assets List (COE)
KAL Keywords and Learning (AIE)
KAL Korean Air Lines Co. Ltd. [*ICAO designator*] (FAAC)
KAL Korean Air Lines, Inc.
KALA Davenport, IA [*FM radio station call letters*]
KALAM Kalamazoo, MI [*American Association of Railroads railroad junction routing code*]
KALB Albany/Albany [*New York*] [*ICAO location identifier*] (ICLI)
KALB-TV Alexandria, LA [*Television station call letters*]
KALC Denver, CO [*FM radio station call letters*]
KALC Krypton Absorption in Liquid Carbon Dioxide [*Nuclear energy*] (NRCH)
KALCC Korean Airlift Control Center (SAUO)
KALD Kalamein [*Trademark*] Door
KALDAS Kidsgrove ALGOL [*Algorithmic Language*] Digital Analogue Simulation [*Computer science*] [*British*]
KALE Richland, WA [*AM radio station call letters*]
KALF Red Bluff, CA [*FM radio station call letters*]
KALG Chadron, NE [*FM radio station call letters*] (RBYB)
KALI Alice/International [*Texas*] [*ICAO location identifier*] (ICLI)
KALI San Gabriel, CA [*AM radio station call letters*]
KALI West Covina, CA [*AM radio station call letters*] (BROA)
KALI-FM Santa Ana, CA [*FM radio station call letters*] (RBYB)
KALK Winfield, TX [*FM radio station call letters*]
KALL Kallio Company [*NCIC trailer make code*]
KALL Salt Lake City, UT [*AM radio station call letters*]
KALM Thayer, MO [*AM radio station call letters*]
KALN Iola, KS [*AM radio station call letters*]
KALO Honolulu, HI [*Television station call letters*] (BROA)
KALO Port Arthur, TX [*AM radio station call letters*]
KALP Alpine, TX [*FM radio station call letters*]
KAL PPT Kali Praeparatum [*Prepared Kali*] [*Carbonate of potash*] [*Pharmacy*] (ROG)
KALQ Alamosa, CO [*FM radio station call letters*]
KALR Hot Springs, AR [*FM radio station call letters*]
KalR Kallah Rabbati (BJA)
KALS Kalispell, MT [*FM radio station call letters*]
KALT Atlanta, TX [*AM radio station call letters*]
KALT-FM Alturas, CA [*FM radio station call letters*] (BROA)
KALU Langston, OK [*FM radio station call letters*]
KALV Alva, OK [*AM radio station call letters*]
KALW San Francisco, CA [*FM radio station call letters*]
KALX Berkeley, CA [*FM radio station call letters*]
KALY Kalyn Company [*NCIC trailer make code*]
KALY Los Ranchos de Albuquerque, NM [*AM radio station call letters*]
KALZ-FM Fresno, CA [*FM radio station call letters*] (BROA)
KAM Benedictine College, South Campus, Atchison, KS [*Library symbol*] [*Library of Congress*] (LCLS)
KAM Kama [*NCIC motorcycle make code*]
KAM Kamaran Island [*South Arabia (Yemen)*] [*Airport symbol*] (AD)

kam.......... Kamba [*MARC language code*] [*Library of Congress*] (LCCP)
Kam......... Kames' Dictionary of Decisions, Scotch Court of Session [*A publication*] (DLA)
Kam......... Kames' Remarkable Decisions, Scotch Court of Session [*2 vols.*] [*1716-52*] [*A publication*] (DLA)
KAM......... Kameyama [*Japan*] [*Seismograph station code, US Geological Survey*] (SEIS)
KAM......... Kansas Association of Mappers (SAUO)
KAM......... Kaupapa Atawhai Manager (SAUO)
KAM......... Keep-Alive Memory [*Computer science*]
KAM......... Kehillath Anshe Mayriv (BJA)
KAM......... Kenya African Movement
KAM......... Key Account Management (FOTI)
KAM......... Keyboard Attach Machine [*Computer science*] (TIMI)
KAM......... Kinematic Analysis Method
KAM......... Knudsen Absolute Manometer [*Physics*]
KAM......... Kolmogorov-Arnold-Moser [*Statistical mechanics*]
KAMA........ Amarillo/Amarillo Air Terminal [*Texas*] [*ICAO location identifier*] (ICLI)
KAMA........ El Paso, TX [*AM radio station call letters*]
KAMA........ Kamp-a-While Industries [*NCIC trailer make code*]
KAMA........ Korean-American Medical Association (EA)
Kaman...... Kaman Corp. [*Associated Press*] (SAG)
KAMB........ Merced, CA [*FM radio station call letters*]
KAMC........ Komatsu America Manufacturing Corp. [*Chattanooga, TN*]
KAMC........ Lubbock, TX [*Television station call letters*]
KAMD........ Camden, AR [*AM radio station call letters*]
KAMD-FM... Camden, AR [*FM radio station call letters*] (RBYB)
KAME........ Reno, NV [*Television station call letters*]
Kam Eluc... Kames' Elucidation of the Laws of Scotland [*A publication*] (DLA)
Kam Eq..... Kames' Principles of Equity [*A publication*] (DLA)
Kames....... Kames' Dictionary of Decisions, Scotch Court of Session [*A publication*] (DLA)
Kames....... Kames' Remarkable Decisions, Scotch Court of Session [*2 vols.*] [*1716-52*] [*A publication*] (DLA)
Kames Dec... Kames' Dictionary of Decisions, Scotch Court of Session [*A publication*] (DLA)
Kames Dict Dec... Kames' Dictionary of Decisions, Scotch Court of Session [*A publication*] (DLA)
Kames Elucid... Kames' Elucidation of the Laws of Scotland [*A publication*] (DLA)
Kames Eq... Kames' Principles of Equity [*A publication*] (DLA)
Kames Rem......... Kames' Remarkable Decisions, Scotch Court of Session [*2 vols.*] [*1716-52*] [*A publication*] (DLA)
Kames Rem Dec... Kames' Remarkable Decisions [*Scotland*] [*A publication*] (DLA)
Kames Sel Dec... Kames' Select Decisions [*Scotland*] [*A publication*] (DLA)
KAMF........ Kansas Motor Freight [*Common carrier symbol*]
KAMFES..... Kentucky Association of Milk, Food, and Environmental Sanitarians (SRA)
KAMFR...... Kinesthetic Application of Mechanical Force Reflection
KAMFT...... Kansas Association of Marriage and Family Therapy (SRA)
KAMFT...... Kentucky Association for Marriage and Family Therapy (SRA)
KAMG....... Victoria, TX [*AM radio station call letters*]
KAMI........ Cozad, NE [*AM radio station call letters*]
KAMI........ Kasatuan Aksi Mahasiswa Indonesia [*Political party*] (BARN)
KAMI-FM.... Cozad, NE [*FM radio station call letters*]
KAMJ........ Gosnell, AR [*FM radio station call letters*] (RBYB)
KAMK........ National Council for Quality and Accreditation (SAUO)
KAMK-FM... Forest City, IA [*FM radio station call letters*] (RBYB)
KAML........ Gillette, WY [*FM radio station call letters*]
KAML........ Kenedy-Karnes City, TX [*AM radio station call letters*]
KamLAND... Kamioka Liquid Scintillator Anti-Neutrino Detector
KAMLO...... Kamloops, BC [*American Association of Railroads railroad junction routing code*]
Kam L Tr.... Kames' Historical Law Tracts [*Scotland*] [*A publication*] (DLA)
KAMM....... Karlsruhe Atmospheric Mesoscale Model (SAUO)
KAMM....... Madison, SD [*FM radio station call letters*] (RBYB)
KAMN....... Kaman Corp. [*NASDAQ symbol*] (NQ)
KAMNA..... Kaman Corp. Cl'A' [*NASDAQ symbol*] (TTSB)
KAMNZ..... Kaman Cp $3.25 Ser 2 Cv Dep Pfd [*NASDAQ symbol*] (TTSB)
KAMO....... Korean Airlift Management Office (SAUO)
KAMO....... Rogers, AR [*AM radio station call letters*]
KAMO-FM... Rogers, AR [*FM radio station call letters*]
KAMOPAC... Kamo Electric Cooperative Inc. PAC [*Vinita, OK*] (PACS)
KAMP........ El Centro, CA [*AM radio station call letters*]
KAMP........ Kampers Kabin [*NCIC trailer make code*]
KAMPI....... Supporters of the Free Philippines [*Political party*] (PSAP)
KAMQ....... Carlsbad, NM [*AM radio station call letters*]
KAMR....... Amarillo, TX [*Television station call letters*]
Kam Rem... Kames' Remarkable Decisions, Scotch Court of Session [*2 vols.*] [*1716-52*] [*A publication*] (DLA)
KAMS........ Korea Ammunition Management System (MCD)
KAMS........ Mammoth Spring, AR [*FM radio station call letters*]
Kam Sel.... Kames' Select Decisions [*Scotland*] [*A publication*] (DLA)
Kam Sel Dec... Kames' Select Decisions [*Scotland*] [*A publication*] (DLA)
KAMT........ Juneau, AK [*FM radio station call letters*] (RBYB)
KAMT........ Keeping Abreast of Medical Transcription (SAUO)
KAMU....... Chameleon Containers [*Intermodal shipping container symbol*] (TVRC)
KAMU....... College Station, TX [*FM radio station call letters*]
KAMU-TV... College Station, TX [*Television station call letters*]
KAMX........ Luling, TX [*FM radio station call letters*] (RBYB)
KAMY........ Lubbock, TX [*FM radio station call letters*]
KAMZ........ Koch Asphalt Materials [*Federal Railroad Administration identification code*]
KAMZ........ Tahoka, TX [*FM radio station call letters*] (BROA)
KAN.......... Kanazawa [*Japan*] [*Seismograph station code, US Geological Survey*] (SEIS)
kan........... Kannada [*MARC language code*] [*Library of Congress*] (LCCP)
KAN.......... Kannapolis, NC [*Amtrak rail station code*]
KAN.......... Kano [*Nigeria*] [*Airport symbol*] (OAG)
Kan.......... Kansas (ODBW)
KAN.......... Kansas
KAN.......... Kansas Power & Light Co. (SAUO)
Kan.......... Kansas Supreme Court Reports [*A publication*] (DLA)
Kan.......... Kantorei [*Record label*] [*Germany*]
KAN.......... Kriegsausruestungsnachweisung [*Table of Basic Allowances*] [*German military - World War II*]
KANA........ Kamut Association of North America (NTPA)
KANA........ Kana Software [*NASDAQ symbol*]
Kan Admin Regs... Kansas Administration Regulations [*A publication*] (DLA)
Kan Ann..... Vernon's Kansas Statutes, Annotated [*A publication*] (DLA)
Kan App..... Kansas Appeals Reports [*A publication*] (DLA)
KANAU...... Kanauga, OH [*American Association of Railroads railroad junction routing code*]
Kanb......... Kaneb Services, Inc. [*Associated Press*] (SAG)
Kan City L Rep... Kansas City Law Reporter [*A publication*] (DLA)
Kan City L Rev... Kansas City Law Review [*A publication*] (DLA)
Kan Civ Pro Stat Ann... Vernon's Kansas Statutes, Annotated, Code of Civil Procedure [*A publication*] (DLA)
Kan Civ Pro Stat Ann (Vernon)... Vernon's Kansas Statutes, Annotated, Code of Civil Procedure [*A publication*] (DLA)
Kan CL & IWC... Kansas Commission of Labor and Industry Workmen's Compensation Department Reports [*A publication*] (DLA)
Kan CL Rep... Kansas City Law Reporter [*A publication*] (DLA)
Kan Crim Code & Code of Crim Proc... Criminal Code and Code of Criminal Procedure [*Kansas*] [*A publication*] (DLA)
Kan Crim Code & Code of Crim Proc (Vernon)... Vernon's Kansas Statutes, Annotated, Criminal Code and Code of Criminal Procedure [*A publication*] (DLA)
Kan Ct App... Kansas Appellate Reports [*A publication*] (DLA)
KANCY...... Kansas City, KS [*American Association of Railroads railroad junction routing code*]
KAND........ Corsicana, TX [*AM radio station call letters*]
K&B.......... Kaufman & Broad Home (EFIS)
k & b........ Kitchen and Bathroom (ODA)
K & B........ Kotze and Barber's Transvaal (High Court) Reports [*1885-88*] [*A publication*] (DLA)
K & B Dig... Kerford and Box's Victorian Digest [*A publication*] (DLA)
K & CL...... Kensington and Chelsea Law Group [*British*]
K&D......... Kaselaan & d'Angelo Associates, Inc. (EFIS)
K & D....... Kitchen and Dining Room [*Real estate terminology*]
K&E.......... Kirkland & Ellis
K & E Conv... Key and Elphinstone's Conveyancing [*15th ed.*] [*1953-54*] [*A publication*] (DLA)
K & F NSW... Knox and Fitzhardinge's New South Wales Reports [*A publication*] (DLA)
K & G....... Keane and Grant's English Registration Appeal Cases [*1854-62*] [*A publication*] (DLA)
K & G....... Kerbing and Guttering [*British*] (ADA)
K & Gr...... Keane and Grant's English Registration Appeal Cases [*1854-62*] [*A publication*] (DLA)
K & GRC.... Keane and Grant's English Registration Appeal Cases [*1854-62*] [*A publication*] (DLA)
K&H......... Memory Time Value (SAUS)
KANDIDATS... Kansas Digital Data System
KANDIDATS... Kansas Digital Image Data System (SAUO)
KANDIDATS... University of Kansas Landsat Software System (SAUO)
Kan Dig..... Hatcher's Kansas Digest [*A publication*] (DLA)
K & J........ Kay and Johnson's English Vice-Chancellors' Reports [*69, 70 English Reprint*] [*A publication*] (DLA)
K & J........ Kenrick & Jefferson (DGA)
K&M......... Kane-Miller Corp. (EFIS)
K & O....... Knapp and Ombler's English Election Cases [*A publication*] (DLA)
K & R....... Kent and Radcliff's Law of New York, Revision of 1801 [*A publication*] (DLA)
K&R......... Kernighan & Ritchie (VLIE)
K&R......... Kernighan + Ritchie (SAUO)
K and R...... Kidnaping and Ransom [*Insurance policy*]
K&S.......... Kulicke & Soffa Industries (EFIS)
K&SEAFA... Korea and South East Asia Forces Association of Australia (SAUO)
K & W....... Kames and Woodhouselee's Folio Dictionary, Scotch Court of Session [*A publication*] (DLA)
K & W Dic... Kames and Woodhouselee's Folio Dictionary, Scotch Court of Session [*A publication*] (DLA)
K & Z........ Kipp and Zonen Recorders
KANE........ Kane, PA [*American Association of Railroads railroad junction routing code*]
KANE........ Kane Trailers [*NCIC trailer make code*]
KANE........ New Iberia, LA [*AM radio station call letters*]
Kaneb....... Kaneb Services, Inc. [*Associated Press*] (SAG)
Kanex....... Kansai Agricultural Commodities Exchange (NUMA)
KANG........ Kangaroo Express [*Common carrier symbol*]
KANGA...... Kangaroo (DSUE)
KANG-FM... Carrington, ND [*FM radio station call letters*] (RBYB)
KANG-FM... lake Havasu City, AZ [*FM radio station call letters*] (BROA)
KANH........ Emporia, KS [*FM radio station call letters*] (BROA)
KANH........ Kan Haul Trailer Sales [*NCIC trailer make code*]
KANI......... Wharton, TX [*AM radio station call letters*]
KANJ-FM.... Giddings, TX [*FM radio station call letters*] (RBYB)

KANKA ...... Kankakee, IL [*American Association of Railroads railroad junction routing code*]
KankakB .... Kankakkee Bancorp, Inc. [*Associated Press*] (SAG)
KANL .... Baker City, OR [*FM radio station call letters*] (BROA)
KANL .... Elko, NV [*Television station call letters*] (RBYB)
Kan Law .... Kansas Lawyer [*A publication*] (DLA)
Kan LJ ...... Kansas Law Journal [*A publication*] (DLA)
KANM .... Modesto, CA [*AM radio station call letters*] (BROA)
KANM .... Winnemucca, NV [*Television station call letters*] (RBYB)
KANN .... El Kane [*Common carrier symbol*]
KANN .... Kentucky Nurses Association (SAUO)
KANN .... Roy, UT [*AM radio station call letters*]
KANO-FM ... Hilo, HI [*FM radio station call letters*] (BROA)
KANOP ...... Kanolpolis, KS [*American Association of Railroads railroad junction routing code*]
KANP .... St. Charles, MN [*FM radio station call letters*] (RBYB)
KanPip ...... Kaneb Pipe Line Partners Ltd. [*Associated Press*] (SAG)
KanPipSn ... Kaneb Pipe Line Partners LP [*Associated Press*] (SAG)
KANQ .... Grand Marais, MN [*FM radio station call letters*] (RBYB)
KANR .... Belle Plaine, KS [*FM radio station call letters*]
KANr .... Kanamycin Resistant [*Genetics*]
KANS .... Kansas (AFM)
Kans .... Kansas (ODBW)
Kans .... Kansas Reports [*A publication*] (DLA)
KANS .... Larned, KS [*AM radio station call letters*]
KANS .... Osage City, KS [*FM radio station call letters*] (RBYB)
Kans App ... Kansas Appeals Reports [*A publication*] (DLA)
Kansas LJ .. Kansas Law Journal [*A publication*] (DLA)
Kansas R ... Kansas Reports [*A publication*] (DLA)
Kans BA..... Kansas City Bar Journal [*A publication*] (DLA)
Kan SCC .... Kansas State Corporation Commission Reports [*A publication*] (DLA)
Kansenshogaku Zasshi... Kansenshogaku Zasshi. Journal of the Japanese Association for Infectious Diseases (SAUO)
Kan Sess Laws... Session Laws of Kansas [*A publication*] (DLA)
Kans R...... Kansas Reports [*A publication*] (DLA)
Kans St U... Kansas State University of Agriculture and Applied Science (GAGS)
Kan Stat .... Kansas Statutes [*A publication*] (DLA)
Kan Stat Ann... Kansas Statutes Annotated [*A publication*] (AAGC)
Kan St LJ... Kansas State Law Journal [*A publication*] (DLA)
Kan Subject Ann Vernon's... Vernon's Kansas Statutes, Annotated [*A publication*] (DLA)
KANT .... Roseau, MN [*FM radio station call letters*] (RBYB)
KANU .... Kenya African National Union [*Political party*] (PPW)
KANU .... Lawrence, KS [*FM radio station call letters*]
Kan UCC Ann (Vernon)... Vernon's Kansas Statutes, Annotated, Uniform Commercial Code [*A publication*] (DLA)
Kan U Lawy... Kansas University Lawyer [*A publication*] (DLA)
Kan Univ Lawy... Kansas University Lawyer [*A publication*] (DLA)
KANUPP .... Karachi Nuclear Power Plant [*Pakistan*] (ODA)
KANW .... Albuquerque, NM [*FM radio station call letters*]
KAN-WIN.... Korean American Women in Need (MHID)
KANX .... Sheridan, AR [*FM radio station call letters*] (BROA)
KANX-FM ... Pine Bluff, AR [*FM radio station call letters*] (RBYB)
KANZ .... Garden City, KS [*FM radio station call letters*]
KANZ .... Kanzol Enterprises [*NCIC trailer make code*]
KANZUS..... Korea, Australia, New Zealand, and the United States
kao........... Kaolin (BARN)
KAO.......... Kappa Alpha Order
KAO.......... Key Account Owner (FOTI)
KAO.......... Kinesthetic Anharmonic Oscillator [*Facetious term for a swing*]
KAO.......... Kirtland Area Office [*Department of Energy*]
KAO.......... Knee-Ankle Orthosis [*Medicine*] (DAVI)
KAO.......... Knights of Aquarius Order (EAIO)
KAO.......... Kuiper Airborne Observatory [*NASA*]
KAO.......... Kuusamo [*Finland*] [*Airport symbol*] (OAG)
KAOA EXP STN... New Orleans, LA [*Radio expansion station*] (RBYB)
KAOB .... Devils Lake, ND [*FM radio station call letters*] (RBYB)
KAOC .... Cavalier, ND [*FM radio station call letters*] (RBYB)
KAOD .... Babbitt, MN [*FM radio station call letters*] (RBYB)
KAOE .... Hilo, HI [*FM radio station call letters*]
KAOG .... Jonesboro, AR [*FM radio station call letters*] (RBYB)
KAOH-FM ... Lompoc, CA [*FM radio station call letters*] (RBYB)
KAOI .... Kihei, HI [*AM radio station call letters*]
KAOI-FM .... Wailuku, HI [*FM radio station call letters*]
KAOK .... De Ridder, LA [*FM radio station call letters*] (BROA)
KAOK .... Lake Charles, LA [*AM radio station call letters*]
KAOL .... Carrollton, MO [*AM radio station call letters*]
KAOM .... Kansas Association of Osteopathic Medicine (SRA)
KAON .... Canadian high energy physics project (SAUO)
KAOR .... Vermillion, SD [*FM radio station call letters*]
KAOS .... Killer as an Organized Sport [*Campus game*]
KAOS .... Olympia, WA [*FM radio station call letters*]
KAOW-FM... Fort Smith, AR [*FM radio station call letters*] (RBYB)
KAOX-FM ... Kemmerer, WY [*FM radio station call letters*] (RBYB)
KAOY .... Kealakekua, HI [*FM radio station call letters*]
KAP.......... CapMAC Holdings [*NYSE symbol*] (SAG)
KAP.......... Hyannis Air Service, Inc. [*ICAO designator*] (FAAC)
KAP.......... Kaphearst Resources [*Vancouver Stock Exchange symbol*]
KAP.......... Kapitan [*NCIC car model code*]
KAP.......... Keyboard Automation Program [*Computer science*] (TIMI)
KAP.......... Khalistan Armed Police (SAUO)
KAP.......... Kids Against Pollution
KAP.......... Kinematical Analysis Program
KAP.......... Kluwer Academic Publishers
KAP.......... Knowledge, Aptitudes, and Practices [*Fertility*] (STED)
KAP.......... Knowledge, Attitudes, and Practice [*Sociology*]
KAP.......... Kuwait Action Plan [*Advisory Committee on Pollution of the Sea*]
KAPA .... Hilo, HI [*FM radio station call letters*] (BROA)
KAPA .... Kaneohe, HI [*TV station call letters*] (RBYB)
KAPA .... Potassium Aminopropylamide [*Organic chemistry*]
KAPAC....... Korean American Political Action Committee [*Washington, DC*] [*National Association of Korean Americans*] (PACS)
KAPB .... Marksville, LA [*AM radio station call letters*]
KAPB-FM ... Marksville, LA [*FM radio station call letters*]
KAPC-FM ... Butte, MT [*FM radio station call letters*] (RBYB)
KAPCS....... Kansas Association of Private Career Schools (SRA)
KAPE .... Cape Girardeau, MO [*AM radio station call letters*]
KAPE .... Kansas Association of Public Employees (SRA)
KAPE .... Keeping the Army in the Public Eye [*British military*] (DMA)
KAPE .... Kentucky Association of Professional Educators (EARSL)
KAPES....... Knowledge-Aided Process Planning and Estimation (VLIE)
KAPF-FM.... Taos, NM [*FM radio station call letters*] (RBYB)
KAPG .... Bentonville, AR [*FM radio station call letters*] (BROA)
KAPG .... Kluwer Academic Publishers Group (SAUO)
KAPI .... Kasatuan Aksi Peladjar Indonesia [*Political party*] (BARN)
KAPI-FM .... Ruston, LA [*FM radio station call letters*] (RBYB)
KAPK-FM ... Grants Pass, OR [*FM radio station call letters*] (RBYB)
KAPL .... Kaplan Industries Inc. (SAUO)
KAPL .... Kennedy Approved Parts List [*NASA*] (KSC)
KAPL .... Knolls Atomic Power Laboratory [*Schenectady, NY*] [*Department of Energy*]
KAPL .... KSC Approved Parts List (SAUS)
KAPL .... Phoenix, OR [*AM radio station call letters*] (RBYB)
K-APM....... Kennedy Space Center Automated Payloads Plan/Requirement (NAKS)
K-APM....... KSC Automated Payloads Plan/Requirement (SAUS)
KAPM-FM... Alexandria, LA [*FM radio station call letters*] (RBYB)
KAPMO...... Kent Apple and Pear Marketing Organization (SAUO)
K-APN .... KSC [*Kennedy Space Center*] Automated Payloads Notice [*NASA*] (NASA)
KAPN .... Salt Lake City, UT [*AM radio station call letters*]
KAPO .... Kameradschaftpolizei (BJA)
KAPP .... Key Asset Protection Plan [*National Guard*] (INF)
KAPP .... Kimberley Aboriginal Pastoralists Project (SAUO)
KAPP .... Knolls Atomic Power Plant
KAPP .... Yakima, WA [*Television station call letters*]
kappa........ A Light Chain of Human Immunoglobulins [*Medicine*] (EDAA)
KAPPA....... Kappa Networks, Inc. (SAUO)
KAPPA....... Kappa Site (SAUO)
K-APPS...... KSC [*Kennedy Space Center*] Automated Payloads Project Specification [*NASA*] (NASA)
KAPR .... Douglas, AZ [*AM radio station call letters*]
KAPS .... Kawasaki Automatic Power-Drive System [*Kawasaki Motors Corp.*]
KAPS .... Kentucky Association of Land Surveyors (SAUO)
KAPS .... Kuopio Atherosclerosis Prevention Study
KAPS .... Mount Vernon, WA [*AM radio station call letters*]
KAPSE....... Kernel Ada Programming Support Environment (SAUO)
KAPSE....... Kernel APSE [*ADA Program Support Environment*] [*Computer science*]
KapsnSn .... Kapson Senior Quarters Corp. [*Associated Press*] (SAG)
KAPU-FM ... Amarillo, TX [*FM radio station call letters*] (RBYB)
KAPV-FM.... Elma, WA [*FM radio station call letters*] (RBYB)
KAPWA...... Kite Aerial Photography Worldwide Association (SAUO)
KAPWR...... Keep-Alive Power [*Automotive engineering*]
KAPX .... Albuquerque, NM [*Television station call letters*] (BROA)
KAPY .... Port Angeles, WA [*AM radio station call letters*]
KAPZ .... Bald Knob, AR [*AM radio station call letters*]
KAQ.......... King and Queen [*Telegraphy*] (PCTE)
KAQA-FM ... Kilauea, HI [*FM radio station call letters*] (RBYB)
KAQD-FM ... Abilene, TX [*FM radio station call letters*] (RBYB)
KAQE-FM ... St. Martinville, LA [*FM radio station call letters*] (RBYB)
KAQF-FM ... Clovis, NM [*FM radio station call letters*] (RBYB)
KAQQ .... Spokane, WA [*AM radio station call letters*]
KAQR-FM ... Helena, MT [*FM radio station call letters*] (RBYB)
KAQS .... Shawnee, OK [*TV station call letters*] (RBYB)
KAQU .... Huntington, TX [*FM radio station call letters*]
KAQX .... Long Beach, WA [*FM radio station call letters*] (BROA)
KAQX-FM ... Bonanza, OR [*FM radio station call letters*] (RBYB)
KAQY .... Columbia, LA [*Television station call letters*] (BROA)
Kar........... Indian Law Reports, Karachi Series [*A publication*] (DLA)
KAR.......... Kamarang [*Guyana*] [*Airport symbol*] (OAG)
KAR.......... Kansas Administrative Regulations [*A publication*]
KAR.......... Kap Resources [*Vancouver Stock Exchange symbol*]
KAR.......... Karabiner [*Carbine*] [*German military - World War II*]
KAR.......... Karachi [*Pakistan*] [*Seismograph station code, US Geological Survey*] (SEIS)
KAR.......... Kar-Air OY [*Finland*] [*ICAO designator*] (FAAC)
kar .... Karen [*MARC language code*] [*Library of Congress*] (LCCP)
KAR.......... Karmann [*NCIC car model code*]
KAR.......... Karmann Ghia [*NCIC car model code*]
Kar........... Karolus de Tocco [*Flourished, 13th century*] [*Authority cited in pre-1607 legal work*] (DSA)
KAR.......... Kars [*Turkey*] [*Airport symbol*] (AD)
KAR.......... Keilschrifttexte aus Assur Religioesen Inhalts [*A publication*] (BJA)
KAR.......... Kentucky Administrative Regulations [*A publication*] (AAGC)
KAR.......... King's African Rifles [*Military unit*] [*British*]
KAR.......... Knot Area Ratio (PDAA)
KAR.......... Kodak Automated Registration [*Eastman Kodak Co.*] (CIST)

KAR......... Kodak Automated Retrieval [*Kodak*] [*Microfilm office information system*] (NITA)
Kar......... Pakistan Law Reports, Karachi Series [*A publication*] (DLA)
K/Ar......... Potassium/Argon (SAUS)
KARA......... Karavan Trailers [*NCIC trailer make code*]
KARA......... Santa Clara, CA [*FM radio station call letters*]
KARA......... Williams, CA [*FM radio station call letters*] (BROA)
KARAC...... Kustoms and Rodders Association of Canada
Karachi Univ J Sci... Karachi University Journal of Science (SAUO)
KARB......... Price, UT [*FM radio station call letters*]
KARD......... West Monroe, LA [*Television station call letters*]
KARE......... Kat Adoption Rescue Education (EARSL)
KARE......... Koala Corp. [*NASDAQ symbol*] (SAG)
KARE......... Korean Americans Reaching for Excellence [*Association*] (EA)
KARE......... Minneapolis, MN [*Television station call letters*]
KARF......... Washington [*District of Columbia*] [*ICAO location identifier*] (ICLI)
KARF-FM... Independence, KS [*Television station call letters*] (BROA)
KARG-FM... Poteau, OK [*Television station call letters*] (BROA)
KARH-FM... Forrest City, AR [*FM radio station call letters*] (BROA)
KARI......... Blaine, WA [*AM radio station call letters*]
KARI......... Kari Cool Trailer [*NCIC trailer make code*]
KARI......... Keilschrifttexte aus Assur Religioesen Inhalts [*A publication*] (BJA)
KARI......... Ketol-Acid Reductoisomerase [*An enzyme*]
KARI......... Korea Aerospace Research Institute (SAUO)
KARK......... Little Rock, AR [*Television station call letters*]
KARL......... Karlsruhe Architectural Language [*Computer science*] (CSR)
KARL......... Tracy, MN [*FM radio station call letters*]
KARLAA..... Kansas Agriculture and Rural Leadership Alumni Association (EARSL)
KARM......... Visalia, CA [*FM radio station call letters*]
Karman Inst Fluid Dynam Lecture Ser... Von Karman Institute for Fluid Dynamics Lecture Series (SAUS)
KARMEN.... Karlsruhe-Rutherford Medium-Energy Neutrino Experiment
KARN......... Humnoke, AR [*FM radio station call letters*] (RBYB)
KARN......... Little Rock, AR [*AM radio station call letters*]
KARNA...... Karnak, IL [*American Association of Railroads railroad junction routing code*]
KARO......... Caldwell, ID [*FM radio station call letters*] (RBYB)
KARO......... Jordan Valley, OR [*FM radio station call letters*] (BROA)
KARO......... Kar-Go Metal Stamping [*NCIC trailer make code*]
KARP......... Dassel, MN [*FM radio station call letters*] (BROA)
KARP......... Glencoe, MN [*FM radio station call letters*]
KARP......... Korea Association for Radiation Protection (SAUO)
KARPEN..... Karyawan Pegawai Negeri [*Indonesia*]
KARQ......... Ashdown, AR [*FM radio station call letters*]
KARQ......... Lendell Karnes [*Common carrier symbol*]
KARQ......... Mesquite, NV [*FM radio station call letters*] (BROA)
KARR......... Karrington Health, Inc. [*NASDAQ symbol*] (SAG)
KARR......... Kar-Rite Corporation [*NCIC trailer make code*]
KARR......... Kirkland, WA [*AM radio station call letters*]
KarrHlth...... Karrington Health, Inc. [*Associated Press*] (SAG)
KARS......... Belen, NM [*AM radio station call letters*]
KARS......... Kansas Applied Remote Sensing Program [*University of Kansas*] [*Research center*] (RCD)
KARS......... Karson Industries [*NCIC trailer make code*]
KARS......... Kennedy Athletic Recreation and Social [*NASA*] (KSC)
KARS......... Laramie, WY [*FM radio station call letters*] (BROA)
KART......... Jerome, ID [*AM radio station call letters*]
KART......... Kartote [*NCIC trailer make code*]
KART......... Watertown/International [*New York*] [*ICAO location identifier*] (ICLI)
KARV......... Russellville, AR [*AM radio station call letters*]
KARV-FM... Ola, AR [*FM radio station call letters*] (BROA)
KARW......... Cut Bank, MT [*FM radio station call letters*] (BROA)
KARW......... Longview, TX [*AM radio station call letters*]
KARX......... Claude, TX [*FM radio station call letters*]
KARY......... Grandview, WA [*FM radio station call letters*]
KARY......... Prosser, WA [*AM radio station call letters*]
KARZ......... Burney, CA [*FM radio station call letters*]
KARZ-FM... Marshall, MN [*FM radio station call letters*] (BROA)
KAS......... Benedictine College, North Campus, Atchison, KS [*Library symbol*] [*Library of Congress*] (LCLS)
KAS......... Kansas [*Obsolete*] (ROG)
Kas......... Kansas Reports [*A publication*] (DLA)
kas......... Kashmiri [*MARC language code*] [*Library of Congress*] (LCCP)
KAS......... Kaskada Resources Ltd. [*Vancouver Stock Exchange symbol*]
KAS......... Kasler Corp. (SAUO)
KAS......... Kasler Holdings [*NYSE symbol*] (SPSG)
KAS......... Kastamonu [*Turkey*] [*Seismograph station code, US Geological Survey*] (SEIS)
KAS......... Katz Adjustment Scales [*Psychology*]
KAS......... Keep-Alive Signal [*Military*]
KAS......... Kentucky Academy of Science (SAUO)
KAS......... Kenya-Australia Society
KAS......... Ketoacyl-ACP Synthase [*An enzyme*]
KAS......... Killed on Active Service (SAUS)
KAS......... Kingston Air Services [*Canada*] [*ICAO designator*] (FAAC)
KAS......... Kiva Administrative Server [*Computer science*]
KAS......... Knowledge Access System [*Interface*]
KAS......... Knowledge Acquisition System
KAS......... Knowledge, Attitude, Skills (BB)
KAS......... Knowledge, Attitudes, Skills [*Training term*] (LPT)
KAS......... Konrad Adenauer Stiftung [*Germany*] [*Political party*]
KAS......... Kroeber Anthropological Society (EA)
KAS......... Kulanka Afka Somalyed
KASA......... Kentucky Association of School Administrators (SRA)
KASA......... Phoenix, AZ [*AM radio station call letters*]
KASA......... Santa Fe, NM [*Television station call letters*]
KASB......... Bellevue, WA [*FM radio station call letters*]
KASB......... Kansas Association of School Boards (SRA)
KASC......... Knowledge Availability Systems Center [*University of Pittsburgh*]
KASE......... Austin, TX [*FM radio station call letters*]
KASE......... Kasey [*NCIC trailer make code*]
KASF......... Alamosa, CO [*FM radio station call letters*]
KASH......... Anchorage, AK [*FM radio station call letters*]
Kash......... Kashmir (VRA)
KASH......... Kash n'Karry Food Stores [*NASDAQ symbol*] (TTSB)
KASH......... Kash n Karry Food Stores, Inc. [*NASDAQ symbol*] (SAG)
KASH......... Knowledge, Abilities, Skills, and Habits (STED)
KASH......... Knowledge, Attitude, Skills, Habits [*Formula*] [*LIMRA*]
Kashmir LJ... Kashmir Law Journal [*India*] [*A publication*] (DLA)
KashrK...... Kash n Karry Food Stores, Inc. [*Associated Press*] (SAG)
KASI......... Ames, IA [*AM radio station call letters*]
KASI......... Kesatuan Aksi Sardjana Indonesia [*Action Front of Indonesian Scholars*]
KASK-FM... Fairfield, CA [*FM radio station call letters*] (BROA)
KASL......... Kansas Association of School Librarians (or Libraries) (SAUO)
KASL......... Kasler Corp. (SAUO)
KASL......... Newcastle, WY [*AM radio station call letters*]
Kasler Holding Co.... Kasler Corp. [*Associated Press*] (SAG)
KASM......... Albany, MN [*AM radio station call letters*]
KASM-FM... Albany, MN [*FM radio station call letters*]
KASMS...... Korean Air Support Management System (SAUO)
KASN......... Pine Bluff, AR [*Television station call letters*]
KASO......... Minden, LA [*AM radio station call letters*]
KASO-FM... Minden, LA [*FM radio station call letters*]
KASP......... Kasper A.S.L., Ltd. [*NASDAQ symbol*] (NASQ)
KASP......... Kehr-Activated Sludge Process (PDAA)
KAS/P....... Kroeber Anthropological Society Papers. University of California. Berkeley (SAUO)
Kas R......... Kansas Reports [*A publication*] (DLA)
KASR......... Perry, OK [*AM radio station call letters*]
KASR-FM... Conway, AR [*FM radio station call letters*] (BROA)
KASR-FM... Perry, OK [*FM radio station call letters*]
KASRP...... Kaiser Steel Corp. Pfd (SAUO)
KASS......... Casper, WY [*FM radio station call letters*] (RBYB)
KASS......... Kagan Affective Sensitivity Scales [*Psychology*] (DHP)
KASS......... Kassborth [*NCIC truck make code*]
KASS......... Kassborth [*NCIC trailer make code*]
Kass......... Kassinin [*Biochemistry*]
KASS......... Kent Automated Serials System [*Kent State University*] [*Automated library system*] (NITA)
KASSP....... Kentucky Association of Secondary School Principals (SRA)
KASSR...... Kalmyk Autonomous Soviet Socialist Republic (SAUO)
KA SSR..... Kazakh Soviet Socialist Republic (SAUO)
KASSR...... Komi Autonomous Soviet Socialist Republic (SAUO)
KAST......... Astoria, OR [*AM radio station call letters*]
KAST......... Kalman Automatic Sequential TMA [*Military*] (CAAL)
KAST......... Kindergarten Auditory Screening Test [*Otorhinolaryngology*] (DAVI)
KAST-FM.... Astoria, OR [*FM radio station call letters*]
KASU......... Jonesboro, AR [*FM radio station call letters*]
KASV-FM.... Borger, TX [*FM radio station call letters*] (BROA)
KASW......... Phoenix, AZ [*Television station call letters*]
KASX-FM... Pine Bluffs, WY [*FM radio station call letters*] (BROA)
KASY......... Albuquerque, NM [*FM radio station call letters*]
KASY-TV.... Albuquerque, NM [*Television station call letters*]
KASZ......... Gatesville, TX [*FM radio station call letters*] (BROA)
KAT......... Asbury Theological Seminary, Wilmore, KY [*OCLC symbol*] (OCLC)
KAT......... Die Keilinschriften und das Alte Testament [*A publication*] (BJA)
KAT......... Kaitaia [*New Zealand*] [*Airport symbol*] (OAG)
KAT......... Kanamycin Acetyltransferase [*An enzyme*]
KAT......... Kappa Alpha Theta [*Sorority*]
kat......... Katal [*Unit of enzyme activity*]
KAT......... Kattegat Air, AS [*Denmark*] [*ICAO designator*] (FAAC)
KAT......... Kenosha Auto Transport (SAUO)
KAT......... Key-to-Address Transformation [*Computer science*] (PDAA)
KAT......... Kizyl-Arvat [*Former USSR*] [*Seismograph station code, US Geological Survey*] (SEIS)
KAT......... Kommentar zum Alten Testament [*A publication*] (BJA)
KATA......... Arcata, CA [*AM radio station call letters*]
KATB......... Anchorage, AK [*FM radio station call letters*]
KATC......... Katz Digital Technologies [*NASDAQ symbol*] (TTSB)
KATC......... Katz Digital Technologies, Inc. [*NASDAQ symbol*] (SAG)
KATC......... Kentucky Association of Technology Coordinators
KATC......... Korean Army Training Center
KATC......... Lafayette, LA [*Television station call letters*]
KATCA....... Korean-American Technical Cooperation Association
Katch Pr Law... Katchenovsky's Prize Law [*2nd ed.*] [*1867*] [*A publication*] (DLA)
KATD......... Pittsburg, CA [*AM radio station call letters*]
KATE......... Albert Lea, MN [*AM radio station call letters*]
KATE......... Knowledge Based Automatic Test Equipment (ACAE)
KatechBR... Katechetische Blaetter [*Berlin-Grunewald*] [*A publication*] (BJA)
KATF......... Dubuque, IA [*FM radio station call letters*]
KATH......... Bozeman, MT [*FM radio station call letters*]
KATH-FM.... El Paso, TX [*FM radio station call letters*] (BROA)
KathM....... Die Katholischen Missionen (BJA)
KATI......... California, MO [*FM radio station call letters*] (RBYB)
KATIE....... Killer Alert Threat Identification & Evasion (SAUS)
KATJ......... George, CA [*FM radio station call letters*]

KATJ......... Victorville, CA [*AM radio station call letters*] (BROA)
KATK......... Carlsbad, NM [*AM radio station call letters*]
KATK-FM.... Carlsbad, NM [*FM radio station call letters*]
KATL......... Atlanta/The William B. Hartsfield Atlanta International [*Georgia*] [*ICAO location identifier*] (ICLI)
KATL......... Miles City, MT [*AM radio station call letters*]
KATM........ Katmai National Monument
KATM........ Modesto, CA [*FM radio station call letters*]
KATN........ Fairbanks, AK [*Television station call letters*]
KATO........ Safford, AZ [*AM radio station call letters*]
KATP......... Amarillo, TX [*FM radio station call letters*]
KATQ......... Plentywood, MT [*AM radio station call letters*]
KATQ-FM.... Plentywood, MT [*FM radio station call letters*]
KATR......... Wray, CO [*FM radio station call letters*]
KATS......... Campus Antenna Television System (SAUS)
KATS......... Kennedy Avionics Test Set (SAUO)
KATS......... Kennedy Space Center Avionics Test Set [*NASA*] (NASA)
KATS......... Yakima, WA [*FM radio station call letters*]
KatShing.... Katorikku Shingaku [*Catholic Theology*] [*Tokyo*] [*A publication*] (BJA)
KATSI........ Kommentar zum Alten Testament [*E. Sellin*] [*A publication*] (BJA)
KATT......... Oklahoma City, OK [*FM radio station call letters*]
KATU......... Kato Aromatic [*Intermodal shipping container symbol*] (TVRC)
KATU......... Portland, OR [*Television station call letters*]
KATU-DT.... Portland, OR [*Television station call letters*] (BROA)
KATUSA...... Korean Augmentation to the United States Army
KATUSA...... Korean Augmentee to U.S. Army
KATV......... Little Rock, AR [*Television station call letters*]
KATW......... Lewiston, ID [*FM radio station call letters*]
KATX......... Eastland, TX [*FM radio station call letters*] (BROA)
KATY......... Idyllwild, CA [*FM radio station call letters*]
KatyInd...... Katy Industries, Inc. [*Formerly, Missour-Kansas-Texas R.R. Co., with Wall Street slang name of "Kathy"*] [*Associated Press*] (SAG)
KATYP....... Kallitype (VRA)
KATZ......... Alton, IL [*FM radio station call letters*] (BROA)
KATZ......... St. Louis, MO [*AM radio station call letters*]
KatzDig...... Katz Digital Technologies, Inc. [*Associated Press*] (SAG)
KATZ-FM.... Alton, IL [*FM radio station call letters*] (BROA)
KatzM........ Katz Media Group, Inc. [*Associated Press*] (SAG)
kau........... Kanuri [*MARC language code*] [*Library of Congress*] (LCCP)
KAU........... Kaohsiung [*Takao*] [*Republic of China*] [*Seismograph station code, US Geological Survey*] (SEIS)
KAU........... Kauhava [*Finland*] [*Airport symbol*] (AD)
KAU........... Kenya African Union [*1944*] [*Political party*] (PPW)
KAU........... Kenya Africa Union (SAUO)
KAU........... Kerala Agricultural University (SAUO)
KAU........... Keystation Adapter Unit [*Computer science*]
KAU........... Kilo Accounting Units (NASA)
KAU........... Kind-of-Activity-Unit (EURO)
KAU........... King-Armstrong Unit [*Clinical chemistry*]
KAUB-FM.... Reedsport, OR [*FM radio station call letters*] (BROA)
KAUF......... Kaufan Trailers [*NCIC trailer make code*]
KaufBH....... Kaufman & Broad Home Corp. [*Associated Press*] (SAG)
KAUF-FM.... Kennett, MO [*FM radio station call letters*] (BROA)
KaufHW...... Kaufman [*H. W.*] Financial Group [*Associated Press*] (SAG)
Kauf Mack... Kaufmann's Edition of Mackeldey's Civil Law [*A publication*] (DLA)
Kaufm Mackeld Civ Law... Kaufmann's Edition of Mackeldey's Civil Law [*A publication*] (DLA)
KAUFX....... Kaufmann Fund [*Mutual fund ticker symbol*] (SG)
KAUG......... Augusta [*Maine*] [*ICAO location identifier*] (ICLI)
KAUG-FM.... El Dorado, AR [*FM radio station call letters*] (BROA)
KAUI.......... Kekaha, HI [*FM radio station call letters*]
KAUJ......... Grafton, ND [*FM radio station call letters*] (BROA)
KAUJ-FM.... Walhalla, ND [*FM radio station call letters*] (BROA)
KAUL-FM.... Ellington, MO [*FM radio station call letters*] (BROA)
KAUM........ Colorado City, TX [*FM radio station call letters*]
KAUN......... Sioux Falls, SD [*Television station call letters*] (BROA)
KAUO......... Santa Fe, NM [*Television station call letters*] (BROA)
KAUP......... Pendleton, OR [*Television station call letters*] (BROA)
KAUQ-FM.... Omak, WA [*FM radio station call letters*] (BROA)
KAUR......... Sioux Falls, SD [*FM radio station call letters*]
KAUS......... Austin, MN [*AM radio station call letters*]
KAUS......... Austin/Robert Mueller Municipal [*Texas*] [*ICAO location identifier*] (ICLI)
KAUS-FM.... Austin, MN [*FM radio station call letters*]
KAUT......... Oklahoma City, OK [*Television station call letters*] (GDPB)
KAUT-TV.... Oklahoma City, OK [*Television station call letters*] (BROA)
KAUV-FM.... Viola, AR [*FM radio station call letters*] (BROA)
KAUY-FM.... LaJunta, CO [*FM radio station call letters*] (BROA)
KAUZ......... Wichita Falls, TX [*Television station call letters*]
KAV........... Cambourne Resources [*Vancouver Stock Exchange symbol*]
KAV........... Katukina [*Language symbol*] (ETLW)
KAV........... Kavieng [*New Ireland*] [*Seismograph station code, US Geological Survey*] [*Closed*] (SEIS)
KAV........... Keilschrifttexte aus Assur Verschiedenen Inhalts [*A publication*] (BJA)
KAVA......... Burney, CA [*AM radio station call letters*]
KAVA......... Pueblo, CO [*AM radio station call letters*] (BROA)
KAVAS....... Knowledge Acquisition Visualization and Assessment Study (SAUO)
KAVC......... Mojave, CA [*AM radio station call letters*] (BROA)
KAVC......... Rosamond, CA [*FM radio station call letters*]
KAVD-FM.... Limon, CO [*FM radio station call letters*] (BROA)
KAVE......... Oakridge, OR [*FM radio station call letters*]
KAVG-FM.... Beulah, ND [*FM radio station call letters*] (BROA)
KAVH-FM.... Eudora, AR [*FM radio station call letters*] (BROA)
KAVI.......... Keilschrifttexte aus Assur Verschiedenen Inhalts [*A publication*] (BJA)
KAVJ-FM.... Sutherlin, OR [*FM radio station call letters*] (BROA)
KAVK-FM.... Many, LA [*FM radio station call letters*] (BROA)
KAVL......... Kavli's Truck Line [*Common carrier symbol*]
KAVL......... Lancaster, CA [*AM radio station call letters*]
KAVLICO.... Fred Kavli Company [*Automotive industry*]
KAVO-FM.... Borger, TX [*FM radio station call letters*] (BROA)
KAVP-AM.... Colona, CO [*AM radio station call letters*] (BROA)
KAVS......... Mojave, CA [*FM radio station call letters*]
KAVT-AM.... Fresno, CA [*AM radio station call letters*] (BROA)
KAVU......... Victoria, TX [*Television station call letters*]
KAVV......... Benson, AZ [*FM radio station call letters*]
KAVW-FM.... Amarillo, TX [*FM radio station call letters*] (BROA)
KAVX-FM.... Lufkin, TX [*FM radio station call letters*] (BROA)
KAW.......... Kawthaung [*Myanmar*] [*Airport symbol*] (OAG)
KAWA........ Floydada, TX [*AM radio station call letters*]
KAWAD...... Karnataka Watersheds Development
KAWB........ Brainerd, MN [*Television station call letters*]
KAWC........ Yuma, AZ [*AM radio station call letters*]
KAWC-FM.... Yuma, AZ [*FM radio station call letters*]
KAWD-FM.... Tahoka, TX [*FM radio station call letters*] (BROA)
KAWE........ Bemidji, MN [*Television station call letters*]
KAWF-FM.... Los Molinos, CA [*FM radio station call letters*] (BROA)
KAWJ......... Hutchinson, KS [*Television station call letters*] (BROA)
KAWJ......... Korrespondenzblatt des Vereins zur Gruendung und Erhaltung der Akademie fuer dieWissenschaft des Judentums [*A publication*] (BJA)
KAWK........ Kawasaki [*NCIC motorcycle make code*]
KAWK-FM.... Custer, SD [*FM radio station call letters*] (RBYB)
KAWL......... York, NE [*AM radio station call letters*]
KAWN......... Carswell [*Texas*] [*ICAO location identifier*] (ICLI)
KAWOL....... Knowledgeable, Absent Without Leave
KAWOL....... Knowledge, Absent Without Leave [*Army*] (ADDR)
KAWQ-FM.... Bridgeport, NE [*FM radio station call letters*] (BROA)
KAWS......... Hemphill, TX [*AM radio station call letters*]
KAWT-FM.... Princeville, HI [*FM radio station call letters*] (BROA)
KAWU-FM.... Newberry Springs, CA [*FM radio station call letters*] (BROA)
KAWV-FM.... Lihue-Kauai, HI [*FM radio station call letters*] (BROA)
KAWW........ Heber Springs, AR [*AM radio station call letters*]
KAWW-FM.... Heber Springs, AR [*FM radio station call letters*]
KAWX-FM.... Weaverville, CA [*FM radio station call letters*] (BROA)
KAWY-FM.... Denver City, TX [*FM radio station call letters*] (BROA)
KAWZ......... Twin Falls, ID [*FM radio station call letters*]
KAX........... Kalbarri [*Australia*] [*Airport symbol*] (OAG)
KAXA-FM.... Pioche, NV [*FM radio station call letters*] (BROA)
KAXB-FM.... Tuba City, AZ [*FM radio station call letters*] (BROA)
KAXE......... Grand Rapids, MN [*FM radio station call letters*]
KAXF......... Conroe, TX [*FM radio station call letters*] (BROA)
KAXF-FM.... Huntsville, TX [*FM radio station call letters*] (BROA)
KAXG-FM.... Gillette, WY [*FM radio station call letters*] (BROA)
KAXH-FM.... Pampa, TX [*FM radio station call letters*] (BROA)
KAXI-FM..... Willcox, AZ [*FM radio station call letters*] (BROA)
KAXJ-FM.... Sunrise Beach, MO [*FM radio station call letters*] (BROA)
KAXL......... Green Acres, CA [*FM radio station call letters*]
KAXM........ Agana, Guam [*Television station call letters*] (BROA)
KAXR-FM.... Arkansas City, KS [*FM radio station call letters*] (BROA)
KAXT......... Hollister, CA [*FM radio station call letters*] (RBYB)
KAXV-FM.... Bastrop, LA [*FM radio station call letters*] (BROA)
KAXW-AM.... Merced, CA [*AM radio station call letters*] (BROA)
KAXX......... Ventura, CA [*FM radio station call letters*]
KAXX-AM.... Eagle River, AK [*AM radio station call letters*] (BROA)
KAXY-AM.... Waco, TX [*AM radio station call letters*] (BROA)
KAY........... Katlanovo [*Yugoslavia*] [*Seismograph station code, US Geological Survey*] (SEIS)
Kay........... Kay's English Vice-Chancellors' Reports [*69 English Reprint*] [*A publication*] (DLA)
KAY........... Wakaya [*Fiji*] [*Airport symbol*] [*Obsolete*] (OAG)
KAYA-FM.... Hubbard, NE [*FM radio station call letters*] (BROA)
Kay & J...... Kay and Johnson's English Vice-Chancellors' Reports [*69, 70 English Reprint*] [*A publication*] (DLA)
Kay & J (Eng)... Kay and Johnson's English Vice-Chancellors' Reports [*69, 70 English Reprint*] [*A publication*] (DLA)
Kay & John... Kay and Johnson's English Vice-Chancellors' Reports [*69, 70 English Reprint*] [*A publication*] (DLA)
Kay & Johns... Kay and Johnson's English Vice-Chancellors' Reports [*69, 70 English Reprint*] [*A publication*] (DLA)
KAYB-FM.... Sunnyside, WA [*FM radio station call letters*] (BROA)
KAYC......... Beaumont-Port Arthur, TX [*AM radio station call letters*] (GDPB)
KAYC-FM.... Durant, OK [*FM radio station call letters*] (BROA)
KAYD......... Beaumont, TX [*AM radio station call letters*] (RBYB)
KAYD......... Kaydel [*NCIC trailer make code*]
KAYD......... Silsbee, TX [*FM radio station call letters*] (BROA)
KAYD-FM.... Beaumont, TX [*FM radio station call letters*]
Kaydon....... Kaydon Corp. [*Associated Press*] (SAG)
KAYE......... Kaye Group [*NASDAQ symbol*] (TTSB)
KAYE......... Kaye Group, Inc. [*NASDAQ symbol*] (SAG)
KAYE......... Tonkawa, OK [*FM radio station call letters*]
KayeGrp..... Kaye Group, Inc. [*Associated Press*] (SAG)
KayeK........ Kaye Kotts Associates, Inc. [*Associated Press*] (SAG)
Kay (Eng).... Kay's English Vice-Chancellors' Reports [*69 English Reprint*] [*A publication*] (DLA)
KAYF......... Kayout-Forester Travel Trailer [*NCIC trailer make code*]
KAYF-FM.... Starbuck, MN [*FM radio station call letters*] (BROA)
KAYG-FM.... Camp Wood, TX [*FM radio station call letters*] (BROA)
KAYH-FM.... Fayetteville, AR [*FM radio station call letters*] (BROA)

KAYI-FM .... Princeville, HI [*FM radio station call letters*] (BROA)
KAYK .... Victoria, TX [*FM radio station call letters*] (BROA)
KAYK-AM ... Arvada, CO [*AM radio station call letters*] (BROA)
KAYL......... Storm Lake, IA [*AM radio station call letters*]
KAYL-FM.... Storm Lake, IA [*FM radio station call letters*]
KAYM-FM... Weatherford, OK [*FM radio station call letters*] (BROA)
KAYO .... Elma, WA [*FM radio station call letters*] (BROA)
KAYO .... Kayot [*NCIC truck make code*]
KAYO .... Kayot [*NCIC trailer make code*]
KAYO-FM ... Aberdeen, WA [*FM radio station call letters*]
KAYP .... Burlington, IA [*FM radio station call letters*] (BROA)
KAYP-FM.... Mount Pleasant, IA [*FM radio station call letters*] (BROA)
KAYQ .... Warsaw, MO [*FM radio station call letters*]
KAYR .... Van Buren, AR [*AM radio station call letters*]
KAYS .... Hays, KS [*AM radio station call letters*]
KAYSEE ..... Kansas City [*Missouri*] [*Slang*]
Kay Ship.... Kay. Shipmasters, and Seamen [*2nd ed.*] [*1894*] [*A publication*] (DLA)
KAYT-FM.... Jena, LA [*FM radio station call letters*] (BROA)
KAYU .... Spokane, WA [*Television station call letters*]
KAYW........ Kaywood Homes [*NCIC trailer make code*]
KAYW-FM... Meeker, CO [*FM radio station call letters*] (BROA)
KAYX .... Richmond, MO [*FM radio station call letters*]
KAYY-FM.... Clearwater, KS [*FM radio station call letters*] (BROA)
KAZ .... Karuizawa [*Also, KRZ*] [*Japan*] [*Seismograph station code, US Geological Survey*] (SEIS)
kaz........... Kazakh [*MARC language code*] [*Library of Congress*] (LCCP)
KAZ .... Kazakhstan (ADWA)
Kaz........... Kazakstan (MILB)
KAZ .... Keio Advanced ZEV (Zero Emissions Vehicle) [*Automotive engineering*]
KAZ .... Knight Arnold [*Federal Railroad Administration identification code*]
KAZA .... Gilroy, CA [*AM radio station call letters*]
KAZAIR...... Kazakhstan Airlines [*ICAO designator*] (FAAC)
KAZB-FM.... Coalinga, CA [*FM radio station call letters*] (BROA)
KAZC-FM.... Tishomingo, OK [*FM radio station call letters*] (BROA)
KAZD-FM ... Montrose, CO [*FM radio station call letters*] (BROA)
KAZE......... Ore City, TX [*FM radio station call letters*] (BROA)
KAZE-FM.... Coalgate, OK [*FM radio station call letters*] (BROA)
KAZF-FM.... Hebronville, TX [*FM radio station call letters*] (BROA)
KAZG .... Ogden, UT [*Television station call letters*] (BROA)
KAZG-AM ... Scottsdale, AZ [*AM radio station call letters*] (BROA)
KAZH .... Baytown, TX [*Television station call letters*] (BROA)
KAZI .... Austin, TX [*FM radio station call letters*]
KAZJ......... Seattle, WA [*AM radio station call letters*] (BROA)
KAZL......... Castle Rock, WA [*FM radio station call letters*]
KAZM........ Sedona, AZ [*AM radio station call letters*]
KAZN .... Pasadena, CA [*AM radio station call letters*]
KAZP-AM ... Bellevue, NE [*AM radio station call letters*] (BROA)
KAZQ .... Albuquerque, NM [*Television station call letters*]
KAZR-FM ... Pella, IA [*FM radio station call letters*] (RBYB)
KazSSR ..... Kazakh Soviet Socialist Republic
KAZT-AM... Redding, CA [*AM radio station call letters*] (BROA)
KAZU .... Pacific Grove, CA [*FM radio station call letters*]
KAZW-AM... College Station, TX [*AM radio station call letters*] (BROA)
KAZX-FM.... Kirtland, NM [*FM radio station call letters*] (BROA)
KAZY .... Woodward, OK [*FM radio station call letters*] (BROA)
KAZY-FM.... Winfield, KS [*FM radio station call letters*] (BROA)
KAZZ......... Deer Park, WA [*FM radio station call letters*]
KB............ Bermuda [*IYRU nationality code*] (IYR)
KB............ Burnthills [*ICAO designator*] (AD)
KB............ Construction Bureau (SAUO)
KB............ Contribute [*Telegraphy*] (PCTE)
KB............ English Law Reports, King's Bench Division [*1901-52*] [*A publication*] (DLA)
KB............ Kashin-Bek Disease [*Medicine*] (DMAA)
KB............ Kaufman & Broad, Inc. (MHDW)
KB............ Kauri-Butanol Value [*Measure of relative solvent power*]
KB............ Keel Bending (SSD)
KB............ Keilinschriftliche Bibliothek [*Berlin*] [*A publication*] (BJA)
KB............ Kelly Bushing [*Drilling*] (DICI)
KB............ Kelp Bay [*Alaska*] (ALAC)
KB............ Ketone Bodies [*Clinical chemistry*]
KB............ Keyboard [*Computer science*]
KB............ Kickback (MHDB)
kb .... Kilobar
kb .... Kilobase
KB............ Kilobaud (IAA)
kb .... KiloBIT [*Binary Digit*] [*Computer science*]
KB............ Kilobit (NAKS)
Kb............ Kilobit (DCOM)
KB............ Kilo BTU [*British Thermal Unit*]
kb .... Kilobyte (ELAL)
Kb............ Kilobyte (NFD)
KB............ Kilobyte [*10^3 bytes*] [*Computer science*]
KB............ Kimball International Inc. (SAUO)
KB............ Kincheng Banking Corp. [*Hong Kong*]
KB............ King's Bench [*of law courts*] [*British*]
KB............ King's Bishop [*Chess*]
KB............ Kitchen and Bathroom
KB............ Kitchen Biddy [*Female kitchen worker*] [*Restaurant slang*]
KB............ Kite Balloon [*Air Force*]
K-B........... Kleihauer-Betke [*Stain*] [*Medicine*] (MEDA)
KB............ Knee Bearing [*Prosthesis*]
KB............ Knee Brace [*Technical drawings*]
KB............ Knight Bachelor [*or Knight Companion*] of the Order of the Bath [*British*]
KB............ Knight of the Bath (SAUO)
Kb............ Knit into Back of Stitch [*Knitting*] (BARN)
KB............ Knockback (WDAA)
KB............ Knowledgeability Brief (MCD)
KB............ Knowledge Base [*Computer science*] (IAA)
KB............ Knuckle-Bender Splint [*Orthopedics*] (DAVI)
KB............ Komercni Bank [*Czech Republic Bank*]
KB............ Komercni Banka AS [*Czech Republic*] [*Banking*]
KB............ Kommanditbolaget [*Limited Partnership*] [*German*] (ILCA)
KB............ Koninklijk Besluit [*Royal Decree*] [*Dutch*] (ILCA)
Kb............ Kontrabass [*Double Bass*] [*German*] [*Music*] (WDAA)
KB............ Kontrabass [*Double Bass*] [*Music*]
KB............ Korbach [*German license plate city code*]
KB............ Korpus Bezpieczenstwa (BJA)
KB............ Korrespondenz-Blatt des Verbandes der Deutschen Juden [*A publication*] (BJA)
KB............ Kredietbank N.V. (EFIS)
KB............ Kuiper Belt [*Planetary science*]
KB............ Kulturbund
KB............ Kunstgeschichte in Bildern [*A publication*] (OCD)
KBA.......... Barbados [*IYRU nationality code*] (IYR)
KBA.......... Beni Abbes [*Algeria*] [*Airport symbol*] (AD)
KBA.......... Kabala [*Sierra Leone*] [*Airport symbol*] (OAG)
KBA.......... Kansas Bankers Association (SRA)
KBA.......... Kansas Bar Association (SRA)
KBA.......... Kenn Borek Air Ltd. [*Canada*] [*ICAO designator*] (FAAC)
KBA.......... Kentucky Bar Association (SRA)
KBA.......... Kentucky Broadcasters Association (SRA)
KBA.......... Ketobutyraldehyde Dimethyl Acetal [*Biochemistry*]
KBA.......... Keyboard Assembly (DWSG)
KBA.......... Killed by Action [*In reference to the enemy*] [*Vietnam*] (VNW)
KBA.......... Killed by Air [*Military*]
KBA.......... Killed by Artillery [*In reference to the enemy*] [*Vietnam*] (VNW)
KBA.......... Kleinwort Benson Aus [*NYSE symbol*] (TTSB)
KBA.......... Kleinwort Benson Australian Income Fund, Inc. [*NYSE symbol*] (SPSG)
KBA.......... Knight of St. Benedict of Avis
KBA.......... Koenig & Bauer-Albert AG (EFIS)
KBAB .... Marysville/Beale Air Force Base [*California*] [*ICAO location identifier*] (ICLI)
KBAB-FM ... Kerrville, TX [*FM radio station call letters*] (BROA)
KBAC .... Kennedy Booster Assembly Contractor (MCD)
KBAC .... Las Vegas, NM [*FM radio station call letters*]
KBAC .... Santa Fe, NM [*FM radio station call letters*] (BROA)
KBAD .... Shreveport/Barksdale Air Force Base [*Louisiana*] [*ICAO location identifier*] (ICLI)
KBAD-AM ... Las Vegas, NV [*AM radio station call letters*] (BROA)
KBAE .... Llano, TX [*FM radio station call letters*] (RBYB)
KBAH-FM ... Plainview, TX [*FM radio station call letters*] (BROA)
KBAI .... Bellingham, WA [*AM radio station call letters*] (BROA)
KBAI .... Morro Bay, CA [*AM radio station call letters*]
KBAJ-FM.... Deer River, MN [*FM radio station call letters*] (BROA)
KBAK .... Bakersfield, CA [*Television station call letters*]
KBAL .... Kimball International, Inc. [*NASDAQ symbol*] (NQ)
KBAL .... Kleine Beitraege zum Assyrischen Lexikon [*A publication*]
KBAL .... San Saba, TX [*AM radio station call letters*]
KBALB....... Kimball Intl Cl'B' [*NASDAQ symbol*] (TTSB)
KBAL-FM.... San Saba, TX [*FM radio station call letters*] (RBYB)
K-BALL...... Cannibalize (MCD)
KBAM........ Longview, WA [*AM radio station call letters*]
KBAN .... De Ridder, LA [*FM radio station call letters*] (BROA)
KB&TS ...... Kuwait Broadcasting and Television Service (SAUO)
KBAO .... Lewistown, MT [*Television station call letters*] (BROA)
KBAP-FM ... King City, CA [*FM radio station call letters*] (BROA)
KBAQ .... Phoenix, AZ [*FM radio station call letters*]
KBAR .... Burley, ID [*AM radio station call letters*]
KBAR .... K-Bar Industries [*NCIC trailer make code*]
kbar.......... Kilobar (ABAC)
KBAR .... Kilobar
KBART....... Kings Bay Army Terminal
KBAS .... Bullhead City, AZ [*AM radio station call letters*]
KBASSR..... Kabardino-Balkar Autonomous Soviet Socialist Republic (SAUO)
KBAT......... Midland, TX [*FM radio station call letters*]
KBAU .... Big Sandy, TX [*FM radio station call letters*] (RBYB)
KBAust ...... Kleinwort Benson Australian Income Fund, Inc. [*Associated Press*] (SAG)
KBAW-FM... Zapata, TX [*FM radio station call letters*] (BROA)
KBAX .... Fallbrook, CA [*FM radio station call letters*]
KBAY .... Gilroy, CA [*FM radio station call letters*] (BROA)
KBAY .... San Jose, CA [*FM radio station call letters*]
KBAZ .... Hamilton, MT [*FM radio station call letters*] (BROA)
KBB.......... Baker University, Baldwin City, KS [*Library symbol*] [*Library of Congress*] (LCLS)
KBB.......... Bear Stearns Companies, Inc. [*AMEX symbol*] (SAG)
KBB.......... Bear Stearns Cos.'CUBS"98 [*AMEX symbol*] (TTSB)
KBB.......... King's Bad Bargain [*Undesirable serviceman*] [*Slang*] [*British*] (DSUE)
KBB.......... Kitchens, Bedrooms, and Bathrooms Equipment Exhibition [*British*] (ITD)
KBB.......... Koninklijke Bijenkorf Beheer (EFIS)
KBBA .... Abilene, TX [*AM radio station call letters*]
KBBB-FM ... Billings, MT [*FM radio station call letters*] (RBYB)
KBBC .... Lake Havasu City, AZ [*FM radio station call letters*]
KBBE .... McPherson, KS [*FM radio station call letters*]

KBBF .... Santa Rosa, CA [*FM radio station call letters*]
KBBG .... Waterloo, IA [*FM radio station call letters*]
KBBI .... Homer, AK [*AM radio station call letters*]
KBBJ .... Havre, MT [*Television station call letters*] (BROA)
KBBK .... Lincoln, NE [*FM radio station call letters*] (BROA)
KBBK .... Rupert, ID [*AM radio station call letters*]
KBBL .... Cabot, AR [*AM radio station call letters*]
KBBL-FM.... Cabot, AR [*FM radio station call letters*]
KBBN .... Broken Bow, NE [*FM radio station call letters*]
KBBO .... Yakima, WA [*AM radio station call letters*]
KBBQ .... Fort Smith, AR [*FM radio station call letters*]
KBBR .... North Bend, OR [*AM radio station call letters*]
KBBS .... Buffalo, WY [*AM radio station call letters*]
KBBT .... Portland, OR [*AM radio station call letters*]
KBBT .... Schertz, TX [*FM radio station call letters*] (BROA)
KBBT-FM.... Banks, OR [*FM radio station call letters*] (BROA)
KBBV .... Big Bear Lake, CA [*AM radio station call letters*]
KBBV-AM ... Loma Linda, CA [*AM radio station call letters*] (BROA)
KBBW .... Waco, TX [*AM radio station call letters*]
KBBX .... Nebraska City, NE [*FM radio station call letters*] (BROA)
KBBX .... Omaha, NE [*AM radio station call letters*]
KBBY-FM.... Ventura, CA [*FM radio station call letters*]
KBBZ .... Kalispell, MT [*FM radio station call letters*]
KBC .... Bellarmine College, Louisville, KY [*OCLC symbol*] (OCLC)
KBC .... Birch Creek [*Alaska*] [*Airport symbol*] (OAG)
KBC .... K-Band Circulator
KBC .... King's Bench Court [*British*]
KBC .... Kiowa Business Committee [*An association*]
KBC .... Kredietbank NV (EFIS)
KBC .... Kyushu Asahi Broadcasting (SAUO)
KBCA .... Elk City, OK [*Television station call letters*] (BROA)
KBCA .... Keystone Bituminous Coal Association
KBCB .... Bellingham, WA [*Television station call letters*]
KBCC .... Helena, MT [*Television station call letters*] (BROA)
KBCD .... Newport Beach, CA [*FM radio station call letters*]
KBCE .... Boyce, LA [*FM radio station call letters*]
KBCH .... Kings Beach, CA [*FM radio station call letters*] (RBYB)
KBCH .... Lincoln City, OR [*AM radio station call letters*]
KBCI .... Boise, ID [*Television station call letters*]
KBCJ .... Vernal, UT [*Television station call letters*] (BROA)
KBCK .... Deer Lodge, MT [*AM radio station call letters*] (BROA)
KBCK .... Diamondville, WY [*FM radio station call letters*]
KBCL .... Bossier City, LA [*AM radio station call letters*] (BROA)
KBCL .... Shreveport, LA [*AM radio station call letters*]
KBCM .... Blytheville, AR [*FM radio station call letters*] (BROA)
KBCM .... Fort Worth, TX [*AM radio station call letters*] (BROA)
KBCN .... Marshall, AR [*FM radio station call letters*]
KBCO .... Boulder, CO [*AM radio station call letters*]
KBCO-FM ... Boulder, CO [*FM radio station call letters*]
KBCQ .... Roswell, NM [*FM radio station call letters*]
KBCR .... Steamboat Springs, CO [*AM radio station call letters*]
KBCR-FM ... Steamboat Springs, CO [*FM radio station call letters*] (RBYB)
KBCS .... Bellevue, WA [*FM radio station call letters*]
KBCT .... Boca Raton [*Florida*] [*ICAO location identifier*] (ICLI)
KBCT-FM.... Waco, TX [*FM radio station call letters*] (RBYB)
KBCU .... North Newton, KS [*FM radio station call letters*]
KBCV .... Hollister, MO [*AM radio station call letters*] (BROA)
KBCV-FM.... Paris, TX [*FM radio station call letters*] (BROA)
KBCW-FM... McAlester, OK [*FM radio station call letters*] (BROA)
KBCX-FM ... Big Spring, TX [*FM radio station call letters*] (BROA)
KBCY .... Tye, TX [*FM radio station call letters*]
KBCZ .... Holbrook, AZ [*Television station call letters*] (BROA)
KBCZ .... Kelley Bean [*Federal Railroad Administration identification code*]
KBD .... Contributed [*Telegraphy*] (PCTE)
KBD .... Kaschin-Beck Disease [*Medicine*]
kbd .... Keyboard (WDAA)
KBD .... Keyboard
KBD .... King's Bench Division [*of law courts*] [*British*] (ROG)
KBD .... Thousand Barrels per Day [*Also, TBD*]
KBDA-FM ... Great Bend, KS [*FM radio station call letters*] (BROA)
KBDC .... King's Bench Divisional Court [*British*]
KBDC-FM ... Mason City, IA (BROA)
KBDD-FM ... Winfield, KS [*FM radio station call letters*] (BROA)
KBDE .... Baudette [*Minnesota*] [*ICAO location identifier*] (ICLI)
KBDE .... Temple, TX [*FM radio station call letters*] (BROA)
KBDE-FM ... Gatesville, TX [*FM radio station call letters*] (BROA)
KBDG .... Turlock, CA [*FM radio station call letters*]
KBDH-FM ... San Ardo, CA [*FM radio station call letters*] (BROA)
KBDI .... Broomfield, CO [*Television station call letters*]
KB Div'l Ct... King's Bench Divisional Court [*England*] (DLA)
KBDJ-FM.... Ruston, LA [*FM radio station call letters*] (BROA)
KBDK .... Hoisington, KS [*Television station call letters*] (BROA)
KBDL .... Windsor Locks/Bradley International [*Connecticut*] [*ICAO location identifier*] (ICLI)
KBDM .... Yreka City, CA [*Television station call letters*] (BROA)
KBDN .... Bandon, OR [*FM radio station call letters*] (RBYB)
KBDO-FM ... Des Arc, AR [*FM radio station call letters*] (BROA)
KBDQ-FM ... Owensville, MO [*FM radio station call letters*] (BROA)
KBDR .... Mirando City, TX [*FM radio station call letters*]
KBDS .... Taft, CA [*FM radio station call letters*] (BROA)
KBDS-FM ... Arvin, CA [*FM radio station call letters*] (BROA)
KBDT-FM.... Oraibi, AZ [*FM radio station call letters*] (BROA)
KBDU-FM ... Hayden, CO [*FM radio station call letters*] (BROA)
KBDX .... Blanding, UT [*FM radio station call letters*] (BROA)
KBDZ .... Perryville, MO [*FM radio station call letters*]
KBE .... Bell Island, AK [*Location identifier*] [*FAA*] (FAAL)
KBE .... Berea College, Berea, KY [*OCLC symbol*] (OCLC)
KBE .... Keyboard Encoder [*Computer science*]
KBE .... Keyboard Entry [*Computer science*]
KBE .... Key British Enterprises [*Dun & Bradstreet Ltd.*] [*Information service or system*] (IID)
KBE .... Knight Commander of the [*Order of the*] British Empire
KBE .... Knight of the Black Eagle [*Russia*] [*Obsolete*]
KBE .... Knowledge-Based Economy (FOTI)
KBE .... Knowledge-Based Engineering [*Expert systems*] [*Computer-aided design*]
KBE .... Knowledge Base Environment
KBEA .... Muscatine, IA [*FM radio station call letters*] (BROA)
KBEB .... Rayne, LA [*FM radio station call letters*] (BROA)
KBEB-FM.... Hamilton, MT [*FM radio station call letters*] (BROA)
KBEC .... Kent, Barry, Eaton Connecting Railway [*Federal Railroad Administration identification code*]
KBEC .... Waxahachie, TX [*AM radio station call letters*]
KBED .... Bedford/Laurence G. Hanscom Field [*Massachusetts*] [*ICAO location identifier*] (ICLI)
KBED-FM ... Shreveport, LA [*FM radio station call letters*] (BROA)
KBEE .... Modesto, CA [*AM radio station call letters*]
KBEE .... Salt Lake City, UT [*FM radio station call letters*] (RBYB)
KBEF .... Minden, LA [*FM radio station call letters*] (GDPB)
KBEF-FM.... Gibsland, LA [*FM radio station call letters*] (BROA)
KBEG .... Clovis, CA [*AM radio station call letters*] (BROA)
KBEH .... Bellevue, WA [*Television station call letters*]
KBEI .... Durango, CO [*Television station call letters*] (BROA)
KBEJ .... Fredericksburg, TX [*Television station call letters*] (BROA)
KBEK .... Mora, MN [*FM radio station call letters*]
KBEL .... Idabel, OK [*AM radio station call letters*]
KBEL-FM.... Idabel, OK [*FM radio station call letters*]
KBEM .... Minneapolis, MN [*FM radio station call letters*]
KBEN .... Carrizo Springs, TX [*AM radio station call letters*]
KBENC .... Keyboard Encoder (NITA)
KB (Eng) .... English Law Reports, King's Bench Division [*1901-52*] [*A publication*] (DLA)
KBEO .... Jackson, WY [*Television station call letters*] (BROA)
KBEQ .... Blue Springs, MO [*AM radio station call letters*]
KBEQ .... Kansas City, MO [*FM radio station call letters*]
KBER .... Ogden, UT [*FM radio station call letters*]
KBES .... Ceres, CA [*FM radio station call letters*]
KBES .... Knowledge-Based Expert System
KBET .... Canyon Country, CA [*AM radio station call letters*]
KBET .... Pocatello, ID [*AM radio station call letters*] (BROA)
KBEV .... Dillon, MT [*FM radio station call letters*] (GDPB)
KBEV-FM.... Dillon, MT [*FM radio station call letters*] (BROA)
KBEW .... Blue Earth, MN [*AM radio station call letters*]
KBEW-FM... Blue Earth, MN [*FM radio station call letters*]
KBEX-FM.... Billings, MT [*FM radio station call letters*] (BROA)
KBEZ .... Tulsa, OK [*FM radio station call letters*]
KBF .... K-Band Feed
KBF .... Kyburz Flat [*California*] [*Seismograph station code, US Geological Survey*] (SEIS)
KBFA .... Wolfforth, TX [*Television station call letters*] (BROA)
KBFB .... Dallas, TX [*FM radio station call letters*] (BROA)
KBFB-FM.... Dallas, TX [*FM radio station call letters*] (BROA)
KBFC .... Forrest City, AR [*FM radio station call letters*]
KBFC .... Karen Brooks Fan Club (EA)
KBFC .... Kippe Brannon Fan Club [*Defunct*] (EA)
KBFD .... Honolulu, HI [*Television station call letters*]
KBFE-FM.... Grand Junction, CO [*FM radio station call letters*] (BROA)
KBFF-FM.... Gallup, NM [*FM radio station call letters*] (BROA)
KBFG-FM ... Santa Fe, NM [*FM radio station call letters*] (BROA)
KBFH-FM ... Moose Lake, MN [*FM radio station call letters*] (BROA)
KBFI .... Bonners Ferry, ID [*AM radio station call letters*]
KBFI .... Seattle Boeing Field/King Country International [*Washington*] [*ICAO location identifier*] (ICLI)
KBFJ-FM.... Mountain Home, AR [*FM radio station call letters*] (BROA)
KBFL .... Bakersfield/Meadows Field [*California*] [*ICAO location identifier*] (ICLI)
KBFL .... Buffalo, MO [*FM radio station call letters*]
KBFM .... Edinburg, TX [*FM radio station call letters*]
KBFM .... Mobile/Aerospace [*Alabama*] [*ICAO location identifier*] (ICLI)
KBFN-FM ... Big Sky, MT [*FM radio station call letters*] (BROA)
KBFO-FM ... Aberdeen, SD [*FM radio station call letters*] (BROA)
KBFQ .... Enid, OK [*AM radio station call letters*] (BROA)
KBFR .... Bismarck, ND [*FM radio station call letters*] (BROA)
KBFR-FM ... Bridgeport, TX [*FM radio station call letters*] (BROA)
KBFS .... Belle Fourche, SD [*AM radio station call letters*]
KBFS .... K and B Freight Systems [*Common carrier symbol*]
KBFV-FM.... Carlsbad, NM [*FM radio station call letters*] (BROA)
KBFW .... Bellingham-Ferndale, WA [*AM radio station call letters*]
KBFX .... Anchorage, AK [*FM radio station call letters*]
KBFZ-FM.... Kimball, NE [*FM radio station call letters*] (BROA)
KBG .... Contributing [*Telegraphy*] (PCTE)
KBG .... Khamba [*Language symbol*] (ETLW)
KBGA-FM ... Missoula, MT [*FM radio station call letters*] (RBYB)
KBGC .... Pullman, WA [*Television station call letters*] (BROA)
KBGD .... Farwell, TX [*Television station call letters*] (BROA)
KBGE .... Bellevue, WA [*Television station call letters*] (RBYB)
KBGE-AM ... Kilgore, TX [*AM radio station call letters*] (BROA)
KBGF .... Douglas, AZ [*Television station call letters*] (BROA)
KBGG .... Des Moines, IA [*AM radio station call letters*] (BROA)

KBGG........ San Francisco, CA [*FM radio station call letters*] (RBYB)
KBGH........ Filer, ID [*Television station call letters*]
KBGIS....... Knowledge Based Geographical Information System (SAUO)
KBGJ-FM.... Marble Hill, MO [*FM radio station call letters*] (BROA)
KBGL........ Larned, KS [*FM radio station call letters*] (BROA)
KBGM-FM... Park Hills, MO [*FM radio station call letters*] (BROA)
KBGN........ Caldwell, ID [*AM radio station call letters*]
KBGO-FM... Las Vegas, TX [*FM radio station call letters*] (RBYB)
KBGP-FM... Bellview, MN [*FM radio station call letters*] (BROA)
KBGQ-FM... Harrisburg, AR [*FM radio station call letters*] (BROA)
KBGR........ Bangor/International [*Maine*] [*ICAO location identifier*] (ICLI)
KBGR........ Beebe, AR [*FM radio station call letters*] (BROA)
KBGR........ Belview, MN [*FM radio station call letters*] (BROA)
KBGS........ Big Spring/Webb Air Force Base [*Texas*] [*ICAO location identifier*] (ICLI)
KBGT-FM.... Hastings, NE [*FM radio station call letters*] (BROA)
KBGU-FM... Ingalls, KS [*FM radio station call letters*] (BROA)
KBGV-FM... Clear Lake, SD [*FM radio station call letters*] (BROA)
KBGX-FM... Newport, OR [*FM radio station call letters*] (BROA)
KBGY-FM.... Fairbault, MN [*FM radio station call letters*] (BROA)
KBGZ-FM... Galena, KS [*FM radio station call letters*] (BROA)
KBH.......... Kaufman & Broad Home [*NYSE symbol*] (TTSB)
KBH.......... Kaufman & Broad Home Corp. [*NYSE symbol*] (SPSG)
KBH.......... KB Home [*Company symbol*]
KBH.......... Killed by Helicopter [*In reference to the enemy*] [*Vietnam*]
KBHA-FM... Wake Village, TX [*FM radio station call letters*] (BROA)
KBHB........ Sturgis, SD [*AM radio station call letters*]
KBHC........ Nashville, AR [*AM radio station call letters*]
KBHD-FM... Gregory, TX [*FM radio station call letters*] (BROA)
KBHE........ Rapid City, SD [*FM radio station call letters*]
KBHE-TV.... Rapid City, SD [*Television station call letters*]
KBHG........ Alexandria, MN [*FM radio station call letters*] (BROA)
KBHH-FM... Kerman, CA [*FM radio station call letters*] (BROA)
KBHI-FM.... Miner, MO [*FM radio station call letters*] (BROA)
KBHJ-FM.... Jackson, WY [*FM radio station call letters*] (BROA)
KBHK........ San Francisco, CA [*Television station call letters*]
KBHL........ Osakis, MN [*FM radio station call letters*]
KBHM........ Birmingham [*Alabama*] [*ICAO location identifier*] (ICLI)
KBHM-FM... Johannesburg, CA [*FM radio station call letters*] (BROA)
KBHN-FM... Hydesville, CA [*FM radio station call letters*] (BROA)
KBHO-FM... Boonville, MO [*FM radio station call letters*] (BROA)
KBHP........ Bemidji, MN [*FM radio station call letters*]
KBHQ-FM... Moapa Valley, NV [*FM radio station call letters*] (BROA)
KBHR........ Big Bear City, CA [*FM radio station call letters*]
KBHS........ Hot Springs, AR [*AM radio station call letters*]
KBHT........ Crockett, TX [*FM radio station call letters*]
KBHU........ Spearfish, SD [*FM radio station call letters*]
KBHV-FM... Wellton, AZ [*FM radio station call letters*] (BROA)
KBHW........ International Falls, MN [*FM radio station call letters*]
KBHX-FM... Shingletown, CA [*FM radio station call letters*] (BROA)
KBHY-FM.... Atkins, AR [*FM radio station call letters*] (BROA)
KBHZ-FM... Willmar, MN [*FM radio station call letters*] (RBYB)
KBI........... Kawecki Berylco Industries (ACAE)
KBI........... Keyboard Immortals [*Recording label*]
KBI........... Key Buying Influence (WDMC)
KBI........... Kill Before Intercept [*Military*] (ACAE)
Kb/i.......... Kilobits per Inch (VLIE)
KBI........... Klan Bureau of Investigation (SAUO)
KBI........... Kribi [*Cameroon*] [*Airport symbol*] (OAG)
KBIA........ Columbia, MO [*FM radio station call letters*]
KBIA........ Kansas Building Industry Association (EARSL)
KBIA........ Kent Barlow Information Associates [*British*] (NITA)
KBIB........ Marion, TX [*AM radio station call letters*]
KBIC........ Raymondville, TX [*FM radio station call letters*] (RBYB)
KBID........ Bakersfield, CA [*AM radio station call letters*]
KBIE........ Fountain Hills, AZ [*FM radio station call letters*] (BROA)
KBIE-FM.... Ingalls, KS [*FM radio station call letters*] (BROA)
KBIF........ El Paso/Biggs Air Force Base [*Texas*] [*ICAO location identifier*] (ICLI)
KBIF........ Fresno, CA [*AM radio station call letters*]
KBIG........ Los Angeles, CA [*FM radio station call letters*]
KBIH-FM.... Coeur d'Alene, ID [*FM radio station call letters*] (BROA)
KBII-FM.... Hatfield, AR [*FM radio station call letters*] (BROA)
KBIJ-FM.... Mena, AR [*FM radio station call letters*] (BROA)
KBIL........ Billings, MT [*FM radio station call letters*] (BROA)
KBIL........ Breckenridge, TX [*AM radio station call letters*]
KBIL-FM.... Grand Isle, LA [*FM radio station call letters*] (BROA)
KBIM........ Keyboard Interface Module (MCD)
KBIM........ Roswell, NM [*AM radio station call letters*]
KBIM-FM.... Roswell, NM [*FM radio station call letters*]
KBIM-TV.... Roswell, NM [*Television station call letters*]
KBIN........ Council Bluffs, IA [*Television station call letters*]
KBIO-FM.... Natchitoches, LA [*FM radio station call letters*] (BROA)
KBIQ........ Fountain, CO [*FM radio station call letters*]
KBIQ-FM.... Manitou Springs, CO [*FM radio station call letters*] (RBYB)
KBIS........ Kitchen and Bath Industry Show West (ITD)
KBIS-AM.... Highland Park, TX [*AM radio station call letters*] (BROA)
KBISKK...... Kodak Business Information Services K.K. (EFIS)
K-bit........ 1024 bits (128 bytes) [*Communications term*] (DCT)
Kbit.......... Kilobit
KBIT........ Knowledge Based Intelligent Tracking (ACAE)
KBIT/S....... KiloBITS [*Binary Digits*] per Second [*Transmission rate*] [*Computer science*] (TEL)
Kbit/s........ Kilobits/Second (VLIE)
KBIU........ Lake Charles, LA [*FM radio station call letters*]
KBIV........ El Paso, TX [*AM radio station call letters*] (BROA)
KBIX........ Biloxi/Keesler Air Force Base [*Mississippi*] [*ICAO location identifier*] (ICLI)
KBIX........ Muskogee, OK [*AM radio station call letters*]
KBIY-FM.... Van Buren, MO [*FM radio station call letters*] (BROA)
KBIZ........ Ottumwa, IA [*AM radio station call letters*]
KBJ.......... Kentucky State Bar Journal [*A publication*] (DLA)
KBJA........ Sandy, UT [*AM radio station call letters*] (BROA)
KBJC........ Kansas City, KS [*AM radio station call letters*] (BROA)
KBJD........ Denver, CO [*AM radio station call letters*] (BROA)
KBJE........ Monroe, LA [*AM radio station call letters*] (BROA)
KBJF-FM.... Shelby, MT [*FM radio station call letters*] (BROA)
KBJG-FM.... Mesquite, NV [*FM radio station call letters*] (BROA)
KBJJ........ Marshall, MN [*FM radio station call letters*]
KBJL........ Sheridan, WY [*Television station call letters*] (BROA)
KBJM........ Lemmon, SD [*AM radio station call letters*]
KBJN........ Ely, NV [*Television station call letters*] (BROA)
KBJO........ Avalon, CA [*Television station call letters*] (BROA)
KBJQ-FM.... Bronson, KS [*FM radio station call letters*] (BROA)
KBJR........ Superior, WI [*Television station call letters*]
KBJS........ Jacksonville, TX [*FM radio station call letters*]
KBJT........ Fordyce, AR [*AM radio station call letters*]
KBJU-FM.... Bagdad, AZ [*FM radio station call letters*] (BROA)
KBJX........ Shelley, ID [*FM radio station call letters*] (BROA)
KBJY........ Ennis, MT [*FM radio station call letters*] (BROA)
KBK.......... KBK Capital [*AMEX symbol*] (TTSB)
KBK.......... KBK Capital Corp. [*AMEX symbol*] (SAG)
KBK.......... Kirkjubaejar [*Iceland*] [*Airport symbol*] (AD)
KBKB........ Fort Madison, IA [*AM radio station call letters*]
KBKB-FM... Fort Madison, IA [*FM radio station call letters*]
KBKC........ KBK Capital Corp. [*NASDAQ symbol*] (SAG)
KBK Cap.... KBK Capital Corp. [*Associated Press*] (SAG)
KBKC-FM... Moberly, MO [*FM radio station call letters*] (BROA)
KBKF-FM.... Snyder, OK [*FM radio station call letters*] (BROA)
KBKG........ Corning, AR [*FM radio station call letters*]
KBKH........ Shamrock, TX [*FM radio station call letters*] (BROA)
KBKH-FM... Ilwaco, WA [*FM radio station call letters*] (BROA)
KBKI........ Walla Walla, WA [*Television station call letters*] (BROA)
KBKK........ Spanish Fork, UT [*FM radio station call letters*] (RBYB)
KBKK-FM... Pillager, MN [*FM radio station call letters*] (BROA)
KBKL........ Grand Junction, CO [*FM radio station call letters*]
KBKN........ Lamesa, TX [*FM radio station call letters*] (BROA)
KBKO........ Billings, MT [*FM radio station call letters*] (RBYB)
KBKO-AM... Santa Barbara, CA [*AM radio station call letters*] (BROA)
KBKR........ Baker City, OR [*AM radio station call letters*]
KBKS-FM... Tacoma, WA [*FM radio station call letters*] (RBYB)
KBKW........ Aberdeen, WA [*AM radio station call letters*] (RBYB)
KBKY........ Merced, CA [*FM radio station call letters*] (BROA)
KBKZ........ Raton, NM [*FM radio station call letters*] (BROA)
KBL.......... Design, Development and Implementation of a Knowledge-Based Leitstand (SAUO)
KBL.......... Hebraeisches und Aramaeisches Lexikon zum Alten Testament [*L. Koehler and W. Baumgarther*] [*A publication*] (BJA)
KBL.......... Kabul [*Afghanistan*] [*Airport symbol*] (OAG)
KBL.......... Kabul [*Afghanistan*] [*Seismograph station code, US Geological Survey*] (SEIS)
KBL.......... Keebler Foods [*NYSE symbol*] (SG)
KBL.......... Keyboard Listener [*Computer science*] (MHDI)
KBL.......... Kill Before Launch [*Military*] (ACAE)
KBL.......... Kilusan ng Bangong Lipunan [*New Society Movement*] [*Philippines*] (PD)
KBL.......... Kraft Black Liquor [*Pulping technology*]
KBL.......... Kredietbank Luxembourgeoise [*Luxembourg*]
KBL.......... Lexicon in Veteris Testamenti Libros. Supplementum [*L. Koehler and W. Baumgartner*] [*A publication*] (BJA)
KBL.......... New Society Movement (Philippines) [*Political party*] (PSAP)
KBLA........ Santa Monica, CA [*AM radio station call letters*]
KBLB........ Nisswa, MN [*FM radio station call letters*] (BROA)
KBLD-FM... Kennewick, WA [*FM radio station call letters*] (BROA)
KBLE........ Seattle, WA [*AM radio station call letters*] (BROA)
KBLF........ Red Bluff, CA [*AM radio station call letters*]
KBLG........ Billings, MT [*AM radio station call letters*]
KBLH........ Keel Blade Height [*Botany*]
KBLI........ Bellingham/International [*Washington*] [*ICAO location identifier*] (ICLI)
KBLI........ Blackfoot, ID [*AM radio station call letters*] (BROA)
KBLJ........ La Junta, CO [*FM radio station call letters*]
KBLK........ Burnet, TX [*FM radio station call letters*]
KBLL........ Helena, MT [*AM radio station call letters*]
KBLL........ Keel Blade Length [*Botany*]
KBLL-FM.... Helena, MT [*FM radio station call letters*]
KBLP........ Lindsay, OK [*FM radio station call letters*]
KBLPS....... Knowledge-Based Logistics Planning Shell
KBLQ........ Logan, UT [*FM radio station call letters*]
KBLR........ Blair, NE [*FM radio station call letters*] (BROA)
KBLR........ Paradise, NV [*Television station call letters*]
KBLS........ North Fort Riley, KS [*FM radio station call letters*]
KBLT-FM.... Leakey, TX [*FM radio station call letters*] (BROA)
KBLU........ Yuma, AZ [*AM radio station call letters*]
KBLUP....... Kootenay/Boundary Land Use Plan (SAUO)
KBLUPHLP... Kootenay/Boundary Land Use Plan Higher Level Plan (SAUO)
KBLV........ Bellerville/Scott Air Force Base [*Illinois*] [*ICAO location identifier*] (ICLI)
KBLV........ Bellevue, WA [*AM radio station call letters*]
KBLX........ Berkeley, CA [*FM radio station call letters*] (RBYB)
KBLZ........ Kaneohe, HI [*FM radio station call letters*]

KBLZ......... Winona, TX [*FM radio station call letters*] (BROA)
KBM......... Kabwum [*Papua New Guinea*] [*Airport symbol*] (OAG)
KBM......... Karissimo Bene Merenti [*To the Most Dear and Well-Deserving*] [*Correspondence*]
KBM......... Keyboard Monitor [*Computer science*]
KBM......... Knowledge-Based Manufacturing
KBM......... Knowledge Base Machine [*Computer science*]
KBMA........ Bryan, TX [*FM radio station call letters*]
KBMB-FM... Sacramento, CA [*FM radio station call letters*] (BROA)
KBMC........ Bozeman, MT [*FM radio station call letters*]
KBMD........ Marble Falls, TX [*FM radio station call letters*] (BROA)
KBME........ Bismarck, ND [*Television station call letters*]
KBME........ Houston, TX [*AM radio station call letters*] (BROA)
KBMEDM.... Knowledge Based Model of the Experienced Decision Maker (VLIE)
KBME-DT... Bismarck, ND [*Television station call letters*] (BROA)
KBMG........ Hamilton, MT [*FM radio station call letters*]
KBMH........ Holbrook, AZ [*FM radio station call letters*] (BROA)
KBMI........ Roma, TX [*FM radio station call letters*]
KBMJ........ Hardin, MT [*FM radio station call letters*]
KBMJ........ Heber Springs, AR [*FM radio station call letters*] (BROA)
KBMM........ Odessa, TX [*FM radio station call letters*] (BROA)
KBMO........ Benson, MN [*AM radio station call letters*] (GDPB)
KBMO-AM.. Benson, MN [*AM radio station call letters*] (BROA)
KBMO-TV... Tonopah, NV [*Television station call letters*] (BROA)
KBMP........ Enterprise, KS [*FM radio station call letters*] (BROA)
KBMQ........ Monroe, LA [*FM radio station call letters*] (BROA)
KBMR........ Bismarck, ND [*AM radio station call letters*]
KBMS........ Knowledge Based Management System
KBMS........ Knowledge Base Management System [*Computer science*]
KBMS........ Vancouver, WA [*AM radio station call letters*]
KBMT........ Beaumont, TX [*Television station call letters*]
KBMT........ Knowledge-Based Machine Translation [*Computer science*]
KBMU........ BPO Minudobrenia [*Intermodal shipping container symbol*] (TVRC)
KB-MUSICA-2671... Knowledge-Based Multi-Sensor Systems in CIM Applications (SAUO)
KBMV........ Birch Tree, MO [*AM radio station call letters*]
KBMV-FM... Birch Tree, MO [*FM radio station call letters*]
KBMW........ Breckenridge, MN [*AM radio station call letters*]
KBMX........ Eldon, MO [*FM radio station call letters*]
KBMX........ Proctor, MN [*FM radio station call letters*] (BROA)
KBMY........ Bismarck, ND [*Television station call letters*]
KBN.......... Contribution [*Telegraphy*] (PCTE)
KBN.......... Kill Bad Name [*Marketing*] (WDMC)
KBNA........ El Paso, TX [*AM radio station call letters*]
KBNA........ Nashville/Metropolitan [*Tennessee*] [*ICAO location identifier*] (ICLI)
KBNA-FM... El Paso, TX [*FM radio station call letters*]
KBNB-AM... Gilmer, TX [*AM radio station call letters*] (RBYB)
KBND........ Bend, OR [*AM radio station call letters*]
KBNF-FM... Chester, CA [*FM radio station call letters*] (BROA)
KBNG........ Silverton, CO [*FM radio station call letters*] (BROA)
KBNH........ Homedale, ID [*FM radio station call letters*] (BROA)
KBNJ........ Corpus Christi, TX [*FM radio station call letters*]
KBNL........ Laredo, TX [*FM radio station call letters*]
KBNM........ Sheridan, WY [*Television station call letters*] (BROA)
KBNN........ Springfield, MO [*AM radio station call letters*] (GDPB)
KBNN-AM... Lebanon, MO [*AM radio station call letters*] (BROA)
KBNO........ Denver, CO [*AM radio station call letters*]
KBNO........ White Salmon, WA [*FM radio station call letters*] (BROA)
KBNP........ Portland, OR [*AM radio station call letters*]
KBNR........ Brownsville, TX [*FM radio station call letters*]
KBNT........ San Diego, CA [*Television station call letters*] (GDPB)
KBNU-FM... Uvalde, TX [*FM radio station call letters*] (RBYB)
KBNV........ Fayetteville, AR [*FM radio station call letters*] (BROA)
KBNWR...... Klamath Basin National Wildlife Refuges (SAUO)
KBNX........ Goldfield, NV [*Television station call letters*] (BROA)
KBNY........ Ely, NV [*Television station call letters*] (BROA)
KBNZ........ Tremonton, UT [*FM radio station call letters*] (BROA)
KBNZ-AM... Honolulu, HI [*AM radio station call letters*] (BROA)
KBO.......... Kabalo [*Zaire*] [*Airport symbol*] (AD)
KBO.......... Keep Buggering On [*Perseverance*] [*Slang*] [*British*] (DSUE)
KBo.......... Keilschrifttexte aus Boghazkoi [*A publication*] (BJA)
KBO.......... Kite and Balloon Officer [*Navy*]
KBO.......... Kommunistischer Bund Oesterreichs [*Communist League of Austria*] [*Political party*] (PPW)
KBO.......... Kuiper Belt Objects [*Planetary science*]
KBO.......... Organization for the Management and Development of the Kagera River Basin (EA)
KBOA........ Kennett, MO [*AM radio station call letters*]
KBOA........ Piggott, AR [*FM radio station call letters*] (RBYB)
KBOB........ Geneseo, IL [*FM radio station call letters*] (BROA)
KBOB........ Muscatine, IA [*FM radio station call letters*]
KBOC........ Bridgeport, TX [*FM radio station call letters*]
KBOE........ Oskaloosa, IA [*AM radio station call letters*]
KBOE-FM... Oskaloosa, IA [*FM radio station call letters*]
KBOF........ Washington/Bolling Air Force Base [*District of Columbia*] [*ICAO location identifier*] (ICLI)
KBOI........ Boise/Boise Air Terminal [*Idaho*] [*ICAO location identifier*] (ICLI)
KBOI........ Boise, ID [*AM radio station call letters*]
KBOJ........ Worthington, MN [*FM radio station call letters*] (BROA)
KBOK........ Malvern, AR [*AM radio station call letters*]
KBOK-FM... Malvern, AR [*FM radio station call letters*]
KBOM........ Los Alamos, NM [*FM radio station call letters*]
KBOM........ Santa Fe, NM [*FM radio station call letters*] (BROA)
KBON-FM... Mamou, LA [*FM radio station call letters*] (BROA)
KBOO........ Portland, OR [*FM radio station call letters*]
KBOP........ Pleasanton, TX [*AM radio station call letters*]
KBOP-FM... Jourdanton, TX [*FM radio station call letters*] (BROA)
KBOQ........ Carmel, CA [*FM radio station call letters*] (RBYB)
KBOR........ Brownsville, TX [*AM radio station call letters*]
KBOR........ Mission, TX [*FM radio station call letters*] (BROA)
KBOS........ Boston/Logan International [*Massachusetts*] [*ICAO location identifier*] (ICLI)
KBOS........ Tulare, CA [*FM radio station call letters*]
KBOT........ Kansas City Board of Trade
KBOT........ Pelican Rapids, MN [*FM radio station call letters*]
KBOV........ Bishop, CA [*AM radio station call letters*]
KBOW........ Butte, MT [*AM radio station call letters*]
KBOX........ Lompoc, CA [*FM radio station call letters*]
KBOY........ Medford, OR [*FM radio station call letters*]
KBOZ........ Bozeman, MT [*AM radio station call letters*]
KBP.......... Kainate-Binding Protein [*Biochemistry*]
KBP.......... Kappa Beta Pi [*Society*]
KBP.......... Kent-Barlow Publications Ltd. [*Information service or system*] (IID)
KBP.......... Keyboard Process [*Computer science*]
KBP.......... Kiev Borispol Airport [*Former USSR*] [*Airport symbol*] (OAG)
kbp.......... Kilobase Pairs [*Genetics*]
KBP.......... King's Bishop's Pawn [*Chess*] (IIA)
KBP.......... Kite Balloon Pilot
KBP.......... Koala Bear Park [*Adelaide*] [*Airport symbol*] (AD)
KBPA........ Knowledge-Based Programming Assistant (PDAA)
KBPA-AM... Palo Alto, CA [*AM radio station call letters*] (BROA)
KBPAP...... Kidney Bean Purple Acid Phosphatase [*An enzyme*]
KBPB........ Harrison, AR [*FM radio station call letters*] (BROA)
KBPD........ La Grande, OR [*Television station call letters*] (BROA)
KBPG........ Montevideo, MN [*FM radio station call letters*] (BROA)
KBPI........ Denver, CO [*FM radio station call letters*]
KBPK........ Buena Park, CA [*FM radio station call letters*]
KBPL........ Communist League Proletarian Left [*Netherlands*] [*Political party*] (PPW)
KBPM........ Moreno Valley, CA [*AM radio station call letters*] (BROA)
KBPN........ Brainerd, MN [*FM radio station call letters*] (BROA)
KBPR........ Brainerd, MN [*FM radio station call letters*]
KBPRC...... Keyboard and Printer Controller [*Computer science*] (NITA)
KBPS........ Kilobits per Second (NAKS)
Kbps........ Kilobits per Second [*Computer science*]
KBps........ Kilobytes per Second [*Computer science*] (DOM)
KBPS........ Portland, OR [*AM radio station call letters*]
Kbps........ thousand bits per second (SAUS)
Kbps........ Thousands of Bits Per Second (bps) [*Communications term*] (DCT)
KBPS-FM... Portland, OR [*FM radio station call letters*]
KBPT........ Beaumont Port-Arthur/Jefferson County [*Texas*] [*ICAO location identifier*] (ICLI)
KBPU........ De Queen, AR [*FM radio station call letters*] (BROA)
KBPW........ Hampton, AR [*FM radio station call letters*] (BRO)
KBPX........ Flagstaff, AZ [*Television station call letters*] (BROA)
KBQC........ Independence, KS [*FM radio station call letters*] (BROA)
KBQI........ Albuquerque, NM [*FM radio station call letters*] (BROA)
KBQQ........ Minot, ND [*FM radio station call letters*]
KBR.......... Kaaba Resources [*Vancouver Stock Exchange symbol*]
KBR.......... Kafa [*Language symbol*] (ETLW)
KBR.......... Kota Bharu [*Malaysia*] [*Airport symbol*] (OAG)
KBr.......... Potassium Bromide [*An anticonvulsant and sedative*] (DAVI)
KBRA-FM... Freer, TX [*FM radio station call letters*] (BROA)
KBRB........ Ainsworth, NE [*AM radio station call letters*]
KBRB-FM... Ainsworth, NE [*FM radio station call letters*]
KBRC........ Mount Vernon, WA [*AM radio station call letters*]
KBRD........ Lacey, WA [*AM radio station call letters*] (RBYB)
KBRE........ Atwater, CA [*FM radio station call letters*] (BROA)
KBRE........ Cedar City, UT [*AM radio station call letters*]
KBRE-FM... Cedar City, UT [*FM radio station call letters*]
KBRF........ Fergus Falls, MN [*AM radio station call letters*]
KBRG........ Fremont, CA [*FM radio station call letters*]
KBRG........ San Jose, CA [*FM radio station call letters*] (BROA)
KBRH........ Baton Rouge, LA [*AM radio station call letters*]
KBRI........ Brinkley, AR [*AM radio station call letters*]
KBRJ........ Anchorage, AK [*FM radio station call letters*]
KBRK........ Brookings, SD [*AM radio station call letters*]
KBRK-FM... Brookings, SD [*FM radio station call letters*]
KBRL........ McCook, NE [*AM radio station call letters*]
KBRN........ Boerne, TX [*AM radio station call letters*]
KBRO........ Bremerton, WA [*AM radio station call letters*]
KBRO........ Brownsville/International [*Texas*] [*ICAO location identifier*] (ICLI)
KBRQ........ Hillsboro, TX [*FM radio station call letters*]
KBRR........ Thief River Falls, MN [*Television station call letters*]
KBRS........ Springdale, AR [*FM radio station call letters*]
KBRT........ Avalon, CA [*AM radio station call letters*]
KBRU........ Fort Morgan, CO [*FM radio station call letters*]
KBRV........ Soda Springs, ID [*AM radio station call letters*]
KBRW........ Barrow, AK [*AM radio station call letters*]
KBRW-FM... Barrow, AK [*FM radio station call letters*] (RBYB)
KBRX........ O'Neill, NE [*AM radio station call letters*]
KBRX-FM... O'Neill, NE [*FM radio station call letters*]
KBRZ........ Freeport, TX [*AM radio station call letters*]
KBS.......... Bo [*Sierra Leone*] [*Airport symbol*] [*Obsolete*] (OAG)
KBS.......... Contributes [*Telegraphy*] (PCTE)
KBS.......... Gamair Ltd. [*Gambia*] [*ICAO designator*] (FAAC)
KBS.......... Kellogg Biological Station [*Michigan State University*]

kbs .... KiloBITS [*Binary Digits*] per Second [*Transmission rate*] [*Computer science*]
Kb/s .... Kilobits per Second (VLIE)
KBS .... Kilobytes per Second [*Computer science*]
KBS .... Kinematic Bombing System
KBS .... Kingsbay [*Spitsbergen*] [*Seismograph station code, US Geological Survey*] (SEIS)
KBS .... Kinki Broadcasting System (SAUO)
KBS .... Kluver-Bucy Syndrome [*Psychiatry*] (DAVI)
KBS .... Knight of the Blessed Sacrament
KBS .... Knowledge-Based System [*Computer model*] [*Computer science*]
KBS .... Korea Base Section (SAUO)
KBS .... Korean Broadcasting System [*South Korea*] (FEA)
KBS .... Korean Bureau of Standards, Seoul (SAUO)
KBS .... Stites, McElwain & Fowler, Bellarmine College Library, Louisville, KY [*OCLC symbol*] (OCLC)
KBSA .... El Dorado, AR [*FM radio station call letters*]
KBSA .... Kassian Benevolent Society in America (EA)
KBSA .... Knowledge-Based Software Assistant [*Computer science*]
KBSB .... Bemidji, MN [*FM radio station call letters*]
KBSC .... Knowledge-Based Systems Centre [*Polytechnic of the South Bank*] [*British*] (CB)
KBSD .... Ensign, KS [*Television station call letters*]
KBSE .... Knowledge-Based Software Engineering (RALS)
KBSEA .... Bulletin. Kyoto Educational University. Series B. Mathematics and Natural Science (journ.) (SAUS)
KBSF .... Springhill, LA [*AM radio station call letters*]
KBSG .... Auburn, WA [*AM radio station call letters*]
KBSG .... Tacoma, WA [*FM radio station call letters*]
KBSH .... Hays, KS [*Television station call letters*]
KBSI .... Cape Girardeau, MO [*Television station call letters*]
KBSJ .... Jackpot, NV [*FM radio station call letters*] (BROA)
KBSK .... McCall, MD [*FM radio station call letters*] (BROA)
KBSL .... Goodland, KS [*Television station call letters*]
KBSL .... Knowledge Base Services Ltd. (SAUO)
KBSM .... Austin/Bergstrom Air Force Base [*Texas*] [*ICAO location identifier*] (ICLI)
KBSM .... McCall, ID [*FM radio station call letters*]
KBSN .... Moses Lake, WA [*AM radio station call letters*]
KBSO .... Corpus Christi, TX [*FM radio station call letters*]
KBSP .... Salem, OR [*Television station call letters*]
KBSQ .... McCall, ID [*FM radio station call letters*] (BROA)
KBSR .... Kankakee, Beaverville & Southern Railroad Co. [*AAR code*]
KBSR .... Laurel, MT [*AM radio station call letters*]
KBSS .... Sun Valley, ID [*FM radio station call letters*] (BROA)
KBST .... Big Spring, TX [*AM radio station call letters*]
KBST-FM .... Big Spring, TX [*FM radio station call letters*]
KBSU .... Boise, ID [*AM radio station call letters*]
KBSU-FM .... Boise, ID [*FM radio station call letters*]
KBSV-TV .... Ceres, CA [*TV station call letters*] (RBYB)
KBSW .... Twin Falls, ID [*FM radio station call letters*]
KBSX-FM .... Boise, ID [*FM radio station call letters*] (BROA)
KBSY-FM .... Burley, ID [*FM radio station call letters*] (BROA)
KBSZ .... Kankakee Beaverville and Southern Railroad [*Intermodal trailer symbol*]
KBSZ .... Wickenburg, AZ [*FM radio station call letters*] (RBYB)
KBT .... Kerry Blue Terrier (ROAS)
KBTA .... Batesville, AR [*AM radio station call letters*]
KBTA-FM .... Batesville, AR [*FM radio station call letters*] (BROA)
KBTC .... Houston, MO [*AM radio station call letters*]
KBTC .... Knoxville Building Trades Council (SAUO)
KBTC .... Tacoma, WA [*FM radio station call letters*]
KBTC-TV .... Tacoma, WA [*Television station call letters*]
KBTD .... Knee Board Training Device [*Military*] (MCD)
KBTE-FM .... Rockport, TX [*FM radio station call letters*] (BROA)
KBTG .... Keep Britain Tidy Group (DCTA)
KBTK-AM .... Corrales, NM [*AM radio station call letters*] (BROA)
KBTL-FM .... El Dorado, KS [*FM radio station call letters*] (BROA)
KBTM .... Jonesboro, AR [*AM radio station call letters*]
KBTN .... Neosho, MO [*AM radio station call letters*]
KBTN-FM .... Neosho, MO [*FM radio station call letters*] (RBYB)
KBTO .... Bottineau, ND [*FM radio station call letters*]
KBTR .... Baton Rouge/Ryan Field [*Louisiana*] [*ICAO location identifier*] (ICLI)
KBTS .... Big Spring, TX [*FM radio station call letters*]
KBTT .... Bridgeport, TX [*FM radio station call letters*]
KBTT .... Haughton, LA [*FM radio station call letters*] (BROA)
KBTU .... Carmel, CA [*FM radio station call letters*] (BROA)
KBTU .... Kilo British Thermal Unit (WDAA)
KBTV .... Burlington/International [*Vermont*] [*ICAO location identifier*] (ICLI)
KBTV-TV .... Port Arthur, TX [*Television station call letters*] (BROA)
KBTW .... Lenwood, CA [*FM radio station call letters*] (BROA)
KBTX .... Bryan, TX [*Television station call letters*]
KBTZ .... Butte, MT [*Television station call letters*] (BROA)
KBU .... Keyboard Unit [*Computer science*] (NASA)
KBU .... Knuckle Buster University [*Facetious term*]
KBU .... Kotabaru [*West Irian, Indonesia*] [*Airport symbol*] (AD)
KBUA-FM .... San Fernando, CA [*FM radio station call letters*] (BROA)
KBUB .... Brownwood, TX [*FM radio station call letters*] (GDPB)
KBUB-FM .... Brownwood, TX [*FM radio station call letters*] (BROA)
KBUC .... Jourdanton, TX [*FM radio station call letters*] (BROA)
KBUC .... Pleasonton, TX [*FM radio station call letters*] (BROA)
KBUC .... Upper Canada King's Bench Reports [*A publication*] (DLA)
KBUD .... Sardis, MS [*FM radio station call letters*] (BROA)
KBUE .... Long Beach, CA [*FM radio station call letters*] (RBYB)
KBUF .... Buffalo/Greater Buffalo International [*New York*] [*ICAO location identifier*] (ICLI)
KBUF .... Holcomb, KS [*AM radio station call letters*]
KBUG .... Malin, OR [*FM radio station call letters*] (BROA)
KBUG .... Osceola, MO [*FM radio station call letters*]
KBUK .... La Grange, TX [*FM radio station call letters*]
KBUL .... Billings, MT [*AM radio station call letters*] (BROA)
KBUL .... Carson City, NV [*FM radio station call letters*]
KBUL-AM .... Modesto, CA [*AM radio station call letters*] (BROA)
KBUL-FM .... Carson City, NV [*FM radio station call letters*] (BROA)
KBUN .... Bemidji, MN [*AM radio station call letters*]
KBUQ-FM .... Paradise Valley, AZ [*FM radio station call letters*] (RBYB)
KBUR .... Burbank/Hollywood-Burbank [*California*] [*ICAO location identifier*] (ICLI)
KBUR .... Burlington, IA [*AM radio station call letters*]
KBUS .... Paris, TX [*FM radio station call letters*]
KBUT .... Crested Butte, CO [*FM radio station call letters*]
KBUW-FM .... Buffalo, WY [*FM radio station call letters*] (BROA)
KBUX .... Quartzsite, AZ [*FM radio station call letters*]
KBUY .... Ruidoso, NM [*AM radio station call letters*]
KBUY-FM .... Amarillo, TX [*FM radio station call letters*]
KBUZ .... Topeka, KS [*FM radio station call letters*]
KBV .... Kobold Resources Ltd. [*Vancouver Stock Exchange symbol*]
KBV .... Kustbevakningen [*Sweden*] [*ICAO designator*] (FAAC)
KBVA .... Bella Vista, AR [*FM radio station call letters*]
KBVC-FM .... Buena Vista, CO [*FM radio station call letters*] (BROA)
KBVI .... Boulder, CO [*AM radio station call letters*] (RBYB)
KBVL .... Pawhuska, OK [*FM radio station call letters*] (BROA)
KBVM .... Portland, OR [*FM radio station call letters*]
KBVR .... Corvallis, OR [*FM radio station call letters*]
KBVS .... Billings, MT [*FM radio station call letters*] (BROA)
KBVU .... Eureka, CA [*Television station call letters*]
KBVU-FM .... Alta, IA [*FM radio station call letters*] (BROA)
KBVV .... Enid, OK [*FM radio station call letters*]
KBW .... Klan Border Watch (SAUO)
KBW .... Kommunistischer Bund Westdeutschland [*Communist League of West Germany*] [*Political party*] (PPW)
KBWB .... San Francisco, CA [*Television station call letters*] (BROA)
KBWC .... Marshall, TX [*FM radio station call letters*]
KBWD .... Brownwood, TX [*AM radio station call letters*]
KBWI .... Baltimore/Baltimore-Washington International [*Maryland*] [*ICAO location identifier*] (ICLI)
KBWS .... Sisseton, SD [*FM radio station call letters*]
KBXB-FM .... Sikeston, MO [*FM radio station call letters*] (RBYB)
KBXG .... Lake Charles, LA [*FM radio station call letters*] (BROA)
KBXL .... Caldwell, ID [*FM radio station call letters*]
KBXR .... Ashland, MO [*FM radio station call letters*]
KBXR .... Columbia, MO [*FM radio station call letters*] (BROA)
KBXX .... Houston, TX [*FM radio station call letters*]
KBXY .... Baker, CA [*FM radio station call letters*]
KBY .... Streaky Bay [*Australia*] [*Airport symbol*] (OAG)
KBYB .... El Dorado, AR [*FM radio station call letters*]
KBYE .... Dolan Springs, AZ [*FM radio station call letters*] (BROA)
KBYE .... Oklahoma City, OK [*AM radio station call letters*]
KBYG .... Big Spring, TX [*AM radio station call letters*]
KBYG .... Coahoma, TX [*FM radio station call letters*]
KBYH .... Blytheville Air Force Base [*Arkansas*] [*ICAO location identifier*] (ICLI)
KBYI .... Rexburg, ID [*FM radio station call letters*] (BROA)
KBYN .... Arnold, CA [*FM radio station call letters*]
KBYO .... Tallulah, LA [*AM radio station call letters*]
KBYO-FM .... Tallulah, LA [*FM radio station call letters*]
KBYR .... Anchorage, AK [*AM radio station call letters*]
KBYR .... Rexburg, ID [*FM radio station call letters*] (BROA)
kbyte/sec .... kilobytes per second (SAUS)
Kbytes/sec .... Kilobytes per Second [*Computer science*] (IGQR)
KBYU .... Provo, UT [*FM radio station call letters*]
KBYU-TV .... Provo, UT [*Television station call letters*]
KBYZ .... Bismarck, ND [*FM radio station call letters*]
KBZB .... Pioche, NV [*FM radio station call letters*] (BROA)
KBZD .... Amarillo, TX [*FM radio station call letters*] (BROA)
KBZE .... Berwick, LA [*FM radio station call letters*]
KBZG-FM .... Payson, AZ [*FM radio station call letters*] (BROA)
KBZI .... Deerfield, MO [*FM radio station call letters*] (BROA)
KBZK .... Bozeman, MT [*Television station call letters*] (BROA)
KBZK-FM .... Morro Bay, CA [*FM radio station call letters*] (BROA)
KBZN .... Ogden, UT [*FM radio station call letters*]
KBZO .... Lubbock, TX [*AM radio station call letters*] (RBYB)
KBZQ .... Lawton, OK [*FM radio station call letters*]
KBZR .... Coolidge, AZ [*FM radio station call letters*] (RBYB)
KBZS .... Palo Alto, CA [*AM radio station call letters*] (BROA)
KBZS-AM .... Grand Junction, CO [*AM radio station call letters*] (RBYB)
KBZT .... San Diego, CA [*FM radio station call letters*]
KBZU .... Albuquerque, NM [*FM radio station call letters*] (BROA)
KBZX-FM .... Paso Robles, CA [*FM radio station call letters*] (BROA)
KBZY .... Salem, OR [*AM radio station call letters*]
KBZZ .... La Junta, CO [*AM radio station call letters*]
KBZZ .... Morgan City, LA [*FM radio station call letters*] (BROA)
KBZZ-AM .... Sparks, NV [*AM radio station call letters*] (BROA)
KC .... Canada [*IYRU nationality code*] (IYR)
KC .... Concentrate [*Telegraphy*] (PCTE)
KC .... Cook Islands International [*ICAO designator*] (AD)
KC .... Kalamazoo College (SAUO)
KC .... [*The*] Kanawha Central Railway Co. [*AAR code*]
KC .... Kangaroo Care [*Medicine*] (MELL)

KC .... Kansas Central Railways (SAUO)
KC .... Kansas City [*Missouri*] [*Slang*]
KC .... Kansas City Area Office (SAUO)
KC .... Kansas City Chiefs [*National Football League*] [*1963-present*] (NFLA)
KC .... Kansas City Plant (SAUO)
KC .... Kansas City-St. Joseph [*Diocesan abbreviation*] [*Missouri*] (TOCD)
KC .... Karman Constant [*Physics*]
KC .... Kartell Convent Deutscher Studenten Juedischen Glaubens (BJA)
KC .... Kathodal Closing [*Medicine*]
KC .... Keble College (SAUO)
KC .... Keep-Clean [*Fuels and lubricants*]
KC .... Kendall College (SAUO)
KC .... Kennedy Center (SAUO)
KC .... Kennel Club
KC .... Kennel Cough [*Infectious tracheobronchitis*] (SPVS)
KC .... Kent Chemical Co. Ltd. (SAUO)
KC .... Kenyon College (SAUO)
KC .... Keratoconjunctivitis [*Ophthalmology*]
KC .... Keratoconus [*Ophthalmology*] (DAVI)
KC .... Keratoma Climacterium [*Dermatology*] (DAVI)
KC .... Kerr Cell [*Optics*]
KC .... Keston College (SAUO)
KC .... Ketocyclazocine [*Biochemistry*]
KC .... Keuka College (SAUO)
KC .... Key Company (SAUO)
KC .... Keystone Center [*An association*] (EA)
KC .... Keystone College (SAUO)
KC .... Kilgore College (SAUO)
kc .... Kilocalorie
KC .... Kilocharacter (BUR)
kC .... Kilocoulomb [*Medicine*] (EDAA)
KC .... Kilocurie (IAA)
kc .... Kilocurie (IDOE)
KC .... Kilocycle (AEBE)
kc .... Kilocycle [*Radio*]
kc .... Kilograms per Square Centimeter (DS)
K-C .... Kimberly-Clark Corporation (EFIS)
KC .... King's Colonials [*British military*] (DMA)
KC .... Kings Council (SAUO)
KC .... King's Counsel [*British*]
KC .... Kings County [*Sussex, New Brunswick*] (DAS)
KC .... King's Cross [*British*] (ADA)
KC .... Kirksville College (SAUO)
KC .... Kiting Check [*Investment*] (MHDB)
KC .... Knees to Chest [*Position*] [*Medicine*] (DAVI)
KC .... Knickerbocker Conference (PSS)
KC .... Knight Club (EA)
KC .... Knight Commander
KC .... Knight of the Crescent [*Turkey*]
KC .... Knights of Columbus
KC .... Knowledge Community (GART)
KC .... Knox College (SAUO)
KC .... Knoxville College (SAUO)
KC .... Knuckle Cracking [*Orthopedics*] (DAVI)
Kc .... Koruna [*Czech Coin*] (BARN)
KC .... Krishna Consciousness [*Medicine*] (EDAA)
KC .... Kronach [*German license plate city code*]
Kc .... Kupffer Cell [*Histology*]
KC .... Kyle Classification [*Library science*]
KC .... Strikeout, Called [*Baseball term*] (NDBD)
KC .... King's College (ODA)
KC-10 .... Extender (SAUS)
KC-10A .... Extender McDonnell Douglas [*Aerial tanker and transport aircraft*] [*Air Force*] (POLM)
KC-130 .... Hercules Aerial Tanker and Transport Aircraft [*Navy*] (POLM)
KC-135 .... Stratotanker [*Tanker aircraft*] [*Military*] (POLM)
KCA .... Kansas Chiropractic Association (SRA)
KCA .... Kansas Contractors Association (SRA)
KCA .... Keeshond Club of America (EA)
KCA .... Keesings Contemporary Archives [*A publication*] [*Also, an information service or system*]
KCA .... Kentucky Callers Association (EA)
KCA .... Kentucky Cattlemen's Association (SRA)
KCA .... Kentucky Coal Association (SRA)
KCA .... Kidney Cancer Association (EA)
KCA .... Kikuyu Central Association (SAUO)
KCA .... Kindness Club of Africa (SAUO)
KCA .... Kiowa-Comanche-Apache
KCA .... Kitchen Cabinet Association (SAUO)
KCA .... Komondor Club of America (EA)
KCA .... Kuvasz Club of America (EA)
KCAA .... Keuka College Alumni Association (EA)
KCAA .... Loma Linda, CA [*AM radio station call letters*] (BROA)
KCAB .... Dardanelle, AR [*AM radio station call letters*]
KCAC .... Camden, AR [*FM radio station call letters*]
KCAC .... Kansas Collegiate Athletic Conference (PSS)
KCAC .... Korean Civil Assistance Command (SAUO)
KCAD-FM .... Dickinson, ND [*FM radio station call letters*] (RBYB)
KCAG .... Korean Civil Action Group (SAUO)
KCAH .... Watsonville, CA [*Television station call letters*]
KCAILUC .... Kiowa-Commanche-Apache Intertribal Land Use Committee
KCAJ-FM .... Roseau, MN [*FM radio station call letters*] (BROA)
Kcal .... Kilcalorie (NTIO)
Kcal .... Kilocalorie (SHCU)
kcal .... Kilocalorie
KCAL .... Redlands, CA [*AM radio station call letters*] (RBYB)
KCAL-FM .... Redlands, CA [*FM radio station call letters*]
KCAL-TV .... Los Angeles, CA [*Television station call letters*]
KCAM .... Glennallen, AK [*AM radio station call letters*]
KCAN .... Albion, NE [*Television station call letters*]
KC&C .... Kembla Coal and Coke (SAUO)
KCAO .... Kansas City Area Office [*Energy Research and Development Administration*]
KCAP .... Helena, MT [*AM radio station call letters*]
KCAQ .... Oxnard, CA [*FM radio station call letters*]
KCAR .... Caribou [*Maine*] [*ICAO location identifier*] (ICLI)
KCAR .... Clarksville, TX [*AM radio station call letters*]
KCAR-FM .... Galena, KS [*FM radio station call letters*] (BROA)
KCAS .... Knots Calibrated Airspeed (MCD)
KCAS-FM .... McCook, TX [*FM radio station call letters*] (BROA)
KCAT .... Kemptville College of Agricultural Technology [*Canada*] (ARC)
KCAT .... Pine Bluff, AR [*AM radio station call letters*]
KCAU .... Sioux City, IA [*Television station call letters*]
KCAW .... Sitka, AK [*FM radio station call letters*]
KCAY .... Russell, KS [*FM radio station call letters*]
KCAZ .... Mission, KS [*AM radio station call letters*] (RBYB)
KCB .... Kansas City Ballet
KCB .... Kartell Convent Blaetter (BJA)
KCB .... Kenya Commercial Bank (SAUO)
KCB .... Keyboard Change Button [*Computer science*]
KCB .... Knight Commander of the [*Order of the*] Bath [*British*] (GPO)
KCBA .... King County Bar Association (SAUO)
KCBA .... Salinas, CA [*Television station call letters*]
KCBC .... Riverbank, CA [*AM radio station call letters*]
KCBD .... Lubbock, TX [*Television station call letters*]
KCBF .... Fairbanks, AK [*AM radio station call letters*]
KCBI .... Dallas, TX [*FM radio station call letters*]
KCBL-AM .... Fresno, CA [*AM radio station call letters*] (BROA)
KCBM .... Columbus Air Force Base [*Mississippi*] [*ICAO location identifier*] (ICLI)
KCBN .... Reno, NV [*AM radio station call letters*]
KCBNAY .... Annals. Kurashiki Central Hospital (journ.) (SAUS)
KCBQ .... San Diego, CA [*AM radio station call letters*]
KCBQ-FM .... San Diego, CA [*FM radio station call letters*]
KCBR .... Monument, CO [*AM radio station call letters*]
KCBS .... Los Angeles, CA [*FM radio station call letters*]
KCBS .... San Francisco, CA [*AM radio station call letters*]
KCBS-TV .... Los Angeles, CA [*Television station call letters*]
KCBT .... Board of Trade of Kansas City, MO (EA)
KCBX .... KCBX Terminals [*Federal Railroad Administration identification code*]
KCBX .... San Luis Obispo, CA [*FM radio station call letters*]
KCBY .... Coos Bay, OR [*Television station call letters*]
KCBZ .... Cannon Beach, OR [*FM radio station call letters*] (RBYB)
KCC .... Centre College of Kentucky, Danville, KY [*OCLC symbol*] (OCLC)
KCC .... Coffman Cove, AK [*Location identifier*] [*FAA*] (FAAL)
KCC .... Kaiser Cement Corporation (EFIS)
KCC .... Kansas City Connecting Railroad Co. [*AAR code*]
KCC .... Kansas Co-Operative Council (SRA)
KCC .... Karamea Consultative Committee (SAUO)
KCC .... Kathodal Closure Contraction [*Medicine*]
KCC .... Kellogg Community College (SAUO)
KCC .... Kenai Community College (SAUO)
KCC .... Kennedy Cultural Center (SAUO)
KCC .... Kentucky Chamber of Commerce (SRA)
KCC .... Keokuk Community College [*Iowa*]
KCC .... Kernel Command & Control (SAUS)
KCC .... Ketchikan Community College (SAUO)
KCC .... Keyboard Common Contact [*Computer science*]
KCC .... Key Control Characteristic
KCC .... K-III Communications [*NYSE symbol*] (TTSB)
KCC .... K-III Communications Corp. [*NYSE symbol*] (SPSG)
KCC .... Kingsborough Community College (SAUO)
KCC .... Kiwi Conservation Club (SAUO)
KCC .... Knapp Communications Corporation (SAUO)
KCC .... Knife Collectors Club (EA)
KCC .... Knight Commander of the [*Order of the*] Crown [*Belgium*]
KCC .... Knowledge Collaboration Center [*Army*]
KCC .... Knowledge Consistency Checker [*Computer science*] (MWOL)
KCC .... Kona Coffee Council [*Defunct*] (EA)
KCC .... Koplar Communications Center [*St. Louis, MO*] [*Telecommunications*] (TSSD)
KCC .... Korea Church Coalition for Peace, Justice and Reunification (EA)
KCC .... Korean Chamber of Commerce (SAUO)
KCC .... Kulchitsky Cell Carcinoma [*Medicine*] (RAWO)
KCC .... Lubila [*Language symbol*] (ETLW)
KCCA .... Colorado City, AZ [*FM radio station call letters*]
KCCA .... Korean Chamber of Commerce in America (SAUO)
KCCB .... Corning, AR [*AM radio station call letters*]
KCCC .... Carlsbad, NM [*AM radio station call letters*]
KCCC .... Kansas City Computer Center (ALAC)
KCCC .... Key Chain Collectors Club (EA)
KCCD .... Kentucky Council on Crime and Delinquency (SAUO)
KCCD .... Moorhead, MN [*FM radio station call letters*]
KCCE .... Keystone Center for Continuing Education (SAUO)
KCCF .... Cave Creek, AZ [*AM radio station call letters*]
KCCF .... Ferndale, WA [*AM radio station call letters*] (BROA)
KCCG-FM .... Ingleside, TX [*FM radio station call letters*] (BROA)
KCCH .... Knight Commander of Court of Honor [*British*]

KCCI .... Des Moines, IA [*Television station call letters*]
KCCI .... Kansas Chamber of Commerce and Industry (SRA)
KCCI .... Korean Chamber of Commerce and Industry (SAUO)
KCCK .... Cedar Rapids, IA [*FM radio station call letters*]
KCCL-FM.... Shingle Springs, CA [*FM radio station call letters*] (BROA)
KCCM........ Kupffer Cell Conditioned Medium
KCCM........ Moorhead, MN [*FM radio station call letters*]
KCCN .... Honolulu, HI [*AM radio station call letters*]
KCCN .... Monterey, CA [*Television station call letters*]
KCCN-FM ... Honolulu, HI [*FM radio station call letters*]
KCCO .... Alexandria, MN [*Television station call letters*]
KCCO .... Kansas City Commodity Office (SAUO)
KCCO .... Saint Louis Park, MN [*AM radio station call letters*] (BROA)
KCCPr .... K-III Commun$2.875SrExPfd [*NYSE symbol*] (TTSB)
KCCQ .... Ames, IA [*FM radio station call letters*]
KCCR .... Pierre, SD [*AM radio station call letters*]
KCCS .... Salem, OR [*AM radio station call letters*]
KCCT .... Corpus Christi, TX [*AM radio station call letters*]
KCCT .... Kaolin Cephalin Clotting Time (PDAA)
KCCU .... Lawton, OK [*FM radio station call letters*]
KCCV .... Overland Park, KS [*AM radio station call letters*]
KCCV-FM.... Olathe, KS [*FM radio station call letters*]
KCCW .... Walker, MN [*Television station call letters*]
KCCX-FM ... Lexington, MO [*FM radio station call letters*] (BROA)
KCCY .... Pueblo, CO [*FM radio station call letters*]
KCCZ .... Kaiser Cement [*Federal Railroad Administration identification code*]
KCD.......... Concentrated [*Telegraphy*] (PCTE)
KCD.......... Kinestatic Charge Detector [*Medicine*] (RAWO)
KCD.......... Knock Center Detection [*Automotive engineering*]
KCDA .... Coeur D'Alene, ID [*FM radio station call letters*]
KCDA-FM ... Post Falls, ID [*FM radio station call letters*] (BROA)
KCDC .... Longmont, CO [*FM radio station call letters*]
KCDC-FM ... Wellton, AZ [*FM radio station call letters*] (BROA)
KCDD .... Hamlin, TX [*FM radio station call letters*]
KCDI .... Oro Valley, AZ [*FM radio station call letters*]
KCDI-FM.... Bryant, AR [*FM radio station call letters*] (BROA)
KCDL .... Cordell, OK [*FM radio station call letters*]
KCDMA...... Kiln, Cooler, and Dryer Manufacturers Association (SAUO)
KCDQ .... Douglas, AZ [*FM radio station call letters*] (BROA)
KCDQ .... Key Centre for Design Quality (SAUO)
KCDQ .... Monahans, TX [*FM radio station call letters*]
KCDR .... Turlock, CA [*AM radio station call letters*] (RBYB)
KCDS .... Angwin, CA [*FM radio station call letters*]
KCDS .... Childress [*Texas*] [*ICAO location identifier*] (ICLI)
KCDT .... Coeur D'Alene, ID [*Television station call letters*]
KCDU .... Kali Chemie [*Intermodal shipping container symbol*] (TVRC)
KCDU-FM ... Hollister, CA [*FM radio station call letters*] (RBYB)
KCDV-FM ... Cordova, KS [*FM radio station call letters*] (RBYB)
KCDX .... San Carlos, AZ [*FM radio station call letters*]
KCDX-FM ... Florence, AZ [*FM radio station call letters*] (BROA)
KCDY .... Carlsbad, NM [*FM radio station call letters*]
KCDZ .... Twentynine Palms, CA [*FM radio station call letters*]
KCE .... Collinsville [*Australia*] [*Airport symbol*] (OAG)
KCE .... Key Configuration Element (DNAB)
KCE .... Kickapoo Cultural Exchange (EARSL)
KCEA .... Atherton, CA [*FM radio station call letters*]
KCEC .... Denver, CO [*Television station call letters*]
KCEC .... Wellton, AX [*FM radio station call letters*] (BROA)
KCED .... Centralia, WA [*FM radio station call letters*]
KCEE......... Tucson, AZ [*AM radio station call letters*]
KCEF......... Chicopee Falls/Westover Air Force Base [*Massachusetts*] [*ICAO location identifier*] (ICLI)
KCEL-FM.... California City, CA [*FM radio station call letters*] (BROA)
KCEM........ Kansas Certified Emergency Manager [*Emergency Management*] (EMA)
KCEN .... Temple, TX [*Television station call letters*]
KCEO .... Vista, CA [*AM radio station call letters*]
KCEP .... Las Vegas, NV [*FM radio station call letters*]
KCER .... Kananaskis Centre for Environmental Research [*University of Calgary*] [*Research center*] (RCD)
KCES .... Eufaula, OK [*FM radio station call letters*]
KCET......... Los Angeles, CA [*Television station call letters*]
KCET-DT .... Los Angeles, CA [*Television station call letters*] (BROA)
KCEW........ Crestview/Bob Sikes [*Florida*] [*ICAO location identifier*] (ICLI)
KCEY .... Huntsville, TX [*FM radio station call letters*]
KCEZ......... Corning, CA [*FM radio station call letters*]
KCEZ-FM.... Los Molinos, CA [*FM radio station call letters*] (BROA)
KCF .... Key-Click Filter
KCF .... Key Clinical Finding [*Medicine*] (HCT)
KCF .... Khalistan Commando Force (SAUO)
KCF .... Thousand Cubic Feet
KCFA......... Amold, CA [*FM radio station call letters*]
KCFB .... King City Federal Savings Bank (SAUO)
KCFB .... St. Cloud, MN [*FM radio station call letters*]
KCFC .... Boulder, CO [*AM radio station call letters*] (BROA)
KCFC .... Karen Carpenter Fan Club [*Defunct*] (EA)
KCFD .... Bryan/Coulter Field [*Texas*] [*ICAO location identifier*] (ICLI)
KCFE......... Eden Prairie, MN [*FM radio station call letters*]
KCFF......... Korean Cultural and Freedom Foundation (EA)
KCFG .... Flagstaff, AZ [*Television station call letters*] (BROA)
KCFMC ...... Kevin Collins Foundation for Missing Children (EA)
KCFM-FM ... Levan, UT [*FM radio station call letters*] (BROA)
KCFM-FM ... Okmulgee, OK [*FM radio station call letters*] (BROA)
KCFN .... Wichita, KS [*FM radio station call letters*]
KCFO .... Tulsa, OK [*AM radio station call letters*]
KCFP-FM.... Pueblo, CO [*FM radio station call letters*] (RBYB)
KCFR .... Denver, CO [*FM radio station call letters*]
KCFS .... Sioux Falls, SD [*FM radio station call letters*]
KCFV .... Ferguson, MO [*FM radio station call letters*]
KCFW........ Kalispell, MT [*Television station call letters*]
KCFX .... Harrisonville, MO [*FM radio station call letters*]
KCFY .... Yuma, AZ [*FM radio station call letters*]
KCG.......... Chignik, AK [*Location identifier*] [*FAA*] (FAAL)
KCG.......... Concentrating [*Telegraphy*] (PCTE)
KCG.......... Key Calling [*Telecommunications*] (IAA)
KCG.......... Kinetocardiogram [*Cardiology*]
KCGB .... Hood River, OR [*FM radio station call letters*]
KCGL .... Diamondville (SAUS)
KCGL .... Kyocera Graphic Language (SAUS)
KCGL .... Powell, WY [*FM radio station call letters*] (BROA)
KCGM .... KCGM Transport [*Common carrier symbol*]
KCGM .... Scobey, MT [*FM radio station call letters*]
KCGN........ Sioux Falls, SD [*AM radio station call letters*]
KCGN-FM ... Ortonville, MN [*FM radio station call letters*]
KCGQ........ Cape Girardeau, MO [*AM radio station call letters*]
KCGQ-FM ... Gordonville, MO [*FM radio station call letters*]
KCGR .... Cottage Grove, OR [*FM radio station call letters*]
KCGS .... Marshall, AR [*AM radio station call letters*]
KCGS .... United States Army, Command and General Staff College Library, Fort Leavenworth (SAUS)
KCGX .... Broken Bow, OK [*FM radio station call letters*] (RBYB)
KCGX .... Kaiser Cement and Gypsum [*Private rail car owner code*]
KCGY .... Laramie, WY [*FM radio station call letters*]
KCH.......... Ketch
KCH.......... Ketchum & Co. , Inc. (SAUO)
kch........... Kilocharacter (MHDB)
KCH.......... King's College Hospital
KCH.......... Knight Commander of the Guelphic Order of Hanover [*British*]
KCH.......... Kuching [*Malaysia*] [*Airport symbol*] (OAG)
KCHA .... Charles City, IA [*AM radio station call letters*]
KCHA .... Chattanooga/Lovell [*Tennessee*] [*ICAO location identifier*] (ICLI)
KCHA-FM ... Charles City, IA [*FM radio station call letters*]
KCHC .... Conroe, TX [*AM radio station call letters*] (BROA)
KCHC .... Kings County Hospital Center [*New York*] [*Medicine*] (EDAA)
KCHC .... Willows, CA [*FM radio station call letters*] (BROA)
KCHC-FM ... Conroe, TX [*FM radio station call letters*] (RBYB)
KCHD .... Chandler/Williams Air Force Base [*Arizona*] [*ICAO location identifier*] (ICLI)
KCH-DMC... Kings County Hospital-Downtown Medical Center [*New York*] [*Medicine*] (EDAA)
KCHE .... Cherokee, IA [*AM radio station call letters*]
KCHE-FM ... Cherokee, IA [*FM radio station call letters*]
KCHF .... Santa Fe, NM [*Television station call letters*]
KCHG .... Somerset, TX [*AM radio station call letters*]
KCHI......... Chicago/Metropolitan Area [*Illinois*] [*ICAO location identifier*] (ICLI)
KCHI......... Chillicothe, MO [*AM radio station call letters*]
KCHI-FM.... Chillicothe, MO [*FM radio station call letters*]
KCHJ .... Delano, CA [*AM radio station call letters*]
KCHK .... New Prague, MN [*AM radio station call letters*]
KCHK-FM ... New Prague, MN [*FM radio station call letters*]
KCHL .... San Antonio, TX [*AM radio station call letters*]
KCHN .... Brookshire, TX [*AM radio station call letters*] (BROA)
KCHN-AM... Liberty, TX [*AM radio station call letters*] (BROA)
KCHO .... Chico, CA [*FM radio station call letters*]
KCHQ .... Altamont, OR [*FM radio station call letters*]
KCHQ .... Driggs, ID [*FM radio station call letters*] (BROA)
KCHQ-FM ... Santa Fe, NM [*FM radio station call letters*] (BROA)
KCHR .... Charleston, MO [*AM radio station call letters*]
kchr.......... Kilocharacter (MHDB)
KCHS .... Charleston/Municipal and Air Force Base [*South Carolina*] [*ICAO location identifier*] (ICLI)
KCHS .... Kilo Characters per Second (IAA)
KCHS .... Knight Commander of the Holy Sepulchre
KCHS .... Truth or Consequences, NM [*AM radio station call letters*]
KCHT .... Astoria, OR [*AM radio station call letters*] (BROA)
KCHT .... Kechabta [*Tunisia*] [*Seismograph station code, US Geological Survey*] (SEIS)
KCHT-AM ... Selah, WA [*AM radio station call letters*] (RBYB)
KCHU........ Valdez, AK [*AM radio station call letters*]
KCHX........ Midland, TX [*FM radio station call letters*]
KCHY-FM.... Hope, ND [*FM radio station call letters*] (BROA)
KCHZ .... Kerley Chemical [*Federal Railroad Administration identification code*]
KCHZ-FM ... Ottawa, KS [*FM radio station call letters*] (RBYB)
KCI........... Aeromech Commuter Airlines (SAUS)
KCI........... Key Club International (EA)
KCI........... Key Collectors International (EA)
kCi........... Kilocurie (DEN)
KCI........... Kit Collectors International (EA)
KCI........... Potassium Chloride (MELL)
KCIA .... Korean Central Intelligence Agency (SAUO)
KCIA .... Medford, OR [*FM radio station call letters*]
KCIA .... South Korean Central Intelligence Agency [*Later, Agency for National Security Planning*] (PD)
KCIB .... Milan, NM [*AM radio station call letters*] (RBYB)
KCIC .... Grand Junction, CO [*FM radio station call letters*]
KCID .... Caldwell, ID [*AM radio station call letters*]
KCID-FM.... Caldwell, ID [*FM radio station call letters*]
KCIE .... Dulce, NM [*FM radio station call letters*]

KCIE .... Knight Commander of the [*Order of the*] Indian Empire [*British*]
KCIF-FM .... Hilo, HI [*FM radio station call letters*] (BROA)
KCII .... Washington, IA [*AM radio station call letters*]
KCII-FM ..... Washington, IA [*FM radio station call letters*]
KCIJ .... North Fort Polk, LA [*FM radio station call letters*]
KCIL .... Houma, LA [*FM radio station call letters*]
KCIM .... Carroll, IA [*AM radio station call letters*]
KCIN .... Tacoma, WA [*FM radio station call letters*] (RBYB)
KCIN-FM .... Cedar City, UT [*FM radio station call letters*] (BROA)
KCIO .... King's Commissioned Indian Officer [*British military*] (DMA)
KCIO .... Potassiun Hypochlorite [*Medicine*] (EDAA)
KCIPAC ...... Kinetic Concepts Inc. PAC [*San Antonio, TX*] (PACS)
KCIR .... Twin Falls, ID [*FM radio station call letters*]
KCIS .... Edmonds, WA [*AM radio station call letters*]
KCIT .... Amarillo, TX [*Television station call letters*]
K-CITEM .... Kennedy Space Center Cite Plan/Requirement (NAKS)
K-CITEM .... KSC CITE Plan (or Requirement) (SAUS)
KCITY .... Kansas City, MO [*American Association of Railroads railroad junction routing code*]
KCIU .... Kali Chemie-Iberia [*Intermodal shipping container symbol*] (TVRC)
KCIV .... Mount Bullion, CA [*FM radio station call letters*]
KCIX .... Garden City, ID [*FM radio station call letters*]
KCIX .... Nova Chemicals [*Private rail car owner code*]
KCIY .... Liberty, MO [*FM radio station call letters*] (RBYB)
KCJ .... Kolel Chibas Jerusalem [*An association*] (EA)
KCJB .... Minot, ND [*AM radio station call letters*]
KCJC .... Dardanelle, AR [*FM radio station call letters*] (RBYB)
KCJF .... Earle, AR [*FM radio station call letters*] (BROA)
KCJH .... Stockton, CA [*FM radio station call letters*]
KCJH-FM .... Livingston, CA [*FM radio station call letters*] (BROA)
KCJJ .... Iowa City, IA [*AM radio station call letters*]
KCJK .... Iowa City, IA [*AM radio station call letters*] (BROA)
KCJZ .... Terrell Hills, TX [*FM radio station call letters*] (RBYB)
KCK .... Kansas City, KS [*Location identifier*] [*FAA*] (FAAL)
KCKA .... Centralia, WA [*Television station call letters*]
KCKC .... Concord, CA [*AM radio station call letters*] (BROA)
KCKC .... San Bernardino, CA [*AM radio station call letters*]
KCKI .... Henryetta, OK [*FM radio station call letters*]
KCKK .... Lakewood, CO [*AM radio station call letters*] (BROA)
KCKK-FM .... Longmont, CO [*FM radio station call letters*] (BROA)
KCKL .... Malakoff, TX [*FM radio station call letters*]
KCKN .... Roswell, NM [*AM radio station call letters*]
KCKN-AM .... Kansas City, KS [*AM radio station call letters*] (BROA)
KCKR .... Waco, TX [*FM radio station call letters*]
KCKS .... Concordia, KS [*FM radio station call letters*]
KCKT-FM .... Crockett, TX [*FM radio station call letters*] (BROA)
KCKX .... Stayton, OR [*AM radio station call letters*]
KCKY .... Coolidge, AZ [*AM radio station call letters*]
KCL .... Chignik, AK [*Location identifier*] [*FAA*] (FAAL)
KCL .... Conciliate [*Telegraphy*] (PCTE)
KCL .... Keystation Control Language [*Computer science*] (MHDI)
KCL .... King's College, London
KCL .... Kirchhoff's Current Law [*Electronics*] (IAA)
KCL .... Kitchen, Company Level
KCL .... Klamath County Library, Klamath Falls, OR [*OCLC symbol*] (OCLC)
KCL .... Knitting Cylinder Lubrication (PDAA)
KCL .... Knudsen Cosine Law [*Physics*]
KCL .... Potassium Chloride [*Medicine*] (BCRP)
KCLA .... Pine Bluff, AR [*AM radio station call letters*]
KCLB .... Coachella, CA [*AM radio station call letters*]
KCLB-FM .... Coachella, CA [*FM radio station call letters*]
KCLC .... Kinder-Care Learning Centers, Inc. [*NASDAQ symbol*] (SAG)
KCLC .... Kinder-Care Learning Ctrs [*NASDAQ symbol*] (TTSB)
KCLC .... St. Charles, MO [*FM radio station call letters*]
KCLCW .... Kinder-Care Lrng Ctr Wrrt [*NASDAQ symbol*] (TTSB)
KCLD .... Conciliated [*Telegraphy*] (PCTE)
KCLD .... St. Cloud, MN [*FM radio station call letters*]
KCLE .... Cleburne, TX [*AM radio station call letters*]
KCLE .... Cleveland/Cleveland-Hopkins International [*Ohio*] [*ICAO location identifier*] (ICLI)
KCLE .... Continuing Legal Education, University of Kentucky College of Law (DLA)
KCLE .... Glen Rose, TX [*FM radio station call letters*] (RBYB)
KCLG .... Conciliating [*Telegraphy*] (PCTE)
KCLH .... Caledonia, MN [*FM radio station call letters*] (BROA)
KCLH-FM .... Yankton, SD [*FM radio station call letters*] (BROA)
KCLI .... Clinton, OK [*FM radio station call letters*]
KCLI .... Kansas City Life Ins [*NASDAQ symbol*] (TTSB)
KCLI .... Kansas City Life Insurance Co. [*NASDAQ symbol*] (NQ)
KCLI-AM ..... Clinton, OK [*AM radio station call letters*] (RBYB)
KCLJ .... Knight Commander of the Order of St. Lazarus of Jerusalem (DD)
KCLJ .... Knight Commander, Order of St. Lazarus of Jerusalem [*British*] (WA)
KCLK .... Asotin, WA [*AM radio station call letters*]
KCLK .... Clarkston, WA [*FM radio station call letters*]
KCLL .... College Station/Easterwood Field [*Texas*] [*ICAO location identifier*] (ICLI)
KCLL .... Lompoc, CA [*AM radio station call letters*]
KCLM .... Newport, OR [*FM radio station call letters*]
KCLN .... Clinton, IA [*FM radio station call letters*]
KCLN .... Conciliation [*Telegraphy*] (PCTE)
KCLO .... Rapid City, SD [*Television station call letters*]
KCLQ .... Lebanon, MO [*FM radio station call letters*]
KCLR .... Boonville, MO [*FM radio station call letters*]
KCLR .... Ralls, TX [*AM radio station call letters*]
KCLR-FM .... Boonville, MO [*FM radio station call letters*] (BROA)
KCLS .... Conciliates [*Telegraphy*] (PCTE)
KCLS .... Flagstaff, AZ [*AM radio station call letters*]
KCLS .... Kern County Library System [*Library network*]
KCLS .... Knight Commander of the Lion and the Sun
KCLS-FM .... Ely, NV [*FM radio station call letters*] (BROA)
KCLT .... West Helena, AR [*FM radio station call letters*]
KCLU .... Korean Council of Organization [*South Korea*]
KCLU .... Thousand Oaks, CA [*FM radio station call letters*]
KCLV .... Clovis, NM [*AM radio station call letters*]
KCLV-FM .... Clovis, NM [*FM radio station call letters*]
KCLW .... Hamilton, TX [*AM radio station call letters*]
KCLX .... Colfax, WA [*AM radio station call letters*]
KCLY .... Clay Center, KS [*FM radio station call letters*]
KCLY .... Kent and County of London Yeomanry [*Military unit*] [*British*]
KCM .... Kam Creed Mines Ltd. [*Vancouver Stock Exchange symbol*] [*Toronto Stock Exchange symbol*]
KCM .... Kansas City Museum (SAUO)
KCM .... Keratinocyte-Conditioned Medium [*Biochemistry*]
KCM .... Key Center for Mines [*University of Wollongong*] [*Australia*]
KCM .... Kilenge Mission [*New Britain*] [*Seismograph station code, US Geological Survey*] (SEIS)
KCM .... Kirchhoff Coda Migration [*For seismic wave imaging*]
KCM .... Kupffer Cell Medium
KCMA .... Holdenville, OK [*FM radio station call letters*] (RBYB)
KCMA .... Kitchen Cabinet Manufacturers Association (EA)
KCM & B .... Kansas City, Memphis & Birmingham Railroad
KCMB .... Baker City, OR [*FM radio station call letters*]
KCMC .... Texarkana, TX [*AM radio station call letters*]
KCME .... Kuznetsk Commodity and Raw Materials Exchange [*Russian Federation*] (EY)
KCME .... Manitou Springs, CO [*FM radio station call letters*]
KCMF-FM .... Fergus Falls, MN [*FM radio station call letters*] (BROA)
KCMG .... Knight Commander of St. Michael and St. George [*Facetiously translated, "Kindly Call Me God"*] [*British*]
KCMG .... Mountain Grove, MO [*AM radio station call letters*]
KCMG-FM .... Los Angeles, CA [*FM radio station call letters*] (BROA)
KCMG-FM .... Mountain Grove, MO [*FM radio station call letters*]
KCMH .... Columbus/Port Columbus International [*Ohio*] [*ICAO location identifier*] (ICLI)
KCMH .... Mountain Home, AR [*FM radio station call letters*]
KCMI .... Terrytown, NE [*FM radio station call letters*]
KCMJ .... Indio, CA [*FM radio station call letters*]
KCMJ .... Palm Springs, CA [*AM radio station call letters*]
KCMJ-AM .... Thousand Palms, CA [*AM radio station call letters*] (BROA)
KCML-FM .... St. Joseph, MN [*FM radio station call letters*] (BROA)
KCMLN .... Kansas City Metropolitan Library Network Council [*Library network*]
KCMM-FM .. Belgrade, MT [*FM radio station call letters*] (BROA)
KCMN .... Colorado Springs, CO [*AM radio station call letters*]
KCMO .... Kansas City, Mexico & Orient [*AAR code*]
KCMO .... Kansas City, MO [*AM radio station call letters*]
KCMO-FM .... Kansas City, MO [*FM radio station call letters*]
KCMQ .... Columbia, MO [*FM radio station call letters*]
KCMR .... Mason City, IA [*FM radio station call letters*]
KCMS .... Edmonds, WA [*FM radio station call letters*]
KCMS .... Kodak Color Management System [*Eastman Kodak Co.*] (PCM)
KCMT .... Chester, CA [*FM radio station call letters*]
KCMT-FM .... Billings, MT [*FM radio station call letters*] (BROA)
KCMT-FM .... Oro Valley, AZ [*FM radio station call letters*] (BROA)
KCMU .... Seattle, WA [*FM radio station call letters*]
KCMW .... Warrensburg, MO [*FM radio station call letters*]
KCMX .... Ashland, OR [*AM radio station call letters*]
KCMX .... Keyset Central Multiplexer
KCMX .... Phoenix, OR [*AM radio station call letters*] (BROA)
KCMX-FM .... Ashland, OR [*FM radio station call letters*]
KCMY .... Sacramento, CA [*Television station call letters*]
KCMZ .... Kindall Coal Mine [*Federal Railroad Administration identification code*]
KCN .... Chernofski Harbor, AK [*Location identifier*] [*FAA*] (FAAL)
KCN .... Concentration [*Telegraphy*] (PCTE)
KCN .... Intetnational Colin Energy [*NYSE symbol*] (SAG)
KCN .... Intl Colin Energy [*NYSE symbol*] (TTSB)
KCN .... Kids' Clubs Network (AIE)
KCN .... Kit Configuration Notice (MCD)
KCN .... Kit Control Number [*Navy*] (NG)
KCN .... Nubi [*Language symbol*] (ETLW)
KCN .... Potassium Cyanide (SAUS)
KCNA .... Cave Junction, OR [*FM radio station call letters*]
KCNA .... Korean Central News Agency [*North Korea*]
KCNB-AM .... Holdenville, OK [*AM radio station call letters*] (BROA)
KCNC .... Denver, CO [*Television station call letters*]
KCND .... Bismarck, ND [*FM radio station call letters*]
KCNE .... Chadron, NE [*FM radio station call letters*]
KCNF .... Fort Worth [*Texas*] [*ICAO location identifier*] (ICLI)
KCNI .... Broken Bow, NE [*AM radio station call letters*]
KCNL-FM .... Fremont, CA [*FM radio station call letters*] (BROA)
KCNM .... Carlsbad/Cavern City Air Terminal [*New Mexico*] [*ICAO location identifier*] (ICLI)
KCNM .... San Jose, Philippines [*AM radio station call letters*]
KCNM-FM .... Garapan-Saipan, NP [*FM radio station call letters*] (BROA)
KCNN .... East Grand Forks, MN [*AM radio station call letters*]
KCNO .... Alturas, CA [*AM radio station call letters*]
KCNO-FM .... Alturas, CA [*FM radio station call letters*] (RBYB)
KCNP .... Kings Canyon National Park (SAUO)

KCNP........ Ku-ring-gai Chase National Park (SAUO)
KCNQ........ Kernville, CA [*FM radio station call letters*]
KCNR........ Salt Lake City, UT [*AM radio station call letters*]
KCNR........ Shasta, CA [*AM radio station call letters*] (BROA)
KCNS........ San Francisco, CA [*Television station call letters*]
KCNT........ Hastings, NE [*FM radio station call letters*]
KCNW........ Fairway, KS [*AM radio station call letters*]
KCNW........ Kelly's Creek & Northwestern Railroad Co. [*AAR code*]
KCNW........ Waco/James Connally [*Texas*] [*ICAO location identifier*] (ICLI)
KCNZ........ Cedar Falls, IA [*AM radio station call letters*] (RBYB)
KCO.......... Keep Cost Order [*Telecommunications*] (TEL)
KCOB........ Newton, IA [*AM radio station call letters*]
KCOBE....... Knight Commander-Order of the British Empire (SAUO)
KCOB-FM... Newton, IA [*FM radio station call letters*]
KCOE........ Johnson, NE [*FM radio station call letters*] (GDPB)
KCOF........ Cocoa/Patrick Air Force Base [*Florida*] [*ICAO location identifier*] (ICLI)
KCOG........ Centerville, IA [*AM radio station call letters*]
KCOH........ Houston, TX [*AM radio station call letters*]
KCOIC....... Korean Combat Operations Intelligence Center (SAUO)
KCOL........ Fort Collins, CO [*AM radio station call letters*]
KCOL........ Groves, TX [*FM radio station call letters*] (BROA)
KCOL-AM... Wellington, CO [*AM radio station call letters*] (BROA)
KCoIC........ Colby Community College, Colby, KS [*Library symbol*] [*Library of Congress*] (LCLS)
KCole........ Kenneth Cole Productions, Inc. [*Associated Press*] (SAG)
KColePd..... Kenneth Cole Productions, Inc. [*Associated Press*] (SAG)
KCOM........ Comanche, TX [*AM radio station call letters*]
KCOM........ Kirksville College of Osteopathic Medicine (MHID)
KCOMZ...... Korean Communications Zone [*Military*]
KCON........ Conway, AR [*AM radio station call letters*]
KCOO-FM... Shafter, CA [*FM radio station call letters*] (BROA)
KCOP........ Kencope Energy Companies (SAUO)
KCOP........ Los Angeles, CA [*Television station call letters*]
KCOP-DT.... Los Angeles, CA [*Television station call letters*] (BROA)
KCOR........ San Antonio, TX [*AM radio station call letters*]
KCOR-FM... Comfort, TX [*FM radio station call letters*] (BROA)
KCOS........ Colorado Springs/Peterson Field [*Colorado*] [*ICAO location identifier*] (ICLI)
KCOS........ El Paso, TX [*Television station call letters*]
KCOT........ Cotulla/Municipal [*Texas*] [*ICAO location identifier*] (ICLI)
KCOT........ San Augustine, TX [*FM radio station call letters*]
KCOU........ Columbia, MO [*FM radio station call letters*]
KCOU........ Kokkola Chemicals [*Intermodal shipping container symbol*] (TVRC)
KCOW........ Alliance, NE [*AM radio station call letters*]
KCOY........ Santa Maria, CA [*Television station call letters*]
KCOZ........ Point Lookout, MO [*FM radio station call letters*] (RBYB)
KCP.......... Kansas City Plant [*Department of Energy*] [*Kansas City, MO*] (GAAI)
KCP.......... Kansas City Public Library, Kansas City, MO [*OCLC symbol*] (OCLC)
KCP.......... Keene's Cement Plaster [*Technical drawings*]
KCP.......... Kenneth Cole Productions'A' [*NYSE symbol*] (TTSB)
KCP.......... Kenneth Cole Productions, Inc. [*NYSE symbol*] (SAG)
KCP.......... Keyboard-Controlled Phototypesetter (NITA)
KCP.......... Key Crude Prices [*Database*] [*Petroleum Intelligence Weekly*] [*Information service or system*] (CRD)
KCP.......... Kirghiz Communist Party [*Political party*]
KCP.......... Knee-Chest Position (MELL)
KCP.......... Knight Commander of [*the Order of*] Pius IX
KCP.......... Korean Communist Party [*Political party*] [*North Korea*] (FEA)
KCPA........ Kaolin Clay Producers Association (DGA)
KCPA........ Kennedy Center for the Performing Arts (SAUO)
KCPA........ Kentucky College Placement Association (SAUO)
KCP & G.... Kansas City, Pittsburgh & Gulf Railroad
KCPB........ Thousand Oaks, CA [*FM radio station call letters*]
KCPC........ Keene's Cement Plaster Ceiling [*Technical drawings*]
KCPCA....... Kansas Committee for Prevention of Child Abuse (EDAC)
KCPI........ Albert Lea, MN [*FM radio station call letters*]
KCPL........ Kansas City Power & Light Co. [*Associated Press*] (SAG)
KCPL........ Kansas City Public Library (SAUO)
KCPL........ Olympia, WA [*AM radio station call letters*]
KCPM........ Chico, CA [*Television station call letters*]
KCPM........ Grand Forks, ND [*Television station call letters*] (BROA)
KCPO........ Kansas City Philharmonic Orchestra (SAUO)
KCPP........ Casper, WY [*FM radio station call letters*] (BROA)
KCPQ........ Tacoma, WA [*Television station call letters*]
KCPR........ San Luis Obispo, CA [*FM radio station call letters*]
KCPS........ Burlington, IA [*AM radio station call letters*]
KCPS........ Kansas City Public Service R. R. [*AAR code*]
kcps........ Kilocycles per Second
KCPT........ Kansas City, MO [*Television station call letters*]
KCPT-DT.... Kansas City, MO [*Television station call letters*] (BROA)
KCPUG...... Kentuckiana Contingency Planners Users Group [*Emergency Management*] (EMA)
KCPW........ Salt Lake City, UT [*FM radio station call letters*]
KCPX........ Centerville, UT [*FM radio station call letters*]
KCPX-AM... Centerville, UT [*AM radio station call letters*] (RBYB)
KCQL........ Aztec, NM [*AM radio station call letters*]
KCQQ........ Davenport, IA [*FM radio station call letters*] (RBYB)
KCQV........ Arthur, ND [*FM radio station call letters*]
KCR.......... Colorado Creek, AK [*Location identifier*] [*FAA*] (FAAL)
KCR.......... Kansas City Law Review [*A publication*] (DLA)
KC r.......... Kansas City Terminal Railway Co. (SAUO)
KCR.......... Key Call Receiver [*Telecommunications*] (TEL)
KCR.......... Knowledge-Centric Re-Engineering (GART)
KCR.......... [*The*] Kowloon Canton Railway [*Hong Kong*] (DCTA)
KCR.......... Reports Tempore Chancellor King [*A publication*] (DLA)
KCRA........ Sacramento, CA [*Television station call letters*]
KCRABB..... Annual Report. Cancer Research Institute. Kanazawa University (journ.) (SAUS)
KCRB........ Bemidji, MN [*FM radio station call letters*]
KCRC........ Enid, OK [*AM radio station call letters*]
KCRC........ Kansas City Records Center [*Military*]
KCRC........ Kowloon-Canton Railway Corp. [*Commercial firm*] [*Hong Kong*]
KCRCC...... Korean Combined Rescue Coordination Center (SAUO)
KCRCHE..... Kansas City Regional Council for Higher Education [*Library network*]
KCRE........ Crescent City, CA [*FM radio station call letters*]
KCRF........ Korean Conflict Research Foundation [*Defunct*]
KCRF........ Newport, OR [*FM radio station call letters*] (RBYB)
KCRF-FM... Lincoln City, OR [*FM radio station call letters*] (BROA)
KCRG........ Cedar Rapids, IA [*AM radio station call letters*]
KCRG-TV.... Cedar Rapids, IA [*Television station call letters*]
KCRH........ Hayward, CA [*FM radio station call letters*]
KCRI-FM.... Mojave, CA [*FM radio station call letters*] (BROA)
KCRK........ Colville, WA [*FM radio station call letters*]
KCRL........ Rayne, LA [*FM radio station call letters*]
KCRL-FM... Sunrise Beach, MO [*FM radio station call letters*] (BROA)
KCRM-FM... Lubbock, TX [*FM radio station call letters*] (BROA)
KCRN........ San Angelo, TX [*AM radio station call letters*]
KCRN-FM... San Angelo, TX [*FM radio station call letters*]
KCRO........ Omaha, NE [*AM radio station call letters*]
KCRP........ Corpus Christi/International [*Texas*] [*ICAO location identifier*] (ICLI)
KCRR........ Grundy Center, IA [*FM radio station call letters*] (RBYB)
KCRS........ Midland, TX [*AM radio station call letters*]
KCRS-FM... Midland, TX [*FM radio station call letters*]
KCRT........ KCR Technology, Inc. (SAUO)
KCRT........ Keyboard Cathode Ray Tube (MCD)
KCRT........ Trinidad, CO [*AM radio station call letters*]
KCRT-FM.... Trinidad, CO [*FM radio station call letters*]
KCRU........ Oxnard, CA [*FM radio station call letters*]
KCRV........ Caruthersville, MO [*AM radio station call letters*]
KCRW........ Santa Monica, CA [*FM radio station call letters*]
KCRX........ Kootenay Central Rail Services [*Private rail car owner code*]
KCRX........ Roswell, NM [*AM radio station call letters*]
KCRX-FM... Seaside, OR [*FM radio station call letters*] (BROA)
KCRY........ Indio, CA [*FM radio station call letters*]
KCRY........ Kentucky Central Railway [*Federal Railroad Administration identification code*]
KCRZ........ Tucson, AZ [*FM radio station call letters*]
KCRZ-FM... Tipton, CA [*FM radio station call letters*] (BROA)
KCS.......... Concentrates [*Telegraphy*] (PCTE)
KCS.......... Conston Corp. (SAUO)
KCS.......... [*The*] Kansas City Southern Railway Co. [*AAR code*]
KCS.......... Kansas City Standard [*Audio tape technology*] (EECA)
KCS.......... KCS Energy [*NYSE symbol*]
KCS.......... KCS Energy, Inc. [*Formerly, KCS Group, Inc.*] [*NYSE symbol*] (SPSG)
KCS.......... Keratoconjunctivitis Sicca [*Ophthalmology*]
KCS.......... Keyboard Configuration Studies (NASA)
KCS.......... Keyboard Controlled Sequencer [*Computer science*]
KCS.......... Keyboards, Computers, and Software [*A publication*]
KCS.......... Key Configuration Studies (NASA)
KCS.......... Kilocharacters per Second (IAA)
kc/s.......... Kilocycles per Second (MIST)
KCS.......... King's College School [*British*]
KCS.......... Kinki Chemical Society (SAUO)
KCS.......... Knight of [*the Order of*] Charles III of Spain
KCS.......... Knight of the Order of Charles XIII of Sweden [*Freemasonry*]
KCS.......... Knoxville Air Courier Service, Inc. (SAUO)
KCS.......... Kockums Computer Systems AB (SAUO)
KCS.......... Korean Chemical Society
KCS.......... Krishna Consciousness Society [*Medicine*] (EDAA)
KCS.......... Thousand Characters per Second
KC/SO........ Kilocycles per Second (SAUS)
KCSA........ Kentucky Crushed Stone Association (EARSL)
KCSA........ Kerr Center for Sustainable Agriculture [*Research center*] (RCD)
KCSA........ Kimberly-Clark Corporation (EFIS)
KCSAAC..... Kansas Center for Sustainable Agriculture and Alternative Crops [*Kansas State University*] (RCD)
KCSB........ Santa Barbara, CA [*FM radio station call letters*]
KCSC........ Edmond, OK [*FM radio station call letters*]
KCSC........ Kansas City Service Center [*IRS*]
KCSC........ Kansas Cosmosphere and Space Center [*Hutchinson, KS*]
KCSC........ Kidde Computer Services Company (SAUO)
KCSC........ Korean Cold Store Corporation (SAUO)
KCSD........ Sioux Falls, SD [*FM radio station call letters*]
KCSD-TV.... Sioux Falls, SD [*Television station call letters*] (RBYB)
KCSE-FM... Ballinger, TX [*FM radio station call letters*] (RBYB)
KCSE-FM... Sterling City, TX [*FM radio station call letters*] (BROA)
KCSF........ Stanton Foundation (EA)
KCSG........ Cedar City, UT [*Television station call letters*] (BROA)
KCSG........ KCS Group, Inc. [*NASDAQ symbol*] (COMM)
KCSG........ Knight Commander of Saint Gregory the Great (SAUO)
KCSG........ Knight Commander of [*the Order of*] St. Gregory [*British*]
KCSH-FM... Ellensburg, WA [*FM radio station call letters*] (BROA)
KCSI........ Kansas City Southern Industries, Inc.
KCSI........ Knight Commander of the [*Order of the*] Star of India [*British*]
KCSI........ Red Oak, IA [*FM radio station call letters*]
KCSJ........ Pueblo, CO [*AM radio station call letters*]

KCSLA Kansas City School Library Association
KCSM San Mateo, CA [*FM radio station call letters*]
KCSM-TV San Mateo, CA [*Television station call letters*]
KCSN Northridge, CA [*FM radio station call letters*]
KCSo Kansas City Southern Industries, Inc. [*Associated Press*] (SAG)
KCSO Kansas City Support Office (SAUO)
KCSO Kansas City Symphony Orchestra (SAUO)
KCSO Modesto, CA [*Television station call letters*]
KCSou Kansas City Southern Industries, Inc. [*Associated Press*] (SAG)
KCSP Casper, WY [*FM radio station call letters*]
KCSR Chadron, NE [*AM radio station call letters*]
KCSRy Kansas City Southern Railway Co. (SAUO)
KCSS Kentucky Center for School Safety (RCD)
KCSS Key Center for Statistical Services [*Deakin University*] [*Australia*]
KCSS Knight Commander of [*the Order of*] St. Sylvester
KCSS Korean Combat Support System (SAUO)
KCSS Turlock, CA [*FM radio station call letters*]
KCS/SO Keyboard Class Select / Statistics Output [*Computer science*] (MHDI)
KCST Florence, OR [*AM radio station call letters*]
KCST-FM Florence, OR [*FM radio station call letters*]
KCStJ & CB Kansas City, St. Joseph & Council Bluffs Railroad
KCSU Fort Collins, CO [*FM radio station call letters*]
KCSU Kansas City Southern Railway [*Intermodal shipping container symbol*] (TVRC)
KCSWF Kunz Center for the Study of Work and Family [*University of Cincinnati*] (RCD)
KCSX Kasten Rail Car Service [*Federal Railroad Administration identification code*]
KCSX-FM Moberly, MO [*FM radio station call letters*] (BROA)
KCSZ Kansas City Southern Railway [*Intermodal trailer symbol*]
KCT Kansas City Terminal Railway Co. [*AAR code*]
KCT Kaolin Cephalin Time [*Clinical chemistry*]
KCT Kaolin Clotting Time [*Clinical chemistry*]
KCT Kathodal Closing Tetanus [*Medicine*]
KCT Kelvin Circulation Theorem [*Physics*]
KCT Knight Commander of the Temple [*Freemasonry*] (ROG)
KCT Knox's Cube Test [*Short-term memory and attention span test*]
KCTA Corpus Christi, TX [*AM radio station call letters*]
KCTA Kootenay Christmas Tree Association (SAUO)
KCTAX Kemper State TF Inc. Ser: Cal. Cl.A [*Mutual fund ticker symbol*] (SG)
KCTB Cut Bank [*Montana*] [*ICAO location identifier*] (ICLI)
KCTC Sacramento, CA [*AM radio station call letters*]
KCTD-AM Los Angeles, CA [*AM radio station call letters*] (BROA)
KCTE Independence, MO [*AM radio station call letters*]
KCTE Kathodal Closure Tetanus [*Medicine*]
KCTE/LA Kentucky Council of Teachers of English/Language Arts (EARSL)
KCTF Waco, TX [*Television station call letters*]
KCTG Ozark, MO [*FM radio station call letters*] (RBYB)
KCTI Gonzales, TX [*AM radio station call letters*]
KCTI-FM Gonzales, TX [*FM radio station call letters*] (RBYB)
KCTK-AM Phoenix, AZ [*AM radio station call letters*] (BROA)
KCTM Rio Grande City, TX [*FM radio station call letters*]
KCTMLPCC Key Chain Tag and Mini License Plate Collectors Club [*Later, LP-KCMLPCC*] (EA)
KCTN Garnavillo, IA [*FM radio station call letters*]
KCTO Columbia, LA [*AM radio station call letters*]
KCTO-FM Columbia, LA [*FM radio station call letters*]
KCTR Billings-Hardin, MT [*FM radio station call letters*] (GDPB)
KCTR-FM Billings, MT [*FM radio station call letters*]
KCTS Knight Commander of the Tower and Sword [*Portugal*] (ROG)
KCTS Seattle, WA [*Television station call letters*]
KCTT Yellville, AR [*FM radio station call letters*]
KCTV Kansas City, MO [*Television station call letters*]
KCTV KCT Railway [*Federal Railroad Administration identification code*]
KCTX Childress, TX [*AM radio station call letters*]
KCTY Salinas, CA [*AM radio station call letters*]
KCTY-FM Plattsmouth, NE [*FM radio station call letters*] (BROA)
KCtyPL Kansas City Power & Light Co. [*Associated Press*] (SAG)
KCTZ Bozeman, MT [*Television station call letters*]
KCTZ KCT Elevator [*Federal Railroad Administration identification code*]
KCU Keyboard Control Unit
KCU Kilocurie (IAA)
KCUA Coalville, UT [*FM radio station call letters*]
KCUB Stephenville, TX [*FM radio station call letters*]
KCUB Tucson, AZ [*AM radio station call letters*]
KCUE Red Wing, MN [*AM radio station call letters*]
KCUI Pella, IA [*FM radio station call letters*]
KCUK Chevak, AK [*FM radio station call letters*]
KCUL Tyler-Longview-Jacksonville, TX [*AM radio station call letters*] (GDPB)
KCUL Tyler-Longview-Jacksonville, TX [*FM radio station call letters*] (GDPB)
KCUL-AM Marshall, TX [*AM radio station call letters*] (BROA)
KCUL-FM Marshall, TX [*FM radio station call letters*] (BROA)
KCUR Kansas City, MO [*FM radio station call letters*]
KCUS Columbus/Municipal [*New Mexico*] [*ICAO location identifier*] (ICLI)
KCUV Englewood, CO
KCUZ Clifton, AZ [*AM radio station call letters*]
KCV Kancana Ventures Ltd. [*Vancouver Stock Exchange symbol*]
KCV Knight of Gustavus Vasa (SAUO)
KCVG Cincinnati/Greater Cincinnati [*Ohio*] [*ICAO location identifier*] (ICLI)
KCVI Blackfoot, ID [*FM radio station call letters*]
KCVJ-FM Osceola, MO [*FM radio station call letters*] (BROA)
KCVK Otterville, MO [*FM radio station call letters*] (BROA)
KCVL Colville, WA [*AM radio station call letters*]
KCVL Kentucky Commonwealth Virtual Library
KCVM-FM Hudson, IA [*FM radio station call letters*] (BROA)
KCVO Camdenton, MO [*FM radio station call letters*]
KCVO Knight Commander of the Royal Victorian Order [*British*]
KCVP Konservativ-Christlichsoziale Volkspartei [*Conservative Christian-Social Party*] [*Switzerland*] [*Political party*] (PPE)
KCVQ-FM Knob Noster, MO [*FM radio station call letters*] (BROA)
KCVR Columbia, CA [*FM radio station call letters*] (BROA)
KCVR Lodi, CA [*AM radio station call letters*]
KCVS Clovis/Cannon Air Force Base [*New Mexico*] [*ICAO location identifier*] (ICLI)
KCVS Salina, KS [*FM radio station call letters*]
KCVT-FM Silver Lake, KS [*FM radio station call letters*] (RBYB)
KCVU Paradise, CA [*Television station call letters*]
KCVW-FM Kingman, KS [*FM radio station call letters*] (RBYB)
KCVZ Dixon, MO [*FM radio station call letters*] (BROA)
KCW Kentucky Commission on Women (EARSL)
KCWA Arnold, MO [*FM radio station call letters*]
KCWA Kern County Water Agency (SAUO)
KCWB Kansas City Westport Belt [*AAR code*]
KCWB-TV Kansas City, MO [*TV station call letters*] (RBYB)
KCWC Lander, WY [*Television station call letters*]
KCWC Riverton, WY [*FM radio station call letters*]
KCWC-TV Lander, WY [*Television station call letters*] (BROA)
KCWD Harrison, AR [*FM radio station call letters*]
KCWD Kaleidoscope: Current World Data [*ABC-CLIO*] [*Information service or system*] (IID)
KCWE Kansas City, MO [*Television station call letters*] (BROA)
KCWJ-AM Blue Springs, MO [*AM radio station call letters*] (BROA)
KCWM Hondo, TX [*AM radio station call letters*] (RBYB)
KCWM-FM Hondo, TX [*FM radio station call letters*] (RBYB)
KCWN New Sharon, IA [*FM radio station call letters*]
KCWR Bakersfield, CA [*AM radio station call letters*]
KCWS Merkel, TX [*FM radio station call letters*]
KCWT Wenatchee, WA [*Television station call letters*]
KCWU-FM Ellensburg, WA [*FM radio station call letters*] (BROA)
KCWW Tempe, AZ [*AM radio station call letters*]
KCWX Columbia Falls, MT [*FM radio station call letters*]
KCWY Casper, WY [*Television station call letters*] (BROA)
KCX Conscious [*Telegraphy*] (PCTE)
KCXL Calexico/International [*California*] [*ICAO location identifier*] (ICLI)
KCXL Liberty, MO [*AM radio station call letters*] (RBYB)
KCXN Consciousness [*Telegraphy*] (PCTE)
KCXX Lake Arrowhead, CA [*FM radio station call letters*] (RBYB)
KCXY Camden, AR [*FM radio station call letters*]
KCY Kansas City, MO [*Amtrak rail station code*]
KCY Korandje [*Language symbol*] (ETLW)
KCYC King's Cheshire Yeomanry Cavalry [*British military*] (DMA)
KCYL Lampasas, TX [*AM radio station call letters*]
KCYN-FM Moab, UT [*FM radio station call letters*] (RBYB)
KCYO-FM Ozark, MO [*FM radio station call letters*] (BROA)
KCYQ-FM Richfield, UT [*FM radio station call letters*] (BROA)
KCYS Cheyenne [*Wyoming*] [*ICAO location identifier*] (ICLI)
KCYS-FM Seaside, OR [*FM radio station call letters*] (BROA)
KCYT-FM Houston, AK [*FM radio station call letters*] (RBYB)
KCYT-FM Lead, SD [*FM radio station call letters*] (BROA)
KCYY San Antonio, TX [*FM radio station call letters*]
KCZ Kochi [*Japan*] [*Airport symbol*] (OAG)
KCZE New Hampton, IA [*FM radio station call letters*]
KCZN-FM Santa Paula, CA [*FM radio station call letters*] (BROA)
KCZO Carrizo Springs, TX [*FM radio station call letters*]
KCZQ Cresco, IA [*FM radio station call letters*]
KCZY Osage, IA [*FM radio station call letters*]
KCZZ British Island Airways Ltd. (SAUO)
KCZZ Mission, KS [*AM radio station call letters*] (BROA)
KD Batch Distribution Coefficient (SAUS)
KD Cathodal Duration [*Medicine*] (DMAA)
KD Christian Democrats (Sweden) [*Political party*] (PSAP)
Kd Coefficient of Soil-Water Absorption (GNE)
K_d Dissociation Constant [*Physics*] (DAVI)
K_d Distribution Coefficient [*Partition coefficient*] [*Physics*] (DAVI)
KD Kallidin [*Biochemistry*]
KD Kappa Delta (EA)
KD Kathodal Duration [*Medicine*]
KD Kawasaki Disease [*Also, KS, MLNS*] [*Medicine*]
KD Keep It Dark [*Say nothing about it*] [*Slang*]
KD Kendell Airlines [*ICAO designator*] (AD)
KD Kennnedy Disease [*Medicine*] (DMAA)
KD Kentucky Dam [*TVA*]
KD Keto-Diastix [*Miles Inc.*] [*Pharmacology*] (DAVI)
KD Kettledrum
KD Keyboard and Display [*Computer science*] (MHDB)
K/D Keyboard/Display (ACRL)
KD Key Definition (MHDB)
KD Keyed to Differ [*Locks*] (ADA)
KD Khaki Drill [*British military*] (DMA)
KD Kick-Down [*Automotive engineering*]
KD Kidderpore Docks (SAUO)
KD Kidney Donor (STED)
KD Killed (AABC)
KD Kiln-Dried [*Lumber*]
kd Kilodalton (STED)
kD Kilodalton [*Molecular mass measure*]
KD Kilter Diagram

KD .... Kind [*Telegraphy*] (PCTE)
KD .... Klinge [*Germany*] [*Research code symbol*]
KD .... Knee Disarticulation [*Medicine*]
KD .... Knitted Dacron (MEDA)
kd .... Knocked Down (EBF)
KD .... Knocked Down [*i.e., disassembled*]
KD .... Known-Distance [*Range*] [*Weaponry*] (INF)
KD .... Kohler Disease (MELL)
KD .... Komitet Domowy. Warsaw Ghetto (BJA)
KD .... Korsakoff's Disease [*Medicine*]
KD .... Kriegs Dekoration [*War Decoration*] [*German*]
KD .... Kuwaiti Dinar [*Monetary unit*] (BJA)
KD .... Pilotless Aerial Target [*Navy*]
KDA .... Kansas Dental Association (SAUO)
KDA .... Kendall Airlines [*Australia*] [*ICAO designator*] (FAAC)
kDa .... Kilodalton [*Physics*] [*Chemistry*] (DOG)
KDA .... Kit Design Approach
KDA .... Known Drug Allergies [*Medicine*] (DMAA)
KDA .... Kolda [*Senegal*] [*Airport symbol*] (AD)
KDA .... Kuranda [*Australia*] [*Seismograph station code, US Geological Survey*] [*Closed*] (SEIS)
KDA .... Potassium Dihydrogen Arsenate (SAUS)
KDAA .... Rolla, MO [*FM radio station call letters*] (RBYB)
KDAB .... Prairie Grove, AR [*FM radio station call letters*]
KDAC .... Fort Bragg, CA [*AM radio station call letters*]
KDAE .... Sinton, TX [*AM radio station call letters*]
KDAF .... Dallas, TX [*Television station call letters*]
KDAG .... Farmington, NM [*FM radio station call letters*]
KDAK .... Carrington, ND [*AM radio station call letters*]
KDAL .... Dallas/Dallas-Love Field [*Texas*] [*ICAO location identifier*] (ICLI)
KDAL .... Duluth, MN [*AM radio station call letters*]
kdal .... Kilodalton (STED)
KDAL-FM ... Duluth, MN [*FM radio station call letters*]
KDAM .... Monroe City, MO [*FM radio station call letters*]
KDAO .... Marshalltown, IA [*AM radio station call letters*]
KDAO-FM ... Eldora, IA [*FM radio station call letters*]
KDAP .... Douglas, AZ [*AM radio station call letters*]
KDAP-FM ... Douglas, AZ [*FM radio station call letters*]
KDAQ .... Shreveport, LA [*FM radio station call letters*]
KDAR .... Oxnard, CA [*FM radio station call letters*]
KDAT .... Cedar Rapids, IA [*FM radio station call letters*] (RBYB)
KDAT .... Kiln-Dried After Treatment [*Lumber*]
KDAV .... Lubbock, TX [*AM radio station call letters*] (BROA)
KDAY .... Dayton/James M. Coxdayton Municipal [*Ohio*] [*ICAO location identifier*] (ICLI)
KDAY .... Independence, CA [*FM radio station call letters*]
KDAZ .... Albuquerque, NM [*AM radio station call letters*]
KDB .... Kambalda [*Australia*] [*Airport symbol*] (OAG)
KDB .... Keller-Dorian, Berthon [*Method*] [*Photography*]
KDB .... Kelvin Double Bridge [*Physics*]
KDB .... Konedobu [*Papua New Guinea*] [*Seismograph station code, US Geological Survey*] (SEIS)
KDB .... Korea Development Bank
KDB .... Santa Barbara, CA [*FM radio station call letters*]
KDBB .... Bonne Terre, MO [*FM radio station call letters*]
KDBC .... El Paso, TX [*Television station call letters*]
KDBH .... Natchitoches, LA [*FM radio station call letters*]
KDBL .... Toppenish, WA [*FM radio station call letters*] (BROA)
KDBM .... Dillon, MT [*AM radio station call letters*]
KDBM-FM ... Dillon, MT [*FM radio station call letters*]
KDBN .... Haltom City, TX [*FM radio station call letters*] (BROA)
KDBR .... Kalispell, MT [*FM radio station call letters*]
KDBS .... KENNYBASE Database Service [*Database*] (GDD)
KDBS-AM ... Alexandria, LA [*AM radio station call letters*] (RBYB)
KDBV .... Salinas, CA [*AM radio station call letters*] (BROA)
KDBX .... Banks, OR [*FM radio station call letters*]
KDBX-FM ... Clear Lake, SD [*FM radio station call letters*] (BROA)
KDBZ .... Anchorage, AK [*FM radio station call letters*] (BROA)
KDBZ-AM ... Portland, OR [*AM radio station call letters*] (BROA)
KDC .... Conduct [*Telegraphy*] (PCTE)
KDc .... Dodge City Public Library, Dodge City, KS [*Library symbol*] [*Library of Congress*] (LCLS)
KDC .... Kathodal Duration Contraction [*Medicine*]
KDC .... KD Air Corp. [*ICAO designator*] (FAAC)
KDC .... Keil and Delitzsch Commentaries [*A publication*] (BJA)
KDC .... Kerberos key Distribution Center (SAUO)
KDC .... Key Distribution Center (MCD)
KDC .... Keyed Display Console
KDC .... Kidney Disease Treatment Center (DMAA)
KDC .... Kodak Digital Camera [*Image format*] (AAEL)
KDC .... Kodiak [*Alaska*] [*Seismograph station code, US Geological Survey*] (SEIS)
KDC .... Kosher Dining Club (BJA)
KDC .... Knocked-Down Condition [*Commerce*] (ODA)
KDCA .... Washington/National [*District of Columbia*] [*ICAO location identifier*] (ICLI)
KDCC .... Dodge City, KS [*AM radio station call letters*]
KDCC .... Washington [*District of Columbia*] [*ICAO location identifier*] (ICLI)
KDCD .... Conducted [*Telegraphy*] (PCTE)
KDCD .... San Angelo, TX [*FM radio station call letters*]
KDCE .... Espanola, NM [*AM radio station call letters*]
KDCG .... Conducting [*Telegraphy*] (PCTE)
KDCG .... San Diego Coast Guard Air Base [*California*] [*ICAO location identifier*] (ICLI)
KDCI .... Key Display Call Indicator
KDCK .... Cadec Systems, Inc. (SAUO)
KDCK .... Dodge City, KS [*Television station call letters*] (BROA)
KDCL .... Knocked Down, in Carloads
KDCP .... Kidney Disease Control Program [*Public Health Service*]
KDCQ .... Coos Bay, OR [*FM radio station call letters*] (RBYB)
KDCR .... Conductor [*Telegraphy*] (PCTE)
KDCR .... Sioux Center, IA [*FM radio station call letters*]
KDCV .... Blair, NE [*FM radio station call letters*]
KDD .... Knowledge Discovery in Databases (RALS)
KDD .... Kokusai Denshin Denwa Co. Ltd. [*Telegraph & Telephone Corp.*] [*Tokyo, Japan*] [*Telecommunications*]
KDDA .... Dumas, AR [*AM radio station call letters*]
KDDB .... Paso Robles, CA [*FM radio station call letters*]
KDDB-FM ... Waipahu, HI [*FM radio station call letters*] (BROA)
KDDD .... Dumas, TX [*AM radio station call letters*]
KDDG-FM ... Albany, MN [*FM radio station call letters*] (BROA)
KDDJ-FM ... Globe, AZ [*FM radio station call letters*] (BROA)
KDDK .... Jacksonville, AR [*FM radio station call letters*]
KDDK-FM ... Benton, AR [*FM radio station call letters*] (BROA)
KDDQ .... Comanche, OK [*FM radio station call letters*]
KDDR .... Oakes, ND [*AM radio station call letters*]
KDDS .... Duluth,MN-Superior,WI [*AM radio station call letters*] (GDPB)
KDDS-AM ... Duluth, MN [*AM radio station call letters*] (BROA)
KDDX .... Spearfish, SD [*FM radio station call letters*] (RBYB)
KDDZ .... Arvada, CO [*AM radio station call letters*] (BROA)
KDDZ-AM ... San Diego, CA [*AM radio station call letters*] (RBYB)
KDE .... 4 Kids Entertainment [*NYSE symbol*]
KDE .... 4Kids Entertainment [*NYSE symbol*]
KDe .... Derby Public Library, Derby, KS [*Library symbol*] [*Library of Congress*] (LCLS)
KDE .... Kappa Delta Epsilon [*An association*] (NTPA)
KDE .... K-Desktop Environment [*Linux*] (RALS)
KDE .... Keyboard Data Entry
KDE .... Kidde, Inc. (SAUO)
KDE .... Kinetic Depth Effect [*Cognitive science*]
KDE .... Koroba [*Papua New Guinea*] [*Airport symbol*] [*Obsolete*] (OAG)
KDEA .... New Iberia, LA [*FM radio station call letters*]
KDEB .... Springfield, MO [*Television station call letters*]
KDEC .... Decorah, IA [*AM radio station call letters*]
KDEC-FM ... Decorah, IA [*FM radio station call letters*]
KDEDC ...... Kaslo and District Economic Development Committee (SAUO)
KDEF .... Albuquerque, NM [*AM radio station call letters*]
KDEI-AM .... Port Arthur, TX [*AM radio station call letters*] (BROA)
KDEL .... Arkadelphia, AR [*FM radio station call letters*]
KDEM .... Deming, NM [*FM radio station call letters*]
KDEM .... Kansas Division of Emergency Management [*Emergency Management*] (EMA)
KDEM .... Kurzweil Data Entry Machine [*for optical character recognition*]
KDEN .... Denver/Stapleton International [*Colorado*] [*ICAO location identifier*] (ICLI)
KDEN-TV .... Longmont, CO [*TV station call letters*] (RBYB)
KDEO-FM ... Waipahu, HI [*FM radio station call letters*]
KDEP .... Kansas Division of Emergency Preparedness [*Emergency Management*] (EMA)
KDEP .... Kentucky Department of Environmental Protection
KDEP .... Smoke Layer Estimated (Feet) Deep [*Meteorology*] (FAAC)
KDEP-FM ... Depoe Bay, OR [*FM radio station call letters*] (RBYB)
KDES .... Palm Springs, CA [*AM radio station call letters*] (RBYB)
KDES-FM ... Palm Springs, CA [*FM radio station call letters*]
KDET .... Center, TX [*AM radio station call letters*]
KDET .... Detroit/Detroit City [*Michigan*] [*ICAO location identifier*] (ICLI)
KDET-FM .... Center, TX [*FM radio station call letters*]
KDEW .... De Witt, AR [*AM radio station call letters*] (RBYB)
KDEW-FM ... De Witt, AR [*FM radio station call letters*] (RBYB)
KDEX .... Dexter, MO [*AM radio station call letters*]
KDEX .... GLNX [*Private rail car owner code*]
KDEX-FM ... Dexter, MO [*FM radio station call letters*]
KDEZ .... Jonesboro, AR [*FM radio station call letters*]
KDF .... Kalamein [*Trademark*] Door and Frame
KDF .... Knob Door Fastener
KDF .... Knocked Down Flat
KDF .... Kraft durch Freude [*Strength through Joy Movement*] [*Pre-World War II*] [*German*]
KDFC .... Kenny Dale Fan Club (EA)
KDFC .... Korea Development Finance Corp.
KDFC .... Palo Alto, CA [*AM radio station call letters*]
KDFC .... San Francisco, CA [*FM radio station call letters*]
KDFI .... Dallas, TX [*Television station call letters*]
KDFM-FM ... Falfurrias, TX [*FM radio station call letters*] (BROA)
KDFN .... Doniphan, MO [*AM radio station call letters*]
KDFO .... Bakersfield, CA [*AM radio station call letters*] (BROA)
KDFO-FM ... Delano, CA [*FM radio station call letters*] (BROA)
KDFR .... Des Moines, IA [*FM radio station call letters*]
KDFT .... Ferris, TX [*AM radio station call letters*]
KDFW .... Dallas-Fort Worth/Regional Airport [*Texas*] [*ICAO location identifier*] (ICLI)
KDFW .... Dallas, TX [*Television station call letters*]
KDFW-DT ... Dallas, TX [*Television station call letters*] (BROA)
KDFX .... Dallas, TX [*AM radio station call letters*] (RBYB)
KDG .... Kedougou [*Senegal*] [*Seismograph station code, US Geological Survey*] [*Closed*] (SEIS)
KDG .... King's Dragoon Guards [*Later, QDG*] [*Military unit*] [*British*]
KDG .... Knowledge [*Telegraphy*] (PCTE)
KDGB .... Dodge City, KS [*FM radio station call letters*]
KDGB-FM ... Pratt, KS [*FM radio station call letters*] (BROA)

KDGE .... Gainesville, TX [*FM radio station call letters*]
KDGE-FM ... Fort Worth, TX [*FM radio station call letters*] (BROA)
KDGNBX .... Annual Report. Kinki University. Atomic Energy Research Institute (journ.) (SAUS)
KDGO .... Durango, CO [*AM radio station call letters*]
KDGS .... Andover, KS [*FM radio station call letters*] (RBYB)
KDH .... Christian Democratic Movement (Slovakia) [*Political party*] (PSAP)
KDH .... Kandahar [*Afghanistan*] [*Airport symbol*] (OAG)
KDH .... Key Depression per Hour [*Computer science*] (IAA)
KDH .... Korean Direct Hire
KDH .... Kosher Dining Hall (BJA)
KDHE .... Kansas Department of Health and Environment (SAUO)
KDHI .... Twentynine Palms, CA [*FM radio station call letters*]
KDHI-FM .... Joshua Tree, CA [*FM radio station call letters*] (BROA)
KDHL .... Faribault, MN [*AM radio station call letters*]
KDHN .... Dimmitt, TX [*AM radio station call letters*]
KDHN .... Dothan [*Alabama*] [*ICAO location identifier*] (ICLI)
KDHNM ..... Kill Devil Hill National Memorial (SAUO)
KDHT .... Dalhart [*Texas*] [*ICAO location identifier*] (ICLI)
KDHX .... St. Louis, MO [*FM radio station call letters*]
KDI .... KDI Corp. [*NYSE symbol*] (COMM)
KDI .... Kendari [*Indonesia*] [*Airport symbol*] (OAG)
KDI .... Knowledge and Distributed Intelligence
KDI .... Korea Development Institute (ECON)
KDI .... Kuwaiti Dinar [*Monetary unit*] (DS)
KDIA .... Korea Defense Industry Association (SAUO)
KDIA .... Oakland, CA [*AM radio station call letters*]
KDIA .... Vallejo, CA [*AM radio station call letters*] (BROA)
KDIC .... Grinnell, IA [*FM radio station call letters*]
KDIF .... Riverside, CA [*AM radio station call letters*]
KDIG .... Orland, CA [*FM radio station call letters*]
KDII .... Key Defense Intelligence Issue (MCD)
KDIN .... Des Moines, IA [*Television station call letters*]
KDIO .... Ortonville, MN [*AM radio station call letters*]
KDIS .... Los Angeles (Corona & San Bernardino), CA [*AM radio station call letters*] (GDPB)
KDIS-AM .... Los Angeles, CA [*AM radio station call letters*] (BROA)
KDIU .... Dimmitt, TX [*FM radio station call letters*]
KDIX .... Dickinson, ND [*AM radio station call letters*]
KDIZ .... Minneapolis-St. Paul, MN [*AM radio station call letters*] (GDPB)
KDIZ-AM .... Golden Valley, MN [*AM radio station call letters*] (RBYB)
KDJ .... Karamojong [*Language symbol*] (ETLW)
KDJ .... Njdole [*Gabon*] [*Airport symbol*] (AD)
KDJI .... Holbrook, AZ [*AM radio station call letters*]
KDJK .... Oakdale, CA [*FM radio station call letters*]
KDJK-FM .... Mariposa, CA [*FM radio station call letters*] (BROA)
KDJM .... Broomfield, CO [*FM radio station call letters*] (BROA)
KDJM-FM ... Greeley, CO [*FM radio station call letters*] (BROA)
KDJR .... De Soto, MO [*FM radio station call letters*]
KDJS .... Willmar, MN [*AM radio station call letters*]
KDJS-FM .... Willmar, MN [*FM radio station call letters*]
KDJW .... Amarillo, TX [*AM radio station call letters*]
KDK .... Khodzhikent [*Former USSR*] [*Seismograph station code, US Geological Survey*] [*Closed*] (SEIS)
KDK .... Knit de Knit Texturing (IAA)
KDK .... Kodiak Airways Inc. (SAUO)
KDK .... Kodiak [*Alaska*] Municipal Airport [*Airport symbol*] [*Obsolete*] (OAG)
KDKA .... Pittsburgh, PA [*First station to broadcast a baseball game, August 5, 192 1*] [*AM radio station call letters*]
KDKA-DT .... Pittsburgh, PA [*Television station call letters*] (BROA)
KDKA-TV .... Pittsburgh, PA [*Television station call letters*]
KDKB .... Mesa, AZ [*FM radio station call letters*] (GDPB)
KDKB-FM ... Mesa, AZ [*FM radio station call letters*] (RBYB)
KDKD .... Clinton, MO [*AM radio station call letters*]
KDKD-FM ... Clinton, MO [*FM radio station call letters*]
KDKF .... Klamath Falls, OR [*Television station call letters*]
KDKK .... Park Rapids, MN [*FM radio station call letters*]
KDKO .... Littleton, CO [*AM radio station call letters*]
KDKR-FM ... Decatur, TX [*FM radio station call letters*] (RBYB)
KDKS-FM ... Blanchard, LA [*FM radio station call letters*] (BROA)
KDKS-FM ... Haughton, LA [*FM radio station call letters*]
KDL .... Kerrisdale Resources Ltd. [*Vancouver Stock Exchange symbol*]
KDL .... Kinshasa-Dilolo-Lubumbashi Railway Co. (SAUO)
KDL .... Koronadal [*Mindanao, Philippines*] [*Airport symbol*] (AD)
KDL .... Kreisinger Development Laboratory (KSC)
KDLA .... De Ridder, LA [*AM radio station call letters*]
KDLB .... Henryetta, OK [*AM radio station call letters*]
KD lcl .... Knocked Down in Less Than Carload Lots (EBF)
KDLCL .... Knocked Down, in Less than Carloads
KDLF .... Del Rio/Laughlin Air Force Base [*Texas*] [*ICAO location identifier*] (ICLI)
KDLG .... Dillingham, AK [*AM radio station call letters*]
KDLH .... Duluth/International [*Minnesota*] [*ICAO location identifier*] (ICLI)
KDLH .... Duluth, MN [*Television station call letters*]
KDLK .... Del Rio, TX [*AM radio station call letters*] (RBYB)
KDLK-FM ... Del Rio, TX [*FM radio station call letters*]
KDLL .... Kenai, AK [*FM radio station call letters*] (RBYB)
KDLM .... Detroit Lakes, MN [*AM radio station call letters*]
KDLO .... Watertown, SD [*FM radio station call letters*]
KDLO-TV .... Florence, SD [*Television station call letters*]
KDLP .... Bayou Vista, LA [*AM radio station call letters*]
KDLR .... Devils Lake, ND [*AM radio station call letters*]
KDLS .... Perry, IA [*AM radio station call letters*]
KDLS-FM ... Perry, IA [*FM radio station call letters*]
KDLT .... Mitchell, SD [*Television station call letters*]
kdlth .... Kodalith (VRA)
KDLT-TV ..... Sioux Falls, SD [*Television station call letters*] (BROA)
KDLV .... Sioux Falls, SD [*Television station call letters*] (BROA)
KDLV-TV .... Mitchell, SD [*Television station call letters*] (BROA)
KDLX .... Makawao, HI [*FM radio station call letters*]
KDLY .... Lander, WY [*FM radio station call letters*]
KDM .... K Display Manager (SAUS)
KDM .... Key Decision Memorandum (ACAE)
KDM .... Kingdom (WGA)
KDM .... Kyrgyzstan Democratic Movement [*Political party*]
KDMA .... Montevideo, MN [*AM radio station call letters*]
KDMA .... Tucson/Davis Monthan Air Force Base [*Arizona*] [*ICAO location identifier*] (ICLI)
KDMD .... Anchorage, AK [*Television station call letters*]
KDMG .... Burlington, IA [*FM radio station call letters*]
KDMI .... Des Moines, IA [*FM radio station call letters*]
KDMI .... Thousands of Delivered Machine Instructions [*Computer science*]
KDMI-AM ... Des Moines, IA [*AM radio station call letters*] (RBYB)
KDMM .... Herington, KS [*FM radio station call letters*]
KDMM .... Highland Park, TX [*AM radio station call letters*]
KDMN .... Buena Vista, CO [*AM radio station call letters*]
KDMO .... Carthage, MO [*AM radio station call letters*]
KDMS .... El Dorado, AR [*AM radio station call letters*]
KDMS .... Kennedy Space Center Data Management System [*NASA*] (NASA)
KDMS .... Kork Digital Mapping System (SAUO)
KDMV.OB ... Kingdom Ventures [*OTCBB symbol*]
KDMX .... Dallas, TX [*FM radio station call letters*]
KDN .... Kaydon Corp. [*NYSE symbol*] (SAG)
K/DN .... Kickdown [*Automotive engineering*]
KDN .... Kindness [*Telegraphy*] (PCTE)
KDN .... Kinetically Designed Nozzle (NASA)
KDN .... Knocked Down [*Construction term*] (MIST)
KdN .... Koninkrijk der Nederlanden [*Kingdom of the Netherlands*] [*Dutch*] (BARN)
KDN .... N'Dende [*Gabon*] [*Airport symbol*] (OAG)
K-DNA .... Deoxyribonucleic Acid - Kinetoplast [*Biochemistry, genetics*]
kDNA .... Kinetoplast DNA[*Deoxyribonucleic Acid*] [*Genetics*] (DOG)
KDNA .... Yakima, WA [*FM radio station call letters*]
KDND .... Sacramento-Stockton, CA [*FM radio station call letters*] (GDPB)
KDND-FM ... Sacramento, CA [*FM radio station call letters*] (BROA)
KDNE .... Crete, NE [*FM radio station call letters*]
KDNI .... Duluth, MN [*FM radio station call letters*]
KDNK .... Carbondale, CO [*FM radio station call letters*]
KDNL .... St. Louis, MO [*Television station call letters*]
KDNN-FM ... Honolulu, HI [*FM radio station call letters*] (BROA)
KDNO .... Delano, CA [*FM radio station call letters*]
KDNO-FM ... Thermopolis, WY [*FM radio station call letters*] (BROA)
KDNP .... Keresztenydemokrata Neppart [*Christian Democratic People's Party*] [*Hungary*] [*Political party*] (EY)
KDNR .... Los Lunas, NM [*FM radio station call letters*] (RBYB)
KDNS .... Downs, KS [*FM radio station call letters*]
KDNW .... Duluth, MN [*FM radio station call letters*]
KDNY .... Home Intensive Care Inc. (SAUO)
KDNZ .... Cedar Falls, IA [*AM radio station call letters*] (BROA)
KDO 3-Deoxy-D-Manno-2-Octulosonate-8-Phosphate
KDO .... Ketodeoxyoctonate [*Biochemistry*]
KDO .... Ketodeoxyoctonic Acid (STED)
KDO .... Key District Office [*IRS*]
KDOC .... Anaheim, CA [*Television station call letters*]
K-DODM .... Kennedy Space Center Department of Defense Plan/Requirement (NAKS)
K-DODM .... KSC DOD Plan/Requirement (SAUS)
KDOG .... North Mankato, MN [*FM radio station call letters*]
KDOK .... Tyler, TX [*FM radio station call letters*]
KDOL .... Henderson, NV [*AM radio station call letters*]
KDOM .... Windom, MN [*AM radio station call letters*]
KDOM-FM .. Windom, MN [*FM radio station call letters*]
KDON .... Kaydon Corp. (SAUO)
KDON .... Salinas, CA [*FM radio station call letters*]
KDOR .... Bartlesville, OK [*Television station call letters*]
KDOS .... Corsicana, TX [*FM radio station call letters*] (BROA)
KDOS .... Key Display Operating System
KDOS .... Key to Disk Operating System
KDOS .... Laredo, TX [*AM radio station call letters*]
KDOS-FM ... Gainesville, TX [*FM radio station call letters*] (BROA)
KDOT .... Reno, NV [*FM radio station call letters*] (GDPB)
KDOT-FM ... Reno, NV [*FM radio station call letters*] (RBYB)
KDOV .... Dover Air Force Base [*Delaware*] [*ICAO location identifier*] (ICLI)
KDOV .... Medford, OR [*FM radio station call letters*] (RBYB)
KDOX .... Henderson, NV [*AM radio station call letters*] (BROA)
KDP .... Deuterated Potassium dideuterium phosphate (SAUS)
KDP .... Kalabagh Dam Project (SAUO)
KDP .... Kandep [*Papua New Guinea*] [*Airport symbol*] [*Obsolete*] (OAG)
KDP .... Kappa Delta Pi [*Honor society*] (AEE)
KDP .... Keyboard, Display, and Printer [*Computer science*]
KDP .... Key Data Points (MCD)
KDP .... Key Decision Point [*USCG*] (TAG)
KDP .... Key Development Plan [*Telecommunications*] (TEL)
KDP .... Known Datum Point
KDP .... Korean Democratic Party [*North Korea*] [*Political party*] (FEA)
KDP .... Kurdish Democratic Party [*Iran*] [*Political party*]
KDP .... Potassium Dideuterium Phosphate
KDP .... Potassium [*Kalium*] Dihydrogen Phosphate [*Inorganic chemistry*]

KDPA .... Knitgoods Dyers and Processors Association
KDPA .... West Chicago/Du Page County [*Illinois*] [*ICAO location identifier*] (ICLI)
KDPI .... Kurdish Democratic Party of Iran [*Political party*] (PPW)
K-DPM ...... Kennedy Space Center Department of Defense Payloads Plan/ Requirement (NAKS)
K-DPM ...... KSC DOD Payloads Plan (or Requirement) (SAUS)
K-DPN .... Kennedy Space Center Department of Defense Payloads Notice (NAKS)
K-DPN .... KSC [*Kennedy Space Center*] DOD Payloads Notice [*Department of Defense*] [*NASA*] (NASA)
KDPP .... Keyboard/Display/Printer/Punch (ACAE)
K-DPPS ..... Kennedy Space Center Department of Defense Payloads Project Specification (NAKS)
K-DPPS ..... KSC DOD Payloads Project Specification (SAUS)
K-DPPS ..... KSC [*Kennedy Space Center*] DOD Payloads Projects Specification [*Department of Defense*] [*NASA*] (NASA)
KDPR .... Dickinson, ND [*FM radio station call letters*]
KDPS .... Des Moines, IA [*FM radio station call letters*]
KDPS .... Kurdish Democratic Party of Syria [*Political party*]
KDQN .... De Queen, AR [*AM radio station call letters*]
KDQN-FM ... De Queen, AR [*FM radio station call letters*]
KDR .... Kandrian [*Papua New Guinea*] [*Airport symbol*] (OAG)
KDR .... Kangeld Resources Ltd. [*Vancouver Stock Exchange symbol*]
KDR .... Kappa Delta Rho [*Fraternity*]
KDR .... Keyboard Data Recorder [*Computer science*]
KDR .... Key Descriptor Record (TIMI)
KDR .... Kidderminster [*British depot code*]
KDR .... Kill/Detection Ratio (SAUS)
K/DR .... Kitchen/Dining Room [*Classified advertising*] (ADA)
KDR .... Knockdown Resistance [*Pesticide technology*]
KDRE .... North Little Rock, AR [*FM radio station call letters*]
KDRG .... Deer Lodge, MT [*AM radio station call letters*]
KDRH .... Glenwood Springs, CO [*FM radio station call letters*]
KDRH-FM ... King City, CA [*FM radio station call letters*] (BROA)
KDRK .... Dishman, WA [*AM radio station call letters*] (BROA)
KDRK .... Spokane, WA [*FM radio station call letters*]
KDRM .... Moses Lake, WA [*FM radio station call letters*]
KDRNBK .... Annual Report. Noto Marine Laboratory (journ.) (SAUS)
KDRO .... Sedalia, MO [*AM radio station call letters*]
KDRQ .... Wishek, ND [*AM radio station call letters*]
KDRS .... Paragould, AR [*AM radio station call letters*]
KDRSM ...... Democratic Committee To Support the Malagasy Socialist Revolution (SAUS)
KDRT .... Del Rio/International [*Texas*] [*ICAO location identifier*] (ICLI)
KDRV .... Medford, OR [*Television station call letters*]
KDRY .... Alamo Heights, TX [*AM radio station call letters*]
KDS .... Christian Democratic Party (Czech Rep.) [*Political party*] (PSAP)
KDS .... K2 Del Aire SA de CV [*Mexico*] [*ICAO designator*] (FAAC)
KDS .... Kamad Silver Co. Ltd. [*Vancouver Stock Exchange symbol*]
KDS .... Kathode Dark Space
KDS .... Kaufman Developmental Scale [*Child development test*]
KDS .... Kedougou [*Senegal*] [*Seismograph station code, US Geological Survey*] (SEIS)
KDS .... Keel Depth Simulator
KDS .... Keyboard Display Station [*Computer science*] (DA)
KDS .... Key Data Station (NITA)
KDS .... Key Display System [*Computer science*] (MDG)
KDS .... Key to Disc System
KDS .... Khuzistan Development Service (SAUO)
KDS .... King-Denborough Syndrome [*Medicine*] (EDAA)
KDS .... Kiting Detection System (HGAA)
KDS .... Knowledge Directory Server
KDS .... Kocher-Debre-Semelaigne [*Syndrome*] [*Medicine*] (EDAA)
KDS .... Komma Dimokratikou Sosialismou [*Party for Democratic Socialism*] [*Greek*] [*Political party*] (PPE)
KDS .... Kristen Demokratisk Samling [*Christian Democratic Union*] [*Sweden*] [*Political party*] (PPE)
KDSD .... Aberdeen, SD [*Television station call letters*]
KDSD .... Pierpont, SD [*FM radio station call letters*]
KDSE .... Dickinson, ND [*Television station call letters*]
kd/sec .... Kilocycles per Second [*Measurement*] (DAVI)
KDSI .... Alice, TX [*AM radio station call letters*]
KDSI .... Knowledge Data System Inc. (SAUO)
KDSI .... Thousands of Delivered Source Instructions [*Computer science*]
KDSJ .... Deadwood, SD [*AM radio station call letters*]
KDSK-FM ... Grants, NM [*FM radio station call letters*] (BROA)
KDSL .... Thousands of Delivered Source Lines of Code [*Computer science*]
KDSM .... Des Moines [*Iowa*] [*ICAO location identifier*] (ICLI)
KDSM .... Des Moines, IA [*Television station call letters*]
KDSM .... Keratinizing Desquamative Squamous Metaplasia [*Medicine*]
KDSN .... Denison, IA [*AM radio station call letters*]
KDSN-FM ... Denison, IA [*FM radio station call letters*]
KDSR .... Williston, ND [*FM radio station call letters*]
KDSRA2 ..... Annals of Science. Kanazawa University. Part 2. Biology-Geology (journ.) (SAUS)
KDSS .... Ely, NV [*FM radio station call letters*]
KDSS .... Key-to-Disk Subsystem [*Computer science*] (MHDB)
KDST .... Dyersville, IA [*FM radio station call letters*]
KDSU .... Fargo, ND [*FM radio station call letters*]
KDSX .... Denison-Sherman, TX [*AM radio station call letters*]
KDT .... Kammer der Technik
KDT .... Kathodal Duration Tetanus [*Medicine*]
KDT .... Keyboard and Display Test (MCD)
KDT .... Keyboard Definition Table [*Computer science*] (MWOL)
KDT .... Keyboard Display Terminal (MCD)
KDT .... Key Data Terminal
KDT .... Key Definition Table [*Computer science*] (PCM)
KDT .... Key-to-Disk-to-Tape (MCD)
KDT .... Knowledge Discovery in Text (IDAI)
KDTA .... Delta, CO [*AM radio station call letters*]
KDTB .... Keg and Drum Trade Board (SAUO)
KDTE .... Kathodal Duration Tetanus [*Medicine*] (ROG)
KDTH .... Dubuque, IA [*AM radio station call letters*]
KDTK .... Prescott Valley, AZ [*FM radio station call letters*]
KDTL-FM .... Lake Village, AR [*FM radio station call letters*] (RBYB)
KDTN .... Denton, TX [*Television station call letters*]
KDTP .... Phoenix, AZ [*Television station call letters*] (BROA)
KDTV .... San Francisco, CA [*Television station call letters*]
KDTW .... Detroit/Metropolitan Wayne County [*Michigan*] [*ICAO location identifier*] (ICLI)
KDTX .... Dallas, TX [*Television station call letters*]
KDTX .... Tomco Railway Car [*Private rail car owner code*]
KDU .... Christian Democratic Union [*Czechoslavakia*] [*Political party*] (ECON)
KDU .... Conduce [*Telegraphy*] (PCTE)
KDU .... Kadaru [*Language symbol*] (ETLW)
KDU .... Keyboard Display Unit (MCD)
KDU .... Kidney Dialysis Unit (MELL)
KDU .... Skardu [*Pakistan*] [*Airport symbol*] (AD)
KDUC .... Barstow, CA [*FM radio station call letters*]
KDUD .... Conduced [*Telegraphy*] (PCTE)
KDUG .... Conducing [*Telegraphy*] (PCTE)
KDUG .... Douglas/Bisbee International [*Arizona*] [*ICAO location identifier*] (ICLI)
KDUH .... Scottsbluff, NE [*Television station call letters*]
KDUK .... Eugene, OR [*AM radio station call letters*]
KDUK .... Florence, OR [*FM radio station call letters*]
KDUN .... Reedsport, OR [*AM radio station call letters*]
KDUP .... Portland, OR [*AM radio station call letters*] (GDPB)
KDUQ .... Ludlow, CA [*FM radio station call letters*]
KDUR .... Durango, CO [*FM radio station call letters*]
KDUS .... Cadus Pharmaceutical Corp. [*NASDAQ symbol*] (SAG)
KDUS .... Conduces [*Telegraphy*] (PCTE)
KDUS-AM ... Tempe, AZ [*AM radio station call letters*] (BROA)
KDUV .... Visalia, CA [*FM radio station call letters*]
KDUW-FM ... Douglas, WY [*FM radio station call letters*] (BROA)
KDUX .... Aberdeen, WA [*FM radio station call letters*]
KDUZ .... Hutchinson, MN [*AM radio station call letters*]
KDV .... Kandavu [*Fiji*] [*Airport symbol*] (OAG)
KdV .... Korteweg-deVries [*Equation*] [*Mathematics*]
KDVA-FM ... Buckeye, AZ [*FM radio station call letters*] (BROA)
kDVC .... Kilovolts, Direct Current (KSC)
KDVE .... Pittsburg, TX [*FM radio station call letters*] (BROA)
KDVE-FM ... Denison-Sherman, TX [*FM radio station call letters*] (RBYB)
KDVE-FM ... Tatum, TX [*FM radio station call letters*] (BROA)
KDVL .... Devils Lake, ND [*FM radio station call letters*]
KDVR .... Denver, CO [*Television station call letters*]
KDVS .... Davis, CA [*FM radio station call letters*]
KDVV .... Topeka, KS [*FM radio station call letters*]
KDW .... Keep Digging, Watson (SAUS)
KDWA .... Hastings, MN [*AM radio station call letters*]
KDWB .... Richfield, MN [*FM radio station call letters*]
KDWD .... Spencer, IA [*FM radio station call letters*] (GDPB)
KDWD-FM .. Emmetsburg, IA [*FM radio station call letters*] (BROA)
KDWG .... Billings, MT [*AM radio station call letters*] (RBYB)
KDWG-FM .. Dillon, MT [*FM radio station call letters*] (BROA)
KDWN .... Las Vegas, NV [*AM radio station call letters*]
KDWY .... Diamondville, WY [*FM radio station call letters*] (BROA)
KDX .... Klondex Mines [*Vancouver Stock Exchange symbol*]
KDX .... Klondex Mines Ltd [*VS, exchange symbol*] (TTSB)
KDX .... Knock Down Export [*Automotive engineering*]
KDX .... Korea Defence Experiment (SAUO)
KDXE .... Sulphur Springs, TX [*FM radio station call letters*]
KDXI .... Center, TX [*FM radio station call letters*] (GDPB)
KDXL .... St. Louis Park, MN [*FM radio station call letters*]
KDXT-FM .... Granbury, TX [*FM radio station call letters*] (BROA)
KDXU .... St. George, UT [*AM radio station call letters*]
KDXX .... Dallas, TX [*AM radio station call letters*] (BROA)
KDXX .... Lewisville, TX [*FM radio station call letters*] (BROA)
KDXX-FM ... Corsicana, TX [*FM radio station call letters*] (BROA)
KDXY-FM .... Lake City, AR [*FM radio station call letters*] (RBYB)
KDY .... Kennedy Resources [*Vancouver Stock Exchange symbol*]
KDY .... Kindly [*Telegraphy*] (PCTE)
KDYA .... Vallejo, CA [*AM radio station call letters*] (BROA)
KDYL .... Salt Lake City, UT [*AM radio station call letters*]
KDYN .... Ozark, AR [*AM radio station call letters*]
KDYN-FM ... Ozark, AR [*FM radio station call letters*]
KDYS .... Abilene/Dyess Air Force Base [*Texas*] [*ICAO location identifier*] (ICLI)
KDYS-AM ... Lafayette, LA [*AM radio station call letters*] (RBYB)
KdyWils ..... Kennedy Wilson, Inc. [*Associated Press*] (SAG)
KDZ .... Kurdzhali [*Bulgaria*] [*Seismograph station code, US Geological Survey*] (SEIS)
KDZA .... Pueblo, CO [*AM radio station call letters*]
KDZA-FM ... Pueblo, CO [*FM radio station call letters*] (RBYB)
KDZN .... Glendive, MT [*FM radio station call letters*]
KDZY-FM ... McCall, ID [*FM radio station call letters*] (BROA)
KDZZ .... Albuquerque, NM [*AM radio station call letters*]
K_e .... Exchangeable Body Potassium [*Biochemistry*] (DAVI)
KE .... Kagel Exercise (MELL)

KE... Kaiser Engineers (NRCH)
KE... Kansas Eastern Railroad [*Federal Railroad Administration identification code*]
Ke... Keen's English Rolls Court Reports [*48 English Reprint*] [*A publication*] (DLA)
KE... Kempten [*Allgaeu*] [*German license plate city code*]
KE... Kendall's Compound E [*Cortisone*]
KE... Kenya [*ANSI two-letter standard code*] (CNC)
ke... Kenya [*MARC country of publication code*] [*Library of Congress*] (LCCP)
KE... Kerr Effect [*Optics*]
KE... Kessering Site Office (SAUO)
KE... Key Equipment [*Telecommunications*] (TEL)
KE... Kinetic Energy
KE... King Edward (ROG)
KE... Kitchen Exhaust (OA)
KE... Knight of the Eagle
KE... Knight of the Elephant [*Denmark*]
KE... Knights of Equity (EA)
KE... Knowledge Engineer [*Computer science*]
KE... Koger Equity [*AMEX symbol*] (TTSB)
KE... Koger Equity, Inc. [*AMEX symbol*] (CTT)
KE... Korea Fund [*NYSE symbol*] (TTSB)
KE... Korean Air [*Airline flight code*] (ODBW)
KE... Korean Air Lines [*ICAO designator*] (AD)
KE... Korean AirLines, Inc. (SAUO)
KE... Kroger Equity [*NYSE symbol*] (SG)
KEA... Carcino Embryonales Antigen (SAUS)
KEA... Kanada Esperanto-Asocio [*Canadian Esperanto Association*]
KEA... Kealakomo [*Hawaii*] [*Seismograph station code, US Geological Survey*] [*Closed*] (SEIS)
KEA... Keane Healthcare Services Div [*OTCBB symbol*]
KEA... Keane, Inc. [*AMEX symbol*] (SPSG)
KEA... Kent Executive Aviation Ltd. [*British*] [*ICAO designator*] (FAAC)
KEA... Kentucky Education Association (SAUO)
KEA... Kinetic Enzyme Analyzer [*Medicine*] (EDAA)
KEA... Kiwifruit Exporters Association (SAUO)
KEA... Knitwear Employers Association (EA)
KEA... Kuba Esperanto-Asocio (SAUO)
KEA... Kubota Engine America [*Automotive supplier*]
KEAG... Anchorage, AK [*FM radio station call letters*]
KEAH... Kill Everyone After Hours (SAUS)
KEAL... Tucson, AZ [*FM radio station call letters*] (GDPB)
KEAL-FM... Douglas, AZ [*FM radio station call letters*] (RBYB)
KEAN... Abilene, TX [*AM radio station call letters*]
KEAN... Keane, Inc. [*NASDAQ symbol*] (COMM)
Kean C NJ.. Kean College of New Jersey (GAGS)
Keane... Keane, Inc. [*Associated Press*] (SAG)
Keane & Gr... Keane and Grant's English Registration Appeal Cases [*1854-62*] [*A publication*] (DLA)
Keane & GRC... Keane and Grant's English Registration Appeal Cases [*1854-62*] [*A publication*] (DLA)
KEANE PAC. Keane Inc Pac [*Boston, MA*] (PACS)
KEAN-FM... Abilene, TX [*FM radio station call letters*]
KEAR... San Francisco, CA [*FM radio station call letters*]
KEARN... Kearney, NE [*American Association of Railroads railroad junction routing code*]
KEAS... Eastland, TX [*AM radio station call letters*]
KEAS... Knots Equivalent Airspeed (MCD)
KEASAT... Kinetic Energy Anti-Satellite
KEAS-FM... Eastland, TX [*FM radio station call letters*]
Keat Fam Sett... Keatinge's Family Settlements [*1810*] [*A publication*] (DLA)
KEAZ... De Ridder, LA [*FM radio station call letters*]
KEB... English Bay, AK [*Location identifier*] [*FAA*] (FAAL)
KEB... Keban [*Turkey*] [*Seismograph station code, US Geological Survey*] (SEIS)
Keb... Keble's English King's Bench Reports [*83, 84 English Reprint*] [*A publication*] (DLA)
KEB... Korea Exchange Bank (IMH)
KEBC... Oklahoma City, OK [*FM radio station call letters*]
KEB COLL... Keble College [*Oxford University*] (ROG)
KEBE... Jacksonville, TX [*AM radio station call letters*]
KEBI... Kentucky Enterprise Bancorp [*NASDAQ symbol*] (SAG)
Keb J... Keble's Justice of the Peace [*A publication*] (DLA)
KEBK... Korea Exchange Bank (SAUO)
Kebl... Keble's English King's Bench Reports [*83, 84 English Reprint*] [*A publication*] (DLA)
Keble... Keble College (SAUO)
Keble... Keble's English King's Bench Reports [*83, 84 English Reprint*] [*A publication*] (DLA)
Keble (Eng)... Keble's English King's Bench Reports [*83, 84 English Reprint*] [*A publication*] (DLA)
KEBN... Salem, OR [*Television station call letters*]
KEBR... North Highlands, CA [*FM radio station call letters*]
KEBR... Rocklin, CA [*AM radio station call letters*]
Keb Stat... Keble's Statutes [*A publication*] (DLA)
KEBV... Salinas, CA [*FM radio station call letters*] (BROA)
KEBX... Manufacturers Leasing [*Private rail car owner code*]
KEC... KDD Engineering and Consulting Inc. (NITA)
KEC... Kecskemet [*Hungary*] [*Seismograph station code, US Geological Survey*] (SEIS)
KEC... Kent Electronics Corp. [*AMEX symbol*] (COMM)
KEC... Klebsiella, Enterobacter, Citrobacter [*Bacteriae*] [*Microbiology*] (DAVI)
KEC... Korea Explosives Co. Ltd. (SAUO)
KECC... Keystone Empire Collegiate Conference (PSS)
KECC... Miles City, MT [*FM radio station call letters*]
KECG... El Cerrito, CA [*FM radio station call letters*]
KECG... Elizabeth City Coast Guard Air Base (SAUS)
KECG... Elizabeth City Coast Guard Air Base/Municipal [*North Carolina*] [*ICAO location identifier*] (ICLI)
KECH... Sun Valley, ID [*FM radio station call letters*]
KECI... Korean Existing Chemicals Inventory (SAUO)
KECI... Missoula, MT [*Television station call letters*]
KECME... Kuzbass Commodity and Raw Materials Exchange [*Russian Federation*] (EY)
KECN... Blackfoot, ID [*AM radio station call letters*] (GDPB)
KECN-AM... Blackfoot, ID [*AM radio station call letters*] (RBYB)
KECO... Elk City, OK [*FM radio station call letters*]
KECO... Kent Electronics Corporation (SAUO)
KECO... Korea Electric Company (SAUO)
KECP... Kit Engineering Change Proposal (KSC)
KECR... El Cajon, CA [*AM radio station call letters*]
KECS... Gainesville, TX [*FM radio station call letters*] (RBYB)
KECY... El Centro, CA [*Television station call letters*] (RBYB)
KECZ... Kellogg [*Federal Railroad Administration identification code*]
KED... Kaedi [*Mauritania*] [*Airport symbol*] (OAG)
KED... Kedougou [*Senegal*] [*Seismograph station code, US Geological Survey*] [*Closed*] (SEIS)
KED... Kendrick Extrication Device (SAUS)
KED... Kill Enhancement Device [*Military*] (ACAE)
KED... Known Enemy Dead [*Military*]
KEDA... Ken E. Davis Associates, Inc. (EFIS)
KEDA... San Antonio, TX [*AM radio station call letters*]
KEDD-FM... Johannesburg, CA [*FM radio station call letters*] (BROA)
KEDDS... Kansas Education Dissemination/Diffusion System (EDAC)
KEDG... Las Vegas, NV [*FM radio station call letters*]
KEDG-FM... Alexandria, LA [*FM radio station call letters*] (BROA)
KEDI... Korean Education Development Institute (BUAC)
KEDJ... Gilbert, AZ [*FM radio station call letters*] (BROA)
KEDJ... Sun City, AZ [*FM radio station call letters*]
KEDM... Monroe, LA [*FM radio station call letters*]
KEDO... Korea Energy Development Organisation [*A consortium formed by the US, North Korea, and South Korea to finance and build reactors*] (ECON)
KEDO... Longview, WA [*AM radio station call letters*]
KEDP... Las Vegas, NM [*FM radio station call letters*]
KEDR... Sacramento, CA [*FM radio station call letters*]
KEDS... Knowledge Express Data Systems
KEDT... Corpus Christi, TX [*FM radio station call letters*]
KEDT-TV... Corpus Christi, TX [*Television station call letters*]
KEDW... Edwards Air Force Base [*California*] [*ICAO location identifier*] (ICLI)
KEE... Emporia State University, School of Library Science, Emporia, KS [*OCLC symbol*] (OCLC)
KEE... Kelle [*Congo*] [*Airport symbol*] (OAG)
KEE... Kerr Electro-Optical Effect [*Optics*]
KEE... Kewanee, IL [*Amtrak rail station code*]
KEE... Keychart Educational Equipment [*for use with an electronic typewriter*]
KEE... Keystone Air Services Ltd. [*Canada*] [*ICAO designator*] (FAAC)
KEE... Knowledge Engineering Environment [*An artificial intelligence system*]
KEED... Eugene, OR [*AM radio station call letters*] (RBYB)
KEEE... Nacogdoches, TX [*AM radio station call letters*]
KEEF... Los Angeles, CA [*Television station call letters*]
KEEH... Spokane, WA [*FM radio station call letters*]
KEEI... Key Energy Enterprises, Incorporated (SAUO)
KEEL... Kent European Enterprises Ltd. [*British*]
KEEL... Shreveport, LA [*AM radio station call letters*]
Keen... Keen's English Rolls Court Reports [*48 English Reprint*] [*A publication*] (DLA)
KEEN... Kids Enjoy Exercise Now
KEEN... Palmer, AK [*FM radio station call letters*] (RBYB)
Keen Ch... Keen's English Rolls Court Reports [*48 English Reprint*] [*A publication*] (DLA)
Keen (Eng)... Keen's English Rolls Court Reports [*48 English Reprint*] [*A publication*] (DLA)
Keener Quasi Contr... Keener's Cases on Quasi Contracts [*A publication*] (DLA)
Keene St C... Keene State College (GAGS)
KEEP... Bandera, TX [*FM radio station call letters*]
KEEP... Kamehameha Early Education Program [*Hawaii*] (EDAC)
KEEP... Kentucky Environmental Education Program (EDAC)
KEEP... Kidney Early Education Program
KEEP... Knowledge Enhancement Exchange Program
KEEP... Kuroshio Edge Exchange Processes (SAUO)
KEEP... Kyosato Education Experiment Project [*Self-help program for Japanese farmers established by Americans in 1948*]
KEEPS... Kodak Ektaprint Electronic Publishing System [*Hardware and software components*] [*Eastman Kodak Co.*]
KEES... Gladewater, TX [*AM radio station call letters*]
KEET... Eureka, CA [*Television station call letters*]
Keet... Parakeet [*Bird*]
KEEX... Kee Exploration, Inc. (SAUO)
KEEY... St. Paul, MN [*FM radio station call letters*]
KEEZ... Mankato, MN [*FM radio station call letters*]
KEF... Keflavik [*Iceland*] [*Airport symbol*] (AD)
KEF... Korea Equity Fund [*NYSE symbol*] (SPSG)
KEF... Kpessi [*Language symbol*] (ETLW)
KEF... Reykjavik [*Iceland*] Keflavik Airport [*Airport symbol*] (OAG)
KEFD... Houston/Ellington Air Force Base [*Texas*] [*ICAO location identifier*] (ICLI)

KEFE......... Los Alamos, NM [*FM radio station call letters*]
KEFH-FM.... Clarendon, TX [*FM radio station call letters*] (BROA)
KEFM......... Omaha, NE [*FM radio station call letters*]
KEFR......... Le Grand, CA [*FM radio station call letters*]
KEFX-FM.... Twin Falls, ID [*FM radio station call letters*] (BROA)
KEG.......... Keg Restaurants Ltd. [*Toronto Stock Exchange symbol*] [*Vancouver Stock Exchange symbol*]
KEG.......... Key Energy Group [*AMEX symbol*] (SPSG)
KEG.......... Key Gap [*Computer science*] (MHDI)
KEGE......... Richfield, MN [*AM radio station call letters*]
KEGEAC..... Japanese Journal of Plastic and Reconstructive Surgery (journ.) (SAUS)
KEGE-FM.... Minneapolis, MN [*FM radio station call letters*]
KEGG......... Daingerfield, TX [*AM radio station call letters*]
KEGG......... Kyoto Encyclopedia of Genes and Genomes [*Computer network*]
KEGK-FM... Julesburg, CO [*FM radio station call letters*] (BROA)
KEGL......... Fort Worth, TX [*FM radio station call letters*]
KEGP......... Eagle Pass/Municipal [*Texas*] [*ICAO location identifier*] (ICLI)
KEGQ......... James P. Keegan [*Common carrier symbol*]
KEGR......... Fort Dodge, IA [*FM radio station call letters*] (BROA)
KEGR......... Red Bluff, CA [*FM radio station call letters*] (RBYB)
KEGS......... Kenworth Engine Governing System [*Automotive engineering*]
KEGS......... King Edward VI Grammar School (SAUO)
KEGT......... Lake Village, AR [*FM radio station call letters*]
KEGX......... Richland, WA [*FM radio station call letters*]
KEH.......... Kaiser Engineers Hanford (SAUO)
KEH.......... Kelheim [*German license plate city code*]
KEH.......... King Edward's Horse Regiment [*Military unit*] [*British*]
KEH.......... Kurzgefasstes Exegetisches Handbuch zum Alten Testament [*Leipzig*] [*A publication*] (BJA)
KEHK-FM... Brownsville, OR [*FM radio station call letters*] (RBYB)
KEI........... Keithley Instruments [*NYSE symbol*] (TTSB)
KEI........... Keithley Instruments, Inc. [*AMEX symbol*] (SPSG)
KEI........... Kepi [*Indonesia*] [*Airport symbol*] (OAG)
KEI........... Kresge Eye Institute
KEI........... Lorin E. Kerr Ergonomics Institute [*University of Massachusetts Lowell*] (RCD)
KEIA......... Korea Economic Institute of America (EA)
KEIA......... Korea Electronics Industries Association (SAUO)
KEIDANREN... Federation of Economic Organizations, Japan (SAUO)
Keil.......... Keilway's English King's Bench Reports [*72 English Reprint*] [*A publication*] (DLA)
KEIL......... Key Essential Item List [*Defense Supply Agency*]
Keilw........ Keilway's English King's Bench Reports [*72 English Reprint*] [*A publication*] (DLA)
Keilway..... Keilway's English King's Bench Reports [*72 English Reprint*] [*A publication*] (DLA)
Keilw (Eng)... Keilway's English King's Bench Reports [*72 English Reprint*] [*A publication*] (DLA)
KEIN......... Great Falls, MT [*AM radio station call letters*]
KEIN-FM.... Conrad, MT [*FM radio station call letters*] (BROA)
KEIS......... Kentucky Economic Information System [*University of Kentucky*] [*Lexington*] [*Database producer*] [*Information service or system*]
Keith Ch PA... Registrar's Book, Keith's Court of Chancery [*Pennsylvania*] [*A publication*] (DLA)
Keithly...... Keithley Instruments, Inc. [*Associated Press*] (SAG)
KEJB......... El Dorado, AR [*Television station call letters*] (BROA)
KEJB......... Jack B. Kelley [*Common carrier symbol*]
KEJC......... Modesto, CA [*FM radio station call letters*] (RBYB)
KEJJ-FM.... Gunnison, CO [*FM radio station call letters*] (BROA)
KEJL-FM.... Eunice, NM [*FM radio station call letters*] (BROA)
KEJO......... Corvallis, OR [*FM radio station call letters*]
KEJO......... Kelly-Johnston Enterprises (SAUO)
KEJS......... Lubbock, TX [*FM radio station call letters*]
KEK.......... Ekwok [*Alaska*] [*Airport symbol*] (OAG)
KEK.......... Kappa Eta Kappa [*Fraternity*]
KEK.......... Kinetic Energy Kill (SAUS)
KEK.......... Konferenz Europaeischer Kirchen [*Conference of European Churches - CEC*] (EA)
KEK.......... Koo Energy Ken
KEK.......... Kypriakon Ethnikon Komma [*Cypriot National Party (1944-1960)*] [*Greek Cypriot*] [*Political party*] (PPE)
KEKA......... Eureka, CA [*FM radio station call letters*]
KEKB......... Fruita, CO [*FM radio station call letters*]
Ke/Kg........ Exchangeable Potassium per Kilogram of Body Weight [*Biochemistry*] (DAVI)
KEKL......... East Sonora, CA [*FM radio station call letters*] (BROA)
KEKO-FM.... Hebronville, TX [*FM radio station call letters*] (BROA)
KEL.......... Karntner Einheitsliste [*Carinthian Unity List*] [*Austria*] [*Political party*] (PPE)
KEL.......... Keles [*Later, TKT*] [*Former USSR*] [*Geomagnetic observatory code*]
Kel........... Kelim (BJA)
KEL.......... Kell Blood Group System [*Immunology*] (QSUL)
KEL.......... Kelsey-Hayes Canada Ltd. [*Toronto Stock Exchange symbol*]
KEL.......... Kelso, WA [*Amtrak rail station code*]
KEL.......... Kelud [*Java*] [*Seismograph station code, US Geological Survey*] [*Closed*] (SEIS)
KEL.......... Known Enemy Location [*Military*]
KEL.......... Koroska Enotna Lista [*Carinthian Unity List*] [*Austria*] [*Political party*] (PPE)
KEL.......... Kroatia Esperanto-Ligo (SAUO)
KELA......... Centralia-Chehalis, WA [*AM radio station call letters*]
Kel An........ Kelly's Life Annuities [*1835*] [*A publication*] (DLA)
Kel Cont.... Kelly on Contracts of Married Women [*A publication*] (DLA)
KELD......... El Dorado, AR [*AM radio station call letters*]
KELD......... El Dorado/Goodwin Field [*Arkansas*] [*ICAO location identifier*] (ICLI)
Kel Draft.... Kelly's Draftsman [*14th ed.*] [*1978*] [*A publication*] (DLA)
KELE......... Kelley Manufacturing [*NCIC trailer make code*]
KELE-AM.... Mountain Grove, MO [*AM radio station call letters*] (RBYB)
KELE-FM.... Mountain Grove, MO [*FM radio station call letters*] (BROA)
Kel-f......... Polymonochlorotrifluoroethylene (IDOE)
KELG......... Elgin, TX [*AM radio station call letters*]
Kel GA...... Kelly's Reports [*1-3 Georgia*] [*A publication*] (DLA)
Kelh.......... Kelham's Norman French Law Dictionary [*A publication*] (DLA)
Kelham...... Kelham's Norman French Law Dictionary [*A publication*] (DLA)
Kelh Dict.... Kelham's Norman French Law Dictionary [*A publication*] (DLA)
KELI......... Kristana Esperantista Ligo Internacia [*International Christian Esperanto Association*] (EAIO)
KELI......... San Angelo, TX [*FM radio station call letters*]
KELIM....... Kelim, CO [*American Association of Railroads railroad junction routing code*]
K-ELISA..... Kinetic Measurement of Enzyme-Linked Immunosorbant Assay
KELK......... Elko, NV [*AM radio station call letters*]
Kelk Jud Acts... Kelke's Judicature Acts [*A publication*] (DLA)
KELL......... CC Kelley & Sons [*NCIC trailer make code*]
KELL......... Keller Trucking Company [*Common carrier symbol*]
KELL......... Kellstrom Industries [*NASDAQ symbol*] (TTSB)
KELL......... Kellstrom Industries, Inc. [*NASDAQ symbol*] (SAG)
Kellen....... Kellen's Reports [*146-55 Massachusetts*] [*A publication*] (DLA)
Kel Life Ann... Kelly on Life Annuities [*A publication*] (DLA)
KellOG....... Kelley Oil and Gas Corp. [*Associated Press*] (SAG)
Kellogg...... Kellogg Co. [*Associated Press*] (SAG)
KELLOGG.... W.K. Kellogg Foundation Institute (SAUO)
KELLW....... Kellstrom Inds Wrrt [*NASDAQ symbol*] (TTSB)
Kellwood.... Kellwood Co. [*Associated Press*] (SAG)
Kelly......... Kelly's Reports [*1-3 Georgia*] [*A publication*] (DLA)
Kelly & C... Kelly and Cobb's Reports [*4, 5 Georgia*] [*A publication*] (DLA)
Kelly & Cobb... Kelly and Cobb's Reports [*4, 5 Georgia*] [*A publication*] (DLA)
KELLYPAC... Kelly Services Inc. PAC [*Troy, MI*] (PACS)
KellyRus.... Kelly Russell Studios, Inc. [*Associated Press*] (SAG)
KellyS....... Kelly Services, Inc. [*Associated Press*] (SAG)
KELN......... Kell Negative [*Hematology*] (DAVI)
KELN......... North Platte, NE [*FM radio station call letters*]
KELO......... Sioux Falls, SD [*AM radio station call letters*]
KELO-FM.... Sioux Falls, SD [*FM radio station call letters*]
KELO-TV.... Sioux Falls, SD [*Television station call letters*]
KELOW...... Kelowna, BC [*American Association of Railroads railroad junction routing code*]
KELP......... Coronal Emission Line Polarimeter (SAUS)
KELP......... El Paso/International [*Texas*] [*ICAO location identifier*] (ICLI)
KELP......... El Paso, TX [*AM radio station call letters*]
KELP......... Kindergarten Evaluation for Learning Potential [*McGraw Hill*]
KELP......... Mesquite, NM [*FM radio station call letters*] (BROA)
KELR......... Chariton, IA [*FM radio station call letters*]
KELS......... Kelson Engineering Company [*NCIC trailer make code*]
KELS......... Kohlman Evaluation of Living Skills [*Occupational therapy*]
Kel Sc Fac... Kelly's Scire Facias [*2nd ed.*] [*1849*] [*A publication*] (DLA)
Kelstr........ Kellstrom Industries, Inc. [*Associated Press*] (SAG)
Kelstrm..... Kellstrom Industries, Inc. [*Associated Press*] (SAG)
KELT-FM.... Riverside, CA [*FM radio station call letters*] (BROA)
KELTY....... Keltys, TX [*American Association of Railroads railroad junction routing code*]
KELU......... Kelian Equatorial Mining [*Intermodal shipping container symbol*] (TVRC)
KELU......... Kuching Employees and Labourers' Union [*Sarawak*]
Kel Us....... Kelly on Usury [*1835*] [*A publication*] (DLA)
KELY......... Ely, NV [*AM radio station call letters*]
KELY......... Kelly Services, Inc. [*NASDAQ symbol*] (NQ)
KELYA....... Kelly Services'A' [*NASDAQ symbol*] (TTSB)
KELYB....... Kelly Services [*NASDAQ symbol*]
KELYB....... Kelly Services'B' [*NASDAQ symbol*] (TTSB)
KELY-FM.... Ely, NV [*FM radio station call letters*]
KELYOG..... Kelley Oil & Gas Partnership Ltd. (SAUO)
KEm.......... Emporia Public Library, Emporia, KS [*Library symbol*] [*Library of Congress*] (LCLS)
KEM.......... Kemi [*Finland*] [*Airport symbol*] (OAG)
KEM.......... Kemper Corp. [*NYSE symbol*] (SPSG)
KEM.......... Kinetic Energy Missile (INF)
KEMA......... Kansas Emergency Management Association [*Emergency Management*] (EMA)
KEMA......... Kitchen Equipment Manufacturers Association (SAUO)
KEMA-FM... Three Rivers, TX [*FM radio station call letters*] (BROA)
KEMAR...... Knowles Electronics Manikin for Acoustic Research
KEMB......... Emmetsburg, IA [*FM radio station call letters*]
Kemble Sax... Kemble's The Saxons in England [*A publication*] (DLA)
KEMC......... Billings, MT [*FM radio station call letters*]
KEmC......... College of Emporia, Emporia, KS [*Library symbol*] [*Library of Congress*] (LCLS)
KEMC......... Kaiserslautern Equipment Maintenance Center (SAUO)
KEMC......... Kemper Corp. (MHDW)
KEMEDB..... Infection, Inflammation and Immunity (journ.) (SAUS)
Kemet....... Kemet Corp. [*Associated Press*] (SAG)
KEMM......... Commerce, TX [*FM radio station call letters*]
KEMO......... Kennesaw Mountain National Battlefield Park
Kemo Tx.... Chemical Therapy [*or Chemotherapy*] [*Pharmacology*] (DAVI)
KEMP......... Kempf Car Hauler [*NCIC trailer make code*]
Kemper..... Kemper Corp. [*Associated Press*] (SAG)
KEMR......... San Francisco, CA [*FM radio station call letters*] (BROA)
KEMRI....... Kenya Medical Research Institute (BUAC)

KEMRI....... Kenyan Medical Research Institute (SAUO)
KEMS........ Kaiser Engineers Management System (SAUO)
KEmT........ Kansas State Teachers College, Emporia, KS [*Library symbol*] [*Library of Congress*] [*Obsolete*] (LCLS)
KEmU........ Emporia State University, Emporia, KS [*Library symbol*] [*Library of Congress*] (LCLS)
KEMU........ Kemira Polargas [*Intermodal shipping container symbol*] (TVRC)
KEM-V....... Kinetic Energy Missile Vehicle [*Army*]
KEMV........ Mountain View, AR [*Television station call letters*]
KEMX........ Locust Grove, OK [*FM radio station call letters*]
Ken.......... Kendall [*Record label*]
KEN.......... Kenema [*Sierra Leone*] [*Airport symbol*] (OAG)
KEN.......... Kenridge Mineral [*Vancouver Stock Exchange symbol*]
KEN.......... Ken Trailer [*NCIC trailer make code*]
Ken.......... Kentucky (ODBW)
KEN.......... Kentucky
KEN.......... Kenya [*ANSI three-letter standard code*] (CNC)
Ken.......... Kenya (VRA)
KEN.......... Kenyon College, Gambier, OH [*OCLC symbol*] (OCLC)
Ken.......... Kenyon's English King's Bench Reports [*A publication*] (DLA)
KEN.......... National Mental Health Services Knowledge Exchange Network (SAUO)
KENA........ Kenai Corp. (SAUO)
KENA........ Kenosha Auto Transport Corporation [*Common carrier symbol*]
KENA........ Mena, AR [*AM radio station call letters*]
KENA-FM... Mena, AR [*FM radio station call letters*]
Kenan....... Kenan's Reports [*76-91 North Carolina*] [*A publication*] (DLA)
Kenan....... Kenan Transportation Co. [*Associated Press*] (SAG)
KENATCO... Kenya National Transport Co. (BUAC)
KENC........ Kden-Craft Products [*NCIC trailer make code*]
KENC........ Kennecott Copper [*Federal Railroad Administration identification code*]
KENC........ Kentucky Central Life Insurance Co. (SAUO)
KENCLIP.... Kentucky Cooperative Library and Information Project [*Library network*]
KENCO...... Kendrick & Co. [*Telecommunications service*] (TSSD)
KEND........ Enid/Vance Air Force Base [*Oklahoma*] [*ICAO location identifier*] (ICLI)
KEND........ Roswell, NM [*FM radio station call letters*]
KENDA...... Kenya National Democratic Alliance Party (SAUO)
Ken Dec..... Kentucky Decisions (Sneed) [*2 Kentucky*] [*A publication*] (DLA)
KENE........ Toppenish, WA [*AM radio station call letters*]
Kenetech.... Kenetech Corp. [*Associated Press*] (SAG)
KENGO...... Kenya Energy and Environment Organisations (BUAC)
KENI......... Anchorage, AK [*AM radio station call letters*]
Kenkyu Hokoku Sci Pap Cent Res Inst Jap Tob Salt Public Corp... Kenkyu Hokoku. Scientific Papers. Central Research Institute. Japan Tobacco and Salt Public Corporation (SAUO)
Ken LR...... Kentucky Law Reporter [*A publication*] (DLA)
Ken L Re... Kentucky Law Reporter [*A publication*] (DLA)
KENN........ Farmington, NM [*AM radio station call letters*]
KENN........ Kennecott Co. Railroad [*AAR code*]
KENN........ Kennewick School District (SAUO)
KENN........ Kennington Ltd. (SAUO)
KENN........ Kenron Corporation [*NCIC trailer make code*]
Kenn Ch..... Kennedy's Chancery Practice [*2nd ed.*] [*1852-53*] [*A publication*] (DLA)
Kenn C Mar... Kennedy on Courts-Martial [*A publication*] (DLA)
KENNECOTT PAC... Kennecott Holdings Corporation PAC [*Magna, UT*] (PACS)
Kennett...... Kennett's Glossary [*A publication*] (DLA)
Kennett...... Kennett upon Impropriations [*A publication*] (DLA)
Kennett Gloss... Kennett's Glossary [*A publication*] (DLA)
Kennett Par Ant... Kennett's Parochial Antiquities [*A publication*] (DLA)
Kenn Gloss... Kennett's Glossary [*A publication*] (DLA)
Kenn Imp... Kennett upon Impropriations [*A publication*] (DLA)
Kenn Jur... Kennedy on Juries [*A publication*] (DLA)
Kennmtl..... Kennametal, Inc. [*Associated Press*] (SAG)
Kenn Par Antiq... Kennett's Parochial Antiquities [*A publication*] (DLA)
Kenn Pr..... Kennedy's Chancery Practice [*2nd ed.*] [*1852-53*] [*A publication*] (DLA)
keno......... Empty [*Prefix Meaning*] [*Medicine*] (EDAA)
KENO......... Kenskill Trailer Corporation [*NCIC trailer make code*]
KENO......... Las Vegas, NV [*AM radio station call letters*]
Ken Opin.... Kentucky Opinions [*A publication*] (DLA)
Kenora...... Keewatin, Norman, and Rat Portage [*Communities that merged to form town in Ontario, Canada*]
KENOV...... Kenova, WV [*American Association of Railroads railroad junction routing code*]
KENPRO..... Kenyan Committee on Trade Procedures (BUAC)
KENR........ Hudson, TX [*AM radio station call letters*]
Ken R........ Kenyon Review [*A publication*] (BRI)
KENS........ Kenilworth Systems Corp. (SAUO)
KENS........ Kensington [*West London*] (ROG)
KENS........ Kensington [*NCIC truck make code*]
KENS........ San Antonio, TX [*AM radio station call letters*]
KENSE....... Kensett, AR [*American Association of Railroads railroad junction routing code*]
KenseyN.... Kensey Nash Corp. [*Associated Press*] (SAG)
KENSI....... Kensington, IL [*American Association of Railroads railroad junction routing code*]
KENS-TV.... San Antonio, TX [*Television station call letters*]
KENT........ Honolulu, HI [*AM radio station call letters*] (BROA)
KENT........ Kent Financial Services [*NASDAQ symbol*] (SPSG)
KENT........ Kent Financial Svcs [*NASDAQ symbol*] (TTSB)
KENT........ Kent, OH [*American Association of Railroads railroad junction routing code*]
Kent......... Kent's Commentaries on American Law [*A publication*] (DLA)
KENT........ Kentucky Manufacturing Company [*NCIC trailer make code*]
KENT........ Odessa, TX [*AM radio station call letters*]
Kent & R St... Kent and Radcliff's Law of New York, Revision of 1801 [*A publication*] (DLA)
Kentch....... Kenetech Corp. [*Associated Press*] (SAG)
Kent Com... Kent's Commentaries on American Law [*A publication*] (DLA)
Kent Comm... Kent's Commentaries on American Law [*A publication*] (DLA)
Kentekl...... Kentek Information Systems, Inc. [*Associated Press*] (SAG)
KentEl....... Kent Electronics [*Associated Press*] (SAG)
KentEnt...... Kentucky Enterprise Bancorp [*Associated Press*] (SAG)
KENT-FM.... Odessa, TX [*FM radio station call letters*]
KentFn...... Kent Financial Services, Inc. [*Associated Press*] (SAG)
KENTING.... Kenting Earth Sciences (SAUS)
KENTL....... Kentland, IN [*American Association of Railroads railroad junction routing code*]
Kent's Commen... Kent's Commentaries on American Law [*A publication*] (DLA)
Kent St U... Kent State University (GAGS)
KENU........ Enumclaw, WA [*AM radio station call letters*]
KENV........ Wendover Auxiliary Air Base (SAUS)
KENV........ Wendover/Wendover Auxiliary Air Base [*Utah*] [*ICAO location identifier*] (ICLI)
KENV-TV.... Elko, NV [*TV station call letters*] (RBYB)
KENW........ Kenway Campers [*NCIC trailer make code*]
KENW........ Portales, NM [*FM radio station call letters*]
KENWIN..... Kenwin Shops, Inc. (SAUO)
KENW-TV... Portales, NM [*Television station call letters*]
Ke:nx........ Connects [*Macintosh*] [*Computer science*]
Keny......... Kenyon's English King's Bench Reports [*A publication*] (DLA)
KENYA....... Kenney Yark, PA [*American Association of Railroads railroad junction routing code*]
Kenya LR... Kenya Law Reports [*A publication*] (DLA)
Keny Ch..... Chancery Cases [*2 Notes of King's Bench Cases*] [*England*] [*A publication*] (DLA)
KENZ........ Kennesaw [*Federal Railroad Administration identification code*]
KENZ-FM.... Orem, UT [*FM radio station call letters*] (RBYB)
KEO.......... Keld'Or Resources, Inc. [*Vancouver Stock Exchange symbol*]
KEO.......... King Edward's Own [*British military*] (DMA)
KEO.......... Odienne [*Ivory Coast*] [*Airport symbol*] (OAG)
KEOC........ King Edward's Own Cavalry [*British military*] (DMA)
KEOG........ King Edward VII Own Gurkhas (SAUO)
KEOJ........ Caney, KS [*FM radio station call letters*]
KEOK........ Tahlequah, OK [*FM radio station call letters*]
KEOKU...... Keokuk, IA [*American Association of Railroads railroad junction routing code*]
KEOL........ King Edward's Own Lancers [*British military*] (DMA)
KEOL........ La Grande, OR [*FM radio station call letters*]
KEOM........ Mesquite, TX [*FM radio station call letters*]
KEOR........ Atoka, OK [*AM radio station call letters*]
KEOS........ College Station, TX [*FM radio station call letters*] (RBYB)
KEOT-FM.... St. George, UT [*FM radio station call letters*] (BROA)
KEP.......... Kaneb Energy Partners Ltd. (MHDW)
KEP.......... Kellner Eye Piece
KEP.......... Key Entry Processing
KEP.......... King Edward Point [*South Georgia Island*] [*Seismograph station code, US Geological Survey*] (SEIS)
KEP.......... Knight of the Eagle and Pelican [*Freemasonry*]
KEP.......... Korea Electric Power ADS [*NYSE symbol*] (TTSB)
KEP.......... Korea Electric Power Corp. [*NYSE symbol*] (SAG)
KEP.......... Nepalganj [*Nepal*] [*Airport symbol*] (OAG)
KEPA........ Kansas Emergency Preparedness Association [*Emergency Management*] (EMA)
KEPB........ Eugene, OR [*Television station call letters*]
KE/PB....... Kaiser Engineers, Inc./Parsons Brinckerhoff Quade & Douglas, Inc. (SAUO)
KEPC........ Colorado Springs, CO [*FM radio station call letters*]
KEPCO...... Korea Electric Power Corp.
KEPCO...... Kyushu Electric Power Company (SAUO)
KEPD........ Kinetic Energy Penetrator Destructor (SAUS)
KEPE........ Kentron Programmatismou kai Oikonomikon Ereunon [*Centre of Planning and Economic Research*] [*Greece*]
KEPG........ Victoria, TX [*FM radio station call letters*]
kephal...... Head [*Prefix Meaning*] [*Medicine*] (EDAA)
KEPI......... Eagle Pass, TX [*FM radio station call letters*] (RBYB)
KEPOA...... Keep This Office Advised
KEPR........ Pasco, WA [*Television station call letters*]
KEPROM.... Keyed-Access, Erasable, Programmable Read-Only Memory [*Computer science*]
KEPRU...... Keele European Parties Research Unit [*Keele University*] [*United Kingdom*] (RCD)
KEPS........ Eagle Pass, TX [*AM radio station call letters*]
KEPT........ Kempter Trailer [*NCIC trailer make code*]
KEPX........ Eagle Pass, TX [*FM radio station call letters*]
KEPZ........ Kaohsiung Export Processing Zone [*Reexport manufacturing complex*] [*Taiwan*]
KEPZ........ Kentucky Powder [*Federal Railroad Administration identification code*]
KEQ.......... Kamar [*Language symbol*] (ETLW)
KEQ.......... Kebar [*Indonesia*] [*Airport symbol*] (OAG)
KEQU........ Kewaunee Scientific [*NASDAQ symbol*] (TTSB)
KEQU........ Kewaunee Scientific Corp. [*Formerly, Kewaunee Science Equipment*] [*NASDAQ symbol*] (NQ)
Ker.......... Indian Law Reports, Kerala Series [*A publication*] (DLA)

Ker .... Kerithoth (BJA)
Ker .... Keritot [*Religion*] [*Judaism*]
KER .... Kerman [*Iran*] [*Airport symbol*] (OAG)
KER .... Kermanshah [*Iran*] [*Seismograph station code, US Geological Survey*] (SEIS)
KER .... Kerr-Addison Mines [*TS, exchange symbol*] (TTSB)
KER .... Kerr Addison Mines Ltd. [*Toronto Stock Exchange symbol*]
KER .... Kerry [*County in Ireland*] (ROG)
KER .... Kinetic Energy Release
KERA .... Dallas, TX [*FM radio station call letters*]
KERA .... Kentucky Education Reform Act
Kera .... Keratitis [*Ophthalmology*] (DAVI)
KERA .... KeraVision, Inc. [*NASDAQ symbol*] (SAG)
Kerala .... All Indian Law Reports, Kerala Series [*A publication*] (DLA)
Kerala LJ ... Kerala Law Journal [*A publication*] (DLA)
KERA-TV .... Dallas, TX [*Television station call letters*]
KeraVis ..... KeraVision, Inc. [*Associated Press*] (SAG)
KeraVs ...... KeraVision, Inc. [*Associated Press*] (SAG)
KERB .... Kermit, TX [*AM radio station call letters*]
KERB-FM ... Kermit, TX [*FM radio station call letters*]
KERC .... Marked Tree, AR [*FM radio station call letters*]
KERD .... Kinetic Energy Release Distribution [*Of ions for spectral studies*]
KERE .... Atchison, KS [*AM radio station call letters*]
KERE .... Kuroshio Extension Regional Experiment (SAUO)
KERE-FM.... Horton, KS [*FM radio station call letters*]
KEREN-OR... Jerusalem Institutions for the Blind (EA)
KERI .... Kia Economic Research Institute
KERI .... Wasco, CA [*AM radio station call letters*]
KERIS .... Kiel Ecosystem Research Information System (SAUO)
KERIS .... Korea Education and Research Information Service
KERKHFF ... Kerkhoff Industries Inc. (SAUO)
KERM........ Torrington, WY [*FM radio station call letters*]
KERMA...... Kinetic Energy Released in Materials (ACAE)
KERMA...... Kinetic Energy Released per Unit Mass (DEN)
KERN .... Bakersfield, CA [*AM radio station call letters*]
Kern .... Kernan's Reports [*11-14 New York*] [*A publication*] (DLA)
Kern .... Kern's Reports [*100-116 Indiana*] [*A publication*] (DLA)
KERN-FM ... Bakersfield, CA [*FM radio station call letters*]
KERO .... Bakersfield, CA [*Television station call letters*]
KERO .... Kerosine [*British*]
KERO .... Kuwait Emergency Recovery Office (SAUO)
KERP .... Kuwait Emergency Recovery Programme (SAUS)
KERP .... Pueblo, CO [*FM radio station call letters*]
Kerr.......... Kerr Group [*Associated Press*] (SAG)
KERR .... Kerrier [*England*]
Kerr.......... Kerr's New Brunswick Reports [*A publication*] (DLA)
Kerr.......... Kerr's Reports [*18-22 Indiana*] [*A publication*] (DLA)
Kerr.......... Kerr's Reports [*27-29 New York Civil Procedure*] [*A publication*] (DLA)
KERR .... Kerr, TX [*American Association of Railroads railroad junction routing code*]
KERR .... Kinetic Energy Recovery Rope (SAUS)
KERR .... Polson, MT [*AM radio station call letters*]
Kerr Act..... Kerr's Actions at Law [*3rd ed.*] [*1861*] [*A publication*] (DLA)
Kerr Anc L... Kerr on Ancient Lights [*A publication*] (DLA)
Kerr Black... Kerr's Blackstone [*12th ed.*] [*1895*] [*A publication*] (DLA)
Kerr Disc ... Kerr's Discovery [*1870*] [*A publication*] (DLA)
Kerr Ext ..... Kerr on Inter-State Extradition [*A publication*] (DLA)
Kerr F & M... Kerr's Fraud and Mistake [*7th ed.*] [*1952*] [*A publication*] (DLA)
Kerr Fr ...... Kerr's Fraud and Mistake [*7th ed.*] [*1952*] [*A publication*] (DLA)
KerrGp ...... Kerr Group [*Associated Press*] (SAG)
Kerr Inj...... Kerr on Injunctions [*A publication*] (DLA)
KerrMc...... Kerr McGee Corp. [*Associated Press*] (SAG)
Kerr (NB) ... Kerr's New Brunswick Reports [*A publication*] (DLA)
Kerr Rec .... Kerr on Receivers [*A publication*] (DLA)
Kerr Stu Black... Kerr's Student's Blackstone [*A publication*] (DLA)
Kerr W & M Cas... Kerr's Water and Mineral Cases [*A publication*] (DLA)
Kerse........ Kerse's Manuscript Decisions, Scotch Court of Session [*A publication*] (DLA)
KERU .... Kerr Steamship [*Intermodal shipping container symbol*] (TVRC)
KERU .... Kerr Steamship Company [*Common carrier symbol*]
KERUK-NASI... Kerukunan Nasional [*Campaign for National Harmony*] [*Indonesia*]
KERV .... Kentucky Equine Respiratory Virus [*Veterinary science*] (DMAA)
KERV .... Kerrville, TX [*AM radio station call letters*]
Kerwin ...... Kerwin Shops, Inc. [*Associated Press*] (SAG)
KERX .... Kentucky River Coal [*Federal Railroad Administration identification code*]
KERX .... Paris, AR [*FM radio station call letters*]
KERZ .... Kerr Steamship [*Common carrier symbol*]
KES .... Karg-Elert Society (BUAC)
KES .... Key Element Search (MCD)
KES .... Keystone Consolidated Industries, Inc. [*NYSE symbol*] (SPSG)
KES .... Keystone Consol Ind [*NYSE symbol*] (TTSB)
KES .... Knigovedenie: Entsiklopedicheskil Slovar [*A publication*]
KES .... Knowledge Engineering System [*Software Architecture and Engineering Inc.*] (NITA)
KES .... Ksar Es Souk [*Seismograph station code, US Geological Survey*] [*Closed*] (SEIS)
KES .... Kvakera Esperantista Societo [*Quaker Esperanto Society - QES*] (EAIO)
KESAB....... Keep South Australia Beautiful (SAUO)
KESC .... Karachi Electric Supply Corporation (SAUO)
KESC-FM.... Wilburton, OK [*FM radio station call letters*] (BROA)
KESCO....... Kowloon Electricity Supply Company (SAUO)
KESD .... Brookings, SD [*FM radio station call letters*]
KESD-TV .... Brookings, SD [*Television station call letters*]
KESE......... Bentonville-Bella Vista, AR [*AM radio station call letters*] (RBYB)
KESF......... Alexandria/Esler Field [*Louisiana*] [*ICAO location identifier*] (ICLI)
KESFF .... Kinetic Energy Self Forging Fragments (ACAE)
KESH .... State Electricity Cooperative of Albania (BUAC)
KESI .... Kentucky Electric Steel [*NASDAQ symbol*] (TTSB)
KESI .... Kentucky Electric Steel Co. [*NASDAQ symbol*] (SAG)
KESI .... Kurzweil Educational Systems, Inc.
KESM........ El Dorado Springs, MO [*AM radio station call letters*]
KESM-FM... El Dorado Springs, MO [*FM radio station call letters*]
KESN .... Allen, TX [*FM radio station call letters*] (BROA)
KESO-FM ... South Padre Island, TX [*FM radio station call letters*] (BROA)
KESP-AM ... Modesto, CA [*AM radio station call letters*] (BROA)
KESP-FM.... Payson, AZ [*FM radio station call letters*] (BROA)
KESQ .... Indio, CA [*AM radio station call letters*] (BROA)
KESQ .... Keystone Lawrence Express [*Common carrier symbol*]
KESQ .... Palm Springs, CA [*Television station call letters*]
KESR .... Shasta Lake City, CA [*FM radio station call letters*] (BROA)
KESS .... Fort Worth, TX [*AM radio station call letters*]
KESS .... Kesselring Site [*Knolls Atomic Power Laboratory*] (GAAI)
KESS .... Kinetic Energy Storage System
KEST......... Kestrel Energy [*NASDAQ symbol*] (TTSB)
KEST......... Kestrel Energy, Inc. [*NASDAQ symbol*] (SAG)
KEST......... San Francisco, CA [*AM radio station call letters*]
Kestrel ...... Kestrel Energy, Inc. [*Associated Press*] (SAG)
KESY .... Cuba, MO [*FM radio station call letters*] (BROA)
KESY .... Omaha, NE [*FM radio station call letters*]
KESZ......... Phoenix, AZ [*FM radio station call letters*]
KET .... Cat Kargo Hava Tasima, AS [*Turkey*] [*FAA designator*] (FAAC)
KET .... Kengtung [*Myanmar*] [*Airport symbol*] (OAG)
KET .... Keravat [*New Britain*] [*Seismograph station code, US Geological Survey*] [*Closed*] (SEIS)
KET .... Ketamine [*An anesthetic*]
Ket........... Kethuboth (BJA)
Ket........... Ketubbot [*Religion*] [*Judaism*]
KET .... Kiel Electron Telescope
KET .... Krypton Exposure Technique (MCD)
KETA......... Kenya External Trade Authority (BUAC)
KETA......... Oklahoma City, OK [*Television station call letters*]
KETAL .... Kalamazoo Area Library Consortium [*Library network*]
KET BD...... Ketone Bodies [*Endocrinology*] (DAVI)
KETC......... Kealy Trucking Company [*Common carrier symbol*]
KETC......... St. Louis, MO [*Television station call letters*]
KETD .... Darren Kent Trucking Company [*Common carrier symbol*]
KETG .... Arkadelphia, AR [*Television station call letters*]
KETH .... Houston, TX [*Television station call letters*]
Keth .... Kethuboth (BJA)
KETK......... Jacksonville, TX [*Television station call letters*]
keto.......... Ketosteroid [*Endocrinology*]
KETO-AM ... Rupert, ID [*AM radio station call letters*] (BROA)
KE-TP........ Kinetic Energy-Training Projectile (MCD)
KETR .... Commerce, TX [*FM radio station call letters*]
KETRI........ Kenya Trypanosomiasis Research Institute
KETS......... Little Rock, AR [*Television station call letters*]
K'ETTE ...... Kitchenette [*Classified advertising*] (ADA)
KETV......... Omaha, NE [*Television station call letters*]
KETX......... Livingston, TX [*AM radio station call letters*]
KETX-FM.... Livingston, TX [*FM radio station call letters*]
KEU .... Eastern Kentucky University, Richmond, KY [*OCLC symbol*] (OCLC)
KEUG-FM ... Cottage Grove, OR [*FM radio station call letters*] (BROA)
KEUL-FM.... Girdwood, AK [*FM radio station call letters*] (BROA)
KEUN .... Eunice, LA [*AM radio station call letters*]
KEV .... Kevo [*Finland*] [*Seismograph station code, US Geological Survey*] (SEIS)
keV .... Kiloelectron Unit (ADWA)
KEV .... Kilo Electron Volt (AAEL)
KeV .... Kiloelectron Volt (ABAC)
KEV .... Kinetic Energy Vehicle (ACAE)
KEV .... King's Empire Veterans [*British military*] (DMA)
KEV .... Komisarstvo za Evreiskiie Vuprosi [*Bulgaria*] (BJA)
KEVA......... Evanston, WY [*AM radio station call letters*]
KEVAS....... Key Educational Vocational Assessment System (TES)
KEVEVAPI... Kenyan Veterinary Vaccines Production Institute (SAUO)
KEVII .... King Edward VII [*British*]
KEVIII........ King Edward VIII [*British*]
Kevlin .... Kevlin Corp. [*Associated Press*] (SAG)
KEVN .... Kimmins Environmental Service Corp. (SAUO)
KEVN .... Rapid City, SD [*Television station call letters*]
KEVR .... La Junta, CO [*FM radio station call letters*] (BROA)
KEVT......... Cortaro, AZ [*AM radio station call letters*]
KEVU .... Eugene, OR [*Television station call letters*]
KEVX .... Kevex Corp. (SAUO)
KEW .... Kew [*England*] [*Seismograph station code, US Geological Survey*] [*Closed*] (SEIS)
KEW .... Kewatin
keW.......... Kiloelectron Watt
KEW .... Kinetic Energy Weapons [*Military*] (RDA)
KEWAU...... Kewaunee, WI [*American Association of Railroads railroad junction routing code*]
KEWB........ Anderson, CA [*FM radio station call letters*]
KEWB........ Kinetic Experiment on Water Boiler [*Nuclear reactor*]
Kew Bull.... Kew Bulletin (SAUO)

KEWC........ Kinetic Energy Weapon, Chemically Propelled (ACAE)
KEWE........ Kinetic Energy Weapon, Electromagnetically Propelled (ACAE)
KEWE........ Oroville, CA [*FM radio station call letters*]
KEWG........ Kinetic Energy Weapon, Ground (ACAE)
KEWH........ Kewash Railroad [*Federal Railroad Administration identification code*]
KEWI........ Benton, AR [*AM radio station call letters*]
KEWL........ New Boston, TX [*FM radio station call letters*] (RBYB)
KEWL........ Texarkana, TX [*AM radio station call letters*] (BROA)
KEWN........ New Bern/Simmons-Nott [*North Carolina*] [*ICAO location identifier*] (ICLI)
KewnSc..... Kewaunee Scientific Corp. [*Associated Press*] (SAG)
KEWO........ Kinetic Energy Weapon, Orbital (ACAE)
KEWR........ Newark/International [*New Jersey*] [*ICAO location identifier*] (ICLI)
KEWS........ Koger Equity Wrrt [*AMEX symbol*] (TTSB)
KEWS-AM... Portland, OR [*AM radio station call letters*] (BROA)
KEWS-FM... Arlington, TX [*FM radio station call letters*] (RBYB)
KEWU........ Cheney, WA [*FM radio station call letters*]
KEX.......... Kanabea [*Papua New Guinea*] [*Airport symbol*] (OAG)
KEX.......... Kirby Corp. [*AMEX symbol*] (SPSG)
KEX.......... Portland, OR [*AM radio station call letters*]
KEXD........ Kirby Exploration Co. , Inc. (SAUO)
KEXL........ Norfolk, NE [*FM radio station call letters*]
KEXO........ Grand Junction, CO [*AM radio station call letters*]
KEXP-FM.... Seattle, WA [*FM radio station call letters*] (BROA)
KEXS........ Excelsior Springs, MO [*AM radio station call letters*]
KEXT........ Bosque Farms, NM [*FM radio station call letters*] (RBYB)
KEXX-FM.... Llano, TX [*FM radio station call letters*] (BROA)
KEY.......... Key [*Commonly used*] (OPSA)
KEY.......... Key Anacon Mines Ltd. [*Toronto Stock Exchange symbol*]
KEY.......... KeyCorp [*NYSE symbol*] (SPSG)
Key.......... Keyes' New York Court of Appeals Reports [*A publication*] (DLA)
Key.......... Of Illicit Drug [*Medicine*] (EDAA)
KEYA........ Belcourt, ND [*FM radio station call letters*]
Key & Elph Conv... Key and Elphinstone's Conveyancing [*15th ed.*] [*1953-54*] [*A publication*] (DLA)
KEYB........ Altus, OK [*FM radio station call letters*]
KEYB........ Keyboard Carriage [*Common carrier symbol*]
KEYBBE..... foreign language KEYBoard program-BElgium (SAUS)
KEYBBR..... Foreign language KEYBoard program - Brazil (SAUS)
KEYBCF..... foreign language KEYBoard program-Canadian-French (SAUS)
KEYBCZ..... Foreign language KEYBoard program - Czechoslovakia (Czech) (SAUS)
KEYBD....... Keyboard [*Computer science*]
KEYBDF..... foreign language KEYBoard program-Denmark (SAUS)
KEYBDK..... Foreign language KEYBoard program-Denmark (SAUS)
KEYBFR..... foreign language KEYBoard program-FRance (SAUS)
KEYBGR..... Foreign language KEYBoard program - Germany (SAUS)
KEYBHU..... foreign language KEYBoard program-HUngary (SAUS)
KEYBIT...... Foreign language KEYBoard program - Italy (SAUS)
KEYBLA..... foreign language KEYBoard program-Latin America (SAUS)
KEYBNL..... Foreign language KEYBoard program - Netherlands (SAUS)
KEYBNO..... foreign language KEYBoard program-NOrway (SAUS)
KEYBPL..... Foreign language KEYBoard program - Poland (SAUS)
KEYBPO..... foreign language KEYBoard program-Portugal (SAUS)
KEYBSF..... Foreign language KEYBoard program - Swiss-French (SAUS)
KEYBSG..... foreign language KEYBoard program-Swiss-German (SAUS)
KEYBSL..... Foreign language KEYBoard program - Czechoslovakia (Slovak) (SAUS)
KEYBSP..... foreign language KEYBoard program-SPain (SAUS)
KEYBSU..... Foreign language KEYBoard program - Finland (SAUS)
KEYBSV..... foreign language KEYBoard program-Sweden (SAUS)
KEYBUK..... Foreign language KEYBoard program - United Kingdom (SAUS)
KEYBUS..... foreign language KEYBoard program-United States (SAUS)
KEYBYU..... Foreign language KEYBoard program - Yugoslavia (SAUS)
KEYC........ Key Centurion Bancshares (EFIS)
KEYC........ Key Centurion Bancshares, Inc. (SAUO)
KEYC........ Mankato, MN [*Television station call letters*]
KEYCA....... Keystone Camera Products Corp. (SAUO)
Key Ch...... Keyes on Future Interest in Chattels [*A publication*] (DLA)
KeyCon...... Keystone Consolidated Industries [*Associated Press*] (SAG)
Keycorp..... Keycorp [*Associated Press*] (SAG)
Keycp....... Keycorp [*Associated Press*] (SAG)
KEYE........ Perryton, TX [*AM radio station call letters*]
KEYE-FM.... Perryton, TX [*FM radio station call letters*]
KeyEng...... Key Energy Group [*Associated Press*] (SAG)
Keyes........ Keyes' New York Court of Appeals Reports [*A publication*] (DLA)
KEYE-TV.... Austin, TX [*Television station call letters*] (RBYB)
KEYF........ Cheney, WA [*FM radio station call letters*]
KEYF........ Dishman, WA [*AM radio station call letters*]
KeyFn....... Keyston Financial, Inc. [*Associated Press*] (SAG)
KEYG........ Grand Coulee, WA [*AM radio station call letters*]
KEYG-FM... Grand Coulee, WA [*FM radio station call letters*]
KEYH........ Houston, TX [*AM radio station call letters*]
KEYI......... Key Industries [*NCIC trailer make code*]
KEYI......... San Marcos, TX [*FM radio station call letters*]
KeyInt....... Keystone International [*Associated Press*] (SAG)
KEYJ......... Abilene, TX [*FM radio station call letters*]
Keyl.......... Keylway's [*or Keilway's*] English King's Bench Reports [*A publication*] (DLA)
KEYL......... Long Prairie, MN [*AM radio station call letters*]
Key Lands... Keyes on Future Interest in Lands [*A publication*] (DLA)
Keylway..... Keylway's [*or Keilway's*] English King's Bench Reports [*A publication*] (DLA)
KEYMA...... Keymar, MD [*American Association of Railroads railroad junction routing code*]
KEYMAT..... Keying Material [*Computer science*] (NVT)
KEYN........ Wichita, KS [*FM radio station call letters*]
KEYO........ Keystone Trailer & Equipment Company [*NCIC trailer make code*]
KEY PAC.... Key Plastics LLC PAC [*Northville, MI*] (PACS)
KEYPAC..... Keyspan Energy PAC [*Brooklyn, NY*] (PACS)
keypal....... Internet Penpal (ADWA)
KEYPER..... Keywords Permuted (DIT)
KEYPrA...... KeyCorp 10% cm Dep Pfd [*NYSE symbol*] (TTSB)
KeyPrd...... Key Production Co., Inc. [*Associated Press*] (SAG)
KEYPWR.... Key Power [*Automotive engineering*]
KEYQ........ Fresno, CA [*AM radio station call letters*]
KEYR........ Marlin, TX [*FM radio station call letters*]
Key Rem.... Keyes on Remainders [*A publication*] (DLA)
KEYS........ Corpus Christi, TX [*AM radio station call letters*]
KEYS........ FFTF access control keycard system (SAUS)
KEYS........ Keys [*Commonly used*] (OPSA)
KEYS........ Keystone Automotive Industries, Inc. [*NASDAQ symbol*] (SAG)
KEYS........ Keystone Coach [*NCIC trailer make code*]
KeysAut..... Keystone Automotive Industries, Inc. [*Associated Press*] (SAG)
KeysHer..... Keystone Heritage Group, Inc. [*Associated Press*] (SAG)
Keys St Ex... Keyser's Stock Exchange [*1850*] [*A publication*] (DLA)
KeystFn..... Keystone Financial [*Associated Press*] (SAG)
KEYSTN..... Keystone
KEYSTONE PAC... Keystone Consolidated Industries Inc. PAC [*Peoria, IL*] (PACS)
KEYT......... Santa Barbara, CA [*Television station call letters*]
KeyTech..... Key Technology, Inc. [*Associated Press*] (SAG)
KEYTECT.... Keyword Detection (NITA)
Key Trn...... Key Tronics Corp. [*Associated Press*] (SAG)
KEYV........ Las Vegas, NV [*FM radio station call letters*]
KEYW........ Key West/Key West International [*Florida*] [*ICAO location identifier*] (ICLI)
KEYW........ Pasco, WA [*FM radio station call letters*]
KEYY........ Provo, UT [*AM radio station call letters*]
KEYZ......... Williston, ND [*AM radio station call letters*]
KEZ.......... Kiester Elevator [*Federal Railroad Administration identification code*]
KEZA........ Fayetteville, AR [*FM radio station call letters*]
KEZB........ Hempstead, TX [*FM radio station call letters*]
KEZC........ Yuma, AZ [*AM radio station call letters*]
KEZD........ Windsor, CA [*AM radio station call letters*]
KEZE........ Spokane, WA [*FM radio station call letters*] (GDPB)
KEZE-FM.... Spokane, WA [*FM radio station call letters*] (RBYB)
KEZF......... Tigard, OR [*AM radio station call letters*]
KEZF-FM.... Albuquerque, NM [*FM radio station call letters*] (BROA)
KEZG........ Lincoln, NE [*FM radio station call letters*]
KEZH........ Hastings, NE [*FM radio station call letters*]
KEZI......... Eugene, OR [*Television station call letters*]
KEZJ......... Twin Falls, ID [*AM radio station call letters*]
KEZJ-FM.... Twin Falls, ID [*FM radio station call letters*]
KEZK........ St. Louis, MO [*FM radio station call letters*]
KEZL......... Fowler, CA [*FM radio station call letters*]
KEZM........ Sulphur, LA [*AM radio station call letters*]
KEZN........ Palm Desert, CA [*FM radio station call letters*]
KEZO........ Omaha, NE [*AM radio station call letters*]
KEZO-FM.... Omaha, NE [*FM radio station call letters*]
KEZP......... Bunkie, LA [*FM radio station call letters*]
KEZQ........ Little Rock, AR [*AM radio station call letters*] (RBYB)
KEZQ........ Sheridan, AR [*FM radio station call letters*]
KEZQ-FM.... Island Park, ID [*FM radio station call letters*] (BROA)
KEZQ-FM.... West Yellowstone, MT [*FM radio station call letters*] (BROA)
KEZR........ San Jose, CA [*FM radio station call letters*]
KEZS........ Cape Girardeau, MO [*FM radio station call letters*]
KEZT......... Ames, IA [*FM radio station call letters*]
KEZU........ Booneville, AR [*FM radio station call letters*]
KEZW........ Aurora, CO [*AM radio station call letters*]
KEZX........ Seattle, WA [*AM radio station call letters*]
KEZY........ Anaheim, CA [*FM radio station call letters*]
KEZY-AM.... San Bernardino, CA [*AM radio station call letters*] (BROA)
KEZZ........ Aitkin, MN [*FM radio station call letters*]
KEZZ........ Estes Park, CO [*AM radio station call letters*] (BROA)
KF............ Catskill Airways [*ICAO designator*] (AD)
KF............ Confer [*Telegraphy*] (PCTE)
KF............ Cooperative Movement (Sweden) [*Political party*] (PSAP)
KF............ Family Key (SAUS)
KF............ Fiji [*IYRU nationality code*] (IYR)
kf............ Flocculation Speed in Antigen-Antibody Reactions [*Immunology*] (DAVI)
KF............ Gold Coast Judgments and the Masai Cases, by King-Farlow [*1915-17*] [*Ghana*] [*A publication*] (DLA)
KF............ Karl Fischer [*Reagent*] [*Analytical chemistry*]
KF............ Kaufbeuren [*German license plate city code*]
KF............ Kellogg Foundation (SAUO)
KF............ Kenner-Fecal Medium [*Organic chemistry*] (DAVI)
KF............ Kent Foundation (SAUO)
KF............ Keramos Fraternity [*An association*] (NTPA)
KF............ Kerr-Fourier [*Imaging*]
KF............ Key Field
KF............ Key File [*Computer science*] (ELAL)
KF............ Kidney Foundation (SAUO)
KF............ Kidney Function [*Nephrology*] (DAVI)
KF............ KIDS Fund (EA)
KF............ Kleine Flote [*Piccolo*] [*German*]
KF............ Klenow Fragment [*Genetics*]

KF Klippel-Feil [*Syndrome*] [*Neurology*] (DAVI)
KF Knight of Ferdinand [*Spain*]
KF Knudsen Flow [*Physics*]
KF Koff [*Type of ship*] (DS)
KF Koinonia Foundation (EA)
KF Konservative Folkeparti [*Conservative People's Party (Commonly called the Conservative Party)*] [*Denmark*] [*Political party*] (PPE)
KF Kontrafagott [*Double Bassoon*] [*Organ stop*] [*Music*]
KF Korea Fund, Inc. [*NYSE symbol*] (SPSG)
KF Kosciuszko Foundation (EA)
KF Kossuth Foundation (EA)
K+F Kummerly + Frey AG (SAUS)
KF Potassium Fluoride (SAUS)
KF Rhine Air AG [*Sweden*] [*ICAO designator*] (ICDA)
KFA Keep Fit Association [*British*]
KFA Kelowna Flightcraft Air Charter Ltd. [*Canada*] [*ICAO designator*] (FAAC)
KFA Kenya Farmers Association (BUAC)
KFA Kernforschungsanlage [*Julich, Germany*]
KFA Kershner Family Association (EA)
KFA Kiffa [*Mauritania*] [*Airport symbol*] (OAG)
KFA Kilts Family Association (EA)
KFA Kinesthetic Figural Aftereffects [*Also, KFAE*] [*Psychometrics*]
KFA Kjaerulf Family Association (EA)
KFA Krishnamurti Foundation of America (EA)
KFAA Rogers, AR [*Television station call letters*]
KFAB Kidney-Fixing Antibody [*Immunology*]
KFAB Kindred, ND [*FM radio station call letters*] (BROA)
KFAB Omaha, NE [*AM radio station call letters*]
KFAC Santa Barbara, CA [*FM radio station call letters*]
KFAD Alexandria, LA [*FM radio station call letters*]
KFAE Kinesthetic Figural Aftereffects [*Also, KFA*] [*Psychometrics*]
KFAE Richland, WA [*FM radio station call letters*]
KFAED Kuwait Fund for Arab Economic Development
KFAI Minneapolis, MN [*FM radio station call letters*]
KFAL Fulton, MO [*AM radio station call letters*]
KFAM Keyed File Access Method [*Computer science*] (PDAA)
KFAM North Salt Lake City, UT [*AM radio station call letters*]
KFAN Johnson City, TX [*FM radio station call letters*]
KFAN Minneapolis, MN [*AM radio station call letters*]
KF&R Knight, Frank & Rutley (WDAA)
KFAO Knee-Foot-Ankel Orthosis [*Orthopedics*] (DAVI)
KFAQ Tulsa, OK [*AM radio station call letters*] (BROA)
KFAR Fairbanks, AK [*AM radio station call letters*]
KFAS Casa Grande, AZ [*AM radio station call letters*]
KFAS Keyed File Access System
KFAS Kuwait Foundation for the Advancemenent of Sciences (SAUO)
KFAS Kuwait Foundation for the Advancement of Science (BUAC)
KFASSR Karelo-Finnish Autonomous Soviet Socialist Republic (SAUO)
K-FAST Kaufman Functional Academic Skills Test (TMMY)
KFAT Corvallis, OR [*FM radio station call letters*]
KFAT Fresno/Fresno Air Terminal [*California*] [*ICAO location identifier*] (ICLI)
KFAT National Union of Knitwear, Footwear and Apparel Trades [*United Kingdom*] (EAIO)
KFAT-FM Anchorage, AK [*FM radio station call letters*] (BROA)
KFAV Warrenton, MO [*FM radio station call letters*]
KFAX San Francisco, CA [*AM radio station call letters*]
KFAY Bentonville, AR [*FM radio station call letters*] (RBYB)
KFAY Farmington, AR [*AM radio station call letters*]
KFB Air Botnia OY, AB, Finland [*FAA designator*] (FAAC)
KFB Bethany College, Lindsborg, KS [*OCLC symbol*] (OCLC)
KFB Kuwait French Bank
KFB Northwestern Kolami [*Language symbol*] (ETLW)
KFBB Great Falls, MT [*Television station call letters*]
KFBC Cheyenne, WY [*AM radio station call letters*]
KFBD Waynesville, MO [*FM radio station call letters*]
KFBG Fort Bragg/Simons Auxiliary Air Base [*North Carolina*] [*ICAO location identifier*] (ICLI)
KfBH Kaufman & Broad Home Corp. [*Associated Press*] (SAG)
KFBI Klamath First Bancorp [*NASDAQ symbol*] (TTSB)
KFBI Klamath First Bancorp, Inc. [*NASDAQ symbol*] (SAG)
KFBI Pahrump, NV [*FM radio station call letters*]
KFBK Sacramento, CA [*AM radio station call letters*]
KFBN Lincoln, NE [*FM radio station call letters*]
KFBN-FM Fargo, ND [*FM radio station call letters*] (BROA)
KFBQ Cheyenne, WY [*FM radio station call letters*]
KFBT Las Vegas, NV [*Television station call letters*]
KFBZ K & F Brick [*Federal Railroad Administration identification code*]
KFBZ-FM Haysville, KS [*FM radio station call letters*] (BROA)
KFC Conference [*Telegraphy*] (PCTE)
KFC Kajagoogoo Fan Club [*Defunct*] (EA)
KFC Katholieke Film-Centrale [*Netherlands*]
KFC Kentfield [*California*] [*Seismograph station code, US Geological Survey*] (SEIS)
KFC Kentucky Fried Chicken Corp. [*Later, KFC Corp.*] (ADA)
KFC Korea Friendship Committee [*British*] (EAIO)
KFC Kropp Forge Company (SAUO)
KFCA Conway, AR [*AM radio station call letters*]
KFCB Concord, CA [*Television station call letters*]
KFCC Bay City, TX [*AM radio station call letters*] (RBYB)
KFCF Fresno, CA [*FM radio station call letters*]
KFCI Knife and Fork Club International (EA)
KFCM Cherokee Village, AR [*FM radio station call letters*]
KFCR Custer, SD [*AM radio station call letters*]
KFCT Fort Collins, CO [*FM radio station call letters*]
KFCX-FM Weston, ID [*FM radio station call letters*] (BROA)
KFCZ Kent Feed [*Federal Railroad Administration identification code*]
KFD Conferred [*Telegraphy*] (PCTE)
KFD Key Financial Data (ADA)
KFD Kinetic Family Drawing [*Psychology*]
KFD Kyasanur Forest Disease
KFDA Amarillo, TX [*Television station call letters*]
KFDC Washington/National Flight Data Center [*District of Columbia*] [*ICAO location identifier*] (ICLI)
KFDF Van Buren, AR [*AM radio station call letters*]
KFDI Wichita, KS [*AM radio station call letters*]
KFDI-FM Wichita, KS [*FM radio station call letters*]
KFDM Beaumont, TX [*Television station call letters*]
KFDN Lakewood, CO [*FM radio station call letters*] (BROA)
KfdO Komitee fuer den Osten (BJA)
KFDT Kinetic Family Drawing Test [*Psychology*] (DAVI)
KFDX Wichita Falls, TX [*Television station call letters*]
KFE Conferee [*Telegraphy*] (PCTE)
KFE Kathode Flicker Effect
KFEA Korean Federation of Education Associations
KFEB-FM Campbell, MO [*FM radio station call letters*] (BROA)
KFEG-FM Klamath Falls, OR [*FM radio station call letters*] (BROA)
KFEL Pueblo, CO [*AM radio station call letters*]
KFEQ St. Joseph, MO [*AM radio station call letters*]
KFER Santa Cruz, CA [*FM radio station call letters*]
KFEZ Kansas City, MO [*AM radio station call letters*]
KFF Kiplinger Finance & Forecasts [*Database*] (GDD)
KFF Kvinnenes Frie Folkevalgte [*Women's Freely Elected Representatives*] [*Norway*] [*Political party*] (PPE)
KFFA Helena, AR [*AM radio station call letters*]
KFFA-FM Helena, AR [*FM radio station call letters*] (RBYB)
KFFB Fairfield Bay, AR [*FM radio station call letters*]
KFFG Los Altos, CA [*FM radio station call letters*] (RBYB)
KFFLBA Konglomerati Florida Foundation for Literature and the Book Arts (EA)
KFFM Yakima, WA [*FM radio station call letters*]
KFFN Tucson, AZ [*AM radio station call letters*] (GDPB)
KFFN-AM Tucson, AZ [*AM radio station call letters*] (RBYB)
KFFO Dayton/Wright-Patterson Air Force Base [*Ohio*] [*ICAO location identifier*] (ICLI)
KFFR Eagle River, AK [*AM radio station call letters*]
KFFW Cabool, MO [*FM radio station call letters*] (BROA)
KFFX Emporia, KS [*FM radio station call letters*]
KFFX-TV Pendleton, OR [*Television station call letters*] (BROA)
KFG Conferring [*Telegraphy*] (PCTE)
KFGA-FM Clayton, LA [*FM radio station call letters*] (BROA)
KFGE Lincoln, NE [*FM radio station call letters*]
KFGE-FM Milford, NE [*FM radio station call letters*] (BROA)
KFGG Corpus Christi, TX [*FM radio station call letters*]
KFGI-FM Brainerd, MN [*FM radio station call letters*] (RBYB)
KFGO Fargo, ND [*AM radio station call letters*]
KFGO-FM Fargo, ND [*FM radio station call letters*]
KFGQ Boone, IA [*AM radio station call letters*]
KFGQ-FM Boone, IA [*FM radio station call letters*]
KFGX-FM Detroit Lakes, MN [*FM radio station call letters*] (RBYB)
KFGY Santa Rosa, CA [*FM radio station call letters*] (GDPB)
KFGY-FM Healdsburg, CA [*FM radio station call letters*] (RBYB)
KFH Clearwater, KS [*FM radio station call letters*] (BROA)
KFH Fort Hays State University, Hays, KS [*OCLC symbol*] (OCLC)
KFH Kaiser Foundation Hospital (SAUO)
KFH Ku-Band Feed Horn
KFH Kuwait Finance House (BUAC)
KFH Wichita, KS [*AM radio station call letters*]
KFHD KFH Delivery Service [*Common carrier symbol*]
KFHP Kaiser Foundation Health Plan [*Medicine*] (EDAA)
KFI Kinetic Fluid Induction
KFI Krause's Furniture [*AMEX symbol*] (SG)
KFI Los Angeles, CA [*AM radio station call letters*]
KFIA Carmichael, CA [*AM radio station call letters*]
KFIA Kentucky Forest Industries Association (EARSL)
KFIA King Fahd International Airport [*Saudi Arabia*]
KFIE Merced, CA [*FM radio station call letters*]
KFIF Soda Springs, ID [*FM radio station call letters*] (BROA)
KFIG Fresno, CA [*AM radio station call letters*]
KFIL Preston, MN [*AM radio station call letters*]
KFIL-FM Preston, MN [*FM radio station call letters*]
KFIN Jonesboro, AR [*FM radio station call letters*]
KFIR Sweet Home, OR [*AM radio station call letters*]
KFIS Soda Springs, ID [*FM radio station call letters*]
KFIS Tillamook, OR [*FM radio station call letters*] (BROA)
KFIT Lockhart, TX [*AM radio station call letters*]
KFIT-EX San Antonio, TX [*AM radio station call letters*] (BROA)
KFIT EXP STN San Antonio, TX [*Radio expansion station*]
KFIV Modesto, CA [*AM radio station call letters*]
KFIX-FM Plainville, KS [*FM radio station call letters*] (RBYB)
KFIZ Fond Du Lac, WI [*AM radio station call letters*]
KFIZ-FM Fond du Lac, WI [*FM radio station call letters*] (RBYB)
KFJB Marshalltown, IA [*AM radio station call letters*]
KFJC Los Altos, CA [*FM radio station call letters*]
KFJM Grand Forks, ND [*AM radio station call letters*]
KFJM-FM Grand Forks, ND [*FM radio station call letters*]
KFJO Concord, CA [*FM radio station call letters*] (GDPB)

KFJO-FM .... Walnut Creek, CA [*FM radio station call letters*] (BROA)
KFJY .... Grand Forks, ND [*FM radio station call letters*] (RBYB)
KFJZ .... Fort Worth, TX [*AM radio station call letters*]
KFK .... Korn-Og Foderstof Kompagniet (EFIS)
KFKA .... Greeley, CO [*AM radio station call letters*]
KFKF .... Kansas City, KS [*FM radio station call letters*]
KFKQ .... New Holstein, WI [*FM radio station call letters*]
KFKX-FM .... Hastings, NE [*FM radio station call letters*] (RBYB)
KFL .... Kenya Federation of Labour
KFL .... Kenya Flamingo Airways Ltd. [*ICAO designator*] (FAAC)
KFL .... Key Facilities List [*AEC*]
KFL .... Lifestream Technologies [*AMEX symbol*]
KFL .... University of Kansas, Law Library, Lawrence, KS [*OCLC symbol*] (OCLC)
KFLA .... Scott City, KS [*AM radio station call letters*]
KFIAH .... United States Army Hospital, Fort Leavenworth, KS [*Library symbol*] [*Library of Congress*] (LCLS)
KFLB .... Odessa, TX [*AM radio station call letters*] (BROA)
KFLB .... Odessa, TX [*FM radio station call letters*] (BROA)
KFLD .... Pasco, WA [*AM radio station call letters*] (RBYB)
KFLG .... Bullhead City, AZ [*AM radio station call letters*]
KFLG-FM .... Bullhead City, AZ [*FM radio station call letters*]
KFLG-FM .... Kingman, AZ [*FM radio station call letters*] (BROA)
KFIGS .... United States Army, Command and General Staff College Library, Fort Leavenworth,KS [*Library symbol*] [*Library of Congress*] (LCLS)
KFLH-FM .... Chama, NM [*FM radio station call letters*] (BROA)
KFLL .... Floydada, TX [*FM radio station call letters*]
KFLL .... Fort Lauderdale/Fort Lauderdale-Hollywood International [*Florida*] [*ICAO location identifier*] (ICLI)
KFLL .... Great Falls, MT [*FM radio station call letters*] (BROA)
KFLN .... Baker, MT [*AM radio station call letters*]
KFLO .... Florence/Municipal [*South Carolina*] [*ICAO location identifier*] (ICLI)
KFLO .... Shreveport, LA [*AM radio station call letters*]
KFLOPS .... Kilo Floating Point Operations per Second [*Computer science*] (CIST)
KFLP .... Floydada, TX [*AM radio station call letters*] (GDPB)
KFLP .... Floydada, TX [*FM radio station call letters*] (GDPB)
KFLP-AM .... Floydada, TX [*AM radio station call letters*] (RBYB)
KFLQ .... Albuquerque, NM [*FM radio station call letters*]
KFLR .... Phoenix, AZ [*FM radio station call letters*]
KFLS .... Klamath Falls, OR [*AM radio station call letters*]
KFLS .... Tulelake, CA [*FM radio station call letters*]
KFLT .... Tucson, AZ [*AM radio station call letters*]
KFLV-FM .... Wilber, NE [*FM radio station call letters*] (BROA)
KFLW .... St. Robert, MO [*FM radio station call letters*] (RBYB)
KFLX .... Kachina Village, AZ [*FM radio station call letters*]
KFLX-FM .... Kachina Village, AZ [*FM radio station call letters*] (BROA)
KFLY .... Corvallis, OR [*FM radio station call letters*]
KFLZ .... Bishop, TX [*FM radio station call letters*]
KFM .... Conform [*Telegraphy*] (PCTE)
KFM .... K File Manager (SAUS)
KFM .... Khunsari [*Language symbol*] (ETLW)
KFM .... Klystron Frequency Multiplier
KFM .... Knight of St. Ferdinand and Merit [*Italy*]
KFMA-FM .... Green Valley, AZ [*FM radio station call letters*] (RBYB)
KFMB .... San Diego, CA [*AM radio station call letters*]
KFMB-DT .... Sand Diego, CA [*Television station call letters*] (BROA)
KFMB-FM .... San Diego, CA [*FM radio station call letters*]
KFMB-TV .... San Diego, CA [*Television station call letters*]
KFMC .... Fairmont, MN [*FM radio station call letters*]
KFMD .... Conformed [*Telegraphy*] (PCTE)
KFMD .... Delta, UT [*FM radio station call letters*]
KFMD-FM .... Denver, CO [*FM radio station call letters*] (BROA)
KFME .... Fargo, ND [*Television station call letters*]
KFME .... Garden City, MO [*FM radio station call letters*] (BROA)
KFMF .... Chico, CA [*FM radio station call letters*]
KFMG .... Conforming [*Telegraphy*] (PCTE)
KFMG .... Pella, IA [*FM radio station call letters*]
KFMG-FM .... Juneau, AK [*FM radio station call letters*] (BROA)
KFMH .... Belle Fourche, SD [*FM radio station call letters*] (BROA)
KFMH .... Falmouth/Otis Air Force Base [*Massachusetts*] [*ICAO location identifier*] (ICLI)
KFMI .... Eureka, CA [*FM radio station call letters*]
KFMJ-FM .... Ketchikan, AK [*FM radio station call letters*] (RBYB)
KFMK .... Winton, CA [*FM radio station call letters*]
KFMK-FM .... Round Rock, TX [*FM radio station call letters*] (BROA)
KFML .... Kommunistiska Foerbundet Marxist-Leninisterna [*Communist League of Marxist-Leninists*] [*Sweden*] [*Political party*] (PPE)
KFML .... Little Falls, MN [*FM radio station call letters*]
KFMM .... Thatcher, AZ [*FM radio station call letters*]
KFMN .... Farmington [*New Mexico*] [*ICAO location identifier*] (ICLI)
KFMN .... Lihue, HI [*FM radio station call letters*]
KFMO .... Park Hills, MO [*AM radio station call letters*]
KFMQ-FM .... Gallup, NM [*FM radio station call letters*] (RBYB)
KFMR-FM .... Winslow, AZ [*FM radio station call letters*] (RBYB)
KFMS .... Conforms [*Telegraphy*] (PCTE)
KFMS-FM .... Las Vegas, NV [*FM radio station call letters*]
KFMT .... Fremont, NE [*FM radio station call letters*]
KFMU .... Oak Creek, CO [*FM radio station call letters*]
KFMV .... Franklin, LA [*FM radio station call letters*]
KFMW .... Waterloo, IA [*FM radio station call letters*]
KFMX .... Lubbock, TX [*FM radio station call letters*]
KFMY .... Conformity [*Telegraphy*] (PCTE)
KFMY .... Fort Myers/Page Field [*Florida*] [*ICAO location identifier*] (ICLI)
KFMY-FM .... Raymond, WA [*FM radio station call letters*] (BROA)
KFMY-FM .... South Bend, WA [*FM radio station call letters*] (RBYB)
KFMZ .... Brookfield, MO [*AM radio station call letters*] (BROA)
KFMZ .... Columbia, MO [*FM radio station call letters*]
KFNA .... El Paso, TX [*AM radio station call letters*]
KFNB .... Casper, WY [*Television station call letters*]
KFNE .... Riverton, WY [*Television station call letters*]
KFNF .... Oberlin, KS [*FM radio station call letters*]
KFNI .... Pleasanton, TX [*AM radio station call letters*] (BROA)
KFNK-FM .... Eatonville, WA [*FM radio station call letters*] (BROA)
KFNN .... Mesa, AZ [*AM radio station call letters*]
KFNO .... Fresno, CA [*FM radio station call letters*]
KFNP .... Kaieteur Falls National Park (SAUO)
KFNR .... Rawlins, WY [*Television station call letters*]
KFNS .... Wood River, IL [*AM radio station call letters*]
KFNS-FM .... Troy, MO [*FM radio station call letters*] (BROA)
KFNV .... Ferriday, LA [*AM radio station call letters*]
KFNV-FM .... Ferriday, LA [*FM radio station call letters*]
KFNW .... West Fargo, ND [*AM radio station call letters*]
KFNW-FM .... Fargo, ND [*FM radio station call letters*]
KFNX .... Cave Creek, AZ [*AM radio station call letters*] (BROA)
KFNZ .... Salt Lake City, UT [*AM radio station call letters*] (GDPB)
KFNZ-AM .... Salt Lake, UT [*AM radio station call letters*] (RBYB)
KFO .... Killing Federal Officer
KFO .... King Solomon Resources [*Vancouver Stock Exchange symbol*]
KFO .... Klamath Falls [*Oregon*] [*Seismograph station code, US Geological Survey*] (SEIS)
KFOC .... Kaiser-Frazer Owners Clubs of America [*Later, KFOCI*] (EA)
KFOCI .... Kaiser-Frazer Owners Club International (EA)
KFOE .... Topeka/Forbes Air Force Base [*Kansas*] [*ICAO location identifier*] (ICLI)
KFOG .... San Francisco, CA [*FM radio station call letters*]
KFOK .... West Hampton Beach/Suffolk County [*New York*] [*ICAO location identifier*] (ICLI)
KFON .... Austin, TX [*AM radio station call letters*]
KFOR .... Lincoln, NE [*AM radio station call letters*]
KFOR-TV .... Oklahoma City, OK [*Television station call letters*]
KFOS .... Korean Fragmentary Order System (SAUO)
KFOX .... Redondo Beach, CA [*FM radio station call letters*]
KFOX-AM .... Torrance, CA [*AM radio station call letters*] (BROA)
KFOX-TV .... El Paso, TX [*Television station call letters*]
KFP .... False Pass [*Alaska*] [*Airport symbol*] (OAG)
KFP .... Kenya Freedom Party (SAUO)
KFP .... Konstitutionella Folkpartiet [*Constitutional People's Party*] [*Finland*] [*Political party*] (PPE)
KFP .... Korean Fighter Program
KFP .... Pittsburg State University, Pittsburg, KS [*OCLC symbol*] (OCLC)
KF PAC .... Kraft Food Inc. PAC [*Northfield, IL*] (PACS)
KFPB-FM .... Chino Valley, AZ [*FM radio station call letters*] (BROA)
KFPC .... Kansas Foundation for Private Colleges (SAUO)
KFPR .... Redding, CA [*FM radio station call letters*]
KFPW .... Fort Smith, AR [*AM radio station call letters*]
KFPX .... Newton, IA [*Television station call letters*] (BROA)
KFQC .... Davenport, IA [*AM radio station call letters*]
KFQD .... Anchorage, AK [*AM radio station call letters*]
KFQX-FM .... Anson, TX [*FM radio station call letters*] (BROA)
KFQX-FM .... Merkel, TX [*FM radio station call letters*] (BROA)
KFQX-TV .... Grand Junction, CO [*TV station call letters*] (RBYB)
KFR .... Kayser-Fleischer Ring [*Medicine*] (DMAA)
KFR .... Keefer Resources, Inc. [*Vancouver Stock Exchange symbol*]
KFRA .... Franklin, LA [*AM radio station call letters*]
KFRB-FM .... Bakersfield, CA [*FM radio station call letters*] (RBYB)
KFRC .... San Francisco, CA [*AM radio station call letters*]
KFRC-FM .... San Francisco, CA [*FM radio station call letters*]
KFRD .... Bellville, TX [*AM radio station call letters*]
KFRD .... Butte, MT [*FM radio station call letters*] (BROA)
KFRE .... Fresno, CA [*AM radio station call letters*]
KFRG .... San Bernardino, CA [*FM radio station call letters*]
KFRJ .... China Lake, CA [*FM radio station call letters*] (BROA)
KFRL .... Kansas Flight Research Laboratory
KFRM .... Salina, KS [*AM radio station call letters*]
KFRN .... Long Beach, CA [*AM radio station call letters*]
KFRO .... Gilmer, TX [*FM radio station call letters*]
KFRO .... Longview, TX [*AM radio station call letters*]
KFRQ .... Harlingen, TX [*FM radio station call letters*]
KFRQ-FM .... Harlingen, TX [*FM radio station call letters*]
KFRR .... Woodlake, CA [*FM radio station call letters*]
KFRS-FM .... Soledad, CA [*FM radio station call letters*] (BROA)
KFRST .... Killing Frost [*NWS*] (FAAC)
KFRU .... Columbia, MO [*AM radio station call letters*]
KFRX .... Lincoln, NE [*FM radio station call letters*]
KFRY-FM .... Manteca, CA [*FM radio station call letters*] (BROA)
KFRZ-FM .... Green River, WY [*FM radio station call letters*] (BROA)
KFS .... Confers [*Telegraphy*] (PCTE)
KFS .... Kalitta Flying Service, Inc. [*FAA designator*] (FAAC)
KFS .... Kalman Filtering System
KFS .... Keyed File System [*Computer science*]
KFS .... Kingsway Financial Services [*NYSE symbol*]
KFS .... Klamath Falls, OR [*Amtrak rail station code*]
KFS .... Klippel-Feil Syndrome [*Medicine*]
KFS .... Kohles, F. S., Montebello CA [*STAC*]
KFS .... University of Kansas, Spencer Library, Lawrence, KS [*OCLC symbol*] (OCLC)
KFSA .... Fort Smith, AR [*AM radio station call letters*]

KFSA .... Keep Fit South Australia
KFSB .... Joplin, MO [*AM radio station call letters*]
KFSB .... Korean Federation of Small Businesses (BUAC)
KFSB .... Ontario, CA [*FM radio station call letters*] (BROA)
KFSD .... Keratosis Follicularis Spinulosa Decalvans [*Medicine*] (DMAA)
KFSD .... San Diego, CA [*FM radio station call letters*]
KFSD-FM ... Escondido, CA [*FM radio station call letters*] (BROA)
KFSG .... Los Angeles, CA [*FM radio station call letters*]
KFSG .... Redondo Beach, CA [*FM radio station call letters*] (BROA)
KFSH .... Anaheim, CA [*FM radio station call letters*] (BROA)
KFSH-AM ... Seward, AK [*AM radio station call letters*] (BROA)
KFSH & RC... King Faisal Specialist Hospital and Research Center [*Saudi Arabia*]
KFSI .... Rochester, MN [*FM radio station call letters*]
KFSK .... Petersburg, AK [*FM radio station call letters*]
KFSM .... Fort Smith, AR [*Television station call letters*]
KFSM .... Fort Smith/Municipal [*Arkansas*] [*ICAO location identifier*] (ICLI)
KFSN .... Fresno, CA [*Television station call letters*]
KFSO .... Visalia, CA [*FM radio station call letters*]
KFSR .... Fresno, CA [*FM radio station call letters*]
KFSR .... Karakul Fur Sheep Registry [*Later, AKFSR*] (EA)
KFST .... Fort Stockton, TX [*AM radio station call letters*]
KFST-FM .... Fort Stockton, TX [*FM radio station call letters*]
KFT .... Conflict [*Telegraphy*] (PCTE)
KFT .... Kalman Filter Theory
KFT .... Kidney Function Test [*Medicine*] (MELL)
KFT .... Kraft Foods [*Company symbol*]
KFTA .... Rupert, ID [*AM radio station call letters*] (GDPB)
KFTA-AM .... Rupert, ID [*AM radio station call letters*] (BROA)
KFTC .... Bemidji, MN [*Television station call letters*] (BROA)
KFTCIC ...... Kuwait Foreign Trade (or Trading) Contracting and Investment Company (SAUO)
KFTCIC ...... Kuwait Foreign Trading, Contracting & Investment Co.
KFTD .... Conflicted [*Telegraphy*] (PCTE)
KFTE .... Breaux Bridge, LA [*FM radio station call letters*]
KFTG .... Conflicting [*Telegraphy*] (PCTE)
KFTG .... Pasadena, TX [*FM radio station call letters*] (RBYB)
KFTH .... Marion, AR [*FM radio station call letters*]
KFTI-AM .... Wichita, KS [*AM radio station call letters*] (BROA)
KFTK-FM .... Florissant, MO [*FM radio station call letters*] (BROA)
KFTL .... Keptel, Inc. (SAUO)
KFTL .... Stockton, CA [*Television station call letters*]
KFTM .... Fort Morgan, CO [*AM radio station call letters*]
KFTS .... Conflicts [*Telegraphy*] (PCTE)
KFTS .... Klamath Falls, OR [*Television station call letters*]
KFTU .... Korean Federation of Trade Unions [*North Korea*]
KFTV .... Hanford, CA [*Television station call letters*]
KFTW .... Fort Worth/Meacham [*Texas*] [*ICAO location identifier*] (ICLI)
KFTW .... Fredericktown, MO [*AM radio station call letters*]
KFTX .... Kingsville, TX [*FM radio station call letters*] (RBYB)
KFTY .... Santa Rosa, CA [*Television station call letters*]
KFTZ .... Idaho Falls, ID [*FM radio station call letters*]
KFU .... Friends University, Wichita, KS [*OCLC symbol*] (OCLC)
KFU .... King Fahd University (SAUO)
KFU .... King Faisal University [*Saudi Arabia*] (BUAC)
KFUK .... Kristelig Forening for Unge Kvinder [*Young Women's Christian Associations - YWCA*] [*Denmark*]
KFUM .... Kristelig Forening for Unge Maend [*Young Men's Christian Associations - YMCA*] [*Denmark*]
KFUN .... Las Vegas, NM [*AM radio station call letters*]
KFUO .... Clayton, MO [*AM radio station call letters*]
KFUO-FM ... Clayton, MO [*FM radio station call letters*]
KFV .... Quest for Value Dual Fd [*NYSE symbol*] (TTSB)
KFV .... Quest for Value Fund [*NYSE symbol*] (SAG)
KFVE .... Honolulu, HI [*Television station call letters*]
KFVPr .... Quest For Value Income Shrs [*NYSE symbol*] (TTSB)
KFVR .... Crescent City, CA [*AM radio station call letters*]
KFVR-FM ... Nephi, UT [*FM radio station call letters*] (BROA)
KFVS .... Cape Girardeau, MO [*Television station call letters*]
KFW .... Confer With [*Telegraphy*] (PCTE)
KfW .... Kreditanstalt fur Wiederaufbau [*Finance*] [*Germany*]
KFW .... Wichita Public Library, Wichita, KS [*OCLC symbol*] (OCLC)
KFWB .... Los Angeles, CA [*AM radio station call letters*]
KFWD .... Fort Worth, TX [*Television station call letters*]
KFWH .... Fort Worth/Carswell Air Force Base [*Texas*] [*ICAO location identifier*] (ICLI)
KFWJ .... Lake Havasu City, AZ [*AM radio station call letters*]
KFWU .... Fort Bragg, CA [*Television station call letters*]
KFX .... KFX Inc. [*AMEX symbol*] (TTSB)
KFX .... Korean Foreign Exchange (IMH)
KFX .... Kullu Pahari [*Language symbol*] (ETLW)
KFXA .... Cedar Rapids, IA [*Television station call letters*] (RBYB)
KFXB .... Dubuque, IA [*Television station call letters*] (RBYB)
KFXD .... Nampa, ID [*AM radio station call letters*]
KFXD-FM ... Nampa, ID [*FM radio station call letters*]
KFXE .... Cuba, MO [*AM radio station call letters*]
KFXE .... Fort Lauderdale/Executive [*Florida*] [*ICAO location identifier*] (ICLI)
KFXE-FM .... Cuba, MO [*FM radio station call letters*] (BROA)
KFXF .... Fairbanks, AK [*Television station call letters*] (RBYB)
KFXI .... KFx, Inc. [*NASDAQ symbol*] (SAG)
KFXI .... Marlow, OK [*FM radio station call letters*]
KFX Inc ..... KFx, Inc. [*Associated Press*] (SAG)
KFXJ .... Abilene, TX [*FM radio station call letters*]
KFXJ .... Augusta, KS [*FM radio station call letters*] (BROA)
KFXJ-FM .... Nampa, ID [*FM radio station call letters*] (BROA)
KFXK .... Longview, TX [*Television station call letters*]
KFXN .... Houma, LA [*FM radio station call letters*] (BROA)
KFXN .... Minneapolis, MN [*AM radio station call letters*] (BROA)
KFXP .... Pocatello, ID [*Television station call letters*] (BROA)
KFXR .... Chinle, AZ [*FM radio station call letters*] (RBYB)
KFXR .... Dallas, TX [*AM radio station call letters*] (BROA)
KFXS .... Rapid City, SD [*FM radio station call letters*] (RBYB)
KFXT .... Sulphur, OK [*FM radio station call letters*]
KFXX .... Hugoton, KS [*FM radio station call letters*]
KFXX .... Oregon City, OR [*AM radio station call letters*]
KFXX .... Vancouver, WA [*AM radio station call letters*] (BROA)
KFXY .... Morgan City, LA [*FM radio station call letters*]
KFXY-AM .... Houma, LA [*AM radio station call letters*] (BROA)
KFXZ .... Maurice, LA [*FM radio station call letters*]
KFY .... KISS [*Knights in the Service of Satan*] - Flaming Youth [*Defunct*] (EA)
KFY .... Korn/Ferry Intl. [*NYSE symbol*] (SG)
KFYE .... Kingsburg, CA [*FM radio station call letters*] (BROA)
KFYI .... Phoenix, AZ [*AM radio station call letters*]
KFYN .... Bonham, TX [*AM radio station call letters*]
KFYO .... Lubbock, TX [*AM radio station call letters*]
KFYR .... Bismarck, ND [*AM radio station call letters*]
KFYR-TV .... Bismarck, ND [*Television station call letters*]
KFYV .... Fayetteville/Drake Field [*Arkansas*] [*ICAO location identifier*] (ICLI)
KFYX .... Texarkana, AR [*FM radio station call letters*] (BROA)
KFYZ .... Bonham, TX [*FM radio station call letters*]
KFZX .... Monahans, TX [*FM radio station call letters*] (BROA)
KG .... Bad Kissingen [*German license plate city code*]
KG .... Catalina Airlines [*ICAO designator*] (AD)
KG .... Center of Gravity above Keel (MCD)
KG .... Kammergericht [*District Court, Berlin*] [*German*] (DLA)
KG .... Kampfgeschwader [*Bombardment wing*] [*German military - World War II*]
KG .... Karmann-Ghia [*Volkswagen model designation*]
kg .... Keg (MIST)
KG .... Keg
KG .... Keratoglobus [*Medicine*] (MELL)
KG .... Ketoglutarate (DMAA)
KG .... Ketoglutaric [*Biochemistry*]
KG .... Key Generator (MCD)
kG .... Kilogauss
Kg .... Kilogram [*Medicine*] (BCRP)
KG .... Kilogram (GAVI)
kg .... Kilogram [*Also, k*] [*Symbol*] [*SI unit for mass*]
KG .... Kindergarten
KG .... Kinder, Gentler [*America*] [*In a George Bush speech during the 1989 Republican Convention*]
KG .... King
KG .... King Pharmaceuticals [*NYSE symbol*]
KG .... Kininogen [*Biochemistry*]
KG .... Knifemakers Guild (EA)
KG .... Knight of [*the Order of*] the Garter [*British*]
KG .... Known Gambler [*Police slang*]
KG .... Kommanditgesellschaft [*Limited Partnership*] [*German*]
KG .... Kultusgemeinde (BJA)
KG .... Kumagai Gumi Co. (EFIS)
KG .... Kyrgyzstan [*Internet country code*]
KG .... Orion Airways Ltd. (SAUO)
KG-1 .... Koeffler Golde-1 [*Cell line*] [*Cytology*] (DAVI)
KG5 .... HMS King George V [*British military*] (DMA)
KGA .... Kananga [*Zaire*] [*Airport symbol*] (OAG)
KGA .... Ketoglutaric Acid (MELL)
KGA .... King's German Artillery [*British military*] (DMA)
KGA .... Kitchen Guild of America
KGA .... Kyrghyzstan Airlines [*ICAO designator*] (FAAC)
KGA .... Spokane, WA [*AM radio station call letters*]
KGAB-AM ... Orchard Valley, WY [*AM radio station call letters*] (BROA)
KGAC .... Kentucky Guild of Artists and Craftsmen (EARSL)
KGAC .... St. Peter, MN [*FM radio station call letters*]
KGAF .... Gainesville, TX [*AM radio station call letters*]
KGAG .... Gage [*Oklahoma*] [*ICAO location identifier*] (ICLI)
KgAG .... Kurzgefasste Assyrische Grammatik [*A publication*] (BJA)
KGAK .... Gallup, NM [*AM radio station call letters*]
KGAL .... Lebanon, OR [*AM radio station call letters*] (RBYB)
KGAL/MIN... Kilogallons per Minute (MCD)
kgal/min .... Kilogallons per Minute (NAKS)
KGAM-AM... Palm Springs, CA [*AM radio station call letters*] (BROA)
KGAN .... Cedar Rapids, IA [*Television station call letters*]
KGAP .... Clarksville, TX [*FM radio station call letters*]
KGAR-FM ... Garden City, MO [*FM radio station call letters*] (BROA)
KGAS .... Carthage, TX [*AM radio station call letters*]
KGAS-FM ... Carthage, TX [*FM radio station call letters*]
KGB .... Committee for State Security (SAUS)
KGB .... Kewaunee, Green Bay & Western R. R. [*AAR code*]
KGB .... Kindly Gunn Bunch [*Refers to the Metropolitan Transit Authority of New York City; Gunn is the MTA chairman*]
KGB .... Known Good Board (AAEL)
KGB .... Komitet Gosudarstvennoi Bezopasnosti [*Committee of State Security*] [*Russian Secret Police*] [*Also satirically interpreted as Kontora Grubykh Banditov, or "Office of Crude Bandits"*]
KGB .... Konge [*Papua New Guinea*] [*Airport symbol*] (OAG)
KGB .... San Diego, CA [*FM radio station call letters*]
KGBA .... Holtville, CA [*FM radio station call letters*]

KGBA........ Kinder Goat Breeders Association (EA)
KGbB........ Barton County Community College, Great Bend, KS [*Library symbol*] [*Library of Congress*] (LCLS)
KGBB........ Temecula, GA [*FM radio station call letters*] (BROA)
KGBC........ Galveston, TX [*AM radio station call letters*]
KGBI........ Omaha, NE [*FM radio station call letters*]
KGbLS........ Central Kansas Library System, Great Bend, KS [*Library symbol*] [*Library of Congress*] (LCLS)
KGBM........ Randsburg, CA [*FM radio station call letters*] (BROA)
KGbMC........ Central Kansas Medical Center, Great Bend, KS [*Library symbol*] [*Library of Congress*] (LCLS)
KGBR........ Gold Beach, OR [*FM radio station call letters*]
KGBS........ Krypton Gas Bottling Station [*Nuclear energy*] (NRCH)
KGBT........ Harlingen, TX [*AM radio station call letters*]
KGBT........ McAllen, TX [*FM radio station call letters*] (BROA)
KGBT-TV.... Harlingen, TX [*Television station call letters*]
KGBW........ Kewaunee, Green Bay and Western (SAUO)
KGBX........ Nixa, MO [*FM radio station call letters*]
KGBY........ Sacramento, CA [*FM radio station call letters*]
KGBZ........ Harwood, ND [*FM radio station call letters*] (BROA)
KGC........ Keflin, Gentamicin, and Carbenicellin [*Antibiotics*] (DAVI)
kgc........ Kilogram-Calorie (IDOE)
KGC........ King City, CA [*Amtrak Busline code*]
KGC........ Kingscote [*Australia*] [*Airport symbol*] (OAG)
KGC........ Kinross Gold [*NYSE symbol*] (TTSB)
KGC........ Kinross Gold Corp. [*NYSE symbol*] (SAG)
KGC........ Kiwi Growers of California (EA)
KGC........ Knight Grand Commander
KGC........ Knight of the Golden Circle
KGC........ Knight of the Grand Cross
KGC........ Knights of the Golden Circle (SAUO)
KGC........ W. M. Krogman Center for Research in Child Growth and Development [*University of Pennsylvania*] [*Research center*] (RCD)
kgcal........ Kilogram-Calorie
KGCB........ Knight Grand Cross of the [*Order of the*] Bath [*British*]
KGCB........ Prescott, AZ [*FM radio station call letters*]
KGCF........ Kahlil Gibran Centennial Foundation (EA)
KGCHS........ Knight Grand Cross of the Equestrian Order of the Holy Sepulchre of Jerusalem
KGCK........ Garden City [*Kansas*] [*ICAO location identifier*] (ICLI)
KGCR........ Goodland, KS [*FM radio station call letters*]
KGCSG........ Knight Grand Cross of the Order of Saint Gregory the Great (SAUO)
KGCSG........ Knight Grand Cross of the Order of St. Gregory the Great [*British*] (ADA)
KGCU........ Kamigumi [*Intermodal shipping container symbol*] (TVRC)
kg/cum........ Kilograms per Cubic Meter
KGCZ........ Kokomo Grain [*Federal Railroad Administration identification code*]
KGD........ Congratulated [*Telegraphy*] (PCTE)
KGD........ Karaganda [*Former USSR*] [*Geomagnetic observatory code*]
KGD........ Known Good Die [*Electronics manufacturing*]
KGDC........ Walla Walla, WA [*AM radio station call letters*] (RBYB)
KGDD........ Paris, TX [*AM radio station call letters*]
KGDE........ Lincoln, NE [*FM radio station call letters*] (RBYB)
KGDN........ Pasco, WA [*FM radio station call letters*]
KGDP........ Orcutt, CA [*AM radio station call letters*]
KGDP-FM.... Orcutt, CA [*FM radio station call letters*] (BROA)
KGE........ Kansas Gas and Electric Co. (SAUO)
KGE........ King-Errington Resources Ltd. [*Vancouver Stock Exchange symbol*]
KGE........ Klein-Gordon Equation [*Physics*]
KGE........ Knights of the Golden Eagle (EA)
KGEB........ Tulsa, OK [*Television station call letters*] (BROA)
KGEE........ Monahans, TX [*FM radio station call letters*]
KGEG........ Spokane/International [*Washington*] [*ICAO location identifier*] (ICLI)
KGEM........ Boise, ID [*AM radio station call letters*]
KGEN........ Hanford, CA [*FM radio station call letters*] (RBYB)
KGEN........ Tulare, CA [*AM radio station call letters*]
KGEO........ Bakersfield, CA [*AM radio station call letters*]
KGER........ Long Beach, CA [*AM radio station call letters*]
KGER-AM.... Yakima, WA [*AM radio station call letters*] (BROA)
KGER-FM.... Quincy, WA [*FM radio station call letters*] (BROA)
KGET........ Bakersfield, CA [*Television station call letters*]
KGEZ........ Kalispell, MT [*AM radio station call letters*]
KGEZ........ Kansas Gas & Electric [*Federal Railroad Administration identification code*]
KGF........ Keilinschriften und Geschichtsforschung [*A publication*] (BJA)
KGF........ Keratinocyte Growth Factor [*Biochemistry*]
kg-f........ Kilogram-Foot
kgf........ Kilogram-Force [*Unit of force*]
KGF........ Knight of the Golden Fleece [*Spain and Austria*]
KGF........ Kriegsgefangener [*Prisoner of War*] [*German*]
KGFA........ Great Falls/Malmstrom Air Force Base [*Montana*] [*ICAO location identifier*] (ICLI)
KGFC-FM.... Great Falls, MT [*FM radio station call letters*] (RBYB)
KGF/CM².... Kilogram Force per Square Centimeter
KGFE........ Grand Forks, ND [*Television station call letters*]
KGFF........ Shawnee, OK [*AM radio station call letters*]
KGFJ........ Los Angeles, CA [*AM radio station call letters*]
KGFJ-FM.... Markham, TX [*FM radio station call letters*] (BROA)
KGFK........ Grand Forks/International [*North Dakota*] [*ICAO location identifier*] (ICLI)
KGFL........ Clinton, AR [*AM radio station call letters*]
KGFM........ Bakersfield, CA [*FM radio station call letters*]
KGF/M........ Kilogram Force per Meter
KGF/M².... Kilogram Force per Square Meter
KGFR........ Keratinocyte Growth Factor Receptor [*Biochemistry*]
KGFR........ Kidney Glomerular Filtration Rate [*Medicine*] (ODA)
KGFS........ King George's Fund for Sailors [*British*]
KGFST........ Korean General Federation of Science and Technology (SAUO)
KGFT........ Pueblo, CO [*FM radio station call letters*]
KGFW........ Kearney, NE [*AM radio station call letters*]
KGFX........ Pierre, SD [*AM radio station call letters*]
KGFX-FM.... Pierre, SD [*FM radio station call letters*]
KGFY........ Stillwater, OK [*FM radio station call letters*]
KGG........ Congratulating [*Telegraphy*] (PCTE)
KGG........ Consolidated Goldwest [*Vancouver Stock Exchange symbol*]
KGG........ Kedougou [*Senegal*] [*Airport symbol*] (OAG)
KGG........ Knight of the Guelphic Order of Hanover (SAUO)
KgGBAS........ Kurzgefasste Grammatik der Biblisch Aramaeischen Sprache [*A publication*] (BJA)
KGGF........ Coffeyville, KS [*AM radio station call letters*]
KGGF-FM.... Fredonia, KS [*FM radio station call letters*] (BROA)
KGGG........ Longview/Gregg County [*Texas*] [*ICAO location identifier*] (ICLI)
KGGG........ Sterling, KS [*FM radio station call letters*] (RBYB)
KGGI........ Riverside, CA [*FM radio station call letters*]
KGGK-FM.... Winner, SD [*FM radio station call letters*] (RBYB)
KGGL........ Missoula, MT [*FM radio station call letters*] (RBYB)
KGGM........ Delhi, LA [*FM radio station call letters*] (RBYB)
KGGN........ Gladstone, MO [*AM radio station call letters*]
KGGO........ Des Moines, IA [*FM radio station call letters*]
KGGR........ Dallas, TX [*AM radio station call letters*]
KGGY........ Dubuque, IA [*FM radio station call letters*]
KGH........ Kidney Goldblatt Hypertension Scale
KGH........ Knight of the Guelphic Order of Hanover [*British*]
KGHF........ Pueblo, CO [*AM radio station call letters*]
KGHL........ Billings, MT [*AM radio station call letters*]
KGHO-AM.... Olympia, WA [*AM radio station call letters*] (RBYB)
KGHO-FM.... Hoquiam, WA [*FM radio station call letters*]
KGHP........ Gig Harbor, WA [*FM radio station call letters*]
KG/HR........ Kilograms per Hour (WDAA)
KGHR........ Tuba City, AZ [*FM radio station call letters*]
KGHS........ International Falls, MN [*AM radio station call letters*]
KGHT........ Kidney Goldblatt Hypertension [*Medicine*] (DAVI)
KGHT........ Sheridan, AR [*AM radio station call letters*]
KGHY........ Kings Highway [*NCIC truck make code*]
KGHY........ Kings Highway [*NCIC trailer make code*]
KGI........ Cryderman Gold, Inc. [*Vancouver Stock Exchange symbol*]
KGI........ Kalgoorlie [*Australia*] [*Airport symbol*] (OAG)
KGI........ Kellogg [*Idaho*] [*Seismograph station code, US Geological Survey*] (SEIS)
KGI........ Kuala Lumpur Sign Language [*Language symbol*] (ETLW)
KGII........ King George II [*British*]
KGIL-AM.... Beverly Hills, CA [*AM radio station call letters*] (BROA)
KGIM........ Aberdeen, SD [*AM radio station call letters*]
KGIM-FM.... Redfield, SD [*FM radio station call letters*] (BROA)
KGIN........ Grand Island, NE [*Television station call letters*]
KGIR........ Paducah, KY-Cape Girardeau, MO-Marion, IL [*AM radio station call letters*] (GDPB)
KGIR-AM.... Cape Giradeau, MO [*AM radio station call letters*] (RBYB)
KGIU........ Kamigumi USA [*Intermodal shipping container symbol*] (TVRC)
KGIW........ Alamosa, CO [*AM radio station call letters*]
KGJ........ Karonga [*Malawi*] [*Airport symbol*] (OAG)
KG/J........ Kilograms per Joule
KGJ........ King Jack Resources [*Vancouver Stock Exchange symbol*]
KGK........ Kabushiki Goshi Kaisha [*Partnership*] [*Japan*]
KGK........ Koliganek [*Alaska*] [*Airport symbol*] (OAG)
KGKL........ San Angelo, TX [*AM radio station call letters*]
KGKL-FM.... San Angelo, TX [*FM radio station call letters*]
KGKS-FM.... Scott City, MO [*FM radio station call letters*] (BROA)
KGL........ Kaufel Group Ltd. [*Toronto Stock Exchange symbol*]
KGL........ Key Geographic Location (SAUS)
KGL........ Kigali [*Rwanda*] [*Airport symbol*] (OAG)
kg/L........ Kilogram Per Liter (STED)
KGL........ King's German Legion [*British military*] (DMA)
KGL........ Koeniglich [*Royal*] [*German*]
KGL........ Port-Aux-Francais [*Formerly, Kerguelen*] [*France*] [*Geomagnetic observatory code*]
KGLA........ Gretna, LA [*AM radio station call letters*]
KGLB........ Okmulgee, OK [*Television station call letters*]
KGLC........ Miami, OK [*FM radio station call letters*]
KGLD........ Tyler, TX [*AM radio station call letters*]
KGLE........ Glendive, MT [*AM radio station call letters*]
KGLE........ South Lake Tahoe, CA [*FM radio station call letters*]
KGLF........ Robstown, TX [*AM radio station call letters*]
KGLI........ Sioux City, IA [*FM radio station call letters*]
KGLL........ Greeley, CO [*FM radio station call letters*]
KGLM........ Anaconda, MT [*FM radio station call letters*]
KGLN........ Glenwood Springs, CO [*AM radio station call letters*]
KGLO........ Mason City, IA [*AM radio station call letters*]
KGLP........ Gallup, NM [*FM radio station call letters*]
KGLQ-FM.... Phoenix, AZ [*FM radio station call letters*] (BROA)
KGLS........ Galveston/Scholes Field [*Texas*] [*ICAO location identifier*] (ICLI)
KGLS........ Pratt, KS [*FM radio station call letters*]
KGLT........ Bozeman, MT [*FM radio station call letters*]
KGLW........ San Luis Obispo, CA [*AM radio station call letters*]
KGLX........ Gallup, NM [*FM radio station call letters*]
KGLY........ Tyler, TX [*FM radio station call letters*]
KGM........ Keratinocyte Growth Medium [*Cell culture*]
KGM........ Kerr Glass Manufacturing Corp. (SAUO)
KGM........ Kerr Glass Mfg. (EFIS)

KGM .... Kerr Group [*NYSE symbol*] (SPSG)
KGM .... Key Generator Module
KGM .... Kiena Gold Mines Ltd. [*Toronto Stock Exchange symbol*]
kgm .... Kilogram [*Also, k, kg*] [*SI unit for mass*] (DAVI)
kg-m .... Kilogram-Meter (ADWA)
kgm .... Kilogram-Meter (IDOE)
KGM .... Kingdom [*Telegraphy*] (PCTE)
KGM .... Kluang [*Malaysia*] [*Seismograph station code, US Geological Survey*] (SEIS)
KG/M² .... Kilograms per Square Meter
kg/m³ .... Kilograms per Cubic Meter (IDOE)
KG/M³ .... Kilograms per Cubic Meter
KGMB .... Honolulu, HI [*Television station call letters*]
KGMC .... Clovis, CA [*Television station call letters*]
KGMD .... Hilo, HI [*Television station call letters*]
KGME .... Glendale, AZ [*AM radio station call letters*]
KGME-AM ... Phoenix, AZ [*AM radio station call letters*] (BROA)
KGMens ..... K & G Mens Center, Inc. [*Associated Press*] (SAG)
KGMF .... K & G Manufacturing [*NCIC trailer make code*]
KGMG .... Oracle, AZ [*FM radio station call letters*] (BROA)
KGMI .... Bellingham, WA [*AM radio station call letters*]
KGMM .... Abilene, TX [*AM radio station call letters*] (BROA)
KGMN .... Kingman, AZ [*FM radio station call letters*]
KGMO .... Cape Girardeau, MO [*FM radio station call letters*]
KGMS .... Green Valley, AZ [*FM radio station call letters*]
KGMS-AM ... Tucson, AZ [*AM radio station call letters*] (BROA)
KGMT .... Fairbury, NE [*AM radio station call letters*]
KGMV .... Wailuku, HI [*Television station call letters*]
KGMX .... Lancaster, CA [*FM radio station call letters*]
KGMY .... Aurora, MO [*FM radio station call letters*]
KGMY .... Springfield, MO [*AM radio station call letters*]
KGMZ .... Aiea, HI [*FM radio station call letters*]
KGN .... Congratulation [*Telegraphy*] (PCTE)
Kgn .... Kingsman (SAUS)
Kgn .... Kininogen [*Medicine*] (EDAA)
KGNA .... Arnold, MO [*FM radio station call letters*] (BROA)
KGNB .... New Braunfels, TX [*AM radio station call letters*]
KGNC .... Amarillo, TX [*AM radio station call letters*]
KGNC-FM ... Amarillo, TX [*FM radio station call letters*]
KGND .... Ketchum, OK [*FM radio station call letters*]
KGNM .... St. Joseph, MO [*AM radio station call letters*]
KGNN .... Cuba, MO [*AM radio station call letters*]
KGNN-FM ... Cuba, MO [*FM radio station call letters*] (RBYB)
KGNO .... Dodge City, KS [*AM radio station call letters*]
KGNP .... Kalahari Gemsbok National Park (SAUO)
KGNP .... Katherine Gorge National Park (SAUO)
KGNS .... Laredo, TX [*Television station call letters*]
KGNT .... Grants/Grants-Milan [*New Mexico*] [*ICAO location identifier*] (ICLI)
KGNT-FM ... Smithfield, UT [*FM radio station call letters*] (BROA)
KGNU .... Boulder, CO [*FM radio station call letters*]
KGNV .... Gainesville [*Florida*] [*ICAO location identifier*] (ICLI)
KGNV .... Washington, MO [*FM radio station call letters*]
KGNW .... Burien-Seattle, WA [*AM radio station call letters*]
KGNZ .... Abilene, TX [*FM radio station call letters*]
KGO .... Kasongo [*Zaire*] [*Airport symbol*] (AD)
KGO .... King's Gurkha Officer [*British military*] (DMA)
KGO .... San Francisco, CA [*AM radio station call letters*]
KGO-DT ..... San Francisco, CA [*Television station call letters*] (BROA)
KGOE .... Eureka, CA [*FM radio station call letters*]
KGOK .... Pauls Valley, OK [*FM radio station call letters*]
KGOL .... Humble, TX [*AM radio station call letters*]
KGON .... Portland, OR [*FM radio station call letters*]
KGOR .... Omaha, NE [*FM radio station call letters*]
KGOS .... Torrington, WY [*AM radio station call letters*]
KGOT .... Anchorage, AK [*FM radio station call letters*]
KGO-TV ..... San Francisco, CA [*Television station call letters*]
KGOU .... Norman, OK [*FM radio station call letters*]
KGOY .... Raton, NM [*FM radio station call letters*] (BROA)
KGOZ .... Gallatin, MO [*FM radio station call letters*]
KGP .... Komma Georgiou Papandreou [*Party of George Papandreou*] [*Greek*] [*Political party*] (PPE)
KG/(PA S M²)... Kilograms per Pascal Second Square Meter
KGPE .... Fresno, CA [*Television station call letters*] (BROA)
KGPL .... Dermott, AR [*AM radio station call letters*]
KGPQ-FM ... Monticello, AR [*FM radio station call letters*] (RBYB)
KGPR .... Great Falls, MT [*FM radio station call letters*]
KGPS .... Kilograms per Second (GOBB)
kgps .... Kilograms per Second
KGPS .... Kinematic Geographic Positioning System [*Mapping and navigation systems*]
KGPS .... Kinematic GPS (SAUS)
KGPX .... Spokane, WA [*Television station call letters*] (BROA)
KGPZ .... Coleraine, MN [*FM radio station call letters*]
KGR .... Kanonengranate [*Shell for a gun*] [*German military - World War II*]
KGR .... Kengate Resources [*Vancouver Stock Exchange symbol*]
KGR .... Key Generator Receiver (MCD)
kgr .... Kilograin (BARN)
kgr .... Kirghiz Soviet Socialist Republic [*MARC country of publication code*] [*Library of Congress*] (LCCP)
KGR .... Klydonograph Type Gradient Recorder (IAA)
KGRA .... Jefferson, IA [*FM radio station call letters*]
KGRA .... Known Geothermal Resource Area [*Department of the Interior*]
KGRAX ...... Kemper Growth Cl.A [*Mutual fund ticker symbol*] (SG)
KGRB .... Greenbay/Austin Straubel [*Wisconsin*] [*ICAO location identifier*] (ICLI)
KGRB .... West Covina, CA [*AM radio station call letters*]
KGRBX ...... Kemper Growth Cl.B [*Mutual fund ticker symbol*] (SG)
KGRC .... Hannibal, MO [*FM radio station call letters*]
KGRD .... Orchard, NE [*FM radio station call letters*]
KGRE .... Greeley, CO [*AM radio station call letters*]
KGRG .... Auburn, WA [*FM radio station call letters*]
KGRI .... Henderson, TX [*FM radio station call letters*]
KGRK .... Killeen/Robert Gray Army Air Field [*Texas*] [*ICAO location identifier*] (ICLI)
KGRM .... Grambling, LA [*FM radio station call letters*]
KGRN .... Grinnell, IA [*AM radio station call letters*]
KGRO .... Pampa, TX [*AM radio station call letters*]
KGRP-FM ... Calistoga, CA [*FM radio station call letters*] (BROA)
KGRR .... Epworth, IA [*FM radio station call letters*]
KGRR .... Grand Rapids/Kent County Cascade [*Michigan*] [*ICAO location identifier*] (ICLI)
KGRS .... Burlington, IA [*FM radio station call letters*]
KGRT .... Las Cruces, NM [*AM radio station call letters*]
KGRT-FM .... Las Cruces, NM [*FM radio station call letters*]
KGRV .... Winston, OR [*AM radio station call letters*]
KGRW .... Friona, TX [*FM radio station call letters*]
KGRX .... Kasgro Rail [*Private rail car owner code*]
KGRZ .... Missoula, MT [*AM radio station call letters*]
KGS .... Kansas Geological Society (SAUO)
KGS .... Kansas Geological Survey (SAUO)
KGS .... Kate Greenaway Society (EA)
KGS .... Kentucky Genealogical Society (EARSL)
KGS .... Kentucky Geological Survey (SAUO)
KGS .... Ketogenic Steroid [*Endocrinology*]
KGS .... Kigezi Gorilla Sanctuary (SAUO)
kg/s .... Kilograms per Second
Kgs .... Kings [*Old Testament book*]
KGS .... Known Geological Structure (ODA)
KGS .... Kos [*Greece*] [*Airport symbol*] (OAG)
KGSB .... Goldsboro/Seymour-Johnson Air Force Base [*North Carolina*] [*ICAO location identifier*] (ICLI)
KGSG-FM ... Pasco, WA [*FM radio station call letters*] (BROA)
KGSLD ...... Kingsland, GA [*American Association of Railroads railroad junction routing code*]
KGSP .... Parkville, MO [*FM radio station call letters*]
KGSR .... Bastrop, TX [*FM radio station call letters*]
KGST .... Fresno, CA [*AM radio station call letters*]
kgst .... Kilograms Static Thrust (DOMA)
KGStJ .... Knight of Grace of the Order of Saint John of Jerusalem (SAUO)
KGStJ .... Knight of Grace, Order of St. John of Jerusalem
KGT .... Kemper Intermediate Government Trust [*NYSE symbol*] (SPSG)
KGT .... Kemper Interm Gvt Tr [*NYSE symbol*] (TTSB)
KGT .... Somyewe [*Language symbol*] (ETLW)
KGTF .... Agana, GU [*Television station call letters*]
KGTF .... Great Falls/International [*Montana*] [*ICAO location identifier*] (ICLI)
KGTL .... Homer, AK [*AM radio station call letters*]
KGTM .... Rexburg, ID [*FM radio station call letters*]
KGTO .... Tulsa, OK [*AM radio station call letters*]
KGTR .... Larned, KS [*FM radio station call letters*] (RBYB)
KGTS .... College Place, WA [*FM radio station call letters*]
KGTV .... San Diego, CA [*Television station call letters*]
KGTV-DT ... San Diego, CA [*Television station call letters*] (BROA)
KGTW .... Ketchikan, AK [*FM radio station call letters*]
KGU .... Congratulate [*Telegraphy*] (PCTE)
KGU .... Honolulu, HI [*AM radio station call letters*]
KGU .... Keningau [*Malaysia*] [*Airport symbol*] (OAG)
KGU .... Kobe Gakuin University [*UTLAS symbol*]
KGUL .... Port Lavaca, TX [*AM radio station call letters*]
KGUL-FM ... Edna, TX [*FM radio station call letters*] (BROA)
KGUM .... Agana, GU [*AM radio station call letters*]
KGUM-FM ... Dededo, GU [*FM radio station call letters*] (BROA)
KGUN .... Tucson, AZ [*Television station call letters*]
KGUS .... Peru/Grisson Air Force Base [*Indiana*] [*ICAO location identifier*] (ICLI)
KGUY-AM ... Milwaukee, OR [*AM radio station call letters*] (BROA)
KGV .... King George V [*British*]
KGV .... Knight of Gustavus Vasa [*Sweden*]
KGVA .... Fort Belknap Agency, MT [*FM radio station call letters*] (RBYB)
KGVE .... Grove, OK [*FM radio station call letters*]
KGVL .... Greenville, TX [*AM radio station call letters*]
KGVM .... Gardnerville-Minden, NV [*FM radio station call letters*]
KGVO .... King George the Fifth's Own [*British military*] (DMA)
KGVO .... Missoula, MT [*AM radio station call letters*]
KGVT .... Greenville/Majors Field [*Texas*] [*ICAO location identifier*] (ICLI)
KGVW .... Belgrade, MT [*AM radio station call letters*]
KGVW .... Grandview/Richards-Gebaur Air Force Base [*Missouri*] [*ICAO location identifier*] (ICLI)
KGVY .... Green Valley, AZ [*AM radio station call letters*]
KGW .... Kagi [*Papua New Guinea*] [*Airport symbol*] (OAG)
KGW .... Kreeger, George W., Atlanta GA [*STAC*]
KGW .... Portland, OR [*Television station call letters*]
KGWA .... Enid, OK [*AM radio station call letters*]
KGWB .... Wahpeton, ND [*FM radio station call letters*]
KGWB-TV ... Burlington, IA [*Television station call letters*] (BROA)
KGWC .... Casper, WY [*Television station call letters*]
KGWC .... Offutt Air Force Base, Omaha [*Nebraska*] [*ICAO location identifier*] (ICLI)
KGW-DT ..... Portland, OR [*Television station call letters*] (BROA)
KGWL .... Lander, WY [*Television station call letters*]
KGWN .... Cheyenne, WY [*Television station call letters*]

KGWO .... Greenwood-Leflore [*Mississippi*] [*ICAO location identifier*] (ICLI)
KGWR .... Rock Springs, WY [*Television station call letters*]
KGWS .... Keoladeo Ghana Wildlife Sanctuary (SAUO)
KGWT .... Kilogram Weight (IAA)
KGWY .... Gillette, WY [*FM radio station call letters*]
KGX .... Grayling [*Alaska*] [*Airport symbol*] (OAG)
KGXL-AM ... Costa Mesa, CA [*AM radio station call letters*] (BROA)
KGXY .... Lenwood, CA [*FM radio station call letters*]
KGY .... Congratulatory [*Telegraphy*] (PCTE)
kGy .... Kilo Gray [*Absorbed dose*] [*Radiology*]
KGY .... Kingaroy [*Australia*] [*Airport symbol*] (OAG)
KGY .... Olympia, WA [*AM radio station call letters*]
KGY-FM ..... McCleary, WA [*FM radio station call letters*]
KGYN .... Guymon, OK [*AM radio station call letters*]
kg/yr .... Kilograms per Year (COE)
KGZ .... Glacier Creek, AK [*Location identifier*] [*FAA*] (FAAL)
KGZ .... Kyrgyzstan (ADWA)
Kgz .... Kyrgyzstan (MILB)
KGZC .... Folsom, LA [*FM radio station call letters*]
KGZF .... Emporia, KS [*FM radio station call letters*]
KGZH .... Nyssa, OR [*FM radio station call letters*]
KGZO-FM ... Shafter, CA [*FM radio station call letters*] (RBYB)
KH .... Bad Kreuznach [*German license plate city code*]
KH .... Cambodia [*ANSI two-letter standard code*] (CNC)
KH .... Cook Islandair [*ICAO designator*] (AD)
KH .... Cook Island Airways Ltd. (SAUO)
KH .... Hong Kong [*IYRU nationality code*] (IYR)
KH .... Hungary [*License plate code assigned to foreign diplomats in the US*]
KH .... Kadosh [*Freemasonry*] (ROG)
KH .... Kawasaki Heavy Industries Ltd. [*Japan*] [*ICAO aircraft manufacturer identifier*] (ICAO)
KH .... Kelvin-Helmholtz [*Waves*] [*Meteorology*]
KH .... Kelvin Hughes A/S (SAUO)
KH .... Keren Hayesod (BJA)
KH .... Kersten Hurik Group [*Commercial firm*] [*British*]
KH .... Ketogenic Hormone [*Medicine*] (EDAA)
KH .... Key Hole [*Reconnaissance satellite series*] (DOMA)
KH .... Keyhole Series [*Optical reconnaissance satellites*]
Kh .... Khirbet (BJA)
KH .... Kilohenry
kH .... Kilohertz
kh .... Kilohour (ELAL)
Kh .... Kilohour (VLIE)
KH .... King's Hussars [*Military unit*] [*British*]
KH .... Kneller Hall [*British military*] (DMA)
KH .... Knight of Honor
KH .... Knight of the Guelphic Order of Hanover [*British*]
KH .... Know-How (FOTI)
KH .... Kramers-Henneberger [*Coordinate frame for electron movement*] [*Physics*]
KH .... Krebs-Henseleit [*Cycle*] [*or Ornithine cycle*] [*Analytical biochemistry*] (DAVI)
KH .... Krebs-Henseleit Buffer [*Analytical biochemistry*] (DMAA)
KH .... Kupat Holim (BJA)
KH3 .... Geriatricum [*Drug containing procaine hydrochloride and hematoprophyrin base*] [*Medicine*] (EDAA)
KHA .... Kansas Hospital Association (SRA)
KHA .... Khamsin [*NCIC car model code*]
KHA .... Khancoban [*Australia*] [*Seismograph station code, US Geological Survey*] (SEIS)
kha .... Khasi [*MARC language code*] [*Library of Congress*] (LCCP)
KHA .... Killed by Hostile Action [*Military*]
KHA .... Kitty Hawk Airways, Inc. [*ICAO designator*] (FAAC)
KHAA .... Kansas Hearing Aid Association (EARSL)
KHAC .... Tse Bonito, NM [*AM radio station call letters*]
KHAD .... De Soto, MO [*AM radio station call letters*]
KhAI .... Kharkov Aviation Institute (SAUO)
KHAK .... Cedar Rapids-Waterloo-Dubuque, IA [*FM radio station call letters*] (GDPB)
KHAK-FM ... Cedar Rapids, IA [*FM radio station call letters*]
KHalH .... Hertzler Research Foundation, Halstead, KS [*Library symbol*] [*Library of Congress*] (LCLS)
KHAM-FM ... Saint Ansgar, IA [*FM radio station call letters*] (BROA)
KHAP .... Chico, CA [*FM radio station call letters*]
KHAR .... Anchorage, AK [*AM radio station call letters*]
KHAR .... Harrisburg/Capital City [*Pennsylvania*] [*ICAO location identifier*] (ICLI)
KHAS .... Hastings, NE [*AM radio station call letters*]
KHAS-TV .... Hastings, NE [*Television station call letters*]
KHAT .... Kurzer Handkommentar zum Alten Testament [*Tuebingen*] [*A publication*] (BJA)
KHAT .... Laramie, WY [*FM radio station call letters*] (BROA)
KHAT .... Lincoln, NE [*AM radio station call letters*]
KHAW .... Hilo, HI [*Television station call letters*]
KHAY .... Ventura, CA [*FM radio station call letters*]
KHayF .... Fort Hays State University, Hays, KS [*Library symbol*] [*Library of Congress*] (LCLS)
KHayv .... Haysville Community Library, Haysville, KS [*Library symbol*] [*Library of Congress*] (LCLS)
KHAZ .... Hays, KS [*FM radio station call letters*]
KHB .... Keyhole Bypass [*Medicine*] (EDAA)
KHB .... Khabarovsk [*Former USSR*] [*Geomagnetic observatory code*]
KHB .... King's Hard Bargain [*British military slang for undesirable sailor or soldier*]
KHB .... Korea Housing Bank (IMH)
KHB .... Krebs-Henseleit Bicarbonate [*A buffer*] [*Analytical biochemistry*]
KHB .... Krebs-Henseleit Buffer [*Medicine*] (EDAA)
KHB .... KSC [*Kennedy Space Center*] Handbook [*NASA*] (KSC)
KHB .... Kurzgefasstes Exegetisches Handbuch zum Alten Testament [*Leipzig*] [*A publication*] (BJA)
KHb .... Potassium Hemoglobinate (AAMN)
KHBC .... Hilo, HI [*Television station call letters*]
KHBG .... Healdsburg, CA [*FM radio station call letters*] (RBYB)
KHBM .... Monticello, AR [*AM radio station call letters*]
KHBM-FM ... Monticello, AR [*FM radio station call letters*]
KHBR .... Hillsboro, TX [*AM radio station call letters*]
KHBR .... Hobart [*Oklahoma*] [*ICAO location identifier*] (ICLI)
KHBS .... Fort Smith, AR [*Television station call letters*]
KHBT .... Humboldt, IA [*FM radio station call letters*]
KHBX-FM ... El Dorado, AR [*FM radio station call letters*] (BROA)
KHByF .... Fort Hays State University (SAUO)
KHBZ .... Oklahoma City, OK [*FM radio station call letters*] (BROA)
KHBZ-AM ... Honolulu, HI [*AM radio station call letters*] (BROA)
KHC .... 135 Airways [*FAA designator*] (FAAC)
KHC .... Karen Horney Clinic (EA)
KHC .... Karen Horney Psychoanalytic Clinic (SAUO)
KHC .... Kasperske Hory [*Czechoslovakia*] [*Seismograph station code, US Geological Survey*] (SEIS)
KHC .... Kinesin Heavy Chain [*Physiology*]
KHC .... Kinetic Hemolysis Curve [*Biochemistry*] (DAVI)
KHC .... King's Honorary Chaplain [*British*]
KHCA .... Wamego, KS [*FM radio station call letters*]
KHCB .... Galveston, TX [*AM radio station call letters*]
KHCB .... Houston, TX [*FM radio station call letters*]
KHCC .... Hutchinson, KS [*FM radio station call letters*]
KHCCC ...... Kokomo - Howard County Chamber of Commerce (EARSL)
KHCD .... Kenya High Court Digest [*A publication*] (DLA)
KHCD .... Salina, KS [*FM radio station call letters*]
KHCE .... Khabarovsk Commodity Exchange [*Russian Federation*] (EY)
KHCE .... San Antonio, TX [*Television station call letters*]
KHCH .... Huntsville, TX [*AM radio station call letters*] (BROA)
KHCJ .... Jefferson, TX [*FM radio station call letters*] (BROA)
KHCK .... Dallas, TX [*AM radio station call letters*] (BROA)
KHCK .... Denton, TX [*FM radio station call letters*] (RBYB)
KHCL .... Arcadia, LA [*FM radio station call letters*] (BROA)
KHCME ...... Kharkov Commodity and Raw Materials Exchange [*Ukraine*] (EY)
KHCP .... Paris, TX [*FM radio station call letters*] (BROA)
KHCR .... Potosi, MO [*FM radio station call letters*]
KHCS .... Palm Desert, CA [*FM radio station call letters*]
KHCT .... Great Bend, KS [*FM radio station call letters*]
KHCV .... Seattle, WA [*Television station call letters*]
KHCX .... Chief Petty Paper [*Private rail car owner code*]
KHCZ .... Koch Carbon [*Federal Railroad Administration identification code*]
KHD .... Kinky Hair Disease [*Medicine*] (DMAA)
KHD .... Klockner-Humboldt-Deutz (EFIS)
KHDC .... Chualar, CA [*FM radio station call letters*]
KHDN .... Hardin, MT [*AM radio station call letters*] (RBYB)
KHDR-FM ... Victorville, CA [*FM radio station call letters*] (BROA)
KHDS .... Honorary Dental Surgeon to the King (SAUS)
KHDS .... King's Honorary Dental Surgeon [*British*]
KHDT .... Caldwell, ID [*Television station call letters*]
KHDV .... King City, CA [*FM radio station call letters*] (BROA)
KHDX .... Conway, AR [*FM radio station call letters*]
KHDY-FM ... Plainview, TX [*FM radio station call letters*] (RBYB)
KHE .... Kanfey-Ha'Emek Aviation [*Israel*] [*FAA designator*] (FAAC)
KHE .... Kheis [*Former USSR*] [*Seismograph station code, US Geological Survey*] (SEIS)
KHE .... Kherson [*USSR*] [*Airport symbol*] (AD)
KHE .... Korowai [*Language symbol*] (ETLW)
KHEP .... Phoenix, AZ [*AM radio station call letters*]
KHER .... Crystal City, TX [*FM radio station call letters*]
KHET .... Honolulu, HI [*Television station call letters*]
KHEY .... El Paso, TX [*AM radio station call letters*]
KHEY-FM .... El Paso, TX [*FM radio station call letters*]
KHF .... Know How Fund [*European economic development fund*]
KHF .... Korean Hemorrhagic Fever [*Medicine*]
KHFD .... Hartford/Brainard Field [*Connecticut*] [*ICAO location identifier*] (ICLI)
KHFD-FM ... Hereford, TX [*FM radio station call letters*] (BROA)
KHFI .... Georgetown, TX [*FM radio station call letters*]
KHFM .... Albuquerque, NM [*FM radio station call letters*]
KHFM .... Santa Fe, NM [*FM radio station call letters*] (BROA)
KHFN .... Los Ranchos de Albuquerque, NM [*AM radio station call letters*] (RBYB)
KHFS-AM ... Fort Smith, AR [*AM radio station call letters*] (BROA)
KHFT .... Hobbs, NM [*Television station call letters*]
KHFX-FM ... Ball, LA [*FM radio station call letters*] (BROA)
KHG .... Kashi [*China*] [*Airport symbol*] (OAG)
KHG .... Keystone Heritage Group [*AMEX symbol*] (TTSB)
KHG .... Keystone Heritage Group, Inc. [*AMEX symbol*] (SAG)
K hgb .... Potassium Hemoglobinate [*Organic chemistry*] (DAVI)
KHGG .... Fort Smith, AR [*AM radio station call letters*] (GDPB)
KHGG-AM ... Van Buren, AR [*AM radio station call letters*] (BROA)
KHGI .... Kearney, NE [*Television station call letters*]
KHGI .... Keystone Heritage Group, Incorporated (SAUO)
KHGN-FM ... Kirksville, MO [*FM radio station call letters*] (BROA)
KHH .... Kaohsiung [*Taiwan*] [*Airport symbol*] (OAG)
KHH .... Kirchoff, H. H., St. Paul MN [*STAC*]
KHHA .... Kentucky Home Health Association (EARSL)
KHHK .... Yakima, WA [*FM radio station call letters*] (BROA)

KHHK-FM... Naches, WA [*FM radio station call letters*] (RBYB)
KHHL........ Leander, TX [*FM radio station call letters*] (BROA)
KHHO-AM... Tacoma, WA [*AM radio station call letters*] (RBYB)
KHHT........ Killeen, TX [*FM radio station call letters*]
KHHT........ Los Angeles, CA [*FM radio station call letters*] (BROA)
KHHZ........ Oroville, CA [*FM radio station call letters*] (BROA)
KHI........... Kakhk [*Iran*] [*Seismograph station code, US Geological Survey*] (SEIS)
KHi........... Kansas State Historical Society, Topeka, KS [*Library symbol*] [*Library of Congress*] (LCLS)
KHI........... Karachi [*Pakistan*] [*Airport symbol*] (OAG)
KHI........... Kawasaki Heavy Industries (ACAE)
KHI........... Kawasaki Heavy Industries Ltd (SAUS)
KHI........... Kelvin-Helmholtz Instability (PDAA)
KHI........... Kemper High Income [*NYSE symbol*] (SPSG)
KHIB......... Durant, OK [*FM radio station call letters*]
KHIB......... Hibbing/Chisholm-Hibbing [*Minnesota*] [*ICAO location identifier*] (ICLI)
KHID......... McAllen, TX [*FM radio station call letters*]
KHIF......... Keeping House of Ill Fame
KHIF......... Ogden/Hill Air Force Base [*Utah*] [*ICAO location identifier*] (ICLI)
KHIH-FM.... Denver, CO [*FM radio station call letters*] (RBYB)
KHII.......... Cloudcroft, NM [*FM radio station call letters*] (BROA)
KHII.......... Security, CO [*FM radio station call letters*]
KHIL.......... Willcox, AZ [*AM radio station call letters*]
KHILS........ Kill-vehicle In-the-Loop Simulator (SAUS)
KHiIT........ Tabor College, Hillsboro, KS [*Library symbol*] [*Library of Congress*] (LCLS)
KHIMA....... Kentucky Health Information Management Association (EARSL)
KHIM-FM.... Mangum, OK [*FM radio station call letters*] (BROA)
KHIM-TV.... Conroe, TX [*TV station call letters*] (RBYB)
KHIN......... Red Oak, IA [*Television station call letters*]
KHIP......... Felton, CA [*FM radio station call letters*]
KHIS......... Bakersfield, CA [*AM radio station call letters*]
KHIS-FM.... Bakersfield, CA [*FM radio station call letters*]
KHIT......... Reno, NV [*FM radio station call letters*]
KHIT-AM.... Reno, NV [*AM radio station call letters*] (RBYB)
KHIX......... Carlin, NV [*FM radio station call letters*] (BROA)
KHIX-FM.... Ely, NV [*FM radio station call letters*] (BROA)
KHIZ......... Barstow, CA [*Television station call letters*]
KHJ.......... Los Angeles (Corona & San Bernardino), CA [*AM radio station call letters*] (GDPB)
KHJ-AM..... Los Angeles, CA [*AM radio station call letters*] (BROA)
KHJC......... Lihue, HI [*FM radio station call letters*] (BROA)
KHJJ......... Lancaster, CA [*AM radio station call letters*]
KHJM........ Taft, OK [*FM radio station call letters*]
KHJP-FM.... Leone, AS [*FM radio station call letters*] (BROA)
KHJQ-FM... Susanville, CA [*FM radio station call letters*] (BROA)
KHJR......... Gooding, ID [*FM radio station call letters*] (BROA)
KHJS-FM.... Pago Pago, AS (BROA)
KHK.......... Khark [*Iran*] [*Airport symbol*] [*Obsolete*] (OAG)
KHK.......... Kurzer Handkommentar zum Alten Testament [*A publication*] (BJA)
KHKC......... Atoka, OK [*FM radio station call letters*]
KHKE......... Cedar Falls, IA [*FM radio station call letters*]
KHKI.......... Des Moines, IA [*FM radio station call letters*]
KHKK-FM... Modesto, CA [*FM radio station call letters*] (RBYB)
KHKL......... Laytonville, CA [*FM radio station call letters*] (BROA)
KHKN......... Benton, AR [*FM radio station call letters*] (BROA)
KHKR......... East Helena, MT [*AM radio station call letters*]
KHKR-FM... East Helena, MT [*FM radio station call letters*]
KHKS......... Denton, TX [*FM radio station call letters*]
KHKV......... Kerrville, TX [*FM radio station call letters*] (BROA)
KHKX......... Odessa, TX [*FM radio station call letters*] (BROA)
KHKY......... Hickory/Municipal [*North Carolina*] [*ICAO location identifier*] (ICLI)
KHL........... Kennedy-Heaviside Layer [*Electronics*]
KHL........... Kentron Hawaii [*Federal Railroad Administration identification code*]
KHL........... Keren Hajesod Ljisroel (BJA)
KHL........... Khulna [*Bangladesh*] [*Airport symbol*] (AD)
KHL........... Kupat Holim Le-'Ovdim Le'umiyim [*A publication*] (BJA)
KHLA......... Jennings, LA [*FM radio station call letters*] (BROA)
KHLA......... Lake Charles, LA [*FM radio station call letters*]
KHLB......... Burnet, TX [*AM radio station call letters*]
KHLB-FM... Burnet, TX [*FM radio station call letters*]
KHLL......... Richwood, LA [*FM radio station call letters*]
KHLO......... Hilo, HI [*AM radio station call letters*]
KHLOS....... Kilo High Level Language Operations per Second (CCCA)
KHLP......... Omaha, NE [*AM radio station call letters*] (BROA)
KHLR......... Cameron, TX [*FM radio station call letters*]
KHLR......... Kahler Corp. [*NASDAQ symbol*] (NQ)
KHLR......... KahlerRealty [*NASDAQ symbol*] (TTSB)
KHLS......... Blytheville, AR [*FM radio station call letters*]
KHLT......... Hallettsville, TX [*AM radio station call letters*] (RBYB)
KHM.......... Cambodia [*ANSI three-letter standard code*] (CNC)
KHM.......... Khamtis [*Myanmar*] [*Airport symbol*] (OAG)
KHM.......... King's Harbour Master [*Obsolete*] [*British*]
KH-M........ Yad V'Kidush Hashem, House of Martyrs (EA)
KHMA........ Kentucky Hotel and Motel Association (SRA)
KHMB........ Hamburg, AR [*FM radio station call letters*]
KHMC........ Goliad, TX [*FM radio station call letters*]
KHME........ Winona, MN [*FM radio station call letters*]
KHMG........ Barrigada, GU [*FM radio station call letters*] (RBYB)
KHMN........ Alamogordo/Holloman Air Force Base [*New Mexico*] [*ICAO location identifier*] (ICLI)
KHMO........ Hannibal, MO [*AM radio station call letters*]
KHMS........ Victorville, CA [*FM radio station call letters*]
KHMT........ Hardin, MT [*Television station call letters*] (RBYB)
KHMX........ Houston, TX [*FM radio station call letters*]
KHMY........ Wichita-Hutchinson, KS [*FM radio station call letters*] (GDPB)
KHN.......... Knoop Hardness Number
KHN.......... Nanchang [*China*] [*Airport symbol*] (OAG)
KHN.......... Northern Kentucky University, Highland Heights, KY [*OCLC symbol*] (OCLC)
KHNC........ Johnstown, CO [*AM radio station call letters*]
KHND........ Harvey, ND [*AM radio station call letters*]
KHNE........ Hastings, NE [*FM radio station call letters*]
KHNE-TV.... Hastings, NE [*Television station call letters*]
KHNL........ Honolulu, HI [*Television station call letters*]
KHNN........ Kuehn and Nagel [*Common carrier symbol*]
KHNR........ Honolulu, HI [*AM radio station call letters*]
KHNS........ Haines, AK [*FM radio station call letters*]
KHNS........ Honorary Nursing Sister to the King (SAUS)
KHNS........ King's Honorary Nursing Sister [*British*]
KHO.......... Khorog [*Former USSR*] [*Seismograph station code, US Geological Survey*] (SEIS)
KHO.......... Khors Aircompany [*Ukraine*] [*FAA designator*] (FAAC)
kho........... Khotanese [*MARC language code*] [*Library of Congress*] (LCCP)
KHOB........ Hobbs/Les County [*New Mexico*] [*ICAO location identifier*] (ICLI)
KHOB........ Hobbs, NM [*AM radio station call letters*]
KHOC-FM... Casper, WY [*FM radio station call letters*] (BROA)
KHOE........ Fairfield, IA [*FM radio station call letters*]
KHOG........ Fayetteville, AR [*Television station call letters*]
KHOK........ Hoisington, KS [*FM radio station call letters*]
KHOL........ Beulah, ND [*AM radio station call letters*]
KHOM........ Houma, LA [*FM radio station call letters*]
KHOM........ Salem, AR [*FM radio station call letters*] (BROA)
KHON........ Honolulu, HI [*Television station call letters*]
KHOP........ Hopkinsville/Campbell Army Air Field [*Kentucky*] [*ICAO location identifier*] (ICLI)
KHOP........ Modesto, CA [*FM radio station call letters*]
KHOP........ Oakdale, CA [*FM radio station call letters*] (BROA)
KHOS........ Sonora, TX [*AM radio station call letters*]
KHOS-FM... Sonora, TX [*FM radio station call letters*]
KHOT........ Globe, AZ [*FM radio station call letters*] (RBYB)
KHOT........ Madera, CA [*AM radio station call letters*]
KHOT........ Paradise Valley, AZ [*FM radio station call letters*] (BROA)
KHOU........ Houston, TX [*Television station call letters*]
KHOU........ Houston/William P. Hobby [*Texas*] [*ICAO location identifier*] (ICLI)
KHOU-DT... Houston, TX [*Television station call letters*] (BROA)
KHOV........ Wickenburg, AZ [*FM radio station call letters*] (BROA)
KHOW........ Denver, CO [*AM radio station call letters*]
KHOX........ Hoxie, AR [*FM radio station call letters*]
KHOY........ Laredo, TX [*FM radio station call letters*]
KHOZ........ Harrison, AR [*AM radio station call letters*]
KHOZ-FM... Harrison, AR [*FM radio station call letters*]
KHP.......... Honorary Physician to the King [*British*]
KHP.......... Kapori [*Language symbol*] (ETLW)
KHP.......... Koppers Hydrate Process
KHP.......... Potassium Hydrogen Phthalate (SAUS)
KHPA........ Hope, AR [*FM radio station call letters*]
KHPC........ Karen Horney Psychoanalytic Clinic (SAUO)
KHPE........ Albany, OR [*FM radio station call letters*]
KHPN........ Loveland, CO [*AM radio station call letters*] (BROA)
KHPN........ White Plains/Westchester [*New York*] [*ICAO location identifier*] (ICLI)
KHPQ........ Clinton, AR [*FM radio station call letters*]
KHPR........ Honolulu, HI [*FM radio station call letters*]
KHPS........ Kilo Hops per Second (CCCA)
KHPT........ Conroe, TX [*FM radio station call letters*] (BROA)
KHPU-FM... Brownwood, TX [*FM radio station call letters*] (BROA)
KHPX........ El Paso, TX (Las Cruces, NM) [*FM radio station call letters*] (GDPB)
KHPY........ Moreno Valley, CA [*AM radio station call letters*]
KHQ.......... Spokane, WA [*Television station call letters*]
KHQA........ Hannibal, MO [*Television station call letters*]
KHQN........ Spanish Fork, UT [*AM radio station call letters*]
KHQT........ Las Cruces, NM [*FM radio station call letters*] (BROA)
KHR.......... Khanai-Hindubagh Railway [*Indian Railway*] (TIR)
KHR.......... Khazar [*Turkmenistan*] [*ICAO designator*] (FAAC)
KHR.......... Khorongon [*Former USSR*] [*Seismograph station code, US Geological Survey*] [*Closed*] (SEIS)
KHRA........ Honolulu, HI [*AM radio station call letters*] (BROA)
KHRD........ Weaverville, CA [*FM radio station call letters*] (BROA)
KHRI......... Hollister, Ca [*FM radio station call letters*] (BROA)
KHRI......... Kresge Hearing Research Institute [*University of Michigan*] [*Research center*]
KHRL........ Harlingen/Industrial Airpack [*Texas*] [*ICAO location identifier*] (ICLI)
KHRN........ Hearne, TX [*FM radio station call letters*] (RBYB)
KHRO........ El Paso, TX [*FM radio station call letters*] (BROA)
KHRO........ Harrison/Boone County [*Arkansas*] [*ICAO location identifier*] (ICLI)
KHRP........ Kurdish Human Rights Project (BUAC)
KHRR........ Tucson, AZ [*Television station call letters*]
KHRT........ Mary Esther/Eglin Air Field Auxiliary [*Florida*] [*ICAO location identifier*] (ICLI)
KHRT........ Minot, ND [*AM radio station call letters*]
KHS.......... Honorary Surgeon to the King [*British*]
KHS.......... Kelly Highway Steer [*Tire marketing*]
KHS.......... Kennedy High School (SAUO)
KHS.......... King's Honorary Surgeon [*Medicine*] (EDAA)
KHS.......... Kinky Hair Syndrome [*Medicine*] (DMAA)
KHS.......... Knight of the Holy Sepulchre
KHS.......... Knight of the Holy Sepulchre of Jerusalem (DD)

KHS Korean Hemorrhagic Fever [*Medicine*] (QSUL)
KHS Krebs-Henseleit Solution (DB)
KHS Kushtia [*Bangladesh*] [*Airport symbol*] (AD)
KHSA Kentucky Human Services Association (SRA)
KHSC Ontario, CA [*Television station call letters*]
KHSD Lead, SD [*Television station call letters*]
KHSH Alvin, TX [*Television station call letters*]
KHSL Paradise, CA [*FM radio station call letters*]
KHSL-TV Chico, CA [*Television station call letters*]
KHSN Coos Bay, OR [*AM radio station call letters*]
KHSP Ashdown, AR [*FM radio station call letters*]
KHSP Kein Hung Shipping Company [*Common carrier symbol*]
KHSP Texarkana, TX [*AM radio station call letters*]
KHSR-FM Crescent City, CA [*FM radio station call letters*] (BROA)
KHSS Walla Walla, WA [*FM radio station call letters*]
KHST Homestead/Homestead Air Force Base [*Florida*] [*ICAO location identifier*] (ICLI)
KHST Lamar, MO [*FM radio station call letters*]
KHSU Arcata, CA [*FM radio station call letters*]
KHSX Irving, TX [*Television station call letters*]
KHT Kathode Heating Time
KHT Khost [*Afghanistan*] [*Airport symbol*] [*Obsolete*] (OAG)
KHTA Wake Village, TX [*FM radio station call letters*] (BROA)
KHTC Phoenix, AZ [*FM radio station call letters*] (RBYB)
KHTE-AM England, AR [*AM radio station call letters*] (BROA)
KHTE-FM Lonoke, AR [*FM radio station call letters*] (BROA)
KHTH Dillon, CO [*AM radio station call letters*]
KHTK Sacramento, CA [*AM radio station call letters*]
KHTL Albuquerque, NM [*AM radio station call letters*] (RBYB)
KHTL Houghton Lake/Roscommon [*Michigan*] [*ICAO location identifier*] (ICLI)
KHTN Los Banos, CA [*FM radio station call letters*]
KHTO Mount Vernon, MO [*FM radio station call letters*]
KHTQ Hayden, ID [*FM radio station call letters*] (RBYB)
KHTR Pullman, WA [*FM radio station call letters*]
KHTS El Cajon, CA [*FM radio station call letters*] (RBYB)
KHTT Muskogee, OK [*FM radio station call letters*]
KHTTA Kanata High Technology Training Association [*Canada*] (EDAC)
KHTV Houston, TX [*Television station call letters*]
KHTW-FM Caledonia, MN [*FM radio station call letters*] (BROA)
KHTX Salinas, CA [*AM radio station call letters*] (RBYB)
KHTY Santa Barbara, CA [*FM radio station call letters*]
KHTZ Albuquerque, NM [*AM radio station call letters*] (BROA)
KHTZ Cameron, TX [*FM radio station call letters*] (BROA)
KHu Hutchinson Public Library, Hutchinson, KS [*Library symbol*] [*Library of Congress*] (LCLS)
KHU Kahuku [*Hawaii*] [*Seismograph station code, US Geological Survey*] (SEIS)
KHUB Fremont, NE [*AM radio station call letters*]
KHuC Hutchinson Community Junior College, Hutchinson, KS [*Library symbol*] [*Library of Congress*] (LCLS)
KHUG Rocky Ford, CO [*FM radio station call letters*]
KHUG-FM England, AR [*FM radio station call letters*] (BROA)
KHUI Honolulu, HI [*FM radio station call letters*] (BROA)
KHUL Houlton/International [*Maine*] [*ICAO location identifier*] (ICLI)
KHUL Kanab, UT [*FM radio station call letters*] (BROA)
KHUL-FM Waipahu, HI [*FM radio station call letters*] (BROA)
KHUM Garberville, CA [*FM radio station call letters*] (RBYB)
KHUT Hutchinson, KS [*FM radio station call letters*]
KHV Khabarovsk [*Former USSR*] [*Airport symbol*] (OAG)
KhV Khranit' Vechno [*To be Kept in Perpetuity*] [*KGB file status*]
KhV Khristianski Vostok (BJA)
KHVH Honolulu, HI [*AM radio station call letters*]
KHVL Huntsville, TX [*AM radio station call letters*] (GDPB)
KHVL-AM Huntsville, TX [*AM radio station call letters*] (BROA)
KHVN Fort Worth, TX [*AM radio station call letters*]
KHVO Hilo, HI [*Television station call letters*]
KHVO-DT Hilo, HI [*Television station call letters*] (BROA)
KHVR Havre [*Montana*] [*ICAO location identifier*] (ICLI)
KHWB Houston, TX [*Television station call letters*] (BROA)
KHWG Quincy, CA [*FM radio station call letters*] (BROA)
KHWG-FM Kings Beach, CA [*FM radio station call letters*] (RBYB)
KHWI Hilo, HI [*FM radio station call letters*]
KHWK Tonopah, NV [*FM radio station call letters*]
KHWO Hollywood/North Perry [*Florida*] [*ICAO location identifier*] (ICLI)
KHWS-FM North Pole, AK [*FM radio station call letters*] (BROA)
KHWY Essex, CA [*FM radio station call letters*]
KHWZ-FM Ludlow, CA [*FM radio station call letters*] (RBYB)
KHX Hugo Rizzuto [*ICAO designator*] (FAAC)
KHXR-FM Sun Valley, NV [*FM radio station call letters*] (BROA)
KHXS Abilene, TX [*FM radio station call letters*]
KHXS Merkel, TX [*FM radio station call letters*] (BROA)
KHYAX Kemper High Yield Cl.A [*Mutual fund ticker symbol*] (SG)
KHYB Kupat Holim Year Book [*A publication*] (BJA)
KHYBX Kemper High Yield Cl.B [*Mutual fund ticker symbol*] (SG)
KHYF Know How You Feel (ADWA)
KHYF-FM Taos, NM [*FM radio station call letters*] (BROA)
KHYI Howe, TX [*FM radio station call letters*]
KHYL Auburn, CA [*FM radio station call letters*]
KHYM Gilmer, TX [*AM radio station call letters*]
KHYM-FM Copeland, KS [*FM radio station call letters*] (BROA)
KHYS Abilene, TX [*FM radio station call letters*] (BROA)
KHYS Port Arthur, TX [*FM radio station call letters*]
KHYT-FM Tucson, AZ [*FM radio station call letters*] (RBYB)
KHYZ Mountain Pass, CA [*FM radio station call letters*]
KHZ Kilohertz [*FAA*] (TAG)
KHz Kilohertz (VLIE)
kHz Kilohertz [*Electronics*]
KHZL Shingletown, CA [*FM radio station call letters*] (RBYB)
KI Absorption index for the daylight end of a day-night electromagnetic transmission path (SAUS)
KI Kach International (EA)
KI Kanaanaeische Inschriften [*A publication*] (BJA)
KI Kangaroo Island (SAUO)
KI Karyopyknotic Index [*Cytology*] (MAE)
KI Karyotype Instability [*Genetics*]
KI Kennarasamband Islands [*Iceland*] (BUAC)
KI Keyette International (EA)
KI Key Industry [*Business term*]
KI Khmer Insurgents [*Cambodian rebel force*]
KI Kiel [*German license plate city code*]
KI Kill [*Telegraphy*] (PCTE)
KI Kilo (WDAA)
KI Kinase Insert
Ki Kings [*Old Testament book*]
KI Kiribati [*Internet country code*]
KI Kirtland Area Office (SAUO)
KI Kitchen (AABC)
KI Kiwanis International (EA)
KI Knesset Israel (BJA)
KI Know, Incorporated (SAUO)
KI Knowledge Initiative (FOTI)
KI Knowledge Integrity [*Electronic information*] (IT)
KI Kovats [*Retention*] Index
KI Krama Inggil [*Linguistics*] (IEL)
KI Kroenig's Isthmus [*Of resonance*] [*Medicine*]
KI Potassium Iodide (AAMN)
Ki Secret Identity Key (CGWS)
KiA Die Keilinschriften der Achaemeniden [*A publication*] (BJA)
KIA Kachin Independence Army [*Myanmar*] [*Political party*] (EY)
KIA Kaiapit [*New Guinea*] [*Airport symbol*] (AD)
KIA Kansai International Airport [*Japan*]
KIA Kent International Airport [*British*]
KIA Kenya Institute of Administration (BUAC)
KIA Kia [*NCIC car make code*]
KIA Kibbutz Industries Association [*Israel*] (BUAC)
KIA Killed in Action [*Military*]
KIA Kim [*Language symbol*] (ETLW)
KIA KIWI International Air Lines, Inc. [*ICAO designator*] (FAAC)
KIA Kligler Iron Agar [*Medium*]
KIA Know It All [*Usually the captain*] [*Nautical term*] (NTA)
KIA Korean Inferior Automobile (SAUO)
KIA Kotoka International Airport [*Ghana*]
KIAA Kangaroo Industries Association of Australia
KIAA Korea Industrial Advancement Administration (SAUO)
KIAB Wichita/McConnell Air Force Base [*Kansas*] [*ICAO location identifier*] (ICLI)
KIA - BNR Killed in Action - Body Not Recovered (MCD)
KIAC Kansai International Airport Co. [*Japan*]
KIAC Kansai International Airport Company (SAUO)
KIAC Kerr Industrial Applications Center [*Southeastern Oklahoma State University*] [*Durant*] [*Information service or system*] (IID)
KIAD Washington/Dulles International [*District of Columbia*] [*ICAO location identifier*] (ICLI)
KIAG Niagara Falls/International [*New York*] [*ICAO location identifier*] (ICLI)
KIAH Houston/Intercontinental [*Texas*] [*ICAO location identifier*] (ICLI)
KIAI Mason City, IA [*FM radio station call letters*]
KIAK Fairbanks, AK [*AM radio station call letters*]
KIAK-FM Fairbanks, AK [*FM radio station call letters*]
KIAL Unalaska, AK [*AM radio station call letters*]
KIAM Nenana, AK [*AM radio station call letters*]
KIAQ Clarion, IA [*FM radio station call letters*]
KIAR Kiwanis International Accredited Representative
KIAR Kuzell Institute for Arthritis Research [*Medical Research Institute at Pacific Medical Center*] [*Research center*] (RCD)
KIAS Knots Indicated Airspeed (MCD)
KIAS Korea Advanced Institute of Science
KIB Ivanof Bay, AK [*Location identifier*] [*FAA*] (FAAL)
KIB Kansas Inspection Bureau (SAUO)
KiB Keilinschriftliche Bibliothek [*A publication*] (BJA)
KIB Kentucky Inspection Bureau (SAUO)
kib Kilopounds (NAKS)
KIB Kirchheimbolanden [*German license plate city code*]
KIBB-FM Los Angeles, CA [*FM radio station call letters*] (RBYB)
KIBC Burney, CA [*FM radio station call letters*]
KIBG-FM Merced, CA [*FM radio station call letters*] (RBYB)
KIBIC Karolinska Institutets Bibliotek och Informationscentral [*Karolinska Institute Library and Information Center*] [*Sweden*] [*Information service or system*] (IID)
KIBL Beeville, TX [*AM radio station call letters*]
KIBN Wichita, KS [*FM radio station call letters*]
KIBO Knowledge In, Bullshit Out (SAUO)
KIBR-FM Sandpoint, ID [*FM radio station call letters*] (BROA)
KIBS Bishop, CA [*FM radio station call letters*]
KIBX Bonners Ferry, ID [*FM radio station call letters*] (BROA)
KIBZ Lincoln, NE [*FM radio station call letters*]
KIC Kansas Information Circuit [*Library network*]
KIC Karlsruhe Isochronous Cyclotron

KIC.......... Kart Industry Council
KIC.......... Kellogg International Corporation (SAUO)
KIC.......... Kenya Indian Congress (SAUO)
KIC.......... Kernal Input Controller [*Computer science*] (CIST)
KIC.......... Ketoisocaproate [*Biochemistry*]
KIC.......... Keto Isocaproic Acid (DMAA)
KIC.......... King City, CA [*Location identifier*] [*FAA*] (FAAL)
KIC.......... Knight of the Iron Crown [*British*] (ROG)
KIC.......... Kollsman Instrument Corporation (SAUO)
KIC.......... Kosan Boka [*Ivory Coast*] [*Seismograph station code, US Geological Survey*] (SEIS)
KIC.......... Kurdistan Information Centre (BUAC)
KIC.......... Kuwait Insurance Co. (BUAC)
KICA........ Clovis, NM [*AM radio station call letters*]
KICA........ Farwell, TX [*FM radio station call letters*]
KICAX...... Kemper Inc. Cap. Pres. Cl.A [*Mutual fund ticker symbol*] (SG)
KICB........ Fort Dodge, IA [*FM radio station call letters*]
KICB........ Killed Intracellular Bacteria [*Microbiology*] (DAVI)
KICD........ Spencer, IA [*AM radio station call letters*]
KICD-FM.... Spencer, IA [*FM radio station call letters*]
KICE........ Bend, OR [*FM radio station call letters*]
KICF........ Kentucky Independent College Foundation (SAUO)
KICI........ Corsicana, TX [*FM radio station call letters*] (RBYB)
KICI........ Denton, TX [*AM radio station call letters*] (RBYB)
KICK........ Master Glaziers Karate Intl. [*NASDAQ symbol*] (SAG)
KICK........ Palmyra, MO [*FM radio station call letters*]
KICKW...... Master Glaziers Karate Wrrt'A' [*NASDAQ symbol*] (TTSB)
KICKZ...... Master Glaziers Karate Wrrt'B' [*NASDAQ symbol*] (TTSB)
KICM........ Healdton, OK [*FM radio station call letters*]
KICN........ Idaho Falls, ID [*AM radio station call letters*]
KICO........ Calexico, CA [*AM radio station call letters*]
KICR........ Coeur d'Alene, ID [*FM radio station call letters*] (BROA)
KICR........ Oakdale, LA [*AM radio station call letters*]
KICR-FM.... Oakdale, LA [*FM radio station call letters*]
KICS........ Hastings, NE [*AM radio station call letters*]
KICS........ Kansas Individualized Curriculum Sequencing (EDAC)
KICS........ Kids in Crisis Support (EARSL)
KICT........ Wichita, KS [*FM radio station call letters*]
KICT........ Wichita/Mid-Continent [*Kansas*] [*ICAO location identifier*] (ICLI)
KICU........ Keyboard Interface Control Unit [*Computer science*]
KICU........ San Jose, CA [*Television station call letters*]
KICX........ McCook, NE [*FM radio station call letters*]
KICY........ Nome, AK [*AM radio station call letters*]
KICY-FM.... Nome, AK [*FM radio station call letters*]
KID.......... Idaho Falls, ID [*AM radio station call letters*]
KID.......... Kent Infant Development Scale (EDAC)
KID.......... Keratitis, Ichthyosis, and Deafness Syndrome [*Medicine*] (DMAA)
KID.......... Keyboard Input Device (MCD)
KID.......... Key Industry [*Business term*] (DS)
KID.......... Khmer Institute of Democracy [*Phnom Penh, Cambodia*]
KID.......... Kiddie
KID.......... Kidd Resources Ltd. [*Vancouver Stock Exchange symbol*]
Kid.......... Kiddushin (BJA)
KID.......... Kidnaping [*FBI standardized term*]
KID.......... Kidney [*Anatomy*] (DAVI)
KID.......... Kildare [*County in Ireland*] (ROG)
KID.......... Killed [*Telegraphy*] (PCTE)
KID.......... Kinase-Inducible Domain [*Biochemistry*]
KID.......... Kristianstad [*Sweden*] [*Airport symbol*] (OAG)
KIDA........ Ida Grove, IA [*FM radio station call letters*]
KIDA........ Korea Institute for Defence Analyses (SAUO)
KIDA........ Korean International Development Agency (BUAC)
KIDA........ Sun Valley, ID [*Television station call letters*] (BROA)
KidAlnt...... Kiddie Academy International, Inc. [*Associated Press*] (SAG)
KIDC........ Kentucky Industrial Development Council (SRA)
KIDC........ Kiowa Industrial Development Commission
KIDD........ First Yars Inc. (The) [*NASDAQ symbol*] (SAG)
KIDD........ First Years [*NASDAQ symbol*] (TTSB)
KIDD........ Kiddie Products, Inc. [*NASDAQ symbol*] (NQ)
KIDD........ Monterey, CA [*AM radio station call letters*]
KiddAcInt... Kiddie Academy International, Inc. [*Associated Press*] (SAG)
KIDDCOS.... Kitchens Design Drawing and Costing [*Kitchens International DMS Electronics Ltd.*] [*Software package*] (NCC)
KIDE........ 4 Kids Entertainment [*NASDAQ symbol*] (TTSB)
KIDE........ For Kids Entertainment, Inc. [*NASDAQ symbol*] (SAG)
KIDE........ Hoopa, CA [*FM radio station call letters*]
Kideo........ Kideo Productions [*Associated Press*] (SAG)
KID-FM..... Idaho Falls, ID [*FM radio station call letters*]
KIDH........ Eagle, ID [*AM radio station call letters*]
KIDI........ Guadalupe, CA [*FM radio station call letters*]
KIDK........ Idaho Falls, ID [*Television station call letters*]
KIDM........ Kids Mart [*OTCBB symbol*]
KIDN........ Hayden, CO [*FM radio station call letters*]
KIDN-TV.... Avalon, CA [*Television station call letters*] (BROA)
KIDO........ Boise, ID [*AM radio station call letters*]
KIDO........ Kideo Productions [*NASDAQ symbol*] (SAG)
KIDQ........ New Horizon Kids Quest [*NASDAQ symbol*] (TTSB)
KIDQ........ New Horizon Kids Quest, Inc. [*NASDAQ symbol*] (SAG)
KIDR........ Phoenix, AZ [*AM radio station call letters*]
KIDS........ Children's Comprehensive Services [*NASDAQ symbol*] (SAG)
KIDS........ Children's Comp Svcs [*NASDAQ symbol*] (TTSB)
KIDS........ Kent Infant Development Scale [*Neonatology*] (DAVI)
KIDS........ Kestrel Interactive Development System [*Computer science*]
KIDS........ Kids in a Drug-Free Society [*Association*] (EA)
KIDS........ Kids Informed in Drugs and Safety (EARSL)
KIDS........ Kids in Integrated Day Care Settings (MELL)
KIDS........ Kindergarten Inventory of Developmental Skills [*Child development test*]
KIDS........ Knowledge-Based Integrated Design System (DOMA)
KIDS........ Magic Years Child Care & Learning Centers, Inc. (SAUO)
KIDS........ Springfield, MO [*AM radio station call letters*]
Kidult....... Kid-Adult [*Television viewer aged 12-34*]
KIDWE...... Direct Connect Intl Wrrt [*NASDAQ symbol*] (TTSB)
KIDX........ Billings, MT [*FM radio station call letters*]
KIDX........ Ruidoso, NM [*FM radio station call letters*] (BROA)
KIDY........ Kindersley Transport [*Common carrier symbol*]
KIDY........ San Angelo, TX [*Television station call letters*]
KIDZ........ Direct Connect International [*OTCBB symbol*]
KIDZ........ Direct Connection International, Inc. (SAUO)
KIE.......... Kenia Industrial Estates Limited (SAUO)
KIE.......... Kennedy Institute of Ethics, Washington, DC [*OCLC symbol*] (OCLC)
KIE.......... Kieta [*Papua New Guinea*] [*Airport symbol*] (OAG)
KIE.......... Kinetic Isotope Effect [*Physical chemistry*]
KIE.......... Kirklees Information Exchange [*Formerly, Huddersfield and District Information*] (NITA)
KIE.......... Kodak Image Enhancement
KIEE........ Knoxville International Energy Exposition [*1982*]
KIEE........ Korean Institute of Electrical Engineers
KIEF........ Kiefer Built [*NCIC trailer make code*]
KI-EF....... Kiwanis International - European Federation [*An association*]
KIEI........ Kundu Introversion-Extraversion Inventory [*Personality development test*] [*Psychology*]
KIEM........ Eureka, CA [*Television station call letters*]
KIEMP...... Kenya Industrial Energy Management Program (BUAC)
KIER........ Korea Institute of Energy and Resources (BUAC)
KIESEC..... Korea International Exchange Society for Education and Culture (SAUO)
KIET........ Korea Institute for Economics and Technology (BUAC)
KIET........ Korea Institute for Industrial Economics and Technology (SAUO)
KIET........ Korea Institute for Industrial Economics and Trade (ECON)
KIEV........ Burbank, CA [*AM radio station call letters*] (BROA)
KIEV........ Glendale, CA [*AM radio station call letters*]
KIEZ........ Carmel Valley, CA [*AM radio station call letters*]
KIF.......... Key Index File [*Computer science*] (VLIE)
KIF.......... Kiwanis International Foundation [*An association*]
KIF.......... Knitting Industries Federation (BUAC)
KIF.......... Knitting Industries Foundation [*British*] (DBA)
KIF.......... Knowledge Interchange Format [*Computer-oriented language*] (NETL)
KIF.......... Kodak Industrial Film
KIF.......... Korean Investment Fund [*NYSE symbol*] (SAG)
KIF.......... Name and Address Key Index File [*IRS*]
Kif Aus...... Kiffa Australis [*Constellation*] (WDAA)
Kif Bor...... Kiffa Borealis [*Constellation*] (WDAA)
KIFG........ Iowa Falls, IA [*AM radio station call letters*]
KIFG-FM.... Iowa Falls, IA [*FM radio station call letters*]
KIFI........ Idaho Falls, ID [*Television station call letters*]
KIFIS........ Kollsman Integrated Flight Instrumentation System [*Aviation*]
KIFM........ San Diego, CA [*FM radio station call letters*]
KIFO........ Pearl City, HI [*AM radio station call letters*]
KIFP........ Korean Institute for Family Planning (BUAC)
KIFS........ Ashland, OR [*FM radio station call letters*] (BROA)
KIFTSG...... Kiftsgate [*England*]
KIFV........ Korean Infantry Fighting Vehicle (SAUS)
KIFW........ Sitka, AK [*AM radio station call letters*]
KIFX........ Roosevelt, UT [*FM radio station call letters*]
KIG.......... Killing [*Telegraphy*] (PCTE)
KIG.......... Koingnaas [*South Africa*] [*Airport symbol*] (OAG)
KIGAM...... Korean Institute of Geology, Mining and Minerals (SAUO)
KIGB........ King Breslin Trucking [*Common carrier symbol*]
KIGC........ Oskaloosa, IA [*FM radio station call letters*]
KIGL........ Seligman, MO [*FM radio station call letters*] (BROA)
KIGL........ Spencer, IA [*FM radio station call letters*]
KIGN........ Burns, WY [*FM radio station call letters*] (BROA)
KIGN-FM.... Cheyenne, WY [*FM radio station call letters*] (RBYB)
KIGO........ St. Anthony, ID [*AM radio station call letters*]
KIGS........ Hanford, CA [*AM radio station call letters*]
KIH.......... Coast Independent Hi-Tech [*Vancouver Stock Exchange symbol*]
KIH.......... Kaisar-I-Hind [*Indian medal*]
KIH.......... Kilometres in the Hour [*Rate of march*] [*Military*] [*British*]
KIH.......... Kish Island [*Iran*] [*Airport symbol*] (OAG)
KIHA........ Kodiak Island Housing Authority (SAUO)
KIHASA..... Korea Institute for Health and Social Affairs (BUAC)
KIHK-FM.... Rock Valley, IA [*FM radio station call letters*] (BROA)
KIHM-AM... Reno, NV [*AM radio station call letters*] (BROA)
KIHM-AM... Sun Valley, NV [*AM radio station call letters*] (BROA)
KIHN........ Hugo, OK [*AM radio station call letters*]
KIHR........ Hood River, OR [*AM radio station call letters*]
KIHR........ Korean Institute for Human Rights (EA)
KIHS........ Adel, IA [*FM radio station call letters*] (BROA)
KIHT........ St. Louis, MO [*FM radio station call letters*]
K-II.......... Karyovirus-II (ECON)
KII.......... Keystone International, Inc. [*NYSE symbol*] (SPSG)
KII.......... Kuder Interest Inventory [*Occupational information*] (OICC)
KIIC........ Kuwait International Investment Company (SAUO)
KIIC-FM..... Lamoni, IA [*FM radio station call letters*] (BROA)
KIID-AM.... Sacramento, CA [*AM radio station call letters*] (BROA)
KIII.......... Corpus Christi, TX [*Television station call letters*]

K-III.......... K-III Communications Corp. [*Associated Press*] (SAG)
KIIK.......... Fairfield, IA [*FM radio station call letters*]
KIIM.......... Tucson, AZ [*FM radio station call letters*]
KIIN.......... Iowa City, IA [*Television station call letters*]
KIIS.......... Keller Industries Ltd. (SAUO)
KIIS.......... Korean Institute of International Studies
KIIS.......... Los Angeles, CA [*AM radio station call letters*]
KIIS-AM..... Canyon Country, CA [*AM radio station call letters*] (BROA)
KIIS-FM..... Los Angeles, CA [*FM radio station call letters*]
KIIX.......... Koppers Industries [*Private rail car owner code*]
KIIX.......... Wellington, CO [*AM radio station call letters*]
KIIX-AM..... Fort Collins, CO [*AM radio station call letters*] (BROA)
KIIZ.......... Killeen, TX [*FM radio station call letters*]
KIJ.......... Independence Community Junior College, Independence, KS [*Library symbol*] [*Library of Congress*] (LCLS)
KIJ.......... Kawah Idjen [*Java*] [*Seismograph station code, US Geological Survey*] [*Closed*] (SEIS)
KIJ.......... Niigata [*Japan*] [*Airport symbol*] (OAG)
KIJK.......... Prineville, OR [*FM radio station call letters*]
KIJN.......... Farwell, TX [*AM radio station call letters*]
KIJN-FM.... Farwell, TX [*FM radio station call letters*]
KIJV.......... Huron, SD [*AM radio station call letters*]
KIK.......... Kentucky's Individualized Kindergartens (EDAC)
kik.......... Kikuyu [*MARC language code*] [*Library of Congress*] (LCCP)
KIK.......... Kirkuk [*Iraq*] [*Airport symbol*] (AD)
KIK.......... Kozawa, Iwatsuru, and Kawaguchi [*Factor involving injection of cancerous gastric juices into rabbits, named for its discoverers*] [*Medicine*]
KIK.......... Kuwait Intertiational Investment Co. (SAUO)
KIKC.......... Forsyth, MT [*AM radio station call letters*]
KIKC-FM.... Forsyth, MT [*FM radio station call letters*]
KIKD-FM.... Lake City, IA [*FM radio station call letters*] (BROA)
KIKF.......... Cascade, MT [*FM radio station call letters*] (BROA)
KIKF.......... Garden Grove, CA [*FM radio station call letters*]
KIKI.......... Honolulu, HI [*AM radio station call letters*]
KIKI-FM..... Honolulu, HI [*FM radio station call letters*]
KIKK.......... Pasadena, TX [*AM radio station call letters*]
KIKK-FM.... Houston, TX [*FM radio station call letters*]
KIKM.......... Sherman, TX [*FM radio station call letters*]
KIKN.......... Port Angeles, WA [*AM radio station call letters*] (BROA)
KIKN.......... Salem, SD [*FM radio station call letters*]
KIKO.......... Claypool, AZ [*FM radio station call letters*]
KIKO.......... Miami, AZ [*AM radio station call letters*]
KIKR.......... Asbury, IA [*FM radio station call letters*]
KIKR.......... Beaumont, TX [*AM radio station call letters*] (BROA)
KIKS.......... Iola, KS [*FM radio station call letters*]
KIKT.......... Greenville, TX [*FM radio station call letters*]
KIKU.......... Honolulu, HI [*Television station call letters*]
KIKV.......... Alexandria, MN [*FM radio station call letters*]
KIKX.......... Manitou Springs, CO [*FM radio station call letters*]
KIKX-FM.... Ketchum, ID [*FM radio station call letters*] (BROA)
KIKY.......... Hutto, TX [*FM radio station call letters*] (RBYB)
KIKY-FM..... Hutto, TX [*FM radio station call letters*] (RBYB)
KIKZ.......... Seminole, TX [*AM radio station call letters*]
KIL.......... Kariya [*Language symbol*] (ETLW)
KIL.......... Keyed Input Language
KIL.......... Keystone Intl [*NYSE symbol*] (TTSB)
Kil.......... Kil'aim (BJA)
KIL.......... Kilderkin [*Unit of measurement*] [*British*] (ROG)
KIL.......... Kilembe Resources Ltd. [*Vancouver Stock Exchange symbol*]
KIL.......... Killeen, TX [*Amtrak Busline code*]
KIL.......... Kilogram
KIL.......... Kilometer
KIL.......... Krypton Ion LASER
KILA.......... Las Vegas, NV [*FM radio station call letters*]
Kilamco..... Kilwa Ammonia Co. [*Tanzania*] (BUAC)
Kilb.......... Kilburn's English Magistrates' Cases [*A publication*] (DLA)
KILBY........ Kilby, VA [*American Association of Railroads railroad junction routing code*]
KILC.......... Kile Transfer Corporation [*Common carrier symbol*]
KILD.......... Kildare [*County in Ireland*] (ROG)
KILD.......... Kilderkin [*Unit of measurement*] [*British*]
KILE.......... Bellaire, TX [*AM radio station call letters*] (BROA)
KILE.......... Kile Technology Corp. (SAUO)
KILE-AM.... Port Lavaca, TX [*FM radio station call letters*] (RBYB)
Kilern........ Killearn Properties, Inc. [*Associated Press*] (SAG)
KILG.......... Kilgore Industries [*NCIC trailer make code*]
KILG.......... Wilmington/Greater Wilmington [*Delaware*] [*ICAO location identifier*] (ICLI)
KILJ.......... Mount Pleasant, IA [*AM radio station call letters*]
KILJ-FM..... Mount Pleasant, IA [*FM radio station call letters*]
KILK.......... Kilkenny [*County in Ireland*]
Kilk.......... Kilkerran's Scotch Court of Session Decisions [*A publication*] (DLA)
Kilkerran.... Kilkerran's Scotch Court of Session Decisions [*A publication*] (DLA)
KILL.......... Kill Brothers [*NCIC trailer make code*]
kill.......... Kilowatt (NAKS)
KILLS........ Ka-Inertial Launch and Leave System
KILM.......... Raymondville, TX [*FM radio station call letters*] (BROA)
KILM.......... Wilmington/New Hannover County [*North Carolina*] [*ICAO location identifier*] (ICLI)
KILN.......... Kirlin Holding [*NASDAQ symbol*] (TTSB)
KILN.......... Kirlin Holding Corp. [*NASDAQ symbol*] (SAG)
KILO.......... Colorado Springs, CO [*FM radio station call letters*]
kilo.......... Kilogram (ADWA)
KILO.......... Kilogram
KILO.......... Kilometer
KILOBAUD... One Thousand Bits per Second (AGLO)
KILOL........ Kiloliter
KILOM........ Kilometer
KILOPAC.... Thousand Packages (SAUS)
KILOPACS... Thousand Package Switchings (SAUS)
kilovar....... Kilovolt-Ampere Reactive Hour (BARN)
KILR.......... Estherville, IA [*AM radio station call letters*]
KILR-FM.... Estherville, IA [*FM radio station call letters*]
KILS.......... Minneapolis, KS [*FM radio station call letters*]
KILT.......... Houston, TX [*AM radio station call letters*]
KILT-FM..... Houston, TX [*FM radio station call letters*]
KILU.......... Paauilo, HI [*FM radio station call letters*] (RBYB)
KILV.......... Castana, IA [*FM radio station call letters*] (BROA)
KILX.......... Hatfield, AR [*FM radio station call letters*] (BROA)
KIM.......... Joint Struggle Committee (SAUS)
KIM.......... Kenya Independence Movement (SAUO)
KIM.......... Kenya Institute of Management (BUAC)
KIM.......... Keyboard Input Matrix [*Computer science*]
KIM.......... Kimberley [*South Africa*] [*Airport symbol*] (OAG)
KIM.......... Kimberley [*South Africa*] [*Seismograph station code, US Geological Survey*] (SEIS)
KIM.......... Kimco Realty [*NYSE symbol*] (SPSG)
KIM.......... Kinetic Impact Munition (ACAE)
KIM.......... Knowledge-Based Integrated Machine [*Computer science*]
KIMA.......... Yakima, WA [*Television station call letters*]
KIMB.......... Kimball, NE [*AM radio station call letters*]
KIMB.......... Kimbark Oil & Gas Co. (SAUO)
KIMBA........ Kimball, OH [*American Association of Railroads railroad junction routing code*]
Kimbal....... Kimball International, Inc. [*Associated Press*] (SAG)
KimbClk..... Kimberly Clark [*Associated Press*] (SAG)
KIMBR........ Kimbrough, AL [*American Association of Railroads railroad junction routing code*]
KIMC.......... Kimberly Clark [*Federal Railroad Administration identification code*]
KIMC.......... Kimco Energy Corp. (SAUO)
Kimc.......... Kimco Realty Corp. [*Associated Press*] (SAG)
Kimco........ Kimco Realty Corp. [*Associated Press*] (SAG)
KIMCO........ Koehring International Marketing (EFIS)
KIMCODE... Kimble Method for Controlled Devacuation
KimEnv...... Kimmins Environmental Services [*Associated Press*] (SAG)
KIMG.......... Key Image Systems Inc. (SAUO)
KIMI.......... King Midget [*NCIC car make code*]
KIML.......... Gillette, WY [*AM radio station call letters*]
KIMM.......... Rapid City, SD [*AM radio station call letters*]
KIMMA....... Kongres Indian Muslim Malaysia [*Malaysia Indian Moslem Congress*] [*Political party*] (PPW)
KIMN.......... Denver, CO [*FM radio station call letters*] (BROA)
KIMN.......... Fort Collins, CO [*FM radio station call letters*]
KIMO.......... Anchorage, AK [*Television station call letters*]
KIMO.......... Kings Mountain National Military Park
KIMP.......... Mount Pleasant, TX [*AM radio station call letters*]
KIMPrA...... Kimco Rlty 7.75% Sr'A'Dep Pfd [*NYSE symbol*] (TTSB)
KIMPrB...... Kimco Rlty 8.50% Sr'B'Dep Pfd [*NYSE symbol*] (TTSB)
KIMPrC...... Kimco Rlty 8.375% Sr'C'Dep [*NYSE symbol*] (TTSB)
KIMS.......... Kennedy Inventory Management System [*NASA*] (SSD)
KIMS.......... Kodak Image Management System (HGAA)
KIMSA........ Kirsten Murine Sarcoma [*Virus*] [*Oncology*] (DAVI)
KiMSV........ Kirsten Murine Sarcoma Virus
KIMT.......... Mason City, IA [*Television station call letters*]
KI MUSV.... Kirsten Murine Sarcoma Virus
KIMX.......... Laramie, WY [*FM radio station call letters*]
KIMY.......... Watonga, OK [*FM radio station call letters*]
KIN.......... Association of Kinsmen Clubs (EA)
KIN.......... Keyboard Input [*Computer science*] (VLIE)
KIN.......... Kinark Corp. [*AMEX symbol*] (SPSG)
KIN.......... Kinescope
kin.......... Kinetic (VRA)
Kin.......... Kinetics (SAUS)
KIN.......... Kingston [*Jamaica*] [*Airport symbol*] (OAG)
KIN.......... Kingston [*Jamaica*] [*Seismograph station code, US Geological Survey*] (SEIS)
KIN.......... Kingston, RI [*Amtrak rail station code*]
KIN.......... Kingswood [*NCIC car model code*]
Kin.......... Kinnim (BJA)
KIN.......... Kinross-Shire [*Former county in Scotland*] (WGA)
kin.......... Kinyarwanda [*MARC language code*] [*Library of Congress*] (LCCP)
KIN.......... K Mart Information Network (EFIS)
KINA.......... King Fish Boat Trailer [*NCIC trailer make code*]
KINA.......... Salina, KS [*AM radio station call letters*]
Kinark........ Kinark Corp. [*Associated Press*] (SAG)
KINC.......... King Homes [*NCIC trailer make code*]
KINC.......... Las Vegas, NV [*Television station call letters*] (RBYB)
KINCA........ Kincaid, ND [*American Association of Railroads railroad junction routing code*]
KIND.......... Independence, KS [*AM radio station call letters*]
KIND.......... Indianapolis/International [*Indiana*] [*ICAO location identifier*] (ICLI)
KIND.......... Kinder-Care Learning Centers, Inc. (SAUO)
KIND.......... Kindergarten (WDAA)
KIND.......... Kindness in Nature's Defense [*Elementary school course*]
KIND.......... Kindred Healthcare (MHID)
KIND.......... King Richards [*NCIC trailer make code*]
KINDERGTN... Kindergarten

KIND-FM.... Independence, KS [*FM radio station call letters*]
KINE......... Honolulu, HI [*FM radio station call letters*]
KINE......... Kinescope
KINE......... Kingsville, TX [*AM radio station call letters*] (RBYB)
KINE......... King Trailer Company [*NCIC trailer make code*]
Kinetic...... Kinetic Concepts, Inc. [*Associated Press*] (SAG)
KINF......... King-Co [*NCIC trailer make code*]
KINF......... Roswell, NM [*AM radio station call letters*] (BROA)
KINF-AM.... Denton, TX [*AM radio station call letters*] (RBYB)
KING......... Kinetic Intense Neutron Generator
KING......... King Pharmaceuticals, Inc. [*NASDAQ symbol*] (NASQ)
King......... King's Reports [*5, 6 Louisiana*] [*A publication*] (DLA)
King......... Select Cases in Chancery Tempore King, Edited by Macnaghten [*1724-33*] [*England*] [*A publication*] (DLA)
King Cas.... Cases in King's Colorado Civil Practice [*A publication*] (DLA)
King Cas Temp... Select Cases in Chancery Tempore King [*1724-33*] [*England*] [*A publication*] (DLA)
KINGD....... Kingdom
King Dig.... King's Tennessee Digest [*A publication*] (DLA)
KING-DT.... Seattle, WA [*Television station call letters*] (BROA)
King-Farlow... Gold Coast Judgments and the Masai Cases, by King-Farlow [*1915-17*] [*Ghana*] [*A publication*] (DLA)
KING-FM.... Seattle, WA [*FM radio station call letters*]
King-Kong... Barbiturate or Other Sedative Pill [*Medicine*] (EDAA)
KINGMAP... King's Music Analysis Package [*King's College*] [*University of London*] [*British*] (NITA)
Kings........ Kingsway [*Record label*]
KINGSBR.... Kingsbridge [*England*]
King's Con Cs... King's Conflicting Cases [*Texas*] [*A publication*] (DLA)
King's Conf Ca... King's Conflicting Cases [*Texas*] [*A publication*] (DLA)
KINGT....... Kingston, RI [*American Association of Railroads railroad junction routing code*]
KINGTEL.... Kingston upon Thames Viewdata Service (SAUO)
KING-TV..... Seattle, WA [*Television station call letters*]
KingWd..... King World Productions [*Associated Press*] (SAG)
KINI......... Crookston, NE [*FM radio station call letters*]
KINIT........ Korea Institute of Industry & Technology Information [*South Korea*] (DDC)
KINK......... Portland, OR [*FM radio station call letters*]
KINK......... Wink/Winkler County [*Texas*] [*ICAO location identifier*] (ICLI)
KINL......... Eagle Pass, TX [*FM radio station call letters*]
KINL......... International Falls [*Minnesota*] [*ICAO location identifier*] (ICLI)
KINN......... Alamogordo, NM [*AM radio station call letters*]
KINN......... Kinnard Investments [*NASDAQ symbol*] (TTSB)
KINN......... Kinnard Investments, Inc. [*NASDAQ symbol*] (NQ)
Kinnard..... Kinnard Investments, Inc. [*Associated Press*] (SAG)
Kinney Law Dict & Glos... Kinney's Law Dictionary and Glossary [*A publication*] (DLA)
KINO......... King Ocean Lines [*Common carrier symbol*]
KINO......... Winslow, AZ [*AM radio station call letters*]
KINQ......... King Distribution and Transfer [*Common carrier symbol*]
Kinross...... Kinross Gold Corp. [*Associated Press*] (SAG)
KINS......... Eureka, CA [*AM radio station call letters*]
KINS......... Indian Springs/Indian Springs Army Air Field [*Nevada*] [*ICAO location identifier*] (ICLI)
KINS......... Kingston Horse Trailer [*NCIC trailer make code*]
KINSA....... Kodak International Newspaper Snapshot Awards
KINST....... Kinston, NC [*American Association of Railroads railroad junction routing code*]
KINSYM..... Kinematic Synthesis (PDAA)
KINT......... El Paso, TX [*Television station call letters*]
KINT......... King Transfer [*Common carrier symbol*]
KINT......... Koninklijk Instituut voor het duurzame beheer van de Natuurlijke rijkdommen en de bevordering van schone Technologie (SAUO)
KINT......... Winston Salem/Smith-Reynolds [*North Carolina*] [*ICAO location identifier*] (ICLI)
KINTB....... Kintbury [*England*]
KINT-FM.... El Paso, TX [*FM radio station call letters*]
KINV........ Kentucky Investors Inc. (SAUO)
KINX......... Great Falls, MT [*FM radio station call letters*] (BROA)
KINY......... Juneau, AK [*AM radio station call letters*]
KINY......... Kinney System Inc. (SAUO)
KINZ-FM.... Humboldt, KS [*FM radio station call letters*] (BROA)
KINZ-TV..... Arlington, TX [*TV station call letters*] (RBYB)
KIo........... Iola Free Public Library, Iola, KS [*Library symbol*] [*Library of Congress*] (LCLS)
KIO........... Kachin Independence Organization [*Myanmar*] [*Political party*] (EY)
KIO........... Kenya Information Office (BUAC)
KIO........... Kick It Off [*Slang*] (DOMA)
KIO........... Kili [*Marshall Islands*] [*Airport symbol*] (OAG)
KIO........... Kraiaero [*Russian Federation*] [*ICAO designator*] (FAAC)
KIO........... Kuwait Investment Office (BUAC)
KIO3......... Potassium Iodate [*Emergency Management*] (EMA)
KIOA......... Des Moines, IA [*AM radio station call letters*]
KIOA-FM.... Des Moines, IA [*FM radio station call letters*]
KIOC......... Orange, TX [*FM radio station call letters*]
KIOD-FM.... McCook, NE [*FM radio station call letters*] (BROA)
KIOI.......... San Francisco, CA [*FM radio station call letters*]
KIOK......... Richland, WA [*FM radio station call letters*]
KIOL......... Lamesa, TX [*FM radio station call letters*]
KION......... Monterey, CA [*Television station call letters*] (BROA)
KIOO......... Porterville, CA [*FM radio station call letters*]
KIOPI........ Kienzle Input/Output Peripheral Interface
KIOPI........ Kienzle Input/Output Processor Interface (NITA)
KIOQ......... Folsom, CA [*AM radio station call letters*]
KIOS......... Omaha, NE [*FM radio station call letters*]
KIoS......... Southeast Kansas Library System, Iola, KS [*Library symbol*] [*Library of Congress*] (LCLS)
KIOT......... Los Lunas [*FM radio station call letters*]
KIOU......... Shreveport, LA [*AM radio station call letters*]
KIOV......... Payette, ID [*AM radio station call letters*]
KIOW......... Forest City, IA [*FM radio station call letters*]
KIOX......... El Campo, TX [*FM radio station call letters*]
KIOZ......... Oceanside, CA [*FM radio station call letters*]
KIOZ......... San Diego, CA [*FM radio station call letters*] (BROA)
KIP........... Keep Alone if Possible [*Travel industry*] (TRID)
KIP........... Keyboard Input Processor [*Computer science*] (NASA)
KIP........... Key Indigenous Personnel (MCD)
KIP........... Key Intelligence Position (AFM)
KIP........... Key Intermediary Proteins (DAVI)
KIP........... Kilopound (IAA)
KIP........... Kinetics Internet Protocol (GART)
KIP........... Kipapa [*Hawaii*] [*Seismograph station code, US Geological Survey*] (SEIS)
KIP........... Kit, Individual Protection [*British army*] (INF)
KIP........... Knowledge Industry Publications
KIP........... Knowledge Industry Publications, Inc. [*Telecommunications*]
KIP........... Knowledge Information Processing [*Computer science*]
KIP........... Knowledge Is Powerful (EARSL)
KIP........... Korean Industry Participation (SAUS)
KIP........... Thousand Pounds
KIPA......... Hilo, HI [*AM radio station call letters*]
KIPC......... Kipco [*NCIC trailer make code*]
KIP-FT....... Thousand Foot-Pounds
KIPI.......... Knowledge Industry Publications, Inc. [*White Plains, NY*] [*Telecommunications*] [*Information service or system*]
KIPI.......... PBI Media (IID)
KIPIC........ Kuwait International Petroleum Investment Co. (BUAC)
KIPL......... Imperial/Imperial County [*California*] [*ICAO location identifier*] (ICLI)
Kiplinger.... Kiplinger's Personal Finance Magazine [*A publication*] (BRI)
KIPO......... Honolulu, HI [*FM radio station call letters*]
KIPO......... Keyboard Input Printout [*Computer science*] (IEEE)
KIPR......... Pine Bluff, AR [*FM radio station call letters*]
KIPRC....... Kentucky Injury Prevention and Research Center [*University of Kentucky*] (RCD)
KIPS......... 10^3 (K) of Instructions Per Second [*Unit of computer processing speed*] (NITA)
KIPS......... Kaufman Infant and Preschool Scale [*Child development test*] [*Psychology*]
KIPS......... Key Indicators, Probes, and a Scoring Method [*Health care*] (HCT)
KIPS......... Kilo-Instructions per Second
KIPS......... Kilowatt Isotope Power System (IEEE)
KIPS......... Knowledge Information Processing Systems [*Computer science*]
KIPT......... Kharkov Institute for Science and Technology (SAUO)
KIPT......... Twin Falls, ID [*Television station call letters*]
KIQ........... Key Intelligence Question [*CIA*]
KIQ........... Key Intelligence Requirement [*Military*] (MUSM)
KIQ........... Kira [*Papua New Guinea*] [*Airport symbol*] (OAG)
KIQI.......... San Francisco, CA [*AM radio station call letters*]
KIQK......... Rapid City, SD [*FM radio station call letters*]
KIQN......... Tooele, UT [*AM radio station call letters*] (BROA)
KIQO......... Atascadero, CA [*FM radio station call letters*]
KIQQ......... Barstow, CA [*AM radio station call letters*]
KIQQ......... Newberry Springs, CA [*FM radio station call letters*] (BROA)
KIQS......... Willows, CA [*AM radio station call letters*]
KIQX......... Durango, CO [*FM radio station call letters*]
KIQZ......... Rawlins, WY [*FM radio station call letters*]
KIR........... Key Intelligence Requirement (MCD)
KIR........... Killer-Cell Inhibitory Receptor [*Immunology*]
Kir........... Kirby's Connecticut Reports and Supplement [*1785-89*] [*A publication*] (DLA)
kir........... Kirghiz [*MARC language code*] [*Library of Congress*] (LCCP)
KIR........... Kiruna [*Sweden*] [*Seismograph station code, US Geological Survey*] (SEIS)
KIR........... Knight's Industrial Reports [*A publication*] (DLA)
KIR........... Kyocera Image Refinement (SAUS)
Kirb.......... Kirby's Connecticut Reports and Supplement [*1785-89*] [*A publication*] (DLA)
KIRBS....... Korean Institute for Research in the Behavioral Sciences
Kirby......... Kirby Exploration Co., Inc. [*Associated Press*] (SAG)
Kirby......... Kirby's Connecticut Reports and Supplement [*1785-89*] [*A publication*] (DLA)
Kirby's Conn R... Kirby's Connecticut Reports [*A publication*] (DLA)
Kirby's R.... Kirby's Connecticut Reports [*A publication*] (DLA)
Kirby's Rep... Kirby's Connecticut Reports [*A publication*] (DLA)
KIRC......... Seminole, OK [*FM radio station call letters*]
KIRDI........ Kenya Industrial Research and Development Institute (BUAC)
KirinBr...... Kirin Brewery Co. Ltd. [*Associated Press*] (SAG)
KIRIS........ Kentucky Instructional Results Information System
KIRK......... Kirkcaldy [*Seaport in Scotland*]
KIRK......... Lebanon, MO [*FM radio station call letters*]
KIRK......... Macon, MO [*FM radio station call letters*] (BROA)
KIRK-AM.... Bethany, MO [*AM radio station call letters*] (BROA)
KIRKCUDB... Kirkcudbrightshire [*County in Scotland*]
KIRL......... St. Charles, MO [*AM radio station call letters*]
Kirlin........ Kirlin Holding Corp. [*Associated Press*] (SAG)
KIRN......... Los Angeles, CA [*AM radio station call letters*] (GDPB)
KIRN-AM.... Simi Valley, CA [*AM radio station call letters*] (BROA)
KIRO......... Seattle, WA [*AM radio station call letters*]
KIRO-DT.... Seattle, WA [*Television station call letters*] (BROA)

KIRO-FM .... Seattle, WA [*FM radio station call letters*]
KIRO-TV .... Seattle, WA [*Television station call letters*]
KIRP .... Kodak Infrared Phosphor
KIRQ .... Lawton, OK [*FM radio station call letters*] (RBYB)
KIRS .... Kodak Infrared Scope
KIRS .... Kris's Truck Transport [*Common carrier symbol*]
KIRS .... Sun Valley, NV [*AM radio station call letters*] (RBYB)
KirSeph .... Kirjath Sepher [*Jerusalem*] (BJA)
KirSSR ...... Kirghiz Soviet Socialist Republic
KIRT .... Mission, TX [*AM radio station call letters*]
KIRTAK ...... Kirghiz Telegraph Agency, Frunze (BUAC)
Kirt Sur Pr... Kirtland on Practice in Surrogates' Courts [*A publication*] (DLA)
KIRU .... RB Kirkconnell and Brothers [*Intermodal shipping container symbol*] (TVRC)
KIRV .... Fresno, CA [*AM radio station call letters*]
KIRVL .... Kirksville, MO [*American Association of Railroads railroad junction routing code*]
KIRX .... Kirksville, MO [*AM radio station call letters*]
KIS .... Contactair Flugdienst & Co. [*Germany*] [*ICAO designator*] (FAAC)
KIS .... Keep it Short (ELAL)
KIS .... Keep It Simple (ADA)
KIS .... Kenny Information Systems [*Database producer*] (IID)
KIS .... Kenya Independent Squadron [*British military*] (DMA)
KIS .... Kenya Inspection Service (BUAC)
KIS .... Keyboard Input Simulation [*Computer science*]
KIS .... Kills [*Telegraphy*] (PCTE)
KIS .... Kishinev [*Former USSR*] [*Seismograph station code, US Geological Survey*] (SEIS)
KIS .... Kissimmee, FL [*Amtrak rail station code*]
KIS .... Kisumu [*Kenya*] [*Airport symbol*] (OAG)
KIS .... Kitting Instruction Sheet [*NASA*] (NASA)
KIS .... Knowbot Information Service (VLIE)
KIS .... Kodak Infrared Scope
KIS .... Krankenhaus Information System (DAVI)
KISA .... Honolulu, HI [*AM radio station call letters*]
KISA .... Karaoke International Sing-Along Association (EA)
KISA .... Korean International Steel Associates (BUAC)
KISA .... Korean International Steel Association (SAUO)
KISA .... Voluntary International Service Assignments [*of the Society of Friends*]
Kisb Ir Land L... Kisbey on the Irish Land Law [*A publication*] (DLA)
KISC .... Kimmins Corporation (SAUO)
KISC .... Knowledge Industry Systems Concept [*Publishing and education*] [*Pronounced "kiss"*]
KISC .... Knowledge Information Skills and Curriculum [*Project*] (AIE)
KISC .... Spokane, WA [*FM radio station call letters*]
KISD .... Pipestone, MN [*FM radio station call letters*]
KISE-FM .... Seaside, CA [*FM radio station call letters*] (RBYB)
KISEH .... Kent Incorporated Society for Experiments in Horticulture (SAUO)
KISF .... Lexington, MO [*FM radio station call letters*]
KISF-FM .... Las Vegas, NV [*FM radio station call letters*] (BROA)
KISI .... Malvern, AR [*FM radio station call letters*]
KISK-FM .... Shasta Lake City, CA [*FM radio station call letters*] (BROA)
KISL .... Avalon, CA [*FM radio station call letters*]
KISM .... Kismet Manufacturing Company [*NCIC trailer make code*]
KISM-FM.... Bellingham, WA [*FM radio station call letters*] (RBYB)
KISMIF ...... Keep It Simple, Make It Fun
KISN .... Salt Lake City, UT [*AM radio station call letters*]
KISN .... Williston/International [*North Dakota*] [*ICAO location identifier*] (ICLI)
KISN-FM .... Salt Lake City, UT [*FM radio station call letters*]
KISNOPI..... Keyboard Input Stimulation Noise Problem Input (IAA)
KISO .... Kol Israel Symphony Orchestra (SAUO)
KISO .... Phoenix, AZ [*AM radio station call letters*]
KISP .... Blair, NE [*FM radio station call letters*]
KISP .... Islip/MacArthur Field [*New York*] [*ICAO location identifier*] (ICLI)
KISQ-FM .... San Francisco, CA [*FM radio station call letters*] (BROA)
KISR .... Fort Smith, AR [*FM radio station call letters*]
KISR .... Kuwait Institute for Science Research (SAUO)
KISR .... Kuwait Institute for Scientific Research (BUAC)
KISS .... Kanton Island Sounding System (SAUS)
KISS .... Keep It Safe and Simple (VLIE)
KISS .... Keep It Short and Simple (MCD)
KISS .... Keep It Short and Sweet [*Radio messages*]
KISS .... Keep It Simple, Sir (SAA)
KISS .... Keep It Simple, Stupid [*Bridge bidding term*]
KISS .... Keep It Simple Sweetie
KISS .... Keep It Straight and Simple [*Computer science*]
KISS .... Keyed Indexed Sequential Search
KISS .... Key Integrative Social Systems
KISS .... Knights in the Service of Satan [*Rock music group*]
KISS .... Knowledge-Based Interactive Signal Monitoring System (SAUO)
KISS .... Knowledge Integrating Simulation System
KISS .... Korean Information Science Society (SAUO)
KISS .... Korean Intelligence Support System (DOMA)
KISS .... Potassium Iodide Saturated Solution [*Medicine*] (EDAA)
KISS .... San Antonio, TX [*FM radio station call letters*]
KISS .... Saturated Solution of Potassium Iodide [*Pharmacology*] (DAVI)
KI SSR ...... Kirgiz Soviet Socialist Republic (SAUO)
KIST .... Keyword Index to Serial Titles [*A publication*]
KIST .... Korean Institute for Science and Technology
KIST .... Santa Barbara, CA [*AM radio station call letters*]
KIST-FM.... Santa Barbara, CA [*FM radio station call letters*] (BROA)
KISU .... Kelvin International Services [*Intermodal shipping container symbol*] (TVRC)
KISU .... Pocatello, ID [*Television station call letters*]
KISU-FM .... Pocatello, ID [*FM radio station call letters*] (BROA)
KiSV .... Kirsten Sarcoma Virus
KISV-FM .... Bakersfield, CA [*FM radio station call letters*] (BROA)
KISW .... Seattle, WA [*FM radio station call letters*]
KISX .... Whitehouse, TX [*FM radio station call letters*]
KISZ .... Cortez, CO [*FM radio station call letters*]
KISZ .... Kommunista Ifjusagi Szovetseg [*Communist Youth Organization*] [*Hungary*]
KISZAR...... Japanese Journal of Parasitology (journ.) (SAUS)
KIT .... Kahn Intelligence Test (DMAA)
KIT .... KAPSE Interface Team (SAUO)
KIT .... Kaufman Ion Thrustor
KIT .... Keep in Touch [*Slang*] (DNAB)
KIT .... Kent Information Technology Conference (NITA)
KIT .... Kentucky & Indiana Terminal Railroad Co. [*AAR code*]
KIT .... Kermit [*Texas*] [*Seismograph station code, US Geological Survey*] (SEIS)
KIT .... Key Intelligence Topic (AAEL)
KIT .... Key Issue Tracking [*Database*]
KIT .... Kitchen (ADA)
kit .... Kitchen (ADWA)
Kit .... Kitchin's Retourna Brevium [*4 eds.*] [*1581-92*] [*A publication*] (DLA)
KIT .... Kithira [*Greece*] [*Airport symbol*] (OAG)
KIT .... Kit House Trailer [*NCIC trailer make code*]
KIT .... Kit Manufacturing Co. [*AMEX symbol*] (SPSG)
KIT .... Kit Mfg [*AMEX symbol*] (TTSB)
KIT .... Kittrell Junior College, Kittrell, NC [*Inactive*] [*OCLC symbol*] (OCLC)
KIT .... Knowledge-based Information Tutorial (SAUO)
KIT .... Korean International Telecommunications (SAUO)
KIT .... KWIC Interactive Tagger [*University of Minnesota*] [*Text editing system*] (NITA)
KIT .... Yakima, WA [*AM radio station call letters*]
KITA .... Kesatuan Insaf Tanah Air [*National Consciousness Party*] [*Malaysia*] [*Political party*] (PPW)
KITA .... Kick in the Afterdeck [*Bowdlerized version*]
KITA .... Little Rock, AR [*AM radio station call letters*]
KITC .... Kentucky-Indiana-Tennessee Conference (PSS)
kitch .... Kitchen (BARN)
KITCH .... Kitchener, ON [*American Association of Railroads railroad junction routing code*]
Kitch......... Kitchin on Jurisdictions of Courts-Leet, Courts-Baron, Etc. [*A publication*] (DLA)
Kitch Courts... Kitchin on Jurisdictions of Courts-Leet, Courts-Baron, Etc. [*A publication*] (DLA)
Kitch Cts.... Kitchin on Courts [*A publication*] (DLA)
Kitchen...... Griqualand West Reports [*Cape Colony, South Africa*] [*A publication*] (DLA)
KITCO .... Kenala Industry and Technical Consultancy Organisation [*India*] (BUAC)
KITCO .... Kerala Industry and Technical Consultancy Organization (SAUO)
Kit Ct........ Kitchin on Jurisdictions of Courts-Leet, Courts-Baron, Etc. [*A publication*] (DLA)
KITE .... Kerrville, TX [*FM radio station call letters*]
KITE .... Kinetic energy kill vehicle Integrated Technology Experiments (SAUS)
KITE .... Kinetic Energy Weapon Integrated Test Experiment (MCD)
KITE .... Kinetic Isolation Tether Experiment (SAUS)
KITE .... Kuiper Infrared Technology Experiment (ACAE)
KITE .... Port Lavaca, TX [*FM radio station call letters*] (BROA)
Kite .... Spinnaker [*Slang*] [*Nautical term*] (NTA)
KITES....... Kinescope Image Test and Evaluation System (MCD)
KITG .... Kiting (ABBR)
KITH .... Kapaa, HI [*FM radio station call letters*] (BROA)
KITI .... Centralia-Chehalis, WA [*AM radio station call letters*]
KITI .... Winlock, WA [*FM radio station call letters*] (RBYB)
KITIA .... KAPSE Interface Team for Industry and Academia (SAUO)
Kit Jur....... Kitchin on Jurisdictions of Courts-Leet, Courts-Baron, Etc. [*A publication*] (DLA)
KITK .... Kit Karson Corp. (SAUO)
KITK .... Kit Kat [*NCIC motorcycle make code*]
KITL .... King International Corp. (SAUO)
KITLV....... Royal Institute of Linguistics and Anthropology (SAUO)
KITM......... Kit Manufacturing [*NCIC truck make code*]
KITM......... Kit Manufacturing [*NCIC trailer make code*]
Kit Mfg ...... Kit Manufacturing Co. [*Associated Press*] (SAG)
KITN .... Kitten (ABBR)
KITN .... Worthington, MN [*FM radio station call letters*] (RBYB)
KITO .... Vinita, OK [*AM radio station call letters*]
KITO-FM .... Vinita, OK [*FM radio station call letters*]
KITR .... Creston, IA [*FM radio station call letters*]
Kit Rd Trans... Kitchin's Road Transport Law [*19th ed.*] [*1978*] [*A publication*] (DLA)
KITS .... Campus Instructional Television System (SAUS)
KITS .... Meridian Diagnostics [*NASDAQ symbol*] (TTSB)
KITS .... Meridian Diagnostics, Inc. (SAUO)
KITS .... San Francisco, CA [*FM radio station call letters*]
KITT .... Kinetic Tree Theory (PDAA)
KITT .... Knight Industries Two Thousand [*Acronym is name of computerized car in TV series "Knight Rider"*]
KITT .... Korean International Telephone & Telegraph
KITT .... Parowan, UT [*AM radio station call letters*] (BROA)
KITT .... Shreveport, LA [*FM radio station call letters*]
KITTY....... Kentucky-Illinois-Tennessee League [*Old baseball league*]
KittyHk ...... Kitty Hawk, Inc. [*Associated Press*] (SAG)
KITU .... Beaumont, TX [*Television station call letters*]

KITV .... Honolulu, HI [*Television station call letters*]
KITV-DT ..... Honolulu, HI [*Television station call letters*] (BROA)
KITX .... Hugo, OK [*FM radio station call letters*]
KITY .... Llano, TX [*FM radio station call letters*] (BROA)
KITZ .... Silverdale, WA [*AM radio station call letters*]
KIU .... Kainantu [*New Guinea*] [*Airport symbol*] (AD)
KIU .... Kallikrein Inactivator Unit [*Analytical biochemistry*]
KIU .... Kallikrein-Inhibiting Unit [*Analytical biochemistry*] (DAVI)
KIU .... Krein Inactivator Unit (DB)
KIUL .... Garden City, KS [*AM radio station call letters*]
KIUN .... Pecos, TX [*AM radio station call letters*]
KIUP .... Durango, CO [*AM radio station call letters*]
K-IUSM ...... KSC IUS Plan (or Requirement) (SAUS)
K-IUSN ...... KSC IUS Notice (SAUS)
K-IUSPS ..... KSC IUS Project Specification (SAUS)
KIV .... Air Kiev [*Ukraine*] [*FAA designator*] (FAAC)
KIV .... Kali Venture Corp. [*Vancouver Stock Exchange symbol*]
KIV .... Keep in View
KIV .... Ketoisovalerate [*Biochemistry*]
KIV .... Kiev [*Former USSR*] [*Geomagnetic observatory code*]
KIV .... Kishinev [*Former USSR*] [*Airport symbol*] (OAG)
KIVA .... Albuquerque, NM [*AM radio station call letters*] (BROA)
KIVA .... Corrales, NM [*AM radio station call letters*]
KIVA .... Keto Isovaleriec Acid [*Medicine*] (EDAA)
Kiva .... Kiva. University of Arizona. Arizona Archaeological and Historical Society. Arizona State Museum. Tucson (SAUO)
KIVA .... Workgroup for Indians of North America [*Acronym is based on foreign phrase*] [*Netherlands*]
KIVA-AM .... Albuquerque, NM [*AM radio station call letters*] (BROA)
KIVI .... Koninklijk Instituut van Inginieurs [*Netherlands*] (ACII)
KIVI .... Nampa, ID [*Television station call letters*]
KIvI .... Royal Institution of Engineers in the Netherlands (SAUO)
KIVV .... Lead, SD [*Television station call letters*]
KIVY .... Crockett, TX [*AM radio station call letters*]
KIVY-FM ..... Crockett, TX [*FM radio station call letters*]
KIW .... Kitwe [*Zambia*] [*Airport symbol*] (OAG)
KIW .... Northeast Kiwai [*Language symbol*] (ETLW)
KIW .... Royal New Zealand Air Force [*FAA designator*] (FAAC)
KIWA .... Keuringsinstituut voor Waterleidingartikelen
KIWA .... Sheldon, IA [*AM radio station call letters*]
KIWA-FM .... Sheldon, IA [*FM radio station call letters*]
KIWD .... Las Vegas, NV [*FM radio station call letters*] (GDPB)
KIWI .... Bakersfield, CA [*FM radio station call letters*]
KIWI-A ...... Nuclear Rocket Propulsion Experiments (SAUO)
KIWR .... Council Bluffs, IA [*FM radio station call letters*]
KIWU .... Fabryka Wagonow Swidnica [*Intermodal shipping container symbol*] (TVRC)
KIWW .... Harlingen, TX [*FM radio station call letters*]
KIX .... Kerkhoff Industries, Inc. (SAUO)
KIXA .... Lucerne Valley, CA [*FM radio station call letters*]
KIXB .... El Dorado, AR [*FM radio station call letters*]
KIXC .... Quanah, TX [*FM radio station call letters*]
KIXD-FM .... Oracle, AZ [*FM radio station call letters*] (BROA)
KIXE .... Redding, CA [*Television station call letters*]
KIXF .... Baker, CA [*FM radio station call letters*]
KIXF .... Kodak Industrial X-Ray Film
KIXI .... Mercer Island-Seattle, WA [*AM radio station call letters*]
KIXK .... Canton, SD [*FM radio station call letters*] (RBYB)
KIXK-FM .... Linden, TX [*FM radio station call letters*] (BROA)
KIXL .... Del Valle, TX [*AM radio station call letters*]
KIXN .... Hobbs, NM [*FM radio station call letters*] (RBYB)
KIXO-FM .... Sulphur, OK [*FM radio station call letters*] (BROA)
KIXQ .... Webb City, MO [*FM radio station call letters*]
KIXR .... Ponca City, OK [*FM radio station call letters*]
KIXS .... Victoria, TX [*FM radio station call letters*]
KIXT .... Bellingham-Ferndale, WA [*AM radio station call letters*] (BROA)
KIXT-FM ..... Grover City, CA [*FM radio station call letters*]
KIXV .... Brady, TX [*FM radio station call letters*]
KIXW .... Apple Valley, CA [*AM radio station call letters*] (RBYB)
KIXW .... Lenwood, CA [*FM radio station call letters*]
KIXX .... Watertown, SD [*FM radio station call letters*]
KIXY .... San Angelo, TX [*FM radio station call letters*]
KIXZ .... Amarillo, TX [*AM radio station call letters*]
KIXZ .... Opportunity, WA [*FM radio station call letters*] (BROA)
KIY .... Kilwa [*Tanzania*] [*Airport symbol*] (OAG)
KIY .... Kiyosumi [*Japan*] [*Seismograph station code, US Geological Survey*] [*Closed*] (SEIS)
KIYS .... Jonesboro, AR [*FM radio station call letters*]
KIYU .... Galena, AK [*AM radio station call letters*]
KIYX-FM .... Sageville, IA [*FM radio station call letters*] (RBYB)
KIZ .... Kanaf-Arkia Airlines Ltd. [*Israel*] [*ICAO designator*] (FAAC)
KIZ .... Kemira Industries [*Federal Railroad Administration identification code*]
KIZ .... Kunming Institute of Zoology (BUAC)
KIZN .... Boise, ID [*FM radio station call letters*]
KIZS .... Broken Arrow, OK [*FM radio station call letters*] (BROA)
KIZZ .... Minot, ND [*FM radio station call letters*]
KJ .... Air Guyane [*ICAO designator*] (AD)
KJ .... Complain [*Telegraphy*] (PCTE)
KJ .... Crescent Air Transport (SAUS)
KJ .... Jamaica [*IYRU nationality code*] (IYR)
KJ .... Karaoke Jockey
kJ .... Kilojoule
KJ .... King James [*Version of the Bible*] (WDAA)
KJ .... Kirchenmusikalisches Jahrbuch [*A publication*]
KJ .... Knee Jerk [*Medicine*]
KJ .... Knight of St. Joachim
KJ .... Knights of Jurisprudence
KJA .... Avistar (Cyprus) Ltd. [*ICAO designator*] (FAAC)
KJAA .... Globe, AZ [*AM radio station call letters*]
KJAB .... Mexico, MO [*FM radio station call letters*]
KJAC .... Port Arthur, TX [*Television station call letters*]
KJAE .... Leesville, LA [*FM radio station call letters*]
KJAK .... Slaton, TX [*FM radio station call letters*]
KJAM .... Madison, SD [*AM radio station call letters*]
KJAM-FM ... Madison, SD [*FM radio station call letters*]
KJAN .... Atlantic, IA [*AM radio station call letters*]
KJAN .... Jackson/Allen C. Thompson Field [*Mississippi*] [*ICAO location identifier*] (ICLI)
KJAS-FM .... Jasper, TX [*FM radio station call letters*] (RBYB)
KJAT .... Yermo, CA [*FM radio station call letters*] (BROA)
KJAV .... Alamo, TX [*FM radio station call letters*]
KJAX .... Jacksonville/International [*Florida*] [*ICAO location identifier*] (ICLI)
KJAX .... Jackson, WY [*FM radio station call letters*] (BROA)
KJAX .... Stockton, CA [*AM radio station call letters*]
KJAY .... Sacramento, CA [*AM radio station call letters*]
KJAZ .... McFarland, CA [*AM radio station call letters*]
KJAZ .... San Rafael, CA [*AM radio station call letters*] (BROA)
KJAZ-AM .... Beverly Hills, CA [*AM radio station call letters*] (BROA)
KJB .... Kinder- und Jugendlichenberatung (SAUO)
KJB .... Korea-Japan Board (SAUO)
KJBB .... Watertown, SD [*FM radio station call letters*] (BROA)
KJBC .... Midland, TX [*AM radio station call letters*]
KJBN .... Little Rock, AR [*AM radio station call letters*]
KJBR-FM .... Marked Tree, AR [*FM radio station call letters*] (RBYB)
KJBX-FM .... Trumann, AR [*FM radio station call letters*] (BROA)
KJBZ .... Laredo, TX [*FM radio station call letters*]
KJc .... fracture toughness calculated from the J-integral Jc at the point of cleavage (SAUS)
KJC .... Jefferson Community College, Louisville, KY [*OCLC symbol*] (OCLC)
KJC .... Kaiser Jeep Corporation (SAUO)
KJC .... Keystone Junior College [*Pennsylvania*]
KJCB .... Lafayette, LA [*AM radio station call letters*]
KJCC .... Lake Havasu City, AZ [*FM radio station call letters*]
KJCCC ...... Kansas Jayhawk Community College Conference (PSS)
KJCD .... Longmont, CO [*FM radio station call letters*] (BROA)
KJCE .... Rollingwood, TX [*AM radio station call letters*]
KJCF .... Festus, MO [*AM radio station call letters*]
KJCK .... Junction City, KS [*AM radio station call letters*]
KJCK-FM .... Junction City, KS [*FM radio station call letters*]
KJCM .... Snyder, OK [*FM radio station call letters*] (BROA)
KJCPL ...... Koninklijke Java-China-Paketvaart Lijnen
KJCR .... Keene, TX [*FM radio station call letters*]
KJCS .... Nacogdoches, TX [*FM radio station call letters*]
KJCT .... Grand Junction, CO [*Television station call letters*]
KJCV .... Country Club, MO [*FM radio station call letters*] (BROA)
KJCY .... Saint Ansgar, IA [*FM radio station call letters*] (BROA)
KJD .... Complained [*Telegraphy*] (PCTE)
KJDJ .... San Luis Obispo, CA [*AM radio station call letters*]
KJDX .... Susanville, CA [*FM radio station call letters*]
KJDY .... John Day, OR [*AM radio station call letters*]
KJDY-FM .... Canyon City, OR [*FM radio station call letters*] (RBYB)
KJEE .... Montecito, CA [*FM radio station call letters*]
KJEF .... Jennings, LA [*AM radio station call letters*]
KJEF-FM .... Jennings, LA [*FM radio station call letters*]
KJEL .... Lebanon, MO [*AM radio station call letters*]
KJEM .... Seligman, MO [*FM radio station call letters*] (RBYB)
KJEO .... Fresno, CA [*Television station call letters*]
KJET .... Hoquiam, WA [*AM radio station call letters*] (RBYB)
KJET .... South Bend, WA [*FM radio station call letters*] (BROA)
KJEZ .... Poplar Bluff, MO [*FM radio station call letters*]
KJF .... Kajaani [*Finland*] [*Seismograph station code, US Geological Survey*] (SEIS)
KJF .... Karl-Jaspers Foundation (EA)
KJF .... Kutta-Joukowski Force
KJFA .... Grass Valley, CA [*FM radio station call letters*]
KJFF .... St. Louis, MO (Mt. Vernon, IL) [*AM radio station call letters*] (GDPB)
KJFF-AM .... Festus, MO [*AM radio station call letters*] (RBYB)
KJFK .... New York/John F. Kennedy International [*New York*] [*ICAO location identifier*] (ICLI)
KJFK-FM .... Lampasas, TX [*FM radio station call letters*] (BROA)
KJFM .... Louisiana, MO [*FM radio station call letters*]
KJFX .... Fresno, CA [*FM radio station call letters*]
KJG .... Complaining [*Telegraphy*] (PCTE)
KJGC .... KJG Cartage [*Common carrier symbol*]
KJGM .... Fredonia, KS [*FM radio station call letters*] (RBYB)
KJH .... Khakas [*Language symbol*] (ETLW)
KJHA-FM .... Houston, AK [*FM radio station call letters*] (BROA)
KJHK .... Lawrence, KS [*FM radio station call letters*]
KJHY .... Emmett, ID [*FM radio station call letters*]
KJI .... Kay Jewelels Inc. (SAUO)
KJI .... Kay Jewelers, Incorporated (SAUO)
KJIA .... Spirit Lake, IA [*FM radio station call letters*] (BROA)
KJIB .... South Padre Island, TX [*FM radio station call letters*]
KJIL .... Copeland, KS [*FM radio station call letters*]
KJIM .... Sherman, TX [*AM radio station call letters*]
KJIN .... Houma, LA [*AM radio station call letters*]
KJIR .... Hannibal, MO [*FM radio station call letters*] (BROA)

KJIW......... West Helena, AR [*AM radio station call letters*]
KJIW-FM.... West Helena, AR [*FM radio station call letters*]
KJJ........... Kuhner, J. J., Cleveland OH [*STAC*]
KJJB......... Eunice, LA [*FM radio station call letters*]
KJJC......... Osceola, IA [*FM radio station call letters*]
KJJD-AM.... Windsor, CO [*AM radio station call letters*] (BROA)
KJJJ......... Lake Havasu City, AZ [*FM radio station call letters*] (BROA)
KJJJ-FM.... Seligman, AZ [*FM radio station call letters*] (RBYB)
KJJK......... Fergus Falls, MN [*AM radio station call letters*]
KJJK-FM.... Fergus Falls, MN [*FM radio station call letters*]
KJJL-AM.... Cheyenne, WY [*AM radio station call letters*] (RBYB)
KJJM-FM... Baker, MT [*FM radio station call letters*] (BROA)
KJJO......... St. Louis Park, MN [*AM radio station call letters*]
KJJQ......... Volga, SD [*AM radio station call letters*]
KJJR......... Whitefish, MT [*AM radio station call letters*]
KJJY......... Ankeny, IA [*FM radio station call letters*]
KJJZ......... Kodiak, AK [*FM radio station call letters*]
KJJZ-FM.... Indio, CA [*FM radio station call letters*] (BROA)
KJKB-FM.... Jacksboro, TX [*FM radio station call letters*] (RBYB)
KJKI......... Leupp, AZ [*FM radio station call letters*] (BROA)
KJKJ......... Grand Forks, ND [*FM radio station call letters*]
KJKL......... Selma, OR [*FM radio station call letters*] (BROA)
KJKS......... Cameron, TX [*FM radio station call letters*]
KJKT......... Joplin, MO [*FM radio station call letters*]
KJL........... Kenneth J. Lane [*Jewelry designer*]
KJLA......... Ventura, CA [*Television station call letters*] (BROA)
KJLF......... El Paso, TX [*Television station call letters*]
KJLH......... Compton, CA [*FM radio station call letters*]
KJLL......... South Tucson, AZ [*AM radio station call letters*] (BROA)
KJLO......... Monroe, LA [*FM radio station call letters*]
KJLS......... Hays, KS [*FM radio station call letters*]
KJLT......... North Platte, NE [*AM radio station call letters*]
KJLT-FM..... North Platte, NE [*FM radio station call letters*]
KJLU......... Jefferson City, MO [*FM radio station call letters*]
KJLV......... Hoxie, AR [*FM radio station call letters*] (BROA)
KJLY......... Blue Earth, MN [*FM radio station call letters*]
KJMB......... Blythe, CA [*FM radio station call letters*]
KJMC......... Des Moines, IA [*FM radio station call letters*] (BROA)
KJMD......... Pukalani, HI [*FM radio station call letters*] (BROA)
KJME......... Denver, CO [*AM radio station call letters*]
KJMG......... Bastrop, LA [*FM radio station call letters*] (BROA)
KJMH......... Burlington, IA [*Television station call letters*]
KJMJ-AM... Alexandria, LA [*AM radio station call letters*] (BROA)
KJMK-FM... Webb City, MO [*FM radio station call letters*] (BROA)
KJML-FM... Columbus, KS [*FM radio station call letters*] (BROA)
KJMM......... Bixby, OK [*FM radio station call letters*]
KJMN-FM... Castle Rock, CO [*FM radio station call letters*] (RBYB)
KJMO......... Jefferson City, MO [*FM radio station call letters*]
kJ mol....... Kilojoule Mole [*Chemistry*] (MEC)
KJMP......... Pierce, CO [*AM radio station call letters*] (BROA)
KJMS......... Memphis, TN [*FM radio station call letters*]
KJMX......... Reedsport, OR [*FM radio station call letters*] (BROA)
KJMX......... Tulia, TX [*FM radio station call letters*]
KJMY......... Seaside, CA [*FM radio station call letters*] (RBYB)
KJMZ......... Henderson, NV [*FM radio station call letters*] (RBYB)
KJMZ-FM... Lawton, OK [*FM radio station call letters*] (RBYB)
KJN........... Conjunction [*Telegraphy*] (PCTE)
KJN........... Kajaani [*Finland*] [*Seismograph station code, US Geological Survey*] [*Closed*] (SEIS)
KJNA......... Jena, LA [*AM radio station call letters*]
KJNA-FM.... Jena, LA [*FM radio station call letters*]
KJNB......... Collegeville, MN [*FM radio station call letters*] (GDPB)
KJNO......... Juneau, AK [*AM radio station call letters*]
KJNP......... North Pole, AK [*AM radio station call letters*]
KJNP-FM.... North Pole, AK [*FM radio station call letters*]
KJNP-TV.... North Pole, AK [*Television station call letters*]
KJNT......... Hempsted [*New York*] [*ICAO location identifier*] (ICLI)
KJNZ......... Hereford, TX [*FM radio station call letters*] (BROA)
KJO........... Kommunistische Jugend Oesterreich [*Communist Youth of Austria*]
KJOC......... Davenport, IA [*AM radio station call letters*]
KJOE......... Slayton, MN [*FM radio station call letters*] (RBYB)
KJOI......... Dinuba, CA [*FM radio station call letters*]
KJOJ......... Conroe, TX [*AM radio station call letters*]
KJOJ-FM.... Freeport, TX [*FM radio station call letters*]
KJOK......... Yuma, AZ [*FM radio station call letters*]
KJOL......... Grand Junction, CO [*FM radio station call letters*]
KJON-AM... Anadarko, OK [*AM radio station call letters*] (BROA)
KJOP......... Lemoore, CA [*AM radio station call letters*]
KJOT......... Boise, ID [*FM radio station call letters*]
KJOV-FM.... Woodward, OK [*FM radio station call letters*] (RBYB)
KJOX......... Selah, WA [*AM radio station call letters*] (BROA)
KJOX-AM... Yakima, WA [*AM radio station call letters*] (RBYB)
KJOY......... Stockton, CA [*FM radio station call letters*]
KJPN......... Waipahu, HI [*AM radio station call letters*]
KJPW......... Waynesville, MO [*AM radio station call letters*]
KJPW-FM... Waynesville, MO [*FM radio station call letters*]
KJQI-AM.... San Rafael, CA [*AM radio station call letters*] (BROA)
KJQN......... Brigham City, UT [*FM radio station call letters*] (BROA)
KJQN-FM... Stockton, CA [*FM radio station call letters*] (BROA)
KJQS......... Murray, UT [*AM radio station call letters*] (BROA)
KJQY......... Rocky Ford, CO [*FM radio station call letters*] (BROA)
KJQY......... San Diego, CA [*FM radio station call letters*]
KJR........... Kiski Junction Railroad [*Federal Railroad Administration identification code*]
KJR........... Seattle, WA [*AM radio station call letters*]
KJRB......... Spokane, WA [*AM radio station call letters*]
KJRE......... Ellendale, ND [*Television station call letters*]
KJRF......... Lawton, OK [*FM radio station call letters*] (BROA)
KJR-FM..... Seattle, WA [*FM radio station call letters*]
KJRG......... Newton, KS [*AM radio station call letters*]
KJRH......... Tulsa, OK [*Television station call letters*]
KJRL......... Herington, KS [*FM radio station call letters*] (BROA)
KJRR......... Jamestown, ND [*Television station call letters*]
KJRT......... Amarillo, TX [*FM radio station call letters*]
KJRY......... Keokuk Junction Railway [*Federal Railroad Administration identification code*]
KJS........... East Kewa [*Language symbol*] (ETLW)
KJS........... Kansas Journal of Sociology
KJS........... Karl-Jaspers Stiftung [*Karl-Jaspers Foundation - KJF*] (EA)
KJS........... Kiva Java Server [*Computer science*]
KJS........... Kodak Job Sheet
KJS........... V-Groove on One Side [*Lumber*]
KJSA......... Mineral Wells, TX [*AM radio station call letters*]
KJSK......... Columbus, NE [*AM radio station call letters*]
KJSL......... St. Louis, MO [*AM radio station call letters*]
KJSN......... Modesto, CA [*FM radio station call letters*]
KJSR......... Tulsa, OK [*FM radio station call letters*] (RBYB)
KJStJ........ Knight of Justice, Order of St. John of Jerusalem
KJT........... Complaint [*Telegraphy*] (PCTE)
KJTA......... Flagstaff, AZ [*FM radio station call letters*]
KJTL......... Wichita Falls, TX [*Television station call letters*]
KJTT......... Oak Harbor, WA [*AM radio station call letters*]
KJTV......... Lubbock, TX [*Television station call letters*]
KJTX......... Jefferson, TX [*FM radio station call letters*]
KJTY......... Topeka, KS [*FM radio station call letters*]
KJU........... Kamiraba [*Papua New Guinea*] [*Airport symbol*] [*Obsolete*] (OAG)
KJUD......... Juneau, AK [*Television station call letters*]
KJUG......... Tulare, CA [*AM radio station call letters*]
KJUG-FM... Tulare, CA [*FM radio station call letters*]
KJUL......... North Las Vegas, NV [*FM radio station call letters*]
KJUN......... Eatonville, WA [*FM radio station call letters*]
KJUN......... Puyallup, WA [*AM radio station call letters*]
KJUN-FM... Tillamook, OR [*FM radio station call letters*] (BROA)
KJUS......... Beaumont, TX [*AM radio station call letters*] (RBYB)
KJV........... King James Version [*or Authorized Version of the Bible, 1611*]
KJVC......... Mansfield, LA [*FM radio station call letters*]
KJVD......... Kommunistischer Jugendverband Deutschlands [*Communist Youth Club of Germany*]
KJVH......... Longview, WA [*FM radio station call letters*]
KJVI......... Jackson, WY [*Television station call letters*]
KJWA......... Grand Junction, CO [*Television station call letters*]
KJWL......... Fresno, CA [*FM radio station call letters*]
KJWY-TV.... Jackson, WY [*TV station call letters*] (RBYB)
KJYE......... Grand Junction, CO [*FM radio station call letters*]
KJYL......... Eagle Grove, IA [*FM radio station call letters*]
KJYO......... Oklahoma City, OK [*FM radio station call letters*]
KJZA......... Drake, AZ [*FM radio station call letters*] (BROA)
KJZS......... Sparks, NV [*FM radio station call letters*] (BROA)
KJZY......... Sebastopol, CA [*FM radio station call letters*] (RBYB)
KJZZ......... Phoenix, AZ [*FM radio station call letters*]
KJZZ-TV.... Salt Lake City, UT [*Television station call letters*]
KK............ Arab International Aviation Co. (SAUO)
KK............ Confirmed [*Travel industry*] (TVEL)
KK............ Die Welt der Bibel. Kleinkommentare zur Heiligen Schrift [*Duesseldorf*] [*A publication*] (BJA)
KK............ Kabushiki Kaishi [*Joint stock company*] [*Japan*]
KK............ Kahal Kadosh. Holy Congregation (BJA)
KK............ Kallikrein (DB)
KK............ Kaluza-Klein [*Theories*] [*Physics*]
KK............ Kaplan-Klaskin [*Syndromes*] [*Medicine*] (QSUL)
KK............ Kar-Kraft [*Automotive industry supplier*]
KK............ Karnataka-Kerala Express [*Indian Railway*] (TIR)
KK............ Kenya [*IYRU nationality code*] (IYR)
KK............ Keren Kayemeth (BJA)
KK............ Key-Encrypting Key [*Computer science*] (VLIE)
kK............ Kilokayser
KK............ Kilokelvin
KK............ Kings
KK............ Kingston Korner (EA)
K-K........... Kirov-Kiev [*Former USSR*]
KK............ Kleinkaliber [*Small Caliber*] [*German military*]
KK............ Knee Kick [*Neurology*]
KK............ Knock-for-Knock (MARI)
KK............ Know That You Know (VLIE)
KK............ Kokusai Koryu [*Japan Foundation*] (EAIO)
KK............ Komisja Koordynacyjna. Zydowskie Instytucje Opiekuncze (BJA)
KK............ Kosher Kitchen (BJA)
KK............ Kremlin Kommandant
KK............ Kulutusosuuskuntien Keskusliitto [*Co-Operative Union*] [*Finland*] (EY)
KK............ Kurtis-Kraft [*US racecar maker*]
KK............ Kurzgefasster Kommentar zu den Heiligen Schriften Alten und Neuen Testaments [*Munich*] [*A publication*] (BJA)
KKA.......... Benedictine College, Atchison, KS [*OCLC symbol*] (OCLC)
KKA.......... Kelsey Kindred of America (EA)
KKA.......... Kitchen Klutzs of America [*Inactive*] (EA)
KKA.......... Knights of King Arthur (EA)
KKA.......... Koyukuk [*Alaska*] [*Airport symbol*] (OAG)
KKAA........ Aberdeen, SD [*AM radio station call letters*]

KKAC .... Vandalia, Mo [*FM radio station call letters*] (BROA)
KKAG .... Porterville, CA [*Television station call letters*]
KKAJ........ Ardmore-Ada, OK [*FM radio station call letters*] (GDPB)
KKAJ-FM.... Ardmore, OK [*FM radio station call letters*]
KKAL .... Arroyo Grande, CA [*AM radio station call letters*]
KKAL .... Morro Bay, CA [*FM radio station call letters*] (BROA)
KKAM........ Lubbock, TX [*AM radio station call letters*]
KKAN .... Phillipsburg, KS [*AM radio station call letters*]
KKAP .... Little Rock, AR [*Television station call letters*] (BROA)
KKAQ .... Thief River Falls, MN [*AM radio station call letters*]
KKAR .... Omaha, NE [*AM radio station call letters*]
KKAS .... Julesburg, CO [*FM radio station call letters*] (BROA)
KKAS .... Silsbee, TX [*AM radio station call letters*]
KKASSR..... Kara-Kalpak Autonomous Soviet Socialist Republic (SAUO)
kkat.......... Kilokatal [*Medicine*] (EDAA)
KKAT......... Ogden, UT [*FM radio station call letters*]
KKAW-FM... Albin, WY [*FM radio station call letters*] (BROA)
KKAY .... Donaldsonville, LA [*FM radio station call letters*]
KKAY .... White Castle, LA [*AM radio station call letters*]
KKAZ .... Cheyenne, WY [*FM radio station call letters*]
KKB.......... Baker University, Baldwin City, KS [*OCLC symbol*] (OCLC)
KKB .... Kitoi [*Alaska*] [*Airport symbol*] (OAG)
KKBA .... Kingsville, TX [*FM radio station call letters*] (RBYB)
KKBB .... Bakersfield, CA [*FM radio station call letters*]
KKBC .... Baker City, OR [*FM radio station call letters*]
KKBC .... Korea Kuwait Banking Corp.
KKBD .... Sallisaw, OK [*FM radio station call letters*] (BROA)
KKBE .... Los Angeles (Corona & San Bernardino), CA [*FM radio station call letters*] (GDPB)
KKBE-FM.... Ojai, CA [*FM radio station call letters*] (BROA)
KKBG .... Hilo, HI [*FM radio station call letters*]
KKBH .... San Diego, CA [*FM radio station call letters*] (RBYB)
KKBI .... Broken Bow, OK [*FM radio station call letters*]
KKBJ......... Bemidji, MN [*AM radio station call letters*]
KKBJ-FM.... Bemidji, MN [*FM radio station call letters*]
KKBL .... Monett, MO [*FM radio station call letters*]
KKBN .... Twain Harte, CA [*FM radio station call letters*]
KKBQ .... Houston, TX [*AM radio station call letters*]
KKBQ .... Pasadena, TX [*FM radio station call letters*]
KKBR .... Billings, MT [*FM radio station call letters*]
KKBS .... Guymon, OK [*FM radio station call letters*]
KKBT .... Los Angeles, CA [*FM radio station call letters*]
KKBX .... Fargo, ND [*FM radio station call letters*] (BROA)
KKBY-AM.... Puyallup, WA [*AM radio station call letters*] (RBYB)
KKBY-FM.... Eatonville, WA [*FM radio station call letters*] (RBYB)
KKBZ .... Clarinda, IA [*FM radio station call letters*]
KKC.......... Kansas City Public Library, Kansas City, KS [*OCLC symbol*] (OCLC)
KKC.......... Khon Kaen [*Thailand*] [*Airport symbol*] (OAG)
KKC.......... Knox College Library, University of Toronto [*UTLAS symbol*]
KKCA .... Fulton, MO [*FM radio station call letters*]
KKcB......... Central Baptist Theological Seminary, Kansas City, KS [*Library symbol*] [*Library of Congress*] (LCLS)
KKCB-FM ... Duluth, MN [*FM radio station call letters*] (RBYB)
KKcBM ...... Bethany Medical Center, Kansas City, KS [*Library symbol*] [*Library of Congress*] (LCLS)
KKcD .... Donnelly College, Kansas City, KS [*Library symbol*] [*Library of Congress*] (LCLS)
KKCD .... Omaha, NE [*FM radio station call letters*]
KKCH-FM ... Glenwood Springs, CO [*FM radio station call letters*] (BROA)
KKCI .... Goodland, KS [*FM radio station call letters*]
KKcJS .... Jensen-Salsbery Laboratories, Kansas City, KS [*Library symbol*] [*Library of Congress*] (LCLS)
KKCK .... Marshall, MN [*FM radio station call letters*]
KKCL .... Lorenzo, TX [*FM radio station call letters*]
KKCM........ Shakopee, MN [*AM radio station call letters*]
KKCN........ Ballinger, TX [*FM radio station call letters*] (BROA)
KKCN .... Trumann, AR [*FM radio station call letters*] (RBYB)
KKCN-FM ... Sterling City, TX [*FM radio station call letters*] (BROA)
KKCO-TV.... Grand Junction, CO [*TV station call letters*] (RBYB)
kKCP......... Koala Conservation Program (SAUO)
KKcP......... Providence - Saint Margaret Health Center, Kansas City, KS [*Library symbol*] [*Library of Congress*] (LCLS)
KKcPS....... Kansas City Kansas Public Schools, Kansas City, KS [*Library symbol*] [*Library of Congress*] (LCLS)
KKCQ .... Bagley, MN [*FM radio station call letters*] (BROA)
KKCQ .... Fosston, MN [*AM radio station call letters*]
KKCQ-FM ... Fosston, MN [*FM radio station call letters*]
KKCR-FM ... Hanalei, HI [*FM radio station call letters*] (RBYB)
KKCS .... Colorado Springs, CO [*AM radio station call letters*]
KKCS-FM ... Colorado Springs, CO [*FM radio station call letters*]
KKCT .... Bismarck, ND [*FM radio station call letters*]
KKCV .... Cedar Falls, IA [*FM radio station call letters*]
KKCW .... Beaverton, OR [*FM radio station call letters*]
KKCY .... Colusa, CA [*FM radio station call letters*]
KKD.......... Kinuku [*Language symbol*] (ETLW)
KKD.......... Kokoda [*Papua New Guinea*] [*Airport symbol*] (OAG)
KKD.......... Korintji-Kaba-Dempo [*Sumatra*] [*Seismograph station code, US Geological Survey*] [*Closed*] (SEIS)
KKDA .... Dallas, TX [*FM radio station call letters*]
KKDA .... Grand Prairie, TX [*AM radio station call letters*]
KKDD........ Katalog Kandidatskikh i Doktorskikh Dissertatsii [*A bibliographic publication*]
KKDD .... North Las Vegas, NV [*AM radio station call letters*] (RBYB)
KKDD .... San Bernardino, CA [*AM radio station call letters*] (BROA)
K K-D-H..... Knight Kadosch [*Freemasonry*]
KKDJ .... Delano, CA [*FM radio station call letters*] (BROA)
KKDJ .... Fresno, CA [*FM radio station call letters*]
KKDKA ...... Bulletin. Kyushu Institute of Technology (journ.) (SAUS)
KKDL .... Detroit Lakes, MN [*FM radio station call letters*]
KKDM .... Des Moines, IA [*FM radio station call letters*]
KKDQ........ Thief River Falls, MN [*FM radio station call letters*]
KKDS .... South Salt Lake, UT [*AM radio station call letters*]
KKDU........ El Dorado, AR [*FM radio station call letters*] (BROA)
KKDV .... San Francisco, CA [*FM radio station call letters*] (BROA)
KKDY .... West Plains, MO [*FM radio station call letters*]
KKDZ .... Seattle, WA [*AM radio station call letters*]
KKE.......... Kerikeri [*New Zealand*] [*Airport symbol*] (OAG)
KKE.......... Kleena Kleene Gold Mines [*Vancouver Stock Exchange symbol*]
KKE.......... Kommunistiko Komma Ellados [*Communist Party of Greece*] [*Political party*] (PPW)
KKEA .... Honolulu, HI [*AM radio station call letters*] (GDPB)
KKED-FM ... Fairbanks, AK [*FM radio station call letters*] (BROA)
KKEE......... Astoria, OR [*FM radio station call letters*] (BROA)
KKEE......... Long Beach, WA [*FM radio station call letters*]
KKEes .... Kommunistiko Komma Ellados - Esoterikou [*Communist Party of Greece - Interior*] [*Political party*] (PPE)
KKEex .... Kommunistiko Komma Ellados - Exoterikou [*Communist Party of Greece - Exterior*] [*Political party*] (PPE)
KKEG .... Fayetteville, AR [*FM radio station call letters*]
KKE-Interior... Greek Communist Party of the Interior [*Political party*] (PSAP)
KKEL......... Hobbs, NM [*AM radio station call letters*]
KKEN .... Duncan, OK [*AM radio station call letters*] (BROA)
KKEN-FM ... Duncan, OK [*FM radio station call letters*] (BROA)
KKEQ .... Fosston, MN [*FM radio station call letters*] (GDPB)
KKEQ-FM ... Fosston, MN [*FM radio station call letters*] (RBYB)
KKER-FM ... Kerrville, TX [*FM radio station call letters*] (BROA)
KKES .... Kommunistiko Komma Ellados - Esoterikou [*Communist Party of Greece - Interior*] [*Political party*] (PPW)
KKEX .... Preston, ID [*FM radio station call letters*]
KKEY .... Harrisburg, AR [*FM radio station call letters*] (BROA)
KKEY .... Portland, OR [*AM radio station call letters*]
KKEZ......... Fort Dodge, IA [*FM radio station call letters*]
KKFC .... Coalgate, OK [*FM radio station call letters*] (BROA)
KKFC .... KISS [*Knights in the Service of Satan*] Konnection Fan Club (EA)
KKFG .... Bloomfield, NM [*FM radio station call letters*]
KKFI .... Kansas City, MO [*FM radio station call letters*]
KKFJ......... Alturas, CA [*AM radio station call letters*] (GDPB)
KKFJ-AM.... Alturas, CA [*AM radio station call letters*] (RBYB)
KKFM........ Colorado Springs, CO [*FM radio station call letters*]
KKFN .... Denver, CO [*AM radio station call letters*]
KKFO .... Coalinga, CA [*AM radio station call letters*]
KKFR .... Glendale, AZ [*FM radio station call letters*]
KKFS .... Dunnigan, CA [*FM radio station call letters*] (BROA)
KKG.......... Kappa Kappa Gamma [*Sorority*]
KKG.......... Konawaruk [*Guyana*] [*Airport symbol*] [*Obsolete*] (OAG)
KKG.......... Kootenay King Resources [*Vancouver Stock Exchange symbol*]
KKG.......... Thousand Kilograms (EG)
KKGB .... Sulphur, LA [*FM radio station call letters*]
KKGD .... Silt, CO [*AM radio station call letters*] (GDPB)
KKGJ .... Grand Junction, CO [*AM radio station call letters*] (BROA)
KKGL-FM ... Nampa, ID [*FM radio station call letters*] (BROA)
KKGM .... Grand Junction, CO [*AM radio station call letters*] (RBYB)
KKGO .... Frazier Park, CA [*AM radio station call letters*]
KKGO-FM ... Los Angeles, CA [*FM radio station call letters*]
KKGR-AM ... East Helena, MT [*AM radio station call letters*] (BROA)
KKGT .... Portland, OR [*AM radio station call letters*] (BROA)
KKH.......... Kailua-Kona [*Hawaii*] [*Seismograph station code, US Geological Survey*] (SEIS)
KKH.......... Karakoram Highway [*Asia*]
KKH.......... Kongiganak [*Alaska*] [*Airport symbol*] (OAG)
KKHB-FM ... Eureka, CA [*FM radio station call letters*] (RBYB)
KKHG .... Flandreau, SD [*FM radio station call letters*] (BROA)
KKHG .... Tucson, AZ [*FM radio station call letters*]
KKHI .... Laramie, WY [*AM radio station call letters*] (BROA)
KKHI .... San Rafael, CA [*AM radio station call letters*]
KKHI-FM .... San Rafael, CA [*FM radio station call letters*]
KKHJ .... Los Angeles, CA [*AM radio station call letters*]
KKHJ .... Pago Pago, AS [*FM radio station call letters*] (BROA)
KKHK .... Kansas City, KS [*AM radio station call letters*] (BROA)
KKHK-FM ... Denver, CO [*FM radio station call letters*] (RBYB)
KKHL .... Klung Kidney-Heart-Lung [*Machine*]
KKHN-FM ... Naipahu, HI [*FM radio station call letters*] (BROA)
KKHQ .... Odem, TX [*FM radio station call letters*]
KKHR .... Abilene, TX [*FM radio station call letters*] (BROA)
KKHR .... Anson, TX [*FM radio station call letters*]
KKHT .... Conroe, TX [*FM radio station call letters*] (RBYB)
KKHT-AM ... Houston, TX [*AM radio station call letters*] (BROA)
KKHU .... Kani Kommerz [*Intermodal shipping container symbol*] (TVRC)
KKI........... Akiachak [*Alaska*] [*Airport symbol*] (OAG)
KKI........... Kankakee, IL [*Amtrak rail station code*]
KKI........... Karkar Island [*Papua New Guinea*] [*Seismograph station code, US Geological Survey*] (SEIS)
KKI........... Kenpo Karate International (EA)
KKIA .... Ida Grove, IA [*FM radio station call letters*] (BROA)
KKIC .... Boise, ID [*AM radio station call letters*]
KKID .... Salem, MO [*FM radio station call letters*] (BROA)
KKID .... Sallisaw, OK [*AM radio station call letters*]
KKIFC........ Kris Kristofferson International Fan Club (EA)
KKIH .... King Khalid International Hospital [*Saudi Arabia*] (WDAA)

KKIK .... Temple, TX [*FM radio station call letters*] (RBYB)
KKIK-FM .... La Junta, CO [*FM radio station call letters*] (BROA)
KKIM .... Albuquerque, NM [*AM radio station call letters*]
KKIN .... Aitkin, MN [*AM radio station call letters*]
KKIN-FM .... Aitkin, MN [*FM radio station call letters*] (RBYB)
KKIQ .... Livermore, CA [*FM radio station call letters*]
KKIS .... Concord, CA [*AM radio station call letters*]
KKIS .... Soldotna, AK [*FM radio station call letters*]
KKIT .... Angel Fire, NM [*FM radio station call letters*] (BROA)
KKIT .... Taos, NM [*AM radio station call letters*]
KKIX .... Fayetteville, AR [*FM radio station call letters*]
KKJ .... Kita Kyushu [*Japan*] [*Airport symbol*] [*Obsolete*] (OAG)
KKJG .... San Luis Obispo, CA [*FM radio station call letters*]
KKJI .... Gallup, NM [*FM radio station call letters*]
KKJJ-FM .... Ashland, OR [*FM radio station call letters*] (RBYB)
KKJL .... San Luis Obispo, CA [*AM radio station call letters*] (RBYB)
KKJM .... St Joseph, MN [*FM radio station call letters*]
KKJO .... St. Joseph, MO [*FM radio station call letters*]
KKJQ .... Garden City, KS [*FM radio station call letters*]
KKJR .... Hutchison, MN [*FM radio station call letters*]
KKJT .... Joshua Tree, CA [*FM radio station call letters*]
KKJT .... Twentynine Palms, CA [*FM radio station call letters*] (BROA)
KKJW-FM ... Stanton, TX [*FM radio station call letters*] (BROA)
KKJX .... Klamath Falls, OR [*AM radio station call letters*] (GDPB)
KKJX-AM .... Klamath Falls, OR [*AM radio station call letters*] (BROA)
KKJY .... Albuquerque, NM [*AM radio station call letters*] (BROA)
KKJY-AM .... Lake Oswego, OR [*AM radio station call letters*] (BROA)
KKJZ .... Lake Oswego, OR [*FM radio station call letters*]
KKK .... Invisible Empire Knights of the Ku Klux Klan (EA)
KKK .... Kissel Kar Klub (EA)
KKK .... Knight of the Ku Klux Klan (EA)
KKK .... Kolmer, Kline, Kahn [*Test for syphilis*] [*Medicine*] (DAVI)
KKK .... Kuehnle, Kopp, & Kausch [*Auto industry supplier*]
KKK .... Ku Klux Klan [*White supremacist organization*] (EMA)
KKKIS .... K.K. Kodak Information Systems (EFIS)
KKKK .... Knights of the Ku Klux Klan (BUAC)
KKKK .... Odessa, TX [*FM radio station call letters*]
KKKK .... White Knights of the Ku-Klux-Klan (SAUO)
KKKK-FM ... Crane, TX [*FM radio station call letters*] (BROA)
KKKUK ...... Ku-Klux-Klan in the United Kingdom (SAUO)
KKL .... Kam-Kotia Mines Ltd. [*Toronto Stock Exchange symbol*]
KKL .... Karluk Lake, AK [*Location identifier*] [*FAA*] (FAAL)
KKL .... Keren Kayemeth Leisrael (BJA)
KKL .... Kol-Kol Airlines Ltd. [*Nigeria*] [*FAA designator*] (FAAC)
KKLA .... Los Angeles, CA [*FM radio station call letters*]
KKLA .... San Bernardino, CA [*AM radio station call letters*] (RBYB)
KKLB .... Elgin, TX [*FM radio station call letters*]
KKLD-FM ... Prescott Valley, az [*FM radio station call letters*] (RBYB)
KKLE .... Winfield, KS [*AM radio station call letters*]
KKLF .... Denison-Sherman, TX [*AM radio station call letters*] (BROA)
KKLH-FM ... Marshfield, MO [*FM radio station call letters*] (RBYB)
KKLI .... Widefield, CO [*FM radio station call letters*]
KKLK-FM .... Daingerfield, TX [*FM radio station call letters*] (BROA)
KKLL .... Kirk Line [*Common carrier symbol*]
KKLL .... Webb City, MO [*AM radio station call letters*]
KKLL-FM .... Webb City, MO [*FM radio station call letters*]
KKLN-FM ... Atwater, MN [*FM radio station call letters*] (BROA)
KKLO .... Leavenworth, KS [*AM radio station call letters*]
KKLP .... La Pine, OR [*FM radio station call letters*] (BROA)
KKLQ .... Oceanside, CA [*AM radio station call letters*] (RBYB)
KKLQ-FM ... San Diego, CA [*FM radio station call letters*]
KKLQ-FM ... Vancouver, WA [*FM radio station call letters*] (BROA)
KKLR .... Poplar Bluff, MO [*FM radio station call letters*]
KKLS .... Rapid City, SD [*AM radio station call letters*]
KKLS-FM .... Sioux Falls, SD [*FM radio station call letters*]
KKLT .... Phoenix, AZ [*FM radio station call letters*]
KKLU .... Kawasaki Kisen Kaisha [*Common carrier symbol*]
KKLU .... Kawasaki Kisen Kaisha (K-Line) [*Intermodal shipping container symbol*] (TVRC)
KKLV .... Honolulu, HI [*FM radio station call letters*]
KKLV-FM .... Bismarck, ND [*FM radio station call letters*] (BROA)
KKLV-FM .... Turrell, AR [*FM radio station call letters*] (BROA)
KKLX .... Worland, WY [*FM radio station call letters*]
KKLY-FM .... Pecos, TX [*FM radio station call letters*] (RBYB)
KKLZ .... K Line [*Intermodal trailer symbol*]
KKLZ .... Las Vegas, NV [*FM radio station call letters*]
KKM .... Kota Kinabalu [*Malaysia*] [*Seismograph station code, US Geological Survey*] (SEIS)
KKM .... Kreiskoblenmotor [*Circulating Piston Engine*] [*Automotive engineering*]
KKM .... North Central Kansas Library, Manhattan, KS [*OCLC symbol*] (OCLC)
KKMA .... Le Mars, IA [*FM radio station call letters*]
KKMC .... Gonzales, CA [*AM radio station call letters*]
KKMC .... King Khalid Military City [*Saudi Arabia*] (DOMA)
KKMG .... Pueblo, CO [*FM radio station call letters*]
KKMI .... Burlington, IA [*FM radio station call letters*]
KKMJ .... Austin, TX [*FM radio station call letters*]
KKMK .... Rapid City, SD [*FM radio station call letters*]
KKMN .... Kirkman Trucking [*Common carrier symbol*]
KKMO .... Tacoma, WA [*AM radio station call letters*]
KKMR .... Arizona City, AZ [*FM radio station call letters*] (BROA)
KKMR-FM ... Haltom City, TX [*FM radio station call letters*] (BROA)
KKMS-AM ... Richfield, MN [*AM radio station call letters*] (BROA)
KKMT-FM ... Columbia Falls, MT [*FM radio station call letters*] (BROA)
KKMV .... Rupert, ID [*FM radio station call letters*]
KKMX .... Tri City, OR [*FM radio station call letters*]
KKMY .... Orange, TX [*FM radio station call letters*]
KKMZ .... Kokomo Range [*Federal Railroad Administration identification code*]
KKN .... Kansas Newman College, Wichita, KS [*OCLC symbol*] (OCLC)
KKN .... Kirkenes [*Norway*] [*Airport symbol*] (OAG)
KKNB .... Crete, NE [*FM radio station call letters*]
KKND .... Tucson, AZ [*AM radio station call letters*] (RBYB)
KKND-FM ... Port Sulphur, LA [*FM radio station call letters*] (RBYB)
KKNG .... Laramie, WY [*FM radio station call letters*]
KKNG-FM ... Newcastle, OK [*FM radio station call letters*] (BROA)
KKNL .... New London, IA [*FM radio station call letters*] (BROA)
KKNN .... Delta, CO [*FM radio station call letters*] (RBYB)
KKNO .... Gretna, LA [*AM radio station call letters*]
KKNU .... Springfield-Eugene, OR [*FM radio station call letters*]
KKNW .... Seattle, WA [*AM radio station call letters*] (BROA)
KKNW-AM ... Port Angeles, WA [*AM radio station call letters*] (BROA)
KKNX-AM ... Eugene, OR [*AM radio station call letters*] (RBYB)
KKO .... Kaikohe [*New Zealand*] [*Airport symbol*] [*Obsolete*] (OAG)
KKO .... Karko [*Language symbol*] (ETLW)
KKO .... National Citizens' Committee [*Poland*] [*Political party*]
KKO .... Ottawa University, Ottawa, KS [*OCLC symbol*] (OCLC)
KKOA .... Kustom Kemps of America (EA)
KKOA .... Volcano, HI [*FM radio station call letters*]
KKOB .... Albuquerque, NM [*AM radio station call letters*]
KKOB-EX .... Santa Fe, NM [*AM radio station call letters*] (BROA)
KKOB Exp Stn ... Santa Fe, NM [*Radio expansion station*] (RBYB)
KKOB-FM ... Albuquerque, NM [*FM radio station call letters*]
KKOH .... Reno, NV [*AM radio station call letters*] (RBYB)
KKOJ .... Jackson, MN [*AM radio station call letters*]
KKOK .... Morris, MN [*FM radio station call letters*]
KKOL .... Hampton, AR [*FM radio station call letters*]
KKOL-AM ... Seattle, WA [*AM radio station call letters*] (BROA)
KKOM .... Arroyo Grande, CA [*AM radio station call letters*] (BROA)
KKON .... Kealakekua, HI [*AM radio station call letters*]
KKOR .... Gallup, NM [*FM radio station call letters*]
KKOS-FM ... Palacios, TX [*FM radio station call letters*] (RBYB)
KKOT .... Columbus, NE [*FM radio station call letters*]
KKOW .... Pittsburg, KS [*AM radio station call letters*]
KKOW-FM ... Pittsburg, KS [*FM radio station call letters*]
KKOY .... Chanute, KS [*AM radio station call letters*]
KKOY-FM .... Chanute, KS [*FM radio station call letters*]
KKOZ .... Ava, MO [*AM radio station call letters*]
KKOZ-FM ... Ava, MO [*FM radio station call letters*]
KKP .... Canadian Communist Party [*Political party*]
KKP .... Chinese Communist Party [*Political party*]
KKP .... Cuban Communist Party [*Political party*]
KKP .... Cypriot Communist Party [*Political party*]
KKP .... Kappa Kappa Psi [*Society*]
KKP .... Kina Kommunista Partja [*Communist Party of China*] [*Political party*]
KKP .... King's Knight's Pawn [*Chess*] (IIA)
KKP .... Komisja Kontroli Partyjnej (SAUO)
KKp .... University of Kansas Medical Library (SAUO)
KKP .... University of Kansas, Medical Library, Kansas City, KS [*OCLC symbol*] (OCLC)
KKPC .... Pueblo, CO [*FM radio station call letters*]
KKPC-AM ... Pueblo, CO [*AM radio station call letters*] (RBYB)
KKPL .... Cheyenne, WY [*FM radio station call letters*] (BROA)
KKPL .... Opportunity, WA [*AM radio station call letters*]
KKPL-FM .... Los Alamos, NM [*FM radio station call letters*] (BROA)
KKPN-FM ... Houston, TX [*FM radio station call letters*] (BROA)
KKPN-FM ... Rockport, TX [*FM radio station call letters*] (BROA)
KKPR .... Kearney, NE [*AM radio station call letters*]
KKPR-FM ... Kearney, NE [*FM radio station call letters*]
KKPS .... Brownsville, TX [*FM radio station call letters*]
KKPT .... Little Rock, AR [*FM radio station call letters*]
KKPW-FM ... Kerman, CA [*FM radio station call letters*] (BROA)
KKPX .... San Jose, CA [*Television station call letters*] (BROA)
KKPZ .... Portland, OR [*AM radio station call letters*] (RBYB)
KKQ .... Sterling College, Sterling, KS [*OCLC symbol*] (OCLC)
KKQQ .... Volga, SD [*FM radio station call letters*]
KKQY-FM .... HillCity, KS [*FM radio station call letters*] (RBYB)
KKR .... Emporia State University, Emporia, KS [*OCLC symbol*] (OCLC)
KKR .... Kaukura [*French Polynesia*] [*Airport symbol*] (OAG)
KKR .... Kohlberg Kravis Roberts (BUAC)
KKR .... Kohlberg Kravis Roberts & Co.
KKR .... Kokanee Resources Ltd. [*Vancouver Stock Exchange symbol*]
KKR .... Kurtis-Kraft Register [*Defunct*] (EA)
KKR .... Kurukshetra [*India*] [*Seismograph station code, US Geological Survey*] (SEIS)
KKRB .... Klamath Falls, OR [*FM radio station call letters*]
KKRC .... Granite Falls, MN [*FM radio station call letters*]
KKRD .... Wichita, KS [*FM radio station call letters*]
KKRF .... Stuart, IA [*FM radio station call letters*]
KKRG .... Albuquerque, NM [*FM radio station call letters*] (BROA)
KKRH .... Salem, OR [*FM radio station call letters*] (RBYB)
KKRI .... Pocola, OK [*FM radio station call letters*] (BROA)
KKrJS .... Jensen-Salsbery Laboratories, Kansas City (SAUS)
KKRK .... Douglas, AZ [*FM radio station call letters*]
KKRK-FM ... Coffeyville, KS [*FM radio station call letters*] (BROA)
KKRL .... Carroll, IA [*FM radio station call letters*]
KKRN-FM ... Cabot, AR [*FM radio station call letters*] (RBYB)
KKRN-FM ... Humnoke, AR [*FM radio station call letters*] (BROA)
KKRO .... Anchorage, AK [*FM radio station call letters*]

KKRO........ Koo Koo Roo [*NASDAQ symbol*] (TTSB)
KKRO........ Koo Koo Roo, Inc. [*NASDAQ symbol*] (SAG)
KKRO........ Redding, CA [*FM radio station call letters*] (BROA)
KKRQ........ Iowa City, IA [*FM radio station call letters*]
KKRR........ Knox & Kane Railroad [*Federal Railroad Administration identification code*]
KKRR-FM... Casper, WY [*FM radio station call letters*] (BROA)
KKRR-FM... Laramie, WY [*FM radio station call letters*] (BROA)
KKRS-FM... Davenport, WA [*FM radio station call letters*] (BROA)
KKRT........ Wenatchee, WA [*AM radio station call letters*]
KKRV........ Wenatchee, WA [*AM radio station call letters*] (GDPB)
KKRV-FM... Wenatchee, WA [*FM radio station call letters*]
KKRW........ Houston, TX [*FM radio station call letters*]
KKRX........ Lawton, OK [*AM radio station call letters*]
KKRX-FM... Lawton, OK [*FM radio station call letters*]
KKRY........ Miles City, MT [*FM radio station call letters*] (GDPB)
KKRY-FM.... Miles City, MT [*FM radio station call letters*] (BROA)
KKRZ........ Portland, OR [*FM radio station call letters*]
KKS.......... Kallikrein-Kinin System [*Medicine*] (EDAA)
KKS.......... Kansas State University, Farrell Library, Manhattan, KS [*OCLC symbol*] (OCLC)
KKS.......... Konstanta Kongresa Sekretario (SAUO)
KKSA........ Keith Keating Society for the Arts [*Defunct*] (EA)
KKSA........ San Angelo, TX [*AM radio station call letters*] (RBYB)
KKSB-FM... Goleta, CA [*FM radio station call letters*] (BROA)
KKSC........ Brawley, CA [*AM radio station call letters*] (BROA)
KKSC........ Plattsmouth, NE [*AM radio station call letters*] (BROA)
KKSD-FM... Milbank, SD [*FM radio station call letters*] (BROA)
KKSF........ San Francisco, CA [*FM radio station call letters*]
KKSI........ Eddyville, IA [*FM radio station call letters*]
KKSJ........ San Jose, CA [*AM radio station call letters*]
KKSL........ Lake Oswego, OR [*AM radio station call letters*] (RBYB)
KKSM-AM... Oceanside, CA [*AM radio station call letters*] (RBYB)
KKS-MTSH... National Committee for the Liberation and Protection of Albanian Lands [*Government term*] (GA)
KKSN........ Oregon City, OR [*AM radio station call letters*] (BROA)
KKSN........ Portland, OR [*FM radio station call letters*]
KKSN........ Vancouver, WA [*AM radio station call letters*]
KKSO........ Des Moines, IA [*AM radio station call letters*]
KKSR........ Sartell, MN [*FM radio station call letters*]
KKSS........ Santa Fe, NM [*FM radio station call letters*]
KKST........ Alexandria, LA [*FM radio station call letters*] (GDPB)
KKST-FM.... Oakdale, LA [*FM radio station call letters*] (BROA)
KKSU........ Manhattan, KS [*AM radio station call letters*]
KKSY........ Bald Knob, AR [*FM radio station call letters*]
KKT.......... King's Knight [*Chess*]
KKTA........ Kent Kartage [*Common carrier symbol*]
KKTK........ Texarkana, TX [*AM radio station call letters*] (BROA)
KKTK-AM... Waco, TX [*AM radio station call letters*] (RBYB)
KKTL........ Casper, WY [*AM radio station call letters*] (BROA)
KKTL-FM.... Cleveland, TX [*FM radio station call letters*] (BROA)
KKTO-FM... Tahoe City, CA [*FM radio station call letters*] (RBYB)
KKTP........ King's Knight's Pawn [*Chess*] (IIA)
KKTR........ Fresno, CA [*AM radio station call letters*]
KKTR........ Kushalgarh-Kohat-Thal Railway [*Indian Railway*] (TIR)
KKTR-FM... Kirksville, MO [*FM radio station call letters*] (BROA)
KKTT-FM.... Eugene, OR [*FM radio station call letters*] (BROA)
KKTU........ Cheyenne, WY [*Television station call letters*]
KKTU........ Kerr Steamship [*Intermodal shipping container symbol*] (TVRC)
KKTV........ Colorado Springs, CO [*Television station call letters*]
KKTX........ Corpus Christi, TX [*AM radio station call letters*] (BROA)
KKTX........ Kilgore, TX [*AM radio station call letters*]
KKTX-FM.... Kilgore, TX [*FM radio station call letters*]
KKTY........ Douglas, WY [*AM radio station call letters*]
KKTY-FM.... Douglas, WY [*FM radio station call letters*]
KKTZ........ Mountain Home, AR [*FM radio station call letters*]
KKTZ-FM.... Lakeview, AR [*FM radio station call letters*] (BROA)
KKU.......... Ekuk [*Alaska*] [*Airport symbol*] (OAG)
KKU.......... Keanakolu [*Hawaii*] [*Seismograph station code, US Geological Survey*] (SEIS)
KKU.......... Khon Kaen University (SAUO)
KKU.......... University of Kansas, Lawrence, KS [*OCLC symbol*] (OCLC)
KKUA........ Wailuku, HI [*FM radio station call letters*]
KKUB........ Brownfield, TX [*AM radio station call letters*]
KKUH........ King Khalid University Hospital [*Saudi Arabia*]
KKUL........ King Kullen Grocery Co. Inc. (SAUO)
KKUL-FM... Lincoln, NE [*FM radio station call letters*] (RBYB)
KKUP........ Cupertino, CA [*FM radio station call letters*]
KKUS........ Tyler, TX [*FM radio station call letters*]
KKUU-FM... Indio, CA [*FM radio station call letters*] (BROA)
KKUZ........ Sallisaw, OK [*FM radio station call letters*]
KKUZ-AM... Sallisaw, OK [*AM radio station call letters*] (RBYB)
KKV.......... Central Kansas Library System, Book Processing Center, Great Bend, KS [*OCLC symbol*] (OCLC)
KKV.......... Kinetic-Kill Vehicle [*Military*] (SDI)
KKVI........ Twin Falls, ID [*Television station call letters*]
KKVO........ Altus, OK [*FM radio station call letters*]
KKVS........ El Paso, TX (Las Cruces, NM) [*FM radio station call letters*] (GDPB)
KKVS-FM... Truth or Consequences, NM [*FM radio station call letters*] (BROA)
KKVV........ Las Vegas, NV [*AM radio station call letters*]
KKW.......... Kainokawa [*Japan*] [*Seismograph station code, US Geological Survey*] (SEIS)
KKW.......... Kikwit [*Zaire*] [*Airport symbol*] (OAG)
KKW.......... Kinetic Kill Weapon (SAUS)
KKW.......... Washburn University of Topeka, Topeka, KS [*OCLC symbol*] (OCLC)
KKWB........ El Paso, TX [*Television station call letters*] (BROA)
KKWD-FM... Edmond, OK [*FM radio station call letters*] (BROA)
KKWK-FM... Cameron, MO [*FM radio station call letters*] (BROA)
KKWM........ Winfield, KS [*FM radio station call letters*]
KKWQ........ Warroad, MN [*FM radio station call letters*]
KKWS........ Wadena, MN [*FM radio station call letters*]
KKWV........ San Francisco, CA [*FM radio station call letters*] (BROA)
KKWY........ Fox Farm, WY [*AM radio station call letters*] (BROA)
KKWZ........ Richfield, UT [*FM radio station call letters*]
KKX.......... Kikaiga Shima [*Japan*] [*Airport symbol*] (OAG)
KKX.......... Southwestern College, Winfield, KS [*OCLC symbol*] (OCLC)
KKXI........ K and K Distribution Services [*Common carrier symbol*]
KKXK........ Montrose, CO [*FM radio station call letters*]
KKXL........ Grand Forks, ND [*AM radio station call letters*]
KKXL-FM.... Grand Forks, ND [*FM radio station call letters*]
KKXO........ Eugene, OR [*AM radio station call letters*]
KKXS........ Shingletown, CA [*FM radio station call letters*] (BROA)
KKXX........ Delano, CA [*FM radio station call letters*]
KKXX........ Paradise, CA [*AM radio station call letters*]
KKXX-FM... Bakersfield, CA [*FM radio station call letters*] (BROA)
KKYA........ Yankton, SD [*FM radio station call letters*]
KKYC........ Muleshoe, TX [*FM radio station call letters*]
KKYC-FM... Clovis, NM [*FM radio station call letters*] (BROA)
KKYD........ Denver, CO [*AM radio station call letters*]
KKYK-TV.... El Dorado, AR [*Television station call letters*] (BROA)
KKYN........ Plainview, TX [*AM radio station call letters*]
KKYN-FM... Plainview, TX [*FM radio station call letters*]
KKYR........ Texarkana, AR [*AM radio station call letters*]
KKYR-FM... Texarkana, TX [*FM radio station call letters*]
KKYS........ Bryan, TX [*FM radio station call letters*]
KKYT........ McCook, NE [*FM radio station call letters*]
KKYT-FM.... Holyoke, CO [*FM radio station call letters*] (BROA)
KKYX........ San Antonio, TX [*AM radio station call letters*]
KKYY........ Blair, NE [*FM radio station call letters*] (BROA)
KKYY........ Gunnison, CO [*FM radio station call letters*]
KKYZ........ Sierra Vista, AZ [*FM radio station call letters*]
KKZ.......... Kaska [*Language symbol*] (ETLW)
KKZIS........ Komisja Koordynacyjna Zydowskich Instytucji Spolecznych (BJA)
KKZN........ Thornton, CO [*AM radio station call letters*] (BROA)
KKZN-FM... Haltom City, TX [*FM radio station call letters*] (BROA)
KKZQ........ Lowell, AR [*FM radio station call letters*]
KKZQ-FM... Tehachapi, CA [*FM radio station call letters*] (BROA)
KKZX........ Spokane, WA [*FM radio station call letters*]
KKZY-FM.... Bemidji, MN [*FM radio station call letters*] (BROA)
KKZZ........ Santa Paula, CA [*AM radio station call letters*]
KL............ Air Atlantique [*ICAO designator*] (AD)
KL............ Collect [*Telegraphy*] (PCTE)
KL............ Confirmed Waitlist [*Travel industry*] (TVEL)
KL............ Kahunen-Loeve [*Mathematics*] (CCCA)
KL............ Kaiserslautern [*German license plate city code*]
KL............ Kaliszer Leben (BJA)
KL............ Kansalaisvallen Liitto [*League of Civil Power*] [*Finland*] [*Political party*] (PPW)
K-L.......... Kansas State Library, Law Department, Topeka, KS [*Library symbol*] [*Library of Congress*] (LCLS)
KL............ Karl Lagerfeld [*Fashion designer*]
K-L.......... Karl-Lorimar Home Video, Inc.
KL............ Keel (ROG)
KL............ Keller's Language [*1977*] [*Computer science*] (CSR)
KL............ Kelly [*Tire casing code*]
KL............ Kelvin Law [*Physics*]
KL............ Kerley Lines [*Radiology*]
KL............ Key Length [*Computer science*] (BUR)
KL............ Key Lever (IAA)
KL............ Key Locker
KL............ Kidney Lobe
kL............ Kilolambert
kl............ Kiloliter (MIST)
kL............ Kiloliter
KL............ Klaeger [*Plaintiff*] [*German*] (ILCA)
kl............ Klang [*Musical Overtone*] [*German*]
Kl............ Klarinette [*Clarinet*] [*German*] [*Music*] (WDAA)
KL............ Klebs-Loeffler [*Bacteriology*]
KL............ Kleine-Levin [*Syndrome*] [*Medicine*] (DAVI)
KL............ Kleinmann-Low [*Astronomy*]
KL............ Klemm Flugzeugbau GmbH & Apparatebau Nabern [*Germany*] [*ICAO aircraft manufacturer identifier*] (ICAO)
KL............ KLM [*Koninklijke Luchtvaart Maatschappij*] Royal Dutch Airlines [*ICAO designator*] (OAG)
KL............ Knight of Leopold [*Austria, Belgium*] (ROG)
KL............ Knight of [*the Order of*] Leopold of Austria
KL............ Knights of Lithuania
KL............ Konzentrationslager [*Concentration Camp*] [*German*] (BJA)
KL............ Kuala Lumpur [*Malaysia*]
KL............ Kullback-Leibler [*Mathematics*]
KLA.......... Air Lietuva [*Lithuania*] [*ICAO designator*] (FAAC)
KLA.......... Ka-Ahari Resources [*Vancouver Stock Exchange symbol*]
KLA.......... Kampala [*Uganda*] [*Airport symbol*] (AD)
KLA.......... Kansas Library Association
KLA.......... Karachi Library Association [*Pakistan*] (BUAC)
KLA.......... Kentucky Library Association (SAUO)
KLA.......... Kenya Library Association (BUAC)
KLA.......... Key Learning Area [*Education*]

KLA .... Kingdom of Libya Airways, Bengasi (SAUO)
KLA .... KLA Instruments Corp. [*Associated Press*] (SAG)
KLA .... KLA Tencor Corporation (EFIS)
KLA .... Klystron Amplifier
KLA .... Knight of [*the Order of*] Leopold of Austria
KLA .... Korean Library Association (BUAC)
KLA .... Kosovo Liberation Army [*Yugoslavia*]
KLAA .... Tioga, LA [*FM radio station call letters*]
KLAC .... KLA Instruments [*NASDAQ symbol*] (TTSB)
KLAC .... KLA Instruments Corp. [*NASDAQ symbol*] (NQ)
KLAC .... KLA-Tencor Corp. [*NASDAQ symbol*] (SG)
KLAC .... Los Angeles, CA [*AM radio station call letters*]
KLAD .... Klamath Falls, OR [*AM radio station call letters*]
KLAD-FM ... Klamath Falls, OR [*FM radio station call letters*]
KLAE .... Klassen Homes [*NCIC trailer make code*]
KLAFS .... Klamath Falls, OR [*American Association of Railroads railroad junction routing code*]
KLAK .... Durant, OK [*FM radio station call letters*]
KLAL-FM .... Wrightsville, AR [*FM radio station call letters*] (BROA)
KLAM .... Cordova, AK [*AM radio station call letters*]
Klamath ..... Klamath First Bancorp, Inc. [*Associated Press*] (SAG)
KLAN .... Glasgow, MT [*FM radio station call letters*]
KLAN .... Lansing/Capital Region [*Michigan*] [*ICAO location identifier*] (ICLI)
KLANSS ..... Keep That Local Area Network Simple, Stupid [*Telecommunications*]
KLAQ .... El Paso, TX [*FM radio station call letters*]
KLAR .... Laredo, TX [*AM radio station call letters*]
KLAS .... Keystone Library Automation System [*Keystone Systems*] (IID)
KLAS .... Klassic Trailer Manufacturing [*NCIC trailer make code*]
KLAS .... Las Vegas/McCarran International [*Nevada*] [*ICAO location identifier*] (ICLI)
KLAS .... Las Vegas, NV [*Television station call letters*]
KLaSH .... Larned State Hospital, Larned, KS [*Library symbol*] [*Library of Congress*] (LCLS)
Klass Phil Stud ... Klassische Philologische Studien [*A publication*] (OCD)
KLAT .... Houston, TX [*AM radio station call letters*]
KLAT .... Winnie, TX [*FM radio station call letters*] (BROA)
KLAV .... Las Vegas, NV [*AM radio station call letters*]
KLaw .... Lawrence Free Public Library, Lawrence, KS [*Library symbol*] [*Library of Congress*] (LCLS)
KLAW .... Lawton, OK [*FM radio station call letters*]
K Law Rep ... Kentucky Law Reporter [*A publication*] (DLA)
KLAX .... East Los Angeles, CA [*FM radio station call letters*] (BROA)
KLAX .... Long Beach, CA [*FM radio station call letters*]
KLAX .... Los Angeles/International [*California*] [*ICAO location identifier*] (ICLI)
KLAX-TV .... Alexandria, LA [*Television station call letters*]
KLAY .... Lakewood, WA [*AM radio station call letters*]
KLAZ .... Hot Springs, AR [*FM radio station call letters*]
KLB .... Audio Book Club (SG)
KLB .... Kalabo [*Zambia*] [*Airport symbol*] (OAG)
KLB .... Kilopound (MCD)
KLB .... Knight of [*the Order of*] Leopold [*Belgium*]
KLB .... Korea Longterm Credit Bank (BUAC)
KLBA .... Albia, IA [*AM radio station call letters*]
KL Bac ...... Klebs-Loeffler Bacillus (AAMN)
KLBA-FM .... Albia, IA [*FM radio station call letters*] (BROA)
KLBB .... Lubbock/Regional [*Texas*] [*ICAO location identifier*] (ICLI)
KLBB .... St. Paul, MN [*AM radio station call letters*]
KLBC .... Durant, OK [*FM radio station call letters*]
KL-BET ...... Kleihauer-Betke [*Medicine*] (EDAA)
KLBF .... Kilopound-Force (WDAA)
KLBG .... Alexandria, LA [*AM radio station call letters*] (RBYB)
KLBJ .... Austin, TX [*AM radio station call letters*]
KLBJ-FM .... Austin, TX [*FM radio station call letters*]
KLBK .... Lubbock, TX [*Television station call letters*]
KLBM .... La Grande, OR [*AM radio station call letters*]
KLBN .... Auberry, CA [*FM radio station call letters*] (RBYB)
KLBO .... Monahans, TX [*AM radio station call letters*]
KLBP-AM ... Brooklyn Park, MN [*AM radio station call letters*] (BROA)
KLBQ .... El Dorado, AR [*FM radio station call letters*]
KLBS .... Los Banos, CA [*AM radio station call letters*]
KLBY .... Colby, KS [*Television station call letters*]
KLC .... Kaingaroa Logging Company (SAUO)
KLC .... Kansas Library Catalog [*Database*] (GDD)
KLC .... Kaolack [*Senegal*] [*Airport symbol*] (AD)
KLC .... Kern County Library System, Bakersfield, CA [*OCLC symbol*] (OCLC)
KLC .... Kinesin Light Chain [*Cytology*]
KLC .... Kirkland Lake [*Ontario*] [*Seismograph station code, US Geological Survey*] [*Closed*] (SEIS)
KLC .... KLM Cityhopper BV [*Netherlands*] [*ICAO designator*] (FAAC)
KLC .... Kodiak Launch Complex (ISAK)
KLCA-FM .... Tahoe City, CA [*FM radio station call letters*] (BROA)
KLCB .... Libby, MT [*AM radio station call letters*]
KLCC .... Eugene, OR [*FM radio station call letters*]
KLCC .... Kuala Lumpur City Center [*Malaysia*] (ECON)
KLCCL .... Kilocycle (ABBR)
KLCD .... Decorah, IA [*FM radio station call letters*]
KLCE .... Blackfoot, ID [*FM radio station call letters*]
KLCE .... Kuala Lumpur Commodity Exchange [*Malayia*] (NUMA)
KLCH .... Lake Charles/Lake Charles [*Louisiana*] [*ICAO location identifier*] (ICLI)
KLCH .... Lake City, MN [*FM radio station call letters*] (BROA)
KLCI .... Nampa, ID [*FM radio station call letters*]
KLCI-FM .... Princeton, MN [*FM radio station call letters*] (BROA)
KLCK .... Goldendale, WA [*AM radio station call letters*]
KLCK .... Rickenbacker Air Force Base [*Ohio*] [*ICAO location identifier*] (ICLI)
KLCL .... Lake Charles, LA [*AM radio station call letters*]
KLCM .... Lewistown, MT [*FM radio station call letters*]
KLCN .... Blytheville, AR [*AM radio station call letters*]
KLCO .... Newport, OR [*FM radio station call letters*]
KLCQ .... Healdsburg, CA [*FM radio station call letters*]
KLCR .... Cedar Rapids-Waterloo-Dubuque, IA [*FM radio station call letters*] (GDPB)
KLCR-FM ... Lakeview, OR [*FM radio station call letters*] (BROA)
KLCS .... Los Angeles, CA [*Television station call letters*]
KLCU .... IBJ Leasing [*Intermodal shipping container symbol*] (TVRC)
KLCU-FM ... Ardmore, OK [*FM radio station call letters*] (BROA)
KLCV-FM .... Lincoln, NE [*FM radio station call letters*] (RBYB)
KLCX .... Indio, CA [*FM radio station call letters*] (RBYB)
KLCX-FM .... St. Charles, MN [*FM radio station call letters*] (BROA)
KLCY .... East Missoula, MT [*AM radio station call letters*]
KLCY-FM .... Vernal, UT [*FM radio station call letters*]
KLCZ .... Corcoran, CA [*FM radio station call letters*]
KLD .... Collected [*Telegraphy*] (PCTE)
KLD .... Kelly, Douglas & Co. Ltd. [*Toronto Stock Exchange symbol*]
KLD .... King's Light Dragoons [*British military*] (DMA)
KLD .... Kongres Liberalno-Demokratyczny [*Liberal Democratic Congress*] [*Poland*] [*Political party*] (EY)
KLDC .... Commerce City, CO [*AM radio station call letters*] (RBYB)
KLDC-AM ... Brighton, CO [*AM radio station call letters*] (RBYB)
KLDE .... Houston, TX [*FM radio station call letters*]
KLDE-FM .... Lake Jackson, TX [*FM radio station call letters*] (BROA)
KLDG .... Liberal, KS [*FM radio station call letters*]
KLDI .... Laramie, WY [*AM radio station call letters*]
KLDJ-FM .... Duluth, MN [*FM radio station call letters*] (RBYB)
KLDN .... Lufkin, TX [*FM radio station call letters*]
KLDO .... Laredo, TX [*Television station call letters*]
KLDR .... Harbeck-Fruitdale, OR [*FM radio station call letters*]
KLDR .... Killdeer (ABBR)
KLDS-AM ... Falfurrias, TX [*AM radio station call letters*] (BROA)
KLDSOP ..... Kaleidoscope (ABBR)
KLDSOPC .... Kaleidoscopic (ABBR)
KLDT .... Lake Dallas, TX [*Television station call letters*]
KLDU .... Koala Lines [*Intermodal shipping container symbol*] (TVRC)
KLDV-FM .... Morrison, CO [*FM radio station call letters*] (BROA)
KLDY-AM .... Lacey, WA [*AM radio station call letters*] (BROA)
KLDZ .... Lincoln, NE [*FM radio station call letters*]
KLDZ-FM .... Fremont, CA [*FM radio station call letters*] (BROA)
KLDZ-FM .... Medford, OR [*FM radio station call letters*] (BROA)
KLE .... Kaele [*Cameroon*] [*Airport symbol*] (AD)
KLE .... Kala Explorations [*Vancouver Stock Exchange symbol*]
KLE .... Kleve [*German license plate city code*]
KLe .... Leavenworth Public Library, Leavenworth, KS [*Library symbol*] [*Library of Congress*] (LCLS)
KLEA .... Lovington, NM [*AM radio station call letters*]
KLEA-FM .... Lovington, NM [*FM radio station call letters*]
KLEB .... Golden Meadow, LA [*AM radio station call letters*]
Kleb .... Klebsiella [*Genus of microorganisms*] (MAH)
KleBl .... Klerusblatt [*Munich*] [*A publication*] (BJA)
Klebs .... Klebsiella [*A genus of bacteria*]
KLEC-FM .... Lonoke, AR [*FM radio station call letters*] (BROA)
KLEE .... Ottumwa, IA [*AM radio station call letters*]
KleerVu ..... Kleer-Vu Industries, Inc. [*Associated Press*] (SAG)
KLEF .... Anchorage, AK [*FM radio station call letters*]
KLEH .... Anamosa, IA [*AM radio station call letters*]
KLEI .... Kailua-Kona, HI [*AM radio station call letters*]
Kleinrt .... Kleinert's, Inc. [*Associated Press*] (SAG)
KLEL .... San Jose, CA [*FM radio station call letters*]
KLEM .... Le Mars, IA [*AM radio station call letters*]
KLEN .... Cheyenne, WY [*FM radio station call letters*]
KLEO .... Kahaluu, HI [*FM radio station call letters*]
KLEP .... Newark, AR [*Television station call letters*]
KLEPTO ..... Kleptomania (ABBR)
KLER .... Orofino, ID [*AM radio station call letters*]
KLER-FM .... Orofino, ID [*FM radio station call letters*]
KLERW ...... Kleer-Vu Industries, Inc. (SAUO)
KLeS .... Saint Mary College, Leavenworth, KS [*Library symbol*] [*Library of Congress*] (LCLS)
KLES-FM .... Mabton, WA [*FM radio station call letters*] (BROA)
KLEU-FM .... Lewistown, MT [*FM radio station call letters*] (BROA)
KLeVA .... United States Veterans Administration Center, Leavenworth, KS [*Library symbol*] [*Library of Congress*] (LCLS)
KLEW .... Lewiston, ID [*Television station call letters*]
KLEX .... Lexington, MO [*AM radio station call letters*]
KLEY .... Wellington, KS [*AM radio station call letters*]
KLEY-FM .... Floresville, TX [*FM radio station call letters*] (BROA)
KLF .... Kips per Lineal Foot [*Construction term*] (MIST)
KLF .... Kopyright Liberation Front (SAUO)
KLFA .... King City, CA [*FM radio station call letters*]
KLFB .... Lubbock, TX [*AM radio station call letters*]
KLFC .... Branson, MO [*FM radio station call letters*]
KLFD .... Litchfield, MN [*AM radio station call letters*]
KLFE .... Seattle, WA [*AM radio station call letters*] (RBYB)
KLFF .... Arroyo Grande, CA [*AM radio station call letters*] (BROA)
KLFF .... San Luis Obispo, CA [*FM radio station call letters*] (RBYB)
KLFI .... Hampton/Langley Air Force Base [*Virginia*] [*ICAO location identifier*] (ICLI)
KLFJ .... Springfield, MO [*AM radio station call letters*]
KLFK .... Lufkin/Angelina County [*Texas*] [*ICAO location identifier*] (ICLI)

KLFM........ Great Falls, MT [*FM radio station call letters*]
KLFN-FM.... Sunburg, MN [*FM radio station call letters*] (BROA)
KLFO........ Florence, OR [*FM radio station call letters*] (BROA)
KLFR........ Reedsport, OR [*FM radio station call letters*] (BROA)
KLFS........ Kelly Freight Services [*Common carrier symbol*]
KLFS........ Van Buren, AR [*FM radio station call letters*] (BROA)
KLFT........ Lafayette/Regional [*Louisiana*] [*ICAO location identifier*] (ICLI)
KLFU........ Kawasaki Kisen Kaisha (K-Line) [*Intermodal shipping container symbol*] (TVRC)
KLFV-FM.... Grand Junction, CO [*FM radio station call letters*] (BROA)
KLFX........ Nolanville, TX [*FM radio station call letters*] (RBYB)
KLFY........ Lafayette, LA [*Television station call letters*]
KLG.......... Collecting [*Telegraphy*] (PCTE)
KLG.......... Kalgoorlie [*Australia*] [*Seismograph station code, US Geological Survey*] (SEIS)
KLG.......... Kalskag [*Alaska*] [*Airport symbol*] (OAG)
KLG.......... Kenelm Lee Guinness (SAUO)
KLG.......... Keto-Laevo-Gulonic Acid [*Organic chemistry*]
KLG.......... Keto-L-glutonic (Acid) [*Biochemistry*]
KLG.......... Killing (ABBR)
KLG.......... Knudsen Leaf Gauge [*Physics*]
KLG.......... University of Louisville, Louisville, KY [*OCLC symbol*] (OCLC)
KLGA........ Algona, IA [*AM radio station call letters*]
KLGA........ New York/La Guardia [*New York*] [*ICAO location identifier*] (ICLI)
KLGA-FM... Algona, IA [*FM radio station call letters*]
KLGB........ Long Beach [*California*] [*ICAO location identifier*] (ICLI)
KLGD-FM... Tulia, TX [*FM radio station call letters*] (BROA)
KLGH........ Kingfisher, OK [*FM radio station call letters*] (BROA)
KLGL........ Richfield, UT [*FM radio station call letters*] (BROA)
KLGM........ Kilogram (ABBR)
KLGN........ Logan, UT [*AM radio station call letters*]
KLGR........ Knight's Local Government Reports [*A publication*] (DLA)
KLGR........ Redwood Falls, MN [*AM radio station call letters*]
KLGR-FM... Redwood Falls, MN [*FM radio station call letters*]
KLGT........ Buffalo, WY [*FM radio station call letters*]
KLGT........ Kellogg Transfer [*Common carrier symbol*]
KLGT-TV.... Minneapolis, MN [*Television station call letters*]
KLH.......... Kapapala Ranch [*Hawaii*] [*Seismograph station code, US Geological Survey*] (SEIS)
KLH.......... Keyhole Limpet Hemocyanin [*Immunology*]
KLH.......... Kingdom of Lesotho Handicrafts (BUAC)
KLH.......... KLH Computers, Inc. (SAUO)
KLH.......... KLM Helicopters NV [*Netherlands*] [*ICAO designator*] (FAAC)
KLH.......... Kloss, Low, and Hofmann [*Initialism is name of electronics company and brand name of its products*]
KLH.......... Knight of the Legion of Honor [*France*]
KLH.......... Knight of the Legion of Honour (DD)
KLH.......... Long Akha [*Malaysia*] [*Airport symbol*] (AD)
KLH.......... Minister of State for Population and Research Environment, Indonesia (SAUO)
KLHB-FM... Odem, TX [*FM radio station call letters*] (RBYB)
KLHI.......... Lahaina, HI [*FM radio station call letters*]
KLHK-FM... Shelby, MT [*FM radio station call letters*] (BROA)
KLHS........ Kelly Line Haul Steer [*Tire marketing*]
KLHS........ Lewiston, ID [*FM radio station call letters*]
KLHS-FM... Lewiston, ID [*FM radio station call letters*] (BROA)
KLHT........ Honolulu, HI [*AM radio station call letters*]
KLI........... Collide [*Telegraphy*] (PCTE)
KLI........... Kaliber Resources Ltd. [*Vancouver Stock Exchange symbol*]
KLI........... King's Light Infantry [*Military unit*] [*British*]
KLI........... K Line Trailer [*NCIC trailer make code*]
KLI........... Klingon Language Institute
KLI........... Kolyma-Avia [*Former USSR*] [*FAA designator*] (FAAC)
Kliatt........ Kliatt Young Adult Paperback Book Guide [*A publication*] (BRI)
KLIAU........ Korea Land Improvement Association Union (BUAC)
KLIB.......... Roseville, CA [*AM radio station call letters*] (BROA)
KLIC.......... Keyletter-in-Context [*Computer science*]
KLIC.......... Kulicke & Soffa Ind [*NASDAQ symbol*] (TTSB)
KLIC.......... Kulicke & Soffa Industries, Inc. [*NASDAQ symbol*] (NQ)
KLIC.......... Kulicke & Soffia Industries, Inc. (SAUO)
KLIC.......... Monroe, LA [*AM radio station call letters*]
KLID.......... Collided [*Telegraphy*] (PCTE)
KLID.......... Poplar Bluff, MO [*AM radio station call letters*]
KLIF.......... Dallas, TX [*AM radio station call letters*]
KLIG.......... Colliding [*Telegraphy*] (PCTE)
KLIH-AM.... Little Rock, AR [*AM radio station call letters*] (BROA)
KLIK.......... Jefferson City, MO [*AM radio station call letters*]
KLIL.......... Moreauville, LA [*FM radio station call letters*]
KLIM.......... Limon, CO [*AM radio station call letters*] (RBYB)
KLiMN........ Alamogordo/Holloman Air Force Base (SAUS)
KLIN.......... Klinger Products [*NCIC trailer make code*]
KLIN.......... Lincoln, NE [*AM radio station call letters*]
KLINA........ K, Li, and Na [*For the chemical elements potassium, lithium, and sodium*] [*Beckman flame system*] [*Trademark*]
KLindB...... Bethany College, Lindsborg, KS [*Library symbol*] [*Library of Congress*] (LCLS)
K Line....... Kawasaki Kisen Kaisha Ltd (EFIS)
KLIP.......... Monroe, LA [*FM radio station call letters*]
KLIPS........ Kilo Logical Inferences Per Second (SAUS)
KLIPS........ Thousands of Logical Inferences Per Second (SAUS)
KLIQ-FM.... Hastings, NE [*FM radio station call letters*] (BROA)
KLIR.......... Columbus, NE [*FM radio station call letters*]
KLIS.......... Palestine, TX [*FM radio station call letters*]
KLIS-FM.... Frankston, TX [*FM radio station call letters*] (BROA)
KLIT.......... Little Rock/Adams Field [*Arkansas*] [*ICAO location identifier*] (ICLI)
KLIT-FM.... Avalon, CA [*FM radio station call letters*] (BROA)
KLIV.......... San Jose, CA [*AM radio station call letters*]
KLIX.......... Twin Falls, ID [*AM radio station call letters*]
KLIX-FM.... Twin Falls, ID [*FM radio station call letters*]
KLIZ.......... Brainerd, MN [*AM radio station call letters*]
KLIZ.......... Korea Limited Identification Zone
KLIZ.......... Limestone/Loring Air Force Base [*Maine*] [*ICAO location identifier*] (ICLI)
KLIZ-FM.... Brainerd, MN [*FM radio station call letters*]
KLJ........... Jewish Hospital, Louisville, KY [*OCLC symbol*] (OCLC)
KLJ........... Knight of [*the Order of*] St. Lazarus of Jerusalem [*British*]
KLJ........... Knight of the Military and Hospitalier Order of St. Lazarus (DD)
KLJB.......... Davenport, IA [*Television station call letters*]
KLJC.......... Kansas City, MO [*FM radio station call letters*]
KLJH-FM.... Silverton, CO [*FM radio station call letters*] (BROA)
KLJT-FM.... Jacksonville, TX [*FM radio station call letters*] (BROA)
KLJY.......... Killjoy (ABBR)
KLJZ.......... Port Sulphur, LA [*FM radio station call letters*] (RBYB)
KLJZ.......... Yuma, AZ [*FM radio station call letters*] (BROA)
KLJZ-FM.... Yuma, AZ [*FM radio station call letters*] (BROA)
KLK........... Kalkaska, MI [*Amtrak Busline code*]
KLK........... Kealakekua [*Hawaii*] [*Seismograph station code, US Geological Survey*] [*Closed*] (SEIS)
KLK........... Killick Gold Co. [*Vancouver Stock Exchange symbol*]
KLK........... Kono [*Language symbol*] (ETLW)
KLKC.......... Parsons, KS [*AM radio station call letters*]
KLKC-FM.... Parsons, KS [*FM radio station call letters*]
KLKE.......... Albion, NE [*Television station call letters*] (RBYB)
KLKI........... Anacortes, WA [*AM radio station call letters*]
KLKK.......... Clear Lake, IA [*FM radio station call letters*]
KLKL.......... Benton, LA [*FM radio station call letters*]
KLKL.......... Minden, LA [*FM radio station call letters*] (BROA)
KLKN-TV.... Lincoln, NE [*TV station call letters*] (RBYB)
KLKO.......... Elko, NV [*FM radio station call letters*]
KLKS.......... Breezy Point, MN [*FM radio station call letters*]
KLKX.......... Rosamond, CA [*FM radio station call letters*]
KLKY.......... Milton-Freewater, OR [*AM radio station call letters*]
KLKY-FM.... Milton-Freewater, OR [*FM radio station call letters*] (RBYB)
KLL........... Kalltalsperre [*Federal Republic of Germany*] [*Seismograph station code, US Geological Survey*] (SEIS)
KLL........... Levelock [*Alaska*] [*Airport symbol*] (OAG)
KLLA.......... Leesville, LA [*AM radio station call letters*]
KLLB.......... West Jordan, UT [*AM radio station call letters*]
KLLC.......... San Francisco-Oakland-San Jose [*FM radio station call letters*] (GDPB)
KLLC-FM.... San Francisco, CA [*FM radio station call letters*] (RBYB)
KLLF.......... Wichita Falls, TX [*AM radio station call letters*]
KLLI........... Hooks, TX [*FM radio station call letters*]
KLLK.......... Fort Bragg, CA [*FM radio station call letters*]
KLLK.......... Willits, CA [*AM radio station call letters*]
KLLL.......... Lubbock, TX [*AM radio station call letters*]
KLLL-FM.... Lubbock, TX [*FM radio station call letters*]
KLLM.......... Forks, WA [*FM radio station call letters*]
KLLM.......... Kent Line [*Common carrier symbol*]
KLLM.......... KLLM Transport Services, Inc. [*NASDAQ symbol*] (NQ)
KLLM.......... KLLM Transport Sv [*NASDAQ symbol*] (TTSB)
KLLN.......... Newark, AR [*FM radio station call letters*]
KLLP-FM.... Chubbuck, ID [*FM radio station call letters*] (BROA)
KLLR.......... Amarillo, TX [*FM radio station call letters*] (RBYB)
KLLR.......... Keller Transport [*Common carrier symbol*]
KLLS.......... Augusta, KS [*FM radio station call letters*]
KLLT.......... Vinton, IA [*FM radio station call letters*]
KLLT-FM.... Spencer, IA [*FM radio station call letters*] (BROA)
KLLU-AM... Reedsport, OR [*AM radio station call letters*] (BROA)
KLLV.......... Breen, CO [*AM radio station call letters*]
KLLY.......... Oildale, CA [*FM radio station call letters*]
KLLZ.......... Kone-Landell Lead [*Federal Railroad Administration identification code*]
KLLZ.......... Walker, MN [*AM radio station call letters*]
KLLZ-FM.... Walker, MN [*FM radio station call letters*]
KL/M.......... Kiloliters per Minute
KLM........... Kilometer
KLM........... KLM Royal Dutch Air [*NYSE symbol*] (TTSB)
KLM........... KLM [*Koninklijke Luchtvaart Maatschappij*] Royal Dutch Airlines [*NYSE symbol*] (SPSG)
KLM........... KLM Royal Dutch Airlines [*Netherlands*] [*ICAO designator*] (FAAC)
KLM........... Koninklijke Luchtvaart Maatschappij [*Royal Dutch Airlines*]
KLM........... Kuala Lumpur [*Malaysia*] [*Seismograph station code, US Geological Survey*] (SEIS)
KLM........... University of Louisville, School of Music Library, Louisville, KY [*OCLC symbol*] (OCLC)
KLMA.......... Hobbs, NM [*FM radio station call letters*]
KLMB-FM.... Bastrop, LA [*FM radio station call letters*] (RBYB)
KLMC.......... Knights of Life Motorcycle Club (EA)
KLME.......... Kuala Lumpur Metal Exchange (BUAC)
KLMJ.......... Hampton, IA [*FM radio station call letters*]
KLMK.......... Klimek Welding & Manufacturing [*NCIC trailer make code*]
KLMM-FM.... Morro Bay, CA [*FM radio station call letters*] (BROA)
KLMN.......... Amarillo, TX [*FM radio station call letters*]
KLMN.......... Great Falls, MT [*Television station call letters*] (BROA)
KLMO.......... Longmont, CO [*AM radio station call letters*]
KLMO-FM.... Dilley, TX [*FM radio station call letters*] (BROA)
KLMP.......... Rapid City, SD [*FM radio station call letters*]
KLMR.......... Lamar, CO [*AM radio station call letters*]

KLMS-AM... Lincoln, NE [*AM radio station call letters*] (BROA)
KLMT........ Billings, MT [*FM radio station call letters*] (BROA)
KLMTR...... Kilometer (ABBR)
KLMX........ Clayton, NM [*AM radio station call letters*] (GDPB)
KLMX-AM... Clayton, NM [*AM radio station call letters*] (RBYB)
KLMY........ Seaside, CA [*FM radio station call letters*]
KLMZ-FM... Stamps, AR [*FM radio station call letters*] (BROA)
KLN.......... Collection [*Telegraphy*] (PCTE)
KLN.......... Kelan Resources [*Vancouver Stock Exchange symbol*]
KLN.......... Larsen Bay [*Alaska*] [*Airport symbol*] (OAG)
KLN.......... Norton-Children's Hospital Medical Library, Louisville, KY [*OCLC symbol*] (OCLC)
KLNA........ West Palm Beach/Palm Beach County Park [*Florida*] [*ICAO location identifier*] (ICLI)
KLNA-FM... Dunnigan, CA [*FM radio station call letters*] (RBYB)
KLNC-FM... Killeen, TX [*FM radio station call letters*] (BROA)
KLND........ Little Eagle, SD [*FM radio station call letters*] (RBYB)
KLNE........ HO Kline [*Common carrier symbol*]
KLNE........ Lexington, NE [*FM radio station call letters*]
KLNE-TV.... Lexington, NE [*Television station call letters*]
KLNG........ Council Bluffs, IA [*AM radio station call letters*]
KLNI........ Decorah, IA [*FM radio station call letters*]
KLNITE...... Knitting, Lace, and Net Industry Training Board (BUAC)
KLNK........ Lincoln/Municipal [*Nebraska*] [*ICAO location identifier*] (ICLI)
KLNO-FM... Fort Worth, TX [*FM radio station call letters*] (BROA)
KLNQ-FM... Des Moines, IA [*FM radio station call letters*] (BROA)
KLNR........ Panaca, NV [*FM radio station call letters*]
KLNT........ Clinton, IA [*AM radio station call letters*]
KLNT........ Laredo, TX [*AM radio station call letters*] (BROA)
KLNV-FM.... San Diego, CA [*FM radio station call letters*] (BROA)
KLNZ-FM.... Glendale, AZ [*FM radio station call letters*] (BROA)
KLO.......... Kalibo [*Philippines*] [*Airport symbol*] (OAG)
KLO.......... Klystron Oscillator
KLO.......... Ogden, UT [*AM radio station call letters*]
KLOA........ Ridgecrest, CA [*AM radio station call letters*]
KLOA-FM... Ridgecrest, CA [*FM radio station call letters*]
KLOB........ Thousand Palms, CA [*FM radio station call letters*]
KLOC........ Ceres, CA [*AM radio station call letters*]
KLOC........ Kilo Lines of Code [*Computer science*] (IGQR)
KLOC........ Kush Locke [*NASDAQ symbol*] (SAG)
KLOC........ Kushner-Locke [*NASDAQ symbol*] (TTSB)
KLOC........ [*The*] Kushner-Locke Co. [*NASDAQ symbol*] (NQ)
KLOC........ Kushner-Locke Company (SAUO)
KLOC........ Thousand Lines of Code (SAUS)
KLOC........ Thousands of Lines of Code (SAUS)
KLOCW...... Kushner-Locke Wrrt [*NASDAQ symbol*] (TTSB)
KLOD........ Shafter, CA [*FM radio station call letters*]
KLOD-FM... Flagstaff, AZ [*FM radio station call letters*] (BROA)
KLOE........ Goodland, KS [*AM radio station call letters*]
KLOF........ Kloof Gold Mining Co. Ltd. [*NASDAQ symbol*] (NQ)
KLOFFE..... Kuala Lumpur Options and Financial Futures Exchange [*Maylaysia*] (NUMA)
KLOFY....... Kloof Gold Mining ADR [*NASDAQ symbol*] (TTSB)
KLOG........ Kelso, WA [*AM radio station call letters*]
KLOH........ Pipestone, MN [*AM radio station call letters*]
KLOI-FM.... Silsbee, TX [*FM radio station call letters*] (BROA)
KLOK........ San Jose, CA [*AM radio station call letters*]
KLOK-FM... Greenfield, CA [*FM radio station call letters*] (RBYB)
KLOL........ Houston, TX [*FM radio station call letters*]
KLOM........ Lompoc, CA [*AM radio station call letters*]
KLON........ Long Beach, CA [*FM radio station call letters*]
KLOO........ Corvallis, OR [*AM radio station call letters*]
KloofG....... Kloof Gold Mining Co. Ltd. [*Associated Press*] (SAG)
KLOO-FM... Corvallis, OR [*FM radio station call letters*] (BROA)
KLOQ........ Merced, CA [*AM radio station call letters*]
KLOQ-FM... Winton, CA [*FM radio station call letters*] (RBYB)
KLOR........ Ponca City, OK [*FM radio station call letters*]
KLOS........ Kloss Video Corp. (SAUO)
KLOS........ Los Angeles, CA [*FM radio station call letters*]
KloS......... Southeast Kansas Library System, Iola (SAUS)
KLOU........ Louisville/Bowman [*Kentucky*] [*ICAO location identifier*] (ICLI)
KLOU........ St. Louis, MO [*FM radio station call letters*]
KLOV........ Loveland, CO [*AM radio station call letters*]
KLOV-FM.... Winchester, OR [*FM radio station call letters*] (BROA)
KLOW........ Caruthersville, MO [*FM radio station call letters*]
KLOZ........ Eldon, MO [*FM radio station call letters*]
KLP.......... Korean Labor Party [*Political party*]
KLP.......... Louisville Free Public Library, Louisville, KY [*OCLC symbol*] (OCLC)
KLP.......... Redding Aero Enterprises, Inc. [*FAA designator*] (FAAC)
KLPA........ Alexandria, LA [*Television station call letters*]
KLPA........ Khan-Lewis Phonological Analysis [*Speech evaluation test*]
KLPA........ Knuckeys Lagoon Protected Area (SAUO)
Kl Pauly..... Der Kleine Pauly [*A publication*] (OCD)
KLPB........ Lafayette, LA [*Television station call letters*]
KLPC........ Krypton Laser Photocoagulation [*Medicine*] (MELL)
KLPI........ Ruston, LA [*FM radio station call letters*]
KLPL........ Lake Providence, LA [*AM radio station call letters*]
KLPL-FM.... Lake Providence, LA [*FM radio station call letters*]
KLPQ........ Sherweeod, AR [*FM radio station call letters*]
KLPQ-FM... Arkansas City, KS [*FM radio station call letters*] (BROA)
KLPR........ Lincoln-Hastings-Kearney, NE [*FM radio station call letters*] (GDPB)
KLPR-FM... Keamey, NE [*FM radio station call letters*] (RBYB)
KLPS........ Collapse [*Telegraphy*] (PCTE)
KLPSD....... Collapsed [*Telegraphy*] (PCTE)
KLPSG....... Collapsing [*Telegraphy*] (PCTE)
KLPTMN.... Kleptomania (ABBR)
KLPTMNC... Kleptomaniac (ABBR)
KLPW........ Union, MO [*AM radio station call letters*]
KLPW-FM... Union, MO [*FM radio station call letters*]
KLPX........ Tucson, AZ [*FM radio station call letters*]
KLPZ........ Parker, AZ [*AM radio station call letters*]
KLQB........ Oracle, AZ [*FM radio station call letters*]
KLQL........ Luverne, MN [*FM radio station call letters*]
KLQP........ Madison, MN [*FM radio station call letters*]
KLQV-FM.... San Diego, CA [*FM radio station call letters*] (BROA)
KLQZ........ Paragould, AR [*FM radio station call letters*]
KLR.......... Collector [*Telegraphy*] (PCTE)
KLR.......... Columbus Air Transport, Inc. [*ICAO designator*] (FAAC)
KLR.......... Kalmar [*Sweden*] [*Airport symbol*] (OAG)
KLR.......... Kathiawar Law Reports [*India*] [*A publication*] (DLA)
KLR.......... Kentucky Law Reporter [*A publication*] (DLA)
KLRA........ England, AR [*AM radio station call letters*]
KLRA-FM... England, AR [*FM radio station call letters*]
KLRA-TV.... Little Rock, AR [*Television station call letters*] (BROA)
KLRB........ Aurora, NE [*FM radio station call letters*]
KLRC........ Siloam Springs, AR [*FM radio station call letters*]
KLRD........ Laredo/International [*Texas*] [*ICAO location identifier*] (ICLI)
KLRD........ Yucaipa, CA [*FM radio station call letters*]
KLRE........ Little Rock, AR [*FM radio station call letters*]
KLRF........ Brownsville, OR [*FM radio station call letters*]
KLRF........ Jacksonville/Little Rock Air Force Base [*Arkansas*] [*ICAO location identifier*] (ICLI)
KLRF-FM.... Milton-Freewater, OR [*FM radio station call letters*] (BROA)
KLRG........ North Little Rock, AR [*AM radio station call letters*]
KLRK........ Vandalia, MO [*FM radio station call letters*]
KLRK-FM... Marlin, TX [*FM radio station call letters*] (BROA)
KLRL........ Collateral [*Telegraphy*] (PCTE)
KLRM-FM... San Luis Obispo, CA [*FM radio station call letters*] (BROA)
KLRN........ San Antonio, TX [*Television station call letters*]
KLRO-FM... Nile, WA [*FM radio station call letters*] (BROA)
KLRQ........ Clinton, MO [*FM radio station call letters*]
KLRR........ Redmond, OR [*FM radio station call letters*]
KLRS........ Chico, CA [*FM radio station call letters*]
KLRT........ Kleinert's, Inc. [*NASDAQ symbol*] (NQ)
KLRT........ Little Rock, AR [*Television station call letters*]
KLRU........ Austin, TX [*Television station call letters*]
KLRU-DT.... Austin, TX [*Television station call letters*] (BROA)
KLRV........ Park City, MT [*FM radio station call letters*] (BROA)
KLRX-FM... Madrid, IA [*FM radio station call letters*] (BROA)
KLRZ........ Larose, LA [*FM radio station call letters*]
KLS.......... Collects [*Telegraphy*] (PCTE)
KLS.......... Faculty of Library and Information Science, University of Toronto [*UTLAS symbol*]
KLS.......... Karlskrona [*Sweden*] [*Seismograph station code, US Geological Survey*] [*Closed*] (SEIS)
KLS.......... Kaskaskia Library System [*Library network*]
KLS.......... Kelso Resources [*Vancouver Stock Exchange symbol*]
KLS.......... Kelso, WA [*Location identifier*] [*FAA*] (FAAL)
KLS.......... Key Lock Switch
KLS.......... Kidney, Liver, Spleen [*Medicine*]
KLS.......... Kleine-Levin Syndrome [*Medicine*] (MELL)
Kls........... Kloster (SAUO)
KLS.......... Knight of the Lion and Sun [*Persia*] (ROG)
KLS.......... Knotted List Structure (BUR)
KLS.......... Kreuzbein Lipomatous Syndrome [*Medicine*] (DMAA)
KLS.......... Kreuzbein's Lipomatous Syndrome [*Medicine*] (DB)
KLS.......... Krypton LASER System
KLSA........ Alexandria, LA [*FM radio station call letters*]
KLSB........ Nacogdoches, TX [*Television station call letters*]
KLSC........ Kalamazoo, Lake Shore & Chicago Railway [*Federal Railroad Administration identification code*]
KLSC........ Korean Logistic Service Corps (CINC)
KLSC-FM.... Fayette, MO [*FM radio station call letters*] (RBYB)
KLSC-FM.... Malden, MO [*FM radio station call letters*] (BROA)
Kl Schr...... Kleine Schriften [*of various authors*] [*Classical studies*] (OCD)
KLSD........ Kiribati Land and Survey Division (SAUO)
KLSE........ Kuala Lumpur Stock Exchange
KLSE........ Rochester, MN [*FM radio station call letters*]
KLSIFC...... Kathy Lynn Sacra International Fan Club (EA)
KLSI-FM.... Hutchinson, KS [*FM radio station call letters*] (BROA)
KLSK........ Las Vegas, NM [*FM radio station call letters*] (BROA)
KLSK........ Santa Fe, NM [*FM radio station call letters*]
KLSN........ Collision [*Telegraphy*] (PCTE)
KLSN........ Hudson, TX [*FM radio station call letters*] (BROA)
KLSN........ New London, MO [*FM radio station call letters*] (RBYB)
KLSN-FM... Santa Cruz, CA [*FM radio station call letters*] (BROA)
KLSP........ Angola, LA [*FM radio station call letters*]
KLSQ........ Laughlin, NV [*AM radio station call letters*] (RBYB)
KLSQ-EX... East Las Vegas, NV [*AM radio station call letters*] (BROA)
KLSQ EXP STN... East Las Vegas, NV [*Radio expansion station*] (RBYB)
KLSR........ Memphis, TX [*AM radio station call letters*]
KLSR-FM... Memphis, TX [*FM radio station call letters*]
KLSR-TV.... Eugene, OR [*Television station call letters*] (BROA)
KLSS........ Korean Library Science Society (BUAC)
KLSS-FM.... Mason City, IA [*FM radio station call letters*]
KLST........ Kindergarten Language Screening Test
KLST........ San Angelo, TX [*Television station call letters*]
KLSU........ Baton Rouge, LA [*FM radio station call letters*]

KLSV........ Las Vegas/Nellis Air Force Base [*Nevada*] [*ICAO location identifier*] (ICLI)
KLSX........ Los Angeles, CA [*FM radio station call letters*]
KLSY........ Bellevue, WA [*FM radio station call letters*]
KLSZ........ Van Buren, AR [*FM radio station call letters*]
KLT........ Kansas City Power & Light Co. [*NYSE symbol*] (SPSG)
KLT........ Kansas City Pwr & Lt [*NYSE symbol*] (TTSB)
KLT........ Karhunen-Loeve Transform [*Mathematics*]
KLT........ Killington, VT [*Amtrak Busline code*]
KLT........ Kiloton [*Nuclear equivalent of 1000 tons of high explosives*] (AAG)
KIT........ Kleine Texte fuer Theologische und Philosophische Vorlesungen [*A publication*] (BJA)
KLT........ Klystron Life Test
KLTA........ Breckenridge, MN [*FM radio station call letters*]
KLTB........ Boise, ID [*FM radio station call letters*]
KLTC........ Dickinson, ND [*AM radio station call letters*]
KLTC........ Superior, MT [*FM radio station call letters*] (BROA)
KLTCB........ Korean Long Term Credit Bank
KLTD........ Temple, TX [*FM radio station call letters*]
KLTE........ Kirksville, MO [*FM radio station call letters*]
KLTF........ Little Falls, MN [*AM radio station call letters*]
KLTG........ Corpus Christi, TX [*FM radio station call letters*]
KLTH........ Kansas City, MO [*FM radio station call letters*]
KLTH........ Lake Oswego, OR [*FM radio station call letters*] (BROA)
KLTI........ Ames, IA [*FM radio station call letters*] (BROA)
KLTI........ Macon, MO [*AM radio station call letters*]
KLTI-FM........ Ames, IA [*FM radio station call letters*] (BROA)
KLTJ........ Galveston, TX [*Television station call letters*]
KLTK........ South West City, MO [*AM radio station call letters*]
KLTL........ Lake Charles, LA [*Television station call letters*]
KLTM........ Monroe, LA [*Television station call letters*]
KLTN........ Kiloton (ABBR)
KLTN........ Port Arthur, TX [*FM radio station call letters*]
KLTN-FM........ Houston, TX [*FM radio station call letters*] (BROA)
KLTO........ Crystal Beach, TX [*FM radio station call letters*] (BROA)
KLTO........ Knurling Tool
KLTO........ Rosenberg, TX [*FM radio station call letters*] (RBYB)
KLTO-FM........ Galveston, TX [*FM radio station call letters*] (BROA)
KLTP-FM........ Galveston, TX [*FM radio station call letters*] (RBYB)
KLTPrA........ Kansas City P&L 3.80% Pfd [*NYSE symbol*] (TTSB)
KLTPrD........ Kansas City P&L 4.35% Pfd [*NYSE symbol*] (TTSB)
KLTPrE........ Kansas City P&L 4.50% Pfd [*NYSE symbol*] (TTSB)
KLTQ........ Lincoln, NE [*FM radio station call letters*] (BROA)
KLTQ........ Sparta, MO [*FM radio station call letters*]
KLTR........ Franklin, TX [*FM radio station call letters*] (RBYB)
KLTR........ Kilter (ABBR)
KLTR-FM........ Caldwell, TX [*FM radio station call letters*] (BROA)
KLTS........ Altus Air Force Base [*Oklahoma*] [*ICAO location identifier*] (ICLI)
KLTS........ Shreveport, LA [*Television station call letters*]
KLTT........ Brighton, CO [*AM radio station call letters*]
KLTT........ Commerce City, CO [*AM radio station call letters*] (BROA)
KLTU........ Kawasaki Kisen Kaisha (K-Line) [*Intermodal shipping container symbol*] (TVRC)
KLTV........ Tyler, TX [*Television station call letters*]
KLTW-AM........ Sierra Vista, AZ [*AM radio station call letters*] (RBYB)
KLTW-FM........ Rayne, LA [*FM radio station call letters*] (BROA)
KLTX........ Harker Heights, TX [*FM radio station call letters*]
KLTX........ Long Beach, CA [*AM radio station call letters*] (BROA)
KLTY........ Fort Worth, TX [*FM radio station call letters*]
KLTY-FM........ Arlington, TX [*FM radio station call letters*] (BROA)
KLTZ........ Glasgow, MT [*AM radio station call letters*]
KLU........ Kaiser Aluminum [*NYSE symbol*] (TTSB)
KLU........ Kaiser Aluminum & Chemical Corp. [*NYSE symbol*] (SPSG)
KLU........ Kaisertech Ltd. [*NYSE symbol*] (COMM)
KLU........ Key and Lamp Units [*Telecommunications*]
KLU........ Klagenfurt [*Austria*] [*Airport symbol*] (OAG)
KLU........ Klutina [*Alaska*] [*Seismograph station code, US Geological Survey*] (SEIS)
KLUA........ Kailua-Kona, HI [*FM radio station call letters*]
KLUB........ Bloomington, TX [*FM radio station call letters*]
KLUC-FM........ Las Vegas, NV [*FM radio station call letters*]
KLUE........ Knowledge Legacy of the Unavailable Expert [*Computer science*] (BTTJ)
KLUE........ Soledad, CA [*FM radio station call letters*]
KLUF........ Phoenix/Luke Air Force Base [*Arizona*] [*ICAO location identifier*] (ICLI)
KLUH........ Poplar Bluff, MO [*FM radio station call letters*]
KLUJ........ Harlingen, TX [*Television station call letters*]
KLUK........ Cincinnati/Municipal-Lunken Field [*Ohio*] [*ICAO location identifier*] (ICLI)
KLUK........ Laughlin, NV [*FM radio station call letters*] (RBYB)
KLUK-FM........ Needles, CA [*FM radio station call letters*] (BROA)
KLUN-FM........ Paso Robles, CA [*FM radio station call letters*] (BROA)
KLUP........ Terrell Hills, TX [*AM radio station call letters*]
KLUPrD........ Kaiser Alum 8.255% 'PRIDES' [*NYSE symbol*] (TTSB)
KLUR........ Wichita Falls, TX [*FM radio station call letters*]
KLUV........ Dallas, TX [*FM radio station call letters*]
KLUX........ Robstown, TX [*FM radio station call letters*]
KLUZ........ Albuquerque, NM [*Television station call letters*]
KLV........ Collective [*Telegraphy*] (PCTE)
KLV........ Karlovy Vary [*Former Czechoslovakia*] [*Airport symbol*] (OAG)
KLV........ Maskelynes [*Language symbol*] (ETLW)
KLVA........ Casa Grande, AZ [*FM radio station call letters*] (RBYB)
KLVB-AM........ Medford, OR [*AM radio station call letters*] (BROA)
KLVB-FM........ Red Bluff, CA [*FM radio station call letters*] (BROA)
KLVC........ Magalia, CA [*FM radio station call letters*]
KLVE........ Los Angeles, CA [*FM radio station call letters*]
KLVF........ Las Vegas, NM [*FM radio station call letters*]
KLVG........ Garberville, CA [*FM radio station call letters*] (RBYB)
KLVH-FM........ Leavenworth, WA [*FM radio station call letters*] (BROA)
KLVH-FM........ San Luis Obispo, CA [*FM radio station call letters*] (BROA)
KLVI........ Beaumont, TX [*AM radio station call letters*]
KLVJ........ Mountain Home, ID [*AM radio station call letters*]
KLVJ-FM........ Julian, CA [*FM radio station call letters*] (BROA)
KLVJ-FM........ Mountain Home, ID [*FM radio station call letters*]
KLVK........ Dimmitt, TX [*FM radio station call letters*] (RBYB)
KLVK-FM........ Coalinga, CA [*FM radio station call letters*] (BROA)
KLVK-FM........ Kingsburg, CA [*FM radio station call letters*] (BROA)
KLVL........ Pasadena, TX [*AM radio station call letters*]
KLVM........ Prunedale, CA [*FM radio station call letters*]
KLVN........ Chowchilla, CA [*FM radio station call letters*] (RBYB)
KLVN-FM........ Livingston, CA [*FM radio station call letters*] (BROA)
KLVO........ Belen, NM [*FM radio station call letters*] (RBYB)
KLVP........ Tigard, OR [*AM radio station call letters*] (BROA)
KLVP-FM........ Cherryville, OR [*FM radio station call letters*] (BROA)
KLVQ........ Athens, TX [*AM radio station call letters*]
KLVR........ Santa Rosa, CA [*FM radio station call letters*]
KLVS........ Las Vegas [*New Mexico*] [*ICAO location identifier*] (ICLI)
KLVS-FM........ Grass Valley, CA [*FM radio station call letters*] (BROA)
KLVS-FM........ Kingsburg, CA [*FM radio station call letters*] (RBYB)
KLVT........ Levelland, TX [*AM radio station call letters*]
KLVT-FM........ Levelland, TX [*FM radio station call letters*]
KLVU........ Haynesville, LA [*AM radio station call letters*]
KLVU-FM........ Sweet Home, OR [*FM radio station call letters*] (BROA)
KLVV........ Ponca City, OK [*FM radio station call letters*]
KLVW........ Julian, CA [*FM radio station call letters*] (RBYB)
KLVW-FM........ Odessa, TX [*FM radio station call letters*] (BROA)
KLVX........ Las Vegas, NV [*Television station call letters*]
KLVY........ Powell, WY [*AM radio station call letters*] (GDPB)
KLVY-FM........ Fairmead, CA [*FM radio station call letters*] (BROA)
KLVZ-AM........ Denver, CO [*AM radio station call letters*] (BROA)
KLW........ Claw Resources Ltd. [*Vancouver Stock Exchange symbol*]
KLW........ Faculty of Law Library, University of Toronto [*UTLAS symbol*]
KLW........ Klawock [*Alaska*] [*Airport symbol*] (OAG)
KLWD-FM........ Gillette, WY [*FM radio station call letters*] (BROA)
KLWJ........ Umatilla, OR [*AM radio station call letters*]
KLWN........ Lawrence, KS [*AM radio station call letters*]
KLWS-FM........ Moses Lake, WA [*FM radio station call letters*] (BROA)
KLWT........ Kilowatt (ABBR)
KLWT........ Kirsch Laser Welding Technique [*Medicine*] (MELL)
KLWT........ Lebanon, MO [*AM radio station call letters*]
KLWU........ Kleinwachter [*Intermodal shipping container symbol*] (TVRC)
KLWV........ Chugwater, WY [*FM radio station call letters*] (BROA)
KLWY........ Cheyenne, WY [*Television station call letters*]
KLX........ Kalamata [*Greece*] [*Airport symbol*] (OAG)
KLX........ Kalix Air [*Nigeria*] [*FAA designator*] (FAAC)
KLX........ Kidney and Lung Extract
KLXK........ Duluth, MN [*FM radio station call letters*]
KLXK-FM........ Breckenridge, TX [*FM radio station call letters*] (BROA)
KLXM-FM........ Salinas, CA [*FM radio station call letters*] (BROA)
KLXO........ El Centro, CA [*Television station call letters*]
KLXQ........ Hot Springs, AR [*FM radio station call letters*]
KLXQ-FM........ Hot Springs, AR [*FM radio station call letters*] (BROA)
KLXR........ Redding, CA [*AM radio station call letters*]
KLXS........ Pierre, SD [*FM radio station call letters*]
KLXU........ Hans Klaeser Luxembourg [*Intermodal shipping container symbol*] (TVRC)
KLXV........ San Jose, CA [*Television station call letters*]
KLXV-FM........ Glenwood Springs, CO [*FM radio station call letters*] (BROA)
KLXX........ Bismarck-Mandan, ND [*AM radio station call letters*]
KLY........ Kalima [*Zaire*] [*Airport symbol*] (AD)
KLY........ Kelley Oil & Gas Partners, Ltd. [*AMEX symbol*] (NASQ)
KLY........ Klyuchi [*Former USSR*] [*Seismograph station code, US Geological Survey*] (SEIS)
KLYC........ McMinnville, OR [*AM radio station call letters*]
KLYD........ Shafter, CA [*FM radio station call letters*] (RBYB)
KLYF........ Des Moines, IA [*FM radio station call letters*]
KLYF........ Thousand Oaks, CA [*AM radio station call letters*] (BROA)
KLYF-FM........ Ankeny, IA [*FM radio station call letters*] (BROA)
KLYK........ Longview, WA [*FM radio station call letters*]
KLYN........ Lynden, WA [*FM radio station call letters*]
KLYQ........ Hamilton, MT [*AM radio station call letters*]
KLYR........ Clarksville, AR [*AM radio station call letters*]
KLYR........ Smoke Layer Aloft [*Meteorology*] (FAAC)
KLYR-FM........ Clarksville, AR [*FM radio station call letters*]
KLYT........ Albuquerque, NM [*FM radio station call letters*]
KLYV........ Dubuque, IA [*FM radio station call letters*]
KLYY-FM........ Arcadia, CA [*FM radio station call letters*] (RBYB)
KLZ........ Denver, CO [*AM radio station call letters*]
KLZ........ Kalispell Line [*Federal Railroad Administration identification code*]
KLZ........ Kleinzee [*South Africa*] [*Airport symbol*] (OAG)
KLZA-FM........ Falls City, NE [*FM radio station call letters*] (BROA)
KLZE........ Owensville, MO [*FM radio station call letters*]
KLZK........ Brownfield, TX [*FM radio station call letters*]
KLZR........ Lawrence, KS [*FM radio station call letters*]
KLZX-FM........ Brigham City, UT [*FM radio station call letters*] (RBYB)
KLZY........ Powell, WY [*FM radio station call letters*]
KLZZ........ Waite Park, MN [*FM radio station call letters*]
KM........ Air Malta [*ICAO designator*] (AD)

KM .... Communicate [*Telegraphy*] (PCTE)
KM .... Comoros [*ANSI two-letter standard code*] (CNC)
KM .... Draepelin-Morel [*Disease*] [*Psychiatry*] (DAVI)
KM .... Ha-Kibbuts ha-Me'uhad (BJA)
KM .... Kabataang Makabayan [*Nationalist Youth*] [*Philippines*]
KM .... Kabelmetal Aktiengesellschaft (EFIS)
KM .... Kaffrarian Museum (SAUO)
KM .... Kamenz [*German license plate city code*]
KM .... Kanamycin [*Antibacterial compound*]
KM .... [*The*] Kansas & Missouri Railway & Terminal Co. [*Formerly, KMRT*] [*AAR code*]
KM .... Kansas Mapper (SAUO)
KM .... Kerr-McGee Corporation (EFIS)
KM .... Kia [*Society of Automotive Engineers auto manufacturer code for service information interchange*]
kM .... Kilomega
Km .... Kilometer (TBD)
km .... Kilometer
KM .... K-Immunoglobulin Light Chains [*Immunology*] (DAVI)
KM .... Kinetic Momentum
KM .... King and Martyr [*Church calendars*]
KM .... Kingdom
KM .... King's Medal [*or Medallist*] [*British*]
KM .... King's Messenger [*British*] (ROG)
KM .... Kirchoff Method [*Telecommunications*] (OA)
KM .... Kirk-Mayer, Inc. (SAUO)
KM .... Kitchen Mechanic [*Restaurant slang*]
KM .... Klystron Mount
KM .... Kmart [*NYSE symbol*] (TTSB)
KM .... K Mart Corp. [*NYSE symbol*] (SPSG)
KM .... K mart Financing Trust I [*NYSE symbol*] (SAG)
KM .... Kneading Massage (MELL)
KM .... Knight of Malta
KM .... Knight of the Sovereign and Military Order of Malta (DD)
KM .... Knowledge Management (NETL)
KM .... Knowledge Manager
KM .... Knowledge Module (GART)
KM .... Kraepelin-Morel [*Disease*] [*Psychiatry*] (DAVI)
KM .... Kubelka-Munk [*Optics*]
KM .... Kurram Militia [*British military*] (DMA)
KM .... Manhattan Public Library, Manhattan, KS [*Library symbol*] [*Library of Congress*] (LCLS)
Km .... Michaelis Constant [*In enzyme assays*] (STED)
Km .... Michaelis-Menten Dissociation Constnat (DAVI)
KM2 .... Kermit [*Texas*] [*Seismograph station code, US Geological Survey*] (SEIS)
km2 .... Square Kilometer
K M^2/W .... Kelvin Square Meters per Watt
KM^3 .... Cubic Kilometer
KM5 .... Kermit [*Texas*] [*Seismograph station code, US Geological Survey*] (SEIS)
KM6 .... Kermit [*Texas*] [*Seismograph station code, US Geological Survey*] (SEIS)
KM9 .... Kermit [*Texas*] [*Seismograph station code, US Geological Survey*] (SEIS)
KMA .... Kansas Museums Association (EARSL)
KMA .... Kentucky Medical Association [*Medicine*] (EDAA)
KMA .... Kerema [*Papua New Guinea*] [*Airport symbol*] (OAG)
KMA .... Ketchikan Management Area [*Alaska*] [*USDA Forest Service*] (ALAC)
KMA .... Kinematograph Manufacturers Association, Inc. (SAUO)
KMA .... Korea Military Academy
KMA .... Ku-Band Multiple Access (MCD)
KMA .... Royal Military Academy for Army & Air Force (SAUO)
KMA .... Shenandoah, IA [*AM radio station call letters*]
KMAA .... Kart Marketing Association of America (EA)
KMAC .... Gainesville, MO [*FM radio station call letters*]
KMAC .... Kushi Macrobiotic Corp. [*NASDAQ symbol*] (SAG)
KMAC .... Kushi Macrobiotics [*NASDAQ symbol*] (TTSB)
KMACW .... Kushi Macrobiotics Wrrt [*NASDAQ symbol*] (TTSB)
KMAD .... Madill, OK [*AM radio station call letters*]
KMAD-FM .... Madill, OK [*FM radio station call letters*]
KMAF .... Midland/Regional Air Terminal [*Texas*] [*ICAO location identifier*] (ICLI)
KMAG .... Fort Smith, AR [*FM radio station call letters*]
KMAG .... Komag, Inc. [*NASDAQ symbol*] (NQ)
KMAG .... Korea Military Advisory Group [*United States*]
KMAGV .... Korean Military Assistance Group, Vietnam (VNW)
KMAJ .... Topeka, KS [*AM radio station call letters*]
KMAJ-FM .... Topeka, KS [*FM radio station call letters*]
KMAK .... Orange Cove, CA [*FM radio station call letters*]
KMAL .... Malden, MO [*FM radio station call letters*]
KMAM .... Butler, MO [*AM radio station call letters*]
KMAN .... Manhattan, KS [*AM radio station call letters*]
KMAN .... R Kuntzman [*Common carrier symbol*]
KMAP-AM .... Frazier Park, CA [*AM radio station call letters*] (BROA)
KMAP-FM .... Castana, IA [*FM radio station call letters*] (BROA)
KMAQ .... Marquoketa, IA [*AM radio station call letters*]
KMAQ-FM .... Maquoketa, IA [*FM radio station call letters*]
KMAR .... Kmart Camper Foldup [*NCIC trailer make code*]
KMAR .... Winnsboro, LA [*AM radio station call letters*]
KMAR-FM .... Winnsboro, LA [*FM radio station call letters*]
K mart .... K Mart Corp. [*Associated Press*] (SAG)
KmartF .... K mart Financing Trust I [*Associated Press*] (SAG)
KMAS .... Korean Medical Association of America (EA)
KMAS .... Shelton, WA [*AM radio station call letters*]
KMAS-TV .... Steamboat Springs, CO [*Television station call letters*] (BROA)
KMAT-FM .... Seadrift, TX [*FM radio station call letters*] (BROA)
KMAU .... Wailuku, HI [*Television station call letters*]
KMAU-DT .... Wailuku, HI [*Television station call letters*] (BROA)
KMAV .... Mayville, ND [*AM radio station call letters*]
KMAV-FM .... Mayville, ND [*FM radio station call letters*]
KMAX .... Arcadia, CA [*FM radio station call letters*]
KMAX .... Colfax, WA [*AM radio station call letters*] (BROA)
KMAX-AM .... Opportunity, WA [*AM radio station call letters*] (RBYB)
KMAX-TV .... Sacramento, CA [*Television station call letters*] (BROA)
KMAY .... Billings, MT [*AM radio station call letters*]
KMAZ .... Las Cruces, NM [*Television station call letters*] (BROA)
KMB .... Kimbe [*New Britain*] [*Seismograph station code, US Geological Survey*] [*Closed*] (SEIS)
KMB .... Kimberly-Clark [*NYSE symbol*] (TTSB)
KMB .... Kimberly-Clark Corp. [*NYSE symbol*] (SPSG)
KMB .... Koinambe [*Papua New Guinea*] [*Airport symbol*] (OAG)
KMBAX .... Kemper Municipal Bond Cl.A [*Mutual fund ticker symbol*] (SG)
KMBC .... Kansas City, MO [*Television station call letters*]
KMBD .... Tillamook, OR [*AM radio station call letters*]
KMBH .... Harlingen, TX [*Television station call letters*]
KMBH-FM .... Harlingen, TX [*FM radio station call letters*]
KMBI .... Spokane, WA [*AM radio station call letters*]
KMBI-FM .... Spokane, WA [*FM radio station call letters*]
KMBL .... Junction, TX [*AM radio station call letters*]
KMBN-FM .... Las Cruces, NM [*FM radio station call letters*] (BROA)
KMBO .... Keith Martin Ballet Oregon
KMBQ .... Wasilla, AK [*FM radio station call letters*]
KMBR .... Butte, MT [*FM radio station call letters*] (GDPB)
KMBR-FM .... Butte, MT [*FM radio station call letters*] (BROA)
KMBS .... West Monroe, LA [*AM radio station call letters*]
KMBV .... Navasota, TX [*FM radio station call letters*]
KMBX .... Soledad, CA [*AM radio station call letters*] (BROA)
KMBY .... Capitola, CA [*AM radio station call letters*] (RBYB)
KMBY-FM .... Gonzales, CA [*FM radio station call letters*] (RBYB)
KMBZ .... Kansas City, MO [*AM radio station call letters*]
KMC .... Kamloops CableNet [*Vancouver Stock Exchange symbol*]
KMC .... Kane-Miller Corp. (EFIS)
KMC .... Kenya Meat Commission (BUAC)
KMC .... Kernel Migration Coefficient (PDAA)
kMc .... Kilomegacycle
KMC .... Kinetic Monte Carlo [*Simulation*]
KMC .... Knowledge Management Consortium (SAUO)
KMC .... Knowledge Management Network (SAUO)
KMC .... Korean Marine Corps [*North Korea*]
KMC .... Manhattan Christian College, Manhattan, KS [*Library symbol*] [*Library of Congress*] (LCLS)
KMCA-AM .... Burney, CA [*AM radio station call letters*] (BROA)
KMCA-AM .... Shasta, CA [*AM radio station call letters*] (BROA)
KMCC .... Lake Havasu City, AZ [*Television station call letters*] (BROA)
KMCC .... Sacremento/McClellan Air Force Base [*California*] [*ICAO location identifier*] (ICLI)
KMCD .... Fairfield, IA [*AM radio station call letters*]
KMCF .... Tampa/MacDill Air Force Base [*Florida*] [*ICAO location identifier*] (ICLI)
KMCG .... Casper, WY [*AM radio station call letters*] (BROA)
KMCG-FM .... Carlsbad, CA [*FM radio station call letters*] (BROA)
KMCH .... Manchester, IA [*FM radio station call letters*]
KMCI .... Kansas City/International [*Missouri*] [*ICAO location identifier*] (ICLI)
KMCI .... Lawrence, KS [*Television station call letters*]
KMCJ .... Colstrip, MT [*FM radio station call letters*] (BROA)
KMCK .... Siloam Springs, AR [*FM radio station call letters*]
KMCL .... Donnelly, ID [*AM radio station call letters*] (BROA)
KMCL .... McCall, ID [*AM radio station call letters*]
KMCL-FM .... McCall, ID [*FM radio station call letters*]
KMCM .... Miles City, MT [*FM radio station call letters*]
K-MCM .... Potassium-Containing Minimal Capacitation Medium [*Medicine*] (BABM)
KMCM-FM .... Odessa, TX [*FM radio station call letters*] (BROA)
KMCO .... Kemco Trucking [*Common carrier symbol*]
KMCO .... McAlester, OK [*FM radio station call letters*]
KMCO .... Orlando/McCoy Air Force Base [*Florida*] [*ICAO location identifier*] (ICLI)
KMCP .... Kodak Metal Clad Plate (IAA)
KMC PAC .... KMC Telecom Holdings Inc. PAC [*Bedminster, NJ*] (PACS)
KMcpC .... McPherson College, McPherson, KS [*Library symbol*] [*Library of Congress*] (LCLS)
kMcps .... Kilomegacycle per Second (STED)
kMcps .... Kilomegacycles per Sound [*Measurement*] (DAVI)
KMCQ .... The Dalles, OR [*FM radio station call letters*]
KMCR .... Montgomery City, MO [*FM radio station call letters*]
kMcs .... Kilomegacycles per Second (AABC)
KMCT .... KMC Telecom Holdings [*NASDAQ symbol*]
KMCT .... West Monroe, LA [*Television station call letters*]
KMCU .... Mitsui Osaka Shosen Kaisha Lines [*Intermodal shipping container symbol*] (TVRC)
KMCU .... Wichita Falls, TX [*FM radio station call letters*] (BROA)
KMCV-FM .... High Point, MO [*FM radio station call letters*] (BROA)
KMCX .... Knappen Milling [*Private rail car owner code*]
KMCX .... Ogallala, NE [*FM radio station call letters*]
KMCY .... Minot, ND [*Television station call letters*]
KMCZ .... Kellermeyer [*Federal Railroad Administration identification code*]
KMD .... Communicated [*Telegraphy*] (PCTE)
KMD .... Kamlode Resources, Inc. [*Vancouver Stock Exchange symbol*]
KMD .... Kentucky Manpower Development (SAUO)
KMDAT .... KeyMath Diagnostic Arithmetic Test

KMDC .... Kirschner Medical Corporation (SAUO)
KMDG .... Nephi, UT [*FM radio station call letters*] (BROA)
KMDL .... Kaplan, LA [*FM radio station call letters*]
KMDO .... Fort Scott, KS [*AM radio station call letters*]
KMDO .... Komodo, Inc. [*NASDAQ symbol*] (QUAN)
KMDR .... Pearl City, HI [*AM radio station call letters*] (BROA)
KMDT .... Middletown/Harrisburg International-Olmsted Field [*Pennsylvania*] [*ICAO location identifier*] (ICLI)
KMDW .... Chicago/Chicago Midway [*Illinois*] [*ICAO location identifier*] (ICLI)
KMDX-FM ... San Angelo, TX [*FM radio station call letters*] (BROA)
KMDY-FM ... Keokuk, IA [*FM radio station call letters*] (BROA)
KMDZ-FM ... Las Vegas, NM [*FM radio station call letters*] (BROA)
KME .... Kansas Missouri Elevator [*Federal Railroad Administration identification code*]
KME .... Kappa Mu Epsilon [*Society*]
KME .... Kermit [*Texas*] [*Seismograph station code, US Geological Survey*] [*Closed*] (SEIS)
KME .... Kerr Magneto-Optical Effect [*Optics*]
KME .... KM-Europa Metal Aktiengelsellschaft (EFIS)
KME .... Kraft Mill Effluent [*Pulp and paper processing*]
KME .... Media Center, Audio Visual Library, University of Toronto [*UTLAS symbol*]
KMEA .... Kansas Music Educators Association (SAUO)
KMEA .... Kentucky Music Educators Association (SAUO)
KMEB .... Wailuku, HI [*Television station call letters*]
KMEC .... Keystone Medical Corporation (SAUO)
KMED .... K MED Centers, Inc. (SAUO)
KMED .... Medford, OR [*AM radio station call letters*]
KMEF .... Keratin, Myosin, Epidermin, Fibrin [*Biochemistry*]
KMEG .... Sioux City, IA [*Television station call letters*]
KMEIA .... Kodaly Music Education Institute of Australia
KMEL .... San Francisco, CA [*FM radio station call letters*]
KMEM .... Lincoln, NE [*AM radio station call letters*]
KMEM .... Memphis/International [*Tennessee*] [*ICAO location identifier*] (ICLI)
KMEM .... Memphis, MO [*FM radio station call letters*]
KMEN .... San Bernardino, CA [*AM radio station call letters*]
KMEN-FM ... Mendota, CA [*FM radio station call letters*] (BROA)
KMEO-FM ... Flower Mound, TX [*FM radio station call letters*] (BROA)
KMER .... Kemmerer, WY [*AM radio station call letters*]
KMER .... Kodak Metal Etch Resist
KMER .... Merced/Castle Air Force Base [*California*] [*ICAO location identifier*] (ICLI)
KMET .... Banning, CA [*AM radio station call letters*]
KMET .... Kemet Corp. [*NASDAQ symbol*] (SAG)
KMEU .... K Line [*Intermodal shipping container symbol*] (TVRC)
KMEX .... Los Angeles, CA [*Television station call letters*]
KMEZ .... Belle Chasse, LA [*FM radio station call letters*]
KMEZ .... Kerr-McGee Chemical [*Federal Railroad Administration identification code*]
KMF .... Kamina [*Papua New Guinea*] [*Airport symbol*] (OAG)
KMF .... Koussevitzky Music Foundation (EA)
KMFA .... Austin, TX [*FM radio station call letters*]
KMFB .... Mendocino, CA [*FM radio station call letters*]
KMFC .... Centralia, MO [*FM radio station call letters*]
KMFC .... Kimberly McCullough Fan Club (EA)
KMFE .... McAllen/Miller International [*Texas*] [*ICAO location identifier*] (ICLI)
KMFG-FM ... Nashwauk, MN [*FM radio station call letters*] (BROA)
KMFM .... Premont, TX [*FM radio station call letters*]
KMFR-FM ... Hondo, TX [*FM radio station call letters*] (BROA)
KMFX .... Lake City, MN [*FM radio station call letters*]
KMFX .... Wabasha, MN [*AM radio station call letters*]
KMFY .... Grand Rapids, MN [*FM radio station call letters*]
KMG .... Communicating [*Telegraphy*] (PCTE)
KMG .... Kate [*Language symbol*] (ETLW)
KMG .... Kerr-McGee [*NYSE symbol*] (TTSB)
KMG .... Kerr-McGee Corp. [*NYSE symbol*] [*Toronto Stock Exchange symbol*] (SPSG)
KMG .... Kumagaya [*Japan*] [*Seismograph station code, US Geological Survey*] (SEIS)
KMG .... Kunming [*China*] [*Airport symbol*] (OAG)
KMGA .... Albuquerque, NM [*FM radio station call letters*]
KMGB .... KMG Chemicals [*NASDAQ symbol*]
KMGC .... Camden, AR [*FM radio station call letters*] (RBYB)
KMGDP .... Kinam Gold [*OTCBB symbol*]
KMGE .... Eugene, OR [*FM radio station call letters*]
KMGE .... Marietta/Dobbins Air Force Base [*Georgia*] [*ICAO location identifier*] (ICLI)
KMGG .... Monte Rio, CA [*FM radio station call letters*]
KMGH .... Denver, CO [*Television station call letters*]
KMGI .... Pocatello, ID [*FM radio station call letters*]
KMGJ .... Grand Junction-Durango, CO [*FM radio station call letters*] (GDPB)
KMGJ-FM ... Grand Junction, CO [*FM radio station call letters*] (BROA)
KMGK .... Glenwood, MN [*FM radio station call letters*]
KMGL .... Oklahoma City, OK [*FM radio station call letters*]
KMGM .... Montevideo, MN [*FM radio station call letters*]
KMGN .... Flagstaff, AZ [*FM radio station call letters*]
KMGO .... Centerville, IA [*FM radio station call letters*]
KMGP .... Knowledge Mechanics Group, Inc. [*NASDAQ symbol*] (QUAN)
KMGPrD ..... Kerr Group $1.70 Cv Pfd [*NYSE symbol*] (TTSB)
KMGQ .... Goleta, CA [*FM radio station call letters*]
KMGQ-FM ... Santa Barbara, CA [*FM radio station call letters*] (BROA)
KMGR .... Delta, UT [*FM radio station call letters*] (BROA)
KMGR .... Murray, UT [*AM radio station call letters*]
KMGT .... Waimanalo, HI [*Television station call letters*] (BROA)
KMGV-FM ... Fresno, CA [*FM radio station call letters*] (BROA)
KMGW .... Casper, WY [*FM radio station call letters*]
KMGX .... Rio Dell, CA [*FM radio station call letters*] (RBYB)
KMGX-FM ... Bend, OR [*FM radio station call letters*] (BROA)
KMGZ .... Lawton, OK [*FM radio station call letters*] (RBYB)
kmh .... Kilometers per Hour
KMH .... Kleinhans Music Hall (SAUO)
KMH .... Knight of Merit of Holstein
KMHA .... Four Bears, ND [*FM radio station call letters*]
KMHCA .... Kentucky Mental Health Counselors Association (SEAT)
KMHD .... Gresham, OR [*FM radio station call letters*]
KMHF-FM ... Bastrop, TX [*FM radio station call letters*] (BROA)
KMHI .... Kentucky Manufactured Housing Institute (EARSL)
KMHI-AM ... Mountain Home, ID [*AM radio station call letters*] (BROA)
KMHK-FM ... Hardin, MT [*FM radio station call letters*] (RBYB)
KMHL .... Marshall, MN [*AM radio station call letters*]
KMHM-FM ... Lutesvile, MO [*FM radio station call letters*] (RBYB)
KM/HR ...... Kilometers per Hour
KMHR .... Sacramento/Mather Air Force Base [*California*] [*ICAO location identifier*] (ICLI)
KMHS-AM ... Coos Bay, OR [*AM radio station call letters*] (BROA)
KMHT .... Marshall, TX [*AM radio station call letters*]
KMHX-FM ... Windsor, CA [*FM radio station call letters*] (BROA)
kMHZ .... Kilomega Hertz (MCD)
KMI .... Keilschrifttexte Medizinischen Inhalts [*A publication*] (BJA)
KMI .... Kentucky Military Institute (SAUO)
KMI .... Kessler Marketing Intelligence [*Information service or system*] (IID)
KMI .... Kinder Morgan [*Company symbol*]
KMI .... Kirk-Mayer, Inc. (SAUO)
KMI .... KSC [*Kennedy Space Center*] Management Instruction [*NASA*] (KSC)
KMI .... Miyazaki [*Japan*] [*Airport symbol*] (OAG)
KMIA .... Jasper, TX [*FM radio station call letters*]
KMIA .... Miami/International [*Florida*] [*ICAO location identifier*] (ICLI)
KMIB .... Minot/Minot Air Force Base [*North Dakota*] [*ICAO location identifier*] (ICLI)
KMIC .... Kentucky Medical Insurance Company (EFIS)
KMIC-AM ... Houston, TX [*AM radio station call letters*] (BROA)
KMID .... Midland, TX [*Television station call letters*]
KMIDC .... Korean Marine Industry Development Corporation (SAUO)
KMIH .... Mercer Island, WA [*FM radio station call letters*]
KMiJ .... Johnson County Mental Health Center, Mission, KS [*Library symbol*] [*Library of Congress*] (LCLS)
KMIK .... Tempe, AZ [*AM radio station call letters*] (BROA)
KMIL .... Cameron, TX [*AM radio station call letters*]
KMIN .... Grants, NM [*AM radio station call letters*]
KMIP .... Key Management Interface Processor (ACAE)
KMIPS .... Kaist Map and Image Processing Station (SAUO)
KMIQ .... Robstown, TX [*FM radio station call letters*]
KMIR .... Palm Springs, CA [*Television station call letters*]
KMIS .... New Madrid, MO [*FM radio station call letters*]
KMIS .... Portageville, MO [*AM radio station call letters*]
KMIT .... Mitchell, SD [*FM radio station call letters*]
KMIV .... Millville/Millville [*New Jersey*] [*ICAO location identifier*] (ICLI)
KMIX .... Tracy, CA [*FM radio station call letters*] (RBYB)
KMixer ...... Kernel Mixer (MWOL)
KMIZ .... Columbia, MO [*Television station call letters*]
KMJ .... Fresno, CA [*AM radio station call letters*]
KMJ .... Knight of Maximilian Joseph [*Bavaria*]
KMJ .... Kumamoto [*Japan*] [*Airport symbol*] (OAG)
KMJ .... Kume Jima [*Ryukyu Islands*] [*Seismograph station code, US Geological Survey*] (SEIS)
KMJC .... Mount Shasta, CA [*AM radio station call letters*] (RBYB)
KMJC-FM ... Mount Shasta, CA [*FM radio station call letters*] (RBYB)
KMJE-FM ... Gridley, CA [*FM radio station call letters*] (RBYB)
KMJG-FM ... Homer, AK [*FM radio station call letters*] (BROA)
KMJI .... Sacramento, CA [*AM radio station call letters*] (RBYB)
KMJI-FM ... Ashdown, AR [*FM radio station call letters*] (BROA)
KMJJ .... Shreveport, LA [*FM radio station call letters*]
KMJK .... Buckeye, AZ [*FM radio station call letters*]
KMJK-FM ... Lexington, MO [*FM radio station call letters*] (BROA)
KMJM .... Cedar Rapids, IA [*AM radio station call letters*] (BROA)
KMJM .... St. Louis, MO [*FM radio station call letters*]
KMJM-FM ... Columbia, IL [*FM radio station call letters*] (BROA)
KMJO-FM ... Marina, CA [*FM radio station call letters*] (BROA)
KMJQ .... Houston, TX [*FM radio station call letters*]
KMJR .... Portland, TX [*FM radio station call letters*] (BROA)
KMJR-FM ... Redondo Beach, CA [*FM radio station call letters*] (BROA)
KMJV .... Soledad, CA [*FM radio station call letters*] (BROA)
KMJX .... Conway, AR [*FM radio station call letters*]
KMJY .... Newport, WA [*AM radio station call letters*]
KMJY-FM ... Newport, WA [*FM radio station call letters*]
KMJZ .... Prineville, OR [*FM radio station call letters*] (BROA)
KMJZ-FM ... St. Louis Park, MN [*FM radio station call letters*] (RBYB)
KMK .... Kamakura [*Japan*] [*Seismograph station code, US Geological Survey*] [*Closed*] (SEIS)
KMK .... Kansas State University, Manhattan, KS [*Library symbol*] [*Library of Congress*] (LCLS)
KMK .... Keren Mif'alim Konstruktiviyim [*Constructive Enterprises Fund*] (BJA)
KMK .... Konyvtartudomanyi es Modszertani Kozpont [*Center for Library Science and Methodology*] [*Hungary*] [*Information service or system*] (IID)
KMK .... Makabana [*Congo*] [*Airport symbol*] (AD)
KMK .... Perhaps...Kids Meeting Kids Can Make A Difference [*An association*] (EA)

KMKC........ Kansas City/Kansas City [*Missouri*] [*ICAO location identifier*] (ICLI)
KMKE........ Grand Junction, CO [*FM radio station call letters*]
KMKE........ Milwaukee/General Mitchell Field [*Wisconsin*] [*ICAO location identifier*] (ICLI)
KMKF........ Manhattan, KS [*FM radio station call letters*]
KMKI........ Plano, TX [*AM radio station call letters*] (BROA)
KMKL........ North Branch, MN [*FM radio station call letters*] (BROA)
KMKM........ Kansas City [*Missouri*] [*ICAO location identifier*] (ICLI)
KMKO........ Muskogee/Davis [*Oklahoma*] [*ICAO location identifier*] (ICLI)
KMKP-FM... Honolulu, HI [*FM radio station call letters*] (BROA)
KMKRY...... Kvutzat Mesahake Kadur Regel Yehudit (BJA)
KMKS........ Bay City, TX [*FM radio station call letters*]
KMKT-FM... Bells, TX [*FM radio station call letters*] (BROA)
KMK-V........ Kansas State University, Veterinary Medicine Library, Manhattan, KS [*Library symbol*] [*Library of Congress*] (LCLS)
KMKX........ San Diego, CA [*FM radio station call letters*] (RBYB)
KMKX-FM... Rock Springs, WY [*FM radio station call letters*] (BROA)
KMKX-FM... Willits, CA [*FM radio station call letters*] (BROA)
KMKY........ Oakland, CA [*AM radio station call letters*] (BROA)
KMKZ........ Lahoma, OK [*FM radio station call letters*]
KMKZ-FM... Enid, OK [*FM radio station call letters*] (BROA)
KML......... Carmel Container Sys [*AMEX symbol*] (TTSB)
KML......... Carmel Container Systems Ltd. [*AMEX symbol*] (SPSG)
KML......... Criminal [*Telegraphy*] (PCTE)
KML......... Kamileroi [*Australia*] [*Airport symbol*] [*Obsolete*] (OAG)
KML......... Kamuela [*Hawaii*] [*Seismograph station code, US Geological Survey*] [*Closed*] (SEIS)
KML......... Keys Marine Laboratory [*Florida Institute of Oceanography*] (RCD)
KMLA-FM... El Rio, CA [*FM radio station call letters*] (RBYB)
KMLB........ Melbourne/Cape Kennedy Regional [*Florida*] [*ICAO location identifier*] (ICLI)
KMLB........ Monroe, LA [*AM radio station call letters*]
KMLC........ McAlester/Municipal [*Oklahoma*] [*ICAO location identifier*] (ICLI)
KMLD-FM... Casper, WY [*FM radio station call letters*] (BROA)
KMLE........ Chandler, AZ [*FM radio station call letters*]
KMLK-FM... El Dorado, AR [*FM radio station call letters*] (BROA)
KMLM........ Odessa, TX [*Television station call letters*]
KMLO-FM... Lowry, SD [*FM radio station call letters*] (RBYB)
KMLT........ Millinocket/Millinocke [*Maine*] [*ICAO location identifier*] (ICLI)
KMLT-FM.... Thousand Oaks, CA [*FM radio station call letters*] (BROA)
KMLU........ Monroe/Monroe Municipal [*Louisiana*] [*ICAO location identifier*] (ICLI)
KMLV-FM... Ralston, NE [*FM radio station call letters*] (BROA)
KMLW........ Moses Lake, WA [*FM radio station call letters*] (RBYB)
KMLY........ Criminally [*Telegraphy*] (PCTE)
KMM......... Kamigamo [*Japan*] [*Seismograph station code, US Geological Survey*] [*Closed*] (SEIS)
KMM......... Kemper Multi-Market Income [*NYSE symbol*] (SPSG)
KMM......... Kimam [*Indonesia*] [*Airport symbol*] (OAG)
KMM......... Knight of the Order of Military Merit [*Prussia*] (ROG)
KMM......... Koffel Machine & Metal Fabricating [*NCIC trailer make code*]
KMM......... Kumpulan Mujahidin Malaysia [*Government term*] (GA)
KMM......... Morehead State University, Morehead, KY [*OCLC symbol*] (OCLC)
KMMA........ Knitting Machine Manufacturers Association [*Defunct*] (EA)
KMMA........ Korean Merchant Marine Academy (SAUO)
KMMC........ K & M Manufacturing Company [*NCIC trailer make code*]
KMMC........ Kangaroo Marketing and Management Committee [*Australia*]
KMMC........ Kerala Minerals and Metals Corp. [*India*] (BUAC)
KMMC........ Salem, MO [*FM radio station call letters*]
KMMG........ Pearsall, TX [*FM radio station call letters*] (BROA)
KMMG-FM... Santa Fe, NM [*FM radio station call letters*] (BROA)
KMMJ........ Grand Island, NE [*AM radio station call letters*]
KMML........ Amarillo, TX [*FM radio station call letters*]
KMMM........ Madera, CA [*FM radio station call letters*]
KMMO........ Marshall, MO [*AM radio station call letters*]
KMMO-FM... Marshall, MO [*FM radio station call letters*]
KMMPI....... Khatena-Morse Multitalent Perception Inventory [*Test*] (TMMY)
KMMR........ Malta, MT [*FM radio station call letters*]
KMMS........ Bozeman, MT [*AM radio station call letters*]
K-MMSEM... KSC MMSE Plan (or Requirement) (SAUS)
K-MMSEN... KSC [*Kennedy Space Center*] MMSE Notice [*Multiuse Mission Support Equipment*] [*NASA*] (NASA)
K-MMSEPS... KSC [*Kennedy Space Center*] MMSE Project Specification [*Multiuse Mission Support Equipment*] [*NASA*] (NASA)
KMMS-FM... Bozeman, MT [*FM radio station call letters*]
KMMT........ Mammoth Lakes, CA [*FM radio station call letters*]
KMMX........ Lamesa, TX [*FM radio station call letters*]
KMMX-FM... Tahoka, TX [*FM radio station call letters*] (BROA)
KMMY........ Muskogee, OK [*FM radio station call letters*]
KMMZ-AM... Enid, OK [*AM radio station call letters*] (BROA)
KMN......... Communication [*Telegraphy*] (PCTE)
KMN......... Kamina [*Zaire*] [*Airport symbol*] (OAG)
KMN......... Kumano [*Japan*] [*Seismograph station code, US Geological Survey*] (SEIS)
KMNA-FM... Prosser, WA [*FM radio station call letters*] (BROA)
KMNC........ North Central Kansas Libraries, Manhattan, KS [*Library symbol*] [*Library of Congress*] (LCLS)
KMND........ Kluckman Delivery [*Common carrier symbol*]
KMND........ Midland, TX [*AM radio station call letters*]
KMNE........ Bassett, NE [*FM radio station call letters*]
KMNE-TV... Bassett, NE [*Television station call letters*]
KMNL........ Kinetic Minerals, Inc. (SAUO)
KMNO........ Kimono (ABBR)
KMnO........ Potassium Permanganate [*Pharmacology*] (DAVI)
KMNR........ Rolla, MO [*FM radio station call letters*]
KMNS........ Sioux City, IA [*AM radio station call letters*]
KMNT........ Centralia, WA [*FM radio station call letters*]
KMNY........ Pomona, CA [*AM radio station call letters*]
KMNZ........ Oklahoma City, OK [*Television station call letters*]
KMO......... Kobe Marine Observatory (BARN)
KMO......... Manokotak [*Alaska*] [*Airport symbol*] (OAG)
KMOB........ Mobile/Bates Field [*Alabama*] [*ICAO location identifier*] (ICLI)
KMOC........ Wichita Falls, TX [*FM radio station call letters*]
KMOD........ Kuwait Ministry of Defence (SAUO)
KMOD........ Tulsa, OK [*FM radio station call letters*]
KMOE........ Butler, MO [*FM radio station call letters*]
KMOG........ Payson, AZ [*AM radio station call letters*]
KMOH........ Kingman, AZ [*Television station call letters*]
KMOJ........ Minneapolis, MN [*FM radio station call letters*]
KMOK........ Lewiston, ID [*FM radio station call letters*]
KMOL........ San Antonio, TX [*Television station call letters*]
KMOM........ Monticello, MN [*AM radio station call letters*]
KMOM-FM... Fountain, CO [*FM radio station call letters*] (BROA)
KMON........ Great Falls, MT [*AM radio station call letters*]
KMON........ Keyboard Monitor [*Digital Equipment Corp.*]
KMON-FM... Great Falls, MT [*FM radio station call letters*]
KMOO........ Tyler-Longview-Jacksonville, TX [*FM radio station call letters*] (GDPB)
KMOO-FM... Mineola, TX [*FM radio station call letters*]
KMOQ........ Baxter Springs, KS [*FM radio station call letters*]
KMOR........ Scottsbluff, NE [*FM radio station call letters*]
KMOS........ Sedalia, MO [*Television station call letters*]
KMOT........ Minot/International [*North Dakota*] [*ICAO location identifier*] (ICLI)
KMOT........ Minot, ND [*Television station call letters*]
KMOU........ Roswell, NM [*FM radio station call letters*]
KMOV........ St. Louis, MO [*Television station call letters*]
KMOV-DT... St. Louis, MO [*Television station call letters*] (BROA)
KMOX........ St. Louis, MO [*AM radio station call letters*]
KMOZ........ Rolla, MO [*AM radio station call letters*]
KMOZ-FM... Grand Junction, CO [*FM radio station call letters*] (BROA)
KMP......... Compare [*Telegraphy*] (PCTE)
KMP......... Kaiser Metal Products (SAUO)
KMP......... Kangaroo Management Program [*Australia*]
KMP......... Keetmanshoop [*South-West Africa*] [*Airport symbol*] (OAG)
KMP......... Kent Mathematics Project [*British*] (AIE)
KMP......... Key Management Protocol [*Communications term*] (DCT)
KMP......... Key Measurement Point (FOTI)
KMP......... Kilusang Mabubukid ng Pilipnas [*Philippine Peasant Federation*] [*Political party*]
KMP......... Kommunistak Magyarorszagi Partja [*Communist Party of Hungary*] [*Political party*] (PPE)
KMP......... Policy and Regulations Division, Information Resources Management Service (AAGC)
KMPA........ Korean Maritime and Port Administration (SAUO)
KMPC........ Abilene, TX [*AM radio station call letters*] (BROA)
KMPC........ Los Angeles, CA [*AM radio station call letters*]
KMPD........ Compared [*Telegraphy*] (PCTE)
KMPD........ Kingston Military Products Division (SAA)
KMPG........ Comparing [*Telegraphy*] (PCTE)
KMPG........ Hollister, CA [*AM radio station call letters*]
KMPH........ Hanford, CA [*FM radio station call letters*]
kmph........ Kilometers per Hour (AABC)
KMPH........ Visalia, CA [*Television station call letters*]
KmpHi....... Kemper High Income Trust [*Associated Press*] (SAG)
KmpIGv...... Kemper Intermediate Government Trust [*Associated Press*] (SAG)
KMPL........ Sikeston, MO [*AM radio station call letters*]
KmpMI....... Kemper Multi-Market Income Trust [*Associated Press*] (SAG)
KmpMu....... Kemper Municipal Income Fund [*Associated Press*] (SAG)
KMPO........ Modesto, CA [*FM radio station call letters*]
KMPP........ Kisan Mazdoor Praja Party [*India*] [*Political party*]
KMPQ........ Rosenberg-Richmond, TX [*AM radio station call letters*]
KMPQ-FM... Woodward, OK [*FM radio station call letters*] (BROA)
KMPR........ Minot, ND [*FM radio station call letters*]
KMPS........ Kernel Multiple Processing System [*Computer science*]
KMPS........ Kilometers per Second (GOBB)
kmps........ Kilometers per Second
KMPS........ Seattle, WA [*AM radio station call letters*]
KMPS-FM... Seattle, WA [*FM radio station call letters*]
KmpSInc.... Kemper Strategic Income Fund [*Associated Press*] (SAG)
KmpStr...... Kemper Strategic Municipal Income Trust [*Associated Press*] (SAG)
KMP-TUCP... Katipunang Manggagawang Pilipino [*Trade Union Congress of the Philippines*] (EY)
KMPV........ Comparative [*Telegraphy*] (PCTE)
KMPV........ Montpelier/Edward F. Knapp [*Vermont*] [*ICAO location identifier*] (ICLI)
KMPX........ Decatur, TX [*Television station call letters*]
KMQ......... Komatsu [*Japan*] [*Airport symbol*] (OAG)
KMQA........ West Covina, CA [*FM radio station call letters*]
KMQA-FM... East Porterville, CA [*FM radio station call letters*] (BROA)
KMQT........ Marquette/Marquette County [*Michigan*] [*ICAO location identifier*] (ICLI)
KMQUT....... Kumquat (ABBR)
KMQX........ Springtown, TX [*FM radio station call letters*] (RBYB)
KMR......... Cambria Resources Ltd. [*Vancouver Stock Exchange symbol*]
KMR......... Central Khmer [*Language symbol*] (ETLW)
KMR......... Kafrarian Mounted Rifles [*British military*] (DMA)
KMR......... Karimui [*Papua New Guinea*] [*Airport symbol*] (OAG)
KMR......... Kremsmuenster [*Austria*] [*Seismograph station code, US Geological Survey*] (SEIS)

KMR .... Kwajalein Missile Range (AABC)
KMR .... Western Pacific Airlines, Inc. [*FAA designator*] (FAAC)
KMRA .... Knitwear Mill Representatives Association [*Defunct*] (EA)
KMRB .... San Gabriel, CA [*AM radio station call letters*] (BROA)
KMRC .... Morgan City, LA [*AM radio station call letters*]
KMRE .... Dumas, TX [*FM radio station call letters*]
KMRF .... Keyswitch Magic Relay Finder (IAA)
KMRF .... Marshfield, MO [*AM radio station call letters*]
KMRI .... Salt Lake City, UT [*AM radio station call letters*] (GDPB)
KMRI-AM ... West Valley City, UT [*AM radio station call letters*] (BROA)
KMrJ .... Johnson County Library, Merriam, KS [*Library symbol*] [*Library of Congress*] (LCLS)
KMRJ-FM ... Rancho Mirage, CA [*FM radio station call letters*] (RBYB)
KMRK .... Odessa, TX [*FM radio station call letters*]
KMRL .... Buras, LA [*FM radio station call letters*] (RBYB)
KMRN .... Cameron, MO [*AM radio station call letters*]
KMRO .... Camarillo, CA [*FM radio station call letters*]
KMRQ-FM ... Manteca, CA [*FM radio station call letters*] (BROA)
KMRR .... Globe, AZ [*FM radio station call letters*] (BROA)
KMRR .... South Tucson, AZ [*AM radio station call letters*]
KMRR-FM ... Sanger, TX [*FM radio station call letters*] (BROA)
KMRS .... Morris, MN [*AM radio station call letters*]
KMrS .... Shawnee Mission Medical Center, Merriam, KS [*Library symbol*] [*Library of Congress*] (LCLS)
KMRT .... Dallas, TX [*AM radio station call letters*]
KMRT .... [*The*] Kansas & Missouri Railway & Terminal Co. [*Later, KM*] [*AAR code*]
KMRT-FM ... Granbury, TX [*FM radio station call letters*] (RBYB)
KMRU .... Administrazione della Regione de Kemerovo [*Intermodal shipping container symbol*] (TVRC)
KMRV-FM ... Blair, NE [*FM radio station call letters*] (RBYB)
KMRX-FM ... Collinsville, OK [*FM radio station call letters*] (BROA)
KMRY .... Cedar Rapids, IA [*AM radio station call letters*]
KMRY .... Kettle Moraine Railway [*Federal Railroad Administration identification code*]
KMRZ-AM ... San Bernadino, CA [*AM radio station call letters*] (BROA)
KMS .... Camas Resources Ltd. [*Vancouver Stock Exchange symbol*]
KMS .... Kabuki Make-Up Syndrome [*Medicine*] (DMAA)
KMS .... Kansas Medical Society (SAUO)
KMS .... Karitane Mothercraft Society [*Australia*]
KMS .... Key Management System [*Communications term*] (DCT)
KMS .... Keysort Multiple Selector
km/s .... Kilometers per Second
KMS .... King's Magnetic Ore Separator (ROG)
KMS .... Knowledge Management System [*Computer science*]
KMS .... Komatsu Mining Systems [*Automotive supplier*]
KMS .... Kumasi [*Ghana*] [*Airport symbol*] (OAG)
KMS .... Kwashiorkormarasmus Syndrome [*Medicine*] (DMAA)
KMS .... K-Words Times Millions of Seconds [*Unit of measure*] (GFGA)
KMS .... Murray State University, Murray, KY [*OCLC symbol*] (OCLC)
KMSA .... Grand Junction, CO [*FM radio station call letters*]
KMSB .... Committee for Public Opinion Information (SAUS)
KMSB .... Tucson, AZ [*Television station call letters*]
KMSC .... Sioux City, IA [*FM radio station call letters*]
KMSD .... Milbank, SD [*AM radio station call letters*]
KMSE-FM ... Rochester, MN [*FM radio station call letters*] (BROA)
KMSG .... Sanger, CA [*Television station call letters*]
KMSI .... Kelly Miller Smith Institute on Black Church Studies [*Vanderbilt University*] (RCD)
KMSI .... KMS Industries, Inc. (SAUO)
KMSI .... Moore, OK [*FM radio station call letters*]
KMSK .... Austin, MN [*FM radio station call letters*]
KMSL .... Great Falls, MT [*AM radio station call letters*]
KMSL .... Ontario, CA [*AM radio station call letters*] (BROA)
KMSM .... Butte, MT [*FM radio station call letters*]
KMSM .... Communism [*Telegraphy*] (PCTE)
KMSN .... Madison/Truax Field [*Wisconsin*] [*ICAO location identifier*] (ICLI)
KMSO .... Missoula, MT [*FM radio station call letters*]
KMSP .... Minneapolis/Minneapolis-St. Paul International [*Minnesota*] [*ICAO location identifier*] (ICLI)
KMSP .... Minneapolis, MN [*Television station call letters*]
KMSR .... Kamasura [*NCIC motorcycle make code*]
KMSR .... Sauk Centre, MN [*FM radio station call letters*]
KMSS .... Massena/Richards Field [*New York*] [*ICAO location identifier*] (ICLI)
KMSS .... Shreveport, LA [*Television station call letters*]
KMST .... Communist [*Telegraphy*] (PCTE)
KMSU .... Mankato, MN [*FM radio station call letters*]
KMSV .... Kirsten Murine Sarcoma Virus [*Medicine*] (DB)
KMSW-FM ... The Dalles, OR [*FM radio station call letters*] (BROA)
KMSX-FM ... Carlsbad, CA [*FM radio station call letters*] (BROA)
KMSY .... New Orleans/International [*Louisiana*] [*ICAO location identifier*] (ICLI)
KMT .... Kennametal, Inc. [*NYSE symbol*] (SPSG)
KMT .... Kinomoto [*Japan*] [*Seismograph station code, US Geological Survey*] [*Closed*] (SEIS)
KMT .... Knight of St. Maria Theresa [*Austria*] (ROG)
KMT .... Kraus Messtechnik und Telemetry [*Kraus Measurement Technology and Telemetry*]
KMT .... Kuomintang [*Nationalist Party of Taiwan*] [*Political party*] (PD)
KMT .... Nationalist Party (Taiwan) [*Political party*] (PSAP)
KMTA .... Miles City, MT [*AM radio station call letters*]
KMTB .... Kibris Milli Turk Birligi [*Cypriot National Turkish Union*] (PPE)
KMTB .... Murfreesboro, AR [*FM radio station call letters*]
KMTC .... Korea Marine Transport Company (SAUO)
KMTC .... Mount Clemens/Selfridge Air Force Base [*Michigan*] [*ICAO location identifier*] (ICLI)
KMTC .... Russellville, AR [*FM radio station call letters*]
KMTF .... Helena, MT [*Television station call letters*] (BROA)
KMTG .... San Jose, CA [*FM radio station call letters*] (BROA)
KMTH .... Maljamar, NM [*FM radio station call letters*]
KMTI .... Manti, UT [*AM radio station call letters*]
KMTK-FM ... Bend, OR [*FM radio station call letters*] (BROA)
KMTL .... Sherwood, AR [*AM radio station call letters*]
KMTN .... Jackson, WY [*FM radio station call letters*]
KMTNC ...... King Mahendra Trust for Nature Conservation [*Nepal*] (BUAC)
KMTP .... San Francisco, CA [*Television station call letters*]
KMTPS ...... Key Makers' Trade Protection Society [*A union*] [*British*]
KMTR .... Eugene, OR [*Television station call letters*]
KMTS .... Glenwood Springs, CO [*FM radio station call letters*]
KMTT .... Tacoma, WA [*AM radio station call letters*]
KMTT-FM ... Tacoma, WA [*FM radio station call letters*]
KMTU .... Korea Marine Transport [*Intermodal shipping container symbol*] (TVRC)
KMTV .... Omaha, NE [*Television station call letters*]
KMTX .... Helena, MT [*AM radio station call letters*]
KMTX-FM ... Helena, MT [*FM radio station call letters*]
KMTX-TV .... Roseburg, OR [*Television station call letters*]
KMTY .... Holdrege, NE [*FM radio station call letters*] (GDPB)
KMTY-FM ... Holdrege, NE [*FM radio station call letters*] (RBYB)
KMTZ .... Coos Bay, OR [*Television station call letters*]
KMTZ .... Hyundai Merchant Marine [*Intermodal trailer symbol*]
KMU .... Kamikineusu Station [*Japan*] [*Seismograph station code, US Geological Survey*] (SEIS)
KMU .... Kansas Municipal Utilities (EARSL)
KMU .... Karl Marx University (SAUO)
KMU .... Kilusang Mayo Uno [*May First Movement*] [*Philippines*] [*Political party*]
KMU .... Kismayu [*Somalia*] [*Airport symbol*] (OAG)
KMU .... Kit Munition Unit [*Air Force*] (MCD)
KMUD .... Garberville, CA [*FM radio station call letters*]
KMUE-FM ... Eureka, CA [*FM radio station call letters*] (RBYB)
KMUFA ...... Central Technological Development Fund (SAUS)
KMUL .... Muleshoe, TX [*FM radio station call letters*]
KMUN .... Astoria, OR [*FM radio station call letters*]
KMUO .... Mountain Home/Mountain Home Air Force Base [*Idaho*] [*ICAO location identifier*] (ICLI)
KMUR .... Pryor, OR [*AM radio station call letters*] (BROA)
KMUS .... Burns, WY [*FM radio station call letters*]
KMUS-AM ... Muskogee, OK [*AM radio station call letters*] (RBYB)
KMUT .... Salt Lake City, UT [*FM radio station call letters*] (GDPB)
KMUW .... Wichita, KS [*FM radio station call letters*]
KMUZ .... Gresham, OR [*AM radio station call letters*] (RBYB)
KMV .... Kalemyo [*Myanmar*] [*Airport symbol*] (OAG)
KMV .... Keen Mountain [*Virginia*] [*Seismograph station code, US Geological Survey*] [*Closed*] (SEIS)
KMV .... Killed Measles-Virus Vaccine
KMVC .... Marshall, MO [*FM radio station call letters*]
KMVI .... Wailuku, HI [*AM radio station call letters*]
KMVI-FM ... Pukalani, HI [*FM radio station call letters*]
KMVK .... Benton, AR [*FM radio station call letters*]
KMVL .... Madisonville, TX [*AM radio station call letters*]
KMVL-FM ... Madisonville, TX [*FM radio station call letters*] (RBYB)
KMVP-AM ... Phoenix, AZ [*AM radio station call letters*] (BROA)
KMVR .... Mesilla Park, NM [*FM radio station call letters*]
KMVT .... Twin Falls, ID [*Television station call letters*]
KMVU .... Medford, OR [*Television station call letters*]
KMVX .... Jerome, ID [*FM radio station call letters*]
KMW .... Communicate With [*Telegraphy*] (PCTE)
kmw .... Kilomegawatt (WGA)
KMW .... KMW Systems Corp. (SAUO)
KMWB .... Minneapolis, MN [*Television station call letters*] (BROA)
kmwh .... Kilomegawatt-Hour (WGA)
KMWL .... Mineral Wells [*Texas*] [*ICAO location identifier*] (ICLI)
KMWR .... Brookings, OR [*FM radio station call letters*] (BROA)
KMWX .... Yakima, WA [*AM radio station call letters*]
KMWZ .... Kenmore Warehouse [*Federal Railroad Administration identification code*]
KMX .... Carmax Group [*Company symbol*]
KMX .... Circuit City Strs-CarMx Grp [*NYSE symbol*] (SG)
KMXA .... Englewood, CO [*AM radio station call letters*] (GDPB)
KMXA-AM ... Aurora, CO [*AM radio station call letters*] (RBYB)
KMXA-FM ... Minot, ND [*FM radio station call letters*] (RBYB)
KMXB .... Orem, UT [*FM radio station call letters*]
KMXB-FM ... Henderson, NV [*FM radio station call letters*] (BROA)
KMXC .... Sioux Falls, SD [*FM radio station call letters*]
KMXD .... Ankeny, IA [*FM radio station call letters*]
KMXD-FM ... Des Moines, IA [*FM radio station call letters*] (BROA)
KMXE .... Red Lodge, MT [*FM radio station call letters*]
KMXF .... Montgomery/Maxwell Air Force Base [*Alabama*] [*ICAO location identifier*] (ICLI)
KMXF-FM ... Lowell, AR [*FM radio station call letters*] (BROA)
KMXG .... Clinton, IA [*FM radio station call letters*]
KMXI .... Chico, CA [*FM radio station call letters*] (RBYB)
KMXJ-FM ... Amarillo, TX [*FM radio station call letters*] (BROA)
KMXJ-FM ... Sallisaw, OK [*FM radio station call letters*] (RBYB)
KMXK .... Cold Spring, MN [*FM radio station call letters*]
KMXL .... Carthage, MO [*FM radio station call letters*]
KMXM-FM .. Gooding, ID [*FM radio station call letters*] (RBYB)

KMXN .... Santa Rosa, CA [*AM radio station call letters*]
KMXN-AM .. Ontario, CA [*AM radio station call letters*] (BROA)
KMXN-FM... Garden Grove, CA [*FM radio station call letters*] (BROA)
KMXO .... Merkel, TX [*AM radio station call letters*]
KMXP........ Phoenix (Kingman, Prescott), AZ [*FM radio station call letters*] (GDPB)
KMXP-FM... Phoenix, AZ [*FM radio station call letters*] (BROA)
KMXQ .... Socorro, NM [*FM radio station call letters*]
KMXR .... Corpus Christi, TX [*FM radio station call letters*]
KMXS........ Anchorage, AK [*FM radio station call letters*] (RBYB)
KMXT........ Kodiak, AK [*FM radio station call letters*]
KMXU .... Manti, UT [*FM radio station call letters*]
KMXV .... Kansas City, MO [*FM radio station call letters*]
KMXW-FM... Newton, KS [*FM radio station call letters*] (BROA)
KMXX........ Imperial, CA [*FM radio station call letters*]
KMXY-FM... Grand Junction, CO [*FM radio station call letters*] (RBYB)
KMXZ........ Tucson, AZ [*FM radio station call letters*] (GDPB)
KMXZ-FM... Tucson, AZ [*FM radio station call letters*] (RBYB)
KMY .... Community [*Telegraphy*] (PCTE)
KMY .... Moser Bay [*Alaska*] [*Airport symbol*] (OAG)
kmy........... square kilometer (or kilometre) (SAUS)
KMYC........ Marysville, CA [*AM radio station call letters*]
KMYF........ Kiss Me You Fool (SAUS)
KMYI .... Kirtland, NM [*FM radio station call letters*]
KMYI .... San Diego, CA [*FM radio station call letters*] (BROA)
KMYL........ Phoenix, AZ [*AM radio station call letters*] (GDPB)
KMYL-AM... Tolleson, AZ [*AM radio station call letters*] (BROA)
KMYL-FM... Wickenburg, AZ [*FM radio station call letters*] (BROA)
KMYR .... Myrtle Beach/Myrtle Beach Air Force Base [*South Carolina*] [*ICAO location identifier*] (ICLI)
KMYR .... Wichita, KS [*AM radio station call letters*] (BROA)
KMYX........ Taft, CA [*AM radio station call letters*]
KMYX-FM... Arvin, CA [*FM radio station call letters*] (BROA)
KMYX-FM... Taft, CA [*FM radio station call letters*]
KMYY........ Monroe, LA [*FM radio station call letters*]
KMYZ........ Pryor, OK [*AM radio station call letters*]
KMYZ-FM... Pryor, OK [*FM radio station call letters*]
KMZ .... Kangaroo Management Zone
KMZ .... Kerr-McGee [*Federal Railroad Administration identification code*]
KMZA........ Seneca, KS [*FM radio station call letters*]
KMZE........ Woodward, OK [*FM radio station call letters*]
KMZK-AM... Billings, MT [*AM radio station call letters*] (BROA)
KMZL-FM... Missoula, MT [*FM radio station call letters*] (BROA)
KMZN........ Farwell, TX [*Television station call letters*]
KMZQ........ Henderson, NV [*FM radio station call letters*]
KMZT........ Los Angeles (Corona & San Bernardino), CA [*FM radio station call letters*] (GDPB)
KMZT-FM .. Los Angeles, CA [*FM radio station call letters*] (BROA)
KMZU........ Carrollton, MO [*FM radio station call letters*]
KMZX........ Lonoke, AR [*FM radio station call letters*]
KN .... Air Kentucky [*ICAO designator*] (AD)
KN .... GKN Group Services Ltd. [*British*] [*ICAO designator*] (ICDA)
KN .... Kennecott Copper Corporation (SAUO)
KN .... Kenya Navy
KN .... Khan (ABBR)
kN............ Kilonewton
KN .... Kinetics of Neutralization [*Chemistry*]
KN .... King's Knight [*Chess*] (GOBB)
KN .... Kings Norton Mint [*British*]
KN .... Kitting Notice [*NASA*] (NASA)
KN .... Klamath Northern Railway Co. [*Later, KNOR*] [*AAR code*]
Kn............ Knapp's Privy Council Appeal Cases [*1829-36*] [*England*] [*A publication*] (DLA)
kn............ Knee
KN .... Knight (ABBR)
KN .... Knops Blood Group System [*Immunology*] (QSUL)
KN .... Knot
kn............ Knot
kn............ Known (VRA)
KN .... Known
KN .... Know-Nothing [*American political party, 1855-60*]
Kn............ Knudsen Number [*IUPAC*]
KN .... Kol Nidre (BJA)
KN .... Konstanz [*German license plate city code*]
kn .... Korea, North [*MARC country of publication code*] [*Library of Congress*] (LCCP)
KN .... Krone (ABBR)
KN .... Kronen (ABBR)
KN .... KSC [*Kennedy Space Center*] Notice [*NASA*] (NASA)
KN .... St. Christopher-Nevis [*ANSI two-letter standard code*] (CNC)
KN .... Temsco Airlines [*ICAO designator*] (AD)
KNA.......... Katholische Nachrichten-Agentur [*Catholic Press Agency*] [*Germany*]
KNA.......... Kenar Resources [*Vancouver Stock Exchange symbol*]
KNA.......... Kentucky Nurses Association (SAUO)
KNA.......... Kenya News Agency
KNA.......... Kex National Association (EA)
KNA.......... Killed; Not Enemy Action [*Military*]
KNA.......... Knight Air Ltd. [*Canada*] [*ICAO designator*] (FAAC)
KNA.......... Knogo North America [*AMEX symbol*] (TTSB)
KNA.......... Knogo North America, Inc. [*AMEX symbol*] (SAG)
KNA.......... Korean National Airlines
KNA.......... Korean National Association (EA)
KNA.......... Kuki National Assembly [*India*] [*Political party*] (PPW)
KNA.......... Kununurra [*Australia*] [*Seismograph station code, US Geological Survey*] (SEIS)
KNA.......... St. Christopher-Nevis [*ANSI three-letter standard code*] (CNC)
KNAA-FM ... Show Low, AZ [*FM radio station call letters*] (BROA)
KNAB .... Albany/Albany Naval Air Station [*Georgia*] [*ICAO location identifier*] (ICLI)
KNAB .... Burlington, CO [*AM radio station call letters*]
KNAB-FM ... Burlington, CO [*FM radio station call letters*]
KNAC .... Earlimart, CA [*FM radio station call letters*] (RBYB)
Kn AC .... Knapp's Privy Council Appeal Cases [*1829-36*] [*England*] [*A publication*] (DLA)
KNAD-FM ... Page, AZ [*FM radio station call letters*] (BROA)
KNAF .... Fredricksburg, TX [*AM radio station call letters*]
KNAG-FM ... Grand Canyon, AZ [*FM radio station call letters*] (BROA)
KNAI .... Phoenix, AZ [*FM radio station call letters*]
KNAIR .... Kuehne & Nagel Air Cargo Ltd. [*British*]
KNAK .... Delta, UT [*AM radio station call letters*]
KNAL .... Victoria, TX [*AM radio station call letters*]
Kn & O....... Knapp and Ombler's English Election Cases [*A publication*] (DLA)
Kn & Omb... Knapp and Ombler's English Election Cases [*A publication*] (DLA)
KNAP .... Knape & Vogt Manufacturing Co. [*NASDAQ symbol*] (NQ)
KNAP .... Knape & Vogt Mfg [*NASDAQ symbol*] (TTSB)
KNAP .... Knapwell [*England*]
KnapeV...... Knape & Vogt Manufacturing Co. [*Associated Press*] (SAG)
Knapp .... Knapp's Privy Council Reports [*England*] [*A publication*] (DLA)
Knapp & O... Knapp and Ombler's English Election Cases [*A publication*] (DLA)
KNAQ .... Flagstaff, AZ [*FM radio station call letters*] (RBYB)
KNAQ .... Prescott, AZ [*FM radio station call letters*] (BROA)
KNAR .... Kinard Trucking [*Common carrier symbol*]
KNAS .... Kenya National Academy of Arts and Sciences (BUAC)
KNAS .... Nashville, AR [*FM radio station call letters*]
KNASW...... National Association of Social Workers, Kansas Chapter (EARSL)
KNAT .... Albuquerque, NM [*Television station call letters*]
KNAU .... Flagstaff, AZ [*FM radio station call letters*]
KNAU .... Knauers Express and Storage [*Intermodal shipping container symbol*] (TVRC)
KNAX .... Fresno, CA [*FM radio station call letters*]
KNAX-AM ... Fort Worth, TX [*AM radio station call letters*] (BROA)
KNAY-FM.... Fredonia, AZ [*FM radio station call letters*] (BROA)
KNAZ .... Flagstaff, AZ [*Television station call letters*]
KNB.......... Kanab [*Utah*] [*Airport symbol*] (OAG)
KNB.......... Kanab [*Utah*] [*Seismograph station code, US Geological Survey*] (SEIS)
KNB.......... Kanab, UT [*Location identifier*] [*FAA*] (FAAL)
KNB.......... Kansas-Nebraska Natural Gas Company, Inc. (SAUO)
KNB.......... Kita-Nihon Broadcasting (SAUO)
KNBA-FM ... Anchorage, AK [*FM radio station call letters*] (RBYB)
KNBB-FM ... Ruston, LA [*FM radio station call letters*] (BROA)
KNBC .... Beaufort/Beaufort Marine Corps Air Station [*South Carolina*] [*ICAO location identifier*] (ICLI)
KNBC .... Los Angeles, CA [*Television station call letters*]
KNBC-DT.... Los Angeles, CA [*Television station call letters*] (BROA)
KNBE .... Dallas/Hensley Field Naval Air Station [*Texas*] [*ICAO location identifier*] (ICLI)
KNBG........ New Orleans/Alvin Callender Naval Air Station [*Louisiana*] [*ICAO location identifier*] (ICLI)
KNBJ .... Bemidji, MN [*FM radio station call letters*]
KNBL .... Knife Blade
KNBN........ Rapid City, SD [*Television station call letters*] (BROA)
KNBO........ New Boston, TX [*AM radio station call letters*]
KNBR........ Knobbier (ABBR)
KNBR........ San Francisco, CA [*AM radio station call letters*]
KNBR-FM ... Haltom City, TX [*FM radio station call letters*] (RBYB)
KNBST....... Knobbiest (ABBR)
KNBT .... New Braunfels, TX [*FM radio station call letters*]
KNBU........ Baldwin City, KS [*FM radio station call letters*]
KNBW .... Kirin Brewery Co. Ltd. [*NASDAQ symbol*] (NQ)
KNBWY...... Kirin Brewery ADS [*NASDAQ symbol*] (TTSB)
KNBY .... Knobby (ABBR)
KNBY .... Newport, AR [*AM radio station call letters*]
KNBZ-FM ... Redfield, SD [*FM radio station call letters*] (BROA)
KNC.......... Canadian Crew Energy [*Vancouver Stock Exchange symbol*]
KNC.......... Conscience [*Telegraphy*] (PCTE)
KNC.......... Kalamazoo Nature Center (SAUO)
KNC.......... Kamerun National Congress
KNC.......... Kansas Newman College [*Formerly, Sacred Heart College*] [*Wichita*]
KNC.......... Karenni National Council [*Burma*] (BUAC)
KNC.......... Ken Craft Trailer [*NCIC trailer make code*]
KNC.......... Kenuzi-Dongola [*Language symbol*] (ETLW)
KNC.......... Kingcome Navigation [*AAR code*]
KNC.......... Korea Network Corporation (EFIS)
KNCA .... Burney, CA [*FM radio station call letters*]
KNCA .... Jacksonville/New River Marine Corps Air Station [*North Carolina*] [*ICAO location identifier*] (ICLI)
KNCB .... Vivian, LA [*AM radio station call letters*]
KNCB-FM ... Vivian, LA [*FM radio station call letters*]
KNCC .... Elko, NV [*FM radio station call letters*]
KNCCI........ Kenya National Chamber of Commerce and Industry (BUAC)
KNCD........ Kincaid Furniture Co., Inc. (SAUO)
KNCG........ Kinsella Cartage [*Common carrier symbol*]
KNCI......... Kinetic Concepts [*NASDAQ symbol*] (TTSB)
KNCI......... Kinetic Concepts, Inc. [*NASDAQ symbol*] (NQ)
KNCI......... Sacramento, CA [*FM radio station call letters*]
KNCIAWPRC... Korean National Committee of the International Association on Water Pollution Research and Control (EAIO)

KNCIAWPRC... Kuwaiti National Committee of the International Association on Water Pollution Research and Control (EAIO)
Kn Civ Proc... Knox on Civil Procedure in India [*A publication*] (DLA)
KNCK........ Concordia, KS [*AM radio station call letters*]
KNCK-AM... Concordia, KS [*AM radio station call letters*] (BROA)
KNCKBT..... Knockabout (ABBR)
KNCKDN.... Knockdown (ABBR)
KNCKKN..... Knock-knee (ABBR)
KNCKOT..... Knockout (ABBR)
KNCKR...... Knocker (ABBR)
KNCM-FM... Appleton, MN [*FM radio station call letters*] (RBYB)
KNCN........ Sinton, TX [*FM radio station call letters*]
KNCO........ Grass Valley, CA [*AM radio station call letters*]
KNCO........ Quonset Point/Quonset Point Naval Air Station [*Rhode Island*] [*ICAO location identifier*] (ICLI)
KNCO-FM... Grass Valley, CA [*FM radio station call letters*]
KNCQ........ Redding, CA [*FM radio station call letters*]
KNCR........ Fortuna, CA [*AM radio station call letters*] (BROA)
KNCR........ Paso Robles, CA [*FM radio station call letters*] (RBYB)
Kn Cr Law... Knox on Bengal Criminal Law [*A publication*] (DLA)
KNCT........ Belton, TX [*Television station call letters*]
KNCT........ Killeen, TX [*FM radio station call letters*]
KnCtyL...... Kansas City Life Insurance [*Associated Press*] (SAG)
KNCU........ Kilimanjaro Native Cooperation Union (SAUO)
KNCU........ Newport, OR [*FM radio station call letters*] (BROA)
KNCW-FM... Omak, WA [*FM radio station call letters*] (BROA)
KNCY........ Nebraska City, NE [*AM radio station call letters*]
KNCY-FM.... Auburn, NE [*FM radio station call letters*] (RBYB)
KNCZ........ Knox County Co-Operative [*Federal Railroad Administration identification code*]
KND.......... Candidate [*Telegraphy*] (PCTE)
KND.......... Kindu [*Zaire*] [*Airport symbol*] (OAG)
KNDA........ Alice, TX [*FM radio station call letters*] (RBYB)
KNDC........ Hettinger, ND [*AM radio station call letters*]
KNDC........ KwaNdebele National Development Corporation (SAUO)
KNDD........ Seattle, WA [*FM radio station call letters*]
KNDE........ Knight's Delivery Service [*Common carrier symbol*]
KNDGTN.... Kindergarten (ABBR)
KNDHTD.... Kindhearted (ABBR)
KNDHTDNS... Kindheartedness (ABBR)
KNDI......... Honolulu, HI [*AM radio station call letters*]
KNDK........ Langdon, ND [*AM radio station call letters*]
KNDK-FM... Langdon, ND [*AM radio station call letters*]
KNDL........ Kendle International, Inc. [*NASDAQ symbol*] (NASQ)
KNDL........ Kindle (ABBR)
KNDLD...... Kindled (ABBR)
KNDLES..... Kindless (ABBR)
KNDL-FM... Angwin, CA [*FM radio station call letters*] (BROA)
KNDLG...... Kindling (ABBR)
KNDLIR..... Kindlier (ABBR)
KNDLNS..... Kindliness (ABBR)
KNDLST..... Kindliest (ABBR)
KNDLY...... Kindly (ABBR)
KNDN........ Farmington, NM [*AM radio station call letters*]
KNDN-FM... Sacramento, CA [*FM radio station call letters*] (BROA)
KNDNS...... Kindness (ABBR)
KNDO........ Karen National Defense Organization [*Burma*]
KNDO........ Yakima, WA [*Television station call letters*]
KNDP........ Kamerun National Democratic Party [*Later, UNC*]
KNDQ........ Nashville, AR [*FM radio station call letters*] (BROA)
KNDR........ Kinder (ABBR)
KNDR........ Kinder-Care Learning Centers, Inc. (SAUO)
KNDR........ Mandan, ND [*FM radio station call letters*]
KNDRD...... Kindred (ABBR)
KNDRG...... Kindergarten (ABBR)
KNDRGR.... Kindergartener (ABBR)
KndrL........ Kinder-Care Learning Centers, Inc. [*Associated Press*] (SAG)
KndrLr....... Kinder-Care Learning Centers, Inc. [*Associated Press*] (SAG)
KNDST...... Kindest (ABBR)
KNDU........ Kuehne and Nagel Overseas [*Intermodal shipping container symbol*] (TVRC)
KNDU........ Richland, WA [*Television station call letters*]
KNDX........ Bismarck, ND [*Television station call letters*] (BROA)
KNDY........ Candidacy [*Telegraphy*] (PCTE)
KNDY........ Kindly (ABBR)
KNDY........ Marysville, KS [*AM radio station call letters*]
KNDY-FM... Marysville, KS [*FM radio station call letters*]
KNE.......... KN Energy [*NYSE symbol*] (TTSB)
KNE.......... KN Energy, Inc. [*NYSE symbol*] (SPSG)
KNE.......... Knie Resources, Inc. [*Vancouver Stock Exchange symbol*]
KNEA........ Brunswick/Glynco Naval Air Station [*Georgia*] [*ICAO location identifier*] (ICLI)
KNEA........ Jonesboro, AR [*AM radio station call letters*]
K-NEA....... Kansas-National Education Association (SAUO)
KNEA........ Kentucky Negro Education Association (SAUO)
KNEB........ Scottsbluff, NE [*AM radio station call letters*]
KNEB-FM... Scottsbluff, NE [*FM radio station call letters*]
KNEB-TV.... Ketchikan, AK [*Television station call letters*] (RBYB)
KNEC-FM... Yuma, CO [*FM radio station call letters*] (BROA)
KNECP....... Kneecap (ABBR)
KNED........ Knife Edge
KNED........ McAlester, OK [*AM radio station call letters*]
KNEDP...... Kneedeep (ABBR)
KNEEH....... Kneehill, AB [*American Association of Railroads railroad junction routing code*]
KNEI......... Waukon, IA [*AM radio station call letters*]
KNEI-FM.... Waukon, IA [*FM radio station call letters*]
KNEK........ Washington, LA [*AM radio station call letters*]
KNEK-FM... Washington, LA [*FM radio station call letters*]
KNEL........ Brady, TX [*AM radio station call letters*]
KNEL........ Lakehurst/Lakehurst Naval Air Station [*New Jersey*] [*ICAO location identifier*] (ICLI)
KNEL-FM.... Brady, TX [*FM radio station call letters*] (RBYB)
KNELG....... Kneeling (ABBR)
KNELR....... Kneller (ABBR)
KNEM........ Nevada, MO [*AM radio station call letters*]
KNEN........ Norfolk, NE [*FM radio station call letters*]
KN Engy..... KN Energy, Inc. [*Associated Press*] (SAG)
KNEO........ Neosho, MO [*FM radio station call letters*]
KNeo......... W. A. Rankin Memorial Library, Neodesha, KS [*Library symbol*] [*Library of Congress*] (LCLS)
KNES........ Fairfield, TX [*FM radio station call letters*]
Knet......... Knowledge Management on Networks [*Computer science*] (HODG)
KNET........ Palestine, TX [*AM radio station call letters*]
KNET-FM.... Lincoln, NE [*FM radio station call letters*] (RBYB)
KNEU........ Roosevelt, UT [*AM radio station call letters*]
KNEV........ Reno, NV [*FM radio station call letters*]
KNEW........ New Orleans [*Louisiana*] [*ICAO location identifier*] (ICLI)
KNEW........ Oakland, CA [*AM radio station call letters*]
KNEX-FM... Laredo, TX [*FM radio station call letters*] (BROA)
KNEZ-AM... Creedmoor, TX [*AM radio station call letters*] (BROA)
KNF.......... Klein-Nishina Formula [*Physics*]
KNF.......... Knife (ABBR)
KNF.......... Konjunktive Normalform (SAUO)
KNFC........ Kenya National Federation of Cooperatives (BUAC)
KNFD........ Knifed (ABBR)
KNFG........ Knifing (ABBR)
KNFL........ Fillmore, UT [*AM radio station call letters*] (BROA)
KNFL........ Tremonton, UT [*AM radio station call letters*]
KNFL-FM.... Tremonton, UT [*FM radio station call letters*]
KNFLK....... Kinfolk (ABBR)
KNFLK....... Knifelike (ABBR)
KNFM........ Midland, TX [*FM radio station call letters*]
KNFO........ Basalt, CO [*FM radio station call letters*] (RBYB)
KNFP........ Kellogg National Fellowship Program
KNFR........ Opportunity, WA [*FM radio station call letters*]
KNFT........ Bayard, NM [*AM radio station call letters*]
KNFT-FM.... Bayard, NM [*FM radio station call letters*]
KNFX........ Austin, MN [*AM radio station call letters*]
KNFX........ Bryan, TX [*FM radio station call letters*] (BROA)
KNFX-FM... Spring Valley, MN [*FM radio station call letters*]
KNG.......... Kaimana [*Indonesia*] [*Airport symbol*] (OAG)
KNG.......... Kaliningrad [*Former USSR*] [*Geomagnetic observatory code*]
KNG.......... King Aviation [*British*] [*ICAO designator*] (FAAC)
KNG.......... King Horse Trailer [*NCIC trailer make code*]
KNG.......... Kingman, AZ [*Amtrak rail station code*]
KNG.......... Kininogen (DMAA)
KNG.......... Konigsberg [*Kaliningrad*] [*Former USSR*] [*Seismograph station code, US Geological Survey*] [*Closed*] (SEIS)
KNG.......... Kraftwerks und Netzgesellschaft (EFIS)
KNGA........ St. Peter, MN [*FM radio station call letters*]
KNGDM..... Kingdom (ABBR)
KNGDM..... Kinhdom
KNGFSH..... Kingfish (ABBR)
KNGFSHR... Kingfisher (ABBR)
KNGH........ Kingham [*NCIC trailer make code*]
KNGHT...... Knight
KnghtR...... Knight Ridder, Inc. [*Associated Press*] (SAG)
KNGL........ McPherson, KS [*AM radio station call letters*]
KNGLNS..... Kingliness (ABBR)
KNGLR....... Kinglier (ABBR)
KNGLST..... Kingliest (ABBR)
KNGLY....... Kingly (ABBR)
KNGM........ Emporia, KS [*FM radio station call letters*]
KNGN........ McCook, NE [*AM radio station call letters*]
KNGP........ Corpus Christi/Corpus Christi Naval Air Station [*Texas*] [*ICAO location identifier*] (ICLI)
KNGPN...... Kingpin (ABBR)
KNGR........ Kangaroo (ABBR)
KNGR........ Kruger National Game Reserve (SAUO)
KNGS........ Coalinga, CA [*FM radio station call letters*]
KNGS........ Kingsway Travel Trailer [*NCIC trailer make code*]
KngsRd...... Kings Road Entertainment, Inc. [*Associated Press*] (SAG)
KNGSZ...... Kingsize (ABBR)
KNGT........ Jackson, CA [*FM radio station call letters*]
KNGT........ Knight (ABBR)
KNGT........ Knight Transportation [*NASDAQ symbol*] (SAG)
KNGTHD.... Knighthood (ABBR)
KNGTLY.... Knightly (ABBR)
KNGT-RNT... Knight-Errant (ABBR)
KNGU........ Norfolk/Norfolk Naval Air Station [*Virginia*] [*ICAO location identifier*] (ICLI)
KNGY........ Kingly (ABBR)
KNGZ........ Alameda/Alameda Naval Air Station [*California*] [*ICAO location identifier*] (ICLI)
KNH.......... Kipuka Nene [*Hawaii*] [*Seismograph station code, US Geological Survey*] (SEIS)

KNHC........ Seattle, WA [*FM radio station call letters*]
KNHD-AM... Camden, AR [*AM radio station call letters*] (BROA)
KNHK........ Patuxent River/Patuxent River Naval Air Station [*Maryland*] [*ICAO location identifier*] (ICLI)
KNHK-FM... Reno, NV [*FM radio station call letters*] (BROA)
KNHN........ Kansas City, KS [*AM radio station call letters*]
KNHT........ Knight (ABBR)
KNHT........ Rio Dell, CA [*FM radio station call letters*] (BROA)
KNHZ........ Brunswick/Brunswick Naval Air Station [*Maryland*] [*ICAO location identifier*] (ICLI)
KNI........... Centaur Resources Ltd. (SAUO)
KNI........... Kalallit Niuerfiat [*Greenland Trade*] (EY)
KNI........... Kantorberita Nasional Indonesia [*News service*] [*Indonesia*] (EY)
KNI........... Katmai New Instructions [*Computer science*]
KNI........... Knight-Ridder Newspapers Incorporated (SAUO)
KNI........... Koyna Nagar [*India*] [*Seismograph station code, US Geological Survey*] [*Closed*] (SEIS)
KNI........... Kyodo News International, Inc. [*Information service or system*] (IID)
KNIA......... Knoxville, IA [*AM radio station call letters*]
KNIC......... [*The*] Knickerbocker [*L.L.*] Company, Inc. [*NASDAQ symbol*] (SAG)
Knick......... [*The*] Knickerbocker [*L. L.*] Co., Inc. [*Associated Press*] (SAG)
KnickL....... [*The*] Knickerbocker [*L. L.*] Company, Inc. [*Associated Press*] (SAG)
KNID......... Enid, OK [*FM radio station call letters*]
KNID......... Lahoma, OK [*FM radio station call letters*] (BROA)
Knight Mech Dict... Knight's American Mechanical Dictionary [*A publication*] (DLA)
Knight's Ind... Knight's Industrial Reports [*A publication*] (DLA)
KnightTr..... Knight Transportation [*Associated Press*] (SAG)
KNIK......... Anchorage, AK [*FM radio station call letters*]
KNIL......... Koninklijk Nederlandsch-Indisch Leger [*Royal Dutch Indies Army*]
KNIM......... Maryville, MO [*AM radio station call letters*]
KNIM-FM... Maryville, MO [*FM radio station call letters*]
KNIN......... Dallas-Fort Worth, TX [*FM radio station call letters*] (GDPB)
KNIN-FM... Wichita Falls, TX [*FM radio station call letters*]
KNIN-TV.... Caldwell, ID [*TV station call letters*] (RBYB)
KNIP......... Jacksonville/Jacksonville Naval Air Station [*Florida*] [*ICAO location identifier*] (ICLI)
KNIR......... Beeville/Chase Field Naval Air Station [*Texas*] [*ICAO location identifier*] (ICLI)
KNIR......... New Iberia, LA [*AM radio station call letters*]
KNIS......... Carson City, NV [*FM radio station call letters*]
KNIT......... Techknits, Inc. [*NASDAQ symbol*] (SAG)
KNITG....... Knitting (ABBR)
KNITR....... Knitter (ABBR)
KNIX......... Phoenix, AZ [*FM radio station call letters*]
KNJ........... Kindamba [*Congo*] [*Airport symbol*] (OAG)
KNJK......... El Centro Naval Air Station [*California*] [*ICAO location identifier*] (ICLI)
KNJO......... Thousand Oaks, CA [*FM radio station call letters*]
KNJP......... Sargent, NE [*FM radio station call letters*]
KNJU......... Raton, NM [*FM radio station call letters*]
KNJY......... Spokane, WA [*FM radio station call letters*]
KNJZ......... Alton, IL [*FM radio station call letters*]
KNK........... Compact Sodium-Cooled Nuclear Reactor Plant, Karlsruhe (SAUS)
KNK........... Kakhonak [*Alaska*] [*Airport symbol*] (OAG)
KNK........... Kankakee Bancorp [*AMEX symbol*] (TTSB)
KNK........... Kankakee Bancorp, Inc. [*AMEX symbol*] (SAG)
KNK........... Klondike Air, Inc. (SAUO)
KNK........... Knik Glacier [*Alaska*] [*Seismograph station code, US Geological Survey*] (SEIS)
KNKA......... Kansas City [*Missouri*] [*ICAO location identifier*] (ICLI)
KNKE......... Jasper, TX [*FM radio station call letters*]
KNKI-FM... Sherman, TX [*FM radio station call letters*] (BROA)
KNKK-FM... Needles, CA [*FM radio station call letters*] (BROA)
KNKL......... Knuckle (ABBR)
KNKLD....... Knuckled (ABBR)
KNKLG....... Knuckling (ABBR)
KNKN......... Pueblo, CO [*FM radio station call letters*]
KNKR......... Kinkier (ABBR)
KNKRS....... Knickers (ABBR)
KNKST....... Kinkiest (ABBR)
KNKT......... Armijo, NM [*FM radio station call letters*] (RBYB)
KNKT......... Cherry Point Marine Corps Air Station [*North Carolina*] [*ICAO location identifier*] (ICLI)
KNKX......... Miramar Naval Air Station [*California*] [*ICAO location identifier*] (ICLI)
KNL........... Centaur Resources Ltd. [*Vancouver Stock Exchange symbol*]
KNL........... Darrow's Solution [*For antidiarrhea potassium therapy*] (DAVI)
KNL........... Keller, N. L., Washington DC [*STAC*]
KNL........... Kennel (ABBR)
KNL........... Knight of the Netherlands Lion
KNL........... Knoll (ABBR)
KNLA......... Karen National Liberation Army [*Myanmar*] [*Political party*]
KNLA......... White Rock, NM [*FM radio station call letters*]
KNLB......... Lake Havasu City, AZ [*FM radio station call letters*]
KNLC......... Hanford/Lemorre Naval Air Station [*California*] [*ICAO location identifier*] (ICLI)
KNLC......... St. Louis, MO [*Television station call letters*]
KNLD......... Duluth, MN [*Television station call letters*]
KNLD......... Kenneled (ABBR)
KNLE......... Round Rock, TX [*FM radio station call letters*]
KNLF......... Karen National Liberation Front [*Myanmar*] [*Political party*] (PD)
KNLF......... Quincy, CA [*FM radio station call letters*]
KNLG......... Kenneling (ABBR)
KNLG-FM... New Bloomfield, MO [*FM radio station call letters*] (BROA)
Kn LGR...... Knight's Local Government Reports [*A publication*] (DLA)
KNLH-FM... Cedar Hill, MO [*FM radio station call letters*] (BROA)
KNLJ......... Jefferson City, MO [*Television station call letters*]
KNLM-FM... Marshfield, MO [*FM radio station call letters*] (BROA)
KNLN......... Vienna, MO [*FM radio station call letters*] (BROA)
KNLP-FM... Potosi, MO [*FM radio station call letters*] (BROA)
KNLR......... Bend, OR [*FM radio station call letters*]
KNLS......... Kenya National Library Service (BUAC)
KNLS......... Knolls (MCD)
KNLT......... Walla Walla, WA [*FM radio station call letters*]
KNLU......... Monroe, LA [*FM radio station call letters*]
KNLU......... Ned-Lloyd Lines [*Intermodal shipping container symbol*] (TVRC)
KNLV......... Ord, NE [*AM radio station call letters*]
KNLV-FM.... Ord, NE [*FM radio station call letters*]
KNM.......... Katmai National Monument (SAUO)
KNM.......... Keene State College, Keene, NH [*OCLC symbol*] (OCLC)
KNM.......... Kenya National Museum
KNM.......... Mennonite Historical Society, Newton, KS [*Library symbol*] [*Library of Congress*] (LCLS)
KNMA-FM... Reserve, NM [*FM radio station call letters*] (BROA)
KNMB......... Cloudcroft, NM [*FM radio station call letters*] (BROA)
KNMC......... Havre, MT [*FM radio station call letters*]
KNMC......... Knutson Mortgage Corporation (SAUO)
KNME......... Albuquerque, NM [*Television station call letters*]
KNMH......... Coast Guard Station, Washington [*District of Columbia*] [*ICAO location identifier*] (ICLI)
KNMI......... Farmington, NM [*FM radio station call letters*]
KNML-AM... Los Ranchos de Albuquerque, NM [*AM radio station call letters*] (RBYB)
KNMO......... Nevada, MO [*FM radio station call letters*]
KNMR......... Kenai National Moose Range (SAUO)
KNMT......... Portland, OR [*Television station call letters*]
KNMTCS.... Kinematics
KNMvD....... Royal Netherlands Veterinary Association (GVA)
KNMX......... Las Vegas, NM [*AM radio station call letters*]
KNMZ......... K & N Meats [*Federal Railroad Administration identification code*]
KNMZ-FM... Alamogordo, NM [*FM radio station call letters*] (RBYB)
KNN........... Gan Chinese [*Language symbol*] (ETLW)
KNN........... Kankan [*Guinea*] [*Airport symbol*] (AD)
KNN........... Kenton Natural Resources Corp. [*Vancouver Stock Exchange symbol*]
KNN........... K-Nearest-Neighbor [*Algorithm*]
KNnB......... Bethel College, North Newton, KS [*Library symbol*] [*Library of Congress*] (LCLS)
KNNB......... Whiteriver, AZ [*FM radio station call letters*]
KNNC......... Georgetown, TX [*FM radio station call letters*]
KNND......... Cottage Grove, OR [*AM radio station call letters*]
KNNG......... Sterling, CO [*FM radio station call letters*]
KNNK-FM... Dimmitt, TX [*FM radio station call letters*] (RBYB)
KNNL......... K and L Trucking [*Common carrier symbol*]
KNNN......... Central Valley, CA [*FM radio station call letters*]
KNNS......... Beverly Hills, CA [*AM radio station call letters*] (RBYB)
KNNS......... Larned, KS [*AM radio station call letters*] (BROA)
Kn NSW..... Knox's New South Wales Reports [*A publication*] (DLA)
KNNT......... Farmington, NM [*AM radio station call letters*] (BROA)
KNNW......... Kenworth Northwest [*NCIC truck make code*]
KNNZ......... Cedar City, UT [*AM radio station call letters*] (BROA)
KNNZ......... Costa Mesa, CA [*AM radio station call letters*] (RBYB)
KNO........... Beginn der Knospenbildung (SAUS)
KNO........... Kano, Nigeria [*Remote site*] [*NASA*] (NASA)
KNO........... Keep Needle Open [*Reference to intravenous fluid lines*] (DAVI)
KNO........... Kennedy Space Center Notice (NAKS)
KNO........... Knogo Corp. (SAUO)
KNO........... Knox Ranch [*California*] [*Seismograph station code, US Geological Survey*] [*Closed*] (SEIS)
KNO........... Koch, Neff, Oetlinger [*Germany*] (NITA)
KNO........... Korrespondenzblatt der Nachrichtenstelle fuer den Orient [*A publication*] (BJA)
KNOB......... San Rafael, CA [*AM radio station call letters*] (RBYB)
KNOBA....... Knowledge-Based Real-Time Systems for Fault Diagnosis of Flexible Manufacturing Systems (SAUO)
KNOBS....... Knowledge-Based System
KNOC......... Natchitoches, LA [*AM radio station call letters*]
KNOD......... Harlan, IA [*FM radio station call letters*]
KNOE......... Monroe, LA [*AM radio station call letters*]
KNOE-FM... Monroe, LA [*FM radio station call letters*]
KNOE-TV.... Monroe, LA [*Television station call letters*]
KNOF......... St. Paul, MN [*FM radio station call letters*]
KNOG-FM... Nogales, AZ [*FM radio station call letters*] (RBYB)
KnogNA...... Knogo North America, Inc. [*Associated Press*] (SAG)
KNOL......... Knoll [*Commonly used*] (OPSA)
KNOLL....... Knoll [*Commonly used*] (OPSA)
KNOLLS..... Knolls [*Commonly used*] (OPSA)
KNOM......... Nome, AK [*FM radio station call letters*]
KNOM-FM... Nome, AK [*FM radio station call letters*]
KNON......... Dallas, TX [*FM radio station call letters*]
KNOOM....... Knowledge Orientated Office Model (SAUO)
KNOP......... North Platte, NE [*Television station call letters*]
KNOR......... Klamath Northern Railway Co. [*AAR code*]
KNOR......... Norman, OK [*AM radio station call letters*]
KNOR......... Pauls Valley, OK [*FM radio station call letters*] (BROA)
knork......... Knife and Fork [*Pharmacology*] (DAVI)
KNOS......... Albuquerque, NM [*AM radio station call letters*] (RBYB)
KNOS-FM... Omaha, NE [*FM radio station call letters*] (RBYB)
KNoSH....... Norton State Hospital, Norton, KS [*Library symbol*] [*Library of Congress*] (LCLS)

KNOT — Knot, Inc. (The) [*NASDAQ symbol*] (QUAN)
KNOT — Prescott, AZ [*AM radio station call letters*]
Knot — Speed Measure of One Nautical Mile Per Hour [*Nautical term*] (NTA)
KNOT-FM — Prescott, AZ [*FM radio station call letters*]
KNOU — Empire, LA [*FM radio station call letters*] (BROA)
Know — Knowledge [*Record label*]
KNOW — Knowledge Ware Inc. (SAUO)
KNOW — Knowles Manufacturing Company [*NCIC trailer make code*]
KNOW — Port Angeles Coast Guard Air Station [*Washington*] [*ICAO location identifier*] (ICLI)
KNOW-FM — Minneapolis-St. Paul, MN [*FM radio station call letters*]
Knowl — Knowledge (DIAR)
Knowl Eng Rev — Knowledge Engineering Review [*A publication*] (PABS)
Knowles — Knowles' Reports [*3 Rhode Island*] [*A publication*] (DLA)
KNOWLT — Knowlton [*England*]
KNOW-NET — Knowledege Network of Washington (EDAC)
KNOX — Grand Forks, ND [*AM radio station call letters*]
KNOX — Knox Homes Corporation [*NCIC trailer make code*]
KNOX — Knox Metals [*Private rail car owner code*]
Knox — Knox's New South Wales Reports [*A publication*] (DLA)
Knox & F — Knox and Fitzhardinge's New South Wales Reports [*A publication*] (DLA)
KNOX-FM — Grand Forks, ND [*FM radio station call letters*]
KNOZ — Cameron, MO [*FM radio station call letters*]
KNP — Contemplate [*Telegraphy*] (PCTE)
KNP — Kafue National Park (SAUO)
KNP — Kakadu National Park (SAUO)
KNP — Kalahari National Park (SAUO)
KNP — Kalbarri National Park (SAUO)
KNP — Kanha National Park (SAUO)
KNP — Katholieke Nationale Partij [*Catholic National Party*] [*Netherlands*] [*Political party*] (PPE)
KNP — Katholisk Nederlands Persbureau [*Catholic Netherlands Press Agency*] [*Netherlands*]
KNP — Kejimkujik National Park (SAUO)
KNP — Kenya National Party (SAUO)
KNP — Kinabalu National Park (SAUO)
KNP — Kinchega National Park (SAUO)
KNP — Kinetics of Nonhomogeneous Processes
KNP — King's Knight's Pawn [*Chess*] (BARN)
KNP — Kootenay National Park (SAUO)
KNP — Korea National Party [*South Korea*] [*Political party*] (PPW)
KNP — Korean National Police (SAUO)
KNP — Kosciuszko National Park (SAUO)
KNP — Koshkonong Nuclear Plant (NRCH)
KNP — Kruger National Park (SAUO)
KNPA — Pensacola/Pensacola Naval Air Station [*Florida*] [*ICAO location identifier*] (ICLI)
KNPB — Reno, NV [*Television station call letters*]
Kn PC — Knapp's Privy Council Appeal Cases [*1829-36*] [*England*] [*A publication*] (DLA)
KNPC — Korea National Party [*Political party*] (BUAC)
KNPC — Kuwait National Petroleum Co.
KNPD — Contemplated [*Telegraphy*] (PCTE)
KNPG — Contemplating [*Telegraphy*] (PCTE)
KNPI — Kundu's Neurotic Personality Inventory [*Psychology*]
KNPN — Contemplation [*Telegraphy*] (PCTE)
KNPP — Karenni National Progressive Party [*Myanmar*] [*Political party*] (EY)
KNPP — Kewaunee Nuclear Power Plant (NRCH)
KNPP — Kola Nuclear Power Plant (SAUO)
KNPR — Las Vegas, NV [*FM radio station call letters*]
KNPS — Contemplates [*Telegraphy*] (PCTE)
KNPSK — Knapsack (ABBR)
KNPT — Newport, OR [*AM radio station call letters*]
KNQ — Kone [*New Caledonia*] [*Airport symbol*] [*Obsolete*] (OAG)
KNQI — Kingsville Naval Air Station [*Texas*] [*ICAO location identifier*] (ICLI)
KNQX — Key West/Key West Naval Air Station [*Florida*] [*ICAO location identifier*] (ICLI)
KNR — Kalaallit Nunaata Radioa [*Greenland*] (EY)
KNR — Kidnap and Ransom [*Insurance terminology*]
KNR — King's National Roll
KNR — Kinki Nippon Railway (SAUO)
KNR — Klamath Northern Railway (MHDW)
KNR — Korean National Railroad (DCTA)
KNRB — Atlanta, TX [*FM radio station call letters*] (BROA)
KNRB — Mayport/Mayport Naval Station [*Florida*] [*ICAO location identifier*] (ICLI)
KNRC — Littleton, CO [*AM radio station call letters*] (BROA)
KNRC — Reno, NV [*AM radio station call letters*] (RBYB)
KNRG — New Ulm, TX [*FM radio station call letters*] (BROA)
KNRIS — Kentucky Natural Resources Information System (SAUO)
KNRJ — Payson, AZ [*FM radio station call letters*] (BROA)
KNRK — Camas, WA [*FM radio station call letters*] (RBYB)
KNRK — Kirsten Sarcoma Virus in Normal Rat Kidney [*Medicine*] (DMAA)
KNRL — Kernel (ABBR)
KNRL — Knurl [*Engineering*]
KNRO — Redding, CA [*AM radio station call letters*]
KNRQ — Eugene, OR [*FM radio station call letters*] (BROA)
KNRQ — K and R Express Systems [*Common carrier symbol*]
KNRQ — Springfield, OR [*AM radio station call letters*] (RBYB)
KNRQ-FM — Creswell, OR [*FM radio station call letters*] (RBYB)
KNRR — Pembina, ND [*Television station call letters*]
KNRS — Salt Lake City, UT [*AM radio station call letters*] (BROA)
KNRV-FM — Harker Heights, TX [*FM radio station call letters*] (RBYB)
KNRX — Castle Rock, CO [*FM radio station call letters*] (RBYB)
KNRX — Kingwood Northern Railroad [*Federal Railroad Administration identification code*]
KNRX-FM — Oklahoma City, OK [*FM radio station call letters*] (RBYB)
KNRY — Monterey, CA [*AM radio station call letters*]
KNS — Converse [*Telegraphy*] (PCTE)
KNS — Kazan [*Formerly, Kazanskaya*] [*Former USSR*] [*Geomagnetic observatory code*]
KNS — Kenuz Airlines Ltd. [*Nigeria*] [*ICAO designator*] (FAAC)
KNS — King Island [*Tasmania*] [*Airport symbol*] (OAG)
KNS — Kinney Services, Inc. (SAUO)
KNS — Knight of [*the Order of*] the Royal Northern Star [*Sweden*]
KNS — Korean Nuclear Society (SAUO)
KNSA — Unalakleet, AK [*AM radio station call letters*]
KNSCP — Kinescope (ABBR)
KNSD — Conversed [*Telegraphy*] (PCTE)
KNSD — San Diego, CA [*Television station call letters*]
KNSD-DT — San Diego, CA [*Television station call letters*] (BROA)
KNSE — Ontario, CA [*AM radio station call letters*]
KNSF — Washington Naval Air Facility [*District of Columbia*] [*ICAO location identifier*] (ICLI)
KNSG — Conversing [*Telegraphy*] (PCTE)
KNSG — Springfield, MN [*FM radio station call letters*] (RBYB)
KNSHP — Kinship (ABBR)
KNSI — San Nicolas Auxiliary Air Base (SAUS)
KNSI — San Nicolas Island/San Nicolas Auxiliary Air Base [*California*] [*ICAO location identifier*] (ICLI)
KNSI — St. Cloud, MN [*AM radio station call letters*]
KNSJA — Journal. Korean Nuclear Society (journ.) (SAUS)
KNSMN — Kinsman (ABBR)
KNSN — Atlanta, LA [*FM radio station call letters*] (BROA)
KNSN — Chico, CA [*AM radio station call letters*] (RBYB)
KNSN — Conversation [*Telegraphy*] (PCTE)
KNSO — Merced, CA [*Television station call letters*]
KNSP — Staples, MN [*AM radio station call letters*]
KNSP-FM — Staples, MN [*FM radio station call letters*]
KNSQ — Mount Shasta, CA [*FM radio station call letters*]
KNSR — Collegeville, MN [*FM radio station call letters*]
KNSS — Wichita, KS [*AM radio station call letters*]
KNST — Tucson, AZ [*AM radio station call letters*]
KNSU — Kenya National Shipping Line [*Intermodal shipping container symbol*] (TVRC)
KNSU — Thibodaux, LA [*FM radio station call letters*]
KNSW — Knife Switch
KNSWMN — Kinswoman (ABBR)
KNSX-FM — Steelville, MO [*FM radio station call letters*] (BROA)
KNSY — Kensey Nash [*NASDAQ symbol*] (TTSB)
KNSY — Kensey Nash Corp. [*NASDAQ symbol*] (SAG)
KNSY-FM — Amarillo, TX [*FM radio station call letters*] (BROA)
KNT — Kent Electronics [*NYSE symbol*] (TTSB)
KNT — Kent Electronics Corp. [*NYSE symbol*] (SPSG)
knt — Knight (GEAB)
KNT — Knight [*British title*]
KNT — Knight-Knott Hotels Corp. (SAUO)
KNT — Knightway Air Charter Ltd. [*British*] [*ICAO designator*] (FAAC)
KNT — Knitting
KNT — Sanandaj [*Iran*] [*Airport symbol*] (AD)
KNT — Short-Cycle Gas Nitriding (SAUS)
KNTA — Santa Clara, CA [*AM radio station call letters*]
KNTB — Lakewood, WA [*AM radio station call letters*] (BROA)
KNTB — Los Alamitos/Los Alamitos Naval Air Station [*California*] [*ICAO location identifier*] (ICLI)
KNTB-FM — Lakewood, WA [*FM radio station call letters*] (RBYB)
KNTC — Kenya National Trading Company (SAUO)
KNTC — Kenya National Trading Corp. (BUAC)
KNTC — Kinetic (ABBR)
KNTC — Kinetic [*NCIC motorcycle make code*]
KNTC — Korea National Tourism Corp. (BUAC)
KNTC — Korean National Tourism Corporation (SAUO)
KntckyEl — Kentucky Electric Steel Co. [*Associated Press*] (SAG)
KNTD — Knotted (ABBR)
KNTD — Point Mugu Naval Air Station [*California*] [*ICAO location identifier*] (ICLI)
KNTE — Lakewood, WA [*AM radio station call letters*]
KNTG — Knotting (ABBR)
KNTHL — Knothole (ABBR)
KNTI — Kent Industries [*NCIC trailer make code*]
KNTI — Lakeport, CA [*FM radio station call letters*]
KNTK — Kentek Information Sys [*NASDAQ symbol*] (TTSB)
KNTK — Kentek Information Systems, Inc. [*NASDAQ symbol*] (SAG)
KNTL — Bethany, OK [*FM radio station call letters*]
KNtl — Kinetic Concepts, Inc. (SAUO)
KNTLK — Knotlike (ABBR)
KNTLS — Knotless (ABBR)
KNTN — Thief River Falls, MN [*FM radio station call letters*]
KNTO — Chowchilla, CA [*FM radio station call letters*] (BROA)
KNTO — Livingston, CA [*FM radio station call letters*]
KNTR — Ferndale, WA [*AM radio station call letters*]
KNTR-AM — Lake Havasu City, AZ [*AM radio station call letters*] (BROA)
KNTS — Abilene, TX [*AM radio station call letters*]
KNTTD — Knitted
KNTU — Denton, TX [*FM radio station call letters*]
KNTU — Kanto [*Intermodal shipping container symbol*] (TVRC)
KNTU — McKinney, TX [*FM radio station call letters*] (BROA)

KNTU .... Virginia Beach/Oceana Naval Air Station [*Virginia*] [*ICAO location identifier*] (ICLI)
KNTV .... San Jose, CA [*Television station call letters*]
KNTWR...... Knitwear
KNTX .... Wichita Falls, TX-Lawton, OK [*AM radio station call letters*] (GDPB)
KNTX-AM ... Bowie, TX [*AM radio station call letters*] (BROA)
KNTY .... Knotty (ABBR)
KNU.......... Kanpur [*India*] [*Airport symbol*] (OAG)
KNU.......... Karen National Union [*Myanmar*] (PD)
KnU.......... Knowledge Utility (SAUS)
KNU.......... Knuckle [*Automotive engineering*]
KNU.......... Kyungpook National University (SAUO)
KNUC........ Smithfield, UT [*FM radio station call letters*]
KNUDO...... Kore Nationality Union Democratic Organization (SAUO)
KNUE........ Tyler, TX [*FM radio station call letters*]
KNUFNS..... Kampuchean National United Front for National Salvation (PD)
KNUI.......... Kahului, HI [*AM radio station call letters*]
KNUI-FM.... Kahului, HI [*FM radio station call letters*]
KNUJ .... New Ulm, MN [*AM radio station call letters*]
KNUJ .... Sleepy Eye, MN [*FM radio station call letters*]
KNUP........ Karen National Unity Party [*Burma*]
KNUQ........ Mountain View/Moffett Naval Air Station [*California*] [*ICAO location identifier*] (ICLI)
KNUQ-FM... Paauilo, HI [*FM radio station call letters*] (RBYB)
KNUR........ Knox Nursery, Inc. [*NASDAQ symbol*] (QUAN)
KNUS........ Denver, CO [*AM radio station call letters*]
KNUT........ Kenya National Union of Teachers [*Political party*] (PSAP)
KNUU........ Knutsen Lines [*Intermodal shipping container symbol*] (TVRC)
KNUU........ Paradise, NV [*AM radio station call letters*]
KNUW........ Santa Clara, NM [*FM radio station call letters*] (BROA)
KNUW........ Whidbey Island/Whidbey Island Naval Air Station [*Washington*] [*ICAO location identifier*] (ICLI)
KNUW-FM... Central, NM [*FM radio station call letters*] (RBYB)
KNUZ........ Bellville, TX [*AM radio station call letters*] (BROA)
KNUZ........ Houston, TX [*AM radio station call letters*]
KNUZ Exp Stn... Houston, TX [*Radio expansion station*]
KNV.......... Knave (ABBR)
KNVA........ Austin, TX [*Television station call letters*]
KNVC........ Consolidated Nevada Goldfields Corp. [*NASDAQ symbol*] (SAG)
KNVCF...... Consolidated Nev Goldfields [*NASDAQ symbol*] (TTSB)
KNVH........ Knavish (ABBR)
KNVHLY..... Knavishly (ABBR)
KNVN........ Chico, CA [*Television station call letters*] (BROA)
KNVO........ McAllen, TX [*Television station call letters*]
KNVQ........ South Lake Tahoe, CA [*FM radio station call letters*] (BROA)
KNVR........ Beatty, NV [*FM radio station call letters*] (BROA)
KNVRY...... Knavery (ABBR)
KNW......... Konawaena [*Hawaii*] [*Seismograph station code, US Geological Survey*] [*Closed*] (SEIS)
KNW......... New Stuyahok [*Alaska*] [*Airport symbol*] (OAG)
KNWA........ Bellefonte, AR [*AM radio station call letters*]
KNWB........ Hilo, HI [*FM radio station call letters*] (RBYB)
KNWB........ Knowable (ABBR)
KNWC........ Sioux Falls, SD [*AM radio station call letters*]
KNWC-FM... Sioux Falls, SD [*FM radio station call letters*]
KNWD........ Natchitoches, LA [*FM radio station call letters*]
KNWDV...... Knickerbocker L L Wrrt [*NASDAQ symbol*] (TTSB)
KNWF........ Fergus Falls, MN [*FM radio station call letters*] (BROA)
KNWG........ Knowing (ABBR)
KNWGNS.... Knowingness (ABBR)
KNWGY..... Knowingly (ABBR)
KNWHW..... Know-How (ABBR)
KNWJ........ Gosnell, AR [*FM radio station call letters*] (BROA)
KNWJ........ Leone, AS [*FM radio station call letters*] (BROA)
KNWL........ Knowledge (ABBR)
KNWLB...... Knowledgeable (ABBR)
KNWLDG.... Knowledge (ABBR)
KNWLDGB... Knowledgeable (ABBR)
KNWNTHG... Know-Nothing (ABBR)
KNWO........ Cottonwood, ID [*FM radio station call letters*]
KNWP-FM... Port Angeles, WA [*FM radio station call letters*] (BROA)
KNWQ-AM... Palm Springs, CA [*AM radio station call letters*] (BROA)
KNWR........ Ellensburg, WA [*FM radio station call letters*] (RBYB)
KNWR........ Kirwin National Wildlife Refuge (SAUO)
KNWR........ Knower (ABBR)
KNWS........ Kwame Nkrumah Welfare Society (SAUO)
KNWS........ Waterloo, IA [*AM radio station call letters*]
KNWS-FM... Waterloo, IA [*FM radio station call letters*]
KNWS-TV... Katy, TX [*Television station call letters*]
KNWV-FM... Clarkston, WA [*FM radio station call letters*] (RBYB)
KNWX........ Seattle, WA [*AM radio station call letters*] (RBYB)
KNWY........ Yakima, WA [*FM radio station call letters*]
KNWZ........ Thousand Palms, CA [*AM radio station call letters*]
KNWZ-AM... Coachella, CA [*AM radio station call letters*] (BROA)
KNWZ-FM... Yucca Valley, CA [*FM radio station call letters*]
KNX.......... Conscientious [*Telegraphy*] (PCTE)
KNX.......... Knighthawk Air Express Ltd. [*Canada*] [*ICAO designator*] (FAAC)
KNX.......... Knoxville [*Diocesan abbreviation*] [*Tennessee*] (TOCD)
KNX.......... Kununurra [*Australia*] [*Airport symbol*] (OAG)
KNX.......... Los Angeles, CA [*AM radio station call letters*]
KNXN........ Sierra Vista, AZ [*AM radio station call letters*]
KNXR........ Rochester, MN [*FM radio station call letters*]
KNXT........ Knoxville Transport [*Common carrier symbol*]
KNXT........ Visalia, CA [*Television station call letters*]
KNXV........ Knoxville [*Tennessee*] (ABBR)
KNXV........ Phoenix, AZ [*Television station call letters*]
KNXV-DT.... Phoenix, AZ [*Television station call letters*] (BROA)
KNXVL....... Knoxville, TN [*American Association of Railroads railroad junction routing code*]
KNXX........ Donaldsonville, LA [*FM radio station call letters*] (BROA)
KNXX........ Willow Grove/Willow Grove Naval Air Station [*Pennsylvania*] [*ICAO location identifier*] (ICLI)
KNY.......... Conscientiously [*Telegraphy*] (PCTE)
KNY.......... Kanoya [*Japan*] [*Geomagnetic observatory code*]
KNY.......... Kanyok [*Language symbol*] (ETLW)
KNY.......... Kearney National, Inc. (SAUO)
KNY.......... Kenergy Resource Corp. [*Vancouver Stock Exchange symbol*]
KNYC........ New York (City) [*New York*] [*ICAO location identifier*] (ICLI)
KNYD........ Broken Arrow, OK [*FM radio station call letters*]
KNYE........ Pahrump, NV [*FM radio station call letters*] (BROA)
KNYL........ Yuma/Vincent Marine Corps Air Station [*Arizona*] [*ICAO location identifier*] (ICLI)
KNYN........ Santa Fe, NM [*FM radio station call letters*]
KNYN-FM... Fort Bridger, WY [*FM radio station call letters*] (BROA)
KNZ.......... Kanozan [*Japan*] [*Geomagnetic observatory code*]
KNZ.......... Kenieba [*Mali*] [*Airport symbol*] (OAG)
KNZA........ Hiawatha, KS [*FM radio station call letters*]
KNZJ........ El Toro Marine Corps Air Station [*California*] [*ICAO location identifier*] (ICLI)
KNZR........ Bakersfield, CA [*AM radio station call letters*]
KNZS........ Montecito, CA [*AM radio station call letters*]
KNZW........ South Weymouth/South Weymouth Naval Air Station [*Massachusetts*] [*ICAO location identifier*] (ICLI)
KNZY........ San Diego/North Island Naval Air Station [*California*] [*ICAO location identifier*] (ICLI)
KNZZ........ Grand Junction, CO [*AM radio station call letters*]
Ko............ C. H. Boehringer Sohn, Ingelheim [*Germany*] [*Research code symbol*]
KO............ [*The*] Coca-Cola Co. [*NYSE symbol*] (SPSG)
KO............ Coca Cola Co. [*NYSE symbol*]
KO............ Commanding Officer [*Military slang*]
KO............ Contracting Officer [*Also, CO, CONTRO*]
KO............ Kashrut Observance (BJA)
KO............ Kattoo [*Ship's rigging*] (ROG)
KO............ Keep Off [*i.e., avoid assuming the risk on an application, pending further investigation*] [*Insurance*]
KO............ Keep On [*Continue*] [*Medicine*] (DAVI)
K/O........... Keep Open [*Medicine*]
KO............ Key Output (SAUS)
KO............ Kickoff (MSA)
KO............ Killarney Oscillation [*Climatology*]
KO............ Killed Organism [*Medicine*] (DMAA)
KO............ Kilogram (ROG)
KO............ Kilohm (ABBR)
KO............ King's Own [*Military unit*] [*British*]
KO............ Klystron Oscillator
KO............ Knee Open [*Therapy term*] (CTAA)
KO............ Knee Orthosis [*Medicine*]
K/O........... Knocked Out [*To write or produce something quickly*] [*Also called knock off*] (WDMC)
ko............ Knock Out [*Boxing*] (WA)
KO............ Knockout [*Partly cut out or loosened area which can be easily removed, as in a junction box*] [*Technical drawings*]
KO............ Knockout [*Boxing*]
KO............ Koblenz [*German license plate city code*]
KO............ Kodiak-Western Alaska Airlines, Inc. [*CAB official abbreviation*]
Ko............ Korea (SAUO)
ko............ Korea, South [*MARC country of publication code*] [*Library of Congress*] (LCCP)
KO............ Kraus-Thomson Organization [*Publisher*]
ko............ Keep Out (ODA)
KOA.......... Communications on Alternatives in Education [*Defunct*] (EA)
KOA.......... Denver, CO [*AM radio station call letters*]
KOA.......... Kailua-Kona, HI [*Location identifier*] [*FAA*] (FAAL)
KOA.......... Kampground Owners Association [*Phoenix, AZ*] (EA)
KOA.......... Kampgrounds of America
KOA.......... Kansas Optometric Association (EARSL)
KOA.......... Kentucky Opera Association (SAUO)
KOA.......... Kentucky Optometric Association (SRA)
KOA.......... Knocked-on-Atom
KOA.......... Koala Technologies Corp. (SAUO)
KOA.......... Kobuan [*Solomon Islands*] [*Seismograph station code, US Geological Survey*] [*Closed*] (SEIS)
KOA.......... Kona [*Hawaii*] [*Airport symbol*] (OAG)
KOA.......... Kone Air Ltd. [*Finland*] [*ICAO designator*] (FAAC)
KOA.......... Korean Operation Area (SAUO)
KOA.......... Kustoms of America [*Association*] (EA)
KOAA........ Pueblo, CO [*Television station call letters*]
KOAB........ Bend, OR [*FM radio station call letters*]
KOAB-TV.... Bend, OR [*Television station call letters*]
KOAC........ Corvallis, OR [*AM radio station call letters*]
KOAC-TV.... Corvallis, OR [*Television station call letters*]
KOAI......... Fort Worth, TX [*FM radio station call letters*]
KOAI A...... Koala Technologies Corp. (SAUO)
KOAK........ Oakland/Metropolitan Oakland International [*California*] [*ICAO location identifier*] (ICLI)
KOAK........ Red Oak, IA [*AM radio station call letters*]
KOAL........ Price, UT [*AM radio station call letters*]

KOALA........ Keyfile Open Access Layer [*Workflow automation software*] (PCM)
Koala........ Koala Corp. [*Associated Press*] (SAG)
KOALAS..... Knowledgeable Observation Analysis Advisory System (SAUO)
KOAM .... Korean-American Oil Co.
KOAM .... Pittsburg, KS [*Television station call letters*]
KO & G....... Kansas, Oklahoma & Gulf Railway Co.
KO&G........ Kansas, Oklahoma & Gulf Railway Company (SAUO)
KOAP .... Lakeview, OR [*FM radio station call letters*] (BROA)
KOAQ .... Terrytown, NE [*AM radio station call letters*]
KOAS .... Broken Arrow, OK [*FM radio station call letters*] (RBYB)
KOAT .... Albuquerque, NM [*Television station call letters*]
KOAZ .... Oro Valley, AZ [*FM radio station call letters*] (BROA)
KOAZ-FM ... Glendale, AZ [*FM radio station call letters*] (RBYB)
KOB.......... Albuquerque, NM [*Television station call letters*]
KOB.......... King's Own Borderers [*British military*] (DMA)
KOB.......... Kob Air Ltd. [*Uganda*] [*ICAO designator*] (FAAC)
KOB.......... Kobe [*Japan*] [*Seismograph station code, US Geological Survey*] (SEIS)
KoB .... Koehler and Baumgartner Lexikon in Veteris Testamenti Libros [*Leiden*] [*A publication*] (BJA)
KOB.......... Koutaba [*Cameroon*] [*Airport symbol*] (OAG)
KOB.......... Kriegsoffizier-Bewerber [*Applicant for Wartime Commission*] [*German military - World War II*]
KOBB .... Bozeman, MT [*AM radio station call letters*]
KOBC .... Joplin, MO [*FM radio station call letters*]
KOBE .... Las Cruces, NM [*AM radio station call letters*]
Kobe UL Rev... Kobe University. Law Review [*A publication*] (DLA)
KOBF .... Farmington, NM [*Television station call letters*]
KOBI......... Medford, OR [*Television station call letters*]
KOBN........ Honolulu, HI [*Television station call letters*]
KOBO .... Yuba City, CA [*AM radio station call letters*]
KOBOL ...... Keystation On-Line Business-Oriented Language [*Computer science*]
KOBR .... Roswell, NM [*Television station call letters*]
KOBU .... Ter Haak Koelbox [*Intermodal shipping container symbol*] (TVRC)
Koc .... Coefficient of Organic Carbon Partition (GNE)
KOC.......... Kathodal Opening Contraction [*Medicine*]
KOC.......... Key Operational Capability [*Military*] (RDA)
KOC.......... Knight of the [*Order of the*] Oak Crown
KOC.......... Kochi [*Japan*] [*Seismograph station code, US Geological Survey*] (SEIS)
KOC.......... Kollmorgen Optical Corporation (SAUO)
KOC.......... Koumac [*New Caledonia*] [*Airport symbol*] (OAG)
KOC.......... Kuwait Oil Co.
Koc .... Measure of Soil Absorption (GNE)
KOC.......... Occupational and Environmental Health Unit, University of Toronto [*UTLAS symbol*]
KOC.......... TCC Beverages Ltd. [*Toronto Stock Exchange symbol*]
KOCB .... Oklahoma City, OK [*Television station call letters*]
KOCC .... Oklahoma City, OK [*FM radio station call letters*]
KOCCCG..... Kenya Operations Control Center Coordination Group (SAUO)
KOCCCG..... Kunia Operations Control Center Coordination Group (CINC)
KOCD .... Columbus, KS [*FM radio station call letters*]
KOCE .... Huntington Beach, CA [*Television station call letters*]
KOCE .... Komi Commodity Exchange [*Russian Federation*] (EY)
Koch .... Koch's Supreme Court Decisions [*Ceylon*] [*A publication*] (DLA)
KOCH........ Koch, TX [*American Association of Railroads railroad junction routing code*]
KOCHPAC... Koch Industries Inc. PAC [*Washington, DC*] (PACS)
KOCL .... Carlsbad, CA [*FM radio station call letters*] (BROA)
KOCL-FM ... Arthur, ND [*FM radio station call letters*] (BROA)
KOCM .... Norman, OK [*Television station call letters*] (BROA)
KOCN........ Pacific Grove, CA [*FM radio station call letters*]
KOCO .... Korea Oil Corporation (SAUO)
KOCO .... Oklahoma City, OK [*Television station call letters*]
KOCP .... Camarillo, CA [*FM radio station call letters*] (RBYB)
KOCR .... Joplin, MO-Pittsburg, KS [*AM radio station call letters*] (GDPB)
KOCR-AM... Joplin, MO [*AM radio station call letters*] (BROA)
KOCT .... Carlsbad, NM [*Television station call letters*]
KOCU .... Altus, OK [*FM radio station call letters*] (BROA)
KOCV .... Odessa, TX [*FM radio station call letters*]
KOCV-TV.... Odessa, TX [*Television station call letters*]
KOCX .... Keith Oil [*Private rail car owner code*]
KOCY-FM.... Hoxie, AR [*FM radio station call letters*] (RBYB)
KOCZ .... Koch Refining [*Federal Railroad Administration identification code*]
KOD.......... Kick-Off Drift [*Navigation*] (ODA)
KO'd .... Knocked Out [*Boxing*] (DAVI)
KOD.......... Knockout Drops [*Medicine*] (EDAA)
KOD.......... Kodaikanal [*India*] [*Seismograph station code, US Geological Survey*] (SEIS)
KOD.......... Kodaikanal [*India*] [*Geomagnetic observatory code*]
KODA........ Houston, TX [*FM radio station call letters*]
KODA........ Kodiak Transfer [*Common carrier symbol*]
KODC........ Korea Oceanographic Data Center [*Marine science*] (OSRA)
KODCH ...... Kodachrome (VRA)
KODCO ...... Korean Overseas Development Co. [*Korean government agency*]
KODE .... Joplin, MO [*Television station call letters*]
KODI......... Cody, WY [*AM radio station call letters*]
KODI......... Kodiak [*NCIC truck make code*]
KODI......... Kodiak Coach & Manufacturing [*NCIC trailer make code*]
KODJ .... Salt Lake City, UT [*FM radio station call letters*]
KODL .... The Dalles, OR [*AM radio station call letters*]
KODM .... Odessa, TX [*FM radio station call letters*]
KODR........ King's Overseas Dominions Regiment [*British military*] (DMA)
KODS........ Carnelian Bay, CA [*FM radio station call letters*]
KODY........ North Platte, NE [*AM radio station call letters*]
KODZ........ Eugene, OR [*FM radio station call letters*]
KOE.......... Kilograms Oil Equivalent [*Petroleum industry*]
kOe .... Kilooersted
KOE.......... Koppel [*Federal Republic of Germany*] [*Seismograph station code, US Geological Survey*] (SEIS)
KOE.......... Kupang [*Indonesia*] [*Airport symbol*] (OAG)
KOE.......... MER Leasing [*FAA designator*] (FAAC)
KOE.......... Northland Aviation, Inc. [*ICAO designator*] (FAAC)
KOEA .... Doniphan, MO [*FM radio station call letters*]
KOEBES ..... Koelner Bibliothekserschliessungssystem [*Automated library system*] (NITA)
KOED .... Tulsa, OK [*Television station call letters*]
KOEL .... Oelwein, IA [*AM radio station call letters*]
KOEL-FM.... Oelwein, IA [*FM radio station call letters*]
KOEN .... Koenig, Inc. (SAUO)
KOEO .... Key On, Engine Off [*Automotive engineering*]
KOEO .... Key-On Engine-Off [*Automotive engineering*]
KOEOST..... Key On, Engine Off Self-Test [*Automotive engineering*]
KOER .... Key On, Engine Running [*Automotive engineering*]
KOER .... Key-On Engine-Running [*Automotive engineering*]
KOERST..... Key On, Engine Running Self-Test [*Automotive engineering*]
KOES-FM ... Stamford, TX [*FM radio station call letters*] (BROA)
KOET .... Eufaula, OK [*Television station call letters*]
KOeT .... Koethen [*Anhalt*] [*German license plate city code*]
KOEX .... Korea Exhibition Center (SAUO)
KOEX .... Oklahoma City [*Oklahoma*] [*ICAO location identifier*] (ICLI)
KOEZ .... Newton, KS [*FM radio station call letters*]
KOEZ .... Saint George, UT [*FM radio station call letters*] (GDPB)
KOF.......... Coca-Cola FEMSA [*NYSE symbol*] (SPSG)
KOF.......... Coca-Cola FEMSA ADS [*NYSE symbol*] (TTSB)
KOF.......... Knitted Outerwear Foundation (EA)
KOF.......... Kofu [*Japan*] [*Seismograph station code, US Geological Survey*] (SEIS)
KOFC .... Fayetteville, AR [*AM radio station call letters*]
K of C .... Knights of Columbus (EA)
K of E .... Knights of Equity (SAUO)
KOFE .... St. Maries, ID [*AM radio station call letters*]
KOFF .... Koffel Machine & Metal Fabricating [*NCIC trailer make code*]
KOFF .... Offutt Air Force Base, Omaha [*Nebraska*] [*ICAO location identifier*] (ICLI)
K of H....... Knight of Hanover
KOFH-FM ... Nogales, AZ [*FM radio station call letters*] (BROA)
KOFI......... Kalispell, MT [*AM radio station call letters*]
KOFI-FM .... Kalispell, MT [*FM radio station call letters*]
K of L .... Knights of Labor
K of L .... Knights of Lithuania (EA)
KOFM........ Enid, OK [*FM radio station call letters*]
KOFO .... Ottawa, KS [*AM radio station call letters*]
K of P .... Knights of Pythias
KOFR-FM ... Post, TX [*FM radio station call letters*] (BROA)
KOFS .... Key Officers of Foreign Service Posts [*A publication*]
KOFSE....... Kuwait Oil-Fire Smoke Experiment (SAUO)
KOFST....... Korean Federation of Science and Technology
KOFT .... Farmington, NM [*Television station call letters*] (BROA)
KOFT .... Gallup, NM [*Television station call letters*]
KOFX .... El Paso, TX [*FM radio station call letters*]
KOFX .... Kofax Image Products, Inc. [*NASDAQ symbol*] (NASQ)
KOFY .... San Francisco, CA [*Television station call letters*]
KOFY .... San Mateo, CA [*AM radio station call letters*]
KOFY-AM.... Gilmer, TX [*AM radio station call letters*] (BROA)
KOG.......... Kansas, Oklahoma & Gulf Railway Co. [*AAR code*]
KOG.......... Kindly Old Gentleman [*Slang*]
KOG.......... Koger Properties Inc. (SAUO)
KOGA........ Kentucky Oil and Gas Association (EARSL)
KOGA........ Ogallala, NE [*AM radio station call letters*]
KOGA-FM ... Ogallala, NE [*FM radio station call letters*]
KOGC .... Kelley Oil and Gas Corp. [*NASDAQ symbol*] (SAG)
KOGCC ...... Kelley Oil & Gas [*NASDAQ symbol*] (SG)
KogEq ...... Koger Equity, Inc. [*Associated Press*] (SAG)
KOGG........ Wailuku, HI [*Television station call letters*]
KOGM .... Opelousas, LA [*FM radio station call letters*]
KOGO........ San Diego, CA [*AM radio station call letters*]
KOGO........ Temecula, CA [*FM radio station call letters*] (BROA)
KogrEq ...... Koger Equity, Inc. [*Associated Press*] (SAG)
KOGS........ Ogdensburg [*New York*] [*ICAO location identifier*] (ICLI)
KOGT .... Orange, TX [*AM radio station call letters*]
KOH.......... King's Own Hussars [*British military*] (DMA)
KOH.......... Kohala [*Hawaii*] [*Seismograph station code, US Geological Survey*] (SEIS)
Koh .... Kohelet (BJA)
KOH.......... Koolatah [*Australia*] [*Airport symbol*] [*Obsolete*] (OAG)
KOH.......... Potassium Hydroxide [*Organic chemistry*]
KOHEMA .... Korean Heavy Machinery Industries (SAUO)
KOHEPFC ... King of Our Hearts Elvis Presley Fan Club (EA)
KOHI......... St. Helens, OR [*AM radio station call letters*]
KOHL .... Fremont, CA [*FM radio station call letters*]
KOHL .... Kohler Transfer [*Common carrier symbol*]
Kohls .... Kohls Corp. [*Associated Press*] (SAG)
KOHM .... Kilohm (MCD)
KOHM .... Lubbock, TX [*FM radio station call letters*]
KOHN........ Sells, AZ [*FM radio station call letters*] (BROA)
KOHO........ Honolulu, HI [*AM radio station call letters*]
KOHO........ Leavenworth, WA [*FM radio station call letters*] (BROA)

KohR .... Kohelet Rabbah (BJA)
KOHS .... Orem, UT [*FM radio station call letters*]
KOHT .... Marana, AZ [*FM radio station call letters*]
KOHU .... Hermiston, OR [*AM radio station call letters*]
KOHYNO .... Nordic Coordinating Committee of Hydrology (SAUO)
KOI .... Kennedy Operating Instructions [*NASA*] (KSC)
K-OI .... Keren-OR, Inc. [*An association*] (EA)
KOI .... Kirkwall [*Orkney Islands*] [*Airport symbol*] (OAG)
KOI .... KSC [*Kennedy Space Center*] Operation Instruction [*NASA*] (NASA)
KOI .... Olathe Public Library (SAUS)
KOI .... Ontario Institute for Studies in Education Library [*UTLAS symbol*]
KOICA .... Korea International Cooperation Agency (BUAC)
KOIL .... Bellevue, NE [*AM radio station call letters*]
KOIL .... Kelley Oil (EFIS)
KOIL .... Kelley Oil Corp. (SAUO)
KOIN .... Portland, OR [*Television station call letters*]
KOIN-DT .... Portland, OR [*Television station call letters*] (BROA)
KOIR .... Edinburg, TX [*FM radio station call letters*]
KOIS .... Kuder Occupational Interest Survey [*Aptitude and skills test*]
KOIT .... San Francisco, CA [*AM radio station call letters*]
KOIT-FM .... San Francisco, CA [*FM radio station call letters*]
KOJ .... Kagoshima [*Japan*] [*Airport symbol*] (OAG)
KOJ .... Keen on the Job (ADA)
KOJ .... Sara Dunjo [*Language symbol*] (ETLW)
KOJI .... Okoboji, IA [*FM radio station call letters*] (BROA)
KOJJ .... East Porterville, CA [*FM radio station call letters*]
KOJM .... Havre, MT [*AM radio station call letters*]
KOJO .... Lake Charles, LA [*FM radio station call letters*]
KOJW .... Amarillo, TX [*AM radio station call letters*] (GDPB)
KOJY .... Bloomfield, IA [*FM radio station call letters*] (GDPB)
KOK .... Horizon Cargo Transport, Inc. [*ICAO designator*] (FAAC)
KOK .... Kansallinen Kokoomus [*National Coalition Party*] [*Finland*] [*Political party*] (EAIO)
KOK .... Kokkola [*Finland*] [*Airport symbol*] (OAG)
kok .... Konkani [*MARC language code*] [*Library of Congress*] (LCCP)
KOKA .... Shreveport, LA [*AM radio station call letters*]
KOKB .... Blackwell, OK [*AM radio station call letters*]
KOKC .... Guthrie, OK [*AM radio station call letters*]
KOKC .... Oklahoma City/Will Rogers World [*Oklahoma*] [*ICAO location identifier*] (ICLI)
KOKE .... Giddings, TX [*FM radio station call letters*]
KOKE .... Koschkee Transfer [*Common carrier symbol*]
KOKE .... Pflugerville, TX [*AM radio station call letters*] (BROA)
KOKF .... Edmond, OK [*FM radio station call letters*]
KOKH .... Oklahoma City, OK [*Television station call letters*]
KOKI .... Tulsa, OK [*Television station call letters*]
KOKK .... Huron, SD [*AM radio station call letters*]
KOKL .... Okmulgee, OK [*AM radio station call letters*]
KOKO .... Kerman, CA [*FM radio station call letters*] (BROA)
KO-KO .... Kommerzielle Koordination [*Former East German political party*]
KOKO .... Warrensburg, MO [*AM radio station call letters*]
KOKOM ...... Kokomo, IN [*American Association of Railroads railroad junction routing code*]
KOKP .... Perry, OK [*AM radio station call letters*] (BROA)
KOKR .... Newport, AR [*FM radio station call letters*] (BROA)
KOKS .... Poplar Bluff, MO [*FM radio station call letters*]
KOKU .... Agana, GU [*FM radio station call letters*]
KOKX .... Keokuk, IA [*AM radio station call letters*]
KOKX-FM ... Keokuk, IA [*FM radio station call letters*]
KOKY-FM ... Sherwood, AR [*FM radio station call letters*] (BROA)
KOKZ .... Waterloo, IA [*FM radio station call letters*]
KOL .... Column [*Telegraphy*] (PCTE)
KOL .... King's College, Wilkes-Barre, PA [*OCLC symbol*] (OCLC)
KOL .... Knights of Lithuania (EA)
KOL .... Kollmorgen Corp. [*NYSE symbol*] (SPSG)
KOl .... Olathe Public Library, Olathe, KS [*Library symbol*] [*Library of Congress*] (LCLS)
KOLA .... Keep Old Los Angeles (SAUO)
KOLA .... San Bernardino, CA [*FM radio station call letters*]
KOLAS .... Korean Laboratory Accreditation Scheme (SAUO)
KOLD .... Tucson, AZ [*Television station call letters*]
KOLE .... Port Arthur, TX [*AM radio station call letters*]
KOLF .... Kolff Medical, Inc. (SAUO)
KOLH .... Olathe Commumity Hospital (SAUS)
KOlH .... Olathe Commumity Hospital, Olathe, KS [*Library symbol*] [*Library of Congress*] (LCLS)
KOLI .... King's Own Light Infantry [*Military unit*] [*British*]
KOLI-FM .... Electra, TX [*FM radio station call letters*] (BROA)
KOLIN .... Consortium of East Slovakian Libraries (SAUO)
KOLJL .... Johnson County Law Library Olathe (SAUS)
KOlJL .... Johnson County Law Library, Olathe, KS [*Library symbol*] [*Library of Congress*] (LCLS)
KOLK-FM ... Onawa, IA [*FM radio station call letters*] (RBYB)
KOLL .... Maumelle, AR [*FM radio station call letters*]
KollRE .... Koll Real Estate Group [*Associated Press*] (SAG)
KollRI .... Koll Real Estate Group [*Associated Press*] (SAG)
KOLM .... Rochester, MN [*AM radio station call letters*]
KOlMN ...... Mid-America Nazarene College, Olathe, KS [*Library symbol*] [*Library of Congress*] (LCLS)
Kolmor ...... Kollmorgen Corp. [*Associated Press*] (SAG)
KOLN .... Lincoln, NE [*Television station call letters*]
KOLO .... Reno, NV [*Television station call letters*]
KOLR .... Springfield, MO [*Television station call letters*]
KOLS .... Dodge City, KS [*FM radio station call letters*]
KOLS .... Nogales/International [*Arizona*] [*ICAO location identifier*] (ICLI)
KOLT .... Bridgeport, NE [*FM radio station call letters*] (BROA)
KOLT .... Scottsbluff, NE [*AM radio station call letters*]
KOLT-FM .... Gering, NE [*FM radio station call letters*] (BROA)
KOLT-FM .... Santa Fe, NM [*FM radio station call letters*]
KOLU .... Pasco, WA [*FM radio station call letters*]
KOLV .... Olivia, MN [*FM radio station call letters*]
KOLX .... Barling, AR [*FM radio station call letters*]
KOLY .... Mobridge, SD [*AM radio station call letters*]
KOLY-FM .... Mobridge, SD [*FM radio station call letters*]
Kolze .... Transvaal Reports, by Kolze [*A publication*] (DLA)
KOLZ-FM .... Cheyenne, WY [*FM radio station call letters*] (BROA)
KOM .... Common [*Telegraphy*] (PCTE)
KOM .... Kansas-Oklahoma-Missouri League [*Old baseball league*]
KOM .... Kennedy Space Center Operation instruction (SAUO)
KOM .... Kennedy Space Center Organizational Manual (SAUO)
KOM .... Kentucky, Ohio, Michigan [*Medical library network*]
KOM .... Kilometric Wavelength [*Radio astronomy*]
KOM .... Knight of the Order of Malta (WDAA)
KOM .... Komaba [*Japan*] [*Seismograph station code, US Geological Survey*] [*Closed*] (SEIS)
KOM .... Kombi [*NCIC car model code*]
KOM .... Komitet Opiekunczy Miejski (BJA)
KOM .... Komo-Manda [*Papua New Guinea*] [*Airport symbol*] [*Obsolete*] (OAG)
KoM .... Korea Microforms, Seoul, Korea [*Library symbol*] [*Library of Congress*] (LCLS)
KOM .... KSC [*Kennedy Space Center*] Organizational Manual [*NASA*] (NASA)
KOMA .... Oklahoma City, OK [*AM radio station call letters*]
KOMA .... Omaha/Eppley Air Field [*Nebraska*] [*ICAO location identifier*] (ICLI)
KOMA-FM ... Oklahoma City, OK [*FM radio station call letters*]
Komag ...... Komag, Inc. [*Associated Press*] (SAG)
KOMB .... Fort Scott, KS [*FM radio station call letters*]
KomBeiANT ... Kommentare und Beitraege zum Alten und Neuen Testament [*Duesseldorf*] [*A publication*] (BJA)
KOMC .... Branson, MO [*AM radio station call letters*]
KOMC-FM ... Kimberking City, MO [*FM radio station call letters*] (BROA)
KOME .... San Jose, CA [*FM radio station call letters*]
KOME-AM ... Clovis, CA [*AM radio station call letters*] (BROA)
KOMF .... Komfort Travel Trailer [*NCIC trailer make code*]
KOMG .... Komag [*NASDAQ symbol*]
KOMG .... Ozark, MO [*FM radio station call letters*] (BROA)
KOMH-AM ... Pawhuska, OK [*AM radio station call letters*] (RBYB)
KOMJ-AM ... Omaha, NE [*AM radio station call letters*] (BROA)
KOMO .... Seattle, WA [*AM radio station call letters*]
KOMO-DT ... Seattle, WA [*Television station call letters*] (BROA)
KOMO-TV ... Seattle, WA [*Television station call letters*]
KOMP .... Kompak Camping Trailer [*NCIC trailer make code*]
KOMP .... Las Vegas, NV [*FM radio station call letters*]
KOMPAC .... Keep Our Majority PAC [*Alexandria, VA*] (PACS)
KOMR .... Komar [*NCIC motorcycle make code*]
KOMR .... Sun City, AZ [*FM radio station call letters*] (BROA)
KOMRML ... Kentucky, Ohio, Michigan Regional Medical Library (SAUO)
KOMRMLN ... Kentucky-Ohio-Michigan Regional Medical Library [*Library network*]
KOMS .... Poteau, OK [*FM radio station call letters*]
KOMSAT .... Korean Multi-Purpose Satellite System (SAUO)
KOMSOMOL ... Communist Youth League [*From the Russian*]
KOMT .... Mountain Home, AR [*FM radio station call letters*] (BROA)
KOMU .... Columbia, MO [*Television station call letters*]
KOMW .... Omak, WA [*AM radio station call letters*]
KOMW-FM ... Omak, WA [*FM radio station call letters*]
KOMX .... Pampa, TX [*FM radio station call letters*]
KOMY-AM ... Watsonville, CA [*AM radio station call letters*] (BROA)
KON .... Kongcha [*Publisher*]
kon .... Kongo [*MARC language code*] [*Library of Congress*] (LCCP)
KON .... Kongsberg [*Norway*] [*Seismograph station code, US Geological Survey*] (SEIS)
KON .... Kontum [*South Vietnam*] [*Airport symbol*] (AD)
KONA .... Kennewick, WA [*AM radio station call letters*]
KONA-FM ... Kennewick, WA [*FM radio station call letters*]
KOND-FM ... Cleveland, TX [*FM radio station call letters*] (RBYB)
KONE .... Lubbock, TX [*FM radio station call letters*]
KONG .... Everett, WA [*Television station call letters*]
KONI .... Lanai City, HI [*FM radio station call letters*]
KONJC ...... Kona Junction, NC [*American Association of Railroads railroad junction routing code*]
KONK .... Kon Kwest Manufacturing [*NCIC trailer make code*]
KONO .... Helotes, TX [*FM radio station call letters*] (BROA)
KONO .... San Antonio, TX [*AM radio station call letters*]
KONO-FM ... Fredricksburg, TX [*FM radio station call letters*]
KONP .... Port Angeles, WA [*AM radio station call letters*]
KONQ .... Dodge City, KS [*FM radio station call letters*]
Konst & W Rat App ... Konstam and Ward's Rating Appeals [*1909-12*] [*A publication*] (DLA)
Konst Rat App ... Konstam's Rating Appeals [*1904-08*] [*A publication*] (DLA)
KONT .... Kontiki Camper Trailer [*NCIC trailer make code*]
KONT .... Kooken Trucking [*Common carrier symbol*]
KONT .... Ontario/International [*California*] [*ICAO location identifier*] (ICLI)
KONX .... Elkonix Corp. (SAUO)
KONY .... Saint George, UT [*FM radio station call letters*] (BROA)
KONY .... Washington, UT [*AM radio station call letters*]
KONY-FM ... Kanab, UT [*FM radio station call letters*]
KONZ .... Arizona City, AZ [*FM radio station call letters*]
KOO .... Kongolo [*Zaire*] [*Airport symbol*] (OAG)
KOOC .... Belton, TX [*FM radio station call letters*]

KOOD........ Hays, KS [*Television station call letters*]
KOOG........ Ogden, UT [*Television station call letters*]
KOOI........ Jacksonville, TX [*FM radio station call letters*]
KOOJ........ New Iberia, LA [*FM radio station call letters*] (BROA)
KOOJ........ Riverside, CA [*FM radio station call letters*]
KOOK-FM... Junction, TX [*FM radio station call letters*] (BROA)
KOOKR...... Kookier (ABBR)
KooKR...... Koo Koo Roo, Inc. [*Associated Press*] (SAG)
KOOKST..... Kookiest (ABBR)
KOOL........ Insta Cool Inc. of North America (SAUO)
KOOL........ Phoenix, AZ [*AM radio station call letters*]
KOOL........ Thermagenesis Corp. [*NASDAQ symbol*] (SAG)
KOOL........ Thermogenesis Corp. [*NASDAQ symbol*] (SAG)
KOOL-FM... Phoenix, AZ [*FM radio station call letters*]
KOOO-AM... Dallas, TX [*AM radio station call letters*] (BROA)
KOOP........ drkoop.com, Inc. [*NASDAQ symbol*] (SG)
KOOP........ Hornsby, TX [*FM radio station call letters*]
KOOQ........ North Platte, NE [*AM radio station call letters*]
KOOR........ Clovis, CA [*AM radio station call letters*] (BROA)
Koor........ Koor Industries Ltd. [*Associated Press*] (SAG)
KOOS........ North Bend, OR [*FM radio station call letters*]
KOOT........ Pecos, NM [*FM radio station call letters*] (BROA)
KOOU........ Hardy, AR [*FM radio station call letters*]
KOOV........ Copperas Cove, TX [*FM radio station call letters*]
KOOZ........ Great Falls, MT [*FM radio station call letters*]
KOOZ........ Myrtle Point, OR [*FM radio station call letters*] (BROA)
KOP.......... Cooperate [*Telegraphy*] (PCTE)
KOP.......... Kansallis-Osake-Pankki [*National Capital Stock Bank*] [*Finland*]
KOP.......... Kickoff Point [*Diamond drilling*]
KOP.......... Klippfontain Organic Product Corporation (SAUO)
KOP.......... Kohlensaure-Produktions-Gesellschaft MBH (EFIS)
KOP.......... Kopeck [*Monetary unit in Russia*]
KOP.......... Koppers Co., Inc. (SAUO)
KOP.......... Nakhon Phanom [*Thailand*] [*Airport symbol*] [*Obsolete*] (OAG)
KOPA........ Scottsdale, AZ [*AM radio station call letters*]
KOPB........ Portland, OR [*FM radio station call letters*]
KOPB-TV.... Portland, OR [*Television station call letters*]
KOPC........ Koppers [*Federal Railroad Administration identification code*]
KOPCC...... Kunzang Odsal Palyul Changchub Choling [*An association*] (EA)
KOPD........ Cooperated [*Telegraphy*] (PCTE)
KOPE........ Medford, OR [*FM radio station call letters*]
KOPEC....... Korea National Committee for Pacific Economic Cooperation
KOPF........ Miami/Opa Locka [*Florida*] [*ICAO location identifier*] (ICLI)
KOPG........ Cooperating [*Telegraphy*] (PCTE)
Kopin........ Kopin Corp. [*Associated Press*] (SAG)
KOPN........ Columbia, MO [*FM radio station call letters*]
KOPN........ Cooperation [*Telegraphy*] (PCTE)
KOPN........ Kopin Corp. [*NASDAQ symbol*] (SAG)
KOPP........ Kopperud Transportation [*Common carrier symbol*]
KOPR........ Butte, MT [*FM radio station call letters*]
KOPS........ K (10^3) Operations Per Second (NITA)
KOPS........ Keep Off Pounds Sensibly [*Club*]
KOPS........ Thousands of Operations per Second (NASA)
KOPX........ Oklahoma City, OK [*Television station call letters*] (BROA)
KOPY........ Alice, TX [*AM radio station call letters*] (GDPB)
KOPY........ Alice, TX [*FM radio station call letters*] (GDPB)
KOPY-AM... Alice, TX [*AM radio station call letters*] (RBYB)
KOPY-FM.... Alice, TX [*FM radio station call letters*] (RBYB)
KOQI........ Soquel, CA [*AM radio station call letters*]
KOQL........ Ashland, MO [*FM radio station call letters*] (BROA)
KOQL........ Columbia, MO [*FM radio station call letters*]
KOQO........ Clovis, CA [*AM radio station call letters*]
KOQO........ Fresno, CA [*FM radio station call letters*]
KOR.......... Air Koryo [*North Korea*] [*ICAO designator*] (FAAC)
KOR.......... Contracting Officer
KOR.......... King's Own Royal [*Military unit*] [*British*]
KOR.......... Klein Offset Rotation [*Typography*] (DGA)
KOR.......... Knowledge of Results [*Visual monitoring*]
KOR.......... Koala Resources Ltd. [*Vancouver Stock Exchange symbol*]
KOR.......... Kodak Ortho Resist
KOR.......... Kokoro [*Papua New Guinea*] [*Airport symbol*] (OAG)
KOR.......... Koor Indus Ltd ADS [*NYSE symbol*] (TTSB)
KOR.......... Koor Industries Ltd. [*NYSE symbol*] (SAG)
KOR.......... Koracorp Industries, Inc. (SAUO)
KOR.......... Koran (ROG)
KOR.......... Korando [*NCIC car model code*]
Kor.......... Korea (VRA)
Kor.......... Korean (DIAR)
kor.......... Korean [*MARC language code*] [*Library of Congress*] (LCCP)
KOR.......... Koror [*Palau Islands*] [*Seismograph station code, US Geological Survey*] [*Closed*] (SEIS)
KOR.......... Republic of Korea [*ANSI three-letter standard code*] (CNC)
KOR.......... Seaplane [*Russian symbol*]
KOR.......... Social Self-Defense Committee [*Also, SSDC*] [*Poland*] (PD)
KORA........ Bryan, TX [*FM radio station call letters*]
KORB........ Bettendorf, IA [*FM radio station call letters*] (RBYB)
KORBL...... Korblex, CA [*American Association of Railroads railroad junction routing code*]
KORC........ Waldport, OR [*AM radio station call letters*]
KORD........ Chicago/O'Hare [*Illinois*] [*ICAO location identifier*] (ICLI)
KORD-FM... Richland, WA [*FM radio station call letters*]
KORDI....... Korea Ocean Research and Development Institute (USDC)
KORE........ Kinetic Analysis Using Over-Relaxation [*FORTRAN computer program*] [*Physical chemistry*]
KORE........ Springfield-Eugene, OR [*AM radio station call letters*]
Korea........ Korea Fund, Inc. [*Associated Press*] (SAG)
KoreaElc.... Korea Electric Power Corp. [*Associated Press*] (SAG)
KoreaEqt.... Korea Equity Fund [*Associated Press*] (SAG)
Korea Inf Sci Soc Rev... Korea Information Science Society Review (SAUO)
KoreaInv.... Korean Investment Fund [*Associated Press*] (SAG)
Korea LR... Korea Law Review [*A publication*] (DLA)
KoreaM..... Korea Mobile Telecommunications [*Associated Press*] (SAG)
Korean J Comp L... Korean Journal of Comparative Law [*A publication*] (DLA)
Korean J Int'l L... Korean Journal of International Law [*A publication*] (DLA)
Korean J of Internat L... Korean Journal of International Law [*A publication*] (DLA)
Korean L.... Korean Law [*A publication*] (DLA)
KorEIN....... Korea Electric Power Corp. [*Associated Press*] (SAG)
KORF........ Norfolk/Norfolk Regional Airport [*Virginia*] [*ICAO location identifier*] (ICLI)
KORG........ Anaheim, CA [*AM radio station call letters*]
KORI........ Mansfield, LA [*FM radio station call letters*]
KORK........ Las Vegas, NV [*AM radio station call letters*]
KORL........ Honolulu, HI [*AM radio station call letters*]
KORL........ Orlando [*Florida*] [*ICAO location identifier*] (ICLI)
KORL-FM... Honolulu, HI [*FM radio station call letters*] (RBYB)
KORMEX.... Korea Monsoon Experiment (SAUO)
KORN........ Mitchell, SD [*AM radio station call letters*]
KORO........ Corpus Christi, TX [*Television station call letters*]
KOROC....... Keep Out of Reach of Children (DI)
KORP........ Charles, [*J. W.*] Financial Services [*NASDAQ symbol*] (SAG)
KORP........ Charles (JW) Finl Svcs [*NASDAQ symbol*] (TTSB)
KORP........ Corporate Management Group, Inc. (SAUO)
KORQ........ Winters, TX [*FM radio station call letters*] (BROA)
KORQ-FM... Abilene, TX [*FM radio station call letters*]
KORR........ American Falls, ID [*FM radio station call letters*] (RBYB)
KORR........ King's Own Royal Regiment [*Military unit*] [*British*]
KORSTIC.... Korea Scientific and Technical Information Centre (NITA)
KORSTIC.... Korea Scientific and Technological Information Center [*INSPEC operator*]
KORT........ Grangeville, ID [*AM radio station call letters*]
KORT-FM.... Grangeville, ID [*FM radio station call letters*]
KORV........ Oroville, CA [*AM radio station call letters*]
KORY........ Kory Farm Equipment [*NCIC trailer make code*]
KOS.......... Kent University On-Line System [*Computer science*] (PDAA)
KO's......... Knockout Drops [*A drug producing unconsciousness*] [*Slang*]
KOS.......... Kosmodemyansk [*Former USSR*] [*Seismograph station code, US Geological Survey*] [*Closed*] (SEIS)
KOS.......... Kosovaair [*Yugoslavia*] [*ICAO designator*] (FAAC)
KOSA........ Odessa, TX [*Television station call letters*]
KOSAA....... Korea Shipping Agencies Association (SAUO)
KOSAMI..... Korea Society for the Advancement of Machine Industry (SAUO)
KOSAMP.... Kuwait Oil-Fire Smoke Atmospheric Measurements Program (SAUO)
KOSB........ King's Own Scottish Borderers [*Military unit*] [*British*]
KOSB-FM... Perry, OK [*FM radio station call letters*] (BROA)
KOSC........ Oscoda/Wurtsmith Air Force Base [*Michigan*] [*ICAO location identifier*] (ICLI)
KOSCO...... Korea Oil Storage Company (SAUO)
KOSCOT..... Cosmetics for the Community of Tomorrow [*Acronym used as brand name*]
KOSE........ Osceola, AR [*AM radio station call letters*]
KOSE........ Wilson, AR [*AM radio station call letters*] (BROA)
KOSEF....... Korea Science and Engineering Foundation (SAUO)
KOSE-FM... Osceola, AR [*FM radio station call letters*]
KOSG........ Camden, AR [*AM radio station call letters*]
KOSH........ Osawatomie State Hospital, Osawatomie, KS [*Library symbol*] [*Library of Congress*] (LCLS)
KOSI........ Denver, CO [*FM radio station call letters*]
KOSI........ Kaiser Optical Systems Inc. (SAUO)
KOSJ........ Nebraska City, NE [*FM radio station call letters*] (RBYB)
KOSM........ Cascade International Inc. (SAUO)
KOSN........ Kosan Biosciences [*NASDAQ symbol*]
KoSNU...... Seoul National University, Seoul, Korea [*Library symbol*] [*Library of Congress*] (LCLS)
KOSO........ Patterson, CA [*FM radio station call letters*]
KOSP........ Kos Pharmaceuticals
KOSP........ Willard, MO [*FM radio station call letters*]
KOSR-AM... Omaha, NE [*AM radio station call letters*] (RBYB)
KOSS........ Koss Corp. [*NASDAQ symbol*] (SAG)
KOSS-FM... Rosamond, CA [*FM radio station call letters*] (BROA)
KOST........ Koster Manufacturing [*NCIC trailer make code*]
KOST........ Los Angeles, CA [*FM radio station call letters*]
KOSU........ Stillwater, OK [*FM radio station call letters*]
KOSY........ Texarkana, AR [*AM radio station call letters*] (BROA)
KOSY-FM.... Spanish Fork, UT [*FM radio station call letters*] (BROA)
KoSYU...... Yonsei University, Seoul, Korea [*Library symbol*] [*Library of Congress*] (LCLS)
KOSZ........ Rio Rancho, NM [*FM radio station call letters*] (BROA)
KOSZ........ Vermillion, SD [*AM radio station call letters*]
KOSZ-FM... Idaho Falls, ID [*FM radio station call letters*]
KOT.......... Kitchener, Ontario, Canada [*Amtrak rail station code*]
KOT.......... Knowledge of Occupations Test [*Psychology*] (DAVI)
KOT.......... Kotlik [*Alaska*] [*Airport symbol*] (OAG)
KOTA........ Kota Shipping Corporation [*Common carrier symbol*]
KOTA........ Rapid City, SD [*AM radio station call letters*]
KOTAR....... Korean Tactical Range (SAUO)
KOTA-TV.... Rapid City, SD [*Television station call letters*]
KOTB........ Evanston, WY [*FM radio station call letters*]
KOTC........ Keep on Trucking Company [*Common carrier symbol*]

KOTC .... Kennett, MO [*AM radio station call letters*] (RBYB)
KOTC .... Kuwait Oil Tanker Co. (BUAC)
KOTD .... Plattsmouth, NE [*AM radio station call letters*]
KOTD-FM ... Plattsmouth, NE [*FM radio station call letters*]
KOTE .... Eureka, KS [*FM radio station call letters*]
KOTI .... Klamath Falls, OR [*Television station call letters*]
KOTK .... Portland, OR [*AM radio station call letters*] (RBYB)
KOTL .... Kiss on The Lips (SAUS)
KOTM .... Ottumwa, IA [*FM radio station call letters*]
KOTN .... Keep on Truckin' News [*A publication*] (EAAP)
KOTN .... Pine Bluff, AR [*AM radio station call letters*]
KOTO .... Telluride, CO [*FM radio station call letters*]
KOTR .... Cambria, CA [*FM radio station call letters*]
KOTR .... King of the Road Trailer Company [*NCIC trailer make code*]
KOTRA ...... Korea Trade Promotion Center (EA)
KOTRA ...... Korea Trade Promotion Co. (BUAC)
KOTS .... Deming, NM [*AM radio station call letters*]
KOTT .... Otterville, MO [*FM radio station call letters*]
KOtU .... Ottawa University, Ottawa, KS [*Library symbol*] [*Library of Congress*] (LCLS)
KOTV .... Tulsa, OK [*Television station call letters*]
KOTY .... Mason, TX [*FM radio station call letters*] (BROA)
KOTZ .... Kotzebue, AK [*AM radio station call letters*]
Kotze .... Kotze's Transvaal High Court Reports [*South Africa*] [*A publication*] (DLA)
Kotze & B... Supreme Court Reports, Transvaal [*1885-88*] [*South Africa*] [*A publication*] (DLA)
Kotze & Barb... Supreme Court Reports, Transvaal [*1885-88*] [*South Africa*] [*A publication*] (DLA)
Kotze & Barber... Transvaal Court Reports [*A publication*] (DLA)
KOU .... Koke [*Language symbol*] (ETLW)
KOU .... Koula Moutou [*Gabon*] [*Airport symbol*] (OAG)
KOU .... Koumac [*New Caledonia*] [*Seismograph station code, US Geological Survey*] (SEIS)
KOUL .... Sinton, TX [*FM radio station call letters*]
KOUN .... Kountryaire Travel Trailer [*NCIC trailer make code*]
KOUNT ...... Kountze, TX [*American Association of Railroads railroad junction routing code*]
KOURIR ..... Association for Parents of Children with Juvenile Chronic Arthritis (SAUO)
KOUT .... Rapid City, SD [*FM radio station call letters*]
KOUU .... American Falls, ID [*FM radio station call letters*]
KOUU .... Pocatello, ID [*AM radio station call letters*] (BROA)
KOUZ .... Alexandria, LA [*FM radio station call letters*] (RBYB)
KOV .... Key Operated Valve
KOV .... Knock Out Vessel (EEVL)
Kov .... N. A. Kovach, Los Angeles, CA [*Library symbol*] [*Library of Congress*] (LCLS)
KOVA-FM ... Rosenberg, TX [*FM radio station call letters*] (BROA)
KOVC .... Valley City, ND [*AM radio station call letters*]
KOVC-FM ... Valley City, ND [*FM radio station call letters*]
KOVE .... Galveston, TX [*FM radio station call letters*] (BROA)
KOVE .... Lander, WY [*AM radio station call letters*]
KOVE-FM ... Port Arthur, TX [*FM radio station call letters*] (BROA)
KOVO .... Provo, UT [*AM radio station call letters*]
KOvpJ .... Johnson County Community College, Overland Park, KS [*Library symbol*] [*Library of Congress*] (LCLS)
KovpST ...... St. Thomas High School, Overland Park, KS [*Library symbol*] [*Library of Congress*] (LCLS)
KOVR .... Stockton, CA [*Television station call letters*]
KOVT .... Silver City, NM [*Television station call letters*]
Kow .... Coefficient of Octanolwater Partition (GNE)
KOW .... Ghanzhou [*China*] [*Airport symbol*] (OAG)
KOW .... Keen on Waller [*A coterie of women admirers of British stage actor, Lewis Waller (1860-1915)*] (ROG)
KOW .... Knock-Off Wheels [*Automotive accessory*]
KOW .... Kowkash Gold [*Vancouver Stock Exchange symbol*]
KOWACO .... Korea Water Resources Development Corporation (SAUO)
KOWB .... Laramie, WY [*AM radio station call letters*]
KOWF .... Escondido, CA [*FM radio station call letters*]
KOWL .... South Lake Tahoe, CA [*AM radio station call letters*]
KOWO .... Waseca, MN [*AM radio station call letters*]
KOWS .... Texarkana, TX [*AM radio station call letters*] (BROA)
KOWS-FM... Ashdown, AR [*FM radio station call letters*] (BROA)
KOWW-AM... Blue Springs, MO [*AM radio station call letters*] (RBYB)
KOWZ .... Waseca, MN [*AM radio station call letters*] (GDPB)
KOWZ-FM... Blooming Prairie, MN [*FM radio station call letters*] (RBYB)
KOX .... Keyboard Operated Transmission [*Computer science*] (VLIE)
KoX .... Knights of Xenu (SAUO)
KOX .... Kokonao [*West Irian, Indonesia*] [*Airport symbol*] (AD)
KOXE .... Brownwood, TX [*FM radio station call letters*]
KOXR .... Oxnard, CA [*AM radio station call letters*]
KOXZ-FM ... Comanche, TX [*FM radio station call letters*] (BROA)
KOY .... Koyama [*Japan*] [*Seismograph station code, US Geological Survey*] [*Closed*] (SEIS)
KOY .... Olga Bay [*Alaska*] [*Airport symbol*] (OAG)
KOY .... Phoenix, AZ [*AM radio station call letters*]
KOYE .... Frankston, TX [*FM radio station call letters*] (BROA)
KOYE .... Laredo, TX [*FM radio station call letters*]
KOYL .... Plainview, TX [*AM radio station call letters*] (GDPB)
KOYLI ...... King's Own Yorkshire Light Infantry [*Military unit*] [*British*]
KOYN .... Paris, TX [*FM radio station call letters*]
KOYT .... Tucson, AZ [*FM radio station call letters*] (BROA)
KOZ .... Kozyrevsk [*Former USSR*] [*Seismograph station code, US Geological Survey*] (SEIS)
KOZ .... Ouzinkie, AK [*Location identifier*] [*FAA*] (FAAL)
KOZA .... Odessa, TX [*AM radio station call letters*]
KOZE .... Lewiston, ID [*AM radio station call letters*]
KOZE-FM.... Lewiston, ID [*FM radio station call letters*]
KOZI .... Chelan, WA [*AM radio station call letters*]
KOZI-FM .... Chelan, WA [*FM radio station call letters*]
KOZJ .... Joplin, MO [*Television station call letters*]
KOZK .... Springfield, MO [*Television station call letters*]
KOZL-FM.... New Boston, TX [*FM radio station call letters*] (BROA)
KOZN .... Bellevue, NE [*AM radio station call letters*] (BROA)
KOZN-FM ... Kansas City, MO [*FM radio station call letters*] (BROA)
KOZO-FM ... Branson, MO [*FM radio station call letters*] (RBYB)
KOZQ .... Waynesville, MO [*AM radio station call letters*]
KOZT .... Fort Bragg, CA [*FM radio station call letters*]
KOZX .... Cabool, MO [*FM radio station call letters*]
KOZY .... Gering, NE [*FM radio station call letters*] (BROA)
KOZY .... Grand Rapids, MN [*AM radio station call letters*]
KOZY .... Kozy Coach Company [*NCIC trailer make code*]
KOZZ .... Reno, NV [*AM radio station call letters*]
KOZZ-FM.... Reno, NV [*FM radio station call letters*]
Kp .... Body Potassium [*Medicine*] (EDAA)
KP .... Commission Percentage [*Travel industry*] (TVEL)
KP .... Democratic People's Republic of Korea [*ANSI two-letter standard code*] (CNC)
kp .... geomagnetic planetary index (SAUS)
KP .... Hot Pack [*Medicine*] (EDAA)
K-P .... Kaiser-Permanente [*Diet*]
kp .... Kaliophilite [*CIPW classification*] [*Geology*]
KP .... Kaufmann-Peterson Base [*Medicine*] (DMAA)
KP .... Keep [*Telegraphy*] (PCTE)
KP .... Kensington Palace [*British*]
KP .... Keogh Plan [*Business term*]
KP .... Keratic Precipitate (SAUS)
KP .... Keratitic Precipitate [*Ophthalmology*]
KP .... Keratitis Punctata [*Ophthalmology*]
KP .... Keskustapuolue [*Center Party of Finland*] [*Political party*] (PPW)
KP .... Keyboard Perforator
KP .... Key Personnel
KP .... Key Production Co. [*NYSE symbol*] (SAG)
KP .... Key Pulsing
KP .... Keypunch [*Computer science*]
KP .... Kickpipe [*Building construction*]
KP .... Kick Plate
KP .... Kidder, Peabody & Co. (EFIS)
KP .... Kidney Pore
KP .... Kidney Protein [*Nephrology*] (DAVI)
KP .... Kidney Punch [*Medicine*] (DAVI)
KP .... Kids of Preachers
KP .... Killed Parenteral [*Vaccine*] [*Immunology*] (DAVI)
KP .... Kill Probability (MCD)
KP .... Kilometer Post
KP .... Kilopond
kp .... Kilopulse
KP .... Kinetic Percolation
KP .... Kinetic Potential
KP .... King Post
KP .... King's Parade [*British*] (DSUE)
KP .... King's Pawn [*Chess*] (ADA)
KP .... King's Pleasure [*British*]
KP .... King's Proctor [*British*]
KP .... Kitchen Patrol [*Army*]
KP .... Kitchen Police [*Kitchen helpers*] [*Military*]
KP .... Kitchen Punishment (SAUO)
KP .... Klebsiella Pneumoniae [*Genus of microorganism*] (DAVI)
KP .... Klein Paradox [*Physics*]
KP .... Knight of Pius IX
KP .... Knight of St. Patrick [*British*]
KP .... Knights of Pythias (EA)
KP .... Knotty Pine
KP .... Knowledge Park at Penn State Erie (RCD)
KP .... Kodak Process Resist [*Photography*] (DICI)
KP .... Komma Proodeftikon [*Progressive Party*] [*Greek*] [*Political party*] (PPE)
KP .... Kommunistesch Partei [*Communist Party*] [*Luxembourg*] [*Political party*] (PPE)
KP .... Kommunistische Partei [*Communist Party*] [*German*] [*Political party*]
KP .... Korsakoff's Psychosis [*Medicine*] (EDAA)
KP .... Kurdish Heritage Foundation of America
KP .... Kurdish Program (EA)
KP .... Kurie Plot [*Physics*]
kp .... low magnetic activity (SAUS)
KP .... North Korea [*Internet country code*]
KP .... Papua New Guinea [*IYRU nationality code*] (IYR)
KP .... Safair [*ICAO designator*] (AD)
KPA .... Innkeepers USA Trust [*NYSE symbol*] (SAG)
KPA .... Kalenjin Political Alliance (SAUO)
KPA .... Kansas Pharmaceutical Association (SAUO)
KPA .... Kansas Press Association (EARSL)
KPA .... Kappa Networks, Inc. [*AMEX symbol*] (COMM)
KPA .... Kentucky Pharmaceutical Association (SAUO)
KPA .... Key Personnel Analysis (TIMI)
KPA .... Key-Process Area (AAEL)
KPA .... Key Pulse Adapter [*Telecommunications*] (TEL)
KPA .... Kidney Plasminogen Activator [*Anticlotting agent*]

kPa .... Kilopascal
KPA .... Klystron Power Amplifier
KPA .... Kopiago [*Papua New Guinea*] [*Airport symbol*] (OAG)
KPA .... Korean People's Army [*Democratic People's Republic of Korea*] (BUAC)
KPA .... Korea Procurement Agency
KPA .... Kraft Paper Association [*Later, API*] (EA)
KPAB .... Keep Port Aransas Beautiful (EARSL)
KPAC .... KPAC [*Dallas, TX*] (PACS)
KPAC .... San Antonio, TX [*FM radio station call letters*]
KPAE .... Erwinville, LA [*FM radio station call letters*]
KPAE .... Everett/Snohomish County-Paine Field [*Washington*] [*ICAO location identifier*] (ICLI)
KPAG .... Pagosa Springs, CO [*AM radio station call letters*]
KPAK .... Alva, OK [*FM radio station call letters*] (BROA)
KPAL-AM .... North Little Rock, AR [*AM radio station call letters*] (RBYB)
KPAM .... Panama City/Tyndall Air Force Base [*Florida*] [*ICAO location identifier*] (ICLI)
KPAM .... Troutdale, OR [*AM radio station call letters*] (BROA)
KPAN .... Hereford, TX [*AM radio station call letters*]
KP & D .... Kick Plate and Drip (AAG)
KPAN-FM .... Hereford, TX [*FM radio station call letters*]
KPAR .... Granbury, TX [*AM radio station call letters*]
KParSH .... Parsons State Hospital, Parsons, KS [*Library symbol*] [*Library of Congress*] (LCLS)
KPAS .... Fabens, TX [*FM radio station call letters*]
KPAT .... Orcutt, CA [*FM radio station call letters*] (BROA)
KPAT-FM .... San Luis Obispo, CA [*FM radio station call letters*] (BROA)
KPAW .... Fort Collins, CO [*FM radio station call letters*] (RBYB)
KPAWU .... Kenya Plantation and Agricultural Workers Union (BUAC)
KPAX .... Missoula, MT [*Television station call letters*]
KPAY .... Chico, CA [*AM radio station call letters*]
KPAZ .... Phoenix, AZ [*Television station call letters*]
KPB .... Kalium [*Potassium*] Phosphate Buffer [*Biochemistry*] (DAVI)
KPB .... Kenai Peninsula Borough [*Alaska*]
KPB .... Kenya Pyrethrum Board (BUAC)
KPB .... Ketophenylbutazone [*or Kebuzone*] [*An antirheumatic*] (DAVI)
KPB .... Kommunistische Partij van Belgie [*Communist Party of Belgium*] [*See also PCB*] [*Political party*] (PPE)
KPB .... Party of Communists of Belarus [*Political party*] (PSAP)
KPB .... Point Baker, AK [*Location identifier*] [*FAA*] (FAAL)
KPBA .... Pine Bluff, AR [*AM radio station call letters*]
KPBB .... Brownfield, TX [*FM radio station call letters*] (BROA)
KPBC .... Garland, TX [*AM radio station call letters*]
KPBC-AM .... Lake Oswego, OR [*AM radio station call letters*] (BROA)
KPBE-FM .... Brownwood, TX [*FM radio station call letters*] (BROA)
KPBF .... Pine Bluff/Grider Field [*Arkansas*] [*ICAO location identifier*] (ICLI)
KPBG .... Plattsburg/Plattsburg Air Force Base [*New York*] [*ICAO location identifier*] (ICLI)
KPBI .... Greenwood, AR [*AM radio station call letters*]
KPBI .... West Palm Beach/Palm Beach International [*Florida*] [*ICAO location identifier*] (ICLI)
KPBL .... Hemphill, TX [*AM radio station call letters*] (GDPB)
KPBL-AM .... Hemphill, TX [*AM radio station call letters*] (BROA)
KPBM-FM .... McCamey, TX [*FM radio station call letters*] (BROA)
KPBQ .... Pine Bluff, AR [*FM radio station call letters*]
KPBRS .... Korean Peace Bioreserves System
KPBS .... San Diego, CA [*Television station call letters*]
KPBS-FM .... San Diego, CA [*FM radio station call letters*]
KPBX .... Spokane, WA [*FM radio station call letters*]
KPC .... Kappa Resources [*Vancouver Stock Exchange symbol*]
KPC .... Kembata People's Congress [*Ethiopia*]
KPC .... Kentucky Power Co. [*NYSE symbol*] (SAG)
KPC .... Kentucky Pwr 8.72% Sr'A'Debs [*NYSE symbol*] (TTSB)
KPC .... Keratinocyte Precursor Cell
KPC .... Keratoconus Posticus Circumscriptus [*Medicine*] (DMAA)
KPC .... Ketchikan Pulp Corporation (ALAC)
KPC .... Keyboard/Printer Control [*Computer science*]
KPC .... Keyboard Priority Controller [*Computer science*] (HGAA)
KPC .... Key Personnel Course (MCD)
KPC .... Key Product Characteristic
KPC .... Keypunch Cabinet [*Computer science*]
KPC .... Khapcheranga [*Former USSR*] [*Seismograph station code, US Geological Survey*] (SEIS)
kpc .... Kiloparsec [*Astronomy*]
KPC .... Kilo Parsecs [*Astronomy*] (GOBB)
KPC .... Kinetic Process Control
KPC .... Klystron Phase Control
KPC .... Knights of Peter Claver (EA)
KPC .... Koblenz Procurement Center [*Federal Republic of Germany*] [*Military*] (NATG)
KPC .... Kodak Photofabrication Center
KPC .... Kohn Problem Checklist (TES)
KPC .... Korean Productivity Center (SAUO)
KPC .... Korean Productivity Council (SAUO)
KPC .... Korea Productivity Centre (BUAC)
KPC .... Kuwait Petroleum Corporation (SAUO)
KPC .... Paducah Junior College, Paducah, KY [*OCLC symbol*] (OCLC)
KPC .... Port Clarence [*Alaska*] [*Airport symbol*] (OAG)
KPC .... Port Clarence, AK [*Location identifier*] [*FAA*] (FAAL)
KPCB-TV .... Snyder, TX [*TV station call letters*] (RBYB)
KPCC .... Pasadena, CA [*FM radio station call letters*]
KPCH .... Dubach, LA [*FM radio station call letters*]
KPCI .... Key Production [*NASDAQ symbol*] (TTSB)
KPCI .... Key Production Co., Inc. [*NASDAQ symbol*] (NQ)
KPCK .... Kopeck (ABBR)
KPC/KSC .... Kohn Problem Checklist/Kohn Social Competence Scale [*Test*] (TMMY)
KPCL .... Farmington, NM [*FM radio station call letters*]
KPCMS .... Kodak Precision Color Management System (SAUS)
KPCO .... Quincy, CA [*AM radio station call letters*]
KPCR .... Bowling Green, MO [*AM radio station call letters*]
KPCR-FM .... Bowling Green, MO [*FM radio station call letters*]
KPCU .... Kenyan Planters Co-Operative Union (BUAC)
KPCW .... Park City, UT [*FM radio station call letters*]
KPCZ .... K and P Cartage [*Intermodal trailer symbol*]
KPD .... Comprehend [*Telegraphy*] (PCTE)
KPD .... Kennedy Program Directive [*NASA*] (NASA)
KPD .... Knowledge-Based Producibility Decision-Maker [*Productivity technology*] (RDA)
KPD .... Kommunistische Partei Deutschlands [*Communist Party of Germany*] [*Political party*] (PPW)
KPDB .... Big Lake, TX [*FM radio station call letters*] (BROA)
KPDES .... Kentucky Pollutant Discharge Elimination System (SAUO)
KPDL .... Kyocera Page Description Language (SAUS)
KPDL .... Kyocera Printer Description Language [*Computer science*] (VLIE)
KPD-ML .... Kommunistische Partei Deutschlands/Marxisten-Leninisten [*Communist Party of Germany/Marxists-Leninists*] [*Political party*] (PPW)
KPDQ .... Portland, OR [*AM radio station call letters*]
KPDQ-FM .... Portland, OR [*FM radio station call letters*]
KPDR .... Korean People's Democratic Republic (BUAC)
KPDR .... Wheeler, TX [*FM radio station call letters*]
KPDU .... Kaffa People's Democratic Union [*Ethiopia*] [*Political party*] (EY)
KPDX .... Portland/International [*Oregon*] [*ICAO location identifier*] (ICLI)
KPDX .... Vancouver, WA [*Television station call letters*]
KPE .... Kelman Phakoemulsification [*Ophthalmology*] (DAVI)
KPE .... Key Point Error [*Computer science*] (IAA)
KPE .... Kilman Phacoemulsification [*Medicine*] (MEDA)
kpe .... Kpelle [*MARC language code*] [*Library of Congress*] (LCCP)
KPEB .... Huntsville, UT [*FM radio station call letters*] (BROA)
KPEJ .... Odessa, TX [*Television station call letters*]
KPEK-FM .... Albuquerque, NM [*FM radio station call letters*] (RBYB)
KPEL .... Abbeville, LA [*FM radio station call letters*] (BROA)
KPEL .... Lafayette, LA [*AM radio station call letters*]
KPEL-FM .... Erath, LA [*FM radio station call letters*]
KPEN .... Homer, AK [*FM radio station call letters*] (GDPB)
KPENC .... Korean Centre of International PEN (EAIO)
KPEN-FM .... Soldotna, AK [*FM radio station call letters*]
KPER .... Hobbs, NM [*FM radio station call letters*]
KPET .... Lamesa, TX [*AM radio station call letters*]
KPEZ .... Austin, TX [*FM radio station call letters*]
KPF .... Kangaroo Protection Foundation (EA)
KPF .... Katadyn Pocket Filter
KPF .... Kenya Patriotic Front [*Political party*] (BUAC)
KPF .... Key Pulse on Front Cord [*Telecommunications*] (TEL)
KPF .... Knowledge Presentation Format [*Computer science*] (GART)
KPF .... Kohn Pedersen Fox [*New York, NY*] [*Architectural firm*]
KPF .... Komba [*Language symbol*] (ETLW)
KPFA .... Berkeley, CA [*FM radio station call letters*]
KPFA .... Knackery and Pet Food Association [*Australia*]
KPFB .... Berkeley, CA [*FM radio station call letters*]
KPFC .... Kuwait Pacific Finance Company (SAUO)
KPFC-FM .... Callisburg, TX [*FM radio station call letters*] (BROA)
KPFK .... Los Angeles, CA [*FM radio station call letters*]
KPFM .... Mountain Home, AR [*FM radio station call letters*]
KPFN-FM .... Seward, AK [*FM radio station call letters*] (BROA)
KPFR .... Pine Grove, OR [*FM radio station call letters*] (BROA)
KPFSM .... King's Police and Fire Services Medal for Distinguished Service [*British*]
KPFSM .... King's Police & Fire Services Medal for Gallantry [*British*] (WDAA)
KPFT .... Houston, TX [*FM radio station call letters*]
KPFX .... Fargo, ND [*FM radio station call letters*]
KPG .... Keeping
KPG .... King Power Intl. [*AMEX symbol*] (SG)
KPG .... Kurupung [*Guyana*] [*Airport symbol*] (OAG)
KPGA .... Kansas Personnel and Guidance Association (SAUO)
KPGA .... Kentucky Personnel and Guidance Association (SAUO)
KPGA .... Kentucky Propane Gas Association (EARSL)
KPGB .... Pryor, MT [*FM radio station call letters*] (BROA)
KPGE .... Page, AZ [*AM radio station call letters*]
KPGG .... Ashdown, AR [*FM radio station call letters*] (BROA)
KPGM .... Pawhuska, OK [*AM radio station call letters*] (BROA)
KPGR .... Pleasant Grove, UT [*FM radio station call letters*]
KPGX .... Kentucky Processing [*Private rail car owner code*]
KPH .... Kaena Point [*Hawaii*] [*Seismograph station code, US Geological Survey*] [*Closed*] (SEIS)
KPH .... Keystrokes Per Hour (NITA)
kph .... Kilometers per Hour
KPH .... Know Problems of Hydrocephalus (EA)
KPH .... Komunisticka Partija Hrvatske [*Communist Party of Croatia*] [*Political party*]
KPH .... Ktav Publishing House, Inc. [*New York*] (BJA)
KPH .... Pauloff Harbor/Sanak Island, AK [*Location identifier*] [*FAA*] (FAAL)
KPhA .... Kansas Pharmacists Association (SRA)
KPHA .... Kansas Public Health Association (SAUO)
KPhA .... Kentucky Pharmacists Association (SRA)
KPHF .... Newport News/Patrick Henry [*Virginia*] [*ICAO location identifier*] (ICLI)
KPHF .... Phoenix, AZ [*FM radio station call letters*]

KPHL .... Philadelphia/International [*Pennsylvania*] [*ICAO location identifier*] (ICLI)
KPHN .... Kansas City, MO [*AM radio station call letters*] (BROA)
KPHN .... Pittsburg, KS [*AM radio station call letters*]
KPHN .... Port Huron [*Michigan*] [*ICAO location identifier*] (ICLI)
KPHO .... Phoenix, AZ [*Television station call letters*]
KPHO-DT .... Phoenix, AZ [*Television station call letters*] (BROA)
KPHR .... Milbank, SD [*FM radio station call letters*]
KPHR-FM ... Ortonville, MN [*FM radio station call letters*] (BROA)
KPHS-FM ... Plains, TX [*FM radio station call letters*] (RBYB)
KPHT .... Kindred, ND [*FM radio station call letters*] (RBYB)
KPHX .... Phoenix, AZ [*AM radio station call letters*]
KPHX .... Phoenix/Sky Harbor International [*Arizona*] [*ICAO location identifier*] (ICLI)
KPHZ .... Holbrook, AZ [*Television station call letters*] (BROA)
KPI .... Kallikrein-Protease Inhibitor [*Medicine*] (EDAA)
KPI .... Kapit [*Malaysia*] [*Airport symbol*] (OAG)
KPI .... Karyopyknotic Index [*Cytology*]
KPI .... Kernel Programming Interface [*Computer science*]
KPI .... Key Performance Indicator (EBF)
KPI .... Killearn Properties, Inc. [*AMEX symbol*] (SPSG)
KPI .... King Pin Inclination [*Automotive engineering*]
kpi .... Kips [*Thousands of Pounds*] per Square Inch
KPI .... Kontron Personal Instrumentation [*Kontron Electronics*] (NITA)
KPI .... Kunitz Protease Inhibitor [*Medicine*]
KPI .... Kuwait Petroleum International (BUAC)
KPI .... KWIK Products International Corp. [*Vancouver Stock Exchange symbol*]
KPIB .... Key Points Intelligence Branch (SAUO)
KPIC .... Key Phrase in Context
KPIC .... Roseburg, OR [*Television station call letters*]
KPICO .... Kuwait Pharmaceutical Industries Co. (BUAC)
KPIE .... St. Petersburg/Clearwater International [*Florida*] [*ICAO location identifier*] (ICLI)
KPIG .... Freedom, CA [*FM radio station call letters*]
KPIK .... Beebe, AR [*FM radio station call letters*]
KPIN-FM .... Pinedale, WY [*FM radio station call letters*] (RBYB)
KPIR .... Granbury, TX [*AM radio station call letters*] (BROA)
KPIT .... Pittsburgh/Greater Pittsburgh [*Pennsylvania*] [*ICAO location identifier*] (ICLI)
KPIX .... San Francisco, CA [*AM radio station call letters*] (RBYB)
KPIX-DT .... San Francisco, CA [*Television station call letters*] (BROA)
KPIX-FM .... San Francisco, CA [*FM radio station call letters*] (RBYB)
KPIX-TV ..... San Francisco, CA [*Television station call letters*]
KPJ .... Komunisticka Partija Jugoslavije [*Communist Party of Yugoslavia*] [*Political party*] (PPE)
KPJC-AM .... Paris, TX [*AM radio station call letters*] (BROA)
KPK .... Communist Party of Kazakhstan [*Political party*] (BUAC)
KPK .... Kanaka Peak [*California*] [*Seismograph station code, US Geological Survey*] (SEIS)
KPK .... Kapok (ABBR)
KPK .... Kappa Phi Kappa [*Fraternity*]
KPK .... Parks [*Alaska*] [*Airport symbol*] (OAG)
KPK .... Parks, AK [*Location identifier*] [*FAA*] (FAAL)
KPKE .... Gunnison, CO [*AM radio station call letters*] (GDPB)
KPKE-AM ... Gunnison, CO [*AM radio station call letters*] (RBYB)
KPKK .... Oakley, UT [*FM radio station call letters*] (BROA)
KPKX .... Livingston, MT [*FM radio station call letters*] (RBYB)
KPKY .... Pocatello, ID [*FM radio station call letters*]
KPL .... Compel [*Telegraphy*] (PCTE)
KPL .... Copeland Resources [*Vancouver Stock Exchange symbol*]
KPL .... Kalamazoo Public Library
KPL .... Key Personnel Locator (SAUO)
KPL .... Khao San Pathet Lao [*News agency*] [*Laos*] (FEA)
KPL .... Kick Plate [*Building construction*]
KPL .... Killearn Properties [*AMEX symbol*] (TTSB)
KPL .... Knoxville Public Library (SAUO)
KPL .... Kommunistisch Partei vu Leetzebuerg [*Communist Party of Luxembourg*] [*Political party*] (PPW)
KPl .... Kuwait Petroleum Corporation (SAUO)
K-PL .... Potassium-Plasma [*Biochemistry*] (DAVI)
KPLA .... Columbia, MO [*FM radio station call letters*] (RBYB)
KPLC .... Lake Charles, LA [*Television station call letters*]
KPLG-FM ... Plains, MT [*FM radio station call letters*] (BROA)
KPLM .... Palm Springs, CA [*FM radio station call letters*]
KPLN .... San Diego, CA [*FM radio station call letters*] (GDPB)
KPLN-FM ... Plains, TX [*FM radio station call letters*]
KPLN-FM ... San Diego, CA [*FM radio station call letters*] (BROA)
KPLO .... Reliance, SD [*FM radio station call letters*]
KPLO-TV ... Reliance, SD [*Television station call letters*]
KPLR .... St. Louis, MO [*Television station call letters*]
KPLS .... Key Pulsing (MSA)
KPLS .... Orange, CA [*AM radio station call letters*]
KPLT .... Paris, TX [*AM radio station call letters*]
KPLT-FM .... Paris, TX [*FM radio station call letters*]
KPLU .... K Line [*Intermodal shipping container symbol*] (TVRC)
KPLU .... Tacoma, WA [*FM radio station call letters*]
KPLV .... Idaho Falls, ID [*FM radio station call letters*] (BROA)
KPLV .... Port Lavaca, TX [*FM radio station call letters*]
KPLW-FM ... Wenatchee, WA [*FM radio station call letters*] (RBYB)
KPLX .... Fort Worth, TX [*FM radio station call letters*]
KPLY .... Sparks, NV [*AM radio station call letters*]
KPLZ .... Seattle, WA [*FM radio station call letters*]
KPM .... Kahler Process Model [*Computer science*]
KPM .... Kathode Pulse Modulation
KPM .... Kensington Palace Gardens [*British interrogation center*]
Kpm .... Kilopondmeter
KPM .... Kilo/Pound/Meters (STED)
KPM .... King's Police Medal
KPM .... King's Police Medal for Distinguished Service [*British*]
KPM .... King's Police Medal for Gallantry [*British*]
KPM .... Kronig-Penny Model
KPMA .... Kentucky Podiatric Medical Association (EARSL)
KPMB .... Pembina [*North Dakota*] [*ICAO location identifier*] (ICLI)
KPMB .... Plainview, TX [*FM radio station call letters*] (BROA)
KPMC .... Kenai Peninsula Marketing Council [*An association*] [*Alaska*] (ALAC)
KPMD .... Palmdale/Air Force Plant No. 42 [*California*] [*ICAO location identifier*] (ICLI)
KPMG .... Klynveld Peat Marwick Goerdeler [*Commercial firm*] [*British*]
KPMG .... KPMG Peat Marwick (SAUO)
KPMI .... Kraner Preschool Math Inventory [*Educational test*]
KPMO .... Mendocino, CA [*AM radio station call letters*]
KPMR .... Santa Barbara, CA [*Television station call letters*] (BROA)
KPMW .... Hallimaile, HI [*FM radio station call letters*]
KPMX .... Sterling, CO [*FM radio station call letters*]
KPN .... Competition [*Telegraphy*] (PCTE)
KPN .... Confederation for an Independent Poland (PD)
KPN .... Kipnuk [*Alaska*] [*Airport symbol*] (OAG)
KPN .... Kipnuk, AK [*Location identifier*] [*FAA*] (FAAL)
KPN .... Koninklijke PTT Nederland [*Post and telecommunications company*] (ECON)
KPN .... KPN [*NYSE symbol*] (SAG)
KPN .... Kupiano [*Papua New Guinea*] [*Seismograph station code, US Geological Survey*] (SEIS)
KPN .... Royal PTT Nederland ADS [*NYSE symbol*] (TTSB)
KPNC .... Ponca City [*Oklahoma*] [*ICAO location identifier*] (ICLI)
KPNC .... Ponca City, OK [*FM radio station call letters*]
KPND .... Sandpoint, ID [*FM radio station call letters*]
KPNE .... North Platte, NE [*Television station call letters*]
KPNE .... Philadelphia/North Philadelphia [*Pennsylvania*] [*ICAO location identifier*] (ICLI)
KPNE-FM ... North Platte, NE [*FM radio station call letters*]
KPNLF .... Khmer People's National Liberation Front [*Cambodia*] [*Political party*] (PD)
KPNO .... Kitt Peak National Observatory [*Tucson, AZ*] [*National Science Foundation*]
KPNO .... Norfolk, NE [*FM radio station call letters*]
KPNOB ...... Kitt Peak National Observatory [*Tucson, AZ*]
KPNS .... Pensacola/Regional [*Florida*] [*ICAO location identifier*] (ICLI)
KPNT .... St. Louis, MO (Mt. Vernon, IL) [*FM radio station call letters*] (GDPB)
KPNT-FM .... Ste. Genevieve, MO [*FM radio station call letters*] (RBYB)
KPNW .... Eugene, OR [*AM radio station call letters*]
KPNWR ..... Kern-Pixley National Wildlife Refuge (SAUO)
KPNX .... Phoenix (Kingman, Prescott), AZ [*Television station call letters*] (GDPB)
KPNX-DT .... Mesa, AZ [*Television station call letters*] (BROA)
KPNX-TV .... Mesa, AZ [*Television station call letters*]
KPNY .... Alliance, NE [*FM radio station call letters*]
KPO .... Key Performance Objectives (VLIE)
KPO .... Keypunch Operator [*Computer science*]
KPO .... King Pin Offset [*Automotive engineering*]
KPO .... Kitt Peak National Observatory, Tucson, AZ [*OCLC symbol*] (OCLC)
KPO .... Kommunistische Partei Oesterreichs [*Communist Party of Austria*] [*Political party*] (PPW)
KPO .... Korean Post Office (SAUO)
KPOA .... Lahaina, HI [*FM radio station call letters*]
KPOB .... Fayetteville/Pope Air Force Base [*North Carolina*] [*ICAO location identifier*] (ICLI)
KPOB .... Poplar Bluff, MO [*Television station call letters*]
KPOC .... Key Prep on Campus [*Slang*]
KPOC .... Pocahontas, AR [*AM radio station call letters*]
KPOC-FM ... Pocahontas, AR [*FM radio station call letters*]
KPOD .... Crescent City, CA [*AM radio station call letters*]
KPOD-FM ... Crescent North, CA [*FM radio station call letters*]
KPOF .... Denver, CO [*AM radio station call letters*]
KPOI .... Honolulu, HI [*FM radio station call letters*]
KPOK .... Bowman, ND [*AM radio station call letters*]
KPOM .... Fort Smith, AR [*Television station call letters*]
KPOO .... San Francisco, CA [*FM radio station call letters*]
KPOP .... Kerberized Post Office Protocol (SAUS)
KPOP .... San Diego, CA [*AM radio station call letters*]
KPOR .... Emporia, KS [*FM radio station call letters*] (BROA)
KPOS .... Post, TX [*AM radio station call letters*]
KPOS-FM ... Post, TX [*FM radio station call letters*]
KPOW .... Powell, WY [*AM radio station call letters*]
KPOW-FM ... La Monte, MO [*FM radio station call letters*] (BROA)
KPOWU ...... Kenya Petroleum and Oil Workers' Union
KPOZ-AM ... San Antonio, TX [*AM radio station call letters*] (BROA)
KPP .... Kaneb Pipeline Partnership LP [*NYSE symbol*] (SPSG)
KPP .... Kaneb Pipe Line Partners LP [*NYSE symbol*]
KPP .... Kaneb Pipe Line PtnrsL.P. [*NYSE symbol*] (TTSB)
KPP .... Keeper of the Privy Purse [*British*]
KPP .... Key Performance Parameter
KPP .... Komunistyczna Partia Polski [*Communist Party of Poland (1925-1938)*] [*Political party*] (PPE)
KPP .... Korean Pacific Press (SAUO)
KPP .... K-Profile Parameterization scheme (SAUS)
KPPA .... Kosovo Patriotic and Political Association (BUAC)
KPPC .... Kansas Pork Producers Council (EARSL)
KPPC .... Kentucky Pollution Prevention Center (RCD)

KPPC .... Pasadena, CA [*AM radio station call letters*]
KPPL .... Colusa, CA [*FM radio station call letters*]
KPPL .... Poplar Bluff, MO [*FM radio station call letters*] (BROA)
KPPR .... Williston, ND [*FM radio station call letters*]
KPPS .... Kilopackets per Second [*Telecommunications*]
KPPS .... Kilopulses per Second (NAKS)
kpps .... Kilopulses per Second
KPPT .... Newport, OR [*AM radio station call letters*] (GDPB)
KPPT .... Newport, OR [*FM radio station call letters*] (GDPB)
KPPT-AM.... Toledo, OR [*AM radio station call letters*] (BROA)
KPPT-FM.... Toledo, OR [*FM radio station call letters*] (BROA)
KPPV .... Prescott Valley, AZ [*FM radio station call letters*]
KPPX .... Tolleson, AZ [*Television station call letters*] (BROA)
KPQ.......... Korupun-Sela [*Language symbol*] (ETLW)
KPQ.......... Wenatchee, WA [*AM radio station call letters*]
KPQ-FM..... Wenatchee, WA [*FM radio station call letters*]
KPQI......... Presque Isle/Presque Isle [*Maine*] [*ICAO location identifier*] (ICLI)
KPQX .... Havre, MT [*FM radio station call letters*]
KPQZ-FM ... Amarillo, TX [*FM radio station call letters*] (BROA)
KPR.......... Conspire [*Telegraphy*] (PCTE)
KPR.......... Keeper (ABBR)
KPR.......... Kenya Police Reserve
KPR.......... Key Pulse Rate [*Cardiology*] (DAVI)
KPR.......... Keypunch Replacement [*Computer science*] (MHDI)
KPR.......... Knight of Polonia Restituta [*British*]
KPR.......... Knots per Revolution
KPR.......... Kodak Photo Resist
KPR.......... Krasnaya Polyana [*Former USSR*] [*Seismograph station code, US Geological Survey*] [*Closed*] (SEIS)
KPR.......... Kuder Preference Record [*Psychology*] (DAVI)
KPR.......... Port Williams [*Alaska*] [*Airport symbol*] (OAG)
KPR.......... Port Williams, AK [*Location identifier*] [*FAA*] (FAAL)
KPRA .... Ukiah, CA [*FM radio station call letters*]
KPRB-FM ... Brush, CO [*FM radio station call letters*] (BROA)
KPRC .... Houston, TX [*AM radio station call letters*]
KPRC-DT.... Houston, TX [*Television station call letters*] (BROA)
KPRC-TV.... Houston, TX [*Television station call letters*]
KPRD .... Conspired [*Telegraphy*] (PCTE)
KPRD .... Hays, KS [*FM radio station call letters*] (RBYB)
KPRD .... KSC [*Kennedy Space Center*] Program Requirements Document [*NASA*] (NASA)
KPRE .... Vail, CO [*FM radio station call letters*] (RBYB)
KPRF .... Amarillo, TX [*FM radio station call letters*] (BROA)
KPRG .... Agana, GU [*FM radio station call letters*] (RBYB)
KPRG .... Conspiring [*Telegraphy*] (PCTE)
KPRH-FM ... Montrose, CO [*FM radio station call letters*] (BROA)
KPRI .... Encinitas, CA [*FM radio station call letters*] (BROA)
KPRI .... Fagaitua, AS [*FM radio station call letters*] (RBYB)
KPRI .... Kinshasa Peace Research Institute (SAUO)
KPRJ .... Jamestown, ND [*FM radio station call letters*]
KPRK .... Livingston, MT [*AM radio station call letters*]
KPRL .... Paso Robles, CA [*AM radio station call letters*]
KPRM .... Park Rapids, MN [*AM radio station call letters*]
KPRN .... Grand Junction, CO [*FM radio station call letters*]
KPRNA ...... Konza Prairie Research Natural Area (SAUO)
KPRO .... Kentucky Peer Review Organization [*Medicine*] (EDAA)
KPRO .... Riverside, CA [*AM radio station call letters*]
KPRP .... Kampuchean [*or Khmer*] People's Revolutionary Party [*Political party*] (PD)
KPR-P .... Kuder Preference Record - Personal [*Psychology*]
KPRQ .... Price, UT [*FM radio station call letters*]
KPRR .... El Paso, TX [*FM radio station call letters*]
KPRS .... Kansas City, MO [*FM radio station call letters*]
KPRT .... Kansas City, MO [*AM radio station call letters*]
KPRU-FM ... Delta, CO [*FM radio station call letters*] (BROA)
KPRV .... Heavener, OK [*FM radio station call letters*]
KPR-V .... Kuder Preference Record - Vocational [*Psychology*] (DAVI)
KPRV .... Poteau, OK [*AM radio station call letters*]
KPRV-FM ... Heavener, OK [*FM radio station call letters*] (BROA)
KPRW-FM... Perham, MN [*FM radio station call letters*] (RBYB)
KPRX .... Bakersfield, CA [*FM radio station call letters*]
KPRY .... Pierre, SD [*Television station call letters*]
KPRZ .... San Marcos, CA [*AM radio station call letters*]
KPRZ-FM ... Fountain, CO [*FM radio station call letters*] (RBYB)
KPS.......... Karnofsky Performance Status [*Medicine*] (EDAA)
KPS.......... Keeper of the Privy Seal (SAUO)
KPS.......... Kempsey [*Australia*] [*Airport symbol*] (OAG)
KPS.......... Keypunch Performance System [*Computer science*] (PDAA)
KPS.......... Kilometers per Second (NASA)
KPS.......... Kirbati Philatelic Society (EA)
KPS.......... Klystron Power Supply
KPS.......... Knight of the (Order of the) Polar Star [*Sweden*] (ROG)
KPS.......... Knowledge Processing System [*Expert system shell*] (NITA)
KPS.......... Kommunistische Partei der Schweiz [*Communist Party of Switzerland*] [*Political party*] (PPE)
KPS.......... Kommunistische Partij Suriname [*Communist Party of Surinam*] [*Political party*] (PPW)
KPS.......... Korean Physical Society (SAUO)
KPS.......... One Thousand Pulses per Second (KSC)
KPSA .... Alamogordo, NM [*AM radio station call letters*]
KPSA .... Carlsbad, NM [*FM radio station call letters*] (BROA)
KPSA .... La Luz, NM [*FM radio station call letters*]
KPSA-AM ... Roswell, NM [*AM radio station call letters*] (BROA)
KPSC .... Palm Springs, CA [*FM radio station call letters*]
KPSD .... Faith, SD [*FM radio station call letters*]
KPSD-TV.... Eagle Butte, SD [*Television station call letters*]
KPSG .... Oklahoma City, OK [*Television station call letters*] (BROA)
KPSH .... Kepco Power Supply Handbook (SAUO)
KPSI .... Kip [*Thousands of Pounds*] per Square Inch
KPSI .... Palm Springs, CA [*AM radio station call letters*]
KPSI-FM .... Palm Springs, CA [*FM radio station call letters*]
KPSK .... Keepsake (ABBR)
KPSL .... Oxnard, CA [*FM radio station call letters*] (BROA)
KPSL .... Thousand Palms, CA [*AM radio station call letters*]
KPSM........ Brownwood, TX [*FM radio station call letters*]
KPSM........ Klystron Power Supply Modulator
KPSM........ Portsmouth/Pease Air Force Base [*New Hampshire*] [*ICAO location identifier*] (ICLI)
KPSNSW .... Koala Preservation Society of New South Wales [*Australia*]
KPSO .... Falfurrias, TX [*AM radio station call letters*]
KPSO-FM ... Falfurrias, TX [*FM radio station call letters*]
KPSQ .... Kapson Senior Quarters Corp. [*NASDAQ symbol*] (SAG)
KPSS .... Kommunisticheskaya Partiya Sovietskogo Soyuza [*Communist Party of the Soviet Union*] [*Political party*]
KPST .... Vallejo, CA [*Television station call letters*]
KPSU .... Goodwell, OK [*FM radio station call letters*]
KPSX .... Palacios [*Texas*] [*ICAO location identifier*] (ICLI)
KPT.......... Compete [*Telegraphy*] (PCTE)
KPT.......... Kaena Point Station [*Hawaii*] [*Military*]
KPT.......... Kai's Power Tools for Windows [*HSC Software*] (PCM)
KPT.......... Karpatair [*Hungary*] [*ICAO designator*] (FAAC)
KPT.......... Keeprite, Inc. [*Toronto Stock Exchange symbol*]
KPT.......... Kenner Parker Toys, Inc. (SAUO)
KPT.......... Kidney Punch Test [*or Murphy's test*] (DAVI)
KPT.......... Konover Property [*Formerly, FAC Realty Trust*] [*NYSE symbol*]
KPT.......... Konover Property Trust [*NYSE symbol*]
KPT.......... Kuder Performance Test [*Psychology*] (DAVI)
KPT.......... Pittsburgh State University (SAUS)
KPT.......... Pittsburg State University, Pittsburg, KS [*Library symbol*] [*Library of Congress*] (LCLS)
KPT3......... Kai's Power Tools [*Computer science*]
KPTB .... Lubbock, TX [*Television station call letters*] (RBYB)
KPTC .... Kuwait Public Transport Co. (BUAC)
KPTD .... Competed [*Telegraphy*] (PCTE)
KPTE-FM.... Durango, CO [*FM radio station call letters*] (BROA)
KPTF......... Farwell, TX [*Television station call letters*] (BROA)
KPTG .... Competing [*Telegraphy*] (PCTE)
KPTH .... Sioux City, IA [*Television station call letters*] (BROA)
KPTI .... Alameda, CA [*FM radio station call letters*] (BROA)
KPTI .... Kunitz Pancreatic Trypsin Inhibitor [*Medicine*] (MAE)
KPTL......... Carson City, NV [*AM radio station call letters*]
KPTL......... Keptel, Inc. [*NASDAQ symbol*] (COMM)
KPTM........ Omaha, NE [*Television station call letters*]
KPTR .... Competitor [*Telegraphy*] (PCTE)
KPTS .... Hutchinson, KS [*Television station call letters*]
KPTT......... Kaolin Partial Thromboplastin Time [*Clinical chemistry*] (MAE)
KPTT......... Reno, NV [*AM radio station call letters*] (BROA)
KPTV .... Competitive [*Telegraphy*] (PCTE)
KPTV .... Portland, OR [*Television station call letters*]
KPTX .... Pecos, TX [*FM radio station call letters*]
KPTY .... Missouri City, TX [*FM radio station call letters*] (BROA)
KPTY-FM.... Gilbert, AZ [*FM radio station call letters*] (BROA)
KPU.......... Kaneb Pipe Line Partners LP [*NYSE symbol*] (SAG)
KPU.......... Kaneb Pipe Ln Ptnrs LP Pref Ut [*NYSE symbol*] (TTSB)
KPU.......... Kaszubian Pomeranian Union [*Poland*] [*Political party*] (BUAC)
KPU.......... Kenya People's Union [*Political party*] (PSAP)
KPU.......... Ketchikan Public Utilities (SAUO)
KPU.......... Keyboard Printer Unit (SAUS)
KPU.......... Khapalu [*Pakistan*] [*Airport symbol*] (AD)
KPU.......... Kommunisticheskaia Partiia Ukrainy [*Communist Party of the Ukraine*] [*Political party*]
KPUA .... Hilo, HI [*AM radio station call letters*]
KPUB .... Flagstaff, AZ [*FM radio station call letters*] (BROA)
KPUB .... Pueblo Memorial [*Colorado*] [*ICAO location identifier*] (ICLI)
KPUB-FM ... Prescott, AZ [*FM radio station call letters*] (BROA)
KPUC .... Korean Presidential Unit Citation [*Military award*]
KPUG .... Bellingham, WA [*AM radio station call letters*]
KPUP .... Amargosa Valley, NV [*FM radio station call letters*] (BROA)
KPUP .... Key Personnel Upgrade Program [*National Guard*]
KPUR........ Amarillo, TX [*AM radio station call letters*]
KPUR-FM ... Canyon, TX [*FM radio station call letters*]
KPUS .... Gregory, TX [*FM radio station call letters*] (BROA)
KPUZ .... Kommunisticheskaia Partiia Uzbekistana [*Communist Party of Uzbekistan*] [*Political party*]
KPV.......... Comprehensive [*Telegraphy*] (PCTE)
KPV.......... Key Process Variable [*Medicine*] (EDAA)
KPV.......... Keypunch Verifier (VLIE)
KPV.......... Kid-Powered Vehicle
KPV.......... Killed Parenteral Vaccine [*Immunology*] (DAVI)
KPV.......... Killed Polio Vaccine [*Medicine*] (STED)
KPVD .... Providence/Theodore Francis Greene State [*Rhode Island*] [*ICAO location identifier*] (ICLI)
KPV HMG... Krupnokalibernyi Pulemyoy Vladimirova Heavy Machine Gun [*Soviet-made weaponry used extensively by the People's Army of North Vietnam*] (VNW)
KPVI .... Pocatello, ID [*Television station call letters*]
KPVS .... Hilo, HI [*FM radio station call letters*]
KPVU .... Prairie View, TX [*FM radio station call letters*]

KPVW .... Aspen, CO [*FM radio station call letters*] (BROA)
KPVY .... Amarillo, TX [*FM radio station call letters*]
KPW .... North Korean Won (SAUS)
KPWA .... Korean Patriotic Women's Association in America [*Defunct*] (EA)
KPWB .... Piedmont, MO [*AM radio station call letters*]
KPWB-FM ... Piedmont, MO [*FM radio station call letters*]
KPWB-TV ... Ames, IA [*Television station call letters*] (BROA)
KPWB-TV ... Sacramento, CA [*Television station call letters*] (RBYB)
KPWIN ...... KnowledgePro Windows [*Computer science*] (HODG)
KPWM .... Portland/International Jetport [*Maine*] [*ICAO location identifier*] (ICLI)
KPWR .... Los Angeles, CA [*FM radio station call letters*]
KPWS .... Crowley, LA [*AM radio station call letters*]
KPWU .... Korean Port Worker's Union (BUAC)
KPWW-FM ... Hooks, TX [*FM radio station call letters*] (BROA)
KPX .... Conspicuous [*Telegraphy*] (PCTE)
KPXA .... Sisters, OR [*FM radio station call letters*]
KPXB .... Conroe, TX [*Television station call letters*] (BROA)
KPXC .... Indian Springs, NV [*FM radio station call letters*]
KPXC-TV ... Denver, CO [*Television station call letters*] (BROA)
KPXD .... Arlington, TX [*Television station call letters*] (BROA)
KPXE .... Kansas City, MO [*Television station call letters*] (BROA)
KPXE .... Liberty, TX [*AM radio station call letters*]
KPXF .... Lacombe, LA [*FM radio station call letters*]
KPXF .... Porterville, CA [*Television station call letters*] (BROA)
KPXG .... Salem, OR [*Television station call letters*] (BROA)
KPXH .... Garapan-Saipan, MP [*FM radio station call letters*]
KPXI .... Mount Pleasant, TX [*FM radio station call letters*]
KPXI .... Overton, TX [*FM radio station call letters*] (BROA)
KPXJ .... Minden, LA [*Television station call letters*] (BROA)
KPXK .... Odessa, TX [*Television station call letters*] (BROA)
KPXL .... Uvalde, TX [*Television station call letters*] (BROA)
KPXM .... St. Cloud, MN [*Television station call letters*] (BROA)
KPXN .... San Bernardino, CA [*Television station call letters*] (BROA)
KPXO .... Kaneohe, HI [*Television station call letters*] (BROA)
KPXP .... Garapan-Saipan, MP [*FM radio station call letters*]
KPXQ .... Phoenix, AZ [*AM radio station call letters*] (GDPB)
KPXQ-AM ... Glendale, AZ [*AM radio station call letters*] (BROA)
KPXQ-AM ... Phoenix, AZ [*AM radio station call letters*] (RBYB)
KPXR .... Cedar Rapids, IA [*Television station call letters*] (BROA)
KPXX .... Progress Rail Services [*Private rail car owner code*]
KPY .... Conspiracy [*Telegraphy*] (PCTE)
KPY .... Port Bailey [*Alaska*] [*Airport symbol*] (OAG)
KPY .... Port Bailey, AK [*Location identifier*] [*FAA*] (FAAL)
KPYK .... Terrell, TX [*AM radio station call letters*]
KPYN .... Atlanta, TX [*FM radio station call letters*]
KPZA .... Espanola, NM [*FM radio station call letters*] (RBYB)
KQ .... Air South, Inc. [*Airline code*]
KQ .... Kenya Airways [*Airline flight code*] (ODBW)
KQ .... Kenya Airways Ltd. (SAUO)
KQ .... Line Squall [*Meteorology*] (WDAA)
KQA .... Akutan [*Alaska*] [*Airport symbol*] (OAG)
KQA .... Akutan, AK [*Location identifier*] [*FAA*] (FAAL)
KQA .... Kenya Airways Ltd. [*ICAO designator*] (FAAC)
KQAA .... Aberdeen, SD [*FM radio station call letters*]
KQAB-AM ... Lake Isabella, CA [*AM radio station call letters*] (BROA)
KQAC .... Amarillo, TX [*FM radio station call letters*]
KQAD .... Luverne, MN [*AM radio station call letters*]
KQAK .... Bend, OR [*FM radio station call letters*]
KQAL .... Winona, MN [*FM radio station call letters*]
KQAM .... Wichita, KS [*AM radio station call letters*]
KQAR-FM ... Jacksonville, AR [*FM radio station call letters*] (BROA)
KQAY .... Tucumcari, NM [*FM radio station call letters*]
KQAZ .... Springerville-Eager, AZ [*FM radio station call letters*]
KQB .... Kovai [*Language symbol*] (ETLW)
KQBA .... Los Alamos, NM [*FM radio station call letters*] (BROA)
KQBB .... Center, TX [*FM radio station call letters*] (BROA)
KQBE .... Ellensburg, WA [*FM radio station call letters*]
KQBL .... Bethany, Ok [*FM radio station call letters*] (BROA)
KQBR .... Davis, CA [*FM radio station call letters*]
KQBR .... Lubbock, TX [*FM radio station call letters*] (BROA)
KQBT-FM ... Taylor, TX [*FM radio station call letters*] (BROA)
KQBU .... Port Arthur, TX [*FM radio station call letters*] (BROA)
KQBZ .... Seattle, WA [*FM radio station call letters*] (BROA)
KQC .... Convince [*Telegraphy*] (PCTE)
KQC .... King's College London [*British*] (IRUK)
KQCA .... Stockton, CA [*Television station call letters*] (RBYB)
KQCD .... Convinced [*Telegraphy*] (PCTE)
KQCD .... Dickinson, ND [*Television station call letters*]
KQCG .... Convincing [*Telegraphy*] (PCTE)
KQCH .... Omaha, NE [*FM radio station call letters*] (BROA)
KQCL .... Faribault, MN [*FM radio station call letters*]
KQCP .... King's and Queen's College of Physicians [*Ireland*]
KQCR .... Parkersburg, IA [*FM radio station call letters*] (BROA)
KQCT .... Davenport, IA [*Television station call letters*]
KQCV .... Oklahoma City, OK [*AM radio station call letters*]
KQCV .... Shawnee, OK [*FM radio station call letters*] (BROA)
KQD .... Convicted [*Telegraphy*] (PCTE)
KQDD .... Osceola, AR [*FM radio station call letters*] (BROA)
KQDI .... Great Falls, MT [*AM radio station call letters*] (BROA)
KQDI-FM ... Great Falls, MT [*FM radio station call letters*]
KQDJ .... Jamestown, ND [*AM radio station call letters*]
KQDJ-FM ... Valley City, ND [*FM radio station call letters*] (RBYB)
KQDS .... Duluth, MN [*AM radio station call letters*]
KQDS-FM ... Duluth, MN [*FM radio station call letters*]
KQDY .... Bismarck, ND [*FM radio station call letters*]
KQED .... San Francisco, CA [*FM radio station call letters*]
KQED-DT ... San Francisco, CA [*Television station call letters*] (BROA)
KQED-TV ... San Francisco, CA [*Television station call letters*]
KQEG .... La Crescent, MN [*FM radio station call letters*]
KQEN .... Roseburg, OR [*AM radio station call letters*]
KQEO .... Idaho Falls, ID [*FM radio station call letters*] (BROA)
KQEO-FM ... Grants, NM [*FM radio station call letters*] (BROA)
KQEP .... Rock Valley, IA [*FM radio station call letters*]
KQEQ .... Fowler, CA [*AM radio station call letters*] (RBYB)
KQEW .... Fordyce, AR [*FM radio station call letters*]
KQEX .... Fortuna, CA [*FM radio station call letters*]
KQEZ-FM ... Houston, AK [*FM radio station call letters*] (BROA)
KQF .... Krupp Quick-Firing Gun
KQFC .... Boise, ID [*FM radio station call letters*]
KQFE .... Springfield, OR [*FM radio station call letters*]
KQFM .... Hermiston, OR [*FM radio station call letters*]
KQFN .... Fargo, ND [*AM radio station call letters*] (RBYB)
KQFX .... Borger, TX [*FM radio station call letters*]
KQG .... Convicting [*Telegraphy*] (PCTE)
KQH .... Kiloquadergy Hour [*Electric utility company*]
KQHA .... Kansas Quarter Horse Association (EARSL)
KQHC-FM ... Burns, OR [*FM radio station call letters*] (RBYB)
KQHN .... Nederland, TX [*AM radio station call letters*]
KQHR .... Hood River, OR [*FM radio station call letters*] (BROA)
KQHT .... Crookston, MN [*FM radio station call letters*]
KQIB-FM ... Idabel, OK [*FM radio station call letters*] (BROA)
KQIC .... Willmar, MN [*FM radio station call letters*]
KQID .... Alexandria, LA [*FM radio station call letters*]
KQIK .... Lakeview, OR [*AM radio station call letters*]
KQIK-FM ... Lakeview, OR [*FM radio station call letters*]
KQIL .... Grand Junction, CO [*AM radio station call letters*]
KQIP .... Odessa, TX [*FM radio station call letters*]
KQIS-FM ... Basile, LA [*FM radio station call letters*] (BROA)
KQIX .... Grand Junction, CO [*FM radio station call letters*]
KQIZ .... Amarillo, TX [*FM radio station call letters*]
KQJD .... West Fargo, ND [*AM radio station call letters*] (BROA)
KQJM .... King, Queen, Jack Meld [*Canasta*]
KQJZ-FM ... Grover City, CA [*FM radio station call letters*] (BROA)
KQKD .... Redfield, SD [*AM radio station call letters*]
KQKD-FM ... Redfield, SD [*FM radio station call letters*]
KQKI .... Bayou Vista, LA [*FM radio station call letters*]
KQKK-FM ... Walker, MN [*FM radio station call letters*] (BROA)
KQKL .... Selma, CA [*FM radio station call letters*] (BROA)
KQKQ .... Council Bluffs, IA [*FM radio station call letters*]
KQKS .... Lakewood, CO [*FM radio station call letters*] (BROA)
KQKS .... Longmont, CO [*FM radio station call letters*]
KQKY .... Kearney, NE [*FM radio station call letters*]
KQL .... Kol [*Papua New Guinea*] [*Airport symbol*] (OAG)
KQLA .... Ogden, KS [*FM radio station call letters*]
KQLB .... Los Banos, CA [*FM radio station call letters*]
KQLF .... Cheyenne, WY [*FM radio station call letters*] (BROA)
KQLI-FM ... Geneseo, IL [*FM radio station call letters*] (BROA)
KQLL .... Owasso, OK [*FM radio station call letters*]
KQLL .... Tulsa, OK [*AM radio station call letters*]
KQLM-FM ... Odessa, TX [*FM radio station call letters*] (RBYB)
KQLO .... Reno, NV [*AM radio station call letters*]
KQLQ .... Columbia, LA [*FM radio station call letters*] (BROA)
KQLQ-AM ... Sun Valley, NV [*AM radio station call letters*] (BROA)
KQLS .... Colby, KS [*FM radio station call letters*]
KQLT .... Casper, WY [*FM radio station call letters*]
KQLV-FM ... Grants, NM [*FM radio station call letters*] (BROA)
KQLX .... Lisbon, ND [*AM radio station call letters*]
KQLX-FM ... Lisbon, ND [*FM radio station call letters*]
KQM .... Khisa [*Language symbol*] (ETLW)
KQM .... Kolson Quick Modality Test [*Education*]
KQMA .... Phillipsburg, KS [*FM radio station call letters*]
KQMB-FM ... Midvale, UT [*FM radio station call letters*] (RBYB)
KQMC .... Brinkley, AR [*FM radio station call letters*]
KQMG .... Independence, IA [*AM radio station call letters*]
KQMG-FM ... Independence, IA [*FM radio station call letters*]
KQML .... Knowledge and Query Management Language [*Computer science*] (GART)
KQML .... Knowledge Query and Manipulation Language [*Computer science*]
KQMN .... Thief River Falls, MN [*FM radio station call letters*]
KQMO .... Shell Knob, MO [*FM radio station call letters*] (BROA)
KQMO-FM ... Ash Grove, MO [*FM radio station call letters*] (RBYB)
KQMQ .... Honolulu, HI [*AM radio station call letters*]
KQMQ-FM ... Honolulu, HI [*FM radio station call letters*]
KQMR .... Indian Springs, NV [*FM radio station call letters*] (BROA)
KQMS .... Redding, CA [*AM radio station call letters*]
KQMT .... Denver, CO [*FM radio station call letters*] (BROA)
KQMX-FM ... Clinton, OK [*FM radio station call letters*] (RBYB)
KQN .... Conviction [*Telegraphy*] (PCTE)
KQNA .... Prescott Valley, AZ [*AM radio station call letters*]
KQNC .... Quincy, CA [*FM radio station call letters*]
KQNG .... Lihue, HI [*AM radio station call letters*]
KQNG-FM ... Lihue, HI [*FM radio station call letters*]
KQNK .... Norton, KS [*AM radio station call letters*]
KQNK-FM ... Norton, KS [*FM radio station call letters*]
KQNN .... Alice, TX [*FM radio station call letters*]
KQNS .... Lindsborg, KS [*FM radio station call letters*]
KQNV .... Sparks, NV [*FM radio station call letters*] (RBYB)

KQOD........ Stockton, CA [*FM radio station call letters*]
KQOK........ Shawnee, OK [*Television station call letters*] (BROA)
KQOL........ Boulder City, NV [*FM radio station call letters*] (RBYB)
KQOL........ Las Vegas, NV [*FM radio station call letters*] (BROA)
KQOR........ Mena, AR [*FM radio station call letters*] (BROA)
KQPD........ Ardmore, OK [*FM radio station call letters*] (BROA)
KQPM........ Ukiah, CA [*FM radio station call letters*]
KQPR........ Albert Lea, MN [*FM radio station call letters*]
KQPT........ Colusa, CA [*FM radio station call letters*] (BROA)
KQPT........ Sacramento, CA [*FM radio station call letters*]
KQQA........ Creedmoor, TX [*AM radio station call letters*] (BROA)
KQQK........ Beaumont, TX [*FM radio station call letters*] (BROA)
KQQK........ Galveston, TX [*FM radio station call letters*]
KQQL........ Anoka, MN [*FM radio station call letters*]
KQQQ........ Pullman, WA [*AM radio station call letters*]
KQQQ-FM..... Hutto, TX [*FM radio station call letters*] (BROA)
KQQT........ Gonzales, TX [*FM radio station call letters*] (BROA)
KQR......... Cobequid Resources Ltd. [*Vancouver Stock Exchange symbol*]
KQR......... Kit Quotation Request (MCD)
KQRA........ Brookline, MO [*FM radio station call letters*] (BROA)
KQRB........ Windom, MN [*FM radio station call letters*] (BROA)
KQRC-FM..... Leavenworth, KS [*FM radio station call letters*]
KQRD........ Sulphur, OK [*FM radio station call letters*] (BROA)
KQRI........ Lubbock, TX [*FM radio station call letters*] (BROA)
KQRK........ Ronan, MT [*FM radio station call letters*]
KQRN........ Mitchell, SD [*FM radio station call letters*]
KQRQ........ Rapid City, SD [*FM radio station call letters*] (BROA)
KQRS........ Golden Valley, MN [*AM radio station call letters*]
KQRS-FM..... Golden Valley, MN [*FM radio station call letters*]
KQRV-FM..... Deer Lodge, MT [*FM radio station call letters*] (BROA)
KQRX........ Midland, TX [*FM radio station call letters*]
KQS......... Convicts [*Telegraphy*] (PCTE)
KQSB........ Santa Barbara, CA [*AM radio station call letters*]
KQSC........ Willows, CA [*FM radio station call letters*]
KQSD........ Lowry, SD [*Television station call letters*]
KQSI........ San Augustine, TX [*FM radio station call letters*] (BROA)
KQSK........ Chadron, NE [*FM radio station call letters*]
KQSN........ Naches, WA [*FM radio station call letters*] (BROA)
KQSN-FM..... Toppenish, WA [*FM radio station call letters*] (BROA)
KQSR-FM..... Oklahoma City, OK [*FM radio station call letters*] (BROA)
KQSS........ Miami, AZ [*FM radio station call letters*]
KQST........ Sedona, AZ [*FM radio station call letters*]
KQSW........ Rock Springs, WY [*FM radio station call letters*]
KQSY........ Nowata, OK [*FM radio station call letters*] (RBYB)
KQT......... Convict [*Telegraphy*] (PCTE)
KQT......... Konkordanz zu den Qumrantexten [*A publication*] (BJA)
KQTL........ Sahuarita, AZ [*AM radio station call letters*]
KQTN-FM..... Lordsburg, NM [*FM radio station call letters*] (BROA)
KQTP........ St. Marys, KS [*FM radio station call letters*]
KQTV........ St. Joseph, MO [*Television station call letters*]
KQTY........ Borger, TX [*AM radio station call letters*]
KQTZ........ Hobart, OK [*FM radio station call letters*]
KQUA........ Lutesville, MO [*FM radio station call letters*]
KQUE........ Houston, TX [*FM radio station call letters*]
KQUL........ Lake Ozark, MO [*FM radio station call letters*] (BROA)
KQUR........ Laredo, TX [*FM radio station call letters*] (BROA)
KQUS........ Hot Springs, AR [*FM radio station call letters*]
KQUY........ Butte, MT [*FM radio station call letters*]
KQV......... Pittsburgh, PA [*AM radio station call letters*]
KQVO........ Calexico, CA [*FM radio station call letters*]
KQVT........ Victoria, TX [*FM radio station call letters*] (BROA)
KQWB........ Fargo, ND [*AM radio station call letters*] (BROA)
KQWB........ Moorhead, MN [*FM radio station call letters*]
KQWC........ Webster City, IA [*AM radio station call letters*]
KQWC-FM..... Webster City, IA [*FM radio station call letters*]
KQWK-FM..... Wallace, ID [*FM radio station call letters*] (BROA)
KQWS-FM..... Omak, WA [*FM radio station call letters*] (BROA)
KQX......... Mser [*Language symbol*] (ETLW)
KQXC........ Wichita Falls, TX [*FM radio station call letters*]
KQXI........ Aruada, CO [*AM radio station call letters*]
KQXL........ New Roads, LA [*FM radio station call letters*]
KQXR........ Payette, ID [*FM radio station call letters*] (RBYB)
KQXS........ Stephenville, TX [*FM radio station call letters*] (BROA)
KQXT........ San Antonio, TX [*FM radio station call letters*]
KQXX........ Brownsville, TX [*AM radio station call letters*] (BROA)
KQXX........ McAllen, TX [*FM radio station call letters*]
KQXY........ Beaumont, TX [*FM radio station call letters*]
KQYB........ Spring Grove, MN [*FM radio station call letters*]
KQYN........ Twentynine Palms, CA [*FM radio station call letters*]
KQYX........ Joplin, MO [*AM radio station call letters*]
KQZE........ St. Johns, AZ [*FM radio station call letters*]
KQZX........ Markham, TX [*FM radio station call letters*] (BROA)
KQZZ-FM..... Devils Lake, ND [*FM radio station call letters*] (RBYB)
KR.......... Color [*Telegraphy*] (PCTE)
KR.......... Contractor [*Navy*]
KR.......... Kabinenroller [*Cabin scooter*] [*Automobile model designation-Messerschmitt*]
KR.......... Kallah Rabbati (BJA)
KR.......... Kar-Air [*ICAO designator*] (AD)
KR.......... Karat (ABBR)
KR.......... Keesom Relationship
KR.......... Kennedy Round
K-R......... Kent-Rosanoff Free Association Test [*Psychology*]
KR.......... Kenya Railways
KR.......... Kenya Regiment (SAUO)
KR.......... Ketoaldonate Reductase [*An enzyme*]
KR.......... Ketoreductase [*An enzyme*]
KR.......... Keying Relay
KR.......... Key Records [*Record label*]
KR.......... Key Register
KR.......... Khmer Rouge (BARN)
kR.......... Kilorayleigh
kR.......... Kiloroentgen
KR.......... Kimberley Regiment (SAUO)
KR.......... Kinetic Reaction
KR.......... King's Regiment [*Military unit*] [*British*]
KR.......... King's Regulations for the Army and the Army Reserves [*British*]
KR.......... King's Remembrancer [*British*]
KR.......... King's Rook [*Chess*]
KR.......... Kipp Relay
KR.......... Kirkus Review [*A publication*] (BRI)
KR.......... Knight of the [*Order of the*] Redeemer [*Greece*]
KR.......... Knight-Ridder
KR.......... Knight-Ridder Newspapers, Inc. (EFIS)
KR.......... Knowledge of Results
KR.......... Knowledge Representation [*Computer science*]
KR.......... Koloniale Rundschau (BJA)
KR.......... Konkan Railway [*Indian Railway*] (TIR)
KR.......... Kopper Reppart [*Medium*] [*Biochemistry*] (DAVI)
KR.......... Korean Register of Shipping (SAUO)
KR.......... Krefeld [*German license plate city code*]
KR.......... Kreuzer [*Monetary unit*] [*German*]
KR.......... Kroger Co. [*NYSE symbol*] (TTSB)
KR.......... Krona [*Crown*] [*Monetary unit*] [*Iceland, Sweden*] (EY)
KR.......... Krone [*Crown*] [*Monetary unit*] [*Denmark, Norway*] (EY)
K-R......... Krueger-Ringier [*Book manufacturer*]
Kr.......... Krypton [*Chemical element*]
K-R......... Kuder-Richardson Formula [*Education*] (AEE)
KR.......... Republic of Korea [*ANSI two-letter standard code*] (CNC)
KR20........ Kuder-Richardson Formula 20
KR21........ Kuder-Richardson Formula 21
KRA......... Contractor Responsible Action (MCD)
KRA......... Karenni Revolutionary Army [*Myanmar*] [*Political party*] (EY)
KRA......... Kentucky Restaurant Association (EARSL)
KRA......... Kerang [*Victoria, Australia*] [*Airport symbol*] (AD)
KRA......... Key Recovery Alliance (VLIE)
KRA......... Key Result Area
KRA......... Kickback Racket Act
KRA......... Klinefelter-Reifenstein-Albright [*Syndrome*] [*Medicine*] (DAVI)
KRA......... Kraftco Corp. (SAUO)
KRA......... Kraft, Inc. [*NYSE symbol*] (COMM)
KRA......... Krakow [*Poland*] [*Seismograph station code, US Geological Survey*] (SEIS)
KRA......... Waft, Inc. (SAUO)
KRAB........ Greenacres, CA [*FM radio station call letters*]
KRAC........ Kaiserslautern Community Relations Advisory Committee (SAUO)
KRAD........ Kilorad (WDAA)
KRAD........ Portland, TX [*FM radio station call letters*]
KRAE........ Cheyenne, WY [*AM radio station call letters*]
KRAE........ Krager [*NCIC truck make code*]
KRAE........ Krager Kustom Koach [*NCIC trailer make code*]
KRAF........ Holdenville, OK [*AM radio station call letters*]
KRAG-JORG........ Krag-Jorgensen Rifle
KRAI........ Craig, CO [*AM radio station call letters*]
KRAI-FM..... Craig, CO [*FM radio station call letters*]
KR Air...... King's Regulations and Orders for the Royal Canadian Air Force
KRAJ........ Johannesburg, CA [*FM radio station call letters*]
KRAK........ Sacramento-Stockton, CA [*FM radio station call letters*] (GDPB)
KRAK-AM..... Hesperia, CA [*AM radio station call letters*] (BROA)
KRAK-FM..... Sacramento, CA [*FM radio station call letters*]
KRAL........ Rawlins, WY [*AM radio station call letters*]
KRAM........ St. Louis, MO [*AM radio station call letters*] (RBYB)
KRAM........ West Klamath, OR [*AM radio station call letters*] (BROA)
KRAN........ Krantor Corp. [*NASDAQ symbol*] (SAG)
KRAN-AM..... Merced, CA [*AM radio station call letters*] (BROA)
KR & ACI.... King's Regulations and Air Council Instructions [*British military*] (DMA)
KR & AI..... King's Regulations and Admiralty Instructions [*Navy*] [*British*]
KR & O (Can)... King's Regulations and Orders for the Royal Canadian Army
Krantor..... Krantor Corp. [*Associated Press*] (SAG)
Krantr...... Krantor Corp. [*Associated Press*] (SAG)
KRANW....... Krantor Corp.Wrrt'A' [*NASDAQ symbol*] (TTSB)
Kranzc...... Kranzco Realty Trust [*Associated Press*] (SAG)
KRAO........ Colfax, WA [*FM radio station call letters*]
KRAQ........ Jackson, MN [*FM radio station call letters*]
KRAR-FM..... Brigham City, UT [*FM radio station call letters*] (BROA)
KRAS........ Keyworded References to Archaeological Science [*Department of Archaeology*] [*University of Leicester British*] [*Database*] (NITA)
KRAT-FM..... Altamont, OR [*FM radio station call letters*] (BROA)
KRAU........ Kellogg Rural Adjustment Center, University of New England (SAUO)
KRAU........ Production Amalgamation Krasitel [*Intermodal shipping container symbol*] (TVRC)
Krause...... Krauses Furniture, Inc. [*Associated Press*] (SAG)
KrauseF..... Krauses Furniture, Inc. [*Associated Press*] (SAG)
KRAV........ Tulsa, OK [*FM radio station call letters*]
KRAW-FM..... Lake Arthur, LA [*FM radio station call letters*] (BROA)

KRAY .... Salinas, CA [*FM radio station call letters*]
KRAZ .... Santa Ynez, CA [*FM radio station call letters*] (BROA)
KRAZ .... Sutter Creek, CA [*FM radio station call letters*]
KRB .... Corroborate [*Telegraphy*] (PCTE)
KRB .... Kansas River Basin
KRB .... Kariba [*Zimbabwe*] [*Seismograph station code, US Geological Survey*] [*Closed*] (SEIS)
KRB .... Karumba [*Australia*] [*Airport symbol*] (OAG)
KRB .... Krebs-Ringer-Bicarbonate [*Buffer solution*]
KRB .... Krebs-Ringer Bicarbonate Buffer [*Biochemistry*] (DAVI)
KRB .... MBNA Corp. [*NYSE symbol*] (SPSG)
KRBA .... Lufkin, TX [*AM radio station call letters*]
KRBB .... Krebs-Ringer Bicarbonate Buffer [*Biochemistry*] (DAVI)
KRBB .... Wichita, KS [*FM radio station call letters*]
KRBC .... Abilene, TX [*Television station call letters*]
KRBD .... Corroborated [*Telegraphy*] (PCTE)
KRBD .... Ketchikan, AK [*FM radio station call letters*]
KRBE .... Houston, TX [*FM radio station call letters*]
KRBF .... Bonners Ferry, ID [*FM radio station call letters*]
KRBFC .... Kenny Roberts and Bettyanne Fan Club [*Defunct*] (EA)
KRBG .... Canadian, TX [*FM radio station call letters*]
KRBG .... Corroborating [*Telegraphy*] (PCTE)
KRBG .... Krebs-Ringer Bicarbonate Buffer [*Containing*] Glucose (DAVI)
KRBG .... Krebs-Ringer Bicarbonate Buffer with Glucose [*Medicine*] (DMAA)
KRB-GA ..... Krebs-Ringer-Bicarbonate Glucose-Albumin [*Buffer solution*]
KRBH-FM ... Hondo, TX [*FM radio station call letters*] (RBYB)
KRBI .... St. Peter, MN [*AM radio station call letters*]
KRBI-FM .... St. Peter, MN [*FM radio station call letters*]
KRBK .... Booneville, AR [*FM radio station call letters*] (BROA)
KRBL .... Idalou, TX [*FM radio station call letters*] (RBYB)
KRBM .... Pendleton, OR [*FM radio station call letters*]
KRBN .... Boston [*Massachusetts*] [*ICAO location identifier*] (ICLI)
KRBN .... Corroboration [*Telegraphy*] (PCTE)
KRBO .... Las Vegas, NV [*FM radio station call letters*]
KRBPrA ..... MBNA Corp.7.50% Sr'A'Pfd [*NYSE symbol*] (TTSB)
KRBR .... Duluth, MN [*FM radio station call letters*] (GDPB)
KRBR-FM ... Superior, WI [*FM radio station call letters*] (RBYB)
KRBS .... Corroborates [*Telegraphy*] (PCTE)
KRBS .... Krebs-Ringer Bicarbonate Solution
KRBSG ...... Krebs-Ringer Bicarbonate Solution with Glucose
KRBT .... Eveleth, MN [*AM radio station call letters*] (BROA)
KRBT .... Fresno, CA [*FM radio station call letters*]
KRBV .... Dallas, TX [*FM radio station call letters*] (RBYB)
KRBW-FM... Ottawa, KS [*FM radio station call letters*] (BROA)
KRBZ .... Kansas City, MO [*FM radio station call letters*] (BROA)
KRBZ .... Reedsport, OR [*FM radio station call letters*]
KRC .... Keweenaw Research Center [*Houghton, MI*] [*Army*] [*Research center*] (GRD)
KRC .... Kilroy Realty [*NYSE symbol*] (SG)
KRC .... King Ranch [*California*] [*Seismograph station code, US Geological Survey*] [*Closed*] (SEIS)
KRC .... Knight of the Red Cross [*Freemasonry*]
KRC .... Knowledge Resource Center [*Computer-based information delivery system in libraries*] [*Generic term*]
KRC .... Knowledge, Responsibility, Control (SAUO)
KRC .... Kodak Reflex Camera
KRC .... Regis College Library, University of Toronto [*UTLAS symbol*]
KRCA .... Rapid City/Ellsworth Air Force Base [*South Dakota*] [*ICAO location identifier*] (ICLI)
KRCA .... Riverside, CA [*Television station call letters*]
KRCB .... Santa Rosa, CA [*FM radio station call letters*]
KRCB-TV .... Cotati, CA [*Television station call letters*]
KRCC .... Colorado Springs, CO [*FM radio station call letters*]
KRCC .... Kingston Regional Cancer Center [*Canada*] (PDAA)
KRCD .... Chubbuck, ID [*AM radio station call letters*]
KRCD .... Inglewood, CA [*FM radio station call letters*] (BROA)
KRCG .... Jefferson City, MO [*Television station call letters*]
KRCH .... Rochester, MN [*FM radio station call letters*]
KRCHF ...... Kerchief (ABBR)
KRCI .... Avalon, CA [*FM radio station call letters*]
KRCI .... Bagdad, AZ [*FM radio station call letters*] (BROA)
KRCK .... Burbank, CA [*AM radio station call letters*]
KRCK .... Mecca, CA [*FM radio station call letters*] (BROA)
KRCL .... Konkan Railway Corporation, Ltd [*Indian Railway*] (TIR)
KRCL .... Salt Lake City, UT [*FM radio station call letters*]
KRCM .... Beaumont, TX [*AM radio station call letters*] (BROA)
KRCN .... King's Regulations and Orders for the Royal Canadian Navy
KRCO .... Prineville, OR [*AM radio station call letters*]
KRCQ .... Detroit Lakes, MN [*FM radio station call letters*] (RBYB)
KRCR .... Redding, CA [*Television station call letters*]
KRCRA ...... Known Recoverable Coal Resource Area (PDAA)
KRCS .... Sturgis, SD [*FM radio station call letters*]
KRCU .... Cape Girardeau, MO [*FM radio station call letters*]
KRCV .... West Covina, CA [*FM radio station call letters*] (BROA)
KRCW .... Royal City, WA [*FM radio station call letters*]
KRCX .... Kokomo Rail [*Federal Railroad Administration identification code*]
KRCX .... Marysville, CA [*FM radio station call letters*] (BROA)
KRCX .... Roseville, CA [*AM radio station call letters*]
KRCY .... Kingman, AZ [*FM radio station call letters*]
KRCZ .... Knife River Coal [*Federal Railroad Administration identification code*]
KRD .... Colored [*Telegraphy*] (PCTE)
KRD .... Kourday [*Former USSR*] [*Seismograph station code, US Geological Survey*] [*Closed*] (SEIS)
KRD .... Krieger Data International Corp. [*Vancouver Stock Exchange symbol*]
KRDC .... Konkan Railway Development Corporation [*Indian Railway*] (TIR)
KRDC .... St. George, UT [*FM radio station call letters*]
KRDD .... Roswell, NM [*AM radio station call letters*]
KRDE .... Denver [*Colorado*] [*ICAO location identifier*] (ICLI)
KRDF .... Spearman, TX [*FM radio station call letters*]
KRDG .... Redding, CA [*AM radio station call letters*]
KRDG-FM ... Shingletown, CA [*FM radio station call letters*] (BROA)
KRDL .... Kreidler [*NCIC motorcycle make code*]
KRDO .... Colorado Springs, CO [*AM radio station call letters*]
KRDO-FM ... Colorado Springs, CO [*FM radio station call letters*]
KRDO-TV ... Colorado Springs, CO [*Television station call letters*]
KRDR .... Red River/Grand Forks Air Force Base [*North Dakota*] [*ICAO location identifier*] (ICLI)
KRDR-FM ... Red River, NM [*FM radio station call letters*] (BROA)
KRDS .... New Prague, MN [*FM radio station call letters*] (BROA)
KRDS .... Tolleson, AZ [*AM radio station call letters*]
KRDS .... Wickenburg, AZ [*FM radio station call letters*]
KRDU .... Dinuba, CA [*AM radio station call letters*]
KRDU .... Raleigh/Raleigh-Durham [*North Carolina*] [*ICAO location identifier*] (ICLI)
KRDZ .... Wray, CO [*AM radio station call letters*]
KRE .... Aerosucre, SA [*Colombia*] [*FAA designator*] (FAAC)
KRE .... Capital Re [*NYSE symbol*] (TTSB)
KRE .... Capital Real Estate [*NYSE symbol*] (SPSG)
KRE .... Capital Re Corp. [*NYSE symbol*]
KRE .... Capital Re Corporation1 [*NYSE symbol*] (SAG)
KRE .... Consolidated Regal Resources Ltd. [*Vancouver Stock Exchange symbol*]
KRE .... Knight of the Red Eagle [*Prussia*]
KRE .... Kobe Rubber Exchange (NUMA)
KRE .... Kure [*Japan*] [*Seismograph station code, US Geological Survey*] [*Closed*] (SEIS)
KREA .... Ontario, CA [*FM radio station call letters*]
KREA-AM ... Honolulu, HI [*AM radio station call letters*] (BROA)
KREB .... Huntsville, AR [*FM radio station call letters*]
KREB-AM ... Bentonville-Bella Vista, AR [*AM radio station call letters*] (BROA)
KREC .... Brian Head, UT [*FM radio station call letters*]
KRED .... Eureka, CA [*FM radio station call letters*] (GDPB)
KRED-FM ... Eureka, CA [*FM radio station call letters*]
KREE .... Lubbock/Reese Air Force Base [*Texas*] [*ICAO location identifier*] (ICLI)
KREEP .... Potassium and Rare-Earth Elements and Phosphorus (SAUS)
KREEP .... Potassium [*Chemical symbol: K*], Rare-Earth Elements, and Phosphorus [*Acronym used to describe crust material brought from the moon by astronauts*]
KREEP .... Potassium, Rare Earth Elements, Phosphorus (SAUS)
KREF-AM ... Norman, OK [*AM radio station call letters*] (BROA)
KREG .... Glenwood Springs, CO [*Television station call letters*]
KREG .... Koll Real Estate Group [*NASDAQ symbol*] (SAG)
KREG .... Koll Real Estate Grp [*NASDAQ symbol*] (TTSB)
KREGP ...... Koll Real Estate Cv'A'Pfd [*NASDAQ symbol*] (TTSB)
KREH .... Oakdale, LA [*AM radio station call letters*]
KREH .... Pecan Grove, TX [*AM radio station call letters*] (BROA)
KREI .... Farmington, MO [*AM radio station call letters*]
KREIC .... Kuwait Real Estate Investment Consortium (BUAC)
Kreislr .... Kreisler Manufacturing Co. [*Associated Press*] (SAG)
KREJ .... Medicine Lodge, KS [*FM radio station call letters*]
KREK .... Bristow, OK [*FM radio station call letters*]
KREL .... California, MO [*AM radio station call letters*] (RBYB)
KREM .... Krispy Kreme Doughnuts [*NASDAQ symbol*] (SG)
KREM .... Spokane, WA [*Television station call letters*]
KREMS ...... Kiernan Reentry Measurement Site
KREMU ...... Kenya Department of Resources Surveys and Remote Sensing (BUAC)
KREMU ...... Kenya Rangeland Ecological Monitoring Unit
KREN .... Kings Road Entertainment, Inc. [*NASDAQ symbol*] (NQ)
KREN .... Kings Road Entmt [*NASDAQ symbol*] (TTSB)
KREN .... Reno, NV [*Television station call letters*]
KREO-FM ... Superior, MT [*FM radio station call letters*] (BROA)
KREP .... Belleville, KS [*FM radio station call letters*]
KREPrL ...... Capital Re LLC'MIPS' [*NYSE symbol*] (TTSB)
KRES .... Moberly, MO [*FM radio station call letters*]
KRESS .... Kinetic Ring Energy Storage System
Kress .... Kress' Reports [*2-12 Pennsylvania Superior Court*] [*166-194 Pennsylvania*] [*A publication*] (DLA)
Krestintern ... International Farmer and Peasant Council (SAUO)
KREU-FM ... Roland, OK [*FM radio station call letters*] (RBYB)
KREUZ .... Kreuzer [*Monetary unit*] [*German*] (ROG)
KREV .... Lakeville, MN [*FM radio station call letters*]
KREW .... Sunnyside, WA [*AM radio station call letters*]
KREW-FM ... Sunnyside, WA [*FM radio station call letters*]
KREX .... Grand Junction, CO [*Television station call letters*]
KREX .... Keel Blade Tip Reflex [*Botany*]
KREY .... Montrose, CO [*Television station call letters*]
KREZ .... Durango, CO [*Television station call letters*]
KREZ .... Marble Hill, MO [*FM radio station call letters*] (BROA)
KRF .... Kathode Ray Furnace
KRF .... Kentucky Research Foundation (SAUO)
KRF .... Kerf Petroleums [*Vancouver Stock Exchange symbol*]
KRF .... Knowledge of Results Feedback
KRF .... Kramfors [*Sweden*] [*Airport symbol*] (OAG)
KrF .... Kristelig Folkpartiet [*Christian People's Party*] [*Norway*] [*Political party*] (PPE)

KrF.......... Kristeligt Folkeparti [*Christian People's Party*] [*Denmark*] [*Political party*] (PPE)
KRF.......... No. 32 (The Royal) Squadron [*British*] [*FAA designator*] (FAAC)
KRFA........ Moscow, ID [*FM radio station call letters*]
KRFC........ KISS [*Knights in the Service of Satan*] Rocks Fan Club (EA)
KRFE........ Lubbock, TX [*AM radio station call letters*] (RBYB)
KRFM........ Show Low, AZ [*FM radio station call letters*]
KRFN........ Knight-Ridder Financial News [*Database*] (IT)
KRFO........ Owatonna, MN [*AM radio station call letters*]
KRFO-FM... Owatonna, MN [*FM radio station call letters*]
KRFR........ Shafter, CA [*FM radio station call letters*] (BROA)
KRFS........ Superior, NE [*AM radio station call letters*]
KRFS-FM... Superior, NE [*FM radio station call letters*]
KRFT........ Knowledge of Results Feedback Task (SAA)
KRFT-AM.... De Soto, MO [*AM radio station call letters*] (BROA)
KRFW........ Fort Worth [*Texas*] [*ICAO location identifier*] (ICLI)
KRFX........ Denver, CO [*FM radio station call letters*]
KRG.......... Coloring [*Telegraphy*] (PCTE)
KRG.......... Kakapo Recovery Group (SAUO)
KRG.......... Karasabai [*Guyana*] [*Airport symbol*] (OAG)
KRG.......... Kerema [*Papua New Guinea*] [*Seismograph station code, US Geological Survey*] [*Closed*] (SEIS)
KRG.......... Kiwi Recovery Group (SAUO)
KRG.......... Knight of the Redeemer of Greece (ROG)
KRG.......... Kokako Recovery Group (SAUO)
KRG.......... Krebs-Ringer-Glucose [*Buffer solution and growth medium*]
KRG.......... KRG Management, Inc. [*Toronto Stock Exchange symbol*]
KrG.......... Kriegsgericht [*War Tribunal*] [*German*]
KRG.......... Krug International Corp. [*AMEX symbol*] (SAG)
KRG.......... Quantum Restaurant Group, Inc. [*NYSE symbol*] (SPSG)
KRGC........ Chicago [*Illinois*] [*ICAO location identifier*] (ICLI)
KRGD-FM... Burlington, CO [*FM radio station call letters*] (BROA)
KRGE........ Weslaco, TX [*AM radio station call letters*]
KRGI........ Grand Island, NE [*AM radio station call letters*]
KRGI-FM.... Grand Island, NE [*FM radio station call letters*]
KRGN........ Amarillo, TX [*FM radio station call letters*]
KRGO........ Fowler, CA [*AM radio station call letters*]
KRGO........ Kargo Trailers [*NCIC trailer make code*]
KRGQ........ West Valley City, UT [*AM radio station call letters*]
KRGQ-FM... Roy, UT [*FM radio station call letters*]
KRGS........ Rifle, CO [*AM radio station call letters*]
K Rgt........ Kenya Regiment (SAUO)
KRGV........ Weslaco, TX [*Television station call letters*]
KRGY........ Aurora, NE [*FM radio station call letters*] (BROA)
Krh.......... Karachi (SAUO)
KRH.......... Redhill [*England*] [*Airport symbol*]
KRHCF...... Rich Coast Res Ltd [*NASDAQ symbol*] (TTSB)
KRHCF...... Rich Coast Resouces [*NASDAQ symbol*] (SAG)
KRHD........ Duncan, OK [*AM radio station call letters*]
KRHD-FM... Duncan, OK [*FM radio station call letters*]
KRHS........ Overland, MO [*FM radio station call letters*]
KRHT-AM... Concord, CA [*AM radio station call letters*] (RBYB)
KRHV........ Big Pine, CA [*FM radio station call letters*] (RBYB)
KRHW........ Sikeston, MO [*AM radio station call letters*] (GDPB)
KRHW-AM.. Sikeston, MO [*AM radio station call letters*] (BROA)
KRI.......... Karin Lake Explorations [*Vancouver Stock Exchange symbol*]
KRI.......... Kikori [*Papua New Guinea*] [*Airport symbol*] (OAG)
KRI.......... King Research, Inc. [*Computer consultant*] [*Information service or system*] (IID)
KRI.......... King's Royal Irish [*Military unit*] [*British*]
KRI.......... Knight-Ridder, Inc. [*NYSE symbol*] (SPSG)
KRI.......... Krilo [*Former USSR*] [*FAA designator*] (FAAC)
KRI.......... Krio [*Language symbol*] (ETLW)
KRIB........ Mason City, IA [*AM radio station call letters*]
KRIC........ Korean Reinsurance Company (SAUO)
KRIC........ Rexburg, ID [*FM radio station call letters*]
KRIC........ Richmond/Richard Evelyn Byrd International [*Virginia*] [*ICAO location identifier*] (ICLI)
K-RIDE...... Rail Infrastructure Development Corporation [*Indian Railway*] (TIR)
KRIG........ Nowata, OK [*FM radio station call letters*]
KRIG........ Pawhuska, OK [*AM radio station call letters*] (RBYB)
KRIH........ King's Royal Irish Hussars [*British military*] (DMA)
KRII.......... International Falls, MN [*Television station call letters*] (BROA)
KRII.......... Knight-Ridder Information Inc.
KRIL........ Odessa, TX [*AM radio station call letters*]
KRIM........ Payson, AZ [*FM radio station call letters*]
KRIN........ Waterloo, IA [*Television station call letters*]
KRIO........ Floresville, TX [*FM radio station call letters*]
KRIO........ McAllen, TX [*AM radio station call letters*]
KRIPA....... Korean Research Institute of Public Administration (BUAC)
KRIPES..... K-Resolved Inverse Photoelectron Spectroscopy
KRIPES..... K-Resolved Inverse Photoemission Spectroscopy (SAUS)
KRIPO....... Kriminalpolizei [*Ordinary Criminal Police*] [*German*]
KRIS........ Corpus Christi, TX [*Television station call letters*]
KRIS........ Kentucky Resources Information System (SAUO)
KRIS........ Kris Kraft Mobile Homes [*NCIC trailer make code*]
KRISO....... Korea Research Institute of Ship and Ocean (BUAC)
KRISP....... Kenya Rift International Seismic Project
KRISS....... Korean Research Institute of Standards and Science (SAUO)
KRISS....... Korea Research Institute of Standards and Science (SAUO)
KRIST....... Konkan Railway Institute for Staff Training [*Indian Railway*] (TIR)
KRITIC...... Knowledge Representation and Inference Techniques in Industrial Control (SAUO)
KRITIC...... Knowlege based Review and Intervention to Impose Constraints (SAUO)
KRIV........ Houston, TX [*Television station call letters*]
KRIV........ Riverside/March Air Force Base [*California*] [*ICAO location identifier*] (ICLI)
KRIV-DT.... Houston, TX [*Television station call letters*] (BROA)
KRIX........ General Electric Railcar Services [*Private rail car owner code*]
KRIZ........ Kramer Industries [*Federal Railroad Administration identification code*]
KRIZ........ Renton, WA [*AM radio station call letters*]
KRJ.......... Kamimuroga [*Japan*] [*Seismograph station code, US Geological Survey*] (SEIS)
KRJB........ Ada, MN [*FM radio station call letters*]
KRJC........ Elko, NV [*FM radio station call letters*]
KRJM........ Mahnomen, MN [*FM radio station call letters*] (BROA)
KRJO-AM... Monroe, LA [*AM radio station call letters*] (BROA)
KRJT........ Bowie, TX [*AM radio station call letters*]
KRJT-FM... Bowie, TX [*FM radio station call letters*]
KRJY........ St. Louis, MO (Mt. Vernon, IL) [*FM radio station call letters*] (GDPB)
KRK.......... Kirkenes [*Norway*] [*Seismograph station code, US Geological Survey*] [*Closed*] (SEIS)
KRK.......... Krakow [*Poland*] [*Airport symbol*] (OAG)
KRKA........ Erath, LA [*FM radio station call letters*] (BROA)
KRKC........ Kansas City [*Missouri*] [*ICAO location identifier*] (ICLI)
KRKC........ King City, CA [*AM radio station call letters*]
KRKC-FM... King City, CA [*FM radio station call letters*]
KRKD........ Dermott, AR [*FM radio station call letters*] (BROA)
KRKE........ Aspen, CO [*AM radio station call letters*]
KRKH-FM... Harwood, ND [*FM radio station call letters*] (BROA)
KRKI........ Estes Park, CO [*AM radio station call letters*]
KRKI........ Newcastle, WY [*FM radio station call letters*] (BROA)
KRKK........ Rock Springs, WY [*AM radio station call letters*]
KRKL........ Yountville, CA [*AM radio station call letters*]
KRKM........ Kremmling, CO [*FM radio station call letters*]
KRKN........ Eldon, IA (RBYB)
KRKN........ Kraken (ABBR)
KRKO........ Everett, WA [*AM radio station call letters*]
KRKQ........ Des Moines, IA [*FM radio station call letters*] (GDPB)
KRKQ-FM... Boone, IA [*FM radio station call letters*] (RBYB)
KRKR-FM... Lincoln, NE [*FM radio station call letters*] (BROA)
KRKR-FM... Roy, UT [*FM radio station call letters*] (RBYB)
KRKS........ Boulder, CO [*FM radio station call letters*]
KRKS........ Denver, CO [*AM radio station call letters*]
KRKT........ Albany, OR [*AM radio station call letters*]
KRKT-FM.... Albany, OR [*FM radio station call letters*]
KRKU........ McCook, NE [*FM radio station call letters*] (BROA)
KRKX........ Billings, MT [*FM radio station call letters*]
KRKY........ Granby, CO [*AM radio station call letters*]
KRKZ........ Altus, OK [*FM radio station call letters*]
KRL.......... Karlsruhe [*Federal Republic of Germany*] [*Seismograph station code, US Geological Survey*] (SEIS)
KRL.......... Kathode Ray Lamp
KRL.......... Kingdom Resources Ltd. [*Vancouver Stock Exchange symbol*]
KRL.......... Kirchhoff Radiation Law [*Physics*]
KRL.......... Knowledge Representation Language
KRL.......... Korla [*China*] [*Airport symbol*] (OAG)
KRL.......... Kryla [*Ukraine*] [*FAA designator*] (FAAC)
KRLA........ Glendale, CA [*AM radio station call letters*] (BROA)
KRLA........ Los Angeles [*California*] [*ICAO location identifier*] (ICLI)
KRLA........ Pasadena, CA [*AM radio station call letters*]
KRLB........ Lubbock, TX [*FM radio station call letters*]
KRLC........ Lewiston, ID [*AM radio station call letters*]
KRLD........ Dallas, TX [*AM radio station call letters*]
KRLDA...... Kansas Association of Beverage Retailers (EARSL)
KRLF........ Pullman, WA [*FM radio station call letters*]
KRLI........ Malta Bend, MO [*FM radio station call letters*]
KRLJ........ La Junta, CO [*FM radio station call letters*] (BROA)
KRLK........ Cassville, MO [*FM radio station call letters*]
KRLK........ Kreilkamp Trucking [*Common carrier symbol*]
KRLK........ Stockton, MO [*FM radio station call letters*] (BROA)
KRLN........ Canon City, CO [*AM radio station call letters*]
KRLN-FM... Canon City, CO [*FM radio station call letters*]
KRLR........ Las Vegas, NV [*Television station call letters*]
KRLS........ Keweenaw Rocket Launch Site [*University of Michigan*]
KRLS........ Knoxville, IA [*FM radio station call letters*]
KRLT........ South Lake Tahoe, CA [*FM radio station call letters*]
KRLV........ Las Vegas, NV [*AM radio station call letters*] (RBYB)
KRLW........ Walnut Ridge, AR [*AM radio station call letters*]
KRLW-FM... Walnut Ridge, AR [*FM radio station call letters*]
KRLX........ Northfield, MN [*FM radio station call letters*]
KRLz........ Krelitz Industries, Inc. (SAUO)
KRM.......... Karma (ABBR)
KRM.......... Kentucky Railway Museum [*Federal Railroad Administration identification code*]
KRM.......... Klein-Rydberg Method [*Physics*]
KRM.......... Kurmenty [*Former USSR*] [*Seismograph station code, US Geological Survey*] (SEIS)
KRM.......... Kurzweil Reading Machine
KRM.......... Royal Ontario Museum Library [*UTLAS symbol*]
KRMA........ Denver, CO [*Television station call letters*]
KRMB-FM... Bisbee, AZ [*FM radio station call letters*] (RBYB)
KRMC........ Douglas, AZ [*FM radio station call letters*] (RBYB)
KRMC........ Karmic (ABBR)
KRMC........ K.R.M. Petroleum Corp. [*NASDAQ symbol*] (COMM)
KRMD........ Shreveport, LA [*AM radio station call letters*]

KRMD-FM... Shreveport, LA [*FM radio station call letters*]
KRME........ Rome/Griffiss Air Force Base [*New York*] [*ICAO location identifier*] (ICLI)
KRME-FM... Shafter, CA [*FM radio station call letters*] (RBYB)
KRMG....... Tulsa, OK [*AM radio station call letters*]
KRMH....... Colorado Springs-Pueblo, CO [*AM radio station call letters*] (GDPB)
KRMH....... Colorado Springs-Pueblo, CO [*FM radio station call letters*] (GDPB)
KRMH-FM... Red Mesa, AZ [*FM radio station call letters*] (BROA)
KRMJ........ Grand Junction, CO [*Television station call letters*] (BROA)
KRMJ-FM... Grand Junction, CO [*FM radio station call letters*] (RBYB)
KRML........ Carmel, CA [*AM radio station call letters*]
KRMN-FM... Shamrock, TX [*FM radio station call letters*] (BROA)
KRMO....... Cassville, MO [*AM radio station call letters*] (BROA)
KRMO....... Monett, MO [*AM radio station call letters*]
KRMP....... Anadarko, OK [*AM radio station call letters*] (GDPB)
KRMP-FM... Portland, TX [*FM radio station call letters*] (BROA)
KRMR....... Hayden, CO [*FM radio station call letters*] (BROA)
KRMS....... Osage Beach, MO [*AM radio station call letters*]
KRMS-FM... Osage Beach, MO [*FM radio station call letters*] (BROA)
KRMT........ Denver, CO [*Television station call letters*] (RBYB)
KRMX....... Kershaw Manufacturing [*Federal Railroad Administration identification code*]
KRMX....... Pueblo, CO [*AM radio station call letters*]
KRMY....... Kileen, TX [*AM radio station call letters*]
KRN.......... Food Magazine (journ.) (SAUS)
KRN.......... Kiruna [*Sweden*] [*Airport symbol*] (OAG)
KRN.......... Knight Ridder Newspapers [*Viewdata Corp.*] [*Videotex producer*] (NITA)
KRNA........ Iowa City, IA [*FM radio station call letters*]
KRNB........ Decatur, TX [*FM radio station call letters*] (RBYB)
KRNC-FM... Fresno, CA [*FM radio station call letters*] (BROA)
KRND........ San Antonio/Randolf Air Force Base [*Texas*] [*ICAO location identifier*] (ICLI)
KRNE........ Merriman, NE [*FM radio station call letters*]
KRNE-TV.... Merriman, NE [*Television station call letters*]
KRNG........ Fallon, NV [*FM radio station call letters*] (RBYB)
KRNH........ Comfort, TX [*FM radio station call letters*]
KRNH........ Kerrville, TX [*FM radio station call letters*] (BROA)
KRNI......... Mason City, IA [*AM radio station call letters*]
KRNL........ Kernel (ABBR)
KRNL........ Mount Vernon, IA [*FM radio station call letters*]
KRNM-FM... Saipan, MP [*FM radio station call letters*] (BROA)
KRNN-AM... North Little Rock, AR [*AM radio station call letters*] (RBYB)
KRNO........ Reno/International [*Nevada*] [*ICAO location identifier*] (ICLI)
KRNO........ Reno, NV [*FM radio station call letters*]
KRNQ-FM... Keokuk, IA [*FM radio station call letters*] (RBYB)
KRNR........ Roseburg, OR [*AM radio station call letters*]
KRNT........ Des Moines, IA [*AM radio station call letters*]
KRNU........ Lincoln, NE [*FM radio station call letters*]
KRNV........ Reno, NV [*Television station call letters*]
KRNV-FM... Reno, NV [*FM radio station call letters*] (RBYB)
KRNW....... Chillicothe, MO [*FM radio station call letters*]
KRNX-AM... Victoria, TX [*AM radio station call letters*] (BROA)
KRNY........ Kearney, NE [*FM radio station call letters*]
KRNY........ New York [*New York*] [*ICAO location identifier*] (ICLI)
KRO.......... Alibiu Airways SpA [*Italy*] [*ICAO designator*] (FAAC)
KRO.......... Congress of Russian Communities [*Political party*] (PSAP)
KRO.......... Kathode Ray Oscilloscope
KRO.......... Katholieke Radio Omroep [*Catholic Broadcasting Association*] [*Netherlands*]
KRO.......... Kreis Resident Officer (SAUO)
kro........... Kru [*MARC language code*] [*Library of Congress*] (LCCP)
KROA........ Grand Island, NE [*FM radio station call letters*]
KROAG...... Committee for the Revolution in Oman and the Arabian Gulf [*Denmark*]
KROB........ Robstown, TX [*AM radio station call letters*] (GDPB)
KROC........ Keg Ran Out Club (EARSL)
KROC........ Rochester, MN [*AM radio station call letters*]
KROC........ Rochester/Rochester-Monroe County [*New York*] [*ICAO location identifier*] (ICLI)
KROC-FM... Rochester, MN [*FM radio station call letters*]
KROD........ El Paso, TX [*AM radio station call letters*]
KROE........ Sheridan, WY [*AM radio station call letters*]
Kroeber Anthr Soe Pap... Kroeber Anthropological Society Papers. Berkeley (SAUO)
KROE-FM... Sheridan, WY [*FM radio station call letters*]
KROF........ Abbeville, LA [*AM radio station call letters*]
KROF-FM... Abbeville, LA [*FM radio station call letters*]
KROG........ Grants Pass, OR [*FM radio station call letters*] (BROA)
KROG........ Kroll-O'Gara [*Stock market symbol*]
KROG........ Kroll O'Gara Co. [*NASDAQ symbol*]
KROG........ Phoenix, OR [*FM radio station call letters*]
Kroger....... [*The*] Kroger Co. [*Associated Press*] (SAG)
KROJ........ Vinton, IA [*FM radio station call letters*] (BROA)
KROK........ De Ridder, LA [*FM radio station call letters*]
KROL........ Las Cruces, NM [*FM radio station call letters*]
KROM....... Kromag [*NCIC motorcycle make code*]
KROM....... San Antonio, TX [*FM radio station call letters*]
KRON........ Kronos, Inc. [*NASDAQ symbol*] (SAG)
KRON........ San Francisco, CA [*Television station call letters*]
KRON-DT... San Francisco, CA [*Television station call letters*] (BROA)
Kronos...... Kronos, Inc. [*Associated Press*] (SAG)
KROO........ Breckenridge, TX [*FM radio station call letters*]
KROP........ Brawley, CA [*AM radio station call letters*]
KROP........ Kropf Manufacturing Company [*NCIC trailer make code*]
KROPAC..... Kroger PAC [*Cincinnati, OH*] (PACS)
KROQ........ Pasadena, CA [*FM radio station call letters*]
KROR-FM... Hastings, NE [*FM radio station call letters*] (BROA)
KROS........ Clinton, IA [*AM radio station call letters*]
KROS........ Kross Kountry [*NCIC trailer make code*]
KROTOS..... Test facility at Joint Research Center Ispra for studying steam explosions (SAUO)
KROU........ Spencer, OK [*FM radio station call letters*]
KROW....... Krown Camper [*NCIC trailer make code*]
KROW....... Mariposa, CA [*FM radio station call letters*]
KROW....... Roswell/Industrial Air Center [*New Mexico*] [*ICAO location identifier*] (ICLI)
KROW-FM... Huntsville, MO [*FM radio station call letters*] (BROA)
KROX........ Crookston, MN [*AM radio station call letters*]
KROX-FM... Giddings, TX [*FM radio station call letters*] (RBYB)
KROY........ Kroy Inc. (SAUO)
KROY........ Palacios, TX [*FM radio station call letters*] (BROA)
KROY........ Victorville, CA [*AM radio station call letters*] (RBYB)
KROZ........ Roseburg, OR [*Television station call letters*]
KRP.......... Corrupt [*Telegraphy*] (PCTE)
KRP.......... Karapiro [*New Zealand*] [*Seismograph station code, US Geological Survey*] (SEIS)
KRP.......... Karup [*Denmark*] [*Airport symbol*] (OAG)
KRP.......... Key Resource People [*US Chamber of Commerce*]
KRP.......... Kinesin-Related Polypeptide [*Biochemistry*]
KRP.......... King's Rook's Pawn [*Chess*]
KRP.......... Known Reference Point
KRP.......... Kodak Relief Plate
KRP.......... Kolmer [*Test with*] Reiter Protein [*Serology*]
KRP.......... Krebs-Ringer-Phosphate [*Buffer solution*]
KRP.......... Kurdistan Revolutionary Party [*Iraq*] [*Political party*] (PPW)
KRPA........ Rancho Palos Verdes, CA [*Television station call letters*]
KRPB........ Krebs-Ringer-Phosphate Buffer [*Solution*]
KRPD........ Corrupted [*Telegraphy*] (PCTE)
KRPG........ Corrupting [*Telegraphy*] (PCTE)
KRPH-FM... Dodge City, KS [*FM radio station call letters*] (BROA)
KRPI......... Kinshasa Peace Research Institute (SAUO)
KRPL........ Moscow, ID [*AM radio station call letters*]
KRPM....... Houston, AK [*FM radio station call letters*] (BROA)
KRPM....... Tacoma, WA [*FM radio station call letters*]
KRPM-AM... Seattle, WA [*AM radio station call letters*] (RBYB)
KRPN........ Corruption [*Telegraphy*] (PCTE)
KRPQ........ Rohnert Park, CA [*FM radio station call letters*]
KRPR........ Rochester, MN [*FM radio station call letters*]
KRPS........ Corrupts [*Telegraphy*] (PCTE)
KRPS........ Krebs-Ringer-Phosphate Buffer Solution (MAE)
KRPS........ Pittsburg, KS [*FM radio station call letters*]
KRPT........ Anadarko, OK [*AM radio station call letters*]
KRPT-FM.... Anadarko, OK [*FM radio station call letters*]
KRPU........ Karlander [*Intermodal shipping container symbol*] (TVRC)
KRPV........ Roswell, NM [*Television station call letters*]
KRPX........ Price, UT [*AM radio station call letters*]
KRQ.......... Crimsonstar Resources [*Vancouver Stock Exchange symbol*]
KRQC........ Bennington, NE [*FM radio station call letters*] (BROA)
KRQC........ Marina, CA [*FM radio station call letters*]
KRQE........ Albuquerque, NM [*Television station call letters*]
KRQK........ Lompoc, CA [*FM radio station call letters*]
KRQQ........ Tucson, AZ [*FM radio station call letters*]
KRQR........ San Francisco, CA [*FM radio station call letters*]
KRQS........ Pagosa Springs, CO [*FM radio station call letters*]
KRQS........ Santa Fe, NM [*FM radio station call letters*] (BROA)
KRQT-FM... Castle Rock, WA [*FM radio station call letters*] (RBYB)
KRQU........ Laramie, WY [*FM radio station call letters*]
KRQX........ Mexia, TX [*AM radio station call letters*]
KRQZ........ Lompoc, CA [*FM radio station call letters*] (BROA)
KRQZ-FM... Wagoner, OK [*FM radio station call letters*] (RBYB)
KRR.......... Kansai Research Reactor [*Japan*]
KRR.......... Karoi [*Zimbabwe*] [*Seismograph station code, US Geological Survey*] (SEIS)
KRR.......... Kettle River Resources Ltd. [*Vancouver Stock Exchange symbol*]
KRR.......... Kiamichi Railroad [*Federal Railroad Administration identification code*]
KRR.......... King's Royal Rifles [*Military unit*] [*British*]
KRR.......... Krasnodar [*Former USSR*] [*Airport symbol*] (OAG)
KRRA........ Newport, OR [*FM radio station call letters*] (BROA)
KRRA-AM... West Covina, CA [*AM radio station call letters*] (BROA)
KRRB........ Dickinson, ND [*FM radio station call letters*]
KRRB........ Perry, KS [*FM radio station call letters*] (BROA)
KRRC........ King's Royal Rifle Corps [*Military unit*] [*British*]
KRRC........ Portland, OR [*FM radio station call letters*]
KRRD........ Dickinson, ND [*FM radio station call letters*]
KRRE........ Davis, CA [*FM radio station call letters*] (BROA)
KRRE-FM... Shingle Springs, CA [*FM radio station call letters*] (BROA)
KRRF-AM... Denver, CO [*AM radio station call letters*] (RBYB)
KRRG........ Laredo, TX [*FM radio station call letters*]
KRRK........ Bennington, NE [*FM radio station call letters*]
KRRK-FM... Lake Havasu City, AZ [*FM radio station call letters*] (BROA)
KRRM....... Rogue River, OR [*FM radio station call letters*]
KRRN........ Las Vegas, NV [*FM radio station call letters*] (BROA)
KRRNY...... King's Royal Regiment of New York (GEAB)
KRRO........ Sioux Falls, SD [*FM radio station call letters*]
KRRP........ Coushatta, LA [*AM radio station call letters*]
KRRQ........ Lafayette, LA [*FM radio station call letters*]

KRRR-FM ... Cheyenne, WY [*FM radio station call letters*] (RBYB)
KRRS .... Karnataka State Farmers' Association (India) [*Political party*] (PSAP)
KRRS .... Kinetic Resonance Raman Spectroscopy (DAVI)
KRRS .... Santa Rosa, CA [*AM radio station call letters*]
KRRT .... Kerrville, TX [*Television station call letters*]
KRRU .... Pueblo, CO [*AM radio station call letters*]
KRRV .... Alexandria, LA [*AM radio station call letters*]
KRRV-FM ... Alexandria, LA [*FM radio station call letters*]
KRRW .... Dallas, TX [*FM radio station call letters*]
KRRW-FM .. St. James, MN [*FM radio station call letters*] (BROA)
KRRX .... Chico-Redding, CA [*FM radio station call letters*] (GDPB)
KRRX-FM ... Burney, CA [*FM radio station call letters*] (BROA)
KRRY .... Canton, MO [*FM radio station call letters*] (RBYB)
KRRZ .... Minot, ND [*AM radio station call letters*]
KRS .... Colors [*Telegraphy*] (PCTE)
KRS .... Kearney State College, Kearney, NE [*OCLC symbol*] (OCLC)
KRS .... Kentucky Revised Statutes [*A publication*]
KRS .... Kerato-Refractive Society (EA)
KRS .... Kernighan + Ritchie Standard (SAUO)
KRS .... Kinematograph Renter's Society
KRS .... Knowledge-based Replanning System (SAUO)
KRS .... Knowledge Retrieval System [*KnowledgeSet Corp.*]
KRS .... Korsar [*Russian Federation*] [*ICAO designator*] (FAAC)
KRS .... Krasnogorka [*Former USSR*] [*Seismograph station code, US Geological Survey*] [*Closed*] (SEIS)
KRS .... Kristiansand [*Norway*] [*Airport symbol*] (OAG)
KRSA .... Petersburg, AK [*AM radio station call letters*]
KRSB .... Roseburg, OR [*FM radio station call letters*]
KRSC .... Claremore, OK [*Television station call letters*]
KRSC .... Kaiser Resources, Inc. [*NASDAQ symbol*] (SAG)
KRSC .... Kaiser Ventures [*NASDAQ symbol*] (TTSB)
KRSC .... Kaiser Ventures, Inc. [*NASDAQ symbol*] (SAG)
KRSC .... Othello, WA [*AM radio station call letters*]
KRSC-FM ... Claremore, OK [*FM radio station call letters*] (RBYB)
KRSD .... Sioux Falls, SD [*FM radio station call letters*]
KRSE .... Seattle [*Washington*] [*ICAO location identifier*] (ICLI)
KRSE .... Yakima, WA [*FM radio station call letters*]
KRSEN ...... Kerosene (ABBR)
KRSH .... Healdsburg, CA [*FM radio station call letters*] (BROA)
KRSH .... Middletown, CA [*FM radio station call letters*]
KRSHB ...... Annals of Science. Kanazawa University (journ.) (SAUS)
KRSI .... Garapan-Saipan, MP [*FM radio station call letters*]
KRSI .... Kelly Russell Studios, Inc. [*NASDAQ symbol*] (SAG)
KRSI .... Kreisler Mfg [*NASDAQ symbol*] (TTSB)
KRSJ .... Durango, CO [*FM radio station call letters*]
KRSK-FM ... Salem, OR [*FM radio station call letters*] (BROA)
KRSL .... Kreisler Manufacturing Co. [*NASDAQ symbol*] (NQ)
KRSL .... Kreisler Manufacturing Corp. [*NASDAQ symbol*]
KRSL .... Russell, KS [*AM radio station call letters*]
KRSM .... Dallas, TX [*FM radio station call letters*]
KRSN .... Kerosene (MSA)
KRSN .... Los Alamos, NM [*AM radio station call letters*]
KRS-ONE.... Knowledge Reigns Supreme Over Nearly Everyone [*Rap recording artist*]
KRSP .... Salt Lake City, UT [*FM radio station call letters*]
KRSQ .... Laurel, MT [*FM radio station call letters*]
KRSR .... Coos Bay, OR [*AM radio station call letters*]
KRSR-FM ... Santa Rosa, NM [*FM radio station call letters*] (BROA)
KRSS .... Chubbuck, ID [*FM radio station call letters*]
KRSS .... Tarkio, MO [*FM radio station call letters*] (BROA)
KRST .... Albuquerque, NM [*FM radio station call letters*]
KRSTL .... Knowledge Representation Systems Trials Laboratory [*Pronounced "crystal"*] [*Artificial intelligence*]
KRSU .... Appleton, MN [*FM radio station call letters*]
KRSV .... Afton, WY [*AM radio station call letters*]
KRSV-FM ... Afton, WY [*FM radio station call letters*]
KRSW .... Worthington-Marshall, MN [*FM radio station call letters*]
KRSX .... Kayen Rail Car Service [*Federal Railroad Administration identification code*]
KRSY .... La Luz, NM [*FM radio station call letters*] (BROA)
KRSY .... Roswell, NM [*AM radio station call letters*]
KRSY-AM ... Alamogordo, NM [*AM radio station call letters*] (BROA)
KRT .... Cretan Airlines SA [*Greece*] [*ICAO designator*] (FAAC)
KRT .... Karate
KRT .... Kathode Ray Tube (AAG)
KRT .... Keratin (DMAA)
KRT .... Keravat [*New Britain*] [*Seismograph station code, US Geological Survey*] [*Closed*] (SEIS)
KRT .... Khartoum [*Sudan*] [*Airport symbol*] (OAG)
KRT .... Knight-Ridder, Inc. (EFIS)
KRT .... Kranzco Realty Trust [*NYSE symbol*] (SPSG)
KRT .... Tumari Kanuri [*Language symbol*] (ETLW)
KRTA .... K and R Transportation [*Common carrier symbol*]
KRTA .... Kentucky Retired Teachers Association (EARSL)
KRTA .... Medford, OR [*AM radio station call letters*] (RBYB)
KRTBN ...... Knight-Ridder/Tribune Business News [*Database*] (GDD)
KRTD .... K and R Transportation [*Common carrier symbol*]
KRTE .... Karate (ABBR)
KRTH .... Los Angeles, CA [*FM radio station call letters*]
KRTI .... Grinnell, IA [*FM radio station call letters*]
KRTK .... Chubbuck, ID [*AM radio station call letters*] (BROA)
KRTL .... Atlanta [*Georgia*] [*ICAO location identifier*] (ICLI)
KRTM .... Temecula, CA [*FM radio station call letters*]
KRTN .... Karatin (ABBR)
KRTN .... Raton, NM [*AM radio station call letters*]
KRTN-FM ... Raton, NM [*FM radio station call letters*]
KRTO .... Kathode Ray Tube Oscillograph
KRTO-FM ... West Covina, CA [*FM radio station call letters*] (RBYB)
KRTR .... Kailua, HI [*FM radio station call letters*]
KRTR-AM ... Honolulu, HI [*AM radio station call letters*] (BROA)
KRTS .... Kathode Ray Tube Shield
KRTS .... Seabrook, TX [*FM radio station call letters*]
KRTT .... Kathode Ray Tube Tester
KRTU .... San Antonio, TX [*FM radio station call letters*]
KRTV .... Great Falls, MT [*Television station call letters*]
KRTX .... Galveston, TX [*FM radio station call letters*]
KRTX .... Kanawha River Terminal [*Federal Railroad Administration identification code*]
KRTX .... Rosenberg-Richmond, TX [*AM radio station call letters*] (BROA)
KRTY .... Kirtley Trucking Company [*Common carrier symbol*]
KRTY .... Los Gatos, CA [*FM radio station call letters*]
KRTZ .... Cortez, CO [*FM radio station call letters*]
KRU .... Crusade [*Telegraphy*] (PCTE)
KRU .... Karasu [*Former USSR*] [*Seismograph station code, US Geological Survey*] (SEIS)
KRU .... Krueger Brewing Company (SAUO)
kru .... Kurukh [*MARC language code*] [*Library of Congress*] (LCCP)
KRUA .... Anchorage, AK [*FM radio station call letters*]
KRUC-FM ... Las Cruces, NM [*FM radio station call letters*] (BROA)
KRUD .... Honolulu, HI [*AM radio station call letters*] (BROA)
KRUE .... W.A. Krueger Co. [*NASDAQ symbol*] (COMM)
KRUE .... Waseca, MN [*FM radio station call letters*]
KRUF .... Shreveport, LA [*FM radio station call letters*] (GDPB)
KRUF-FM ... Shreveport, LA [*FM radio station call letters*] (RBYB)
KRUG .... KRUG International [*NASDAQ symbol*] (TTSB)
KRUG .... KRUG International Corp. [*NASDAQ symbol*] (NQ)
KRUGW ..... KRUG Intl Wrrt [*NASDAQ symbol*] (TTSB)
KRUI .... Iowa City, IA [*FM radio station call letters*]
KRUI .... Ruidoso Downs, NM [*AM radio station call letters*]
Krummeck .. Decisions of the Water Courts [*1913-36*] [*South Africa*] [*A publication*] (DLA)
KRUN .... Ballinger, TX [*AM radio station call letters*]
KRUN-FM ... Ballinger, TX [*FM radio station call letters*]
KRUP .... Dillingham, AK [*FM radio station call letters*] (RBYB)
KRUS .... Ruston, LA [*AM radio station call letters*]
KRUU .... Boone, IA [*FM radio station call letters*]
KRUX .... Las Cruces, NM [*FM radio station call letters*]
KRUZ .... Europa Cruises [*NASDAQ symbol*] (TTSB)
KRUZ .... Europa Cruises Corp. [*NASDAQ symbol*] (SAG)
KRUZ .... Santa Barbara, CA [*FM radio station call letters*]
KRV .... Kilham Rat Virus [*Medicine*]
KRV .... Kirovabad [*Former USSR*] [*Seismograph station code, US Geological Survey*] (SEIS)
KRVA .... Cockrell Hill, TX [*AM radio station call letters*]
KRVA .... McKinney, TX [*FM radio station call letters*]
KRVB .... Nampa, ID [*FM radio station call letters*] (BROA)
KRVC .... Medford, OR [*AM radio station call letters*]
KRVE .... Brusly, LA [*FM radio station call letters*]
KRVF .... Terrell, TX [*FM radio station call letters*] (BROA)
KRVG .... Glenwood Springs, CO [*FM radio station call letters*] (BROA)
KRVH .... Rio Vista, CA [*FM radio station call letters*]
KRVI .... Detroit Lakes, MN [*FM radio station call letters*] (BROA)
KRVK-FM ... Midwest, WY [*FM radio station call letters*] (BROA)
KRVL .... Kerrville, TX [*FM radio station call letters*]
KRVM .... Eugene, OR [*FM radio station call letters*]
KRVN .... Lexington, NE [*AM radio station call letters*]
KRVN-FM ... Lexington, NE [*FM radio station call letters*]
KRVO .... Vancouver, WA [*FM radio station call letters*] (BROA)
KRVQ-FM ... Blanchard, LA [*FM radio station call letters*] (BROA)
KRVR .... Copperopolis, CA [*FM radio station call letters*] (RBYB)
KRVS .... Lafayette, LA [*FM radio station call letters*]
KRVT-AM ... Claremore, OK [*AM radio station call letters*] (BROA)
KRVV .... Bastrop, LA [*FM radio station call letters*]
KRVY .... Starbuck, MN [*FM radio station call letters*] (BROA)
KRVZ .... Springerville-Eager, AZ [*AM radio station call letters*]
KRW .... Karlsruhe - West [*Federal Republic of Germany*] [*Seismograph station code, US Geological Survey*] (SEIS)
KRWA .... Waldron, AR [*FM radio station call letters*]
KRWA .... Washington [*District of Columbia*] [*ICAO location identifier*] (ICLI)
KRWB .... Roseau, MN [*AM radio station call letters*]
KRWB-FM ... Roseau, MN [*FM radio station call letters*] (RBYB)
KRWC .... Buffalo, MN [*AM radio station call letters*]
KRWF .... Redwood Falls, MN [*Television station call letters*]
KRWG .... Las Cruces, NM [*FM radio station call letters*]
KRWG-TV ... Las Cruces, NM [*Television station call letters*]
KRWM .... Bremerton, WA [*FM radio station call letters*]
KRWN .... Farmington, NM [*FM radio station call letters*]
KRWP .... Beaumont, TX [*FM radio station call letters*] (BROA)
KRWQ .... Gold Hill, OR [*FM radio station call letters*]
KRWV-FM ... Emporia, KS [*FM radio station call letters*] (BROA)
KRX .... Christina Exploration [*Vancouver Stock Exchange symbol*]
KRX .... Kar Kar [*Papua New Guinea*] [*Airport symbol*] (OAG)
KRXB .... Beeville, TX [*FM radio station call letters*] (BROA)
KRXE .... Opelousas, LA [*FM radio station call letters*] (BROA)
KRXI .... Reno, NV [*Television station call letters*]
KRXK .... Rexburg, ID [*AM radio station call letters*]
KRXL .... Kirksville, MO [*FM radio station call letters*]
KRXO .... Oklahoma City, OK [*FM radio station call letters*]

KRXQ........ Roseville, CA [*FM radio station call letters*]
KRXQ........ Sacramento, CA [*FM radio station call letters*] (BROA)
KRXR........ Gooding, ID [*AM radio station call letters*]
KRXS........ Globe, AZ [*FM radio station call letters*]
KRXT........ Rockdale, TX [*FM radio station call letters*]
KRXV........ Yermo, CA [*FM radio station call letters*]
KRXX........ Kodiak, AK [*FM radio station call letters*] (GDPB)
KRXX-FM... Kodiak, AK [*FM radio station call letters*] (RBYB)
KRXY........ Shelton, WA [*FM radio station call letters*] (BROA)
KRXZ........ Ardmore, OK [*FM radio station call letters*] (RBYB)
KRXZ-FM... Erath, LA [*FM radio station call letters*] (BROA)
KRY.......... Crystallex Intl. [*AMEX symbol*] (SG)
KRY.......... Karamay [*China*] [*Airport symbol*] (OAG)
KRYD........ Telluride, CO [*FM radio station call letters*]
KRYK........ Chinook, MT [*FM radio station call letters*]
KRYL........ Gatesville, TX [*FM radio station call letters*]
KRYPN...... Krypton (ABBR)
KRYS........ Corpus Christi, TX [*AM radio station call letters*]
KRYS........ Krystal Co. [*NASDAQ symbol*] (SAG)
KRYS-FM... Corpus Christi, TX [*FM radio station call letters*]
KRYSQ...... Krystal Company [*NASDAQ symbol*] (TTSB)
Krystal...... Krystal Co. [*Associated Press*] (SAG)
KRZ.......... Karuizawa [*Japan*] [*Also, KAZ*] [*Seismograph station code, US Geological Survey*] (SEIS)
KRZ.......... Kiri [*Zaire*] [*Airport symbol*] (OAG)
KRZA........ Alamosa, CO [*FM radio station call letters*]
KRZB........ Archer City, TX [*FM radio station call letters*] (BROA)
KRZB-FM... Olney, TX [*FM radio station call letters*] (BROA)
KRZE........ Farmington, NM [*AM radio station call letters*]
KRZI........ Waco, TX [*AM radio station call letters*]
KRZK........ Branson, MO [*FM radio station call letters*]
KRZN........ Albuquerque, NM [*FM radio station call letters*]
KRZN........ Billings, MT [*FM radio station call letters*] (BROA)
KRZQ........ Sparks, NV [*FM radio station call letters*] (BROA)
KRZQ........ Tahoe City, CA [*FM radio station call letters*]
KRZR........ Hanford, CA [*FM radio station call letters*]
KRZX-AM... Waco, TX [*AM radio station call letters*] (BROA)
KRZY........ Albuquerque, NM [*AM radio station call letters*]
KRZY-FM.... Santa Fe, NM [*FM radio station call letters*] (RBYB)
KRZZ........ Derby, KS [*FM radio station call letters*]
KS............ Conserve [*Telegraphy*] (PCTE)
KS............ Directorate of Mission Support (SAUO)
KS............ Kafus Environmental Industries [*AMEX symbol*] [*Formerly, Kafus Capital*] (SG)
KS............ Kallmann's Syndrome [*Medicine*] (MELL)
KS............ Kansas [*Postal code*]
KS............ Kansas City Star [*Federal Railroad Administration identification code*]
KS............ Kansas Reports [*A publication*] (DLA)
KS............ Kaposi's Sarcoma [*Medicine*]
KS............ Kartagener's Syndrome [*Medicine*] (DAVI)
KS............ Kassel [*German license plate city code*]
KS............ Katoptric System [*Optics*]
KS............ Kawasaki Syndrome [*Also, KD, MLNS*]
KS............ Keep Type Standing [*Printing*]
KS............ Kehr's Sign [*Medicine*] (MELL)
KS............ Kelly-Springfield Tire Co.
KS............ Keltic Society (SAUO)
KS............ Keltic Society and the College of Druidism (EA)
KS............ Kentucky State College (SAUO)
KS............ Kernig's Sign [*Medicine*] (MELL)
KS............ Kerr Stuart [*Indian Railway*] [*Stoke-on-Trent*] [*UK*] (TIR)
KS............ Ketosteroid [*Medicine*] (MELL)
KS............ Key Seated [*Freight*]
KS............ Keyset [*Navy*] (NVT)
KS............ Key Stage [*Of National Curriculum*] [*British*] (AIE)
KS............ Keystone (IAA)
K/S........... Kick Stage [*NASA*] (NASA)
KS............ Kidney Sac
KS............ Kilostere
KS............ King Solomon [*Freemasonry*] (ROG)
KS............ King's Scholar [*British*]
KS............ King's Serjeant [*British*] (ROG)
KS............ King's Speech [*British*]
KS............ Kipling Society of North America - USA and Canada (EA)
KS............ Kirjath Sepher [*Jerusalem*] (BJA)
KS............ Kitchener Scholar (ODA)
KS............ Kiting Stock [*Investment term*]
KS............ Klima-Service GmbH (EFIS)
KS............ Klinefelter's Syndrome [*Medicine*]
KS............ Knee Society (SAUO)
KS............ Knife Switch
KS............ Knight of the Sword [*of Sweden*]
KS............ Knock Sensor [*Automotive engineering*]
KS............ Knowledge Source (IAA)
KS............ Kodak Standard [*Photography*]
KS............ Kokoxili Suture [*Paleogeography*]
KS............ Kolmogorov-Smirnoff Tests (DIPS)
KS............ Kolmogorov - Smirnov Test [*Statistics*]
KS............ Konungariket Sverige [*Kingdom of Sweden*] (BARN)
KS............ Koplik's Spots [*Medicine*] (MELL)
KS............ Korean Bureau of Standards (SAUO)
KS............ Korea Shipping (SAUO)
KS............ Korea Society (EA)
KS............ Korsakoff Syndrome [*Medicine*] [*Medicine*] (DMAA)
KS............ Krackow Suture [*Medicine*] (MELL)
KS............ Kraemer System
KS............ Kugel-Stoloff [*Syndrome*] [*Medicine*] (DAVI)
KS............ Kurze Sicht [*Short Sight*] [*German*]
Ks............ Kush (BJA)
KS............ Kveim-Seltzback (Test) [*Medicine*]
KS............ Peninsula Airways [*ICAO designator*] (AD)
ks............ Potassium Metasilicate [*CIPW classification*] [*Geology*]
KS............ Session Key (SAUS)
KS............ Singapore [*IYRU nationality code*] (IYR)
KS............ Storm of Drifting Snow [*Meteorology*] (WDAA)
KS............ Strikeout, Swinging [*Baseball term*] (NDBD)
KS............ King's School (ODA)
KSA.......... Kafka Society of America (EA)
KSA.......... Kaiserslautern Support Activity (SAUO)
KSA.......... Kalman Saffran Associates (SAUO)
KSA.......... Kansas Motor Carriers Association, Topeka KS [*STAC*]
KSA.......... Kansas Statutes, Annotated [*A publication*]
K-SA......... Keats-Shelley Association of America (SAUO)
KSA.......... Kindle, Stone & Associates, Inc. (EFIS)
KSA.......... Kitchen Specialists Association [*British*] (DBA)
KSA.......... Kite-Supported Antenna
KSA.......... Klinefelter's Syndrome Association (BUAC)
KSA.......... Klinefelter Syndrome and Associates (EA)
KSA.......... Knight of St. Anne [*Russia*] [*Obsolete*]
KSA.......... Knowledge, Skills, and Abilities [*Psychology*] (DAVI)
KSA.......... Ksara [*Lebanon*] [*Seismograph station code, US Geological Survey*] (SEIS)
KSA.......... Ku-Band Single Access (MCD)
KSA.......... Kwajalein Standard Atmosphere
KSA.......... St. Augustine's Seminary Library, University of Toronto [*UTLAS symbol*]
KSAA........ Keats-Shelley Association of America (EA)
KSAB........ Robstown, TX [*FM radio station call letters*]
KSAC........ Kingston and Saint Andrew Corp. [*Jamaica*] (BUAC)
KSAC........ Sacramento/Executive [*California*] [*ICAO location identifier*] (ICLI)
KSAC........ Sutter Creek, CA [*FM radio station call letters*] (RBYB)
KSAE........ Kansas Society of Association Executives (SRA)
KSAE........ Kentucky Society of Association Executives (SRA)
KSAF........ K-Band, Single Access Forward (SSD)
KSAF........ Santa Fe [*New Mexico*] [*ICAO location identifier*] (ICLI)
KSAH........ Universal City, TX [*AM radio station call letters*]
KSAI........ Saipan, MP [*AM radio station call letters*]
KSAJ........ Abilene, KS [*FM radio station call letters*]
KSAK........ Royal Aero Club of Sweden (SAUO)
KSAK........ Walnut, CA [*FM radio station call letters*]
KSAL........ Salina, KS [*AM radio station call letters*]
KSAL........ Salina Public Library (SAUS)
KSal.......... Salina Public Library, Salina, KS [*Library symbol*] [*Library of Congress*] (LCLS)
KSalM....... Marymount College, Salina, KS [*Library symbol*] [*Library of Congress*] (LCLS)
KSalW....... Kansas Wesleyan University, Salina, KS [*Library symbol*] [*Library of Congress*] (LCLS)
KSAM........ Huntsville, TX [*AM radio station call letters*]
KSAM........ Keyed Sequential Access Method [*Computer science*] (CMD)
KSAM........ Key Field Sequential Access Method (NITA)
KSAM-FM... Huntsville, TX [*FM radio station call letters*]
KSAMI....... Korea Society for the Advancement of Machine Industry (SAUO)
KSAN........ San Diego/International-Lindbergh Field [*California*] [*ICAO location identifier*] (ICLI)
KSAN........ San Francisco, CA [*FM radio station call letters*]
KSAN........ San Mateo, CA [*FM radio station call letters*] (BROA)
KSANG...... Kansas Air National Guard (MUSM)
KSAQ........ San Antonio (Kerrville), TX [*FM radio station call letters*] (GDPB)
KSAR........ K-Band, Single Access Return (SSD)
KSAR........ Salem, AR [*FM radio station call letters*]
KSAR........ Thayer, MO [*FM radio station call letters*] (BROA)
KSAS........ Caldwell, ID [*FM radio station call letters*] (BROA)
KSAS........ Wichita, KS [*Television station call letters*]
KSAT........ San Antonio/International [*Texas*] [*ICAO location identifier*] (ICLI)
KSAT........ San Antonio, TX [*Television station call letters*]
KSAU........ Nacogdoches, TX [*FM radio station call letters*]
KSAV........ KS Bancorp [*NASDAQ symbol*] (TTSB)
KSAV........ KS Bancorp, Inc. [*NASDAQ symbol*] (SAG)
KSAV........ Savannah/Municipal [*Georgia*] [*ICAO location identifier*] (ICLI)
KSAW........ Gwinn/K. I. Sawyer Air Force Base [*Michigan*] [*ICAO location identifier*] (ICLI)
KSAX........ Alexandria, MN [*Television station call letters*]
KSAY........ Fort Bragg, CA [*FM radio station call letters*]
KSAZ........ Tucson, AZ [*AM radio station call letters*]
KSAZ-TV.... Phoenix, AZ [*Television station call letters*]
KSB.......... Keyboard Status Block [*Computer science*] (TIMI)
KSB.......... Klein Schanzlin & Becker (EFIS)
KSB.......... Knowledge, Skill, and Behavioral
KSB.......... Kradschuetzen-Bataillon [*Motorcycle Battalion*] [*German military - World War II*]
KSBA........ Coos Bay, OR [*FM radio station call letters*]
KSBA........ Kentucky School Boards Association (SAUO)
KSB Bc...... KSB Bancorp [*Associated Press*] (SAG)
KSBC........ Hot Springs, AR [*FM radio station call letters*]
KS Bcp...... KS Bancorp, Inc. [*Associated Press*] (SAG)
KSBD........ San Bernardino/Norton Air Force Base [*California*] [*ICAO location identifier*] (ICLI)

KSBEMS .... Kansas Board of Emergency Medical Services (MHID)
KSBH .... Coushatta, LA [*FM radio station call letters*]
KSBHA ...... Kansas State Board of Healing Arts (MHID)
KSBI .... Oklahoma City, OK [*Television station call letters*]
KS BIRP..... Kansas Business and Industry Recycling Program (EARSL)
KSBJ.......... Humble, TX [*FM radio station call letters*]
KSBK .... KSB Bancorp [*NASDAQ symbol*] (SAG)
KSBL .... Carpinteria, CA [*FM radio station call letters*]
KSBN .... Spokane, WA [*AM radio station call letters*]
KSBN .... Springdale, AR [*Television station call letters*]
KSBQ .... Santa Maria, CA [*AM radio station call letters*]
KSBR .... Mission Viejo, CA [*FM radio station call letters*]
KSBS .... Pago Pago, AS [*FM radio station call letters*]
KSBS .... Steamboat Springs, CO [*Television station call letters*]
KSBT .... Steamboat Springs, CO [*FM radio station call letters*]
KSBV .... Salida, CO [*FM radio station call letters*] (BROA)
KSBW .... Salinas, CA [*Television station call letters*]
KSBY .... Salisbury/Wicomico County [*Maryland*] [*ICAO location identifier*] (ICLI)
KSBY .... San Luis Obispo, CA [*Television station call letters*]
KSBZ .... Sitka, AK [*FM radio station call letters*]
KSC.......... Council of State Governments, Lexington, KY [*OCLC symbol*] (OCLC)
KSC.......... Kagoshima Space Center [*Japan*]
KSC.......... Kansas State College of Applied Sciences (SAUO)
KSC.......... Kathodal Closing Contraction [*Medicine*] (DAVI)
KSC.......... Kennedy Space Center [*NASA*]
KSC.......... Kentucky State College (SAUO)
KSC.......... King's School, Canterbury (ROG)
KSC.......... Knight of St. Columba
KSC.......... Knights of St Columbanus (BUAC)
KSC.......... Kohn Social Competence Scale [*Psychology*] (DHP)
KSC.......... Komunisticka Strana Ceskoslovenska [*Communist Party of Czechoslovakia*] [*Political party*] (PPW)
KSC.......... Korean Service Corps
KSC.......... Kosice [*Former Czechoslovakia*] [*Airport symbol*] (OAG)
KSC.......... KSC, Inc. (SAUO)
KSC.......... Kutztown State College (SAUO)
KSCA........ Glendale, CA [*FM radio station call letters*]
KSCAP....... Kennedy Space Center Area Permit [*NASA*] (MCD)
KSCAX....... Kemper Small Cap. Equity Cl.A [*Mutual fund ticker symbol*] (SG)
KSCB .... Khe Sanh Combat Base [*Vietnam*] [*Marine Corps*] (VNW)
KSCB .... Liberal, KS [*AM radio station call letters*]
KSCB-FM ... Liberal, KS [*FM radio station call letters*]
KSCC .... Hutchinson, KS [*Television station call letters*] (BROA)
KSCC .... Kansas Society for Crippled Children (EARSL)
KSCE .... El Paso, TX [*Television station call letters*]
KSCF .... Thousand Standard Cubic Feet
KSCH .... Sulphur Springs, TX [*FM radio station call letters*] (BROA)
KSch (Alt)... Kleine Schriften zur Geschichte de Volkes Israel [*A. Alt*] [*A publication*] (BJA)
KSCI .... Long Beach, CA [*Television station call letters*] (BROA)
KSCI .... San Bernardino, CA [*Television station call letters*]
KSCI .... San Clemente Naval Auxiliary Air Base [*California*] [*ICAO location identifier*] (ICLI)
KSCJ......... Sioux City, IA [*AM radio station call letters*]
KSCK .... Stockton/Stockton Metropolitan [*California*] [*ICAO location identifier*] (ICLI)
KSCL .... Shreveport, LA [*FM radio station call letters*]
KSCM........ Communist Party of Bohemia and Moravia-Left Bloc (Czech Rep.) [*Political party*] (PSAP)
KSCN .... Pittsburg, TX [*FM radio station call letters*] (BROA)
KSCN .... Potassium Thiocyanate [*Broth*] [*A reagent*] [*Pharmacology*] (DAVI)
KSCO......... Santa Cruz, CA [*AM radio station call letters*]
KSCQ........ Silver City, NM [*FM radio station call letters*]
KSCR........ Benson, MN [*AM radio station call letters*]
KSCR........ Eugene, OR [*AM radio station call letters*] (BROA)
KSCR-FM ... Benson, MN [*FM radio station call letters*]
KSCS......... Fort Worth, TX [*FM radio station call letters*]
KSCU........ Korea Shipping [*Intermodal shipping container symbol*] (TVRC)
KSCU........ Santa Clara, CA [*FM radio station call letters*]
KSC/ULO.... Kennedy Space Center/Unmanned Launch Operations [*NASA*]
KSCV .... Kearney, NE [*FM radio station call letters*]
KSCV .... Springfield, MO [*FM radio station call letters*] (BROA)
KSC-WTROD ..... Kennedy Space Center - Western Test Range Operations Division [*NASA*]
KSCY .... Belgrade, MT [*FM radio station call letters*]
KSCZ .... Korea Shipping [*Intermodal trailer symbol*]
KSD.......... C. H. Boehringer Sohn, Ingelheim [*Germany*] [*Research code symbol*]
KSD.......... Conserved [*Telegraphy*] (PCTE)
KSD.......... Karlstad [*Sweden*] [*Airport symbol*] (OAG)
KSD.......... St Louis, MO [*AM radio station call letters*]
KSDA........ Agat, GU [*FM radio station call letters*]
KSDA........ Korean Securities Dealers' Association (ECON)
KSDB........ Kommunal Statistisk DataBank [*Danmarks Statistik*] [*Denmark*] [*Information service or system*] (CRD)
KSDB........ Manhattan, KS [*FM radio station call letters*]
KSD-FM..... St. Louis, MO [*FM radio station call letters*]
KSDG........ Julian, CA [*AM radio station call letters*] (BROA)
KSDIC .... Kerala State Industrial Development Corp. [*India*] (BUAC)
KSDJ......... Brookings, SD [*FM radio station call letters*]
KSDK........ St. Louis, MO [*Television station call letters*]
KSDL......... Sedalia, MO [*FM radio station call letters*]
KSDM .... International Falls, MN [*FM radio station call letters*]
KSDN........ Aberdeen, SD [*AM radio station call letters*]
KSDN........ Kennedy Switched Data Network (SAUO)
KSDN-FM ... Aberdeen, SD [*FM radio station call letters*]
KSDO........ San Diego, CA [*AM radio station call letters*]
KSDP........ Sand Point, AK [*AM radio station call letters*]
KSDR........ Watertown, SD [*AM radio station call letters*]
KSDR-FM ... Watertown, SD [*FM radio station call letters*]
KSDS........ Kansas Specialty Dog Service (EARSL)
KSDS........ Key Sequenced Data Set (CMD)
KSDS........ San Diego, CA [*FM radio station call letters*]
KSDT .... Hemet, CA [*AM radio station call letters*] (RBYB)
KSDZ .... Gordon, NE [*FM radio station call letters*]
KSE.......... Karachi Stock Exchange [*Pakistan*]
KSE.......... Kasese [*Uganda*] [*Airport symbol*] (OAG)
KSE.......... Kewdale Structural Engineers (SAUS)
KSE.......... KeySpan Corp. [*NYSE symbol*]
KSE.......... Keyspan Energy [*NYSE symbol*] [*Formerly, Brooklyn Union Gas*] (SG)
KSE.......... Kids for Saving Earth [*An association*] (EA)
KSE.......... Kisbee Air Ltd. [*New Zealand*] [*ICAO designator*] (FAAC)
KSE.......... Knight of Saint-Esprit [*France*]
KSE.......... Knight of the Star of the East (ROG)
KSE.......... Knowledge Sharing Effort [*Computer science*] (GART)
KSE.......... Korea Stock Exchange (ECON)
KSE.......... Kuni [*Language symbol*] (ETLW)
KSEA .... Greenfield, CA [*FM radio station call letters*]
KSEA .... Korean Scientists and Engineers Association in America (EA)
KSEA .... Seattle/Seattle-Tacoma International [*Washington*] [*ICAO location identifier*] (ICLI)
KSEAFA ..... Korea and South-East Asia Forces Association (SAUO)
KSEC .... Bentonville, AR [*FM radio station call letters*] (BROA)
KSEC .... Korea Shipbuilding and Engineering Corporation (SAUO)
KSEC .... Lamar, CO [*FM radio station call letters*]
KSED .... Sedona, AZ [*FM radio station call letters*]
KSEE......... Fresno, CA [*Television station call letters*]
KSEG .... Sacramento, CA [*FM radio station call letters*]
KSEI .... Pocatello, ID [*AM radio station call letters*]
KSEK .... Girard, KS [*FM radio station call letters*]
KSEK .... Pittsburg, KS [*AM radio station call letters*] (BROA)
KSEL......... Portales, NM [*AM radio station call letters*]
KSEL-FM.... Portales, NM [*FM radio station call letters*]
KSEM........ Selma/Craig Air Force Base [*Alabama*] [*ICAO location identifier*] (ICLI)
KSEM........ Seminole, TX [*FM radio station call letters*]
KSEN .... Shelby, MT [*AM radio station call letters*]
KSEO .... Durant, OK [*AM radio station call letters*]
KSEQ .... Visalia, CA [*FM radio station call letters*]
KSER .... Everett, WA [*FM radio station call letters*]
KSES .... Seaside, CA [*FM radio station call letters*] (BROA)
KSES .... Selma/Selfield [*Alabama*] [*ICAO location identifier*] (ICLI)
KSES-AM ... Soledad, CA [*AM radio station call letters*] (BROA)
KSES-FM.... Yucca Valley, CA [*FM radio station call letters*] (RBYB)
KSET......... El Paso, TX [*FM radio station call letters*]
KSET-AM.... Silsbee, TX [*AM radio station call letters*] (BROA)
KSEV .... Tomball, TX [*AM radio station call letters*]
KSEY .... Seymour, TX [*AM radio station call letters*]
KSEY-FM.... Seymour, TX [*FM radio station call letters*]
KSEZ......... Sioux City, IA [*FM radio station call letters*]
KSF.......... Karen Silkwood Fund (EA)
KSF.......... Kashmiri Students Federation (BUAC)
KSF.......... Kassel [*Germany*] [*Airport symbol*] (OAG)
KSF.......... K-Band Shuttle Forward (SSD)
KSF.......... Keel Shock Factor (NATG)
KSF.......... Key Success Factor (VLIE)
ksf .... Kips [*Thousands of Pounds*] per Square Foot
KSF.......... Knight of San Fernando [*Spain*]
KSF.......... Knight of St. Ferdinand [*Sicily*] (ROG)
KSF.......... Kulkyne State Forest (SAUO)
KSF.......... Quaker State Corp. [*NYSE symbol*] (SPSG)
KSFA......... Nacogdoches, TX [*AM radio station call letters*]
KSFB .... Palo Alto, CA [*AM radio station call letters*] (BROA)
KSFB .... San Rafael, CA [*FM radio station call letters*] (BROA)
KSFC .... Karnataka State Financial Corp. [*India*] (BUAC)
KSFC .... Keith Sewell Fan Club (EA)
KSFC .... Spokane, WA [*FM radio station call letters*]
KSFF......... Spokane/Felts [*Washington*] [*ICAO location identifier*] (ICLI)
KSFF-FM.... Caledonia, MN [*FM radio station call letters*] (BROA)
KSFH .... Mountain View, CA [*FM radio station call letters*]
KSFI .... Salt Lake City, UT [*FM radio station call letters*]
KSFM........ Knight of St. Ferdinand and Merit [*Italy*]
KSFM........ Woodland, CA [*FM radio station call letters*]
KSFN-AM ... North Las Vegas, NV [*AM radio station call letters*] (BROA)
KSFO .... San Francisco, CA [*AM radio station call letters*]
KSFO .... San Francisco/International [*California*] [*ICAO location identifier*] (ICLI)
KSFQ-FM ... White Rock, NM [*FM radio station call letters*] (BROA)
KSFR .... Santa Fe, NM [*FM radio station call letters*]
KSFS .... San Francisco Coast Guard Air Station [*California*] [*ICAO location identifier*] (ICLI)
KSFS .... Sioux Falls, SD [*AM radio station call letters*] (BROA)
KSFT......... St. Joseph, MO [*AM radio station call letters*]
KSFT-FM.... South Sioux City, NE [*FM radio station call letters*] (RBYB)
KSFUS....... Korean Student Federation of the United States (EA)
KSFX .... Roswell, NM [*FM radio station call letters*]

KSFY .... Sioux Falls, SD [*Television station call letters*]
KSG .... Conserving [*Telegraphy*] (PCTE)
KSG .... Harvard University, Kennedy School for Government, Cambridge, MA [*OCLC symbol*] (OCLC)
KSG .... Kniest Syndrome Group (NRGU)
KSG .... Knight of St. George [*Russia*] [*Obsolete*]
KSG .... Knight of St. Gregory
KSGB .... Kite Society of Great Britain (BUAC)
KSGC .... Kentucky Space Grant Consortium (RCD)
KSGC .... Tusayan, AZ [*FM radio station call letters*]
KSGF .... Springfield, MO [*AM radio station call letters*] (BROA)
KSGI .... Cedar City, UT [*Television station call letters*]
KSGI .... St. George, UT [*AM radio station call letters*]
KSGI-FM .... St George, UT [*FM radio station call letters*]
KSGL .... Wichita, KS [*AM radio station call letters*]
KSGM .... Chester, IL [*AM radio station call letters*]
KSGN .... Riverside, CA [*FM radio station call letters*]
KSGO .... Centerville, UT [*AM radio station call letters*] (BROA)
KSGR .... Portland, TX [*FM radio station call letters*] (BROA)
KSGS .... Minneapolis, MN [*AM radio station call letters*] (GDPB)
KSGS-AM ... St. Louis Park, MN [*AM radio station call letters*] (RBYB)
KSGT .... Jackson, WY [*AM radio station call letters*]
KSGW .... Sheridan, WY [*Television station call letters*]
KSH .... K-Band Shuttle (SSD)
KSH .... Kenya Shilling [*Monetary unit*] (IMH)
KSh .... Kenya Shilling [*Monetary unit*] (ODBW)
KSH .... Kermanshah [*Iran*] [*Airport symbol*] (AD)
ksh .... Key Strokes per Hour (VLIE)
KSH .... Key Strokes per Hour
KSH .... Knight of St. Hubert [*Bavaria*]
KSH .... Kolel Shomre Hachomos [*An association*] (EA)
ksh .... Korn Shell [*Written by David Korn of Bell Labs, a standard Unix shell*] (DCDG)
KSH .... Kuh Shi [*Republic of China*] [*Seismograph station code, US Geological Survey*] (SEIS)
KSHA .... Kansas Speech-Language-Hearing Association (EARSL)
KSHA .... Kentucky Speech-Language-Hearing Association (EARSL)
KSHA .... Redding, CA [*FM radio station call letters*]
KSHB .... Kansas City, MO [*Television station call letters*]
KSHE .... Crestwood, MO [*FM radio station call letters*]
KSHI .... Zuni, NM [*FM radio station call letters*]
KSHK .... Kekaha, HI [*FM radio station call letters*] (BROA)
KSHL .... Gleneden Beach, OR [*FM radio station call letters*]
KshLc .... Kush Locke [*Associated Press*] (SAG)
KShm .... Johnson County Public Library, Shawnee Mission, KS [*Library symbol*] [*Library of Congress*] (LCLS)
KSHN .... Liberty, TX [*FM radio station call letters*]
KSHO .... Lebanon, OR [*AM radio station call letters*]
KSHP-AM ... North Las Vegas, Nv [*AM radio station call letters*] (RBYB)
KSHR .... Coquille, OR [*FM radio station call letters*]
KSHR .... Kosher (ABBR)
KSH/RMBH . Kolel Shomre Hachomos/Reb Meir Baal Haness (EA)
KSHS .... Kansas State Historical Society (BUAC)
KSHS .... Kansas State Horticultural Society (SAUO)
KSHSR ...... Kentucky State Historical Society Register (SAUO)
KSHU .... Huntsville, TX [*FM radio station call letters*]
KSHV .... Kaposi's Sarcoma Associated Herpesvirus [*Medicine*]
KSHV .... Shreveport, LA [*Television station call letters*] (RBYB)
KSHV .... Shreveport/Regional Airport [*Louisiana*] [*ICAO location identifier*] (ICLI)
KSHY .... Cheyenne, WY [*AM radio station call letters*]
KSI .... Karsanskaya [*Later, TFS*] [*Former USSR*] [*Geomagnetic observatory code*]
KSI .... Kemgas Sydney, Inc. [*Vancouver Stock Exchange symbol*]
KSI .... Kilopounds per Square Inch (SAA)
KSI .... Kips [*Thousands of Pounds*] per Square Inch (MCD)
KSI .... Kissidougou [*Guinea*] [*Airport symbol*] (AD)
KSI .... Kleine Schriften zur Geschichte des Volkes Israel [*A. Alt*] [*A publication*] (BJA)
KSI .... Knight of [*the Order of*] the Star of India [*British*]
KSIB .... Creston, IA [*AM radio station call letters*]
KSIB-FM .... Creston, IA [*FM radio station call letters*] (BROA)
K sicca ...... Keratoconjunctivitis sicca (SAUS)
KSID .... Sidney, NE [*AM radio station call letters*]
KSIDC .... Kerala State Industrial Development Corporation (SAUO)
KSID-FM .... Sidney, NE [*FM radio station call letters*]
KSIE .... Kinetic Solvent Isotope Effect [*Chemistry*] (ODA)
KSIG .... Basile, LA [*FM radio station call letters*]
KSIG .... Crowley, LA [*AM radio station call letters*]
KSII .... El Paso, TX [*FM radio station call letters*] (RBYB)
KSIIMK ...... Kratkie Soobshcheniia o Dokladakh i Polevykh Issledovaniiakh Instituta Istorii Materialnoi Kulturi [*A publication*] (BJA)
KSIL-FM .... Wallace, ID [*FM radio station call letters*] (BROA)
K-SIM .... K-Band Simulation (SSD)
KSIM .... Sikeston, MO [*AM radio station call letters*]
KSIN .... Sioux City, IA [*Television station call letters*]
KSIP .... Kent Scientific & Industrial Projects Ltd. [*University of Kent*] [*Research center*] [*British*] (IRUK)
KSIQ .... Brawley, CA [*FM radio station call letters*]
KSIR .... Brush, CO [*AM radio station call letters*]
KSIR-FM .... Brush, CO [*FM radio station call letters*]
KSIS .... Sedalia, MO [*AM radio station call letters*]
KSIT .... Rock Springs, WY [*FM radio station call letters*]
KSIV .... Clayton, MO [*AM radio station call letters*]
KSIV-FM .... St. Louis, MO [*FM radio station call letters*] (RBYB)
KSIW .... Woodward, OK [*AM radio station call letters*]
KSIX .... Corpus Christi, TX [*AM radio station call letters*]
KSIZ .... Jacksonville, TX [*FM radio station call letters*]
KSIZ-FM .... Maumelle, AR [*FM radio station call letters*] (BROA)
KSJ .... Kashima [*Japan*] [*Seismograph station code, US Geological Survey*] (SEIS)
KSJ .... Kasos Island [*Greece*] [*Airport symbol*] (OAG)
KSJ .... Knight of St. Januarius [*Naples*]
KSJ .... Knights of St. John (EA)
KSJB .... Jamestown, ND [*AM radio station call letters*]
KSJC .... Stockton, CA [*FM radio station call letters*]
KSJD .... Cortez, CO [*FM radio station call letters*]
KSJE .... Farmington, NM [*FM radio station call letters*]
KSJJ .... Redmond, OR [*FM radio station call letters*]
KSJK .... Talent, OR [*AM radio station call letters*]
KSJL .... Devine, TX [*FM radio station call letters*] (BROA)
KSJL .... San Antonio, TX [*FM radio station call letters*]
KSJL .... Somerset, TX [*AM radio station call letters*] (BROA)
KSJM-FM ... Oro Valley, AZ [*FM radio station call letters*] (RBYB)
KSJN .... Minneapolis, MN [*FM radio station call letters*]
KSJO .... San Jose, CA [*FM radio station call letters*]
KSJQ .... Savannah, MO [*FM radio station call letters*]
KSJR .... Collegeville, MN [*FM radio station call letters*]
KSJS .... San Jose, CA [*FM radio station call letters*]
KSJSC .... Knights of St. John Supreme Commandery (EA)
KSJT .... San Angelo/Mathis Field [*Texas*] [*ICAO location identifier*] (ICLI)
KSJT .... San Angelo, TX [*FM radio station call letters*]
KSJV .... Fresno, CA [*FM radio station call letters*]
KSJX .... San Jose, CA [*AM radio station call letters*]
KSJY .... Lafayette, LA [*FM radio station call letters*]
KSJZ .... Jamestown, ND [*FM radio station call letters*]
KSK .... Alcohol-free variety of ethyl iodoacetate (SAUS)
KSK .... Kappa Sigma Kappa [*Later, Theta Xi*] [*Fraternity*]
KSK .... Karlskoga [*Sweden*] [*Airport symbol*] (OAG)
KSK .... Kathodenschliessungs-Kontaktion [*or kathodal closing contraction*] [*Medicine*] (DAVI)
KSK .... Kiosk (ABBR)
KSKA .... Anchorage, AK [*FM radio station call letters*]
KSKA .... Spokane/Fairchild Air Force Base [*Washington*] [*ICAO location identifier*] (ICLI)
KSKB .... Brooklyn, IA [*FM radio station call letters*]
KSKD .... Livingston, CA [*FM radio station call letters*] (BROA)
KSKD .... Sweet Home, OR [*FM radio station call letters*]
KSKD-FM ... Chowchilla, CA [*FM radio station call letters*] (BROA)
KSKE .... Vail, CO [*AM radio station call letters*]
KSKE-FM.... Vail, CO [*FM radio station call letters*]
KSKF .... Klamath Falls, OR [*FM radio station call letters*]
KSKF .... San Antonio/Kelly Air Force Base [*Texas*] [*ICAO location identifier*] (ICLI)
KSKG .... Salina, KS [*FM radio station call letters*]
KSKI .... Sun Valley, ID [*FM radio station call letters*]
KSKJ .... American Slovenian Catholic Union of the USA (EA)
KSKK .... Staples, MN [*FM radio station call letters*]
KSKL .... Scott City, KS [*FM radio station call letters*]
KSKN .... Spokane, WA [*Television station call letters*]
KSKO .... McGrath, AK [*AM radio station call letters*]
KSKS .... Fresno, CA [*FM radio station call letters*]
KSKU .... Hutchinson, KS [*FM radio station call letters*] (BROA)
KSKU .... Lyons, KS [*FM radio station call letters*]
KSKX .... Colorado Springs-Pueblo, CO [*FM radio station call letters*] (GDPB)
KSKX-FM ... Security, CO [*FM radio station call letters*] (RBYB)
KSKY .... Balch Springs, TX [*AM radio station call letters*]
KSKY .... Sandusky/Griffing [*Ohio*] [*ICAO location identifier*] (ICLI)
KSKZ .... Leoti, KS [*FM radio station call letters*] (RBYB)
KSL .... Kanadska Slovenska Liga [*Canadian Slovak League - CSL*]
KSL .... Kassala [*Sudan*] [*Airport symbol*] (OAG)
KSL .... Keio University [*EDUCATSS*] [*UTLAS symbol*]
KSL .... Kentucky Department of Libraries, Library Extension Division, Frankfort, KY [*OCLC symbol*] (OCLC)
KSL .... Keyboard Simulated Lateral Telling [*Computer science*]
KSL .... Kinsel Drug Company (SAUO)
KSL .... Knight of the Sun and Lion [*Persia*]
KSL .... Salt Lake City, UT [*AM radio station call letters*]
KSLA .... Shreveport, LA [*Television station call letters*]
KSLC .... McMinnville, OR [*FM radio station call letters*]
KSLC .... Salt Lake City/International [*Utah*] [*ICAO location identifier*] (ICLI)
KSLD .... Soldotna, AK [*AM radio station call letters*]
KSLE .... Wewoka, OK [*FM radio station call letters*] (BROA)
KSLG .... Hydesville, CA [*FM radio station call letters*] (BROA)
KSLG-AM ... Saint Louis, MO [*AM radio station call letters*] (BROA)
KSLI .... Crete, NE [*FM radio station call letters*] (BROA)
KSLI .... King's Shropshire Light Infantry [*Military unit*] [*British*]
KSLJ .... Knight of [*the Order of*] St. Lazarus of Jerusalem [*British*]
KSLK .... Visalia, CA [*FM radio station call letters*]
K-SLM .... Kennedy Space Center Spacelab Plan/Requirement (NAKS)
K-SLM .... KSC Spacelab Plan (or Requirement) (SAUS)
KSLM .... Salem, OR [*AM radio station call letters*]
K-SLN .... KSC [*Kennedy Space Center*] Spacelab Notice [*NASA*] (NASA)
KSLNRC .... Knowledge Systems Laboratory of the National Research Council (SAUO)
KSLO .... Opelousas, LA [*AM radio station call letters*]
KSLOC ...... Thousands of Source Lines of Code (SAUS)
K-SLPS ..... KSC [*Kennedy Space Center*] Spacelab Project Specification [*NASA*] (NASA)
KSLQ .... Washington, MO [*AM radio station call letters*]

KSLQ-FM ... Washington, MO [*FM radio station call letters*]
KSLR .... San Antonio, TX [*AM radio station call letters*]
KSLS .... Liberal, KS [*FM radio station call letters*]
KSLT .... Spearfish, SD [*FM radio station call letters*]
KSL-TV ...... Salt Lake City, UT [*Television station call letters*]
KSLU .... Hammond, LA [*FM radio station call letters*]
KSLU .... Kiribati Shipping Services [*Intermodal shipping container symbol*] (TVRC)
KSLV .... Monte Vista, CO [*AM radio station call letters*]
KSLV-FM .... Monte Vista, CO [*FM radio station call letters*]
KSLX .... Scottsdale, AZ [*FM radio station call letters*]
KSLY .... San Luis Obispo, CA [*FM radio station call letters*]
KSLZ-FM .... St. Louis, MO [*FM radio station call letters*] (BROA)
KSM .... Conservatism [*Telegraphy*] (PCTE)
KSM .... Kane Security Monitor [*Computer security device*]
KSM .... Katubsanan sa Mamumio [*Philippine United Labor Congress*]
KSM .... Kemper Strategic Municipal Trust [*NYSE symbol*] (SPSG)
KSM .... Kemper Strategic Muni Tr [*NYSE symbol*] (TTSB)
KSM .... Kooperative Serbaguna Malaysia [*Bank*]
KSM .... Korean Service Medal [*Military decoration*]
K-SM .... KSC [*Kennedy Space Center*] Shuttle Management [*Document*] [*NASA*] (NASA)
KSM .... Saint Mary's [*Alaska*] [*Airport symbol*] (OAG)
KSM .... Saint Mary's, AK [*Location identifier*] [*FAA*] (FAAL)
KSM .... Shawnee Medical Center Medical Library, Shawnee Mission, KS [*OCLC symbol*] (OCLC)
KSM .... St. Michael's College Library, University of Toronto [*UTLAS symbol*]
Ksm .... thousand square meters (SAUS)
KSMA .... Keats-Shelley Memorial Association (BUAC)
KSMA .... Kentucky School Media Association
KSMA .... Kentucky State Medical Association (SAUO)
KSMA .... Osage, IA [*FM radio station call letters*] (BROA)
KSMA .... Santa Maria, CA [*AM radio station call letters*]
KSM & SG ... Knight of Saint Michael and Saint George [*Ionian Islands*]
KSMB .... Lafayette, LA [*FM radio station call letters*]
KSMC .... Moraga, CA [*FM radio station call letters*]
KSME .... Greeley, CO [*FM radio station call letters*] (BROA)
KSMF .... Ashland, OR [*FM radio station call letters*]
KSMF .... Sacramento/Sacramento Metropolitan [*California*] [*ICAO location identifier*] (ICLI)
KSMG .... Seguin, TX [*FM radio station call letters*]
KSMH .... Auburn, CA [*AM radio station call letters*] (BROA)
KSMJ .... Shafter, CA [*FM radio station call letters*] (BROA)
KSMJ .... Winfield, KS [*FM radio station call letters*] (BROA)
KSMJ-FM ... Bakersfield, CA [*FM radio station call letters*] (BROA)
KSML .... Diboll, TX [*AM radio station call letters*] (RBYB)
KSML .... Kosher Meal [*Airline notation*]
KSMM .... Shakopee, MN [*AM radio station call letters*] (BROA)
KSMMP ..... Kind Seeking Missing Military Personnel (SAUO)
KSMMP ..... Kin Seeking Missing Military Personnel [*Organization of parents with sons missing in action with purpose of supplementing US government search for missing personnel*] [*Post-World War II*]
KSMN .... Worthington, MN [*Television station call letters*] (RBYB)
KSMO .... Kansas City, MO [*Television station call letters*]
KSMO .... Salem, MO [*AM radio station call letters*]
KSMQ .... Austin, MN [*Television station call letters*]
KSMR .... Winona, MN [*FM radio station call letters*]
KSMS .... Point Lookout, MO [*FM radio station call letters*]
KSMS-TV ... Monterey, CA [*Television station call letters*]
KSMT .... Breckenridge, CO [*FM radio station call letters*]
KSMT .... Kismet (ABBR)
KSMU .... Komunistycha Spilka Molodi Ukrainy
KSMU .... Springfield, MO [*FM radio station call letters*]
KSMW .... West Plains, MO [*FM radio station call letters*] (BROA)
KSMX .... Clovis, NM [*FM radio station call letters*] (RBYB)
KSMX .... Kosmos Portland Cement [*Private rail car owner code*]
KSMY .... Lompoc, CA [*FM radio station call letters*] (BROA)
KSN .... Conservation [*Telegraphy*] (PCTE)
KSN .... Kansas State Network, Inc. (EFIS)
KSN .... Kassan Resources [*Vancouver Stock Exchange symbol*]
KSN .... Kit Serial Number (SAUO)
KSN .... Kit Shortage Notice
KSN .... Sam Neua [*Laos*] [*Airport symbol*] (AD)
KSNA .... Kansas State Nurses Association (SAUO)
KSNA .... Shasta Lake City, CA [*AM radio station call letters*] (BROA)
KSNA-FM ... Laramie, WY [*FM radio station call letters*] (BROA)
K-SNAP ..... Kaufman Short Neuropsychological Assessment Procedure [*Test*] (TMMY)
KSNB .... Superior, NE [*Television station call letters*]
KSNC .... Great Bend, KS [*Television station call letters*]
KSND .... Lincoln City, OR [*FM radio station call letters*]
KSNE-FM ... Las Vegas, NV [*FM radio station call letters*] (RBYB)
KSNF .... Joplin, MO [*Television station call letters*]
KSNG .... Garden City, KS [*Television station call letters*]
KSNI .... Santa Maria, CA [*FM radio station call letters*]
KSNK .... McCook, NE [*Television station call letters*]
KS/NLS ...... Keyword Search/Natural Language Search [*Computer science*] (GART)
KSNM .... Thousands of square nautical miles (SAUS)
KSNM .... Truth or Consequences, NM [*FM radio station call letters*]
KSNM-AM ... Las Cruces, NM [*AM radio station call letters*] (BROA)
KSNN .... Arlington, TX [*FM radio station call letters*]
KSNN-FM ... St. George, UT [*FM radio station call letters*] (BROA)
KSNO .... Snowmass Village, CO [*FM radio station call letters*]
KSNOPI ..... Keyboard Input Simulation-Noise-Problem Input [*Computer science*] (SAA)
KSNP .... Burlington, KS [*FM radio station call letters*]
KSNP .... Khao Salob National Park (SAUO)
KSNR .... Thief River Falls, MN [*FM radio station call letters*]
KSNS-FM ... Medicine Lodge, KS [*FM radio station call letters*] (BROA)
KSNT .... Topeka, KS [*Television station call letters*]
KSNU-FM ... Roy, UT [*FM radio station call letters*] (BROA)
KSNW .... Wichita, KS [*Television station call letters*]
KSNX-FM ... Show Low, AZ [*FM radio station call letters*] (BROA)
KSNY .... Snyder, TX [*AM radio station call letters*]
KSNY-FM .... Snyder, TX [*FM radio station call letters*]
KSNZ .... Lamar, CO [*FM radio station call letters*] (BROA)
KSO .... Kalamazoo Symphony Orchestra (SAUO)
KSO .... Kansas City Support Office (SAUO)
KSO .... Kastoria [*Greece*] [*Airport symbol*] (OAG)
KSO .... Knoxville Symphony Orchestra (SAUO)
KSOB-FM ... Dell Rapids, SD [*FM radio station call letters*] (BROA)
KSOC .... Gainesville, TX [*FM radio station call letters*] (BROA)
KSoc .... Kamashastra Society (SAUO)
KSOC .... Key Symbol Out of Context [*Computer science*] (DIT)
KSOF .... Caledonia, MN [*FM radio station call letters*]
KSOF-FM ... Dinuba, CA [*FM radio station call letters*] (BROA)
KSOH .... Wapato, WA [*FM radio station call letters*]
KS/OI .... Kaposi's Sarcoma and Opportunistic Infection [*Infectious disease*] (DAVI)
KSOK .... Arkansas City, KS [*AM radio station call letters*]
KSOK-FM ... Winfield, KS [*FM radio station call letters*] (RBYB)
KSOL .... San Francisco, CA [*FM radio station call letters*]
KSOL .... Santa Clara, CA [*FM radio station call letters*] (BROA)
KSOM .... Audubon, IA [*FM radio station call letters*] (RBYB)
KSON .... San Diego, CA [*AM radio station call letters*]
KSON-FM ... San Diego, CA [*FM radio station call letters*]
KSOO .... Sioux Falls, SD [*AM radio station call letters*]
KSOP .... Salt Lake City, UT [*FM radio station call letters*]
KSOP .... South Salt Lake, UT [*AM radio station call letters*]
KSOR .... Ashland, OR [*FM radio station call letters*]
KSOR .... "Republic" Coordinating Council of Public Associations (Kazakhstan) [*Political party*] (PSAP)
KSOS .... Brigham City, UT [*AM radio station call letters*]
KSOS .... Kernelized Secure Operating System (CCCA)
KSOS-FM ... Brigham City, UT [*FM radio station call letters*]
KSOU .... Sioux City, IA [*AM radio station call letters*] (GDPB)
KSOU .... Sioux City, IA [*FM radio station call letters*] (GDPB)
KSOU-AM ... Sioux Center, IA [*AM radio station call letters*] (RBYB)
KSOU-FM ... Sioux Center, IA [*FM radio station call letters*] (RBYB)
KSOX .... Raymondville, TX [*AM radio station call letters*]
KSOX-FM ... Raymondville, TX [*FM radio station call letters*]
KSP .... Farmer's and Worker's Party (Bangladesh) [*Political party*] (PSAP)
KSP .... Kaba [*Language symbol*] (ETLW)
KSP .... Karolinska Scales of Personality [*Medicine*] (DMAA)
KSP .... Kentucky Department of Libraries, Processing Center, Frankfort, KY [*OCLC symbol*] (OCLC)
KSP .... Kerala Socialist Party (SAUO)
KSP .... Keyset Panel
KSP .... Kidney-Specific Protein [*Medicine*] (DAVI)
KSP .... Knight of Saint Patrick (SAUO)
KSP .... Knight of Saint Stanislaus of Poland (SAUO)
KSP .... Knight of St. Stanislaus of Poland
KSP .... Kodak Special Plate
KSP .... Ksiaz [*Poland*] [*Seismograph station code, US Geological Survey*] (SEIS)
Ksp .... Potassium Solubility Product [*Biochemistry*] (DAVI)
KSP .... Servicios Aereos Especializados en Transportes Petroleros [*Colombia*] [*ICAO designator*] (FAAC)
KSPA .... Escondido, CA [*AM radio station call letters*]
KSPB .... Pebble Beach, CA [*FM radio station call letters*]
KSPC .... Claremont, CA [*FM radio station call letters*]
KSPC .... Kuwait Spanish Petroleum Co. (BUAC)
KSPD .... Boise, ID [*AM radio station call letters*]
KSPE .... Kentucky Society of Professional Engineers (SAUO)
KSPE .... Santa Barbara, CA [*AM radio station call letters*]
KSPE-FM .... Ellwood, CA [*FM radio station call letters*] (RBYB)
KSPG .... Clearwater, KS [*FM radio station call letters*]
KSPG .... St. Petersburg/Albert Whitted [*Florida*] [*ICAO location identifier*] (ICLI)
KSPI .... Stillwater, OK [*AM radio station call letters*]
KSPI-FM .... Stillwater, OK [*FM radio station call letters*]
KSPK .... Walsenburg, CO [*FM radio station call letters*]
KSPL .... Bakersfield, CA [*FM radio station call letters*] (GDPB)
KSPL-FM .... Kalispell, MT [*FM radio station call letters*] (RBYB)
KSPM .... Keystrokes Per Minute (SAUS)
KSPN .... Aspen, CO [*FM radio station call letters*]
K-SPN .... KSC [*Kennedy Space Center*] Shuttle Project Notice [*NASA*] (NASA)
KSPN-AM ... Pasadena, CA [*AM radio station call letters*] (BROA)
KSPO .... Dishman, WA [*FM radio station call letters*] (BROA)
KSPO .... Spokane, WA [*FM radio station call letters*]
KSPQ .... West Plains, MO [*FM radio station call letters*]
KSPR .... Springfield, MO [*Television station call letters*]
KSPS .... Kilo Symbols per Second (MCD)
K-SPS .... KSC [*Kennedy Space Center*] Shuttle Project Specification [*NASA*] (NASA)
KSPS .... Spokane, WA [*Television station call letters*]
KSPS .... Wichita Falls/Sheppard Air Force Base and Municipal [*Texas*] [*ICAO location identifier*] (ICLI)
KSPT .... KSP Truck Lines [*Common carrier symbol*]

K-SPT .... Potassium-Urine [*Spot*] [*Biochemistry*] (DAVI)
KSPT .... Sandpoint, ID [*AM radio station call letters*]
KSPT-FM.... Sandpoint, ID [*FM radio station call letters*] (RBYB)
KSPW .... Sparta, MO [*FM radio station call letters*] (BROA)
KSPX .... Sacramento, CA [*Television station call letters*] (BROA)
KSPY .... Quincy, CA [*FM radio station call letters*]
KSPY .... Williston, ND [*FM radio station call letters*] (BROA)
KSPZ .... Colorado Springs, CO [*FM radio station call letters*]
KSQA .... Wallace, ID [*FM radio station call letters*]
KSQB .... Dell Rapids, SD [*FM radio station call letters*] (BROA)
KSQB-AM ... Sioux Falls, SD [*AM radio station call letters*] (BROA)
KSQB-FM ... Flandreau, SD [*FM radio station call letters*] (BROA)
KSQD .... Lowry, SD [*FM radio station call letters*]
KSQQ .... Morgan Hill, CA [*FM radio station call letters*]
KSQR .... Sacramento, CA [*AM radio station call letters*] (RBYB)
KSQX .... Springtown, TX [*FM radio station call letters*] (BROA)
KSQY .... Deadwood, SD [*FM radio station call letters*]
KSR .... Kaiser (ABBR)
KSR .... Kalka Simla Railway [*Indian Railway*] (TIR)
KSR .... K-Band Shuttle Return (SSD)
KSR .... Keyboard Select Routing Send/Receive [*Communications term*] (DCT)
KSR .... Keyboard Send and Receive [*Computer science*]
KSR .... Knowledge of Stock Remaining [*Machine tools*]
KSR .... Koster [*South Africa*] [*Seismograph station code, US Geological Survey*] (SEIS)
KSR .... Sandy River, AK [*Location identifier*] [*FAA*] (FAAL)
KSRA .... Salmon, ID [*AM radio station call letters*]
KSRA-FM ... Salmon, ID [*FM radio station call letters*]
KSRB .... Seattle, WA [*AM radio station call letters*] (BROA)
KSRC .... Kansas City, MO [*FM radio station call letters*] (BROA)
KSRC .... Kuwait Shipbuilding & Repairyard Company (SAUO)
KSRD .... Saint Joseph, MO [*FM radio station call letters*] (BROA)
KSRE .... Minot, ND [*Television station call letters*]
KSRF .... Poipu, HI [*FM radio station call letters*]
KSRG .... Ashland, OR [*FM radio station call letters*] (RBYB)
KSRH .... San Rafael, CA [*FM radio station call letters*]
KSRI .... Korea Standards Research Institute, Seoul (SAUO)
KSRI .... Santa Cruz, CA [*FM radio station call letters*] (BROA)
KSRJ .... Juneau, AK [*FM radio station call letters*] (BROA)
KSRK-AM ... Carmel Valley, CA [*AM radio station call letters*] (BROA)
KSRM .... Soldotna, AK [*AM radio station call letters*]
KSRN .... Kings Beach, CA [*FM radio station call letters*] (BROA)
KSRN .... Sparks, NV [*FM radio station call letters*]
KSRO .... Santa Rosa, CA [*AM radio station call letters*]
KSRQ .... Thief River Falls, MN [*FM radio station call letters*]
KSRR .... Provo, UT [*AM radio station call letters*]
KSRS .... Roseburg, OR [*FM radio station call letters*]
KSR/T .... Keyboard Send/Receive Terminal [*Computer science*] (MHDI)
KSRT .... Point Arena, CA [*FM radio station call letters*] (BROA)
KSRTC....... Karnataka State Road Transport Corp. [*India*] (BUAC)
KSR terminal... Keyboard Send Receive Terminal [*Computer science*]
KSRV .... Ontario, OR [*AM radio station call letters*]
KSRV-FM ... Ontario, OR [*FM radio station call letters*]
KSRW .... Childress, TX [*FM radio station call letters*]
KSRX .... El Dorado, KS [*AM radio station call letters*]
KSRX .... Koscuisko & Southwestern Railway [*Federal Railroad Administration identification code*]
KSRZ .... Omaha, NE [*FM radio station call letters*] (GDPB)
KSRZ-FM ... Omaha, NE [*FM radio station call letters*] (BROA)
KSS .... Kearns-Sayre Syndrome [*Ophthalmology*]
KSS .... Keep Sunday Special [*Campaign*] (BUAC)
KSS .... Kellogg Switchboard and Supply
KSS .... Kent State University, School of Library Science, Kent, OH [*OCLC symbol*] (OCLC)
KSS .... Keying Switching Station
Kss.......... Kilo-Samples per Second (MWOL)
KSS .... Knee Signature System [*Orthopedics*]
KSS .... Knight of St. Sylvester
KSS .... Knight of the Southern Star [*Brazil*]
KSS .... Knight of the Sword of Sweden
KSS .... Knock Sensor System [*Automotive engineering*]
KSS .... Kohl's Corp. [*NYSE symbol*] (SPSG)
KSS .... Komunisticka Strane Slovenska [*Communist Party of Slovakia*] [*Former Czechoslovakia*] [*Political party*] (PPW)
KSS .... Korea Stamp Society (EA)
KSSA .... Ingalls, KS [*FM radio station call letters*] (BROA)
KSSB .... Calipatria, CA [*FM radio station call letters*]
KSSB .... Kissable (ABBR)
KSSC .... KSC [*Kennedy Space Center*] Security Steering Committee [*NASA*] (SSD)
KSSC .... Santa Monica, CA [*FM radio station call letters*] (BROA)
KSSC .... Sumter/Shaw Air Force Base [*South Carolina*] [*ICAO location identifier*] (ICLI)
KSSD .... Cedar City, UT [*FM radio station call letters*]
KSSD .... Newport Beach, CA [*FM radio station call letters*] (BROA)
KSSE .... Kurdish Students' Society in Europe (BUAC)
KSSE-FM.... Riverside, CA [*FM radio station call letters*] (BROA)
KSSI .... China Lake, CA [*FM radio station call letters*]
KSSJ........ Fair Oaks, CA [*FM radio station call letters*] (BROA)
KSSJ........ Shingle Springs, CA [*FM radio station call letters*]
KSSK .... Honolulu, HI [*AM radio station call letters*]
KSSK .... Waipahu, HI [*FM radio station call letters*]
KSSM........ Cooperas Cove, TX [*FM radio station call letters*] (BROA)
KSSM........ Sault Ste. Marie/Sault Ste. Marie Municipal [*Michigan*] [*ICAO location identifier*] (ICLI)
KSSN .... Little Rock, AR [*FM radio station call letters*]
KSSP-AM ... Greenwood, AR [*AM radio station call letters*] (BROA)
KSSQ .... Conroe, TX [*AM radio station call letters*]
KSSR .... Kazakh Soviet Socialist Republic (SAUO)
KSSR .... Kirghizian Soviet Socialist Republic (SAUO)
KSSR .... Kisser (ABBR)
KSSR .... Santa Rosa, NM [*AM radio station call letters*]
KSSS .... Bismarck, ND [*FM radio station call letters*]
KSSS .... Kennedy Space Center Station Set Specification (SAUO)
K-SSS .... KSC [*Kennedy Space Center*] Shuttle Project Station Set Specification [*NASA*] (NASA)
KSST .... KSS Transportation [*Common carrier symbol*]
KSST .... Sulphur Springs, TX [*AM radio station call letters*]
KSSU .... Kerr Steamship [*Intermodal shipping container symbol*] (TVRC)
KSSU .... Kerr Steamship Company [*Common carrier symbol*]
KSSU .... Kiev T.G. Shevchenko State University (SAUO)
KSSU-FM ... Durant, OK [*FM radio station call letters*] (RBYB)
KSSZ .... Fayette, MO [*FM radio station call letters*] (BROA)
KST .... Christ [*Telegraphy*] (PCTE)
KST .... Kallistatin (DMAA)
KST .... Kathodenschilessungs-Tetanus [*or Kathodal closing tetanus*] [*Medicine*] (DAVI)
KST .... Keilinschriftliche Studien [*A publication*] (BJA)
KST .... Kemper Strategic Income [*AMEX symbol*] (TTSB)
KST .... Kemper Strategic Income Fund [*NYSE symbol*] (SAG)
KST .... Keyboard Skills Test (TES)
KST .... Keyseat (KSC)
KST .... Key Station Terminal [*Computer science*]
KST .... King-Seeley Thermos Company (SAUO)
KST .... King Solomon's Temple [*Freemasonry*]
KST .... Known Segment Table [*Computer science*] (IAA)
KST .... Kolcsonos Segito Takarekpenztarak [*Mutual Savings Banks*] [*Hungarian*]
KST .... Korean Society of Translators, Seoul (SAUO)
KST .... Kosti [*Sudan*] [*Airport symbol*] (AD)
KSTA........ Coleman, TX [*AM radio station call letters*]
KSTA-FM.... Coleman, TX [*FM radio station call letters*]
K-State...... Kansas State University (SAUO)
KSTB-FM.... Crystal Beach, TX [*FM radio station call letters*] (RBYB)
KSTC .... Sterling, CO [*AM radio station call letters*]
KSTC-TV .... Minneapolis, MN [*Television station call letters*] (BROA)
KSTE........ Rancho Cordova, CA [*AM radio station call letters*]
KSteC........ Sterling College, Sterling, KS [*Library symbol*] [*Library of Congress*] (LCLS)
KSTF........ Scottsbluff, NE [*Television station call letters*]
KSTG .... Sikeston, MO [*FM radio station call letters*]
KStJ .... Knight Commander of [*the Order of*] St. John of Jerusalem [*British*]
KStJ .... Knight of the Order of St. John of Jerusalem (DD)
KStJ .... Knight Venerable, Order of St. John of Jerusalem [*Decoration*] (CMD)
KSTJ-FM.... Boulder City, NV [*FM radio station call letters*] (BROA)
K ST J of J... Knight of St. John of Jerusalem [*Freemasonry*] (ROG)
KSTK .... Wrangell, AK [*FM radio station call letters*]
KSTKBO..... Clean Air. Special Edition (journ.) (SAUS)
KSTL........ St. Louis/Lambert-St. Louis International [*Missouri*] [*ICAO location identifier*] (ICLI)
KSTL........ St. Louis, MO [*AM radio station call letters*]
KSTM........ Indianola, IA [*FM radio station call letters*]
KSTN .... Christian [*Telegraphy*] (PCTE)
KSTN .... Keystone Financial [*NASDAQ symbol*] (TTSB)
KSTN .... Keystone Financial, Inc. [*NASDAQ symbol*] (NQ)
KSTN .... Kriegsstaerke-Nachweisung [*Table of Organization*] [*German military - World War II*]
KSTN .... Stockton, CA [*AM radio station call letters*]
KSTN-FM ... Stockton, CA [*FM radio station call letters*]
KSTO .... Agana, GU [*FM radio station call letters*]
K stoff....... Chloromethyl Chloroformate [*Organic chemistry*] (DAVI)
KSTON ...... Kingston, ON [*American Association of Railroads railroad junction routing code*]
KSTP .... St. Paul, MN [*AM radio station call letters*]
KSTP-FM.... St. Paul, MN [*FM radio station call letters*]
KSTP-TV .... St. Paul, MN [*Television station call letters*]
KSTQ .... Alexandria, MN [*FM radio station call letters*]
KSTR .... Montrose, CO [*FM radio station call letters*]
KSTR-AM ... Grand Junction, CO [*AM radio station call letters*] (BROA)
KSTRL....... Kestrel (ABBR)
KSTR-TV .... Irving, TX [*Television station call letters*] (BROA)
KSTS .... San Jose, CA [*Television station call letters*]
K-STSM ..... KSC [*Kennedy Space Center*] Space Transportation System Management [*Document*] [*NASA*] (NASA)
K-STSN...... KSC [*Kennedy Space Center*] Shuttle Test Station Notice [*NASA*] (GFGA)
K-STSPS .... KSC [*Kennedy Space Center*] Shuttle Test Station Project Specification [*NASA*] (GFGA)
KSTT........ Los Osos-Baywood Park, CA [*FM radio station call letters*]
KSTU .... Salt Lake City, UT [*Television station call letters*]
KSTV .... Stephenville, TX [*AM radio station call letters*]
KSTV .... Ventura, CA [*Television station call letters*]
KSTV-FM.... Dublin, TX [*FM radio station call letters*] (BROA)
KSTW........ Tacoma, WA [*Television station call letters*]
KSTX .... San Antonio, TX [*FM radio station call letters*]
KSTY .... Canon City, CO [*FM radio station call letters*]
KSTZ........ Des Moines, IA [*FM radio station call letters*]

KSU .... C-14 dates produced by Kyoto Sangyo University (SAUS)
KSU .... Consummate [*Telegraphy*] (PCTE)
ksu .... Kansas [*MARC country of publication code*] [*Library of Congress*] (LCCP)
KSU .... Kansas City So. Ind. [*NYSE symbol*] (TTSB)
KSU .... Kansas City Southern [*NYSE symbol*]
KSU .... Kansas City Southern Industries, Inc. [*NYSE symbol*] (SPSG)
KSU .... Kansas State University
KSU .... Kent State University, Kent, OH [*OCLC symbol*] (OCLC)
KSU .... Key Service Unit (IEEE)
KSU .... Key System Control Unit [*Telecommunications*]
KSU .... Kharkov State University (SAUO)
KSU .... Kousour [*Djibouti*] [*Seismograph station code, US Geological Survey*] (SEIS)
KSU .... Kristiansund [*Norway*] [*Airport symbol*] (OAG)
KSU .... Kyoto Sangyo University [*UTLAS symbol*]
KSUA .... College, AK [*FM radio station call letters*]
KSUA .... Fairbanks, AK [*FM radio station call letters*] (BROA)
KSUA .... Fairbranks, AK [*FM radio station call letters*] (BROA)
KSUAA .... Kent State University Alumni Association (EA)
KSUAAS ...... Kansas State University of Agriculture and Applied Science (SAUO)
KSUB .... Cedar City, UT [*AM radio station call letters*]
KSUD .... Consummated [*Telegraphy*] (PCTE)
KSUD .... West Memphis, AR [*AM radio station call letters*]
KSUE .... Susanville, CA [*AM radio station call letters*]
KSUG .... Consummating [*Telegraphy*] (PCTE)
KSUH .... Puyallup, WA [*AM radio station call letters*] (BROA)
KSUI .... Iowa City, IA [*FM radio station call letters*]
KSUM .... Fairmont, MN [*AM radio station call letters*]
KSUN .... Consummation [*Telegraphy*] (PCTE)
KSUN .... Phoenix, AZ [*AM radio station call letters*]
KSUP .... Juneau, AK [*FM radio station call letters*]
KSUPr .... Kansas City So. Ind 4% Pfd [*NYSE symbol*] (TTSB)
KSUR .... Beverly Hills, CA [*AM radio station call letters*] (BROA)
KSUT .... Ignacio, CO [*FM radio station call letters*]
KSUU .... Cedar City, UT [*FM radio station call letters*]
KSUU .... Fairfield/Travis Air Force Base [*California*] [*ICAO location identifier*] (ICLI)
KSUV-FM ..... McFarland, CA [*FM radio station call letters*]
KSUW-FM ..... Sheridan, WY [*FM radio station call letters*] (BROA)
KSUX .... Sioux City [*Iowa*] [*ICAO location identifier*] (ICLI)
KSUX .... Winnebago, NE [*FM radio station call letters*]
KSV .... Conservative [*Telegraphy*] (PCTE)
KSV .... Knight of Saint Vladimir (SAUO)
KSVA .... Corrales, NM [*FM radio station call letters*]
KSVA-AM ..... Albuquerque, NM [*AM radio station call letters*] (BROA)
KSVC .... Richfield, UT [*AM radio station call letters*]
KSVE .... El Paso, TX [*AM radio station call letters*]
KSVI .... Billings, MT [*Television station call letters*]
KSVL .... Smith, NV [*FM radio station call letters*] (BROA)
KSVN .... Ogden, UT [*AM radio station call letters*]
KSVOAD ...... Kansas Voluntary Organizations Active in Disaster [*Emergency Management*] (EMA)
KSVP .... Artesia, NM [*AM radio station call letters*]
KSVR .... Mount Vernon, WA [*FM radio station call letters*]
KSVY .... Opportunity, WA [*AM radio station call letters*]
KSW .... C. H. Boehringer Sohn, Ingelheim [*Germany*] [*Research code symbol*]
KSW .... Kansas Southwestern Railway [*Federal Railroad Administration identification code*]
KSW .... Keeping Scientology Working (SAUO)
KSW .... Knight of Saint Wladimir (SAUO)
KSW .... Wichita State University, Wichita, KS [*OCLC symbol*] (OCLC)
KSWA .... Graham, TX [*AM radio station call letters*]
KSWA .... Swan Islands [*ICAO location identifier*] (ICLI)
KSWB .... Seaside, OR [*AM radio station call letters*] (RBYB)
KSWB-TV ..... San Diego, CA [*TV station call letters*] (RBYB)
KSWC .... Winfield, KS [*FM radio station call letters*]
KSWD .... Seward, AK [*AM radio station call letters*]
KSWF .... Newburgh/Stewart [*New York*] [*ICAO location identifier*] (ICLI)
KSWG .... Wickenburg, AZ [*FM radio station call letters*] (GDPB)
KSWG-FM ..... Wickenburg, AZ [*FM radio station call letters*] (RBYB)
KSWH .... Arkadelphia, AR [*FM radio station call letters*]
KSWI .... Atlantic, IA [*FM radio station call letters*] (BROA)
K Swiss ..... K Swiss, Inc. [*Associated Press*] (SAG)
KSWK .... Lakin, KS [*Television station call letters*]
KSWM .... Aurora, MO [*AM radio station call letters*]
KSWN-FM ..... McCook, NE [*FM radio station call letters*] (BROA)
KSWO .... Lawton, OK [*AM radio station call letters*]
KSWO-TV ..... Lawton, OK [*Television station call letters*]
KSWP .... Lufkin, TX [*FM radio station call letters*]
KSWR .... Clinton, OK [*FM radio station call letters*]
KSWS .... K Swiss, Inc. [*NASDAQ symbol*] (SAG)
KSWS .... K Swiss Inc. 'A' [*NASDAQ symbol*] (TTSB)
KSWS .... Sisseton, SD [*FM radio station call letters*]
KSWT .... Yuma, AZ [*Television station call letters*]
KSWV .... Santa Fe, NM [*AM radio station call letters*]
KSWW .... Elma, WA [*FM radio station call letters*] (BROA)
KSWW .... Raymond, WA [*FM radio station call letters*]
KSXR .... Worthington, MN [*FM radio station call letters*] (BROA)
KSXX .... Marysville, CA [*FM radio station call letters*]
KSXX .... Roseville, CA [*AM radio station call letters*] (BROA)
KSXY .... Middletown, CA [*FM radio station call letters*] (BROA)
KSXZ .... McCall, ID [*FM radio station call letters*] (BROA)
KSYB .... Shreveport, LA [*AM radio station call letters*] (BROA)
KSYC .... Yreka, CA [*AM radio station call letters*]
KSYC-FM ..... Yreka, CA [*FM radio station call letters*] (RBYB)
KSYD .... Reedsport, OR [*FM radio station call letters*]
KSYE .... Frederick, OK [*FM radio station call letters*]
KSYG .... Little Rock, AR [*AM radio station call letters*] (RBYB)
KSYG-FM ..... Little Rock, AR [*FM radio station call letters*] (RBYB)
KSYL .... Alexandria, LA [*AM radio station call letters*]
KSYM .... San Antonio, TX [*FM radio station call letters*]
KSYM .... Smyrna/Sewart Air Force Base [*Tennessee*] [*ICAO location identifier*] (ICLI)
KSYN .... Joplin, MO [*FM radio station call letters*]
KSYR .... Benton, LA [*FM radio station call letters*] (BROA)
KSYR .... Syracuse/Hancock International [*New York*] [*ICAO location identifier*] (ICLI)
KSYR-FM ..... Minden, LA [*FM radio station call letters*] (BROA)
KSYS .... Medford, OR [*Television station call letters*]
KSYSA .... Kansas State Youth Soccer Association (EARSL)
KSYU .... Corrales, NM [*FM radio station call letters*] (BROA)
KSYV .... Solvang, CA [*FM radio station call letters*]
KSYY-FM ..... Fallbrook, CA [*FM radio station call letters*] (RBYB)
KSYZ .... Grand Island, NE [*FM radio station call letters*]
KSZL .... Barstow, CA [*AM radio station call letters*]
KSZL .... Knobnoster/Whiteman Air Force Base [*Missouri*] [*ICAO location identifier*] (ICLI)
KSZZ .... San Bernardino, CA [*AM radio station call letters*] (RBYB)
KT .... British Airtours Ltd. [*British*] [*ICAO designator*] (ICDA)
KT .... Canadian-Tech Industries, Inc. [*Vancouver Stock Exchange symbol*]
kt .... Cassiterite (SAUS)
KT .... Contain [*Telegraphy*] (PCTE)
KT .... Contract [*Navy*]
KT .... Cretaceous-Tertiary [*Geology*]
K/T .... Cretaceous/Tertiary boundary (SAUO)
KT .... Kahn Test [*Medicine*] (EDAA)
KT .... Kangmar Thrust [*Geophysics*]
kt .... Karat (NTIO)
KT .... Karat [*Also, CT*]
KT .... Karuna Trust [*Multinational association based in England*] (EAIO)
KT .... Katy Indus [*NYSE symbol*] (TTSB)
KT .... Katy Industries, Inc. [*Formerly, Missouri-Kansas-Texas R. R. Co., with Wall Street slang name of "Kathy"*] [*NYSE symbol*] (SPSG)
KT .... Keel Torsion (SSD)
KT .... Kelling's Test [*Medicine*] (MELL)
KT .... Kentucky & Tennessee Railway [*AAR code*]
KT .... Kenya Times [*A publication*]
KT .... Kermit [*Texas*] [*Seismograph station code, US Geological Survey*] (SEIS)
KT .... Kerner's Test [*Medicine*] (MELL)
KT .... Ketamine [*An anesthetic*]
KT .... Keying Time [*Computer order entry*]
KT .... Key Tape (ELAL)
KT .... Khaksar Tehrik [*Pakistan*] [*Political party*] (FEA)
KT .... Khotanese Texts (BJA)
KT .... Kidney Transplant [*Medicine*] (DMAA)
KT .... Killian's Test [*Medicine*] (MELL)
KT .... Kiloton (MILB)
kt .... Kiloton [*Nuclear equivalent of 1000 tons of high explosives*]
KT .... Kinberg's Test [*Medicine*] (MELL)
KT .... Kinetic Theory
KT .... Kinetin [*Plant growth regulator*]
KT .... Kingston-upon-Thames [*Postcode*] (ODBW)
KT .... Kit
KT .... Kitzingen [*German license plate city code*]
KT .... Klimow's Test [*Medicine*] (MELL)
KT .... Klippel-Trenaunay [*Syndrome*] [*Medicine*] (DAVI)
KT .... Knapp's Test [*Medicine*] (MELL)
Kt .... Knight [*British title*] (WA)
KT .... Knight [*British title*]
KT .... Knight [*Chess*]
Kt .... Knight Bachelor (SAUO)
KT .... Knighted
KT .... Knight of Tabor [*Freemasonry*] (ROG)
KT .... Knight of the Thistle [*British*]
KT .... Knights Templar
kt .... Knot (COE)
KT .... Knots [*Also, K*] [*Nautical speed unit*]
KT .... Kober Test [*Medicine*] (MELL)
KT .... Koopman's Theorem
K-T .... Kosterlitz-Thouless Theory [*Physics*]
KT .... Kuder Test [*Psychology*] (DAVI)
KT .... Kungtang [*Labor party*] [*Taiwan*] [*Political party*] (EY)
KT .... Potassium Titanate (SAUS)
KT .... Topeka Public Library, Topeka, KS [*Library symbol*] [*Library of Congress*] (LCLS)
KT .... Trinidad and Tobago [*IYRU nationality code*] (IYR)
KT .... Turtle Airways [*ICAO designator*] (AD)
KTA .... Journal. Korean Physical Society (journ.) (SAUS)
KTA .... Kansas Telecommunications Association (SRA)
KTA .... Karratha [*Australia*] [*Airport symbol*] (OAG)
KTA .... Katua [*Language symbol*] (ETLW)
KTA .... Kentucky Telephone Association (SRA)
KTA .... Kentucky Thoroughbred Association (SRA)
KTA .... Keyboard Teachers Association (EA)
KTA .... Key Telephone Adapter [*Telecommunications*] (TEL)
KTA .... Kindergarten Teachers Association (BARN)

KTA .... Kite Trade Association International (EA)
KTA .... Knitted Textile Association (EA)
KTA .... Knots True Airspeed
KTA .... Korean Telecommunication Authority (SAUO)
KTA .... Korean Traders Association, Seoul (SAUO)
KTA .... Korea Tourist Association (EAIO)
KTA .... Kotzebue [*Alaska*] [*Seismograph station code, US Geological Survey*] (SEIS)
KTA .... Potassium Turbo-Alternator
KTAA .... Big Sandy, TX [*FM radio station call letters*] (BROA)
KTAA .... Kerman, CA [*FM radio station call letters*]
KTAAK .... Korea Trading Agents Association (SAUO)
KTAB .... Abilene, TX [*Television station call letters*]
KTAC .... Ephrata, WA [*FM radio station call letters*] (RBYB)
KTACS .... Korean Tactical Air Control System (SAUO)
KTAE .... Taylor, TX [*AM radio station call letters*]
KTAG .... Cody, WY [*FM radio station call letters*]
KTAG .... Korea Trade Advisory Group [*British Overseas Trade Board*] (DS)
KTAI .... Keyboard Teachers Association International (NTPA)
KTAI .... Kingsville, TX [*FM radio station call letters*]
KTAI .... Kingsway Transport of America [*Common carrier symbol*]
KTAI .... Kite Trade Association International [*Later, KTA*] (EA)
KTAJ .... St. Joseph, MO [*Television station call letters*]
KTAK .... Riverton, WY [*FM radio station call letters*]
KTAL .... Texarkana, TX [*FM radio station call letters*]
KTAL-TV ...... Texarkana, TX [*Television station call letters*]
KTAM .... Bryan, TX [*AM radio station call letters*]
KTAN .... Sierra Vista, AZ [*AM radio station call letters*]
KTAO .... Taos, NM [*FM radio station call letters*]
KTAP .... Santa Maria, CA [*AM radio station call letters*]
KTAQ .... Greeneville, TX [*Television station call letters*]
KTAR .... Phoenix, AZ [*AM radio station call letters*]
KTAS .... Kjoebenhauns Telefon Aktieselskab [*Communications term*] (DCT)
KTAS .... Knots True Airspeed [*Navy*] (NVT)
KTAS .... San Luis Obispo, CA [*Television station call letters*] (BROA)
KTAT .... Frederick, OK [*AM radio station call letters*]
KTAX .... Kaye Kotts Associates, Inc. [*NASDAQ symbol*] (SAG)
KTAX .... Kay Kotts Assoc [*NASDAQ symbol*] (TTSB)
KTAXW ...... Kaye Kotts Assoc Wrrt [*NASDAQ symbol*] (TTSB)
KTB .... Cretaceous-Tertiary Boundary [*German*] [*Astronomy term*]
KTB .... German continental deep-drilling project (SAUS)
KTB .... Kosterlitz-Thouless-Berezinskii Layers [*Physics*]
KTB .... Kriegstagebuch [*War Diary*] [*German military - World War II*]
KTB .... Thorne River, AK [*Location identifier*] [*FAA*] (FAAL)
KTBA .... Ketothiomethylbutyric Acid [*Organic chemistry*]
KTBA .... Tuba City, AZ [*AM radio station call letters*]
Kt Bach ..... Knight Bachelor
KTBB .... Tyler, TX [*AM radio station call letters*]
KTBC .... Austin, TX [*Television station call letters*]
KTBG .... Warrensburg, MO [*FM radio station call letters*] (BROA)
KTBI .... Ephrata, WA [*AM radio station call letters*]
KTBJ-FM ..... Festus, MO [*FM radio station call letters*] (RBYB)
KTBK .... Denison-Sherman, TX [*AM radio station call letters*] (BROA)
KTBK .... Sherman, TX [*AM radio station call letters*] (BROA)
KTBL-AM .... Los Ranchos de Albuquerque, NM [*AM radio station call letters*] (BROA)
KTBL-FM .... Albuquerque, NM [*FM radio station call letters*] (RBYB)
KTBN .... Santa Ana, CA [*Television station call letters*]
KTBO .... Oklahoma City, OK [*Television station call letters*]
KTBQ .... Nacogdoches, TX [*FM radio station call letters*]
KTBR .... Roseburg, OR [*AM radio station call letters*]
KTBR-FM ... Myrtle Point, OR [*FM radio station call letters*] (BROA)
KTBS .... Shreveport, LA [*Television station call letters*]
KTBT .... Collinsville, OK [*FM radio station call letters*] (BROA)
KTBT-FM .... New Iberia, LA [*FM radio station call letters*] (BROA)
KTBU .... Conroe, TX [*Television station call letters*] (BROA)
KTBW .... Tacoma, WA [*Television station call letters*]
KTBY .... Anchorage, AK [*Television station call letters*]
KTBZ .... Houston, TX [*FM radio station call letters*] (BROA)
KTBZ .... Lake Jackson, TX [*FM radio station call letters*] (RBYB)
KTBZ .... Tulsa, OK [*AM radio station call letters*] (BROA)
KTC .... Kellogg Telecommunications Corp. [*Littleton, CO*] [*Telecommunications*] (TSSD)
KTC .... Kentucky Tourism Council (SRA)
KTC .... Kettleman City, CA [*Amtrak Busline code*]
KTC .... Keystone Tankship Corporation (SAUO)
KTC .... Kindergarten Teachers College (SAUO)
KTC .... Kodiak Tracking Station (SAUO)
KTC .... Korea Technologies Corp. (SAUS)
KTC .... Korea Telecom ADS [*NYSE symbol*] (SG)
KTC .... Kutchino [*Later, MOS*] [*Former USSR*] [*Geomagnetic observatory code*]
KTC .... Somerset Community College, Somerset, KY [*OCLC symbol*] (OCLC)
KTC .... Trinity College Library, University of Toronto [*UTLAS symbol*]
KTCA .... St. Paul, MN [*Television station call letters*]
KTCAX .... Kemper Technology Cl.A [*Mutual fund ticker symbol*] (SG)
KTCB .... Malden, MO [*AM radio station call letters*]
KTCC .... Colby, KS [*FM radio station call letters*]
KTCC .... Key Tronic Corp. [*NASDAQ symbol*] (TTSB)
KTCC .... Key Tronics Corp. [*NASDAQ symbol*] (NQ)
KTCC .... Tucumcari [*New Mexico*] [*ICAO location identifier*] (ICLI)
KTCCA .... Kotwali Thana Central Cooperative Association [*Bangladesh*] (BUAC)
KTCE .... Payson, UT [*FM radio station call letters*]
KTCF .... Crosby, MN [*FM radio station call letters*]
KTCF .... Dolores, CO [*FM radio station call letters*] (BROA)
ktch .... Kitchen (ADWA)
KTCH .... Wayne, NE [*AM radio station call letters*]
KTCH-FM ... Wayne, NE [*FM radio station call letters*]
KTCHN .... Kitchen
KTCHP .... Ketchup (ABBR)
KTCI .... St. Paul, MN [*Television station call letters*]
KTCI-DT ..... St. Paul, MN [*Television station call letters*] (BROA)
KTCJ .... Centerville, TX [*FM radio station call letters*] (BROA)
KTCJ .... Minneapolis, MN [*AM radio station call letters*]
KTCK .... Dallas, TX [*AM radio station call letters*]
KTCL .... Fort Collins, CO [*FM radio station call letters*]
KTCM .... Kingman, KS [*FM radio station call letters*]
KTCM .... Tacoma/McChord Air Force Base [*Washington*] [*ICAO location identifier*] (ICLI)
KTCN .... Eureka Springs, AR [*FM radio station call letters*]
KTCN .... Kitchen (ABBR)
KTCNET ..... Kitchennette (ABBR)
KTCNWR .... Kitchenware (ABBR)
KTCO .... Duluth, MN [*FM radio station call letters*]
KTCO .... Kenan Transport [*NASDAQ symbol*] (TTSB)
KTCO .... Kenan Transportation Co. [*NASDAQ symbol*] (NQ)
KTCO .... Kenan Transport Company (SAUO)
KTCOOTN ... Keep This Crap Out of This Newsgroup (SAUO)
KTCR .... Kennewick, WA [*AM radio station call letters*]
KTCS .... Fort Smith, AR [*AM radio station call letters*]
KTCS .... Truth Or Consequences/Municipal [*New Mexico*] [*ICAO location identifier*] (ICLI)
KTCS-FM .... Fort Smith, AR [*FM radio station call letters*]
KTCT-AM .... San Mateo, CA [*AM radio station call letters*] (BROA)
KTCU .... Fort Worth, TX [*FM radio station call letters*]
KTCU .... Kuskokwim Transportation [*Intermodal shipping container symbol*] (TVRC)
KTCV .... Kennewick, WA [*FM radio station call letters*]
KTCWAO .... Kenya Thirsty Child and Women Aid Organisation (BUAC)
KTCX .... Klamath Gas [*Private rail car owner code*]
KTCX-FM .... Beaumont, TX [*FM radio station call letters*] (RBYB)
KTCY .... Denison, TX [*FM radio station call letters*]
KTCY .... Pilot Point, TX [*FM radio station call letters*] (BROA)
KTCZ .... Minneapolis, MN [*FM radio station call letters*]
KTD .... Contained [*Telegraphy*] (PCTE)
KTD .... Killed Target Detector [*Military*] (PDAA)
KTD .... Kita-Daito [*Japan*] [*Airport symbol*] (OAG)
KTDA .... Kenya Tea Development Authority (BUAC)
KT/DA .... Kidney Transplant/Dialysis Association (SAUO)
KTDB .... Ramah, NM [*FM radio station call letters*]
KTDC .... Kenya Tourist Development Corp. (BUAC)
KTDD .... San Bernardino, CA [*AM radio station call letters*] (BROA)
KTDE .... Gualala, CA [*FM radio station call letters*] (BROA)
KTDK .... Sanger, TX [*FM radio station call letters*] (BROA)
KTDO .... Columbia, CA [*FM radio station call letters*] (RBYB)
KTDR .... Del Rio, TX [*FM radio station call letters*]
KTDS .... Key to Disk Software
KTDU .... Trimble, CO [*FM radio station call letters*] (BROA)
KTDX .... Mountain Pine, AR [*FM radio station call letters*] (RBYB)
KTDY .... Lafayette, LA [*FM radio station call letters*]
KTE .... Kennedy-Thorndike Experiment
KTE .... Kermit [*Texas*] [*Seismograph station code, US Geological Survey*] (SEIS)
KTE .... Scientific Society for Transport (SAUO)
K-TEA .... Kaufman Test of Educational Achievement
KTEB .... Teterboro [*New Jersey*] [*ICAO location identifier*] (ICLI)
KTEC .... Key Technologies, Inc. [*NASDAQ symbol*] (SAG)
KTEC .... Key Technology [*NASDAQ symbol*] (TTSB)
KTEC .... Klamath Falls, OR [*FM radio station call letters*]
KTEE .... Seaside, CA [*FM radio station call letters*] (BROA)
KTEF .... Knights Templar Educational Foundation (SAUO)
KTEG .... Albuquerque, NM [*FM radio station call letters*] (RBYB)
KTEG .... Bosque Farms, NM [*FM radio station call letters*] (BROA)
KTEH .... San Jose, CA [*Television station call letters*]
KTEI .... Placerville, CO [*FM radio station call letters*] (BROA)
KTEJ .... Jonesboro, AR [*Television station call letters*]
KTEK .... Alvin, TX [*AM radio station call letters*]
K-TEL .... Kives-Television [*In company name K-Tel International. Derived from name of company president and fact that it markets its products on television*]
KTEL .... K-Tel International [*NASDAQ symbol*] (TTSB)
K-Tel .... K-tel International, Inc. [*Associated Press*] (SAG)
KTEL .... K-tel International, Inc. [*NASDAQ symbol*] (SAG)
KTEL .... Walla Walla, WA [*AM radio station call letters*]
KTEL-FM ... Walla Walla, WA [*FM radio station call letters*]
KTEL-TV .... Carlsbad, NM [*Television station call letters*] (BROA)
KTEM .... Temple, TX [*AM radio station call letters*]
KTEN .... Ada, OK [*Television station call letters*]
KTEO .... Wichita Falls, TX [*FM radio station call letters*]
KTEP .... El Paso, TX [*FM radio station call letters*]
KTEQ .... Rapid City, SD [*FM radio station call letters*]
KTER .... Rudolph, TX [*FM radio station call letters*] (BROA)
KTEX .... Brownsville, TX [*FM radio station call letters*]
KTEZ .... Kock Carbon Terminal [*Federal Railroad Administration identification code*]
KTEZ .... Mount Enterprise, TX [*FM radio station call letters*] (BROA)
KTF .... Kansas Turfgrass Foundation (EA)
KTF .... Kauai Test Facility [*AEC*]

KTF .... Kemper Municipal Income Fund [*NYSE symbol*] (CTT)
KTF .... Kemper Muni Income [*NYSE symbol*] (TTSB)
KTF .... Kuwaiti [*Civil Affairs*] Task Force (DOMA)
KTFA .... Groves, TX [*FM radio station call letters*]
KTFC .... Sioux City, IA [*FM radio station call letters*]
KTFG .... Sioux Rapids, IA [*FM radio station call letters*]
KTFH .... Conroe, TX [*Television station call letters*]
KTFI .... Twin Falls, ID [*AM radio station call letters*]
KTFJ .... Dakota City, NE [*AM radio station call letters*]
KTFL .... Flagstaff, AZ [*Television station call letters*] (BROA)
KTFM .... San Antonio, TX [*FM radio station call letters*]
KTFN-AM ... Merced, CA [*AM radio station call letters*] (BROA)
KTFO .... Tulsa, OK [*Television station call letters*]
KTFR .... Chelsea, OK [*FM radio station call letters*] (BROA)
KTFR .... Claremore, OK [*FM radio station call letters*]
KTFR .... Kodak Thin-Film Resist [*Cathode coating*]
KTFS .... Shreveport, LA-Texarkana, TX [*AM radio station call letters*] (GDPB)
KTFS-AM .... Texarkana, TX [*AM radio station call letters*] (RBYB)
KTFW .... Glen Rose, TX [*FM radio station call letters*] (BROA)
KTFW .... Waco, TX [*AM radio station call letters*] (BROA)
KTFW-FM ... Stamford, TX [*FM radio station call letters*] (BROA)
KTFX .... Sand Springs, OK [*FM radio station call letters*] (RBYB)
KTFX .... Warner, OK [*FM radio station call letters*] (BROA)
KTG .... Containing [*Telegraphy*] (PCTE)
KTG .... Kap Tobin [*Greenland*] [*Seismograph station code, US Geological Survey*] (SEIS)
KTG .... Ketapang [*Indonesia*] [*Airport symbol*] (OAG)
KTG .... Nuclear Technical Society of the German Atomic Forum, Inc. (SAUO)
KTGA .... Kenya Tea Growers Association (BUAC)
KTGE .... Salinas, CA [*AM radio station call letters*]
KTGF .... Great Falls, MT [*Television station call letters*]
KTGF .... Keratinocyte T-Cell Growth Factor [*Immunology*]
KTGG .... Spring Arbor, MI [*AM radio station call letters*]
KTGIFC ...... Karen Taylor-Good International Fan Club [*Defunct*] (EA)
KTGL .... Beatrice, NE [*FM radio station call letters*]
KTGM .... Tamuning, GU [*Television station call letters*]
KTGO .... Tioga, ND [*AM radio station call letters*]
KTGP-FM ... Pawhuska, OK [*FM radio station call letters*] (RBYB)
KTGR .... Columbia, MO [*AM radio station call letters*]
KTGS-FM ... Ada, OK [*FM radio station call letters*] (BROA)
KTGW .... Fruitland, NM [*FM radio station call letters*] (BROA)
KTH .... Kungliga Tekniska Hoegskolan [*Royal Institute of Technology*] [*Stockholm, Sweden*] (ARC)
KTHB .... Kungliga Tekniska Hogskolans Bibliotek [*Royal Institute of Technology Library*] [*Information service or system*] (IID)
KTHC .... Sidney, MT [*FM radio station call letters*] (RBYB)
KTHE .... Thermopolis, WY [*AM radio station call letters*]
KTHI .... Caldwell, ID [*FM radio station call letters*] (BROA)
KTHK .... Okmulgee, OK [*FM radio station call letters*]
KTHK-FM ... Milton-Freewater, OR [*FM radio station call letters*] (BROA)
KTHN .... La Junta, CO [*FM radio station call letters*] (BROA)
KTHN-FM ... Hooks, TX [*FM radio station call letters*] (BROA)
KTHO .... South Lake Tahoe, CA [*AM radio station call letters*]
KTHP .... Hemphill, TX [*FM radio station call letters*] (BROA)
KTHQ-FM ... Eagar, AZ [*FM radio station call letters*] (RBYB)
KTHR .... Gallup, NM [*AM radio station call letters*] (BROA)
KTHR-FM ... Grants, NM [*FM radio station call letters*] (RBYB)
KTHS .... Berryville, AR [*AM radio station call letters*]
KTHS-FM ... Berryville, AR [*FM radio station call letters*]
KTHT .... Cleveland, TX [*FM radio station call letters*] (BROA)
KTHT .... Fresno, CA [*FM radio station call letters*]
KTHU .... Corning, CA [*FM radio station call letters*] (BROA)
KTHU-FM ... Los Molinos, CA [*FM radio station call letters*] (BROA)
KTHV .... Little Rock, AR [*Television station call letters*]
KTHX .... Dayton, WV [*FM radio station call letters*] (BROA)
KTHX .... Visalia, CA [*AM radio station call letters*]
KTHX-FM ... Carson City, NV [*FM radio station call letters*]
KTHY .... Mount Vernon, WA [*FM radio station call letters*] (BROA)
KTI .... Kalingrad Technological Institute (SAUO)
KTI .... Kallikrein-Trypsin Inhibitor (DB)
KTI .... Kano Transport International Ltd. KATI Air [*Nigeria*] [*ICAO designator*] (FAAC)
KTI .... Keyboard Training, Incorporated (SAUO)
KTI .... Kinai Technologies, Inc. [*Formerly, Kinai Resources Corp.*] [*Vancouver Stock Exchange symbol*]
KTI .... Kirsch Technologies, Inc. [*Software manufacturer*] [*St. Clair, MI*]
KTI .... Kitchen Table International [*David D. Busch's vaporware software company*]
KTI .... Knowledge Technologies International Ltd. (IID)
KTI .... Kratie [*Cambodia*] [*Airport symbol*] (AD)
KTI .... KTI, Inc. [*Associated Press*] (SAG)
KTI .... Kunitz Trypsin Inhibitor (DB)
KTIB .... Thibodaux, LA [*AM radio station call letters*]
KTIC .... West Point, NE [*AM radio station call letters*] (RBYB)
KTIE .... Bakersfield, CA [*FM radio station call letters*]
KTIE .... KTI, Inc. [*NASDAQ symbol*] (SAG)
KTIEE .... KTI [*NASDAQ symbol*]
KTIG .... Pequot Lakes, MN [*FM radio station call letters*]
KTII .... K-Tron International, Inc. [*NASDAQ symbol*] (NASQ)
KTII .... K-Tron Intl [*NASDAQ symbol*] (TTSB)
KTIJ .... Elk City, OK [*FM radio station call letters*]
KTIK .... Nampa, ID [*AM radio station call letters*]
KTIK .... Oklahoma City/Tinker Air Force Base [*Oklahoma*] [*ICAO location identifier*] (ICLI)
KTIL .... Tillamook, OR [*FM radio station call letters*] (GDPB)
KTIL-FM ..... Tillamook, OR [*FM radio station call letters*]
KTIM .... Wickenburg, AZ [*AM radio station call letters*]
KTIN .... Fort Dodge, IA [*Television station call letters*]
KTIP .... Porterville, CA [*AM radio station call letters*]
KTIQ .... Merced, CA [*AM radio station call letters*] (BROA)
KTIS .... Minneapolis, MN [*AM radio station call letters*]
KTIS-FM .... Minneapolis, MN [*FM radio station call letters*]
KTIU .... Kozraktarosazi Kozpont [*Intermodal shipping container symbol*] (TVRC)
KTIV .... Sioux City, IA [*Television station call letters*]
KTIX .... Pendleton, OR [*AM radio station call letters*]
KTJC .... Rayville, LA [*FM radio station call letters*]
KTJJ .... Farmington, MO [*FM radio station call letters*]
KTJK .... Del Rio, TX [*AM radio station call letters*] (BROA)
KTJM .... Port Arthur, TX [*FM radio station call letters*] (BROA)
KTJN .... Mercedes, TX [*FM radio station call letters*]
KTJO .... Ottawa, KS [*FM radio station call letters*]
KTJS .... Hobart, OK [*AM radio station call letters*]
KTJX .... Mission, TX [*FM radio station call letters*]
KTKA .... Topeka, KS [*Television station call letters*]
KTKB .... Agana, GU [*FM radio station call letters*] (BROA)
KTKC .... Springhill, LA [*FM radio station call letters*]
KTKK .... Sandy, UT [*AM radio station call letters*]
KTKL .... K Truck Lines [*Common carrier symbol*]
KTKL .... Stigler, OK [*FM radio station call letters*] (BROA)
KTKN .... Ketchikan, AK [*AM radio station call letters*]
KTKO .... Beeville, TX [*FM radio station call letters*]
KTKR .... San Antonio, TX [*AM radio station call letters*]
KTKS .... Savannah, GA [*AM radio station call letters*] (BROA)
KTKS .... Versailles, MO [*FM radio station call letters*]
KTKT .... Tucson, AZ [*AM radio station call letters*]
KTKU .... Juneau, AK [*FM radio station call letters*]
KTKX .... Crystal Beach, TX [*FM radio station call letters*]
KTKY-FM .... Refugio, TX [*FM radio station call letters*] (BROA)
KTKZ .... Sacramento, CA [*AM radio station call letters*] (BROA)
ktl .... Kai ta Loipa [*And the Rest, And So Forth*]
KTL .... Kettle (ABBR)
KTL .... Key-Edit Terminal Language [*Computer science*] (MHDI)
KTL .... Kitale [*Kenya*] [*Airport symbol*] (AD)
KTL .... Koroshi [*Language symbol*] (ETLW)
KTL .... K-Tel International, Inc. [*Toronto Stock Exchange symbol*] (SPSG)
KTL .... Kuratorium fuer Technik in der Landwirtschaft
KTLA .... Los Angeles, CA [*Television station call letters*]
KTLA-DT .... Los Angeles, CA [*Television station call letters*] (BROA)
KTLB .... Twin Lakes, IA [*FM radio station call letters*]
KTLC .... Oklahoma City, OK [*Television station call letters*]
KTLC-FM .... Canon City, CO [*FM radio station call letters*] (BROA)
KTLD .... Pineville, LA [*AM radio station call letters*]
KTLDR .... Kettledrum (ABBR)
KTLE .... Tooele, UT [*FM radio station call letters*]
KTLF .... Colorado Springs, CO [*FM radio station call letters*]
KTLG .... Fowler, CO [*FM radio station call letters*] (BROA)
KTLH .... Tallahassee/Dale Mabry Field [*Florida*] [*ICAO location identifier*] (ICLI)
KTLI .... El Dorado, KS [*FM radio station call letters*]
KTLK .... Santa Barbara-Santa Maria-San Luis Obispo, CA [*AM radio station call letters*] (GDPB)
KTLK .... Thornton, CO [*AM radio station call letters*]
KTLM .... Rio Grande City, TX [*Television station call letters*] (BROA)
KTLN .... Thibodaux, LA [*FM radio station call letters*] (RBYB)
KTLN-TV .... Novato, CA [*Television station call letters*] (BROA)
KTLO .... Mountain Home, AR [*AM radio station call letters*]
KTLO-FM .... Mountain Home, AR [*FM radio station call letters*]
KTLP .... KTL [*Common carrier symbol*]
KTLQ .... Tahlequah, OK [*AM radio station call letters*]
KTLR .... Terrell, TX [*FM radio station call letters*]
KTLR-AM ... Oklahoma City, OK [*AM radio station call letters*] (BROA)
KTLS .... Ada, OK [*FM radio station call letters*]
KTLS .... Holdenville, OK [*FM radio station call letters*] (BROA)
KTLT .... Wichita Falls, TX [*FM radio station call letters*]
KTLU .... Rusk, TX [*AM radio station call letters*]
KTLV .... Midwest City, OK [*AM radio station call letters*]
KTLW .... Lancaster, CA [*FM radio station call letters*] (RBYB)
KTLX .... Columbus, NE [*FM radio station call letters*]
KTLZ .... Cuero, TX [*FM radio station call letters*] (BROA)
KTM .... Katmai [*Alaska*] [*Seismograph station code, US Geological Survey*] (SEIS)
KTM .... Katmandu [*Nepal*] [*Airport symbol*] (OAG)
KTM .... Keep to Top of Mast (RIMS)
KTM .... Ketema, Inc. (SAUO)
KTM .... Key Transport Module
KTM .... Menninger Clinic Library, Topeka, KS [*Library symbol*] [*Library of Congress*] (LCLS)
KTM .... Thomas More College, Fort Mitchell, KY [*OCLC symbol*] (OCLC)
KTMA .... Ketema, Inc. (SAUO)
KT MAR SC... Knight Mareschal of Scotland (ROG)
KT MAR SC... Knight Marschal of Scotland (SAUO)
KTMB .... Miami/New Tamiami [*Florida*] [*ICAO location identifier*] (ICLI)
KTMC .... McAlester, OK [*AM radio station call letters*]
KTMC-FM ... McAlester, OK [*FM radio station call letters*]
KTMD .... Galveston, TX [*Television station call letters*]
KTME .... Lompoc, CA [*AM radio station call letters*]
KTMF .... Missoula, MT [*Television station call letters*]

KTMG........ Deer Trail, CO [*AM radio station call letters*]
KTMH........ Colona, CO [*FM radio station call letters*] (BROA)
KTMI........ KAT Transportation [*Common carrier symbol*]
KTMI........ West Hartford, CT [*AM radio station call letters*] (BROA)
KTMM........ Grand Junction-Durango, CO [*AM radio station call letters*] (GDPB)
KTMM-AM... Grand Junction, CO [*AM radio station call letters*] (BROA)
KTMN........ Cloudcroft, NM [*FM radio station call letters*] (BROA)
KTMN........ Los Alamos, NM [*FM radio station call letters*]
KTMO........ Kennett, MO [*FM radio station call letters*]
KTMO........ New Madrid, MO [*FM radio station call letters*] (BROA)
KTMP........ Heber City, UT [*AM radio station call letters*]
KTMR........ Edna, TX [*AM radio station call letters*]
KTMS........ Knapp Time Metaphor Scale
KTMS........ Knowledge-Based Tank Management System (VLIE)
KTMS........ Santa Barbara, CA [*AM radio station call letters*]
KTMT........ Ashland, OR [*AM radio station call letters*] (BROA)
KTMT........ Medford, OR [*FM radio station call letters*]
KTMT........ Phoenix, OR [*AM radio station call letters*]
KTMW........ Salt Lake City, UT [*Television station call letters*] (BROA)
KTMX........ York, NE [*FM radio station call letters*]
KTN.......... Cotton Valley Resources Corp. [*AMEX symbol*] (NASQ)
KTN.......... Keltic, Inc. [*Toronto Stock Exchange symbol*]
KTN.......... Ketchikan [*Alaska*] [*Airport symbol*] (OAG)
KTN.......... Ketchikan, AK [*Location identifier*] [*FAA*] (FAAL)
KTN.......... Kitten (ABBR)
KTN.......... Kuratorium fuer die Tagungen der Nobelpreistrager [*Standing Committee for Nobel Prize Winners' Congresses - SCNPWC*] [*Germany*] (EA)
KTN.......... Potassium Tantalate Niobate (MCD)
KTNA........ Talkeetna, AK [*FM radio station call letters*]
KTNC........ Falls City, NE [*AM radio station call letters*]
KTNC-TV.... Concord, CA [*TV station call letters*] (RBYB)
KTND........ Georgetown, TX [*FM radio station call letters*] (BROA)
KTND........ Ojai, CA [*FM radio station call letters*] (RBYB)
KTNE........ Alliance, NE [*FM radio station call letters*]
KTNE-TV.... Alliance, NE [*Television station call letters*]
KTNF........ Kodak Timing Negative Film
KTNH........ Kittenish (ABBR)
KTNI........ Kansas Neurological Institute, Topeka, KS [*Library symbol*] [*Library of Congress*] (LCLS)
KTNL........ Sitka, AK [*Television station call letters*]
KTNM........ Tucumcari, NM [*AM radio station call letters*]
KTNN........ Window Rock, AZ [*AM radio station call letters*]
KTNO........ Denton, TX [*AM radio station call letters*] (BROA)
KTNO........ Fort Worth, TX [*AM radio station call letters*]
KTNP-FM... Bennington, NE [*FM radio station call letters*] (RBYB)
KTNQ........ Los Angeles, CA [*AM radio station call letters*]
KTNR........ Kenedy, TX [*FM radio station call letters*]
KTNS........ Oakhurst, CA [*AM radio station call letters*]
KTNT........ Edmund, OK [*FM radio station call letters*]
KTNT........ Eufaula, OK [*FM radio station call letters*] (BROA)
KTNT........ Miami/Dade-Collier Training and Transition Airport [*Florida*] [*ICAO location identifier*] (ICLI)
KTNV........ Las Vegas, NV [*Television station call letters*]
KTNV........ Washbuni University of Topeka (SAUO)
KTNW........ Richland, WA [*Television station call letters*]
KTNY........ Libby, MT [*FM radio station call letters*]
KTNZ........ Amarillo, TX [*AM radio station call letters*] (RBYB)
KTO.......... K2, Inc. [*NYSE symbol*] [*Formerly, Anthony Industries*] (SG)
KTO.......... Kato [*Guyana*] [*Airport symbol*] (OAG)
KTO.......... Kraus-Thomson Organization [*Publishing*]
KtO.......... KTO Microform, Millwood, NY [*Library symbol*] [*Library of Congress*] (LCLS)
KTO.......... Kuwaiti Theatre of Operation [*Operation Desert Storm*]
KTO.......... Kuwait Theater (or Theatre) of Operations (SAUO)
KTO.......... Kuwait Theatre of Operations (SAUS)
KTOB........ Petaluma, CA [*AM radio station call letters*]
KTOC........ Jonesboro, LA [*AM radio station call letters*]
KTOC-FM... Jonesboro, LA [*FM radio station call letters*]
KTOD........ Conway, AR [*FM radio station call letters*]
KTOE........ Mankato, MN [*AM radio station call letters*]
KTOF........ Cedar Rapids, IA [*FM radio station call letters*]
KTOH........ Kalaheo, HI [*FM radio station call letters*] (BROA)
KTOK........ Oklahoma City, OK [*AM radio station call letters*]
KTOL........ Lacey, WA [*AM radio station call letters*]
KTOM........ Salinas, CA [*AM radio station call letters*]
KTOM-FM... Salinas, CA [*FM radio station call letters*]
KTON........ Belton, TX [*AM radio station call letters*]
KTON........ Ketone [*Organic chemistry*] (ABBR)
KTOO........ Juneau, AK [*FM radio station call letters*]
KTOO-TV.... Juneau, AK [*Television station call letters*]
KTOP........ Topeka, KS [*AM radio station call letters*]
KTOQ........ Rapid City, SD [*AM radio station call letters*]
KTOR........ Chester, CA [*FM radio station call letters*] (BROA)
KTOS........ Kratos, Inc. (SAUO)
KTOT........ Spearman, TX [*FM radio station call letters*] (BROA)
KTOW........ Sand Springs, OK [*AM radio station call letters*]
KTOW-FM... Sand Springs, OK [*FM radio station call letters*]
KTOX........ Needles, CA [*AM radio station call letters*]
KTOZ........ Marshfield, MO [*FM radio station call letters*]
KTOZ........ Pleasant Hope, MO [*FM radio station call letters*] (BROA)
KTOZ........ Springfield, MO [*AM radio station call letters*]
KTP.......... Keep This Private [*Internet lingo*] (NETL)
KTP.......... Kentucky Truck Plant [*Ford Motor Co.*]
KTP.......... Keyboard Typing Perforator (NITA)
KTP.......... Kingstip, Inc. (SAUO)
KTP.......... Kingston-Tinson [*Jamaica*] [*Airport symbol*] (OAG)
KT P.......... Knight's Pawn [*Chess*] (ROG)
KTP.......... Kommunistinen Tyovaenpuolue [*Communist Workers' Party*] [*Finland*] [*Political party*] (EY)
KTP.......... Potassium Titanyl Phosphate (SAUS)
KTPA........ Prescott, AR [*AM radio station call letters*]
KTPA........ Tampa/International [*Florida*] [*ICAO location identifier*] (ICLI)
KTPB........ Kilgore, TX [*FM radio station call letters*]
KTPC........ Korea Trade Promotion Corporation (SAUO)
KTPH........ Tonopah, NV [*FM radio station call letters*]
KTPI........ Indonesian Party of High Ideals (Suriname) [*Political party*] (PSAP)
KTPI........ Kaum-Tani Persatuan Indonesia [*Indonesian Farmers' Party*] [*Surinam*] [*Political party*] (PPW)
KTPI........ Tehachapi, CA [*FM radio station call letters*]
KTPK........ Topeka, KS [*FM radio station call letters*]
KTPP........ Potassium Tripolyphosphate (SAUS)
KTPR........ Fort Dodge, IA [*FM radio station call letters*]
KTPS........ Pagosa Springs, CO [*FM radio station call letters*] (BROA)
KTPW........ Sanger, TX [*FM radio station call letters*] (BROA)
KTPX........ Okmulgee, OK [*Television station call letters*] (BROA)
KTPZ-FM.... Mountain Home, ID [*FM radio station call letters*] (BROA)
KTQM........ Clovis, NM [*FM radio station call letters*]
KTQX........ Bakersfield, CA [*FM radio station call letters*]
KTR.......... Contractor
KTR.......... Helikoptertransport AB [*Sweden*] [*ICAO designator*] (FAAC)
KTR.......... K-2 Resources, Inc. [*Vancouver Stock Exchange symbol*]
KTR.......... Katherine [*Northern Territory, Australia*] [*Airport symbol*] (AD)
KTR.......... Katuura [*Japan*] [*Later, HTY*] [*Geomagnetic observatory code*]
KTR.......... Kauai Test Range (SAUO)
KTR.......... Keyboard Typing Reperforator [*Computer science*]
KTR.......... Kingstree, SC [*Amtrak rail station code*]
KTR.......... Knowledge Template Repository (VLIE)
KTRA........ Farmington, NM [*FM radio station call letters*]
KTRA-AM... Dallas, TX [*AM radio station call letters*] (BROA)
KTRAX....... Kemper Total Return Cl.A [*Mutual fund ticker symbol*] (SG)
KTRB........ Modesto, CA [*AM radio station call letters*]
KTRBX....... Kemper Total Return Cl.B [*Mutual fund ticker symbol*] (SG)
KTRC........ Santa Fe, NM [*AM radio station call letters*]
KTRE........ Lufkin, TX [*Television station call letters*] (GDPB)
KTRE-TV.... Lufkin, TX [*Television station call letters*]
KTRF........ Thief River Falls, MN [*AM radio station call letters*]
KTRG........ Del Rio, TX [*Television station call letters*]
KTRH........ Houston, TX [*AM radio station call letters*]
KTRI........ Mansfield, MO [*FM radio station call letters*]
KTRJ-AM.... Frazier Park, CA [*AM radio station call letters*] (RBYB)
KTRK........ Houston, TX [*Television station call letters*]
KTRK-DT.... Houston, TX [*Television station call letters*] (BROA)
KTRL........ Keller Transfer Line [*Common carrier symbol*]
KTRL........ Las Vegas, NM [*FM radio station call letters*] (BROA)
KTRM-FM... Kirksville, MO [*FM radio station call letters*] (BROA)
KTRN........ Silverton, CO [*FM radio station call letters*]
KTRN-FM... White Hall, AR [*FM radio station call letters*] (BROA)
KTRO........ Port Hueneme, CA [*AM radio station call letters*]
KTron........ K-Tron International, Inc. [*Associated Press*] (SAG)
KTRQ-FM... Brinkley, AR [*FM radio station call letters*] (BROA)
KTRQ-FM... Quincy, WA [*FM radio station call letters*] (RBYB)
KTRR........ Loveland, CO [*FM radio station call letters*]
KTRS........ Casper, WY [*FM radio station call letters*]
KTRS........ St. Louis, MO [*AM radio station call letters*] (BROA)
KTRT........ Claremore, OK [*AM radio station call letters*]
KTRU........ Houston, TX [*FM radio station call letters*]
KTRV........ Nampa, ID [*Television station call letters*]
KTRW........ Spokane, WA [*AM radio station call letters*]
KTRX........ Dickson, OK [*FM radio station call letters*] (BROA)
KTRX........ Tarkio, MO [*FM radio station call letters*]
KTRY........ Bastrop, LA [*AM radio station call letters*]
KTRY-FM.... Bastrop, LA [*FM radio station call letters*]
KTRZ........ Riverton, WY [*FM radio station call letters*]
KTS.......... Brevig Mission [*Alaska*] [*Airport symbol*] (OAG)
KTS.......... Contains [*Telegraphy*] (PCTE)
KTS.......... Kagoshima Television Station (SAUO)
KTS.......... Kelvin Temperature Scale
KTS.......... Kethoxal Thiosemicarbazone [*An antiviral*] [*Pharmacology*] (DAVI)
KTS.......... Key Telephone System [*Telecommunications*] (AAG)
KTS.......... Kiersley Temperament Sorter [*Psychiatry*] (DAVI)
KTS.......... Klippel-Trenaunay Syndrome [*Medicine*] (DMAA)
KTS.......... Knight of the Tower and Sword [*Portugal*]
KTS.......... Knots (ADA)
KTS.......... Kodiak Tracking Station [*NASA*] (MCD)
KTS.......... Korea National Tourist Service (SAUO)
KTS.......... Kotas Joint Civil Aviation Enterprise [*Former USSR*] [*FAA designator*] (FAAC)
KTS.......... Kumbheshwor Technical School (SAUO)
KTS.......... Kwajalein Test Site (MCD)
KTS.......... Southern Baptist Theological Seminary, Louisville, KY [*OCLC symbol*] (OCLC)
KTS.......... Teller Mission, AK [*Location identifier*] [*FAA*] (FAAL)
KTSA........ Kahn Test of Symbol Arrangement [*Psychology*]
KTSA........ San Antonio, TX [*AM radio station call letters*]
KTSB........ Sioux Center, IA [*FM radio station call letters*]
KTSC........ Kitsch (ABBR)
KTSC........ Pueblo, CO [*FM radio station call letters*]

KTSCHOOL... Karnali Technical School (SAUO)
KTSC-TV.... Pueblo, CO [*Television station call letters*]
KTSD........ Reliance, SD [*FM radio station call letters*]
KTSD-TV.... Pierre, SD [*Television station call letters*]
KTSE......... Patterson, CA [*FM radio station call letters*] (BROA)
KTSF......... San Francisco, CA [*Television station call letters*]
KTSG........ Klippel-Trenaunay Support Group (EA)
KTSH........ Tishomingo, OK [*FM radio station call letters*]
KTSH........ Topeka State Hospital, Topeka, KS [*Library symbol*] [*Library of Congress*] (LCLS)
KTSJ......... Pomona, CA [*AM radio station call letters*]
KTSL......... Medical Lake, WA [*FM radio station call letters*]
KTSM........ El Paso, TX [*AM radio station call letters*]
KTSM-FM... El Paso, TX [*FM radio station call letters*]
KTSM-TV.... El Paso, TX [*Television station call letters*]
KTSN-AM... Elko, NV [*AM radio station call letters*] (RBYB)
KTSO........ Okmulgee, OK [*FM radio station call letters*] (BROA)
KTSP........ St. George, UT [*AM radio station call letters*] (BROA)
KTSR........ College Station, TX [*FM radio station call letters*]
KTST......... Oklahoma City, OK [*FM radio station call letters*] (RBYB)
KTSU........ Houston, TX [*FM radio station call letters*]
KTSV........ Stormont-Vail Hospital, Topeka, KS [*Library symbol*] [*Library of Congress*] (LCLS)
KTSW........ San Marcos, TX [*FM radio station call letters*]
KTSY........ Caldwell, ID [*FM radio station call letters*]
KTT.......... Kermit [*Texas*] [*Seismograph station code, US Geological Survey*] [*Closed*] (SEIS)
KTT.......... Key to Tape (VLIE)
KTT.......... Kittila [*Finland*] [*Airport symbol*] (OAG)
KTTA-FM.... Esparto, CA [*FM radio station call letters*] (BROA)
KTTB......... Glencoe, MN [*FM radio station call letters*] (BROA)
KTTC......... Keesler Technical Training Center
KTTC......... Kids to the Cup [*Association*] (EA)
KTTC......... Kingston-upon-Thames Technical College (SAUO)
KTTC......... Rochester, MN [*Television station call letters*]
KTTF-AM.... Springfield, MO [*AM radio station call letters*] (BROA)
KTTG........ Mena, AR [*FM radio station call letters*] (RBYB)
KTTI......... Yuma, AZ [*FM radio station call letters*]
KTTK......... Lebanon, MO [*FM radio station call letters*] (GDPB)
KTTL......... Alva, OK [*FM radio station call letters*]
KTTL......... Korea Tactical Target List (MCD)
KTTM........ Huron, SD [*Television station call letters*]
KTTN........ Trenton/Mercer County [*New Jersey*] [*ICAO location identifier*] (ICLI)
KTTN........ Trenton, MO [*AM radio station call letters*] (BROA)
KTTN-FM.... Trenton, MO [*FM radio station call letters*]
KTTP-AM.... Pineville, LA [*AM radio station call letters*] (BROA)
KTTR........ Kita Transport [*Common carrier symbol*]
KTTR........ Rolla, MO [*AM radio station call letters*]
KTTR........ St. James, MO [*FM radio station call letters*]
KTTS......... Springfield, MO [*AM radio station call letters*]
KTTS-FM.... Springfield, MO [*FM radio station call letters*]
KTTT......... Columbus, NE [*AM radio station call letters*]
KTTU........ Tucson, AZ [*Television station call letters*]
KTTV......... Los Angeles, CA [*Television station call letters*]
KTTV-DT.... Los Angeles, CA [*Television station call letters*] (BROA)
KTTW........ Sioux Falls, SD [*Television station call letters*]
KTTX......... Brenham, TX [*FM radio station call letters*]
KTTY......... Kitty Hawk, Inc. [*NASDAQ symbol*] (NASQ)
KTTY......... San Diego, CA [*Television station call letters*]
KTTZ......... Ajo, AZ [*FM radio station call letters*]
KTU.......... Key Telephone Unit
KTU.......... Kidney Transplant Unit [*National Health Service*] [*British*] (DI)
KTU.......... Kota [*India*] [*Airport symbol*] (OAG)
KTU.......... Kutaisi [*USSR*] [*Airport symbol*] (AD)
KTU.......... Kyushu Tokai University (SAUO)
KTU.......... Transylvania University (SAUO)
KTU.......... Transylvania University, Lexington, KY [*OCLC symbol*] (OCLC)
KTUB........ Farmersville, TX [*AM radio station call letters*] (BROA)
KTUC........ Kiribati Trades Union Congress (BUAC)
KTUC........ Tucson, AZ [*AM radio station call letters*]
KTUE........ Tulia, TX [*AM radio station call letters*]
KTUF........ Kirksville, MO [*FM radio station call letters*]
KTUH........ Honolulu, HI [*FM radio station call letters*]
KTUI......... Sullivan, MO [*AM radio station call letters*]
KTUI-FM.... Sullivan, MO [*FM radio station call letters*]
KTUL........ Tulsa/International [*Oklahoma*] [*ICAO location identifier*] (ICLI)
KTUL........ Tulsa, OK [*Television station call letters*]
KTUM........ Tatum, NM [*FM radio station call letters*] (BROA)
KTUN........ Avon, CO [*FM radio station call letters*] (GDPB)
KTUN-FM... Eagle, CO [*FM radio station call letters*] (RBYB)
KTUO........ Sonora, CA [*FM radio station call letters*]
KTUR........ Tooele, UT [*AM radio station call letters*]
KTUS........ Tucson/International [*Arizona*] [*ICAO location identifier*] (ICLI)
KTUU-TV.... Anchorage, AK [*Television station call letters*]
KTUX........ Carthage, TX [*FM radio station call letters*]
KTUZ........ Okarche, OK [*FM radio station call letters*] (BROA)
KTUZ-FM.... Chickasha, OK [*FM radio station call letters*] (BROA)
KTV.......... Controvert [*Telegraphy*] (PCTE)
KTV.......... Kamarata [*Venezuela*] [*Airport symbol*] (OAG)
KTV.......... Kuwait Television
KTVA......... Anchorage, AK [*Television station call letters*]
KTVA......... United States Veterans Administration Hospital, Topeka, KS [*Library symbol*] [*Library of Congress*] (LCLS)
KTVB........ Boise, ID [*Television station call letters*]
KTVC........ Cedar Rapids, IA [*Television station call letters*]
KTVC........ Roseburg, OR [*Television station call letters*] (BROA)
KTVD........ Denver, CO [*Television station call letters*]
KTVE......... El Dorado, AR [*Television station call letters*]
KTVF......... Fairbanks, AK [*Television station call letters*]
KTVF-DT.... Fairbanks, AK [*Television station call letters*] (BROA)
KTVG........ Grand Island, NE [*Television station call letters*]
KTVH........ Helena, MT [*Television station call letters*]
KTVI......... St. Louis, MO [*Television station call letters*]
KTVI-DT..... St. Louis, MO [*Television station call letters*] (BROA)
KTVJ......... Boulder, CO [*Television station call letters*]
KTVK........ Phoenix, AZ [*Television station call letters*]
KTVL......... Medford, OR [*Television station call letters*]
KTVM........ Butte, MT [*Television station call letters*]
KTVN........ Reno, NV [*Television station call letters*]
KTVO........ Kirksville, MO [*Television station call letters*]
KTVQ........ Billings, MT [*Television station call letters*]
KTVR........ La Grande, OR [*Television station call letters*]
KTVS........ Keystone Telebinocular Visual Survey (STED)
KTVS........ Sterling, CO [*Television station call letters*]
KTVT......... Fort Worth, TX [*Television station call letters*]
KTVT-DT.... Fort Worth, TX [*Television station call letters*] (BROA)
KTVU........ Oakland, CA [*Television station call letters*]
KTVU-DT.... Oakland, CA [*Television station call letters*] (BROA)
KTVW........ Phoenix, AZ [*Television station call letters*]
KTVX........ Salt Lake City, UT [*Television station call letters*]
KTVZ......... Bend, OR [*Television station call letters*]
KTW.......... Katowice [*Poland*] [*Airport symbol*] (OAG)
KTW.......... Klippel-Trenaunay-Weber Syndrome [*Medicine*] (DMAA)
KTW.......... Washburn University of Topeka, Topeka, KS [*Library symbol*] [*Library of Congress*] (LCLS)
KTWA........ Ottumwa, IA [*FM radio station call letters*]
KTWB........ Sioux Falls, SD [*FM radio station call letters*]
KTWB-TV... Seattle, WA [*Television station call letters*] (BROA)
KTWC........ Glendale, AZ [*FM radio station call letters*]
KTWD........ Wallace, ID [*FM radio station call letters*] (BROA)
KTWG........ Agana, GU [*AM radio station call letters*]
KTWI......... Warm Springs, OR [*FM radio station call letters*]
KTWK........ Colorado Springs, CO [*AM radio station call letters*]
KTW-L....... Washburn University of Topeka, School of Law, Topeka, KS [*Library symbol*] [*Library of Congress*] (LCLS)
KTWN........ Texarkana, TX [*AM radio station call letters*]
KTWN-FM... Texarkana, AR [*FM radio station call letters*]
KTWO........ Casper, WY [*AM radio station call letters*]
KTWO........ K2 Design, Inc. [*NASDAQ symbol*] (SAG)
KTWO-TV... Casper, WY [*Television station call letters*]
KTWS........ Bend, OR [*FM radio station call letters*]
KTWS........ Klippel-Trenaunay-Weber Syndrome [*Medicine*] (DMAA)
KTWU........ Topeka, KS [*Television station call letters*]
KTWV........ Los Angeles, CA [*FM radio station call letters*]
KTWY-FM... Walla Walla, WA [*FM radio station call letters*] (RBYB)
KTX.......... Kaxarari [*Language symbol*] (ETLW)
KTX.......... Keith Railway Equipment Co. [*AAR code*]
KTX.......... Kermit [*Texas*] [*Seismograph station code, US Geological Survey*] (SEIS)
KTXA........ Arlington, TX [*Television station call letters*]
KTXB........ Beaumont, TX [*FM radio station call letters*]
KTXC........ Cuero, TX [*AM radio station call letters*] (RBYB)
KTXC........ Lamesa, TX [*FM radio station call letters*] (BROA)
KTXH........ Houston, TX [*Television station call letters*]
KTXI-FM.... Ingram, TX [*FM radio station call letters*] (BROA)
KTXJ......... Jasper, TX [*AM radio station call letters*]
KTXK........ Texarkana/Municipal-Webb Field [*Arkansas*] [*ICAO location identifier*] (ICLI)
KTXK........ Texarkana, TX [*FM radio station call letters*]
KTXL......... Sacramento, CA [*Television station call letters*]
KTXM-FM... Hallettsville, TX [*FM radio station call letters*] (BROA)
KTXN........ Victoria, TX [*FM radio station call letters*]
KTXO........ Hope, AR [*FM radio station call letters*] (BROA)
KTXP........ Bushland, TX [*FM radio station call letters*] (BROA)
KTXQ........ Fort Worth, TX [*FM radio station call letters*]
KTXR........ Springfield, MO [*FM radio station call letters*]
KTXS........ Sweetwater, TX [*Television station call letters*]
KTXT......... Lubbock, TX [*FM radio station call letters*]
KTXT-TV.... Lubbock, TX [*Television station call letters*]
KTXV........ Frankston, TX [*AM radio station call letters*] (BROA)
KTXX........ Devine, TX [*FM radio station call letters*]
KTXX........ Salinas, CA [*AM radio station call letters*] (BROA)
KTXY........ Jefferson City, MO [*FM radio station call letters*]
KTXZ......... West Lake Hills, TX [*AM radio station call letters*]
KTY.......... Controversy [*Telegraphy*] (PCTE)
KTY.......... Kitty (ABBR)
KTY.......... Terror Bay [*Alaska*] [*Airport symbol*] (OAG)
KTY.......... Terror Bay, AK [*Location identifier*] [*FAA*] (FAAL)
KTYB.OB.... Kentucky Bancshares [*OTCBB symbol*]
KTYCR....... Kitty-Corner (ABBR)
KTYD........ Katydid (ABBR)
KTYD........ Santa Barbara, CA [*FM radio station call letters*]
KTYL......... Tyler, TX [*FM radio station call letters*]
KTYM........ Inglewood, CA [*AM radio station call letters*]
KTYN........ Minot, ND [*AM radio station call letters*]
KTYR........ Tyler/Pounds Field [*Texas*] [*ICAO location identifier*] (ICLI)
KTYS........ Knoxville/McGee Tyson [*Tennessee*] [*ICAO location identifier*] (ICLI)
KTYX-FM.... Jonesville, LA [*FM radio station call letters*] (BROA)

KTZ .... Katz Media [*AMEX symbol*] (TTSB)
KTZ .... Katz Media Group, Inc. [*AMEX symbol*] (SAG)
KTZ .... Kutztown [*Pennsylvania*] [*Seismograph station code, US Geological Survey*] (SEIS)
KTZA......... Artesia, NM [*FM radio station call letters*]
KTZN .... Anchorage, AK [*AM radio station call letters*] (BROA)
KTZO .... Albuquerque, NM [*FM radio station call letters*] (BROA)
KTZR .... Tucson, AZ [*AM radio station call letters*]
KTZU .... Kazakhstan Railway [*Intermodal shipping container symbol*] (TVRC)
KTZZ......... Conrad, MT [*FM radio station call letters*] (BROA)
KTZZ......... Seattle, WA [*Television station call letters*]
KU .... Continue [*Telegraphy*] (PCTE)
KU .... Kallikrein Unit (DMAA)
KU .... Kalmar Union (SAUO)
KU .... Kanazawa University (SAUO)
KU .... Kansas University (SAUO)
KU .... Kapuskasing Uplift [*Geology*] [*Canada*]
KU .... Karachi University (SAUO)
KU .... Karmen Unit [*Medicine*] (MAE)
KU .... Kasetsart University (SAUO)
KU .... Keep Up [*Typography*] (DGA)
KU .... Keio University (SAUO)
KU .... Kentucky University (PDAA)
KU .... Kentucky Utilities Co. (EFIS)
KU .... Keyboard Unit [*Computer science*] (NASA)
KU .... Kilourane (ABBR)
KU .... Kimbel Unit (AAMN)
KU .... Kimbrel Unit (STED)
KU .... Kinski University (SAUO)
KU .... Kitvei Ugarit (BJA)
KU .... Knightsbridge University [*Denmark*] (ECON)
KU .... Knowledge Universe
KU .... Kobe University (SAUO)
KU .... Kochi University (SAUO)
KU .... Kogakuin University (SAUO)
KU .... Kogoshima University (SAUO)
KU .... Kokushukan University (SAUO)
K-U .... Kremers-Urban Co. (DAVI)
KU .... KU Energy [*NYSE symbol*] (TTSB)
KU .... KU Energy Co. [*NYSE symbol*] (SPSG)
KU .... Kulmbach [*German license plate city code*]
KU .... Kumamoto University (SAUO)
KU .... Kumho [*Tire casing code*]
Ku............ Kurchatovium [*See also Rf*] [*Proposed name for chemical element 104*]
Ku............ Kurtosis [*The relative degree of flatness in the region about the mode of a frequency curve*]
ku .... Kuwait [*MARC country of publication code*] [*Library of Congress*] (LCCP)
KU .... Kuwait Airways [*ICAO designator*] (AD)
KU .... Kuwait Airways Corp. (SAUO)
KU .... Kyoto University (SAUO)
KU .... Kyushu University (SAUO)
KU .... Unit Key (SAUS)
KU .... University of Kansas, Lawrence, KS [*Library symbol*] [*Library of Congress*] (LCLS)
KUA........... Kit Upkeep Allowance [*British*]
KUA........... Kuantan [*Malaysia*] [*Airport symbol*] (OAG)
KUAB-FM ... Fairbanks, AK [*FM radio station call letters*] (BROA)
KUAC .... Fairbanks, AK [*FM radio station call letters*]
KUAC-TV.... Fairbanks, AK [*Television station call letters*]
KUAD......... Windsor, CO [*FM radio station call letters*]
KUAF .... Fayetteville, AR [*FM radio station call letters*]
KUAI.......... Eleele, HI [*AM radio station call letters*]
KUAL .... Crosby, MN [*FM radio station call letters*] (BROA)
KUAM .... Agana, GU [*AM radio station call letters*]
KUAM-FM... Agana, GU [*FM radio station call letters*]
KUAM-TV ... Agana, GU [*Television station call letters*]
KUAP......... Pine Bluff, AR [*FM radio station call letters*]
KUAR......... Little Rock, AR [*FM radio station call letters*]
KUAS......... Tucson, AZ [*Television station call letters*]
KUAT .... Tucson, AZ [*AM radio station call letters*]
KUAT-FM.... Tucson, AZ [*FM radio station call letters*]
KUAT-TV .... Tucson, AZ [*Television station call letters*]
KUAU......... Haiku, HI [*AM radio station call letters*]
KUAV .... Annual Reports. Research Reactor Institute. Kyoto University (journ.) (SAUS)
KUAZ .... Tucson, AZ [*FM radio station call letters*]
KUB........... Keilschrifturkunden aus Boghazkoi [*A publication*] (BJA)
KUB........... Kidney and Upper Bladder
KUB........... Kidney and Urinary Bladder (STED)
KUB........... Kidney Ultrasound Biopsy [*Medicine*] (MELL)
KUB........... Kidney, Ureter, Bladder [*X-ray*]
KUB........... Kubota Corp. ADR [*NYSE symbol*] (SPSG)
KUB........... Kubota Motor (SAUS)
KUBA......... Yuba City, CA [*AM radio station call letters*]
KuBand...... Satellite to Satellite communication frequency (SAUS)
KUBB .... Mariposa, CA [*FM radio station call letters*]
KUBC .... Montrose, CO [*AM radio station call letters*]
KUBD......... Denver, CO [*Television station call letters*]
KUBD......... Ketchikan, AK [*Television station call letters*] (BROA)
KUBE .... Seattle, WA [*FM radio station call letters*]
KUBL .... Salt Lake City, UT [*FM radio station call letters*] (RBYB)
KUBL-AM ... Colorado Springs, CO [*AM radio station call letters*] (BROA)
KUBO......... Calexico, CA [*FM radio station call letters*]
Kubota ...... Kubota Corp. [*Associated Press*] (SAG)
KUBQ......... La Grande, OR [*FM radio station call letters*]
KUBR......... San Juan, TX [*AM radio station call letters*]
KUBS .... Newport, WA [*FM radio station call letters*]
KUBU......... Kube and Kubenz International Speditions [*Intermodal shipping container symbol*] (TVRC)
KUC........... Continuance [*Telegraphy*] (PCTE)
KUC........... Kucino [*Former USSR*] [*Seismograph station code, US Geological Survey*] [*Closed*] (SEIS)
KUC........... Kuria [*Kiribati*] [*Airport symbol*] (OAG)
KUCA......... Conway, AR [*FM radio station call letters*]
KUCB......... Des Moines, IA [*FM radio station call letters*]
KUCD......... Pearl City, HI [*FM radio station call letters*]
KUCE .... Kiev Universal Commodity Exchange [*Ukraine*] (EY)
KUCI.......... Irvine, CA [*FM radio station call letters*]
KUCOG...... Kunia Coordinating Group (SAA)
KUCR......... Riverside, CA [*FM radio station call letters*]
KUCU-AM... Hobbs, NM [*AM radio station call letters*] (RBYB)
KUCV .... Lincoln, NE [*FM radio station call letters*]
KUD........... Continued [*Telegraphy*] (PCTE)
KUD........... Keokuk Union Depot [*Federal Railroad Administration identification code*]
KUD........... Kudat [*Malaysia*] [*Airport symbol*] (OAG)
KUDD......... Roy, UT [*FM radio station call letters*] (BROA)
KUDL......... Kansas City, KS [*FM radio station call letters*]
KUDO......... Anchorage, AK [*AM radio station call letters*] (BROA)
KUDU-FM... Tok, AK [*FM radio station call letters*] (RBYB)
KUDY......... Spokane, WA [*AM radio station call letters*]
KUED......... Kodak Unitized Engineering Data
KUED......... Salt Lake City, UT [*Television station call letters*]
KUEL .... Fort Dodge, IA [*FM radio station call letters*]
KUeN......... Kuenzelsau [*German license plate city code*]
KU Engy..... KU Energy Corp. [*Associated Press*] (SAG)
KUER......... Salt Lake City, UT [*FM radio station call letters*]
KUES .... Richfield, UT [*Television station call letters*] (BROA)
KUET .... Black Canyon, AZ [*AM radio station call letters*] (RBYB)
KUEW .... Saint George, UT [*Television station call letters*] (BROA)
KUEZ .... Lufkin, TX [*FM radio station call letters*]
KUF........... Kabul Union of Furriers [*Afghanistan*] (BUAC)
KUF........... Kidney Ultrafiltration Rate [*Nephrology*] (DAVI)
KUFM......... Missoula, MT [*FM radio station call letters*]
KUFM-TV ... Missoula, MT [*Television station call letters*]
KUFNCD..... Kampuchean United Front for National Construction and Defence [*Political party*] (PPW)
KUFN-FM ... Hamilton, MT [*FM radio station call letters*] (RBYB)
KUFNS ...... Kampuchean National United Front for National Salvation
KUFO......... Portland, OR [*FM radio station call letters*]
KUFPEC...... Kuwait Foreign Petroleum Exploration Co. (BUAC)
KUFR......... Salt Lake City, UT [*FM radio station call letters*]
KUFX .... Gilroy, CA [*FM radio station call letters*]
KUFX .... San Jose, CA [*FM radio station call letters*] (BROA)
KUG........... Continuing [*Telegraphy*] (PCTE)
KUG........... Kupang [*Timor*] [*Seismograph station code, US Geological Survey*] (SEIS)
KUGB......... Karate Union of Great Britain
KUGBNC .... Karate Union of Great Britain National Championship
KUGN......... Eugene, OR [*AM radio station call letters*]
KUGN-FM... Eugene, OR [*FM radio station call letters*]
KUGR......... Green River, WY [*AM radio station call letters*]
KUGS......... Bellingham, WA [*FM radio station call letters*]
KUGT .... Jackson, MO [*AM radio station call letters*]
KUH........... Kaapuna [*Hawaii*] [*Seismograph station code, US Geological Survey*] (SEIS)
KUH........... Kuhlman Corp. [*NYSE symbol*] (SPSG)
KUH........... Kushiro [*Japan*] [*Airport symbol*] (OAG)
KUHB......... St. Paul, AK [*AM radio station call letters*] (BROA)
KUHB......... St. Paul Island, AK [*FM radio station call letters*]
KUHCA ...... Journal. Korean Institute of Metals (journ.) (SAUS)
KUHD......... Port Neches, TX [*AM radio station call letters*]
KUHF .... Houston, TX [*FM radio station call letters*]
KUHG......... Milford, NE [*FM radio station call letters*]
KUHL......... Santa Maria, CA [*AM radio station call letters*]
Kuhlm .... Kuhlman Corp. [*Associated Press*] (SAG)
KUHM-FM... Helena, MT [*FM radio station call letters*] (RBYB)
KUHT .... Houston, TX [*Television station call letters*]
KUI............ Kuikuro-Kalapalo [*Language symbol*] (ETLW)
KUIC.......... Vacaville, CA [*FM radio station call letters*]
KUID.......... Moscow, ID [*Television station call letters*]
KUIK.......... Hillsboro, OR [*AM radio station call letters*]
KUIP.......... Kernel User Interface Package (VLIE)
KUIPNET.... Kyoto University Information Processing Network (SAUO)
KUIS .... Kentucky Union List of Serials (SAUO)
KUISA .... Japanese Journal of Aerospace Medicine and Psychology (journ.) (SAUS)
KUJ........... Walla Walla, WA [*AM radio station call letters*]
KUJ-FM ..... Walla Walla, WA [*FM radio station call letters*] (BROA)
KUJZ.......... Creswell, OR [*FM radio station call letters*] (BROA)
KUK........... College of Universal Knowledge (SAUO)
KUK........... Kasigluk [*Alaska*] [*Airport symbol*] (OAG)
KUK........... University of Kentucky, Lexington, KY [*OCLC symbol*] (OCLC)
KUKA......... San Diego, TX [*FM radio station call letters*]
KUKI.......... Ukiah, CA [*AM radio station call letters*]
KUKI-FM.... Ukiah, CA [*FM radio station call letters*]

KUKL .... Kalispell, MT [*FM radio station call letters*] (RBYB)
KUKN .... Kelso, WA [*FM radio station call letters*]
KUKQ .... Tempe, AZ [*AM radio station call letters*]
KUKU .... Kube and Kubenz International Speditions [*Intermodal shipping container symbol*] (TVRC)
KUKU .... Willow Springs, MO [*AM radio station call letters*]
KUKU-FM ... Willow Springs, MO [*FM radio station call letters*]
KUL .... Continual [*Telegraphy*] (PCTE)
KUL .... Kabul University Library (SAUO)
KUL .... Karachi University Library (SAUO)
KUL .... Kinjo Gakuin University Library [*UTLAS symbol*]
KUL .... Kuala Lumpur [*Malaysia*] [*Airport symbol*] (OAG)
KUL .... Kulyab [*Former USSR*] [*Seismograph station code, US Geological Survey*] (SEIS)
KUL .... Kyoto University Library (SAUO)
KUL .... Sterling Central Union List of Serials, Sterling, KS [*OCLC symbol*] (OCLC)
KU-L .... University of Kansas, School of Law, Lawrence (SAUS)
KU-L .... University of Kansas, School of Law, Lawrence, KS [*Library symbol*] [*Library of Congress*] (LCLS)
KULA .... Maunawili, HI [*AM radio station call letters*]
KULC .... Ogden, UT [*Television station call letters*]
Kulcke .... Kulicke & Soffa Industries, Inc. [*Associated Press*] (SAG)
KULE .... Ephrata, WA [*AM radio station call letters*]
KULE-FM .... Ephrata, WA [*FM radio station call letters*]
KULF .... Brenham, TX [*FM radio station call letters*]
KULH-FM ... Wheeling, MO [*FM radio station call letters*] (BROA)
KULL-FM .... Abilene, TX [*FM radio station call letters*] (BROA)
KULM .... Columbus, TX [*FM radio station call letters*]
KULP .... El Campo, TX [*AM radio station call letters*]
Kulp .... Kulp's Luzerne Legal Register Reports [*Pennsylvania*] [*A publication*] (DLA)
KULR .... Billings, MT [*Television station call letters*]
KULS .... Kentucky Union List of Serials [*Library network*]
KULSAA ..... Karachi University Library Science Alumni Association (SAUO)
KULV .... Ukiah, CA [*FM radio station call letters*] (BROA)
KULY .... Ulysses, KS [*AM radio station call letters*]
KUM .... Cape Kumukahi, Hawaii (SAUS)
KUM .... Kumamoto [*Japan*] [*Seismograph station code, US Geological Survey*] (SEIS)
KU-M .... University of Kansas, School of Medicine, Kansas City, KS [*Library symbol*] [*Library of Congress*] (LCLS)
KUM .... University of Kentucky, Medical Center, Lexington, KY [*OCLC symbol*] (OCLC)
KUM .... Yaku Shima [*Japan*] [*Airport symbol*] (OAG)
KUMA .... Pendleton, OR [*AM radio station call letters*]
KUMA-FM ... Pendleton, OR [*FM radio station call letters*]
KUMBX ...... Kemper U.S. Mtge Cl.B [*Mutual fund ticker symbol*] (SG)
KUMC .... Kansas University Medical Center [*Medicine*] (EDAA)
KUMD .... Duluth, MN [*FM radio station call letters*]
KUMM .... Morris, MN [*FM radio station call letters*]
KUMMI .... Kobe University Medical Mission to Indonesia
KUMR .... Rolla, MO [*FM radio station call letters*]
KuMSIC ..... Kuwait Medical Student International Committee (SAUO)
KUMT .... Centerville, UT [*FM radio station call letters*]
KUMU .... Honolulu, HI [*AM radio station call letters*]
KUMU-FM ... Honolulu, HI [*FM radio station call letters*]
KUMV .... Williston, ND [*Television station call letters*]
KU-MW ...... University of Kansas, School of Medicine-Witchita, Witchita, KS [*Library symbol*] [*Library of Congress*] (LCLS)
KUMX .... North Fort Polk, LA [*FM radio station call letters*] (BROA)
KUMX-FM ... Houma, LA [*FM radio station call letters*] (BROA)
KUN .... Continuation [*Telegraphy*] (PCTE)
KUN .... Kunia, Oahu, HI [*Location identifier*] [*FAA*] (FAAL)
KUN .... Kunming [*Republic of China*] [*Seismograph station code, US Geological Survey*] (SEIS)
KUNA .... Indio, CA [*AM radio station call letters*]
KUNA .... Kuwait News Agency (BUAC)
KUNA-FM ... La Quinta, CA [*FM radio station call letters*]
KUNC .... Greeley, CO [*FM radio station call letters*]
KUND .... Grand Forks, ND [*AM radio station call letters*] (GDPB)
KUND-AM ... Grand Forks, ND [*AM radio station call letters*] (BROA)
KUND-FM ... Grand Forks, ND [*FM radio station call letters*] (BROA)
KUNF-AM ... Washington, UT [*AM radio station call letters*] (BROA)
KUNI .... Cedar Falls, IA [*FM radio station call letters*]
KUNM .... Albuquerque, NM [*FM radio station call letters*]
KUNO .... Corpus Christi, TX [*AM radio station call letters*]
KUNQ .... Houston, MO [*FM radio station call letters*]
KUNR .... Reno, NV [*FM radio station call letters*]
KUNV .... Las Vegas, NV [*FM radio station call letters*]
KUNX .... Ventura, CA [*AM radio station call letters*] (BROA)
KUNY .... Mason City, IA [*FM radio station call letters*]
KUO .... Kuopio [*Finland*] [*Airport symbol*] (OAG)
KUOA .... Siloam Springs, AR [*AM radio station call letters*]
KUOI .... Moscow, ID [*FM radio station call letters*]
KUOL .... San Marcos, TX [*AM radio station call letters*]
Kuom .... Kuomintang (SAUO)
KUOM .... Minneapolis, MN [*AM radio station call letters*]
KUON .... Lincoln, NE [*Television station call letters*]
KUOO .... Spirit Lake, IA [*FM radio station call letters*]
KUOP .... Stockton, CA [*FM radio station call letters*]
KUOR .... Redlands, CA [*FM radio station call letters*]
KUOW .... Seattle, WA [*FM radio station call letters*]
KUP .... Catholic People's Party (Netherlands) [*Political party*] (PSAP)
KUP .... Kupang [*Timor*] [*Seismograph station code, US Geological Survey*] [*Closed*] (SEIS)
KUP .... Kupiano [*Papua New Guinea*] [*Airport symbol*] (OAG)
KUP .... Kwacha United Press [*Angola*] (BUAC)
KUP .... University of Kentucky, Plestonburg Community College (SAUO)
KUP .... University of Kentucky, Prestonburg Community College, Prestonburg, KY [*OCLC symbol*] (OCLC)
KUPB .... Midland, TX [*Television station call letters*] (BROA)
KUPC .... Carlsbad, NM [*Television station call letters*] (BROA)
KUPD .... Tempe, AZ [*FM radio station call letters*]
KUPH-FM ... Mountain View, MO [*FM radio station call letters*] (BROA)
KUPI .... Idaho Falls, ID [*AM radio station call letters*]
KUPI-FM .... Idaho Falls, ID [*FM radio station call letters*]
KUPK-TV .... Garden City, KS [*Television station call letters*]
KUPL .... Portland, OR [*AM radio station call letters*] (BROA)
KUPL-FM ... Portland, OR [*FM radio station call letters*]
KUPN .... Las Vegas, NV [*Television station call letters*] (RBYB)
KUPN .... Mission, KS [*AM radio station call letters*] (BROA)
KUPR .... Alamogordo, NM [*FM radio station call letters*] (BROA)
KUPR .... Carlsbad, CA [*FM radio station call letters*] (RBYB)
KUPS .... Tacoma, WA [*FM radio station call letters*]
KUPT .... Wolfforth, TX [*Television station call letters*] (BROA)
KUPX .... Provo, UT [*Television station call letters*] (BROA)
KUQL .... Wessington Springs, SD [*FM radio station call letters*] (BROA)
KUQQ-FM ... Milford, IA [*FM radio station call letters*] (RBYB)
KUR .... Kit Use Ratio [*Statistics*]
kur .... Kurdish [*MARC language code*] [*Library of Congress*] (LCCP)
KUR .... Kurilsk [*Former USSR*] [*Seismograph station code, US Geological Survey*] (SEIS)
KUR .... Kyoto University Reactor
KURA .... Ouray, CO [*FM radio station call letters*]
KURB .... Little Rock, AR [*AM radio station call letters*]
KURB-FM ... Little Rock, AR [*FM radio station call letters*]
KURCHATOV ... Kurchatov Institute-Russia (SAUO)
KURE .... KURE Foundation
KURE-FM ... Ames, IA [*FM radio station call letters*] (RBYB)
KUREX ...... Kursk Experiment (SAUO)
KURK .... Imperial, NE [*FM radio station call letters*] (BROA)
KURL .... Billings, MT [*AM radio station call letters*]
KURM .... Kurmann Trailer Company [*NCIC trailer make code*]
KURM .... Kurzweil MusicSystems, Inc. (SAUO)
KURM .... Rogers, AR [*AM radio station call letters*]
KURM .... South West City, MO [*FM radio station call letters*] (BROA)
KURQ .... Grover Beach, CA [*FM radio station call letters*] (BROA)
KURR-FM ... Bountiful, UT [*FM radio station call letters*] (RBYB)
KURRI .... Kyoto University Research Reactor Institute [*Japan*] (BUAC)
KURS .... San Diego, CA [*AM radio station call letters*]
KURT .... Kurtis Kraft [*NCIC car make code*]
KURV .... Edinburg, TX [*AM radio station call letters*]
KURY .... Brookings, OR [*AM radio station call letters*]
KURY-FM ... Brookings, OR [*FM radio station call letters*]
KURZ .... Kurzweil Applied Intelligence, Inc. [*NASDAQ symbol*] (SAG)
Kurzweil .... Kurzweil Applied Intelligence, Inc. [*Associated Press*] (SAG)
KUS .... Continues [*Telegraphy*] (PCTE)
KUS .... Kidney, Ureter, and Spleen [*Anatomy*] (MAH)
KUS .... Kulusuk Island [*Greenland*] [*Airport symbol*] (AD)
KUS .... Kursk State Air Enterprise [*Former USSR*] [*FAA designator*] (FAAC)
KUS .... Kusel [*German license plate city code*]
KUS .... Kushiro [*Japan*] [*Seismograph station code, US Geological Survey*] (SEIS)
KU-S .... University of Kansas, Kenneth Spencer Research Library, Lawrence, KS [*Library symbol*] [*Library of Congress*] (LCLS)
KUS .... University of Kentucky, Southeast Center, Cumberland, KY [*OCLC symbol*] (OCLC)
KUSA .... Denver, CO [*Television station call letters*]
KUSAX ...... Kemper U.S. Govt. Secs. Cl.A [*Mutual fund ticker symbol*] (SG)
KUSC .... Los Angeles, CA [*FM radio station call letters*]
KUSD .... Vermillion, SD [*AM radio station call letters*]
KUSD-FM ... Vermillion, SD [*FM radio station call letters*]
KUSD-TV .... Vermillion, SD [*Television station call letters*]
KUSF .... San Francisco, CA [*FM radio station call letters*]
KUSG .... St. George, UT [*Television station call letters*]
KUSH .... Cushing, OK [*AM radio station call letters*]
Kush .... Kushan (VRA)
Kushi .... Kushi Macrobiotic Corp. [*Associated Press*] (SAG)
KushLc ...... Kush Locke [*Associated Press*] (SAG)
KushLc ...... [*The*] Kushner-Locke Co. [*Associated Press*] (SAG)
KushLk ...... Kush Locke [*Associated Press*] (SAG)
KushLk ...... [*The*] Kushner-Locke Co. [*Associated Press*] (SAG)
KUSI .... San Diego, CA [*Television station call letters*]
KUSJ .... Harker Heights, TX [*FM radio station call letters*] (BROA)
KUSK .... Prescott, AZ [*Television station call letters*]
KUSM .... Bozeman, MT [*Television station call letters*]
KUSN .... Coffeyville, KS [*FM radio station call letters*]
KUSN .... Dearing, KS [*FM radio station call letters*] (BROA)
KuSNU ...... Seoul National University (SAUO)
KUSO .... Albion, NE [*FM radio station call letters*] (BROA)
KUSP .... Ku-Band Signal Processor (MCD)
KUSP .... Ku-Band Single Processor (MCD)
KUSP .... Santa Cruz, CA [*FM radio station call letters*]
KUSR .... Ames, IA [*FM radio station call letters*]
KUSR .... Logan, UT [*FM radio station call letters*] (BROA)
KUST .... Kustom Electronics Inc. (SAUO)
KUST .... Kustom Kraft [*NCIC trailer make code*]

KUST-FM.... Huntsville, TX [*FM radio station call letters*] (BROA)
KUSU........ Logan, UT [*FM radio station call letters*]
KUSZ........ Proctor, MN [*FM radio station call letters*] (RBYB)
KUT.......... Austin, TX [*FM radio station call letters*]
KUT.......... Kutahya [*Turkey*] [*Airport symbol*] (AD)
kut........... Kutenai [*MARC language code*] [*Library of Congress*] (LCCP)
KUT.......... Kutsu-Ga-Hara [*Japan*] [*Seismograph station code, US Geological Survey*] (SEIS)
Kut........... Kuttim (BJA)
KUT.......... Lexington Technical Institute, Lexington, KY [*OCLC symbol*] (OCLC)
KUT.......... Peere [*Language symbol*] (ETLW)
KUT.......... University of Toronto Union Catalogue Section [*UTLAS symbol*]
KUTA........ Blanding, UT [*AM radio station call letters*]
Kutch........ All India Reporter, Kutch [*1949-56*] [*A publication*] (DLA)
KUTD........ Keep Up to Date (KSC)
KUTE-FM.... Ignacio, CO [*FM radio station call letters*] (BROA)
KUTGW....... Keep Up the Good Work
KUTH........ Logan, UT [*Television station call letters*] (BROA)
KUTI......... Selah, WA [*AM radio station call letters*]
KUTI......... Yakima, WA [*AM radio station call letters*] (BROA)
KUTO........ Kids Under Twenty One (MHID)
KUTO........ San Francisco-Oakland-San Jose [*AM radio station call letters*] (GDPB)
KUTP........ Phoenix, AZ [*Television station call letters*]
KUTQ........ Bountiful, UT [*FM radio station call letters*]
KUTR........ Kutzler Express [*Common carrier symbol*]
KUTT........ Fairbury, NE [*FM radio station call letters*]
KUTV........ Salt Lake City, UT [*Television station call letters*]
KUTX........ San Angelo, TX [*FM radio station call letters*] (RBYB)
KUTY........ Palmdale, CA [*AM radio station call letters*]
KUTZ........ Lampasas, TX [*FM radio station call letters*]
Kutztown U... Kutztown University of Pennsylvania (GAGS)
KUU.......... Kulu [*India*] [*Airport symbol*] (AD)
KUUG........ Karlsruher UNIX User Group (SAUO)
KUUL........ Davenport, IA [*FM radio station call letters*]
KUUL-FM... East Moline, IL [*FM radio station call letters*] (BROA)
KUUU........ Tooele, UT [*FM radio station call letters*] (BROA)
KUUY........ Orchard Valley, WY [*AM radio station call letters*]
KUUY-FM... Glendo, WY [*FM radio station call letters*] (BROA)
KUUZ........ Lake Village, AR [*FM radio station call letters*]
KUVA........ Uvalde, TX [*FM radio station call letters*]
KUVI......... Bakersfield, CA [*Television station call letters*] (BROA)
KUVN........ Garland, TX [*Television station call letters*]
KUVO........ Denver, CO [*FM radio station call letters*]
KUVR........ Holdrege, NE [*AM radio station call letters*]
KUVR-FM... Holdrege, NE [*FM radio station call letters*]
KUVS........ Modesto, CA [*Television station call letters*] (BROA)
KUW.......... Kuwait (ABBR)
Kuw.......... Kuwait (VRA)
KUWA-FM... Afton, WY [*FM radio station call letters*] (BROA)
Kuwait J Sci Eng... Kuwait Journal of Science & Engineering [*A publication*] (PABS)
KUWB........ Ogden, UT [*Television station call letters*] (BROA)
KUWC-FM... Casper, WY [*FM radio station call letters*] (BROA)
KUWD........ Sundance, WY [*FM radio station call letters*] (BROA)
KUWG-FM... Gillette, WY [*FM radio station call letters*] (BROA)
KUWJ........ Jackson, WY [*FM radio station call letters*]
KUWL........ College, AK [*FM radio station call letters*] (BROA)
KUWL........ Fairbanks, AK [*FM radio station call letters*]
KUWN-FM... Newcastle, WY [*FM radio station call letters*] (BROA)
KUWP........ Powell, WY [*FM radio station call letters*] (BROA)
KUWR........ Laramie, WY [*FM radio station call letters*]
KUWS........ Superior, WI [*FM radio station call letters*]
KUWT........ Themopolis, WY [*FM radio station call letters*] (BROA)
KUWT........ Thermopolis, WY [*FM radio station call letters*] (BROA)
KUWX........ Pinedale, WY [*FM radio station call letters*] (BROA)
KUWZ........ Rock Springs, WY [*FM radio station call letters*]
KUX.......... Kumix Resources Corp. [*Vancouver Stock Exchange symbol*]
KUY.......... Continually [*Telegraphy*] (PCTE)
KUY.......... Kuyper [*Indonesia*] [*Later, TNG*] [*Geomagnetic observatory code*]
KUY.......... Uyak [*Alaska*] [*Airport symbol*] (OAG)
KUY.......... Uyak, AK [*Location identifier*] [*FAA*] (FAAL)
KUYI-FM.... Holevilla, AZ [*FM radio station call letters*] (BROA)
KUYL........ Sacramento-Stockton, CA [*AM radio station call letters*] (GDPB)
KUYL-AM... Stockton, CA [*AM radio station call letters*] (BROA)
KUYO........ Evansville, WY [*AM radio station call letters*]
KUZZ........ Bakersfield, CA [*FM radio station call letters*]
KUZZ-TV.... Bakersfield, CA [*Television station call letters*]
KV............ British Virgin Island [*IYRU nationality code*] (IYR)
KV............ Convert [*Telegraphy*] (PCTE)
KV............ Kanamycin-Vancomycin [*An antibiotic*] (DAVI)
KV............ Karnaugh Veitch (SAUO)
KV............ Kerr Vector [*Optics*]
KV............ Key Verifier [*Computer science*]
KV............ Kidney Valve
KV............ Killed Vaccine [*Immunology*] (MAE)
KV............ Killed Virus [*Pharmacology*] (DAVI)
KV............ Kill Vehicle
KV............ Kilovolt (AAEL)
kv............ Kilovolt (MIST)
kV............ Kilovolt
KV............ Kinematic Viscosity
KV............ Knights of Vartan (EA)
KV............ Knutson Vandenberg Act [*Trust fund for timber sale area*] (ALAC)
KV............ Kochel-Verzeichnis [*List of Mozart's works*] (IIA)
KV............ Kriegsverwendungsfaehig [*Fit for Active Service*] [*German military - World War II*]
KV............ K-V Pharmaceutical Co. [*AMEX symbol*] (SPSG)
KV............ Transkei Airways [*ICAO designator*] (AD)
KV1.......... Kalanchoe Virus 1 [*Plant pathology*]
KVA.......... Convey [*Telegraphy*] (PCTE)
KVA.......... Karavia [*Zaire*] [*Geomagnetic observatory code*]
KVA.......... Kavala [*Greece*] [*Airport symbol*] (OAG)
KVA.......... Kill Vehicle Assembly [*Military*] (ACAE)
KVA.......... Kilovolt Ampere [*Electric utility company*]
kVA.......... Kilovolt Ampere
KVA.......... Kilovolt-Ampere (VLIE)
KVA.......... Korean Veterans Association (SAUO)
KVA.......... Royal Academy of Science (SAUS)
KVAB-FM.... Clarkston, WA [*FM radio station call letters*] (RBYB)
KVAC........ Conveyance [*Telegraphy*] (PCTE)
KVAC........ Forks, WA [*AM radio station call letters*]
KVAC........ Kilovolt Alternating Current (IAA)
KVAD........ Conveyed [*Telegraphy*] (PCTE)
KVAD........ Valdosta/Moody Air Force Base [*Georgia*] [*ICAO location identifier*] (ICLI)
KVAG........ Conveying [*Telegraphy*] (PCTE)
KVAG-FM... Rugby, ND [*FM radio station call letters*] (RBYB)
KVAH........ Kilovolt Ampere-Hour [*Electric utility company*]
kVAH........ Kilovolt-Ampere Hour
kVAhm....... Kilovolt-Ampere Hour Meter (MSA)
KVAK........ Valdez, AK [*AM radio station call letters*]
KVAK-FM.... Valdez, AK [*FM radio station call letters*] (BROA)
KVAL......... Eugene, OR [*Television station call letters*]
kVAM........ Kilovolt-Ampere Meter
KVAN........ Korean Voice Alerting Network (SAUO)
KVAN........ Vancouver, WA [*AM radio station call letters*]
kvar.......... Kilovar
KVAR........ Kilovolt Ampere Reactive [*Electric utility company*]
kVAr......... Kilovolt-Ampere Reactive
KVAR........ Riverside, CA [*FM radio station call letters*]
kvarh........ Kilovar-Hour
kVARh....... [*Reactive*] Kilovolt-Ampere-Hour (IDOE)
KVAS........ Astoria, OR [*AM radio station call letters*]
KVAS........ Ilwaco, WA [*FM radio station call letters*] (BROA)
KVAW........ Eagle Pass, TX [*Television station call letters*]
KVAY........ Lamar, CO [*FM radio station call letters*]
KVAZ........ Henryetta, OK [*FM radio station call letters*]
KVB.......... Convertible [*Telegraphy*] (PCTE)
KVB.......... KV Pharmaceutical Co. [*NYSE symbol*]
KVBA........ Kanamycin-Vancomycin Blood Agar [*Microbiology*]
KVBC........ Las Vegas, NV [*Television station call letters*]
KVBC-FM... Las Vegas, NV [*FM radio station call letters*] (RBYB)
KVBG........ Lompoc/Vandenberg Air Force Base [*California*] [*ICAO location identifier*] (ICLI)
KVBL........ Visalia, CA [*AM radio station call letters*] (BROA)
KVBM........ Minneapolis, MN [*Television station call letters*]
KVBR........ Brainerd, MN [*AM radio station call letters*]
KVBR-FM... Brainerd, MN [*FM radio station call letters*]
KVC.......... King Cove [*Alaska*] [*Airport symbol*] (OAG)
KVC.......... King Cove, AK [*Location identifier*] [*FAA*] (FAAL)
KVCA-AM... Simi Valley, CA [*AM radio station call letters*] (BROA)
KVCE........ Fallon, NV [*FM radio station call letters*]
KVCI......... Canton, TX [*AM radio station call letters*] (BROA)
KVCI......... Mineola, TX [*AM radio station call letters*]
KVCK........ Wolf Point, MT [*AM radio station call letters*]
KVCK-FM... Wolf Point, MT [*FM radio station call letters*]
KVCL........ Winnfield, LA [*AM radio station call letters*]
KVCL-FM.... Winnfield, LA [*FM radio station call letters*]
KVCM........ Helena, MT [*FM radio station call letters*]
KVCO........ Concordia, KS [*FM radio station call letters*]
KVCO........ Kevco, Inc. [*NASDAQ symbol*] (NASQ)
KVCOQ....... Kevco [*OTCBB symbol*]
kVcp......... Kilovolt Constant Potential (STED)
kVCP......... Kilovolt Constant Potential
KVCQ........ Cuero, TX [*FM radio station call letters*] (RBYB)
KVCR........ San Bernardino, CA [*FM radio station call letters*]
KVCR-TV.... San Bernardino, CA [*Television station call letters*]
KVCS........ KXE6S Verein Chess Society (EA)
KVCS-AM... Perry, OK [*AM radio station call letters*] (RBYB)
KVCS-FM... Perry, OK [*FM radio station call letters*] (RBYB)
KVCT........ Victoria, TX [*Television station call letters*]
KVCU........ Boulder, CO [*AM radio station call letters*] (BROA)
KVCV........ Victorville/George Air Force Base [*California*] [*ICAO location identifier*] (ICLI)
KVCX........ Gregory, SD [*FM radio station call letters*]
KVCY........ Fort Scott, KS [*FM radio station call letters*]
KVD.......... Converted [*Telegraphy*] (PCTE)
KVDA........ San Antonio, TX [*Television station call letters*]
KVDB........ Sioux Center, IA [*AM radio station call letters*]
kVdc......... Kilovolt Direct Current (IEEE)
KVDL........ Quanah, TX [*AM radio station call letters*]
KVDP........ Dry Prong, LA [*FM radio station call letters*]
KVDT........ Keyboard Visual Display Terminal (MCD)
KVDW........ England, AR [*AM radio station call letters*] (BROA)
KVE.......... Kalabakan [*Language symbol*] (ETLW)
KVE.......... Kaposi's Varicelliform Eruption [*Medicine*] [*Medicine*] (DMAA)
KVEA........ Corona, CA [*Television station call letters*]

KVEC .... San Luis Obispo, CA [*AM radio station call letters*]
KVEE .... Lake Arthur, LA [*FM radio station call letters*] (BROA)
KVEG .... Mesquite, NV [*FM radio station call letters*] (BROA)
KVEG .... North Las Vegas, NV [*AM radio station call letters*]
KVEL .... Vernal, UT [*AM radio station call letters*]
KVEN .... Ventura, CA [*AM radio station call letters*]
KVEO .... Brownsville, TX [*Television station call letters*]
KVER .... El Paso, TX [*FM radio station call letters*]
KVET .... Austin, TX [*AM radio station call letters*]
KVET-FM .... Austin, TX [*FM radio station call letters*]
KVEW .... Kennewick, WA [*Television station call letters*]
KVEZ-FM .... Parker, AZ [*FM radio station call letters*] (RBYB)
KVF .... Kent Volunteer Fencibles [*British military*] (DMA)
KVFC .... Cortez, CO [*AM radio station call letters*]
KVFD .... Fort Dodge, IA [*AM radio station call letters*]
KVFG .... Victorville, CA [*FM radio station call letters*] (BROA)
KVFM .... Beeville, TX [*FM radio station call letters*] (BROA)
KVFM .... Logan, UT [*FM radio station call letters*]
KVFR .... Daytonville, CA [*FM radio station call letters*] (BROA)
K-V Funds .. Knutson-Vandenberg Funds (WPI)
KVFX .... Manteca, CA [*FM radio station call letters*]
KVFX-FM .... Logan, UT [*FM radio station call letters*] (BROA)
KVG .... Converting [*Telegraphy*] (PCTE)
KVG .... Kavieng [*New Ireland*] [*Airport symbol*] (AD)
KVG .... Kavieng [*Papua New Guinea*] [*Airport symbol*] (OAG)
KVG .... Kavieng [*Papua New Guinea*] [*Seismograph station code, US Geological Survey*] (SEIS)
KVG .... Keyed Video Generator
KVG .... Key Variable Generator (COE)
KVGB .... Great Bend, KS [*AM radio station call letters*]
KVGB-FM ... Great Bend, KS [*FM radio station call letters*]
KVGO-FM ... Spring Valley, MN [*FM radio station call letters*] (RBYB)
KVGS .... Laughlin, NV [*FM radio station call letters*] (BROA)
KVH .... Kilovolt Hour [*Electric utility company*]
KVH .... Kits Van Heyningen [*Automotive industry*]
KVH .... Kreditverwaltungsgesellschaft Hamburg (EFIS)
KVHI .... KVH Industries [*NASDAQ symbol*] (TTSB)
KVHI .... KVH Industries, Inc. [*NASDAQ symbol*] (SAG)
KVHInd ...... KVH Industries, Inc. [*Associated Press*] (SAG)
KVHP .... Lake Charles, LA [*Television station call letters*]
KVHP2 .... Lake Charles, LA [*Television station call letters*] (GDPB)
KVHS .... Concord, CA [*FM radio station call letters*]
KVHS .... Kanawha Valley Historical Society (SAUO)
KVHT .... Vermillion, SD [*FM radio station call letters*]
KVI .... Carlsbad Ventures [*Vancouver Stock Exchange symbol*]
KVI .... Known Value Item (VLIE)
KVI .... Korean Veterans International (EA)
KVI .... Seattle, WA [*AM radio station call letters*]
KVIA .... El Paso, TX [*Television station call letters*]
KVIC .... Khadi & Village Industries Commission (SAUO)
KVIC .... Victoria, TX [*FM radio station call letters*]
KVIE .... Sacramento, CA [*Television station call letters*]
KVIH .... Clovis, NM [*Television station call letters*]
KVII .... Amarillo, TX [*Television station call letters*]
KVIK .... Decorah, IA [*FM radio station call letters*] (RBYB)
KVIL-FM .... Highland Park, TX [*FM radio station call letters*]
KVIN-AM .... Turlock, CA [*AM radio station call letters*] (BROA)
KVIP .... Redding, CA [*AM radio station call letters*]
KVIP-FM .... Redding, CA [*FM radio station call letters*]
KVIQ .... Eureka, CA [*Television station call letters*]
KVIS .... Miami, OK [*AM radio station call letters*]
KVIV .... El Paso, TX [*AM radio station call letters*]
KViWM ...... Wesley Medical Center, Wichita (SAUS)
KVJM .... Waco-Temple-Bryan, TX [*FM radio station call letters*] (GDPB)
KVJM-FM ... Hearme, TX [*FM radio station call letters*] (BROA)
KVJY .... Pharr, TX [*AM radio station call letters*]
KVJZ .... Ankeny, IA [*FM radio station call letters*] (BROA)
KVK .... Kriegsverdienstkreuz [*War Service Cross*] [*German military decoration - World War II*]
KVKI .... Shreveport, LA [*FM radio station call letters*]
KVL .... Kingsvale Resources [*Vancouver Stock Exchange symbol*]
KVL .... Kirchhoff's Voltage Law (PDAA)
KVL .... Kivalina [*Alaska*] [*Airport symbol*] (OAG)
KVL .... Kivalina, AK [*Location identifier*] [*FAA*] (FAAL)
KVLA .... Vidalia, LA [*AM radio station call letters*]
KVLBA .... Kanamycin-Vancomycin Labeled Blood Agar [*Microbiology*]
KVLC .... Hatch, NM [*FM radio station call letters*] (RBYB)
KVLD .... Atkins, AR [*FM radio station call letters*] (BROA)
KVLD .... Valdez, AK [*AM radio station call letters*]
KVLE .... Gunnison, CO [*FM radio station call letters*]
KVLF .... Alpine, TX [*AM radio station call letters*]
KVLG .... La Grange, TX [*AM radio station call letters*]
KVLH .... Pauls Valley, OK [*AM radio station call letters*]
KVLI .... Lake Isabella, CA [*AM radio station call letters*]
KVLI-FM .... Lake Isabella, CA [*FM radio station call letters*]
KVLL .... Woodville, TX [*AM radio station call letters*]
KVLL-FM .... Woodville, TX [*FM radio station call letters*]
KVLM .... Kevlin Corp. [*NASDAQ symbol*] (NQ)
KVLO-FM ... Sheridan, AR [*FM radio station call letters*] (RBYB)
KVLR .... Twisp, WA [*FM radio station call letters*]
KVLT .... Victoria, TX [*FM radio station call letters*]
KVLU .... Beaumont, TX [*FM radio station call letters*]
KVLV .... Fallon, NV [*AM radio station call letters*]
KVLV-FM .... Fallon, NV [*FM radio station call letters*]
KVLY .... Edinburg, TX [*FM radio station call letters*]
KVLY-TV .... Fargo, ND [*Television station call letters*] (RBYB)
KVM .... Keyboard Video Monitor
KVM .... Keyboard-Video-Mouse [*Computer science*]
kVM .... Kilovolt Meter
KVM .... K Virtual Machine (SAUS)
KVM .... Rusaerolizing Airling [*Former USSR*] [*FAA designator*] (FAAC)
KVMA .... Kansas Veterinary Medical Association (GVA)
KVMA .... Kentucky Veterinary Medical Association (GVA)
KVMA .... Magnolia, AR [*AM radio station call letters*]
KVMA-FM ... Magnolia, AR [*FM radio station call letters*]
KVMC .... Colorado City, TX [*AM radio station call letters*]
KVMD-TV ... Twentynine Palms, CA [*TV station call letters*] (RBYB)
KVMI .... Arthur, ND [*FM radio station call letters*] (BROA)
KVML .... Sonora, CA [*AM radio station call letters*]
KV/mm ...... Kilovolt per Millimeter (VLIE)
KVMR .... Nevada City, CA [*FM radio station call letters*]
KVMT .... Montrose, CO [*FM radio station call letters*] (BROA)
KVMV .... McAllen, TX [*FM radio station call letters*]
KVMX .... Banks, OR [*FM radio station call letters*] (BROA)
KVMX .... Eastland, TX [*FM radio station call letters*]
KVN .... Conversion [*Telegraphy*] (PCTE)
KVN .... Kaiserville [*Nevada*] [*Seismograph station code, US Geological Survey*] (SEIS)
KVN .... Kimmins Corp. [*NYSE symbol*] (TTSB)
KVN .... Kimmins Environmental Services [*NYSE symbol*] (SPSG)
KVNA .... Flagstaff, AZ [*AM radio station call letters*]
KVNA-FM ... Flagstaff, AZ [*FM radio station call letters*]
KVNE .... Tyler, TX [*FM radio station call letters*]
KVNF .... Paonia, CO [*FM radio station call letters*]
KVNI .... Coeur D'Alene, ID [*AM radio station call letters*]
KVNM .... Kimmins Corp. [*OTCBB symbol*]
KVNO .... Omaha, NE [*FM radio station call letters*]
KVNP .... Kidepo Valley National Park (SAUO)
KVNR .... Santa Ana, CA [*AM radio station call letters*] (BROA)
KVNU .... Logan, UT [*AM radio station call letters*]
KVO .... Keep Vein Open [*Medicine*]
KVO .... Kraftverkehrsordnung fuer den Gueterfernverkehr mit Kraftfahrzeugen [*Regulation for the Carriage of Goods by Motor Vehicles*] [*German*] [*Business term*] (ILCA)
KVOA .... Tucson, AZ [*Television station call letters*]
KVOC .... Casper, WY [*AM radio station call letters*]
KVO C D5W .... Keep Vein Open Cum [*with*] Dextrose 5% in Water [*Pharmacology*] (DAVI)
KVOD .... Denver, CO [*FM radio station call letters*]
KVOE .... Emporia, KS [*AM radio station call letters*]
KVOE-FM ... Emporia, KS [*FM radio station call letters*]
KVOI .... Oro Valley, AZ [*AM radio station call letters*]
KVOI .... Tucson, AZ [*AM radio station call letters*] (BROA)
KVOK .... Kodiak, AK [*AM radio station call letters*]
KVOL .... Lafayette, LA [*AM radio station call letters*]
KVOL .... Opelousas, LA [*FM radio station call letters*]
KVOM .... Morrilton, AR [*AM radio station call letters*]
KVOM-FM ... Morrilton, AR [*FM radio station call letters*]
KVON .... Napa, CA [*AM radio station call letters*]
KVOO .... Tulsa, OK [*AM radio station call letters*]
KVOO-FM ... Tulsa, OK [*FM radio station call letters*]
KVOP .... Plainview, TX [*AM radio station call letters*]
KVOP-FM ... Plainview, TX [*FM radio station call letters*] (BROA)
KVOR .... Colorado Springs, CO [*AM radio station call letters*]
KVOS .... Seattle-Tacoma (Bellingham), WA [*Television station call letters*] (GDPB)
KVOS-TV ... Bellingham, WA [*Television station call letters*]
KVOU .... Uvalde, TX [*AM radio station call letters*]
KVOV .... Glenwood Springs, CO [*FM radio station call letters*] (BROA)
KVOW .... Riverton, WY [*AM radio station call letters*]
KVOX .... Moorhead, MN [*AM radio station call letters*]
KVOX-FM ... Moorhead, MN [*FM radio station call letters*]
KVOY .... Mojave, CA [*AM radio station call letters*]
KVOZ .... Del Mar Hills, TX [*AM radio station call letters*] (BROA)
KVOZ .... Laredo, TX [*AM radio station call letters*]
KVP .... Katholieke Volkspartij [*Catholic People's Party*] [*Netherlands*] [*Political party*] (PPE)
kVP .... Kilovolt Peak
KVP .... Kodak Vacuum Probe
KVP .... Kodak Versamat Processor
KVP .... Kompane [*Language symbol*] (ETLW)
KVPA .... Port Isabel, TX [*FM radio station call letters*]
KVPC .... San Joaquin, CA (RBYB)
KVPC-FM ... San Joaquin, CA [*FM radio station call letters*] (BROA)
KV Ph .... K-V Pharmaceutical Co. [*Associated Press*] (SAG)
KVPI .... Ville Platte, LA [*AM radio station call letters*]
KVPI-FM .... Ville Platte, LA [*FM radio station call letters*]
KVPR .... Fresno, CA [*FM radio station call letters*]
KVPS .... Valparaiso/Eglin Air Force Base [*Florida*] [*ICAO location identifier*] (ICLI)
KVPT .... Fresno, CA [*Television station call letters*]
KVPX .... KVP [*Private rail car owner code*]
KVR .... Kangra Valley Railway [*Indian Railway*] (TIR)
KVRB .... Vero Beach/Vero Beach [*Florida*] [*ICAO location identifier*] (ICLI)
KVRC .... Arkadelphia, AR [*AM radio station call letters*]
KVRD .... Cottonwood, AZ [*AM radio station call letters*]
KVRD-FM ... Cottonwood, AZ [*FM radio station call letters*]
KVRE .... Hot Springs Village, AR [*FM radio station call letters*]

KVRG .... Seaside, CA [*FM radio station call letters*]
KVRG .... Soledad, CA [*AM radio station call letters*] (RBYB)
KVRH .... Kilovolt Ampere Reactive Hour [*Electric utility company*]
KVRH .... Salida, CO [*AM radio station call letters*]
KVRH-FM ... Salida, CO [*FM radio station call letters*]
KVRI-AM .... Blaine, WA [*AM radio station call letters*] (BROA)
KVRN-FM ... Marvell, AR [*FM radio station call letters*] (BROA)
KVRO-FM ... Stillwater, OK [*FM radio station call letters*] (BROA)
KVRP .... Haskell, TX [*FM radio station call letters*]
KVRP .... Stamford, TX [*AM radio station call letters*]
KVRQ .... Atwater, CA [*FM radio station call letters*]
KVRR .... Fargo, ND [*Television station call letters*]
KVRS .... Lawton, OK [*FM radio station call letters*]
KVRT .... Victoria, TX [*FM radio station call letters*] (RBYB)
KVRW .... Lawton, OK [*FM radio station call letters*]
KVRX .... Austin, TX [*FM radio station call letters*]
KVRY .... Mesa, AZ [*FM radio station call letters*]
KVS .... Converts [*Telegraphy*] (PCTE)
KVS .... Kansanvalistusseura [*Society for Culture and Education*] [*Finland*] (EAIO)
KVS .... Kelvin-Varley Slide [*Electronics*]
KVS .... Keyboard/Video Switch [*Computer science*]
KVS .... Kurzweil VoiceSystem [*Voice-recognition computer device*]
KVSA .... McGehee, AR [*AM radio station call letters*]
KVSC .... St. Cloud, MN [*FM radio station call letters*]
KVSF .... Santa Fe, NM [*AM radio station call letters*]
KVSH .... Valentine, NE [*AM radio station call letters*]
KVSI .... Montpelier, ID [*AM radio station call letters*]
KVSL .... Show Low, AZ [*AM radio station call letters*]
KVSN .... Tumwater, WA [*AM radio station call letters*]
KVSO .... Ardmore, OK [*AM radio station call letters*] (RBYB)
KVSP .... Oklahoma City, OK [*AM radio station call letters*]
KVSR-FM ... Fresno, CA [*FM radio station call letters*] (BROA)
KVSS .... Omaha, NE [*FM radio station call letters*] (BROA)
KVST .... Huntsville, TX [*FM radio station call letters*]
KVST .... Keystone Visual Survey Test [*Ophthalmology*]
KVST .... Willis, TX [*FM radio station call letters*] (BROA)
KVSV .... Beloit, KS [*AM radio station call letters*]
KVSV-FM.... Beloit, KS [*FM radio station call letters*]
KVT .... Kavak [*Turkey*] [*Seismograph station code, US Geological Survey*] (SEIS)
KVTA......... Port Hueneme, CA [*AM radio station call letters*] (BROA)
KVTF......... Williams, AZ [*FM radio station call letters*]
KVTH .... Hot Springs, AR [*Television station call letters*] (RBYB)
KVTI .... Tacoma, WA [*FM radio station call letters*]
KVTJ-TV..... Jonesboro, AR [*TV station call letters*] (RBYB)
KVTK .... Yankton, SD [*AM radio station call letters*] (GDPB)
KVTK-AM ... Vermillion, SD [*AM radio station call letters*] (BROA)
KVTN .... Pine Bluff, AR [*Television station call letters*]
KVTO .... Berkeley, CA [*AM radio station call letters*]
KVTT......... Dallas, TX [*FM radio station call letters*]
KVTV .... Laredo, TX [*Television station call letters*]
KVTY-FM.... Lewiston, ID [*FM radio station call letters*] (BROA)
KVU .... Kleer-Vu Industries [*AMEX symbol*] (TTSB)
KVU .... Kleer-Vu Industries, Inc. [*AMEX symbol*] (SPSG)
KVU .... Victoria University Library, University of Toronto [*UTLAS symbol*]
KVUE .... Austin, TX [*Television station call letters*]
KVUT .... Little Rock, AR [*Television station call letters*]
KVUU .... Pueblo, CO [*FM radio station call letters*]
KVVA .... Phoenix, AZ [*AM radio station call letters*]
KVVA-FM.... Apache Junction, AZ [*FM radio station call letters*]
KVVN .... Santa Clara, CA [*AM radio station call letters*] (BROA)
KVVP .... Leesville, LA [*FM radio station call letters*]
KVVQ .... Hesperia, CA [*AM radio station call letters*]
KVVQ .... Victorville, CA [*FM radio station call letters*]
KVVR .... Dutton, MT [*FM radio station call letters*] (BROA)
KVVS .... Mojave, CA [*FM radio station call letters*] (BROA)
KVVS .... Windsor, CO [*AM radio station call letters*]
KVVU .... Henderson, NV [*Television station call letters*]
KVVV .... Baytoun, TX [*Television station call letters*]
KVVY .... Merced, CA [*AM radio station call letters*] (BROA)
KVW .... Kansas City, Kaw Valley R. R., Inc. [*AAR code*]
KVW .... Kurzweil Voice Writer
KVWB .... Las Vegas, NV [*Television station call letters*] (BROA)
KVWC .... Vernon, TX [*AM radio station call letters*]
KVWC-FM... Vernon, TX [*FM radio station call letters*]
KVWG .... Pearsall, TX [*AM radio station call letters*]
KVWG-FM... Pearsall, TX [*FM radio station call letters*]
KVWM........ Show Low, AZ [*AM radio station call letters*]
KVWM-FM... Show Low, AZ [*FM radio station call letters*]
KVY .... CAI [*Compagnia Aeronautica Italiana SpA*] [*Italy*] [*ICAO designator*] (FAAC)
KVY.......... Convertibly [*Telegraphy*] (PCTE)
KVYE-TV .... El Centro, CA [*TV station call letters*] (RBYB)
KVYF .... Wilson Creek, WA [*FM radio station call letters*]
KVYN .... St. Helena, CA [*FM radio station call letters*]
KVYS .... St. George, UT [*FM radio station call letters*]
KVYY-FM.... Ventura, CA [*FM radio station call letters*] (RBYB)
KVZK-2 ...... Pago Pago, AS [*Television station call letters*]
KVZK-4 ...... Pago Pago, AS [*Television station call letters*]
KVZK-5 ...... Pago Pago, AS [*Television station call letters*]
KW........... Afrikan Airlines Ltd. (SAUO)
K_w........... Dissociation Constant of Water [*Physics*] (DAVI)
KW........... Dorado Wings [*Airline code*]
KW........... Kaiser Wilhelm [*King William*] [*Name of two Prussian kings and emperor of Germany*] (ROG)
KW........... Kaliszer Woch (BJA)
KW........... Kampfwagen [*Tank*] [*German military - World War II*]
KW........... Katabatic Wind
KW........... Keith-Wagener [*Ophthalmology*]
KW........... Kenworth [*NCIC truck make code*]
KW........... Kenworth Truck Co.
KW........... Key West [*Florida*]
KW........... Key Word [*Online database field identifier*]
KW........... Killer Weed [*Slang for phencyclidine; also called PCP and Sernyl*] (DAVI)
kW .... Kilohm [*Formerly, K*] [*Unit of electrical resistance*] (DAVI)
KW........... Kilowaft [*Electric utility company*]
Kw .... Kilowatt (EBF)
kw............ Kilowatt (ELAL)
kW .... Kilowatt
KW........... Kiloword (BUR)
KW........... Kimmelstiel-Wilson [*Medicine*]
KW........... Kirkwall, Orkney [*Postcode*] (ODBW)
KW........... Knight of William [*Netherlands*]
KW........... Knight of Windsor (ROG)
KW........... Knitwise [*Knitting*]
KW........... Know (ADWA)
KW........... Korean War
KW........... Kraftwagen [*Motor Vehicle*] [*German*]
KW........... Kruskal-Wallis Test [*Fisheries*]
KW........... Kugelberg-Welander Disease (DAVI)
KW........... Kuwait [*ANSI two-letter standard code*] (CNC)
Kw .... Weighted Kappa [*Medicine*] (EDAA)
KWA .... Kama [*Language symbol*] (ETLW)
KWA .... Key West Airport, FL [*Amtrak Busline code*]
KWA .... Keyword Adapted [*Computer science*]
KWA .... Kodiak Western Alaska Airlines (SAUO)
KWA .... Kwajalein [*Marshall Islands*] [*Airport symbol*] (OAG)
KWA .... Kwantlen College Library [*UTLAS symbol*]
KWA .... Kweiyang [*Republic of China*] [*Seismograph station code, US Geological Survey*] (SEIS)
KWAB........ Big Spring, TX [*Television station call letters*]
KWAB........ Boulder, CO [*AM radio station call letters*] (BROA)
KWAC........ Bakersfield, CA [*AM radio station call letters*]
KWAC........ Keyword and Context [*Indexing*] (DIT)
KWAD .... Wadena, MN [*AM radio station call letters*]
KWADE...... Key Word as a Dictionary Entry [*IBM*] [*Indexing system*] (NITA)
K-W AG ..... Kitchener-Waterloo Art Gallery (SAUO)
KWAI .... Honolulu, HI [*AM radio station call letters*]
KWAJ........ Kwajalein Atoll (AABC)
KWAK........ Stuttgart, AR [*AM radio station call letters*]
KWAK-FM... Stuttgart, AR [*FM radio station call letters*]
KWAL........ Wallace, ID [*AM radio station call letters*]
KWAL........ Wallops Island/Wallops Station [*Virginia*] [*ICAO location identifier*] (ICLI)
KWAM....... Memphis, TN [*AM radio station call letters*]
KWAN .... Gualala, CA [*FM radio station call letters*]
Kwansei Gak L Rev... Kwansei Gakuin University. Law Review [*A publication*] (DLA)
Kwansei Gakuin Univ Annual Stud... Kwansei Gakuin University. Annual Studies. Kwansei Gakuin University, Nishinomiya (SAUO)
KWAR .... Waverly, IA [*FM radio station call letters*]
KWAS........ Joplin, MO [*AM radio station call letters*]
KWAT........ Watertown, SD [*AM radio station call letters*]
KWAU .... Korea Women's Associations United (BUAC)
KWAV........ Monterey, CA [*FM radio station call letters*]
KWAW....... Garapan-Saipan, NP [*FM radio station call letters*] (BROA)
KWAX........ Eugene, OR [*FM radio station call letters*]
KWAY........ Waverly, IA [*AM radio station call letters*]
KWAY-FM ... Waverly, IA [*FM radio station call letters*]
KWAZ........ Needles, CA [*FM radio station call letters*]
KWB .... Keith, Wagener, Barker [*Ophthalmology*]
KWB .... Koch-Weeks Bacillus [*Medicine*] (MELL)
KWBA .... Sierra Vista, AZ [*Television station call letters*] (BROA)
KWBC .... Navasota, TX [*AM radio station call letters*]
KWBC .... Washington [*District of Columbia*] [*ICAO location identifier*] (ICLI)
KWBE........ Beatrice, NE [*AM radio station call letters*]
KWBF........ Flagstaff, AZ [*Television station call letters*] (RBYB)
KWBF........ Katholische Welt-Bibelfoderation [*World Catholic Federation for the Biblical Apostolate - WCFBA*] (EAIO)
KWBG .... Boone, IA [*AM radio station call letters*]
KWBH .... Rexburg, ID [*FM radio station call letters*]
KWBI .... Great Bend, KS [*FM radio station call letters*] (BROA)
KWBI .... Morrison, CO [*FM radio station call letters*]
KWBJ........ Baton Rouge, LA [*Television station call letters*] (GDPB)
KWBK-AM.... Beaumont, TX [*AM radio station call letters*] (BROA)
KWBM....... Harrison, AR [*Television station call letters*] (BROA)
KWBN .... Honolulu, HI [*Television station call letters*] (BROA)
KWBP .... Salem, OR [*Television station call letters*] (RBYB)
KWBQ .... Santa Fe, NM [*Television station call letters*] (BROA)
KWBR .... Pismo Beach, CA [*FM radio station call letters*]
KWBS-TV ... Eureka Springs, AR [*Television station call letters*] (BROA)
KWBT........ Muskogee, OK [*Television station call letters*] (BROA)
KWBU .... Waco, TX [*FM radio station call letters*]
KWBW....... Hutchinson, KS [*AM radio station call letters*]
KWBX .... Salem, OR [*FM radio station call letters*] (BROA)
KWBY .... Woodburn, OR [*AM radio station call letters*]

KWBZ........ Monroe City, MO [*FM radio station call letters*] (BROA)
KWC........ K-Band Waveguide Circulator
KWC........ Kentucky Wesleyan College [*Owensboro*]
KWC........ Kierownictwo Walki Cywilnej (BJA)
KWC........ Wycliffe College Library, University of Toronto [*UTLAS symbol*]
KWCA....... Weaverville, CA [*FM radio station call letters*] (BROA)
KWCB....... Floresville, TX [*FM radio station call letters*]
KWCC....... Kootenay Weed Control Committee (SAUO)
KWCC....... KTACS Warning and Control Center (SAUO)
KWCC-FM... Muscatine, IA [*FM radio station call letters*] (RBYB)
KWCD....... Bisbee, AZ [*FM radio station call letters*]
KWCH....... Hutchinson, KS [*Television station call letters*]
KWCK....... Searcy, AR [*AM radio station call letters*]
KWCK-FM... Searcy, AR [*FM radio station call letters*]
KWCL....... Oak Grove, LA [*FM radio station call letters*]
KWCM....... Appleton, MN [*Television station call letters*]
KWCO....... Chickasha, OK [*AM radio station call letters*]
KWCR....... Ogden, UT [*FM radio station call letters*]
KWCU....... World Container Leasing [*Intermodal shipping container symbol*] (TVRC)
KWCV....... Wichita, KS [*Television station call letters*]
KWCW....... Walla Walla, WA [*FM radio station call letters*]
KWCX....... Wilcox, AZ [*FM radio station call letters*]
KWCY-FM... Glendale, AZ [*FM radio station call letters*] (BROA)
KWD........ Consolidated Westrex Development [*Vancouver Stock Exchange symbol*]
KWD........ Draco [*Sweden*] [*Research code symbol*]
KWD........ Kellwood Co. [*NYSE symbol*] (SPSG)
KWD........ Kirkwood, MO [*Amtrak rail station code*]
KWD........ Kugelberg-Welander Disease [*Chronic childhood spinal muscular atrophy*] [*Medicine*] (EDAA)
KWDA....... White Hall, AR [*FM radio station call letters*]
KWDB-AM... Oak Harbor, WA [*AM radio station call letters*] (BROA)
KWDF....... Ball, LA [*AM radio station call letters*]
KWDJ....... Ridgecrest, CA [*AM radio station call letters*] (BROA)
KWDK....... Tacoma, WA [*Television station call letters*]
KWDM....... West Des Moines, IA [*FM radio station call letters*]
KWDO....... Waldo, AR [*FM radio station call letters*] (BROA)
KWDQ....... Woodward, OK [*FM radio station call letters*]
KWDT....... KW Dart [*NCIC truck make code*]
KWDX....... Silsbee, TX [*FM radio station call letters*]
KWE........ Guiyang [*China*] [*Airport symbol*] (OAG)
KWE........ Keith-Welti-Ernst [*Method*] [*Radiology*] (DAVI)
KWE........ Kilowatt Electric [*DOE*] (TAG)
kWe........ Kilowatts of Electric Energy
KWE........ Kintetsu World Express Pte Ltd (EFIS)
KWE........ Knight of the White Eagle [*Poland*]
KWE........ Kumar, Welti, and Ernst [*Medicine*] [*Method*] (RAWO)
KWE........ Kweiyang [*China*] [*Airport symbol*] (AD)
KWEB....... Rochester, MN [*AM radio station call letters*]
KWED....... Seguin, TX [*AM radio station call letters*]
KWEG-FM... Warm Springs, OR [*FM radio station call letters*] (BROA)
KWEI....... Weiser, ID [*AM radio station call letters*]
KWEI-FM... Fruitland, ID [*FM radio station call letters*] (RBYB)
KWEL....... Midland, TX [*AM radio station call letters*]
KWEN....... Tulsa, OK [*FM radio station call letters*]
KWEO....... Garberville, CA [*FM radio station call letters*]
KWES....... Ruidoso, NM [*FM radio station call letters*]
KWES-TV... Odessa, TX [*Television station call letters*]
KWET....... Cheyenne, OK [*Television station call letters*]
KWEX....... San Antonio, TX [*Television station call letters*]
KWEY....... Weatherford, OK [*AM radio station call letters*]
KWEY-FM... Weatherford, OK [*FM radio station call letters*]
KWEZ-FM... Santa Margarita, CA [*FM radio station call letters*] (BROA)
KWF........ Kirschner Wire Fixation (MELL)
KWF........ Waterfall, AK [*Location identifier*] [*FAA*] (FAAL)
KWFC....... Kelli Warren Fan Club [*Defunct*] (EA)
KWFC....... Springfield, MO [*FM radio station call letters*]
KWFH....... Parker, AZ [*FM radio station call letters*]
KWFJ....... Roy, WA [*FM radio station call letters*]
KWFL....... Roswell, NM [*FM radio station call letters*]
KWFM....... Green Valley, AZ [*FM radio station call letters*] (BROA)
KWFM....... Kurt Weill Foundation for Music (EA)
KWFM-FM... Tucson, AZ [*FM radio station call letters*]
KWFR....... San Angelo, TX [*FM radio station call letters*] (RBYB)
KWFS....... Wichita Falls, TX [*FM radio station call letters*]
KWFS-FM... Wichita Falls, TX [*FM radio station call letters*] (RBYB)
KWFT....... Kilowatt Foot (IAA)
KWFT....... Wichita Falls, TX [*AM radio station call letters*]
KWFX....... Woodward, OK [*FM radio station call letters*]
KWG........ Kerguelen Working Group (SAUO)
KWG........ Knowing [*Telegraphy*] (PCTE)
KWG........ Kunststoffwerk Gessmann GmbH & Co. (EFIS)
KWG........ Stockton, CA [*AM radio station call letters*]
KWGB-FM... Colby, KS [*FM radio station call letters*] (BROA)
KWGDF...... KWG Resources, Inc. [*NASDAQ symbol*] (SAG)
KWGL....... Ouray, CO [*FM radio station call letters*] (BROA)
KWGN....... Denver, CO [*Television station call letters*]
KWG Rs..... KWG Resources, Inc. [*Associated Press*] (SAG)
KWGS....... Tulsa, OK [*FM radio station call letters*]
KWH........ Kilowatt Hour [*Electric utility company*]
Kwh........ Kilowatt Hour (EBF)
KWH........ Kilowatt Hour [*DOE*] (TAG)
KWh........ Kilowatt-Hour (VLIE)
kWh........ Kilowatt-Hour
KWHB....... Tulsa, OK [*Television station call letters*]
KWHD....... Castle Rock, CO [*Television station call letters*]
KWHE....... Honolulu, HI [*Television station call letters*]
kWhe....... Kilowatt-Hour Electric
KWHH....... Hilo, HI [*Television station call letters*]
KWHI....... Brenham, TX [*AM radio station call letters*]
KWHI....... WH Kent [*Common carrier symbol*]
KWHL....... Anchorage, AK [*FM radio station call letters*]
KWHM....... Kilowatt-Hour Meter
KWHM....... Wailuku, HI [*Television station call letters*]
KWHN....... Fort Smith, AR [*AM radio station call letters*]
KWHN....... Haynesville, LA [*FM radio station call letters*]
KWHO....... Weed, CA [*FM radio station call letters*]
KWHQ....... Kenai, AK [*FM radio station call letters*]
kW-hr...... Kilowatt-Hour (ADWA)
kwhr....... Kilowatt-Hour (MIST)
kWhr....... Kilowatt-Hour
KWHR....... Kilowatthour (ABBR)
KWHT....... Pendleton, OR [*FM radio station call letters*]
KWHW....... Altus, OK [*AM radio station call letters*]
KWHY....... Los Angeles, CA [*Television station call letters*]
KWHY-DT... Los Angeles, CA [*Television station call letters*] (BROA)
KWI........ Karst Waters Institute Inc. (RCD)
KWI........ Kosher Wine Institute (EA)
KWI........ Kuwait [*Airport symbol*] (OAG)
KWi........ Wichita Public Library, Wichita, KS [*Library symbol*] [*Library of Congress*] (LCLS)
KWiB....... Boeing Co., Wichita Division Library (SAUO)
KWiB....... [*The*] Boeing Co., Wichita Division Library, Wichita, KS [*Library symbol*] [*Library of Congress*] (LCLS)
KWIC....... Kennedy Wilson, Inc. [*NASDAQ symbol*] (SAG)
KWIC....... Kentucky Women's Intercollegiate Conference (PSS)
KWIC....... Keyword in Context [*Indexing*]
KWIC....... Topeka, KS [*FM radio station call letters*]
KWiF....... Friends University, Wichita, KS [*Library symbol*] [*Library of Congress*] (LCLS)
KWiGS...... Church of Jesus Christ of Latter-Day Saints Genealogical Society Library, Wichita Branch (SAUO)
KWiGS...... Church of Jesus Christ of Latter-Day Saints, Genealogical Society Library, Wichita Branch, Wichita, KS [*Library symbol*] [*Library of Congress*] (LCLS)
KWiIL...... Institute of Logopedics, Wichita, KS [*Library symbol*] [*Library of Congress*] (LCLS)
KWiK....... Kansas Newman College, Wichita, KS [*Library symbol*] [*Library of Congress*] (LCLS)
KWIK....... KWIK Products International Corp. (SAUO)
KWIK....... Pocatello, ID [*AM radio station call letters*]
KWIL....... Albany, OR [*AM radio station call letters*]
KWiIL...... Institute of Logopedics, Wichita (SAUS)
KWIM....... Window Rock, AZ [*FM radio station call letters*]
KWIN....... Lodi, CA [*FM radio station call letters*]
KWIP....... Dallas, OR [*AM radio station call letters*]
KWIP....... Keyword Word in Permutation [*Indexing*] (PDAA)
KWIPS...... Kilo Whetstones Per Second (SAUO)
KWIQ....... Moses Lake, WA [*AM radio station call letters*]
KWIQ-FM... Moses Lake, WA [*FM radio station call letters*]
K-wire..... Kirschner wire (SAUS)
KWiSF...... Saint Francis Hospital, Wichita, KS [*Library symbol*] [*Library of Congress*] (LCLS)
KWiSJ...... Saint Joseph Hospital, Wichita, KS [*Library symbol*] [*Library of Congress*] (LCLS)
KWIT....... Keyword in Title [*Indexing*]
KWIT....... Sioux City, IA [*FM radio station call letters*]
KWiU....... Wichita State University, Wichita, KS [*Library symbol*] [*Library of Congress*] (LCLS)
KWiVA...... United States Veterans Administration Hospital, Wichita, KS [*Library symbol*] [*Library of Congress*] (LCLS)
KWiWC...... Wichita Clinic, Wichita, KS [*Library symbol*] [*Library of Congress*] (LCLS)
KWiWM...... Wesley Medical Center, Wichita, KS [*Library symbol*] [*Library of Congress*] (LCLS)
KWIX....... Moberly, MO [*AM radio station call letters*]
KWIZ....... Santa Ana, CA [*AM radio station call letters*]
KWIZ-FM... Santa Ana, CA [*FM radio station call letters*]
KWJC....... Liberty, MO [*FM radio station call letters*]
KWJG-FM... Kasilof, AK [*FM radio station call letters*] (BROA)
KWJJ....... Portland, OR [*AM radio station call letters*]
KWJJ-FM... Portland, OR [*FM radio station call letters*]
KWJL....... Lancaster, CA [*AM radio station call letters*] (BROA)
KWJM....... Farmerville, LA [*FM radio station call letters*]
KWJZ....... Seattle, WA [*FM radio station call letters*] (RBYB)
KWK........ Kampfwagenkanone [*Tank Gun*] [*German military - World War II*]
KWK........ Kwigillingok [*Alaska*] [*Airport symbol*] (OAG)
KWK........ Kwigillingok, AK [*Location identifier*] [*FAA*] (FAAL)
KWK........ Quicksilver Resources, Inc. [*AMEX symbol*] (NASQ)
KWKA....... Clovis, NM [*AM radio station call letters*]
KWKB-TV... Iowa City, IA [*TV station call letters*] (RBYB)
KWKC....... Abilene, TX [*AM radio station call letters*] (BROA)
KWKH....... Shreveport, LA [*AM radio station call letters*]
KWKH-FM... Shreveport, LA [*FM radio station call letters*]
KWKJ....... Windsor, MO [*FM radio station call letters*] (BROA)
KWKK....... Dardanelle, AR [*FM radio station call letters*]
KWKK....... Russellville, AR [*FM radio station call letters*] (BROA)
KWKL....... Grandfield, OK [*FM radio station call letters*] (BROA)

KWKM-FM ... St. Johns, AZ [*FM radio station call letters*] (BROA)
KWKQ .... Graham, TX [*FM radio station call letters*]
KWKT .... Waco, TX [*Television station call letters*]
KWKU-AM ... Pomona, CA [*AM radio station call letters*] (BROA)
KWKW .... Los Angeles, CA [*AM radio station call letters*]
KWKY .... Des Moines, IA [*AM radio station call letters*]
KWKZ .... Charleston, MO [*FM radio station call letters*]
KWL .... Guilin [*China*] [*Airport symbol*] (OAG)
KWL .... Kofyar [*Language symbol*] (ETLW)
KWLA .... Many, LA [*AM radio station call letters*]
KWLC .... Decorah, IA [*AM radio station call letters*]
KWLD .... Plainview, TX [*FM radio station call letters*]
KWLF .... Fairbanks, AK [*FM radio station call letters*]
KWLF .... Kodak Wratten Light Filter
KWLL .... Casa Grande, AZ [*AM radio station call letters*]
KWLM .... Willmar, MN [*AM radio station call letters*]
KWLN .... Wilson Creek, WA [*FM radio station call letters*] (BROA)
KWLO .... Waterloo, IA [*AM radio station call letters*]
KWLR .... Maurmelle, AR [*FM radio station call letters*] (BROA)
KWLS .... Pratt, KS [*AM radio station call letters*]
KWLT .... North Crossett, AR [*FM radio station call letters*]
KWLV .... Many, LA [*FM radio station call letters*]
KWLW .... North Salt Lake City, UT [*AM radio station call letters*] (BROA)
KWLZ .... Warm Springs, OR [*FM radio station call letters*] (BROA)
kWm .... Kilowatt Meter
KWM .... Korean War Memorial (EA)
KWM .... Kowanyama [*Australia*] [*Airport symbol*] (OAG)
KWM .... K Window Manager (SAUS)
KW/M² .... Kilowatts per Square Meter
KWMC .... Del Rio, TX [*AM radio station call letters*]
KWME .... Wellington, KS [*FM radio station call letters*]
KWMH .... K & K Mobile Homes [*NCIC trailer make code*]
KWMJ .... Tulsa, OK [*Television station call letters*]
KWMM .... Osage, IA [*FM radio station call letters*] (GDPB)
KWMM-FM ... Osage, IA [*FM radio station call letters*] (BROA)
KWMO .... Washington, MO [*AM radio station call letters*] (BROA)
KWMQ .... Southwest City, MO [*FM radio station call letters*]
KWMR-FM ... Point Reyes Station, CA [*FM radio station call letters*] (BROA)
KWMT .... Fort Dodge, IA [*AM radio station call letters*]
KWMU .... St. Louis, MO [*FM radio station call letters*]
KWMW .... Maljamar, NM [*FM radio station call letters*]
KWMX .... Lakewood, CO [*FM radio station call letters*]
KWMX-FM ... Williams, AZ [*FM radio station call letters*] (BROA)
KWN .... Kenwin Shops [*AMEX symbol*] (TTSB)
KWN .... Kenwin Shops, Inc. [*AMEX symbol*] (SPSG)
KWN .... Korean Wideband Network [*Communications*] [*Military*] (MCD)
KWN .... Quinhagak [*Alaska*] [*Airport symbol*] (OAG)
KWN .... Quinhagak, AK [*Location identifier*] [*FAA*] (FAAL)
KWNA .... Winnemucca, NV [*AM radio station call letters*]
KWNA-FM .. Winnemucca, NV [*FM radio station call letters*]
KWNB .... Hayes Center, NE [*Television station call letters*]
KWNC .... Quincy, WA [*AM radio station call letters*]
KWND .... Kenetech Corp. [*NASDAQ symbol*] (SAG)
KWND .... Springfield, MO [*FM radio station call letters*]
KWNDZ ...... KENETECH Cp 8.25% Cv Dep Pfd [*NASDAQ symbol*] (TTSB)
KWNE .... Ukiah, CA [*FM radio station call letters*]
KWNG .... Red Wing, MN [*FM radio station call letters*]
KWNK .... Simi Valley, CA [*AM radio station call letters*]
KWNN .... Turlock, CA [*FM radio station call letters*] (RBYB)
KWNO .... Rushford, MN [*FM radio station call letters*]
KWNO .... Winona, MN [*AM radio station call letters*]
KWNR .... Henderson, NV [*FM radio station call letters*]
KWNS .... Kensington Welding & Trailer [*NCIC trailer make code*]
KWNS .... Winnsboro, TX [*FM radio station call letters*]
KWNV-TV ... Winnemucca, NV [*TV station call letters*] (RBYB)
KWNWR ..... Key West National Wildlife Refuge (SAUO)
KWNX .... Keyword Index Subsystem (SAUO)
KWNX .... Taylor, TX [*AM radio station call letters*] (BROA)
KWNZ .... Carson City, NV [*FM radio station call letters*]
KWOA .... Worthington, MN [*AM radio station call letters*]
KWOA-FM ... Worthington, MN [*FM radio station call letters*]
KWOC .... Keyword out of Context [*Indexing*]
KWOC .... Poplar Bluff, MO [*AM radio station call letters*]
KWOCA ...... Key Word Online Catalogue Access
KWOD .... Sacramento, CA [*FM radio station call letters*]
KWOF .... Hiawatha, IA [*FM radio station call letters*] (BROA)
KWOF .... Waterloo, IA [*AM radio station call letters*] (BROA)
KWOG .... Bellevue, WA [*Television station call letters*] (BROA)
KWOI .... Carroll, IA [*FM radio station call letters*] (BROA)
KWOK .... Novato, CA [*Television station call letters*] (BROA)
KWOK-AM ... Hoquiam, WA [*AM radio station call letters*] (BROA)
KWOL .... San Joaquin, CA [*FM radio station call letters*] (BROA)
KWOM .... Watertown, MN [*AM radio station call letters*] (RBYB)
KWON .... Bartlesville, OK [*AM radio station call letters*]
KWOR .... Worland, WY [*AM radio station call letters*]
KWOS .... Jefferson City, MO [*AM radio station call letters*]
KWOT .... Keyword out of Title [*Indexing*]
KWOT .... Kilometer-Wave Orbiting Telescope [*NASA*]
KWOW .... Clifton, TX [*FM radio station call letters*]
KWOX .... Woodward, OK [*FM radio station call letters*]
KWOZ .... Mountain View, AR [*FM radio station call letters*]
KWP .... Kierowinctwo Walki Podziemnej (BJA)
KWP .... King World Prod'ns [*NYSE symbol*] (TTSB)
KWP .... King World Productions, Inc. [*NYSE symbol*] (SPSG)
KWP .... Korean Workers' Party [*North Korea*] [*Political party*] (PD)
KWP .... West Point [*Alaska*] [*Airport symbol*] (OAG)
KWP .... West Point, AK [*Location identifier*] [*FAA*] (FAAL)
KWPA-AM ... Pomona, CA [*AM radio station call letters*] (RBYB)
KWPC .... Muscatine, IA [*AM radio station call letters*]
KWPK .... Sisters, OR [*FM radio station call letters*] (BROA)
KWPL .... Kitchener-Waterloo Public Library (SAUO)
KWPM .... West Plains, MO [*AM radio station call letters*]
KWPN .... Omaha, NE [*FM radio station call letters*] (GDPB)
KWPN-FM ... West Point, NE [*FM radio station call letters*]
KWPR .... Lund, NV [*FM radio station call letters*] (BROA)
KWPT .... Fortuna, CA [*FM radio station call letters*] (BROA)
KWPX .... Bellevue, WA [*Television station call letters*] (BROA)
KWPZ .... Lynden, WA [*FM radio station call letters*] (GDPB)
KWPZ-FM ... Lynden, WA [*FM radio station call letters*] (RBYB)
KWQC .... Davenport, IA [*Television station call letters*]
KWQH-FM ... San Luis Obispo, CA [*FM radio station call letters*] (RBYB)
KWQJ-FM ... Anchorage, AK [*FM radio station call letters*] (RBYB)
KWQL .... Dishman, WA [*FM radio station call letters*]
kWr .... Kilowatts Reactive
KWR .... KW Resources Ltd. [*Vancouver Stock Exchange symbol*]
KWR .... Quaker Chemical [*NYSE symbol*]
KWRB .... Bisbee, AZ [*FM radio station call letters*] (RBYB)
KWRB .... Macon/Robins Air Force Base [*Georgia*] [*ICAO location identifier*] (ICLI)
KWRD .... Henderson, TX [*AM radio station call letters*]
KWRD .... Highland Village, TX [*FM radio station call letters*] (BROA)
KWRD-FM ... Arlington, TX [*FM radio station call letters*] (BROA)
KWRE .... Warrenton, MO [*AM radio station call letters*]
KWRF .... Warren, AR [*AM radio station call letters*]
KWRF-FM ... Warren, AR [*FM radio station call letters*]
KWRI .... Bartlesville, OK [*FM radio station call letters*] (BROA)
KWRI .... Wrightstown/McGuire Air Force Base [*New Jersey*] [*ICAO location identifier*] (ICLI)
KWRK .... Window Rock, AZ [*FM radio station call letters*]
KWRL .... La Grande, OR [*FM radio station call letters*]
KWRM .... Corona, CA [*AM radio station call letters*]
KWRN .... Apple Valley, CA [*AM radio station call letters*] (RBYB)
KWRO .... Coquille, OR [*AM radio station call letters*]
KWRP .... San Jacinto, CA [*FM radio station call letters*]
KWRQ .... Clifton, AZ [*FM radio station call letters*] (RBYB)
KWRR-FM ... Ethete, WY [*FM radio station call letters*] (RBYB)
KWRRI ...... Kansas Water Resources Research Institute [*Kansas State University*] [*Department of the Interior*] [*Research center*] (RCD)
KWRRI ...... Kentucky Water Resources Research Institute [*University of Kentucky*] [*Lexington, KY*] [*Department of the Interior*] [*Research center*] (RCD)
KWRS .... Spokane, WA [*FM radio station call letters*]
KWRT .... Boonville, MO [*AM radio station call letters*]
KWRU .... Fresno, CA [*AM radio station call letters*] (GDPB)
KWRU-AM ... Fresno, CA [*AM radio station call letters*] (BROA)
KWRV .... Sun Valley, ID [*FM radio station call letters*]
KWRW .... Rusk, TX [*FM radio station call letters*]
KWRX .... Redmond, OR [*FM radio station call letters*] (BROA)
KWRZ .... Eaton, CO [*FM radio station call letters*] (BROA)
KWS .... Kaziranga Wildlife Sanctuary (SAUO)
KWS .... Kenya Wildlife Service
KWS .... Knows [*Telegraphy*] (PCTE)
KWS .... Korean Welfare Society [*Australia*]
KWS .... Southwestern College, Winfield, KS [*Library symbol*] [*Library of Congress*] (LCLS)
KWSA .... West Klamath, OR [*AM radio station call letters*]
KWSB .... Gunnison, CO [*FM radio station call letters*]
KWSC .... Wayne, NE [*FM radio station call letters*]
KWSD .... White Sands/Condron Army Air Field [*New Mexico*] [*ICAO location identifier*] (ICLI)
KWSE .... Williston, ND [*Television station call letters*]
KWSH .... Wewoka, OK [*AM radio station call letters*]
KWSH-FM ... Wewoka, OK [*FM radio station call letters*] (BROA)
KWSJ .... Saint John's College, Winfield, KS [*Library symbol*] [*Library of Congress*] (LCLS)
KWSJ-AM ... Kansas City, KS [*AM radio station call letters*] (BROA)
KWSJ-FM ... Haysville, KS [*FM radio station call letters*] (RBYB)
KWSK-FM ... Daingerfield, TX [*FM radio station call letters*] (RBYB)
KWSL .... Sioux City, IA [*AM radio station call letters*] (RBYB)
KWSM .... Korean War Service Medal (SAUO)
KWSM .... Sherman, TX [*FM radio station call letters*]
KWSN .... Sioux Falls, SD [*AM radio station call letters*]
KWSO .... Warm Springs, OR [*FM radio station call letters*]
KWSP .... Santa Margarita, CA [*FM radio station call letters*]
KWSR .... Paso Robles, CA [*FM radio station call letters*] (BROA)
KWST .... Brawley, CA [*FM radio station call letters*]
KWST-AM ... El Centro, CA [*AM radio station call letters*] (BROA)
KWSU .... Pullman, WA [*AM radio station call letters*]
KWSU-TV ... Pullman, WA [*Television station call letters*]
KWSW .... Eureka, CA [*AM radio station call letters*]
KWSWA ..... Kansas Wine and Spirits Wholesalers Association (SRA)
KWSZ .... Lompoc, CA [*FM radio station call letters*] (BROA)
kWt .... Kilowatt, Thermal
KWT .... Kuwait [*ANSI three-letter standard code*] (CNC)
Kwt .... Kuwait (MILB)
KWT .... Kwethluk [*Alaska*] [*Airport symbol*] (OAG)
KWT .... Kwethluk, AK [*Location identifier*] [*FAA*] (FAAL)

KWT .... KWT Railway [*Federal Railroad Administration identification code*]
KWTD .... Ridgecrest, CA [*FM radio station call letters*] (BROA)
kW(th)...... Kilowatt, Thermal
KWTM....... June Lake, CA [*FM radio station call letters*] (BROA)
KWTO .... Springfield, MO [*AM radio station call letters*]
KWTO-FM... Springfield, MO [*FM radio station call letters*]
KWTR .... Georgetown, TX [*AM radio station call letters*]
KWTR-FM... Big Lake, TX [*FM radio station call letters*] (BROA)
KWTS........ Canyon, TX [*FM radio station call letters*]
KWTU .... W Kobrunner [*Intermodal shipping container symbol*] (TVRC)
KWTV........ Oklahoma City, OK [*Television station call letters*]
KWTW....... Bishop, CA [*FM radio station call letters*] (BROA)
KWTX....... Waco, TX [*AM radio station call letters*]
KWTX-FM... Waco, TX [*FM radio station call letters*]
KWTX-TV ... Waco, TX [*Television station call letters*]
KWTY........ Cartago, CA [*FM radio station call letters*]
KWU......... Kansas Wesleyan University [*Salina*]
KWU......... Kawau Island [*New Zealand*] [*Airport symbol*] (AD)
KWU......... Kraftwerksunion [*Germany*]
KWUA .... Clovis, NM [*FM radio station call letters*]
KWUC .... Keyword and Universal Decimal Classification (PDAA)
KWUD .... Woodville, TX [*AM radio station call letters*] (BROA)
KWUF .... Pagosa Springs, CO [*AM radio station call letters*] (GDPB)
KWUF .... Pagosa Springs, CO [*FM radio station call letters*] (GDPB)
KWUF-AM... Pagosa Springs, CO [*AM radio station call letters*] (BROA)
KWUF-FM... Pagosa Springs, CO [*FM radio station call letters*] (BROA)
KWUN-AM... Murray, UT [*AM radio station call letters*] (BROA)
KWUR .... Clayton, MO [*FM radio station call letters*]
KWVA........ Eugene, OR [*FM radio station call letters*]
KWVA........ Korean War Veterans Association (EA)
KWVE........ San Clemente, CA [*FM radio station call letters*]
KWVM....... Korean War Veterans Memorial [*Defunct*] (EA)
KWVR .... Enterprise, OR [*AM radio station call letters*]
KWVR-FM... Enterprise, OR [*FM radio station call letters*]
KWVU .... Ko-operative Wijnbouwers ver Van Afrika Beperkt [*Intermodal shipping container symbol*] (TVRC)
KWVV .... Homer, AK [*FM radio station call letters*]
KWVZ........ Florence, OR [*FM radio station call letters*] (BROA)
KWW .... Asbury College, Wilmore, KY [*OCLC symbol*] (OCLC)
KWW .... Kwinti [*Language symbol*] (ETLW)
KWWC....... Columbia, MO [*FM radio station call letters*]
KWWD ...... Wildwood/Cape May County [*New Jersey*] [*ICAO location identifier*] (ICLI)
KWWF....... Waterloo, IA [*Television station call letters*] (BROA)
KWWF-FM... West Yellowstone, MT [*FM radio station call letters*] (RBYB)
KWWJ........ Baytown, TX [*AM radio station call letters*]
KWWK....... Rochester, MN [*FM radio station call letters*]
KWWL....... Waterloo, IA [*Television station call letters*]
KWWR ...... Mexico, MO [*FM radio station call letters*]
KWWS-FM... Walla Walla, WA [*FM radio station call letters*] (RBYB)
KWwUT ..... United Telecommunications/U.S. Sprint, Westwood, KS [*Library symbol*] [*Library of Congress*] (LCLS)
KWWV....... Morro Bay, CA [*FM radio station call letters*]
KWWV....... Santa Margarita, CA [*FM radio station call letters*] (BROA)
KWWW...... Quincy, WA [*FM radio station call letters*]
KWWX....... Wenatchee, WA [*AM radio station call letters*]
KWWY....... Fort Collins, CO [*FM radio station call letters*] (BROA)
KWX .... Kiwai Island [*Papua New Guinea*] [*Airport symbol*] (OAG)
KWXA .... Durango, CO [*FM radio station call letters*]
KWXD .... Asbury, MO [*FM radio station call letters*]
KWXE........ Glenwood, AR [*FM radio station call letters*]
KWXH .... Sun City, CA [*FM radio station call letters*]
KWXI .... Glenwood, AR [*AM radio station call letters*]
KWXI-AM ... Glenwood, AR [*AM radio station call letters*] (RBYB)
KWXP .... KW Express [*Common carrier symbol*]
KWXT........ Dardanelle, AR [*AM radio station call letters*]
KWXX .... Hilo, HI [*FM radio station call letters*]
KWXY .... Cathedral City, CA [*AM radio station call letters*]
KWXY-FM... Cathedral City, CA [*FM radio station call letters*]
KWY......... Key Way
KWYB .... Butte, MT [*Television station call letters*]
KWYD .... Colorado Springs, CO [*AM radio station call letters*]
KWYI .... Kawaihae, HI [*FM radio station call letters*]
KWYK .... Aztec, NM [*FM radio station call letters*]
KWYL........ Sun Valley, NV [*FM radio station call letters*] (BROA)
KWYN .... Wynne, AR [*AM radio station call letters*]
KWYN-FM... Wynne, AR [*FM radio station call letters*]
KWYO .... Sheridan, WY [*AM radio station call letters*]
KWYO-FM... Sheridan, WY [*FM radio station call letters*]
KWYR .... Winner, SD [*AM radio station call letters*]
KWYR-FM... Winner, SD [*FM radio station call letters*]
KWYS .... Island Park, ID [*FM radio station call letters*] (BROA)
KWYS .... West Yellowstone, MT [*AM radio station call letters*]
KWYW....... Lost Cabin, WY [*FM radio station call letters*] (BROA)
KWYX .... Jasper, TX [*FM radio station call letters*]
KWYY-FM... Casper, WY [*FM radio station call letters*] (BROA)
KWYZ........ Everett, WA [*AM radio station call letters*]
KWZ .... Kolwezi [*Zaire*] [*Airport symbol*] (AD)
KX........... Cayman Airways [*Airline flight code*] (ODBW)
KX........... Cayman Airways Ltd. (SAUO)
KX........... [*The*] Holy Bible (1955) [*R.A. Knox*] [*A publication*] (BJA)
KXA......... Kasaan, AK [*Location identifier*] [*FAA*] (FAAL)
KXAA .... Cle Elum, WA [*FM radio station call letters*] (BROA)
KXAA .... Rock Island, WA [*FM radio station call letters*]
KXAC .... St. James, MN [*FM radio station call letters*]
KXAL .... Pittsburg, TX [*FM radio station call letters*]
KXAL .... Tatum, TX [*FM radio station call letters*] (BROA)
KXAM........ Mesa, AZ [*AM radio station call letters*]
KXAM-TV ... Llano, TX [*Television station call letters*]
KXAN .... Austin, TX [*Television station call letters*]
KXAR .... Hope, AR [*AM radio station call letters*]
KXAR-FM ... Hope, AR [*FM radio station call letters*]
KXAS .... Fort Worth, TX [*Television station call letters*]
KXAS-DT.... Fort Worth, TX [*Television station call letters*] (BROA)
KXAX .... St. James, MN [*FM radio station call letters*]
KXAZ .... Page, AZ [*FM radio station call letters*]
KXBA-FM ... Nikiski, AK [*FM radio station call letters*] (BROA)
KXBJ......... Victoria, TX [*FM radio station call letters*]
KXBK .... Bryan, TX [*FM radio station call letters*] (BROA)
KXBL .... Henryetta, OK [*FM radio station call letters*] (BROA)
KXBR........ International Falls, MN [*FM radio station call letters*] (BROA)
KXBR-AM ... Minneapolis, MN [*AM radio station call letters*] (BROA)
KXBS .... Santa Paula, CA [*FM radio station call letters*]
KXBT .... Vallejo, CA [*AM radio station call letters*]
KXBX .... Lakeport, CA [*AM radio station call letters*]
KXBX-FM ... Lakeport, CA [*FM radio station call letters*]
KXBZ-FM.... Manhattan, KS [*FM radio station call letters*] (RBYB)
KXC.......... Construct [*Telegraphy*] (PCTE)
KXC.......... Keleket X-Ray Corp.
KXCA .... Lawton, OK [*AM radio station call letters*] (BROA)
KXCC .... Rockport, TX [*FM radio station call letters*]
KXCD-AM ... Duncan, OK [*AM radio station call letters*] (BROA)
KXCI .... Tucson, AZ [*FM radio station call letters*]
KXCL .... Yuba City, CA [*FM radio station call letters*]
KXCR........ El Paso, TX [*FM radio station call letters*]
KXCS .... Cameron, TX [*FM radio station call letters*] (BROA)
KXCT .... Coleman, TX [*FM radio station call letters*] (BROA)
KXCV .... Maryville, MO [*FM radio station call letters*]
KXD.......... Constructed [*Telegraphy*] (PCTE)
KXDA .... Las Cruces, NM [*FM radio station call letters*] (RBYB)
KXDC .... Carmel, CA [*FM radio station call letters*] (RBYB)
KXDC .... Estes Park, CO [*FM radio station call letters*] (BROA)
KXDD .... Yakima, WA [*FM radio station call letters*]
KXDG........ Webb City, MO [*FM radio station call letters*] (RBYB)
KXDL .... Browerville, MN [*FM radio station call letters*]
KXDR........ Hamilton, MT [*FM radio station call letters*] (BROA)
KXDZ .... Templeton, CA [*FM radio station call letters*] (BROA)
KXEB .... Sherman, TX [*AM radio station call letters*]
KXED .... Los Angeles, CA [*AM radio station call letters*]
KXEG .... Phoenix, AZ [*AM radio station call letters*] (BROA)
KXEG .... Tolleson, AZ [*AM radio station call letters*]
KXEI .... Havre, MT [*FM radio station call letters*]
KXEL......... Waterloo, IA [*AM radio station call letters*]
KXEM........ Bakersfield, CA [*AM radio station call letters*] (RBYB)
KXEM........ Tolleson, AZ [*AM radio station call letters*] (BROA)
KXEM-AM... Roswell, NM [*AM radio station call letters*] (BROA)
KXEN .... Festus-St. Louis, MO [*AM radio station call letters*]
KXEO .... Mexico, MO [*AM radio station call letters*]
KXEQ .... Reno, NV [*AM radio station call letters*]
KXEW........ South Tucson, AZ [*AM radio station call letters*]
KXEX .... Fresno, CA [*AM radio station call letters*]
KXEZ......... Los Angeles, CA [*FM radio station call letters*]
KXEZ-FM.... Farmersville, TX [*FM radio station call letters*] (BROA)
KXF .... Kodak X-Ray Film
KXF .... Koro [*Fiji*] [*Airport symbol*] (OAG)
KXFE......... Dumas, AR [*FM radio station call letters*]
KXFF......... Cedar City, UT [*FM radio station call letters*] (BROA)
KXFG-FM ... Sun City, CA [*FM radio station call letters*] (RBYB)
KXFM........ Santa Maria, CA [*FM radio station call letters*]
KXFS .... Ventura, CA [*AM radio station call letters*] (BROA)
KXFX .... Santa Rosa, CA [*FM radio station call letters*]
KXG.......... Constructing [*Telegraphy*] (PCTE)
KXGA .... Glennallen, AK [*FM radio station call letters*] (RBYB)
KXGE-FM ... Dubuque, IA [*FM radio station call letters*] (BROA)
KXGF .... Great Falls, MT [*AM radio station call letters*]
KXGJ .... Bay City, TX [*FM radio station call letters*]
KXGL-FM ... San Diego, CA [*FM radio station call letters*] (BROA)
KXGM .... Muenster, TX [*FM radio station call letters*]
KXGN .... Glendive, MT [*AM radio station call letters*]
KXGN-TV.... Glendive, MT [*Television station call letters*]
KXGO .... Arcata, CA [*FM radio station call letters*]
KXGR........ Green Valley, AZ [*Television station call letters*]
KXGT .... Fargo, ND [*FM radio station call letters*] (GDPB)
KXGT-FM.... Jamestown, ND [*FM radio station call letters*] (RBYB)
KXH.......... Karo [*Language symbol*] (ETLW)
KXHA .... Shafter, CA [*FM radio station call letters*]
KXHR........ Knoxville & Holston River Railroad [*Federal Railroad Administration identification code*]
KXHT-FM.... Marion, AR [*FM radio station call letters*] (BROA)
KXHV .... Sacramento, CA [*FM radio station call letters*]
KXIA .... Marshalltown, IA [*FM radio station call letters*]
KXIC .... Iowa City, IA [*AM radio station call letters*]
KXII .... Sherman, TX [*Television station call letters*]
KXIL-FM .... Sanger, TX [*FM radio station call letters*] (BROA)
KXIO .... Clarksville, AR [*FM radio station call letters*]
KXIT .... Dalhart, TX [*AM radio station call letters*]
KXIT-FM..... Dalhart, TX [*FM radio station call letters*]

KXIX .... Bend, OR [*FM radio station call letters*]
KXJB .... Valley City, ND [*Television station call letters*]
KXJH .... Linton, IN [*FM radio station call letters*] (BROA)
KXJK .... Forrest City, AR [*AM radio station call letters*]
KXJM .... Portland, OR [*FM radio station call letters*] (BROA)
KXJZ .... Sacramento, CA [*FM radio station call letters*]
KXKB .... Tahoe City, CA [*FM radio station call letters*]
KXKC .... New Iberia, LA [*FM radio station call letters*]
KXKK .... Lordsburg, NM [*FM radio station call letters*]
KXKK-FM ... Park Rapids, MN [*FM radio station call letters*] (BROA)
KXKL .... Denver, CO [*AM radio station call letters*]
KXKL-FM .... Denver, CO [*FM radio station call letters*]
KXKM .... McCarthy, AK [*FM radio station call letters*] (RBYB)
KXKQ .... Safford, AZ [*FM radio station call letters*]
KXKS .... Albuquerque, NM [*AM radio station call letters*]
KXKS .... Shreveport, LA [*FM radio station call letters*] (BROA)
KXKT .... Atlantic, IA [*FM radio station call letters*]
KXKT .... Glenwood, IA [*FM radio station call letters*] (BROA)
KXKU .... Lyons, KS [*FM radio station call letters*] (BROA)
KXKX .... Knob Noster, MO [*FM radio station call letters*]
KXKZ .... Ruston, LA [*FM radio station call letters*]
KXL .... Portland, OR [*AM radio station call letters*]
KXLA .... Rayville, LA [*AM radio station call letters*]
KXLB .... Livingston, MT [*FM radio station call letters*] (BROA)
KXLC .... La Crescent, MN [*FM radio station call letters*]
KXLE .... Ellensburg, WA [*AM radio station call letters*]
KXLE-FM .... Ellensburg, WA [*FM radio station call letters*]
KXLF .... Butte, MT [*Television station call letters*]
KXL-FM ..... Portland, OR [*FM radio station call letters*] (BROA)
KXLI .... St. Cloud, MN [*Television station call letters*]
KXLI-AM .... Opportunity, WA [*AM radio station call letters*] (BROA)
KXLK .... Haysville, KS [*FM radio station call letters*]
KXLM .... Oxnard, CA [*FM radio station call letters*]
KXLN .... Rosenburg, TX [*Television station call letters*]
KXLO .... Lewistown, MT [*AM radio station call letters*]
KXLP .... New Ulm, MN [*FM radio station call letters*]
KXLQ .... Indianola, IA [*AM radio station call letters*] (RBYB)
KXLR .... Fairbanks, AK [*FM radio station call letters*]
KXLS .... Alva, OK [*FM radio station call letters*]
KXLT .... Eagle, ID [*FM radio station call letters*]
KXLT-TV ..... Rochester, MN [*Television station call letters*]
KXLU .... Los Angeles, CA [*FM radio station call letters*]
KXLV .... Amarillo, TX [*FM radio station call letters*] (BROA)
KXLY .... Spokane, WA [*AM radio station call letters*]
KXLY-DT ..... Spokane, WA [*Television station call letters*] (BROA)
KXLY-FM .... Spokane, WA [*FM radio station call letters*]
KXLY-TV ..... Spokane, WA [*Television station call letters*]
KXMA .... Dickinson, ND [*Television station call letters*]
KXMB .... Bismarck, ND [*Television station call letters*]
KXMC .... Minot, ND [*Television station call letters*]
KXMD .... Williston, ND [*Television station call letters*]
KXME-FM ... Kaneohe, HI [*FM radio station call letters*] (BROA)
KXMG .... Cedar Park, TX [*FM radio station call letters*] (BROA)
KXMG-AM .. Los Angeles, CA [*AM radio station call letters*] (RBYB)
KXMO .... Owensville, MO [*FM radio station call letters*] (BROA)
KXMR .... Bismarck, ND [*AM radio station call letters*] (RBYB)
KXMS .... Joplin, MO [*FM radio station call letters*]
KXMT .... Taos, NM [*FM radio station call letters*] (BROA)
KXMX .... Cedar Rapids, IA [*FM radio station call letters*] (RBYB)
KXMX-AM ... Anaheim, CA [*AM radio station call letters*] (BROA)
KXN .... Construction [*Telegraphy*] (PCTE)
KXNA .... Springdale, AR [*FM radio station call letters*] (BROA)
KXND .... Minot, ND [*Television station call letters*] (BROA)
KXNE .... Norfolk, NE [*FM radio station call letters*]
KXNE-TV .... Norfolk, NE [*Television station call letters*]
KXNO .... Des Moines, IA [*AM radio station call letters*] (BROA)
KXNO .... North Las Vegas, NV [*AM radio station call letters*]
KXNP .... North Platte, NE [*FM radio station call letters*]
KXNT .... North Las Vegas, NV [*AM radio station call letters*] (BROA)
KXO .... El Centro, CA [*AM radio station call letters*]
KXOA .... Roseville, CA [*FM radio station call letters*] (BROA)
KXOA .... Sacramento, CA [*AM radio station call letters*]
KXOA-FM ... Sacramento, CA [*FM radio station call letters*]
KXOF .... Bloomfield, IA [*FM radio station call letters*]
KXO-FM ..... El Centro, CA [*FM radio station call letters*]
KXOI .... Crane, TX [*AM radio station call letters*]
KXOJ .... Sapulpa, OK [*AM radio station call letters*]
KXOJ-FM .... Sapulpa, OK [*FM radio station call letters*]
KXOK .... Florissant, MO [*FM radio station call letters*]
KXOL .... Brigham City, UT [*AM radio station call letters*] (BROA)
KXOL .... Clinton, OK [*AM radio station call letters*]
KXOL .... Los Angeles [*FM radio station call letters*] (BROA)
KXOO .... Elk City, OK [*FM radio station call letters*] (RBYB)
KXOQ .... Kennett, MO [*FM radio station call letters*] (RBYB)
KXOR .... Thibodaux, LA [*FM radio station call letters*]
KXOW .... Hot Springs, AR [*AM radio station call letters*]
KXOX .... Sweetwater, TX [*AM radio station call letters*]
KXOX-FM ... Sweetwater, TX [*FM radio station call letters*]
KXOZ .... Mountain View, MO [*FM radio station call letters*]
KXPA .... Bellevue, WA [*AM radio station call letters*] (BROA)
KXPA-AM ... Pasadena, CA [*AM radio station call letters*] (RBYB)
KXPC .... Lebanon, OR [*FM radio station call letters*]
KXPH .... Seattle-Tacoma (Bellingham), WA [*AM radio station call letters*] (GDPB)
KXPK .... Evergreen, CO [*FM radio station call letters*]
KXPL-AM ... El Paso, TX [*AM radio station call letters*] (BROA)
KXPN .... Lincoln-Hastings-Kearney, NE [*AM radio station call letters*] (GDPB)
KXPO .... Grafton, ND [*AM radio station call letters*]
KXPO-FM ... Grafton, ND [*FM radio station call letters*]
KXPR .... Sacramento, CA [*FM radio station call letters*]
KXPS .... Thousand Palms, CA [*AM radio station call letters*] (BROA)
KXPT .... Las Vegas, NV [*FM radio station call letters*]
KXPW .... Belle Plaine, IA [*FM radio station call letters*]
KXPX .... Stillwater, OK [*FM radio station call letters*] (RBYB)
KXPZ .... Lytle, TX [*FM radio station call letters*]
KXRA .... Alexandria, MN [*AM radio station call letters*]
KXRA-FM ... Alexandria, MN [*FM radio station call letters*]
KXRB .... Sioux Falls, SD [*AM radio station call letters*]
KXRD .... Victorville, CA [*FM radio station call letters*]
KXRE .... Manitou Springs, CO [*AM radio station call letters*]
KXRI .... Amarillo, TX [*FM radio station call letters*] (BROA)
KXRJ .... Russellville, AR [*FM radio station call letters*]
KXRK .... Provo, UT [*FM radio station call letters*]
KXRM .... Colorado Springs, CO [*Television station call letters*]
KXRO .... Aberdeen, WA [*AM radio station call letters*]
KXRQ-FM ... Roosevelt, UT [*FM radio station call letters*] (BROA)
KXRR .... Rayville, LA [*FM radio station call letters*] (BROA)
KXRS .... Hemet, CA [*FM radio station call letters*]
KXRT .... Idabel, OK [*FM radio station call letters*] (BROA)
KXRX .... Walla Walla, WA [*FM radio station call letters*]
KXRZ .... Alexandria, MN [*FM radio station call letters*] (BROA)
KXS .... Constructs [*Telegraphy*] (PCTE)
KXS .... Kangjia [*Language symbol*] (ETLW)
KXS .... Kiva Executive Server [*Computer science*]
KXSA .... Monticello, AR [*FM radio station call letters*] (GDPB)
KXSA-FM ... Dermott, AR [*FM radio station call letters*]
KXSB .... Big Bear Lake, CA [*FM radio station call letters*] (RBYB)
KXSM .... Saint Mary College, Xavier, KS [*Library symbol*] [*Library of Congress*] (LCLS)
KXSP .... Ventura, CA [*AM radio station call letters*] (RBYB)
KXSR .... Groveland, CA [*FM radio station call letters*]
KXSS .... Waite Park, MN [*AM radio station call letters*]
KXST-FM .... Oceanside, CA [*FM radio station call letters*] (RBYB)
KXTA .... Los Angeles, CA [*AM radio station call letters*] (BROA)
KXTC .... Thoreau, NM [*FM radio station call letters*]
KXTD .... Wagoner, OK [*AM radio station call letters*]
KXTE-FM .... Rahrump, NV [*FM radio station call letters*] (RBYB)
KXTF .... Twin Falls, ID [*Television station call letters*] (BROA)
KXTJ .... Beaumont, TX [*FM radio station call letters*]
KXTK-AM ... Des Moines, IA [*AM radio station call letters*] (RBYB)
KXTL .... Butte, MT [*AM radio station call letters*]
KXTN .... San Antonio, TX [*AM radio station call letters*]
KXTN-FM ... San Antonio, TX [*FM radio station call letters*]
KXTO .... Reno, NV [*AM radio station call letters*]
KXTP .... Superior, WI [*AM radio station call letters*]
KXTQ .... Lubbock, TX [*AM radio station call letters*]
KXTQ-FM ... Lubbock, TX [*FM radio station call letters*]
KXTR .... Kansas City, MO [*FM radio station call letters*]
KXTS .... Calistoga, CA [*FM radio station call letters*] (BROA)
KXTU .... Kawasaki Kisen Kaisha (K-Line) [*Intermodal shipping container symbol*] (TVRC)
KXTV .... Sacramento, CA [*Television station call letters*]
KXTX .... Dallas, TX [*Television station call letters*]
KXTZ .... San Luis Obispo, CA [*FM radio station call letters*] (GDPB)
KXTZ-FM .... Pismo Beach, CA [*FM radio station call letters*] (BROA)
KXU .... Kastamonu [*Turkey*] [*Airport symbol*] (AD)
KXU .... Keyword Transformation Unit [*Computer science*] (MHDI)
KXUA .... Fayetteville, AR [*FM radio station call letters*] (BROA)
KXUL .... Monroe, LA [*FM radio station call letters*] (BROA)
KXUM .... Minot-Bismarck-Dickinson, ND-Glendive, MT [*AM radio station call letters*] (GDPB)
KXUS .... Springfield, MO [*FM radio station call letters*]
KXUX .... Bend, OR [*AM radio station call letters*]
KXVA .... Abilene, TX [*Television station call letters*] (BROA)
KXVI .... Dallas-Fort Worth, TX [*FM radio station call letters*] (GDPB)
KXVO .... Omaha, NE [*Television station call letters*] (RBYB)
KXXI .... Gallup, NM [*FM radio station call letters*]
KXXK .... Chickasha, OK [*FM radio station call letters*]
KXXK .... Hoquiam-Aberdeen, WA [*FM radio station call letters*] (BROA)
KXXL .... Crane, TX [*FM radio station call letters*]
KXXL-FM ... Sun Valley, NV [*FM radio station call letters*] (BROA)
KXXM-FM ... San Antonio, TX [*FM radio station call letters*] (BROA)
KXXO .... Olympia, WA [*FM radio station call letters*]
KXXQ .... Milan, NM [*FM radio station call letters*] (BROA)
KXXR .... Minneapolis, MN [*FM radio station call letters*] (GDPB)
KXXR-FM ... Minneapolis, MN [*FM radio station call letters*] (BROA)
KXXS .... Marble Falls, TX [*FM radio station call letters*] (BROA)
KXXS .... Toppenish, WA [*FM radio station call letters*]
KXXT .... Santa Barbara, CA [*AM radio station call letters*] (BROA)
KXXV .... Waco, TX [*Television station call letters*]
KXXX .... Colby, KS [*AM radio station call letters*]
KXXY .... Oklahoma City, OK [*AM radio station call letters*]
KXXY-FM ... Oklahoma City, OK [*FM radio station call letters*]
KXXZ .... Barstow, CA [*FM radio station call letters*]
KXYL .... Brownwood, TX [*AM radio station call letters*]
KXYL-FM .... Brownwood, TX [*FM radio station call letters*]
KXYQ .... Milwaukie, OR [*AM radio station call letters*]
KXYZ .... Houston, TX [*AM radio station call letters*]

KXZN-FM ... Sanger, TX [*FM radio station call letters*] (BROA)
KXZX .... El Dorado, AR [*FM radio station call letters*] (BROA)
KXZZ......... Lake Charles, LA [*AM radio station call letters*]
KY............ [*A Sterile*] Lubricating Jelly [*Medicine*] (EDAA)
KY............ Cayman Islands [*ANSI two-letter standard code*] (CNC)
KY............ Kabaka Yekka [*The King Alone*] [*Uganda*] [*Suspended*] [*Political party*]
KY............ Kabaka Yekka Party (SAUO)
KY............ Kapustin Yar [*Test Facility*] [*US prefix for Soviet-Russian developmental missiles*] (DOMA)
KY............ Kentucky [*Postal code*] (AFM)
Ky............ Kentucky (ODBW)
Ky............ Kentucky Department of Libraries, Frankfort, KY [*Library symbol*] [*Library of Congress*] (LCLS)
Ky............ Kentucky Reports [*A publication*] (AAGC)
KY............ Kentucky Supreme Court Reports [*1879-1951*] [*A publication*] (DLA)
KY............ Kent Yeomanry [*Military unit*] [*British*]
KY............ Key
KY............ Keyhole [*United States reconnaissance satellite*] (DOMA)
KY............ Keying (VLIE)
KY............ Keying Devices [*JETDS nomenclature*] [*Military*] (CET)
KY............ Kol Yisroel [*Israeli Broadcasting Service*]
Ky............ Kyrie (GROV)
KY............ Kyrie [*Liturgical*]
KY............ R-S Truck Body Company RSTB Allen [*NCIC trailer make code*]
KY............ Sun West [*ICAO designator*] (AD)
KY............ thousand years (SAUS)
KyA .... Ashland Public Library, Ashland, KY [*Library symbol*] [*Library of Congress*] (LCLS)
Kya .... Kenya (MILB)
KYA .... Konya [*Turkey*] [*Airport symbol*] (AD)
KYA .... Kyakhta [*Former USSR*] [*Seismograph station code, US Geological Survey*] [*Closed*] (SEIS)
kya........... thousands of years ago (SAUO)
KYA .... Yana Air Cargo (Kenya) Ltd. [*ICAO designator*] (FAAC)
KYAA .... Soquel, CA [*AM radio station call letters*] (BROA)
KY Admin Reg... Kentucky Administrative Register [*A publication*] (DLA)
KY Admin Regs... Kentucky Administration Regulations Service [*A publication*] (DLA)
Ky Admin Regs... Kentucky Administrative Regulations [*A publication*] (AAGC)
KYAJ......... Merced, CA [*FM radio station call letters*]
KYAK .... Anchorage, AK [*AM radio station call letters*]
KYAK .... Yakima, WA [*AM radio station call letters*] (BROA)
KYAL......... Tulsa (Bartlesville), OK [*AM radio station call letters*] (GDPB)
Ky-Ar .... Kentucky Department of Libraries and Archives, Kentucky State Archives, Frankfort, KY [*Library symbol*] [*Library of Congress*] (LCLS)
KYAT......... Keokuk, IA [*FM radio station call letters*]
KYAX .... Alturas, CA [*FM radio station call letters*]
KYB .... Kayaba Industry Co. [*Auto industry supplier*]
KYB .... Know Your Body (DAVI)
KYBA .... Stewartville, MN [*FM radio station call letters*]
KyBB......... Berea College, Berea, KY [*Library symbol*] [*Library of Congress*] (LCLS)
KYBB-FM ... Canton, SD [*FM radio station call letters*] (BROA)
KYBC .... Cottonwood, AZ [*AM radio station call letters*] (GDPB)
KYBC-AM ... Cottonwood, AZ [*AM radio station call letters*] (RBYB)
KYBD .... Copeland, KS [*FM radio station call letters*]
KYBD .... Keyboard (MSA)
KYBE .... Frederick, OK [*FM radio station call letters*]
KYBG .... Aurora, CO [*AM radio station call letters*]
KyBgW ...... Western Kentucky University, Bowling Green, KY [*Library symbol*] [*Library of Congress*] (LCLS)
KyBgW-K.... Western Kentucky University, Kentucky Library, Bowling Green, KY [*Library symbol*] [*Library of Congress*] (LCLS)
KYBI-FM .... Huntington, TX [*FM radio station call letters*] (RBYB)
KYBJ......... Lake Jackson, TX [*FM radio station call letters*] (RBYB)
KYBN .... Bend, OR [*FM radio station call letters*] (BROA)
Ky-BPH...... Kentucky Library for the Blind and Physically Handicapped, Frankfort, KY [*Library symbol*] [*Library of Congress*] (LCLS)
KYBR .... Espanola, NM [*FM radio station call letters*] (BROA)
KYBRD ...... Keyboard
KYBR-FM ... Espanola, NM [*FM radio station call letters*] (RBYB)
KyBrU .... Union College, Barbourville (SAUO)
KyBvU .... Union College, Barbourville, KY [*Library symbol*] [*Library of Congress*] (LCLS)
KYC .... HCL Aviation, Inc. [*ICAO designator*] (FAAC)
KYC .... Keystone Camera Products Corp. (SAUO)
KYC .... Klan Youth Corps (SAUO)
KYC........... Knickerbocker Yacht Club (SAUO)
KYC .... Know Your Customer [*Investment term*] (DFIT)
KYCA .... Prescott, AZ [*AM radio station call letters*]
KyCambC ... Campbellsville College, Campbellsville, KY [*Library symbol*] [*Library of Congress*] (LCLS)
KyCarD ...... Dow Corning Corp., TIS Library, Carrollton, KY [*Library symbol*] [*Library of Congress*] (LCLS)
KYCC .... Stockton, CA [*FM radio station call letters*] (BROA)
KYCC-FM ... Livingston, CA [*FM radio station call letters*] (BROA)
KYCE .... Hams Station, CA [*FM radio station call letters*] (BROA)
KYCH .... Convent General of the Knights York Cross of Honour (EA)
KYCK .... Crookston, MN [*FM radio station call letters*]
KYCM-FM... Bastrop, TX [*FM radio station call letters*] (BROA)
KYCN .... Wheatland, WY [*AM radio station call letters*]
KYCN-FM ... Wheatland, WY [*FM radio station call letters*]
KyColW ..... Lindsey Wilson College, Columbia, KY [*Library symbol*] [*Library of Congress*] (LCLS)
KY Comment'r... Kentucky Commentator [*A publication*] (DLA)
KyCov .... Kenton County Public Library, Covington, KY [*Library symbol*] [*Library of Congress*] (LCLS)
KyCovStE ... Saint Elizabeth Medical Center, Covington, KY [*Library symbol*] [*Library of Congress*] (LCLS)
KYCP .... Keystone Camera Products Corporation (SAUO)
KYCR .... Golden Valley, MN [*AM radio station call letters*]
KYCS .... Rock Springs, WY [*FM radio station call letters*]
KYCU .... Clinton, OK [*FM radio station call letters*] (BROA)
KYCW .... Seattle, WA [*FM radio station call letters*]
KYCX .... Mexia, TX [*FM radio station call letters*]
KYCY .... San Francisco, CA [*FM radio station call letters*]
KYD.......... Karey [*Language symbol*] (ETLW)
KYD.......... Kilo Yard
Kyd .... Kyd on Bills of Exchange [*A publication*] (DLA)
Kyd Aw...... Kyd on Awards [*A publication*] (DLA)
Kyd Bills.... Kyd on Bills of Exchange [*A publication*] (DLA)
KyDC .... Centre College of Kentucky, Danville, KY [*Library symbol*] [*Library of Congress*] (LCLS)
Kyd Corp.... Kyd on Corporations [*A publication*] (DLA)
KYDE .... Pine Bluff, AR [*AM radio station call letters*]
KY Dec ...... Sneed's Kentucky Decisions [*2 Kentucky*] [*A publication*] (DLA)
KYDKAJ ..... Annual Report. Kyoritsu College of Pharmacy (journ.) (SAUS)
KYDS .... Kiloyards (MCD)
KYDS .... Sacramento, CA [*FM radio station call letters*]
KYDT-FM.... Sundance, WY [*FM radio station call letters*] (RBYB)
KYDZ .... Cody, WY [*FM radio station call letters*]
KYEA .... West Monroe, LA [*FM radio station call letters*]
KYEE......... Alamogordo, NM [*FM radio station call letters*]
KYEG-FM ... Canadian, TX [*FM radio station call letters*] (RBYB)
KyeKtts..... Kaye Kotts Associates, Inc. [*Associated Press*] (SAG)
KYEL......... Danville, AR [*FM radio station call letters*] (BROA)
KYERI .... Know Your Endorsers - Require Identification [*Advice to business-men and others who cash checks for the public*]
KyErP........ Seminary of Saint Pius X, Erlanger, KY [*Library symbol*] [*Library of Congress*] (LCLS)
KYES .... Anchorage, AK [*Television station call letters*]
KYET......... Williams, AZ [*AM radio station call letters*]
KYEZ......... Salina, KS [*FM radio station call letters*]
KYF .... Kentucky First Bancorp [*AMEX symbol*] (TTSB)
KYF .... Kentucky First Bancorp, Inc. [*AMEX symbol*] (NASQ)
KYF .... Kyffhaeuserkreis [*German license plate city code*]
KYF .... Yeelirie [*Australia*] [*Airport symbol*] (OAG)
KYFA......... Amarillo, TX [*FM radio station call letters*]
KYFC .... Kansas City, MO [*Television station call letters*]
KyFc .... United States Army, Fort Campbell Post Library (R. F. Sink Memorial Library), Fort Campbell, KY [*Library symbol*] [*Library of Congress*] (LCLS)
KyFCE .... Kentucky Council on Higher Education, Frankfort, KY [*Library symbol*] [*Library of Congress*] (LCLS)
KyFkAS...... United States Army Armor School, Fort Knox, KY [*Library symbol*] [*Library of Congress*] (LCLS)
KYFL......... Monroe, LA [*FM radio station call letters*]
KyFLR .... Legislative Research Commission, Library, Frankfort, KY [*Library symbol*] [*Library of Congress*] (LCLS)
KYFM......... Bartlesville, OK [*FM radio station call letters*]
KyFmTM .... Thomas More College, Fort Mitchell, KY [*Library symbol*] [*Library of Congress*] (LCLS)
KYFO .... Ogden, UT [*AM radio station call letters*]
KYFO-FM ... Ogden, UT [*FM radio station call letters*]
Ky For Lang Q... Kentucky Foreign Language Quarterly. University of Kentucky. Lexington (SAUO)
KYFP-FM.... Palestine, TX [*FM radio station call letters*] (BROA)
KYFR .... Shenandoah, IA [*AM radio station call letters*]
KYFS .... San Antonio, TX [*FM radio station call letters*]
KyFSC .... Kentucky State University, Frankfort, KY [*Library symbol*] [*Library of Congress*] (LCLS)
KY Fst....... Kentucky First Bancorp, Inc. [*Associated Press*] (SAG)
KY FstB ..... Kentucky First Bancorp, Inc. [*Associated Press*] (SAG)
KYFT......... Lubbock, TX [*FM radio station call letters*]
KYFV .... Victoria, TX [*AM radio station call letters*] (BROA)
KYFW......... Wichita, KS [*FM radio station call letters*]
KYFX .... Little Rock, AR [*FM radio station call letters*]
Ky-G .... Kentucky Department of Libraries and Archives, Kentucky Guide Project, Frankfort, KY [*Library symbol*] [*Library of Congress*] (LCLS)
KyGeC .... Georgetown College, Georgetown, KY [*Library symbol*] [*Library of Congress*] (LCLS)
KYGL .... Texarkana, AR [*FM radio station call letters*] (RBYB)
KYGO .... Lakewood, CO [*AM radio station call letters*]
KYGO-FM ... Denver, CO [*FM radio station call letters*]
KYHAFTY ... Keep Your Hands and Feet to Yourselves (BB)
KyHaHi...... Harrodsburg Historical Society, Harrodsburg, KY [*Library symbol*] [*Library of Congress*] (LCLS)
KyHhN....... Northern Kentucky University, Highland Heights, KY [*Library symbol*] [*Library of Congress*] (LCLS)
KyHhN-L .... Northern Kentucky University, B. P. Chase College of Law, Coving-ton (SAUS)
KyHhN-L .... Northern Kentucky University, B. P. Chase College of Law, Coving-ton, KY [*Library symbol*] [*Library of Congress*] (LCLS)
KyHi .... Kentucky Historical Society, Frankfort, KY [*Library symbol*] [*Library of Congress*] (LCLS)
KYHL .... Keyhole (ABBR)
KYHN-AM... Fort Smith, AR [*AM radio station call letters*] (BROA)

KyHopC ..... Hopkinsville Community College, Hopkinsville, KY [*Library symbol*] [*Library of Congress*] (LCLS)
KYHT .... Yermo, CA [*FM radio station call letters*]
KyHzC .... Hazard Community College, Hazard, KY [*Library symbol*] [*Library of Congress*] (LCLS)
KYI E .... Kyle Technology Corp. (SAUO)
KYIN .... Mason City, IA [*Television station call letters*]
KYIP .... Detroit/Willow Run [*Michigan*] [*ICAO location identifier*] (ICLI)
KYIS .... Oklahoma City, OK [*FM radio station call letters*]
KYIX .... South Oroville, CA [*FM radio station call letters*] (RBYB)
KYIZ .... Renton, WA [*AM radio station call letters*] (BROA)
KYJC-FM.... Grants Pass, OR [*FM radio station call letters*]
KYJT......... Yuma, AZ [*FM radio station call letters*] (RBYB)
KYJY-AM.... Albuquerque, NM [*AM radio station call letters*] (BROA)
KYK.......... Karluk [*Alaska*] [*Airport symbol*] (OAG)
KYK.......... Karluk, AK [*Location identifier*] [*FAA*] (FAAL)
KYK.......... Kayak (ABBR)
KYK.......... Kayak Island [*Alaska*] [*Seismograph station code, US Geological Survey*] (SEIS)
KYK.......... Kelley-Kerr Energy [*Vancouver Stock Exchange symbol*]
KYKA .... Naches, WA [*FM radio station call letters*]
KYKC .... Byng, OK [*FM radio station call letters*]
KYKD .... Bethel, AK [*FM radio station call letters*]
KYKF .... San Fernando, CA [*FM radio station call letters*]
KYKK .... Hobbs, NM [*AM radio station call letters*]
KYKL .... Tracy, CA [*FM radio station call letters*] (BROA)
KYKM......... Yoakum, TX [*FM radio station call letters*] (RBYB)
KYKN .... Keizer, OR [*AM radio station call letters*]
KYKN .... Nephi, UT [*FM radio station call letters*]
KYKN .... Pkynocytes [*Hematology*] (DAVI)
KYKR .... Beaumont, TX [*FM radio station call letters*]
KYKS .... Lufkin, TX [*FM radio station call letters*]
KYKX .... Longview, TX [*FM radio station call letters*]
KYKY .... Kyokuyo Company [*Common carrier symbol*]
KYKY .... St. Louis, MO [*FM radio station call letters*]
KYKZ .... Lake Charles, LA [*FM radio station call letters*] (BROA)
KY L .... Kentucky Law Reporter [*A publication*] (DLA)
KYL........... Key Largo, FL [*Amtrak Busline code*]
KYL........... Kyle Resources, Inc. [*Vancouver Stock Exchange symbol*]
KYLA-FM.... Homer, LA [*FM radio station call letters*] (BROA)
KY Law Rep... Kentucky Law Reporter [*A publication*] (DLA)
KYLC .... Lake Charles, LA [*FM radio station call letters*] (BROA)
KYLC .... Osage Beach, MO [*FM radio station call letters*]
KYLD .... San Francisco, CA [*FM radio station call letters*] (BROA)
KYLD .... San Mateo, CA [*FM radio station call letters*]
KYLE......... Bryan, TX [*Television station call letters*]
KYLE......... Kyle Railroad [*Federal Railroad Administration identification code*]
KYLM........ Yuma Marine Corps Air Station (SAUS)
KyLo......... Louisville Free Public Library, Louisville, KY [*Library symbol*] [*Library of Congress*] (LCLS)
KyLoB .... Bellarmine College, Louisville, KY [*Library symbol*] [*Library of Congress*] (LCLS)
KyloB-M..... Bellarmine College, Thomas Merton Studies Center (SAUS)
KyLoB-M.... Bellarmine College, Thomas Merton Studies Center, Louisville, KY [*Library symbol*] [*Library of Congress*] (LCLS)
KyLoBW..... Brown & Williamson Tobacco Corp., Research Department Library, Louisville, KY [*Library symbol*] [*Library of Congress*] (LCLS)
KyLoC .... Courier-Journal & Louisville Times Co., Inc., Louisville, KY [*Library symbol*] [*Library of Congress*] (LCLS)
KyLoF .... Filson Club, Louisville, KY [*Library symbol*] [*Library of Congress*] (LCLS)
KyloJ .... Jefferson Community College, Louisville (SAUS)
KyLoJ........ Jefferson Community College, Louisville, KY [*Library symbol*] [*Library of Congress*] (LCLS)
KyLoL .... Louisville Presbyterian Seminary, Louisville, KY [*Library symbol*] [*Library of Congress*] (LCLS)
KyLoM....... Louisville Medical Library, Louisville, KY [*Library symbol*] [*Library of Congress*] (LCLS)
KyLoN .... Spalding College, Louisville, KY [*Library symbol*] [*Library of Congress*] (LCLS)
KyLoS .... Southern Baptist Theological Seminary, Louisville, KY [*Library symbol*] [*Library of Congress*] (LCLS)
KyLoU .... University of Louisville, Louisville, KY [*Library symbol*] [*Library of Congress*] (LCLS)
KyLoU-Ar ... University of Louisville, University Archives and Records Center, Louisville, KY [*Library symbol*] [*Library of Congress*] (LCLS)
KyLoU-HS... University of Louisville, Health Sciences Library, Louisville, KY [*Library symbol*] [*Library of Congress*] (LCLS)
KyLoU-L..... University of Louisville, Law Library, Louisville,KY [*Library symbol*] [*Library of Congress*] (LCLS)
KyLoU-Mu... University of Louisville, Dwight Anderson Music Library, Louisville, KY [*Library symbol*] [*Library of Congress*] (LCLS)
KyLoV .... United States Veterans Administration Hospital, Louisville, KY [*Library symbol*] [*Library of Congress*] (LCLS)
KYLR .... Huntsville, TX [*AM radio station call letters*]
KY LR .... Kentucky Law Reporter [*A publication*] (DLA)
KY L Rep ... Kentucky Law Reporter [*A publication*] (DLA)
KY L Rev ... Kentucky Law Review [*A publication*] (DLA)
KY L Rptr... Kentucky Law Reporter [*A publication*] (DLA)
KYLS .... Farmington, MO [*AM radio station call letters*] (GDPB)
KYLS-AM ... Fredericktown, MO [*AM radio station call letters*] (BROA)
KYLS-FM.... Ironton, MO [*FM radio station call letters*] (BROA)
KYLT......... Missoula, MT [*AM radio station call letters*]
KYLU .... NYK Line [*Intermodal shipping container symbol*] (TVRC)
KYLV-FM.... Oklahoma City, OK [*FM radio station call letters*] (BROA)
KyLx......... Lexington Public Library, Lexington, KY [*Library symbol*] [*Library of Congress*] (LCLS)
KyLxCB...... Lexington Theological Seminary, Lexington, KY [*Library symbol*] [*Library of Congress*] (LCLS)
KyLxCS...... Council of State Governments, State Information Center, Lexington, KY [*Library symbol*] [*Library of Congress*] (LCLS)
KyLxI .... IBM Corp., Office Products Division, Lexington, KY [*Library symbol*] [*Library of Congress*] (LCLS)
KyLxIMM.... Institute for Mining and Minerals Research, Lexington, KY [*Library symbol*] [*Library of Congress*] (LCLS)
KyLxK .... Keeneland Association, Inc., Lexington, KY [*Library symbol*] [*Library of Congress*] (LCLS)
KyLxT........ Transylvania University, Lexington, KY [*Library symbol*] [*Library of Congress*] (LCLS)
KyLxTI....... Lexington Technical Institute, Lexington, KY [*Library symbol*] [*Library of Congress*] (LCLS)
KyLxV .... United States Veterans Administration Hospital, Lexington, KY [*Library symbol*] [*Library of Congress*] (LCLS)
KYLZ......... Los Lunas, NM [*FM radio station call letters*] (BROA)
KYLZ......... Santa Cruz, CA [*FM radio station call letters*]
KYMA........ Yuma, AZ [*Television station call letters*]
KyMadC..... Madisonville Community College, Media Center, Madisonville, KY [*Library symbol*] [*Library of Congress*] (LCLS)
KyMan....... Clay County Public Library, Manchester, KY [*Library symbol*] [*Library of Congress*] (LCLS)
KYMC........ Ballwin, MO [*FM radio station call letters*]
KYMD .... Kentucky Medical Insurance Co. [*NASDAQ symbol*] (NQ)
KyMdC ...... Midway Junior College and Pinkerton High School, Midway, KY [*Library symbol*] [*Library of Congress*] (LCLS)
KyMed....... Kentucky Medical Insurance Co. [*Associated Press*] (SAG)
KYMG .... Anchorage, AK [*FM radio station call letters*]
KYMI .... Los Ybanez, TX [*FM radio station call letters*]
KYMN........ Northfield, MN [*AM radio station call letters*]
KYMO .... East Prairie, MO [*AM radio station call letters*]
KYMO .... Kymograph (ABBR)
KYMO-FM... East Prairie, MO [*FM radio station call letters*]
KyMoreU.... Morehead State University (SAUO)
KyMoreU.... Morehead State University, Morehead, KY [*Library symbol*] [*Library of Congress*] (LCLS)
KYMR .... Salem, MO [*FM radio station call letters*] (BROA)
KYMS........ Keep Your Mouth Shut
KYMS........ Santa Ana, CA [*FM radio station call letters*]
KyMurT...... Murray State University, Murray, KY [*Library symbol*] [*Library of Congress*] (LCLS)
KYMV........ Kennedya Yellow Mosaic Virus [*Plant pathology*]
KYMX........ Sacramento, CA [*FM radio station call letters*]
KyMyC....... Maysville Community College, Maysville, KY [*Library symbol*] [*Library of Congress*] (LCLS)
KYN.......... Kentuckian [*Telegraphy*] (PCTE)
KYN.......... Kynurenic Acid (DMAA)
KYN.......... Kynurenine [*Biochemistry*]
KYN.......... Kyrnair [*France*] [*ICAO designator*] (FAAC)
KyNaM ...... Nazareth Mother House Archives, Nazareth, KY [*Library symbol*] [*Library of Congress*] (LCLS)
KYND .... Cypress, TX [*AM radio station call letters*]
KYNE .... Omaha, NE [*Television station call letters*]
KYNG .... Dallas, TX [*FM radio station call letters*]
KYNG .... Youngstown [*Ohio*] [*ICAO location identifier*] (ICLI)
KYNO .... Fresno, CA [*AM radio station call letters*]
KYNP .... Khao Yai National Park (SAUO)
KYNR .... Toppenish, WA [*AM radio station call letters*] (BROA)
KYNT .... Keynote (ABBR)
KYNT .... Yankton, SD [*AM radio station call letters*]
KYNTG ...... Keynoting (ABBR)
KYNU .... Carrington, ND [*FM radio station call letters*] (BROA)
KYNU .... Jamestown, ND [*FM radio station call letters*]
KYNZ .... Lone Grove, OK [*FM radio station call letters*]
KYO.......... Kelon [*Language symbol*] (ETLW)
KYO.......... Kyocera Corp. [*NYSE symbol*] (SPSG)
KYO.......... Kyocera Corp.ADR [*NYSE symbol*] (TTSB)
KYO.......... Kyoeera Corp. (SAUO)
KYO.......... Kyoto [*Japan*] [*Seismograph station code, US Geological Survey*] (SEIS)
Kyocer....... Kyocera Corp. [*Associated Press*] (SAG)
KYOD........ Glendo, WY [*FM radio station call letters*] (BROA)
KYOD-FM ... Casper, WY [*FM radio station call letters*] (BROA)
KYOK........ Houston, TX [*AM radio station call letters*]
KYOK........ Kyokuyo Shipping Company [*Common carrier symbol*]
KYOK-AM ... Conroe, TX [*AM radio station call letters*] (BROA)
KYOO........ Bolivar, MO [*AM radio station call letters*]
KYOO-FM ... Halfway, MO [*FM radio station call letters*]
KY Op .... Kentucky Court of Appeals Opinions [*A publication*] (DLA)
KY Opin..... Kentucky Opinions [*A publication*] (DLA)
KYOR-FM... Yucca Valley, CA [*FM radio station call letters*] (BROA)
KYOS .... Merced, CA [*AM radio station call letters*]
KYOT .... Phoenix (Kingman, Prescott), AZ [*FM radio station call letters*] (GDPB)
KYOT-FM.... Phoenix, AZ [*FM radio station call letters*]
Kyoto L Rev... Kyoto Law Review [*A publication*] (DLA)
Kyot Univ ... Kyoto University (SAUO)
KYOU........ Wendover, NV [*FM radio station call letters*]
KYOU-TV.... Ottumwa, IA [*Television station call letters*]
KyOw .... Owensboro-Daviess County Public Library, Owensboro, KY [*Library symbol*] [*Library of Congress*] (LCLS)
KyOwB ...... Brescia College, Owensboro, KY [*Library symbol*] [*Library of Congress*] (LCLS)

KyOwC ...... Owensboro Community College, Owensboro, KY [*Library symbol*] [*Library of Congress*] (LCLS)
KyOwK ...... Kentucky Wesleyan College, Owensboro, KY [*Library symbol*] [*Library of Congress*] (LCLS)
KYOX .... Comanche, TX [*FM radio station call letters*] (BROA)
KYP .... Kyaukpyu [*Myanmar*] [*Airport symbol*] (OAG)
KYPA-AM ... Los Angeles, CA [*AM radio station call letters*] (RBYB)
KyPad .... Paducah Public Library, Paducah, KY [*Library symbol*] [*Library of Congress*] (LCLS)
KyPadC...... Paducah Community College, Paducah, KY [*Library symbol*] [*Library of Congress*] (LCLS)
KyParF ...... John Fox, Jr. Memorial Library, Paris, KY [*Library symbol*] [*Library of Congress*] (LCLS)
kyph .... Kyphosis [*Orthopedics*] (DAVI)
KyPikC ...... Pikeville College, Pikeville, KY [*Library symbol*] [*Library of Congress*] (LCLS)
KYPL-FM.... Yakima, WA [*FM radio station call letters*] (RBYB)
KyPpA .... Alice Lloyd College, Pippa Passes, KY [*Library symbol*] [*Library of Congress*] (LCLS)
KyPrbC ...... Prestonburg Community College, Prestonsburg, KY [*Library symbol*] [*Library of Congress*] (LCLS)
KYPT .... Seattle, WA [*FM radio station call letters*] (BROA)
KyPw25 ..... Kentucky Power Co. [*Associated Press*] (SAG)
KYPX .... Camden, AR [*Television station call letters*] (BROA)
KYPX .... Little Rock, AR [*Television station call letters*] (BROA)
KYQQ .... Arkansas City, KS [*FM radio station call letters*]
KYQX .... Weatherford, TX [*FM radio station call letters*] (RBYB)
KY R .... Kentucky Reports [*A publication*] (DLA)
Kyr .... Kiloyear (SAUS)
KYR .... Kyber Resources [*Vancouver Stock Exchange symbol*]
KyRE......... Eastern Kentucky University, Richmond, KY [*Library symbol*] [*Library of Congress*] (LCLS)
KY Rev Stat... Kentucky Revised Statutes [*A publication*] (DLA)
KY Rev Stat & Rules Serv... Kentucky Revised Statutes and Rules Service (Baldwin) [*A publication*] (DLA)
KY Rev Stat Ann... Baldwin's Kentucky Revised Statutes, Annotated [*A publication*] (DLA)
Kyrgyz........ Kyrgyzstani (DIAR)
KYRK-FM ... Eunice, NM [*FM radio station call letters*] (RBYB)
KYRM-FM... Yuma, AZ [*FM radio station call letters*] (BROA)
KYRO .... Potosi, MO [*AM radio station call letters*]
KYRS .... Atwater, NM [*FM radio station call letters*]
KYRV-FM ... Concordia, MO [*FM radio station call letters*] (BROA)
KYRX .... Chaffee, MO [*FM radio station call letters*] (BROA)
KYRX .... Louisville Scrap Material [*Private rail car owner code*]
KYS .... Kayes [*Mali*] [*Airport symbol*] (OAG)
KYS .... Kentucky State University, Frankfort, KY [*OCLC symbol*] (OCLC)
KYS .... Keycorp Industries [*Vancouver Stock Exchange symbol*]
KYS .... Keys
KYS .... Kiyosumi - Telemeter [*Japan*] [*Seismograph station code, US Geological Survey*] (SEIS)
KY SBJ...... Kentucky State Bar Journal [*A publication*] (DLA)
KYSC .... Fairbanks, AK [*FM radio station call letters*] (BROA)
KYSC .... Yakima, WA [*FM radio station call letters*]
KYSF .... Bonanza, OR [*FM radio station call letters*] (BROA)
KYSG .... Coos Bay, OR [*FM radio station call letters*] (RBYB)
Kyshe........ Kyshe's Reports [*1808-90*] [*A publication*] (DLA)
KYSL .... Frisco, CO [*FM radio station call letters*]
KYSM........ Mankato, MN [*AM radio station call letters*]
KYSM-FM... Mankato, MN [*FM radio station call letters*]
KYSN .... East Wenatchee, WA [*FM radio station call letters*]
KySoC .... Somerset Community College, Somerset, KY [*Library symbol*] [*Library of Congress*] (LCLS)
Kysor .... Kysor Industrial Corp. [*Associated Press*] (SAG)
KYSR .... Los Angeles, CA [*FM radio station call letters*]
KYSS .... Missoula, MT [*FM radio station call letters*] (GDPB)
KYSS-FM ... Missoula, MT [*FM radio station call letters*]
kyst .... Keystone (VRA)
KYST .... Texas City, TX [*AM radio station call letters*]
KY St BJ .... Kentucky State Bar Journal [*A publication*] (DLA)
kysth......... Vagina [*Prefix meaning*] [*Medicine*] (EDAA)
KY St Law... Morehead and Brown. Digest of Kentucky Statute Laws [*A publication*] (DLA)
KYSTN....... Keystone (ABBR)
KYSY-FM.... Ankeny, IA [*FM radio station call letters*] (BROA)
KYT .... Corporate High Yield Fd II [*NYSE symbol*] (TTSB)
KYT .... Corporate High Yield II [*NYSE symbol*] (SAG)
KYT .... Keystone Explorations [*Vancouver Stock Exchange symbol*]
KYT .... Kyauktaw [*Myanmar*] [*Airport symbol*] (OAG)
KYTC .... Northwood, IA [*FM radio station call letters*]
KYTE......... Newport, OR [*FM radio station call letters*]
KYTI .... Sheridan, WY [*FM radio station call letters*] (GDPB)
KYTI-FM .... Sheridan, WY [*FM radio station call letters*] (BROA)
KYTN .... Wrightsville, AR [*FM radio station call letters*]
kyto .... Cell [*or Hollow*] [*Prefix meaning*] [*Medicine*] (EDAA)
KYTOON..... Kite Balloon [*Air Force*]
KyTrA .... Abbey of Gethsemani, Trappist, KY [*Library symbol*] [*Library of Congress*] (LCLS)
KYTT......... Coos Bay, OR [*FM radio station call letters*]
KYTT......... Key Trucking [*Common carrier symbol*]
KYTV .... Springfield, MO [*Television station call letters*]
KYTX .... Beeville, TX [*FM radio station call letters*]
KYTZ......... Walhalla, ND [*FM radio station call letters*] (BROA)
kyu........... Kentucky [*MARC country of publication code*] [*Library of Congress*] (LCCP)
KYU.......... Koyukuk [*Alaska*] [*Airport symbol*] (OAG)
KYU.......... Koyukuk, AK [*Location identifier*] [*FAA*] (FAAL)
KyU .... University of Kentucky (SAUO)
KyU .... University of Kentucky, Chemistry/Physics Library (SAUO)
KyU .... University of Kentucky, Lexington, KY [*Library symbol*] [*Library of Congress*] (LCLS)
KyU-A .... University of Kentucky, Ashland Community College, Ashland, KY [*Library symbol*] [*Library of Congress*] (LCLS)
KyU-ASC .... University of Kentucky, Agricultural Science Center, Lexington, KY [*Library symbol*] [*Library of Congress*] (LCLS)
KYUC .... Roland, OK [*FM radio station call letters*]
KyU-C .... University of Kentucky, Southeast Center, Cumberland, KY [*Library symbol*] [*Library of Congress*] (LCLS)
KyU-E........ University of Kentucky, Elizabethtown Community College, Elizabethtown, KY [*Library symbol*] [*Library of Congress*] (LCLS)
KyU-F........ University of Kentucky, Fort Knox Center, Fort Knox, KY [*Library symbol*] [*Library of Congress*] (LCLS)
KYUF .... Uvalde, TX [*FM radio station call letters*]
KyU-H .... University of Kentucky, Northwest Center, Henderson, KY [*Library symbol*] [*Library of Congress*] (LCLS)
KYUK........ Bethel, AK [*AM radio station call letters*]
KYUK-TV.... Bethel, AK [*Television station call letters*]
KyU-L........ University of Kentucky, Law Library, Lexington, KY [*Library symbol*] [*Library of Congress*] (LCLS)
KYUL-FM ... Harker Heights, TX [*FM radio station call letters*] (BROA)
KyU-M....... University of Kentucky, Medical Center, Lexington, KY [*Library symbol*] [*Library of Congress*] (LCLS)
KYUM .... Yuma/Yuma Marine Corps Air Station, Yuma International [*Arizona*] [*ICAO location identifier*] (ICLI)
KyU-N .... University of Kentucky, Northern Center, Covington, KY [*Library symbol*] [*Library of Congress*] (LCLS)
KYUNGHEE... KYUNG Hee Nepal Friendship Medical Center (SAUS)
KyU-P .... University of Kentucky, Prestonburg Community College, Prestonburg, KY [*Library symbol*] [*Library of Congress*] (LCLS)
KYUS .... Miles City, MT [*Television station call letters*]
KYUU .... Liberal, KS [*AM radio station call letters*]
KYV .... Kibris Turk Hava Yollari Ltd. [*Turkey*] [*FAA designator*] (FAAC)
KYVA .... Gallup, NM [*AM radio station call letters*]
KYVA .... Grants, NM [*FM radio station call letters*] (BROA)
KYVE .... Yakima, WA [*Television station call letters*]
KYVT .... Yakima, WA [*FM radio station call letters*] (BROA)
KYVU .... Kentucky Virtual University
KYW .... Philadelphia, PA [*AM radio station call letters*]
KyWA........ Asbury College, Wilmore, KY [*Library symbol*] [*Library of Congress*] (LCLS)
KyWAT....... Asbury Theological Seminary, Wilmore, KY [*Library symbol*] [*Library of Congress*] (LCLS)
KyWAT12.... Asbury Theological Seminary, Wilmore (SAUS)
KyWavH..... Waverly Hills Tuberculosis Sanatorium, Waverly Hills, KY [*Library symbol*] [*Library of Congress*] (LCLS)
KY WC Dec. Kentucky Workmen's Compensation Board Decisions [*A publication*] (DLA)
KYW-DT..... Philadelphia, PA [*Television station call letters*] (BROA)
KyWilC ...... Cumberland College, Williamsburg, KY [*Library symbol*] [*Library of Congress*] (LCLS)
KYWL........ Spokane, WA [*FM radio station call letters*] (BROA)
KyWn .... Clark County Public Library, Winchester, KY [*Library symbol*] [*Library of Congress*] (LCLS)
KyWnS ...... Southeastern Christian College, Winchester, KY [*Library symbol*] [*Library of Congress*] (LCLS)
KYW-TV..... Philadelphia, PA [*Television station call letters*]
KYX.......... Yalumet [*Papua New Guinea*] [*Airport symbol*] (OAG)
KYXE .... Selah, WA [*AM radio station call letters*]
KYXK .... Gurdon, AR [*FM radio station call letters*]
KYXS .... Mineral Wells, TX [*FM radio station call letters*]
KYXX .... Ozona, TX [*FM radio station call letters*]
KYXY .... San Diego, CA [*FM radio station call letters*]
KYYA .... Billings, MT [*FM radio station call letters*]
KYYD .... Abilene, TX [*AM radio station call letters*]
KYYI .... Burkburnett, TX [*FM radio station call letters*]
KYYK .... Palestine, TX [*FM radio station call letters*]
KYYS .... Kansas City, MO [*FM radio station call letters*]
KYYT .... Goldendale, WA [*FM radio station call letters*]
KYYX .... Minot, ND [*FM radio station call letters*]
KYYY .... Bismarck, ND [*FM radio station call letters*]
KYYZ .... Williston, ND [*FM radio station call letters*]
KYZ .... Kayabi [*Language symbol*] (ETLW)
KYZ .... Kayseri [*Turkey*] [*Airport symbol*] (AD)
Kyzen........ Kyzen Corp. [*Associated Press*] (SAG)
KYZK .... Sun Valley, ID [*FM radio station call letters*] (BROA)
KYZN .... Kyzen Corp. [*NASDAQ symbol*] (SAG)
KYZN .... Kyzen Corp.'A' [*NASDAQ symbol*] (TTSB)
KYZNW..... Kyzen Corp.Wrrt'A' [*NASDAQ symbol*] (TTSB)
KYZS .... Tyler, TX [*AM radio station call letters*]
KYZX .... Pueblo, CO [*FM radio station call letters*]
KYZZ......... San Angelo, TX [*FM radio station call letters*]
KZ............ Consult [*Telegraphy*] (PCTE)
KZ............ Dust/Sand Storm [*Meteorology*] (WDAA)
kZ .... duststorm (SAUS)
KZ............ Kaplan-Zuelzer [*Syndrome*] (DAVI)
KZ............ Kazakhstan [*Internet country code*]
KZ............ Ketoconazole (DMAA)
KZ............ Killing Zone [*Military*] [*British*]
KZ............ Kilohertz [*Preferred form is kHz*] [*Electronics*] (MCD)

KZ .... Konzentrationslager [*Concentration Camp*] [*Initials also used in medicine to indicate a psychiatric syndrome found in surviving victims of the World War II camps*] [*German*]
KZ .... Kuhns Zeitschrift fuer Vergleichende Sprachforschung [*A publication*] (BJA)
Kz .... Kwanza [*Monetary Unit*][*Angola*] (BARN)
KZ .... Kysor Indl [*NYSE symbol*] (TTSB)
KZ .... Kysor Industrial Corp. [*NYSE symbol*] (SPSG)
KZ .... New Zealand [*IYRU nationality code*] (IYR)
KZ .... Oriens & King [*ICAO designator*] (AD)
KZA .... Kazakhstan Airlines [*ICAO designator*] (FAAC)
KZAB .... Albuquerque [*New Mexico*] [*ICAO location identifier*] (ICLI)
KZAC .... Esparto, CA [*FM radio station call letters*] (RBYB)
KZAK .... Incline Village, NV [*FM radio station call letters*]
KZAL .... Desert Center, CA [*FM radio station call letters*]
KZAM-FM .... Ganado, TX [*FM radio station call letters*] (RBYB)
KZAN .... Hays, KS [*FM radio station call letters*] (BROA)
KZAP .... Paradise, CA [*FM radio station call letters*] (RBYB)
KZAR-AM .... Rogers, AR [*AM radio station call letters*] (BROA)
KZAR-TV .... Provo, UT [*Television station call letters*] (RBYB)
KZAT .... Kommentar zum Alten Testament [*A publication*] (BJA)
KZAT-FM .... Belle Plaine, IA [*FM radio station call letters*] (BROA)
KZAU .... Chicago, Aurora [*Illinois*] [*ICAO location identifier*] (ICLI)
KZAZ .... Bellingham, WA [*FM radio station call letters*]
KZB .... Zachar Bay [*Alaska*] [*Airport symbol*] (OAG)
KZB .... Zachar Bay, AK [*Location identifier*] [*FAA*] (FAAL)
KZBA .... Shafter, CA [*FM radio station call letters*]
KZBB .... Poteau, OK [*FM radio station call letters*]
KZBE .... Pleasant Hope, MO [*FM radio station call letters*] (RBYB)
KZBE-FM .... Omak, WA [*FM radio station call letters*] (BROA)
KZBK .... Brookfield, MO [*AM radio station call letters*]
KZBK-FM .... Brookfield, MO [*FM radio station call letters*]
KZBL .... Natchitoches, LA [*FM radio station call letters*]
KZBN .... Santa Barbara, CA [*AM radio station call letters*] (BROA)
KZBQ .... Idaho Falls-Pocatello, ID [*AM radio station call letters*] (GDPB)
KZBQ .... Idaho Falls-Pocatello, ID [*FM radio station call letters*] (GDPB)
KZBQ-FM .... Pocatello, ID [*FM radio station call letters*]
KZBR-FM .... Mountain Pine, AR [*FM radio station call letters*] (RBYB)
KZBW .... Boston, Nashua [*New Hampshire*] [*ICAO location identifier*] (ICLI)
KZBZ .... Salina, KS [*FM radio station call letters*]
KZCD .... Lawton, OK [*FM radio station call letters*]
KZCO .... Sacramento, CA [*FM radio station call letters*] (GDPB)
KZCO-FM .... Oroville, CA [*FM radio station call letters*] (RBYB)
KZCR .... Fergus Falls, MN [*FM radio station call letters*]
KZCY-FM .... Cheyenne, WY [*FM radio station call letters*] (BROA)
KZD .... Consulted [*Telegraphy*] (PCTE)
KZDC .... San Antonio, TX [*AM radio station call letters*] (RBYB)
KZDC .... Washington, Leesburg [*Virginia*] [*ICAO location identifier*] (ICLI)
KZDF-FM .... McKinney, TX [*FM radio station call letters*] (BROA)
KZDG .... Greeley, CO [*FM radio station call letters*]
KZDL-FM .... Terrell, TX [*FM radio station call letters*] (BROA)
KZDV .... Denver, Longmont [*Colorado*] [*ICAO location identifier*] (ICLI)
KZDX .... Burley, ID [*FM radio station call letters*]
KZDY-FM .... Cawker City, KS [*FM radio station call letters*] (BROA)
KZEE .... Weatherford, TX [*AM radio station call letters*]
KZEG .... Clinton, IA [*FM radio station call letters*] (GDPB)
KZEG-FM .... Clinton, IA [*FM radio station call letters*] (BROA)
KZEL .... Eugene, OR [*FM radio station call letters*]
KZEN .... Central City, NE [*FM radio station call letters*]
KZEP-FM .... San Antonio, TX [*FM radio station call letters*]
KZEW .... Wheatland, WY [*FM radio station call letters*] (GDPB)
KZEW-FM .... Wheatland, WY [*FM radio station call letters*] (BROA)
KZEY .... Tyler, TX [*AM radio station call letters*]
KZEY-FM .... Marshall, TX [*FM radio station call letters*]
KZEZ .... St. George, UT [*FM radio station call letters*]
KZF .... Kaintiba [*Papua New Guinea*] [*Airport symbol*] (OAG)
KZFM .... Corpus Christi, TX [*FM radio station call letters*]
KZFN .... Moscow, ID [*FM radio station call letters*]
KZFO .... Clovis, CA [*FM radio station call letters*] (BROA)
KZFO .... Madera, CA [*FM radio station call letters*]
KZFR .... Chico, CA [*FM radio station call letters*]
KZFT .... Merced, CA [*FM radio station call letters*] (RBYB)
KZFW .... Fort Worth, Euless [*Texas*] [*ICAO location identifier*] (ICLI)
KZFX-FM .... Lincoln, NE [*FM radio station call letters*] (BROA)
KZG .... Consulting [*Telegraphy*] (PCTE)
KZGL .... Cottonwood, AZ [*FM radio station call letters*]
KZGO .... Glenwood Springs, CO [*FM radio station call letters*] (RBYB)
KZGT .... Great Falls [*Montana*] [*ICAO location identifier*] (ICLI)
KZGZ .... Agana, GU [*FM radio station call letters*]
KZHE .... Stamps, AR [*FM radio station call letters*]
KZHK-FM .... St. George, UT [*FM radio station call letters*] (BROA)
KZHR .... Dayton, WA [*FM radio station call letters*]
KZHT .... Provo, UT [*FM radio station call letters*]
KZHU .... Houston, Humble [*Texas*] [*ICAO location identifier*] (ICLI)
KZI .... Kozani [*Greece*] [*Airport symbol*] (OAG)
KZIA .... Las Cruces, NM [*Television station call letters*]
KZIA-FM .... Cedar Rapids, IA [*FM radio station call letters*] (BROA)
KZID .... Indianapolis [*Indiana*] [*ICAO location identifier*] (ICLI)
KZIG .... Cave City, AR [*FM radio station call letters*]
KZII .... Lubbock, TX [*FM radio station call letters*]
KZIM .... Cape Girardeau, MO [*AM radio station call letters*]
KZIN .... Shelby, MT [*FM radio station call letters*]
KZIO .... Superior, WI [*FM radio station call letters*]
KZIO-FM .... Two Harbors, MN [*FM radio station call letters*] (BROA)
KZIP .... Amarillo, TX [*AM radio station call letters*]
KZIQ .... Ridgecrest, CA [*AM radio station call letters*]
KZIQ-FM .... Ridgecrest, CA [*FM radio station call letters*]
KZIZ .... Sumner, WA [*AM radio station call letters*]
KZJC .... Flagstaff, AZ [*Television station call letters*]
KZJG .... Longmont, CO [*Television station call letters*]
KZJH .... Jackson, WY [*FM radio station call letters*]
KZJL .... Houston, TX [*Television station call letters*]
KZJM-FM .... Rockport, TX [*FM radio station call letters*] (BROA)
KZJX .... Jacksonville Hillard [*Florida*] [*ICAO location identifier*] (ICLI)
KZJZ .... St. Louis, MO [*AM radio station call letters*] (BROA)
KZK .... Kazukuru [*Language symbol*] (ETLW)
KZKC .... Kansas City Olathe [*Kansas*] [*ICAO location identifier*] (ICLI)
KZKE .... Seligman, AZ [*FM radio station call letters*] (RBYB)
KZKI .... San Bernardino, CA [*Television station call letters*]
KZKK .... Huron, SD [*FM radio station call letters*]
KZKL .... Rio Rancho, NM [*FM radio station call letters*]
KZKL-AM .... Milan, NM [*AM radio station call letters*] (BROA)
KZKS .... Rifle, CO [*FM radio station call letters*]
KZKX .... Seward, NE [*FM radio station call letters*]
KZKZ .... Greenwood, AR [*FM radio station call letters*]
KZLA .... Los Angeles, CA [*FM radio station call letters*]
KZLA .... Los Angeles Palmdale [*California*] [*ICAO location identifier*] (ICLI)
KZLC .... Salt Lake City [*Utah*] [*ICAO location identifier*] (ICLI)
KZLE .... Batesville, AR [*FM radio station call letters*]
KZLG .... Mansura, LA [*FM radio station call letters*] (BROA)
KZLK .... Rapid City, SD [*FM radio station call letters*] (BROA)
KZLN .... Othello, WA [*FM radio station call letters*]
KZLO .... Bozeman, MT [*AM radio station call letters*]
KZLO-FM .... Bozeman, MT [*FM radio station call letters*] (BROA)
KZLS .... Great Bend, KS [*FM radio station call letters*]
KZLT .... East Grand Forks, MN [*FM radio station call letters*]
KZLV .... Lytle, TX [*FM radio station call letters*] (BROA)
KZLZ .... Keamy, AZ [*FM radio station call letters*]
KZMA .... Miami [*Florida*] [*ICAO location identifier*] (ICLI)
KZMA .... Poplar Bluff, MO [*FM radio station call letters*]
KZME .... Hudson, IA [*FM radio station call letters*]
KZME .... Memphis [*Tennessee*] [*ICAO location identifier*] (ICLI)
KZMG .... New Plymouth, ID [*FM radio station call letters*]
KZMI .... San Jose, MP [*FM radio station call letters*]
KZMK .... Sierra Vista, AZ [*FM radio station call letters*]
KZML .... Quincy, WA [*FM radio station call letters*] (BROA)
KZMM .... Troy, MO [*FM radio station call letters*]
KZMP .... Azle, TX [*FM radio station call letters*] (BROA)
KZMP .... Fort Worth, TX [*AM radio station call letters*] (BROA)
KZMP .... Minneapolis, Farmington [*Minnesota*] [*ICAO location identifier*] (ICLI)
KZMP-AM .... University Park, TX [*AM radio station call letters*] (BROA)
KZMQ .... Greybull, WY [*AM radio station call letters*]
KZMQ-FM .... Greybull, WY [*FM radio station call letters*]
KZMR .... Santa Cruz, CA [*FM radio station call letters*] (BROA)
KZMS .... Patterson, CA [*FM radio station call letters*]
KZMT .... Helena, MT [*FM radio station call letters*]
KZMU .... Moab, UT [*FM radio station call letters*]
KZMX .... Hot Springs, SD [*AM radio station call letters*]
KZMX-FM .... Hot Springs, SD [*FM radio station call letters*]
KZMY .... Bozeman, MT [*FM radio station call letters*] (BROA)
KZMZ .... Alexandria, LA [*FM radio station call letters*]
KZN .... Consultation [*Telegraphy*] (PCTE)
KZN .... Kazan [*Former USSR*] [*Airport symbol*] (OAG)
KZN .... Kozani [*Greece*] [*Seismograph station code, US Geological Survey*] (SEIS)
KZN .... KwaZulu Natal [*South Africa*]
KZN .... Zaimische [*Later, KNS*] [*Former USSR*] [*Geomagnetic observatory code*]
KZNA .... Hill City, KS [*FM radio station call letters*]
KZNC .... Huron, SD [*FM radio station call letters*]
KZNE-AM .... College Station, TX [*AM radio station call letters*] (BROA)
KZNG .... Hot Springs, AR [*AM radio station call letters*]
KZNI .... Idaho Falls, ID [*AM radio station call letters*] (BROA)
KZNM .... Grants, NM [*FM radio station call letters*]
KZNM .... Los Alamos, NM [*FM radio station call letters*] (BROA)
KZNN .... Rolla, MO [*FM radio station call letters*]
KZNO .... Nogales, AZ [*FM radio station call letters*] (RBYB)
KZNR .... Blackfoot, ID [*AM radio station call letters*] (BROA)
KZNR-FM .... Lakeville, MN [*FM radio station call letters*] (BROA)
KZNS .... Salt Lake City, UT [*AM radio station call letters*] (BROA)
KZNT-FM .... Cambridge, MN [*FM radio station call letters*] (BROA)
KZNU .... Saint George, UT [*AM radio station call letters*] (BROA)
KZNX-FM .... Astoria, OR [*FM radio station call letters*] (BROA)
KZNY .... New York, Ronkonkoma [*New York*] [*ICAO location identifier*] (ICLI)
KZNZ .... Colorado City, AZ [*FM radio station call letters*] (BROA)
KZNZ-FM .... Eden Prairie, MN [*FM radio station call letters*] (BROA)
KZOA .... KZ Owners' Association [*Defunct*] (EA)
KZOA .... Oakland, Freemont [*California*] [*ICAO location identifier*] (ICLI)
KZOB .... Cleveland, Oberlin [*Ohio*] [*ICAO location identifier*] (ICLI)
KZOE .... Longview, WA [*FM radio station call letters*]
KZOK .... Seattle, WA [*FM radio station call letters*]
KZOL .... Merced, CA [*FM radio station call letters*] (BROA)
KZOL-FM .... Santa Cruz, CA [*FM radio station call letters*] (RBYB)
KZON .... Phoenix, AZ [*FM radio station call letters*]
KZOO .... Honolulu, HI [*AM radio station call letters*]
KZOQ .... Missoula, MT [*FM radio station call letters*]
KZOR .... Hobbs, NM [*FM radio station call letters*]
KZOT .... Marianna, AR [*AM radio station call letters*]

KZOZ .... San Luis Obispo, CA [*FM radio station call letters*]
KZP .... Kwartalnik dla Historji Zydow w Polsce [*A publication*] (BJA)
KZPA......... Fort Yukon, AK [*AM radio station call letters*]
KZPD .... Ash Grove, MO [*FM radio station call letters*]
KZPE......... Ford City, CA [*FM radio station call letters*]
KZPH .... Cashmere, WA [*FM radio station call letters*]
KZPI-FM .... Deming, NM [*FM radio station call letters*] (RBYB)
KZPK .... Paynesville, MN [*FM radio station call letters*]
KZPM........ Bakersfield, CA [*AM radio station call letters*]
KZPN .... Bayside, CA [*FM radio station call letters*]
KZPO .... Lindsay, CA [*FM radio station call letters*]
KZPR .... Minot, ND [*FM radio station call letters*]
KZPS .... Dallas, TX [*FM radio station call letters*]
KZPT-FM.... Tucson, AZ [*FM radio station call letters*] (BROA)
KZQD .... Liberal, KS [*FM radio station call letters*]
KZQQ .... Abilene-Sweetwater, TX [*AM radio station call letters*] (GDPB)
KZQQ-AM ... Abilene, TX [*AM radio station call letters*] (BROA)
KZQZ-FM.... San Francisco, CA [*FM radio station call letters*] (BROA)
kzr .... Kazakh Soviet Socialist Republic [*MARC country of publication code*] [*Library of Congress*] (LCCP)
KZR........... Khuzdar [*Pakistan*] [*Airport symbol*] (AD)
KZRA......... Springdale, AR [*AM radio station call letters*]
KZRB .... New Boston, TX [*FM radio station call letters*]
KZRC .... Markham, TX [*FM radio station call letters*] (BROA)
KZRI.......... Welches, OR [*FM radio station call letters*] (BROA)
KZRK .... Canyon, TX [*AM radio station call letters*] (RBYB)
KZRK-FM ... Canyon, TX [*FM radio station call letters*] (RBYB)
KZRO .... Dunsmuir, CA [*FM radio station call letters*]
KZRQ .... Ash Grove, MO [*FM radio station call letters*] (BROA)
KZRQ .... Santa Fe, NM [*FM radio station call letters*]
KZRR .... Albuquerque, NM [*FM radio station call letters*]
KZRV .... Billings, MT [*FM radio station call letters*] (BROA)
KZRX .... Dickinson, ND [*FM radio station call letters*] (BROA)
KZRZ .... West Monroe, LA [*FM radio station call letters*] (BROA)
KZS .... Consults [*Telegraphy*] (PCTE)
KZS .... Kutztown State College, Kutztown, PA [*OCLC symbol*] (OCLC)
KZSA .... Placerville, CA [*FM radio station call letters*]
KZSC .... Santa Cruz, CA [*FM radio station call letters*]
KZSD .... Martin, SD [*FM radio station call letters*]
KZSD-TV .... Martin, SD [*Television station call letters*]
KZSE......... Rochester, MN [*FM radio station call letters*]
KZSE......... Seattle, Auburn [*Washington*] [*ICAO location identifier*] (ICLI)
KZSF......... Alameda, CA [*FM radio station call letters*] (RBYB)
KZSF......... San Jose, CA [*AM radio station call letters*] (BROA)
KZSJ......... San Martin, CA [*AM radio station call letters*] (RBYB)
KZSN .... Hutchinson, KS [*FM radio station call letters*]
KZSN .... Wichita, KS [*AM radio station call letters*]
KZSP .... South Padre Island, TX [*FM radio station call letters*]
KZSQ .... Sonora, CA [*FM radio station call letters*]
KZSR .... Onawa, IA [*FM radio station call letters*] (BROA)
KZSR .... Reno, NV [*FM radio station call letters*]
KZSS .... Albuquerque, NM [*AM radio station call letters*]
KZST......... Santa Rosa, CA [*FM radio station call letters*]
KZSU .... Stanford, CA [*FM radio station call letters*]
KZTA......... Naches, WA [*FM radio station call letters*] (BROA)
KZTA......... Yakima, WA [*AM radio station call letters*]
KZTA-FM.... Yakima, WA [*FM radio station call letters*]
KZTB......... Yakima, WA [*FM radio station call letters*] (GDPB)
KZTB-FM.... Sunnyside, WA [*FM radio station call letters*] (RBYB)
KZTK......... Bakersfield, CA [*AM radio station call letters*] (BROA)
KZTL......... Atlanta, Hampton [*Georgia*] [*ICAO location identifier*] (ICLI)
KZTO .... Ottawa, KS [*FM radio station call letters*]
KZTQ .... Laredo, TX [*FM radio station call letters*]
KZTR-FM.... Franklin, TX [*FM radio station call letters*] (BROA)
KZTS......... Yakima, WA [*AM radio station call letters*] (GDPB)
KZTS-AM.... Sunnyside, WA [*AM radio station call letters*] (BROA)
KZTS-AM.... Tacoma, WA [*AM radio station call letters*] (BROA)
KZTU .... Eugene, OR [*AM radio station call letters*] (RBYB)
KZTU .... Junction City, OR [*AM radio station call letters*] (BROA)
KZTU-AM ... Eugene, OR [*AM radio station call letters*] (RBYB)
KZTV......... Corpus Christi, TX [*Television station call letters*]
KZTW......... Fairview, OR [*AM radio station call letters*] (RBYB)
KZTX......... Refugio, TX [*FM radio station call letters*]
KZTY......... Winchester, NV [*AM radio station call letters*]
KZUA .... Holbrook, AZ [*FM radio station call letters*]
KZUB .... Tahoka, TX [*FM radio station call letters*]
KZUE .... El Reno, OK [*AM radio station call letters*]
KZUL .... Lake Havasu City, AZ [*FM radio station call letters*]
KZUM........ Lincoln, NE [*FM radio station call letters*]
KZUN .... Zuni Pueblo/Blackrock [*New Mexico*] [*ICAO location identifier*] (ICLI)
KZUS .... Toledo, OR [*AM radio station call letters*]
KZUS-FM ... Toledo, OR [*FM radio station call letters*]
KZUU .... Pullman, WA [*FM radio station call letters*]
KZV.......... Kartell Zionistischer Verbindungen (BJA)
KZW .... Kariri-Xoco [*Language symbol*] (ETLW)
KZWA........ Lake Charles, LA [*FM radio station call letters*]
KZWA........ Moss Bluff, LA [*FM radio station call letters*] (BROA)
KZWC........ Walnut Creek, CA [*FM radio station call letters*]
KZWY........ Sheridan, WY [*FM radio station call letters*] (GDPB)
KZWY-FM ... Sheridan, WY [*FM radio station call letters*] (BROA)
KZXA .... Santa Fe, NM [*FM radio station call letters*]
KZXB .... Homer, LA [*FM radio station call letters*]
KZXC .... Anchorage, AK [*Television station call letters*]
KZXR .... Prosser, WA [*FM radio station call letters*]
KZXV .... Seminole, OK [*FM radio station call letters*] (BROA)
KZXX .... Kenai, AK [*AM radio station call letters*]
KZXY .... Victorville, CA [*FM radio station call letters*] (GDPB)
KZXY-FM.... Apple Valley, CA [*FM radio station call letters*]
KZYP .... Pine Bluff, AR [*FM radio station call letters*]
KZYQ .... Lake Village, AR [*FM radio station call letters*] (BROA)
KZYQ-FM ... Lake Village, AR [*FM radio station call letters*] (BROA)
KZYR .... Avon, CO [*FM radio station call letters*]
KZYX .... Philo, CA [*FM radio station call letters*]
KZYZ......... Willits, CA [*FM radio station call letters*] (RBYB)
KZZB......... Beaumont, TX [*AM radio station call letters*]
KZZC-FM.... Tipton, CA [*FM radio station call letters*] (RBYB)
KZZD-FM.... Wichita, KS [*FM radio station call letters*] (BROA)
KZZE......... Eagle Point, OR [*FM radio station call letters*] (RBYB)
KZZF-FM.... South Lake Tahoe, CA [*FM radio station call letters*] (RBYB)
KZZI .... Belle Fourche, SD [*FM radio station call letters*] (RBYB)
KZZJ......... Rugby, ND [*AM radio station call letters*] (RBYB)
KZZK-FM.... New London, MO [*FM radio station call letters*] (RBYB)
KZZL......... Pullman, WA [*FM radio station call letters*]
KZZM-FM ... Dayton, WA [*FM radio station call letters*] (BROA)
KZZN .... Littlefield, TX [*AM radio station call letters*]
KZZO-FM.... Sacramento, CA [*FM radio station call letters*] (BROA)
KZZOKY ..... Sacramento-Stockton, CA [*FM radio station call letters*] (GDPB)
KZZP......... Winner, SD [*FM radio station call letters*] (RBYB)
KZZP-FM.... Mesa, AZ [*FM radio station call letters*] (BROA)
KZZQ .... Winterset, IA [*FM radio station call letters*] (RBYB)
KZZR .... Burns, OR [*AM radio station call letters*]
KZZS......... Thermopolis, WY [*FM radio station call letters*] (BROA)
KZZT......... Moberly, MO [*FM radio station call letters*]
KZZU .... Spokane, WA [*FM radio station call letters*]
KZZX......... Alamogordo, NM [*FM radio station call letters*]
KZZY......... Devils Lake, ND [*FM radio station call letters*]
KZZZ......... Kingman, AZ [*FM radio station call letters*]
KZZZ-AM.... Bullhead City, AZ [*AM radio station call letters*] (BROA)

L
By Acronym

L .... Angle

L .... Angular Momentum [*Symbol*] [*IUPAC*]

l---- .... Atlantic Ocean [*MARC geographic area code*] [*Library of Congress*] (LCCP)

L .... Avogadro Constant [*Symbol*] [*IUPAC*]

l .... Azimuthal Quantum Number [*or Orbital Angular Momentum Quantum Number*] [*Symbol*]

L .... Azimuthal Quantum Number [*or Orbital Angular Momentum Quantum Number*] - Total [*Symbol*]

L .... Cleared to Land (SAUS)

L .... Coefficient of Induction [*Medicine*] (EDAA)

L .... Coefficient of Physics [*Physics*] (DAVI)

L .... Concerts and Recitals of Serious Music (Permits) [*Public-performance tariff class*] [*British*]

L .... Countermeasures [*JETDS nomenclature*]

L .... Days before Launch [*Usually followed by a number*] [*NASA*] (KSC)

L .... Difference of Latitude [*Navigation*]

L .... Diffusion Length [*Medicine*] (EDAA)

L .... Drizzle [*Meteorology*]

L .... Electrical [*in British naval officers' ranks*]

L .... Electromagnet Radiance [*Astronomy*] (BARN)

L .... Element

L .... Elevated [*Railway*] [*Also, EL*]

L .... Equipped with Search Light [*Suffix to plane designation*] [*Navy*]

L .... extra insulation (SAUS)

L .... Fifty [*Roman numeral*]

L .... Finland [*IYRU nationality code*] (IYR)

L .... Glider Aircraft [*When first letter in Navy aircraft designation*]

L .... Inductance [*Symbol*] (AAG)

L .... Induction (SAUS)

L .... Inductor (SAUS)

L .... Kinetic Potential [*Symbol*]

L .... Labaz [*Belgium, France*] [*Research code symbol*]

L .... Label (MDG)

L .... Labetalol [*Pharmacology*]

L .... Labor

L .... Laboratory

L .... Laboratory Attendant [*Ranking title*] [*British Royal Navy*]

l .... Labor Only (MIST)

L .... Lactobacillus

L .... Lacuna [*Medicine*] (EDAA)

L .... Ladestreifen [*Ammunition Clip*] [*German military - World War II*]

L .... Ladinian [*Geology*]

L .... Lady [*or Ladyship*]

L .... Lagrange [*Lagrange points L1-L5*] [*Astronomy term*]

L .... Lagrangian Function

l .... Lah [*Music*] (ODA)

L .... Lake [*Maps and charts*]

L .... Lambda (WDAA)

L .... Lambda Index (DIPS)

L .... Lambert [*Unit of luminance*] [*Preferred unit is lx, Lux*]

L .... Lamellar Lipid Phase [*Biochemistry*] (QSUL)

L .... Lameness [*Used by immigration officials*] [*Obsolete*]

L .... Laminated

L .... Lamp

L .... Lancashire Flats [*British*] (DCTA)

L .... Lancers

L .... Lancet [*Medicine*] (EDAA)

L .... Land

L .... Landing

L .... Landplane

L .... Land Transportation [*FCC*] (NTCM)

L .... Landulfus Acconzaioco [*Flourished, 13th century*] [*Authority cited in pre-1607 legal work*] (DSA)

L .... Lane

L .... Langmuir [*Unit of measure*]

L .... Language

L .... Language Score (DIPS)

L .... Lansing's New York Supreme Court Reports [*A publication*] (DLA)

L .... Lansing's Select Cases in Chancery [*1824, 1826*] [*New York*] [*A publication*] (DLA)

L .... Lanthanum [*Chemical element; symbol is La*]

L .... Larceny [*FBI standardized term*]

l .... Large (WDMC)

L .... Large [*Size designation for clothing, etc.*]

L .... Larva [*Biology*]

L .... Laser

L .... Laser Research and Technology Division (SAUO)

L .... L-Asparaginase [*Also, A, L-ase, L-asnase, L-Asp*] [*An enzyme, an antineoplastic*]

L .... Lat [*Monetary unit*] [*Latvia*]

L .... Latching [*Electronics*]

l .... Late (WDMC)

L .... Late

L .... Latent Heat

L .... Lateral (IAA)

L .... Latex (DMAA)

L .... Latin

L .... Latitude

L .... Laudatur [*Latin*]

L .... Launch [*or Launcher*]

L .... Laurentius Hispanus [*Deceased, 1248*] [*Authority cited in pre-1607 legal work*] (DSA)

L .... Lavender [*Botany*]

L .... Law

L .... Lawson's Notes of Decisions, Registration [*A publication*] (DLA)

L .... Layer [*Officer's rating*] [*British Royal Navy*]

L .... "Lay" Source (BJA)

L .... Leader (ADA)

L .... Leader Sequence (DMAA)

L .... Lead Sheath (AAG)

L .... Leaf [*Bibliography*] [*Botany*]

L .... Leaflet

L .... League

L .... Learner

L .... Learning [*Denotes learning drivers before they receive their automobile driving licenses*] [*British*]

L .... Leasehold (ROG)

L .... Leather

L .... Leave

L .... Leave without pay (SAUO)

L .... Lederle Laboratories [*Research code symbol*]

L .... Leeward

l .... Left (WDMC)

L .... Left [*Politics*]

L .... Left [*Direction*]

L .... Left Eye [*Opthalmology*] (DAVI)

L .... Left Hand [*Music*] (ROG)

L .... Legal Division [*Coast Guard*]

L .... Leges [*Laws*] [*Latin*] (ROG)

L .... Legge [*Law, Act, Statute*] [*Italian*] (ILCA)

L .... Legionella [*A bacteria*] (DAVI)

L .... Legitimate

L .... Lehrregiment (SAUO)

L .... Leipzig [*German license plate city code*]

L .... Leishmania [*Microbiology*] (MAE)

L .... Lek [*Monetary unit*] [*Albania*] (BARN)

L .... Lempira [*Monetary unit*] [*Honduras*]

L .... Lenad Subgroup [*Leucite, nephelite, halite, thenardite*] [*CIPW classification*] [*Geology*]

L .... Length [*or Lengthwise*]

l .... Length [*Symbol*] [*IUPAC*]

L .... Lens

L .... Lente Insulin [*Pharmacology*] (DAVI)

L .... Leo (WDAA)

L .... Lepetit [*Italy*] [*Research code symbol*]

L .... Lepidocrocite [*A mineral*]

L .... Leptin (MELL)

L .... Leptospira [*A bacteria*] (DAVI)

L .... Leptotrichia [*A bacteria*] (DAVI)

L .... Lesser (DAVI)

L .... Lethal

L .... Letter

L .... Leu [*Monetary unit*] [*Romania*]

L .... Leucine [*One-letter symbol; see Leu*] [*An amino acid*]

L .... Leuconostoc [*An algae*] [*Biochemistry*] (DAVI)

L .... Leukemia Abstracts [*Medicine*] (EDAA)

L .... Leukocyte (MELL)

L .... Lev [*Monetary unit*] [*Bulgaria*]

L .... Level (KSC)

L .... Lever

L .... Levo [*or Laevo*] [*Configuration in chemical structure*]

l .... Levorotary [*or Levorotatory*] [*Chemistry*]

L .... Levorotatory [*Organic chemistry*] (DIPS)

L .... Lewisite [*War gas*] [*Army symbol*]

L .... Lexical Rule [*Linguistics*]

L .... Liaison [*Airplane designation*]
L .... Liber [*Book*] [*Latin*]
L .... Liberal [*Politics*]
L .... Liberty Financial Companies, Inc. [*NYSE symbol*] (SAG)
L .... Liberty Financial Cos. [*NYSE symbol*] (TTSB)
L .... Liberty Media Corp. [*NYSE symbol*]
L .... Libra [*Pound*]
L .... Library
L .... Libration [*Space exploration*]
L .... Licenciatus [*Academic Qualification*] [*Latin*]
L .... License
L .... Licensed to Practice [*Medicine*]
L .... Licentiate
L .... Lidocaine [*Topical anesthetic*]
L .... Lidoflazine [*A vasodilator*]
L .... Lies [*Read*] [*German*]
L .... Lieutenant [*Navy*] [*British*]
L .... Life [*Insurance*]
L .... Lifestyle [*Wire service code*] (NTCM)
L .... Lift
L .... Ligament [*or Ligamentum*]
L .... Ligand [*Chemistry*]
L .... Light [*Chain*] [*Biochemistry, immunochemistry*]
L .... Lighting [*As part of a code*]
L .... Lightning [*Meteorology*]
L .... Light Sense
L .... Lignite (WDAA)
L .... Lilac
L .... Lilangeni [*Monetary unit*] [*Swaziland*] (BARN)
L .... Lima [*Phonetic alphabet*] [*International*] (DSUE)
L .... Lime
L .... Limen or Threshold [*Psychology*]
L .... Limes [*Boundary*] [*Pharmacology*] (DAVI)
L .... Limes Death [*Medicine*] (EDAA)
L .... Limestone [*Petrology*]
L .... Limit
L .... Limited (DLA)
L .... Limited security clearance (SAUO)
L .... Lincoln and Welland Regiment (SAUO)
L .... Lincomycin (STED)
l .... Line (WDMC)
L .... Line
L .... Line Assembly (AAG)
L .... Line Drive [*Baseball term*] (NDBD)
L .... Linen [*Deltiology*]
L .... Line (of Print) [*Publishing*] (NTCM)
L .... Liner [*Nautical*]
L .... Lines Dose [*Medicine*]
L .... Lingual [*Dentistry*]
L .... Link
L .... Linnaean
L .... Lip
L .... Lipoid [*Biochemistry*]
(l) .... Liquid [*Chemistry*]
L .... Liquidity [*Business term*]
L .... Liquor (STED)
L .... Lira [*Monetary unit*] [*Italy*]
L .... List (MSA)
L .... Listed [*Stock exchange term*]
L .... Listening Post [*In symbol only*]
L .... Listeria [*A bacteria*] (DAVI)
L .... Lit
L .... Litas [*Monetary unit*] [*Lithuania*]
L .... Liter [*Also, l*] [*Metric measure of volume*]
l .... Liter
L .... Literate
L .... Lithium [*Chemical element*] (ROG)
L .... Lithuania (MILB)
L .... Little
L .... Live [*Wiring code*] [*British*]
L .... Liver (MAE)
L .... Liverpool [*Postcode*] (ODBW)
L .... Living (DAVI)
L .... Living Room (ROG)
L .... Livre [*Monetary unit*] [*Obsolete*] [*French*]
L .... Load (MDG)
L .... Loam [*Agronomy*]
L .... Lobe [*Of a leaf*] [*Botany*]
L .... Loblaw Companies Ltd. [*Toronto Stock Exchange symbol*] [*Vancouver Stock Exchange symbol*]
L .... Loblaw Cos. [*TS, exchange symbol*] (TTSB)
L .... Local [*Broadcasting program*] (NTCM)
l .... Local (WDMC)
L .... Location [*Linguistics*] (IEL)
l .... Locative (Case) [*Linguistics*]
L .... Locator [*Compass*]
L .... Locator Beacon
L .... Loch
L .... Lockheed Aircraft Corp. [*ICAO aircraft manufacturer identifier*] (ICAO)
L .... Locking [*Lamp base type*] (NTCM)
L .... Locus [*Place*] [*Latin*]
L .... Lodge
L .... Logarithm [*Mathematics*]
L .... London (ODA)
L .... Long
L .... Longacre [*James B.*] [*Designer's mark, when appearing on US coins*]
L .... Longitude
L .... Longo Catalogue [*A. Scarlatti*] (GROV)
L .... Long, Rolling Sea [*Meteorology*]
L .... Loop [*Fingerprint description*]
L .... Looper [*Computer science*] (MDG)
L .... LORAN [*Long-Range Navigation*] (IAA)
L .... Lorazepam [*A tranquilizer*]
L .... Lord [*or Lordship*]
L .... Lorentz Unit [*Electronics*]
L .... Losing Pitcher [*Baseball term*] (NDBD)
L .... loss (WDAA)
L .... Lost [*RADAR*]
L .... Lost [*Sports statistics*]
L .... Loti [*Monetary unit*] [*Lesotho*] (BARN)
L .... Lough [*Maps and charts*]
L .... Louisiana Reports [*A publication*] (DLA)
L .... Louisiana State Library, Baton Rouge, LA [*Library symbol*] [*Library of Congress*] (LCLS)
L .... Louisville [*Diocesan abbreviation*] [*Kentucky*] (TOCD)
L .... Love [*Phonetic alphabet*] [*World War II*] (DSUE)
l .... Low (IDOE)
L .... Low [*or Lower*]
L .... Low Altitude (PIPO)
L .... Lower Bow [*Music*] (ROG)
l .... Lower Limit of a Class Interval [*Psychology*]
L .... Lowest (IDYL)
L .... Low Season [*Airline fare code*]
L .... Loyalty
L .... Luer [*Medicine*] (EDAA)
L .... Lues [*or Syphilis*] [*Medicine*] (DAVI)
L .... Luitingh [*Holland*]
L .... Lumbar [*Medicine*]
l .... Lumen (IDOE)
L .... Lumen [*Unit of luminous flux*]
L .... Luminance (DMAA)
L .... Lunch (CDAI)
L .... Lung [*Anatomy*] (DAVI)
L .... Luteolin [*Botany*]
L .... Luxembourg
L .... Luxury [*In automobile model name "Cordia L"*]
L .... Lygranum Antigen [*Medicine*] (EDAA)
L .... Lying Down [*Medicine*] (EDAA)
L .... Lymph [*A fluid*] [*Biochemistry*] (DAVI)
L .... Lymphocyte [*Biochemistry*] (DAVI)
L .... Lymphocyte Antibody [*Medicine*] (EDAA)
L .... Lymphogranuloma [*Pathology*] (DAVI)
L .... Lysosome [*Biochemistry*] (DAVI)
l .... Lyxose [*As substituent on nucleoside*] [*Biochemistry*]
l .... Mean Free Path [*Symbol*] [*IUPAC*]
L .... Merck & Co., Inc. [*Research code symbol*]
l .... Orbital Angular Momentum Quantum Number [*Physics*] (ODA)
L .... Promotional Fare [*Also, K, Q, V*] [*Airline fare code*]
L .... Quinquaginta [*Fifty*] [*Latin*]
L .... Radiance [*Symbol*] [*IUPAC*]
L .... Requires Fuel and Oil [*Search and rescue symbol that can be stamped in sand or snow*]
L .... Sandoz Pharmaceuticals [*Research code symbol*]
L .... San Francisco [*Branch in the Federal Reserve regional banking system*] (BARN)
L .... Searchlight Control [*JETDS nomenclature*]
L .... Self-Inductance [*Symbol*] [*IUPAC*]
L .... Shape Descriptor [*Dining el, for example. The shape resembles the letter for which it is named*]
L .... Silo Launched [*Missile launch environment symbol*]
L .... Single Acetate (AAG)
L .... Timber [*Lumber*] [*Vessel load line mark*]
L .... Time of Launch [*NASA*]
l .... Laevorotatory [*Chemistry*] (ODA)
L0 .... Raw SAR data (SAUS)
L1 .... First language (SAUS)
L1 .... First Language (ADA)
L_1 .... First Lumbar Nerve [*Second lumbar nerve is L_2, etc., through L_5*] [*Medicine*] (DAVI)
L_1 .... First Lumbar Vertebra [*Second lumbar vertebra is L_2, etc., through L5*] [*Medicine*]
L1A .... Processed SAR data (SAUS)
L1B .... Processed and Geocoded SAR data (SAUS)
L1 cache .... Level 1 Cache [*Computer science*] (FOTI)
L1TC .... Level 1 Trauma Center [*Medicine*] (DMAA)
L-2 .... Launch Minus 2 Days (SAUS)
L02 .... Liquid Oxygen (NAKS)
L2 .... Second Language [*Linguistics*] (IEL)
L2 cache .... Level 2 Cache (L2) [*Computer science*] (FOTI)
L2D2 .... Lightweight Loran Digital Dropsonde (SAUS)
L2F .... Layer 2 Forwarding [*Computer science*] (HODG)
L2TP .... Layer Two Tunneling Protocol [*Computer science*] (DCOM)
L3 .... Line Three-cylinder [*Automotive engineering*]
L/3 .... Lower Third [*Referring to long bones*] [*Orthopedics*] (DAVI)
L3S .... LNG [*Liquefied Natural Gas*] Seabed Supported System
L4 .... Automatic Lockup Four Speed [*DOE*] (TAG)
L4 .... Fourth lumbar vertebra (SAUS)

L4 .... Line Four-cylinder [*Automotive engineering*]
L5 .... Fifth of five lumbar vertebra (SAUS)
L5 .... Line Five-cylinder [*Automotive engineering*]
L5 .... Long Quinto [*Pt. 10 of Year Books*] [*A publication*] (DSA)
L-5HTP ...... L-5-Hydroxytryptophan [*Pharmacology*] (DAVI)
L6 .... Laboratories Low-Level Linked List Language [*Bell Systems*] (DIT)
L6 .... Line Six-cylinder [*Automotive engineering*]
L8 .... Line Eight-cylinder [*Automotive engineering*]
L-10-W ...... Levulose (10 Percent) in Water
L15 .... Leibovitz 15 (SAUS)
L123UA ..... Lotus 1-2-3 Users' Association
LA .... Concerts and Recitals of Serious Music (Annual Licence) [*Public-performance tariff class*] [*British*]
LA .... Fighter [*Russian aircraft symbol*]
LA .... Hoffmann-La Roche, Inc. [*Research code symbol*]
La .... [*The*] Holy Bible from Ancient Eastern Manuscripts [*G. M. Lamsa*] [*A publication*] (BJA)
LA .... Lab. Aron [*France*] [*Research code symbol*]
La .... Labial [*Dentistry*]
LA .... Labor Administration (SAUO)
LA .... Labor Arbitration Reports [*A publication*] (DLA)
LA .... Labor Area
LA .... Laboratory Analytical procedure (SAUO)
LA .... Laboratory Animals [*Medicine*] (EDAA)
LA .... Laboratory of Anthropology (SAUO)
La .... Laches [*of Plato*] [*Classical studies*] (OCD)
LA .... Lactalbumin [*Biochemistry*]
La .... Lactate [*Blood*] [*Medicine*] (EDAA)
LA .... Lactic Acid [*Biochemistry*]
LA .... Lactic Acidosis [*Medicine*] (MELL)
LA .... Lag Amplifier
LA .... Lag Angle (IAA)
LA .... LA Gear, Inc. [*NYSE symbol*] (CTT)
La .... Lagulanda (BJA)
LA .... Laira [*Plymouth*] [*British depot code*]
LA .... Lake Aircraft [*ICAO aircraft manufacturer identifier*] (ICAO)
LA .... Lama Foundation (EA)
LA .... Lambda Alpha
La .... Lambert [*Unit of luminance*] [*Preferred unit is lx, Lux*] (ADA)
La .... Lamellar Phase [*Physical chemistry*]
La .... Lamentations [*Old Testament book*] (BJA)
LA .... LAN Analyzer (SAUS)
LA .... Lancaster [*Postcode*] (ODBW)
LA .... Lancastrian [*Of the royal house of Lancaster*] [*British*] (ROG)
LA .... Lan Chile [*Airline flight code*] (ODBW)
LA .... Land Agent [*Ministry of Agriculture, Fisheries, and Food*] [*British*]
L/A .... Landing Account [*Shipping*]
LA .... Landscape Architect (ALAC)
LA .... Landshut [*Bayern*] [*German license plate city code*]
La .... Landulfus Acconzaioco [*Flourished, 13th century*] [*Authority cited in pre-1607 legal work*] (DSA)
LA .... Lane
La .... Lane's English Exchequer Reports [*1605-12*] [*A publication*] (DLA)
La .... Lanfrancus [*Deceased, 1089*] [*Authority cited in pre-1607 legal work*] (DSA)
La .... Lanfrancus Cremensis [*Deceased, 1229*] [*Authority cited in pre-1607 legal work*] (DSA)
LA .... Langley Alloys Limited (SAUO)
LA .... Language [*Online database field identifier*]
LA .... Language Age [*Score*]
LA .... Language Arts [*A publication*] (BRI)
LA .... Lanthanum (NAKS)
La .... Lanthanum [*Chemical element*]
LA .... Laos [*or Lao People's Democratic Republic*] [*ANSI two-letter standard code*] (CNC)
La .... Lapus de Castiglionchio [*Flourished, 1353-81*] [*Authority cited in pre-1607 legal work*] (DSA)
La .... Lapus Tatti [*Flourished, 14th century*] [*Authority cited in pre-1607 legal work*] (DSA)
LA .... Lard Association (BUAC)
LA .... Large Amount [*Medicine*]
LA .... Large Aperture [*Photography*] (ROG)
LA .... Laryngeal Atresia [*Medicine*] (MELL)
LA .... LASER Altimeter [*NASA*]
LA .... LASER Angioplasty [*Cardiology*] (DMAA)
LA .... LASER [*Gyro*] Axis (IEEE)
LA .... Last [*Wool weight*]
la .... Late (VRA)
LA .... Late Abortion [*Medicine*] (DMAA)
LA .... Late Antigen [*Biochemistry*] (DAVI)
LA .... Latex Agglutination [*Test*] [*Clinical chemistry*]
LA .... Latex Allergy (MELL)
LA .... Lathe [*Division in the county of Kent*] [*British*]
La .... Latin [*Linguistics*] (IEL)
LA .... Latin America
La .... Latvian [*Linguistics*] (IEL)
LA .... Launch Abort [*NASA*] (KSC)
LA .... Launch Aft
LA .... Launch Analyst [*Aerospace*] (AAG)
LA .... Launch Area [*NASA*] (KSC)
LA .... Launch Azimuth [*NASA*] (KSC)
LA .... Laureate in Arts
La .... Laurentius Hispanus [*Deceased, 1248*] [*Authority cited in pre-1607 legal work*] (DSA)
LA .... Lava [*Maps and charts*]
LA .... Lavatory (DSUE)
LA .... Lavochkin [*USSR aircraft type*] [*World War II*]
LA .... Law Agent
LA .... Law Association (SAUO)
LA .... Lawyers' Reports, Annotated [*A publication*] (DLA)
LA .... Lead Adapter [*Electric equipment*]
LA .... Lead Agent (COE)
LA .... Lead Amplifier
LA .... Lead Angle (MSA)
LA .... Leading Aircraftsman [*RAF*] [*British*]
LA .... Leading Article (ROG)
LA .... Leaf Abscission [*Botany*]
LA .... Learning Activity (ADA)
LA .... Leasehold Area (ADA)
L/A .... Leave Address (DNAB)
L/A .... Leave Advance [*Military*]
LA .... Lebanese Army (BUAC)
LA .... Lebensalter [*Chronological Age*] [*Psychology*]
LA .... Ledger Account (ROG)
LA .... Ledger Asset
LA .... Left Angle
LA .... Left Angulation [*Orthopedics*] (DAVI)
LA .... Left Arm [*Medicine*]
LA .... Left Ascension
LA .... Left Atrial [*or Avricular*] Appendage [*Cardiology*] (DAVI)
LA .... Left Atrium [*Anatomy*]
LA .... Left Auricle [*Anatomy*]
LA .... Left Axilla (KSC)
LA .... Leftist Alliance (Finland) [*Political party*] (PSAP)
LA .... Legal Adviser
LA .... Legal Advisor (SAUO)
LA .... Legal Asset [*Business term*]
LA .... Lege Artis [*According to the Art*] [*Pharmacy*]
LA .... Legislative Affairs
LA .... Legislative Assembly
LA .... Legislative Assistant [*US Congress*]
LA .... Legitimate Access [*British police term*]
LA .... Legum Allegoriae [*Philo*] (BJA)
LA .... LeMans America (EA)
LA .... Lemko Association [*Poland*] (BUAC)
LA .... Lemko Association of US and Canada (EA)
LA .... Lenticular Astigmatism (MELL)
LA .... Lesbian Activities (WDAA)
LA .... Leschetizky Association (EA)
LA .... Lethal Area [*Of indirect-fire weapon systems*] [*Military*]
LA .... Letter of Activation [*Military*]
L/A .... Letter of Authority (EBF)
LA .... Letter of Authorization (ALAC)
LA .... Letters Abroad (EA)
L/A .... Lettre d'Avis [*Letter of Advice*] [*French*]
LA .... Leucinamide (MELL)
LA .... Leucine Aminopeptidase [*Also, LP, LPAP*] [*An enzyme*]
LA .... Leukemia Antigen [*Immunochemistry*] (DAVI)
LA .... Leukoagglutinating [*Immunochemistry*]
LA .... Leukogglutination (DMAA)
LA .... Leuprolide Acetate (DMAA)
LA .... Levator Ani [*Anatomy*]
LA .... Level Absolute (SSD)
LA .... Level Alarm [*Engineering*]
LA .... Level Amplifier (IAA)
LA .... Levulinic Acid [*Organic chemistry*]
LA .... Liberal Arts
LA .... Liberator Atlanta [*An association*] (EA)
LA .... Libertarian Alliance [*British*] (EAIO)
LA .... Library Administrator (SAUO)
LA .... Library Association [*British*] (NITA)
LA .... Library Automation
LA .... Library of Art [*A publication*]
LA .... License Application (SAUO)
LA .... Licensing Act (DLA)
LA .... Licensing Assistant (NRCH)
LA .... Licensing Authority (DCTA)
LA .... Licentiate in Arts
LA .... Lichen Amyloidosis [*Dermatology*] (DAVI)
LA .... Lieutenant-at-Arms [*British*]
LA .... Light Ale (ADA)
LA .... Light Alloy
LA .... Light Armor [*Telecommunications*] (TEL)
LA .... Light Artillery
LA .... Lighter Association (EA)
LA .... Lighter-than-Air [*Aircraft*]
LA .... Lighter Than Air Airship (PIPO)
LA .... Lighting Association (SAUO)
LA .... Lightning Arrester
LA .... Lightwood-Albright [*Syndrome*] [*Nephrology*] (DAVI)
LA .... Limited Area
LA .... Limited Availability [*Tire design*]
LA .... Linea Aerea Nacional de Chile [*Chilean airline*] [*ICAO designator*] (OAG)
LA .... Linea Aspera (MELL)
LA .... Line Adapter [*Computer science*] (CMD)
LA .... Line Adaptor (NITA)
LA .... Linear Arithmetic [*Computer science*]
LA .... Linear Assembly

LA .... Line Art (ELAL)
LA .... Linguistic Area [*Linguistics*] (IEL)
LA .... Linguoaxial [*Dentistry*]
LA .... Link Address (IAA)
LA .... Link Allotter
LA .... Link Analysis
LA .... Link Aviation, Inc. (SAUO)
LA .... Linnaean Society
LA .... Linoleic Acid (AAMN)
LA .... Linolenic Acid (MELL)
LA .... Liquid Asset [*Business term*]
LA .... Listed Address [*Telecommunications*] (TEL)
LA .... Listing Agent [*Classified advertising*] (ADA)
la .... Listing Agent [*Real estate*] (REAL)
LA .... Literate in Arts
LA .... Lithuanian National Accreditation Bureau (SAUO)
LA .... Live Action (NTCM)
L/A .... Liver/Aorta [*Medicine*] (RAWO)
LA .... Liverpool Academy [*British*]
LA .... Living Allowance
L/A .... Lloyd's Agent
LA .... Load Address (IAA)
LA .... Load Adjuster (CET)
LA .... Load Allocation [*Environmental science*] (FFDE)
LA .... Loan Amount [*Dialog*] [*Searchable field*] [*Information service or system*] (NITA)
LA .... Lobuloalveolar [*Medicine*] (DAVI)
LA .... Local Address
LA .... Local Agent
LA .... Local Alarm (NRCH)
LA .... Local Anesthetic [*Medicine*]
LA .... Local Association (ODA)
LA .... Local Authority
LA .... Location Area (SAUO)
LA .... Lock Actuator (MCD)
LA .... Locomotor Ataxia [*Medicine*] (MELL)
LA .... Locus Allowed (ROG)
LA .... Lodging Allowance [*British military*] (DMA)
LA .... Log Analyzer (SAUO)
LA .... Log Analyzer Processor [*Computer science*]
LA .... Logarithmic Amplifier
LA .... Logical Address
LA .... Logical Area (ELAL)
LA .... Logistics Assistance (SAUO)
LA .... Loners of America [*An association*] (EA)
LA .... Long-Acting [*Pharmacy*]
LA .... Long-Arm [*Cast*] [*Orthopedics*] (DAVI)
LA .... Longitudinal Acoustic [*Spectroscopy*]
LA .... Look Ahead (IAA)
LA .... Look Angle (ACAE)
LA .... Loop Antenna (DEN)
LA .... Lord Advocate of Scotland (DLA)
LA .... Los Alamos Scientific Laboratory [*USAEC*] (MCD)
LA .... Los Angeles [*California*] [*Slang*]
LA .... Louisiana [*Postal code*] (AFM)
La .... Louisiana (BEE)
LA .... Louisiana & Arkansas (SAUO)
LA .... Louisiana & Arkansas Railway Co. [*AAR code*]
LA .... Louisiana Reports [*A publication*] (DLA)
LA .... Louisiana Supreme Court Reports [*A publication*] (DLA)
LA .... Louvain Association (SAUO)
LA .... Low Alcohol [*Trademark of Anheuser-Busch, Inc.*]
LA .... Low Altitude
LA .... Low Angle [*RADAR*] (DEN)
LA .... Low Anxiety (MAE)
LA .... Lower Arm
LA .... Ludwig's Angina [*Medicine*] (DAVI)
LA .... Lunula (MELL)
LA .... Lupus Anticoagulant [*Medicine*] (MELL)
LA .... Luscombe Association (EA)
LA .... Lyme Arthritis (MELL)
LA .... Lymphadenopathy [*Medicine*]
LA .... National Leukemia Association (SAUO)
La .... Old Latin Version (BJA)
LA .... Linear Accelerator [*Physics*] (ODA)
LA 2000 ..... Los Alamos 2000 Strategic Planning and Allocation (SAUO)
LAA .... Amphibious Assault Ship [*Military*]
LAA .... International Legal Aid Association (SAUO)
LAA .... Jamahiriya Libyan Arab Airlines [*ICAO designator*] (FAAC)
LAA .... Laboratory Animal Allergy (HEAS)
LAA .... Lamar [*Colorado*] [*Airport symbol*] (OAG)
LAA .... Lamar, CO [*Location identifier*] [*FAA*] (FAAL)
LAA .... Large Active Area [*Automotive energy systems*]
LAA .... Laser Association of America [*Later, LEMA*] (EA)
LAA .... LASER Attenuator Assembly
LAA .... Lateral Accelerometer Assembly (MCD)
LAA .... Latex Advisors Association (NTPA)
LAA .... Latin American Association (BUAC)
LAA .... Launch Area Antenna (MCD)
LAA .... Laundrette Association of Australia
LAA .... Lead Agency Attorney (EPAT)
LAA .... League of Advertising Agencies [*New York, NY*] (EA)
LAA .... Leather Apparel Association (EA)
LAA .... Left Atrial Abnormality [*Medicine*] (STED)
LAA .... Left Atrial Appendage [*Medicine*] (STED)
LAA .... Left Auricular Appendage [*Medicine*] (STED)
LAA .... Legal Assistance Association [*Medicine*] (EDAA)
LAA .... Leukemia-Associated Antigen [*Medicine*] (STED)
LAA .... Leukocyte Ascorbic Acid [*Clinical chemistry*] (AAMN)
LAA .... Library Association of Alberta [*Canada*] (BUAC)
LAA .... Library Association of Australia (BUAC)
LAA .... Libyan Arab Airlines (BUAC)
LAA .... Licentiate of the Central Association of Accountants (SAUO)
LAA .... Lieutenant-at-Arms [*British*] (DMA)
LAA .... Life Insurance Advertisers Association [*Later, LCA*] (EA)
LAA .... Light Antiaircraft [*Guns*]
LAA .... Light Army Aircraft
LAA .... Lighterage Assembly Area
LAA .... Limited Access Authorization [*Military*] (GFGA)
LAA .... Lipizzan Association of America (EA)
LAA .... Lithuanian Agriculture Academy (BUAC)
LAA .... Lithuanian Alliance of America (EA)
LAA .... Little America [*Antarctica*] [*Seismograph station code, US Geological Survey*] [*Closed*] (SEIS)
LAA .... Little Athletics Association [*Australia*]
LAA .... Live Assembly Area (MCD)
LAA .... Liverpool Academy of Arts [*England*]
LAA .... Local Administration Bill (Zambia) [*Political party*] (PSAP)
LAA .... Local Airport Advisory [*Aviation*] (FAAC)
LAA .... Locally Administered Address [*Computer science*] (CIST)
LAA .... Longest Available Agent (DINT)
LAA .... Los Angeles Airways, Inc.
LA A .... Louisiana Annual Reports [*A publication*] (DLA)
LA A .... Louisiana Courts of Appeal Reports [*A publication*] (DLA)
LAA .... Low-Altitude Attack
LAA .... Lymphoedema Association of Australia (SAUO)
LAAA .... Latin American Association of Archives [*See also ALA*] (EAIO)
LAAAAS ..... Latin American Association for Afro-Asian Studies [*Mexico*] (EAIO)
LAAAS .... Low-Altitude Airfield Attack System (MCD)
LAAB .... Landscape Architectural Accreditation Board (GAGS)
LAAB .... Light Armored Assault Battalion [*Marine Corps*]
LAABAM .... Latin American Association of Behavior Analysis and Modification [*Uruguay*] (EAIO)
LAABF .... Ladies' Auxiliary of the American Beekeeping Federation (EA)
LAABNMS... Latin American Association of Biological and Nuclear Medicine Societies [*Medicine*] (EDAA)
LAAC .... Library Association's Annual Conference [*British*]
LAAC .... Lord Chancellor's Legal Aid Advisory Committee [*British*] (DLA)
LAACC .... Light Antiaircraft Control Center (NATG)
LAACG .... Los Alamos Accelerator Code Group (SAUO)
LAACP .... Local Alcohol Abuse Control Program (SAUO)
LAACT .... Legislative Assembly of the Australian Capital Territory
LA Acts ...... State of Louisiana: Acts of the Legislature [*A publication*] (DLA)
LAAD .... Latin American Agribusiness Development Corp.
LAAD .... Los Angeles Aircraft Division [*Rockwell International*]
LAAD .... Low Altitude Air Defense (SAUO)
LAADBN ..... Low Altitude Air Defense Battalion [*Navy*] (ANA)
LAADIW ..... Latin American Association for the Development and Integration of Women [*See also ALADIM*] [*Chile*] (EAIO)
LA Admin Code... Louisiana Administrative Code [*A publication*] (DLA)
LA Admin Reg... Louisiana Administrative Register [*A publication*] (DLA)
LAADS .... Los Angeles Air Defense Sector [*ADC*]
LAADS .... Low Altitude Aircraft Detection System (SAUS)
LAADS .... Low-Altitude Air Defense [*or Delivery*] System
LAADS .... Low-Altitude Air Dropped Stores (MCD)
LAAEMCTS... Latin American Association of Environmental Mutagens, Carcinogens, and Teratogens Societies [*Mexico*] (EAIO)
LAAF .... Lawson Army Airfield [*Fort Benning, GA*] (MCD)
LAAF .... Libby Army Airfield
LAAF .... Libyan Arab Air Force (BUAC)
LAAFS .... Los Angeles Air Force Station
LAAG .... Latin American Anthropology Group (EA)
LAAG .... Light Anti-Aircraft Gun (SAUS)
LAAGOWRNAFE... Local Authority Associations Group of Work Related Non-Advanced Further Education (AIE)
LAAI .... Licentiate of the Institute of Administrative Accountants [*British*] (DBQ)
LAAIB .... Latin American Air Intelligence Brief (MCD)
LAAL .... Life After Assault League [*Association*] (EA)
LAAM .... L and L Motor Freight [*Common carrier symbol*]
LAAM .... Large-Animal Anesthesia Machine [*Instrumentation*]
LAAM .... Levo-alpha-Acetylmethadol [*Drug alternative to methadone*]
LAAM .... Light Antiaircraft Missile
LAAMBN .... Light Antiaircraft Missile Battalion (MUGU)
LAAME ...... Large Antenna Assembly & Measurement Experiment (SAUO)
LAAMM ..... London Association in Aid of Moravian Missions (SAUO)
LAAMS ...... Land Armaments Movement Model (SAUO)
LAAMSF ..... Latin American Association of Medical Schools and Faculties [*See also ALAFEM*] [*Ecuador*] (EAIO)
La An .... Lawyers' Reports, Annotated [*A publication*] (DLA)
LA & LR .... Livonia Avon & Lakeville Railroad (MHDB)
LA & M ..... Library Administration and Management
LAANG ...... Louisiana Air National Guard (MUSM)
LA Ann ..... Louisiana Annual Reports [*A publication*] (DLA)
LA Ann Reps... Louisiana Annual Reports [*A publication*] (DLA)
LA An R .... Louisiana Annual Reports [*A publication*] (DLA)
LA An Rep.. Louisiana Annual Reports [*A publication*] (DLA)
L A Ant ..... Latin America Antiquity [*A publication*]

LA Ant .... Latin American Antiquity [*A publication*] (BRI)
LAAO .... L-Amino Acid Oxidase [*An enzyme*]
LA/Ao .... Left Atria/Arotic [*Ratio*] [*Medicine*] (EDAA)
LAAO .... Los Alamos Area Office [*Energy Research and Development Administration*]
LAAO-ES&H... Los Alamos Area Office/Environment, Safety & Health Branch (SAUO)
LAAO-FOB... Los Alamos Area Office/Facilities Operations Branch (SAUO)
LAAO-PMB... Los Alamos Area Office/Project Management Branch (SAUO)
LA A (Orleans)... Louisiana Court of Appeals (Parish of Orleans) (DLA)
LAAP .... Language Arts Assessment Portfolio [*Test*] (TMMY)
LAAP .... Law Association for Asia and the Pacific [*Australia*]
LAAP .... Longhorn Army Ammunition Plant (MCD)
LAAP .... Louisiana Army Ammunition Plant (AABC)
LAAPD....... Los Angeles Air Procurement District
LAAPI........ Latin American Association of Pharmaceutical Industries [*See also ALIFAR*] (EAIO)
LA App ...... Louisiana Courts of Appeal Reports [*A publication*] (DLA)
LA App (Orleans)... Louisiana Court of Appeals (Parish of Orleans) (DLA)
LAAPS....... Laptop Automated Aid Positioning System [*Coast Guard*] [*Computer science*] (DOMA)
LAAPS....... Latin American Association of Physiological Sciences (SAUO)
LA/AR .... Left Atrium/Aortic Root [*Medicine*] (RAWO)
LAAR .... Liquid Air Accumulator Rocket
LAAR .... Low-Altitude Air Refuelling (SAUS)
LAARD ...... Long-Acting Antirheumatic Drug [*Medicine*] (STED)
LAA Regt ... Light Anti-Aircraft Regiment (SAUO)
LAARS....... LASER-Augmented Air-Rescue System (PDAA)
LAAS .... Latin American Association for Afro-Asian Studies (SAUO)
LAAS .... Light Armor Antitank System (MCD)
LAAS .... Lincolnshire Architectural and Archaeological Society (SAUO)
LAAS .... Local Area Augmentation System (HLLA)
LAAS .... London Amateur Aviation Society (SAUO)
LAAS .... Los Angeles Air Service, Inc.
LAAS .... Low Altitude Airfield Attack System (SAUO)
LAAS .... Low Altitude Airway Structure (LDOE)
LAAS .... Low-Altitude Alerting System
LAAS .... Low Altitude Alert System [*Aviation*] (PIPO)
LAASCA ..... Long-Range Antisubmarine Capability Aircraft
LAASH....... LITEF Analogue Air data System for Helicopters (SAUS)
LAASL....... Latin American Association for the Study of the Liver [*Mexico*] (EAIO)
LAASP....... Latin American Association for Social Psychology [*Formerly, Latin American Social Psychology Committee*] (EA)
LAAT......... Laser Augmented Airborne TOW (SAUS)
LAAT......... LASER-Augmented Airborne TOW Sight [*Army*] (MCD)
LAAT......... LASER-Augmented Airborne Track
LAAT......... Logistics Assessment and Assistance Team (MCD)
LAATC .... Latin American Association of Trading Companies [*Brazil*] (BUAC)
LAAUW...... Los Alamos Area United Way (SAUO)
LAAV......... Light Airborne ASW [*Antisubmarine Warfare*] Vehicle
LA Avgas... Los Alamos Aviation Gas Association (SAUO)
LAAW........ Legal Automated Army-Wide
LAAW........ Light Assault Antitank Weapon
LAAW........ Local Antiair Warfare (NVT)
LAAWC ...... Local Antiair Warfare Commander (NVT)
LAAWC ...... Local Anti-Air Warfare Co-ordinator (SAUS)
LAAWS ...... Legal Automation Army-Wide Systems
LAB .... CIE color space, Laboratory (SAUS)
Lab .... Labatt's California District Court Reports [*1857-58*] [*A publication*] (DLA)
LAB .... Label [*or Labelling*] (IAA)
LAB .... Lablab [*Papua New Guinea*] [*Airport symbol*] (OAG)
LAB .... Labmin Resources Ltd. [*Toronto Stock Exchange symbol*]
Lab .... Labor (MIST)
LAB .... Labor
LAB .... Labor Advisory Board [*New Deal*]
LAB .... Laboratories for Applied Biology Ltd. (WDAA)
Lab .... Laboratory (AL)
lab .... Laboratory (WDMC)
LAB .... Laboratory
LAB .... Laboratory Animals Bureau (BUAC)
LAB .... Laboratory Automation Based (VLIE)
LAB .... Laboratory for Applied Biophysics [*MIT*] (MCD)
LAB .... Labor Officer [*Foreign service*]
LAB .... Labour Party [*British*] [*Political party*]
Lab .... Labrador (NTIO)
LAB .... Labrador [*Canada*]
LAB .... Labrador Retriever [*Dog breed*]
LAB .... Labuan [*Island in Malaysia*] (ROG)
LAB .... Lactic Acid Bacteria [*Food microbiology*]
Lab .... Lambertus de Ramponibus [*Deceased, 1304*] [*Authority cited in pre-1607 legal work*] (DSA)
LAB .... Land Air Battle (ACAE)
LAB .... Language Assessment Battery (SAUO)
LAB .... Latin America Bureau [*British*] (EAIO)
LAB .... Latrobe, PA [*Amtrak rail station code*]
LAB .... Lead Acid Battery
LAB .... Leave Authorization Balance [*Air Force*] (AFM)
LAB .... Legal Advisory Board (TELE)
LAB .... Legal Aid Board (BUAC)
LAB .... Leisure Activities Blank [*Vocational guidance test*]
LAB .... Level of Aspiration Board [*Psychology*]
LAB .... Liber Antiquitatum Biblicarum. Pseudo-Philo (BJA)
LAB .... Library Association of Barbados (BUAC)
LAB .... Library of American Biography (SAUO)
LAB .... Licentiate of the Associated Board (SAUO)
LAB .... Licentiate of the Associated Board of Royal Schools of Music [*British*]
LAB .... Licquor Administration Board (SAUO)
LAB .... Light Assault Bridge [*Military program*] (INF)
LAB .... Light Attack Battalion (INF)
LAB .... Line Adapter Base (VLIE)
LAB .... Linear Alkylbenzene [*Organic chemistry*]
LAB .... Lithosphere-Asthenosphere Boundary [*Geology*]
LAB .... Live Animals Board [*IATA*] (DS)
LAB .... Lloyd Aereo Boliviano SA [*Lloyd Bolivian Air Line*]
LAB .... Local Area Broadcast (NVT)
LAB .... Logic Array Block (SAUS)
LAB .... Los Angeles Branch [*AEC*]
LAB .... Low-Altitude Bombing [*Military*]
LAB .... Nichols Institute [*AMEX symbol*] (COMM)
Lab .... Lightness, Red-Green Axis (A), Yellow-Blue Axis (B) [*Computing*] (ODA)
LAB .... Load Aboard Barge (ODA)
LABA .... Laboratory Animal Breeders Association (EA)
Lab AC .... Labour Appeal Cases [*India*] [*A publication*] (DLA)
LABAC....... Licentiate Member of the Association of Business and Administrative Computing [*British*] (DBQ)
LABAD....... Laboratory Based Automated Diagnosis [*Medicine*] (EDAA)
LABAN....... Lakas ng Bayan [*Peoples' Power Movement - Fight*] [*Philippines*] [*Political party*] (PPW)
Lab & Auto Bull... Labor and Automation Bulletin [*A publication*] (DLA)
LA Bar....... Louisiana Bar. Official Publication of the Louisiana State Bar Association [*A publication*] (DLA)
Lab Arb ..... Labor Arbitration Reports [*Bureau of National Affairs*] [*A publication*] (DLA)
Lab Arb & Disp Settl... Labor Arbitration and Dispute Settlements [*A publication*] (DLA)
Lab Arb Awards... Labor Arbitration Awards [*Commerce Clearing House*] [*A publication*] (DLA)
LaBarg ...... La Barge, Inc. [*Associated Press*] (SAG)
LABB .... Beauty Labs, Inc. [*NASDAQ symbol*] (COMM)
LABB .... Laboratory for Applied Biotelemetry and Biotechnology [*Texas A&M University at Galveston*] (RCD)
LABB .... Legal Abbreviations [*Database*]
LABBS....... Ladies Association of British Barbershop Singers (BUAC)
LABC .... Local Automatic Brightness Control (ACAE)
LABC .... Lymphadenosis Benigna Cutis [*Medicine*]
LabChile .... Laboratorio Chile SA [*Associated Press*] (SAG)
LABCOM .... Laboratory Command [*Adelphi, MD*] [*Army*] (RDA)
LABCOM .... US Army Laboratory Command (SAUS)
LAB-CO-OP... Labour and Co-Operative Party [*British*]
LabCp .... Laboratory Corp. of America Holdings [*Associated Press*] (SAG)
LABD .... Labored [*Telegraphy*] (PCTE)
LABE......... Lady Bea Trailers [*NCIC trailer make code*]
LABE......... Lava Beds National Monument
LABE......... Louisiana Association of Business Educators (EDAC)
LABECO .... Laboratory Equipment Corp. [*Auto industry supplier*]
Lab Econ.... Labour Economics [*A publication*] (JLIT)
LABEL .... Law Students Association for Buyers' Education in Labeling [*Student legal action organization*]
LABELS ..... Region 3 Mail Labels System (SAUS)
LABEX....... International Laboratory Apparatus and Material Exhibition (SAUO)
LABEX....... Laboratory Equipment Exhibition (TSPED)
LABF......... Latin American Banking Federation [*Bogota, Colombia*] (EA)
LABG .... Laboring [*Telegraphy*] (PCTE)
LABH .... Lab Holdings [*NASDAQ symbol*] (SG)
Lab His ..... Labour History [*A publication*]
LABI .... Louisiana Association of Business and Industry (EARSL)
LABIB........ LASER Bibliography (MCD)
LABIL........ Light Aircraft Binary Information Link
LABIM .... Licentiate, American Board of International Medicine (CMD)
Lab Ind...... Labour and Industry [*A publication*]
LabInd....... Labour Independent (SAUO)
LABIS........ Laboratory Information Systems (DNAB)
Lab J Aust... Laboratory Journal of Australasia [*A publication*]
LABK .... Lafayette American Bank & Trust [*NASDAQ symbol*] (SAG)
LABK .... Lafayette American Bk & Tr [*NASDAQ symbol*] (TTSB)
LABL......... Australian Co. Secretary's Business Law Manual [*A publication*]
LABL......... Multi-Color Corp. [*NASDAQ symbol*] (NQ)
Lab L Rep.. Labor Law Reporter [*Commerce Clearing House*] [*A publication*] (DLA)
LABMIS ..... Laboratories Management Information System
LABN .... Lake Ariel Bancorp [*NASDAQ symbol*] (SAG)
LABNET ..... Los Alamos National Laboratory Network (SAUO)
LABO .... Licentiate, American Board of Ophthalmology (CMD)
LabOne...... LabOne, Inc. [*Associated Press*] (SAG)
LABOOH..... Like a Bat Out of Hell [*Internet lingo*] (NETL)
Labor C ..... Labor Code [*A publication*] (DLA)
LABORDOC... International Labour Documentation [*International Labour Office*] [*Geneva, Switzerland*] [*Bibliographic database*]
LABORERS LOCAL 427 PAC... Heavy and General Construction Laborers Local Union [*Newark, NJ*] (PACS)
LABORF ..... La Teko Resources Ltd. [*NASDAQ symbol*] (COMM)
LABORINFO... Labour Information Database [*International Labour Office*] [*Information service or system*] (IID)
LABORSTAT... International Labor Organization, Bureau of Statistics Database (GFGA)
LABP .... Latin American Book Programs [*Defunct*]

LABP .... Lethal Aid for Bomber Penetration (MCD)
LABP .... Licentiate, American Board of Pediatrics (CMD)
LABPIE .... Low-Altitude Bombing Position Indicator Equipment [*Military*]
LABPR....... Local Advisory Board Procedural Regulation (Office of Rent Stabilization) [*Economic Stabilization Agency*] [*A publication*] (DLA)
LAB PROC... Laboratory Procedure [*Medicine*] (BABM)
Lab proc.... Laboratory Procedure [*Medicine*] (EDAA)
LabProg..... Labour Progressive (SAUO)
LABPROP... Laboratory Property Management System (SAUO)
LabPty....... Labour Party (SAUO)
LabPU....... Labour Party of Ukraine [*Political party*] (BUAC)
labr .... Laborer (GEAB)
LABR .... Laborer
LABR .... Licentiate, American Board of Radiology (CMD)
L Abr .... Lilly's Abridgment [*England*] [*A publication*] (DLA)
LABRAPS ... Laboratoire de Recherche en Administration et Politique Scolaires [*Canada*]
Lab Rel Guide (P-H)... Labor Relations Guide (Prentice-Hall, Inc.) [*A publication*] (DLA)
LABREV ..... Laboratoire de Recherche sur l'Emploi, la Repartition, et la Securite du Revenu [*University of Quebec at Montreal*] [*Research center*] (RCD)
LABROC..... Laboratory Rocket
LABRV....... Large Advanced Ballistic Re-entry Vehicle (SAUS)
LABS .... LabOne, Inc. [*NASDAQ symbol*] (SAG)
LABS .... Laboratories [*United States Postal Service last word addressing abbreviation*]
LABS .... Laboratory Admission Baseline Studies
Labs .... Laboratory classes (SAUS)
LABS .... Labors [*Telegraphy*] (PCTE)
LABS .... LASER Active Boresight System (PDAA)
LABS .... Learning about Basic Science [*Education program*]
LABS .... Linear Alkylbenzene Sulfonate (EDCT)
LABS .... Los Alamos Bright Source (SAUO)
LABS .... Low-Altitude Bombing System [*Air Force*]
LABSAP ..... Laboratoire des Sciences de l'Activite Physique [*Laval University*] [*Canada*] [*Research center*] (RCD)
LABS I/II .... Los Alamos Bright Source Laser Facility (SAUO)
LabSpc...... Laboratory Specialists of America, Inc. [*Associated Press*] (SAG)
LabSpec ..... Laboratory Specialists of America, Inc. [*Associated Press*] (SAG)
LABSTAT .... Labor Statistics [*Database*] [*Department of Labor*]
LABSTAT .... United States Bureau of Labor Statistics (SAUO)
LabStatBull... United States Bureau of Labor Statistics Bulletin (SAUO)
LABT......... Labtec, Inc. [*NASDAQ symbol*] (NASQ)
LAB TECH... Laboratory Technologies Corp. (PCM)
LABU .... Latin American Blind Union [*See also ULAC*] [*Uruguay*] (EAIO)
LA Bus ...... Los Alamos Bus System (SAUO)
LABUT....... Labor Utilization (MCD)
LABV .... Left Atrial Ball Valve [*Medicine*] (EDAA)
LAbV......... Vermilion Parish Library, Abbeville, LA [*Library symbol*] [*Library of Congress*] (LCLS)
LabVIEW.... Laboratory Virtual Instrument Engineering Workbench
LABVT....... Left Atrial Ball-Valve Thrombus [*Medicine*] (STED)
LABY .... Laboratory [*Telegraphy*] (PCTE)
LABZ......... Laboratory Specialists Amer [*NASDAQ symbol*] (TTSB)
LABZ......... Laboratory Specialists of America, Inc. [*NASDAQ symbol*] (SAG)
LABZW ...... Laboratory Specialists Wrrt [*NASDAQ symbol*] (TTSB)
LAC .... AB Bofors [*Sweden*] [*Research code symbol*]
LAC .... Fort Lewis, WA [*Location identifier*] [*FAA*] (FAAL)
LaC .... Labiocervical [*Dentistry*]
LAC .... Laboratory Accreditation Committee (SAUO)
LAC .... Laboratory Animals Centre (BUAC)
LAC .... Labour Appeal Cases [*India*] [*A publication*] (ILCA)
LAC .... Labour Arbitration Cases [*Canada Law Book, Inc.*] [*Information service or system*] [*A publication*] [*A publication*] (CRD)
Lac........... Laceration [*Medicine*] (AMHC)
LAC .... Laceration [*Medicine*]
Lac........... Lacerta [*Constellation*]
LAC .... Lac Minerals Ltd. (SAUO)
lac .... Lacquer (VRA)
LAC .... Lacquer (WDAA)
LAC .... La Crosse [*A bunyavirus*]
LAC .... Lactation (WDAA)
LAC .... Lactose [*Cardiology*] (DAVI)
LAC .... Lae-City [*Papua New Guinea*] [*Airport symbol*] (OAG)
LAC .... Landers [*California*] [*Seismograph station code, US Geological Survey*] (SEIS)
LAC .... Landscape Advisory Committee (BUAC)
LAC .... Language Across the Curriculum
LAC .... Large Acrocentric Chromosome [*Medicine*]
LAC .... Large Anechoic Chamber (ACAE)
LAC .... Large-Area-Counter [*Astronomy*] [*Instrumentation*]
LAC .... Large Area Counter on Ginga (SAUO)
LAC .... Large Area Coverage [*Marine science*] (OSRA)
LAC .... LASER Amplifier Chain
LAC .... Latin American Center (BUAC)
LAC .... Latvian Academy of Culture (BUAC)
LAC .... Launch Analyst's Console [*Aerospace*] (AAG)
LAC .... Launcher Assignment Console
LAC .... Law-abiding Citizen (BARN)
LAC .... Lead Angle Compensator (ACAE)
LAC .... Leading Aircraftsman [*RAF*] [*British*]
LAC .... League of Arab Countries (SAUO)
LAC .... Learning Assistance Center [*Stanford University*]
LAC .... Left Atrial Contraction [*Cardiology*] (DAVI)
LAC .... Legal Advice Centre (SAUO)
LAC .... Legal Advisory Committee [*of NYSE*]
LAC .... Legislative Action Conference (SAUO)
LAC .... Lemon Administrative Committee (EA)
LAC .... Less Active [*Telegraphy*] (PCTE)
LAC .... Liberal Academic Complex
LAC .... Liberated Areas Committee [*World War II*]
LAC .... Liberty Amendment Committee of the USA (EA)
LAC .... Library Advisory Council [*Department of Education and Science*] [*British*] (NITA)
LAC .... Library Assistants Certificate [*City and Guilds Institute*] [*British*] (NITA)
LAC .... Library Association of China (BUAC)
LAc .... Licensed Acupuncturist [*Medicine*]
LAC .... Licentiate of the Apothecaries' Company [*British*]
LAC .... Light Armored Car [*Police and security equipment*]
LAC .... Lights Advisory Committee [*General Council of British Shipping*] (DS)
LAC .... Limited Area Coverage [*Data*]
LAC .... Limiting Admissible Concentration
LAC .... Limits of Acceptable Change [*USDA Forest Service*]
LAC .... Limits to Acceptable Change [*Park tourism management*]
LAC .... Lindamood Auditory Conceptualization Test [*Psychology*] (DAVI)
LAC .... Linear Absorption Coefficient
LAC .... Linear Aeronautical Chart (BARN)
LAC .... Linear Amplitude-Continuous (PDAA)
LAC .... Linguoaxiocervical [*Dentistry*]
LAC .... Liposome-Antibody-Complement [*Immunochemistry*]
LAC .... Liquid Affinity Chromatography
LAC .... List of Assessed Contractors [*Military*] (RDA)
LAC .... Lithuanian American Community (EA)
LAC .... Lithuanian American Council
LAC .... Live Action Camera (WDMC)
LAC .... Livestock Advisory Committee (SAUO)
LAC .... Load Accumulator
LAC .... Local Advisory Council [*British labor*]
LAC .... Local Agency Check (AFM)
LAC .... Local Area Controller (SAUO)
LAC .... Local Area Coverage [*Meteorology*]
LAC .... Local Arrangements Committee [*National Court Reporters Association*]
LAC .... Local Authority Circular (HEAS)
LAC .... Lockheed Aircraft Corp. [*ICAO designator*] (FAAC)
LAC .... Logistics Area Coordinator (MCD)
LAC .... London Assembly Centre (SAUO)
LAC .... Long Arm Cast [*Medicine*] (MEDA)
LAC .... Longitudinal Aerodynamic Characteristics
LAC .... Long-Run Average Cost Curve [*Economics*]
LAC .... Loop Assignment Center (VLIE)
LA-C .... Los Alamos Conference (SAUO)
LAC .... Los Alamos County (SAUO)
LAC .... Los Angeles Chargers [*National Football League*] [*1960*] (NFLA)
LAC .... Lotus Authorized Consultants (SAUS)
LAC .... Louisiana Accelerator Center [*University of Louisiana at Lafayette*] (RCD)
LAC .... Low-Altitude Cruise (MCD)
LAC .... Low Amplitude Contraction [*Neurology*] (DAVI)
LAC .... Lunar Aeronautical Chart [*Air Force*]
LAC .... Lunar Atlas Chart [*Aerospace*] (SAA)
LAC .... Lung Adenocarcinoma Cell [*Medicine*] (STED)
LAC .... Lupus Anticoagulant [*Immunochemistry*]
LAC .... London Athletic Club (ODA)
LACA .... Ladies Apparel Contractors Association (EA)
LACA .... Latin America Coffee Agreement (BUAC)
LACA .... Latin American Coffee Agreement (SAUO)
LACA .... Life Agency Cashiers Association of the United States and Canada (EA)
LACA .... Local Authority Caterers Association (BUAC)
LACA .... London Association of Certified Accountants (SAUO)
LACA .... Low-Altitude Control Area
LACAC....... Latin American Civil Aviation Commission [*See also CLAC*] (EAIO)
lac & cont... Lacerations and Contusions [*Medicine*] (STED)
LACAP....... Latin American Cooperative Acquisitions Program [*or Project*]
LACAP....... Los Alamos Civil Air Patrol (SAUO)
LaCARP ..... Louisiana Community AIDS Research Program [*Tulane University Health Sciences*] (MHID)
LACAS....... LASER Applications in Close Air Support [*Air Force*]
LACas .... Latin American Casinos, Inc. [*Associated Press*] (SAG)
LACAS....... Lineas Aereas Costarricenses SA [*Costa Rica*] [*ICAO designator*] (FAAC)
LACAS....... Local Authority Catering Advisory Service (AIE)
LACAS....... Low Altitude Close Aircraft Support (SAUO)
LACAS....... Low-Altitude Close Air Support [*Military*]
LACASA ..... Latin American and Caribbean Solidarity Association (EA)
LACAT .... Legislative Alliance of Creative Arts Therapies [*Defunct*] (EA)
LACATA...... Laundry and Cleaners Allied Trades Association [*Later, TCATA*] (EA)
LACATE...... Low Atmospheric Composition and Temperature Experiment (SAUO)
LACATE...... Lower Atmosphere Composition and Temperature Experiment [*National Science Foundation*]
LACB .... Landing Aids Control Building [*NASA*] (NASA)
LACB .... Look Angles of Celestial Bodies (KSC)
LACBWR .... LaCrosse Boiling Water Reactor [*Also, LCBWR*]
LACC .... Latin American and Caribbean Center [*Florida International University*] [*Research center*] (RCD)
LACC .... Latin-American Council of Churches (BUAC)

LACC .... Lloyd's Aviation Claims Centre (AIA)
LACC .... Local Area Control Center (VLIE)
LACC .... Los Angeles City College [*California*]
l'ACCAB .... L'Association Canadienne des Centres d'Action Benevole (AC)
LACCB .... Latin American Confederation of Clinical Biochemistry [*Colombia*] (EAIO)
LACCD .... Los Angeles Community College District (ACAE)
LACCSM .... Latin American and Caribbean Council for Self-Management (EAIO)
LACD .... Left Apexcardiogram, Calibrated Displacement [*Medicine*] (RAWO)
LACD .... Limited-Amplitude, Controlled-Decay (PDAA)
LACDC .... Life Action Community Development Corp. of Middle Georgia (EARSL)
LACDE .... Local Authorities Confronting Disasters and Emergencies [*Emergency Management*] (EMA)
LACDL .... Louisiana Association of Criminal Defense Lawyers (SRA)
LACE .... Alpine Lace Brands [*NASDAQ symbol*] (SPSG)
LACE .... Landline Air defense Communications Encryption (SAUS)
LACE .... Language for ALGOL [*Algorithmic Language*] Compiler Extension [*Computer science*] (CSR)
LACE .... LASER Aerospace Communications Experiment
LACE .... Laser Communication Experiment (ACAE)
LACE .... Launch Angle Condition Evaluator
LACE .... Launch Automatic Checkout Equipment
LACE .... Library Advisory Council for England (NITA)
LACE .... [*The*] Lingerie and Corsetry Exhibition [*British*] (ITD)
LACE .... Linkage Assistance and Cooperation for the European Border Regions (BUAC)
LACE .... Liquid Air Collection Engine
LACE .... Liquid Air Cycle Engine [*Aerospace plane engine concept*]
LACE .... Local Automatic Circuit Exchange [*Telecommunications*]
LACE .... Low-Power Atmospheric Compensation Experiment [*Strategic Defense Initiative*]
LACE .... Low-power Atmospheric Compensation Experiment satellite (SAUS)
LACE .... Lunar Atmospheric Composition Experiment [*Apollo*] [*NASA*]
LACE .... Luton Analogue Computing Engine [*British*] (DEN)
LACE .... Lysergic Acid Cryptoethelane (IIA)
LACEF .... Los Alamos Critical Experiments Facility (SAUO)
LACES .... London Airport Cargo Electronic-Data-Processing Scheme
LACES .... Los Angeles Council for Engineering Societies (SAUO)
Lacey Dig ... Lacey's Digest of Railroad Decisions [*A publication*] (DLA)
LACF .... Low Acid Canned Food
LACFD .... Los Alamos County Fire Department (SAUO)
LACFFP ..... Latin-American Commission on Forestry and Forest Products (SAUO)
LACFFP ..... Latin-American Commission on Forestry and Forestry Products (BUAC)
Lach .... Laches [*of Plato*] [*Classical studies*] (OCD)
LACH .... Lightweight Amphibious Container Handler (MCD)
LACHESIS ... Laterally Archiving Containment, Health, Environment & Safety System (SAUO)
LACHEX ..... Los Alamos Chess Experiment (SAUO)
LACI .... Land Air Campaign Initiative (SAUO)
LACI .... Latin Amer Casinos [*NASDAQ symbol*] (TTSB)
LACI .... Latin American Casinos, Inc. [*NASDAQ symbol*] (SAG)
LACI .... Lipoprotein-Associated Coagulation Inhibitor [*Hematology*]
LACI .... Lockheed Aeromod Centers Inc. (SAUO)
LACI .... London Association of Conference Interpreters (SAUO)
LACIE .... Large Area Crop Inventory Experiment [*NASA*]
LACIM .... Latin American and Caribbean International Moving [*Panama*] (EAIO)
LACIP .... Large Area Crop Inventory Program [*NASA*] (NASA)
LACIR .... Laboratory for Automation, Communication, and Information Systems Research [*University of Victoria*] [*Canada*] (RCD)
LACIRS ...... Latin American Communications Information Retrieval System (SAUO)
LA Civ Code Ann (West) ... West's Louisiana Code of Civil Procedure, Annotated [*A publication*] (DLA)
LACIW .... Latin Amer Casinos Wrrt [*NASDAQ symbol*] (TTSB)
LACJ .... Los Angeles County Jail (SAUO)
L'ACJE ...... L'Association Canadienne pour les Jeunes Enfants (AC)
LACKA .... Lackawanna, NY [*American Association of Railroads railroad junction routing code*]
Lacka Leg News ... Lackawanna Legal News [*Pennsylvania*] [*A publication*] (DLA)
Lackawanna B ... Lackawanna Bar Reporter [*Pennsylvania*] [*A publication*] (DLA)
Lack Bar R ... Lackawanna Bar Reporter [*Pennsylvania*] [*A publication*] (DLA)
Lack Co (PA) ... Lackawanna County Reports [*Pennsylvania*] [*A publication*] (DLA)
Lack Leg N ... Lackawanna Legal News [*Pennsylvania*] [*A publication*] (DLA)
Lack Leg News (PA) ... Lackawanna Legal News [*Pennsylvania*] [*A publication*] (DLA)
Lack Leg R ... Lackawanna Legal Record [*Pennsylvania*] [*A publication*] (DLA)
Lack Leg Rec ... Lackawanna Legal Record [*Pennsylvania*] [*A publication*] (DLA)
Lack LN ..... Lackawanna Legal News [*Pennsylvania*] [*A publication*] (DLA)
Lack LR ..... Lackawanna Legal Record [*Pennsylvania*] [*A publication*] (DLA)
LACL .... Latin American Citizens League (SAUO)
LACLA .... Latin American Constitutional Law Association [*Argentina*] (EAIO)
LacledeSt ... Laclede Steel Co. [*Associated Press*] (SAG)
LaclGas ..... Laclede Gas Co. [*Associated Press*] (SAG)
LACM .... Latin America Common Market [*Proposed*]
LACM .... Latin American Common Market (SAUO)
LACM .... Load Accumulator with Magnitude (HGAA)
LACM .... Los Angeles County Museum (SAUO)
LACM .... Los Angeles County Museum of Natural History [*California*]
LACMA ...... Latin American and Caribbean Movers Association (EAIO)
LACMA ...... Los Angeles Conservatory of Music and Arts (SAUO)
LACMA ...... Los Angeles County Medical Association (SAUO)
LACMA ...... Los Angeles County Museum of Art
LACMedA ... Los Angeles County Medical Association (SAUO)
LACMN ...... Leading Aircrewman [*British military*] (DMA)
LACMNH/Q ... Quarterly. Los Angeles County Museum of Natural History. Los Angeles (SAUS)
lac-mRNA ... Ribonucleic Acid, Messenger - lac operon [*Biochemistry, genetics*]
Lac-mRNA ... Ribonucleic Acid, Messenger-Lac operon (SAUS)
LACN .... Local Area Communications Network (DMAA)
LACNSW .... Legal Aid Commission of New South Wales [*Australia*]
LACNT .... Legal Aid Commission of the Northern Territory [*Australia*]
LACO .... Erich Lacher Co.
LACO .... Lakes Gaming, Inc. [*NASDAQ symbol*] (NASQ)
LACO .... LASER Communication (SSD)
LACO .... Liberty American Corporation (SAUO)
LACO .... Los Angeles Chamber Orchestra (SAUO)
LACO .... Los Angeles College of Optometry [*California*]
LA Co Art Mus ... Los Angeles County Art Museum (SAUO)
LA Code Civ Pro Ann ... West's Louisiana Code of Civil Procedure, Annotated [*A publication*] (DLA)
LA Code Crim Pro Ann ... West's Louisiana Code of Criminal Procedure, Annotated [*A publication*] (DLA)
LAC of AMFC ... Library Affairs Committee of the Associated Mid-Florida Colleges [*Library network*]
LACOM ...... Low-Altitude Contour Matching (MCD)
LACONIQ .... Laboratory Computer Online Inquiry
LA Const Art ... Louisiana Constitution [*A publication*] (DLA)
LACOTS ..... Local Authorities' Coordinating Body on Training Standards [*British*]
LACP .... Large Area Coverage Processor (ACAE)
LACP .... Latin American Co-operative Acquisition Project (SAUO)
LACP .... Lignes Aeriennes Canadiennes Pacifiques
LA-CP .... Los Alamos Controlled Publication (SAUO)
LACPA .... Los Angeles County Purchasing Agent (ACAE)
LACQ .... Lacquer
LACQLD ..... Legal Aid Commission of Queensland [*Australia*]
Lacr .... Lacerta [*Constellation*]
lacr .... Lacrimal [*Ophthalmology*] (DAVI)
LACR .... La Crosse [*NCIC trailer make code*]
LACR .... Lancer Corp. (SAUO)
LACR .... Low-Altitude Coverage RADAR
LACRC .... Locally Assigned Convoy Route Carrier Code
LAC REC .... Lactis Recentis [*New Milk*] [*Pharmacy*] (ROG)
LaCrose ..... LaCrosse Footwear, Inc. [*Associated Press*] (SAG)
Lac RR Dig ... Lacey's Digest of Railroad Decisions [*A publication*] (DLA)
LACRS .... La Crosse, VA [*American Association of Railroads railroad junction routing code*]
LACS .... Laboratory Automated Calibration System (MCD)
LACS .... Large-Area Chemical Sensor (ABAC)
LACS .... League Against Cruel Sports (EA)
LACS .... Liberal Arts Career Services
LACS .... Listener Active State (IAA)
LACS .... Lithuanian-American Catholic Services [*Defunct*] (EA)
LACS .... Los Angeles Catalyst Study [*Environmental Protection Agency*]
LACS .... Los Angeles Copyright Society (EA)
LACSA .... Lineas Aereas Costarricenses Sociedad Anonima [*Airline*] [*Costa Rica*]
LACSAB ..... Local Authorities' Conditions of Service Advisory Board [*British*] (DCTA)
LACSD .... Los Angeles County Sanitation District (SAUO)
L'ACSQ ...... Association Canadienne des Cinq Quilles [*Formerly, Canadian Bowling Congress*] (AC)
LACST .... Lancaster, SC [*American Association of Railroads railroad junction routing code*]
lact .... Lactate [*or Lactating*] (AAMN)
lact .... Lactating [*Medicine*] (MAE)
LACT .... Lactic Acid [*Biochemistry*] (DAVI)
LAC T .... Lactose Tolerance [*Gastroenterology*] (DAVI)
LACT .... Lease Automatic Custody Transfer
LACT .... Legal Aid Commission of Tasmania [*Australia*]
LACT .... Library of Anglo-Catholic Theology [*A publication*] (ODCC)
LACT .... Lindamood Auditory Conceptualization Test [*Psychology*] (STED)
LACT .... London Association of Classical Teachers (SAUO)
LACT .... Los Angeles County Transportation Commission [*Federal Railroad Administration identification code*]
LACT .... Low-Affinity Choline Transport
LACT-ART ... Lactate Arterial (STED)
LACTC .... Los Angeles County Transportation Commission (ACAE)
lact hyd ..... Lactalbumin Hydrolysate (STED)
LACTOZ ..... Laboratory Studies of the Chemistry of Atmospheric Ozone (SAUO)
LACUNY .... Library Association of the City University of New York (EARSL)
LACUS ...... Linguistic Association of Canada and the United States (EA)
LACUSA .... Liberty Amendment Committee of the USA (EA)
LACUSA .... Lithuanian-American Community of the USA [*Later, LAC*] (EA)
LAC/USC .... Los Angeles County/University of Southern California Medical Center (DAVI)
LACV .... Light Amphibious Cargo Vehicle (MCD)
LACV .... Light Armored Combat Vehicle
LACV .... Lighter, Air-Cushion Vehicle [*Usually used in combination with numerals*] [*Military*] (RDA)
LACV-30 .... Lighter, Air Cushion Vehicle, 30 Tons [*Military*] (MCD)
LACW .... Leading Aircraft Woman [*RAF*] [*British*]
LACWA ...... Legal Aid Commission of Western Australia
LACX .... Goodyear Tire & Rubber [*Federal Railroad Administration identification code*]
LACY .... WE Lacey & Sons [*NCIC trailer make code*]
LACYMCA ... Latin American Confederation of YMCAs [*See also CLACJ*] (EAIO)

LACZ Los Angeles County Transportation Commission [*Federal Railroad Administration identification code*]
LAD Laboratory Astrophysics Division (SAUO)
LAD Lactate Dehydrogenase [*Also, LD, LDH*] [*An enzyme*]
LAD Lactic Acid Dehydrogenase [*See also LDH*] [*An enzyme*]
LAD Ladder (MSA)
lad Ladino [*MARC language code*] [*Library of Congress*] (LCCP)
LAD Ladron Mountain [*New Mexico*] [*Seismograph station code, US Geological Survey*] (SEIS)
LAD Landing Assist Device [*Aviation*] (NG)
LAD Language Acquisition Device
LAD Large Area Detector [*Instrumentation*]
LAD Large Area Display
LAD LASER Acoustic Delay
LAD LASER Acquisition and Direction
LAD LASER Acquisition Device (MCD)
LAD LASER Air Defense
LAD Last Appearance Datum [*Geology*]
LAD Last Appearance of Date (or Datum) (SAUO)
LAD Lateral Awareness and Directionality Test [*Sensorimotor skills test*]
LAD Latest Arrival Date (AABC)
LAD Launch Assist Device (SAUS)
LAD Leaf Area Duration [*Botany*]
LAD Least Absolute Deviation (IDAI)
LAD Lebanon Airport Development Corp. [*ICAO designator*] (FAAC)
LAD Left Anterior Descending [*Artery*]
LAD Left Anterior Digestive [*Gland*]
LAD Left Axis Deviation [*Medicine*]
LAD Leukocyte Adhesion Deficiency [*Medicine*]
LAD Liberation Army Daily (SAUS)
LAD Library Administration Division [*American Library Association*] [*Later, LAMA*] (EA)
LAD Ligament Augmentation Device [*Sports medicine*]
LAD Light Aid Detachment [*Military*] [*British*]
LAD Light Area Defense (MCD)
LAD Linoleic Acid Depression [*Clinical chemistry*] (AAMN)
LAD Lipoamide Dehydrogenase [*An enzyme*]
LAD Liquid Agent Detector (AABC)
LAD Lithia Motors'A' [*NYSE symbol*] (SG)
LAD Lithium Aluminum Deuteride [*Inorganic chemistry*]
L-AD Liver Alcohol Dehydrogenase [*Medicine*] (EDAA)
LAD Lloyd's Aviation Department (AIA)
LAD Load Address (IAA)
LAD Local Air Defence (SAUS)
LAD Local Area Disk (VLIE)
LAD Location Aid Device (MCD)
LAD Logical Analysis Device
LAD Logical Aptitude Device (BUR)
LAD Logic and Adder (IAA)
LAD Logistic Approval Data
LAD Logistics Anchor Desk [*Military*]
LAD Lookout Assist Device [*Navigation*] (OA)
LAD Low-Accuracy Data/Designation [*System*] (MUGU)
LAD Low Alcohol Drinking [*Rat strain*]
LAD Low Altitude Dispenser (SAUO)
LAD Low-Altitude Dispenser
LAD Low-Angle Dolly
LAD Luanda [*Angola*] [*Airport symbol*] (OAG)
LAD Lunar Atmosphere Detector [*Aerospace*]
LAD Lymphocyte-Activating Determinant (DAVI)
LAD Lymphocyte-Activating Determinate (STED)
LAD Our Lady of Angels College, Aston, PA [*OCLC symbol*] (OCLC)
LADA Laboratory Animal Dander Allergy (DAVI)
LADA Lada [*NCIC car make code*]
LADA Left Acromio-Dorso-Anterior [*A fetal position*] [*Obstetrics*]
LADA Left Anterior Descending Artery [*Anatomy*] (DAVI)
LADA Lesson Analysis Design Approach
LADA Light Air Defense Artillery [*Army*]
LADA London Air Defence Area [*British military*] (DMA)
LADA London Alley Dwelling Authority (SAUO)
LADAPT Lookup Dictionary Adaptor Program (IEEE)
LADAR LASER Detection and Ranging
LADAR LASER Doppler RADAR (MCD)
LADB Laboratory Animal Data Bank [*Battelle Memorial Institute*] [*Columbus, OH*] [*No longer available online*] [*Information service or system*] (IID)
LADB Latin American Data Bank [*University of Florida*] (IID)
LADB Latin American Data Base [*An association*] (EA)
LADB Lesotho Agricultural Development Bank (BUAC)
LADC LASER Advanced Development Center (IAA)
L'ADC L'Association Dentaire Canadienne (AC)
LADC Left Anterior Descending Coronary Artery [*Anatomy*]
LADC Local Area Data Channel [*Communications term*] (DCT)
LADC Los Alamos Document Center (SAUO)
LADCA Left Anterior Descending Coronary Artery [*Medicine*] (STED)
LADCP Lowered Acoustic Doppler Current Profiler (SAUS)
Ladd Ladd's Reports [*59-64 New Hampshire*] [*A publication*] (DLA)
LADD Left Anterior Descending Diagonal [*Branch of coronary artery*] [*Anatomy*] (DAVI)
LADD Lens Antenna Deployment Demonstration (ACAE)
LADD Low-Altitude Drogue Delivery (AFM)
LADD Lowest Acceptable Daily Dose (EPAT)
LADDER Language Access to Distributed Data with Error Recovery
LaddFr Ladd Furniture, Inc. [*Associated Press*] (SAG)
LADDR Layered Device Driver Architecture [*Microsoft Corp.*] [*Computer science*] (PCM)
LADDS Laundry and Decontamination Drycleaning System [*Military*] (DWSG)
LADE Language Definition Environment (SAUO)
LADE Lineas Aereas del Estada [*Argentine Air Force airline*]
La de Castigl Lapus de Castiglionchio [*Flourished, 1353-81*] [*Authority cited in pre-1607 legal work*] (DSA)
LADECO Linea Aerea del Cobre SA [*Chile*] (EY)
La de Rampo Lambertus de Ramponibus [*Deceased, 1304*] [*Authority cited in pre-1607 legal work*] (DSA)
LADF Ladd Furniture [*NASDAQ symbol*] (SAG)
LADF Ladd Furniture, Inc. (SAUO)
LADFU Large Area Detector Flight Unit (SAUS)
LADGA Layered Acrylic Directed Graph with Attributes (VLIE)
LADH Lactic Acid Dehydrogenase [*An enzyme*] (DAVI)
LADH Liver Alcohol Dehydrogenase [*An enzyme*]
LADIES Lapan Digital Image Evaluation System (SAUO)
LADIES Life after Divorce Is Eventually Sane (EA)
LADIES Los Alamos Digital Image Enhancement Software (PDAA)
LADIES Los Alamos Digital Image Enhancement System (SAUO)
LADIES Low-Altitude Air Defense Identification and Engagement Study
LADIR Low-Cost Arrays for Detection of Infrared (PDAA)
LADIZ Leaving Air Defense Identification Zone
LADLE Librarians Antidefamation League
LAD-LOMS Library Administration Division, Library Organization and Management Section [*American Library Association*] (AEBS)
LADM Laboratory Automated Data Management
LADME Liberation, Absorption, Distribution, Metabolism, and Excretion [*Medicine*] (STED)
LADME Liberation, Absorption, Distribution, Metabolism, Excretion [*Medicine*] (DAVI)
LAD-MIN Left Axis Deviation Minimal [*Cardiology*] (DAVI)
LADMIS Low Altitude Air Defense Missile (ACAE)
LADMS Lightweight Air Defense Missile System (SAUS)
LADO Latin American Defense Organization (SAUO)
LADO Latin American Development Organization (SAUO)
LADO Los Angeles District Office (SAUO)
LADOG Low-Altitude Drive on Ground (IAA)
Ladp Ladyship (BARN)
LADP Leadership Assessment and Development Program [*Army*] (INF)
LADP Left Acromio-Dorso-Posterior [*A fetal position*] [*Obstetrics*]
LADP Locally-Acting Drug Product [*Drug evalution*]
LA/DP Office of Development Programs, Bureau for Latin America (SAUO)
LADPOP Lethal Agent Disposal Process Optimization Program (MCD)
LADR Linear Accelerator-Driven Reactor (BARN)
LADRAP Lethal Area Data Reduction and Plotting (SAA)
LADS LASER Actuator Director System [*DoD*]
LADS LASER Airborne Depth Sounder
LADS LASER Air Defense System
LADS Light Air Defense System (SAUS)
LADS Light Area Defense System (MCD)
LADS Lightweight Actuator Detector Weapons System (SAUO)
LADS Lightweight Air Defense System (MCD)
LADS Limited Attack Defense System
LADS Linear Analysis and Design of Structure (IAA)
LADS Listener Addressed State (IAA)
LADS Literary and Debating Society (SAUO)
LADS Local Area Data Service [*Telecommunications*] (ACRL)
LADS Local Area Data Set
LADS Logic Automation Documentation System (VLIE)
LADS Low-Altitude Defense System (MCD)
LADS Low-Altitude Detection System [*Air Force*]
LADS Low-Altitude Dispensing System [*Missiles*]
LADSIRLAC Liverpool and District Scientific Industrial and Research Library Advisory Council [*Library cooperative scheme*] [*British*] (NITA)
LADSR Low Altitude Defense System Radar (ACAE)
LADT Local Access Data Transport (SAUO)
LADT Local Area Data Transport [*AT & T*]
LADT Local Area Digital Transmission (WGA)
LADT Low-Altitude Drop Test [*NASA*]
LADTAC Light Area Defense Technical Assistance Control (ACAE)
LADu Lobuloalveolar-Ductal (STED)
LADV Laboratoires d'Applications Dermatologiques de Vichy (EFIS)
L Adv Lord Advocate [*British*] (DAS)
L Advertiser Law Advertiser [*1823-31*] [*A publication*] (DLA)
LADWP Los Angeles Department of Water and Power (SAUO)
LADY Tennis Lady, Inc. (SAUO)
LadyLuck Lady Luck Gaming Corp. [*Associated Press*] (SAG)
Lady Snow Cocaine [*Medicine*] (EDAA)
LAE Lae [*Papua New Guinea*] [*Airport symbol*] (OAG)
LAE Lae [*Papua New Guinea*] [*Seismograph station code, US Geological Survey*] [*Closed*] (SEIS)
LAE La Grande, OR [*Amtrak Busline code*]
LAE Launcher Adapter Electronics (MCD)
LAE Lead Angle Error
LAE Leadership Ability Evaluation [*Psychology*]
LAE Left Arithmetic Element
LAE Left Atrial Enlargement [*Cardiology*]
LAE Lethal Area Estimate
LAE Linear Alcohol Ethoxylate [*Surfactant*]
LAE Lineas Aereas Colombianas Ltd. [*Colombia*] [*ICAO designator*] (FAAC)
LAE London Association of Engineers [*England*] (BUAC)

LAE .... Long Above-Elbow [*Cast*] (STED)
LAE .... "Love Is All" for Enge (EA)
LAE .... Low Altitude Extraction (SAUS)
LAEA .... LA Xpress Assembly and Distribution [*Common carrier symbol*]
LAEADA ..... Alabama. Agricultural Experiment Station. Leaflet (SAUS)
LAEC .... Los Angeles Electric Club (SAUO)
LAEC .... Los Angeles Electronic Club (SAUO)
LAEC .... Lotus Authorized Education Center (SAUO)
LAECC .... Groupe International Laicat et Communaute Chretienne [*International Laity and Christian Community Group - ILCCG*] [*Defunct*] (EA)
LAECG .... Local Aboriginal Education Consultative Group [*Australia*]
LAED .... Large Area Electronic Display
LAED .... Low Angle Electron Diffraction (PDAA)
LAEDP .... Large Area Electronic Display Panel
LAEDV .... Left Atrial End-Diastolic Volume [*Medicine*] (STED)
LAEDV .... Left Atrial Volume in End Diastole [*Medicine*] (DMAA)
LAEE .... Lithuanian Association for Energy Economics (BUAC)
LAEF .... Luso-American Education Foundation (EA)
LAEI .... Left Atrial Emptying Index [*Medicine*] (STED)
LAE NOTE ... Licensed Aircraft Engineers' Notice (DNAB)
LAEO .... Low-Altitude Electro-Optical (SAUS)
LAEP .... Large Area Electronic Panel
LAEPC .... Local Aboriginal Employment Promotion Committee [*Australia*]
LAER .... Largest Achievable Emissions Reduction (FOTI)
LAER .... Lowest Achievable Emission Rate [*Environmental Protection Agency*]
LAERF .... Lewisville Aquatic Ecosystem Research Facility [*Texas*]
LAEs .... Aircraft Engineers (SAUS)
LAES .... Latin American Economic System
LAESV .... Left Atrial End-Systolic Volume [*Medicine*] (STED)
LAET .... Limiting Actual Exposure Time (KSC)
LAETRILE ... Laevo-Mandelonitrile-beta-glucuronic Acid [*Possible anticancer compound*]
LAEU .... Launching Adapter Electronic Unit (ACAE)
LAEV .... Laevus [*Left*] [*Pharmacy*]
Laeve .... Left [*or Counterclockwise*] [*Prefix meaning*] [*Medicine*] (EDAA)
LAF .... AAUW Legal Advocacy Fund [*Association*] (EA)
LAF .... Lafarge Corp. [*NYSE symbol*] (SPSG)
LAF .... Lafarge North America [*Company symbol*]
LAF .... Lafayette [*Indiana*] [*Airport symbol*] (OAG)
LAF .... Lafayette [*Rhode Island*] [*Seismograph station code, US Geological Survey*] [*Closed*] (SEIS)
LAF .... Lafayette [*Diocesan abbreviation*] [*Louisiana*] (TOCD)
LAF .... Lafayette (automobile) [*NCIC car model code*]
LAF .... Lafayette College, Easton, PA [*OCLC symbol*] (OCLC)
LAF .... Lafayette, IN [*Location identifier*] [*FAA*] (FAAL)
LAF .... Lake Acidification and Fisheries (SAUO)
LAF .... Laminar Airflow (KSC)
LAF .... Land Acquisition Fund (SAUO)
LAF .... Landscape Architecture Foundation (EA)
Laf .... Lanfrancus [*Deceased, 1089*] [*Authority cited in pre-1607 legal work*] (DSA)
Laf .... Lanfrancus Cremensis [*Deceased, 1229*] [*Authority cited in pre-1607 legal work*] (DSA)
LAF .... Latin American Female [*Classified advertising*] (DMAA)
LAF .... Laugh [*Telegraphy*] (PCTE)
LAF .... Left Anterior Fascicle [*Anatomy*]
LAF .... Legal Aid Fund (SAUO)
LAF .... Legislative Action Fund [*Federal political committee terminology*] (PACS)
LAF .... Leukocyte-Activating Factor [*Immunochemistry*]
LAF .... Leukocyte-/Lymphocyte-Activating Factor [*Medicine*] (EDAA)
LAF .... Light Assault Ferry (SAUS)
LAF .... Limited Amplifier Filter
LAF .... Limits and Fits [*System*] [*Precision of tolerance*] [*Automotive engineering*]
LAF .... Live Aid Foundation (EA)
LAF .... Living Arts Foundation (EA)
LAF .... Load Alleviation Function (ACAE)
LAF .... Logistic Availability Factor (CAAL)
LAF .... Long Address Form (NITA)
LAF .... Low Animal Fat (STED)
LAF .... Low Frequency Active System (SAUS)
LAF .... Luteal Angiogenic Factor [*Biochemistry*]
LAF .... Lymphocyte Activating Factor [*Immunology*]
LAF .... Lyophilized Allantoic Fluid [*Endocrinology*]
Lafarge ...... Lafarge Corp. [*Associated Press*] (SAG)
LAFAY .... Lafayette, IN [*American Association of Railroads railroad junction routing code*]
Lafay .... Lafayette Industries, Inc. [*Associated Press*] (SAG)
LafayABk .... Lafayette American Bank & Trust [*Associated Press*] (SAG)
Lafaye .... Lafayette Industries, Inc. [*Associated Press*] (SAG)
LAFB .... Langley Air Force Base (MCD)
LAFB .... Left Anterior Fascicular Block [*Cardiology*]
LAFB .... Libyan Arab Foreign Bank
LAFB .... Light Assault Floating Bridge [*British military*] (DMA)
LAFB .... Lincoln Air Force Base (AAG)
LAFB .... Local Authority Fire Brigade [*British*]
LAFB .... Lockland Air Force Base (SAUO)
LAFB .... Lowry Air Force Base (SAA)
LAFB .... Luke Air Force Base (SAUO)
LAFC .... Latin-American Forestry Commission
LAFC .... Loan America Financial Corporation (SAUO)
LAFC .... Lynn Anderson Fan Club (EA)
LAFD .... Los Alamos Fire Department (SAUO)
LAFD .... Los Angeles Fire Department (SAUO)
LAFF .... Lafferty Banking, Insurance and Professional Services Intelligence [*Database*] [*United Kingdom*] (GDD)
LAFF .... Launcher Air Filtration Facility
LAFF .... Luso-American Fraternal Federation (EA)
LAFFX .... Lord Abbett: Affiliated Cl.A [*Mutual fund ticker symbol*] (SG)
LAFI .... Lafayette Industries, Inc. [*NASDAQ symbol*] (SAG)
Lafico .... Libyan Arab Foreign Investment (BUAC)
LAFIE .... Lafayette Industries [*NASDAQ symbol*] (TTSB)
LAFIS .... Local Authority Financial Information System (PDAA)
LAFIS .... Local Authority Financial Institution System (AIE)
LAFL .... Latin American Football League [*British*]
LAFM .... Limited-Area Fine Mesh
LAFM .... Los Alamos Fuel Model [*Department of Energy*] (GFGA)
LAFO .... Los Alamos Field Office (SAUO)
LAFO .... Los Angeles Foundation of Otology (SAUO)
LA FONT .... La Fontaine [*French author, 1621-1695*] (ROG)
LAFR .... American La France [*NCIC truck make code*]
LAFR .... Laminar Air Flow Room (STED)
LaFr .... Laminar Airflow Room [*Medicine*] (DAVI)
LAFS .... Los Angeles Funeral Society (SAUO)
LAFTA .... Latin American Association of Freight and Transport Agents [*Paraguay*] (EAIO)
LAFTA .... Latin American Free Trade Association (SAUO)
LAFTA .... Latin-American Free Trade Association [*Later, LAIA*]
LAFTC .... Latin American Federation of Thermalism and Climatism [*See also FLT*] [*Argentina*] (EAIO)
LAFTO .... Latin American Confederation of Tourist Organizations [*Argentina*] (EAIO)
LAFTS .... LASER and FLIR [*Forward-Looking Infrared*] Test Set [*Air Force*]
LAFTS .... Los Alamos Fourier Transform Spectrometer [*Department of Energy*] (GRD)
LAFU .... Ladies Amateur Fencing Union [*British*] (DBA)
LAFU .... Laminar Airflow Unit [*Medicine*] (DAVI)
LAFUC .... Los Alamos Fleet Users Committee (SAUO)
LAFUS .... Latvian Association of Foresters in the United States [*Defunct*] (EA)
LAFV .... Light Armoured Fighting Vehicle [*British military*] (DMA)
LAFWE .... Lafayette Industries Wrrt [*NASDAQ symbol*] (TTSB)
LAFY .... Lafayette (trucks) [*NCIC truck make code*]
LAFY .... Lafayette United (SAUO)
LAFZ .... Lathrop Facility [*Federal Railroad Administration identification code*]
LAG .... Aerovias de Lagos SA de CV [*Mexico*] [*ICAO designator*] (FAAC)
Lag .... Flask [*or Bottle*] [*Medicine*] (EDAA)
LaG .... Labiogingival [*Dentistry*]
Lag .... Lagena [*Flask*] [*Latin*]
LAG .... Lagging [*Engineering*]
LAG .... Lagonda [*NCIC car model code*]
LAG .... Lagoon [*Maps and charts*]
LAG .... Lagrange Road, IL [*Amtrak rail station code*]
LAG .... La Guaira [*Venzuela*] [*Airport symbol*] (AD)
LAG .... LaGuardia Community College Library [*UTLAS symbol*]
LAG .... Langila [*Cape Gloucester*] [*New Britain*] [*Seismograph station code, US Geological Survey*] (SEIS)
LAG .... Language [*Telegraphy*] (PCTE)
LAG .... LASER Absolute Gravimeter
LAG .... Laser Advisory Group (SAUO)
LAG .... Lastenausgleichsgesetz (BJA)
LAG .... Layton Art Gallery (SAUO)
LAG .... Legal Action Group [*British*] (DBA)
LAG .... Legislative Advisory Group (SAUO)
LAG .... Librarians Automation Group [*Australia*] (NITA)
LAG .... Liga Armada Gallega [*Armed Galician League*] [*Spain*] (PD)
LAG .... Line of Arrested Growth [*Biology*]
LAG .... Linguoaxiogingival [*Dentistry*]
LAG .... Listen Address Group (SAUO)
LAG .... [*A*] Literary Atlas and Gazetteer of the British Isles [*A publication*]
LAG .... Livermore Action Group [*Defunct*] (EA)
LAG .... Load and Go (NITA)
LAG .... Load and Go Assembler (BUR)
LAG .... Local Address Group (VLIE)
LAG .... Logical Address Group (SAUO)
LAG .... Logical Applications Group [*Social Security Administration*]
LAG .... London Amusement Guide
LAG .... Lympangiosium [*Medicine*]
LAG .... Lymphangiogram [*or Lymphangiography*]
LAGAP .... LASER-Guided Artillery Projectile (TIMI)
LAGB .... Linguistics Association of Great Britain
LAGB .... Linhas Aereas da Guine-Bissau [*Airline*] [*Guinea-Bissau*]
LAGD .... Louisiana Academy of General Dentistry (SAUO)
LAGE .... Los Angeles Grain Exchange (EA)
LA Gear ..... LA Gear, Inc. [*Associated Press*] (SAG)
LAGEO .... LASER Geodynamic Satellite [*NASA*] (PDAA)
LAGEOS ..... Laser Geodetic Satellite (SAUO)
LAGEOS ..... LASER Geodynamic Satellite [*NASA*]
LAGER .... Layout Generating Routine (VLIE)
LAGER .... Lesbian and Gay Employment Rights (BUAC)
LAGER .... Liberal Action Group for Electoral Reform [*British*] (DI)
LAGEX .... Lord Abbett: Global Equity Cl.A [*Mutual fund ticker symbol*] (SG)
LAGG .... Fighter [*Russian aircraft symbol*]
LAGG .... Langley Traffic Services [*Common carrier symbol*]
LAGIC .... Life and General Insurance Committee (SAUO)
LAGIC .... Louisiana Geographic Information Center (SAUO)
LaGIN .... Louisiana Government Information Network [*Louisiana State Library*] [*Baton Rouge*] [*Information service or system*] (IID)

LAGIX .... Lord Abbett: Global Income Cl.A [*Mutual fund ticker symbol*] (SG)
LAGLG .... Library Association Government Libraries Group (PDAA)
LAGMA .... Lawn and Garden Manufacturers Association [*Defunct*] (EA)
LAGN .... Lagoon [*Board on Geographic Names*]
LAGO .... Lagonda [*NCIC car make code*]
LAGO .... Light Atomic Gas Oil [*Petroleum product*]
Lagos HCR ... Lagos High Court Reports [*A publication*] (DLA)
Lagos R ..... Judgments in the Supreme Court, Lagos [*1884-92*] [*Nigeria*] [*A publication*] (DLA)
LAGR .... L.A. Gear, Inc. [*NASDAQ symbol*] (COMM)
LAGR .... Los Angeles Gear, Inc. (SAUO)
LAGRA ...... La Grange, IL [*American Association of Railroads railroad junction routing code*]
LaGrange C ... LaGrange College (GAGS)
LAGS .... LASER-Activated Geodetic Satellite [*AFCRL*]
LAGS .... Launch Abort Guide Simulation [*NASA*] (NASA)
LAGS .... Los Angeles Geographic Society (SAUO)
LAGU .... Lagusa [*NCIC truck make code*]
LAGUMS .... LASER-Guided Missile System (MCD)
LAGVX .... Lord Abbett: U.S. Govt. Secs. Cl.A [*Mutual fund ticker symbol*] (SG)
LAGWX ...... Lord Abbett: Developing Growth Cl.A [*Mutual fund ticker symbol*] (SG)
Lah .... Indian Law Reports, Lahore Series [*A publication*] (DLA)
Lah .... Indian Rulings, Lahore Series [*A publication*] (DLA)
LAH .... Labuha [*Indonesia*] [*Airport symbol*] (OAG)
LAH .... Lactalbumin Hydrolysate [*Biochemistry*] (MAE)
LAH .... LA Helicopter, Inc. [*ICAO designator*] (FAAC)
lah .... Lahnda [*MARC language code*] [*Library of Congress*] (LCCP)
LAH .... Lahore [*Pakistan*] [*Seismograph station code, US Geological Survey*] [*Closed*] (SEIS)
LAH .... Lahu [*Language symbol*] (ETLW)
LAH .... Latex Agglutination-Inhibition (DB)
LAH .... Launch Axis, Horizontal (MCD)
LAH .... Lebanon, NH [*Location identifier*] [*FAA*] (FAAL)
LAH .... Left Anterior Hemiblock [*Cardiology*]
LAH .... Left Atrial Hypertrophy [*Cardiology*]
LAH .... Licentiate of Apothecaries (SAUO)
LAH .... Licentiate of the Apothecaries' Hall [*Dublin*]
LAH .... Light-Armed Helicopter [*Military*] (PDAA)
LAH .... Lithium Aluminum Hydride [*Inorganic chemistry*]
LAH .... Logical Analyzer of Hypothesis (IEEE)
LA-H .... Los Alamos History (SAUO)
LAH .... Low-Altitude Hold [*Military*] (CAAL)
Lah .... Pakistan Law Reports, Lahore Series [*A publication*] (DLA)
LAH .... Pakistan Law Repos, Lahore Series (SAUS)
LAHA .... La Habra Products [*Common carrier symbol*]
LAHA .... Linear Array Hybrid Assembly (PDAA)
LAHAWS .... LASER Homing and Warning System [*Military*] (PDAA)
LAHB .... Left Anterior Hemiblock [*Medicine*] (STED)
LAHB .... Local Authorities Historic Buildings Act [*Town planning*] [*British*]
LAHBR ...... Los Angeles Harbor, CA [*American Association of Railroads railroad junction routing code*]
LAHC .... Los Angeles Harbor College (SAUO)
LAHC .... Los Angeles Harbor Commission (SAUO)
LAHC .... Low Affinity-High Capacity [*Medicine*] (DMAA)
Lah Cas ..... Lahore Cases [*India*] [*A publication*] (DLA)
LAHCG ...... Look Ahead Carry Generator [*Computer science*] (NITA)
LAHCP .... Los Alamos Health Care Plan (SAUO)
LAHD .... Los Angeles Harbor Department (SAUO)
LAHF .... Latin American Hospital Federation [*Mexico*] (EAIO)
Lahhs .... Large Hydrofoil Hybrid Ship
LAHIVE ...... Low-Altitude/High-Velocity Experiment
Lah LJ .... Lahore Law Journal [*India*] [*A publication*] (DLA)
Lah LT .... Lahore Law Times [*India*] [*A publication*] (DLA)
LAHM .... Limited Area HIBU [*Hydrological Institute and Belgrade University*] (USDC)
Lahore ...... All India Reporter, Lahore Series [*A publication*] (ILCA)
Lahore L Times ... Lahore Law Times [*India*] [*A publication*] (DLA)
LAHP .... L and H Trucking Company [*Common carrier symbol*]
LAHPERD ... Louisiana Association for Health, Physical Education, Recreation, and Dance (SRA)
LAHRC ...... Libyan Arab Human Rights Committee (BUAC)
LAHS .... Leicestershire Archaeological and Historical Society (SAUO)
LAHS .... Local Authority Health Services [*British*]
LAHS .... Los Alamos High School (SAUO)
LAHS .... Low-Altitude, High-Speed
LAHSO ...... Land and Hold Short Operation (SAUO)
LAHV .... Leukocyte-Associated Herpesvirus [*Medicine*] (STED)
LAHV .... Leukocyte-Associates Herpes Virus [*Medicine*] (DAVI)
LAHX .... Transportation Equipment [*Private rail car owner code*]
LAI .... LaBat-Anderson, Inc. (EFIS)
LAI .... Labioincisal [*Dentistry*]
LAI .... Laboratory Audit Inspection [*Environmental Protection Agency*] (EPAT)
LAI .... Lact-Aid International [*Commercial firm*] (EA)
LAI .... Lamb Associates Incorporated (SAUO)
LAI .... LAN [*Linked Access Network*] Automatic Inventory [*Brightwork Development, Inc.*] [*Computer science*] (PCM)
LAI .... Lannion [*France*] [*Airport symbol*] (OAG)
LAI .... Lasir Gold, Inc. [*Vancouver Stock Exchange symbol*]
LAI .... Latex Agglutination-Inhibition (PDAA)
LAI .... Latin American Institute [*University of New Mexico*] [*Research center*] (RCD)
LAI .... Leaf Area Index [*Forestry*]
LAI .... Lean Aerospace Initiative [*Massachusetts Institute of Technology*] (RCD)
LAI .... Lean Aircraft Initiative (SAUS)
LAI .... Left Atrial Involvement [*Medicine*] (STED)
LAI .... Lesotho Airways Corp. [*ICAO designator*] (FAAC)
LAI .... Lesson Administrative Instructions [*Military*]
LAI .... Leukocyte Adherence Inhibition [*Immunochemistry*]
LAI .... Library Association of Ireland (EAIO)
LAI .... Life Adjustment Inventory [*Psychology*]
LAI .... Light Armored Infantry [*Marine Corps*] (DOMA)
L-A-I .... Linkage, Ability, Interest [*Fundraising term*] (NFD)
LAI .... Load Address Immediate (BUR)
LAI .... Loaded Applicator Impedance
LAI .... Location-Activity Inventory (DB)
LAI .... Location Area Identification
LAI .... Love Attitudes Inventory [*Premarital relations test*] [*Psychology*]
LAI .... Low Airspeed Indicator
LAI .... Low-Altitude Indicator
LAIA .... Latin American Industrialists Association [*Uruguay*] (EAIO)
LAIA .... Latin American Integration Association [*Formerly, LAFTA*] [*See also ALADI*] [*Uruguay*] (EAIO)
LAIC .... Latin America Information Centre (BUAC)
LAIC .... Lesbian Archive and Information Centre (BUAC)
LAIC .... Lithuanian-American Information Center [*Defunct*]
LA-ICP-MS ... LASER Ablation-Inductively Coupled Plasma-Mass Spectrometry [*Analytical chemistry*]
LAICS .... Los Alamos Integrated Communications System (SAUO)
LAID .... Left Anterior Internal Diameter [*Medicine*] (RAWO)
LaidlwA ..... Laidlaw, Inc. [*Associated Press*] (SAG)
LaidlwB ..... Laidlaw, Inc. [*Associated Press*] (SAG)
LAIEC .... Latin American Institute of Educational Communication [*Mexico*] (EAIO)
LAIF .... Leukocyte Adherence Inhibition Factor (DAVI)
LAIFS .... Los Angeles International Fern Society (EA)
LAIG .... LA Industrial Group (NITA)
LAIG .... Library Association Industrial Group (BUAC)
LAII .... Land-Atmosphere-Ice-Interactions (SAUO)
LAIICS ...... Latin American Institute for Information and Computer Sciences [*Chile*] (PDAA)
LAILA .... Latin American Indian Literatures Association (EA)
LAIMP .... Lunar-Anchored Interplanetary Monitoring Platform [*Aerospace*] (MCD)
LAINS .... Low-Altitude Inertial Navigation System [*Air Force*]
LAIR .... Laser & Atomic Research & Development (SAUS)
LAIR .... Letterman Army Institute of Research [*San Francisco, CA*]
LAIR .... Liquid Air (NASA)
LAIRS .... Labor Agreement Information Retrieval System [*Office of Management and Budget*]
LAIRS .... Land-Air Integrated Reduction System (MUGU)
LAIRS .... Laser Imaging and Ranging System (ACAE)
LAIRS .... Light Aircraft Reconnaissance System (SAUS)
LAIRS .... Lightweight Advanced Inertial Reference Sphere
LAIRTS ...... Large Aperture Infrared Telescope System
LAIS .... Advanced Interventional Systems (SAUS)
LAIS .... Labor Arbitration Information System [*LRP Publications*] [*Information service or system*] (CRD)
LAIS .... Labyrinth Air Induction Silencer [*Automotive engineering*]
LAIS .... Labyrinth Air Induction System [*Automotive engineering*]
LAIS .... Leiter Adult Intelligence Scale [*Intelligence test*] [*Psychology*]
LAIS .... Library Acquisitions Information System
LAIS .... Lithium Aluminium Iron Sulphide (SAUS)
LAIS .... Loan Accounting Information System [*Agency for International Development*]
LAIS .... Local Automatic Intercept System (VLIE)
LAIS .... Logistics Attrition Information System (SAUO)
LAISDSS .... Latin American Institute of Social Doctrine and Social Studies [*Chile*] (EAIO)
LAISPS ...... Los Angeles Institute and Society for Psychoanalytic Studies (SAUO)
LAIT .... Laboratory for Advanced Information Technology [*University of Maryland, Baltimore County*] (RCD)
LAIT .... Langdon Adult Intelligence Test (TES)
LAIT .... Latex Agglutination Inhibition Test [*for pregnancy*] [*Medicine*]
LAIT .... Library Association Information Technology Group [*British*] (NITA)
LAIT .... Logistics Assistance and Instruction Team [*Military*] (AABC)
LAITG .... Library Association Information Technology Group (AIE)
LAITS .... Latin American Institute for Transnational Studies (EA)
LAIU .... Launch Abort Interface Unit [*NASA*] (MCD)
LAIV .... Loss Adjusters Institute of Victoria (SAUO)
LAIWS .... Land-Air White Sands (MUGU)
LAIX .... LAI Worldwide, Inc. [*NASDAQ symbol*] (NASQ)
LAJ .... British Mediterranean Airways Ltd. [*FAA designator*] (FAAC)
LAJ .... Lajes [*Brazil*] [*Airport symbol*] (OAG)
LAJ .... La Junta, CO [*Amtrak rail station code*]
LAJ .... London Airtours Ltd. [*British*] [*ICAO designator*] (FAAC)
LAJ .... Los Angeles Junction Railway Co. [*AAR code*]
LAJC .... Latin American Jewish Congress (BUAC)
LAJC .... London Agreement Joint Committee (SAUO)
LAJD .... La Jolla Diagnostics [*NASDAQ symbol*]
LaJollPh .... La Jolla Pharmaceutical [*Associated Press*] (SAG)
LaJolP .... La Jolla Pharmaceutical [*Associated Press*] (SAG)
LAJPEL ...... Latin American Journal of Politics, Economics, and Law [*A publication*] (DLA)
LAK .... Aklavik [*Canada*] [*Airport symbol*] (OAG)
LAK .... Lakeland, FL [*Amtrak rail station code*]
LAK .... Laker Resources [*Vancouver Stock Exchange symbol*]

LAK .... Lennox Airways [*Kenya*] [*ICAO designator*] (FAAC)
LAK .... Leukocyte-Activated Killer [*Cells*] [*Oncology*] (DAVI)
LAK .... Lightweight Antenna Kit
LAK .... Lymphokine-Activated Killer [*Cells*] [*Immunotherapy*]
LAKAS-NCUD ... People's Power-National Union of Christian Democrats (Philippines) [*Political party*] (PSAP)
LAKBC .... Los Angeles Kings Booster Club (EA)
LAKE .... Clean Lakes Database (SAUO)
LAKE .... Lake [*Commonly used*] (OPSA)
LAKE .... Lakeland Indus [*NASDAQ symbol*] (TTSB)
LAKE .... Lakeland Industries, Inc. [*NASDAQ symbol*] (SAG)
LAKE .... Lakeside Industries [*NCIC trailer make code*]
LakeAriel ... Lake Ariel Bancorp [*Associated Press*] (SAG)
LakehdP .... Lakehead Pipe Line Partners Ltd. [*Associated Press*] (SAG)
Lake-ICE .... Lake-Induced Convection Experiment (SAUO)
Lakelnd ..... Lakeland Industries, Inc. [*Associated Press*] (SAG)
LAKEL .... Lakeland, MI [*American Association of Railroads railroad junction routing code*]
LAKES .... Lakes [*Commonly used*] (OPSA)
Lakes Lett ... Lakes Letter [*A publication*] (PABS)
LakevwF .... Lakeview Financial Corp. [*Associated Press*] (SAG)
LAKFC .... Los Angeles Kings Fan Club (EA)
LAKL .... Lakeland Camper [*NCIC trailer make code*]
LakldFt ...... Lakeland First Fianancial Group, Inc. [*Associated Press*] (SAG)
LAKU .... Ceylon Shipping [*Intermodal shipping container symbol*] (TVRC)
Lal .... Labioincisal [*Medicine*] (EDAA)
LaL .... Labiolingual [*Dentistry*]
LAL .... Labrador Airways Ltd. [*Canada*] [*ICAO designator*] (FAAC)
LAL .... Lakeland [*Florida*] [*Airport symbol*] (AD)
LAL .... Lakeland, FL [*Location identifier*] [*FAA*] (FAAL)
LAL .... Lana Gold Corp. [*Vancouver Stock Exchange symbol*]
LAL .... Landcare Australia Limited (SAUO)
LAL .... Langley Aeronautical Laboratory [*NASA*]
LAL .... Launch and Leave [*Military*] (MUSM)
LAL .... Left Axillary Line [*Medicine*] (DMAA)
LAL .... Light-Adjusting Lens [*Medicine*] (EDAA)
LAL .... Limulus Amebocyte Lysate [*Medicine*]
LAL .... Livonia, Avon & Lakeville Railroad Corp. [*AAR code*]
LAL .... Local Adjunct Language (PDAA)
LAL .... Los Almos Laboratory (SAUO)
LAL .... Loudspeaker Acoustical Labyrinth
LAL .... Low Air Loss
LAL .... Lower Acceptance Level
LAL .... Lysinoalanine [*An amino acid*]
LAL .... Lysosomal Acid Lipase [*Medicine*] (EDAA)
L-Ala .... L-Alanine [*Biochemistry*] (DAVI)
LALA .... Large Amplitude Late Arrival [*Seismology*]
LALA .... Linoletic Acid-Like Activity (PDAA)
LA(L)A .... Local Authorities (Land) Act [*Town planning*] [*British*]
LALA .... Low-Altitude Alert [*Air traffic control*]
LaLand ...... Louisiana Land & Exploration Co. [*Associated Press*] (SAG)
LALD .... Low-Angle Low-Drag
L Alem ...... Law of the Alemanni [*A publication*] (DLA)
LALF .... Light Aviation & Land Forces (SAUO)
LALI .... Labiolingual [*Dentistry*]
LALI .... Latin American-Caribbean Labor Institute (EA)
LALI .... Lymphocyte Antibody-Lymphocytolytic Interaction [*Medicine*] (DMAA)
La Ligue .... Ligue nationale contre le cancer (SAUO)
LA line ...... Left Atrial Line [*Medicine*] (BCRP)
LALIS .... Luso-American Life Insurance Society
LA LJ .... Louisiana Law Journal [*New Orleans*] [*A publication*] (DLA)
LALL .... LaSalle [*NCIC car make code*]
LALL .... Longest Allowed Lobe Length (SAUO)
LALLL .... Low-Altitude Low-Light Level
LALLS .... Low-Angle LASER Light Scattering
LALM .... Limulus Amebocyte Lysate Method
LALO .... Low-Altitude Observation
LALOC ...... Laser Locator (ACAE)
Lalor .... Lalor's Supplement to Hill and Denio's New York Reports [*A publication*] (DLA)
Lalor Pol Econ ... Lalor's Cyclopaedia of Political Science, Political Economy, Etc. [*A publication*] (DLA)
Lalor's Supp ... Lalor's Supplement to Hill and Denio's New York Reports [*A publication*] (DLA)
Lalor's Supp (Hill and Denio) ... Lalor's Supplement to Hill and Denio's New York Reports [*A publication*] (DLA)
Lalor Supp ... Lalor's Supplement to Hill and Denio's New York Reports [*A publication*] (DLA)
LALP .... Longest Activity from Longest Project
LALP .... Los Alamos Laboratory Publication (SAUO)
LALR .... Latin American Literary Review. Carnegie-Mellon University, Department of Modern Languages. Pittsburgh (SAUO)
LALR .... Lookahead Left to Right [*Computer science*]
LALR .... Rapides Parish Library, Alexandria (SAUS)
LAIR .... Rapides Parish Library, Alexandria, LA [*Library symbol*] [*Library of Congress*] (LCLS)
Lal RP ...... Lalor's Law of Real Property [*A publication*] (DLA)
LALS .... LaGuardia Automated Library System [*LaGuardia Community College*] [*Information service or system*] (IID)
LALS .... LASER Alarm Locator System
LALS .... Linkless Ammunition Loading System (MCD)
LALSD ...... Language for Automated Logic and System Design [*Computer science*] (CSR)
LALU .... Overseas Containers Bahamas [*Intermodal shipping container symbol*] (TVRC)
LALUC .... Local Authority Land Use Classification (PDAA)
LALV .... Lucerne Australian Latent Virus [*Plant pathology*]
L'AM .... L'Alliance Monarchiste (EA)
Lam .... Lamarck [*Biology*] (BARN)
lam .... Lamba [*MARC language code*] [*Library of Congress*] (LCCP)
Lam .... Lambert [*Unit of luminance*] [*Preferred unit is lx, Lux*]
Lam .... Lambertus de Ramponibus [*Deceased, 1304*] [*Authority cited in pre-1607 legal work*] (DSA)
Lam .... Lamentations [*Old Testament book*]
LAM .... Lamina [*Medicine*] (DAVI)
Lam .... Lamina (STED)
LAM .... Laminate (MSA)
LAM .... Laminated (MIST)
lam .... Laminated (WDMC)
Lam .... Laminectomy [*Medicine*] (AMHC)
LAM .... Laminectomy [*Medicine*]
lam .... Laminogram (MAE)
LAM .... Land Attack Mode [*Navy*] (CAAL)
LAM .... Laramide Resources Ltd. [*Vancouver Stock Exchange symbol*]
LAM .... LASER [*Light Amplification by Stimulated Emission of Radiation*] Aiming Module
LAM .... L-Asparaginase and Methotrexate [*Antineoplastic drug regimen*] (DAVI)
LAM .... Late Ambulatory Monitoring [*Medicine*]
LAM .... Latin America Inv Fd [*NYSE symbol*] (TTSB)
LAM .... Latin America Mission (EA)
LAM .... Latin American Investment Fund [*NYSE symbol*] (SPSG)
LAM .... Latin American Male (DAVI)
LAM .... Latin American Mission [*Air Force*]
LAM .... Leading Air Mechanic [*British military*] (DMA)
LAM .... Learner-Approved Motorcycle
LAM .... Left Anterior Measurement [*Medicine*] (STED)
LAM .... Left Artial Myxoma [*Cardiology*] (DAVI)
LAM .... Left Atrial Myxoma [*Medicine*] (STED)
LAM .... Levator Ani Muscle (MELL)
LAM .... Liberal Alliance of Montenegro (BUAC)
LAM .... Liberalium Artium Magister [*Master of the Liberal Arts*]
LAM .... Library Association of Malaysia (BUAC)
LAM .... Life Action Ministries (EA)
LAM .... Light-Absorbing Molecules
LAM .... Lightweight Analog Motor (MCD)
LAM .... Limited Area Model [*Marine science*] (OSRA)
LAM .... Limpet Assembly Modular [*Navy*] (CAAL)
LAM .... Linhas Aereas de Mocambique [*Mozambique*] [*ICAO designator*] (FAAC)
LAM .... Lipoarabinomannan [*Biochemistry*]
LAM .... Liquid Apogee Motor (ACAE)
LAM .... Lithuanian Academy of Music (BUAC)
LAM .... Load Acceptance Module
LAM .... Load Accumulator with Magnitude
LAM .... Lobe Attachment Module [*Computer science*]
LAM .... Lobe Attachment Unit [*Computer science*] (ACRL)
LAM .... Local Area Missile (ACAE)
LAM .... Logical Acknowledgement Message [*Aviation*] (DA)
LAM .... London Academy of Music
LAM .... Long Aerial Mine [*Military*]
LAM .... Longitudinal Acoustic [*or Acoustical*] Mode [*Spectroscopy*]
LAM .... Look at Me (IAA)
LAM .... Loop Access Module (TIMI)
LAM .... Loop Adder and Multiplier (NITA)
LAM .... Loop Addition and Modification [*Computer science*]
LAM .... Los Alamos [*New Mexico*] [*Airport symbol*] (OAG)
LAM .... Los Alamos Airport (SAUO)
LA-M .... Los Alamos Manual (SAUO)
LAM .... Los Alamos, NM [*Location identifier*] [*FAA*] (FAAL)
LAM .... Louisiana Motor Freight Bureau [*STAC*]
LAM .... Lousiana Maneuvers [*Military*]
LAM .... Low-Altitude Missile (MCD)
LAM .... Low-Attack Mode (MCD)
LAM .... Lunar Excursion Module (ACAE)
LAM .... Lymphangioleiomyomatosis [*Medicine*]
LAM .... Master of Liberal Arts
LAMA .... Laboratory Animal Management Association (EA)
LAMA .... Laminin A (DMAA)
LAMA .... Large Array for Millimeter Astronomy
LAMA .... Laser-Assisted Microanastomosis [*Medicine*] (MELL)
LAMA .... Latin American Manufacturers Association [*Washington, DC*] (EA)
LAMA .... Lead Air Materiel Area [*Air Force*]
LAMA .... Legal Assistant Management Association (EA)
LAMA .... Library Administration and Management Association (EA)
LAMA .... Light Aircraft Manufacturers' Association (EA)
LAMA .... Livestock Auction Markets Association (EA)
LAMA .... Local Authority Members Association [*Ireland*] (BUAC)
LAMA .... Local Automatic Message Accounting [*Telecommunications*] (TEL)
LAMA .... Locomotive and Allied Manufacturers' Association [*British*] (BI)
LAMA .... Los Angeles Maintainability Association (SAUO)
LAMA BES ... LAMA [*Library Administration and Management Association*] Buildings and Equipment Section
LAMACHA ... Louisiana-Alabama-Mississippi Automated Clearing House Association
LAMA FRFDS ... LAMA [*Library Administration and Management Association*] Fund Raising and Financial Development Section
LAMAHRS ... Human Resources Section

LAMA LOMS.. LAMA [*Library Administration and Management Association*] Library Organization and Management Section
LaMan....... LaMan Corp. [*Associated Press*] (SAG)
lam & fus... Laminectomy and Fusion [*Medicine*] (DAVI)
LAMA PAS... LAMA [*Library Administration and Management Association*] Personnel Administration Section
LAMA PRS.. LAMA [*Library Administration and Management Association*] Public Relations Section
LAMAR...... Lamar, MO [*American Association of Railroads railroad junction routing code*]
Lamar....... Lamar's Reports [*25-40 Florida*] [*A publication*] (DLA)
LAMAR...... Large Amplitude Modular Array (SAUS)
LAMAR...... Large Area Modular Array of Reflectors [*Astronomy*]
LAMAR...... Linear-Elastic Matrix Analysis Routine
LAMARPAC... Lamar Corporation PAC [*Baton Rouge, LA*] (PACS)
LAMARS.... Large Amplitude Multimode Aerospace Research Simulator
Lamar U.... Lamar University (GAGS)
LAMAS...... Location and Movement Analysis System (MCD)
LAMAS...... London and Middlesex Archaeological Society [*England*] (BUAC)
LAMA SASS........ LAMA [*Library Administration and Management Association*] Systems and Services Section
LAMA SS... LAMA [*Library Administration and Management Association*] Statistics Section
LAMA SSS.. LAMA [*Library Administration and Management Association*] Systems and Services Section
LA-MAX..... Maximal Left Atrial [*Dimension*] [*Medicine*] (STED)
Lamb........ Lambard's Archaionomia [*A publication*] (DLA)
Lamb........ Lambard's Archeion [*1635*] [*A publication*] (DLA)
Lamb........ Lambard's Eirenarcha [*A publication*] (DLA)
Lamb........ Lambard's Explication [*A publication*] (DLA)
LAMB........ Lambeth [*Degrees granted by Archbishop of Canterbury*] [*British*] (ROG)
LAMB........ Lambourne [*England*]
LAMB........ Lambretta [*NCIC motorcycle make code*]
Lamb........ Lamb's Reports [*103-105 Wisconsin*] [*A publication*] (DLA)
LAMB........ Lentigines, Atrial Myxoma, Mucocutaneous Myxomas, and Blue Nevi [*Medicine*] [*Syndrome*] (PALA)
LAMB........ Light Armoured Motor Brigade [*British military*] (DMA)
LAMB........ Lively Arts Market Builder (ACAE)
LAMB........ Local Area Multiuser Board [*American Micronics*] [*Computer science*]
LAMB........ Los Alamos Water Boiler (NRCH)
LAMB........ Low-Altitude Multiburst Code (MCD)
LAMBADA... Amazon Basin Experiment (SAUO)
Lamb Arch... Lambard's Archaionomia [*A publication*] (DLA)
Lamb Arch... Lambard's Archeion [*1635*] [*A publication*] (ILCA)
Lamb Archaion... Lambard's Archaionomia [*A publication*] (DLA)
LAMBC...... Los Angeles Motor Boat Club (SAUO)
Lamb Const... Lambard's Duties of Constables, Etc. [*A publication*] (DLA)
LAMBDA.... Language for Manufacturing Business and Distribution Activity (IAA)
LAMBDA.... Least-squares Ambiguity Decorrelation Adjustment
Lamb de Ramp... Lambertus de Ramponibus [*Deceased, 1304*] [*Authority cited in pre-1607 legal work*] (DSA)
Lamb Dow... Lambert's Law of Dower [*A publication*] (DLA)
Lamb Eir.... Lambard's Eirenarcha [*A publication*] (DLA)
Lamb Eiren... Lambard's Eirenarcha [*A publication*] (DLA)
Lamber de Sal... Lambertus de Salinis [*Flourished, 14th century*] [*Authority cited in pre-1607 legal work*] (DSA)
Lamb Explic... Lambard's Explication [*A publication*] (DLA)
Lam Bk Rpt... Lambda Book Report [*A publication*] (BRI)
LAMBR...... Laminin B Receptor (DMAA)
LAMBS...... Laboratory Animal Management and Business Systems [*Computer science*]
LAMC........ Laminin C (DMAA)
LAMC........ Language and Mode Converter [*Computer science*] (TEL)
LAMC........ Last Maneuver Calculation [*Orbit identification*]
LAMC........ Letterman Army Medical Center (AABC)
LAMC........ Lima Army Modification Center (RDA)
LAMC........ Livestock Auctioneers' Market Committee [*British*] (DBA)
LAMC........ Livestock Auctioneers Market Committee for England and Wales (BUAC)
LAMC........ Los Alamos Medical Center (SAUO)
LAMC........ Los Angeles Metropolitan College (SAUO)
LAMC........ Los Angeles Music Center (SAUO)
LAMCIS..... Los Angeles Multiple Corridor Identification System (SAA)
LAMCO...... Liberian American-Swedish Minerals Co.
LAMCS...... Latin American-American Communications Systems (PDAA)
LAMCS...... Latin American Military Communications System
LAMD........ London Association of Master Decorators (SAUO)
LAMDA...... [*The*] London Academy of Music and Dramatic Art
LAME........ Lake Mead National Recreation Area
LAME........ Lange Motor Express [*Common carrier symbol*]
LAME........ Licensed Aircraft Maintenance Engineer (ADA)
LAMEF...... Los Alamos Medium Energy Facility
La Mennais Brothers... Brothers of Christian Instruction of Ploermel (SAUO)
LAMG........ Laban Art of Movement Guild [*Later, LG*] (EA)
LAMI......... Laminectomy [*Medicine*] (MELL)
lami......... Laminotomy [*Medicine*] (STED)
LAMIDA..... Lancashire and Merseyside Industrial Development Association (SAUO)
Lamin....... Laminating Technologies, Inc. [*Associated Press*] (SAG)
LAMINAR... Low Altitude, Mapping, Interception, Navigation (ACAE)
Laminat..... Laminating Technologies, Inc. [*Associated Press*] (SAG)
LAMIS....... Local Authority Management Information System (SAUO)
LAMIS....... Los Angeles Municipal Information System (SAUO)
LAMIT....... Local Authorities' Mutual Investment Trust [*British*]
LAMM....... Land Armament Manpower and Material Data Base (SAUO)
LAMM....... Los Angeles Master Morticians (SAUO)
LAMM....... Lutheran-American Melancthon Movement (SAUO)
LAMMA..... LASER Microprobe Mass Analyzer [*Spectrometry*]
LAMMP..... Fight of the Free Filipino Masses Party [*Political party*] (PSAP)
LAMMP..... Lower Acceptable Mean Maximum Pressure (SAA)
LAMMR..... Large Antenna Multichannel Microwave Radiometer (SAUS)
LAMMR..... Large Antenna Multifrequency Microwave Radiometer (MCD)
LAMMS..... LASER Microprobe Mass Spectrometry [*or Spectroscopy*]
LAMN........ La Man Corp. [*NASDAQ symbol*] (TTSB)
LAMO........ La Mark Transport [*Common carrier symbol*]
LAMO........ Lamborghini [*NCIC car make code*]
LAMOPH.... Ladies Auxiliary, Military Order of the Purple Heart (SAUO)
LAMOPH.... Ladies Auxiliary, Military Order of the Purple Heart, United States of America (EA)
LAMOST.... Large Area Multi Object Fiber Spectroscopic Telescope [*Proposed, China*]
LAMOST.... Large Sky Area Multi-Objects Fiber Spectoscopic Telescope [*China*]
LAMP........ Center for the Study of Legal Authority and Mental Patient Status (EA)
LAMP........ Center for the Study of the Authority and Mental Patient Status (SAUS)
LAMP........ Lake Acidification Mitigation Project [*Environmental Protection Agency*] (GFGA)
LAMP........ Lakewide Management Plan [*Great Lakes*] [*Environmental Protection Agency*]
LAMP........ Lanier Academic Motivational Program [*Military*]
LAMP........ Laos Ammunition Procedures (CINC)
LAMP........ Large Advanced Mirror Program [*Military*] (SDI)
LAMP........ LASER and MASER Patents
LAMP........ LASER and Mixing Program
LAMP........ Laser Microbeam Program [*Research center*] (RCD)
LAMP........ Laser Modulation Program (ACAE)
LAMP........ Latin America Mass Media Project (BUAC)
LAMP........ Latin American Maize Project (SAUO)
LAMP........ Latin American Market Planning Centre (BUAC)
LAMP........ Leap and Stamp [*Dance terminology*]
LAMP........ Library Addition and Maintenance Program
LAMP........ Life Agency Management Program [*GAMC*]
LAMP........ Light Airborne Multipurpose System [*Navy*] (MCD)
LAMP........ Lighthouse Automation and Modernization Project [*US Coast Guard*] (PDAA)
LAMP........ Linux, Apache, MySQL, PHP (SAUS)
LAMP........ Lockheed Adaptive Modular Payload (SAUS)
LAMP........ Logic Analysis for Maintenance Planning (MHDB)
LAMP........ Logistics Automation Master PLan [*Military*]
LAMP........ Louis Armstrong Memorial Project
LAMP........ Low-Altitude Manned Penetrator
LAMP........ Low Altitude Mapping Photogrammetry (SAUO)
LAMP........ Lunar Analysis and Mapping Program [*NASA*] (IAA)
LAMP........ Lysosome-Associated Membrane Protein [*Biochemistry*]
LAMP........ SOI Industries, Inc. (SAUO)
LAMP-1..... Lysosomal Membrane Glycoprotein-1 [*Medicine*] (PALA)
LAMP-2..... Lysosomal Membrane Glycoprotein-2 [*Medicine*] (PALA)
LAMP-2..... Lysosome-Associated Membrane Protein-2
LAMPEX..... Large Area Marine Productivity-Pollution Experiments (SAUO)
LAMPF...... Los Alamos Meson Physics Facility [*Later, Clinton P. Anderson Meson Physics Facility at Los Alamos*] [*Department of Energy*]
LAMP-H..... Lighter, Amphibian Heavy Lift
LAMPP...... Los Alamos Molten Plutonium Program
LAMPRE.... Los Alamos Molten Plutonium Reactor Experiment
LAMPS...... Large Amplitude SLOSH [*Sea, Lake, Overland Surge from Hurricanes*] [*NASA*]
LAMPS...... Light Airborne Multiple Package System
LAMPS...... Light Airborne Multipurpose System [*Navy*]
LAMPS...... Limited Area Mesoscale Prediction System (MCD)
LAMPS...... Logistics Assessment of Modifications Program (SAUO)
LAMPS...... London Area Mobile Physiotherapy Service (SAUO)
LAMPSOP... Light Airborne Multipurpose System Standard Operating Procedures Manual [*Navy*] (DNAB)
LA/MPSS.... Large Area/Mobile Projected Smoke System [*Military*] (RDA)
LAMR........ Lamar Advertising 'A' [*NASDAQ symbol*] (SG)
LAMR........ Lamar Advertising Co. [*NASDAQ symbol*] (NASQ)
LamR........ Lamentations Rabbah (BJA)
LAMR........ Large Aperture Microwave Radiometer (SSD)
LAMRDT.... Large Aperture Microwave Radiometer Development Test (SAUO)
LAMRL...... Logistic Area Material Readiness List [*Military*] (AFIT)
LamRsch.... Lam Research Corp. [*Associated Press*] (SAG)
LAMRTPI.... Legal Associate Member of the Royal Town Planning Institute [*British*] (DBQ)
LAMS........ Lake Analysis Management System (SAUO)
LAMS........ Land Acoustical Monitoring System [*NASA*]
LAMS........ Land Acquisition and Management Schemes [*British*]
LAMS........ Large Atypical Mole Syndrome [*Medicine*]
LAMS........ Light Aircraft Maintenance Schedule (PIAV)
LAMS........ Lightweight Artillery Meteorological System (SAUO)
LAMS........ Limited Area Models (SAUO)
LAMS........ Load Alleviation and Mode Stabilization
LAMS........ Local Area Missile System (SAUO)
LAMS........ Local Asset Management System (ACAE)
LAMS........ London Aero Motor Services
LA-MS....... Los Alamos Manuscript (SAUO)
LAMS........ Los Alamos Scientific Laboratory [*USAEC*] (MCD)

LAMS .... Launch Acoustic Measuring System (ODA)
LAMSA ...... Lineas Aereas Mexicana, Sociedad Anonima
LAMSAC .... Local Authorities' Management Services and Computer Committee [*British*]
LAMSAC Committee... Local Authorities Management Services and Computer Committee (SAUO)
LAMSAS .... Linguistic Atlas of the Middle and South Atlantic States
LamSes ..... [*The*] Lamson & Sessions Co. [*Associated Press*] (SAG)
LAMSIM..... Launcher and Missile Simulator
L Am Soc... Law in American Society [*A publication*] (DLA)
L Am Soc'y... Law in American Society [*A publication*] (DLA)
LAMSS ...... Laser Air Motion Sensing System (SAUS)
LAMT........ Laminating Technologies, Inc. [*NASDAQ symbol*] (SAG)
LAmT........ Tangihoa Parish Library, Amite (SAUS)
LAmT........ Tangipahoa Parish Library, Amite, LA [*Library symbol*] [*Library of Congress*] (LCLS)
LAMTD ...... Laminated
LAMTPI ..... Legal Associate Member of the Town Planning Institute (SAUO)
LAMTS ...... Launcher Adapter Missile Test Set
LAMU......... Almar Maritime Services [*Intermodal shipping container symbol*] (TVRC)
LAN.......... Inland [*Aviation code*]
LAN.......... Laboratory Automation News (SAUO)
LAN.......... Lanarkshire [*County in Scotland*]
LAN.......... Lancer [*NCIC car model code*]
LAN.......... Lancer Corp. [*AMEX symbol*] (SPSG)
LAN.......... Lanchow [*Republic of China*] [*Seismograph station code, US Geological Survey*] [*Closed*] (SEIS)
LAN.......... Landall [*NCIC car model code*]
LAN.......... Landau [*Automotive classified advertising*]
LAN.......... Landing Aid [*Navigation*] (IAA)
Lan .... Landulfus Acconzaioco [*Flourished, 13th century*] [*Authority cited in pre-1607 legal work*] (DSA)
LAN.......... Lane Flatbed Trailer [*NCIC trailer make code*]
Lan .... Lanfrancus [*Deceased, 1089*] [*Authority cited in pre-1607 legal work*] (DSA)
Lan .... Lanfrancus Cremensis [*Deceased, 1229*] [*Authority cited in pre-1607 legal work*] (DSA)
LAN.......... Langley [*Unit of sun's heat*] (IAA)
lan........... Langue d'Oc [*MARC language code*] [*Library of Congress*] (LCCP)
LAN.......... Lanos [*NCIC car model code*]
LAN.......... Lansing [*Michigan*] [*Airport symbol*] (OAG)
LAN.......... Lansing, MI [*Location identifier*] [*FAA*] (FAAL)
Lan .... Lanthionine (DB)
LAN.......... Lateral Access Network (NITA)
LAN.......... Latin American Newsletters [*British*] [*Information service or system*] (IID)
LAN.......... Latin American Newsletters Ltd. (SAUO)
LAN.......... Library Advocacy Now [*American Library Association*]
LAN.......... Library Automation and Networks
LAN.......... Lime-Ammonium-Nitrate [*Fertilizer*]
LAN.......... Linea Aerea Nacional [*National Airline*] [*Chile*]
LAN.......... Linea Aerea Nacional de Chile [*ICAO designator*] (FAAC)
LAN.......... Linked Access Network
LAN.......... Local Apparent Noon [*Navigation*]
LAN.......... Local Area Network [*Computer science*] (NETL)
LAN.......... Local Area Networks [*Information Gatekeepers, Inc.*] [*No longer available online*] [*Information service or system*] (CRD)
LAN.......... Long-Acting Neuroleptic [*Pharmacology*] (DAVI)
LAN.......... Longitude of the Ascending Node
LAN.......... Los Alamos National Laboratory (SAUO)
LAN.......... Louisianian [*Telegraphy*] (PCTE)
LAN.......... Lymphadenopathy (STED)
LAN.......... Mesa Public Library, Los Alamos, NM [*OCLC symbol*] (OCLC)
LAN.......... Panorama Air Tour, Inc. (SAUO)
LANA .... Lancer Mobile Homes [*NCIC trailer make code*]
LANA .... Language Analog [*Project*]
LANA .... Lipizzan Association of North America (NTPA)
LANA .... Liquid Air Corp. (SAUO)
LANA .... Lithuanian American National Alliance (EA)
LANA .... Llama Association of North America (EA)
LANA .... Local Area Network Accelerator [*Computer science*] (CIST)
LANA .... Low-Altitude Night Attack (DOMA)
LANABS..... Light Attack Navigation and Bombing System (MCD)
LANAC....... Laminar Air Navigation and Anticollision [*Air Force*]
LANAC....... Lawyers Alliance for Nuclear Arms Control [*Later, LAWS*] (EA)
Lan Acon ... Landulfus Acconzaioco [*Flourished, 13th century*] [*Authority cited in pre-1607 legal work*] (DSA)
LANAP....... Latin American Natural Areas Program (BUAC)
Lanarks ..... Lanarkshire (GROV)
LANBY....... Large Automatic Navigational Buoy [*Shipping*] (DS)
LANC .... Lancaster [*England*] (ROG)
LANC .... Lancaster Colony [*NASDAQ symbol*] (SAG)
LANC .... Lancaster Colony Corp. [*NASDAQ symbol*]
Lanc.......... Lancellottus [*Authority cited in pre-1607 legal work*] (DSA)
LANC .... Lancer [*Military*] [*British*] (ROG)
LANC .... Lanchester [*NCIC car model code*]
LANC .... Liga Apararii Nationale Crestine [*League of National Christian Defense*] [*Romania*] [*Political party*] (PPE)
LANC .... Local Application Control Bus System (SAUS)
LANC .... Local Application Numerical Control [*Sony Corp.*] (DOM)
LANC .... Long-Arm Navicular Cast [*Orthopedics*] (DAVI)
Lancastr .... Lancaster Colony [*Associated Press*] (SAG)
LANCC....... Local Area Network Communications Controller (SAUO)
LANCC....... Local Area Network Control Center (SAUO)
LANCC/SM... Local Area Network Control Center and Security Monitor (SAUO)
LANCE....... Ballistic Missile with Self Contained Guidance (SAUO)
Lance........ Lance, Inc. [*Associated Press*] (SAG)
LANCE....... Local Area Network Controller for Ethernet [*Mostek*] (NITA)
Lance Cpl... Lance Corporal (SAUO)
Lance FDS... Lance Fire Direction System (SAUO)
Lancell Galiaul... Lancellottus Galiaula [*Flourished, 16th century*] [*Authority cited in pre-1607 legal work*] (DSA)
Lancer....... Lancer Corp. [*Associated Press*] (SAG)
Lancet....... Lancet [*UK Journal*] [*Medicine*] (EDAA)
LANCET ..... Library Association National Council for Educational Technology (NITA)
LanChile .... Linea Aerea Nacional de Chile
Lancit .... Lancit Media Productions Ltd. [*Associated Press*] (SAG)
Lanc Law Rev... Lancaster Law Review [*A publication*] (DLA)
Lanc L Rev... Lancaster Law Review [*A publication*] (DLA)
LANCO ...... Landscape Nursery Council (EA)
LANCRA..... Landing Craft
LANCRAB ... Landing Craft and Bases [*Military*]
LANCRABEU... Landing Craft and Bases, Europe [*Navy*]
LANCRABNAW... Landing Craft and Bases, Northwest African Waters [*World War II*] [*Navy*]
Lan Cre ..... Lanfrancus Cremensis [*Deceased, 1229*] [*Authority cited in pre-1607 legal work*] (DSA)
Lanc Rev ... Lancaster Review [*Pennsylvania*] [*A publication*] (DLA)
Lancs........ Lancashire (ADWA)
LANCS....... Lancashire [*County in England*]
LAND .... Land [*Postal Service standard*] (OPSA)
LAND .... Landair Services [*NASDAQ symbol*] (SAG)
LAND .... Landcraft Corporation [*NCIC trailer make code*]
LAND .... Landman's Association of North Dakota (EARSL)
LAND .... League Against Nuclear Dangers [*Defunct*] (EA)
LAND .... Local Access Network Directory [*Frye Computer Systems*] [*Telecommunications*] (PCM)
LANDA ...... Ladies Auxiliary to the National Dental Association [*Later, ANDA*] (EA)
LANDA ...... LAN [*Local Area Network*] Dealers Association (CDE)
L & A........ Landing and Ascent [*NASA*]
L & A........ Leembruggen and Asirvatham's Appeal Court Reports [*Ceylon*] [*A publication*] (DLA)
L & A........ Light and Accommodation [*Ophthalmology*] (DAVI)
L & A........ Living and Active (DAVI)
L & A........ Louisiana & Arkansas Railway Co.
LANDAC..... Land Development Accounting System (MHDB)
Landair...... Landair Services [*Associated Press*] (SAG)
LANDASSESS... CSIRO Program to assess land degradation (SAUS)
LANDATA.... Land Division Data Base [*Australia*] (BUAC)
Landaur..... Landauer, Inc. [*Associated Press*] (SAG)
L & B........ Leadam and Baldwin's Select Cases before the King's Council [*England*] [*A publication*] (DLA)
L & B........ Left and Below [*Medicine*]
L & B........ Lothians and Border Horse [*British military*] (DMA)
L & Bank ... Lawyer and Banker [*A publication*] (DLA)
L & B Bull... Daily Law and Bank Bulletin [*Ohio*] [*A publication*] (DLA)
L & B Fin ... L & B Financial, Inc. [*Associated Press*] (SAG)
L & B Ins Dig... Littleton and Blatchley's Insurance Digest [*A publication*] (DLA)
LandBnc .... Landmark Bancshares [*Associated Press*] (SAG)
L & B Prec... Leake and Bullen's Precedents of Pleading [*A publication*] (DLA)
L & BR...... London & Blackwall Railway [*British*] (ROG)
L&C.......... Laboratory and Checkout (NAKS)
L & C........ Laboratory and Checkout (NASA)
L & C........ Laxatives and Cathartics (MELL)
L & C........ Lefroy and Cassel's Practice Cases [*1881-83*] [*Ontario*] [*A publication*] (ILCA)
L & C........ Leigh and Cave's English Crown Cases Reserved [*1861-65*] [*A publication*] (DLA)
LANDCARE... CSIRO Program on management improvement to prevent degradation (SAUS)
L&CC .... Lewis and Clark College (SAUO)
L & CCC .... Leigh and Cave's English Crown Cases Reserved [*1861-65*] [*A publication*] (DLA)
LANDCENT... Allied Land Forces Central Europe [*NATO*]
L & CM ..... Lime and Cement Mortar (DAC)
L&CMPS .... London and Counties Medical Protection Society (SAUO)
L & Comm... Law and Communication [*A publication*] (DLA)
Land Comp Rep... Land Reports, by Roche, Dillon, and Kehoe [*1881-82*] [*Ireland*] [*A publication*] (DLA)
L & Computer Tech... Law and Computer Technology [*A publication*] (DLA)
Land Com Rep... Land Reports, by Roche, Dillon, and Kehoe [*1881-82*] [*Ireland*] [*A publication*] (DLA)
L & CONTEM PROB... Law and Contemporary Problems [*A publication*] (LWAP)
LANDCRA... Landing Craft and Bases [*Military*] (AFIT)
LANDCRAB... Landing Craft and Bases [*Military*] (AABC)
L & D........ Labor and Delivery [*Area of a hospital*]
L & D........ Landing and Deceleration [*NASA*] (NASA)
l&d........... Loans and Discounts (EBF)
L & D........ Loans and Discounts [*Banking*]
l&d........... Loss and Damage (EBF)
L & D........ Loss and Damage
L & D Conv... Leigh and Dalzell. Conversion of Property [*1825*] [*A publication*] (DLA)
Land Dec ... Land Decisions, United States [*A publication*] (DLA)
L & E........ English Law and Equity Reports [*American Reprint*] [*A publication*] (DLA)

LANDE....... Landers, IL [*American Association of Railroads railroad junction routing code*]
Land Econ... Land Economics [*A publication*] (JLIT)
LANDENMARK... Allied Land Forces Denmark [*NATO*]
L & Eq Rep... Law and Equity Reporter [*United States*] [*A publication*] (DLA)
L & E Rep... English Law and Equity Reports [*American Reprint*] [*A publication*] (DLA)
Land Est C... Landed Estates Court [*England*] (DLA)
LANDEX..... Landing Exercise [*Navy*] (CAAL)
L&F.......... Liver and Iron [*Medicine*] (EDAA)
LANDFAE.... Large Area Nozzle Delivery of Fuel Air Explosive (RDA)
LANDFOR... Landing Force [*Military*]
LANDFORASCU... Landing Force Air Support Control Unit [*Navy*]
L & G Temp Plunk... Lloyd and Goold's Irish Chancery Reports Tempore Plunkett [*A publication*] (DLA)
L & G Temp Sugd... Lloyd and Goold's Irish Chancery Reports Tempore Sugden [*1835*] [*A publication*] (DLA)
L & GTP.... Lloyd and Goold's Irish Chancery Reports Tempore Plunkett [*A publication*] (DLA)
L & GT Plunk... Lloyd and Goold's Irish Chancery Reports Tempore Plunkett [*A publication*] (DLA)
L & GTS.... Lloyd and Goold's Irish Chancery Reports Tempore Sugden [*1835*] [*A publication*] (DLA)
L & GT Sug... Lloyd and Goold's Irish Chancery Reports Tempore Sugden [*1835*] [*A publication*] (DLA)
L & H........ Lamport & Holt Line [*Steamship*] (MHDB)
L & H........ Laurel and Hardy [*The film comedy team of Stan Laurel and Oliver Hardy*]
L&H.......... Lernout & Hauspie [*A speech products manufacturer*] (PCM)
L&H.......... Light and Heat (MIST)
L&H.......... Lungs and Heart (SAUS)
L & HR...... [*The*] Lehigh & Hudson River Railway Co. [*Absorbed into Consolidated Rail Corp.*]
L & HTC.... Line and Halftone Combined [*Illustration*] (DGA)
L & I......... Launch and Impact (AFM)
L&I.......... Liver and Iron (DMAA)
L & ID........ London and India Docks [*Shipping*] [*British*] (ROG)
LANDING.... Landing [*Commonly used*] (OPSA)
LANDIS...... Low-Approach Navigation Director System [*Aircraft landing aid*] [*Air Force*]
L&J.......... Law and Justice (SAFN)
L & J Tr Mar... Ludlow and Jenkyns on the Law of Trade-Marks [*A publication*] (DLA)
LANDJUT... Allied Land Forces Schleswig-Holstein and Jutland [*NATO*] (NATG)
L & K........ Love and Kisses [*Correspondence*]
L & L........ Latch and Lock (DAC)
L&L.......... Launch and Landing [*Aerospace*] (NAKS)
L & L........ Leave and Liberty (WDAA)
L & L........ Legislative and Liaison [*Military*]
L&L.......... Lerner and Loewe [*Composers*]
L & L........ Lewd and Lascivious
L & L........ Love and Liquor (IIA)
L&L.......... Lyrics and Lyricists [*Long running New York show*]
L & LC...... Leeds and Liverpool Canal [*Shipping*] [*British*] (ROG)
L & LC...... Lift and Lift Cruise (MCD)
LANDLD..... Landlord (ROG)
L & Leg GDR... Law and Legislation in the German Democratic Republic [*A publication*] (DLA)
L & Legis in GDR... Law and Legislation in the German Democratic Republic [*A publication*] (DLA)
L & LeM.... Leigh and Le Marchant. Elections [*4th ed.*] [*1885*] [*A publication*] (DLA)
L & Lib...... Law and Liberty [*A publication*] (DLA)
L&LS........ Londonderry and Lough Swilly (SAUO)
L & M....... Labor and Material Bond
L&M.......... L&M Drafting Service (SAUO)
L & M....... Layout and Manuscript [*Advertising*] (WDMC)
L&M.......... Layout and Manuscript [*Publishing*] (WDMC)
L & M....... Legal and Magnanimous Side [*Sarcastic reference to the government of Vietnam and its allies*] (VNW)
L & M....... [*The*] Librarian and the Machine [*A publication*]
L&M.......... Linotype and Machinery (SAUO)
L&M.......... Logistics and Maintenance (FOTI)
L & M....... Lowndes and Maxwell's English Practice Cases [*1852-54*] [*A publication*] (DLA)
LANDMARC... International Land Management Research Centre (SAUO)
L&MM....... Logistics and Materiel Management (SAUO)
L&N.......... Leeds & Northrup (SAUO)
L&N.......... Lomas & Nettleton Financial Corp. (EFIS)
L & N........ Louisville & Nashville Railroad Co.
L & NE...... Lehigh & New England Railway Co. [*Absorbed into Consolidated Rail Corp.*]
LANDNON... Allied Land Forces North Norway [*NATO*] (NATG)
LANDNON... Land Forces North Norway (SAUO)
LANDNOR... Allied Land Forces, North Norway (SAUO)
LANDNORTH... Allied Land Forces Northern Europe [*NATO*] (NATG)
LANDNORTH... Land Forces Northern Europe (SAUO)
LANDNORWAY... Allied Land Forces Norway [*NATO*]
L & NRR.... Louisville & Nashville Railroad Co.
L&NWRy.... London and North-Western Railway (SAUO)
L&O.......... Lead and Oil (MIST)
L&OD........ Leadership & Organization Development (SAUO)
L & OD...... Lester & Orpen Dennys [*Canadian publisher*]
L&OG........ Logistics and Operations Group (SAUO)
L & Order... Law and Order [*A publication*] (DLA)
L&P.......... Labor and Population Program [*RAND*] (RCD)
L & P........ Latch and Plaster (DAC)
L&P.......... Lath and Plaster [*Construction term*] (MIST)
L&P.......... Leggett and Platt, Inc. (EFIS)
L & P........ Lighting and Power
L&P.......... Literature and Psychology [*A publication*] (ANEX)
L & PA...... Lodging and Pay Allowance [*British military*] (DMA)
L & PP...... Lunar and Planetary Program
L & Psychology Rev... Law and Psychology Review [*A publication*] (DLA)
L & Psych Rev... Law and Psychology Review [*A publication*] (DLA)
L & R........ Lake and Rail
L & R........ Landing and Recovery (KSC)
L & R........ Larceny and Receiving
L & R........ Left and Right
L & R........ Loring and Russell's Election Cases in Massachusetts [*A publication*] (DLA)
L & R Election Cases... Loring and Russell's Election Cases in Massachusetts [*A publication*] (DLA)
LANDREST... CSIRO Program on cost effective restoration technologies (SAUS)
L&RScRgt... Lanark and Renfrew Scottish Regiment (SAUO)
Landrys..... Landrys Seafood Restaurants, Inc. [*Associated Press*] (SAG)
L&S.......... College of Letters and Science (SAUS)
L&S.......... Language and Speech (SAUO)
L & S........ Launch and Servicing (AAG)
L & S........ Laurinburg & Southern Railroad Co. (IIA)
L & S........ Laverne and Shirley [*Television program*]
L&S.......... Ligation and Stripping [*Medicine*] (BCRP)
L&S.......... Liver and Spleen (SAUS)
L & S........ Logistics and Support (NASA)
L&SA........ Law and Society Association (SAUO)
Landsat..... Land Remote Sensing Satellite (EOSA)
LANDSAT... Land Remote Sensing Satellite System (GFGA)
LANDSAT... Land Satellite [*Marine science*] (OSRA)
LANDSC..... Landscape
Landsc Ecol... Landscape Ecology (SAUO)
Landsc J.... Landscape Journal (SAUO)
LANDSCPG... Landscaping
Landsc Urban Plan... Landscape and Urban Planning (SAUO)
LandsE...... Land's End, Inc. [*Associated Press*] (SAG)
LANDSONOR... Allied Land Forces South Norway [*NATO*] (NATG)
LANDSOUTH... Allied Land Forces Southern Europe [*NATO*]
LANDSOUTHEAST... Allied Land Forces Southeastern Europe [*NATO*]
LANDSS..... Lightweight Advanced Night/Day Surveillance System (SAUO)
Landstr...... Landstar Systems, Inc. [*Associated Press*] (SAG)
L & SWR... London & South-Western Railway (ROG)
L & T........ Laboratories and Test (NASA)
L&T.......... Laboratory and Test (SAUO)
L & T........ Landlord and Tenant [*A publication*] (DLA)
L & T........ Line and Terminal [*Telecommunications*] (TEL)
L & T........ Longfield and Townsend's Irish Exchequer Reports [*1841-42*] [*A publication*] (DLA)
L&T Camp... Leave and Transit Camp (SAUO)
L & TH...... Lethality and Target Hardening [*Military*] (SDI)
L & U........ Loading and Unloading
L & U........ Lower and Upper [*Anatomy*]
LANDUP..... Alberta Land Use Planning Data Bank [*Alberta Municipal Affairs*] [*Information service or system*] [*Defunct*] (IID)
Land U Pl Rep... Land Use Planning Reports [*A publication*] (DLA)
Land Use & Env't L Rev... Land Use and Environment Law Review [*A publication*] (DLA)
L & W....... Living and Well
L & W....... Lloyd and Welsby's English Commercial and Mercantile Cases [*1829-30*] [*A publication*] (DLA)
Land Water... Land and Water [*A publication*] (PABS)
L & Welsb.. Lloyd and Welsby's English Commercial and Mercantile Cases [*1829-30*] [*A publication*] (DLA)
L&WV....... Lackawanna and Wyoming Valley Railroad Co. (SAUO)
L&YR........ Lancashire and Yorkshire Railway (SAUO)
LANDZEALAND... Allied Land Forces Zealand [*NATO*] (NATG)
LANE........ Lane [*Commonly used*] (OPSA)
LANE........ Lane Horse Trailer [*NCIC trailer make code*]
Lane........ Lane's English Exchequer Reports [*1605-12*] [*A publication*] (DLA)
LANE........ Lane Transfer [*Common carrier symbol*]
LANE........ Local Area Network Emulation [*Telecommunications*] (ACRL)
LANES....... Lane [*Commonly used*] (OPSA)
LANES....... League for the Advancement of New England Storytelling
LANET....... Lanett, AL [*American Association of Railroads railroad junction routing code*]
LANFLTMATCONOFF... Atlantic Fleet Material Control Office (SAUS)
LANFORTRACOMLANT... Landing Force Training Command, Atlantic [*Navy*]
LANFORTRAU... Landing Force Training Unit [*Marine Corps*] (DNAB)
LANFOX..... Local Area Network Fiber Optic Transceiver (ACAE)
LANFZT..... Latin American Nuclear Free Zone Treaty (SAUO)
LANG........ Langley [*England*]
LANG........ Language (AFM)
Lang......... Language (AL)
lang.......... Language (WDAA)
Lang Ca Cont... Langdell's Cases on Contracts [*A publication*] (DLA)
Lang Ca Sales... Langdell's Cases on the Law of Sales [*A publication*] (DLA)
Lang Cont... Langdell's Cases on Contracts [*A publication*] (DLA)
Lang Cont... Langdell's Summary of the Law of Contracts [*A publication*] (DLA)
Langd Cont... Langdell's Cases on Contracts [*A publication*] (DLA)
Langd Cont... Langdell's Summary of the Law of Contracts [*A publication*] (DLA)

Lang Eq Pl... Langdell's Cases in Equity Pleading [*A publication*] (DLA)
Lang Eq Pl... Langdell's Summary of Equity Pleading [*A publication*] (DLA)
Langer...... [*The*] Langer Biomechanics Group, Inc. [*Associated Press*] (SAG)
Lang Sales... Langdell's Cases on the Law of Sales [*A publication*] (DLA)
Lang Soc... Language in Society [*A publication*] (BRI)
Lang Sum Cont... Langdell's Summary of the Law of Contracts [*A publication*] (DLA)
Lang Tr...... Langley's Trustees' Act [*A publication*] (DLA)
Language... Language. Journal of the Linguistic Society of America. Baltimore (SAUO)
LANH........ Landola Homes [*NCIC trailer make code*]
LANH........ Launch (MSA)
LANI........ Landair Corp. [*NASDAQ symbol*] (NASQ)
LANIC....... LAN [*Local Area Network*] Interface Card (PCM)
LANIC....... Latin American Network Information Center [*Internet resource*]
LANICA...... Lineas Aereas de Nicaragua, SA [*Nicaraguan airline*]
LANIS....... Landisville, PA [*American Association of Railroads railroad junction routing code*]
LANL........ Landoll [*NCIC trailer make code*]
LANL........ Los Alamos National Laboratory [*Los Alamos, NM*] [*Department of Energy*]
LANM........ Landmaster [*NCIC trailer make code*]
LANMAS.... Local Area Network Material Accounting System (SAUO)
LANN........ Lannett Co. [*OTCBB symbol*]
L Ann........ Louisiana Annual Reports [*A publication*] (DLA)
Lannet........ Lannet Data Communictions Ltd. [*Associated Press*] (SAG)
LANNET..... Large Artificial Nerve [*or Neuron*] Network
LANO........ Lancaster Northern Railway [*Federal Railroad Administration identification code*]
LANO........ Lights are not on (BB)
Lanoptic.... Lanoptics Ltd. [*Associated Press*] (SAG)
LANP........ Lanes Pacesetter Trailer [*NCIC trailer make code*]
LANP........ Leucine-Rich Acidic Nuclear Protein [*Biochemistry*]
LAnP......... Louisiana State Penitentiary, Angola, LA [*Library symbol*] [*Library of Congress*] (LCLS)
LANP........ Plaintree Systems Inc. [*NASDAQ symbol*] (SAG)
LAN/PDL.... Local Area Network / Program Design Language (LAIN)
LANPF....... Plaintree Systems [*NASDAQ symbol*] (TTSB)
LANR........ Lancer [*NCIC motorcycle make code*]
LANRAC..... Land Army Reunion Association Committee (SAUO)
Lan Reg..... Lancashire Regiment (SAUO)
LANRES..... LAN Resource Extension and Services [*Communications term*] (DCT)
LANRES..... Linked Access Network Resource Extension and Service
LANRES..... Local Network Resource Extension [*Computer science*] (CIST)
LAN/RM..... Local Area Network Reference Model
LANS........ Landis Steel Company [*NCIC trailer make code*]
Lans......... Lansing's New York Supreme Court Reports [*A publication*] (DLA)
LANS........ Large Atypical Nevus Syndrome [*Medicine*]
LANS........ Latin America News Service (BUAC)
LANS........ Lightweight Airborne Navigation System (MCD)
LANS........ Local Area Network Services (SAUO)
LANS........ Local Area Network System [*Telecommunications*]
LANS........ LORAN Airborne Navigation System (IEEE)
LANSA....... Latin American Paper Money Society (EA)
LANSA....... Lineas Aereas Nacionales Consolidadas Sociedad Anonima
LANSCE..... Los Alamos Neutron Scattering Center
LANSCE..... Los Alamos Neutron Science Center (SAUO)
Lans Ch..... Lansing's Select Cases in Chancery [*1824, 1826*] [*New York*] [*A publication*] (DLA)
LANSF....... Lansford, ND [*American Association of Railroads railroad junction routing code*]
LANSG...... Lansing, MI [*American Association of Railroads railroad junction routing code*]
Lansg........ New York Supreme Court Reports (Lansing) [*A publication*] (DLA)
LANSHIPRON... Landing Ship Squadron (CINC)
Lansing..... New York Supreme Court Reports (Lansing) [*A publication*] (DLA)
LANSL....... Los Alamos National Scientific Laboratories [*New Mexico*]
Lans Sel Cas... Lansing's Select Cases in Chancery [*1824, 1826*] [*New York*] [*A publication*] (DLA)
LANSW...... Laryngectomee Association of New South Wales [*Australia*]
LANSW...... Legislative Assembly of New South Wales [*Australia*]
LANSW...... Lupus Association of New South Wales [*Australia*]
LANSX....... Lord Abbett: Tax Free Inc.: National Cl.A [*Mutual fund ticker symbol*] (SG)
LANt......... Atlanten (SAUS)
LANT........ Atlantic
LANT........ Atlantic Area (SAUO)
LANT........ Lange Truck Line [*Common carrier symbol*]
LANT........ Lanheim [*NCIC trailer make code*]
LANT........ Lannet Data Communications Ltd. [*NASDAQ symbol*] (SAG)
L ANT....... Left Anterior (STED)
LANT........ Legislative Assembly of the Northern Territory [*Australia*]
LANTCOM... Atlantic Command [*Navy*]
LANTCOMINSGEN... Atlantic Command Inspector General (DNAB)
LANTCOMMBPO... Atlantic Command Military Blood Program Office (DNAB)
LANTCOMOPCONCEN... Atlantic [*Fleet*] Commander Operational Control Center [*Navy*]
LANTCOMOPSUPPFAC... Atlantic Command Operations Support Facility (DNAB)
LANTDAC... Atlantic Command Defense Analysis Center (SAUO)
LANTDIS.... Atlantic Command Deployable Intelligence System (SAUS)
LANTDIS.... US Atlantic Command Deployable Intelligence System (SAUO)
LANTFAP.... Allied Command Atlantic Frequency Allocation Panel [*Obsolete*] [*NATO*] (NATG)
LANTFAST... Atlantic Forward Area Support Team [*Military*] (DNAB)
LANTFLEASWTACSCOL... Atlantic Fleet Antisubmarine Warfare Tactical School [*Navy*]
LANTFLEASWTASCOL... Atlantic Fleet Antisubmarine Warfare Tactical School (SAUS)
LANTFLT.... Atlantic Fleet
LANTFLTHEDSUPPACT... Atlantic Fleet Headquarters Support Activity [*Navy*] (DNAB)
LANTFLTMATCONOFF... Atlantic Fleet Material Control Office [*Navy*] (DNAB)
LANTFLTPEB... Atlantic Fleet Propulsion Examining Board [*Navy*] (DNAB)
LANTFLTRANSUPPFAC... Atlantic Fleet Training Support Facilities
LANTFLTWPNRAN... Atlantic Fleet Weapons Range [*Later, AFRSF*] [*Navy*]
LANTFLTWPNTRAFAC... Atlantic Fleet Weapons Training Facility [*Navy*] (DNAB)
L Anti........ Antilles (VRA)
L Anti........ Lesser Antilles (VRA)
LANTICOMIS... LANTCOM Integrated Command and Control Management Information System (MCD)
LANTINCEN... Atlantic Intelligence Center (SAUS)
LANTINTCEN... Atlantic Intelligence Center [*Navy*]
LANTIRN.... Low-Altitude Navigation and Targeting Infrared [*System*] for Night [*Aviation*]
LANTMS.... Linked Access Network Transport Management System [*Telecommunications*]
LANTNAVFACENGCOM... Atlantic Division Naval Facilities Engineering Command
LANTOPS... Atlantic Operations Supply Facilities (MCD)
LANTOPSSUPFAC... Atlantic Operations Supply Facilities
LANTREADEX... Atlantic Readiness Exercise (MCD)
LANTREPCNAVRES... Atlantic Fleet Chief of Naval Reserve Representative (DNAB)
LANTREPCOMNAVSURFRES... Atlantic Representative for Commander Naval Surface Reserve Force (DNAB)
LANTRESFLT... Atlantic Reserve Fleet
LANTSAR... Atlantic International Air and Surface Search and Rescue Seminar (PDAA)
LANTSOC... Atlantic Fleet Signals Security Operations Center [*Navy*] (DNAB)
LANTWWMCCS... Atlantic Fleet Worldwide Military Command Control System [*Navy*] (DNAB)
LANU........ Catu Containers [*Intermodal shipping container symbol*] (TVRC)
LANU........ Landau [*NCIC truck make code*]
LANUG...... Los Alamos Next Users Group (SAUO)
LANV........ LanVision Systems [*NASDAQ symbol*] (TTSB)
LANV........ Left Atrial Neovascularization [*Cardiology*] (DAVI)
LANWR...... Laguna Atascosa National Wildlife Refuge (SAUO)
LANWR...... Lake Andes National Wildlife Refuge (SAUO)
LANX........ Local Area Network Exchange
LANY........ Linseed Association of New York (SAUO)
LANYX....... Lord Abbett: Tax Free Inc.: N.Y. Cl.A [*Mutual fund ticker symbol*] (SG)
LANZ........ Lancer Orthodontics [*NASDAQ symbol*] (TTSB)
LANZ........ Lancer Orthodontics, Inc. [*NASDAQ symbol*] (SAG)
LAO.......... Laboratory Assessment Office (SAUO)
lao........... Lao [*MARC language code*] [*Library of Congress*] (LCCP)
LAO.......... Laoag [*Philippines*] [*Airport symbol*] (OAG)
LAO.......... Lao Aviaton [*Laos*] [*ICAO designator*] (FAAC)
LAO.......... Laos [*or Lao People's Democratic Republic*] [*ANSI three-letter standard code*] (CNC)
Lao.......... Laos (MILB)
LAO.......... Large Assembly Order (MCD)
LAO.......... Lasa Array [*Montana*] [*Seismograph station code, US Geological Survey*] (SEIS)
LAO.......... La Teko Resources Ltd. [*Vancouver Stock Exchange symbol*]
LAO.......... Lateral Anterior Oblique (DB)
LAO.......... Lead Agency Official (MHDB)
LAO.......... Left Anterior Oblique [*Cardiology*]
LAO.......... Left Anterior Occipital [*Medicine*] (STED)
LAO.......... Left Atrial Overloading [*Cardiology*] (DAVI)
LAO.......... Legal Aid Office
LAO.......... Legal Assistance Officer
LAO.......... Legislative Analyst's Office (AGLO)
LAO.......... Licensing Authorities Office
LAO.......... Licentiate in Obstectric Science (DAVI)
LAO.......... Licentiate of the Art of Obstetrics [*British*]
LAO.......... Limited Attack Option (COE)
LAO.......... Local Area Office (SAUO)
LAO.......... Local Area Operations (SAUO)
LAO.......... Location Administrative Officer (SARE)
LAO.......... Logistics Area Officer (MCD)
LAO.......... Logistics Assistance Office [*or Officer*] [*Army Materiel Command*]
LAOAR...... Latin American Office of Aerospace Research [*Air Force*]
LAOCIF..... Logistic Assistance Office Command Interest Flasher [*Military*] (AABC)
LAOCP....... Limited Amateur Operator's Certificate of Proficiency [*Radio*]
LAOD........ Los Angeles Ordnance District [*Military*] (AAG)
LAOF........ Longitudinal Arch of Foot (MELL)
LAOL........ Los Alamos Opacity Library (SAUO)
LAOOC...... Los Angeles Olympic Organizing Committee (EA)
LAOR........ La Teko Resources Ltd. [*NASDAQ symbol*] (SAG)
LAORF....... La Teko Resources Ltd [*NASDAQ symbol*] (TTSB)
LAOS........ Laymen's Overseas Service [*Acronym is now used as official name of the organization*]
LAOSA....... Librarianship and Archives Old Students' Association (DGA)
LAOSC....... Local Authorities Ordnance Survey Committee [*British*]
LAOT........ La Otto Metal Fabricating Company [*NCIC trailer make code*]
LAOT........ Los Angeles Opera Theater (SAUO)
LAP.......... Laboratory Accreditation Program [*Department of Commerce*]
LAP.......... Laboratory of Advertising Performance [*McGraw-Hill*]

LAP .... Laboratory of Architecture and Planning [*Massachusetts Institute of Technology*] [*Research center*] (RCD)
LAP .... Laboratory of Atmospheric Physics (SAUO)
LAP .... Laboratory of Aviation Psychology (SAUO)
LAP .... Labour Action for Peace [*Political party*] (BUAC)
LAP .... Lakewood Public Library, Lakewood, OH [*OCLC symbol*] (OCLC)
LAP .... Landsat Applications Program (SAUO)
lap .... Laparoscopy [*Medicine*]
Lap .... Laparotomy [*Medicine*] (AMHC)
LAP .... Laparotomy [*Sponges*] (DAVI)
LAP .... La Paz [*Mexico*] [*Airport symbol*] (OAG)
LAP .... La Paz [*Mexico*] [*Seismograph station code, US Geological Survey*] (SEIS)
LAP .... Lapland
LAP .... La Plata, MO [*Amtrak rail station code*]
lap .... Lapp [*MARC language code*] [*Library of Congress*] (LCCP)
Lap .... Lapus de Castiglionchio [*Flourished, 1353-81*] [*Authority cited in pre-1607 legal work*] (DSA)
LAP .... Large Area Panel
LAP .... Large-Area Processing [*For fabricating multichip modules*]
LAP .... Large Scale Advanced Propeller (ACAE)
LAP .... Last Appearance (SAUO)
LAP .... Latin American Parliament [*See also PLA*] [*Colombia*] (EAIO)
LAP .... Lattice Assessment Program [*Civil Defense*]
LAP .... Launch Analyst Panel [*Aerospace*] (AAG)
LAP .... Launch Assist Platform [*Space launch term*] (ISAK)
LAP .... Launcher Adaptable Platform (ACAE)
LAP .... Launcher Avionics Package (ACAE)
LAP .... Learning Ability Profile [*Margarita Henning*] (TES)
LAP .... Learning Accomplishment Profile [*Psychology*]
LAP .... Learning Activity Package (EDAC)
LAP .... Learning Activity Packet (AEE)
LAP .... Learning Assistance Program
LAP .... Leased Attached Pallet (SSD)
LAP .... Left Arterial Pressure [*Cardiology*] (DAVI)
LAP .... Left Atrial Pressure [*Cardiology*]
LAP .... Lend-a-Paw Relief Organization (EARSL)
LAP .... Lesson Assembly Program (IEEE)
LAP .... Lethality Assessment Program
LAP .... Leucine Aminopeptidase [*Also, LA, LP*] [*An enzyme*]
LAP .... Leukocyte Adhesion Stimulator [*Medicine*] (MELL)
LAP .... Leukocyte Alkaline Phosphatase [*An enzyme*]
LAP .... Liberation Action Party [*Trinidad and Tobago*] [*Political party*] (PPW)
LAP .... Liberian Action Party [*Political party*] (BUAC)
LAP .... Library Access Program
LAP .... Library Awareness Program [*FBI*]
LAP .... Line Access Point [*Telecommunications*] (TEL)
LAP .... Linear Arithmetic Processor (IAA)
LAP .... Lineas Aereas Paraguayas [*Paraguay*] [*ICAO designator*] (FAAC)
LAP .... Lingual Antimicrobial Peptide [*Biochemistry*]
LAP .... Link Access Procedure [*Telecommunications*] (TEL)
LAP .... Link Access Protocol [*Telecommunications*]
LAP .... Link Asynchronous Protocol [*Telecommunications*]
LAP .... Linux Application Platform (VLIE)
LAP .... List Assembly Programming [*Computer science*]
LAP .... Load, Assemble, Pack [*Army*] (AABC)
LAP .... Loading Assembling and Packing
LAP .... Local Access Port [*Telecommunications*] (ACRL)
LAP .... Local Air Picture (SAUS)
LAP .... Local Analysis and Prediction [*Marine science*] (OSRA)
LAP .... Local Area Power [*Computer science*] (CIST)
LAP .... Location Audit Program [*Navy*] (NG)
LAP .... Logistics Assistance Program
LAP .... Loide Aereo Nacional, SA [*Brazilian airline*]
LAP .... London Airport
LAP .... London Artid Plastics Ltd. (SAUO)
LAP .... Lord's Acre Plan (EA)
LA-P .... Los Alamos Proposal (SAUO)
LAP .... Loudspeaker Acoustical Phase-Inverter
L Ap .... Louisiana Courts of Appeal Reports [*A publication*] (DLA)
LAP .... Low Achievers Project [*Education*] (AIE)
LAP .... Low-Altitude Penetration
LAP .... Low-Altitude Performance
LAP .... Low Altitude Program (ACAE)
LAP .... Low Atmospheric Pressure (DAVI)
LAP .... Lyophilized Anterior Pituitary [*Endocrinology*]
LAPA .... Latin America Parents Association (EA)
LAPA .... Leukocyte Alkaline Phosphatase Activity [*Biochemistry*]
LAPA .... Lightweight Aggregate Producers Association (EA)
LAPA .... Los Angeles Procurement Agency [*Army*]
LAPAC .... Life Amendment Political Action Committee [*Defunct*] (EA)
LaPac .... Louisiana-Pacific Corp. [*Associated Press*] (SAG)
LAPADA ..... London and Provincial Antique Dealers Association [*England*] (BUAC)
LAPADS ..... Lightweight Acoustic Processing and Display System [*British military*] (DMA)
LAPAM ...... Low-Altitude Penetrating Attack Missile [*Proposed*]
LAPAN .... Institute of Aeronautics and Space (SAUS)
LAPAN .... National Aeronautics and Space Agency (SAUS)
LAPAR .... Large Phased-Array RADAR
LAPB .... Laboratories' Applied Physiology Branch [*Army*]
LAPB .... Light Armored Police Bus [*Police and security equipment*]
LAPB .... Link Access Procedure [*or Protocol*] Balanced [*Telecommunications*]
LAPB .... Link Access Procedure for Balanced Mode (SAUO)
LAP-B .... Link Access Protocol-Balanced (MLOA)
LAPB .... Link Access Protocol, B Channel [*Telecommunications*]
LAPB .... Local Analysis and Prediction Branch (SAUO)
LAPC .... Land and Agriculture Policy Centre [*South Africa*]
LAPC .... Landmarks of American Popular Culture [*A publication*]
LAPC .... Large Area Proportional Counter Array (SAUO)
LAPC .... Los Angeles Pacific College [*California*]
LAPC .... Los Angeles Pierce College (SAUO)
LAPCO .... Lavan Petroleum Co. [*Iran*] (BUAC)
LAPD .... Latin American Pollen Database (QUAC)
LAPD .... Limited Axial Power Distribution (IEEE)
LAPD .... Link Access Procedure-D [*Telecommunications*] (DOM)
LAPD .... Link Access Procedure Direct (SAUO)
LAPD .... Link Access Procedure for the D Channel (SAUO)
LAPD .... Link Access Protocol, D Channel [*Telecommunications*]
LAPD .... Los Alamos Police Department (SAUO)
LAPD .... Los Angeles Air Procurement District
LAPD .... Los Angeles Police Department (WDAA)
LAPD .... Los Angeles Police District (SAUO)
LAPD .... Los Angeles Procurement District (SAUO)
Lap Dec ..... Laperriere's Speaker's Decisions [*Canada*] [*A publication*] (DLA)
LAPDis ...... Los Angeles Procurement District (SAUO)
LAPDOG ..... Low-Altitude Pursuit Dive on Ground (MCD)
LAPDP .... Laboratory for Automation Psychology and Decision Processes [*University of Maryland at College Park*] (RCD)
LAPDRY ..... Lapidary
LAPE .... Lineas Aereas Postales Espanoles [*Airline*] [*Spain*]
LAPE .... Low Altitude Parachute Extraction System (SAUO)
LAPERS ..... Labor and Production Effectiveness Reporting System [*DoD*]
LAPES .... Low-Altitude Parachute Extraction System [*Military*]
LAPF .... Link Access Procedure to Frame Mode Bearer Services [*Telecommunications*] (ACRL)
LAPF .... Low-Affinity Platelet Factor (STED)
LAPFA .... Laminated Plastics Fabricators Association (SAUO)
LAPF-Core ... Core Aspects of the Link Access Procedure to Frame Mode Bearer Services (SAUS)
LAPFO .... Los Angeles Procurement Field Office
LAPH .... Lithium Aluminum Pentahydride (MCD)
LAPIC .... Local Advanced Programmable Interrupt Controller (SAUS)
lapid .... Lapideum [*Stony*] [*Latin*] (MAE)
LAPIS .... LASER Photoionization Spectroscopy
LAPIS .... Legislative Authorization Program Information System [*General Accounting Office*] [*Defunct*] (IID)
LAPIS .... Local Automated Personnel Information System (DNAB)
LAPIS .... Locality and Practice Information (SAUO)
LAPL .... Lead Allowance Parts List
LAPL .... Library Association Publishing Ltd. [*British*]
LAPL .... Los Angeles Public Library
LaPL .... Louisiana Power & Light Co. [*Associated Press*] (SAG)
LAPLA .... La Plata, MO [*American Association of Railroads railroad junction routing code*]
LAPLS .... Lead Allowance Parts List System (DNAB)
LAPM .... Last Premidcourse Orbit
LAPM .... Link Access Procedure for MODEMs [*Communications protocol*] [*Computer science*] (PCM)
LAPM .... Link Access Protocol for Modems [*Computer science*] (DCOM)
LAPMS ...... Latin American Paper Money Society (EA)
LAPMS ...... Long Arm Posterior Molded Splint [*Medicine*] (MEDA)
LAPO .... Los Angeles Philharmonic Orchestra (SAUO)
LAPOCA ..... L-Asparaginase, Prednisone, Oncovin [*Vincristine*], Cytarabine, Adriamycin [*Antineoplastic drug regimen*]
La Pol Inst ... Louisiana Polytechnical Institute (SAUO)
LAPOR ...... La Porte, IN [*American Association of Railroads railroad junction routing code*]
LAPP .... Land Arctic Physical Processes (SAUO)
LAPP .... Lappish [*Language, etc.*] (ROG)
LAPP .... Lower Achieving Pupils Project [*British*]
LAPPES ..... Large Power Plant Effluent Study (NRCH)
Lappie .... Live-Alone Person [*Lifestyle classification*]
LAPR .... Life Assurance Premium Relief [*Business term*]
LAPR .... Los Alamos Power Reactor
LA-PR .... Los Alamos Progress Report (SAUO)
LAPRE .... Los Alamos Power Reactor Experiment
LAPS .... LASER Profile System
LAPS .... Latin American Philatelic Society (EA)
LAPS .... Latin American, Portuguese, and Spanish [*Division*] [*Library of Congress*]
LAPS .... Launcher Avionics Packages (MCD)
LAPS .... Left Aft Propulsion System [*or Subsystem*] (NASA)
LAPS .... Light-Addressable Potentiometric Sensor [*Semiconductor*]
LAPS .... Literary, Artistic, Political, or Scientific [*Value*] [*In obscenity law, a criterion established by the 1973 case of Miller Versus California*]
LAPS .... Loan Application Processing System
LAPS .... Local Analysis and Prediction System [*Marine science*] (OSRA)
LAPS .... Louis-Allen Power Supply
LAPS .... Lovelace Aerosol Particle Separator [*Lovelace Foundation for Medical Education and Research*] (PDAA)
LAPS .... Low-Altitude Proximity Sensor (MCD)
LAPS .... Low Attaining Pupils in Secondary Schools (AIE)
LAPSA .... Lineas Aereas Paraguayas Sociedad Anonima [*Airline*] [*Paraguay*]
LAPSE .... Longterm Ambulatory Physiological Surveillance Equipment (PDAA)
LAPSS .... Large Area Pulsed Solar Simulator (ACAE)
LAPSS .... LASER Airborne Photographic Scanning System [*Navy*]
LAPSS .... Low-Angle Polycrystalline Silicon Sheet [*Photovoltaic energy systems*]

LAPT........ La Porte Transit Company [*Common carrier symbol*]
LAPT........ Library Acquisitions: Practice and Theory [*A publication*]
LAPT........ Local Apparent Time (MSA)
LAPT........ London Association for the Protection of Trade (SAUO)
LAPT........ Los Angeles Union Passenger Terminal [*AAR code*]
LAPTA....... Local Authorities Passenger Transport Association (SAUO)
LAPTC....... Lucas Aerospace Power Transmission Corp. (SAUO)
LAPUT....... Light-Activated Programmable Unijunction Transistor
LAPW....... Left Atrial Posterior Wall [*Cardiology*] (DAVI)
LAPW....... Linear Augmented Plane-Wave [*Physics*]
LAPW....... Linearized Augmented Plane Wave [*Physical chemistry*]
LAPX........ Labelle Point Railroad [*Federal Railroad Administration identification code*]
LAPX........ Link Access Procedure Half-Duplex [*Telecommunications*] (ACRL)
LAQ......... Al Bayda [*Libya*] [*Airport symbol*] (AD)
LAQ......... Beida [*Libya*] [*Airport symbol*] (OAG)
LAQ......... Lacquer (KSC)
LAQ......... Latin America Equity Fd [*NYSE symbol*] (TTSB)
LAQ......... Latin America Equity Fund [*NYSE symbol*] (SPSG)
LAQ......... Leathercrafters' Association of Queensland [*Australia*]
LAQ......... Lebanese Air Transport [*ICAO designator*] (FAAC)
LAQ......... Legislative Assembly of Queensland [*Australia*]
L'AQORCD... L'Association Quebecoise des Organismes Regionaux de Concertation et de Developpement (AC)
LAQ STNS... Laquer Stains
LAQT........ Low-Altitude Qualification Test [*Balloon*]
LaQuinta.... La Quinta Motor Inns Ltd. [*Associated Press*] (SAG)
LAR......... Division of Labor Relations (SAUO)
LAR......... Labor Arbitration Reports [*Bureau of National Affairs*] [*A publication*] (DLA)
LAR......... Laboratory Animal Resources
LAR......... Land Registry [*British*]
LAR......... Laramie [*Wyoming*] [*Airport symbol*] (OAG)
LAR......... Laramie [*Wyoming*] [*Seismograph station code, US Geological Survey*] (SEIS)
LAR......... Laramie, WY [*Location identifier*] [*FAA*] (FAAL)
LAR......... Larceny [*Legal shorthand*] (LWAP)
LAR......... Large-Account Reseller (GART)
LAR......... Lariat Oil & Gas Ltd. [*Toronto Stock Exchange symbol*]
LAR......... Lark (automobile) [*NCIC car model code*]
LAR......... Laryngology
lar......... Larynx [*Anatomy*] (DAVI)
LAR......... LASER-Aided Rocket (MCD)
LAR......... Last Address Register (TIMI)
LAR......... Late Asthmatic Response [*Medicine*] (DAVI)
LAR......... Late Reaction [*Medicine*] (DMAA)
LAR......... Launch Acceptability Region (MCD)
LAR......... Launch Alert Receiver (DNAB)
LAR......... Launcher Adapter Rail (MCD)
LAR......... Lawrence Aviation, Inc. [*ICAO designator*] (FAAC)
LAR......... Leaf Area Ratio [*Botany*]
LAR......... Leaflet Artillery Round [*PSYOP*] (RDA)
LAR......... Left Arm Reclining [*or Recumbent*] [*Medicine*]
LAR......... Leukocyte Adhesion Receptor [*Immunology*]
LAR......... Leukocyte Antigen-Related [*Medicine*] (DMAA)
LAR......... Library Association of Rhodesia (SAUO)
LAR......... Library Association Record [*A publication*] (BRI)
LAR......... Libyan Arab Republic (BUAC)
LAR......... Life Assurance Relief [*British*]
LAR......... Ligase Amplification Reaction [*Biochemistry*] (QSUL)
LAR......... Light Artillery Rocket (MCD)
LAR......... Light Attendant Station [*Coast Guard*]
LAR......... Light Automatic Rifle (SAUS)
LAR......... Limit Address Register [*Computer science*]
LAR......... Limited Access Required (ACAE)
LAR......... Linhas Aereas Regionais SA [*Portugal*] [*ICAO designator*] (FAAC)
LAR......... Liquid Air Rocket
LAR......... Load Access Rights (VLIE)
LAR......... Local Acquisition RADAR (CET)
LAR......... Locus Activation Region [*Genetics*]
LAR......... Logistic Assessment Review (ACAE)
LAR......... Logistics Assessment Review (SAUO)
LAR......... Logistics Assistance Representative [*Army*] (DOMA)
LAR......... Loita Armada Revolucionaria [*Armed Revolutionary Struggle*] [*Spain*] (PD)
LAR......... Long-Range Aircraft Rocket (NG)
LAR......... Long-Range Assessments and Research [*Program*] [*Department of State*] [*Washington, DC*]
LAR......... Los Angeles Raiders [*National Football League*] [*1982-94*] (NFLA)
LAR......... Lot Age Report (AAEL)
L-Ar......... Louisiana Department of State, State Archives and Records, Baton Rouge, LA [*Library symbol*] [*Library of Congress*] (LCLS)
LA R......... Louisiana Reports [*A publication*] (DLA)
LAR......... Low-Altitude Release
LAR......... Low-Angle Reentry [*Aerospace*] (MCD)
LAR......... Low-Aspect Ratio
LARA........ Land Access Rights Association (BUAC)
LARA........ Larado Mobile Homes [*NCIC trailer make code*]
LARA........ Latin American Railways Association (EA)
LARA........ League of Americans Residing Abroad (SAUO)
LARA........ Licensed Agencies for Relief in Asia (SAUO)
LARA........ Light Armed Reconnaissance Aircraft [*Air Force*]
LARA........ Local Acquisition Radar (ACAE)
LARA........ Low-Altitude RADAR Altimeter [*Air Force*]
LARAC....... Local Authority Recycling Advisory Council (BUAC)
LARAM...... Line Accessed Random-Accesed Memory [*Medicine*] (EDAA)
LARAM...... Line Addressable Random Access Memory [*Computer science*] (MDG)
LArB........ Bienville Parish Library, Arcadia, LA [*Library symbol*] [*Library of Congress*] (LCLS)
LArbG....... Landesarbeitsgericht [*Provincial Labor Court of Appeal*] [*German*] (ILCA)
LARC........ Association for Library Automation Research Communications (EA)
LARC........ Lambda Amateur Radio Club (EA)
LaRC........ Langley Research Center [*Hampton, VA*] (NAKS)
LARC........ Langley Research Center [*NASA*]
LARC........ Larceny [*FBI standardized term*]
LARC........ Large Automatic Research Computer [*or Calculator*]
LARC........ LASER-Activated Recession Compensator (MCD)
LARC........ LASER Applications Research Center (RCD)
LARC........ Latin American Research Centre [*University of Calgary*] [*Canada*] (RCD)
LARC........ Legal Aid Review Committee
LARC........ Leukocyte Automatic Recognition Computer [*Blood counting*]
LARC........ Library Automation Research and Consulting Association (NITA)
LARC........ Library Automation Research and Consulting Services (IAA)
LARC........ Libyan-American Reconstruction Commission
LARC........ Light Amphibious Resupply Craft
LARC........ Lighter, Amphibious, Resupply, Cargo [*Army ship designation*] (POLM)
LARC........ Lindheimer Astronomical Research Center [*Northwestern University*]
LARC........ Livermore Atomic Research Computer
LARC........ Livermore Automatic Research Calculator (VLIE)
LARC........ Livermore Automatic Research Computer (RALS)
LARC........ Local Alcoholism Reception Center
LARC........ Locally Assigned Reporting Code [*Munitions reports*] (AFM)
LARC........ Loose Actors Revolving Company [*for producing plays; members include actors George C. Scott and Rod Steiger*]
LARC........ Low-Altitude Ride Control [*Shock-absorbing system*] [*Aviation*] (MCD)
LARC........ Luse Asbestos Removal Company (EFIS)
LaRC........ NASA Langley Research Center (SAUO)
LARC........ Regional Conference for Latin America [*UN Food and Agriculture Organization*]
LARCCH..... Latin America Resource Center and Clearinghouse [*Defunct*] (EA)
LARCEF..... Latin American Council for Cosmic Radiation & Physical (SAUO)
LARCF....... Lithuanian American Roman Catholic Federation (EA)
LARCH...... Larch, MI [*American Association of Railroads railroad junction routing code*]
LARC Services... Library Automation Research and Consulting Services (SAUO)
LARCT....... Last Radio Contact [*Aviation*]
LARC-V...... Lighter, Amphibious, Resupply, Cargo-Five Ton [*Vessel*] (DNAB)
LARD........ Lacrimo-Auriculo-Radio-Dental [*Syndrome*] [*Medicine*] (EDAA)
LARD........ Load Adjuster Reference Datum (IAA)
LarDav...... Larson-Davis [*Associated Press*] (SAG)
LARDS...... Low-Accuracy RADAR Data Transmission System
LARE........ Local Asymptotic Relative Efficiency [*Statistics*]
LARED....... Laredo, TX [*American Association of Railroads railroad junction routing code*]
LAREHS..... Laboratory of Research in Human and Social Ecology [*University of Quebec at Montreal*] [*Canada*] [*Research center*] (RCD)
LA Rep...... Louisiana Reports [*A publication*] (DLA)
LA Rev Stat Ann (West)... West's Louisiana Revised Statutes, Annotated [*A publication*] (DLA)
LARF........ Latin American Reserve Fund (BUAC)
LARF........ Lebanese Armed Revolutionary Faction
LARF........ Low-Altitude RADAR Fuzing (CET)
LARG........ Largamente [*Easily*] [*Music*]
LARG........ Largo [*Very Slow*] [*Music*] (ROG)
LARG........ Library-Anthropology Resource Group
LARGE....... Laboratory of Regional Geodynamics (SAUO)
LARGE....... Moscow Laboratory of Regional Geodynamics (SAUS)
LARGO...... Larghetto [*Slow*] [*Music*] (ROG)
LARGOS..... LASER-Activated Reflecting Geodetic Optical Satellite
LARIA....... Local Authorities Research and Intelligence Association [*British*]
LARIAT...... LASER RADAR Intelligence Acquisition Technology
LARIAT...... Long-Range Area RADAR for Intrusion Detection and Tracking
LARIS....... Louisiana Areal Resource Information System (SAUO)
LARIS....... Low-Altitude RADAR Interface System (MCD)
Larizz....... Larizza Industries, Inc. [*Associated Press*] (SAG)
LARK........ Landmark Bancshares [*NASDAQ symbol*] (TTSB)
LARK........ Lark Trailer [*NCIC trailer make code*]
LARL........ Laurel Cap Group [*NASDAQ symbol*] (TTSB)
LARL........ Laurel Capital Group [*NASDAQ symbol*] (SAG)
LARL........ Laurel Savings Assn. [*NASDAQ symbol*] (COMM)
LARM........ Logistics Assets Requirements Model (PDAA)
LARM........ Low-Angle Re-Entry Maneuvering Re-Entry Vehicle (PDAA)
LARMC....... Landstuhl Army Regional Medical Center [*Germany*]
LARO........ Larson Machine [*NCIC trailer make code*]
LARO........ Latin American Regional Office [*United Nations Food and Agricultural Organization*] (BARN)
LAROO...... Lackland Aircraft Reactors Operations Office (SAA)
LARP........ Launch and Recovery Platform (DNAB)
LARP........ Line Automatic Reperforator (CET)
LARP........ Live-Action Role Playing (ADWA)
LARP........ Local and Remote Printing [*Computer science*]
LARP........ Local Approvals Review Program
LARPS....... Large Aircraft Robotic Paint-Stripping System (SAUS)
LARPS....... Local and Remote Printing Station [*Computer science*]
LARR........ Large Area Record Reader (IAA)

LARR .... Latin American Research Review. University of North Carolina Press for the Latin American Studies Association. Chapel Hill (SAUO)
LARR .... Linear Accelerator Regenerator Reactor (BARN)
LARRIE ...... Local Authorities Race Relations Information Exchange (BUAC)
LARRL .... Fort Keogh Livestock and Range Research Laboratory [*Miles City, MT*] [*Department of Agriculture*] (GRD)
LARRS ...... Livestock and Range Research Station [*Department of Agriculture*] (GRD)
LARRS ...... Low-Altitude Retro Rocket System (DWSG)
LARS .... Laboratory for Agricultural Remote Sensing
LARS .... Laboratory for Applications of Remote Sensing [*Purdue University*] [*Research center*] (RCD)
LARS .... Laminar Angular Rate Sensor [*Navy*]
LARS .... Language-Structured Auditory Retention Span Test
LARS .... Large Animal Research Station [*University of Alaska Fairbanks*] (RCD)
LARS .... Larscom Inc. [*NASDAQ symbol*] (SAG)
LARS .... Larsen Lapline Trailer [*NCIC trailer make code*]
LARS .... LASER-Aided Rocket System [*Military*] (CAAL)
LARS .... LASER Angular Rate Sensor [*or Scanner*]
LARS .... LASER-Articulated Robotic System
LARS .... Launch and Recovery System [*NASA*]
LARS .... Learning and Recognition System [*GTE*]
LARS .... Left Add, Right Subtract [*Army field artillery technique*] (INF)
LARS .... Leucyl-Transfer Ribonucleic Acid [*Biochemistry*] (DAVI)
LARS .... Light Artillery Rocket System (NATG)
LARS .... Living Aquatic Resources Sector [*Aquaculture*]
LARS .... Low-Altitude RADAR System (NATG)
LARS .... Lower Airspace RADAR Advisory Service [*British*] (DA)
LARS .... Lower Atmosphere Research Satellite (SSD)
LARSA .... Latin American Rural Sociological Association (EAIO)
Larscom .... Larscom Inc. [*Associated Press*] (SAG)
LARSFRIS ... Laboratory for Applications of Remote Sensing Forest (SAUO)
LARSI .... Laboratoire de Recherche en Sciences Immobilieres [*University of Quebec at Montreal*] [*Research center*] (RCD)
LA RSIS ..... LA Reference, Special and Information Section [*British*] (NITA)
LARSIS ...... Library Association Reference and Special Information Section (PDAA)
LARSP .... Language Assessment Remediation and Screening Procedure [*for the language impaired*]
LARSSYAA ... Laboratory for Applications of Remote Sensing System for Aircraft Analysis [*NASA*] (GFGA)
LARSYS ..... Laboratory of Applications of Remote Sensing Image Data Processing System (SAUO)
LARSYSAA ... Laboratory for Applications of Remote Sensing System for Aircraft Analysis (SAUO)
LART .... Larsen Trucking [*Common carrier symbol*]
LART .... Lateral Acceleration Response Time
LART .... Los Angeles Rapid Transit (SAUO)
LART .... Loser Attitude Readjustment Tool [*Internet lingo*] (NETL)
LART .... Luser Attitude Re-adjustment Tool (SAUS)
LARTS .... LOGAIR Real-Time Terminal System (SAUO)
LARU .... Lanan [*Intermodal shipping container symbol*] (TVRC)
LARU .... Latin American Research Unit (SAUO)
LARV .... Light Armoured Reconnaissance Vehicle (SAUS)
LARV .... Low-Altitude Research Vehicle (IAA)
LARVA .... Low-Altitude Research Vehicular Advancements
LARWS ...... Lightweight Airborne Radar Warning System (SAUO)
LARX .... Larsen Farms [*Private rail car owner code*]
LARX .... Lewistown & Auburn Railroad [*Federal Railroad Administration identification code*]
laryn .... Laryngeal [*Medicine*] (STED)
laryn .... Laryngitis [*Otorhinolaryngology*] (DAVI)
laryn .... Laryngoscopy [*Otorhinolaryngology*] (DAVI)
Laryng .... Laryngologist/ogy [*Medicine*] (EDAA)
Laryng .... Laryngology
Laryng .... Laryngoscope [*Medicine*] (EDAA)
Laryng .... Laryngoscope/py [*Medicine*] (EDAA)
LARYNGLGST ... Laryngologist
LARYNGLGY ... Laryngology
Laryngol .... Laryngologist (DAVI)
LARYNGOL ... Laryngology
LARZ .... Lanan [*Intermodal trailer symbol*]
LARZ .... Little America Refinery [*Federal Railroad Administration identification code*]
LAS .... Almirall [*Spain*] [*Research code symbol*]
LAS .... Label as Such [*Pharmacology*] (CDAI)
las .... Label as Such [*Medicine*] (WDAA)
LAS .... Labor Area Summary [*Employment and Training Administration*] [*Department of Labor*]
LAS .... Laboratories of Applied Sciences [*University of Chicago*] (MCD)
LAS .... Laboratory Analytical Services (SAUO)
LAS .... Laboratory Animal Sciences
LAS .... Laboratory Automation System
LAS .... Laboratory of Atmospheric Sciences [*National Science Foundation*]
LAS .... LAGEOS Apogee Stage (SAUS)
LAS .... Lama [*Language symbol*] (ETLW)
LAS .... Land Agents' Society [*British*] (DI)
LAS .... Land Analysis Software (ACAE)
LAS .... Land Analysis System (ACAE)
LAS .... Landing Approach Simulator
LAS .... Landsat Assessment System (ACAE)
LAS .... LANDSAT [*Land Remote Sensing Satellite System*] Sensor [*NASA*] (SSD)
LAS .... Lane Awareness System [*Automotive electronics*]
LAS .... Language Assessment Scales [*Test*]
LAS .... Lapidus Airfloat System (DAVI)
LAS .... Large Amplitude Simulator
LAS .... Large Astronomical Satellite [*ESRO*]
LAS .... Large-Probe Atmospheric Structure [*NASA*]
LAS .... La Salle College, Philadelphia, PA [*OCLC symbol*] (OCLC)
LAS .... LASER Absorption Spectrometer
LAS .... LASER Antiflash System
LAS .... LASER Attack System
LAS .... Laser (automobile) [*NCIC car model code*]
LAS .... Laser Indus Ltd, Ord [*AMEX symbol*] (TTSB)
LAS .... Laser Industries Ltd. [*AMEX symbol*] (SPSG)
LAS .... Last [*Telegraphy*] (PCTE)
LAS .... Las Vegas [*Nevada*] [*Airport symbol*] (OAG)
LAS .... Las Vegas, NV [*Location identifier*] [*FAA*] (FAAL)
LAS .... Lateral Amyotrophic Sclerosis [*Medicine*] (STED)
LAS .... Launch Area Supervisor (AFM)
LAS .... Launch Auxiliary System
las .... Laxative [*Medicine*] (DAVI)
LAS .... Laxative Abuse Syndrome [*Medicine*] (DAVI)
LAS .... Leader Authenticity Scale [*Psychology*] (EDAC)
LAS .... Leadership Appraisal Survey [*Interpersonal skills and attitudes test*]
LAS .... League of Arab States [*Tunis, Tunisia*]
LAS .... Lebanese-American Society of Greater New York [*Defunct*] (EA)
LAS .... Left Anterior-Superior [*Anatomy*] (DAVI)
LAS .... Left Arm Sitting [*Blood pressure and pulse measurement*] [*Cardiology*] (DAVI)
LAS .... Legal Aid Service (SAUO)
LAS .... Legal Aid Society (WDAA)
LAS .... Leipziger Aegyptologische Studien [*A publication*] (BJA)
LAS .... Leisure Attitude Scale (IDYL)
LAS .... Leucine Acetylsalicylate [*Biochemistry*] (DAVI)
LAS .... Liberal Arts and Sciences (FOTI)
LAS .... Library Access System (SAUO)
LAS .... Library Association of Singapore (BUAC)
LAS .... Library Automation Services [*Oxford University*]
LAS .... Life Assurance of Scotland [*Commercial firm*]
LAS .... Light-Activated Switch
LAS .... Lignes Aerienne Seychelles [*ICAO designator*] (FAAC)
LAS .... Limited Assignment Status [*Military*]
LAS .... Limited Assortment Store (WDMC)
LAS .... Line Apparatus Shop [*Telecommunications*] (OA)
LAS .... Linear Alkylbenzene Sulfonate [*Surfactant*]
LAS .... Linear Alkyl Sulfonate (STED)
LAS .... Link Active Scheduler (ACII)
LAS .... Litha-Alumina-Silicate [*Inorganic chemistry*]
LAS .... Lithuanian Academy of Sciences (BUAC)
LAS .... Liturgical Arts Society (EA)
LAS .... Liverpool Architectural Society (SAUO)
LAS .... Local Adaptation Syndrome [*Medicine*]
LAS .... Local Address Space
LAS .... Local Alignment System [*Optics*]
LAS .... Local Area Screening
LAS .... Location Addressable Storage [*Computer science*] (VLIE)
LAS .... Lockheed Aircraft Services Co. (SAUO)
LAS .... Locum Appointment Service (SAUO)
LAS .... Logical Address Strobe
LAS .... Logical Compare Accumulator with Storage (SAA)
LAS .... Logic Analysis System [*Rohde and Schwartz*] [*Germany*] (NITA)
LAS .... London Appreciation Society
LAS .... Long-Arm Splint [*Orthopedics*] (DAVI)
LAS .... Longitudinal Air Spring
LAS .... Long-Range Assistance Strategy (CINC)
LAS .... Look-Out Aiming Sight [*Military*] (PDAA)
LAS .... Loop Actuating Signal (SAA)
LAS .... Lord Advocate of Scotland
LAS .... Los Alamos Science (SAUO)
LAS .... Los Angeles Shop (SAUO)
LAS .... Louisiana Academy of Sciences (SAUO)
LAS .... Low Air Speed (MCD)
LAS .... Low-Alloy Steel
LAS .... Low-Altitude Satellite
LAS .... Low-Angle Scattering [*Physics*] (ODA)
LAS .... Low Apgar Score [*Medicine*] (MELL)
LAS .... Lower Abdominal Surgery (DAVI)
LAS .... Lower Airspace (WDAA)
LAS .... Lunar Attitude System [*Aerospace*]
LAS .... Lung Alveolar Surfactant (SAUS)
LAS .... Lupus Anticoagulant Syndrome [*Medicine*] (MELL)
LAS .... Lutheran Academy for Scholarship [*Defunct*] (EA)
LAS .... Lymphadenopathy Syndrome [*Medicine*]
LAS .... Lymphangioscintigraphy (STED)
LAS .... Lysine Acetylsalicylate [*Biochemistry*]
LAS .... McCarran International Airport [*FAA*] (TAG)
LAS .... Saskatchewan Libraries Retrospective Conversion [*UTLAS symbol*]
LAS .... London Archaeological Service (ODA)
LASA .... Laboratory Animal Science Association [*British*]
LASA .... Large Aperture Seismic Array [*Nuclear detection device*]
LASA .... Large Area Solar Array
LASA .... La Salle [*NCIC trailer make code*]
LASA .... LASER Anti-Satellite Weapon (LAIN)
LASA .... Latin American Shipowners Association (BUAC)
LASA .... Latin American Student Association (SAUO)
LASA .... Latin American Studies Association (EA)

LA(SA) ...... Latvian Association of South Australia
LASA .... LIDAR [*Light Detection and Ranging*] Atmospheric Sounder and Altimeter
LASA .... Linear-Analogue Self Assessment (DMAA)
LASA .... London Advice Services Alliance [*England*] (BUAC)
LASAIL ...... Land-Sea-Air Interaction Laboratory (SAUO)
LASAL .... LaSalle, IL [*American Association of Railroads railroad junction routing code*]
La Salette Missionaries... Missionaries of Our Lady of La Salette (SAUO)
LaSalle...... La Salle Re Holdings Ltd. [*Associated Press*] (SAG)
LASAM ...... Laser Anti Tank Semi Active Missile (ACAE)
LASAM ...... LASER Semiactive Missile
LASAN....... Los Alamos Systems Analysis (SAUO)
LASA-P...... Linear-Analogue Self-Assessment-Pristman (DMAA)
LASAR....... Logic Automated Stimulus and Response (MCD)
LASARS ..... Low Probability of Intercept Antijam Secure Airborne Radio System (MCD)
LASAS....... Latin American Secretariat for Academic Services [*Defunct*]
LASA-S...... Linear-Analogue Self-Assessment-Selby (DMAA)
LASAT .... Laser Antisatellite Satellite (ACAE)
LASB .... Lackawaxen & Stourbridge Railroad Corp. [*AAR code*]
LASBO....... Louisiana Association of School Business Officials (SAUO)
LASC .... Light Armored Squad Carrier
LASC .... Lockheed Aeronautical Systems Corporation (ACAE)
LASC .... Los Angeles State College (SAUO)
LASCA....... Large Area Solar Cell Array
LASCA....... Los Angeles State and County Arboretum (SAUO)
LASCAR ..... Language for Simulation of Computer Architecture (CSR)
Lasc H War... Lascelles' Horse Warranty [*2nd ed.*] [*1880*] [*A publication*] (DLA)
Lasc Juv Off... Lascelles on Juvenile Offenders [*A publication*] (DLA)
LASCO....... Laher Spring & Electric Car Corp. (EFIS)
LASCO....... Large Angle and Spectrometric Coronagraph Experiment [*For observation of the sun*]
LASCO....... Large-Angle Spectrometric Coronagraph [*Marine science*] (OSRA)
LASCO....... Large-Angle Spectroscopic Coronagraph [*Instrumentation*]
LASCo .... Larkin Aircraft Supply Company (SAUO)
LASCO....... Latin American Science Cooperation Office (SAUO)
LASCO....... Latin America Science Cooperation Office (MSC)
LASCODOCS... Linguistic Analysis of Spanish Colonial Documents
LASCOM .... Laser Communication (SAUS)
LASCOT ..... Large Screen Color Television System (NASA)
LASCR....... Light-Activated Silicon-Controlled Rectifier
LASCS....... Light-Activated Silicon-Controlled Switch (MCD)
LASD .... Labor Agreement Settlement Data [*Cast Metals Association*] [*A publication*]
LASD .... Large Area Screen Display (VLIE)
LASD .... Latin American Serial Documents
LASE......... LAMPS Shipboard Element (MCD)
LASE......... Large Aperture Seismic Experiment [*Geophysical survey*]
LASE......... Laser [*NCIC car make code*]
LASE......... Laser Adjustable Synethetic Epikeratoplasty (SAUS)
LASE......... Laser Atmospheric Sensing Experiment (ACAE)
LASE......... Laser-Scan International, Inc. (SAUO)
LASE......... Laser Sight, Inc. [*NASDAQ symbol*] (SAG)
L-Ase........ L-Asparaginase [*Also, A, L, L-Asp, L-asnase*] [*An enzyme, an antineoplastic*]
LASE......... LIDAR [*Light Detection and Ranging*] Atmosphere Sensing Experiment
LASE......... Lidar Atmospheric Sensing Experiment (SAUO)
LASE......... Logistics Asset Support Estimate
LASED....... Latin Americans for Social and Economic Development (SAUO)
LASEDECO... Land Settlement and Development Corp. [*Philippines*] (BUAC)
LASEK....... Laser Epithelial Keratomileusis [*Medicine*]
LASEORS ... London and South Eastern Operational Research Society (SAUO)
LASER....... Laboratory for Advanced Software Engineering Research [*University of Massachusetts at Amherst*] (RCD)
Laser........ Laser Industries Ltd. [*Associated Press*] (SAG)
LASER....... League for the Advancement of States' Equal Rights (EA)
LASER....... Learning About Science, Engineering, and Research (SAUS)
LASER....... Learning Achievement through Saturated Educational Resources
LASER....... Light Amplification by Stimulated Emission of Radiation [*Acronym was coined in 1957 by scientist Gordon Gould*]
LASER....... London and South East Advisory Council [*England*] (BUAC)
LASER....... London and South Eastern Library Region [*Information service or system*] (IID)
LASER....... London and South Eastern Library Region cooperative (SAUO)
LASERCOM... LASER Communications (MCD)
LASERCOM... Light Amplification by Stimulated Emission of Radiation Computer Output Microfilm (EECA)
Lasergte .... Lasergate Systems, Inc. [*Associated Press*] (SAG)
LASERS ..... Learning about Science Easily and Readily (SAUS)
LaserSt...... Laser Storm, Inc. [*Associated Press*] (SAG)
Lasertech... Laser Technics [*Associated Press*] (SAG)
LA Sess Law Serv... Louisiana Session Law Service [*A publication*] (DLA)
LASFB....... Left Anterior-Superior Fascicular Block [*Medicine*] (STED)
LASGAM .... Laser Semi-Active Guided Anti Tank Missile (ACAE)
LASH .... Lake & Shore [*NCIC truck make code*]
LASH .... LASER Antitank Semiactive Homing
LASH .... Latin American Society of Hepatology [*See also SLH*] (EAIO)
LASH .... Left Anterior-Superior Hemiblock [*Medicine*] (STED)
LASH .... Left Anterosuperior Hemiblock [*Cardiology*] (DAVI)
LASH .... Legislative Action on Smoking and Health (EA)
LASH .... Lighter Aboard Ship [*Barge-carrying ship*]
LASH .... Locking Action Safety Holster [*Police and security equipment*]
LASHAR..... Laser System Hardware (ACAE)
LASHE....... Low Altitude Simultaneous HAWK Engagement (SAUS)
LASHST..... Latin American Society for the History of Sciences and Technology (BUAC)
LASHUP..... Land-Air Synergic Homogeneous Ultra-Processor (SAA)
LASI .... Landing-Site Indicator [*Aviation*]
LASI .... Laser Industries Ltd. (SAUO)
LASI .... Library of Ancient Semitic Inscriptions (BJA)
LASI .... Licentiate of the Ambulance Service Institute [*British*] (DBQ)
LASI .... Lockheed Aircraft Service, Incorporated (SAUO)
LASIC........ Laser Application Specific Integrated Circuit (SAUS)
LASIE........ Information Bulletin. Library Automated Systems Information Exchange (journ.) (SAUS)
LASIE........ Library Automated Systems Information Exchange [*Australia*] (NITA)
LASIK........ Laser Assisted In-Situ Keratomileusis [*Ophthalmology*]
LASIK........ Laser In-situ Keratomileusis (SAUS)
LASIK........ Laser in Situ Keratomileusis [*A combination of laser and lamellar corneal surgery*] [*Medicine*] (EDAA)
LASIL........ Land and Sea Interaction Laboratory [*Environmental Science Services Administration*]
LASIM....... LASER Aiming Simulation (PDAA)
LASIM....... Los Angeles Society of Internal Medicine (BUAC)
LASINT...... LASER Intelligence (MCD)
LASJ......... Latin American Society of Japan (SAUO)
LASJC....... La Salle Junction, IL [*American Association of Railroads railroad junction routing code*]
LASL......... La Salle Homes [*NCIC trailer make code*]
LASL......... Los Alamos Scientific Laboratory [*USAEC*]
LASLA....... Laboratoire d'Analyse Statistique des Langues Anciennes [*Laboratory for the Statistical Analysis of Ancient Languages*] [*University of Liege, Belgium*]
LASLA....... Laboratory for the Statistical Analysis of Ancient Languages (SAUO)
LASM........ Laboratories for Applied Superconductivity and Magnetism [*Ohio State University*] (RCD)
LASM........ Land-Attack Standard Missile
LASM........ LASER Semiactive Missile (DNAB)
LASMCO .... Liberian American-Swedish Minerals Company (SAUO)
LASMEC..... Local Authorities School Meals Equipment Consortium
Lasmo....... Lasmo Ltd. [*Associated Press*] (SAG)
LASMO....... London & Scottish Marine Oil [*British*]
L-Asnase.... L-Asparaginase [*Also, A, L, L-ase, L-Asp*] [*An enzyme, an antineoplastic*]
LASO .... Latin American Solidarity Organization (BUAC)
LASO .... Los Angeles Society of Ophthalmology (SAUO)
LASO .... Low-Altitude Search Option [*Search mode of the BOMARC guidance system*]
L A social econ trans... Proceedings of the Conference on Latin America in Social and Economic Transition. Inter-American Short Papers. The University of New Mexico Press. (SAUO)
LA-SOP...... Los Alamos Standard Operating Procedure (SAUO)
LASOR ...... Laser Airborne Simulated Optical Range Tester (ACAE)
LASOR ...... LASER Spillover and Reflectivity (MCD)
LASP .... Laboratory for Atmosphere and Space Physics (SAUS)
LASP .... Laboratory for Atmospheric and Space Physics [*University of Colorado*] [*Research center*]
L-Asp........ L-Asparaginase [*Also, A, L, L-ase, L-asnase*] [*An enzyme, an antineoplastic*]
LASP .... Local Attached Support Processor
LASP .... Logistics Analysis Simulation Program (VLIE)
LASP .... Low-Altitude Space Platform (MCD)
LASP .... Low-Altitude Surveillance Platform (MCD)
LASPAC ..... Landing Gear, Avionics Systems Package (MCD)
LaSPACE.... Louisiana Space Consortium (RCD)
LASPAU ..... Latin American Scholarship Program of American Universities (EA)
LasPMd ..... Laser Pacific Media Corp. [*Associated Press*] (SAG)
LASPOL ..... Leningrad Association of Soviet Polar Explorers (SAUO)
LASR .... Laboratories for Astrophysics and Space Research [*University of Chicago*] [*Research center*]
LASR .... Laser Precision Corp. (SAUO)
LASR .... Letter Writing with Automatic Send-Receive (IAA)
LASR .... Library Access, Search and Retrieval (SAUO)
LA-SR .... Los Alamos Status Report (SAUO)
LASR .... Low-Altitude Surveillance RADAR
LASR-2...... Litton Airborne Search RADAR Mark Two [*Canada*] (PDAA)
LASRA....... Leather and Shoe Research Association [*New Zealand*] (BUAC)
LASRAM .... Low-Altitude Short-Range Missile
LasrCp ...... Laser Corp. [*Associated Press*] (SAG)
LASRE....... Lightweight Advanced Super-Responsive Engine [*Automotive engineering*]
LASREF ..... Los Alamos Spallation Radiation Effects Facility (SAUO)
Lasrgt .... Lasergate Systems, Inc. [*Associated Press*] (SAG)
LASRM...... Low-Altitude Short-Range Missile
LASRM...... Low Altitude Supersonic Ramjet Missile (ACAE)
LASRM...... Low-Altitude Supersonic Research Missile
LasrmTc.... LaserMaster Technologies, Inc. [*Associated Press*] (SAG)
Lasrscp ..... Laserscope, Inc. [*Associated Press*] (SAG)
Lasrtch..... Laser Technics, Inc. [*Associated Press*] (SAG)
LASS .... Labile Aggregation-Stimulating Substance [*Hematology*]
LASS .... Land Applications Satellite System (ACAE)
LASS .... Language and Assembly Language [*Computer science*] (DNAB)
LASS .... Laptop Avionics Support System (SAUS)
LASS .... Large Aircraft Start System (DWSG)
LASS .... Large Amplitude Space Simulator (SAUS)
LASS .... Large Aperture Solenoid Spectrometer [*Stanford Linear Accelerator Center*]

LASS .... Large Area Screening Systems (MCD)
LASS .... Large Area Sky Survey
LASS .... Large Area Smoke Screening (SAUS)
LASS .... Large Area Space Simulator (ACAE)
LASS .... LASER-Activated Semiconductor Switch (IAA)
LASS .... LASER-Activated Silicon Switch (MCD)
LASS .... LASER Applications System Study [*Military*]
LASS .... Laser Scanning System (ACAE)
LASS .... Lateral Acceleration Sensing System (PDAA)
LASS .... Latin American Sleep Society (SAUO)
LASS .... Launch Area Support Ship
LASS .... Leisure Accident Surveillance System (HEAS)
LASS .... Liaoning Academy of Social Sciences (BUAC)
LASS .... Library Access and Sixth-Form Studies [*British*] (AIE)
LASS .... Library Automated Service System (IAA)
LASS .... Light-Activated Silicon Switch
LASS .... Lighter-than-Air Submarine Simulator
LASS .... Line Amplifier and Super Sync Mixer
LASS .... Linguistic Analysis of Speech Samples (DAVI)
LASS .... Linked Administrative Statistical Sample [*Social Security Administration*] (GFGA)
LASS .... Local Area Sensor System [*Military*] (LAIN)
LASS .... Local Area Signaling Service [*Bell Laboratories*]
LASS .... Local Area Signaling Services [*Telecommunications*] (ACRL)
LASS .... Local Area Sounding System (SAUO)
LASS .... Local Authority Social Services [*British*]
LASS .... Lockheed Airline System Simulation (PDAA)
LASS .... Logistic-Automated Support System (SSD)
LASS .... Logistics Activities Status System (SAUO)
LASS .... Logistics Analysis Simulation System
LASS .... Logistics Automated Supply System
LASS .... Los Angeles Special Services (SAUO)
LASS .... Low-Altitude Space Surveillance System [*Military*] (MUSM)
LASS .... Low Altitude Surveillance System (SAUS)
LASS .... Low-Angle Silicon Sheet [*Photovoltaic energy systems*]
LASS .... Lunar Applications of a Spent Stage [*Aerospace*] (MCD)
LASSA .... Licensed Animal Slaughter and Salvage Association (SAUO)
LASSA .... Licensed Animal Slaughterers and Salvage Association [*British*] (BI)
LASSC .... Latin American Social Sciences Council [*Argentina*] [*Database producer*] (EA)
LASSC .... Los Alamos Space and Science Committee (SAUO)
LASSCO ..... Los Angeles Steamship Company (SAUO)
LASSI .... Latin American Secretariat of the Socialist International (BUAC)
LASSI-HS ... Learning and Study Strategies Inventory-High School Version [*Test*] (TMMY)
LASSII ...... Low-Altitude Satellite Studies of Ionospheric Irregularities
LASSM ...... Line Amplifier and Super Sync Mixer (MSA)
LASSO ...... Landing and Approach System, Spiral-Oriented
LASSO ...... LASER Search and Secure Observer (CET)
LASSO ...... LASER Synchronization from Stationary Orbit (IEEE)
LASSO ...... Latin American Student Studies Organization (SAUO)
LASSO ...... Library Acquisition Services System Online [*Suggested name for the Library of Cogress computer system*]
LASSO ...... Light Air-to-Surface Semiautomatic Optical [*French missile*]
LASSO ...... Light Anti-Surface Semi-automatic Optical missile (SAUS)
LASSO ...... Light Aviation Special Support Operations
LASSO ...... Linguistic Association of the Southwest (SAUO)
LASSO ...... Lunar Applications of a Spent Stage in Orbit [*Aerospace*] (MCD)
LASSOS ..... Library Automation Systems and Services Options Study [*Advisory committee*] (NITA)
LASSP .... Laboratory for Atomic and Solid State Physics [*Cornell University*] [*Research center*] (RCD)
LASSP .... Los Alamos Students in Science Program (SAUO)
LA SSR ...... Latvian Soviet Socialist Republic (SAUO)
LASST .... Laboratory for Surface Science and Technology [*University of Maine at Orono*] [*Research center*] (RCD)
LASSV .... Land and Approach System for Space Vehicles [*NASA*] (KSC)
LAST .... Labor and Sample Tracking (SAUO)
LAST .... Lactic Acidosis Support Trust [*British*] (NRGU)
LAST .... Language and Systems Together [*Programming language*] [*Baytec*] [*Bay City, MI*]
LAST .... Large Aperture Scanning Telescope (TEL)
LAST .... La Salle Trucking Company [*Common carrier symbol*]
LAST .... Laser Aided Search and Track (ACAE)
LAST .... Last Satellite Position [*Navy Navigation Satellite System*] (DNAB)
LAST .... Left Anterior Small Thoracotomy [*Medicine*] (DMAA)
LAST .... Leukocyte-Antigen Sensitivity Testing [*Medicine*] (MEDA)
LAST .... Light Applique System Technique (SAUS)
LAST .... Local Area Storage Transport (SAUO)
LAST .... Local Area System Transport [*Computer science*] (CIST)
LAST .... Logic Analysis and Simulation Technique (VLIE)
LAST .... London Association of Science Teachers (SAUO)
LAST .... Low-Altitude Supersonic Target (RDA)
LASTCHP ... Last Paging Channel (CGWS)
LASTE .... Low-Altitude Safety and Targeting Equipment (DWSG)
LASTport ... Local Area Storage Transport [*Computer science*] (VLIE)
LASU .... Large Aircraft Sector Understanding (SAUO)
LASU .... Local Air Supply Unit [*British military*] (DMA)
LASU .... Socomat [*Intermodal shipping container symbol*] (TVRC)
LA SUQ ..... Louisiana State University. Quarterly [*A publication*] (DLA)
LASUSSR ... Library of the Academy of Science of the USSR (SAUO)
LASV .... Low-Altitude Supersonic Vehicle [*Formerly, SLAM*] [*Air Force*]
LASV .... Low-Altitude Surface Vehicle (WDAA)
LasVDsc .... Las Vegas Discount Golf & Tennis, Inc. [*Associated Press*] (SAG)
LasVE .... Las Vegas Entertainment Network [*Associated Press*] (SAG)
LasVEE ...... Las Vegas Entertainment Network [*Associated Press*] (SAG)
LASVEM ..... Lightly Armored Structure Vulnerability Estimation Methodology (MCD)
LasVEnt ..... Las Vegas Entertainment Network [*Associated Press*] (SAG)
LasVMaj .... Las Vegas Major League Sports [*Associated Press*] (SAG)
LASW .... Licensed Advanced Social Worker (SEAT)
LASW .... Lightweight Anti-Submarine Weapons (SAUS)
LASWMMR ... London Association of Scale and Weighing Machine Manufacturers and Repairers [*England*] (BUAC)
LASX .... Laser Technics [*NASDAQ symbol*] (SAG)
LASX .... Lasertechnics Inc. [*NASDAQ symbol*] (TTSB)
LAT .... Aviation Legere de l'Armee de Terre [*France*] [*ICAO designator*] (FAAC)
LAT .... Laboratory Assessment Team (SAUO)
LaT .... Lactate Threshold [*Biochemistry*]
LAT .... Lae [*Papua New Guinea*] [*Seismograph station code, US Geological Survey*] (SEIS)
LAT .... Language Aptitude Test [*Military*] (AFM)
LAT .... Large Angle Tagger (MCD)
LAT .... Large Angle Torque (MCD)
LAT .... LASER Acquisition and Tracking (OA)
LAT .... Latch (NASA)
Lat .... Latch's English King's Bench Reports [*1625-28*] [*A publication*] (DLA)
LAT .... Latent
Lat .... Lateral [*Medicine*] (AMHC)
LAT .... Lateral (KSC)
lat .... Lateral (VRA)
LAT .... Latex Agglutination Test [*Clinical chemistry*]
LAT .... Lathwell Resources Ltd. [*Vancouver Stock Exchange symbol*]
Lat .... Latin (BEE)
lat .... Latin [*MARC language code*] [*Library of Congress*] (LCCP)
LAT .... Latin
lat .... Latissimus [*Dorsi*] (STED)
lat .... Latitude (ELAL)
Lat .... Latitude (WA)
LAT .... Latitude
LAT .... Latitude of Target
LAT .... Latrine (DSUE)
LAT .... Latshaw Enterprises, Inc. [*AMEX symbol*] (COMM)
LAT .... Lattice (MIST)
lat .... Latus [*Broad*] [*Latin*] (EES)
LAT .... Latus [*Wide*] [*Pharmacy*]
Lat .... Latvia (MILB)
LAT .... Latvia
LAT .... Learning Ability Test [*Military*] (AFM)
LAT .... Learning by Advanced Telecommunications (SAUO)
LAT .... Left Anterior Thigh [*Medicine*]
LAT .... Left Atrial Thrombosis [*Medicine*] (EDAA)
LAT .... Less Active Tetragonal (PDAA)
LAT .... Level above Threshold
LAT .... Licensing Appeals Tribunal [*Australia*]
LAT .... Lidocaine, Adrenaline and Tetracaine (SAUS)
LAT .... Light Anti-Tank (SAUS)
LAT .... Light Artillery Tractor [*British military*] (DMA)
LAT .... Linear Accelerator Tube
LAT .... Linseed Association Terms [*Shipping*]
LAT .... Local Access Transport (AGLO)
LAT .... Local Apparent Time
LAT .... Local Area Transport [*Telecommunications*]
LAT .... Lockheed Air Terminal, Inc. [*Subsidiary of Lockheed Aircraft Corp.*]
LAT .... Locum Appointment for Training (SAUO)
LAT .... Logistics Assistance Team (MCD)
LAT .... Long-Acting Theophylline [*Pharmacology*]
LA-T .... Los Alamos Thesis (SAUO)
LAT .... Los Angeles Tiger [*Automotive accessories*]
LAT .... Los Angeles Times [*A publication*]
LAT .... Lot Acceptance Test (NASA)
LAT .... Lovely and Talented [*Internet lingo*] (NETL)
LAT .... Low-Altitude Tactics (DOMA)
LAT .... Low-Angle Track (CAAL)
LAT .... Lowest Astronomical Tide (PDAA)
LAT .... Lumbermen's Association of Texas (SRA)
LAT .... Lysolecithin Acyltransferase [*Medicine*] (EDAA)
Lat .... Valsts Biblioteka [*State Library of Latvia*], Riga, Latvia [*Library symbol*] [*Library of Congress*] (LCLS)
LAT-A .... Latrunculin-A [*A toxin*]
LATA .... Local Access and Transport Area
LATA .... Local Access Transport Area [*Telecommunications*]
LATA .... Local Area and Transport Area (CCCA)
LATA .... Local-Area Telephone Authority [*Telecommunications*]
LATA .... London Amenity and Transport Association
LATA .... Los Alamos Technical Associates, Inc. (SAUO)
LatACas ..... Latin American Casinos, Inc. [*Associated Press*] (SAG)
LatADis ..... Latin American Discovery Fund [*Associated Press*] (SAG)
LatADIr ..... Latin America Dollar Income Fund [*Associated Press*] (SAG)
LAT AD-MOV .... Lateri Admoveatum [*Let It Be Applied to the Side*] [*Pharmacy*]
LatAEqt ..... Latin America Equity Fund [*Associated Press*] (SAG)
LATAF .... Logistics Activation Task Force [*Air Force*] (MCD)
LATAG .... LASER Air-to-Air Gunnery Simulator [*Military*] (CAAL)
LATAG .... Latin American Trade Advisory Group [*British Overseas Trade Board*] (DS)
LatAInv ...... Latin American Investment Fund [*Associated Press*] (SAG)
LATAK .... Latvian National Accreditation Bureau (SAUO)

LatAm .... Index to Latin American Periodicals (journ.) (SAUS)
Lat Am Antiq... Latin American Antiquity. Society for American Archaeology. Washington (SAUO)
Lat Am Stud/NISC... Latin American Studies. National Information Services Corporation. Baltimore (SAUO)
lat & loc .... Lateralizing and Localizing [*Medicine*] (STED)
LATAR .... LASER-Augmented Target Acquisition and Recognition System (MCD)
LATAS .... LASER-Augmented Target Acquisition System
LAT-B .... Latrunculin-B [*A toxin*]
LATB .... Lithium Aluminum Tri-tert-Butoxyhydride [*Organic chemistry*]
LATBR .... Los Angeles Times Book Review [*A publication*] (BRI)
LATC .... Lateral Talocalcaneal [*Medicine*] (RAWO)
LATC .... Los Angeles Theater Center [*California*]
LATCC .... London Air-Traffic Control Center
LATCC .... London Air Traffic Control Centre (SAUO)
Latch .... Latch's English King's Bench Reports [*1625-28*] [*A publication*] (DLA)
LATCH .... Literature Attached to Charts [*Nursing program*]
LATCH .... Lower Anchors and Tethers for Children [*Car seat safety term*]
LATCRS ...... London Air Traffic Control Radar Station (SAUO)
LATD .... Large Area Transmission Density (MCD)
LATD .... Latitude (ADA)
LATD .... Latitude Communications, Inc. [*NASDAQ symbol*] (NASQ)
LATDISP .... Lateral Dispersion (MCD)
LAT DOL .... Lateri Dolente [*To the Painful Side*] [*Pharmacy*]
LATE .... Late Assessment of Thrombolytic Efficacy [*Cardiology study*]
LATE .... Legal Assistance for the Elderly
LATE .... London Association for the Teaching of English [*British*] (AIE)
La Tech U... Louisiana Tech University (GAGS)
LaTeko ...... La Teko Resources Ltd. [*Associated Press*] (SAG)
LATER .... Ladies' After Thoughts on Equal Rights [*Acronym is used as name of association*] [*Defunct*] (EA)
LATER .... [*The*] Life and Times of Eddie Roberts [*TV program*]
Later Rom Emp... [*The*] Later Roman Empire [*A publication*] (OCD)
Latex .... Latex Resources [*Associated Press*] (SAG)
LATEX .... Louisiana-Texas Experiment [*Gulf Marine Minerals Management*] [*Marine science*] (OSRA)
LatexRs ..... Latex Resources [*Associated Press*] (SAG)
LATF .... Legal Aid Task Force
LATF .... Lloyd's American Trust Fund (AIA)
LATF .... Low Altitude Tactical Formation (ACAE)
LATG .... Laboratory Automation Trials Group (SAUO)
LATH .... Laos and Thailand Military Assistance
La Th .... La Themis [*A publication*] (DLA)
Lath .... Lather (MIST)
Lath .... Lathrop's Reports [*115-145 Massachusetts*] [*A publication*] (DLA)
LATH .... Libraries of Affiliated Teaching Hospitals - School of Medicine [*Library network*]
LATH .... Long-Wavelength Above the Horizon (ACAE)
La Them LC... La Themis (Lower Canada) [*A publication*] (DLA)
LATHES ..... LASER Terminal Homing Engagement Simulator (PDAA)
Lathrop ...... Lathrop's Reports [*115-145 Massachusetts*] [*A publication*] (DLA)
Lath Wind L... Latham on the Law of Window Lights [*A publication*] (DLA)
LATI .... Linee Aeree Transcontinentali Italiane
Latin .... American Confederation of Clinical Biochemistry (SAUO)
LatinAGr .... Latin America Growth Fund, Inc. [*Associated Press*] (SAG)
LATINAH .... Latin America Human Settlements Information Network (BUAC)
LATIS .... Lightweight Airborne Thermal Imaging System (MCD)
LATIS .... Loop Activity Tracking Information System [*Telecommunications*] (TEL)
LATIX .... Lord Abbett: Tax Free Inc: Texas Cl.A [*Mutual fund ticker symbol*] (SG)
Lat Jus ...... Latrobe's Justice [*A publication*] (DLA)
LATK .... Local Administrative Tool Kit [*AT & T*] [*Software development and integration tools*] (NITA)
LATKWEPSCOLPAC... Light Attack Weapons School, Pacific (DNAB)
LATL .... Lateral (MSA)
LATLI .... Latin American Tax Law Institute [*Uruguay*] (EAIO)
LATM .... Local Asynchronous Transfer Mode (SAUO)
lat men ..... Lateral Meniscectomy [*Orthopedics*] (DAVI)
LATN .... Low-Altitude Tactical Navigation
LATNET ...... Latvian Academic Network (TELE)
LATNS .... Los Angeles Times News Service
LATO .... List of Applicable Technical Orders [*Military*] (AFIT)
LATO .... Los Alamos Technical Office (SAUO)
LATO .... Los Alamos Technology Office (SAUO)
LATOFF ...... Lowest Astronomical Tide of the Foreseeable Future (PDAA)
LATOM ...... Lowest Astronomical Tide of the Month (PDAA)
LATOY .... Lowest Astronomical Tide of the Year (PDAA)
LATP .... League of American Theatres and Producers (EA)
LATP .... Left Atrial Transmural Pressure [*Medicine*] (DMAA)
LATP .... Lima Army Tank Plant [*Ohio*]
LATPT .... Left Atrial Transesophageal Pacing Test [*Medicine*] (DMAA)
LATR .... Lateral (DNAB)
Latr .... Locator [*Compass*] (DA)
LATR .... Los Alamos Translation (SAUO)
LA TR .... Louisiana Term Reports (Martin) [*A publication*] (DLA)
LATR .... Low Altitude Threat Radar (ACAE)
LATREC ..... LASER-Acoustic Time Reversal Expansion and Compression (MCD)
lat Rin ...... Lactated Ringer [*Solution*] (STED)
LATRL .... Lateral
LA TR (NS)... Louisiana Term Reports, New Series (Martin) [*1823-30*] [*A publication*] (DLA)
LATRS .... Logistic Air Terminal Reporting System (ACAE)
LATS .... Latin American Thyroid Society (SAUO)
LATS .... Latin-America Thyroid Society (BUAC)
LATS .... L.A. T Sportswear [*NASDAQ symbol*] (TTSB)
LATS .... LA T Sportswear, Inc. [*NASDAQ symbol*] (SAG)
LATS .... LDEF [*Long-Duration Exposure Facility*] Assembly and Transportation System [*NASA*] (NASA)
LATS .... Leather and Associated Trades Show [*British*] (ITD)
LATS .... Light Armored Turret System (MCD)
LATS .... Light Attack Turbofan Single Aircraft [*Aviation*]
LATS .... Lightweight Antenna Terminal Seeker
LATS .... Long-Acting Thyroid Stimulator [*Endocrinology*]
LATS .... Long-Acting Transmural Stimulator [*Medicine*] (STED)
LATS .... Long Duration Exposure Facility Assembly and Transportation System (SAUO)
LATS-P ...... Long Acting Thyroid Stimulator-Protector [*Endocrinology*]
LA T Spt .... LA T Sportswear, Inc. [*Associated Press*] (SAG)
LatSSR ...... Latvian Soviet Socialist Republic
LATT .... LASER Atmospheric Transmission Test
LATT .... Library Association of Trinidad and Tobago (BUAC)
LATTC .... Los Angeles Trade-Technical College (SAUO)
Lattice .... Lattice Semiconductor Corp. [*Associated Press*] (SAG)
Latt Pr C Pr... Lattey's Privy Council Practice [*1869*] [*A publication*] (DLA)
LATTU .... Latin American Table Tennis Union (BUAC)
LATu .... Lobuloalveolar Tumor [*Medicine*] (DB)
LATU .... Unitrans [*Intermodal shipping container symbol*] (TVRC)
LATUF .... Latin America Trade Union Federation (NATG)
Latv .... Latvia (VRA)
Latv .... Latvian
LATWING ... Light Attack Wing [*Navy*] (NVT)
LATWPNS... Los Angeles Times Washington Post News Service (SAUO)
LATX .... Latex Res Inc. [*NASDAQ symbol*] (TTSB)
LATX .... Latex Resources, Inc. [*NASDAQ symbol*] (SAG)
LAU .... Lamu [*Kenya*] [*Airport symbol*] (OAG)
LAU .... Lauder [*New Zealand*] [*Geomagnetic observatory code*]
LAU .... Laufer [*NCIC car model code*]
LAU .... Lauf [*Pegnitz*] [*German license plate city code*]
LAU .... Laumontite [*A zeolite*]
LAU .... Launcher Aircraft Unit
LAU .... Launcher Armament Unit [*Navy*] (DOMA)
LAU .... Laundry (MSA)
LAU .... Laurel, MS [*Amtrak rail station code*]
LAU .... Laurentian [*NCIC car model code*]
LAU .... Laurentian University Library [*UTLAS symbol*]
Lau .... Laurentius Hispanus [*Deceased, 1248*] [*Authority cited in pre-1607 legal work*] (DSA)
LAU .... Lebanese American University (SAUO)
LAU .... Line Access Unit (NITA)
LAU .... Line Adapter Unit [*Computer science*]
LAU .... Linear Accelerometer Unit (PDAA)
LAU .... Lineas Aereas Suramericanas Ltd. [*Colombia*] [*ICAO designator*] (FAAC)
LAU .... Lithuanian Artists' Union (BUAC)
LAU .... Local Authority Unit (HEAS)
lau .... Louisiana [*MARC country of publication code*] [*Library of Congress*] (LCCP)
LAU .... Lower Arithmetic Unit (IAA)
LAUA .... Lloyd's Aviation Underwriters Association [*British*] (DBA)
LAUBAG ..... Lausitzer Braunkohle Aktiengesellschaft (EFIS)
LAUD .... Layered Access User Diversification (SAUS)
LAUD .... League of Americans of Ukrainian Descent (EA)
Lau de Pin... Laurentius de Pinu [*Deceased, 1397*] [*Authority cited in pre-1607 legal work*] (DSA)
Lauder ...... Fountainhall's Session Cases [*1678-1712*] [*Scotland*] [*A publication*] (DLA)
LAUK .... Library Association of the United Kingdom
Lau Lib ...... Laurentian Library (SAUO)
LAUM .... Linguistic Atlas of the Upper Midwest
LAUN .... Launch Media [*NASDAQ symbol*] (SG)
Laun .... Laundry Room (ADWA)
LAUNC ...... Launceston [*Municipal borough in England*]
LAUND ...... Laundry [*Classified advertising*]
La Univ ..... Louisiana State University (SAUO)
LAUNS ...... Local Area Underwater Navigation System (SAUS)
LAUP .... LASER-Assisted Uvulopalatoplasty [*Medicine*] (DMAA)
LAUR .... Laurel Bancorp, Inc. [*NASDAQ symbol*] (SAG)
LAUR .... Laurel Entertainment, Inc. [*NASDAQ symbol*] (COMM)
Laur .... Laurentian Library [*Classical studies*] (OCD)
Laur .... Laurentius Hispanus [*Deceased, 1248*] [*Authority cited in pre-1607 legal work*] (DSA)
LA-UR .... Los Alamos Unlimited Release (SAUO)
LA-UR .... Los Alamos-XXXX Report (SAUO)
Laur .... Reports of the High Court of Griqualand [*1882-1910*] [*South Africa*] [*A publication*] (DLA)
LAURA ...... Low-Altitude Unmanned Reconnaissance Aircraft (DOMA)
Laur de Palat... Laurentius de Pallatis [*Flourished, 16th century*] [*Authority cited in pre-1607 legal work*] (DSA)
LAURE .... Laurel, MS [*American Association of Railroads railroad junction routing code*]
LaurelBc .... Laurel Bancorp, Inc. [*Associated Press*] (SAG)
Lauren ...... Laurentius Hispanus [*Deceased, 1248*] [*Authority cited in pre-1607 legal work*] (DSA)
Laurence.... Laurence's Reports of the High Court of Griqualand [*1882-1910*] [*South Africa*] [*A publication*] (DLA)
Lauren de Rodul... Laurentius de Rodulphis [*Flourished, 15th century*] [*Authority cited in pre-1607 legal work*] (DSA)

Laur HC Ca... Lauren's High Court Cases [*South Africa*] [*A publication*] (DLA)
LAURI .... Laurinburg, NC [*American Association of Railroads railroad junction routing code*]
LAURIN ..... Libraries and Archives collecting newpaper clippings Unified for their integration into Networks (SAUO)
LaurlCa ..... Laurel Capital Group [*Associated Press*] (SAG)
Laur Prim... Laurence's Primogeniture [*1878*] [*A publication*] (DLA)
LAUS .... Local Area Unemployment Statistics (OICC)
LAUSC....... Linguistic Atlas of the United States and Canada [*1930*]
LAUSD ...... Los Angeles United School District (SAUO)
Lauss Eq.... Laussat's Equity Practice in Pennsylvania [*A publication*] (DLA)
LAUTRO..... Life Assurance and Unit Trust Regulatory Authority (SAUS)
LAUTRO..... Life Assurance and Unit Trust Regulatory Organisation [*British*]
LAUW .... London Associaton of University Women (SAUO)
LAV .... Las Vegas [*Diocesan abbreviation*] [*Nevada*] (TOCD)
lav .... Latvian [*MARC language code*] [*Library of Congress*] (LCCP)
LAV .... Launch Axis, Vertical (MCD)
LAV .... Lavaliere [*Lapel microphone*] (NTCM)
Lav........... Lavatory (ADWA)
LAV .... Lavatory (KSC)
lav .... Lavender [*Philately*]
LAV .... Lavish [*Telegraphy*] (PCTE)
LAV .... Law Association of Victoria [*Australia*]
LAV .... Leafhopper A Virus [*Medicine*] (DMAA)
LAV .... Legislative Assembly of Victoria [*Australia*]
LAV .... Leisure Activity Vehicle
LAV .... Lifting Ascent Vehicle
LAV .... Light Armored Vehicle [*Army*] (RDA)
LAV .... Light Assault Vehicle (SAUS)
LAV .... Linea Aeropostal Venezolana [*Venezuela*] [*ICAO designator*] (FAAC)
LAV .... Load Average (SAUS)
LAV .... Luxury Activity Vehicle [*Automotive industry*]
LAV .... Lymphadenopathy-Associated Virus
LAV .... Lymphocyte-Associated Virus
LAV .... Varah [*L. A.*] Ltd. [*Toronto Stock Exchange symbol*]
LAVA......... Laboratory for Computer Architecture [*University of Virginia*] (RCD)
LAVA......... Linear Acoustic Vernier Analyzer (CAAL)
LAVA......... Linear Amplifier for Various Applications (IEEE)
LAVA......... Local Authorities Videotex Association (BUAC)
LAVA......... Local Authority Valuers Association [*British*] (DBA)
LAVA......... Look Ahead Variable Acceleration [*Computer science*] (MHDB)
LAVA......... Los Alamos Vulnerability Assessment (SAUO)
LAVA......... Low-Frequency Acoustic Vernier Analyzer (NVT)
LAVA......... Low-profile Adaptive Vehicular Antenna (SAUS)
LAVAC .... LASER Atmospheric Visibility and Contamination (PDAA)
LAV/AD ...... Light Armored Vehicle / Air Defense [*Army*] (DWSG)
LAV-AD ...... Light Armoured Vehicle-Air Defence (SAUS)
LAV/ADS .... Light Armored Vehicle/Air Defense System [*Army*]
LAV-AF ...... Light Armored Vehicle, Air Force (LAIN)
LAV-AG ...... Light Armored Vehicle-Assault Gun [*Marine Corps*] (DOMA)
LAV-AG ...... Light Armoured Vehicle-Assault Gun (SAUS)
LAVALIN..... Lavalin Transport (SAUS)
LavalTPh.... Laval Theologique et Philosophique [*Quebec*] [*A publication*] (BJA)
LAV-AT ...... Light Armored Vehicle - Antitank [*Canada*]
LAVB......... Light Armored Vehicle Battalion [*Marine Corps*] (DOMA)
LAVC......... Local Area VAX Cluster (SAUO)
LAVc......... Local Area Vaxcluster (USDC)
LAVC......... Los Angeles Valley College (SAUO)
LAVD .... Lavished [*Telegraphy*] (PCTE)
LAVE......... Association Vocanologique Europeenne [*European Volcanological Association*] [*Paris, France*] (EAIO)
LAVE......... Laverda [*NCIC motorcycle make code*]
LaVeLe...... LandesverbindungslehrerIn (SAUO)
LAVEND ..... Lavendula [*Lavender*] [*Pharmacology*] (ROG)
LAVEPA...... Local Administration of Vocational Education and Practical Arts (OICC)
LAVERS ..... Lake Vessel Reporting System
LAVFWUS... Ladies Auxiliary to the Veterans of Foreign Wars of the United States (EA)
LAVG .... Lavishing [*Telegraphy*] (PCTE)
LAVH .... Laparoscopically-Assisted Vaginal Hysterectomy [*Medicine*]
LAVH .... Leparoscopically Assisted Vaginal Hysterectomy [*Medicine*]
LAVI .... Lymphadenopathy-Associated Virus (PDAA)
LAVIP........ Landsurface-Atmosphere (or Atmospheric)-Vegetation Interaction Programme (SAUO)
LAVLX .... Lord Abbett Mid-Cap Value Cl.A [*Mutual fund ticker symbol*] (SG)
LAVM........ LORAN [*Long-Range Navigation*] Automatic Vehicle Monitoring (PDAA)
LAVM........ Los Alamos Voice Messaging (SAUO)
LAVM........ Low-Altitude Vulnerability Model [*Aerospace*] (MCD)
LAVMS ...... Los Alamos Voice Messaging System (SAUO)
LAVO .... Lassen Volcanic National Park
LAVO .... Lavatory [*Slang*] (DSUE)
Lav Pall..... Lavacrum Palladis [*of Callimachus*] [*Classical studies*] (OCD)
LAVV......... Left Atrioventricular Valve [*Medicine*] (MELL)
LAVY......... Lavishly [*Telegraphy*] (PCTE)
LAW .... Ladies Against Women (EA)
LAW .... Land Authority for Wales
LAW .... LASER Absorption Wave (PDAA)
LAW .... Lawrence [*Kansas*] [*Seismograph station code, US Geological Survey*] (SEIS)
LAW .... Lawter International, Inc. [*NYSE symbol*] (SPSG)
LAW .... Lawter Intl [*NYSE symbol*] (TTSB)
LAW .... Lawton [*Oklahoma*] [*Airport symbol*] (OAG)
LAW .... Lawton, OK [*Location identifier*] [*FAA*] (FAAL)
LAW .... Lawyer (ADA)
LAW .... Leading Aircraft Woman [*RAF*] [*British*]
LAW .... League of American Wheelmen
LAW .... Left Atrial Wall [*Medicine*] (STED)
LAW .... Left Attack Wing [*Women's lacrosse position*]
LAW .... Left-Handers Against the World [*Defunct*] (EA)
LAW .... Legal Action for Women [*An association*] (BUAC)
LAW .... Legal Advocates for Women (EA)
LAW .... Legal Aid Warranty [*Fund providing legal services in case of arrest*]
LAW .... Library, Amphibious Warfare (DNAB)
LAW .... Light Antiarmor Weapon [*Military*] (RDA)
LAW .... Light Antitank Weapon
LAW .... Light Area Weapon
LAW .... Light Assault Weapon
LAW .... Light Attack Weapon
LAW .... Link Airways of Australia [*Australia*] [*ICAO designator*] (FAAC)
LAW .... Local Air Warning
LAW .... Local Air Wing (DNAB)
LAW .... Local Authority Workstation (SAUO)
LAW .... Logistics Action Worksheet
LAW .... Low-Acid Waste [*Nuclear energy*] (NRCH)
LAW .... Low Active Waste [*Nuclear energy*]
LAW .... Low-Altitude Warning (MCD)
LAW .... Loyalist Association of Workers [*Trade union*] [*Northern Ireland*]
LAW .... Lubricant, Arctic, Weapon [*Military*] (INF)
LAW .... Quaere Legal Resources Ltd. [*UTLAS symbol*]
LAW .... United States Supreme Court Library, Washington, DC [*OCLC symbol*] (OCLC)
LAWA........ Legislative Assembly of Western Australia
Law Advert... Law Advertiser [*1823-31*] [*A publication*] (DLA)
Law Alm .... Law Almanac [*New York*] [*A publication*] (DLA)
Law Amdt J... Law Amendment Journal [*1855-58*] [*A publication*] (DLA)
Law Am Jour... Law Amendment Journal [*1855-58*] [*A publication*] (DLA)
Law & Bank... Lawyer and Banker [*New Orleans*] [*A publication*] (DLA)
Law & Bank... Lawyers' and Bankers' Quarterly [*A publication*] (DLA)
Law & Banker... Lawyer and Banker and Central Law Journal [*A publication*] (DLA)
Law & Bk Bull... Weekly Law and Bank Bulletin [*Ohio*] [*A publication*] (DLA)
Law & Eq Rep... Law and Equity Reporter [*New York*] [*A publication*] (DLA)
Law & Hist Rev... Law and History Review [*A publication*] (DLA)
Law & Legisl in the German Dem Rep... Law and Legislation in the German Democratic Republic [*A publication*] (DLA)
Law & Lib... Law and Liberty [*A publication*] (DLA)
Law & Mag... Lawyer and Magistrate Magazine [*1898-99*] [*Dublin*] [*A publication*] (DLA)
Law & Magis Mag... Lawyer's and Magistrate's Magazine [*A publication*] (DLA)
Law & Mag Mag... Lawyer and Magistrate Magazine [*1898-99*] [*Dublin*] [*A publication*] (DLA)
Law & Psychology Rev... Law and Psychology Review [*A publication*] (DLA)
Law & Soc... Law and Social Change [*A publication*] (DLA)
Law & Soc Inquiry... Law & Social Inquiry: Journal of the American Bar Foundation (SAUO)
LAWASIA.... LAWASIA. Journal of the Law Association for Asia and the Western Pacific [*A publication*] (DLA)
LAWASIA.... Law Association for Asia and the Western Pacific (BUAC)
LAWASIA HRB... LAWASIA [*Law Association for Asia and the Pacific*] Human Rights Bulletin [*A publication*]
LAWASIA LJ... LAWASIA [*Law Association for Asia and the Pacific*] Law Journal [*A publication*] (DLA)
LAWB........ Lawrenceburg Transfer [*Common carrier symbol*]
LAWB........ Los Alamos Water Boiler [*Nuclear reactor*] (NRCH)
LAW BBS ... Legal Access in Washington Bulletin Board System (SAUO)
LAWBG...... Lawrenceburg, IN [*American Association of Railroads railroad junction routing code*]
Law Bk Rev Dig... Law Book Review Digest and Current Legal Bibliography [*A publication*] (DLA)
Law Bul & Br... Law Bulletin and Brief [*A publication*] (DLA)
Law Bul IA... Law Bulletin. State University of Iowa [*A publication*] (DLA)
Law Bull .... Law Bulletin [*Zambia*] [*A publication*] (DLA)
Law Bull .... Weekly Law Bulletin [*Ohio*] [*A publication*] (DLA)
LAW/BUSA.. League of American Wheelman/Bicycle USA (EA)
LAWC........ Land Air Warfare Committee [*Military*]
LAWC........ LA Woods Company [*NCIC trailer make code*]
Law Cas Wm I... Law Cases, William I to Richard I [*England*] [*A publication*] (DLA)
Law Ch Bdg Soc... Law on Church Building Societies [*A publication*] (DLA)
Law Ch P ... Lawes on Charterparties [*1813*] [*A publication*] (DLA)
Law Chr..... Law Chronicle [*England*] [*A publication*] (DLA)
Law Chr..... Law Chronicle [*South Africa*] [*A publication*] (ILCA)
Law Chr & Auct Rec... Law Chronicle and Auction Record [*A publication*] (DLA)
Law Chr & Jour Jur... Law Chronicle and Journal of Jurisprudence [*A publication*] (DLA)
Law Ch Ward... Law on Church Wardens [*A publication*] (DLA)
Law Cl ...... Law Clerk (DLA)
Law Cl Rec... Law Clerk Record [*1910-11*] [*A publication*] (DLA)
Law Com ... Law Commission (DLA)
Law Com ... Law Commission Report [*A publication*] (DLA)
Law Comm... Law Commission [*Great Britain*] (SAFN)
Law Committee News... Lawyers' Committee News [*A publication*] (DLA)
Law Con .... Lawson on Contracts [*A publication*] (DLA)
Law cont prob... Law and Contemporary Problems. School of Law. Duke University. Durham (SAUO)
Law Dept Bull... Law Department Bulletin, Union Pacific Railroad Co. [*A publication*] (DLA)

LAWDS...... LORAN-Aided Weapons Delivery System
LAWEB...... Lake Warning [*or Weather*] Bulletin [*National Weather Service*] [*A publication*]
Law Ecc Law... Law's Ecclesiastical Law [*2nd ed.*] [*1844*] [*A publication*] (DLA)
Law Ed...... Lawyer's Edition, United States Supreme Court Reports [*A publication*] (DLA)
Law Ed 2d.. United States Supreme Court Reports, Lawyers' Edition, Second Series [*A publication*] (DLA)
Law Ed Adv Op... United States Supreme Court Reports, Lawyers' Edition, Advance Opinions [*A publication*] (DLA)
Lawes Ch... Lawes on Charterparties [*1813*] [*A publication*] (DLA)
Lawes Pl.... Lawes on Pleading [*A publication*] (DLA)
Law Ex J.... Law Examination Journal [*A publication*] (DLA)
Law Ex Rep... Law Examination Reporter [*A publication*] (DLA)
Law Fr Dict... Law French Dictionary [*A publication*] (DLA)
LAWG........ Latin American Working Group [*Canada*] (CROSS)
Law Gaz.... Law Gazette [*A publication*] (DLA)
Law Guild M... Lawyers Guild Monthly [*A publication*] (DLA)
Law in Cont... Law in Context [*A publication*]
Law Int...... Law Intelligencer [*United States*] [*A publication*] (DLA)
Law J........ Law Journal Reports [*A publication*] (DLA)
Law J Ch... Law Journal, New Series, Chancery [*A publication*] (DLA)
Law J Exch... Law Journal, New Series, Exchequer [*A publication*] (DLA)
Law Jour.... Law Journal Reports [*A publication*] (DLA)
Law Jour (M & W)... Morgan and Williams' Law Journal [*London*] [*A publication*] (DLA)
Law JPD.... Law Journal, Probate Division [*A publication*] (DLA)
Law JPD & A... Law Journal Reports, New Series, Probate, Divorce, and Admiralty [*1875-1946*] [*A publication*] (DLA)
Law JQB.... Law Journal, New Series, English Queen's Bench [*A publication*] (DLA)
Law Jr QB... Law Journal, New Series, English Queen's Bench [*A publication*] (DLA)
Law Jur.... Law's Jurisdiction of the Federal Courts [*A publication*] (DLA)
Law Lat Dic... Law Latin Dictionary [*A publication*] (DLA)
Law Lib N.. Law Library News [*A publication*] (DLA)
Law Lib NS... Law Library, New Series [*Philadelphia, PA*] [*A publication*] (DLA)
Law LJ...... Lawrence Law Journal [*A publication*] (DLA)
LAW M...... Law Magazine and Review [*A publication*] (ROG)
LawM........ Lawrence Microfilming Service, Fuquay-Varina, NC [*Library symbol*] [*Library of Congress*] (LCLS)
LAWM....... Light All-Weather Missile (MCD)
Law Mag.... Law Magazine [*A publication*] (DLA)
Law Mag & Law Rev... Law Magazine and Law Review [*A publication*] (DLA)
Law Mag & R... Law Magazine and Review [*A publication*] (DLA)
Law Mag & Rev... Law Magazine and Review [*A publication*] (DLA)
Law Mo..... Western Law Monthly (Reprint) [*Ohio*] [*A publication*] (DLA)
LAWN........ Lawndale Homes [*NCIC trailer make code*]
Law N........ Law News [*A publication*] (DLA)
LAWN........ Local Area Wireless Network [*O'Neill Communications, Inc.*] [*Computer science*] (PCM)
Law of Trusts Tiff & Bul... Tiffany and Bullard on Trusts and Trustees [*A publication*] (DLA)
Law Pat..... Law's United States Patent Cases [*A publication*] (DLA)
Law Pat Dig... Law's Digest of United States Patent Cases [*A publication*] (DLA)
Law Pl...... Lawes' Pleading in Assumpsit [*1810*] [*A publication*] (DLA)
Law Pl...... Lawes' Pleading in Civil Actions [*1806*] [*A publication*] (DLA)
Law Pr...... Law's Practice in United States Courts [*A publication*] (DLA)
Law Q Rev... Law Quarterly Review [*A publication*] (BRI)
Lawr......... Lawrence High Court Reports [*Griqualand*] [*A publication*] (DLA)
LAWR........ Lawrence Trailer [*NCIC trailer make code*]
LAWRC....... Limited Air Weather Reporting Certificate (IAA)
Law Rec.... Ceylon Law Recorder [*A publication*] (DLA)
Law Rec.... Ceylon Law Recorder (journ.) (SAUS)
Law Rec.... Irish Law Recorder [*1827-38*] [*A publication*] (ILCA)
Law Rec.... Law Recorder [*1827-31*] [*Ireland*] [*A publication*] (DLA)
Law Rec (NS)... Law Recorder, New Series [*Ireland*] [*A publication*] (DLA)
Law Rec (OS)... Law Recorder, First Series [*Ireland*] [*A publication*] (DLA)
Law Ref Com... Law Reform Committee (DLA)
Law Ref Cttee... Law Reform Committee (DLA)
Law Reg.... American Law Register [*Philadelphia*] [*A publication*] (DLA)
Law Reg.... Law Register, Chicago [*A publication*] (DLA)
Law Reg Cas... Lawson's Registration Cases [*England*] [*A publication*] (DLA)
LAWREMS... Land and Water Resources and Economic Models System (SAUO)
Lawrence... Lawrence's Reports [*20 Ohio*] [*A publication*] (DLA)
Lawrence Comp Dec... Lawrence's First Comptroller's Decisions [*United States*] [*A publication*] (DLA)
Lawrence Compt Dec... Lawrence's First Comptroller's Decisions [*United States*] [*A publication*] (DLA)
Law Rep.... Law Reporter [*England*] [*A publication*] (DLA)
Law Rep.... Law Reporter (Ramsey and Morin) [*Canada*] [*A publication*] (DLA)
Law Rep.... Law Reports [*England*] [*A publication*] (DLA)
Law Rep.... Louisiana Reports [*A publication*] (DLA)
Law Rep.... New Zealand Law Reports [*A publication*] (DLA)
Law Rep.... Ohio Law Reporter [*A publication*] (DLA)
Law Rep A & E... Law Reports, Admiralty and Ecclesiastical Cases [*1865-75*] [*A publication*] (DLA)
Law Rep App Cas... Law Reports, Appeal Cases [*England*] [*A publication*] (DLA)
Law Rep CC... Law Reports, Crown Cases [*A publication*] (DLA)
Law Rep Ch... Law Reports, Chancery Appeal Cases [*England*] [*A publication*] (DLA)
Law Rep Ch App... Law Reports, Chancery Appeal Cases [*England*] [*A publication*] (DLA)
Law Rep Ch D... Law Reports, Chancery Division [*A publication*] (DLA)
Law Rep CP... Law Reports, Common Pleas [*England*] [*A publication*] (DLA)
Law Rep CPD... Law Reports, Common Pleas Division [*England*] [*A publication*] (DLA)
Law Rep Dig... Law Reports Digest [*A publication*] (DLA)
Law Rep Eq... Law Reports, Equity Cases [*A publication*] (DLA)
Law Rep Ex... Law Reports, Exchequer [*A publication*] (DLA)
Law Rep Ex D... Law Reports, Exchequer Division [*England*] [*A publication*] (DLA)
Law Rep HL... Law Reports, House of Lords, English and Irish Appeal Cases [*A publication*] (DLA)
Law Rep HL Sc... Law Reports, Scotch and Divorce Appeal Cases, House of Lords [*A publication*] (DLA)
Law Rep Ind App... Law Reports, Indian Appeals [*A publication*] (DLA)
Law Rep Ir... Law Reports, Irish [*A publication*] (DLA)
Law Rep Misc D... Law Reports, Miscellaneous Division [*A publication*] (DLA)
Law Rep NS... Law Reports, New Series [*New York*] [*A publication*] (DLA)
Law Repos... Carolina Law Repository [*North Carolina*] [*A publication*] (DLA)
Law Rep P... Law Reports, Probate [*A publication*] (DLA)
Law Rep P & D... Law Reports, Probate and Divorce Cases [*A publication*] (DLA)
Law Rep PC... Law Reports, Privy Council, Appeal Cases [*England*] [*A publication*] (DLA)
Law Rep QB... Law Reports, Queen's Bench [*A publication*] (DLA)
Law Rep QBD... Law Reports, Queen's Bench Division [*A publication*] (DLA)
Law Repr... Law Reporter (Ramsey and Morin) [*Canada*] [*A publication*] (DLA)
Law Rep (Tor)... Law Reporter (Toronto) [*A publication*] (DLA)
Law Rev & Qu J... Law Review and Quarterly Journal [*London*] [*A publication*] (DLA)
Law Rev J... Law Review Journal [*A publication*] (DLA)
Law Rev Qu... Law Review Quarterly [*Albany, NY*] [*A publication*] (DLA)
Law Rev U Det... Law Review. University of Detroit [*A publication*] (DLA)
LawrG....... Lawrence Insurance Group, Inc. [*Associated Press*] (SAG)
LAWRS....... Limited Aviation Weather Reporting Station [*FAA*] (TAG)
LawrSB...... Lawrence Savings Bank [*Associated Press*] (SAG)
Lawr Wh.... Lawrence's Edition of Wheaton on International Law [*A publication*] (DLA)
LAWS........ Land and Water Systems [*Michigan*]
LAWS........ Laser Atmospheric Wind Sound (SAUS)
LAWS........ LASER Atmospheric Wind Sounder [*NASA*]
LAWS........ Laser Weapon Simulator (ACAE)
LAWS........ Lawson Products [*NASDAQ symbol*] (SAG)
LAWS........ Lawson Products, Inc. (SAUO)
LAWS........ Lawyers Alliance for World Security (EA)
LAWS........ Leadership and World Society [*Defunct*]
LAWS........ Lidar Atmospheric Wind Sounder (SAUS)
LAWS........ Light Antitank Weapon System (LAIN)
LAWS........ Low-Altitude Warning System (NVT)
Law School Rec... Law School Record [*Chicago*] [*A publication*] (DLA)
Law School Rev... Law School Review. Toronto University [*A publication*] (DLA)
Laws Cont... Lawson on Contracts [*A publication*] (DLA)
Law Ser MO Bull... University of Missouri. Bulletin. Law Series [*A publication*] (DLA)
Lawsn....... Lawson Products, Inc. [*Associated Press*] (SAG)
LAWSO...... Lockheed Antisubmarine Warfare Systems Organization
Law Soc ACT NL... Law Society of the Australian Capital Territory. Newsletter [*A publication*]
Law Soc G.. Law Society. Gazette [*A publication*]
Law Soc J.. Law Society Journal (SAUO)
Law Soc Jo... Law Society of Massachusetts. Journal [*A publication*] (DLA)
Law Soc Tas NL... Law Society of Tasmania. Newsletter [*A publication*]
Law Soc'y Scotl... Law Society of Scotland. Journal [*A publication*] (DLA)
Lawson Exp Ev... Lawson on Expert and Opinion Evidence [*A publication*] (DLA)
Lawson Pres Ev... Lawson on Presumptive Evidence [*A publication*] (DLA)
Lawson Rights Rem & Pr... Lawson on Rights, Remedies, and Practice [*A publication*] (DLA)
Lawson Usages & Cust... Lawson on the Law of Usages and Customs [*A publication*] (DLA)
Laws Reg Cas... Lawson's Registration Cases, Irish [*1885-1914*] [*A publication*] (DLA)
Law Stud... Law Student [*A publication*] (ILCA)
Law Stud Mag... Law Students' Magazine [*A publication*] (DLA)
Law Stud Mag NS... Law Students' Magazine. New Series [*A publication*] (DLA)
Law Stu H... Law Students' Helper [*A publication*] (ILCA)
Law Stu Mag... Law Students' Magazine [*A publication*] (DLA)
Laws Wom... Laws of Women [*A publication*] (DLA)
Law T........ Law Times Reports [*A publication*] (DLA)
Law Tchr.... Law Teacher [*A publication*] (DLA)
LAWTE...... Laboratory Animal Welfare Training Exchange (GVA)
Law Tenn Rep... Tennessee Reports [*A publication*] (DLA)
Lawter....... Lawter International, Inc. [*Associated Press*] (SAG)
Law Times (NS)... Law Times. New Series [*Pennsylvania*] [*A publication*] (DLA)
Law Times (OS)... Law Times, Old Series [*Luzerne, PA*] [*A publication*] (DLA)
Law T NS... Law Times. New Series [*Pennsylvania*] [*A publication*] (DLA)
Law T NS... Law Times Reports, New Series [*England*] [*A publication*] (DLA)
Law Tr....... Law Tracts [*A publication*] (DLA)
Law T Rep NS... Law Times Reports, New Series [*England*] [*A publication*] (DLA)
Law T Rep OS... Law Times Reports, Old Series [*England*] [*A publication*] (DLA)
Law US Cts... Law's Practice in United States Courts [*A publication*] (DLA)
LAWV........ [*The*] Lorain & West Virginia Railway Co. [*AAR code*]
Law V & S... Lawrence's Visitation and Search [*A publication*] (DLA)
LAWVL...... Lawrenceville, IL [*American Association of Railroads railroad junction routing code*]
Law W...... Law Weekly [*A publication*] (DLA)

Law Wheat... Lawrence's Edition of Wheaton on International Law [*A publication*] (DLA)
LAWXN...... Lackawaxen, PA [*American Association of Railroads railroad junction routing code*]
Lawy......... Lawyer (DLA)
Lawyer & Banker... Lawyer and Banker and Central Law Journal [*A publication*] (DLA)
Lawyers Co-Op... Lawyers Co-Operative Publishing Co. (DLA)
Lawyers guild rev... Lawyers Guild Review with which is combined International Juridical Association Bulletin. Washington (SAUO)
Lawyers' Rep Ann... Lawyers' Reports, Annotated [*A publication*] (DLA)
Lawyers' Rep Annotated... Lawyers' Reports, Annotated [*A publication*] (DLA)
Lawyers' Rev... Lawyers' Review [*A publication*] (DLA)
Lawy Mag... Lawyers' Magazine [*A publication*] (DLA)
Lawy Rep Ann... Lawyers' Reports, Annotated [*A publication*] (DLA)
Lawy Rev... Lawyers' Review [*A publication*] (DLA)
LAX.......... Bahia De Los Angeles [*Mexico*] [*Seismograph station code, US Geological Survey*] (SEIS)
LAX.......... Lacrosse [*British*] (ROG)
LAX.......... Laurel Explorations Ltd. [*Vancouver Stock Exchange symbol*]
Lax........... Laxative [*Medicine*] (AMHC)
lax........... Laxative [*Pharmacy*]
lax........... Laxity (STED)
LAX.......... Limited Area automatic Extraction (SAUS)
LAX.......... Los Angeles [*California*] [*Airport symbol*] (OAG)
LAXRAY..... Large X-Ray Survey Experiment (PDAA)
LAXS........ Large-Angle X-Ray Scattering
LAXS........ Low-Angle X-Ray Scattering (MCD)
LAXSM...... Large Area X-ray Spectroscopy Mission (SAUS)
LAXV........ Land-Air Express of Vermont [*Common carrier symbol*]
LAY.......... Ladysmith [*South Africa*] [*Airport symbol*] (OAG)
LAY.......... Lanyu [*Republic of China*] [*Seismograph station code, US Geological Survey*] (SEIS)
Lay........... Lay's English Chancery Reports [*A publication*] (DLA)
LAY.......... Look After Yourself Project Centre (BUAC)
LAYB........ Library Association Year Book [*A publication*] (DGA)
LAYCAN..... Layday Cancelling Date (RIMS)
LAYDET..... Layer Detection (SAA)
LAYGEN..... Layout Generator [*Ergonomics*]
LAYM........ Los Angeles-Yuma Freight Lines [*Common carrier symbol*]
LAYN........ Layne Christensen Co. [*NASDAQ symbol*] (SAG)
LAYN........ Layne, Inc. [*NASDAQ symbol*] (SAG)
Layne........ Layne Christensen Co. [*Associated Press*] (SAG)
Layne........ Layne, Inc. [*Associated Press*] (SAG)
Layos........ Layos, Hollywood [*Record label*]
LAYT........ Layton Homes [*NCIC trailer make code*]
LAZ.......... Balkan-Bulgarian Airlines [*ICAO designator*] (FAAC)
LAZ.......... Bom Jesus Da Lapa [*Brazil*] [*Airport symbol*] (OAG)
LAZ.......... La Luz Mines Ltd. [*Toronto Stock Exchange symbol*]
LAZ.......... Los Angeles Zoo (SAUO)
LaZ Boy..... La-Z Boy Chair Co. [*Associated Press*] (SAG)
LAZE........ Lazer [*NCIC motorcycle make code*]
LAZE........ Lazer Truck Lines [*Common carrier symbol*]
LAZJ........ Lazy J Horse Trailer [*NCIC trailer make code*]
LazKap...... Lazare Kaplan International, Inc. [*Associated Press*] (SAG)
LAZR........ Laser Storm [*NASDAQ symbol*] (TTSB)
LAZR........ Laser Storm, Inc. [*NASDAQ symbol*] (SAG)
LAZRU...... Laser Storm Unit [*NASDAQ symbol*] (TTSB)
LAZRW...... Laser Storm Wrrt [*NASDAQ symbol*] (TTSB)
LAZU........ Lazer Line [*Intermodal shipping container symbol*] (TVRC)
LB........... Baccalaureus Literarum [*Bachelor of Literature*] [*Latin*]
LB........... Farbwerke Hoechst AG [*Germany*] [*Research code symbol*]
LB........... Graduate in Letters
LB........... LaBarge, Inc. [*AMEX symbol*] (SPSG)
LB........... Laboratory (MAE)
LB........... Laboratory Bulletin
LB........... Labrador [*Postal code*] [*Canada*]
LB........... Lactose Broth [*Microbiology*]
LB........... Ladies of Bethany (TOCD)
LB........... Lady Boss
LB........... Lag Bolt [*Technical drawings*]
LB........... Lamellar Body [*Physiology*]
LB........... Land Based
LB........... Landesbank Rheinland-Pfalz (EFIS)
LB........... Landing Barge
LB........... Landing Beach [*Navy*]
L/B.......... Landing Book [*Tea trade*] (ROG)
LB........... Lane Bryant, Inc.
LB........... Langmuir-Blodgitt Technique [*Optics*] (EECA)
LB........... Large Bowel [*Anatomy*]
LB........... Lasa B Ring [*Montana*] [*Seismograph station code, US Geological Survey*] (SEIS)
LB........... Last Brochure
LB........... Late Babylonian (BJA)
LB........... Late Bronze [*Age*] (BJA)
LB........... Lateral Bending (STED)
LB........... Latin Bibliography
LB........... Launch Boost (MCD)
LB........... Launch Bunker (MUGU)
LB........... Launch Bus (NASA)
LB........... Laurentian Bank of Canada [*Toronto Stock Exchange symbol*]
LB........... Lavatory Basin
LB........... Leaky Bucket [*Training term*] (LPT)
LB........... Lebanon [*ANSI two-letter standard code*] (CNC)
LB........... Lectori Benevolo [*To the Kind (or Gentle) Reader*] [*Latin*]
LB........... Lecture Bottle [*Shipment of gas products*] [*Union Carbide Corp.*]
LB........... Lederer-Brill [*Syndrome*] [*Medicine*] (DB)
LB........... Left Back [*Football*] (WDAA)
LB........... Left Base [*Aviation*] (FAAC)
LB........... Left Border [*Genetics*]
LB........... Left Breast [*Medicine*] (DMAA)
LB........... Left Bundle [*Cardiology*] (DMAA)
LB........... Left Buttock [*Medicine*]
LB........... Left Button (SAUO)
LB........... Left Fullback [*Soccer*]
LB........... Left on Base [*Baseball*]
LB........... Legal Bond [*Investment term*]
LB........... Leg Bye [*Cricket*]
LB........... Legum Baccalaureus [*Bachelor of Laws*]
LB........... Leiomyoblastoma [*Medicine*]
L/B.......... Length/Beam Ratio (DNAB)
Lb........... Leptosphaerulinia briosiana [*A fungus*]
L/B.......... Lesion-to-Brain [*Medicine*] (RAWO)
LB........... Letterbook (SAUO)
LB........... Letter Box
LB........... Levobunolol [*Also, LBUN*] [*Biochemistry*]
LB........... Liaison Branch [*BUPERS*]
lb........... Liberia [*MARC country of publication code*] [*Library of Congress*] (LCCP)
Lb........... Liberia (MILB)
lb........... Libra [*Pound*] [*Latin*] (AAG)
LB........... Library Bookseller (NITA)
LB........... Library Buckram (SAUO)
LB........... Library Bulletin
LB........... Library Bureau (SAUO)
L-B.......... Liebermann-Burchard [*Reaction*] [*Medicine*] (MEDA)
LB........... Lifeboat (AAG)
LB........... Lifeboat Station [*Coast Guard*]
LB........... Ligand Binding Domain [*Genetics*]
LB........... Light Battalion [*British military*] (DMA)
LB........... Light Bombardment [*Air Force*]
LB........... Light Bomber [*Air Force*]
LB........... Light Bracket (AAG)
LB........... Lighted Buoy [*USCG*] (TAG)
LB........... Limited Base [*Air Force*] (AFM)
LB........... Limited Benefits [*Unemployment insurance*] (OICC)
LB........... Limited Partner in Brokers Firm [*London Stock Exchange*]
LB........... Linebacker [*Football*]
LB........... Line Block (SAUO)
LB........... Line Buffer [*Computer science*]
LB........... Line Busy
LB........... Link Babler [*Telecommunications*] (ECII)
LB........... Linoleum Base [*Technical drawings*]
LB........... Lipid Body [*Biochemistry*] (MAE)
LB........... Lithium Bromide (DNAB)
LB........... Litterarum Baccalaureus [*Bachelor of Letters or Literature*] [*Latin*]
LB........... Litter Bearer (AABC)
LB........... Live Birth
LB........... Liver Biopsy [*Medicine*] (STED)
LB........... Living Bank (EA)
LB........... Lloyd Aereo Boliviano [*ICAO designator*] (AD)
LB........... Load Bank [*Computer science*] (KSC)
LB........... Local Batch (IAA)
LB........... Local Battery [*Radio*]
LB........... Local Board
LB........... Logan Brothers Book Co.
LB........... Log Book
LB........... Logical Block
LB........... London Borough [*England*]
LB........... London Bridge
Lb........... Long Bill (EBF)
LB........... Long Bill [*Business term*]
LB........... Long Binh [*Vietnam*]
LB........... Long-Bout
LB........... Loose Body [*Medicine*]
LB........... Low Back [*Disorder*] [*Medicine*]
LB........... Low Band (AAG)
LB........... Low Battery [*Modem status information light*] [*Computer science*] (IGQR)
LB........... Low Bay (KSC)
LB........... Low Breakage (STED)
LB........... Lower Bearing
LB........... Lower Berth [*Indian Railway*] (TIR)
LB........... Lower Body (IDYL)
LB........... Lower Bound [*Computer science*]
LB........... Lower Brace (MCD)
LB........... Lower, But [*Telegraphy*] (PCTE)
LB........... Ludwigsburg [*German license plate city code*]
LB........... Lunch Break
LB........... Lung Biopsy [*Medicine*] (STED)
LB........... Luria Broth [*For cultivation of cells*]
LB........... Photographic Laboratory Specialist [*Navy*]
lb........... Pound [*Libra*] [*Unit of weight*]
lb........... Link Belt (ODA)
LBA.......... Bus Adapter (SAUS)
LBA.......... Lahr/Bader Area [*Germany*]
LBA.......... Lambada-Baterista and Ambiace (SAUS)

LBA .... Large Scale Biological-Atmosphere Experiment Amazonia (SAUS)
LBA .... Large-scale Biosphere-Atmosphere Field Experiment in Amazonia (SAUS)
LBA .... LASER Beam Analyzer (IAA)
LBA .... Latin Business Association (NTPA)
LBA .... Leeds/Bradford [*England*] [*Airport symbol*] (OAG)
LBA .... Left Basal Artery [*Medicine*] (DMAA)
LBA .... Left Brachial Artery [*Medicine*] (MELL)
LBA .... Lifting-Body Airship (PDAA)
LBA .... Ligand-Binding Assay [*Analytical biochemistry*]
LBA .... Lima Bean Agar [*Microbiology*]
LBA .... Limas Bulgarian Airlines [*ICAO designator*] (FAAC)
LBA .... Limit of Basic Aircraft (MCD)
LBA .... Linear Boom Actuator (ACAE)
LBA .... Linear-Bounded Automaton
LBA .... Little Books on Art [*A publication*]
LBA .... Load-Bearing Axis
LBA .... Local Battery Apparatus
LBA .... Local Bus Adapter [*Computer science*]
LBA .... Local Bus Adaptor (NITA)
LBA .... Logical Block Address [*Computer science*]
LBA .... Logical Block Addressing [*Computer science*] (VLIE)
LBA .... London Boroughs Association [*British*] (DCTA)
LBA .... London Building Acts (SAUO)
LBA .... Longbow Apache [*Helicoptor*] [*Army*] (RDA)
LBA .... Louisiana Bankers Association (SRA)
LBA .... Lutheran Benevolent Association (EA)
LBA .... Luxembourg Brotherhood of America (EA)
LBAB .... Lima Bean Advisory Board [*Superseded by California Dry Bean Advisory Board*] (EA)
LBAD .... Lexington-Blue Grass Army Depot [*Kentucky*] (AABC)
LBAF .... Line Width, Black-to-White-Ratio, Area, Fixation Point
LBAK .... Lightweight Broadband Antenna Kit
L-BAND .... 390 to 1,550 MHz (SAUS)
LB&A .... Legislative Budget and Audit (SAUO)
LB&A .... Lever Brothers & Associates Ltd. (SAUO)
LB&AL .... Lever Brothers and Associates Limited (SAUO)
lb ap .... Apothecaries' Pound (BARN)
Lb Ap .... Pound, Apothecaries (SAUS)
LBAT .... Late Babylonian Astronomical and Related Texts (BJA)
LBAT .... Leukocyte Bactericidal Assay Test [*Medicine*] (MELL)
LBA-TESS .... Longbow Apache-Tactical Engagement Simulation System
LBAU .... Laboratory Automation System (SAUO)
lb av .... Pound Avoirdupois (BARN)
LBB .... Lancaster Bible College, Lancaster, PA [*OCLC symbol*] (OCLC)
LBB .... Landesbank Berlin (EFIS)
LBB .... Leak before Burst (LDOE)
LBB .... Left Breast Biopsy [*Medicine*] (STED)
LBB .... Left Bundle-Branch [*Cardiology*] (DAVI)
Lbb .... Leishmania braziliensis braziliensis [*Microbiology*]
LBB .... Life Blower Bearing
LBB .... Linear Ball Bushing
LBB .... [*The*] Little Black Book [*Cygnet Technologies, Inc.*] [*Database software*]
LBB .... Logic Building Block (SAUS)
LBB .... Low Back Bend (STED)
LBB .... Low Back Bending (DMAA)
LBB .... Low Band Basic (TIMI)
LBB .... Lubbock [*Texas*] [*Airport symbol*] (OAG)
LBB .... Lubbock, TX [*Location identifier*] [*FAA*] (FAAL)
LBBA .... London Bacon Buyers' Association Ltd. [*British*]
LBBB .... Left Bundle Branch Block [*Cardiology*]
LBBG .... Burgas [*Bulgaria*] [*ICAO location identifier*] (ICLI)
LBBM .... Ludlow Bone Bed Member [*England*] [*Geology*]
LBBP .... Laboratory of Blood and Blood Products [*Public Health Service*]
LBBSB .... Left Bundle Branch System Block [*Cardiology*]
LBB/W .... Locks, Bolts & Bars/Windows (WDAA)
LBBX .... Left Breast Biopsy Examination [*Medicine*] (AAMN)
LBBY .... Lobby
LBC .... Albanian Airline Co. [*ICAO designator*] (FAAC)
LBC .... Laboratoires Bruneau & Cie [*France*] [*Research code symbol*]
LBC .... Laboratorio Chile ADS [*NYSE symbol*] (TTSB)
LBC .... Laboratorio Chile SA [*NYSE symbol*] (SAG)
LBC .... Land Bank Commission
LBC .... Landmark Bancshares Corporation (SAUO)
LBC .... Large Bobbin Core (SAUS)
LBC .... Large Bore Cannon (MCD)
LBC .... LASER Beam Cutting [*Welding*]
LBC .... Launcher Battery Charger (ACAE)
LBC .... Law Book Company (SAUO)
LBC .... Layman's Bible Commentary [*London*] [*A publication*] (BJA)
LBC .... Left Book Club [*Founded in the 1930's by publisher Victor Gollancz*] [*Defunct*] [*British*]
LBC .... Left Bounded Context [*Computer science*] (MHDB)
LBC .... Letter Book Copy (GEAB)
LBC .... Levesque, Beaubien & Co. [*Toronto Stock Exchange symbol*]
LBC .... Liberian Broadcasting Corporation (SAUO)
LBC .... Liberty Baptist College [*Virginia*]
LBC .... Liberty Bell Communications, Inc. [*Detroit, MI*] [*Telecommunications*] (TSSD)
LBC .... Lidocaine Blood Concentration [*Medicine*] (STED)
LBC .... Lilliputian Bottle Club (EA)
LBC .... Line Balance Converter
LBC .... Little British Car
LBC .... Load Bus Contactor [*Aviation*]
LBC .... Local Baggage Committee [*IATA*] (DS)
LBC .... Local Bus Controller
LBC .... Logistical Base Command [*Korea*]
LBC .... London Ballet Circle
LBC .... London Bankruptcy Court
LBC .... London Bradcasting Company (SAUO)
LBC .... London Brick Co. (WDAA)
LBC .... London Broadcasting Co.
LBC .... Long Beach, CA [*Amtrak Busline code*]
LBC .... Loose Bladder Construction [*Ball*] (DICI)
LBC .... Lothian and Berwick Cavalry [*British military*] (DMA)
LBC .... Lowband Color [*Broadcasting*] (NTCM)
LBC .... Lubudi [*Zaire*] [*Seismograph station code, US Geological Survey*] (SEIS)
LBC .... Lummer-Brodhun Cube [*Physics*]
LBC .... Lymphadenosis Benigna Cutis [*Medicine*] (DMAA)
LBC-A .... LASER Beam Cutting - Air
LB CAL .... Pound Calorie (WDAA)
LBCC .... Long Beach City College [*California*]
LBC/CML .... Lymphoid Blast Crisis of Chronic Myeloid Leukemia [*Oncology*]
LBCD .... Left Border Cardiac Dullness [*Cardiology*]
LBC-EV .... LASER Beam Cutting - Evaporative
LBCF .... Laboratory Branch Complement Fixation [*Clinical chemistry*]
Lb CHU .... Pound Centigrade Heat Unit (SAUS)
LBCI .... Liberty Bancorp, Inc. [*NASDAQ symbol*] (SAG)
LBC-IG .... LASER Beam Cutting - Inert Gas
LBCL .... Liberty Baptist College (SAUO)
LBCL .... Louisville Behavior Check List [*Psychology*]
LBCL .... Lymphoblastoid B-Cell Line [*Genetics*]
LBCM .... Licentiate of the Bandsmen's College of Music (WDAA)
LBCM .... Locator at Back Course Marker (PDAA)
LBCM .... London Board of Congregational Ministers (SAUO)
Lb Co .... Labour Company (SAUO)
LBCO .... Lanthanum-Barium-Copper-Oxide [*Inorganic chemistry*]
LBC-O .... LASER Beam Cutting - Oxygen
LBcS .... Belle Chasse State School, Belle Chasse, LA [*Library symbol*] [*Library of Congress*] (LCLS)
LBCS .... Land-Based Classification Standard (PA)
Lb/cu ft .... Pound per Cubic Foot (SAUS)
Lb/cu in .... Pound per Cubic Inch (SAUS)
Lb/cu yd .... Pound per Cubic Yard (SAUS)
LBCV .... Left Brachiocephalic Vein [*Medicine*] (MELL)
LBCX .... Lewisburg & Buffalo Creek [*Federal Railroad Administration identification code*]
LBD .... Lamellar Body Density [*Medicine*] (MELL)
LBD .... Large Bile Duct [*Medicine*] (DMAA)
LBD .... Laser Beam Detector (ADWA)
LBD .... Laser Beam Directors (SAUO)
LBD .... Left Border of Dullness [*Cardiology*]
LBD .... Letter Bomb Detector [*Police and security equipment*]
LBD .... Licensed Beverage Distributors (SRA)
LBD .... Lifting Body Development
LBD .... Ligand-Binding Domain [*Biology*]
LBD .... Light Beam Deflection
LBD .... Little Black Devils [*Nickname given to the 90th Battalion of the Winnipeg Rifles during the Northwest Rebellion in 1885*]
LBD .... Little Black Dress [*Women's fashions*]
LBD .... Logic Block Diagram (IAA)
LBD .... Low Band Difference (TIMI)
LBD .... Lower Back Disability [*Medicine*]
LBDA .... Lexington Bluegrass Depot Activity [*Kentucky*] [*Army*]
LBDI .... Liberian Bank for Development and Investment (BUAC)
LBDQ .... Leader Behavior Description Questionnaire [*Psychology*]
L/Bdr .... Lance-Bombardier [*British military*] (DMA)
LBDS .... Laser Beam Diagnostic Scanner (ACAE)
LBDS .... Leiden-Berkeley Deep Survey [*Astronomy*]
LBDT .... Low Bay Dolly Tug (NASA)
LBDU .... Lombardia [*Intermodal shipping container symbol*] (TVRC)
LBE .... Lak [*Language symbol*] (ETLW)
LBE .... Lakewood Board of Education, Lakewood, OH [*Inactive*] [*OCLC symbol*] (OCLC)
LBE .... Lambada-Bateristа Experiment (SAUS)
LBE .... Lance-Bubbling-Equilibrium [*Steelmaking*]
LBE .... Land-Bearing Equipment [*Military*] (INF)
LBE .... Landing Barge, Emergency Repair
LBE .... Language Based Editor (VLIE)
LBE .... Latrobe [*Pennsylvania*] [*Airport symbol*] (OAG)
LBE .... Latrobe, PA [*Location identifier*] [*FAA*] (FAAL)
LBE .... Libra Energy, Inc. [*Vancouver Stock Exchange symbol*]
LBE .... Load-Bearing Equipment (INF)
LBE .... Local Business Entities (TIMI)
LBE .... Location-Based Entertainment
LBE .... Long Below-Elbow [*Cast*] (STED)
LBE .... Long Bill of Exchange [*Business term*] (MHDW)
LBE .... Lower Band Edge (VLIE)
LBEA .... Lutheran Braille Evangelism Association (EA)
LBeB .... Bossier Parish Library, Benton, LA [*Library symbol*] [*Library of Congress*] (LCLS)
LBEB .... Laboratory of Brain Evolution and Behavior [*National Institute of Mental Health*]
LBEF .... Land-Based Evaluation Facility [*Military*] (CAAL)
LBEFM .... Low Background Epifluorescence Microscopy
LBEI .... Licentiate of the Institution of Body Engineers [*British*] (DBQ)

LBEN Low-Byte Enable
Lber Literaturbericht (BJA)
LBES Laboratory of Biomedical and Environmental Sciences [*Research center*] (RCD)
LBES Lifeboat Enthusiasts Society (BUAC)
LBETV Les Brown's Encyclopedia of Television [*A publication*]
LB Eur Lehman Brothers, Inc. [*Associated Press*] (SAG)
LBF Botanical Society of Lund (SAUO)
LBF Lactobacillus bulgaricus Factor [*Biochemistry*]
LBF Landing Barge Flak [*British military*] (DMA)
LBF Latin America Dollar Inc.Fd [*NYSE symbol*] (TTSB)
LBF Latin America Dollar, Inc. Fund [*NYSE symbol*] (SPSG)
LBF Les Buteaux [*France*] [*Seismograph station code, US Geological Survey*] (SEIS)
LBF Limb Blood Flow (AAMN)
LBF Lithuanian Basketball Federation (BUAC)
LBF Liver Blood Flow [*Physiology*]
LBF Load Bit Field [*Computer science*] (IAA)
LBF London Book Fair [*England*]
LBF Louis Braille Foundation for Blind Musicians [*Defunct*] (EA)
LBF Lyme Borreliosis Foundation (EA)
LBF North Platte [*Nebraska*] [*Airport symbol*] (OAG)
LBF North Platte, NE [*Location identifier*] [*FAA*] (FAAL)
lbf Pound-Force (WPI)
LBF Pounds, Force (MCD)
LBFA Landau/Bain Fan Association (SAUO)
LBFA Official Martin Landau-Barbara Bain Fan Association (EA)
LBFC Landmark Financial Corporation (SAUO)
LBFC Lane Brody Fan Club (EA)
LBFC Laura Branigan Fan Club (EA)
LBFC Lauralee Bell Fan Club (EA)
LBFC Long Beach Finl'. [*NASDAQ symbol*] (SG)
LBFCR Longbow Fire Control RADAR (DWSG)
LBFE Lower Back Flexion Exercise [*Therapy term*] (CTAA)
lbf-ft Pound Force Foot (STED)
LBFI L & B Financial, Inc. [*NASDAQ symbol*] (SAG)
LBF/IN^2 Pound-Force per Square Inch (WDAA)
LBFL L&B Financial [*NASDAQ symbol*] (TTSB)
LBF-S Pound-Force per Second
$LBF\ S/FT^2$ Pound-Force Seconds per Square Foot
Lbf s/fty Pound-Force Seconds per Square Foot (SAUS)
lb-ft Pound-Feet (STED)
Lb-Ft Pound-Foot (SAUS)
Lb/ft Pound per Foot (SAUS)
LB/FT Pounds per Foot
LB/FT^2 Pounds per Square Foot
Lb/ft3 Pound per Cubic Foot (SAUS)
lb/ft3 Pounds Per Cubic Foot [*Industrial hygiene term*] (OHS)
LB/FT^3 Pounds per Cubic Foot
LB/(FT H) Pounds per Foot-Hour
LB/(FT S) Pounds per Foot-Second
Lb/fty Pound per Square Foot (SAUS)
Lb/fty Pounds per Square Foot (SAUS)
LBFZ LB Foster [*Federal Railroad Administration identification code*]
LBG Le Bourget Airport [*France*]
LBG Left Buccal Ganglion [*Medicine*]
LBG Load Balancing Group [*Computer science*] (ELAL)
LBG Local Battle Group (ACAE)
LBG Locust Bean Gum (OA)
LBG Loss of Bowel Gas [*Medicine*] (EDAA)
LBG Low BTU Gas (MCD)
LBG Lucky Break Gold [*Vancouver Stock Exchange symbol*]
LB/GAL Pounds per Gallon
LBGC Columbia Lesbian, Bisexual and Gay Coalition (EA)
LBGO Gorna Orechovitsa [*Bulgaria*] [*ICAO location identifier*] (ICLI)
LBH Laker Airways (Bahamas) Ltd. [*ICAO designator*] (FAAC)
LBH Late Biblical Hebrew [*Linguistics*] (IEL)
LBH LB Ltd. [*FAA designator*] (FAAC)
LBH Leased Bachelor Housing [*Military*] (DNAB)
LBH Length, Breadth, Height
LBH Local Board of Health [*British*]
LBH Lyman-Birge-Hopfield [*System*] [*Physics*] (MUGU)
LB/H Pounds per Hour
LBH Sydney [*Australia*] [*Airport symbol*] (OAG)
LBHA Little Big Horn Associates (EA)
LBHASA London Business Houses Amateur Sports Association (SAUO)
LBHB Low-Barrier Hydrogen Bond [*Enzymology*]
LBHD Long Beach Harbor Department (SAUO)
LB Horse Lothians and Border Horse (SAUO)
Lb/HP Pound-Force per Horsepower (SAUS)
LB/(HP H) Pounds per Horsepower-Hour
Lb/hphr Pound per Horsepower-Hour (SAUS)
lb/hr Pounds per Hour (MIST)
LBHS Long Beach High School (SAUO)
LBHS Longbow Hellfire Seeker (DWSG)
LBHS Luther Burbank High School (SAUO)
LBHY Lothians and Border Horse Yeomanry (SAUO)
LBI Albi [*France*] [*Airport symbol*] (OAG)
LBI Land Based Interceptor (ACAE)
LBI Last Byte In (ECII)
LBI Leisure Barriers Inventory (IDYL)
LBI Leo Baeck Institute (EA)
LBI Liberte Investors [*Formerly, Lomas & Nettleton Mortgage Investors*] [*NYSE symbol*] (SPSG)
LBI Libra Industries, Inc. [*Vancouver Stock Exchange symbol*]
LBI Library Bibliographies and Indexes [*A publication*]
LBI Library Binding Institute (EA)
LBI Licensed Beverage Industries [*Later, DISCUS*] (EA)
LBI Lima Bean (trypsin) Inhibitor [*Biochemistry*]
LBI Limited Background Investigation (EAGT)
LBI Little Barrier Island (SAUS)
LBI Lloyds & BOLSA [*Bank of London & South America*] International Bank Ltd. [*British*]
LBI Lloyds Bank International (ADA)
LBI Long-Baseline Interferometer [*or Interferometry*] (PDAA)
LBI Lost by Inventory (DNAB)
LBI Low Back Injury [*Medicine*] (DMAA)
LBI Low Serum-Bound Iron (MAE)
LBI Luftbehandling AB (EFIS)
LBIA Archives of the Leo Baeck Institute (SAUO)
LBIAC Left Brains in Airport Carpark (BB)
LBI-ALA Library Binding Institute-American Library Association (SAUO)
LBIB Bulletin des Leo Baeck Instituts (SAUS)
LBIB Bulletin of the Leo Baeck Instituts (SAUO)
LBibel Im Lande der Bibel [*Berlin-Dahlem*] [*A publication*] (BJA)
LBIC Licensed Beverage Information Council (EA)
Lb/imp gall Pound per Imperial Gallon (SAUS)
LBIMS Laban/Bartenieff Institute of Movement Studies (EA)
LBIN Pound-Force per Inch (MSA)
Lb-in Pound-Inch (SAUS)
Lb/in Pound per Inch (SAUS)
LB/IN^2 Pounds per Square Inch
Lb/in3 Pound per Cubic Inch (SAUS)
LB/IN^3 Pounds per Cubic Inch
Lb-in/s Pound-Inch per Second (SAUS)
Lb/iny Pound per Square Inch (SAUS)
LBIPP Licentiate of the British Institute of Professional Photography (DBQ)
LBIR Laser Beam Image Recorder (ACAE)
LBIR LASER Beam Image Reproducer
LBIR Low Background Infrared Radiometry
LBIST Licentiate of the British Institute of Surgical Technologists (DBQ)
LBIX Leading Brands [*NASDAQ symbol*]
LBIY Yearbook of the Leo Baeck Institute (SAUO)
LBIZ Labarge Industries [*Federal Railroad Administration identification code*]
LBJ Lady Bird Johnson [*Mrs. Lyndon Baines Johnson*]
LBJ Little Brown Job [*Unidentified bird, to a bird watcher*]
LBJ Load Bank and Jump [*Computer science*]
LBJ Long Binh Jail [*Vietnam*]
LBJ Lower Ball Joint [*Automotive engineering*]
LBJ Lyndon Baines Johnson [*US president, 1908-1973*]
LBJL Lyndon B. Johnson Library
LBJSC Lyndon B. Johnson Space Center (MSC)
LBJSHP Lyndon B. Johnson State Historic Park (SAUO)
LBJTMC Lyndon B. Johnson Tropical Medical Center (SAUO)
LBK Landing Barge, Kitchen
LBK Left Bank
LBL Ernest Orlando Lawrence Berkeley National Laboratory
lbl Label (ELAL)
LBL Label (MSA)
LBL Labeled Lymphoblast [*Oncology*] (DMAA)
LBL Laminar Boundary Layer
LBL Lawrence Berkeley Laboratories (or Laboratory) (SAUO)
LBL Lawrence Berkeley Laboratory [*Berkeley, CA*] [*Department of Energy*] (GRD)
LBL Left Buttock Line (MCD)
LBL Liberal [*Kansas*] [*Airport symbol*] (OAG)
LBL Liberal [*Telegraphy*] (PCTE)
LBL Liberal, KS [*Location identifier*] [*FAA*] (FAAL)
LBL Limited Broadcasting License [*Australia*]
LBL Line by Line (ARMP)
LBL Lloyds Bank Limited (SAUO)
LBL Low Brightness Laser (ACAE)
LBL Lymphoblastic Lymphoma [*Oncology*]
lb/LF Pounds per Linear Foot (MIST)
LBLG Large Blast Load Generator (PDAA)
LBLS Laminar Boundary-Layer Separation
LBLTY Liability
LBLU Lloyd-Bermuda [*Intermodal shipping container symbol*] (TVRC)
LBM Deluxe Paint image format (SAUS)
LBM LASER Beam Machine (IAA)
LBM Last Bowel Movement [*Medicine*] (BCRP)
LBM Lean Body Mass [*Exercise*]
LBM Left Buffer Memory (GFGA)
LBM Liberty-Bell Mines, Inc. [*Vancouver Stock Exchange symbol*]
LBM Liquid Boost Module (MCD)
LBM Little Brown Mushroom (LDT)
LBM Little Butte [*Montana*] [*Seismograph station code, US Geological Survey*] [*Closed*] (SEIS)
LBM Load Balance Module [*Communications term*] (DCT)
LBM Load Buffer Memory [*Computer science*]
LBM Local Battle Manager (ACAE)
LBM Local Board Memoranda
LBM Locator Back Marker [*Aviation*] (DA)
LBM Logic Bus Monitor [*Computer science*] (CET)
LBM Loose Bowel Movement [*Medicine*] (CPH)
LBM Lowband Monochrome [*Broadcasting*] (NTCM)
LBM Lunar Breaking Module [*NASA*] (IAA)

LBM .... Lung Basement Membrane [*Medicine*] (DMAA)
LBM .... Morehouse Parish Library, Bastrop, LA [*Library symbol*] [*Library of Congress*] (LCLS)
LbM.......... Pound Mass (SAUS)
LBM .... Pounds, Mass (MCD)
LB/M......... Pounds per Minute (AAG)
LBMA........ London Bullion Market Association
LBMC........ Liberty Bell Matchcover Club (EA)
LBMCTX..... Local Battery Magneto Call Telephone Exchange (IAA)
LBMI......... Lease Base Machine Inventory (MHDB)
LB/MIN...... Pounds per Minute
LBMM....... Lifetime Book of Money Management [*A publication*]
Lb Mol ...... Pound Molecule (SAUS)
LBMP........ Land-Based Marine Pollution
LBMS........ Learmonth & Burchett Management Systems [*British*] (NITA)
LBMS........ London Boroughs Management Services (SAUO)
LBM/S-IN2... Pounds of Mass per Second per Square Inch
Lbm/s-iny... Pounds of Mass per Second per Square Inch (SAUS)
LBMSU...... London Boroughs Management Service Unit (SAUO)
LBMSY...... Learmouth & Burchett Management Systems, Inc. [*NASDAQ symbol*] (SAG)
LBMSY...... Learmouth & Burchett Mgt ADS [*NASDAQ symbol*] (TTSB)
LbN.......... Labial Nerve [*Anatomy*]
LBN.......... Lawrence Berkeley Laboratory (SAUO)
LBN.......... Lebanon [*ANSI three-letter standard code*] (CNC)
LBN.......... Le Baron [*NCIC car model code*]
LBN.......... Letter Box Number [*Viet Cong equivalent to the US APO*]
LBN.......... Lewis x Brown Norway [*Rat strain*]
LBN.......... Liberty Broadcasting Network [*Cable-television system*]
LBN.......... Line Balancing Network [*Telecommunications*] (TEL)
LBN.......... Logical Bibliographic Network [*Library science*] (TELE)
LBN.......... Logical Block Numer [*Computer science*] (CIST)
LBN.......... Logic Bucket Number (NITA)
LBNA........ Liberty Bancorp, Inc., Oklahoma [*NASDAQ symbol*] (SAG)
LBNA........ Liberty Bancorp(OK) [*NASDAQ symbol*] (TTSB)
LBNDX...... Lord Abbett: Bond Debenture Cl.A [*Mutual fund ticker symbol*] (SG)
LBNL......... Lawrence Berkeley National Laboratory (HGEN)
LBNON...... Lebanon, OR [*American Association of Railroads railroad junction routing code*]
LBNP........ Lower Body Negative Pressure [*Boots*] [*Space flight equipment*] [*NASA*]
LBNPD...... Lower Body Negative Pressure Device [*Space flight equipment*] [*NASA*]
LBNS........ Long Beach Naval Shipyard (DNAB)
LBNSY...... Long Beach Naval Shipyard (MUGU)
LBO.......... Lamp Burnout (LDOE)
LBO.......... Landing Barge Oiler [*British military*] (DMA)
LBO.......... Lanthanum Boron Oxide [*Inorganic chemistry*]
LBO.......... Large Bowel Obstruction [*Medicine*]
LBO.......... Lebanon, MO [*Location identifier*] [*FAA*] (FAAL)
LBO.......... Leveraged Buy-Out
LBO.......... Liberal Bosnian Organization (BUAC)
LBO.......... Light Beam Oscillograph
LBO.......... Line Building Out
LBO.......... Line Build Out [*Telecommunications*] (MLOA)
LBO.......... Line Build-Out [*Computer science*] (VLIE)
LBO.......... Lithium Boron Oxide [*Inorganic chemistry*]
LBocNS..... Northwest State School, Bier City (SAUS)
LBocNS..... Northwest State School, Bossier City, LA [*Library symbol*] [*Library of Congress*] (LCLS)
LBOE........ Local Board of Education (SAUO)
LBOM........ Local Area Network-Based Object Management (SAUO)
L Book Adviser... Law Book Adviser [*A publication*] (DLA)
Lboro........ Email address for Loughborough University (SAUO)
LBOS........ Leveraged Buyouts [*Business term*]
LBOT........ Logical Beginning of Tape (VLIE)
LBP.......... Laboratory of Biochemical Physiology [*National Cancer Institute*] (RCD)
LBP.......... Land-Based Plant (NRCH)
LBP.......... Laser Beam Printer (NITA)
LBP.......... Lead-Based Paint (LDOE)
LBP.......... Length Between Perpendiculars [*Technical drawings*]
LBP.......... Leucine-Binding Protein [*Biochemistry*]
LBP.......... Light Beam Pickup
LBP.......... Line Binder Post (IAA)
LBP.......... Lipopolysaccharide-Binding Protein [*Biochemistry*]
LBP.......... Local Batch Processing [*Computer science*] (VLIE)
LBP.......... London Borough Polytechnic (SAUO)
LBP.......... Louisiana Board of Pharmacy (EARSL)
LBP.......... Low-Back Pain [*Medicine*]
LBP.......... Low Band Processor (TIMI)
LBP.......... Low Blood Pressure [*Medicine*]
LBP.......... Low Body Pain [*Medicine*] (EDAA)
LBP.......... Lumbar Back Pain [*Medicine*] (DMAA)
LBP.......... Personnel Landing Boat [*Navy symbol*] [*Obsolete*]
LBPA........ Lysobisphosphatidic Acid [*Biochemistry*]
LBPC........ London Building Productivity Committee (SAUO)
Lb p cu ft... Pounds per Cubic Foot (SAUS)
LBPD........ Plovdiv [*Bulgaria*] [*ICAO location identifier*] (ICLI)
LBPF........ Long Bone or Pelvic Fracture [*Medicine*] (DMAA)
Lb p gal..... Pounds per Gallon (SAUS)
LBPH........ Libraries for the Blind and Physically Handicapped [*Automated system*]
LBPH........ Library for the Blind and Physically Handicapped (SAUO)
L-BPH....... Louisiana State Library, Department for the Blind and Physically Handicapped, Baton Rouge, LA [*Library symbol*] [*Library of Congress*] (LCLS)
LBPI......... LASER Beam Position Indicator
LBPIS........ LASER Beam Position Indicator System
LBPL......... Long Beach Public Library (SAUO)
LBPO........ Lifting Body Program Office [*NASA*]
LBPPPA..... Lead-Based Paint Poisoning Prevention Act [*Industrial hygiene term*] (OHS)
LBPQ........ Low Back Pain Questionnaire [*Medicine*] (DMAA)
LBPR........ Lumped Burnable Poison Rod [*Assembly*] [*Nuclear energy*] (NRCH)
LBPS........ Lead-Based Paint Survey [*Environmental science*] (COE)
LBPX........ Labelle Point Railroad [*Federal Railroad Administration identification code*]
Lb p yd...... Pounds per Yard (SAUS)
LBQ.......... Lambarene [*Gabon*] [*Airport symbol*] (OAG)
LBQS........ Large Bright Quasar Survey [*Astronomy*]
LBr........... East Baton Rouge Parish Public Library, Baton Rouge, LA [*Library symbol*] [*Library of Congress*] (LCLS)
Lbr........... Labor
LBR.......... Laborer
LBR.......... Labor Room (MELL)
LBR.......... Labrea [*Brazil*] [*Airport symbol*] (AD)
LBR.......... Large Business Remote [*Computer science*] (CIST)
LBR.......... LASER Beam Recorder [*or Recording*]
LBR.......... LASER Beam Rider (RDA)
LBR.......... L-Band Radiometer (MCD)
LBR.......... Legislative Budget Request [*Emergency Management*] (EMA)
LBR.......... Liberia [*ANSI three-letter standard code*] (CNC)
LBR.......... Librarian (WDAA)
LBR.......... Line of Bomb Release (NATG)
LBR.......... Little Bear Resources [*Vancouver Stock Exchange symbol*]
LBR.......... Little Books on Religion [*A publication*]
LBR.......... Living Benefits Rider [*Insurance*] (WYGK)
LBR.......... Local Base Rescue [*Air Force*] (AFM)
LBR.......... Low Birth Rate
LBR.......... Low BIT [*Binary Digit*] Rate [*Computer science*] (MCD)
LBR.......... Lower Burma Rulings [*India*] [*A publication*] (DLA)
LBR.......... Low Rurning Rate (KSC)
LBR.......... [*The*] Lowville & Beaver River Railroad Co. [*AAR code*]
LBR.......... Lumber (KSC)
Lbr........... Lumber (MIST)
LBRA........ Laboratory of Biochemical Risk Analysis (GNE)
LBrAg........ Louisiana State Department of Agriculture, Research Library, Baton Rouge, LA [*Library symbol*] [*Library of Congress*] (LCLS)
LBRC........ Loft Bomb Release Computer (MCD)
LBrC......... Louisiana Commerce Department, Research Library, Baton Rouge, LA [*Library symbol*] [*Library of Congress*] (LCLS)
LBrCJIS..... Commission on Law Enforcement and Criminal Justice, Criminal Justice InformationSystem, Baton Rouge, LA [*Library symbol*] [*Library of Congress*] (LCLS)
LBrcTI....... Louisiana Training Institute, Bridge City Library, Bridge City, LA [*Library symbol*] [*Library of Congress*] (LCLS)
LBrE......... Ethyl Corp., Chemical Development Library, Baton Rouge, LA [*Library symbol*] [*Library of Congress*] (LCLS)
LBrEd........ Louisiana Education Department, Baton Rouge, LA [*Library symbol*] [*Library of Congress*] (LCLS)
LBRF........ Louse-Borne Relapsing Fever [*Medicine*] (AAMN)
LBRF........ Lower Branchial Filament
LBrG......... Gulf South Research Institute, Baton Rouge, LA [*Library symbol*] [*Library of Congress*] (LCLS)
LBRG........ LASER Beam Rider Guidance (MCD)
LBRG........ Laser Beam-Riding Guidance (SAUS)
LBrGS....... Church of Jesus Christ of Latter-Day Saints, Genealogical Society Library, Baton Rouge (SAUO)
LBrGS....... Church of Jesus Christ of Latter-Day Saints, Genealogical Society Library, BatonRouge Branch, Baton Rouge, LA [*Library symbol*] [*Library of Congress*] (LCLS)
LBrHR....... Louisiana Department of Health and Human Resources, Policy Planning and Evaluation Office, Baton Rouge, LA [*Library symbol*] [*Library of Congress*] (LCLS)
LBrHR-Y.... Louisiana Department of Health and Human Resources, Office of Youth Services, Baton Rouge, LA [*Library symbol*] [*Library of Congress*] (LCLS)
LBRI......... Lake Biwa Research Institute (BUAC)
LBrIPA....... Louisiana Information Processing Authority, Baton Rouge, LA [*Library symbol*] [*Library of Congress*] (LCLS)
LBrJ......... Louisiana Justice Department, Huey P. Long Library, Baton Rouge, LA [*Library symbol*] [*Library of Congress*] (LCLS)
LBrJS........ Jimmy Swaggart Bible College Library, Baton Rouge, LA [*Library symbol*] [*Library of Congress*] (LCLS)
LBrL......... Labor Department, Research Library, Baton Rouge, LA [*Library symbol*] [*Library of Congress*] (LCLS)
LBrLAS...... Louisiana Arts and Science Center, Baton Rouge, LA [*Library symbol*] [*Library of Congress*] (LCLS)
LBrLC........ Louisiana Legislative Council, Reference Division, Baton Rouge, LA [*Library symbol*] [*Library of Congress*] (LCLS)
LBrLH....... Earl K. Long Hospital, Medical Library, Baton Rouge, LA [*Library symbol*] [*Library of Congress*] (LCLS)
LBRM........ Large Basin Runoff Model [*Marine science*] (OSRA)
LBRM........ Laser Beam Rider Missile (ACAE)
LBrNR....... Natural Resources Department, Research and Development Library, Baton Rouge, LA [*Library symbol*] [*Library of Congress*] (LCLS)
LBrNR-F..... Natural Resources Department, Office of Forestry, Baton Rouge, LA [*Library symbol*] [*Library of Congress*] (LCLS)

LBrPS .... Public Service Commission, Baton Rouge, LA [*Library symbol*] [*Library of Congress*] (LCLS)
LBrR .... Louisiana Revenue Department, Research Department, Baton Rouge, LA [*Library symbol*] [*Library of Congress*] (LCLS)
LBRS .... Low Background Reference System
LBRS .... Rousse [*Bulgaria*] [*ICAO location identifier*] (ICLI)
LBrSP .... State Planning Office, Library, Baton Rouge, LA [*Library symbol*] [*Library of Congress*] (LCLS)
Lbr Svc ...... Labor Service (SAUO)
LBRT .... Liberate Technologies [*NASDAQ symbol*] (SG)
LBRT .... Liberty
LBrTD-Av .... Department of Transportation and Development, Aviation (SAUS)
LBrTD-Av .... Department of Transportation and Development, Aviation Office, Baton Rouge, LA [*Library symbol*] [*Library of Congress*] (LCLS)
LBrTD-H ..... Department of Transportation and Development, Office of Highways, Research and Development Library, Baton Rouge, LA [*Library symbol*] [*Library of Congress*] (LCLS)
LBrTD-Pw ... Department of Transportation and Development, Office of Public Works, Baton Rouge, LA [*Library symbol*] [*Library of Congress*] (LCLS)
LBRTY .... Liberty
LBRU .... Companhia de Navegacao Lloyd Brasileiro [*Intermodal shipping container symbol*] (TVRC)
LBrUC .... Department of Urban and Community Affairs, Office of Planning and Technical Assistance, Baton Rouge, LA [*Library symbol*] [*Library of Congress*] (LCLS)
LBRV .... Lifting Body Research Vehicle
LBRV .... Low BIT [*Binary Digit*] Rate Voice [*Telecommunications*]
LBrWF-S .... Department of Wildlife and Fisheries, Louisiana Stream Control Commission, BatonRouge, LA [*Library symbol*] [*Library of Congress*] (LCLS)
LBRY .... Library (MSA)
LBS .... Labasa [*Fiji*] [*Airport symbol*] (OAG)
LBS .... Lactobacillus Selector [*Microbiology*] (DAVI)
LBS .... Laminar Boundary-Layer Separation
LBS .... Land-Based Sources [*of Marine Pollution*] [*Marine science*] (OSRA)
LBS .... Land-Based Sources of Marine Pollution (USDC)
LBS .... Landesbank Hessen-Thuringen Girozentrale (EFIS)
LBS .... Landing Boat, Support [*Navy symbol*]
LBS .... Large Blast Simulator
LBS .... Large Bulb Ship
LBS .... LASER Beam Surgery
LBS .... LASER Bombing System
LBS .... Launch Base Support [*Air Force*]
LBS .... Launch Blast Simulator (MUGU)
LBS .... Lead Belly Society (EA)
LBS .... Lecithin Bile State [*Medicine*]
LBS .... Lectori Benevolo Salutem [*To the Kind (or Gentle) Reader, Greeting*] [*Latin*]
LBS .... Liberation Broadcasting Station (CINC)
LBS .... Life Boat Station (SAUO)
LBS .... Lifeboat Stations (SAUO)
LBS .... Light Bomber Strike [*Air Force*] (NATG)
LBS .... Line Buffer System [*Computer science*]
LBS .... Liquid Bipropellant System (ACAE)
LBS .... Lithuanian Boy Scouts (EA)
LBS .... Load Balance System [*Telecommunications*] (TEL)
LBS .... Load-Bearing Surface (MCD)
LBS .... Load Bearing System
LBS .... Local Battery Signaling [*Telecommunications*] (IAA)
LBS .... Local Battery Supply [*Telecommunications*] (IAA)
LBS .... Local Battery Switchboard [*Telecommunications*] (IAA)
LBS .... Local Battery System [*Telecommunications*] (IAA)
LBS .... Location-Based Services [*Navigation systems*]
LBS .... Loire Base Section [*World War II*]
LBS .... London Boroughs Association (SAUO)
LBS .... London Business Aviation [*British*] [*ICAO designator*] (FAAC)
LBS .... London Business School [*England*]
LBS .... London Graduate School of Business Studies (SAUO)
LBS .... Low Back Strain (DAVI)
LBS .... Low Back Syndrome [*Medicine*] (DMAA)
LBS .... Lumbar Back Strain [*Medicine*] (DMAA)
LBS .... Lysine-Binding Site [*Hematology*]
LB/S .... Pounds per Second
LBS .... Libyan Broadcasting Service (ODA)
LBSA .... Libraries Board of South Australia
LBSA .... Lipid-Bound Sialic Acid [*Analytical biochemistry*]
LBSA .... Long Binh Subarea [*Vietnam*]
LBSC .... Licentiate of the British Society of Commerce (DBQ)
LBSC .... London, Brighton and South Coast Railway (SAUO)
LBSC .... Long Beach State College (SAUO)
LBSC .... LSB Bancshares Inc. of South Carolina [*NASDAQ symbol*] (COMM)
LBSCR .... London, Brighton & South Coast Railway [*British*]
LBSD .... Lightweight Battlefield Surveillance Device
LBSF .... Lions Blind Sports Foundation (EA)
LBSF .... Little Brothers of Saint Francis (TOCD)
LBSF .... Sofia [*Bulgaria*] [*ICAO location identifier*] (ICLI)
LBSG .... Letter Box Study Group [*British*] (DBA)
LBSM .... Licentiate of Birmingham and Midland Institute School of Music (SAUO)
Lb/sq ft ..... Pound per Square Foot (SAUS)
Lb/sq in ..... Pound per Square Inch (SAUS)
Lb/sq yd .... Pound per Square Yard (SAUS)
LBSR .... Lightweight Battleweight Surveillance Radar (ACAE)
LBSS .... Lightweight Battlefield Surveillance System (SAUS)
LBSS .... Local Boards of the Selective Service System
lbst .... Pounds [*Libra in Latin*] Static Thrust (DOMA)
LBSTR .... Lobster
LBSW .... L and B Swift Express [*Common carrier symbol*]
LBSZ .... Stara Zagora [*Bulgaria*] [*ICAO location identifier*] (ICLI)
LBT .... Air Liberte Tunisie [*Tunisia*] [*ICAO designator*] (FAAC)
LBT .... Chemical Laboratory Technician [*or Technology*] [*Navy*]
LBT .... Labatt [*John*] Ltd. [*Toronto Stock Exchange symbol*] [*Vancouver Stock Exchange symbol*]
LBT .... Labete [*Solomon Islands*] [*Seismograph station code, US Geological Survey*] (SEIS)
LBT .... Lachi [*Language symbol*] (ETLW)
LBT .... Land-Based Tanker [*Aircraft*] (DOMA)
LBT .... Large Binocular Telescope
LBT .... Launch Base Test (ACAE)
LBT .... L-Band Tetrode
LBT .... L-Band Transmitter
LBT .... LBT [*NCIC trailer make code*]
LBT .... Lean Best Torque [*Automotive engineering*]
lbt .... Librettist [*MARC relator code*] [*Library of Congress*] (LCCP)
LBT .... Light-Beam Transmissometer (PDAA)
LBT .... Linear Beam Tube
LBT .... Listen Before Talk (SAUO)
LBT .... Local Battery Telephone [*Telecommunications*] (IAA)
LBT .... Local Bus Target (SAUO)
LBT .... Long-Baseline Tiltmeter [*For earthquake study*]
LBT .... Low Back Tenderness [*Medicine*] (DMAA)
LBT .... Low Bandpass Transformer
LBT .... Low BIT [*Binary Digit*] Test [*Computer science*] (IEEE)
LBT .... Lumberton, NC [*Location identifier*] [*FAA*] (FAAL)
LBT .... Lupus Band Test [*Medicine*]
LBT .... Lutheran Bible Translators (EA)
LBT .... Pounds Thrust [*NASA*] (KSC)
LBT .... Pound Troy
LBT CBS .... Local-Battery Talking, Common-Battery Signaling [*Telecommunications*] (TEL)
Lb t/cu ft .... Pound Troy per Cubic Foot (SAUS)
Lb t/cu in .... Pound Troy per Cubic Inch (SAUS)
Lb t/cu yd ... Pound Troy per Cubic Yard (SAUS)
LBTF .... Land-Based Test Facility (DNAB)
LBTF .... Langmuir-Blodgett Trough Facility (SAUS)
LBTF .... Long Beach Test Facility [*Missiles*]
Lb t/ft .... Pound Troy per Foot (SAUS)
Lb t/ft3 ...... Pound Troy per Cubic Foot (SAUS)
Lb t/fty ...... Pound Troy per Square Foot (SAUS)
LBTI .... Lima Bean Trypsin Inhibitor (DB)
LBTI .... Long-Burning Target Indicator [*British military*] (DMA)
Lb t/in .... Pound Troy per Inch (SAUS)
Lb t/in3 ..... Pound Troy per Cubic Inch (SAUS)
Lb t/iny ..... Pound Troy per Square Inch (SAUS)
LBTMA .... Listen Before Transmission Multiple Access (PDAA)
LBTP .... Launch Base Test Plan (ACAE)
lb tr .... Pound Troy [*Medicine*] (EDAA)
LBTS .... Land-Based Test Site
LBTS .... Land-Based Test System (SAUS)
LBTS .... Local Battery Telephone Set [*Telecommunications*] (IAA)
LBTS .... Local Battery Telephone Switchboard [*Telecommunications*] (IAA)
LBTS .... London Blood Transfusion Service (SAUO)
Lb t/sq ft .... Pound Troy per Square Foot (SAUS)
Lb t/sq yd ... Pound Troy per Square Yard (SAUS)
Lb t/sy in ... Pound Troy per Square Inch (SAUS)
LbtTrm .... Liberty Term Trust [*Associated Press*] (SAG)
Lb t Weight ... Pound Troy Weight (SAUS)
LBTX .... Local Battery Telephone Exchange [*Telecommunications*] (IAA)
LBTY .... Liberty Petroleum Co. (SAUO)
LBTY .... Tele-Communications Class A [*NASDAQ symbol*] (SAG)
LBTYA .... Liberty Media Group [*NASDAQ symbol*]
LBTYA .... Tele-Comm Inc. 'A' Liberty Media [*NASDAQ symbol*] (TTSB)
LbtyASE ..... Liberty All-Star Equity [*Associated Press*] (SAG)
LbtyASG ..... Liberty All Star Growth [*Associated Press*] (SAG)
LBTYB .... Tele-Comm'B'Liberty Media [*NASDAQ symbol*] (TTSB)
LbtyBc .... Liberty Bancorp, Inc. [*Associated Press*] (SAG)
Lb t/yd ...... Pound Troy per Yard (SAUS)
Lb t/yd3 ..... Pound Troy per Cubic Yard (SAUS)
Lb t/ydy ..... Pound Troy per Square Yard (SAUS)
LbtyH .... Liberty Homes, Inc. [*Associated Press*] (SAG)
LBU .... Labuan [*Malaysia*] [*Airport symbol*] (OAG)
LBU .... Large Base Unit [*Telecommunications*]
LBU .... Launcher Booster Unit
LBUN .... Levobunolol [*Also, LB*] [*Biochemistry*]
LBuP .... Plaquemines Parish Library, Buras, LA [*Library symbol*] [*Library of Congress*] (LCLS)
LBUR .... Library Bureau, Inc. (SAUO)
LBUTX .... Federated Utility Cl.A [*Mutual fund ticker symbol*] (SG)
LBV .... La Belle, FL [*Location identifier*] [*FAA*] (FAAL)
LBV .... Landing Boat, Vehicle [*Navy symbol*] [*Obsolete*]
LBV .... Lateral Boundary Value (QUAC)
LBV .... Left Brachial Vein [*Cardiology*] (DAVI)
LBV .... Left Bundle to Venticular [*Medicine*] (EDAA)
LBV .... Libreville [*Gabon*] [*Airport symbol*] (OAG)
LBV .... Load-Bearing Vest [*Military*] (INF)
LBV .... Local Bus Video
LBV .... Luminous Blue Variables [*Astronomy*]
LBV .... Lung Blood Volume [*Medicine*] (EDAA)

LBVAH....... Long Beach Veterans' Administration Hospital [*California*] [*Medicine*] (EDAA)
LBW......... Landing Barge Water [*British military*] (DMA)
LBW......... LASER Beam Welding
LBW......... Lean Body Weight [*Medicine*] (DMAA)
lbw.......... Leg before Wicket [*Cricket*] (WA)
LBW......... Leg before Wicket [*Cricket*]
LBW......... Long Bawan [*Indonesia*] [*Airport symbol*] (OAG)
LBW......... Long Wheelbase [*Automotive term*] (GOBB)
LBW......... Low Birth Weight [*Obstetrics*]
LBW......... Low Body Weight
LBW......... Low-Speed Black and White [*Photography*]
LBW......... Lutheran Braille Workers (EA)
LBW......... Live Body Weight (ODA)
LBWBUZCALTX... Local Battery with Buzzer Calling Telephone Exchange [*Telecommunications*] (IAA)
LBWI........ Low-Birth-Weight Infant [*Obstetrics*] (MAE)
LBWL........ Lansing Board of Water & Light [*Federal Railroad Administration identification code*]
LBWMABCTX... Local Battery with Magneto and Buzzer Calling Telephone Exchange [*Telecommunications*] (IAA)
LBWN........ Varna [*Bulgaria*] [*ICAO location identifier*] (ICLI)
LBWOC...... Level Bombing Wind Offset Computer [*Military*] (IAA)
LBWR........ Lung-Body Weight Ratio [*Medicine*] (MAE)
Lb Wt........ Pound-Weight (SAUS)
Lb wt/cu ft... Pound-Weight per Cubic Foot (SAUS)
Lb wt/cu in... Pound-Weight per Cubic Inch (SAUS)
Lb wt/cu yd... Pound-Weight per Cubic Yard (SAUS)
Lb wt/ft...... Pound-Weight per Foot (SAUS)
Lb wt/ft3.... Pound-Weight per Cubic Foot (SAUS)
Lb wt/fty.... Pound-Weight per Square Foot (SAUS)
Lb wt/hp.... Pound-Weight per Horsepower (SAUS)
Lb wt/in..... Pound-Weight per Inch (SAUS)
Lb wt/in3.... Pound-Weight per Cubic Inch (SAUS)
Lb wt/iny.... Pound-Weight per Square Inch (SAUS)
Lb wt/sq ft... Pound-Weight per Square Foot (SAUS)
Lb wt/sq in... Pound-Weight per Square Inch (SAUS)
Lb wt/sq yd... Pound-Weight per Square Yard (SAUS)
Lb wt/yd.... Pound-Weight per Yard (SAUS)
Lb wt/yd3... Pound-Weight per Cubic Yard (SAUS)
Lb wt/ydy... Pound-Weight per Square Yard (SAUS)
LBX.......... Laborious [*Telegraphy*] (PCTE)
LBX.......... Lake Jackson, TX [*Location identifier*] [*FAA*] (FAAL)
LBX.......... Local Bus Accelerator (VLIE)
LBX.......... Low Band with X (SAUO)
LBY.......... Hattiesburg, MS [*Location identifier*] [*FAA*] (FAAL)
LBY.......... La Baule [*France*] [*Airport symbol*] (AD)
LBY.......... Libbey, Inc. [*NYSE symbol*] (SPSG)
LBY.......... Liberty Fabrics of New York (SAUO)
LBY.......... Libya [*ANSI three-letter standard code*] (CNC)
Lb/yd........ Pound per Yard (SAUS)
LB/YD^2...... Pounds per Square Yard
Lb/yd3....... Pound per Cubic Yard (SAUS)
LB/YD^3...... Pounds per Cubic Yard
Lb/ydy....... Pound per Square Yard (SAUS)
Lb/ydy....... Pounds per Square Yard (SAUS)
LBYR........ Labyrinth [*Engineering*]
LBYRPK..... Labyrinth Pack [*Engineering*]
LC........... Addressee Left City [*Telegraphy*] (PCTE)
LC........... Convention on the Prevention of Marine Pollution by Dumping of Wastes and other Matter (SAUS)
LC........... Co-ordinating Committee for the Liberation of Africa (SAUO)
LC........... Deferred Cable (EBF)
LC........... Ewell's Leading Cases on Infancy, Etc. [*A publication*] (DLA)
L/C.......... Inductance/Capacitance (AAG)
LC........... Inductor Capacitor circuit (SAUS)
LC........... Label Clause
LC........... Laboratory Counsel (SAUO)
LC........... Laboratory Craftsman (ADA)
LC........... Labor Cases [*A publication*] (DLA)
LC........... Labor Code (DNAB)
LC........... Labour Canada [*See also TRAVC*]
LC........... Labour Corps [*British military*] (DMA)
LC........... Lackawanna College (SAUO)
LC........... La Crosse [*Diocesan abbreviation*] [*Wisconsin*] (TOCD)
LC........... Lactation Consultant [*Medicine*] (MEDA)
LC........... Ladycliff College (SAUO)
LC........... Laennec's Cirrhosis [*Medicine*] (MAE)
LC........... Lafayette College (SAUO)
LC........... Lagonda Club, US Section (EA)
LC........... Lake Central Airlines
LC........... Lake Current (COE)
LC........... Lakehead College (SAUO)
LC........... Lakeland College (SAUO)
LC........... Lakey Clinic Medical Center [*Burlington, MA*]
LC........... Lamb Committee (EA)
LC........... Lambuth College (SAUO)
LC........... Lancaster & Chester Railway Co. [*AAR code*]
LC........... Lance Corporal
LC........... Land Commission [*British*]
LC........... Land Court [*Legal*] [*British*]
L/C.......... Land Cover (CARB)
LC........... Lander College (SAUO)
LC........... Landing Craft
LC........... Lane College (SAUO)
LC........... Langerhans' Cells [*Medicine*]
LC........... Langmuir Circulation [*Geophysics*]
LC........... Language Code [*Online database field identifier*]
LC........... Lannois-Cleret [*Syndrome*] [*Medicine*] (DB)
LC........... Laredo College (SAUO)
LC........... Large Case [*Indicator*] [*IRS*]
LC........... Large Cell [*Lymphoma classification*]
LC........... Large Chromophobe [*Medicine*] (EDAA)
LC........... Large Cleaved Cell (DB)
LC........... Larval Chamber [*Botany*]
LC........... Lasa C Ring [*Montana*] [*Seismograph station code, US Geological Survey*] (SEIS)
LC........... Lassen College (SAUO)
LC........... Last Card
LC........... Late Clamped [*Umbilical cord*]
LC........... Late Commitment [*Reason for missed interception*] [*Military*]
LC........... Lateral Component
LC........... Latvia's Way [*Political party*] (PSAP)
LC........... Launch Center
LC........... Launch Complex
LC........... Launch Conference [*Aerospace*] (AAG)
L/C.......... Launch Control [*Aerospace*] (AAG)
LC........... Launch Coordinator [*NASA*]
LC........... Launch Corridor [*Aerospace*] (AAG)
LC........... Launch Cost [*Aerospace*]
LC........... Launch Count [*NASA*] (KSC)
LC........... Launch Countdown [*NASA*] (NASA)
LC........... Launch Critical (MCD)
LC........... Launching Control [*Military*]
LC........... Laundry Chute (MSA)
LC........... Laureate of Arts
LC........... Laureate of Letters
LC........... Law Commission (DLA)
LC........... Law Court (SAUO)
LC........... Law Courts
LC........... Lawrence College (SAUO)
LC........... Lead Covered [*or Coated*]
LC........... Leading Cases (DLA)
LC........... League of Communists [*Former Yugoslavia*]
LC........... League of Composers (EA)
LC........... League of the Cross [*Roman Catholic religious order*] (ROG)
LC........... Leander Club (SAUO)
LC........... Learning Curve (MSA)
LC........... Least Count
LC........... Lecithin Cholesterol Acyltransferase (DB)
LC........... Lee College (SAUO)
LC........... Leesona Corp. (KSC)
LC........... Leesona Corporation (SAUO)
lc............ Left Center (WDAA)
LC........... Left Center [*A stage direction*]
LC........... Left Chest [*Medicine*] (KSC)
LC........... Left Circumflex (Artery) [*Anatomy*]
LC........... Left Ear, Cold Stimulus [*Medicine*] (MEDA)
LC........... Legal Committee (MCD)
LC........... Legal Currency (ADA)
lc............ Legionaries of Christ (TOCD)
LC........... Legionaries of Christ [*Roman Catholic men's religious order*]
LC........... Legislative Council [*British*]
LC........... Legitimate Child
LC........... Leisure Counseling [*Medicine*] (MEDA)
LC........... Length of Chord (MSA)
LC........... Lesley College (SAUO)
LC........... Lethal Concentration
L/C.......... Lettera di Credito [*Letter of Credit*] [*Italian*] [*Business term*]
LC........... Letter Contract
l/c........... Letter of Credit (EBF)
LC........... Letter of Credit
LC........... Letters and Cards [*US Postal Service*]
LC........... Lettre de Credit [*Letter of Credit*] [*Business term*] [*French*]
lc............ Leucite [*CIPW classification*] [*Geology*]
LC........... Level Control
LC........... Level Crossing
LC........... Leverage Contract [*Business term*]
LC........... Lewis College (SAUO)
LC........... Leydig's Cells [*Endocrinology*]
LC........... Leyland Cars [*Leyland Daf Ltd.*]
LC........... Liaison-Cargo [*Air Force*]
LC........... Liaison Committee of Rector's Conferences of Member States of the European Communities (BUAC)
LC........... Liaison/Communicator (COE)
LC........... Liberal Conservative
LC........... Liberalt Centrum [*Liberal Center*] [*Denmark*] [*Political party*] (PPE)
LC........... Liberty Corp. [*NYSE symbol*] (SPSG)
LC........... Library of Congress
LC........... Library of Congress Card Number (NITA)
LC........... Library of Congress Classification
LC........... License Cancelled
LC........... License Condition (HEAS)
L/C.......... License to Cut (SAUO)
LC........... Licensing Committee (SAUO)
LC........... Licensing Country [*Dialog*] [*Searchable field*] [*Information service or system*] (NITA)
LC........... Lieutenant Commander

LC........... Life Care [*Medicine*] (BABM)
LC........... Light Car [*British*]
LC........... Light Case [*Military*] (NATG)
LC........... Light Chain [*Immunoglobulin*]
LC........... Light Company [*British military*] (DMA)
LC........... Light Control [*Technical drawings*]
LC........... Light Current (IAA)
LC........... Lightly Canceled
LC........... Lightweight Computer (SAUS)
LC........... Limestone College (SAUO)
LC........... Limited Coordinating (NG)
LC........... Limp Cloth [*Bookbinding*] (DGA)
LC........... Lincoln College (SAUO)
LC........... Lindenwood College (SAUO)
LC........... Linear Chair [*Chemistry*] (ODA)
LC........... Linear Combination
LC........... Line-Carrying
LC........... Line Circuit [*Telecommunications*]
LC........... Line Collector
LC........... Line Concentrator
LC........... Line Connection
LC........... Line Connector (NITA)
LC........... Line Construction Tools [*JETDS nomenclature*] [*Military*] (CET)
LC........... Line Contractor (MCD)
LC........... Line Control
LC........... Line Crosser [*Deserter*] [*Military*]
LC........... Line Length Ciceros [*Typography*] (DGA)
LC........... Line of Communication [*Military*]
LC........... Line of Contact [*Military*]
L/C........... Line of Credit [*Business term*]
LC........... Linfield College (SAUO)
LC........... Linguocervical [*Dentistry*]
LC........... Link Circuit
LC........... Link Control [*Telecommunications*] (OSI)
LC........... Links and Chargers (NATG)
LC........... Linux Computer (SAUS)
LC........... Lions Club (SAUO)
LC........... Lipid Cytosome [*Biochemistry*] (MAE)
LC........... Liquid Capacity
LC........... Liquid Chromatography
LC........... Liquid Cooled [*Mechanical engineering*]
LC........... Liquid Crystal
LC........... Literature Criticism from 1400 to 1800 [*A publication*]
LC........... Lithocholate [*Biochemistry*]
LC........... Lithocolic Acid [*Biochemistry*] (DB)
LC........... Liturgical Conference (EA)
LC........... Live Clinic [*Medicine*] (EDAA)
LC........... Liver Cirrhosis [*Medicine*]
LC........... Livestock Commission (SAUO)
LC........... Living Children
LC........... Livingstone College (SAUO)
LC........... Load Carrier
LC........... Load Cell
LC........... Load Center (MSA)
LC........... Load-Compensating (MSA)
LC........... Load Computer [*or Controller*] (MCD)
LC........... Load Contactor
LC........... Load Control [*Hydraulics*]
L/C........... Load Crew (SAUO)
LC........... Loading Capacity (RIMS)
LC........... Loading Coil [*Telecommunications*] (TEL)
LC........... Loan Capital [*Business term*]
LC........... Loan Crowd [*Investment term*]
LC........... Local Call [*Followed by telephone number*]
LC........... Local Changes (SAUS)
LC........... Local Channel (CET)
LC........... Localization Code (IAA)
LC........... Localized Corrosion (PDAA)
LC........... Location Counter [*Computer science*]
LC........... Locked Closed
lc........... Loco Citato [*At the Place Cited*] [*Latin*] (EES)
LC........... Loco Citato [*In the Place Cited*] [*Latin*]
LC........... Locomotive and Carriage Institute (BUAC)
LC........... Locus Ceruleus [*Brain anatomy*]
LC........... Locus of Control [*Psychology*]
LC........... Loganair [*ICAO designator*] (AD)
LC........... Logical Channel (PDAA)
LC........... Logical Choice (ELAL)
LC........... Logical Comparison (ELAL)
LC........... Logic Cell (IAA)
LC........... Logic Circuit (ELAL)
LC........... Logic Corp.
LC........... Logistics Command (IAA)
LC........... London Clause [*Business term*]
LC........... London Club (EA)
LC........... Long-Chain [*Triglyceride*] [*Biochemistry*] (MAE)
LC........... Long Clear [*Telegraphy*] (PCTE)
LC........... Long Colt [*Gunnery*]
LC........... Longwood College (SAUO)
LC........... Loopback Capability (SAUS)
L/C........... Loop Check (MUGU)
LC........... Loop Circuit (ELAL)
LC........... Loose Coupler
LC........... Loras College (SAUO)
LC........... Lord Chamberlain [*British*]
LC........... Lord Chancellor [*British*]
LC........... Los Californianos (EA)
LC........... Loss of Contact (IAA)
LC........... Lotta Continua [*Continuous Struggle*] [*Italy*] [*Political party*] (PPE)
LC........... Loud and Clear
LC........... Loudness Control (ELAL)
LC........... Louisburg College (SAUO)
LC........... Louisiana College (SAUO)
LC........... [*A*] Lover's Complaint [*Shakespearean work*]
LC........... Low Calorie (AAMN)
LC........... Low Carbon [*Content, as low-carbon steel*]
L/C........... Low Compression [*Automotive engineering*]
LC........... Low Conditioners [*Psychology*]
LC........... Low Cost (ELAL)
LC........... Low Cost Color [*Computer science*] (CDE)
LC........... Lower California
LC........... Lower Canada
lc........... Lowercase (WDMC)
LC........... Lowercase [*i.e., small letters*] [*Typography*]
LC........... Lower Character (IAA)
LC........... Lower Control (IAA)
LC........... Lower Court (SAUO)
LC........... Lower Cylinder
LC........... LOX [*Liquid Oxygen*] Clean
LC........... Loyola College (SAUO)
LC........... Lubrication Chart
LC........... Luminosity Class [*Astronomy*] (IAA)
LC........... Lumped Constant [*Electronics*] (ODA)
LC........... Lutheran Council [*British*] (DBA)
LC........... Lutheran Council of Great Britain (BUAC)
LC........... Luther College (SAUO)
LC........... Luzon College (SAUO)
LC........... Lycoming College (SAUO)
LC........... Lyman Continuum [*Spectroscopy*] (OA)
LC........... Lymphocyte-Mediated Cytotoxicity [*Also, LMC*] [*Immunology*]
LC........... Lynchburg College (SAUO)
LC........... Lytic Capacity [*Clinical chemistry*]
LC........... Scottish Land Court Reports [*A publication*] (DLA)
L/C........... Single Acetate Single Cotton [*Wire insulation*] (AAG)
LC........... St. Lucia [*ANSI two-letter standard code*] (CNC)
LC........... United States Public Health Service Hospital, Carville (SAUS)
LC .... Cross of Leo (ODA)
lc .... Letter Card (ODA)
LC3 .... Logistics Command, Control and Communications (SAUO)
LC-39........... Launch Complex 39 (SAUS)
LC_{50}........... Lethal Concentration, Median [*Lethal for 50% of test group*]
LCA .... Laboratory for Computer Architecture [*University of Texas at Austin*] (RCD)
LCA .... Lacana Mining Corp. [*Toronto Stock Exchange symbol*]
LCA .... La Crescenta, CA [*Amtrak Busline code*]
LCA .... Lake Carriers' Association (EA)
LCA .... Lake Central Airlines
LCA .... Lamborghini Club America (EA)
LCA .... Laminate Council of America [*Defunct*] (EA)
LCA .... Land Compensation Act [*Town planning*] [*British*]
LCA .... Landing Craft, Armored [*Used in Vietnam by the French to transport their engineer units*] (VNW)
LCA .... Landing Craft, Assault [*Navy ship symbol*]
LCA .... Larnaca [*Cyprus*] [*Airport symbol*] (OAG)
LCA .... Last Chance for Animals [*Association*] (EA)
LCA .... Last Common Ancestor [*Evolution*]
LCA .... Latent Class Analysis
LCA .... Launch Control Amplifier [*NASA*] (NASA)
LCA .... Launch Control Analyst [*NASA*] (AAG)
LCA .... Launch [*or Launcher*] Control Area [*Missiles*]
LCA .... Lead Contractors Association [*British*] (EAIO)
LCA .... Leadership Councils of America (EA)
LCA .... Leading Cases, Annotated [*A publication*] (DLA)
LCA .... Leading Catering Accountant [*British military*] (DMA)
LCA .... Learning Corporation of America (SAUO)
LCA .... Leber's Congenital Amaurosis [*Medicine*] (DAVI)
LCA .... LeConte Airlines [*ICAO designator*] (FAAC)
LCA .... Left Carotid Artery [*Cardiology*] (DAVI)
LCA .... Left Circumflex Artery [*Medicine*] (DB)
LCA .... Left Coronary Angiography [*Medicine*] (RAWO)
LCA .... Left Coronary Artery [*Cardiology*]
LCA .... Lesson Content Analysis
LCA .... Leukocyte Common Antigen [*Immunochemistry*]
LCA .... Leveling Control Amplifier
LCA .... Ley de Comunidad Aut"noma (SAUO)
LCA .... Library Club of America [*Defunct*] (EA)
LCA .... Library-College Associates [*Defunct*] (EA)
LCA .... Library of Congress Authority File [*Source file*] [*UTLAS symbol*]
LCA .... Licensed Company Auditor [*British*]
LCA .... Life Communicators Association [*Des Moines, IA*] (EA)
LCA .... Life Cycle Analysis [*or Assessment*] [*Environmental science*]
LCA .... Life Cycle Assessment (ADWA)
LCA .... Light Combat Aircraft [*Military*]
LCA .... Light Contact Assist (STED)
LCA .... Lighting Control Assembly [*NASA*] (KSC)
LCA .... Lightweight Ceramic Armor [*Police and security equipment*]
LCA .... Line Clearance Airdrome [*Air Force*]
LCA .... Line Control Adapter

LCA .... Liquid Crystal Analog
LCA .... Lithocholic Acid [*Biochemistry*]
LCA .... Lithuanian Catholic Alliance (EA)
LCA .... Liverpool Cotton Association (BUAC)
LCA .... Living Centers of America [*NYSE symbol*] (SAG)
LCA .... Lns Culinaris [*Plant lectins*] (QSUL)
LCA .... Load-Carrying Ability (IAA)
LCA .... Load Control Assembly (SAUS)
LCA .... Load Controller Assembly (NASA)
LCA .... Local Communications Adapter [*IBM Corp.*]
LCA .... Local Communications Area (KSC)
LCA .... Local Cooperation Agreement [*Army Corps of Engineers*]
LCA .... Local Core Alignment [*Telecommunications*] (NITA)
LCA .... Log Cabin [*Alabama*] [*Seismograph station code, US Geological Survey*] (SEIS)
LCA .... Logic Cell Array (IAA)
LCA .... Logistic Control Activity (AABC)
LCA .... Logistics Control Area (IAA)
LCA .... London City Airport [*British*]
LCA .... Longitudinal Chromatic Aberration
LCA .... Losely Coupled Architecture (SAUO)
LCA .... Lotus Communications Architecture (SAUO)
LCA .... Louisiana Cattlemen's Association (SRA)
LCA .... Louisiana Chemical Association (SRA)
LCA .... Low Cost Aircraft (ACAE)
LCA .... Low-Cost Automation (WDAA)
LCA .... Lowercase Alphabet
lca .... Lowercase-Alphabet Length [*Typesetting*] (WDMC)
LCA .... Lussazione Congenita dell'Anca [*Congenital Hip Dislocation*] [*Italian*] [*Medicine*]
LCA .... Lutheran Church in America [*Later, ELCA*]
LCA .... Lutheran Collegiate Association [*Defunct*] (EA)
LCA .... Lymphocytotoxic Antibody [*Medicine*] (STED)
LCA .... St. Lucia [*ANSI three-letter standard code*] (CNC)
LCAA .... Licensed Clubs Association of Australia
LCAACT .... Licensed Clubs Association of the Australian Capital Territory
LCAAJ .... Language and Culture Atlas of Ashkenazic Jewry [*A publication*] (BJA)
LCAAP .... Lake City Army Ammunition Plant (AABC)
LCABLS Bull ... Law Council of Australia. Business Law Section. Bulletin [*A publication*]
LCaC .... Cameron Parish Library, Cameron, LA [*Library symbol*] [*Library of Congress*] (LCLS)
LCAC .... La Ligue des Cadets de l'Armee du Canada [*Association*] [*Canada*] (EAIO)
LCAC .... Landing Craft, Air Cushion [*Navy symbol*]
LCAC .... Landing Craft, Air Cushioned (SAUO)
LCAC .... Library of Congress Classification - Additions and Changes [*A publication*]
LCAC .... Light Craft, Air Cushion (ACAE)
LCAC .... Ligue des Cadets de l'Air du Canada [*Association*] [*Canada*] (EAIO)
LCAC .... Listed Company Advisory Committee [*of NYSE*]
LCAC .... Low-Cost Automation Centre [*British*]
LCACCC .... Laymen's Commission of the American Council of Christian Churches (EA)
LCACM .... Liaison Committee of Architects of the Common Market (SAUO)
LCACT .... Law Council of the Australian Capital Territory
LCAD .... Logistics Cost Analysis Data (MCD)
LC-ADD .... Library of Congress - American Doctoral Dissertations [*A bibliographic publication*]
LCAF .... Lutheran Church in America Foundation
LCA(FT) .... Landing Craft, Assault (Flamethrower) [*British military*] (DMA)
LCA-GB .... Lightweight Cycle Association of Great Britain (BUAC)
LCA(H) .... Landing Craft, Assault (Hedgerow)
LCAH .... London and Continental Advertising Holdings [*British*]
LCAJ .... Low-Cost Anti-Jam system (SAUS)
LCAL .... Lower Conformance Altitude (SAA)
LCAM .... Liver Cell Adhesion Molecule [*Cytology*]
LCAMIMS ... Logistics Capability Assessment Models Information Management System (SAUO)
LCAMOS .... Loop Cable Maintenance Operation System (VLIE)
LCAN .... Lockheed Canada Inc. (SAUO)
LC & M Gaz ... Lower Courts and Municipal Gazette [*Canada*] [*A publication*] (DLA)
LC&TPA .... Lighting Column and Transmission Pole Association (BUAC)
LCANSW .... Landscape Contractors' Association of New South Wales [*Australia*]
LCANSW .... Licensed Clubs Association of New South Wales [*Australia*]
LCAO .... Leadership Council of Aging Organizations (EA)
LCAO .... Limited Configuration Atomic Orbital (MCD)
LCAO .... Linear Combination of Atomic Orbitals [*Physical chemistry*]
LCA(OC) .... Landing Craft, Assault (Obstacle Clearance) [*British military*] (DMA)
LCAofGB .... Lightweight Cycle Association of Great Britian (DBA)
LCAO-MO ... Linear Combination of Atomic Orbital-Molecular Orbital (DB)
LCAO-MO-SCF ... Linear Combination of Atomic Orbitals to Form Molecular Orbitals by a Self-Consistent Field [*Quantum mechanics*]
LCAP .... Linear Control Analysis Program (ACAE)
LCAP .... Local Combat Air Patrol
LCAP .... Loop Carrier Analysis Program [*Bell System*]
LCAP .... Low Cost Accurate Programmer (ACAE)
LCAR .... Late Cutaneous Anaphylactic Reaction [*Immunology*]
LCAR .... Launch Complex Assessment Report [*NASA*] (KSC)
LCAR .... Local Capability Assessment for Readiness [*Emergency Management*] (EMA)
LCAR .... Lotus Cortina of America Register [*Defunct*] (EA)
LCAR .... Low-Cost Attack RADAR
LCAR .... Low-Coverage Acquisiton RADAR (PDAA)
LCAR .... Luxury Car (TRID)
LCar .... United States Public Health Service Hospital, Carville, LA [*Library symbol*] [*Library of Congress*] (LCLS)
LCARC .... Lake County Amateur Radio Club (SAUO)
LCARS .... Library Computer Access Retrieval System (VLIE)
LCAS .... Land Capability Assessment Strategy (SAUO)
LCAS .... Light Close Air Support (SAUS)
LCAS .... Lithuanian Catholic Academy of Sciences (EA)
LCASA .... Licensed Clubs Association of South Australia
LCAT .... Laser Communications Airborne Testbed (ACAE)
LCAT .... Lecithin-Cholesterol Acyltransferase [*An enzyme*]
LCAT .... Licensed Clubs Association of Tasmania [*Australia*]
LCAT .... Lifts and Cranes Appeals Tribunal [*Australia*]
LCATA .... Laundry and Cleaners Allied Trades Association [*Later, TCATA*]
LCATS .... Large Capacity Automated Telecommunications System (SAUO)
LCATS .... Laser Communications Airborne Test Set (ACAE)
LCAUE .... Liaison Committee of the Architects of United Europe [*EC*] (ECED)
LCAUS .... Latvian Choir Association of the United States (SAUO)
LCAV .... Landscape Contractors Association of Victoria [*Australia*]
LCAV .... LCA-Vision [*NASDAQ symbol*] (TTSB)
L Cav .... Lucy Cavendish Collegiate Society, Cambridge (SAUO)
LCAVAT .... Landing Craft and Amphibious Vehicle Assignment Table
LCAW .... Low-Cost Anti-Submarine Weapon (SAUS)
LCAX .... Lake City Army Ammunition Plant [*Federal Railroad Administration identification code*]
LCAX .... Landing Craft, Assault, Experimental [*Navy ship symbol*]
LCB .... Laboratory Coordinating Board (SAUO)
LCB .... Landing Craft, Vehicle [*Navy symbol*]
LCB .... Language Control Board (TIMI)
LCB .... Launch Control Building [*NASA*]
LCB .... Least-Common Bigram [*Computer science*] (BYTE)
LCB .... Least Common BIT [*Binary Digit*] (MCD)
LCB .... Left Cornerback [*Football*]
LCB .... Liefdezusters van de H. Carolus Borromeus [*Sisters of Charity of St. Charles Borromeo - SCSCB*] (EAIO)
LCB .... Limited Capability Buoy
LCB .... Line Control Block [*Computer science*]
LCB .... Line to Computer Buffer (VLIE)
LCB .... Link Control Block [*Computer science*] (ELAL)
LCB .... Liquor Control Board [*Canada*]
LCB .... Living Country Blues [*A publication*]
LCB .... Logic Control Block
LCB .... London and Continental Bankers (SAUO)
LCB .... London Centre for Biotechnology [*British*] (IRUK)
LCB .... Long-Chain Branching [*Organic chemistry*]
LCB .... Longitudinal Centre of Buoyancy (SAUO)
LCB .... Longitudinal Position of Center of Buoyancy
LCB .... Lord Chief Baron [*British*]
LCB .... Low Cost Bipolar (VLIE)
LCBA .... Loyal Christian Benefit Association [*Erie, PA*] (EA)
LCBB .... "Life Can Be Beautiful" [*Old radio program; nicknamed "Elsie Beebee"*]
LCBBC .... Liquor Control Board of British Columbia (SAUO)
LCBC .... Lake Chad Basin Commission [*Chad*] (BUAC)
LCBF .... Local Cerebral Blood Flow [*Medicine*]
LCBIV .... Landmark/Community Bancorp, Inc. [*NASDAQ symbol*] (COMM)
LCBM .... Lifecore Biomedical [*NASDAQ symbol*] (TTSB)
LCBM .... LifeCore Biomedical, Inc. [*NASDAQ symbol*] (SAG)
LCBM .... Liquor Control Board of Manitoba (SAUO)
LCBO .... Linear Combination of [*Semi-localized*] Band Orbitals [*Atomic physics*]
LCBO .... Liquor Control Board of Ontario (SAUO)
LC/BPL .... Laboratory Counsel/Business & Patent Law (SAUO)
LCBR .... Laboratory for Cognitive Brain Research [*University of California, Irvine*] (RCD)
LCBRA .... Laboratory of Computational Biology and Risk Analysis [*National Institute of Environmental Health Sciences*] (RCD)
LCBS .... Liquor Control Board of Saskatchewan (SAUO)
LCBS .... London Classification of Business Studies [*Library classification scheme*] [*British*] (NITA)
LCBU .... Lake Chelan Boat [*Intermodal shipping container symbol*] (TVRC)
LCBWR .... LaCrosse Boiling Water Reactor [*Also, LACBWR*]
LCBX .... Large Computerized [*Private*] Branch Exchange (MHDI)
LCC .... Amphibious Command Ship [*Formerly, AGC*] [*Navy symbol*]
LCC .... Cameron Parish Library (SAUS)
LCC .... Charles A. Lindbergh Collectors Club (EA)
LCC .... Laboratory of Computer Chemistry (VLIE)
LCC .... Labor Case Comments [*Cast Metals Association*] [*A publication*]
LCC .... Labor Class Code (DNAB)
LCC .... Labour Coordinating Committee [*British*]
LCC .... Lactose Coliform Count [*Medicine*] (BABM)
LCC .... Land Capability Classes [*Agriculture*]
LCC .... Land Component Commander (MCD)
LCC .... Land Court Cases [*New South Wales*] [*A publication*] (DLA)
LCC .... Landing Control Center
LCC .... Landing Craft, Control
LCC .... Lands Conservation Council (SAUO)
LCC .... Langley Complex Coordination [*Device*] [*NASA*]
LCC .... Language for Conversational Computing (MDG)
LCC .... Lansing Community College (SAUO)
LCC .... Large Capacity Cassette [*Electronic printing*] (DGA)
LCC .... Large Cavitation Channel [*Pressurized water tunnel to test submarines and ship models*] [*Navy*]
LCC .... Large Compressor Colorimeter (MCD)

LCC .... Last Clear Chance [*Legal shorthand*] (LWAP)
LCC .... Late Choice Call (NITA)
LCC .... Launch Command and Control
LCC .... Launch Commit Criteria (MCD)
LCC .... Launch Committee Criteria (SAUO)
LCC .... Launch Control Car (SAUS)
LCC .... Launch Control Center [*NASA*]
LCC .... Launch Control Console
LCC .... Laurie Cox Conference (PSS)
LCC .... Leach's English Crown Cases [*1730-1815*] [*A publication*] (DLA)
LCC .... Lead-Coated Copper (OA)
LCC .... Lead Covered Cable [*Telecommunications*] (TEL)
LCC .... Leaded Chip Carrier [*Electronics*] (AAEL)
LCC .... Leadless Ceramic Carrier (TIMI)
LCC .... Leadless Chip Carrier [*Motorola, Inc.*]
LCC .... League of California Cities (SAUO)
LCC .... Le Cercle Concours d'Elegance (EA)
LCC .... Ledger Card Computer (MHDB)
LCC .... Left Circumflex Coronary Artery [*Medicine*] (DMAA)
LCC .... Left Coronary Cusp [*Medicine*] (STED)
LCC .... Legacy Coordinating Council [*Australia*]
LCC .... Legalise Cannabis Campaign [*British*] (DBA)
LCC .... Legalize Cannabis Campaign (SAUO)
LCC .... Lesser of Costs or Charges [*Medicine*] (GFGA)
LCC .... Levo-Carnitine Chloride [*Biochemistry*]
LCC .... Leyland Cars Council (SAUO)
LCC .... Liang-Chow [*Republic of China*] [*Seismograph station code, US Geological Survey*] [*Closed*] (SEIS)
LCC .... Libertarian Council of Churches [*Defunct*] (EA)
LCC .... Libraries Consultative Committee [*Australia*]
LCC .... Libraries Copyright Committee [*Australia*]
LCC .... Library of Congress Classification
LCC .... Libreville Construction Company (SAUO)
LCC .... Life Cycle Center (SAUO)
LCC .... Life Cycle Cost (ADWA)
LCC .... Life-Cycle Cost [*Military*]
LCC .... Life-Cycle Costing [*or Costs*] [*DoD*]
LCC .... Light of Cambodian Children [*Association*] (EA)
LCC .... Lignin-Carbohydrate Complex [*Organic chemistry*]
LCC .... Ligue Canadienne des Composeurs [*Canadian League of Composers - CLC*]
LCC .... Limited Capability Configuration [*Army*] (DOMA)
LCC .... Lincoln Capital Corp. [*Toronto Stock Exchange symbol*]
LCC .... Linear Cutting Cord [*Aircraft escape technology*] (PDAA)
LCC .... Linecaster Control (DGA)
LCC .... Link Control Standard Controller [*Telecommunications*] (ECII)
LCC .... Liquid Column Chromatography (EDCT)
LCC .... Liquid Crystal Cell (IEEE)
LCC .... Liquid-Cushion Electroplating Cell [*Steel production*]
LCC .... Liquor Control Commission
LCC .... Lithophane Collectors Club (EA)
LCC .... Little Carter Cay [*NASA*] (KSC)
LCC .... Liver Cell Carcinoma [*Medicine*] (DB)
LCC .... Load-Carrying Capability [*Electrical Engineering*] (ODA)
LCC .... Load Controlling Crewman [*Helicopter*] [*Navy*]
LCC .... Loading Coil Case [*Telecommunications*] (TEL)
LCC .... Local Command Centre (SAUO)
LCC .... Local Communications Complex
LCC .... Local Communications Console
LCC .... Local Control Center (SAUO)
LCC .... Local Control Console (CAAL)
LCC .... Local Coordinating Committee
LCC .... Lockheed-California Co. [*Division of Lockheed Aircraft Corp.*]
LCC .... Lockheed California Company (SAUO)
LCC .... Lockheed Corporation of California (SAUO)
LCC .... Logistic Control Code [*Military*] (AABC)
LCC .... Logistics Control Center [*Military*] (INF)
LCC .... Logistics Coordination Center [*NATO*]
LCC .... Logistics Co-ordination Centre (SAUO)
LCC .... London Chamber of Commerce [*British*] (DAS)
LCC .... London City Council (SAUO)
LCC .... London Communication Committee (SAUO)
LCC .... London Communications Committee [*World War II*]
LCC .... London County Council [*or Councillor*] [*Later, GLC*]
LCC .... London Cycling Campaign [*England*] (BUAC)
LCC .... Lost Calls Cleared [*Telecommunications*] (NITA)
LCC .... Lost Chord Clubs (EA)
LCC .... Low-Cement Castable [*Ceramics*]
LCC .... Low-Cost Classifier (MCD)
LCC .... Lower Columbia College (SAUO)
LCC .... Lundy Collectors Club (EA)
LCCA .... Late Cortical Cerebellar Atrophy [*Neurology*]
LCCA .... Lawyers Committee on Central America [*Defunct*] (EA)
LCCA .... Lead Contamination Control Act of 1988 (COE)
LCCA .... Left Circumflex Coronary Artery [*Anatomy*]
LCCA .... Left Common Carotid Artery [*Cardiology*] (DAVI)
LCCA .... Leukocytoelastic Angitis [*Cardiology*] (DAVI)
LCCA .... Life Cycle Cost Analysis (MCD)
LCCA .... Lionel Collectors Club of America (EA)
LCCA .... Lithuanian Chamber of Commerce of America (EA)
LCCA .... Load Current Contacting Aiding
LCCA .... London Church Choir Association
LCCA .... Low-Cost Computer Attachment (IAA)
LCCB .... Local Change Control Board (MCD)
LCCB .... Local Configuration Control Board (AABC)
LCCB .... Low-Cost Controllable Booster (MCD)
LCCC .... Latvian Canadian Cultural Centre (EAIO)
LCCC .... Launch Control Centre Computer (SAUO)
LCCC .... Leadless Ceramic Chip Carrier [*Electronics*]
LCCC .... Library of Congress Catalogue Card (WDAA)
LCCC .... Library of Congress Computer Catalog (NITA)
LCCC .... Life Care Communities Corporation (SAUO)
LCCC .... Lorain County Community College (SAUO)
LCCC .... Low-Cost Chip Carrier (TIMI)
LCCC .... Lower Canada Civil Code [*A publication*] (DLA)
LCCC .... Lucas County Corrections Center (SAUO)
LCCC .... Luzerne County Community College [*Nanticoke, PA*] (TSSD)
LCCC .... Nicosia [*Cyprus*] [*ICAO location identifier*] (ICLI)
LCCCN .... Library of Congress Catalog Card Number (NITA)
LCCD .... Launch Commit Criteria Document [*NASA*] (NASA)
LCCD .... Launch Committee Criteria Document (SAUO)
LCCD .... Low Complexity Color Display [*Video technology*] (EECA)
LCC/DTC .... Life Cycle Cost / Design to Cost
LCCE .... Lee County Central Electric [*AAR code*]
LCCE .... Life-Cycle Cost Estimate (AABC)
LCCEB .... London Chamber of Commerce Examinations Board [*British*] (AIE)
LCCEP .... Logistics Civilian Career Enhancement Program [*Military*]
LCCEV .... Low Cost Cryogenic Expendable Vehicle (SAUS)
LCCEWG .... Large-Core Code Evaluation Working Group (SAUO)
LCCFC .... Launch Control Complex Facility Console [*NASA*] (IAA)
LCCFCO ..... Lake Cowichan Combined Fire Control Organization (SAUO)
LCCH .... London College of Clinical Hypnosis (SAUO)
LCCH .... London County Council Hospital (SAUO)
LCCI .... LCC International, Inc. [*NASDAQ symbol*] (NASQ)
LCCI .... London Chamber of Commerce and Industry [*British*] (DCTA)
LCCID .... Life Cycle Cost in Design [*Computer program released by US Army Construction Engineering Research Laboratory*] (RDA)
LCCIEB ...... London Chamber of Commerce and Industry Examinations Board
LCCIS .... Local Common Channel Interoffice Signaling (VLIE)
LCCIW .... Life Cycle Cost Impact Worksheet (SPST)
LCCJ .... Louisiana Council on Criminal Justice (SAUO)
LCCL .... Line Card Cable (VLIE)
LCCLN .... Line Card Cable Narrative (VLIE)
LCCM .... LanClient Control Manager [*Computer science*]
LCCM .... Late Choice Call Meter [*Telecommunications*] (NITA)
LCCM .... Life Cycle Cost Management (SPST)
LCCM .... Life Cycle Cost Model (ACAE)
LCCMARC ... Library of Congress Current MARC [*Machine-Readable Catalog*] File (NITA)
LCCMD ...... Low Cost Cruise Missile Defense [*Defense Advanced Research Projects Agency*] (RCD)
LCCMS ...... Launch Control Center Measuring Station [*NASA*] (KSC)
LCCN .... Library of Congress Catalog-Card Number
LCCO .... Lamar Capital Corp. [*NASDAQ symbol*] (NASQ)
LCCO .... Landing Craft Control Officer [*Military*]
LCCO .... Leadership Career Counseling Officer (DNAB)
LCCO .... Life Cycle Cost of Ownership (MCD)
LCCOGA ..... Liaison Committee of Cooperating Oil and Gas Associations (EA)
LC Cont ..... Langdell's Cases on Contracts [*A publication*] (DLA)
LCCP .... Landing Craft Control Primary [*Military*]
LCCP .... LASER Code Control Panel (MCD)
LCCP .... Launch Captain's Control Panel [*Navy*] (CAAL)
LCCP .... Lower Canada Civil Procedure [*A publication*] (DLA)
LCC-PDR .... League of Communists of Croatia - Party of Democratic Reform [*Political party*]
LCCPMP .... Life Cycle Computer Program Management Plan (VLIE)
LCCPT .... Low-Cost Cockpit Procedures Trainer (MCD)
LCCR .... Laboratory for Computer and Communications Research [*Simon Fraser University*] [*Canada*] [*Research center*] (RCD)
LCCR .... Leadership Conference on Civil Rights (EA)
LCCRUL ..... Lawyers' Committee for Civil Rights under Law (EA)
LCCS .... Laboratory Customer Communications System (SAUO)
LCCS .... Land Capability Classification System (COE)
LCCs .... Land Care Committees (SAUO)
LCCS .... Landing Craft Control Secondary (SAUS)
LCCS .... Large Capacity Core Storage [*Computer science*] (MDG)
LCCS .... Launch Checkout and Countdown System [*Aerospace*] (IAA)
LCCS .... Launch Control and Checkout System [*Aerospace*] (IAA)
LCCS .... Launcher Captain Control System [*Military*] (NVT)
LCCS .... Library of Congress Classification Schedules [*A publication*]
LCCS .... Life Cycle Contractor Support
LCCS .... Logistics Control Center System
LCCS .... London County Council Service (SAUO)
LCCS .... Low Cervical Caesarean Section
LCCS .... Lucy Cavendish Collegiate Society (SAUO)
LCCTS .... Life Cycle Cost Tracking System [*Social Security Administration*]
LCCU .... Lightweight Crewman Communication Umbilical (MCD)
LCCV .... Large-Component Cleaning Vessel [*Nuclear energy*] (NRCH)
LCCW .... Low-Cost Composite Weapon (MCD)
LCD .... Land Conservation District (SAUO)
LCD .... Language for Computer Design (CSR)
LCD .... Launch Control Design [*NASA*] (AAG)
LCD .... Launch Countdown [*NASA*] (NASA)
LCD .... Least [*or Lowest*] Common Denominator [*or Divisor*] [*Mathematics*]
lcd .... Least Common Denominator (NTIO)
LCD .... Left Crus of Diaphragm [*Medicine*] (MELL)
LCD .... Lesotho Congress for Democracy [*Political party*] (PSAP)
LCD .... Letter Carrier Depot (DD)

LCD .... Light-Chain Deposition (MELL)
LCD .... Lightweight Ceramic Dome
LCD .... Line Control Definer (VLIE)
LCD .... Line Current Disconnect (HGAA)
LCD .... Lipochondral Degeneration [*Medicine*] (PALA)
LCD .... Liquid Crystal Device (SAUS)
LCD .... Liquid Crystal Digital [*Battery-powered wristwatch*]
LCD .... Liquid Crystal Diode
LCD .... Liquid Crystal Display
LCD .... Liquor Carbonis Detergens [*Coal tar solution*] [*Medicine*]
LCD .... LISP Code Directory (SAUS)
LCD .... List of Chosen Descriptors (PDAA)
LCD .... Liver Cell Dysplasia [*Medicine*]
LCD .... LM [*Lunar Module*] Change Directive [*NASA*] (KSC)
LCD .... Load Classification Group (SAUO)
LCD .... Lobster-Claw Deformity (MELL)
LCD .... Local Climatological Data [*A publication*]
LCD .... Localized Collagen Dystrophy [*Medicine*] (DAVI)
LCD .... Logistics Communications Division [*Military*]
LCD .... London College of Divinity
LCD .... London Dumping Convention (SAUO)
LCD .... Lord Chancellor's Department [*British*]
LCD .... Loss of Cell Delineation (MLOA)
LCD .... Loss of Clock Detector
LCD .... Louis Trichardt [*South Africa*] [*Airport symbol*] (OAG)
LCD .... Low Calorie Diet (MELL)
LCD .... Low Cost Drifter [*Marine science*] (OSRA)
LCD .... Lower Court Decisions (ODA)
LCD .... Lowest Common Denominator (GOBB)
lcd .... Lowest Common Denominator
LCD .... Lumped Constant Dispersion
LCD .... Ohio Lower Court Decisions [*A publication*] (DLA)
LCD .... Lord Chamberlain's Department (ODA)
LCDB .... Land Cover Database (SAUO)
LCDC .... Laboratory Centre for Disease Control [*Canada*]
LCDC .... Land Conservation and Development (SAUO)
LCDC .... Land Conservation District Committee (SAUO)
LCDC .... Licensed Chemical Dependency Counselor (NUJO)
LC-DCP ...... Low-Contact Dynamic Compression Plate [*Medicine*] (RAWO)
LCDD .... Light Chain Deposition Disease [*Medicine*] (DMAA)
LCDDS ...... Leased Circuit Digital Data Service [*British Telecom*] (EECA)
LCDHWIU ... Laundry, Cleaning, and Dye House Workers' International Union [*Later, Textile Processors, Service Trades, Health Care, Professional, and Technical Employees International Union*] (EA)
LCDLVC ..... Library of Congress Digital Library Visiotrs' Center (WDAA)
LCDM .... Large Component Development Management (SAUO)
LCDM .... Life-Cycle Document Management (SAUO)
LCDM .... Low Collateral-Damage Munitions (SAUS)
LCDN .... Last Called Directory Number (ROAS)
LCDOSEM ... Local Civil Defense Operating Systems Evaluation Model (PDAA)
LCDP .... Local Career Development Panels (HEAS)
LCDR .... Lieutenant Commander (AAG)
LCdr .... Lieutenant-Commander (SAUO)
LCDR .... London, Chatham & Dover Railway [*British*]
LCDS .... Lefschetz Center for Dynamical Systems [*Brown University*] [*Research center*] (RCD)
LCDS .... Line-Conditioned Data Stream [*Computer science*] (GART)
LCDS .... Liquid-Crystal Displays [*Computer science*]
LCDS .... Low-Cost Development System [*National Semiconductor Corp.*]
LCDT .... London Contemporary Dance Theatre [*Defunct*]
LCDTL .... Load-Compensated Diode Transistor Logic [*Computer science*]
LCDTL .... Low Current Diode Transistor Logic [*Electronics*] (IAA)
LCDU .... Pennwalt-Lucidol [*Intermodal shipping container symbol*] (TVRC)
LCE .... La Ceiba [*Honduras*] [*Airport symbol*] (OAG)
LCE .... Lance (WGA)
LCE .... Land-Covered Earth (OA)
LCE .... Landing Craft, Emergency Repair
LCE .... Latest Cost Estimate (NATG)
LCE .... Launch Complex Engineer [*NASA*] (KSC)
LCE .... Launch Complex Equipment
LCE .... Launch Control Equipment (AAG)
LCE .... Launch Countdown Exercise [*NASA*] (AFM)
LCE .... Left Center Entrance [*Theater*] (WDMC)
LCE .... Legal Counsel for the Elderly (EA)
LCE .... Licentiate in Civil Engineering (WDAA)
LCE .... Life Cycle Energy
LCE .... Load-Carrying Equipment (MCD)
LCE .... Load Circuit Efficiency
LCE .... Logistic Capability Estimate (MCD)
LCE .... Logistics Capability Estimator (COE)
LCE .... London Commodity Exchange (NUMA)
LCE .... Lone Star Cement Corp. (SAUO)
LCE .... Lone Star Indus [*NYSE symbol*] (TTSB)
LCE .... Lone Star Industries, Inc. [*Formerly, Lone Star Cement Corp.*] [*NYSE symbol*] (SPSG)
LCE .... Low-Cost Expendable [*Refers to payload type*] [*NASA*]
LCE .... Lyapunov Characteristic Exponent [*Mathematics*]
LCE.WS ..... Lone Star Indus Wrrt [*NYSE symbol*] (TTSB)
LCEA .... Licentiate of the Association of Cost and Executive Accountants [*British*] (DBQ)
LCEAPL ..... Lawyers Committee for the Enforcement of Animal Protection Law (EA)
LCEB .... Launch Control Equipment Building (AFM)
LCEBM ...... Liaison Committee of European Bicycle Manufacturers [*Belgium*] (EAIO)
LCEC .... Liquid Chromatographs with Electrochemical Detection
LCED .... Low-Cost Encryption Device [*Military*] (GFGA)
LCEE .... Louisiana Council on Economic Education (EDAC)
LCEE .... Low Cost Emplacement Excavator (SAUS)
LCEECSTI ... Liaison Committee of the European Economic Community Steel Tube Industry [*Defunct*] (EAIO)
LCEF .... Leadership Conference Education Fund [*Association*] (EA)
LCEHV .... Low-Cost Expendable Harassment Vehicle [*Air Force*] (MCD)
LCEM .... Leading Control Electrical Mechanic [*British military*] (DMA)
LCEMD ...... Low Cost Expendable Mine Destructor (SAUS)
LCEMM ...... Liaison Committee of European Motorcycle Manufacturers [*Belgium*] (EAIO)
LCEOP .... Landing Craft, Engine Overhaul Parties
LCEP .... Lower Critical End Points [*Supercritical extraction*]
LCEPS .... Labor Cooperative Educational and Publishing Society [*Defunct*] (EA)
LC Eq .... White and Tudor's Leading Cases in Equity [*A publication*] (DLA)
LCER .... Labour Campaign Electoral Reform [*British*] [*An association*] (DBA)
LCES .... Least Cost Estimating and Scheduling (IAA)
LCES .... Lightweight Communications Equipment Subsystem (ACAE)
LCETB .... Linen and Cotton Embroidery Trade Board (SAUO)
LCEU .... FMC-Industrial Chemical [*Intermodal shipping container symbol*] (TVRC)
LCEWS ...... Low-Cost Electronic Warfare Suite (NVT)
LCEZ .... Lasfage Cement [*Federal Railroad Administration identification code*]
LCF .... Labour Co-operative Farms (SAUO)
LCF .... Landing Craft, Flak
LCF .... Language Central Facility [*Computer science*] (IEEE)
LCF .... Large Core Fibre (SAUS)
LCF .... Last Chance Filter (MCD)
LCF .... Last Chance Forever (EA)
LCF .... Latent Cancer Fatalities (PDAA)
LCF .... Launch Control Facility
LCF .... Law Centres Federation [*British*] (DBA)
LCF .... Lawyers Christian Fellowship (EA)
LCF .... Learning Curve Factor
LCF .... Least [*or Lowest*] Common Factor [*Mathematics*]
LCF .... Least Cost Feed Formulation System (ADA)
LCF .... Lederberg-Coxeter-Frucht [*Notation*] [*Graph theory, mathematics*]
LCF .... Left Circumflex Artery [*Anatomy*]
LCF .... Left Common Femoral [*Artery*] [*Anatomy*] (DAVI)
LCF .... Leonard Cheshire Foundation (WDAA)
LCF .... Level Control Function [*Computer science*]
LCF .... Librarians' Christian Fellowship [*British*] (DBA)
LCF .... Library of Congress Films [*Source file*] [*UTLAS symbol*]
LCF .... Lightweight Client Framework [*Computer science*] (GART)
LCF .... Lime, Cement, and Flyash (PDAA)
LCF .... Lincomycin Cosynthetic Factor [*Biochemistry*]
LCF .... Liquid, Complex Fertilizer (PDAA)
LCF .... Little City Foundation (EA)
LCF .... Living Church Foundation (EA)
LCF .... Local area network File System (SAUO)
LCF .... Local Control Facility [*FAA*] (TAG)
LCF .... Local Cycle Fatigue (IEEE)
LCF .... Log Cabin Federation (EA)
LCF .... Log Control Function [*Open Systems Interconnection*] (ODAA)
LCF .... Logical Channel Fill
LCF .... London College of Fashion [*England*] (WDAA)
LCF .... Longitudinal Centre of Flotation (SAUO)
LCF .... Longitudinal Position of Center of Flotation
LCF .... Low Cab Forward [*Truck configuration*]
LCF .... Low-Carbon Ferrochrome [*Metallurgy*]
LCF .... Low Coefficient of Friction [*Aerodynamics*]
LCF .... Low-Cycle Fatigue [*Rocket engine*]
lcf .... Lowest Common Factor [*Mathematics*] (ODA)
LCF .... Lymphocyte Chemoattractant Factor [*Biochemistry*]
LCFA .... Lithuanian Catholic Federation Ateitis (EA)
LCFA .... Long-Chain Fatty Acids [*Organic chemistry*]
LCFA .... Lower California Fisheries Association (SAUO)
LCFB .... Lahey Clinic Foundation Bulletin [*Medicine*] (EDAA)
LCFC .... Launch Complex Facility Console [*NASA*] (IAA)
LCFC .... Leslie Charleson Fan Club (EA)
LCFC .... Linear Combination of Fragment Configuration (DB)
LCFC .... Living Colour Fan Club (EA)
LCFC .... Lou Christie Official Fan Club (EA)
LCFC .... Low-Cycle Fatigue Counter (PDAA)
LCFDU .... Laser Countermeasure Frequency Double Unit (ACAE)
LC(FF) ...... Landing Craft, Infantry (Flotilla Flagship) [*Navy symbol*]
LCFIX .... Lord Abbett: Cal. Tax-Free Inc. Cl.A [*Mutual fund ticker symbol*] (SG)
LCFLOLS .... Laterally Compounded Fresnel Lens Optical Landing System
LCFLOTSPAC ... Landing Craft, Flotilla, Pacific Fleet
LCFM .... Left Circumflex Marginal [*Medicine*] (EDAA)
LCFNM ...... Lawyers' Campaign to Free Nelson Mandela [*Defunct*] (EA)
LCFR .... Life Cycle Fuel Requirement
LCFS .... Last-Come, First-Served
LCFS .... Launch Control Facility Simulator [*NASA*] (IAA)
LCFSPR ..... Last Come, First Served Preemptive Resume (PDAA)
LCFU .... Laboratory Configured Fire Units (MCD)
LCFU .... Leukocyte Colony-Forming Unit [*Medicine*] (EDAA)
LCG .... Harvard Laboratory for Computer Graphics (SAUS)
LCG .... Laboratory for Computer Graphics (SAUO)
LCG .... La Coruna [*Spain*] [*Airport symbol*] (OAG)

LCG .... Landing Craft Gun (MCD)
LCG .... Landing Craft, Gunboat
LCG .... Langerhans' Cell Granule [*Anatomy*]
LCG .... Langerhans' Cell Granulomatosis [*Oncology*]
LCG .... Laser-Assisted Catalytic Growth
LCG .... Lead Computing Gyro (MCD)
LCG .... Left Cerebral Ganglion [*Medicine*]
LCG .... Leon Cerro Gordo [*Mexico*] [*Seismograph station code, US Geological Survey*] (SEIS)
LCG .... Liquefied Compressed Gas (LDOE)
LCG .... Liquid-Cooled Garment [*Spacesuit*]
LCG .... Liquid Cooling Garment (SAUS)
LCG .... Load Classification Group (DA)
LCG .... Loads Control Group [*Prepares supplies to be airlifted*] [*Military*]
LCG .... Logistics Control Group [*Air Materiel Command*] (AAG)
LCG .... London Capital Group (SAUO)
LCG .... Longitudinal Position of Center of Gravity
LCG .... Lookahead Carry Generator [*Computer science*] (IAA)
LCG .... Low Center of Gravity [*Tractor engineering*]
LCG .... Low-Cost Generator
LCG .... Lower Courts Gazette [*Ontario*] [*A publication*] (DLA)
LCG .... Wayne, NE [*Location identifier*] [*FAA*] (FAAL)
LCGB .... Letzeburger Chreschtliche Gewerkschaftsbond [*Confederation of Christian Trade Unions of Luxembourg*]
LCGB .... Locomotive Club of Great Britain (BI)
LCGF .... Longitudinal Ciliated Groove of Filament
LCGI .... Local Common Graphics Interface (SAUS)
LCGIL .... Libera Confederazione Generale Italiana dei Lavoratori [*Free Italian General Confederation of Workers*]
LC/GL .... Laboratory Counsel/General Law (SAUO)
LCG(L) ...... Landing Craft, Gun (Large)
LCGL .... Large-Cell Granulocytic Leukemia [*Medicine*] (EDAA)
LCG(M) ...... Landing Craft, Gun (Medium)
LCGMD ...... Library of Congress Geography and Map Division (SAUO)
LCGME ...... Liaison Committee on Graduate Medical Education
LCGN .... Logical Channel Group Number [*Telecommunications*] (OSI)
LCGO .... Linear Combination of Gaussian Orbitals [*Atomic physics*]
LCGP .... Landing Craft, Group
LCG(S) ...... Landing Craft, Gun (Small) [*British military*] (DMA)
LCGS .... Lead Computing Gun Sight
LCGT .... Listening Comprehension Group Test
LCGT/IGS ... Low-Cost Graphics Terminal/Interactive Graphics System (PDAA)
LCGU .... Lead Computing Gyroscope Unit (MCD)
LCGU .... Lesser Curve Gastric Ulcer (MELL)
LCGU .... Local Cerebral Glucose Utilization [*Biochemistry*]
LCGU .... Local Rates of Glucose Utilization (DB)
LCH .... Lake Charles [*Louisiana*] [*Airport symbol*] (OAG)
LCH .... Lake Charles, LA [*Location identifier*] [*FAA*] (FAAL)
LCH .... Landing Craft Headquarters [*British military*] (DMA)
LCH .... Landing Craft (Heavy) (ADA)
LCH .... Landing Craft Hospital [*British military*] (DMA)
LCH .... Langerhans Cell Histiocytosis [*Medicine*] (EDAA)
LCH .... Larch Resources Ltd. [*Vancouver Stock Exchange symbol*]
LCH .... Latch (MSA)
LCH .... Launch
LCH .... Launching Charging Header
LCh .... Licentiate of the Institute of Chiropodists [*British*]
L Ch .... Licentiatus Chirurgiae [*Licentiate in Surgery*]
LCH .... Life Cycle Hypothesis [*Economics*]
LCH .... Load Channel (IAA)
LCH .... Local City Hospital (DAVI)
LCH .... Logical Channel Queue [*Computer science*]
LCH .... London Clearing House (SAUO)
L CH .... Lord Chancellor [*British*] (ROG)
LCH .... Lost Calls Held [*Telecommunications*] (NITA)
LCH .... Luchazi [*Language symbol*] (ETLW)
Lch .... Lunch
LCH .... Lynch Flying Service, Inc. [*ICAO designator*] (FAAC)
LCHA .... Lens Culinaris Hemagglutinin A [*Medicine*] (EDAA)
LCHA .... Love Canal Homeowners Association (EA)
LChaMC ..... Louisiana Universities Marine Consortium, Chauvin, LA [*Library symbol*] [*Library of Congress*] (LCLS)
LCHB .... Lens Culinaris Hemagglutinin B [*Medicine*] (EDAA)
LCHC .... Laboratory of Comparative Human Cognition [*University of California, San Diego*] (RCD)
LCHC .... Life Cycle Hydrocarbons
LCHD .... Lake Charles Harbor District [*Federal Railroad Administration identification code*]
LCHE .... Luton College of Higher Education (AIE)
LCHIP .... Late-Cycle High Injection Pressure [*Automotive fuel systems*]
LCHM .... Life Chemistry, Inc. (SAUO)
LCH/M/T/U/VP ... Landing Craft, Heavy/Merchanised/Tank/Utility/Vehicles and Personnel (MILB)
LCHP .... Local Control Hydraulic Panel
LCHQ .... Local Command Headquarters [*NATO*] (NATG)
LCHR .... Launcher (AAG)
L Chr .... Law Chronicle [*England*] [*A publication*] (DLA)
LCHR .... Lawyers Committee for Human Rights (EA)
LChr .... Liberte Chretienne [*A publication*] (BJA)
L Chron ..... Law Chronicle [*England*] [*A publication*] (DLA)
L Chron & L Stud Mag ... Law Chronicle and Law Students' Magazine [*A publication*] (DLA)
L Chron & L Stud Mag (NS) ... Law Chronicle and Law Students' Magazine (New Series) [*A publication*] (DLA)
LCHS .... Large Component Handling System [*Nuclear energy*] (NRCH)
LCHS .... Lund Centre for Habitat Studies (SAUO)
LChSt .... Saint Bernard Parish Library, Chalmette, LA [*Library symbol*] [*Library of Congress*] (LCLS)
LCHTF .... Low-Cycle High-Temperature Fatigue [*Rocket engine*]
LCHU .... Low Cost Home User (SAUO)
LCHX .... Laporte County Historical Steam Society [*Federal Railroad Administration identification code*]
LCI .... Laboratory of Cellular Immunology [*University of Arizona*] [*Research center*] (RCD)
LCI .... Laboratory of Clinical Investigation [*National Center for Complementary and Alternative Medicine*] (RCD)
LCI .... Labor Cost Index
LCI .... Laconia [*New Hampshire*] [*Airport symbol*] (OAG)
LCI .... Laconia, NH [*Location identifier*] [*FAA*] (FAAL)
LCI .... Lafarge Canada, Inc. [*Toronto Stock Exchange symbol*]
LCI .... Landing Craft, Infantry [*Obsolete*]
LCI .... Launch Complex Instrumentation (IAA)
LCI .... Launcher Control Indicator [*Missiles*] (AABC)
LCI .... LCI International [*NYSE symbol*] (SAG)
LCI .... Leadership Competency Inventory [*Test*] (TMMY)
LCI .... Learner-Centered Instruction (PDAA)
LCI .... Legally Correct Interpretation [*of the ABM treaty*]
LCI .... Life Cycle Inventory [*Environmental engineering*]
LCI .... Liga Comunista Internacionalista [*International Communist League*] [*Portugal*] [*Political party*] (PPE)
LCI .... Lions Clubs International (EA)
LCI .... Liquid Crystal Institute [*Kent State University*] (PDAA)
LCI .... Literary Criticism Index [*A publication*]
LCI .... Livestock Conservation, Incorporated (SAUO)
LCI .... Livestock Conservation Institute (EA)
LCI .... Local Cerebral Ischemia [*Medicine*] (MELL)
LCI .... Locus of Control Interview [*Psychology*]
LCI .... Logical Channel Indentifier (SAUO)
LCI .... Low-Cost Inertial
LCI .... Lummus Crest, Inc. [*Telecommunications service*] (TSSD)
LCI .... United States Central Intelligence Agency, McLean, VA [*OCLC symbol*] (OCLC)
LCI(A) .... Landing Craft, Infantry (Ammunition)
LCIA .... Life Cycle Impact Assessment [*Recycling*]
LCIA .... London Court of International Arbitration
LCIB .... Library of Congress. Information Bulletin [*A publication*]
LCIC .... Leisure Concepts [*NASDAQ symbol*] (SAG)
LCIC .... Leisure Concepts, Incorporated (SAUO)
LCICD .... Liquid Crystal Induced Circular Dichroism [*Spectroscopy*]
LCID .... Laboratory Corporate Information Directory (SAUO)
LCI(D) .... Landing Craft, Infantry (Demolition) [*British military*] (DMA)
LCIDIV ...... Landing Craft, Infantry, Division
LCIE .... Large Carnivore Initiative Europe (SAUO)
LCIFC .... Lou Christie International Fan Club (EA)
LCIFLOT .... Landing Craft, Infantry, Flotilla [*Obsolete*]
LCI(G) .... Landing Craft, Infantry, Gunboat [*Obsolete*]
LCIGB .... Locomotive and Carriage Institution of Great Britain and Eire (BI)
LCIGB .... Locomotive and Carriage Institution of Great Britain and Ireland (SAUO)
LCIGRP ..... Landing Craft, Infantry, Group
LCIGS .... Low-Cost Inertial Guidance Subsystem (MCD)
LCIHR .... Lawyers Committee for International Human Rights (EA)
LCII .... Laser Craft Industries, Incorporated (SAUO)
LCII .... Laser Master International, Incorporated (SAUO)
LCI Int ...... LCI International [*Associated Press*] (SAG)
LCIL .... Landing Craft, Infantry, Large [*Obsolete*]
LCILFLOT ... Landing Craft, Infantry, Large, Flotilla [*Obsolete*]
LCI(M) .... Landing Craft, Infantry (Medium) [*British military*] (DMA)
LCI(M) .... Landing Craft, Infantry (Mortar Ship) [*Obsolete*]
LCINS .... Low Cost Inertial Navigation System (SAUS)
LC Intl ...... LCI International [*Associated Press*] (SAG)
LCIOB .... Licentiate of the Chartered Institute of Building [*British*] (DI)
LC/IP .... Laboratory Counsel/Intellectual Property (SAUO)
LCIPr .... LCI Intl 5% Cv Exch Pfd [*NYSE symbol*] (TTSB)
LCI(R) .... Landing Craft, Infantry (Rocket Ship) [*Obsolete*]
LC/IR .... Liquid Chromatography/Infrared
LCIR .... London Centre of International Relations [*University of Kent at Canterbury*] [*British*]
LCI(S) .... Landing Craft, Infantry (Small) [*British military*] (DMA)
LCIS .... Library of Computer and Information Sciences (SAUO)
LCIS .... Lighter Collectors' International Society [*Defunct*] (EA)
LCIS .... Lobular Carcinoma in Situ [*Medicine*] (AAMN)
LCISA .... Lockheed Corporation International SA (SAUO)
LCISC .... Laundry and Cleaning Industry Sports Club (SAUO)
LCIU .... International Commercial Leaders [*Intermodal shipping container symbol*] (TVRC)
LCIX .... Praxair [*Private rail car owner code*]
LCJ .... Lawyers for Civil Justice (EA)
LCJ .... Lord Chief Justice [*British*]
LCJ .... Low Cost Junction [*Optical fibre equipment*] (NITA)
LCJ .... Lower Canada Jurist, Montreal [*1848-91*] [*A publication*] (DLA)
LCJC .... Lake City Junior College (SAUO)
LCJC .... Lower Columbia Junior College (SAUO)
LC Jur ...... Lower Canada Jurist [*A publication*] (DLA)
LCK .... Columbus, OH [*Location identifier*] [*FAA*] (FAAL)
LCK .... Landing Craft, Kitchen
L Ck .... Leading Cook [*British military*] (DMA)
LCK .... Legion of Christ the King [*Defunct*] (EA)
LCK .... Library Construction Kit [*Microsoft Corp.*] [*Computer science*] (PCM)

LCK .... Lock [*Postal Service standard*] (OPSA)
LCKR .... Locker
LCKS .... Locks
LCKU .... Locatank [*Intermodal shipping container symbol*] (TVRC)
LCKY .... Lucky
LCL .... Labor Congress of Liberia
LCL .... Labor Congress of Liberia, Inc. (SAUO)
LCL .... Lambert Cosine Law [*Physics*]
LCL .... Landing Craft, Logistic [*British military*] (DMA)
LCL .... Laser Centreline Localiser (SAUS)
LCL .... Lateral Capsular Ligament [*Medicine*] (MELL)
LCL .... Lateral Collateral Ligament [*Anatomy*]
LCL .... Leading Catholic Layman
LCL .... Lens Culinaris Lectin
Lcl .... Less than Carload (EBF)
LCL .... Less-than-Carload [*Under 60,000 pounds*]
LCL .... Less-than-Carload Lot (DFIT)
lcl .... Less than Carload Lots (WPI)
LCL .... Less-than-Container Load [*Shipping*]
LCL .... Levinthal-Coles-Lillie Bodies [*Microbiology*]
LCL .... Liberal and Country League (SAUO)
LCL .... Liberal Country League [*Australia*] (BARN)
LCL .... Library Control Language (OA)
LCL .... Library of Congress, Interlibrary Loan Department [*UTLAS symbol*]
LCL .... Licentiate in Common Law (SAUO)
LCL .... Licentiate of Canon Law [*British*]
LCL .... Licentiate of Civil Law
LCL .... Lifting Condensation Level [*Meteorology*]
LCL .... Light Center Length
LCL .... Limited Channel Logout
LCL .... Linkage Control Language [*Computer science*] (BUR)
LCL .... Liquid Control Line [*Emergency Management*] (EMA)
LCL .... Liverpool Central Library (SAUO)
LCL .... Local (AFM)
LCL .... Localizer (CET)
LCL .... Loeb Classical Library. Harvard University Press [*A publication*] (BJA)
LCL .... Logical Comparative LOFAR
LCL .... Loose Container Load [*Shipping*] (IMH)
LCL .... Lot-Car Load
LCL .... Loughborough Consultants Ltd. (SAUO)
LCL .... Low-Capacity Link [*Telecommunications*] (OA)
LCL .... Lower Confidence Limit [*Statistics*]
LCL .... Lower Control Limit [*QCR*]
LCL .... Lower of Cost or Market (TDOB)
LCL .... Lumbocostal Ligament [*Medicine*] (MELL)
LCL .... Lymphoblastoid Cell Line
LCL .... Lymphocytic Leukemia (MAE)
LCL .... Lymphocytic Lymphosarcoma [*Oncology*]
LCL .... Lymphoma Cell Line [*Oncology*]
LCL .... Mala Services Ltd. [*British*] [*FAA designator*] (FAAC)
LCLA .... Lutheran Church Library Association (EA)
LCLAA .... Labor Council for Latin American Advancement (EA)
LCLC .... Large Cell Lung Carcinoma [*Oncology*] (DAVI)
LCLC .... Las Cumbres Learning Center (SAUO)
LCL/CI .... Limited Calendar Life, Controlled Item
LCLD .... Laclede Steel [*NASDAQ symbol*] (TTSB)
LCLD .... Laclede Steel Co. [*NASDAQ symbol*] (SAG)
LCLDQ .... Laclede Steel Co. [*OTCBB symbol*]
LCli .... Audubon Regional Library, Clinton, LA [*Library symbol*] [*Library of Congress*] (LCLS)
LCLJ .... Lower Canada Law Journal [*A publication*] (DLA)
LCL Jo .... Lower Canada Law Journal [*A publication*] (DLA)
LCLK .... Larnaca [*Cyprus*] [*ICAO location identifier*] (ICLI)
LCLM .... Low-Cost Lightweight Missile (MCD)
LCLO .... Lethal Concentration Low [*Environmental science*] (COE)
LC^{Lo} .... Lethal Concentration Low (ERG)
LCLo .... Lowest Published Lethal Concentration [*Medicine*] (EDAA)
LCLOC .... Line Card Location (VLIE)
LCLQ .... International and Comparative Law Quarterly [*A publication*] (SAFN)
LCLS .... Lewis and Clark Library System [*Library network*]
LCLS .... Livestock Commission Levy Scheme (SAUO)
LCLSC .... Life-Cycle Logistic Support Cost (PDAA)
LCLS-SLT ..... Low Cost Low Speed-Solid Logic Technology (VLIE)
LCLU .... Landing Control Logic Unit [*Aviation*] (OA)
LCLV .... Liberace Club of Las Vegas (EA)
LCLV .... Lilac Chlorotic Leafspot Virus [*Plant pathology*]
LCLV .... Liquid-Crystal Light Valve (IEEE)
LCLV .... Low-Cost Launch Vehicle [*NASA*] (KSC)
LCLW .... Lincoln Trail Towing and Storage [*Common carrier symbol*]
LCLZR .... Localizer (IAA)
LCM .... Laboratory Contract Manager (MCD)
LCM .... La Cumbre [*Argentina*] [*Airport symbol*] (AD)
LCM .... Lagos Church Missions (SAUO)
LCM .... Lake Champlain & Moriah Rail Road Co. [*AAR code*]
LCM .... Land Combat Missile
LCM .... Landing Craft, Mechanized [*Navy symbol*]
LCM .... Landing Craft, Medium [*Navy*]
LCM .... Lane Change-Merge [*Automotive safety*]
LCM .... Large-Core Memory [*Computer science*]
LCM .... Laser Capture Microdissection [*Biochemistry*]
LCM .... LASER Cloud Mapper
LCM .... LASER Countermeasure
LCM .... Last Calls Meter [*Telecommunications*] (NITA)
LCM .... Late Change Message [*Aviation*] (DA)
LCM .... Latent Cardiomyopathy [*Medicine*] (STED)
LCM .... Launch Control Monitor (MCD)
LCM .... Launch Crew Member (AAG)
LCM .... Lead-Coated Metal [*Technical drawings*]
lcm .... Least Common Multiple (SHCU)
LCM .... Least Common Multiple [*Mathematics*]
LCM .... Least Concave Majorant [*Statistics*]
LCM .... Left Costal Margin [*Medicine*]
LCM .... Legis Comparativae Magister [*Master of Comparative Law*] [*Latin*] (WGA)
LCM .... Leisure Competency Measure (IDYL)
LCM .... Leukocyte-Conditioned Medium [*Microbiology*]
LCM .... Library of Congress Maps [*Source file*] [*UTLAS symbol*]
LCM .... Life Cycle Management (EEVL)
LCM .... Life Cycle Manager (MCD)
LCM .... Lighting Control Module [*Automotive engineering*]
LCM .... Lightning Creek Mines Ltd. [*Vancouver Stock Exchange symbol*]
LCM .... Line Concentrator Module
LCM .... Line Control Module [*Telecommunications*] (TEL)
LCM .... Liquid Composite Molding [*Plastics*]
LCM .... Liquid Crystal Module (SAUS)
LCM .... Liquid Curing Medium
LCM .... Little Company of Mary, Nursing Sisters [*Roman Catholic religious order*]
LCM .... Liverpool Classical Monthly [*A publication*] (ABAR)
LCM .... LOCA [*Loss-of-Coolant Accident*] Core Melt [*Nuclear energy*] (NRCH)
LCM .... Local Coordination Module [*Traffic engineering*]
LCM .... Loer, C. M., Reno NV [*STAC*]
LCM .... Logical Connection Manager (VLIE)
LCM .... Logistics Capability Model (SAUO)
LCM .... London City Mission
LCM .... London College of Music (ROG)
LCM .... Longhaul Customer Modem [*Telecommunications*] (NITA)
LCM .... Loose Cubic Meter (DAC)
LCM .... Lost Circulation Material [*Oil well drilling*]
LCM .... Low Cost Module (IAA)
LCM .... Lower Costal Margin (STED)
LCM .... Lower of Cost or Market
LCM .... Lowest Common Multiple [*Mathematics*]
LCM .... Lymphocyte Conditioned Medium [*Hematology*]
LCM .... Lymphocytic Choriomeningitis [*Medicine*]
LCM(2) .... Landing Craft, Mechanized, MKII [*Navy symbol*]
LCM(3) .... Landing Craft, Mechanized, MKIII [*Navy symbol*]
LCM6 .... Landing Craft, Mechanized, MKVI [*Navy symbol*]
LCM8 .... Landing Craft, Mechanized, MKVIII [*Navy symbol*]
LCMA .... Lightweight Cycle Manufacturers Association [*British*] (DBA)
LCMA .... Longhaul Customer Modem Adapter [*Telecommunications*] (NITA)
LCMA .... Lutheran Campus Ministry Association [*Defunct*] (EA)
LCMA .... Lutheran Church Men of America
LC MARC ...... Library of Congress Machine Readable Catalog [*Washington, DC*] [*Bibliographic database*] [*Library of Congress*]
LC-MARC ...... Library of Congress MARC (SAUO)
LCMARC .... Library of Congress MARC [*Machine-Readable Catalog*] Files (NITA)
LCMCFC .... Liaison Committee for Mediterranean Citrus Fruit Culture [*See also CLAM*] [*Madrid, Spain*] (EAIO)
LCMCS .... Liquid Conditioned Microclimate System [*Army*] (RDA)
LCMD .... Laser Countermeasures Materials Development (ACAE)
LCMD .... Low-Cost Motor Demonstration (MCD)
LCME .... Large Climate-Moderating Envelope [*Energy-conserving form of architecture*]
LCME .... Liaison Committee on Medical Education (EA)
LCM(G) .... Landing Craft, Mechanised (Gun) [*British military*] (DMA)
LCMG .... Long-Chain Monoglyceride [*Biochemistry*] (MAE)
LCMH .... Lake Charles Memorial Hospital [*Lake Charles, LA*]
LCMI .... Left Ventricular Mass Index [*Medicine*] (RAWO)
LCMI .... Licentiate Cost and Management Institute (SAUO)
LCMI .... Licentiate of Cost and Management Institute [*British*]
LCML .... Library of Congress Minimal Level Cataloguing [*Source file*] [*UTLAS symbol*]
LCML .... Low-Capacity Microwave Link
LC(ML)C ...... Ligue Communiste (Marxiste-Leniniste) du Canada [*Canadian Communist League (Marxist-Leninist)*]
LCMM .... Life-Cycle Management Model (AABC)
LCMM .... Life Cycle Material Manager (MCD)
LCMMD .... Laser Countermeasures Material Development (ACAE)
LCMO .... Lanthanum/Calcium/Manganese/Oxygen [*Inorganic chemistry*]
LCMP .... Launcher Control and Monitoring Panel
LCMP .... Life Cycle Management Planning [*Army*]
LCMP .... Local Commandant, Military Police [*British military*] (DMA)
LCM-PDR ...... League of Communists of Macedonia - Party for Democratic Reform [*Political party*]
LCM(R) .... Landing Craft, Mechanised (Rocket) [*British military*] (DMA)
LCMR .... Local Cerebral Metabolic Rate (DB)
LCMRGlc ...... Local Cerebral Metabolic Rate for Glucose [*Brain research*]
LCMS .... Lake County Medical Society (SAUO)
LCMS .... Lancaster Moving and Storage Company [*Common carrier symbol*]
LCMS .... Laser Cavity Mode Spacing (ACAE)
LCMS .... LASER Countermeasure System [*Military*] (INF)
LCMS .... Launch Control and Monitoring System [*NASA*] (AAG)
LCMS .... Library Collection Management System (NITA)
LCMS .... LifeCare Management Services, LLC (MHID)
LCMS .... Life-Cycle Management System
LC/MS .... Liquid Chromatography/Mass Spectrometry
LCMS .... Logistics Capability Measurement System (SAUO)

LCMS .... Logistics Command Management System
LCMS .... Longshore Case Management System [*Department of Labor*] (GFGA)
LCMS .... Low-Cost Modular Spacecraft [*NASA*]
LCMS .... Lutheran Church - Missouri Synod
LCMSDS .... Laurier Centre for Military Strategic and Disarmament Studies [*Wilfrid Laurier University*] [*Canada*] (RCD)
LCMSO ...... Landing Craft, Material Supply Officer
LCMT .... London Centre for Marine Technology [*British*] (IRUK)
LCMU .... L and C Marine [*Intermodal shipping container symbol*] (TVRC)
LCMU .... Load Current Monitoring Unit (ACAE)
LCMV .... Lymphocytic Choriomeningitis Virus
LCMWG ..... Life Cycle Management Working Group (SAUO)
LC-MY .... League of Communists - Movement for Yugoslavia [*Political party*]
LCN .... Laboratory for Cognitive Neuroscience [*Salk Institute for Biological Studies*] (RCD)
LCN .... Labor Collection Network (ACAE)
LCN .... La Cosa Nostra [*Our Thing*]
LCN .... Landing Craft, Navigation [*Obsolete*]
LCN .... Large Co-Ops Network [*British*]
LCN .... Lateral Cervical Nucleus (STED)
LCN .... Lateral Cutaneous Nerve [*Medicine*] (EDAA)
LCN .... Left Caudate Nucleus [*Medicine*] (DMAA)
LCN .... Liaison Change Notice
LCN .... Library of Congress Number (MCD)
LCN .... Lineas Aereas Canarias SA [*Spain*] [*ICAO designator*] (FAAC)
LCN .... Linked Cluster Network [*Chemistry*]
LCN .... Load Classification Number (AFM)
LCN .... Local Civil Noon (ADA)
LCN .... Local Communication Network (ACRL)
LCN .... Local Communications Network (GAVI)
LCN .... Local Computer Network (VLIE)
LCN .... Local Control Network (SAUS)
LCN .... Local Control Number (MCD)
LCN .... Logical Channel Number [*Computer science*] (TNIG)
LCN .... Logistics Change Notice (SAUS)
LCN .... Logistics Control Number (MCD)
LCN .... Loosely Coupled Network [*Telecommunications*] (OSI)
LCNA .... Lacana Mining Corp. (SAUO)
LCNA .... Lewis Carroll Society of North America (EA)
LC/NA .... Lutherans Concerned/North America (EA)
LCNADE ..... Liquid-Cooled Naturally Aspirated Diesel Engine
LCNB .... Lincoln Bancorp. [*NASDAQ symbol*] (COMM)
LCNC .... Local Cartage National Conference [*Later, LSHCNC*]
LCNC .... Nicosia [*Cyprus*] [*ICAO location identifier*] (ICLI)
LC NGO-EC... Liaison Committee of Development Non-Governmental Organizations to the European Communities [*Belgium*] (EAIO)
LCNI .... IA Lacina [*Common carrier symbol*]
LCNI .... Landmark Communications, Inc. (EFIS)
LCNM .... Lehman Caves National Monument (SAUO)
LCNN .... Land Commander Northern Norway (SAUO)
LCNN .... Land Commander, North Norway [*NATO*] (NATG)
LCNP .... Lawyers' Committee on Nuclear Policy (EA)
LCNP .... Licentiate of the National Council of Psychotherapists [*British*]
LCNR .... Liquid Core Nuclear Rocket
LCNSD ...... Licensed
LCNSW ...... Labor Council of New South Wales [*Australia*]
LCNSW ...... Legislative Council of New South Wales [*Australia*]
LCNT .... Link Celestial Navigation Trainer
LCNTR .... Location Counter [*Computer science*]
LCNU .... Loconav [*Intermodal shipping container symbol*] (TVRC)
LC/NUC ...... Library of Congress and National Union Catalog Author Lists, 1942-1962 [*A publication*]
LCNVA .... Low-Cost Night Vision Aid (MCD)
LCNVG ...... Low-Cost Night Vision Goggles (MCD)
LCNY .... Linguistic Circle of New York (SAUO)
LCNYC .... Lincoln Center New York City (SAUO)
LCNY/W Word... Journal of the Linguistic Circle of New York (journ.) (SAUS)
LCO .... Laboratory of Cellular Oncology [*National Cancer Institute*] (RCD)
LCO .... Land Conservation Officer (SAUO)
LCO .... Landing Craft Officer [*British*] (ADA)
LCO .... Latching Contract Operate (VLIE)
LCO .... Launch Control Officer (SAUO)
LCO .... Launch Control Operation (MCD)
LCO .... Launching Control Office [*or Officer*] [*Military*]
LCO .... Lee Conservancy Office (SAUO)
LCO .... Libraries Connect Ohio
LCO .... Light Cycle Oil [*Petrochemical technology*]
LCO .... Limiting Conditions for Operation [*Nuclear energy*] (NRCH)
LCO .... Linea Aerea del Cobre Ltda. [*Chile*] [*ICAO designator*] (FAAC)
LCO .... Lipo-Chitooligosaccharide [*Botany*]
LCO .... Logistics Control Office [*Military*] (AABC)
LCO .... London College of Osteopathy (SAUO)
LCO .... Lord Chancellor's Office [*British*] (DLA)
LCO .... Low Cardiac Output [*Cardiology*]
LCO .... Lower Cost of Ownership (GART)
LCO .... Lowest Cost of Ownership
LCO .... MMC Uniform Central Number (SAUS)
LCOA .... Logistics Control Office, Atlantic [*Military*]
LCOC .... Launch Control Officer's Console (AAG)
LCOC .... Lincoln and Continental Owners Club (EA)
LCOC .... Lincoln Continental Owners Club (EA)
LCOCC .... Atlantic [*Fleet*] Commander Operational Control Center [*Navy*]
LCOCC .... Atlantic Command Operational Control Center (SAUO)
LCOCU ...... Landing Craft, Obstruction Clearance Unit
LCOD .... Last Cutoff Date (ACAE)
LC OFC ...... Linear Crystal Oxygen Free Copper [*Cable component*] (NITA)
L/COH .... Lance-Corporal of Horse [*British military*] (DMA)
L/Col .... Lieutenant Colonel (SAUO)
LCOL .... Lieutenant Colonel
LColC .... Caldwell Parish Library, Columbia, LA [*Library symbol*] [*Library of Congress*] (LCLS)
LColfG .... Grant Parish Library, Colfax, LA [*Library symbol*] [*Library of Congress*] (LCLS)
LCOLNT ..... Low Coolant
LCOM .... Lieutenant Commander (GOBB)
LCOM .... Local Committee Operations Manual [*A publication*] (EAAP)
LCOM .... Logic Control Output Module (MCD)
LCOM .... Logistics Composite Model
LCOMM ..... Library Council of Metropolitan Milwaukee [*Wisconsin*] [*Library network*]
L Comment... Law Commentary [*A publication*] (DLA)
L Comment'y... Law Commentary [*A publication*] (DLA)
L COMP RAM... Licentiate in Composition, Royal Academy of Music [*British*] (ROG)
L/COMPT .... Luggage Compartment [*Automotive engineering*]
LCOP .... Launch Control Officer's Panel (AAG)
LCOP .... Logistics Control Office, Pacific [*Military*] (AABC)
LCOR .... Laboratory for Comparative Orthopaedic Research [*Michigan State University*] (RCD)
LCOR .... Langley Corporation (SAUO)
LCOR .... Lincoln Cosmopolitan Owners Registry [*Defunct*] (EA)
LCOR .... Load Character with Offset Register (VLIE)
L-CORP ..... Lance-Corporal [*Military*] [*British*] (ROG)
LCOS .... Launch Checkout Stations (ACAE)
LCOS .... Lead Computing Optical Sight
LCOS .... Limiting Conditions for Operations Specification (SAUO)
LCOS .... Liquid Crystal on Silicon (AEBE)
LCOS .... Low Cardiac Output Syndrome [*Medicine*] (DMAA)
LCOS .... Lycos Inc. [*NASDAQ symbol*] (TTSB)
LCOSE .... Launch Complex Operational Support Equipment
LCOSS .... Lead Computing Optical Sighting System (MCD)
LCOSS .... Lead Computing Optical Sight System (SAUS)
LCOT .... Lower Critical Ordering Transition [*Polymer physics*]
LCOTA .... Licensed Certified Occupational Therapy Assistant [*Therapy term*] (CTAA)
LCouRR ..... Red River Parish Library, Coushata, LA [*Library symbol*] [*Library of Congress*] (LCLS)
LCovD .... Delta Regional Primate Research Center, Science Information Service, Covington (SAUS)
LCovD .... Delta Regional Primate Research Center, Science Information Service, Covington, LA [*Library symbol*] [*Library of Congress*] (LCLS)
LCovSt ...... Saint Tammany Parish Library, Covington, LA [*Library symbol*] [*Library of Congress*] (LCLS)
LCP .... Galbraith Lake Camp, AK [*Location identifier*] [*FAA*] (FAAL)
LCP .... Laboratory for Crustal Petrology [*University of Maryland at College Park*] (RCD)
LCP .... Landing Craft, Personnel
LCP .... Language Conversion Program [*Computer science*] (BUR)
LCP .... Large Coil Program [*Physics*]
LCP .... Large Computer Project (IAA)
LCP .... Last Card Program Start (IAA)
LCP .... Last Complete Program (WDAA)
LCP .... Lateral Choroid Plexus (PDAA)
LCP .... Launch Control Panel
LCP .... Launch Control Post (MCD)
LCP .... Laws for Construction of Programs (MHDB)
LCP .... Lawyers Co-Operative Publishing Co. [*Rochester, NY*]
LCP .... Leader, Company Procurement [*Military*] (AFIT)
LCP .... League of Canadian Poets [*Canada*] (EAIO)
LCP .... Lebanese Communist Party [*Political party*] (PSAP)
LCP .... Left Circular Polarization
LCP .... Left-Handed Circular Polarization (VLIE)
L-C-P .... Leg-Calve-Perthes Disease [*Medicine*]
LCP .... Legg-Calve-Perthes [*Disease*] [*Medicine*] (DB)
LCP .... Legislative Council for Photogrammetry [*Later, MAPPS*] (EA)
LCP .... Lehndorff Canadian Prop. [*Limited Partnership Units*] [*Toronto Stock Exchange symbol*]
LCP .... Letter Carrier Presort [*Canadian postal term*] (NFD)
LCP .... Liberal and Country Party (SAUO)
LCP .... Liberal Country Party [*Australia*] (BARN)
LCP .... Library Company of Philadelphia (SAUO)
LCP .... Licensed Clinical Psychologist
LCP .... Licentiate of the College of Preceptors [*British*]
LCP .... Light Compact Performance [*Filtration systems*] [*Automotive engineering*]
LCP .... Link Control Procedure [*Telecommunications*]
LCP .... Link Control Protocol [*Telecommunications*] (ACRL)
LCP .... Liquid-Crystal Polymer [*Organic chemistry*]
LCP .... Liquid Cyclone Process [*for making high-protein edible cottonseed flour*]
LCP .... Little Computer Person [*Activision computer game*]
LCP .... Liverpool Court of Passage (SAUO)
LCP .... Load Cell Platform
LCP .... Loading Control Program (IAA)
LCP .... Local Calibration Procedure
LCP .... Local Coastal Program (SAUO)

LCP .... Local Collaborative Projects [*Between business and education*] [*British*]
LCP .... Local Contigency Plan (SAUO)
LCP .... Local Control Panel (CAAL)
LCP .... Local Control Point [*Telecommunications*] (TEL)
LCP .... Location Characterization Plan (SAUO)
LCP .... Loews Cineplex Entertainment Corp. [*NYSE symbol*]
LCP .... Loews Cineplex Entertain't. [*NYSE symbol*] (SG)
LCP .... Logistic Capability Plan [*Navy*]
LCP .... London College of Printing
LCP .... Long-Chain Polysaturated Fatty Acid [*Biochemistry*] (MAE)
LCP .... Lost Cause Press, Louisville, KY [*Library symbol*] [*Library of Congress*] (LCLS)
LCP .... Low-Calcium Pyroxene [*Mineralogy*]
LCP .... Low-Cost Production (WDAA)
LCP .... Lower Control Panel [*Automotive engineering*]
LCP .... Lower Cost Processor (MCD)
LCP .... Lymphocyte Cytosol Polypeptide [*Medicine*] (DMAA)
LCP .... Lymphocytophoresis [*Medicine*] (EDAA)
LCPA .... Lincoln Center for the Performing Arts (EA)
LC-PAD ...... Liquid Chromatography plus Pulsed Amperometric Detection [*Analytical chemistry*]
LCP & SA ... Licentiate of Physicians and Surgeons of America
LCP&SA ..... Licentiate of the College of Physicians and Surgeons of America (SAUO)
LCP&SO ..... Licentiate of the College of Physicians and Surgeons of Ontario (SAUO)
LCPC .... Lancashire and Cheshire Provincial Council (SAUO)
LCPC .... Liquid Cyclone Processed Cottonseed Flour
LCPC .... Low-Cost-to-Produce Classifier (MCD)
LCP-FY ...... Logistic Capability Plan - Fiscal Year [*Navy*] (NG)
LCPG .... Logic Clock Pulse Generator [*Computer science*]
LCPH .... Paphos [*Cyprus*] [*ICAO location identifier*] (ICLI)
LCPIS .... Low-Cost Propulsion Integration Study (MCD)
LCPK .... Low Cost Precision Kill [*Military*]
LCPL .... Lance Corporal
L/Cpl .... Lance-Corporal (WDAA)
LCPL .... Landing Craft, Personnel, Large [*Navy symbol*]
LCPL .... Left Circularly Polarized Light
LCPL .... Leon-Jefferson Library System [*Library network*]
LCPLR .... Landing Craft, Personnel Leader
LCP(M) ...... Landing Craft, Personnel (Medium)
LCP(N) ...... Landing Craft, Personnel (Nested) [*Obsolete*]
LCPO .... Leading Chief Petty Officer (DNAB)
LCPP .... Land Capability Planning Program (SAUO)
LCP(P) ...... Landing Craft, Personnel (Plastic)
LCPR .... Landing Craft, Personnel, Ramped [*Navy symbol*]
LCPRC .... Liquid Crystalline Polymer Research Center [*University of Connecticut*] [*Research center*] (RCD)
LCP(S) ...... Landing Craft, Personnel (Small) [*British military*] (DMA)
LCPS .... Large Cloud Particle-Size Spectrometer
LCPS .... Licentiate of the College of Physicians and Surgeons [*British*]
LCPS .... Lithuanian Catholic Press Society (EA)
LCPS .... London Carthorse Parade Society (SAUO)
LCP(SY) ..... Landing Craft, Personnel (Survey)
LCPT .... Lightweight Collapsible Pillolo Tank
LCPTT .... Low-Cost Part Task Trainer (MCD)
LCP(U) ...... Landing Craft, Personnel (Utility) [*British military*] (DMA)
LCPUFA ..... Long-Chain Polyunsaturated Fatty Acids
LCPVC .... Life Cycle Present Value Costs (SAUO)
LCQ .... Launch Crew Quarters (AFM)
LCQ .... Learning Climate Questionnaire [*Medicine*] (DMAA)
LCQ .... Liquid Crystal Quartz (WGA)
LCQ .... Logical Channel Queue [*Computer science*] (BUR)
LCR .... Inductance-Capacitance-Resistance (CET)
LCR .... Lake County Railroad [*Federal Railroad Administration identification code*]
LCR .... La Lucha [*Costa Rica*] [*Seismograph station code, US Geological Survey*] (SEIS)
LCR .... Landcare Reserach Limited Lease (SAUO)
LCR .... Land Compensation Reports [*A publication*] (ILCA)
LCR .... Land Cruiser [*NCIC car model code*]
LCR .... Landing Craft, Raiding [*British*]
LCR .... Landing Craft, Rocket [*British military*] (DMA)
LCR .... Landing Craft, Rubber
LCR .... Las Cruces, NM [*Location identifier*] [*FAA*] (FAAL)
LCR .... Late Cutaneous Reaction [*Immunology*]
LCR .... Launch Control Rack (ACAE)
LCR .... Launch Control Room (MCD)
LCR .... Least-Cost Routing [*Telecommunications*]
LCr .... Letter of Credit
L/CR .... Lettre de Credit [*Letter of Credit*] [*French*]
LCR .... Leurocristine [*Oncovin, Vincristine*] [*Also, O, V, VC, VCR*] [*Antineoplastic drug*]
LCR .... Level Crossing Rate (IAA)
LCR .... Level Crossing Resonance [*Physical chemistry*]
LCR .... Libyan Arab Company for Air Cargo [*ICAO designator*] (FAAC)
LCr .... Lieutenant Commander [*Navy*] [*British*]
LCR .... Ligase Chain Reaction [*Genetics*]
LCR .... Light Chopping Reticle
LCR .... Ligue Communiste Revolutionnaire [*Revolutionary Communist League*] [*France*] [*Political party*] (PPW)
LCR .... Limit Control Register [*Navy Navigation Satellite System*] (DNAB)
LCR .... Liquid Chromatographic Reactor
LCR .... Liquide Cephalo-Rachidien [*Cerebrospinal Fluid*] [*French*]
LCR .... Liquido Cefalloraquideo [*Cerebrospinal Fluid*] [*Spanish*]
LCR .... Load Complement Register (IAA)
LCR .... Local Content Requirement (JAGO)
LCR .... Locus Control Region [*Genetics*]
LCR .... Logarithmic Correlators Ratiometer (PDAA)
LCR .... Log Cabin Republicans (EA)
LCR .... Log Count Rate [*Nuclear energy*] (NRCH)
LCR .... Logistic Change Report [*Military*] (AFM)
LCR .... London & Continental Railways Ltd.
LCR .... Low Compression Ratio [*Automotive engineering*] (IAA)
LCR .... Low Cost Range
LCR .... Low-Cost Reusable [*Refers to payload type*] [*NASA*]
LCR .... Low Count Range [*Nuclear energy*] (NUCP)
LCR .... Low Cross Range
LCR .... Lower Canada Reports [*A publication*] (DLA)
LCR .... Lower Circulating Reflux [*Chemical engineering*]
LCR .... Lowest Current Rate (RIMS)
LCR .... Low Pass Coaxial Relay (ACAE)
LCR .... Lucero Resources Corp. [*Vancouver Stock Exchange symbol*]
LCR .... Lung Configuration Recorder
LCR .... Lutheran Churches of the Reformation
LCR .... Revolutionary Communist League (France) [*Political party*] (PSAP)
LCR .... The Radical-Cause (Venezuela) [*Political party*] (PSAP)
LCrA .... Acadia Parish Library, Crowley, LA [*Library symbol*] [*Library of Congress*] (LCLS)
LCRA .... Akrotiri [*Cyprus*] [*ICAO location identifier*] (ICLI)
LCRA .... Labour Cost Research Associates Ltd. [*British*] (ECON)
LCRA .... Lackawanna County Railroad Authority [*Federal Railroad Administration identification code*]
LCRA .... Lithuanian Catholic Religious Aid (EA)
LCRA .... Lower Colorado River Authority
LCRC .... Lake Champlain Research Consortium [*Marine science*] (OSRA)
LCRC .... Laotian Cultural and Research Center (EA)
LCRC .... Lenawee County Railroad Co., Inc. [*AAR code*]
LCRC .... Lenawee County Railroad Company, Inc. (SAUO)
LCRDP ...... Laboratory/Campus Research and Development Program (SAUO)
LCRE .... LCR Truck and Equipment Company [*Common carrier symbol*]
LCRE .... Lithium Cooled Reactor Experiment
LC Rep S Qu ... Lower Canada Seignorial Questions Reports [*A publication*] (DLA)
LCRES .... Letter Carrier Route Evaluation System [*Postal Service*]
LCRF .... L'Association Canadienne des Ludotheques et des Centres de Ressources pour la Famille [*Canadian Association of Toy Libraries and Parent Resource Centers*] [*See also TLRC*] (EAIO)
LCRI .... Library of Congress Rule Interpretations [*A publication*]
LCRIS .... Loop Cable Record Inventory System (MCD)
LCR(L) ...... Landing Craft, Rubber (Large) [*Obsolete*]
LCRL .... Lewis and Clark Regional Library [*Library network*]
LCRM .... Launch Control Room (AAG)
LCRM .... Linear Count Rate Meter (NRCH)
LCRO .... Episkopi [*Cyprus*] [*ICAO location identifier*] (ICLI)
LCRO .... Linear Combination of Rydberg Orbitals [*Atomic physics*]
LCRO .... Low Cross-Range Orbiter (KSC)
LCROS ...... La Crosse, WI [*American Association of Railroads railroad junction routing code*]
LCR PAC .... Log Cabin Republicans PAC [*Washington, DC*] (PACS)
LCRPM ...... Large-Capacity Reciprocating Pultrusion Machine [*Plastics*]
LCR(R) ...... Landing Craft, Rubber (Rocket)
LCRR .... Low-Cost Risk Reduction (PDAA)
LCRR .... Nicosia [*Cyprus*] [*ICAO location identifier*] (ICLI)
Lcrs .... Lancers (SAUO)
LCR(S) ...... Landing Craft, Rubber (Small) [*Obsolete*]
LCRS .... Leachate Collection and Removal System (SAUO)
LCRS .... Leachate Control and Removal System [*Environmental science*] (COE)
LCRS .... Low-Cost Readout Station [*NASA*]
LCRSMEEC ... Liaison Committee of the Rice Starch Manufacturers of the EEC [*Belgium*] (EAIO)
LCRT .... L-Cart [*NCIC trailer make code*]
LCRT .... Lincoln Center Repertory Theater (SAUO)
LCRT .... Low-Contrast Resolution Test [*Optics*]
LCRU .... Landing Craft, Recovery Unit
LCRU .... Lunar Communications Relay Unit [*Apollo*] [*NASA*]
LCRV .... Length of Curve (MSA)
LCRX .... Luzerne County Rail [*Federal Railroad Administration identification code*]
LCRY .... LeCroy Corp. [*NASDAQ symbol*] (SAG)
LCRZ .... Lower Colorado River Authority [*Federal Railroad Administration identification code*]
LCS .... Ann Arbor Laboratory Computer System (SAUS)
LCS .... Laboratory-Certifying Scientist [*Analytical chemistry*]
LCS .... Laboratory Computer System (SAUO)
LCS .... Laboratory Control Sample (ABAC)
LCS .... Laboratory for Computational Statistics [*Stanford University*] (PDAA)
LCS .... Laboratory for Computer Science [*Massachusetts Institute of Technology*] [*Research center*] (RCD)
LCS .... Laboratory for Computer Systems [*Carnegie Mellon University*] (RCD)
LCS .... Labor Collection System (TIMI)
LCS .... Lancaster, CA [*Amtrak Busline code*]
LCS .... Lancaster Resources [*Vancouver Stock Exchange symbol*]
LCS .... Land Combat System
LCS .... Landing Craft, Support
LCS .... Landsat Customer Services (SAUO)
LCS .... Landscape Creation Series [*Off-Highway equipment*]
LCS .... Lane Control Signal

LCS Large Capacity [*or Core*] Storage [*Computer science*]
LCS Large Core Storage [*Computer science*] (OA)
LCS Laser Communications Subsystem (SAUS)
LCS LASER Communications System
LCS Laser Cross Section (ACAE)
LCS LASER Crosswind System (RDA)
LCS Last Cast Syndrome [*Fictitious fishing malady*]
LCS Lateral Channel Stop (IAA)
LCS Lateral Control System (MUGU)
LCS Lathe Control System
LCS Launch Complex Set
LCS Launch Control Sequence (AAG)
LCS Launch Control Shelter (ACAE)
LCS Launch Control Simulator
LCS Launch Control Station
LCS Launch Control System [*or Subsystem*]
LCS Law of Corresponding States [*Physics*]
LCS LCS Industries, Inc. [*Associated Press*] (SAG)
LCS League Championship Series [*Baseball*]
LCS League of Communists of Yugoslavia (Slovenia) [*Political party*] (PSAP)
LCS Leakage Collection System [*Nuclear energy*] (NRCH)
LCS Leak Control System [*Nuclear energy*] (NRCH)
LCS Learning Classifier System [*Computer science*]
LCS Leukocyte Complement System [*Immunology*] (QSUL)
LCS Leveling Control System
LCS Liaison Call Sheet
LCS Library Call Society (SAUO)
LCS Library Cat Society (EA)
LCS Library Circulation System (SAUO)
LCS Library Computer System [*University of Illinois*] [*Library network*]
LCS Library Control System [*Ohio State Library*] [*Columbus*] [*Information service or system*] (IID)
LCS Lichen Chronicus Simplex [*Dermatology*] (DAVI)
LCS Life Care Services
LCS Life Cycle Support (SAUO)
LCS Life-Cycle Survivability (MSA)
LCS Light Cruiser Squadron [*British military*] (DMA)
LCS Light Curtain Scanner [*Electronics*]
LCS Limiting Control Settings (SAUO)
LCS Lincoln Calibration Sphere
LCS Linear Collision Sequence (MCD)
LCS Line Coding Storage
LCS Link Control Station [*Telecommunications*] (ECII)
LCS Linked Cross Sectional (PDAA)
LCS Linux Compatibility Standard (SAUS)
LCS Liquid Controlled Solid (KSC)
LCS Liquid Cooling System
LCS Liquid Crystal Shutter [*Epson*] [*Printer technology*]
LCS List of Command Signals (MCD)
LCS Lithuanian Cultural Society [*Defunct*] (EA)
LCS Litton Computer Services [*Information service or system*] (IID)
LCS Litton Enterprise Solutions (IID)
LCS Lladro Collectors Society (EA)
LCS Loadable Control Storage [*Computer science*] (NITA)
LCS Loamy Coarse Sand [*Soil biology*] [*Soil texture*] (QSUL)
LCS Local Communications Services [*British*]
LCs Local Councils (Uganda) [*Political party*] (PSAP)
LCS London Controlling Section [*British military*] (DMA)
LCS Loop Control System [*Nuclear energy*] (NRCH)
LCS LOPO [*Local Post*] Collectors Society (EA)
LCS Lottery Collectors Society (EA)
LCS Lotus Communications Server [*Computer science*] (HODG)
LCS Loudness Contour Selector
LCS Low Constant [*or Continuous*] Suction [*Surgical procedure*] (DAVI)
LCS Low-Cost LASER Seeker (MCD)
LCS Low Cost Seeker (SAUS)
LCS Low-Cost Sonobuoy (DOMA)
LCS Lyon Court, Scotland (SAUO)
LCS Region 10 Library Circulation System (SAUS)
LCS Statewide Library Computer System [*University of Illinois*] [*Information service or system*] (IID)
LCSA Legislative Council of South Australia
LCSA Lewis and Clark Society of America (EA)
LCSA Lotteries Commission of South Australia
LCSAJ Linear Code Sequence and Jump [*Computing*] (ODA)
LC Sales Langdell's Cases on the Law of Sales [*A publication*] (DLA)
LCSB Launch Control Support Building [*Missiles*]
LCSC Legislative Council Select Committee (SAUO)
LCSC London Child Study Centre (SAUO)
LCS/CMF Library Control System/Change Management Facility [*Computer science*] (HODG)
LCSCU Launch Coolant System Control Unit (AAG)
LCSD Laminate Chip Signal Diode (SAUS)
LC-SDP League of Communists-Social Democratic Party [*Bosnia-Hercegovina*] [*Political party*] (BUAC)
LCSE Laboratory for Computational Science and Engineering [*University of Minnesota*] (RCD)
LCSE LASER Communication Satellite Experiment [*NASA*]
LCSE Life-Cycle Software Engineering [*Army*] (RDA)
LCSEC Life-Cycle Software Engineering Center [*Army*]
LCSEFE Labor Committee for Safe Energy and Full Employment [*Defunct*] (EA)
LCSFP Low Cerebrospinal Fluid Pressure [*Medicine*] (MELL)
LCSG London Construction Safety Group (SAUO)
LCSG Lung Cancer Study Group (ADWA)
LC/SG Scientific Group (SAUO)
LCSH Library of Congress National Union Catalogue Subject Headings (TELE)
LCSH Library of Congress Subject Headings [*Formerly, SHDC*] [*A publication*]
LCSI Launch Critical Support Items [*NASA*] (KSC)
LCSI LCS Industries [*NASDAQ symbol*] (SAG)
LCSI Licentiate of the Construction Surveyors' Institute [*British*] (DBQ)
LCSI Logistic Control Shipping Instruction (AAG)
LCSIE Liquid-Cooled Spark Ignition Engine
LCS/IS Local Communications Services/Information Services (NITA)
LCS(L) Landing Craft, Support (Large) [*Obsolete*]
LCSL Lightwave Communication Systems Laboratory [*University of Kansas*] (RCD)
LCSLT Low-Cost Solid Logic Technology (IAA)
LCS(M) Landing Craft, Support (Medium)
LCSM Launch Control and Status Monitor
LCSMM Life-Cycle Systems Management Model
LCSN Local Circuit Switched Network
LCSO Launch Complex Safety Officer (IAA)
LCSO Launch Control Safety Officer (MCD)
LCSO Leon County Sheriffs Association [*Emergency Management*] [*Florida*] (EMA)
LCSO Local Communications Service Order
LCSO Low-Cost Systems Office [*NASA*] (PDAA)
LCSP Logical Channels Switching Program (MHDB)
LCSP London and Counties Society for Psychologists (SAUO)
LCSP Lowell Center for Sustainable Production [*University of Massachusetts Lowell*] (RCD)
LCS-PDR League of Communists of Slovenia - Party of Democratic Reform [*Political party*]
LCSPL Launch Critical Spare Parts List [*NASA*] (KSC)
LCSR Laboratory for Computer Science Research [*Rutgers University*] [*Research center*] (RCD)
LCS(R) Landing Craft, Support (Rocket)
LCSR Landing Craft, Swimmer Reconnaissance [*Navy symbol*]
LCSR Large Caliber Soft Recoil [*Weaponry*] (MCD)
LCSR Leadville, Colorado & Southern Railroad [*Federal Railroad Administration identification code*]
LCSR(L) Landing Craft, Swimmer Recovery (Light) [*Navy symbol*] (NVT)
LCSRM Loop Current Step Response Method (IEEE)
LCSS Land Combat Support Set (NATG)
LCSS Land Combat Support System (DWSG)
LCSS Land Combat System Study (AFIT)
LCS(S) Landing Craft, Support (Small), MKI [*Navy symbol*] [*Obsolete*]
LCSS Launch Control and Sequencer System
LCSS Launch Control System Simulator [*NASA*] (IAA)
LCSS Life Cycle Software Support
LCSS Lightweight Camouflage Screen System (MCD)
LCSs Local Conservation Strategies (SAUO)
LCSS London Council of Social Service
LCSS Low Cost Sonobuoy System (SAUS)
LCSSAP Low-Cost Silicon Solar Array Project
LCSSC Life-Cycle Software Support Center [*Army*]
LCSSE Life-Cycle Software Support Environment [*Army*]
LCSSP Laboratory of Chemical and Solid-State Physics [*MIT*] (MCD)
LCSSP Laboratory of Chemistry and Solid-State Physics (SAUO)
LCST LecStar Corp. [*NASDAQ symbol*] (QUAN)
LCST Licentiate of the College of Speech Therapists [*British*]
LCST Lower Critical-Solution-Temperature
LCSU Lao Civil Servants' Union
LCSU Local Concentrator Switching Unit [*Telecommunications*] (TEL)
LCSVF Logistics Combat Support Vehicle Family (MCD)
LCSW Latch Checking Switch (MSA)
LCSW Licensed Clinical Social Worker [*Medicine*]
LCSX Laclede Steel [*Private rail car owner code*]
LCT Landing Craft, Tank [*Navy symbol*]
LCT Laplace-Carson Transform [*Mathematics*]
LCT Last Card Total (IAA)
LCT Last Compliance Time
LCT Latest Closing Time
LCT Launch Control Trailer
LCT Launch Countdown [*NASA*] (NASA)
L Ct Law Court (DLA)
LCT Legislative Council of Tasmania [*Australia*]
LCT Lencourt Ltd. [*Toronto Stock Exchange symbol*]
LCT Less than Truckload Lot [*Under 24,000 pounds*] (MHDW)
LCT Licensing Commission of Tasmania [*Australia*]
LCT Life Component Tester
LCT Light Capital Technology (PDAA)
LCT Light Crawler Tractor (SAUS)
LCT Ligue Communiste des Travailleurs [*Communist Workers' League*] [*Senegal*] [*Political party*] (PPW)
LCT Linear Combination Technique [*Nuclear science*] (OA)
LCT Linkage Control Table [*Telecommunications*] (IAA)
LCT Liquid Crystal Thermography
LCT Listening Comprehension Test (TES)
LCT Liver Cell Tumor [*Medicine*] (DMAA)
LCT Local Civil Time
LCT Local Correlation-Tracking [*Instrumental technique*]
LCT Locate (MSA)
LCT Location, Command, and Telemetry (IAA)
LCT Locust (MSA)
LCT Logical Channel Termination

LCT .... Long Calcined Ton [*Bauxite, etc.*]
LCT .... Long-Chain Triglyceride [*Biochemistry*]
LCT .... Loughsborough College of Technology (SAUO)
LCT .... Louis Comfort Tiffany [*Signature on the art glass designed by Tiffany*]
LCT .... Low Cervical Transverse [*Position*] [*Obstetrics*] (DAVI)
LCT .... Low-Cost Technology (PDAA)
LCT .... Low Cost Terminal [*Telecommunications*] (LAIN)
LCT .... Luscher Color Test [*Psychology*] (DAVI)
LCT .... Lymphocytotoxicity [*Medicine*] (DMAA)
LCT .... Lymphocytotoxicity Test [*Hematology*]
LCT .... Shidler Center for Law, Commerce, and Technology [*University of Washington*] (RCD)
LCT-1 .... Lunar Cycle Test One [*Aerospace*]
LCt50 .... Exposure to a Vapor or Gas That Will Reliably Cause Death in 50 Percent of the Exposed Population [*Emergency Management*] (EMA)
LCTA .... Land Condition-Trend Analysis [*Army*] (RDA)
LCT(A) .... Landing Craft, Tank (Armored)
LCTA .... London Corn Trade Association
LCTA .... Lungs Clear to Auscultation (SAUS)
LCTA .... Lymphocytotoxic Antibodies [*Immunochemistry*]
LCTB .... Launch Control Training Building [*NASA*] (IAA)
LC/TC .... Livonia Career/Technical Center
LCTCDE ..... Liquid-Cooled Turbocharged Diesel Engine
LCTD .... Located (AFM)
LCTF .... Large Coil Test Facility (MCD)
LCTF .... Lloyd's Canadian Trust Fund (AIA)
LCTGM ...... Library of Congress Thesaurus for Graphic Materials (TELE)
LCT(H) .... Landing Craft, Tank (Hospital) [*British military*] (DMA)
LCTHF .... Lewis and Clark Trail Heritage Foundation (EA)
LCTI .... Large Components Test Installation [*Nuclear energy*] (NRCH)
LCTL .... Large Component Test Loop [*Nuclear energy*]
LCTL .... Less Commonly Taught Languages Project [*Association*] (EA)
LCTLs .... Less Commonly Taught Languages
LCTMP ...... Little Change in Temperature [*NWS*] (FAAC)
LCTN .... Location
LCTP .... Launcher Control Test Panel
LCT(R) .... Landing Craft, Tank (Rocket)
LCTR .... Locator
LCTS .... Lagos City Transport Services (SAUO)
LCT(S) .... Landing Craft, Tank (Slow)
LCTS .... LASER Coherence Techniques Section
LCTSU .... Launch Control Transfer Switching Unit [*Aerospace*] (AAG)
LCTT .... Launch Complex Telemetry Trailer
LCTT .... Low-Cost Tow Target (SAUS)
LCTU .... Locatainers [*Intermodal shipping container symbol*] (TVRC)
LCTV .... Liquid Crystal Television (CIST)
LCU .... Lac-Coated Urea Fertilizer
LCU .... Lancashire Congregational Union (SAUO)
LCU .... LAN CID Utility (SAUS)
LCU .... Landing Craft, Utility [*Navy symbol*]
LCU .... Laparoscopic Contact Ultrasonography [*Medicine*] (RAWO)
LCU .... Large Close-Up (ADA)
LCU .... Laser Coding Unit (ACAE)
LCU .... LASER Cooling Unit (MCD)
LCU .... Last Cluster Used (VLIE)
LCU .... Launch Control Unit (MCD)
LCU .... Level Converter Unit [*Computer science*] (CIST)
LCU .... Library of Congress Music [*Source file*] [*UTLAS symbol*]
LCU .... Life Change Unit [*Psychometrics*]
LCU .... Lightweight Computer Unit [*Computer science*] (CIST)
LCU .... Line Control Unit [*Data communications*]
LCU .... Line Converter Unit (ACAE)
LCU .... Line Coupling Unit (NASA)
LCU .... Link Control Unit [*Telecommunications*] (TEL)
LCU .... Liquid Cooling Undersuit [*Police and security equipment*]
LCU .... Local Control Unit (IAA)
LCU .... London Congregational Union (SAUO)
LCU .... Loop Control Unit [*Computer science*] (ELAL)
LCU .... Lower Control Unit (WDAA)
LCU .... Loyal Citizens of Ulster (SAUO)
LCU .... Lucin, UT [*Location identifier*] [*FAA*] (FAAL)
LCUC .... Letter Carriers' Union of Canada
LCuC .... Liver Copper Concentration [*Physiology*]
LCUG .... Liquid-Cooled Undergarment (MCD)
LCUG .... Liquid Cooling under Garment (SAUS)
LCUP .... Least Cost Utility Planning (SAUO)
LCUSA .... Ladies of Charity of the United States of America [*An association*] (EA)
LC/USA ...... Lutheran Council in the USA [*Defunct*] (EA)
LCUT .... Lifetime Hoan [*NASDAQ symbol*] (TTSB)
LCUT .... Lifetime Hoan Corp. [*NASDAQ symbol*] (SAG)
LCV .... Labor Cost Variance (ACAE)
LCV .... La Cueva [*New Mexico*] [*Seismograph station code, US Geological Survey*] (SEIS)
LCV .... Landing Craft, Vehicle [*Navy symbol*]
LCV .... Large Capacity Vehicle
LCV .... Large Compound Vesicle [*Biochemistry*]
LCV .... LASER Compatible Vidicon
LCV .... League of Conservation Voters (EA)
LCV .... Legislative Council of Victoria [*Australia*]
LCV .... Level Control Valve (MCD)
LCV .... Licentiate of the College of Violinists (SAUO)
LCV .... Light Commercial Vehicle
LCV .... Light Contingency Vehicle (SAUS)
LCV .... Line Coding Violation (SAUS)
LCV .... Llymphocryptovirus
LCV .... Load Control Valve [*Engineering*]
LCV .... Local Control Valve [*Nuclear energy*] (NRCH)
LCV .... Long Combination Vehicle
LCV .... Longer Combination Vehicle [*Trucks hauling multiple trailers*]
LCV .... Lorry Command Vehicle [*British military*] (DMA)
LCV .... Lorry Company Vehicle (SAUO)
LCV .... Low Calorific Value [*of a fuel*]
LCV .... Low Cervical Vertical [*Incision*] [*Obstetrics*] (DAVI)
LCV .... Low Cost Visual (ACAE)
LCV .... Low-Cost Visual (SAUS)
LCV .... Lymphocytic Choriomeningitis Virus [*Medicine*] (DB)
LCVA .... Light Commercial Vehicle Association (EA)
LCVAO .... Linear Combination of Virtual Atomic Orbitals [*Physical chemistry*]
LCVASI ...... Low-Cost Visual-Approach Slope Indicator (DNAB)
LCVD .... Laser-Assisted Chemical Vapor Deposition [*Coating technology*]
LCVD .... LASER Chemical Vapor Deposition [*Coating technology*]
LCVD .... Least Coincidence Voltage Detection (MDG)
LCV EARTH FUND ... League of Conservation Voters Action Fund [*Washington, DC*] (PACS)
LCVG .... Liquid Cooling and Ventilation Garment [*NASA*] (NASA)
LCVIP .... Licensee Contractor Vendor Inspection Report Program [*Nuclear energy*] (NRCH)
LCVM .... Log Conversion Voltmeter
LCVP .... Landing Craft, Vehicle, Personnel [*Navy symbol*] [*NATO*]
LCW .... Limited Conventional War [*Description of Vietnam War*] [*DoD*] (VNW)
LCW .... Line Control Word
LCW .... Lithuanian American Roman Catholic Women's Alliance
LCW .... Lithuanian Catholic Women (EA)
LCW .... Lutheran Church Women [*Defunct*] (EA)
LCWA .... Legislative Council of Western Australia
LCWA .... Lotteries Commission of Western Australia
LCWDS ...... Low-Cost Weapon Delivery System (MCD)
LCWE .... Lausanne Committee for World Evangelization (SAUO)
LCWF .... Launch Complex Work Flow (IAA)
LCWHN .... Latin American and Caribbean Women's Health Network (EAIO)
LCWI .... Left Ventricular Cardiac Work Index [*Physiology*]
LCWIO .... Liaison Committee of Women's International Organisations [*British*] (DI)
LCWP .... Law Commission Working Paper [*A publication*] (DLA)
LCWR .... Leadership Conference of Women Religious of the United States of America (SAUO)
LCWS .... Land and Water Conservation Fund (SAUO)
LCWSL ...... Large Caliber Weapon Systems Laboratory [*ARRADCOM*] (RDA)
LCX .... Higginsville, MO [*Location identifier*] [*FAA*] (FAAL)
LCX .... Launch Complex
LCx .... Left Circumflex [*Artery*] [*Medicine*] (DB)
LCX .... Left Circumflex Coronary Artery [*Cardiology*] (DAVI)
LCXT .... Large Cosmic X-Ray Telescope (PDAA)
LCY .... Guthrie, OK [*Location identifier*] [*FAA*] (FAAL)
LCY .... League of Communists of Yugoslavia [*Savez Komunista Jugoslavije*] [*Political party*] (PPW)
LCY .... Loose Cubic Yard (DAC)
LCYC .... Lemon Creek Yacht Club (SAUO)
LCZ .... Lauhoff [*Federal Railroad Administration identification code*]
LCZ .... Laws of the Canal Zone [*A publication*] (DLA)
LCZR .... Localizer
LD .... Decisions Lost [*Boxing*]
LD .... Doctor of Letters
LD .... Lab. Dausse [*France*] [*Research code symbol*]
LD .... Label Definition (IAA)
LD .... Labor and Delivery [*Obstetrics*] (DAVI)
LD .... Laboratory Data (MAE)
LD .... Labor Daily [*A publication*]
LD .... Labor Department
LD .... Labor Dispute (DLA)
LD .... Labyrinthine Defect [*Physiology*] (MAE)
LD .... Labyrinthine Dysfunction [*Medicine*] (MELL)
LD .... Lactase Deficiency [*Medicine*] (MELL)
LD .... Lactate Dehydrogenase [*Also, LAD, LDH*] [*An enzyme*]
LD .... Lady Day [*March 25, the Feast of the Annunciation*] [*British*]
LD .... Lamina Densa [*Dermatology*]
LD .... Lamp Driver
LD .... Land
LD .... Landau [*Pfalz*] [*German license plate city code*]
LD .... Land Disposal (EPAT)
LD .... Landing Distance [*Aviation*] (IAA)
LD .... Land Office Decisions, United States [*A publication*] (DLA)
LD .... Language Disordered
LD .... Large Date [*Numismatic term*]
LD .... Large Dollar [*Indicator*] [*IRS*]
LD .... Lasa D Ring [*Montana*] [*Seismograph station code, US Geological Survey*] (SEIS)
LD .... Laser Designator (ACAE)
LD .... LASER Desorption [*of ions for analysis*]
LD .... LASER Diode
LD .... LASER Disc (DCOM)
LD .... LASER Discectomy [*Spinal surgery*]
LD .... Last Dose (MELL)
LD .... Lated Dude [*Internet lingo*] (NETL)
LD .... Lateral Direction (MCD)

LD .... Lateral Dorsal [*Anatomy*]
LD .... Lateral Drift
LD .... Lateralis Dorsalis [*Neuroanatomy*]
LD .... Launch Director [*NASA*] (KSC)
LD .... Launching Division [*Missiles*] (MUGU)
LD .... Laus Deo [*Praise to God*] [*Latin*]
LD .... Law Dictionary [*A publication*] (DLA)
LD .... Layer Depth
ld .... Lead (WDMC)
LD .... Lead [*or Leads*] [*Publishing*]
LD .... Leading (MSA)
ld .... Leading (WDMC)
LD .... Leading Edge Delay [*Aviation*] (IAA)
LD .... Leak Detection [*Nuclear energy*] (IAA)
LD .... Learning Disabilities/Differences
LD .... Learning Disability [*or Learning-Disabled*]
LD .... Learning Disabled (NTIO)
LD .... Learning Disorder (DB)
LD .... Least Depth [*Nautical charts*]
LD .... Lectio Divina [*Paris*] [*A publication*] (BJA)
LD .... Left Defense
LD .... Left Deltoid [*Medicine*]
LD .... Left Door [*Theater*]
LD .... Legal Deposit (ADA)
LD .... Legal Discriminator (MCD)
LD .... Legal Division (SAUO)
LD .... Legionnaire's Disease
LD .... Legion of Decency (SAUO)
LD .... Legislative Department [*Generic term*] (ROG)
LD .... Leigh's Disease [*Medicine*] (MELL)
LD .... Leipzig Declaration (SAUO)
L-D .... Leishman-Donovan (Bodies) [*Microbiology*]
LD .... Length-Diameter Ratio
LD .... Lepide Dictum [*Wittily Said*] [*Latin*] (ADA)
LD .... Letdown [*Nuclear energy*] (NRCH)
LD .... Lethal Dose
LD .... Let's Discuss
LD .... Letter Description (PDAA)
L/D .... Letter of Deposit [*Banking*]
LD .... Leukodystrophy [*Medicine*] (MELL)
LD .... Level Detector
LD .... Level Discriminator
LD .... Levodopa [*Obstetrics*] (DAVI)
LD .... Liberal Democrat (WA)
LD .... Library of Devotion [*A publication*]
LD .... Libyan Dinar [*Monetary unit*] (BJA)
LD .... Licensed Dietician [*Therapy term*] (CTAA)
LD .... Licentiate in Dentistry [*British*] (ROG)
LD .... Licentiate in Divinity (DAS)
LD .... Lifeboat Deck
L:D .... Lift-Drag [*Ratio*]
L/D .... Lift-Drag Ratio [*Aerodynamics*]
L/D .... Lift to Drag Ratio (PIPO)
LD .... Light-Dark [*Cycles*]
L/D .... Light-Dark [*Ratio*] [*Ophthalmology*] (DAVI)
LD .... Light Demand [*Telegraphy*] (PCTE)
LD .... Light Detail (ELAL)
LD .... Light Difference [*Difference between amounts of light perceptible to the two eyes*] [*Ophthalmology*]
LD .... Light Dragoons [*Military unit*] [*British*]
LD .... Light Driver (IAA)
L/D .... Light Duty [*Automotive engineering*]
LD .... Lighting Designer (NTCM)
LD .... Lighting Director (NTCM)
LD .... Light on Dark
LD .... Limited
LD .... Limited Disease [*Medicine*]
LD .... Limited Partner in Dual Capacity Firm [*London Stock Exchange*]
LD .... Linear Decision
LD .... Linear Dichroism [*Spectra*]
LD .... Line Delete [*Computer science*] (VLIE)
LD .... Line Dolly (MCD)
LD .... Line Drawing (MSA)
LD .... Line Driver
LD .... Line of Departure [*Military*]
LD .... Line of Duty [*Military*]
LD .... Linguodistal [*Dentistry*]
LD .... Linkage Disequlilibrium [*Genetics*]
LD .... Linker Directive [*Telecommunications*] (TEL)
LD .... Linz and Donawetz [*Furnace*] [*Metallurgy*] [*Named after two plant sites in Austria*]
LD .... Lipodystrophy [*Medicine*] (MELL)
LD .... Liquid Drop
LD .... Lisfranc Dislocation [*Medicine*] (MELL)
LD .... List Down
LD .... List of Drawings [*USN*] (MCD)
LD .... Litera Dominicalis [*Sunday Letter*]
LD .... Litterarum Doctor [*Doctor of Letters or Literature*] [*Latin*] (ROG)
ID .... Liver Disease [*Gastroenterology*] (DAVI)
LD .... Living Donor [*Medicine*]
LD .... Load [*or Loader*] (AAG)
ld .... Load (WDAA)
LD .... Load Draught (IAA)
LD .... Loaded Deployability [*Posture*] [*Military*] (DOMA)
LD .... Loaded Deployability Posture (SAUO)
LD .... Loading Dock (MCD)
LD .... Loading Dose
LD .... Local Delivery
LD .... Local Director (DCTA)
LD .... Local Directory (ACRL)
LD .... Loft Dried Paper (DGA)
LD .... Logical Design
LD .... Logical Diagram (ELAL)
LD .... Logic Driver [*Computer science*]
LD .... Logistics Demonstration (MCD)
LD .... Logistics Document (MCD)
LD .... Lombard-Dowell [*Broth medium*] [*Microbiology*]
LD .... London [*Telegraphy*] (PCTE)
LD .... London Division (SAUO)
LD .... London Docks
LD .... Long Day [*Botany*]
LD .... Long Delay
LD .... Long Distance
LD .... Long Duration
LD .... Longitudinal Diameter
LD .... Longitudinal Division [*Cytology*]
LD .... Loop Diagram
LD .... Loop-Disconnect [*Telecommunications*] (TEL)
LD .... Lord
LD .... Loss and Damage (IAA)
LD .... Louis Dreyfus Natural Gas [*NYSE symbol*] (TTSB)
LD .... Louis Dreyfus Natural Gas Holdings Corp. [*NYSE symbol*] (SPSG)
LD .... Low Density
LD .... Low Dispersion [*Optics*]
LD .... Low Door (WDAA)
LD .... Low Dose [*Medicine*]
LD .... Low Drag
LD .... Low Dust
LD .... Low Dutch [*Language, etc.*]
LD .... Low Dynamic
LD .... Lower Deck
LD .... Lubricating Dutchman [*Automotive oil*]
LD .... Lucey-Driscoll [*Syndromes*] [*Medicine*] (QSUL)
LD .... Luminance-Defined (SAUS)
LD .... Luminescence Detector (SSD)
LD .... Luminescence Diode (IAA)
LD .... Lunar Day (KSC)
LD .... Lunar Docking [*NASA*] (IAA)
LD .... Lunar Drill [*NASA*] (KSC)
LD .... Lyme Disease [*Medicine*]
LD .... Lymphocyte Defined [*Immunology*]
LD .... Lymphocyte Depleted [*Medicine*]
LD .... Lymphocyte Depletion [*Hematology*]
LD .... Lymphocytical Determined [*Hematology*] (DAVI)
LD .... Vietnam [*License plate code assigned to foreign diplomats in the US*]
LD 1 .... Isoenzyme of Lactate Dehydrogenase [*Found in the heart, erythrocytes, and kidneys*] [*Medicine*] (EDAA)
LD 2 .... Isoenzyme of Lactate Dehydrogenase [*Found in the lungs*] [*Medicine*] (EDAA)
LD 3 .... Isoenzyme of Lactate Dehydrogenase [*Found in the lungs*] [*Medicine*] (EDAA)
LD 4 .... Isoenzyme of Lactate Dehydrogenase [*Found in the liver*] [*Medicine*] (EDAA)
LD 5 .... Isoenzyme of Lactate Dehydrogenase [*Found in the liver and muscles*] [*Medicine*] (EDAA)
LD-7a .... Lymphocyte Determinant [*Medicine*] (EDAA)
LD50 .... Lethal Dose 50
LD_{50} .... Lethal Dose, Median [*Also, MLD*] [*Lethal for 50% of test group*]
LD50 .... Lethal Dose of a Liquid Agent That Will Reliably Cause Death in 50 Percent of an Exposed Population [*Emergency Management*] (EMA)
LD-50 .... Lethal Dose So That 50 Percent of the Exposed Population Dies [*Emergency Management*] (EMA)
LD 50 .... Low Dose, Fifty Percent Fatality [*Environmental science*] (COE)
LD 50/60 .... Median Radiological Lethal Dose Such That 50 Percent of the Population Will Die Within 60 Days [*Emergency Management*] (EMA)
LDA .... Ascension Parish Library, Donaldsonville, LA [*Library symbol*] [*Library of Congress*] (LCLS)
LDA .... Laboratory Designated Area (AFIT)
LDA .... Labor Developments Abroad [*A publication*]
LDA .... Ladies Darts Association (SAUO)
LDA .... Land Development Aircraft (PDAA)
LDA .... Landing Directional Aid [*FAA*] (TAG)
LDA .... Landing Distance Available [*ICAO*] (FAAC)
LDA .... Laser Disc Association (NTPA)
LDA .... LASER Doppler Anemometry
LDA .... Last Day of Attendance
LDA .... Late-Differentiation Antigen [*Immunology*]
LDA .... Lauda Air [*Austria*] [*ICAO designator*] (FAAC)
LDA .... Lauryl Diethanolamide [*Also, LDE*] [*Organic chemistry*]
LDA .... Lead Development Association [*British*] (EAIO)
LDA .... Leadership Analysis (SAUO)
LDA .... Learning Disabilities Association (SAUO)
LDA .... Learning Disabilities Association of America (EA)
LDA .... Left Dorso-Anterior [*A fetal position*] [*Obstetrics*]
LDA .... Legitimacy Declaration Act [*British*] (ROG)
LDA .... Lesson Design Approach (MCD)

LDA.......... Lightweight Decontamination Apparatus [*Military*] [*Chemical warfare*]
LDA.......... Limited Depository Account
LDA.......... Limiting Dilution Analyses [*Analytical biochemistry*]
LDA.......... Linc Development Assistant [*Computer science*] (HODG)
LDA.......... Linear Discriminant Analysis
LDA.......... Linear Displacement Analysis (DAVI)
LDA.......... Linear Dynamic Analyzer (IAA)
LDA.......... Line Driving Amplifier
LDA.......... Lithium Diisopropylamide [*Organic chemistry*]
LDA.......... Local Data Acquisition
LDA.......... Local Data Administrator
LDA.......... Local-Density (Functional) Approximation [*Physical chemistry*]
LDA.......... Local Design Agency (MCD)
LDA.......... Local Display Adapter (MHDB)
LDA.......... Local Distribution Accesses (ACAE)
LDA.......... Localizer Directional Aid [*Aviation*]
LDA.......... Localizer Type Directional Aid (PIPO)
LDA.......... Locate Drum Address (CET)
LDA.......... Logical Device Address [*Computer science*] (IBMDP)
LDA.......... Logic Design Automation (AAEL)
LDA.......... Lord's Day Alliance of the United States (EA)
LDA.......... Louisiana Dental Association (SAUO)
LDA.......... Low-Density Amorph [*Materials science*]
LDA.......... Lower-Deck Attitude [*British military*] (DMA)
LDA.......... Lowest Designated Assembly
LDA.......... Lutheran Deaconess Association (EA)
LDA.......... Lymphocyte-Dependent Antibody [*Immunology*]
LDA-AL...... Learning Disabilities Association of Alabama (EARSL)
LDAC........ Learning Disabilities Association of Canada (EAIO)
LDAC........ Low-Dose Cytosine Arabinoside [*Medicine*] (EDAA)
LDAC........ Lunar Surface Data Acquisition Camera [*Aerospace*]
LDA-CA...... Learning Disabilities Association of California (EARSL)
LDAD........ Local Data Acquisition and Dissemination (SAUO)
LDAI........ Low-Dose Oral Alpha Interferon [*Medicine*] (TAD)
LDAK........ Lidak Pharmaceuticals [*NASDAQ symbol*] (SAG)
LDAKA....... LIDAK Pharmaceuticals'A' [*NASDAQ symbol*] (TTSB)
LDAM........ Local Damage Assessment Model (PDAA)
LDAM........ Logical Data Access Method [*Computer science*] (VLIE)
LD & B...... Lyme Disease and Babesiosis [*Medicine*] (MELL)
LDAO........ Lauryldimethylamine Oxide [*Detergent*]
LDAP........ Light Directory Access Protocol [*Computer science*] (VLIE)
LDAP........ Lightweight Directory Access Protocol [*Computer utility tool*] (PCM)
LDAPAPI.... Lightweight Directory Access Protocol Application Program Interface (SAUS)
LDAPS....... Long-Duration Auxiliary Power System (NG)
LDAQ........ Association Quebecoise pour les Troubles d'Apprentissage (AC)
LDAQ........ Learning Disabilities Association of Quebec (AC)
LDAR........ Latex Direct Agglutination Reaction [*Medicine*] (EDAA)
LDAR........ Leak Detection and Repair [*Chemical engineering*]
LDAR........ Lightning Detection and Ranging System [*Meteorology*]
LDAS........ LASER Detection and Analysis System (MCD)
LDA-SD..... Learning Disabilities Association of South Dakota (EARSL)
LDASE....... Large Deployable Antenna Shuttle Experiment [*NASA*] (PDAA)
LDAT........ Learning Disabilities Association of Texas (EARSL)
Ldata........ Life Data (DIPS)
LDAU........ Laboratory Data Adapter Unit (ACAE)
LDAZ........ Lazy Daze [*NCIC truck make code*]
LdB.......... Das Land der Bibel (BJA)
LDB.......... Genetic Location Database (SAUO)
LDB.......... Lamb Dysentery Bacillus [*Medicine*] (DMAA)
LDB.......... Launch Data Bus [*Computer science*] (MCD)
LDB.......... L. D. Brinkman & Co. (EFIS)
LDB.......... LDBrinkman Corporation (EFIS)
LDB.......... Leader Dogs for the Blind (EA)
LDB.......... Legionnaires Disease Bacillus [*Medicine*] (DMAA)
LDB.......... Legionnaire's Disease Bacterium
LDB.......... Legislative Data Base [*Department of Energy*] [*Information service or system*] (IID)
LDB.......... Leisure Diagnostic Battery [*Psychology*] (EDAC)
LDB.......... Lexington Development Branch (SAA)
LDB.......... Light Distribution Box (AAG)
LDB.......... Limited Data Block (KSC)
LDB.......... Liquidity Data Bank (NUMA)
LDB.......... Load Determining Bolt
LDB.......... Local Data Buffer (IAA)
LDB.......... Logical Database
LDB.......... Logistics Data Bank (NASA)
LDB.......... Londrina [*Brazil*] [*Airport symbol*] (OAG)
LDB.......... Lordsburg, NM [*Amtrak rail station code*]
LDB.......... Low-Drag Bomb
LDBC........ LDB Corp. (EFIS)
LDBC........ LD Brinkman Corporation (SAUO)
LDBCD....... LDB Corp. [*NASDAQ symbol*] (COMM)
LDBE........ London Diocesan Board of Education
LDBHS....... Louis D. Brandeis High School (SAUO)
Ld Birk...... Lord Birkenhead's Judgments, House of Lords [*England*] [*A publication*] (DLA)
LDBLC....... Low-Drag Boundary Layer Control [*Military*]
LDBOS....... LASER Designation Battlefield Obscuration Simulator (RDA)
Ld Br Sp.... Lord Brougham's Speeches [*A publication*] (DLA)
LDBS........ Land Data Bank System (SAUO)
LDBS........ Local Data Base System (MHDI)
LDC.......... Laboratory Data Control [*Commercial firm*]
LDC.......... Labor Data Collection (MCD)
LDC.......... Labor Day Committee [*Australia*]
LDC.......... Ladeco Cargo, SA [*Chile*] [*FAA designator*] (FAAC)
LDC.......... Lancashire Dynamo & Crypto Ltd. (SAUO)
LDC.......... Land Defense of CONUS (SAUO)
LDC.......... Large Diameter Core (SAA)
LDC.......... Lasco Development [*Federal Railroad Administration identification code*]
LDC.......... LASER Discharge Capacitor (IAA)
LDC.......... Latitude Data Computer
LDC.......... Launch Detection System (SAUS)
LDC.......... Laundry and Dry Cleaning International Union
LDC.......... Laydown Code Development (ACAE)
LDC.......... Learning Disability Center
LDC.......... Learning Disordered Children
LDC.......... Least Developed Countries (SAUO)
LDC.......... Le Dain Commission [*Medicine*] (EDAA)
LDC.......... Less Developed Countries (or Country) (SAUO)
LDC.......... Less Developed Country (JAGO)
LDC.......... Leukocyte Differential Count [*Medicine*] (MEDA)
LDC.......... Level Decision Circuit
LDC.......... Libertarian Defense Caucus [*Defunct*] (EA)
LDC.......... Library Development Center [*Columbia University*]
LDC.......... Library Development Consultants, Inc. [*Information service or system*] (IID)
LDC.......... Light Direction Center [*Military*]
LDC.......... Lightweight Deployable Communications System [*Army*]
LDC.......... Limiting Dilution Cloning [*Biochemistry*]
LDC.......... Linde Digital Control [*Automotive electronics*]
LDC.......... Lindeman Island [*Australia*] [*Airport symbol*]
LDC.......... Linear Detonating Cord (MSA)
LDC.......... Line Directional Coupler
LDC.......... Line-Drop Compensator (MSA)
LDC.......... Linguistic Data Consortium [*Defense Advanced Research Projects Agency*]
LDC.......... Linguistics Documentation Center [*University of Ottawa*] [*Database*] [*Canada*] (NITA)
LDC.......... Link Data Channel [*Communications term*] (DCT)
LDC.......... Load Drawer Computer (MCD)
LDC.......... Local Damping Control [*Automotive engineering*]
LDC.......... Local Data Concentrator [*Telecommunications*]
LDC.......... Local Defense Center
LDC.......... Local Dental Committee (SAUO)
LDC.......... Local Departmental Committee [*British labor*]
LDC.......... Local Development Company
LDC.......... Local Display Controller
LDC.......... Local Distribution Center (CCCA)
LDC.......... Local Distribution Center Telephone (SAUO)
LDC.......... Local Distribution Company
LDC.......... Location Dependent Code (VLIE)
LDC.......... Logical Device Coordinates (VLIE)
LDC.......... Logistics Data Center [*Army*] (AABC)
LDC.......... London Diagnostic Centre [*England*] (WDAA)
LDC.......... London Diocesan Council (SAUO)
LDC.......... London Dumping Convention [*Sets standards for disposal of wastes in oceans*]
LDC.......... Long Day Care
LDC.......... Long-Distance Call
LDC.......... Long Distance Carrier (VLIE)
LDC.......... Long-Distance Communications
LDC.......... Lotus Development Corporation (SAUO)
LDC.......... Low Density Center (VLIE)
LDC.......... Lower Dead Center
LDC.......... Low-Speed Data Channel
LDC.......... Lutheran Deaconess Conference (EA)
LDC.......... Lymphoid Dendritic Cell [*Medicine*] (EDAA)
LDC.......... Lysine Decarboxylase [*Medicine*] (EDAA)
LDCA........ Land Development Contractors' Association [*Australia*]
LDCC........ Laboratory Data Communications Center (SAUO)
LDCC........ Large Diameter Component Cask [*Nuclear energy*] (NRCH)
LDCC........ Lectin-Dependent Cell-Mediated Cytotoxicity [*Biochemistry*]
LDCC........ Local Disease Control Centre (SAUO)
LD-CELP.... Long Delay-Code Excited Linear Prediction
LD-CELP.... Low-Delay Code Excited Linear Prediction (SAUS)
LDCF........ Lymphocyte Derived Chemotactic Factor [*Biochemistry*]
LDCI........ Low-Dose Continuous Infusion [*Medicine*] (EDAA)
LDCIU....... Laundry and Dry Cleaning International Union (NTPA)
LDCL........ Loudcloud [*NASDAQ symbol*]
LDCM........ LANDesk Client Manager Technology [*Intel*] [*Computer science*]
LDCMMA.... Laundry and Dry Cleaners Machinery Manufacturers Association (SAUO)
LDCMWW... London Diocesan Council for Moral Welfare Work (SAUO)
LDCO........ Laundry and Dry Cleaning Operations [*Military*]
LDCO........ Leader Development Corporation (SAUO)
LDCP........ Landing Dynamics Computer Program [*NASA*]
LDCR........ Light-Duty Common Rail [*Automotive fuel systems*]
LDCR........ Lucas Diesel Common Rail [*Automotive engines*]
LDCRS....... Leachate Detection, Collection, and Removal System (EEVL)
LDCS........ Long-Distance Control System (IEEE)
LDC/SG...... Scientific Group on Dumping (SAUO)
LDCT........ Late Distal Cortical Tubule [*Medicine*] (DMAA)
LDCT........ Linear Discriminant Classification Tree [*Mathematics*]
LDCV........ Large Dense-Core Vesicle [*Neurobiology*]
LDCZ........ Louis-Dreyfus [*Federal Railroad Administration identification code*]
LDD.......... LASER Detector Diode

LDD LASER Diode Driver
LDD Late Dedifferentiation (DB)
LDD Letter of Determination of Dependency
LDD Light-Dark Discrimination [*Ophthalmology*]
LDD Light-Dependent Diode [*Instrumentation*]
LDD Light Duty Diesel (COE)
LDD Lightly Doped Drain (MCD)
LDD Little Diomede Island, AK [*Location identifier*] [*FAA*] (FAAL)
LDD Loaded
LDD Local Data Distribution
LDD Local Development District
LDD Logical Database Designer [*Computer science*]
LDD Logic Design Data [*Telecommunications*] (TEL)
LDD Long-Distance Dispersal [*Botany*]
LDD Low-Density Data (KSC)
LDD Luminaire Dirt Depreciation [*Floodlighting*]
LDD Lunar Dust Detector [*NASA*]
LDDB London Neurogenetics Database [*United Kingdom*] (GDD)
LDDC Least-Developed Developing Country [*Trade status*]
LDDC Liquid Distribution for Dust Control [*Highway safety*]
LDDC London Docklands Development Corp. [*British*] (ECON)
LDDC Long-Distance Dialing Center (IAA)
LDDC Long Distance Direct Current [*Telecommunications*] (CIST)
LDDCS Laundry and Decontamination Drycleaning System [*Military*] (DWSG)
LDDI Less Developed Defence Industrial nation (SAUO)
LDDI Local Distributed Data Interface [*Telecommunications*]
LDDL Logical Data Definition Language (IAA)
LDDM LASER Doppler Displacement Meter (AAEL)
LDDMWG LGSOWG Data Distribution and Marketing Working Group (SAUO)
LDDO Long-Distance Diesel Oil (PDAA)
LDDO Long-Drain Diesel Oil [*Fuels and lubricants*]
LDDS LDDS Communications, Inc. (SAUO)
LDDS Licentiate Doctor of Dental Surgery [*Medicine*] (EDAA)
LDDS Light Division Direct Support [*Artillery system*] (MCD)
LDDS Limited Distance Data Service [*Telecommunications*]
LDDS Limited Distance Data Set [*Modem*] (NITA)
LDDS Local Dentist (DAVI)
LDDS Local Digital Data Service [*Communications term*] (DCT)
LDDS Local Digital Distribution Subsystem
LDDS Local Doctor of Dental Surgery (MAE)
LDDS Long-Distance Discount Service [*Telecommunications*]
LDDS Long Distance Discount Services Co. (SAUO)
LDDS Low-Density Data System
LDDT Light-Duty Diesel Truck [*Automotive emissions*]
LDDV Light Duty Diesel Vehicle [*VDOT*] (TAG)
LDDVX Lindner Dividend [*Mutual fund ticker symbol*] (SG)
LDE Lagrange Differential Equation
LDE Laminar Defect Examination (IEEE)
LDE Laser Detection Equipment
LDE Lauryl Diethanolamide [*Also, LDA*] [*Organic chemistry*]
LDE Les Dames d'Escoffier (EA)
LDE Lighting Director Engineer (NTCM)
LDE Linear Differential Equation
LDE Lineas Aereas del Estado [*Argentina*] [*ICAO designator*] (FAAC)
LDE Local Dynamics Experiment [*Marine science*] (MSC)
LDE Long-Delayed Echo
LDE Long-Duration Exposure
LDE Lourdes/Tarbes [*France*] [*Airport symbol*] (OAG)
LDeB Beauard Parish Library, DeRidder (SAUS)
LDeB Beauregard Parish Library, DeRidder, LA [*Library symbol*] [*Library of Congress*] (LCLS)
L Dec Land Office Decisions, United States [*A publication*] (DLA)
LDEC Lunar Docking Events Controller [*NASA*] (MCD)
LDEF Long-Duration Exposure Facility [*NASA*]
LDEG Laus Deo et Gloria [*Praise and Glory Be to God*] [*Latin*]
LDEI Les Dames d'Escoffier [*Association*] (EA)
LDentSc Licentiate in Dental Science (SAUO)
L Dent Sci Licentiate in Dental Science (SAUO)
L-DEO Lamont-Doherty Earth Observatory (SAUO)
LDEO Lamont-Doherty Earth Observatory of Columbia University (SAUO)
LDEP Lancashire Dynamo Electronic Products (SAUO)
LDEQ Louisiana Department of Environmental Quality (SAUO)
LDERRY Londonderry [*County in Ireland*] (ROG)
LDET Level Detector (MSA)
LDEX Landing Exercise [*Navy*] (NVT)
LD-EYA Lombard-Dowell Egg Yolk Agar [*Microbiology*]
LDF Laboratory Directors Funds (ACAE)
LDF Land Disposal Facility
LDF Landed Duty Free
LDF Laser Demonstration Facility (SAUO)
LDF Laser Doppler Flowmetry (RAWO)
LDF Latin American Discovery Fund [*NYSE symbol*] (SPSG)
LDF Legal Defense and Educational Fund (SAUO)
LDF Legal Defense Fund (SAUO)
LDF Light Digital FACSIMILE [*Machine*]
LDF Light Distillate Feedstock (PDAA)
LDF Lightweight Digital Facsimile (SAUS)
LDF Linear Discriminant Function [*Mathematics*]
LDF Linear Driving Force
LDF Liquid Drop Experiment Facility (SAUS)
LDF Load Division Fault
LDF Load Factor (IAA)
LDF Local Defense Forces
LDF Local-Density Functional Equation (MCD)
LDF Local Density Functional Theory [*Chemistry*]
LDF London Diocesan Fund
LDF Lyme Disease Foundation
LDF NAACP [*National Association for the Advancement of Colored People*] Legal Defense and Educational Fund (EA)
LDFC Lew DeWitt Fan Club [*Defunct*] (EA)
LDFS London District Friendly Society (SAUO)
LDFSTN Landing Direction Finding Station [*Aviation*] (IAA)
LDG Lactic Dehydrogenase (DMAA)
LDG Lading (WDAA)
LDG Landing [*Maps and charts*] (AFM)
LDG Leading
LDG Left Digestive Gland
LDG Lexington Design Group (SAA)
LDG Libyan Desert Glass [*Archeology*]
LDG Linear Displacement Gauge
LDG Lingual Developmental Groove (DMAA)
LDG Loading
LDG Lodge [*or Lodging*] (MCD)
LDG Logistics Data Gateway (SAUO)
LDG Longs Drug Stores [*NYSE symbol*] (TTSB)
LDG Longs Drug Stores Corp. [*NYSE symbol*] (SPSG)
LDG Low-Density Gas
Ldg & Dly Landing and Delivery [*Shipping*] (DS)
LDGE LEM [*Lunar Excursion Module*] Dummy Guidance Equipment [*NASA*] (KSC)
LDGE Lodge [*Commonly used*] (OPSA)
LDGLT Leading Light [*Navigation signal*]
LDGN Lawrence Lindgren [*Common carrier symbol*]
LDGO Lamont Doherty Geological Observatory [*Marine science*] (OSRA)
L-DGO Lamont-Doherty Geological Observatory [*Formerly, LGO*] [*Columbia University*]
LDGP Liverpool Division of General Practice (SAUO)
LDGP Low-Drag, General Purpose (SAUO)
LDGPS Local DGPS [*Differential*][*Global Positioning System*] (GAVI)
LDGSPTBN Landing Support Battalion (DNAB)
Ld Gt Land Grant (MHDB)
LDGT Light-Duty Gasoline-fueled Truck [*Automotive engineering*]
LDGT Light-Duty Gasoline Truck (EPAT)
Ldg Tel Leading Telegraphist
LDGV Light-Duty Gasoline Vehicle
LDGX Lodgistix, Inc. [*NASDAQ symbol*] (COMM)
LDH Lactate Dehydrogenase [*Also, LAD, LD*] [*An enzyme*]
LDH Lactic Dehydrogenase
LDH Lacto Dehydrogenase [*Medicine*] (BCRP)
L d'H Legion d'Honneur [*French decoration*]
LDH Ligue des Droits de l'Homme [*France*]
LDH Limiting Dome Height [*Automotive metal stamping*]
LDH London District Headquarters (SAUO)
LDH Lord Howe Island [*Australia*] [*Airport symbol*] (OAG)
LDHA Lactic Dehydrogenase A (DB)
LDHB Lactic Dehydrogenase B (DB)
LDHC Lactic Dehydrogenase-C (DMAA)
LDHC Locker Door Hydraulic Cylinder
LDHD Lymphocyte-Depletion Hodgkin's Disease [*Medicine*]
LDHI Lactic Dehydrogenase Isoenzymes (DAVI)
LDHILS Laser Designator Hardware in the Loop Simulation (ACAE)
LDHK Lactic Dehydrogenase-K (DMAA)
LDHM London Diocesan Home Mission [*or Missionary*]
LDHRR League for the Defense of Human Rights in Romania [*Paris, France*] (EAIO)
LDI Lacy Diversified Industries, Inc. (EFIS)
LDI Landing Direction Indicator [*ICAO*] (FAAC)
LDI LASER Desorption Ionization [*Spectroscopy*]
LDI Lauda Air [*Italy*] [*ICAO designator*] (FAAC)
LDI Life Detection Instrument
LDI Lindi [*Tanzania*] [*Airport symbol*] (OAG)
LDI Linear Displacement Indicator
LDI Load Indicator
LDI Lockheed DataPlan, Inc. [*Information service or system*] (IID)
LDI Loredi Resources Ltd. [*Vancouver Stock Exchange symbol*]
LDI Lossless Digital Integrator (IAA)
LDI Low-Density Indication (MCD)
LDIC LDI Corp. [*NASDAQ symbol*] (SAG)
LDI Cp LDI Corp. [*Associated Press*] (SAG)
L Dict Law Dictionary [*A publication*] (DLA)
LDID Logical Disk Identifier (SAUS)
LDIH Left Direct Inguinal Hernia [*Medicine*] (DMAA)
LDII Larson Davis [*NASDAQ symbol*] (TTSB)
LDIM Luminescence Digital Imaging Microscopy
LDIN Lead-In Lighting [*or Lights*] [*Aviation*]
LDIN Lead in Lighting System (PIPO)
LDIN Lead-in-Light System [*FAA*] (TAG)
L-Dink Lower Class - Double [*or Dual*] Income, No Kids [*Lifestyle classification*]
LDIP Laboratory Data Integrity Program [*Environmental Protection Agency*] (GFGA)
LDIR Low-Dose Ionizing Radiation (MELL)
LDIS Low-data-rate Distributorless Ignition System [*Automotive engineering*]
L-DISC Late Direct Injection Stratified Charge
LDISCR Level Discriminator (MSA)
LD Is FFD Line of Departure Is Friendly Forward Disposition [*Army*] (AABC)
LDISO Lactic Dehydrogenase Isoenzymes (DAVI)

LD Is PPOS ... Line of Departure Is Present Positions [*Military*] (AABC)

LDIU ... Launch Data Interface Unit (MCD)

L Div ... Law Division (DLA)

L Div ... Licentiate in Divinity

LDJ ... Linden, NJ [*Location identifier*] [*FAA*] (FAAL)

LDJ ... Load D-Bank and Jump [*Computer science*]

LDJU ... Lovers of David Jones United (SAUO)

LDJU ... Luvers of David Jones United (EA)

LDK ... Lahn-Dill-Kreis [*German license plate city code*]

LDK ... Leelau [*Language symbol*] (ETLW)

LDK ... Lower Deck

Ld Ken ... Lord Kenyon's English King's Bench Reports [*1753-59*] [*A publication*] (DLA)

Ld Kenyon ... Lord Kenyon's English King's Bench Reports [*1753-59*] [*A publication*] (DLA)

Ld Kenyon (Eng) ... Lord Kenyon's English King's Bench Reports [*1753-59*] [*A publication*] (DLA)

LDL ... Lactate [*Medicine*] (EDAA)

LDL ... Lactic Dehydrogenase [*Medicine*] (EDAA)

LDL ... Lambda Delta Lambda (EA)

LDL ... Landing Direction Light [*Aviation*] (IAA)

LDL ... Language Description Language [*Computer science*]

LDL ... Learned Doctor of Laws

LDL ... Lighting Design Lumen (PDAA)

LDL ... Liquid Delay Line

LDL ... Logical Data Language [*Computer science*] (IAA)

LDL ... Logical Display List (MCD)

LDL ... Long Distance Love [*An association*] (EA)

LDL ... Loudness Discomfort Level (MAE)

LDL ... Low-Density Lipoprotein [*Biochemistry*]

LDL ... Lower Detectable Limit [*Chemical analysis*]

LDL ... Lower Detection Limit (AAEL)

LDL ... Lower Deviation Level (AABC)

LDL ... Lydall, Inc. [*NYSE symbol*] (SPSG)

LDL ... University of Nebraska, Lincoln, Lincoln, NE [*OCLC symbol*] (OCLC)

LDLA ... Limited Distance Line Adapter

LDLA ... Low-Density Lipoprotein Apheresis [*Medicine*] (DMAA)

LD/LC ... Line of Departure/Line of Contact [*Army*] (ADDR)

LDL-C ... Low-Density Lipoprotein-Cholesterol [*Biochemistry*]

LDLE ... Light-Duty Lathe Engine

LdLew ... Lewisville Public Library, Lewisville, ID [*Library symbol*] [*Library of Congress*] (LCLS)

LDLF ... LDL Transfer [*Common carrier symbol*]

LD-LISC ... Ligand-Driven Light-Induced Spin Changes [*Physics*]

LD LMT ... Load Limit (WDAA)

LDLN ... Long Distance Learning Network (SAUO)

LDLO ... Lethal Dose Low [*Environmental science*] (COE)

LD^{Lo} ... Lethal Dose Low (ERG)

LDLP ... Lithuanian Democratic Labor Party [*Political party*] (PSAP)

LDLP ... Low Density Lipoprotein [*Biochemistry*]

LDLR ... Land Development Law Reporter [*A publication*] (DLA)

LDLR ... Low-Density Lipoprotein Receptor [*Biochemistry*]

LDLR ... Low Density Lipoprotein Receptor Database (MHID)

LDLS ... Lesotho Department of Lands, Surveys and Physical Planning (SAUO)

Ldlw COO ... Laidlaw One, Inc. [*Associated Press*] (SAG)

LdlwOOO ... Laidlaw One, Inc. [*Associated Press*] (SAG)

LDM ... Laidlaw Transportation Ltd. [*Toronto Stock Exchange symbol*]

LDM ... LASER Drilling Machine

LDM ... Last Day of the Month (AFM)

LDM ... Lee, David M., Los Angeles CA [*STAC*]

LDM ... Libby Dam [*Montana*] [*Seismograph station code, US Geological Survey*] (SEIS)

LDM ... Licentiate of Dental Medicine

LDM ... Limited-Distance MODEM [*Computer science*]

LDM ... Linear Delta Modulation

LDM ... Load Distribution Matrix (IAA)

LDM ... Local Data Management (SAUO)

LDM ... Local Data Manager

LDM ... Logical Data Model (VLIE)

LDM ... Long-Delay Monostable [*Circuitry*]

LDM ... Long Distance Modem (VLIE)

LDM ... Lord Mayor

LDM ... Low-Density Microsome [*Cytology*]

LDM ... Ludington, MI [*Location identifier*] [*FAA*] (FAAL)

LDm ... Median Lethal Time (EES)

LDMA ... London Discount Market Association [*British*] (MHDW)

L/Dmax ... Point of Maximum Lift to Drag Ratio [*Aviation*] (PIPO)

LDME ... LASER Distance Measuring Equipment (DNAB)

LDMFA ... Laidlaw Transportation Ltd. (Class A) [*NASDAQ symbol*] (COMM)

LDMFB ... Laidlaw Transportation Ltd. (Class B) [*NASDAQ symbol*] (COMM)

LDMI ... LASER Distance Measuring Instrument

LDMK ... Landmark (KSC)

LDMK ... Landmark Bank for Savings (Massachusetts) [*NASDAQ symbol*] (COMM)

LDMK ... Landmark Systems Corp. [*NASDAQ symbol*] (NASQ)

LdmkBc ... Landmark Bancorp [*Associated Press*] (SAG)

LdmkGph ... Landmark Graphics Corp. [*Associated Press*] (SAG)

LDMM ... Leadville Mining & Milling Corp. (SAUO)

LDMOS ... Lateral Double-Diffused Metal-Oxide Semiconductor (MCD)

LDMOS ... Laterally Diffused Metal Oxide Semiconductor [*Electronics*]

LDMOS ... Laterally Diffused Metal-Oxide Semiconductor (AAEL)

LDMOS ... Latterally Diffused MOS (SAUS)

LD-MPT ... Ligue Democratique - Mouvement pour le Parti des Travailleurs [*Democratic League - Movement for the Workers' Party*] [*Senegal*] [*Political party*] (PPW)

LDMS ... Laboratory Data Management System [*IBM Corp.*]

LDMS ... LASER Desorption Mass Spectrometry

LDMS ... LASER Distance Measuring System

LDMS ... Lunar Distance Measuring System [*Aerospace*]

LDMS ... Region 2, Lab Data Management System (SAUS)

LDMTS ... Long Distance Message Telecommunications Service (VLIE)

LDMWA ... Low Drag Multi/Wire Antenna (CCCA)

LDMWR ... Limited Depot Maintenance Work Requirements

LDMX ... Local Digital Message Exchange (AABC)

Ldn ... Average Day-Night Sound Level [*Industrial hygiene term*] (OHS)

LDN ... Greater London (SAUS)

LDN ... Lamidanda [*Nepal*] [*Airport symbol*] (OAG)

LDN ... Lightning Detection Network [*Electric Power Research Institute*]

LDN ... Linden, VA [*Location identifier*] [*FAA*] (FAAL)

LDN ... Listed Directory Number [*Bell System*]

LDN ... Local Data Network (SAUS)

LDN ... Locally Defined Neighborhood

LDN ... London [*Ontario*] [*Seismograph station code, US Geological Survey*] (SEIS)

LDN ... London [*England*]

LDN ... London Silver Corp. [*Vancouver Stock Exchange symbol*]

LDNA ... Long-Distance Navigation Aid

LD-NEYA ... Lombard-Dowell Neomycin Egg Yolk Agar [*Microbiology*]

LDNF ... London Foundation (SAUO)

LDNG ... Loading

LDNRX ... Lindner Growth Fund [*Mutual fund ticker symbol*] (SG)

LDNS ... Laser Doppler Navigation System (SAUS)

LDNS ... Lightweight Doppler Navigation System (MCD)

LDO ... Ladouanie [*Suriname*] [*Airport symbol*] (OAG)

LDO ... Laminated Diatom Ooze [*Oceanography*]

LDO ... Language Dependent Objects (VLIE)

LDO ... Laredo, TX [*Amtrak Busline code*]

LDO ... Launch Division Officer [*Missiles*] (MUGU)

LDO ... Licensed Deck Officer (SAUO)

LDO ... Light Diesel Oil (IAA)

LDO ... Limited Duties (or Duty) Officer (SAUO)

LDO ... Limited Duty Officer [*Navy*]

LDO ... Linear Diophantine Object

LDO ... Local Dental Officer

LDO ... Logical Device Order [*Computer science*] (IBMDP)

LDO ... Long-Distance Oil [*Service mark*] [*Amoco Oil Co.*]

LDO ... Low-Density Oil [*Petroleum industry*]

LDO ... Low-Density Overlay [*Plywood*]

LDO ... Low Drop Out

LDO ... St. Mary's Dominican College, New Orleans, LA [*OCLC symbol*] (OCLC)

LDOCE ... Longman's Dictionary of Contemporary English [*A publication*]

LDOCF ... Long Distance Operational Control Facility (SAUS)

LDOE ... Longitude Drift/Orbit Eccentricity (ACAE)

LDOM ... Lorenz Domination [*Statistics*]

L-DOPA ... Levo-Dihydroxyphenylalanine [*Pharmacology*]

L-dopa ... Levodopa (WDAA)

LDOS ... Leather Dressers' Old Society [*A union*] [*British*]

LDOS ... Local Density of Electron States [*Physical chemistry*]

LDOS ... Local Density of States [*Solid state physics*]

LDOS ... Lord's Day Observance Society [*British*]

LDP ... Laban ng Demokratikong Pilipino [*Democratic Filipino's Struggle*] [*Political party*]

LDP ... Label Distribution Protocol (VLIE)

LDP ... Laboratory Data Processor (IAA)

LDP ... Laboratory Data Products (VLIE)

LDP ... Laboratory Distribution Panel

LDP ... Lactate [*Medicine*] (EDAA)

LDP ... Lactic Dehydrogenase [*Medicine*] (EDAA)

LDP ... Ladyship [*or Lordship*]

LDP ... Landed Duty Paid [*Military*]

LDP ... Langmuir Diffusion Pump [*Engineering*]

LDP ... Language Data Processing (MSA)

LDP ... Large Developmental Plant [*Project*] [*Department of Energy*]

LDP ... Laser Designator Pod (SAUS)

LDP ... Leadership Development Projects [*National Science Foundation*]

LDP ... Leaflet Dispensing Pod

LDP ... League for Democracy and Peace [*Myanmar*] [*Political party*] (EY)

LDP ... Leak Detection Pump [*Automotive engineering*]

LDP ... Left Dorso-Posterior [*A fetal position*] [*Obstetrics*]

LDP ... Lesotho Democratic Party (SAUO)

LDP ... Liberal Democratic Party [*Slovenia*] [*Political party*] (EY)

LDP ... Liberal-Democratic Party of Japan [*Jiyu-Minshuto*] [*Political party*] (PPW)

LDP ... Liberal Demokratische Partei [*Liberal Democratic Party*] [*Germany*] [*Political party*] (PPE)

LDP ... Lietuviy Demokraty Partija [*Lithuanian Democratic Party*] [*Political party*] (PPE)

LDP ... Limited Denial of Participation (SAUO)

LDP ... Linux Documentation Project (SAUO)

LDP ... Lithuanian Democratic Party (SAUO)

L/DP ... Living/Dying Project (EA)

LDP ... Local Data Package (KSC)

LDP ... Local Data Processor (AABC)

LDP ... Local Distribution Point (SAUS)

LDP ... Logistics Data Package

LDP ... Logistics Development Program (DOMA)

LDP Lomas Data Products [*Marlboro, MA*] [*Computer manufacturer*]
LDP London Daily Price [*British*]
LDP Long-Day Plant [*Botany*]
LDP Lordship [*British*]
LDP Lorentz Doppler Profile [*Physics*]
LDP Low Density Plasma (AAEL)
LDP Lumbo-Dorsal Pain (SAUS)
LDP Lung Damaging Particle
LDPC Logistic Data Processing Centre (SAUO)
LDPD Liberal-Demokratische Partei Deutschlands [*Liberal Democratic Party of Germany*] [*Political party*] (PPW)
LDPE Low-Density Polyethylene [*Polymer*]
LDP Group Laboratory Data Products Group (SAUO)
LDPHDN Lead Additive Report for Refineries and Importers and for Manufacturing (SAUO)
LDPN Low-Density Phenolic Nylon [*Polymer*]
LDPR Liberal Democratic Party of Russia [*Political party*] (PSAP)
LDPS L-Band Digital Phase Shifter
LDPT Load Point (VLIE)
LDQ Laboratory and Data Quality (SAUO)
LDQ Leaders Equity Corp. [*Vancouver Stock Exchange symbol*]
LDQ Lobe-Dominated Quasar [*Astronomy*]
LDR Aero Lider SA de CV [*Mexico*] [*ICAO designator*] (FAAC)
LDR County Londonderry (SAUS)
LDR Labor, Delivery, Recovery Room [*Medicine*]
LDR Labor Distribution Record
LDR Landauer, Inc. [*AMEX symbol*] (SPSG)
LDR Land Disposal Restriction (COE)
LDR Land Disposal Restrictions [*Environmental Protection Agency*]
LDR Landmark Resources Ltd. [*Vancouver Stock Exchange symbol*]
LDR Large Deployable Reflector [*Astronomy*]
LDR LASER Designator Range (MCD)
LDR Laser Designator Receiver (ACAE)
LDR Latest Date of Release (WDAA)
ldr Leader (GEAB)
LDR Leader
LDR Leading Deep Recess [*Rotary automotive engine*]
LDR Ledger (ADA)
LDR Length-Diameter Ratio
LDR Level Distribution Recorder
LDR Liberal, Democratic, and Reformist Group [*European political movement*] (ECON)
Ldr Lidar (SAUS)
LDR Light Dependent Resistor
LDR Light Detect Resistor (SAUS)
LDR Light-to-Dark Ratio
LDR Limited Distribution Reports (SAUO)
LDR Limiting Drawing Ratio (MCD)
LDR Linear Decision Rule
LDR Linear Depolarization Ratio
LDR Linear Dynamic Range
LDR Line Driver-Receiver [*Computer communication*] (TEL)
LDR Link Loader (VLIE)
LDR Liquid Droplet Radiator (MCD)
LDR Llandore [*Welsh depot code*]
LDR Loader (MSA)
LDR Loan Default Rate [*Banking term*]
LDR Lodar [*South Arabia*] [*Airport symbol*] (AD)
LDR Log Dose Response [*Biochemical analysis*]
LDR Long Distance Relationship [*Internet lingo*] (NETL)
LDR Lorentz Double Refraction [*Physics*]
L/DR Lounge/Dining Room [*Classified advertising*] (ADA)
LDR Low Data Rate [*RADAR*]
LDR Low Data Rate [*Automotive engineering*]
LDR Low Data Register [*Computer science*]
LDR Low-Density, Recorder
LDR Low Dose Rate [*Medicine*]
LDR Lutheran Disaster Response [*Emergency Management*] (EMA)
LDRA Low Data Rate Auxiliary [*RADAR*]
Ld Ray Lord Raymond's King's Bench and Common Pleas Reports [*1694-1732*] [*A publication*] (DLA)
Ld Raym Lord Raymond's King's Bench and Common Pleas Reports [*1694-1732*] [*A publication*] (DLA)
LDRC Libel Defense Resource Center (EA)
LDRC Lumber Dealers Research Council [*Defunct*] (EA)
LDRD Laboratory-Directed Research and Development (SAUO)
LDRDA Long Distance Running Directors Association (EA)
LDRER Launderer
LDRF Long-Distance Range Finder (SSD)
LDRG Liberal, Democratic and Reformist Group [*See also GLDR*] (EAIO)
LDRI Learning Disabilities Research Institute [*University of Virginia*] (EDAC)
LDRI Low Data Rate Input [*RADAR*]
LDRIACS Low Data Rate Integrated Acoustic Communications System [*Military*] (CAAL)
LDRL Landstar TLC [*Common carrier symbol*]
LDRM LASER Designator Rangefinding Module (RDA)
LDRN Lode Runner [*Common carrier symbol*]
LDRP Labor, Delivery, Recovery, Post-Partum [*Medicine*] (MEDA)
LDRP Learning Disability Rating Procedure [*Educational test*]
LDRPS Labor-Delivery-Recovery-Postpartum Suite (HCT)
LDRR Laboratory of Diagnostic Radiology Research (ADWA)
LDRR Louisiana & Delta Railroad [*Federal Railroad Administration identification code*]
LDRRDDB Land Disposal Restrictions Rule Development (SAUO)
LDRRIM Low-Density Reinforced Reaction Injection Molding [*Plastics*]
LDRS Labor-Delivery-Recovery Suite (HCT)
LDRS LASER Discrimination RADAR System
L/DRS Level and Density Recorder Switch [*Nuclear energy*] (NRCH)
LDRSHP Leadership
LDRSP Leadership (AFM)
LDRT [*The*] Lake Front Dock & Railroad Terminal Co. [*Formerly, LDT*] [*AAR code*]
LDRT Low Data Rate [*RADAR*] (IAA)
LDRTF Land Disposal Restrictions Task Force [*Environmental Protection Agency*] (GFGA)
LDRY Landry's Seafood Restaurants [*NASDAQ symbol*] (TTSB)
LDRY Landrys Seafood Restaurants, Inc. [*NASDAQ symbol*] (SAG)
LDRY Laundry (AFM)
LDryNG Louis Dreyfus Natural Gas [*Associated Press*] (SAG)
LDS Church of Jesus Christ and Latter Day Saints (SAUO)
LDS Havre, MT [*Location identifier*] [*FAA*] (FAAL)
LDS Labor Distribution System (TIMI)
LDS Lakeland Dialect Society (SAUO)
LDS Lancashire Dialect Society (SAUO)
LDS Landing/Deceleration Subsystem [*NASA*] (NASA)
LDS Landing, Deservicing, and Safing [*NASA*] (KSC)
LDS Landkreis Dahme-Spreewald [*German license plate city code*]
LDS Langmuir Dark Space [*Electronics*]
LDS Language for Description and Functional Specification (VLIE)
LDS Large Disk Storage [*Computer science*] (IEEE)
LDS Laser Dazzle Sight (SAUS)
LDS LASER Deep Space
LDS LASER Designator System [*Rangefinder*] (MCD)
LDS Laser Detecting Set (SAUS)
LDS Laser Detection System
LDS Laser Docking Sensor (SAUS)
LDS LASER Drilling System
LDS Last Data Sample (IAA)
LDS Latter-Day Saints [*Mormons*]
LDS Launch Data System [*NASA*] (KSC)
LDS Launch Detection Satellite [*Former USSR*]
LDS Laus Deo Semper [*Praise to God Always*] [*Latin*]
LDS Layered Defense System (MCD)
LDS Lead Design Supervisor [*Engineering*]
LDS Leader Development Study [*Army*]
LDS Leads (VLIE)
LDS Leak Detection System [*Nuclear energy*] (NRCH)
LDS Lethal Defense System (MCD)
LDS Lexington Developmental Scales [*Child development test*]
LDS Liberal Democracy of Slovenia [*Political party*] (PSAP)
LDS Licentiate in Dental Surgery
LDS Lietuviu Darbininku Susivienijimas [*Association of Lithuanian Workers*] (EA)
LDS Ligating and Dividing Stapler [*Used surgical procedures*] (DAVI)
LDS Light Distillate Spirit (PDAA)
LDS Lightweight Decontamination System (INF)
LDS Linear Dynamic System
LDS Liquid, Diesel-Cycle, Supercharged
LDS Loads [*Military*]
LDS Local Dependant Services (SAUO)
LDS Local Development Scheme (SAUO)
LDS Local Digital Switch [*Telecommunications*] (TEL)
LDS Local Distribution Service [*Cable TV network*] (NITA)
LDS Local Distribution System [*or Service*] [*Cable television*] (MDG)
LDS Locked Door Seclusion [*Medicine*] (DMAA)
LDS Logistics Data Sheet
LDS Logistics Data System (SAUO)
LDS Long Distance Savers
LDS Long Distance Swimmer
LDS Longitudinal Direct Substitution Imputation Procedure [*Bureau of the Census*] (GFGA)
LDS Loral Defense Systems Corp. (SAUO)
LDS Louis Douglas Serrurier [*Motorsports*]
LDS Lucey-Driscoll Syndrome [*Medicine*] (MELL)
LDS Lunar Drill System [*NASA*]
LDSA Logistics Doctrine and Systems Agency [*Army*] (MCD)
LDSBCAA LDS Business College Alumni Association (EA)
LDSC Layered Defense Systems Countermeasures (ACAE)
LDSc Licentiate in Dental Science [*British*]
ldscp Landscape (VRA)
LDSD LeadingSide [*OTCBB symbol*]
LDSD LeadingSide, Inc. [*NASDAQ symbol*] (QUAN)
LDSD Lookdown/Shootdown (MCD)
LDSD Low Dimensional Structures and Devices [*British*]
LDSFE Fuel Economy (SAUO)
LDSG Long Distance Signal Group (SAUO)
LDSH Ladish Co. [*NASDAQ symbol*] (SG)
LDSI Licentiate in Dental Surgery, Ireland (SAUO)
LDSJ Little Daughters of St. Joseph [*Roman Catholic religious order*]
LDSO Logistics Doctrine and Systems Office [*Army*]
LDSP Lietuvos Socialdemokratu Partija [*Social Democratic Party of Lithuania*] [*Political party*] (EAIO)
LDSR League of Distilled Spirits Rectifiers [*Defunct*]
LDSRA Logistics Doctrine Systems and Readiness Agency [*Army*] (AABC)
LDSRCPS Licentiate in Dental Surgery of the Royal College of Physicians and Surgeons (SAUO)

LDSRCPS Glas... Licentiate in Dental Surgery of the Royal College of Physicians and Surgeons of Glasgow [*British*]
LDSRCS..... Licentiate in Dental Surgery of the Royal College of Surgeons [*British*]
LDSRCSEd... Licentiate in Dental Surgery of the Royal College of Surgeons of Edinburgh (DI)
LDSRCS Edin... Licentiate in Dental Surgery of the Royal College of Surgeons of Edinburgh [*British*]
LDSRC-SEng........ Licentiate in Dental Surgery of the Royal College of Surgeons in England (SAUO)
LDSRCS Eng... Licentiate in Dental Surgery of the Royal College of Surgeons of England
LDSRCSI.... Licentiate in Dental Surgery of the Royal College of Surgeons in Ireland (SAUO)
LDSRCS Irel... Licentiate in Dental Surgery of the Royal College of Surgeons in Ireland
LD-SRIM.... Low-Density Structural Reaction Injection Molding [*Plastics*]
LDSS........ LASER Designator Search System
LDSS........ Lunar Deep Seismic Sounding [*Aerospace*] (MCD)
LDSSIG...... Learning Disabled Student SIG [*Special Interest Group*] (EA)
LDST........ Landis Transportation [*Common carrier symbol*]
LDST........ Letdown Storage Tank [*Nuclear energy*] (NRCH)
LDSU........ Local Digital Service Unit [*Communications term*] (DCT)
LDSU........ Local Distribution Service Unit (IAA)
LDSU2....... Local Digital Service Unit-Model 2 [*Communications term*] (DCT)
LDT.......... [*The*] Lake Front Dock & Railroad Terminal Co. [*Later, LDRT*] [*AAR code*]
LDT.......... Language Dependent Translator
LDT.......... Laser Detector Tracker (SAUS)
LDT.......... LASER Discharge Tube
LDT.......... Lateral Dorsal Tract [*Neuroanatomy*]
LDT.......... L-DOPA Test [*Endocrinology*]
LDT.......... Left Dorsotransverse [*Medicine*] (DMAA)
LDT.......... Level Delay Time
LDT.......... Level Detector (KSC)
LDT.......... Library Development Team
LDT.......... Licensed Deposit-Taking Institution [*British*]
LDT.......... Light Displacement Ton [*MARAD*] (TAG)
LDT.......... Light-Duty Truck
LDT.......... Lightning Data Transport
LDT.......... Linear Differential Transformer
LDT.......... Linear Displacement Transduced (MCD)
LDT.......... Local Daylight Saving Time
LDT.......... Local Descriptor Table [*Computer science*]
LDT.......... Logical Design Translator (NITA)
LDT.......... Logical Device Table (IAA)
LDT.......... Logic Design Translator [*Computer science*]
LDT.......... Logistic Delay Time (CAAL)
LDT.......... London Dipole Theory
LDT.......... Long Distance Transmission (BUR)
LDT.......... Long Dry Ton
LDT.......... Lowest Dose Tested [*Environmental science*] (EPAT)
LDT.......... Lubbock, TX [*Location identifier*] [*FAA*] (FAAL)
LDTA........ Leak Detection Technology Association (EA)
LDTC........ Lawndale Transportation Co. [*AAR code*]
LDTC........ Learning Disabilities Teacher Consultant
LDTD........ Lousiana Department of Transportation and Development (SAUO)
LD/TE....... Line Driver/Terminal Equipment (MCD)
LDTEL....... Long Distance Telephone [*Telecommunications*] (IAA)
LDTF........ Large Dynamic Test Facility (SAUO)
LDTF........ Light of Divine Truth Foundation (EA)
LDTM........ Lander Dynamic Test Model [*NASA*]
LDTM........ Light-Duty Tank Target Mechanism (SAUS)
LDTO........ Long-Distance Telegraph Office (SAUO)
LDTOF....... LASER Desorption Time-of-Flight [*Spectrometry*]
LDTR........ Load Descriptor Table Register (SAUO)
LDTR........ Long Dwell Time RADAR (NATG)
LDTRC....... Local Descriptor Table Register Cache (SAUO)
LDTS........ Laser Designator Targeting System (ACAE)
LDTS........ Laser Designator Tracker System (ACAE)
LDT/SCAM... Laser Detector & Tracker-Strike Camera (SAUS)
LDTTWA..... Let's Do the Time Warp Again [*Internet lingo (reference to the movie "Rocky Horror Picture Show")*] (NETL)
LDTTY....... Landing Line Teletype
LDU.......... Lahad Datu [*Malaysia*] [*Airport symbol*] (OAG)
LDU.......... Lamp Dimmer Unit (MCD)
LdU.......... Landesring der Unabhaengigen [*Independent Party*] [*Switzerland*] [*Political party*] (PPE)
LDU.......... Launcher Display Unit (SAUS)
LDU.......... Leather Dressers' Union [*British*]
LDU.......... Line Driver Unit [*Computer communication*] (MCD)
LDU.......... Local Defence Union (SAUO)
LDU.......... Local Delivery Unit
LDUA........ Light-Duty Utility Arm (ABAC)
LDUB........ Long Double Upright Brace [*Medicine*]
LDUF........ Leduff Trucking [*Common carrier symbol*]
LDUH........ Low-Dose Unfractionated Heparin [*Medicine*] (DMAA)
LD/USA..... Long Distance/USA, Inc. [*Honolulu, HI*] [*Telecommunications*] (TSSD)
LDV.......... Lactic Dehydrogenase Virus
LDV.......... Large Dense-Cored Vesicle [*Medicine*] (DMAA)
LDV.......... LASER Doppler Velocimeter
LDV.......... Laser Doppler Velocimetry [*Medicine*] (MELL)
LDV.......... Leadville [*Nevada*] [*Seismograph station code, US Geological Survey*] [*Closed*] (SEIS)
LDV.......... League of Disabled Voters (EA)
LDV.......... Lectus Developments Ltd. [*Vancouver Stock Exchange symbol*]
LDV.......... Leyland DAF (van Doorne Automobiel Fabriek) Vans [*Vehicle manufacturer*]
LDV.......... Light Delivery Vehicle
LDV.......... Light-Duty Vehicle
LDV.......... Linear Differential Vector
LDV.......... Local Defence Volunteers [*Later called Home Guards*] [*British*] [*World War II*]
LDV.......... Low-Dollar Value
LDVA........ Lodi District Vintners Association (EA)
LDVE........ Linear Differential Vector Equation
LDVS........ Logistics Data Validation System (SAUO)
LDW.......... Laidlaw Inc. [*NYSE symbol*] (SAG)
LDW.......... Lane Departure Warning [*Automotive electronics*]
LDW.......... Left Defense Wing [*Women's lacrosse position*]
LDW.......... Liability Damage Waiver [*Insurance*]
LDW.......... Licensed Driver's Waiver (BARN)
LDW.......... Loss Damage Waiver [*Insurance*] (TVEL)
LDWA........ Long Distance Walkers Association [*British*] (DBA)
LDWSS...... LASER Designator Weapon System Simulation (RDA)
LDWY........ Landstar Inway [*Common carrier symbol*]
LDX.......... Long-Distance Xerography [*Xerox Corp.*] [*Communications facsimile system*]
LDXL........ Large Diameter Extended Length [*Space launch term*] (ISAK)
LDY.......... Lancashire and Derbyshire Yeomanry (SAUO)
LDY.......... Laundry
LDY.......... Leicestershire and Derbyshire Yeomanry [*Military unit*] [*British*]
LDY.......... Londonderry [*Northern Ireland*] [*Airport symbol*] (OAG)
LDZ.......... Lodz [*Poland*] [*Airport symbol*] (AD)
LDZ.......... St. Louis, MO [*Location identifier*] [*FAA*] (FAAL)
LE............ Antenna Effective Length for Electric-Field Antennas (IEEE)
LE............ Caribbean Council of Legal Education (SAUO)
LE............ Eunice Public Library, Eunice, LA [*Library symbol*] [*Library of Congress*] (LCLS)
LE............ Laboratory Essential (SAUO)
LE............ Laboratory Evaluation (MUGU)
LE............ Laboratory of Electronics [*Rockefeller University*] [*Research center*] (RCD)
LE............ Labor Exchange
LE............ Labour Exchange (SAUO)
LE............ Lacrosse Encephalitis [*Emergency Management*] (EMA)
LE............ Lactate Extraction [*Medicine*] (DMAA)
LE............ Lafayette Escadrille (ACAE)
LE............ Lands' End [*NYSE symbol*] (SPSG)
LE............ LAN [*Local Area Network*] Emulation [*Computer science*]
LE............ Large End (OA)
LE............ LASER Electronics (MCD)
LE............ Latent Heat (SAUS)
LE............ Lateral Element
LE............ Lateral Epicondyle [*Anatomy*]
LE............ Latest Estimate [*Business term*]
LE............ Launch Eject
LE............ Launch Electronics
L/E........... Launch Encounter [*NASA*] (KSC)
LE............ Launch Escape [*NASA*] (KSC)
LE............ Launching Equipment
LE............ Law Enforcement
LE............ Laws of Eshnunna (BJA)
LE............ Lawyers' Edition, United States Supreme Court Reports [*A publication*] (DLA)
LE............ Lazy Eye (MELL)
LE............ Lead Engineer (AAG)
LE............ Leading Edge [*Aerospace*]
LE............ Lease
LE............ Leave Edge (DGA)
LE............ Lebanese International Airways (SAUO)
le............ Lebanon [*MARC country of publication code*] [*Library of Congress*] (LCCP)
LE............ Lector
Le............ Ledge
LE............ Lee-Enfield [*British military*] (DMA)
LE............ Left Ear (DMAA)
LE............ Left End
LE............ Left Extremity
LE............ Left Eye
LE............ Leg Exercise [*Sports medicine*]
LE............ Length (IAA)
Le............ Leonard [*Unit for cathode rays*]
LE............ Leone [*Monetary unit*] [*Sierra Leone*]
LE............ Less or Equal (SAUO)
LE............ Less than or Equal
LE............ Leucine Enkephalin [*Biochemistry*]
LE............ Leucocyte Elastase [*An enzyme*]
LE............ Leukemia [*Oncology*]
LE............ Leukocyte Esterase (MELL)
LE............ Leukoerythrogenetic (MAE)
LE............ Levy Industries Ltd. [*Toronto Stock Exchange symbol*]
Le............ Lewis [*Blood group*]
Le............ Lewis Number [*IUPAC*]
LE............ Library Edition (ADA)
LE............ Life Expectancy (MELL)
LE............ Lifting Eye
LE............ Light Equipment
LE............ Limited Edition (ADA)

LE........... Limit of Endurance [*Materials testing*]
LE........... Limits of Error
LE........... Linear Expansion [*Physics*]
LE........... Line Equipment [*Telecommunications*] (TEL)
LE........... Linkage Editor (IAA)
LE........... Linkage Equilibrium [*Genetics*]
LE........... Link Encapsulation (MLOA)
L-E........... List/Enumerate (SAUS)
LE........... Local Area Network Emulation [*Computer science*] (DDC)
LE........... Local Exchange [*Telecommunications*] (TEL)
LE........... Locally Engaged
LE........... Locally Excited [*Physical chemistry*]
LE........... Logic Element
LE........... Logistic Effectiveness (CAAL)
LE........... Logistic Evaluation
LE........... London Electricity (ODA)
LE........... Long-Evans Rat
LE........... Loop Error [*Computer science*] (ELAL)
LE........... Loop Extender [*Telecommunications*] (TEL)
LE........... Louisiana Eastern Railroad [*AAR code*]
LE........... Low Efficiency
LE........... Low Energy (CAAL)
LE........... Low Entry [*Truck cab*]
LE........... Lower Epidermis [*Botany*]
LE........... Lower Extremity [*Medicine*]
LE........... Low Explosive [*Military*]
LE........... Low Exposure (MELL)
LE........... Lugalbanda and Enmerkar (BJA)
LE........... Lugalbanda Epos (BJA)
LE........... Lunar Ephemeris
LE........... Lupus Erythematosus [*Hematology*]
LE........... Luxury Edition [*Automobile model designation*]
LE........... Magnum Airlines [*ICAO designator*] (AD)
Le........... [*The*] Twenty-Four Books of the Holy Scriptures (1853) [*I. Leeser*] (BJA)
LE 2d........ Lawyer's Edition, United States Supreme Court Reports, Second Series [*A publication*] (DLA)
LE 29060... Vinblastine Sulfate [*Medicine*] (EDAA)
LEA.......... Laborista Esperanto-Asocio (SAUO)
LEA.......... Labour Education Authority (SAUO)
LEA.......... Landes-Entschaedigungsamt (BJA)
LEA.......... Language Experience Approach [*Education*]
LEA.......... Latest Epicardial Activation [*Cardiology*]
LEA.......... Launch Enable Alarm (MCD)
LEA.......... Launcher Electronics Assembly (ACAE)
LEA.......... Launch Escape Assembly [*NASA*] (KSC)
LEA.......... Law Enforcement Agencies (DOMA)
LEA.......... Law Enforcement Agency (SAUO)
LEA.......... Law Enforcement Assistance (SAUO)
LEA.......... Law Enforcement Assistance Program (EA)
LEA.......... Lead [*South Dakota*] [*Seismograph station code, US Geological Survey*] [*Closed*] (SEIS)
LEA.......... Lead Air Jet Service [*France*] [*ICAO designator*] (FAAC)
LEA.......... Leader Resources, Inc. [*Vancouver Stock Exchange symbol*]
LEA.......... Leaf (SAUS)
lea.......... League (WDAA)
LEA.......... League [*Unit of measurement*]
LEA.......... Lear Corp. [*NYSE symbol*] [*Formerly, Lear Seating*] (SG)
LEA.......... Learmonth [*Australia*] [*Airport symbol*] (OAG)
LEA.......... Learning Experience Approach [*Education*] (EDAC)
LEA.......... Lear Seating Co. [*NYSE symbol*] (SAG)
Lea.......... Lea's Tennessee Reports [*A publication*] (DLA)
lea.......... Leather (VRA)
LEA.......... Leather
LEA.......... Leave
LEA.......... Letter Enjoyers Association (EA)
LEA.......... Librarians, Editors, Authors. Pan American Union. Washington (SAUO)
LEA.......... Light-Emitting Array
LEA.......... Limited Exclusion Area (SAUO)
LEA.......... Linear Embedding Algorithm (PDAA)
LEA.......... Line Equalizing Amplifier (AFM)
LEA.......... Load Effective Address [*Computer science*]
LEA.......... Local Education Agency [*School district*] [*HEW*] (OICC)
LEA.......... Local Educational Agency (SAUO)
LEA.......... Local Education Area (SAUO)
LEA.......... Local Education Authority [*British*] (WDAA)
LEA.......... Local Employment Act [*Town planning*] [*British*]
LEA.......... Local Enforcement Agency (SARE)
LEA.......... Local Enterprise Agency (EURO)
LEA.......... Local Examination Authority (SAUO)
LEA.......... Locomotive Engineers Association (SAUO)
LEA.......... Logistic Evaluation Agency [*Army*]
LEA.......... Logistics Engineering Analysis (NASA)
LEA.......... Logistics Evaluation Activity [*Army*]
LEA.......... Logistics Evaluation Agency (SAUO)
LEA.......... Long-Endurance Aircraft
LEA.......... Longitudinally Excited Atmosphere [*LASER technology*] (EECA)
LEA.......... Loop Extension Amplifier
LEA.......... Loss Executives Association [*Parsippany, NJ*] (EA)
LEA.......... Lower Excess Air [*Combustion technology*]
LEA.......... Lower Extremity Amputation [*Medicine*] (DMAA)
LEA.......... Low-Excess-Air [*Combustion technology*]
LEA.......... Lumbar Epidural Anesthesia [*Medicine*] (EDAA)
LEA.......... Lutheran Education Association (EA)
LEAA......... Lace and Embroidery Association of America [*Later, Lace Importers Association*] (EA)
LEAA......... Law Enforcement Alliance of America Inc. Fund for Responsible Government [*Falls Church, VA*] (PACS)
LEAA......... Law Enforcement Assistance Act
LEAA......... Law Enforcement Assistance Administration [*Closed, functions transferred to Office of Justice Assistance, Research, and Statistics*] [*Department of Justice*]
LEAA Legal Op... Law Enforcement Assistance Administration. Legal Opinions [*A publication*] (DLA)
LEAB......... Albacete [*Spain*] [*ICAO location identifier*] (ICLI)
LEA/BZ...... Vessel Leased to Brazil [*Navy*]
LEAC......... Levelized Energy Adjustment Clause (NRCH)
LEAC......... Madrid [*Spain*] [*ICAO location identifier*] (ICLI)
Leach......... Leach's English Crown Cases [*1730-1815*] [*A publication*] (DLA)
LEA/CH...... Vessel Leased to China [*Navy*]
Leach CC... Leach's Crown Cases, King's Bench [*England*] [*A publication*] (DLA)
Leach CL... Leach's Cases in Crown Law [*A publication*] (DLA)
Leach Cl Cas... Leach's Club Cases [*London*] [*A publication*] (DLA)
Leach Cr Cas... Leach's English Crown Cases [*1730-1815*] [*A publication*] (DLA)
LEA/CR...... Vessel Leased to Greece (SAUS)
LEAD........ Law Enforcement Activities Division [*National Rifle Association*]
LEAD........ Law Students Exposing Advertising Deceptions [*Student legal action organization*]
LEAD........ Lead Education Abatement Design Group (SAUO)
LEAD........ Leader Effectiveness and Adaptability Description [*Test*]
LEAD........ Leader Horse Trailer [*NCIC trailer make code*]
Lead........ Leader Law Reports [*Ceylon*] [*A publication*] (DLA)
LEAD........ Leadership and Excellence in Alzheimer's Disease Award Program [*Department of Health and Human Services*] (GFGA)
LEAD........ Leadership, Education, and Development [*US Army Corps of Engineers*]
LEAD........ Leadership for Environment and Development Institute [*Non-profit organization*] (ECON)
LEAD........ Leadership in Educational Administration Development
LEAD........ Leadville Corp. [*NASDAQ symbol*] (SAG)
LEAD........ Learn, Execute, and Diagnose
LEAD........ Lens Electronic Automatic Design (IAA)
LEAD........ Letterkenny Army Depot [*Pennsylvania*] (AABC)
LEAD........ Low-Cost Encryption Authentication Devices (SAUO)
Lead-acid battery... Car battery (SAUS)
Leadam..... Leadam's Select Cases before King's Council in the Star Chamber [*Selden Society Publications, Vols. 16, 25*] [*A publication*] (DLA)
Leadam Req... Select Cases in the Court of Requests, Edited by I. S. Leadam [*Selden Society Publications, Vol. 12*] [*A publication*] (DLA)
Lead Cas Am... American Leading Cases, Edited by Hare and Wallace [*A publication*] (DLA)
Lead Cas Eq... Leading Cases in Equity, by White and Tudor [*A publication*] (DLA)
Lead Cas in Eq... Leading Cases in Equity, by White and Tudor [*A publication*] (DLA)
Lead Cas in Eq (Eng)... Leading Cases in Equity, by White and Tudor [*England*] [*A publication*] (DLA)
LEADER..... Lehigh Automatic Device for Efficient Retrieval [*Center for Information Sciences, Lehigh University*] [*Bethlehem, PA*] [*Computer science*]
LEADER..... Logistics Echelons above Division in Europe (MCD)
LEADER..... Low Emissions Advanced Engine Range [*Automotive engineering*]
LEADER..... Low-Emissions Advanced Engine Range [*Automotive engineering*]
LEADERMART.... LEADER Mechanical Analysis and Retrieval of Text (NITA)
LEADEX..... Arctic Leads Dynamics Experiment (SAUO)
LEADEX..... Lead Dynamics Experiment (SAUS)
LEADEX..... Lead Experiment [*Marine science*] (OSRA)
Lead LR..... Leader Law Reports [*South Africa*] [*A publication*] (DLA)
LEAD PAC... Greater Cleveland Automobile Dealers Legislative Empowerment Automobile Dealers PAC [*Brecksville, OH*] (PACS)
LEAD PAC... Leadership for America's Future PAC [*Alexandria, VA*] (PACS)
LEADR....... Lawyers Engaged in Alternative Dispute Resolution [*Australia*] [*An association*]
LeadrFn..... Leader Financial Corp. [*Associated Press*] (SAG)
LEADS....... Law Enforcement Automated Data System (IEEE)
LEADS....... Leigh Airborne Data Acquisition System (SAUO)
LEADS....... Library Experimental Automated Demonstration System [*Computer science*]
LEADS....... Line Equipment Assignment and Display System [*GTE Corp.*]
LEAD USA... Leadership Education and Development USA (EA)
Leadvle..... Leadville Corp. [*Associated Press*] (SAG)
LEA/EC...... Vessel Leased to Ecuador [*Navy*]
LEAF......... Interleaf, Inc. [*Cambridge, MA*] [*NASDAQ symbol*] (NQ)
LEAF......... Land Educational Associates Foundation [*Defunct*] (EA)
LEAF......... Law Enforcement Access Field [*Telecommunications*]
LEAF......... Law, Equality and Freedom (SAUO)
LEAF......... Lea-Francis [*NCIC car make code*]
LEAF......... Legal Education and Action Fund (SAUO)
LEAF......... Legal Environmental Assistance Foundation (EA)
LEAF......... Liberal Education for Adoptive Families (EA)
LEAF......... LISP Extended Algebraic Facility
LEAF......... Lotus Extended Applications Facility
LEAF......... Women's Legal Education and Action Fund [*Canada*]
LEAFAC...... Local Employment Acts Financial Advisory Committee (SAUO)
LEA/FR...... Vessel Leased to France [*Navy*]
LEAFS....... LASER-Excited Atomic Fluorescent Spectrometry
LEAG........ Legislative Extended Assistance Group [*University of Iowa*] [*Research center*] (RCD)
LEA/GR...... Vessel Leased to Greece [*Navy*]

LEAGUE..... Lesbian, Bisexual, and Gay United Employees at AT & T
League of Nations Off J... League of Nations. Official Journal [*A publication*] (DLA)
League of Nations OJ... League of Nations. Official Journal [*A publication*] (DLA)
League of Nations OJ Spec Supp... League of Nations. Official Journal. Special Supplement [*A publication*] (DLA)
LEAH........ Lulov, Esrog, Arrovos, Hadassim (BJA)
LEAHS....... Lifetime Evaluation and Analysis of Heterogeneous System (PDAA)
LEAJ........ Law Enforcement and Administration of Justice (SAUO)
LEAK........ Leak-X Environmental [*NASDAQ symbol*] (TTSB)
LEAK........ Leak-X Environmental Corp. [*NASDAQ symbol*] (SAG)
LEAK........ Liposome-Encapsulated Amikacin [*Bactericide*]
Leake........ Leake on Contracts [*1861-1931*] [*A publication*] (DLA)
Leake........ Leake's Digest of the Law of Property in Land [*A publication*] (DLA)
Leake Cont... Leake on Contracts [*1861-1931*] [*A publication*] (DLA)
Leake Land... Leake's Digest of the Law of Property in Land [*A publication*] (DLA)
LEAKW...... Leak-X Environmental Wrrt [*NASDAQ symbol*] (TTSB)
LeakX....... Leak-X Environmental Corp. [*Associated Press*] (SAG)
LEAL........ Alicante [*Spain*] [*ICAO location identifier*] (ICLI)
LEAL........ Al Lewis Trucking [*Common carrier symbol*]
LEAM........ Almeria [*Spain*] [*ICAO location identifier*] (ICLI)
LEAM........ Lunar Ejecta and Meteorites [*Experiment*] [*NASA*]
Leam & Spic... Leaming and Spicer's Laws, Grants, Concessions, and Original Constitutions [*New Jersey*] [*A publication*] (DLA)
LEAMI....... Leamington, ON [*American Association of Railroads railroad junction routing code*]
LEAMS....... Law Enforcement Automated Management Subsystem (SAUO)
LEA/MX..... Vessel Leased to Mexico [*Navy*]
LEAN........ Law Enforcement Agency Network (SAUO)
LEAN........ Low-Fat Eating for America Now
Le & Ca..... Leigh and Cave's English Crown Cases Reserved [*1861-65*] [*A publication*] (DLA)
LE&S........ Logistics Engineering and Support (SAUS)
LE&WRR.... Lake Erie and Western Railroad Co. (SAUO)
LEA/NE...... Vessel Leased to Netherlands [*Navy*]
LEA/NO...... Vessel Leased to Norway [*Navy*]
LEANON..... Lupus Erythematosus Anonymous (EA)
LEANS....... Lehigh Analog Simulator (IAA)
LEAO........ Almagro [*Spain*] [*ICAO location identifier*] (ICLI)
LEAO........ Law Enforcement Aerial Observation (SAUO)
LEAP........ International Brotherhood of Boilermakers, Iron Ship Builders, Blacksmiths, Forgers & Helpers Legislative Education Fund [*Kansas City, KS*] (PACS)
LEAP........ Laboratory Education Advancement Program [*Department of Labor*]
LEAP........ Laboratory Evaluation and Accreditation Program
LEAP........ Laboratory Evening Academic Program (SAA)
LEAP........ Labor Education Advancement Program
LEAP........ Lambda Efficiency Analysis Program (VLIE)
LEAP........ Landcare and Environment Action Plan (SAUO)
LEAP........ Landcare and Environment Action Program (SAUO)
LEAP........ Language for Expressing Associative Procedures [*Computer science*]
LEAP........ Language for the Expression of Associative Procedures (VLIE)
LEAP........ Large Einsteinium Activation Program
LEAP........ Large Experimental Aquifer Program [*Oregon Graduate Institute of Science and Technology*] [*Research center*] (RCD)
LEAP........ Lasers and Electro-Optics Applications Program
LEAP........ Leadership and Education for Advancement of Phoenix [*Arizona*]
LEAP........ Leadership and Performance
LEAP........ Leading Edge Airborne PANAR
LEAP........ Leap Group, Inc. (The) [*NASDAQ symbol*] (SAG)
LEAP........ Leapnet, Inc. [*NASDAQ symbol*] (NASQ)
LEAP........ Legal and Educational Aid to the Poor [*Center*]
LEAP........ Legislative Evaluation and Accountability Program Committee (SAUO)
LEAP........ Lennox Employee Advocacy Program [*Dallas, TX*] (PACS)
LEAP........ Lewis Expandable Adjustable Prosthesis [*Orthopedics*]
LEAP........ Lifetime Element Advancing Program
LEAP........ Lift-Off Elevation and Azimuth Programmer
LEAP........ Light Exo-Atmospheric Projectile [*Formerly, Lightweight*] (DOMA)
LEAP........ Lightweight Exoatmospheric Advanced Projectile [*Military*] (SDI)
LEAP........ Limited Education Assistance Program (SAUO)
LEAP........ Linear-Elastic Analysis Program [*SIA Computer Services*] [*Software package*] (NCC)
LEAP........ Liquid Engine Air-Augmented Package (MCD)
LEAP........ Loan and Educational Aid Programme (SAUO)
LEAP........ Loaned Executives Assignment Program [*American Association of Advertising Agencies lobbying group*]
LEAP........ Local Education Authorities Project for School Management Training (AIE)
LEAP........ Lockheed Electronics Assembly Program
LEAP........ Logistic Element Action Proposal (MCD)
LEAP........ Logistic Element Alternatives Process (MCD)
LEAP........ Logistic Event and Assessment Program
LEAP........ Logistics Efficiencies to Increase Army Power (MCD)
LEAP........ Logistics Event and Assessment Program (SAUO)
LEAP........ Long-Term Equity Anticipations [*Business term*]
LEAP........ Louisiana Educational Assessment Program
LEAP........ Low Emissions, Advanced Performance [*Automotive engineering*]
LEAP........ Low-Energy All-Purpose (Collimator) [*Radiology*]
LEAP........ Lower Eastside Action Project [*New York City*]
LEAP........ Lower-Extremity Amputation Protocol [*Orthopedics*]
LEAP........ Low-Power Embedded Application Processor (VLIE)
LEAP........ Low-Power Enhanced at Portable (VLIE)
LEAP........ Lunar Escape Ambulance Pack [*Aerospace*]
LEAP........ Life Education for the Autistic Person (ODA)
LEA/PA...... Vessel Leased to Panama [*Navy*]
LEA/PE...... Vessel Leased to Peru [*Navy*]
LEA/PG...... Vessel Leased to Paraguay [*Navy*]
LeapGrp..... Leap Group, Inc. (The) [*Associated Press*] (SAG)
Leap Rom Civ L... Leapingwell on the Roman Civil Law [*A publication*] (DLA)
LEAPS....... LASER Electro-Optical Alignment Pole for Surveying [*NASA*]
LEAPS....... LASER Engineering and Application of Prototype System (MCD)
LEAPS....... Law Enforcement Agencies Processing System (SAUO)
LEAPS....... Local Exchange Area Planning Simulation [*Bell Laboratories*]
LEAPS....... Long-Term Equity Anticipation Securities [*Investment term*] (DFIT)
LEAPS....... Low Electron Attachment Potential Species (SAUO)
LEAR........ Learn [*Database*]
LEAR........ Lear Petroleum Corp. (SAUO)
LEAR........ Logistics Evaluation and Review
LEAR........ Low-Energy Antiproton Ring [*Particle physics*]
LEAR........ Low Erucic Acid Rapeseed [*Plant variety*]
LearBur..... Learmouth & Burchett Management Systems, Inc. [*Associated Press*] (SAG)
LEARN....... Laboratory Experience in Atmospheric Research at NCAR (SAUO)
LEARN....... Learnng
LEARN....... Literacy Education Acts Right Now (EARSL)
LEARN....... Literacy Education and Reading Network [*Tucson, AZ*]
LEARN....... Los Angeles Educational Alliance for Restructuring Now [*Education-reform project*] (ECON)
Learn & L... Learning and the Law [*A publication*] (DLA)
Learn & Law... Learning and the Law [*A publication*] (DLA)
Learnl....... LeaRonal, Inc. [*Associated Press*] (SAG)
LEARPAC.... Lear Corporation [*Southfield, MI*] (PACS)
LEARS....... Long [*Term*] Equity Anticipation Securities [*Finance*]
LearSeat.... Lear Seating Co. [*Associated Press*] (SAG)
LEARSYN... Logistics Evaluation and Review Synchronization (IAA)
LEA/RU...... Vessel Leased to Russia [*Navy*]
LEAS........ Aviles/Asturias [*Spain*] [*ICAO location identifier*] (ICLI)
LEAS........ Lata Equal Access System (VLIE)
LEAS........ Lease Electronic Accounting System (IEEE)
LEAs........ Local Education Agencies (PAZ)
LEAS........ Local Education Authorities (ECON)
LEAS........ Lower Echelon Automatic Switchboard
LEAS........ Pride Automotive Gp [*NASDAQ symbol*] (TTSB)
LEAS........ Pride Automotive Group, Inc. [*NASDAQ symbol*] (SAG)
LEA SAT..... Leased Communications Satellite (SAUO)
LEASAT...... Leased Satellite (NITA)
LEASAT...... Leased Satellite Communications (NVT)
LEASAT...... Leased Satellite Communications System (SAUO)
LEASATCOM... Leased Satellite Communications (SAUO)
Leasco...... Leasco Corporation (SAUO)
LEASCO..... Leasing Company-Equipment [*Transportation company classification code*]
LEASE....... Leasing
LeasEd...... Leasing Edge Corp. [*Associated Press*] (SAG)
LEASESAT... Leased Satellite (SAUS)
LEAS-FACS... Lease-Financial Accounting Control System (MHDB)
LEASI........ Leaside, ON [*American Association of Railroads railroad junction routing code*]
LEASIB...... Local Education Authorities and Schools Item Banking [*Project*] (AIE)
LEAST....... Learning Systems Standardization (SAUO)
L East Eur... Law in Eastern Europe [*A publication*] (DLA)
LEASW...... Pride Automotive Gp Wrrt [*NASDAQ symbol*] (TTSB)
LEATGS..... Local Education Authority Training Grants Scheme (AIE)
LEATH....... Leather (ROG)
LEATH....... Leatherhead [*City in England*]
LeathFac.... Leather Factory, Inc. [*Associated Press*] (SAG)
LEA/UK...... Vessel Leased to United Kingdom [*Navy*]
LEA/UR...... Vessel Leased to Uruguay [*Navy*]
LEAVE....... Leavenworth, KS [*American Association of Railroads railroad junction routing code*]
LEAVERATS... Leave Rations [*Military*]
LEAVI........ Leavittsburg, OH [*American Association of Railroads railroad junction routing code*]
LEAZ........ Leaseway [*Federal Railroad Administration identification code*]
LEB.......... East Baton Rouge Parish Public Library, Baton Rouge, LA [*OCLC symbol*] (OCLC)
LEB.......... Lateral Efferent Bundle [*Neuroanatomy*]
Leb.......... Lebanese (DIAR)
LEB.......... Lebanon [*New Hampshire*] [*Airport symbol*] (OAG)
Leb.......... Lebanon (VRA)
LEB.......... Lebanon, NH [*Location identifier*] [*FAA*] (FAAL)
LEB.......... Lebap [*Turkmenistan*] [*ICAO designator*] (FAAC)
LEB.......... Le Baron [*NCIC car model code*]
LEB.......... LeBaron [*Automotive classified advertising*]
LEB.......... Local Ethernet Bridge [*RAD Network Devices, Inc.*]
LEB.......... London Electricity Board
LEB.......... Low-Emissions Bus
LEB.......... Lower Equipment Bay [*Apollo*] [*NASA*]
Leb.......... Lupus Erythematosus Body [*Medicine*] (EDAA)
LEBA........ Cordoba [*Spain*] [*ICAO location identifier*] (ICLI)
LEBA........ Long Endurance Breathing Apparatus (PDAA)
Lebanese... Hashish [*Medicine*] (EDAA)
Lebanon.... Lebanon County Legal Journal [*Pennsylvania*] [*A publication*] (DLA)
Lebanon Co LJ (PA)... Lebanon County Legal Journal [*Pennsylvania*] [*A publication*] (DLA)
LeBAU....... American University of Beirut, Beirut, Lebanon [*Library symbol*] [*Library of Congress*] (LCLS)

LEBB......... Bilbao [*Spain*] [*ICAO location identifier*] (ICLI)
LEBC......... Letchworth Indep Bancshares [*NASDAQ symbol*] (TTSB)
LEBC......... Letchworth Independent Bancshares Corp. [*NASDAQ symbol*] (SAG)
LEBCW...... Letchworth Indep Bcshs Wrrt [*NASDAQ symbol*] (TTSB)
LEBFO....... Lorin Elias Bassett Family Organization [*Association*] (EA)
LEBG......... Burgos [*Spain*] [*ICAO location identifier*] (ICLI)
LEBI......... Lebarnold [*Common carrier symbol*]
LEBL......... Barcelona [*Spain*] [*ICAO location identifier*] (ICLI)
LEBNAP..... Lebanese Kidnap [*Victims*] [*American hostages held in Beirut*]
LEBR......... Bardenas Reales [*Spain*] [*ICAO location identifier*] (ICLI)
LEBS......... London Emergency Bed Service (SAUO)
LEBS......... Low Emission Boiler Systems (SAUO)
LebSeels.... Lebendige Seelsorge (BJA)
LEBT......... Betera [*Spain*] [*ICAO location identifier*] (ICLI)
LEBU......... Large Eddy Breakup Device [*Aerodynamics*]
LEBZ......... Badajoz/Talavera La Real [*Spain*] [*ICAO location identifier*] (ICLI)
LEC.......... Lake City, FL [*Amtrak rail station code*]
LEC.......... Lake Erie College, Painesville, OH [*OCLC symbol*] (OCLC)
LEC.......... LAMPS [*Light Airborne Multipurpose System*] Element Coordinator [*Navy*] (CAAL)
LEC.......... Landed Estates Courts Commission [*England*] (DLA)
LEC.......... Landmarks of Early Cartography (SAUO)
LEC.......... LAN [*Local Area Network*] Emulation Client [*Telecommunications*] (ACRL)
LEC.......... LANTCOM ELINT Center (MCD)
LEC.......... LASER Electronic Computer
LEC.......... Launceston Environment Centre (SAUO)
LEC.......... Launch Escape Control [*NASA*] (KSC)
LEC.......... Law and Economics Center (SAUO)
LEC.......... Law Enforcement Center (SAUO)
LEC.......... Le Car [*NCIC car model code*]
LEC.......... Lec Refrigeration Ltd. [*British*] [*ICAO designator*] (FAAC)
LEC.......... Lecture
LEC.......... Leukoencephalitis [*Medicine*] (DB)
LEC.......... Levelized Energy Cost
LEC.......... Library of English Classics [*A publication*]
LEC.......... Ligand Exchange Chromatography (DB)
LEC.......... Light-Emitting Chemical Compound [*Marking agent for equipment used in night operations*] [*Military*] (VNW)
LEC.......... Light-Emitting Electrochemical Cell [*Chemistry*]
LEC.......... Light Energy Converter [*Telecommunications*] (TEL)
LEC.......... Lignite Energy Council (EARSL)
LEC.......... Limited Editions Club
LEC.......... Liquid Encapsulated Czochralski [*Crystal growing technique*] (IEEE)
LEC.......... List Execution Condition (IAA)
LEC.......... Little East Conference (PSS)
LEC.......... Livestock Equipment Council [*Defunct*] (EA)
LEC.......... Local Emergency Coordinator (SARE)
LEC.......... Local Employment Committee [*Department of Employment*] [*British*]
LEC.......... Local Engineering Change [*DoD*]
LEC.......... Local Exchange Carrier [*Telecommunications*] (PCM)
LEC.......... Local Exchange Company [*Computer science*] (FOTI)
LEC.......... Local Export Control [*British*] (DS)
LEC.......... Lockheed Electronics Company (SAUO)
LEC.......... Lockheed Electronics Corp. [*Subsidiary of Lockheed Aircraft Corp.*]
LEC.......... Locking Escape Character [*Computer science*] (VLIE)
LEC.......... London Education Classification [*Library classification system*] (NITA)
LEC.......... London Environment Centre [*London Guildhall University*] [*United Kingdom*] (RCD)
LEC.......... London Executive Council (SAUO)
LEC.......... Low-Echo-Centroid [*Geology*]
LEC.......... Low Emitter Concentration (PDAA)
LEC.......... Lower East Coast
LEC.......... Lower Epidermal Cell [*Botany*]
LEC.......... Lower Esophageal Contractility [*Medicine*] (EDAA)
LEC.......... Low Exchange Carriers (SAUS)
LEC.......... Lumped Element Circulator
LEC.......... Lunar Equipment Conveyor [*Aerospace*]
LEC.......... Local Enterprise Company (ODA)
LECA......... Landed Estate Companies Association [*British*] (BI)
LECA......... Launch Escape Control Area [*NASA*] (KSC)
LECA......... Left External Cartoid Artery [*Medicine*] (EDAA)
LECA......... Lehman Caves National Monument
LECA......... Light European Combat Aircraft (PDAA)
LECA......... Light-Expanded Clay Aggregate (DAC)
LECA......... Madrid [*Spain*] [*ICAO location identifier*] (ICLI)
LECAM...... Lectin Adhesion Molecule [*Biochemistry*]
LECAM...... Lectin-Cellular Adhesion Molecule [*Biochemistry*]
LECAPSR... Llano Estacado Center for Advanced Professional Studies and Research [*Eastern New Mexico University*] [*Research center*] (RCD)
LECB......... Barcelona [*Spain*] [*ICAO location identifier*] (ICLI)
LECC......... Lake Erie Cleanup Committee [*Defunct*] (EA)
LECC......... Linear Error Correcting Code (IAA)
LECCAM..... Leukocyte Endothelial Cell-Cell Adhesion Molecule [*Cytology*]
LECCE....... Left Extracapsular Cataract Extraction (MELL)
LECE......... Leasing Edge [*NASDAQ symbol*] (TTSB)
LECE......... Leasing Edge Corp. [*NASDAQ symbol*] (SAG)
LECEL....... Leasing Edge Wrrt'B' [*NASDAQ symbol*] (TTSB)
LECEP....... Leasing Edge cm Cv'A'Pfd [*NASDAQ symbol*] (TTSB)
LECEZ....... Leasing Edge Wrrt'A' [*NASDAQ symbol*] (TTSB)
LECH......... Calamocha [*Spain*] [*ICAO location identifier*] (ICLI)
LECH......... Lechmere Construction [*NCIC trailer make code*]
LECH......... Lechters, Inc. [*NASDAQ symbol*] (SAG)
Lechters.... Lechters, Inc. [*Associated Press*] (SAG)
LECL......... Linkage Editor Control Language [*Computer science*] (VLIE)
LECL......... Valencia [*Spain*] [*ICAO location identifier*] (ICLI)
LECLU....... Law Enforcement Civil Liberties Unit (SAUO)
LECM......... Laboratory of Environmental Carcinogenesis and Mutagenesis [*National Institute of Environmental Health Sciences*] (RCD)
LECM......... Madrid [*Spain*] [*ICAO location identifier*] (ICLI)
LECNA....... Lutheran Educational Conference of North America (EA)
LECO......... La Coruna [*Spain*] [*ICAO location identifier*] (ICLI)
LECO......... Leeco Diagnostics, Inc. (SAUO)
LECO......... Lincoln Electric [*NASDAQ symbol*] (TTSB)
LECO......... [*The*] Lincoln Electric Co. [*NASDAQ symbol*] (SAG)
LECO......... Lincoln Electric Holdings [*NASDAQ symbol*] [*Formerly, Lincoln Electric*]
LECO......... Local Engineering Control Office [*Telecommunications*] (TEL)
LECO......... London Engineering Congress (SAUO)
LECOA....... Lincoln Electric 'A' [*NASDAQ symbol*] (TTSB)
LECOM....... Lake Erie College of Osteopathic Medicine (MHID)
LEconSc..... License Economic Sciences [*Canada*] (DD)
LECOS....... Light Electronic Control System (SAUS)
LECOS....... Lunar-Environment Construction and Operations Simulator [*NASA*] (IAA)
LECP......... Low-Energy Charged Particle [*Atomic physics*]
LECP......... Palma [*Spain*] [*ICAO location identifier*] (ICLI)
LECR......... Law Enforcement Candidate Record [*Test*] (TMMY)
LeCroy...... LeCroy Corp. [*Associated Press*] (SAG)
LECS......... LAN [*Local Area Network*] Emulation Configuration Server [*Telecommunications*] (ACRL)
LECS......... Launching Equipment Checkout Set
LECS......... Local Economic Consequences Study [*Military*]
LECS......... Local Enterprise Companies [*Scotland*] (ECON)
LECS......... Sevilla [*Spain*] [*ICAO location identifier*] (ICLI)
LECT......... League for the Exchange of Commonwealth Teachers (EA)
LECT......... LecTec Corp. [*NASDAQ symbol*] (SAG)
LECT......... Lectern (ROG)
LECT......... Lectracan [*NCIC motorcycle make code*]
Lect.......... Lecture (DIAR)
LECT......... Lecture [*or Lecturer*]
Lect.......... Lecturer (AL)
Lectec....... LecTec Corp. [*Associated Press*] (SAG)
Lect LSUC... Special Lectures. Law Society of Upper Canada [*A publication*] (DLA)
lectn......... Lectionary (VRA)
Lect Notes Earth Sci... Lecture Notes in Earth Sciences (SAUS)
LECTO....... Lectotype
LECTR....... Lecturer
Lect y V..... Lectura y Vida [*A publication*]
LECU......... Champion-Scandinavian Cargo Equipment [*Intermodal shipping container symbol*] (TVRC)
LECV......... Colmenar Viejo [*Spain*] [*ICAO location identifier*] (ICLI)
LECZ......... Loveland Elevator [*Federal Railroad Administration identification code*]
LED.......... Large Electronic Display
LED.......... Law Enforcement Division [*National Park Service*]
L Ed......... Lawyers' Edition, United States Supreme Court Reports [*A publication*] (DLA)
LED.......... Leaded
LED.......... League for Ecological Democracy (EA)
Led.......... Ledger (EBF)
led........... Ledger (WDAA)
LED.......... Ledger
LED.......... Leningrad [*Former USSR*] [*Airport symbol*] (OAG)
LED.......... Library Education Division [*American Library Association*] [*Defunct*]
LED.......... License Expiry Date (WDAA)
LED.......... Light-Emitting Diode [*Display component*]
LED.......... Line Embossing Device [*Computer science*]
LED.......... Liquid Element Display
LED.......... Logical Error Detection
LED.......... Logistics Engineering Directorate [*ARRCOM*] (RDA)
LED.......... London Engine Drivers (SAUO)
LED.......... Longitudinal Establishment Data [*Bureau of the Census*] (GFGA)
LED.......... Low Echo Defense (ACAE)
LED.......... Low Endoatmospheric Defence (SAUS)
LED.......... Low-Energy Detector
LED.......... Low-Energy Diffraction
LED.......... Lower Emissions Dispatch [*Environmental Protection Agency*]
LED.......... Lowest Effective Dose [*Medicine*] (DB)
LED.......... Lowest Emitting Dose [*Medicine*] (DMAA)
LED.......... Lupus Erythematosus Disseminatus [*Medicine*]
LED.......... North Platte, NE [*Location identifier*] [*FAA*] (FAAL)
L Ed 2d..... Lawyers' Edition, United States Supreme Court Reports, Second Series [*A publication*] (DLA)
LEDA......... LANDSAT Earthnet Data Availability [*ESA-Earthnet Programme Office*] [*Database*]
LEDA......... Lawn Equipment Dealers Association [*California*] (EARSL)
LEDA......... Lee Data Corporation (SAUO)
LEDA......... Library of Efficient Data Types and Algorithms (VLIE)
LEDA......... Local Employment Development Action (SAUO)
LEDA......... Low-Energy Deasphalting [*Petroleum refining*]
LEDA......... On-line Earthnet Data Access (SAUS)
L Ed (Adv Ops)... United States Supreme Court Reports, Lawyers' Edition, Advance Opinions [*A publication*] (DLA)
LEDC......... League for Emotionally Disturbed Children
LEDC......... Local Economic Development Corp.
LEDC......... Logistics Executive Development Course [*Army*]

LEDC — Low-Energy Detonating Cord (SAA)
LEDD — Light-Emitting Diode Display
LEDET — Law Enforcement Detachment [*Coast Guard*]
LED FO — Ledger Folio (ROG)
LEDG — Ledger Capital Corp. [*NASDAQ symbol*]
LEDI — Local Employment Development Initiative [*Australia*]
LEDI — Low Endo-Atmospheric Defense Interceptor (ACAE)
LEDM — Valladolid [*Spain*] [*ICAO location identifier*] (ICLI)
LEDO — Laboratory Emergency Duty Officer (SAUO)
LEDO — Long-Term Effects of Dredging Operations [*Coastal Engineering Research Center*]
LEDP — Large Electronic Display Panel
LEDR — Laboratory for Environmental Data Research [*National Oceanic and Atmospheric Administration*]
LEDR — Light-Emitting Diode Recorder (MCD)
LEDS — Law Enforcement Data System
LEDS — Light-Emitting Diodes
LEDS — Liquid Effluents Data System [*Environmental Protection Agency*] (GFGA)
LEDSHP — Leadership
LEDT — Limited Entry Decision Table
LEDU — Local Employment Development Unit (SAUO)
L Ed (US) — Lawyers' Edition, United States Supreme Court Reports [*A publication*] (DLA)
L Ed US — Supreme Court Reports, Lawyer's Edition [*A publication*] (NTCM)
LEDVL — Leadville, CO [*American Association of Railroads railroad junction routing code*]
LEDW — Ledwell & Son [*NCIC trailer make code*]
LEE — [*The*] Lake Erie & Eastern Railroad Co. [*AAR code*]
LEE — LASER Energy Evaluator (PDAA)
LEE — Launch Electronics Equipment
LEE — Leading Edge Environment
LEE — Lee [*NCIC trailer make code*]
LEE — Leeds [*Utah*] [*Seismograph station code, US Geological Survey*] (SEIS)
LEE — Lee Enterprises [*NYSE symbol*] (TTSB)
LEE — Lee Enterprises, Inc. [*NYSE symbol*] (SPSG)
LEE — Leesburg, FL [*Location identifier*] [*FAA*] (FAAL)
Lee — Lee's English Ecclesiastical Reports [*A publication*] (DLA)
Lee — Lee's Reports [*9-12 California*] [*A publication*] (DLA)
LEE — Lee's Summit, MO [*Amtrak rail station code*]
LEE — Life and Earth Environment (SAUO)
LEE — Logistics Evaluation Exercise
LEE — London Electrical Engineers (SAUO)
LEEA — Law Enforcement Education Agency (SAUO)
LEEA — Lifting Equipment Engineers Association [*British*] (EAIO)
Lee Abs — Lee's Abstracts of Title [*1843*] [*A publication*] (DLA)
Lee & H — Lee's English King's Bench Reports Tempore Hardwicke [*1733-38*] [*A publication*] (DLA)
Lee Bank — Lee's Law and Practice of Bankruptcy [*3rd ed.*] [*1887*] [*A publication*] (DLA)
LEEBI — Low-Energy Electron Beam Irradiation [*Physics*]
LEEC — LASER-to-Electric Energy Conversion (SSD)
LEEC — Lee Coaches [*NCIC trailer make code*]
LEEC — London Environmental Economics Centre (SAUO)
LEEC — Sevilla-El Copero Base [*Spain*] [*ICAO location identifier*] (ICLI)
Lee Cap — Lee on Captures [*A publication*] (DLA)
LEED — LASER-Energized Explosive Device
LEED — Longitudinal Employer-Employee Data File [*Social Security Administration*]
LEED — Low-Energy Electron Diffraction [*Spectroscopy*]
Lee Dict — Lee's Dictionary of Practice [*A publication*] (DLA)
LEEDS — Low-Energy Electron Diffraction Spectroscopy (DB)
LeedsFdl — Leeds FSB [*Associated Press*] (SAG)
LEEE — Madrid [*Spain*] [*ICAO location identifier*] (ICLI)
Lee Eccl — Lee's English Ecclesiastical Reports [*A publication*] (DLA)
LeeEnt — Lee Enterprises, Inc. [*Associated Press*] (SAG)
LEEGS — Law Enforcement Explorer Girls (SAUO)
Lee I — Leeward Islands (SAUO)
LE-EIA — Leukocyte Esterase Enzyme Immunoassay
LEEIXS — Low-Energy-Electron-Induced X-Ray Spectrometry
LEEM — Low-Energy Electron Microscopy
LEEN — L & E Enterprises [*NCIC trailer make code*]
LEEP — Law Enforcement Education Program [*Department of Justice*]
LEEP — Law Enforcement Explorer Post [*Boy Scouts*]
LEEP — Left End-Expiratory Pressure [*Medicine*] (MELL)
LEEP — Library Education Experimental Project [*Syracuse University*]
LEEP — Loop Electrosurgical Excision Procedure [*Medicine*]
LEEPE — Leading-Edge Earth Products, Inc. [*NASDAQ symbol*] (QUAN)
LeePhr — Lee Pharmaceuticals [*Associated Press*] (SAG)
LEER — Leer [*NCIC trailer make code*]
LEER — Low-Energy Electron Reflection (IEEE)
LEERS — Long-Endurance Experimental Research Submarine (SAA)
LEES — Laboratory for Electromagnetic and Electronic Systems [*Massachusetts Institute of Technology*] [*Research center*] (RCD)
LEES — Lake Erie Environmental Studies
LEES — Launch Equipment Evaluation Set (MCD)
LEES — Leesburg [*NCIC trailer make code*]
Leese — Leese's Reports [*26 Nebraska*] [*A publication*] (DLA)
Lee Ship — Lee's Laws of Shipping [*A publication*] (DLA)
LEET — Limiting Equivalent Exposure Time (MUGU)
Lee T Hard — Lee's English King's Bench Cases Tempore Hardwicke [*1733-38*] [*England*] [*A publication*] (DLA)
Lee T Hardw — Lee's English King's Bench Cases Tempore Hardwicke [*1733-38*] [*England*] [*A publication*] (DLA)
LEE W — Lee White Tritium [*Clotting Time*] [*Hematology*] (DAVI)
LEF — Lake Erie, Franklin & Clarion Railroad Co. [*AAR code*]
LEF — Landpower Education Fund
LEF — LASER Excited Fluorescence
LEF — Leading Edge Flap [*Aviation*]
LEF — Left-In Telephone [*Telecommunications*] (TEL)
LEF — Leukokinesis-Enhancing Factor [*Medicine*] (DMAA)
LEF — Library Exchange Format (SAUO)
LEF — Licentiate in Economics and Finance
LEF — Life Extension Foundation (EA)
LEF — Light-Emitting Film (IEEE)
LEF — Lighting Effectiveness Factor (LDOE)
LEF — Lincoln Educational Foundation [*Defunct*] (EA)
LEF — Linear-Energy Spectrophotofluorometry
LEF — Line Expansion Function
LEF — Liquid Expanded Film
LEF — Lobby Europeen des Femmes [*European Women's Lobby*] [*Belgium*] (EAIO)
LEF — Local Education Fund
LEF — Loss Entry Form [*Insurance*]
LEF — Lupus Erythematosus Factor [*Medicine*] (DMAA)
LEF — Lupus Erythematosus Foundation [*Medicine*] [*Inc.*] (EDAA)
LEF — Luquillo Experimental Forest (RCD)
LEF — Lymphoid-Enhanced Binding Factor [*Medicine*] (DMAA)
LEF — Lymphoid Enhancer Factor [*Biochemistry*]
Lef & Cas — Lefroy and Cassel's Practice Cases [*1881-83*] [*Ontario*] [*A publication*] (DLA)
LEFC — L-Band Electronic Frequency Converter
Lef Cr L — Lefroy's Irish Criminal Law [*A publication*] (DLA)
LEFCS — Leading Edge Flap Control System [*Aviation*]
Lef Dec — Lefevre's Parliamentary Decisions, by Bourke [*England*] [*A publication*] (DLA)
LEFE — Linear Electric Field Effect (PDAA)
LEFI — Local Electrical Field Instrument (EOSA)
LEFM — Linear-Elastic Fracture Mechanics
LEFO — Land's End for Order [*Shipping*]
Lefroy — Lefroy's Railroad and Canal Cases [*England*] [*A publication*] (DLA)
LEFTA — Labour Economic, Finance and Taxation Association (SAUO)
LEFU — Light Ends Fractionating Unit [*Petroleum technology*]
LEFW — Lake Erie & Fort Wayne Railroad Co. [*AAR code*]
LEG — Aleg [*Mauritania*] [*Airport symbol*] (AD)
LEG — Cabinet Legislation Committee (SAUO)
Leg — De Legibus [*of Cicero*] [*Classical studies*] (OCD)
LEG — Language of Functions and Graphs (AIE)
LEG — Law Enforcement Group (WDAA)
LEG — Legacy [*NCIC car model code*]
LEG — Legal (AFM)
leg — Legal (SHCU)
LEG — Legal Committee (SAUO)
LEG — Legal Department (SAUO)
LEG — Legal Questions Relating to Scientific Investigations in the Ocean (SAUO)
LEG — Leganza [*NCIC car model code*]
leg — Legate (WDAA)
LEG — Legate
Leg — Legatio ad Gaium [*of Philo Judaeus*] [*Classical studies*] (OCD)
leg — Legato (NTIO)
LEG — Legato [*Smoothly and Connectedly*] [*Music*]
LEG — Legend [*Numismatics*]
LEG — Legend (automobile) [*NCIC car model code*]
Leg — Leges [*Laws*] [*Latin*] (ILCA)
LEG — Leggett & Platt [*NYSE symbol*] (TTSB)
LEG — Leggett & Platt, Inc. [*NYSE symbol*] (SPSG)
LEG — Leggett, CA [*Amtrak Busline code*]
LEG — Legislation [*or Legislature*]
Leg — Legislative (PHSD)
LEG — Legislative Library of British Columbia [*UTLAS symbol*]
LEG — Legislature (GOBB)
Leg — Legislature (WDAA)
LEG — Legit [*He, or She, Reads*] [*Latin*]
LEG — Legunt [*They Read*] [*Latin*] (ADA)
LEG — Lengua [*Language symbol*] (ETLW)
LEG — Library Education Group of the Library Association (NITA)
LEG — Liquefied Energy Gas
LEG — Logistical Expediting Group
LEG — Logistic Evaluation Group
LEGA — Granada/Armilla [*Spain*] [*ICAO location identifier*] (ICLI)
Legacy — Legacy: A Journal of American Women Writers [*A publication*] (BRI)
Leg Adv — Legal Adviser [*Chicago*] [*A publication*] (DLA)
Leg Agr — De Lege Agraria [*of Cicero*] [*Classical studies*] (OCD)
LEGAL — League for Equitable General Aviation Legislation (EA)
Legal Adv — Legal Advertiser [*Chicago*] [*A publication*] (DLA)
Legal Adv — Legal Adviser [*Denver*] [*A publication*] (DLA)
Legal Asp Med Prac — Legal Aspects of Medical Practice [*A publication*] (DLA)
Leg Alfred — Leges Alfredi [*Laws of King Alfred*] [*Latin*] [*A publication*] (DLA)
Legal Gaz (PA) — Legal Gazette (Pennsylvania) [*A publication*] (DLA)
Legal Int — Legal Intelligencer [*A publication*] (DLA)
Legal Intel — Legal Intelligencer [*A publication*] (DLA)
Legal Intell — Legal Intelligencer [*A publication*] (DLA)
Legal Obser — Legal Observer [*London*] [*A publication*] (DLA)
Legal Observer — New York Legal Observer [*A publication*] (DLA)
LegalR — Legal Research Center, Inc. [*Associated Press*] (SAG)
Legal Rep — Legal Reporter [*Australia*] [*A publication*]
Legal Rep — Legal Reporter, New Series [*Tennessee*] [*A publication*] (DLA)

Legal Resp Child Adv Protection... Legal Response; Child Advocacy and Protection [*A publication*] (DLA)
Leg & Ins R... Legal and Insurance Reporter [*Pennsylvania*] [*A publication*] (DLA)
Leg & Ins Rep... Legal and Insurance Reporter [*Philadelphia, PA*] [*A publication*] (DLA)
Leg & Ins Rept... Legal and Insurance Reporter [*Philadelphia, PA*] [*A publication*] (DLA)
Legat........ De Lagatione ad Caium [*Philo*] (BJA)
LEGAT....... Legal Attache [*FBI agent posted at an American embassy*]
Legato....... Legato Systems, Inc. [*Associated Press*] (SAG)
LEGATT...... Legal Attache [*Foreign service*]
Leg Bibl..... Legal Bibliography [*A publication*] (DLA)
Leg Canut... Leges Canuti [*Laws of King Canute or Knut*] [*Latin*] [*A publication*] (DLA)
Leg Ch Forms... Leggo's Chancery Forms [*Ontario*] [*A publication*] (DLA)
Leg Ch Pr... Leggo's Chancery Practice [*Ontario*] [*A publication*] (DLA)
Leg Chron... Legal Chronicle Reports, Edited by Foster [*Pennsylvania*] [*A publication*] (DLA)
Leg Chron Rep... Legal Chronicle Reports [*Pottsville, PA*] [*A publication*] (DLA)
Legco........ Legislative Council [*Hong Kong*] (ECON)
LEG COM... Legally Committed (BABM)
legd.......... Legend
LEGE......... Gerona/Costa Brava [*Spain*] [*ICAO location identifier*] (ICLI)
Leg Edm.... Leges Edmundi [*Laws of King Edmund*] [*Latin*] [*A publication*] (DLA)
LEGEN....... Liposome-Encapulated Gentamicin [*Bactericide*]
LEGEND..... Legal Electronic Network and Database (IID)
Legend...... Legend Properties, Inc. [*Associated Press*] (SAG)
Leg Ethel... Leges Ethelredi [*Laws of King Ethelred*] [*Latin*] [*A publication*] (DLA)
Leg Exam... Legal Examiner [*London or New York*] [*1831-35; 1862-68; 1869-72*] [*A publication*] (DLA)
Leg Exam & LC... Legal Examiner and Law Chronicle [*London*] [*A publication*] (DLA)
Leg Exam & Med J... Legal Examiner and Medical Jurist [*London*] [*A publication*] (DLA)
Leg Exam NS... Legal Examiner, New Series [*England*] [*A publication*] (DLA)
Leg Exam WR... Legal Examiner Weekly Reporter [*A publication*] (DLA)
Leg Exch.... Legal Exchange [*Des Moines, IA*] [*A publication*] (DLA)
LEGG........ Launch Eject Gas Generator
Leg G........ Legal Guide [*A publication*] (DLA)
Legg......... Leggett's Reports [*India*] [*A publication*] (DLA)
LEGG........ Leggiero [*Light and Rapid*] [*Music*]
Leg Gaz..... Legal Gazette [*A publication*] (DLA)
Leg Gaz R... Campbell's Legal Gazette Reports [*Pennsylvania*] [*A publication*] (DLA)
Leg Gaz Re... Campbell's Legal Gazette Reports [*Pennsylvania*] [*A publication*] (ILCA)
Leg Gaz Rep... Campbell's Legal Gazette Reports [*Pennsylvania*] [*A publication*] (DLA)
Legg Bills L... Leggett on Bills of Lading [*A publication*] (DLA)
LeggMas.... Legg Mason, Inc. [*Associated Press*] (SAG)
Leggo....... Leggiero [*Light and Rapid*] [*Music*]
Legg Out.... Legge on Outlawry [*A publication*] (DLA)
LEGGS....... Loyal Escorts of the Green Garters (EA)
LEGH........ Leighton's Express [*Common carrier symbol*]
Leg HI....... Laws of King Henry the First [*A publication*] (DLA)
Leg Inf Bul... Legal Information Bulletin [*A publication*] (DLA)
Leg Inq...... Legal Inquirer [*London*] [*A publication*] (DLA)
Leg Int...... Legal Intelligencer [*A publication*] (DLA)
Leg Intel.... Legal Intelligencer [*A publication*] (DLA)
Leg Intell... Legal Intelligencer [*A publication*] (DLA)
Leg Intl..... Legal Intelligencer [*A publication*] (DLA)
Legis......... Legislative (AL)
LEGIS........ Legislative [*or Legislature*]
LEGIS........ Legislative Information and Status System [*for House of Representatives*]
LEGISL...... Legislative (ADA)
LEGISLN.... Legislation
LEGISN...... Legislation [*Legal shorthand*] (LWAP)
LEGISNET... National Legislative Network [*National Conference of State Legislatures*] [*Information service or system*] (IID)
LEGISOR.... Legislator [*Legal shorthand*] (LWAP)
Legis Stud Q... Legislative Studies Quarterly [*A publication*] (DLA)
Leg Issues... Legal Issues of European Integration [*A publication*] (ILCA)
LEGISURE... Legislature [*Legal shorthand*] (LWAP)
LEGISV...... Legislative [*Legal shorthand*] (LWAP)
LEGIT........ Legitimate (DSUE)
legit.......... Legitimate (SHCU)
LEGIW....... Co. Counsel Inc. Wrrt [*NASDAQ symbol*] (TTSB)
Leg J......... Pittsburgh Legal Journal [*Pennsylvania*] [*A publication*] (DLA)
Leg Jour.... Pittsburgh Legal Journal [*Pennsylvania*] [*A publication*] (DLA)
LEGL......... Co-Counsel, Inc. [*NASDAQ symbol*] (SAG)
LEGM........ Low-Energy Gamma Monitor
Leg Misc.... Legal Miscellany [*Ceylon*] [*A publication*] (DLA)
Leg Misc & Rev... Legal Miscellany and Review [*India*] [*A publication*] (DLA)
Leg News... Legal News [*Canada*] [*A publication*] (DLA)
Leg Notes.. Legal Notes on Local Government [*New York*] [*A publication*] (DLA)
LEGO........ Leg Godt [*Play Well*] [*Acronym is brand of child's building toy*] [*Denmark*]
Leg Obs..... Legal Observer [*London*] [*A publication*] (DLA)
Leg Obs..... Legal Observer and Solicitor's Journal [*London*] [*A publication*] (DLA)
LEGOL....... Legally Oriented Language [*Programming language project*] [*British*] (NITA)
Leg Oler.... Laws of Oleron [*Maritime law*] [*A publication*] (DLA)
Leg Op...... Legal Opinion [*Pennsylvania*] [*A publication*] (DLA)
Leg Ops (PA)... Legal Opinion [*Pennsylvania*] [*A publication*] (DLA)
Leg Out..... Legge on Outlawry [*A publication*] (DLA)
LegPlat...... Leggett & Platt, Inc. [*Associated Press*] (SAG)
Leg Port.... Leges Portuum [*A publication*] (DLA)
Leg Pract & Sol J... Legal Practitioner and Solicitor's Journal [*1846-47, 1849-51*] [*A publication*] (DLA)
LEGR........ Granada [*Spain*] [*ICAO location identifier*] (ICLI)
Leg R........ Legal Record Reports [*Pennsylvania*] [*A publication*] (DLA)
Leg Rec..... Legal Record [*Detroit, MI*] [*A publication*] (DLA)
Leg Rec Rep... Legal Record Reports [*Pennsylvania*] [*A publication*] (DLA)
Leg Ref..... Legal Reformer [*1819-20*] [*A publication*] (DLA)
Leg Rem.... Legal Remembrancer [*Calcutta*] [*A publication*] (DLA)
Leg Rep..... Legal Reporter [*1840-43*] [*Ireland*] [*A publication*] (DLA)
Leg Rep (Ir)... Legal Reporter, Irish Courts [*A publication*] (DLA)
Leg Rep SL... Legal Reporter Special Leave Supplement [*A publication*]
Leg Rev..... Legal Review [*1812-13*] [*London*] [*A publication*] (DLA)
LEGRI....... Low Energy Gamma-Ray Imager (SAUS)
Leg R (Tenn)... Legal Reporter Parallel to Shannon Cases [*Tennessee*] [*A publication*] (DLA)
LEGS........ Database Program to write reports with leg (SAUS)
LEGS........ Lateral Electronic Guidance System [*Automotive engineering*]
LEGS........ Learning Experience Guides for Nursing Students [*Series of films, games, slides, etc.*]
LEGS........ Legacies (ROG)
LEGS........ Legislative Effort Group System [*AMA*] [*Medicine*] (EDAA)
LEGS........ Lethality End Game Simulation (MCD)
LEGS........ Lighter Electronics Guidance System (MCD)
LEGS........ Lightweight Engine Generator Set (SAUS)
LEGS........ Logistic Engine Generator Set (DWSG)
LEGT......... Lycee d'Enseignement General et Technologique [*High School for General and Technical Studies*] [*French*] (BARN)
LEGT......... Madrid/Getafe [*Spain*] [*ICAO location identifier*] (ICLI)
Leg T Cas... Legal Tender Cases [*A publication*] (DLA)
Legul........ Leguleian [*1850-65*] [*A publication*] (DLA)
LEG (UN)... Department of Legal Affairs of the United Nations
Legve........ Legislative
Leg W........ Legal World [*India*] [*A publication*] (DLA)
Leg Wisb... Laws of Wisby [*Maritime law*] [*A publication*] (DLA)
LEG WT..... Legal Weight (WDAA)
LEGY........ Legacy (ROG)
Leg YB...... Legal Year Book [*London*] [*A publication*] (DLA)
LEH.......... Launch/Entry Helmet (MCD)
LEH.......... Leeds Central Helicopters [*British*] [*FAA designator*] (FAAC)
LEH.......... Le Havre [*France*] [*Airport symbol*] (OAG)
Leh.......... Lehigh County Law Journal [*Pennsylvania*] [*A publication*] (DLA)
LEH.......... Lehigh Valley Industries, Inc. (SAUO)
LEH.......... Lehman Br Holdngs [*NYSE symbol*] (TTSB)
LEH.......... Lehman Brothers [*NYSE symbol*] (SAG)
LEH.......... Licentiate in Ecclesiastical History (SAUO)
LEH.......... Linear Enamel Hypoplasia (SAUO)
LEH.......... Linear Enamel Hypoplasias (QUAC)
LEH.......... Liposome Encapsulated Hemoglobin [*Biochemistry*]
LehAMGN... Lehman Brothers Holdings, Inc. [*Associated Press*] (SAG)
LehBr35.... Lehman Brothers [*Associated Press*] (SAG)
LEHC........ Huesca [*Spain*] [*ICAO location identifier*] (ICLI)
Leh Co LJ (PA)... Lehigh County Law Journal [*Pennsylvania*] [*A publication*] (DLA)
LehGTel..... Lehman Brothers, Inc. [*Associated Press*] (SAG)
LEHI......... Hinojosa Del Duque [*Spain*] [*ICAO location identifier*] (ICLI)
LEHI......... Lehame Herut Israel [*Fighters of the Freedom of Israel*]
LEHI......... Lehigh University (SAUO)
Lehigh....... Lehigh Valley Law Reporter [*Pennsylvania*] [*A publication*] (DLA)
Lehigh Co LJ... Lehigh County Law Journal [*Pennsylvania*] [*A publication*] (DLA)
LehighGp... Lehigh Group, Inc. [*Formerly, LUI Group*] [*Associated Press*] (SAG)
Lehigh LJ... Lehigh County Law Journal [*Pennsylvania*] [*A publication*] (DLA)
Lehigh U.... Lehigh University (GAGS)
Lehigh Val Law Rep... Lehigh Valley Law Reporter [*Pennsylvania*] [*A publication*] (DLA)
Lehigh Val LR... Lehigh Valley Law Reporter [*Pennsylvania*] [*A publication*] (DLA)
Lehigh Val L Rep... Lehigh Valley Law Reporter [*Pennsylvania*] [*A publication*] (DLA)
LEHI PAC... Lehigh Cement Company PAC [*Allentown, PA*] (PACS)
LeHK........ Lehman Brothers, Inc. [*Associated Press*] (SAG)
Leh LJ....... Lehigh County Law Journal [*A publication*] (DLA)
Lehman C (CUNY)... Herbert H. Lehman College of The City University of New York (GAGS)
LehmBr..... Lehman Brothers [*Associated Press*] (SAG)
LEHMIC..... Lumped Element Hybrid Microwave Integrated Circuit [*Electronics*] (LAIN)
LehMU...... Lehman Brothers, Inc. [*Associated Press*] (SAG)
LehORCL.... Lehman Brothers Holdings, Inc. [*Associated Press*] (SAG)
LEHPZ....... Lower Esophageal High Pressure Zone [*Gastroenterology*] (DAVI)
LEHR........ Laboratory for Energy-Related Health Research [*University of California-D avis*] [*Department of Energy*] (GRD)
LehRgBk.... Lehman Brothers, Inc. [*Associated Press*] (SAG)
LehSTc...... Lehman Brothers [*Associated Press*] (SAG)
Leh VLR (PA)... Lehigh Valley Law Reporter [*Pennsylvania*] [*A publication*] (DLA)
LEI........... Air UK (Leisure) Ltd. [*British*] [*ICAO designator*] (FAAC)
LEI........... Almeria [*Spain*] [*Airport symbol*] (OAG)
LEI........... Laboratory Engineering Instruction (ACAE)
LEI........... LASER-Enhanced Ionization [*Spectrometry*]
LEI........... Leading Economic Indicator
LEI........... Lehigh Group [*NYSE symbol*] (TTSB)
Lei........... Leijona [*Record label*] [*Finland*]

LEI .... Leipzig [*German Democratic Republic*] [*Seismograph station code, US Geological Survey*] [*Closed*] (SEIS)
lei .... Leisure (IDYL)
LEI .... Libertarian Education Institute (EA)
LEI .... Library Equipment Institute [*American Library Association*]
LEI .... Life Events [*or Expectancy*] Inventory
LEI .... Literacy and Evangelism International (EA)
LEI .... Lloyd's Electronics, Inc. (EFIS)
LEI .... Local Engineering Instruction (DNAB)
LEI .... Locher Evers International Ltd.
LEI .... Lotus Enterprise Integrator (GART)
LEI .... Raleigh, NC [*Location identifier*] [*FAA*] (FAAL)
LEIA .... Luminescence Enzyme Immunoassay [*Clinical chemistry*]
LEIAC .... Livestock Export Industry Advisory Committee (SAUO)
LEIB .... Ibiza [*Spain*] [*ICAO location identifier*] (ICLI)
LEIC .... Leicestershire [*County in England*] (ROG)
Leics .... Leicestershire (DIAR)
LEICS .... Leicestershire [*County in England*]
LEICSC .... Legal Education Institute, United States Civil Service Commission (DLA)
LEID .... Limit of Error on Inventory Difference
LEID .... Low-Energy Ion Detector
LEIDS .... Logistics Electronic Information Delivery System
LeIF .... Leukocyte Interferon [*Genetics*]
LEIFS .... Lake Erie Information Forecasting System [*Marine science*] (OSRA)
LEIFX .... Federated Equity Income Cl.A [*Mutual fund ticker symbol*] (SG)
Leigh .... Leigh's Virginia Supreme Court Reports [*1829-42*] [*A publication*] (DLA)
Leigh .... Ley's English King's Bench Reports [*1608-29*] [*A publication*] (DLA)
Leigh Abr .... Leigh's Abridgment of the Law of Nisi Prius [*1838*] [*A publication*] (DLA)
Leigh & C .. Leigh and Cave's English Crown Cases Reserved [*1861-65*] [*A publication*] (DLA)
Leigh & CCC... Leigh and Cave's English Crown Cases Reserved [*1861-65*] [*A publication*] (DLA)
Leigh & D Conv... Leigh and Dalzell. Conversion of Property [*1825*] [*A publication*] (DLA)
Leigh & LM Elec... Leigh and Le Marchant. Elections [*4th ed.*] [*1885*] [*A publication*] (DLA)
Leigh GA.... Leigh's Game Act [*A publication*] (DLA)
Leigh NP.... Leigh's Abridgment of the Law of Nisi Prius [*1838*] [*A publication*] (DLA)
Leigh (VA)... Leigh's Virginia Supreme Court Reports [*1829-42*] [*A publication*] (DLA)
LEIJC .... Leipsic Junction, OH [*American Association of Railroads railroad junction routing code*]
LEIM .... Law Enforcement Information Management Section [*An association*] (EA)
LEIN .... Law Enforcement Information Network
LEINS R .... Leinster Regiment [*Military unit*] [*British*] (ROG)
leio .... Leiomyoma [*Gynecology*] (DAVI)
LEIP .... Leipzig [*City in East Germany*] (ROG)
LEIP .... Link Eleven Improvement Program (DOMA)
LEIPS .... Leipsic, OH [*American Association of Railroads railroad junction routing code*]
Leipz Stud... Leipziger Studien zur Klassischen Philosophie [*A publication*] (OCD)
LEIR .... Leisure Craft [*NCIC trailer make code*]
LEIR .... Low Energy Ion Ring
LEIS .... Lander Electrical Interface Simulator [*NASA*]
LEIS .... LASER-Enhanced Ionization Spectroscopy (MEC)
Le Is .... Leeward Islands (BARN)
LEIS .... Legislative Environmental Impact Statement (SAUO)
LEIS .... LEISURE: Australian Leisure Index (SAUO)
LEIS .... LeisureLine [*Footscray Institute of Technology Library*] [*Database*] [*Information service or system*] (IID)
LEIS .... Leisuretime [*NCIC truck make code*]
LEIS .... Low-Energy Ion Scattering [*For study of surfaces*]
LEISA .... Low External Input and Sustainable Agriculture (SAUO)
LeisMkt .... Leisureways Marketing [*Associated Press*] (SAG)
LEISS .... Low-Energy Ion Scattering Spectroscopy
LEIT .... Leisure Home Trailer [*NCIC trailer make code*]
LEIT .... Leitchfield Transfer Company [*Common carrier symbol*]
LEIT .... Leitrim [*County in Ireland*] (ROG)
LEIT .... Light Emission via Inelastic Tunnelling (IAA)
LEITH .... Leithton, IL [*American Association of Railroads railroad junction routing code*]
Leith Black... Leith. Blackstone on Real Property [*2nd ed.*] [*1880*] [*A publication*] (DLA)
Leith R Pr... Leith's Real Property Statutes [*Ontario*] [*A publication*] (DLA)
LEITR .... Leitrim [*County in Ireland*] (ROG)
LEIU .... Law Enforcement Intelligence Units [*An association*] (EA)
LEIU .... Leisure Products [*NCIC trailer make code*]
LEIU .... Leitner International Transport Spedition [*Intermodal shipping container symbol*] (TVRC)
LEIX .... Lowrance Electronics [*NASDAQ symbol*] (SAG)
LEIX .... Lowrance Electronics, Inc. (SAUO)
LEJ .... Leipzig [*Germany*] [*Airport symbol*] (OAG)
LEJ .... Ligation of the Esophagogastric Junction [*Medicine*] (EDAA)
LEJ .... Longitudinal Expansion Joint [*Technical drawings*]
LEJR .... Jerez [*Spain*] [*ICAO location identifier*] (ICLI)
LeJY .... Lehman Brothers, Inc. [*Associated Press*] (SAG)
LEK .... Labe [*Guinea*] [*Airport symbol*] (AD)
LEK .... Laiko Enotiko Komma [*Populist Union Party*] [*Greece*] [*Political party*] (PPE)
LEK .... LASER Experimental Package
LEK .... Lexington [*Kentucky*] [*Seismograph station code, US Geological Survey*] (SEIS)
LEK .... Liquid Encapsulated Kyropoulos [*Crystal growing technique*]
Leknas .... National Institute for Economic and Social Research (SAUO)
LEKOTEK.... Leksaker, Bibliotek [*Program providing meaningful toys for mentally disturbed children; operates on the same principle as a lending library.*] [*Name formed from Swedish words for "playthings" and "library"*]
LEKT .... Lektracycle [*NCIC motorcycle make code*]
lekyt .... Lekythos (VRA)
LEL .... Labor Electoral League (SAUO)
LEL .... Lake Evella [*Australia*] [*Airport symbol*] (OAG)
LEL .... Lancashire Enterprise Ltd. [*British*] (ECON)
LEL .... Large Engineering Loop [*NASA*] (NRCH)
LEL .... Laureate in English Literature
LEL .... League of Empire Loyalists [*British*]
LEL .... Learning Expectancy Level [*Education*]
LEL .... Lens-End-Lamp
LEL .... Letitia Elizabeth Landon [*English poet and novelist, 1802-1839*]
LEL .... Link-Edit Language [*Computer science*]
LEL .... Low Energy LASER [*Light Amplification by Stimulated Emission of Radiation*] [*Military*]
LEL .... Lower Earnings Limit (MHDB)
LEL .... Lower Electrical Limit (NRCH)
LEL .... Lower Explosive Limit [*of fuel vapor*]
LEL .... Lower Exposure Limit (of a Gas Mixture) [*Medicine*] (EDAA)
LEL .... Lowest Effect Level [*Toxicology*]
LELA .... Leland Engineering [*NCIC trailer make code*]
LELC .... Murcia/San Javier [*Spain*] [*ICAO location identifier*] (ICLI)
LELL .... Sabadell [*Spain*] [*ICAO location identifier*] (ICLI)
LELN .... Leon [*Spain*] [*ICAO location identifier*] (ICLI)
LELO .... Logrono [*Spain*] [*ICAO location identifier*] (ICLI)
LELS .... Low-Energy LASER System
LELS/OR .... Odyssey Review. A quarterly of modern Latin American and European literature in English translation. Latin American and European Literary Society (SAUO)
LELTS .... Lightweight Electronic Locating and Tracking System
LELU .... Launch Enable Logic Unit
LELU .... Lugo [*Spain*] [*ICAO location identifier*] (ICLI)
Lely & F Elec... Lely and Foulkes' Elections [*3rd ed.*] [*1887*] [*A publication*] (DLA)
Lely & F Jud Acts... Lely and Foulkes' Judicature Acts [*4th ed.*] [*1883*] [*A publication*] (DLA)
Lely & F Lic Acts... Lely and Foulkes' Licensing Acts [*3rd ed.*] [*1887*] [*A publication*] (DLA)
Lely Railw... Lely's Regulation of Railway Acts [*1873*] [*A publication*] (DLA)
LEM .... Antenna Effective Length for Magnetic-Field Antennas (IEEE)
LEM .... Laboratory Environment Model (MCD)
LEM .... Laboratory of Electro-Modeling [*Former USSR*]
LEM .... Lake Exploration Module [*University of Wisconsin*]
LEM .... Language Extension Module (SAUO)
LEM .... LASER Energy Monitor
LEM .... LASER Exhaust Measurement
LEM .... Lateral Eye Movement
LEM .... Launch Enclosure Maintenance [*Aerospace*] (IAA)
LEM .... Launcher Electronic Module [*Military*] (RDA)
LEM .... Launch Escape Monitor (MCD)
LEM .... Launch Escape Motor [*NASA*]
LEM .... Law Enforcement Manual [*IRS*]
LEM .... Leading Electrical Mechanician
LEM .... Legacy Encapsulation Methodology
LEM .... Lehman Corp. (SAUO)
LEM .... Leibovitz-Emory Medium [*Microbiology*]
LEM .... LeMans [*NCIC car model code*]
LEM .... Lembang [*Java*] [*Seismograph station code, US Geological Survey*] (SEIS)
LEM .... Lemmon, SD [*Location identifier*] [*FAA*] (FAAL)
lem .... Lemon [*Philately*]
LEM .... Lemoyne [*NCIC car model code*]
LEM .... Length of Effectiveness for Magnetic-Field Antennae
LEM .... Leukocytic Endogenous Mediator [*Immunochemistry*]
LEM .... Leukoencephalomalacia [*Veterinary medicine*]
LEM .... Library Education and Manpower (SAUO)
LEM .... Light Effector Mediator System [*Plant physiology*]
LEM .... Light Electron/Emission Microscope/py [*Medicine*] (EDAA)
LEM .... Light Emission Microscopy (MELL)
LEM .... Light Equipment Maintenance (MCD)
LEM .... Linear Electric Motor [*Magnetic rapid-transit car*] (PS)
LEM .... Liquid Emulsion Membrane [*Separation technology*]
LEM .... Logical End of Media
LEM .... Logic Enhanced Memory
LEM .... Logistic Element Manager
LEM .... Logistics Element Manager (SAUO)
LEM .... Lower Explosive Mixture (SAUS)
LEM .... Luminescences Emission Monitor
LEM .... Lunar Excursion Module [*Later, LM*] [*NASA*]
LEM .... Lunar Exploration Module [*NASA*] (IAA)
LEMA .... Laser and Electro-Optics Manufacturers' Association (EA)
LEM(A) .... Leading Electrical Mechanic (Air) [*British military*] (DMA)
LEMA .... Lifting Equipment Manufacturers Association [*British*] (BI)
LEMA .... Lighting Equipment Manufacturers' Association (DAC)
LEMA .... Long-term Ecological Modelling Activity (SAUO)
LEMAC .... Leading Edge Mean Aerodynamic Chord
LEMAG .... Laboratory Equipment and Methods Advisory Group (SAUO)
LEMAR .... Legalize Marijuana [*Acronym is used for name of an organization*]

Le Mar ...... Le Marchant's Gardner Peerage Case [*A publication*] (DLA)
LEMAR ...... Le Mars, IA [*American Association of Railroads railroad junction routing code*]
LEMARS .... Law Enforcement Management Reporting System (ALAC)
LEM(AW).... Leading Electrical Mechanic (Air Weapon) [*British military*] (DMA)
LEMC .... Lemco Tool Corporation [*NCIC trailer make code*]
LEMCA ...... Low-Echelon Maneuver Control Application (SAUS)
LEMCO ...... Light Equipment Maintenance Co. (MCD)
LEMD........ Madrid/Barajas [*Spain*] [*ICAO location identifier*] (ICLI)
LEMDA ...... Lighting-Electrical Materials Distributors Association (EA)
LEMDE ...... Lunar Excursion Module Descent Engine [*NASA*] (MCD)
LEMES ...... Low-Energy Magnetic Electron Spectrum (IAA)
LEMF .... Labour Exchange Managers' Federation [*A union*] [*British*]
LEMF .... Law Enforcement Memorial Foundation (EA)
LEMF .... Local Effective Mole Fraction [*Chemistry*]
LEMG........ Lockyer Resource Management Group (SAUO)
LEMG........ Malaga [*Spain*] [*ICAO location identifier*] (ICLI)
LEMH........ Mahon/Menorca [*Spain*] [*ICAO location identifier*] (ICLI)
LEML & AIA... Locomotive Engineers Mutual Life and Accident Insurance Association (EA)
LEMM .... Madrid [*Spain*] [*ICAO location identifier*] (ICLI)
LEMO........ Local Emergency Management Officer
LEMO........ Lowest Empty Molecular Orbital [*Medicine*] (DMAA)
LEMO........ Sevilla/Moron [*Spain*] [*ICAO location identifier*] (ICLI)
LEMOC ...... Local Emergency Management Operations Course [*Emergency Management*] (EMA)
LEMOY ...... Lemoyne, IL [*American Association of Railroads railroad junction routing code*]
LEMP........ Lightning Electromagnetic Pulse (SAUO)
LEMP........ Logistics Element Manager Plan (SAUO)
LEMPA ...... Low-Energy Magnetospheric Particle Analyzer [*Atomic physics*]
LEMRAS .... Law Enforcement Manpower Resource Allocation System (SAUO)
LEMRAS .... Law Enforcement Manpower Resources Allocation [*IBM program product*]
LEMRP ...... Law Enforcement Memorial Research Project (EA)
LEMS........ Laboratory for Engineering Man/Machine Systems [*Brown University*] (RCD)
LEMS........ Lambert-Eaton Myasthenic Syndrome [*Medicine*] (DB)
LEMS........ Linear Econometric Modeling System (BUR)
LEMS........ Low-Energy Molecular Scattering (MCD)
LEMSCO .... Lockheed Engineering and Management Services Company Inc. (SAUO)
LEMSIP ..... Laboratory for Experimental Medicine and Surgery in Primates [*New York University*] [*Research center*]
LEMT .... Lunar Excursion Module Track [*NASA*] (IAA)
LEMU........ Hans Lechner Spedition [*Intermodal shipping container symbol*] (TVRC)
LEMUF ...... Limits of Error on Material Unaccounted For
LEN .... [*The*] Lake Erie & Northern Railway Co. [*AAR code*]
LEN .... Large Extension Node [*Telecommunications*] (LAIN)
LEN .... Large Extension Node. Communications (SAUS)
LEN .... Length
LEN .... Leninakan [*Former USSR*] [*Seismograph station code, US Geological Survey*] (SEIS)
LEN .... Lennar Corp. [*NYSE symbol*] (SPSG)
LEN .... Lenora Explorations Ltd. [*Toronto Stock Exchange symbol*]
LEN .... Lentini Aviation, Inc. [*ICAO designator*] (FAAC)
LEN .... Leon [*Mexico*] [*Airport symbol*] (OAG)
LEN .... Library of Early Novelists [*A publication*]
LEN .... Light-Emitting Numerics
LEN .... Ligue Europeenne de Natation [*European Swimming Federation*] [*Sweden*] (EAIO)
LEN .... Linear Electrical Network
LEN .... Line Equipment Number (SAUS)
LEN .... Living Economy Network (SAUO)
LEN .... Load Equalization Net [*Aircraft arresting barrier*] [*Trademark*]
LEN .... Local Employment Network (AIE)
LEN .... Local Entry Network (NITA)
LEN .... Low Entry Networking (MCD)
LENA .... Lower Eastside Neighborhoods Association (SAUO)
LEND .... Credit Depot [*NASDAQ symbol*] (TTSB)
LEND .... Credit Depot Corp. [*NASDAQ symbol*] (SAG)
L en D....... Licencie en Droit [*Licentiate in Law*] [*French*]
LEND .... Lockheed Engineers for National Deployment (SAA)
LENGTH ..... Length
LENGTHD ... Lengthened (ROG)
LENI .... Leon's Trucking Service [*Common carrier symbol*]
LENIT........ Leniter [*Gently*] [*Pharmacy*]
LENJC .... Lenawee Junction, MI [*American Association of Railroads railroad junction routing code*]
Lennar ...... Lennar Corp. [*Associated Press*] (SAG)
LENNI .... Local area network Emulation Network Node Interface (SAUS)
Lennk........ Low Endoatmospheric Non Nuclear Kill [*Military*] (ACAE)
LENS .... Concord Camera Corp. [*NASDAQ symbol*] (NQ)
LENS .... Large Enthalpy National Shock (SAUO)
LENS .... Large Extension Node Switch. Communications (SAUS)
LENS .... LASER-Engineered Net Shaping [*Army*]
LENS .... Late-Bound Encapsulated Name Spaces [*Computer science*] (HODG)
LENS .... Lockheed Expendable Neutralization System (SAUS)
LENSCE ..... Limited Enemy Situation Correlation Element (SAUO)
LENT......... Late Effects of Normal Tissue [*Medicine*] (RAWO)
LEntA........ London Enterprise Agency
LENTO....... Lentando [*With Increasing Slowness*] [*Music*] (ROG)
LENWID..... Length to Width Ratio [*Of a leaf*] [*Botany*]
LENZ......... Vision Sciences, Inc. (SAUO)
LEO .... Dreyfus Strategic Municipals [*NYSE symbol*] (SPSG)
LEO .... Law Enforcement Officer (MCD)
LEO .... Law Enforcement Online [*Emergency Management*] (EMA)
LEO .... Lear Oil & Gas Corp. [*Vancouver Stock Exchange symbol*]
Leo .... Leonard's King's Bench Reports [*1540-1615*] [*England*] [*A publication*] (DLA)
Leo .... Leonardus [*Authority cited in pre-1607 legal work*] (DSA)
LEO .... Leoncito [*Argentina*] [*Seismograph station code, US Geological Survey*] (SEIS)
LEO .... Leone [*NCIC car model code*]
LEO .... Leopair SA [*Switzerland*] [*ICAO designator*] (FAAC)
LEO .... Leopoldville (SAUO)
LEO .... Liaison Engineering Order
LEO .... Library Entrance Online
LEO .... Librating Equidistant Observer
LEO .... Link Everything Online (SAUO)
LEO .... Littoral Environment Observation [*Program*] [*Oceanography*]
LEO .... Local Elected Official (OICC)
LEO .... Low Earth Orbit
LEO .... Lunar Exploration Office [*NASA*]
LEO .... Lyons Electronic Office [*J. Lyons & Co*] [*British*] (NITA)
Leoc .... Against Leocrates [*of Lycurgus*] [*Classical studies*] (OCD)
LEOC .... Local Emergency Operations Controller
LEOC .... Ocana [*Spain*] [*ICAO location identifier*] (ICLI)
LEOCOMM... Low Earth Orbit Mobile Data Communications
LEOD .... Lens Extraction, Oculus Dexter [*Right eye*] [*Ophthalmology*] (DAVI)
LEOMA ...... LASER and Electro-Optics Manufacturers' Association
LEOMA ...... LASER/Electro/Optic Measurement Alignment System
Leon......... Leonard's King's Bench, Common Pleas, and Exchequer Reports [*England*] [*A publication*] (DLA)
LEON .... Leoni Motor Express [*Common carrier symbol*]
Leon LA Dig... Leonard's Louisiana Digest of United States Cases [*A publication*] (DLA)
Leon Prec .. Leonard's Precedents in County Courts [*1869*] [*A publication*] (DLA)
LEOP .... Launch and Early Operations Phase (ACAE)
LEOP .... Local Emergency Operations Plan [*Emergency Management*] (EMA)
LEOPARD ... Lentigines, EKG Abnormalities, Ocular Hypertelorism, Pulmonary Stenosis, Abnormalities of Genitalia, Retardation of Growth, and Deafness Syndrome [*Medicine*] (DMAA)
LEOPCID .... Local Elected Officials Project of the Center for Innovative Diplomacy [*Defunct*] (EA)
LEOS .... IEEE [*Institute of Electrical and Electronics Engineers*] LASERS and Electro-Optics Society (EA)
LEOS .... Large Erectable Optical System (ACAE)
LEOS .... Lasers and Electro-Optics Society (SAUO)
LEOS .... Loral Electro-Optical Systems (SAUS)
LEOS .... Loral Electro-Optical Systems Corp.
LEOS .... Low Earth Orbit Satellite (MCD)
LEOS .... Low Earth Orbit Satellites (ACRL)
LEOSAR..... Low Earth Orbit Search and Rescue (SAUO)
LEOT......... Left-End-of-Tape
LEOV......... Oviedo [*Spain*] [*ICAO location identifier*] (ICLI)
LEP .... Air West Airlines, Inc. [*ICAO designator*] (FAAC)
LEP .... Laboratory Evaluation Program [*Environmental Protection Agency*] (GFGA)
LEP .... Laboratory of Experimental Pathology [*National Institute of Environmental Health Sciences*] (RCD)
LEP .... Large Electronic Panel
LEP .... Large Electron-Positron [*Accelerator*] [*in Europe*]
LEP .... Laser Eye Protection (ACAE)
LEP .... Leadership for Performance (ACAE)
LEP .... Least Energy Principle
Lep .... Lepidoptera [*Entomology*]
Lep .... Lepus [*Constellation*]
LEP .... Lethal Effective Phase [*Medicine*] (DB)
LEP .... Library of Exact Philosophy
LEP .... Light Emitting Polymer (SAUS)
LEP .... Light-Emitting Polymer
LEP .... Light Evaluation Plan (MCD)
LEP .... Light External Pintle (SAUS)
LEP .... Lightning-Induced Electron Precipitation [*Atmospheric physics*]
LEP .... Limited English Proficiency
LEP .... Limited English Proficient (SAUO)
LEP .... Lipoprotein Electrophoresis [*Biochemistry*]
LEP .... List of Effective Pages (NVT)
LEP .... Local Enterprise Program
LEP .... Local Field Potential [*Neurobiology*]
LEP .... Locally Enlisted Personnel [*British military*] (DMA)
LEP .... Logistics Excellence Program (SAUO)
LEP .... Low Egg Passage [*Rabies vaccine*]
LEP .... Low Emissions Partnership
LEP .... Low-Energy Photon (ABAC)
LEP .... Lower End Plug (IEEE)
LEP .... Lower Esophageal [*Medicine*] (DB)
LEP .... Lowest Effective Power
LEP .... Lowest Evaluated Price (ACAE)
LEP .... Low-Frequency Prediction [*Marine science*] (OSRA)
LEP .... Lupus Erythematosus Preparation [*Hematology*] (DAVI)
LEP .... Lycee d'Enseignement Professionel [*Professional Secondary School for AdvancedStudies*] [*French*] (BARN)
LEPA......... Laboratoire d'Etudes Politiques et Administratives [*Universite Laval, Quebec*] [*Canada*]
LEPA......... Law Enforcement Planning Agency (SAUO)
LEPA......... Palma De Mallorca [*Spain*] [*ICAO location identifier*] (ICLI)
LEPC......... Law Enforcement Planning Commission

LEPC......... Local Education Agency [*Environment term*] (EGA)
LEPC......... Local Emergency Planning Commission (SAUO)
LEPC......... Local Emergency Planning Committee [*Hazardous waste*]
LEPC......... Local Energy Planning Committee (SAUO)
LEPC......... Low Emissions Paint Consortium
LEPC......... Low Energy Proportional Counter [*Spectrum-X-Gamma*] (HCJD)
LEPD......... Legal Enforcement Policy Division [*Environmental Protection Agency*] (GFGA)
LEPD......... Low-Energy Photon Detector [*Environmental Protection Agency*]
LEPEDEA.... Low-Energy Proton-Electron Differential Energy Analyzer [*NASA*]
LEPG......... Lep Group Ltd. [*NASDAQ symbol*] (SAG)
LE/PH........ Local Exchange/Packet Handler (ACRL)
LEPI......... Litton Educational Publishing, Inc.
LEPMA...... Lithographic Engravers and Plate Makers Association (EA)
LEPO......... LEP Express [*Common carrier symbol*]
LEPO......... Low Exercise Price Options (NUMA)
LEPO......... Pollensa [*Spain*] [*ICAO location identifier*] (ICLI)
LEPOR........ Long-Range and Expanded Oceanic Research (SAUO)
LEPOR........ Long-Term and Expanded Program of Oceanic Exploration and Research
LEPORE..... Long-Term and Expanded Program of Oceanic Research and Exploration (BARN)
LEPP......... Pamplona/Noain-Pamplona [*Spain*] [*ICAO location identifier*] (ICLI)
LEPR......... LASER Electron Paramagnetic Resonance
LEPRA........ British Leprosy Relief Association (IRUK)
LEPRA........ Leprosy Relief Association [*British*] (DI)
LE Prep..... Lupus Erythematosus Preparation [*Hematology*] (CPH)
LEPS......... Launch Escape Propulsion System [*NASA*]
Leps......... Lepus [*Constellation*]
LEPS......... Light-Emitting Polymers [*Computer science*] [*Polymer light-emitting diodes*]
LEPS......... London-Eyring-Polanyi-Sato Method [*Reaction dynamics*]
LEPS......... Low-Energy Photon Spectroscopy (ABAC)
LEPSOC..... Lepidopterists' Society (EA)
Lept.......... Against Leptines [*of Demosthenes*] [*Classical studies*] (OCD)
LEPT......... Leptocytes [*Biochemistry*] (DAVI)
Lept.......... Leptospira [*Genus of bacteria*]
LEPT......... Long-Endurance Patrolling Torpedo
LEPT......... Low-Energy Particle Telescope
LEPTOS..... Leptospirosis Agglutinins [*Biochemistry*] (DAVI)
LEPV......... Low Egg Passage Virus [*Virology*] (QSUL)
LEPW......... Longitudinal Electric Pressure Wave
LEQ.......... Lehman Br Hldg 8.30%'QUICS' [*NYSE symbol*] (TTSB)
LEQ.......... Lehman Brothers [*NYSE symbol*] (SAG)
LEQ.......... Level Equivalent (SSD)
LEQ.......... Life Events Questionnaire [*Psychology*] (EDAC)
LEQ.......... Line Equalizer [*Communications term*] (DCT)
LEQ.......... Line Equipped [*Telecommunications*] (TEL)
LEQ.......... Line of Equipment [*Telecommunications*] (TEL)
Leq.......... Loudness Equivalent [*Medicine*] (DMAA)
LER.......... Land Equivalent Ratio [*Agriculture*]
LER.......... LANSCE/Energy Research Programs (SAUO)
LER.......... Launcher Equipment Room [*Missiles*]
LER.......... Leading Edge Radius (MSA)
LER.......... Lease Expenditure Request (MCD)
LER.......... Leer [*Ostfriesland*] [*German license plate city code*]
LER.......... Leinster [*Australia*] [*Airport symbol*] (OAG)
LER.......... Lenkau [*Language symbol*] (ETLW)
LER.......... Lerner Stores Corp. (SAUO)
LER.......... Lerwick [*United Kingdom*] [*Geomagnetic observatory code*]
LER.......... Licensee Event Report [*Nuclear energy*] (NRCH)
LER.......... Life Elongation Ratio (DB)
LER.......... Life Extension Refit (SAUS)
LER.......... Light Efficiency Radiator [*General Motors Corp.*] [*Automotive engineering*]
LER.......... Light-Emitting Resistor [*Computer hacker terminology*] (NHD)
LER.......... Lissajous Electron Plasma (AAEL)
LER.......... Logansport & Eel River Short Line [*Federal Railroad Administration identification code*]
LER.......... London Eastern Railway (SAUO)
LER.......... London Electric Railway
LER.......... Long Eye Relief (MCD)
LER.......... Loss Exchange Ratio (MCD)
LER.......... Lysozomal Enzyme Release (DB)
LER.B....... Leroux Steel [*Toronto Stock Exchange symbol*] [*Canada*]
LERA......... Limited Employee Retirement Account (IEEE)
LERAM...... Littoral Ecosystem Risk Assessment Model (SAUO)
LERAM...... Littoral Ecosystem Risk Assessment Model for Prediction of Risk of Chemical Stressors Entering the Aquatic Environment [*Environmental Protection Agency*] (AEPA)
LERB......... Line Error Recording Block (MCD)
LERC......... Laboratory Environmental Review Committee (SAUO)
LERC......... Language for Export Research Center [*University of Western Sydney*] [*Australia*]
LERC......... Laramie Energy Research Center [*Department of Energy*]
LERC......... Law Enforcement Resource Center (SAUO)
LERC......... Lean Enterprise Research Centre [*Cardiff University*] [*United Kingdom*] (RCD)
LERC......... Lewis Research Center [*NASA*] (KSC)
LeRC......... Lewis Research Center [*Cleveland, OH*] (NAKS)
LERC......... Local Emergency Response Committee (EPAT)
LERC......... London Electric Railway Company (SAUO)
LERF......... Laboratory Experimental Research Facility [*Army*] (RDA)
LERG......... Local Electroretingogram (DB)
LERH......... Leerhoff Trucking [*Common carrier symbol*]
LERI......... Murcia/Alcantarilla [*Spain*] [*ICAO location identifier*] (ICLI)
LERIS........ Low-Energy Recoil Ion Spectroscopy
LERK......... LASER Experimental Research Kit
LERM......... Logansport & Eel River Museum [*Federal Railroad Administration identification code*]
LERMISTOR... Learning Materials Information Store (PDAA)
LERN......... Learning Resources Network (EA)
LERN......... Learning Technology, Inc. (SAUO)
LERNA....... Lerns, IL [*American Association of Railroads railroad junction routing code*]
LERP......... Labor Education and Research Project (EA)
LERP......... Linear Interpolation [*Computer science*] (NHD)
LERS......... Reus [*Spain*] [*ICAO location identifier*] (ICLI)
LERSC....... Location Evaluation Recognition and Statistical Comparison (PDAA)
LERSO....... Low Erucic Acid Rapeseed Oil (PDAA)
LERT......... Lockheed Emergency Reset Timer (IAA)
LERT......... Rota [*Spain*] [*ICAO location identifier*] (ICLI)
LERTCON... Alert Condition [*Military*] (AABC)
LERTCON... Alert Condition System (SAUO)
LERTS........ Laboratoire d'Etudes et de Recherches en Teledetection Spatiale [*France*] (EOSA)
LERX......... Leading Edge Root Extension [*Aviation*]
L-ERX....... Leukoerythroblastic Reaction [*Biochemistry*] (DAVI)
LERX......... PSI Energy [*Private rail car owner code*]
LERY......... LeRoi [*NCIC trailer make code*]
LERY......... Leroy Pharmacies, Inc. (SAUO)
LES.......... Automotors Salta SACYF [*Argentina*] [*ICAO designator*] (FAAC)
LES.......... Laboratory for Environmental Studies [*Ohio State University*] [*Research center*] (RCD)
LES.......... Lambert-Eaton Myasthenic Syndrome [*Medicine*]
LES.......... Land Earth Station (SAUO)
LES.......... LAN [*Local Area Network*] Emulation Server [*Telecommunications*] (ACRL)
LES.......... Large Eddy Simulation [*For modelling fluid flow*]
LES.......... Laser Engagement System (ACAE)
LES.......... LASER Excitation Spectroscopy
LES.......... Lateral Epithelial Space [*Anatomy*] (DAVI)
LES.......... Launch Effects Simulator
LES.......... Launch Enabling System
LES.......... Launch/Entry Suit [*NASA*]
LES.......... Launch Environmental Simulator (MCD)
LES.......... Launch Equipment Shop (MCD)
LES.......... Launch Escape System [*or Subsystem*] [*NASA*]
LES.......... Law Enforcement Squadron
LES.......... Lawrence Experiment Station [*Agar*] [*Medicine*] (BABM)
LES.......... Leading Edge Slats (MCD)
LES.......... Leave and Earnings Statement [*Military*] (AABC)
LES.......... Le Sabre [*NCIC car model code*]
LES.......... Lesbian (DSUE)
LES.......... Leslie Fay Companies (SAUO)
LES.......... Lesobeng [*Lesotho*] [*Airport symbol*] (OAG)
LES.......... Lesozavodsk [*Former USSR*] [*Seismograph station code, US Geological Survey*] [*Closed*] (SEIS)
LES.......... Licensing Executive Society (SAUO)
LES.......... Licensing Executives Society (EA)
LES.......... Licensing Executives Society International (SAUO)
LES.......... Life Experiences Survey [*Psychology*]
LES.......... Life Extension Society (SAUO)
LES.......... Light-Emitting Switch [*Electronics*] (OA)
LES.......... Light Experimental Supercruiser (MCD)
LES.......... Light Exposure Speed [*Photography*] (OA)
LES.......... Lilliput Edison Screw
LES.......... Limited Early Site [*Nuclear energy*] (NRCH)
LES.......... Limited English Speaking (OICC)
LES.......... Lincoln Experimental Satellite [*Lincoln Laboratory, MIT*]
LES.......... Lincoln Laboratory Experimental Satellite (SAUO)
LES.......... Line Errored Seconds (SAUS)
LES.......... Loaded Equipment Section
LES.......... Local Engineering Specifications [*DoD*]
LES.......... Local Engineering Standard (IAA)
LES.......... Local Excitatory State
LES.......... Locally Engaged Staff
LES.......... Locke Egg Serum [*Medicine*] (MAE)
LES.......... Logistics Execution System (GART)
LES.......... Loop Error Signal
LES.......... Louisiana Engineering Society (SAUO)
LES.......... Low-Energy Sputter
LES.......... Lower Esophageal Sphincter [*Medicine*]
LES.......... Lunar Escape System [*NASA*]
LES.......... Lupus Erythematosus, Systemic [*Medicine*] (MAE)
LES.......... Support Landing Boat [*Navy symbol*] [*Obsolete*]
LES-9........ Lincoln Experimental Satellite-9 (SAUS)
LES 8/9..... Lincoln Laboratories Experimental Satellites Number 8 and 9 (SAUO)
LESA......... Lake Erie Steam Association [*Defunct*]
LESA......... Land Evaluation and Site Assessment System [*Department of Agriculture*]
LESA......... Lunar Exploration System for Apollo [*NASA*]
LESA......... Salamanca [*Spain*] [*ICAO location identifier*] (ICLI)
LESAP....... Law Enforcement Security Access Position
LESAR....... Linear Elastic Structural Analysis Routine (ACAE)
LESAT....... Leased Satellite [*Military*] (CAAL)
LESAT....... Lockheed Environmental Systems and Technologies Co. (SAUO)
LESC......... Launch Escape System Control [*NASA*] (KSC)
LESC......... Leschago [*Common carrier symbol*]

LESC .... LE [*Lupus Erythematosus*] Support Club (EA)
LESC .... Liberty Equipment and Supply Company (SAUO)
LESC .... Life and Environmental Sciences Committee (SAUO)
LESC .... Light-Emitting Switch Control [*Electronics*] (OA)
LESC .... Lockheed Electronic Systems Company (SPST)
LESC .... Lockheed Engineering & Sciences Co. (SAUS)
LESC .... Lunar-Environment Sample Container [*Apollo*] [*NASA*]
Lesco .... Lesco, Inc. [*Associated Press*] (SAG)
LESCS .... Launch Escape Stabilization and Control System [*NASA*] (IAA)
LESD .... Letterer-Siwe Disease [*Medicine*] (DMAA)
LESEM .... Low Energy Scanning Electron Microscope (ACAE)
LESG .... Late Effects Study Group [*for Hodgkins disease*]
Lesh .... Leshonenu [*Jerusalem*] (BJA)
LESI .... Leif Ericson Society International (EA)
LESJ .... Son San Juan Air Force Base [*Spain*] [*ICAO location identifier*] (ICLI)
LESL .... Law Enforcement Standards Laboratory [*National Institute of Standards and Technology*]
LESL .... Leslie's Poolmart [*NASDAQ symbol*] (TTSB)
L es L .... Licencie es Lettres [*Licentiate in Letters*] [*French*] (EY)
Lesli .... List of Eligible Surplus Line Insurers
LESM .... Longman's Elementary Science Manuals [*A publication*]
LESM .... Murcia [*Spain*] [*ICAO location identifier*] (ICLI)
Les Miz .... Les Miserables [*Musical based on Victor Hugo's novel*]
LESNW .... Lesnwith [*England*]
LESO .... Lifting Engineering Stop Order (ACAE)
LESO .... San Sebastian [*Spain*] [*ICAO location identifier*] (ICLI)
LESOC .... Lincoln Experimental Satellite Operations Center (MCD)
LESOP .... Leveraged Employee Stock Ownership Plan [*Procter & Gamble Co.*]
LESP .... Law Enforcement Standards Program [*National Institute of Law Enforcement and Criminal Justice*]
LESP .... Lower Esophageal Sphincter Pressure [*Medicine*]
LESP .... Madrid [*Spain*] [*ICAO location identifier*] (ICLI)
LesPol .... Leslie's Poolmart, Inc. [*Associated Press*] (SAG)
L'Esprit .... L'Esprit Createur [*A publication*] (BRI)
LESR .... Leisure Manor [*NCIC trailer make code*]
LESR .... Limited Early Site Review [*Nuclear energy*] (NRCH)
LESS .... La Esperanto-Spiritista Societo (SAUO)
LESS .... LASER-Excited Shpol'skii Spectrometry
LESS .... Lateral Electrical Spine Stimulation [*Orthopedics*] (DAVI)
LESS .... Launch Escape System Simulator [*NASA*] (IAA)
LESS .... Law Encounter Severity Scale [*Personality development test*] [*Psychology*]
LESS .... Leading Edge Structure Subsystem [*Aviation*] (NASA)
LESS .... Leading Edge Subsystem (NAKS)
LESS .... Least-Cost Estimating and Scheduling System
LesS .... Licencie es Sciences [*Licentiate in Science*] [*French*] (BARN)
L/ESS .... Loads/Environmental Spectra Survey (MCD)
LESS .... Lunar Escape System Simulator [*NASA*]
L es SC .... Licencie es Sciences [*Licentiate of Sciences*] [*French*]
LesSc .... Licencie es Sciences [*Licentiate of Sciences*] [*French*] (ASC)
lessy .... lesbian [*Psychology*] (DAVI)
LEST .... John Lestician Trucking [*Common carrier symbol*]
LEST .... Large Earth-Based [*formerly, European*] Solar Telescope
LEST .... Large Earth Survey Telescope
LEST .... Launch Electronics System Test
LEST .... Launch Enable System Turret (IAA)
Lest .... Licencie es Lettres [*Licentiate in Letters*] [*French*] (BARN)
LEST .... Low-Energy Speech Transmission
LEST .... Santiago [*Spain*] [*ICAO location identifier*] (ICLI)
Lest & But ... Lester and Butler's Supplement to Lester's Georgia Reports [*A publication*] (DLA)
Lester .... Lester's Reports [*31-33 Georgia*] [*A publication*] (DLA)
Lester & B ... Lester and Butler's Supplement to Lester's Georgia Reports [*A publication*] (DLA)
Lester Supp ... Lester and Butler's Supplement to Lester's Georgia Reports [*A publication*] (DLA)
Lest PL .... Lester's Decisions in Public Land Cases [*A publication*] (DLA)
LESTR .... Leukocyte-Expressed Seven-Transmembrane-Domain Receptor [*Biochemistry*]
LESU .... Law Enforcement Study Unit [*of the American Topical Association*] (EA)
LESU .... Seo De Urgel [*Spain*] [*ICAO location identifier*] (ICLI)
LET .... Aerolineas Ejecutivas SA [*Mexico*] [*ICAO designator*] (FAAC)
LET .... Laboratory Electronics Technician (IAA)
LET .... Laboratory of Electromagnetic Theory (SAUO)
LET .... Launch & Escape Time (SAUS)
LET .... Launch Effects Trainer [*Weaponry*] (MCD)
LET .... Launch Eject Test
LET .... Launch Equipment Test
LET .... Launch Escape Tower [*NASA*] (MCD)
LET .... Leader Effectiveness Training [*A course of study*]
LET .... Leading Edge Tracker
LET .... Learning Efficiency Test [*Educational test*]
LET .... Legacy Encapsulation Technology
LET .... Leonard Euler Telescope (SAUO)
LET .... Leticia [*Colombia*] [*Airport symbol*] (OAG)
LET .... Letter
LET .... Lettish [*Latvian*] (ROG)
LET .... Leukocyte Esterase Test [*Medicine*] (PALA)
LET .... Lidocaine, Epinephrine and Tetracaine (SAUS)
LET .... Lidocaine, Epinephrine, and Tetracaine Solution [*Medicine*] (DMAA)
LET .... Life Environmental Testing (IAA)
LET .... Light Equipment Transporter (MCD)
LET .... Limited Environmental Test (MCD)
LET .... Lincoln Experimental Terminal [*NASA*]
LET .... Linear Energy Transfer [*Radiology*]
LET .... Lithium Excretion Test [*Clinical chemistry*]
LET .... Live Environment Testing
LET .... Live Environment Training [*Military*] (ADDR)
LET .... Local Enterprise Trust [*British*]
LET .... Logical Equipment Table
LET .... Logistic Escape Trunk (CAAL)
LET .... London and Edinburgh Trust [*British*]
LET .... Low-Emissions Truck
LET .... Low-End Torque [*Automotive engineering*]
LET .... Low-Energy Telescope [*Geophysics*]
LET .... Lux e Tenebris [*Light Out of Darkness*] [*Freemasonry*] [*Latin*]
LETA .... Latvian Telegraph Agency (EY)
LETA .... Sevilla/Tablada [*Spain*] [*ICAO location identifier*] (ICLI)
LETAC .... Law Enforcement Training Advisory Council (SAUO)
LET&D .... Liquid Effluent Treatment and Disposal Liability Act (SAUO)
LETATA .... Light Edge Tool and Allied Trades Association [*British*] (BI)
LETB .... Local Exchange Test Bed [*Telecommunications*] (TEL)
LETC .... Laramie Energy Technology Center [*Department of Energy*] (GRD)
Letch .... Letchworth Independent Bancshares Corp. [*Associated Press*] (SAG)
LetchInd .... Letchworth Independent Bancshares Corp. [*Associated Press*] (SAG)
LETCO .... Law Engineering Testing Co. (EFIS)
LETCO .... Law Environmental Testing Company (EFIS)
LETCS .... Launch Escape Tower Canard System [*NASA*] (IAA)
Let D .... Doctor of Letters
LETD .... Lowest Effective Toxic Dose [*Medicine*] (DMAA)
LE-TE .... Leading Edge - Trailing Edge [*Aerodynamics*]
LETEC .... London East Training and Enterprise Council [*British*] (AIE)
LETF .... Launch Equipment Exposure Facility (SAUS)
LETF .... Launch Equipment Test Facility [*NASA*] (NASA)
LETFO .... Letter Follows (NOAA)
LETGS .... Low Energy Transmission Grating Spectrometer (SAUS)
leth .... Lethal [*Pharmacology*] (DAVI)
LETHR .... Leather
LETI .... Leningrad Electrotechnical Institute (SAUO)
LETIS .... Leicestershire Technical Information Service [*British*] (NITA)
LETL .... Lewis Truck Lines [*Common carrier symbol*]
LETM .... Lake Evaporation and Thermodynamics Model [*Marine science*] (OSRA)
LETN .... Law Enforcement Television Network
LETO .... Madrid/Torrejon [*Spain*] [*ICAO location identifier*] (ICLI)
LETRI .... Leihua Electronic Technology Research Institute (SAUO)
LETS .... Large, External Transformation Sensitive [*Glycoprotein*] [*Also known as CSP*] [*Cytochemistry*]
LETS .... Large, External Transformation-Sensitive Fibronectin [*Medicine*] (PALA)
LETS .... Launch Equipment Test Set (MCD)
LETS .... Law Enforcement Teletype [*or Teletypewriter*] Service [*Phoenix, AZ*]
LETS .... Law Enforcement Teletypewriter System (SAUO)
LETS .... Leading Edge Tracker System
LETS .... Learning Experience for Technical Students [*NASA*]
Lets .... Letter Rulings
LETS .... Linear-Energy Transfer Spectrometer [*Radiology*] (KSC)
LETS .... Linear-Energy Transfer System [*Radiology*]
LETS .... Live Environment Testing with SAGE (MCD)
LETS .... Local Exchange Trading Scheme (WDAA)
LETS .... Low-Energy Telescope System [*Geophysics*]
LETS .... Lunar Experiment Telemetry System [*Aerospace*]
LETS .... Local Entertainment and Trade System (ODA)
LETT .... Letters
LETT .... Lettish [*Latvian*] (ROG)
LETTS .... Lettsworth, LA [*American Association of Railroads railroad junction routing code*]
LETU .... Gilmar Leasing [*Intermodal shipping container symbol*] (TVRC)
LEU .... Emory University, Division of Librarianship, Atlanta, GA [*OCLC symbol*] (OCLC)
LEU .... Laser Electronic Unit (SAUS)
LEU .... Launch Enable Unit
LEU .... Launcher Electronic Unit (MCD)
leu .... Leucine [*An amino acid*] (DOG)
Leu .... Leucine [*Also, L*] [*An amino acid*]
LEU .... Leucovorin (DMAA)
LEU .... Leukocyte Equivalent Unit (DMAA)
LEU .... Lewis, IN [*Location identifier*] [*FAA*] (FAAL)
LEU .... License to Export Uranium (NRCH)
LEU .... Lions-Air, AG [*Switzerland*] [*FAA designator*] (FAAC)
LEU .... Low-Enriched Uranium [*Nuclear energy*]
LEU .... Seo De Urgel [*Spain*] [*Airport symbol*] (OAG)
LEUC .... Leucotomy [*European term for lobotomy*] (DSUE)
leuc .... Leuk [*Medicine*] (EDAA)
LeucNtl .... Leucadia National Corp. [*Associated Press*] (SAG)
Leuk .... Leukemia [*Medicine*]
LEUK .... Leukocyte [*Biochemistry*] (DAVI)
LEUKAP .... Leukocyte Alkaline Phosphatase [*Biochemistry*] (DAVI)
leuko .... Leukocyte [*Hematology*]
LEUP .... Leuprlide [*Antineoplastic drug*] (CDI)
LEV .... Bureta [*Fiji*] [*Airport symbol*] (OAG)
LEV .... Grand Isle, LA [*Location identifier*] [*FAA*] (FAAL)
LEV .... Launch Escape Vehicle [*NASA*]
LEV .... Leavenworth, WA [*Amtrak Busline code*]
LEV .... Leibovitz-Emory Medium for Viral Cultures [*Microbiology*]
LEV .... Leichtverwundet; Leichtverwundeter [*Slightly wounded; minor casualty*] [*German military - World War II*]

LEV .... Levamisole [*Antineoplastic drug*] (CDI)
LEV .... Levant
lev .... Levator [*Muscle*] [*Medicine*] (MEDA)
LEV .... Level
LEV .... Lever
LEV .... Leverkusen [*German license plate city code*]
LEV .... Leviathan Gas PL Partners Ltd. [*NYSE symbol*] (SPSG)
LEV .... Leviathan Gas PLPtnrs LP [*NYSE symbol*] (TTSB)
Lev .... Levinz's King's Bench and Common Pleas Reports [*1660-97*] [*England*] [*A publication*] (DLA)
LEV .... Levis [*Light*] [*Pharmacy*]
Lev .... Leviticus [*Old Testament book*]
LEV .... Levitz Furniture Corp. (SAUO)
lev .... Levorotatory [*Optics*] [*Chemistry*] (DOG)
LEV .... Lev Scientific Industries Ltd. [*Vancouver Stock Exchange symbol*]
LEV .... Levyne [*A zeolite*]
LEV .... Lifting Entry Vehicle
LEV .... Loader/Editor/Verifier [*Telecommunications*] (TEL)
LEV .... Local Exhaust Ventilation [*Hazardous material control*]
LEV .... Logistics Entry Vehicle
LEV .... Lolium Enation Virus [*Plant pathology*]
LEV .... Low-Emissions Vehicle
LEV .... Loyal Edinburgh Volunteers [*British military*] (DMA)
LEV .... Lunar Escape Vehicle (IAA)
LEV .... Lunar Excursion Vehicle [*Aerospace*]
LEVC .... Levco Manufacturers [*NCIC trailer make code*]
LEVC .... Valencia [*Spain*] [*ICAO location identifier*] (ICLI)
LEVCB .... Low-Emission Vehicle Certification Board [*Terminated, 1980*] [*Environmental Protection Agency*]
LEVD .... Valladolid [*Spain*] [*ICAO location identifier*] (ICLI)
LevelOne ... Level One Communications, Inc. [*Associated Press*] (SAG)
Lev Ent .... Levinz's Entries [*England*] [*A publication*] (DLA)
LEVER .... Levert, LA [*American Association of Railroads railroad junction routing code*]
LevGas .... Leviathan Gas Pipeline [*Associated Press*] (SAG)
LE-VGF .... Liquid Encapsulation-Vertical Gradient Freeze (PDAA)
Levi Com L... Levi's International Commercial Law [*2nd ed.*] [*1863*] [*A publication*] (DLA)
Levi Merc L... Levi's Mercantile Law [*1854*] [*A publication*] (DLA)
LEVIT .... Leviter [*Lightly*] [*Pharmacy*]
LEVIT .... Leviticus [*Old Testament book*] (ROG)
Levitz .... Levitz Furniture, Inc. [*Associated Press*] (SAG)
Lev JP .... Levinge's Irish Justice of the Peace [*A publication*] (DLA)
LEVL .... Level One Communications [*NASDAQ symbol*] (TTSB)
LEVL .... Level One Communications, Inc. [*NASDAQ symbol*] (SAG)
LEVM .... Valencia [*Spain*] [*ICAO location identifier*] (ICLI)
LEVMETR ... Levelometer
LEVN .... Levin Computer Corp. (SAUO)
LEVONORG... Levonorgestrel (SAUS)
LevR .... Leviticus Rabbah (BJA)
LEVS .... Leaves
LEVS .... Lev Scientific Industries Ltd. (SAUO)
LEVS .... Madrid/Cuatro Vientos [*Spain*] [*ICAO location identifier*] (ICLI)
LEVT .... Left Extremity Venous Tracing [*Cardiology*] (DAVI)
LEVT .... Levitt Corporation (SAUO)
LEVT .... Lower Extremity Venous Tracing [*Cardiology*] (DAVI)
LEVT .... Vitoria [*Spain*] [*ICAO location identifier*] (ICLI)
LEVTAB .... Level Table (MHDB)
LEVVA .... Lunar Extravehicular Visor Assembly [*NASA*] (KSC)
LEVX .... Level Energy [*Private rail car owner code*]
LEVX .... Vigo [*Spain*] [*ICAO location identifier*] (ICLI)
Levy WTM... Woerterbuch ueber die Talmudim und Midraschim [*J. Levy*] [*A publication*] (BJA)
LEW .... Auburn-Lewiston [*Maine*] [*Airport symbol*] (AD)
LEW .... Auburn/Lewiston, ME [*Location identifier*] [*FAA*] (FAAL)
LEW .... Lech-Elektrizitatswerke AG (EFIS)
Lew .... Lewin's English Crown Cases Reserved [*1822-38*] [*A publication*] (DLA)
LEW .... Lewis [*Rat strain*]
Lew .... Lewis' Reports [*Nevada*] [*A publication*] (DLA)
Lew .... Lewis' Reports [*Missouri*] [*A publication*] (DLA)
LEW .... Lewiston [*Maine*] [*Airport symbol*] (OAG)
LEW .... Lewistown, PA [*Amtrak rail station code*]
LEW .... Logical Early Warning (GART)
LEW .... Lyttleton Engineering Works (SAUO)
LEWA .... Lewaub Trailer Manufacturing [*NCIC trailer make code*]
Lew App .... Lewin's Appportionment [*1869*] [*A publication*] (DLA)
Lew B & S... Lewis on Bonds and Securities [*A publication*] (DLA)
Lew CC .... Lewin's English Crown Cases [*A publication*] (DLA)
Lew CL .... Lewis' Criminal Law [*A publication*] (DLA)
Lew Conv ... Lewis' Principles of Conveyancing [*A publication*] (DLA)
LEWDD .... Lightweight Early Warning Detection Device (SAUS)
LEWDI .... Light Weight Early Warning Detection Device (ACAE)
Lew Dig Cr L... Lewis' Digest of United States Criminal Law [*A publication*] (DLA)
Lew Elec .... Lewis' Election Manual [*A publication*] (DLA)
Lew Eq Dr... Lewis on Equity Drafting [*A publication*] (DLA)
LEWEX .... Labrador Extreme Waves Experiment (SAUO)
LEWI .... Lewis-Shepard [*NCIC truck make code*]
LEWIB .... Lewisburg, PA [*American Association of Railroads railroad junction routing code*]
Lewin .... Lewin on Trusts [*A publication*] (DLA)
Lewin CC ... Lewin's English Crown Cases Reserved [*1822-38*] [*A publication*] (DLA)
Lewin CC (Eng)... Lewin's English Crown Cases [*A publication*] (DLA)
Lewin Cr Cas... Lewin's English Crown Cases Reserved [*A publication*] (DLA)
Lew Ind Pen... Lewis' East India Penal Code [*A publication*] (DLA)
Lewis .... Lewis' Appeals Reports [*29-35 Missouri*] [*A publication*] (DLA)
Lewis .... Lewis' Kentucky Law Reporter [*A publication*] (DLA)
Lewis .... Lewis' Reports [*Nevada*] [*A publication*] (DLA)
Lewis & Clark C... Lewis and Clark College (GAGS)
Lewis Em Dom... Lewis on Eminent Domain [*A publication*] (DLA)
Lewis Perp... Lewis' Law of Perpetuities [*A publication*] (DLA)
Lew L Cas... Lewis' Leading Cases on Public Land Law [*A publication*] (DLA)
Lew LT .... Lewis on Land Titles in Philadelphia [*A publication*] (DLA)
LEWP .... Line Echo Wave Pattern
Lew Perp ... Lewis' Law of Perpetuities [*A publication*] (DLA)
Lew St .... Lewis on Stocks, Bonds, Etc. [*A publication*] (DLA)
Lew Tr .... Lewin on Trusts [*A publication*] (DLA)
LEWU .... Lanka Estate Workers' Union [*Ceylon*]
LEWU .... Norman Lewis Tankers [*Intermodal shipping container symbol*] (TVRC)
Lew US Cr L... Lewis' Digest of United States Criminal Law [*A publication*] (DLA)
LEWWG .... Land Electonic Warfare Working Group (SAUO)
LEX .... Cary Memorial Library, Lexington, MA [*OCLC symbol*] (OCLC)
LEX .... Land Exercise [*Marine Corps*]
LEX .... Leading Edge Extension [*Aviation*]
LEX .... Letter Exchange (EA)
Lex .... Lexical (BJA)
LEX .... Lexicographer (ABBR)
Lex .... Lexicon (DIAR)
lex .... Lexicon (WDAA)
LEX .... Lexicon
LEX .... Lexington [*Virginia*] [*Seismograph station code, US Geological Survey*] [*Closed*] (SEIS)
LEX .... Lexington [*Diocesan abbreviation*] [*Kentucky*] (TOCD)
LEX .... Lexington/Frankfort [*Kentucky*] [*Airport symbol*] (OAG)
LEX .... L'Express, Inc. [*ICAO designator*] (FAAC)
LEX .... Line Exchange [*Telecommunications*]
LEX .... Listing Exchange
LEx .... Liver Extract [*Protein/lipid substance*] [*Immunology*]
LEXB .... Lexington Savings Bank (SAUO)
LexBLF .... Lexington B & L Financial Corp. [*Associated Press*] (SAG)
LexCrpP .... Lexington Corporate Properties [*Associated Press*] (SAG)
Lex Cust .... Lex Custumaria [*Latin*] [*A publication*] (DLA)
LEXD .... Lexden [*England*]
LEXD .... Lexidata Corp. (SAUO)
LEXG .... Lexicon Genetics [*NASDAQ symbol*] (SG)
LexGlbl .... Lexington Global Asset Managers, Inc. [*Associated Press*] (SAG)
LEXI .... Lexical (ABBR)
LEXI .... Lexicon Corp. (SAUO)
LEXICO .... Lexicographer (ABBR)
lexicog .... Lexicography (WDAA)
LEXICOG .... Lexicography
LEXIN .... Lexington, KY [*American Association of Railroads railroad junction routing code*]
LEXIS .... Legal Exchange Information Service (SAUO)
LEXIS .... Legal Research Service [*Registered service mark*] (IID)
LEXIS .... Lexicography Information Service [*Germany*] [*Computer science*]
LEXJ .... Santander [*Spain*] [*ICAO location identifier*] (ICLI)
Lex Man .... Lex Maneriorum [*Latin*] [*A publication*] (DLA)
Lex Mer Am... Lex Mercatoria Americana [*Latin*] [*A publication*] (DLA)
Lex Mess ... Lexicon Messanense [*Classical studies*] (OCD)
Lexmrk .... Lexmark International Group [*Associated Press*] (SAG)
LEXN .... Lexicon (ABBR)
LEXOG .... Lexicology (ABBR)
LEXOGL .... Lexicological (ABBR)
LEXOGT .... Lexicologist (ABBR)
LEXP .... Language Experience
Lex Parl .... Lex Parliamentaria [*Latin*] [*A publication*] (DLA)
LEXPHR .... Lexicographer (ABBR)
LEXPHY .... Lexicography (ABBR)
LEXS .... Lexus [*NCIC truck make code*]
LEXS .... Lexus [*NCIC car make code*]
LEXSWG .... Lunar Exploration Science Working Group [*NASA*]
LexSyr .... Lexicon Syriacum [*A publication*] (BJA)
LEXT .... Lexitech International Documentation Network, Inc. (SAUO)
L/EXT .... Lower Extremity [*Medicine*]
Ley .... Ley's English Court of Wards Reports [*A publication*] (DLA)
Ley .... Ley's English King's Bench Reports [*1608-29*] [*A publication*] (DLA)
LEY .... Liberal European Youth
LEYD .... Leyden [*Netherlands*] (ROG)
LEYL .... Leyland [*NCIC truck make code*]
Ley Wards... Ley's English Court of Wards Reports [*A publication*] (DLA)
LEZ .... Lunar Equatorial Zone [*Army Map Service*]
LEZA .... Zaragoza [*Spain*] [*ICAO location identifier*] (ICLI)
LEZG .... Zaragoza [*Spain*] [*ICAO location identifier*] (ICLI)
LEZL .... Sevilla [*Spain*] [*ICAO location identifier*] (ICLI)
LEZOR .... Liquid Encapsulation Zone-Refining (PDAA)
LF .... Fighter Aircraft Fitted with Engine Rated for Low-Altitude Performance (SAUS)
LF .... Labile Factor (DB)
LF .... Lacrimatory Factor [*Food technology*]
LF .... Lacrosse Foundation (EA)
LF .... Lactoferrin [*Biochemistry*]
LF .... La Fosse Platinum Group, Inc. [*Toronto Stock Exchange symbol*]
LF .... Lakser Foundation (SAUO)
LF .... Lama Foundation (EA)
LF .... Laminar Flow (AAEL)

LF .... [*The*] Lancashire Fusiliers [*Military unit*] [*British*]
LF .... Land Forces [*Military*] [*British*]
LF .... Landing Force [*Navy*] (NVT)
LF .... Largest Frame (ACRL)
LF .... Laryngofissure (MAE)
LF .... Lassa Fever [*Medicine*] (MELL)
LF .... Latex Fixation [*Test*] [*Medicine*]
LF .... Lathe Fixture (MCD)
LF .... Laucks Foundation (EA)
LF .... Launch Facility
LF .... Launch Forward
LF .... Law French (DLA)
LF .... Lawn Faucet (MSA)
LF .... Laws of Florida [*Emergency Management*] (EMA)
L/F .... Leader/Follower (ACAE)
LF .... Lead Fabricators Ltd. (SAUO)
LF .... Lead-Free
LF .... Leaf [*Bibliography*] (ROG)
lf .... Leaf (VRA)
LF .... Leaflet (WGA)
LF .... League of Friendship [*Defunct*] (EA)
LF .... Leapfrog Configuration [*Circuit theory*] (IEEE)
LF .... Least Favourable (FOTI)
LF .... Least Frequent (AEBS)
LF .... Lebanese Forces
LF .... Lederer Foundation (EA)
LF .... Ledger Folio
LF .... Left (ECII)
lf .... Left Field [*Baseball term*] (NDBD)
LF .... Left Field [*or Fielder*] [*Baseball*]
LF .... Left Foot
LF .... Left Fore (SPVS)
LF .... Left Forward [*Football*]
LF .... Left Front
LF .... Left Fullback [*Soccer*]
LF .... Legion of Frontiersmen [*British military*] (DMA)
LF .... Leslie Fay Companies, Inc. (EFIS)
LF .... Lethal Factor (MELL)
LF .... Lettering Faded
LF .... Leukotactic Factor [*Medicine*] (MELL)
LF .... Lexical Function [*Linguistics*] (IEL)
LF .... Liberal Forum (Austria) [*Political party*] (PSAP)
LF .... Liberty Federation (EA)
LF .... Library of Fathers [*A publication*] (ODCC)
LF .... Liederkranz Foundation (EA)
LF .... Life (ABBR)
LF .... Life Float
LF .... Lifeline Foundation (EA)
LF .... Lifting Fan [*Hovercraft*]
LF .... Ligamenta Flava [*Medicine*] (MELL)
LF .... Lightface [*Type*]
lf .... Lightface Type (WDMC)
LF .... Light Fastness Ink (DGA)
lf .... Light Framing [*Construction term*] (MIST)
LF .... Ligue de Foyer [*Salvation Army Home League - SAHL*] (EAIO)
Lf .... Limes Flocculation [*Medicine*] (PALA)
LF .... Limiting Fragmentation [*Physics*] (OA)
LF .... Limit of Flocculation
LF .... Lineal Feet
LF .... Linear File [*Computer file*] (NITA)
LF .... Linear Filter
LF .... Linear Foot
LF .... Linear Fracture (SAUS)
LF .... Line Feed [*Control character*] [*Computer science*]
LF .... Line Finder [*Teletype*]
L/F .... Linen-Faced Paper (DGA)
LF .... Linjeflyg [*ICAO designator*] (AD)
LF .... Linoleum Floor [*Technical drawings*]
LF .... Lisle Fellowship (EA)
LF .... Listener Function (IAA)
LF .... Lituanus Foundation (EA)
LF .... Live Fire
LF .... Live Flying (NATG)
LF .... Liver Fluke [*Medicine*] (MELL)
LF .... Load Factor
LF .... Loaf
LF .... Loan Forgiveness (DICI)
LF .... Local Film
LF .... Local Force [*Viet Cong combat force*]
LF .... Local Forces (SAUS)
LF .... Locally Funded (AFM)
LF .... Lock Forward
LF .... Logical File [*Computer science*] (BUR)
LF .... Logical Form [*Linguistics*] (IEL)
LF .... Logic Function
LF .... Long Form (SAUS)
LF .... Loss Factor (ELAL)
LF .... Lost on Foul [*Boxing*]
LF .... Lovelace Foundation for Medical Education and Research [*Reorganized to form Lovelace Medical Foundation and Lovelace Biomedical and Environmental Research Institute*]
Lf .... Lower Left (ACAE)
LF .... Low Fat [*Diet*]
LF .... Low Fidelity (ACAE)
LF .... Low Filter (ELAL)
LF .... Low Flange (DICI)
LF .... Low-Fluence [*Physics*]
LF .... Low Foliage Forager [*Ecology*]
LF .... Low Food Density [*Ecology*]
LF .... Low Force
LF .... Low Forceps [*Delivery*] [*Obstetrics*]
lf .... Low Frequency (WDMC)
LF .... Low Frequency
lf .... Low Rate Forward [*Ecology*]
LF .... Lung Fluke [*Medicine*] (MELL)
LF .... Siebelwerke ATG GmbH [*Germany*] [*ICAO aircraft manufacturer identifier*] (ICAO)
LF1 .... Long Flashing Light [*Nautical term*] (NTA)
LFA .... Air Alfa Hava Yollari Ve Tec, AS [*Turkey*] [*FAA designator*] (FAAC)
LFA .... Klamath Falls, OR [*Location identifier*] [*FAA*] (FAAL)
LFA .... Land Force Adriatic [*British Royal Marines*] [*World War II*]
LFA .... Land Force, Airmobility [*NATO*] (NATG)
LFA .... Land Freedom Army (SAUO)
LFA .... Landing Force Aviation
LFA .... Language Foundation of Australia
LFA .... Large Families of America [*Defunct*] (EA)
LFA .... Lasher Family Association (EA)
LFA .... Last Field Address (IAA)
LFA .... Lavage Fluid Analysis [*Medicine*] (MELL)
LFA .... Lead Federal Agency (COE)
LFA .... Leading Field Activity (MCD)
LFA .... Left Femoral Artery [*Anatomy*]
LFA .... Left Forearm (SAUS)
LFA .... Left Frontal Craniotomy [*Medicine*] (DMAA)
LFA .... Left Frontoanterior [*A fetal position*] [*Obstetrics*]
LFA .... Less Favored Areas (WDAA)
LFA .... Less Favoured Area (SAUO)
LFA .... Leukocyte Function-Associated Antigen [*Immunology*]
LFA .... Leukotactic Factor Activity [*Medicine*] (DMAA)
LFA .... Light Freight Agent (ADA)
LFA .... Lillard Family Association (EA)
LFA .... Lime Fly Ash [*Aggregate*] (DICI)
LFA .... Link Field Address (SAUS)
LFA .... Littlefield, Adams [*AMEX symbol*] (TTSB)
LFA .... Littlefield, Adams & Co. [*AMEX symbol*] (SPSG)
LFA .... Lobster Fishing Area (FOTI)
LFA .... Local Feature Analysis (VLIE)
LFA .... Local File Access [*Computer science*] (VLIE)
LFA .... Local Flying Area [*Aviation*] (DA)
LFA .... Local Freight Agent
LFA .... Logical Framework Analysis (FOTI)
LFA .... London Football Association (SAUO)
LFA .... Louisiana Forestry Association (WPI)
LFA .... Louks/Loucks Family Association [*Canada*] (EAIO)
LFA .... Low Flow Alarm (IEEE)
LFA .... Low-Flying Area (SAUS)
LFA .... Low Frequency Active (DOMA)
LFA .... Low Friction Arthroplasty [*Orthopedics*] (DAVI)
LFA .... Low Functioning Autism
LFA .... Lupus Foundation of America (EA)
LFA .... Lutheran Fraternities of America (EA)
LFA .... Luther Family Association
LFA .... Lymphocyte Function-Associated Antigen [*Immunochemistry*]
LFAA .... Ambleteuse [*France*] [*ICAO location identifier*] (ICLI)
LFAAV .... Landing Force Assault Amphibious Vehicle (MCD)
LFAB .... Dieppe/Saint-Aubin [*France*] [*ICAO location identifier*] (ICLI)
LFAC .... Calais/Dunkerque [*France*] [*ICAO location identifier*] (ICLI)
LFACS .... Light Future Armored Combat System [*Tank*]
LFACS .... Loop Facilities Assignment and Control System (VLIE)
LFAD .... Compiegne/Margny [*France*] [*ICAO location identifier*] (ICLI)
LFAE .... Eu-Mers/Le Treport [*France*] [*ICAO location identifier*] (ICLI)
LFAF .... Laon/Chambry [*France*] [*ICAO location identifier*] (ICLI)
LFAF .... Low-Frequency Accelerometer Flutter (MCD)
LFAG .... Leafage (ABBR)
LFAG .... Peronne/Saint-Quentin [*France*] [*ICAO location identifier*] (ICLI)
LFAH .... Soissons/Cuffies [*France*] [*ICAO location identifier*] (ICLI)
LFAI .... Lifting Fair Air Intake [*Hovercraft*]
LFAI .... Nangis/Les Loges [*France*] [*ICAO location identifier*] (ICLI)
LFAJ .... Argentan [*France*] [*ICAO location identifier*] (ICLI)
LFAK .... Dunkerque-Ghyvelde [*France*] [*ICAO location identifier*] (ICLI)
LFAL .... La Fleche/Thoree-Les-Pins [*France*] [*ICAO location identifier*] (ICLI)
LFAL .... Lutheran Fraternities of America Life
LFAM .... Berck-Sur-Mer [*France*] [*ICAO location identifier*] (ICLI)
LFAM .... Life of America Insurance Corporation of Boston (SAUO)
LFAM .... Low-Frequency Accelerometer Modes (MCD)
LFAN .... Conde-Sur-Noireau [*France*] [*ICAO location identifier*] (ICLI)
LFA-NYST .... Lupus Foundation of America - New York Southern Tier Chapter (EARSL)
LFAO .... Bagnole-De-L'Orne [*France*] [*ICAO location identifier*] (ICLI)
LFAP .... Lightweight Flow Admission Protocol (SAUS)
LFAP .... Low-Frequency Accelerometer POGO [*Polar Orbiting Geophysical Observatory*] [*NASA*] (NASA)
LFAP .... Rethel-Perthes [*France*] [*ICAO location identifier*] (ICLI)
LFAQ .... Albert/Bray [*France*] [*ICAO location identifier*] (ICLI)
LFAR .... Last Frame Address Register
LFAR .... Libertarians for Animal Rights (EA)
LFAR .... Montdidier [*France*] [*ICAO location identifier*] (ICLI)
LFAS .... Falaise-Monts-D'Eraines [*France*] [*ICAO location identifier*] (ICLI)

LFAS........ League of Finnish-American Societies (EAIO)
LFAS........ Licentiate of Faculty of Architects and Surveyors (SAUO)
LFAS........ Low-Frequency Active Sonar (DOMA)
LFASU....... Let's Face It USA [*Association*] (EA)
LFASV....... Landing Force Amphibious Support Vehicle (SAA)
LFAT........ Le Touquet/Paris-Plage [*France*] [*ICAO location identifier*] (ICLI)
LFATDS...... Light Field Artillery Tactical Data System (GFGA)
LFaU........ Union Parish Library, Farmerville, LA [*Library symbol*] [*Library of Congress*] (LCLS)
LFAU........ Vauville [*France*] [*ICAO location identifier*] (ICLI)
LFAV........ Valenciennes/Denain [*France*] [*ICAO location identifier*] (ICLI)
LFAW........ Villerupt [*France*] [*ICAO location identifier*] (ICLI)
LFAX........ Mortagne-Au-Perche [*France*] [*ICAO location identifier*] (ICLI)
LFAY........ Amiens/Glisy [*France*] [*ICAO location identifier*] (ICLI)
LFAY........ Leslie Fay Co. [*OTCBB symbol*]
LFB......... Lafayette, TN [*Location identifier*] [*FAA*] (FAAL)
LFB......... Landing Force Bulletin [*Marine Corps*]
LFB......... Lateral Forebrain Bundle
LFB......... Left Fullback [*Soccer*]
LFB......... Leverage Fund of Boston (SAUO)
LFB......... Licensed Fishing Boat
LFB......... Life Boat [*Telegraphy*] (PCTE)
LFB......... Light Field Battery [*British military*] (DMA)
LFB......... Limited Frequency Band
LFB......... Linear Frame Buffer [*Computer science*] (VLIE)
LFB......... London Festival Ballet
LFB......... London Fire Brigade
LFB......... Longview Fibre [*NYSE symbol*] (TTSB)
LFB......... Longview Fibre Co. [*NYSE symbol*] (CTT)
LFB......... Loop Fluidized Bed [*Chemical engineering*]
LFB......... Low-Frequency Beacon
LFB......... Luxol Fast Blue [*Biological stain*]
LFB2........ London Festival Ballet's Ensemble Group
LFBA........ Agen/La Garenne [*France*] [*ICAO location identifier*] (ICLI)
LFBA........ Licentiate of the Corporation of Executives and Administrators [*British*] (DBQ)
LFBB........ Bordeaux [*France*] [*ICAO location identifier*] (ICLI)
LFBC........ Cazaux [*France*] [*ICAO location identifier*] (ICLI)
LFBD........ Bordeaux/Merignac [*France*] [*ICAO location identifier*] (ICLI)
LFBD........ Letters of the First Babylonian Dynasty [*A publication*] (BJA)
LFBD........ Lifeblood (ABBR)
LFBE........ Bergerac/Roumaniere [*France*] [*ICAO location identifier*] (ICLI)
LFBF........ Louisiana Farm Bureau Federation (SRA)
LFBF........ Toulouse/Francazal [*France*] [*ICAO location identifier*] (ICLI)
LFBG........ Cognac/Chateau Bernard [*France*] [*ICAO location identifier*] (ICLI)
LFBH........ La Rochelle/Laleu [*France*] [*ICAO location identifier*] (ICLI)
LFBI........ Little Falls Bancorp [*NASDAQ symbol*] (TTSB)
LFBI........ Poitiers/Biard [*France*] [*ICAO location identifier*] (ICLI)
LFBJ........ Saint-Junien [*France*] [*ICAO location identifier*] (ICLI)
LFBK........ Lincoln First Banks (SAUO)
LFBK........ Montlucon-Gueret [*France*] [*ICAO location identifier*] (ICLI)
LFBL........ Limoges/Bellegarde [*France*] [*ICAO location identifier*] (ICLI)
LFBM........ Mont-De-Marsan [*France*] [*ICAO location identifier*] (ICLI)
LFBN........ Niort/Souche [*France*] [*ICAO location identifier*] (ICLI)
LFBO........ Toulouse/Blagnac [*France*] [*ICAO location identifier*] (ICLI)
LFBP........ Pau/Pont-Long-Uzein [*France*] [*ICAO location identifier*] (ICLI)
LFBQ........ Toulouse [*France*] [*ICAO location identifier*] (ICLI)
LFBR........ LASER Fusion Breeder Reactor
LFBR........ Liquid Fluidized Bed Reactor
LFBR........ Longview Fibre Co. (SAUO)
LFBR........ Muret/Lherm [*France*] [*ICAO location identifier*] (ICLI)
LFBR-CX..... Liquid Fluidized Bed Reactor Critical Experiment
LFBS........ Biscarosse/Parentis [*France*] [*ICAO location identifier*] (ICLI)
LFBT........ Lifeboat (ABBR)
LFBT........ Tarbes/Ossun-Lourdes [*France*] [*ICAO location identifier*] (ICLI)
LFBU........ Angouleme/Brie-Champniers [*France*] [*ICAO location identifier*] (ICLI)
LFBV........ Brive/La Roche [*France*] [*ICAO location identifier*] (ICLI)
LFBW........ Mont-De-Marsan [*France*] [*ICAO location identifier*] (ICLI)
LFBX........ Perigeux/Bassillac [*France*] [*ICAO location identifier*] (ICLI)
LFBY........ Dax/Seyresse [*France*] [*ICAO location identifier*] (ICLI)
LFBZ........ Biarritz-Bayonne/Anglet [*France*] [*ICAO location identifier*] (ICLI)
LFC......... Aero Control Air Ltd. [*Canada*] [*ICAO designator*] (FAAC)
LFC......... Concordia Parish Library, Ferriday, LA [*Library symbol*] [*Library of Congress*] (LCLS)
LFC......... Lafayette Flying Corps [*World War I*]
LFC......... Lake Forest College [*Illinois*]
LFC......... Lake Fork Canyon [*New Mexico*] [*Seismograph station code, US Geological Survey*] (SEIS)
LFC......... Laminar Flow Control [*Aerodynamics*]
LFC......... Lands and Forests Commission [*Australia*]
LFC......... Large Format Camera [*Space exploration*]
LFC......... Laser Film Corporation (SAUO)
LFC......... Lateral Femoral Condyle [*Anatomy*]
LFC......... L-Band Frequency Converter
LFC......... Left Frontal Craniotomy [*Medicine*] (EDAA)
LFC......... Level of Free Convection [*Meteorology*]
LFC......... Levitz Furniture Incorporated (EFIS)
LFC......... Liberty Financial Corp. (EFIS)
LFC......... Liberty Football Conference (PSS)
LFC......... Light Fighter Course [*Army*]
LFC......... Line Feed Character [*Computer science*] (VLIE)
LFC......... Liquids from Coal
LFC......... Live Fire Component (MCD)
LFC......... Living Female Child [*Medicine*] (DMAA)
LFC......... Load Frequency Control (IEEE)
LFC......... Local Files Check
LFC......... Local Forms Control [*Computer science*] (CMD)
LFC......... Local Function Capabilities (VLIE)
LFC......... Logic Flow Chart [*Computer science*]
LFC......... Logo Forum on Compuserve [*Defunct*] (EA)
LFC......... Lomas Financial Corp. [*NYSE symbol*] (SPSG)
LFC......... Longview Fibre [*Federal Railroad Administration identification code*]
LFC......... Loverboy Fan Club (EA)
LFC......... Lowest-Feasible Concentration (ABAC)
LFC......... Low Fan Control (HAWK)
LFC......... Low Fat and Cholesterol Diet (DMAA)
LFC......... Low-Frequency Choke (DEN)
LFC......... Low-Frequency Correction (CET)
LFC......... Low-Frequency Current
LFC......... Lucio Fan Club [*Association*] (EA)
LFC......... Lunar Facsimile Capsule [*NASA*] (KSC)
LFC......... Lunar Farside Chart [*Air Force*]
LFC......... Lutheran Free Church (WDAA)
LFCA........ Chatellerault/Targe [*France*] [*ICAO location identifier*] (ICLI)
LFCA........ La Federation Canado-Arabe [*Association*] [*Canada*] (EAIO)
LFCB........ Bagneres De Luchon [*France*] [*ICAO location identifier*] (ICLI)
LFCB........ Legal Fees and Costs Board [*Australia*]
LFCC........ Cahors/Lalbenque [*France*] [*ICAO location identifier*] (ICLI)
LFCC........ Linux Federation for Commercial Customers (SAUO)
LFCD........ Andernos-Les-Bains [*France*] [*ICAO location identifier*] (ICLI)
LFCDA....... London Fire and Civil Defence Authority (HEAS)
LFCE........ Gueret/Saint-Laurent [*France*] [*ICAO location identifier*] (ICLI)
LFCF........ Figeac/Livernon [*France*] [*ICAO location identifier*] (ICLI)
LFCG........ Saint-Girons/Antichan [*France*] [*ICAO location identifier*] (ICLI)
LFCH........ Arcachon/La Teste De Buch [*France*] [*ICAO location identifier*] (ICLI)
LFCI........ Albi/Le Sequestre [*France*] [*ICAO location identifier*] (ICLI)
LFCI........ Licentiate of the Faculty of Commerce and Industry [*British*] (DBQ)
LFCJ........ Jonzac/Neulles [*France*] [*ICAO location identifier*] (ICLI)
LFCK........ Castres/Mazamet [*France*] [*ICAO location identifier*] (ICLI)
LFCL........ Less Than Full Container Load
LFCL........ Toulouse/Lasbordes [*France*] [*ICAO location identifier*] (ICLI)
LFCM........ Liquid-Fed Ceramic Melter (ABAC)
LFCM........ Low-Frequency Cross-Modulation [*Electronics*] (OA)
LFCM........ Millau/Larzac [*France*] [*ICAO location identifier*] (ICLI)
LFCN........ Nogaro [*France*] [*ICAO location identifier*] (ICLI)
LFCO........ Oloron/Herrere [*France*] [*ICAO location identifier*] (ICLI)
LFCOp....... Leading Fire Control Operator (WDAA)
LFCP........ Pons/Avy [*France*] [*ICAO location identifier*] (ICLI)
LFCQ........ Graulhet/Mondragon [*France*] [*ICAO location identifier*] (ICLI)
LFCR........ Rodez/Marcillac [*France*] [*ICAO location identifier*] (ICLI)
LFCS........ Bordeaux/Saucats [*France*] [*ICAO location identifier*] (ICLI)
LFCS........ Laboratory for Foundations of Computer Science [*University of Edinburgh*] [*United Kingdom*] (RCD)
LFCS........ Land Forces Classification System (AABC)
LFCS........ LASER Fire Control System
LFCS........ Licentiate of the Faculty of Secretaries [*British*] (DBQ)
LFCS........ Low-Flow Cooling System [*Automotive engineering*]
LFCT........ Leader Financial [*NASDAQ symbol*] (TTSB)
LFCT........ Leader Financial Corp. [*NASDAQ symbol*] (SAG)
LFCT........ Thouars [*France*] [*ICAO location identifier*] (ICLI)
LFCU........ Ussel/Thalamy [*France*] [*ICAO location identifier*] (ICLI)
LFCV........ Villefranche-De-Rouergue [*France*] [*ICAO location identifier*] (ICLI)
LFCW........ Villeneuve-Sur-Lot [*France*] [*ICAO location identifier*] (ICLI)
LFCX........ Castelsarrasin/Moissac [*France*] [*ICAO location identifier*] (ICLI)
LFCY........ Royan/Medis [*France*] [*ICAO location identifier*] (ICLI)
LFCZ........ Lyon Farm Center [*Federal Railroad Administration identification code*]
LFCZ........ Mimizan [*France*] [*ICAO location identifier*] (ICLI)
LFD......... Lactose-Free Diet
LFD......... Laser Flow Diagnostics Laboratory [*State University of New York at Buffalo*] (RCD)
LFD......... Lateral Facial Dysplasia [*Medicine*] (MELL)
LFD......... Latest Finish Date
LFD......... Launch and Flight Division [*Ballistic Research Laboratory*] (RDA)
LFD......... Least Fatal Dose
LFD......... Line Fault Detector [*Telecommunications*] (TEL)
LFD......... Line Feed (VLIE)
LFD......... Litchfield, MI [*Location identifier*] [*FAA*] (FAAL)
LFD......... Local Frequency Distribution
LFD......... Longford [*County in Ireland*] (ROG)
LFD......... Low-Fat Diet
LFD......... Low Fiber Diet (MELL)
LFD......... Low-Forceps Delivery [*Obstetrics*]
LFD......... Low-Frequency Decoy
LFD......... Low-Frequency Disturbance
LFD......... Lutheran Foundation for Religious Drama (EA)
LFDA........ Aire-Sur-L'Addour [*France*] [*ICAO location identifier*] (ICLI)
LFDA........ Land and Facilities Development Administration [*HUD*]
LFDB........ Montauban [*France*] [*ICAO location identifier*] (ICLI)
LFDC........ Montendre/Marcillac [*France*] [*ICAO location identifier*] (ICLI)
LFDE........ Egletons [*France*] [*ICAO location identifier*] (ICLI)
LFDF........ Low-Frequency Direction Finder (MCD)
LFDF........ Sainte-Foy-La-Grande [*France*] [*ICAO location identifier*] (ICLI)
LFDG........ Gaillac/Lisle Sur Tarn [*France*] [*ICAO location identifier*] (ICLI)
LFDH........ Auch/Lamothe [*France*] [*ICAO location identifier*] (ICLI)
LFDI........ FD Lia [*Common carrier symbol*]
LFDI........ Libourne/Artiques De Lussac [*France*] [*ICAO location identifier*] (ICLI)
LFDJ........ Pamiers/Les Pujols [*France*] [*ICAO location identifier*] (ICLI)

LFDK .... Soulac-Sur-Mer [*France*] [*ICAO location identifier*] (ICLI)
LFDL........ Loudun [*France*] [*ICAO location identifier*] (ICLI)
LFDM........ Low Flyer, Defense Mode
LFDM........ Marmande/Virazeil [*France*] [*ICAO location identifier*] (ICLI)
LFDN .... Rochefort/Saint-Agnant [*France*] [*ICAO location identifier*] (ICLI)
LFDO .... Bordeaux/Souge [*France*] [*ICAO location identifier*] (ICLI)
LFDP .... Saint-Pierre D'Oleron [*France*] [*ICAO location identifier*] (ICLI)
LFDQ .... Castelnau-Magnoac [*France*] [*ICAO location identifier*] (ICLI)
LFDR .... La Reole/Floudes [*France*] [*ICAO location identifier*] (ICLI)
LFDS .... Sarlat/Domme [*France*] [*ICAO location identifier*] (ICLI)
LFDT........ Tarbes/Laloubere [*France*] [*ICAO location identifier*] (ICLI)
LFDU .... Lesparre/St. Laurent Du Medoc [*France*] [*ICAO location identifier*] (ICLI)
LFDV .... Couhe/Verac [*France*] [*ICAO location identifier*] (ICLI)
LFDW........ Chauvigny [*France*] [*ICAO location identifier*] (ICLI)
LFDX .... Fumel/Montayral [*France*] [*ICAO location identifier*] (ICLI)
LFDY .... Bordeaux-Yvrac [*France*] [*ICAO location identifier*] (ICLI)
LFDZ........ Condat-Sur-Vezere [*France*] [*ICAO location identifier*] (ICLI)
LFE .... Brotherhood of Locomotive Firemen and Enginemen [*Later, United Transportation Union*] [*AFL-CIO*]
LFE .... Laboratory for Electronics (DNAB)
LFE .... Laboratory for Electronics, Inc. (SAUO)
LFE .... Laminar Flow Element [*Engineering*]
LFE .... Large Flight Envelope (MCD)
LFE .... LFE Corp. (SAUO)
LFE .... Logarithmic Feedback Element [*Computer science*]
LFE .... London Fixtures Exchange (SAUO)
LFE .... London Fur Exchange (SAUO)
LFEA........ Delle-Ile [*France*] [*ICAO location identifier*] (ICLI)
LFEB........ Dinan/Trelivan [*France*] [*ICAO location identifier*] (ICLI)
LFEB........ Launch Facility Equipment Building [*Missiles*]
LFEC........ Ouessant [*France*] [*ICAO location identifier*] (ICLI)
Lfecore...... LifeCore Biomedical, Inc. [*Associated Press*] (SAG)
LFED........ Leeds Federal Svgs Bk [*NASDAQ symbol*] (TTSB)
LFED........ Leeds FSB [*NASDAQ symbol*] (SAG)
LFED........ Pontivy [*France*] [*ICAO location identifier*] (ICLI)
LFEE........ Reims [*France*] [*ICAO location identifier*] (ICLI)
LFEF........ Amboise/Dierre [*France*] [*ICAO location identifier*] (ICLI)
LFEG........ Argenton-Sur-Creuse [*France*] [*ICAO location identifier*] (ICLI)
LFEH........ Aubigny-Sur-Nere [*France*] [*ICAO location identifier*] (ICLI)
LFEI........ Briare/Chatillon [*France*] [*ICAO location identifier*] (ICLI)
LFEJ........ Chateauroux/Villers [*France*] [*ICAO location identifier*] (ICLI)
LFEK........ Issoudun/Le Fay [*France*] [*ICAO location identifier*] (ICLI)
LFEL........ Le Blanc [*France*] [*ICAO location identifier*] (ICLI)
LfelneS...... Lifeline Systems, Inc. [*Associated Press*] (SAG)
LFEM........ Montargis/Vimory [*France*] [*ICAO location identifier*] (ICLI)
LfeMd....... Life Medical Sciences [*Associated Press*] (SAG)
LfeMed...... Life Medical Sciences [*Associated Press*] (SAG)
LFEN........ Laboratorio de Fisica e Engenharia Nucleores [*Portugal*]
LFEN........ Tours/Sorigny [*France*] [*ICAO location identifier*] (ICLI)
LFEO........ Saint-Malo/Saint-Servan [*France*] [*ICAO location identifier*] (ICLI)
LFEP........ Pouilly-Maconge [*France*] [*ICAO location identifier*] (ICLI)
LFEPA....... London Fire and Emergency Planning Authority [*Emergency Management*] (EMA)
LFEQ........ Quiberon [*France*] [*ICAO location identifier*] (ICLI)
LfeQst...... LifeQuest Medical, Inc. [*Associated Press*] (SAG)
LFER........ Linear Free Energy Relationship
LFER........ Redon/Bains-Sur-Oust [*France*] [*ICAO location identifier*] (ICLI)
LFES........ Guiscriff-Scaer [*France*] [*ICAO location identifier*] (ICLI)
LFET........ Lifetime Custom Coach [*NCIC trailer make code*]
LFET........ Til-Chatel [*France*] [*ICAO location identifier*] (ICLI)
LfeTch...... Life Technologies, Inc. [*Associated Press*] (SAG)
LFETS....... Live Fire Evasive Target System [*Army*] (INF)
LFEU........ Bar-Le-Duc [*France*] [*ICAO location identifier*] (ICLI)
LfeUSA...... Life USA Holding, Inc. [*Associated Press*] (SAG)
LFEV........ Gray-Saint-Adrien [*France*] [*ICAO location identifier*] (ICLI)
LFEW........ Saulieu-Liernais [*France*] [*ICAO location identifier*] (ICLI)
LF-EX....... Life Expectancy [*Military*]
LFEX........ Nancy-Azelot [*France*] [*ICAO location identifier*] (ICLI)
LFEY........ Ile-D'Yeu/Le Grand Phare [*France*] [*ICAO location identifier*] (ICLI)
LFEZ........ Nancy-Malzeville [*France*] [*ICAO location identifier*] (ICLI)
LFF .... La Frestal [*France*] [*Seismograph station code, US Geological Survey*] (SEIS)
LFF .... Large Formation Flyer (SSD)
LFf .... Leading Firefighter (WDAA)
LFF .... Libraries for the Future [*Association*] (EA)
LFF .... Light Filter Factor
LFF .... Limited Fanout-Free (MHDB)
LFF .... Logistic Factors File (DOMA)
LFF .... London Film Festival
LFF .... Low-Frequency Filter (IAA)
LFFA........ CORTA (Orly Ouest) [*France*] [*ICAO location identifier*] (ICLI)
LFFB........ Buno-Bonnevaux [*France*] [*ICAO location identifier*] (ICLI)
LFFC........ Mantes-Cherence [*France*] [*ICAO location identifier*] (ICLI)
LFFD........ Saint-Andre-De L'Eure [*France*] [*ICAO location identifier*] (ICLI)
LFFE........ Enghien-Moisselles [*France*] [*ICAO location identifier*] (ICLI)
LFFET....... Low-Frequency Field-Effect Transistor [*Electronics*] (OA)
LFFEZ....... Large Force Fighter Employment Zone (SAUS)
LFFF........ Paris [*France*] [*ICAO location identifier*] (ICLI)
LFFG........ La Ferte-Gaucher [*France*] [*ICAO location identifier*] (ICLI)
LFFH........ Chateau-Thierry-Belleau [*France*] [*ICAO location identifier*] (ICLI)
LFFI........ Ancenis [*France*] [*ICAO location identifier*] (ICLI)
LFFJ........ Joinville-Mussey [*France*] [*ICAO location identifier*] (ICLI)
LFFK........ Fontenay-Le-Conte [*France*] [*ICAO location identifier*] (ICLI)
LFFL........ Bailleau-Armenonville [*France*] [*ICAO location identifier*] (ICLI)
LFFM........ La Motte-Beuvron [*France*] [*ICAO location identifier*] (ICLI)
LFFN........ Brienne-Le-Chateau [*France*] [*ICAO location identifier*] (ICLI)
LFFO........ Tonnerre-Moulins [*France*] [*ICAO location identifier*] (ICLI)
LFFP........ LASER Fusion Feasibility Project [*Nuclear fusion*]
LFFP........ Pithiviers [*France*] [*ICAO location identifier*] (ICLI)
LFFQ........ La Ferte-Alais [*France*] [*ICAO location identifier*] (ICLI)
LFFR........ Bar-Sur-Seine [*France*] [*ICAO location identifier*] (ICLI)
LFFS........ Suippes [*France*] [*ICAO location identifier*] (ICLI)
LFFT........ Left Front Fluid Temperature [*Brake system*] [*Automotive engineering*]
LFFT........ Neufchateau-Roucaux [*France*] [*ICAO location identifier*] (ICLI)
LFFU........ Chateauneuf-Sur-Cher [*France*] [*ICAO location identifier*] (ICLI)
LFFU........ Special Equipment Transport [*Intermodal shipping container symbol*] (TVRC)
LFFV........ Vierzon-Mereau [*France*] [*ICAO location identifier*] (ICLI)
LFFW........ Montaigu-Saint-Georges [*France*] [*ICAO location identifier*] (ICLI)
LFFX........ Tournus-Cuisery [*France*] [*ICAO location identifier*] (ICLI)
LFFY........ Etrepagny [*France*] [*ICAO location identifier*] (ICLI)
LFFZ........ Sezanne-Saint-Remy [*France*] [*ICAO location identifier*] (ICLI)
LFG .... Landamerica Financial Grp. [*NYSE symbol*] (SG)
LFG .... Landfill Gas
LFG .... Lead-Free Glass
LFG .... Lexical Functional Grammar [*Artificial intelligence*]
LFG .... Liberty Financial Group, Inc. (SAUO)
LFG .... Low-Frequency Generator
LFGA .... Colmar/Houssen [*France*] [*ICAO location identifier*] (ICLI)
LFGB .... Mulhouse/Habsheim [*France*] [*ICAO location identifier*] (ICLI)
LFGC .... Strasbourg/Neuhof [*France*] [*ICAO location identifier*] (ICLI)
LFGD .... Arbois [*France*] [*ICAO location identifier*] (ICLI)
LFGE........ Avallon [*France*] [*ICAO location identifier*] (ICLI)
LFGF........ Beaune/Challanges [*France*] [*ICAO location identifier*] (ICLI)
LFGG .... Belfort/Chaux [*France*] [*ICAO location identifier*] (ICLI)
LFGG .... Low-Frequency Gravity Gradiometer
LFGH .... Cosne-Sur-Loire [*France*] [*ICAO location identifier*] (ICLI)
LFGI .... Dijon/Val Suzon [*France*] [*ICAO location identifier*] (ICLI)
LFGJ........ Dole/Tavaux [*France*] [*ICAO location identifier*] (ICLI)
LFGK .... Joigny [*France*] [*ICAO location identifier*] (ICLI)
LFGL........ Lons Le Saunier/Courlaoux [*France*] [*ICAO location identifier*] (ICLI)
LFGM........ Montceau Les Mines/Pouilloux [*France*] [*ICAO location identifier*] (ICLI)
LFGN .... Paray Le Monial [*France*] [*ICAO location identifier*] (ICLI)
LFGO .... Pont-Sur-Yonne [*France*] [*ICAO location identifier*] (ICLI)
LFGP .... Saint-Florentin/Cheu [*France*] [*ICAO location identifier*] (ICLI)
LFGQ .... Semur-En-Auxois [*France*] [*ICAO location identifier*] (ICLI)
LFGR .... Doncourt-Les-Conflans [*France*] [*ICAO location identifier*] (ICLI)
LFGRD ...... Lifeguard (ABBR)
LFGS .... Longuyon/Villette [*France*] [*ICAO location identifier*] (ICLI)
LFGT........ Sarrebourg/Buhl [*France*] [*ICAO location identifier*] (ICLI)
LFGU .... Sarreguemines/Neunkirch [*France*] [*ICAO location identifier*] (ICLI)
LFGV .... Thionville/Yutz [*France*] [*ICAO location identifier*] (ICLI)
LFGW........ Verdun/Rozelier [*France*] [*ICAO location identifier*] (ICLI)
LFGX .... Champagnole/Crotenay [*France*] [*ICAO location identifier*] (ICLI)
LFGY .... Saint-Die/Remoneix [*France*] [*ICAO location identifier*] (ICLI)
LFGZ........ Nuits-Saint-Georges [*France*] [*ICAO location identifier*] (ICLI)
LFH .... Left Femoral Hernia [*Medicine*]
LFH .... Lower Fascial Height [*Medicine*]
LFH .... Low Fire Hazard (SAUS)
LFH .... Lunar Far Horizon (KSC)
LFHA .... Issoire/Le Broc [*France*] [*ICAO location identifier*] (ICLI)
LFHB .... Moulins/Avermes [*France*] [*ICAO location identifier*] (ICLI)
LFHC .... Perouges/Meximieux [*France*] [*ICAO location identifier*] (ICLI)
LFHD .... Pierrelatte [*France*] [*ICAO location identifier*] (ICLI)
LFHE........ Romans/Saint-Paul [*France*] [*ICAO location identifier*] (ICLI)
LFHF........ Ruoms [*France*] [*ICAO location identifier*] (ICLI)
LFHG .... Saint-Chamond/L'Horme [*France*] [*ICAO location identifier*] (ICLI)
LFHH .... Vienne/Reventin [*France*] [*ICAO location identifier*] (ICLI)
LFHI .... Morestel [*France*] [*ICAO location identifier*] (ICLI)
LFHJ........ Lyon/Corbas [*France*] [*ICAO location identifier*] (ICLI)
LFHK .... Camp De Canjuers [*France*] [*ICAO location identifier*] (ICLI)
LFHL........ Langogne/L'Esperon [*France*] [*ICAO location identifier*] (ICLI)
LFHL........ Low-Frequency Hearing Loss (DMAA)
LFHM........ Megeve [*France*] [*ICAO location identifier*] (ICLI)
LFHN .... Bellegarde/Vouvray [*France*] [*ICAO location identifier*] (ICLI)
LFHO .... Aubenas-Vals-Lanas [*France*] [*ICAO location identifier*] (ICLI)
LFHP .... Le Puy/Loudes [*France*] [*ICAO location identifier*] (ICLI)
LFHQ .... Saint-Flour/Coltines [*France*] [*ICAO location identifier*] (ICLI)
LFHR .... Brioude-Beaumont [*France*] [*ICAO location identifier*] (ICLI)
LFHS .... Bourg/Ceyreziat [*France*] [*ICAO location identifier*] (ICLI)
LFHSC....... London Foot Hospital School of Chiropody (SAUO)
LFHT........ Ambert-Le-Poyet [*France*] [*ICAO location identifier*] (ICLI)
LFHU .... L'Alpe D'Huez [*France*] [*ICAO location identifier*] (ICLI)
LFHV .... Villefrance/Tarare [*France*] [*ICAO location identifier*] (ICLI)
LFHW........ Belleville-Villie-Morgon [*France*] [*ICAO location identifier*] (ICLI)
LFHX .... Lapalisse-Perigny [*France*] [*ICAO location identifier*] (ICLI)
LFHY .... Moulins/Montbeugny [*France*] [*ICAO location identifier*] (ICLI)
LFHZ........ Sallanches-Mont-Blanc [*France*] [*ICAO location identifier*] (ICLI)
LFI .... Hampton, VA [*Location identifier*] [*FAA*] (FAAL)
LFI .... Last File Indicator (VLIE)
LFI .... Last Frame Indicator
LFI .... Left Front Inside-Drive [*Tire maintenance*]
LFI .... Lethal Force Institute (SAUO)
LFI .... Let's Face It [*Later, AFLFI*] [*An association*] (EA)
LFI .... Levitz Furniture [*NYSE symbol*] (TTSB)

LFI .... Levitz Furniture, Inc. [*NYSE symbol*] (SPSG)
LFI .... Licensed Financial Institution
LFI .... Licentiate of the Faculty of Insurance (SAUO)
LFI .... Life Insurance [*Telegraphy*] (PCTE)
LFI .... Lifting Fan Intake [*Hovercraft*]
LFI .... Linear Function Interpolator
L-FI .... Live-Free, Inc. [*An association*] (EA)
LFI .... Long Fiber Injection
LFI .... Low-Frequency Inductor
LFIA .... Luminescence and Fluorescence Immunoassay [*Clinical chemistry*]
LFIB .... Belves-Saint-Pardoux [*France*] [*ICAO location identifier*] (ICLI)
LFIC .... Cross Corsen [*France*] [*ICAO location identifier*] (ICLI)
LFIC .... Landing Force Intelligence Center [*Navy*] (DNAB)
LFICS .... Landing Force Integrated Communications System [*Marine Corps*]
LFID .... Condom-Valence-Sur-Baise [*France*] [*ICAO location identifier*] (ICLI)
LF-ID .... Logical Frame Identifier (VLIE)
LFIE .... Cross Etel [*France*] [*ICAO location identifier*] (ICLI)
LFIF .... Saint-Afrique-Belmont [*France*] [*ICAO location identifier*] (ICLI)
LFIG .... Cassagnes-Begonhes [*France*] [*ICAO location identifier*] (ICLI)
LFIH .... Chalais [*France*] [*ICAO location identifier*] (ICLI)
LFIINST .... Life Fellow Imperial Institute [*British*] (ROG)
LFIJ .... Cross Jobourg [*France*] [*ICAO location identifier*] (ICLI)
LFIK .... Riberac-Saint-Aulaye [*France*] [*ICAO location identifier*] (ICLI)
LFIL .... Rion-Des-Landes [*France*] [*ICAO location identifier*] (ICLI)
LFILIE .... Libera Federazione Italiana Lavoratori Industrie Estrattive [*Free Italian Federation of Workers in Mining Industries*]
LFIM .... Low-Frequency Instruments and Measurement (MCD)
LFIM .... Saint Gaudens Montrejeau [*France*] [*ICAO location identifier*] (ICLI)
LFIN .... Cross Gris-Nez [*France*] [*ICAO location identifier*] (ICLI)
LFIN .... Lincoln Financial Corp. [*NASDAQ symbol*] (COMM)
LFIN .... Local Financial [*NASDAQ symbol*] (SG)
LFINT .... Low-Frequency Intersection
LFIP .... Peyresourde-Balestas [*France*] [*ICAO location identifier*] (ICLI)
LFIPA .... Laminated Fiberglass Insulation Producers Association [*Defunct*] (EA)
LFIR .... Revel-Montgey [*France*] [*ICAO location identifier*] (ICLI)
LFIRSS .... Louis Finkelstein Institute for Religious and Social Studies (EA)
LFISWB .... Loyal, Free, Industrious Society of Wheelwrights and Blacksmiths [*A union*] [*British*]
LFIT .... Toulouse-Bourg-Saint-Bernard [*France*] [*ICAO location identifier*] (ICLI)
LFIV .... Vendays-Montalivet [*France*] [*ICAO location identifier*] (ICLI)
LFIX .... Itxassou [*France*] [*ICAO location identifier*] (ICLI)
LFIY .... Saint-Jean-D'Angely [*France*] [*ICAO location identifier*] (ICLI)
LFIZ .... Litchfield Industrial Railroad [*Federal Railroad Administration identification code*]
LFJ .... Local Feed Junctor [*Telecommunications*] (NITA)
LFJ .... Low-Frequency Jammer
LFJ .... Lumbar Facet Joints [*Medicine*] (MELL)
LFJG .... Cross La Garde [*France*] [*ICAO location identifier*] (ICLI)
LFJV .... Low Frequency Jet Ventilation [*Medicine*]
LFK .... Lufkin/Nacogdoches [*Texas*] [*Airport symbol*] (OAG)
LFK .... Lufkin, TX [*Location identifier*] [*FAA*] (FAAL)
LFKA .... Albertville [*France*] [*ICAO location identifier*] (ICLI)
LFKB .... Bastia/Poretta, Corse [*France*] [*ICAO location identifier*] (ICLI)
LFKC .... Calvi/Sainte-Catherine, Corse [*France*] [*ICAO location identifier*] (ICLI)
LFKD .... Sollieres-Sardieres [*France*] [*ICAO location identifier*] (ICLI)
LFKE .... Saint-Jean-En-Royans [*France*] [*ICAO location identifier*] (ICLI)
LFKF .... Figari, Sud-Corse [*France*] [*ICAO location identifier*] (ICLI)
LFKG .... Ghisonaccia-Alzitone [*France*] [*ICAO location identifier*] (ICLI)
LFKH .... Saint-Jean-D'Avelanne [*France*] [*ICAO location identifier*] (ICLI)
LFKJ .... Ajaccio/Campo Dell'Oro, Corse [*France*] [*ICAO location identifier*] (ICLI)
LFKL .... Lyon-Brindas [*France*] [*ICAO location identifier*] (ICLI)
LFKM .... Saint-Galmier [*France*] [*ICAO location identifier*] (ICLI)
LFKO .... Propriano [*France*] [*ICAO location identifier*] (ICLI)
LFKP .... La Tour-Du-Pin-Cessieu [*France*] [*ICAO location identifier*] (ICLI)
LFKS .... Solenzara, Corse [*France*] [*ICAO location identifier*] (ICLI)
LFKT .... Corte [*France*] [*ICAO location identifier*] (ICLI)
LFKY .... Belley-Peyrieu [*France*] [*ICAO location identifier*] (ICLI)
LFKZ .... Saint-Claude-Pratz [*France*] [*ICAO location identifier*] (ICLI)
LFL .... Lan Chile ADS [*NYSE symbol*] [*Formerly, Linea Aerea Nac'l. Chile ADS*]
LFL .... LASER Flash Lamp
LFL .... League for Liberty (EA)
LFL .... Left Frontolateral [*Medicine*] (EDAA)
LFL .... Length of Flowering Period [*Botany*]
LFL .... Lesbian Feminist Liberation (EA)
LFL .... Leukocyte Feeder [*Medicine*] (EDAA)
LFL .... Leukocyte Feeder Layer [*Medicine*] (DMAA)
LFL .... Libertarians for Life (EA)
LFL .... Linear Field Line
LFl .... Long Flashing Light [*Navigation signal*]
LFL .... Lower Flammability Limit (EEVL)
LFL .... Lower Flammable Limit [*Medicine*] (EDAA)
LFL .... Lower Flexibility Limit [*Environmental science*] (COE)
LFL .... Lower Frequency Limit (ACAE)
LFL .... Lutherans for Life (EA)
LFLA .... Auxerre/Moneteau [*France*] [*ICAO location identifier*] (ICLI)
LFLA .... Landing Force Logistics Afloat (MCD)
LFIAA .... Laut-und Formenlehre des Aegyptisch-Aramaeisch [*A publication*] (BJA)
LFLB .... Chambery/Aix-Les-Bains [*France*] [*ICAO location identifier*] (ICLI)
LFLC .... Clermont-Ferrand/Aulnat [*France*] [*ICAO location identifier*] (ICLI)
LFLD .... Bourges [*France*] [*ICAO location identifier*] (ICLI)
LFLE .... Chambery/Challes-Les-Eaux [*France*] [*ICAO location identifier*] (ICLI)
LFLEN .... Leaf Length [*Botany*]
LFLF .... Orleans [*France*] [*ICAO location identifier*] (ICLI)
LFLG .... Grenoble/Le Versoud [*France*] [*ICAO location identifier*] (ICLI)
LFLGTH .... Leaf Length [*Botany*]
LFLH .... Chalon/Champforgeuil [*France*] [*ICAO location identifier*] (ICLI)
LFLI .... Annemasse [*France*] [*ICAO location identifier*] (ICLI)
LFLID .... Long Focal Length Imaging Demonstration (ACAE)
LFLJ .... Courchevel [*France*] [*ICAO location identifier*] (ICLI)
LFLK .... Lifelike (ABBR)
LFLK .... Oyonnax/Arbent [*France*] [*ICAO location identifier*] (ICLI)
LFLL .... Lyon/Satolas [*France*] [*ICAO location identifier*] (ICLI)
LFLM .... Macon/Charnay [*France*] [*ICAO location identifier*] (ICLI)
LFLN .... Lifeline (ABBR)
LFLN .... Saint-Yan [*France*] [*ICAO location identifier*] (ICLI)
LFLO .... Roanne/Renaison [*France*] [*ICAO location identifier*] (ICLI)
LFLOW .... Linearized High-Resolution Wind-Field Flow [*Model*] [*Marine science*] (OSRA)
LFLP .... Annecy/Meythet [*France*] [*ICAO location identifier*] (ICLI)
LFLPU .... Libyan Federation of Labor and Professional Unions
LFLQ .... Montelimar/Ancone [*France*] [*ICAO location identifier*] (ICLI)
LFLR .... Saint-Rambert-D'Albon [*France*] [*ICAO location identifier*] (ICLI)
LFLRASP .... Lifwynn Foundation for Laboratory Research in Analytical and Social Psychiatry (SAUO)
LFLS .... Grenoble/Saint-Geoirs [*France*] [*ICAO location identifier*] (ICLI)
LFLS .... Leafless (ABBR)
LFLSY .... Lifelessly (ABBR)
LFLT .... Left Front Lining Temperature [*Brake system*] [*Automotive engineering*]
LFLT .... Montlucon/Domerat [*France*] [*ICAO location identifier*] (ICLI)
LFLU .... Valence/Chabeuil [*France*] [*ICAO location identifier*] (ICLI)
LFLV .... Vichy/Charmeil [*France*] [*ICAO location identifier*] (ICLI)
LFLW .... Aurillac [*France*] [*ICAO location identifier*] (ICLI)
LFLWP .... Land Forces Logistics Working Party (MCD)
LFLX .... Chateauroux/Deols [*France*] [*ICAO location identifier*] (ICLI)
LFLY .... Lyon/Bron [*France*] [*ICAO location identifier*] (ICLI)
LFLZ .... Feurs/Chambeon [*France*] [*ICAO location identifier*] (ICLI)
LFM .... Franklin and Marshall College, Lancaster, PA [*OCLC symbol*] (OCLC)
LFM .... Landing Force Manual [*Marine Corps, Navy*]
LFM .... Large Function Modules (ACAE)
LFM .... LASER Feedback Microscope
LFM .... LASER Force Microscope
LFM .... Lateral Force Microscopy [*Morphology*]
LFM .... Launch First Motion
LFM .... Leaders for Manufacturing Program [*Massachusetts Institute of Technology*] (RCD)
LFM .... Lieutenant Field Marshal
LFM .... Limited-Area Fine-Mesh Model [*Marine science*] (OSRA)
LFM .... Limited Fine Mesh
Lfm .... Linear Feet Per Minute [*Industrial hygiene term*] (OHS)
LFM .... Linear Feet per Minute
LFM .... Linear Frequency Modulation (CAAL)
LFM .... Link Framing Module (VLIE)
LFM .... Live Firing Monitor (SAUS)
LFM .... Local File Manager
LFM .... Longitudinal Field Modulator
LFM .... Loss Frequency Method [*Insurance*]
LFM .... Lower Figure of Merit
LFM .... Low Fat Milk [*Medicine*] (AMHC)
LFM .... Low-Field Magnetometer [*Instrumentation*]
LFM .... Low-Frequency Magnetic [*Field*]
LFM .... Low-Frequency Modulation
LFM .... Low-Powered Fan Marker (MUGU)
LFM .... Lubrecht Forest [*Montana*] [*Seismograph station code, US Geological Survey*] [*Closed*] (SEIS)
LFMA .... Aix-Les-Milles [*France*] [*ICAO location identifier*] (ICLI)
LFMA .... Laminated Foil Manufacturers' Association [*Defunct*]
LFMB .... Aix-En-Provence [*France*] [*ICAO location identifier*] (ICLI)
LFMC .... Le Luc/Le Cannet [*France*] [*ICAO location identifier*] (ICLI)
LFMD .... Cannes/Mandelieu [*France*] [*ICAO location identifier*] (ICLI)
LfMd .... Life Medical Sciences [*Associated Press*] (SAG)
LFME .... Nimes/Courbessac [*France*] [*ICAO location identifier*] (ICLI)
LFMER .... Lovelace Foundation for Medical Education and Research [*Reorganized to form Lovelace Medical Foundation and Lovelace Biomedical and Environmental Research Institute*] (MCD)
LFMF .... Fayence [*France*] [*ICAO location identifier*] (ICLI)
LF/MF .... Low Frequency, Medium Frequency
LFMG .... La Montagne Noire [*France*] [*ICAO location identifier*] (ICLI)
LFMH .... Saint-Etienne/Boutheon [*France*] [*ICAO location identifier*] (ICLI)
LFMI .... Istres/Le Tube [*France*] [*ICAO location identifier*] (ICLI)
LFMI .... Lasers for Medicine, Incorporated (SAUO)
LFMJ .... Nice/Mont Agel [*France*] [*ICAO location identifier*] (ICLI)
LFMK .... Carcassonne/Salvaza [*France*] [*ICAO location identifier*] (ICLI)
LFML .... Little Flower Mission League (EA)
LFML .... Marseille/Marignane [*France*] [*ICAO location identifier*] (ICLI)
LFMM .... Aix-En-Provence [*France*] [*ICAO location identifier*] (ICLI)
LFMM .... Liquid-Fed Minimelter (ABAC)
LFMN .... Nice/Cote D'Azur [*France*] [*ICAO location identifier*] (ICLI)
LFMO .... Orange/Caritat [*France*] [*ICAO location identifier*] (ICLI)
LFMOP .... Linear Frequency Modulation on Pulse (MCD)
LFMP .... Perpignan/Rivesaltes [*France*] [*ICAO location identifier*] (ICLI)
LFM/PD .... Local Flow Management/Profile Descent
LFMQ .... Le Castellet [*France*] [*ICAO location identifier*] (ICLI)

LFMR........ Barcelonnette/Saint-Pons [*France*] [*ICAO location identifier*] (ICLI)
LFMR........ Low-Frequency Microwave Radiometer
LFMS........ Ales/Deaux [*France*] [*ICAO location identifier*] (ICLI)
LFMS........ Laminated Ferrite Memory System (MCD)
LFMT........ Montpellier/Frejorgues [*France*] [*ICAO location identifier*] (ICLI)
LFMU........ Beziers/Vias [*France*] [*ICAO location identifier*] (ICLI)
LFMV........ Avignon/Caumont [*France*] [*ICAO location identifier*] (ICLI)
LFMW........ Castelnaudary/Villeneuve [*France*] [*ICAO location identifier*] (ICLI)
LFMX........ Chateau-Arnoux/Saint-Auban [*France*] [*ICAO location identifier*] (ICLI)
LFMX........ Lufkin Foundry & Machine [*Federal Railroad Administration identification code*]
LFMY........ Salon [*France*] [*ICAO location identifier*] (ICLI)
LFMZ........ Lezignan-Corbieres [*France*] [*ICAO location identifier*] (ICLI)
LFN.......... Lactoferrin [*Biochemistry*] (MAE)
LFN.......... Libraries for Nursing (SAUO)
LFN.......... Logical File Name
LFN.......... Logical File Number [*Computer science*] (MCD)
LFN.......... Long Filename (PCM)
LFN.......... Louisburg, NC [*Location identifier*] [*FAA*] (FAAL)
LFNA........ Gap/Tallard [*France*] [*ICAO location identifier*] (ICLI)
LFNB........ Mende/Brenoux [*France*] [*ICAO location identifier*] (ICLI)
LFNBK....... Long File Name BacKup (SAUS)
LFNC........ Mont-Dauphin/Saint-Crepin [*France*] [*ICAO location identifier*] (ICLI)
LFND........ Pont-Saint-Esprit [*France*] [*ICAO location identifier*] (ICLI)
LFNE........ Salon/Eyguieres [*France*] [*ICAO location identifier*] (ICLI)
LFNF........ Vinon [*France*] [*ICAO location identifier*] (ICLI)
LFNG........ Montpellier/L'Or [*France*] [*ICAO location identifier*] (ICLI)
LFNGFT..... Landing Force Naval Gunfire Team
LFNH........ Carpentras [*France*] [*ICAO location identifier*] (ICLI)
LFNI........ Conqueyrac [*France*] [*ICAO location identifier*] (ICLI)
LFNJ........ Aspres-Sur-Buech [*France*] [*ICAO location identifier*] (ICLI)
LFNK........ Vars-Les-Crosses-Et-Les-Tronches [*France*] [*ICAO location identifier*] (ICLI)
LFNL........ Saint-Martin-De-Londres [*France*] [*ICAO location identifier*] (ICLI)
LFNM........ La Mole [*France*] [*ICAO location identifier*] (ICLI)
LFNO........ Florac-Sainte-Enimie [*France*] [*ICAO location identifier*] (ICLI)
LFNP........ Pezenas-Nizas [*France*] [*ICAO location identifier*] (ICLI)
LFNQ........ Mont-Louis-La-Quillane [*France*] [*ICAO location identifier*] (ICLI)
LFNR........ Berre-La-Fare [*France*] [*ICAO location identifier*] (ICLI)
LFNS........ Leafiness (ABBR)
LFNS........ Low-Frequency Navigation System (NG)
LFNS........ Sisteron-Theze [*France*] [*ICAO location identifier*] (ICLI)
LFNT........ Avignon-Pujaut [*France*] [*ICAO location identifier*] (ICLI)
LFNT........ Low Frequency Intersection (FAAC)
LFNU........ Uzes [*France*] [*ICAO location identifier*] (ICLI)
LFNV........ Valreas-Visan [*France*] [*ICAO location identifier*] (ICLI)
LFNW........ Puivert [*France*] [*ICAO location identifier*] (ICLI)
LFNX........ Bedarieux-La-Tour-Sur-Orb [*France*] [*ICAO location identifier*] (ICLI)
LFNY........ Saint-Etienne-En-Devoluy [*France*] [*ICAO location identifier*] (ICLI)
LFNZ........ Le Mazet-De-Romanin [*France*] [*ICAO location identifier*] (ICLI)
LFO.......... Large Follow-On
LFO.......... LASER/Fiber-Optic (MCD)
LFO.......... Left Front Outside-Drive
LFO.......... Light Fuel Oil (BARN)
LFO.......... Low-Frequency Oscillator
LFOA........ Avord [*France*] [*ICAO location identifier*] (ICLI)
LFOA........ Last Frame of Action [*Cinematography*] (WDMC)
LFOB........ Beauvais/Tille [*France*] [*ICAO location identifier*] (ICLI)
LFOC........ Crateaudun [*France*] [*ICAO location identifier*] (ICLI)
LFOC........ Landing Force Operation Center [*Navy*] (CAAL)
LFOC........ Lea-Francis Owners Club [*British*] (EAIO)
LFOD........ Saumur/Saint-Florent [*France*] [*ICAO location identifier*] (ICLI)
LFOE........ Evreux/Fauville [*France*] [*ICAO location identifier*] (ICLI)
LFOF........ Alencon/Valframbert [*France*] [*ICAO location identifier*] (ICLI)
LFOG........ Flers/Saint-Paul [*France*] [*ICAO location identifier*] (ICLI)
LFOH........ Le Havre/Octeville [*France*] [*ICAO location identifier*] (ICLI)
LFOI........ Abbeville [*France*] [*ICAO location identifier*] (ICLI)
LFOJ........ Orleans/Bricy [*France*] [*ICAO location identifier*] (ICLI)
LFOK........ Chalons/Vatry [*France*] [*ICAO location identifier*] (ICLI)
LFOL........ L'Aigle/Saint-Michel [*France*] [*ICAO location identifier*] (ICLI)
LFOM........ Lessay [*France*] [*ICAO location identifier*] (ICLI)
LFOM........ Low-Frequency Outer Marker (MSA)
LFON........ Dreux/Vernouillet [*France*] [*ICAO location identifier*] (ICLI)
LFOO........ Les Sables D'Olonne/Talmont [*France*] [*ICAO location identifier*] (ICLI)
LFOP........ Landing and Ferry Operations Panel [*NASA*] (NASA)
LFOP........ Rouen/Boos [*France*] [*ICAO location identifier*] (ICLI)
LFOQ........ Blois/Le Breuil [*France*] [*ICAO location identifier*] (ICLI)
LFOR........ Chartres/Champhol [*France*] [*ICAO location identifier*] (ICLI)
LFORM...... Landing Force Operational Reserve Material [*Navy*] (NVT)
LFOS........ Launch and Flight Operations System
LFOS........ Saint-Valery/Vittefleur [*France*] [*ICAO location identifier*] (ICLI)
LFOT........ Tours/Saint-Symphorien [*France*] [*ICAO location identifier*] (ICLI)
LFOU........ Cholet/Le Pontreau [*France*] [*ICAO location identifier*] (ICLI)
LFOV........ Large Field of View [*Radiology*] (DAVI)
LFOV........ Large Field-Of-View (SAUS)
LFOV........ Laval/Entrammes [*France*] [*ICAO location identifier*] (ICLI)
LFOW........ Saint-Quentin/Roupy [*France*] [*ICAO location identifier*] (ICLI)
LFOX........ Etampes/Mondesir [*France*] [*ICAO location identifier*] (ICLI)
LFOY........ Le Havre/Saint-Romain [*France*] [*ICAO location identifier*] (ICLI)
LFOZ........ Orleans/Saint-Denis-De-L'Hotel [*France*] [*ICAO location identifier*] (ICLI)
LFP.......... Labor-Force Participation
LFP.......... Large Flat Plate
LFP.......... LASER Flash Photolysis (MEC)
LFP.......... Late Flight Plan
LFP.......... Left Frontoposterior [*A fetal position*] [*Obstetrics*]
LFP.......... LFP Holdings, Inc. [*Toronto Stock Exchange symbol*]
LFP.......... Liberala Folkpartiet [*Liberal People's Party*] [*Finland*] [*Political party*] (PPE)
LFP.......... Libraries for Prisons [*An association*] (EA)
LFP.......... Life Point, Inc. [*AMEX symbol*] (SG)
LFP.......... Light Floor Pintle (SAUS)
LFP.......... Lindbergh Field Plant (SAUO)
LFP.......... Listen for Pleasure [*Audio books*]
LFP.......... Livestock Feed Program
LFP.......... Local Facilities Plan (SAUO)
LFP.......... Local Field Potential [*Electrophysiology*]
LFP.......... Low-Frequency Prediction (USDC)
LFP.......... Low Fuel Pump (HAWK)
LFPA........ Persan-Beaumont [*France*] [*ICAO location identifier*] (ICLI)
LFPAG...... Live Firing Program Analysis Group [*Military*] (CAAL)
LFPB........ Paris/Le Bourget [*France*] [*ICAO location identifier*] (ICLI)
LFPC........ Creil [*France*] [*ICAO location identifier*] (ICLI)
LFPC........ Louisiana Foundation for Private Colleges (SAUO)
LFPD........ Bernay/Saint-Martin [*France*] [*ICAO location identifier*] (ICLI)
LFPE........ Meaux/Esbly [*France*] [*ICAO location identifier*] (ICLI)
LFPEF....... Low-Frequency Pulsed Electromagnetic Field
LFPER...... Leaf Persistence [*Botany*]
LFPF........ Beynes/Thiverval [*France*] [*ICAO location identifier*] (ICLI)
LFPG........ Paris/Charles-De-Gaulle [*France*] [*ICAO location identifier*] (ICLI)
LFPH........ Chelles/Le Pin [*France*] [*ICAO location identifier*] (ICLI)
LFPI........ Paris/Issy-Les-Moulineaux [*France*] [*ICAO location identifier*] (ICLI)
LFPJ........ Taverny [*France*] [*ICAO location identifier*] (ICLI)
LFPK........ Coulommiers/Voisins [*France*] [*ICAO location identifier*] (ICLI)
LFPL........ Lewis Flight Propulsion Laboratory [*NASA*]
LFPL........ Lognes/Emerainville [*France*] [*ICAO location identifier*] (ICLI)
LFPM........ Melun/Villaroche [*France*] [*ICAO location identifier*] (ICLI)
LFPN........ Toussus-Le-Noble [*France*] [*ICAO location identifier*] (ICLI)
LFPO........ Paris/Orly [*France*] [*ICAO location identifier*] (ICLI)
LFPP........ Le Plessis-Belleville [*France*] [*ICAO location identifier*] (ICLI)
LFPP........ Low Fuel-pump Pressure [*Automotive engineering*]
LFPPV...... Low-Frequency Positive Pressure Ventilation [*Medicine*] (DMAA)
LFPQ........ Fontenay-Tresigny [*France*] [*ICAO location identifier*] (ICLI)
LFPR........ Guayancourt [*France*] [*ICAO location identifier*] (ICLI)
LFPRI....... London Female Preventive and Reformatory Institution (SAUO)
LFPRL...... Lewis Flight Propulsion Research Laboratory [*NASA*] (MUGU)
LFPS........ Licentiate of the Faculty of Physicians and Surgeons [*British*]
LFPS........ Low-Frequency Phase Shifter [*Telecommunications*]
LFPS........ Paris [*France*] [*ICAO location identifier*] (ICLI)
LFPSG...... Licentiate of the Faculty of Physicians and Surgeons, Glasgow (ROG)
LFPT........ Pontoise/Cormeilles-En-Vexin [*France*] [*ICAO location identifier*] (ICLI)
LFPU........ Lion Ferry Portland [*Intermodal shipping container symbol*] (TVRC)
LFPU........ Moret/Episy [*France*] [*ICAO location identifier*] (ICLI)
LFPUB...... Leaf Pubescence [*Botany*]
LFPV........ Villacoublay/Velizy [*France*] [*ICAO location identifier*] (ICLI)
LFPW........ Low-Frequency Plasma Wave
LFPW........ Paris, Centre Meteorologique [*France*] [*ICAO location identifier*] (ICLI)
LFPX........ Chavenay/Villepreux [*France*] [*ICAO location identifier*] (ICLI)
LFPY........ Bretigny-Sur-Orge [*France*] [*ICAO location identifier*] (ICLI)
LFPZ........ Saint-Cyre-L'Ecole [*France*] [*ICAO location identifier*] (ICLI)
LFQ.......... Light Foot Quantizer
LFQ.......... Limited Flying Quality
LFQA........ Reims/Prunay [*France*] [*ICAO location identifier*] (ICLI)
LFQB........ Troyes/Barberey [*France*] [*ICAO location identifier*] (ICLI)
LFQC........ Luneville/Croismare [*France*] [*ICAO location identifier*] (ICLI)
LFQD........ Arras/Roclincourt [*France*] [*ICAO location identifier*] (ICLI)
LFQE........ Etain/Rouvres [*France*] [*ICAO location identifier*] (ICLI)
LFQF........ Autun/Bellevue [*France*] [*ICAO location identifier*] (ICLI)
LFQG........ Nevers/Fourchambault [*France*] [*ICAO location identifier*] (ICLI)
LFQH........ Chatillon-Sur-Seine [*France*] [*ICAO location identifier*] (ICLI)
LFQI........ Cambrai/Epinoy [*France*] [*ICAO location identifier*] (ICLI)
LFQJ........ Maubeuge/Elesmes [*France*] [*ICAO location identifier*] (ICLI)
LFQK........ Chalons/Ecury-Sur-Coole [*France*] [*ICAO location identifier*] (ICLI)
LFQL........ Lens/Benifontaine [*France*] [*ICAO location identifier*] (ICLI)
LFQM........ Besancon-La-Veze [*France*] [*ICAO location identifier*] (ICLI)
LFQN........ Saint-Omer/Wizernes [*France*] [*ICAO location identifier*] (ICLI)
LFQO........ Lille/Marcq-En-Baroeul [*France*] [*ICAO location identifier*] (ICLI)
LFQP........ Phalsbourg/Bourscheid [*France*] [*ICAO location identifier*] (ICLI)
LFQQ........ Lille/Lesquin [*France*] [*ICAO location identifier*] (ICLI)
LFQR........ Romilly-Sur-Seine [*France*] [*ICAO location identifier*] (ICLI)
LFQS........ Vitry-En-Artois [*France*] [*ICAO location identifier*] (ICLI)
LFQT........ Merville/Calonne [*France*] [*ICAO location identifier*] (ICLI)
LFQU........ Sarre-Union [*France*] [*ICAO location identifier*] (ICLI)
LFQV........ Charleville/Mezieres [*France*] [*ICAO location identifier*] (ICLI)
LFQW........ Vesoul-Frotey [*France*] [*ICAO location identifier*] (ICLI)
LFQY........ Saverne-Steinbourg [*France*] [*ICAO location identifier*] (ICLI)
LFQZ........ Dieuze-Gueblange [*France*] [*ICAO location identifier*] (ICLI)
L FR......... Franc [*Monetary unit*] [*Luxembourg*]
LFR.......... Inshore Fire Support Ship [*Navy symbol*]
LFR.......... Laboratory Facilities Request (MCD)
LFR.......... La Fria [*Venezuela*] [*Airport symbol*] (OAG)
LFR.......... Laminar-Flow Reactor [*Engineering*]
LFR.......... LASERgraphics Film Recorder (PCM)

LFR .... Laughter [*Telegraphy*] (PCTE)
L Fr .... Law French (DLA)
LFR .... Leafier (ABBR)
LFR .... Less-Favoured Region (EURO)
LFR .... Lifer (ABBR)
LFR .... Linear Flow Reactor [*Chemical engineering*]
LFR .... Line Frequency Rejection (IAA)
LFR .... Logical Forms Recognition [*Computer science*]
LFR .... Lowest Fare Routing [*Travel industry*]
LFR .... Low-Flux Reactor
LFR .... Low Frequency Radio Range (TAG)
LFR .... Low-Frequency Range (MCD)
LFR .... Low Frequency Receiver (ACAE)
LFR .... Lymphoid Follicular Reticulosis [*Medicine*] (DB)
LFr .... Saint Mary Parish Library, Franklin, LA [*Library symbol*] [*Library of Congress*] (LCLS)
LFRA .... Angers/Avrille [*France*] [*ICAO location identifier*] (ICLI)
LFRA .... League of Federal Recreation Associations (EA)
LFRA .... Leatherhead Food Research Association [*British*] (ARC)
LFRAP .... Long Feeder Route Analysis Program [*Bell System*]
LFRB .... Brest/Guipavas [*France*] [*ICAO location identifier*] (ICLI)
LFRC .... Cherbourg/Maupertus [*France*] [*ICAO location identifier*] (ICLI)
LFRC .... Latex Foam Rubber Council [*Defunct*] (EA)
LFRC .... Laurentian Forest Research Center [*Canadian Forestry Service*] [*Research center*] (RCD)
LFRC .... Library Fundraising Resource Center [*American Library Association*]
LFRD .... Dinard/Pleurtuit-Saint-Malo [*France*] [*ICAO location identifier*] (ICLI)
LFRD .... Lot Fraction Reliability Deviation [*Quality control*]
LFRE .... La Baule/Escoublac [*France*] [*ICAO location identifier*] (ICLI)
LFRED .... Liquid-Fueled Ramjet Engine Demonstration [*Navy*] (MCD)
LFRED .... Liquid-Fuelled Ramjet Engine Development (SAUS)
LFRF .... Granville [*France*] [*ICAO location identifier*] (ICLI)
LFRG .... Deauville/Saint-Gatien [*France*] [*ICAO location identifier*] (ICLI)
LFRH .... Lorient/Lann-Bihoue [*France*] [*ICAO location identifier*] (ICLI)
LFRI .... La Roche-Sur-Yon/Les Ajoncs [*France*] [*ICAO location identifier*] (ICLI)
LFRJ .... Landivisiau [*France*] [*ICAO location identifier*] (ICLI)
LFRJ .... Liquid-Fueled Ramjet [*Navy*] (MCD)
LFRK .... Caen/Carpiquet [*France*] [*ICAO location identifier*] (ICLI)
LFRL .... Lanveoc/Poulmic [*France*] [*ICAO location identifier*] (ICLI)
LFRM .... Le Mans/Arnage [*France*] [*ICAO location identifier*] (ICLI)
LFRN .... Lavender Families Resource Network [*An association*] (EA)
LFRN .... Rennes/Saint-Jacques [*France*] [*ICAO location identifier*] (ICLI)
LFRO .... Lannion/Servel [*France*] [*ICAO location identifier*] (ICLI)
LFRP .... Ploermel-Loyat [*France*] [*ICAO location identifier*] (ICLI)
LFRQ .... Quimper/Pluguffan [*France*] [*ICAO location identifier*] (ICLI)
LFRR .... Brest [*France*] [*ICAO location identifier*] (ICLI)
LFRR .... Low-Frequency Radio Range (MCD)
LFRS .... Nantes/Chateau Bougon [*France*] [*ICAO location identifier*] (ICLI)
LFRSB .... Loose Fuel-Rod Shipping Basket (GAAI)
LFRT .... Long-fiber Reinforced Thermoplastic [*Plastics*]
LFRT .... Long Film-Reinforced Thermoplastic
LFRT .... Saint-Brieuc Armor [*France*] [*ICAO location identifier*] (ICLI)
LFrtW .... Washington Parish Library (SAUO)
LFrtW .... Washington Parish Library, Franklinton (SAUS)
LFrtW .... Washington Parish Library, Franklinton, LA [*Library symbol*] [*Library of Congress*] (LCLS)
LFRU .... Morlaix/Ploujean [*France*] [*ICAO location identifier*] (ICLI)
LFRV .... Vannes/Meucon [*France*] [*ICAO location identifier*] (ICLI)
LFRW .... Avranches/Le Val Saint-Pere [*France*] [*ICAO location identifier*] (ICLI)
LFRX .... Brest [*France*] [*ICAO location identifier*] (ICLI)
LFRY .... Cherbourg [*France*] [*ICAO location identifier*] (ICLI)
LFRZ .... Saint-Nazaire/Montoir [*France*] [*ICAO location identifier*] (ICLI)
LFS .... Amphibious Fire Support Ship [*Navy symbol*]
LFS .... Labour Force Survey [*Canada*]
LFS .... Lancaster Finishing School [*British military*] (DMA)
LFS .... LASER Fluorescence Spectroscopy
LFS .... Lateral Facet Syndrome [*Medicine*] (EDAA)
LFS .... Launch Facility Simulator
LFS .... League of Filipino Students
LFS .... Leather Finishers' Society [*A union*] [*British*]
LFS .... Libertarian Futurist Society (EA)
LFS .... Licentiate of the Faculty of Architects and Surveyors [*British*] (DBQ)
LFS .... Licentiate Surveyor of the Faculty of Architects and Surveyors (SAUO)
LFS .... Li-Fraumeni Syndrome [*Oncology*]
LFS .... Limbic Forebrain Structure [*Medicine*] (EDAA)
LFS .... Liquid Filter System
LFS .... Liquid Filtration System
LFS .... Liquid Flow System
LFS .... Liver Function Series [*Clinical chemistry*]
LFS .... Loamy Fine Sand [*Soil biology*] [*Soil texture*] (QSUL)
LFS .... Local Format Storage
LFS .... Logical File Structure [*Computer science*] (OA)
LFS .... Logical File System (IAA)
LFS .... Logic Fault Simulator [*Computer science*]
LFS .... Logistics Feasibility System
LFS .... Logistics/Ferry Station
LFS .... London Financial Studies
LFS .... London Fire Service (SAUO)
LFS .... Loop Feedback Signal
LFS .... Low-Frequency Stimulation [*Neurophysiology*]
LFS .... Low Frequency Synchronization (ACAE)
LFS .... Lubrication Filtration System [*Automotive lubricants*]
LFS .... Luftfahrzeug Service - Aircraft Service [*Austria*] [*ICAO designator*] (FAAC)
LFSA .... Besancon/Thise [*France*] [*ICAO location identifier*] (ICLI)
LFSA .... First Federal S&L Assn. of Lenawee County [*NASDAQ symbol*] (COMM)
LFSA .... Law Firm Services Association (EA)
LFSA .... List of Frequently Seen Acronyms (SAUO)
LFSA .... Logistical Force Structure Assessment (MCD)
LFSB .... Bale/Mulhouse [*France/Switzerland*] [*ICAO location identifier*] (ICLI)
LFSB .... LFS Bancorp [*NASDAQ symbol*] (SAG)
LFS Bcp .... LFS Bancorp [*Associated Press*] (SAG)
LFSC .... Colmar/Meyenheim [*France*] [*ICAO location identifier*] (ICLI)
LFSC .... Life Sciences, Inc. (SAUO)
LFSC .... Limited First-Strike Capability
LFSC .... London Fire Salvage Corps (SAUO)
LFSC .... Louisville Fear Survey for Children [*Psychology*]
LFSCWW .... Live Food Singles Club - World Wide [*Defunct*] (EA)
LFSD .... Dijon/Longvic [*France*] [*ICAO location identifier*] (ICLI)
LFSE .... Epinal/Dogneville [*France*] [*ICAO location identifier*] (ICLI)
LFSF .... Metz/Frescaty [*France*] [*ICAO location identifier*] (ICLI)
LFSG .... Epinal/Mirecourt [*France*] [*ICAO location identifier*] (ICLI)
LFSH .... Haguenau [*France*] [*ICAO location identifier*] (ICLI)
LFSI .... Saint-Dizier/Robinson [*France*] [*ICAO location identifier*] (ICLI)
LFSID .... Local Form Session Identifier (ACRL)
LFSJ .... Sedan/Douzy [*France*] [*ICAO location identifier*] (ICLI)
LFSK .... Vitry-Le-Francois/Vauclerc [*France*] [*ICAO location identifier*] (ICLI)
LFSL .... Toul/Rosieres [*France*] [*ICAO location identifier*] (ICLI)
LFSM .... Montbeliard/Courcelles [*France*] [*ICAO location identifier*] (ICLI)
LFSMS .... Logistics Force Structure Management Support (ACAE)
LFSMT/S .... Liquid Fuel Systems Maintenance Technician/Specialist [*Aerospace*] (AAG)
LFSN .... Lipomyelomeningocele Family Support Network [*Founded in 1997*] (NRGU)
LFSN .... Nancy/Essey [*France*] [*ICAO location identifier*] (ICLI)
LFSO .... Nancy/Ochey [*France*] [*ICAO location identifier*] (ICLI)
LFSP .... Landing Force Support Party [*Navy*] (ANA)
LFSP .... Pontarlier [*France*] [*ICAO location identifier*] (ICLI)
LFSPT .... Long Form System Performance Test (ACAE)
LFSQ .... Belfort/Fontaine [*France*] [*ICAO location identifier*] (ICLI)
LFSR .... Linear Feedback Shift Register [*Computer science*] (CIST)
LFSR .... Reims/Champagne [*France*] [*ICAO location identifier*] (ICLI)
LFSS .... Landing Force Support Ship [*Navy*]
LFSS .... Launch Facility Security System [*NASA*] (KSC)
LFST .... Largest Feasible Steerable Telescope
LFST .... Lifestyle (ABBR)
LFST .... Linder's Four Seasons Transportation [*Common carrier symbol*]
LFST .... Strasbourg/Entzheim [*France*] [*ICAO location identifier*] (ICLI)
LFSTK .... Leafstalk (ABBR)
LFSU .... Rolampont [*France*] [*ICAO location identifier*] (ICLI)
LFSV .... Landing Force Support Vehicle (MCD)
LFSV .... Lifesaver (ABBR)
LFSV .... Pont-Saint-Vincent [*France*] [*ICAO location identifier*] (ICLI)
LFSW .... Epernay/Plivot [*France*] [*ICAO location identifier*] (ICLI)
LFSW .... Landing Force Support Weapon
LFSX .... Luxeuil/Saint-Sauveur [*France*] [*ICAO location identifier*] (ICLI)
LFSY .... Chaumont-La Vendue [*France*] [*ICAO location identifier*] (ICLI)
lf sz .... Life Size (VRA)
LFSZ .... Lifesize (ABBR)
LFSZ .... Vittel/Champ De Courses [*France*] [*ICAO location identifier*] (ICLI)
LFT .... Aerolift Philippines Corp. [*ICAO designator*] (FAAC)
LFT .... Ladd-Franklin Theory [*Color vision*]
LFT .... Lafayette [*Louisiana*] [*Airport symbol*] (OAG)
LFT .... Lafayette [*Diocesan abbreviation*] [*Indiana*] (TOCD)
LFT .... Lafayette, LA [*Location identifier*] [*FAA*] (FAAL)
LFT .... Laminar Flow Torch [*For plasma generation*]
LFT .... LASER Flash Tube
LFT .... Late Finish Time
LFT .... Latest Finish Time
LFT .... Latex Fixation Test [*Medicine*]
LFT .... Latex Flocculation Test [*Clinical chemistry*]
LFT .... Launch Facility Trainer
LFT .... Law Foundation of Tasmania [*Australia*]
LFT .... Leafiest (ABBR)
LFT .... Leaflet (ADA)
LFT .... Leap-Frog Test
LFT .... Left (ABBR)
lft .... Left (VRA)
LFT .... Left Frontotransverse [*A fetal position*] [*Obstetrics*]
LFT .... Left Half Indicators, Off Test (SAA)
LFT .... Lexford Residential TR SBI [*NYSE symbol*] (SG)
LFT .... Lifetime Corporation (SAUO)
LFT .... Lifting (MSA)
LFT .... Ligand-Field Theory [*Physical chemistry*]
LFT .... Light Fire Team [*Military*] (CINC)
LFT .... Linear Flash Tube
LFT .... Linear Foot (ADA)
LFT .... Live Fire Test
LFT .... Live Fire Testing (SAUS)
LFT .... Liver Function Test [*Medicine*]
LFT .... Long-Fiber Thermoplastic
LFT .... Long-term Fuel Trim [*Automotive engineering*]
LFT .... Low-Frequency Tetanus [*Medicine*] (DMAA)
LFT .... Low-Frequency Transduction
LFT .... Low-Frequency Transfer [*Sex factor*] (DB)

L/FT^2 .... Lumens per Square Foot (WDAA)
LFTA .... London Fur Trade Association (SAUO)
LFTA .... Low-Frequency Timing Assembly (IAA)
LFT & E ..... Live Fire Test and Evaluation [*Required testing for major weapon system and munition programs*] [*Military*] (RDA)
LFTB .... Lace Finishing Trade Board (SAUO)
LFTB .... Liquid Fuels Trust Board (SAUO)
LFTC .... Landing Force Training Command [*Navy*] (NVT)
LFTC .... Toulon [*France*] [*ICAO location identifier*] (ICLI)
LFTCPAC .... Landing Force Training Command, Pacific [*Navy*] (DNAB)
LFTDWP .... Land Force Tactical Doctrine Working Party [*NASA*] (MCD)
LFTEG .... Liquid-Fuelled Thermo-Electric Generator (PDAA)
L-F test ..... Latex Fixation Test [*Medicine*] (EDAA)
LFTF .... Cuers/Pierrefeu [*France*] [*ICAO location identifier*] (ICLI)
LFTF .... Liftoff (ABBR)
LFTF .... London Furniture Trades Federation (SAUO)
LFTH .... Hyeres/Le Palyvestre [*France*] [*ICAO location identifier*] (ICLI)
LFTHDD ..... Lefthanded (ABBR)
LFTHDY ..... Lefthandedly (ABBR)
LFTINS ...... Loftiness (ABBR)
LFTIR .... Loftier (ABBR)
LFTIT .... Loftiest (ABBR)
LFTL .... Lafayette [*NCIC trailer make code*]
LFTM .... Lifetime (ABBR)
LFTM .... Lifetime Communities (SAUO)
LFTN .... La Grand'Combe [*France*] [*ICAO location identifier*] (ICLI)
LFTOV .... Leftover (ABBR)
LFtp .... Library Program, Cataloging Department, Recreation Service (SAUO)
LFtp .... Library Program, Cataloging Department, Recreation Service, Fort Polk, LA [*Library symbol*] [*Library of Congress*] (LCLS)
LFTPR .... Long Fiber Thermoplastic Resin
LFTR .... Toulon/Saint-Mandrier [*France*] [*ICAO location identifier*] (ICLI)
LFTS .... Low Frequency Test Station (ACAE)
LFTS .... Toulon [*France*] [*ICAO location identifier*] (ICLI)
LFTT .... Leftist (ABBR)
LFTU .... Frejus/Saint-Raphael [*France*] [*ICAO location identifier*] (ICLI)
LFTU .... Landing Force Training Unit [*Marine Corps*]
LFTU .... LFT Internationale Fachspedition [*Intermodal shipping container symbol*] (TVRC)
LFTW .... Nimes/Garons [*France*] [*ICAO location identifier*] (ICLI)
LFTWF .... Luftwaffe (ABBR)
LFTWG ...... Leftwing (ABBR)
LFTWR ...... Leftwinger (ABBR)
LFTY .... Lofty (ABBR)
LFU .... Laser Firing Unit (ACAE)
LFU .... Least Frequency Unit (NITA)
LFU .... Least Frequently Used [*Computer science*]
LFU .... Leonhartsberger Fluguntemchmen GmbH [*Austria*] [*ICAO designator*] (FAAC)
LFU .... LFU Leonhartsberger Flugunternehmen Gesellschaft MbH [*Austria*] [*FAA designator*] (FAAC)
LFU .... Limit Flocculation Unit [*Medicine*] (EDAA)
LFU .... Lipid Fluidity Unit (DB)
LFU .... Lost to Followup (HVTR)
LFU .... Lunar Flying Unit [*NASA*]
LFU Memory ... Least Frequency Used Memory [*Computer science*] (ITCA)
LFUS .... Littelfuse, Inc. [*NASDAQ symbol*] (SAG)
LFUSS .... Landing Force Organizational Systems Study
LFUSW ...... Littelfuse Inc. Wrrt'A' [*NASDAQ symbol*] (TTSB)
LFV .... Large Field of View [*Radiology*] (DAVI)
LFV .... Lassa-Fever Virus
LFV .... Light Forces Vehicle (SAUS)
LFV .... Low-Frequency Vibration
LFV .... Lunar Flying Vehicle [*NASA*]
LFV .... Northhampton, MA [*Location identifier*] [*FAA*] (FAAL)
LFVLF .... Low Frequency, Very Low Frequency (IAA)
LFVM .... Miquelon [*France*] [*ICAO location identifier*] (ICLI)
LFVO .... Library Foundation for Voluntary Organizations [*Defunct*] (EA)
LFVP .... Saint-Pierre, Saint-Pierre-Et Miquelon [*France*] [*ICAO location identifier*] (ICLI)
LFW .... Liberal Federation of Wales (SAUO)
LFW .... Linear Friction Welding [*Environmental science*]
LFW .... Lome [*Togo*] [*Airport symbol*] (OAG)
LFW .... Looking for Work
LFWB .... Sccom Sud-Ouest [*France*] [*ICAO location identifier*] (ICLI)
LFWD .... Location of Four-Wheel Drive [*Automotive emissions*]
LFWID .... Length of Leaf at Widest Portion [*Botany*]
LFWK .... Lifework (ABBR)
LFX .... Limited output Full area automatic Extraction (SAUS)
LFX .... Live Fire Exercise [*Army*] (INF)
LFX .... Live-Fire Exercises [*Army*] (INF)
LFXA .... Amberieu [*France*] [*ICAO location identifier*] (ICLI)
LFXB .... Saintes/Thenac [*France*] [*ICAO location identifier*] (ICLI)
LFXC .... Contrexeville [*France*] [*ICAO location identifier*] (ICLI)
LFXD .... Doullens/Lucheux [*France*] [*ICAO location identifier*] (ICLI)
LFXE .... Camp De Mourmelon [*France*] [*ICAO location identifier*] (ICLI)
LFXF .... Limoges/Romanet [*France*] [*ICAO location identifier*] (ICLI)
LFXG .... Camp De Bitche [*France*] [*ICAO location identifier*] (ICLI)
LFXH .... Camp Du Valdahon [*France*] [*ICAO location identifier*] (ICLI)
LFXI .... Apt/Saint-Christol [*France*] [*ICAO location identifier*] (ICLI)
LFXJ .... Bordeaux [*France*] [*ICAO location identifier*] (ICLI)
LFXK .... Camp De Suippes [*France*] [*ICAO location identifier*] (ICLI)
LFXL .... Mailly-Le-Camp [*France*] [*ICAO location identifier*] (ICLI)
LFXM .... Mourmelon [*France*] [*ICAO location identifier*] (ICLI)
LFXN .... Narbonne [*France*] [*ICAO location identifier*] (ICLI)
LFXO .... Tours/Cinq-Mars La Pile [*France*] [*ICAO location identifier*] (ICLI)
LFXP .... Camp De Sissonne [*France*] [*ICAO location identifier*] (ICLI)
LFXQ .... Camp De Coetquidan [*France*] [*ICAO location identifier*] (ICLI)
LFXR .... Rochefort/Soubise [*France*] [*ICAO location identifier*] (ICLI)
LFXS .... Camp De La Courtine [*France*] [*ICAO location identifier*] (ICLI)
LFXT .... Camp De Caylus [*France*] [*ICAO location identifier*] (ICLI)
LFXU .... Les Mureaux [*France*] [*ICAO location identifier*] (ICLI)
LFXV .... Lyon/Mont-Verdun [*France*] [*ICAO location identifier*] (ICLI)
LFXW .... Camp Du Larzac [*France*] [*ICAO location identifier*] (ICLI)
LFY .... Leafy (ABBR)
LFYA .... Drachenbronn [*France*] [*ICAO location identifier*] (ICLI)
LFYD .... Damblain [*France*] [*ICAO location identifier*] (ICLI)
LFYF .... Centre Meteorologique de Concentration et de Diffusion, French Air Force [*France*] [*ICAO location identifier*] (ICLI)
LFYG .... Cambrai/Niergnies [*France*] [*ICAO location identifier*] (ICLI)
LFYH .... Broye-Les-Pesmes [*France*] [*ICAO location identifier*] (ICLI)
LFYL .... Lure/Malbouhans [*France*] [*ICAO location identifier*] (ICLI)
LFYM .... Marigny-Le-Grand [*France*] [*ICAO location identifier*] (ICLI)
LFYO .... Villacoublay [*France*] [*ICAO location identifier*] (ICLI)
LFYR .... Romorantin/Pruniers [*France*] [*ICAO location identifier*] (ICLI)
LFYS .... Sainte-Leocadie [*France*] [*ICAO location identifier*] (ICLI)
LFYT .... Saint-Simon/Clastres [*France*] [*ICAO location identifier*] (ICLI)
LFYX .... Paris [*France*] [*ICAO location identifier*] (ICLI)
LFZ .... Laminar Flow Zone
LFZA .... Laforza [*NCIC truck make code*]
LG .... Directorate of Logistics Systems (SAUO)
LG .... Guidotti & C. [*Italy*] [*Research code symbol*]
LG .... Laban Guild [*Formerly, LAMG*] (EA)
LG .... Laboratory of Genetics (GNE)
LG .... Laclede Gas [*NYSE symbol*] (TTSB)
LG .... Laclede Gas Co. [*NYSE symbol*] (SPSG)
LG .... Laclede Group [*NYSE symbol*]
LG .... Lady [*of the Order of the*] Garter (BARN)
LG .... Lagoon [*Maps and charts*] (ROG)
LG .... Landed Gentry
LG .... Landgericht [*Regional Court*] [*German*] (ILCA)
L/G .... Land Grant (DLA)
LG .... L & G Trailer [*NCIC trailer make code*]
LG .... Landing Gear [*Aircraft*]
LG .... Landing Ground [*Navy*]
LG .... Landing Group [*Navy*] (NVT)
LG .... Lane Grader [*Slang for an army instructor*] (VNW)
LG .... Language [*Online database field identifier*]
lg .... Large (BEE)
Lg .... Large (DIAR)
LG .... Large
LG .... Large Grain
LG .... Laryngectomy [*Medicine*] (MAE)
LG .... LASER Gyro (MCD)
LG .... Lateral Gastrocnemius
LG .... Lateral Geniculate [*Medicine*] (MELL)
LG .... Launcher Group [*Army*]
LG .... Laurens Glass [*Federal Railroad Administration identification code*]
LG .... Law Glossary (DLA)
L-G .... Lawson Gould [*Publisher*]
LG .... Leathercraft Guild (EA)
LG .... Leaving Group
LG .... Lecture Guide [*Training term*] (LPT)
LG .... Left Gluteus [*Medicine*]
LG .... Left Guard [*Football*]
LG .... Leg (IAA)
LG .... Leichtgeschuetz [*Light gun for airborne operations*] [*German military - World War II*]
lg .... Length (MIST)
LG .... Length (MSA)
LG .... Leucylglycine (DB)
LG .... Level Gauge
LG .... Lewis Gun
LG .... Lieutenant General [*British*] (ROG)
LG .... Life Guards [*Military unit*] [*British*]
LG .... Light Green
LG .... Light Gun
LG .... Linear Gate
LG .... Line Generator [*Computer science*]
LG .... Line Graph (OA)
LG .... Line-to-Ground (IAA)
LG .... Linguogingival [*Dentistry*]
LG .... Lining
LG .... Linkage Group [*Genetics*] (OA)
LG .... Lipoglycopeptide (DB)
LG .... Liquid Gas
LG .... Liquid Gold (WDAA)
LG .... [*The*] Literary Guild
LG .... Little Guides [*A publication*]
LG .... Local Government (ADA)
LG .... Local Ground (ACAE)
LG .... Loganiar Ltd. [*British*]
LG .... Logistics Group [*Military*]
LG .... London Group (SAUO)
LG .... Long (KSC)
LG .... Longold Resources, Inc. [*Vancouver Stock Exchange symbol*]
LG .... Longwood Gardens [*Kennett Square, PA*]
LG .... Loop Gain

LG........... Low German [*Language, etc.*]
LG........... Low Glucose [*Medicine*]
LG........... Lucky-Goldstar (EFIS)
LG........... Lueneburg [*German license plate city code*]
LG........... Lumen Gentium [*Dogmatic Constitution on the Church*] [*Vatican II document*]
LG........... Lymph Glands [*Medicine*]
LG .... London Gazette (ODA)
LGA.......... Elgaz [*Poland*] [*ICAO designator*] (FAAC)
LGA.......... Flight Ground Attack Fighter (ACAE)
LGA.......... LaGuardia Airport [*New York*] (CDAI)
LGA.......... Large for Gestational Age [*Pediatrics*]
LGA.......... Left Gastric Artery [*Medicine*] (MELL)
LGA.......... LGA: Local Government Administration [*A publication*]
LGA.......... Light-Gun Amplifier
LGA.......... Liptako-Gourma Integrated Development Authority (SAUO)
LGA.......... Local Government Act (SAUO)
LGA.......... Local Government Administration
LGA.......... Local Government Agency (SAUO)
LGA.......... Local Government Area (ADA)
LGA.......... Local Government Association (GVA)
LGA.......... Local Government Audit [*British*]
LGA.......... Local Government Authority (SAUO)
LgA.......... Lodging Allowance [*British military*] (DMA)
LGA.......... Lower Grades Advanced [*Telegraphy*] (PCTE)
LGA.......... Low-Gain Antenna
LGA.......... New York [*New York*] La Guardia [*Airport symbol*] (OAG)
LGAA......... Local Government Auditors Association (SAUO)
LGAANSW... Local Government Auditors' Association of New South Wales [*Australia*]
LGAB........ Local Government Advisory Board [*Tasmania, Australia*]
LGAB........ Local Government Auditors' Board [*Queensland, Australia*]
LGAC........ Athinai [*Greece*] [*ICAO location identifier*] (ICLI)
LgacySft.... Legacy Software, Inc. [*Associated Press*] (SAG)
LGAD........ Andravida [*Greece*] [*ICAO location identifier*] (ICLI)
LGAES....... Lesbian and Gay Associated Engineers and Scientists [*Later, NOGLSTP*] (EA)
LGAF........ Flight Ground-Attack Fighter (SAUS)
LGAF........ Light Ground-Attack Fighter
LGAG........ Agrinion [*Greece*] [*ICAO location identifier*] (ICLI)
LGAG........ Luggage (ABBR)
LGAL........ Alexandroupolis [*Greece*] [*ICAO location identifier*] (ICLI)
LGAM........ Amphiali [*Greece*] [*ICAO location identifier*] (ICLI)
LGAM........ Lexington Global Asset Managers, Inc. [*NASDAQ symbol*] (SAG)
LGAM........ Lexington Global Assets Mgrs [*NASDAQ symbol*] (TTSB)
LGAN........ Logan Transportation Company [*Common carrier symbol*]
LG&E........ Louisville Gas and Electric Co. (EFIS)
LGANSW.... Local Government Association of New South Wales [*Australia*]
LGANT....... Local Government Association of the Northern Territory [*Australia*]
LGAR........ Ladies of the Grand Army of the Republic (EA)
LGAS........ Louisville Gas & Electric Co. [*NASDAQ symbol*] (SAG)
LGAS........ Low-G Accelerometer System [*NASA*]
LGASA....... Local Government Association of South Australia
LGASP....... Louiseville G&E 5% Pfd [*NASDAQ symbol*] (TTSB)
LGAT........ Athinai [*Greece*] [*ICAO location identifier*] (ICLI)
LGAT........ Local Government Appeals Tribunal (SAUO)
LGAX........ Alexandria [*Greece*] [*ICAO location identifier*] (ICLI)
L Gaz........ Law Gazette [*A publication*] (DLA)
LGB.......... Landry-Guillain-Barre (Syndrome) [*Medicine*]
LGB.......... LASER-Guided Bomb
LGB.......... Lateral Geniculate Body
LGB.......... Legible (ABBR)
LGB.......... Local Government Board
LGB.......... Long Beach [*California*] [*Airport symbol*] (OAG)
LGB.......... Long Beach, CA [*Location identifier*] [*FAA*] (FAAL)
LGBA........ Lesbian and Gay Bands of America (EA)
LGBC........ Local Government Boundaries Commission [*New South Wales, Australia*]
LGBC........ Local Government Boundary Commission (SAUO)
LGBCE....... Local Government Boundary Commission for England
LGBCH...... Long Beach, CA [*American Association of Railroads railroad junction routing code*]
LGBL........ Nea Anghialos [*Greece*] [*ICAO location identifier*] (ICLI)
LGBO........ Local Government Board Office [*British*]
LGBPM...... Lesbian, Gay, and Bisexual People in Medicine (EA)
LGBR........ Loganberry (ABBR)
LGBRPCV... Lesbian, Gay, and Bisexual Returned Peace Corps Volunteers (EA)
LGBRU...... Lugubrious (ABBR)
LGBRUY..... Lugubriously (ABBR)
LGBS........ Landry-Guillain-Barre Syndrome [*Medicine*] (DMAA)
LGBT........ Legibility (ABBR)
LGBT........ Lesbian, Gay, Bisexual, and Transgendered [*Lifestyle classifications*]
LGBTA....... Lesbian Gay Bisexual Transgender Association
LGBY........ Legibly (ABBR)
LGC.......... Laboratory of the Government Chemist [*Research center*] [*British*] (IRC)
LGC.......... La Grange, GA [*Location identifier*] [*FAA*] (FAAL)
LGC.......... Lakewood Golf Course [*California*] [*Seismograph station code, US Geological Survey*] (SEIS)
LGC.......... Large Diameter Gravity Corer [*Nuclear energy*] (NUCP)
LGC.......... Large-Probe Gas Chromatograph [*NASA*]
LGC.......... Launch Guidance Computer
LGC.......... Laurentian Group Corp. [*Toronto Stock Exchange symbol*]
LGC.......... Leafy Greens Council (EA)
LGC.......... Left Giant Cell [*Medicine*] (STED)
LGC.......... Line Group Controller (ACRL)
LGC.......... LM [*Lunar Module*] Guidance Computer [*NASA*]
LGC.......... Local Government Center [*Database producer*] (EA)
LGC.......... Local Government Chronicle [*1855*] [*A publication*] (DLA)
LGC.......... Local Government Commission [*Victoria, Australia*]
LGC.......... Local Government Contact (SAUO)
LGC.......... Local Government Council
L-G C........ Lockheed-Georgia Company (SAUO)
LGC.......... Logic (MSA)
LGC.......... Longitude Grid Control (ACAE)
LGC.......... Lord Great Chamberlain [*British*] [*A publication*] (DLA)
LGC.......... Lorry with Gas Containers [*British*]
LGC.......... Lunar Gas Chromatograph
LGC.......... Lunar Geological Camera [*NASA*] (KSC)
LGCA........ Land-Grant College of Agriculture
LGCA........ Late Great Chevrolet Association (EA)
LGCA........ Local Government Clerks' Association [*Australia*]
LGCA........ London Gregorian Choral Association
LGCANSW... Local Government Clerks' Association of New South Wales [*Australia*]
LGCB........ Local Government Clerks' Board [*Queensland, Australia*]
LGCC........ Letchworth Garden City Corporation (SAUO)
LGCC........ Local Government Clerks' Certificate
LGCH........ Long Chih Industrial Company [*NCIC trailer make code*]
LGCL........ Licentiate of the Guild of Cleaners and Launderers [*British*] (DBQ)
LGCL........ Logical (ABBR)
LGCLT....... Logicality (ABBR)
LGCLY....... Logically (ABBR)
LGCM........ Lesbian & Gay Christian Movement (WDAA)
LGCN........ Logician (ABBR)
LGCOMB.... Large Combatant (DNAB)
LGCP........ Lexical-Graphical Composer Printer [*Photocomposition*]
LGCPHW.... Lesbian and Gay Caucus of Public Health Workers (EA)
LGCS........ Limited Generation Certification Scheme (SAUO)
LGCY........ Legacy (ABBR)
LGCY........ Legacy Software [*NASDAQ symbol*] (TTSB)
LGCY........ Legacy Software, Inc. [*NASDAQ symbol*] (SAG)
LGD.......... Compagnie Aerienne du Languedoc [*France*] [*ICAO designator*] (FAAC)
LGd.......... Dorsal Lateral Geniculate Nucleus [*Also, dLGN*] [*Anatomy*]
LGD.......... Laboratory of Genomic Diversity [*National Cancer Institute*] (RCD)
LGD.......... La Grande, OR [*Location identifier*] [*FAA*] (FAAL)
LGD.......... Lambda Gamma Delta [*Society*]
LGD.......... Large Group Display (MCD)
LGD.......... Leaderless Group Discussion
lgd........... Legend (VRA)
LGD.......... Limb Guide Dystrophy [*Medicine*] (EDAA)
LGD.......... Local Government Development (SAUO)
LGD.......... Local Government Division (SAUO)
LGD.......... Local Government Division, Department of Internal Affairs (SAUS)
LGD.......... Longed [*Telegraphy*] (PCTE)
LGD.......... Lou Gehrig Disease [*Medicine*] (MELL)
LGD.......... Low-Grade Dysplasia [*Medicine*]
LGDA........ Lawn and Garden Distributors Association (SAUO)
LGDA........ National Lawn and Garden Distributors Association (EA)
LGDG........ Lightning Drayage Company [*Common carrier symbol*]
LGDHC...... Ligue Guineenne des Droits de l'Homme [*Guinea*] [*Political party*] (EY)
LGDM....... LASER-Guided Dispenser Munition (PDAA)
LGDMN..... Legerdemain (ABBR)
LGDR........ Labor of Genetic Disease Research [*National Institutes of Health*]
LGDT........ Load Global Descriptor Table (SAUO)
LGE.......... Landing Ground, Emergency [*British military*] (DMA)
LGE.......... Large (MSA)
lge........... Large (REAL)
LGE.......... Laser Guidance Element (ACAE)
LGE.......... League (WDAA)
LGE.......... LEM [*Lunar Excursion Module*] Guidance Equipment [*NASA*] (KSC)
LGE.......... LG & E Energy [*NYSE symbol*] (SPSG)
LGE.......... Light Generation Efficiency (AAEL)
LGE.......... Local Government Engineer
LGE.......... Logic Gate Expander [*Computer science*]
LGE.......... Low Grade Fever [*Medicine*] (EDAA)
LGE.......... Lunar Geological Equipment [*NASA*]
LGEA........ Local Government Electricity Association (SAUO)
LGEANSW.. Local Government Electricity Association of New South Wales [*Australia*]
LGEANSW... Local Government Engineers' Association of New South Wales [*Australia*]
LGEB........ Local Government Examination Board (SAUO)
LGEC........ Lunar Geological Exploration Camera (PDAA)
LGEEQC..... Local Government Electrical Engineering Qualifications Committee [*Australia*]
LGEIES...... Local Government Environmental Information Exchange Scheme (SAUO)
LGEL........ Elefsis [*Greece*] [*ICAO location identifier*] (ICLI)
LGEME...... Legion of Greeks from Egypt and the Middle East [*Australia*] [*An association*]
LGEMP...... Local Government Energy Management Program
LGEN........ Lieutenant General (GOBB)
LGen........ Lieutenant General [*Navy*] [*British*]
LGEQC....... Local Government Engineering Qualifications Committee [*Australia*]
LGER........ Low German [*Language, etc.*] (ROG)

LGEU .... Catu Containers [*Intermodal shipping container symbol*] (TVRC)
LGEZ......... LG Everest [*Federal Railroad Administration identification code*]
LGF .... LAAS (Local Area Augmentation Service) Ground Facility [*Navigation systems*]
LGF .... Lateral Giant Fiber (DB)
LGF .... Light Guiding Film [*Adhesives*]
LGF .... Light Guiding Film [*Plastics*]
LGF .... Lions Gate Entertainment [*AMEX symbol*] (SG)
LGF .... Lions Gate Entertainment Corp. [*Toronto Stock Exchange symbol*] [*Canada*]
LGF .... Lions Gate Entertainment Corp. [*AMEX symbol*]
LGF .... Yuma/Yuma Proving Ground, AZ [*Location identifier*] [*FAA*] (FAAL)
LGFA......... Lattice Girder Floor Association [*British*] (DBA)
LGFC .... Lesley Gore Fan Club (EA)
LGFPP...... Long Glass Fiber Polypropylene [*Plastics*]
LGFS .... Local Government Financial System (MHDB)
LGFSTF ..... Liquified Gaseous Fuels Spill Test Facility [*Department of Energy*]
LGFSTP ..... Liquefied Gaseous Fuels Spill Test Facility (USDC)
LGG.......... Least General Generalization (IDAI)
LGG.......... Legging (ABBR)
LGG.......... Liege [*Belgium*] [*Airport symbol*] (OAG)
LGG.......... Light Gas Gun
LGG.......... Light-Gun Pulse Generator
LGG.......... Longing [*Telegraphy*] (PCTE)
LGGBFC..... Larry Gatlin and the Gatlin Brothers Fan Club (EA)
LGGBIFC .... Larry Gatlin and the Gatlin Brothers International Fan Club (EA)
LGGC .... Local Government Grants Commission
LGGE .... Laboratory of Glaciology and Geophysics of the Environment [*France*]
LGGG .... Athinai [*Greece*] [*ICAO location identifier*] (ICLI)
LGGR........ Logger (ABBR)
LGGRHD .... Loggerhead (ABBR)
LGH.......... Lactogenic Hormone [*Also, LTH, PR, PRL*] [*Endocrinology*]
LGH.......... Laghuu [*Language symbol*] (ETLW)
LGH.......... Lansing General Hospital [*Michigan*]
LGH.......... Laugh (ABBR)
LGH.......... Launch Grapnel Hook
LGH.......... Leigh Creek [*Australia*] [*Airport symbol*] (OAG)
LGH.......... Length
LGH.......... Letterman General Hospital (SAUO)
LGH.......... Liberty Godparent Home [*An association*] (EA)
LGH.......... Little Growth Hormone [*Medicine*] (STED)
LGH.......... Logarithmic Histogram Scanning [*Mass spectrometry*]
LGHB .... Laughable (ABBR)
LGHBY .... Laughably (ABBR)
LGHCS ...... Lutheran General Health Care System (EA)
LGHD .... Laughed (ABBR)
LGHET....... Larghetto (ABBR)
LGHG .... Laughing (ABBR)
LGHGY ...... Laughingly (ABBR)
LGHI .... Khios [*Greece*] [*ICAO location identifier*] (ICLI)
LGHL .... Porto Heli [*Greece*] [*ICAO location identifier*] (ICLI)
LGHN .... Leghorn (ABBR)
LGHP .... Large Group Health Plan [*Department of Health and Human Services*] (GFGA)
LGHR......... Laugher (ABBR)
LGHS .... Louisiana Genealogical and Historical Society (EARSL)
LGHTR ...... Laughter (ABBR)
LGHTR ...... Lighter
LGI........... Deadman's Cay [*Bahamas*] [*Airport symbol*] (OAG)
LGI........... Large Glucagon Immunoreactivity [*Immunochemistry*]
LGI........... Laser Glidescope Indicator (SAUS)
LGI........... Lateral Giant Interneuron [*Neurobiology*]
LGI........... Linear Gate and Integrator (MHDB)
LGI........... Locally Generated Income (MCD)
LGI........... Lower Gastrointestinal [*Medicine*] (STED)
LGI........... Lunar Geology Investigation [*NASA*]
LGI........... Lynx Geosystems Incorporated (SAUO)
LGIB .... Local Government International Bureau (EURO)
LGIB .... Lower Gastrointestinal Bleeding (SAUS)
LGIEE........ Liaison Group for International Educational Exchange (EA)
LGIO .... Ioannina [*Greece*] [*ICAO location identifier*] (ICLI)
LGIO .... Local Government Information Office (SAUO)
LGIOM....... Lieutenant-Governor of the Isle of Man (SAUO)
LGIR.......... Iraklion [*Greece*] [*ICAO location identifier*] (ICLI)
LGISC .... Louisiana Geographic Information Systems Council (SAUO)
LGITIT .... Legitimist (ABBR)
LGITIZ....... Legitimize (ABBR)
LGITIZD ..... Legitimized (ABBR)
LGITIZG ..... Legitimizing (ABBR)
LGITMA ..... Legitimate (ABBR)
LGITMAD ... Legitimated (ABBR)
LGITMAG ... Legitimating (ABBR)
LGITMC ..... Legitmacy (ABBR)
LGITMY ..... Legitimately (ABBR)
LGIU .... LASER Gyro Interface Unit (NASA)
LGIU .... Local Government Information Unit [*British*]
LGIX.......... Elders Grain [*Private rail car owner code*]
LGJ .... Local Government Journal [*A publication*] (ROG)
LGK.......... Langkawi [*Malaysia*] [*Airport symbol*] (OAG)
LGk .... Late Greek [*or Low Greek*] [*Language*] (BARN)
LGKA .... Kastoria [*Greece*] [*ICAO location identifier*] (ICLI)
LGKC .... Kithira [*Greece*] [*ICAO location identifier*] (ICLI)
LGKF .... Kefallinia [*Greece*] [*ICAO location identifier*] (ICLI)
LGKJ......... Kastelorizo [*Greece*] [*ICAO location identifier*] (ICLI)
LGKL .... Kalamata [*Greece*] [*ICAO location identifier*] (ICLI)
LGKM........ Kavala/Amigdhaleon [*Greece*] [*ICAO location identifier*] (ICLI)
LGKO .... Kos [*Greece*] [*ICAO location identifier*] (ICLI)
LGKP .... Karpathos [*Greece*] [*ICAO location identifier*] (ICLI)
LGKR .... Kerkira [*Greece*] [*ICAO location identifier*] (ICLI)
LGKS .... Kasos [*Greece*] [*ICAO location identifier*] (ICLI)
LGKV .... Kavala/Khrisoupolis [*Greece*] [*ICAO location identifier*] (ICLI)
LGKZ .... Kozani [*Greece*] [*ICAO location identifier*] (ICLI)
LGL .... Labioglossolaryngeal [*Dentistry*] (DAVI)
LGL .... La Gloria [*Colombia*] [*Airport symbol*] (AD)
LGL .... Large Granular Leukocyte [*Hematology*]
LGL .... Large Granular Lymphocyte [*Hematology*]
LGL .... Legal (ABBR)
Lgl .... Legal (TBD)
LGL .... Lobular Glomerulonephritis [*Medicine*] (STED)
LGL .... Local Government Library [*A publication*]
LGL .... Local Graphics Library [*Cambridge Computer Graphics Ltd.*] [*Software package*] (NCC)
LGL .... Long Lellang [*Malaysia*] [*Airport symbol*] (OAG)
LGL .... Lown-Ganong-Levine [*Syndrome*] [*Medicine*]
LGL .... Luxair-Societe Luxembourgeoise de Navigation Aerienne SA [*Germany*] [*ICAO designator*] (FAAC)
LGL .... Lynch Corp. [*AMEX symbol*] (SPSG)
LGLA .... Legislate (ABBR)
LGLAD....... Legislated (ABBR)
LGLAG....... Legislating (ABBR)
LGLAN....... Legislation (ABBR)
LGLAR....... Legislator (ABBR)
LGLAR....... Legislature (ABBR)
LGLAY....... Legislative (ABBR)
LGLC .... Libertarians for Gay and Lesbian Concerns (EA)
LGLE......... Leros [*Greece*] [*ICAO location identifier*] (ICLI)
LGLM........ Legalism (ABBR)
LGLPFA ..... London and Greater London Playing Fields Association (SAUO)
LGLR .... Larissa [*Greece*] [*ICAO location identifier*] (ICLI)
LGLST .... Legalist (ABBR)
LGLSTC ..... Legalistic (ABBR)
LGLSTCY.... Legalistically (ABBR)
LGLT .... Legality (ABBR)
LGLTC .... Legalistic (ABBR)
LGLY......... Legally (ABBR)
LGLZ......... Legalize (ABBR)
LGLZD .... Legalized (ABBR)
LGLZG....... Legalizing (ABBR)
LGLZN....... Legalization (ABBR)
LGM .... LASER Ground Mapper
LGM .... LASER-Guided Munition
LGM .... Last Glacial Maximum [*Climatology*]
LGM .... Liberty Godparent Ministry (EA)
LGM .... Little Green Men [*British term for space signals*]
LGM .... Little Green Mountain [*Idaho*] [*Seismograph station code, US Geological Survey*] [*Closed*] (SEIS)
LGM .... Lloyd's Gold (ODA)
LGM .... Local Government Management [*A publication*]
LGM .... Logistic Guidance Memorandum
LGM .... Logistics Module [*Simulation games*] [*Army*] (SSD)
LGM .... Longmont, CO [*Amtrak Busline code*]
LGM .... Loop Ground Multiplexer (MCD)
LGM .... Loop Group Multiplexer. Communications (SAUO)
LGM .... Lymphogranuloma [*Medicine*] (MELL)
LGM .... Silo-Launched surface attack Guided Missile (SAUS)
LGM-30G .... Minuteman III [*Military*] [*Intercontinental ballistic missile*] (POLM)
LGM-118..... Peacekeeper [*Air Force*] [*Intercontinental ballistic missile*] (POLM)
LGMA........ Lesbian and Gay Medical Association [*Defunct*] (EAIO)
LGMAC ...... Laboratory for Global Marine and Atmospheric Chemistry [*University of East Anglia*] [*United Kingdom*] (RCD)
LGMB........ Lady Godiva Marching Band (SAUO)
LGMB........ Local Government Management Board (AIE)
LGMD .... Limb Girdle Muscular Dystrophy [*Medicine*]
LGMD .... Lobular Giant Movement Detector (PDAA)
LGMG .... Lipid and Glycopeptide Modified Derivative (DB)
LGMG .... Megara [*Greece*] [*ICAO location identifier*] (ICLI)
LGMK........ Mikonos [*Greece*] [*ICAO location identifier*] (ICLI)
LGML........ Milos [*Greece*] [*ICAO location identifier*] (ICLI)
LGMN .... Ligament (ABBR)
LGMR .... Laser Guided Magnetical Recording (SAUS)
LGMR .... Marathon [*Greece*] [*ICAO location identifier*] (ICLI)
LGMS........ LASER Ground Mapping System
LGMS........ Laser Guided Missile System (SAUO)
LGMT........ Mitilini [*Greece*] [*ICAO location identifier*] (ICLI)
LGMTA ...... LogiMetrics [*OTCBB symbol*]
LGN.......... Lagoon (ADA)
LGN.......... Lagunillas [*Venezuela*] [*Seismograph station code, US Geological Survey*] (SEIS)
LGN.......... Lateral Geniculate Nucleus
LGN.......... Left Green Network [*An association*] (EA)
LGN.......... Legion (ABBR)
LGN.......... Legion Resources Ltd. [*Vancouver Stock Exchange symbol*]
LGN.......... Line Gate Number [*Computer science*]
LGN.......... Lobular Glomerulonephritis [*Medicine*] (MAE)
LGN.......... Local Government Network [*Emergency Management*] (EMA)
LGN.......... Lodgian [*AMEX symbol*]
LGN.......... Logical Group Node (SAUO)

LGN .... Logical Group Number [*Computer science*] (IBMDP)
LGN .... Logicon, Inc. [*NYSE symbol*] (SPSG)
LGNAP ...... Lagniappe (ABBR)
LGNAR ...... Legionaire (ABBR)
LGNBRY ..... Loganberry (ABBR)
LGND .... Lateral Geniculate Nucleus Dorsal [*Neuroanatomy*]
LGND .... Legend (ABBR)
LGND .... Ligand Pharmaceuticals, Inc. [*NASDAQ symbol*] (SAG)
LGND .... Ligand Pharmaceuticals 'B' [*NASDAQ symbol*] (TTSB)
LGNDY ...... Legendary (ABBR)
LGNMVTE ... Lignum Vitae [*Botany*]
LGNQ .... WL Logan [*Common carrier symbol*]
LGNS .... Largeness (ABBR)
LGNS .... Leggoons Inc. [*NASDAQ symbol*] (TTSB)
LGNT .... LEGENT Corp. (SAUO)
LGNY .... Legionary (ABBR)
LGNZ .... Local Government New Zealand (SAUO)
LGO .... Lamont Geological Observatory [*Later, L-DGO*] [*Columbia University*]
LGO .... Largo (ABBR)
LGO .... Light Gas Oil [*Fuel technology*]
LGO .... Local Government Office
LGO .... Logo Resources Ltd. [*Vancouver Stock Exchange symbol*]
LGO .... Low Gravity Orbit
LGO .... Lunar Geoscience Observer (MCD)
LGOC .... London General Omnibus Co. [*British*] (DCTA)
LGOFC ...... Linda Gray's Official Fan Club (EA)
LGON .... Lagoon (ABBR)
LGOR .... Langor (ABBR)
LGORU ...... Langorous (ABBR)
LGORU ...... Local Government Operational Research Unit [*British*] (DI)
LGORUY .... Langorously (ABBR)
LGP .... Labioglossopharyngeal [*Dentistry*] (DAVI)
LGP .... Laboratory Graduate Participation [*Oak Ridge National Laboratory*]
LGP .... LASER-Guided Projectile (MCD)
LGP .... Legaspi [*Philippines*] [*Airport symbol*] (OAG)
LGP .... Legaspi [*Philippines*] [*Seismograph station code, US Geological Survey*] (SEIS)
LGP .... Low G Projectile (ACAE)
LGP .... Low Ground Pressure
LGP .... Lummer-Gehreke Plate [*Physics*]
LGPA .... Livestock and Grain Producers Association (SAUO)
LGPA .... Paros [*Greece*] [*ICAO location identifier*] (ICLI)
LGPANSW ... Livestock and Grain Producers' Association of New South Wales [*Australia*]
LGPIM ...... Lesbian and Gay People in Medicine [*Later, LGBPM*] (EA)
LGPL .... Lesser General Public License (SAUO)
LGPL .... Library General Public License (SAUO)
LGPN .... International Leather Goods, Plastic, and Novelty Workers' Union (EA)
LGPO .... Local Group Policy Object (SAUO)
LGPZ .... Preveza [*Greece*] [*ICAO location identifier*] (ICLI)
LGQ .... Lago Agrio [*Ecuador*] [*Airport symbol*] (OAG)
LGQ .... Linear Gaussian Quadratic (AAEL)
LGQB .... Local Government Qualifications Board [*Victoria, Australia*]
LGR .... Knight's Local Government Reports [*A publication*] (DLA)
LGR .... Lager (ABBR)
LGR .... Laird Group, Inc. [*Toronto Stock Exchange symbol*]
LGR .... Larger (WGA)
lgr .... Larger
LGR .... Laser Guidance Receiver (SAUS)
LGR .... Leasehold Ground Rent (ROG)
LGR .... Lethal Ground Range (MCD)
LGR .... Letter of General Representation (PDAA)
LGR .... Light-Water-Cooled, Graphite-Moderated Reactor (NRCH)
LGR .... Local Government Radio [*Emergency Management*] (EMA)
LGR .... Local Government Reorganization [*British*]
LGR .... Local Government Reports [*England*] [*A publication*] (DLA)
LGR .... Local Governments Reimbursement Program (SAUO)
LGR .... Localized Gain Region (PDAA)
LGR .... Logrono [*Spain*] [*Seismograph station code, US Geological Survey*] (SEIS)
LGR .... London Grand Rank [*Freemasonry*]
lgr .... Longer (MIST)
LGR .... Longer (WGA)
LGR .... Loop Gap Resonator [*Spectrometry*]
LGR .... Low Greek [*Language, etc.*]
LGR .... Low Group Receiving Unit
LGra .... Grambling State University, Grambling, LA [*Library symbol*] [*Library of Congress*] (LCLS)
LGRD .... Laggard (ABBR)
LGRD .... Rodos/Maritsa [*Greece*] [*ICAO location identifier*] (ICLI)
LGR (Eng) ... Local Government Reports [*England*] [*A publication*] (DLA)
LGRF .... Loan Guaranty Revolving Fund
LGrJ .... Jefferson Parish Public Library, Gretna, LA [*Library symbol*] [*Library of Congress*] (LCLS)
LGR Laser ... Localized Gain Region Laser (SAUO)
LGRMG ...... Lesbian/Gay Rights Monitoring Group (EA)
LGRP .... Rodos/Paradisi [*Greece*] [*ICAO location identifier*] (ICLI)
LGR Unit .... Low Group Receiving Unit (SAUO)
LGRX .... Araxos [*Greece*] [*ICAO location identifier*] (ICLI)
LGS .... Grambling State University, Grambling, LA [*OCLC symbol*] (OCLC)
LGS .... Lagoons [*Maps and charts*] (ROG)
LGS .... Landing Guidance System [*Aerospace*]
LGS .... Large Gray Ship [*Slang*] [*Navy*]
LGS .... Large Green Soft [*Stool*] [*Gastroenterology*] (DAVI)
LGS .... LASER Guidance System (MCD)
LGS .... Last Glacial Stage (QUAC)
LGS .... Late Glacial Stage [*Paleontology*]
LGS .... Lega dei Giovani Somali [*Somali Youth League*]
LGS .... Lennox-Gastaut Syndrome [*Medicine*] (EDAA)
LGS .... Limb Girdle Sydrome [*Medicine*] (EDAA)
LGS .... Limerick Generation Station [*Nuclear energy*] (NRCH)
LGS .... Liquid Asset and Government Securities (ADA)
LGS .... Lithogenic Grain Size [*An indicator of wind intensity*]
LGS .... Litton Graphics Standard (MCD)
LGS .... Load Generator System [*Computer science*] (HODG)
LGS .... Longs [*Telegraphy*] (PCTE)
LGS .... Louisiana General Services, Inc. (SAUO)
LGS .... Louisiana Geological Survey (SAUO)
LGS .... Lower Group Stop (NRCH)
LGS .... Lunar Geophysical Surface
LGS .... Lunar Gravity Simulator [*Aerospace*]
LGSA .... Khania/Souda [*Greece*] [*ICAO location identifier*] (ICLI)
LGSA .... Langer-Giedion Syndrome Association (NRGU)
LGSA .... Leinster Guild of Shop Assistants (SAUO)
LGSB .... Local Government Services Bureau [*South Australia*]
LGSB .... Local Government Superannuation Board [*Queensland, Australia*]
LGSC .... Large Scale (ABBR)
LGSC .... Linear Glideslope Capture (SAUS)
LGSD .... Sedes [*Greece*] [*ICAO location identifier*] (ICLI)
L/GSE .... Launch and Ground Support Equipment
LGS/GJ ...... Geological Journal. Liverpool Geological Society and the Manchester Geological Association. Liverpool (SAUO)
LGSI .... Logistics Insight Corporation [*Common carrier symbol*]
LGSIL .... Low Grade Squamous Intraepithelial Lesions [*Medicine*] (WDAA)
LGSK .... Skiathos [*Greece*] [*ICAO location identifier*] (ICLI)
LGSL .... Lugsail (ABBR)
LGSM .... Licentiate of Guildhall School of Music [*British*]
LGSM .... Light Ground Station Module
LGSM .... Samos [*Greece*] [*ICAO location identifier*] (ICLI)
LGSOWG .... Landsat Ground Station Operations (or Operators) Working Group (SAUO)
LGSOWOG ... Landsat Ground Station Operations Working Group (SAUO)
LGSP .... Sparti [*Greece*] [*ICAO location identifier*] (ICLI)
LGSR .... Santorini [*Greece*] [*ICAO location identifier*] (ICLI)
LGsSH ...... Greenwell Springs State Hospital, Greenwell Springs, LA [*Library symbol*] [*Library of Congress*] (LCLS)
LGST .... Sitia [*Greece*] [*ICAO location identifier*] (ICLI)
lgstc .... Linguistic (ADWA)
LGSTC ...... Logistic (ABBR)
LGSTCL ..... Logistical (ABBR)
LGSTCN .... Logistician (ABBR)
Lgstcs ...... Linguistics (ADWA)
LGSV .... Stefanovikion [*Greece*] [*ICAO location identifier*] (ICLI)
LGSX .... Mid-American Energy [*Private rail car owner code*]
LGSY .... Skyros [*Greece*] [*ICAO location identifier*] (ICLI)
LGT .... Laboratoire Generale des Telecommunications (EFIS)
LGT .... Langat Encephalitis [*Medicine*]
LGT .... Largest (ABBR)
LGT .... Late Generalized Tuberculosis [*Medicine*]
LGT .... Legate (ABBR)
LGT .... Legitimate [*Telegraphy*] (PCTE)
LGT .... Liechtenstein Global Trust
LGT .... Light
lgt .... Light
lgt .... Lighting (MIST)
LGT .... Liquid Gas Tank
LGT .... Local Geomagnetic Time
LGT .... Logistec Corp. [*Toronto Stock Exchange symbol*]
LGT .... Longitudinal Survey of Work Experience (SAUO)
LGT .... Low Gelling Temperature [*Analytical biochemistry*]
LGT .... Low Group Transmit (SAUO)
LGT .... Low Group Transmitting Unit
LGTA .... Ligue Generale des Travailleurs Angolais [*General League of Angolan Workers in Exile*]
LGTB .... Local Government Training Board [*British*]
LGTD .... Lighted
LGTE .... Legatee (ABBR)
LGTFGR .... Lightfingered (ABBR)
LGTFTD .... Lightfooted (ABBR)
LGTFTY .... Lightfootedly (ABBR)
LGTG .... Lighting (ABBR)
LGTG .... Tanagra [*Greece*] [*ICAO location identifier*] (ICLI)
LGTH .... Length (AFM)
lgth .... Length (VRA)
LGTH .... Lexington Group in Transportation History (EA)
LGTH .... Lightning Hole [*Electronics*]
LGTHCOLM ... Length of Column [*Military*] (GFGA)
LGTHD ...... Lightheaded (ABBR)
LGTHDY .... Lightheadedly (ABBR)
LGTHIY ..... Lengthily (ABBR)
LGTHN ...... Lengthen (ABBR)
LGTHND .... Lengthened (ABBR)
LGTHNG .... Lengthening (ABBR)
LGTHNS .... Lengthiness (ABBR)
LGTHR ...... Lengthier (ABBR)
LGTHRTD ... Lighthearted (ABBR)

LGTHRTNS ... Lightheartedness (ABBR)
LGTHRTY ... Lightheartedly (ABBR)
LGTHS ... Lighthouse (ABBR)
LGTHT ... Lengthiest (ABBR)
LGTHWS ... Lengthwise (ABBR)
LGTHY ... Lengthy (ABBR)
LGTI ... Lower Genital Tract Infection [*Medicine*] (DMAA)
LGTIC ... Logistic (ABBR)
LGTICL ... Logistical (ABBR)
LGTK ... Logitek, Inc. (SAUO)
LGTL ... Kasteli [*Greece*] [*ICAO location identifier*] (ICLI)
LGTMDD ... Lightminded (ABBR)
LGTMDY ... Lightmindedly (ABBR)
LGTN ... Legation (ABBR)
LGTN ... Lighten (ABBR)
LG TN ... Long Ton [*2240 pounds*] (WDAA)
LGTNG ... Lightning (ABBR)
LGTO ... Legato (ABBR)
LGTO ... Legato Systems [*NASDAQ symbol*] (TTSB)
LGTO ... Legato Systems, Inc. [*NASDAQ symbol*] (SAG)
LGTP ... Tripolis [*Greece*] [*ICAO location identifier*] (ICLI)
LGTPB ... Local Government Town Planners' Board [*Queensland, Australia*]
LG TPR ... Long Taper (WDAA)
LGTQ ... Long's Transfer and Storage [*Common carrier symbol*]
LGTR ... Ligature (ABBR)
LGTR ... Lightener (ABBR)
LGTRD ... Ligatured (ABBR)
LGTRG ... Ligaturing (ABBR)
LGTS ... Lights [*Postal Service standard*] (OPSA)
LGTS ... Thessaloniki [*Greece*] [*ICAO location identifier*] (ICLI)
LGTT ... Dekeleia/Tatoi [*Greece*] [*ICAO location identifier*] (ICLI)
LGTU ... Liquid and Gas Transport [*Intermodal shipping container symbol*] (TVRC)
LGTUD ... Longitude (ABBR)
LGTUDL ... Longitudinal (ABBR)
LGTUDY ... Longitudinally (ABBR)
LGT Unit ... Low Group Transmitting Unit (SAUO)
LGTWT ... Lightweight (ABBR)
LGTY ... Lightly (ABBR)
LGTY ... Logility, Inc. [*NASDAQ symbol*] (NASQ)
LGTYR ... Lightyear (ABBR)
LGU ... Ladies Golf Union
LGU ... Land-Grant University
LGU ... League (ABBR)
LGU ... Legume (ABBR)
LGU ... Local Glucose Utilization [*Physiology*]
LGU ... Local Government Union (SAUO)
LGU ... Local Government Unit (SAUO)
LGU ... Logan [*Utah*] [*Airport symbol*] (OAG)
LGU ... Logan, UT [*Location identifier*] [*FAA*] (FAAL)
L Guard ... Law Guardian [*A publication*] (DLA)
LGUD ... Leagued (ABBR)
LGUG ... Leaguing (ABBR)
LGUM ... Legume, Inc. (SAUO)
LGUNU ... Leguminous (ABBR)
LGUs ... Local Government Units (SAUS)
LGV ... Large Goods Vehicle (SAUO)
LGV ... Large Granular Vesicle (OA)
LGV ... Long Goods Vehicle (SAUO)
LGV ... Lymphogranuloma Venereum [*Medicine*]
LGVA ... Longview Air Freight [*Common carrier symbol*]
LGVC ... Local Government Valuers' Committee [*New South Wales, Australia*]
LGVD ... Large Group View Display (MCD)
LGVHD ... Lethal Graft-Versus-Host Disease [*Medicine*] (DMAA)
LGVMA ... Lesbian & Gay Veterinary Medical Association (GVA)
LGVO ... Volos [*Greece*] [*ICAO location identifier*] (ICLI)
LGVU ... STMI [*Intermodal shipping container symbol*] (TVRC)
LGW ... Landing Gear Warning
LGW ... Laser-Guided Weapon (DOMA)
LGW ... London-Gatwick [*England*] [*Airport symbol*] (OAG)
LGW ... Longines-Wittnauer Watch Company (SAUO)
LGW ... Love Games Won [*Tennis*]
LGW ... Lufttarhtgesellschaft Walter GmbH [*Germany*] [*ICAO designator*] (FAAC)
LGW/CAS ... Laser Guided Weapons in Close Air Support (SAUO)
LGWCM ... LASER-Guided Weapons Counter-Measure (PDAA)
LGWD ... Large Group Wall Display (SAUO)
LGWF ... Libyan General Workers' Federation
LGWS ... LASER-Guided Weapons Systems (IEEE)
LGWV ... Long Wave (FAAC)
LGWX ... Logic Works [*NASDAQ symbol*] (TTSB)
LGWX ... Logic Works, Inc. [*NASDAQ symbol*] (SAG)
LGX ... Lovington, NM [*Location identifier*] [*FAA*] (FAAL)
LgX ... Lymphogranulomatosis X [*Medicine*] (EDAA)
LGY ... Lagunillas [*Venezuela*] [*Airport symbol*] (AD)
LGY ... Largely (ABBR)
LGY ... Legally [*Telegraphy*] (PCTE)
LGY ... Leggy (ABBR)
LGZ ... Legalize [*Telegraphy*] (PCTE)
LGZA ... Zakinthos [*Greece*] [*ICAO location identifier*] (ICLI)
LH ... Deutsche Lufthansa AG [*Germany*] [*ICAO designator*] (OAG)
LH ... Laboratory Corp. Amer Hldgs Wrrt [*NYSE symbol*] (TTSB)
LH ... Laboratory Corp. of America Holdings [*NYSE symbol*] (SAG)
LH ... Labor Historians [*Defunct*] (EA)
LH ... Labor Hour [*In contract work*]
LH ... Laetolil Hominid
LH ... Lamphole (ABBR)
LH ... Langmuir-Hinshelwood Mechanism [*Chemistry*]
LH ... Lanugo Hair (MELL)
LH ... Laparoscopic Herniorrhaphy [*Medicine*] (MELL)
LH ... Large Heavy Seeds [*Botany*]
LH ... Larval Heart
LH ... Las Hermanas [*Later, LH-USA*] (EA)
LH ... Last Half [*of month*] [*Business term*] (DS)
LH ... Last Harvest [*An association*] (EA)
LH ... Last Hope [*Facetious name for Chrysler's 1993 sedans*]
LH ... Late Helladic (BJA)
LH ... Latent Heat (IAA)
LH ... Lateral Hypothalamic [*or Hypothalamus*]
L-H ... Learned Helplessness [*Psychology*] (QSUL)
LH ... Learning Handicapped
LH ... Learning How [*An association*] (EA)
L/H ... Leasehold [*Legal term*] (DLA)
LH ... Left Half (WDAA)
LH ... Left Halfback [*Soccer*]
LH ... Left Hand
LH ... Left Hemisphere (DB)
LH ... Left Hind (SPVS)
LH ... Left Hyperphoria [*Ophthalmology*]
LH ... Legal Holiday (MHDW)
LH ... Legion d'Honneur [*French decoration*]
LH ... Lewisite-Mustard Gas Mix [*for land mines*] [*Army symbol*]
Lh ... Lhasa [*Linguistics*] (IEL)
LH ... L. Hungerford [*Record label*] [*Great Britain*]
LH ... Liberty House (SAUO)
LH ... Licentiate of Hygiene (SAUO)
LH ... Lidocaine Hydrochloride [*Medicine*] (MELL)
lh ... Liechtenstein [*MARC country of publication code*] [*Library of Congress*] (LCCP)
LH ... Light-Harvesting (MEC)
LH ... Lighthawk [*An association*] (EA)
LH ... Light Helicopter [*Military*] (RDA)
LH ... Light Horse [*Cavalry*]
LH ... Lighthouse [*Maps and charts*]
LH ... Lightly Hinged [*Philately*]
LH ... Limited Hold
LH ... Linear Hybrid
LH ... Link Header (ACRL)
LH ... Link House Books [*Publisher*] [*British*]
LH ... Lipid Hydrocarbon [*Biochemistry*]
LH ... Liquid Helium (IAA)
LH ... Liquid Hydrogen
LH ... Litter Hook
LH ... Little House (WDAA)
LH ... Load-High [*Computer science*] (PCM)
LH ... Local Horizontal
LH ... Locating Head [*Engineering*] (OA)
LH ... Loch's Horse [*British military*] (DMA)
LH ... Long Haul (ACAE)
LH ... Loop of Henle (MEC)
LH ... Lower Half
LH ... Lower Hemispherical (MCD)
LH ... Lower Hold [*Shipping*]
LH ... Low Head [*Nuclear energy*] (NRCH)
L/H ... Low-to-High (MDG)
LH ... Lues Hereditaria [*Medicine*]
LH ... Lufthansa (ABBR)
LH ... Lufthansa German Airlines [*ICAO designator*] (AD)
LH ... Luteinizing-Hormone [*Also, ICSH, LSH*] [*Endocrinology*]
LH ... Licensing Hours (ODA)
LH.WS ... Laboratoy Corp. Amer Hldgs Wrrt [*NYSE symbol*] (TTSB)
LH2 ... Liquid Hydrogen (NAKS)
LH_2 ... Liquid Hydrogen [*NASA*]
LHA ... Amphibious Assault Carrier [*or Ship*] (Landing Helicopter Assault Ship) [*Navy symbol*]
LHA ... Ladies' Hermitage Association (EA)
LHA ... Laha [*Language symbol*] (ETLW)
LHA ... Lake Havasu City, AZ [*Amtrak Busline code*]
LHA ... Landing Helicopter Assault
LHA ... Lanham Housing Act (DLA)
LHA ... Lateral Hypothalamic Area
LHA ... Lay Helpers' Association [*British*]
LHA ... Left Heart Assistance [*Cardiology*]
LHA ... Left Hepatic Artery [*Medicine*] (DMAA)
LHA ... Leisure & Hotel Appointments [*Recruitment for the hotel, leisure, and travel industries*] [*British*]
LHA ... Lhasa [*Tibet*] [*Seismograph station code, US Geological Survey*] [*Closed*] (SEIS)
LHA ... Libertarian Humanist Association (EA)
LHA ... Licentiate of the Australian Institute of Hospital Administration (SAUO)
LHA ... Licentiate of the Institute of Health Service Administrators [*British*] (DBQ)
LHA ... Light Helicopter, Attack [*Computer test vehicle*]
LHA ... Lincoln Highway Association [*Motoring history organization*]
LHA ... Livestock Husbandry Adviser [*Ministry of Agriculture, Fisheries, and Food*] [*British*]
LHA ... Local Health Authority [*British*]
LHA ... Local Highway Authority (SAUO)

LHA .... Local Hour Angle [*Navigation*]
LHA .... Local Housing Authority
LHA .... Lord High Admiral [*British*]
LHA .... Louisiana Hospital Association (EARSL)
LHA .... Lower-Half Assembly
LHA .... Lower Hour Angle [*Navigation*]
LHA .... Lutheran Hospital Association of America (EA)
LHA .... McNeese State University, Lake Charles, LA [*OCLC symbol*] (OCLC)
LHAA .... Budapest [*Hungary*] [*ICAO location identifier*] (ICLI)
LHAAP .... Longhorn Army Ammunition Plant (AABC)
LHAD .... Left Heart Assist Device (SAUS)
L/Hadr .... Lance Havidar [*Military*] [*British*]
LHAL .... Lethal (ABBR)
LHAMS ...... Local Hour Angle of Mean Sun
LH&HS ...... Lutheran Hospitals and Homes Society of America (SAUO)
LHAR .... London-Hamburg-Antwerp-Rotterdam (SAUO)
LHAR .... London, Havre, Antwerp, Rouen [*Shipping route*] (ROG)
LHAR .... London, Hull, Antwerp, or Rotterdam [*Shipping route*]
LHAR .... Lothario (ABBR)
LHarC .... Catahoula Parish Library, Harrisonburg, LA [*Library symbol*] [*Library of Congress*] (LCLS)
LHAS .... Luteinizing Hormone Antiserum [*Endocrinology*]
LHASA .... Logic and Heuristic Applied to Synthetic Analysis (VLIE)
LHaSC .... Saint Charles Parish Library, Hahnville, LA [*Library symbol*] [*Library of Congress*] (LCLS)
LHAT .... League of Historic American Theatres (EA)
LHATS .... Local Hour Angle of True Sun
LHAW .... Liquid High Activity Waste [*Nuclear energy*] (NUCP)
LHAWS ...... Laser Homing and Warning System (SAUO)
LHB .... Bachelor of Humane Letter (SAUO)
LHB .... Bachelor of Humane Letters [*or Bachelor of Literature or Bachelor of the More Humane Letters*]
LHB .... Bachelor of Literature (SAUO)
LHB .... Bachelor of the More Humane Letters (SAUO)
LHB .... Laboratory Hazards Bulletin [*Royal Society of Chemistry*] [*Information service or system*] (IID)
LHB .... Late Heavy Bombardment [*Planetary history*]
LHb .... Lateral Habenular (Nucleus) [*Neuroanatomy*]
LHB .... Left Halfback [*Soccer*]
LHB .... Left-Handed Batter [*Baseball term*] (NDBD)
LHB .... Line History Block (SAUS)
LHB .... Linke Hoffman Busch GmbH [*Indian Railway*] [*Germany*] (TIR)
LHB .... Long Head of Biceps [*Medicine*] (RAWO)
LHB .... Lost Heartbeat [*An attractive girl*] [*Slang*]
LHBANA ..... Log House Builder's Association of North America (EA)
LHBMA ...... Let's Have Better Mottoes Association [*A mythical association*] (EA)
LHBP .... Budapest/Ferihegy [*Hungary*] [*ICAO location identifier*] (ICLI)
LHBV .... Left Heart Blood Volume [*Medicine*] (DB)
LHC .... Arlington, TN [*Location identifier*] [*FAA*] (FAAL)
LHC .... Heavy Salvage Ship [*Navy symbol*] (VNW)
LHC .... Lakehead University [*Thunder Bay*] [*Ontario*] [*Seismograph station code, US Geological Survey*] (SEIS)
LHC .... L & N Housing Corporation (SAUO)
LHC .... Langerhans Cell Histiocytosis [*Medicine*] (EDAA)
LHC .... Large Hadron Collider [*Nuclear physics*] (ECON)
LHC .... Lease Housing Coordinator (SAUO)
LHC .... Left-Hand Chain (MHDI)
LHC .... Left-Hand Circular [*Polarization*] (IEEE)
LHC .... Left Heart [*Medicine*] (EDAA)
LHC .... Left Hypochondrium [*Medicine*]
LHC .... Light Harvesting Complex
LHC .... Light Hydrocarbon [*Organic chemistry*]
LHC .... Lignin-Hemicellulose-Cellulose [*A complex found in plants*]
LHC .... Lined Hollow Charge
LHC .... Liquid Hydrogen Container
LHC .... LNH Real Estate Investment Trust (SPSG)
LHC .... LNH REIT, Inc. [*NYSE symbol*] (SAG)
LHC .... Local Health Councils [*Scotland*] (DAVI)
LHC .... Local Host Computer (VLIE)
LHC .... Log Homes Council (EA)
LHC .... London Housing Consortium (SAUO)
LHC .... Lord High Chancellor [*British*]
LHC .... Loretto Heights College [*Denver, CO*]
LHC .... Louis, Holland, Callaway [*Advertising agency*]
LHC .... Lovers of the Holy Cross Sisters (TOCD)
LHC .... Lutheran Historical Conference (EA)
LHCA .... Longshoremen's and Harbor Workers' Compensation Act (DLA)
LHCC .... Budapest [*Hungary*] [*ICAO location identifier*] (ICLI)
LHCCBA ..... London and Home Counties Contract Bridge Association (SAUO)
LHCCBCI .... London and Home Counties Conciliation Board of the Cinematograph Industry (SAUO)
LHCGACS ... Lord High Commissioner to the General Assembly of the Church of Scotland (SAUO)
LHCIMA ..... Licentiate of the Hotel, Catering, and Institutional Management Association [*British*] (DBQ)
LHCJEA ..... London and Home Counties Joint Electricity Authority (SAUO)
LHCN .... Long Haul Communication Network (SAUO)
LHCP .... Left-Hand Circularly Polarized [*LASER waves*]
LHCP .... Less Hazardous Cigarette Program [*Medicine*] (EDAA)
LHCP .... Light-Harvesting Chlorophyll A/B-Binding Protein (DB)
LHCRC ...... Lapheld Computer Requirements Contract (SAUO)
LHCTL .... Left-Hand Control (IAA)
LHCU .... Leif Hoegh [*Intermodal shipping container symbol*] (TVRC)
LHCX .... Louisville, Harrods Creek & Westport Railroad [*Federal Railroad Administration identification code*]
LHD .... Amphibious Assault Ship [*Navy designation*] (POLM)
LHD .... Anchorage, AK [*Location identifier*] [*FAA*] (FAAL)
LHD .... Doctor of Humane Letters (DD)
LHD .... Doctor of Humanities (SAUO)
LHD .... Doctor of Letters (SAUO)
LHD .... Doctor of Letters of Humanity (SAUO)
LHD .... Doctor of Literature (DD)
LHD .... Doctor of Polite Literature (SAUO)
LHD .... Doctor of the Humanities (DD)
LHD .... Doctor of the More Humane Letters (SAUO)
LHD .... Lakehead University Library [*UTLAS symbol*]
LHD .... Large Helical Device [*Plasma physics*]
LHD .... Lateral Head Displacement [*Sperm*] [*Medicine*] (DMAA)
LHD .... Left-Hand Drive [*AEC*]
LHD .... Licentiate in Health, Dublin (ROG)
LHD .... Light Heavy-Duty [*Automotive engineering*]
LHD .... Litterarum Humaniorum Doctor [*Doctor of Humane Letters*] [*Latin*]
LHD .... Load, Haul, Dump [*Mining*]
LHD .... Local Health Department (SAUO)
LHD .... Long Haired Domestic [*Non-pedigree cat*] (SPVS)
LHD .... Multipurpose Amphibious Assault Ship
LHDA .... Lesotho Highlands Development Authority (ECON)
LHDC .... Debrecen [*Hungary*] [*ICAO location identifier*] (ICLI)
LHDC .... Lateral Homing Depth Charge
LHDDE ...... Light Heavy-Duty Diesel Engine [*Motor vehicle specifications*]
LHDDV ...... Light Heavy-Duty Diesel Vehicle (EPAT)
LHDLC .... Logical High-Level Data Lead Control (SAUO)
LHDPE .... Linear High-Density Polyethylene (EDCT)
LHDR .... Left-Hand Drive [*AEC*]
LHDS .... LASER Hole Drilling System
LHE .... Lagrange-Helmholtz Equation
LHE .... Lahore [*Pakistan*] [*Airport symbol*] (OAG)
LHE .... Lateral Humeral Epicondylalgia [*Medicine*] (MELL)
LHE .... Lateral Humeral Epicondylitis [*Medicine*] (MELL)
LHe .... Liquid Helium (NAKS)
LHE .... Liquid Helium
LHEA .... Laboratory for High Energy Astrophysics [*Greenbelt, MD*] [*NASA*] (GRD)
LHEAA .... Low-Income Home Energy Assistance Act of 1981 (COE)
LHeb .... Late Hebrew (ADWA)
L HEB .... Late Hebrew (WDAA)
LHEB .... Left-Hand Equipment Bay [*NASA*] (KSC)
LHEF .... Lesbian Herstory Educational Foundation (EA)
LHEG .... Local Healthcare Executive Group (HCT)
LHeT .... Liquid Helium Temperature (PDAA)
LHF .... Labor Heritage Foundation (EA)
LHF .... Lamp Heat Flux
LHF .... Left Heart Failure [*Medicine*]
LHF .... Lighthouse, Fixed [*Maps and charts*] (ROG)
LHF .... List Handling Facility
LHF .... Long Hood Forward [*Indian Railway*] (TIR)
LHFA .... Lung Hageman Factor Activator [*Medicine*] (DMAA)
LHFC .... Laura Hendler Fan Club (EA)
LHFCS .... Long Haul Fuel Conservation System
LHFEB .... Left-Hand Forward Equipment Bay [*NASA*] (KSC)
LHFI .... Lighthouse, Floating [*Maps and charts*] (ROG)
LHFS .... Ligand Hyperfine Structure
LH-FSH ...... Luteinizing Hormone-Follicle-Stimulating Hormone [*Medicine*] (MTAA)
LHFT .... Light Helicopter Fireteam [*Navy*] (NVT)
LHFX .... Lehigh Heavy Forge [*Private rail car owner code*]
LHG .... Left Hand Grip (DMAA)
LHG .... Library History Group (SAUO)
LHG .... Licentiate of the Institute of Heraldic and Genealogical Studies [*British*] (DBQ)
LHG .... Live Hogs [*Telegraphy*] (PCTE)
LHG .... Local Hemolysis in Gel (PDAA)
LHGR .... Linear Heat Generation Rate [*Nuclear energy*] (NRCH)
LHGX .... Griffing Tank Car Line [*Private rail car owner code*]
LHH .... League of Home Help [*Australia*] [*An association*]
LHH .... League of the Helping Hand (SAUO)
LHH .... Left-Hand Head
LHH .... Left Homonymous Hemianopsia [*Medicine*] (EDAA)
LHH .... Lower Hybrid Resonance Heating (MCD)
LHHS .... Lutheran Hospitals and Homes Society of America (EA)
LHHW .... Langmuir-Hinshelwood-Hougen-Watson Rate Equation [*Chemical kinetics*]
LHI .... Fort Lauderdale, FL [*Location identifier*] [*FAA*] (FAAL)
LHI .... Leadership Housing, Incorporated (SAUO)
LHI .... Leasing fur Handel und Industrie GmbH (EFIS)
LHI .... Lefthanders International (EA)
LHI .... Leigh Instruments Ltd. [*Toronto Stock Exchange symbol*]
LHI .... Library of the Hoover Institution (SAUO)
LHI .... Lighthouse, Intermittent [*Maps and charts*] (ROG)
LHI .... Lipid Hydrocarbon Inclusions [*Biochemistry*] (DAVI)
LHi .... Louisiana Historical Society, New Orleans, LA [*Library symbol*] [*Library of Congress*] (LCLS)
LHIA .... Logistics Horizontal Integration Analysis (SAUO)
LHID .... Logical Hardware Interface Description [*Computer science*]
LHIMA .... Louisiana Health Information Management Association (EARSL)
LHITA .... Long Haul Information Transfer Architecture (SAUO)
LHL .... Fort Lauderdale (SAUS)
LHL .... Left Hemisphere Lesion [*Neurology*] (DAVI)
LHL .... Left Hepatic Lobe [*Anatomy*]
LHL .... Leigh Instruments Limited (SAUO)

LHL .... Line and Half Line [*Illustration*] (DGA)
LHL .... Long Haul Link (VLIE)
LHL .... Long Hood Leading [*Indian Railway*] (TIR)
LHLW .... Liquid High Level Waste [*Nuclear energy*] (NUCP)
LHM .... Lake Helena [*Montana*] [*Seismograph station code, US Geological Survey*] [*Closed*] (SEIS)
LHM .... Laser Hardened Materials (ACAE)
LHM .... Laser-Hardened Materials (SAUS)
LHM .... Left-Hand Circularly Polarized Mode (IAA)
LHM .... Licensed Hotel Motel
LHM .... Lisuride Hydrogen Maleate [*Pharmacology*]
LHM .... Loop Handling Machine [*Nuclear energy*] (NRCH)
LHM .... Lysuride Hydrogen Maleate [*Medicine*] (EDAA)
LHM .... Master of Humane Letters [*or Master of the More Humane Letters*]
LHM .... Master of the More Humane Letters (SAUO)
LHMC .... London Hospital Medical College [*British*] (DI)
LHME .... LASER HELLFIRE Missile Evaluation (MCD)
LHMEL .... LASER-Hardened Materials Evaluation Laboratory
LHMM .... Laymen's Home Missionary Movement (EA)
LHMN .... Lehman Cartage [*Common carrier symbol*]
LHMO .... Local Hazard Mitigation Officer [*Department of Emergency Management*] (DEMM)
LHMP .... Life Health Monitoring Program (BABM)
LHMU .... Ladies' Home Mission Union [*British*] (BI)
LHN .... Express One International, Inc. [*ICAO designator*] (FAAC)
LHN .... Lateral Hypothalamic Nucleus (STED)
LHN .... Lillehammer [*Norway*] [*Seismograph station code, US Geological Survey*] (SEIS)
LHN .... Load Half Name (VLIE)
LHN .... Localized Hypertrophic Neuropathy [*Medicine*]
LHN .... Long-Haul Network (RDA)
LHNCBC ...... Lister Hill National Center for Biomedical Communications [*National Library of Medicine*] [*Information service or system*] (IID)
LHNT .... Lehn Trucking [*Common carrier symbol*]
LHO .... LaSalle Hotel Properties [*NYSE symbol*] (SG)
LHO .... Lemko Housing Organization [*Association*] (EA)
LHO .... Local Head Office [*British*] (DCTA)
LHOB .... Longworth House Office Building
LHoC .... Clairborne Parish Library, Homer, LA [*Library symbol*] [*Library of Congress*] (LCLS)
LHOLD .... Leasehold (ROG)
LHON .... Leber's Hereditary Optic Neuropathy [*Ophthalmology*]
LHOR .... Load Halfword with Offset Register (VLIE)
LHO ratio ... Library Holdings Ratio per Inhabitant
LHOTS .... Long-Haul Optical Transmission Set [*Telecommunications*] (EECA)
LHouT .... Terrebonne Parish Library, Houma, LA [*Library symbol*] [*Library of Congress*] (LCLS)
LHOX .... Low- and High-Pressure Oxygen
LHP .... Lakehead Pipe Line Partners Ltd. [*NYSE symbol*] (SPSG)
LHP .... Lakehead Pipe Line Ptrs L.P. [*NYSE symbol*] (TTSB)
LHP .... Lamp of Hope Project [*An association*] (EA)
LHP .... Larval Hemolymph Protein [*Entomology*]
LHP .... Late Hyperpolarizing Potential [*Neurophysiology*]
LHP .... Launcher Handling Procedure
LHP .... Left Half Plane (IAA)
LHP .... Left-Handed Pitcher [*Baseball*]
LHP .... Left-Hand Page (DGA)
lhp .... Left-Hand Page (WDMC)
LHP .... Left-Hand Panel
LHP .... Left Hemiparesis [*Medicine*] (MEDA)
LHP .... Left Hemiplegia (STED)
LHP .... Lehu [*Papua New Guinea*] [*Airport symbol*] (OAG)
LHPC .... Light-Harvesting Chlorophyll Protein Complex [*Botany*]
LHPC .... Lipomatous Hemangiopericytoma [*Medicine*] (PALA)
LHPG .... LASER-Heated Pedestal Growth [*Crystal growing technology*]
LHPG .... Liverpool HIV Pharmacology Group [*University of Liverpool*] [*United Kingdom*] (RCD)
LHPR .... Laboratory for Human Performance Research [*Medicine*] (EDAA)
LHPS .... Lead Hydrogen Purge System [*Nuclear energy*] (IEEE)
LHPT .... LHP Transportation Services [*Common carrier symbol*]
LHPT .... Loculated Hydropneumothorax [*Medicine*] (MELL)
LHPZ .... Lower Esophageal High-Pressure Zone [*Medicine*] (STED)
LHQ .... Allied Land Headquarters [*World War II*]
LHQ .... Lancaster, OH [*Location identifier*] [*FAA*] (FAAL)
LHQ .... Life History Questionnaire [*Psychology*] (DAVI)
LHR .... Launcher (ACAE)
LHR .... Lawyers for Human Rights (SAFN)
LHR .... Left-Hand Rule
LHR .... [*The*] Lehigh & Hudson River Railway Co. [*Absorbed into Consolidated Rail Corp.*] [*AAR code*]
LHR .... Leukocyte Histamine Release [*Test*]
LHR .... Life History Recorder (ACAE)
LHR .... Lighthouse, Revolving [*Maps and charts*] (ROG)
LHR .... Liquid-Holding Recovery [*of bacterial cells*]
LHR .... Load Halfword Register (VLIE)
LHR .... London-Heathrow [*England*] [*Airport symbol*] (OAG)
LHR .... Long-Term Heart Rate (PDAA)
LHR .... Lower Hybrid Resonance
LHR .... Low-Heat-Rejection Engine [*Mechanical engineering*] (RDA)
LHR .... Low heat Release [*Adiabatic engines*] [*Automotive engineering*]
LHR .... Lumen Hour (ADA)
l-hr .... Lumen-Hour [*Unit quantity of light*] (STED)
LHRAA .... Lutheran Human Relations Association of America (EA)
LHRBI .... Luteinizing Hormone Receptor Binding Inhibitor [*Endocrinology*]
LHRE .... Low Heat Rejection Engine [*Mechanical engineering*]
LHRF .... Luteinizing Hormone-Releasing Factor [*Medicine*] (STED)
LH-RF .... Luteinizing-Hormone Releasing Factor [*Also, GnRF, GnRH, LH-RH, LH-RH/FSH-RH, LRF, LRH*] [*Endocrinology*]
LHRF .... Luteotropin Hormone-Releasing Factor [*Medicine*] (STED)
LHRFDS ...... Large Heterogeneous Reference Fuel Design Study (SAUO)
LHRH .... Left Hand, Right Hand (IAA)
LHRH .... Luteinizing Hormone-Releasing Hormone [*Medicine*] (STED)
LH-RH .... Luteinizing-Hormone Releasing Hormone [*Also, GnRF, GnRH, LH-RF, LH-RH/FSH-RH, LRF, LRH*] [*Endocrinology*]
LH-RH/FSH-RH ... Luteinizing-Hormone Releasing Hormone/Follicle-Stimulating Hormone Releasing Hormone [*Also, GnRF, GnRH, LH-RF, LH-RH, LRF, LRH*] [*Endocrinology*]
LHRR .... Longhorn Railroad [*Federal Railroad Administration identification code*]
LHRR .... Longhorn Railway [*Federal Railroad Administration identification code*]
LHRS .... Life History Recorder Set [*or System*] (MCD)
LHRT .... Library History Round Table [*American Library Association*]
LHS .... Lafayette High School (SAUO)
LHS .... Lake Hughes, CA [*Location identifier*] [*FAA*] (FAAL)
LHS .... Lawrence Hall of Science
LHS .... Layered Half Space
LHS .... Left-Hand Side
LHS .... Left-Hand Steering [*Automotive engineering*]
LHS .... Left Heart Strain [*Medicine*]
LHS .... Left Heel Strike (STED)
LHS .... Liberty Hill [*South Carolina*] [*Seismograph station code, US Geological Survey*] (SEIS)
LHS .... Library History Seminar
LHS .... Lightweight Hydraulic System [*Navy aviation*]
LHS .... Line Haul Steer [*Tire design*]
LHS .... Load Handling System (SAUS)
LHS .... Loop Handling System [*Nuclear energy*] (NRCH)
LHS .... Lunar Horizon Sensor [*Aerospace*]
LHS .... Lymphatic and Hematopoietic System (STED)
LHS .... Southeastern Louisiana University, Hammond, LA [*Library symbol*] [*Library of Congress*] (LCLS)
LHSC .... Lateral Horn of Spinal Cord [*Medicine*] (MELL)
LHSC .... Left-Hand Side Console [*NASA*] (KSC)
LHSC .... Liquid Hydrogen System Complex [*NASA*] (KSC)
LHSC .... Lock Haven State College (SAUO)
LHSC .... Luther Hospital Sentence Completions [*Nursing school test*]
LHSI .... Low-Head Safety Injection [*Nuclear energy*] (NRCH)
LHSLG .... Lincoln Health Sciences Library Group [*Library network*]
LHSP .... Lernout & Hauspie Speech Products [*NASDAQ symbol*] (SAG)
LHSPF .... Lernout & Hauspie Speech Pds [*NASDAQ symbol*] (TTSB)
LHSSC .... Left-Hand Side Storage Container [*NASA*] (KSC)
LHSV .... Liquid Hourly Space Velocity [*Fluid dynamics*]
LHSX .... Lake Hubbard Steam & Electric [*Federal Railroad Administration identification code*]
LHT .... Left Hypertropia [*Ophthalmology*]
LHT .... Library Hi Tech [*Pierian Press, Inc.*] [*Information service or system*] [*A publication*] (IID)
LHT .... Light (ABBR)
LHT .... Lighthouse Tender
LHT .... Line and Halftone [*Illustration*] (DGA)
LHT .... Line-Haul Tractor (DOMA)
LHT .... Long Holding Time (VLIE)
LHT .... Lord High Treasurer [*British*]
LHT .... Luboil Hydrotreater [*Petroleum engineering*]
LHT .... Lunar Hand Tool [*NASA*]
LHTD .... Lighted (ABBR)
LHTEC .... Light Helicopter Turbine Engine Co. [*US Army contractor*]
LHTEN .... Lighten (ABBR)
LHTEND ...... Lightened (ABBR)
LHTENG ...... Lightening (ABBR)
LHTF .... Lincoln Heritage Trail Foundation (EA)
LHTG .... Lighting (ABBR)
LHTH .... Left-Hand Thread
L-HTL .... L-Histidinol [*Biochemistry*]
LHTL .... Luxury Class Hotel (TVEL)
LHTL .... Luxury Hotel (TRID)
LHTN .... Library Hi Tech News [*A publication*]
LHTNG .... Lightning (ABBR)
LHTR .... Lighter (ABBR)
LHTR .... Lighthouse Transmitter Receiver (IAA)
LHTST .... Lightest (ABBR)
LHTX .... Larsen Farms Hay Terminal [*Private rail car owner code*]
LHTY .... Lightly (ABBR)
LHU .... Lake Havasu City [*Arizona*] [*Airport symbol*] (OAG)
LHUS .... Literary History of the United States (SAUO)
LH-USA ...... Las Hermanas-United States of America (EA)
LHUSA .... Likud-Herut USA (EA)
LHV .... Left Hepatic Vein [*Medicine*] (RAWO)
LHV .... Light Horse Volunteers [*British military*] (DMA)
LHV .... Liquid Hydrogen Vessel
LHV .... Lock Haven [*Pennsylvania*] [*Airport symbol*] (AD)
LHV .... Lock Haven, PA [*Location identifier*] [*FAA*] (FAAL)
LHV .... Lower Heating Value (CARB)
LHV .... Low Heat [*or Heating*] Value (MCD)
LHV .... Luchtvaart Historische Vereniging [*Society of Aeronautical Historians*] [*Netherlands*] Defunct] (EAIO)
LHW .... Hinesville, GA [*Location identifier*] [*FAA*] (FAAL)
LHW .... Lanzhou [*China*] [*Airport symbol*] (OAG)
LHW .... Laser-Homing Weapon (SAUS)

LHW .... League of Hispanic Women (SAUO)
LHW .... Lees-Hromas-Webb [*Theory*]
LHW .... Left Half Word
LHW .... Left Hand World [*British*] [*An association*] (DBA)
LHW .... Lehman Brothers, Inc. [*AMEX symbol*] (SAG)
LHW .... Length, Height, and Width [*Automotive engineering*]
LHW .... Lower High-Water [*Tides and currents*]
LHWCA ...... Longshore and Harbor Workers' Compensation Act (AAGC)
LHWI .... Lower High-Water Interval [*Tides and currents*]
LHWP .... Lesotho Highlands Water Project (ECON)
LHX .... La Junta [*Colorado*] [*Airport symbol*] (AD)
LHX .... La Junta, CO [*Location identifier*] [*FAA*] (FAAL)
LHX .... Light Helicopter, Experimental [*Army*] (RDA)
LHX .... Light Helicopters [*Army*] (RDA)
LHX .... Lochiel Exploration Ltd. [*Toronto Stock Exchange symbol*]
LHY .... Lancashire Hussars Yeomanry [*British military*] (DMA)
LHY .... Lohame Herut Yisrael (BJA)
L Hy .... Registered Hypnotist
LHY .... Wilkes-Barre, PA [*Location identifier*] [*FAA*] (FAAL)
LI .... Current License [*Motor vehicle violation driver status code in state of North Dakota*] (MVRD)
LI .... Icelandic Medical Association (SAUO)
LI .... Labeling Index [*Measurement of cell labeling*]
L/I .... Labindustries [*Commercial firm*]
LI .... Labor Intensive (MHDW)
LI .... Lactose Intolerance [*Medicine*] (MELL)
LI .... Land Institute [*An association*] (EA)
LI .... Landscape Institute [*British*]
LI .... Langelier Index (EEVL)
LI .... LAN Interface (SAUS)
LI .... Large Intestine [*Medicine*] (DB)
L/I .... Laser Imager (ACAE)
LI .... LASER Interferometry (AAEL)
LI .... Laser Interrogator (SAUS)
LI .... Laser Iridotomy [*Medicine*] (MELL)
LI .... Late Iron [*Age*] (BJA)
LI .... Launch Instructions (SAA)
LI .... Lawn Institute (EA)
LI .... (Laws of) Lipit-Ishtar (BJA)
LI .... Leadership Institute (EA)
LI .... Lead In (VLIE)
LI .... Leakage of Information [*British*] [*World War II*]
LI .... Learned Information [*Database originator and marketer*] (NITA)
LI .... Leeward Islands (BARN)
LI .... Leeward Islands Air Transport Ltd. (SAUO)
LI .... Left In (VLIE)
LI .... Left in Place [*Telecommunications*] (TEL)
LI .... Legal Intelligencer [*A publication*] (DLA)
LI .... Legislative Instrument [*Ghana*] [*1960-*] [*A publication*] (ILCA)
LI .... Leitender Ingenieur [*Chief Engineer*] [*German military - World War II*]
LI .... Length Indicator [*Computer science*] (TNIG)
LI .... Leptospirosis Icterohemorrhagica [*Medicine*] (DB)
L/I .... Letter of Indemnity (DS)
L/I .... Letter of Intent (ACAE)
LI .... Letter of Introduction (ADA)
LI .... Level Indicator
LI .... Liability [*Insurance*]
LI .... Liberal International [*World Liberal Union*] [*British*] (EAIO)
LI .... Liberia (ABBR)
LI .... Libertarian International (EA)
LI .... License Inquiry [*Police*]
LI .... Licentiate of Instruction [*or Licentiate Instructor*]
LI .... Liechtenstein [*ANSI two-letter standard code*] (CNC)
LI .... Lifegain Institute (EA)
LI .... Lifted Index (ARMP)
LI .... Lifting Index [*Ergonometrics*]
LI .... Liga International (EA)
LI .... Light Infantry
LI .... Lightly Included [*Colored gemstone grade*]
LI .... Lignin Institute (NTPA)
LI .... Ligue Internationale de la Representation Commerciale [*International League of Commercial Travelers and Agents - ILCTA*] (EAIO)
LI .... Lilac (ROG)
LI .... Lilly Industries, Inc. [*NYSE symbol*] (SAG)
LI .... Lilly Industries'A' [*NYSE symbol*] (TTSB)
LI .... Lincoln's Inn [*London*] [*One of the Inns of Court*]
LI .... Lindau [*Bodensee*] [*German license plate city code*]
LI .... Linear Interpolator (IAA)
LI .... Line Item (AABC)
li .... Lines per Vertical Inch (WDMC)
LI .... Linguoincisal [*Dentistry*]
Li .... Link (ADWA)
LI .... Link
LI .... Lions International [*Later, LCI*] (EA)
LI .... Liquid Ionization [*Spectrometric instrumentation*]
LI .... List Item (SAUS)
LI .... Litchfield Institute (EA)
LI .... Liter [*Metric measure of volume*] (MCD)
LI .... Lithic [*Soil biology*] (QSUL)
Li .... Lithium [*Chemical element*]
LI .... Lithograph [*or Lithography*] (WDAA)
LI .... Lithographer [*Navy rating*]
Li .... Lithuanian [*Linguistics*] (IEL)
LI .... Liver Infarct [*Medicine*] (MELL)
LI .... Load Index [*Tires*] [*Automotive engineering*]
LI .... Local Interneuron [*Neuroanatomy*]
LI .... Local Intraconnect (SAUO)
LI .... Location Identifier (IAA)
LI .... Logistic Index (CAAL)
LI .... Logistics Instructions [*Military*]
LI .... Loglan Institute (EA)
LI .... Loitering with Intent [*British*] (DSUE)
LI .... London International [*Record label*] [*Great Britain, USA, etc.*]
LI .... Long Island
LI .... [*The*] Long Island Rail Road Co. [*AAR code*]
LI .... Long Istand Rail Road Co. (SAUO)
LI .... Longitudinal Interval (ADA)
LI .... Loop of Intestine
LI .... Lot Indices
LI .... Low Impulsiveness (MAE)
LI .... Low Inertia [*Automotive engineering*]
LI .... Low Intensity
LI .... Lubrication Instructions [*Marine Corps*]
LI .... Lubricity Index (IAA)
LI .... Lues I [*Primary syphilis*] [*Infectious diseases*] (DAVI)
LI .... Lukens, Inc. (EFIS)
LI .... Luteinization Inhibitor [*Endocrinology*]
LI .... Lymphoid Cellular Infiltration [*Oncology*]
LI1 .... Lithographer, First Class [*Navy rating*]
LI2 .... Lithographer, Second Class [*Navy rating*]
LI3 .... Lithographer, Third Class [*Navy rating*]
LIA .... International Union of Life Insurance Agents
LIA .... Label Information Area (CMD)
LIA .... Land Improvement Agreement (SAUO)
LIA .... Land Information and Analysis [*Program*] [*Department of the Interior*]
LIA .... Land Information and Analysis office (SAUO)
LIA .... Laser Industry (or Industries) Association (SAUO)
LIA .... Laser Institute of America (EA)
LIA .... Lead Industries Association [*New York, NY*] (EA)
LIA .... Leasinggesellschaft fur Immobilien und Anlageguter (EFIS)
LIA .... Leather Industries of America (EA)
LIA .... Lebanese International Airways
LIA .... Leeward Islands Air Transport (1974) Ltd. [*Antigua and Barbuda*] [*ICAO designator*] (FAAC)
LIA .... Leukemia-Associated Inhibiting Activity [*Medicine*]
LIA .... Leukemia Cell-Derived Inhibitory Activity [*Hematology*] (DAVI)
LIA .... Level Indicating Alarm [*Engineering*]
LIA .... Liability [*Telegraphy*] (PCTE)
LIA .... Liaison
LIA .... Liberian International Airways (SAUO)
LIA .... Licensing Industry Association [*Later, ILMA*] (EA)
LIA .... Licentiate in Accountancy (DD)
LIA .... Licentiate Institute of the Accountants and Auditors of Province of Quebec (SAUO)
LIA .... Life Insurance Act [*Australia*]
LIA .... Life Insurance Association [*British*] (DBA)
LIA .... Lima [*Ohio*] [*Airport symbol*] (OAG)
LIA .... Limited Intelligent Agent [*Virtual reality technology*] (PS)
LIA .... Limiting Interval Availability
LIA .... Linear Induction Accelerator (MCD)
LIA .... Liposome Immunoassay [*Clinical chemistry*]
LIA .... Lithographic Institute of Australia
LIA .... Little Ice Age [*Geoscience*]
LIA .... Liver Infusion Agar [*Germination medium*]
LIA .... Livestock Improvement Association (SAUO)
LIA .... Livestock Industry Act (SAUO)
LIA .... Localized Induction Approximation [*Mathematics*]
LIA .... Lock-In Amplifier (MAE)
LIA .... Long Island Association (SAUO)
LIA .... Loop Interface Address
LIA .... Low-Impact Aerobics
LIA .... Low Intensity Area (SAUO)
LIA .... Luminescence Immunoassay [*Clinical chemistry*]
LIA .... Lymphocyte-Induced Angiogenesis [*Immunology*]
LIA .... Lysine Iron Agar [*Microbiology*]
LIAA .... Library and Information Association of Australia (SAUO)
LIAA .... Life Insurance Association of America [*Later, ACLI*] (EA)
LIAA .... Louisiana Independent Administrators Association (SRA)
Liab .... Liability (TBD)
LIAB .... Liability
LIAB .... Life Insurance Adjustment Bureau [*Defunct*] (EA)
LIABT .... Liability (ABBR)
LIAC .... Legal Industry Advisory Council (EA)
LIAC .... Liberian International American Corporation [*New York*]
LIAC .... Light-Induced Absorbance Change
LIAC .... Local Industry Advisory Committee [*Civil defense*]
LIADA .... Liga Ibero-Americana de Astronomia [*Ibero-American Astronomy League*] (EAIO)
LIADA .... Louisiana Independent Automobile Dealers Association (SRA)
LIAFI .... Late Infantile Amaurotic Familial Idiocy [*Medicine*] (MAE)
LIAI .... Licensing Industry Association International (SAUO)
LIAI .... Love in Action International (EA)
LIALS .... Long Island Airport Limousine Service (SAUO)
LIAMA .... Life Insurance Agency Management Association [*Later, LIMRA*]
LIAR .... Lexicon of Inconspicuously Ambiguous Recommendations [*Term coined by Robert J. Thornton of Lehigh University*]

LIAR .... Report Labrador Inuit Association (SAUS)
LIAS .... Liabilities [*Telegraphy*] (PCTE)
LIAS .... Library Information Access System [*Pennsylvania State University Libraries*] [*University Park*] [*Information service or system*] (IID)
LIAS .... Pennsylvania State University (IID)
LIASAR ...... LASER Inertial Aided Synthetic Aperture RADAR (MCD)
LIASE .... Linking Industry and School Education (AIE)
LIAT .... Leeward Islands Air Transport Services Ltd. [*Humorous interpretation: Luggage in Another Town*] [*Airline*]
LIB .... Air Liberte [*France*] [*ICAO designator*] (FAAC)
LIB .... Federal Liberal Agency of Canada Library [*UTLAS symbol*]
LIB .... Harlan Hatcher Graduate Library (SAUS)
LIB .... Laboratory Information Bulletin (GNE)
LIB .... Left Inboard (MCD)
LIB .... Left in Bottle (MAE)
LIB .... Libby, MT [*Amtrak rail station code*]
LIB .... Liber [*Book*] [*Latin*]
lib .... Liberal (SHCU)
LIB .... Liberal
Lib .... Liberal Party (SAUO)
lib .... Liberation (SHCU)
LIB .... Liberation
LIB .... Liberator Bomber Aircraft [*British*] (DSUE)
Lib .... Liberia
LIB .... Liberty [*Telegraphy*] (PCTE)
lib .... Liberty (WDAA)
LIB .... Liberty [*Geographical division*] [*British*]
LIB .... Liberty Aviation, Inc. (SAUO)
LIB .... Liberty, NC [*Location identifier*] [*FAA*] (FAAL)
LIB .... LibertyOne Ltd. [*Australian Stock Exchange symbol*]
LIB .... Libra [*Pound*]
Lib .... Libra [*Constellation*]
Lib .... Librarian (DLA)
LIB .... Library (AFM)
Lib .... Library [*A publication*] (BRI)
lib .... Library (GEAB)
lib .... Libretto (WDAA)
LIB .... Libretto [*Music*]
LIB .... Light Infantry Brigade (SAUO)
LIB .... Light Ion Beam (PDAA)
LIB .... Line Interface Base [*Telecommunications*]
LIB .... London Infantry Brigade (SAUO)
LIB .... Loudspeaker Intercom Box (SAUS)
LIB-2 .... EC 12-part study on new information technologies in libraries 1988 (SAUS)
LIBA .... Amendola [*Italy*] [*ICAO location identifier*] (ICLI)
LIBA .... Leeds Institute for Plant Biotechnology and Agriculture [*University of Leeds*] [*United Kingdom*] (RCD)
LIBA .... Liberty Coach Company [*NCIC trailer make code*]
LIBA .... Licentiate of the Institute of Business Administration
LIBA .... Long Island Biological Association
LIBA .... Long Island Biological Association Inc. (SAUO)
LIBACC ...... Library Acquisition Program [*Computer program*]
LIBACT1 ..... Impact CR-ROM project for National Libraries (SAUS)
Lib & Cult ... Libraries & Culture [*A publication*] (BRI)
LIB & SL .... Libel and Slander [*Legal term*] (DLA)
LIBANOR .... Lebanese Standards Institution (SAUO)
Lib Ass ...... Liber Assisarum [*Book of Assizes, or pleas of the crown*] [*Pt. 5 of Year Books*] [*A publication*] (DLA)
LIBB .... Brindisi [*Italy*] [*ICAO location identifier*] (ICLI)
LIBBA .... Long Island Beach Buggy Association (SAUO)
Libbey .... Libbey, Inc. [*Associated Press*] (SAG)
LIBBKS ...... Headquarters Book System (SAUO)
LIBC .... Cray C library (SAUO)
LIBC .... Crotone [*Italy*] [*ICAO location identifier*] (ICLI)
LIBC .... Latent Iron-Binding Capacity [*Clinical chemistry*]
LIBC .... Liberty National Bank [*NASDAQ symbol*] (SAG)
LIBC .... Lloyd's Insurance Brokers Committee (AIA)
LIB CAT ..... Library Catalogue (WDAA)
LIBCEPT ..... LIBRIS Intercept [*Sweden*] (NITA)
LIBCO .... Liberty Equipment Co. (EFIS)
LIBCO .... Liberty Investors Benefit Insurance Company (SAUO)
Lib Colon ... Libri Coloniarum [*Classical studies*] (OCD)
LIBCON ...... Libertarian Conservative
LIBCON ...... Library of Congress
LIBCON/E ... Library of Congress/English [*Database on English language monographs*] (NITA)
LIB CONG ... Library of Congress (WDAA)
Lib Cong Q ... Library of Congress. Quarterly Journal [*A publication*] (DLA)
LI Bcp .... Long Island Bancorp, Inc. [*Associated Press*] (SAG)
LIBD .... Bari/Palese Macchie [*Italy*] [*ICAO location identifier*] (ICLI)
Lib-Dem .... Liberal Democrat (WDAA)
LIBE .... Liberty Travel Trailers [*NCIC trailer make code*]
LIBE .... Library Editor (MHDI)
LIBE .... Ligo Internacia de Blindaj Esperantistoj [*International League of Blind Esperantists - ILBE*] (EAIO)
LIBE .... Monte S. Angelo [*Italy*] [*ICAO location identifier*] (ICLI)
LIBEC .... Light Behind Camera [*Photographic technique*]
LIBECON .... Monitor of Library Economics (SAUO)
LIBEDIT ..... Library Editor (MHDI)
LIBEL .... Liberal, KS [*American Association of Railroads railroad junction routing code*]
Lib Ent ...... Old Books of Entries [*A publication*] (DLA)
Liber .... Liberia (VRA)
LIBER .... Ligue des Bibliotheques Europeennes de Recherche [*League of European Research Libraries*] (EAIO)
LIBERATION ... Libraries: Electronic Remote Access to Information over Networks (SAUO)
LIBERATOR ... Libraries in European Regions-Access to Telematics and Other Resources (SAUO)
LIBERD ...... Liberated (ABBR)
LIBERG ...... Liberating (ABBR)
LIBERN ...... Liberation (ABBR)
LIBERR ...... Liberator (ABBR)
LIBERTAS ... Automated library system marketed by SLS Ltd (SAUS)
Liberte ...... Liberte Investors, Inc. [*Associated Press*] (SAG)
LIBF .... Foggia [*Italy*] [*ICAO location identifier*] (ICLI)
Lib Feud .... Liber Feudorum [*Book of Feuds*] [*At the end of the Corpus Juris Civilis*] [*A publication*] (DLA)
LibFin .... Liberty Financial Companies, Inc. [*Associated Press*] (SAG)
LIBG .... Grottaglie [*Italy*] [*ICAO location identifier*] (ICLI)
LIBG .... SC Linebaugh [*Common carrier symbol*]
LIBGIS ...... Library General Information Survey [*of the National Center for Educational Statistics*]
LIBH .... Liberty Homes [*NCIC trailer make code*]
LIBH .... Liberty Homes, Inc. [*NASDAQ symbol*] (SAG)
LIBH .... Marina Di Ginosa [*Italy*] [*ICAO location identifier*] (ICLI)
LIBHA .... Liberty Homes Cl'A' [*NASDAQ symbol*] (TTSB)
LIBHB .... Liberty Homes Cl'B' [*NASDAQ symbol*] (TTSB)
LIBI .... Vieste [*Italy*] [*ICAO location identifier*] (ICLI)
Libid .... London interbank bid or deposit rate (SAUO)
LIBID .... London Interbank Bid Rate [*Finance*] [*British*]
LibInt(BG) ... Liberal International (British Group) [*World Liberal Union*] (EAIO)
LIBISAC ..... Livres Bibliotheque Saclay Database [*Commissariat a l'Energie Atomique*] [*France*] [*Information service or system*] (CRD)
LIBJ .... Vibo Valentia [*Italy*] [*ICAO location identifier*] (ICLI)
LIBK .... Caraffa Di Catanzaro [*Italy*] [*ICAO location identifier*] (ICLI)
LIBL .... Liable (ABBR)
LIBL .... Liberal
LIBL .... Palascia [*Italy*] [*ICAO location identifier*] (ICLI)
Lib-Lab ...... Liberal-Labour (SAUO)
LIB LAB ..... Liberal-Labour Alliance [*British*] (DSUE)
Lib L & Eq ... Library of Law and Equity [*A publication*] (DLA)
Liblit .... Library Literature
LIBLZG ...... Liberalizing (ABBR)
LIBM .... Grottammare [*Italy*] [*ICAO location identifier*] (ICLI)
LIBMAN ..... Library Management (MHDB)
LIBMAS ..... Library Master File [*FORTRAN program*]
LIBMISH .... Liberia Military Mission [*US*]
LIBMISH .... United States Military Mission, Liberia (SAUO)
LIBMRG ..... Library Merge Program [*Computer program*]
LIBN .... Lecce [*Italy*] [*ICAO location identifier*] (ICLI)
LIBN .... Liberty National Corp. (SAUO)
LIBN .... Librarian (WGA)
LibNat .... Liberal National (SAUO)
LIBNAT ...... Library Network Analysis Theory
LibNBk ...... Liberty National Bank [*Huntington Beach, CA*] [*Associated Press*] (SAG)
LIBO .... Lincoln Boyhood National Memorial
LIBO .... London Interbank Offered [*Rate*] [*Reference point for syndicated bank loans*]
LIBO .... Ortanova [*Italy*] [*ICAO location identifier*] (ICLI)
LIB/OL .... Librarian/Online [*Database*] (MHDI)
LIBOL .... Litton Business-Oriented Language (IAA)
LibOp .... Libraries Operator (SAUO)
LIBOR .... London Interbank Offered Rate [*Reference point for syndicated bank loans*]
LIBORS ...... LASER Ionization Based on Resonant Saturation [*Physics*]
LIBP .... Pescara [*Italy*] [*ICAO location identifier*] (ICLI)
Lib Parl ..... Library of Parliament (SAUO)
Lib Plac ..... Lilly's Assize Reports [*1688-93*] [*A publication*] (DLA)
LIBQ .... Monte Scuro [*Italy*] [*ICAO location identifier*] (ICLI)
LIBR .... Brindise/Casale [*Italy*] [*ICAO location identifier*] (ICLI)
Libr .... Libra [*Constellation*]
LIBR .... Librarian (EY)
libr .... Library (VRA)
LIBR .... Library
LIBR .... Librium [*Pharmacology*] (DAVI)
LIBR .... RTP Library (SAUS)
LIBRA .... Laboratory for Ion Beam Research and Applications [*University of Maryland at College Park*] (RCD)
LIBRA .... Living in the Buff Recreational Associates (SAUO)
LIBRARY .... Tape Library and Workload Management System (SAUO)
LIBRE .... Living in the Buff Residential Enterprises (SAUO)
Lib Reg ..... Register Book [*A publication*] (DLA)
LIBRI .... Literary Information Bases for Research and Instruction [*American Philological Association*] [*An association*] (NITA)
LIBRIME .... Library and Information Management in Europe (TELE)
LIBRIS .... Land Image-Based Resource Information System (SAUO)
LIBRIS .... Library Information Service [*or System*] [*The Royal Library*] [*Database*] [*Information service or system*] (IID)
LIBRLZ ...... Liberalize (ABBR)
LIBRN .... Librarian
LIBROS ...... Library Outreach in Spanish [*Program*]
Libr quart ... Library Quarterly. University of Chicago (SAUO)
LibrtyTc ..... Liberty Technologies, Inc. [*Associated Press*] (SAG)
LIBRY .... Library (ABBR)
LIBS .... Campobasso [*Italy*] [*ICAO location identifier*] (ICLI)
LIBS .... LASER-Induced Breakdown Spectroscopy

LIBS .... Liberties [*Telegraphy*] (PCTE)
LIBS .... Library Internet Browsing Software
LIBSET .... Library Set [*Computer program*]
LibSIG .... Libertarian SIG [*Special Interest Group*] (EA)
LIBSM .... Low Inertia Beam Steering Minor (ACAE)
Lib Soc Sci... Library of Social Science (SAUO)
LIBSOFT .... Library Software Archives [*Computer science*] (TNIG)
Libsp .... Librarianship (DIAR)
LibSt .... Libyan Studies [*A publication*] (ABAR)
LIBSTAD .... Working Party on Library and Book Trade Relations [*British*]
Libs Unl ..... Libraries Unlimited (SAUO)
LIBSYS ...... Library System [*Computer program*]
LIBT .... Liability (ABBR)
LIBT .... Liberty (ABBR)
LIBT .... Liberty Technologies [*NASDAQ symbol*] (TTSB)
LIBT .... Liberty Technologies, Inc. [*NASDAQ symbol*] (SAG)
LIBT .... Termoli [*Italy*] [*ICAO location identifier*] (ICLI)
LibtProp ..... Liberty Property Trust [*Associated Press*] (SAG)
LibtyCp ...... Liberty Corp. [*Associated Press*] (SAG)
LIBU .... Latronico [*Italy*] [*ICAO location identifier*] (ICLI)
LIBU .... Lib Leasing [*Intermodal shipping container symbol*] (TVRC)
LIB (UN) .... Headquarters Library of the United Nations
Lib UN ...... Library of the United Nations (SAUO)
LIBV .... Gioia Del Colle [*Italy*] [*ICAO location identifier*] (ICLI)
LibVT .... Libri Veteris Testamenti (BJA)
LIBW .... Bonifati [*Italy*] [*ICAO location identifier*] (ICLI)
LIBX .... Little Beaver Creek Valley [*Federal Railroad Administration identification code*]
LIBX .... Martina Franca [*Italy*] [*ICAO location identifier*] (ICLI)
LIBY .... Santa Maria Di Leuca [*Italy*] [*ICAO location identifier*] (ICLI)
LIBZ .... Potenza [*Italy*] [*ICAO location identifier*] (ICLI)
LIC .... Chief Lithographer [*Navy rating*]
LIC .... Lacquer Insulating Compound
LIC .... Lamto [*Ivory Coast*] [*Seismograph station code, US Geological Survey*] (SEIS)
LIC .... Lands Improvement Company (SAUO)
LIC .... Language Identity Code [*Army*] (INF)
LIC .... Large Integrated Circuit [*Electronics*]
LIC .... LASER Image Converter
LIC .... LASER-Induced Chemistry (RDA)
LIC .... LASER Intercept Capability [*Military*] (CAAL)
LIC .... Last in Chain (ELAL)
LIC .... Last Instruction Cycle (IAA)
LIC .... Launcher Interchange Circuit (IAA)
LIC .... Law in Context [*Australia*] [*A publication*]
LIC .... Lawson, I. C., St. Paul MN [*STAC*]
LIC .... League International for Creditors (DCTA)
LIC .... Least Incompatible [*Laboratory science*] (DAVI)
LIC .... Lecturer in Charge (ADA)
LIC .... Left Iliac Crest [*Anatomy*] (DAVI)
LIC .... Left Internal Carotid [*Artery*] [*Anatomy*] (DAVI)
LIC .... Leisure-Interest Class (MEDA)
LIC .... Less Industrialized Country (MHDW)
LIC .... Level Indicator Controller (NRCH)
LIC .... Library and Information Commission [*British*] (TELE)
LIC .... Library Information Center [*Lunar and Planetary Institute*] [*Information service or system*] (IID)
Lic .... Licenciado [*Lawyer*] [*Spanish*] (WA)
lic .... License (BEE)
LIC .... License (KSC)
LIC .... Licensed Internal Code (SAUO)
Lic .... Licentiate [*Medicine*] (EDAA)
LIC .... Licentiate
LIC .... Life Insurers Conference [*Richmond, VA*] (EA)
LIC .... Limiting Isorrheic Concentration [*Medicine*]
LIC .... Limon, CO [*Location identifier*] [*FAA*] (FAAL)
LIC .... Linear Integrated Circuit
LIC .... Lineas Aereas del Caribe [*Colombia*] [*ICAO designator*] (FAAC)
LIC .... Line Integrity Check (SAUS)
LIC .... Liquor Industry Council (SAUO)
LIC .... List of Instruments and Controls (DNAB)
LIC .... Lithuanian Information Center [*Defunct*] (EA)
LIC .... Load Interface Circuit (MCD)
LIC .... Local Import Control [*British*] (DS)
LIC .... Local Indigenous Civilian [*Military*]
LIC .... Local Intelligence Committee (SAUO)
LIC .... Local Interstellar Cloud [*Astronomy*]
LIC .... Logical Link Control (SAUO)
LIC .... Logistics Indoctrination Course [*Military*] (DNAB)
LIC .... London International College [*British*]
LIC .... Loop Insertion Cell [*Nuclear energy*] (NRCH)
LIC .... Louisiana Insurers' Conference (SRA)
LIC .... Love in Christ [*Internet lingo*] (NETL)
LIC .... Lower Incisor Cavity [*Linguistics*] (IEL)
LIC .... Low Income Country
LIC .... Low Inertia Clutch
LIC .... Low Intensity Conflict (SAUO)
LIC .... Low-Intensity Conflict [*Military*]
LIC .... Lunar Instrument Carrier [*NASA*] (KSC)
LICA .... International League Against Racism and Antisemitisme (SAUO)
LICA .... Lamezia/Terme [*Italy*] [*ICAO location identifier*] (ICLI)
LICA .... Land Improvement Contractors of America (EA)
LICA .... Left Internal Carotid Artery [*Anatomy*] (DAVI)
LICA .... Licentiate, International College of Anesthetists (CMD)
LICA .... Ligue Internationale Contre le Racisme et l'Antisemitisme [*International League Against Racism and Antisemitism*]
LICA .... Lithium Isopropylcyclohexylamide [*Organic chemistry*]
LicAc .... Licentiate in Acupuncture [*British*]
Lic Agro ..... Licentiate in Agronomy [*British*]
LICALM ..... LORAN Inertial Command Air-Launched Missile
LICAP .... LASER-Induced Cut and Patch
LICAS .... Low Intensity Conflict Aircraft System (SAUS)
LICB .... Comiso [*Italy*] [*ICAO location identifier*] (ICLI)
LICB .... Laboratory of Immune Cell Biology [*National Cancer Institute*] (RCD)
LICB .... Licensable (ABBR)
LICB .... Long Island Financial Corp. [*NASDAQ symbol*] (NASQ)
LICC .... Catania/Fontanarossa [*Italy*] [*ICAO location identifier*] (ICLI)
LICC .... Land Information Co-ordinating Committee (SAUO)
LICC .... League for Innovation in the Community College (EA)
LICC .... Litton Industries, Inc. (EFIS)
LICC .... Local Interagency Coordinating Council
LICC .... London Institute for Contemporary Christianity (SAUO)
LICC .... Long Island Council of Churches (SAUO)
LiCCA .... Languages in Contact and Conflict in Africa (SAUO)
LICCB .... Laboratory Information Calibration Control Board (SAUO)
LICCD .... Ligue Internationale Contre la Concurrence Deloyale [*International League Against Unfair Competition*] (EAIO)
LICCRE ...... Laboratory of Ice Core and Cold Regions Environment (SAUO)
LICCS .... Laboratory Information Calibration Control System (SAUO)
LICD .... Lampedusa [*Italy*] [*ICAO location identifier*] (ICLI)
LICD .... Licensed (ROG)
LicD .... Licentiate in Theology, Malta (SAUO)
LICE .... Enna [*Italy*] [*ICAO location identifier*] (ICLI)
LICE .... LASER Interface Control Electronics (MCD)
LICE .... License (ROG)
LIC ECON ... Licentiate in Economic Sciences (WDAA)
Lic en Der ... Licenciado en Derecho [*Licentiate in Law*] [*Spanish*]
LICENDOR ... License Endorsements [*National Highway Traffic Safety Administration Fatal Accident Recording System code*]
Lic en Fil ... Licenciado en Filosofia [*Licentiate in Philosophy*] [*Spanish*]
LICeram ..... Licentiate of the Institute of Ceramics (SAUO)
LICET .... Library of Industrial and Commercial Education and Training
LICF .... Laser-Induced Chlorophyll Fluorescence [*Analytical biochemistry*]
LICF .... Long Island City Financial Corp. [*NASDAQ symbol*] (COMM)
LICF .... Messina [*Italy*] [*ICAO location identifier*] (ICLI)
LICG .... Licensing (ABBR)
LICG .... Pantelleria [*Italy*] [*ICAO location identifier*] (ICLI)
LICGF .... Land Information & Computer Graphics Facility (SAUO)
LICGS .... Lightweight Intermediate Caliber Gun System (MCD)
LICH .... Capo Spartivento [*Italy*] [*ICAO location identifier*] (ICLI)
LICh .... Licentiate of the Institute of Chiropodists (SAUO)
LICH .... Lichfield [*City in England*] (ROG)
LICH .... Little Champ Camper [*NCIC trailer make code*]
LICI .... Finale [*Italy*] [*ICAO location identifier*] (ICLI)
LICI .... Lilly Industrial Coatings, Incorporated (SAUO)
LICIA .... Lilly Industries, Incorporated (SAUO)
LICIT .... Labor-Industry Coalition for International Trade [*Washington, DC*] (EA)
LICITA .... Life Insurance Co. Income Tax Act of 1959
LICJ .... Palermo/Punta Raisi [*Italy*] [*ICAO location identifier*] (ICLI)
LICK .... Lightweight Communication Kit (MCD)
LICK .... Lightweight Communications Kit (SAUO)
LICL .... Gela [*Italy*] [*ICAO location identifier*] (ICLI)
LICM .... Calopezzati [*Italy*] [*ICAO location identifier*] (ICLI)
LICM .... Left Intercostal Margin [*Anatomy*]
LICM .... Master Chief Lithographer [*Navy rating*]
Lic Med ..... Licentiate in Medicine
LICND .... Life Insurance Committee for a Nuclear Disarmament (EA)
LICNWF ..... Life Insurance Committee for a Nuclear Weapons Freeze [*Later, LICND*] (EA)
LICO .... Cozzo Spadaro [*Italy*] [*ICAO location identifier*] (ICLI)
LICO .... Lifesurance Corp. [*NASDAQ symbol*] (COMM)
LICO .... Linco Trailer Home [*NCIC trailer make code*]
LICO .... Low Income Cut-Off [*Canada*]
$LiCO_3$ .... Lithium Carbonate [*Pharmacology*] (DAVI)
LICOF .... Land Lines Communications Facilities (FAAC)
LICOR .... Lightning Correlation
LICP .... Lead Inventory Control Point (NG)
LICP .... Palermo/Boccadifalco [*Italy*] [*ICAO location identifier*] (ICLI)
Lic Phil ..... Licentiate in Philosophy [*British*]
LICR .... Lloyd's Information Casualty Report [*A publication*]
LICR .... Reggio Calabria [*Italy*] [*ICAO location identifier*] (ICLI)
LICRA .... Ligue Internationale Contre le Racisme et l'Antisemitisme [*France*]
LICROSS .... League of International Red Cross Societies
LiCrOx .... Lithium/Chromium-Oxide [*Type of battery*]
LICS .... Left Intercostal Space [*Cardiology*] (MAE)
L-ICS .... Level I Controlled Shipping [*Automotive engineering*]
LICS .... Licenses [*Telegraphy*] (PCTE)
Lic S .... Licentiate in Surgery [*Academic degree*] (WDAA)
LICS .... Lotus international Character Set [*Printer technology*] (PCM)
LICS .... Sciacca [*Italy*] [*ICAO location identifier*] (ICLI)
LICS .... Senior Chief Lithographer [*Navy rating*]
LICSR .... Life Insurance Committee for Social Responsibility (EA)
LICSW .... Licensed Independent Clinical Social Worker (SEAT)
LICT .... Laser Imaging Component Technology (ACAE)
LICT .... Trapani/Birgi [*Italy*] [*ICAO location identifier*] (ICLI)
LICTA .... Life Insurance Co. Tax Act of 1955
Lic Tech ..... Licentiate in Technology [*British*]

Lic Theol ... Licentiate in Theology [*British*]
LICU .... Laparoscopic Intracorporeal Ultrasound [*Medicine*] (RAWO)
LICU .... League of IBM [*International Business Machines Corp.*] Employee Credit Unions (EA)
LICU .... Ustica [*Italy*] [*ICAO location identifier*] (ICLI)
LICVD .... LASER-Induced Chemical Vapor Deposition [*Photovoltaic energy systems*]
LICW .... Licentiate of the Institute of Clerks of Works of Great Britain, Inc. (DBQ)
LICX .... Prizzi [*Italy*] [*ICAO location identifier*] (ICLI)
LICZ .... Sigonella [*Italy*] [*ICAO location identifier*] (ICLI)
LID .... Alidaunia SRL [*Italy*] [*ICAO designator*] (FAAC)
LID .... Doctor of Letters of Journalism (SAUS)
LID .... Laboratory of Infectious Diseases [*Later, Laboratory of Viral Diseases*] [*NIAID*]
LID .... Labor Information Database [*International Labor Office*] [*Information service or system*] (IID)
LID .... Land Information Division (SAUO)
LID .... Laser Illuminator Detector (ACAE)
LID .... LASER Image Display (MCD)
LID .... LASER Injection Diode
LID .... LASER Intrusion Detector
LID .... LASER Intrusion Device (MCD)
LID .... Laser Irradiation Detector (SAUS)
LID .... LASER Isotope Dating
LID .... Late Immunoglobulin Deficiency [*Medicine*] (DB)
LID .... Leadless Inverted Device
LID .... League for Industrial Democracy (EA)
LID .... Letters in Digit Strings [*Psychology*]
LID .... Library Issue Document (NVT)
LID .... Lidco Industries, Inc. [*Toronto Stock Exchange symbol*]
LID .... Lido [*NCIC car model code*]
LID .... Lift Improvement Device (MCD)
LID .... Light Infantry Division [*Army*] (INF)
LID .... Limited Instrument Departure (MCD)
LID .... Linear Imaging Device (MCD)
LID .... Line Isolation Device [*Telecommunications*] (NITA)
LID .... Line Item Description (MCD)
LID .... Liquid Immersion Development [*Reprography*]
LID .... Liquid Interface Diffusion
LID .... Literaturdienst Medizin und Umwelt [*Literature Service in Medicine and Environment*] [*Austrian National Institute for Public Health*] [*Information service or system*] (IID)
LID .... Local Issue Data [*Telecommunications*] (TEL)
LID .... Locked-In Device (MSA)
LID .... Logical Identification (MCD)
LID .... Logistics Identification Document (NASA)
LID .... Low-Iodine Diet [*Medicine*]
LID .... Lunar Ionosphere Detector (PDAA)
LIDA .... Ligue Internationale des Droits de l'Animal [*International League for Animal Rights*] (EAIO)
LIDA .... Lodzer Idishe Dramatishe Aktyorn (BJA)
Lidak .... Lidak Pharmaceuticals [*Associated Press*] (SAG)
LIDAR .... Atmospheric Light Detection and Ranging Facility [*Los Alamos, NM*] [*Los Alamos National Laboratory*] [*Department of Energy*] (GRD)
LIDAR .... Laser Induced Differential Absorption Radar (ACAE)
LIDAR .... LASER Infrared RADAR (IEEE)
LIDAR .... LASER Intensity Direction and Ranging (IEEE)
LIDAR .... Light Detection and Range (SAUO)
LIDAR .... Light Detection and Ranging
LIDAR .... Light Detection and Ranging Instrument (SAUO)
LIDAS .... Laboratory Instrument Data Acquisition
LIDASE ...... Lecturer in Design and Analysis of Scientific Experiments (SAUO)
LIDB .... Line Information Database [*Telecommunications*] (ACRL)
LIDB .... Logistics Intelligence Data Base (AABC)
LIDC .... Lead Industries Development Council [*British*] (DAS)
LIDC .... Ligue Internationale du Droit de la Concurrence [*International League for Competition Law*] [*Paris, France*] (EA)
LIDC .... Livestock Industry Development Council (SAUO)
LIDC .... Low Intensity - Direct Current
LIDD .... Laydown Initialization Data Document (SAUS)
LIDE .... LED Light-Emittng Diode Indirect Exposure [*Canon*]
LIDEX .... Labrador Ice Dynamics Experiment (SAUO)
LIDF .... Line Intermediate Distributing Frame
LIDI .... Lions-International Diabetes Institute (SAUO)
LIDIA .... Learning in Dialog (PDAA)
LIDIA .... Liaison Internationale des Industries de l'Alimentation [*International Liaison for the Food Industries*]
LIDM .... Line Impact Dot Matrix (GART)
LIDO .... Lidocaine (SAUS)
LIDO .... Logic In, Documents Out (PDAA)
LIDO .... Logistics Inventory Disposition Order (AAG)
LIDOC .... Lidocaine [*Topical anesthetic*] (WDAA)
LIDQA .... Landsat Image Data Quality and Analysis (SAUO)
LIDS .... Laboratory for Information and Decision Systems [*Massachusetts Institute of Technology*] [*Research center*] (RCD)
LIDS .... LASER Illumination Detection System
LIDS .... LASER Infrared Countermeasures Demonstration System [*Air Force*]
LIDS .... Laser Instrumentation Detection System (ACAE)
LIDS .... Listener Idle State (IAA)
LIDS .... Lithium Ion Drift Semiconductor
LIDS .... Local Inmate Database System (WDAA)
LIDS .... Logistics Item Data Systems [*DoD*]
LIDT .... LASER-Induced Damage Testing
LIDT .... Load Interrupt Descriptor Table (SAUO)
LIDUS .... Liberal-Demokratische Union der Schweiz [*Liberal Democratic Union of Switzerland*] [*Political party*] (PPE)
LIE .... Laterally Inclined Engine
LIE .... Left Inboard Elevon [*Aviation*] (MCD)
LIE .... Lessio Intellectuale Europeo [*Research Institute*] [*Consiglio Nationale delle Richerche*] [*Italy*] (NITA)
LIE .... Libenge [*Zaire*] [*Airport symbol*] [*Obsolete*] (OAG)
LIE .... Liechtenstein [*ANSI three-letter standard code*] (CNC)
LIE .... Limited Information Estimation
LIE .... Line Islands Experiment [*National Science Foundation*]
LIE .... Long Island Expressway (BARN)
LIEA .... Alghero [*Italy*] [*ICAO location identifier*] (ICLI)
LIEA .... Low Income Energy Assistance [*Later, LIHEAP*] [*Block grant*]
LIEB .... Capo Bellavista [*Italy*] [*ICAO location identifier*] (ICLI)
LIEB .... Lieber Industries [*NCIC trailer make code*]
LIEB .... Liebert Corporation (SAUO)
Lieber Civ Lib... Lieber on Civil Liberty and Self Government [*A publication*] (DLA)
Lieb Herm... Lieber's Hermeneutics [*A publication*] (DLA)
Liebigs Ann Chem... Liebigs Annalen der Chemie (MEC)
LIEC .... Capo Carbonara [*Italy*] [*ICAO location identifier*] (ICLI)
LIECH .... Liechtenstein (ABBR)
Liech .... Liechtenstein (SHCU)
Liecht .... Liechtenstein
LIECU .... League of IBM [*International Business Machines Corp.*] Employee Credit Unions [*Later, LICU*] (EA)
LIED .... Decimomannu [*Italy*] [*ICAO location identifier*] (ICLI)
LIED .... Large Industrial Engineering Development (SAUO)
LIED .... LASER Initiating Explosive Device
LIED .... Linkage Editor [*Computer science*]
LIEE .... Cagliari/Elmas [*Italy*] [*ICAO location identifier*] (ICLI)
LIEE .... Law in Eastern Europe [*A publication*] (DLA)
LIEF .... Capo Frasca [*Italy*] [*ICAO location identifier*] (ICLI)
LIEF .... Launch Information Exchange Facility [*NASA*]
LIEFC .... Long Island Early Fliers Club (EA)
LIEG .... Guardiavecchia [*Italy*] [*ICAO location identifier*] (ICLI)
LIEH .... Capo Caccia [*Italy*] [*ICAO location identifier*] (ICLI)
LIEJA .... Long Island Equal Justice Association (SAUO)
LIEL .... Capo S. Lorenzo [*Italy*] [*ICAO location identifier*] (ICLI)
LIEM .... Macomer [*Italy*] [*ICAO location identifier*] (ICLI)
LIEMA .... Long Island Electronics Manufacturers Association (SAUO)
LIEMC .... Long Island Electronics Manufacturers Council (SAUO)
LIEN .... Fonni [*Italy*] [*ICAO location identifier*] (ICLI)
LIENS .... Ligue Europeenne pour une Nouvelle Societe [*European League for a New Society - ELNS*] [*Paris, France*] (EAIO)
LIEO .... Olbia/Costa Smeralda [*Italy*] [*ICAO location identifier*] (ICLI)
LIEP .... Large Internet Exchange Packet (VLIE)
LIEP .... LORAN Integrated Engineering Program
LIEP .... Perdasdefogu [*Italy*] [*ICAO location identifier*] (ICLI)
LIEPS .... LORAN Integrated Engineering Program, Shed Light
lierr .... Spleen [*Prefix Meaning*] [*Medicine*] (EDAA)
LIES .... LASER-Induced Emission Spectroscopy (MEC)
LIES .... Library Information and Enquiry System
LIESA .... Long Island Episcopal Schools Association (SAUO)
LIESST ...... Light-Induced Excited Spin State Trapping [*Physics*]
LIET .... Liedtka Trucking [*Common carrier symbol*]
Liet .... Lieutenant (SAUS)
LIETS .... Land Integrated Equipment for Tactical Systems (MCD)
LIEUT .... Lieutenant (EY)
lieut .... Lieutenant (GEAB)
Lieut .... Lieutenant (WDAA)
LIEUTC ...... Lieutenancy (ABBR)
Lieut Col .... Lieutenant Colonel (SAUO)
Lieut-Col .... Lieutenant-Colonel [*British military*] (DMA)
Lieut Comdr... Lieutenant Commander (SAUO)
LIEUTE ...... Lieutenancy (ABBR)
Lieut Gen ... Lieutenant General (SAUO)
Lieut-Gen ... Lieutenant-General [*British military*] (DMA)
Lieut Gov .... Lieutenant Governor (SAUO)
Lieut Jg ...... Lieutenant Junior Grade [*Navy*]
LIF .... Large Isothermal Furnace (SAUS)
LIF .... LASER-Induced Fluorescence [*Physical chemistry*]
LIF .... LASER Interference Filter
LIF .... Latino Issues Forum [*Association*] (EA)
LIF .... Layaway of Industrial Facilities (AABC)
LIF .... Left Iliac Fossa [*Medicine*]
LIF .... Left Index Finger (MELL)
LIF .... Leukemia Inhibitory Factor [*Oncology*]
LIF .... Leukocyte Inhibition Factor [*Hematology*]
LIF .... Leukocytosi-Inducing Factor [*Hematology*] (DAVI)
LIF .... Lichtenfels [*German license plate city code*]
LIF .... Lief (ABBR)
LIF .... Lifestyle Restaurants, Inc. (SAUO)
LIF .... Lifu [*Loyalty Islands*] [*Airport symbol*] (OAG)
LIF .... Lighting Industry Federation [*British*] (DBA)
LIF .... Limbu [*Language symbol*] (ETLW)
LIF .... Line Interface Feature [*Computer science*] (ELAL)
LIF .... Linking Interface [*Electronics*]
LiF .... Lithium Fluoride [*Medicine*] (RAWO)
LIF .... Location Interoperability Forum [*Communications standards*]
LIF .... Logical Interchange Format (SAUS)
LIF .... Logistics Intelligence File (AABC)

LIF .... Lone Indian Fellowship [*Later, Lone Indian Fellowship and Lone Scout Alumni*] (EA)
LIF .... Low Insertion Force (AAEL)
LIF .... Low-Ionization Filament Component [*Galactic science*]
LIFA .... Licentiate of the International Faculty of Arts [*British*]
LIFB .... Life Bancorp [*NASDAQ symbol*] (TTSB)
LIFB .... Life Bancorp, Inc. [*NASDAQ symbol*] (SAG)
LIFC .... Lifecell Corp. [*NASDAQ symbol*] (SAG)
LIFD .... Last In First Drop (SAUS)
LIFE .... Laboratory for International Fuzzy Engineering (SAUO)
LIFE .... Laboratory for International Fuzzy Engineering Research [*Japan*]
LIFE .... Ladies Involved For Education (SAUO)
LIFE .... La Grange International Friendship Exchange (EARSL)
LIFE .... Language Improvement to Facilitate Education of Hearing-Impaired Children [*A project of NEA*]
LIFE .... Language Institute for English (EFIS)
LIFE .... LASER-Induced Fluorescence Emission
LIFE .... Leadership and Investment for Fighting an Epidemic [*Initiative*]
LIFE .... Leadership & Investment in Fighting an Epidemic (SAUO)
LIFE .... League for International Food Education [*Defunct*] (EA)
LIFE .... League of Independent Ferret Enthusiasts (EA)
LIFE .... Lear Integrated Flight Equipment (MCD)
LIFE .... Learning in a Free Environment [*Education program*]
LIFE .... Less Infant Fatality Everywhere [*In association name, Project LIFE*]
LIFE .... Let's Improve Future Environment
LIFE .... Liberia International Foundation for Elevation
LIFE .... Life Issues in Formal Education (EA)
LIFE .... Lifeline Systems [*NASDAQ symbol*] (TTSB)
LIFE .... Lifeline Systems, Inc. (SAUO)
LIFE .... Lifetime [*Cable television channel*]
LIFE .... Likelihood Function Estimation (ACAE)
LIFE .... Living in Family Environments
LIFE .... Logistics Evaluation and Review Integrated Flight Equipment [*Aviation*] (IAA)
LIFE .... Logistics Intelligence File Europe
LIFE .... Logistics Interface for a Factory Environment [*Computer science*] (VLIE)
LIFE .... London International Futures Exchange (SAUO)
LIFE .... Long Instruction Format Engine [*Computer science*] (CIST)
LIFE .... Longitudinal Interval Follow-Up Evaluation (MEDA)
LIFE .... Love Is Feeding Everyone (EA)
LIFE .... Low Income Family Emancipation Society
LIFE .... Low Income Family Emergency Center
LIFE .... Lung-Imaging Fluorescent Endoscope [*Medicine*] (ECON)
Life and Acc Ins R... Bigelow's Life and Accident Insurance Reports [*A publication*] (DLA)
LIFE at UCF... Learning Institute for Elders at University of Central Florida (EARSL)
Life Bcp .... Life Bancorp, Inc. [*Associated Press*] (SAG)
Life C .... Life (Health and Accident) Cases [*Commerce Clearing House*] [*A publication*] (DLA)
Life Cas .... Life (Health and Accident) Cases [*Commerce Clearing House*] [*A publication*] (DLA)
Life Cas 2d... Life (Health and Accident) Cases, Second Series [*Commerce Clearing House*] [*A publication*] (DLA)
Lifecell .... Lifecell Corp. [*Associated Press*] (SAG)
LifeHoan .... Lifetime Hoan Corp. [*Associated Press*] (SAG)
LIFEL .... Limited Functional English Literacy
LIFEMAN .... Live Fire Evaluation Manikin [*Perceptronics, Inc.*] [*Military*]
LifePart .... Life Partners [*Associated Press*] (SAG)
LIFER .... Language Interface Facility with Ellipsis and Recursion [*Computer science*] (MHDI)
LifeRe .... Life Re Corp. [*Associated Press*] (SAG)
LifeRte .... LifeRate Systems, Inc. [*Associated Press*] (SAG)
LIFES .... LASER-Induced Fluorescence and Environmental Sensing [*NASA*]
LifeSpir .... [*The*] Life of the Spirit [*London*] [*A publication*] (BJA)
LIFESTA .... Lifeboat Station [*Coast Guard*]
LIFETECH... Long-term Funding for the Environment Through Technology (SAUO)
Lifeway .... Lifeway Foods, Inc. [*Associated Press*] (SAG)
LIFF .... Lifschultz Inds [*NASDAQ symbol*] (TTSB)
LIFF .... Lifschultz Industries, Inc. [*NASDAQ symbol*] (SAG)
LIFF .... Line Impact Fully Formed (GART)
Liffe .... London and International Financial Futures Exchange (SAUO)
Liffe .... London International Financial Futures & Options Exchange
LIFFE .... London International Financial Futures and Options Exchange (NUMA)
LIFFE .... London International Financial Futures Exchange (EBF)
LIFFE .... London International Financial Futures Exchange Ltd. [*London, England*]
LIFFOE .... London International Financial Futures and Options Exchange (EBF)
LiFHAS .... Libertarian Foundation for Human Assistance (EAIO)
LIFI .... Life of Indiana Corp. (SAUO)
LIFireE .... Licentiate of the Institute of Fire Engineers (SAUO)
LI Fire Eng... Licentiate of the Institute of Fire Engineers (SAUO)
LIFLSA .... Lone Indian Fellowship and Lone Scout Alumni (EA)
LIFMA .... Leather Importers, Factors and Merchants Association (SAUO)
LIFMOP .... Linearly Frequency-Modulated Pulse
LIFO .... Last In, First Out [*Queuing technique*] [*Accounting*]
LIFO .... Life Orientation (Survey)
LIFPL .... Ligue Internationale de Femmes pour la Paix et la Liberte [*Women's International League for Peace and Freedom - WILPF*] (EAIO)
LIFPL/SF .... Ligue Internationale de Femmes pour la Paix et la Liberte, Section Francaise (EAIO)
LIFR .... Leukemia Inhibitory Factor Receptor [*Biochemistry*]
LIFRAM .... Liquid-Fueled Ramjet [*Navy*] (MCD)
LIFS .... LASER-Induced Fluorescence Spectroscopy
LIFS .... London International Furniture Show [*British*] (ITD)
LIFS .... Lowell Institution for Savings (SAUO)
Lifschlt .... Lifschultz Industries, Inc. [*Associated Press*] (SAG)
LIFSUM .... Airlift Summary (SAUS)
LIFSUM .... Airlift Summary Report [*Air Force*]
LIFT .... Aviation Group, Inc. (SAUO)
LIFT .... Bereavement Services & Community Education (AC)
LIFT .... Labor Investing for Tomorrow [*Department of Labor*]
LIFT .... Lead-In Fighter Training (SAUS)
LIFT .... Lead-In Flight Training [*Air Force*] (DOMA)
LIFT .... Link Intellectual Functions Tester
LIFT .... Literacy Involves Families Together [*Arizona*]
LIFT .... Logically Integrated FORTRAN Translator [*UNIVAC*]
LIFT .... Logistics Improvement Facility Technology (SAUO)
LIFT .... London International Festival of Theatre [*British*]
LIFT .... London International Freight Terminal (DS)
LIFT .... Long Island Forum for Technology [*New York*] (EARSL)
LIFT .... Lower Inventories for Tomorrow (SAUO)
LIFT .... Lower Inventory for Tomorrow [*A program of the Canadian government to bring heavy stocks of wheat into line with demand by paying farmers not to produce*]
LIFT .... Low Interfacial Tension [*Physical chemistry*]
LIFT .... Lymphocyte Immunofluorescence Test (STED)
LIFTG .... Lifting (ABBR)
LIFU .... Igorel Lineas Feeder [*Intermodal shipping container symbol*] (TVRC)
LIFU .... Liquid Fuel
LIFUM .... Airlift Summary Report (SAUS)
LIG .... Laboratory Implementation Guidance (SAUO)
LIG .... Landcare Liaison Group (SAUO)
LIG .... LASER Image Generator (MCD)
LIG .... LASERS in Graphics (DGA)
LIG .... Last Interglacial (SAUO)
LIG .... Last Interglacial Period [*Climatology*]
LIG .... Leichte Infanteriegeschuetz [*Light Infantry Howitzer*] [*German military - World War II*]
LIG .... Liege (ABBR)
LIG .... Ligament [*Anatomy*] (DAVI)
lig .... Ligamentum (STED)
LIG .... Ligated [*or Ligation*] [*Medicine*]
lig .... Ligation (STED)
LIG .... Ligature (DGA)
LIG .... Liggett Group, Inc. [*NYSE symbol*] (COMM)
LIG .... Limoges [*France*] [*Airport symbol*] (OAG)
LIG .... London Industrial Group [*British*]
Lig .... Pro Ligario [*of Cicero*] [*Classical studies*] (OCD)
LIGA .... Liquid Granule Applicator [*Device used to disperse pesticides*]
LIGA .... Lithographic Galvanoforming Abformung [*Materials science*]
Ligand .... Ligand Pharmaceuticals, Inc. [*Associated Press*] (SAG)
LIGCM .... Licentiate of the Incorporated Guild of Church Musicians [*British*] (ROG)
Lig Dig .... Ligon's Digest [*Alabama*] [*A publication*] (DLA)
LIGG .... Lanzhou Institute of Glaciology and Geocryology (SAUO)
ligg .... Ligaments (STED)
LIGG .... Ligaments [*or Ligamenti*]
ligg .... Ligature [*Surgery*] (DAVI)
LIGH .... Light Equipment [*NCIC trailer make code*]
LIGHT .... Lifecycle Global HyperText [*Computer science*] (VLIE)
LIGHT .... Light [*Commonly used*] (OPSA)
LIGHT .... Light Industrial Gas Heat Transfer
LIGHT .... Lighting (ABBR)
LIGHT .... Lightning (ABBR)
LIGHTEX .... Searchlight Illumination Exercise [*Also, LITEX*] [*Military*] (NVT)
LightP .... LightPath Technologies, Inc. [*Associated Press*] (SAG)
LIGHTPHOTORON... Light Photographic Squadron
LIGHTS .... Lights [*Commonly used*] (OPSA)
LightSav .... Light Savers USA, Inc. [*Associated Press*] (SAG)
LIGL .... Legal Institute of the Great Lakes [*University of Toledo*] (RCD)
Lign .... Lignum [*Wood*] [*Latin*]
LIGNITE PAC... Lignite Energy Council PAC [*Bismarck, ND*] (PACS)
LIGO .... Laser Interferometer Gravitational Wave Observatory (SAUO)
LIGO .... LASER Interferometry Gravitational Wave Observatory [*Proposed*]
LIG PAC .... Lincoln Insurance Group [*Lincoln, NE*] (PACS)
LIGS .... Landstar Ligon [*Common carrier symbol*]
LIGT .... Lighter-Bilt Trailers [*NCIC trailer make code*]
LIH .... LASER Interferometric Holography
LIH .... Left Inguinal Hernia [*Medicine*]
LIH .... Letters and Inscriptions of Hammurabi [*A publication*] (BJA)
LIH .... Leucine-Induced Hypoglycemia [*Medicine*] (MELL)
LIH .... Leukocyte Inhibiting Factor [*Medicine*] (MELL)
LIH .... Licensed Industrial Hygienist (SARE)
LIH .... Light Intensity High
LIH .... Lihue [*Hawaii*] [*Airport symbol*] (OAG)
LIH .... Line Interface Handler
LiH .... Lithium Hydride
LIHA .... Low Impulsiveness, High Anxiety (MAE)
LIHDC .... Low Income Housing Development Corp. [*North Carolina*] (EA)
LIHE .... Lutheran Institute of Human Ecology (EA)
LIHEAP .... Low Income Home Energy Assistance Program [*Formerly, LIEA*] [*Block grant*]
LIHG .... Ligue Internationale de Hockey sur Glace [*International Ice Hockey Federation*]
LihirGld .... Lihir Gold Ltd. [*Associated Press*] (SAG)
LIHIS .... Low Income Housing Information Service (EA)

LIHM .... Licentiate of the Institute of Housing Managers [*British*] (DI)
LIHN .... Hieronymi Liber Interpretationis Hebraicorum Nominum (BJA)
LIHPRHA.... Low Income Housing Preservation and Resident Homeownership Act of 1990
LIHREC...... Long Island Horticultural Research Extension Center [*Cornell University*] (RCD)
LIHRY .... Lihir Gold ADS [*NASDAQ symbol*] (TTSB)
LIHRY .... Lihir Gold Ltd. [*NASDAQ symbol*] (SAG)
LIHS .... Long Island Horticultural Society (SAUO)
LIHTC........ Low Income Housing Tax Credit
LII............ Flight Research Institute, M. Gromov [*Former USSR*] [*FAA designator*] (FAAC)
LII............ Land Information Infrastructure (SAUO)
LII............ Larizza Industries (SAUO)
LII............ Larizza Industries, Inc. [*AMEX symbol*] (SPSG)
LII............ Leisure Interest Inventory (STED)
LII............ Lennox Intl. [*NYSE symbol*] (SG)
LII............ Life Insurance Index [*A publication*]
LII............ Light Image Intensifier (SAUS)
LII............ Linux Internationalisation Inititative (SAUO)
LII............ Livestock Industry Institute (EA)
LII............ London Insurance Institute (SAUO)
LII............ Lues II [*or Secondary syphilis*] [*Infectious diseases*] (DAVI)
LII............ Mulia [*Indonesia*] [*Airport symbol*] (OAG)
LII............ The Legal Information Institute [*Cornell University*] [*Law School*] (IID)
LI/IA .... Ibero Americana. Scandinavian Association for Research on Latin America. Stockholm (SAUO)
LIIA .... Italy International NOTAM Office [*Italy*] [*ICAO location identifier*] (ICLI)
LIIB .... Roma [*Italy*] [*ICAO location identifier*] (ICLI)
LIIC .... Italy Military International NOTAM Office [*Italy*] [*ICAO location identifier*] (ICLI)
LIICC .... Land Information and Inventory Co-ordinating Committee (SAUO)
L-IICS .... Level II Controlled Shipping [*Automotive engineering*]
LIIG .... Logistics Item Identification Guide [*Military*] (AFM)
LIII .... Lues III [*Teritiary syphilis*] [*Infectious diseases*] (DAVI)
LIII .... Roma [*Italy*] [*ICAO location identifier*] (ICLI)
li-ion .... Lithium Ion
LIIP .... LASER-Induced Infrared Photochemistry
LIIR .... Italian Agency for Air Navigation Services [*Italy*] [*ICAO location identifier*] (ICLI)
LIJ .... Lawyers for an Independent Judiciary [*Defunct*] (EA)
LIJ .... Left Internal Jugular Vein [*Medicine*] (DMAA)
LIJJ .... Roma [*Italy*] [*ICAO location identifier*] (ICLI)
LIK........... Leichte Infanteriekolonne [*Light Infantry Supply Column*] [*German military - World War II*]
LIK........... Likiep [*Marshall Islands*] [*Airport symbol*] (OAG)
LIKE .... Learning Inventory of Kindergarten Experience [*Owigns, Mills, and O'Dell*] (TES)
LIKONA...... Limburgse Koepel voor Natuurstudie (SAUO)
LIL........... Laboratory Interface Language [*Programming language*]
LIL........... Laporte Industries Limited (SAUO)
LIL........... Large Immersion Lens
LIL........... Large-Ion Lithophile
LIL........... Law of the Iterated Logarithm (PDAA)
LIL........... Lead-In Light-System [*Aviation*]
LIL........... Light Intensity Low
LIL........... Lilac (ROG)
LIL........... Li'L Hustler [*NCIC car model code*]
LIL........... Lille [*France*] [*Airport symbol*] (OAG)
LIL........... Lille [*France*] [*Seismograph station code, US Geological Survey*] [*Closed*] (SEIS)
LIL........... Lilliputian (ABBR)
Lil............ Lilly's English Assize Reports [*1688-93*] [*A publication*] (DLA)
LIL........... Lily-Tulip Cup Corporation (SAUO)
LIL........... Lincoln's Inn Library [*A publication*] (DLA)
LIL........... Linguaphone Institute Limited (SAUO)
LIL........... Lithuanian Airlines [*ICAO designator*] (FAAC)
LIL........... Little (ABBR)
LIL........... Live-In Lover [*Slang*] (DSUE)
LIL........... Log-Inject-Log [*Petroleum technology*]
LIL........... Long Island Light'g [*NYSE symbol*] (TTSB)
LIL........... Long Island Lighting Co. [*Formerly, LLT*] [*NYSE symbol*] (SPSG)
LIL........... Low-Input Landscaping
LIL........... Lunar International Laboratory
LILA .... Life Insurance Logistics Automated (SAUO)
LILA .... Ligue Internationale de la Librairie Ancienne [*International League of Antiquarian Booksellers - ILAB*] (EAIO)
LILA .... Lilac [*NCIC motorcycle make code*]
LILA .... Low Impulsiveness, Low Anxiety (MAE)
Lil Abr....... Lilly's Abridgment [*England*] [*A publication*] (DLA)
LILAC........ Low-Intensity Large Area [*Headlight*]
LILACS ...... Latin American and Caribbean Health Sciences Literature (IID)
LILAM .... Licentiate of the Institute of Leisure and Amenity Management [*British*] (DBQ)
LILBO........ Libourn, MO [*American Association of Railroads railroad junction routing code*]
LILC .... Annual Long Island Library Conference
LILC .... Lil' Cat [*NCIC trailer make code*]
LILCo .... Long Island Lighting Co. [*Associated Press*] (SAG)
Lil Conv..... Lilly's Conveyancer [*A publication*] (DLA)
LILE.......... Large Ion Lithophile Element [*Geochemistry*]
LILIT......... Lilita, AL [*American Association of Railroads railroad junction routing code*]
Lill Ent ...... Lilly's Entries [*England*] [*A publication*] (DLA)
Lilly.......... Lilly [*Eli*] and Co. [*Associated Press*] (SAG)
Lilly.......... Lilly Endowment, Inc. [*Medicine*] (EDAA)
Lilly.......... Lilly's Reports and Pleadings of Cases in Assize [*170 English Reprint*] [*1688-93*] [*A publication*] (DLA)
Lilly Abr .... Lilly's Abridgment [*England*] [*A publication*] (DLA)
Lilly Assize... Lilly's Reports and Pleadings of Cases in Assize [*170 English Reprint*] [*1688-93*] [*A publication*] (DLA)
Lilly Assize (Eng)... Lilly's Reports and Pleadings of Cases in Assize [*170 English Reprint*] [*1688-93*] [*A publication*] (DLA)
LillyE........ Lilly [*Eli*] & Co. [*Associated Press*] (SAG)
LillyEli ...... Lilly [*Eli*] [*Associated Press*] (SAG)
LillyInd...... Lilly Industries, Inc. [*Associated Press*] (SAG)
LILN .... Lil Indian [*NCIC motorcycle make code*]
LILO .... Last-In, Last-Out [*Accounting*]
LILO .... Link Loader (IAA)
LILO .... Linux Loader (RALS)
LILOC........ Light Lyne Optical Correlation (MCD)
LILPrA....... Long Island Ltg 7.95% Pfd [*NYSE symbol*] (TTSB)
LILPrB....... Long Island Ltg 5% B Pfd [*NYSE symbol*] (TTSB)
LILPrC....... Long Island Ltg 7.66% Pfd [*NYSE symbol*] (TTSB)
LILPrE....... Long Island Ltg 4.35% Cv E Pfd [*NYSE symbol*] (TTSB)
LILPrI........ Long Island Ltg, 5.75% Cv I Pfd [*NYSE symbol*] (TTSB)
LILPrQ....... Long Island Ltg 7.05% Pfd [*NYSE symbol*] (TTSB)
LILRC........ Long Island Library Resources Council [*Bellport, NY*] [*Library network*]
Lil Reg...... Lilly's Practical Register [*A publication*] (ILCA)
LILU .... Laporte Industries [*Intermodal shipping container symbol*] (TVRC)
LilVern ...... Lillian Vernon Corp. [*Associated Press*] (SAG)
LILZ.......... Lil'Z [*NCIC trailer make code*]
LIM .... BVBA Lucorp [*Belgium*] [*FAA designator*] (FAAC)
LIM .... Compass Locator of Inner Marker Site
LIM .... Laboratory Institute of Merchandising [*New York, NY*]
LIM .... Laminate Insert Molding [*Plastics*]
LIM .... Land Information Management (SAUO)
LIM .... Land Inventory and Management Program (SAUO)
LIM .... Language Interface Module (NITA)
LIM .... Language Interpretation Module
LIM .... Latent Image Memory
LIM .... Leg-Inducing Membrane [*Entomology*]
LIM .... Leisure Interest Measure (IDYL)
LIM .... Leningrad Institute of Metals [*Former USSR*] (MCD)
LIM .... Licentiate of the Institution of Metallurgists (SAUO)
LIM .... Light Intensity Medium
LIM .... Lima [*Peru*] [*Airport symbol*] (OAG)
LIM .... Lima [*Peru*] [*Seismograph station code, US Geological Survey*] (SEIS)
LIM .... Lima [*NCIC car model code*]
LIM .... Lima Public Library, Lima, OH [*OCLC symbol*] (OCLC)
LIM .... Limber (MSA)
LIM .... Limerick [*County in Ireland*] (ROG)
lim........... Limes [*Limit*] [*Latin*]
lim........... Limit (ELAL)
LIM .... Limit
lim........... Limitation (STED)
LIM .... Limited (automobile) [*NCIC car model code*]
LIM .... Limiter [*Electronics*] (ECII)
LIM .... Limonene [*Organic chemistry*]
LIM .... Limousine (automobile) [*NCIC car model code*]
LIM .... Linear Induction Motor [*Magnetic rapid-transit car*]
LIM .... Line Insulation Monitor (PDAA)
LIM .... Line Interface Module
LIM .... Line Isolation Monitor [*Medicine*] (EDAA)
LIM .... Liquid Injection Molding
LIM .... Locator Inner Marker [*Aviation*] (DA)
LIM .... Logic Interface Module (TIMI)
LIM .... Losing Inventory Manager [*Army*] (AABC)
LIM .... Lotus/Intel/Microsoft [*Computer science*]
LIM .... Lower Inlet Module [*Nuclear energy*] (NRCH)
LIM .... Low-Inclination Mission (SAUS)
LIMA......... Langkawi International Maritime & Aerospace Exhibition (SAUO)
LIMA......... LASER-Induced Ion-Mass Analyzer [*Instrumentation*]
LIMA......... LASER-Induced Mass Analysis (AAEL)
LIMA......... Left Internal Mammary Artery [*Anatomy*] (AAMN)
LIMA......... Licentiate of the Institute of Mathematics and Its Applications [*British*] (DBQ)
LIMA......... Light Induced Modulation of Absorption (VLIE)
LIMA......... Lima, OH [*American Association of Railroads railroad junction routing code*]
LIMA......... Logic-in-Memory Array
LIMA......... Long Island Museum Association (SAUO)
LIMA......... Lotus/Intel/Microsoft/Ast (SAUO)
LIMA......... Torino [*Italy*] [*ICAO location identifier*] (ICLI)
LIMAC....... Large Integrated Monolithic Array Computer (MCD)
LIMAC....... Linden Industrial Mutual Aid Council (SAUO)
LIM ACT .... Limitation of Action [*Legal term*] (DLA)
LIMAD....... Linear Magnetic Drive (SAUS)
LIMAP....... Landsat Imagery Analysis Package (SAUO)
LIMAS....... Lightweight Marking System [*British Army*]
LIMB......... Library Instruction Materials Bank [*Loughborough University of Technology*] [*Information service or system*] (IID)
LIMB......... Limestone Injection/Multistage Burner
LIMB......... Liquid Metal Breeder [*Reactor*]
LiMB......... Listing of Molecular Biology Databases (SAUO)
LIMB......... Look In Mail Box (VLIE)

LIMB......... Milano/Bresso [*Italy*] [*ICAO location identifier*] (ICLI)
LIMBT....... Large Injection-Molded Body Technology [*Automotive plastics*]
LIMC......... Milano/Malpensa [*Italy*] [*ICAO location identifier*] (ICLI)
LIMD......... Grigna Settentrionale [*Italy*] [*ICAO location identifier*] (ICLI)
LIMD......... Limited (ROG)
LIMDAT..... Limiting Date
LIMDIS...... Limited Distribution [*Military*] (AFIT)
LIMDOW.... Light Intensity Modulation Direct OverWrite [*Computer science*]
LIMDU....... Limited Duty (MCD)
LIME......... Bergamo/Orio Al Serio [*Italy*] [*ICAO location identifier*] (ICLI)
LIME......... Laser Inducted Microwave Emissions (ADWA)
LIME......... Low-Iron, Manganese-Enriched [*Meteorite*]
LIMEA....... Low-Iron-Content Monoethanolamine
LIMEAN..... London Interbank Median Average Rate
LIMED....... Limedale, IN [*American Association of Railroads railroad junction routing code*]
LIM-EMS.... Lotus-Intel-Microsoft Expanded Memory Specification [*Computer science*] (BTTJ)
LIMESCO.... Line Memory Scan Converter
limest....... Limestone [*Petrology*]
LIMEX....... Labrador Ice Margin Experiment (SAUO)
LIMF......... Land Information Management Framework (SAUO)
LIMF......... Licentiate of the Institute of Metal Finishing [*British*] (DBQ)
LIMF......... Linden Motor Freight Company [*Common carrier symbol*]
LIMF......... Torino/Caselle [*Italy*] [*ICAO location identifier*] (ICLI)
LIMFAC...... Limiting Factor (MCD)
LIMG......... Albenga [*Italy*] [*ICAO location identifier*] (ICLI)
LIMH......... Pian Rosa [*Italy*] [*ICAO location identifier*] (ICLI)
LIMI.......... Colle Del Gigante [*Italy*] [*ICAO location identifier*] (ICLI)
LIMI.......... Leningrad International Management Institute [*Joint Venture between Bocconi University, Italy and Leningrad University*] (ECON)
LIMIRIS..... LASER-Induced Modulation of Infrared in Silicon
LIMIT........ Leicester Intravenous Magnesium Intervention Trial [*Cardiology study*]
LIMIT........ Lot-Size Inventory Management Interpolation Technique (BUR)
Limitd....... [*The*] Limited, Inc. [*Associated Press*] (SAG)
Limit Ed..... Limited Edition
LIMITS...... Development and Evaluation of a New Generation of Real Time Software Engineering Design Tools for Handling the Temporal Aspects of Industrial Applications of Information Technology (SAUO)
LIMJ......... Genova/Sestri [*Italy*] [*ICAO location identifier*] (ICLI)
LIMK......... Torino/Bric Della Croce [*Italy*] [*ICAO location identifier*] (ICLI)
LIML......... Limited Information Maximum Likelihood [*Econometrics*]
LIML......... Milano/Linate [*Italy*] [*ICAO location identifier*] (ICLI)
LIMM......... Milano [*Italy*] [*ICAO location identifier*] (ICLI)
LIMN......... Cameri [*Italy*] [*ICAO location identifier*] (ICLI)
LIMNET..... London Insurance Market Network (SAUO)
LIMNOL..... Limnology
LIMNURP... Lippincott Manual of Nursing Practice (SAUO)
LIMO......... Land Information Management Office (SAUO)
LIMO......... Least Input for the Most Output [*Business term*]
LIMO......... Limousine (DSUE)
Limo.......... Limousine
LIMO......... Limousine Industry Manufacturers Organization (EA)
LIMO......... Monte Bisbino [*Italy*] [*ICAO location identifier*] (ICLI)
LIMON....... Limon, CO [*American Association of Railroads railroad junction routing code*]
LIMON....... Limonis [*Of Lemon*] [*Pharmacy*] (ROG)
LIMOS....... Laser Intensity Modulation System [*Computer science*]
LIMOSO..... Limitation of Supplies Order [*World War II*]
LIMP......... Laboratory Instrument Maintenance Program (SAUO)
LIMP......... Language-Independent Macro Processor (PDAA)
LIMP......... Life-Injury-Money-Problems (SAUO)
LIMP......... Louis XIV, James II, Mary, Prince of Wales [*Jacobite toast*]
LIMP......... Lunar-Anchored Interplanetary Monitoring Platform [*Aerospace*]
LIMP......... Lunar Interplanetary Monitoring Probe (IAA)
LIMP......... Parma [*Italy*] [*ICAO location identifier*] (ICLI)
LIMPES..... Logistics Interactive Mobilization/Planning and Execution System (SAUO)
LIMPS....... Linear Induction Motor Propulsion System
LIMQ......... Govone [*Italy*] [*ICAO location identifier*] (ICLI)
LIMR......... Lankenau Institute for Medical Research (RCD)
LIMR......... Limiter
LIMR......... Novi Ligure [*Italy*] [*ICAO location identifier*] (ICLI)
LIMRA....... Life Insurance Marketing and Research Association [*Hartford, CT*] (EA)
LIMRC....... LRU [*Line Replaceable Unit*] Identification and Maintenance Requirements Catalog (NASA)
LIMRF....... Life Insurance Medical Research Fund [*Defunct*]
LIMRIC...... LRU Identification and Maintenance Requirements Catalog (SAUS)
LIMRV....... Linear Induction Motor Research Vehicle [*Magnetic rapid-transit car*]
LIMS......... Laban Institute of Movement Studies [*Later, LBIMS*] (EA)
LIMS......... Laboratory Information Management System
LIMS......... LASER-Induced Mass Spectrometry (AAEL)
LIMS......... LASERInduced Microgrough Structures [*Surface Technology*]
LIMS......... Laser Ionization Mass Spectrometer (ACAE)
LIMS......... Lewis Information Management System (SAUO)
LIMS......... Library Information Management System [*University of Maryland*]
LIMS......... Light Ion Mass Spectrometer (SAUS)
LIMS......... Limb Infrared Monitor of the Stratosphere
LIMS......... Limb-Motion Sensor [*System*]
LIMS......... Limb Sounder (SSD)
LIMS......... Liquid Injection Molding Simulation [*Plastics*]
LiMS......... Lithium Metal Sulfide
LIMS......... Logistic Inventory Management System [*North American Rockwell*]
LIMS......... Logistics Information Management System (SAUO)
LIMS......... Logistics Inventory Management System (SAUO)
LIMS......... Lotus Intel Microsoft Specifications (VLIE)
LIMS......... Piacenza/San Damiano [*Italy*] [*ICAO location identifier*] (ICLI)
LIMSS....... Logistics Information Management Support System [*Military*]
LIMSW...... Limit Switch (NRCH)
LIMT......... Passo Della Cisa [*Italy*] [*ICAO location identifier*] (ICLI)
LIMTN....... Little Mountain, UT [*American Association of Railroads railroad junction routing code*]
LIMTV....... Linear Induction Motor Test Vehicle [*Magnetic rapid-transit car*]
LIMU......... Capo Mele [*Italy*] [*ICAO location identifier*] (ICLI)
LIMU......... LASER Inertial Measurement Unit (MCD)
LIMV......... Lilac Mottle Virus [*Plant pathology*]
LIMV......... Passo Dei Giovi [*Italy*] [*ICAO location identifier*] (ICLI)
LIMW........ Aosta [*Italy*] [*ICAO location identifier*] (ICLI)
LIMY......... Monte Malanotte [*Italy*] [*ICAO location identifier*] (ICLI)
LIMZ......... Levaldigi [*Italy*] [*ICAO location identifier*] (ICLI)
LIN........... Law Institute News [*Australia*] [*A publication*]
LIN........... Linair-Hungarian Regional Airlines [*FAA designator*] (FAAC)
LIN........... Lincoln [*Nebraska*] [*Seismograph station code, US Geological Survey*] [*Closed*] (SEIS)
LIN........... Lincoln [*Diocesan abbreviation*] [*Nebraska*] (TOCD)
Lin............ Lincolnshire Regiment (SAUO)
Lin............ Linden [*Record label*]
LIN........... Linden, CA [*Location identifier*] [*FAA*] (FAAL)
LIN........... Line (WDAA)
lin............ Lineal (MIST)
LIN........... Lineal (MSA)
LIN........... Linear (KSC)
lin............ Linear (STED)
LIN........... Line Item Number (ACAE)
LIN........... Linen (ADA)
lin............ Linen (VRA)
LIN........... Linens'n Things [*NYSE symbol*] (SG)
lin............ Liniment (STED)
LIN........... Liniment
LIN........... Liquid Nitrogen (AFM)
LIN........... Local Interconnect Network (SAUO)
LIN........... Massachusetts Institute of Technology, Lincoln Laboratory, Lexington, MA [*OCLC symbol*] (OCLC)
LIN........... Milan [*Italy*] Forlanini-Linate [*Airport symbol*] (OAG)
LIN........... Nitlyn Airways, Inc. (SAUO)
LINA......... Learning Information Network Association [*United Kingdom*] (EAIO)
LINA......... Liberian News Agency (EY)
LINA......... Literaturnachweise [*Literature Compilations Database*] [*Fraunhofer Society*] (IID)
LINABOL.... Lineas Navieras Bolivianas [*Shipping line*] [*Bolivia*] (EY)
LINAC....... Linear [*Electron*] Accelerator
LINAS....... LASER Inertial Navigation Attack System (IAA)
LINAS....... LASER-Integrated Navigation/Attack System (MCD)
LINB......... LIN Broadcasting Corp. (SAUO)
LINC......... Laboratory Instrument Computer [*Medical analyzer*]
LINC......... Language Information Network Coordination [*Education*] (AIE)
LINC......... Language in the National Curriculum [*Project*] (WDAA)
LINC......... Learning Institute of North Carolina
LINC......... Legislative Information Network Corp. [*Information service or system*] (IID)
LINC......... Lewis & Clark Railroad [*Federal Railroad Administration identification code*]
LINC......... Library & Information Consultants Ltd. [*Information service or system*] (IID)
LINC......... Library and Information Cooperation Council (SAUO)
LINC......... Lincoln [*NCIC car make code*]
LINC......... Lincolnshire [*County in England*]
LINC......... Lincoln (trucks) [*NCIC truck make code*]
LINC......... Lindas Diversified Holdings [*NASDAQ symbol*] (SAG)
LINC......... Lucas Industries Noise Centre [*Research center*] [*British*] (IRUK)
LINCA....... Linda's Flame Roasted Chicken [*NASDAQ symbol*] (TTSB)
L'INCA....... L'Institut National Canadien pour les Aveugles (AC)
Lincare...... Lincare Holdings, Inc. [*Associated Press*] (SAG)
LINCE....... LASER-Improved Naval Combat Equipment (PDAA)
LincEl....... [*The*] Lincoln Electric Co. [*Associated Press*] (SAG)
LincElA...... Lincoln Electric Co. (The) [*Associated Press*] (SAG)
LINCLOE.... Lightweight Individual Combat Clothing and Equipment (AABC)
LinCMOS.... Linear CMOS [*Complementary Metal Oxide Semiconductor*] [*Texas Instruments*] (NITA)
LINCMOS... Linear Complementary Metal-Oxide Semiconductor [*Electronics*] (EECA)
LincN........ Lincoln National Corp. [*Associated Press*] (SAG)
LincN........ Lincoln National Corp. Capital I [*Associated Press*] (SAG)
LincN........ Lincoln National Corp. Capital II [*Associated Press*] (SAG)
LincNatl..... Lincoln National Corp. [*Associated Press*] (SAG)
LincNIF..... Lincoln National Income Fund, Inc. [*Associated Press*] (SAG)
LINCO....... Linear Composition (PDAA)
LINCO....... Linearly Organized Chemical Code for Use in Computer Systems (DIT)
Lincoln U... Lincoln University (GAGS)
LINCOMPEX... Linked Compressor and Expander (NATG)
LINCOS...... Lingua Cosmica [*Artificial language consisting of radio signals of varying lengths and frequencies*]
LINCOTT.... Liaison, Interface, Coupling, Technology Transfer
LINC PAC... Leadership in the New Century [*Washington, DC*] (PACS)

LINCS .... Language Information Network and Clearinghouse System [*Center for Applied Linguistics*] [*Washington, DC*]
LINCS .... Leased Interfacility Nas Communications System [*FAA*] (TAG)
LINCS .... LeTourneau Integrated Network Control System [*Automotive engineering*]
Lincs .... Lincolnshire (DIAR)
LINCS .... Lincolnshire [*County in England*]
LINCS .... Literacy Information and Communication System
LinCS .... Local Independents Collaborating with Stations (SAUO)
LincSB ...... Lincoln Savings Bank [*Associated Press*] (SAG)
LincSnk ..... Lincoln Snacks Co. [*Associated Press*] (SAG)
LINCSS ...... Local Integrated Navigation and Communications Satellite System
LINCT .... Linctus [*Tincture*] [*Pharmacy*] (ROG)
LincTel ...... Lincoln Telecommunications Co. [*Associated Press*] (SAG)
LINCW .... Linda's Flame Rstd Ckn Wrrt'A' [*NASDAQ symbol*] (TTSB)
LINCZ .... Linda's Flame Rstd Ckn Wrrt'B' [*NASDAQ symbol*] (TTSB)
LIND .... Lindberg Corp. [*NASDAQ symbol*] (SAG)
LIND .... Lindbergh Corporation (SAUO)
LIND .... Linde [*NCIC trailer make code*]
Linda .... Lindas Flame Roasted Chicken, Inc. [*Associated Press*] (SAG)
Linda .... Lindasw Diversified Holdings [*Associated Press*] (SAG)
LINDA .... Line Drawing Analyzer [*Cybernetics*]
LindasCh .... Lindas Flame Roasted Chicken, Inc. [*Associated Press*] (SAG)
LindasDiv ... Lindas Diversified Holdings [*Associated Press*] (SAG)
Lindbrg ...... Lindberg Corp. [*Associated Press*] (SAG)
LINDE .... Linden, AL [*American Association of Railroads railroad junction routing code*]
LINDI .... Line-to-Disk [*Computer science*] (MHDI)
Lind Jur ..... Lindley's Study of Jurisprudence [*A publication*] (DLA)
Lindl Copartn ... Lindley on Partnership [*A publication*] (DLA)
Lindley ...... Lindley's Law of Companies [*A publication*] (DLA)
Lindley Comp ... Lindley's Law of Companies [*A publication*] (DLA)
Lindley P ... Lindley on Partnership [*A publication*] (DLA)
Lindley Part ... Lindley on Partnership [*A publication*] (DLA)
LindlH .... Lindal Cedar Homes, Inc. [*Associated Press*] (SAG)
Lindl Partn ... Lindley on Partnership [*A publication*] (DLA)
LINDN .... Linden, IN [*American Association of Railroads railroad junction routing code*]
Lind Part .... Lindley on Partnership [*A publication*] (DLA)
Lind Pr ...... Lindewoode's Provinciales [*A publication*] (DLA)
Lind Prob ... Lindsay on Probates [*A publication*] (DLA)
LINDS .... Lindsay, ON [*American Association of Railroads railroad junction routing code*]
Lindsy .... Lindsay Manufacturing Co. [*Associated Press*] (SAG)
lindwd .... Lindenwood (VRA)
LINE .... Lightweight Inertial Northseeking Equipmet (SAA)
LINE .... Linear Corp. (SAUO)
LINE .... Line Ministries (SAUO)
LINE .... Long Interspersed Element Sequence [*Genetics*]
LINE .... Long Interspersed Nuclear Element [*Genetics*]
LINEAR ...... Lincoln Near-Earth Asteroid Research
LinearT ...... Linear Technology Corp. [*Associated Press*] (SAG)
L in Eastern Eur ... Law in Eastern Europe [*A publication*] (DLA)
LINED .... Line Editor [*Computer science*] (MHDI)
LINEII .... Logic and Information Network Compiler II [*Computer science*] (HGAA)
LINER .... Low-Ionization Nuclear Emission-Line Region [*Spectroscopy*]
LINES .... Library Information Network Exchange Services [*Australia*] [*A publication*]
LINEs .... Long Interspered Nuclcotide Elements [*Genetics*]
LINES .... Long-Interspersed Repeated Segments [*of DNA*] [*Genetics*] (DAVI)
LINF .... Lincraft Industries [*NCIC trailer make code*]
Linfield C ... Linfield College (GAGS)
lin ft .... Lineal Feet (MIST)
linft .... Linear Foot (WPI)
LINFT .... Linear Foot
Ling .... De Lingua Latina [*of Varro*] [*Classical studies*] (OCD)
LING .... Learning Independence Through Computers, Inc.
Ling .... Lingual [*Medicine*] (EDAA)
Ling .... Linguistics (BEE)
ling .... Linguistics (SHCU)
LING .... Linguistics
LINGO .... Linguistic Operation (VLIE)
LINGUA ..... Linguistic Analysis System (ECII)
Linim .... Liniment [*Medicine*] (EDAA)
LINIM .... Liniment
Lin Ins ...... De Lineis Insecabilibus [*of Aristotle*] [*Classical studies*] (OCD)
Linium ...... Linium Technology Corp. [*Associated Press*] (SAG)
LINJC .... Linden Junction, NJ [*American Association of Railroads railroad junction routing code*]
LINJET ...... Liquid Injection Electric Thruster [*NASA*] (NASA)
LINK .... Data Link (SAUS)
LINK .... Interlink Electronics [*NASDAQ symbol*] (TTSB)
LINK .... Interlink Electronics, Inc. [*NASDAQ symbol*] (SAG)
LINK .... International Leisure Information Network (SAUO)
LINK .... Lambeth Information Network [*Information service or system*] [*British*] (NITA)
LINK .... Library and Information Network [*Planned Parenthood Federation of America, Inc.*] [*Information service or system*] (IID)
LINK .... Link Trucking [*Common carrier symbol*]
LINK .... Literature in Nursing Kardex
LINK .... McCormick Library [*Planned Parenthood Federation of America*] [*Education Department*] (IID)
LINK-PAC ... PAC of the Satellite Broadcasting & Communications Association of America [*Alexandria, VA*] (PACS)
LINKW .... Interlink Electrs Wrrt [*NASDAQ symbol*] (TTSB)
LINLOG ...... Linear-Logarithmic (IEEE)
LINMH .... Linear Meters per Hour (IAA)
LINMOS ..... Laser Intensity Modulation (SAUO)
LINN .... Lincoln Foodservice Products, Inc. (SAUO)
LINN .... Linnaeus
LINN .... LION, Inc. [*NASDAQ symbol*] (QUAN)
Linn Ind ..... Linn's Index of Pennsylvania Reports [*A publication*] (DLA)
Linn Laws Prov PA ... Linn on the Laws of the Province of Pennsylvania [*A publication*] (DLA)
LINO .... Liaison Officer [*Military*]
lino .... Linocut (VRA)
Lino .... Linoleum (ADWA)
lino .... Linoleum (MIST)
LINO .... Linoleum
Lino .... Linotronic [*Computer science*]
LINO .... Linotype
Linoco .... Libyan National Oil Corporation (SAUO)
LINOL .... Linoleum (MSA)
LINOSCO .... Libraries in North Staffordshire and South Cheshire in Cooperation [*British*] (NITA)
LINOSCO .... Libraries of North Staffordshire in Cooperation (SAUO)
LINP .... Lincoln Park Mobile Homes [*NCIC trailer make code*]
LINPEX ...... London International Invention and New Products Exhibition (SAUO)
LINQ .... Ling Transfer [*Common carrier symbol*]
LINQ .... Literature in North Queensland [*A publication*]
LINR .... Linear Instruments Corp. (SAUO)
LINS .... Labrador Institute of Northern Studies [*Memorial University of Newfoundland*] [*Canada*] [*Research center*] (RCD)
LINS .... LASER Inertial Navigation System (MCD)
LINS .... Lightweight Inertial Navigation System [*Air Force*]
LINS .... Lindsey's Express [*Common carrier symbol*]
LINS .... LORAN Inertial System
L in Soc'y ... Law in Society [*A publication*] (DLA)
LInstBB ...... Licentiate of the Institute of British Bakers (DBQ)
LInstBCA .... Licentiate of the Institute of Burial and Cremation Administration [*British*] (DBQ)
L Inst P ..... Licentiate of the Institute of Physics [*British*]
L Inst Phys ... Licentiate of the Institute of Physics (SAUO)
LInstPRA .... Licentiate of the Institute of Park and Recreation Administration [*British*] (DI)
LINSU .... Liberian National Student Union (SAUO)
LINT .... Lintzcraft Travel Trailer [*NCIC trailer make code*]
Lint .... L Linteum [*An absorbent dressing material*] [*Medicine*] (EDAA)
LINTAS ...... Lever International Advertising Service (SAUO)
LINTEL ...... Lincoln Telecommunications Co. (EFIS)
LinTelev ..... Lin Television Corp. [*Associated Press*] (SAG)
L Intell ...... Law Intelligencer [*United States*] [*A publication*] (DLA)
LINTN .... Lincolnton, NC [*American Association of Railroads railroad junction routing code*]
L in Trans J ... Law in Transition Journal [*A publication*] (DLA)
L in Trans Q ... Law in Transition Quarterly [*A publication*] (DLA)
LINU .... Linde [*Intermodal shipping container symbol*] (TVRC)
LINUS .... Local Independently Nucleated Units of Structure (MELL)
LINUS .... Local Information Network for Universal Service [*Telecommunications service*] (TSSD)
LINUS .... Logical Inquiry and Update System
LINV .... Life Investors, Inc. (SAUO)
LINV .... Linville Horse Trailer [*NCIC trailer make code*]
LINW .... Linwood Manufacturing [*NCIC trailer make code*]
LINWR ...... Lake Ilo National Wildlife Refuge (SAUO)
LINX .... Logistics Information Exchange [*Computer science*] (CIST)
LINZ .... Land Information New Zealand (SAUO)
LINZ .... Lindsay Manufacturing [*NASDAQ symbol*] (SAG)
LINZ .... Lindsay Manufacturing Co. (SAUO)
LINZ .... Lindsay Mfg [*NASDAQ symbol*] (TTSB)
LINZ .... Lingoe Elevator [*Federal Railroad Administration identification code*]
LIO .... Air Charter Ltd. (Leiguflug Isleifs Ottesen) [*Iceland*] [*FAA designator*] (FAAC)
LIO .... Laser Indirect Ophthalmoscope [*Medicine*] (MELL)
LIO .... Left Inferior Oblique [*Anatomy*] (DAVI)
LIO .... Legislative Information Office (SAUO)
LIO .... Lesser Included Offense
LIO .... Liberian Iron Ore Ltd. [*Toronto Stock Exchange symbol*]
LIO .... Limon [*Costa Rica*] [*Airport symbol*] (OAG)
LIO .... Lionel Corporation (SAUO)
LIO .... Lions International Organization (SAUO)
LIO .... Liottite [*A zeolite*]
LiO .... Lithium Organic Battery
LIO .... Livestock Improvement Organization (SAUO)
LIO .... Local Interconnect Option [*Wang Laboratories, Inc.*] (BYTE)
LIO .... National Restaurant Association Large Independent Operators [*Defunct*] (EA)
LIOAS .... LASER-Induced Optoacoustic Spectroscopy
LIOB .... Licentiate of the Institute of Builders (or Building) (SAUO)
LIOB .... Licentiate of the Institute of Building (SAUO)
LIOC .... Lighted Independent of Computer
LIOCS .... Logical Input/Output Control System [*Computer science*]
LIOD .... Lightweight Optronic Detector (SAUS)
LIOD .... Lightweight Optronic Director (MCD)
LIODD .... LASER In-Flight Obstacle Detection Device
LiOH .... Lithium Hydroxide (NASA)
LIOJ .... Language Institute of Japan (SAUO)

LIOL .... Legal Information On-Line [*Ministry of Labour*] [*Hamilton, ON*] [*Information service or system*] (IID)
LION .... Fidelity National [*NASDAQ symbol*] (TTSB)
LION .... Fidelity National Corp. [*NASDAQ symbol*] (SAG)
LION .... Fidelity Southern Corp. [*NASDAQ symbol*]
LION .... Lehman Investment Opportunity Note
LION .... Library Information OnLine [*International Atomic Energy Agency*] [*United Nations*] (DUND)
LION .... Literature Online [*Chadwyck-Healey*]
LION .... Local Input/Output Nozzle [*Computer science*]
LION .... Local Integrated Optical Network (SAUO)
LI/ON .... Logicon Input/Output Network
LION .... Low Energy Ion and Electron Instrument (ADWA)
LION .... Lunar International Observer Network [*NASA*]
LionBrw ..... Lion Brewery, Inc. (The) [*Associated Press*] (SAG)
Lion-Club ... Liberty, Intelligence, Our Nations Safety (SAUO)
LIONS .... Library Information and On-Line Network Service [*New York Public Library*] [*Information service or system*] (IID)
LIOP .... Life in One Position [*Telecommunications*] (TEL)
LIOP .... Limited Initial Operating Production (MCD)
LIOU .... Lion Ferry [*Intermodal shipping container symbol*] (TVRC)
LIP .... Boston, MA [*Location identifier*] [*FAA*] (FAAL)
LIP .... Laboratory for Image Processing (SAUO)
LIP .... Large Igneous Province [*Geochemistry*]
LIP .... Large Internet Packet [*Computer science*] (PCM)
LIP .... LASER-Induced Plasma [*Spectroscopy*]
LIP .... Latent Information Parameter
LIP .... Lateral Intraparietal Area [*Anatomy*]
LIP .... Launch in Process [*NASA*] (IAA)
LIP .... Legal Inverse Path [*Physics*]
LIP .... Letter Input Procesing [*Printing*] (DGA)
LIP .... Library Information Plan (AIE)
LIP .... Life Insurance Policy
LIP .... Limited Implementation Program [*FAA*] (TAG)
Lip .... Lipase [*Medicine*] (EDAA)
lip .... Lipemic [*Cardiology*] (DAVI)
Lip .... Lipid [*Medicine*] (EDAA)
LIP .... Lipkovo [*Yugoslavia*] [*Seismograph station code, US Geological Survey*] (SEIS)
Lip .... Lipoate [*Also called Lipoic acid*] [*Biochemistry*] (DAVI)
Lip .... Lipoic [*Acid*] [*Medicine*] (EDAA)
LIP .... Lippe [*German license plate city code*]
LIP .... Lithium-Induced Polydipsia (DB)
LIP .... Lithographer (Pressman) [*U.S. Navy enlisted rating*] (AUER)
LIP .... Local Initiatives Program [*Canada*]
LIP .... Local Interested Party (SAUO)
LIP .... London International Press, Ltd. (SAUO)
LIP .... Loop Initialization Protocol (SAUS)
LIP .... Low Internal Phase [*Emulsion chemistry*]
LIP .... Low Involvement Product (BB)
LIP .... Lunar Impact Probe [*Aerospace*]
LIP .... Lymphoid Interstitial Pneumonitis [*Medicine*]
LIPA .... Aviano [*Italy*] [*ICAO location identifier*] (ICLI)
LIPA .... Labor Institute of Public Affairs (EA)
LIPA .... Lauric [*or Lauroyl or Lauryl*] Isopropanolamide [*Also, LPA*] [*Organic chemistry*]
LIPA .... Ligue panafricaine contre le tribalisme, le sectarianisme et le racisme (SAUO)
LIPA .... List of Interchangeable Parts and Assemblies
LIPA .... Liverpool Institute of Performing Arts [*England*] (WDAA)
LIPA .... Louisiana Independent Physicians Association, Inc.
LIPAD .... Ligue Patriotique pour le Developpement [*Burkina Faso*] [*Political party*] (EY)
LIPAS .... LASER-Induced Photoacoustic Spectroscopy
LIPB .... Bolzano [*Italy*] [*ICAO location identifier*] (ICLI)
LIPB .... Lipase B (DMAA)
LIPB .... Lloyd's International Private Banking [*Finance*]
Lip Bib Jur ... Lipenius' Bibliotheca Juridica [*A publication*] (DLA)
LIPC .... Cervia [*Italy*] [*ICAO location identifier*] (ICLI)
LIPC .... Levenson's Internal, Powerful Others, and Chance Scales (EDAC)
LIPC .... Livestock Industry Promotion Corporation (SAUO)
LIPC .... Livestock Industry Promotion Council [*Australia*]
LIPD .... Lipase D (DMAA)
LIPD .... Udine/Campoformido [*Italy*] [*ICAO location identifier*] (ICLI)
LIPE .... Bologna/Borgo Panigale [*Italy*] [*ICAO location identifier*] (ICLI)
LIPE .... Guinean League for the Protection of the Environment [*Political party*] (PSAP)
LIPE .... Lipe-Rollway Corp. (SAUO)
LIPES .... LASER-Induced Plasma Emission Spectroscopy (MEC)
LIPF .... Ferrara [*Italy*] [*ICAO location identifier*] (ICLI)
LIPF .... LASER-Induced Photodissociation and Fluorescence [*Coal technology*]
LIPFS .... Laser-Induced Plasma Fluorescence Spectroscopy (MEC)
LIPG .... Gorizia [*Italy*] [*ICAO location identifier*] (ICLI)
LIPH .... Treviso/San Angelo [*Italy*] [*ICAO location identifier*] (ICLI)
LIPHE .... Life Interpersonal History Enquiry [*Test*] [*Psychology*]
LIPI .... Indonesian Institute of Sciences [*Marine science*] (OSRA)
LIPI .... Marine Pollution Monitoring Center (SAUO)
LIPI .... Rivolto [*Italy*] [*ICAO location identifier*] (ICLI)
LIPID .... Logical Page Identifier
LIPJ .... Bassano Del Grappa [*Italy*] [*ICAO location identifier*] (ICLI)
LIPK .... Forli [*Italy*] [*ICAO location identifier*] (ICLI)
LIPL .... Ghedi [*Italy*] [*ICAO location identifier*] (ICLI)
LIPL .... Linear Information Processing Language [*High-order programming language*] [*Computer science*] (IEEE)
LIPLAFCO ... Liberia Plastic Footwear Corporation (SAUO)
LIPN .... Verona/Boscomantico [*Italy*] [*ICAO location identifier*] (ICLI)
LIPO .... Liposome Co. [*NASDAQ symbol*] (SAG)
LIPO .... Liposome Co., Inc. (SAUO)
Lipo .... Liposuction (ADWA)
LIPO .... Montichiari [*Italy*] [*ICAO location identifier*] (ICLI)
LIPOC .... Language-Independent Preferred Order of Constituents [*Linguistics*] (IEL)
Liposm ...... [*The*] Liposome Co., Inc. [*Associated Press*] (SAG)
LIPOZ .... Liposome $1.9375 Cv Dep'A'Pfd [*NASDAQ symbol*] (TTSB)
LIPP .... LASER-Induced Pressure Pulse [*Medicine*] (DMAA)
LIP P .... Lipid Profile [*Cardiology*] (DAVI)
LIPP .... Padova [*Italy*] [*ICAO location identifier*] (ICLI)
Lipp Cr L ... Lippitt's Massachusetts Criminal Law [*A publication*] (DLA)
LIPQ .... Ronchi De'Legionari [*Italy*] [*ICAO location identifier*] (ICLI)
LIPR .... Little Prospector [*NCIC truck make code*]
LIPR .... Rimini [*Italy*] [*ICAO location identifier*] (ICLI)
LIPS .... Jerry Lipps [*Common carrier symbol*]
LIPS .... Laboratory Information Processing System (SAUO)
LIPS .... Laboratory Interface Peripheral Subsystem [*Computer science*]
LIPS .... Lanthanide Ion Probe Spectroscopy
LIPS .... Laser Image Processing Scanner (ACAE)
LIPS .... Laser Intensify Profile System (ACAE)
LIPS .... Late-Inning Pressure Situation [*Baseball term*] (NDBD)
LIPS .... Leiter International Performance Scale [*Psychology*]
LIPS .... Library and Information Plans [*British*]
LIPS .... Lightweight Internet Person Schema [*Computer science*] (HODG)
LIPS .... Linear Inferences per Second (ADWA)
LIPS .... Litton Industries Privacy System
LIPS .... Logical Inferences per Second [*Processing power units*] [*Computer science*]
LIPS .... Logic Inference per Second (IAA)
Lips .... Low Income, Parents Supporting [*Lifestyle classification*]
LIPS .... Treviso/Istrana [*Italy*] [*ICAO location identifier*] (ICLI)
Lipsm .... [*The*] Liposome Co., Inc. [*Associated Press*] (SAG)
LIPT .... Leiter International Performance Test [*Psychology*] (DAVI)
LIPT .... Vicenza [*Italy*] [*ICAO location identifier*] (ICLI)
LIPU .... Padova [*Italy*] [*ICAO location identifier*] (ICLI)
LIPV .... Venezia/San Nicolo [*Italy*] [*ICAO location identifier*] (ICLI)
LIPX .... Large Internetwork Packet Exchange (SAUO)
LIPX .... Villafranca [*Italy*] [*ICAO location identifier*] (ICLI)
LIPY .... Ancona/Falconara [*Italy*] [*ICAO location identifier*] (ICLI)
LIPZ .... Lakeview Industry Park [*Federal Railroad Administration identification code*]
LIPZ .... Venezia/Tessera [*Italy*] [*ICAO location identifier*] (ICLI)
LIQ .... Athens, TX [*Location identifier*] [*FAA*] (FAAL)
LIQ .... Left Inner Quadrant (SAUS)
LIQ .... Libido [*Language symbol*] (ETLW)
LIQ .... Liquest International Marketing [*Vancouver Stock Exchange symbol*]
liq .... Liqueur [*Solution*] [*Pharmacy*]
LIQ .... Liquid (AAG)
liq .... Liquid (ELAL)
LIQ .... Liquidation (MCD)
LIQ .... Liquids of all types (SAUS)
liq .... Liquor (NTIO)
LIQ .... Liquor
LIQ .... Lisala [*Zaire*] [*Airport symbol*] (OAG)
LIQ .... Lower Inner Quadrant [*Anatomy*]
LIQB .... Arezzo [*Italy*] [*ICAO location identifier*] (ICLI)
LIQB .... Liqui-Box Corp. [*NASDAQ symbol*] (SAG)
LIQC .... Capri [*Italy*] [*ICAO location identifier*] (ICLI)
LIQD .... Liquid (ECII)
LIQD .... Passo Della Porretta [*Italy*] [*ICAO location identifier*] (ICLI)
LIQDTE ...... Liquidate (ROG)
LIQFRKT .... Liquid Fuel Rocket (IAA)
LIQI .... Gran Sasso [*Italy*] [*ICAO location identifier*] (ICLI)
LIQJ .... Civitavecchia [*Italy*] [*ICAO location identifier*] (ICLI)
LIQK .... Capo Palinuro [*Italy*] [*ICAO location identifier*] (ICLI)
LIQM .... Rifredo Mugello [*Italy*] [*ICAO location identifier*] (ICLI)
LIQN .... Rieti [*Italy*] [*ICAO location identifier*] (ICLI)
LIQO .... Monte Argentario [*Italy*] [*ICAO location identifier*] (ICLI)
LIQOR .... Liquidator (ROG)
LIQP .... Palmaria [*Italy*] [*ICAO location identifier*] (ICLI)
LIQQ .... Monte Cavo [*Italy*] [*ICAO location identifier*] (ICLI)
LIQR .... Radicofani [*Italy*] [*ICAO location identifier*] (ICLI)
LIQS .... Siena [*Italy*] [*ICAO location identifier*] (ICLI)
LIQSS .... Liquid Steady State (PDAA)
LIQT .... Circeo [*Italy*] [*ICAO location identifier*] (ICLI)
LIQT .... Liquid Transient (PDAA)
LIQU .... Liquid & Bulk Tank [*NCIC trailer make code*]
LiquiBox .... Liqui-Box Corp. [*Associated Press*] (SAG)
LIQUID ...... Liquidus [*Liquid*] [*Pharmacy*] (ROG)
LIQUON ...... Liquidation
Liquor Cont L Serv (CCH) ... Liquor Control Law Service (Commerce Clearing House) [*A publication*] (DLA)
LIQV .... Volterra [*Italy*] [*ICAO location identifier*] (ICLI)
LIQW .... Liquidation World, Inc. [*NASDAQ symbol*] (NASQ)
LIQW .... Sarzana/Luni [*Italy*] [*ICAO location identifier*] (ICLI)
LIQWF .... Liquidation World [*OTCBB symbol*]
LIQZ .... Ponza [*Italy*] [*ICAO location identifier*] (ICLI)
LIR .... Dover, DE [*Location identifier*] [*FAA*] (FAAL)
LIR .... Laboratory for Insulation Research [*MIT*] (MCD)
LIR .... Laboratory Implementation Requirements (SAUO)
LIR .... Laser Intercept Receiver (SAUS)

LIR .... Leader Internode Ratio [*Botany*]
LIR .... Left Iliac Region [*Medicine*] (MAE)
LIR .... Left Inferior Rectus [*Muscle*] [*Ophthalmology and surgery*] (DAVI)
LIR .... Level Indicator Recorder [*Electronics*] (ECII)
LIR .... Liberia [*Costa Rica*] [*Airport symbol*] (OAG)
LIR .... Library and Information Resources (NITA)
LIR .... Library of International Relations (SAUO)
LIR .... Licentiate of the Institute of Population Registration [*British*] (DBQ)
LIR .... Limiting Interval Reliability
LIR .... Line Integral Refractometer
LIR .... Lionair SA [*Luxembourg*] [*ICAO designator*] (FAAC)
lir .... Lira [*Monetary unit*] [*Italy*]
lir .... Lithuanian Soviet Socialist Republic [*MARC country of publication code*] [*Library of Congress*] (LCCP)
LIR .... Load-Indicating Relay (IAA)
LIR .... Load-Indicating Resistor (IAA)
LIR .... Location Inventory Report (AAEL)
LIR .... London Irish Rifles (SAUO)
LIR .... Longitude Independent Reset
LIR .... Lost Item Replacement (MCD)
LIRA .... Lambeg Industrial Research Association [*British*] (IRUK)
LIRA .... Liberal Industrial Relations Association [*British*]
LIRA .... Linen Industry Research Association [*British*] (BI)
LIRA .... Literature Retrieval Agent (SAUO)
LIRA .... Lithospheric Investigation in the Ross Sea Area (SAUO)
LIRA .... Little Italy Restoration Association
LIRA .... Logging Industry Research Association (SAUO)
LIRA .... Low Intensity Reconnaissance Aircraft (SAUS)
LIRA .... Roma/Ciampino [*Italy*] [*ICAO location identifier*] (ICLI)
LIRAD .... Lidar/Radiometer (CARB)
LIRAQ .... Livermore Regional Air Quality Model (SAUO)
LIRB .... Liability Insurance Research Bureau (NTPA)
LIRB .... Vigna Di Valle [*Italy*] [*ICAO location identifier*] (ICLI)
LIRBM .... Liver, Iron, Red Bone Marrow
LIRC .... Centocelle [*Italy*] [*ICAO location identifier*] (ICLI)
LIRC .... Lebanese Information and Research Center (EA)
LIRC .... Leisure Industries Research Centre [*United Kingdom*] (RCD)
LIRC .... Level Indicator Recorder Controller [*Electronics*] (ECII)
LIRC .... Ligue Internationale de la Representation Commerciale [*International League of Commercial Travelers and Agents - ILCTA*] (EAIO)
LIRC .... Louisville & Indiana Railroad [*Federal Railroad Administration identification code*]
LIRC .... Low Interest Rate Currency (MHDW)
LIRD .... Laser & Infra-red Irradiation Detector (SAUS)
LIRDP .... Luangwa Integrated Resource Development Project [*China*] (BUAC)
LIRE .... Lincoln Institute for Research and Education (EA)
LIRE .... Pratica Di Mare [*Italy*] [*ICAO location identifier*] (ICLI)
LIRES .... Literature Retrieval System [*Computer science*]
LIRES-MC .... Literature Retrieval System - Multiple Searching, Complete Text [*Computer science*]
LIRF .... Low-Intensity Reciprocity Failure [*Of photographic emulsions*]
LIRF .... Roma/Fiumicino [*Italy*] [*ICAO location identifier*] (ICLI)
LIRG .... Guidonia [*Italy*] [*ICAO location identifier*] (ICLI)
LIRG .... Landesverband der Israelitischen Religionsgemeinde (BJA)
LIRG .... Library and Information Research Group [*Bristol Polytechnic Library*] [*British*] [*Information service or system*] (IID)
LIRH .... Frosinone [*Italy*] [*ICAO location identifier*] (ICLI)
LIRI .... Leather Industries Research Institute [*South Africa*] (BUAC)
LIRI .... Licentiate of the Institution of the Rubber Industry (SAUO)
LIRI .... Salerno/Pontecagnano [*Italy*] [*ICAO location identifier*] (ICLI)
LIRIC .... Language Instruction for Recent Immigrants through Computer Technology (EDAC)
LIRJ .... Marina Di Campo [*Italy*] [*ICAO location identifier*] (ICLI)
LIRK .... Monte Terminillo [*Italy*] [*ICAO location identifier*] (ICLI)
LIRL .... Latina [*Italy*] [*ICAO location identifier*] (ICLI)
LIRL .... Low Intensity Runway Edge Lights [*FAA*] (TAG)
LIRL .... Low-Intensity Runway Lighting
LIRLY .... Load-Indicating Relay (MSA)
LIRM .... Grazzanise [*Italy*] [*ICAO location identifier*] (ICLI)
LIRMA .... London Insurance and Reinsurance Market Association (ECON)
LIRN .... Library and Information for the Northwest [*Program of the Fred Meyer Charitable Trust*]
LIRN .... Library and Information Research News [*A publication*] (NITA)
LIRN .... Library Information Enquiry and Referral Network (TELE)
LIRN .... Napoli/Capodichino [*Italy*] [*ICAO location identifier*] (ICLI)
LIROC .... Last Instruction Readout Cycle (IAA)
LIROD .... Lightweight Radar Optronic Director (SAUS)
LIRP .... Pisa [*Italy*] [*ICAO location identifier*] (ICLI)
LIRQ .... Firenze [*Italy*] [*ICAO location identifier*] (ICLI)
LIRR .... [*The*] Long Island Rail Road Co.
LIRR .... Luoyang Institute of Refractories Research [*China*] (BUAC)
LIRR .... Roma [*Italy*] [*ICAO location identifier*] (ICLI)
LIRRTP .... Lao-IRRI Rice Research and Training Project (SAUO)
LIRS .... Grosseto [*Italy*] [*ICAO location identifier*] (ICLI)
LIRS .... Lance Information Retrieval System
LIRS .... Laser Inertial Reference System (SAUS)
LIRS .... Legal Information and Reference Services [*General Accounting Office*] (IID)
LIRS .... Level Indicator Recording Switch (NRCH)
LIRS .... Library Information Retrieval Service [*Oregon State University*] [*Information service or system*]
LIRS .... Library Information Retrieval System [*California Institute of Technology*] [*Pasadena, CA*]
LIRS .... Low Impact Resistant Supports [*FAA*] (TAG)
LIRS .... Lutheran Immigration and Refugee Service (EA)
LIRS .... Texto Refundido del Impuesto General sobre la Renta de las Sociedades (SAUO)
LIRSH .... List of Items Requiring Special Handling
LIRT .... Library Instruction Round Table [*American Library Association*]
LIRT .... Low Input Reduced Tillage [*Cropping systems*] (GNE)
LIRT .... Trevico [*Italy*] [*ICAO location identifier*] (ICLI)
LIRTS .... Large Infrared Telescope
LIRU .... Roland [*Intermodal shipping container symbol*] (TVRC)
LIRU .... Roma/Urbe [*Italy*] [*ICAO location identifier*] (ICLI)
LIRV .... Viterbo [*Italy*] [*ICAO location identifier*] (ICLI)
LIRZ .... Perugia [*Italy*] [*ICAO location identifier*] (ICLI)
LIS .... Airlis SA [*Spain*] [*ICAO designator*] (FAAC)
LIS .... Laboratory Information Systems
LIS .... Laboratory Integrated System (ACAE)
LIS .... Land Information System (ACAE)
LIS .... Land Inventory System (SAUO)
LIS .... Landsat Information System (SAUO)
LIS .... Language Implementation System (IAA)
LIS .... Lanthanide-Induced Shift [*Spectroscopy*]
LIS .... Lanthanide-Ion Induced Chemical Shift [*Spectroscopy*]
LIS .... LARC Instruction Simulator
LIS .... Large Interactive Surface [*Automated drafting table that serves as a computer input and output device*]
LIS .... Laser Ignition System [*Military*]
LIS .... LASER Illuminator System
LIS .... LASER-Induced Separation (MCD)
LIS .... LASER Interferometer System
LIS .... LASER Isotope Separation
LIS .... Lateral Intercellular Space (PDAA)
LIS .... Launch Instant Selector
LIS .... Laurentide Ice Sheet [*Climatology*]
LIS .... Left Intercostal Space [*Cardiology*]
LIS .... Legislative Information Service [*New Jersey State Legislature*] [*Trenton*] [*Information service or system*] (IID)
LIS .... Legislative Information System [*Illinois State Legislature*] (IID)
LIS .... Legislative Information System [*National Conference of State Legislatures*] [*Information service or system*] (IID)
LIS .... Lesbian Information Service (BUAC)
LIS .... Libertarian Information Service [*An association*] (EA)
LIS .... Library and Information Science
LIS .... Library and Information Service
LIS .... Library and Information Services [*Institution of Mining and Metallurgy*] [*British*] [*Information service or system*] (IID)
LIS .... Library and Information Systems (SAUO)
LIS .... Library Information System [*Georgetown University*] [*Information service or system*]
LIS .... Libyan Intelligence Service (CARL)
lis .... licensed (SAUS)
LIS .... Licensing Information Service (IID)
LIS .... Licensure Information System [*Public Health Service*] [*Georgetown University Medical Center*] (IID)
LIS .... Light Industries Services [*Singapore*] (BUAC)
LIS .... Light Industry Services (SAUO)
LIS .... Lightning Imaging Sensor (CARB)
LIS .... Line Information Store [*Telecommunications*] (TEL)
LIS .... Line Isolation Switch [*Reactor level switch*] (IEEE)
LIS .... Link Information Sciences (BUR)
LIS .... Liposome Immunosensor [*Electrochemistry*]
LIS .... Lisbon [*Portugal*] [*Airport symbol*] (OAG)
LIS .... Lisbon [*Portugal*] [*Seismograph station code, US Geological Survey*] (SEIS)
LIS .... List and Index Society [*British*] (NITA)
LIS .... Lithium Diodosalicylate [*Organic chemistry*]
LIS .... Lithium Ion Storage (SAUS)
LIS .... LM [*Lunar Module*] Interface Control Specification [*NASA*] (KSC)
LIS .... Load I-Bank and Jump [*Computer science*]
LIS .... Lobular in Situ [*Medicine*]
LIS .... Local Implementation Strategy (SAUO)
LIS .... Local Interface Station (TIMI)
LIS .... Locate in Scotland [*Investment group*] (ECON)
LIS .... Locked-in Syndrome [*Medicine*] (MELL)
LIS .... Lockheed Information Systems (NITA)
LIS .... Logistic Information System (VLIE)
LIS .... Logistics Information System (SAUO)
LIS .... Loop Input Signal
LIS .... Loss Information Service [*Insurance*]
LIS .... Low-Impact Switch (MCD)
LIS .... Low Inductance Stripline (IAA)
LIS .... Low-Intensity Sonication [*Chemistry*]
LIS .... Low Intermittent Suction [*Medicine*] (MEDA)
LIS .... Low Ionic Strength (DB)
LIS .... Lutheran Immigration Service [*Later, LIRS*] (EA)
LIS .... Luxembourg Income Study [*Economics*]
LISA .... Laboratory for Information Science in Agriculture [*Research center*] [*Defunct*] (RCD)
LISA .... Land Information System for Agriculture (SAUO)
LISA .... LARC Instruction Assembly
LISA .... Large Installations Systems Administration (SAUO)
LISA .... Large Installation Systems Administration (VLIE)
LISA .... LASER Indirect Fire Semiactive
LISA .... Laser Interferometer Space Antenna (SAUS)
LISA .... Lateral Integrated Silicon Accelerometer
LISA .... Lead-in-Steel Analyser (PDAA)
LISA .... Leather Industry Suppliers Associates [*British*] (DBA)

LISA .... Leather Industry Suppliers Association (BUAC)
LISA .... Library & Science Abstracts
LISA .... Library Systems Analysis
LISA .... Licht Sammler [*Light Collector*] [*Fluorescent plastic used in commercial displays*] [*German*]
LISA .... Life Insurance Society of America (EA)
LISA .... Linear Systems Analysis
LISA .... Linear Systems Analysis Programme (SAUO)
LISA .... Line Impedance Stabilization Network
LISA .... Linked Indexed Sequential Access
LISA .... Linux Installation & System Administration (SAUS)
LISA .... Locally Integrated Software Architecture [*Apple microcomputer*] [*Computer science*]
LISA .... Logistics Information Systems Analysis (SAUO)
LISA .... London and International School of Acting [*British*]
LISA .... Long Island Schizophrenia Association (SAUO)
LISA .... Low-Input Sustainable Agriculture
LISA .... Seaman Apprentice, Lithographer, Striker [*Navy rating*]
LISAN .... Librarians on the Information Superhighway Advocacy Network (AL)
LISAN .... Libraries on the Information Superhighway Advocacy Network (TELE)
LISARD...... Latest Information Selected and Abstracted for Researchers and Decision-Makers [*Database*]
LISARD...... Library and Information Service Automated Retrieval of Data (NITA)
LISARD...... Library Information Search and Retrieval Data System [*US Navy*] (NITA)
LISARDS.... Library Information Search and Retrieval Data System (VLIE)
LISB .... Lithium Ion Storage Battery (PCM)
LISB .... Long Island Bancorp [*NASDAQ symbol*] (TTSB)
LISB .... Long Island Bancorp, Inc. [*NASDAQ symbol*] (SAG)
LISBMS ..... Laboratory Integrated Standards Based Management System (SAUO)
Lisbon Union... Union for the Protection of Appellations of Origin and their International Registration (SAUO)
LISB PAC ... Long Island Savings Bank FSB PAC [*Lake Success, NY*] (PACS)
LISC .... Land Information Strategic Council (SAUO)
LISC .... Land Information System Committee (SAUO)
LISC .... Library and Information Services Council [*British*]
LISC .... Lions International Stamp Club (EA)
LISC .... Local Initiatives Support Corp. (EA)
LISC .... London Institute for the Study of Conflict (SAUO)
LIS/CIV ...... Logistics Information System/Critical Item Visibility Systems (SAUO)
LISCO .... Liberian Iron and Steel Corp. (BUAC)
LISD .... Latest Information Selected and Abstracted for Researchers and Decision-Makers [*Database*]
LISD .... Library and Information Services Division [*National Oceanic and Atmospheric Administration*] (NITA)
LISD .... Liechtenstein Institute on Self-Determination [*Princeton University*] (RCD)
LISD .... Logistics Information Systems Division (SAUO)
LISDOK...... Literaturinformationssystem [*Literature Information System*] [*North Rhine-Westphalia Institute for Air Pollution Control*] [*Information service or system*] (IID)
LISDP .... LOAD [*Low-Altitude Defense*] Interceptor Subsystem Development Plan
LISE .... Laser Integrated Space Experiment (ACAE)
LISE .... Librarians of Institutes and Schools of Education [*British*] (DBA)
LISFA......... Lost in Space Fannish Alliance (EA)
LISFAN...... Lost in Space Fannish Alliance (EA)
LISH .... Last In, Still Here [*Accounting*] (ADA)
LISI .... LASER-Induced Surface Improvement [*Metallurgical engineering*]
LISI .... Library Interface Systems, Inc. [*Information service or system*] (IID)
LISIC .... Library and Information Service to Industry and Commerce (NITA)
LISK .... Liskeard [*Municipal borough in England*]
LISL .... Amsterdam Studies in the Theory and History of Linguistic Science. Series V. Library and Information Sourees in Linguistics (journ.) (SAUS)
LISI .... Library Interface Systems, Incorporated (SAUO)
LISL .... Lislet Foundries [*NCIC trailer make code*]
LISM......... Licentiate, Institute of Sales and Marketing Executives (ADA)
LISM......... Licentiate of Incorporated Society of Musicians (SAUO)
LISM......... Licentiate of the Incorporated Society of Musicians (ROG)
LISM......... Local Interstellar Medium
LISN .... Library Services Network [*Library network*]
LISN .... Line Impedance Stabilization Network
LISN .... Load Impedance Stabilization Network [*Electrical engineering*]
LISN .... Long Island Sports Network [*Cable-television system*]
LISN .... Seaman, Lithographer, Striker [*Navy rating*]
LISNY .... Life Insurance Society of New York (SRA)
LISP .... LASER Isotope Separation Program
LISP .... Library and Information Software Package (PDAA)
LISP .... License Suspended [*Motor vehicle violation driver status code in state of North Dakota*] (MVRD)
LISP .... Lightweight Individual Special Purpose [*Weaponry*]
LISP .... Liquid Injector Spray Pattern (MCD)
LISP .... List-Oriented Processing [*Computer science*] (VLIE)
LISP .... List Processing [*Programming language*] [*Facetious translation: "Lots of Insane, Stupid Parentheses"*] [*Computer science*]
LISP .... List Processor [*Standard programming language*] [*1958*] [*Computer science*]
LISP .... Local Initiatives Support Project (VLIE)
LISP .... Lots of Irritating Superfluous (SAUO)
LISP .... Lots of Isolated Silly Parentheses (SAUS)
LISPA........ Long Island Sound Pilots Association (SAUO)
LISPB........ Lithospheric Seismic Profile in Britain (PDAA)
LISPER...... Limited Speech Recognition (PDAA)
LISPO .... License Suspended-Occupational Permit [*Motor vehicle violation driver status code in state of North Dakota*] (MVRD)
LISPOP...... Laurier Institute for the Study of Public Opinion and Policy [*Wilfrid Laurier University*] [*Canada*] (RCD)
LISR .... Line Information Storage and Retrieval [*Information service or system*] (NITA)
LISRB .... Life Insurance Sales Research Bureau [*Later, LIMRA*]
LISREL ...... Linear Structural Relationships (NITA)
LISREL ...... Popular Cross-Sectional Structural Equation Modeling Program [*Psychology*] (QSUL)
LISRES-A ... Life Stressors and Social Resources Inventory-Adult Form [*Test*] (TMMY)
LISRES-Y ... Life Stressors and Social Resources Inventory Youth-Form [*Test*] (TMMY)
LI SRR ...... Lithuanian Soviet Socialist Republic (SAUO)
LISS .... Laser Illuminator Subsystem (ACAE)
LISS .... Lightweight Integrated Shelter System (DWSG)
LISS .... Linear/Imaging Self-Scanner Sensor (MCD)
LISS .... Linked Intersection Signal System [*Traffic management*]
LISS .... London Institute of Strategic Studies (SAUO)
LISS .... Los-Ionic-Strength Saline Solution [*Medicine*] (MEDA)
LISS .... Low-Ionic-Strength Saline [*Medicine*] (DMAA)
LISSADA .... Library and Information Science Students Attitudes, Demographics, and Aspirations Survey [*American Libraries Association*]
LISST........ Laser In Situ Scattering and Transmissometery (SAUS)
LISST........ Library and Information Scholarship Today [*A publication*]
LIST .... Centre for Living Information Systems Thinking [*Brunel University*] [*United Kingdom*] (RCD)
LIST .... Last In, Still There [*Accounting*]
LIST .... Library and Information Science Trends
LIST .... Library & Information Selective Targeting (WDAA)
LIST .... Library and Information Services, Tees-Side (IEEE)
LIST .... Library and Information Services Today [*A publication*]
LIST .... Library Index Search and Transcribe
LIST .... List-Oriented Interactive Language [*Computer science*] (TIMI)
LIST .... Low Isotonic Strength Titrator
LISTAR ...... Lincoln Information Storage and Associative Retrieval System [*Lincoln Laboratory*] [*Massachusetts Institute of Technology*] (NITA)
LISTAR ...... Lincoln Information Storage and Retrieval [*MIT*]
LISTD......... Licentiate of the Imperial Society of Teachers of Dancing [*British*]
LISTED ...... Library Integrated Systems for Telematics-Based Education (TELE)
LISTEN ...... Low-Income-Schools Teacher Education (SAUO)
LISTS......... Library Information System Time-Sharing
LISTSERV... Apparently, the term is a registered trademark licensed to L-Soft international, Inc. (SAUO)
LISTSERV... List Server [*Computer science*] (VLIE)
LISU .... Library and Information Statistics Unit (AIE)
LISV .... Loyal Independent Sheffield Volunteers [*British military*] (DMA)
LISW .... Licensed Independent Social Worker (ADWA)
LISWG........ Land Interface Sub-Working Group [*NATO*] (NATG)
LIT .... Adams Field [*FAA*] (TAG)
LIT .... Air Littoral [*France*] [*ICAO designator*] (FAAC)
LIT .... Language Imitation Test
LIT .... Language Inventory for Teachers [*Child development test*]
LIT .... Lawrence Institute of Technology [*Later, Lawrence Technological University*]
LIT .... Lead-In Training [*Air Force*] (DOMA)
LIT .... Leukocyte Immunization Therapy [*Medicine*]
LIT .... Librarians Inquiry Terminal (IT)
Lit............ Lietuvos TSR Valstybine Respublikine Biblioteka [*National Library of Lithuania*], Vilnius, Lithuania [*Library symbol*] [*Library of Congress*] (LCLS)
LIT .... Life Insurance Trust (DLA)
LIT .... Light Interface Technology [*Signal transmission*]
LIT .... Light Intratheater Transport [*Air Force*]
LIT .... Light Ion Trough
LIT .... Line Impedance Tester [*Police and security equipment*]
LIT .... Line Insulation Test [*Telecommunications*]
LIT .... Liquid Injection Technique (IEEE)
Lit............ Lire Italiane [*Italian Lire*] [*Monetary unit*]
lit .... Litany (GROV)
LIT .... Liter [*Metric measure of volume*]
LIT .... Literacy
lit .... Literal (ELAL)
LIT .... Literal
lit .... Literally (ELAL)
Lit............ Literary (WA)
LIT .... Literary
Lit............ Literature (AL)
lit .... Literature (WDMC)
LIT .... Literature
LIT .... Lithographer (Cameraman and Platemaker) [*U.S. Navy enlisted rating*] (AUER)
lit .... Lithuanian [*MARC language code*] [*Library of Congress*] (LCCP)
LIT .... Lithuanian Apostolate for Lithuanian Catholics [*Diocesan abbreviation*] (TOCD)
Lit............ Littell's Kentucky Reports [*A publication*] (DLA)
LIT .... Litter (WDAA)
LIT .... Litterae [*Letters*] [*Latin*] (ADA)
LIT .... Little [*Telegraphy*] (PCTE)
Lit............ Little
LIT .... Little Rock [*Arkansas*] [*Airport symbol*] (OAG)
Lit............ Littleton's English Common Pleas Reports [*A publication*] (DLA)
Lit............ Littleton's Tenures [*A publication*] (DLA)

LIT .... Litton Indus [*NYSE symbol*] (TTSB)
LIT .... Litton Industries, Inc. [*NYSE symbol*] (SPSG)
LIT .... Liturgy
LIT .... Load Initial Table [*Computer science*] (ELAL)
LIT .... Local Inclusive Tour (DCTA)
LIT .... Local Income Tax (PDAA)
LIT .... Local Information Transfer (SAUO)
LIT .... Location/Identification Transmitter [*NASA*]
LIT .... Logical Interface Tape (VLIE)
LIT .... London Investment Trust [*British*]
LIT .... Low-Impedance Transmission
LITA .... Library and Information Technology Association (EA)
LITA .... LIbrary and Information Technology Associaton of the ALA (NITA)
LITA .... Local Information Transfer Architecture (SAUO)
LITA .... Low Income Tax Advisors (EARSL)
LITACS ...... Lightweight Integrated Tactical Artillery Command & Control System (SAUO)
LITADLIG ... Library & Information Technology Associaton Distance Learning Interest Group
LITAEPEJIG ... Library & Information Technology Association Electronic Publishing/Electronic Journals Interest Group
LITAETIG ... Library & Information Technology Association Emerging Technologies Interest Group
LITAIRIG ... Library & Information Technology Association Internet Resources Interest Group
LITA/ISAS ... Library and Information Technology Association/Information Science and Automation Section (SAUO)
LITAMUIG ... Library & Information Technology Association Microcomputer Users Interest Group
Lit & Bl Dig ... Littleton and Blatchley's Insurance Digest [*A publication*] (DLA)
LITAOSSIG ... Library & Information Technology Association Open Source Systems Interest Group
LITAS .... Low Intensity Two-Color Approach Slope Indicator [*Aviation*] (DA)
LITASSIG ... Library & Information Technology Association Secure Systems Interest Group
LITASTOR ... Light Tapping Storage (IAA)
LITATIG ...... Library & Information Technology Association Telecommunications Interest Group
LITA/VCCS ... Library and Information Technology Association/Video and Cable Communication-Section (SAUO)
Lit B .... Bachelor of Literature (SAUS)
Lit B .... Litterarum Baccalaureus [*Bachelor of Letters or Literature*] [*Latin*]
LITBIEL ...... Lithuania & Byelorussia (SAUS)
LITBL .... Long Island Talking Book Library (MHID)
Lit Brooke ... Brooke's New Cases, English King's Bench [*1515-58*] [*A publication*] (DLA)
LITC .... Library Information Technology Centre [*British*] (TELE)
LITC .... Little Chum Manufacturing [*NCIC trailer make code*]
LITCA .... International Licensing, Innovation and Technology Consultants Association (SAUO)
LITCA .... Licensing Innovation Technology Consultants Association (BUAC)
LitchFin ..... Litchfield Financial Corp. [*Associated Press*] (SAG)
LITCO .... Lebanese International Trading Company (SAUO)
LITCO .... Lockheed Idaho Technologies Company (SAUO)
LITCO .... Long Island Trust Co. (EFIS)
Lit Crit ...... Literary Criticism (ADWA)
Lit D .... Doctor of Literature (SAUS)
LITD .... Laser-Induced Thermal Desorption
Lit D .... Litterarum Doctor [*Doctor of Letters or Literature*] [*Latin*]
LITD .... Little Dude Trailer Company [*NCIC trailer make code*]
LITDL .... Link-16 Interoperable Tactical Data Link (SAUS)
LitDokAB .... Literaturdokumentation zur Arbeitsmarkt- und Berufsforschung [*Deutsche Bundesanstalt fuer Arbeit*] [*Germany*] [*Information service or system*] (CRD)
LITE .... BMC International Corp. (SAUO)
LITE .... Laptop Imagery Transmission System (SAUS)
LITE .... LASER Illuminator Targeting Equipment
LITE .... Laser Infrared Tracking Experiment (ACAE)
LITE .... LASER In-Space Technology Experiment
LITE .... Legal Information Through Electronics [*Air Force*]
LITE .... Let's Improve Today's Education [*Newsletter*]
LITE .... Lidar In-Space Technology Experiment (EOSA)
LITE .... Vari-Lite International, Inc. [*NASDAQ symbol*] (NASQ)
LITEF .... Litton Technische Werke (EFIS)
Litelfuse .... Littelfuse, Inc. [*Associated Press*] (SAG)
LITES .... Ladies in Technical Electronic Servicing (SAUO)
LITES .... LASER Initiated Transfer Energy Subsystem [*Detonator, developed by US Navy*]
LITES .... LASER Intercept and Technical Exploitation System (MCD)
LITEX .... Searchlight Illumination Exercise [*Also, LIGHTEX*] [*Military*] (NVT)
LITFASS ..... Lindenberg Inhomogeneous Terrain, Fluxes between Atmosphere and Surface (SAUS)
LitfldAd ...... Littlefield, [*Adams*] & Co. [*Associated Press*] (SAG)
Litfse .... Littelfuse, Inc. [*Associated Press*] (SAG)
LITFUND .... Fund for the Relief of Russian Writers and Scientists in Exile (EA)
litg .... Liturgy (VRA)
LITH .... Lithium [*Pharmacy*] (DAVI)
LITH .... Lithograph [*or Lithography*] (ROG)
lith .... Lithograph (WDMC)
lith .... Lithographic (WDMC)
lith .... Lithography (WDMC)
LITH .... Lithuania (ROG)
Lith .... Lithuania (VRA)
LITH .... Lithuanian [*Language, etc.*]
LITH BRO ... Lithium Bromide (DNAB)
LITHD .... Lithographed (ROG)
LITHO .... Lithograph (AABC)
litho .... Lithograph (VRA)
litho .... Lithographic (WDMC)
litho .... Lithography (WDMC)
litho .... Lithotripsy [*Medicine*] (DAVI)
LITHOC ...... Lithographic
lithog .... Lithograph (WDMC)
lithog .... Lithographic (WDMC)
LITHOG ..... Lithographing
lithog .... Lithography (WDMC)
LITHOG ..... Lithography
lithol .... Lithology (BARN)
LITHOR ..... Lithographer
LITHOT ..... Lithotomy [*Medicine*]
LITHOY ..... Lithography
LITHP .... Link Type Description Language for Hypertext Processing [*Computer science*] (VLIE)
LithSSR ..... Lithuanian Soviet Socialist Republic
LITHUAN .... Lithuanian
Lit Hum ..... Literae Humaniores [*Faculty of Classics and Philosophy, Oxford*] [*British*] (WA)
LIT HUM .... Litterae Humaniores [*Classic literature*] [*Latin*] (ROG)
Litig .... Litigation [*A publication*] (DLA)
LITIGON ..... Litigation (ROG)
LITINT .... Literacy International
LITINT .... Literature Intelligence (MCD)
LITIR .... Literary Information and Retrieval [*Computer science*]
LITIR .... Literature Information and Retrieval [*Database on Victorian studies literature*] [*University of Alberta*] [*Canada*] (NITA)
LIT-LIT ...... Committee on World Literacy and Christian Literature [*Later, Intermedia*] (EA)
LITM .... London International Trade Market (SAUO)
Lit M .... Master of Literature
LitMo .... Liturgie und Moenchtum [*A publication*] (BJA)
LITON .... Littleton, CO [*American Association of Railroads railroad junction routing code*]
LITP .... Ley del Impuesto sobre Transmisiones Patrimoniales y Actos Jur!dicos Documentados (SAUO)
LITP .... Little Prince Travel Trailer [*NCIC trailer make code*]
LITPrB .... Litton Indus,$2 B Pfd [*NYSE symbol*] (TTSB)
Litprog ...... Literate Programming [*Computer science*] (VLIE)
LITR .... Low-Cost Indirect-Fire Training Round [*Army*] (INF)
LITR .... Low-Intensity Test Reactor [*ORNL*]
LITRO .... Little Rock, AR [*American Association of Railroads railroad junction routing code*]
LITRONIC ... Light Electronic [*Automotive engineering*]
LITS .... Laboratory for Information Transmission Systems (SAUO)
LITS .... Laboratory Information Tracking System
LITS .... Lighted Infantry Telescope System [*Police and security equipment*]
LITS .... Light Interface Technology System (SAUO)
LITS .... Litigation Support System (EAGT)
LITS .... Little Sport Enterprises [*NCIC trailer make code*]
LITS .... Local Information Transfer System (SAUO)
LITS .... Logistics Information Technology Strategy (SAUO)
Lit Sel Ca ... Littell's Select Kentucky Cases [*A publication*] (DLA)
LITSUR ...... Litigation Survey System (SAUO)
LITT .... Laser-Induced Thermography [*Medicine*] (RAWO)
Litt .... Littell's Kentucky Supreme Court Reports [*1822-24*] [*A publication*] (DLA)
LITT .... Litterateur [*French*] (ROG)
LITT .... Littleford Brothers [*NCIC trailer make code*]
Litt .... Littleton's English Common Pleas Reports [*A publication*] (DLA)
Litt & S St Law ... Littell and Swigert's Digest of Statute Law [*Kentucky*] [*A publication*] (DLA)
LittB .... Bachelor of Letters or Literature (SAUO)
Litt B .... Litterarum Baccalaureus [*Bachelor of Letters or Literature*] [*Latin*]
Litt Comp Laws ... Littell's Statute Law [*Kentucky*] [*A publication*] (DLA)
LittD .... Doctor of Letters (SAUO)
LittD .... Doctor of Literature (SAUO)
Litt D .... Litterarum Doctor [*Doctor of Letters or Literature*] [*Latin*]
LittD(Econ) ... Doctor of Letters in Economic Studies (ADA)
Littell .... Littell's Kentucky Reports [*A publication*] (DLA)
LittHD .... Doctor of Hebrew Letters (BJA)
Litt (KY) ..... Littell [*Kentucky*] [*A publication*] (DLA)
Litt L .... Licentiate in Letters
Little Brooke ... Brooke's New Cases, English King's Bench [*1515-58*] [*A publication*] (DLA)
Littleton ..... Littleton's English Common Pleas and Exchequer Reports [*A publication*] (DLA)
Litt M .... Master of Letters
Litton .... Litton Industries, Inc. [*Associated Press*] (SAG)
Litt Rep ..... Littleton's English Common Pleas and Exchequer Reports [*A publication*] (DLA)
LITTS .... Large Inventory Top-Tier Site [*Industrial hazard designation*] [*British*]
Litt Sel Cas ... Littell's Select Kentucky Cases [*A publication*] (DLA)
LITTT .... Luoyang Institute of Tracking and Telecommunication Technology [*China*] (BUAC)
Litt Ten ...... Littleton's Tenures [*A publication*] (DLA)
LITTY .... Libraries of Idaho Teletype Network - Academics [*Library network*]
LITU .... Liral Trading International [*Intermodal shipping container symbol*] (TVRC)
Litur Arts ... Liturgical Arts. Liturgical Arts Society. Concord, New Hampshire (SAUO)
Liturg .... Liturgical (DIAR)

LITURG...... Liturgies (ROG)
LITVC........ Liquid Injection Thrust Vector Control
LITW........ Longitudinally in Homogeneous Traveling Waves (MCD)
LITZ.......... Litzendraht [*Wire*] [*German*]
LIU........... LAN Interface Unit (SAUS)
LIU........... Launcher Interface Unit (SAUS)
LIU........... Library and Information Unit
LIU........... Line Interface Unit [*Data communications*]
LIU........... Line Isolation Unit [*Electronics*]
LIU........... Link Interface Unit [*Telecommunications*] (ECII)
LIU........... Littlefield, TX [*Location identifier*] [*FAA*] (FAAL)
LIU........... Long Island University [*Brooklyn, NY*]
LIU........... Wood, Wire, and Metal Lathers' International Union [*Later, UBC*]
LIUNA....... Laborers' International Union of North America (EA)
LIUP......... Long Island University Press (DGA)
Liuski........ Liuski International, Inc. [*Associated Press*] (SAG)
LIV........... Law of Initial Value [*Joseph Wilder*]
LIV........... Left Innominate Vein [*Medicine*] (MAE)
LIV........... Legislative Indexing Vocabulary
LIV........... Light Infantry Volunteers [*Military unit*] [*British*]
LIV........... Linear, Invariant (PDAA)
LIV........... Line Item Value
LIV........... Lived [*or Living*]
LIV........... Livengood, AK [*Location identifier*] [*FAA*] (FAAL)
LIV........... Liver Battery Test [*Gastroenterology*] (DAVI)
LIV........... Livermore, CA [*Amtrak Busline code*]
LIV........... Liverpool (ROG)
Liv........... Liverpool University (SAUO)
LIV........... Living (DAVI)
LIV........... Livingstone Energy [*Vancouver Stock Exchange symbol*]
Liv........... Livingston's Mayor's Court Reports [*New York*] [*A publication*] (DLA)
LIV........... Livorno [*Italy*] [*Seismograph station code, US Geological Survey*] [*Closed*] (SEIS)
LIV........... Livraison [*Delivery*] [*French*]
LIV........... Livre [*Book or Pound*] [*French*]
LIV........... Livy [*Roman historian, c. 10BC*] (ROG)
LIV........... Low-Input Voltage (KSC)
LIV........... Low Investment Vehicle
LIV........... Lunar and Interplanetary Vehicle [*Aerospace*] (AFM)
Liv Ag....... Livermore on Principal and Agent [*A publication*] (DLA)
LIVB......... Passo Del Brennero [*Italy*] [*ICAO location identifier*] (ICLI)
LIV-BP....... Leucine, Isoleucine, and Valine Binding Protein [*Biochemistry*] (DMAA)
LIVC......... Left Inferior Vena Cava [*Medicine*] (EDAA)
LIVC......... Low-Input Voltage Converter
LIVC......... Monte Cimone [*Italy*] [*ICAO location identifier*] (ICLI)
Liv Cas...... Livingston's Cases in Error [*New York*] [*A publication*] (DLA)
LIVCR........ Low-Input Voltage Conversion and Regulation
LIVD......... Dobbiaco [*Italy*] [*ICAO location identifier*] (ICLI)
Liv Dis...... Livermore's Dissertation on the Contrariety of Laws [*A publication*] (DLA)
LIVE......... Laboratory for Image and Video Engineering [*University of Texas at Austin*] (RCD)
LIVE......... Learning through Industry and Voluntary Educators [*Community education program*]
LIVE......... Liquid Inertia Vibration Eliminator (SAUS)
LIVE......... Live Entertainment [*NASDAQ symbol*] (TTSB)
LIVE......... Lunar Impact Vehicle [*NASA*] (KSC)
LIVE......... Passo Resia [*Italy*] [*ICAO location identifier*] (ICLI)
LiveEn....... LIVE Entertainment, Inc. [*Associated Press*] (SAG)
LiveEnt...... LIVE Entertainment, Inc. [*Associated Press*] (SAG)
LIVEN........ Linear Inflammatory Verrucous Epidermal Nevus [*Medicine*] (EDAA)
Livent....... Livent, Inc. [*Associated Press*] (SAG)
LIVEP........ Live Entmt cm Cv'B' Pfd [*NASDAQ symbol*] (TTSB)
Liverm Ag... Livermore on Principal and Agent [*A publication*] (DLA)
Livermore Ag... Livermore on Principal and Agent [*A publication*] (DLA)
LIVEX........ Live Exercise [*Military exercise in which live forces participate*] (NATG)
LIVF......... Frontone [*Italy*] [*ICAO location identifier*] (ICLI)
LIVG......... Monte Grappa [*Italy*] [*ICAO location identifier*] (ICLI)
LIVID........ Language Identification and Voice Identification (SAUS)
Livingston U... Livingston University (GAGS)
Liv Jud Cas... Livingston's Judicial Opinions [*New York*] [*A publication*] (DLA)
Liv Judic Op... Livingston's Judicial Opinions [*New York*] [*A publication*] (DLA)
Liv Jud Op... Livingston's Judicial Opinions [*New York*] [*A publication*] (DLA)
Liv La Cr Code... Livingston's Louisiana Criminal Code [*A publication*] (DLA)
Liv Law Mag... Livingston's Law Magazine [*New York*] [*A publication*] (DLA)
Liv L Mag... Livingston's Law Magazine [*New York*] [*A publication*] (DLA)
Liv L Reg... Livingston's Law Register [*New York*] [*A publication*] (DLA)
LIVM......... Marino Di Ravenna [*Italy*] [*ICAO location identifier*] (ICLI)
LivngCtr..... Living Centers of America, Inc. [*Associated Press*] (SAG)
LIVO......... Tarvisio [*Italy*] [*ICAO location identifier*] (ICLI)
LIVP......... Paganella [*Italy*] [*ICAO location identifier*] (ICLI)
LivPro....... Liver Profile [*Medicine*] (EDAA)
LIVR......... Low-Input Voltage Regulation
LIVR......... Passo Rolle [*Italy*] [*ICAO location identifier*] (ICLI)
liv rm........ Living Room (BARN)
livrm......... Living Room (REAL)
LIVT......... Trieste [*Italy*] [*ICAO location identifier*] (ICLI)
Liv US Pen Co... Livingston's System of United States Penal Codes [*A publication*] (DLA)
LIVV......... Monte Venda [*Italy*] [*ICAO location identifier*] (ICLI)
LIW.......... Letters in Words [*Psychology*]
LIW.......... Lightweight Individual Weapon (PDAA)
LIW.......... Loikaw [*Myanmar*] [*Airport symbol*] (OAG)
LIW.......... Long Instruction Word [*Teraplex*] [*Computer science*]
LIW.......... Loss in Weight
LIW.......... Lyttleton Engineering Works (SAUO)
LIWAP....... Low-Income Weatherization Assistance Program (SAUO)
LIWB........ Livermore Water Boiler [*Nuclear reactor*] [*Dismantled*]
LIWC........ Linguistic Inquiry and Word Count
LIWHA....... Laura Ingalls Wilder Home Association (EARSL)
LIWMS....... Laura Ingalls Wilder Memorial Society (EA)
LIWY........ Li-Way Transfer and Storage [*Common carrier symbol*]
LIX.......... Expired License [*Motor vehicle violation driver status code in state of North Dakota*] (MVRD)
LIX.......... Liquid Crystal (IDOE)
Lix........... Legal Information Exchange [*Computing*] (ODA)
LIXISCOPE... Low-Intensity X-Ray Imaging Scope
LIY.......... Leicestershire Imperial Yeomanry [*British military*] (DMA)
LIY.......... Limay [*Nicaragua*] [*Seismograph station code, US Geological Survey*] (SEIS)
LIYP........ Legacy International Youth Program [*Later, LIYTP*] (EA)
LIYTP....... Legacy International Youth Training Program (EA)
LIYV........ Lettuce Infectious Yellows Virus
LIYW........ Aviano [*Italy*] [*ICAO location identifier*] (ICLI)
LIZ.......... Limestone, ME [*Location identifier*] [*FAA*] (FAAL)
LIZ.......... Lizard (MSA)
LIZ.......... Liz Claiborne [*NYSE symbol*] (TTSB)
LIZ.......... Liz Claiborne, Inc. [*NYSE symbol*] (SAG)
LIZARDS.... Library Information Search and Retrieval Data System (IEEE)
Lizars....... Lizar's Scotch Exchequer Cases [*A publication*] (DLA)
LIZC........ Liz Claiborne, Inc. (SAUO)
LizClab...... Claiborne [*Liz*], Inc. [*Associated Press*] (SAG)
LIZ EI....... London Initiative Zone Educational Incentives (SAUO)
Liz Sc Exch... Lizar's Scotch Exchequer Cases [*A publication*] (DLA)
LJ........... British Guiana Limited Jurisdiction (Official Gazette) [*1899-1955*] [*A publication*] (DLA)
LJ........... Hall's American Law Journal [*A publication*] (DLA)
LJ........... House of Lords Journals [*England*] [*A publication*] (DLA)
LJ........... Jennings Public Library, Jennings, LA [*Library symbol*] [*Library of Congress*] (LCLS)
LJ........... Joullie [*France*] [*Research code symbol*]
LJ........... Larsen-Johansson [*Disease*] [*Medicine*] (DB)
LJ........... Law Journal Newspaper [*1866-1965*] [*A publication*]
LJ........... Law Judge (DLA)
LJ........... Lawson & Jones Ltd. [*Toronto Stock Exchange symbol*]
LJ........... Left Justified (TIMI)
LJ........... Lennard-Jones [*Physical chemistry*]
LJ........... Library Journal [*A publication*] (BRI)
LJ........... Life Jacket
LJ........... Limited Partner in Jobbers Firm [*London Stock Exchange*]
LJ........... Line Judge [*Football*]
LJ........... Little Joe [*Early developmental spacecraft*] [*NASA*]
LJ........... Little John [*Rocket*] [*Military*] (AABC)
LJ........... Lockjaw (MELL)
LJ........... Long Jump
LJ........... Lord Justice
L-J.......... Lowenstein-Jensen [*Growth medium*]
LJ........... Lower Canada Law Journal [*A publication*] (DLA)
LJ........... Ohio State Law Journal (SAUS)
LJ........... Sierra Leone Airways [*ICAO designator*] (AD)
LJ........... University of California, San Diego, La Jolla (SAUO)
LJA.......... Lady Jockeys Association [*British*] (DBA)
LJA.......... Lodja [*Zaire*] [*Airport symbol*] (OAG)
LJA.......... London Jute Association [*England*] (BUAC)
LJA.......... Lord Justice of Appeal
L JaD........ Dixon Correctional Institute, Jackson (SAUS)
LJaD......... Dixon Correctional Institute, Jackson, LA [*Library symbol*] [*Library of Congress*] (LCLS)
LJ Adm...... Law Journal, New Series, Admiralty [*A publication*] (DLA)
LJ Adm NS... Law Journal Reports, Admiralty, New Series [*1865-75*] [*A publication*] (DLA)
LJ Adm NS (Eng)... Law Journal Reports, New Series, Admiralty [*England*] [*A publication*] (DLA)
LJ App....... Law Journal Reports, New Series, Appeals [*A publication*] (DLA)
LJ Bank...... Law Journal Reports, Bankruptcy [*A publication*] (DLA)
LJ Bank NS... Law Journal Reports, New Series, Bankruptcy [*A publication*] (DLA)
LJ Bankr..... Law Journal Reports, Bankruptcy [*A publication*] (DLA)
LJ Bankr NS (Eng)... Law Journal Reports, New Series, Bankruptcy [*England*] [*A publication*] (DLA)
LJ Bcy....... Law Journal Reports, New Series, Bankruptcy [*A publication*] (DLA)
LJBF......... Let's Just Be Friends [*Online dialog*]
LJ Bk........ Law Journal Reports, Bankruptcy [*A publication*] (DLA)
LJC.......... Lackawanna Junior College (SAUO)
LJC.......... La Jolla [*California*] [*Seismograph station code, US Geological Survey*] [*Closed*] (SEIS)
LJC.......... La Jolla Bancorp [*AMEX symbol*] (COMM)
LJC.......... Lamar Junior College (SAUO)
LJC.......... Laredo Junior College [*Texas*]
LJC.......... Lasell Junior College [*Newton, MA*]
LJC.......... Law Journal Reports, New Series, Common Pleas [*England*] [*A publication*] (DLA)
LJC.......... Lees Junior College [*Jackson, KY*]
LJC.......... Lincoln Junior College (SAUO)
LJC.......... London Joint Committee on Graduate and Student Engineers (SAUO)
LJC.......... London Juvenile Court (DAS)

LJC .... Lord Jesus Christ (ROG)
LJC .... Loretto Junior College [*Kentucky*]
LJC .... Louisville, KY [*Location identifier*] [*FAA*] (FAAL)
LJCBDP ..... Local Joint Control Boards for Dock Pilots (SAUO)
LJCC......... Law Journal, County Courts Reporter [*A publication*] (DLA)
LJCC......... Local Joint Consultative Committee [*British*] (DCTA)
LJCCA .... Law Journal Newspaper, County Court Appeals [*England*] [*A publication*] (DLA)
LJCCR .... Law Journal Reports, New Series, Crown Cases Reserved [*England*] [*A publication*] (DLA)
LJCCR (NS)... Law Journal Reports, New Series, Crown Cases Reserved [*England*] [*A publication*] (DLA)
LJ Ch .... Law Journal Reports, New Series, Chancery [*A publication*] (DLA)
LJ Ch (Eng)... Law Journal Reports, New Series, Chancery [*England*] [*A publication*] (DLA)
LJ Ch NS (Eng)... Law Journal Reports, New Series, Chancery [*England*] [*A publication*] (DLA)
LJ Ch (OS)... Law Journal Reports, Chancery, Old Series [*1822-31*] [*England*] [*A publication*] (DLA)
LJCP......... Law Journal Reports, Common Pleas Decisions [*England*] [*A publication*] (DLA)
LJCPD....... Law Journal Reports, Common Pleas Decisions [*England*] [*A publication*] (DLA)
LJCP (Eng)... Law Journal Reports, Common Pleas Decisions [*England*] [*A publication*] (DLA)
LJCP NS .... Law Journal Reports, Common Pleas Decisions, New Series [*1831-75*] [*A publication*] (DLA)
LJCP NS (Eng)... Law Journal Reports, Common Pleas, New Series [*England*] [*A publication*] (DLA)
LJCP (OS) .. Law Journal Reports, Common Pleas, Old Series [*England*] [*A publication*] (DLA)
LJCRF .... La Jolla Cancer Research Foundation [*Research center*] (RCD)
LJCS......... Lord Justice Clerk of Scotland (DAS)
LJD .... Doctor of Letters of Journalism
LJD & M.... Law Journal Reports, New Series, Divorce and Matrimonial [*England*] [*A publication*] (DLA)
LJDFC .... Lacy J. Dalton Fan Club (EA)
LJE.......... Local Job Entry
LJ Ecc .... Law Journal Reports, New Series, Ecclesiastical Cases [*A publication*] (DLA)
LJ Eccl ...... Law Journal Reports, New Series, Ecclesiastical Cases [*A publication*] (DLA)
LJED......... Large Jet Engine Department [*NASA*] (KSC)
LJeL......... LaSalle Parish Library, Jena, LA [*Library symbol*] [*Library of Congress*] (LCLS)
LJ Eq .... Law Journal Reports, Chancery, New Series [*1831-1946*] [*A publication*] (DLA)
LJEWU ...... Lanka Jatika Estate Workers' Union [*Ceylon National Estate Workers' Union*]
LJ Ex .... Law Journal Reports, New Series, Exchequer Division [*England*] [*A publication*] (DLA)
LJ Exch ..... Law Journal Reports, New Series, Exchequer Division [*England*] [*A publication*] (DLA)
LJ Exch (Eng)... Law Journal Reports, New Series, Exchequer Division [*England*] [*A publication*] (DLA)
LJ Exch in Eq (Eng)... English Law Journal. Exchequer in Equity [*A publication*] (DLA)
LJ Exch NS... Law Journal Reports, New Series, Exchequer [*1831-75*] [*A publication*] (DLA)
LJ Exch NS (Eng)... Law Journal Reports, New Series, Exchequer Division [*England*] [*A publication*] (DLA)
LJ Exch (OS)... Law Journal Reports, Exchequer, Old Series [*A publication*] (DLA)
LJ Ex D ..... Law Journal Reports, New Series, Exchequer Division [*England*] [*A publication*] (DLA)
LJ Ex Eq .... Law Journal, Exchequer in Equity [*England*] [*A publication*] (DLA)
LJFC......... Leon Jordan Fan Club (EA)
LJG .... Leading Jewelers Guild (NTPA)
LJG .... Levend Joods Geloof (Liberaal Joodse Gemeente) (BJA)
LJG .... Lord Justice General [*British*]
LjGI......... TIGR [*The Institute of Genomic Research*] Lotus japonicus Gene Index [*Database*] (GDD)
LJHL......... Law Journal Reports, New Series, House of Lords [*England*] [*A publication*] (DLA)
LJI .... Laiyolo [*Language symbol*] (ETLW)
LJI .... Legal Journals Index [*Information service or system*] (IID)
LJI .... Library of Jewish Information (BJA)
LJI .... List of Journals Indexed (DMAA)
LJI .... List of Journals Indexed in Index Medicus (SAUO)
LJIF......... Ludmila Jivkova International Foundation (SAUO)
LJIFS .... Law Journal, Irish Free State [*1931-32*] [*A publication*] (DLA)
LJ Ir .... Law Journal, Irish [*1933-34*] [*A publication*] (DLA)
LJJ.......... Jefferson Davis Parish Library, Jennings, LA [*Library symbol*] [*Library of Congress*] (LCLS)
LJJ.......... Long Josephson Junction (ACAE)
LJJ.......... Lords Justices
LJK .... Ashland, VA [*Location identifier*] [*FAA*] (FAAL)
LJKB......... Law Journal Reports, King's Bench [*A publication*] (DLA)
LJKB (Eng)... Law Journal Reports, King's Bench [*England*] [*A publication*] (DLA)
LJKB NS .... Law Journal Reports, King's Bench, New Series [*A publication*] (DLA)
LJKB NS (Eng)... Law Journal Reports, King's Bench, New Series [*England*] [*A publication*] (DLA)
LJKB OS .... Law Journal, King's Bench, Old Series [*England*] [*A publication*] (DLA)
LJL.......... Lateral Joint Line [*Orthopedics*] (DAVI)
LJL.......... Little John Launcher [*Military*]
LJLB......... LJL BioSystems, Inc. [*NASDAQ symbol*] (NASQ)
LJLC......... Law Journal (Lower Canada) [*A publication*] (DLA)
LJLT......... Law Journal (Law Tracts) [*England*] [*A publication*] (DLA)
LJLV .... Little Joe Launch Vehicle [*NASA*]
LJM.......... Limited Joint Mobility [*Medicine*] (DMAA)
LJM.......... Lowenstein-Jensen Growth Medium (MAE)
LJ Mag...... Law Journal, New Series, Common Law, Magistrates Cases (Discontinued) [*A publication*] (DLA)
LJ Mag Cas... Law Journal Reports, Magistrates' Cases [*1822-31*] [*A publication*] (DLA)
LJ Mag Cas (Eng)... Law Journal Reports, Magistrates' Cases [*England*] [*A publication*] (DLA)
LJ Mag Cas NS... Law Journal Reports, Magistrates' Cases, New Series [*1831-96*] [*A publication*] (DLA)
LJ Mag Cas NS (Eng)... Law Journal Reports, Magistrates' Cases, New Series [*England*] [*A publication*] (DLA)
LJM & W ... Morgan and Williams' Law Journal [*London*] [*A publication*] (DLA)
LJ Mat ...... Law Journal, Matrimonial [*England*] [*A publication*] (DLA)
LJ Mat Cas... Law Journal, New Series, Divorce and Matrimonial [*England*] [*A publication*] (DLA)
LJ Mat (Eng)... Law Journal, Matrimonial [*England*] [*A publication*] (DLA)
LJMC........ Law Journal Reports, New Series, Magistrates' Cases [*England*] [*A publication*] (DLA)
LJMCA ...... La Jolla Museum of Contemporary Art (SAUO)
LJM Cas .... Law Journal Reports, New Series, Magistrates' Cases [*England*] [*A publication*] (DLA)
LJMCOS..... Law Journal Reports, Old Series, Magistrates' Cases [*England*] [*A publication*] (DLA)
LJMPA....... Law Journal Reports, Matrimonial, Probate, and Admiralty [*England*] [*A publication*] (DLA)
LJMX .... LJ Laplace [*Private rail car owner code*]
LJN .... Lake Jackson [*Texas*] [*Airport symbol*] (OAG)
LJNC......... Law Journal, Notes of Cases [*A publication*] (DLA)
LJNCCA ..... Law Journal Newspaper, County Court Appeals [*England*] [*A publication*] (DLA)
LJNCCR ..... Law Journal Newspaper, County Court Reports [*England*] [*A publication*] (DLA)
LJNC (Eng)... Law Journal, Notes of Cases [*England*] [*A publication*] (DLA)
LJ News .... Law Journal Newspaper [*1866-1965*] [*A publication*] (DLA)
LJ News (Eng)... Law Journal Newspaper [*England*] [*A publication*] (DLA)
LJ Newsp ... Law Journal Newspaper [*1866-1965*] [*A publication*] (DLA)
LJ NS........ Law Journal, New Series [*England*] [*A publication*] (DLA)
LJo.......... Jackson Parish Library, Jonesboro, LA [*Library symbol*] [*Library of Congress*] (LCLS)
L Jo.......... Law Journal Newspaper [*England*] [*A publication*] (DLA)
LJ of the Marut Bunnag Internat L Off... Law Journal. Marut Bunnag International Law Office [*A publication*] (DLA)
L Jo NC ..... Law Journal, Notes of Cases [*England*] [*A publication*] (DLA)
LJ OS........ Law Journal, Old Series [*1822-31*] [*London*] [*A publication*] (DLA)
LJ OS Ch ... Law Journal, Old Series, Chancery [*1822-23*] [*A publication*] (DLA)
LJ OS CP ... Law Journal, Old Series, Common Pleas [*1822-31*] [*A publication*] (DLA)
LJ OS Ex.... Law Journal, Old Series, Exchequer [*1830-31*] [*A publication*] (DLA)
LJ OS KB ... Law Journal, Old Series, King's Bench [*1822-31*] [*A publication*] (DLA)
LJOSMC..... Law Journal, Old Series, Magistrates' Cases [*1826-31*] [*A publication*] (ILCA)
LJP .... Law Journal Reports, New Series, Privy Council [*England*] [*A publication*] (DLA)
LJP .... Law Journal Reports, Probate, Divorce, and Admiralty [*England*] [*A publication*] (DLA)
LJP .... Liquid Junction Potential
LJP .... Localized Juvenile Periodontitis [*Dentistry*]
LJP .... Local Job Processing (IAA)
LJP & M.... Law Journal, Probate and Matrimonial [*England*] [*A publication*] (DLA)
LJPC......... La Jolla Pharmaceutical [*NASDAQ symbol*] (SAG)
LJPC......... Law Journal Reports, Privy Council [*England*] [*A publication*] (DLA)
LJ PC (Eng)... Law Journal Reports, Privy Council [*England*] [*A publication*] (DLA)
LJ PC NS ... Law Journal Reports, New Series, Privy Council [*England*] [*A publication*] (DLA)
LJPCW ...... La Jolla Pharmaceutical Wrrt [*NASDAQ symbol*] (TTSB)
LJPD & A... Law Journal Reports, New Series, Probate, Divorce, and Admiralty [*1875-1946*] [*A publication*] (DLA)
LJPD & Adm... Law Journal Reports, New Series, Probate, Divorce, and Admiralty [*England*] [*A publication*] (DLA)
LJPM & A... Law Journal Reports, New Series, Probate, Matrimonial, and Admiralty [*England*] [*A publication*] (DLA)
LJ Prob ..... Law Journal Reports, New Series, Probate and Matrimonial [*1858-59, 1866-75*] [*A publication*] (DLA)
LJ Prob & Mat... Law Journal, Probate and Matrimonial [*England*] [*A publication*] (DLA)
LJ Prob (Eng)... Law Journal, Probate and Matrimonial [*England*] [*A publication*] (DLA)
LJ Prob NS... Law Journal Reports, New Series, Probate and Matrimonial [*1858-59, 1866-75*] [*A publication*] (DLA)
LJ Prob NS (Eng)... Law Journal, Probate and Matrimonial, New Series [*England*] [*A publication*] (DLA)
LJQB......... Law Journal Reports, New Series, Queen's Bench [*England*] [*A publication*] (DLA)
LJQBD....... Law Journal Reports, New Series, Queen's Bench Division [*England*] [*A publication*] (DLA)
LJQBD NS... Law Journal Reports, New Series, Queen's Bench Division [*England*] [*A publication*] (DLA)
LJQB (Eng)... Law Journal Reports, New Series, Queen's Bench [*England*] [*A publication*] (DLA)

LJQB NS .... Law Journal Reports, New Series, Queen's Bench [*1831-1946*] [*A publication*] (DLA)
LJQB NS (Eng)... Law Journal Reports, Queen's Bench, New Series [*England*] [*A publication*] (DLA)
LJR .... Larkana-Jacobabad Railway [*Indian Railway*] (TIR)
LJR .... Law Journal Reports [*A publication*]
LJR .... Lead Joint Runner
LJR .... Little John Rocket [*Military*]
LJR .... Lone Jack Resources Ltd. [*Vancouver Stock Exchange symbol*]
LJR .... Low Jet Route (ADA)
LJR (Eng)... Law Journal Reports [*England*] [*A publication*] (DLA)
LJ Rep ...... Law Journal Reports [*A publication*] (DLA)
LJ Rep NS... Law Journal Reports, New Series [*A publication*] (DLA)
LJRTC .... London Joint Road Transport Council (SAUO)
LJS .... Lap Joint Strength
LJS .... Lithuanian Journalists' Society (BUAC)
LJSI.......... L.J. Simone, Inc. [*NASDAQ symbol*] (COMM)
LJ Sm .... Smith's Law Journal [*London*] [*A publication*] (DLA)
LJST .... Library of Japanese Science and Technology [*England*] (BUAC)
LJSU......... Local Junction Switching Unit [*Telecommunications*] (TEL)
LJTSA .... Library of the Jewish Theological Seminary of America (SAUO)
LJU .... La Jolla University (SAUO)
LJU .... Lithuanian Journalists' Union (BUAC)
LJU .... Ljubljana [*Slovenia*] [*Airport symbol*] (OAG)
LJU .... Ljubljana [*Slovenia*] [*Seismograph station code, US Geological Survey*] (SEIS)
LJU .... Oscoda, MI [*Location identifier*] [*FAA*] (FAAL)
LJUC......... Law Journal of Upper Canada [*A publication*] (DLA)
LJV .... Louisville-Jeffersonville, IN [*Amtrak rail station code*]
LJWG........ Logistic Joint Work Group [*DoD*]
LJZ........... Lajes [*Brazil*] [*Airport symbol*] (AD)
LK............ Arawak Airlines (OAG)
LK............ Laiko Komma [*Populist Party*] [*Greece*] [*Political party*] (PPE)
Lk............ Lake (SHCU)
LK............ Lake
LK............ Lamellar Keratoplasty [*Medicine*] (MELL)
LK............ Landry-Kussmaul [*Syndrome*] [*Medicine*] (DB)
LK............ Leak (KSC)
LK............ Left Kidney [*Medicine*]
LK............ Lek [*Monetary unit*] [*Albania*]
Lk............ Leptosphaeria korrea [*A fungus*]
LK............ Letaba Airways [*ICAO designator*] (AD)
LK............ Lichenoid Keratosis [*Medicine*] (DMAA)
LK............ Liederkranz [*Type of cheese*] (BJA)
LK............ Like [*Telegraphy*] (PCTE)
L-K.......... Linguistic-Kinesic [*Psychiatry*]
LK............ Link (KSC)
Lk............ Linking Number [*Molecular biology*] (QSUL)
LK............ Lock [*Automotive engineering*]
LK............ Lockheed Aircraft Corp. (SAUO)
LK............ Lockheed Corp. (SAUO)
LK............ Loehr-Kindberg [*Syndrome*] [*Medicine*] (DB)
LK............ Looking for Party [*Telecommunications*] (TEL)
LK............ Lord Keeper [*of the Great Seal*] [*British*] (ROG)
LK............ Lowenfeld Kaleidoblocs [*Psychological testing*]
LK............ Low-Priority Key [*Computer science*]
LK............ Lucas Air Societies (SAUO)
Lk............ Luke [*New Testament book*]
LK............ Lymphokine [*Immunochemistry*]
LK............ Sri Lanka [*ANSI two-letter standard code*] (CNC)
LK1 .... Ladies' Kayak, Single Person (ADA)
LK2 .... Ladies' Kayak, Two Person (ADA)
LK4 .... Ladies' Kayak, Four Person (ADA)
LKA .... Alkair Flight Operations APS [*Denmark*] [*ICAO designator*] (FAAC)
LKA .... Amphibious Cargo Ship [*Navy symbol*]
LKA .... Attack Cargo Ship [*Navy symbol*]
LKA .... Ladies Kennel Association [*British*] (BI)
LKA .... Larantuka [*Indonesia*] [*Airport symbol*] (OAG)
LKA .... Last Known Address (LAIN)
LKA .... Lazare-Klerman-Armour [*Personality inventory*] (STED)
LKA .... Lighthouse Keepers Association (EA)
LKA .... Literarische Keilschrifttexte aus Assur [*A publication*] (BJA)
LKA .... Miraloma, CA [*Location identifier*] [*FAA*] (FAAL)
LKA .... Sri Lanka [*ANSI three-letter standard code*] (CNC)
LKAA .... Ladies Kennel Association of America (EA)
LKAA .... Praha [*Former Czechoslovakia*] [*ICAO location identifier*] (ICLI)
LKAAAN..... Annual Report. Laboratory of Algology (journ.) (SAUS)
LK & PRR... Lahaina-Kaanapali & Pacific Railroad [*Hawaii*]
LK&PRR .... Lahaina-Kaanapali & Pacific Railroad Co. (SAUO)
LKA of A.... Ladies Kennel Association of America (EA)
LKartB....... Landeskartellbehoerde [*Provincial Cartel Authority*] [*German*] (DLA)
LKB .... Lakeba [*Fiji*] [*Airport symbol*] (OAG)
LKB .... Lockwood, Kessler & Bartlett Inc. (SAUO)
LKBB .... Bratislava [*Former Czechoslovakia*] [*ICAO location identifier*] (ICLI)
LKBUT....... Lake Butler, FL [*American Association of Railroads railroad junction routing code*]
LKC .... Lake Chabot [*California*] [*Seismograph station code, US Geological Survey*] (SEIS)
LKC .... Lake Charles [*Diocesan abbreviation*] [*Louisiana*] (TOCD)
LKC .... Lancaster County Library, Lancaster, PA [*OCLC symbol*] (OCLC)
LKC .... Lekana [*Congo*] [*Airport symbol*] (OAG)
Lkc........... Leukocyte (MELL)
LKCHA....... Lake Charles, LA [*American Association of Railroads railroad junction routing code*]
LKCL......... LASER Kit Combination Lock
LKCT......... Lukasik Cartage [*Common carrier symbol*]
LKCY .... Lake City, FL [*American Association of Railroads railroad junction routing code*]
LKD .... Liked [*Telegraphy*] (PCTE)
LKD .... Locked (KSC)
LKDM........ Low K Dielectric Material (AAEL)
LKDP .... Lietuviu Krikscioniu Demokratu Partija [*Lithuanian Christian Democratic Party*] [*Political party*] (PPE)
LKDS .... Farmer's Union/Christian Democratic Union/Latgale/Democratic Party Coalition (Latvia) [*Political party*] (PSAP)
LKED .... Linkage Editor [*Computer science*] (CIST)
LKESTR ..... Leukocyte Esterase (STED)
LKF .... Linear Kalman Filter
LKFN .... Lakeland Financial Corp. [*NASDAQ symbol*] (NASQ)
LKG .... Lake Geneva, WI [*Amtrak rail station code*]
LKG .... League of the Kingdom of God [*Church of England*]
LKG .... Leakage (MSA)
LKG .... Liking [*Telegraphy*] (PCTE)
LKG .... Linking (IAA)
LKG .... Locking (KSC)
LKG .... Looking (MSA)
LKG .... Loop Key Generator (MCD)
LKGABKG ... Leakage and Breakage (IAA)
LKG & BKG... Leakage and Breakage (WDAA)
LKGE .... Linkage (MSA)
LKGR .... Lake Kyle Game Reserve (SAUO)
LKHAR ...... Lake Harbor, FL [*American Association of Railroads railroad junction routing code*]
LKHO .... Holesov [*Former Czechoslovakia*] [*ICAO location identifier*] (ICLI)
LKI .... Duluth, MN [*Location identifier*] [*FAA*] (FAAL)
LKI .... Lazare Kaplan International, Inc. [*AMEX symbol*] (SPSG)
LKI .... Lazare Kaplan Intl [*AMEX symbol*] (TTSB)
LKI .... Loki Gold Corp. [*Vancouver Stock Exchange symbol*]
LKIB .... Bratislava/Ivanka [*Former Czechoslovakia*] [*ICAO location identifier*] (ICLI)
LKID .... Left Kidney [*Anatomy*] (DAVI)
LKJ .... Linton Kwesi Johnson [*British musician*]
LKK .... Kulik Lake, AK [*Location identifier*] [*FAA*] (FAAL)
LKK .... Lake Shore Mines Ltd. [*Toronto Stock Exchange symbol*]
LKK .... Loka Kongresa Komitato (SAUO)
LKKS .... Liver, Kidneys, and Spleen (STED)
LKKV .... Karlovy Vary [*Former Czechoslovakia*] [*ICAO location identifier*] (ICLI)
LKKZ......... Kosice [*Former Czechoslovakia*] [*ICAO location identifier*] (ICLI)
LKL .... Lakeland Aviation [*ICAO designator*] (FAAC)
LKL .... Lakselv [*Norway*] [*Airport symbol*] (OAG)
LKLF......... Lung Kruppel-Like Factor [*Immunology*]
LKLY......... Likely (FAAC)
LKM .... Lafayette, LA [*Location identifier*] [*FAA*] (FAAL)
LKM .... Liver-Kidney Microsomal [*Antibody*] [*Medicine*] (DMAA)
LKM .... Locke Rich Minerals [*Vancouver Stock Exchange symbol*]
LKM .... Low-Key Maintenance
LKM .... Nekempt [*Ethiopia*] [*Airport symbol*] (AD)
LKMT......... Ostrava [*Former Czechoslovakia*] [*ICAO location identifier*] (ICLI)
LKMU........ Lakespan Marine [*Intermodal shipping container symbol*] (TVRC)
LKN.......... Leknes [*Norway*] [*Airport symbol*] (OAG)
LKN.......... Lock-In
LK-NDV ..... Newcastle Disease Virus, L-Kansas Strain
LKNPOS..... Last Known Position (MCD)
LKNPT....... Last Known Port (MCD)
LKNT .... Locknut (MSA)
LKO .... Billings, MT [*Location identifier*] [*FAA*] (FAAL)
LKO .... Lucknow [*India*] [*Airport symbol*] (OAG)
LKP .... Lahaina, Kaanapoli & Pacific [*Federal Railroad Administration identification code*]
LKP .... Lake Placid, NY [*Location identifier*] [*FAA*] (FAAL)
LKP .... Lamellar Keratoplasty [*Ophthalmology*]
LKP .... Landelijke Knokplogen [*Netherlands Regional Action Groups*] [*World War II*]
LKP .... Last Known Position [*Aviation*] (NVT)
LKP .... Liberaalinen Kansanpuolue [*Liberal People's Party*] [*Finland*] [*Political party*] (PPE)
LKP .... Lietuvos Komunisty Partija [*Communist Party of Lithuania*] [*Political party*] (PPE)
LKP .... Local Knowledge Pool (SAUS)
LKPP .... Piestany [*Former Czechoslovakia*] [*ICAO location identifier*] (ICLI)
LKPR .... Praha/Ruzyne [*Former Czechoslovakia*] [*ICAO location identifier*] (ICLI)
LKQ .... Like Kind and Quality (Metal) [*Auto repair*]
LKQCPI...... Licentiate of the King's and Queen's College of Physicians of Ireland
LKR .... Lake Air Helicopters Ltd. [*British*] [*ICAO designator*] (FAAC)
LKR .... Lancaster, SC [*Location identifier*] [*FAA*] (FAAL)
LKR .... Left Knee Right [*Guitar playing*]
LKR .... LK Resources Ltd. [*Toronto Stock Exchange symbol*]
LKR .... Locker (KSC)
LKROT....... Locked Rotor
LKRR .... Little Kanawha River Rail [*Federal Railroad Administration identification code*]
LKRT......... Loyal Knights of the Round Table (EA)
LKS .... Lakes
LKS .... Lakeside Aviation Ltd. [*British*] [*ICAO designator*] (FAAC)
LKS .... Lambda Kappa Sigma (EA)
LKS .... Landau-Kleffer Syndrome [*Medicine*]

LKS .... Landau-Kleffler Syndrome
LKS .... Liberation Kanake Socialiste [*Socialist Kanak Liberation*] [*New Caledonia*] (PD)
LKS .... Likes [*Telegraphy*] (PCTE)
LKS .... Liver, Kidney, Spleen [*Medicine*]
LKS .... Logan-Keck-Stickney [*Method*]
LKS .... Louisville, KY [*Location identifier*] [*FAA*] (FAAL)
LKS .... Lucky 7 Exploration [*Vancouver Stock Exchange symbol*]
LKS .... Lucky Stores, Inc. (SAUO)
LKSB .... Liver, Kidney, Spleen, Bladder [*Medicine*] (DMAA)
LKSCR .... Lockscrew
LKSL .... Sliac [*Former Czechoslovakia*] [*ICAO location identifier*] (ICLI)
LKS NP .... Liver, Kidneys, and Spleen Not Palpable [*On physical examination*] (DAVI)
LKT .... Lakota [*Language symbol*] (ETLW)
LKT .... Locket (ROG)
LKT .... Lookout (MSA)
LKT .... Salmon, ID [*Location identifier*] [*FAA*] (FAAL)
LKTT .... Poprad/Tatry [*Former Czechoslovakia*] [*ICAO location identifier*] (ICLI)
LKTW .... Leek Transfer Company [*Common carrier symbol*]
LKTYP .... Like Type (FAAC)
LKU .... Literarische Keilschrifttexte aus Uruk [*A publication*] (BJA)
LKUP .... Lockup
LKV .... Laked Kanamycin-Vancomycin [*Agar*] [*Microbiology*]
LKV .... Lake Ventures Ltd. [*Vancouver Stock Exchange symbol*]
LKV .... Lakeview, OR [*Location identifier*] [*FAA*] (FAAL)
LKV .... Left Knee Vertical [*Guitar playing*]
LKV .... Lengyel-Kerman-Vargar [*Rating*] [*Psychology*] (DAVI)
LKVL .... Lakeville Motor Express [*Common carrier symbol*]
LKVY .... Lykens Valley Railroad Co. [*AAR code*]
LKW .... Lake Wisdom [*Papua New Guinea*] [*Seismograph station code, US Geological Survey*] (SEIS)
LKW .... Lakewood Mining [*Vancouver Stock Exchange symbol*]
LKW .... Larkana [*Pakistan*] [*Airport symbol*] (AD)
LK/WA .... Lock Washer [*Automotive engineering*]
LKWASH .... Lock Washer [*Automotive engineering*]
LKWD .... Lakewood [*NCIC trailer make code*]
LKWR .... Lackland Western Railroad [*Federal Railroad Administration identification code*]
LKX .... La Pryor, TX [*Location identifier*] [*FAA*] (FAAL)
LKY .... Likely [*Telegraphy*] (PCTE)
LKY .... Lucky Strike Resources [*Vancouver Stock Exchange symbol*]
LKZ .... Letaba Airways [*South Africa*] [*ICAO designator*] (FAAC)
LL .... Aero Lloyd Flugreisen GmbH & Co. KG (SAUO)
LL .... All Is Well [*Search and rescue symbol that can be stamped in sand or snow*]
LL .... Bell-Air [*ICAO designator*] (AD)
LL .... Continuous Light [*Plant physiology*] (QSUL)
LL .... Double-Loop Magnetic Mine Sweep [*Navy*] [*British*]
LL .... International Convention on Load Lines (SAUO)
LL .... Lab. Lafon [*France*] [*Research code symbol*]
LL .... Labor Letter [*Cast Metals Association*] [*A publication*]
LL .... Lamina Lucida [*Dermatology*]
LL .... Land-Line [*Telecommunications*] (TEL)
LL .... Landline [*Aviation*]
LL .... Land Lines (SAUO)
LL .... Land Locomotion Division [*Army Tank-Automotive Command*] [*Warren, MI*]
LL .... Land Locomotion Laboratory [*Army*]
LL .... Landlord [*Legal shorthand*] (LWAP)
LL .... Landsberg [*Lech*] [*German license plate city code*]
LL .... Language Laboratory (SAUO)
ll .... Lapis Lazuli (VRA)
LL .... Large Letter
LL .... Large Light Seeds [*Botany*]
LL .... Large Lymphocyte [*Medicine*]
LL .... Last (ROG)
LL .... Late Latin [*Language, etc.*]
LL .... Latent Lethality [*Radiation casualty criterion*] [*Army*]
LL .... Lateral Lemniscus [*Neuroanatomy*]
LL .... Lateral Line [*Invertebrate zoology*]
LL .... Lateral Lip
L/L .... Latitude/Longitude (IEEE)
LL .... Laugh Lovers (EA)
LL .... Launch and Landing [*NASA*] (NASA)
LL .... Launch Left (MCD)
LL .... Laurentian Life Insurance Co., Inc. [*Toronto Stock Exchange symbol*]
LL .... Law Latin
L-L .... Law Library of Louisiana, New Orleans, LA [*Library symbol*] [*Library of Congress*] (LCLS)
LL .... Law List (ILCA)
LL .... Laws (ROG)
LL .... Laymen's League (EA)
LL .... League (ROG)
LL .... Lean Line (EA)
LL .... Leased Line [*Private telephone or Teletype line*] [*Telecommunications*]
LL .... Lease or Loan
LL .... Leaves [*Bibliography*]
LL .... Lederle Laboratories [*Research code symbol*]
LL .... Left Lateral [*Anatomy*] (DAVI)
LL .... Left Leg (MAE)
LL .... Left Lower [*Medicine*]
LL .... Left Lung [*Medicine*]
LL .... Legal Letter (WDAA)
LL .... Lega Lombarda [*Italy*] [*Political party*] (ECED)
LL .... Leges [*Laws*] [*Latin*]
LL .... Legislative Liaison
LL .... Legum [*Of Laws*] [*Latin*] (ADA)
L/L .... Leigh Light [*British military*] (DMA)
LL .... Lending Library
LL .... Lend-Lease [*Bill*] [*World War II*]
LL .... Lepromatous-Type Leprosy [*Animal pathology*]
LL .... Lessons Learned
LL .... Level Lock (SAUS)
LL .... Lever Lock (MCD)
LL .... Lewandowsky-Lutz [*Syndrome*] [*Medicine*] (DB)
LL .... Liberty Lobby (EA)
L/L .... Library Labels [*Antiquarian book trade*]
LL .... License in Civil Law
LL .... Lighterage Limits
LL .... Light Line [*Military*]
LL .... Light Load (AAG)
LL .... Light Lock
LL .... Light Lorry [*British*]
LL .... Limited Liability [*Finance*]
LL .... Limiting Level
LL .... Lincoln Laboratories (or Laboratory) (SAUO)
LL .... Lincoln Laboratory [*MIT*] (MCD)
LL .... Lincoln Libraries (ACAE)
LL .... Lincoln Library of Essential Information
L/L .... Line for Line [*Typesetting*] (WDMC)
LL .... Line Leg [*Telegraph*] [*Telecommunications*] (TEL)
LL .... Line Link (IAA)
ll .... Lines (WDMC)
LL .... Lines
LL .... Lines Layout (MCD)
L-L .... Line-to-Line (MCD)
LL .... Linking Loader (IAA)
LL .... Link Level [*Telecommunications*]
LL .... Lipoprotein Lipase (DB)
LL .... Liquid Level (ECII)
LL .... Liquid Limit (IEEE)
L/L .... Liquid/Liquid Extraction [*Laboratory procedure*]
LL .... Liquor Law
L-L .... List/Leave (SAUS)
LL .... List of Lights [*Nautical term*] (HRNC)
LL .... Literary Lives [*A publication*]
LL .... Lithic [*Soil biology*] [*Soil phases*] (QSUL)
LL .... Litre (ROG)
LL .... Little League [*Baseball*]
LL .... Live Load
LL .... Load Limiter [*Automotive engineering*]
LL .... Load Line [*Shipping*] (DS)
LL .... Load List (MSA)
LL .... Local Lesion [*Pathology*]
LL .... Local Line [*Telecommunications*]
LL .... Local Linearization
LL .... Local Loopback (MHDB)
LL .... Locator Lists [*Army*]
LL .... Loco Laudato [*In the Place Quoted*] [*Latin*]
LL .... Lodges [*Freemasonry*] (ROG)
LL .... Loft Line (MSA)
LL .... London Library (ODA)
LL .... London Lyceum (SAUO)
LL .... Longest Lobe [*Communications term*] (DCT)
LL .... Long Lead (NASA)
LL .... Long Line [*Telecommunications*] (MCD)
LL .... Loose Leaf
LL .... Lord Lieutenant
LL .... Lords
LL .... Loudness Level
LL .... Lower Laterals [*Botany*]
LL .... Lower Left
LL .... Lower Leg
LL .... Lower Lid [*Ophthalmology*]
LL .... Lower Limb [*Lower edge of sun, moon, etc.*] [*Navigation*]
LL .... Lower Limen [*Psychology*]
LL .... Lower Limit
LL .... Lower Lip [*Anatomy*] (DAVI)
LL .... Lower Lobe [*Medicine*]
LL .... Low Latin [*Language, etc.*]
LL .... Low Level
LL .... Low Load [*Finance*]
LL .... Lumbar Laminectomy [*Medicine*] (IDYL)
LL .... Lumbar Length [*Anatomy*] (DAVI)
LL .... Lunar Landing [*NASA*] (KSC)
LL .... Luther League [*Defunct*] (EA)
LL .... Lutlag [*Limited Company*] [*Norwegian*]
LL .... Lymphoblastic Lymphoma [*Oncology*] (DAVI)
LL .... Lymphoid Leukemia [*Medicine*] (DB)
L/L .... Lymphoma/Leukemia [*Oncology*]
LL .... Lysolecithin [*Biochemistry*]
LL .... Linear-Linear [*Mathematics*] (ODA)
LLA .... Lady Licentiate of Arts [*Scotland*]
LLA .... Lady Literate in Arts [*British*]
LLA .... Lakeland Aviation (SAUO)

LLA .... Language and Literary Agency (SAUO)
LLA .... Latin Liturgy Association (EA)
LLA .... Latitude, Longitude, Altitude (SAUS)
LLA .... Laubach Literacy Action (EA)
LLA .... Leased Line Adapter [*Telecommunications*]
LLA .... Leased Line Adaptor (NITA)
LLA .... Lebanese Library Association (BUAC)
LLA .... Lend-Lease Administration [*Defunct*]
LLA .... Lesotho Liberation Army (PD)
LLA .... Limited Locus Allowed [*Legal*] (ROG)
LLA .... Limiting Lines of Approach [*Navy*] (NVT)
LLA .... Limulus Lysate Assay (DMAA)
LLA .... Link Level Access (SAUO)
LLA .... Literary Landmarks Association (EA)
LLA .... Little Library [*A publication*]
LLA .... Llanada [*California*] [*Seismograph station code, US Geological Survey*] (SEIS)
LLA .... Local Lighthouse Authority (SAUO)
LLA .... Louisiana Library Association (BUAC)
LLA .... Lower Left Abdomen [*Injection Site*]
LLA .... Low-Level Analog (MCD)
LLA .... Low Low Alarm (ECII)
LLA .... Lulea [*Sweden*] [*Airport symbol*] (OAG)
LLA .... Luther League of America [*Later, LL*]
LLA .... Servicio Leo Lopez SA de CV [*Mexico*] [*ICAO designator*] (FAAC)
LLA .... White Lake, LA [*Location identifier*] [*FAA*] (FAAL)
LLAA .... Israel Airports Authority Headquarters [*Israel*] [*ICAO location identifier*] (ICLI)
LLAAII .... Leurs Altesses Imperiales [*Their Imperial Highnesses*] [*French*]
LLAARR .... Leurs Altesses Royales [*Their Royal Highnesses*] [*French*]
LLAB .... Laser Lines [*Common carrier symbol*]
LLABL .... Liberation Academy Bonded Labourers (SAUO)
LLAD .... Ben Gurion [*Israel*] [*ICAO location identifier*] (ICLI)
LLAD .... Linear Log-Analog-to-Digital [*Converter*] [*Medicine*] (EDAA)
LLAD .... Low-Level Air Defence [*Navy*] [*British*]
LLADI .... Low Level Air Defense Interface (SAUS)
LLADS .... Low Level Air Defence System (SAUS)
LLafL .... Lafayette Public Library, Lafayette, LA [*Library symbol*] [*Library of Congress*] (LCLS)
LLafS .... University of Southwestern Louisiana, Lafayette, LA [*Library symbol*] [*Library of Congress*] (LCLS)
LL Alfredi ... Leges Alfredi [*Laws of King Alfred*] [*Latin*] [*A publication*] (DLA)
Llam .... Lumbar Laminectomy [*Medicine*] (DAVI)
LLAMA .... Low-Level Acceleration Measurement Apparatus
LLAN .... Llandaff (ROG)
LL & B ...... Latch, Lock, and Bolt (DAC)
LL&E .... Louisiana Land and Exploration Company (EFIS)
Ll & GTP .... Lloyd and Goold's Irish Chancery Reports Tempore Plunkett [*A publication*] (DLA)
Ll & GT Pl ... Lloyd and Goold's Irish Chancery Reports Tempore Plunkett [*A publication*] (DLA)
Ll & GTS .... Lloyd and Goold's Irish Chancery Reports Tempore Sugden [*1835*] [*A publication*] (DLA)
LL & N ...... Language, Literacy and Numeracy Skills Taskforce [*Australia*]
Ll & W ...... Lloyd and Welsby's English Mercantile Cases [*A publication*] (DLA)
Ll & Wels ... Lloyd and Welsby's English Commercial Cases [*A publication*] (DLA)
LLAP .... LocalTalk Link Access Protocol [*Computer science*] (ACRL)
LLap .... Saint John Parish Library, La Place, LA [*Library symbol*] [*Library of Congress*] (LCLS)
LLAR .... Local Loop Access Ring [*Telecommunications*] (ACRL)
LLAT .... Law Latin
LLAT .... Lawrence Lowery Apperception Test
LLAT .... Left Lateral [*Radiology*] (DAVI)
LLAT .... Lysolecithin-Lecithin Acyltransferase (ADWA)
LL Athelst ... Laws of Athelstan [*A publication*] (DLA)
LLATIS .... Low Light and Thermal Imaging System (PDAA)
LLAW .... Liquid Low Activity Waste [*Nuclear energy*] (NUCP)
LLB .... Bachelor of Laws (DD)
LLB .... Computrac, Inc. [*AMEX symbol*] (SPSG)
LLB .... Lawyers' Law Books [*1977*] [*A publication*] (ILCA)
LLB .... Left Lateral Bending (SAUS)
LLB .... Left Lateral Border [*Medicine*] (DMAA)
LLB .... Left Linebacker (WGA)
LLB .... Legum Baccalaureus [*Bachelor of Laws*] [*Latin*]
LLB .... Line Loop Back [*Telecommunications*] (ITD)
LLB .... Liquor Licensing Board [*Australian Capital Territory*]
LLB .... Little League Baseball (EA)
LLB .... Live Letter-Box (CARL)
LLB .... Lloyd Aereo Boliviano SA [*Bolivia*] [*ICAO designator*] (FAAC)
LLB .... Local Licensing Bench (SAUO)
LLB .... Long Leg Brace [*Orthopedics*]
LLB .... Long Lower Brace (IDYL)
LLB .... Lower Leg Brace [*Medicine*]
LLB .... Luluabourg [*Zaire*] [*Airport symbol*] (AD)
LLBA .... Language and Language Behavior Abstracts [*Sociological Abstracts*] [*Database*] (NITA)
LLBA .... Linguistics and Language Behavior Abstracts (ADWA)
LLBAM .... Lincoln Laboratory Boolean Algebra Minimizer (IAA)
LLBBMA ..... Loose Leaf and Blank Book Manufacturers Association [*Later, ABPM*] (EA)
LLBC .... Liquid Large-Bore Cannon (MCD)
LLBCD .... Left Lower Border of Cardiac Dullness [*Cardiology*]
LLBD .... Meteorological Service [*Israel*] [*ICAO location identifier*] (ICLI)
LLBG .... Tel Aviv/D. Ben Gurion [*Israel*] [*ICAO location identifier*] (ICLI)
LLBO .... Liquor License Board of Ontario (SAUO)
LL brace .... Long Leg Brace (AMHC)
LLBS .... Beersheba/Teyman [*Israel*] [*ICAO location identifier*] (ICLI)
LLBS .... Low-Level Bombsight (NATG)
LLBU .... Lloyd Brasileiro Line [*Intermodal shipping container symbol*] (TVRC)
LL Burgund ... Laws of Burgundians [*A publication*] (DLA)
LLC .... Laboratory Leadership Council (SAUO)
LLC .... Lac Minerals Ltd. (SAUO)
LLc .... Lake Charles Public Library, Lake Charles, LA [*Library symbol*] [*Library of Congress*] (LCLS)
LLC .... Lakeland Library Cooperative [*Library network*]
LLC .... La Lucha Farm [*Costa Rica*] [*Seismograph station code, US Geological Survey*] (SEIS)
LLC .... Lankalink Aircargo (Pvp) Ltd. [*Sri Lanka*] [*FAA designator*] (FAAC)
LLC .... Laparoscopic Laser Cholecystectomy [*Medicine*] (MELL)
LLC .... Law Certificate
LLC .... Left Line Contactor (MCD)
LLC .... Lessons-Learned Committee (SAUO)
LLC .... Lewis Lung Carcinoma [*Medicine*] (DB)
LLC .... Libertarian Law Council (SAUO)
LLC .... Liberty Loan Corp. (EFIS)
LLC .... Library Learning Center (AL)
LLC .... Light Salvage Ship [*Navy symbol*] (VNW)
LLC .... Lightweight Leader Computer [*Army*] (INF)
LLC .... Limited Liability Company
LLC .... Limited Life Component (MCD)
LLC .... Linde Load Control [*Automotive electronics*]
LLC .... Line Land Control (SAUO)
LLC .... Liquid Level Control
LLC .... Liquid Level Controller (ECII)
LLC .... Liquid-Liquid Chromatography
LLC .... Live from the Lost Continent (SAUO)
LLC .... Living Learning Center (SAUO)
LLC .... Local Level Control [*Electronics*]
LLC .... Local Liaison Committee (HEAS)
LLC .... Logical Link Control [*Telecommunications*]
LLC .... Logic Link Control [*Network interfacing*] (NITA)
LLC .... Long Leg Cast [*Orthopedics*]
LLC .... Long-Life Coolant [*Automotive engineering*]
LLC .... Long Lines Coordination (NATG)
LLC .... Long-Linking Carbon
LLC .... Low Level Code (VLIE)
LLC .... Low Liquid Cutoff
LLC .... Loyola University, Career Information Center, New Orleans, LA [*OCLC symbol*] (OCLC)
LLC .... Luneberg Lens Commutator [*Physics*]
LLC .... Lymphocytic Leukemia, Chronic (MAE)
LLC .... Lyotropic Liquid Crystals [*Physical chemistry*]
LLC1 .... Logical Link Control [*Open Systems Interconnection*] (ODAA)
LLC2 .... Logical Link Control Class 2 (SAUO)
LL Canuti R ... Laws of King Canute [*or Knut*] [*A publication*] (DLA)
LLCB .... Long-Link Carbon Tire [*Tire engineering*]
LLcC .... Calcasieu Parish Public Library, Lake Charles, LA [*Library symbol*] [*Library of Congress*] (LCLS)
LLCC .... Leadless Chip Carrier (AAEL)
LLCC .... Long-Leg Cylinder Cast [*Medicine*] (MELL)
LLCCA .... Low Life Cycle Cost Avionics (ACAE)
LLC/CC .... Low Level Code/Continuity Check (VLIE)
Ll CC Pr ..... Lloyd's County Courts Practice [*A publication*] (DLA)
LLCF .... Launch and Landing Computational Facilities [*NASA*] (NASA)
LLCFR .... Lobbyists and Lawyers for Campaign Finance Reform (EA)
LLCLINK .... Logical Layer Control Link [*Computer science*] (VLIE)
LLCM .... Licentiate of the London College of Music [*British*] (DBQ)
LLCM .... Low Level Control Module [*NASA*] (SPST)
LLCM .... Master of Comparative Law (DLA)
LLcM .... McNeese State University, Lake Charles, LA [*Library symbol*] [*Library of Congress*] (LCLS)
LLCM(TD) ... Licentiate of the London College of Music (Teacher's Diploma) [*British*]
LLCO .... Licentiate of the London College of Osteopathy
Ll Comp ..... Lloyd's Compensation for Lands, Etc. [*6th ed.*] [*1895*] [*A publication*] (DLA)
LL COOL J ... Ladies Love Cool James [*Rap recording artist, James Todd Smith*]
LLCS .... Link Level Communications Subsystem [*NCR Corp.*]
LLCS .... Liquid Level Control Switch
LLCS .... Logical Link Control Security [*Computer science*] (VLIE)
LLCS .... Low-Level Compaction Station [*Nuclear energy*] (NRCH)
LLCSC .... Lower Level Computer Software Component
LLCT .... Last Line Control (VLIE)
LLCUNAE ... Law Library of Congress United Association of Employees
LLD .... Deep Laterolog (SAUS)
LLD .... Doctor of Laws (CMD)
LLD .... Lactobacillus Lactis Dorner Factor [*Vitamin B_{12}*] [*Also, APA, APAF, EF*]
LLD .... Lamp Lumen Depreciation
LLD .... Language Learning Disorder
LLD .... LASER Light Detector
LLD .... Laser Locator Designator (ACAE)
LLD .... Late-Life Depression (MELL)
LLD .... Launcher Load Dolly
LLD .... Law and Legal Information Directory [*A publication*]
LLD .... Left Lateral Decubitus [*Muscle*] [*Medicine*] (EDAA)
LLD .... Leg Length Discrepancy [*Orthopedics*] (DAVI)
LLD .... Legum Doctor [*Doctor of Laws*] [*Latin*]

LLD .... Lipid-Lowering Drug (MELL)
LLD .... Live Letter-Drop [*Espionage*]
LLD .... Logic Level Driver [*Computer science*] (MCD)
LLD .... Long-Lasting Depolarization [*Neurophysiology*]
LLD .... Loveland, CO [*Amtrak Busline code*]
LLD .... Lower Level Discriminator (ACAE)
LLD .... Lower Limit of Detection [*Spectrometry*]
LLD .... Lowest Lethal Dose [*Medicine*] (LDT)
LLD .... Low-Level Detector (IEEE)
LLD .... Low-Level Dose [*Nuclear energy*] (NRCH)
LLDB .... Luc Luong Dac Biet [*South Vietnam*]
LLDC .... Lesser Developed Country (SAUO)
LLDCs ...... Least Developed Countries (SAUO)
LLDEF ...... Lambda Legal Defense and Education Fund (EA)
LLDF .... Lactobacillus Lactis Dormer Factor [*Vitamin B12*] (STED)
LLDH .... Liver Lactate Dehydrogenase [*An enzyme*] (DAVI)
LLDL .... Low-Level Differential Logic (IAA)
LLDPE ...... Linear Low-Density Polyethylene [*Plastics technology*]
LLD/R ...... Laser Locator Designator/Rangefinder (ACAE)
LLDR .... Lightweight LASER [*Light Amplification by Stimulated Emission of Radiation*] Designator Range Finder [*DoD*]
LLDS .... Low-Level Weapons Delivery System (MCD)
Llds .... Lloyd's [*Insurance*] (ODA)
LLDT .... Light Light-Duty Truck
LLDT .... Load Local Descriptor Table (VLIE)
LLDV .... Light Light-Duty Vehicle [*Automotive emissions*]
LLDV .... Luc-Luong Dac-Viet [*Vietnamese special forces*]
LLE .... Laboratory for LASER Energetics [*University of Rochester*] [*Research center*]
LLE .... Large Local Exchange [*Telecommunications*] (TEL)
LLE .... Lead Lead Engineer (SAUO)
LLE .... Left Lower Extremity [*Medicine*]
LLE .... Lessons-Learned Evaluation (SAUO)
LLE .... Lightning Loss Exclusion [*Insurance*]
LLE .... Liquid-Liquid Equilibria [*Physical chemistry*]
LLE .... Liquid-Liquid Extraction
LLE .... Load List Element (VLIE)
LLE .... Long Line Effect
LLE .... Long Line Equipment [*Telecommunications*] (TEL)
LLE .... Lower Left Extremity [*Therapy term*] (CTAA)
LLE .... West Bend, WI [*Location identifier*] [*FAA*] (FAAL)
LLEA .... Local Law Enforcement Agency
LLEC .... Long Lake Energy Corporation (SAUO)
LLECR ...... Lessons-Learned Evaluation Condition Report (SAUO)
LL Edw Conf ... Laws of Edward the Confessor [*A publication*] (DLA)
LLEE .... Leurs Eminences [*Their Eminences*] [*French*]
LLEE .... Leurs Excellences [*Their Excellencies*] [*French*]
LLEGO ...... National Latina/o Lesbian, Gay Bisexual and Transgender Organization [*Association*] (EA)
LLEI .... Lincoln Library of Essential Information (SAUO)
LLEIS ...... Lower Level End Item Subdivision [*Army*] (AABC)
LLER .... Lessons-Learned Evaluation Request (SAUO)
LLE Ry ...... LL & E Royalty Trust [*Associated Press*] (SAG)
LLES .... Eyn-Shemer [*Israel*] [*ICAO location identifier*] (ICLI)
LLeS .... Leesville State School, Leesville, LA [*Library symbol*] [*Library of Congress*] (LCLS)
LLET .... Elat/J. Hozman [*Israel*] [*ICAO location identifier*] (ICLI)
L LETT ...... Licentiate of Letters (WDAA)
LLETZ ...... Large Loop Excision of the Transformation Zone [*Medicine*]
LLEU .... Lailon Container Leasing [*Intermodal shipping container symbol*] (TVRC)
LLeV .... Vernon Parish Library, Leesville, LA [*Library symbol*] [*Library of Congress*] (LCLS)
LLF .... Fibrin-Stabilizing Factor [*Hematology*] (DAVI)
LLF .... Lag Line Filter
LLF .... Laki-Lorand Factor [*Factor XIII*] [*Also, FSF*] [*Hematology*]
LLF .... Land Level Facility [*Navy*]
LLF .... Land Loss Fund [*Association*] (EA)
LLF .... Latin American Growth Fd [*NYSE symbol*] (TTSB)
LLF .... Laubach Literacy Fund [*Later, LLI*] (EA)
LLF .... Left Lateral Femoral [*Site of injection*] [*Medicine*]
LLF .... Left Lateral Flexion [*Medicine*] (DMAA)
LLF .... Left Little Finger (SAUS)
LLF .... Lehman Brothers Latin American Growth Fund [*NYSE symbol*] (SAG)
LLF .... Light Loss Factor [*Floodlighting*]
LLF .... Line Link Frame [*Telecommunications*] (TEL)
LLF .... Little League Foundation (EA)
LLF .... Load List File (AFIT)
LLF .... London Liberal Federation (SAUO)
LLF .... Lower Limb Fracture (MELL)
LLF .... Low Layer Functions [*Communications term*] (DCT)
LLF .... Low Level Format (VLIE)
LLFA .... Low-Low Frequency Acoustics (DOMA)
LLFC .... Laryssa Lauret Fan Club (EA)
LLFC .... Loretta Lynn Fan Club (EA)
LLFET ...... Linear-Load Field Effect Transistor [*Electronics*] (PDAA)
LLFM .... Land Line Frequency Modulation (AAG)
LLFM .... Low-Level Flux Monitor [*Nuclear energy*] (NRCH)
LLFPB ...... Linear, Lumped, Finite, Passive, Bilateral
LLG .... Chillagoe [*Australia*] [*Airport symbol*] [*Obsolete*] (OAG)
LLG .... Labour Life Group (BUAC)
LLG .... Landcare Liaison Group (BUAC)
LLG .... Linear Light Guide [*Automotive electronics*]
LLG .... Line-to-Line to Ground (IAA)
LLG .... Logical Language Group [*An association*] (EA)
LLG .... Logical Line Group [*Computer science*] (IBMDP)
LLG .... Loose Lug [*Tire maintenance*]
LLG .... Lower Limb Girdle [*Medicine*] (EDAA)
LLG .... Luggage and Leather Goods Salesmen's Association of America (EA)
LLGA .... Leadless Land Grid Array [*Electronics*] (EECA)
LLGAF ...... Leslie-Lohman Gay Art Foundation (EA)
LLGDS ...... Landlocked and Geographically Disadvantaged States [*Developing countries*]
LLGF .... Leather, Leather Goods, Fur [*Department of Employment*] [*British*]
LLGL .... Low-Level Graphical Language (PDAA)
LLGMA ...... Luggage and Leather Goods Manufacturers of America (EA)
LLGs .... Logical Line Groups (SAUO)
LLGSA ...... Luggage and Leather Goods Salesmen's Association of America (NTPA)
LL-GXT ...... Low-Level Graded Exercise Test [*Cardiology*] (DAVI)
LLH .... Ladies Left Handed
LLH .... Lahore Light Horse [*British military*] (DMA)
LLH .... Library of Literary History [*A publication*]
LLH .... Light Liaison Helicopter (SAUS)
LLH .... Light Lift Helicopter (ACAE)
LLH .... Linked-List Histogrammers (ACAE)
LLH .... Low-Level Heating [*Nuclear energy*] (OA)
LLHA .... Haifa/U. Michaeli [*Israel*] [*ICAO location identifier*] (ICLI)
LL Hen I .... Laws of Henry I [*A publication*] (DLA)
LLHZ .... Herzlia [*Israel*] [*ICAO location identifier*] (ICLI)
LLI .... Lalibella [*Ethiopia*] [*Airport symbol*] (OAG)
LLI .... Language-Based Learning Impairment [*Neurology*]
LLI .... Late Latent Infection [*Medicine*]
LLI .... Latitude and Longitude Indicator
LLI .... Laubach Literacy International (EA)
LLI .... Life Line International (EA)
LLI .... Ligula Length Index
LLI .... Limited Life Item (MCD)
LLI .... Link Layer Interface [*Computer science*] (PCM)
LLI .... Lipari [*Lipari Islands*] [*Seismograph station code, US Geological Survey*] (SEIS)
LLI .... Liquid Level Indicator
LLI .... Logical Link Identifier (ACRL)
LLI .... Longitude and Latitude Indicator
LLI .... Long Lead Item (MUGU)
LLI .... Lord Lieutenant of Ireland
LLI .... Lower Large Intestine (ABAC)
LLI .... Lower Layer Information (SAUO)
LLI .... Low-Level Interface
LLIAC-IV .... Illinois Integrator & Automatic Computer (SAUO)
LLIB .... Load Module Librarian (MHDB)
LLIB .... Rosh Pina/Mahanaim-I. Ben-Yaakov [*Israel*] [*ICAO location identifier*] (ICLI)
LLIBC ...... Lotus Lantern International Buddhist Center [*South Korea*] (EAIO)
LLIC .... Lamar Life Corporation (SAUO)
LLIL .... Long Lead Item List
LLIL .... Long Lead Time Items List (NASA)
LLiLi .... Livingston Parish Library, Livingston, LA [*Library symbol*] [*Library of Congress*] (LCLS)
LL Inse ...... Laws of Ina [*A publication*] (DLA)
LLIT .... Liquid-Like Intermediate Transistory
LLIU .... Launch and Landing Interface Unit (MCD)
LLIV .... Low-Level Input Voltage
LLJ .... Challis, ID [*Location identifier*] [*FAA*] (FAAL)
LLJ .... Lahore Law Journal [*India*] [*A publication*] (DLA)
LLJ .... Lalmonirhat [*Bangladesh*] [*Airport symbol*] (AD)
LLJ .... LaTrobe Library Journal [*A publication*]
LLJ .... Leaf Library of Judaica (SAUO)
LLJ .... Liberation of the Lingonberry Juice (SAUO)
LLJ .... Low-Level Jet [*Marine science*] (OSRA)
LLJJ .... Lords Justices
LLJM .... Ministry of Transport [*Israel*] [*ICAO location identifier*] (ICLI)
Ll Jud Act ... Lloyd's Supreme Court of Judicature Acts [*1875*] [*A publication*] (DLA)
LLK .... Liberator Lake, AK [*Location identifier*] [*FAA*] (FAAL)
LLK .... Little Lake Resources Ltd. [*Vancouver Stock Exchange symbol*]
LLK .... Louis Leakey - Korongo [*Anthropological skull*]
LLL .... L-3 Communications Hldgs. [*NYSE symbol*] (SG)
LLL .... L 3 Communications Corp. [*NYSE symbol*]
LLL .... Labour Left Liaison [*An association*] (BUAC)
LLL .... Lake Lynn Laboratory [*National Institute for Occupational Safety and Health*] (RCD)
LLL .... La Leche League [*Local affiliates of LLLI*] (EA)
LLL .... Land Locomotion Laboratory [*Army*]
LLL .... Last Look Logic (VLIE)
LLL .... Latitude/Longitude Locator (SAUS)
LLL .... Lawrence Livermore Laboratory [*Also, LLNL*] [*University of California*]
LLL .... Lawrence Livermore National Laboratories (SAUO)
LLL .... Lawyers, Layers, and Limos [*Television broadcasting industry*]
LLL .... Left Liver Lobe (STED)
LLL .... Left Lower Eyelid [*Medicine*]
LLL .... Left Lower Leg (STED)
LLL .... Left Lower Lid (MELL)
LLL .... Left Lower Limb [*Anatomy*] (DAVI)
LLL .... Left Lower Lobe [*of lung*] [*Medicine*]
LLL .... Left Lower Lung (STED)
LLL .... Liberal Liberty League (SAUO)

LLL .... Liberte, Liberation, et Liberation Nationale [*French resistance movement*] [*World War II*]
LLL .... Licence en Droit [*Licentiate in Law*] [*French*] (ASC)
LLL .... Licentiate in Laws
LLL .... Light Living Library (EA)
LLL .... Lillooet [*British Columbia*] [*Seismograph station code, US Geological Survey*] [*Closed*] (SEIS)
LLL .... Localized Leishmania Lymphadenitis [*Medicine*] (PALA)
LLL .... Long Lead List (MCD)
LL/L.......... Long Leadtime/Items List
LLL .... Long Line Loiter [*Aircraft*]
LLL .... Loose Leaf Ledger
LLL .... Love's Labour's Lost [*Shakespearean work*]
LLL .... Lower Left Lobe [*Therapy term*] (CTAA)
LLL .... Lower Lip Length [*Medicine*]
LLL .... Low Level Language [*Computer programming*] (NTCM)
LLL .... Low-Level Logic
LLL .... Low Light Level
LLL .... Low Liquid Level [*Engineering*]
LLL .... Loyal Lusitanian League [*British military*] (DMA)
LLL .... Lutheran Laymen's League [*Later, ILLL*] (EA)
LLL .... University of Nebraska, Lincoln College of Law, Lincoln, NE [*OCLC symbol*] (OCLC)
LLLB......... Left Long Leg Brace [*Medicine*]
L LL brace... Left Long-Leg Brace (STED)
LLLE......... Lower Lid, Left Eye [*Medicine*] (EDAA)
LLLE......... Low-Level Lead Exposure (MELL)
LLLGB....... Low-Level-LASER Guided Bomb
LLLI.......... La Leche League International (EA)
Ll List LR... Lloyd's List Law Reports [*England*] [*A publication*] (DLA)
LLLLL .... Laboratories Low Level Linked List (NITA)
LLLLLL .... Laboratories Low-Level Linked List Language [*Bell Systems*] (MCD)
Ll LLR....... Lloyd's List Law Reports [*England*] [*A publication*] (DLA)
LLLM .... Low Liquid Level Monitor (STED)
LLLNR....... Left Lower Lobe, No Rales [*Medicine*] (STED)
LLLO......... Lend-Lease Liaison Office [*World War II*]
LL Longobard... Laws of the Lombards [*A publication*] (DLA)
Ll L Pr Cas... Lloyd's List Prize Cases Reports [*England*] [*A publication*] (DLA)
Ll LR .... Lloyd's List Law Reports [*England*] [*A publication*] (DLA)
Ll L Rep ..... Lloyd's List Law Reports [*England*] [*A publication*] (DLA)
Ll LRep ..... Lloyds List Law Reports [*A publication*] (SAFN)
LLLT .... Low Level Laser Therapy (SAUO)
LLLT .... Low-Light-Level Television [*Night vision device*] [*Military*] (RDA)
LLLTV........ Low-Level LASER Television
LLLTV........ Low-Light-Level Television [*Night vision device*] [*Military*]
LLLW .... Liquid Low Level Waste [*Nuclear energy*] (NUCP)
LLLW .... Low Level Liquid Waste [*Nuclear energy*] (NUCP)
LLLWT....... Low-Level Liquid Waste Tank [*Nuclear energy*] (NRCH)
LLLX......... Louisiana Leasing [*Private rail car owner code*]
LLM.......... Launcher Loader Module
LLM.......... Lawyers Linked by MODEM [*Computer bulletin board system*] [*FIDO*]
LLM.......... Layer Laminate Manufacturing (SAUS)
LLM.......... Legum Magister [*Master of Laws*] [*Latin*]
LLM.......... Life and Liberty Movement (SAUO)
LLM.......... Limb Load Monitor
LLM.......... Linear Learning Machine [*Data analysis*]
LLM.......... Load Line Method
LLM.......... Localized Leukocyte Mobilization
LLM.......... Local Linear Model (AAEL)
LLM.......... Long Lama [*Malaysia*] [*Airport symbol*] (AD)
LLM.......... Low-Level Multiplexer
LLM.......... Loyola University, New Orleans, LA [*OCLC symbol*] (OCLC)
LLM.......... Lunar Landing Mission [*NASA*]
LLM.......... Lunar Landing Module [*NASA*] (MCD)
LLM.......... Master of Law (GAGS)
LLM.......... Master of Laws
LLMA........ Leavers Lace Manufacturers of America [*Defunct*] (EA)
LL Malcom R Scott... Laws of Malcolm, King of Scotland [*A publication*] (DLA)
Ll Mar LN... Lloyd's Maritime Law Newsletter [*A publication*] (DLA)
LLMC........ Convention on Limitation of Liability for Maritime Claims (SAUS)
LLMC........ International Convention on Limitation of Liability for Maritime Claims (SAUO)
LLM (CL) ... Master of Laws in Comparative Law
LLM Com ... Master of Commercial Law
LLMD........ Lifeline Healthcare Group, Ltd. (SAUO)
LLME......... Leuo Leucine Methylester [*Biochemistry*]
LLMFC ...... Laura Lee McBride Fan Club (EA)
LLMH......... Loyal Legion of the Medal of Honor (EA)
LLMI......... Local Labour Market Information/Intelligence [*British*] (AIE)
LLM (Int L)... Master of Laws in International Law
LLMM .... Leurs Majestes [*Their Majesties*] [*French*]
LLMPP ...... Liquid Level Monitor Port Plug [*Nuclear energy*] (NRCH)
LLMR......... Mitzpe-Ramon [*Israel*] [*ICAO location identifier*] (ICLI)
LLMRCP .... Licentiate and Licentiate in Midwifery of the Royal College of Physicians (SAUO)
LLMRCS .... Licentiate and Licentiate in Midwifery of the Royal College of Surgeons (SAUO)
LLMS........ Longitudinal Layer of Muscles of Stomach (MELL)
LLMW .... Low Level Mixed Waste [*Environmental science*] (COE)
LLMZ........ Metzada/I. Bar Yehuda [*Israel*] [*ICAO location identifier*] (ICLI)
LLN.......... Language, Literacy and Numeracy
LLN.......... League for Less Noise
LLN.......... Levelland, TX [*Location identifier*] [*FAA*] (FAAL)
LLN.......... Line Link Network [*Bell System*]
LLN.......... Local Line Network [*Telecommunications*] (NITA)
LLN.......... Lower Limit of Normal [*Medicine*] (MELL)
LLNE......... Law Librarians of New England (BUAC)
LLNL......... Lawrence Livermore National Laboratory [*Also, LLL*] [*Livermore, CA*] [*Department of Energy*] (GRD)
LLNL......... Lawrence Livermore National Library [*Industrial hygiene term*] (OHS)
LLNNR .... Loch Leven National Nature Reserve (SAUO)
LLNO .... Low-Level Night Operations [*Aviation*]
LLNQ .... Least Lots Next Queue (AAEL)
LL NS .... Law Library, New Series [*Philadelphia Reprint of English Treatises*] [*A publication*] (DLA)
LLNWR...... Long Lake National Wildlife Refuge (SAUO)
LLO.......... Eliadamello SPA [*Italy*] [*ICAO designator*] (FAAC)
LLO.......... Khlor [*Language symbol*] (ETLW)
LLO.......... Lead Laboratory Office (SAUO)
LLO.......... Legionella-Like Organisms [*Medicine*]
LLO.......... Legislative Liaison Office (AAGC)
LLO.......... Lifer Liaison Officer (WDAA)
LLO.......... Llano, TX [*Location identifier*] [*FAA*] (FAAL)
LLO.......... Local Lockout (IAA)
LLO.......... Low Lunar Orbit
LLOC .... Land Line of Communications [*Military*]
LLOC .... Land Lines of Communications (SAUO)
LLOD .... Lloyd's Trailer Finishing [*NCIC trailer make code*]
LLOD .... Lowe Limit of Detection [*Also, LLD*] [*Analytical chemistry*]
LLOD .... Lower Lid, Right Eye [*L. oculus dextra*] [*Medicine*] (EDAA)
LLOE......... Louisiana Land & Offshore Explorations (SAUO)
LLOG .... Lincoln Logs Ltd. (SAUO)
LLOPS........ Law Librarians of Puget Sound (SAUO)
LLOS .... Landmark Line of Sight (KSC)
LLOS .... Lower Lid, Left Eye [*L oculus sinistra*] [*Medicine*] (EDAA)
LLOV .... Low-Level Output Voltage
LLOV .... Ovda [*Israel*] [*ICAO location identifier*] (ICLI)
LLOY .... Lloyd [*NCIC car make code*]
Lloyd & Goold (T Plunkett) (Ir)... Lloyd and Goold's Irish Chancery Reports Tempore Plunkett [*A publication*] (DLA)
Lloyd & Goold (T Sugden) (Ir)... Lloyd and Goold's Irish Chancery Reports Tempore Sugden [*A publication*] (DLA)
Lloyd & W... Lloyd and Welsby's English Mercantile Cases [*A publication*] (DLA)
Lloyd LR.... Lloyd's List Law Reports [*England*] [*A publication*] (DLA)
Lloyd Pr Cas... Lloyd's List Prize Cases Reports [*England*] [*A publication*] (DLA)
Lloyd Pr Cas NS... Lloyd's List Prize Cases Reports, Second Series [*1939-53*] [*A publication*] (DLA)
Lloyds Bank Rev... Lloyds Bank Review [*A publication*] (JLIT)
Lloyd's List LR... Lloyd's List Law Reports [*England*] [*A publication*] (DLA)
Lloyd's Mar LN... Lloyd's Maritime Law Newsletter [*A publication*] (DLA)
Lloyd's Pr Cas... Lloyd's List Prize Cases Reports [*England*] [*A publication*] (DLA)
Lloyd's Prize Cas... Lloyd's List Prize Cases Reports [*London*] [*A publication*] (DLA)
Lloyd's Rep... Lloyd's List Law Reports [*England*] [*A publication*] (DLA)
LLP .... Lambda Limiting Process
LLP .... LASER Light Pump
LLP .... Late Luteal Phase (DB)
LLP .... Launch and Landing Project [*NASA*] (NASA)
LLP .... Law and Liberty Project [*Defunct*] (EA)
LLP .... Leased Long Lines Program (NATG)
LLP .... Liberian Liberal Party [*Political party*] (EY)
LLP .... Lightning Location and Protection (SAUS)
LLP .... Linear Log Potentiometer
LLP .... Line Link Pulsing [*Telecommunications*]
LLP .... Link Layer Protocol (SAUO)
LLP .... Link Level Protocol (SAUS)
LLP .... Literacy and Learning Program
LLP .... Live Load Punch
LLP .... Lloyd's of London Press [*British*]
LLP .... Local Language Program
LLP .... Lollipop Daycare [*Vancouver Stock Exchange symbol*]
LLP .... London Labour Party [*British*] [*Political party*]
LLP .... Long-Lasting Potentiation (DB)
LLP .... Long Lead Part
LLP .... Long Line Program (SAUO)
LLP .... Lower Layer Protocol (SAUO)
LLP .... Lowest Level Processor [*Computer science*] (CIST)
LLP .... Lunar Landing Program [*NASA*]
LLP .... Lyman Laboratory of Physics [*Harvard*] (MCD)
LLPA......... Low Level Waste Policy Act [*1980*] (NUCP)
LLPDD....... Late Luteal Phase Dysphoric Disorder [*Gynecology*]
LLPDU....... Logical Link Protocol Data Unit [*Open Systems Interconnection*] (ODAA)
LLPE......... Labor's League for Political Education [*AFL*] [*Later merged into Committee on Political Education of AFL-CIO*]
LLpEC .... East Carroll Parish Library, Lake Providence, LA [*Library symbol*] [*Library of Congress*] (LCLS)
LLPI .... Linen and Lace Paper Institute [*Later, SSI*] (EA)
LLPL......... Low Low Pond Level (IEEE)
LLPMS ...... Long Leg Posterior Molded Splint [*Medicine*] (MEDA)
LLPN .... Lumped, Linear, Parametric Network
LLPO .... Launch and Landing Project Office [*NASA*] (NASA)
Ll Pr......... Lloyd on Prohibition [*1849*] [*A publication*] (DLA)
Ll Pr Cas ... Lloyd's List Prize Cases Reports [*England*] [*A publication*] (DLA)
Ll Pr Cas NS... Lloyd's List Prize Cases Reports, New Series [*1939-53*] [*A publication*] (DLA)
LLPS......... Low-Level Pumping Station (ADA)

LL-PTC ...... Liquid Liquid Phase Transfer Catalysis [*Physical chemistry*]
LLPX .... Locomotive Leasing Partners [*Private rail car owner code*]
LLQ .... Left Lower Quadrant [*of abdomen*] [*Medicine*]
LLQA .... Limiting Lines of Quiet Approach [*Navy*] (NVT)
LLR .... High Court of Lagos Law Reports [*Nigeria*] [*A publication*] (ILCA)
LLR .... Lancaster Law Review [*A publication*] (DLA)
LLR .... Large Lattice Relaxation (AAEL)
LLR .... Large Local Reaction [*Medicine*] (DMAA)
LLR .... Lawyer Legal Research OnLine (SAUO)
LLR .... Leader Law Reports [*South Africa*] [*A publication*] (DLA)
LLR .... Left Lateral Rectus [*Eye muscle*] (BABM)
LLR .... Left Lateral Rotation [*Medicine*]
LLR .... Left Lumbar Region [*Medicine*] (MAE)
LLR .... Lender of Last Resort
LLR .... Leukemia-Like Reaction [*Hematology*]
LLR .... Liberian Law Reports [*A publication*] (ILCA)
LLR .... Line Length Remainder [*Graphic arts*] (DGA)
LLR .... Line of Least Resistance
LLR .... Load-Limiting Resistor
LLR .... LOFT [*Loss-of-Fluid Test*] Lead Rod (GAAI)
LLR .... Log-Likelihood Ratio (PDAA)
LLR .... Long Latency Response [*Neurology*]
LLR .... Long Length Record (IAA)
LLR .... Low-Level Radiation
LLR .... Low-Level Resistance [*to disease*]
LLR .... Lunar LASER Ranging [*Aerospace*]
LLRA .... LapLink Remote Access [*Traveling Software, Inc.*] [*Computer science*] (PCM)
LLRC .... Luneberg Lens Rapid Commutator [*Physics*]
LLRDS .... Long Life Recording and Data Storage (MCD)
Ll Rep .... Lloyd's List Law Reports [*England*] [*A publication*] (DLA)
LLRES .... Load-Limiting Resistor (MSA)
LLRF .... Low-Level Radio Frequency
LLRF .... Lunar Landing Research Facility [*Aerospace*]
LLRF .... Lunar LASER Range-Finder [*Aerospace*]
LLRI .... Low-Level-Run-In (MCD)
LLRM .... Low-Level Radio Modulator
LLRMW ..... Low-Level Radioactive Mixed Waste (ABAC)
LLRP .... Long Lead Repair Part
Ll R Pr Cas ... Lloyd's List Prize Cases Reports, Second Series [*1939-53*] [*A publication*] (DLA)
LLRR .... Log-Likelihood Ratio Representation (MHDB)
LLRR .... Lowest Level Remove-Replace (SAA)
LLRS .... LASER Lightning Rod System (PDAA)
LLRT .... Local Leak Rate Test [*Nuclear energy*] (NRCH)
LLRT .... Low-Level Reactor Test (IEEE)
LLRU .... Leadership and Learning Research Unit [*University of Glamorgan*] [*United Kingdom*] (RCD)
LLRV .... Lunar Landing Research Vehicle [*Aerospace*]
LLRW .... Low-Level Radiological Waste [*U.S. Army Corps of Engineers*]
LLRWPA .... Low-Level Radioactive Waste Policy Act (SAUO)
LLRWPA .... Low-Level Radioactive Waste Policy Act of 1980 (GAAI)
LLRWPAA ... Low-Level Radioactive Waste Policy Amendments Act (SAUO)
LLRWPAA ... Low-Level Radioactive Waste Policy Amendments Act of 1985 (GAAI)
LLS .... Land Laws Service [*Australia*] [*A publication*]
LLS .... LASER Light Scattering [*Physical chemistry*]
LLS .... LASER Light Source
LLS .... LASER Line Scanner
LLS .... Later-Life Sexuality (MELL)
LLS .... Launch and Landing Site (MCD)
LLS .... Lazy Leukocyte Syndrome [*Medicine*]
LLS .... Linear Least Squares [*Mathematics*]
LLS .... Liquid Level Sensor
LLS .... Liquid Level Switch (IAA)
LLS .... Little League Shoulder (MELL)
LLS .... Localized Light Scatterer (AAEL)
LLS .... Local Library System [*OCLC*]
LLS .... Longitudinal Leaf Spring [*Automotive engineering*]
LLS .... Long Left Shift (SAA)
LLS .... Long Leg Splint [*Orthopedics*] (DAVI)
LLS .... Louisiana State University, Graduate School of Library Science, Baton Rouge, LA [*OCLC symbol*] (OCLC)
LLS .... Low-Level Sensor (KSC)
LLS .... Low-Level Service [*Computer science*]
LLS .... Low-Level Solid [*Nuclear energy*] (NRCH)
LLS .... Lunar Landing Simulator [*Aerospace*] (AAG)
LLS .... Lunar Logistics System [*NASA*]
LLS .... Lyman Limit System [*Spectroscopy*]
LLSA .... Land Lines Assembly [*Ground Communications Facility, NASA*]
LLSA .... Latin Languages Speaking Allergists [*See also GAILL*] (EAIO)
LLSA .... Limiting Lines of Surfaced Approach [*Navy*] (NVT)
LLSAC .... LASER Line Scanner Aerial Camera
LLSAGW .... Low-Level Surface-to-Air Guided Weapon (IAA)
LLSB .... Left Lower Scapular Border [*Medicine*] (DMAA)
LLSB .... Left Lower Sternal Border [*Anatomy*] (DAVI)
LLSBA .... Leicester Longwool Sheep Breeders Association [*England*] (BUAC)
LLSC .... Israel South Control Area Control Center Unit [*Israel*] [*ICAO location identifier*] (ICLI)
LLSD .... Tel Aviv/Sde Dov [*Israel*] [*ICAO location identifier*] (ICLI)
LLSI .... Laser Light Scattering Instrument (SAUS)
LLSI .... LSI Logic Corp. [*NASDAQ symbol*] (COMM)
LLSIL .... Lower Living Standard Income Level [*CETA*] [*Department of Labor*]
LLSL .... Lakeland Savings & Loan Association (SAUO)
LLSNA .... Limiting Lines of Snorkel Approach [*Navy*] (NVT)
LLSP .... Law Library Service to Prisoners [*Minnesota State Law Library*]
LLSPT .... Licentiateship of the London School of Polymer Technology [*British*] (DBQ)
LLSS .... LASER Light Scattering Spectroscopy
LLSS .... LASER Light Source Station
LLSS .... Long Life Space System (IAA)
LLSS .... Low-Level Sounding System [*for measuring weather conditions*]
Ll St .... Lloyd's Statutes of Practical Utility [*A publication*] (DLA)
LLSU .... Lilley Construction [*Intermodal shipping container symbol*] (TVRC)
LLSU .... Low-Level Signaling Unit [*Telecommunications*] (TEL)
LLSUA .... Limiting Lines of Submerged Approach [*Navy*] (NVT)
Ll Suc .... Lloyd on Succession Laws [*1877*] [*A publication*] (DLA)
LLSV .... Low-Level Storage Vault [*Nuclear energy*] (NRCH)
LLSV .... Lunar Logistics Supply Vehicle [*NASA*] (IAA)
LLSV .... Lunar Logistics System Vehicle [*NASA*]
LLSWCP .... Low-Level Solid Waste Certification Plan (SAUO)
LLSWV ...... Low-Level Solid Waste Storage Vault [*Nuclear energy*] (NRCH)
LLT .... Lahore Law Times [*India*] [*A publication*] (DLA)
LLT .... Lander Local Time [*NASA*]
LLT .... Land-Line Teletypewriter [*Military*] (IAA)
LLT .... Left Lateral [*Anatomy*] (DAVI)
LLT .... Left Lateral Thigh [*Medicine*]
LLT .... Library of Living Thought [*A publication*]
LLT .... London Landed Terms [*Shipping*]
LLT .... Long Lead Time
LLT .... Low-Level Terminal
LLT .... Low-Level Turbulence
LLT .... Low-Light Television
LLT .... Loyola University, Law Library, New Orleans, LA [*OCLC symbol*] (OCLC)
LLT .... Lysolecithin (DMAA)
LLTA .... Tel Aviv [*Israel*] [*ICAO location identifier*] (ICLI)
LLTC .... Linear Technology Corp. [*NASDAQ symbol*] (TTSB)
LLTC .... Linear Technology Corporation (SAUO)
LLTCS .... Low-Limit Temperature Control Systems
LLTD .... Lightweight LASER Target Designator
LLTDS .... Launch Landing Test Data System (MCD)
LLTFR .... Loop Line Transfer, ON [*American Association of Railroads railroad junction routing code*]
LLTI .... Long Lead Time Items (AAG)
LLTIL .... Long Lead Time Items List [*Military*] (CAAL)
LLTM .... Long Lead Time Material (DNAB)
LLTR .... L & L Trailers [*NCIC trailer make code*]
LLTR .... Large Leak Test Rig [*Nuclear energy*] (NRCH)
LLTR .... Low-Level Transit Route (SAUO)
LLTR .... Low-Level Transit Time
Ll Tr M ...... Lloyd on Trade-Marks [*A publication*] (DLA)
LLTT .... Landline Teletypewriter [*Military*]
LLTTY .... Landline Teletypewriter [*Military*]
LLTV .... Low-Light-Level Television [*Night vision device*] [*Military*]
LLTV .... Low Light Television (ACAE)
LLTV .... Lunar Landing Training Vehicle [*Aerospace*]
LLTWP ...... Low-Level Tritiated Water Processing Subsystem (MCD)
LLU .... Lamar, MO [*Location identifier*] [*FAA*] (FAAL)
LLU .... Lending Library Unit
LLU .... Lithuanian Liberal Union (BUAC)
LLU .... Loma Linda University, Loma Linda, CA [*OCLC symbol*] (OCLC)
LLu .... Saint James Parish Library, Lutcher, LA [*Library symbol*] [*Library of Congress*] (LCLS)
LLUSM ...... Loma Linda University School of Medicine [*Medicine*] (EDAA)
LLV .... Large Launch Vehicle Planning Group (SAUO)
LLV .... Lockheed Launch Vehicle (ISAK)
LLV .... Long Life Valve
LLV .... Long Life Vehicle [*Automotive engineering*]
LLV .... Long-Life Vehicle [*Automotive engineering*]
LLV .... Lonicera Latent Virus [*Plant pathology*]
LLV .... Low Level Vault (ABAC)
LLV .... Loyal London Volunteers [*British military*] (DMA)
LLV .... Lunar Landing Vehicle [*NASA*]
LLV .... Lunar Logistics Vehicle [*NASA*]
LLV .... Lymphocytic Leukemia Virus
LLVIR .... Long Line Voice Interface Rack (SSD)
LLVP .... Left Lateral Ventricular Preexcitation [*Medicine*] (DMAA)
LLVPG .... Large Launch Vehicle Planning Group [*NASA*]
LLW .... Lilongwe [*Malawi*] [*Airport symbol*] (OAG)
LLW .... Lower Low Water [*Tides and currents*]
LLW .... Low-Level Radioactive Waste
LLW .... Low-Level Waste [*Nuclear energy*] (NRCH)
LLWAS ...... Low-Level Windshear Alert System (USDC)
LLWC .... Long-Leg Walking Cast [*Orthopedics*] (DAVI)
LLWCP ...... Low Level Waste Certification Plan (SAUO)
LLWD .... Lower Low Water Datum [*Nautical term*] (HRNC)
LLWD .... Low-Level Weapons Delivery (SAUS)
LLWDDD .... Low-Level Waste Disposal Development and Demonstration
LLWDF ...... Low-Level Waste Disposal Facilities (SAUO)
LLWI .... Lower Low-Water Interval [*Tides and currents*]
LL Wisegotho ... Laws of the Visigoths [*A publication*] (DLA)
LLWM .... Low-Level Waste Management (SAUO)
LL Wm Conq ... Laws of William the Conqueror [*A publication*] (DLA)
LL Wm Noth ... Laws of William the Bastard [*A publication*] (DLA)
LLWMP ...... Low-Level Waste Management Program (GAAI)
LLWPA ...... Low-Level Waste Policy Act (SAUO)
LLWPAA .... Low-Level Waste Policy Amendment Act (SAUO)

LLWPSS..... Low-level Waste Processing and Shipping System (SAUO)
LLWQAPP... Low Level Waste Quality Assurance Program Plan (SAUO)
LLWS........ Low Level Wind Shear [*Aviation*] (FAAC)
LLWSV...... Low-Level Waste Storage Vault [*Nuclear energy*] (NRCH)
LLX.......... Left Lower Extremity (SAUS)
LLX.......... Louisiana Land & Exploration Co. [*NYSE symbol*] [*Toronto Stock Exchange symbol*]
LLX.......... Louisiana Land/Exp [*NYSE symbol*] (TTSB)
LLX.......... Lyndonville, VT [*Location identifier*] [*FAA*] (FAAL)
LLY.......... Eli Lilly and Co. [*NYSE symbol*]
LLY.......... Lilly [*Eli*] & Co. [*NYSE symbol*] (SPSG)
LLY.......... Lilly (Eli) [*NYSE symbol*] (TTSB)
LLY.......... Llanelly [*Welsh depot code*]
LLYP......... Long Leaf Yellow Pine [*Lumber*]
LLYU......... Lily Marine Services [*Intermodal shipping container symbol*] (TVRC)
LLZ.......... Left Lower Zone [*Medicine*] (DMAA)
LLZ.......... Localizer [*ICAO designator*] (CET)
LM........... Labiomental [*Lip and chin*] [*Dentistry*] (DAVI)
LM........... Laboratory Manager
LM........... Laboratory Microscope
LM........... Laboratory Module (MCD)
LM........... Labour Mobility [*British*]
LM........... Lactic Acid Mineral (DMAA)
LM........... Lactose Malabsorption [*Gastroenterology*]
LM........... Lacus Mortis [*Lunar area*]
Lm........... Lamentations (ADWA)
LM........... Lamentations [*Old Testament book*]
LM........... Landmark (KSC)
LM........... Land Mine [*Military*]
LM........... Land Mobile
LM........... Land Mobility (TIMI)
LM........... Landsdale Microelectronics (SAUO)
LM........... Language Minority (SAUO)
LM........... Laramie Projects Office (SAUO)
LM........... Large Memory [*Computer science*]
LM........... Large Momentum (ACAE)
LM........... Large Mouth Bass [*Pisciculture*]
LM........... Laryngeal Mask [*Medicine*] (DMAA)
LM........... Laryngeal Muscle (BABM)
LM........... LASER Machine (IAA)
LM........... Late Midcourse (ACAE)
LM........... Late Model [*Class of racing cars*]
LM........... Lateral Malleolus [*Anatomy*]
LM........... Lateral Meniscus [*Anatomy*]
LM........... Laufenden Monats [*Of the Current Month*] [*German*]
LM........... Launch Module
LM........... Launch Mount (AFM)
LM........... Layer Management [*Communications term*] (DCT)
LM........... Leading Mechanician
LM........... Leave Message [*Word processing*]
LM........... Lee-Metford [*British military*] (DMA)
LM........... Left Male (MSA)
LM........... Left Mid (NASA)
LM........... Legal Medicine
LM........... Legg Mason, Inc. [*NYSE symbol*] (SPSG)
LM........... Legion of Merit [*Military decoration*]
LM........... Leg Multiple [*Telegraph*] [*Telecommunications*] (TEL)
LM........... Lemniscus Medialis (DB)
LM........... Lentigo Maligna [*Oncology*]
LM........... Leprosy Mission [*Australia*] [*An association*]
LM........... Leptomeningeal Metastasis
LM........... Lethal Material
LM........... Level Meter
LM........... Liability Management (EBF)
LM........... Licentiate in Medicine
LM........... Licentiate in Midwifery
LM........... Licentiate in Music (WDAA)
LM........... Light Machine Gun
LM........... Light Maintenance
LM........... Light Metal
LM........... Light Microscope
LM........... Light Microscopy (AAEL)
LM........... Light Minimum [*Medicine*]
lm........... Light-Minute
LM........... Light Music [*Canadian Broadcasting Corp. record series prefix*]
LM........... Limburg [*Lahn*] [*German license plate city code*]
LM........... Lime Mortar (DAC)
LM........... Limit (IAA)
LM........... Limitation [*Dialog*] [*Searchable field*] [*Information service or system*] (NITA)
LM........... Lincoln Memorial (SAUO)
LM........... Lincoln Mercury [*Division of Ford Motor Co.*]
LM........... Linear Meter
LM........... Linear Mile
LM........... Linear Modulation
LM........... Line Mark (IAA)
l/m.......... Lines per Minute (IDOE)
L/M.......... Lines per Minute [*Computer science*]
LM........... Linguomesial [*Dentistry*]
LM........... Link Manager
LM........... Lipid Mobilizing Hormone [*Endocrinology*]
LM........... Liquidity-Money Supply [*Economics*]
LM........... Liquid Membrane
LM........... Liquid Metal
Lm........... [*Maltese*] Lira [*Monetary Unit*][*Malta*] (BARN)
LM........... Listeria Monocytogenes [*Microorganism*]
LM........... List of Material [*DoD*]
L/M.......... List of Materials (AAG)
LM........... Litchfield & Madison [*AAR code*]
LM........... Literary Mongolian [*Linguistics*] (IEL)
l/m.......... Liters per Minute (IDYL)
L/M.......... Liters per Minute
LM........... Liturgie und Moenchtum [*A publication*] (BJA)
LM........... Load Management (ODA)
LM........... Load Master (SAUO)
LM........... Load Module (MCD)
LM........... Load Multiple [*Computer command*] (PCM)
LM........... Local Manufacture (AAG)
LM........... Local Memory
LM........... Local Militia [*British military*] (DMA)
LM........... Lockheed Martin Corp. (SAUO)
LM........... Locus Monumenti [*Place of the Monument*] [*Latin*]
LM........... Logical Module (NITA)
LM........... Logic Module [*Computer science*] (MCD)
LM........... Logistics Manager (MCD)
LM........... Logistics Module [*Simulation games*] [*Army*] (SSD)
LM........... London Museum (SAUO)
LM........... Longitudinal Muscle [*Anatomy*]
LM........... Long March [*Launch vehicle*]
LM........... Long Measure (ROG)
LM........... Long Meter [*Music*]
LM........... Longmile [*Tire retread brand*]
LM........... Long Module (MCD)
LM........... Loop Multiplexer
LM........... Looser-Milkman [*Syndrome*] [*Medicine*] (DB)
LM........... Lord Marquis (ODA)
LM........... Lord Mayor
LM........... Loss Margin (IAA)
LM........... Lost Motion
LM........... Louisiana Midland Railway Co. (IIA)
L-M.......... Louisiana State Museum, New Orleans, LA [*Library symbol*] [*Library of Congress*] (LCLS)
LM........... Lower Magazine [*Typography*]
LM........... Lower Motor [*Neurology*]
LM........... Low Meaningfulness [*Psychology*]
L/M.......... Low/Medium (MCD)
LM........... Low-Melting (OA)
LM........... Low Middling [*Telegraphy*] (PCTE)
LM........... Low Modulus [*Mechanical engineering*]
LM........... Low Molecular [*Chemistry*]
LM........... Luftmine [*Aerial mine*] [*German military - World War II*]
lm........... Lumen (IDOE)
LM........... Lumen [*Symbol*] [*SI unit of luminous flux*]
L/M.......... Luminosity to Mass [*Ratio*] [*Astronomy*]
LM........... Lunar Mission
LM........... Lunar Module [*Formerly, LEM*] [*NASA*]
LM........... Maestretti [*Italy*] [*Research code symbol*]
LM........... Middle Latitude [*Navigation*]
LM1A......... Late Minoan 1A [*Archaeology*]
LM1B......... Late Minoan 1B [*Archaeology*]
LM2.......... Lima [*Magdalena*] [*Peru*] [*Seismograph station code, US Geological Survey*] (SEIS)
LM2.......... Liver Microsomal Band 2
L/(M² D)... Liters per Square Meter Day
LMA......... Labor Market Area
LMA......... Lake Minchumina [*Alaska*] [*Airport symbol*] (OAG)
LMA......... Laminating Materials Association [*Oradell, NJ*] (EA)
LMA......... Land Mammal Ages [*Paleontology*]
LMA......... Large Model Access (MCD)
LMA......... Laryngeal Mask Airway (SAUS)
LMA......... LASER Microspectral Analysis
LMA......... Last Manufacturers Association [*Defunct*] (EA)
LMA......... Latvian Maritime Academy (BUAC)
LMA......... Leading Medical Assistant [*British military*] (DMA)
LMA......... League for Mutual Aid [*Defunct*] (EA)
LMA......... Leased Management Agreement [*Radio*] [*Television*] (WDMC)
LMA......... Leave Me Alone (SAUS)
LMA......... Lebanese Management Association (BUAC)
LMA......... Lebanese Moslem Association [*Australia*]
LMA......... Left Mentoanterior [*A fetal position*] [*Obstetrics*]
LMA......... Liberian Marketing Association (SAUO)
LMA......... Licensed Merchandisers' Association [*Later, ILMA*] (EA)
LMA......... Limbic Midbrain Area (STED)
LMA......... Lingerie Manufacturers Association [*Later, IAMA*] (EA)
LMA......... Linoleum Manufacturers Association (BUAC)
LMA......... Liquor Merchants' Association [*Australia*]
LMA......... Little More Active [*Telegraphy*] (PCTE)
LMA......... Liver Membrane Antibody [*Medicine*] (STED)
LMA......... Liver Membrane Autoantibody [*Immunochemistry*]
LMA......... Livestock and Meat Authority [*Queensland, Australia*]
LMA......... Livestock Marketing Association (EA)
LMA......... L. Mike Association (EA)
LMA......... Local Marshalling Areas (MCD)
LMA......... Lock Museum of America (EA)
LMA......... Logsplitter Manufacturers Association [*Defunct*] (EA)
LMA......... London Mayors Association [*England*] (BUAC)
LMA......... London Metropolitan Archives (SAUO)
LMA......... London-Midlands Association (SAUO)

LMA .... Low Moisture Activity [*Brake system*] [*Automotive engineering*]
LMA .... Lumina APV [*NCIC car model code*]
LMA .... Lunar Meteoroid Analyzer [*NASA*]
LMA .... Lunar Module Adapter [*NASA*] (MCD)
LMA .... Lybarger Memorial Association (EA)
LMAA .... Liquor Merchants' Association of Australia
LMAA .... Logistics Management Association of Australia
LMAB .... London Munitions Assignments Board [*World War II*]
LMAC .... Labor-Management Advisory Committee [*Terminated, 1974*] [*Cost of Living Council*] (EGAO)
LMAC .... Labor Market Advisory Council (SAUO)
LMAC .... Labor Market Advisory Councils [*Department of Labor and Department of Health, Education, and Welfare*] [*Terminated, 1982*] (EGAO)
LMAC .... Lockheed Martin Aeronautics Company (SAUO)
LMaD .... DeSoto Parish Library, Mansfield, LA [*Library symbol*] [*Library of Congress*] (LCLS)
LMAD .... Let's Make a Deal [*TV program*]
LMAE .... Lunar Module Ascent Engine [*NASA*]
LMAES ...... Lockheed Martin Advanced Environmental Systems (SAUO)
LMAF .... Live Missile Assembly Facility
LMAF .... Live Motor Assembly Facility (SAUO)
LMAFS ...... Lookout Mountain Air Force Station
LM-Ag .... Liver Membrane Antigen [*Immunochemistry*]
L Mag & LR... Law Magazine and Law Review [*A publication*] (DLA)
L Mag & Rev... Law Magazine and Review [*A publication*] (DLA)
LMAGB ...... Locomotive Manufacturers Association of Great Britain (BUAC)
LMA II ...... Lightspeed Memory Architecture II
LMAL .... Langley Memorial Aeronautical Laboratory [*NASA*] (AAG)
LMAMA ..... Louisa May Alcott Memorial Association (EA)
LMAN .... Lieberman Enterprises, Inc. (SAUO)
LmAN .... Limited Area Networks (NITA)
LM & LR .... Law Magazine and Law Review [*A publication*] (DLA)
LM & P ..... Lowndes, Maxwell, and Pollock's English Bail Court Practice Reports [*1850-51*] [*A publication*] (DLA)
LM & Sc R... London, Midland & Scottish Railway [*British*] (DCTA)
LManyS ..... Sabine Parish Library, Many, LA [*Library symbol*] [*Library of Congress*] (LCLS)
LMA-PAC .... Livestock Marketing Association PAC [*Kansas City, MO*] (PACS)
LMAQ .... Liquor Merchants Association of Queensland [*Australia*]
LMAQ .... Livestock and Meat Authority of Queensland [*Australia*]
LMAR .... Lorimar-Telepictures Corp. (SAUO)
LMarA .... Avoyelles Parish Library, Marksville, LA [*Library symbol*] [*Library of Congress*] (LCLS)
l-marking ... Marking a Lexical Category [*Linguistics*] (IEL)
LMARS ...... Library Management and Retrieval System [*Navy*] [*Information service or system*] (IID)
LMAS .... London and Middlesex Archaeological Society (SAUO)
LM/ATM .... Lunar Module Apollo Telescope Mount [*NASA*] (MCD)
LMAU .... Land Marine Cargo [*Intermodal shipping container symbol*] (TVRC)
LMAV .... LASER Maverick (MCD)
LMAV .... Lumber Manufacturers Association of Virginia (WPI)
LMAW .... Light Multi-purpose Assault Weapon (SAUS)
LMAW .... Liquid Medium Active Waste (NUCP)
LMB .... Laboratory of Molecular Biophysics (GNE)
LMB .... Laboratory of Muscle Biology [*National Institute of Arthritis and Musculoskeletal and Skin Diseases*] (RCD)
LMB .... Labor Market Bulletin (OICC)
LMB .... Laurence-Moon-Biedl [*Medicine*]
LMB .... League of Michigan Bicyclists (EARSL)
LMB .... Left Main-Stem Bronchus [*Medicine*] (MEDA)
LMB .... Left Most BIT [*Binary Digit*] [*Computer science*] (MHDB)
LMB .... Left Mouse Button (VLIE)
LMB .... Leiomyblastoma [*Pathology*] (DAVI)
LMB .... Le Mans Berlinetta [*Le Mans Small car*] [*Automobile model designation-Ferrari*]
LMB .... Leptomycin B [*A cytotoxin*]
LMB .... Linear Motion Bearing
LMB .... Liquidation and Manpower Board (SAUO)
LMB .... Local Marine Board (SAUO)
LMB .... Local Master Browser (SAUS)
LMB .... Local Message Box (NATG)
LMB .... Low-Maintenance Battery (MCD)
LMBATA .... Lace Machine Builders and Allied Trades Association (SAUO)
LMBB .... Laurence-Moon-Bardet-Biedl Syndrome [*Medicine*] (DMAA)
LMBBS ...... Laurence-Moon-Bardet-Biedl Syndrome [*Medicine*]
LMBBSN .... Laurence-Moon-Bardet-Biedl Syndrome Network [*An association*] (EA)
LMBC .... Lady Margaret Boat Club [*of St. John's College, Cambridge*] [*British*]
LMBC .... Landmark Bancorp [*NASDAQ symbol*] (SAG)
LMBC .... Liverpool Marine Biological Committee [*British*] (BARN)
LMBC .... Liverpool Marine Biology Committee (SAUO)
LMBCS ...... Lotus Multi-Byte Character Set [*Computer science*] (VLIE)
LMBD .... Lingular Mandibular Bony Defect [*Medicine*] (RAWO)
LMBDA ...... Language for Manufacturing Business and Distribution Activities (SAUO)
LMBF .... Low and Medium Bleeding Frequency [*Medicine*]
LMBI .... Local Memory Bus Interface [*Computer science*]
LMBnyS ..... Sabine Parish Library, Many (SAUS)
LMBO .... Leveraged Management Buy-Out
LMBP .... Lake Manyara Bird Paradise (SAUO)
LMBR .... Lumber
LMBS .... Laurence-Moon-Biedl Syndrome [*Medicine*]
LMC .... Cleveland-Marshall College of Law, Cleveland, OH [*OCLC symbol*] (OCLC)
LMC .... Laboratory of Molecular Carcinogensis (GNE)
LMC .... Labor Market Characteristics (OICC)
LMC .... Labour Management Committee (SAUO)
LMC .... Lake Michigan College (SAUO)
LMC .... Lake Michigan Conference (PSS)
LMC .... Lamacarena [*Colombia*] [*Airport symbol*] [*Obsolete*] (OAG)
LMC .... Lamina Monopolar Cell [*Cytology*]
LMC .... Lamocks [*Republic of China*] [*Seismograph station code, US Geological Survey*] (SEIS)
LMC .... Lancia Motor Club [*Ledbury, Herefordshire, England*] (EAIO)
LMC .... Land Management Code (PA)
LMC .... Lanzhou Medical College [*China*] (BUAC)
LMC .... Large Magellanic Cloud [*Astronomy*]
LMC .... Large Monopolar Cell [*Anatomy*]
LMC .... large Motile Cell [*Medicine*] (STED)
LMC .... LASER Mirror Coating
LMC .... Late Mid Course (ACAE)
LMC .... Lateral Motor Column [*of the spinal cord*] [*Neurobiology*]
LMC .... Latex-Modified Concrete (PDAA)
LMC .... Launch Monitor Console [*or Control*] [*NASA*] (IAA)
LMC .... Least Material Condition (MSA)
LMC .... Left Main Coronary [*Artery*] [*Medicine*] (STED)
LMC .... Left Middle Cerebral [*Artery*] [*Medicine*] (STED)
LMC .... Lemoore, CA [*Amtrak Busline code*]
LMC .... Library Media Center
LMC .... Ligue Monarchiste du Canada [*Monarchist League of Canada*] (EAIO)
LMC .... Lime-Magnesium Carbonate
LMC .... Liquid Media Concentrate [*Cell culture*]
LMC .... Liquid Metal Cycle
LMC .... Living Male Child [*Medicine*] (DMAA)
LMC .... Lloyd's Machinery Certificate [*Shipping*]
LMC .... LMC [*NCIC trailer make code*]
LMC .... Local Management Committee
LMC .... Local Mate Competition [*Entomology*]
LMC .... Local Medical Committee [*British*]
LMC .... Lockheed Martin Corporation (SAUO)
LMC .... Logistical Maintenance Computer (VLIE)
LMC .... Logistic Movement Center [*Military*] (CAAL)
LMC .... Logistics Management Center [*Army*] (MCD)
LMC .... Lomas Mortgage Corp. (SAUO)
LMC .... London Montessori Centre [*British*] (AIE)
LMC .... Long-Run Marginal Cost Curve [*Economics*]
LMC .... Lon Morris College [*Texas*]
LMC .... Loss of Mesodermal Competence [*Developmental biology*]
LMC .... Louisville Municipal College [*Kentucky*]
LMC .... Low Middling Clause [*Business term*]
LMC .... Low Middling Close [*Telegraphy*] (PCTE)
LMC .... Low-Pressure Molding Compound (MCD)
LMC .... Lutheran Medical Center (SAUO)
LMC .... Lymphocyte-Mediated Cytolysis [*Medicine*] (STED)
LMC .... Lymphocyte-Mediated Cytotoxicity [*Also, LC*] [*Immunology*]
LMC .... Lymphocyte Microcytotoxicity [*Medicine*] (STED)
LMC .... Lymphomyeloid Complex [*Medicine*]
LMc .... Morgan City Public Library, Morgan City, LA [*Library symbol*] [*Library of Congress*] (LCLS)
LMCA .... Laboratory Materiel Control Activity (AFIT)
LMCA .... Land Management Cooperative Agreement (SAUO)
LMCA .... Left Main Coronary Artery [*Anatomy*]
LMCA .... Left Middle Cerebral Artery [*Medicine*] (MAE)
LMCA .... Logistics Management Course for Auditors [*Army*]
LMCA .... Logistics Material Control Activity [*Military*]
LMCA .... Long-Term Medical Conditions Alliance (BUAC)
LMCA .... Lorry-Mounted Crane Association [*British*] (BI)
LMCAD ...... Left Main Coronary Artery Disease
LMCAT ...... Left Middle Cerebral Artery Thrombosis [*Medicine*] (EDAA)
LMCB .... Laboratory of Molecular Cell Biology [*National Cancer Institute*] (RCD)
LMCC .... Land Mobile Communications Council (EA)
LMCC .... Licentiate of Medical Council of Canada
LMCC .... Licentiate of the Medical College of Canada (DD)
LMCC .... Logistic Movement Coordination Center [*Navy*] (ANA)
LMCC .... Low-Mintage Coin Club (EA)
LMCD .... Liquid Metal Cooled Demonstration (IAA)
LMCFP ...... Life Member, College of Family Physicians (CMD)
LMCl .... Left Midclavicular Line [*Medicine*] (EDAA)
LMCLQ ...... Lloyds Maritime and Commercial Law Quarterly [*A publication*] (DLA)
LMCM .... Land Mine Countermeasures (ACAE)
LM/CM² ..... Lumens per Square Centimeter
LMCMS ..... Licentiate Ministers and Certified Mediums Society (EA)
LMCN .... Laboratory of Molecular and Cellular Neuroscience [*Medicine*] (EDAA)
LMCN .... Launch Maintenance Conference Network [*Aerospace*] (AAG)
LMCN .... Launch Missile Control Network (IAA)
LMCNI .... Livestock Marketing Commission for Northern Ireland (BUAC)
LMCO .... Lockheed Martin Corporation and Ericsson (SAUO)
LMCP .... Laboratory Module Computer Program
LMCPA ...... London Motor Cab Proprietors Association [*England*] (BUAC)
LMCR .... Liquid Metal Cooled Reactor
LMCS .... Laboratory Measurement-Control System (SAUO)
LMCS .... Leeds Medico-Chirurgical Society (SAUO)
LMCSS ...... Letter Mail Code Sort System [*Postal Service*]
LMCT .... Licensed Motor Car Trader (SAUO)
LMCT .... Ligand-to-Metal Charge Transfer [*Physical chemistry*]

LMCTF Land Managers Cooperative Task Force (SAUO)
LMCU Ignazio Messina [*Intermodal shipping container symbol*] (TVRC)
LMD Laboratory Management Division
LMD Laboratory Managers Division (SAUO)
LMD Laboratory of Meteorological Dynamics (SAUO)
LMD Labor Mobility Demonstration
LMD Lamda Airlines [*Greece*] [*ICAO designator*] (FAAC)
LMD LASER Microwave Division [*Army*]
LMD Last Modification Date (SAUS)
LMD Lead Military Department (SAUO)
LMD Leaf-Mold (ROG)
LMD Left Main Disease [*Cardiology*] (DB)
LMD Left Medial Deltoid [*Injection Site*]
LMD Left Medline Deviation (SAUS)
LMD Library Macro-Definition (VLIE)
LMD Licensed Motor Dealer
LMD Light Mobile Digger (SAUS)
LMD Linear Magnetic Drive (CCCA)
LMD Lipid-Moiety Modified Derivative (DB)
LMD Liquid Metal Detector
L/(M D) Liter per Meter Day
LMD Local Medical Doctor
LMD Logistics Maintenance Data (ACAE)
LMD Logistics Management Data [*Military*] (MCD)
LMD Long Meter Double [*Music*]
LMD Louisiana Midland Railway Co. [*Later, LMT*] [*AAR code*]
LMD Low Modulus Direction [*Mechanical testing*]
LMD Low-Molecular-Weight Dextran [*Medicine*]
LMD Lunar Meteoroid Detector [*NASA*]
LMDA Lee's Multidifferential Agar [*Brewery bacteria culture medium*]
LMDA Literary Managers and Dramaturgs of the Americas (NTPA)
LMDA Lunar Meteoroid Detector-Analyzer [*NASA*]
LMDC Leadership and Management Development Center [*Maxwell Air Force Base, AL*]
LMDC Leadership Management Development Course (SAUO)
LMDE Limpet Mine Disposal Equipment (SAUS)
LMDE Lunar Module Descent Engine [*NASA*]
LMDH Mauritanian Human Rights League (BUAC)
LMDL Longitudinal Mode Delay Line (VLIE)
LMDM Little Mission for the Deaf-Mute [*See also PMS*] [*Rome, Italy*] (EAIO)
LMDS Lightweight Module Display System (ACAE)
LMDS Local Multipoint Distribution Service [*Telecommunications*]
LMDS Local Multipoint Distribution System [*Telecommunications*] (ACRL)
LMDS Local Multipoint Distribution Systems [*Broadcasting term*]
LM/DUP Launch Module / Defense Unit Platform
LMDW LMD Warehouse and Distribution [*Common carrier symbol*]
LMDX Low-Molecular-Weight Dextran (MAE)
LME Labor Market Exposure [*Work Incentive Program*]
LME Lambda Mercantile Corp. [*Toronto Stock Exchange symbol*]
LME Large Marine Ecosystem
LME Launch Monitor Equipment [*NASA*] (KSC)
LME Layer Management Entity [*Telecommunications*]
LME Left Mediolateral Episiotomy [*Obstetrics*] (MAE)
LME Light Mitochondrial Extract (OA)
LME Link Monitor Equipment (MCD)
LME Liquid Membrane Extraction [*Separation science and technology*]
LME Liquid Mercury Engine
LME Liquid Metal Embrittlement (MCD)
LME Liquid Motion Experiment (SAUS)
LME Locally Manufactured Equipment
LME Logistics Management Engineering, Inc. [*Annapolis, MD*] [*Telecommunications*] (TSSD)
LME London Metal Exchange
LME Lunar Module Engine [*NASA*]
LME Lysine Methyl Ester [*Biochemistry*]
LMEA Louisiana Music Educators Association (SAUO)
LMEC Labour Middle East Council (BUAC)
LMEC Lambda Mercantile Corporation (SAUO)
LMEC Line Map Editing Console
LMEC Liquid Metal Engineering Center [*Energy Research and Development Administration*]
L Med Licentiate in Medicine (SAUO)
LMED Light Military Electronics Department (SAUO)
LMED LyphoMed, Inc. [*NASDAQ symbol*] (COMM)
LMed & Ch Licentiate in Medicine and Surgery (DAVI)
LMEE Left Middle Ear Exploration [*Otorhinolaryngology*] (DAVI)
LMEE Light Military Electronics Equipment
LMEED Light Military Electronics Equipment Department (SAUO)
LMEIC Life Member of Engineering Institute of Canada
LMEP Language MOS Evaluation Program [*Army*]
LMER Land Margin Ecosystem Research [*Marine science*] (OSRA)
LMER Lockheed Martin Energy Research Corp. (SAUO)
LMer London Mercury (SAUO)
LMES Laboratory for Meteorology and Earth Sciences [*NASA*]
LMES Laboratory of Meteorology and Earth Sciences (SAUO)
LMES Lockheed Martin Energy Systems, Inc. (GAAI)
LMET Leadership and Management Education and Training [*Navy*]
L-Meter Induction Meter (SAUS)
LMetJ Jefferson Parish Library, Metairie, LA [*Library symbol*] [*Library of Congress*] (LCLS)
LMetR Jefferson Parish Recreation Department, Metairie, LA [*Library symbol*] [*Library of Congress*] (LCLS)
LMF Laboratory Microfusion Facility (SAUO)
LMF Lack of Moral Fibre [*British military*] (DMA)
LMF Ladle Metallurgy Furnace
LMF Lake Michigan Federation (EA)
LMF Language Media Format (CET)
LMF Large Melt Facility, Sandia National Laboratories (SAUO)
LMF Large Myelinated Fiber [*Neuroanatomy*]
LMF Large-Scale Melt Facility [*Nuclear reactor test unit*]
LMF Last Meal Furnished
LMF Last Month's Forecast (MCD)
LMF Left Middle Finger (DMAA)
LMF Le Mans [*France*] [*Seismograph station code, US Geological Survey*] [*Closed*] (SEIS)
LMF Leukeran [*Chlorambucil*], Methotrexate, Fluorouracil [*Antineoplastic drug regimen*]
LMF Leukocyte Mitogenic Factor [*Medicine*]
LMF Levitation Microfurnace (SAUS)
LMF Linear Matched Filter (IEEE)
LMF Linear Multistep Formula (PDAA)
LMF Liquid Metal Fuel
LMF Logical Mainframe (COE)
LMF London Musical Festival (SAUO)
LMF Low and Medium Frequency
LMF Lower Mid Fuselage (NASA)
L/MF Low/Medium Frequency (PIPO)
LMF Lymphocyte Mitogenic Factor [*Endocrinology, hematology*]
LMF South Lembata [*Language symbol*] (ETLW)
LMFA Light Metal Founders Association [*British*] (DBA)
LMFA Lucky Mee Family Association (EA)
LMFB Liquid-Metal Fast Breeder (MEC)
LMFBR Liquid Metal Fast Breeder Reactor
LMFC Leigh McCloskey Fan Club (EA)
LMFC Liza Minnelli Fan Club (EA)
LMFC Louise Mandrell Fan Club (EA)
LMFE London Meat Futures Exchange [*British*]
LMFR Liquid Metal Fueled Reactor
LMFRE Liquid Metal Fueled Reactor Experiment
LMFS Lockheed Martin Fairchild Systems (SAUO)
LMFT Licensed Marriage and Family Therapist (SEAT)
LM/FT^2 Lumen per Square Foot (WDAA)
lm/ft^2 Lumens per Square Foot (IDOE)
LMG Labial Minor Salivary Gland [*Medicine*] (EDAA)
LMG Laboratory of Molecular Genetics (GNE)
LMG Lactic Esters of Mono/Diglycerides
LMG Lamington [*Papua New Guinea*] [*Seismograph station code, US Geological Survey*] (SEIS)
LMG LASER Milling Gauge
LMG Lauerer Markin Gibbs, Inc. [*Maumee, OH*] [*Telecommunications*] (TSSD)
LMG Lawson Mardon Group (EFIS)
LMG Left Main Gear (MCD)
LMG Lethal Midline Granuloma [*Medicine*] (EDAA)
LMG Liberty Management Group (MHID)
LMG Light Machine Gun
LMG Liquid Methane Gas
LMG London Medical Group (SAUO)
LMG Louisiana Mining Corp. [*Vancouver Stock Exchange symbol*]
LMGC Lunar Module Guidance Computer [*NASA*] (KSC)
LMGEN Load Module Generator (IAA)
LMGR Liberation Movement of the German Reich [*An association*] (EAIO)
LMGSM Latin and Mediterranean Group for Sport Medicine (EA)
LMGTP Le Mans Grand Touring Prototype [*Motorsports*]
LMGTS Le Mans Grand Touring Sports [*Motorsports*]
LMH Lady Margaret Hall [*Oxford University*]
LMH Lewis, M. H., Winchester VA [*STAC*]
LMH Light Metal Hydride
LMH Light Military Hovercraft (PDAA)
LMH Lipid Mobilizing Hormone [*Endocrinology*]
LMH Lumen Hour (IAA)
LMHA Lay Mission-Helpers Association (EA)
LMHA Louisiana Manufactured Housing Association (EARSL)
LMHC Licensed Mental Health Counselor (SEAT)
LMHC Lockheed Martin Hanford Corp. (SAUO)
LMHCA Louisiana Mental Health Counselors Association (SEAT)
LMHF Lauritz Melchior Heldentenor Foundation (EA)
LMHI Liga Medicorum Homoeopathica Internationalis [*International Homoeopathic Medical League*] (EA)
LMHR Lumen Hour (IAA)
lm-hr Lumen-Hour (IDOE)
LMHS Lancaster Mennonite Historical Society (EA)
LMHX Liquid Metal Heat Exchanger (NRCH)
LMI Collaboration Market Interest (SAUS)
LMI Labor Market Information [*Department of Labor*]
LMI Laurentian Mutual Insurance (SAUO)
LMI Lawn Mower Institute [*Later, OPEI*]
LMI Layer Management Interface [*Open Systems Interconnection*] (ODAA)
LMI Leeds Medical Information [*University of Leeds*] (IID)
LMi Leo Minor [*Constellation*]
LMI Leukocyte Migration Inhibition [*Hematology*]
LMI Lewis Management Instruction (SAUO)
LMI Liberation Movement of Iran [*Political party*] (PSAP)
LMI Life Management Institute [*Life Office Management Association*]
LMI Linkage Macro Instruction (VLIE)
LMI Link Management Interface [*Computer science*]
LMI Liquid Mercury Isolator

LMI .... Liquid Metal Ionization [*Spectrometry*]
LMI .... Livestock Merchandising Institute [*Later, LII*] (EA)
LMI .... Loaded Motional Impedance
LMI .... Load Moment Indicator [*Off-Highway equipment*]
LMI .... Local Management Interface [*Telecommunications*] (ACRL)
LMI .... Local Memory Image
LMI .... Logistics Management Information (SAUO)
LMI .... Logistics Management Institute [*Bethesda, MD*] [*Research center*] (AFM)
LMI .... Lower Middle Income (SAUO)
LMI .... Low-Molecular-Weight Inhibitor [*of protease activity*]
LMI .... Lumi [*Papua New Guinea*] [*Airport symbol*] (OAG)
LMI .... Luthiers Mercantile International [*Healdsburg, CA*] [*Commercial firm*]
LMI .... Lymphocyte Migration Index
LMIA .... LMI Aerospace, Inc. [*NASDAQ symbol*] (NASQ)
LMIA .... Louisiana Meat Industry Association (SRA)
LMIAA .... Licentiate Architect Member of the Incorporated Association of Architects and Surveyors [*British*] (DAS)
LMIAS .... Licentiate Surveyor Member of the Incorporated Association of Architects and Surveyors [*British*] (DAS)
LMI-ATS ..... Labor Market Information - Analytical Table Series [*Department of Labor - Employment and Training Administration*] (OICC)
LMIB .... Light Motorized Infantry Battalion (INF)
LMIC .... Land Management Information Center (SAUO)
LMIC .... Liberty Mutual Insurance Co.
LMIC .... Liquid Metal Information Center (SAUO)
LMIC .... Liquid Metals Information Center [*AEC*]
LMIC .... Lower Middle Income Country
LMIF .... Leukocyte Migration Inhibition Factor [*Hematology*] (DMAA)
LMIG .... Liquid Metal Ion Gun [*Surface analysis*]
LMIN .... Laboratory of Molecular and Integrative Neuroscience (GNE)
LMIN .... Lastminute.com plc ADS [*NASDAQ symbol*] (SG)
LMin .... Leo Minor [*Constellation*]
L/min .... Liters per Minute (ADWA)
L/MIN .... Liters per Minute
LMIS .... Labor Market Information System [*Department of Labor*]
LMIS .... Liquid Metal Ion Source
LMIS .... Lloyd's Maritime Information Services (IID)
LMIS .... Lloyd's Maritime Information Services Ltd. [*Information service or system*] (IID)
LMIS .... Logistics Management Information System [*Marine Corps*] (GFGA)
LMIT .... Lockheed Martin Idaho Technologies (GAAI)
LMiW .... Webster Parish Library, Minden, LA [*Library symbol*] [*Library of Congress*] (LCLS)
LMJ .... Greer, SC [*Location identifier*] [*FAA*] (FAAL)
LMK .... Landmark (NASA)
LMK .... Landmark Corp. [*Toronto Stock Exchange symbol*]
LMK .... Let Me Know (SAUS)
LML .... Lae [*Marshall Islands*] [*Airport symbol*] (OAG)
LML .... Landmark Land Co., Inc. (SAUO)
LML .... Lankard Materials Laboratory (SAUO)
LML .... Large and Medium Lymphocytes [*Medicine*]
LML .... Lean Misfire Limb (PDAA)
LML .... Lean Misfire Limit [*Automotive engine testing*]
LML .... Leesona Moos Laboratory
LML .... Left Mediolateral [*Episiotomy*] [*Obstetrics*]
LML .... Left Mentolateral [*Episiotomy*] [*Obstetrics*]
LML .... Left Middle Lobe [*of lung*] (DAVI)
LML .... Lerner Marine Laboratory (SAUO)
LML .... Lightweight Multiple Launcher (SAUS)
LML .... Line Message Log (SAUS)
LML .... Load Module Library [*Computer science*] (VLIE)
LML .... Logical Memory Level
LML .... Lookout Mountain Laboratories [*California*] (SAA)
LML .... Lowest Maintenance Level (MCD)
LMLA .... Leisureways Marketing [*NASDAQ symbol*] (SAG)
LMLA .... Lizzadro Museum of Lapidary Arts (SAUO)
LMLAF .... Leisureways Marketing Ltd [*NASDAQ symbol*] (TTSB)
LMLC .... Low Mobility Load Carrier (SAUS)
LMLE .... Left Mediolateral Episiotomy [*Medicine*] (STED)
LMLE .... Local Maximum Likelihood Estimates [*Statistics*]
LMLE .... Long Magazine Lee-Enfield [*British military*] (DMA)
LMLI .... Liberty Mutual Life Insurance (SAUO)
LMLR .... Load Memory Lockout Register
LM/LRV ..... Lunar Module/Lunar Roving Vehicle [*NASA*]
LMLSA .... Language Monography of the Linguistic Society of America (SAUO)
LML scar w/h ... Lower Midline Scar with Hernia [*Medicine*] (STED)
LMLV .... Lockheed Martin Launch Vehicle
LMLW .... Liquid Medium Level Waste [*Nuclear energy*] (NUCP)
LMM .... Lactobacillus Maintenance Medium [*Microbiology*]
LMM .... Laser Mortgage Mgmt. [*NYSE symbol*] (SG)
LMM .... Lemming Resources, Inc. [*Vancouver Stock Exchange symbol*]
LMM .... Lentigo Maligna Melanoma [*Oncology*]
LMM .... Library Microfilm & Materials Co.
LMM .... Light Meromyosin [*Biochemistry*]
LMM .... Lights Monitor Module [*Automotive engineering*]
LMM .... Linear Multi-Step Method (PDAA)
LMM .... Lines per Millimeter (AAG)
LMM .... Liquid Money Market [*Banking*]
LMM .... Living Masters of Music [*A publication*]
LMM .... Llanelly & Mynydd Mawr Railway [*Wales*]
LMM .... Local Modifications Memory [*Computer science*] (GART)
LMM .... Locator at Middle Marker [*Aviation*]
LMM .... Los Mochis [*Mexico*] [*Airport symbol*] (OAG)
LMM .... Lourenco Marques [*Mozambique*] [*Seismograph station code, US Geological Survey*] (SEIS)
LMM .... Lumbar Motion Monitor [*Ergonometrics*]
LMM .... Lutheran Men in Mission [*An association*] (EA)
LM/M^2 .... Lumen per Square Meter (WDAA)
lm/m^2 .... Lumens per Square Meter (IDOE)
LMMA .... LASER Microprobe Mass Analysis (AAEL)
LMMA .... Lutheran Medical Mission Association [*Defunct*] (EA)
LMMC .... L & M Trailer Manufacturing [*NCIC trailer make code*]
LMMCI ...... Labor Management Maritime Committee, Inc. (EA)
lmmd .... Low Molecular Weight Dextran [*Medicine*] (MELL)
LMMF .... Lederer Messianic Ministries (EA)
LMMF .... Lisa Madonia Memorial Fund [*An association*] (EA)
LMMF .... Local Maintenance and Management of Facilities [*Military*] (AABC)
LMMFHR .... Letelier-Moffitt Memorial Fund for Human Rights [*Later, LMMFHR/IPS*] (EA)
LMMFHR/IPS ... Letelier-Moffitt Memorial Fund for Human Rights/Institute for Policy Studies (EA)
LMMHD ..... Liquid Metal Magnetohydrodynamics
LMM IRSTS ... Lightweight Mast-Mounted IRST System (SAUS)
LMML .... Malta/Luqa [*Malta*] [*ICAO location identifier*] (ICLI)
LMMM ...... Malta [*Malta*] [*ICAO location identifier*] (ICLI)
LMMS .... LASER Microprobe Mass Spectrometry [*or Spectroscopy*]
LMMS .... Library Materials Management System
LMMS .... Lightweight Multipurpose Missile System (MCD)
LMMS .... Local Message Metering Service [*Telecommunications*] (TEL)
LMMS .... Logistics Maintenance Management System (SAUO)
LMMSA ..... Lightweight Modular Multi-purpose Spanning Assembly (SAUS)
LMMU .... Latin Mediterranean Medical Union [*See also UMML*] [*Mantua, Italy*] (EAIO)
LMMV .... Lamium Mild Mosaic Virus [*Plant pathology*]
LMN .... Lamoni, IA [*Location identifier*] [*FAA*] (FAAL)
LMN .... Lanthanum Magnesium Double Nitrate
LMN .... Lateral Mesencephalic Nucleus [*Brain anatomy*]
LMN .... Lateral Motoneuron [*Neurobiology*]
LMN .... Letter of Medical Necessity
LMN .... Library Management Network, Inc. [*Information service or system*] (IID)
LMN .... Library Micromation News (NITA)
LMN .... Limbang [*Malaysia*] [*Airport symbol*] (OAG)
LMN .... Lineman (AABC)
LMN .... Load Matching Network
LMN .... Locomotor Neuron [*Neurology*]
LMN .... Lornex Mining Corp. [*Vancouver Stock Exchange symbol*]
LMN .... Lost Music Network [*Defunct*] (EA)
LMN .... Lower Motor Neuron [*Anatomy*]
LMN .... Low Molecular Number [*Weight*] [*Medicine*] (EDAA)
LMN .... Northeast Louisiana University, Monroe, LA [*Library symbol*] [*Library of Congress*] (LCLS)
LMNA .... Label Manufacturers National Association [*Defunct*]
LMNA .... Land-Based Multimission Naval Aircraft (MCD)
LMNA .... Long-Range Multipurpose Naval Aircraft (HGAA)
LMND .... Lower Motor Neurone Degeneration [*Medicine*] (EDAA)
LMNDF .... Lesbian Mothers National Defense Fund (EA)
LMNE .... Luminent, Inc. [*NASDAQ symbol*]
LMNED .... Laboratories for Molecular Neuroendocrinology and Diabetes [*Tulane University*] [*Research center*] (RCD)
LMNL .... Lower Motor Neuron Lesion [*Medicine*]
LMNP .... Lake Manyara National Park (SAUO)
LMNRA .... Lake Mead National Recreation Area (SAUO)
LMNT .... Laminate
LMNTNG ..... Laminating
LMNVL .... Lemonville, TX [*American Association of Railroads railroad junction routing code*]
LMNW .... Lower Motor Neurone Weakness [*Medicine*] (EDAA)
LMNX .... Luminex Corp. [*NASDAQ symbol*] (SG)
LMO .... LASER Master Oscillator
LMO .... Lasmo Canada, Inc. [*Toronto Stock Exchange symbol*]
LMO .... Lens-Modulated Oscillator
LMO .... Light Machine Oil [*Petroleum engineering*]
LMO .... Lincoln Manufacturing Organization [*Automotive manufacturing*]
LMO .... Linear Master Oscillator
LMO .... Living Modified Organism
LMO .... Living Modified Organisms (SAUS)
LMO .... Localized Molecular Orbital (DB)
LMO .... Logistics Management Office [*Army*]
LMO .... London Meteorological Office (SAUO)
LMO .... Lookout Mountain Observatory [*California*] [*Seismograph station code, US Geological Survey*] [*Closed*] (SEIS)
LMO .... Ouachita Parish Public Library, Monroe, LA [*Library symbol*] [*Library of Congress*] (LCLS)
LMOA .... Locomotive Maintenance Officers' Association (EA)
LMOAC .... Local Medical Officers Advisory Committee (SAUO)
LMOAC .... Local Medical Officers Advisory Committee (SAUS)
LMOE .... Larson's Motor Express [*Common carrier symbol*]
LMOF .... Local Media Output Format (SAUO)
LMOI .... Labor Market and Occupational Information (OICC)
L/mole ...... Liters per Mole [*Chemistry*] (MEC)
LMOP .... Landfill Methane Outreach Program [*Environmental Protection Agency*] (EPAT)
LMOS .... Lake Michigan Ozone Study (SAUO)
LMOS .... Line-Maintenance Operating System [*Telecommunications*] (ITD)
LMOs .... Living Modified Organisms (SAUS)
LMOS .... Loop Maintenance Operations System [*Formerly, MLR*] [*Bell System*]

LMOTS ...... Launcher Maintenance & Operational Training System (SAUS)
LMP .... Labor Mobility Project [*Department of Labor*]
LMP .... Lamap [*New Hebrides*] [*Seismograph station code, US Geological Survey*] (SEIS)
LMP .... Laminated Metal Part
LMP .... Lampedusa [*Italy*] [*Airport symbol*] (OAG)
LMP .... Land Management Plan (ALAC)
LMP .... Land Management Planning (SAUO)
LMP .... LANTCOM Modernization Program (SAUO)
LMP .... Large Multifunctional Protease [*Medicine*] (DMAA)
lmp .... Last Menstrual Period [*Medicine*] (BCRP)
LMP .... Last Menstrual Period [*Medicine*]
LMP .... Late Middle Paleolithic
LMP .... Latent Membrane Potential [*Medicine*] (DMAA)
LMP .... Latent Membrane Protein [*Genetics*]
LMP .... Lawson Mardon Group Ltd. [*Toronto Stock Exchange symbol*]
LMP .... Layered Metal Phosphates [*Physical chemistry*]
LMP .... Left Mentoposterior [*A fetal position*] [*Obstetrics*]
LMP .... Le Mans Prototype [*Motorsports*]
LMP .... Library Material Processed
LMP .... Light Marching Pack [*Military*]
LMP .... Light Metal Products
LMP .... Linguistic Minorities Project [*Education*] (AIE)
LMP .... Liquid Metal Plasma Valve (IAA)
LMP .... Liquid Monopropellant
LMP .... Liquid Oxygen Maintenance Panel (AAG)
LMP .... List of Measurement Points (NASA)
LMP .... Literary Market Place [*A publication*]
LMP .... LM [*Lunar Module*] Mission Programmer [*NASA*] (KSC)
LMP .... London Metropolitan Police (CARL)
LMP .... Longitudinal Muscles of Pinnule
LMP .... Loopback Mirror Protocol [*Communications term*] (DCT)
LMP .... Low Malignant Potential [*Medicine*] (MELL)
LMP .... Low Melting Point
LMP .... Low-Molecular-Weight Polypeptide [*Biochemistry*]
LMP .... Lumbar Puncture [*Medicine*]
LMP .... Lunar Module Pilot [*Apollo*] [*NASA*]
LMP-1 .... Latent Membrane Protein-1 Expression [*Medicine*] (PALA)
LMPA .... Library and Museum of the Performing Arts (SAUO)
LMPA .... Methodist Local Preachers Mutual Aid Association (BUAC)
LMPA .... Qualified Member of the Master Photographers Association [*British*] (DBQ)
LMPB .... Labor-Management Public Board (SAUO)
LMPBLK ..... Lampblack
LMPCR ...... Ligation-Mediated Polymerase Chain Reaction [*Genetics*]
LMPEO ...... Large Message Performance Enhancement Outbound [*Communications term*] (DCT)
LMPG .... Light Mobile Protected Gun (INF)
LMPM .... Library Material Preservation Manual
LMPRT ...... Locally Most Powerful Rank Test [*Statistics*]
LMPS .... Lift Manufacturers Product Section - Material Handling Institute (NTPA)
LMPS .... Lunar Module Procedures Simulator [*NASA*]
LMPT .... Laboratory Material Property Transfer (SAUO)
LMPT .... Logistics and Material Planning Team (NATG)
LMQ .... La Malbaie [*Quebec*] [*Seismograph station code, US Geological Survey*] (SEIS)
LMQ .... Lamarque, TX [*Amtrak Busline code*]
LMQ .... Lamatuka [*Language symbol*] (ETLW)
LMQ .... Marsa Brega [*Libya*] [*Airport symbol*] (AD)
LMR .... Laboratory for Molecular Robotics [*University of Southern California*] (RCD)
LMR .... Labor-Management Relations
LMR .... Lamar, CO [*Amtrak rail station code*]
LMR .... La Maur, Inc. (SAUO)
LMR .... La Mourre [*France*] [*Seismograph station code, US Geological Survey*] (SEIS)
LMR .... Land Mobile Radio (NITA)
LMR .... LASER Magnetic Resonance (MCD)
LMR .... Launch Mission Rules [*NASA*] (KSC)
LMR .... Launch Monitor Room [*NASA*] (MCD)
LMR .... Left Medial Rectus [*Eye muscle*] (BABM)
LMR .... Library Maintenance Routine (IAA)
LMR .... Licensed Motor Repairer
LMR .... Light Modulation Recording
LMR .... Ligue Marxiste Revolutionnaire [*Revolutionary Marxist League*] [*Switzerland*] [*Political party*] (PPW)
LMR .... Linear Multiple Regression (IAA)
LMR .... Line Monitor/Recorder (MCD)
LMR .... Linguomandibular Reflex (STED)
LMR .... Lipman Management Resources Ltd. (NITA)
LMR .... Liquid Metal Reactor
LMR .... Liquid Molding Resin [*Organic chemistry*]
LMR .... Literary Magazine Review [*A publication*] (BRI)
LMR .... Liverpool & Manchester Railway (SAUO)
LMR .... Living Marine Resource [*Marine science*] (OSRA)
LMR .... Localized Magnetic Resonance (DAVI)
LMR .... Log Magnitude Ratio (STED)
LMR .... Longitudinal Medical Record (GART)
LMR .... Long Message Recovery (SAUO)
LMR .... Longmoor Military Railway [*British military*] (DMA)
LMR .... Louisiana Midland Railway [*Federal Railroad Administration identification code*]
LMR .... Lowest Maximum Range
LMR .... Lymphocytic Meningpolyradiculitis [*Medicine*] (DMAA)
LMR .... St. Louis, MO [*Location identifier*] [*FAA*] (FAAL)
LMRA .... Labor-Management Relations Act [*1947*]
LMRA .... Land Mobile Radio Architecture (SAUO)
LMRC .... London Medical Research Council (SAUO)
LMRCP ...... Licenciate in Midwifery of the Royal College of Physicians [*British*]
LMRD .... Launch Mission Rules Document [*NASA*] (KSC)
LMRDA ...... Labor-Management Reporting and Disclosure Act [*1959*]
LMRDA-IM ... Labor-Management Reporting and Disclosure Act - Investigative Matter [*FBI standardized term*]
LMRDFS .... Lightweight Man-Transportable Radio Direction-Finding System [*Army*]
LMREP ...... Lower Mississippi River Environmental Program (SAUO)
LMRI .... Living Marine Resources, Inc. (SAUO)
LMRK .... Landmark Graphics [*NASDAQ symbol*] (SAG)
LMRP .... Lunar Module Replaceable Package [*NASA*] (KSC)
LMRPC ...... Linear-Motor Resonant-Piston Compressor [*Navy*]
LMRR .... Lunar Module Rendezvous RADAR [*NASA*]
LMRS .... Labor-Management Relations Service (SAUO)
LMRS .... Labor-Management Relations Service of the US Conference of Mayors (EA)
LMRS .... Labor-Management Relations Staff [*Department of Agriculture*] (GFGA)
LMRS .... Land Mobile Radio Service [*Telecommunications*] (CIST)
LMRS .... Livestock Market Reporting Service (SAUO)
LMRS .... Lockheed Maintenance Recording System
LMRS .... London Military Radar Services (SAUO)
LMRS .... Lunar Module Rendezvous Simulator [*NASA*] (IAA)
LMRSH ...... Licentiate Member of the Royal Society for the Promotion of Health (SAUO)
LMRSH ...... Licentiate Member of the Royal Society of Health [*British*]
LMRT .... Logistics Management Responsibility Transfer (SAUS)
LMRTPI ..... Legal Member of the Royal Town Planning Institute [*British*] (DBQ)
LMRU .... Transports Lemarecha [*Intermodal shipping container symbol*] (TVRC)
LMS .... Laboratory for Mathematics and Statistics [*University of California at San Diego*] [*Research center*] (RCD)
LMS .... Laboratory Management System (SAUO)
LMS .... Laboratory of Molecular Structure [*Massachusetts Institute of Technology*]
LMS .... Labor Management System (GART)
LMS .... Lamsn & Sessions [*NYSE symbol*] (TTSB)
LMS .... [*The*] Lamson & Sessions Co. [*NYSE symbol*] (SPSG)
LMS .... Land Mass Simulator
LMS .... Land Mobile Service (DA)
LMS .... Lapel Microphone Scrambler [*Police and security equipment*]
LMS .... LASER Bank Management System [*Computer science*]
LMS .... LASER Magnetic Stage
LMS .... LASER Magnetic Storage International
LMS .... LASER Mapping System
LMS .... LASER Mass Spectrometer
LMS .... LASER Mass Spectroscopy (EDCT)
LMS .... Laser Monitoring System [*Police and security equipment*]
LMS .... Lateral Medullary Syndrome [*Medicine*] (MELL)
LMS .... Latin Mass Society (EAIO)
LMS .... Laurence-Moon Syndrome [*Medicine*]
LMS .... Lawer Mapping System (SAUO)
LMS .... Learning Management System [*Training term*] (LPT)
LMS .... Least Mean Square (IEEE)
LMS .... Least Median Squares (ARMP)
LMS .... Leave Management System (SAUO)
LMS .... Leiomyosarcoma [*Oncology*]
LMS .... Leisure Motivation Scale (IDYL)
LMS .... Lelean Memorial School (SAUO)
LMS .... LEM [*Lunar Excursion Module*] Mission Simulator [*NASA*]
LMS .... Levator Muscle of Scapula [*Medicine*] (MELL)
LMS .... Levator Muscle Syndrome [*Medicine*] (MELL)
LMS .... Level Measuring Set [*for test signals*] [*Telecommunications*] (TEL)
LMS .... Library Maintenance System (PDAA)
LMS .... Library Management System
LMS .... License Management Service (SAUO)
LMS .... Licentiate in Medicine and Surgery [*British*]
LMS .... Licentiate in/of Medicine and Surgery (SAUO)
LMS .... Lightning Mapper Sensor [*NASA*]
LMS .... Lightweight Multi-purpose Shelter (SAUS)
LMS .... Limestone [*Technical drawings*]
LMS .... Limited Mass Search [*Chromatography*]
LMS .... Linear Measuring System
LMS .... Liquid Measuring System
LMS .... Liquid Metal System
LMS .... List Management System
LMS .... Literature Management System
LMS .... Little More Steady [*Telegraphy*] (PCTE)
LMS .... Loadmaster Systems, Inc. [*Vancouver Stock Exchange symbol*]
LMS .... Load Matching Switch
LMS .... Load Measurement System (NASA)
LMS .... Local Management of Schools [*British*]
LMS .... Local Measured Service [*Telecommunications*] (TEL)
LMS .... Local Missile Selector (IAA)
LMS .... Local Mitigation Strategy [*Emergency Management*] (EMA)
LMS .... Local Monitoring Station (SAUO)
LMS .... Location and Monitoring Service [*Telecommunications*] (OTD)
LMS .... Lockheed Marine Services (SAUO)
LMS .... Lockheed Martin Services (SAUO)
LMS .... Lockheed Missile System (MCD)

LMS .... Logistics Management Specialist (MCD)
LMS .... Logistics Management Systems (ACAE)
LMS .... Logistics Master Schedules (MCD)
LMS .... Lomas Helicopters Ltd. [British] [ICAO designator] (FAAC)
Lms .... London, Madrigal Society (SAUO)
LMS .... London Malacological Society (SAUO)
LMS .... London Mathematical Society [England] (BUAC)
LMS .... London Medical Schools (SAUO)
LMS .... London Medical Society (SAUO)
LMS .... London Medieval Society [England] (BUAC)
LMS .... London Mendicity Society (SAUO)
LmS .... London Microfilming Services Ltd., London, ON, Canada [Library symbol] [Library of Congress] (LCLS)
LMS .... London, Midland & Scottish Railway [British]
LMS .... London Missionary Society
LMS .... London Municipal Society (SAUO)
LMS .... Lookout Mountain Observatory [California] [Seismograph station code, US Geological Survey] (SEIS)
LMS .... Lotto Management Services (SAUO)
LMS .... Lotus Messaging Switch [Communications term] (DCT)
LMS .... Louisville, MS [Location identifier] [FAA] (FAAL)
LMS .... Low Moisture Silage (SAUO)
LMS .... Lubrication Management System [Automotive engineering]
LM/S......... Lumens per Second (MCD)
LMS .... Lunar Mass Spectrometer [NASA]
LMS .... Lunar Measuring System [Aerospace]
LMS .... Lunar Module Simulator [NASA] (SSD)
LMS .... Lutheran Mission Societies (EA)
LMSA........ Labor-Management Services Administration [Department of Labor]
LMSA........ Large Metoscale Area (PDAA)
LMSA........ Large Millimeter and Submillimeter Array (SAUS)
LMSA........ Large Millimetre and Submillimetre Array
LMSA........ Silber-Messing-Lot (SAUS)
LMSAL ...... Lockheed-Martin Solar and Astrophysics Laboratory
LMSC........ LAN/MAN Standards Committee (SAUO)
LMSC........ Let Me See Correspondence [Business term]
LMSC........ Liquid Metals Safety Committee [AEC] (MCD)
LMSC........ Little Missionary Sisters of Charity (TOCD)
LMSC........ Lockheed Missiles and Space Company (SAUO)
LMSC........ Lockheed Missiles & Space Corp. [Subsidiary of Lockheed Aircraft Corp.]
LMSC........ Logistics Management Systems Center [Military]
LMSD........ Lockheed Missile and Space Division (IAA)
LMSD........ Lockheed Missile System Division (SAUO)
LMSE........ Laboratory Module Simulation Equipment
LMSE........ Liquid Metal Slip Ring
LMSEC ...... Lumen Second (IAA)
LMSEO ...... Labor-Management Standards Enforcement Service (SAUO)
lm/sf......... Lumen per Square Foot (MIST)
LMSFX ...... Federated Municipal Securities Cl.A [Mutual fund ticker symbol] (SG)
LMSG........ Lockheed Martin Services Group (SAUO)
LMSG........ Low Magnetic Saturation Garnet
LMSI......... Association of Lithuanian Foresters in Exile [Defunct] (EA)
LMSI......... Local Mobile Station Identity (SAUO)
LMSI......... Lockheed Martin Services, Incorporated (SAUO)
LMSN........ Local Message Switched Network
LMSQFT..... Lumen per Square Foot (IAA)
LMSR........ Large, Medium Speed RO/RO [Roll On/Roll Off] [Navy]
LMSR........ London, Midland & Scottish Railway [British]
LMSR........ London, Midland & Scottish Railway Co. (SAUO)
LMSS........ Land Mobile Satellite Service [Rockwell International Corp.]
LMSS........ LANTIRN Mobility Shelter Set (SAUS)
LMSS........ Lockheed Martin Space Systems
LMSS........ Lunar Mapping and Survey System [NASA] (MCD)
LMSSA ...... Licentiate in Medicine and Surgery of the Society of Apothecaries [British]
LMST........ Learning of Middle Size Task [Psychology]
lmst.......... Limestone (VRA)
LMSV........ Left Maximal Spatial Voltage [Medicine] (EDAA)
LMSW........ Load Machine Status Word (SAUO)
LMSWA ..... Land Management Society of Western Australia
LMT.......... Air Limousin TA [France] [ICAO designator] (FAAC)
LMT.......... Klamath Falls [Oregon] [Airport symbol] (OAG)
LMT.......... Laboratory of Molecular Toxicology [National Institute of Environmental Health Sciences] (RCD)
LMT.......... Large Millimeter Telescope [US-Mexico project] [Proposed, 1994]
LMT.......... LASER Marksmanship Trainer (MCD)
LMT.......... Launch Motor Test
LMT.......... Leadership and Management Training [Navy] (NVT)
LMT.......... Learning Methods Test [Mills] [Education]
LMT.......... Left Mentotransverse [A fetal position] [Obstetrics]
LMT.......... Lemonthyme [Tasmania] [Seismograph station code, US Geological Survey] [Closed] (SEIS)
LMT.......... Length, Mass, Time [Physics]
LMT.......... Length of Mean Turn
LMT.......... Levtech Medical Technologies Ltd. [Vancouver Stock Exchange symbol]
LMT.......... Licensed Massage Therapist [Medicine]
LMT.......... Lifetime Medical Television
LMT.......... Limit (AFM)
LMT.......... Local Mean Time (AFM)
LMT.......... Lockheed Martin [NYSE symbol] (TTSB)
LMT.......... Lockheed Martin Corp. [NYSE symbol] (SAG)
LMT.......... Logical Mapping Table
LMT.......... Logic Master Tape (IAA)
LMT.......... Logic Module Tester (ACAE)
LMT.......... Logistic Management of the Turnaround (MCD)
LMT.......... Logistics Management Team [Navy]
LMT.......... Log Mean Temperature
LMT.......... Louisiana Midland Transport [AAR code]
LMT.......... Lowenfeld Mosaic Test [Psychology]
LMTA .... Language Modalities Test for Aphasia [Psychology]
LMTA .... Library/Media Technical Assistant
LMTA .... Light Microscopy Trace Analysis
LMTA .... Louisiana Motor Transport Association (SRA)
LMTAS ...... Lockheed Martin Tactical Aircraft Systems
LMTBR ...... Liquid Metal Thorium Breeder Reactor
LMTBS ...... Lightweight Multifunction Tactical Beacon System (MCD)
LMTC .... Launcher Maintenance Trainer Course
lmtd .... Limited (AAMN)
LMTD .... Logarithmic Mean Temperature Difference
LMTDNS .... Launch Environment, Mission, Type, Design Number, and Series [Missiles] (AFM)
LMTEC ...... L'Association des Media et de la Technologie en Education du Canada [Canada] (EAIO)
LMTG........ Limiting (MSA)
LMTI......... Louisiana Training Institute, Monroe, LA [Library symbol] [Library of Congress] (LCLS)
LMTLSS..... Limitless
LMTN........ Labor Market Training Needs
LMTN........ Leamington [British depot code]
LMTO........ Linear Combination of Muffin Tin Orbitals [Atomic physics]
LMTPI .... Legal Member of the Town Planning Institute [British] (DLA)
LMTR........ Limiter [Electronics]
LMTS .... LaserMaster Technologies [NASDAQ symbol] (TTSB)
LMTS .... LaserMaster Technologies, Inc. [NASDAQ symbol] (SAG)
LMTS .... Liquid-Mirror Telescopes
LMTU........ Lehnkering Montan Transport [Intermodal shipping container symbol] (TVRC)
LMTV........ Light Medium Tactical Vehicle [Army] (RDA)
LMTVT....... Light Medium Tactical Vehicle Trailer (SAUS)
LMU .... Lake Mountain [Utah] [Seismograph station code, US Geological Survey] (SEIS)
LMU .... Land Management Unit (SAUO)
LMU .... LAN Manager for Unix [Computer science] (HODG)
LMU .... Latin Monetary Union [Established in 1865]
LMU .... Lifer Management Unit (WDAA)
LMU .... Lincoln Memorial University [Tennessee]
LMU .... Line Monitor Unit
LMU .... Location Messaging Unit [Communications]
LMU .... Logical Network Management Unit (SAUO)
LMU .... Loyola Marymount University [Los Angeles, CA]
LMU .... University of Missouri, Law School, Columbia, MO [OCLC symbol] (OCLC)
LMUA........ Lloyd's Motor Underwriters Association [British] (DBA)
L Mus .... Licentiate in Music (SAUO)
LMUS........ Licentiate in Music, University of Saskatchewan (SAUO)
LMus .... Licentiate of Music
LMusLCM... Licentiate in Music, London, College of Music (SAUO)
LMusLCM... Licentiate in Music of the London College of Music [British] (DBQ)
LMusTCL.... Licentiate in Music, Trinity College of Music, London [British] (DBQ)
LMUU........ Landmark Union [Intermodal shipping container symbol] (TVRC)
LMV .... Larva Migrans Visceralis [Medicine] (MELL)
LMV .... Lettuce Mosaic Virus
LMV .... Light Motor Vehicle
LMV .... Long Market Value [Investment term]
LMV .... Low Mass Vehicle
LMVD........ Licensed Motor Vehicle Dealer (SAUO)
LMVD........ Lower Mississippi Valley Division [Army Engineers]
LMVE........ Linear, Minimum Variance Estimation (PDAA)
LMVUS ...... League of Men Voters of the United States (SAUO)
LMW......... Ladd Mountain [Washington] [Seismograph station code, US Geological Survey] (SEIS)
LMW......... Lands, Minerals, & Watershed [Regional office of USDA Forest Service] (ALAC)
LMW......... LASER Microwelder
LMW......... Lower Midwest
LMW......... Low-Molecular Weight [Chemistry]
lm/W .... Lumens per Watt
LMWA .... Low-Molecular-Weight Organic Acid (ABAC)
LMWAGS.... Local Medical Workforce Advisory Groups (SAUO)
lmwd .... Limewood (VRA)
LMWD........ Low-Molecular-Weight Dextran [Medicine] (AAMN)
LMWH........ Low-Molecular-Weight Heparin [Biochemistry]
LMWHC ..... Low-Molecular-Weight Hydrocarbon (MCD)
LMWK........ Low Molecular-Weight Kininogen [Biochemistry]
LMWP........ Labor-Management Welfare-Pension [Reports] [Department of Labor]
LMWP........ Low-Molecular-Weight Proteinuria [Medicine]
LMWU........ Railway Marketing [Intermodal shipping container symbol] (TVRC)
LMX .... Aerolineas Mexicanas JS SA de CV [Mexico] [ICAO designator] (FAAC)
LM/X......... LAN Manager for Unix (SAUO)
LMX .... LMX Resources Ltd. [Vancouver Stock Exchange symbol]
LMX .... London Market Excess of Loss [British] (BUAC)
LMX .... L-Type Multiplex [Telecommunications] (TEL)
LMXB........ Low-Mass X-Ray Binary [Star system]
LMXE........ Leonard Motor Express [Common carrier symbol]
LMY .... Lake Murray [Papua New Guinea] [Airport symbol] (OAG)

LMY .... Lamy, NM [*Amtrak rail station code*]
LN .... Background Noise Level (CAAL)
ln .... Central and Southern Line Islands [*gb (Gilbert Islands) used in records cataloged after October 1978*] [*MARC country of publication code*] [*Library of Congress*] (LCCP)
LN .... Jamahiriya Libyan Arab Airlines (SAUO)
LN .... Labionasal [*lip and nose*] [*Otorhinolaryngology*] (DAVI)
ln .... Lane (ELAL)
Ln .... Lane (PROS)
LN .... Lane (MCD)
Ln .... Lanthanide [*Chemical element*] (WGA)
LN .... Large Node (SAUS)
LN .... Large-Probe Nephelometer [*NASA*]
LN .... LASER Nephelometry [*Analytical biochemistry*]
LN .... Last Name [*Linguistics*] (IEL)
LN .... Lateen [*Ship's rigging*] (ROG)
LN .... Lateral Neuropil [*Neurology*]
LN .... Law Notes, American Bar Association Section of General Practice [*A publication*] (DLA)
LN .... Law Notes, London [*A publication*] (DLA)
LN .... Leading Note [*Music*] (ROG)
LN .... League of Nations [*1919-1946*]
LN .... Legalman [*Military*] (POLM)
LN .... Legal News [*Canada*] [*A publication*] (DLA)
LN .... Legal Notice (OICC)
LN .... Legal Notification [*Ghana*] [*A publication*] (DLA)
LN .... Lepista Nuda [*A fungus*]
L-N .... Lesch-Nyhan [*Medicine*]
LN .... Lesion Number [*Pathology*]
L/N .... Letter-Numerical [*system*] (DAVI)
LN .... Liaison (AFM)
LN .... Liber Niger [*Black Book*] [*A publication*] (DLA)
Ln .... Librarian (AL)
LN .... Libyan Arab Airlines [*ICAO designator*] (AD)
LN .... Licensed Nurse
Ln .... Lien (EBF)
LN .... Lien
LN .... Line (AAG)
ln .... Line (VRA)
LN .... Link Number (MHDB)
LN .... Lip Nerve
LN .... Lipoid Nephrosis (DB)
LN .... Liquid Nitrogen
LN .... Lira Nuova [*Monetary unit*] [*Italy*] (ROG)
LN .... Lithuanian Navigation (BUAC)
LN .... Load Number
Ln .... Loan (TBD)
LN .... Loan
LN .... Local National
LN .... Local Network (FOTI)
ln .... Logarithm (Natural) [*Mathematics*]
LN .... Logical Network (SAUO)
LN .... Logistics Needs (SAUO)
LN .... Lot Number
LN .... Louisville & Nashville Railroad [*Federal Railroad Administration identification code*]
LN .... Love Notes [*An association*] (EA)
LN .... Low Foliage Nester [*Ecology*]
LN .... Low Noise (IAA)
LN .... Luminometer Number [*Hydrocarbon fuel rating*]
LN .... Lupus Network (EA)
LN .... Lymph Node [*Medicine*]
LN .... New Orleans Public Library, New Orleans, LA [*Library symbol*] [*Library of Congress*] (LCLS)
ln--- .... North Atlantic Ocean [*MARC geographic area code*] [*Library of Congress*] (LCCP)
LN .... Northern League (Italy) [*Political party*] (PSAP)
LN .... Norway [*Civil aircraft markings - international*] (PIPO)
LN_2 .... Liquid Nitrogen [*NASA*] (NASA)
LNA .... Airlen [*Russian Federation*] [*ICAO designator*] (FAAC)
LNA .... Lahu National Army [*Myanmar*] [*Political party*] (EY)
LNA .... Launch Numerical Aperture [*Telecommunications*] (TEL)
LNA .... Leading National Advertiser
LNA .... Leading National Advertisers, Inc.
LNA .... League for National Advancement [*Papua New Guinea*] [*Political party*] (EY)
LNA .... League of the Norden Associations (EA)
LNA .... Leucine Nitroanilide [*Biochemistry*]
LNA .... Liberation News Agency [*Vietnam*]
LNA .... Liberian National Airways (SAUO)
LNA .... Libyan National Alliance (BUAC)
LNA .... Lithium Nitrate Ammoniate [*Inorganic chemistry*]
LNA .... Lithographers National Association
LNA .... Lithuanian Numismatic Association (EA)
LNA .... Local Navy Authority
LNA .... Local Numbering Area [*Telecommunications*] (TEL)
LnA .... London Allowance [*British military*] (DMA)
LNA .... Love-N-Addiction [*An association*] (EA)
LNA .... Low-Noise Amplifier [*Satellite communications*]
LNA .... Low-Noise Antenna
LNA .... Lunar Resources Ltd. [*Vancouver Stock Exchange symbol*]
LNA .... New Orleans City Archives, New Orleans, LA [*Library symbol*] [*Library of Congress*] (LCLS)
LNA .... West Palm Beach, FL [*Location identifier*] [*FAA*] (FAAL)
LNAA .... Large Neutral Amino Acid [*Biochemistry*] (DB)
LNAA .... Licentiate of the National Association of Auctioneers, House Agents, Rating Surveyors and Valuers (SAUO)
LNAC .... Amistad Research Center Library, New Orleans, LA [*Library symbol*] [*Library of Congress*] (LCLS)
LNAC .... Librarians for Nuclear Arms Control [*Defunct*] (EA)
LNAC .... Limited National Agency Check (AFM)
LNAC .... Louisville, New Albany & Corydon Railroad Co. [*AAR code*]
LNA/DC ...... Low Noise Amplifier/Downconverter (ACAE)
LNADW ...... Lower North Atlantic Deep Water [*Oceanography*]
LNAH .... League of Night Adoration in the Home [*Later, NAH*] (EA)
LNAH .... Licentiate of National Association of Auctioneers and House Agents (SAUO)
LNAL .... Louisville, New Albany & Corydon Railroad [*Federal Railroad Administration identification code*]
LNaN .... Northwestern State University of Louisiana, Natchitoches, LA [*Library symbol*] [*Library of Congress*] (LCLS)
LNaNa ...... Natchitoches Parish Library, Natchitoches, LA [*Library symbol*] [*Library of Congress*] (LCLS)
LNAP .... Low Nonessential Air Pressure (IEEE)
LNapA ...... Assumption Parish Library, Napoleonville, LA [*Library symbol*] [*Library of Congress*] (LCLS)
LNAPL ...... Light Non-Aqueous Phase Liquids
LNAR .... Lippold and Arnett [*Common carrier symbol*]
LNAV .... Lateral Navigation [*Provides computer description of aircraft's planned lateral flight path*] (GAVI)
lnaz- .... Azores Islands [*MARC geographic area code*] [*Library of Congress*] (LCCP)
LNB .... Lamen Bay [*Vanuata*] [*Airport symbol*] (OAG)
LNB .... Large Automated Navigational Buoy [*Nautical term*] (HRNC)
LNB .... Large Navigation Buoy [*Marine science*] (MSC)
LNB .... Liberty National Bancorp, Inc. (EFIS)
LNB .... Lithium Niobate (PDAA)
LNB .... Local Name Base [*Computer science*]
LNB .... Louisiana National Bank [*Baton Rouge*] (TSSD)
LNB .... Low Nitrogen Oxide Burner [*Combustion technology*]
LNB .... Low-Noise Block [*Satellite communications*]
LNB .... Low Noise Block Converter (SAUO)
LNB .... Lumbar Nerve Block [*Medicine*] (MELL)
LNB .... Lymph Node Biopsy [*Medicine*] (MELL)
LNB .... New Orleans Baptist Theological Seminary, New Orleans, LA [*Library symbol*] [*Library of Congress*] (LCLS)
LNBA .... Bell Aerospace Co., New Orleans, LA [*Library symbol*] [*Library of Congress*] (LCLS)
LNBA .... Laymen's National Bible Association (EA)
LNBC .... Laymen's National Bible Committee [*Formerly, LNC*] [*Later, LNBA*] (EA)
LNBC .... Liberty National Bancorp, Inc. (SAUO)
LNBD .... Lens Board [*Mechanical engineering*]
LNBF .... Low-Noise Block Feed [*Satellite communications*]
LNBK .... Lane Financial, Inc. (SAUO)
lnbm- .... Bermuda [*MARC geographic area code*] [*Library of Congress*] (LCCP)
LNBpA ...... Assumption Parish Library, Napoleonville (SAUS)
LNBS .... Lesotho National Broadcasting Service [*South Africa*]
LNC .... Lancaster, PA [*Amtrak rail station code*]
LNC .... Lancaster, TX [*Location identifier*] [*FAA*] (FAAL)
LNC .... Lance
LNC .... Lancer Resources [*Vancouver Stock Exchange symbol*]
LNC .... Landscape Nursery Council (EA)
LNC .... Languedocien [*Language symbol*] (ETLW)
LNC .... Laymen's National Committee [*Later, LNBC*] (EA)
LNC .... League of Nations Covenant (SAUO)
LNC .... Legal Nurse Consultant (NUJO)
LNC .... Leith Nautical College (SAUO)
LNC .... Leonard Nimoy Club (EA)
LNC .... Libertarian National Committee (SAUO)
LNC .... Lincoln National Corp. [*NYSE symbol*] (SPSG)
LNC .... Lincoln National Corp. Capital I [*NYSE symbol*] (SAG)
LNC .... Lincoln National Corp. Capital II [*NYSE symbol*] (SAG)
LNC .... Lincoln Natl Corp. [*NYSE symbol*] (TTSB)
LNC .... Local Naval Commander
LNC .... LORAN Navigation Chart [*Air Force*]
LNC .... Low-Noise Cable
LNC .... Low Noise Converter (SAUO)
LNC .... Low-Noise Converter [*Satellite communications*]
LNC .... Lunacharskoye [*Former USSR*] [*Seismograph station code, US Geological Survey*] [*Closed*] (SEIS)
LNC .... Lymph Node Cell [*Medicine*]
LNC .... New Orleans Public Library, New Orleans, LA [*OCLC symbol*] (OCLC)
lnca- .... Canary Islands [*MARC geographic area code*] [*Library of Congress*] (LCCP)
LNCB .... Lincoln Bancorp [*NASDAQ symbol*] (NASQ)
LNCC .... LINC Capital [*NASDAQ symbol*]
LNCC .... LINC Capital, Inc. [*NASDAQ symbol*] (NASQ)
LNCE .... Lance, Inc. [*NASDAQ symbol*] (SAG)
LNCE .... Lance Truck-Mount Camper [*NCIC trailer make code*]
LNCFS ...... Low Nitric Oxide [*Combustion technology*]
LNCH .... Launch (AAG)
LNCHR ...... Launcher
LNCI .... Lancia [*NCIC car make code*]
LNCLN ...... Lincoln, NE [*American Association of Railroads railroad junction routing code*]
LNCM .... Licentiate, National College of Music (SAUO)

LncNtC .... Lincoln National Convertible Securities Fund, Inc. [*Associated Press*] (SAG)
LNCO .... Lincoln Electric Company [*NCIC trailer make code*]
L-NCP .... Liberal-National Country Party [*Australia*] [*Political party*] (PPW)
LNCPr .... Lincln Natl $3.00 Cv Pfd [*NYSE symbol*] (TTSB)
LNCR .... Lincare Holdings [*NASDAQ symbol*] (TTSB)
LNCR .... Lincare Holdings, Inc. [*NASDAQ symbol*] (SAG)
LNCR .... Lincoln Resources, Inc. (SAUO)
LncrOrt .... Lancer Orthodontics, Inc. [*Associated Press*] (SAG)
LNCRT .... Licentiate of the National College of Rubber Technology [*British*] (DI)
LNCT .... Lancit Media Productions [*NASDAQ symbol*] (TTSB)
LNCT .... Lancit Media Productions Ltd. [*NASDAQ symbol*] (SAG)
LNCU .... Large Node Computer Unit (SAUS)
lncv- .... Cape Verde [*Islands*] [*MARC geographic area code*] [*Library of Congress*] (LCCP)
LNCY .... Lunacy [*FBI standardized term*]
LND .... Dillard University, New Orleans, LA [*Library symbol*] [*Library of Congress*] (LCLS)
LND .... Lander, WY [*Location identifier*] [*FAA*] (FAAL)
LND .... Lawyers for Nuclear Disarmament [*Defunct*] (EAIO)
LND .... Lesch-Nyhan Disease [*Medicine*] (EDAA)
LND .... Light-Near Dissociation [*Medicine*] (EDAA)
LND .... Limiting Nose Dive [*Aerospace*]
LND .... Lincoln National Direct Placement Fund (SAUO)
LND .... Lincoln National Income Fund, Inc. [*Formerly, Lincoln National Direct Placement Fund, Inc.*] [*NYSE symbol*] (SPSG)
LND .... Lincoln Natl Income Fd [*NYSE symbol*] (TTSB)
LND .... Lined
LND .... Loaned [*Telegraphy*] (PCTE)
LND .... Local Number Dialed [*Telecommunications*] (TEL)
LND .... Local Number Dialling [*Telecommunications*] (NITA)
LND .... London [*Ontario*] [*Seismograph station code, US Geological Survey*] (SEIS)
LND .... Lymph Node Dissection [*Medicine*]
LND .... Skargardsflyg, AB, Finland [*FAA designator*] (FAAC)
LNDA .... Lindatech, Inc. [*NASDAQ symbol*] (QUAN)
LNDB .... Landmark Bancshares (SAUO)
LNDB .... Lesotho National Development Bank (BUAC)
LNDBG ...... Lindsborg, KS [*American Association of Railroads railroad junction routing code*]
LNDC .... Delgado Community College, New Orleans, LA [*Library symbol*] [*Library of Congress*] (LCLS)
LNDC .... Landec Corp. [*NASDAQ symbol*] (TTSB)
LNDC .... Lesotho National Development Corp.
LNDCF .... Locally-Normalized Discrete Correlation Function [*Mathematics*]
LNDF .... Linear Natural Density Filter (AAEL)
LNDFLL ..... Landfill
LNDG .... Landing [*Maps and charts*] (KSC)
Lndg .... Lending (TBD)
LNDH .... Local Nationals, Direct Hire [*Military*] (AABC)
LNDI .... Lotus Notes Document Imaging (SAUO)
LN-DI .... Lotus Notes-Document Imaging (VLIE)
LNDL .... Least Negative Down Level (IAA)
LNDL .... Lindal Cedar Homes [*NASDAQ symbol*] (SAG)
LNDMRK ..... Landmark
LNDNG ...... Landing [*Commonly used*] (OPSA)
LNDO .... Local Neglect of Differential Overlap [*Physical chemistry*]
LNDR .... Land Rover [*NCIC truck make code*]
LNDR .... Land Rover [*NCIC car make code*]
Lndr .... Lender (TBD)
LNDRMT .... Laundromat
LNDRY ...... Laundry
LNDSCP .... Landscape
LndsPc ...... Landsing Pacific Fund [*Associated Press*] (SAG)
LNDSPTPLT ... Landing Support Platoon [*Navy*] (DNAB)
LNDY .... Lindley Trucking Service [*Common carrier symbol*]
LNE .... Late Network Entry (SAUS)
LNE .... Lehigh & New England Railway Co. [*Absorbed into Consolidated Rail Corp.*] [*AAR code*]
LNE .... Liquid Nitrogen Evaporator
LNE .... Local Network Emulator
LNE .... Lonorore [*Vanuata*] [*Airport symbol*] (OAG)
LNE .... Lymph Node Enlargement [*Medicine*] (DMAA)
LNE .... Northeast Louisiana University, Monroe, LA [*OCLC symbol*] (OCLC)
LNEP .... Low-Noise Emission Product (GFGA)
LNER .... Linear Films, Inc. (SAUO)
LNER .... London & North Eastern Railway [*British*]
LNERG ...... London & North Eastern Railway Group [*British*]
LNESC ...... LULAC [*League of United Latin American Citizens*] National Educational Service Centers (EA)
LneSStk ..... Lone Star Steakhouse & Saloon, Inc. [*Associated Press*] (SAG)
LNET .... LodgeNet Entertainment [*NASDAQ symbol*] (TTSB)
LNET .... Lodgenet Entertainment Corp. [*NASDAQ symbol*] (SAG)
LNewr .... Pointe Coupee Parish Library, New Roads, LA [*Library symbol*] [*Library of Congress*] (LCLS)
LNF .... Latvian National Foundation [*Stockholm, Sweden*] (EAIO)
LNF .... Leon's Furniture Ltd. [*Toronto Stock Exchange symbol*]
LNF .... Linfen [*Republic of China*] [*Seismograph station code, US Geological Survey*] (SEIS)
LNF .... Liposoluble Neutral Fraction (OA)
LNF .... Lithuanian National Foundation (EA)
LNF .... Little-Known Fan [*of science fiction or fantastic literature*] [*See also BNF*]
LNF .... Local National Forces [*SEATO*] (CINC)
LNF .... Lomas & Nettleton Financial Corp. (SAUO)
LNF .... London Flights (Biggin Hill) Ltd. [*British*] [*ICAO designator*] (FAAC)
LNF .... Low-Noise Feed [*Satellite communications*]
LNFC .... Leonard Nimoy Fan Club (EA)
LNFCS ...... Leonard Nimoy Fan Club, Spotlight (EAIO)
LNFM .... Louisiana Masonic Grand Lodge, New Orleans, LA [*Library symbol*] [*Library of Congress*] (LCLS)
LNG .... Lateral Nasal Gland [*Anatomy*]
LNG .... Length (IAA)
LNG .... Lese [*Papua New Guinea*] [*Airport symbol*] (OAG)
Lng .... Linging (MIST)
LNG .... Lining (MSA)
LNG .... Liquefied Natural Gas
LNG .... Liquid Natural Gas [*BTS*] [*DOE*] (TAG)
LNG .... Liste de Noms Geographiques [*A publication*] (BJA)
LNG .... Loaning [*Telegraphy*] (PCTE)
LNG .... Long
LNG .... Lounge
LNG .... Luning [*Nevada*] [*Seismograph station code, US Geological Survey*] [*Closed*] (SEIS)
Lnge .... Lounge [*Classified advertising*] (ADA)
LNGR .... Lingerie
LngStk ...... Longhorn Steaks, Inc. [*Associated Press*] (SAG)
LNH .... Large Number Hypothesis [*Medicine*] (DMAA)
LNH .... Lengeh [*Iran*] [*Airport symbol*] (AD)
LNH .... LNH REIT [*Real Estate Investment Trust*], Inc. [*Associated Press*] (SAG)
LNH .... Lunar Near Horizon [*NASA*] (KSC)
LNHA .... Louisiana Historical Association, Memorial Hall, New Orleans, LA [*Library symbol*] [*Library of Congress*] (LCLS)
LNHiC .... [*The*] Historic New Orleans Collection, New Orleans, LA [*Library symbol*] [*Library of Congress*] (LCLS)
LNHS .... London Natural History Society (SAUO)
LNI .... Inland Library System, Redlands, CA [*OCLC symbol*] (OCLC)
LNI .... Local Network Interface [*Communications term*] (DCT)
LNI .... Log Neutralization Index [*Microbiology*]
LNI .... Lonely, AK [*Location identifier*] [*FAA*] (FAAL)
LNIAC .... Los Ninos International Adoption Center (EA)
LNIB .... Like New in Box [*Watch collecting*]
LNIB .... Loch Ness Investigation Bureau [*Inactive*] (EA)
LNil .... Iberia Parish Library, New Iberia (SAUS)
LNil .... Iberia Parish Library, New Iberia, LA [*Library symbol*] [*Library of Congress*] (LCLS)
LNIM .... Latvian National Indepedence Movement (CARL)
LNIS .... Atlantic Naval Intelligence Summary (MCD)
LNIT .... Local Nasal Immunotherapy
lnjn- .... Jan Mayen [*MARC geographic area code*] [*Library of Congress*] (LCCP)
LNK .... Airlink Airlines (Pty) Ltd. [*South Africa*] [*ICAO designator*] (FAAC)
LNK .... Air Link Corp. (SAUO)
LNK .... Clublink Corp. [*Toronto Stock Exchange symbol*] (SG)
L/Nk .... Lance-Naik [*British military*] (DMA)
LNK .... Lenkoran [*Former USSR*] [*Seismograph station code, US Geological Survey*] (SEIS)
LNK .... Lincoln [*Nebraska*] [*Airport symbol*] (OAG)
LNK .... Lincoln, NE [*Amtrak rail station code*]
LNK .... Link
LNKEDT ..... Linkage Editor [*Computer science*] (IAA)
LNKPSC ..... Link Performance Assessment Program (SAUO)
LNL .... Land O'Lakes [*Wisconsin*] [*Airport symbol*] (AD)
LNL .... Land O' Lakes, WI [*Location identifier*] [*FAA*] (FAAL)
LNL .... Law Library of Louisiana, New Orleans, LA [*OCLC symbol*] (OCLC)
LNL .... Let Nicaragua Live [*An association*] [*Defunct*] (EA)
LNL .... Loyal North Lancashire Regiment (SAUO)
LNL .... Loyola University, Law Library, New Orleans (SAUO)
LNL .... Loyola University, New Orleans, LA [*Library symbol*] [*Library of Congress*] (LCLS)
LNL .... Lymph Node Lymphocyte [*Medicine*] (DMAA)
LNLA .... Lithuanian National League of America (EA)
LNLC .... Ladies' Naval Luncheon Club (WDAA)
LNLI .... League for National Labor in Israel (EA)
LNL-L .... Loyola University, Law Library, New Orleans, LA [*Library symbol*] [*Library of Congress*] (LCLS)
LNLM .... Linoleum
LNLM .... Low-Noise Level Margin
LNLM .... United States Bureau of Land Management, New Orleans Outer Continential Shelf Office, New Orleans, LA [*Library symbol*] [*Library of Congress*] (LCLS)
LNL-Phar ... Loyola University, Pharmacy Library, New Orleans, LA [*Library symbol*] [*Library of Congress*] (LCLS)
LNLU .... Ruedas y Tornos [*Intermodal shipping container symbol*] (TVRC)
LNM .... Langimar [*Papua New Guinea*] [*Airport symbol*] (OAG)
LNM .... LAN [*Linked Access Network*] Network Manager
LNM .... Lansdowne Minerals [*Vancouver Stock Exchange symbol*]
LNM .... Lebanese National Movement [*Political party*] (PPW)
LNM .... Leon [*Mexico*] [*Seismograph station code, US Geological Survey*] (SEIS)
LNM .... Level of No Motion [*Oceanography*]
LNM .... Library Cooperative of Macomb [*Library network*]
LNM .... Lithium Nuclear Microprobe
LNM .... Local Notice to Mariners
LNM .... Logical Network Machine (MHDB)
LNM .... Lumen Technologies [*NYSE symbol*] [*Formerly, BEC Group*]
LNM .... Lymph Node Metastases [*Oncology*]
LNM .... Margaret C. Hanson Normal School, New Orleans, LA [*Library symbol*] [*Library of Congress*] [*Obsolete*] (LCLS)

lnma-........ Madeira Islands [*MARC geographic area code*] [*Library of Congress*] (LCCP)
LNMA........ New Orleans Museum of Art, New Orleans, LA [*Library symbol*] [*Library of Congress*] (LCLS)
LNMC........ Monaco [*Monaco*] [*ICAO location identifier*] (ICLI)
LNME........ Mobil Exploration and Producing U.S., Inc., New Orleans, LA [*Library symbol*] [*Library of Congress*] (LCLS)
LNMMS ..... McMain Magnet Secondary School, New Orleans, LA [*Library symbol*] [*Library of Congress*] (LCLS)
LNMP........ Last Normal Menstrual Period [*Medicine*]
LNMR .... Laboratory of Nutritional and Molecular Regulation [*National Cancer Institute*] (RCD)
LNMRB...... Laboratory of Nuclear Medicine and Radiation Biology
LNMS........ Large-Probe Neutral Mass Spectrometer [*NASA*]
LNMU .... Medeur Line [*Intermodal shipping container symbol*] (TVRC)
LNN.......... Leningrad [*Former USSR*] [*Seismograph station code, US Geological Survey*] [*Closed*] (SEIS)
LNN.......... Leningrad [*Former USSR*] [*Geomagnetic observatory code*]
LNN.......... Lincoln Resources, Inc. [*Vancouver Stock Exchange symbol*]
LNN.......... Lindsay Manufacturing Co. [*NYSE symbol*]
LNN.......... Lindsay Mfg. [*NYSE symbol*] (SG)
LNN.......... Linear Nearest Neighbor (MHDB)
LNN.......... Lower Nephron Nephrosis [*Medicine*] (MELL)
LNN.......... Willoughby, OH [*Location identifier*] [*FAA*] (FAAL)
LNNB .... Luria-Nebraska Neuropsychological Battery
LNND .... Notre Dame Seminary, New Orleans, LA [*Library symbol*] [*Library of Congress*] (LCLS)
LNNI .... LAN Emulation Network Node Interface (SAUS)
LNNI .... LAN Emulation Network-to-Network Interface [*Communications term*] (DCT)
LNNK .... Latvian National Conservative Party and Green Party [*Political party*] (PSAP)
LNNP .... Lake Nakuru National Park (SAUO)
LNNR........ Lindisfarne National Nature Reserve (SAUO)
LNO.......... Laona & Northern Railway Co. [*AAR code*]
LNO.......... Leonora [*Australia*] [*Airport symbol*] (OAG)
LNO.......... Liaison Officer [*Military*]
LNO.......... Limited Nuclear Option [*Military*] (MCD)
LNO.......... Local Network Operations [*Computer science*] (VLIE)
LNOC .... Libya National Oil Co.
LNOP .... Lanoptics Ltd. [*NASDAQ symbol*] (SAG)
LNOP .... Orleans Parish Medical Society, New Orleans, LA [*Library symbol*] [*Library of Congress*] (LCLS)
LNOPF....... LanOptics Ltd [*NASDAQ symbol*] (TTSB)
L Notes ..... Law Notes, England [*A publication*] (DLA)
L Notes Gen Pract... Law Notes for the General Practitioner [*A publication*] (DLA)
LNP.......... Bibliotheca Parsoniana, New Orleans, LA [*Library symbol*] [*Library of Congress*] [*Obsolete*] (LCLS)
LNP.......... Chieftain Aviation PC [*South Africa*] [*ICAO designator*] (FAAC)
LNP.......... Laboratory of Neuropathology [*Temple University*] (RCD)
LNP.......... Lamington National Park (SAUO)
LNP.......... Large Neuronal Polypeptide [*Medicine*] (DMAA)
LNP.......... Least Newtonian Path (IAA)
LNP.......... Leg Negative Pressure (PDAA)
LNP.......... Lehn & Fink Products Corporation (SAUO)
LNP.......... Liberal/National Party [*Political party*] [*Australia*]
LNP.......... Libertarian Party [*Australia*] [*Political party*]
LNP.......... Lincoln National Park (SAUO)
LNP.......... Liquefied Natural Petroleum
LNP.......... Liquid Nitrogen Processing
LNP.......... Local Network Protocol (SAUO)
LNP.......... Local Number Portability [*Telecommunications*] (GART)
LNP.......... Logistics Network Planning (GART)
LNP.......... London Northern Polytechnic (SAUO)
LNP.......... Loss of Normal Power (IEEE)
LNP.......... Low Needle Position [*on dial*]
LNP.......... Lunar Neutron Probe [*NASA*] (KSC)
LNP.......... Lunping [*Taiwan*] [*Geomagnetic observatory code*]
LNP.......... Wise, VA [*Location identifier*] [*FAA*] (FAAL)
LNPA .... Low-Noise Pre-Amplifier (SAUS)
LNP & W ... Laramie, North Park & Western Railroad (IIA)
LNPC .... Liberian National Petroleum Company (SAUO)
LNPF .... Lebanese National Patriotic Forces [*Political party*]
LNPF .... Lymph Node Permeability Factor [*Immunology*]
LNPIB .... Loch Ness Phenomena Investigation Bureau [*Later, LNIB*]
LNPo .... Polyanthos, New Orleans, LA [*Library symbol*] [*Library of Congress*] (LCLS)
LNPP .... Leningrad Nuclear Power Plant (SAUO)
LNPU .... Linea Navieria Pan Atlantica [*Intermodal shipping container symbol*] (TVRC)
LNPW .... Laramie, North Park & Western [*Federal Railroad Administration identification code*]
LNQ.......... Longest Queue
LNR.......... Lagos Notes and Records [*A publication*]
LNR.......... Last Number Redial [*Telecommunications*] (VLIE)
LNR.......... Leeds Northern Railway (SAUO)
LNR.......... Linamar Machine (SAUO)
LNR.......... Linamar Machine Ltd. [*Toronto Stock Exchange symbol*]
LNR.......... Line Number (SAUO)
LNR.......... Liner
LNR.......... Line Ring [*Telecommunications*] (VLIE)
LNR.......... Liquid Natural Rubber
LNR.......... Liquid Nitrogen Refrigeration
LNR.......... LNR Property [*NYSE symbol*] (SG)
LNR.......... Local Nature Reserve (PDAA)
LNR.......... Lone Rock, WI [*Location identifier*] [*FAA*] (FAAL)
LNR.......... Lonorore [*New Hebrides*] [*Seismograph station code, US Geological Survey*] (SEIS)
LNR.......... Loteni Nature Reserve (SAUO)
LNR.......... Louisiana Numerical Register [*Louisiana State Library*] [*Baton Rouge, LA*] [*Library network*]
LNR.......... Low-Noise Receiver
LNR.......... Luftnachrichten-Regiment [*Air forces signal regiment*] [*German military - World War II*]
LNR.......... Lymph Node Region [*Medicine*] (DAVI)
LNR.......... Sky Liners Air Services Ltd. [*Suriname*] [*ICAO designator*] (FAAC)
LNRA .... Linear Nested Region Analysis (PDAA)
LNRC .... Little Nash Rambler Club (EA)
LNRD........ Land and Natural Resources Division (SAUO)
LNRS .... Limited Night Recovery System (PDAA)
LNS.......... East Lansing, MI [*Amtrak rail station code*]
LNS.......... Laboratory for Nuclear Science [*MIT*] (MCD)
LNS.......... Laboratory of Neurosciences [*National Institute on Aging*] (RCD)
LNS.......... Labour and National Service (SAUO)
LNS.......... Lancaster [*Pennsylvania*] [*Airport symbol*] (OAG)
LNS.......... Land Nationalization Society (SAUO)
LNS.......... Land Navigation System
LNS.......... Lansco Resources [*Vancouver Stock Exchange symbol*]
LNS.......... Lanslevillard [*France*] [*Seismograph station code, US Geological Survey*] (SEIS)
LNS.......... LASER Night Sensor
LNS.......... Lateral Nuclear Stratum [*Medicine*] (DMAA)
LNS.......... Lesch-Nyhan Syndrome [*Medicine*]
LNS.......... Liberation News Service (EA)
LNS.......... Loans [*Telegraphy*] (PCTE)
LNS.......... London and Northern Securities (SAUO)
LNS.......... London Normal School
LNS.......... Long Normal Superchron [*Geology*]
LNS.......... Lutheran News Service [*Lutheran Church in America*] [*Information service or system*] (IID)
LNS.......... Lymph Node Seeking [*Medicine*] (DB)
LNS.......... Nicholls State University, Ellender Memorial Library (SAUO)
LNS.......... Nicholls State University, Ellender Memorial Library, Thibodaux, LA [*OCLC symbol*] (OCLC)
LNSA .... Local Navy Supervising Activity
LNSB .... Lincoln Savings Bank (SAUO)
lnsb-......... Svalbard and Jan Mayen [*MARC geographic area code*] [*Library of Congress*] (LCCP)
LNSC .... Laboratory for Natural and Simulated Cognition [*McGill University*] [*Canada*] (RCD)
lnscp .... Landscaped (REAL)
lnsd.......... Linseed Oil (VRA)
LNSF .... Light Night Striking Force [*British military*] (DMA)
Lnship....... Librarianship (AL)
LNSL .... Liberia National Shipping Line (EY)
LNSL .... Southeast Louisiana Library Network Cooperative (SEALLING), New Orleans, LA [*Library symbol*] [*Library of Congress*] (LCLS)
LNSM........ Saint Mary's Dominican College, New Orleans, LA [*Library symbol*] [*Library of Congress*] (LCLS)
LNSN .... Local Non-Switched Network
LNsN .... Northwestern State University of Louisiana, Natehitoches (SAUO)
LNSO .... Shell Oil Co., New Orleans, LA [*Library symbol*] [*Library of Congress*] (LCLS)
LNSP .... Lens Speed [*Mechanical engineering*]
LNSTAT...... Line Status (VLIE)
LnStr .... Lone Star Industries [*Associated Press*] (SAG)
LnStrInd..... Lone Star Industries [*Associated Press*] (SAG)
LNSU .... Library Network of SIBIL Users (EAIO)
LNSU .... United States Department of Agriculture, Southern Utilization and Development Division, Agricultural Research Service, New Orleans, LA [*Library symbol*] [*Library of Congress*] (LCLS)
LNT .... Aerolineas Internacionales, SA de CV [*Mexico*] [*FAA designator*] (FAAC)
LNT.......... Alliant Energy [*NYSE symbol*] (SG)
LNT.......... Alliant Energy Corp. [*NYSE symbol*]
LNT.......... Launch Network Test
LNT.......... Leave No Trace [*An association*]
LNT.......... Linear No-Threshold [*Risk model*]
LNT.......... Liquid Nitrogen Temperature (IAA)
LNT.......... Low Noise Tape (ELAL)
LNT.......... Millinocket, ME [*Location identifier*] [*FAA*] (FAAL)
LNT.......... Tulane University, New Orleans, LA [*Library symbol*] [*Library of Congress*] (LCLS)
LNT-BA...... Tulane University, Graduate School of Business Administration, New Orleans, LA [*Library symbol*] [*Library of Congress*] (LCLS)
LNTC .... International House, Cunningham Library, New Orleans, LA [*Library symbol*] [*Library of Congress*] (LCLS)
LNTC .... Lymph Node T Cells [*Immunology*]
LNTE........ Lante Corp. [*NASDAQ symbol*] (SG)
LNTex........ Texas, Inc., New Orleans, LA [*Library symbol*] [*Library of Congress*] (LCLS)
LNTF......... Lipid Nurse Task Force (NTPA)
LNTG .... Liberian National Transitional Government [*Political party*] (PSAP)
LNTL......... Lane Telecommunications, Inc. (SAUO)
LNTL......... Lintel
LNT-L........ Tulane University, Law Library, New Orleans, LA [*Library symbol*] [*Library of Congress*] (LCLS)
LNT-M....... Tulane University, Medical Library, New Orleans, LA [*Library symbol*] [*Library of Congress*] (LCLS)
LNT-MC ..... Greater New Orleans Microform Cooperative, Tulane University, New Orleans, LA [*Library symbol*] [*Library of Congress*] (LCLS)

LNTO .... Lento [*Very Slow*] [*Music*] (ROG)
LNTON ...... Linton, IN [*American Association of Railroads railroad junction routing code*]
LNTP .... New Orleans Times-Picayune, New Orleans, LA [*Library symbol*] [*Library of Congress*] (LCLS)
LNTS .... League of Nations Treaty Series [*A publication*] (DLA)
LNTS .... Liquid Nitrogen Transfer System
LNTT......... Line Nonimpact Thermal Transfer (GART)
LNTV .... Lin Television Corp. [*NASDAQ symbol*] (SAG)
LNTWA...... Low-Noise Traveling Wave Amplifier
LNTWTA..... Low-Noise Traveling Wave Tube Amplifier (IAA)
LNTY .... L90, Inc. [*NASDAQ symbol*] (SG)
LNU.......... Last Name Unknown
LNU.......... League of Nations Union
LNU.......... University of New Orleans, New Orleans, LA [*Library symbol*] [*Library of Congress*] [*OCLC symbol*] (LCLS)
LNUCA ...... United States Circuit Court of Appeals, Fifth Circuit Law Library, New Orleans, LA [*Library symbol*] [*Library of Congress*] (LCLS)
LNUG........ Eugene Lindsey [*Common carrier symbol*]
LNUrs .... Ursuline Academy, New Orleans, LA [*Library symbol*] [*Library of Congress*] (LCLS)
LNV.......... Lanvin-Parfums, Inc. (SAUO)
LNV.......... Last Normal Vertebra [*Medicine*] (RAWO)
LNV.......... Laughlin, NV [*Amtrak Busline code*]
LNV.......... Limit of Night Visibility (SAUS)
LNV.......... Lincln Natl Cv Sec [*NYSE symbol*] (TTSB)
LNV.......... Lincoln National Convertible Securities Fund, Inc. [*NYSE symbol*] (SPSG)
LNV.......... Londolovit [*Papua New Guinea*] [*Airport symbol*] [*Obsolete*] (OAG)
LNV.......... Longovilo [*Chile*] [*Seismograph station code, US Geological Survey*] (SEIS)
LNV.......... Lonvest Corp. [*Toronto Stock Exchange symbol*] [*Vancouver Stock Exchange symbol*]
LNVA........ United States Veterans Administration Hospital, New Orleans, LA [*Library symbol*] [*Library of Congress*] (LCLS)
lNVALY...... Union Valley Corp. (SAUO)
LNVT........ Launch Network Verification Test (IAA)
LNW.......... [*The*] Louisiana & North West Railroad Co. [*AAR code*]
LNWR........ Lacassine National Wildlife Refuge (SAUO)
LNWR........ Lacreek National Wildlife Refuge (SAUO)
LNWR........ London & North Western Railway [*British*]
LNWR........ London & North Western Railway Co. (SAUO)
LNWR........ Lostwood National Wildlife Refuge (SAUO)
LNWR........ Loxahatchee National Wildlife Refuge (SAUO)
LNWS........ Large Node Work Station (SAUS)
LNX.......... Lenex [*Poland*] [*ICAO designator*] (FAAC)
LNX.......... Lenox, Incorporated (SAUO)
LNX.......... London Executive Aviation Ltd. [*British*] [*FAA designator*] (FAAC)
LNX.......... Xavier University, New Orleans, LA [*Library symbol*] [*Library of Congress*] [*OCLC symbol*] (LCLS)
LNXC........ Lenox Bancorp, Inc. [*NASDAQ symbol*] (QUAN)
LNY.......... Lanai City [*Hawaii*] [*Airport symbol*] (OAG)
LNY.......... Lane Bryant, Incorporated (SAUO)
LNY.......... Laws of New York [*A publication*] (DLA)
LNYD........ Lanyard
LNYL........ Leksikon fun der Nayer Yidisher Literatur [*New York*] [*A publication*] (BJA)
LNYT........ League of New York Theaters (SAUO)
LNYT........ League of New York Theatres [*Later, LNYTP*] (EA)
LNYTP...... League of New York Theatres and Producers (EA)
LNYV........ Lettuce Necrotic Yellows Virus
LNZ.......... Linz [*Austria*] [*Airport symbol*] (OAG)
LNZ.......... Litag K.G. [*Austria*] [*FAA designator*] (FAAC)
LNZ.......... Lonzo [*Language symbol*] (ETLW)
LO............ Laboratory Outfitting (SSD)
LO............ Lamp Oil
LO............ Landelijke Organistatie [*Netherlands underground organization*] [*World War II*]
LO............ Land Office (SAUO)
LO............ Landsorganisasjonen i Norge [*Norwegian Federation of Trade Unions*]
LO............ Landsorganisationen i Sverige [*Swedish Federation of Trade Unions*]
LO............ Larval Operculum
LO............ Laser Optical (RALS)
LO............ Lateral Oblique [*X-ray view*] (DAVI)
LO............ Launch Operations [*or Operator*] [*NASA*]
LO............ Launch Operator (SAUO)
LO............ Law Observer [*1872*] [*India*] [*A publication*] (DLA)
LO............ Law Officer
LO............ Law Opinions [*A publication*] (DLA)
LO............ Lay Observer (ILCA)
LO............ Layout [*Graphic arts*]
LO............ Learning Objective
LO............ Left On [*Baseball term*] (NDBD)
LO............ Left Out (TIMI)
LO............ Left Outboard (MCD)
LO............ Legal Observer [*British*]
LO............ Legal Officer
LO............ Legal Opinion [*1870-73*] [*A publication*] (DLA)
LO............ Lenticular Opacity [*Ophthalmology*] (DAVI)
lo............ Lesotho [*MARC country of publication code*] [*Library of Congress*] (LCCP)
L/O.......... Letter of Offer
LO............ Letter Orders
LO............ Leucine Oxidation (STED)
LO............ Level Off
LO............ Leverage Out (VLIE)
LO............ Liaison Office [*or Officer*]
LO............ Licensed Officer [*US Merchant Marine*]
LO............ Lick Observatory (SAUO)
LO............ [*The*] Lifestyles Organization (EA)
LO............ Lift-Off (AAG)
LO............ Lights Out
LO............ Limerent Object [*One who is the object of obsessional romantic love*]
LO............ Limited Order [*Business term*]
LO............ Line Occupancy
LO............ Line Office (USDC)
LO............ Linguoocclusal [*Dentistry*]
LO............ Liquid Oxygen
LO............ Listing Office [*Real estate*] (REAL)
LO............ Livestock Office (SAUO)
LO............ Loam [*Type of soil*] (ROG)
LO............ Loan Officer [*Banking*] (TBD)
Lo............ Local [*Navy*]
LO............ Local Financial Corp. [*AMEX symbol*] (NASQ)
LO............ Local Office
LO............ Local Order
LO............ Local Origination [*Television programming*]
LO............ Local Oscillator [*Electronics*]
LO............ Locator File [*Information retrieval*]
LO............ Locked Open [*Technical drawings*]
LO............ Locked Oscillator
LO............ Lock-On
LO............ Lock-Out
LO............ Loco [*As Written*] [*Music*]
LO............ Loco [*Place*] [*Latin*]
LO............ Logical Operation (AAG)
LO............ Logistics Offensive
LO............ Log Out [*Computer science*] (VLIE)
LO............ London Office
Lo............ London Regiment (SAUO)
Lo............ London Stock Exchange (SG)
LO............ Longitude
LO............ Longitudinal Optic
LO............ Longitudinal Optical (VLIE)
LO............ Look-Out [*Navy*] [*British*]
Lo............ Lord (WGA)
Lo............ Lotarius [*Flourished, 1191-1212*] [*Authority cited in pre-1607 legal work*] (DSA)
LO............ Louisville Orchestra [*Record label*]
LO............ Louth [*County in Ireland*] (ROG)
LO............ Love Object
lo............ Low (IDOE)
LO............ Low (KSC)
LO............ Lowell Observatory (SAUO)
LO............ Lowest Offer [*Business term*]
LO............ Low Loaders (DCTA)
LO............ Low Oblique [*Aerospace*]
LO............ Low Observable (DOMA)
LO............ Low Order [*Computer science*] (OA)
LO............ Low Ordinary (IAA)
LO............ Lubricating Oil
LO............ Lubrication Order
LO............ Lumber Orthosis (STED)
LO............ Lunar Observer (ACAE)
LO............ Lunar Orbiter [*Aerospace*] (MCD)
LO............ Lutte Ouvriere [*Workers' Struggle*] [*France*] [*Political party*] (PPW)
LO............ Lysyl Oxidase [*An enzyme*]
LO............ Opelousas-Eunice Public Library (SAUS)
LO............ Opelousas-Eunice Public Library, Opelousas, LA [*Library symbol*] [*Library of Congress*] (LCLS)
LO............ Solicitor's Law Opinion, United States Internal Revenue Bureau [*A publication*] (DLA)
LO............ Violation of Local Ordinance [*Motor vehicle violation code used in state of Maryland*] (MVRD)
LO_2.......... Liquid Oxygen [*Also, LOX*] [*NASA*] (KSC)
LO2.......... Pahute Mesa [*Nevada*] [*Seismograph station code, US Geological Survey*] [*Closed*] (SEIS)
LOA.......... Landing Operations Area [*NASA*] (NASA)
LOA.......... LASER Opto-Acoustic
LOA.......... Lateral Osseous Ampulla [*Medicine*] (MELL)
LOA.......... Launch on Assessment [*Military*]
LOA.......... Launch on Attack [*Military*]
LOA.......... Launch Operations Agency [*NASA*] (KSC)
LOA.......... Launch Operations Area (MCD)
LOA.......... Lead Operational Authority (COE)
LOA.......... Leave of Absence
LOA.......... Leber Optic Atrophy (STED)
LOA.......... Leber's Optic Atrophy [*Medicine*] (MELL)
LOA.......... Left Anterior Oblique [*Medicine*] (MELL)
LOA.......... Left Occipitoanterior [*A fetal position*] [*Obstetrics*]
LOA.......... Length of Output Area (VLIE)
LOA.......... Length Over-All [*Technical drawings*]
LOA.......... Leona, TX [*Location identifier*] [*FAA*] (FAAL)
LOA.......... Letter of Acceptance
LOA.......... Letter of Agreement
LOA.......... Letter of Authorization
LOA.......... Letter Officers Association (SAUO)

LOA.......... Letter Offices Association (SAUO)
LOA.......... Letter of Offer and Acceptance (MCD)
LOA.......... Letters of Authorization (SAUO)
LOA.......... Level of Authority [*Military*] (AFIT)
LOA.......... Life Offices' Association [*British*] (DCTA)
LOA.......... Light Observation Aircraft
LOA.......... Limit of Advance [*Army*] (DOMA)
LOA.......... Line of Assurance
LOA.......... List of Acronyms (or Abbreviations) (SAUS)
LOA.......... Lithuanian Organists Alliance (SAUO)
LOA.......... Local Ocean Area (SAUO)
LOA.......... Local Overseas Allowance [*British military*] (DMA)
LOA.......... Log-Out Analysis (NITA)
LOA.......... London Orchestral Association (SAUO)
LOA.......... London Orphan Asylum (ROG)
LOA.......... Loners of America [*An association*] (EA)
LOA.......... Looseness of Associations (STED)
LOA.......... Lorcan Resources Ltd. [*Vancouver Stock Exchange symbol*]
LOA.......... Lorcan Resours Ltd. (SAUO)
LOA.......... Lorraine [*Australia*] [*Airport symbol*] [*Obsolete*] (OAG)
LOA.......... Los Alamos [*New Mexico*] [*Seismograph station code, US Geological Survey*] (SEIS)
LOA.......... Low Oil Agglomeration [*Coal processing*]
LOA.......... Low-Speed Output Adapter (MHDB)
LOAA........ Letter of Agreement and Acceptance
LOAC........ Law of Armed Conflict [*Military*]
LOAC........ Low Accuracy
LOAD........ Laser Optoacoustic Detection (ACAE)
LOAD........ Load Rite Trailers [*NCIC trailer make code*]
LOAD........ Low-Altitude Defense (MCD)
LOAD........ Low Altitude Defense Program (SAUO)
LOADEO..... Loading of Explosive Ordnance (SAUS)
LOADEX..... Loading Exercise [*Military*] (NVT)
LOADS...... Lifting of Aerodynamic Decelerators (PDAA)
LOADS...... Low-altitude Air Defence System (SAUS)
LOADS...... Low-Altitude Defense System
LOAEL....... Lowest Observed Adverse Effect Level (EG)
LOAF........ Large Open-Area Floor
LOAF........ Lesbians Over the Age of Forty (SAUO)
LOAF........ Loaf [*Commonly used*] (OPSA)
LOAK........ Load King Trailer Company [*NCIC trailer make code*]
LOAL........ Lock-On after Launch [*Weaponry*] (CAAL)
LOAL........ Lock-One After Launch [*Military*] (MUSM)
LOAM........ List of Applicable Material (MCD)
LOAMP...... Logarithmic Amplifier (IEEE)
LOAN........ Horizon Bancorp, Inc. (TX) [*NASDAQ symbol*] (SAG)
LOAN........ Horizon Bancorp(TX) [*NASDAQ symbol*] (TTSB)
LOAN........ Local Officials' Administration Network [*An association*]
LOAN/A...... Vessels Loaned to Army [*Navy*]
LOAN/C...... Vessels Loaned to Coast Guard [*Navy*]
LO & DS.... London Operatic and Dramatic Society (ROG)
LOAN/M..... Vessels Loaned to Miscellaneous Activities [*US Maritime Academy, etc.*] [*Navy*]
LOAN/S...... Vessels Loaned to States [*Navy*]
LOAN/W..... Vessels Loaned to War Shipping Administration [*Terminated, 1946*] [*Navy*]
LOANZ....... Life Offices Association of New Zealand (SAUO)
LOAP........ Length of Adjacency Process (MHDB)
LOAP........ List of Applicable Publications [*Air Force*]
LOAPS....... Large Order Assembly Planning System (MCD)
LOAS........ Lift-Off Acquisition System
LOAS........ List of Assessed Spares (MCD)
LOAS........ Loyal Order of Ancient Shepherds [*British*] (BI)
LOAT......... Trausdorf [*Austria*] [*ICAO location identifier*] (ICLI)
LOAV........ Lift Owners' Association of Victoria [*Australia*]
LOAV........ Voslau [*Austria*] [*ICAO location identifier*] (ICLI)
LOAVF....... Lorcan Resources Ltd. (SAUO)
LOAX........ Log On America
LOB.......... Laboratory Office Building
LOB.......... [*The*] Land of the Bible: A Historical Geography [*A publication*] (BJA)
LOB.......... Launch Operations Branch [*NASA*]
LOB.......... Launch Operations Building [*NASA*]
LOB.......... Left of Baseline
LOB.......... Left on Base [*Baseball*]
LOB.......... Left on Bases [*Telegraphy*] (PCTE)
LOB.......... Left Outboard (MCD)
LOB.......... Left Out of Battle [*British*]
LOB.......... Legends of Batman
LOB.......... Limited Operating Base (AFM)
LOB.......... Line of Balance
LOB.......... Line of Bearing [*Navy*] (NVT)
LOB.......... Line of Business [*Used in corporate reports to Federal Trade Commission*]
LOB.......... Lobito [*Angola*] [*Airport symbol*] (AD)
LOB.......... Location of Offices Bureau [*British*]
LOB.......... Logistics Operating Base
LOB.......... Logistics-over-the-Beach Base [*Military*] (VNW)
LOB.......... Low Overbase [*Fuels and lubricants*]
LOB.......... Loyal Order of the Boar (EA)
LOB.......... Lube Oil Balance [*Indian Railway*] (TIR)
LObA........ Allen Parish Library, Oberlin, LA [*Library symbol*] [*Library of Congress*] (LCLS)
LOBA........ Last Offer Binding Arbitration [*Labor negotiations*]
LOBAR...... Long Baseline RADAR
LOBDE....... Lobdell, LA [*American Association of Railroads railroad junction routing code*]
LOBI......... Library Orientation/Bibliographic Instruction [*Florida Library Association caucus*]
LOBI......... Loop Blowdown Investigation (SAUO)
Lobin........ Lobingier's Extra-Territorial Cases [*United States Court for China*] [*A publication*] (DLA)
LOBL........ Lock-On Before Launch [*Missile*] (DOMA)
LOBNAH..... Lights on but Nobody's at Home (BB)
LOBP........ Lubricant Oil Blending Plant [*Petroleum engineering*]
LOBSTER... Long-Term Ocean Bottom Settlement Test for Engineering Research [*Navy project*]
LOBTP....... League of Off-Broadway Theatres and Producers [*Later, OBL*] (EA)
LOBUND.... Laboratories of Bacteriology, University of Notre Dame (SAUO)
LoC.......... Book 6 of the WOT series Lord of Chaos (SAUS)
LOC.......... Landing Operations Center (MCD)
LOC.......... Landsat Oversight Committee (SAUO)
LOC.......... LAN Operations Center (SAUO)
LOC.......... Large Optical Cavity [*LASER design*]
LOC.......... Launch Operations Center [*NASA*]
LOC.......... Launch Operations Complex
LOC.......... Launch Operations Control
LOC.......... Launch Operator's Console [*Aerospace*] (AAG)
LOC.......... Laverda Owner's Club (EA)
LOC.......... Laxative of Choice [*Medicine*]
LOC.......... Le Groupe Opus Communications, Inc. [*Vancouver Stock Exchange symbol*]
LOC.......... LeMoyne-Owen College, Memphis, TN [*OCLC symbol*] (OCLC)
LOC.......... Letter of Comment
LOC.......... Letter of Commitment (FOTI)
LOC.......... Letter of Compliance [*Program*] [*Coast Guard*]
LOC.......... Letter of Consent
LOC.......... Letter of Credit (SAUO)
LOC.......... Letterpress to Offset Conversion (DGA)
LOC.......... Letters of Comment (SAUO)
LOC.......... Letters of Credit
LOC.......... Level of Care [*Medicine*] (GFGA)
LOC.......... Level of Concentration (FOTI)
LOC.......... Level of Concern [*Environmental Protection Agency*] (ERG)
LOC.......... Level of Consciousness [*Medicine*]
LOC.......... Liaison Officer Coordinator [*Air Force*] (AFM)
LOC.......... Libraries and Our Civilizations [*A publication*]
LOC.......... Library of Congress
LoC.......... Library of Congress Classification (TELE)
LOC.......... Light-Off Catalyst [*Exhaust emissions*] [*Automotive engineering*]
LOC.......... Limitation of Cost (AAGC)
LOC.......... Limited Operational Capability (CET)
LOC.......... Limiting Oxygen Concentration [*For ignition*]
LOC.......... Lincoln Owners Club (EA)
LOC.......... Lincoln School [*California*] [*Seismograph station code, US Geological Survey*] (SEIS)
LOC.......... Line of Code
LOC.......... Line of Communication [*Military*]
LOC.......... Line of Contact (MCD)
LOC.......... Line of Correction
LOC.......... Line Office Contact (SAUO)
LOC.......... Lines of Code (SAUO)
LOC.......... Linked Object Code (TEL)
LOC.......... Linked Operational Capability (DOMA)
LOC.......... Liquid Organic Compound
LOC.......... Load Overcurrent
loc........... Local (ELAL)
LOC.......... Local
loc........... Localized (STED)
LOC.......... Localizer (MSA)
LOC.......... Localizer Line of Sight
LOC.......... Locally (SAUS)
LOC.......... Local Operating Company (SAUO)
LOC.......... Local Operations Console (SAUS)
LOC.......... Local Original Channel [*Cable television broadcasting*]
LOC.......... Locate (MSA)
loc........... Located (REAL)
LOC.......... Location (AFM)
loc........... Location (VRA)
LOC.......... Location Counter [*Computer science*]
loc........... Locative [*Linguistics*] (IEL)
LOC.......... Locative (Case) [*Linguistics*]
LOC.......... Locator (PIPO)
LOC.......... Locavia 49 [*France*] [*ICAO designator*] (FAAC)
LOC.......... Lock-On Completed (MCD)
LOC.......... Loco [*Place*] [*Latin*] (WGA)
LOC.......... Loctite Corp. [*NYSE symbol*] (SPSG)
LOC.......... Loctite Corporation (SAUO)
LOC.......... Locus of Control (STED)
LOC.......... Logistical Operations Center (SAUO)
LOC.......... Logistic Operation Center [*Military*]
LOC.......... Logistics Operations Center (SAUO)
LOC.......... Logistics Operations Centre (SAUO)
LOC.......... Loop On-line Control (SAUO)
LOC.......... Lord of Creation
LOC.......... Loss of Consciousness [*Medicine*]
LOC.......... Loss of Coolant (GAAI)
LOC.......... Louisiana Office of Conservation (SAUO)
LOC.......... Low Compression [*Automotive engineering*]

LOC .... Lunar Observer Camera (ACAE)
LOC .... Lyric Opera of Chicago (SAUO)
LOCA .... Late Onset Cerebellar Ataxia [*Medicine*]
LOCA .... Loss-of-Coolant Accident [*Nuclear energy*]
LoCa .... Low Calcium (STED)
LOCA .... Low-Cost Computer Attachment (IAA)
LOCA .... Low Osmolar Contrast Agent [*Medicine*]
LOCAAS ..... Low-Cost Anti-Armor Submunition programme (SAUS)
LOCAAS ..... Low-Cost Anti-Armor Submunitions [*Military*]
LOC ACC .... Location Accuracy [*Environmental science*] (COE)
LOCAE .... List of Classified and Authorised Explosives (HEAS)
LOCAITS .... Low-Cost Airborne Interim Tracking System
LOCAL .... Laboratory Program for Computer-Assisted Learning (IAA)
LOCAL .... Load On-Call [*Computer science*]
lo cal .... Low Calorie (MAE)
Local 464 ... Local 464, Utility Workers Union of America, AFL-CIO and Utility Workers Union of America, AFL-CIO (SAUO)
lo calc .... Low Calcium [*Diet*] (DAVI)
Local Ct & Mun Gaz ... Local Courts and Municipal Gazette [*Toronto, ON*] [*A publication*] (DLA)
Local Gov ... Local Government and Magisterial Reports [*England*] [*A publication*] (DLA)
Local Gov R Aust ... Local Government Reports of Australia [*A publication*] (DLA)
Local Gov't ... Local Government and Magisterial Reports [*England*] [*A publication*] (DLA)
Local Govt Jl WA ... Local Government Journal of Western Australia [*A publication*]
LOCALS ..... Low-Cost Alternate LASER Seeker (MCD)
LOCAM ...... Logistics Cost Analysis Model (MCD)
LOCAN ...... Location of Canisters [*Automotive emissions*]
LOCAP ...... Low Capacitance [*Cable*] [*Bell System*]
LOCAP ...... Low [*Altitude*] Combat Air Patrol (NVT)
LOCAPOR ... Companhia Portuguesa Locacao Financeria Mobiliaria (EFIS)
Locarno Union ... Union for the International Classification for/of Industrial Designs (SAUO)
LOCART ..... Local Cartage Company [*Transportation company classification code*]
LOCAS .... Local Cataloguing Service (NITA)
LOCAT .... Location (DAVI)
LOCAT .... Low-Altitude Clear-Air Turbulence (MCD)
LOCAT .... Low-Cost Aerial Trainer (SAUS)
LOCAT .... Low-Cost Air Target (MCD)
LOCAT .... Low Cost Artillery Trainer (SAUS)
LOCATE ..... Library of Congress Automation Techniques Exchange
LOCATE ..... List of Common Abbreviations in Training and Education (AIE)
LOCATE ..... Local Area Telecommunications, Inc. [*Digital microwave carrier*] [*New York, NY*] (TSSD)
LOCATE ..... LORAN/OMEGA Course and Tracking Equipment (MCD)
LOCATM ..... Low-Cost Advanced Technology Missile (SAUS)
LOCATS ..... Lockheed Optical Communications and Tracking System
LOCB .... London Orchestral Concert Board (SAUO)
LOCC .... Launcher Order and Capture Computer (MCD)
LOCC .... Launch Operations Control Center
LOCC .... Limitation of Cost Clause (AAGC)
Locc .... Loccenius. De Jure Maritimo [*A publication*] (DLA)
LOCC .... Logistical Operations Control Center [*Army*]
LOCCAP ..... Transportation Plans LOCs Capacities and Capabilities (SAUO)
LOCCB .... Lead on Chip with Center Bond (TIMI)
LOC CD ..... Local Carrier Detect [*Communications term*] (DCT)
loc cit .... In the Place Cited [*Loco citato*] [*Latin*] (WDMC)
LOC CIT ..... Loco Citato [*In the Place Cited*] [*Latin*]
LOCCOZO ... Line of Communication Combat Zone [*Military*]
LOCCS .... Letter of Credit Control System [*Department of Housing and Urban Development*] (GFGA)
Loc Ct Gaz ... Local Courts and Municipal Gazette [*Toronto, ON*] [*A publication*] (DLA)
LOCD .... Lines of Communication Designators (MCD)
LOCD .... Local Disease
LOCD .... Loss of Cell Delineation (DINT)
LOC DOL .... Loco Dolenti [*To the Painful Spot*] [*Pharmacy*]
LOCE .... Large Optical Communications Experiment (SAUS)
LOCE .... Last Observation Carried Forward
LOCE .... Limited Operational Capability Europe (SAUO)
LOCE .... Limited Operational Capability for Europe [*DoD*]
LOCE .... Limited Operational Capacity for Europe (SAUO)
LOCE .... Linked Operations/intelligence Centers Europe (SAUO)
LOCE .... Loss-of-Coolant Experiment [*Nuclear energy*]
LOCF .... Location File (MCD)
LOCF .... Loss-of-Coolant Flow [*Nuclear energy*] (NRCH)
Loc Gov Chron ... Local Government Chronicle [*London, England*] [*A publication*] (DLA)
Loc Govt Chr & Mag Rep ... Local Government Chronicle and Magisterial Reporter [*London*] [*A publication*] (DLA)
LOCH .... Loch Exploration, Inc. (SAUO)
LOCH .... London Options Clearing House (NUMA)
LOCI .... Ligue des Originaires de Cote d'Ivoire [*League of Ivory Coast Natives*]
LOCI .... List of Cancelled Items
LOCI .... Local Course Improvement [*National Science Foundation*] (EDAC)
LOCI .... Logarithmic Computing Instrument
LOCI .... Low-Cost Interceptor (MCD)
LOCID .... Location Identifier [*FAA*] (TAG)
LOCIG .... Limited-Overs Cricket Information Group [*British*] (DBA)
LOCIS .... Library of Congress Information System [*Library of Congress*] [*Information service or system*] (IID)
LOCIST ...... Low Cost Improved Sensors Technology (ACAE)
LO CIT ...... Loco Citato [*In the Place Cited*] [*Latin*]
LOCK .... Lock [*Commonly used*] (OPSA)
LOCK .... Logistical Operational Control Key [*Army*] (AABC)
Lock GL ..... Locke's Game Laws [*5th ed.*] [*1866*] [*A publication*] (DLA)
LockhM ..... Lockheed Martin Corp. [*Associated Press*] (SAG)
LOCKN ...... Lockney, TX [*American Association of Railroads railroad junction routing code*]
Lock Rev Ca ... Lockwood's Reversed Cases [*New York*] [*A publication*] (DLA)
Lock Rev Cas ... Lockwood's Reversed Cases [*New York*] [*A publication*] (DLA)
LOCKS .... Locks [*Commonly used*] (OPSA)
LOCKSS ..... Lots of Copies Keeps Stuff Safe
LOCL .... Local Federal Savings & Loan Association (SAUO)
LOCL .... Loyal Order of Catfish Lovers (EA)
LOCLAD ..... Low-Cost Low Altitude Dispenser (SAUS)
LOC LAUD .. Loco Laudato [*In the Place Quoted*] [*Latin*]
LOCLED ..... Low-Operating Current Light-Emitting Diode
LOC LF ...... Local Line Feed [*Telecommunications*] (DNAB)
LOCM .... Low Osmolar Contrast Medium (DB)
LOCMOS .... Locally-Oxidized Complementary Metal-Oxide Semiconductor (PDAA)
LOCN .... Location
LOCO .... Local Copy (VLIE)
LOCO .... Locomobile [*NCIC car make code*]
LOCO .... Locomotion (WDAA)
LOCO .... Locomotive (AABC)
LOCO .... Long Core [*Drilling program*]
LOCO .... Love Oil Company (SAUO)
Loco .... Marijuana [*Medicine*] (EDAA)
Loco .... On the Spot (EBF)
LOCODOSA ... Computer Program [*For calculating dose of implanted radioactive wires*] [*Medicine*] (EDAA)
LOCOM ...... Local Community (ADA)
LOCOM ...... Locomotive
LOCOMOTIVE ... Logistics Chain Multidimensional Design Toolbox with Environmental Assessment (SAUO)
LOCOR ...... Local Coordinator (FAAC)
LOCOS ...... Local Oxidation of Silicon [*Transistor technology*]
LOCOSS ..... Logic of Computers Operating System (MCD)
LOCO TAC ... Low-Cost Tactical RADAR (DNAB)
LOCP .... Launcher Operation Control Panel
LOCP .... Local Operator's Control Panel (ACAE)
LOCP .... Logistics Control Office, Pacific (SAUO)
LOCP .... Loss-of-Coolant Protection [*Nuclear energy*] (NRCH)
LOCPOD ..... Low-Cost Powered Dispenser
LOCPOD ..... Low Cost Powered Off-boresight Dispenser (SAUS)
LOCPORT ... Lines of Communications Ports (AABC)
Loc Primo Cit ... Loco Primo Citato [*In the Place First Cited*] [*Latin*] (ILCA)
LOC PRIUS CIT ... Loco Prius Citato [*In the Place First Cited*] [*Latin*] (ADA)
LOCPURO ... Local Purchase Order
LOCR .... Locker Moving and Storage [*Common carrier symbol*]
LOCREP ..... Location Report (SAUO)
LOCRIS ..... Low-Cost Robot by means of Integrated Servo Control (SAUO)
LOCRV ...... Local Review Program (SAUO)
LOCS .... Land Ocean Climate Satellite (SAUO)
LOCS .... Land-Ocean-Climate Satellite [*Marine science*] (OSRA)
LOCS .... Land Operations Command Systems programme (SAUO)
LOCS .... Librascope Operations Control System
LOCS .... Local Optical Clean-Up System (ACAE)
LOCS .... Local Optical Correction System (ACAE)
LOCS .... Logic and Control Simulation (NITA)
LOCS .... Logic and Control Simulator [*Computer science*] (BUR)
LOCT .... Layered Open Crypto Toolkit (SAUS)
LOCT .... Lockheed Command and Tracking (IAA)
LOC-TFCS ... Letter-of-Credit-Treasury Financial Communications System (SAUO)
Loctite .... Loctite Corp. [*Associated Press*] (SAG)
LOCTRACS ... Lockheed Tracking and Control System
LOCU .... Sachato Distributors [*Intermodal shipping container symbol*] (TVRC)
LOCUS ...... Laser Obstacle Cable Unmasking System (SAUS)
LOCUS ...... Library of Congress Information System [*Communications term*] (DCT)
LOCUSP ..... Low Cost Uncooled Sensor Prototype [*Army*]
Locus Standi ... Locus Standi Reports [*England*] [*A publication*] (DLA)
LOCV .... Loss of Condenser Vacuum [*Environmental science*] (COE)
LOD .... Large Organic Debris [*Pisciculture*]
LOD .... Last Occurrence of Date (QUAC)
LOD .... Last Order Date
LOD .... Launch on Demand (SAUS)
LOD .... Launch Operations Directive [*or Director*] [*NASA*]
LOD .... Launch Operations Directorate (SAUO)
LOD .... Launch Operations Division [*NASA*] (KSC)
LOD .... Law Officers' Department [*British*]
LOD .... Leading Ones Detector [*Computer science*]
LoD .... Legion of Doom (SAUS)
LOD .... Length of Day
LOD .... Letter of Declination (ACAE)
LOD .... Letter of Direction (ACAE)
LOD .... Level of Detail (MCD)
LOD .... Level of Difficulty (FOTI)
LOD .... Light-Off Detector [*Military*] (CAAL)
LOD .... Limit of Detection
LOD .... Limits of Disturbance (PA)
LOD .... Line of Dance
LOD .... Line of Departure [*Military*] (AFM)
LOD .... Line of Direction

LOD .... Line of Duty [*Medicine*] (EDAA)
LOD .... Line of Duty [*Military*]
LOD .... List of Drawings
LOD .... Little Oxford Dictionary [*A publication*]
LOD .... Locally One-Dimensional [*Engineering*] (OA)
LOD .... Location Dependent
LOD .... Lodgian, Inc. [*NYSE symbol*] (SG)
LOD .... Lodi, CA [*Amtrak Busline code*]
LOD .... Lodi Metals, Inc. [*Vancouver Stock Exchange symbol*]
lod .... Logarithm of the Odds [*Favoring linkage*] [*Genetics*] (DOG)
LOD .... Logarithm of the Odds
LOD .... Longana [*Vanuata*] [*Airport symbol*] (OAG)
LOD .... Low Density (IAA)
LOD2 .... Lightweight Omega Digital Dropwindsonde (SAUO)
LODA .... Lodal [*NCIC truck make code*]
LODAC .... Low Dispersion Automatic Cannon (TIMI)
LODACS ...... Longitudinal Fame Developing and Conducting System (PDAA)
LODACS ...... Low-Dispersion Automatic Cannon System
LODC .... Bushog-Loadcraft [*NCIC trailer make code*]
LODC .... Local Defense District Craft
LODCS .... Lunar Orbiter Data Conversion System [*Aerospace*]
LODE .... Comstock Bank [*NASDAQ symbol*] (SAG)
LODE .... Cornstock Bk Carson City Nev [*NASDAQ symbol*] (TTSB)
LODE .... Large Optics Demonstration Experiment [*DoD*]
LODE .... Load Star Corporation [*NCIC trailer make code*]
LODED .... Long Duration Expendable Decoy (SAUS)
LODEM .... Loading Dock Equipment Manufacturers Association (EA)
LODESMP ..... Logistics Data Element Standardization and Management Process (IEEE)
LODESTAR .... Logically Organized Data Entry, Storage, and Recording
LODG .... Lodge [*Commonly used*] (OPSA)
LODG .... Sholodge, Inc. [*NASDAQ symbol*] (SAG)
LODGE .... Lodge [*Commonly used*] (OPSA)
LODGE .... Lodge, IL [*American Association of Railroads railroad junction routing code*]
LodgEnt ..... Lodgenet Entertainment Corp. [*Associated Press*] (SAG)
LODI .... List of Deleted Items (NG)
LODI .... Lodi, CA [*American Association of Railroads railroad junction routing code*]
LODIF .... Long Distance Infrared Flash Camera (PDAA)
LODISNAV .... Long Distance Navigation (FAAC)
LODOR .... Loaded, Waiting Orders or Assignment [*Navy*]
LODP .... Lunar Orbiter Data Printer [*Aerospace*]
LODR .... Loader
LODSB .... Load String Byte [*Computer science*] (VLIE)
LODSC .... Logistics Operations Decision Support Center (SAUO)
LODTM .... Large Optics Diamond Turning Machine (ACAE)
LODUS .... Low Data Rate UHF [*Ultra-High Frequency*] Satellite [*RADAR*] (MCD)
LODYC .... Laboratoire d'Oceanographie Dynamique et de Climatologie [*France*] [*Marine science*] (OSRA)
LODZ .... Load-Eaz Trailer [*NCIC trailer make code*]
LOE .... Late Old English (ADWA)
LOE .... Left Otitis Externa [*Medicine*] (AMHC)
LOE .... Left Outboard Elevon [*Aviation*] (MCD)
LOE .... Letter of Evaluation
LOE .... Letter of Execution (MCD)
LOE .... Level of Effort (KSC)
LOE .... Light-Off Examination [*Navy*] (NVT)
LOE .... Limit of Exploitation (SAUS)
LOE .... Line of Effort (MCD)
LOE .... Line Oriented Evaluation (GAVI)
LOE .... Loei [*Thailand*] [*Airport symbol*] [*Obsolete*] (OAG)
LOe .... Loerrach [*German license plate city code*]
LOE .... Loeser, Luftfarhtgesellschaft GmbH [*Germany*] [*ICAO designator*] (FAAC)
LOE .... Louisiana Eastern Railroad (SAUO)
LOEAT .... Lowest Temperature Equaled for All Time [*NWS*] (FAAC)
LOEC .... List of Effective Cards (NVT)
LOEC .... Lowest Observed Effect Concentration [*Environmental Technology*]
LOEE .... Loyal Order of Overtime Experts (SAUO)
LOEFM .... Lowest Temperature Equaled for the Month [*NWS*] (FAAC)
LOEH .... Loehmann's Inc. [*NASDAQ symbol*] (TTSB)
LOEL .... Lowest-Observed-Effect Level [*Environmental science*] (FFDE)
LOEM(A) ..... Leading Ordnance Electrical Mechanic (Air) [*British military*] (DMA)
LOEP .... List of Effective Pages (NVT)
LOEP .... Loss of Electric Power
LOER .... Laboratory for Oceanographic and Environmental Research [*Texas A&M University at Galveston*] (RCD)
LOER .... Salvador Loera Transportation [*Common carrier symbol*]
LOERO .... Large Orbiting Earth Resources Observatory (IEEE)
LOESE .... Lowest Temperature Equaled So Early [*NWS*] (FAAC)
LOESL .... Lowest Temperature Equaled So Late [*NWS*] (FAAC)
Loewen ...... Loewen Group, Inc. [*Associated Press*] (SAG)
LoewenG ..... Loewen Group Capital LP [*Associated Press*] (SAG)
Loews .... Loew's Corp. [*Formerly, Loew's Theatres, Inc.*] [*Associated Press*] (SAG)
LOEX .... Laboratory of Experimental Tissue Engineering (SAUO)
LOEX .... Library Orientation/Instruction Exchange [*Library network*]
LOF .... Lack of Fusion
LOF .... Lecherous Old Fool [*Slang*]
LOF .... Letter of Finding (GFGA)
LOF .... Libbey-Owens-Ford Glass Co. [*Auto industry supplier*]
LOF .... Lift-Off (SAUS)
LOF .... Limitation of Funds (AAGC)
LOF .... Line of Fire
LOF .... Line-of-Flight (MCD)
LOF .... Line of Force
LOF .... List Overflow (VLIE)
LOF .... Lloyd's Open Form (RIMS)
LOF .... Local Oscillator Filter [*Electronics*]
LOF .... Local Oscillator Frequency [*Electronics*]
LOF .... Lock Off-Line [*Computer science*] (VLIE)
LOF .... Lofexidine (DMAA)
LOF .... London and Overseas Freighter
LOF .... Longest Operation First
LOF .... Look Ahead on Fault [*Computer science*] (MHDB)
LOF .... Loss of Feedwater [*Nuclear energy*] (NRCH)
LOF .... Loss of Flow [*Nuclear energy*] (NRCH)
LOF .... Loss of Fluid (BARN)
LOF .... Loss of Frame (MLOA)
LOF .... Lowest Operating Frequency (IEEE)
LOF .... Low Outlet Forceps [*Delivery*] [*Obstetrics*] (DAVI)
LOF .... Lube and Oil Filter
LOF .... Lube, Oil, and Filter [*Automobile servicing*]
LOF .... Trans States Airlines, Inc. [*ICAO designator*] (FAAC)
LOF .... Loss of Function (ODA)
LOFA .... Leisure and Outdoor Furniture Association [*British*] (DBA)
LOFA .... Loss of Flow Accident [*Nuclear energy*] (NRCH)
LOFAAD ...... Low-Altitude Forward Area Air Defense (AABC)
LOFAADS ..... Low-Altitude Forward Area Anti-Aircraft Defense System [*Army*]
LOFAADS ..... Low Level Forward Area Air Defense System (SAUO)
LOFADS ...... Low-Altitude Forward Air Defense System (PDAA)
LOFAR .... Low-Frequency Acquisition and Ranging
LOFAR .... Low-Frequency Analysis and Recording [*Sonobuoys*] [*Navy*]
LOFAR .... Low Frequency Omnidirectional Acoustic Frequency Analysis & Recording (SAUS)
LOFARGRAM ... Low Frequency Recording & Analysis Gram (SAUS)
LOFAT .... Low-Flying Aerial Target [*Military*] (CAAL)
L of C ...... Library of Congress
L of C ...... Lines of Communication (SAUO)
LOFC .... Loss of Forced Circulation [*Nuclear energy*] (NRCH)
LOFES .... Load Factor Error Sensor (MCD)
LOFEZ .... Low Fighter Engagement Zone (PDAA)
LOFF .... Leakoff [*Mechanical engineering*]
L Off Econ & Mgt ... Law Office Economics and Management [*A publication*] (DLA)
LOFFIRS ..... Low Cost Fire/Forget Infrared Seeker (ACAE)
Lofft .... Lofft's English King's Bench Reports [*1772-74*] [*A publication*] (DLA)
Lofft Append ... Lofft's Maxims, Appended to Lofft's Reports [*A publication*] (DLA)
Lofft Lib ... Lofft on the Law of Libels [*A publication*] (DLA)
Lofft Max ... Maxims Appended to Lofft's Reports [*A publication*] (DLA)
Lofft's Rep ... Lofft's English King's Bench Reports [*1772-74*] [*A publication*] (DLA)
Lofft Un L ... Lofft's Elements of Universal Law [*A publication*] (DLA)
LOFG .... Lofgren Trucking Service [*Common carrier symbol*]
LOFIRE ...... Controllable Fire [*Emergency Management*] (EMA)
L of N ...... League of Nations [*1919-1946*]
LOFO .... Low-Frequency Oscillation (MCD)
L of P ...... Lodge of Perfection [*Freemasonry*] (DAS)
LOFRECO ..... Low Front End Cost [*Engineering*]
LOFS .... Launch Operations Flow Subgroup (SAUO)
Lofs .... London and Overseas Freighters Society (SAUO)
LOFS .... London & Overseas Freightliners [*NASDAQ symbol*] (SAG)
LOFSY .... London & Overseas Freight ADS [*NASDAQ symbol*] (TTSB)
LOFT .... Line Oriented Flight Training (MCD)
Loft .... Lofft's English King's Bench Reports [*1772-74*] [*A publication*] (DLA)
LOFT .... Loss of Flow [*or Fluid*] Test Facility [*Nuclear energy*]
LOFT .... Loss-of-Fluid Test (GAAI)
LOFT .... Low-Frequency Telescope [*NASA*]
LOFTI .... Low-Frequency Transionospheric Satellite
LOFTPS ...... Lube Oil Fill, Transfer, and Purification System (DNAB)
LOFW .... Loss of Feedwater [*Nuclear energy*] (NRCH)
LofX .... Libbey-Owens-Ford Glass [*Private rail car owner code*]
LOG .... Labor Old Guard [*Australia*] [*An association*]
LOG .... Lambda Omicron Gamma Medical Society (NTPA)
LOG .... Lawn-O-Gram [*A publication*] (EAAP)
LOG .... Legion of Guardsmen (EA)
LOG .... Logan [*Utah*] [*Seismograph station code, US Geological Survey*] [*Closed*] (SEIS)
LOG .... Loganair Ltd. [*British*] [*ICAO designator*] (FAAC)
LOG .... Logan Mines Ltd. [*Vancouver Stock Exchange symbol*]
log .... Logarithm (IDOE)
LOG .... Logarithm [*Mathematics*]
log .... log book (SAUS)
log .... Loggia (VRA)
LOG .... Logging
LOG .... Logic
LOG .... LogicaCMG PLC [*London Stock Exchange symbol*]
log .... Logistic (MILB)
LOG .... Logistician
LOG .... Logistics (KSC)
log .... Logogram (BJA)
log .... Logographic (BJA)
LOG .... Pago Pago, AQ [*Location identifier*] [*FAA*] (FAAL)
LOG .... Rayonier Timberlands (SAUO)
LOG .... Rayonier Timberlands Cl'A' [*NYSE symbol*] (TTSB)
LOG .... Rayonier Timberlands LP [*NYSE symbol*] (SPSG)
log10 .... Logarithm to the Base 10 [*Industrial hygiene term*] (OHS)
LOGACS ...... Low-G Accelerometer Calibration System [*NASA*]

LOGAI .... Logical Addressing and Interoperability (SAUO)
LOGAIR ..... Logistics Airlift [*Military*]
LOGAIR ..... Logistics Air Network (SAUO)
Logair .... United States Air Force Logistics Command (SAUO)
LOGAIRNET... Logistics Air Network [*Air Force*]
LOGAIS...... Logistics Automated Information System [*Marine Corps*] (DOMA)
LOGAL....... Logical Algorithmic Language [*Computer science*] (CSR)
LogalEd ..... Logal Educational Software & Systems Ltd. [*Associated Press*] (SAG)
LOGALGOL... Logical Algorithmic Language [*Computer science*]
LOGAM...... Logistics Analysis Model [*Army*] (RDA)
LOGAMP .... Logarithmic Amplifier (IAA)
LOGAMP .... Logistics and Acquisition Management Program [*Army*] (RDA)
LOGANDS... Logical Commands
Logans...... Logan's Roadhouse, Inc. [*Associated Press*] (SAG)
LOGATAK.... Logistics Attack Model [*BDM Corp.*] (MCD)
LOGBALNET... Logistics Ballistic Missile Network [*Air Force*]
LOGC .... Logic Devices [*NASDAQ symbol*] (TTSB)
LOGC .... Logic Devices, Inc. [*NASDAQ symbol*] (SAG)
LOGC .... Logistics Center [*Army*]
LOG-C3...... Logistics Command, Control and Communications (SAUO)
LOG-C3I..... Logistics Command, Control, Communications and Intelligence (SAUO)
LOGCAB..... Logistics Center Advisory Board (MCD)
LOGC-AMIP... Logistics Center Involvement in Army Model Improvement Program
LOGCAP..... Logistic and Command Assessment of Projects [*Army*]
LOGCAP..... Logistics Capability
LOGCAP..... Logistics Civil Augmentation Program [*Army*]
LOGCCIS.... Logistics Command & Control Information System (SAUO)
LOGCCIS.... Logistics Command Central Information System [*British*]
LOGCEN..... Logistics Center (MCD)
LOGCMD.... Logistical Command
Log Com.... Logistical Command (SAUO)
LOGCOM.... Logistic Communications (CET)
LOGCOM.... Logistics Command (MCD)
LOGCOMD.. Logistical Command
LOGCOMNET... AFLC Teletypewriter Communications System (SAUO)
Log Comp .. Logan's Compendium of Ancient Law [*A publication*] (DLA)
LOGCON .... Logic Connection (VLIE)
LOGCON .... Logistics Readiness Condition System [*DARCOM*] (MCD)
LOGCON .... Medical Logistics and Contingency Planning system (SAUO)
LOGCOR .... Logistics Coordination (NVT)
LOGCOST... Logistics Cost Model (PDAA)
LOG CTR.... Logistic Center [*Army*]
LOGDB ...... Logistics Database
LOGDEC..... Logarithmic Decrement (IAA)
LOGDESMAP... Logistics Data Element Dictionary (SAUO)
LOGDESMAP... Logistics Data Element Standardization and Management Program [*DoD*] (AABC)
LOGDESMO... Logistics Data Element Standardization and Management Office [*DoD*] (AABC)
LOGDET..... Logistics Detachment (SAUO)
LOGDET..... Logistics Detail (SAUO)
LOGDIS ..... Logistics Data Integration System (SAUO)
LOGDIV ..... Logistics Division [*Supreme Headquarters, Allied Powers Europe*] (NATG)
log$_e$.......... Logarithm to the Base e [*Mathematics*] (DAVI)
LOGE .... Logetronics, Inc. (SAUO)
LOGEL....... Logic Generating Language [*Computer science*]
LOGEN ...... Aircraft Load Generator (SAUO)
LOGEST ..... Annual Logistic Estimate (NATG)
LOGEX....... Logistical Exercise [*Army*] (AABC)
LOGEX....... Logistic Exercise (SAUS)
LOGFAC ..... Logistics Feasibility Analysis Capability (SAUO)
LOGFACREP... Logistics Factors Report (SAUO)
LOGFED..... Log File Editor (NITA)
LOGFED..... Log File Editor Processor [*Computer science*]
LOGFOR..... Logistics Force [*Military*]
LOGFTC..... Logarithmic Fast Time Constant
LOGHELO... Logistics Helicopter (NVT)
LOGHOLDAIR... Air Logistics Message (SAUS)
LOGI......... Logarithmic Computing Instrument (HGAA)
LOGI......... Logimetrics, Incorporated (SAUO)
LOGI......... Logitech International S.A. [*NASDAQ symbol*] (NASQ)
LOGIC .... LASER Optical Guidance Integration Concept [*Missile guidance*]
LOGIC .... Level of Greatest Item Control [*DoD*]
LOGIC .... Local Government Information Center
Logic .... Logic Works, Inc. [*Associated Press*] (SAG)
LOGIC .... Loveland Geographic Information/ Cartographic System (SAUO)
LogicD ...... Logic Devices, Inc. [*Associated Press*] (SAG)
LOGICOM... Logical Communications, Inc. [*East Norwalk, CT*] [*Telecommunications*] (TSSD)
Logicon ..... Logicon Corp. [*Associated Press*] (SAG)
LOGICON.... Logicon, Inc. (ACAE)
LOGIFAMP... Logarithmic Intermediate Frequency Amplifier (IAA)
LOGIK .... Logical Organizing and Gathering of Information Knowledge (MHDI)
LOGIMP...... Logistic Improvement Program [*Military*]
LOGIN .... Local Government Information Network [*Information service or system*]
LOGIPAC.... Logical Processor and Computer
LOGISTC.... Logistic
Logist Transp Rev... Logistics and Transportation Review [*A publication*] (JLIT)
LOGIT .... Logical Inference Tester [*NASA*]
LOGK .... Kapfenberg [*Austria*] [*ICAO location identifier*] (ICLI)
LOGL .... Logal Educational Software & Systems Ltd. [*NASDAQ symbol*] (SAG)
LOGLAN..... Logical Language
LOGLAND... Logistics Transport by Land [*Military*]
LOGLF....... Logal Educational Softwr&Sys [*NASDAQ symbol*] (TTSB)
LOGLISP .... Prolog and List Processing
LOGMAN.... Logistics & Manpower Division (SAUO)
LOGMAP .... Logistic Master Plan (SAUO)
LOGMAP .... Logistics System Master Plan [*Army*]
LOGMAPS .. Logistics Master Planning System
LOGMARS .. Logistic Applications of Automated Marking and Reading Symbols [*DoD*]
LOGMDS.... Logistics Management Data System (SAUO)
LOGMET .... Logistics Management Engineering Team [*Military*]
Log Mgt Cen... Logistical Management Center (SAUO)
LOGMIS ..... Logistics Management Information System [*USACC*]
LOGMOD.... Logic Model [*Fault isolation device*] [*Army*] (MCD)
LOGMOD.... Logistics Module [*Simulation games*] [*Army*] (INF)
LOGMOD-B... Logistics Module-Base Level (SAUO)
LOGMOD-M... Logistics Module-Major Command Level (SAUO)
LOGMSG.... Log Message [*Computer science*] (VLIE)
LOGMTD .... Logarithmic Mean Temperature Difference (IAA)
LOGN .... Logan Coach [*NCIC trailer make code*]
LOGN .... Logansort Financial [*NASDAQ symbol*] (TTSB)
LOGN .... Logansport Financial Corp. [*NASDAQ symbol*] (SAG)
LOGNET ..... Logistics Data Network (SAUO)
LOGNET ..... Logistics Network (MCD)
LOGNEW .... Logistics Network (SAUO)
Lognspt ..... Logansport Financial Corp. [*Associated Press*] (SAG)
LOGO .... Limitation of Government Obligation (MCD)
LOGO .... Limit of Government Obligation (NAKS)
LOGO .... Logotype [*Advertising*] (DSUE)
LOGOIS ..... Logistics Operating Information System (AABC)
LOGOS ...... Language of Generalized Operational Simulation (VLIE)
LOGP .... Logistics Plans
LOGPAC..... Logistics Package [*Army*] (INF)
LOGPARS ... Logistics Planning & Requirements Simplification (SAUO)
LOGPARS ... Logistics Planning and Requirements Simplification System [*Army*] (RDA)
LOGPLAN ... Logistics Planning Module (SAUO)
LOGPLAN ... Logistics Plans Generation Subsystem (SAUO)
LOG PLAN... Logistics System Plan [*Navy*] [*DoD*]
LOGPT....... Logansport, IN [*American Association of Railroads railroad junction routing code*]
LOGR........ Logistical Ratio [*Army*]
LOGRAM.... Logical Program
LOGRAM.... Logistics Readiness Assessment Model (SAUO)
LOGREADI... Logistics Production/ Maintenance/Readiness (SAUO)
LOGREC..... Log Recording [*Computer science*]
LOGREDI.... Logistics Readiness (SAUO)
LOGREP..... Logistics Replenishment (NVT)
LOGREP..... Logistics Report (SAUO)
LOGREP..... Logistics Representative [*Navy*] (NVT)
LOGREQ..... Logistics Requirements (NVT)
LOGS .... Labor's Old Guard Socialists [*Australia*] [*An association*]
LOGS .... Logistics Supportability (AABC)
LOGS .... Logos Scientific, Inc. (SAUO)
LOGSA ...... Logistics Support Activity [*Army*]
LOGSACS ... Logistics Structure and Composition System (AABC)
LOGSAFE ... Logistics Sustainability Analysis Feasibility Estimator (DOMA)
LOGSAFE ... Logistics Sustainment Analysis and Feasibility Estimator (SAUO)
LOGSAM.... Logistics Support Alternative [*or Analysis*] Model (MCD)
LOGSAR..... Logistics Storage and Retrieval System (MCD)
LOGSARC... Logistics System Acquisition Review Council (ACAE)
LOGSAT ..... Logistics Special Assistance Team (MCD)
LOGSAT ..... Logistics Support Assistance Team (SAUO)
LOGSEA..... Logistics Transport by Sea [*Military*]
LOGSHORE... Logistics Short Report message (SAUS)
LOGSIM ..... Logic Simulator Program (ACAE)
LOGSIM ..... Logistic Simulation (ACAE)
LOGSS ...... Logistics Support Squadron [*Military*]
LOGSTAR ... Logistics Status Report (SAUO)
LOGSTAT.... Logistical Status Report [*Military*] (INF)
LOGSTAT.... Logistics State (SAUO)
LOGSTCN ... Logistician
LOGSUM.... Logistics Summary (NVT)
LOGSUM.... Logistics Summary Data (SAUO)
LOGSUP..... Logistics Support
LOGSUPREP... Logistics Support Report message (SAUS)
LOGSVC..... Logistics Service [*Military*] (NVT)
LOGTAB ..... Logic Tables (IEEE)
LOGTANBG... Logarithm Tangent Bearing (IAA)
LOGTECH ... Logistics Technology (SAUO)
LOGTIES .... Logistic Technology Initiatives for Existing Systems (ACAE)
LOGU .... Societe Logermafer [*Intermodal shipping container symbol*] (TVRC)
LOGWARS .. Logistic Wartime Automated Readiness System (SAUO)
LOgWC ...... West Carroll Parish Library, Oak Grove, LA [*Library symbol*] [*Library of Congress*] (LCLS)
LOGX .... Linden Leasing [*Private rail car owner code*]
LOH.......... "Lady of the House" [*Advertising*] (DOAD)
loh .... Lady of the House [*Telephone marketing*] (WDMC)
LOH.......... League of Housewives [*Also known as HOW*]
LOH.......... Length of Hospitalization

L o H .... Library of Hawaii (SAUO)
LOH .... Light Observation Helicopter
LOH .... Line Overhead (ACRL)
LOH .... Local Osteolytic Hypercalcemia [*Endocrinology*]
LOH .... Loja [*Ecuador*] [*Airport symbol*] (OAG)
LOH .... Loop of Henle [*Medicine*] (DMAA)
LOH .... Loss of Heterozygosity [*Genetics*]
LOHAC ...... Loading and Handling Corrective Action Program
LOHAP ...... Light Observation Helicopter Avionics Package (MCD)
LOHET .... Linear Output Hall Effect Transducer
LOHF .... Late-Onset Hepatic Failure [*Medicine*] (MELL)
LOHO .... Longhorn Steaks [*NASDAQ symbol*] (TTSB)
LOHO .... Longhorn Steaks, Inc. [*NASDAQ symbol*] (SAG)
Lo Ho .... Lower Hold (RIMS)
LOHP .... Labor Occupational Health Program (SAUO)
LOHS .... Loss of Heat Sink [*Nuclear energy*] (NRCH)
LOHTADS ... Light Observation Helicopter Target Acquisition Designation System (MCD)
LOI .... Laboratory Operating Instructions (MCD)
LOI .... Laredo [*Texas*] [*Airport symbol*] (AD)
LOI .... Laredo, TX [*Location identifier*] [*FAA*] (FAAL)
LOI .... Launch-on-Impact [*Military*] (MUSM)
LOI .... Letter of Indemnity (RIMS)
LOI .... Letter of Instruction
LOI .... Letter of Intent (ACAE)
LOI .... Letter of Interest (NG)
LOI .... Letter of Introduction
LOI .... Level of Incompetence (DMAA)
LOI .... Level of Injury [*Neurology*] (DAVI)
LOI .... Limited Oxygen Index [*Safety standards*]
LOI .... Limiting Oxygen Index
LOI .... Limit of Impurities
LOI .... Line of Induction
LOI .... List of Items (AABC)
LOI .... Lock-On Initiated (MCD)
LOI .... Lodge of Instruction [*Freemasonry*]
LOI .... Loss of Imprinting [*Genetics*]
LOI .... Loss-of-Input (COE)
LOI .... Loss on Ignition [*Analytical chemistry*]
LOI .... Loss-on-Ignition (SAUO)
LOI .... Lunar Orbit Insertion [*NASA*]
LOIA .... Liaison Officer for Internal Affairs (SAUO)
LOICZ .... Land-Ocean Interaction in the Costal Zone [*International Geosphere Biosphere Programme*]
LOICZ-SSC.. LOICZ Scientific Steering Committee (SAUO)
LOID .... Location Identifiers [*A publication*] [*FAA*]
LOIH .... Hohenems-Dornbirn [*Austria*] [*ICAO location identifier*] (ICLI)
LOIH .... Left Oblique Inguinal Hernia [*Medicine*] (DMAA)
LOIJ .... St. Johann, Tirol [*Austria*] [*ICAO location identifier*] (ICLI)
LOINC .... Laboratory Observation Identifier Names and Codes (IDYL)
LOINC .... Logical Observation Identifier Names and Codes (RALS)
LOIRA .... Land-Ocean Interactions in the Russian Arctic (SAUO)
LOIS .... Land-Ocean Interaction Study
LOIS .... Langsam Library Online Information Services [*University of Cincinnati*] (OLDSS)
LOIS .... Law Office Information Systems (VLIE)
LOIS .... Legal Office Information System
LOIS .... Lesbians Organising in Solidarity [*An association*]
LOIS .... Library Online Information Services [*Morehead State University*] (OLDSS)
LOIS .... Library Order Information System [*Computer system*] [*Library of Congress*] [*Obsolete*]
LOIS .... Likelihood of Image Shape [*Automotive engineering*]
LOIS .... Loislawcom (IID)
LOIS .... Loss of Interim Status [*Environmental Protection Agency*]
Lois Batim... Lois des Batiments [*A publication*] (DLA)
Lois Rec ..... Lois Recentes du Canada [*A publication*] (DLA)
LOIT .... Loitering [*FBI standardized term*]
LOIUSA...... Loyal Orange Institution of United States of America (EA)
LOIV .... Loyal Orange Institution of Victoria [*Australia*]
LOJ .... Lodge [*Telegraphy*] (PCTE)
LoJack ...... Lo-Jack Corp. [*Associated Press*] (SAG)
LOJN .... LoJack Corp. [*NASDAQ symbol*] (SAG)
LOK.......... Lock [*Telegraphy*] (PCTE)
LOK.......... Lockwood Petroleum, Inc. [*Vancouver Stock Exchange symbol*]
LOKI .... Lock City Trucking [*Common carrier symbol*]
LOKSMTH... Locksmith
LOKTAL ..... Locked Octal (IAA)
LOL .... Laughing Out Loud
LOL .... Laugh Out Loud [*Internet language*] [*Computer science*]
LOL .... League of Lefthanders [*Defunct*] (EA)
LOL .... Left Occipitolateral [*A fetal position*] [*Obstetrics*]
LOL .... Length of Lead [*Actual*] [*Technical drawings*]
LOL .... Limited Operating Life
LOL .... Limit of Liability (MCD)
LOL .... Line of Launch [*Navy*] (CAAL)
LOL .... List of Lists (SAUS)
LOL .... Little Old Lady [*Slang*]
LOL .... Lobitos Oilfields Limited (SAUO)
lol .... Lolo (Bantu) [*MARC language code*] [*Library of Congress*] (LCCP)
LOL .... Loloda [*Language symbol*] (ETLW)
LOL .... London-Oiseau-Lyre [*Record label*] [*Great Britain, USA, etc.*]
LOL .... Longitude of Launch
LOL .... Loss of Learning (SAUO)
LOL .... Loss of Life (SAUS)
LOL .... Lovelock [*Nevada*] [*Airport symbol*] [*Obsolete*] (OAG)
LOL .... Low Order Language (ACAE)
LOL .... Loyal Orange Lodge
LOLA .... Layman-Oriented Language (IAA)
LOLA .... Library On-Line Acquisitions [*Washington State University*] [*Data processing system*]
LOLA .... Light Observation Light-Armored Aircraft
LOLA .... Lola [*NCIC car make code*]
LOLA .... London Online Local Authorities (NITA)
LOLA .... Long Line Azimuth [*Survey*]
LOLA .... Lower Leg Artery [*Anatomy*]
LOLA .... Low-Level Oil Alarm (IAA)
LOLA .... Lunar Orbit and Landing Approach [*Simulator*] [*NASA*]
LOLAD....... Low-Altitude LASER Air Defense System
LOLADS..... Low Altitude Laser Air Defense System (ACAE)
LOLAS....... Location of Launching Site [*Army*]
LOLEX....... Low-Level Extraction [*Military aviation*]
LOLI .... Limited Operational-Life Items [*NASA*] (NASA)
LOLI .... Local Truck Lines [*Common carrier symbol*]
LOLI .... Loyal Orange Ladies Institution (EA)
LOLIT........ Lolita, TX [*American Association of Railroads railroad junction routing code*]
LOLITA ...... Language for the On-Line Investigation and Transformation of Abstractions [*Computer science*]
LOLITA ...... Library On-Line Information and Text Access [*Oregon State University*] [*Corvallis, OR*] [*Data processing system*]
LOLITS ...... Little Old Ladies in Tennis Shoes [*Facetious reference to minor league baseball*]
LO/LO .... Lift-On/Lift-Off
LOLP .... Loss of Load Probability [*Nuclear energy*] (IEEE)
LOLPAC ..... Land O'Lakes Inc./Agriliance LLC PAC [*Formerly known as Land O'Lake Inc. PAC*] [*Saint Paul, MN*] (PACS)
LOLSD....... Liquid Crystal Large Screen Display (ACAE)
LOLV......... Lower Leg Vein [*Anatomy*]
LOLVE .... Lower Leg Venule [*Anatomy*]
LOLW........ Laid Off, Lack of Work [*Unemployment insurance and the Bureau of Labor Statistics*] (OICC)
LOLW........ Wels [*Austria*] [*ICAO location identifier*] (ICLI)
LOM .... Laminated Object Manufacturing [*Desktop manufacturing*]
LOM .... Laminated Object Modeling [*Prototyping*]
LOM .... LASER Optical Modulator
LOM .... Launch Operations Manager [*NASA*]
LOM .... League of Mercy [*Salvation Army*]
LOM .... League of Mothers (SAUO)
LOM .... Left Otitis Media [*Medicine*] (CPH)
LOM .... Legion of Merit [*Military award*]
LOM .... Level of Maintenance (MCD)
LOM .... Light-Optic Microscope (MSA)
LOM .... Limitation of Motion [*Neurology*] (DAVI)
LOM .... Limitation of Movement
LOM .... List of Material (SAUO)
LOM .... List of Materials (CET)
LOM .... List of Modifications (AFM)
LOM .... Little Old Man [*Slang*] (DAVI)
LOM .... Living Operating Module (ACAE)
LOM .... Locator at Outer Marker [*Aviation*]
LOM .... Loewen, Ondaatje, McCutcheon, Inc. [*Toronto Stock Exchange symbol*] [*Vancouver Stock Exchange symbol*]
LOM .... Lomas & Nettleton Mortgage Investors (SAUO)
LOM .... Lombard [*NCIC motorcycle make code*]
LOM .... Lome [*Togo*] [*Seismograph station code, US Geological Survey*] (SEIS)
LOM .... Lompoc, CA [*Amtrak Busline code*]
LOM .... Loss of Motion [*Medicine*]
LOM .... Loss of Movement (SAUO)
LOM .... Low-Frequency Outer Marker
LOM .... Low-Order Memory (CET)
LOM .... Loyal Order of Moose (EA)
LOM .... Lunar Orbital Map [*Air Force*]
LOM .... Lunar Orbital Mission [*NASA*] (KSC)
LOM .... SERTEL [*Servicios Telereservacios SA de CV*] [*ICAO designator*] (FAAC)
LOMA........ Lange Order Matrix Arithmetic (ACAE)
LOMA........ Letter of Map Amendment [*Emergency Management*] (EMA)
LOMA........ Life Office Management Association [*Atlanta, GA*] (EA)
LOMA........ Literature on Modern Art
LOMA........ Louisiana Oil Marketers and Convenience Store Association (EARSL)
LOMA........ Lutheran Outdoors Ministry Association [*Later, NLOMA*] (EA)
LOMAC...... Logical Machine Corporation (SAUO)
LOMAC...... Logistic Management Advisory Committee
Lomaco ..... Lonrho-Mozambique Agroindustrial Company (SAUO)
LOMAD...... Low-to-Medium-Altitude Air Defense (AABC)
LOMADS.... Low Altitude Missile Air Defence System (SAUS)
LOMAH...... Location of Miss and Hit [*Marksmanship training*] [*Army*] (INF)
Lomak....... Lomak Petroleum, Inc. [*Associated Press*] (SAG)
Loma Linda U... Loma Linda University (GAGS)
LOMAR...... Local Manual Attempt Recording (TEL)
LOMAR...... Logistics, Maintenance, and Repair (IAA)
LOMAS...... Law Office Managemnt and Accounting System (HGAA)
Lomax Ex'rs.... Lomax on Executors [*A publication*] (DLA)
LOMB........ Lockheed Missile Beacon (IAA)
LOMC........ Logistics Management Committee (AAGC)
Lom CH Rep... Lomas's City Hall Reporter [*New York*] [*A publication*] (DLA)
Lom Dig .... Lomax's Digest of Real Property [*A publication*] (DLA)

Lome III..... Third ACP-EEC convention (SAUO)
Lom Ex...... Lomax on Executors [*A publication*] (DLA)
LOMEZ...... Low-altitude Missile Engagement Zone (SAUO)
LOMF........ Loss of Main Feedwater [*Nuclear energy*] (NRCH)
LOMI........ Letter of Moral Intent [*Business term*]
LOMI........ Low Oxidation State Metallic Ion [*Nuclear energy*] (NUCP)
LOMIS....... Locator Map in Source (IAA)
LOMJ........ Law Office Management Journal [*A publication*] (SAFN)
LOMK........ Lomak Petroleum [*NASDAQ symbol*] (TTSB)
LOMK........ Lomak Petroleum, Inc. [*NASDAQ symbol*] (SAG)
LOMKS....... Lomax, KS [*American Association of Railroads railroad junction routing code*]
LOMMCA...... Logistics Operations Manpower and Materiel Cost Analysis (SAUO)
LOMMIS...... Land Ordnance Maintenance Management Information System (PDAA)
LOMO........ London Overseas Mail Office
LOMOR....... Long-Distance Medium Frequency Omni Range (IAA)
LOMP........ Local Office Microcomputer Project (NITA)
LOMPT....... Lincoln-Oseretsky Motor [*Medicine*] (EDAA)
LOMR........ Letter of Map Revision [*Emergency Management*] (EMA)
LOMS........ Laboratory for Optomechanics and Multilayer Systems [*University of Maryland at College Park*] (RCD)
LOMS........ Library Organization and Management Section [*Library Administration Division of ALA*]
LOMSA....... Left Otitis Media Suppurative Acute [*Medicine*]
LOMSACh..... Left Otitis Media Suppurative, Chronic [*Medicine*] (MEDA)
LOMSCH...... Left Otitis Media Suppurative Chronic [*Medicine*]
LOMUSS...... Lockheed Multiprocessor Simulation System (IEEE)
LOMV........ Lolium Mottle Virus [*Plant pathology*]
LON......... Avilond, TAC [*Ukraine*] [*FAA designator*] (FAAC)
LON......... League of Nations (SAUO)
LON......... Letter of Notification
LON......... Line of Nodes
LON......... Local Operating Network [*Computer science*] (AGLO)
LON......... London [*England*] [*Airport symbol*] (OAG)
Lon......... London [*Record label*] [*Export issues of English Decca - mainly USA, Canada, etc.*]
LON......... London European Airways PLC [*British*] [*ICAO designator*] (FAAC)
LON......... Longchamp [*NCIC car model code*]
LON......... Longitude (KSC)
LON......... Longmire [*Washington*] [*Seismograph station code, US Geological Survey*] (SEIS)
LON......... Tupelo, MS [*Location identifier*] [*FAA*] (FAAL)
LON......... University College, London, England [*OCLC symbol*] (OCLC)
LONA........ Lonaire Manufacturing [*NCIC trailer make code*]
LoNa........ Low Sodium [*Dietetics*] (DAVI)
LONAL....... Local Off-Net Access Line [*Telecommunications*] (TEL)
LONB........ Lone Star Boat Manufacturing [*NCIC trailer make code*]
LONC........ Lonestar Cement [*Federal Railroad Administration identification code*]
LOND........ London
Lond........ London Encyclopedia [*A publication*] (DLA)
LOND........ London House, Inc. [*NASDAQ symbol*] (COMM)
LOND........ London International Group Ltd. [*NASDAQ symbol*] (SAG)
LOND........ London International Group plc [*NASDAQ symbol*] (NASQ)
LOND........ London Motors [*NCIC car make code*]
LondInt..... London International Group PLC [*Associated Press*] (SAG)
Lond Jur.... London Jurist Reports [*England*] [*A publication*] (DLA)
Lond Jur NS... London Jurist, New Series [*A publication*] (DLA)
Lond LM..... London Law Magazine [*A publication*] (DLA)
LondM....... London Magazine (SAUO)
LondMedSt... London Medical Studies (SAUO)
LONDO....... London, ON [*American Association of Railroads railroad junction routing code*]
LondonP..... London Pacific Group Ltd. [*Associated Press*] (SAG)
LONDON SE........... London Stock Exchange [*England*]
LondOvr..... London & Overseas Freightliners [*Associated Press*] (SAG)
LondQR...... London Quarterly Review (SAUO)
LondTopogRec... London Topographical Record (SAUO)
LONDY....... London Intl Group plc ADS [*NASDAQ symbol*] (TTSB)
LONE........ Lonergan Corporation [*NCIC trailer make code*]
LONEOS...... Lowell Observatory Near-Earth Object Search (SAUO)
LONESHS..... Limited- or Non-English Speaking Handicapped Student
LoneStar.... Lone Star Technologies [*Associated Press*] (SAG)
LONESTARPAC... Lone Star Steel Company [*Lone Star, TX*] (PACS)
LoneStr..... Lone Star Technologies, Inc. [*Associated Press*] (SAG)
LONEX....... Laboratory Office Network Experiment [*DoD*]
LONF........ FA Long [*NCIC trailer make code*]
LONF........ London Financial [*NASDAQ symbol*] (TTSB)
Long........ Longford [*County in Ireland*] (WGA)
LONG........ Longitude (AFM)
long........ Longitude (ELAL)
Long........ Longtitude (WA)
LONG........ Longus [*Long*] [*Pharmacy*]
LONG........ Longwood Group Ltd. [*NASDAQ symbol*] (COMM)
Long & R.... Long and Russell's Election Cases [*Massachusetts*] [*A publication*] (DLA)
Long & T.... Longfield and Townsend's Irish Exchequer Reports [*1841-42*] [*A publication*] (DLA)
Long Beach B Bull... Long Beach Bar Bulletin [*A publication*] (DLA)
LongDr...... Longs Drug Stores Corp. [*Associated Press*] (SAG)
LongDrg..... Longs Drug Stores [*Associated Press*] (SAG)
LONGF....... Longford [*County in Ireland*] (ROG)
Longf & T... Longfield and Townsend's Irish Exchequer Reports [*1841-42*] [*A publication*] (DLA)
LONGFD...... Longford [*County in Ireland*]
Longf Dist... Longfield on Distress and Replevin [*A publication*] (DLA)
LONGFOG..... Long-Range, Fiber-Optic Guided [*Missiles*]
LONGFOG..... Long-range FOG (SAUS)
Long Irr.... Long on Irrigation [*A publication*] (DLA)
longit...... Longitudinal (VRA)
LONG LINES... Long Hydrographic Sections Program (SAUO)
LONGLINES... Long Hydrographic Sections Programme (SAUO)
LONGM....... Longmont, CO [*American Association of Railroads railroad junction routing code*]
LONGN....... Longeron [*Aerospace engineering*]
Long Q...... Long Quinto [*Pt. 10 of Year Books*] [*A publication*] (DLA)
Long Quinto... Year Books, Part X [*5 Edw. 4, 1465*] [*A publication*] (DLA)
LONGRAM..... Long-Range Artillery Missile (SAUS)
Long S...... Long on Sales of Personal Property [*A publication*] (DLA)
LONGT....... Longtree [*England*]
LONGTRUCO... Long Island Trust Co. (EFIS)
LONGV....... Longevity (AFM)
LongvF...... Longview Fibre Co. [*Associated Press*] (SAG)
Longwood C... Longwood College (GAGS)
LONGZ....... Long-Term Terrain Model (SAUO)
LONH........ Longmark Mobile Homes [*NCIC trailer make code*]
LONI........ Library of Neuropsychological Information (SAUO)
LonMag...... London Magazine (SAUO)
LONN........ Lonnie's Trailer Sales [*NCIC trailer make code*]
LONO........ Letter of No Objection [*FDA*]
LONO........ Low Noise
LONPT....... Long Point, TX [*American Association of Railroads railroad junction routing code*]
LONR........ Longrun [*NCIC trailer make code*]
Lon R Bks... London Review of Books [*A publication*] (BRI)
LONRHO...... London and Rhodesian Mining and Land Company (SAUO)
Lonrho...... London-Rhodesia Company (SAUO)
LONS........ Laboratory Office Network System [*DoD*]
LONS........ Light of the Night Sky [*Galaxy*]
LONS........ Local Online Network System
LONS........ Logistic Office Network System (ACAE)
Lons Cr L... Lonsdale's Statute Criminal Law [*A publication*] (DLA)
LONT........ Long Trailer Company [*NCIC trailer make code*]
LONU........ Lonza [*Intermodal shipping container symbol*] (TVRC)
LOO......... Laghouat [*Algeria*] [*Airport symbol*] (AD)
LOO......... Leave One Out at a Time [*Data analysis*]
LOO......... Letter of Offer (ACAE)
LOO......... Loumic Resources Ltd. [*Vancouver Stock Exchange symbol*]
LOO......... Low Observable Office (CARL)
LOOK TR.... Lookout Station, Watch Tower [*Nautical term*] (HRNC)
LOOM........ John R. Loomis [*Common carrier symbol*]
LOOM........ Light Opera of Manhattan
LOOM........ Loyal Order of Moose (EA)
LOOP........ Long-Range Open Ocean Patrol [*Navy*] (NVT)
LOOP........ Loop [*Postal Service standard*] (OPSA)
LOOP........ Loss of Offsite Power [*Nuclear energy*] (NRCH)
LOOP........ Louisiana Offshore Oil Port [*Group of major oil companies*]
LOOPE....... Loop while Equal (VLIE)
LOOPNE...... Loop while Not Equal (VLIE)
LOOPNZ...... Loop while Not Zero (VLIE)
LOOPs....... Locally Organized and Operated Partnerships (SAUO)
LOOPS....... Local Office Online Payment System [*Unemployment insurance*]
LOOPS....... Loop [*Commonly used*] (OPSA)
LOOPZ....... LOOP while Zero (SAUO)
LOOS........ League of Older Students (SAUO)
LOOW........ Lake Ontario Ordnance Works
LOP......... Laboratory Operating Procedures (SAUO)
LOP......... Lactosuria of Pregnancy (MELL)
LOP......... Lake of the Pines Junction, CA [*Amtrak Busline code*]
LOP......... Lake Ontario Cement Ltd. [*Toronto Stock Exchange symbol*]
LOP......... Last Operation Completed [*Computer science*]
LOP......... Launch Operations [*or Operator's*] Panel [*NASA*]
LOP......... Learning Opportunity [*Education*]
LOP......... Least Objectionable Program [*Television*]
LOP......... Leave on Pass
LOP......... Left Occipitoposterior [*A fetal position*] [*Obstetrics*]
LOP......... Left Outside Position [*Dancing*]
LOP......... Letter of Promulgation [*Navy*] (NVT)
LOP......... Letter of Proposal [*Military*] (AFM)
LOP......... Level of Pain (MELL)
LOP......... Level of Performance (ACAE)
LOP......... Levels-of-Processing [*Psychology*]
LOp......... Lex Operator Gene
LOP......... Life of Program
LOP......... Line of Position [*Electronics*]
LOP......... Line of Power (WDAA)
LOP......... Line-Oriented Protocol
LOP......... Linton-on-Ouse FTU [*British*] [*ICAO designator*] (FAAC)
LOP......... Loanda [*Brazil*] [*Airport symbol*] (AD)
LOP......... Locally-Originated Program [*Broadcasting*] (NTCM)
LOP......... Local Office Project [*Department of Health and Social Security*] [*British*]
LOP......... Local Operating Procedures (AFM)
LOP......... Local Operational Plot
LOP......... Local Operations Plot (SAUS)
LOP......... Logic Processor (IAA)

LOP.......... Logistics Officer Program [*Army*]
LOP.......... Lookout Post (IAA)
LOP.......... Loss of Offsite Power [*Nuclear energy*] (NRCH)
LOP.......... Loss of Pointer
LOP.......... Loss of Privileges (WDAA)
LOP.......... Low Oil Pressure (SAUS)
LOP.......... Low-Order Position [*Military*] (AFIT)
LOP.......... Lubricating Oil Panel [*Fuels and lubricants*]
LOP.......... Lubricating Oil Pump (MSA)
LOP.......... Lunar Orbit Plane [*NASA*] (IAA)
LOPA........ Layout of Passenger Accommodation (MCD)
LOPA........ Local Payment of Airline (MCD)
LOPAC....... Load Optimization and Passenger Acceptance Control [*Airport computer*]
LOPAC....... Lorillard Tobacco Company Public Affairs Committee [*Greensboro, NC*] (PACS)
LOPACC..... Late Quaternary Ocean Palaeocirculation and Climate Change (SAUO)
LOPAD....... Logarithmic Outline [*or Online*] Processing System for Analog Data (IEEE)
LOPAIR...... Long Path Infrared
LOP & G.... Live Oak, Perry & Gulf Railroad (IIA)
LOPAR....... Long Baseline Position and Rates [*Guidance and tracking system*] [*Air Force*]
LOPAR....... Low-Power Acquisition RADAR
LOPBS....... List of Organic Persistant and Bioaccumulative Substances (SAUO)
LOPC........ Lunar Orbital Photocraft [*NASA*] (IAA)
LOPC........ Lunar Orbit Plane Change [*NASA*]
LOPE........ Live on Planet Earth (WDAA)
LOPG........ Launch Operations Planning Group
LOPG........ Live Oak, Perry & Gulf Railroad (SAUO)
LOP-GAP.... Liquid Oxygen Petrol, Guided Aircraft Projectile
LOPI......... Loss of Pipe Integrity [*Nuclear energy*] (NRCH)
LOPKGS..... Loose or in Packages [*Freight*]
LOPM........ Liaison Office for Personnel Management (SAUO)
LOPO........ Local Post (EA)
LOPO........ Low-Power Boiler [*US reactor*]
LOPOS...... Local Oxidation of Polysilicon over Silicon [*Transistor technology*]
LOPP........ Lunar Orbiter Photographic Project [*Aerospace*]
LOPPE....... Law of Political Organizations and Electoral Processes (Mexico) [*Political party*] (PSAP)
LOPPLAR... LASER Doppler RADAR (IAA)
LOPR........ Loprofile Boat Trailer [*NCIC trailer make code*]
LOPRA....... Low-Power Reactor Assembly [*University of Illinois*] (NRCH)
lopro......... low probe (SAUS)
LO-PRO..... Low-Profile
LOPRPr..... Santander Overseas Bk'A' Pfd [*NYSE symbol*] (TTSB)
LOPS........ Length of Patient Stay [*Medicine*] (AABC)
LOPS........ Lunar Orbiting Photographic System [*Aerospace*]
LOPSOD..... Long on Promises, Short on Delivery [*Computer slang*] (NETL)
LOPT........ Line Output Transformer (IAA)
LOPT........ Lynx Helicopter Observer Procedure Trainer (SAUS)
LOPU........ Logistics Organization Planning Unit
LOQ.......... Leadership Opinion Questionnaire [*Test*]
LOQ.......... Left Lower Quadrant (SAUS)
LOQ.......... Left Outer Quadrant (SAUS)
LOQ.......... Level of Quantification (SAUO)
LOQ.......... Level of Quantitation (EEVL)
LOQ.......... Limit of Quantitation [*Analytical chemistry*]
LOQ.......... Lobatsi [*Botswana*] [*Airport symbol*] (AD)
LOQ.......... Loquitur [*He, or She, Speaks*] [*Latin*]
LOQ.......... Lower Outer Quadrant [*Anatomy*]
LOQ.......... Lowest Obtainable Quantification (ABAC)
LOQC........ Linear Optics Quantum Computation
LO-QG...... Locked Oscillator-Quadrature Grid [*Computer science*]
LOR.......... Ladies of Retreads (EA)
LOR.......... Large Optical Reflector
LOR.......... League of Remembrance (SAUO)
LOR.......... Lender's Offered Rate [*Banking*]
LOR.......... Letter of Readiness (SAUS)
LOR.......... Letter of Request (AFIT)
LOR.......... Letters of Response (SAUO)
LOR.......... Level of Repair
LOR.......... Licence of Right (DB)
LOr.......... Licentiate in Orientation (SAUO)
LOR.......... Light Output Ratio (WDAA)
LOR.......... Likely Operational Range [*Navy*] (ANA)
LOR.......... Lock-Out Relay [*Electrical engineering*]
LOR.......... Long Open Reading [*Frame*] [*Genetics*]
LOR.......... Loral Corp. [*NYSE symbol*] (SPSG)
LOR.......... Loral Space Communications [*NYS*] (TTSB)
LOR.......... Lorazepam [*A tranquilizer*]
LOR.......... Lorcainide (STED)
LOR.......... Lorcha [*Ship's rigging*] (ROG)
LOR.......... Loricrin (DMAA)
LOR.......... Lormes [*Somee*] [*France*] [*Seismograph station code, US Geological Survey*] (SEIS)
LOR.......... Lorton, VA [*Amtrak rail station code*]
LOR.......... Loss of Righting Reflex [*Medicine*] (DMAA)
LOR.......... Lower Operator Rate [*Telecommunications*] [*British*]
LOR.......... Low-Frequency Omnidirectional Radio Range
LOR.......... Lunar Orbit [*or Orbital*] Rendezvous [*NASA*]
LOR.......... Ozark, Fort Rucker, AL [*Location identifier*] [*FAA*] (FAAL)
LOR-1....... Level of Rehabilitation Scale 1 (STED)
LORA........ Lecturer-Oriented Response Analysis (PDAA)
LOR/A....... Letter of Repair/Analysis (AAGC)
LORA........ Level of Repair Analysis (MCD)
LORA........ Long-Range Adaption (MCD)
LORA........ Long-Range Addition (NVT)
LORA........ Low Out of Range Alarm (ECII)
LORAAS..... Long-Range Airborne ASW [*Antisubmarine Warfare*] System (MCD)
LORAC....... Long-Range Accuracy [*RADAR*]
LORACON... Local Radioactivity Control (SAUO)
LORAD...... Long-Range Active Detection
LORAD...... Long-Range Air Defense (AABC)
LORAD...... Moderate Radiation [*Emergency Management*] (EMA)
LORADAC... Long-Range Active Detection and Communications System
LORADS..... LASER Optical Ranging and Designation System
LORADS..... Long Range Radar & Display System (SAUS)
LORAE....... Long-Range Attitude and Event [*Instrumentation system*]
LORAH...... Long-Range Area Homing
LORA-HOJ... Long-Range - Home on Jam
LORAI....... Lorain, OH [*American Association of Railroads railroad junction routing code*]
LORAINE.... Long-Range Interceptor Experiment (SAUS)
Loral......... Loral Corp. [*Associated Press*] (SAG)
LORAM...... Level of Repair for Aeronautical Material (PDAA)
LORAMS.... Long-Range Automatic Measuring Station [*Meteorology*]
LORAN...... Long-Range Aid to Navigation [*Military*] (DOMA)
LORAN...... Long-Range Area Navigation System (SAUO)
loran......... Long-Range Navigation (IDOE)
LORAN...... Long-Range Navigation
LORAN...... Long-Range Radio Navigation (ACRL)
LORAN D... Long-Range Navigation Doppler Inertial (DNAB)
LORAN DM... Long-Range Navigation Double Master
Lor & Russ... Loring and Russell's Election Cases in Massachusetts [*A publication*] (DLA)
LORAN DS... Long-Range Navigation Double Slave
LORAN M... Long-Range Navigation Master
LORAN S.... Long-Range Navigation Slave
LORAP...... Level of Repair Analysis Program
LORAPH.... Long-Range Passive Homing System
LORAPL..... Long-Range Planning Task Group [*Oversaw military strategy in Vietnam*] (VNW)
LORAS...... Linear Omnidirectional Airspeed System (PDAA)
LORAS...... Long-Range Airborne Surveillance (SAUS)
LORAS...... Low-Range Airspeed System (MCD)
Loras C..... Loras College (GAGS)
LORBAS..... Large Off-Line Retrieval Text Base Access System
LORBI....... Locked-On RADAR Bearing Indicator
LORC........ Lockheed Radio Command (MUGU)
LORCO...... Lionetti Oil Recovery, Inc. (EFIS)
LORCS...... League of Red Cross and Red Crescent Societies
LORCS...... League of Red Cross Societies
LORD........ Licensing Online Retrieval Data (NRCH)
LORD........ List of Required Documents (NVT)
LORD........ Long-Range and Detection RADAR (NATG)
lord......... Lordosis (STED)
LORD........ Lordosis [*Medicine*]
Lord......... Lordotic [*Medicine*] (EDAA)
LORDF...... Loredi Resources Ltd. (SAUO)
LORDS...... Licensing On-Line Retrieval Data System (NRCH)
Lords Jour... Journals of the House of Lords [*England*] [*A publication*] (DLA)
LORE........ Land Ordnance Engineering Branch [*Canada*] [*Military*] (PDAA)
LORE........ Line Oriented Editor (VLIE)
LOREC....... Long-Range Earth Current Communications
LORELCO... Lower Elevated Serum Cholesterol [*Acronym is trade name of Dow Chemical*]
LORELEI.... Long-Range Echo Level Indicator
LOREN...... Lorenzo, IL [*American Association of Railroads railroad junction routing code*]
LORENDAS... Long-Range Energy Development and Supply (PDAA)
Lorenz....... Lorenz's Ceylon Reports [*A publication*] (DLA)
Lorenz App R... Lorenz's Appeal Reports [*Ceylon*] [*A publication*] (DLA)
Lorenz Rep... Lorenz's Ceylon Reports [*A publication*] (ILCA)
LOREOR.... Long Range Electro Optical Reconnaissance (ACAE)
LOREORS... Long-Range, Electro-Optical Reconnaissance System
LORES....... Long-Range Environmental Studies (SAUO)
LORES....... Long-Route Engineering Study [*Bell System*]
LO-RES...... Low Resolution [*Computer science*]
Loreto....... Institute of the Blessed Virgin Mary, Irish Branch (SAUO)
LOREX....... Lomonosov Ridge Experiment (SAUO)
LORI......... Limited Operational Readiness Inspection (MCD)
LORI......... Logistics Operation Readiness Inspection (SAUO)
LoriCp....... Lori Corp. [*Associated Press*] (SAG)
LORINE...... Limited Range Imagery Networks Elements (SAUO)
Loring & Russel El Cases... Loring and Russell's Election Cases in Massachusetts [*A publication*] (DLA)
Loring & Russell... Loring and Russell's Election Cases in Massachusetts [*A publication*] (DLA)
Lor Inst..... Lorimer. Institutes of Law [*A publication*] (ILCA)
LORIS....... Long-Range Infra-red System (SAUS)
LORK........ Lorak [*NCIC trailer make code*]
LORL........ Large Orbital Research Laboratory [*NASA*]
LORMODS... Long-Range Metal Object Detection System (MCD)
LORMONSTA... LORAN Monitor Station
LORO........ Lobe-On Receive Only [*Electronic counter-countermeasures*]
LOROC...... Long-Range Offboard Chaff (SAUS)

LOROC ...... Long-Range Optical Camera (SAUS)
Loronix...... Loronix Information Systems, Inc. [*Associated Press*] (SAG)
LOROP ...... Long-Range Oblique Photography
LORPGAC... Long-Range Proving Ground Automatic Computer (IEEE)
LORRA ...... Lorraine, KS [*American Association of Railroads railroad junction routing code*]
L or RC ..... Leather or Rubber Covered [*Freight*]
LORRE ...... Laboratory of Renewable Resources Engineering [*Purdue University*]
LORROS .... Long-Range Reconnaissance & Observation System (SAUS)
LORS .... Labor Organization Reporting System [*Department of Labor*] (GFGA)
LORS .... LM [*Lunar Module*] Optical Rendezvous System [*NASA*]
LORS .... Long-Range SONAR
LORS .... Lorsbach Trucking [*Common carrier symbol*]
LORS .... Lunar Orbiting Reconnaissance System [*Aerospace*]
LORSA ...... Long-Range Steerable Antenna (MCD)
LORSAC..... Long-Range Submarine Communications (AAG)
Lor Sc L .... Lorimer's Handbook of Scotch Law [*A publication*] (DLA)
LORS-I ..... Level of Rehabilitation Scale-I [*Medicine*] (DAVI)
LORSTA..... LORAN Transmitting Station
LORSU ...... Long-Range Special Unit [*Military*]
LORT .... League of Resident Theaters (EA)
LORTAN..... Long-Range and Tactical Navigation System
LORTID...... Long Range Target Identification (ACAE)
LORTRAP ... Long-Range Training and Rotation Plan
LORU .... Renzlor Securities [*Intermodal shipping container symbol*] (TVRC)
LORV .... Low-Observability Reentry Vehicle
LORW .... Light Output Ratio Working (PDAA)
LORX........ Loronix Information Systems, Inc. [*NASDAQ symbol*] (SAG)
LORX........ Loronix Info Systems [*NASDAQ symbol*] (TTSB)
LOS.......... Laboratory Operating System [*NASA*]
LOS.......... Lagos [*Nigeria*] [*Airport symbol*] (OAG)
LOS.......... Landkreis Oder-Spree [*German license plate city code*]
LOS.......... Land Observation Satellite (PDAA)
LOS.......... Land Ownership Survey
LOS.......... Latin Old Style (ADA)
LOS.......... Launcher Operation Station (MCD)
LOS.......... Launch on Search [*Navy*] (CAAL)
LOS.......... Launch Operations System [*NASA*] (KSC)
LOS.......... Launch Optional Selector (IAA)
LOS.......... Law of the Sea [*United Nations*] (ASF)
LOS.......... Length of Service
LOS.......... Length of Stay
LOS.......... Level of Service [*BTS*] (TAG)
LOS.......... Level of Support (VLIE)
LOS.......... Liaison Office Support
LOS.......... Licentiate in Obstetrical Science
LOS.......... Lift-Off Simulator [*NASA*] (NASA)
LOS.......... Limited Operational Strategy
LOS.......... Limited Operation Strategy [*Automotive engineering*]
LOS.......... Limit Order Switching (PDAA)
LOS.......... Line-Off Simulator (SAUS)
LOS.......... Line of Scrimmage [*Football*]
LOS.......... Line of Service (GART)
LOS.......... Line of Sight
LOS.......... Line of Site (SAUS)
LOS.......... Line of Supply
LOS.......... Line-Oriented Simulation (GAVI)
LOS.......... Line Out of Service [*Telecommunications*] (TEL)
LOS.......... Little Orchestra Society (SAUO)
LOS.......... Live Oak Society (EA)
LOS.......... Local Office System (SAUO)
LOS.......... Local Operating Station (DNAB)
LOS.......... Local Operating System (IAA)
LOS.......... Logistic Operation - Streamline [*Military*] (AABC)
LOS.......... Logistic Oriented Schools [*Army*]
LOS.......... London Orphan School (SAUO)
LOS.......... Loop Output Signal (CET)
Los.......... Los Angeles Rams [*National Football League*] [*1946-94*] (NFLA)
LOS.......... Lossiemouth FTU [*British*] [*ICAO designator*] (FAAC)
LOS.......... Loss of Selectivity (AAEL)
LOS.......... Loss of Sight
LOS.......... Loss of Signal
LOS.......... Loss of Site (STED)
LOS.......... Loss of Sync [*Aerospace*] (NAKS)
LOS.......... Loss of Synchronization
LOS.......... Lost in Space [*Television Program*]
LOS.......... Lower (O)Esophageal Sphincter (STED)
LOS.......... Low Output Syndrome (MAE)
LOS.......... Lunar Orbiting Satellite [*or Spacecraft*] [*Aerospace*] (MCD)
LOS.......... Midwestern Baptist Theological Seminary, Kansas City, MO [*OCLC symbol*] (OCLC)
LOS.......... United Nations Convention on the Law of the Sea (SAUO)
LOSACA..... Liaison Officer to Supreme Allied Commander (ACAE)
LOSACA..... Liaison Officer to the Supreme Allied Commander, Atlantic (SAUO)
LOS-AD ..... Line-of-Sight - Air Defense [*DoD*]
LOSAM ..... Low-Altitude Surface-to-Air Missiles (NATG)
LOSAN ...... Los Angeles, CA [*American Association of Railroads railroad junction routing code*]
Los Angeles BAB... Los Angeles Bar Association. Bulletin [*A publication*] (DLA)
Los Angeles L Rev... Los Angeles Law Review [*A publication*] (DLA)
LOSARP..... Line-of-Sight - Repeater Placement Program (IAA)
LOSAT....... Language-Oriented System Analysis Table (IAA)
LOS-AT...... Line-of-Sight - Antitank [*DoD*]
LOSC .... Laboratory Operations Support Center [*NASA*] (SSD)
LOSC .... Law of the Sea Conference [*United Nations*] (MSC)
LOSC .... Law of the Sea Convention [*Australia*]
LOSC .... Local On-Scene Commander [*Military*] (DNAB)
LOSD .... League of St. Dymphna (EA)
LOSE .... Let Others Share Equally [*Slogan opposing President Gerald R. Ford's anti-inflation WIN campaign*]
LOSE .... Let's Omit Superfluous Expenses [*Slogan opposing President Gerald R. Ford's anti-inflation WIN campaign*]
LOSE .... Line of Sight Equipment (ACAE)
LOSE .... Line-of-Sight Expendables (DNAB)
LOS-F .... Line-of-Sight - Forward [*DoD*]
LOS-FH...... Line-of-Sight - Forward Heavy [*DoD*]
LOS-FL ...... Line of Sight-Forward Light [*DoD*]
LOSH .... Labor Occupational Safety & Health program (SAUO)
LOSI .... Ad hoc Task Team to Study the Implications, for the Commission, of the United Nations Convention on the Law of the Sea and the New Ocean Regime (SAUS)
LOSI .... Line-Of-Sight Indicator (SAUS)
LOSIS .... Law of the Sea Information System (GNE)
LOSL .... Saint Landry Parish Library, Opelousas, LA [*Library symbol*] [*Library of Congress*] (LCLS)
LOSM........ Launch Operations Simulation Model
LOSM........ Launch Operations Support Manager (SAUO)
LOSM........ Lunar Orbital Survey Missions (ACAE)
LOSMAD .... Line of Sight Missile for Air Defense (ACAE)
LOSMS...... Los Mochis, SI [*American Association of Railroads railroad junction routing code*]
LOS of NA.. Ladies Oriental Shrine of North America (EA)
LOSOS ...... Local Oxidation of Silicon on Sapphire [*Transistor technology*] (IAA)
LOSP .... Loss of Offsite Power [*Nuclear energy*] (NRCH)
LOSP .... Loss of System Pressure [*Nuclear energy*] (NRCH)
LOSP .... Lower (O)Esophageal Sphincter Pressure (STED)
LOS(P) ...... Lower O-Esophageal Sphincter Pressure [*Medicine*] (DMAA)
LOSP .... Low Speed channel connector (SAUS)
LOS PrepCom... United Nations Preparatory Commission on the International Sea-Bed Authority and for the international Tribunal for the Law of the Sea (SAUO)
LOSR .... Limit of Stack Register
LOSR .... Line of Sight Range (ACAE)
LOSR .... Line-of-Sight Rate (MCD)
LOS-R .... Line-of-Sight - Rear [*DoD*]
LOSREP..... Loss Report [*Aircrew/aircraft*]
LOSS .... Landing Observer Signal System (MSA)
LOSS .... LAPS Observing System Simulation (USDC)
LOSS .... LAPS [*Local Analysis and Prediction System*] Observing System Stimulation [*Marine science*] (OSRA)
LOSS .... Large Object Salvage System [*Navy*]
LOSS .... Launch Operations Support Services (ACAE)
LOSS .... Line of Sight of Signal [*Open Systems Interconnection*] (ODAA)
LOSS .... Lunar Orbital Survey System [*NASA*] (KSC)
LOSS .... Lunar Orbit Space Station [*NASA*]
Loss & Dam Rev... Loss and Damage Review [*A publication*] (DLA)
Loss Sec Reg... Loss' Security Regulations [*A publication*] (DLA)
LOSSYS..... Landing Observer Signal System
LOST .... Law of the Sea Treaty (MCD)
LOST .... Linear One-Step Transition [*Mathematical model for social grouping*]
LOST .... Lommel and Steinkopf [*German name for mustard gas, taken from two of the chemists who helped develop it as a chemical warfare agent*]
LOST .... Lube Oil Storage Tank (NRCH)
LOST/A...... Vessels Lost by Accident, Collision, or Similar Methods [*Navy*]
LOST/E...... Vessels Lost through Enemy Action [*Navy*]
LOSTF....... Line-of-Sight Test Fixture
LOSTFC ..... Line-of-Sight Task Force Communications [*Military*] (CAAL)
LOSTFCS.... Line-of-Sight Task Force Communications System [*Military*]
LOST/P...... Vessels Lost Due to Weather, Perils of the Sea, or Similar Reasons [*Navy*]
LOSTPED ... Load, Orientation, Speed, Travel, Precision, Environment, and Duty Cycle (VLIE)
LOSTW...... Lostwithiel [*Municipal borough in England*]
LOSU .... Lanng and Stelman [*Intermodal shipping container symbol*] (TVRC)
LOSX .... Locomotive Specialist [*Private rail car owner code*]
LOT.......... Laminated Overlay Transistor [*Electronics*] (IAA)
LOT.......... Lapped Orthogonal Transform [*Telecommunications*]
LOT.......... Large Orbiting Telescope (MCD)
LOT.......... Lateral Olfactory Tract
LOT.......... Leak-Off Test
LOT.......... Left Occipitotransverse [*A fetal position*] [*Obstetrics*]
LOT.......... Left Outer Thigh [*Injection site*]
LOT.......... Lengthened Off Time (STED)
LOT.......... Letter of Transmittal (MCD)
LOT.......... Life of Type (AFIT)
LOT.......... Lift-Off Time [*Aerospace*] (MCD)
LOT.......... Light-Off Temperature [*For steady-state combustion*]
LOT.......... Light-Off Time [*Exhaust emissions*] [*Automotive engineering*]
LOT.......... Light Operated Typewriter
LOT.......... Limited Operational Test
LOT.......... Linear Optical Trajectory [*Vision*]
LOT.......... List on Tape (IAA)
LOT.......... Load on Top [*Oil tankers*]
LOT.......... Lock on Track
LOT.......... Lodestar Energy, Inc. [*Vancouver Stock Exchange symbol*]
LOT.......... Logic Optimization with Testability (VLIE)
LOT.......... London, Ontario, Canada [*Amtrak rail station code*]

Lot .... Lotarius Rosario de Cremona [*Deceased, 1227*] [*Authority cited in pre-1607 legal work*] (DSA)
LOT .... Lotio [*Lotion*] [*Pharmacy*]
lot .... Lotion (STED)
LOT .... Lotru [*Romania*] [*Seismograph station code, US Geological Survey*] (SEIS)
LOT .... Lotus [*NCIC car model code*]
LOT .... Lower Outer Tube
LOT .... Low-Observables Technology (SAUO)
LOT .... Low-Observable Technology (MCD)
LOT .... Lumisis Operations Team (ACAE)
LOT .... Polskie Linie Lotnicze [*Poland*] [*ICAO designator*] (FAAC)
LOT .... Romeoville, IL [*Location identifier*] [*FAA*] (FAAL)
LOTA .... Loss of Target Accident [*Environmental science*] (COE)
LOTADS .... Long Term Air Defense Study (SAUO)
LOTADS .... Long-Term Worldwide Air Defense Study [*Army*] (AABC)
LOTAS .... Large Optical Tracker - Aerospace
LOTAWS .... LASER Obstacle Terrain Avoidance Warning System
LOTC .... London Over-the-Counter Market [*Information service or system*] (IID)
LOTCA .... Loewenstein Occupational Therapy Cognitive Assessment [*Test*] (TMMY)
LOTCIP .... Long-Term Communications Improvement Plan (NATG)
LOTE .... Languages Other than English
LOTE .... Lesser of Two Evils [*Politics*]
LOTEX .... Life-of-Type Extension (SAUO)
LOTH R .... Lotharian Regiment [*Military*] [*British*] (ROG)
LOTIS .... Logical Structure: The Timing and the Sequencing of Synchronous/Asynchronous Machines [*Computer science*] (CSR)
LOTIS .... Logical Timing Sequencing (NITA)
LOTIS .... Logic, Timing, and Sequencing (VLIE)
LOTMP .... Lowest Temperature [*NWS*] (FAAC)
LO-TO .... Longitudinal-Optic-Transverse-Optic [*Spectral characteristic*]
LOTO .... Lottery Enterprises [*NASDAQ symbol*] (TTSB)
LOTON .... Long Tons Discharged or Loaded
LOTOS .... Language of Temporal Ordering of Specifications [*Computer science*]
LOTP .... Logical Operation Time Projection (VLIE)
LOTQ .... Lotz Trucking [*Common carrier symbol*]
LOTR .... Licensed Occupational Therapist Registered [*Therapy term*] (CTAA)
LOTR .... [*The*] Lord of the Rings [*A trilogy*]
LOTREX .... Land-Ocean Interactions in the Coastal Zone (SAUO)
LOTREX .... Land-Surface Traverse Experiment (SAUO)
LOTREX .... Working LORAN (SAUS)
LOTS .... Large Overland Transporter System (MCD)
LOTS .... Late-Onset Tay-Sachs [*Medical term*]
LOTS .... Launch Operations Television System
LOTS .... Launch Optical Trajectory System [*NASA*] (IAA)
LOTS .... LEM [*Lunar Excursion Module*] Optical Tracking System [*NASA*] (KSC)
LOTS .... Lighter, Over-the-Shore [*Missions*] [*For air-cushion vehicles*] (RDA)
LOTS .... Load over the Side
LOTS .... Logistics over the Shore [*Military*]
LOTS .... LORAN Operational Training School
LOTS .... Lotus Development Corp. (SAUO)
LOTS .... Low Overhead Time-Sharing System (CIST)
LOTSF .... Late-Onset Tay-Sachs Foundation [*Association*] (EA)
LOTSS .... Libraries of the Social Sciences [*Australia*] [*An association*]
LotteryE .... Lottery Enterprises, Inc. [*Associated Press*] (SAG)
LottoW .... Lotto World, Inc. [*Associated Press*] (SAG)
LOTU .... Lotus [*NCIC car make code*]
LOTUS .... Ladies Organized to Unfetter Sexuality (SAUO)
LOTUS .... Long-Term Upper Ocean Study
LOTV .... Launch Operations and Test Vehicle [*NASA*] (KSC)
LOTW .... Loaded on Trailers or Wagons [*Freight*]
LOU .... Letter of Understanding [*Nuclear energy*] (NRCH)
LOU .... Letters of Undertaking [*RSPA*] (TAG)
LOU .... Limited Official Use
LOU .... Line Output Unit [*Printing*] (DGA)
LOU .... Linomatic Operating Unit [*Printing*] (DGA)
LOU .... Louisiana
LOU .... Louisville Gas & Electric Co. (SAUO)
LOU .... Louisville, KY [*Location identifier*] [*FAA*] (FAAL)
Lou .... Louth [*County in Ireland*] (WGA)
LOUC .... Louisville Cement [*Federal Railroad Administration identification code*]
LOUD .... Loudeye Tech [*NASDAQ symbol*] (SG)
LouG .... Louisville Gas & Electric Co. [*Associated Press*] (SAG)
LouG 5 .... Louisville Gas & Electric Co. [*Associated Press*] (SAG)
Lough .... Loughborough University of Technology (SAUO)
LOUH .... Light Observation Utility Helicopter (NATG)
LOUI .... Louie's Cartage [*Common carrier symbol*]
LOUIS .... Logical On-Line User Inquiry System (SAUO)
LOUIS .... Louisiana Library Network [*Library science*]
LOUIS .... Louisiana, MO [*American Association of Railroads railroad junction routing code*]
LOUISA .... Lunar Optical-UVIR [*Ultraviolet Infrared*] Synthesis Array [*NASA*]
Louisiana Ann .... Louisiana Annual Reports [*A publication*] (DLA)
Louisiana Ann Rep .... Louisiana Annual Reports [*A publication*] (DLA)
Louisiana Rep .... Louisiana Reports [*A publication*] (DLA)
Louis Rep .... Louisiana Reports [*A publication*] (DLA)
Lou Leg N .... Louisiana Legal News [*A publication*] (DLA)
Lou LJ .... Louisiana Law Journal [*New Orleans*] [*A publication*] (DLA)
Lou L Jour .... Louisiana Law Journal [*A publication*] (DLA)
LOUO .... Limited Official Use Only [*Military*]
Lou R .... Louisiana Reports [*A publication*] (DLA)
Lou Rep NS .... Martin's Louisiana Reports, New Series [*A publication*] (DLA)
Lou Reps .... Louisiana Reports [*A publication*] (DLA)
LOUVL .... Louisville, KY [*American Association of Railroads railroad junction routing code*]
LOV .... Large Opaque Vesicle [*Medicine*] (DMAA)
LOV .... Limit of Visibility
LOV .... London Flight Centre (Stansted) Ltd. [*British*] [*ICAO designator*] (FAAC)
LOV .... Loss of Vehicle (KSC)
LOV .... Loss of Visibility (NASA)
LOV .... Loss of Vision (DAVI)
LOV .... Love [*Telegraphy*] (PCTE)
LOV .... Loveland Area Office (SAUO)
LOV .... Lovo [*Sweden*] [*Geomagnetic observatory code*]
LOV .... Low-Observable Vehicle [*Military*] (MUSM)
LOV .... Monclova [*Mexico*] [*Airport symbol*] (AD)
LOV .... Societe Miniere Louvem, Inc. [*Toronto Stock Exchange symbol*]
LOVA .... Low Vulnerability Ammunition [*Military*] (RDA)
LOVAG .... Low Voltage Agreement Group (SAUO)
Lov Arb .... Lovesy on Arbitration [*1867*] [*A publication*] (DLA)
LOVARC .... Life Options, Vocational and Resource Center (MHID)
LOVB .... Lovebug Travel Trailer [*NCIC trailer make code*]
LOVE .... Language Organization Voicing Esperanto
LOVE .... League of Victims and Emphathizers (SAUO)
LOVE .... Limited Only to Vans in Europe (SAUO)
LOVE .... Linguistics of Visual English [*Sign language system for the hearing impaired*]
Love Bank .... Lovesy's Bankruptcy Act [*1869, 1870*] [*A publication*] (DLA)
LOVEL .... Loveland, CO [*American Association of Railroads railroad junction routing code*]
LOVER .... Lunar Orbiting Vehicle for Emergency Rescue (PDAA)
LOVISIM .... Low-Visibility Landing Simulation [*Program*] [*Air Force*]
LOVL .... Laugh Out Very Loud [*Internet language*] [*Computer science*]
LOVV .... Wien [*Austria*] [*ICAO location identifier*] (ICLI)
LOW .... Last Open Water (RIMS)
LOW .... Launch on Warning [*Missiles*]
LOW .... Laws of War (MCD)
LOW .... League of Welldoers (SAUO)
LOW .... Link Order Wire (SAUO)
LOW .... Link Orderwire Project
LOW .... Loners on Wheels (EA)
LOW .... Low Core Threshold (NITA)
Low .... Lowell's District Court Reports [*United States, Massachusetts District*] [*A publication*] (DLA)
low .... Lower (VRA)
LOW .... Lowe's Companies, Inc. [*NYSE symbol*] (SPSG)
LOW .... Lowe's Cos. [*NYSE symbol*] (TTSB)
LOW .... Tampias Lobu [*Language symbol*] (ETLW)
LOW .... West Yellowstone, MT [*Location identifier*] [*FAA*] (FAAL)
LOWAT .... Low-Observable Weapon Airframe Technology (SAUS)
LOWB .... LowBoy Trailer [*NCIC trailer make code*]
LOWBI .... Low-Birth-Weight Infant [*Obstetrics*]
Low Can .... Lower Canada Reports [*A publication*] (DLA)
Low Can Jur .... Lower Canada Jurist [*A publication*] (DLA)
Low Can Jurist .... Lower Canada Jurist [*A publication*] (DLA)
Low Can LJ .... Lower Canada Law Journal [*A publication*] (DLA)
Low Can R .... Lower Canada Reports [*A publication*] (DLA)
Low Can Rep .... Lower Canada Reports [*A publication*] (DLA)
Low Can Rep SQ .... Lower Canada Seignorial Questions Reports [*A publication*] (DLA)
LOWCAT .... Low Cost Air Target (SAUS)
LOW-COST CONTROL .... Adaptable Low-Cost Shop-Floor Control Systems (SAUO)
Low C Seign .... Lower Canada Seignorial Questions Reports [*A publication*] (DLA)
Low Dec (F) .... Lowell's Decisions [*A publication*] (DLA)
Low Dis .... Lowell's District Court Reports [*United States, Massachusetts District*] [*A publication*] (DLA)
LOWE .... Lowe Industries [*NCIC trailer make code*]
Low-E .... Low-Elevation (CAAL)
LOW-E .... Low-Emissivity [*Glass*]
Lowell .... Lowell's District Court Reports [*United States, Massachusetts District*] [*A publication*] (DLA)
Lower Can Jur .... Lower Canada Jurist [*A publication*] (DLA)
Lower Can SQ .... Lower Canada Seignorial Questions Reports [*A publication*] (DLA)
Lower Ct Dec .... Ohio Lower Court Decisions [*A publication*] (DLA)
Lowes .... Lowe's Companies, Inc. [*Associated Press*] (SAG)
LOWESS .... Locally-Weighted Scatterplot Smoother [*Medicine*]
LOWFAR .... Low-Frequency Analysis and Recording (MCD)
LOWFER .... Low Frequency Experimental Radio (SAUO)
LOWG .... Graz [*Austria*] [*ICAO location identifier*] (ICLI)
LOWG .... Landing Operations Working Group [*NASA*] (NASA)
LOWG .... Launch Operations Working Group (ACAE)
LOWI .... Innsbruck [*Austria*] [*ICAO location identifier*] (ICLI)
LOWK .... Klagenfurt [*Austria*] [*ICAO location identifier*] (ICLI)
LOWL .... Linz [*Austria*] [*ICAO location identifier*] (ICLI)
LOWL .... Low Degree Oscillations Experiment (SAUO)
LOWL .... Low-Level Language [*Computer programming*]
LOWM .... Wien [*Austria*] [*ICAO location identifier*] (ICLI)
Low NA .... Low Sodium [*Medicine*] (BCRP)
Lown & M .... Lowndes and Maxwell's English Bail Court Reports [*1852-54*] [*A publication*] (DLA)
Lownd & M .... Lowndes and Maxwell's English Bail Court Reports [*1852-54*] [*A publication*] (DLA)

Lownd Av Lowndes' General Average [*10th ed.*] [*1975*] [*A publication*] (DLA)
Lownd Col Lowndes on Collisions at Sea [*A publication*] (DLA)
Lownd Cop Lowndes on Copyright [*A publication*] (DLA)
Lowndes & M Lowndes and Maxwell's English Bail Court Reports [*1852-54*] [*A publication*] (DLA)
Lowndes & M (Eng) Lowndes and Maxwell's English Bail Court Reports [*1852-54*] [*A publication*] (DLA)
Lowndes M & P Lowndes, Maxwell, and Pollock's English Bail Court Reports [*1850-51*] [*A publication*] (DLA)
Lownd Ins Lowndes on Insurance [*A publication*] (DLA)
Lownd Leg Lowndes on Legacies [*A publication*] (DLA)
Lownd M & P Lowndes, Maxwell, and Pollock's English Bail Court Reports [*1850-51*] [*A publication*] (DLA)
LownInST P. W. Lown Institute. Brandeis University. Studies and Texts (BJA)
Lown Leg Lowndes on Legacies [*A publication*] (DLA)
Lown M & P Lowndes, Maxwell, and Pollock's English Bail Court Reports [*1850-51*] [*A publication*] (DLA)
LOWP Low Pro Custom Trailer [*NCIC trailer make code*]
LOWPAC Lowe's Companies Inc. PAC [*N. Wilkesboro, NC*] (PACS)
Low Pr Code Lower Provinces Code [*India*] [*A publication*] (DLA)
LOWR Lower
Lowranc Lowrance Electronics, Inc. [*Associated Press*] (SAG)
LOWS Salzburg [*Austria*] [*ICAO location identifier*] (ICLI)
LOWTRAN Low Resolution Transmission (ACAE)
LOWU Lowaco [*Intermodal shipping container symbol*] (TVRC)
LOWW Wien/Schwechat [*Austria*] [*ICAO location identifier*] (ICLI)
LOWZ Zell Am See [*Austria*] [*ICAO location identifier*] (ICLI)
LOX Lipoxygenase [*An enzyme*]
lox Liquid Oxygen (STED)
LOX Liquid Oxygen [*Also, LO_2*]
LOX Liquid Oxygen Expert System (NITA)
LO-X Low Thermal Expansion [*Synthetic ceramic*]
LOXA Aigen/Ennstal [*Austria*] [*ICAO location identifier*] (ICLI)
LOXAT Lowest Temperature Exceeded for All Time [*NWS*] (FAAC)
LOXFM Lowest Temperature Exceeded for the Month [*NWS*] (FAAC)
LOXG Graz [*Austria*] [*ICAO location identifier*] (ICLI)
LOXK Klagenfurt [*Austria*] [*ICAO location identifier*] (ICLI)
LOXL Horsching [*Austria*] [*ICAO location identifier*] (ICLI)
LOX/LH Liquid Oxygen and Liquid Hydrogen
LOXN Wiener Neustadt [*Austria*] [*ICAO location identifier*] (ICLI)
Lox-PLD Loxoseles reclusus - Phospholipase D [*An enzyme*]
LOXS Schwaz, Tirol [*Austria*] [*ICAO location identifier*] (ICLI)
LOXSE Lowest Temperature Exceeded So Early [*NWS*] (FAAC)
LOXSL lowest Temperature Exceeded So Late [*NWS*] (FAAC)
LOXT Langenlebarn [*Austria*] [*ICAO location identifier*] (ICLI)
LOXT Large Orbital X-Ray Telescope [*NASA*]
LOXZ Zeltweg [*Austria*] [*ICAO location identifier*] (ICLI)
LOY Loyale [*NCIC car model code*]
LOY Loyalty (AABC)
LOY Loyola - Notre Dame Library, Inc. (SAUO)
LOY Loyola - Notre Dame Library, Inc., Baltimore, MD [*OCLC symbol*] (OCLC)
LOYA League of Young Adventurers (SAUO)
LOYC Loyola Capital [*NASDAQ symbol*] (SAG)
LOYC Loyola Capital Corp. (SAUO)
Loy Con Prot J Loyola Consumer Protection Journal [*Los Angeles*] [*A publication*] (DLA)
Loy Dig Loyola Digest [*A publication*] (DLA)
Loy LA Ent LJ Loyola of Los Angeles Entertainment Law Journal (SAUO)
Loy LA L Rev Loyola of Los Angeles Law Review (SAUO)
Loy Law Loyola Lawyer [*A publication*] (DLA)
Loy LJ Loyola Law Journal [*New Orleans*] [*1920-32*] [*A publication*] (DLA)
Loy L Rev Loyola Law Review (SAUO)
Loyola Loyola Capital Corp. [*Associated Press*] (SAG)
Loyola C (Md) Loyola College (Maryland) (GAGS)
Loyola Dig Loyola Digest [*A publication*] (DLA)
Loyola LJ Loyola Law Journal [*A publication*] (DLA)
Loyola Marymount U Loyola Marymount University (Los Angeles) (GAGS)
Loyola U Chicago Loyola University of Chicago (GAGS)
Loyola U (La) Loyola University (Louisiana) (GAGS)
Loyola ULJ (Chicago) Loyola University. Law Review (Chicago) [*A publication*] (DLA)
Loyola Univ L Rev Loyola University. Law Review [*Chicago*] [*A publication*] (DLA)
Loy Pov LJ Loyola Poverty Law Journal (SAUO)
LOYU Companhia de Navegacao Lloyd Brasileiro [*Intermodal shipping container symbol*] (TVRC)
Loy U Chi LJ Loyola University Chicago Law Journal (SAUO)
LOZ Liquid Ozone
LOZ London [*Kentucky*] [*Airport symbol*] (OAG)
LOZ Lovozero [*Former USSR*] [*Geomagnetic observatory code*]
LOZ Lozenge [*Pharmacy*] (DAVI)
LP Air Alpes [*ICAO designator*] (AD)
LP Labile Peptide (DB)
LP Labile Protein (DB)
LP Laboratory Port [*NASA*] (SPST)
LP Laboratory Procedure
LP Labor Pain (MELL)
LP Labour Party (SAUO)
LP Labour Party of South Africa [*Political party*] (PPW)
L/P Lactate/Pyruvate [*Ratio*]
LP Lactic Peroxidase [*Medicine*] (MELL)
LP Lactoperoxidase (DB)
LP Ladyship [*or Lordship*]
LP Laminated Polyethylene Film
LP Lamp [*Automotive engineering*]
LP Landing Point [*British military*] (DMA)
LP Land Plane
LP Language Planning [*Linguistics*] (IEL)
LP Large-Paper Edition [*of a book*]
LP Large Particle
LP Large Post
LP Laryngeal Pharyngeal [*Medicine*]
LP Last Paid [*Military*]
LP Last Performance
LP Last Post (WDAA)
LP Latch Pick (VLIE)
LP Latent Period [*Physiology*]
LP Late Pay [*Electric utility company*]
LP Lateral Pyloric [*Neuron*]
LP Launching Platoon [*Army*]
LP Launch Pad (KSC)
LP Launch Panel
LP Launch Platform
LP Laureate of Philosophy
LP Law Pamphlet (ROG)
LP Lay Preacher
LP Leadership Project [*Defunct*] (EA)
LP Lead Poisoning (MELL)
LP Lead Programmer [*Computer science*] (VLIE)
LP Leaf Protein [*Food industry*]
LP Learning Prototype (SAUO)
LP Leathery Pocket [*of pineapple*]
LP Lecturer Practitioner (WDAA)
LP Left Pectoral Fin [*Fish anatomy*]
LP Left Traffic Pattern [*Aviation*] (FAAC)
LP Legal Process [*British*]
LP Legal Procurator (WDAA)
LP Legislative Proposal (GFGA)
LP Lempira [*Monetary unit*] [*Honduras*]
LP Lesson Plan
LP Lettering Piece (ROG)
L/P Letterpress (ADA)
LP Letters Patent (ROG)
LP Leucine Aminopeptidase [*Also, LA, LAP*] [*An enzyme*]
LP Leucocyte Pyrogen [*Immunology*]
LP Leukocyte-Poor [*Hematology*]
LP Liability Policy [*Information service or system*] (DOAD)
LP Liberal Party [*Canada*] (PPW)
LP Liberator Party [*Guyana*] [*Political party*] (PPW)
LP Libertarian Party (EA)
LP Library of Parliament [*Canada*]
LP Library of Philosophy [*A publication*]
LP Lichen Planus (MELL)
L/P Life Policy [*Insurance*]
LP Lighting Panel (IAA)
LP Light Pen
LP Light Perception [*Ophthalmology*]
LP Lightproof [*Technical drawings*]
LP Light Pulse [*Embryology*]
LP Limited Partnership
LP Limited Planning (MCD)
LP Limited Procurement
LP Limited Production (AABC)
LP Limited Proprietorship [*Business term*]
LP Limit of Proportionality [*Mechanics*] (IAA)
LP Limp [*Binding*] [*Publishing*]
LP Linear Phase
LP Linear Polarization
LP Linear Precedence [*Linguistics*] (IEL)
LP Linear Prediction [*Computer science*]
LP Linear Programming [*Computer science*]
LP Linear Programming Language (NITA)
LP Linen Press (ADA)
lp Line Pair [*Philately*]
LP Line Pressure
LP Line Printer [*Computer science*]
LP Linguistic Problems
LP Linguopulpal [*Dentistry*]
LP Linker Polypeptide [*Biochemistry*]
LP Linkport [*Electronics*] (ECII)
LP Link Printer (ACRL)
LP Lipid Pneumonia (MELL)
Lp Lipoprotein [*Biochemistry*]
LP Liquefied Petroleum [*Gas*]
LP Liquidity Preference [*Economics*]
LP Liquid Petroleum (SAUS)
LP Liquid Phase [*Chemistry*]
LP Liquid Propane (ACAE)
LP Liquid Propellant
LP Listening Post
LP List of Publications [*National Institute of Standards and Technology*]
LP List Price (BARN)
LP List Processor [*Standard programming language*] [*1958*] [*Computer science*] (BUR)
LP Lists of Parts (NATG)
LP Litter Patient

LP........... Little Person
LP........... Livens Projector [*Military*]
LP........... Live Preview (ELAL)
LP........... Liverpool [*Telegraphy*] (PCTE)
LP........... Liverpool Prison (SAUO)
LP........... Liver Protein [*Medicine*]
LP........... Liver to Plasma Concentration Ratio (MAE)
LP........... Load Point (BUR)
LP........... Local-Pair [*Superconductivity*]
LP........... Local Pastors [*British*]
LP........... Local Primary (OTD)
LP........... Local Procurement [*Military*]
LP........... Local Purchase (AFM)
LP........... Locating Point [*Optical tooling*]
LP........... Lodge-Pole Pine [*Utility pole*] [*Telecommunications*] (TEL)
LP........... Loewenthal Papers [*Shanghai/Washington, DC*] [*A publication*] (BJA)
LP........... Logical Partition (SAUO)
LP........... Logic Probe
LP........... Logic Programming (SAUS)
LP........... Log Periodic [*Antenna*] (NATG)
LP........... Lollipop Power [*An association*] (EA)
LP........... London Particular [*Marsala*]
LP........... London Police (SAUO)
LP........... Longest Path
LP........... Longest Perpendicular [*IOR*] [*Yacht racing*]
LP........... Longitudinal Parity [*Telecommunications*] (TEL)
LP........... Long-Pass [*Absorption cell*]
LP........... Long Period
LP........... Long Persistence
LP........... Long Picot
LP........... Long Play [*VHS recorder mode*] (NTCM)
LP........... Long Playing [*Phonograph record*]
LP........... Long Position [*Investment term*]
LP........... Long Primer
LP........... Long Provost
LP........... Loop [*Knitting*]
LP........... Lord President of the Court of Session, Scotland (DLA)
LP........... Lord Provost [*British*]
LP........... Lorentz-Polarization [*Optics*]
LP........... Losing Pitcher [*Baseball*]
LP........... Loss of Pay [*Court-martial sentence*] [*Marine Corps*]
LP........... Lost Planes [*An association*] (EA)
LP........... Love Project (EA)
LP........... Lower Panel (IAA)
LP........... Lower Peninsula [*Michigan*]
LP........... Low Pass [*Electronics*]
LP........... Low Performance
LP........... Low Point
LP........... Low Potency (DB)
LP........... Low Pour [*Fuels and lubricants*]
LP........... Low Power [*Microscopy*]
LP........... Low Pressure
LP........... Low-Pressure Cylinder [*Especially, a locomotive cylinder*]
LP........... Low Primary (IAA)
LP........... Low-Profile [*Tire design*]
LP........... Low Protein [*Nutrition*]
LP........... Lumbar-Peritoneal [*Shunt*] (DAVI)
LP........... Lumbar Puncture [*Medicine*]
LP........... Lumboperitoneal (DB)
LP........... Lunar and Planetary [*Aerospace*] (IAA)
LP........... Lunar Prospector [*NASA*]
LP........... Luster Paper [*Photography*] (DGA)
LP........... Lymphocyte Predominant [*Medicine*]
L/P........... Lymphocyte to Polymorph Ratio [*Hematology*]
LP........... Lymphoid Plasma [*Hematology*] (MAE)
LP........... Lymphoid Predominance [*Medicine*] (AAMN)
L/P........... Lymph-Plasma [*Ratio*] [*Laboratory science*] (DAVI)
LP........... Lymph-Plasma Ratio [*Hematology*] (MAE)
LP........... Lythway Press [*British*]
LP........... Popular Concerts [*Public-performance tariff class*] [*British*]
Lp........... Pressure Level [*Sound*] [*Medicine*] (EDAA)
LP-28........ Ligas Populares de 28 de Febrero [*February 28 Popular Leagues*] [*El Salvador*] (PD)
LPA.......... Amphibious Transport [*Navy ship symbol*]
LPA.......... Collaboration Partners Acquired (SAUS)
LPA.......... Laboratory Products Association (NTPA)
LPA.......... Labor Party Association (SAUO)
LPA.......... Labor Policy Association (EA)
LPA.......... Labor Press Association (SAUO)
LPA.......... La Plata [*Argentina*] [*Seismograph station code, US Geological Survey*] (SEIS)
LPA.......... LASER Printer Adapter
LPA.......... Las Palmas [*Canary Islands*] [*Airport symbol*] (OAG)
LPA.......... Latex Particle Agglutination [*Immunochemistry*] (DAVI)
LPA.......... Latvian Privatization Agency
LPA.......... Launcher Plant Assembly (IAA)
LPA.......... Launch Phase Analyst
LPA.......... Lauric [*or Lauroyl or Lauryl*] Isopropanolamide [*Also, LIPA*] [*Organic chemistry*]
LPA.......... Leaky Pipe Antenna
LPA.......... Leather Producers' Association for England, Scotland, and Wales (BI)
LPA.......... Lecithin Palmitic Acid [*Concentration in the amniotic fluid*] [*Medicine*] (EDAA)
LPA.......... Left Pulmonary Artery [*Anatomy*]
LPA.......... Lightning Position Analyser (QUAC)
LPA.......... Light Pulser Array
LPA.......... Limited Period Appointment [*Short-term employment*] [*British*]
LPA.......... Limited Purpose Agency (OICC)
LPA.......... Linear Power Amplifier
LPA.......... Link Pack Area [*Computer science*] (MCD)
LpA.......... Lipoprotein A [*Biochemistry*]
LPA.......... Liquid Propellant Analysis
LPA.......... Literature Primers [*A publication*]
LPA.......... Lithium Perchlorate Ammoniate [*Inorganic chemistry*]
LPA.......... Little People of America (EA)
LPA.......... Load Planning Advisor (SAUS)
LPA.......... Loan Production Office (EBF)
LPA.......... Local Pay Authority (AIE)
LPA.......... Local Planning Assistance (OICC)
LPA.......... Local Planning Authority [*British*] (DCTA)
LPA.......... Local Processing Agency [*Department of Housing and Urban Development*] (GFGA)
LPA.......... Local Public Agency
LPA.......... Logarithmic Periodic Antenna (MCD)
LPA.......... Logistics Pipeline Analysis [*Military*] (MCD)
LPA.......... Log Periodic Antenna
LPA.......... London Academy of Performing Arts [*England*] (WDAA)
LPA.......... Louisiana Pharmacists Association (SRA)
LPA.......... Louisiana Preservation Alliance (EARSL)
LPA.......... Louisiana Press Association (SRA)
LPA.......... Louisiana Psychological Association (SRA)
LPA.......... Low-Power Amplifier (CET)
LPA.......... Low-Pressure Alarm (IEEE)
LPA.......... Lysophosphatidic Acid [*Biochemistry*] (QSUL)
LPA.......... PAL Aerolineas SA de CV [*Mexico*] [*ICAO designator*] (FAAC)
LPAA......... League of Pace Amendment Advocates (EA)
LPAA......... Log Periodic Array Antenna
LPAA......... London Poster Advertising Association (SAUO)
LPAAT....... Lysophosphatidic Acid Acyltransferase [*An enzyme*]
LPAB......... Legal Practitioners' Admission Board [*Australia*]
LPAC......... Labor Policy Advisory Committee for Multilateral Trade Negotiations [*Terminated, 1980*] (EGAO)
LPAC......... Lancer Pacific, Inc. (SAUO)
LPAC......... Laser Pacific Media Corp. [*NASDAQ symbol*] (SAG)
LPAC......... Laser-pac Media [*NASDAQ symbol*] (TTSB)
LPAC......... Libertarian Party Abolitionist Caucus (EA)
LPAI......... La Petite Academy, Incorporated (SAUO)
LPAI......... Ligue Populaire Africaine pour l'Independance [*African People's League for Independence*] [*Djibouti*]
LPAM........ Lisboa [*Portugal*] [*ICAO location identifier*] (ICLI)
L-PAM....... L-Phenylalanine Mustard [*Melphalan*] [*Also, A, M, MPH, MPL*] [*Antineoplastic drug*]
L-PAM....... L-Phenylalanin, Procarbazine, Adriamycin, Methotrexate [*Antineoplastic drug regimen*] (DAVI)
LP & KTF... London Printing and Kindred Trades Federation (DGA)
LP&L........ Louisiana Power and Light (SAUO)
LP&LC....... Louisiana Power & Light Company (SAUO)
LP & M..... Liverpool Post and Mercury [*A publication*] (ROG)
LP & P...... Logistics Policy and Procedures for Contingency Operations [*DARCOM*] (CINC)
LPAR........ Alverca [*Portugal*] [*ICAO location identifier*] (ICLI)
LPAR........ Large Phased-Array RADAR
LPAR........ Logical Partition [*Computer science*] (CIST)
LPAR........ Logistics Partners Company [*Common carrier symbol*]
LPARL....... Lockheed Palo Alto Research Laboratory (SAUO)
LPARM...... Liquid Propellant Applied Research Motor
LPAS......... Luciano Pavarotti Appreciation Society [*British*] (DBA)
LPASA....... Linear Pulse-Height Analyzer Spectrum Analysis (PDAA)
L/PAT........ Legislative/Political Action Team
L/PAT........ Letters Patent (ROG)
LPAT......... Lopat Industries, Inc. (SAUO)
LPATS....... Lightning Position and Tracing System (MCD)
LPAV......... Aveiro [*Portugal*] [*ICAO location identifier*] (ICLI)
LPA-VS...... London and Provincial Anti-Vivisection Society (SAUO)
LPAZ......... Santa Maria, Santa Maria Island [*Portugal*] [*ICAO location identifier*] (ICLI)
LPB.......... La Paz [*Bolivia*] [*Airport symbol*] (OAG)
LPB.......... La Paz [*Bolivia*] [*Seismograph station code, US Geological Survey*] (SEIS)
LPB.......... Launch Pad Building (ACAE)
LPB.......... Lighted Pushbutton (ECII)
LPB.......... Lightweight Passive Binoculars [*Police and security equipment*]
LpB.......... Lipoprotein B [*Biochemistry*]
LPB.......... Lithium Polymer Battery
LPB.......... Load Program Block [*Computer science*] (ELAL)
LPB.......... Loan Policy Board [*of SBA*] [*Abolished, 1965*]
LPB.......... Lollipop Power Books (EA)
LPB.......... [*The*] Louisiana & Pine Bluff Railway Co. [*AAR code*]
LPB.......... Low-Level Penetration Bomb
LPB.......... Low-Probability Behavior
LPB.......... Lunar and Planetary Bibliography [*Lunar and Planetary Institute*] [*Information service or system*] (IID)
LPB.......... Paper Book of Laurence, J., in Lincoln's Inn Library [*A publication*] (DLA)
LPBA........ Lawyer-Pilots Bar Association (EA)
LPBBA....... Log Periodic Broadband Antenna
LPBE......... Beja [*Portugal*] [*ICAO location identifier*] (ICLI)
LPBE......... Linear Poisson-Boltzmann Equation [*Physical chemistry*]

LPBG .... Braganca [*Portugal*] [*ICAO location identifier*] (ICLI)
LPBJ .... Beja [*Portugal*] [*ICAO location identifier*] (ICLI)
LPBP .... Latino Public Broadcasting Project (SAUO)
LPBP .... Low-Profile Bioprosthesis [*Medicine*] (DMAA)
LPBR .... Braga [*Portugal*] [*ICAO location identifier*] (ICLI)
LPBT .... Ladies Professional Bowlers Tour (EA)
LPC .... Acyl Lyso-glycerophosphocholine (SAUS)
LPC .... Laboratory of Pharmacology and Chemistry [*National Institute of Environmental Health Sciences*] (RCD)
LPC .... Laboratory Precision Connector (IAA)
LPC .... Laboratory Pulse Compression
LPC .... Labour Party Conference (SAUO)
LPC .... La Cumbre Peak [*California*] [*Seismograph station code, US Geological Survey*] (SEIS)
LPC .... Lamina Precursor Cell [*Neurology*]
LPC .... Landmarks Preservation Commission [*New York City*]
LPC .... Land Protection Council [*Victoria, Australia*]
LPC .... Large Particle Count (SAUS)
LPC .... LASER Particle Counter (AAEL)
LPC .... Laser Photocoagulation [*Ophthalmology*] (DAVI)
LPC .... Late Positive Component (MAE)
LPC .... Launch Pod Container [*General Support Rocket System*] (MCD)
LPC .... Laurylpyridinium Chloride [*Also, DPC*] [*Organic chemistry*]
LPC .... Leader Preparation Course
LPC .... Leaf Protein Concentrate [*Food industry*]
LPC .... League of Professional Craftsmen [*British*] (DBA)
LPC .... Least-Preferred Co-Worker [*Management term*]
LPC .... Leather Personnel Carriers [*i.e., boots*] [*Slang*] [*Army*]
LPC .... Lehigh Portland Cement [*Federal Railroad Administration identification code*]
LPC .... Less Prosperous Country
LPC .... Leukocyte Particle Counter [*Instrumentation*]
LPC .... Liberal Party of Canada (EAIO)
LPC .... Libertarian Party of California (EARSL)
LPC .... Licensed Professional Counselor
LPC .... Lieberman Plasma Cell (DB)
LPC .... Light Patrol Car [*British*]
LPC .... Limiting Permissible Concentration (EEVL)
LPC .... Linear Power Controller
LPC .... Linear Prediction Code
LPC .... Linear Prediction Coefficient [*Linguistics*] (IEL)
LPC .... Linear Predictive Coding [*Digital coding technique*] [*Telecommunications*]
LPC .... Linkport Controller [*Electronics*] (ECII)
LPC .... Link Priority Change [*NASA*] (KSC)
LPC .... Lipocortin (DMAA)
LpC .... Lipoprotein C [*Biochemistry*]
LPC .... Livermore Projects Committee (SAUO)
LPC .... Livestock and Pastoral Company (SAUO)
LPC .... Livestock Publications Council (EA)
LPC .... Loan Pricing Corporation
LPC .... Local Procedure Call (VLIE)
LPC .... Local Productivity Committee (SAUO)
LPC .... Lockheed Propulsion Co. [*Division of Lockheed Aircraft Corp.*] (KSC)
LPC .... Logical Processing Capabilities (ACAE)
LPC .... Lompoc, CA [*Location identifier*] [*FAA*] (FAAL)
LPC .... London Parochial Charities (SAUO)
LPC .... London Processing Centre (SAUO)
LPC .... London Publicity Club (SAUO)
LPC .... Longitudinal Parity Check [*Telecommunications*] (IAA)
LPC .... Longitudinal Primary Care [*Medicine*] (DMAA)
LPC .... Loop-Control [*Relay*] (IEEE)
LPC .... Loop Preparation Cask [*Nuclear energy*] (NRCH)
LPC .... Lord President's Committee [*British*]
LPC .... Lords of the Privy Council Lower Provinces Code [*India*] [*A publication*] (DLA)
LPC .... Loss and Prevention Council (HEAS)
LPC .... Lottery Promotion Co. [*British*] (ECON)
LPC .... Lower Pump Cubicle (IEEE)
LPC .... Low Particle Concentration
LPC .... Low-Power Channel (IAA)
LPC .... Low-Power Counter
LPC .... Low-Pressure Chamber Technician [*Navy*]
LPC .... Low-Pressure Composite
LPC .... Low Pressure Compressor (SAUS)
LPC .... Low-Pressure Compressor
LPC .... Low Price Center (SAUO)
LPC .... Lumped-Parameter Calorimeter [*Heat measure*]
LPC .... Lysophosphatidylcholine [*Also, Lyso-PC*] [*Biochemistry*]
LPCA .... Licensed Professional Counselors Association of Georgia (SEAT)
LPCA .... Louisiana Pest Control Association (SRA)
LPCA .... Louisiana Primary Care Association (SRA)
LPCA .... Lunar Pyrotechnic Control Assembly [*Aerospace*]
LPCANC ..... Licensed Professional Counselors Association of North Carolina (SEAT)
LPCAT .... Laboratory for Pest Control Application Technology [*Ohio State University*] [*Research center*] (RCD)
LPCC .... Lamb Promotion Coordination Committee (SAUO)
LPCC .... Legal Practitioners Complaints Committee [*South Australia*]
LPCC .... London Propaganda Coordinating Committee (SAUO)
LPCC .... Low-Pressure Combustion Chamber
LPCDF .... Low Profile Combined Distributing Frame (ROAS)
LPCG .... LASER Planning and Coordination Group [*Energy Research and Development Administration*]
LPCH .... Chaves [*Portugal*] [*ICAO location identifier*] (ICLI)
LPCh .... Lateral Posterior Choroidal [*Medicine*] (RAWO)
LPCH .... Local Process Control Host (IAA)
LPCI .... Low Pressure Coolant Injection (SAUS)
LPCI .... Low-Pressure Coolant Injection [*Nuclear energy*] (NRCH)
LPCIS .... Low-Pressure Coolant Injection System [*Nuclear energy*] (NRCH)
LPCL .... Laboratory Pulse Compression Loop
LPCL .... Linear Programming Control Language [*Computer science*] (VLIE)
LPCM .... Linear Phase Code Modulation
LPCM .... Linear Pulse-Code Modulation [*Computer science*]
LPCM .... London Police Court Mission (SAUO)
LPCM .... Low Placed Conus Medullaris [*Medicine*] (DMAA)
LPCM .... Low-Pressure Compression Molding [*Plastics*]
LPCO .... Coimbra [*Portugal*] [*ICAO location identifier*] (ICLI)
LPCO .... Laboratory Policy Coordination Office (SAUO)
LPCO .... Low-Pressure Cut-Off [*Air conditioning system*] [*Automotive engineering*]
LPCOMP .... Logical Physical Comparator (VLIE)
LPCP .... Launcher Preparation Control Panel
LPcP .... Light Perception with Projection [*Medicine*] (EDAA)
LPCR .... Low-Pressure Cooling Recirculation Phase [*Environmental science*] (COE)
LPCRS .... Low-Pressure Coolant Recirculation System [*Nuclear energy*] (IEEE)
LPCS .... Cascais [*Portugal*] [*ICAO location identifier*] (ICLI)
LPCS .... Laterally to the Pedunculus Cerebellaris Superior [*Medicine*]
LPCS .... League for the Prohibition of Cruel Sports (SAUO)
LPCS .... Light Pen Control System [*Medicine*] (EDAA)
LPCS .... Local Post Collectors Society (EA)
LPCS .... Low-Pressure Core Spray [*Environmental science*] (COE)
LPCS .... Low-Pressure Core Spray System [*Nuclear energy*] (NRCH)
LPCT .... Late Proximal Cortical Tubule (DB)
LPCV .... Covilha [*Portugal*] [*ICAO location identifier*] (ICLI)
LPCVD .... Liquid Phase Chemical Vapor Deposition [*Photovoltaic energy systems*]
LPCVD .... Liquid Phase Chemical Vapour Deposition (AAEL)
LPCVD .... Low-Pressure Chemical Vapor Deposition [*Semiconductor technology*]
LP-CW .... Long Pulse - Continuous Wave (NG)
LPD .... Amphibious Transport Dock [*Landing Platform, Dock*] [*Navy ship symbol*]
LPD .... Labelled Plan Display (PDAA)
LPD .... Labelled Position Display (SAUS)
LPD .... Label Plan Display (SAUS)
LPD .... Labour Party of Dominica [*Political party*] (EY)
LPD .... Lake Placid, NY [*Amtrak Busline code*]
LPD .... Landing Platform Dock [*Military vehicles*]
LPD .... Landing Platform, Dock
LPD .... Landing Point Designator [*Apollo*] [*NASA*]
LPD .... Language Processing and Debugging [*Computer science*] (BUR)
LPD .... La Pedrera [*Colombia*] [*Airport symbol*] (OAG)
LPD .... Laredo Petroleums [*Vancouver Stock Exchange symbol*]
LPD .... Large Parallel Databases (SAUO)
LPD .... LASER Polarization Detector
LPD .... LASER Projection Display (AAEL)
LPD .... Lateral Photoelectric Detector (PDAA)
LPD .... Launch Platform Detected [*Navy*] (CAAL)
LPD .... Launch Point Determination
LPD .... Launch Procedure Document [*NASA*] (KSC)
LPD .... Least Perceptible Difference [*Psychology*]
lpd .... Least-Perceptible Difference (DIPS)
LPD .... Legendary Pink Dots (VLIE)
LPD .... Legg-Perthes Disease [*Medicine*] (MELL)
LPD .... Liberal Publications Department (SAUO)
LPD .... Lighting-Power Density
LPD .... Light Pipe Device [*Communications*]
LPD .... Light Point Defect (AAEL)
LPD .... Linear Phasing Device [*Telecommunications*] (OA)
LPD .... Line Printer Daemon (PCM)
LpD .... Lipoprotein D [*Biochemistry*]
LPD .... Liquid-Protein Diet
LPD .... Liters per Day (KSC)
LPD .... Local Power Density (NRCH)
LPD .... Local Procurement Direct [*Military*]
LPD .... Logical Physical Design (VLIE)
LPD .... Log Periodic Dipole
LPD .... Low-Performance Drone
LPD .... Low Period Dipole
LPD .... Low-Power Difference (IEEE)
LPD .... Low-Pressure Difference (IEEE)
LPD .... Low Probability of Detection (ADWA)
LPD .... Low Protein Diet
LPD .... Luteal Phase Defect [*Gynecology*] (DAVI)
LPD .... Lymphoproliferative Disease [*Oncology*]
LPD .... Lymphoproliferative Disorder [*Medicine*] (MELL)
LPDA .... Linear Photodiode Array [*Instrumentation*]
LPDA .... Link Problem Determination Aid [*IBM*] (GART)
LPDA .... Log Periodic Dipole Antenna [*Military*] (CAAL)
LPDA .... Log Periodic Dipole Array
LPDC .... Language Programmes Development Centre (SAUO)
LPDC .... LASER Plasmadynamic Converter
LPDC .... Least Positive Down Count (VLIE)
LPDC .... Leonard Peltier Defense Committee (EA)
LPDC .... London Parcels Delivery Co.
LPDC .... London Parcels Delivery Company (SAUO)
LPDC .... Louisiana Population Data Center [*Louisiana State University*] (RCD)

LPDE .... Leeds Product Data Editor (VLIE)
LPDF .... Lipoprotein-Deficient Fraction [*Medicine*] (DMAA)
LPD/H .... Landing Platform, Dock/Helicopter (MILB)
LpDH .... Lysopine Dehydrogenase [*An enzyme*]
LPDM .... List of Physical Dimensions (NASA)
LPDR .... Lao People's Democratic Republic
LPDR .... Local Public Document Room (GFGA)
LPDS .... Lipoprotein Deficient Human Serum
LPDT .... Legal Practitioners Disciplinary Tribunal [*South Australia*]
LPDT .... Low Power Distress Transmitter [*Aviation*] (DA)
LPDTL .... Low-Power Diode Transistor Logic [*Electronics*] (IAA)
LPDU .... Link Layer Protocol Data Unit [*Telecommunications*] (OSI)
LPDU .... Link Protocol Data Unit (SAUS)
LPE .... Labour Party Executive (SAUO)
LPE .... Lamda Point Experiment (SAUS)
LPE .... Lapeer, MI [*Amtrak rail station code*]
LPE .... Launch Preparation Equipment (AABC)
LPE .... Layer Primitive Equation (MHDI)
LPE .... Lead Piping Engineer
LPE .... Limited Paperback Editions
LPE .... Linear Parameter Estimation [*Physical chemistry*]
LPE .... Linear Polyethylene [*Organic chemistry*]
LPE .... Linkport Extension [*Electronics*] (ECII)
LpE .... Lipoprotein E [*Biochemistry*]
LPE .... Lipoprotein Electrophoresis [*Biochemistry*]
LPE .... Liquid Phase Epitaxy [*Magnetic film*]
LPE .... Local Peripheral Equipment (VLIE)
LPE .... London Petroleum Exchange (SAUO)
LPE .... London Press Exchange
LPE .... London Provision Exchange (SAUO)
LPE .... Loop Preparation Equipment [*Nuclear energy*] (NRCH)
LPE .... Low Probability of Exploitation (PDAA)
LPE .... Lunar and Planetary Ephemerides Assembly [*Space Flight Operations Facility, NASA*]
LPE .... Lysophosphatidylethanolamine [*Biochemistry*]
LPEA .... Luis Palau Evangelistic Association (EA)
LPEC .... Labour Party Education Committee (SAUO)
LPEC .... Launch Preparation Equipment Compartment (AABC)
LPed .... Licentiate in Pedagogy (CPGU)
LPEM .... Launch Preparation Equipment Monitor (MCD)
LPEO .... Local Public Employment Office
LPEP .... Le Peep Restaurants, Inc. (SAUO)
LPER .... Institute for Regional Economic Research (SAUO)
LPerc .... Light Perception [*Ophthalmology*]
LPERE .... Linear Phase with Equal Ripple Error (IAA)
LPES .... Lamda Point Experiment System (SAUS)
LPES .... Launch Preparation Equipment Set (AABC)
LPEV .... Evora [*Portugal*] [*ICAO location identifier*] (ICLI)
LPEV .... Launch Preparation Equipment Vault (MCD)
LPF .... Landsing Pacific Fund [*AMEX symbol*] (CTT)
LPF .... Large Payload Fairing [*Space launch term*] (ISAK)
LPF .... Latvian Popular Front [*Political party Defunct*] (EAIO)
LPF .... Leach-Precipitate Float (BARN)
LPF .... Lead Pipe Fracture (MELL)
LPF .... League for Programming Freedom (EA)
LPF .... Left Posterior Fascicle [*Anatomy*]
LPF .... Le Pertre [*France*] [*Seismograph station code, US Geological Survey*] (SEIS)
LPF .... Leukocytosis-Promoting Factor [*Hematology*]
LPF .... Leukopenia Factor (STED)
LPF .... Life Probability Function
LPF .... Light Patrol Frigate (ADA)
LPF .... Lipopolysaccharide Factor (STED)
LPF .... Liquid Pressure Filter
LPF .... Liver Plasma Flow [*Medicine*] (STED)
LPF .... Localized Plaque Formation [*Dentistry*] (MAE)
LPF .... Logically Passive Function
LPF .... Lowest Possible Airfare
LPF .... Low-Pass Filter [*Electronics*]
LPF .... Low Power Factor (MIST)
lpf .... Low-Power Field (STED)
LPF .... Low-Power Field [*Microscopy*]
LPF .... Low-Profile Flange
LPF .... Lutheran Peace Fellowship (EA)
LPF .... Lymphocytosis-Promoting Factor [*Hematology*] (DAVI)
LPF .... Pop Festivals [*Public-performance tariff class*] [*British*]
LPFA .... Laminated Plastics Fabricators Association [*British*] (BI)
LPFA .... London Potato Futures Association [*London Stock Exchange*]
LPFB .... Left Posterior Fascicular Block [*Cardiology*]
LPFGEN .... Linear Programming File Generator [*Computer science*] (IAA)
LPFL .... Flores, Flores Island [*Portugal*] [*ICAO location identifier*] (ICLI)
LPFL .... Lowpass Filter (MSA)
LPFM .... Low-Powered Fan Marker (MSA)
LPFN .... Low-Pass-Filtered Noise (STED)
LPFO .... London Procurement Field Office
LPFP .... Low-Pressure Fuel Pump (KSC)
LPFR .... Faro [*Portugal*] [*ICAO location identifier*] (ICLI)
LPFR .... Liquid Phase Flow Reactor (KSC)
LPFRS .... Low-Profile Frequency Reference Standard
LPFRT .... Limited Preliminary Flight Rating Test
LPFS .... London Public Fur Sales (SAUO)
LPFS .... Low-Pass-Filtered Signal (STED)
LPFSSB .... Lone Parents' Family Support Service - Birthright [*Australia*]
LPFT .... LOPW Pressure Fuel Turboprop (SAUS)
LPFT .... Low-Pressure Fuel Turbopump
LPFTP .... Low-Pressure Fuel Turbopump (NASA)
LPFU .... Funchal, Madeira Island [*Portugal*] [*ICAO location identifier*] (ICLI)
LPG .... Collaboration Programme (SAUS)
LPG .... Lake Ponask Gold Corp. [*Toronto Stock Exchange symbol*]
LPG .... Langage de Programmation et de Gestion [*French computer language*]
LPG .... La Plata [*Argentina*] [*Airport symbol*] (OAG)
LPG .... Lapping [*Electricity*]
LPG .... Last Page Generator (NASA)
LPG .... Launch Preparations Group [*NASA*]
LPG .... Le Parti de la Guadeloupe [*Political party*] (EY)
LPG .... Library Planning Group (SAUO)
LPG .... Licentiate of the Physicians Guild [*British*]
LPG .... Life Partners Group [*NYSE symbol*] (TTSB)
LPG .... Life Partners Group, Inc. [*NYSE symbol*] (SPSG)
LPG .... Linear Predictive Coder (SAUS)
LPG .... Lipophosphoglycan [*Biochemistry*]
LPG .... Liquefied Petroleum Gas
LPG .... Liquid Propane Gas
LPG .... Liquid Propane-Gas Shutoff [*NFPA pre-fire planning symbol*] (NFPA)
LPG .... Liquid Propellant Gun (NASA)
LPG .... List Program Generator (IAA)
LPG .... Loan Portfolio Guarantee (SAUO)
LPG .... Long Path Gas [*Spectroscopy*]
LPG .... Lousy Paying Guest [*Hotel slang*]
LPG .... Low-Pressure Gas (NRCH)
LPG .... Lysophosphoglyceride [*Medicine*] (EDAA)
LPG .... Petrolane Partners (SAUO)
LPGA .... Ladies Professional Golf Association (EA)
LPGA .... Liquefied Petroleum Gas Association (HEAS)
LPGA .... Living Plant Growers Association (EA)
LPGA .... Louisiana Pecan Growers' Association (EA)
LPGA .... Louisiana Personnel and Guidance Association (SAUO)
LP Gas .... Liquefied Petroleum Gas (SAUO)
LPGE .... LEM [*Lunar Excursion Module*] Partial Guidance Equipment [*NASA*] (KSC)
LPGG .... Liquid Propellant Gas Generator
LPGITA .... Liquefied Petroleum Gas Industry Technical Association [*British*]
LPGITA .... Liquid Petroleum Gas Industry Technical Association (SAUO)
LPGITC .... Liquified Petroleum Gas Industry Technical Committee
LPGL .... London Pacific Group Ltd. [*NASDAQ symbol*] (SAG)
LPGLY .... London Pacific Grp ADS [*NASDAQ symbol*] (TTSB)
LPGM .... Last Pinedale Glacial Maximum [*Climatology*]
LPGR .... Graciosa, Graciosa Island [*Portugal*] [*ICAO location identifier*] (ICLI)
LPGS .... Liquid Pathway Generic Study [*Nuclear energy*] (NRCH)
LPGS .... Liquified Petroleum Gas Report [*American Petroleum Institute*] [*Database*]
LPGTC .... Liquified Petroleum Gas Industry Technical Committee (MCD)
LPH .... Amphibious assault ship, helicopter (SAUS)
LPH .... Amphibious Assault Ship (Landing Platform, Helicopter) [*Navy symbol*]
LPH .... Assault Hospital Ship [*Navy symbol*] (VNW)
LPH .... Laboratory of Physiological Hygiene [*University of Minnesota*] [*Research center*] (RCD)
LPH .... Landing Personnel Helicopter [*British*] (NATG)
LPH .... Landing Platform Helicopter (CCCA)
LPh .... Late Phoenician (BJA)
LPH .... Lee Pharmaceuticals [*AMEX symbol*] (SPSG)
LPH .... Left Posterior Hemiblock [*Cardiology*]
LPH .... Legrest Pin Handle
LPh .... Licentiate of Philosophy
LPH .... Light Pintle Head (SAUS)
LPH .... Line Protocol Handler [*Communications term*] (DCT)
LPH .... Lines per Hour [*Printing*]
LPH .... Lipotropic Hormone (ADWA)
LPH .... Lipotropic Pituitary Hormone [*Lipotropin*] [*Medicine*] (STED)
LPH .... Lipotropin Hormone [*Endocrinology*]
LPH .... Liters per Hour (KSC)
LPH .... Lochgilphead [*Scotland*] [*Airport symbol*] (OAG)
LPHB .... Left Posterior Hemiblock [*Medicine*] (STED)
LPHB .... Low-Pressure Heating Boiler
LPHD .... Lymphocyte-Predominance Hodgkin Disease [*Medicine*] (RAWO)
LPHL .... Leisureplanet Holdings [*NASDAQ symbol*] (SG)
LPHLDR .... Lampholder
LPHM .... Lee Pharmaceuticals [*NASDAQ symbol*] (QUAN)
LPHR .... Horta, Faial Island [*Portugal*] [*ICAO location identifier*] (ICLI)
LPHS .... Lunar and Planetary Horizon Scanner [*Aerospace*]
LPhSoc .... London, Royal Philharmonic Society (SAUO)
LPHSW .... Last Pass Heat Sink Welding [*Nuclear energy*] (NUCP)
LPI .... Collaboration Programme Interest (SAUS)
LPI .... Colorado Springs, CO [*Location identifier*] [*FAA*] (FAAL)
LPI .... La Pointe Industries, Inc. [*AMEX symbol*] (COMM)
LPI .... Laser Peripheral Iridectomy [*Medicine*] (MELL)
LPI .... LASER Peripheral Irridectomy (STED)
LPI .... Latent Photographic Image
LPI .... Launching Position Indicator
LPI .... Leadership Practices Inventory [*Test*] (TMMY)
LPI .... Leaf Plastochron Index [*Botany*]
LPI .... Learning Preference Inventory
LPI .... Lease Plan International (SAUO)
LPI .... Left Posterior-Inferior [*Medicine*] (DMAA)
LPI .... Lifetime Products (EFIS)
LPI .... Lightning Protection Institute (EA)

LPI .... Linear Partial Information (PDAA)
Lpi .... Lines per Inch (ADWA)
LPI .... Lines per Inch [*Printing*]
LPI .... Linkoeping [*Sweden*] [*Airport symbol*] (OAG)
LPI .... Linus Pauling Institute of Science and Medicine [*Research center*] (RCD)
LPI .... Linux Professional Institute (SAUO)
LPI .... List per Inch (IAA)
LPI .... Logistics Performance Indicator (PDAA)
LPI .... Lomond Publications, Inc. [*Telecommunications service*] (TSSD)
LPI .... Longitudinally Applied Paper Insulation [*Telecommunications*] (TEL)
LPI .... Long Process of Incus [*Medicine*] (MELL)
LPI .... Louisiana Polytechnical Institute
LPI .... Low-Power Illuminator (NATG)
LPI .... Low-Power Injection [*Nuclear energy*] (NRCH)
LPI .... Low-Power Interrupt (MCD)
LPI .... Low-Pressure Index
LPI .... Low-Pressure Injection [*Nuclear energy*] (NRCH)
LPI .... Low-Pressure Isolation (AAEL)
LPI .... Low Probability of Intercept (NVT)
LPI .... Low Probability of Interest
LPI .... Lunar and Planetary Institute [*University Space Research Association*] [*Research center*] (RCD)
LPI .... Lysinuric Protein Intolerance [*Medicine*] (DMAA)
LPIA .... Label Printing Industries of America (EA)
LPIA .... Launch Pad Interface Assembly
LPIA .... Liquid Propellant Information Agency [*Johns Hopkins Univeristy*]
LPIB .... Law and Policy in International Business [*ABA*] [*A publication*] (AAGC)
LPIBSS .... Lunar and Planetary Institute Bibliographic Search Service [*University Space Research Association*] [*Information service or system*] (IID)
LPiC .... Central Louisiana State Hospital, Medical Library, Pineville, LA [*Library symbol*] [*Library of Congress*] (LCLS)
LPICBM .... Liquid Propellant Intercontinental Ballistic Missile [*Military*] (IAA)
LPID .... Logical Page Identifier (BUR)
LPI/D .... Low Probability of Intercept/Detection [*Environmental science*] (COE)
LPIH .... Left Posteroinferior Hemiblock [*Medicine*] (EDAA)
LPiL .... Louisiana College, Pineville, LA [*Library symbol*] [*Library of Congress*] (LCLS)
LPI/LPE .... Low Probability of Interception & Exploitation (SAUS)
LPIN .... Espinho [*Portugal*] [*ICAO location identifier*] (ICLI)
LPIR .... Limited Partnership Investment Review [*Information service or system*] (IID)
LPIR .... Low-Probability Intercept RADAR
LPIR .... LPI Radar (SAUS)
LPIRB .... Low Probability of Intercept Radio Brassboard (SAUS)
LPIS .... Land Protection Incentives Scheme (SAUO)
LPIS .... Low-Pressure Injection System [*Nuclear energy*] (NRCH)
LPISM .... Liquid Photo-Imageable Solder Mask [*Electronics*] (AAEL)
LPISS .... Low-Power Illuminator Signal Source (MCD)
LPIU .... Leasing Partners International [*Intermodal shipping container symbol*] (TVRC)
LPIU .... Lithographers and Photoengravers International Union [*Later, Graphic Arts International Union*]
LPIW .... Lumber, Production, and Industrial Workers (WPI)
LPJF .... Leiria [*Portugal*] [*ICAO location identifier*] (ICLI)
LPJO .... Alijo [*Portugal*] [*ICAO location identifier*] (ICLI)
LPK .... Lao Pen Kang [*Laotian Neutralist Party*] (CINC)
LPK .... Liver Pyruvate Kinase [*Medicine*] (DMAA)
LPKCMLPCC .... License Plate, Key Chain, and Mini License Plate Collectors Club (EA)
LPKRR .... Logic Programming in Knowledge Representation and Reasoning (SAUO)
LPKS .... Lone Pine Koala Sanctuary (SAUO)
LPL .... Entergy Louisiana, Inc. [*NYSE symbol*] (SAG)
LPL .... Entergy Louisiana, Inc. Capital I [*NYSE symbol*] (SAG)
LPL .... Laborers Political League (EA)
LPL .... Labour Protection League [*A union*] [*British*]
LPL .... Lambeth Palace Library (SAUO)
LPL .... Lamina Propria Lymphocyte [*Hematology*]
LPL .... Lamp-Pumped LASER (MCD)
LPL .... Large Project Leader
LPL .... LASER-Pumped-LASER
LPL .... Lawton Public Library, Lawton, OK [*OCLC symbol*] (OCLC)
LPL .... Lawyers Professional Liability [*Insurance*]
LPL .... Learning and Planning Laboratory [*University of Texas at Arlington*] (RCD)
LPL .... Lease-A-Plane International [*ICAO designator*] (FAAC)
LPL .... Lethbridge Public Library [*UTLAS symbol*]
LPL .... Lichen Planus-Like Lesion [*Medicine*] (DMAA)
LPL .... Lightproof Louver [*Technical drawings*]
LPL .... Linear Polarised Laser (SAUS)
LPL .... Linear Programming Language [*Intertechnique*] [*French*] [*Computer science*]
LPL .... Lipoprotein Lipase [*An enzyme*]
LPL .... Liquid Plastics Limited (SAUO)
LPL .... List Processing Language [*Computer science*] (IEEE)
LPL .... Liverpool [*England*] [*Airport symbol*] (OAG)
LPL .... Liverpool Public Libraries (SAUO)
LPL .... LM [*Lunar Module*] Plan [*NASA*] (KSC)
LPL .... Local Processor Link
LPL .... London Public Library (SAUO)
LPL .... Long Pulse LASER
LPL .... Lotus Programming Language (SAUO)
LPL .... Louisiana Power and Light (SAUO)
LPL .... Louisiana Power & Light Co. [*NYSE symbol*] (SPSG)
LPL .... Louisville Public Library (SAUO)
LPL .... Low Polar Latitude [*Geophysics*]
LPL .... Low Power Laser (ACAE)
LPL .... Low-Power Logic
LPL .... Lule Saami [*Language symbol*] (ETLW)
LPL .... Lunar and Planetary Laboratory [*University of Arizona*] [*Research center*] (MCD)
LPL .... Lunar Projects Laboratory
LPL .... Lysophospholipase [*An enzyme*]
LPLA .... Lajes, Terceira Island [*Portugal*] [*ICAO location identifier*] (ICLI)
LPLA .... Lao Peoples Liberation Army (CINC)
LPLA .... Lipoprotein Lipase Activity [*Medicine*] (DMAA)
LPLA .... Log-Periodic Loop Antenna (PDAA)
LPlal .... Iberville Parish Library, Plaquemine, LA [*Library symbol*] [*Library of Congress*] (LCLS)
LPLC .... Lift-Plus-Lift/Cruise (SAUS)
LPLC .... Low Pressure Liquid Chromatography [*Medicine*] (EDAA)
LPLDF .... Ley de Proteccion Jurisdiccional de las Libertades Publicas y Derechos Fundamentales (SAUO)
LPLE .... Leukocyte Pepsin-Like Enzyme (DB)
LPLG .... Lagos [*Portugal*] [*ICAO location identifier*] (ICLI)
LPLG .... Left Pleural Ganglion [*Medicine*]
LPLI .... LPL Investment Group, Inc. (SAUO)
LPLIA .... LPL Investment Group, Inc. (Class A) [*NASDAQ symbol*] (COMM)
LPLIS .... Lipoprotein Lipase Inactivation System [*Biochemistry*] (DAVI)
LPLM .... Lowest Planned Level of Maintenance (SAA)
LPLNG .... Low-Pressure Liquefied Natural Gases (NRCH)
LPLP .... Language Problems & Language Planning, The University of Texas Press (SAUO)
LPLPr .... Entergy Louisiana 12.64% cmPfd [*NYSE symbol*] (TTSB)
LPLPrA .... Entergy Louisiana 9.68% cm Pfd [*NYSE symbol*] (TTSB)
LPLR .... Lock Pillar (AAG)
LPL?TMC .... Low-Pressure Low-Temperature Molding Compound
LPLV .... Large Payload Life Vehicle (ACAE)
LPLWS .... Launch Pad Lightning Warning System [*NASA*] (KSC)
LPM .... Labour Party of Malaya (SAUO)
LPM .... Lamap [*Vanuatu*] [*Airport symbol*] (OAG)
LPM .... Landing Party Manual (SAUO)
LPM .... Lane Photograph Method
LPM .... LASER Particle Monitor (PDAA)
LPM .... LASER Phase Macroscope
LPM .... Laser Pointing Mirror (ACAE)
LPM .... LASER Precision Microfabrication (IAA)
LPM .... Lateral Pterygoid Muscle (DMAA)
LPM .... Leading Patrolman [*Navy*] [*British*] (DI)
lpm .... Letters Per Minute (WDMC)
LPM .... Licensing Project Manager [*Nuclear energy*] (NRCH)
LPM .... Light Pulser Matrix
LPM .... Linearly Polarized Mode [*Telecommunications*] (TEL)
LPM .... Linear Power Module [*Computer science*] (CIST)
LPM .... Lines per Millimeter (WDAA)
lpm .... Lines per Minute (IDOE)
LPM .... Lines per Minute [*Computer science*]
LPM .... Liquid Phase Methanation [*Fuel chemistry*]
LPM .... Liquid Propulsion Module (ACAE)
Lpm .... Liter per Minute (EEVL)
LPM .... Liters per Minute (MCD)
LPM .... Liver Plasma Membrane
LPM .... Local Processor Memory (IAA)
LPM .... Long Particular [*or Peculiar*] Metre [*Music*]
LPM .... Los Pinos Mountain [*New Mexico*] [*Seismograph station code, US Geological Survey*] (SEIS)
LPM .... Low-Pressure Molding [*Plastics*]
LPM .... Lunar Payload Module [*Aerospace*] (MCD)
LPM .... Lunar Portable Magnetometer [*Apollo*] [*NASA*]
LPMA .... Lead Pencil Manufacturers Association [*Later, Pencil Makers Association*] (EA)
LPMA .... Loose-Parts-Monitor Assembly [*Nuclear energy*] (NRCH)
LPMAD .... Living Personnel Management Authorization Document [*DoD*]
LPMATGEN .... Linear Programming Matrix Generation (IAA)
LPMC .... Low-Pressure Molding Compound
LPMES .... Logistics Performance Measurement and Evaluation System (AABC)
LPMF .... Monfortinho [*Portugal*] [*ICAO location identifier*] (ICLI)
LPMG .... Liquid Phase Miscibility Gap (SAUS)
LPMG .... Lisboa [*Portugal*] [*ICAO location identifier*] (ICLI)
LPMI .... Mirandela [*Portugal*] [*ICAO location identifier*] (ICLI)
LPMO .... Livestock Promotional Marketing Organisation (SAUO)
LPMOSS .... Linear Programming Mathematical Optimization Subroutine System (IAA)
LPMP .... Low-Pressure Molding Process [*Plastics*]
LPMR .... Monte Real [*Portugal*] [*ICAO location identifier*] (ICLI)
LPM/S .... Liquid Phase Methanation/Shift Reaction [*Fuel chemistry*]
LPMS .... Lock Performance Monitoring System [*DOD*] [*COE*] (TAG)
LPMS .... Logistics Program Management System [*Air Force*] (AFIT)
LPMS .... Loose-Parts Monitoring System [*Nuclear energy*] (NRCH)
LPMT .... Montijo [*Portugal*] [*ICAO location identifier*] (ICLI)
LPN .... Alpenair GmbH & Co. KG [*Austria*] [*ICAO designator*] (FAAC)
LPN .... Laboratory Primate Newsletter [*Medicine*] (EDAA)
LPN .... Language Planning Newsletter (SAUO)
LPN .... La Pine, OR [*Amtrak rail station code*]
LPN .... Licensed Practical Nurse
LPN .... Local Packet Network [*Open Systems Interconnection*] (ODAA)

LPN .... Logical Page Number (BUR)
LPN .... Long Part Number
LPN .... Longview, Portland & Northern Railway Co. [*AAR code*]
LPN .... Low-Pass Network [*Electronics*]
LPN .... Lumped Parameter Network (ACAE)
LPN .... National Federation of Licensed Practical Nurses
LPNA .... Licensed Practical Nurses Association (SAUO)
LPNA .... Lithographers and Printers National Association [*Later, PIA*] (EA)
LPNAF ...... Licensed Practical Nurses Association of Florida (SRA)
LPNAI ...... Licensed Practical Nurses Association of Illinois (EARSL)
LPNAN ...... Licensed Practical Nurse Association of Nebraska (EARSL)
LPNGP ...... Low-Pressure Noble Gas Processing (NRCH)
LPNI .... Labour Party of Northern Ireland (SAUO)
LPNI .... Langley Porter Neuropsychiatric Institute (SAUO)
LPNT .... Lifepoint Hospitals [*Company symbol*]
LPNT .... LifePoint Hospitals, Inc. (MHID)
LPO .... La Palma Observatory
LPO .... La Porte [*Indiana*] [*Airport symbol*] (OAG)
LPO .... Laramie Project Office [*Laramie, WY*] [*Department of Energy*] (GRD)
LPO .... Late Pleistocene Origins [*Ecology*]
LPO .... Lateral Preoptic [*Brain anatomy*]
LPO .... Lattice-Preferred Orientation [*Geophysics*]
LPO .... Lauroyl Peroxide [*Organic chemistry*]
LPO .... Leading Petty Officer (SAUO)
LPO .... Left Posterio Occipital [*A fetal position*] (DAVI)
LPO .... Left Posterior Oblique [*Cardiology*] (MAE)
LPO .... Le Pouchou [*France*] [*Seismograph station code, US Geological Survey*] (SEIS)
LPO .... Liberale Partei Oesterreichs [*Liberal Party of Austria*] [*Political party*] (PPE)
LPO .... Liberal Party Organization [*British*]
LPO .... Light Perception Only [*Ophthalmology*]
LPO .... Likely Preferred Options (ABAC)
LPO .... Limited Production Option [*Automotive engineering*]
LPO .... Liquid Phase Oxidation [*Chemical processing*]
LPO .... Loan Production Office [*Banking*]
LPO .... Lobus Parolfactorius (PDAA)
LPO .... Local Purchase Order
LPO .... Logical Post Office (SAUO)
LPO .... London Philharmonic Orchestra
LPO .... London Post Office (SAUO)
LPO .... Low Power Output (MSA)
LPO .... Low-Pressure Oxygen
LPO .... Lunar Parking Orbit [*Apollo*] [*NASA*]
LPO .... Lunar Polar Orbiter [*NASA*]
LPO .... Lunar Program Office [*NASA*] (IAA)
LPOC .... Labile Particulate Organic Carbon [*Environmental science*]
LPOF .... Low-Pressure Oil-Filled [*Cable*] (DICI)
LpOH .... Lysopine Dehydrogenase (BABM)
LPOL .... Landstar Poole [*Common carrier symbol*]
L/POL .... Life Policy [*Insurance*] (DCTA)
L Pon Co .... Light Pontoon Company (SAUO)
LPOOC ...... Lake Placid Olympic Organizing Committee (SAUO)
L'POOL ...... Liverpool (ROG)
LPOP .... Low-Pressure Oxidizer Turbopump (NASA)
L POST ...... Left Posterior [*Medicine*] (MEDA)
LPOT .... Low-Pressure Oxidizer Turbopump (MCD)
LPOT .... Ota [*Portugal*] [*ICAO location identifier*] (ICLI)
LPOTP .... Low-Pressure Oxidizer Turbopump (NASA)
LPOX .... Low-Pressure Oxygen (AFM)
LPP .... Laboratory of Pulmonary Pathobiology (GNE)
LPP .... Labor Protection Plan
LPP .... Labour Progressive Party [*Canadian communist party*]
LPP .... Lanka Prajatantrawadi Party [*Ceylon*]
LPP .... Lappeenranta [*Finland*] [*Airport symbol*] (OAG)
LPP .... Large Paper Proofs
LPP .... LASER-Produced Plasma
LPP .... Lateral Pterygoid Plate [*Medicine*] (DMAA)
LPP .... Launcher Preparation Control Panel
LPP .... Law of Popular Participation (Bolivia) [*Political party*] (PSAP)
LPP .... Leader Preparation Program
LPP .... Leader Preparations Program (SAUO)
LPP .... Learning Prototype Phase (SAUO)
LPP .... Lear Petroleum Partners (SAUO)
LPP .... Lebowa People's Party [*South Africa*] [*Political party*] (PPW)
LPP .... Length of Perpendiculars
LPP .... Let's Play PET [*Database*] (GDD)
LPP .... Liberian People's Party [*Political party*] (EY)
LPP .... Liberia Peoples Party (SAUO)
LPP .... Licensed Program Product (SAUO)
LPP .... Lightweight Presentation Protocol [*Telecommunications*] (ACRL)
LPP .... Linear Photopolymerization [*Organic chemistry*]
LPP .... Lines per Page
LPP .... Link Peripheral Processor (ACRL)
LPP .... Lipoprotein Lipase [*An enzyme*] (DAVI)
LPP .... Liquid Phase Processing [*Chemistry*]
LPP .... Listed Personal Property (FOTI)
LPP .... Local Patching Panel
LPP .... Location of Peak Pressure [*Automotive engines*]
LPP .... Long Periodic Perturbation
LPP .... Long-Period Pulses [*Volcanology*]
LPP .... Long Plenum Plugs (COE)
LPP .... Low-Power Physics (IEEE)
LPP .... Low-Pressure-Pipe System [*Waste water treatment*]
LPP .... Lunar Precepts Positioner [*Aerospace*]
LPPA .... Licensed Pearl Producers' Association [*Australia*]
LPPC .... Labour Progressive Party of Canada (SAUO)
LPPC .... Lisboa [*Portugal*] [*ICAO location identifier*] (ICLI)
LPPC .... Load Point Photocell
LPPC .... Long-Staying Psychiatric Patient Classes (SAUS)
LPPD .... Ponta Delgada, Sao Miguel Island [*Portugal*] [*ICAO location identifier*] (ICLI)
LPPH .... Late Postpartum Hemorrhage [*Medicine*] (DMAA)
LPPH .... Leningrad Prison Psychiatric Hospital [*Later, LSPH*]
LPPI .... Litton Precision Products International, Incorporated (SAUO)
LPPI .... Pico, Pico Island [*Portugal*] [*ICAO location identifier*] (ICLI)
LPPM .... Low Pressure Permanent Mould (PDAA)
LPPM .... Portimao [*Portugal*] [*ICAO location identifier*] (ICLI)
LPPMUL .... Lawyers Protecting People from Malicious and Unjustified Lawsuits (EA)
LPPO .... Santa Maria [*Portugal*] [*ICAO location identifier*] (ICLI)
LPPP .... Low-Pressure Pump Pad (COE)
LPPR .... Porto [*Portugal*] [*ICAO location identifier*] (ICLI)
LPPS .... Low-Pressure Plasma Sprayed [*Thermal barrier coating*]
LPPS .... Porto Santo, Porto Santo Island [*Portugal*] [*ICAO location identifier*] (ICLI)
LPPT .... Lisboa [*Portugal*] [*ICAO location identifier*] (ICLI)
LPPT .... Low Pressurization Pressure Test Transmitter (IEEE)
LPPTS .... [*The*] Library of the Palestine Pilgrims' Text Society (BJA)
LPPV .... League of Private Property Voters [*Association*] (EA)
LPPV .... Praia Verde [*Portugal*] [*ICAO location identifier*] (ICLI)
LPQ .... Learning Process Questionnaire [*J. Biggs*] (TES)
LPQ .... Luang Prabang [*Laos*] [*Airport symbol*] (AD)
LPR .... Amphibious Transport (Small) [*Navy ship symbol*]
LPR .... Laboratory Property Removal Form (SAUO)
LPR .... Lactate-Pyruvate Ratio (MAE)
LPR .... Lanpar Technologies, Inc. [*Toronto Stock Exchange symbol*]
LPR .... La Peregrina [*Puerto Rico*] [*Seismograph station code, US Geological Survey*] (SEIS)
LPR .... Late Phase Reaction [*or Response*] [*Medicine*]
LPR .... Late Position Report [*Report of a flight which is off flight plan*]
LPR .... Late Procurement Request [*Air Force*] (AFM)
LPR .... Lawful Permanent Resident [*Department of Justice*]
LPR .... Leadership Potential Rating [*Army*] (AABC)
LPR .... Licensed Preacher
LPR .... License Plate Reader
LPR .... License Plate Recognition [*Traffic enforcement*]
LPR .... Lilly's Practical Register [*A publication*] (DLA)
LPR .... Linea Aerea Privadas Argentina [*ICAO designator*] (FAAC)
LPR .... Linear Polarization Resistance (MCD)
LPR .... Line Printer [*Computer science*] (NASA)
LPR .... Line Printer Redirector (AGLO)
LPR .... Line Printer Remote (PCM)
LPR .... Liquid Propellant Rocket [*Air Force*]
lpr .... Liter per Revolution
LPR .... Local Payment Receipt (AABC)
LPR .... London Property Register [*London Research Centre*] [*British*] [*Information service or system*] (IID)
LPR .... Long-Playing Record (IAA)
LPR .... Long-Playing Rocket [*Aerospace*]
LPR .... Looper Position Regulator
LPR .... Low-cost Packet Radio (SAUS)
LPR .... Low Power Radio
LPR .... Low Priority Request (SAUS)
LPR .... Lymphocyte Proliferative Response [*Immunology*]
LPR .... Lynchburg Pool Reactor
LPR-5 .... Lease Production Revenue System - 5 File [*Petroleum Information Corp.*] [*Information service or system*] (CRD)
LPR-10 ..... Lease Production Revenue System - 10 File [*Petroleum Information Corp.*] [*Information service or system*] (CRD)
LPRA .... Laws of Puerto Rico Annotated [*A publication*]
LPRA .... Lost Parts Replacement Authorization (MCD)
LPRB .... Loaded Program Request Block [*Computer science*] (BUR)
LPRC .... Laboratory Process Review Committee (SAUO)
LPRC .... Launch Pitch Rate Control
LPRC .... Library Public Relations Council (EA)
LPRCO ...... Logistics Planning and Reporting Code [*Military*]
LPRD .... Launch Program Requirement Document [*NASA*] (IAA)
LPRE .... Launch Prediction (ACAE)
LPRE .... Liquid Propellant Rocket Engine [*Air Force*]
LPRF .... Low-Power Radio Frequency (MCD)
LPRF .... Low Pulse Recurrence Frequency (MCD)
LPRI .... Licentiate of the Plastics and Rubber Institute [*British*] (DBQ)
LPRINT ...... Lookup Dictionary Print Program (IEEE)
LPRINT ...... Lookup Dictionary Print Programme (SAUO)
LPRL .... Laboratory Property Removal/Loan form (SAUO)
LPRL .... Lentz Peace Research Laboratory (EA)
LPRM .... Local Power Range Monitor (NRCH)
LPRM .... Low-Power Range Monitor [*Nuclear energy*] (NRCH)
LPRO .... Legend Properties, Inc. [*NASDAQ symbol*] (SAG)
LProj .... Light Projection [*Ophthalmology*]
LPRP .... Lao People's Revolutionary Party [*Phak Pasason Pativat Lao*] [*Political party*] (PPW)
LPRPrB ...... Santander Overseas Bk 'B'Pfd [*NYSE symbol*] (TTSB)
LPRR .... Low-Power Research Reactor
LPRRAG ..... Labour Party Race Relations Action Group (SAUO)
LPRS .... Local Primary Reference Source
LPRS .... Low Power Radio Service (SAUO)
LPRS .... Low-Pressure Recirculation System (NRCH)

LPRSVR ..... Life Preserver
LPRSX .... Low-Pressure Recirculation System Heat Exchanger [*Environmental science*] (COE)
LPRT .... Laboratory Project Review Team (SAUO)
LPRT .... Low Power Relay Transmitter
LPRU .... Losinjska Plovidba-Mali Losinj [*Intermodal shipping container symbol*] (TVRC)
LPS .... Laboratory for Planetary Studies (SAUO)
LPS .... Laboratory of Plasma Studies (SAUO)
LPS .... Laboratory Peripheral System
LPS .... Laboratory Program Summary (MCD)
LPS .... Labor Performance System (TIMI)
LPS .... Labour Press Service (SAUO)
LPS .... Landing Performance Score (MCD)
LPS .... Language for Programming-in-the-Small [*Computer science*] (MHDI)
LPS .... Lanterman-Petris-Short Act [*Psychology*] (DAVI)
LPS .... La Palma [*El Salvador*] [*Seismograph station code, US Geological Survey*] (SEIS)
LPS .... Large Pointing System (MCD)
LPS .... Large Processing Stations (SAUO)
LPS .... LASER Particulate Spectrometer [*NASA*]
LPS .... LASER Positioning System [*Navigation systems*]
LPS .... LASER Power Supply
LPS .... Laser Printing System (NITA)
LPS .... Last Papanicolaou Smear [*Gynecology*] (DAVI)
LPS .... Last Period Satisfied [*IRS*]
LPS .... Laterality Preference Schedule [*Psychology*]
LPS .... Lateral Premotor System (DMAA)
LPS .... Launch Phase Simulator [*NASA*]
LPS .... Launch Processing System [*NASA*] (KSC)
LPS .... Launch Processor System (SAUS)
LPS .... Launch Protection System (ACAE)
LPS .... Layered Protocol Structure [*Computer science*] (VLIE)
LPS .... L-Band Phase Shifter
LPS .... Learning Preference Scales [*Test*] (TMMY)
LPS .... Le Play Society (SAUO)
LPS .... Levator Palpebrae Superioris [*Muscle*] [*Anatomy*] (AAMN)
LPS .... Liberale Partei der Schweiz [*Liberal Party of Switzerland*] [*Political party*] (PPE)
LPS .... Liberal Party of Switzerland (SAUO)
LPS .... Liberian Philatelic Society [*Defunct*] (EA)
LPS .... Library Processes System [*Educomp*] [*Information service or system*] (IID)
LPS .... Library Programs Service (SAUO)
LPS .... Licensed Program Support (VLIE)
LPs .... Licentiate in Psychiatry (CMD)
LPS .... Life-Cycle Productivity System
LPS .... Lightning Protection System [*Boating*]
LPS .... Light Photo Squadron (SAUO)
LPS .... Lightproof Shade [*Technical drawings*]
LPS .... Linear Profile Scan [*Medicine*] (DMAA)
LPS .... Linear Programming System [*Computer science*]
LPS .... Linear Pulse Sector (OA)
LPS .... Line Pressure Switch [*Automotive engineering*]
LPS .... Line Procedure Specifications (CMD)
LPS .... Line Program Selector (IAA)
lps .... Lines per Second (VLIE)
LPS .... Lines per Second [*Computer science*]
LPS .... Lipase (MAE)
LPS .... Lipopolysaccharide [*Biochemistry*]
LPS .... Liquid-Phase Sintering (MCD)
LPS .... Liquid Propulsion System (ACAE)
LPS .... Liquid Protein Supplement [*Medicine*] (EDAA)
LPS .... Liters per Second (KSC)
LPS .... Loan Production System [*Department of Veterans Affairs*]
LPS .... Local Positioning System (GART)
LPS .... Local Process Specification (NG)
LPS .... Location Programming Standard [*Computer science*] (VLIE)
LPS .... Logicon Products [*Vancouver Stock Exchange symbol*]
LPS .... Logistic Policy Statement [*Navy*]
LPS .... Logistics Planning Study (MCD)
LPS .... Logistics Planning Support (SAUO)
LPS .... Lompoc-Surf Station, CA [*Amtrak rail station code*]
LPS .... London & Port Stanley Railway Co. [*AAR code*]
LPS .... London Parcels Section (SAUO)
LPS .... London Press Service
Lps........... London, Royal Philharmonic Society (SAUO)
LPS .... Lonergan Philosophical Society [*Association*] (EA)
LPS .... Longfellow Poetry Society (EA)
Lps........... Loops [*Military decoration*] (AABC)
LPS .... Lopez Island [*Washington*] [*Airport symbol*] (OAG)
LPS .... Lord Privy Seal [*British*]
LPS .... Low-Power Schottky [*Electronics*]
LPS .... Low-Pressure Sand [*Casting*] [*Automotive engineering*]
LPS .... Low-Pressure Scram [*Nuclear energy*] (IEEE)
LPS .... Low-Pressure Separator [*Chemical engineering*]
LPS .... Low-Pressure Sodium
LPS .... Low Primary Sequence (VLIE)
LPS .... Lunar Penetrometer System [*Aerospace*]
LPS .... Lunar Pilotage System [*Aerospace*]
LPS .... Lyceum Performing Society (SAUO)
LPS .... Lypopolysaccharide [*Medicine*] (TAD)
LPSA .... Liberal Party of South Africa (SAUO)
LPSA .... Licensed Program Support Agreement [*Computer science*] (CIST)
LPSA .... Linea Peninsular [*Common carrier symbol*]
LPSA .... Lithographic Preparatory Services Association [*Later, GPA*] (EA)
LPSA .... Log Periodic Scattering Array
LPSC .... Local Program Support Charges (VLIE)
LPSC .... Lunar and Planetary Science Conference
LPSC .... Luxembourg Philatelic Study Club [*Defunct*] (EA)
LPSC .... Santa Cruz [*Portugal*] [*ICAO location identifier*] (ICLI)
LPS/CDS .... Launch Processing System / Central Data Subsystem [*Military*]
LPS/CDS .... LPS/Central Data Subsystem (SAUS)
LPSCU....... Ladies Pennsylvania Slovak Catholic Union (EA)
LPSD .... Logically Passive Self-Dual
LPSF......... Lens-Pinhole Spatial Filter (PDAA)
LPSG .... Live Oak, Perry & South Georgia Railway Co. [*AAR code*]
LPSI .... Low-Pressure Safety Injection [*Nuclear energy*] (NRCH)
LPSI .... Sines [*Portugal*] [*ICAO location identifier*] (ICLI)
LPSIP........ Low-Pressure Safety Injection Pump [*Nuclear energy*] (NRCH)
LPSJ......... Sao Jorge, Sao Jorge Island [*Portugal*] [*ICAO location identifier*] (ICLI)
LPSM........ Levenson Phase Shift Mask (AAEL)
LPSN .... Local Packet Switched Network
LPSNY....... Lithuanian Philatelic Society of New York (EA)
LPSO .... Laboratory Procurement Supply Office
LPSO .... Lloyd's Policy Signing Office [*Lloyd's of London*]
LPSOL....... Linear Programming Solution (IAA)
LPS/PIA ..... Lothographic Platemakers Section of Printing Industries of America (SAUO)
LPSR .... Lipopolysaccharide Receptor (DB)
LPSS .... Amphibious Transport Submarine [*Landing Platform, Submarine*] [*Navy ship symbol*]
LPSS .... Law and Political Science Section [*Association of College and Research Libraries*]
LPSS .... Line Protection Switching System [*Bell System*]
LPSS .... Local Population Studies Society [*British*]
LPSSNJ ..... Low-Power Self-Screening Noise Jammer [*Military*] (CAAL)
LPSSR....... Low-Power Spread Spectrum RADAR (PDAA)
LPST......... Latest Possible Start Time (SAUO)
LPST......... Sintra [*Portugal*] [*ICAO location identifier*] (ICLI)
LPSTTL...... Low-Power Schottky Transistor-Transistor Logic [*Electronics*] (IAA)
LPSU .... Launcher Power Supply Unit (SAUS)
LPSV .... Low-Pressure Solenoid Valve
LPSVD....... Linear Prediction with Singular Value Decomposition [*Computer science*]
LPSW........ Load Program Status Word (IAA)
LPSW........ Low-Pressure Service Water [*Nuclear energy*] (NRCH)
LPT .... Laboratory Point and Tracking (ACAE)
LPT .... Lampang [*Thailand*] [*Airport symbol*] (OAG)
LPT .... Lampang [*Thailand*] [*Seismograph station code, US Geological Survey*] (SEIS)
LPT .... Language Proficiency Test [*Military*] (AFM)
LPT .... Largest Processing Time First [*Computer science*] (MHDB)
LPT .... LASER Propulsion Test (SSD)
LPT .... LASER Pyrolysis Technique [*Inorganic synthesis*]
LPT .... Latest Recommended Posting Times [*Business term*] (DCTA)
LPT .... Leading Physical Trainer [*British military*] (DMA)
LPT .... Lear Petroleum Corp. (SAUO)
LPT .... Lehigh Portland Cement Company (SAUO)
LPT .... Licensed Physical Therapist
LPT .... Licensed Psychiatric Technician (NUJO)
LPT .... Light Pen Tracking (MCD)
LPT .... Limited Procurement Test
LP-T .... Limited Production - Test (AABC)
LPT .... Line Printer [*Computer science*]
LPT .... Line Printer Port [*Computer science*] (DCDG)
LPT .... Line Printer Terminal (RALS)
LPT .... Lipotropin (DMAA)
LPT .... Liquid Penetrant Testing [*or Examination*] [*Nuclear energy*] (NRCH)
LPT .... Listed Property Trust
LPT .... Local Point (VLIE)
LPT .... Local Printer Terminal (SAUS)
LPT .... Local Public Transportation
LPT .... Lock Pointer Table
LPT .... Longest Processing Time [*Computer science*] (VLIE)
LPT .... Long-Period Tremor [*Volcanology*]
LPT .... Low Point [*Technical drawings*]
LPT .... Low-Power Test
LPT .... Low-Pressure Test
LPT .... Low-Pressure Transducer
LPT .... Low Pressure Turbine (SAUS)
LPT .... Low-Pressure Turbine [*Nuclear energy*] (NRCH)
LPT .... Low Pressure Turbocharger
LPT .... Low Profile Turret (SAUS)
LPT .... Luminescent Pigment Tattooing
LPT .... Lymphocyte Transfer (DB)
LPT1......... First Parallel Printer Port (SAUS)
LPT3......... Third Parallel Printer Port (SAUS)
LPTA......... Louisiana Parent-Teacher Association (SAUO)
LPtaW....... West Baton Rouge Parish Library, Port Allen, LA [*Library symbol*] [*Library of Congress*] (LCLS)
LPTB......... London Passenger Transport Board
LPTB......... Low-Pressure Turbine [*on a ship*] (DS)
LPTC......... Liquid Propellant Travelling Charge (SAUS)
LPTD .... Linear Programmed Thermal Degradation [*Instrumentation*]
LPTD .... Long Play Talkdown
LPTD-MS ... Linear Programmed Thermal Degradation - Mass Spectroscopy [*Instrumentation*]

LPTF......... Low-Power Test Facility [*Nuclear energy*]
LPTH......... LightPath Technologies, Inc. [*NASDAQ symbol*] (SAG)
LPTHA....... LightPath Technologies'A' [*NASDAQ symbol*] (TTSB)
LPTHU....... LightPath Technologies Unit [*NASDAQ symbol*] (TTSB)
LPTHW...... LightPath Technol Wrrt 'A' [*NASDAQ symbol*] (TTSB)
LPTHZ....... LightPath Technol Wrrt 'B' [*NASDAQ symbol*] (TTSB)
LPTIS........ Laguna Peak Tracking and Injection Station
LPTL......... Lubricant Performance Testing Laboratory [*Fuels and lubricants*]
LPTN......... Tancos [*Portugal*] [*ICAO location identifier*] (ICLI)
LPTR......... Line Printer [*Computer science*] (MSA)
LPTR......... Livermore Pool Type Reactor
LPTS......... Lightweight Protected Turret System (SAUS)
LPTS......... Louisiana Presbyterian Theological Seminary
LPTTL....... Low-Power Transistor-Transistor Logic
LPTTP....... League of Professional Theatre Training Programs [*Defunct*] (EA)
LPTV......... Large Payload Test Vehicle [*Air Force*]
LPTV......... Low-Power Television (GOBB)
LPTW......... Lake Providence, Texarkana & Western R. R. [*AAR code*]
LPU.......... Language Processor Unit
LPu.......... Late Punic (BJA)
LPU.......... League of Prayer for Unity [*Defunct*] (EA)
LPU.......... Least Publishable Unit [*of research data*]
LPU.......... Legal Practices Update [*A publication*]
LPU.......... Life Preserver Unit
LPU.......... Limited Procurement, Urgent (MCD)
LP-U......... Limited Production - Urgent (AABC)
LPU.......... Line Printer Unit (COE)
LPU.......... Line Processing Unit
LPU.......... Lions Philatelic Unit (EA)
LPU.......... Liquid Processing Unit
LPU.......... Local Programming Unit (SAUS)
LPU.......... Low Pay Unit [*British*]
LPU.......... Low-Power Unit (CAAL)
LPUG......... Lasers in Publishing Users Group (EA)
LPUL......... Least Positive Uplevel (IAA)
LPUU......... Linear Programming under Uncertainty [*Computer science*]
LPV.......... Houston, TX [*Location identifier*] [*FAA*] (FAAL)
LPV.......... Landing Platform Vehicle [*Navy*] [*British*]
LPV.......... Landing Pontoon Vehicle [*Military*]
LPV.......... Laser-Protective Visor (DOMA)
LPV.......... Launching Point Vertical (NATG)
LPV.......... Launch Preparation Van [*Space launch term*] (ISAK)
LPV.......... Left Portal View [*Medicine*] (EDAA)
LPV.......... Left Pulmonary Vein [*Anatomy*]
LPV.......... Light Patrol Vehicle [*Police and security equipment*]
LPV.......... Light Pen Value (IAA)
LPV.......... Lightproof Vent [*Technical drawings*]
LPV.......... Limiting Pressure Velocity (PDAA)
LPV.......... Log Periodic V [*Antenna*]
LPV.......... Long Period Variable (ADWA)
LPV.......... Low-Pressure Vent (AAEL)
LPV.......... Lymphopathia Venereum (MAE)
LPV.......... Lymphotropic Papovavirus [*Medicine*] (DB)
LPVP......... Left Posterior Ventricular Preexcitation [*Medicine*] (DMAA)
LPVR......... Vila Real [*Portugal*] [*ICAO location identifier*] (ICLI)
LPVS......... Link Packetized Voice Subsystem [*Telecommunications*] (ACRL)
LPVT......... Large Print Video Terminal
LPVZ......... Viseu [*Portugal*] [*ICAO location identifier*] (ICLI)
LPW.......... Lateral Pharyngeal Wall [*Medicine*] (DMAA)
LPW.......... Liberal Party of Wales [*Political party*]
LPW.......... Linear Polarized Wave
LPW.......... Local Point Warning [*Military*]
LPW.......... Longitudinal Pressure Wave
lp/W......... Lumens per Watt (CET)
LPW.......... Lumens per Watt (NAKS)
LPWA......... Local Public Works Act (OICC)
LPWG......... Logistics Planning Working Group (SAUO)
LPWG......... Lunar and Planetary Working Group [*Aerospace*] (IAA)
LP w/o proj... LP without projection (SAUS)
LP w/ proj... LP with projection (SAUS)
LPWR......... Laser Power Corp. [*NASDAQ symbol*] (NASQ)
LPWS......... Low-Pressure Warning Switch
Lp-X......... Lipoprotein-X [*Biochemistry*] (MAE)
LPX.......... Liquid Plume imaging Experiment (SAUS)
LPX.......... Louisiana Pacific [*NYSE symbol*] (TTSB)
LPX.......... Louisiana-Pacific Corp. [*NYSE symbol*] (SPSG)
LPX.......... Low Profile Extended (SAUS)
LPYS......... Labour Party Young Socialists [*British*] [*Political party*]
LPZ.......... La Paz [*San Calixto*] [*Bolivia*] [*Seismograph station code, US Geological Survey*] (SEIS)
LPZ.......... Leipzig [*City and district in East Germany*] (ROG)
LPZ.......... Low Population Zone (NRCH)
LPZ.......... Ruston, LA [*Location identifier*] [*FAA*] (FAAL)
LPZG......... Lincoln Park Zoological Gardens (SAUO)
LQ........... Argentina [*Civil aircraft markings - international*] (PIPO)
LQ........... Inland Empire Airlines [*ICAO designator*] (AD)
LQ........... Laboratory Quality (SAUO)
LQ........... Last Quarter [*Moon phase*]
LQ........... Laterality Quotient [*Neuropsychology*]
LQ........... Laurentian Capital Corp. (SAUO)
LQ........... Law Quarterly [*A publication*] (SAFN)
LQ........... Learning Quotient
LQ........... Lege Quaeso [*Please Read*] [*Latin*]
LQ........... Lens Quality [*Optics*]
LQ........... Letter Quality (PCM)
LQ........... Library Quarterly [*A publication*] (BRI)
LQ........... Limited Quantity (SAUO)
LQ........... Limiting Quality (IAA)
LQ........... Linacre Quarterly [*Medicine*] (EDAA)
LQ........... Linear Quadratic [*Mathematics*]
lq........... Liquid
LQ........... Liquor [*Telegraphy*] (PCTE)
LQ........... Living Quarters (SAUO)
LQ........... Longevity Quotient [*Demography*]
LQ........... Lordosis Quotients [*Medicine*]
Lq........... Love Wave [*Earthquakes*]
LQ........... Lower Quadrant [*Medicine*] (MELL)
LQ........... Lowest Quadrant
LQ........... Lowest Quadrille
LQA.......... La Quiaca [*Argentina*] [*Seismograph station code, US Geological Survey*] [*Closed*] (SEIS)
LQA.......... La Quiaca [*Argentina*] [*Geomagnetic observatory code*]
LQA.......... Line Quality Analysis [*Communications term*] (DCT)
LQA.......... Link Quality Analysis (PDAA)
LQA.......... Link Quality Assessment (SAUS)
LQA.......... Living Quarters Allowance [*Air Force*] (AFM)
LQD.......... Liquid
LQD.......... Liquidated [*Telegraphy*] (PCTE)
LQD.......... Lowest Quantity Determinable [*Analytical chemistry*]
LQDR......... Liquidator
LQER......... Lesser Quantity Emission Rates (EPAT)
LQFD......... Liquefied
LQG.......... Large Quantity Generator (AUEG)
LQG.......... Linear Quadratic Gaussian (MCD)
LQG.......... Liquidating [*Telegraphy*] (PCTE)
LQG.......... Lorain, OH [*Location identifier*] [*FAA*] (FAAL)
LQGLS........ Liquid in Glass
LQI.......... La Quinta Inns [*NYSE symbol*] (SAG)
LQID......... Liquid Audio [*NASDAQ symbol*] (SG)
LQIV......... Linear, Quasi Invariant (PDAA)
LQK.......... Pickens, SC [*Location identifier*] [*FAA*] (FAAL)
LQL.......... Willoughby, OH [*Location identifier*] [*FAA*] (FAAL)
LQM.......... La Quinta Motor Inns (EFIS)
LQM.......... La Quinta Motor Inns, Inc. (SAUO)
LQM.......... Link Quality Monitoring (SAUO)
LQM.......... Puerto Leguizamo [*Colombia*] [*Airport symbol*] (OAG)
LQMD......... LifeQuest Medical [*NASDAQ symbol*] (TTSB)
LQMD......... LifeQuest Medical, Inc. [*NASDAQ symbol*] (SAG)
LQMETR....... Liquidometer
LQN.......... Boston, MA [*Location identifier*] [*FAA*] (FAAL)
LQN.......... Liquidation [*Telegraphy*] (PCTE)
LQN.......... Qala-Nau [*Afghanistan*] [*Airport symbol*] [*Obsolete*] (OAG)
LQP.......... Fort Collins, CO [*Location identifier*] [*FAA*] (FAAL)
LQP.......... Lac Qui Parle Regional Railroad Authority [*Federal Railroad Administration identification code*]
LQP.......... Letter Quality Printer [*Computer science*]
LQP.......... Linear Quadratic Problem [*Mathematics*]
LQPO......... Laboratory Quality & Planning Office (SAUO)
LQQ.......... Chicago, IL [*Location identifier*] [*FAA*] (FAAL)
LQR.......... Larned, KS [*Location identifier*] [*FAA*] (FAAL)
LQR.......... Law Quarterly Review [*A publication*] (SAFN)
LQR.......... Link Quality Report [*Computer science*] (HODG)
LQR.......... Liquor
LQR.......... Local Qualitative Radio [*Ratings*] (NTCM)
LQRev........ Law Quarterly Review (SAUO)
LQRR......... Laser Qualitative Research Requirements (SAUO)
LQRR......... Low-Quality Recruiting Report (DNAB)
LQS.......... Les Quatre Saisons [*Record label*] [*France*]
LQS.......... Liquors [*Telegraphy*] (PCTE)
LQS.......... Lock Haven State College, Lock Haven, PA [*OCLC symbol*] (OCLC)
LQST......... Leadership Q-Sort Test [*Psychology*]
LQT.......... Linear Quantizer (IAA)
LQT.......... Liquidate [*Telegraphy*] (PCTE)
LQT.......... Liverpool Quay Terms (DS)
LQT.......... Los Queltehues [*Chile*] [*Seismograph station code, US Geological Survey*] (SEIS)
LQTS......... Long QT Syndrome
lqtx......... Liquitex (VRA)
LQU.......... Link Quality Analysis (SAUO)
LQU.......... Quilmes Ind(Quinsa)ADS [*NYSE symbol*] (TTSB)
LQUT......... Queensland Unit and Group Titles Law and Practice [*Australia*] [*A publication*]
LQV.......... Leiurus Quinquestriatus Venom (DB)
LQV.......... Pennington Gap, VA [*Location identifier*] [*FAA*] (FAAL)
LQX.......... Lehighton, PA [*Location identifier*] [*FAA*] (FAAL)
LQY.......... Springfield, IL [*Location identifier*] [*FAA*] (FAAL)
LR........... Dealer
LR........... Division of Licensing and Regulation (SAUO)
Lr........... King Lear [*Shakespearean work*]
LR........... Labeled Release [*Mars life detection experiment*]
LR........... Laboratory Reactor
LR........... Laboratory Reagent
LR........... Laboratory Reference (MAE)
LR........... Laboratory Report
LR........... Labor Reports (OICC)
LR........... Labor Review [*A publication*]
LR........... Labor Room [*Obstetrics*]
LR........... Lacrimation Reflex [*Medicine*] (MELL)

LR........... Lactated Ringer [*Medicine*]
LR........... Ladder Rung (AAG)
LR........... Lady's Realm [*A publication*] (ROG)
Lr........... Lancer [*Military*] [*British*] (DMA)
LR........... Landing RADAR
LR........... Landing Report (WDAA)
LR........... Landisville Railroad [*Federal Railroad Administration identification code*]
LR........... Land Registry (DLA)
LR........... Land Rover [*Society of Automotive Engineers auto manufacturer code for service information interchange*]
LR........... Lapse Ratio [*Insurance*]
LR........... Large Range (RIMS)
LR........... Large Reticulocyte [*Medicine*] (EDAA)
LR........... Large Ring
LR........... LASER-RADAR (MCD)
LR........... Laser Rangefinder (ACAE)
LR........... Laser Retroreflector (EOSA)
LR........... Last Record (IAA)
LR........... Last Renewal
LR........... Last Resort (SAUS)
LR........... Latency Reaction [*Medicine*] (DB)
LR........... Latency Relaxation
LR........... Lateral Rectus [*Muscle*] [*Anatomy*]
LR........... Lateral Reversal [*Typography*] (DGA)
LR........... Lateral Root [*Botany*]
L/R........... Late Run
LR........... Late - Rural Electrification Association [*Electric utility company*]
IR........... Laufend Rechnung [*Current Account*] [*German*] [*Business term*]
L/R........... Launch/Reentry (MCD)
LR........... Launch Reliability (MCD)
LR........... Launch Right (MCD)
LR........... Lawesson Reagent [*Organic chemistry*]
LR........... Law Record [*1911-12*] [*India*] [*A publication*] (DLA)
LR........... Law Recorder [*1827-38*] [*Ireland*] [*A publication*] (DLA)
LR........... Law Register [*1880-1909*] [*A publication*] (DLA)
Lr........... Lawrencium [*Original symbol, Lw, changed in 1963*] [*Chemical element*]
LR........... Law Reporter [*1821-22*] [*A publication*] (DLA)
LR........... Law Reports (MIST)
LR........... Law Review [*A publication*] (SAFN)
LR........... Layer Rating [*British military*] (DMA)
LR........... Lay Reader (ROG)
LR........... Leaching Rate [*Nuclear energy*] (NUCP)
LR........... Leaders of Religion [*A publication*]
LR........... Lead Radial (PIPO)
LR........... Leaf Rust [*Plant Pathology*]
LR........... Lear [*ICAO aircraft manufacturer identifier*] (ICAO)
L/R........... Learning Resources (SAUO)
LR........... Leave Rations [*Military*]
LR........... Leave to Appeal Refused [*Legal term*] (ADA)
LR........... Ledger (ROG)
LR........... Lee Rubber & Tire Corp. (SAUO)
L - R........... Left minus Right [*Stereo signals*] (NTCM)
L + R........... Left plus Right [*Stereo signals*] (NTCM)
LR........... Left Rear
LR........... Left Rudder (MCD)
LR........... Left to Right (MAE)
L/R........... Left to Right [*Ratio*] (DAVI)
LR........... Legal Reserve (MHDW)
LR........... Leicestershire Regiment [*Military unit*] [*British*]
LR........... Lending Rate [*Banking*] (MHDW)
LR........... Lent Reading (ROG)
LR........... Lesion Expansion Rate [*Pathology*]
LR........... Lethal Radius (ACAE)
LR........... Letter [*Online database field identifier*]
LR........... Letter of Requirements (SAUO)
LR........... Letter Report
LR........... Letter Requirement
LR........... Level Recorder
LR........... Level Regulator (NRCH)
LR........... Leviticus Rabbah (BJA)
LR........... Liaison Regiment (SAUO)
LR........... Liaison Report (AAG)
LR........... Liaison Request (AAG)
LR........... Liberia [*ANSI two-letter standard code*] (CNC)
LR........... Library Review [*A publication*] (BRI)
LR........... Licensing Registration [*British*]
L/R........... Life/Revisit [*NASA*] (KSC)
LR........... Lifespan Resources [*An association*] (EA)
LR........... Light Reaction (MAE)
LR........... Light Reflex [*Medicine*] (AAMN)
LR........... Likelihood Ratio [*Statistics*]
LR........... Limb Reduction [*Detect*] [*Medicine*] (EDAA)
Lr........... Limes Reacting Dose of Diphtheria Toxin [*Medicine*] (DMAA)
LR........... Limited Recoverable (IEEE)
LR........... Limited Response [*Emergency Management*] (EMA)
LR........... Limit of Reaction [*Medicine*] (EDAA)
LR........... Limit Register
LR........... Limit Response (ELAL)
LR........... Lincoln Red [*Livestock terminology*]
LR........... Lindblad Resonance [*Planetary science*]
LR........... Linear Regression [*Mathematics*]
LR........... Lineas Aereas Costarricenses, Sociedad Anonima (LACSA) [*Costa Rica*] [*ICAO designator*] (ICDA)
LR........... Line Receiver
LR........... Line Relay
LR........... Link Resources, Inc. [*Vancouver Stock Exchange symbol*]
LR........... Lion Rock Trading Co. (SAUO)
LR........... Lip Rehearsal [*Medicine*] (EDAA)
LR........... Liquid Rocket
LR........... Listing Representative (REAL)
lr........... Listing Representative [*Real estate*] (REAL)
LR........... Listing Requirement [*Investment term*]
LR........... Literary Review [*A publication*] (ANEX)
LR........... Little Rock [*Diocesan abbreviation*] [*Arkansas*] (TOCD)
lr........... Living Room (SHCU)
LR........... Living Room
LR........... Lloyd's Register of Shipping
LR........... Loaded Radius [*Tires*]
LR........... Loading Ramp
LR........... Load Ratio
LR........... Load Rejection (NRCH)
LR........... Load-Resistor Relay (MSA)
LR........... Loan Rate [*Banking*]
LR........... Local Recurrence [*Medicine*] (RAWO)
L/R........... Local/Remote [*Telecommunications*] (TEL)
LR........... Local Review (SAUO)
LR........... Location Register (SAUS)
LR........... Lock Rail
LR........... Lock Range (IAA)
L/R........... Locus of Radius
LR........... Logical Record
LR........... Logistical Reassignment [*Military*] (AFIT)
LR........... Logistical Requirement
LR........... Logistic Regression [*Medicine*]
LR........... Log Run [*Lumber*]
LR........... London Rank [*Freemasonry*]
LR........... London Regiment (SAUO)
LR........... Long Range
LR........... Long Residue [*Petroleum engineering*]
LR........... Long Rifle
LR........... Long Run [*Economics*]
LR........... Louisiana Register [*A publication*] (AAGC)
LR........... Louisiana Reports [*A publication*] (DLA)
LR........... Lower (ADA)
LR........... Lower Rail [*Typography*]
LR........... Lower Right
LR........... Lower Rule
LR........... Low Rate (ACAE)
lr........... Low Rate Reverse [*Ecology*]
LR........... Low Reduction (NITA)
LR........... Low Register (IAA)
LR........... Low Renin [*Medicine*] (MELL)
LR........... Low Resistance (IAA)
LR........... Low Resolution (QUAC)
LR........... Low Rise [*Linguistics*] (IEL)
LR........... Low-Riser [*Automotive engines*]
LR........... Low Risk
LR........... Loyal Regiment [*Military*] [*British*]
LR........... Lugger [*Ship's rigging*] (ROG)
LR........... Lunar Rover (ACAE)
LR........... New Zealand Law Reports [*A publication*] (DLA)
LR........... Ohio Law Reporter [*A publication*] (DLA)
LR........... Radiolocation Land Station [*ITU designation*]
Lr........... Rayleigh Wave [*Earthquakes*]
LR3........... LASER Ranging Retroreflection [*Also, LRRR*] [*Initialism pronounced "LR-cubed"*] [*Apollo 11 experiment*] [*NASA*]
LR^3........... Logistics Readiness Rating Report [*DoD*]
LRA........... Labor Research Associates (SAUO)
LRA........... Labor Research Association (EA)
LRA........... Lace Research Association [*British*]
LRA........... Lagged Reserve Accounting [*Banking*]
LRA........... Landing Rights Airport [*US Customs*]
LRA........... Larissa [*Greece*] [*Airport symbol*] (OAG)
LRA........... LASER [*Gyro*] Reference Axis (IEEE)
LRA........... Laser Retroreflector Array (EOSA)
LRA........... Last Return Amount [*IRS*]
LRA........... Latching Rocker Arm [*Automotive engines*]
LRA........... Launcher Relay Assembly [*Navy*] (CAAL)
LRA........... Lawyers' Reports, Annotated [*A publication*] (DLA)
LRA........... Lease Rental Agreement (MHDB)
LRA........... Least Restrictive Alternative [*For the education of the handicapped*]
LRA........... left Renal Artery [*Anatomy*] (DAVI)
LRA........... Libertarian Republican Alliance (EA)
LRA........... Library of Romance [*A publication*]
LRA........... Light Replaceable Assemblies
LRA........... Lincoln Red Association [*Canada*] (EAIO)
LRA........... Lincoln Road Association (SAUO)
LRA........... Line Receiving Amplifier (MSA)
LRA........... Lithuanian Regeneration Association (EA)
LRA........... Little Red Air Service [*Canada*] [*ICAO designator*] (FAAC)
LRA........... Little Rock [*Arkansas*] [*Seismograph station code, US Geological Survey*] [*Closed*] (SEIS)
LRA........... Load Real Address (HGAA)
LRA........... Load Reference Axis
LRA........... Local Radio Association (SAUO)

LRA .... Local Redevelopment Authority (BCP)
LRA .... Locked-Rotor Amperes (MSA)
LRA .... Logical Record Access [*Computer science*] (MHDB)
LRA .... Logical Record Address (NITA)
LRA .... Long-Range Aircraft (SAUO)
LRA .... Long-Range Aviation [*Army*] (AABC)
LRA .... Lord Ruthven Assembly [*An association*] (EA)
LRA .... Lord's Resistance Army [*Government term*] (GA)
LRA .... Louisiana Realtors Association (SRA)
LRA .... Louisiana Restaurant Association (SRA)
LRA .... Louisiana Retailers Association (SRA)
LRA .... Lower Right Abdomen [*Injection site*]
LRA .... Low Right Atrium [*Anatomy*]
LRA .... North Carolina Union List of Serials for Community Colleges [*Library network*]
LRAA .... Long-Range Air Army [*Former USSR*] (MCD)
LRAACA ..... Long-Range Air Anti-submarine Capability Aircraft (SAUS)
LRAACA ..... Long-Range Air Antisubmarine Warfare Capable Aircraft (MCD)
LRAAM ...... Long Range Air-to-Air Missile [*Air Force*]
LRA & E .... English Law Reports, Admiralty and Ecclesiastical [*A publication*] (DLA)
LRAAS .... Long Range Airborne Air to Surface Systems (ACAE)
LRAC .... English Law Reports, Appeal Cases [*A publication*] (DLA)
LRAC .... Long-Run Average Costs [*Marketing*]
LRAD .... Laboratory for Research on Animal Diseases (SAUO)
LRAD .... Licentiate of the Royal Academy of Dancing [*British*]
LRADM ...... Long-Range Air Defense Missile (MCD)
LR Adm & Ecc ... Law Reports, Admiralty and Ecclesiastical Cases [*1865-75*] [*A publication*] (DLA)
LR Adm & Eccl ... Law Reports, Admiralty and Ecclesiastical Cases [*1865-75*] [*A publication*] (DLA)
LR Adm & Eccl (Eng) ... Law Reports, Admiralty and Ecclesiastical Cases [*England*] [*A publication*] (DLA)
LRADP ...... Long-Range Active Duty Program [*Army*]
LRAF .... Long-Range Air Force
LRAF .... Long-Range Aviation Forces (SAUO)
LRAFB .... Little Rock Air Force Base (SAUO)
LRALS .... Long-Range Approach and Landing System (PDAA)
LRAM .... Licentiate of the Royal Academy of Music [*British*] (EY)
LRAMRP .... Long-Range Army Materiel Requirements Plan (SAUS)
LRAN .... Local Regional Access Node (MCD)
LR Ann ...... Lawyers' Reports, Annotated [*A publication*] (DLA)
LRA NS ..... Lawyers' Reports, Annotated, New Series [*A publication*] (DLA)
LRAO .... Logistics Review and Analysis Office [*US Army Defense Ammunition Center and School*]
LRAOP ...... Long-Range Aerospace Observation Platform
LRAP .... Leucine-Rich Amelogenin Polypeptide [*Biochemistry of dental enamel*]
LRAP .... Long-Range Acoustic Propagation
LRAP .... Long Route Analysis Program (VLIE)
LRAPIS ...... Long Range Advanced Piloted Interceptor System (ACAE)
LR App ...... English Law Reports, Appeal Cases, House of Lords [*A publication*] (DLA)
LRAPP .... Long-Range Acoustic Propagation Project
LR App Cas ... English Law Reports, Appeal Cases, House of Lords [*A publication*] (DLA)
LR App Cas (Eng) ... English Law Reports, Appeal Cases, House of Lords [*A publication*] (DLA)
LRAR .... Arad [*Romania*] [*ICAO location identifier*] (ICLI)
LRaR .... Richland Parish Library, Rayville, LA [*Library symbol*] [*Library of Congress*] (LCLS)
LRARFS ..... Long-Range Airlift Requirements Forecast System (SAUO)
LRAS .... Logistics Requirements Allocation Sheet (SSD)
LRAS .... Long-Range Autonomous Submersible
LRAS .... Lunar Module Replaceable Assembly [*NASA*] (IAA)
LRAS3 .... Long-Range Advanced Scout Surveillance System (SAUS)
LRASM ...... Long-Range Air-to-Surface Missile (MCD)
LRASV ...... Long-Range Air-to-Surface Vessel (IAA)
LRAT .... Large Radar Array Technology (ACAE)
LRAT .... Lecithin-Retinol Acyltransferase [*An enzyme*]
LRAT .... Long-Range Antitank [*Army*] (INF)
LRATC ...... Long-Run Average Total Costs [*Economics*]
LRATGW .... Long-Range Antitank Guided Weapon [*British military*] (DMA)
LRB .... Laboratory of Radiation Biology (SAUO)
LRB .... Labor Research Bureau (SAUO)
LRB .... Labour Relations Board [*Canada*]
LRB .... Legislative Reference Bureau (SAUO)
LRB .... Level Reference Base
LRB .... Liquid Rocket Booster (IGSL)
LRB .... Lissamine Rhodamine B [*Fluorescent dye*]
LRB .... Load Request Block (IAA)
LRB .... Local Reference Beam [*Holography*]
LRB .... London Rifle Brigade [*Military unit*] [*British*]
LRB .... Loyalty Review Board [*Abolished, 1953*] [*Civil Service Commission*]
LRBB .... Bucuresti [*Romania*] [*ICAO location identifier*] (ICLI)
LRBB .... Long-Range, Base Bleed (SAUS)
LRBC .... Bacau [*Romania*] [*ICAO location identifier*] (ICLI)
LRBC .... Left-Right Bounded Context (VLIE)
LRBC .... Lift-Right Bounded-Context [*Computer science*] (MHDI)
LRBC .... Lloyd's Registry Building Certificate
LRBF .... Longitudinal Ridge of Basal Fold
LRBFM ...... National Labor Relations Board Field Manual
LRBG .... Law Reports, British Guiana [*1890-1955*] [*A publication*] (DLA)
LRBM .... Baia Mare/Tauti Magherusi [*Romania*] [*ICAO location identifier*] (ICLI)
LRBM .... Long-Range Ballistic Missile
LRBP .... Long-Range Business Plan
LRBR .... Long-Range Ballistic Rocket
LRBR .... Long-Range Bombardment Round
LRB/RANGERS ... London Rifle Brigade/Rangers (SAUO)
LRBS .... Bucuresti/Baneasa [*Romania*] [*ICAO location identifier*] (ICLI)
LRBS .... LASER Ranging Bombing System
LR Burm .... Law Reports, British Burma [*A publication*] (DLA)
LR Burma ... Law Reports, British Burma [*A publication*] (DLA)
LRC .... Labour Relations Committee (SAUO)
LRC .... Labour Representation Committee [*Northern Ireland*] (PPW)
LRC .... Labrador Retriever Club (EA)
LRC .... Ladies Recreation Club (SAUO)
LRC .... Land Reserve Commission (SAUO)
LRC .... Land Resources Corporation (EFIS)
LRC .... Langley Research Center [*NASA*]
LRC .... Language Research Centre [*University of Calgary*] [*Canada*] (RCD)
LRC .... Launch/Recovery Visual Landing Aid Change (MCD)
LRC .... Law Reform Commission [*Canada*]
LRC .... Law Reform Committee (DLA)
LRC .... Lawrence, KS [*Amtrak rail station code*]
LRC .... Leadership Reaction Course (SAUO)
LRC .... Leaders Reaction Course [*Military training*] (INF)
LRC .... Lead Resistance Compensator
LRC .... Leander Rowing Club (SAUO)
LRC .... Learning Resource Center
LRC .... Learning Resources Center
LRC .... Lenoir Rhyne College [*Hickory, NC*]
LRC .... Lesbian Resource Center (EA)
LRC .... Lesser Regional Conflict (SAUO)
LRC .... Lesser Regional Contingencies (SAUS)
LRC .... Level Recording Controller
LRC .... Lewis Research Center [*NASA*]
LRC .... Liberia Refining Co.
LRC .... Library Research Center [*University of Illinois*] (IID)
LRC .... Library Resource Center (SAUO)
LRC .... Light Rapid Comfortable [*Train system*]
LRC .... Light Reflective Capacitor [*Electronics*] (DA)
LRC .... Light Repair Car [*British*]
LRC .... Limnological Research Center [*University of Minnesota*] [*Research center*] (RCD)
LRC .... Linear Responsibility Charting (PDAA)
LRC .... Lineas Aereas Costarricenses SA [*Costa Rica*] [*ICAO designator*] (FAAC)
LRC .... Line Rectifier Circuit
LRC .... Line Replaceable Components (ACAE)
LRC .... Linguistics Research Center [*University of Texas at Austin*] [*Research center*] (RCD)
LRC .... Lionel Railroader Club (EA)
LRC .... Lipid Research Center [*Washington University*] [*Research center*] (RCD)
LRC .... Lipid Research Clinic (SAUO)
LRC .... Lipid Research Clinics
LRC .... Literature Resource Center [*Database*] (GDD)
LRC .... Load Ratio Control (MSA)
LRC .... Local Register Cache (VLIE)
LRC .... Local Review Committee (WDAA)
LRC .... Locomotor Respiratory Coupling [*Physiology*]
LRC .... Lode Resources Corp. [*Vancouver Stock Exchange symbol*]
LRC .... Logistic Regression Classification [*Computer term*]
LRC .... Logistics Research Center (SAUO)
LRC .... Logistics to Relay Converter (MCD)
LRC .... London Rowing Club
LRC .... London Rubber Company (SAUO)
LRC .... Lone Oak Road [*California*] [*Seismograph station code, US Geological Survey*] (SEIS)
LRC .... Longitude Rotation Convention (ADWA)
LRC .... Longitudinal Redundancy Check [*Computer science*]
LRC .... Long-Range Climb (MCD)
LRC .... Long Range Communications (NTCM)
LRC .... Long-Range Cruise [*Aircraft speed*]
LRC .... Lori Corp. [*AMEX symbol*] (SPSG)
LRC .... Lower Rib Cage [*Anatomy*]
LRC .... Lunar Receiving Center (SAUO)
LRC .... Lunar Resources Company (SAUO)
LRC .... Luneberg Rapid Commutator [*Physics*]
LRC .... Lung Rate Counter
LRC .... Lutheran Resources Commission (EA)
LRCA .... Law Reports, Court of Appeals of New Zealand [*A publication*] (DLA)
LRCA .... Lithuanian Roman Catholic Alliance of America [*Later, LCA*] (EA)
LRCA .... Long-Range Combat Aircraft
LRCA .... Lop Rabbit Club of America (EA)
LRCA-STS ... Long Range Combat Aircraft System Test Station (ACAE)
LRCC .... English Law Reports, Crown Cases Reserved [*2 vols.*] [*1865-75*] [*A publication*] (DLA)
LRCC .... Library Resources Coordinating Committee of the University of London (NITA)
LRCC .... Longitudinal Redundancy Check Character [*Telecommunications*] (TEL)
LRCC (Eng) ... English Law Reports, Crown Cases Reserved [*2 vols.*] [*1865-75*] [*A publication*] (DLA)
LRCCM ...... Long-Range Conventional Cruise Missile (MCD)
LRCCPPT ... Lipid Research Clinics Coronary Primary Prevention Trial [*Cardiology*]
LRCCR ...... Law Reports, Crown Cases Reserved [*England*] [*A publication*] (DLA)
LRCD .... Linear Rule of Cumulative Damage (PDAA)

LRCD .... Lunar Rock Coring Device (ACAE)
LRCE .... LASER Relay Communication Equipment
LRCE .... Little Rock Cotton Exchange [*Defunct*]
LRCFA .... Lithuanian Roman Catholic Federation of America (EA)
LR Ch .... Law Reports, Chancery Appeal Cases [*England*] [*A publication*] (DLA)
LR Ch App... Chancery Appeal Cases [*1865-75*] [*A publication*] (DLA)
LR Ch D..... English Law Reports, Chancery Division [*A publication*] (DLA)
LR Ch D (Eng)... Law Reports, Chancery Division, English Supreme Court of Judicature [*A publication*] (DLA)
LR Ch Div (Eng)... Law Reports, Chancery Division, English Supreme Court of Judicature [*A publication*] (DLA)
LR Ch (Eng)... Law Reports, Chancery Appeal Cases [*England*] [*A publication*] (DLA)
LRCI .... Legal Research Center [*NASDAQ symbol*] (TTSB)
LRCI .... Legal Research Center, Inc. [*NASDAQ symbol*] (SAG)
LRCK .... Constanta/M. Kogalniceau [*Romania*] [*ICAO location identifier*] (ICLI)
LRCL .... Cluj-Napoca/Someseni [*Romania*] [*ICAO location identifier*] (ICLI)
LRCL .... Long-Range Chemical LASER (MCD)
LRCM .... Licentiate of the Royal College of Music [*British*]
LRCM .... Long-Range Cruise Missile [*Navy*]
LRCNSW .... Law Reform Commission of New South Wales [*Australia*]
LRCO .... Lead Range Control Officer (SAUO)
LRCO .... Limited Remoste Communications Outlet (SAUO)
LRCO .... Limited Remote [*or Radio*] Communication Outlet
LRCO .... Long-Range Capability Objective [*Air Force*]
LRCP .... Laboratory Research Cooperative Program [*Scientific Services Program*] [*Army*] (RDA)
LRCP .... Law Reports, Common Pleas [*1865-75*] [*England*] [*A publication*] (DLA)
LRCP .... Licensed Respiratory Care Practitioner (NUJO)
LRCP .... Licentiate of the Royal College of Physicians [*British*]
LRCP .... Licentiate, Royal College of Physicians [*British*] (CMD)
LRCP .... Long-Range Construction Program [*Military*]
LRCP & S... Licentiate of the Royal College of Physicians and the College of Surgeons of Edinburgh, and of the Faculty of Physicians and Surgeons of Glasgow (ROG)
LRCP & SI.. Licentiate of the Royal College of Physicians and Surgeons of Ireland (AAMN)
LRCPD ...... English Law Reports, Common Pleas Division [*A publication*] (DLA)
LRCP Div ... Law Reports, Common Pleas Division [*England*] [*A publication*] (DLA)
LRCP Div (Eng)... English Law Reports, Common Pleas Division [*A publication*] (DLA)
LRCPE .... Licentiate of the Royal College of Physicians (Edinburgh)
LRCPEd ..... Licentiate of the Royal College of Physicians Edinburgh (SAUO)
LRCP (Eng)... Law Reports, Common Pleas [*England*] [*A publication*] (DLA)
LRCPI .... Licentiate of the Royal College of Physicians of Ireland
LRCP Irel ... Licentiate of the Royal College of Physicians of Ireland
LRCPLA ..... Lithuanian Roman Catholic Priests' League of America (EA)
LRCPSGlasg... Licentiate of the Royal College of Physicians and Surgeons of Glasgow (DI)
LRCR .... Longitudinal Redundancy Check Register [*Telecommunications*] (IAA)
LRCR .... Long-Range Chaff Rocket (SAUS)
LR Cr Cas Res... Law Reports, Crown Cases Reserved [*England*] [*A publication*] (DLA)
LRCS .... Caransebes/Caransebes [*Romania*] [*ICAO location identifier*] (ICLI)
LRCS .... LASER RADAR Cross Section
LRCS .... League of Red Cross and Red Crescent Societies [*Switzerland*] (EA)
LRCS .... League of Red Cross Societies
LRCS .... Licentiate of the Royal College of Surgeons [*British*]
LRCS .... Lincoln Red Cattle Society [*British*] (DBA)
LRCS .... Load Relief Control System
LRCS .... Long-Range Communications System (SAUO)
LRCS .... Low Radar Cross-Section (SAUS)
LRCSA .... Lincoln Red Cattle Society of Australia
LRCSE .... Licentiate of the Royal College of Surgeons (Edinburgh)
LRCS (Edin)... Licentiate of the Royal College of Surgeons (Edinburgh) (DI)
LRCSG ...... Licentiate of the Royal College of Surgeons, Glasgow (SAUO)
LRCSI .... Licentiate of the Royal College of Surgeons in Ireland
LRCS Irel ... Licentiate of the Royal College of Surgeons in Ireland
LRCSOW .... Long-Range Conventional Standoff Weapon [*Military*]
LRCSS .... Logistics Resource Control and Support System (SAUO)
LRCSW ...... Long-Range Conventional Standoff Weapon (MCD)
LRCT .... Licensed Respiratory Care Technician (NUJO)
LRCT .... Licentiate of the Royal Conservatory of Toronto [*Canada*]
LRC-TCC .... Logistics Readiness Center-Transportation Control Center (SAUO)
LRCU .... Landing Rollout Control Unit (SAUS)
L/RCU .... Local/Remote Control Unit
LRCU .... Logic Refresh Control Unit
LRCV .... Craiova [*Romania*] [*ICAO location identifier*] (ICLI)
LRCVS .... Licentiate of the Royal College of Veterinary Surgeons [*British*]
LRC-W ...... Lutheran Resources Commission - Washington [*Later, LRC*] (EA)
LRC-W ...... Lutheran Resources Commission-Washington (SAUO)
LRCX .... Lam Research [*NASDAQ symbol*] (TTSB)
LRCX .... Lam Research Corp. [*NASDAQ symbol*] (SAG)
LRD .... Labelled RADAR Display (PDAA)
LRD .... Labour Research Department [*Trade union*] [*British*]
LRD .... Landing and Recovery Division [*NASA*]
LRD .... Land Resources Division (SAUO)
LRD .... Lard [*Telegraphy*] (PCTE)
LRD .... Laredo [*Texas*] [*Airport symbol*] (OAG)
LRD .... Laredo Air, Inc. [*ICAO designator*] (FAAC)
LRD .... Laser Rangefinder/Designator (SAUS)
LRD .... LASER Ranger and Designator (MCD)
LRD .... Launch Readiness Demonstration [*NASA*] (KSC)
LRD .... Lightning and Radio-Emission Detector [*Instrumentation*]
LRD .... Liquid Rocket Division Rocket Propulsion Laboratory (SAUO)
LRD .... Living Related Donor [*Medicine*]
LRD .... Living Renal Donor [*Nephrology*] (DAVI)
LRD .... Logistics Requirements Determination (MCD)
LRD .... London Recruiting Depot (SAUO)
LRD .... Long-Range Data [*RADAR*]
LRD .... Long Range Designator (ACAE)
LRD .... Long-Reach Detonator [*Explosive*]
LRD .... Lord River Gold [*Vancouver Stock Exchange symbol*]
LRD .... Low Rate Demodulator (ACAE)
LRD .... Low-Residue Diet (MELL)
LRD .... Lysinated Rhodamine Dextran [*Cytology*]
LRDC .... Land Resources Development Centre [*British*] (ARC)
LRDC .... Learning Research and Development Center [*University of Pittsburgh*] [*Research center*]
LRDCT .... Linear Rotary Differential Capacitance Transducer [*Instrumentation*]
LRDD .... Limited Rights to Delivered Data
LRDE .... Laboratory for Research and Development of Electronics (SAUO)
LRDE .... Long-Run Deal Effect [*Marketing*]
LRDG .... Learning Resources Development Group [*British*] (DBA)
LRDG .... Long Range Desert Group [*British Army*] [*World War II*]
LR Dig ...... Law Reports Digest [*A publication*] (DLA)
LRDL .... Longitudinal Ridge of Dorsal Lip
LRDMM ..... Long-Range Dual-Mission Missile (MCD)
LRDP .... Long Range Detection Program (CARL)
LRDP .... Long-Range Detection Program [*Air Force*] (CARL)
LRDP .... Long-Range Development Program (IAA)
LRDR .... Last Revision Date Routine
LRDS .... LASER Ranging and Designation System [*Military*] (CAAL)
LRDSB ...... Left Minus Right Double Sideband (IAA)
LRDSS ...... Long Range Decision Support System [*Indian Railway*] (TIR)
LRDT .... Laboratory of Reproductive and Developmental Toxicology (GNE)
LRDT .... Living Related Donor Transplant [*Medicine*] (DMAA)
LRD/T ...... Long Range Designator/Transceiver (ACAE)
LRDU .... Long-Range Development Unit
LRE .... Lafayette Radio Electronics (SAUO)
LRE .... Lafayette Radio Electronics Corp.
LRE .... Laser Ranger Experiment (SAUO)
LRE .... Latest Revised Estimate (MCD)
LRE .... Law-Related Education (AEE)
LRE .... Least Restrictive Environment [*For the education of the handicapped*]
LRE .... Leukemic Reticuloendotheliosis [*Medicine*] (AAMN)
LRE .... Library Resources Exhibition [*British*]
LRE .... Licentiate in Religious Education
LRE .... Life Re [*NYSE symbol*] (TTSB)
LRE .... Life Real Estate [*NYSE symbol*] (SPSG)
LRE .... Light Responsive Element [*Chemistry*]
LRE .... Limited Regular Expression (SAUO)
LRE .... Linguistic Research and Engineering (EURO)
LRE .... Liquid Rocket Engine
LRE .... Local Resource Enhancement [*Biology*]
LRE .... Logistics Readiness Elements (MCD)
LRE .... Longreach [*Australia*] [*Airport symbol*] (OAG)
LRE .... Lossless Reciprocal Embedding (IAA)
LRE .... Low Rate Encoding [*Telecommunications*] (LAIN)
LRE .... Low Risk Enhancement (SAUS)
LRE .... Lunar Retrograde Engine [*NASA*] (KSC)
LRE .... Lymphoreticuloendothelial (DB)
LREA .... Law Reports, East Africa [*A publication*] (DLA)
LREA .... Licensed Real Estate Agent (SAUO)
LRE & I App... Law Reports, House of Lords, English and Irish Appeals [*1866-75*] [*A publication*] (DLA)
LREA PAC... Louisiana Rural Electric Association Inc. PAC [*Lafayette, LA*] (PACS)
LREB .... London Regional Examining Board [*British*] (AIE)
L Rec .... Law Recorder [*Dublin, Ireland*] [*A publication*] (DLA)
LREC .... Liaison Residency Endorsement Committee [*RRCEM*] [*Superseded by*] (EA)
LREC .... Local Research Ethics Committee (SAUO)
LRECL .... Logical Record Length (VLIE)
LRECL .... Logical Records of Fixed Length (MCD)
L Rec NS ... Law Recorder, New Series [*Ireland*] [*A publication*] (DLA)
L Record .... Law Recorder [*Dublin, Ireland*] [*A publication*] (DLA)
L Rec OS ... Law Recorder, First Series [*Ireland*] [*A publication*] (DLA)
LREDA .... Liberal Religious Education Directors Association (SAUO)
LREDA .... Liberal Religious Educators Association (EA)
LREE .... Light Rare Earth Elements [*Chemistry*]
LREG .... Leading Regulator [*British*]
LREH .... Laboratory of Radiobiology and Environmental Health (SAUO)
LREH .... Low-Renin Essential Hypertension [*Medicine*]
LREI .... Life Role Expectations Inventory (EDAC)
LREIS .... Laboratory for Resource and Environmental Information Systems (SAUO)
LREM(A) .... Leading Radio Electrical Mechanic (Air) [*British military*] (DMA)
LR Eng & Ir App... Law Reports, English and Irish Appeals [*1866-75*] [*A publication*] (DLA)
L Rep .... Carolina Law Repository (Reprint) [*North Carolina*] [*A publication*] (DLA)
LREP .... Left-Bracketed Representation [*Computer science*] (VLIE)
LREP .... Light Replica Decay (ACAE)
L Rep Mont... Law Reporter, Montreal [*A publication*] (DLA)

L Repos..... Law Repository [*A publication*] (DLA)
LR Eq........ English Law Reports, Equity [*1866-75*] [*A publication*] (DLA)
LREQ........ Larose Transport [*Common carrier symbol*]
LR Eq (Eng)... English Law Reports, Equity [*1866-75*] [*A publication*] (DLA)
L-RERP...... Long-Range Effects Research Program (USDC)
LRES........ Land Resources Corp. (SAUO)
LRES........ Letters
LRES........ Linear Rocket Engine System (PDAA)
LRES........ Long-Range Earth Sensor
LRES........ Low Rigid Frame (PDAA)
L Rev & Quart J... Law Review and Quarterly Journal [*London*] [*A publication*] (DLA)
L Rev Dig... Law Review Digest [*A publication*] (DLA)
L Rev U Detroit... Law Review. University of Detroit [*A publication*] (DLA)
LREW........ Long-Range Early Warning (NATG)
LREWP...... Long-Range Electronic Warfare Plan [*Military*] (CAAL)
LREWS...... Long-Range Early Warning System (NATG)
LR Ex........ English Law Reports, Exchequer [*1866-75*] [*A publication*] (DLA)
LR Ex Cas... English Law Reports, Exchequer [*1866-75*] [*A publication*] (DLA)
LR Exch..... English Law Reports, Exchequer [*1866-75*] [*A publication*] (DLA)
LR Exch D... English Law Reports, Exchequer Division [*A publication*] (DLA)
LR Exch Div... Law Reports, Exchequer Division [*England*] [*A publication*] (DLA)
LR Exch Div (Eng)... English Law Reports, Exchequer Division [*A publication*] (DLA)
LR Exch (Eng)... English Law Reports, Exchequer [*1866-75*] [*A publication*] (DLA)
LR Ex D..... Law Reports, Exchequer Division [*England*] [*A publication*] (DLA)
LR Ex Div... English Law Reports, Exchequer Division [*A publication*] (DLA)
LREXF........ L Rex International Corp. [*NASDAQ symbol*] (COMM)
LRF.......... Jacksonville, AR [*Location identifier*] [*FAA*] (FAAL)
LRF.......... Ladle Refining Furnace [*Nuclear energy*] (NUCP)
LRF.......... Laogai Research Foundation [*Association*] (EA)
LRF.......... LASER RADAR Fuze
LRF.......... LASER Range-Finder
LRF.......... Laser Resonance Fluorescence (ACAE)
LRF.......... Last Return Filed [*IRS*]
LRF.......... Late Renal Failure [*Medicine*]
LRF.......... Latex and Resorcinol Formaldehyde
LRF.......... Launch Rate Factor
LRF.......... Lepidoptera Research Foundation (EA)
LRF.......... Lesson Reference File (ACAE)
LRF.......... Leukaemia Research Fund [*British*]
LRF.......... Leukemia Research Foundation (SAUO)
LRF.......... Lincoln Realty Fund (SAUO)
LRF.......... Lincoln Resign Formulation
LRF.......... Liquid Rocket Fuel (MCD)
LRF.......... Little Rubber Feet (MLOA)
LRF.......... Liver Residue Factor [*Molybdenum*] [*Medicine*]
LRF.......... London Regional Federation [*League of Nations Union*]
LRF.......... Long-Range Facility [*Telecommunications*] (TEL)
LRF.......... Long-Range Fighter (SAUS)
LRF.......... Long-Range Flight
LRF.......... Low Recoil Force (SAUS)
LRF.......... Low Refraction Layer
LRF.......... Lumber Recovery Factor
LRF.......... Luteinizing-Hormone Releasing Factor [*Also, GnRF, GnRH, LH-RF, LH-RH, LH-RH/FSH-RH, LRH*] [*Endocrinology*]
LRF.......... Lymphatic Research Foundation [*Association*] (EA)
LRF.......... National Farmer's Association (Sweden) [*Political party*] (PSAP)
LRFA......... Lymphoma Research Foundation of America (EA)
LRFAX....... Low-Resolution Facsimile [*Telecommunications*] (TEL)
LRFC........ LASER Range-Finder Controller (MCD)
LRFC........ Lymphoma Research Foundation Canada (NRGU)
LRFD........ Lanter Company [*Common carrier symbol*]
LRF/D....... LASER Range-Finder/Designator (MCD)
LRFD........ Load and Resistance Factor Design (WPI)
LRFD........ Low Resolution Fault Dictionary (ACAE)
LRFG........ Low-Range Force Gauge
LRFI......... League for Religious Freedom in Israel [*Later, American Friends of Religious Freedom in Israel*] (EA)
LRF/MTR.... LASER Range-Finder and Marked Target Receiver (MCD)
LRFPB....... Louisiana Rating and Fire Prevention Bureau (SAUO)
LRFPS....... Licentiate of the Royal Faculty of Physicians and Surgeons [*British*]
LRFPS(G)... Licentiate of the Royal Faculty of Physicians and Surgeons, Glasgow
LRFPWG.... Long Range Fiscal Planning Working Group (SAUO)
LRFS........ Long-Range Forecasting System (TEL)
LRF/SSC.... LASER Ranger Finder/Solid State Computer (MCD)
LRFT......... Left Rear Fluid Temperature [*Brake system*] [*Automotive engineering*]
LRG.......... Laboratory Retirees Group (SAUO)
LRG.......... Land Resources Group
LRG.......... Landscape Research Group [*Lutterworth, Leicestershire, England*] (EAIO)
LRG.......... Language Research Group [*State University of New York at Buffalo*] (RCD)
LRG.......... Large [*Classified advertising*]
LRG.......... Leucine-Rich Glycoprotein
LRG.......... License Review Group [*Nuclear energy*] (NRCH)
LRG.......... Lincoln, ME [*Location identifier*] [*FAA*] (FAAL)
LRG.......... Line Relay Group (SAUO)
LRG.......... Liquefied Refinery Gas
LRG.......... Logistic Review Group [*Military*] (CAAL)
LRG.......... Long Range
LRG.......... Long-Range Guidance (MCD)
LRG.......... Lorgues [*France*] [*Seismograph station code, US Geological Survey*] (SEIS)
LRG.......... Lubricant Recommended Guideline
LRGB........ Long-Range Guided Bomb (MCD)
LRGM........ Long Range Guided Missile (CCCA)
LRGPP...... Long-Range Generation Planning Problem [*Energy*]
LRGR........ Landstar Ranger [*Common carrier symbol*]
LRGS........ Local Readout Ground Stations (SAUO)
LRH.......... La Rochelle [*France*] [*Airport symbol*] (OAG)
LRh.......... Liquid Rheostat
LRH.......... Luteinizing-Hormone Releasing Hormone [*Also, GnRF, GnRH, LH-RF, LH-RH, LH-RH/FSH-RH, LRF*] [*Endocrinology*]
LRHB........ Long-Range, Hollow Base (SAUS)
LRHL........ Law Reports, English and Irish Appeals and Peerage Claims, House of Lords [*England*] [*A publication*] (DLA)
LRHL (Eng)... Law Reports, English and Irish Appeals and Peerage Claims, House of Lords [*England*] [*A publication*] (DLA)
LRHL Sc..... English Law Reports, House of Lords, Scotch and Divorce Appeal Cases [*1866-75*] [*A publication*] (DLA)
LRHL Sc App Cas... Law Reports, House of Lords, Scotch and Divorce Appeal Cases [*1866-75*] [*A publication*] (DLA)
LRHL Sc App Cas (Eng)... English Law Reports, House of Lords, Scotch and Divorce Appeal Cases [*1866-75*] [*A publication*] (DLA)
LRHS........ Large Radioisotope Heat Source [*NASA*] (IAA)
LRHS........ Longitudinal Retirement History Survey [*Social Security Administration*] (GFGA)
LRHSC...... Large Radioisotope Heat Source Capsule [*NASA*] (KSC)
LRI........... Big Lost River [*Idaho*] [*Seismograph station code, US Geological Survey*] [*Closed*] (SEIS)
LRI........... Collaboration Research Interest (SAUS)
LRI........... Labour Research Institute (SAUO)
LRI........... Lawndale Railway & Industrial Co. [*Terminated*] [*AAR code*]
LRI........... Learning Resources Institute (EA)
LRI........... LeaRonal, Inc. [*NYSE symbol*] (SPSG)
LRI........... Least Recently Loaded (SAUO)
LRI........... Leather Research Institute [*Texas Tech University*] (RCD)
LRI........... Left Rear Inside-Drive [*Tire maintenance*]
LRI........... Left-Right Indicator
LRI........... Legal Resource Index [*Information Access Corp.*] [*Bibliographic database*] [*Information service or system*] (IID)
LRI........... Leisure and Recreation Involvement Measurement (IDYL)
LRI........... Library Resources, Inc. [*Subsidiary of Encyclopaedia Britannica*]
Lrl............ Library Resources, Incorporated, Chicago, IL [*Library symbol*] [*Library of Congress*] (LCLS)
LRI........... Life Roles Inventory [*Test*] (TMMY)
LRI........... Lighting Research Institute (EA)
LRI........... Limited Range Intercept [*Telecommunications*] [*Navy*] (ANA)
LRI........... Limited Remedial Investigation (SAUO)
LRI........... Line Replaceable Item (CTAS)
LRI........... Literature and Religion of Israel [*A publication*]
LRI........... Load Register Immediate (VLIE)
LRI........... Longboat Resources, Inc. [*Vancouver Stock Exchange symbol*]
LRI........... Long-Range Indicator
LRI........... Long-Range Input (CET)
LRI........... Long-Range Inspector
LRI........... Long-Range Interceptor
LRI........... Long-Range International (DOMA)
LRI........... Long-Range RADAR Input
LRI........... Lorica [*Colombia*] [*Airport symbol*] (AD)
LRI........... Lower Respiratory Infection [*Medicine*]
LRI........... Low Resolution Imager (SAUS)
LRI........... Lubricants Review Institute [*Fuels and lubricants*]
LRI........... Lymphocyte Reactivity Index (DB)
LRIA......... English Law Reports, Indian Appeals [*A publication*] (DLA)
LRIA......... Iasi [*Romania*] [*ICAO location identifier*] (ICLI)
LRIA......... Level Removable Instrument Assembly [*Nuclear energy*] (IEEE)
LRIBA....... Licentiate of the Royal Institute of British Architects
LRIBA....... Licentiate of the Royal Institute of British Architecture (SAUO)
LRIC......... Licentiate of the Royal Institute of Chemistry [*British*]
LRIC......... Long-Run Incremental Cost [*Business term*] (ADA)
LRIDP....... Land Resources Inventory Demonstration Project (SAUO)
LRIFC....... Lauren Robbins International Fan Club (EA)
LRIICC....... Land and Resource Inventory and Information Co-ordinating Committee (SAUO)
LRIM........ Liquid Reaction Injection Molding (EDCT)
LRIM........ Long-Range Input Monitor [*RADAR*]
LR Ind App... English Law Reports, Indian Appeals [*A publication*] (DLA)
LR Ind App Supp... English Law Reports, Indian Appeals, Supplement [*A publication*] (DLA)
LR Indian App... English Law Reports, Indian Appeals [*A publication*] (DLA)
LR Indian App (Eng)... English Law Reports, Indian Appeals [*A publication*] (DLA)
LRINF....... Longer-Range Intermediate-Range Nuclear Forces
LRIP......... Language Research in Progress (DIT)
LRIP......... Liberia Research and Information Project (EA)
LRIP......... Long-Range Impact Point (MUGU)
LRIP......... Low Rate Industrial Production (ACAE)
LRIP......... Low-Rate Initial Production (RDA)
L Ripuar..... Law of the Ripuarians [*A publication*] (DLA)
LRIr.......... Law Reports, Ireland [*1878-1893*] [*A publication*]
LR Ir......... Law Reports, Irish [*A publication*] (DLA)
LRIR......... Limb Radiance Infrared (SAUS)
LRIR......... Limb Radiance Inversion Radiometer
LRIR......... Low-Resolution Infrared Radiometer
LRIRR....... Low-Resolution Infrared Radiometer (MSA)
LRIS......... Land Registration and Information Service (SAUO)

LRIS......... Low Resolution Imaging Spectrograph [*Instrumentation*]
LR-IST........ Long-Range Infra-Red Search & Track (SAUS)
LRITF........ Land Resources Inventory Task Force (SAUO)
LRIX......... Lake Superior Eastern Rail Industries [*Private rail car owner code*]
LRJ.......... Large [*Telegraphy*] (PCTE)
LRJ.......... Lemars, IA [*Location identifier*] [*FAA*] (FAAL)
LRJC......... Lake Region Junior College (SAUO)
LRK.......... Kenya Law Reports [*A publication*] (DLA)
LRK.......... LASER Research Kit
LRK.......... Little Rock, AR [*Amtrak rail station code*]
LRK.......... Long-Range Kinematic [*Navigation systems*]
LRKB......... English Law Reports, King's Bench Division [*1901-52*] [*A publication*] (DLA)
LRKB......... Quebec Official Reports, King's Bench [*A publication*] (ILCA)
LRL.......... Collaboration Research Level (SAUS)
LRL.......... Laser Relay Link (ACAE)
LRL.......... Lawrence Radiation Laboratory [*Livermore*] [*Later, Lawrence Livermore Laboratory*] [*University of California*]
LRL.......... Leakage Resistance Limit
LRL.......... Least Recently Loaded (VLIE)
LRL.......... Light Railway Loads [*British*]
LRL.......... Lightweight Rocket Launcher (SAUS)
LRL.......... Limited Raman LASER
LRL.......... Lincoln Research Laboratory
LRL.......... Linguistics Research Laboratory [*Gallaudet College*] [*Research center*] (RCD)
LRL.......... Linking Relocating Loader
LRL.......... Livermore Research Laboratory [*University of California*] (KSC)
LRL.......... Location Records List [*Computer science*] (VLIE)
LRL.......... Logical Record Length
LRL.......... Logical Record Location
LRL.......... Lunar Receiving Laboratory [*NASA*]
LRL.......... Lunar Research Laboratory [*NASA*] (DAVI)
LRL.......... Tulane University, Law Library, New Orleans, LA [*OCLC symbol*] (OCLC)
LRLA......... La Raza Legal Alliance (SAUO)
LRLB......... Lawrence Radiation Laboratory-Berkeley (SAUO)
LRLCX........ Lord Abbett Research: Large Cap [*Mutual fund ticker symbol*] (SG)
LR/LD........ Line Receiver/Line Driver (MCD)
LRLEI........ League for Religious Labor in Eretz Israel (EA)
LRLF......... Local Radio Luminosity Function [*Cosmology*]
LRLG......... Long-Range Logistics Guidance [*Air Force*]
LRLI......... Ronald L. Leek [*Common carrier symbol*]
LRL-L........ Lawrence Radiation Laboratory, Livermore [*Later, Lawrence Livermore Laboratory*] [*University of California*]
LRLL......... Longitudinal Ridge of Lateral Lip
LRLM......... Lower Reject Limit Median (SAA)
LRLS......... London Regional Library System (SAUO)
LRLSA........ La Raza Law Students Association (SAUO)
LRLT......... Left Rear Lining Temperature [*Brake system*] [*Automotive engineering*]
LRLTRAN.... Lawrence Radiation Laboratory FORTRAN [*Programming language*] [*1961*] (CSR)
LRLTRAN.... Lawrence Radiation Laboratory Translator (IEEE)
LRM.......... Laboratory for Responsible Manufacturing [*Northeastern University*] (RCD)
LRM.......... Labor Reimbursable Material (ACAE)
LRM.......... Labor Relations Reference Manual [*A publication*] (DLA)
LRM.......... Land Resources Management (MCD)
LRM.......... Language Reference Manual (VLIE)
LRM.......... La Rassegna Musicale [*A publication*]
LRM.......... La Romana [*Dominican Republic*] [*Airport symbol*] (OAG)
LRM.......... Latching Relay Matrix
LRM.......... Lead Reactor Manufacturer (NRCH)
LRM.......... Leaflet Rolling Machine [*PSYOP*] (RDA)
LRM.......... Least Recently Used Master [*Computer science*]
LRM.......... Left Radical Mastectomy [*Medicine*] (MAE)
LRM.......... Lightweight Ramjet Missile (MCD)
LRM.......... Limited Register Machine
LRM.......... Linear Radiating Module (ACAE)
LRM.......... Line Replacement Module
LRM.......... Liquid Reaction Molding
LRM.......... Liquid Rocket Motor (KSC)
LRM.......... Logarithmic Radiation Monitor (NRCH)
LRM.......... Logarithmic Ratio Module
LRM.......... Long-Range Missile Launcher
LRM.......... Long Reach Manipulator (ABAC)
LRM.......... Lower Reject Limit Median
LRM.......... Low Rate Multiplexer (SAUS)
LRM.......... Lunar Reconnaissance [*or Rendezvous*] Mission [*Aerospace*]
LRM.......... Lunar Reconnaissance Module [*Aerospace*]
LR Mad..... Indian Law Reports, Madras Series [*A publication*] (DLA)
LRMC......... Lloyd's Refrigerating Machinery Certificate
LRMC......... Long-Run Marginal Costs
LRMCO........ Long Run, Mill Cuts Out [*Forest industry*] (WPI)
LRMG......... Hughes Lockless Rifle/Machine Gun (MCD)
LR Misc D... Law Reports, Miscellaneous Division [*A publication*] (DLA)
LRML......... Long-Range Missile Launcher [*Military*] (IAA)
LRMP......... Land and Resource Management Plan (SAUO)
LRMP......... Last Regular Menstrual Period [*Gynecology*] (DMAA)
LRMP......... Legacy Resource Management Program (DOMA)
LRMP......... Long-Range Maritime Patrol [*Aircraft*] (NATG)
LRMPA........ Long Range Maritime Patrol Aircraft (ACAE)
LRMS......... Library Routine Management System
LRMS......... Low Resolution Mass Spectroscopy (COE)
LRMTS........ LASER Range-Finder and Marked Target Seeker (MCD)
LRMV......... Lilac Ring Mottle Virus [*Plant pathology*]
LRN.......... Learn [*Telegraphy*] (PCTE)
LRN.......... Learning Resource Interchange
LRN.......... Long-Range Navigation
LRN.......... Long Reference Number
LRN.......... LORAN [*Long-Range Aid to Navigation*]
LRN.......... Lorang [*Language symbol*] (ETLW)
LRN.......... Low Recoil Noricum (SAUS)
LRNA......... Laws Relating to the Navy Annotated [*Military law*]
LRNA......... League of Revolutionaries for a New America [*Association*] (EA)
LRNAV........ Long Range Navigation [*FAA*] (TAG)
LRNBA........ La Raza National Bar Association (EA)
LRNC......... Long Reference Number Code
LRND......... Learned [*Telegraphy*] (PCTE)
LRND......... Left Radical Neck Dissection [*Surgical procedure*] (DAVI)
LRNF......... Longer-Range Nuclear Forces (WDAA)
LRNG......... Learning
LRNG......... Learning Co. [*NASDAQ symbol*] (SAG)
LrngCo....... Learning Co. [*Associated Press*] (SAG)
LrnHaus...... Lernout & Hauspie Speech Products [*Associated Press*] (SAG)
LRNOD........ Long-Range Night Observation Device [*Army*] (AABC)
LRNR......... Low-Resolution Non-Scanning Radiometer (MCD)
LRNRM........ Landowners for Responsible Natural Resource Management [*An association*] (WPI)
LRNS......... Long-Range Navigation System [*Aviation*]
LRNS......... Nova Scotia Law Reports [*A publication*] (DLA)
LRNSW........ Law Reports, New South Wales Supreme Court [*A publication*] (DLA)
LRNTF........ Long Range Intermediate Nuclear Forces (ACAE)
LrnTree...... Learning Tree International, Inc. [*Associated Press*] (SAG)
LRNZ......... Law Reports, New Zealand [*A publication*] (DLA)
LRO.......... Laboratory Review Office [*Army*] (RDA)
LRO.......... Labor Relations Officer (COE)
LRO.......... Large Radio Observatory (KSC)
LRO.......... Lathrop, CA [*Location identifier*] [*FAA*] (FAAL)
LRO.......... Leading Radio Operator [*British military*] (DMA)
LRO.......... Left Rear Outside-Drive [*Tire maintenance*]
LRO.......... Loan Review Officer [*Banking*] (TBD)
LRO.......... Logistics Readiness Officer [*Military*] (AABC)
LRO.......... Long-Range Objectives [*Navy*]
LRO.......... Long-Range Order
LRO.......... Low-Resistance Ohmmeter
LROA......... Land Rover Owners Association (EA)
LROA USA... Land Rover Owners Association, USA (EA)
LROC......... Libertarian Republican Organizing Committee [*Defunct*] (EA)
LROD......... Lightning Rod Software [*OTCBB symbol*]
LROD......... Long-Range Overwater Diffusion [*Experiment*] [*Marine science*] (OSRA)
LROD......... Oradea [*Romania*] [*ICAO location identifier*] (ICLI)
LRO(G)....... Leading Radio Operator (General) [*British military*] (DMA)
LROG......... Long-Range Objectives Group [*Navy*] (MCD)
LROI......... Legal Rate of Interest [*Business term*] (MHDB)
LROL......... Laboratoire de Recherches en Optique et Laser [*Laval University*] [*Canada*] [*Research center*] (RCD)
LROP......... Bucuresti/Otopeni [*Romania*] [*ICAO location identifier*] (ICLI)
LROP......... Long-Range Optical Pod (SAUS)
LROP......... Lower Radicular Obstetrical Paralysis [*Medicine*] (DMAA)
LROR......... Low-Resolution Omnidirectional Radiometer (MCD)
LROS......... Long Range Optical System (ACAE)
LRO(W)....... Leading Radio Operator (Warfare) [*British military*] (DMA)
LROY......... Leroy Properties & Development Corp. (SAUO)
LRP.......... English Law Reports, Probate Division [*A publication*] (DLA)
LRP.......... Lancaster, PA [*Location identifier*] [*FAA*] (FAAL)
LRP.......... Landscape Research Project (SAUO)
LRP.......... Lang Recovery Package (ACAE)
LRP.......... Large Repairs to Hull
LRP.......... Large Rotating Plug [*Nuclear energy*] (NRCH)
LRP.......... LASER Retinal Photocoagulator
LRP.......... Lateralized Readiness Potential [*Neurophysiology*]
LRP.......... Late Receptor Potential [*Photoreceptor*] [*Physiology*]
LRP.......... Latest Reporting Period [*Business term*]
LRP.......... Launching Reference Point
LRP.......... LDI [*Low Density Lipoprotein*] Receptor-Related Protein [*Biochemistry*]
LRP.......... League for the Revolutionary Party (EA)
LRP.......... Lebanese Revolutionary Party [*Political party*] (PD)
LRP.......... Lesbian Rights Project [*Later, NCLR*] (EA)
LRP.......... Lichen Ruber Planus (DMAA)
LRP.......... Limited Rate Production
LRP.......... Limited Reaction Processing [*Semiconductor technology*]
LRP.......... Liporotein Receptor-Related Protein [*Biochemistry*]
LRP.......... Live Role Playing (ADWA)
LRP.......... LM [*Lunar Module*] Replaceable Package [*NASA*]
LRP.......... Loan Repayment Program [*Department of Health and Human Services*] (GFGA)
LRP.......... Logical Record Processor (IAA)
LRP.......... Logical Request Package [*Computer science*] (CIST)
LRP.......... Logistics Recovery Program (SAUO)
LRP.......... Logistics Release Point [*Army*] (INF)
LRP.......... Longe Range Interceptor (ACAE)
LRP.......... Long-Range Path (IEEE)
LRP.......... Long-Range Patrol [*Pronounced "lurp"*] [*Formerly, LRRP*] [*Army*] (AABC)
LRP.......... Long-Range Penetration

LRP .... Long-Range Plans (NVT)
LRP .... Low Rate Production (RDA)
LRP .... Low Rigging Penalty [*IOR*] [*Yacht racing*]
LRP .... Society for Long Range Planning (SAUO)
LRP .... Law Reports, Probate [*Division*] (ODA)
LRPA .... Laser Radar Power Amplifier (ACAE)
LRPA .... Little Rock Port Railroad [*AAR code*]
LRPA .... Long-Range Patrol Aircraft (MCD)
LRP & D .... Probate and Divorce Cases [*1865-75*] [*England*] [*A publication*] (DLA)
LRP & M.... Law Reports, Probate and Matrimonial [*1866-75*] [*A publication*] (DLA)
LRPC .... English Law Reports, Privy Council, Appeal Cases [*1866-75*] [*A publication*] (DLA)
LRPC .... Laboratory Review Process Committee (SAUO)
LRPC .... Liberia Rubber Processing Corporation (SAUO)
LRPC .... Lightweight Remote Procedure Call [*Computer science*]
LRPC .... London Regional Passengers Committee [*British*] (ECON)
LRPC (Eng)... English Law Reports, Privy Council, Appeal Cases [*1866-75*] [*A publication*] (DLA)
LRPD .... Law Reports, Probate Division [*A publication*] (DLA)
LRP Div..... English Law Reports, Probate, Divorce, and Admiralty Division [*A publication*] (DLA)
LRPDS ...... Long-Range Position-Determining System [*Army*] (RDA)
LRPE .... Long-Range Procurement Estimate (PDAA)
LRPE .... Long-Run Price Effect [*Marketing*]
LRPF .... Liberal Religious Peace Fellowship (EA)
LRPG .... Long-Range Penetration Group [*Military*] [*World War II*]
LRPG .... Long-Range Proving Ground [*Air Force*]
LRPGD ...... Long-Range Proving Ground Division [*Air Force*]
LRPGR ...... Long-Range Planning Ground Rules (AAG)
LRP/GWU... Logistics Research Project, George Washington University
LRPL .... Liquid Rocket Propulsion Laboratory [*Army*] (IEEE)
LRPL .... Little Rock Public Library (SAUO)
LRPLS....... Long-Range Passive Location System (PDAA)
LRPO .... Location Radiation Protection Officer (SARE)
LRPP .... Long-Range Propulsion Plan (MCD)
LRPPD ...... Long-Range Planning Purpose Document
LR Prob & M (Eng)... English Law Reports, Probate, Divorce, and Admiralty Division [*A publication*] (DLA)
LR Prob Div... English Law Reports, Probate, Divorce, and Admiralty Division [*A publication*] (DLA)
LR Prob Div (Eng)... English Law Reports, Probate, Divorce, and Admiralty Division [*A publication*] (DLA)
LRPS .... Laser Reliability Prediction Study (ACAE)
LRPS .... Licentiate of the Royal Photographic Society [*British*] (DBQ)
LRPS .... London Railway Preservation Society (SAUO)
LRPS .... Long-Range Planning Service [*Stanford Research Institute*] [*Assists businesses in investment activities*] (IID)
LRPS .... Long-Range Planning System (SAUO)
LRPS .... Long-Range Positioning System
LRPSI .... Long-Range Planning for School Improvement [*Pennsylvania*] (EDAC)
LRPT .... Large Repair Parts Transporter (MCD)
LRPT .... Longest Remaining Processing Time (PDAA)
LRPT .... Low-Resolution Picture Transmission (EOSA)
LRQ.......... Lower Right Quadrant (MAE)
LRQB .... English Law Reports, Queen's Bench Division [*1865-75*] [*A publication*] (DLA)
LRQB .... Quebec Queen's Bench Reports [*Canada*] [*A publication*] (DLA)
LRQBD ...... English Law Reports, Queen's Bench Division [*1865-75*] [*A publication*] (DLA)
LRQB Div... English Law Reports, Queen's Bench Division [*1865-75*] [*A publication*] (DLA)
LRQB Div (Eng)... English Law Reports, Queen's Bench Division [*1865-75*] [*A publication*] (DLA)
LRQB (Eng)... English Law Reports, Queen's Bench Division [*1865-75*] [*A publication*] (DLA)
LR-QR....... Letter Requirement - Quick Reaction [*Army*]
LRR.......... Labyrinthine Righting Reflex [*Physiology*]
LRR.......... Lagged Reserve Requirement [*Finance*]
LRR.......... Land-Rover Register 1947-1951 [*Petersfield, Hampshire, England*] (EAIO)
LRR.......... LASER Radiation Receiver
LRR.......... Launch Readiness Report [*or Review*] [*NASA*] (KSC)
LRR.......... Launch Readiness Review [*Aerospace*] (NAKS)
LRR.......... Leucine-Rich Repeat [*Biochemistry*]
LRR.......... Leucine-Rich Repeats [*Genetics*]
LRR.......... Logistic Readiness Review [*Navy*]
LRR.......... Long-Range RADAR
LRR.......... Long-Range Reconnaissance (MCD)
LRR.......... Long-Range Requirements [*Navy*]
LRR.......... Long-Range Rocket (MUGU)
LRR.......... Longreach Resources Ltd. [*Vancouver Stock Exchange symbol*]
LRR.......... Long Reduced Rate [*Taxation*] (WDAA)
LRR.......... Long Regulatory Region [*Genetics*]
LRR.......... Loop Regenerative Repeater
LRR.......... Loss of Righting Reflex [*Medicine*]
LRR.......... Lot Rejection Rate [*Quality measurement*]
LRR.......... Lot Rejection Report
LRR.......... Lower Receiving Room (SAUS)
LRR & MF... Long-Range Resource and Management Forecast
LRRC .... Labor Relations and Research Center [*University of Massachusetts*]
LRRC .... Land Resource Research Centre [*Canada*] (IRC)
LRRC .... Lionel Railroaders Club (EA)
LRRC .... London Regional Reconstruction Committee (SAUO)
LRRD .... Long-Range Reconnaissance Detachment
LRRDA ...... Long Range Research, Development, and Acquisition (ACAE)
LRRDAP..... Long-Range Research, Development, and Acquisition Plan (RDA)
LRRI .... Land Resources Research Institute [*Agriculture Canada*] [*Formerly, Soil Research Institute*] [*Research center*] (RCD)
LRRI .... Long-Range Reference Retroreflectance Instrument [*Bicycle test*] [*National Institute of Standards and Technology*]
LRRM .... Labor Relations Reference Manual [*Bureau of National Affairs*] [*A publication*] (DLA)
LRRM .... Loss Ratio Reserve Method [*Insurance*]
lrRNA........ Ribonucleic Acid, Light Ribosomal [*Biochemistry, genetics*]
LRRO......... Land Revenue Record Office (SAUO)
LRRO......... Land Revenue Records and Enrollments Office [*British*]
LRRP .... Law Reports, Restrictive Practices Cases [*1958-72*] [*A publication*] (DLA)
LRRP .... Long-Range Reconnaissance Patrol [*Pronounced "lurp"*] [*Later, LRP*] [*Army*] (AABC)
LRRP .... Lowest Required Radiated Power
LRRPC ...... Restrictive Practices Cases [*1958-72*] [*England*] [*A publication*] (DLA)
LRRR .... LASER Ranging Retroreflection [*Also, LR3*] [*Pronounced "LR-cubed"*] [*Apollo 11 experiment*] [*NASA*]
LRRRC ...... Liberia Refugee, Repatriation and Resettlement Commission (SAUO)
LRRS .... Library Reports & Research Service, Inc. [*Information service or system*] (IID)
LRRS .... Limited Remaining Radiation Service [*Unit*] [*Military*]
LRRS .... Long-Range RADAR Site (OA)
LRRS .... Long-Range Radar Station (SAUO)
LRRSA ...... Light Railway Research Society of Australia
LRRT .... Library Research Round Table [*American Library Association*]
LRRT .... Light Rail Rapid Transit [*TRB*] (TAG)
LR/RT........ Long-Range Radiotelephone (DNAB)
LRS.......... Laboratory Recoil Simulator (MCD)
LRS.......... Laboratory Release System (MCD)
LRS.......... Labor Relations Specialist (AAGC)
LRS.......... Lactated Ringer's Solution [*Intravenous solution*]
LRS.......... Lake Reporting Service
LRS.......... Lamb-Retherford Shift [*Physics*]
LRS.......... Lander Radio Subsystem [*NASA*]
LRS.......... Land Registry Stamp (ODA)
LRS.......... Language ReSource (SAUO)
LRS.......... Lanyard Release Switch
LRS.......... Larder Resources, Inc. [*Toronto Stock Exchange symbol*]
LRS.......... Lares [*Puerto Rico*] [*Seismograph station code, US Geological Survey*] (SEIS)
LRS.......... Large Ring Sparger [*Engineering*]
LRS.......... Laser Radiometer System (ACAE)
LRS.......... LASER Raman Scattering
LRS.......... LASER Raman Spectroscopy
LRS.......... Laser Rangefinder Set (ACAE)
LRS.......... LASER Ranging System
LRS.......... LASER Raster Scanner
LRS.......... LASER Reflectance Spectrometer (SSD)
LRS.......... Launch and Recovery Site (COE)
LRS.......... Launch Recoil Simulator
LRS.......... Laurinburg & Southern Railroad Co. [*AAR code*]
LRS.......... Lawyer Referral Service
LRS.......... League of Religious Settlements (EA)
LRS.......... Legislative Reference Service [*Later, Congressional Research Service*] [*Library of Congress*]
LRS.......... Legislative Retrieval System [*Database*] (GDD)
LRS.......... Level Recording Switch (NRCH)
LRS.......... Library Reproduction Service, Microfilm Co. of California, Los Angeles, CA [*Library symbol*] [*Library of Congress*] (LCLS)
L/R/S .... Library Rubber Stamps [*Antiquarian book trade*]
LRS.......... Lifetime Reproductive Success [*Demographics*]
LRS.......... Light Radiation Sensor
LRS.......... Light Repair Section [*British military*] (DMA)
LRS.......... Light's Retention Scale [*Test*]
LRS.......... Lightweight RADAR Set
LRS.......... Limited Resources Specialty (AFM)
LRS.......... Lincoln Record Society (SAUO)
LRS.......... Linear Referencing System [*FHWA*] (TAG)
LRS.......... Linguistics Research System
LRS.......... Liquid RADWASTE System (NRCH)
LRS.......... Lloyd's Register of Shipping
LRS.......... Logistics Requirements System [*Navy*]
LRS.......... London Record Society [*British*] (ILCA)
LRS.......... London Research Station [*British Gas*] (WDAA)
LRS.......... Long-Range Schedule (SAA)
LRS.......... Long-Range Search
LRS.......... Long-Range Study
LRS.......... Long-Range Surveillance [*Military*] (INF)
LRS.......... Long Ranging Subsystem (ACAE)
LRS.......... Long Reversed Superchron [*Geology*]
LRS.......... Long Right Shift
LRS.......... Low-Rate Station
LRS.......... Low Resolution Spectrometer (SAUS)
LRS.......... Low Response System (SAUS)
LRSA .... Laboratoire de Recherche en Sciences de l'Administration [*Laval University*] [*Canada*] [*Research center*] (RCD)
LRSA .... Lamprey River Study Act of 1991 (COE)
LRSA .... Long Range Strategic Aircraft (ACAE)
LRSAGW.... Long-Range Surface-to-Air Guided Weapon (IAA)
LRSAM...... Long-Range Surface-to-Air Missile (NATG)

LRS & D App... Law Reports, Scotch and Divorce Appeals [*1866-75*] [*A publication*] (DLA)
LRS & TP... Long-Range Science and Technology Plan [*Army*]
LRSB .... Low Right Sternal Border [*Medicine*] (MELL)
LRSB .... Sibiu/Turnisor [*Romania*] [*ICAO location identifier*] (ICLI)
LRSC .... Law Reports, New Zealand Supreme Court [*A publication*] (DLA)
LRSC .... Licentiate of the Royal Society of Chemistry [*British*] (DBQ)
LRSC .... Long-Range Surveillance Co. [*Military*] (INF)
LRSCA....... Land Remote Sensing Commercialization Act [*1984*]
LRSCA....... Large Retractable Solar Cell Array
LR Sc & D... English Law Reports, House of Lords, Scotch and Divorce Appeal Cases [*1866-75*] [*A publication*] (DLA)
LR Sc & D App... Scottish and Divorce Appeals [*1866-75*] [*A publication*] (DLA)
LR Sc & D App... Scottish and Divorce Cases before the House of Lords [*A publication*] (DLA)
LR Sc & Div... Scotch and Divorce Appeals [*1866-75*] [*A publication*] (DLA)
LR Sc App... Law Reports, Scotch Appeals [*A publication*] (DLA)
LR Sc Div App... Law Reports, Scotch Appeals [*A publication*] (DLA)
LRSCX....... Lord Abbett Research: Small Cap [*Mutual fund ticker symbol*] (SG)
LRSD .... Long-Range Surveillance Detachment [*Military*] (INF)
LRSDC ...... Lakes Region Sled Dog Club (EA)
LR Sess Cas... English Law Reports, Sessions Cases [*A publication*] (DLA)
LRSF .... Lactating Rat Serum Factor [*Immunology*]
LRSF .... Liver Regenerating Serum Factor [*Medicine*] (DMAA)
LRSF .... Long-Range Systems Forecast
LRSI .... LifeRate Systems [*NQS*] (TTSB)
LRSI .... LifeRate Systems, Inc. [*NASDAQ symbol*] (SAG)
LRSI .... Long-Range SOF [*Special Operation Force*] Insertion (DOMA)
LRSI .... Low-Temperature Reusable Surface Insulation (NASA)
LRSIFC...... Lori Robin Smith International Fan Club (EA)
LRSK .... Long-Range Station Keeping (NG)
LRSL .... Law Reports, Sierra Leone Series [*A publication*] (DLA)
LRSL .... Long-Range Surveillance Leader [*Military*] (INF)
LRSLA....... Long-Range Service Life Analysis (MCD)
LRSLBM .... Long Range Sea Launched Ballistic Missile (ACAE)
LRSLC....... Long Range Surveillance Leaders Course [*Army*]
LRSLP....... Lietuvos Revoliuciniu Socialistu Liaudininkai Partija [*Revolutionary Socialist Populists Party of Lithuania*] [*Political party*] (PPE)
LRSM........ Laboratory for Research on the Structure of Matter [*University of Pennsylvania*]
LRSM........ Licentiate of the Royal School of Music, London [*British*]
LRSM........ Long-Range Seismograph Measurements (MCD)
LRSM........ Long-Range Standoff Missile [*Military*] (MUSM)
LRSM........ Satu Mare [*Romania*] [*ICAO location identifier*] (ICLI)
LRSO .... Long-Range Surveillance Outpost (MCD)
LRSOM...... Long-Range Stand-Off Missile
LRSOW...... Long-Range Conventional Standoff Weapon
LRSP .... Long-Range Strategic Planning (PDAA)
LRSP .... Long-Range Systems Plan (TIMI)
LRSR .... Liquid Redox Sulfur Recovery [*Processes for removing hydrogen sulfide from gases*]
LRSR .... Long-Range Sniper Rifle (PDAA)
LRSR .... Long-Range Storage Requirements (SAUO)
LRSS .... Land Rover Security System [*Automotive safety*]
LRSS .... Logistics Readiness Simulation System (SAUO)
LRSS .... Long-Range Scientific Studies (SAUO)
LRSS .... Long-Range Strategic Studies [*Military*] (AFIT)
LRSS .... Long-Range Surveillance System (SAUS)
LRSS .... Long-Range Survey System [*Military*]
LR Stat...... English Law Reports, Statutes [*A publication*] (DLA)
LRSTPP ..... Long-Range Scientific Technical Planning Program (NG)
LRSU .... Long Range Sensor Unit (SAUO)
LRSU .... Long-Range Surveillance Unit [*Military*] (INF)
LRSUBRS... Long-Range Surveillance Unit Base Radio Station [*Military*] (INF)
LRSV .... Lychnis Ringspot Virus [*Plant pathology*]
LRSV .... Suceava/Salcea [*Romania*] [*ICAO location identifier*] (ICLI)
LRT .... LASER Range-Finder Theodolite
LRT .... Last Resort Target [*Military*]
LRT .... Launch Readiness Test (ACAE)
LRT .... Launch, Recovery, and Transport [*Vehicle*]
LRT .... Lawrenceburg, TN [*Location identifier*] [*FAA*] (FAAL)
LRT .... Licensed Radiological Technician [*Therapy term*] (CTAA)
LRT .... Light Rail Transit
LRT .... Light Rail Transport (SAUO)
LRT .... Light Repair Truck [*British*]
LRT .... Likelihood Ratio Test [*Statistics*]
LRT .... Linear Response Theory [*Physics*]
LRT .... Link Readiness Test (ACAE)
LRT .... Little Round Top (SAUO)
LRT .... LL&E Royalty Tr UBI [*NYSE symbol*] (TTSB)
LRT .... LL&E Royalty Trust (EFIS)
LRT .... LL & E Royalty Trust UBI [*NYSE symbol*] (SPSG)
LRT .... Load Ratio Transformer (IAA)
LRT .... Local Leak Rate Test [*Nuclear energy*] (IEEE)
LRT .... Local Radiotherapy
LRT .... Loki Ranging Transponder
LRT .... London Reading Test [*Educational test*]
LRT .... London Regional Transport
LRT .... Long-Range Radiotelephone
LRT .... Long-Range Transport [*Navy*] [*British*]
LRT .... Long-Range Typhon [*Navy*] (NG)
LRT .... Long Ring Timer
LRT .... Lorentz Reciprocal Theorem
LRT .... Lorient [*France*] [*Airport symbol*] (OAG)
LRT .... Lower Respiratory Tract [*Medicine*]
LRT .... Low Rate Type (SAUS)
LRT .... Lymphoreticular Tissue [*Medicine*] (MELL)
LRTA......... Lath Renders' Trade Association [*A union*] [*British*]
LRTA......... Leisure, Recreation, and Tourism Abstracts [*Database*] [*Commonwealth Agricultural Bureaux International*] [*Information service or system*] (CRD)
LRTA......... Light Rail Transit Association [*Milton, Keynes, England*] (EAIO)
LRTAP....... Long Range Transportation of Air Pollution (EEVL)
LRTAP....... Long-Range Transport of Atmospheric Pollutants
LRTAP....... Long-Range Transport of Atmospheric Pollution (SAUO)
LRTC......... Law Reform Commission of Tasmania [*Australia*]
LRTC......... Local Road Transport Co-ordinator (SAUO)
LRTC......... Tulcea/Cataloi [*Romania*] [*ICAO location identifier*] (ICLI)
LRTD .... Living Relative Transplant Donor (MELL)
LRTF......... Linear Radial Transmission Filter [*Photography*]
LRTF......... Long-Range Technical Forecast (IEEE)
LRTG .... Logistics Reassignment Task Group [*DoD*] (MCD)
LRTGP....... Long-Range Tear Gas Projectile [*Police and security equipment*]
LRTGT....... Last Resort Target [*Military*]
LRThD....... Lateral Reach-Through Device (PDAA)
LRTI .... Lower Respiratory Tract Illness (DAVI)
LRTI .... Lower Respiratory Tract Infection [*Medicine*] (ADA)
LRTIA........ Long-Range Scientific and Technical Intelligence Assessment (SAUO)
LRTL......... Light Railway Transport League [*British*] (DCTA)
LRTM........ Long-Range Training Mission [*Military*]
LRTM........ Tirgu Mures/Vidrasau [*Romania*] [*ICAO location identifier*] (ICLI)
LRTNF....... Long-Range Theater Nuclear Force [*Military*]
LRTNW...... Long-Range Theater Nuclear Weapons [*Military*]
LRTP......... Long-Range Technical Plan (PDAA)
LRTP......... Long-Running Thermal Precipitation (DICI)
LRTPP....... Long-Range Scientific Technical Planning Program (SAUO)
LRTQ .... Larsen Transfer and Storage Company [*Common carrier symbol*]
LRTR .... Timisoara/Giarmata [*Romania*] [*ICAO location identifier*] (ICLI)
LRTRO....... Loaded Radial Tire Run-Out [*Automotive engineering*]
LRTS......... LASER Ranging and Tracking System (RDA)
LRTS......... Library Resources & Technical Services [*Association for Library Collections and Technical Services*] [*American Library Association*]
LRTx......... Living Related Renal Transplantation [*Medicine*]
LRU.......... Landowner Relations Unit (SAUO)
LRU.......... Landscape Response Unit (QUAC)
LRU.......... Las Cruces [*New Mexico*] [*Airport symbol*] (OAG)
LRU.......... Las Cruces, NM [*Location identifier*] [*FAA*] (FAAL)
LRU.......... Laser Rangefinder Unit (ACAE)
LRU.......... Laser Recording Unit (SAUS)
LRU.......... Least Recently Used [*Replacement algorithm*] [*Computer science*]
LRU.......... Least Repairable Unit
LRU.......... Least Replaceable Unit (IAA)
LRU.......... Less than Release Unit [*Army*] (AABC)
LRU.......... Line Removable Unit
LRU.......... Line Replaceable Unit (AFM)
LRU.......... Link Retraction Unit (KSC)
LRU.......... Little Rock University [*Merged with University of Arkansas*]
LRU.......... Lone Replaceable Unit (MCD)
LRU.......... Lowest Repairable Unit (MCD)
LRU.......... Lowest Replaceable Unit (SAUO)
LRU.......... Lowest Replacement Unit (MCD)
LRU.......... Tulane University, New Orleans, LA [*OCLC symbol*] (OCLC)
LRuL......... Louisiana Technical University, Ruston, LA [*Library symbol*] [*Library of Congress*] (LCLS)
LRuLP....... Lincoln Parish Library, Ruston, LA [*Library symbol*] [*Library of Congress*] (LCLS)
LRUP .... La Raza Unida Party (EA)
LRUP .... Local Resource Use Plan (SAUO)
LRUPS ...... Line Replaceable Unit Power Supply (MCD)
LRV .... Labor Rate Variance (TIMI)
LRV .... Lanarkshire Rifle Volunteers [*British military*] (DMA)
LRV .... Lancashire Rifle Volunteers [*British military*] (DMA)
LRV .... Last Received Value (ACAE)
LRV .... Launch & Recovery Vehicle (SAUS)
LRV .... Launch Readiness Verification [*NASA*] (NASA)
LRV .... Left Renal Vein [*Anatomy*] (DAVI)
LRV .... Leirvogur [*Iceland*] [*Geomagnetic observatory code*]
LRV .... Lifting Reentry Vehicle (MCD)
LRV .... Light Rail Vehicle
LRV .... Light Reconnaissance Vehicle [*Military*]
LRV .... Light Recreational Vehicle [*Mitsubishi minivan*]
LRV .... Liquid Radioactive Waste (SAUO)
LRV .... Little Rabbit Valley [*California*] [*Seismograph station code, US Geological Survey*] (SEIS)
LRV .... Little River Railroad [*Federal Railroad Administration identification code*]
LRV .... Local Radio Workshop (SAUO)
LRV .... London Radio Workshop (SAUO)
LRV .... Long-Range Vehicle
LRV .... Long-Range Video (MCD)
LRV .... Low Resolution Visible (SAUO)
LRV .... Lunar Rover [*or Roving*] Vehicle [*NASA*]
LRVEP....... League of Rural Voters Education Project (EA)
LRW .... Labor Ready [*NYSE symbol*] (SG)
LRW .... Labor Relations Week [*Bureau of National Affairs*] [*Information service or system*] (CRD)
LRW .... Liquid Radioactive Waste (SAUS)
LRW .... London Radio Workshop [*Independent Local Radio*] [*British*]

LRWC .... Licensed Residental Wages Council (SAUO)
LRWN .... Little Rock & Western Railway [*Federal Railroad Administration identification code*]
LRWRO ..... Loaded Radial Wheel Run-Out [*Automotive engineering*]
LRWY .... Lackawanna Railway [*Federal Railroad Administration identification code*]
LRY .... Lady Robyn Resources, Inc. [*Vancouver Stock Exchange symbol*]
LRY .... Latching Relay (IAA)
LRY .... Liberal Religious Youth
LRY .... Liberty Property Trust [*NYSE symbol*] (SAG)
LRZ .... Lorazepam [*Medicine*] (EDAA)
LRZR .... Lauritzen Reefers [*Common carrier symbol*]
LS .... Labologists Society [*Farnborough, Hampshire, England*] (EAIO)
LS .... Laboratory System
LS .... Labor Service [*Military*]
L/S .... Lactose/Sucrose [*Ratio*]
LS .... Lacus Somniorum [*Lunar area*]
LS .... Lamb Society (SAUO)
LS .... Lamellar Strip [*Botany*]
LS .... Lamp Show
LS .... Landesschuetzeneinheit [*Regional defense force*] [*German military - World War II*]
LS .... Landing Ship
LS .... Landing Side [*Air Force*]
LS .... Landing Site (KSC)
LS .... Landing System (ACAE)
L/S .... Landsat (SAUO)
LS .... Land Service
LS .... Land Surveying Program [*Association of Independent Colleges and Schools specialization code*]
LS .... Land Surveyor
LS .... Lange Sicht [*Long Sight*] [*German*]
LS .... Language Specification (IEEE)
LS .... LAN Server (SAUS)
LS .... Lantern Slide [*Photography*]
ls .... Laos [*MARC country of publication code*] [*Library of Congress*] (LCCP)
LS .... Lapped Seam (DNAB)
LS .... Larcher's Sign [*Medicine*] (MELL)
LS .... Lasallian Sisters (Vietnam) (TOCD)
LS .... Laser Surgery (MELL)
LS .... LASER System
LS .... Lastensegler; Lastensegelflugzeug [*Cargo transport glider*] [*German military - World War II*]
LS .... Latch Side
LS .... Latent Syphilis (MELL)
LS .... Lateral Septum
LS .... Lateral Subsylvian Cortex [*Neuroanatomy*]
LS .... Lateral Suspensor [*Ligament*] [*Anatomy*] (DAVI)
LS .... Late Scramble [*Reason for missed interception*] [*Military*]
LS .... Late Shock [*Medicine*]
LS .... Late Start (SAUO)
LS .... Launching System
LS .... Launch Sequence (MCD)
LS .... Launch Service
LS .... Launch Set
LS .... Launch Simulator (MUGU)
LS .... Launch Site [*NASA*] (MCD)
LS .... Launch Station (MCD)
LS .... Law Society (WDAA)
LS .... Law Student (DLA)
LS .... Layman Speaks [*Journal*] [*Medicine*] (EDAA)
LS .... Leaders of Science [*A publication*]
LS .... Leading Seaman [*Navy*] [*British*]
LS .... Leading Stoker
LS .... Lead Service (ACAE)
LS .... Lead Sheet [*Military*]
LS .... Lead Survey [*Environmental science*] (COE)
LS .... Leaf Spring [*Automotive engineering*]
L-S .... Leap-Second
LS .... Learning Step
LS .... Lease
LS .... Least Significant (IEEE)
LS .... Least Squares [*Mathematical statistics*]
L/S .... Lecithin/Sphingomyelin [*Ratio*] [*Clinical chemistry*]
LS .... Lecithin Supplement (MELL)
LS .... Lectori Salutem [*Latin*]
LS .... Left Sacrum [*Medicine*] (KSC)
LS .... Left Safety [*Football*] (DICI)
LS .... Left Shift
LS .... Left Side
LS .... Left Sign (IAA)
LS .... Left Socialists (SAUO)
LS .... Legally Separated (MAE)
LS .... Legal Scroll
LS .... Le Gros Scouts [*British military*] (DMA)
LS .... Leichtenstern's Sign [*Medicine*] (MELL)
LS .... Leiomyosarcoma [*Medicine*]
LS .... Length of Stroke
LS .... Lepidopterists' Society
LS .... Lesotho [*ANSI two-letter standard code*] (CNC)
LS .... Less
LS .... Lessing Society (EA)
LS .... Letterer-Siwe [*Disease*] [*Medicine*] (DB)
LS .... Letter Service
ls .... Letter Signed [*Handwritten signature*] (WDMC)
LS .... Letter Signed [*Manuscript descriptions*]
LS .... Letter Stock
LS .... Leukemia Society (SAUO)
LS .... Leukemia Society of America
LS .... Level Setter
LS .... Level Switch
LS .... Liaison Squadron (SAUO)
LS .... Libman-Sacks [*Disease*] [*Medicine*] (DB)
LS .... Library Science
LS .... Library Search
LS .... Library Services
LS .... Licensed Surveyor [*British*] (ADA)
LS .... Licentiate in Science
LS .... Licentiate in Surgery
LS .... Lichen Sclerosis [*Medicine*] (MELL)
LS .... Lichen Simplex [*Medicine*] (MELL)
LS .... Lifesaving Service [*Coast Guard*]
LS .... Life Science (NASA)
LS .... Life Sciences (SAUO)
LS .... Life Sciences Division (SAUO)
LS .... Life Support (AAG)
LS .... Life System (MCD)
LS .... Lighthouse Service [*Coast Guard*]
LS .... Lighting Supervisor [*Television*]
LS .... Lighting System
LS .... Lightning Sensor [*Aviation*]
ls .... Light-Second
LS .... Light Shield (SPST)
LS .... Light Ship
LS .... Light Sleep [*Medicine*] (EDAA)
LS .... Light Source
LS .... Light Sussex [*Poultry*]
LS .... Light Switch
LS .... Lignosulfonate [*Pulp and paper processing*]
LS .... Like-Sexed
LS .... Limbic System [*Brain anatomy*]
LS .... Limestone [*Petrology*] (AAG)
LS .... Liminal [*or Least*] Sensation [*Psychology*]
LS .... Liminal Sensitivity (DIPS)
LS .... Limited Smoking
LS .... Limit Switch [*Electronics*]
LS .... Line Scan (DEN)
LS .... Line-Sequential (IAA)
LS .... Line Speed
L/S .... Lines per Second (WDAA)
LS .... Line Stretcher
LS .... Line Switch [*Telecommunications*] (TEL)
LS .... Linker Scanning [*Mutants*] [*Genetics*]
LS .... Linksozialisten [*Left Socialists*] [*Austria*] [*Political party*] (PPE)
LS .... Link State (ACRL)
LS .... Link Status (AGLO)
LS .... Linnean Society [*Australia*]
LS .... Liquid Scintillation [*Chemical analysis*]
LS .... Liquid Sensor (AAG)
LS .... Listed Securities
LS .... Listing Salesperson [*Real estate*] (REAL)
ls .... Listing Salesperson [*Real estate*] (REAL)
LS .... List of Specifications (NATG)
LS .... List Total [*Banking*]
LS .... Literature Search
l/s .... Liters per Second [*SI symbol*]
LS .... Little Stock (MHDW)
LS .... Liver and Spleen [*Medicine*]
LS .... Liver Scan [*Medicine*] (MELL)
LS .... Livestock (DCTA)
LS .... Lladro Society (EA)
LS .... Loading Splice [*Telecommunications*] (TEL)
LS .... Load Sensing
L/S .... Load System (MCD)
LS .... Loamy Sand [*Soil biology*] [*Soil texture*] (QSUL)
LS .... Lobe Switching (IAA)
LS .... Local Single-Layer [*Open Systems Interconnection*] (ODAA)
LS .... Local Store
LS .... Local Sunset
LS .... Local Sunset Time (WDMC)
LS .... Loca Sancta [*A publication*] (BJA)
LS .... Locked Shut (NRCH)
LS .... Lockheed Standards
LS .... Locus Sepulchri [*Place of the Sepulchre*] [*Latin*]
LS .... Locus Sigilli [*Place of the Seal*] [*Legal term*] [*Latin*]
LS .... Logical Sum [*Computer science*]
LS .... Logic Synthesis (VLIE)
LS .... Logistical Support [*Army*]
LS .... Logistics Squadron [*Military*]
LS .... Logistics Summary (SAUO)
LS .... Log-Skidder [*Tires*] (DICI)
LS .... London Scottish [*Army regiment*]
LS .... London Scottish Regiment (SAUO)
LS .... [*The*] London Sinfonietta
LS .... London Society (SAUO)
LS .... Long and Short [*Telegraphy*] (PCTE)
Ls .... Longear Sunfish [*Ichthyology*]

LS .... Longitudinal Section
LS .... Longitudinal Staggering (IAA)
LS .... Long Service (ADA)
LS .... Long Shot [*A photograph or motion picture sequence taken from a distance*]
LS .... Long Sight (WDAA)
LS .... Long Sleep [*Medicine*] (EDAA)
LS .... Long Sleeves [*Dressmaking*]
LS .... Long Stub (VLIE)
LS .... Longview Switching [*Federal Railroad Administration identification code*]
LS .... Loose Shot
LS .... Lost Seska [*Defunct*] (EA)
LS .... Loudspeaker
LS .... Loudspeaker System [*Automotive engineering*]
LS .... Lovat Scouts [*British military*] (DMA)
LS .... Lower Sprocket (ECII)
LS .... Lower Strength [*Medicine*] (EDAA)
LS .... Lower Structure
LS .... Low-Power Schottky [*Electronics*]
LS .... Low Salt [*Dietetics*]
LS .... Low Secondary (IAA)
LS .... Low Similarity [*Psychology*]
LS .... Low-Sodium Diet (DMAA)
LS .... Low-Speed
LS .... Low Spin (EDCT)
LS .... Luciani Syndrome [*Medicine*] [*Syndromes*] (QSUL)
LS .... Lumbar Spine [*Medicine*] (DMAA)
L/S .... Lumbosacral [*Medicine*] (BCRP)
LS .... Lumbosacral [*Medicine*]
LS .... Lumbosacral Spine [*Medicine*] (IDYL)
LS .... Lump Sum
LS .... Lunar Surface (KSC)
LS .... Lung Sounds [*Medicine*]
LS .... Luteinization Stimulator [*Endocrinology*]
LS .... Lute Society [*Harrow, England*] (EAIO)
LS .... Luxury Sport [*In automobile model name "Cordia LS"*]
LS .... Lymphosarcoma [*Medicine*]
LS .... Marco Island Airways [*ICAO designator*] (AD)
LS .... Sandia Laboratories (SAUO)
ls--- .... South Atlantic Ocean [*MARC geographic area code*] [*Library of Congress*] (LCCP)
LS .... Sudanese Pound (IMH)
LS .... Summer [*Vessel load line mark*]
LS2 .... Lesser Sulphur-Crested Cockatoo [*Bird*]
LS3 .... Life Saving, Life Sustaining, Life Supporting (SAUS)
LS3 .... London Specialist Software Systems (NITA)
LSA .... Labor Services Agency (AABC)
LSA .... Labor Surplus Area
LSA .... Labour Services Association (SAUO)
LSA .... Labour Staff Association [*National Coal Board*] [*British*]
LSA .... Lakota Student Alliance [*Association*] (EA)
LSA .... Lamesa, TX [*Location identifier*] [*FAA*] (FAAL)
LSA .... Landing Ship, Assault [*Navy*] [*British*]
LSA .... Landing Supply Activity
LSA .... Landmark Savings Association (EFIS)
LSA .... Land Service Assistant [*Ministry of Agriculture, Fisheries, and Food*] [*British*]
LSA .... Land Settlement Association [*British*]
LSA .... Language Sampling and Analysis [*Educational test*]
LSA .... Large Science Aperture [*Spectrometer*]
LSA .... Large Southern Array (SAUS)
LSA .... Large Space Antenna (SSD)
LSA .... Large Spherical Array
LSA .... Large Submillimeter Array
LSA .... Laser Seeker Assembly (ACAE)
LSA .... LASER-Supported Absorption (PDAA)
LSA .... Lateral Spherical Aberration
LSA .... Later Stone Age (SAUO)
LSA .... Late Stone Age
LSA .... Launcher Structure Assembly (ACAE)
LSA .... Launch Services Agreement (MCD)
LSA .... Law and Society Association (EA)
LSA .... Law Services Association [*British*] (DBA)
LSA .... Layton School of Art [*Wisconsin*]
LSA .... Leading Stores Accountant [*British military*] (DMA)
LSA .... Leading Supply Assistant (WDAA)
LSA .... Lead Spring Assembly
LSA .... League for Socialist Action [*Canada*]
LSA .... Leaving Scene of an Accident [*Traffic offense charge*]
LSA .... Left Sacroanterior [*A fetal position, the breech position*] [*Obstetrics*]
LSA .... Left Subclavian Artery [*Anatomy*] (AAMN)
LSA .... Leisure Studies Association [*British*]
LSA .... Leominster Sportsmen's Association [*Massachusetts and New Hampshire*] (EARSL)
LSA .... Leukemia Society of America (EA)
LSA .... Leukocyte Specific Activity (DB)
LSA .... Level Shift Amplifier
LSA .... Lhasa [*Tibet*] [*Seismograph station code, US Geological Survey*] (SEIS)
LSA .... Library Science Abstracts [*A publication*]
LSA .... Library Service Association (SAUO)
LSA .... Library Services Act [*1956*]
LSA .... Licentiate in Agricultural Science
LSA .... Licentiate of Science in Agriculture (SAUO)
LSA .... Licentiate of the Society of Apothecaries [*British*]
LSA .... Lichen Sclerosis et Atrophicus [*Dermatology*]
LSA .... Life Saving Appliance [*or Apparatus*] (DS)
LSA .... Life Style Analysis [*Psychology*]
LSA .... Lifetime Savings Account
LSA .... Lighthouse Society of America (SAUO)
LSA .... Light Source Assembly (ACAE)
LSA .... Light Strike Aircraft [*Military*] (PDAA)
LSA .... Limbless Soldiers Association (SAUO)
LSA .... Limited Space-Charge Accumulation [*Electronics*]
LSA .... Linea Aerea Nacional (Lansa) [*Dominican Republic*] [*ICAO designator*] (FAAC)
LSA .... Linear Servo Actuator
LSA .... Line Sensing Amplifier (IAA)
LSA .... Line Sharing Adapter (SAUO)
LSA .... Line-Sharing Adapter
LSA .... Line Sharing Adaptor (NITA)
LSA .... Linguistic Society of America (EA)
LSA .... Link State Algorithm (SAUO)
LSA .... Lipid-Bound Sialic Acid [*Biochemistry*] (DAVI)
LSA .... Liquid Scintillation Analyzer [*Chemistry*]
LSA .... Liquor Stores Association (SAUO)
LSA .... List of Sections Affected (AAGC)
LSA .... Lithuanian Scouts Association (EA)
LSA .... Lithuanian Society of America (SAUO)
LSA .... Lithuanian Students Association (EA)
LSA .... Little Sisters of the Assumption [*See also PSA*] [*France*] (EAIO)
LSA .... Livestock Agent
LSA .... Lobor Surplus Area (SAUO)
LSA .... Local Security Authority [*Computer science*] (MWOL)
LSA .... Local Supervising Authority
LSA .... Locksmith Security Association (EA)
LSA .... Logarithmic Sense Amplifier (VLIE)
LSA .... Logic Sequential Access [*Computer science*] (VLIE)
LSA .... Logic State Analyzer (IAA)
LSA .... Logistical Staging Area [*Emergency Management*] (EMA)
LSA .... Logistics Supply Area
LSA .... Logistics Supportability Analysis (SAUO)
LSA .... Logistics Support Analysis
LSA .... Logistics Systems Applications (SAUO)
LSA .... Logistic Support Agreement [*Military*] (CAAL)
LSA .... Logistic Support Aircraft (MCD)
LSA .... Logistic Support Analysis
LSA .... Logistic Support Area (NVT)
LSA .... Logistic Sustainability Analysis [*Environmental science*] (COE)
LSA .... Logistic System Analysis [*Navy*]
LSA .... London Salvage Association (SAUO)
LSA .... London School of Accountancy (SAUO)
LSA .... Longitudinal Spherical Aberration
LSA .... Loss of Situation Awareness (SAUS)
LSA .... Losuia [*Papua New Guinea*] [*Airport symbol*] (OAG)
LSA .... Lotus Solution Architecture (SAUS)
LSA .... Loudspeaker Amplifier (DWSG)
LSA .... Louisiana Statutes, Annotated [*A publication*] (DLA)
LSA .... Low-Cost Solar Array (IEEE)
LSA .... Lowe's Syndrome Association (EA)
LSA .... Low Sidelobe Antenna (ACAE)
LSA .... Low Specific Activity [*Radioisotope*]
LSA .... Low-Speed Adapter (IAA)
LSA .... Lubricant, Small Arms [*Weaponry*] [*Military*] (VNW)
LSA .... Lumbosacral Agenesis [*Medicine*] (MELL)
LSA .... Luntz, Suleiman and Associates (IID)
LSA .... Lute Society of America (EA)
LSa .... Lymphosarcoma [*Medicine*]
LSA .... University of Arizona, Graduate Library School, Tucson, AZ [*OCLC symbol*] (OCLC)
LSAA .... Library Services Authority Act (NITA)
LSAA .... Linen Supply Association of America [*Later, TRSA*] (EA)
LSAA .... Low Sidelobe Antenna Array (ACAE)
LSAAP .... Lone Star Army Ammunition Plant (AABC)
LSAB .... Learning Systems and Access Branch [*Education*] (AIE)
LSAB .... London Society of Air Britain (SAUO)
LSAC .... Laboratory Studies in Atmospheric Chemistry
LSAC .... Labor Sector Advisory Committee [*Terminated, 1980*] (EGAO)
LSAC .... Latvian Society of Artists in Canada (EAIO)
LSAC .... Law School Admission Council (EDAC)
LSAC .... London Sessions Appeal Committee (SAUO)
LSAC .... London Small Arms Co. [*Military*]
LSAC .... London Small Arms Company (SAUO)
LSAC .... Low-Pressure Suction Air Conveyor (PDAA)
LSAC .... Low-Speed Access to a Computer (PDAA)
LSACECC .... Lutheran South-East Asia Christian Education Curriculum Committee (SAUO)
LSAC/LSAS ... Law School Admission Council/Law School Admission Services (EA)
LSACN .... Logistic Support Analysis Control Number (MCD)
LSAD .... Laboratory for the Study of Anxiety Disorders [*University of Texas at Austin*] (RCD)
LSAD .... Launch Safe-and-Arm Device
LSAG .... Geneve [*Switzerland*] [*ICAO location identifier*] (ICLI)
LSAH .... Launch Site Accommodations Handbook [*NASA*] (NASA)
lsai- .... Ascension Island [*MARC geographic area code*] [*Library of Congress*] (LCCP)

LSA/L........ Language. Journal of the Linguistic Society of America. Baltimore (SAUO)
LSAL......... Left Salivary [*Gland*]
L Salic...... Salic Law [*A publication*] (DLA)
LSA/LSAR... Logistic Support Analysis/Logistic Support Analysis Record [*Army*] (RDA)
LSALT....... Lowest Safe Altitude [*Aviation*] (DA)
LSAM........ Launcher System Angles Matched [*Navy*] (CAAL)
LSAM........ Logistics Support Alternative [*or Analysis*] Model (MCD)
LSAM........ Lumped Shell Analysis Method
LSA mode... Limited Space Charge Accumulation Mode [*Telecommunications*] (NITA)
LSAMP...... Louis Stokes Alliances for Minority Participation [*National Science Foundation*] (RCD)
LSANA....... Leukocyte-Specific Antinuclear Antibody [*Hematology*] (DMAA)
LS & A...... Lichen Sclerosus et Atrophicus [*Medicine*] (EDAA)
LS & GCM... Long Service and Good Conduct Medal [*Military decoration*] [*British*]
LS&I......... Lake Superior & Ishpeming Railroad Co. (SAUO)
LS & MS.... Lake Shore & Michigan Southern Railway
LS and MS... Less Sleep and More Speed [*Hobo slang*]
LS&T........ Laser Science and Technology [*Lawrence Livermore National Laboratory*] (RCD)
LSANSW.... Limbless Soldiers' Association of New South Wales [*Australia*]
LSANSW.... Liquor Stores Association of New South Wales [*Australia*]
LSAO........ Line Station Assembly Order (MCD)
LSAO........ Logistics Systems Analysis Office (ACAE)
LSAP........ Laboratory Space Allocation Plan (MCD)
LSAP........ Launch Sequence Applications Program (MCD)
LSAP........ Letzeburger Sozialistesch Arbechter Partei [*Socialist Workers' Party of Luxembourg*] [*Political party*] (PPE)
LSAP........ Life Space Analysis Profile [*Test*] (TMMY)
LSAP........ Linear Systems Analysis Program [*Statistics*]
LSAP........ Link Layer Service Access Point
LSAP........ Local Service Access Point [*Telecommunications*] (OSI)
LSAP........ Logistics Support Analysis Plan (SAUO)
LSAP........ Logistic Support Analysis Plan [*or Program*] [*Army*]
LSAP........ Logistic Support Analysis Process [*Navy*]
LSAP........ Long Service Access Point [*Computer science*] (VLIE)
LSAPT....... Lunar Sample Analysis Planning Team [*NASA*]
LSAQ........ Limbless Soldiers' Association of Queensland [*Australia*]
LSAR........ Local Storage Address Register (IAA)
LSAR........ Logistics Support Analysis Report (SAUO)
LSAR........ Logistic Support Analysis Record (RDA)
LSAR........ Lymphosarcoma Cell [*Oncology*] (DAVI)
LSA/RCS.... Lymphosarcoma - Reticulum Cell Sarcoma [*Oncology*] (MAE)
LSARS....... West's Louisiana Revised Statutes [*A publication*] (DLA)
LSAS........ Law School Admission Services (EDAC)
LSAS........ Longitudinal Stability Augmentation System [*Aviation*] (DA)
LSASA....... Limbless Soldiers' Association of South Australia
LSAST....... Least-Squares Ambiguity Search Technique
LSAT......... Large Scale Applications Test (ACAE)
LSAT......... Law School Admission Test
LSAT......... Law School Aptitude Test (GAGS)
LSAT......... Legal Scholastic Aptitude Test (HGAA)
LSAT......... Leveling/Sharpening Aggressions Test [*Psychology*] (EDAC)
LSAT......... Logistic Shelter Air Transportable
LSAV......... Limbless Soldiers' Association of Victoria [*Australia*]
LSAV......... Liquor Stores' Association of Victoria [*Aerospace*]
LSAW........ LASER-Supported Absorption-Wave (PDAA)
LSAWA...... Liquor Stores' Association of Western Australia
LSAY........ Longitudinal Study of American Youth [*Northern Illinois University*] [*Education*]
LSAZ......... Zurich [*Switzerland*] [*ICAO location identifier*] (ICLI)
LSB.......... Bachelor of Life Science
LSB.......... Labour Supply Board [*British*]
LSB.......... Landing Ship, Bombardment
LSB.......... L&S Bearing Co. (EFIS)
LSB.......... Large-Scale Bypass [*Telecommunications*] (CIST)
LSB.......... La Sacra Bibbia (BJA)
LSB.......... Launcher Support Building
LSB.......... Launch Service Building
LSB.......... Learned Society Board (ACII)
LSB.......... Leased Spacecraft Bus (SSD)
LSB.......... Least Significant BIT [*or Byte*] [*Data compaction*]
LSB.......... Left Sternal Border
LSB.......... Lensibavia [*Former USSR*] [*FAA designator*] (FAAC)
LSB.......... Library of Standard Biographies [*A publication*]
LSB.......... Life Safety Box
LSB.......... Lifestyle Beverage Corp. [*Vancouver Stock Exchange symbol*]
LSB.......... Line Segment Block [*Computer science*]
LSB.......... Linux Standard Base (SAUS)
LSB.......... List of Successful Bidders [*DoD*]
LSB.......... Lithuanian Boy Scouts [*An association*] (EA)
LSB.......... Logistics Sustaining Base [*Military*] (RDA)
LSB.......... Logistic Support Base (NVT)
LSB.......... London School Board
LSB.......... Longitudinal Studies Branch [*Department of Education*] (GFGA)
LSB.......... Long Span Bridge (SAUS)
LSB.......... Long Spike Burst [*Medicine*] (EDAA)
LSB.......... Lordsburg, NM [*Location identifier*] [*FAA*] (FAAL)
LSB.......... Louisiana School Board (SAUO)
LSB.......... Lower Sideband [*Data transmission*]
LSB.......... Low Silhouette Blade [*Aircraft*]
LSB.......... Low-Speed Breaker Relay (IEEE)
LSB.......... Low-Speed Buffer (CET)
LSB.......... Low-Surface-Brightness [*Galaxies - astronomy*]
LSB.......... LSB Industries [*NYSE symbol*] (TTSB)
LSB.......... LSB Industries, Inc. [*NYSE symbol*] (SAG)
LSB.......... Lucas-Sumitomo Brakes [*Auto industry supplier*]
LSB.......... Lunar Surface Base [*NASA*] (KSC)
LSB.......... Southern University, Library, Baton Rouge, LA [*OCLC symbol*] (OCLC)
LSBA........ LaSalle and Bureau County Railroad Company (SAUO)
LSBA........ Leading Sick Bay Attendant [*Navy*] [*British*]
LSBA........ Louisiana School Boards Association (SAUO)
LSBC........ Large Scale Biology Corp. [*NASDAQ symbol*]
LSBC........ [*The*] La Salle & Bureau County Railroad Co. [*AAR code*]
LSB Fn...... LSB Financial Corp. [*Associated Press*] (SAG)
LSB Fncl.... LSB Financial Corp. [*Associated Press*] (SAG)
LSBGA....... Last Sortie Before Ground Alert (SAUO)
LSBI......... LSB Financial [*NASDAQ symbol*] (TTSB)
LSBI......... LSB Financial Corp. [*NASDAQ symbol*] (SAG)
LSB Ind..... LSB Industries, Inc. [*Associated Press*] (SAG)
LS-BMD..... Lumbar Spine Bone Mineral Density [*Medicine*] (EDAA)
LSB NC..... LSB Bancshares, Inc. of North Carolina [*Associated Press*] (SAG)
LSBPHF..... Library Service to the Blind and Physically Handicapped Forum [*Association of Specialized and Cooperative Library Agencies*]
LSBPrC...... LSB Ind $3.25 Cv Exch Pfd [*NYSE symbol*] (TTSB)
LS BPS...... Laparoscopic Bilateral Partial Salpingectomies [*Gynecology*] (DAVI)
LSBR........ Laboratory for Social and Behavioral Research [*Florida International University*] (RCD)
LSBR........ Laboratory of Structural Biology Research [*National Institute of Arthritis and Musculoskeletal and Skin Diseases*] (RCD)
LSBR........ Large Seed-Blanket Reactor
LSBR........ Liquid Strand Burning Rate (MCD)
LSBRT....... Library Service to the Blind Round Table
lsbv-.......... Bouvet Island [*MARC geographic area code*] [*Library of Congress*] (LCCP)
LSBX........ Lawrence Savings Bank [*NASDAQ symbol*] (SAG)
LSBX........ LSB Corp. [*NASDAQ symbol*]
LSBY........ Least Significant Byte [*Data compaction*] [*Computer science*]
LSBZ......... Chicago Rail Link [*Intermodal trailer symbol*]
LSC.......... Laboratory Support Center (SAUO)
LSC.......... Labor Service Center (SAUO)
LSC.......... Labor Socialist Committee [*Australia*]
LSC.......... Labor Studies Center [*AFL-CIO*]
LSC.......... Labor Supervision Company (SAUO)
LSC.......... Lake Survey Center [*National Oceanic and Atmospheric Administration*]
LSC.......... Landing Ship Carrier [*British military*] (DMA)
LSC.......... Language and Society Centre [*Monash University*] [*Australia*]
LSC.......... Languages Services Centre [*South Australia*]
LSC.......... Large-Scale Computer
LSC.......... Large Single Copy Region [*Of a chromosome*] [*Genetics*]
LSC.......... Large Sized Combatant (ACAE)
LSC.......... Large Solar Concentrator (SSD)
LSC.......... Large Submetacentric Chromosome [*Medicine*]
LSC.......... Las Cruces [*Diocesan abbreviation*] [*New Mexico*] (TOCD)
LSC.......... La Serena [*Chile*] [*Airport symbol*] (AD)
LSC.......... LASER Spectral Control
LSC.......... LASER-Supported Combustion (MCD)
LSC.......... Laser Systems Center (SAUO)
LSC.......... Last Significant Character (ECII)
LSC.......... Late Systolic Click [*Cardiology*] (DAVI)
LSC.......... Latrobe Steel Company (SAUO)
LSC.......... Launch Sequence Control
L/SC......... Launch/Storage Container
L Sc.......... Laureate of Science
LSC.......... Law of the Sea Conference [*United Nations*]
LSC.......... Learning Skills Center Reading and Study Skills Program [*Cornell University*] [*Research center*] (RCD)
LSC.......... Learning Station.com
LSC.......... Least Significant Character (IEEE)
LSC.......... Least Square Center (IAA)
LSC.......... Least Squares Circle [*Manufacturing term*]
LSC.......... Least-Squares Collocation [*Mathematics*]
LSC.......... Left-Sided Colon Cancer [*Oncology*]
LSC.......... Left Stage Center [*A stage direction*]
LSC.......... Legal Services Corp. [*Government agency*]
LSC.......... Legal Services for Children (EA)
LSC.......... Legislative Service Center [*Washington State Legislature*] [*Information service or system*] (IID)
LSC.......... Lens Sign Convention
LSC.......... Liberian Shipowners Council (EA)
LSC.......... Library Service Center (SAUO)
LSC.......... Library Services Center, Midwestern Regional Library System [*UTLAS symbol*]
LSC.......... Library Services Center of Missouri [*Library network*]
LSc.......... Licentiate in Science (DD)
LSC.......... Lichen Simplex Chronicus (DB)
LSC.......... Lid, Sclera, and Conjunctiva [*Opthalmology*] (DAVI)
LSC.......... Life Safety Code (IDYL)
LSC.......... Life Sciences Center (SAUO)
LSC.......... Life Support Cost (SAUO)
LSC.......... Limit Signaling Comparator
LSC.......... Lincoln Sesquicentennial Committee [*Terminated, 1960*] [*Government agency*]
LSC.......... Linear Sequential Circuit
LSC.......... Linear-Shaped Charge

LSC .... Linear Slope Controlled (PDAA)
LSC .... Liquid Scintillation Cocktail [*Analytical chemistry*]
LSC .... Liquid Scintillation Counter [*or Counting*]
LSC .... Liquid Smoke Condensate
LSC .... Liquid Solid Chromatography
LSC .... Liquids Solids Contact
LSC .... Little Sisters of Carmel
LSC .... Littleton System Center (ACAE)
LSC .... LOAD [*Low Altitude Defense*] Simulation Center
LSC .... Load Standardization Crew (MCD)
LSC .... Lobbyist Systems Corp. [*Information service or system*] (IID)
LSc .... Local Scleroderma [*Medicine*] (EDAA)
LSC .... Local Supercluster [*Cosmology*]
LSC .... Local Switching Centre [*Telecommunications*] (NITA)
LSC .... Loco Sub Citato [*In the Place Cited Below*] [*Latin*] (ROG)
LSC .... Loco Supra Citato [*In the Place Cited Above*] [*Latin*]
LSC .... Logistical Support Center [*Army*]
LSC .... Logistics Support Costs (SAUO)
LSC .... Logistic Support Cadre (MCD)
LSC .... Logistic Support Command (SAUO)
LSC .... Logistic Support Cost (ACAE)
LSC .... London Salvage Corps
Lsc .... London, Sion College (SAUO)
LSC .... London Survey Committee (SAUO)
LSC .... Lone Star Conference (PSS)
LSC .... Long Single Cone [*Medicine*] (EDAA)
LSC .... Loop Station Connector (MHDB)
LSC .... Low-Speed Concentrator
LSC .... Low-Speed Connection [*Computer science*] (GART)
LSC .... LSI Logic Corp. of Canada, Inc. [*Toronto Stock Exchange symbol*]
LSC .... Lumbosacral Canal [*Medicine*] (EDAA)
LSC .... Luminescent Solar Concentrator
LSC .... Luminescent Stamp Club [*Defunct*] (EA)
LSC .... Lump-Sum Contract
LSC .... Luxury Sport Coupe
LSC .... Shopco Laurel Centre (SAUO)
LSC .... Shopco Laurel Centre L.P. [*AMEX symbol*] (TTSB)
LSC .... Shopco Laurel Centre Ltd. [*AMEX symbol*] (SPSG)
LSC .... Southern University, Law Library, Baton Rouge, LA [*OCLC symbol*] (OCLC)
LScA .... Left Scapuloanterior [*A fetal position*] [*Obstetrics*]
LSCA .... Left Subclavian Artery [*Anatomy*] (DAVI)
LSCA .... Library Services and Construction Act [*1963*]
LSCA .... Logistics Support Cost Analysis (NASA)
LScAct .... Licentiate of Actuarial Science (SAUO)
LScAdmin .... Licence in Administration [*Canada*] (DD)
LSCC .... L and S Cartage Company [*Common carrier symbol*]
LSCC .... Lattice Semiconductor [*NASDAQ symbol*] (TTSB)
LSCC .... Lattice Semiconductor Corp. [*NASDAQ symbol*] (SAG)
LSCC .... Left Side Colon Cancer [*Medicine*] (EDAA)
LSCC .... Liberty Seated Collectors Club (EA)
LSCC .... Library of the Supreme Court of Canada (SAUO)
LScC .... Licentiate in Commercial Science (DD)
LSCC .... Line-Sequential Color Composite (IEEE)
LSCC .... Local Servicing Control Center [*Telecommunications*] (TEL)
LSCC .... London Scottish Cadet Corps [*British military*] (DMA)
LScCom .... Licentiate in Commercial Science
LScComm .... Licentiate in Commercial Science (DD)
LScCompt .... Licencie en Sciences Comptables [*Licentiate of Accounting*] (DD)
L Sc D .... Doctor of the Science of Law
LSCD .... Large Screen Color Display (ACAE)
LSCD .... Leading Seaman Clearance Diver
LSCE .... Launch Sequence and Control Equipment
LSCE .... Least Square Complex Exponential [*Mathematics*]
LScEco .... Licence in Economics [*Canada*] (DD)
LSc(Econ) .... Licence in Science (Economics) [*British*] (DI)
LSCF .... Least Squares Curve Fitting [*Statistics*] (ODA)
LSCG .... Law School Computer Group [*Defunct*] (EA)
LSCI .... Large-Scale Compound Integration
LSCI .... Lymphosarcoma Cell Leukemia [*Medicine*] (DMAA)
LSCL .... Limit Switch Closed [*Electronics*] (IAA)
LSCL .... Lower Surface Center Line
LSCL .... Lymphosarcome Cell Leukemia [*Medicine*] (EDAA)
LSCM .... LASER-Scan Confocal Microscope
LSCM .... LASER Scanning Confocal Microscopy
LSCM .... Logistic Support Coordination Meeting [*Military*] (MCD)
LSCo .... Labor Service Company (SAUO)
LSCO .... Lanthanum Strontium Copper Oxide [*Inorganic chemistry*]
LSCO .... Lesco, Inc. [*NASDAQ symbol*] (SAG)
LScO .... Licence in the Science of Optometry [*Canada*] (DD)
LScO .... Licentiate of Optometry (SAUO)
LSCP .... Lasco Shipping Company [*Common carrier symbol*]
LSCP .... Laserscope [*NASDAQ symbol*] (SAG)
LSCP .... Launching System Control Panel (SAUS)
LScP .... Left Scapuloposterior [*A fetal position*] [*Obstetrics*]
LSCP .... Logistic Support Control Point [*Military*] (AFM)
LSCP .... Low-Speed Card Punch [*Computer science*] (AABC)
LSCP(Assoc) .... Associate of the London and Counties Society of Physiologists [*British*] (DBQ)
LScPol .... Licence en Science Politique [*French*] (CPGU)
LSCPS .... Logistics Support Concept of Pre-Operational Support (ACAE)
LSCRA .... Lower Saint Croix River Act of 1972 (COE)
LSCRC .... Lapheld Small Computer Requirements Contract (SAUO)
LScRel .... Licentiate in Religion (DD)
LSCRRC .... Law Students Civil Rights Research Council (EA)
LSCRS .... Law School Candidate Referral Service (SAUO)
LSCS .... Lower Segment Caesarean Section [*Medicine*]
LScS .... Southern University, Scotlandville, Baton Rouge, LA [*Library symbol*] [*Library of Congress*] (LCLS)
LScS-N .... Southern University at New Orleans, New Orleans, LA [*Library symbol*] [*Library of Congress*] (LCLS)
LScSoc .... Licence in Social Science [*British*]
LSCSS .... Limited Scale Command and Control System (ACAE)
LSCT .... Lamar State College of Technology (SAUO)
LSCT .... LASER Spectral Control Technique
LSCT .... Loevinger Sentence Completion Test (EDAC)
LSCT .... Low-Speed Compound Terminal (CET)
LSCU .... Conterm Services [*Intermodal shipping container symbol*] (TVRC)
LSCU .... Local Servicing Control Unit [*Telecommunications*] (TEL)
LSCV .... Left Subclavian Vein [*Anatomy*] (DAVI)
LSCVP .... Left Subclavian Central Venous Pressure [*Medicine*] (RAWO)
LSCX .... Laclede Steel [*Private rail car owner code*]
LSCZ .... Liquid Sugar [*Federal Railroad Administration identification code*]
LSD .... Amphibious Ship, Dock
LSD .... d-Lysergic acid Diethylamine (SAUS)
LSD .... Dock Landing Ship (SAUO)
LSD .... Doctor of Library Science
LSD .... Doctor of Life Science
LSD .... Laboratory Services Division (SAUO)
LSD .... Landing Ship Deck
LSD .... Landing Ship, Dock [*Navy symbol*]
LSD .... Landing-Site Determination [*NASA*] (KSC)
LSD .... Landing, Storage, Delivery [*Business term*]
LSD .... Land Surface Datum (SAUO)
LSD .... Language for Systems Development
LSD .... Large Scale Display (ACAE)
LSD .... Large-Scale Dynamics (SAUS)
LSD .... Large Screen Display
LSD .... Large Shallow-Draught [*Bulk carrier*] (PDAA)
LSD .... Large Steel Desk [*Position given to ex-astronauts*]
LSD .... Laryngeal Sound Discrimination [*Medicine*] (DMAA)
LSD .... LASER-Selective Demagnetization [*Analytical technique*]
LSD .... LASER Signal Device
LSD .... LASER-Supported Detonation Waves (MCD)
LSD .... Lashed Secured Dunnage (RIMS)
LSD .... Last Safe Date [*Marine insurance*] (DS)
LSD .... Latching Semiconductor Diode
LSD .... Latest Start Date
LSD .... Launch Support Division [*NASA*] (KSC)
LSD .... Launch Systems Data
LSD .... Law Student Division [*American Bar Association*] (BARN)
LSD .... Leadless Sealed Device (PDAA)
LSD .... Lead Sulfide Detection
LSD .... League for Spiritual Discovery (WDAA)
LSD .... League of Safe Drivers [*British*] (BI)
LSD .... Leased (WGA)
LSD .... Least Separation Distance (MUSM)
LSD .... Least Significant Decade (IAA)
LSD .... Least Significant Difference [*Statistics*]
LSD .... Least Significant Digit [*Data compaction*] (MUGU)
LSD .... Legal Sub-division (SAUO)
LSD .... Lesson Specification Document (MCD)
LSD .... Level Sensor Demonstration
LSD .... Lexington, KY [*Location identifier*] [*FAA*] (FAAL)
Lsd .... Librae, Solidi, Denarii [*Shillings and Pence*] [*British*] (WA)
LSD .... Library Service to the Disadvantaged Committee
LSD .... Life, Sport, and Drama [*A publication*] [*British*]
LSD .... Life-Sustaining Device (MELL)
LSD .... Lightermen, Stevedores, and Dockers
LSD .... Light-Sensing Device (IAA)
LSD .... Lime Juice, Scotch, Drambuie [*A cocktail*] (IIA)
LSD .... Limited Saturation Device (PDAA)
LSD .... Limited-Slip Differential [*Automotive engineering*]
LSD .... Limited Space-Charge Drift [*Electronics*] (IAA)
LSD .... Limitswitch Down [*Electronics*] (IAA)
LSD .... Line-Sharing Device
LSD .... Line Signal Detector
LSD .... Linkage System Diagnostic (IAA)
LSD .... Lipid Storage Disease (MELL)
LSD .... Local Spin Density [*Physics*]
LSD .... Logarithmic Series Distribution [*Statistics*]
LSD .... Logistics Systems Division [*Air Force*]
LSD .... Log-Slope Difference [*Statistics*]
LSD .... Lomir Shoyn Davenen (BJA)
LSD .... Long Side
LSD .... Long, Slow Distance [*Training method for runners*]
LSD .... Lowest Significant Dose [*Toxicology*]
LSD .... Low Salt Diet (MELL)
LSD .... Low-Sodium Diet (DMAA)
LSD .... Low-Speed Data
LSD .... Low-Sulfur Diesel Fuel [*Petroleum marketing*]
LSD .... Lump-Sum Distribution [*Banking*]
LSD .... Lunar Surface Drill [*Aerospace*]
LSD .... Lysergic Acid Diethylamide [*or Lysergsaeure Diethylamid*] [*Hallucinogenic drug*]
LSD .... Lysergide (LDT)
LSD-25 .... Lysergic Acid Diethylamide (STED)
LSDA .... Licentiate of the Speech and Drama Association (ADA)

LSDA .... Louisiana Soft Drink Association (SRA)
LSDAR ...... Local Service Designated Agency Representative [*Communications term*] (DCT)
LSDAS....... Law School Data Assembly Service (GAGS)
LSDDP ...... Library Service to Developmentally Disabled Persons [*ASCLA*] (AL)
LSDF .... Large Sodium Disposal Facility [*Nuclear energy*] (NRCH)
LSDF .... Library Service to the Deaf Forum [*Association of Specialized and Cooperative Library Agencies*]
LSDG .... Latitudinal Species-Diversity Gradient [*Biodiversity*]
LSDH .... Ligue Suisse des Droits de l'Homme [*Switzerland*]
LSD/H/M/T... Landing Ship, Dock/Heavy/Medium/Tank (MILB)
LSDIS .... Light & Special Division Interim Sensor (SAUS)
LSDM........ Lagrangian Stochastic Dispersion Model [*Marine science*] (OSRA)
LSDM........ Logical Systems Design Methodology (NITA)
LSDP .... Landsat Signature Development Program (SAUO)
LSDP .... Lietuvos Socialdemokratu Partija [*Lithuanian Social Democratic Party*] [*Political party*] (PPE)
LSDP .... Lithuanian Social Democratic Party (SAUO)
LSDP .... Lump-Sum Death Payment
LSDR .... Local Store Data Register
LSDRM...... Logistic Support Data Responsibility Matrix (MCD)
LSDS .... Large-Scale Dynamical System (PDAA)
LSDS .... Large Screen Display System
LSDS .... Low-Speed Data Service [*RCA Global Communications, Inc.*] [*Piscataway, NJ*] [*Telecommunications*] (TSSD)
LSDS .... Low-Speed Digital System
LSDSP....... Latvijas Socialdemokratiska Stradnieku Partija [*Lativian Social Democratic Workers' Party*] [*Political party*] (EAIO)
LSDT .... Local Sidereal Time (MSA)
LSDU .... Link Layer Service Data Unit
LSDV .... Link Segment Delay Value (SAUS)
LS/DW....... Life Safety/Disaster Warning [*Environmental science*] (COE)
LSE .... Laboratory Support Equipment (SSD)
LSE .... La Crosse [*Wisconsin*]/Winona [*Minnesota*] [*Airport symbol*] (OAG)
LSE .... Landing Ship, Emergency Repair
LSE .... Landing Signal Enlisted [*Military*]
LSE .... Land Surface Experiment (SAUO)
LSE .... Language-Sensitive Editor [*Computer science*] (CIST)
LSE .... Large-Scale Equipment (MCD)
LSE .... Laser Systems & Electronics, Inc. (SAUO)
LSE .... Latex Sphere Equivalent (AAEL)
LSE .... Lattice Screen Editor [*Program editor*]
LSE .... Launcher Servo Electronics (ACAE)
LSE .... Launch Sequencer Equipment [*NASA*]
LSE .... Launch Station Equipment
LSE .... Launch Support Equipment [*NASA*] (AAG)
LSE .... Laurence, Scott & Electromotors Ltd. (SAUO)
LSE .... Lease (ROG)
Lse........... Lease (TBD)
LSE .... Least Squares Estimator [*Statistics*]
LSE .... Left Second Entrance [*Theater*]
LSE .... Left Sternal Edge [*Cardiology*]
LSE .... Legal Services for the Elderly (EA)
lse .... Licensee [*MARC relator code*] [*Library of Congress*] (LCCP)
LSE .... Life Science Experiment (MUGU)
LSE .... Life Support Equipment (KSC)
LSE .... Life Support Evaluator (SAA)
LSE .... Limited Signed Edition (ADA)
LSE .... Lincoln Space Experiment (CCCA)
LSE .... Linkage Stack Entry [*Computer science*] (CIST)
LSE .... Liquid-Solid Extraction [*Chemistry*]
LSE .... Live Sheep Export (SAUO)
LSE .... Living Skin Equivalent [*Synthetic organ*]
LSE .... Local Security Environment (SAUS)
LSE .... Local Services Environment (SAUO)
LSE .... Local Side Effects [*Pharmacology*] (DAVI)
LSE .... Local Single-Layer Embedded [*Open Systems Interconnection*] (ODAA)
LSE .... Local Subscriber Environment (SAUS)
LSE .... Local System Environment [*Open Systems Interconnection*] (ODAA)
LSE .... Logistics Support Element
LSE .... Logistics Support Equipment [*Military*] (MCD)
LSE .... London School of Economics
LSE .... London School of English (SAUO)
LSE .... London Stock Exchange
LSE .... Longitudinal-Section Electric (IEEE)
LSE .... Loose
lse .... Loose
LSE .... Louisiana Sugar Exchange (EA)
LSE .... Lower Sternal Edge [*Cardiology*]
LSE .... Low Self-Esteem
LSE .... Low-Set Ear (MELL)
LSE .... Low-Speed Encoder (IAA)
LSE .... Low-Styrene Emission
LSE .... Low Surface Energy [*Adhesives*]
LSE .... Low Surface Energy [*Plastics*]
LSE .... Lunar Support Equipment [*Aerospace*] (IAA)
LSE .... Lunar Surface Experiment [*NASA*]
LSE .... Luxembourg Stock Exchange
LSE .... Luxury Sport Euro [*Automobile model designation*] [*General Motors Corp. - Cadillac*]
LSE .... MERANT PLC [*London Stock Exchange symbol*]
LSE .... Queen's Bench Library [*Alberta*] [*UTLAS symbol*]
LSEACN ..... Life Sciences and Environmental Risk Analysis Directorate [*Oak Ridge National Laboratory*] (IID)
LSEAD....... Lethal Sead (ACAE)
LSE&PS..... London School of Economics and Political Science (SAUO)
LSE/BJS..... British Journal of Sociology. Published quarterly for the London School of Economics and Political Sience. London (SAUS)
LSEC......... Australian Company Secretary's Practice Manual [*A publication*]
LSEC......... Life-Cycle Software Engineering Center [*Army*]
l/sec .... Liters per Second [*Respiration*] [*Medicine*] (DAVI)
LSECS .... Life Support and Environmental Control System (IEEE)
LsEd .... Leasing Edge Corp. [*Associated Press*] (SAG)
LSEED....... Launch Support Equipment - Engineering Division [*NASA*] (KSC)
LSEG .... Livestock Export Group (SAUO)
LSEG .... Low Styrene Emission Gelcoat
LSEGR....... Linear Solenoid Exhaust Gas Recirculation [*Automotive emissions*]
LSEIF .... Lodestar Energy, Incorporated (SAUO)
LSEL......... Link Selector (VLIE)
LSEL......... London School of Economics Library (SAUO)
LSELR....... Low-Styrene-Emission Laminating Resin
LSEOS....... Lightweight Shipboard Electro-Optical Sensor (TIMI)
LSEP......... Left Somatosensory Evoked Potential (STED)
LSEP......... Legal Service for the Elderly Poor (SAUO)
LSEP......... Legal Services for the Elderly Poor [*Later, LSE*] (EA)
LSEP......... Lifetime Sports Education Project [*of Lifetime Sports Foundation*]
LSEP......... Limited System Evaluation Program (ACAE)
LSEP......... Lunar Surface Experiment Package [*NASA*]
LSE/PS ...... Population Studies. A journal of demography. London School of Economics, The Population Investigation Committee. London (SAUS)
LSEQ .... Launch Sequencer [*Navy*] (CAAL)
LSER .... Laser Corp. [*NASDAQ symbol*] (SAG)
LSER .... Linear Solvation Energy Relationship [*Physical chemistry*]
LSER .... Raron [*Switzerland*] [*ICAO location identifier*] (ICLI)
LSERA....... ERL-Duluth Financial Management Package (SAUS)
LSERB....... ERL-Duluth Personnel and Payroll (SAUS)
LSES......... Large Surface Effect Ship (PDAA)
LSES......... Life Support and Environmental System (IAA)
LSE SKDS... Loose or on Skids [*Freight*]
LSET......... Life Sciences and Environmental Technologies Directorate [*Oak Ridge National Laboratory*] (IID)
LSET......... Logistics Supportability Evaluation Team [*Military*] (AFIT)
LSEU .... La Salle Extension University (SAUO)
LSEV......... Lunar Surface Exploration Vehicle [*Aerospace*]
LSEW........ Law Society of England and Wales (SAUO)
LSEZ......... Zermatt [*Switzerland*] [*ICAO location identifier*] (ICLI)
LSF .... Fort Benning (Columbus), GA [*Location identifier*] [*FAA*] (FAAL)
LSF .... Laboratory Simulation Facility (MCD)
LSF .... Lande Splitting Factor
LSF .... Landing Ship, Fighter Direction [*British military*] (DMA)
LSF .... Language System FORTRAN [*Computer science*]
LSF .... La Souterraine [*France*] [*Seismograph station code, US Geological Survey*] (SEIS)
LSF .... Last Spring Frost (QUAC)
LSF .... Launch Support Facility [*NASA*] (KSC)
LSF .... Least Square Fit
LSF .... Lesser Sciatic Foramen [*Medicine*] (MELL)
LSF .... Lightship Screen File [*Computer science*]
LSF .... Lightweight Strike Fighter [*NATO Air Forces*]
LSF .... Limit Switch Forward [*Electronics*] (IAA)
LSF .... Line Spread Function (MCD)
LSF .... Line Switch Frame [*Telecommunications*] (TEL)
LSF .... Liquid-State Submerged Fermentation [*Biochemistry*]
LSF .... Literary Society Foundation (EA)
LSF .... Lloyd Shaw Foundation (EA)
LSF .... Load Sheet Fuel [*Aviation*] (DA)
LSF .... Local Security Force (SAUO)
LSF .... Local Selling Fare [*Travel industry*] (TRID)
LSF .... Lock Security Force (SAUO)
LSF .... Logistic Support Force [*Military*]
LSF .... Loss Factor [*Electronics*] (IAA)
LSF .... Lower Side Frequency [*Electronics*] (ECII)
LSF .... Low Saturated Fat [*Diet*] (DAVI)
LSF .... Lumped Selection Filter [*Telecommunications*] (OA)
LSF .... Lunar Scientific Facility [*NASA*] (KSC)
LSF .... Lymphocyte-Stimulating Factor [*Biochemistry*]
LSFA......... Logistic System Feasibility Analysis (AABC)
LSFAE .... Low-Speed Fuel Air Explosive
LSFC......... Langley Space Flight Center (SAUO)
LSFC......... Lennon Sisters Fan Club (EA)
LSFE......... Life Sciences Flight Experiment [*NASA*] (NASA)
LSFF......... Landing Ship, Flotilla Flagship [*Navy symbol*] [*Obsolete*]
LSFFAR ..... Low-Speed Folding-Fin Aircraft Rocket (SAUS)
LSFFAR ..... Low-Spin Folding Fin Aircraft Rocket (IEEE)
LSFIAB ...... Like Shooting Fish In A Barrel (SAUS)
lsfk-.......... Falkland Islands [*MARC geographic area code*] [*Library of Congress*] (LCCP)
LSFN .... List of Selected File Numbers (AABC)
LSFO .... Logistics Support Field Office [*Federal disaster planning*]
LSFO .... Low-Sulfur Fuel Oil
LSFR .... Large-Probe Solar Net Flux Radiometer [*NASA*]
LSFR .... Launch Side Flow Review (SAUS)
LSFR .... Local Storage Function Register
LSFS......... Lateral Separation Focus Sensor (PDAA)
LSFS......... Light Sequence Flasher System (DWSG)

LSFT .... London School of Foreign Trade (SAUO)
LSFT .... Low Steamline Flow Test (IEEE)
LSFZ .... Burlington Northern Santa Fe Railway [*Intermodal trailer symbol*]
LSG .... labial Salivary Gland [*Medicine*] (STED)
LSG .... Lake Shore Gold Corp. [*Toronto Stock Exchange symbol*] [*Canada*]
LSG .... Laminated Safety Glass [*Automotive engineering*]
LSG .... Landing Ship, Gantry
LSG .... Landing Ship, Gun [*British military*] (DMA)
LSG .... Language Structure Group [*CODASYL*]
LSG .... Large-Scale Geostrophic [*Marine science*] (OSRA)
LSG .... Lateral Superior Geniculate Artery [*Anatomy*]
LSG .... Launchable Stun Grenade [*Police and security equipment*]
LSG .... Legal Services Group
LSG .... Legislative Strategy Group [*Reagan administration*]
LSG .... Level Sensor Gradiometer
LSG .... Light Sub-machine Gun [*Police and security equipment*]
LSG .... Ligo Samseksamaj Geesperantistoj [*Richmond, Surrey, England*] (EAIO)
LSG .... Limited Subgroup (NATG)
LSG .... Little Sisters of the Gospel (France) (TOCD)
LSG .... Logistics Support Group (AAG)
LSG .... Logistic Support Group (SAUS)
LSG .... Loh's Sinfully Good Ice Cream & Cookies, Inc. [*Vancouver Stock Exchange symbol*]
LSG .... Lone Star Gas Co. (EFIS)
LSG .... Low-Stress Grinding (DICI)
LSG .... Lufthansa Service Holding AG (EFIS)
LSG .... Lunar Surface Gravimeter [*Apollo*] [*NASA*]
LSGA .... Laminators Safety Glass Association (EA)
LSGA .... Los Angeles Securities Group (SAUO)
LSGaz .... Law Society's Gazette [*A publication*] (SAFN)
LSGC .... Les Eplatures [*Switzerland*] [*ICAO location identifier*] (ICLI)
LSGC .... London and Surrey Gliding Club (SAUO)
LSGC .... Long Service and Good Conduct (ADA)
LSGD .... Lymphocyte Specific Gravity Distribution [*Medicine*]
LSGE .... Ecuvillens [*Switzerland*] [*ICAO location identifier*] (ICLI)
LSGG .... Geneve/Cointrin [*Switzerland*] [*ICAO location identifier*] (ICLI)
LSGK .... Saanen [*Switzerland*] [*ICAO location identifier*] (ICLI)
LSGL .... Lausanne/Blecherette [*Switzerland*] [*ICAO location identifier*] (ICLI)
LSG/LSU .... Landing Support Group/Logistics Support Unit (DNAB)
LSGN .... Neuchatel [*Switzerland*] [*ICAO location identifier*] (ICLI)
LSGP .... La Cote [*Switzerland*] [*ICAO location identifier*] (ICLI)
LSGP .... Large-Scale General Purpose
LSGP .... Lateral Simulated Ground Plane [*Aerodynamics*]
LSGR .... Loose Granular Snow [*Skiing condition*]
LSGS .... Left Stellate Ganglion Stimulation [*Physiology*]
LSGS .... Sion [*Switzerland*] [*ICAO location identifier*] (ICLI)
LsgSolu .... Leasing Solutions, Inc. [*Associated Press*] (SAG)
LSGT .... Gruyeres [*Switzerland*] [*ICAO location identifier*] (ICLI)
L Sgt .... Lance Sargeant (SAUO)
L/Sgt .... Lance Sergeant [*British military*] (DMA)
LSGT .... Lasergate Systems [*NASDAQ symbol*] (TTSB)
LSGT .... Lasergate Systems, Inc. [*NASDAQ symbol*] (SAG)
LSGTW .... Lasergate Sys Wrrt [*NASDAQ symbol*] (TTSB)
LSGU .... Local Spinal Glucose Utilization [*Medicine*]
LSH .... Landing Ship, Headquarters
LSH .... Landing Ship, Heavy
LSH .... LaSalle Re Holdings [*NYSE symbol*] (SG)
LSH .... Lashio [*Myanmar*] [*Airport symbol*] (OAG)
LSH .... Latter-day Saints Hospital (SAUO)
LSH .... Library Services to the Handicapped (SAUO)
LSH .... Library Services to the Handicapped, Alberta Culture [*UTLAS symbol*]
LSH .... Light Ship (IAA)
LSH .... London School of Hygiene
LSH .... Lowland-Southern Hybrid [*Hemoglobin phenotype of Rana pipiens*]
LSH .... Low Section Height [*Automotive engineering*]
LSH .... Loyal Suffolk Hussars [*British military*] (DMA)
LSH .... Lutein-Stimulating Hormone [*Also, ICSH, LH*] [*Endocrinology*]
LSH .... Lymphocytosis-Stimulating Hormone [*Endocrinology*]
LSh .... Shreve Memorial and Caddo Parish Extension Library, Shreveport, LA [*Library symbol*] [*Library of Congress*] (LCLS)
LSH .... Southeastern Louisiana University, Hammond, LA [*OCLC symbol*] (OCLC)
LSHA .... Gstaad-Inn Grund [*Switzerland*] [*ICAO location identifier*] (ICLI)
LSHA .... Louisiana State Horticultural Association (SAUO)
LShC .... Centenary College of Louisiana, Shreveport, LA [*Library symbol*] [*Library of Congress*] (LCLS)
LSHC .... Light-Saturated Hydrocarbon [*Organic chemistry*]
LShCa .... Caddo Parish Library, Shreveport, LA [*Library symbol*] [*Library of Congress*] (LCLS)
LSHCNC .... Local and Short Haul Carriers National Conference (EA)
LSHER .... Load Sheet Reference (VLIE)
LSHG .... Gampel [*Switzerland*] [*ICAO location identifier*] (ICLI)
LSHG .... Lashing [*Engineering*]
LshGI .... TIGR [*The Institute of Genomic Research*] Leishmania Gene Index [*Database*] (GDD)
LSHI .... Large-Scale Hybrid Integration
LSHIP .... Leadership
LSH(L) .... Landing Ship, Headquarters (Large)
Lshld .... Leasehold (EBF)
LSHLD .... Leasehold
LSH/LSF .... Landing Ship, Helicopter/Landing Ship, Fighter Direction (DNAB)
LShN .... R. W. Norton Art Foundation, Shreveport, LA [*Library symbol*] [*Library of Congress*] (LCLS)
LSHQ .... Landing Ship, Headquarters [*British military*] (DMA)
LSH(S) .... Landing Ship, Headquarters (Small)
LSHS .... Low Sulphur Heavy Stock (PDAA)
LSHS .... Sezegnin [*Switzerland*] [*ICAO location identifier*] (ICLI)
LSHSS .... Language, Speech, and Hearing Services in Schools (SAUO)
LShTE .... Texas Eastern Transmission Corp., Shreveport, LA [*Library symbol*] [*Library of Congress*] (LCLS)
LSHTM .... London School of Hygiene and Tropical Medicine (DAVI)
LShUG .... United Gas Corp., Shreveport, LA [*Library symbol*] [*Library of Congress*] (LCLS)
LsHUP .... Pennzoil United, Inc., Shreveport, LA [*Library symbol*] [*Library of Congress*] (LCLS)
LSHV .... Laminated Synthetic High Voltage
LSI .... Alis [*Former USSR*] [*FAA designator*] (FAAC)
LSI .... Labour and Socialist International (SAUO)
LSI .... Labour Supply Inspector [*British*]
LSI .... Lake Superior & Ishpeming Railroad Co. [*AAR code*]
LSI .... Landing Ship, Infantry [*Navy symbol*]
LSI .... Large Scale Integrated (Circuit) [*Communications term*] (DCT)
LSI .... Large-Scale Integration [*of circuits*] [*Electronics*]
LSI .... Large Spark-Ignited [*Automotive engines*]
LSI .... Largest Single Item (AFM)
LSI .... LASER Surface Interaction
LSI .... Lateral Shear Interferometer (PDAA)
LSI .... Launch Success Indicator
LSI .... Law of the Sea Institute (EA)
LSI .... Law-Science Institute (SAUO)
LSI .... Law Society of Ireland (SAUO)
LSI .... Laws of the State of Israel (BJA)
LSI .... Leadership Skills Inventory [*Test*] (TMMY)
LSI .... Lead Systems Integration
LSI .... Learning Style Inventory [*Occupational therapy*]
LSI .... Learning Systems Institute [*Florida State University*] [*Research center*] (RCD)
LSI .... Lear Siegler Inc. (NITA)
LSI .... Legal Support Inspection [*Clean Water Act*] [*Environmental Protection Agency*] (EPA)
LSI .... Leisure Search Inventory [*Test*] (TMMY)
LSI .... Lerwick [*Scotland*] [*Airport symbol*] (OAG)
LSI .... Leukemia Society, Incorporated (SAUO)
LSI .... Life Satisfaction Index [*Medicine*] (DMAA)
LSI .... Life Sciences Institute [*University of Michigan*] (RCD)
LSI .... Life Space Interviewing [*Teaching technique*]
LSI .... Life Support International Inc. (SAUO)
LSI .... Light Scatter Index
LSI .... Light Scattering Index (STED)
LSI .... Listing Site Inspection [*Environmental science*] (FFDE)
LSI .... List of Serials Indexed for Online Users (SAUO)
LSI .... Literacy Support Initiative (SAUO)
LSI .... Little Sitkin Island [*Alaska*] [*Seismograph station code, US Geological Survey*] [*Closed*] (SEIS)
LSI .... Logistic Supportability Index
LSI .... Logistic Support Impact
LSI .... LSI Logic [*NYSE symbol*] (TTSB)
LSI .... LSI Logic Corp. [*NYSE symbol*] (SPSG)
LSI .... Lumbar Spine Index [*Medicine*] (DMAA)
LSI .... Lunar Science Institute [*Houston*]
LSI .... Lunar Surface Instrument [*Aerospace*]
LSIA .... Lamp and Shade Institute of America [*Defunct*] (EA)
LSIA .... Licentiate of the Society of Industrial Artists [*British*]
LSIB .... London Stage Information Bank [*Lawrence University*] [*Information service or system*] (IID)
LSIC .... Large-Scale Integrated Circuit [*Electronics*] (KSC)
LSIC .... Large-Scale Integration Computer
LSIC .... Little Servant Sisters of the Immaculate Conception (TOCD)
LSIC .... Lockheed System Integration Contractor (ACAE)
LSICA .... Liquid and Solid Industrial Control Association (EA)
LSID .... Large Scale Integration Development
LSID .... Launch Sequence and Interlock Document [*NASA*] (NASA)
LSID .... Local Session Identification [*Computer science*] (IBMDP)
LSID .... Local Session Identifier (SAUO)
LSidFW .... United States Fish and Wildlife Service, Sidell, LA [*Library symbol*] [*Library of Congress*] (LCLS)
LSIEF .... Library Service to the Impaired Elderly Forum [*Association of Specialized and Cooperative Library Agencies*]
LSIEL .... Low-Grade Squamous Intrapithelial [*Pap smear*] [*Medicine*] (EDAA)
LSIF .... Large Scale Infrastructure Facility (EURO)
LSI(G) .... Landing Craft, Infantry (Gunboat) [*Navy symbol*] [*Obsolete*]
LSIG .... Least Significant (IAA)
LSIG .... Line Scan Image Generator (OA)
LSI(H) .... Landing Ship, Infantry (Hand-Hoisted Boats) [*British*]
LSI Ind .... LSI Industries, Inc. [*Associated Press*] (SAG)
LSI Inds .... LSI Industries, Inc. [*Associated Press*] (SAG)
LSIL .... Land and Sea Interaction Laboratory [*Environmental Science Services Administration*] (NOAA)
LSI(L) .... Landing Ship, Infantry (Large) [*Obsolete*]
LSIL .... Low-Grade Squamous Intraepithelial Lesion [*Medicine*]
LSI Log .... LSI Logic Corp. [*Associated Press*] (SAG)
LSI(M) .... Landing Craft, Infantry (Mortar) [*Navy symbol*] [*Obsolete*]
LSI(M) .... Landing Ship, Infantry (Medium) [*British*]
LSI-M-CAPS .... Large Scale Integrated-Mobile CAPS (SAUO)
LSIMS .... Liquid Secondary Ion Mass Spectrometry
LSIO .... Lumbosacroiliac Orthosis [*Medicine*]
LSI-P .... Learning Styles Inventory-Primary Version [*Occupational therapy*] (EDAC)

LSI(R) .... Landing Craft, Infantry (Rocket) [*Navy symbol*] [*Obsolete*]
LSIR .... Limb-Scanning Infrared Radiometer
LSIR .... Low-Ship Impact Ranging [*Navy*] (CAAL)
LSI(S) .... Landing Ship, Infantry (Small)
LSIS .... Large-Scale Information System (SAUO)
LSIS .... LASER Scan Inspection System (PDAA)
LSIS .... LASER Shutterable Image Sensor
LSIS .... League of Shut-In Sodalists (EA)
LSIS .... Learning Style Identification Scale [*Educational test*]
LSIT .... Land Securities Investment Trust (SAUO)
LSIT .... Large-Scale Integration Technology (IAA)
LSIT .... Linear Strip Ion Thruster
LSITT .... Let's Stick It to Them [*Acronym used as book title*]
LSITV .... Liquid Secondary Injection Thrust Vector Control (PDAA)
LSIU .... LS Intertank [*Intermodal shipping container symbol*] (TVRC)
LSJ .... La Societe Jersiaise (EAIO)
LSJ .... Liddell and Scott [*Greek-English Lexicon, 9th ed., revised by H. Stuart Jones*] [*A publication*] (OCD)
LSJ .... Little Sisters of Jesus [*See also PSJ*] [*Italy*] (EAIO)
LSJ .... London School of Journalism (SAUO)
LSJM .... Laus Sit Jesu et Mariae [*Praise Be to Jesus and Mary*] [*Latin*]
LSJM .... Little Sisters of Jesus and Mary (TOCD)
LSK .... Lasik Vision Corp. [*Vancouver Stock Exchange symbol*] [*Canada*]
LSK .... Law Society of Kenya (SAUO)
LSK .... Leucosulfakinin [*Biochemistry*]
LSK .... Liquid Sample Kit
LSK .... Liuski International [*NASDAQ symbol*] (TTSB)
LSK .... Liver, Spleen, Kidney [*Medicine*]
LSK .... Lusk, WY [*Location identifier*] [*FAA*] (FAAL)
LSKI .... Liuski International, Inc. [*NASDAQ symbol*] (SAG)
LSKM .... Liver-Spleen-Kidney Megaly [*Medicine*]
LSL .... Ladder Static Logic
LSL .... Landing Ship, Logistic [*British*]
LSL .... Language Studies Limited London (SAUO)
LSL .... Lateral Superlattice [*Physics*]
LSL .... Left Sacrolateral [*A fetal position*] [*Obstetrics*]
LSL .... Left Short Leg (MELL)
LSL .... Life Sciences Laboratory (AAG)
LSL .... Link and Selector Language
LSL .... Link Support Layer
LSL .... Linnaean Society of London
LSL .... Litton Systems Ltd. (MCD)
LSL .... Load Segment Limit (VLIE)
LSL .... Location Systems List (VLIE)
LSL .... Logical Shift Left [*Computer science*]
LSL .... Logistics Spares List (KSC)
LSL .... Logistics Systems Laboratory
LSL .... Long Service Leave (ADA)
LSL .... Los Chiles [*Costa Rica*] [*Airport symbol*] (OAG)
LSL .... Louisiana State Library, Baton Rouge, LA [*OCLC symbol*] (OCLC)
LSL .... Lower Specification Limit (SAUO)
LSL .... Lower Specified Limit
LSL .... Low Sight Lobe
LSL .... Low-Speed Logic (IAA)
LSL .... Lucy Stone League (SAUO)
LSL .... Lump Sum Leave (COE)
LSL .... Lump-Sum Leave Payment [*Military*] (DNAB)
LSL .... Lymphosarcoma Leukemia [*Medicine*] (MELL)
LSL A .... Chemical Storage and Transfer Facility (SAUS)
LSLA .... Lincoln Savings & Loan Association (SAUO)
LSLA .... Low Speed Line Adaptor (NITA)
LSLAB .... Life Sciences Laboratory (SAUO)
LSLB .... Land Surveyors' Licensing Board [*Western Australia*]
LSLB .... Left Short Leg Brace [*Medicine*]
LSLBP .... Lump-Sum Leave Payment, Basic Pay [*Military*] (DNAB)
LSLC .... Loop Side Lobe Canceler (ACAE)
LSLDP .... Lietuvos Socialistu Liaudininkai Demokratu Partija [*Socialist Populists Democratic Party of Lithuania*] [*Political party*] (PPE)
LSLE .... Life Sciences Laboratory Experiment (SAUO)
LSLI .... Large-Scale Linear Integration (IAA)
LSLM .... Low Speed Line Manager [*Computer science*] (VLIE)
LSLP .... Lietuvos Socialistu Liaudininkai Partija [*Socialist Populists Party of Lithuania*] [*Political party*] (PPE)
LSLP .... Lump-Sum Leave Payment [*Air Force*] (AFM)
LSL PMA ..... Lump-Sum Leave Payment, Personal Money Allowance [*Military*] (DNAB)
LSLPU .... Low-Speed Line Processing Unit [*Communications term*] (DCT)
LSL QTRS .... Lump-Sum Leave Payment, Quarters [*Military*] (DNAB)
LSLS .... Lincoln & Southern [*Federal Railroad Administration identification code*]
LSL SUBS .... Lump-Sum Leave Payment, Subsistence [*Military*] (DNAB)
LSLT .... League to Save Lake Tahoe (EA)
LSM .... Laboratory for the Structure of Matter [*Navy*] (PDAA)
LSM .... Lakeside & Marblehead R. R. [*AAR code*]
LSM .... Lancastrian School of Management (SAUO)
LSM .... Landing Ship Mechanized (CCCA)
LSM .... Landing Ship, Medium [*Navy symbol*]
LSM .... Large Solid Motor [*Aerospace*]
LSM .... LASER Scanning Microscope
LSM .... LASER Slicing Machine
LSM .... Late Systolic Murmur (MAE)
LSM .... Launcher Status Multiplexer (MSA)
LSM .... Launching System Module
LSM .... Launch Site Maintenance [*NASA*] (IAA)
LSM .... LAWS Simulation Model (SAUO)
LSM .... Layered Synthetic Microstructure [*For optical instruments*]
LSM .... Learning Subspace Method (IDAI)
LSM .... Learning Systems Model (EDAC)
LSM .... Least Square Mean [*Mathematical statistics*]
LSM .... Legal Services Manager (SAUO)
LSM .... Leisure Satisfaction Measure (IDYL)
LSM .... Letter Sorting Machine [*US Postal Service*]
LSM .... Liberation Support Movement Information Center (EA)
LSM .... Life Science Module [*NASA*] (NASA)
LSM .... Linear Select Memory
LSM .... Linear Sequential Machine
LSM .... Linear Shock Machine
LSM .... Linear Synchronous Motor (IAA)
LSM .... Line-Scanning Mode [*Microscopy*]
LSM .... Line Selection Module [*Telecommunications*] (TEL)
LSM .... Line Select Module (NITA)
LSM .... Line Switch Module [*Computer science*] (CIST)
LSM .... Litera Scripta Manet [*The Written Word Remains*] [*Latin*] (ADA)
LSM .... Lithuanian Sajudis Movement (CARL)
LSM .... Little Skull Mountain [*Nevada*] [*Seismograph station code, US Geological Survey*] (SEIS)
LSM .... Local Service for Mobiles [*Computer science*]
LSM .... Local Switching Module [*Communications term*] (DCT)
LSM .... Logical Storage Manager (SAUS)
LSM .... Logic Selection Module (VLIE)
LSM .... Logistics Support Manager (SAUO)
LSM .... Logistic Support Manager
LSM .... Longitudinal Section Magnetic [*Electronics*] (OA)
LSM .... Long Saltatory Movement(s) [*Medicine*] (EDAA)
LSM .... Long Semado [*Malaysia*] [*Airport symbol*] (OAG)
LSM .... Loop Sampling Module
LSM .... Louisiana State Library, Processing Center, Baton Rouge, LA [*OCLC symbol*] (OCLC)
LSM .... Low-Speed MODEM (IAA)
LSM .... Low-Sulfate Medium [*Microbiology*]
LSM .... Lunar Surface Magnetometer [*NASA*]
LSM .... Lymphocyte Separation Medium [*Medicine*]
LSM .... Lysergic Acid Morpholide
LSM .... Master of Life Science
LSMA .... Low-Speed Multiplexer Arrangement
LSMC .... Launching System Module Console [*Navy*] (CAAL)
LSMC .... Logistics Specialty Management Committee (SAUO)
LSMD .... Dubendorf [*Switzerland*] [*ICAO location identifier*] (ICLI)
LSMDC .... Labor Service Medical Depot Company (SAUO)
LSME .... Emmen [*Switzerland*] [*ICAO location identifier*] (ICLI)
LSME .... Logistic Support Maintenance Equipment (MCD)
LSME .... London Society of Music Engravers [*British*] (DGA)
LS/MFT ...... Lucky Strike Means Fine Tobacco [*Advertising slogan*]
LSMHT .... List of Standard/Modified Hand Tools (MCD)
LSMI .... Lake Superior Mining Institute (SAUO)
LSMI .... Loadmaster Systems, Incorporated (SAUO)
LSMI .... Logistics Support Management Information [*NASA*] (NASA)
LSMIS .... Logistics Support Management Information System (SAUO)
LSMITH ...... Locksmith
LSMLC .... Low-Speed Multiline Controller (MHDB)
L/Smn .... Leading Seaman [*Navy*] [*British*] (DMA)
LSMO .... Local Sample Management Office (SAUO)
LSMP .... Logistics Support and Mobilization Plan (SAUO)
LSMP .... Logistics Systems Modernization Program (SAUO)
LSMP .... Logistic Support and Mobilization Plan [*Military*] (NVT)
LSMP .... Payerne [*Switzerland*] [*ICAO location identifier*] (ICLI)
LSMR .... Lake Superior & Mississippi Railroad [*Federal Railroad Administration identification code*]
LSM(R) ...... Landing Ship, Medium (Rocket) [*Later, LFR*] [*Navy symbol*]
LSMR .... Rocket Ship [*Navy symbol*]
LSMS .... Living Standards Management Study [*International Monetary Fund*]
LSMS .... Louisiana State Medical Society (SRA)
LSMSC .... Lake Superior Mines Safety Council (SAUO)
LSMSO .... Landing Ship, Material Supply Officer
LSMT .... Lake Superior Museum of Transportation [*Federal Railroad Administration identification code*]
LSMT .... Landing Ship Marshalling Team (SAUO)
LSMT .... Land Site Marshalling Team [*Military*]
LSMTP .... ListServ Simple Mail Transport Protocol [*L-Soft International, Inc.*] [*Computer science*]
LSMU .... LASERcom Space Measurement Unit (IEEE)
LSM-USA .... Lutheran Student Movement - USA (EA)
LSMV .... Lettuce Speckles Mottle Virus [*Plant pathology*]
LSMW .... London School of Medicine for Women (ROG)
LSMX .... Louisville Scrap Material [*Private rail car owner code*]
LSN .... Landmine Survivors Network [*Association*] (EA)
LSN .... Large Scale Networking Committee (SAUO)
LSN .... Latent Spontaneous Nystagmus [*Medicine*] (EDAA)
LSN .... Lateral Septal Nucleus [*Medicine*] (EDAA)
LSN .... Leasing Solutions [*NYSE symbol*] (SG)
LSN .... Left Substania Nigra [*Medicine*] (EDAA)
LSN .... Left Substantia Nigra (DB)
LSN .... Lesser Sciatic Notch [*Medicine*] (MELL)
LSN .... Life Services Network of Illinois (SRA)
LSN .... Linear Sequential Network (MUGU)
LSN .... Line Stabilization Network
LSN .... Listen [*Amateur radio shorthand*] (WDAA)
LSN .... Load Sharing Network

LSN .... Local Stock Number
LSN .... Logical Session Number (VLIE)
LSN .... Los Banos, CA [*Location identifier*] [*FAA*] (FAAL)
LSN .... Sachsen [*German license plate city code*]
LSNA .... Louisiana State Nurses Association (SAUO)
LSNB .... Lake Shore Bancorp (EFIS)
LSND .... Liquid Scintillator Neutrino Detector [*Physics*]
LSNLIS .... Lunar Science Natural Language Information System (PDAA)
LSNR .... League of Struggle for Negro Rights (SAUO)
LSNS .... Leasing Solutions [*OTCBB symbol*]
LSNSR .... Line of Bearing Sensor
LSNSW .... Law Society of New South Wales [*Australia*]
LSNT .... Law Society of the Northern Territory [*Australia*]
LSNY .... Linnaean Society of New York (EA)
LSNY .... Linnean Society of New York (SAUO)
LSO .... Aerolineas del Sol, SA de CV [*Mexico*] [*FAA designator*] (FAAC)
LSO .... Kelso, WA [*Location identifier*] [*FAA*] (FAAL)
LSO .... Labour Supply Organization (SAUO)
LSO .... Landing Safety Officer (MCD)
LSO .... Landing Signal Officer
LSO .... Landing Support Officer [*Navy*]
LSO .... Land Surveyors Online (SAUO)
LSO .... Large Solar Observatory [*NASA*]
LSO .... LASER Safety Officer (COE)
LSO .... LASMO plc ADS [*NYSE symbol*] (TTSB)
LSO .... Lasmo PLC [*NYSE symbol*] (SAG)
LSO .... Last Standing Order
LSO .... Lateral Superior Olive [*Brain anatomy*]
LSO .... Launch/Safety Officer [*NASA*]
LSO .... Law Schools On-Line (AAGC)
LSO .... Left Salpingo-Oophorectomy [*Gynecology*] (CPH)
LSO .... Left Superior Oblique [*Medicine*] (EDAA)
LSO .... Leningrad Symphony Orchestra (SAUO)
LSO .... Lesotho [*ANSI three-letter standard code*] (CNC)
LSO .... Licensed Science Officer (SAUO)
lso .... Licensor [*MARC relator code*] [*Library of Congress*] (LCCP)
LSO .... Life Systems Officer [*NASA*] (KSC)
LSO .... Limited Strategic Option (SAUO)
LSO .... Line Stabilized Oscillator
LSO .... Linseed Oil (PDAA)
LSO .... Linux Standards Organization (SAUO)
LSO .... Local Central Office [*Telecommunications*] (ITD)
LSO .... Local Service Office (SAUO)
LSO .... Locke Surname Organization [*Association*] (EA)
LSO .... Logistics Studies Office [*Army*] (RDA)
LSO .... London String Orchestra (SAUO)
LSO .... London Symphony Orchestra
LSO .... Lost Lake Resources Ltd. [*Vancouver Stock Exchange symbol*]
LSO .... Louisiana Southern Railway Co. [*AAR code*]
LSO .... Lumbosacral Orthosis [*Medicine*] (EDAA)
LSO .... Lutetium, Silicon, and Oxygen [*Inorganic chemistry*]
LSOA .... Longitudinal Study of Aging (SAUO)
LSOA .... Longitudinal Study of the Aging [*Department of Health and Human Services*] (GFGA)
LSOAD .... Life Sciences Organizations and Agencies Directory [*A publication*]
LSOC .... Launch Support Operations Contractor (SSD)
LSOC .... Lockheed Space Operations Co.
LSOC .... Logistical Support Operations Center [*Army*]
LSOCE .... Linear Stochastic Optimal Control and Estimation [*Computer program*]
LSOMT .... Large-Scale Operations Management Test (RDA)
LSON .... Lason, Inc. [*NASDAQ symbol*] (SG)
LSOP .... Limit Switch Open [*Electronics*] (IAA)
LSOP .... L-Serine-O-Phosphate [*Biochemistry*]
LSOP .... Lunar Surface Operations Planning [*NASA*] (KSC)
LSOPrA .... LASMO plc Sr'A'Pref ADS [*NYSE symbol*] (TTSB)
LSOT .... Landing Signal Officer Trainer [*Navy*]
LSOV .... Linguistic Survey of the Ottawa Valley [*Carleton University*] [*Canada*] [*Research center*] (RCD)
LSP .... Laboratory Standards Project (SAUO)
LSP .... Laboratory Suggestion Program (SAUO)
LSP .... Laminar Soot Processes (SAUS)
LSP .... Landing Ship Personnel [*British military*] (DMA)
LSP .... Land Surface Parameterization (SAUS)
LSP .... Land Surface Parmeterization [*Environmental science*]
LSP .... Language for Specific Purposes [*Linguistics*] (IEL)
LSP .... Las Mesas [*Puerto Rico*] [*Seismograph station code, US Geological Survey*] (SEIS)
LSP .... Las Piedras [*Venezuela*] [*Airport symbol*] (OAG)
LSP .... Latvian Socialist Party [*Political party*] (PSAP)
LSP .... Launcher Status Panel (MCD)
LSP .... Launch Sequence Plan [*NASA*] (IAA)
LSP .... Learning Service Provider (NETL)
LSP .... Learning Skills Profile [*Test*] (TMMY)
LSP .... Least Significant Portion (MCD)
LSP .... Least Significant Position (CMD)
LSP .... Left Sacroposterior [*Medicine*] (MELL)
LSp .... Left Span (MAE)
LSP .... Less Sensitive Person (SAUS)
LSP .... Level Set Point (NRCH)
LSP .... Levitated Spherator (PDAA)
LSP .... Liberale Staatspartij [*Liberal State Party*] [*Netherlands*] [*Political party*] (PPE)
LSP .... Liberal Socialist Party [*Egypt*] [*Political party*] (PPW)
LSP .... Liberal State Party (SAUO)
LSP .... Library Software Package (ADA)
LSp .... Life Span
LSP .... Lifestyle Segmentation Profile [*Demographics*]
LSP .... Life Support Package [*Diving apparatus*]
LSP .... Light Scattering Photometer
LSP .... Lincoln Society of Philately [*Defunct*] (EA)
LSP .... Linear Selenium Photocell
LSP .... Line Spectrum Pair (IAA)
LSP .... Line Synchronizing Pulse
LSP .... Linked Systems Project [*of the Library of Congress*]
LSP .... Linked Systems Protocol [*Computer science*] (TNIG)
LSP .... Link State Packet [*Telecommunications*]
LSP .... Link State PDU [*Communications term*] (DCT)
lsp .... Liters per Second per Person (ECON)
LSP .... Little Sisters of the Poor [*Roman Catholic religious order*]
LSP .... Liver-Specific [*Membrane*] Lipoprotein (DAVI)
LSP .... Liver-Specific Protein
LSP .... LM [*Lunar Module*] Specification [*NASA*] (KSC)
LSP .... Loan Service Personnel (SAUS)
LSP .... Local Service Provider (SAUO)
LSP .... Local Store Pointer
LSP .... Logical Signal Processor (IAA)
LSP .... Logistics Support Plan
LSP .... Logistics Support Priorities (SAUO)
LSP .... Loop Splice Plate (ELAL)
LSP .... Lot Sensitive Plan (PDAA)
LSP .... Lower Sequential Permissive (NRCH)
LSP .... Lower Solution Point
LSP .... Low-Salinity Plume [*Oceanography*]
LSP .... Low-Speed Printer
LSP .... Low Support Program (OICC)
LSP .... Lucas-Sargent Proposition [*Economics*]
LSP .... Lumbar Spine [*Medicine*] (DHSM)
LSP .... Lumbosacral Plexus [*Medicine*] (MELL)
LSP .... Lunar Spectral Photometrics [*Aerospace*]
LSP .... Lunar Surface Probe [*Aerospace*]
LSP .... Lunar Survey Probe [*NASA*] (IAA)
LSPA .... Amlikon [*Switzerland*] [*ICAO location identifier*] (ICLI)
LSPA .... Learning System Pilot Aiding programme (SAUS)
LSPA .... Lithuanian State Privatisation Agency
LSPAFRO .... Lump-Sum Payment to Air Force Reserve Officers
LSPBP .... Large-Solid Propellant Booster Program [*Aerospace*] (IAA)
LSPBV .... Load-Sensing Proportioning and Bypass Valve
LSPC .... Legal Services for Prisoners with Children (EA)
LSPC .... Lewis Space Flight Center (MCD)
LSPC .... Linear Selenium Photocell
LSPC .... Living Stream Prayer Circle (EA)
LSPC .... Logistics Systems Policy Committee [*Navy*]
LSPC .... Louisiana Sweet Potato Commission
LSPCC .... Logistics Support Planning and Control Center (ACAE)
LSPCJ .... London Society for Promoting Christianity amongst the Jews (SAUO)
LSPD .... Dittingen [*Switzerland*] [*ICAO location identifier*] (ICLI)
LSPD .... Large Screen Plasma Display (SAUS)
LSPD .... Low Speed (VLIE)
LSPDF .... Life Science Payloads Development Facility (MCD)
LSPDS .... Lunar Survey Probe Delivery System [*NASA*] (SAA)
LSPE .... Lunar Seismic Profiling Experiment [*NASA*]
LSPES .... Logistics System Planning and Execution System (SAUO)
LSPET .... Lunar Sample Preliminary Examination Team [*NASA*]
LSPF .... Least Square Polynomial Fit (IAA)
LSPF .... Library Service to Prisoners Forum [*Association of Specialized and Cooperative Library Agencies*]
LSPF .... Schaffhausen [*Switzerland*] [*ICAO location identifier*] (ICLI)
LSPG .... Linnean Society Palynology Specialist Group (SAUO)
LSPGA .... London School of Printing and Graphic Arts (SAUO)
LSPH .... Leningrad Special Psychiatric Hospital [*Formerly, LPPH*]
LSPH .... Winterthur [*Switzerland*] [*ICAO location identifier*] (ICLI)
LSPI .... Laboratory Service Process Instructors (ACAE)
L-spine .... Lumbar Spine [*Medicine*] (AMHC)
LSPK .... Hasenstrick [*Switzerland*] [*ICAO location identifier*] (ICLI)
LSPK .... Loudspeaker (TEL)
LSPL .... Langenthal [*Switzerland*] [*ICAO location identifier*] (ICLI)
LSPN .... Lesser Superficial Petrosal Nerve [*Medicine*] (EDAA)
LSPN .... Lightspan Partnership [*NASDAQ symbol*] (SG)
LSPN .... Triengen [*Switzerland*] [*ICAO location identifier*] (ICLI)
LSPO .... Lunar Surface Project Office [*NASA*] (KSC)
LSPOJC .... La Salle-Peru-Oglesby Junior College (SAUO)
LSPP .... Step-by-Step Precedents and Procedures. Companies, Trusts, Superannuation Funds [*Australia*] [*A publication*]
LSPPO .... Lead Screw Position Pick-Off
LSPPS .... Logistic Support Plan for Preoperational Support (MCD)
LSPR .... Large System Performance Reference (GART)
LSPR .... Library Society of Puerto Rico (SAUO)
LSPR .... Logistics Support Property Representative (ACAE)
LSPR .... Low-Speed Pulse Restorer (MCD)
LSPR .... Lumbosacral Polyradiculopathy [*Medicine*] (EDAA)
LSPS .... Limited Serial Project Slip
LSPS .... Local Service Planning System [*Telecommunications*] (TEL)
LSPS .... Logistic Support Plan Summary
LSPS .... Louisiana Society of Professional Surveyors (SAUO)
LSPSD .... Low-Speed Packet Switched Data [*Computer science*] (ACRL)
LSPT .... Launch Site Performance Test (ACAE)
LSPT .... Limited Scope Performance Test [*Environmental science*] (COE)

LSPT......... Logistics Support Planning Team (ACAE)
LSPT......... London School of Polymer Technology [*British*] (AIE)
LSPTP....... Low-Speed Paper Tape Punch [*Telecommunications*] (AABC)
LSPTR....... Low-Speed Paper Tape Reader [*Telecommunications*] (TEL)
LSPUD...... Lietuvos Socialdemokratu Partijos Uzsienio Delegatura [*Lithuanian Social Democratic Party*] (EAIO)
LSPV........ Load-Sensing Proportioning Valve [*Automotive engineering*]
LSPV........ Wangen-Lachen [*Switzerland*] [*ICAO location identifier*] (ICLI)
LSPVPD..... Library Service to People with Visual or Physical Disabilities Forum [*Association of Specialized and Cooperative Library Agencies*] [*American Library Association*]
LSPVPDF... Library Service to People with Visual or Physical Disabilities Forum [*ASCLA*] (AL)
LSPX........ Lone Star Producing [*Private rail car owner code*]
LSPZ......... Lake Superior Paper [*Federal Railroad Administration identification code*]
LSPZ......... Luzern-Beromunster [*Switzerland*] [*ICAO location identifier*] (ICLI)
LSQ.......... Line Squall [*ICAO*] (FAAC)
LSQ.......... L'Octogone, Bibliotheque Municipale de LaSalle, Quebec [*UTLAS symbol*]
LSQ.......... Newark, NJ [*Location identifier*] [*FAA*] (FAAL)
LSQA........ Local System Queue Area [*Computer science*] (BUR)
LSQCP....... Logistic System Quality Control Program [*Military*] (AFIT)
LSR.......... Alsair Societe [*France*] [*ICAO designator*] (FAAC)
LSR.......... Aruop [*Language symbol*] (ETLW)
LSR.......... Laboratory for Space Research [*Netherlands*]
LSR.......... Laboratory of Sensorimotor Research [*National Eye Institute*] (RCD)
LSR.......... Laboratory Standards and Reference (SAUO)
LSR.......... Landing Ship, Rocket (NATG)
LSR.......... Land Sea Rescue (NASA)
LSR.......... Land Speed Record [*Auto racing*]
LSR.......... Lanthanide Shift Reagent [*Spectroscopy*]
LSR.......... Large Ship Reactor
lsr............ Laser (VRA)
LSR.......... Laser
LSR.......... Laser Technology [*AMEX symbol*] (TTSB)
LSR.......... Laser Technology, Inc. [*AMEX symbol*] (SPSG)
LSR.......... Last Speed Rating [*of a horse*]
LSR.......... Launch Signal Responder (AAG)
LSR.......... Launch Site Recovery [*NASA*] (KSC)
LSR.......... Launch Support Requirement [*NASA*] (KSC)
LSR.......... Launch Support Room (SAUS)
LSR.......... League for Socialist Reconstruction [*Later, IUP*] (EA)
LSR.......... Lecithin/Sphingomyelin Ratio [*Medicine*] (DMAA)
LSR.......... Leelanau Scenic Railroad [*Federal Railroad Administration identification code*]
LSR.......... Left Superior Rectus [*Muscle*] [*Medicine*] (DMAA)
LSR.......... Life Science Research Ltd. [*British*] (IRUK)
LSR.......... Lighthouse Resources, Inc. [*Vancouver Stock Exchange symbol*]
LSR.......... Light-Scattering Response [*Biology*]
LSR.......... Light-Sensitive Relay
LSR.......... Light-Sensitive Resistor
LSR.......... Light Stopping Reticle
LSR.......... Light, Straight Run [*Petroleum technology*]
LSR.......... Limited Style Run
LSR.......... Limited to Searches (MCD)
LSR.......... Limit Switch Reverse [*Electronics*] (IAA)
LSR.......... LINAC Stretcher Ring [*Design for an electron accelerator*]
LSR.......... Linear Seal Ring
LSR.......... Linear Sedimentation Rate [*Geology*]
LSR.......... Line Source Range (IAA)
LSR.......... Lingual Skills Required [*Civil service*]
LSR.......... Liquid Slip Ring
LSR.......... Liver/Spleen Ratio [*Medicine*] (DMAA)
LSR.......... Load Shifting Resistor (MSA)
LSR.......... Load Storage Register
LSR.......... Local Shared Resources [*Computer science*] (IBMDP)
LSR.......... Local Standard of Rest [*Galactic science*]
LSR.......... Local Storage Register (NITA)
LSR.......... Local Sunrise
LSR.......... Location Stack Register
LSR.......... Locus Standi Reports [*A publication*] (DLA)
LSR.......... Logical Shift Right [*Computer science*]
LSR.......... Logistics Service Representatives (ACAE)
LSR.......... Logistics Support Requirements (NG)
LSR.......... Logistic Status Review
LSR.......... Loop Shorting Relay (MCD)
LSR.......... Loose Snow on Runway [*NWS*] (FAAC)
LSR.......... Lost River, AK [*Location identifier*] [*FAA*] (FAAL)
LSR.......... Lovers of the Stinking Rose (EA)
LSR.......... Low-Speed Reader
LSR.......... Low Stocking Rate [*Agriculture*] (OA)
LSR.......... Low-Storage Requirement [*Electric vehicles*]
LSR.......... Luftschutzraum [*Air-Raid Shelter*] [*German military - World War II*]
LSR.......... Lunar Surface Rendezvous [*NASA*] (KSC)
LSR.......... Lynchburg Source Reactor
LSR.WS..... Laser Technology Wrrt [*AMEX symbol*] (TTSB)
LSRA........ Logistic Support Requirement Analysis (MCD)
LSRA........ Low Septal Right Atrium [*Medicine*] (EDAA)
L/S ratio.... Lecithin/Sphingomyelin Ratio (ADWA)
LSRB........ Linear Sound Ranging Base (PDAA)
LSRC........ Lake State Railway [*Federal Railroad Administration identification code*]
LSRC........ Land Settlement Research Centre (SAUO)
LSRC........ Launch Site Recovery Commander [*NASA*] (KSC)
LSRC........ Logistics Systems Review Committee [*DARCOM*] (MCD)
LSRC........ Lunar Surface Return Container [*NASA*] (KSC)
LSRD........ Launch Site Requirements Document (ACAE)
LSRD........ Logistic Support Readiness Date
LSRE........ Leisure
LSREF....... LaSalle Re Holdings Ltd. [*NASDAQ symbol*] (SAG)
LSREF....... LaSall Re Holdings [*NASDAQ symbol*] (TTSB)
LSRF........ LASER Submarine Range-Finder
LSRF........ Life Sciences Research Facility (SAUO)
LSRF........ Logistic Support Resource Funds [*Army*]
LSRgt........ Lake Superior Regiment (SAUO)
LSRI.......... Large Screen RADAR Indicator
LSRI.......... Lumbosacral Root Injury (MELL)
LSRL......... Ley de Sociedades de Responsabilidad Limitada (SAUO)
LSRM........ Life Science Research Module (MCD)
LSRO........ Life Sciences Research Office [*NASA*] (KSC)
LSRP........ Local Switching Replacement Planning [*Telecommunications*] (TEL)
LSR-P........ Loose Snow on Runway-Patchy [*Aviation*] (DNAB)
LSRR........ Lone Star Railroad [*Federal Railroad Administration identification code*]
LSRRTI...... Leningrad Scientific Research Radio Technical Institute (SAUO)
LSRS........ LOAD [*Low Altitude Defense*] System Requirements Simulation
LsrSght...... Laser Sight, Inc. [*Associated Press*] (SAG)
LsrTc......... Laser Technology, Inc. [*Associated Press*] (SAG)
LsrTech..... Laser Technology, Inc. [*Associated Press*] (SAG)
LSRU........ Leisure and Sport Research Unit [*Cheltenham and Gloucester College of Higher Education*] [*United Kingdom*] (RCD)
LsrV......... Laser Video Network, Inc. [*Associated Press*] (SAG)
LSRV........ London and Scottish Rifle Volunteers [*Military*] [*British*] (ROG)
LSRV........ Lunar Surface Roving Vehicle [*Aerospace*]
LsrVd........ Laser Video Network, Inc. [*Associated Press*] (SAG)
LsrVide...... Laser Video Network, Inc. [*Associated Press*] (SAG)
LsrVis....... Laser Vision Centers, Inc. [*Associated Press*] (SAG)
LsrVs........ Laser Vision Centers, Inc. [*Associated Press*] (SAG)
LSRX........ Lake Shore Railway [*Federal Railroad Administration identification code*]
LSS.......... Exec Express II, Inc. [*ICAO designator*] (FAAC)
LSS.......... Laboratory for Student Success [*Temple University*] (RCD)
LSS.......... Laboratory for Surface Studies [*University of Wisconsin, Milwaukee*] [*Research center*] (RCD)
LSS.......... Laboratory Support Service
LSS.......... Ladies Shoemakers' Society [*A union*] [*British*]
LSS.......... Landing, Separation Simulator (MCD)
LSS.......... Landing Ship Sternchute [*British military*] (DMA)
LSS.......... Landing Ship, Support (NATG)
LSS.......... Landing-Site Supervisor
LSS.......... Lane Sensing System [*Automotive engineering*]
LSS.......... Language for Symbolic Simulation
LSS.......... Language Support System (IAA)
LSS.......... Laparoscopic Surgery (MELL)
LSS.......... Large-Scale Standard (IAA)
LSS.......... Large-Scale Structure [*Cosmology*]
LSS.......... Large Space Structure (IEEE)
LSS.......... Large Space Structures (SAUS)
LSS.......... Large Space System (IEEE)
LSS.......... Laser Sizing Study (ACAE)
LSS.......... Lateral Series Servo (MCD)
LSS.......... Lateral Spinal Stenosis [*Medicine*] (MELL)
LSS.......... Launcher Support Structure [*Navy*] (CAAL)
LSS.......... Launch Sequence Simulator
LSS.......... Launch Signature Simulator (MCD)
LSS.......... Launch Status Summarizer
LSS.......... Launch Support Section [*NASA*]
LSS.......... Launch Support Services (SAUS)
LSS.......... Launch Support System [*NASA*] (KSC)
LSS.......... Law Society of Scotland
LSS.......... Leipziger Semitische Studien [*A publication*] (BJA)
LSS.......... Leopold Stokowski Society (EA)
LSS.......... Les Saintes [*Guadeloupe*] [*Airport symbol*] (OAG)
LSS.......... Licensing Support System [*Department of Energy*] (EGAO)
LSS.......... Licentiate of Sacred Scripture (SAUO)
LSS.......... Life Satisfaction Scale (IDYL)
LSS.......... Life Saving Service (WDAA)
LSS.......... Life-Saving Service (SAUO)
LSS.......... Lifesaving Station [*Nautical charts*]
LSS.......... Life Services System [*For the disabled*]
LSS.......... Life-Span Study [*Environmental science*] (FFDE)
LSS.......... Life Support Subsystem (SAUS)
LSS.......... Life Support System [*or Subsystem*]
LSS.......... Lightning Sensor System (ACAE)
LSS.......... Lightning Surge Simulator
LSS.......... Lightship Station [*Nautical term*] (NTA)
LSS.......... Light Spot Scanner
LSS.......... Limb-Salvage Surgery (MELL)
LSS.......... Limited Storage Site (AABC)
LSS.......... Line Scanner System
LSS.......... Linking Segment Subprogram
LSS.......... Liquid Scintillation Spectrometer
LSS.......... Literature Search System (SAUO)
LSS.......... Liver-Spleen Scan [*Medicine*] (MEDA)
LSS.......... Living Situations Survey (SAUO)
LSS.......... Load Sensing Signal [*Hydraulics*]
LSS.......... Load Sensing System (SAUS)

LSS .... Local School System (SAUO)
LSS .... Local Subscriber Switch (CCCA)
LSS .... Local Synchronization Subsystem [*Telecommunications*] (TEL)
LSS .... Lockheed Space Systems (SAUO)
LSS .... Logistics Support Station (SAUO)
LSS .... Logistic Support Squadron (AAG)
LSS .... Logistic Support System (AABC)
LSS .... Lone Star Steel [*Federal Railroad Administration identification code*]
LSS .... Lone Star Technologies [*Company symbol*]
LSS .... Longitudinal Static Stability
LSS .... Longitudinal Studies Section [*National Institute on Aging*] (RCD)
LSS .... Loop Surge Suppresser (ELAL)
LSS .... Loop Switching System [*Telecommunications*]
LSS .... LOT [*Limited Operational Test*] Support Services [*Military*] (DWSG)
LSS .... Lumbar Spinal Stenosis [*Medicine*] (MELL)
LSS .... Lumbosacral Spine [*Medicine*] (MEDA)
LSS .... Lunar Soil Stimulant [*NASA*] (KSC)
LSS .... Lunar Surveying System [*Aerospace*]
LSS .... Lunar Survey Sensor [*NASA*] (KSC)
LSS .... Lung Serum Simulant (PDAA)
LSS .... Lutheran Social Service System [*An association*]
LSS .... Scapholunate Ligament [*Medicine*] (RAWO)
LSSA .... Law Society of South Australia
LSSA .... Leopold Stokowski Society of America (EA)
LSSA .... Limnological Society of Southern Africa (SAUO)
LSSA .... Lipid Soluble Secondary Antioxidants [*Biochemistry*]
LSSA .... Lithuanian Student Scout Association [*Later, Lithuanian Scouts Association College Division*] (EA)
LSSA .... Logistic System Support Activity [*Army*]
LSSA .... Logistic System Support Agency
LSSA .... London Subterranean Survey Association (SAUO)
LSSAS .... Longitudinal Static Stability Augmentation System (MCD)
LSSB .... Bern Radio [*Switzerland*] [*ICAO location identifier*] (ICLI)
LSSB .... Lake Sunapee Savings Bank (SAUO)
LSSB .... Legal Support Services Branch [*General Accounting Office*] [*Information service or system*] (IID)
LSSB .... Light SEAL [*Sea, Air, and Land*] Support Boat [*Navy*] (DNAB)
LSSC .... Lake Superior State College [*Sault Ste. Marie, MI*]
LSSC .... Launch Support Services Contracts (SAUO)
LSSc .... Licentiate in Sacred Scriptures
LSSC .... Licentiate in Sanitary Science [*British*] (ROG)
LSSC .... Light SEAL [*Sea, Air, and Land*] Support Craft [*Navy symbol*]
LSSC .... Load Sensing and Speed Control [*Hydraulics*]
LSSC .... Logistic Support System Characteristics (AAG)
LSSC .... Logistic System Support Center [*Army*]
LSSC .... Lower-Sideband Suppressed Carrier (IDOE)
LSSCV .... Large Scale Structure Control Verification (SAUS)
LSSD .... Level Sensitive Scan Design (MCD)
LSSD .... Level-Sensitive Scan Detector (CIST)
LSSD .... Lower-Speed Service-Deriving [*Telecommunications*] (TSSD)
LSSD .... Lunar Surface Sampling Device [*Aerospace*]
LSSDDPMAG... Library Service to Developmentally Disabled Persons Membership Activity Group [*Association of Specialized and Cooperative Library Agencies*] [*American Library Association*]
LSSDPF ..... Library Service to the Developmentally Disabled Persons Forum [*Association of Specialized and Cooperative Library Agencies*] [*American Library Association*]
LSSE .... Launch Site Support Engineer (SAUO)
LSSE .... Licentiate in Social, Economic, & Political Sciences (DD)
LSSF .... Land Special Security Force [*Army*] (AABC)
LSSF .... Life Sciences Support Facility [*NASA*] (NASA)
LSSF .... Limited Service Storage Facility
LSSG .... Logistics Studies Steering Group (AABC)
LSSG .... Logistics Studies Support Group (SAUO)
LSSGR ...... Local Switching System General Requirement [*Telecommunications*]
LSSI .... Leasing Solutions [*NASDAQ symbol*] (TTSB)
LSSI .... Leasing Solutions, Inc. [*NASDAQ symbol*] (SAG)
LSSI .... Library Systems and Services, Inc. [*Information service or system*] (IID)
LSSI .... Library Systems and Services, LLC (IID)
LSSI .... Lockheed Support Systems Inc. (SAUS)
LSSL .... Landing Ship Support, Large [*Military*] (VNW)
LSSL .... Life Sciences Space Laboratory [*NASA*] (NASA)
LSSL .... Support Landing Ship (Large) MK III
LSSM .... Launch Site Support Manager [*NASA*] (NASA)
LSSM .... Local Scientific Survey Module [*NASA*]
LSSM .... Lunar Surface Scientific Module [*NASA*]
LSSO .... Bern. Office Federal de l'Air [*Switzerland*] [*ICAO location identifier*] (ICLI)
LSSO .... Launch Site System Operations (ACAE)
LSSO .... Library Science Student Organization
LSSP .... Lanka Sama Samaja Party [*Sri Lanka Equal Society Party*] [*Political party*] (PPW)
LSSP .... Latest Scram Set Point (NRCH)
LSSP .... Launch Site Support Plan (MCD)
LSSP .... Lunar Surveying System Program [*Aerospace*]
LSSPO .... Life Support Systems Project Office [*NASA*] (MCD)
LSSPS .... Libraries Serving Special Populations Section [*Association of Specialized and Cooperative Library Agencies*]
LSSPSC ..... Life Sciences Strategic Planning Study Committee [*NASA*]
LSSR .... Amphibious Coastal Reconnaissance Ship [*Navy symbol*]
LSSR .... Berne/Radio Suisse SA [*Switzerland*] [*ICAO location identifier*] (ICLI)
LSSR .... Lessor
LSSRC .... Life Sciences Shuttle Research Centrifuge [*NASA*] (NASA)
LSSS .... Geneve [*Switzerland*] [*ICAO location identifier*] (ICLI)
LSSS .... LASER Source Signature Simulator
LSSS .... Lightweight SHF SATCOM System (SAUO)
LSSS .... Lightweight Ship SATCOM Set [*Navy*] (CAAL)
LSSS .... Lime-Sulphur-Synthetic-Solution [*Hydrometallurgy*]
LSSS .... Limiting Safety System Setting [*Nuclear energy*] (NRCH)
LSSS .... London School of Slavonic Studies (SAUO)
LSST .... Laser Spot Seeker/Tracker (SAUS)
LSST .... Launch Site Support Team (MCD)
lsst .... Lead-Sheathed Steel-Taped
LS/ST .... Light Shield/Star Tracker (NASA)
LSST .... List of Specifications and Standards (MSA)
LSST .... Lone Star Technologies [*NASDAQ symbol*] (SAG)
LSST .... Lone Star Technologies, Inc. (SAUO)
LSSTA .... Low Supersonic Transport (PDAA)
LSSTA .... Lunar Space Tug (PDAA)
LSSU .... Lake Superior State University [*Michigan*]
LSSW .... Zurich [*Switzerland*] [*ICAO location identifier*] (ICLI)
LST .... Amphibious Ship, Tank
LST .... Lake States Transportation [*Federal Railroad Administration identification code*]
LST .... Lakewood Forest Products Ltd. [*Vancouver Stock Exchange symbol*]
LST .... Laminated SONAR Transistor
LST .... Landing Ship, Tank [*Navy symbol*]
LST .... Landing Ship Transport (MCD)
LST .... Land Surface Temperature (SAUO)
LST .... Laplace-Stieltjes Transform
LST .... Large Scale Telescope (ACAE)
LST .... Large Scale Test (SAUS)
LST .... Large Simple Trial [*Statistics*]
LST .... Large Space Telescope [*Later, Space Telescope*] [*NASA*]
LST .... Large Stellar Telescope (KSC)
LST .... Large Subsonic Tunnel [*NASA*]
LST .... LASER Spot Tracker (MCD)
LST .... Last (BUR)
LST .... Lateral Sinus Thrombophlebitis [*Medicine*] (MEDA)
LST .... Lateral Spinothalamic Tract [*Neurology*] (DAVI)
LST .... Late Start Time
LST .... Launceston [*Tasmania*] [*Airport symbol*] (OAG)
LST .... Launch Support Team [*NASA*] (KSC)
LST .... Lauryl Sulfate Tryptose [*Growth medium*]
LST .... Law Society of Tasmania [*Australia*]
LST .... Least Squares Tracking (ACAE)
LST .... Left Sacrotransverse [*A fetal position*] [*Obstetrics*]
LST .... Left Store (SAA)
LST .... Licentiate in Sacred Theology [*British*]
LST .... Life-Sustaining Treatment [*Medicine*] (DMAA)
LST .... Light-Sensitive Tube
LST .... Lightweight Satellite Terminal (SAUO)
LST .... Line Scan Tube
LST .... Linux Support Team (SAUO)
LST .... Liquid Oxygen Start Tank (AAG)
LST .... Liquid Storage Tank (AAG)
LST .... Listing of a Program in a File [*Computer science*]
LST .... Living Structures Tank (WDAA)
LST .... Local Sidereal Time
LST .... Local Solar Time
LST .... Local Standard Time
LST .... Local Summer Time [*Astronomy*] (IAA)
LST .... Logic Service Terminal [*Computer science*] (VLIE)
LST .... Lone Star [*Missouri*] [*Seismograph station code, US Geological Survey*] (SEIS)
LST .... Lone Star, TX [*Location identifier*] [*FAA*] (FAAL)
LST .... Long-Term Stability Test [*Chemistry*]
LST .... Lost (GOBB)
LST .... Loud Speaking Telephone (NITA)
LST .... Low-Solvent Technology (GNE)
LST .... Lunar Surface Telescope [*NASA*]
LST .... Lunar Surface Transponder [*Aerospace*]
LST .... Tank Landing Ship (SAUO)
LSTA .... Library Services and Technology Act (SAUO)
LSTAR .... Limited Scientific and Technical Aerospace Reports [*NASA*] (MCD)
LSTAT .... Life Support for Trauma And Transport [*Northrop Grumman*] (PS)
LSTB .... Bellechasse [*Switzerland*] [*ICAO location identifier*] (ICLI)
LSTB .... Long Shoot Terminal Bud [*Botany*]
LStBA .... Saint Joseph's Abbey, St. Benedict, LA [*Library symbol*] [*Library of Congress*] (LCLS)
LSTC .... London Society of Tie Cutters (SAUO)
LST/CAM .... LASER Spot Tracker/Strike Camera (MCD)
LSTD .... Leading Steward [*British military*] (DMA)
LSTD .... Lunar Satellite Tracking Data [*NASA*] (KSC)
lstd- .... Tristan da Cunha Island [*MARC geographic area code*] [*Library of Congress*] (LCCP)
LSTDM ...... Low Speed Time Division Multiplexer (ACAE)
LSTE .... Large Structure Technology Experiment (SSD)
LSTE .... Launch Site Transportation Equipment [*NASA*] (NASA)
LSTF .... Large Scale Test Facility (SAUO)
LSTF .... Lead Sulfide Thin Film
LST-G .... Large Steam Turbine-Generator
LStgH .... Hunt Correctional Center (Louisiana Correctional Institute for Women), St. Gabriel, LA [*Library symbol*] [*Library of Congress*] (LCLS)
LST(H) ...... Landing Ship, Tank (Casualty Evacuation) [*Navy symbol*] [*Obsolete*]
LST(H) ...... Landing Ship, Tank (Hospital) [*British military*] (DMA)
LSTIS .... Laboratory Scientific and Technical Information System (SAUO)

LSTJ......... La Sarge Trucking [*Common carrier symbol*]
LStjT......... Tensas Parish Library, St. Joseph, LA [*Library symbol*] [*Library of Congress*] (LCLS)
LSTL......... Lake Shore Transportation Lines [*Common carrier symbol*]
LSTL......... Laparoscopic Tubal Ligation [*Gynecology*] (DAVI)
LSTM......... Lander Static Test Model [*NASA*]
LSTM......... Large-Sample Scanning Tunneling Mode [*Microscopy*]
LSTM......... Liverpool School of Tropical Medicine (SAUO)
LSTM......... London School of Tropical Medicine (SAUO)
LSTM......... Low Steam
LStmSM..... St. Martin Parish Library, St. Martinville, LA [*Library symbol*] [*Library of Congress*] (LCLS)
LSTN......... Light Station [*Coast Guard*] (IAA)
LSTNG....... Lasting
LSTO......... Motiers [*Switzerland*] [*ICAO location identifier*] (ICLI)
LSTP......... Logistic Systems Training Program (ACAE)
LSTP......... Low Speed Tape Processor (ACAE)
LSTR......... Landstar System [*NASDAQ symbol*] (TTSB)
LSTR......... Landstar System, Inc. [*NASDAQ symbol*] (SAG)
LSTR......... Lasater Truck Company [*Common carrier symbol*]
LSTR......... Launch System Test Rack (ACAE)
LSTR......... Montricher [*Switzerland*] [*ICAO location identifier*] (ICLI)
LSTS......... Landing Ship (Utility) [*Navy symbol*]
LSTS......... Launch Station Test Set (MCD)
LSTS......... Low-Pressure Side Temperature Sensor [*Air conditioning system*] [*Automotive engineering*]
LSTS......... Lunar Surface Thermal Simulator [*NASA*] (KSC)
LST/SCAM... LASER Spot Tracker / Strike Camera
LSTSRFA.... Launch Station Test Set Radio Frequency Adapter (MCD)
LSTT......... Labor Service Transportation Truck (SAUO)
LSTT......... Lake Superior Terminal & Transfer Railway Co. [*AAR code*]
LSTTL....... Low-Power Schottky Transistor-Transistor Logic [*Electronics*]
L Stud H..... Law Students' Helper [*A publication*] (DLA)
L Stud Helper... Law Students' Helper [*A publication*] (DLA)
L Stud J..... Law Students' Journal [*A publication*] (DLA)
L Stu Mag... Law Students' Magazine [*A publication*] (DLA)
L Stu Mag NS... Law Students' Magazine. New Series [*A publication*] (ILCA)
L Stu Mag OS... Law Students' Magazine. Old Series [*A publication*] (ILCA)
lstwx......... Lost Wax (VRA)
LSTX......... Bex [*Switzerland*] [*ICAO location identifier*] (ICLI)
LSTY......... Yverdon [*Switzerland*] [*ICAO location identifier*] (ICLI)
LSU.......... Institute of Continuing Legal Education, Louisiana State University Law Center (DLA)
LSU.......... Labor Service Unit [*Military*]
LSU.......... Labour Service Unit (SAUO)
LSU.......... Lactose Saccharose Urea [*Cell growth medium*]
LSU.......... Lambda Sensor Unit [*Automotive emissions*]
LSU.......... Lamentation over the Destruction of Sumer and Ur (BJA)
LSU.......... Landing Ship, Utility [*Navy symbol*] [*Obsolete*]
LSU.......... Languages, Sorts, Utilities [*Computer science*] (VLIE)
LSU.......... LAN Service Unit (SAUS)
LSU.......... LASER Scanning Unit [*Computer science*] (CIST)
LSU.......... Launcher Selector Unit
LSU.......... Launcher Switching Unit [*Navy*] (CAAL)
LSU.......... Law Society of Upper Canada [*UTLAS symbol*]
LSU.......... Leading Signal Unit [*Telecommunications*] (TEL)
LSU.......... Liberalsoziale Union [*Liberal Social Union*] [*Germany*] [*Political party*] (PPW)
LSU.......... Library Storage Unit
LSU.......... Life Support Umbilical [*NASA*]
LSU.......... Life Support Unit [*NASA*] (KSC)
LSU.......... Lighthouse Study Unit (EA)
LSU.......... Limit Switch Up [*Electronics*] (IAA)
LSU.......... Line Selection Unit [*Telecommunications*] (IAA)
LSU.......... Line-Sharing Unit
LSU.......... Line Signalling Unit (SAUS)
LSU.......... Livestock Unit
LSU.......... Load Storage Unit [*Computer science*]
LSU.......... Local Storage Unit [*Computer science*]
LSU.......... Local Store Unit (ELAL)
LSU.......... Local Switching Unit [*Telecommunications*] (TEL)
LSU.......... Local Synchronization Utility [*Telecommunications*] (TEL)
LSU.......... Logistics Support Unit [*Military*] (NVT)
LSU.......... Lone Signalling Unit (NITA)
LSU.......... Lone Signal Unit [*Telecommunications*] (TEL)
LSU.......... Long Sukang [*Malaysia*] [*Airport symbol*] (OAG)
LSU.......... Loughborough Students Union (SAUO)
LSU.......... Louisiana State University
LSU.......... Louisiana State University and Agricultural and Mechanical College (GAGS)
LSU.......... Southern University at New Orleans, New Orleans, LA [*OCLC symbol*] (OCLC)
LSU-IES..... Louisiana State University Institute of Environmental Studies (SAUO)
LSU Med Cent... Louisiana State University Medicine Center (GAGS)
LSUN......... Labor Service Unit Navy (SAUO)
LSUNO...... Louisiana State University in New Orleans [*Later, University of New Orleans*]
L Sup......... Lake Superior (BARN)
LSUP......... Loader Storage Unit Support Program [*Computer science*] (MHDI)
LSUP......... Louisiana State University Press (SAUO)
L Sup H & D... Lalor's Supplement to Hill and Denio's New York Reports [*A publication*] (DLA)
LSUR......... Leisure
LSU Shreveport... Louisiana State University Shreveport (GAGS)
LSUV......... Lunar Surface Ultraviolet [*Camera*] [*NASA*]
LSUV......... Luxury Sport Utility Vehicle
LSV.......... Alak [*Former USSR*] [*ICAO designator*] (FAAC)
LSV.......... Landing Ship, Vehicle [*Navy symbol*]
LSV.......... Large Scale Vehicle (ACAE)
LSV.......... Las Vegas, NV [*Location identifier*] [*FAA*] (FAAL)
LSV.......... Lateral Sacral Vein [*Medicine*] (MELL)
LSV.......... Left Sinus of Valsalva [*Medicine*] (MELL)
LSV.......... Left Subclavian Vein [*Anatomy*]
LSV.......... Light Strike Vehicle (SAUS)
LSV.......... Lily Symptomless Virus [*Plant pathology*]
LSV.......... Linear Shift-Varying (PDAA)
LSV.......... Linear Sweep Voltammograms [*Electrochemistry*]
LSV.......... Line Status Verifier [*Telecommunications*] (TEL)
LSV.......... Logistics Support Vessel [*Military*]
LSV.......... Logistic Support Vehicle (SAUS)
LSV.......... Low-Signature Vehicle [*Hazardous materials control*]
LSV.......... Low-Speed Vehicle [*Automotive engineering*]
LSV.......... Lunar Shuttle Vehicle [*Aerospace*] (AAG)
LSV.......... Lunar Surface Vehicle [*Aerospace*]
LSV.......... Lunar Survey Viewfinder [*Aerospace*]
LSVC......... Left Superior Vena Cava [*Medicine*] (STED)
LSVC......... Lunar Surface Vehicle Communications [*Aerospace*]
LSvCo....... Labor Service Company (SAUO)
LSvCtr....... Labor Service Center (SAUO)
LSVG......... Lifesaving (MSA)
LSVI......... Large Size Visual Interface [*Computer science*] (VLIE)
LSVI......... Little Switzerland [*NASDAQ symbol*] (TTSB)
LSVI......... Little Switzerland, Inc. [*NASDAQ symbol*] (SAG)
LSVP......... Landing Ship, Vehicle and Personnel [*Navy symbol*]
LSvRwyMPCo... Labor Service Railway Military Police Company (SAUO)
LSVW......... Logistic Support Vehicle, Wheeled (SAUS)
LSW.......... Detroit, MI [*Location identifier*] [*FAA*] (FAAL)
LSW.......... Labrador Sea Water [*Oceanography*]
LSW.......... Landslide [*Washington*] [*Seismograph station code, US Geological Survey*] [*Closed*] (SEIS)
LSW.......... Large Scale Walleye (ACAE)
LSW.......... LASER Spot Welder
LSW.......... Least Significant Word (MCD)
LSW.......... Left-Sided Weakness [*Medicine*] (STED)
LSW.......... Licensed Shorthand Writer
LSW.......... Lifshitz-Slyozov-Wagner Theory of Mineral Recrystallization
LSW.......... Light Support Weapon (MCD)
LSW.......... Limit Switch [*Electronics*]
LSW.......... Line Switch [*Telecommunications*] (IAA)
LSWA........ Large-Amplitude, Slow Wave Activity [*Encephalography*]
LSWA........ Law Society of Western Australia
LSWMA..... Lutheran Society for Worship, Music, and the Arts [*Later, Liturgical Conference*]
LSWP........ Lump-Sum Wage Payments (MCD)
LSWQ........ Leaseway Trucking [*Common carrier symbol*]
LSWR........ London & South-Western Railway (ROG)
LSWS........ London Society for Women's Service [*British*] (WDAA)
LSWT........ Low-Speed Wind Tunnel (MCD)
LSWTF....... Large Scale Wind Test Facility [*Emergency Management*] (EMA)
LSWY........ League of Socialist Working Youth (SAUO)
LSX.......... Landing Ship, Experimental
LSX.......... Land-surface Transfer Scheme (SAUO)
LSX.......... Luzerene & Susquehanna Railway [*Federal Railroad Administration identification code*]
LSXB......... Balzers/FL [*Switzerland*] [*ICAO location identifier*] (ICLI)
LSXD......... Domat-Ems [*Switzerland*] [*ICAO location identifier*] (ICLI)
LSXE......... Erstfeld [*Switzerland*] [*ICAO location identifier*] (ICLI)
LSXH......... Holziken [*Switzerland*] [*ICAO location identifier*] (ICLI)
lsxj-.......... St. Helena [*MARC geographic area code*] [*Library of Congress*] (LCCP)
LSXL......... Lauterbrunnen [*Switzerland*] [*ICAO location identifier*] (ICLI)
LSXM......... St. Moritz [*Switzerland*] [*ICAO location identifier*] (ICLI)
LSXO......... Gossau SG [*Switzerland*] [*ICAO location identifier*] (ICLI)
LSXS......... Schindellegi [*Switzerland*] [*ICAO location identifier*] (ICLI)
LSXT......... Trogen [*Switzerland*] [*ICAO location identifier*] (ICLI)
LSXU......... Untervaz [*Switzerland*] [*ICAO location identifier*] (ICLI)
LSXV......... San Vittore [*Switzerland*] [*ICAO location identifier*] (ICLI)
LSXW......... Wurenlingen [*Switzerland*] [*ICAO location identifier*] (ICLI)
LSY.......... Lindsay Aviation, Inc. [*ICAO designator*] (FAAC)
LSY.......... Lismore [*Australia*] [*Airport symbol*] (OAG)
LSYC......... League of Socialist Youth of Croatia [*Political party*]
LSZA......... Lugano [*Switzerland*] [*ICAO location identifier*] (ICLI)
LSZB......... Bern/Belp [*Switzerland*] [*ICAO location identifier*] (ICLI)
LSZC......... Bad Ragaz [*Switzerland*] [*ICAO location identifier*] (ICLI)
LSZD......... Ascona [*Switzerland*] [*ICAO location identifier*] (ICLI)
LSZE......... Bad Ragaz [*Switzerland*] [*ICAO location identifier*] (ICLI)
LSZF......... Birrfeld [*Switzerland*] [*ICAO location identifier*] (ICLI)
LSZG......... Grenchen [*Switzerland*] [*ICAO location identifier*] (ICLI)
LSZH......... Zurich [*Switzerland*] [*ICAO location identifier*] (ICLI)
LSZI......... Fricktal-Schupfart [*Switzerland*] [*ICAO location identifier*] (ICLI)
LSZJ......... Courtelary [*Switzerland*] [*ICAO location identifier*] (ICLI)
LSZK......... Speck-Fehraltorf [*Switzerland*] [*ICAO location identifier*] (ICLI)
LSZL......... Locarno [*Switzerland*] [*ICAO location identifier*] (ICLI)
LSZM......... Bale [*Switzerland*] [*ICAO location identifier*] (ICLI)
LSZN......... Hausen Am Albis [*Switzerland*] [*ICAO location identifier*] (ICLI)
LSZP......... Biel/Kappelen [*Switzerland*] [*ICAO location identifier*] (ICLI)
LSZR......... Altenrhein [*Switzerland*] [*ICAO location identifier*] (ICLI)
LSZS......... Samedan [*Switzerland*] [*ICAO location identifier*] (ICLI)

LSZT......... Lommis [*Switzerland*] [*ICAO location identifier*] (ICLI)
LSZU......... Buttwil [*Switzerland*] [*ICAO location identifier*] (ICLI)
LSZV......... Sitterdorf [*Switzerland*] [*ICAO location identifier*] (ICLI)
LSZW......... Thun [*Switzerland*] [*ICAO location identifier*] (ICLI)
LSZX......... Schanis [*Switzerland*] [*ICAO location identifier*] (ICLI)
LSZY......... Porrentruy [*Switzerland*] [*ICAO location identifier*] (ICLI)
LSZZ......... Collective address for NOTAM and SNOWTAM [*Switzerland*] [*ICAO location identifier*] (ICLI)
LT............ Fixed Light [*USCG*] (TAG)
LT............ Great Sierra [*ICAO designator*] (AD)
LT............ Heat-labile Enterotoxin [*Biochemistry*] (DAVI)
LT............ Heat-Labile Toxin (STED)
LT............ Labile Toxin (DB)
LT............ Laboratory Technology (SAUO)
LT............ Laboratory Test (IAA)
LT............ [*The*] Lake Terminal Railroad Co. [*AAR code*]
LT............ Lamaze Technique [*Medicine*] (MELL)
LT............ Laminar Tomography (STED)
LT............ Laminated TEFLON
LT............ Landed Terms
LT............ Landing Team
LT............ Landing Time (SAUO)
L/T........... Landlord/Tenant (SAUO)
LT............ Lands Tribunal [*Legal*] [*British*]
LT............ Language Translation [*Computer science*]
LT............ Laplace Transform [*Mathematics*]
LT............ Lapped Transform [*Telecommunications*]
LT............ Laptop [*Computer*] (BARN)
LT............ Large Tug [*Army*]
LT............ Larsen and Toubro Ltd. [*India*] [*Commercial firm*]
LT............ Laser Transmitter (SAUS)
LT............ LASER Trimming (PDAA)
LT............ Lashkar-e-Tayyiba [*Government term*] (GA)
LT............ Last (ROG)
LT............ Last Telecast (NTCM)
LT............ Lateral Tooth
LT............ Lateral Triceps Brachii [*Medicine*]
LT............ Latest Time [*Business term*]
LT............ Laughter Therapy (EA)
LT............ Launch Test [*NASA*] (IAA)
LT............ Laundry Tray
LT............ Lawn Tennis
LT............ Law Times Journal [*A publication*] (DLA)
LT............ Law Times Newspaper [*A publication*] (DLA)
LT............ Law Times Reports [*British*]
LT............ Layout Template (MCD)
LT............ Leadership Team (ALAC)
L/T........... Leading Telegraphist
LT............ Leading Torpedoman [*Navy*] [*British*]
LT............ Lead Time (NG)
LT............ League of Tarcisians (EA)
LT............ Lease Time (SAUS)
Lt............ Left [*Therapy term*] (CTAA)
LT............ Left
LT............ Left Tackle [*Football*]
LT............ Left Thigh
LT............ Left Triceps [*Anatomy*] (DAVI)
LT............ Left Turn (SAUS)
LT............ Legal Tender [*Currency*]
LT............ Legal Title [*Business term*]
lt............ Legal Training [*Navy*] [*British*]
Lt............ Leptosphaerulina Trifolii [*A fungus*]
LT............ Less Than (IBMDP)
LT............ Lethal Time (STED)
LT............ Letter
LT............ Letter of Transmittal (MCD)
LT............ Letter Telegram
LT............ Leukotriene [*Clinical pharmacology*]
LT............ Level Transmitter (NRCH)
LT............ Level Trigger
LT............ Levin Tube [*Medicine*]
LT............ Levothyroxine [*Pharmacy*]
LT............ Library Talk [*A publication*] (BRI)
LT............ Licentiate in Teaching [*British*]
LT............ Licentiate in Theology
LT............ Lid Tank
LT............ Lieutenant (EY)
Lt............ Lieutenant (WA)
LT............ Light (AAG)
lt............ Light (VRA)
LT............ Light Tank
LT............ Light Terminal (PDAA)
LT............ Light Test (IAA)
L/T........... Light Touch (IDYL)
LT............ Light Transportable (SAUS)
LT............ Light Trap
LT............ Light Truck [*British*]
LT............ Light Truck [*Automotive engineering*]
LT............ Limit (DEN)
LT............ Limited Term Employee (OICC)
L/T........... Line Telecommunications
LT............ Line Telegraphy
LT............ Line Terminator
LT............ Line Traffic Coordinator (SAUO)
LT............ Linked Term [*Online database field identifier*]
LT............ Link Terminal [*Telecommunications*] (TEL)
LT............ Link Testing (NITA)
LT............ Link Trailer (SAUO)
LT............ Link Trainer Instructor
LT............ Liquid Toned [*Copier*] [*Reprography*]
LT............ Lira Toscana [*Tuscany Pound*] [*Monetary unit*] [*Italian*] (ROG)
LT............ Lira Turca [*Turkish Pound*] [*Monetary unit*] [*Italian*] (ROG)
LT............ Liter (ECII)
LT............ Lithuania [*Internet country code*]
LT............ Loader Trainer (MCD)
LT............ Loader-Transporter [*British military*] (DMA)
L/T........... Load Test (MCD)
LT............ Local Time
LT............ Locum Tenens [*In the Place Of*] [*Latin*]
LT............ Logical Terminal (SAUS)
LT............ Logic Theorist [*or Theory*] [*Computer science*]
LT............ Logic Tree
LT............ Logistics Technology
LT............ London-Ducretet-Thomson [*Record label*] [*Great Britain, USA, etc.*]
LT............ London Transport
LT............ Long Term
LT............ Long-Term Stay [*in hospital*] [*British*]
LT............ Long Throw [*Speaker system*]
LT............ Long Ton [*2240 pounds*]
LT............ Long Tour [*Military*] (GFGA)
LT............ Long Treble [*Crocheting*] (ROG)
LT............ Lookthrough (LAIN)
L/T........... Loop Test [*Aerospace*] (AAG)
LT............ Lorentz Transformation [*Physics*] (ODA)
LT............ Lorimar-Telepictures Corp. (SAUO)
LT............ Los Alamos Technical Associates (SAUO)
LT............ Lot
LT............ Lo Ta'aseh (BJA)
LT............ Lot Time (SAA)
LT............ Lotus [*Society of Automotive Engineers auto manufacturer code for service information interchange*]
LT............ Lower Tester [*Open Systems Interconnection*] (ODAA)
LT............ Lower Torso
LT............ Low Temperature
LT............ Low Tension
LT............ Low Torque
LT............ Low Transverse [*incision*] [*Obstetrics*] (DAVI)
LT............ Lucis Trust (EA)
LT............ Lues Test (STED)
LT............ Lug Terminal
LT............ Lumbar Traction [*Orthopedics*] (DAVI)
LT............ Luxury Tax (MHDB)
LT............ Lymphocyte Transformation [*Hematology*]
LT............ Lymphocyte Transitional [*Medicine*] (STED)
LT............ Lymphocytic Thyroiditis [*Medicine*] (STED)
LT............ Lymphocytotoxin [*Medicine*] (STED)
LT............ Lymphoid Tissue [*Biology*]
LT............ Lymphotoxin [*Immunochemistry*]
LT............ Turn Left after Takeoff [*Aviation*] (FAAC)
LT2........... LTD II [*NCIC car model code*]
LTA........... Land Trust Alliance (EA)
LTA........... Large Transport Airplane
LTA........... Laser Training Aid (SAUS)
LTA........... Launch Test Area
LTA........... Launch Tube Assembly
LTA........... Lawn Tennis Association (EAIO)
LTA........... Lead Tetraacetate [*Organic chemistry*]
LTA........... Lead Trial Attorney (SAUO)
LTA........... Leave Travel Allowance
LTA........... Legionarios del Trabajo in America (EA)
LTA........... Leisure Time Activity
LTA........... LEM Test Article (MCD)
LTA........... Less than Adequate (COE)
LTA........... Lettera di Transporto Aereo [*Air Waybill*] [*Italian*] [*Business term*]
LTA........... Lettre de Transport Aerien [*Air Waybill*] [*French*] [*Business term*]
LTA........... Leucotriene A [*Clinical pharmacology*]
LTA........... Leveling Torquer Amplifier
LTA........... Library Technical Assistant
LTA........... Lighter-than-Air [*Aircraft*]
LTA........... Light Transport Aircraft (SAUS)
LTA........... Linea Aerea Tama [*Chile*] [*ICAO designator*] (FAAC)
LTA........... Linear Triaxial Accelerometer (SAUS)
LTA........... Linen Trade Association (EA)
LTA........... Line Turnaround [*Communications term*] (DCT)
LTA........... Lipoate Transacetylase [*An enzyme*]
LTA........... Lipoteichoic Acid [*Biochemistry*]
LTA........... Living Together Arrangement
LTA........... LM [*Lunar Module*] Test Article [*NASA*]
LTA........... Local Training Area (MCD)
LTA........... Logical Transient Area
LTA........... Logic Time Analyzer (IAA)
LTA........... Logic Tree Analysis (SAUO)
LTA........... London Traffic Act (SAUO)
LTA........... Long-Term Arrangement (SAUO)
LTA........... Long-Term Arrangements [*Department of State*]
LTA........... Long-Term Average (CAAL)
LTA........... Lower Torso Assembly [*Aerospace*] (MCD)
LTA........... Low Temperature Aftercooled [*Automotive engineering*]

LTA........... Low Temperature Aftercooling [*Automotive engineering*]
LTA........... Low-Temperature Ashing [*Analytical chemistry*]
LTA........... South Lake Tahoe, CA [*Location identifier*] [*FAA*] (FAAL)
LTA........... Tzaneen [*South Africa*] [*Airport symbol*] (OAG)
LTAA......... Ankara [*Turkey*] [*ICAO location identifier*] (ICLI)
LTAB......... Guvercinlik [*Turkey*] [*ICAO location identifier*] (ICLI)
LTAB......... League to Abolish Billionaires [*Fictitious organization mentioned in Donald Duck comic by Carl Barks*]
LTAC......... Ankara/Esenboga [*Turkey*] [*ICAO location identifier*] (ICLI)
LTAC......... Literary Translators Association of Canada (EAIO)
LTAC......... Long-Term Acute Care (MHCS)
LTACFIRE... Light Tactical Fire (SAUS)
LTACFIRE... Lightweight Tactical Fire Direction System [*Artillery*] [*Army*] (INF)
LTAD......... Ankara/Etimesgut [*Turkey*] [*ICAO location identifier*] (ICLI)
LTADL....... Launcher Tube Azimuth Datum Line
LTAE......... Ankara/Murted [*Turkey*] [*ICAO location identifier*] (ICLI)
LTAE......... Long-Term Agroecosystem Experiment
LTAF......... Adana/Sakirpasa [*Turkey*] [*ICAO location identifier*] (ICLI)
LTAG......... Adana/Incirlik [*Turkey*] [*ICAO location identifier*] (ICLI)
LTAG......... Liaison Training and Advisory Group (SAUO)
LTAH......... Afyon [*Turkey*] [*ICAO location identifier*] (ICLI)
LTAI......... Antalya [*Turkey*] [*ICAO location identifier*] (ICLI)
LTAJ......... Gaziantep [*Turkey*] [*ICAO location identifier*] (ICLI)
LTAK......... Iskenderun [*Turkey*] [*ICAO location identifier*] (ICLI)
LTAL......... Kastamonu [*Turkey*] [*ICAO location identifier*] (ICLI)
LTAL......... Lower Transition Altitude (SAA)
LTALT....... Light Alternating (IAA)
LTAM......... Kayseri [*Turkey*] [*ICAO location identifier*] (ICLI)
LTaM......... Madison Parish Library, Tallulah, LA [*Library symbol*] [*Library of Congress*] (LCLS)
LTAN......... Konya [*Turkey*] [*ICAO location identifier*] (ICLI)
LT & D...... Love, Togetherness, and Devotion [*Rock music group*]
LT & S....... London, Tilbury & Southend Railway [*British*]
LT & SR..... London, Tilbury & Southend Railway [*British*] (ROG)
LTAO......... Malatya/Erhac [*Turkey*] [*ICAO location identifier*] (ICLI)
LTAP......... Merzifon [*Turkey*] [*ICAO location identifier*] (ICLI)
LTAQ......... Samsun [*Turkey*] [*ICAO location identifier*] (ICLI)
LTAR......... Sivas [*Turkey*] [*ICAO location identifier*] (ICLI)
LTAS......... Lead Tetraacetate-Schiff (Reaction) [*Clinical chemistry*]
LTAS......... Lighter than Air Society [*An association*] (PDAA)
LTAS......... Zonguldak [*Turkey*] [*ICAO location identifier*] (ICLI)
LTAT......... Malatya/Erhac [*Turkey*] [*ICAO location identifier*] (ICLI)
LTAU......... Kayseri/Erkilet [*Turkey*] [*ICAO location identifier*] (ICLI)
LTAV......... Sivrihisar [*Turkey*] [*ICAO location identifier*] (ICLI)
LTAVD....... Low-Temperature Arc Vapor Deposition [*Coating technology*]
LTB........... Acute Laryngotracheobronchitis [*Commonly known as croup*] (PAZ)
Lt B.......... Bachelor of Literature
LTB........... Department of Genetics and Human Variation La Trobe University, Melbourne (SAUS)
LTB........... Laboratory Test Bed (SAUS)
LTB........... Laparoscopic Tubal Banding [*Ligation*] (DAVI)
LTB........... Laryngo-Tracheal Bronchitis
LTB........... Laryngotracheobronchitis [*Medicine*] (PALA)
LTB........... Last Trunk Busy [*Telecommunications*] (TEL)
LTB........... La Trobe University Herbarium (SAUO)
LTB........... Laundry Trade Board (SAUO)
LTB........... Lawrence Traffic Bureau Inc., Kansas City MO [*STAC*]
LTB........... Law Times Bankruptcy Reports [*United States*] [*A publication*] (DLA)
LTB........... Lead-Time Bias (MELL)
LTB........... Legal, Tax & Business
LTB........... Length-Time Bias (MELL)
LTB........... Lepers Trust Board (SAUO)
LTB........... Leucotriene B [*Clinical pharmacology*]
LTB........... Light Bay [*Horse racing*]
LTB........... Limited Test Ban [*Nuclear testing*]
LTB........... Line Term Buffer [*Computer science*] (AABC)
LTB........... Local Token-Ring Bridge (CIST)
LTB........... London Tourist Board [*British*] (DCTA)
LTB........... London Transport Board [*British*]
LT(B)......... Low-Tension (Battery) (DEN)
LTBA......... Die Lexikalischen Tafelserien der Babylonier und Assyrer in den Berliner Museen [*A publication*] (BJA)
LTBA......... Istanbul/Yesilkoy [*Turkey*] [*ICAO location identifier*] (ICLI)
LTBA......... Lightweight Tactical Body Armor [*Police and security equipment*]
LTBA......... Louisiana Thoroughbred Breeders Association (SRA)
LTBB......... Istanbul [*Turkey*] [*ICAO location identifier*] (ICLI)
LTBC......... Alasehir [*Turkey*] [*ICAO location identifier*] (ICLI)
LTBC......... Lawn Tennis Ball Convention [*British*] (BI)
LTBD......... Aydin [*Turkey*] [*ICAO location identifier*] (ICLI)
LTBE......... Bursa [*Turkey*] [*ICAO location identifier*] (ICLI)
LTBF......... Balikesir [*Turkey*] [*ICAO location identifier*] (ICLI)
LTBF......... Learn To Be Funny (SAUS)
LTBG......... Bandirma [*Turkey*] [*ICAO location identifier*] (ICLI)
LTBG......... Lightbridge, Inc. [*NASDAQ symbol*] (SG)
LTBH......... Canakkale [*Turkey*] [*ICAO location identifier*] (ICLI)
LTBI......... Eskisehir [*Turkey*] [*ICAO location identifier*] (ICLI)
LTBJ......... Izmir/Cumaovasi [*Turkey*] [*ICAO location identifier*] (ICLI)
LTBK......... Izmir/Gaziemir [*Turkey*] [*ICAO location identifier*] (ICLI)
LTBL......... Izmir/Cigli [*Turkey*] [*ICAO location identifier*] (ICLI)
LtBl......... Light Blend [*Horticulture*]
LTBM......... Isparta [*Turkey*] [*ICAO location identifier*] (ICLI)
LTBMC....... Long-Term Bone Marrow Culture [*Cell culture*]
LTBN......... Kutahya [*Turkey*] [*ICAO location identifier*] (ICLI)
LTBO......... Linear Time Base Oscillator
LTBO......... Usak [*Turkey*] [*ICAO location identifier*] (ICLI)
LTBP......... London Tanker Broker Panel
LTBP......... Yalova [*Turkey*] [*ICAO location identifier*] (ICLI)
LTBQ......... Topel [*Turkey*] [*ICAO location identifier*] (ICLI)
LTBR......... Yenisehir [*Turkey*] [*ICAO location identifier*] (ICLI)
LTBS......... Dalaman [*Turkey*] [*ICAO location identifier*] (ICLI)
LTBS......... Little Traverse Bay Scenic Railroad [*Federal Railroad Administration identification code*]
LTBT......... Akhisar [*Turkey*] [*ICAO location identifier*] (ICLI)
LTBT......... Limited Test Ban Treaty [*Signed in 1963; prohibits testing of nuclear devices in certain environments*]
LTC........... Laboratory for Turbulence and Combustion [*University of Michigan*] (RCD)
LTC........... Laboratory Training Center (SAUO)
LTC........... Lafferty Transportation [*AAR code*]
LTC........... Lafferty Transportation Company (SAUO)
LTC........... Lai [*Chad*] [*Airport symbol*] (AD)
LTC........... Land Tenure Center [*University of Wisconsin*] [*Research center*]
LTC........... Land Tenure Centre, Madison, Wisc. (SAUS)
LTC........... Land Transfer Committee (SAUO)
LTC........... Land Transport Corps [*British military*] (DMA)
LTC........... Land Trust Commission (BARN)
LTC........... Language and Time-sharing Center (SAUO)
LTC........... Language Testing Center [*University of Melbourne*] [*Australia*]
LTC........... Language Tuition Centre (SAUO)
LTC........... Large Transformed Cell [*Medicine*] (DMAA)
LTC........... Last Telecast (WDMC)
LTC........... Latcharter [*Latvia*] [*FAA designator*] (FAAC)
LTC........... Lattice (MSA)
LTC........... Launceston Technical College [*Australia*]
LTC........... Launch Vehicle Test Conductor [*NASA*] (KSC)
LTC........... Lawn Tennis Club [*British*]
LTC........... Lead Telluride Crystal [*Photoconductor*]
LTC........... Lead to Come [*Publishing*] (WDMC)
LTC........... Leaseway Transportation Corp. (WDAA)
LTC........... Leave and Transit Camp (SAUO)
LTC........... Lectric Leopard [*NCIC car model code*]
LTC........... Left to Count (DAVI)
LTC........... Legislative Transportation Committee (SAUO)
LTC........... Lesotho Telecommunications Corp. [*Ministry of Transport and Communications*] [*Lesotho*] (TSSD)
LTC........... Less than Truckload Cargo (MCD)
LTC........... Letdown Terrain Clearance (DNAB)
LTC........... Le Tourneau College (SAUO)
LTC........... Leukotriene C [*Clinical pharmacology*]
LTC........... Level and Timing Controller (ACAE)
LTC........... Leyland Technical Center [*Automotive industry*]
LTC........... Liberia Telecommunications Corp. (IMH)
LTC........... Liberty to the Captives [*Later, ACAT*] (EA)
LTC........... Library of Trinity College (SAUO)
LTC........... Library Technical Centre [*Polytechnic of Central London*] (NITA)
LTC........... Licentiate of Trinity College (SAUO)
LTC........... Lidocaine Tissue Concentration [*Medicine*] (DMAA)
LTC........... Lieutenance Colonel (SAUO)
LTC........... Lieutenant Colonel (AABC)
Ltc........... Lieutenant Colonel
LTC........... Lieutenant Commander (GFGA)
LTC........... Lightly Treated Coated [*Papermaking*]
LTC........... Light Terminal Complexes
LTC........... Ligue Trotskyiste du Canada [*Association*] [*Canada*] (EAIO)
LTC........... Linear Transformation Converter (IAA)
LTC........... Linear Transmission Channel
LTC........... Line Terminal Control (IAA)
LTC........... Line Termination Coordinator (SAUS)
LTC........... Line Time Clock
LTC........... Line Traffic Coordinator (CET)
LTC........... Lithcote [*Federal Railroad Administration identification code*]
LTC........... Lithographic Test Chip (AAEL)
LTC........... Living Tree Center (EA)
LTC........... Livros Tecnicos e Cientificos Editora Ltda. [*Brazil*]
LTC........... Load Tap Changing
LTC........... Local Telephone Circuit [*Telecommunications*] (TEL)
LTC........... Local Terminal Controller
LTC........... Local Time Clock
LTC........... Location Traction Control Switch [*Automotive emissions*]
LTC........... Lockwood Torday & Carlisle Ltd. [*British*]
LTC........... London Trades Council (SAUO)
LTC........... Longitudinal Time Code (NTCM)
LTC........... Longitudinal Time Constant
LTC........... Long-Term Care [*Medicine*]
LTC........... Long-Term Complication (MELL)
LTC........... Long-Term Concentration (EAGT)
LTC........... Long-Term Consequence (MELL)
LTC........... Long Term Contract (SAUS)
LTC........... Long-Term Contract (ADA)
LTC........... Long Term Costing [*Military*] (RDA)
LTC........... Long Time Constant (IEEE)
LTC........... Loop Test Conference [*Aerospace*] (AAG)
LTC........... Lotus Cosmetics International (SAUO)
LTC........... Lotus Cosmetics International Ltd. [*Vancouver Stock Exchange symbol*]
LTC........... Low-Tar Content [*of cigarettes*]
LTC........... Low-Temperature Carbonization
LTC........... Low-Temperature Catalyst

LTC.......... Low-Temperature Coefficient
LTC.......... Low-Temperature Cooling
LTC.......... Low-Tension Current (IAA)
LTC.......... Low Transverse Cervical [*Medicine*] (MELL)
LTC.......... LTC Properties [*NYSE symbol*] (TTSB)
LTC.......... LTC Properties, Inc. [*NYSE symbol*] (SPSG)
LTC.......... Lubricant Technology Center [*Fuels and lubricants*]
LTC.......... Lunar Terrain [*or Topographic*] Camera [*NASA*]
LTC.......... Lynchburg Technology Center (GAAI)
L(TC)........ Tax Cases Leaflets [*Legal*] [*British*]
LTCA......... Elazig [*Turkey*] [*ICAO location identifier*] (ICLI)
LTCAX....... Thornburg Ltd. Term Muni-Cal. Cl.A [*Mutual fund ticker symbol*] (SG)
LTCB......... Agri [*Turkey*] [*ICAO location identifier*] (ICLI)
LTCB......... Long Term Credit Bank [*Japan*] (ECON)
LTCB......... Long-Term Credit Bank of Japan, Ltd. (ECON)
LTCC......... Diyarbakir [*Turkey*] [*ICAO location identifier*] (ICLI)
LTCC......... Language Testing and Curriculum Center [*Griffith University*] [*Australia*]
LTCC......... Long-Term Care Campaign (EA)
LTCC......... Low Temperature Co-Fired Ceramic (AAEL)
LTCC......... LTC Trucking Company [*Common carrier symbol*]
LTCCE........ Long-term Continuous Cropping Experiment (SAUO)
LTCCM....... Loading Training Captive Carry Missile (MCD)
LTCD......... Erzincan [*Turkey*] [*ICAO location identifier*] (ICLI)
LTCDA....... Low Temperature Coal Distillers Association [*British*] (DBA)
Lt Cdr....... Lieutenant Commander (WDAA)
LTCDR....... Lieutenant Commander
LTCE......... Erzurum [*Turkey*] [*ICAO location identifier*] (ICLI)
LTCF......... Kars [*Turkey*] [*ICAO location identifier*] (ICLI)
LTCF......... Long-Term Care Facility [*Medicine*]
LTCG......... Long-Term Capital Gain
LTCG......... Trabzon [*Turkey*] [*ICAO location identifier*] (ICLI)
LTCH......... Litchfield Financial [*NASDAQ symbol*] (TTSB)
LTCH......... Litchfield Financial Corp. [*NASDAQ symbol*] (SAG)
LTCH......... Long-Term Care Hospital (MHCS)
LTCH......... Urfa [*Turkey*] [*ICAO location identifier*] (ICLI)
LTCI.......... Van [*Turkey*] [*ICAO location identifier*] (ICLI)
LTCJ......... Batman [*Turkey*] [*ICAO location identifier*] (ICLI)
LTCL......... Licentiate of Trinity College of Music, London [*British*]
LTCL......... Long-Term Capital Loss
LTCM........ Licentiate of the Toronto Conservatory of Music [*Canada*]
LTCM........ Long-Term Capital Management
Lt Cmdr...... Lieutenant Commander (SAUO)
LTCMDS..... Long-Term Care Minimum Data Set [*Department of Health and Human Services*] (GFGA)
LTCML....... Licentiate of Trinity College of Music, London (SAUO)
LTCO......... Lakeside Transportation [*Federal Railroad Administration identification code*]
LtCol......... Lieutenant Colonel (ASC)
LTCOL....... Lieutenant Colonel
LTCOM...... Lieutenant Commander (DNAB)
LT COMDR... Lieutenant Commander (DNAB)
Lt-Comm.... Lieutenant-Commander [*British military*] (DMA)
LT/COR/WR... Light Corner Wear [*Deltiology*]
LTC Prp..... LTC Properties, Inc. [*Associated Press*] (SAG)
LTCR......... Leelanau Transit [*Federal Railroad Administration identification code*]
LT/CR........ Light Crease [*Deltiology*]
LTCS......... Long-Term Contracting Strategy (COE)
LTCS......... Low Transverse Cesarean Section [*Medicine*] (MEDA)
LTCSB....... Long-Term Care Statistics Branch [*Department of Health and Human Services*] (GFGA)
LTCT......... Lower Thermal Comfort Threshold [*Environmental heating*]
LTCVD....... Low-Temperature Chemical Vapor Deposition (AAEL)
LTCZ......... Lilly-Tulip [*Federal Railroad Administration identification code*]
LTD.......... Collaboration Type Details (SAUS)
LTD.......... Ghadames [*Libya*] [*Airport symbol*] (OAG)
LTD.......... Land Titles Division [*South Australia*]
LTD.......... Land Treatment Demonstration [*Environmental science*] (COE)
LTD.......... Language Training Detachment [*Defense Language Institute*] (DNAB)
LTD.......... Largest Tumor Diameter (SAUS)
LTD.......... Largest Tumor Dimension [*Medicine*] (EDAA)
LTD.......... Laron-Type Dwarfism [*Medicine*]
LTD.......... LASER Target Designator
LTD.......... Launch Test Directive [*NASA*] (KSC)
LTD.......... Letdown [*Nuclear energy*] (NRCH)
LTD.......... Leukotriene D [*Clinical pharmacology*]
LTD.......... Lift-Drag [*Ratio*] (MCD)
LTD.......... Lift-to-Drag [*Aerospace*] (NAKS)
LTD.......... Light Displacement Tonnage (SAUS)
LTD.......... Lightweight Target Designator
ltd............ Limited (DAVI)
LTD.......... Limited
Ltd........... Limited (DIAR)
LTD.......... Limited Brands [*Company symbol*]
LTD.......... Limited Company (SAUO)
LTD.......... [*The*] Limited, Inc. [*NYSE symbol*] (SPSG)
Ltd........... Limited Liability (SAUO)
Ltd........... Limited Liability Co. (SAUO)
LTD.......... Limit to Topographic Development [*Of hillsides*] [*Geology*]
LTD.......... Linear Transport Drive
LTD.......... Linear Tumor Diameter [*Oncology*]
LTD.......... Line Transfer Device
LTD.......... Litchfield, IL [*Location identifier*] [*FAA*] (FAAL)
LTD.......... Live Test Demonstration
LTD.......... Local Data Terminal (ACAE)
LTD.......... Local Test Desk [*Telecommunications*] (KSC)
LTD.......... Logistic Technical Data [*Navy*]
LTD.......... Long Tank Delta
LTD.......... Long Term Debt (SAUO)
LTD.......... Long-Term Depression [*Neurophysiology*]
LTD.......... Long-Term Disability
LTD.......... Lost During Transhipment (SAUO)
LTD.......... Low-Temperature Drying
LTD.......... Lumber Transfer and Distribution
LTD.......... Platinum Resistance Thermometer [*Medicine*] (EDAA)
LTDA......... Licensed Taxi Drivers' Association [*British*] (DBA)
LTDA......... London Taxi Drivers' Association [*England*]
LTD ED...... Limited Edition [*Publishing*]
LTDI.......... Learning Technology Dissemination Initiative (AIE)
LTDL......... Life Test Data Logger (CAAL)
LTDM........ Light Transmittance Difference Meter
LTDP......... Long Term Defense Plan (SAUS)
LTDP......... Long-Term Defense Program [*NATO*] (MCD)
LTDQ......... Limited Quantity [*Refers to a test performed on a scanty specimen*] [*Biochemistry*] (DAVI)
LTDR......... Laser Target Designator Rangefinder (ACAE)
LTD/R........ LASER Target Designator/Ranger (DWSG)
LTDR......... LASER Target Designator Receiver
LTDS......... Laser Target Designator Set (ACAE)
LTDS......... LASER Target Designator System (MCD)
LTDS......... Laser Tracking and Discrimination Study (ACAE)
LTDS......... Launch Tracking [*or Trajectory*] Data System
LTDSS........ LASER Target Designator Scoring System (MCD)
LTDSTD..... Limited Standard (IAA)
LTDT......... Langley Transonic Dynamics Tunnel [*NASA*] (KSC)
LTDT......... Low Temperature Deposit Test [*Fuels and lubricants*]
LTD(U)....... Land Treatment Demonstration [*or Unit*] (GNE)
LTE........... Land Trust Exchange [*Later, LTA*] (EA)
LTE........... Laplace Transformation Estimator
LTE........... Large Table Electroplotter [*Computer science*]
LTE........... Large Terminal Repeats [*Genetics*] (DAVI)
LTE........... Large Thrust per Element
LTE........... Launch to Eject
LTE........... Letter to the Editor
LTE........... Leucotriene E [*Clinical pharmacology*]
LTE........... Levitator Technology Experiment (SAUS)
LT(E)......... Lieutenant (Engineer)
LTE........... Limited Technical Evaluation (MCD)
LTE........... Limited Test Equipment
LTE........... Linear Threshold Element [*Computer science*]
LTE........... Line Termination Equipment [*Telecommunications*] (TEL)
LTE........... Local Telephone Exchange (NITA)
LTE........... Local Thermal Equilibrium [*Physical chemistry*]
LTE........... Local Thermodynamic Equilibrium [*or Equivalent*] [*Astronautics, astrophysics*]
LTE........... Local Truncation Error (VLIE)
LTE........... Long-Term Effect
LTE........... Long-Term Enhancement [*Neurophysiology*]
LTE........... Long-Term Equilibration [*Analytical chemistry*]
LTE........... Low-Thrust Engine
LTE........... LTE International Airways SA [*Spain*] [*FAA designator*] (FAAC)
LTE........... Luxury Touring Edition [*Automobile model designation*]
LTEA......... Leaf Tobacco Exporters Association (EA)
LTeach....... Law Teacher (SAFN)
LTEC......... Lincoln Telecmmun [*NASDAQ symbol*] (TTSB)
LTEC......... Lincoln Telecommunications Company (SAUO)
LTED......... Long-Term Economic Deterioration [*Department of Commerce*]
LT/ED/WR... Light Edge Wear [*Deltiology*]
Ltee.......... Limitee [*Limited*] [*French*]
LTEEC........ Lake Tahoe Environmental Education Consortium (SAUO)
LTEK......... Life Technologies [*NASDAQ symbol*] (TTSB)
LTEK......... Life Technologies, Inc. (SAUO)
LTEL......... Lincoln Telecommunications Co. (SAUO)
LTEL......... Lorain Telecommunications Corp. (SAUO)
LTEMP....... Low Temperature
L T (Eng)... Law Times Journal (England) [*A publication*] (DLA)
LTEP......... Long-Term Equipment Plan [*Military*] (RDA)
LTEP......... Low-Temperature Engine Performance
LTER......... Long Term Ecological Research [*National Science Foundation*]
LTER......... Long-Term Ecological Research Project (SAUO)
LTER/LOME. Long-Term Ecological Research in Land/Ocean Margin Ecosystems [*National Science Foundation*] (RCD)
LTERM....... Logical Terminal (TIMI)
LTERM....... Long-Term Ecosystem Research and Monitoring (SAUO)
LTERR....... Lunar Terrestrial Age
LTEU......... Liquor Trades Employees Union (SAUO)
LTEX......... L. Hags [*Private rail car owner code*]
LTF........... Lactotransferrin [*Medicine*] (EDAA)
LTF........... Landline Telephony [*Aviation*] (DA)
LTF........... Laryngo-Tracheo-Esophagael [*Medicine*] (EDAA)
LTF........... LASER Terrain Follower
LTF........... Latvijas Tautas Fronte [*Popular Front of Latvia*] [*Political party*] (EY)
LTF........... Layman Tithing Foundation (EA)
LTF........... Learning to Fly [*Animal Fell off balcony or similar*] (SPVS)
LTF........... Leucotriene F [*Clinical pharmacology*]
LTF........... Ligand-Responsive Transcription Factor [*Genetics*]
LTF........... Light-Float [*Navigation*]
LTF........... Lightning Training Flight [*British military*] (DMA)

LTF.......... Lipotropic Factor [*Choline*] [*Biochemistry*]
LTF.......... Liquid Thermal Flowmeter
LTF.......... Lithographic Technical Foundation [*Later, GATF*] (MSA)
LTF.......... Lithographic Technical Foundation, Inc. (SAUO)
LTF.......... Local Training Flight
LTF.......... Logical Twin Forward Pointer (MHDI)
LTF.......... Logistic Task Force (SAUO)
LTF.......... Log Transfer Facility [*USDA Forest Service*] (ALAC)
LTF.......... Long-Term Forecasting (FOTI)
LTF.......... Lymphocyte Transforming Factor [*Immunology*]
LTF.......... Nicholls State University, Thibodaux, LA [*Library symbol*] [*Library of Congress*] (LCLS)
LTFC.......... Landing Traffic [*Aviation*] (FAAC)
LTFC.......... Low-Temperature Fuel Cell [*Energy source*]
LTFCS.......... LASER Tank Fire Control System
LTFD.......... Logic and Test Function Drawer [*Computer science*] (MCD)
LT/FM.......... Long-Term/Frequency Modulation
LTFP.......... Long Term Force Programmes (SAUS)
LTFRD.......... Lot Tolerance Fraction Reliability Deviation [*Quality control*]
LTFS.......... LASER Terrain Following System
LTFS.......... London Tax Free Shopping Co. (SAUO)
LTFT.......... Long-Term Fuel Trim [*Automotive engineering, fuel systems*]
LTFT.......... Long Term Full Time Training (ACAE)
LTFT.......... Low-Temperature Filter Test
LTFT.......... Low-Temperature Flow Test [*Lubricant technology*]
LTFV.......... Less Than Fair Value [*Business term*]
LTG.......... Catalina Lighting [*NYSE symbol*] (SAG)
LTG.......... Laboratory Test Group (SAUO)
LTG.......... Legal Technology Group [*Information service or system*] (IID)
LTG.......... Lettering (ADA)
LTG.......... Liaison Task Group (AG)
LTG.......... Lieutenant General (AABC)
LTG.......... Lightening
LTG.......... Lighting
LTG.......... Lightning [*Meteorology*]
LTG.......... Lightning Minerals [*Vancouver Stock Exchange symbol*]
LTG.......... Linear Tangent Guidance (MCD)
LTG.......... Line Termination Group (SAUO)
LTG.......... Line Trunk Group [*Telecommunications*]
ltg.......... Lithographer [*MARC relator code*] [*Library of Congress*] (LCCP)
LTG.......... Little Theatre Guild [*British*] (DBA)
LTG.......... Local Tactical Grid [*Military*] (NVT)
LTG.......... Long-Term Goals (DAVI)
LTG.......... Low Tension Glaucoma (SAUS)
LTG.......... Lunar Traverse Gravimeter [*Experiment*] [*NASA*]
LTGA.......... Left [*or Levo*] Transposition of the Great Arteries [*Also called corrected transposition*] [*Cardiology*] (DAVI)
Lt Ga.......... Light Gauge (MIST)
LTGC.......... Lieutenant Grand Commander [*Freemasonry*]
LTGCA.......... Lightning Cloud-to-Air [*NWS*] (FAAC)
LTGCC.......... Lightning Cloud-to-Cloud [*NWS*] (FAAC)
LTGCCCG.......... Lightning Cloud-to-Cloud, Cloud-to-Ground [*NWS*] (FAAC)
LTGCG.......... Lightning Cloud-to-Ground [*NWS*] (FAAC)
LTGCW.......... Lightning Cloud-to-Water [*NWS*] (FAAC)
LTGE.......... Lighterage
Lt Gen.......... Lieutenant General (WDAA)
LTGEN.......... Lieutenant General
LTGF Newl.......... Lawyers' Title Guaranty Funds Newsletter [*A publication*] (DLA)
LTGH.......... Lightening Hole [*Engineering*]
LTGHE.......... Low-Temperature Gradient Heating Furnace (SAUS)
LTGIC.......... Lightning in Clouds [*NWS*] (FAAC)
LTGL.......... Lee-Tse-Goldberg-Lowe [*Theory*]
LTGL.......... Liteglow Industries, Inc. [*NASDAQ symbol*] (QUAN)
Lt Gov.......... Lieutenant Governor (SHCU)
LT Gov.......... Lieutenant Governor (WGA)
Lt grp fl.......... Light, group-flashing (SAUO)
Lt grp occ.......... Light, group occulting (SAUO)
LTH.......... Enterprise Thesaurus [*Database*]
LTH.......... Laboratory Test Handbook
LTH.......... Lactogenic Hormone [*Also, LGH, PR, PRL*] [*Endocrinology*]
L Th.......... La Themis [*Lower Canada*] [*A publication*] (DLA)
LTH.......... Leather [*Automotive advertising*]
LtH.......... Left-Handed (ADWA)
LTH.......... Less than Honorable Discharge [*Military*] (VNW)
LTH.......... Lethality (ACAE)
LTH.......... Lethality & Target Hardening (SAUS)
L Th.......... Licentiate in Theology
LTH.......... Light Towed Howitzer (SAUS)
LTH.......... Light Training Helicopter (WDAA)
LTH.......... Local Tumor Hyperthermia [*Medicine*] (DB)
LTH.......... Logical Track Header
LTH.......... London Teaching Hospitals [*National Health Service*] [*British*] (DI)
LTH.......... Long-Term Holiday (MHDB)
LTH.......... Low-Temperature Herschel (OA)
LTH.......... Low-Temperature Holding
LTH.......... Low Turret Half
LTH.......... Luteotrophic Hormone [*Also, PR, PRL*] [*Endocrinology*]
Lth.......... Martin Luther's German Version of the Bible [*A publication*] (BJA)
LTHA.......... Long-Term Heat Aging
LTHE.......... Low Temperature Heat Exchanger (EEVL)
L Theol.......... Licentiate in Theology [*British*] (WA)
LTHG.......... Lathing
L Th K.......... Lexikon fuer Theologie und Kirche [*A publication*] (ODCC)
LTHO.......... Lighthouse
LTHR.......... Leather (KSC)
LTHV.......... Lucke Tumor Herpesvirus
LTI.......... Aerotaxis Latinoamericanos SA de CV [*Mexico*] [*ICAO designator*] (FAAC)
LTI.......... Ladder Towers Incorporated (SAUO)
LTI.......... Land Training Installations (NATG)
LTI.......... Language Technologies Institute [*Carnegie Mellon University*] (RCD)
LTI.......... Laser Technology Inc. (SAUS)
LTI.......... Lawyers Tile [*NYSE symbol*] (TTSB)
LTI.......... Lawyers Title Corp. [*NYSE symbol*] (SAG)
LTI.......... Learning and Teaching Institute [*Sheffield Hallam University*] [*United Kingdom*] (RCD)
LTI.......... Licentiate of the Textile Institute [*British*] (DBQ)
LTI.......... Life Technologies, Inc. (HGEN)
LTI.......... Light Tip-In [*Automotive testing*]
LTI.......... Light Transmission Index
LTI.......... Limited to Interrogations (MCD)
LTI.......... Linear Technology, Inc. [*Toronto Stock Exchange symbol*]
LTI.......... Linear Time Invariant (IAA)
LTI.......... Lingua Tertii Imperii [*A study of the abuse of language under Nazism by Viktor Klemperer*]
LTI.......... Liquid Transporters Inc. (EFIS)
LTI.......... Logistic Technical Information (SAUO)
LTI.......... London Taxis International [*Vehicle manufacturer*]
LTI.......... Long-Term Inmate (WDAA)
LTI.......... Long-Term Integration (CAAL)
LTI.......... Lost Time Injuries (SAUO)
LTI.......... Lost Time Injury [*Industrial plant safety*]
LTI.......... Louisiana Training Institute (SAUO)
LTI.......... Lowell Technological Institute [*Massachusetts*]
LTI.......... Lowell Textile Institute (SAUO)
LTI.......... Low-Temperature Isomerization [*Organic chemistry*]
LTI.......... Low-Temperature Isotope
LTI.......... Lupus-Type Inclusions [*Medicine*] (DMAA)
LTIA.......... Lynden Transport [*Common carrier symbol*]
LTIB.......... Lead Technical Information Bureau [*British*] (BI)
LTIC.......... Language Teaching Information Centre [*British*] (CB)
LTID.......... LASER Target Interface Device (RDA)
LTID.......... Light-Intensity Detector (MSA)
LTID.......... Logical Terminal Identifier (SAUS)
Lt Inf.......... Light Infantry [*British military*] (DMA)
LTIOV.......... Latest Time Information of Value [*Military*] (AFM)
LTIP.......... Long-Term Incentive Plan
LTIRF.......... Lowell Technological Institute Research Foundation (MCD)
LTIS.......... LASER Target Interface System
LTIU.......... Lloyd Triestine di Navigazione [*Intermodal shipping container symbol*] (TVRC)
LTIV.......... Lunar Trajectory Injection Vehicle [*NASA*] (KSC)
LTIZ.......... Liposome Technology, Inc. [*NASDAQ symbol*] (COMM)
LTJ.......... Law Times Journal [*A publication*] (DLA)
LTJ.......... Lutheran Theological Journal [*A publication*] (APTA)
LTJC.......... Lyons Township Junior College [*Illinois*]
LTJG.......... Lieutenant Junior Grade [*Navy*]
LTjg.......... Lieutenant, Junior Grade [*Navy*] (GOBB)
LT Jo (Eng).......... Law Times Journal (England) [*A publication*] (DLA)
LTK.......... Laser Thermal Keratoplasty (SAUS)
LTK.......... Latakia [*Syria*] [*Airport symbol*] (OAG)
LTK.......... Lead To Come [*Copyediting*] (WDMC)
LTK.......... Leukocyte Tyrosine Kinase [*An enzyme*]
LTK1.......... Ladies' Touring Kayak, Single Person (ADA)
L Tk Co.......... Light Tank Company (SAUO)
LTL.......... Aerie Airlines (SAUO)
LTL.......... Lafourche Parish Library, Thibodaux, LA [*Library symbol*] [*Library of Congress*] (LCLS)
LTL.......... Laparoscopic Tubal Ligation [*Gynecology*] (DAVI)
LTL.......... Lastourville [*Gabon*] [*Airport symbol*] (OAG)
LTL.......... Latvian Airlines [*ICAO designator*] (FAAC)
LTL.......... Learning Through Listening [*Recording for the blind*]
LTL.......... Learning to Look
LTL.......... Less than Lethal (INF)
LTL.......... Less than Truckload [*Under 24,000 pounds*]
LTL.......... Linear Temporal Logic (RALS)
LTL.......... Line-to-Line
LTL.......... Lintel [*Technical drawings*]
LTL.......... Listing-Time Limit (MSA)
LTL.......... Little
LTL.......... Lot-to-Lot (AAEL)
LTL.......... Lot-Truck Load
LTL.......... Lower Tactile Level [*M*
LTL.......... Low Temperature
LTL.......... Lytton Minera
LTL.......... Lytton Min
St
LTLA.......... Launc
LTLA.......... Louisia
lt lat.......... Left Later
LTLCG.......... Little Chang
LTLDW.......... Less-Than-L
ment]
LTLOG.......... Landsat Technic
LTLP.......... Low Temperature,
LTLS.......... Lincoln Trail Librari
LTLS.......... Long-Term Lapse Su
LTLT.......... Long Time Low Tempe

LTLZ .... Lang Trailer Leasing [*Intermodal trailer symbol*]

LTM .... Laici per il Terzo Mondo [*Italy*]

LTM .... LASER Target Marker (RDA)

LTM .... LASER Transfer Module [*Telecommunications*] (LAIN)

LTM .... Leadership Team Meeting (ALAC)

LTM .... Leading Torpedoman [*Navy*] [*British*]

LTM .... Lead Time Matrix (MCD)

LTM .... Learning to Manage Health information (SAUO)

LTM .... Leave Trapping Mode (SAA)

LTM .... Lethem [*Guyana*] [*Airport symbol*] (OAG)

LTM .... Leverage Transaction Merchant (MHDI)

LTM .... Licentiate in/of Tropical Medicine (SAUO)

LTM .... Licentiate in Tropical Medicine [*British*]

LTM .... Lient Trief Mixed [*Cement*]

LTM .... Life Test Model

LTM .... Limits-to-Throughput Model [*Environmental science*]

LTM .... Line Termination Module (SAUS)

LTM .... Line Transition Monitoring (NITA)

LTM .... Line Type Modulation [*Radio*]

LTM .... Little Maria Mountains [*California*] [*Seismograph station code, US Geological Survey*] (SEIS)

LTM .... Little Theatre Movement (SAUO)

LTM .... Live Traffic Model [*Telecommunications*] (TEL)

LTM .... Load Ton Mile (IAA)

LTM .... Logic Theory Machine (SAA)

LTM .... London Terminal Market (SAUO)

LT/M .... Long Term Memory (IDYL)

LTM .... Long-Term Memory

LTM .... Long-Term Monitoring [*Environmental science*] (BCP)

LTM .... Low Thermal Mass (PDAA)

LTM .... Low-Trajectory Missiles (NRCH)

LTM1 .... Lunar Tele-Operations Model 1 [*Mooncolony modeling*]

LTMA .... Lithium Trimethoxyaluminium (MEC)

LTMAC .... Lauryltrimethylammonium Chloride [*Organic chemistry*]

LTMC .... Lymphoid Tissue Mononuclear Cell [*Physiology*]

LTMED .... Low-Temperature Multieffect Distillation [*Chemical engineering*]

LTMFM .... Low-Temperature Magnetic Force Microscope

LTMFX .... Thornburg Ltd. Term Munic: Natl. Cl.A [*Mutual fund ticker symbol*] (SG)

LTMO .... Laser Target Marking Operator (SAUS)

LTMQ .... Litton Moving and Storage Company [*Common carrier symbol*]

LTMR .... Laser Target Marker & Receiver (SAUS)

LTMR .... LASER Target Marker Ranger [*Aviation*] (OA)

LTMR .... Long-Term Multilineage Reconstituting [*Cytology*]

LTMRSC .... Long-Term Multilineage Reconstituting Stem Cell [*Cytology*]

LTMS .... Lubricant Test Monitoring System [*Automotive engineering*]

LTMS .... Lunar Terrain Measuring System [*Aerospace*]

LTMSH .... Laughing 'Til My Sides Hurt (ADWA)

LTN .... Aerolineas Latinas CA [*Venezuela*] [*ICAO designator*] (FAAC)

LTN .... Alaska Legislative Teleconference Network [*Alaska State Legislative Affairs Agency*] [*Juneau, AK*] [*Telecommunications service*] (TSSD)

LTN .... Liberty Tree Network [*An association*] (EA)

LTN .... Lightning (ADA)

LTN .... Linear Time-Varying Network

LTN .... Listen (IAA)

LTN .... Long-Term Nephelometer [*Instrumentation*]

Ltn .... Long Ton (EBF)

LTN .... Luton [*England*] [*Airport symbol*] (OAG)

LTNG .... Lightning [*Meteorology*]

LTNG .... Lightning Transportation [*Common carrier symbol*]

LTNGARR .... Lightning Arrester (IAA)

LTNGP .... Low-Temperature Noble Gas Process [*Nuclear energy*] (NRCH)

LTNIF .... Low-Temperature Neutron Irradiation Facility [*Oak Ridge, TN*] [*Oak Ridge National Laboratory*] [*Department of Energy*] (GRD)

LTNP .... Long-Term Nonprogessor [*Of the human immune deficiency virus*]

LT NS .... Law Times. New Series [*Pennsylvania*] [*A publication*] (DLA)

LT NS .... Law Times Reports, New Series [*England*] [*A publication*] (DLA)

LTNS .... Long Time, No See [*Computer science*] (DOM)

LT NS (Eng) .... Law Times. New Series [*England*] [*A publication*] (DLA)

LTNV .... Lloyd Triestino [*Common carrier symbol*]

LTNYX .... Rochester Limited Term N.Y. Municipal [*Mutual fund ticker symbol*] (SG)

[illegible]TO .... Laboratory Training Office (SAUO)

[illegible]O .... Landing and Takeoff

[illegible] .... Land Transfer Office (SAUO)

[illegible] .... Leading Torpedoman [*Navy*] [*British*] (DMA)

[illegible] .... Leading Torpedo Operator (SAUO)

[illegible] .... Lead-Tin Overlay [*Automotive engineering*]

[illegible] .... Linear Tape Open [*Computer science*] (DCDG)

[illegible] .... Local Tax Office [*British*]

[illegible] .... Locate to Order [*Automotive sales*]

[illegible] .... Loreto [*Mexico*] [*Airport symbol*] (OAG)

[illegible]ot Time Order

[illegible]w-Temperature Orthorhombic [*Crystallography*]

[illegible]y Temperature Oxidation [*Physical chemistry*]

[illegible] Temperature Oxide (AAEL)

[illegible]g-Takeoff Cycle (COE)

[illegible]ed Technical Operations Co. (SAUO)

[illegible]otal Overall Cost (MHDI)

[illegible]e of Organization and Equipment [*Army*] (INF)

[illegible]ature Optical Facility

[illegible]ded Options Market [*British*] (ECON)

[illegible]d Options Market (SAUO)

LTON .... Long Ton [*2240 pounds*]

LTOOR .... Light Truck On-Off Road

LTOP .... Lease to Ownership Plan

LTOP .... Lease to Purchase (COE)

LTOS .... Law Times, Old Series [*British*]

LT OS .... Law Times Reports, Old Series [*England*] [*A publication*] (DLA)

LTOS .... Long to Short [*Computer utility tool*] (PCM)

LTOT .... Latest Time over Target (AFM)

LTOT .... Long-Term Oxygen Therapy [*Medicine*] (EDAA)

LTP .... Laboratory Test Profile [*Medicine*] (DB)

LT-P .... Large Transmitter Coated with Paraffin

LTP .... Laser Trabeculoplasty (SAUS)

LTP .... Laser Training Pistol [*Police and security equipment*]

LTP .... Latpass [*Latvia*] [*FAA designator*] (FAAC)

LTP .... Leader Training Program [*Army*]

LTP .... Lead, Test, Probe (DWSG)

LTP .... LEM [*Lunar Excursion Module*] Test Procedure [*NASA*] (KSC)

LTP .... Let's Tax Plutocrats [*Humorous interpretation of LTP - Limit on Tax Preferences*]

LTP .... Letterpress

LTP .... Leukocyte Thromboplastin (STED)

LTP .... Library Technology Program [*Formerly, Library Technology Project*] [*ALA*] [*Defunct*]

LTP .... Lient Trief Pure [*Cement*]

LTP .... Life Test Procedure (ACAE)

LTP .... Limit on Tax Preferences

LTP .... Linear Time Plot (MUGU)

LTP .... Line-Throwing Projectile (NG)

LTP .... Line Type Processor [*Radio*] (IAA)

LTP .... Lipid Transfer Protein [*Biochemistry*]

LTP .... Living Together Partner [*Lifestyle classification*]

LTP .... Local Tourism Plan

LTP .... Local Training Plan [*Job Training and Partnership Act*] (OICC)

LTP .... Logical Test Port [*Communications term*] (DCT)

LTP .... Long-Tailed Pair [*Electronics*] (OA)

LTP .... Long-Term Potentiation [*Neurophysiology*]

LTP .... Long Term Preceptoship [*Medicine*] (EDAA)

LTP .... Long Term Projections [*Townsend-Greenspan & Co., Inc.*] [*Database*]

LTP .... Lower Trip Point

LTP .... Low-Temperature Passivation (PDAA)

LTP .... Low-Temperature Phase (PDAA)

LTP .... Low-Temperature Phosphorimetry [*Analytical chemistry*]

LTP .... Low-Temperature Physics

LTP .... Low-Temperature Polymer (IAA)

LTP .... L-Tryptophan (STED)

LTP .... Lunar Tidal Perturbation

LTP .... Lunar Transient Phenomenon

LTPA .... Leisure-Time Physical Activity (MELL)

LTPA .... Louisiana Travel Promotion Association (SRA)

LTPADS .... Liver Tissue Procurement and Distribution System [*National Institute of Diabetes and Digestive and Kidney Diseases*] (RCD)

LTPB .... Lactone Terminated Polybutadiene [*Organic chemistry*] (MCD)

LTPD .... Lot Tolerance Percent Defective [*Quality control*] (MSA)

LTPDS .... Live Train Position Display System [*Indian Railway*] (TIR)

LTPE .... Long-Term Public Expenditure [*British*]

LTPG .... Long Term Planning Guidelines (FOTI)

LTPHOTORON ... Light Photographic Squadron

LTPL .... Long-Term Procedural Language

LTPN .... Long-Term Parenteral Nutrition (PDAA)

LTPO .... LASER Technology Program Office [*Navy*]

LTPP .... Lipothiamide-Pyrophosphate

LTPP .... Long-Term Pavement Performance [*FHWA*] (TAG)

LTPP .... Long Term Planning Project (ACAE)

LTPR .... Lightproof [*Technical drawings*] (IAA)

LTPR .... Long Taper

LTPR .... Long-Term Prime Rate [*Finance*]

LTPS .... Lateral Transitional Phase Shift [*Optics*]

LTPS .... Lincoln Tube Process Specification (SAA)

LTPS .... Long Transportation Services [*Common carrier symbol*]

LTPS .... Low Temperature Polysilicon (SAUS)

LTPSTFT .... Low Temperature Polysilicon Thin Film Transistor (SAUS)

LTPT .... Low-Turbulence Pressure Tunnel [*NASA*]

LTPWG .... LOAD [*Low Altitude Defense*] Test Planning Working Group

LTPWS .... Low Tire-Pressure Warning System [*Automotive engineering*]

LTQ .... Le Touquet [*France*] [*Airport symbol*] (OAG)

LTQ .... Local Track Quality (NVT)

LTQ .... Low Torque

LTQC .... Long-Term Quality-Control [*Analytical chemistry*]

LTR .... Archives of Lithuanian Folklore of the Institute of Lithuanian Literature and Folklore (SAUS)

LTR .... AS Lufttransport [*Norway*] [*ICAO designator*] (FAAC)

LTR .... Centre for Learning, Teaching and Research in Higher Education [*University of Durham*] [*United Kingdom*] (RCD)

LTR .... Lander Trajectory Reconstruction [*Program*] [*NASA*]

LTR .... Lands Tribunal Rules [*Town planning*] [*British*]

LTR .... LASER Tank Range-Finder

LTR .... LASER Target Recognition [*Military*] (CAAL)

LTR .... Lattice Test Reactor

LTR .... Law Times Reports, New Series [*England*] [*A publication*] (DLA)

LTR .... Lead Technical Representative (EEVL)

LTR .... [*The*] Learning Tree [*UTLAS symbol*]

LTR .... Left Test Register (IAA)

LTR .... Left to Right (SAUO)

LTR .... Letter (AFM)
Ltr .... Letter (EBF)
ltr .... Letter (ELAL)
LTR .... Library Technology Reports [*American Library Association*]
L-TR .... Licensing Technical Review [*Nuclear energy*] (NRCH)
LTR .... Lighter
LTR .... Light Tactical Raft
LTR .... Liquid Test Rig [*Apollo*] [*NASA*]
LTR .... List Test Resister (PDAA)
LTR .... Littlerock, CA [*Amtrak Busline code*]
LTR .... Living Together Relationship
LTR .... Load Task Register [*Computer science*] (PCM)
LTR .... Location Transactivating Region [*Medicine*] (DMAA)
LTR .... Lockheed Training Reactor
LTR .... Loew's Corp. [*Formerly, Loew's Theatres, Inc.*] [*NYSE symbol*] (SPSG)
LTR .... London Telecommunications Region (SAUO)
LTR .... Lone Tree Road [*California*] [*Seismograph station code, US Geological Survey*] (SEIS)
LTR .... Longitudinal Triangular Ripples [*Oceanography*]
LTR .... Long Terminal Repeat [*or Redundancy*] [*Genetics*]
LTR .... Long Terminal Repeat Sequence (PALA)
LTR .... Long Term Redevelopment [*Emergency Management*] (EMA)
LTR .... Long-Term Research (SAUO)
LTR .... Long-Term Reserve [*British military*] (DMA)
LTR .... Long-Term Residential
LTR .... Long-Term Revitalization (OA)
LTR .... Long Treble [*Knitting*]
LTR .... Long-Tube Recirculation [*Evaporator*]
LTR .... Loop Transfer Recovery (SAUS)
LTR .... Lord Treasurer's Remembrancer [*British*]
LTR .... Low-Temperature Reactor [*Chemical engineering*]
LTR .... Low Thermal Regime (ACAE)
LTR .... Low Top Ring [*Fuels and lubricants*]
LTR .... Lymphocyte Transfer Reaction (STED)
LTRA .... Lands Tribunal Rating Appeals [*Legal*] [*British*]
LTRA .... Leukotriene Receptor Antagonist [*Biochemistry*]
LTRA .... Long Term Remedial Action (SAUO)
L-TRAN .... Lesson Translator (NVT)
L Trans Q .... Law in Transition Quarterly [*A publication*] (DLA)
LTRAS .... Long Term Research on Agricultural Systems Project [*University of California, Davis*] (RCD)
LTRB .... Long Term Review Board (WDAA)
LTRC .... Louisiana Transportation Research Center [*Louisiana State University*] [*Research center*] (RCD)
LTRCA .... Lawn Tennis Registered Coaches Association [*British*] (BI)
LTRD .... Lettered
LTRE .... Learning Tree Intl. [*NASDAQ symbol*] (TTSB)
LTREB .... Long-Term Research in Environmental Biology (SAUO)
LTren .... Left Trendelenburg [*Position*] [*Surgery*] (DAVI)
LT Rep .... Law Times Reports, New Series [*England*] [*A publication*] (DLA)
LT Rep NS .... Law Times Reports, New Series [*England*] [*A publication*] (DLA)
LTRF .... LASER Tank Range-Finder
LTRF .... Low Temperature Research Facility [*NASA*]
LTRI .... Land Trucking Company [*Common carrier symbol*]
LTRI .... Lightning and Transient Research Institute (SAUO)
LTRI .... Lightning and Transients Research Institute [*St. Paul, MN*] (MCD)
LTRMP .... Long-Term Resource Monitoring Program (SAUO)
LTRN .... Lantern (MSA)
LTRN .... Lantern Slide (VRA)
Lt RN .... Lieutenant-Royal Navy (SAUO)
LTR NS .... Law Times Reports, New Series [*England*] [*A publication*] (DLA)
LTRO .... Lateral Tire Run-Out [*Automotive engineering*]
LTROM .... Linear Transformer Read Only Memory [*Computer science*] (IAA)
LTRP .... Long-Term Requirement Plan (NATG)
LTRPRS .... Letterpress
LTRR .... Laboratory for/of Tree Ring Research. Based at the University of Arizona (SAUO)
LTRRS .... Long-Term Regional Research Site (SAUO)
LTRS .... Ladies' Tea and Rhetoric Society [*Association*] (EA)
LTRS .... LASER Target Recognition System
LTRS .... Letters [*Communications term*] (DCT)
LTRS .... Letters Shift [*Teleprinters*]
LTRS .... Low Temperature Research Station [*British*]
LT Rulings .... Land Tax Rulings [*Australia*] [*A publication*]
LTS .... Altus, OK [*Location identifier*] [*FAA*] (FAAL)
LTS .... Laboratory Test Set
LTS .... Labor Turnover Statistics (OICC)
LTS .... Landfall Technique School [*Navy*]
LTS .... Language Teaching System
LTS .... Language Translation System
LTS .... Laparoscopic Tubal Sterilization [*Medicine*] (STED)
LTS .... LASER Target Simulator (MCD)
LTS .... LASER Test Set (MCD)
LTS .... LASER Time Sharing (PDAA)
LTS .... Laser Tracking System (ACAE)
LTS .... Laser Training System (SAUS)
LTS .... LASER-Triggered Switch (MCD)
LTS .... Lateral Test Simulator (IAA)
LTS .... Launch Telemetry Station
LTS .... Launch Telemetry Stations (SAUO)
LTS .... Launch Telemetry System
LTS .... Launch Test Set
LTS .... Launch Tracking Station
LTS .... Launch Tracking Stations (SAUO)
LTS .... Launch Tracking System
LTS .... Leadership Training School (SAUO)
LTS .... Lethality Test System (ACAE)
LTS .... Levothyroxine Sodium (ACAE)
LTS .... Library Technical Services [*Library network*]
LTS .... Libyan Television Service (SAUO)
LTS .... Lifetrends Behavioral Systems, Inc. [*Vancouver Stock Exchange symbol*]
LTS .... Lift-Off Transmission Subsystem (IAA)
LTS .... Lighting Test Set (KSC)
LTS .... Lights
LTS .... Light Tactile Stimulation [*Neurology*] (DAVI)
LTS .... Light Traffic Station (ACAE)
LTS .... Light Truck Structure [*Automotive engineering*]
LTS .... Linearity Test Set
LTS .... Line Test Set [*Communications term*] (DCT)
LTS .... Line Transient Suppression
LTS .... Link Terminal Simulator
LTS .... Link Translator System (SAUS)
LTS .... Linomatic Tape System [*Typography*] (DGA)
LTS .... Llantrisant [*Welsh depot code*]
LTS .... Load Transfer Switch
LTS .... Logistics Test Squadron [*Military*]
LTS .... Log Tape System (TIMI)
LTS .... London Transport System (SAUO)
LTS .... London Typographical Society (SAUO)
LTS .... Long-Term Stability
LTS .... Long-Term Standard [*Lamp for spectrometry*]
LTS .... Long-Term Storage [*Memory*] [*Computer science*]
LTS .... Long-Term Survival [*Medicine*] (DMAA)
LTS .... Long-Term Surviving (STED)
LTS .... Long Tract Sign [*Neurology*] (STED)
LTS .... Loop Testing System [*Communications term*] (DCT)
LTS .... Love Token Society (EA)
LTS .... Low frequency Transmit Subsystem (SAUS)
LTS .... Low-Frequency Transmit System (DWSG)
LTS .... Low-Temperature Separation
LTS .... Low-Temperature Smoking (PDAA)
LTS .... Low Temperature Superconductor (ACAE)
LTS .... Low Threshold Spike [*Neurochemistry*]
LTS .... LTU [*Lufttransport Unternehmen Sud*] GmbH [*Germany*] [*ICAO designator*] (FAAC)
LTS .... Lufttransport-Sud [*Airline*] [*Germany*]
LTS .... Lunar Touchdown System [*NASA*] (IAA)
LTS .... Luxury Touring Sedan
LTS .... Trinity Lutheran Seminary, Columbus, OH [*OCLC symbol*] (OCLC)
LTSB .... London Trustee Savings Bank (SAUO)
LTSC .... Licentiate in the Technology of Surface Coatings [*British*] (DBQ)
LTSC .... Licentiate of the Tonic Sol-fa College (WDAA)
LTSC .... Low-Temperature Semiconductor [*Electronics*]
LTSCP .... Long Term Ship Communication Plan (SAUO)
LTSDE .... Low-Temperature Superconducting Device Electronics (DOMA)
LTSEM .... Low-Temperature Scanning Electron Microscopy
LTSF .... Lid Tank Shielding Facility [*Nuclear energy*] (NRCH)
LTSG .... LASER-Triggered Spark Gap
LTSH .... League of Tarcisians of the Sacred Heart [*Later, LT*] (EA)
LTSM .... Long-Range Tactical Strike Missile (MCD)
LT(Sp) .... Lieutenant (Special)
LTSPC .... L'Union Territoriale des Syndicats Professionelles Caledoniens [*Territorial Federation of New Caledonian Unions of Private Employees*]
LT-SR .... Large Transmitter Coated with Silicon Rubber
LTSR .... Line Trunk Scanner Register [*Computer science*] (IAA)
LTSS .... Lawrence Timesharing System (CIST)
LTSS .... Livermore Time-Sharing System (SAUO)
LTSS .... Long-Term Scientific Study [*NATO Defense Research Group*] (MCD)
LTSS .... Loral Thermal Sight System (SAUS)
LTSS .... Lotus Translation Services for Sametime
LTSTA .... Light Station [*Coast Guard*]
LTSV .... Light Savers USA [*NASDAQ symbol*] (TTSB)
LTSV .... Light Savers USA, Inc. [*NASDAQ symbol*] (SAG)
LTSV .... Lucerne Transient Streak Virus [*Plant pathology*]
LTSW .... Light Switch
LtSwtz .... Little Switzerland, Inc. [*Associated Press*] (SAG)
LTT .... Lactose Tolerance Test [*Medicine*] (STED)
LTT .... Landline Teletypewriter [*Military*]
LTT .... Land Title Trust (DLA)
LTT .... LASER Target Tracker
LTT .... Laser Thermal Tagger (ACAE)
LTT .... Latakia Type Tobacco [*Shipping*]
LTT .... Less than Truckload [*Under 24,000 pounds*] (WGA)
LTT .... Leucine Tolerance Test [*Clinical chemistry*] (AAMN)
LTT .... Liberty Term Trust-1999 [*NYSE symbol*] (SPSG)
LT T .... Lieutenant of Treasury [*British*]
LTT .... Light Tactical Transport (MCD)
LTT .... Light Tracked Tractor (SAUS)
LTT .... Light-Travel-Time [*Astronomy*]
LTT .... Limited Treadmill Test [*Medicine*] (DMAA)
LTT .... Liquid Toner Transfer [*Typography*] (DGA)
LTT .... Lithium Thallium Tartrate [*Inorganic chemistry*]
LTT .... Long-Term Training (MCD)
LTT .... Long-Term Trend [*Finance*] (MHDI)
LTT .... Long Term Trends (SAUO)

LTT.......... Louis Trichardt [*South Africa*] [*Seismograph station code, US Geological Survey*] (SEIS)
LTT.......... Low Temperature Teatment [*Materials science*]
LTT.......... Low-Temperature Test
LTT.......... Low-Temperature Tetragonal [*Crystallography*]
LTT.......... Lunar Test Table [*Aerospace*]
LTT.......... Lymphoblastic Transformation Test [*Biochemistry*] (DAVI)
LTT.......... Lymphocyte Transformation Test [*Medicine*]
LTTA........ Logic Tree Trouble-Shooting Aid (PDAA)
LTTA........ Long Tank Thrust-Augmented (PDAA)
LTTAD....... Long Tank Thrust-Augmented Delta (PDAA)
LTTAID...... Long Tank Thrust Augmented Improved Thor (ACAE)
LTTAS....... Light Tactical Transport Aircraft System [*Helicopter*] [*Military*] (RDA)
LTTAT....... Long Tank Thrust-Augmented Thor
LTTB........ Listen to the Band (EA)
LTTBT....... Low-Threshold Test Ban Treaty [*Proposed*]
LTTC........ Lawn-Tennis-Tournier-Club (SAUO)
LTTC........ Lowry Technical Training Center [*Air Force*] (AFM)
LTTD........ Letter-Type Technical Directive [*Navy*] (NG)
LTTE........ Liberation Tigers of Tamil Eelam [*Sri Lanka*]
LTTE........ Link Terminal Terminating Equipment (SAUO)
LTTL........ Low-Power Transistor-Transistor Logic (IEEE)
LTTM........ Longterm Terrain Model (SAUO)
LTTMT....... Low-Temperature Thermomechanical Treatment
LTTO........ Lotto World [*NASDAQ symbol*] (TTSB)
LTTO........ Lotto World, Inc. [*NASDAQ symbol*] (SAG)
LTTP........ Long-Term Treatment Plan [*Environmental science*] (COE)
LTTPBA...... Late Third Trimester Partial Birth Abortion (MELL)
LTTR........ Latter
LTTR........ Long-Term Tape Recorder
LTTV........ Launch Transient Test Vehicle (SAUS)
LTU......... Laboratory Test Unit (SAUO)
LTU......... Land Treatment Unit [*Waste disposal*]
LTU......... Laser Tracking Unit (ACAE)
LTU......... Laser Transceiver Unit (SAUS)
LTU......... Lawrence Technological University
LTU......... Less Than
LTU......... Lift-Off Time and Update
LTU......... Line Terminating Unit (CET)
LTU......... Line Termination Unit (NITA)
LTU......... Little Mountain [*Utah*] [*Seismograph station code, US Geological Survey*] (SEIS)
LTU......... Long-Term Unemployed
LTU......... Long Ton Unit
LTU......... Loughborough University of Technology (SAUO)
LTU......... Lufttransport Unternehmen GmbH [*Germany*] [*ICAO designator*] (FAAC)
LTU......... Spencer, IA [*Location identifier*] [*FAA*] (FAAL)
LTUAA....... Lawrence Technological University Alumni Association (EA)
LTUAE....... Life, The Universe, and Everything (SAUS)
LTUI........ Low Transverse Uterine Incision [*Medicine*] (STED)
LTUM........ Line Terminating Unit Module (SAUO)
LTUS........ Garden Fresh Restaurant [*NASDAQ symbol*] (TTSB)
LTUS........ Garden Fresh Restaurant Corp. [*NASDAQ symbol*] (SAG)
LTUSA....... La Trobe University Staff Association [*Australia*]
LTV......... Land Transport Vehicle (NVT)
LTV......... Large Test Vessel [*Nuclear energy*] (NRCH)
LTV......... Launch Test Vehicles
LTV......... Laytonville, CA [*Amtrak Busline code*]
LTV......... Leitch Technology Corp. [*Toronto Stock Exchange symbol*] [*Canada*]
LTV......... Life Test Vehicle
LTV......... Light Tactical Vehicle [*Police and security equipment*]
LTV......... Light Trucks and Vans
LTV......... Light-Vessel [*Navigation*]
LTV......... Linear Velocity Transducer (ACAE)
LTV......... Ling-Temco-Vaught (WDAA)
LTV......... Ling-Temco-Vaught Inc. (SAUO)
LTV......... Ling-Temco-Vought Co.
LTV......... Load Threshold Value (DA)
LTV......... Loan-to-Value Ratio [*Finance*]
LTV......... Local Thickness Variation (AAEL)
LTV......... Long-Term Vibration
LTV......... Long Tube Vertical
LTV......... LTV Corp. [*Formerly, Ling-Temco-Vought, Inc.*] [*NYSE symbol*] (SPSG)
LTV......... Lucke Tumor Virus [*Medicine*] (STED)
LTV......... Lunar Excursion Module Test Vehicle [*NASA*] (IAA)
LTV......... Lung Thermal Volume [*Medicine*] (STED)
LTVC........ Launcher Tube Vertical Centerline
LTVC........ Long-Term Venous Catheter [*Medicine*] (MELL)
LTVCQ....... LTV Corp. [*OTCBB symbol*]
LTVR........ Loan-to-Value Ratio (FOTI)
LTVSM....... Long-Term Visiting Staff Member (SAUO)
LTVX........ LTV Mining [*Federal Railroad Administration identification code*]
LTW......... League of Tasmanian Wheelmen [*Australia*]
LTW......... Leydig-Cell Tumor in Wistar Rat [*Medicine*] (DMAA)
LTW......... Long-Term Waviness [*Metal surface finish*]
LTW......... Los Trancos Woods [*California*] [*Seismograph station code, US Geological Survey*] (SEIS)
LTW......... Low-Tension Winding (IAA)
LTW......... NV Luchtvaartmaatschappij Twente [*Netherlands*] [*ICAO designator*] (FAAC)
LTWA........ Lawn Tennis Writers' Association of America [*Later, USTWA*] (EA)
LTWA........ Log Tape Write Ahead [*Computer science*] (ELAL)
LTWA........ Long Trailing Wire Antenna (MCD)
LTWG........ Landsat Technical Working Group (SAUO)
LTWG........ Launch Test Working Group
LTWO........ Learn2.com, Inc. [*NYSE symbol*] (SG)
Lt Wt....... Lightweight (MIST)
LTWT........ Lightweight
LTWV........ LiteWave Corp. [*NASDAQ symbol*] (QUAN)
LTWW........ Limited Treadwear Warranty [*Tires*]
LTX......... Lap-Top Expansion [*Computer science*]
ltx......... Latex (VRA)
LTX......... Leo Taxi Aereo SA de CV [*Mexico*] [*ICAO designator*] (FAAC)
LTX......... Lintronics International Ltd. [*Vancouver Stock Exchange symbol*]
LTX......... LTX Corp. [*Associated Press*] (SAG)
LTXO........ Leeser Transport [*Common carrier symbol*]
LTXP........ Lifetime Motor Express [*Common carrier symbol*]
LTXRD....... Low-Temperature X-Ray Diffraction [*Instrumentation*]
LTXW........ Latex Resources Wrrt [*NASDAQ symbol*] (TTSB)
LTXX........ LTX Corp. [*NASDAQ symbol*] (SAG)
LTY......... Collaboration Type (SAUS)
LTYR........ Light Year
Lu.......... H. Lundbeck [*Denmark*] [*Research code symbol*]
LU.......... Labor Union (OICC)
LU.......... Lamentations over the Destruction of Ur (BJA)
LU.......... Langston University (SAUO)
LU.......... Laurentian University (SAUO)
LU.......... Laval University (SAUO)
LU.......... Laws of Ur Nammu (BJA)
LU.......... Left Unity Group [*European political movement*] (ECON)
LU.......... Left Upper [*Medicine*]
LU.......... Lehigh University (SAUO)
LU-......... Leningrad University (SAUS)
LU.......... Lethbridge University (SAUO)
LU.......... Lexical Unit [*Linguistics*] (IEL)
LU.......... Liberal Unionist (SAUO)
LU.......... Liberal-Unionist [*British*] (ROG)
LU.......... Libraries Unlimited [*Library network*]
LU.......... Library Utility [*Computer science*]
LU.......... Lieu [*Telegraphy*] (PCTE)
LU.......... Lighting Unit (WDAA)
LU.......... Ligue Universelle [*Esperantiste*]
LU.......... Lincoln University (SAUO)
LU.......... Line Unit (IAA)
LU.......... Line-Up
LU.......... List Up
LU.......... Liverpool University (SAUO)
LU.......... Load Unit
LU.......... Lock Up (ADA)
LU.......... Logical Unit [*Computer science*]
LU.......... Logistical Unit (NATG)
LU.......... London Underground [*United Kingdom*]
LU.......... London University (SAUO)
LU.......... Looking Up [*An association*] (EA)
LU.......... Loudness Unit
LU.......... Louisiana State University, Baton Rouge, LA [*Library symbol*] [*Library of Congress*] (LCLS)
LU.......... Loyola University (SAUO)
LU.......... Lucent Technologies [*NYSE symbol*] (TTSB)
LU.......... Lucent Technologies, Inc. [*NYSE symbol*] (SAG)
LU.......... Ludwigshafen [*Rhein*] [*German license plate city code*]
LU.......... Lues [*Syphilis*] [*Latin*] (WDAA)
Lu.......... Lumbar [*Anatomy*] (DAVI)
Lu.......... Lumen [*Anatomy*]
LU.......... Lund University (SAUO)
lu.......... Lute
Lu.......... Lutetium [*Chemical element*]
Lu.......... Lutheran [*Blood group*]
LU.......... Lutheran Blood Group System [*Immunology*] (QSUL)
LU.......... Luxembourg [*ANSI two-letter standard code*] (CNC)
lu.......... Luxembourg [*MARC country of publication code*] [*Library of Congress*] (LCCP)
LU.......... Lytic Unit (DB)
LU.......... St. Luke's Gospel [*New Testament book*] (ROG)
LU.......... Theron Airways [*ICAO designator*] (AD)
LU.......... Upper Limen [*Psychology*]
LUA......... Launch under Attack [*Nuclear warfare option*]
LUA......... Left Upper Arm [*Medicine*]
LUA......... Lens Users Association (SAUO)
LUA......... Library Users of America (EA)
LUA......... Life Underwriters Association (SAUO)
LUA......... Liverpool Underwriters Association (DS)
LUA......... Lloyd's Underwriters' Association [*British*] (DBA)
LUA......... Local Unit of Administration (SAUO)
LUA......... London Underwriters Association (SAUO)
LU-A........ Louisiana State University in Alexandria, Alexandria, LA [*Library symbol*] [*Library of Congress*] (LCLS)
LUA......... Luanda [*Angola*] [*Seismograph station code, US Geological Survey*] [*Closed*] (SEIS)
LUA......... Luanda Belas [*Angola*] [*Geomagnetic observatory code*]
LUA......... Lukla [*Nepal*] [*Airport symbol*] (OAG)
LUA......... Luray, VA [*Location identifier*] [*FAA*] (FAAL)
LUAA........ Life Underwriters Association of Australia (SAUO)
LUAA........ Lincoln University Alumni Association (EA)
LUAC........ Land Use Advisory Council (SAUO)
LUAC........ Life Underwriters Association of Canada
LUAM........ Land Use Allocation Model (SAUO)

LUAMC ...... Leading Underwriters' Agreement for Marine Cargo Business (DS)
LUAMH ...... Leading Underwriters' Agreement for Marine Hull Business (DS)
LUANZ ...... Life Underwriters Association of New Zealand (SAUO)
LUAP .... Land Use Adjustment Program
LUAQ .... Left Upper Abdominal Quadrant [*Medicine*] (BCRP)
LUAR .... Liga de Uniao e Acao Revolucionaria [*Portugal*]
LU-Ar .... Louisiana State University, Department of Archives and Manuscripts, Baton Rouge,LA [*Library symbol*] [*Library of Congress*] (LCLS)
LUB .... Least [*or Lowest*] Upper Bound
LUB .... Left Upper Lobe Bronchus [*Anatomy*]
LUB .... Logical Unit Block [*Computer science*]
lub .... Luba [*MARC language code*] [*Library of Congress*] (LCCP)
LUB .... Lubbock [*Texas*] [*Seismograph station code, US Geological Survey*] (SEIS)
LUB .... Lubricant (WDAA)
LUB .... Lubricate [*or Lubrication*] (AAG)
LUB .... Luby's Cafeterias [*NYSE symbol*] (TTSB)
LUB .... Luby's Cafeterias, Inc. [*NYSE symbol*] (SPSG)
LUB .... Luby's Inc. [*NYSE symbol*]
LUB .... Lusiana [*Czechoslovakia*] [*ICAO designator*] (FAAC)
LUBA .... Limited Underwater Breathing Apparatus (NG)
LUBB .... Lubbock [*NCIC trailer make code*]
LUBBO ...... Lubbock, TX [*American Association of Railroads railroad junction routing code*]
LUBC .... Banking Centre [*Loughborough University*] [*United Kingdom*] (RCD)
LUBC .... Liberty United Bancorp (SAUO)
LUBE .... AutoSpa Corp. (SAUO)
LUBE .... Lubricate (ADA)
LUBEE .... Lubrication
Lube Eq ..... Lube on Equity Pleading [*A publication*] (DLA)
Lube PL ...... Lube on Equity Pleading [*A publication*] (DLA)
LUBIX .... Lutheran Bro. Income [*Mutual fund ticker symbol*] (SG)
LUBO .... Lubricating Oil
LUBR .... Lubricant
LUBR .... Lubricate (ADA)
LUBRISUR ... Lubricantes del Sur (EFIS)
Lubrizol ..... [*The*] Lubrizol Corp. [*Associated Press*] (SAG)
LUBS .... Large Undisturbed-Bottom Sampler (PDAA)
LUBS .... Loughborough University Business School (SAUO)
LUBT .... Lubricant (MSA)
LUBX .... Cross Oil and Refining [*Private rail car owner code*]
Lubys .... Luby's Cafeterias, Inc. [*Associated Press*] (SAG)
LUBZ .... Luria Brothers [*Federal Railroad Administration identification code*]
LUC .... Land Use Commission (SAUO)
LUC .... Land Use Committee (SAUO)
LUC .... Land Use Concurrence [*Acquisition of real estate for the use of US forces on a rent-free basis*] [*Vietnam*]
LUC .... Large Unstained Cells [*Cytology*]
LUC .... Laucala Island [*Fiji*] [*Airport symbol*] (OAG)
LUC .... League of Ukrainian Catholics of America (EA)
LUC .... Limburg University Centre (SAUO)
LUC .... Living under Canvas [*British military*] (DMA)
LUC .... London Union Catalogue (SAUO)
LU-C .... Louisiana State University, Chemistry Library, Baton Rouge, LA [*Library symbol*] [*Library of Congress*] (LCLS)
LUC .... Louisiana Union Catalog [*Library network*]
LUC .... Louisiana University Center (SAUO)
Luc .... Lucan [*39-65AD*] [*Classical studies*] (OCD)
Luc .... Lucas: an Evangelical History Review [*A publication*] (APTA)
Luc .... Lucas' Reports [*Modern Reports, Part X*] [*A publication*] (DLA)
LUC .... Lucerne [*NCIC car model code*]
LUC .... Lucifer (WDAA)
LUC .... Luciferase [*An enzyme*]
Luc .... Lucullus [*of Plutarch*] [*Classical studies*] (OCD)
Luc .... Lucullus or Academica Posteriora [*of Cicero*] [*Classical studies*] (OCD)
LUC .... Lukens, Inc. [*NYSE symbol*] (SPSG)
LUC .... Lukens Steel Company (SAUO)
Luc .... [*The*] Rape of Lucrece [*Shakespearean work*]
LUCALOX .... Translucent Aluminum Oxide [*Ceramic*]
LUCAS ...... Line Utilization Cable Assignment System (MCD)
Lucas .... Lucas' Reports [*Modern Reports, Part X*] [*A publication*] (DLA)
LucasV ...... Lucasvarity PLC [*Associated Press*] (SAG)
LUCB .... Library of the University of California at Berkeley (SAUO)
LUCB .... Lucas Brothers [*Common carrier symbol*]
LUCC .... Land Use and Climate Change (SAUO)
LUCC .... Land Use and Cover Change [*Environmental studies*] (ECON)
LUCC .... Lehigh University Computing Center [*Pennsylvania*] [*Research center*] (RCD)
LUCCAS ..... Land Use and Cover Change Analysis System (SAUO)
LUCC-CPPC ... LUCC Core Project Planning Committee (SAUO)
LUCCO ...... Land Utilization Coordination Committee (SAUO)
LUCE .... Low Urinary Calcium Excretion [*Medicine*] (MELL)
Lucent .... Lucent Technologies, Inc. [*Associated Press*] (SAG)
LUCF .... Load, Unload, Cool, Fracture (PDAA)
LUCHIP ...... Lutheran Church and Indian People [*An association*] [*Defunct*] (EA)
LUCID .... Language for Utility Checkout and Instrumentation Development
LUCID .... Language Used to Communicate Information System Design
LUCID .... Loughborough University Computerized Information and Drawings Project [*British*]
LUCIE .... Study of circulation north and west of Australia (SAUO)
LUCIFS ...... Land Use and Climate Impacts on Fluvial Systems during the Period of Agriculture (SAUO)
Lucil .... Lucilius [*Second century BC*] [*Classical studies*] (OCD)
Lucile .... Lucille Farms, Inc. [*Associated Press*] (SAG)
LucileFr ..... Lucille Farms, Inc. [*Associated Press*] (SAG)
LUCIS .... London University Central Information Services (SAUO)
Luck .... Indian Law Reports, Lucknow Series [*A publication*] (DLA)
LUCK .... Lady Luck Gaming'A' [*NASDAQ symbol*] (TTSB)
LUCK .... Lady Luck Gaming Corp. [*NASDAQ symbol*] (SAG)
LUCK .... Logical Unit and Checker (NITA)
Luck .... Lucknow University (SAUO)
LUCKN ...... Lucknow [*City in India*] (ROG)
Luck Ser .... Indian Law Reports, Lucknow Series [*A publication*] (DLA)
LUCL .... Lateral Ulnar Collateral Ligament [*Medicine*] (RAWO)
LUCO .... Land-Use Coordination Office (SAUO)
LUCO .... Lloyd's Underwriters Claims Office (AIA)
LUCOLA ..... Lutheran Coalition on Latin America (EA)
LUCOLED ... Luminescence Conversion LED (SAUS)
LUCOLED ... Luminescence Conversion Light-Emitting Diode (AAEL)
LUCOM ...... Lunar Communication [*System*] [*Aerospace*]
Lucor .... Lucor, Inc. [*Associated Press*] (SAG)
LUCP .... League to Uphold Congregational Principles [*Defunct*] (EA)
LUC PRIM ... Luce Primo [*At Daybreak*] [*Pharmacy*]
LUCR .... Lucor, Inc. [*NASDAQ symbol*] (SAG)
LUCR .... Lucor Inc.'A' [*NASDAQ symbol*] (TTSB)
Lucr .... [*The Rape of*] Lucrece [*Shakespearean Work*] (BARN)
LUCR .... Lucretius [*Roman poet, 96-55BC*] [*Classical studies*] (ROG)
LUCRE ...... Lower Unit Costs and Related Earnings (MHDB)
LUCRECES ... Leeds University Centre for Russian, Eurasian and Central European Studies [*University of Leeds*] [*United Kingdom*] (RCD)
LUCS .... Land Use Cost Studies (SAUO)
LUCS .... London University Computer Services (IAA)
LUCS .... London University Computing Services (SAUO)
LUCY .... Lucille Farms [*NASDAQ symbol*] (TTSB)
LUCY .... Lucille Farms, Inc. [*NASDAQ symbol*] (SAG)
LUCYW ...... Luclle Farm Wrrt [*NASDAQ symbol*] (TTSB)
LUD .... Land Use Designation [*US Forest Service*]
LUD .... Lift-Up Door [*Technical drawings*]
LUD .... Luderitz [*South-West Africa*] [*Airport symbol*] (OAG)
LUD .... Ludlow Corporation (SAUO)
LUD .... Lundin Explorations [*Vancouver Stock Exchange symbol*]
LUDA .... Land Use Data
LUDA .... Land Use Development Assistance (SAUO)
LUDA .... USGS Land Use Data Analysis (SAUS)
Lud & J Tr M ... Ludlow and Jenkyns on Trade-Marks [*A publication*] (DLA)
Lud Bolog ... Ludovicus Bologninus [*Deceased, 1508*] [*Authority cited in pre-1607 legal work*] (DSA)
Ludd .... Ludden's Reports [*43, 44 Maine*] [*A publication*] (DLA)
Ludden ...... Ludden's Reports [*43, 44 Maine*] [*A publication*] (DLA)
Lud de Ro .. Ludovicus Pontanus de Roma [*Deceased, 1439*] [*Authority cited in pre-1607 legal work*] (DSA)
Lud EC ...... Luder's Election Cases [*England*] [*A publication*] (DLA)
Lud El Cas ... Luder's Election Cases [*England*] [*A publication*] (DLA)
Luder Elec Cas ... Luder's Election Cases [*England*] [*A publication*] (DLA)
Luders Elec Cas (Eng) ... Luder's Election Cases [*England*] [*A publication*] (DLA)
ludes .... Quaaludes [*Methaqualone*] [*Pharmacology*] (DAVI)
Lud Gozad .. Ludovicus Gozzadini [*Deceased, 1536*] [*Authority cited in pre-1607 legal work*] (DSA)
LUDIN .... Ludington, MI [*American Association of Railroads railroad junction routing code*]
Ludo .... Ludovicus Pontanus de Roma [*Deceased, 1439*] [*Authority cited in pre-1607 legal work*] (DSA)
Ludo Bolog ... Ludovicus Bologninus [*Deceased, 1508*] [*Authority cited in pre-1607 legal work*] (DSA)
Ludo Ro ..... Ludovicus Pontanus de Roma [*Deceased, 1439*] [*Authority cited in pre-1607 legal work*] (DSA)
LUDPAC ..... National Lumber and Building Material Dealers Association PAC [*Washington, DC*] (PACS)
LUE .... Dallas, TX [*Location identifier*] [*FAA*] (FAAL)
LUE .... Left Upper Entrance [*Theater*]
LUE .... Left Upper Extremity [*Anatomy*] (DMAA)
LUE .... Life, the Universe and Everything (SAUO)
LUE .... Linear Unbiased Estimator [*Statistics*]
LUE .... Link Utilization Efficiency
LUE .... Local Unit Establishment (SAUO)
LU-E .... Louisiana State University in Eunice, Eunice, LA [*Library symbol*] [*Library of Congress*] (LCLS)
LU-ECT ...... Louisiana State at Baton Rouge, Eighteenth Century Short Title Catalogue, Baton Rouge, LA [*Library symbol*] [*Library of Congress*] (LCLS)
LUED .... Luedtke Manufacturing [*NCIC trailer make code*]
LUEMA ...... Land Use and Environmental Management Authority (SAUO)
LUEV .... Lucerne Enation Virus [*Plant pathology*]
LUF .... Glendale, AZ [*Location identifier*] [*FAA*] (FAAL)
LUF .... Labour Unity Front (SAUO)
LUF .... Laua [*Language symbol*] (ETLW)
LUF .... Lift Unit Frame [*Shipping*] (DS)
LUF .... Limiting System Utilization Factor (MHDB)
LUF .... Local Utah Freight Bureau, Omaha NE [*STAC*]
LUF .... Lowest Usable [*or Useful*] Frequency [*Radio*]
LUF .... Luteinized Unruptured Follicle [*Medicine*] (DMAA)
LUFK .... Lufkin Industries [*NASDAQ symbol*] (TTSB)
LUFK .... Lufkin Industries, Inc. [*NASDAQ symbol*] (SAG)
LUFK .... Lufkin Trailers [*NCIC trailer make code*]
LUFKI .... Lufkin, TX [*American Association of Railroads railroad junction routing code*]
Lufkin .... Lufkin Industries, Inc. [*Associated Press*] (SAG)
LUFO .... Last Used, First Out (VLIE)

LUFO Least Used, First Out [*Computer science*]
LUFO Longest Unused, First Out (VLIE)
LUFORO London Unidentified Flying Objects Research Organization (SAUO)
LUFR Larfer Freight Lines [*Common carrier symbol*]
LUFS Land Use and Forest Resource Survey of Taiwan (SAUO)
LUFS Luteinized Unruptured Follicle Syndrome [*Medicine*] (DMAA)
LUFT Leaking Underground Fuel Tank (SARE)
LUG Lesbian Until Graduation
LUG Lewisburg, TN [*Location identifier*] [*FAA*] (FAAL)
LUG Light Utility Glider
LUG Linux User Group (SAUO)
LUG LOCAS Users Group (NITA)
LUG Lock-Up Garage
lug Luganda [*MARC language code*] [*Library of Congress*] (LCCP)
LUG Lugano [*Switzerland*] [*Airport symbol*] (OAG)
LUG Lugano Resources Ltd. [*Vancouver Stock Exchange symbol*]
LUG Luganville [*New Hebrides*] [*Seismograph station code, US Geological Survey*] (SEIS)
LUG Luggage
LUG Lugger [*Boat*]
LUG BAT Lugdunum Batavorum [*Leyden*] [*Imprint*] (ROG)
LUGD Lugdunum [*Lyons*] [*Imprint*] (ROG)
LUGG Luggage
LUGL Lumen and Glare Calculations [*Facet Ltd.*] [*Software package*] (NCC)
LUGR Luger Industries [*NCIC trailer make code*]
LUGS Land Use Game Simulation
LUGU Lugdunum Export [*Intermodal shipping container symbol*] (TVRC)
LUH Light Utility Helicopter (SAUS)
LUH Lumen Hour
LUHF Lowest Usable [*or Useful*] High-Frequency [*Radio*]
LUHGLSD Lock-Up Helical Gear Limited-Slip Differential [*Automotive engineering*]
LUI Land Use Intensity (PA)
LUI La Union [*Honduras*] [*Airport symbol*] [*Obsolete*] (OAG)
LUI Load Upper Immediate [*Computer science*]
LUI Logical Unit of Information (IAA)
LUI London United Investments [*British*]
lui Luiseno [*MARC language code*] [*Library of Congress*] (LCCP)
LUIC Local Urban Initiative Centre (EURO)
LUIE Leeds University Institute of Education [*British*] (AIE)
LUIP London University Institute of Psychiatry (SAUO)
LUIS Label Use Information System [*Environmental Protection Agency*] (EPAT)
LUIS Library User Information Service (SAUO)
LUIS Library User Information System [*Detroit, MI*] [*Library network*]
LUIS Library User Interface System
LUIS Low-Dose Urea in Invert Sugar (AAMN)
LUISA Leicester University Interactive Structural Analysis Project (SAUO)
LUISA Project Leicester University Interactive Structural Analysis Project (SAUO)
LUIVL Louisville, NE [*American Association of Railroads railroad junction routing code*]
LUJ Big Lake, TX [*Location identifier*] [*FAA*] (FAAL)
LUJ Lesotho Union of Journalists (EAIO)
LUJB Left Umbilical Junction Box [*Aerospace*] (AAG)
LUJBM London Union of Journeymen Basket Makers (SAUO)
LUK Cincinnati, OH [*Location identifier*] [*FAA*] (FAAL)
LUK Leucadia National [*NYSE symbol*] (TTSB)
LUK Leucadia National Corp. [*NYSE symbol*] (SPSG)
LUK Look [*Telegraphy*] (PCTE)
Lukens Lukens, Inc. [*Associated Press*] (SAG)
LukMed Lukens Medical Corp. [*Associated Press*] (SAG)
LUKN Lukens Med [*NASDAQ symbol*] (TTSB)
LUKN Lukens Medical Corp. [*NASDAQ symbol*] (SAG)
LUKOY Lukoil [*Pink Sheets symbol*]
LUKY Luckey Trucking [*Common carrier symbol*]
LUKY Lucky [*NCIC motorcycle make code*]
LUKY Lucky Chance Mining (SAUO)
LUL Language, Unseamanlike [*Slang*] [*Military*] (DNAB)
LUL Laurel, MS [*Location identifier*] [*FAA*] (FAAL)
LUL Left Upper Eyelid [*Medicine*]
LUL Left Upper Lid (SAUS)
LUL Left Upper Limb [*Medicine*]
LUL Left Upper Lobe [*of lung*] [*Medicine*]
LUL London Underground Ltd. [*British*] (ECON)
LUL London University Library (SAUO)
LU-L Louisiana State University, Law Library, Baton Rouge, LA [*Library symbol*] [*Library of Congress*] (LCLS)
LULA Loyola University of Los Angeles [*Later, Loyola Marymount University*]
LULAC League of United Latin American Citizens (EA)
LULL Loyola University, Law Library (SAUO)
LULOP London Union List of Periodicals
LULS Lunar Logistics System [*NASA*]
LULU Locally Unwanted Land Use [*i.e. garbage incinerators, prisons, roads, etc.*]
LULU Logical Unit to Logical Unit
LULU Overseas Container Leasing [*Intermodal shipping container symbol*] (TVRC)
LUM Bellingham, WA [*Location identifier*] [*FAA*] (FAAL)
LUM Launch Utility Mode
LUM Living Utility Module [*NASA*] (KSC)
LUM Local Urgent Mail [*British*]
LU-M Louisiana State University, Medical Center, New Orleans, LA [*Library symbol*] [*Library of Congress*] (LCLS)
LUM Lumbago (WDAA)
LUM Lumbar [*Medicine*] (WDAA)
LUM Lumber (WDAA)
Lum Lumen [*Record label*] [*France*]
LUM Lumex, Inc. [*AMEX symbol*] (SPSG)
LUM Lumina [*NCIC car model code*]
LUM Luminairs Components (SAUS)
LUM Luminous (MSA)
LUM Lumonics, Inc. [*Toronto Stock Exchange symbol*]
LUM Maputo [*Mozambique*] [*Airport symbol*]
LUM University of Maryland, School of Law, Baltimore, MD [*OCLC symbol*] (OCLC)
LUM Lunar Excursion Module (ODA)
LUMAL Mining Automation Laboratory [*Laurentian University*] [*Canada*] (RCD)
Lum Ann Lumley on the Law of Annuities [*A publication*] (DLA)
LUMAS Lunar Mapping System [*Aerospace*]
lumb Lumbar [*Medicine*] (MAE)
Lum Bast Lumley on Bastardy [*A publication*] (DLA)
Lum BL Lumley on Bye-Laws [*A publication*] (DLA)
LUMC Laval University Medical Center (SAUO)
LUMCON Louisiana Universities Marine Consortium
LUMD Lowest Usual Maintenance Dose [*Medicine*] (MELL)
LUME Light Utilization More Efficient (MCD)
LUMEN Loyola University Medical Education Network
Lumen Vitae International Center for Studies in Religious Education (SAUO)
Lumex Lumex, Inc. [*Associated Press*] (SAG)
LUMF Lockheed Underwater Missile Facilities (SAUO)
LUMF Lockheed Underwater Missile Facility (AAG)
LUMI Lumisys, Inc. [*NASDAQ symbol*] (SAG)
LUMIS Land Use Management Information System [*NASA*]
Lumisys Lumisys, Inc. [*Associated Press*] (SAG)
Lumley PLC Lumley's Poor Law Cases [*1834-42*] [*A publication*] (DLA)
LUMO Lowest Unoccupied Molecular Orbit (SAUS)
LUMO Lowest Unoccupied Molecular Orbital [*Atomic physics*]
LUMP Last Unattached Male Person
Lum Parl Pr Lumley's Parliamentary Practice [*A publication*] (DLA)
Lumpkin Lumpkin's Reports [*59-77 Georgia*] [*A publication*] (DLA)
Lum PLC Lumley's Poor Law Cases [*1834-42*] [*A publication*] (DLA)
Lum PL Cas Lumley's Poor Law Cases [*1834-42*] [*A publication*] (DLA)
Lumps Life-Giving Unselfish Middle-Class Parent Survivors [*Facetious term coine d by columnist Erma Bombeck to describe the Yuppies' progenitors*] [*Lifestyle classification*]
Lum Pub H Lumley's Public Health Acts [*12th ed.*] [*1950-55 and supplements*] [*A publication*] (DLA)
LUMS Land Use Management System (SAUO)
Lum Sett Lumley on the Law of Settlements [*A publication*] (DLA)
LUN Laguna Beach, CA [*Amtrak Busline code*]
LUN League of United Nations (SAUO)
LUN Logical Unit Name [*Emergency Management*] (EMA)
LUN Logical Unit Number
LUN Ludington & Northern Railway [*AAR code*]
LUN Lunar (KSC)
LUN Lund [*Sweden*] [*Seismograph station code, US Geological Survey*] [*Closed*] (SEIS)
lun Lunette (VRA)
LUN Lunette
LUN Lusaka [*Zambia*] [*Airport symbol*] (OAG)
LUNA Language for Users' Needs and Aims (NITA)
LUNA Luna Truck Lines [*Common carrier symbol*]
Lunar Lunar Corp. [*Associated Press*] (SAG)
LUNARG Lunar Gravity Simulator [*Aerospace*] (MCD)
LUNCO Lloyd's Underwriters Non-Marine Claims Office (AIA)
LUND Lundell [*NCIC trailer make code*]
LUND Lund Enterprises, Inc. [*NASDAQ symbol*] (COMM)
LUND Lund International [*NASDAQ symbol*] (TTSB)
LUND Lund International Holdings, Inc. [*NASDAQ symbol*] (SAG)
LundInt Lund International Holdings, Inc. [*Associated Press*] (SAG)
Lund Pat Lund on Patents [*A publication*] (DLA)
Lundqua Rep Lundqua Report (SAUO)
LUNG CA Blockers, Inc. [*NASDAQ symbol*] (COMM)
LUNG Lundgreen Flatbed [*NCIC trailer make code*]
Lung Cancer Lung Cancer (SAUS)
LUNHA Land Use History of North America (SAUO)
LUNK Line/Trunk (MCD)
LUNN Lunn Industries [*NASDAQ symbol*] (SAG)
LUNN Lunn Industries, Inc. (SAUO)
Lunnl Lunn Industries, Inc. [*Associated Press*] (SAG)
LUNO Logical Unit Number (TIMI)
LUNOS Lightweight Universal Night Observation System (SAUS)
LUNR Land Use and Natural Resource Information System (SAUO)
LUNR Lunar Corp. [*NASDAQ symbol*] (SAG)
LUO Laboratory Unit Operation
LUO Left Ureteral Orifice [*Medicine*]
LUO Luena [*Angola*] [*Airport symbol*] (OAG)
LUO Luogo [*As Written*] [*Music*]
LUOQ Left Upper Outer Quadrant [*of abdomen*] [*Medicine*]
LUOTC London University Officers Training Corps [*British military*] (DMA)
LUP Kalaupapa [*Hawaii*] [*Airport symbol*] (OAG)
LUP Land Use and Planning [*British*]
LUP Laying-Up Position [*British military*] (DMA)
LUP Liberia Unification Party [*Political party*]
LUP Liverpool University Press (SAUO)
LUP Low Urethral Pressure [*Medicine*] (RAWO)

LUP......... Loyola University Press (SAUO)
LUP......... Lupenga Air Charters [*Zambia*] [*ICAO designator*] (FAAC)
Lup......... Lupus [*Constellation*]
LUPAC...... Life Underwriters Political Action Committee
LUPF........ Linear Utility Prediction Function [*Mathematics*]
LUPI......... Laser Unequal Path Interferometer (ACAE)
Lupi......... Lupus [*Constellation*]
LUPIN....... Land Use Planning Information Network (SAUO)
LUPIS....... Land Use Planning Information System (SAUO)
LUPS........ Logistics Unit Productivity Study [*or System*] [*Army*]
LUPU........ Atochem Deutschland [*Intermodal shipping container symbol*] (TVRC)
LUPUL...... Lupulus [*Hops*] [*Pharmacy*] (ROG)
LUPWT..... Langley Unitary Plan Wind Tunnel [*NASA*] (KSC)
LUQ......... Laval University, Quebec (SAUO)
LUQ......... Left Upper Quadrant [*of abdomen*] [*Medicine*]
LUQ......... Lucumi [*Language symbol*] (ETLW)
LUQ......... San Luis [*Argentina*] [*Airport symbol*] (OAG)
LUR......... Cape Lisburne [*Alaska*] [*Airport symbol*] (OAG)
LUR......... Land Use Ratio (PA)
LUR......... Laurasia Resources Ltd. [*Toronto Stock Exchange symbol*]
LUR......... Laureate [*Numismatics*]
LUR......... Lineas Aereas Latur SA de CV [*Mexico*] [*ICAO designator*] (FAAC)
LUR......... London Underground Railway
LUR......... Luria [*L.*] & Sons, Inc. [*NYSE symbol*] (SAG)
LUR......... Luria (L)& Son [*NYSE symbol*] (TTSB)
LURD........ Liberians United for Reconciliation and Democracy [*Political group*]
LURE........ Lunar Ranging Experiment [*Aerospace*]
LURGA...... Lurgan, PA [*American Association of Railroads railroad junction routing code*]
Luria......... Luria [*L.*] & Sons, Inc. [*Associated Press*] (SAG)
LURS........ Land Use and Requirements Study (MCD)
LURS........ Land Use Reporting System [*USDA Forest Service*] (ALAC)
LURS........ Logistic Unit Productivity System [*Army*]
LURS........ London Underground Railway Society [*United Kingdom*] (EAIO)
LURTx....... Living Unrelated Renal Transplantation [*Medicine*]
LUS......... Land Utilization Survey (WDAA)
LUS......... Laparoscopic Ultrasonography [*Medicine*]
LUS......... Laparoscopic Ultrasound [*Medicine*] (RAWO)
LUS......... Large Ultimate Size [*Telecommunications*] (TEL)
LUS......... Latch Up Screen
LUS......... Laws of the United States [*A publication*] (DLA)
LUS......... Library of Useful Stories [*A publication*]
LUS......... Liquid Upper Stage (NASA)
LUS......... Load, Update, Subset
LUS......... Local Use Study (SAUO)
LUS......... Lock-Up Solenoid [*Automotive engineering*]
LUS......... London Union of Sailmakers (SAUO)
LUS......... Louisiana State University in Shreveport, Library, Shreveport, LA [*OCLC symbol*] (OCLC)
LU-S........ Louisiana State University in Shreveport, Shreveport, LA [*Library symbol*] [*Library of Congress*] (LCLS)
LUS......... Lusaka [*Zambia*] [*Seismograph station code, US Geological Survey*] (SEIS)
LUS......... Lusitanair-Transportes Aereos Comercials SA [*Portugal*] [*ICAO designator*] (FAAC)
lus.......... Lustre (VRA)
LUSA........ Life USA Holding, Inc. [*NASDAQ symbol*] (SAG)
LUSA........ Life USA Holdings [*NASDAQ symbol*] (TTSB)
LUSB........ Left Upper Sternal Border [*Anatomy*] (DAVI)
LUSCC....... Latymer Upper School Cadet Corps [*British military*] (DMA)
LUSCS....... Lower Uterine Segment Caesarian Section [*Medicine*] (WDAA)
LUSER....... Loser USER (SAUS)
LUSEX....... Lunar Surface Explorer Simulation Program [*Aerospace*] (MCD)
Lush........ Lushington's English Admiralty Reports [*1859-62*] [*A publication*] (DLA)
Lush Adm... Lushington's English Admiralty Reports [*1859-62*] [*A publication*] (DLA)
Lush Pr..... Lush's Common Law Practice [*A publication*] (DLA)
Lush Pr L... Lushington on Prize Law [*A publication*] (DLA)
LUSI......... Lunar Surface Inspection [*Aerospace*]
LUSING...... Lusingando [*Coaxingly*] [*Music*]
LUSK........ Luskin's, Inc. [*NASDAQ symbol*] (COMM)
LUSL........ Loyola University School of Law (DLA)
LU-SM....... Louisiana State University in Shreveport, Medical Center Library, Shreveport, LA [*Library symbol*] [*Library of Congress*] (LCLS)
LUSO........ Luso-American Fraternal Federation
LUSOLT..... Lakehead University School of Library Technology [*Canada*]
LUST........ Latrine Urinal Shower Toilet [*A unit of mobility equipment*] [*Military*]
LUST........ Leaking Underground Storage Tank [*Environmental chemistry*]
LUST........ List Updated Sort and Total (PDAA)
LUST........ Lustrous (WDAA)
LUST........ Wanderlust Interactive [*NASDAQ symbol*] (TTSB)
LUST........ Wanderlust Interactive, Inc. [*NASDAQ symbol*] (SAG)
LUSTER..... Lunar Dust and Earth Return [*NASA*] (IAA)
LUSTW...... Wanderlust Interactive Wrrt [*NASDAQ symbol*] (TTSB)
LUSURF..... Lunar Surface (PDAA)
LUSVC....... Logical Unit Services Manager (MHDB)
LUSX........ Luscar [*Private rail car owner code*]
LUT......... Former abbreviation for Loughborough University of Technology (SAUS)
LUT......... Launcher-Umbilical Tower [*Aerospace*] (NAKS)
LUT......... Launch Umbilical Tower [*NASA*]
LUT......... Laura Station [*Australia*] [*Airport symbol*] [*Obsolete*] (OAG)
LUT......... Limited User Test [*Military*] (RDA)
LUT......... Limited User Testing
LUT......... Line Unit [*Computer science*] (BUR)
LUT......... Lining Up Table (DGA)
LUT......... Local User Terminal
LUT......... Lookup Table [*Computer science*] (BYTE)
LUT......... Loughborough University of Technology [*British*] (IRUK)
LUT......... Luteum [*Yellow*] [*Latin*]
LUT......... Miri [*Malaysia*] [*Airport symbol*] (AD)
LUTA........ Library of the University of Texas at Austin (SAUO)
LUTC........ Life Underwriter Training Council [*Washington, DC*] (EA)
LUTC........ Life Underwriter Training Course
LUTCAM.... Language Used to Conceal Actual Meaning
LUTE........ Language Understander Translator and Editor (NITA)
LUTEA....... Land Use in Temperate East Asia (SAUS)
Lut Elec Cas... Lutwyche's English Election Cases [*A publication*] (DLA)
Lut Ent...... Lutwyche's Entries [*1704; 1718*] [*A publication*] (DLA)
LUTET....... Lutetia Parisiorum [*Paris*] [*Imprint*] (ROG)
LUTFCSUSTC... Librarians United to Fight Costly, Silly, Unnecessary Serial Title Changes [*Defunct*] (EA)
Luth......... Lutheran (WDAA)
LUTH........ Lutheran
LUTH........ Luther Medical Products [*NASDAQ symbol*] (SAG)
LUTH........ Luther Medical Products, Inc. (SAUO)
LUTH........ Luther Med Products [*NASDAQ symbol*] (TTSB)
LuthMed.... Luther Medical Products, Inc. [*Associated Press*] (SAG)
LUTIRO...... Life and Unit Trust Intermediaries Regulatory Organisation [*British*]
LUTIS........ Luton Information Service (NITA)
LUTOM...... Land Use Trade Off Model (DICI)
LUTP........ Land Use and Transport Planning [*British*]
LUT PAR.... Lutetia Parisiorum [*Paris*] [*Imprint*] (ROG)
LUTr......... Lighting Unit Trailer (WDAA)
Lut RC....... Lutwyche's English Registration Appeal Cases [*1843-45*] [*A publication*] (DLA)
LUTS........ Light Units, Times Square [*Electronics*]
LUTS........ Locked-Up Trunk Scan [*Communications term*] (DCT)
LUTT........ Launcher Umbilical Tower Transporter [*NASA*] (KSC)
Lutw E....... Lutwyche's English Common Pleas Reports [*A publication*] (DLA)
Lutw Reg Cas... Lutwyche's English Registration Cases [*A publication*] (DLA)
LUU......... Illumination Unit (MCD)
LUU......... Laura [*Australia*] [*Airport symbol*] [*Obsolete*] (OAG)
LUU......... Louisiana State University, Baton Rouge, LA [*OCLC symbol*] (OCLC)
LUUG........ Lunar UNIX Users Group (SAUO)
LUV......... Langgur [*Indonesia*] [*Airport symbol*] (OAG)
LUV......... Large Unilamellar Vesicle [*Pharmacy*] [*Biochemistry*]
LUV......... Let Us Vote (SAUO)
LUV......... Light Utility Vehicle [*Pickup truck*]
LU-V........ Louisiana State University, School of Veterinary Medicine, Medical Library, Baton Rouge, LA [*Library symbol*] [*Library of Congress*] (LCLS)
LUV......... Southwest Airlines [*NYSE symbol*] (TTSB)
LUV......... Southwest Airlines Co. [*NYSE symbol*] (SPSG)
LUVI......... Luv-It Manufacturing [*NCIC trailer make code*]
LUVO........ Lunar Ultraviolet Observatory [*NASA*]
LUVS........ Southwest Airlines Co. (SAUO)
LUW......... Logical Units of Work [*Computer science*] (BYTE)
LUW......... Luwuk [*Indonesia*] [*Airport symbol*] (OAG)
LUX......... Laurens, SC [*Location identifier*] [*FAA*] (FAAL)
LUX......... Leisure & Technology, Inc. [*NYSE symbol*] (COMM)
LUX......... Lincoln Airlines, Inc. [*ICAO designator*] (FAAC)
LUX......... Luxembourg [*ANSI three-letter standard code*] (CNC)
LUX......... Luxembourg [*Airport symbol*] (OAG)
LUX......... Luxembourg [*Seismograph station code, US Geological Survey*] (SEIS)
Lux......... Luxembourg (VRA)
LUX......... Luxottica Group ADS [*NYSE symbol*] (SPSG)
lux.......... Luxurious (ADWA)
LUX......... Luxurious Room [*Travel industry*] (TVEL)
LUX......... Luxury [*or Luxurious*] [*Classified advertising*] (ADA)
LUX......... Luxury [*Telegraphy*] (PCTE)
LUX......... Luxury (automobile) [*NCIC car model code*]
LUX......... Luxus [*NCIC car model code*]
Luxair....... Luxembourg Airlines (SAUO)
Luxem....... Luxembourg
LuxLBN...... Bibliotheque Nationale de Luxembourg, Service du Pret, Luxembourg, Luxembourg [*Library symbol*] [*Library of Congress*] (LCLS)
LUXO........ Luxor-Leffingwell Coach [*NCIC trailer make code*]
Luxottca.... Luxottica Group [*Associated Press*] (SAG)
LUXT........ Luxtec Corp. [*NASDAQ symbol*] (COMM)
Luxtec....... Luxtec Corp. [*Associated Press*] (SAG)
LUXU........ Luxury Homes [*NCIC trailer make code*]
LUXY........ Cinemastar Luxury Theaters [*NASDAQ symbol*] (TTSB)
LUXY........ CinemaStar Luxury Theaters, Inc. [*NASDAQ symbol*] (SAG)
LUXYW...... Cinemastar Luxry Theaters Wrrt [*NASDAQ symbol*] (TTSB)
LUY......... Lushoto [*Tanzania*] [*Airport symbol*] (AD)
LUZED....... Luzon Engineer District [*Army*] [*World War II*]
Luzerne Leg Obs (PA)... Luzerne Legal Observer [*Pennsylvania*] [*A publication*] (DLA)
Luzerne Leg Reg R (PA)... Luzerne Legal Register Reports [*Pennsylvania*] [*A publication*] (DLA)
Luzerne LJ (PA)... Luzerne Law Journal [*Pennsylvania*] [*A publication*] (DLA)
Luz Law T... Luzerne Law Times [*Pennsylvania*] [*A publication*] (DLA)
Luz Leg Obs... Luzerne Legal Observer [*Pennsylvania*] [*A publication*] (DLA)
Luz Leg Reg Rep... Luzerne Legal Register Reports [*Pennsylvania*] [*A publication*] (DLA)

Luz LJ .... Luzerne Law Journal [*Pennsylvania*] [*A publication*] (DLA)
Luz LO ...... Luzerne Legal Observer [*Pennsylvania*] [*A publication*] (DLA)
Luz L Reg Rep... Luzerne Legal Register Reports (Continuation of Kulp) [*Pennsylvania*] [*A publication*] (DLA)
Luz LT (NS)... Luzerne Law Times. New Series [*Pennsylvania*] [*A publication*] (DLA)
Luz LT (OS)... Luzerne Law Times. Old Series [*Pennsylvania*] [*A publication*] (DLA)
LUZZ......... Luzenac [*Federal Railroad Administration identification code*]
LV............ Argentina [*Civil aircraft markings - international*] (PIPO)
Lv............ Catholic University of Louvain (SAUO)
LV............ Laboratory Vehicle (MCD)
LV............ Lacrosse Victoria [*Australia*] [*An association*]
LV............ Lactobacillus Viridescens [*Biochemistry*] (DAVI)
l/v............ Lake View
LV............ Lancastrian Volunteers [*British military*] (DMA)
LV............ Landing Vehicle
LV............ Land Value (ADA)
LV............ Largest Vessel [*British*] (ADA)
LV............ Laryngeal Vestibule [*Medicine*] (MELL)
LV............ LASER Velocimeter
LV............ LaserVision [*Videodisc system*]
LV............ Last Vehicle [*Railroads*] (ROG)
LV............ Latch Valve (ACAE)
LV............ Latent Variable [*Data analysis*]
LV............ Lateral Ventricle [*Neuroanatomy*]
LV............ Lateral Vestibular Nucleus [*Neuroanatomy*]
LV............ Latino Virus [*Medicine*] (MELL)
LV............ Latvia [*Internet country code*]
LV............ Launch Vehicle (MCD)
LV............ Launch Verification [*NASA*] (IAA)
LV............ Lava (WGA)
LV............ Laverda SpA [*Italy*] [*ICAO aircraft manufacturer identifier*] (ICAO)
LV............ Laws of Virginia [*A publication*] (DLA)
LV............ Leaky Valve [*Nuclear energy*] (NRCH)
LV............ Leave (AFM)
lv............ Leave (STED)
LV............ Leaves (GOBB)
LV............ Lecithovitellin (DB)
LV............ Leeds Volunteers [*British military*] (DMA)
LV............ Left Ventral Fin [*Fish anatomy*]
LV............ Left Ventricle [*Cardiology*]
LV............ Left Ventricular [*Medicine*] (EDAA)
LV............ Legal Volt
LV............ Lehigh Valley Railroad Co. [*Absorbed into Consolidated Rail Corp.*] [*AAR code*]
LV............ Lepromatous Variety [*Medicine*] (EDAA)
LV............ Leucovorin (DB)
LV............ Leukemia Virus [*Hematology*] (MAE)
LV............ Lev [*Monetary unit*] [*Bulgaria*]
LV............ Level (VLIE)
LV............ Level of Study [*Online database field identifier*]
Lv............ Leviticus [*Old Testament book*]
LV............ Licensed Victualer
LV............ Lift Vector (NASA)
LV............ Light and Variable [*Referring to wind*]
LV............ Light Value [*Photography*] (DICI)
LV............ Light Variegated Maize
LV............ Light Vehicle [*British military*] (DMA)
LV............ Light-Vessel [*Navigation*]
LV............ Limited Visibility Study (MCD)
LV............ Limit Value
LV............ Linear Velocity
LV............ Lipovitellin [*Biochemistry*] (QSUL)
LV............ Lipoxin [*Biochemistry*] (QSUL)
LV%.......... Liquid Volume Percent [*Industrial hygiene term*] (OHS)
LV............ Livery
LV............ Live Vaccine [*Medicine*]
LV............ Live Virus [*Medicine*] (MAE)
LV............ Livre [*Monetary unit*] [*Obsolete*] [*French*] (ROG)
LV............ Loading Valve (MCD)
LV............ Load Variable [*Automotive engineering*]
LV............ Load Vertical
L/V........... Loan-to-Value Ratio [*Business term*]
L/V........... Local Vertical (KSC)
LV............ Logical Volume (SAUO)
LV............ Loose Volume
LV............ Louis Vuitton [*Initials used as a pattern on Vuitton luggage, handbags, etc.*]
LV............ Low in Volatiles [*Commercial grading*]
LV............ Low Velocity [*British military*] (DMA)
LV............ Low Volatility [*Lubricants*]
LV............ Low Voltage
LV............ Low Volume
LV............ Lumbar Vertebra [*Medicine*]
LV............ Luncheon Voucher [*British*]
LV............ Lung Volume (MAE)
LV............ Valda [*France*] [*Research code symbol*]
LVA .... Lancashire Volunteer Artillery [*British military*] (DMA)
LVA .... Landing Vehicle, Airfoil
LVA .... Landing Vehicle, Assault [*Navy symbol*]
LVA .... Large Vertical Aperture Antenna [*Aviation*]
LVA .... Large Vertical Aperture radar (SAUS)
LVA .... Launch Vehicle Availability [*NASA*]
LVA .... Lava Capital Corp. [*Toronto Stock Exchange symbol*]
LVA .... Lava Cap Resources Ltd. (SAUO)
LVA .... Left Ventricular Aneurysm [*Cardiology*]
LVA .... Left Ventricular Aneurysmectomy [*Medicine*] (STED)
LVA .... Left Ventricular Assistance [*Cardiology*]
LVA .... Left Vertebral Artery [*Medicine*] (STED)
LVA .... Left Visual Acuity [*Medicine*]
LVA .... Literacy Volunteers of America (EA)
LVA .... Local Vendor Agreement (SAUO)
LVA .... Local Virtual Address
LVA .... Logarithmic Video Amplifier (IAA)
LVA .... Low-Velocity Anomaly [*Seismology*]
LVA .... Low Vision Aid [*Ophthalmology*]
LVA .... Low-Voltage Activated [*Neurochemistry*]
LVA .... Low-Voltage Avalanche [*Electronics*] (IAA)
LVA .... Lucasvarity PLC [*NYSE symbol*] (SAG)
LV (A) (2)... Landing Vehicle, Tracked (Armored) (Mark II) [*"Water Buffalo," Canopy Type*]
LVAD......... Left Ventricle Assist Device [*Cardiology*]
LVAD......... Low Velocity Air Drop [*Military vehicle specifications*]
LVAIC........ Lehigh Valley Association of Independent College Libraries [*Library network*]
LVAL......... Lackawanna Valley Railroad [*Federal Railroad Administration identification code*]
L-VAM....... Leuprolide Acetate, Vinblastine, Adriamycin (Doxorubicin), and Mitomycin (STED)
L-VAM....... Lupron, Vinblastine, Adriamycin, Mutamycin [*Antineoplastic drug*] (CDI)
LVAOO....... Las Vegas Accounting Operations Office (SAUO)
LVAP......... Launch Vehicle and Propulsion [*NASA*] (IAA)
LVAR......... Launch Vehicle Assessment Report [*or Review*] [*NASA*] (KSC)
LVAR......... Lithuanian Veterans Association Remove (SAUO)
LVAS......... Land Valuation Assessors of Scotland (SAUO)
LVAS......... Launch Vehicle Alarm System [*NASA*] (IAA)
LVAS......... Left Ventricle Assist System [*Cardiology*]
LVAS......... Left Ventricular Assist System [*Medicine*] (STED)
LVAS......... Light-Vehicle Animation Simulation [*Accident reconstruction*] [*Automotive engineering*]
LVAT......... Left Ventricular Activation Time [*Medicine*] (STED)
LVB .... Left Ventricular Bypass [*Cardiology*]
LVB .... Liquid-Vapor Bubble [*Chemical engineering*]
LVB .... Livramento [*Brazil*] [*Airport symbol*] (OAG)
LVB .... Low-Voltage Bias
LVBLE........ Laramie Valley Boundary Layer Experiment (SAUO)
LVBP......... Left Ventricle Bypass Pump [*Medicine*] (STED)
LVBR......... Land Valuation Boards of Review [*Australia*]
LVC .... Decisions of the Lands Tribunal (Rating) [*A publication*] (DLA)
LVC .... Enid, OK [*Location identifier*] [*FAA*] (FAAL)
LVC .... Large Vacuum Chamber [*Army*]
LVC .... Large Vehicle Center [*Automotive industry*]
LVC .... Last Vehicle Check [*Indian Railway*] (TIR)
LVC .... Lebanon Valley College, Annville, PA [*OCLC symbol*] (OCLC)
LVC .... Lillian Vernon [*AMEX symbol*] (TTSB)
LVC .... Lillian Vernon Corp. [*AMEX symbol*] (SPSG)
LVC .... Log Voltmeter Converter
LVC .... Low-Viscosity Cement [*Medicine*] (EDAA)
LVC .... Low-Voltage Capacitor
LVC .... Low-Voltage Cutoff [*Battery*]
LVC .... Lutheran Volunteer Corps (EA)
LVCD......... Least Voltage Coincidence Detector
LVCD......... Liquid Volume Charge Density [*Automotive fuel systems*]
LVCERI....... Luncheon Voucher Catering Education Research Institute (SAUO)
LVCI.......... Laser Vision Centers [*NASDAQ symbol*] (TTSB)
LVCI.......... Laser Vision Centers, Inc. [*NASDAQ symbol*] (SAG)
LVCM......... Licentiate of the Victoria College of Music [*London*] (ROG)
LVCM......... Licentiate of Victoria College of Music (SAUO)
LVCP......... Laboratory Vehicle Checkout Procedure
LVCS......... Logility Value Chain Solution
LVCS......... Low Vertical Caesarean Section [*Medicine*] (STED)
LVCT......... Low-Voltage Circuit Tester (MCD)
LVCVA....... Las Vegas Convention & Visitors Authority (SAUO)
LVCX......... Lehigh Valley Co-Operative Association [*Private rail car owner code*]
LVD .... Collaboration Validity Date (SAUS)
LVD .... Laboratory Vehicle Development
lvd .... Leaved
LVD .... Left Ventricular Assist Device [*An artificial organ*]
LVD .... Left Ventricular Dimension (STED)
LVD .... Left Ventricular Dysfunction [*Cardiology*] (DAVI)
LVd.......... Left Ventricular End-Diastolic Pressure [*Cardiology*] (MAE)
LVD .... Level Island, AK [*Location identifier*] [*FAA*] (FAAL)
LVD .... Light Valve Display
LVD .... Liquid Crystal Visual Display [*Electronics*] (EECA)
LVD .... Louvered Door (AAG)
LVD .... Low-Velocity Detonation [*or Drop*]
LVD .... Low Voltage Differential
LVD .... Low-Voltage Drop (CET)
LVD1......... Left Ventricular End-Diastolic Pressure [*Medicine*] (STED)
LVDA......... Launch Vehicle Data Adapter [*NASA*]
LVDA......... Launch Vehicle Deployment Assembly [*NASA*] (MCD)
LVDC......... Launch Vehicle Data Center [*NASA*] (KSC)
LVDC......... Launch Vehicle Digital Computer [*NASA*]
LVDC......... Low-Voltage Direct Current
LVdd......... Left Ventricular Diastolic Dimension [*Medicine*] (RAWO)
LVDd......... Left Ventricular Dimension in Enddiastole [*Cardiology*] (DMAA)

LVDE .... Large Volume Data Exchange (SAUO)
LVDG .... Las Vegas Disc Golf & Tennis [*NASDAQ symbol*] (TTSB)
LVDG .... Las Vegas Discount Golf & Tennis [*NASDAQ symbol*] (SAG)
LVDI .... Left Ventricular Dimension [*Cardiology*] (DMAA)
LVDIFC ...... Leroy Van Dyke International Fan Club (EA)
LVDL .... Licensed Victuallers' Defence League of England and Wales (BI)
LVDP .... Left Ventricular Developed Pressure [*Medicine*] (DMAA)
LVDP .... Left Ventricular Diastolic Pressure [*Cardiology*]
LV dp/dt ..... First Derivation of Left Ventricular Pressure [*Cardiology*] (DAVI)
LVDS .... Light-Vehicle Dynamics Simulation [*Accident reconstruction*] [*Automotive engineering*]
LVDS .... Liquid, Vee, Diesel-Cycle, Supercharged
LVDS .... Low-Voltage Differential Signaling
LVDS .... Low Voltage Differential Swing (SAUS)
LVDT .... Linear Variable Differential Transducer [*Electronics*]
LVDT .... Linear Variable Differential Transformer
LVDT .... Linear Variable Displacement Transducer
LVDT .... Linear Velocity Displacement Transformer (IEEE)
LVDT .... Linear Voltage Differential Transformer (NASA)
LVDT-PRIM ... Linear Variable Differential Transformer - Primary
LVDT-SEC .... Linear Variable Differential Transformer - Secondary
LVDV .... Left Ventricular Diastolic Volume [*Cardiology*] (MAE)
LVE .... Launch Vehicle Engine (IAA)
LVE .... Leave (WGA)
LVE .... Left Ventricular Ejection [*Medicine*] (DMAA)
LVE .... Left Ventricular Enlargement [*Cardiology*]
LVE .... Linear Vector Equation
LVE .... Liquid Vapor Equilibrium
LVE .... Live Video Extensions (MWOL)
LVEA .... Leligh Valley Electronic Association (SAUO)
LVECC .... Light Vehicles Energy Consumption Committee (SAUO)
LVED .... Left Ventricular End-Diastolic [*Cardiology*]
LVEDC .... Left Ventricular End-Diastolic Circumference [*Cardiology*] (MAE)
LVEDD .... Left Ventricular End-Diastolic Dimension [*Cardiology*]
LVEDd .... Left Ventricular End-Diastolic Dimension [*Medicine*]
LVEDI .... Left Ventricular End-Diastolic Volume Index [*Medicine*] (RAWO)
LVEDP .... Left Ventricular End-Diastolic Pressure [*Cardiology*]
LVEDV .... Left Ventricular End-Diastolic Volume [*Cardiology*]
LVEF .... Left Ventricular Ejection Fraction [*Time*] [*Cardiology*]
LVEL .... Level 8 Systems
LVEN .... Las Vegas Entertainment Network [*NASDAQ symbol*] (SAG)
LVEN .... Las Vegas Entmt Ntwk [*NASDAQ symbol*] (TTSB)
LVEndo ...... Left Ventricular Endocardial Half [*Cardiology*] (DAVI)
LVENW .... Las Vegas Entmt Ntwk Wrrt'A' [*NASDAQ symbol*] (TTSB)
LVENZ .... Las Vegas Entmt Ntwk Wrrt'B' [*NASDAQ symbol*] (TTSB)
LVEP .... Left Ventricular End-Diastolic Pressure [*Cardiology*] (MAE)
LVEpi .... Left Ventricular Epicardial Half [*Cardiology*] (DAVI)
LVER .... Liver Fraction Elevated [*Gastroenterology*] (DAVI)
LVER .... Local Veterans Employment Representative [*Department of Labor*]
LVES .... Low-Vision Enhancement System [*Medicine*] (EDAA)
LVES .... Low-Voltage Electrical Stimulation [*Meat treatment*]
LVESD .... Left Ventricular End-Systolic Dimension [*Medicine*] (RAWO)
LVESVI ...... Left Ventricular End-Systolic Volume Index [*Medicine*] (RAWO)
LVET .... Left Ventricular Ejection Time [*Cardiology*]
LVET .... Low Volume Eye Test (DMAA)
LVETI .... Left Ventricular Ejection Time Index [*Cardiology*]
LVF .... Dallas, TX [*Location identifier*] [*FAA*] (FAAL)
LVF .... Left Ventricular Failure [*Cardiology*]
LVF .... Left Ventricular Function [*Medicine*] (AMHC)
LVF .... Left Visual Field [*Psychometrics*]
LVF .... Linear Vector Function
LVF .... Low-Voltage Fast [*Electronics*]
LVF .... Low-Voltage Foci (MAE)
LVF .... Loyalist Volunteer Force [*Government term*] (GA)
LVFA .... Low Velocity Friction Apparatus (PDAA)
LVFC .... Launch Vehicle Flight Control
LVFCS .... Launch Vehicle Flight Control System
LVFEL .... Low Voltage Free Electron Laser (ACAE)
LVFF .... Lloyds Forces Volunteer Fund (WDAA)
LVFMC .... Las Vegas Financial Management Center (SAUO)
LVFP .... Left Ventricular Filling Pressure [*Cardiology*]
LVFS .... Large Volume Filtration System [*Environmental chemistry*]
LVFS .... Left Ventricular Functional Shortening [*Medicine*] (RAWO)
LVFS .... Loamy Very Fine Sand [*Soil biology*] [*Soil texture*] (QSUL)
LVFT2 .... Left Ventricular Slow Filling Time [*Medicine*] (STED)
LVFW .... Left Ventricular Free Wall [*Medicine*] (RAWO)
LVG .... Lauro/Viceroy/Global Joint Service [*Shipping*] (DS)
LVG .... Leaving
LVG .... Left Ventral Gluteal [*Injection site*]
LVG .... Left Ventriculogram [*Medicine*] (RAWO)
LVG .... Left Ventriculography [*Medicine*]
LVG .... Left Ventrogluteal [*Anatomy*] (DAVI)
LVG .... Left Visceral Ganglion [*Medicine*]
LVG .... Levengood Oil & Gas, Inc. [*Vancouver Stock Exchange symbol*]
LVG .... Low Viscosity Gyro (SAUS)
LVG .... Lymphogranuloma Venereum Group [*Medicine*] (EDAA)
LVGC .... Launch Vehicle Guidance Computer [*NASA*]
LVGE .... Village Super Market, Inc. [*NASDAQ symbol*] (COMM)
LVGO .... Light Vacuum Gas Oil [*Petroleum technology*]
lvgrm .... Living Room (REAL)
LVGSE .... Launch Vehicle Ground Support Equipment [*NASA*] (KSC)
LVH .... Landing Vehicle, Hydrofoil
LVH .... Large Vessel Hematocrit (MAE)
LVH .... Left Ventricular Hypertrophy [*Cardiology*]
LVHF .... Low Very High Frequency (IAA)
LVHV .... Low-Volume High-Velocity (IEEE)
LVHX .... Landing Craft, Hydrofoil, Experimental [*Navy symbol*]
LVI .... Laus Verbo Incarnato [*Praise to the Incarnate Word*] [*Latin*]
LVI .... Lavalin Industries, Inc. [*Toronto Stock Exchange symbol*]
LVI .... Left Ventricular Insufficiency [*Cardiology*] (MAE)
LVI .... Left Ventricular Ischemia [*Medicine*] (DMAA)
LVI .... Lehigh Group, Inc. [*Formerly, LUI Group*] [*NYSE symbol*] (SAG)
LVI .... Levi Strauss & Company (SAUO)
LVI .... Liquid Vapor Interface
LVI .... Livingstone [*Zambia*] [*Airport symbol*] (OAG)
LVI .... Local Veterinary Inspector [*British*]
LVI .... Logical Volume Image (GART)
LVI .... Low Viscosity Index [*Fuels and lubricants*]
LVI .... Low-Viscosity Index (IAA)
LVI .... Low-Voltage Inverter [*Electronics*] (AAEL)
LVI .... LVI Group, Inc. (SAUO)
LVIA .... Lay Volunteers International Association
LVID .... Left Ventricle Internal Diameter [*Cardiology*]
LVID .... Left Ventricular Internal Diastolic (STED)
LVID .... Left Ventricular Internal Dimension [*Cardiology*] (DAVI)
LVIDd .... Left Ventricular Internal Dimension Diastole [*Medicine*] (STED)
LVID(ed) .... Left Ventricular Internal Diameter, End Diastole [*Medicine*] (STED)
LVID(es) .... Left Ventricular Internal Diameter, End Systole [*Medicine*] (STED)
LVIDF .... Leitch Technology Corp. [*OTCBB symbol*]
LVIDP .... Left Ventricular Initial Diastolic Pressure [*Cardiology*] (AAMN)
LVIDs .... Left Ventricular Internal Dimension Systole [*Medicine*] (STED)
LVIEW .... Longview, TX [*American Association of Railroads railroad junction routing code*]
LVIN .... Low Viscosity Index-Naphthenic [*Petroleum engineering*]
LVIP .... Low Viscosity Index-Paraffinic [*Petroleum engineering*]
L-VIS .... LASER Viewdata Information Service (NITA)
LVIS .... Launch Vehicle Instrumentation Systems [*NASA*] (KSC)
LVIS .... Low Velocity Intense Source
LVIT .... Linear Variable Inductance Transducer
LVIV .... Left Ventricular Infarct Volume [*Medicine*] (STED)
LVIV .... Left Ventricular Inflow Volume [*Medicine*] (RAWO)
LVIWIG ...... Launch Vehicle Integration Working Group (ACAE)
LVJ .... Cleveland, OH [*Location identifier*] [*FAA*] (FAAL)
LVK .... Livermore, CA [*Location identifier*] [*FAA*] (FAAL)
LVK .... Lovelock [*Nevada*] [*Seismograph station code, US Geological Survey*] [*Closed*] (SEIS)
LVL .... Laminated-Veneer Lumber
LVL .... La Verendrye Line (SAUO)
LVL .... Lawrenceville, VA [*Location identifier*] [*FAA*] (FAAL)
LVL .... Left Vastus Lateralis [*Anatomy*] (DAVI)
LVL .... Level (AAG)
Lvl .... Level (TBD)
lvl .... Level (VRA)
LVL .... Levelland Energy [*Vancouver Stock Exchange symbol*]
LVL .... Lex Vehicle Leasing [*British*]
LVL .... Light Vehicles Limited
LVL .... Linda Vista Library (SAUO)
LVL .... Long Vertical Left
LVL .... Louisville, KY [*Amtrak Busline code*]
LVL .... Low-Velocity Layer [*Geophysics*] (OA)
LVL .... Universite Laval, Bibliotheque [*UTLAS symbol*]
LVLA .... Laser Visual Landing Aid (SAUS)
LVLA .... Las Vegas-Los Angeles Express [*Common carrier symbol*]
LVLB .... Land Valuers' Licensing Board [*Western Australia*]
LVLD .... Very Low-Density Lipoproteins [*Chemistry*] (MEC)
LVLG .... Left Ventrolateral Gluteal [*Site of injection*] [*Medicine*]
LVLH .... Local Vertical/Local Horizontal (NASA)
LVLO .... Local Vehicle Licensing Office [*British*]
LVLOF .... Level Off [*Aviation*] (FAAC)
LVLP .... Large Virus-Like Particle
LVLSH .... Level Shifter (NITA)
LVLT .... Level 3 Communications [*NASDAQ symbol*] (SG)
LVM .... LaSallian Volunteer Movement (EA)
LVM .... LaSallian Volunteers [*An association*] (EA)
LVM .... Lateral Vastus Muscle [*Medicine*] (MELL)
LVM .... Launch Vehicle Material (MCD)
LVM .... Launch Vehicle Monitor
LVM .... Left Ventricular Mass [*Cardiology*]
LVM .... Light Vehicle Mine [*Military*]
LVM .... Line Voltage Monitor
LVM .... Literacy Volunteers of Massachusetts
LVM .... Livingston, MT [*Location identifier*] [*FAA*] (FAAL)
LVM .... Localized Vibrational Mode (PDAA)
LVM .... Local Vibrational Mode (SAUS)
LVM .... Logical Volume Management (SAUS)
LVM .... Logical Volume Manager (SAUO)
LVM .... Low-Value Materiel (MCD)
LVMA .... Louisiana Veterinary Medical Association (SRA)
LVMC .... Low-Variation Medical Condition
LVME .... LME [*Common carrier symbol*]
LVMF .... Left Ventricular Minute Flow [*Medicine*] (DB)
LVMH .... Louis Vuitton Moet-Hennessy [*Commercial firm*] [*Belgium*]
LVMH .... LVMH Moet-Hennessey Louis Vuitton [*NASDAQ symbol*] (SAG)
LVMHY .... LVMH Most Henn Lou Vttn ADS [*NASDAQ symbol*] (TTSB)
LVMM .... Left Ventricular Muscle Mass [*Cardiology*] (DAVI)
LVMP .... Launch Vehicle Mission Peculiar
LVMPD .... Las Vegas Metropolitan Police Department (SAUO)
LVMS .... LEG [*Liquefied Energy Gas*] Volume Measuring System

LVMS .... Limb Volume Measuring System
LVMTAS ..... Low-Visibility, Moving Target Acquisition and Strike [*Military*]
LVN .... Carnegie Public Library, Las Vegas, NM [*OCLC symbol*] (OCLC)
LVN .... Lakeville, MN [*Location identifier*] [*FAA*] (FAAL)
LVN .... Las Vegas [*Nevada*] [*Seismograph station code, US Geological Survey*] (SEIS)
LVN .... Lateral Ventricular Nerve [*Medicine*] (DB)
LVN .... Lateral Vestibular Nucleus [*Medicine*] (DMAA)
LVN .... Levon Resources Ltd. [*Toronto Stock Exchange symbol*] [*Vancouver Stock Exchange symbol*]
LVN .... Library Video Network [*Video producer*]
LVN .... Licensed Visiting Nurse
LVN .... Licensed Vocational Nurse
LVN .... Light Virgin Naphtha (PDAA)
LVN .... Limiting Viscosity Number
LVN .... Low-Voltage Neon
LVN .... Lunda [*Language symbol*] (ETLW)
LVNAT .... Licensed Vocational Nurses Association of Texas (SRA)
LVND .... LASER Variable Neutral Density
LVNDL .... Licensed Victuallers' National Defence League [*British*] (DI)
LVNG .... Living
LVNI .... Laser Video Network [*NASDAQ symbol*] (SAG)
LVNIW .... Laser Video Network Wrrt'A' [*NASDAQ symbol*] (TTSB)
LVNIZ .... Laser Video Network Wrrt'B' [*NASDAQ symbol*] (TTSB)
LVNJ .... Long Valley [*New Jersey*] [*Seismograph station code, US Geological Survey*] (SEIS)
LVNM .... Lava Beds National Monument (SAUO)
LVNP .... Lassen Volcanic National Park (SAUO)
LVNP .... Luangwa Valley National Park (SAUO)
LVNTE .... Livent Inc. [*NASDAQ symbol*] (TTSB)
LVNTF .... Livent, Inc. [*NASDAQ symbol*] (SAG)
LVNV .... Levon Resources Ltd. (SAUO)
LVNVF .... Levon Resources Ltd. [*NASDAQ symbol*] (COMM)
LVO .... Launch Vehicle Operations
LVO .... Laverton [*Australia*] [*Airport symbol*] (OAG)
LVO .... Left Ventricle Outflow [*Medicine*] (DMAA)
LVO .... left Ventricular Overactivity [*Cardiology*] (DAVI)
LVO .... Lieutenant of the Royal Victorian Order [*British*] (WDAA)
LVO .... Lieutenant of the Victorian Order [*Canada*] (DD)
LVO .... Lieutenant, Royal Victorian Order [*British*] (WA)
LVO .... Lithiated Vanadium Oxide [*Battery technology*]
LVO .... Louver Opening
LVOA .... Left Ventricular Overactivity [*Cardiology*] (DAVI)
LVOD .... Launch Vehicle Operations Division [*NASA*] (IAA)
LVOP .... Left Ventricular Outflow Pressure [*Medicine*] (EDAA)
LVOP .... Local Vertical and Orbit Plane
LVOR .... Low-Powered, Very-High-Frequency Omnirange
LVOT .... Left Ventricular Outflow Tract [*Cardiology*] (CPH)
LVOTO .... Left Ventricular Outflow Tract Obstruction [*Medicine*] (MELL)
LVOV .... Left Ventricular Outflow Volume [*Medicine*] (RAWO)
LVP .... Large Volume Parenterals [*Medicine*]
LVP .... Left Ventricular Pressure [*Cardiology*]
LVP .... Left Ventricular Pump [*Cardiology*]
LVP .... Levator Veli Palatini [*Medicine*] (EDAA)
LVP .... Light Valve Projector
LVP .... Low-Value Product
LVP .... Low-Voltage Plate
LVP .... Low-Voltage Protection [*Electronics*]
LVP .... Low-Volume Production (TIMI)
LVP .... Lysine Vasopressin [*Antidiuretic hormone*]
LVPD .... Launch Vehicle Pressure Display [*NASA*] (KSC)
LVpE .... Evangeline Parish Library, Ville Platte, LA [*Library symbol*] [*Library of Congress*] (LCLS)
LVPFR .... Left Ventricular Peak Filling Rate [*Cardiology*] (DMAA)
LVPG .... Launch Vehicle Planning Group [*Aerospace*] (AAG)
LVPL .... Liverpool [*England*]
LVPP .... Launch Vehicle and Propulsion Program [*NASA*]
LVPS .... Laboratory Vehicle Procedure Simulator
LVPS .... Low-Voltage Power Supply
LVPTG .... Lateral Vascularized Patellar Tendon Graft [*Orthopedics*]
LVPW .... Left Ventricular Posterior Wall [*Cardiology*] (DMAA)
LVPWT ...... Left Ventricular Posterior Wall Thickness [*Cardiology*] (DAVI)
LVQ .... Learning Vector Quantization (IDAI)
LVR .... Laboratory of Virology and Rickettsial Diseases
lvr .... Latvian Soviet Socialist Republic [*MARC country of publication code*] [*Library of Congress*] (LCCP)
LVR .... Lever (MSA)
LVR .... Line Voltage Regulator
LVR .... Liverpool [*England*] [*Seismograph station code, US Geological Survey*] [*Closed*] (SEIS)
LVR .... London Volunteer Regiment [*British military*] (DMA)
LVR .... Longitudinal Video Recording
LVR .... Long Vertical Right
LVR .... Louver (MSA)
LVR .... Low-Voltage Rack
LVR .... Low-Voltage Relay
LVR .... Low-Voltage Release [*Electronics*]
LVR .... Low-Volume Ramjet (MCD)
LVRATS ...... Leave Rations [*Military*] (DNAB)
LVRATS SL ... Leave Rations, Sick Leave [*Military*] (DNAB)
LVRATS SPEC ... Leave Rations, Special Leave [*Military*] (DNAB)
LVRC .... Lamoille Valley Railroad Co. [*AAR code*]
LVR(CE) ..... Low-Voltage Release (Continuous Effect) [*Electronics*] (DNAB)
LVRCN .... Lehigh Valley Regional Computing Network (SAUO)
LVRE .... Low-Voltage Release Effect [*Electronics*] (MSA)
LV Rep .... Lehigh Valley Law Reporter [*Pennsylvania*] [*A publication*] (DLA)
LVRIS .... Low-Volume Ramjet Inlet System
LVRJ .... Low-Voltage Ramjet
LVRJ .... Low Volume Ram Jet (ACAE)
LVRJ .... Low-Volume Ramjet
LVRLSE ...... Low-Voltage Release [*Electronics*]
LVRO .... Las Vegas Radiation Operations (SAUO)
LV-ROM ..... LASER Vision Read-Only Memory
LVRR .... Lehigh Valley Railroad Co. [*Absorbed into Consolidated Rail Corp.*]
LVRR .... Lycoming Valley Railroad [*Federal Railroad Administration identification code*]
LVRS .... Launch Vehicle Recovery System [*NASA*] (IAA)
LVRS .... Lightweight Video Reconnaissance System [*Military*] (INF)
LVRS .... Lung Volume Reduction Surgery [*Medicine*] (ADWA)
LVRT .... Land and Valuation Review Tribunal [*Northern Territory, Australia*]
LV/RVV ...... Local Vertical/Relative Velocity Vector
LVS .... Laboratory Ventilation Data System (SAUO)
LVS .... Large-Volume Sampling (CARB)
LVS .... Las Vegas, NM [*Location identifier*] [*FAA*] (FAAL)
LVS .... Launch Vehicle Simulator [*NASA*] (IAA)
LVS .... Launch Vehicle System (ACAE)
LVS .... Layout Verification of Schematic (AAEL)
LVS .... Leaves (MSA)
LVS .... Left Ventricular Strain [*Cardiology*]
LVs .... Left Ventricular Systolic Pressure Mean [*Cardiology*] (MAE)
LVS .... Light Value System [*Photography*] (BARN)
LVS .... Logical Volume Series (GART)
LVS .... Logistical Vehicle System
LVS .... Logistics Vehicle System
LVS .... London Vegetarian Society (SAUO)
LVS .... Low-Velocity Scanning
LVS .... Low-Volume Sampler (CARB)
LVSB .... Lakeview Financial [*NASDAQ symbol*] (TTSB)
LVSB .... Lakeview Financial Corp. [*NASDAQ symbol*] (SAG)
LVSC .... London Voluntary Service Council [*British*]
LVSE .... Launch Vehicle Systems Engineer [*NASA*] (SAA)
LVSEM .... Low-Voltage Scanning Electron Microscopy (AAEL)
LVSEMI ...... Left Ventricular Subendocardia Lischemia [*Cardiology*] (DMAA)
LVSF .... Laboratory Vehicle Support Facility
LVSF .... Left Ventricular Shortening Fraction [*Medicine*]
LVSG .... Launch Vehicle Study Group [*NASA*] (KSC)
LVS/ITS ..... LASER Vibration Sensor Inspection Test System [*Army*] (RDA)
LVSO .... Left Ventricular Systolic Output [*Medicine*] (STED)
LVSP .... Left Ventricular Systolic Pressure [*Cardiology*]
LVSS .... Laboratory Vehicle System Segment
LVSS .... LASER Vector Scoring System (DWSG)
LVSSTS ...... Launch Vehicle Safety System Test Set [*NASA*] (IAA)
LVST .... Lateral Vestibulospinal Tract [*Medicine*] (DMAA)
LVST .... Longitudinal Velocity Sorting Tube
LVSTCK ..... Livestock
LVSTK .... Livestock
LVSU .... Leavesley Container Services [*Intermodal shipping container symbol*] (TVRC)
LVSV .... Left Ventricular Stroke Volume [*Cardiology*]
LVSW .... Left Ventricular Septal Wall [*Cardiology*] (DAVI)
LVSW .... Left Ventricular Stroke Work [*Cardiology*]
LVSWI .... Left Ventricular Stroke Work Index [*Cardiology*]
LVT .... Landing Vehicle, Tracked (Unarmored) [*Navy symbol*]
LVT .... Left Ventricular Tension [*Cardiology*] (MAE)
LVT .... Levitt Corp. [*AMEX symbol*] (COMM)
LVT .... Lexicon Hebraicum et Aramaicum Veteris Testamenti [*Rome*] [*A publication*] (BJA)
LVT .... Licensed Veterinary Technician
LVT .... Linear Velocity Transducer
LVT .... Livingston, TN [*Location identifier*] [*FAA*] (FAAL)
LVT .... Low Voltage Technology (AAEL)
LVT .... Low-Voltage Tubular
LVT .... Lysine Vasotonin [*Adrenergic agent*]
LVT (1) ...... Landing Vehicle, Tracked (Unarmored) (Mark I) ["*Alligator*"] [*Navy symbol*]
LVT1 .... Left Ventricular Fast Filling Time [*Medicine*] (STED)
LVT (2) ...... Landing Vehicle, Tracked (Unarmored) (Mark II) ["*Water Buffalo*"] [*Navy symbol*]
LVT (3) ...... Landing Vehicle, Tracked (Unarmored) (Mark III) [*Navy symbol*]
LVT (4) ...... Landing Vehicle, Tracked (Unarmored) (Mark IV)
LVT (A) ...... Landing Vehicle, Tracked (Armored) [*Turret Type*]
LVTA .... London Vintage Taxi Association - American Section (EA)
LVT (A) (1) ... Landing Vehicle, Tracked (Armored) (Mark I) ["*Water Buffalo,*" *Turret Type*]
LVT (A) (4) ... Landing Vehicle, Tracked (Armored) (Mark IV)
LVT (A) (5) ... Landing Vehicle, Tracked (Armored) (Mark V)
LVTC .... Landing Vehicle, Tracked, Command (NVT)
LVTC .... Launch Vehicle Test Conductor [*NASA*] (KSC)
LVTCX .... Landing Vehicle, Tracked, Command, Experimental (MCD)
LVTD .... Las Vegas Mjr League Sports [*NASDAQ symbol*] (TTSB)
LVTE .... Landing Vehicle, Tracked, Engineer [*Model 1*]
LVTE-1 ...... Landing Vehicle, Tracked, Engineer, model 1 (SAUO)
LVTH .... Landing Vehicle, Tracked, Howitzer [*Model 6*]
LVTK .... LV Trucking [*Common carrier symbol*]
LVTL .... Lexicon in Veteris Testamenti Libros [*A publication*] (BJA)
LVTP .... Landing Vehicle, Tracked, Personnel (AABC)
LVTP-CMD ... Landing Vehicle, Tracked Personnel, Command [*Marine Corps*] (VNW)

LVTPX....... Landing Vehicle, Tracked, Personnel, Experimental (MCD)
LVTR......... Landing Vehicle, Tracked, Recovery (SAUO)
LVTR......... Landing Vehicle, Tracked, Retriever (NVT)
LVT(R)....... Landing Vehicle, Tracked (Rocket) [*British military*] (DMA)
LVTR......... Low-VHF [*Very-High-Frequency*] Transmitter-Receiver
LVTRX....... Landing Vehicle, Tracked, Recovery, Experimental (MCD)
LVTS......... Large Value Transfer System
LVTTL........ Low Voltage Transistor Transistor Level (SAUS)
LVTU......... Landing Vehicle, Tracked (Unarmored)
LVTX......... Landing Vehicle, Tracked, Experimental (ACAE)
LVUPK....... Leave and Upkeep Period [*Military*] (NVT)
LVUSA....... Legion of Valor of the United States of America (EA)
LVV.......... Delavan, WI [*Location identifier*] [*FAA*] (FAAL)
LVV.......... Left Ventricular Volume [*Cardiology*]
LVV.......... Le Veen Valve [*Medicine*] (EDAA)
LVV.......... Live Varicella Vaccine [*Medicine*] (STED)
LVV.......... Live Varicella Vaccine/Virus [*Medicine*] (EDAA)
LVV.......... Lvov [*Ukraine*] [*Seismograph station code, US Geological Survey*] (SEIS)
LVVC......... Lincolnshire Vintage Vehicle Club [*British*] (DCTA)
LVVP......... Chlorambucil, Vinblastine, Vincristine, Prednisone [*Antineoplastic drug regimen*] (DAVI)
LVW.......... Landing Vehicle, Wheeled
LVW.......... Las Vegas [*Nevada*] [*Seismograph station code, US Geological Survey*] (SEIS)
LVW.......... Lateral Vaginal Wall [*Medicine*] (STED)
LVW.......... Lateral Ventricular Width (STED)
LVW.......... Left Ventricular Wall [*Anatomy*]
LVW.......... Left Ventricular Work [*Cardiology*]
LVW.......... Linked Vertical Well [*Coal gastification*] (DICI)
LVW.......... Loaded Vehicle Weight
LVW.......... Longview, TX [*Amtrak rail station code*]
LVW/HW.... Lateral Ventricular Width to Hemispheric Width (STED)
LVWI......... Left Ventricular Work Index [*Cardiology*]
LVWM........ Left Ventricular Wall Motion [*Medicine*] (STED)
LVWMA...... Left Ventricular Wall Motion Abnormality [*Medicine*] (STED)
LVWMI....... Left Ventricular Wall Motion Index [*Medicine*] (EDAA)
LVWT........ Left Ventricular Wall Thickness [*Cardiology*] (DMAA)
LVX.......... Lily Virus X [*Plant pathology*]
LVY.......... La Verendrye Management Corp. [*Toronto Stock Exchange symbol*]
LVY.......... Levy [*Alaska*] [*Seismograph station code, US Geological Survey*] (SEIS)
LVYR........ Laramie Valley Railroad [*Federal Railroad Administration identification code*]
LVZ.......... Low-Velocity Zone
LVZ.......... Low-Viscosity Zone
LVZ.......... Lykens Valley [*Federal Railroad Administration identification code*]
LW........... Air Nevada [*ICAO designator*] (AD)
LW........... Griechische und Lateinische Lehnwoerter im Talmud, Midrasch und Targum [*A publication*] (BJA)
LW........... Lab. Wander [*France*] [*Research code symbol*]
LW........... Lacerated Wound
LW........... Lacerating Wound [*Medicine*] (EDAA)
LW........... Lake Erie & Fort Wayne Railroad Co. (SAUO)
LW........... Landsteiner-Wiener [*Serum*]
L-W.......... Landsverk-Wollan [*Radiation survey meter*]
LW........... Land Warrior [*Military*] [*Army*]
LW........... Lane Wood, Inc. (EFIS)
LW........... Langwelle [*Long Wave*] [*German*] (MCD)
LW........... Last Word (IAA)
LW........... Lateral Wall [*Image on transesophageal echocardiography*] [*Cardiology*] (DAVI)
LW........... Late Warning
LW........... Launch Window [*Aerospace*] (AAG)
LW........... Law [*Telegraphy*] (PCTE)
LW........... Lawrence Welk
Lw........... Lawrencium [*Symbol changed, 1963, to Lr*] [*Chemical element*]
LW........... Law Weekly [*A publication*] (DLA)
LW........... Leave Word [*Telecommunications*] (TEL)
LW........... Leeway (COE)
LW........... Lee-White Method [*Hematology*] (MAE)
LW........... Left Ear, Warm Stimulus [*Medicine*] (MEDA)
LW........... Left Wing
LW........... Leri-Weill [*Syndromes*] [*Medicine*] (QSUL)
LW........... Lethal Weapon [*A motion picture*]
LW........... Light Wall
LW........... Light Warning
L/W.......... Light Weathering
LW........... Light Weight [*Technical drawings*]
LW........... Lightweight RADAR (NATG)
LW........... Limited War
LW........... Limited Warfare (SAUO)
LW........... Literatures of the World [*A publication*]
LW........... Liturgisch Woordenboek [*A publication*] (ODCC)
LW........... Lives With (ADA)
LW........... Living Worlds (SAUO)
lw........... Loan Word (BJA)
LW........... Logical Weakness [*Used in correcting manuscripts, etc.*]
LW........... Logistics Wing [*Military*]
LW........... London Waterguard (SAUO)
LW........... Long Wave [*Radio*]
LW........... Long Wavelength (ACAE)
LW........... Long Wire (SAUS)
LW........... Lotus West (EA)
LW........... Louisville & Wadley Railway Co. [*AAR code*]
LW........... Low [*Automotive advertising*]
Lw........... Lower Hold [*Shipping*] (DS)
LW........... Low Water [*Tides and currents*]
LW........... Low Wave (WDAA)
LW........... Low Wing [*Aviation*] (AIA)
LW........... Lucas Weinschel, Incorporated (ACAE)
LW........... Lumens per Watt (ADA)
l/W........... Lumens per Watt (IDOE)
LW........... Lung Water
LW........... United States Law Week [*A publication*] (NTCM)
LW-3......... Light Weight Three Dimensional Radar (ACAE)
LWA.......... Land Withdrawal Act (SAUO)
LWA.......... Large Warfighting Aircraft (SAUS)
LWA.......... Laser Warning Analyser (SAUS)
LWA.......... Last Word Address
LWA.......... Liberian World Airlines, Inc. [*ICAO designator*] (FAAC)
LWA.......... Lightly Wounded in Action
LWA.......... Lightweight Armor
LWA.......... Limited Work Authorizations [*Nuclear energy*]
LWA.......... Local Welfare Authority [*British*]
LWA.......... London Welsh Association [*United Kingdom*] (EAIO)
LWA.......... Long Wire Antenna
LWA.......... University of Southwestern Louisiana, Lafayette, LA [*OCLC symbol*] (OCLC)
LWAAM...... Light-Weight Air-to-Air Missile (MCD)
LWADS...... Lightweight Air Defense System (SAUS)
LWAR........ Lightweight Attack and/or Reconnaissance (NATG)
LWASR...... Letter Writing with Automatic Send-Receive [*Computer science*] (ELAL)
LWASV...... Lightweight Aircraft-to-Surface Vessel [*Military*]
LWAT........ Lake Whatcom Railway [*Federal Railroad Administration identification code*]
LW/AW...... Light Weight / Air Warning
LWAY........ Lifeway Foods [*NASDAQ symbol*] (SAG)
LWB.......... Greenbrier [*West Virginia*] [*Airport symbol*] (OAG)
LWB.......... Laboratory Workbench
LWB.......... Lewisburg, WV [*Location identifier*] [*FAA*] (FAAL)
LWB.......... Light-Water Breeder [*Reactor*]
LWB.......... Lithography Workbench (AAEL)
LWB.......... Long Wheelbase
LWB.......... Lower Bound [*Computer science*]
LWBR........ Light-Water Breeder Reactor
LWBS........ Loyal Wheelwrights' and Blacksmiths' Society [*A union*] [*British*]
LWC.......... Last Working Configuration (SAUS)
LWC.......... Lawrence [*Kansas*] [*Airport symbol*] (OAG)
LWC.......... League of Women Composers [*Later, ILWC*] (EA)
LWC.......... Lightweight Coated [*Paper*]
LWC.......... Lightweight Concrete [*Technical drawings*]
LWC.......... Lindsey Wilson College [*Columbia, KY*]
LWC.......... Liquid Water Content
LWC.......... Lithuanian World Community (EA)
LWC.......... Little Way Circle [*An association*] (EA)
LWC.......... Living Wage Campaign (SAFN)
LWC.......... Living with Cancer [*An association*] (EA)
LWC.......... London Weather Centre (SAUO)
LWC.......... London Writers Circle (SAUO)
LWC.......... Loop Wiring Concentrator (ELAL)
LWC.......... Lost Workday Case (COE)
LWCA........ Light-Water Critical Assembly [*Nuclear reactor*] [*Japan*]
LWCA........ Longwave Club of America (EA)
LWCF........ Land and Water Conservation Fund [*Department of the Interior*]
LWCFA...... Land and Water Conservation Fund Act of 1965 (COE)
LWCG........ Lightweight Coated Gravure [*Paper*] (DGA)
LWCH........ Lightweight Container Handler (MCD)
LWCHW..... Light-Water-Cooled, Heavy-Water-Moderated Reactor (NRCH)
LWCMD..... Licentiate of the Welsh College of Music and Drama [*British*] (DBQ)
LWCMS...... Lightweight Company Mortar System
LWCN........ Libra Works Consolidator Service [*Common carrier symbol*]
LWCO........ Lightweight Coated Offset [*Paper*] (DGA)
LW-COIN.... Limited War - Counterinsurgency
LWCS........ Limited War Capabilities Study
LWCSS...... Lightweight Camouflage Screen System (MCD)
LWCT........ Lachar-Wrobel Critical Items [*Psychology*] (DAVI)
LWCT........ Leaseway Customized Transport [*Common carrier symbol*]
LWCT........ Lee-White Clotting Time [*Hematology*]
LWD.......... Larger Word [*Computer science*]
LWD.......... Large Woody Debris [*Pisciculture*]
LWD.......... Laser Warning Device (SAUS)
LWD.......... LASER Welder/Driller (PDAA)
LWD.......... Last Work Day (TIMI)
LWD.......... Launch Window Display [*Aerospace*] (MCD)
LWD.......... Left Wing Down [*Aviation*]
LWD.......... Local Work Department (SAUO)
LWD.......... Long-Working Distance [*Microscopy*]
LWD.......... Loomis-Wood Diagram [*Physics*]
LWD.......... Lost Work Day (SAUO)
LWD.......... Low-Water Data [*Marine science*] (OSRA)
LWD.......... Low-Water Datum
LWD.......... Worldwide Airline Services, Inc. [*ICAO designator*] (FAAC)
LWDB........ Land Warfare Data Base (ACAE)
LWDF........ Liquid Waste Derived Fuel (EEVL)
LWDF........ Liquid Waste Disposal Facility (ABAC)
LWDG........ Lightweight Director Group [*Military*] (CAAL)
LWDII........ Lost Workday Injury and Illness (SARE)

LWDM .... Light Weight Dogfight Missile (ACAE)
LWD/MO .... Lead Writing Device/Manual Option (SAUO)
LWDR........ Lightweight Designator/ Rangefinder (SAUS)
LWDS........ Local Weather Dissemination Systems (SAUO)
LWE.......... Allwe [*Former USSR*] [*FAA designator*] (FAAC)
LWE.......... Lawrence Mining [*Vancouver Stock Exchange symbol*]
LWE.......... Liquid Whole Egg
LWECS ...... Low-Wind Energy Conversion System (PDAA)
LWeJ .... Welsh Public Library, Welsh, LA [*Library symbol*] [*Library of Congress*] (LCLS)
LWELJ....... Long Wavelength Expendable Laser Jammer (ACAE)
LWELL....... Lowell, MI [*American Association of Railroads railroad junction routing code*]
LWES........ Longitudinal Work Experience Survey (SAUO)
LWESS ...... Lightweight Weapons Engagement Scoring System (ACAE)
LWEST ...... Low Water Equinoctial Spring Tide (ODA)
LWF.......... Lawful [*Telegraphy*] (PCTE)
LWF.......... Lightweight Fighter [*Air Force*]
LWF.......... Local Welfare Authority Full Time [*British*]
LWF.......... Luminous Wall Firing (DICI)
LWF.......... Lutheran World Federation [*See also FLM*] [*Geneva, Switzerland*] (EAIO)
LWF & C.... Low Water Full and Change [*Tides and currents*]
LWFC........ Lloyd Wood Fan Club [*Defunct*] (EA)
LWFCS ...... Lightweight Fire Control System [*Military*] (CAAL)
LWFI......... WF Landi [*Common carrier symbol*]
LWFJTF ..... Lightweight Fighter Joint Test Force [*Air Force*]
LWFUSANC... Lutheran World Federation United States of America National Committee (EA)
LWG .... Corvallis, OR [*Location identifier*] [*FAA*] (FAAL)
LWG .... Lightweight Gun (NG)
LWG .... Logistics Working Group (NAKS)
LWG .... Logistic Work Group [*NATO*] (NATG)
LWG .... Longwood Gardens Library, Kennett Square, PA [*OCLC symbol*] (OCLC)
LWGCR...... Light-Water Moderated, Gas-Cooled Reactor (IAA)
LWGM .... Lightweight Gun Mount [*Military*] (CAAL)
LWGR........ Light-Water-Cooled, Graphic-Moderated (IAA)
LWH .... Lawn Hill [*Australia*] [*Airport symbol*] [*Obsolete*] (OAG)
LWHS........ Lightweight Headset [*Apollo*] [*NASA*]
LWHSS ...... Lightweight Honeycomb Sandwich Structure (ACAE)
LWHVR...... Lightweight High-Velocity Rifle
LWI .... LASER without Inversion
LWI .... Load Wear Index
LWI .... Long Wavelength Infrared (MCD)
LWI .... Low-Water Interval
LWI .... Lutheran World Information [*A publication*]
LWI .... Lwiro [*Zaire*] [*Seismograph station code, US Geological Survey*] (SEIS)
LWIC......... Lightweight Insulating Concrete [*Technical drawings*]
LWII.......... Long Wavelength Infrared Illuminator
LWIN......... Leap Wireless International
LWinF .... Franklin Parish Library, Winnsboro, LA [*Library symbol*] [*Library of Congress*] (LCLS)
LWIR......... Long-Wave Infrared (MUSM)
LWIR......... Long Wavelength Infrared
LWIR......... Long Wavelength Infrared Jammer (ACAE)
LWIRC....... Limited Warfare Intelligence Reduction Complex
LWIRST ..... Lightweight Infra-Red Search & Track system (SAUS)
LWIU......... Laundry, Dry Cleaning, and Dye House Workers' International Union [*Later, Textile Processors, Service Trades, Health Care, Professional, and Technical Employees International Union*]
LWIU......... Leather Workers International Union of America (EA)
LWiW........ Winn Parish Library, Winnfield, LA [*Library symbol*] [*Library of Congress*] (LCLS)
LWJ.......... Lucas, William J., Albuquerque NM [*STAC*]
LWK.......... Large White Kidney [*Medicine*] (DMAA)
LWK.......... Lerwick [*Scotland*] Tingwall Airport [*Airport symbol*] (OAG)
LWK.......... Live Weight Killed (EEVL)
LWL.......... Lambair Ltd. [*Canada*] [*ICAO designator*] (FAAC)
LWL.......... Land Warfare [*formerly, Limited War*] Laboratory [*Army*]
LWL.......... Lawless [*Telegraphy*] (PCTE)
LWL.......... Learning Without Limits [*Education initiative*]
LWL.......... Length [*of a boat*] at Waterline
LWL.......... Length on the Waterline [*Boating*]
LWL.......... Lightweight Launcher (MCD)
LWL.......... Lightweight Weapon Launch system (SAUS)
LWL.......... Limited War Laboratory [*Military*] (IIA)
LWL.......... Liquid Water, Land (ACAE)
LWL.......... Load Waterline
LWL.......... Long Wavelength (ACAE)
LWL.......... Low Waterline
LWL.......... Ludwigslust [*German license plate city code*]
LWL.......... Waterline Length [*Navy*]
LWL.......... Wells [*Nevada*] [*Airport symbol*] [*Obsolete*] (OAG)
LWLC........ Light-Weight Low-Cost (PDAA)
LWLD........ Lightweight LASER Designator
LWLOJS..... Long Wavelength Optical Jamming Simulator (ACAE)
LWM......... Larrimore, William M., San Francisco CA [*STAC*]
LWM......... Lawrence [*Massachusetts*] [*Airport symbol*] (AD)
LWM......... Lawrence, MA [*Location identifier*] [*FAA*] (FAAL)
LWM......... Leonard Wood Memorial [*American Leprosy Foundation*] (EA)
LWM......... Liquid Waste Monitor [*Nuclear energy*] (IEEE)
LWM......... Low Watermark
LWMB....... Local Works Managing Budget [*British Armed Forces*]
LWMEL...... Leonard Wood Memorial for the Eradication of Leprosy [*Later, LWM*] (EA)
LWML .... Light Weight Multiple Launcher (SAUS)
LWML .... Lutheran Women's Missionary League [*Later, ILWML*] (EA)
LWMP .... Land and Water Management Plan (SAUO)
LWMS .... Light Weight Modular Thermal Sight (SAUS)
LWMS .... Liquid Waste Management System [*Nuclear energy*] (NRCH)
LWN .... Lewiston, ID [*Amtrak Busline code*]
LWN .... Loewen Group Capital Ltd. [*NYSE symbol*] (SAG)
LWN .... Loewen Group, Inc. [*Toronto Stock Exchange symbol*]
LWNA........ Lumber [*Timber*], Winter, North Atlantic [*Vessel load line mark*]
LWNGF...... Loewen Group [*NASDAQ symbol*] (TTSB)
LWNPr....... Loewen Group Cap Ser'A' 'MIPS' [*NYSE symbol*] (TTSB)
LWNWR..... Lake Woodruff National Wildlife Refuge (SAUO)
LWO .... Layout Work Order (MCD)
LWO .... Limited Warning Operation
LWO .... Limited War Office [*Air Force*] (MCD)
LWO .... Liquid Water, Ocean (ACAE)
LWO .... Long-Wavelength Oscillation [*Astrophysics*]
LWO .... Lubavitch Women's Organization (EA)
LWO .... Lwow [*Former USSR*] [*Airport symbol*] (OAG)
LWOB........ Lessons Without Borders (SAUO)
LWOFC...... Lindsay Wagner's Official Fan Club (EA)
LWOP........ Lease with Option to Purchase (COE)
LWOP........ Leave without Pay
L-word ...... Liberal [*Especially in negative political context*]
LWOS........ Low-Water Ordinary Spring [*Tides*]
LWOST ...... Low-Water Ordinary Spring Tides
LWOT........ Left Without Therapy [*Medicine*] (MELL)
LWP.......... Langley Working Paper [*NASA*]
LWP.......... Large Whirlpool [*Medicine*] (EDAA)
LWP.......... Lateral Wall Pressure [*Medicine*] (EDAA)
LWP.......... Leave with Pay (KSC)
LWP.......... Lightweight Process (SAUO)
LWP.......... Light Window Pintle (SAUS)
LWP.......... Limited War Plan
LWP.......... Liquid Waste Processing [*Nuclear energy*] (NRCH)
LWP.......... Liquid-Water Path [*Meteorology*]
LWP.......... Load Water Plane
LWP.......... Low Waterplane (PDAA)
LWPF........ Long-Wave Pass Filter (PDAA)
LWPS........ Liquid Waste Processing System [*Nuclear energy*] (NRCH)
LWPW....... Light-Weight Portable Workstation
LWQ .... Low-Water Quadrature
LWQ .... Walnut Ridge, AR [*Location identifier*] [*FAA*] (FAAL)
LWR .... LASER Warning Receiver (MCD)
LWR .... Launch Warning Receiver [*Electronic countermeasure device*] [*Military*] (VNW)
LWR .... Lawrence Ins. Group [*AMEX symbol*] (TTSB)
LWR .... Lawrence Insurance Group [*AMEX symbol*] (SPSG)
LWR .... Lawyer [*Telegraphy*] (PCTE)
LWR .... Light-Water Reactor
LWR .... Limited War Capability (AAG)
LWR .... Line Width Reduction (AAEL)
LWR .... Liquid Waste Release [*Nuclear energy*] (IEEE)
LWR .... Local Wage Rate
LWR .... Long Wavelength Redundant [*Camera for spectra*]
LWR .... Long-Wave Radiation
LWR .... Long Welded Rail [*Indian Railway*] (TIR)
LWR .... Lower (AAG)
Lwr .... Lower (TBD)
lwr .... Lower
LWR .... Lutheran World Relief (EA)
LWRECCE... Lightweight Reconnaissance Aircraft (NATG)
LWRENAM... Leading WREN [*Women's Royal Naval Service*] Air Mechanic [*British military*] (DMA)
LWRENCINE... Leading WREN [*Women's Royal Naval Service*] Cinema Operator [*British military*] (DMA)
LWRENDHYG... Leading WREN [*Women's Royal Naval Service*] Dental Hygienist [*British military*] (DMA)
LWRENDSA... Leading WREN [*Women's Royal Naval Service*] Dental Surgery Assistant [*British military*] (DMA)
LWRENEDUC... Leading WREN [*Women's Royal Naval Service*] Education Assistant [*British military*] (DMA)
LWRENMET... Leading WREN [*Women's Royal Naval Service*] Meteorologist [*British military*] (DMA)
LWRENMT... Leading WREN [*Women's Royal Naval Service*] Motor Transport Driver [*British military*] (DMA)
LWRENPHOT... Leading WREN [*Women's Royal Naval Service*] Photographer [*British military*] (DMA)
LWRENQA... Leading WREN [*Women's Royal Naval Service*] Quarters Assistant [*British military*] (DMA)
LWRENREM... Leading WREN [*Women's Royal Naval Service*] Radio Electrical Mechanic [*British military*] (DMA)
LWRENRO(M)... Leading WREN [*Women's Royal Naval Service*] Radio Operator (Morse) [*British military*] (DMA)
LWRENS(C)... Leading WREN [*Women's Royal Naval Service*] Stores Assistant (Clothes) [*British military*] (DMA)
LWRENS(S)... Leading WREN [*Women's Royal Naval Service*] Stores Assistant (Stores) [*British military*] (DMA)
LWRENSTD... Leading WREN [*Women's Royal Naval Service*] Steward [*British military*] (DMA)
LWRENS(V)... Leading WREN [*Women's Royal Naval Service*] Stores Assistant (Victualling) [*British military*] (DMA)

LWRENTEL... Leading WREN [*Women's Royal Naval Service*] Telephonist [*British military*] (DMA)
LWRENTSA... Leading WREN [*Women's Royal Naval Service*] Training Support Assistant [*British military*] (DMA)
LWRENWA... Leading WREN [*Women's Royal Naval Service*] Weapon Analyst [*British military*] (DMA)
LWRENWTR(G)... Leading WREN [*Women's Royal Naval Service*] Writer (General) [*British military*] (DMA)
LWRENWTR(P)... Leading WREN [*Women's Royal Naval Service*] Writer (Pay) [*British military*] (DMA)
LWRENWTR(S)... Leading WREN [*Women's Royal Naval Service*] Writer (Shorthand) [*British military*] (DMA)
LWRL........ Light Weight Rail Launcher (ACAE)
LWRM........ Lightweight RADAR Missile (MCD)
LWRO........ Lateral Wheel Run-Out [*Automotive engineering*]
LWRP........ Livermore Water Reclamation Plant (SAUO)
LWRP........ Lukuru Wildlife Research Project (SAUO)
LWRRDC.... Land and Water Resources Research and Development Corporation (SAUO)
LWRRI....... Louisiana Water Resources Research Institute [*Louisiana State University*] [*Department of the Interior*] [*Research center*] (RCD)
LWRS........ Lightweight Weather RADAR Set
LWRU........ Lightweight RADAR Unit (NATG)
LWS.......... Large Wafer Study (AAEL)
LWS.......... Laser Warning System (SAUO)
LWS.......... LASER Weapon System (MCD)
LWS.......... Lavage with Saline [*Medicine*] (MELL)
LWS.......... Lewiston [*Idaho*] [*Airport symbol*] (OAG)
LWS.......... Library Wholesale Services [*Information service or system*] (IID)
LWS.......... Lightning Warning Set [*Air Force*]
LWS.......... Lightning Warning System [*NASA*] (NASA)
LWS.......... Light-Warning RADAR Set (NATG)
LWS.......... Lightweight Sight
LWS.......... Lightweight Sports [*Concept car*] [*Automotive engineering*]
LWS.......... Lightweight System
LWS.......... London Wargames Section (SAUO)
LWS.......... Low Water of Spring Tide
LWS.......... Low-Water Sensitivity [*Brake fluid designation*]
LWS.......... Lutheran Welfare Services [*Australia*]
LWSC........ Liberian Water and Sewer Corporation (SAUO)
LWSC........ Local Wage Survey Committee (SAUO)
LWSD........ LASER Weapon System Demonstrator [*Military*]
LWSF........ Lightweight Strike Fighter [*NATO Air Forces*]
LWSR........ Lightweight Search RADAR (IAA)
LWSR........ Lightweight Strike and Reconnaissance Aircraft (NATG)
LWSR(R)..... Lightweight Strike and Reconnaissance Aircraft (Reconnaissance Role) (NATG)
LWSR(S)..... Lightweight Strike and Reconnaissance Aircraft (Strike Role) (NATG)
LWSS........ Letter-Writing Support System (PDAA)
LWST........ Light Waste Storage Tank (IEEE)
LWST........ Lowest (MSA)
LW(STA)..... Light Warning (Station)
LWSTC...... Liquid Waste and Sludge Transporter Council (EA)
Lw Stu H.... Law Students' Helper [*A publication*] (DLA)
LW-SWC.... Light Weight Sheet Molding Compound
LWSY........ L and W Supply Corporation [*Common carrier symbol*]
LWT.......... Amphibious Warping Tug [*Navy symbol*]
LWT.......... Lamb Weather Type [*Meteorology*]
LWT.......... Launch Window Time (SAUS)
LWT.......... Lewistown [*Montana*] [*Airport symbol*] (OAG)
LWT.......... Lightweight
LWT.......... Light Weight Tank (SAUS)
LWT.......... Lightweight Torpedo [*Now Mk 50*] (DOMA)
LWT.......... Lightweight Transponder
LWT.......... Light Weight Turret (SAUS)
LWT.......... Lightweight Type [*Anchor gear*]
LWT.......... Liquid Waste Treatment (MCD)
LWT.......... Listen While Talk (IAA)
LWT.......... Local Winter Time [*Astronomy*] (IAA)
LWT.......... London Weekend Television [*England*]
LWTA........ LASER Window Test Apparatus [*Air Force*]
LWTAP....... Food Science and Technology (journ.) (SAUS)
LWTF........ Low-Water-Tolerant Brake Fluid [*Automotive engineering*]
LWTMA...... Listen While Transmission Multiple Access [*Telecommunications*] (PDAA)
LWTMA...... London Wool Terminal Market Association (SAUO)
LWTP........ Light Weight Tracking Pedestal (ACAE)
LWTR........ Leading Writer [*British military*] (DMA)
LWTS........ Laundry Waste Treatment System [*Nuclear energy*] (NRCH)
LWTS........ Low-Level Waste Treatment System (ABAC)
LWTT........ Liquid Waste Test Tank [*Nuclear energy*] (IEEE)
LWU.......... LASER Welder Unit
LWU.......... Leather Workers International Union of America
LWUI......... Longshoremen's and Warehousemen's Union International
LWULT....... Least Widely Used and Least Taught Languages (AIE)
LWV.......... Lackawanna & Wyoming Valley (SAUO)
LWV.......... Lackawanna & Wyoming Valley Railway Co. [*Absorbed into Consolidated Rail Corp.*] [*AAR code*]
LWV.......... Landwirtschaftsversorgungsamt [*German Land Economic Supply Office*] [*Post-World War II*]
LWV.......... Lawrenceville [*Illinois*] [*Airport symbol*] [*Obsolete*] (OAG)
LWV.......... League of Women Voters of the United States
LWV.......... Light-Weight Van
LWV.......... Longitudinal Wave Velocity (AAEL)
LWVAZ...... League of Women Voters of Arizona (EARSL)
LWVBAE..... League of Women Voters - Berkeley, Albany and Emeryville (EARSL)
LWVC........ League of Women Voters of California (EARSL)
LWVCT...... League of Women Voters of Connecticut (EARSL)
LWVEF....... League of Women Voters Education Fund (EA)
LWVF........ League of Woman Voters Foundation (SAUO)
LWVIL....... League of Women Voters of Illinois (EARSL)
LWVMO..... League of Women Voters of Missouri (EARSL)
LWVMP...... League of Women Voters - Monterey Peninsula (EARSL)
LWVO........ League of Women Voters of Ohio (EARSL)
LWVSD...... League of Women Voters of South Dakota (EARSL)
LWVSF...... League of Women Voters - San Francisco (EARSL)
LWVUS...... League of Women Voters of the United States (EA)
LWVV........ League of Women Voters of Victoria [*Australia*]
LWW......... Launch Window Width [*Aerospace*]
LWW......... Lightweight Weapon
LWW......... Lippincott Williams & Wilkins
LWWS....... Lightweight Weapons Sight
LWX......... LAN [*Linked Access Network*]/WAN Exchange [*Wide Area Network*] [*Telecommunications*]
LWY.......... Lawas [*Malaysia*] [*Airport symbol*] (OAG)
LWYACC..... Lithuanian World Youth Association Communications Center [*Defunct*] (EA)
LWYR........ Lawyer
LwyrTitl..... Lawyers Title Corp. [*Associated Press*] (SAG)
LX............ Crossair [*ICAO designator*] (AD)
LX............ dyslexic rebus for excel (SAUS)
LX............ La Crosse, WI
lx............. Larynx (MELL)
Lx............ Latex [*Medicine*] (EDAA)
LX............ Linear Executable (SAUS)
LX............ Lipoxin [*Biochemistry*] (QSUL)
LX............ Liver Extract [*Protein/lipid substance*] [*Immunology*]
LX............ Local Irradiation (MAE)
LX............ Lower Extremity [*Anatomy*] (DMAA)
LX............ Low Expansion Foam (WDAA)
LX............ Low Index [*NWS*] (FAAC)
Lx............ Lumpectomy [*Medicine*]
LX............ Lux [*Light*] [*Latin*]
lx............. Lux [*Symbol*] [*SI unit of luminance*]
LX............ Luxe [*NCIC car model code*]
LX............ Luxembourg [*Civil aircraft markings - international*] (PIPO)
LX............ Pounds Sterling [*Telegraphy*] (PCTE)
LXA.......... Lhasa [*China*] [*Airport symbol*] (OAG)
LXA.......... Lipoxin A [*Biochemistry*]
LXA.......... Load Index from Address
LXAD........ Lexington Army Depot [*Kentucky*] (AFIT)
lxb........... Language Textbook
LXB.......... Lipoxin B [*Biochemistry*]
LXB.......... Pittsburgh, PA [*Location identifier*] [*FAA*] (FAAL)
LXBK........ LSB Bancshares, Inc. North Carolina [*NASDAQ symbol*] (SAG)
LXBK........ LSB Bancshares(NC) [*NASDAQ symbol*] (TTSB)
LXBX........ LSB Bancshares, Inc. (North Carolina) [*NASDAQ symbol*] (COMM)
LXC.......... Liquid-Ion Exchange Chromatography (PDAA)
LXD.......... LASER Transceiver Device
LXD.......... Load Index from Decrement
LXE.......... Lightguide Express Entry (VLIE)
LXE.......... LXE, Inc. [*Associated Press*] (SAG)
LXEI......... LXE, Inc. [*NASDAQ symbol*] (SAG)
LXFT........ Linear Xenon Flash Tube
LXG.......... League of Extraordinary Gentlemen [*2003 motion picture*]
LXG.......... Luong Namtha [*Laos*] [*Airport symbol*] (AD)
LXGB........ Gibraltar/North Front [*Gibraltar*] [*ICAO location identifier*] (ICLI)
LXIO........ Lake City Express [*Common carrier symbol*]
LXK.......... Lexmark International Group [*NYSE symbol*] (SAG)
LXK.......... Lexmark Intl Group'A' [*NYSE symbol*] (TTSB)
LXL.......... Little Falls, MN [*Location identifier*] [*FAA*] (FAAL)
LXM.......... Lintex Minerals [*Vancouver Stock Exchange symbol*]
LXMAR...... Load External Memory Address Register
Lxmbrg...... Luxembourg (SAUO)
LXMO........ Lexington B & L Financial Corp. [*NASDAQ symbol*] (SAG)
LXN.......... Lexington, NE [*Location identifier*] [*FAA*] (FAAL)
LXN.......... Lexington Resources Ltd. [*Vancouver Stock Exchange symbol*]
LXOH........ Lexington & Ohio Railroad [*Federal Railroad Administration identification code*]
LXP.......... Lexington Corporate Prop [*NYSE symbol*] (TTSB)
LXP.......... Lexington Corporate Properties [*NYSE symbol*] (SAG)
LXP.......... Lorain Public Library, Lorain, OH [*OCLC symbol*] (OCLC)
LXR.......... Airluxor Ltda. [*Portugal*] [*ICAO designator*] (FAAC)
LXR.......... Luxor [*Egypt*] [*Airport symbol*] (OAG)
LXR.......... LXR Biotechnology [*AMEX symbol*] (TTSB)
LXR.......... LXR Biotechnology, Inc. [*AMEX symbol*] (SAG)
LXRBiot..... LXR Biotechnology, Inc. [*Associated Press*] (SAG)
LXS.......... Lemnos [*Greece*] [*Airport symbol*] (OAG)
LX S.......... Lux Second
LXT.......... Left Exotropia [*Ophthalmology*]
LXT.......... Linear Xenon Tube
LXTON....... Lexington, NC [*American Association of Railroads railroad junction routing code*]
LXU.......... Lukulu [*Zambia*] [*Airport symbol*] (AD)
LXU.......... Luxtec Corp. [*AMEX symbol*] (SAG)
LXV.......... Leadville, CO [*Location identifier*] [*FAA*] (FAAL)
LXVR........ Luxapalila Valley Railroad [*Federal Railroad Administration identification code*]
LXX.......... Septuagint [*Version of the Bible*]

LXY .... Mexia, TX [*Location identifier*] [*FAA*] (FAAL)
LY .... El Al Israel Airlines [*ICAO designator*] (AD)
LY .... Lactoalbumin-Yeastolate [*Cell growth medium*]
LY .... Langley [*Unit of sun's heat*]
LY .... Last Year's Model [*Merchandising slang*]
LY .... League for Yiddish [*Later, LYI*] (EA)
LY .... Leicestershire Yeomanry (SAUO)
LY .... Leicestershire Yeomanry (Prince Albert's Own) [*British military*] (DMA)
LY .... Lethal Yellowing [*Plant pathology*]
LY .... Libya [*ANSI two-letter standard code*] (CNC)
ly .... Libya [*MARC country of publication code*] [*Library of Congress*] (LCCP)
LY .... Light Year
ly .... Light-Year
LY .... Light Yeomanry (SAUO)
LY .... Linear Yard (AFM)
LY .... Lithuania [*Civil aircraft markings - international*] (PIPO)
LY .... Lucifer Yellow [*A dye*] [*Organic chemistry*]
Ly .... Lyman [*Spectrography*]
LY .... Lynngold Resources, Inc. [*Toronto Stock Exchange symbol*]
LY .... Queen's Own Lowland Yeomanry [*Military unit*] [*British*]
LYA .... Lynch, Young & Associates [*Newport Beach, CA*] [*Telecommunications*] (TSSD)
LYA .... Lyon Air [*France*] [*ICAO designator*] (FAAC)
LYB .... Little Cayman [*West Indies*] [*Airport symbol*] (OAG)
LYBA .... Beograd [*Former Yugoslavia*] [*ICAO location identifier*] (ICLI)
LYBB .... Beograd [*Former Yugoslavia*] [*ICAO location identifier*] (ICLI)
LYBE .... Beograd [*Former Yugoslavia*] [*ICAO location identifier*] (ICLI)
LYBK .... Banja Luka [*Former Yugoslavia*] [*ICAO location identifier*] (ICLI)
LYBNT .... Last Year but Not This [*Fundraising*]
LYC .... Larchmont Yacht Club (SAUO)
LYC .... Leicestershire Yeomanry Cavalry (Prince Albert's Own) [*British military*] (DMA)
Lyc .... Lycian [*Linguistics*] (IEL)
LYC .... Lycoming College, Williamsport, PA [*OCLC symbol*] (OCLC)
Lyc .... Lycurgus [*of Plutarch*] [*Fourth century BC*] [*Classical studies*] (OCD)
LYCC .... Lancashire Yorkshire Canary Club (SAUO)
LYCD .... Live Yeast Cell Derivative (DB)
Lycoming .... Lycoming Reporter [*Pennsylvania*] [*A publication*] (DLA)
Lycoming R (PA) .... Lycoming Reporter [*Pennsylvania*] [*A publication*] (DLA)
Lycoph .... Lycophron [*Third century BC*] [*Classical studies*] (OCD)
LYCS .... Liberia Young Christian Students Movement (SAUO)
Lycurg .... Lycurgus [*of Plutarch*] [*Fourth century BC*] [*Classical studies*] (OCD)
LYD .... Houston, TX [*Location identifier*] [*FAA*] (FAAL)
LYD .... Lydney [*British depot code*]
L/yd3 .... Pounds per Cubic Yard (SAUS)
Lydall .... Lydall, Inc. [*Associated Press*] (SAG)
LYDIEA .... Lymphocyte-Detected Immunoglobulin E Antigen [*Medicine*] (DB)
LYDMA .... Lymphocyte Determined Membrane Antigen [*Immunology*]
Lydnbg .... Lydenburg Platinum Ltd. [*Associated Press*] (SAG)
LYDPY .... Lydenburg Platinum Ltd ADR [*NASDAQ symbol*] (TTSB)
LYDU .... Dubrovnik [*Former Yugoslavia*] [*ICAO location identifier*] (ICLI)
LYE .... Lyneham, FTU [*British*] [*FAA designator*] (FAAC)
LYES .... Liver Yang Exuberance Syndrome [*Medicine*] (DMAA)
LYF .... Lutheran Youth Fellowship (EA)
LYFT .... Low-Yield Fallout Trajectory (DNAB)
LYG .... Lying [*Telegraphy*] (PCTE)
LYG .... Lymphomatoid Granulomatosis [*Medicine*]
LYH .... Lynchburg [*Virginia*] [*Airport symbol*] (OAG)
LyHIF .... Lymphoblast Human Interferon (DB)
LYI .... League for Yiddish, Inc. (EA)
LYI .... Libby, MT [*Location identifier*] [*FAA*] (FAAL)
LYKES PAC .... Lykes Brothers Inc. PAC [*Tampa, FL*] (PACS)
LYKL .... Lykes Lines [*Common carrier symbol*]
LYKT .... Lykes Transport [*Common carrier symbol*]
LYKU .... Lykes Bros. Steamship Company [*Common carrier symbol*]
LYKU .... Lykes Brothers Steamship [*Intermodal shipping container symbol*] (TVRC)
LYKZ .... Lykes Brothers Steamship [*Intermodal trailer symbol*]
LYL .... League of Young Liberals [*British*] (ROG)
LYL .... Lima, OH [*Location identifier*] [*FAA*] (FAAL)
LYLE .... Lyle, MN [*American Association of Railroads railroad junction routing code*]
LYLJ .... Ljubljana [*Former Yugoslavia*] [*ICAO location identifier*] (ICLI)
LYM .... Last Year's Model [*Marketing*] (WDAA)
LYM .... Lymph [*or Lymphatic*] (WDAA)
LYM .... Lymphocyte
Lym .... Lymphocytic [*Medicine*] (QSUL)
LYM .... Lympne [*England*] [*Airport symbol*] (AD)
LYMA .... Lyman [*NCIC motorcycle make code*]
LYMB .... Maribor [*Former Yugoslavia*] [*ICAO location identifier*] (ICLI)
LYMBS .... Lodzer Young Men's Benevolent Society (EA)
LYMEC .... Liberal and Radical Youth Movement of the Euorpean Community (SAUO)
LYMO .... Mostar [*Former Yugoslavia*] [*ICAO location identifier*] (ICLI)
LYMP .... Lymphocyte (SAUS)
LYMPH .... Lymphocyte
Lymphos .... Lymphocytes [*Medicine*] (BABM)
Lymphs .... Lymphocytes [*Medicine*] (AMHC)
LYN .... Atlanta, GA [*Location identifier*] [*FAA*] (FAAL)
LYN .... Lamba Youth Network [*An association*] (EA)
LYN .... Lehman Brothers, Inc. [*AMEX symbol*] (SAG)
LYN .... Lynton Aviation [*British*] [*ICAO designator*] (FAAC)
Lyn .... Lynx [*Constellation*]
LYN .... Lynx (automobile) [*NCIC car model code*]
LYNC .... Lyncoach [*NCIC trailer make code*]
LYNCH .... Lynchburg, VA [*American Association of Railroads railroad junction routing code*]
Lynchburg C .... Lynchburg College (GAGS)
LynchC .... Lynch Corp. [*Associated Press*] (SAG)
Lynd .... Lyndwood's Provinciales [*A publication*] (DLA)
Lynd Prov .... Lyndwood's Provinciales [*A publication*] (DLA)
Lyndw Prov .... Lyndwood's Provinciales [*A publication*] (DLA)
Lyne .... Lyne's Irish Chancery Cases (Wallis) [*1766-91*] [*A publication*] (DLA)
LyNeF .... Lytic Nephritic Factor (DB)
Lyne Lea .... Lyne on Leases for Lives [*A publication*] (DLA)
Lyne on Renew .... Lyne on Renewals [*A publication*] (DLA)
Lyne (Wall) .... Wallis' Select Cases, Edited by Lyne [*1766-91*] [*Ireland*] [*A publication*] (DLA)
LYNG .... Lynton Group [*OTCBB symbol*]
LYNH .... Lynch Manufacturing [*NCIC trailer make code*]
LYNN .... Lynnton Manufacturing [*NCIC trailer make code*]
LYNR .... Lynn-Towtruck [*NCIC truck make code*]
LYNX .... Bermudas commercial internet (SAUS)
LYNX .... Lynx Truck Leasing [*Private rail car owner code*]
LYNX GTD .... Lynx Global Telecom Database (GDD)
LYO .... Lubavitch Youth Organization (EA)
LYO .... Lyondell Chemical [*Formerly, Lyondell Petrochem*] [*NYSE symbol*]
LYO .... Lyondell Petrochem [*NYSE symbol*] (TTSB)
LYO .... Lyondell Petrochemical [*NYSE symbol*] (SPSG)
LYO .... Lyons, KS [*Location identifier*] [*FAA*] (FAAL)
LYO .... Lyophilized [*Medicine*] (DMAA)
LYOH .... Ohrid [*Former Yugoslavia*] [*ICAO location identifier*] (ICLI)
LYON .... Liquid-Yield Option Note [*Merrill Lynch & Co.*] [*Finance*]
LYON .... Liquid Yield Option Notes (EBF)
LYON .... Lyons, KS [*American Association of Railroads railroad junction routing code*]
Lyon & R BS .... Lyon and Redman on Bills of Sale [*A publication*] (DLA)
LYONDELL PAC .... Lyondell Chemical Company PAC [*Washington, DC*] (PACS)
Lyondl .... Lyondell Petrochemical Co. [*Associated Press*] (SAG)
Lyon Ind L .... Lyon on the Laws of India [*A publication*] (DLA)
Lyon Just .... Lyon's Institutes of Justinian [*A publication*] (DLA)
LYOS .... Osijek [*Former Yugoslavia*] [*ICAO location identifier*] (ICLI)
lyot .... Layout (VRA)
LYOX .... Lyondell Petrochemical [*Private rail car owner code*]
LYP .... Faisalabad [*Pakistan*] [*Airport symbol*] (OAG)
LYP .... Lactose, Yeast, and Peptone Agar [*Medicine*] (DMAA)
LYP .... Librarian's Yellow Pages [*Database*] (GDD)
LYP .... Lower Yield Point [*Medicine*] (DMAA)
LYP .... Lyallpur [*Pakistan*] [*Airport symbol*] (AD)
Lyp .... Lymphosarcoma [*Medicine*] (AAMN)
LYpAS .... Logicheskii Yazyk dlia Predstavleniya Algoritmov Sinteza Releinykh Ustroistv [*A Programming Language for Logic and Coding Algorithm*] [*Book title*]
lyphs .... Lymphocytes [*Medicine*] (IDYL)
LYPL .... Pula [*Former Yugoslavia*] [*ICAO location identifier*] (ICLI)
LYPR .... Pristina [*Former Yugoslavia*] [*ICAO location identifier*] (ICLI)
LYPW .... Legion of Young Polish Women (EA)
LYPZ .... Portoroz [*Former Yugoslavia*] [*ICAO location identifier*] (ICLI)
LYR .... Lancashire & Yorkshire Railway [*British*]
LYR .... Lancashire & Yorkshire Railway Co. (SAUO)
LYR .... Layer (MSA)
lyr .... Layer
LYR .... Layer Cloud [*Meteorology*] (DA)
LYR .... Leeds & York Railway (SAUO)
LYR .... Longyear [*Norway*] [*Airport symbol*] (OAG)
Lyr .... Lyra [*Constellation*]
LYR .... Lyric [*or Lyrical*]
Lyr .... Lyrichord [*Record label*]
lyr .... Lyricist [*MARC relator code*] [*Library of Congress*] (LCCP)
LYRI .... Rijeka [*Former Yugoslavia*] [*ICAO location identifier*] (ICLI)
LYRIC .... Language for Your Remote Instruction by Computer [*Computer science*] (MDG)
Lys .... De Lysia [*of Dionysius Halicarnassensis*] [*Classical studies*] (OCD)
LYS .... Light of Yoga Society (EA)
LYS .... Like Your Style [*Internet lingo*] (NETL)
LYS .... Lycksele [*Sweden*] [*Geomagnetic observatory code*]
LYS .... Lyon [*France*] [*Airport symbol*] (OAG)
Lys .... Lysander [*of Plutarch*] [*Classical studies*] (OCD)
LYS .... Lysander Gold [*Vancouver Stock Exchange symbol*]
Lys .... Lysias [*Fifth century BC*] [*Classical studies*] (OCD)
LYS .... Lysine (DMAA)
lys .... Lysine [*An amino acid*] (DOG)
Lys .... Lysine [*Also, K*] [*An amino acid*]
Lys .... Lysistrata [*of Aristophanes*] [*Classical studies*] (OCD)
LYS .... Lysodren (DMAA)
Lys .... Lysosome (STED)
LYS .... Lysosome [*Cytology*]
LYS .... Lysozyme [*Also, LZM*] [*An enzyme*]
LYS .... Lysyl [*Enzymology*]
LYS .... Lytes Electrolytes [*Medicine*] (DMAA)
LYS .... Olean, NY [*Location identifier*] [*FAA*] (FAAL)
LYSA .... Sarajevo [*Former Yugoslavia*] [*ICAO location identifier*] (ICLI)
LYSK .... Skopje [*Former Yugoslavia*] [*ICAO location identifier*] (ICLI)
LySLk .... Lymphoma Syndrome Leukemia [*Medicine*] (STED)
Lyso-PC .... Lysophosphatidylcholine [*Also, LPC*] [*Biochemistry*]
LYSP .... Split [*Former Yugoslavia*] [*ICAO location identifier*] (ICLI)

LYSU......... LYS Line [*Intermodal shipping container symbol*] (TVRC)
LYSV......... Leek Yellow Stripe Virus [*Plant pathology*]
LYT........... Layout (MSA)
LYTBT....... Low-Yield Test Ban Treaty
Lytes......... Electrolytes [*Medicine*] (BABM)
LYTES....... Electrolytes (STED)
LYTI.......... Titograd [*Former Yugoslavia*] [*ICAO location identifier*] (ICLI)
LYTS......... LSI Industries [*NASDAQ symbol*] (TTSB)
LYTS......... LSI Industries, Inc. [*NASDAQ symbol*] (SAG)
LYTT......... Lytta [*A Blistering Fly*] [*Pharmacy*] (ROG)
LYTU......... Lykes Brothers Steamship [*Intermodal shipping container symbol*] (TVRC)
LYTV......... Tivat [*Former Yugoslavia*] [*ICAO location identifier*] (ICLI)
LYU.......... Lehigh University, Bethlehem, PA [*OCLC symbol*] (OCLC)
LYV.......... Legume Yellows Virus [*Plant pathology*]
LYVR......... Vrsac [*Former Yugoslavia*] [*ICAO location identifier*] (ICLI)
LYW.......... Lyman [*Washington*] [*Seismograph station code, US Geological Survey*] (SEIS)
LYX.......... Atlantic Rich 9% Exch Nts'97 [*NYSE symbol*] (TTSB)
LYX.......... Atlantic Richfield Co. [*NYSE symbol*] (SAG)
LYX.......... Lydd [*England*] [*Airport symbol*]
LYX.......... Lynx-Canada Explorations Ltd. [*Toronto Stock Exchange symbol*]
Lyx........... Lyxose [*Also, l*] [*A sugar*]
LYXT......... Lynx Transport [*Common carrier symbol*]
LYY.......... Batesville, AR [*Location identifier*] [*FAA*] (FAAL)
LYYY......... Beograd [*Former Yugoslavia*] [*ICAO location identifier*] (ICLI)
LYZ........... Lysozyme [*Medicine*] (DMAA)
LYZA......... Zagreb [*Former Yugoslavia*] [*ICAO location identifier*] (ICLI)
LYZB......... Zagreb [*Former Yugoslavia*] [*ICAO location identifier*] (ICLI)
LYZD......... Zadar [*Former Yugoslavia*] [*ICAO location identifier*] (ICLI)
LZ............ Balkan [*ICAO designator*] (AD)
LZ............ Bulgaria [*Civil aircraft markings - international*] (PIPO)
LZ............ Landing Zone
LZ............ Left Zero (IAA)
LZ............ Lempel Zev [*Computer science*]
LZ............ Leucine Zipper [*Protein structure*]
LZ............ Live Zero (IAA)
LZ............ Loading Zone
LZ............ [*The*] Lubrizol Corp. [*NYSE symbol*] (SPSG)
LZ1.......... Luftschiff Zeppelin 1
LZA.......... Labor Zionist Alliance (EA)
LZB.......... La-Z Boy Chair [*NYSE symbol*] (TTSB)
LZB.......... La-Z Boy Chair Co. [*NYSE symbol*] (SPSG)
LZC.......... Landing Zone Construction (SAUO)
LZCC......... Landing Zone Control Center [*Air Force*] (IAA)
LZCO......... Landing Zone Control Officer [*Air Force*] (AFM)
LZD.......... Launch Zone Display
LZDF......... Launch Zone Display Flag
LZE.......... Luminous-Zone Emissivity (SAUS)
LZEEBE...... Long-Term Zonal Earth Energy Budget Experiment [*Spacecraft*] [*NASA*]
LZF.......... Launch Zone Flag
LZGF......... Lewis Zero Gravity Facility
LZH.......... Lanchow [*Republic of China*] [*Seismograph station code, US Geological Survey*] (SEIS)
LZIF.......... Lyudmila Zhivkova International Foundation (EAIO)
LZL.......... Landing Zone Locator
LZL.......... Launcher, Zero Length [*British military*] (DMA)
lzm........... Lysozyme (STED)
LZM.......... Lysozyme [*An enzyme*]
LZMT........ Landing Zone Marshalling Team (SAUO)
LZO.......... Launch Zone Override
LZOA........ Labor Zionist Organization of America (SAUO)
LZOA........ Labor Zionist Organization of America - Poale Zion [*Later, LZA*] (EA)
LZOC........ Lincoln Zephyr Owner's Club (EA)
LZP.......... Landing Zone Preparation (SAUO)
LZP.......... Latvian Green Party [*Political party*] (EY)
LZP.......... Left Zero Print (IAA)
LZP.......... Lorazepam [*Also, L, LOR*] [*Antiepileptic drug*]
LZPC......... Lead-Zinc Producers Committee (EA)
LZR.......... Lazurus Distributors [*Vancouver Stock Exchange symbol*]
LZR.......... Lizard Island [*Australia*] [*Airport symbol*] (OAG)
LZRC........ TLC The Laser Center, Inc. [*NASDAQ symbol*] (NASQ)
LZSA......... Landing Zone Support Area (COE)
LZSDCP..... Lempel-Ziv-Stac-Data Compression Protocol (SAUS)
LZSU......... Leningrad A.A. Zhdanov State University (SAUO)
LZT.......... Lead Zirconate Titanate [*Ferroelectric material*]
LZT.......... Local Zone Time
LZU.......... Lincoln University, Lincoln University, PA [*OCLC symbol*] (OCLC)
LZV.......... Lazarev [*Later, NVL*] [*Former USSR*] [*Geomagnetic observatory code*]
LZW......... Lempel-Zev-Welch [*Compression*] [*Computer science*] (PCM)
LZW......... Olney-Noble, IL [*Location identifier*] [*FAA*] (FAAL)
LZY.......... Greensboro, NC [*Location identifier*] [*FAA*] (FAAL)
LZZ.......... Lampasas, TX [*Location identifier*] [*FAA*] (FAAL)
LZZ.......... Laz [*Language symbol*] (ETLW)

M
By Acronym

M............ Absolute Magnitude [*Astronomy*]
M............ All India Reporter, Madras Series [*A publication*] (ILCA)
m............ Alveolar Capillary Membrane [*Medicine*] (QSUL)
M............ Angular Momentum [*Symbol*] [*Physics*]
m............ Apparent Magnitude (ODA)
M............ Bending Moment [*Aerospace*] (AAG)
M............ Days before Move Operation [*Usually followed by a number*] [*NASA*] (KSC)
M............ Dynamic Testing Division (SAUO)
M............ Em [*Printing*] (WDMC)
m............ Em [*Printing*] (WDMC)
M............ Emma [*Phonetic alphabet*] [*In use in 1904 and 1914*] (DSUE)
M............ Experimental & Pit Division (SAUO)
M............ Field Goals Missed [*Football, basketball*]
M............ Figure of Merit (SAUS)
M............ First Sergeant [*Army skill qualification identifier*] (INF)
M............ Ground, Mobile [*JETDS nomenclature*]
M............ Human Being Movement [*Rorschach*] [*Psychology*]
M............ Hungary [*IYRU nationality code*] (IYR)
M............ Imperial Chemical Industries [*Great Britain*] [*Research code symbol*]
M............ Indian Law Reports, Madras Series [*A publication*] (DLA)
M............ Instrumental Magnitude [*Earthquakes*]
M............ Intensity of Magnetization [*Symbol*] (DEN)
m----........ Intercontinental Areas (Eastern Hemisphere) [*MARC geographic area code*] [*Library of Congress*] (LCCP)
M............ J. F. Macfarlan & Co. [*Scotland*] [*Research code symbol*]
M............ Lundi [*French*] (ASC)
M............ Macerare [*Macerate*] [*Pharmacy*]
m............ Mach (NAKS)
M............ Mach (SHCU)
M............ Machine
M............ Mach Number
M............ MacNeil [*Herman A.*] [*Designer's mark, when appearing on US coins*]
M............ Macpherson's Scotch Session Cases [*1862-73*] [*A publication*] (DLA)
M............ Macrophage (MELL)
M............ Macula (SAUS)
M............ Magenta (WDMC)
m............ Magenta (WDMC)
M............ Magister [*Master*] [*Latin*]
M............ Magistrate
M............ Magistrate Court (SAUO)
M............ Magnaflux
M............ Magnetic
M............ Magnetic Moment [*Symbol*] (DEN)
M............ Magnetic Polarization [*Symbol*] (DEN)
m............ Magnetic Quantum Number [*Atomic physics*] [*Symbol*]
M............ Magnetization (ODA)
M............ Magnetron (MDG)
M............ Magnification (NTCM)
M............ Magnitude
M............ Maiden
M............ Mail
M............ Main
m............ Main [*Menu*] [*Computer science*] [*Telecommunications*]
M............ Maintainability [*or Maintenance*] (MCD)
m............ Maintainability (NAKS)
M............ Maintenance and Test Assemblies [*JETDS nomenclature*]
m............ Maintenance Coefficient [*Microbiology*] (QSUL)
M............ Majesty
M............ Major [*Cycle*]
m............ Major Cycle (NAKS)
M............ Make
m............ Maker (SAUO)
m............ Male (DD)
M............ Male [*Electronics*]
M............ Malignant [*Medicine*]
M............ Maloti [*Plural of Loti*] [*Monetary Unit*] [*Lesotho*] (BARN)
M............ Malta (MILB)
M............ Mammillary [*Medicine*] (EDAA)
M............ Man
M............ Mandatory (KSC)
m............ Mandatory (NAKS)
M............ Mandible (MELL)
M............ Mane [*Morning*] [*Pharmacy*]
M............ Maneuvering Ship [*In speed triangle of relative movement problems*]
M............ Manichaean Middle Persian
M............ Manila [*Rope*]
M............ Manipulus [*A Handful*] [*Pharmacy*]
M............ Mannitol [*Organic chemistry*]
M............ Mano [*Hand*] [*Spanish*]
M............ Mantissa [*Decimal portion of a logarithm*]
m............ Manual (NAKS)
M............ Manual
M............ Manufacturer (SAUO)
M............ Map
M............ March
M............ Mare [*Thoroughbred racing*]
m............ Marginal Propensity to Import [*Economics*]
M............ Maria [*Mary*]
M............ Marijuana (MELL)
M............ Marine [*FCC*] (NTCM)
M............ Marine [*Insurance*]
M............ Marine Corps [*When used as prefix with plane designation*]
M............ Marinus de Caramanico [*Flourished, 1269-85*] [*Authority cited in pre-1607 legal work*] (DSA)
M............ Maritus [*Bridegroom*] [*Latin*]
M............ Mark [*Monetary unit*] [*German*] (GPO)
M............ Marker [*Beacon*] (AFM)
M............ Markka [*Monetary unit*] [*Finland*]
M............ Marksman [*British military*] (DMA)
M............ Marquis [*or Marquess*]
M............ Married
M............ Mars
M............ Marshal
M............ Marshalling Area (SAUO)
M............ Martial [*Medicine*] (EDAA)
M............ Martin Co. Division [*Martin-Marietta Corp.*] [*ICAO aircraft manufacturer identifier*] (ICAO)
M............ Martinus Gosia [*Authority cited in pre-1607 legal work*] (DSA)
M............ Martinus Zamorensis [*Flourished, 13th century*] [*Authority cited in pre-1607 legal work*] (DSA)
M............ Martyr
M............ Marxist [*Politics*]
m............ Masculine (SHCU)
M............ Masculine
m............ masculinum (SAUS)
M............ Masochism (CDAI)
M............ Mason (ROG)
M............ Mass (GOBB)
m............ Mass [*Symbol*] [*IUPAC*]
M............ Massachusetts State Library, Boston, MA [*Library symbol*] [*Library of Congress*] (LCLS)
M............ Massage
M............ Masseur [*Ranking title*] [*British Royal Navy*]
M............ Massive [*Agriculture*]
M............ Master
M............ Mate [*of a ship*]
M............ Mater [*Mother*] [*Latin*]
M............ Maternal (MELL)
M............ Mathematics [*Secondary school course*] [*British*]
M............ Matinee
M............ Matins [*Early morning prayers*]
m............ Matrix (NAKS)
M............ Matrix
M............ Matron [*British military*] (DMA)
M............ Mature
M............ Mature Audiences [*Movie rating*] [*Replaced by GP*]
M............ Matured Bonds [*Investment term*] (DFIT)
M............ Mauthner [*Cell*] [*Neurology*]
M............ Maxilla (MELL)
M............ Maximal [*or Maximum*] [*Medicine*]

M............ Maximum Value [*Electronics*]
M............ Maxwell [*Electronics*] (DEN)
M............ May
m............ Mean (DIPS)
M............ Mean [*Arithmetic average*]
M............ Mean Active Maintenance Downtime [*Computer science*]
M............ Meaningfulness [*Psychology*]
M............ Mean Square
M............ Measles (MELL)
M............ Measure [*Music*]
M............ Measured Ceiling [*Aviation*]
M............ Meatus (MELL)
M............ Mechanical
M............ Mechlorethamine [*Also, HN, HN2, MBA, NM*] [*Mustargen, nitrogen mustard*] [*Antineoplastic drug*]
M............ Medal (ADA)
M............ Media [*Laboratory*] (AAMN)
M............ Medial (DAVI)
(M).......... Median
M............ Mediator
M............ Medical
M............ Medical Service (SAUO)
M............ Medicare (MELL)
M............ Medicinae [*Of Medicine*] [*Latin*]
M............ Medicine
M............ Medieval
M............ Medium [*Size designation for clothing, etc.*]
m............ Medium [*Spectral*]
M............ Medium [*or 2-engine*] Plane
m............ Mega (NAKS)
M............ Mega [*A prefix meaning multiplied by one million*] [*Symbol*]
M............ Megabyte [*Data storage capacity*] [*Computer science*]
M............ Megaton [*Emergency Management*] (EMA)
M............ Megavolt [*Medicine*] (EDAA)
M............ Megohm (AAG)
M............ Melendus [*Flourished, 1188-1209*] [*Authority cited in pre-1607 legal work*] (DSA)
M............ Melittin [*Bee venom*]
M............ Melphalan [*Also, A, L-PAM, MPH, MPL*] [*Antineoplastic drug*]
M............ Melts At ____ [*Followed by a temperature*]
M............ Member
M............ Member of (SAUO)
M............ Membrana [*Membrane*] [*Anatomy*]
M............ Memorandum
M............ Memoria [*Memory*] [*Latin*]
M............ Memorial; Journal Officiel du Grand Duche de Luxembourg [*A publication*] (ILCA)
M............ Memory
M............ Meningeal (MELL)
M............ Mensura [*By Measure*] [*Pharmacy*] (ROG)
M............ Mentum [*Chin*]
M............ Menzies' Cape Colony Supreme Court Reports [*A publication*] (DLA)
M............ Meperidine [*Also, MEP*] [*An analgesic*]
M............ Mercaptopurine [*Purinethol*] [*Also, MP, P*] [*Antineoplastic drug*]
M............ Mercury [*Chemical symbol is Hg*] (KSC)
m............ Mercury (NAKS)
M............ Merehurst [*Publisher*] [*British*]
M............ Merge [*Computer science*] (IBMDP)
M............ Merides [*Latin*] [*Noon*] (WDMC)
m............ Meridian (Lower Branch)
M............ Meridian (Upper Branch)
M............ Meridies [*Noon*] [*Latin*]
M............ Meridional Part [*Navigation*]
M............ Mesangium [*Anatomy*]
M............ Mesh
M............ Mesial [*Dentistry*]
M............ Mesomeric [*Organic chemistry*]
M............ Mesophyll [*Botany*]
M............ Messier [*M31, M13, M57, etc.*] [*Astronomy term*]
m............ Meta [*Chemistry*]
M............ Metabolite
m............ Metabolized [*Medicine*] (QSUL)
M............ Metacenter
M............ Metal
M............ Metalsmith [*Navy*]
M............ Metamorphosis [*Phylogeny*]
M............ Metaproterenol [*Pharmacology*]
M............ Metastasis [*Oncology*]
M............ Meteorological [*JETDS nomenclature*]
M............ Meter (WDMC)
m............ Meter [*SI unit of length*]
M............ Methionine [*One-letter symbol; see Met*]
M............ Method
M............ Methodist
M............ Methotrexate [*Antineoplastic drug*]
m............ Methyl [*As substituent on nucleoside*] [*Biochemistry*]
M............ Metoclopramide [*An antiemetic*]
M............ Metronome
M............ Metropolitan
M............ Mews
M............ Mezzo [*Moderate*] [*Music*]
M............ Michaelmas Term [*British*] [*Legal term*] (ILCA)
m............ Micro (WGA)
M............ Micrococcus [*Genus of bacteria*]
M............ Microfilaria [*Medicine*] (EDAA)
m............ Micrometer (ABAC)
M............ Micrometer
M............ Microphones [*JETDS nomenclature*] [*Military*] (CET)
M............ Microprocessor
M............ Microsporum [*Genus of fungi*]
M............ Microtubule [*Cytology*]
M............ Mid [*Linguistics*] (IEL)
M............ Midazolan [*An anesthetic*]
M............ Midday (ADA)
m............ Middle (NAKS)
M............ Middle
M............ Middle School [*British*]
M............ Middle Term of a Syllogism [*Logistics*] (WDAA)
M............ Midfield [*Men's lacrosse position*]
M............ Midline
M............ Midnight (ROG)
m............ Midship [*Shipping*] (DS)
M............ Midwest Stock Exchange [*Chicago, IL*]
m............ Mihi [*To Me*] [*Latin*] (EES)
M............ Mike [*Phonetic alphabet*] [*International*] [*World War II*] (DSUE)
M............ Mil [*Monetary unit*] [*Cyprus*]
M............ Mild (DAVI)
M............ Mile (WDMC)
m............ mile (WDMC)
M............ Miles
M............ Miles' Pennsylvania Reports [*A publication*] (DLA)
M............ Military
M............ Militia
M............ Milk (ROG)
M............ Mill
M............ Mille [*Thousand*] [*Roman numeral*]
M............ Milli (DFIT)
m............ Milli- [*A prefix meaning divided by 1000*] [*SI symbol*]
M............ Millime [*Monetary unit*] [*Tunisia*]
M............ Millimicrometer (IAA)
m............ Millimicron (DIPS)
M............ Millimicron (IAA)
m............ Million (NAKS)
M............ Million
m............ Mil[*thousand*] (DAVI)
M............ Mine
M............ Minesweeper [*Navy*]
M............ Miniature [*Horticulture*]
m............ Minim [*Medicine*] (BCRP)
M............ Minim
M............ Minimum (ADA)
M............ Ministry
M............ Minor
M............ Mint [*Condition*] [*Numismatics, etc.*]
M............ Minus
M............ Minute
M............ Miotic [*Biology*]
M............ Mira [*A star*] [*Astronomy*] (OA)
M............ Mired (IAA)
M............ Misce [*Mix*] [*Pharmacy*]
M............ Miscellaneous
M............ Miscible
M............ Mishnah [*Basis of the Talmud*] (BJA)
M............ Missile [*Air Force*]
M............ Missile Carrier Aircraft [*Designation for all US military aircraft*]
m............ Missing (NAKS)
M............ Missing [*Data*]
M............ Missing (Weather Reports Only) [*NWS*] (FAAC)
M............ Mission
M............ Mississippian [*Geological period*] (QSUL)
M............ Mist [*Meteorology*]
M............ Mistura [*Mixture*] [*Pharmacy*]
M............ Mitic Subgroup [*Magnetite, chromite, hematite, ilmenite, titanite, perofskite, rutile*] [*CIPW classification*] [*Geology*]
M............ Mitochondrion [*Cytology*]
M............ Mitomycin [*Also, MC, MT*] [*Antineoplastic drug*]
M............ Mitosis [*Cytology*]
M............ Mitte [*Send*] [*Latin*]
M............ Mix [*or Mixture*]
M............ Mixed School [*British*]

M............ Mobile [*Missile launch environment symbol*] [*Biology*]
M............ Mobilization [*as in M-Day*] [*Military*] (AABC)
M............ Modal (Verb) [*Linguistics*]
M............ Mode
M............ Model [*in military nomenclature*]
M............ MODEM [*Computer science*]
M............ Moderate
M............ Moderate Party (Sweden) [*Political party*] (PSAP)
M............ Moderate Sea or Swell [*Meteorology*]
M............ Modern [*Post-1920*] [*Deltiology*]
M............ Modification [*FCC*] (NTCM)
m............ Modified [*Regulation or order modified*] [*Used in Shepard's Citations*] [*Legal term*] (DLA)
M............ Modiolus (MELL)
m............ Modulation Coefficient (IDOE)
M............ Modulation Depth [*Broadcasting*]
M............ Modulator (IAA)
M............ Modulus
M............ Moisture
M............ Mol [*or Mole*] [*Measurement*] (DAVI)
m............ Molal [*Solute concentration by weight*] [*Chemistry*]
m............ Molality (MELL)
m............ Molar [*Tooth, deciduous*] [*Dentistry*] (DAVI)
M............ Molar [*Permanent*] [*Dentistry*]
M............ Molar [*Solute concentration by volume*] [*Chemistry*]
M............ Molarity (MELL)
M............ Molar Mass [*Symbol*] [*IUPAC*]
M............ Mole
M............ Molecular Weight [*Also, MOL WT, MW*]
M............ Moment
M............ Moment Magnitude [*Emergency Management*] (EMA)
M............ Moment of Force [*Symbol*] [*IUPAC*]
M............ Monastery
M............ Monday
M............ Money
M............ Monitor (MDG)
m............ Monitor (NAKS)
M............ Monkey [*Phonetic alphabet*] [*Royal Navy*] [*World War I*] [*Pre-World War II*] (DSUE)
M............ Monochrome (IAA)
M............ Monoclonal [*Biochemistry*]
M............ Monocyte [*Hematology*]
M............ Monograph
M............ Monophage [*Biology*]
M............ Monoplane
M............ Monotype (DGA)
M............ Monsieur [*Mister*] [*French*]
M............ Monsoon
M............ Mont [*Monte, etc.*] [*Italy and Sicily only*]
M............ Montana (DLA)
M............ Montavit Co. [*Austria*] [*Research code symbol*]
m............ Month (WDMC)
M............ Month
m............ Monthly (RION)
M............ Monthly
M............ Montmorillonite [*A mineral*]
M............ Montreal Stock Exchange
M............ Monumentum [*Monument*] [*Latin*]
M............ Moon
M............ More [*Telegraphy*] (PCTE)
M............ Morgan [*George T.*] [*Designer's mark, when appearing on US coins*]
M............ Morison's Dictionary of Decisions, Scotch Court of Session [*1540-1808*] [*A publication*] (DLA)
m............ Morning (WDMC)
M............ Morning
m............ Morpha [*Form*] [*Biology*]
M............ Morphine [*Slang*]
M............ Morphological Rule [*Linguistics*]
M............ Morphometric Analysis [*Botany*]
M............ Mort [*Dead*] [*French*] (ROG)
M............ Mortar
M............ Mortgage
M............ Mortis [*Of Death*] [*Latin*]
M............ Mot [*Linguistics*] (IEL)
M............ Motel
M............ Mother
m............ Motile [*Sperm*] (MAE)
M............ Motivational Ability
M............ Motor
M............ Motorship (DS)
M............ Motorway [*Traffic sign*] [*British*]
M............ Moulder [*Navy rating*] [*British*]
M............ Mound (MSA)
M............ Mountain
M............ Mouth
M............ Move Being Made [*Computer science*]
M............ Movement [*Neurology*]
M............ Movement Response [*Used in Rorschach test scoring*] (DIPS)
M............ [*Time in Days Before*] Move Operations
M............ Mu [*Twelfth letter of the Greek alphabet*] (DAVI)
M............ Mucoid
M............ Mucoid Colony [*Biochemistry*] (DAVI)
M............ Mucosa [*Medicine*] (EDAA)
M............ Mucous [*Medicine*] (EDAA)
M............ Mucus (MELL)
M............ Mud
M............ Muddy [*Track condition*] [*Thoroughbred racing*]
M............ Muddy [*Quality of the bottom*] [*Nautical charts*]
M............ Muenchen [*German license plate city code*]
M............ Multipara (MAE)
M............ Multiplier
M............ Municipal Premises [*Public-performance tariff class*] [*British*]
M............ Murmur [*Heart*] [*Medicine*]
M............ Muscarinic (DB)
M............ Musculus [*Muscle*] [*Anatomy*]
M............ Music [*Films, television, etc.*]
M............ Mustard Gas [*Also, H, HD, HS, HT*] [*Poison gas*] [*US Chemical Corps symbol*]
M............ Muster
M............ Mutitas [*Dullness*] [*Latin*]
M............ Mutual Companies
M............ Mutual Inductance [*Symbol*] [*IUPAC*]
M............ Mycelium [*Biology*]
M............ Mycobacterium [*Genus of microorganisms*]
M............ Mycoplasma [*Medicine*] (MAE)
M............ Mydriacyl (SAUS)
M............ Myocandida [*Medicine*] (EDAA)
M............ Myopia
M............ Myosin [*Muscle physiology*]
M............ Nautical Mile [*Nautical term*] (HRNC)
M............ New York Miscellaneous Reports [*A publication*] (DLA)
M............ Nomina [*Names*] [*Probably a misprint for NN, by some supposed to denote St. Mary, patron saint of girls*] [*Latin*] (ROG)
M............ Noon [*Meridies*]
M............ Ohio Miscellaneous Reports [*A publication*] (DLA)
M............ One Thousand [*Roman numeral*]
M............ Ordered Multistate [*Botany*]
M............ Pole Strength (SAUS)
M............ Queen Mary (DLA)
M............ Radiant Exitance [*Symbol*] [*IUPAC*]
M............ Reckitt & Sons Ltd. [*Great Britain*] [*Research code symbol*]
M............ Red Star of Prominent Titanium Oxide Intensity [*Astronomy*] (BARN)
M............ Refractive Modulus (IDOE)
m............ Response to Human Being Movement [*Rorschach*] [*Psychology*]
M............ Strength of Pole [*Chemistry*] (DAVI)
M............ Thioinosine [*One-letter symbol; see SIno, Sno*]
/M............ Thousand
M-............ Time in Days Before Move Operations (SAUS)
M............ Time of Maneuver
M............ University of Michigan, Ann Arbor (SAUO)
M/0/0/S ..... Minutes Zero Zero Seconds [*Aerospace*] (AAG)
M/1 .... Method 1 (NITA)
M_1............ Mitral First Sound [*Cardiology*]
M_1............ Money Supply of a Country, Consisting of Currency and Demand Deposits [*Economics*]
M_1............ Sight Dullness [*on Auscultation*] [*Medicine*] (DAVI)
M1S .... Matte One Side [*Aluminum*]
M_2............ Insular Segment of Middle Cerebral Artery [*Cardiology*] (DAVI)
M_2............ Marked Dullness [*on Auscultation*] [*Medicine*] (DAVI)
M2 .... Masterspec 2 [*Production Systems for Architects & Engineers, Inc.*] [*Information service or system*] (IID)
M_2............ Mitral Second Heart Sound [*Cardiology*] (DAVI)
M2 .... Moluccan Cockatoo [*Bird*]
M_2............ Money Supply of a Country, Including M_1 and Commercial Time Deposits [*Economics*]
m2 .... Square Meter
M2C .... Massachusetts Microelectronics Center [*Research center*] (RCD)
M^2C^2......... Multi-Media Communication Control (DOMA)
M2CW .... My Two Cents Worth [*Internet lingo*] (NETL)
M2F2 .... Multimode Fire & Forget (SAUS)
M^2FCS....... Multi-Microprocessor Flight Control System (PDAA)
M2FM .... Modified Modified Frequency Modulation
M^{2H2} .... Mary Hartman, Mary Hartman [*Initialism is shortened form of television program title*] [*Also, MH2*]
M2M......... Manager-to-Manager (ACRL)
M2M......... Manufacturer-to-Manufacturer [*Electronic business*] (NETL)
M2M......... May Second Movement [*1960s Yale University war protest*] (VNW)
M2P2........ Mini-Magnetospheric Plasma Propulsion [*Propulsion prototype*] [*Developed by University of Washington - Seattle*]
M2S .... Matte Two Sides [*Aluminum*]
M^2/S......... Square Meters per Second

M_3 Absolute Dullness [*on Auscultation*] [*Medicine*] (DAVI)
m3 Cubic Meter
M3 Mesoscale and Microscale Meteorology division (SAUO)
M/3 Middle Third [*of long bones*] [*Orthopedics*] (DAVI)
M3 Military Manpower Models
M_3 Money Supply of a Country, Including M_2, Savings and Loan Association Deposits, and Certificates of Deposit [*Economics*]
M-3 APD Military Manpower Models Airborne Personnel Detector [*Device used to collect and test air samples to identify enemy sites*] [*Vietnam*] (VNW)
M3C MAJCOM Manpower Management Computer (SAUO)
M^3/D Cubic Meters per Day
M^3/J Cubic Meters per Joule
M^3/KG Cubic Meters per Kilogram
M^3/(M A) Cubic Meters per Meter Year
M^3/(M D) Cubic Meters per Meter Day
M^3/MIN Cubic Meters per Minute
m3/s Cubic Meter (or Metre) per Second (SAUS)
M^3/S Cubic Meters per Second
M-3 TAP Military Manpower Models Toxicological Agents Protective Suit [*Provided protection from chemical agents*] (VNW)
M-3V Movimiento 3V [*Nicaragua*] [*Political party*] (EY)
M_4 Cortical Segment of Middle Cerebral Artery [*Cardiology*] (DAVI)
M4 Message from Multiple Media Maximizes [*Communications*] (WDMC)
M5 Manual Five Speed [*DOE*] (TAG)
M8 Mate [*Computer slang*] (NETL)
M/10 Tenth Molar [*Solute concentration by volume*] [*Chemistry*] (DAVI)
M12 M12 [*Hawaii*] [*Seismograph station code, US Geological Survey*] [*Closed*] (SEIS)
M-18-X Movimiento 18 de Octubre de Accion Revolucionaria Astra [*Astra 18th October Movement of Revolutionary Action*] [*Ecuador*] [*Political party*] (PD)
M-19 April 19 Movement (SAUO)
M-19 Movimiento 19 de Abril [*April 19 Movement*] [*Colombia*]
M-20 Movimiento-20 [*Panama*] [*Political party*] (EY)
M31 Andromeda Galaxy (SAUS)
M-47 Dragon (SAUS)
M50 Mean of 1950 [*Coordinate system*] [*NASA*] (NASA)
M85 85 Percent/15 Percent Unleaded Gasoline [*BTS*] (TAG)
M/100 Hundredth Molar [*Solute concentration by volume*] [*Chemistry*] (DAVI)
MA Aircraft Stations [*ITU designation*] (CET)
MA Amherst College, Amherst, MA [*Library symbol*] [*Library of Congress*] (LCLS)
ma--- Arab States [*MARC geographic area code*] [*Library of Congress*] (LCCP)
MA Commonwealth of Massachusetts (SAUS)
MA Deputy Commander for Maintenance (SAUO)
MA Division of Military Application (SAUO)
Ma Ma'arbae (BJA)
Ma Ma'aserot (BJA)
MA Machine Accountant [*Navy*]
Ma Mach Number [*IUPAC*]
MA Macroaneurysm (SAUS)
MA Macronutrient Additives [*Fat substituted for food*]
MA Madras Artillery [*British military*] (DMA)
MA Madrid Stock Exchange [*Spain*]
MA Mafenide Acetate [*Medicine*] (EDAA)
MA Magestrol Acetate [*Medicine*] (EDAA)
MA Magister Artium [*Master of Arts*] [*Latin*]
MA Magma Arizona (SAUO)
MA Magma Arizona Railroad Co. [*Later, MAA*] [*AAR code*]
MA Magnesium Association [*Later, IMA*] (EA)
MA Magnetic Amplifier
MA Mahogany Association (EA)
MA Maids of Athena (EA)
MA Maids of Athens (SAUO)
MA Main Alarm (IAA)
MA Main Amplifier (OA)
MA Maintenance
MA Maintenance Ability (KSC)
MA Maintenance Actions
MA Maintenance Agency (SAUO)
MA Maintenance Agreement (ELAL)
M/A Maintenance Analysis (KSC)
MA Maintenance Area [*Military*] [*British*]
MA Maintenance Availability
MA Maize [*Soil biology*] [*Human-introduced crops*] (QSUL)
MA Major (DSUE)
MA Malayan Airways (SAUO)
Ma Male (DAVI)
M/A Male, Altered Animal (DMAA)
MA Maleic Anhydride [*Also, MAH*] [*Organic chemistry*]
MA Malev Hungarian Airlines (SAUO)
MA Malicious Damage (MARI)
MA Malignant Angioendotheliomatosis [*Oncology*]
MA Malignant Arrhythmia [*Medicine*] (DMAA)
MA Malignant Astrocytoma [*Medicine*] (MELL)
MA Malonaldehyde [*Organic chemistry*]
MA Malpractice Association (EA)
MA Malvalic Acid (PDAA)
MA Mamma (DSUE)
MA Mammary Adenocarcinoma [*Medicine*] (DB)
MA Management Administration [*Department of Labor Statistics*] (OICC)
MA Management Adviser
MA Management Area [*USDA Forest Service*] (ALAC)
MA Management Audit [*Branch*] [*Medicine*] (EDAA)
MA Manager of Aviation
MA Manager's Assistant (DCTA)
Ma Manchester Regiment (SAUO)
MA Mandelic Acid [*Organic chemistry*] (AAMN)
MA Manifest Achievement (AAMN)
MA Manifest Anxiety
MA Maniilaq Association (EA)
MA Mannheim [*German license plate city code*]
MA Manpower Administration [*Later, Employment and Training Administration*] [*Department of Labor*]
MA Manual
M/A Manual or Automatic (NRCH)
MA Manufacturing Assembly
MA Manufacturing Authorization (ACAE)
MA Manure (ROG)
MA Manx Airlines Ltd.
MA Map Analysis
MA Marangoni [*Tire retread brand*]
MA March
Ma March's Action for Slander and Arbitrament [*A publication*] (DLA)
MA Margin Account [*Investment term*]
MA Marijuana Anonymous (SAUO)
MA Marine Class
MA Maritime Administration [*Also, MARAD, MARITADMIN*] [*Department of Transportation*]
ma Maritime Antarctic [*Air Mass*] [*Meteorology*] (BARN)
MA Mark [*Coin*] (ROG)
MA Market Administration (HCT)
MA Market Average [*Investment term*]
MA Marketing Assistance (MCD)
MA Marriage Analysis [*Psychology*]
Ma Marsh [*Maps and charts*]
MA Marshaling Area [*Military*]
MA Martin Ablator (SAUS)
MA Martin-Albright [*Syndrome*] [*Medicine*] (DB)
MA Martingana [*Ship's rigging*] (ROG)
Ma Martinus de Caramanico [*Flourished, 1269-85*] [*Authority cited in pre-1607 legal work*] (DSA)
Ma Martinus Gosia [*Authority cited in pre-1607 legal work*] (DSA)
MA Maserati [*Society of Automotive Engineers auto manufacturer code for service information interchange*]
MA Massachusetts [*Postal code*]
MA Massachusetts Reports [*A publication*] (DLA)
MA Mass Analyzer
MA Masseter [*Medicine*] (MELL)
M_a Mass Flow of Air [*Aviation*] (DA)
Ma Mass of Atom (DMAA)
MA Mast Aerial (IAA)
MA Master (MSA)
MA Master Alarm
MA Master Assistant [*British military*] (DMA)
MA Master-at-Arms [*Navy*]
MA Master of Arts
MA Master of Arts in Fine Arts (SAUO)
MA Masurium
MA Matched Angle (OA)
MA Mater [*Mother*] [*Latin*] (ADA)
MA Material Authorization (KSC)
MA Materials Application (SAUO)
MA Mathematical Association [*British*] (BI)
Ma Matheus de Mathesillanis [*Flourished, 1381-1402*] [*Authority cited in pre-1607 legal work*] (DSA)
MA Matrix Antigen [*Biochemistry*]
MA Matt Art [*Paper*] (DGA)
Ma Mattes [*Quality of the bottom*] [*Nautical charts*]
MA Maturational Age [*Also, Development Age*] [*Medical term*] (PAZ)
MA Mature Adult [*Film and video classification*]
MA Mature Australia [*An association*]
MA May
MA May Department Stores Co. [*NYSE symbol*] (SPSG)
MA May Dept Stores [*NYSE symbol*] (TTSB)
MA Mazdaznan Association (EA)
MA Mean Arterial Blood Pressure [*Medicine*] (MAE)
MA Measurement Accuracy
MA Mechanical Accessories (MCD)
MA Mechanical Advantage
MA Mechanical Ambush (VNW)
MA Mechanical Atherectomy [*Medicine*] (MELL)
MA Mechanically Alloyed [*Metallurgy*]
MA Mechanician Apprentice [*British military*] (DMA)
MA Mechanoacoustic
MA Media Alliance (EA)
MA Medicaid (DLA)
MA Medical Abbreviation (AAMN)
MA Medical Assistance [*HEW*]
MA Medical Assistant (DAVI)
MA Medical Audit (MAE)
MA Medical Authority
MA Medical Authorization (DAVI)
M/A Mediterranean/Adriatic [*Shipping*] (DS)
MA Mediterranean Area
MA Medium Artillery

MA .... Mega [*A prefix meaning multiplied by one million*]
Ma .... Megaannum (DOG)
MA .... Megaloblastic Anemia [*Medicine*] (MELL)
MA .... Megampere (IEEE)
MA .... Melanesian Alliance [*Papua New Guinea*] [*Political party*] (FEA)
MA .... Melodious Accord (EA)
MA .... Member of the Academy (SAUO)
MA .... Membrane Antigen [*Immunology*]
MA .... Memory Address [*Computer science*]
MA .... Memory Available [*Computer science*] (IAA)
MA .... Menorah Association [*Defunct*] (EA)
MA .... Menstrual Age [*Medicine*]
MA .... Mental Ability (FOTI)
MA .... Mental Age [*Psychology*]
MA .... Mentum Anterior [*In reference to the chin*]
MA .... Mercenary Association (EA)
MA .... Mercer Associates (EA)
MA .... Mercury Arc (MSA)
MA .... Mercury-Atlas [*Spacecraft*] [*NASA*]
MA .... Meso-American [*Linguistics*] (IEL)
MA .... Message Assembler
M/A .... Mess Attendant
MA .... Messies Anonymous [*Commercial firm*] (EA)
MA .... Messing Allowance [*British military*] (DMA)
MA .... Metabolic Acidosis [*Medicine*] (MELL)
MA .... Metabolic Activity
MA .... Metabolic Analyzer
MA .... Metal Anchor (AAG)
MA .... Metallurgistes Unis d'Amerique [*United Steelworkers of America*] (EAIO)
MA .... Metatarsus Adductus [*Medicine*] (EDAA)
MA .... Meteorological Applications [*Branch*] [*Forecast Systems Laboratory*] (USDC)
MA .... Meter Amplifier
MA .... Meter Angle
M/A .... Meters per Year
MA .... Methamphetamine [*Pharmacology*]
MA .... Methoxylamine [*Organic chemistry*]
MA .... Methyl Acrylate [*Organic chemistry*]
MA .... Methyl Anthranilate [*Organic chemistry*]
MA .... Methylanthranilic Acid
MA .... Metric Association [*Later, USMA*] (EA)
MA .... Metropolitan Area (SAUO)
MA .... Mexican-American
MA .... Michigan Amber [*Variety of wheat*]
MA .... Microadenoma [*Medicine*] (MELL)
MA .... Microagglutination [*Immunochemistry*] (DAVI)
MA .... Microalloy
MA .... Microfilm Address (NITA)
MA .... Microphone Amplifier
MA .... Microscopic Agglutination [*Medicine*] (DMAA)
MA .... Microwave Associates, Inc. [*Later, M/A-Com*] (AAG)
MA .... Middeck Act
MA .... Middeck Aft (MCD)
MA .... Middle Ages
MA .... Middle Assyrian [*Language, etc.*] (BJA)
MA .... Midland Aluminium Limited (SAUO)
MA .... Midmarch Associates (EA)
MA .... Midwest Academy (EA)
MA .... Mike Amplifier (NASA)
MA .... Mikes of America (EA)
MA .... Mileage Allowance
MA .... Miles Laboratories, Inc. [*Research code symbol*]
MA .... Military Academy
MA .... Military Accountant [*British military*] (DMA)
MA .... Military Administration
MA .... Military Adviser (SAUO)
MA .... Military Aircraft
MA .... Military Applications (SAUO)
MA .... Military Assistance [*or Assistant*]
MA .... Military Attache [*Diplomacy*]
MA .... Military Aviator
MA .... Mill Annealed
MA .... Millennium Ecosystem Assessment (SAUO)
MA .... Miller-Abbot (Tube) [*Medicine*]
MA .... Milliammeter (IAA)
ma .... Milliamp (AEBE)
mA .... Milliamp, 1 E-3 A [*Industrial hygiene term*] (OHS)
ma .... Milliampere (MIST)
MA .... Milliampere
mA .... Milliampere [*or Milliamperage*]
MA .... Milliangstrom [*Unit of wavelength of light*] (WGA)
Ma .... Million Years Ago
MA .... Mind Association (EA)
MA .... Minimum Aircraft [*Powered hang gliders, replicas of early flying machines, etc.*] [*British*]
MA .... Mining Association (SAUO)
MA .... Ministry of Aviation [*British*]
MA .... Minnesota [*Obsolete*] (ROG)
MA .... Miscellaneous Adjustment [*Electric utility company*]
MA .... Miscellaneous at Anchor [*Navy*] (NVT)
MA .... Miss Angle
MA .... Missed Appointment
MA .... Missed Approach
MA .... Missile Airframe (AAG)
MA .... Missile Armed (ACAE)
MA .... Missile Away
MA .... Mission Abort (SAUO)
MA .... Mission Accomplished [*Air Force*]
MA .... Mission Analysis (MCD)
MA .... Missionarius Apostolicus [*Missionary Apostolic*] [*Latin*]
MA .... Missionary Apostolic (SAUO)
MA .... Mission Assignment (ACAE)
MA .... Missouri Appeal Reports [*A publication*] (DLA)
MA .... Mistresses Anonymous (EA)
MA .... Mitochondrial Antibody [*Medicine*] (EDAA)
MA .... Mitomycin-C and Adriamycin [*Antineoplastic drug regimen*] (DAVI)
MA .... Mitotic Apparatus [*Cytology*]
MA .... Mitral Annulus [*Cardiology*] (DAVI)
MA .... Mobile Airlock (MCD)
MA .... Mobile Allocation (CGWS)
MA .... Mobilization Augmentee [*Military*] (AFM)
MA .... Mobilization for Animals [*Defunct*] (EA)
MA .... Moderately Advanced (MAE)
MA .... Modern Age [*A publication*] (BRI)
MA .... Modified Atmosphere [*Food technology*]
MA .... Modify Address (IEEE)
MA .... Monarchist Alliance (EA)
MA .... Monarticular Arthritis [*Medicine*]
M/A .... Monetary Allowance
MA .... Monitoring Agency
MA .... Monkeein' Around [*An association*] (EA)
MA .... Monoamine [*Chemistry*]
MA .... Monoclonal Antibody [*Medicine*] (DMAA)
MA .... Monomorphic Adenoma [*Medicine*] (MELL)
MA .... Monte Carlo Resources [*Vancouver Stock Exchange symbol*]
MA .... Months After
M/A .... Mood and/or Affect [*Psychology*] (DAVI)
MA .... Moored Alongside [*Navy*] (NVT)
MA .... Moral Alternatives [*An association*] (EA)
MA .... Moreshet Archives [*Jerusalem*] (BJA)
MA .... Morning After (IIA)
MA .... Morocco [*IYRU nationality code*] [*ANSI two-letter standard code*] (CNC)
MA .... Mortuary Affairs [*Army*] (INF)
MA .... Mother's Aide [*Red Cross Nursing Services*]
MA .... Mothers of Asthmatics (EA)
MA .... Mountain Artillery
MA .... Mountaineering Association [*British*] (BI)
MA .... Moving Average [*Statistics*]
MA .... Multi-chambered Auto-injector (SAUS)
MA .... Multiple Access (NASA)
MA .... Multiple Action [*Medicine*] (EDAA)
MA .... Multiple Application [*Military*] (AFIT)
MA .... Munitionsanstalt [*Ammunition Depot*] [*German military - World War II*]
MA .... Munitions Tribunals Appeals, Great Britain High Court of Justice [*A publication*] (DLA)
MA .... Muscle Activity (MAE)
MA .... Museums' Association (WDAA)
MA .... Musical Appreciation [*Record label*]
MA .... Music Alliance [*Defunct*] (EA)
MA .... Muslim Almanac [*A publication*]
MA .... Mutagenic Activity
MA .... Mutual Age
MA .... My Account [*Business term*]
MA .... Myanma Airways (EY)
MA .... Myelinated Axon [*Medicine*] (EDAA)
ma .... Myria [*A prefix meaning multiplied by 10^4*]
MA .... Office of Management and Administration (SAUO)
MA .... United States Military Academy (AAGC)
MA1 .... Machine Accountant, First Class [*Navy*]
MA2 .... Machine Accountant, Second Class [*Navy*]
MA3 .... Machine Accountant, Third Class [*Navy*]
MAA .... Aerotransportes Mas de Carga SA de CV [*Mexico*] [*ICAO designator*] (FAAC)
MAA .... Maastrichtial [*Paleontology*]
MAA .... Macroaggregated Albumin [*Medicine*]
MAA .... Madras [*India*] [*Airport symbol*] (OAG)
MAA .... Magazine Area A (SAUO)
MAA .... Magma Arizona Railroad Co. [*AAR code*]
MAA .... Major Aircraft Accident (MCD)
MAA .... Major Sync Point Acknowledgment [*Open Systems Interconnection*] (ODAA)
MAA .... Manantiales [*Argentina*] [*Seismograph station code, US Geological Survey*] (SEIS)
MAA .... Mandatory Advertising Association [*Automotive retailing*]
MAA .... Manitoba Association of Architects [*1914*] [*Canada*] (NGC)
MAA .... Manufacturers' Agents Association of Great Britain and Ireland (BI)
MAA .... Manufactures Aircraft Association [*Supersedes AMA*] [*Defunct*] (EA)
MAA .... Marina Association of America [*Defunct*] (EA)
MAA .... Marineartillerieabteilung [*Naval Coast Artillery Battalion*] [*German military - World War II*]
MA A .... Massachusetts Appeals Court Reports [*A publication*] (DLA)
MAA .... Master Army Aviator
MAA .... Master At Arms (SAUS)
MAA .... Master-at-Arms [*Navy*]
MAA .... Master of Administrative Arts (GAGS)
MAA .... Master of Aeronautics and Astronautics (GAGS)

MAA .... Master of Applied Art (GAGS)
MAA .... Master of Applied Arts
MAA .... Material Access Area [*Nuclear energy*] (NRCH)
MAA .... Mathematical Association of America (EA)
MAA .... Mature Age Allowance
MAA .... Maximum Acceptance Angle (VLIE)
MAA .... Maximum Authorized Altitude [*Aviation*]
MAA .... Mecca Minerals Ltd. [*Vancouver Stock Exchange symbol*]
MAA .... Mechanical Arm Assembly (NASA)
MAA .... Mediaeval Academy of America (EA)
MAA .... Medical Administrative Assistant (DAVI)
MAA .... Medical Artists Association (SAUO)
MAA .... Medical Artists Association of Great Britain (PDAA)
MAA .... Medical Assistance for the Aged
MAA .... Medium Antiaircraft Weapon (NATG)
MAA .... Melanoma-Associated Antigen [*Oncology*]
MAA .... Member of the Architectural Association (SAUO)
MAA .... Menthoxyacetic Acid [*Organic chemistry*]
MAA .... Methacrylic Acid [*Organic chemistry*]
MAA .... Methanearsonic Acid [*Organic chemistry*]
MAA .... Methyl Acetoacetate [*Organic chemistry*]
MAA .... Metropolitan Area Acquisition Program (SAUO)
MAA .... Michigan Aggregates Association (EARSL)
MAA .... Microlight Aircrafts Association [*British*] (DI)
MAA .... Mid-Amer Apart Communities [*NYSE symbol*] (TTSB)
MAA .... Mid-America Airlines (SAUO)
MAA .... Mid-America Airways, Inc. (SAUO)
MAA .... [*The*] Mid-America Apartment Communities [*NYSE symbol*] (SPSG)
MAA .... Midlands Association for the Arts (SAUO)
MAA .... Military Advisory Assistance (ACAE)
MAA .... Mission Area Analysis (MCD)
MAA .... Mobilization Against AIDS [*An association*] (EA)
MAA .... Mobilization Automation Appraisal (MCD)
MAA .... Modeling Association of America [*Later, MAAI*]
MAA .... Moderate Angle of Attack
MAA .... Moderate Aplastic Anemia [*Medicine*] (EDAA)
MAA .... Modified Ames Assay [*For toxicology*]
MAA .... Monarticular Arthritis [*Orthopedics*] (DAVI)
MAA .... Monitoring Angle of Attack (SAUS)
MAA .... Moped Association of America [*Defunct*] (EA)
MAA .... Motel Association of America [*Later, National Innkeeping Association*]
MAA .... Motor Agents' Association [*British*]
MAA .... Mouvement Anti-Apartheid [*France*]
MAA .... Municipal Arborist Association [*Later, MAUFS*] (EA)
MAA .... Museum of African Art (SAUO)
MAA .... Mutual Aid Agreement (DEMM)
MAA .... Mutual Assistance Association (SAUO)
MAA .... Myositis Association of America (SAUO)
MAAA .... Master of Arts in Arts Administration (PGP)
MAAA .... Member of the American Academy of Actuaries
MAAA .... Memoirs American Anthropological Association (SAUO)
MAAA .... Metropolitan Area Apparel Association (EA)
MAAAA ...... Mid-Am Antique Appraisers Association (EA)
MAAAA ...... Mid-America Antique Appraisers Association (SAUO)
MAAAP ...... macroaggregated Albumin Arterial Perfusion [*Medicine*] (STED)
MAAAS ...... Member of the American Academy of Arts and Sciences (SAUO)
MAAB .... Maintenance Air Abort [*Air Force*] (AFIT)
MAAB .... Materials Application Advisory Board [*NASA*] (NASA)
MAABR ...... Maintenance Air Abort Rate [*Air Force*] (AFIT)
MAABS ...... Master of Arts in Applied Behavioral Sciences (GAGS)
MAAC .... Mastic Asphalt Advisory Council [*British*] (BI)
MAAC .... Maximum Allowable Actual Charge [*Medicare*]
MAAC .... Medical Assistance Advisory Council (SAUO)
MAAC .... Medical Assistants Advisory Council (DAVI)
MAAC .... Metro Atlantic Athletic Conference (PSS)
MAAC .... Metropolitan Area Advisory Committee (SAUO)
MAAC .... Mid-Atlantic Area Council [*Regional power council*]
MAAC .... Military Assistance Advisory Command (DOMA)
MAAC .... Military Assistance Advisory Committee (SAUO)
MAAC .... Military Assistance Advisory Course (SAUO)
MAAC .... Milliampere Alternating Current (IAA)
MAAC .... Minimum Aft Axial Clearance (ACAE)
MAAC .... Mutual Assistance Advisory Committee
MAACBA .... Middle Atlantic Association of Colleges of Business Administration
MAACE ...... Mississippi Association for Adult and Community Education
MAACL ...... Multiple Affect Adjective Check List [*of Educational and Industrial Testing Service*] [*Psychology*]
MAACP ...... Mediterranean-African Airlift Command Post (SAUO)
MAACP ...... Mediterranean Area Airlift Command Post (AFM)
MAACS ...... Multi Address Asynchronous Communication System
MA ADAM ... Master of Arts in Alcoholism and Drug Abuse Ministry (PGP)
MAADMA ...... Methylaminoacetaldehyde Dimethyl Acetal [*Organic chemistry*]
MAAE .... Master of Aeronautical and Astronomical Engineering (GAGS)
MAAE .... Master of Arts in Applied Economics (GAGS)
MAAF .... Mediterranean Allied Air Force
MAAF .... Mediterranean Army Air Forces
MAAF .... Michael Army Air Field (MCD)
MAAF .... Museum Association of the American Frontier (EA)
MAA-FDI .... Museum of African Art - Frederick Douglass Institute [*Smithsonian Institution*] (EA)
MAAG .... Medical Audit Advisory Group (SAUO)
MAAG .... Military Assistance Advisory Group [*Merged with US Military Assistance Command*]
MAAGAP .... Model Analysis of Agricultural Adjustment in the Philippines (SAUO)
MAAGB ...... Medical Artists Association of Great Britain (DAVI)
MAAGI .... Military Assistance Advisory Group, Indochina [*Later, MAAGV*] (VNW)
MAAG-J ..... Military Assistance Advisory Group, Japan (SAUO)
MAAGP ...... Member, American Academy of General Practice (CMD)
MAAGS ...... Military Assistants Advisory Groups (SAUO)
MAAGV ...... Military Assistance Advisory Group, Vietnam [*Formerly, MAAGI*] (VNW)
MAAH .... Museum of African American History (EA)
MAAH .... Museum of Afro-American History (EA)
MAAI .... Modeling Association of America International (EA)
MAAK .... Movement for All-Macedonian Action [*Political party*]
MAAL .... Massachusetts Alliance of Adult Learners
MAAL .... Monthly Adjustment Acceptance List [*Military*] (AFIT)
MAALOX .... Magnesium-Aluminum Hydroxide [*Commercial antacid*]
MAALT .... Multiple Aircraft Approach and Landing Techniques (MCD)
MAAM .... Medium Antiaircraft Missile
MAAMA ..... Middleton Air Material Agency (SAUO)
MAAMA ..... Middletown Air Materiel Area (SAA)
MAAMC ..... Motor Aircraft and Allied Manufacturing Companies (SAUO)
MAAmSt .... Master of Arts in American Studies (GAGS)
MAAN .... Methyleneaminoacetonitrile [*Organic chemistry*]
MAAN .... Mutual Advertising Agency Network [*Grand Forks, ND*] (EA)
MA & D ..... Mission Analysis and Design
MA & E ..... Mission Analysis and Engineering [*NASA*]
MA&F .... Minister of Agriculture and Fisheries (SAUO)
MA&F .... Ministry of Agriculture and Fisheries (SAUO)
MA & P ..... Maintenance Analysis and Planning (NASA)
MA & T ..... Manufacturing Assembly and Test (MCD)
MA and T ... Missile Assembly and Test [*Building*] (NATG)
MAANPI .... Mutual Aid Association of the New Polish Immigration (EA)
MAANS ...... Midwest Association of Administrative Nursing Supervisors (SAUO)
MAAO .... Massachusetts Association of Assessing Officers (EARSL)
MAAOM ..... Master of Arts in Applied Organizational Management (PGP)
MAAP .... Maintenance and Administration Panel [*Bell System*]
MAAP .... Material Access Authorization Program [*Nuclear energy*] (NRCH)
MAAP .... Member, American Association of Physicians (CMD)
MAAP .... Milan Army Ammunition Plant (AABC)
MAAP .... Minority Association for Animal Protection (SAUO)
MAAP .... More Able Autistic Persons
MAAP .... More Abled Autistic Persons
MAAP4 ...... Modular Accident Analysis Program (SAUO)
MAAPA ...... Massachusetts Aggregates and Asphalt Pavement Association (SRA)
MAAPP ...... Manufacturing Assessment and Planning Package (SPST)
MAAPS ...... Massachusetts Association of 766 Approved Private Schools (SRA)
MAAPSS .... Member of the American Academy of Political and Social Science (SAUO)
MAAR .... Maintenance Action Arrival Rate (ACAE)
MAAR .... Mandatory Annual Audit Requirement (AAGC)
MAAR .... MarCor Development Company, Inc. [*NASDAQ symbol*] (COMM)
MAAR .... Memoirs of the American Academy in Rome (SAUO)
MAAR .... Mojave Antiaircraft Range (SAUO)
MAAR .... Monthly Associate Administrator's Review [*NASA*]
MAARA ...... Midlands Asthma and Allergy Research Association [*British*] (DBA)
MAARC ...... Magnetic Annular Arc (IEEE)
MAARC ...... Mid-Atlantic Antique Radio Club (EARSL)
MA Arch .... Master of Arts in Architecture
MAARM ..... Memory-Aided Antiradiation Missile (MCD)
MAARP ...... Medium Attack Advanced Readiness Program [*Navy*] (DOMA)
Ma'as .... Ma'asroth (BJA)
MAAS .... Machine Assisted Assembly System (ACAE)
MAAS .... Manpower Allocation and Accounting Subsystem [*Air Force*] (AFM)
MAAS .... Manpower Allocations and Accounting System (SAUO)
MAAS .... Meet and Assist [*Travel industry*] (TVEL)
MAAS .... Michigan Association of Ambulance Services (SRA)
MAAS .... More Active And a Shade [*Telegraphy*] (PCTE)
MAAS .... Muhammad Ali Amateur Sports
MAAS .... Multicenter Anti-Atheroma Study [*Medicine*] (EDAA)
MAAS .... Multiple Array Avionics Subsystem
MAASCD .... Massachusetts Association for Supervision and Curriculum Development (EARSL)
MA-ASE ..... Multiple Association Application Service Element [*Telecommunications*] (OSI)
MA(AsianStudies)... Master of Arts (Asian Studies)
MAASL ...... Military Assistance Article and Service List (AFIT)
MAASLA .... Movimiento Argentino Antiimperialista de Solidaridad Latinoamericana
Ma'asSh .... Ma'aser Sheni (BJA)
Ma'as Sh ... Ma'aser Sheni [*Religion*] [*Judaism*]
MAAST ...... Multiple Application Addressable Secure Television (ACAE)
MAAT .... MAC [*McDonnell Aircraft Corporation*] Acquisition and Attack Trainer (MCD)
MAAT .... Management of Advanced Automation Technology Center [*Worcester Polytechnic Institute*] [*Research center*] (RCD)
MAAT .... Master of Arts in Applied Theology (PGP)
MAAT .... Master of Arts in Art Therapy (GAGS)
MAAT .... McCormick Affective Assessment Technique [*Teacher evaluation test*]
MAAT .... Member of the Association of Accounting Technicians [*British*] (DCTA)
MAATAG .... Mission Area Analysis Test Advisory Group [*Army*]
MAATC ...... Mobile Antiaircraft Training Center
MAATE ...... Multiple Application Automatic Test Equipment (ACAE)
MAAU .... Mer Austral [*Intermodal shipping container symbol*] (TVRC)
MAAU .... Mexican-American Affairs Unit [*Office of Education*]
MAAW .... Medium Antitank Assault Weapon

MAAWS ..... Middle Atlantic Association of Women Sailors
MAAX .... Memphis Area Transit Authority [*Federal Railroad Administration identification code*]
MAB .... Eaton Vance Insured Massachusetts Municipal Bond Fund [*AMEX symbol*]
MAB .... Macroaddress Bus
MAB .... Magazine Advertising Bureau [*of MPA*]
MAB .... Magazine Area B (SAUO)
MAB .... Magnetic Amplifier Bridge
MAB .... Mainly about Books [*A publication*]
MAB .... Malfunction Analysis Branch [*NASA*]
MAB .... Man and the Biosphere Program [*UNESCO*] [*Paris, France*]
MAB .... Manganese Alkaline Battery
MAB .... Manhay [*Belgium*] [*Geomagnetic observatory code*]
MAB .... Manual d'Archeologie Biblique [*A publication*] (BJA)
MAB .... Maraba [*Brazil*] [*Airport symbol*] (OAG)
MAB .... Maracaibo Oil Exploration Corp. (SAUO)
MAB .... Marine Air Base
MAB .... Marine Amphibious Brigade
MAB .... Massachusetts Association for the Blind (EARSL)
MAB .... Master Acquisition Bus [*Computer science*] (MCD)
MAB .... Master of Arts in Business (PGP)
MAB .... Material Applications Board
MAB .... Materials Advisory Board [*Later, NMAB*] [*NAS-NRC*]
MAB .... Materials Application Board (SAUS)
MAB .... Materials Applications Board (MCD)
MAB .... Maximum Androgen Blockade [*Oncology*]
MAB .... May Be [*Telegraphy*] (PCTE)
MAB .... Mechanical Automation Breadboard (KSC)
MAB .... Medical Advisory Board
MAB .... Member, Advisory Board
MAB .... Memorial Advisory Bureau [*British*] (CB)
MAB .... Menswear Association of Britain (PDAA)
MAB .... Meteorological Applications Branch (SAUO)
MAB .... Methylaminoazobenzene [*Organic chemistry*]
MAB .... Metropolitan Asylums Board [*British*]
MAB .... Michigan Association of Broadcasters (EARSL)
MAB .... Mid-America Bancorp [*AMEX symbol*] (SPSG)
MAB .... Millardair Ltd. [*Canada*] [*ICAO designator*] (FAAC)
MAB .... Missile Activation Building [*NWA*]
MAB .... Missile Assembly Building (MCD)
MAB .... Mission Analysis Branch [*Manned Spacecraft Center*]
MAB .... Mobile Assault Bridge [*Army*]
MAB .... Modular Array Basing (SAUS)
MAB .... Monetary Affairs Branch (SAUO)
mAb .... Monoclonal Antibody [*Immunology*] (QSUL)
MAb .... Monoclonal Antibody [*Immunochemistry*]
MAB .... Multibase Arithmetic Block (ADA)
MAB .... Munitions Assignment Board [*Anglo-American*] [*World War II*]
MAB .... Mutual Air Board [*Canada*] [*World War II*]
MAB .... Nonoclonal Antibody [*Medicine*] (STED)
MABA .... Meta-Aminobenzoic Acid [*Organic chemistry*]
MABA .... (Methylamino) Benzoic Acid [*Organic chemistry*]
MABAC ...... Member of the Association of Business and Administrative Computing [*British*] (DBQ)
MABAX ...... Merrill Lynch: Basic Value CL.A [*Mutual fund ticker symbol*] (SG)
MABB .... Maximum Achievable Body Burden (PDAA)
MABB .... Michigan Association of Blood Banks (EARSL)
MABC .... Men Against Breast Cancer [*Association*] (EA)
MABCGT .... Mutual Adjustment Bureau of Cloth and Garment Trades [*Defunct*] (EA)
MABDG ...... Marine Aircraft Base Defense Group
MABDW ..... Marine Air Base Defense Wing
MABE .... Master of Agricultural Business and Economics (WGA)
MABE .... Master of Arts in Business Education
MABE .... Member of the Association of Business Executives (DCTA)
MABE .... Mobile Assault Bridge Equipment (SAA)
MABF .... Master of Agricultural Business and Finance
MABF .... Mobile Assault Bridge/Ferry [*Army*] (RDA)
MABFEX ..... Marine Amphibious Brigade Field Exercise (NVT)
MABI .... Mother's Assessment of the Behavior of Her Infant (STED)
MABIE .... Mauna Loa Aerosol Backscatter Intercomparison Experiment (SAUO)
MABIM ...... Member, American Board of Internal Medicine (CMD)
MABL .... Mass Addition Boundary Layer Program [*NASA*]
MABLE ...... Miniature Autonetics Baseline Equipment
MABLE ...... Minnesota Atmospheric Boundary Layer Experiments (SAUO)
MABLEX ..... Marine Amphibious Brigade Landing Exercise (NVT)
MABM .... Master of Agribusiness Management (PGP)
MABM .... Multilayer Absorbing Bottom Layer
MaBn .... Maori Battalion (SAUO)
MABNET .... Global Network for Monitoring the Biosphere [*Marine science*] (MSC)
MAB/NSN ... MAB Northern Sciences Network (SAUO)
MABO .... Marianas-Bonins Group
MABOP ...... Mustargen [*Nitrogen mustard*], Adriamycin, Bleomycin, Oncovin , Prednisone [*Vincristine*] [*Antineoplastic drug regimen*]
MABOPA .... Malaysian Book Publishers' Association (EAIO)
MABP .... Mean Arterial Blood Pressure [*Medicine*]
MABPD ...... Military Assistance Basic Planning Document (CINC)
MABR .... Member, American Board of Radiologists (CMD)
MABRON .... Marine Air Base Squadron
MABS .... Maltese-American Benevolent Society (EA)
MABS .... Marine Air Base Squadron
MABS .... Maritime Application Bridge System (OA)
MABS .... Master of Arts in Behavior Science (GAGS)
MABS .... Master of Arts in Biblical Studies (PGP)
MABS .... Methylmethacrylate-Acrylonitrile-Butadiene-Styrene (EDCT)
MABS .... Mixed Air Battle Simulation
MABS .... Monoclonal Antibodies, Inc. [*NASDAQ symbol*] (COMM)
MABS .... Moored Acoustic Buoy System [*Marine science*] (MSC)
MABSC ...... Management and Behavioral Science Center (SAUO)
MABT .... Malvern Brick & Tile [*Federal Railroad Administration identification code*]
MABU .... Maschinengewehr-Eisenbeton-Unterstand [*Machine-Gun-Iron-Reinforced Concrete Emplacement*] [*German "pill box," battlefield redoubts*] [*World War I*]
MABUS ...... Multi-Access Broadcast Unit System (PDAA)
MABX .... American Biogenetic Sciences, Inc. [*NASDAQ symbol*] (SAG)
MABX .... Ma Bell [*Federal Railroad Administration identification code*]
MABX .... Military Automatic Branch Exchange (SAUS)
MABXA ...... Amer Biogenetic Sciences'A' [*NASDAQ symbol*] (TTSB)
MAC .... Chief Machine Accountant [*Later, DPC*] [*Navy rating*]
MAC .... E. F. MacDonald Company (SAUO)
Mac .... George McClellan [*Nickname for US General*] [*Also seen as Little Mac*] [*Civil War term*]
MAC .... Macadam (ADA)
MAC .... Macalester College, Weyerhaeuser Library, St. Paul, MN [*OCLC symbol*] (OCLC)
MAC .... MacAndrew [*Alcoholism scale*]
Mac .... Macassey's New Zealand Reports [*A publication*] (DLA)
MAC .... Macau [*ANSI three-letter standard code*] (CNC)
Mac .... Macbeth [*Shakespearean work*]
MAC .... Maccabees [*Old Testament book*] [*Roman Catholic canon*] (ROG)
MAC .... MacConkey [*Agar*] [*Microbiology*]
MAC .... MacConkey's [*Broth*] [*Medicine*] (EDAA)
mac .... Macedonian [*MARC language code*] [*Library of Congress*] (LCCP)
MAC .... Macerare [*Macerate*] [*Pharmacy*]
MAC .... Macerated (SAUS)
MAC .... Macerich Co. [*NYSE symbol*] (SAG)
MAC .... Machine-Aided Cognition [*Computer project*] [*Massachusetts Institute of Technology*]
MAC .... MacIntosh [*Blade*] (STED)
Mac .... Macintosh [*Computer science*] (WDMC)
MAC .... Mackerel [*Pimp*] [*Slang*] (DSUE)
MAC .... Mackintosh (DSUE)
Mac .... Maclean's [*A publication*] (BRI)
Mac .... Macnaghten's English Chancery Reports [*A publication*] (DLA)
MAC .... Macomb, IL [*Amtrak rail station code*]
MAC .... Macon, GA [*Location identifier*] [*FAA*] (FAAL)
MAC .... MacPaint (SAUO)
MAC .... Macro Authentication Code [*Computer science*]
MAC .... Macrocytic Erythrocyte (STED)
MAC .... Macrophage (MELL)
MAC .... Macula (MELL)
MAC .... Macule (STED)
MAC .... Madrid Automated Center (ACAE)
MAC .... Magazine Area C (SAUO)
MAC .... Magistrates' Appeal Cases [*A publication*] (DLA)
MAC .... Magnetic Attitude Control
MAC .... Magnetic Automatic Calculator (DEN)
MAC .... Magyar Athletic Club (SAUO)
MAC .... Main Display Console
MAC .... Mainland Affairs Council [*China*]
MAC .... Maintained Anesthesia Care (MELL)
MAC .... Maintaining Arc Consistency (SAUS)
MAC .... Maintenance Advisory Committee [*NSIA*]
MAC .... Maintenance Allocation Chart [*Military*]
MAC .... Maintenance Analysis Center [*FAA*]
MAC .... Maintenance and Construction [*Computer science*] (IAA)
MAC .... Major Activity Center
MAC .... Major Air Command [*Later, MAJCOM*]
MAC .... Major Ambulatory Categories [*Patient classification system*] (DAVI)
MAC .... Malaysia Accreditation Council (SAUO)
MAC .... Malignancy-Associated Changes [*Cancer*]
MAC .... Malta Air Charter Co. Ltd. [*ICAO designator*] (FAAC)
MAC .... Mammary Carcinoma [*Oncology*]
MAC .... Man Against Computer (SAUO)
MAC .... Management Action Center (SAUO)
MAC .... Management Ad Hoc Committee (SAUO)
MAC .... Management Advisory Committee [*Environmental Protection Agency*] (GFGA)
MAC .... Management Analysis Course (SAUO)
MAC .... Management Assessment Coordinator (SAUO)
MAC .... Man and Computer (DIT)
MAC .... Mandatory Access Control [*Computer science*] (IGQR)
MAC .... Maneuver Analysis and Command
MAC .... Maneuver Area Command [*Army*]
MAC .... Manpower Advisory Committee (OICC)
MAC .... Mapping Advisory Committee (SAUO)
MAC .... Mapping and Analysis Center (SAUO)
MAC .... Mapping Applications Center (SAUO)
MAC .... Maricopa Agricultural Center (SAUO)
MAC .... Marine Affairs Council [*Marine science*] (MSC)
MAC .... Marine Amphibious Corps
MAC .... Marine Artillery Consultant (ACAE)
MAC .... Maritime Advisory Committee [*Terminated, 1968*]
MAC .... Maritime Air Command [*Canada*] [*NATO*] (NATG)
MAC .... Marker and Cell [*Computing technique*] [*NASA*]
MAC .... Market Access and Compliance

MAC .... Mark West Springs [*California*] [*Seismograph station code, US Geological Survey*] (SEIS)
MAC .... Martial Arts Commission [*British*] (DI)
MAC .... Martins Air Charter (SAUO)
MAC .... Mass Absorption Coefficient
MAC .... Massive Algebraic Computation [*Programming language*] [*1958*] [*Computer science*] (CSR)
MAC .... Master Acoustical Console [*Army*]
MAC .... Master Addictions Counselor (SAUO)
MAC .... Master Aperture Card (ACAE)
MAC .... Master Control (MCD)
MAc.......... Master of Accountancy (SAUO)
M Ac......... Master of Accounting
M Ac......... Master of Acupuncture (PGP)
MAC .... Master of Arts in Communication (GAGS)
MAC .... Master of Arts in Counseling (PGP)
MAC .... Mastoid Air Cell [*Medicine*] (MELL)
MAC .... Material Accounting Center (ABAC)
MAC .... Material Availability Commitment (AAG)
MAC .... Materials Analysis Co.
MAC .... Materials and Coatings (SSD)
MAC .... Maximal Acid Concentration (STED)
MAC .... Maximal Allowable Concentration (STED)
MAC .... Maximal Allowable Cost (STED)
MAC .... Maximum Acceptable Concentration (LDT)
MAC .... Maximum Acid Concentration [*Clinical chemistry*]
MAC .... Maximum Acquisition Cost (DB)
MAC .... Maximum Admissible [*or Allowable*] Concentration
MAC .... Maximum Allowable Concentration [*Toxicology*]
MAC .... Maximum Allowable Cost [*Medicare, Medicaid*]
MAC .... Maximum Atmospheric Concentration
MAC .... Maximum Concentration of Organics (NAKS)
MAC .... McDonnell Aircraft Co. [*Later, McDonnell Douglas Corp.*] (MCD)
MAC .... McLeod Aerating Cardiac
MAC .... McMaster University [*Hamilton, ON*] (DSUE)
MAC .... Mean Aerodynamic Center
MAC .... Mean Aerodynamic Chord
MAC .... Measurement and Analysis Center [*Telecommunications*] (TEL)
MAC .... Measurement and Control [*A publication*] (IAA)
MAC .... Mechanical Advantage Changer
MAC .... Mechanical Analog Computer (DEN)
MAC .... Media Access Code (RALS)
MAC .... Media Access Control [*Telecommunications*]
MAC .... Media Action Coalition [*Defunct*] (EA)
MAC .... Media Assistance Center (DNAB)
MAC .... Medical Administrative Corps [*Army*] [*World War II*]
MAC .... Medical Advisory Committee [*IATA*] (DS)
MAC .... Medical Alert Center
MAC .... Mediterranean Air Command [*Military*]
MAC .... Mediterranean Air Company (SAUO)
MAC .... Medium Access Control [*Telecommunications*]
MAC .... Medium Armored Car (SAUS)
MAC .... Membership Advisory Committee (SAUO)
MAC .... Membrane Affinity Chromatography
MAC .... Membrane Applications Centre [*University of Bath*] [*British*] (CB)
MAC .... Membrane Attack Complex [*Biochemistry*]
MAC .... Memory Access Command [*Computer science*] (IAA)
MAC .... Memory Access Controller
MAC .... Memory-Address Counter [*Computer science*] (IAA)
MAC .... Men after Christ Band [*R & B recording group*]
MAC .... Merchant Aircraft Carrier [*A ship carrying a cargo of oil or grain and provided with a flight deck for the operation of antisubmarine aircraft*] [*British*] [*World War II*]
MAC .... Message Act Concellation (DA)
MAC .... Message Authentication Code
MAC .... Message Authenticity Check [*Computer science*]
MAC .... Metabolic and Analytical Chemistry
MAC .... Metacarpal Ash per Centimeter
MAC .... Metal Arc Cutting [*Welding*]
MAC .... Methotrexate, Actinomycin D, Cyclophosphamide [*Antineoplastic drug regimen*]
MAC .... Methyl Acetamido Cinnamate [*Organic chemistry*]
MAC .... Methyl Allyl Chloride [*Organic chemistry*]
MAC .... Metric Advisory Committee (SAUO)
MAC .... Miami Aviation Corporation (SAUO)
MAC .... Michigan Apple Committee (EA)
MAC .... Microcystic Adnexal Carcinoma [*Oncology*]
MAC .... Microfilm Aperture Card
MAC .... Microgravity Advisory Committee (SAUO)
MAC .... Microwave-Assisted Curing [*Chemical engineering*]
MAC .... Midair Collision (IIA)
MAC .... Mid-American Car [*Federal Railroad Administration identification code*]
MAC .... Mid-American Conference [*College football*]
MAC .... Midarm Circumference
MAC .... Middle Atlantic Conference, East Riverdale MD [*STAC*]
MAC .... Middle Atmosphere Cooperation (SAUO)
MAC .... Midwest Archives Conference (EA)
MAC .... Military Aid to the Community [*British military*] (DMA)
MAC .... Military Air Command (SAUO)
Mac .... Military Aircraft Command [*Airline call sign*]
MAC .... Military Airlift Command [*Formerly, Military Air Transport Service*]
MAC .... Military/Allied Commission [*World War II*]
MAC .... Military and Administrative Committee (SAUO)
MAC .... Military Armistice Commission (KSC)
MAC .... Military Assistance Command (CINC)
MAC .... Mine Action Centre (SAUO)
MAC .... Mine Advisory Committee [*NAS-NRC*] (MCD)
MAC .... Mineralogical Association of Canada
MAC .... Mini-Accommodation Center [*In MAC-1, a low-cost, plastic sleeping module promoted by Texas businessman Charles McLaren*]
MAC .... Minimal Access Coding [*Computer science*] (VLIE)
MAC .... Minimal Alveolar Concentration [*Anesthesiology*]
MAC .... Minimal Auditory Capability Test [*Medicine*]
MAC .... Minimum Alveolar Concentration [*Physiology*]
MAC .... Mining Association of Canada
MAC .... Missile Activation Circuit
MAC .... Missile Advisory Committee [*Pacific Missile Range*] (MUGU)
MAC .... Mission Assignment Code (NATG)
MAC .... Mission Assignment Coordinator (SAUO)
MAC .... Mitomycin C, Adriamycin, Cyclophosphamide [*Antineoplastic drug regimen*]
MAC .... Mitral Annular Calcification [*Cardiology*]
MAC .... MIUW [*Mobile Inshore Undersea Warfare*] Attack Craft [*Navy symbol*]
MAC .... Mixed Armistice Commission [*Arab-Israel borders*] (BJA)
MAC .... Mobil Air Conditioner (EPAT)
MAC .... Mobile Attenuation Code (SAUS)
MAC .... Mobile Automated Correlator (ACAE)
MAC .... Mobile Inshore Undersea Warfare Attack Craft [*Navy*] (MCD)
MAC .... Model Airplane Club
MAC .... Model Algorithmic Control [*Chemical engineering*] [*Computer science*]
MAC .... Modern Advanced Concrete (EFIS)
MAC .... Modern Arts Criticism [*A publication*]
MAC .... Modern Authors Checklist [*Publication series*]
MAC .... Modulator of Adenylate Cyclase (DB)
MAC .... Monitor and Control [*Computer science*] (IAA)
MAC .... Monitored Anesthesia Care [*Medicine*] (DAVI)
MAC .... Montana Association of Churches (EARSL)
MAC .... Monthly Availability Charge (BUR)
MAC .... Months After Contact (SAUO)
MAC .... Months after Contract Award
MAC .... Moore Action Collectibles (SAUO)
MAC .... Morning-After Call [*Sales*]
MAC .... Mosaic Resources Ltd. [*Vancouver Stock Exchange symbol*]
MAC .... Mothers Against Circumcision (SAUO)
MAC .... Motion Analysis Camera
MAC .... Motor Ambulance Convoy
MAC .... MOUT [*Military Operations on Urbanized Terrain*] Assault Course (INF)
MAC .... Moves, Adds and Changes [*Telecommunications*] (ITD)
MAC .... Movimiento Amplio Colombiano [*Broad-Based Movement of Colombia*] [*Political party*] (PPW)
MAC .... Movimiento Autentico Cristiano [*El Salvador*] [*Political party*] (EY)
MAC .... Movimiento de Autenticidad Colorada [*Paraguay*] [*Political party*] (EY)
MAC .... Mudiad Amdyffyn Cymru [*Welsh Defense Movement*]
MAC .... Multi-Access Computer (VLIE)
MAC .... Multi-Access Computing (NITA)
MAC .... Multiaction Computer
MAC .... Multi-Agency Coordination [*Fire group*] [*USDA Forest Service*] (ALAC)
MAC .... Multi-Analyzer Configuration (IAA)
MAC .... Multi-Application Computer (IAA)
MAC .... Multifunctional Automobile Communication System [*Automotive engineering*]
MAC .... Multi-Instrument Aircraft Campaign
MAC .... Multiphase Atmospheric Chemistry (SAUO)
MAC .... Multiple Access Computer
MAC .... Multiple Access Computing (ELAL)
MAC .... Multiple Access Control [*Computer science*] (DIT)
MAC .... Multiple Access Controller (SAUO)
MAC .... Multiple Address Code
MAC .... Multiple Address Computer (IAA)
MAC .... Multiple Analogue Component [*Satellite Television*]
MAC .... Multiple Aperture Core (VLIE)
MAC .... Multiple Array Correlation (CAAL)
MAC .... Multiplexed Analog Component [*Satellite television*] [*British*]
MAC .... Multiplexed Analog Components [*Satellite television system*]
MAC .... Multiply Accumulate (VLIE)
MAC .... Multiply and Accumulate [*Computer science*] (PCM)
MAC .... Multipurpose Arthritis Center [*Medical University of South Carolina*] [*Research center*]
MAC .... Municipal Assistance Corp. [*New York*] [*Also known as "Big Mac"*]
MAC .... Munitions Assignments Committee [*World War II*]
MAC .... Museum Association of the Caribbean (EAIO)
MAC .... Museums Association of Canada
MAC .... Musical Arts Center (SAUO)
MAC .... Musiciens Amateurs du Canada [*Canadian Amateur Musicians*] (EAIO)
MAC .... Mutual Aid Centre (SAUO)
MAC .... Mycobacterium Avium Complex
MAC .... Mycobacterium Avium-Intracellulare Complex [*Bacteriology*]
MAc......... Russell Memorial Library, Acuhnet, MA [*Library symbol*] [*Library of Congress*] (LCLS)
MACA........ MacDonald Camper [*NCIC trailer make code*]
MACA........ Mammoth Cave National Park
MACA........ Management Assistance Corporation of America (AAGC)

MACA........ Maritime Air Control Authority [*NATO*] (NATG)
MACA........ Maritime Air Co-ordination Authority (SAUS)
MACA........ Master of Arts in Communication Arts
MACA........ Master of Arts in Computer Applications (GAGS)
MAcA........ Master of the Acupuncture Association [*British*] (DBQ)
MAcA........ Member of the Acupuncture Association [*British*]
MACA........ Mental After Care Association [*British*] (EAIO)
MACA........ Mental After-Care Association (SAUO)
MACA........ Mexican-American Correctional Association (OICC)
MACA........ Michigan Association of Children's Alliances (SRA)
MACA........ Military Air Clearance Authority (SAUO)
MACA........ Military Airlift Clearance Authority (AABC)
MACA........ Mini-America's Cup Association (EA)
MACA........ Modular Automatic Conferencing Arranger (SAUO)
MAC(A)...... Munitions Assignments Committee (Air) [*World War II*]
MACABRE... Material Ablation with Chemically Active Boundary Layers in Reentry [*NASA*]
MACADS.... MAC Automated Deployment Reporting System [*Military*] (GFGA)
MACAE...... Minnesota Association of Continuing Adult Education (SAUO)
MACAF...... Mediterranean Allied Coastal Air Forces
MACAF...... Military Airlift Command Numbered Air Force (SAUO)
MacAIMS... McDonnell Aircraft Corporation Advanced Interactive Management System (SAUO)
MACAIR..... Macao Air Transport (SAUO)
MACAIR..... Munitions Assignments Committee Air (SAUO)
MACAL...... Military Airlift Command Airlift Operations Report
Macalp Mon L... Macalpin on Money Lenders [*A publication*] (DLA)
MACALT..... Military Airlift Command Alternate Headquarters (SAUO)
MACAM..... Military Airlift Command Automated Management
Mac & G.... Macnaghten and Gordon's English Chancery Reports [*A publication*] (DLA)
Mac & H.... Cox, Macrae, and Hertslet's Reports, Crown Cases [*1847-58*] [*England*] [*A publication*] (DLA)
Mac & I..... Macrae and Hertslet's English Insolvency Cases [*1847-52*] [*A publication*] (DLA)
Mac & Rob... Maclean and Robinson's Scotch Appeal Cases [*1839*] [*A publication*] (DLA)
MACAP...... Major Appliance Consumer Action Panel (EA)
Mac A Pat Cas... MacArthur's Patent Cases [*District of Columbia*] [*A publication*] (DLA)
MAC-API.... Mordechai Anielewicz Circle of Americans for Progressive Israel (EA)
MacAr........ MacArthur's Patent Cases [*A publication*] (DLA)
MacAr........ MacArthur's Reports [*8-10 District of Columbia*] [*A publication*] (DLA)
MacAr & M... MacArthur and Mackey's District of Columbia Supreme Court Reports [*A publication*] (DLA)
MacAr & Mackey... MacArthur and Mackey's District of Columbia Supreme Court Reports [*A publication*] (DLA)
MACARMS... Military Airlift Command Aircrew Resources Management System (SAUO)
MACARNET... Military Airlift Command Airlift Recovery Network (SAUO)
MacAr Pat Cas... MacArthur's Patent Cases [*District of Columbia*] [*A publication*] (DLA)
MACARS.... Microfilm Aperture Card Automated Retrieval System
MacArth..... MacArthur's Patent Cases [*A publication*] (DLA)
MacArth..... MacArthur's Reports [*8-10 District of Columbia*] [*A publication*] (DLA)
MacArth & M... MacArthur and Mackey's District of Columbia Supreme Court Reports [*A publication*] (DLA)
MacArth & M (Dist Col)... MacArthur and Mackey's District of Columbia Supreme Court Reports [*A publication*] (DLA)
MacArth Ct Mar... MacArthur on Courts-Martial [*A publication*] (DLA)
MacArth Pat Cas... MacArthur's Patent Cases [*United States*] [*A publication*] (DLA)
MacArthur... MacArthur's Patent Cases [*A publication*] (DLA)
MacArthur... MacArthur's Reports [*8-10 District of Columbia*] [*A publication*] (DLA)
MacArthur & M... MacArthur and Mackey's District of Columbia Supreme Court Reports [*A publication*] (DLA)
MacArthur Pat Cas... MacArthur's Patent Cases [*United States*] [*A publication*] (DLA)
Macas........ Macassey's New Zealand Reports [*A publication*] (DLA)
MACAS...... Magnetic Capability and Safety System (NVT)
Macask Ex... Macaskie on Executors, Etc. [*A publication*] (DLA)
MACAT...... Master of Arts in Counseling Psychology: Art Therapy (PGP)
MACAT...... Middle School Alternative Classrooms for the Academically Talented [*Education*]
MA(C)AT.... Motor Accidents (Compensation) Appeal Tribunal [*Northern Territory, Australia*]
MACATS..... MATE Automatic Circuit Analyser Test System (SAUS)
Macaulay Hist Eng... Macaulay's History of England [*A publication*] (DLA)
Macb........ Macbeth [*Shakespearean work*] (BARN)
MACB........ Martial Arts Control Board [*Victoria, Australia*]
MACB........ Michigan Association of Community Bankers (TBD)
MACB........ Missile Assembly Control Building
MACBAA.... Maine/Anjou Cattle Breeders' Association of Australia
MACBANK... Machining Data Bank [*PERA*] [*Software package*] (NCC)
MACBASIC... Measurement and Control BASIC [*Programming language developed by Analog Devices*]
MACBS...... Multi-Access Cable Billing System (VLIE)
Macc........ Maccabees [*Old Testament book*] [*Roman Catholic canon*]
MACC........ MACC Private Equities [*NASDAQ symbol*] (TTSB)
MACC........ MACC Private Equities, Inc. [*NASDAQ symbol*] (SAG)
MACC........ Macro-Ovalocyte [*Biochemistry*] (DAVI)
MACC........ Madison Academic Computing Center [*University of Wisconsin - Madison*] [*Information service or system*] [*Research center*]
MACC........ Madison Area Computing Center (SAUO)
MACC........ Malaysian-American Chamber of Commerce [*Later, AAACC*]
MACC........ Massachusetts Association of Conservation Commissions (EARSL)
M Acc........ Master of Accountancy [*or Accounting*]
MAcc........ Master of Accounting (GAGS)
MACC........ McDonald Camper [*NCIC trailer make code*]
MACC........ McMaster Advanced Control Consortium [*McMaster University*] [*Canada*] (RCD)
MACC........ Methotrexate, Adriamycin, Cyclophosphamide, CCNU [*Lomustine*] [*Antineoplastic drug regimen*]
MACC........ Methotrexate, Adriamycin, Cytoxan, CCNU [*Lomustine*] [*Antineoplastic drug*] (CDI)
MACC........ Mexican-American Cultural Center (SAUO)
MACC........ Micro Asynchronous Communications Controller (MHDI)
MACC........ MidAmerican Communications Corp. [*Telecommunications service*] (TSSD)
MACC........ Midwest Affiliation of Computer Clubs (SAUO)
MACC........ Military Aid to Civil Community [*British*]
MACC........ Military Aid to the Civilian Community (SAUO)
MACC........ Military Area Control Centre (SAUO)
MACC........ Military Assistant to the Civil Community
MACC........ Mobility-Affect-Cooperation-Communication [*Psychiatry*]
MACC........ Modified Acrylic Clear Coat [*Metal finishing*]
MACC........ Modified Air Control Center [*Air Force*] (DOMA)
MACC........ Modular Alter and Compose Console [*Computer science*]
MACC........ Multi-Agency Coordination Center [*Emergency Management*] (EMA)
MACC........ Multiple Applications Control Center (SSD)
MACC........ Multiple Architecture Control Console (MCD)
MACCA...... Michigan Association of Circuit Court Administrators (EARSL)
MacCarthy... MacCarthy's Irish Land Cases [*A publication*] (DLA)
Mac CC...... MacGillivray's Copyright Cases [*1901-49*] [*A publication*] (DLA)
Macc Cas... Maccala's Breach of Promise Cases [*A publication*] (DLA)
MacCHESS... Macromolecular Diffraction Facility at the Cornell High Energy Synchrotron Source [*Cornell University*] (RCD)
Maccl........ Maccala's Reports [*Modern Reports, Part X*] [*1710-25*] [*A publication*] (DLA)
Maccl Tr.... Macclesfield's Trial (Impeachment) [*1725*] [*London*] [*A publication*] (DLA)
Mac CM..... Macomb on Courts-Martial [*A publication*] (DLA)
MACCM2.... Middle Atmosphere Community Climate Model, Version 2 (SAUO)
MACCM3.... Middle Atmosphere Community Climate Model, Version 3 (SAUO)
M Acco...... Master of Accounting
MACCONNET... Military Airlift Command Contingency Network (SAUO)
M-Accounts... Merged Accounts (AAGC)
MACCS...... Manufacturing and Cost Control System (IAA)
MACCS...... Manufacturing Cost Collection System
MACCS...... Marine Air Command and Control System (NVT)
M Accs...... Master of Accounts
MACCS...... Mobile Adaptable Communications Countermeasures System (SAUS)
MACCS...... Molecular Access System [*Computer program*]
MAccSc..... Master in Accounting Science (DD)
MACCSU.... Military Airlift Command Accelerated Command Center System Upgrade (SAUO)
M Acct...... Master of Accountancy (PGP)
M Acct...... Master of Accounting (PGP)
MACCT...... Master of Arts in Community College Teaching (GAGS)
MACCT...... Multiple Assembly Cooling Cask Test [*Nuclear energy*] (NRCH)
M ACCUR.... Misce Accuratissime [*Mix Thoroughly*] [*Pharmacy*]
MACCY...... Mackinaw City, MI [*American Association of Railroads railroad junction routing code*]
M Accy...... Master of Accountancy (PGP)
MACD....... MacDermid, Inc. [*NASDAQ symbol*] (NQ)
MacD........ MacDevitt's Irish Land Commissioner's Reports [*A publication*] (DLA)
MACD....... MacDonald's Mobile Homes [*NCIC trailer make code*]
MACD....... McDonald's Express Line [*Common carrier symbol*]
MACD....... Member of the Australasian College of Dermatologists (SAUO)
MACD....... Member of the Australian College of Dentistry (SAUO)
MACD....... Member of the Australian College of Dermatologists (SAUO)
MACD....... Michigan Association of Conservation Districts (EARSL)
MACDAC.... Machine Communication with Digital Automatic Computer
MACDAC.... Man Communication and Display for an Automatic Computer (PDAA)
MACDAC.... McDonnell Douglas Corp. (KSC)
MACDAC-sys........... MACDAC system (NITA)
MACDATA... Materials and Components Development and Testing Association [*Paisley College of Technology*] [*British*] (IRUK)
MACDC...... Military Assistance Command Director of Construction
MACDD...... Marine and Coastal Data Directory of Australia (SAUO)
MacDermott Commission... Commission on the Isle Of Man Constitution. Report [*1959*] [*A publication*] (DLA)
MacDev..... MacDevitt's Irish Land Cases [*1882-84*] [*A publication*] (DLA)
MACDIF..... Mapping and Charting Data Interchange Format (SAUO)
MACDIS..... Military Assistance for Civil Disturbance [*Department of Defense*] (DEMM)
Macd Jam... Macdougall's Jamaica Reports [*A publication*] (DLA)
MACDP...... Metropolitan Atlanta Congenital Defects Program [*Georgia*] (DMAA)
MacDrmd... MacDermid, Inc. [*Associated Press*] (SAG)
MACDS...... Monitor and Control Display System (MCD)
MACE........ Mace Security International [*NASDAQ symbol*] (SAG)
MACE........ Mace Security Intl [*NASDAQ symbol*] (TTSB)
MACE........ Machine-Aided Composition and Editing
MACE........ Maintenance Analysis Checkout Equipment
MACE........ Management Applications in a Computer Environment (IEEE)
MACE........ Managing Company Expansion [*Manpower Services Commission*] [*British*]
MACE........ Maneuvering Attack Concept Evaluation (ACAE)

MACE........ Marginal Absolute Certainty Equivalent [*Statistics*]
MACE........ Massachusetts Advisory Council on Education (SAUO)
MACE........ Master Control Executive (IAA)
MACE........ Master of Air Conditioning Education (NADA)
MACE........ Master of Air-Conditioning Education (SAUO)
MACE........ Master of Air Conditioning Engineering
MACE........ Master of Air-Conditioning Engineering (SAUO)
MACE........ Master of Arts in Christian Education (PGP)
MACE........ Master of Arts in Civil Engineering
MACE........ Master of Arts in Computer Education (PGP)
MACE........ Mechanical Antenna Control Electronics (MCD)
MACE........ Member of the Association of Conference Executives [*British*] (DBQ)
MACE........ Methylchloroform Chloroacetophenone [*Riot-control gas*]
MACE........ Metropolitan Architectural Consortium for Education (AIE)
MACE........ Mid-America Commodity Exchange [*Chicago, IL*]
MACE........ Military Air Cargo Export [*Subsystem*]
MACE........ Military Airlift Capability Estimator
MACE........ Military Airlift Center, Europe (MCD)
MACE........ Military and Computer Electronics Corp. (SAUO)
MACE........ Minnesota Association for Childhood Education (SAUO)
MACE........ Minority Advisory Committee on Energy [*Terminated, 1982*] (EGAO)
MACE........ Mission Adaptive Combat Ensemble (ACAE)
MACE........ Multi-national Alliance for Criminal Emergencies (SAUO)
MACE........ Multipurpose Automatic Control Equipment (HEAS)
Maced........ Macedonia
MACED...... Macedonian
MACEF...... Mastic Asphalt Council and Employers Federation [*British*] (DBA)
MACEN...... Air Defense Command & First Air Region (SAUO)
MAC Eng.... Master of Air Conditioning Engineering
MAC Eng.... Master of Air-Conditioning Engineering (SAUO)
MACER...... Macerare [*Macerate*] [*Pharmacy*]
Macerich.... Macerich Co. [*Associated Press*] (SAG)
MaceSec.... Mace Security International [*Associated Press*] (SAG)
MACEW..... Military Airlift Command Electronic Warfare (ACAE)
MacF........ MacFarlane's Scotch Jury Court Reports [*1838-39*] [*A publication*] (DLA)
MacF........ MacFarlane's Scotch Jury Trials [*A publication*] (DLA)
MACF........ Mulitple Association Control Function [*Telecommunications*] (OSI)
MACFA...... Mid-Atlantic Collegiate Fencing Association (PSS)
MacFar...... MacFarlane's Scotch Jury Court Reports [*1838-39*] [*A publication*] (DLA)
MacFarl..... MacFarlane's Scotch Jury Trials [*A publication*] (DLA)
MacFarlane... MacFarlane's Scotch Jury Trials [*A publication*] (DLA)
Macf Cop... Macfie on Copyright [*A publication*] (DLA)
Macf Min... Macfarland's Digest of Mining Cases [*A publication*] (DLA)
MacF Pr.... MacFarlane's Practice of the Court of Sessions [*A publication*] (DLA)
MacFrug.... MacFrugals Bargains Close Outs [*Associated Press*] (SAG)
MACG....... MacGregor Sports & Fitness [*NASDAQ symbol*] (TTSB)
MACG....... MacGregor Sports & Fitness, Inc. [*NASDAQ symbol*] (SAG)
MacG........ MacGregor Sports & Fitness, Inc. [*Associated Press*] (SAG)
MACG....... MacGregor Yacht [*NCIC trailer make code*]
MACG....... Maneuver Analysis and Command Group
MACG....... Marine Air Control Group
MACG....... Marshaling Area Control Group [*Military*] (AABC)
MACG....... Military Air Control Group (ACAE)
MAC(G)..... Munitions Assignments Committee (Ground) [*World War II*]
MacG CC.... MacGillivray's Copyright Cases [*1901-49*] [*A publication*] (DLA)
MacGillivray & Parkington... MacGillivray and Parkington's Insurance Law [*6th ed.*] [*1975*] [*A publication*] (DLA)
MacG S..... MacGregor Sports & Fitness, Inc. [*Associated Press*] (SAG)
MacG Sp.... MacGregor Sports & Fitness, Inc. [*Associated Press*] (SAG)
MACGW..... MacGregor Sports&Fitness Wrrt [*NASDAQ symbol*] (TTSB)
MACH....... Machabees [*Old Testament book*] [*Douay version*]
mach........ Machine (ELAL)
MACH....... Machine [*or Machinery*]
MACH....... Machinist (WDAA)
MACH....... Master of Arts in Church History (PGP)
MACH....... Measure of Achieving Tendency [*Test*] (TMMY)
MACH....... Military Air Command Hunter [*In MACH 3, a video game by Mylstar Electronics*]
MACH....... Modular Automated Container Handling [*Shipping*] (DS)
MACH....... Multilayer Actuator Head [*Epson America, Inc.*] [*Computer science*] (PCM)
MACH....... Velocity Relative to the Speed of Sound (SAUS)
MACHA...... Member, American College of Hospital Administration (CMD)
Macha....... Michigan Automated Clearing House Association (TBD)
MACHA...... Michigan Automated Clearing House Association
MACHA...... Mid-Atlantic Clearinghouse Association [*Maryland, Virginia, and Washington, DC*]
MACHA...... Midwest Automated Clearing House Association
MACHA...... Military Armistice Commission Headquarters Area (INF)
MACHALT... Machinery Alteration
MACH D..... Machine Direction Paper (DGA)
MACHDC.... Machinability Data Center [*Computerized search services*] [*Metcut Research Associates, Inc.*]
Mach Des... Machine Design [*A publication*] (CABS)
Macheez.... Macheezmo Mouse Restaurants, Inc. [*Associated Press*] (SAG)
MA Chem... Master of Applied Chemistry
MACHG...... Machining
MACHGR.... Machine Group
MACH III.... Maintenance Aided Computer-HAWK-[*Homing All The Way Killer*]-Intelligence/Institutional/Instructor [*Military*]
MA(ChildLit/Reading)... Master of Arts in Children's Literature and Reading
MACHIS..... Michigan Association of Consumer Health Information Specialists (SAUO)
Mach Learn... Machine Learning [*A publication*] (CABS)
MACHO...... Machismo [*Spanish*] (DSUE)
MACHO...... Massive Compact Halo Object [*Astrophysics*]
MACHO...... Massive Compact Halo Objects [*Astronomy*]
MACHO...... Memphians Against Chest Hair at Operas (SAUO)
Macho....... Movimiento Anticomunista Hondureno [*Honduran Anti-Communist Movement*] [*Political party*] (PD)
MACHPA.... Mid-America Comprehensive Health Planning Agency [*Kansas City*] [*Medicine*] (EDAA)
MACHR...... Machiner
MACH R..... Machine Ruling (DGA)
m-AChr...... Muscarinic Acetylcholine Receptor [*Biochemistry*]
MACHST.... Machinist
MachTool... Machines and Tooling (SAUO)
Mach Vision Appl... Machine Vision and Applications [*A publication*] (CABS)
MACHY...... Machinery
MACI........ Member of the American Concrete Institute
MACI........ Military Adaptation of Command [*or Commercial*] Items [*DoD*] (AABC)
MACI........ Military Adaption of Commercial Items (SAUO)
MACI........ Millon Adolescent Clinical Inventory (DIPS)
MACI........ Mine Anti-Char Indetectable (SAUS)
MACI........ Monitor, Access, and Control Interface (NASA)
MACID....... Media Access Control Identifier (SAUS)
MAC II....... Mica and Chessy [*Acronym is name of interior decorating firm and is taken from first names of owners Mica Ertegun and Chessy Rayner*]
MACII........ Missouri Aptitude and Career Information Inventory [*Vocational guidance test*]
MACIMS.... Military Airlift Command Integrated Management System
MACINTER... International Network of Psychology-Based-Man-Computer Interaction Research (SAUO)
MACINTER... International Network of Psychology-Based Man-Computer International Research (SAUO)
MACIPS..... Military Air Command Information Processing System (ACAE)
MACIPS..... Military Airlift Command Information Processing System (SAUO)
MACIS....... Management and Contracts Information Service
MACISIN.... Military Airlift Command Information Systems Internetting (SAUO)
MACJC...... Minnesota Association of Community and Junior Colleges (SAUO)
MACJC...... Mississippi Association of Community and Junior Colleges (PSS)
MACJC...... Missouri Association of Community and Junior Colleges (SAUO)
MACK........ Mackenzie
MACK........ Mack (trucks) [*NCIC truck make code*]
MACK........ Mack Trucks, Inc. [*NASDAQ symbol*] (COMM)
MAC(K)...... Military Armistice Commission (Korea)
Mack & F Jud A... Mackeson and Forbes' Judicature Acts [*A publication*] (DLA)
Mack BL.... Mackenzie on Bills of Lading [*A publication*] (DLA)
Mack CL.... Mackeldey on Modern Civil Law [*A publication*] (DLA)
Mack Crim.. Mackenzie's Treatise on Criminal Law [*4 eds.*] [*1678-1758*] [*Scotland*] [*A publication*] (DLA)
Mack Cr L... Mackenzie's Treatise on Criminal Law [*4th ed.*] [*1678-1758*] [*Scotland*] [*A publication*] (DLA)
Mack Ct Sess... Mackay. Court of Session Practice [*A publication*] (ILCA)
Mackeld..... Mackeldey on Modern Civil Law [*A publication*] (DLA)
Mackeld..... Mackeldey on Roman Law [*A publication*] (DLA)
Mackeld Civil Law... Mackeldey on Modern Civil Law [*A publication*] (DLA)
Mackeld Rom Law... Mackeldey on Roman Law [*A publication*] (DLA)
Mackey...... Mackey's District of Columbia Reports [*12-20 District of Columbia*] [*A publication*] (DLA)
MackFn..... Mackenzie Financial Corp. [*Associated Press*] (SAG)
MACKI....... Mackinaw, IL [*American Association of Railroads railroad junction routing code*]
Mackie...... Mackie Designs, Inc. [*Associated Press*] (SAG)
Mack Inst... Mackenzie's Institutes of the Law of Scotland [*9 eds.*] [*1684-1758*] [*A publication*] (DLA)
Mack Law of Prop... Mackay's Law of Property [*1882*] [*A publication*] (DLA)
Mack Nat... Mackintosh's Law of Nature and Nations [*5th ed.*] [*1835*] [*A publication*] (DLA)
Mack Obs... Mackenzie's Observations on Acts of Parliament [*1675, etc.*] [*Scotland*] [*A publication*] (DLA)
Mack Rom Law... Mackenzie's Studies in Roman Law [*A publication*] (DLA)
Macl......... Maclaren on Wills and Successions [*A publication*] (DLA)
Macl......... Maclaurin's Scotch Criminal Decisions [*A publication*] (DLA)
MACL........ Master of Arts in Classroom Psychology (PGP)
MACL........ Maximum Approximate Conditional Likelihood [*Statistics*]
MACL........ Minimum Acceptable Compliance Level (IAA)
MACL........ Mood Adjective Check List [*Psychometrics*]
MACL........ Multiple-Aspect Colour-Light Signalling [*Indian Railway*] (TIR)
Macl & R... Maclean and Robinson's Scotch Appeal Cases [*9 English Reprint*] [*A publication*] (DLA)
Macl & Rob... Maclean and Robinson's Scotch Appeal Cases [*9 English Reprint*] [*A publication*] (DLA)
MAC layer... Media Access Control Layer [*Computer science*] (IGQR)
Macl Bank... Macleod's Theory and Practice of Banking [*A publication*] (DLA)
Maclean & R... Maclean and Robinson's Scotch Appeal Cases [*9 English Reprint*] [*A publication*] (DLA)
Maclean & R (Sc)... Maclean and Robinson's Scotch Appeal Cases [*9 English Reprint*] [*A publication*] (DLA)
maclib....... Macrolibrary (MHDI)
MAC LLC.... Media Access Control Logical Link Control [*Computer science*]
MACLO...... Military Airlift Command Liaison Officer (SAUO)
MACLOG.... Metropolitan Atlanta Council of Local Governments (SAUO)
MACLOGFOR... Military Airlift Command Logistics Force Packing System (SAUO)
MACLOS.... Manually Commanded to Line-of-Sight (SAUS)

Macl Rem Cas... Maclaurin's Remarkable Cases [*1670-1773*] [*Scotland*] [*A publication*] (DLA)
MACLS...... Multiple-Aspect Colour-Light Signalling [*Indian Railway*] (TIR)
Macl Sh..... Maclachlan on Merchant Shipping [*A publication*] (DLA)
Macl Shipp... Maclachlan on Merchant Shipping [*A publication*] (DLA)
MACM....... Master Chief Machine Accountant [*Later, DPCM*] [*Navy rating*]
MACM....... Master of Arts in Christian Ministries (PGP)
MACM....... Master of Arts in Church Music (PGP)
MACM....... Member of the Association of Computing Machines (ODA)
MACM....... Military Aid to Civil Ministries [*British military*] (DMA)
MA/CM...... Milliamperes per Centimeter
MACM....... Motorized Air Cycle Machine (MCD)
MACM....... Multi Architecture Cost Model (ACAE)
MACMA..... Mid-Atlantic Construction Management Association (SAUO)
MACMA..... Military Airlift Command Minicomputer Acquisition (SAUO)
MACMA..... Military and Aerospace Connector Manufacturers Association (EA)
MACMA..... Mutual Aid Centre Managing Agency [*British*] (CB)
MACMH..... Altona Community Memorial Health Centre, Manitoba [*Library symbol*] [*National Library of Canada*] (NLC)
MACMIP.... Military Airlift Command Mainframe Internetting Project (SAUO)
MACMIS.... Maintenance and Construction Management Information System [*Computer science*]
MACMIS.... Major Army Command Management Information System
MACMO.... Mobile Acquisition Career Management Office [*Army*]
MACMOL.... Macromolecular
MACMS..... Miniature Arms Collectors/Makers Society (EA)
Macn........ Macnaghten's Hindu Law Cases [*India*] [*A publication*] (DLA)
Macn........ Macnaghten's Nizamut Adalat Cases [*1805-50*] [*Bengal, India*] [*A publication*] (DLA)
Macn........ Macnaghten's Select Cases in Chancery Tempore King [*A publication*] (DLA)
Macn........ Macnaghten's Select Cases, Sadr Diwani Adalat [*1791-1858*] [*Bengal, India*] [*A publication*] (DLA)
MACN....... Mobile Allocation Channel Number (CGWS)
MAC(N)..... Munitions Assignments Committee (Navy) [*World War II*]
Macn & G.. Macnaghten and Gordon's English Chancery Reports [*A publication*] (DLA)
Macn & G (Eng)... Macnaghten and Gordon's English Chancery Reports [*A publication*] (DLA)
Macn CM... Macnaghten on Courts-Martial [*A publication*] (DLA)
Macn Cr Ev... Macnaghten's Criminal Evidence [*A publication*] (DLA)
Macn El Hind L... Macnaghten's Elements of Hindu Law [*A publication*] (DLA)
Macn Ev.... Macnally's Rules of Evidence on Pleas of the Crown [*A publication*] (DLA)
MACNIMAATZ... MacArthur, Nimitz, and Spaatz [*Nickname for World War II command structure of Douglas MacArthur, Chester W. Nimitz, and Carl A. Spaatz*]
Macn NA Beng... Macnaghten's Nizamut Adalat Reports [*Bengal, India*] [*A publication*] (DLA)
Macn Nul... Macnamara's Nullities and Irregularities in Law [*1842*] [*A publication*] (DLA)
MacNSc..... [*The*] MacNeal-Schwendler Corp. [*Associated Press*] (SAG)
Macn SDA... Macnaghten's Select Cases, Sadr Diwani Adalat [*1791-1858*] [*Bengal, India*] [*A publication*] (DLA)
Macn Sel Cas... Select Cases in Chancery Tempore King, Edited by Macnaghten [*1724-33*] [*A publication*] (DLA)
MACNW..... Military Airlift Command Northwest (SAUO)
MACNY...... Manufacturers Association of Central New York (EARSL)
MACNYC.... Men's Apparel Club of New York City (EA)
Mac NZ..... Macassey's New Zealand Reports [*A publication*] (DLA)
MACO....... Macoma Engineering [*NCIC trailer make code*]
MACO....... Major Assembly Checkout [*NASA*] (NASA)
MAC(O)..... Management Analysis Course (Class O) [*Navy*] (DNAB)
MACO....... Marshaling Area Control Officer [*Military*] (AABC)
MACO....... Master of Arts in Counseling (PGP)
MACO....... McCormick, Ashland City & Nashville Railroad [*Federal Railroad Administration identification code*]
MACOI....... MACV [*Military Assistance Command, Vietnam*] Office of Information (VNW)
MACOM..... Maintenance Assembly and Check-Out Model (PDAA)
MACOM..... Major Army Command (AABC)
MACOM..... Major Commands [*Military*]
M Ac OM.... Master of Arts in Acupuncture and Oriental Medicine (PGP)
M/A-Com.... Microwave Associates Communications Co. (EFIS)
Macomb CM... Macomb on Courts-Martial [*A publication*] (DLA)
MA Comm... Master of Arts in Communication (PGP)
MACOMTELNET... Military Airlift Command Teletype Network (SAA)
MACON...... Macon, GA [*American Association of Railroads railroad junction routing code*]
MACON...... Maintenance Console (MCD)
MACON...... Matrix Connector Punched Card Programmer [*Computer science*] (IEEE)
MACONS.... Mid-Atlantic Continental Shelf
MACOP...... Methotrexate, Ara-C, Cyclophosphamide, Oncovin [*Vincristine*], Prednisone [*Antineoplastic drug regimen*]
MACOP-B... Methotrexate, Adriamycin Cyclophosphamide, Oncovin, Prednisone, and Bleomycin [*Medicine*] (EDAA)
MACOPS.... Military Airlift Command Operational Phone System (AFM)
MACOPT.... Machining Optimisation [*PERA*] [*Software package*] (NCC)
Mac OS..... Macintosh Operating System [*Computer science*] (CDE)
MACOS...... Man - A Course of Study [*Title of social-studies course*] [*National Science Foundation*]
MACOS...... Military Airlift Combat Operations Staff
MACOV...... Mechanized and Army Combat Operations Vietnam (AABC)
MACP........ Macro Control Processor [*Computer science*] (IAA)
macp........ Macroprocessor (MHDB)
MACP........ Marine Aviation Campaign Plan
MACP........ Master of Arts in Community Psychology (PGP)
MACP........ Master of Arts in Counseling Psychology (PGP)
MACP........ Michigan Association of Cherry Producers (EA)
MACP........ Michigan Association of Chiefs of Police (SRA)
MACP........ Military Aid to the Civil Power [*British military*] (DMA)
MACP........ Mission Analysis Computer Program
MACP........ Mortuary Affairs Collection Point [*Army*] (INF)
MACP........ Multiple Access Command and Pilot (ACAE)
MACPA...... Maryland Association of Certified Public Accountants (SRA)
MACPA...... Michigan Association of Certified Public Accountants (SRA)
MACPA...... Mid America Crop Protection Association (SRA)
MAC-PAC... Manufacturing, Planning, and Control [*Arthur Anderson & Co.*] [*Software package*] (NCC)
MACPAC.... McGlinchey, Stafford, Mintz, Cellini & Lang PAC [*New Orleans, LA*] (PACS)
Mac-Paps... Mackenzie-Papineau Battalion [*Canada*]
Mac Pat Cas... Macrory's Patent Cases [*England*] [*A publication*] (DLA)
Mac PC..... Macrory's Patent Cases [*England*] [*A publication*] (DLA)
Macph....... Macpherson, Lee, and Bell's Scotch Session Cases [*A publication*] (DLA)
Macph....... Macpherson's Scotch Court of Session Cases [*1862-73*] [*A publication*] (DLA)
Macph Inf... Macpherson on Infancy [*A publication*] (DLA)
Macph Jud Com... Macpherson's Practice of the Judicial Committee of the Privy Council [*A publication*] (DLA)
Macph L & B... Macpherson, Lee, and Bell [*Scotland*] [*A publication*] (DLA)
Macph Pr C... Macpherson's Practice of the Judicial Committee of the Privy Council [*2nd ed.*] [*1873*] [*A publication*] (DLA)
Macph Priv Counc... Macpherson's Privy Council Practice [*A publication*] (DLA)
MACP
MACP........ Military Aid to the Civil Power (SAUO)
MACPOL.... Management, Access Control, Planning & Policy (SAUO)
Macq........ Macqueen's Scotch Appeal Cases, House of Lords [*A publication*] (DLA)
Macq D..... Macqueen's Debates on Life-Peerage Questions [*A publication*] (DLA)
Macq Div... Macqueen's Marriage, Divorce, and Legitmacy [*2nd ed.*] [*1860*] [*A publication*] (DLA)
Macq H & W... Macqueen's Rights and Liabilities of Husband and Wife [*4th ed.*] [*1905*] [*A publication*] (DLA)
Macq HL Cas... Macqueen's Scotch Appeal Cases, House of Lords [*A publication*] (DLA)
Macq Mar... Macqueen's Marriage, Divorce, and Legitimacy [*2nd ed.*] [*1860*] [*A publication*] (DLA)
Macq Sc App Cas... Macqueen's Scotch Appeal Cases, House of Lords [*A publication*] (DLA)
Mac R....... Macdougall's Jamaica Reports [*A publication*] (DLA)
Mac R....... Maclean and Robinson's Scotch Appeal Cases [*1839*] [*A publication*] (DLA)
Macr......... Macrobii [*of Lucian*] [*Classical studies*] (OCD)
Macr......... MacroChem Corp. [*Associated Press*] (SAG)
MACR....... Macrocytosis [*Hematology*] (DAVI)
MACR....... Macromedia, Inc. [*NASDAQ symbol*] (SAG)
Macr......... Macrory's Patent Cases [*England*] [*A publication*] (DLA)
MACR....... Materiel Acquisition Control Record (ACAE)
MACR....... Mean Axillary Count Rate [*Medicine*] (DMAA)
MACR....... Member of the American College of Radiology
MACR....... Methacrolein [*Also, MAL*] [*Organic chemistry*]
MACR....... Military Airlift Command Regulation (SAUO)
MACR....... Minneapolis, Anoka and Cuyuna Range Railroad Company (SAUO)
MACR....... Missing Air Crew Report
MACR....... Multiply, Accumulate, and Round
MAC/RAN... Measurement Analysis Corporation/Random Data (ACAE)
Macr & H... Macrae and Hertslet's English Insolvency Cases [*1847-52*] [*A publication*] (DLA)
MACRAT.... Middle-Atmosphere Chemistry, Radiation, and Transport (SAUS)
MACRAT.... Middle-Atmosphere Chemistry, Radiation and Transport program (SAUO)
Macrch...... MacroChem Corp. [*Associated Press*] (SAG)
MACREC.... Military Airlift Command Technical Services Company (SAUO)
MACRES.... Malaysian Centre for Remote Sensing (SAUO)
MACRI...... Mercantile Atlantic Coastal Routing Instructions
MACrimStudies... Master of Arts in Criminological Studies
MACRIT..... Manpower Authorization Criteria [*Army*]
Macrmd..... Macromedia, Inc. [*Associated Press*] (SAG)
MACRO...... Macroassembler (MHDI)
MACRO...... Macrocytosis [*Hematology*] (DAVI)
MACRO...... Macroinstruction (ECII)
MACRO...... Macroprocessor (MHDI)
MACRO...... Massachusetts Association of Community Rehabilitation Organizations (SRA)
MACRO...... Merge and Correlate Recorded Output [*Computer science*] (NASA)
MACRO...... Military Airlift Command Resource Optimization (SAUO)
MACRO...... Monopole, Astrophysics and Cosmic Ray Observatory [*Italy*]
MACRO...... Monopoles, Astrophysics and Cosmic Ray Observatory (SAUO)
Macrob...... Macrobius [*Late fourth and early fifth century AD*] [*Classical studies*] (OCD)
MACROCAL... [*Enhanced*] Macro Version of Common Assembler Language [*Interdata*] (NITA)
MacroCh.... MacroChem Corp. [*Associated Press*] (SAG)
Macroecon Dynam... Macroeconomic Dynamics [*A publication*] (JLIT)
MACROL.... Macro-Based Display Oriented Language [*Raytheon Co.*]
Macr Pat Cas... Macrory's Patent Cases [*England*] [*A publication*] (DLA)

Macr P Cas ... Macrory's Patent Cases [*England*] [*A publication*] (DLA)
MACRS ...... Modified Accelerated Cost Recovery System [*IRS*]
MacS .... MacSweeney on Mines, Quarries, and Minerals [*5 eds.*] [*1884-1922*] [*A publication*] (DLA)
MACS .... Magnetic Countermine System (SAUS)
MACS .... Mainline Automated Clearance System [*Interstate trucking*] [*Highway safety*]
MACS .... Maintenance Assistance Capability Software (SAUO)
MACS .... Management Administration Control System
MACS .... Management & Computer Services, Inc. [*Information service or system*] (IID)
MACS .... Manned Air Combat Simulation (MCD)
MACS .... Manufacturing Application Control System (SAUS)
MACS .... Marine Air Control Squadron
MACS .... Mass and Charge Spectroscopy
MACS .... Mastoid Air Cell System [*Anatomy*]
MACS .... Maximum Aortic Cusp Separation [*Medicine*] (DMAA)
MACS .... McDonnell Automatic Checkout System [*McDonnell Douglas Corp.*]
MACS .... Media Account Control System (PDAA)
MACS .... Medium-Altitude Communications Satellite
MACS .... Member of the American Chemical Society
MACS .... Merchant Airship Cargo Satellite (PDAA)
MACS .... Metering and Accounting System (NITA)
MACS .... Michigan Association of Christian Schools (SRA)
MACS .... Michigan Association of Convenience Stores (SRA)
MACS .... Micro and Anophthalmic Children's Society [*British*] (NRGU)
MACS .... Micro Anophthalmic Children's Society (WDAA)
MACS .... Microwave Attitude Control Sensor
MACS .... Middle Atmosphere in the Climate System (SAUO)
MACS .... Migrant Advisory Committee
MACS .... Military Aeronautical Communications Service
MACS .... Military Airlift Command Service (NATG)
MACS .... Missile Air-Conditioning System
MACS .... Mississippi Association of Convenience Stores (SRA)
MACS .... Mixed Aloha Carrier Sense (SAUO)
MACS .... Mobile Acoustic Communications System
MACS .... Mobile Acoustic Communication Study (SAUO)
MACS .... Mobile Air Conditioning Society (EA)
MACS .... Modem Access Control System (SAUO)
MACS .... Modular Application Customizing System [*Computer science*] (ELAL)
MACS .... Modular Attitude Control Subsystem (SAUS)
MACS .... Modular Attitude Control System (ACAE)
MACS .... Monitoring and Control Station
MACS .... Multi-Access Computer Switch [*Telecommunications*] (TSSD)
MACS .... Multiagency Coordinating System [*Emergency Management*] (EMA)
MACS .... Multiagency Coordination System [*Emergency Management*] (EMA)
MACS .... Multicenter AIDS [*Acquired Immune Deficiency Syndrome*] Cohort Study [*National Institutes of Health*]
MACS .... Multiline Automatic Calling System (HGAA)
MACS .... Multiple Acceleration Control System (SAUS)
MACS .... Multiple Access Communications System [*West German and Dutch*]
MACS .... Multiple Application Connector System
MACS .... Multiple Applications Control System (SAUS)
MACS .... Multiple-Technique Analytical Computer System
MACS .... Multiproject Automated Control System
MACS .... Multipurpose Acquisition and Control System (IAA)
MACS .... Multipurpose Arcade Combat Simulator [*Marksmanship training*] [*Army*] (INF)
MACS .... Senior Chief Machine Accountant [*Later, DPCS*] [*Navy rating*]
MACSAM .... Military Airlift Command System Architecture Modernization (SAUO)
MACSAT ..... Multiple Access Commercial Satellite (DOMA)
MACSAT ..... Multiple Access Communications Satellite (MED)
MACSBUG .. Motorola Advanced Computer Symbolic Debugger (SAUS)
MACSCO .... Metropolitan Academic Consultants Sales Corp.
MACSEA .... Military Assistance Command, Southeast Asia
MACSIS ..... Multi-Agency Community Services Information System
MAC/SM .... Maintenance Allocation Chart and System Maintenance (MCD)
MACSO ...... Military Airlift Command Support Office (SAUO)
MACSOG .... Military Assistance Command Studies and Observation Group (CINC)
MACSQ ...... Marine Air Control Squadron
MACSRRPCC ... Maxwellian Averaged Cross Section Reactor Physics Computer Code [*Electronics*] (IAA)
MACSS ...... Master of Arts in Church Social Services (PGP)
MACSS ...... Medium-Altitude Communications Satellite System
MACSS ...... Montana Association of County School Superintendents (SAUO)
MACSU ...... Maximum Card Study Unit [*An association*] (EA)
MACSV ...... Multipurpose Airmobile Combat-Support Vehicle (SAA)
MACSYM .... Measurement and Control System (MHDB)
MACSYMA .. MAC [*Massive Algebraic Computation*] Symbolic Manipulator [*Programming language*] [*1969*] (CSR)
MACT .... Master of Arts in College Teaching
MACT .... Maximum Achievable [*or Available*] Control Technology [*Environmental chemistry*]
MACT .... Maximum Available Control Technique [*Air quality standards*]
MACT .... Military Assistance Command, Thailand (VNW)
MACT .... Moral Action Choice Test (EDAC)
MACT .... Multiple-Agent Chemotherapy [*Medicine*] (MELL)
MACTAR .... McMaster-Toronto Arthritis and Rehumatism [*Questionnaire*] [*Medicine*] (DMAA)
MACTEC ..... MAC Technical Services Co. (GAAI)
MACTEC ..... Military Airlift Command Technical Services Company (SAUO)
MACTELNET ... Military Airlift Command Teletype Network (AFM)
MacTEP ..... Mac [*Apple's Mackintosh computer*] Terminal Emulation Program
MACTHAI ... Military Assistance Command Thailand (SAUO)
MACTIS ..... Mine-hunting Action Information Subsystem (SAUS)
MACTM ..... Master of Applied Communication Theory and Methodology (PGP)
MACTRAC ... Military Airlift Command Traffic Reporting and Control System
MACTU ...... Mines and Countermeasures Tactical Unit (SAUO)
MACTU ...... Mines and Countermeasures Technical Unit [*Navy*]
MACTVA ..... Mid-America Cable Telecommunications Association (EARSL)
MACU .... Maintenance Assembly Change Unit (SAUS)
MACU .... Marine Auto and Cargo Services International [*Intermodal shipping container symbol*] (TVRC)
MACU .... Material Cost per Unit (ACAE)
MACU .... Monitor and Control Unit [*Aerospace*] (IAA)
MACUL ...... Michigan Association for Computer Users in Learning (EDAC)
MACV .... Military Assistance Command, Vietnam
MACV .... Multipurpose Airmobile Combat-Support Vehicle
MACVD ...... Microwave-Assisted Chemical Vapor Deposition [*Coating technology*]
MACVNAG ... Military Assistance Command, Vietnam Naval Advisory Group (VNW)
MACVSOG ... Military Assistance Command Vietnam Special Operations Group (INF)
MACV-SOG ... Military Assistance Command, Vietnam Studies and Observations Group (VNW)
MACW .... Midwest Athletic Conference for Women (PSS)
MACW .... Missionary Association of Catholic Women [*Defunct*] (EA)
MACWA ..... Mid-Atlantic Council of Watershed Associations (SAUO)
MACWACC ... Military Airlift Command Washington Area Computer Center (SAUO)
MACX .... MAC Acquisitions [*Private rail car owner code*]
M Acy .... Master of Accountancy (PGP)
MACY .... Master of Arts in Accountancy (PGP)
MACYG ...... Mabys Association for the Care of Young Girls (SAUO)
MACZ .... Maryland Association of Rail Commuters [*Federal Railroad Administration identification code*]
Mad .... All India Reporter, Madras [*A publication*] (DLA)
Mad .... Indian Law Reports, Madras Series [*A publication*] (DLA)
Mad .... Indian Rulings, Madras Series [*A publication*] (DLA)
MAD .... Machine Analysis Display
MAD .... Machine ANSI Data
Mad .... Madagascar
MAD .... Madam
MAD .... Madang [*Papua New Guinea*] [*Seismograph station code, US Geological Survey*] (SEIS)
Mad .... Maddock's English Chancery Reports [*56 English Reprint*] [*1815-22*] [*A publication*] (DLA)
Mad .... Maddock's Reports [*9-18 Montana*] [*A publication*] (DLA)
MAD .... Madeco SA [*NYSE symbol*] (SPSG)
MAD .... Madeco S.A. ADS [*NYSE symbol*] (TTSB)
MAD .... Madison [*Diocesan abbreviation*] [*Wisconsin*] (TOCD)
MAD .... Madison, CT [*Location identifier*] [*FAA*] (FAAL)
MAD .... Madison Fund, Inc. (SAUO)
Mad .... Madras High Court Reports [*India*] [*A publication*] (DLA)
MAD .... Madrid [*Spain*] [*Airport symbol*] (OAG)
MAD .... Magnetic Airborne Detector [*Navy*]
MAD .... Magnetic Anomaly Detection [*or Detector*]
MAD .... Magnetic Azimuth Detector (MCD)
MAD .... Main Assembly Drawing
MAD .... Maintenance Alert Directive [*Aviation*]
MAD .... Maintenance Analysis Data [*or Diagram*] (MCD)
MAD .... Maintenance, Assembly, and Disassembly
MAD .... Major Affective Disorder [*Medicine*] (DMAA)
MAD .... Major Air Disaster (PDAA)
MAD .... Management Analysis Division [*NASA*] (MCD)
MAD .... Management Areas Database (SAUO)
MAD .... Mandibulo-Acral Dysplasia [*Medicine*] (DMAA)
MAD .... Manhunter Assignment Device [*Computer science*]
MAD .... Manufacturing Assembly Drawing
MAD .... Maple Air Services Ltd. [*Canada*] [*ICAO designator*] (FAAC)
MAD .... Marine Air [*or Aviation*] Detachment
MAD .... Marine Air Detection (AFIT)
MAD .... Marine Aviation Detachment (SAUO)
MAD .... Mass-Access Device (GART)
MAD .... Mass Analyzer Detector
MAD .... Master Accession Document [*Computer science*] (BUR)
MAD .... Master Air Data [*Computer*]
M Ad .... Master of Administration (PGP)
MAd .... Master of Arts Administration (GAGS)
MAD .... Material Analysis Data
MAD .... Material Assistance Designated [*Report*] (MCD)
MAD .... Material Availability Date (CET)
MAD .... Materials for the Assyrian Dictionary (BJA)
MAD .... Materiel Acquisition and Delivery [*Military*]
MAD .... Mathematical Analysis of Downtime (DNAB)
MAD .... Maximal Androgen Deprivation
MAD .... Maximum Acceptable Deviation
MAD .... Maximum Acid Output [*Biochemistry*] (DAVI)
MAD .... Maximum Allowable Dose [*Medicine*] (DB)
MAD .... Maximum Applicable Dose [*Environmental chemistry*]
MAD .... Mean Absolute Deviation [*Statistics*]
MAD .... Mean Accumulated Dose [*Radiation*] [*Medicine*] (EDAA)
MAD .... MeCCNU [*Semustine*], Adriamycin [*Antineoplastic drug regimen*]
MAD .... Media Access Device [*Telecommunications*]
MAD .... Median Absolute Deviation [*Statistics*]
MAD .... Memory Access Director [*Computer science*] (IAA)
MAD .... Memory Address Driver strength (SAUS)
MAD .... Memphians Against Degeneracy (SAUO)
MAD .... Message Address Directory (SAUO)

MAD .... Methandriol [*Medicine*] (EDAA)
MAD .... Methylacridone [*Organic chemistry*]
MAD .... Methylandrostenediol [*Methandriol*] [*Endocrinology*]
MAD .... Michigan Algebraic Decoder (RALS)
MAD .... Michigan Algorithmic Decoder [*IBM Corp.*] [*University of Michigan*] [*Programming language*] [*1961*]
MAD .... Mileage Accumulation Dynamometer
MAD .... Militarischer Abschirmdienst [*Military counterintelligence*] [*Germany*]
MAD .... Military Air Distress (LAIN)
MAD .... Military Assistance Division (SAUO)
MAD .... Milk-Alkali Disease [*Medicine*] (MELL)
MAD .... Mind-Altering Drug
MAD .... Mine Assembly Depot [*Navy*]
MAD .... Mini-Attack Drone
MAD .... Minimal Aural Dose
MAD .... Minimum Absolute Deviation [*Statistics*]
MAD .... Minimum Approach Distance (SAA)
MAD .... Minimum Average Dose [*Medicine*] (DMAA)
MAD .... Missile Assembly Data
MAD .... Mission Analysis Division [*NASA*] (KSC)
MAD .... Mission Area Deficiency [*Army*]
MAD .... Mississippians Against Disposal (SAUO)
MAD .... Mitotic Arrest-Deficient [*Cytology*]
MAD .... Mixed Analog and Digital [*Telecommunications*] (TEL)
MAD .... Model A Drivers (EA)
MAD .... Mongolian Asiatic Development (SAUO)
MAD .... More After Dark [*Screen-saver computer program from Berkeley Systems*] (PCM)
MAD .... Morse Automatic Decoder (IAA)
MAD .... Mortar Air Delivery System [*Military*] (VNW)
MAD .... Mosquito Abatement District (DICI)
MAD .... Motor Assembly and Disassembly
MAD .... Motorsport Advanced Display [*Auto racing*]
MAD .... Multifunction Antenna Development (ACAE)
MAD .... Multiple Access Device
MAD .... Multiple Access Drive (NITA)
MAD .... Multiple-Aperture Device (MUGU)
MAD .... Multiple Audio Distribution [*Communications*]
MAD .... Multiple-Wavelength Anomalous Dispersion [*Crystallography*]
MAD .... Multiply and Add
MAD .... Multiwavelength Anomalous Diffraction [*Physics*]
mAD .... Muscle Adenylate Deaminase (DB)
MAD .... Music and Dance [*American Dance Festival project*]
MAD .... Mutual Ability for Defense [*Pentagon defense policy*]
MAD .... Mutual Assured Destruction [*Nuclear warfare*]
MAD .... Mutually Assured Destruction (SAUS)
MAD .... Myoadenylate Deaminase [*An enzyme*]
MADA .... Michigan Automobile Dealers Association (EARSL)
MADA .... Multiple Access Demand Assignment (MCD)
MADA .... Multiple Access - Discrete Address [*Navy tactical voice communication*]
MADA .... Muscle Adenylate Deaminase [*Medicine*] (MELL)
madac .... Madrid Air Defense Automated Center (ACAE)
MADAEC .... Military Application Division of the Atomic Energy Commission
MADAG ...... Madagascar (ROG)
Madag .... Madagascar [*Malagasy Republic*] (VRA)
Madag .... Malagasy Republic (VRA)
MADAIR ..... Magnetic Anomaly Detection and Identification Ranging (MCD)
MADALINE ... Multi-Adaptive Linear Neuron (PDAA)
MADAM ..... Maintenance Diagnostic Assistance Module [*Military*] (CAAL)
MADAM ..... Manchester Automatic Digital Machine [*Manchester University*] [*British*] (DEN)
MADAM ..... Mangrove Dynamics and Management (SAUO)
MADAM ..... Marine Air-Droppable Area Marker (MCD)
MADAM ..... Master Data Acquisition Module (SAUS)
MADAM ..... Mean and Dispersion Additive Model [*Statistics*]
MADAM ..... Moderately Advanced Data Management [*Computer science*]
MADAM ..... Multipurpose Automatic Data Analysis Machine
MADAN ...... Multimission Attitude Determination/Autonomous Navigation (ACAE)
Mad & B .... Maddox and Bach's Reports [*19 Montana*] [*A publication*] (DLA)
Mad & Gel ... Maddock and Geldart's English Chancery Reports [*A publication*] (DLA)
MADAP ...... Maastricht Automatic Data Processing and Display System [*Air traffic control*]
MADAR ...... Malfunction Analysis, Detection, and Recording [*Computer science*]
MADAR ...... Malfunction Analysis, Detection and Reporting (SAUO)
MADAR ...... Malfunction and Data Recorder [*Computer science*] (IAA)
MADARS .... Maintenance Analysis, Detection, and Reporting System [*Computer science*] (AFM)
MADARS .... Malfunction Analysis, Detection, and Recording Subsystem [*Computer science*]
MADARTS ... Malfunction Detection Analysis, Recording, and Training System
MADB .... Madison Bancshares Group [*NASDAQ symbol*] (TTSB)
Mad Bar .... Madox's Barona Anglia [*A publication*] (DLA)
MADC .... Machine-Assisted Detection and Classification (NVT)
MADC .... Maritime Administration of the Department of Commerce (SAUO)
MADC .... Milliampere Direct Current [*Electronics*] (IAA)
MADC .... Miniature Air Data Computer (SAUS)
MADC .... Multiplexer Analog-to-Digital Converter (MCD)
MADCAP .... Mammoth Decimal Arithmetic Program [*NASA*] (KSC)
MADCAP .... Mobilization and Deployment Capability Assurance Concept [*Military*]
MADCAP .... Model of Advection, Diffusion, and Chemistry for Air Pollution [*Environmental Protection Agency*] (GFGA)
MADCAR .... Management Data Charting and Review (IAA)
Mad Ch Pr ... Maddock's English Chancery Practice [*3rd ed.*] [*1837*] [*A publication*] (DLA)
MADCK ...... Marine Aide-de-Camp to the King [*British Admiralty*]
Mad Co ..... Madras Code [*India*] [*A publication*] (DLA)
MAD/CO ..... Mid-America Dance Company [*St. Louis, MO*]
MADD .... Madden's Transfer and Storage [*Common carrier symbol*]
MADD .... Madden Trailer [*NCIC trailer make code*]
Madd .... Maddock's English Chancery Reports [*A publication*] (DLA)
Madd .... Maddox's Reports [*9-18 Montana*] [*A publication*] (DLA)
MADD .... Missile Aerosurface Development Device (ACAE)
MADD .... Module for Automatic Dock and Detumble [*Orbital rescue*] [*NASA*]
MADD .... Mothers Against Drunk Driving (EA)
MADD .... Multichannel Analog-to-Digital Data Decoder (IAA)
MADD .... Multiple Acyl-CoA Dehydrogenation Deficiency (STED)
MADDAM ... Macromodule and Digital Differential Analyzer Machine [*Computer science*]
MADDAM ... Multiplexed Analog to Digital, Digital to Analog Multiplexed [*Computer science*]
Madd & B ... Maddox and Bach's Reports [*19 Montana*] [*A publication*] (DLA)
Madd & G ... Maddock and Geldart's English Chancery Reports [*A publication*] (DLA)
Madd & Gel ... Maddock and Geldart's English Chancery Reports [*A publication*] (DLA)
Madd Ch .... Maddock's English Chancery Reports [*56 English Reprint*] [*1815-22*] [*A publication*] (DLA)
Madd Ch (Eng) ... Maddock's English Chancery Reports [*56 English Reprint*] [*A publication*] (DLA)
Madd Ch Pr ... Maddock's English Chancery Practice [*A publication*] (DLA)
MADDDC .... Manufacturers of Aerial Devices and Digger-Derricks Council (EA)
Madden ..... Madden Steven Ltd. [*Associated Press*] (SAG)
MADDIDA ... Magnetic Drum Digital Differential Analyzer
MADDWU ... Mechanics' Assistants' and Dry Dock Workers' Union [*British*]
MADE .... Magnetic Device Evaluator [*Computer science*]
MADE .... Manufacturing and Automated Design Engineering
MADE .... Master of Agricultural Development Economics
MADE .... Microalloy Diffused Electrode
MADE .... Minimum Airborne Digital Equipment
MADE .... Multichannel Analog-to-Digital Data Encoder
MADE .... Multimedia Application Development Environment (SAUS)
MADEC ...... Martial Arts Development Commission [*United Kingdom*] (EAIO)
Madeco ...... Madeco SA [*Associated Press*] (SAG)
M Ad Ed .... Master of Adult Education (PGP)
MAdEd ...... Master of Arts in Adult Education (GAGS)
MADEL ...... Medical and Dental Education Levy (SAUO)
Ma de Ma ... Matheus de Mathesillanis [*Flourished, 1381-1402*] [*Authority cited in pre-1607 legal work*] (DSA)
Ma de Math ... Matheus de Mathesillanis [*Flourished, 1381-1402*] [*Authority cited in pre-1607 legal work*] (DSA)
MADEN ...... Medical and Dental Education Network (SAUO)
MADEP ...... Massachusetts Department of Environmental Protection
MADEPSQ ... Marine Air Depot Squadron
MADER ...... Management of Atmospheric Data for Evaluation and Research [*Marine science*] (OSRA)
MADERI ..... Mexican-American Documentation and Educational Research Institute
MaderSin ... Maderas y Sinteticos Sociedad Anonima [*Associated Press*] (SAG)
MADEX ...... Magnetic Anomaly Detection Exercise (NVT)
Mad Exch ... Madox's History of the Exchequer [*A publication*] (DLA)
MADF .... Maintenance Action Data Form [*Military*] (CAAL)
Mad Fir Burg ... Madox's Firma Burgi [*A publication*] (DLA)
Mad Form ... Madox's Formulare Anglicanum [*A publication*] (DLA)
Mad Form Angl ... Madox's Formulare Anglicanum [*A publication*] (DLA)
MADG .... Madge Networks N.V. [*NASDAQ symbol*] (NASQ)
MADG .... Madge NV [*NASDAQ symbol*] (SAG)
Madge .... Madge NV [*Associated Press*] (SAG)
MadGE ...... Madison Gas & Electric Co. [*Associated Press*] (SAG)
MADGE ...... Malaysian Air Defence Ground Environment (SAUO)
MADGE ...... Microwave Aircraft Digital Guidance Equipment [*Helicopters*]
MadgeNt .... Madge NV [*Associated Press*] (SAG)
MADGF ...... Madge Networks N.V. [*NASDAQ symbol*] (TTSB)
MADGIC ..... Maps, Data and Government Information Centre [*Carleton University Library*] (IID)
MADH .... Master of Applied Development and Health (PGP)
MADH .... Methylamine Dehydrogenase [*An enzyme*]
Mad HC ..... Madras High Court Reports [*India*] [*A publication*] (DLA)
Mad Hist Exch ... Madox's History of the Exchequer [*A publication*] (DLA)
Madh Pra ... All India Reporter, Madhya Pradesh [*A publication*] (DLA)
Mad I .... Madeira Islands (SAUO)
MADI .... Madison Group Assoc [*NASDAQ symbol*] (TTSB)
MADI .... Management and Distribution of Information (SAUO)
MADI .... Master Data Index
MADIC .... Machinery Acoustic Data Information Center (VLIE)
MADICA ..... Massachusetts Acoustical Drywall-Interior Contractors Association (SRA)
MADICT ..... Modular Advanced Development IC-Tester (VLIE)
MADIS .... Burda-MarketingInfoSystem [*Burda GmbH, Marketing Service Department*] [*Information service or system*] (IID)
MADIS .... Madison, IL [*American Association of Railroads railroad junction routing code*]
MADIS .... Manual Aircraft Data Input System (MCD)
MADIS .... Manual Aircraft Display Information System [*Military*] (CAAL)
MADIS .... Millivolt Analog-Digital Instrumentation System
Mad Isl ...... Madeira Islands (SAUO)
Mad Isls .... Madeira Islands

MADIZ....... Military Air Defense Identification Zone (MCD)
M/ADJ....... Manual Adjusting [*Automotive engineering*]
Mad Jur..... Madras Jurist [*India*] [*A publication*] (DLA)
MADL........ Mason and Dixon Lines [*Common carrier symbol*]
MADL........ Maximum Allowable Defect Level (VLIE)
MADL........ Microwave Acoustic Delay Line
Mad Law Rep... Madras Law Reporter [*India*] [*A publication*] (DLA)
MADLR....... Major Assembly Direct Labor Reporting (MCD)
Mad L Rep... Madras Law Reporter [*India*] [*A publication*] (DLA)
MADLS....... Mobile Air Defence Launching System (SAUS)
Mad LT...... Madras Law Times [*India*] [*A publication*] (DLA)
Mad LW...... Madras Law Weekly [*India*] [*A publication*] (DLA)
MADM........ Maintenance Automated Data Management
MADM........ Manchester Automatic Digital Machine [*Manchester University*] [*British*]
M Adm....... Master of Administration
MADM........ Medium Atomic Demolition Munition [*Military*] (AABC)
MADM........ Multi-Attribute Decision Making (VLIE)
MADMAN... Magnetic Anomaly Detector Contact Man (NVT)
MADMAN... Master Activity Data Management (DNAB)
M Adm E.... Master of Administrative Engineering
MAdmin..... Master of Administration
M Admin.... Master of Administrative Studies
M Adm J.... Master in Administration of Justice (PGP)
M Adm Mgt.......... Master of Administration Management (PGP)
Madn........ Madden Steven Ltd. [*Associated Press*] (SAG)
MADN........ Metropolitan Area Digital Network (NTCM)
MAD-N....... Mid-America Dance Network [*Kansas City, MO*]
MADN........ Mid-American Dance Network
MADO........ Mulliken Approximation for Differential Overlap [*Physics*]
MADOC...... Medical Analysis of Days of Care [*Report*]
MADOM...... Magnetic Acoustic Detection of Mines (DOMA)
Madox....... Madox's Formulare Anglicanum [*A publication*] (DLA)
Madox....... Madox's History of the Exchequer [*A publication*] (DLA)
MADP........ Main Air Display Plot
MADP........ Major Acquisition Decision Point [*Military*] (MCD)
MADP........ Material Acquisition Decision Process [*Military*] (MCD)
MADP........ Mission Area Development Plan [*DoD*]
MADP........ Mutual Aid Defence Programme (SAUO)
MADPA...... Medicaid Antidiscriminatory Drug Pricing [*and Patient Benefit Restoration*]Act
MADPAC.... Materiel Deterioration Prevention and Control [*Program*] [*Army*] (RDA)
Mad Papers... James Madison's Papers [*A publication*] (DLA)
MAD Plan... Mongolian Asiatic Development Plan (SAUO)
MADR........ Madras [*India*] (ROG)
MADR........ Madrid Homes [*NCIC trailer make code*]
MADR........ Madritum [*Madrid*] [*Imprint*] [*Latin*] (ROG)
MADR........ Master Graphics [*NASDAQ symbol*]
MADR........ Master of Arts in Dispute Resolution (PGP)
MADR........ Materiel Acquisition Decision Review [*Army*]
MADR........ Microprogram Address Register
MAD-R....... Multiapertured Device-Resistance (DNAB)
Madr........ University of Madras (SAUO)
MADRA...... Mid Atlantic Disaster Recovery Association [*Emergency Management*] (EMA)
MA(Drama)... Master of Arts (Drama)
MADRAS.... Modular Approach to Definition of RACE Subscriber Premises Network (SAUO)
Madras AgricJ... Madras Agricultural Journal (SAUO)
Madras LJ... Madras Law Journal and Reports [*India*] [*A publication*] (DLA)
MADRE...... Magnetic Drum RADAR Equipment
MADRE...... Magnetic Drum Receiving Equipment
MADRE...... Manufacturing Data Retrieval System (NASA)
MADRE...... Martin Automatic Data-Reduction Equipment
MADREC.... Malfunction Detection and Recording [*Checkout system for aircraft*] [*Air Force*]
Mad Reg.... Madden on Registration of Deeds [*A publication*] (DLA)
Madrid Union... Union for the International Registration of Marks (SAUO)
MADRS...... Montgomery-Asberg Depression Rating Scale (STED)
MADS........ Machine-Aided Drafting System (IEEE)
MADS........ Maintenance and Diagnosis System [*Military*] (CAAL)
MADS........ Manned Airborne Defense Station (ACAE)
MADS........ Mars Atmosphere Density Sensor
MADS........ Meteorological Airborne Data System
MADS........ Military Advanced Disk System (SAUS)
MADS........ Missile Attitude Determination System [*LASER device*] [*Air Force*]
MADS........ Mission Area Deficiency Statement [*Army*] (RDA)
MADS........ Mixed Anxiety/Depression Syndrome [*Medicine*] (MELL)
MADS........ Mobile Airborne Data System (ACAE)
MADS........ Mobile Airborne Defense Station (SAUO)
MADS........ Mobile Airborne Defense Station Concept [*Air Force*]
MADS........ Mobile Air Defense System
MADS........ Modified Air Defence System (SAUS)
MADS........ Modular Air Defense System (MCD)
MADS........ Modular Army Demonstration System (MCD)
MADS........ Modular Auxiliary Data System
MADS........ Modular Auxiliary Data Systems (NASA)
MADs........ Mothers Against Drugs (SAUO)
MADS........ MPS Air Defence Simulator (SAUS)
MADS........ Multiple Access Digital System [*Computer science*] (IAA)
MadsBn..... Madison Bancshares Group [*Associated Press*] (SAG)
Mad SDAR... Madras Sadr Diwani Adalat Reports [*India*] [*A publication*] (DLA)
Mad Sel Dec... Madras Select Decrees [*A publication*] (DLA)
Mad Ser.... Indian Law Reports, Madras Series [*A publication*] (DLA)
MAD-SMS... Movement for Autonomous Democracy-Society for Moravia and Silesia [*Former Czechoslovakia*] [*Political party*] (EY)
MADSN...... Madison, WI [*American Association of Railroads railroad junction routing code*]
MADSO...... Madison, GA [*American Association of Railroads railroad junction routing code*]
MADSPM... Mobilization Against the Draft and Student Peace Mobilization [*An association*] (EA)
MADT........ Mean Administrative Delay Time
MADT........ Micro-Alloy Diffused Base Transistor (NITA)
MADT........ Microalloy Diffused Transistor (MUGU)
MADU........ Magnum Speditionsgesellshaft [*Intermodal shipping container symbol*] (TVRC)
MADU........ Methylaminodeoxyuridine [*Pharmacology*]
MadUniv.... Madison University (SAUO)
MadUniv.... Madras University (SAUO)
MADV........ M and D Transfer [*Common carrier symbol*]
M Ad VE.... Master of Administration in Vocational Education (PGP)
MADVEC.... Magnetic Anomaly Detector Vectoring [*Military*] (CAAL)
MADW........ Military Air Defense Warning Network
Mad WN.... Madras Weekly Notes [*A publication*] (DLA)
MADWN...... Military Air Defense Warning Network (IAA)
Mad WNCC... Madras Weekly Notes, Criminal Cases [*India*] [*A publication*] (DLA)
MADYMO... Mathematical Dynamic Modelling (VLIE)
MAE......... Macintosh Application Environment [*Software*] (IGQR)
MAE......... Madera, CA [*Location identifier*] [*FAA*] (FAAL)
MAE......... Maebashi [*Japan*] [*Seismograph station code, US Geological Survey*] (SEIS)
MAE......... Maersk Commuter IS [*Netherlands*] [*ICAO designator*] (FAAC)
Mae.......... Maestro [*Record label*] [*Belgium, etc.*]
MAE......... Maine Association of Engineers (SRA)
MAE......... Maintenance Engineer
MAE......... Malignant Angioendotheliomatosis [*Oncology*]
MAE......... Manchester Association of Engineers (SAUO)
MAE......... Marine & Aerospace Engineering Pty Ltd. (SAUO)
MAE......... Maritime Advisory Exchange (SAUO)
MAE......... Master Electric (IAA)
MaE.......... Master in Engineering (SAUO)
MAE......... Master of Aeronautical Engineering (WDAA)
M Ae........ Master of Aeronautics
MAE......... Master of Aerospace Engineering (PGP)
MAE......... Master of Agricultural Economics (PGP)
MAE......... Master of Agricultural Education (PGP)
MAE......... Master of Agricultural Engineering (GAGS)
MAE......... Master of Agricultural Extension (GAGS)
MAE......... Master of Art Education
MAE......... Master of Arts in Education
MAE......... Master of Arts in English (PGP)
MAE......... Master of Automotive Engineering (PGP)
MaE.......... Master of Engineering (SAUO)
MA E........ Master of Engineering (WDAA)
MAE......... Material and Equipment [*Nuclear energy*] (IAA)
MAE......... Matrix Arithmetic Expression
MAE......... McDonnell Airborne Evaluator [*McDonnell Douglas Corp.*] (MCD)
MAE......... Mean Absolute Error
MAE......... Mean Area of Effectiveness (CINC)
MAE......... Mechanical and Aerospace Engineering (ACAE)
MAE......... Mechanical and Electrical (IAA)
MAE......... Medical Air Evacuation
MAE......... Medical Association of Eire (SAUO)
MAE......... Medium Altitude Endurance (RDA)
MAE......... Memory Access Extension [*Computer science*] (ELAL)
MAE......... Memory Address Extension [*Computer science*] (CIST)
MAE......... Memory Address Register (NITA)
MAE......... Merit Access Exchange (SAUS)
MAE......... (Methylamino)ethanol [*Organic chemistry*]
MAE......... Metropolitan Area Ethernet [*Computer science*] (NETL)
MAE......... Metropolitan Area Exchange [*Telecommunications*] (ACRL)
MAE......... Micro Aided Engineering (NITA)
MAE......... Mid-America Earthquake [*Emergency Management*] (EMA)
MAE......... Miramar Energy Corp. [*Vancouver Stock Exchange symbol*]
MAE......... Missile Airborne Equipment (IAA)
MAE......... Missile Assembly Equipment (IAA)
MAE......... Mission Accomplishment Estimate [*DoD*]
MAE......... Mississippi Association of Educators (SRA)
MAE......... Mobile Ammunition Evaluation
MAE......... Modified Anglia Engine [*Cosworth racing engines*]
MAE......... Monroe Auto Equipment Company (SAUO)
MAE......... Motion Aftereffect
MAE......... Movement After-Effect (PDAA)
MAE......... Moves All Extremities [*Medicine*] (MAE)
MAE......... Multilingual Aphasia Examination [*Speech and language therapy*] (DAVI)
MAE......... Museum of Atomic Energy (SAUO)
MAE......... Mutual Assistance, Executive [*Military appropriation*] (NG)
MAEB........ Material Application Evaluation Board [*NASA*] (MCD)
MAEBR...... Management of Enlisted Bonus Recipients
MAEC........ Manufacturing Analysis of Engineering Change (MCD)
MAEC........ Master of Arts in Economics
MAEC........ Minimum Adverse Effect Concentration [*Pollution technology*]
MAEC........ Missile Attack Emergency Conference (MCD)

MAECAM.... Micro-Aided Engineering/Computer Aided Manufacturing [*Micro-Aided Engineering Ltd. and Digital Microsystems Ltd.*] [*Software package*] (NCC)
MAECO...... NRA [*National Restaurant Association*] Multi-Unit Architects, Engineers, and Construction Officers (EA)
MA (Econ)... Master of Arts in Economic and Social Studies [*University of Manchester*] [*British*]
MA (Econ)... Master of Arts in Economic Studies [*Universities of Newcastle and Sheffield*] [*British*]
MAECON.... Mid-America Electronics Conference
MAECON.... Mid-America Electronics Convention (SAUO)
MA(Ed)....... Master of Arts in Education (CMD)
MAED........ Micro Area Electron Diffraction [*Surface analysis*]
MAED........ Model Architecture Environment (GART)
MAEDC...... Michigan Association for Emotionally Disturbed Children [*Medicine*] (EDAA)
MAEDOS.... Micro-Aided Engineering/Drawing Office System [*Micro-Aided Engineering Ltd.*] [*Software package*] (NCC)
MAEDS...... Meteosat Argos Extended Dissemination Service (SAUO)
MAEDS...... Multisatellite Applications Extended Dissemination Service (SAUO)
MA EdU..... Master of Arts in Education (PGP)
MAEE........ Marine Aircraft Experimental Establishment
MAeE........ Master of Aeronautical Engineering [*Canada*] (ASC)
MAEE........ Mid-Atlantic Electrical Exhibition (ITD)
M Ae Eng... Master of Aeronautical Engineering
MAEEW..... Moves All Extremities Equally Well [*Neurology*] (DAVI)
MAEF........ Mastic Asphalt Employers' Federation [*British*] (BI)
MAEI......... Malaysian-American Electronics Industry
MAEL........ Marine Aircraft Experimental Laboratory [*British*]
MAEL........ Maximum Allowable Emission Level [*Automotive emissions*]
MAELU...... Mutual Atomic Energy Liability Underwriters [*Chicago, IL*] (EA)
MAEN........ Mays Enterprises [*NCIC trailer make code*]
MAENF...... Miramar Mining [*NASDAQ symbol*] (TTSB)
MAENF...... Miramar Mining Corp. [*NASDAQ symbol*] (SAG)
MAEO........ Master Air Electronics Officer (SAUO)
MAEO........ Medium-Altitude Electro-Optical (SAUS)
MAEO........ Months after Exercise of Option
M Aeor E... Master of Aeronautical Engineering (SAUO)
MAEP........ Measure of Adult English Proficiency (EDAC)
MAEP........ Minimum AUTOLAND [*Automatic Landing*] Entry Point (NASA)
MAE-PAC.... Manufacturer's Association of Northwest Pennsylvania PAC [*Erie, PA*] (PACS)
MAEPS...... Model Adoption Exchange Payment System (EDAC)
MAEQW..... Moves All Extremities Quite Well [*Medicine*] (MELL)
MAER........ Maximum Allowable Emission Rate [*Environmental Protection Agency*] (ERG)
MAER........ Mechanical and Electrical Room (IAA)
MAER........ Mobile Ammunition and Reconditioning Unit [*Military*]
MAERC...... MacArthur Agro-Ecology Research Center [*Archbold Biological Station*] (RCD)
MAERC...... Minority Access to Energy-Related Careers (SAUO)
M Aero E... Master of Aeronautical Engineering
M Aero E... Master of Aerospace Engineering (PGP)
M Aero Eng... Master of Aeronautical Engineering
MAEROSPOPNSMGT... Masters Aerospace Operations Management [*Air Force*]
MAERP...... Mutual Atomic Energy Reassurance Pool
MAERU...... Mobile Ammunition Evaluation and Reconditioning Unit
Maes........ Maestoso [*Majestic*] [*Music*]
MAES........ Maine Agriculture Experiment Station [*University of Maine at Orono*] [*Research center*] (RCD)
MAES........ Maintenance Aircraft Engineering Squadron (SAUO)
MAES........ Manufacturing and Engineering Support (IAA)
MAES........ Massachusetts Agricultural Experiment Station (SAUO)
M Ae S...... Master of Aeronautical Science
MAES........ Master of Arts in Environmental Sciences (PGP)
MAES........ Medical Aid for El Salvador (EA)
MAES........ Mexican-American Engineering Society (EA)
MAES........ [*Society of*] Mexican American Engineers and Scientists (NTPA)
MAES........ Michigan Agricultural Experiment Station [*Michigan State University*] [*Research center*] (RCD)
MAESA...... Measurement for Assessing the Effects of Stratospheric Aircraft [*Marine science*] (OSRA)
MAESA...... Measurements for Assessing the Effects of Stratospheric Aircraft (USDC)
M Ae Sc.... Master of Aeronautical Science
MAESON.... Marxist All-Ethiopian Socialist Movement [*Political party*] (PD)
MAESTO.... Maestoso [*Majestic*] [*Music*]
MAESTRO... Machine-Assisted Educational System for Teaching by Remote Operation (IEEE)
MAESTRO... Mission Analysis Evaluation and Space Trajectory Operations [*NASA*]
MAET........ Master of Arts in English Teaching (PGP)
MAET........ Microwave Amplifier Electron Tube
MAET........ Missile Accident Emergency Team (AFM)
MAETS...... Medical Air Evacuation Transport Squadron [*Army*] [*World War II*]
MAEU........ Maersk Line [*Intermodal shipping container symbol*] (TVRC)
MAEU........ Maersk Lines [*Common carrier symbol*]
MAEVIS..... Micro-Aided Engineering 3D Visualisation [*Micro-Aided Engineering Ltd. and Micro-Aided Engineering Digital Microsystems Ltd.*] [*Software package*] (NCC)
MAEW....... Moves All Extremities Well [*Medicine*] (MEDA)
MAEZ........ Manson Elevator [*Federal Railroad Administration identification code*]
MAF......... Front Militant Autonome [*Autonomous Militant Front*] [*French*] (PD)
MAF......... MacAndrews & Forbes Co. (SAUO)
MAF......... Macrophage Activating Factor [*Biochemistry*]
MAF......... Macrophage-Agglutinating Factor (STED)
MAF......... Magnetic Anisotropy Field
MAF......... Maintenance Action Form
MAF......... Major Academic Field
MAF......... Manpower Authorization File
MAF......... Manual Acquisition Facility (SAUS)
MAF......... Manual Authority File
MAF......... Marine Air Facility
MAF......... Marine Amphibious Force (AABC)
MAF......... Marriage Adjustment Form [*Psychology*]
MAF......... Mass Air Flow [*Automotive engineering*]
MAF......... Master Address File [*US Census Bureau*]
MAF......... Master Appraisal File [*Real estate*]
MAF......... Master Audit File (SSD)
MAF......... Master Facility Tool (MCD)
MAF......... Master of Arts in Finance (PGP)
MAF......... Maximum Amplitude Filter
MAF......... Maximum Atrial Fragmentation [*Medicine*] (EDAA)
MAF......... Medical Assisted Facility (SAUO)
MAF......... Medical Awareness Foundation [*Commercial firm*] (EA)
MAF......... Medic Alert Foundation [*Medicine*] (EDAA)
MAF......... Mesoscale Analysis Forecasting (SAUS)
MAF......... Michigan Architectural Foundation (EARSL)
MAF......... Michoud Assembly Facility [*NASA*] (MCD)
MAF......... Middle Atlantic Fisheries (SAUO)
MAF......... Midland/Odessa [*Texas*] [*Airport symbol*] (OAG)
MAF......... Million Acre Feet [*Hydrology*]
MAF......... Mineral Ash Free (ABAC)
MAF......... Minimal Audible Field (DIPS)
MAF......... Minimum Audible Field
MAF......... Minister of Agriculture and Fisheries (SAUO)
MAF......... Minister of Armed Forces (NATG)
MAF......... Ministry of Agriculture and Fisheries [*British*]
MAF......... Missile Assembly Facility
MAF......... Mission Aviation Fellowship [*Indonesia*] [*ICAO designator*] (FAAC)
MAF......... Mixed Amine Fuel
MAF......... Mobile Air Force (NATG)
MAF......... Mobile Assault Ferry [*Army*]
MAF......... Moisture and Ash Free
MAF......... Morris Animal Foundation (EA)
MAF......... Mouse Amniotic Fluid [*Veterinary science*] (DB)
MAF......... Movable Appendage Factor [*IOR*] [*Yacht racing*]
MAF......... Movement Aftereffect [*Optics*]
MAF......... Multimedia Applications in Furniture (EURO)
MAF......... Multiple Access Facility [*Computer science*]
MAF......... Multiple Access Forward (SSD)
MAF......... Multiply-Add-Fused [*Computer science*] (CIST)
MAF......... Municipal Advantage Fund [*NYSE symbol*] (SAG)
MAF......... Mutual Adjustment Fund (SAUO)
MAF......... Mutual Asset Fund (SAUO)
MAFA........ Manchester Academy of Fine Arts [*British*]
MAFA........ Midarm Fat Area (STED)
MAFA........ Mid Atlantic Fiber Association (EA)
MAFA........ Middle Atlantic Fencing Association (PSS)
MAFA........ Middle Atlantic Fisheries Association (EA)
MAFA........ Movement-Associated Fetal Acceleration [*Medicine*] (MELL)
MAFAB...... Market Favors Buyers [*Telegraphy*] (PCTE)
MAFAC...... Marine Fisheries Advisory Committee [*Department of Commerce*] [*Washington, DC*] (EGAO)
MAFAP...... Minimum Altitude over FAcility on Final Approach Course [*Aviation*] (FAAC)
MAFAS...... Marine Automated Flowcharting Analysis System
MAFAs....... Movement-Associates Fetal [*Heart rate*] Accelerations [*Obstetrics*] (DAVI)
MAFASA..... Marine Amphibious Force Air Support Airfield (MCD)
MAFB........ MAF Bancorp [*NASDAQ symbol*] (SPSG)
MAFB........ MAF Bancorporation [*NASDAQ symbol*]
MAFB........ Malmstrom Air Force Base [*Montana*] (KSC)
MAFB........ Mid America Bank [*NYSE symbol*]
MAFB........ Mitchell Air Force Base
MAF Bcp.... MAF Bancorp, Inc. [*Associated Press*] (SAG)
MAFC........ MAGTF [*Marine Air Ground Task Force*] All-Source Fusion Center (DOMA)
MAFC........ Major Army Field Command (AABC)
MAFC........ Master of Arts in Family Counseling (GAGS)
MAFC........ Mel Anderson Fan Club [*Defunct*] (EA)
MAFC........ Micro Adaptive Flow Control Program [*Defense Advanced Research Projects Agency*] (RCD)
MAFC........ Mythadventures Fan Club (EA)
MAFCA...... Model A Ford Club of America (EA)
MAFCC...... Model A Ford Cabriolet Club (EA)
MAFCO...... MacAndrews & Forbes Co., Inc. (EFIS)
Mafco....... Mafco Consolidated Group [*Associated Press*] (SAG)
MAFCO...... Magnetic Field Code
MAFD........ Manic Affective Disorder [*Medicine*] (DMAA)
MAFD........ Minimum Acquisition Flux Density
MAFE........ Maintenance of Air/FMF [*Fleet Marine Force*] Expeditionary Equipment (NG)
MAFEE...... Metro Alliance for Engineering Education (TIMI)
MAFES...... Mississippi Agricultural and Forestry Experiment Station [*Mississippi State University*] [*Research center*] (RCD)
MAFF........ British Ministry of Agriculture, Food and Fisheries (SAUO)
MAFF........ Minister of Agriculture, Fisheries and Food (SAUO)
MAFF........ Ministry of Agriculture, Fisheries, and Food [*British*]

MAFF........ Ministry of Agriculture, Food and Fisheries (SAUO)
MAFF........ Ministry of Agriculture, Forestry and Fisheries [*Japan*] (ECON)
MAFFC...... Munsters and the Addams Family Fan Club (EA)
MAFFEX..... Marine Amphibious Force Field Exercise [*Military*] (NVT)
Maffies...... Middle-Aged Affluent Folks [*Lifestyle Classification*]
MAFFS...... Modular Airborne Fire Fighting System [*Air Force*]
MAFH........ Macroaggregated Ferrous Hydroxide [*Medicine*] (MAE)
MA/FH....... Maintenance Actions per Flight Hour (MCD)
MAFH........ Multicentric Angiofollicular (Lymph Node) Hyperplasia [*Oncology*]
MAFH........ Museum of American Financial History (EA)
MAFI......... Medic Alert Foundation International [*Also known as Medic Alert*] (EA)
MAFI......... Ministry of Agriculture and Food Industries (SAUO)
MAFI......... Ministry of Agriculture, Forestry and Irrigation (SAUO)
MAFIA....... Marimba and Fife Inspectors Association [*Women's tongue-in-cheek organization*] [*Defunct*]
MAFIA....... Missile Auxiliaries Firing Interlock Assembly (ACAE)
MAFIA....... Morte alla Francia Italia Anelo [*Death to the French is Italy's Cry*] [*When used in reference to the secret society often associated with organized crime, "Mafia" is from the Sicilian word for boldness or lawlessness*]
MAFIA....... Multiaccess Executive with Fast Interrupt Acceptance [*Computer science*] (MHDI)
MAFIS....... Malaysian Aquatic Sciences and Fisheries Information System [*Marine science*] (OSRA)
MAFIS....... Management Farm Information Service (PDAA)
MAFIS....... Master of Accountancy and Financial Information Systems (PGP)
MAFIS....... Mobile Area Field Instrumentation System (SAUO)
MAFIS....... Mobile Automated Field Instrumentation System [*TRADOC*] (RDA)
MAFL........ Manual of Air Force Law [*British*]
MAFL........ Multiaperture Ferrite Logic
MAFLA...... Mississippi, Alabama, and Florida [*Oil industry*]
MAFLEX..... Marine Amphibious Force Landing Exercise [*Military*] (NVT)
MAFLIR..... Modified Advanced Forward-Looking Infrared
MAFLL...... Master of Arts in Foreign Language and Literature (PGP)
MAFLS...... Memoirs of the American Folklore Society (SAUO)
MAFMIC..... Minnesota Association of Farm Mutual Insurance Companies (SRA)
MAFN........ Massachusetts Fincorp, Inc. [*NASDAQ symbol*] (QUAN)
MAFOG...... Mediterranean Area Fighter Operations Grid
MAFOR...... Marine Forecast [*Pronounced "mayfor"*]
MAFP........ Maine Academy of Family Physicians (EARSL)
MAFP........ Michigan Academy of Family Physicians [*Medicine*] (EDAA)
MAFP........ Military and Air Force Police [*British military*] (DMA)
MAFPA...... Mid-America Food Processors Association (SRA)
MAFPG...... Mass Air Flow Power Ground [*Automotive engineering*]
MAFR........ Major Frame (ACAE)
MAFR........ Merged Accountability and Fund Reporting [*Air Force*] (AFM)
MAfr......... Missionaries of Africa (TOCD)
mafr......... Missionaries of Africa (TOCD)
MAFR........ Modified Anarchy Flood Routing (PDAA)
MAfr......... Society of Missionaries of Africa (EAIO)
MAFRA...... MAF Regulatory Authority (SAUS)
MAFRA...... Ministry of Agriculture and Forestry Regulatory Authority (SAUO)
MAFRC...... Middle Atlantic Fisheries Research Center [*National Oceanic and Atmospheric Administration*]
MAFREMO... Malawi Freedom Movement (BUAC)
MAFRTN.... Mass Air Flow Return [*Automotive electronics*]
MAFS........ Management Arrangements Feasibility Study (HEAS)
MAFS........ Manned Aerospace Flight Simulator (ACAE)
MAFS........ Memoirs. American Folklore Society [*A publication*]
MAFS........ Memoirs of the American Folklore Society (SAUO)
MAFS........ Mexico-Albania Friendship Society (EAIO)
MAFS........ Mobilization Air Force Specialty
MAFs........ Movement-Associated Fetal (Heart Rate) Accelerations [*Medicine*] (EDAA)
MAFSC...... Mobilization Air Force Specialty Code
MAFSG...... Mass Air Flow Signal Return [*Automotive engineering*]
MAFSI....... Manufacturers' Agents for Food Service Industry (NTPA)
MAFSI....... Marketing Agents for Food Service Industry (EA)
MAFSS...... Multipoint Airfield Fuel Support System
MAFSX...... Merrill Lynch: Federal Secs. Trust Cl.A [*Mutual fund ticker symbol*] (SG)
MAFT........ Master Carrier [*Common carrier symbol*]
MAFT........ Modified-Adopted-Fernald Technique (EDAC)
MAF/TDC.... Maintenance Action Form / Technical Directives Compliance [*Military*] (DNAB)
MAFTEP..... Method for Analysis of Fleet Tactical Effectiveness Performance [*Navy*] (PDAA)
MAFV........ Mean Ambient Flow Vector [*Geology*]
MAFVA...... Miniature Armoured Fighting Vehicle Association (EA)
MAFWA..... Midwest Association of Fish and Wildlife Agencies (EARSL)
MAG......... Air Margarita [*Venezuela*] [*ICAO designator*] (FAAC)
MAG......... Macrogenerator [*SEMIS*]
MAG......... Madang [*Papua New Guinea*] [*Airport symbol*] (OAG)
MAG......... Magadan [*Former USSR*] [*Seismograph station code, US Geological Survey*] (SEIS)
mag.......... Magahi [*MARC language code*] [*Library of Congress*] (LCCP)
MAG......... Magazine (AFM)
mag.......... Magazine (VRA)
Mag.......... Magazine (DIAR)
MAG......... Magenta (ROG)
MAG......... Maggie Mines [*Vancouver Stock Exchange symbol*]
Mag.......... [*The*] Magistrate [*London*] [*A publication*] (DLA)
MAG......... Magistrate [*Motor vehicle violation code used in state of Maryland*] (MVRD)
Mag.......... Magistrate and Municipal and Parochial Lawyer [*London*] [*A publication*] (DLA)
MAG......... Magistrate Court [*Court type found in state of Virginia*] (MVRD)
MAG......... Magnavox Co. (SAUO)
MAG......... Magnesium [*Chemical symbol is Mg*]
MAG......... MagneTek, Inc. [*NYSE symbol*] (SPSG)
MAG......... Magnetic (AFM)
mag.......... Magnetic (WDMC)
MAG......... Magneto (KSC)
mag.......... Magneto (MIST)
MAG......... Magnetometer [*or Magnetometry*]
MAG......... Magnetosphere Currents (or Fields) (SAUS)
MAG......... Magnetron (CET)
mag.......... Magnetron
MAG......... Magnette [*NCIC car model code*]
Mag.......... Magnificat (GROV)
MAG......... Magnification
MAG......... Magnificent [*Telegraphy*] (PCTE)
MAG......... Magnitude (AFM)
MAG......... Magnum (WDAA)
MAG......... Magnum (automobile) [*NCIC car model code*]
MAG......... Magnus [*Large*] [*Pharmacy*]
Mag.......... Magruder's Reports [*1, 2 Maryland*] [*A publication*] (DLA)
MAG......... Magyar [*Language, etc.*] (ROG)
MAG......... Main Armament Group
MAG......... Maintenance Advisory Group (SAUO)
MAG......... Management Advisory Group [*Environmental Protection Agency*] (GFGA)
MAG......... Management Assistance Group [*Washington, DC*] (EA)
MAG......... Marine Aircraft [*or Aviation*] Group
MAG......... Marine Air Group (VNW)
MAG......... Maritime Action Group [*Non-carrier naval task group*] (DOMA)
MAG......... Maritime Air Group [*Canada*]
MAG......... Marker-Adder Generator
MAG......... Marketing Aids Group
M Ag........ Master of Agriculture
MAG......... Master of Applied Geography (PGP)
MAG......... Maximum Available Gain (IAA)
MAG......... Medical Association of Georgia (SRA)
MAg......... Membrane Antigen (DB)
MAG......... Mesoscale Applications Group [*National Oceanic and Atmospheric Administration*] (RCD)
MAG......... Metal Active Gas (HEAS)
MAG......... Military Advisers Group (SAUO)
MAG......... Military Advisory Group
MAG......... Military Airlift Group [*Air Force*]
MAG......... Military Assistance Group (SAUO)
MAG......... Minnesota Attorney General's Office, St. Paul, MN [*OCLC symbol*] (OCLC)
MAG......... Mississippi Air National Guard [*FAA designator*] (FAAC)
MAG......... Mittelassyrisches Gesetz (BJA)
MAG......... Mobile Arresting Gear (SAUS)
MAG......... Monoammonium Glutamate [*Organic chemistry*]
MAG......... Motorcycle Action Group [*British*] (DBA)
MAG......... Mutation Activation Gene [*Immunology*]
MAG......... Myelin-Associated Glycoprotein [*Biochemistry*]
MAGA....... Medium-Accuracy Gyro Assembly
MAGA....... Mexican-American Grocers Association (NTPA)
MAGAEL.... Madison Gas & Electric Co. (EFIS)
Magal....... Magal Security Systems [*Commercial firm*] [*Associated Press*] (SAG)
Magalog.... Magazine-Catalog [*Advertising*]
magamp.... Magnetic Amplifier (IDOE)
MAGAMP... Magnetic Amplifier
Mag & Con... Magistrate and Constable [*A publication*] (DLA)
Mag & Const... Magistrate and Constable [*A publication*] (DLA)
Mag & E Comp... Magnus and Estrin on Companies [*5th ed.*] [*1978*] [*A publication*] (DLA)
Mag & M & PL... Magistrate and Municipal and Parochial Lawyer [*A publication*] (DLA)
Mag Antiq... Magazine Antiques [*A publication*] (BRI)
Mag Arch... Magister Architecturae [*Master of Architecture*] [*Latin*]
MAGARLM... Military Assistance Advisory Group, Army Branch, Logistics-Medical (CINC)
MagArt...... Magazine of Art (SAUO)
MAGB....... Maltsters Association [*British*] (DBA)
MAGB....... Maltsters Association of Great Britain (BUAC)
MAGB....... Masectomy Association of Great Britain
MAGB....... Microfilm Association of Great Britain
MAGB....... Microform Association of Great Britain (BUAC)
Mag Bl...... Magical Blend [*A publication*]
MAGBNT.... Museums and Art Galleries Board of the Northern Territory [*Australia*]
MAGBRG.... Magnetic Bearing [*Navigation*] (DNAB)
MAG BRIT... Magna Britannia [*Great Britain*] [*Latin*] (ROG)
MAGC....... Magic Tilt Trailer [*NCIC trailer make code*]
MagC........ Magma Copper Co. [*Associated Press*] (SAG)
MAGCAP.... Magazine Capacity [*Military*]
MAGCARD... Magnetic Card [*Electronics*] (ECII)
Mag Cas.... Bittleston, Wise, and Parnell's Magistrates' Cases [*England*] [*A publication*] (DLA)
Mag Cas.... Magisterial Cases [*England*] [*A publication*] (DLA)
Mag Cas.... Magistrates' Cases [*Reprinted from Law Journal Reports*] [*1892-1910*] [*A publication*] (DLA)
Mag Char... Magna Charta [*or Carta*] [*Great Charter*] [*Latin*] [*A publication*] (DLA)

MAGCI....... Magnetic Cast Iron (IAA)
mag cit...... Magnesium Citrate [*Pharmacy*]
MAGCOM... Magnetic Contour Matching (MUSM)
MAGCON.... Magnetized Concentration [*Lunar*]
MagCon..... Magnetospheric Constellation (SAUS)
MagCp...... Magnetech Corp. [*Associated Press*] (SAG)
MAGCS...... Magnetic Cast Steel (IAA)
Mag Ct...... Magistrates' Court (DLA)
MAGD....... Magdalen College [*Oxford University*] (ROG)
Magd........ Magdalen College, Cambridge (SAUO)
Magd........ Magdalen College, Oxford (SAUO)
MAGD....... Magdalene College, Cambridge University [*England*] (ROG)
MAGD....... Master of the Academy of General Dentistry (SAUO)
MAGDA...... Mobility Aid and Guide Dog Alliance (BUAC)
MAGDARR... Magnavox Doppler and Ranging RADAR (NG)
Magd Coll... Magdalen College, Oxford (SAUO)
MAgDevEc... Master of Agricultural Development Economics (ADA)
Mag Dig.... Magrath's South Carolina Digest [*A publication*] (DLA)
Magdl....... Magdalenian (VRA)
MAGE........ Map Authoring and Generalisation Expert (SAUO)
MAGE........ Marine Aerosol and Gas Exchange [*Marine science*] (OSRA)
MAGE........ Marine Aerosol and Gas Exchange Experiment
MAGE........ Marine Arctic Geological Expedition (SAUO)
MAGE........ Marine Arctic Geological Expedition, Murmansk Association Sevmorgeologia (SAUO)
MAGE........ Marine Gas Emissions (SAUS)
MAGE........ Marine Gas Emissions, Atmospheric Chemistry and Climate (SAUO)
MAGE........ Mechanical Aerospace Ground Equipment (TEL)
MAGE........ Mechanical Assembly Ground Equipment (ACAE)
MAGE........ Multiple Access Ground Equipment (ACAE)
MAGEBT.... Tigray Peoples Progressive Association (SAUO)
M Ag Ec.... Master of Agricultural Economics
M Ag Ed.... Master of Agricultural Education
MagelPt..... Magellan Petroleum Corp. [*Associated Press*] (SAG)
MagelRst... Magellan Restauraunt System [*Associated Press*] (SAG)
MAGEN...... Matrix Generating and Reporting System [*Computer science*] (PDAA)
MAGERT.... Map and Geography Round Table [*American Library Association*]
MAGES...... Magnitude Estimation Scaling (MCD)
MAgExt...... Master of Agricultural Extension (GAGS)
MAGF........ Male Accessory Gland Fluid [*Medicine*] (DB)
MAGF........ Margo Transport [*Common carrier symbol*]
MAGF........ Mean Amplitude of Glycemic Excursions [*Medicine*] (EDAA)
MAGFET..... Magnetic Metal-Oxide-Semiconductor Field-Effect Transistor (PDAA)
MAGG....... Maggiore [*Major*] [*Music*]
MAGG....... Microagglutination [*Test*] [*Medicine*] (EDAA)
MAGG....... Modular Alphanumeric Graphics Generator (IEEE)
MAGGE...... Medium-Altitude Gravity Gradient Experiment
MAggF...... Macrophage Agglutination Factor [*Biochemistry*] (MAE)
MAGGI...... Million Ampere Generator [*British*] (DEN)
MagGp...... Magna Group, Inc. [*Associated Press*] (SAG)
MAGGS...... Modular Advanced Graphics Generation System (IEEE)
Magh........ Maghreb (BJA)
MAGI........ Mackenzie Art Gallery [*University of Regina*] [*Canada*] [*Research center*] (RCD)
MAGI........ Magic Touch [*NCIC trailer make code*]
MAGI........ Magna Group, Inc. [*NASDAQ symbol*] (NQ)
MAGI........ Maryland Automated Geographic Information System [*Maryland State Department of State Planning*] [*Information service or system*] (IID)
MAGI........ Master Group Information System [*AT & T*]
MAGI........ Mathematical Applications Group, Inc. (MCD)
MAGI........ McNaughton Apparel Group [*NASDAQ symbol*]
MAGI........ Microscope Assisted Guided Intervention [*Medical technique*]
MAGI........ Military Gamma Irradiator
MAGI........ Multiarray Gamma Irradiator
MAGIC....... Machine-Aided Graphics for Illustration and Composition [*Bell Telephone*]
MAGIC....... Machine for Automatic Graphics Interface to a Computer
MAGIC....... Madison Avenue General Ideas Committee [*New York City*]
MAGIC....... Magic Foundation for Children's Growth (EA)
MAGIC....... Magnetically Actuated Grid for Interactive Correspondance (SAUO)
MAGIC....... Magnetic and Germanium Integer Calculator (DEN)
MAGIC....... Magnetic Immunochemistry [*Laboratory analysis*]
MAGIC....... Manual Assisted Gaming of Integrated Combat (PDAA)
MAGIC....... Map and Geographic Information Center (SAUO)
MAGIC....... Mapping and Geographic Information Centre (SAUO)
MAGIC....... Marine Corps Air-Ground Intelligence Center (MCD)
MAGIC....... Maritime Air-Ground Intelligence Center (SAUO)
MAGIC....... Market Analysis Guide - Intercity Communications [*AT & T*]
MAGIC....... Marketing and Advertising General Information Centre [*Datasolve Ltd.*] [*British*] [*Information service or system*]
MAGIC....... Matrix Algebra General Interpretive Coding (IEEE)
MAGIC....... Media Analysis, Grouping, Inventory Control (SAUO)
MAGIC....... Method for Asynchronous Graphics Integral Control [*Computer science*] (PDAA)
MAGIC....... Methods for Advanced Group Technology Integrated with CAD/CAM (SAUO)
MAGIC....... Michigan Automatic General Integrated Computation (MCD)
MAGIC....... Microcomputer Applications of Graphics with Interactive Communications (SAUS)
MAGIC....... Microprobe Analysis Generalized Intensity Corrections
MAGIC....... Microprocessor Application of Graphic with Interactive Communication
MAGIC....... Military Advisory Group in China (SAUO)
MAGIC....... Mobile and Automotive Geographic Information Consortium
MAGIC....... Model of Acidification of Groundwater in Catchment (SAUO)
MAGIC....... Modern Analytical Generator of Improved Circuits [*Computer science*]
MAGIC....... Modified Action Generated Input Control
MAGIC....... Modular Area Graphics Illustrations Composition (DGA)
MAGIC....... Monodisperse Aerosol Generation Interface [*Physics*]
MAGIC....... Motorola Automatically Generated Integrated Circuits
MAGIC....... Mozambique, Angola, and Guine Information Center [*British*]
MAGIC....... Multiple Aperture Gas Imaging Counter (SAUS)
MAGIC....... Multipurpose and Generalized Interface to COBOL [*Computer science*]
Magic Cap... Magic Communicating Applications Platform [*General Magic*] [*Computer science*]
MAGICS..... Mass Balance of Arctic Glaciers and Ice Sheets in relation to Climate and Sea Level Changes (SAUO)
MAGICS..... Modular Architecture for Graphics & Image Control System (SAUS)
MAGICS..... Multiphase Model for Air, Groundwater, Immiscible Contaminant and Solute Transport [*Computer program for testing water flow*]
MAGIC Telescope... Mayor Atmospheric Gamma-ray Imaging Cherenkov Telescope (SAUO)
MAGID...... Magnetic Intrusion Detector (NVT)
MAGIE....... Midwest Agri Industries Expo [*Illinois Fertilizer and Chemical Association*] (TSPED)
MAGIEC.... Magnavox Government and Industrial Electronics Company (SAUO)
MAGIIC...... Mobile Army Ground Imagery Interpretation Center (MCD)
MAGIIC...... Mobile Army Ground Interpretation Center (SAUO)
MAGIK....... Merit Automated Graphics Interface Kit for simulation system (SAUS)
MAG Inc.... Mathematical Applications Group, Incorporated (SAUO)
Mag Ins..... Magen on Insurance [*A publication*] (DLA)
MAGIS....... Magistrate
MAGIS....... Marine Air Ground Intelligence System
MAGIS....... Megawatt Air-to-Ground Illumination System (MCD)
MAGIS....... Municipal Automated Geographic Information System [*District of Columbia Office of the Mayor*] [*Information service or system*] (IID)
Magis & Const (PA)... Magistrate and Constable [*Pennsylvania*] [*A publication*] (DLA)
Magis Ct.... Magistrates' Court (DLA)
MAGISIAC... Marine AirGround Intelligence System Intelligence Analysis Center (SAUO)
MAGL........ Magline [*NCIC trailer make code*]
MAGL........ Magna-Lab, Inc. [*NASDAQ symbol*] (SAG)
MAGL........ Material Acquisition Guidance Letter (MCD)
MAGLA...... Magna Lab [*OTCBB symbol*]
MAGLA...... Magna-Lab 'A' [*NASDAQ symbol*] (TTSB)
MAGLAD.... Marksman and Gunnery Laser Device (SAUS)
MAGLAD.... Marksmanship and Gunnery LASER Device (RDA)
MAGLATCH... Magnetic Latch (MUGU)
MAG-LEV... Magnetically-Levitated [*High-speed ground transportation*]
maglev...... Magnetic Levitation (TRID)
MAGLL...... Magna-Lab Wrrt 'E' [*NASDAQ symbol*] (TTSB)
MAGLOC.... Magnetic Logic Computer
maglrv...... Magnetic Levitation (ADWA)
MAGLU...... Magna-Lab Unit [*NASDAQ symbol*] (TTSB)
MAGLW..... Magna-Lab Wrrt 'A' [*NASDAQ symbol*] (TTSB)
MAGLZ...... Magna-Lab Wrrt 'B' [*NASDAQ symbol*] (TTSB)
MAGMA..... Magma, AZ [*American Association of Railroads railroad junction routing code*]
MAGMA..... Minimal Architecture for Generalized Markup Applications (SAUS)
Magmc...... Magma Copper Co. [*Associated Press*] (SAG)
Mag (MD)... Magruder's Reports [*1, 2 Maryland*] [*A publication*] (DLA)
MAGMOD... Magnetic Modulator
Mag Mor.... Magna Moralia [*of Aristotle*] [*Classical studies*] (OCD)
Mag Mun Par Law... Magistrate and Municipal and Parochial Lawyer [*A publication*] (DLA)
MAGN....... Magainin Pharmaceuticals [*NASDAQ symbol*] (SPSG)
MAGN....... Magnetic (ROG)
MAGN....... Magnetron [*Electricity*]
MAGN....... Magnolia Mobile Homes [*NCIC trailer make code*]
MAGN....... Magnus [*Great*] [*Latin*] (ADA)
MAGN....... Monoaminoguanidine Nitrate [*Organic chemistry*]
Magna....... Magna-Lab, Inc. [*Associated Press*] (SAG)
MAGNA...... Materially and Geometrically Non-Linear Analysis (SAUS)
MAGNA 8.... Fourth-Generation Software (SAUS)
MagnaBb... Magna Bancorp [*Associated Press*] (SAG)
MagnaI...... Magna International, Inc. [*Associated Press*] (SAG)
MagnaL..... Magna-Lab, Inc. [*Associated Press*] (SAG)
Magna Rot Pip... Magnus Rotulus Pipae [*Great Roll of the Pipe*] [*Latin*] [*A publication*] (DLA)
MAGNA-SID... Magnetic Sensing Intrusion Device [*Remote sensor*] [*Also, M-SID*] [*Military*] (VNW)
MAGNETTOR... Magnetic Modulator (SAA)
magnif...... Magnification
MAGNOLIA... Mississippi Alliance for Gaining New Opportunities through Library Information Access
MAGNOX.... Magnesium Oxide [*Magnesium-based alloy*]
MagnPet.... Magnum Petroleum [*Associated Press*] (SAG)
magns....... Magnesium (VRA)
MAGNT...... Museums and Art Galleries of the Northern Territory [*Australia*]
Magntk...... Magnatek, Inc. [*Associated Press*] (SAG)
MAGNUM... Migraine Awareness Group: A National Understanding for Migraineurs (NRGU)
MAGO....... Magnolia Travel Trailer [*NCIC trailer make code*]

MAGO .... Muslims Against Global Oppression [*Government term*] (GA)
MAGOX ...... Magnesium Oxide [*Acronym is trademark of Basic Chemicals*]
MagP .... Magnum Petroleum [*Associated Press*] (SAG)
MAGP .... Master of Arts in Gerontological Psychology (PGP)
MAGP .... Microfibrillar-Associated Glycoprotein [*Biochemistry*]
MAGp .... Military Airlift Group [*Air Force*] (AFM)
MagPet ...... Magnum Petroleum [*Associated Press*] (SAG)
Mag Pharm. Magister Pharmaciae [*Master of Pharmacy*] [*Latin*]
Mag Phil .... Magister Philosophiae [*Master of Philosophy*] [*Latin*]
Mag Phil Fac Theol... Magister Philosophiae Facultatis Theologicae [*Latin*]
MagPhr ..... Magainin Pharmaceuticals [*Associated Press*] (SAG)
MAGPI .... Meatal Advancement and Glanuloplasty [*Operation*] (ODA)
MAGPIE ..... Machine Automatically Generating Production Inventory Evaluation [*Computer science*] (IEEE)
MAGPIE ..... Magazine Page Interactive Editor (DGA)
MAGPIE ..... Markov Game Planar Intercept-Evasion Package [*Computer science*]
MAGPIE ..... Mega-Ampere Generator for Plasma Implosion Experiments [*Astrophysics*] (ECON)
MagPt .... Magnum Petroleum [*Associated Press*] (SAG)
M Agr .... Master of Agriculture
MAGR .... Miniature Airborne GPS Receiver (SAUS)
MAGRAM ... Magnetic Random Access Memory (SAUS)
MAgrDevEc... Master of Agricultural Development Economics
M Agr E ..... Master of Agricultural Engineering
MAgrEc ...... Master of Agricultural Economics
M Agr Eng... Master of Agricultural Engineering
Mag Rer Nat... Magister Rerum Naturalium [*Latin*]
Mag Rer Soc Oec... Magister Rerum Socialium Oeconomicarumque [*Latin*]
M Agric ..... Master of Agriculture
MAGROCV... Military Advisory Group, Government of the Republic of China, Vietnam
Mag Rot .... Magnus Rotulus [*Great Roll of the Exchequer*] [*Latin*] [*A publication*] (DLA)
M Agr S ..... Master of Agricultural Science
M Agr Sc ... Master of Agricultural Science
MAgrSci ..... Master of Agricultural Science
MAgrSt ...... Master of Agricultural Studies (ADA)
Magruder ... Magruder's Reports [*1, 2 Maryland*] [*A publication*] (DLA)
MAGS .... Magal Security Systems [*NASDAQ symbol*] (SAG)
MAGS .... Magal Security Systems, Ltd. [*NASDAQ symbol*] (NASQ)
MAGS .... Magistrates (ROG)
MAGS .... Medical Action for Global Security (BUAC)
MAGS .... Midwestern Association of Graduate Schools (SAUO)
MAGS .... Multiple Aminoglycosides [*Antibacterial agents*]
Magsat ...... Magnetic Field Satellite (EOSA)
MAGSAT .... Magnetic Field Satellite [*NASA*] (MCD)
MAGSAT .... Magnetometer Satellite (NASA)
MAgSc ...... Master of Agricultural Science (ADA)
MAgSci ...... Master of Agricultural Science
MAGSF ...... Magal Security Systems Ltd [*NASDAQ symbol*] (TTSB)
MagSft ...... Magic Software Enterprises [*Associated Press*] (SAG)
MAGSI .... Minimum Altitude at Glide Slope Intersection Inbound [*Aviation*] (FAAC)
MAGSIM .... Magnetic Shield Simulator (PDAA)
MAgSt .... Master of Agricultural Studies
MAGSTR .... Magistrate
mag sulf .... Magnesium Sulfate [*Pharmacology*] (DAVI)
MAGT .... Magnum Custom Trailer [*NCIC trailer make code*]
MAGTAF ..... Marine Air-Ground Task Force (AFM)
mag tape ... Magnetic Tape (DCOM)
MAGTC ...... Magnetic Tape Controller (NITA)
MagTch ...... Magnetics Technology [*Associated Press*] (SAG)
MAGTD ...... Magnitude
MAGTF ...... Marine Air-Ground Task Force (NVT)
Mag Theol... Magister Theologiae [*Master of Theology*] [*Latin*]
MAG-THOR... Magnesium-Thorium [*Inorganic chemistry*]
MAGTOP .... Management of Traffic Operations [*Federal Highway Administration*]
MAGTRAC... Magnetic Tracker (MUGU)
MAGUK ...... Motorcycle Action Group (BUAC)
MAGW .... Maximum Alternate Gross Weight
Magy .... Magyar Muza [*Record label*] [*Hungary*]
Magz .... Magazine
MAH .... Collection des Tablettes Cuneiformes du Musee d'Art et d'Histoire de Geneve (BJA)
MAH .... Findlay, OH [*Location identifier*] [*FAA*] (FAAL)
MAH .... Hampshire College, Amherst, MA [*Library symbol*] [*Library of Congress*] (LCLS)
MAH .... Hanna [*M. A.*] Co. [*NYSE symbol*] (SPSG)
MAH .... Magnesium Aspartate Hydrochloride [*Antihypertensive*]
MAH .... Mahableshwar [*India*] [*Seismograph station code, US Geological Survey*] [*Closed*] (SEIS)
MAH .... M.A. Hanna Co. (EFIS)
MAH .... Mahogany (MSA)
mah .... Mahogany (VRA)
MAH .... Mahommedanism (ROG)
MAH .... Mahon [*Spain*] [*Airport symbol*] (OAG)
MAH .... Maleic Anhydride [*Also, MA*] [*Organic chemistry*]
MAH .... Malev-Hungarian Airlines [*ICAO designator*] (FAAC)
MAH .... Malignancy-Associated Hypercalcemia [*Oncology*]
MAH .... Massachusetts Historical Society, Boston, MA [*OCLC symbol*] (OCLC)
MAH .... Master of Arts in Humanities (GAGS)
MAH .... Miles an Hour [*Telegraphy*] (PCTE)
mAH .... Milliampere Hour
MAH .... Mothers at Home [*An association*] (PAZ)
MAHA .... Marmon Harrington [*NCIC truck make code*]
MAHA .... Metropolitan Association of Handwriting Analysts (EA)
MAHA .... Microangiopathic Hemolytic Anemia [*Medicine*]
Mah & DRT... Mahaffy and Dodson's Road Traffic [*3rd ed.*] [*1961*] [*A publication*] (DLA)
Maharashtra LJ... Maharashtra Law Journal [*India*] [*A publication*] (DLA)
Mahaska .... Mahaska Investment Co. [*Associated Press*] (SAG)
MAHB .... Major Accident Hazards Bureau (EURO)
MAHC .... Maximum Allowable Housing Cost [*Army*] (AABC)
MAHCD ...... Master of Applied Human and Community Development (PGP)
MAHE .... Master of Arts in Hebrew Education (BJA)
MAHE .... Master of Arts in Human Ecology (GAGS)
MAHE .... Michigan Association for Higher Education (SAUO)
MAHE&FE... Master of Arts in Home Economics and Family Ecology (GAGS)
Mahedco .... Maharish Heaven on Earth Development Corporation (SAUO)
MAHEFE ..... Master of Arts in Home Economics and Family Ecology (PGP)
MAHER TERMINALS PAC... Maher Terminals Inc. PAC [*Jersey City, NJ*] (PACS)
MAHH .... Malignancy-Associated Humoral Hypercalcemia [*Medicine*] (DMAA)
MAHi .... Amherst Historical Society, Amherst, MA [*Library symbol*] [*Library of Congress*] (LCLS)
MAHI .... Monarch Avalon [*NASDAQ symbol*] (TTSB)
MAHI .... Monarch Avalon, Inc. [*NASDAQ symbol*] (NQ)
MAHL .... Master of Arts in Hebrew Letters (PGP)
MAHL .... Master of Hebrew Literature (BJA)
Mah LJ ...... Maharashtra Law Journal [*India*] [*A publication*] (DLA)
MAHLOVS... Middle and High Latitudes Oceanic Variability Study (EOSA)
MAHM .... Mid Atlantic Health Management, Inc. (MHID)
MAHMA ...... Midwest Assisted Housing Management Association (SRA)
MAHMO ..... Maryland Association of Health Maintenance Organizations (SRA)
MAHN .... Mongolian People's Revolutionary Party [*Political party*] (BUAC)
MAHO .... Mahoning Homes [*NCIC trailer make code*]
MAHO .... Mobile Assisted Hand-Over (CGWS)
MAHOC ...... Manual for Administration of the Hands-On Component (MCD)
MAHOG ..... Mahogany (DSUE)
MA(Hons)... Master of Arts with Honours (ADA)
MAHP .... Member of the Association of Hypnotists and Physiotherapists [*British*]
MAHPVDC... Magnesium Alloy High-Pressure Die Casting
MAHR .... Minnesota Advocates for Human Rights (EARSL)
MAHRM ..... Master of Arts in Human Resource Management (GAGS)
MAHRS ...... Microflex Attitude & Heading Reference System (SAUO)
MAHRSI ..... Middle Atmosphere High Resolution Spectrograph Investigation
MAHRT ...... Mahrt, AL [*American Association of Railroads railroad junction routing code*]
MAHRU ..... Microflex Attitude & Heading Reference Unit (SAUS)
MAHS .... Master of Human Services (GAGS)
MAHS .... Medical Aspects of Human Sexuality [*Journal*] [*Medicine*] (EDAA)
MAHSM ..... Master of Arts in Human Service Management (GAGS)
MAHT .... Master of Arts in History Teaching (PGP)
MAI .... Air Moravia [*Czechoslovakia*] [*ICAO designator*] (FAAC)
MAI .... Machine-Aided Index (NITA)
MAI .... Machine-Aided Indexing (KSC)
MAI .... M/A-Com, Inc. [*NYSE symbol*] (COMM)
MAI .... Magister in Arte Ingeniaria [*Master of Engineering*]
MAI .... Mai Manufacturing Company [*NCIC trailer make code*]
Mai .... Maine's Reports [*A publication*] (DLA)
MAI .... Mainline [*NCIC car model code*]
MAI .... Maintenance Administrative Instruction (SAUO)
mai .... Maithili [*MARC language code*] [*Library of Congress*] (LCCP)
MAI .... Maius [*May*] [*Latin*]
MAI .... Maizuru [*Japan*] [*Seismograph station code, US Geological Survey*] [*Closed*] (SEIS)
MAI .... Management Action Indicator (SAUO)
MAI .... Management Analysis Inc. (SAUS)
MAI .... Management Analysis Incorporated (SAUO)
MAI .... Management Assistance, Inc. (EFIS)
MAI .... Management Association of Illinois (EARSL)
MAI .... Mantle Arm Index
MAI .... Manufacturers Association of Israel (BUAC)
MAI .... Mapper Application Interface [*Computer science*]
MAI .... Marianna [*Florida*] [*Airport symbol*] (AD)
MAI .... Marianna, FL [*Location identifier*] [*FAA*] (FAAL)
MAI .... Marriage Adjustment Inventory [*Psychology*]
MAI .... Master of Fine Arts International [*British*]
MAI .... Material Annex Item [*Military*]
MAI .... Maximum Allowable Increase [*Environmental Protection Agency*]
MAI .... Mean Annual Increment
MAI .... Media Associates International [*An association*] (EA)
MAI .... Medical Aid for Indochina [*An association*] (EA)
MAI .... Medical Aid for Iraq
MAI .... Medical Ambassadors International [*Association*] (EA)
MAI .... Medical Assurance [*NYSE symbol*] [*Formerly, MAIC Holdings*] (SG)
MAI .... Member, Appraisal Institute [*American Institute of Real Estate Appraisers of the National Association of Realtors*] [*Designation awarded by*]
MAI .... Member of the Anthropological Institute [*British*]
MAI .... Metropolitan Action Institute [*Formerly, SAI*] (EA)
MAI .... Micanite and Insulators (IAA)
MAI .... Microscopic Aggregation Index (DMAA)
MAI .... Midland Airways Limited (SAUO)
MAI .... Military Assistance Institute [*Air Force*]
MAI .... Minimum Annual Income (WDAA)

MAI .... Ministerium fuer Aussenhandel und Innerdeutschen Handel [*Ministry for Foreign Trade and Domestic German Trade*] [*See also MfAI*]
MAI .... Ministry of Armament Industry (SAUO)
MAI .... Minor Acute Illness [*Medicine*] (EDAA)
MAI .... Mobile Allocation Index (CGWS)
MAI .... Monash Asia Institute [*Monash University*] [*Australia*]
MAI .... Movement Assessment of Infants [*Pediatrics*] (DMAA)
MAI .... Multilateral Agreement of Investment (SAUO)
MAI .... Multilateral Agreement on Investment [*1998*]
MAI .... Multilateral Agreement on/of Investment (SAUS)
MAI .... Multilateral Assistance Initiative (SAUO)
MAI .... Multilevel Assessment Instrument [*Medicine*] (DMAA)
MAI .... Multiple Access Interface
MAI .... Multiple Address Instruction
MAI .... Museum of the American Indian (SAUO)
MAI .... Museums Association of India (BUAC)
MAI .... Music Association of Ireland (DBA)
MAI .... Mycobacterium Avium-Intracellulare [*Medicine*]
MAI .... Myobacterium Avium Intercellare (WDAA)
MAIA .... Magnetic Antibody Immunoassay
MAIA .... Master of Arts in Industrial Arts (PGP)
MAIA .... Master of Arts in International Affairs (GAGS)
MAIA .... Member of the American Institute of Appraisers
MAIA .... Michigan Advertising Industry Alliance (EARSL)
MAIAA .... Member of the American Institute of Aeronautics and Astronautics [*Formerly, MIAS*]
MAIAA .... Mid-America Intercollegiate Athletics Association (PSS)
MAIAC .... Maine Athletic Conference (PSS)
MAIADA ..... Massachusetts Independent Auto Dealers Association (SRA)
Mai Anc L... Maine's Ancient Law [*A publication*] (DLA)
MAIAW ...... Massachusetts Association of Intercollegiate Athletics for Women (PSS)
MAIB .... Marine Accident Investigation Board (BUAC)
MAIB .... Marine Accident Investigation Branch (ODA)
MAIB .... Motor Accidents Insurance Board [*Tasmania, Australia*]
MAIBC .... Member of the Architectural Institute of British Columbia [*Canada*] (DD)
MAIBL .... Midland & International Banks Ltd. [*British*]
MAIC .... MAIC Holdings [*NASDAQ symbol*] (TTSB)
MAIC .... MAIC Holdings, Inc. [*NASDAQ symbol*] (SAG)
MAIC .... Maico [*NCIC motorcycle make code*]
MAIC .... Maine Aquaculture Innovation Center [*University of Maine*] [*Research center*] (RCD)
MAIC .... Major Analytical Instrumentation Center [*University of Florida*] [*Research center*] (RCD)
MAIC .... Michigan Association of Insurance Companies (SRA)
MAIC .... Mid-America International Agricultural Consortium
MAIC .... Mutual Assurance, Inc. (EFIS)
MAICE .... Member of the American Institute of Consulting Engineers
MAICh .... Mediterranean Agronomic Institute of Chania (BUAC)
MAIChE ...... Member of the American Institute of Chemical Engineers
MAIC Hld ... MAIC Holdings, Inc. [*Associated Press*] (SAG)
MAICS .... Master of Arts in Intercultural Studies (PGP)
MAICYA ..... Major Authors and Illustrators for Children and Young Adults [*A publication*]
MAID .... Magnetic Anti-Intrusion Detector (PDAA)
MAID .... Maidstone [*Municipal borough in England*]
MAID .... Maintenance Automatic Integration Director [*Computer science*]
MAID .... Manual Intervention and Display
MAID .... Market Analysis and Information Database [*MAID Systems Ltd.*] [*British*] [*Information service or system*] (IID)
MAID .... Master Area Interest Decks (MCD)
MAID .... Master of Arts in Interior Design (GAGS)
MAID .... Master of Arts in International Diplomacy (GAGS)
MAID .... Merger Acquisition Improved Decision [*Computer science*]
MAID .... Methods Assembly Instruction Development (TIMI)
MAID .... Mobile Autonomous Intelligent Device (SAUS)
MAID .... Monroe Automatic Internal Diagnosis [*Computer science*]
MAID .... Multimedia Assets for Industrial Design (EURO)
MAID .... Multiple Aircraft Identification Display (PDAA)
MAIDA .... Multi-Attribute Identification and Analysis Program [*Jointly developed by Georgia Tech Research Institute and the US Air Force*]
MAID/MILES... Magnetic Anti-Intrusion Detector/Magnetic Intrusion Line Sensor (MCD)
MAIDS .... Machine-Aided Information and Dissemination Systems
MAIDS .... Management Automated Information Display System (KSC)
MAIDS .... Mouse Acquired Immunodeficiency Syndrome [*Medicine*] (DMAA)
MAIDS .... Multipurpose Automatic Inspection and Diagnostic Systems [*Army*]
MAIDS .... Murine-Acquired Immunodeficiency Syndrome [*Animal pathology*]
MAIDY .... M.A.I.D. ADS [*NASDAQ symbol*] (TTSB)
MAIE .... Member of the British Association of Industrial Editors (DBQ)
MAIEE .... Member of the American Institute of Electrical Engineers
MAIF .... Major Analytical Instruments Facility [*Case Western Reserve University*] [*Research center*] (RCD)
MAIF .... Maryland Automobile Insurance Fund [*Motor vehicle violation code used in state of Maryland*] (MVRD)
MAIG .... Matsushita Atomic Industrial Group [*Japan*] (BUAC)
MAII .... Medical Alliance, Inc. [*NASDAQ symbol*] (NASQ)
MAIIC .... Master of Arts in International Communications (PGP)
Mai Inst ..... Maine's History of Institutions [*A publication*] (DLA)
MAIL .... Mail Boxes Etc. [*NASDAQ symbol*] (NQ)
MAIL .... Mail.com
MAIL .... MessageMedia [*NASDAQ symbol*]
MAIL .... MILES [*Multiple Integrated LASER Engagement System*] Action Item Log [*Army*]
MAIL .... Multiple Aperture Interlinked (ACAE)
MAIL .... Muslims Against Illegitimate Leaders [*Government term*] (GA)
MailBx ...... Mail Boxes Etc. [*Associated Press*] (SAG)
MAIL DLV LT... Use of Mail Delivery Lights Outside of Active Mail Transport Service [*Conviction term used in state of Oregon*] (MVRD)
MAIL HANDLERS PAC... National Postal Mail Handlers Union PAC [*Washington, DC*] (PACS)
MAILS .... Materiel Acquisition and Integrated Logistics Support
MAILS .... Mid-America Interlibrary Services [*Library network*]
MAILS .... Mississippi Automated Interlibrary Loan System [*Mississippi State Library Commission*] [*Information service or system*] (IID)
MAILS .... Multiple Antenna Instrument Landing System (ACAE)
MailWell .... Mail-Well, Inc. [*Associated Press*] (SAG)
Maim .... Moses Maimonides [*Spanish Talmudist, 1135-1204*] (BJA)
MAIME ...... Member of the American Institute of Mining and Metallurgical Engineers
MAIME ...... Member of the American Institute of Mining Engineers (ASC)
MAIMH ...... Michigan Association for Infant Mental Health (SAUO)
MAIN .... Main command post for that echelon (SAUS)
MAIN .... Maine Shortline [*Federal Railroad Administration identification code*]
MAIN .... Main St. & Main [*NASDAQ symbol*] (TTSB)
MAIN .... Main St. & Main, Inc. [*NASDAQ symbol*] (SAG)
MAIN .... Maintenance (NASA)
MAIN .... Mark Line Industries [*NCIC trailer make code*]
MAIN .... Material Automated Information System
MAIN .... Material Automated Inventory Network (MCD)
MAIN .... Medical Automation Intelligence [*System*]
MAIN .... Mid-America Interconnected Network [*Regional power council*]
MAIN .... Mid-America Interpool Network (SAUO)
MAIN .... Midwest Alliance in Nursing (SRA)
MAIN .... Military Authorization Identification Number
MAIN .... Multiple Access Internal Network [*Computer science*]
MA, Inc. .... Meniere's Australia, Inc. (NRGU)
MA in Comm... Master of Arts in Communications
MAIND ...... Master of Arts in Interior Design (PGP)
MainDta ..... Mainstream Data, Inc. [*Associated Press*] (SAG)
Maine .... Maine Reports [*A publication*] (DLA)
Maine Anc Law... Maine's Ancient Law [*A publication*] (DLA)
Maine PUR... Maine Public Utilities Commission Reports [*A publication*] (DLA)
Maine R .... Maine Reports [*A publication*] (DLA)
Maine Rep... Maine Reports [*A publication*] (DLA)
Mainlobe ... Major Investigation for Low-Frequency Ocean Bottom Loss Experiments [*Marine science*] (MSC)
MA in LS ... Master of Arts in Liberal Studies (SAUO)
MA in LS ... Master of Arts in Library Science (SAUO)
MAINS .... Marine-Aided Inertial Navigation System (PDAA)
MAINS .... Minehunting Action Information & Navigation System (SAUS)
MAINSAIL... Compiler language used in large computer environments (HODG)
MAINSITE... Modular Automated Integrated Systems / Interoperability Test and Evaluation (PDAA)
MainSt ...... Main St. & Main, Inc. [*Associated Press*] (SAG)
MainStB ..... Main Street BankGroup, Inc. [*Associated Press*] (SAG)
MAINT .... Maintenance (AFM)
maint .... Maintenance (MILB)
Maint .... Maintenance (TBD)
MA/INT ..... Maintenance Actions per Interval (MCD)
MA in T ..... Master of Arts in Teaching (SAUO)
MAINTBN ... Maintenance Battalion (DNAB)
MAINTCE... Maintenance (ROG)
maintd ...... Maintained
Maintex ..... Maintenance Conference and Exhibition (SAUO)
MAINTN ..... Maintenance [*Automotive advertising*]
MAINTNCE... Maintenance [*Freight*]
MAINTRAIN... Maintenance and Training [*in complex equipment*]
MAINTSUPOFC... Maintenance Supply Office (DNAB)
MAINTSUPP... Maintenance and Support (DNAB)
MAINTSUPPORTOFF... Maintenance Support Office [*Navy*]
MA in Urb Pl... Master of Arts in Urban Planning
MAIO .... Mashhad [*Iran*] [*Seismograph station code, US Geological Survey*] (SEIS)
MAIO .... Mobile Allocation Index Offset (CGWS)
MAIP .... Marine Engineering Improvement Programme (SAUS)
MAIP .... Matrix Algebra Interpretive Program (IEEE)
MAIPP .... Mid-Atlantic Independent Power Producers (SRA)
MAIR .... Mair & Son [*NCIC trailer make code*]
MAIR .... Manufacturing and Inspection Record (KSC)
MAIR .... Maritime Air (SAUS)
MAIR .... Master of Arts in Industrial Relations
MAIR .... Master of Arts in International Relations (GAGS)
MAIR .... Mechanical Air Injection Reactor [*Automotive engineering*]
MAIR .... Mesaba Holdings [*NASDAQ symbol*] (TTSB)
MAIR .... Mesaba Holdings, Inc. [*NASDAQ symbol*] (SAG)
MAIR .... Metro Airlines, Inc. [*NASDAQ symbol*] (COMM)
MAIR .... Modular Airborne Intercept RADAR (IAA)
MAIR .... Molecular Airborne Intercept RADAR
MAIREASTLANT... Maritime Air, Eastern Atlantic (DNAB)
MAIREASTLANT... Maritime Air, Eastern Atlantic Command (SAUO)
MAIRMAR... Marine Air Depot, Miramar [*California*]
MAIRMED... Maritime Air Forces Mediterranean [*NATO*] (DNAB)
MAIRMED... Maritime Air Forces Mediterranean Command (SAUO)
MAIRS .... Military Air Integrated Reporting System (MCD)
MAIRS .... Military Airlift Integrated Reporting System (SAUO)
MAIRU ...... Mobile Aircraft Instrument Repair Unit
MAIS .... Maine Association of Independent Schools (SAUO)

MAIS .... Maintenance Analysis Information Sheets (SAUO)
MAIS .... Maintenance Information System [*Military*] (NVT)
MAIS .... Major Automated Information Systems (SAUO)
MAIS .... Management Audit Information System
MAIS .... Master of Accounting Information Systems (PGP)
MAIS .... Master of Arts in Interdisciplinary Studies (GAGS)
MAIS .... Master of Arts in International Studies (GAGS)
MAIS .... Mechanical Aids for the Individual Soldier [*Army*]
MAIS .... Mediterranean Association of International Schools (EA)
MAIS .... Member, Association of Industrial Surgeons (CMD)
MAIS .... Memorandum Approval Information System (SAUO)
MAIS .... Microfilm Alpha Index System
MAIS .... Military Airlift Intelligence System (ACAE)
MAIS .... Minnesota Adaptive Instructional System (EDAC)
MAIS .... Mobile Automated Instrumentation Suite (DWSG)
MAIS .... Multicultural Australia and Immigration Studies (MHID)
MAIS .... Mycobacterium Avium-Intracellulare-Scrofulaceum [*Bacteriology*]
MAISA....... Middle Atlantic Intercollegiate Sailing Association
MAISA....... Multiple Analytical Isoelectrofocusing Scanning Apparatus
MAISAC..... Middle Atlantic Inter-Service Athletic Conference (SAUO)
MAISARC... Major Automated Information System Review Council [*Army*]
MAISE....... Member of the Association of Iron and Steel Engineers (SAUO)
MAISITE..... Modular Automatic Integrated System/Interoperability Test and Evaluation (ACAE)
MAISRC..... Major Automated Information Systems Review Council [*Army*]
MAI Sy...... MAI Systems Corp. [*Associated Press*] (SAG)
MAI Sys..... MAI Systems Corp. [*Associated Press*] (SAG)
MAIT......... Maintenance Assistance and Instruction Team [*Army*] (AABC)
Mait......... Maitland's Select Pleas of the Crown [*A publication*] (DLA)
MAIT......... Matrix Analysis of Insider Threat [*Nuclear energy*] (NRCH)
MAIT......... Methotrexate and Cytosine Arabinoside [*Antineoplastic drug regimen*] (DAVI)
MAIT......... Minimum Autoignition Temperature
MAIT......... Missile Airframe Integration Technology (ACAE)
MAIT......... Mulitdiscipline Accident Investigation Team (SAUO)
MAITA....... Marine and Allied Industries Training Association (AIE)
Mait Gl...... Maitland's Pleas of the Crown, County of Gloucester [*A publication*] (DLA)
Maitland.... Maitland's Manuscript Session Cases [*Scotland*] [*A publication*] (DLA)
Maitland.... Maitland's Pleas of the Crown [*1221*] [*England*] [*A publication*] (DLA)
Maitland.... Maitland's Select Pleas of the Crown [*A publication*] (DLA)
MAIU........ Marine Accident Investigation Unit (BUAC)
MAIU........ Marine Atlantic [*Intermodal shipping container symbol*] (TVRC)
MAIWO...... Member of the Austrlaian Institute of Welfare Officers
MAIZ......... Mediterranean Agronomic Institute of Saragossa (BUAC)
MAJ.......... Jones Library, Amherst, MA [*Library symbol*] [*Library of Congress*] (LCLS)
MAJ.......... Majestic Airlines, Inc. [*ICAO designator*] (FAAC)
MAJ.......... Majestic Electronic Stores, Inc. [*Toronto Stock Exchange symbol*]
MAJ.......... Majolica [*Ceramics*] (ROG)
maj.......... Majolica (VRA)
MAJ.......... Major [*Military*] (AABC)
maj.......... Major (GEAB)
Maj.......... Major (WA)
MAJ.......... Majority (KSC)
MAJ.......... Majuro [*Marshall Islands*] [*Airport symbol*] (OAG)
MAJ.......... Maron [*Java*] [*Seismograph station code, US Geological Survey*] [*Closed*] (SEIS)
MAJ.......... Master of Arts in Journalism (GAGS)
MAJ.......... Medical Association of Jamaica (BUAC)
MAJ.......... Michael Anthony Jewelers [*AMEX symbol*] (TTSB)
MAJ.......... Michael Anthony Jewelers, Inc. [*AMEX symbol*] (SPSG)
MAJ.......... Model Air Jet
MAJA........ Majors Transit [*Common carrier symbol*]
MAJAC....... Maintenance Antijam Console [*Air Force*]
MAJC........ Master of Arts in Journalism and Communication (PGP)
MAJC........ Microprocessor Architecture for Java Computing (SAUS)
MAJC........ Mount Aloysius Junior College [*Pennsylvania*]
MAJC........ Mutual Association of Journeymen Coopers [*A union*] [*British*]
MAJCOM.... Major Command [*Formerly, Major Air Command*] [*Military*]
MAJCON.... Major Air Command Controlled [*Units*]
MAJCS...... Master of Arts in Jewish Communal Service (BJA)
MAJCSSW... Master of Arts in Jewish Communal Studies and Social Work (BJA)
MAJE........ Majestic Corporation [*NCIC trailer make code*]
MAJE........ Master of Arts in Jewish Education (BJA)
MAJECA..... Malaysia-Japan Economic Association (SAUO)
MAJ Ed..... Master of Arts in Jewish Education (PGP)
MAJ GEN... Major General (AFM)
Maj Gen.... Major General (NTIO)
MAJI......... Magestic Agency for Joint Intelligence
MAJI......... Majority Agency for Joint Intelligence
MAJIC....... Maji Controlled [*A security classification*]
MAJO........ Major Way [*NCIC trailer make code*]
MAJO........ Matsushiro [*Japan*] [*Seismograph station code, US Geological Survey*] (SEIS)
MAJOUR.... Modular Application for Journals (SAUS)
MAJR........ Majestic Rides Manufacturing [*NCIC trailer make code*]
MAJR........ Major Realty [*NASDAQ symbol*] (TTSB)
MAJR........ Major Realty Corp. [*NASDAQ symbol*] (SAG)
MajRty...... Major Realty Corp. [*Associated Press*] (SAG)
MAJS........ Master of Arts in Jewish Studies (PGP)
MAJS........ Master of Arts in Judaic Studies (BJA)
MAJSR...... Major State Register (MHDB)
MAJU........ Malaysian International Shipping [*Intermodal shipping container symbol*] (TVRC)
MAJY........ Majority (ROG)
MAK......... Mackinaw City, MI [*Amtrak Busline code*]
MAK......... Makedonski Aviotrnasport-Macedonian Airline [*FAA designator*] (FAAC)
MAK......... Makhachkala [*Former USSR*] [*Seismograph station code, US Geological Survey*] (SEIS)
MAK......... Makhuwa-Meetto [*Language symbol*] (ETLW)
MAK......... Making
MAK......... Makkoth (BJA)
MAK......... Malakal [*Sudan*] [*Airport symbol*] (OAG)
MAK......... Maliair Ltd. [*British*] [*ICAO designator*] (FAAC)
MAK......... Manual Abell-Kendall [*Clinical chemistry*]
mAk.......... Maritime Arctic [*Cold Air*] [*Meteorology*] (BARN)
MAK......... Markway Resources Ltd. [*Vancouver Stock Exchange symbol*]
MAK......... Medical Accessories Kit [*Apollo*] [*NASA*]
MAK......... Meninigitis Awareness Key to Prevention (EARSL)
MAK......... Methyl Amyl Ketone [*Organic chemistry*]
MAK......... Methylated Albumin Kieselguhr [*Chromatography*]
MAK......... Monopulse Antenna Kit
MAKA........ Major Karyotypic Abnormalities [*Medicine*]
MAKETRANS... Make Necessary Transfer [*Military*] (DNAB)
Makh........ Makhshirim [*Religion*] [*Judaism*]
Makhsh..... Makhshirin (BJA)
MAKHU...... Moskovsky Akademichesky Khoreografichesky Uchilishche
MAKI........ Israel Communist Party [*Political party*] (PSAP)
Makita....... Makita Corp. [*Associated Press*] (SAG)
MAKL........ Markel Corp. [*NASDAQ symbol*] (NQ)
makm....... Makimono (VRA)
MAKO....... Mako Marine International, Inc. [*NASDAQ symbol*] (SAG)
MAKO....... Mako Marine Intl. [*NASDAQ symbol*] (TTSB)
MakoM...... Mako Marine International, Inc. [*Associated Press*] (SAG)
MAKOU..... Mako Marine Intl. 'Unit' [*NASDAQ symbol*] (TTSB)
MAKR....... Maker Communications, Inc. [*NASDAQ symbol*] (NASQ)
MAKRO..... Management Analysis of Key Resource Operations [*Military*]
Makromol Chem Symp... Makromoleculare Chemie Symposia (MEC)
Maks........ Makhshirin (BJA)
MAKS........ Multipurpose Aero-Space Plane [*Russian delta-wing orbiter*]
Maksh....... Makhshirin (BJA)
MAKSUTSUB... Make Suitable Substitution
MAKV........ Mark V Trailer [*NCIC trailer make code*]
MAL......... Macroassembly Language [*Computer science*] (BUR)
MAL......... Mad Art Lover
MAL......... Magnetic Armature Loudspeaker
MAL......... Maintain at Least (Altitude) [*Aviation*] (FAAC)
Mal.......... Malachi [*Old Testament book*]
MAL......... Malachias [*Old testament book*] [*Douay version*]
MAL......... Malaga [*Spain*] [*Seismograph station code, US Geological Survey*] (SEIS)
MAL......... Malan Realty Investors [*NYSE symbol*] (SAG)
MAL......... Malariology Technician [*Navy*]
MAL......... Malaspina College Learning Resources Centre [*UTLAS symbol*]
MAL......... Malate
MAL......... Malay (WDAA)
mal.......... Malayalam [*MARC language code*] [*Library of Congress*] (LCCP)
MAL......... Malayan (AABC)
MAL......... Malayan Airways Ltd.
Mal.......... Malaysia (MILB)
MAL......... Malaysia (WDAA)
MAL......... Malaysian Air Lines
MAL......... Malcolm Music [*Publisher*]
Mal.......... Maleyl [*Biochemistry*]
MAL......... Malfunction (KSC)
MAL......... Malibu (automobile) [*NCIC car model code*]
MAL......... Malicious [*FBI standardized term*]
MAL......... Malignant (SAUS)
MAL......... Malleable (MSA)
mal.......... Malonate [*Organic chemistry*]
MAL......... Malone [*New York*] [*Airport symbol*] (AD)
MAL......... Malone College, Canton, OH [*OCLC symbol*] (OCLC)
MAL......... Malone, NY [*Location identifier*] [*FAA*] (FAAL)
MAL......... Malta (WDAA)
MAL......... Malta, MT [*Amtrak rail station code*]
mal.......... Malum [*Ill*] [*Latin*] (MAE)
Mal.......... Malus [*Constellation*] (WDAA)
MAL......... Man and LASER (MCD)
MAL......... Marco Resources [*Vancouver Stock Exchange symbol*]
MAL......... Master Authorization List
MAL......... Materiel Allowance List [*Military*]
MAL......... Maximal Acceptable Load (PDAA)
MAL......... McAlpine Aviation Ltd. [*British*] [*ICAO designator*] (FAAC)
MAL......... Medullary Thick Ascending Limb [*Anatomy*]
MAL......... Memory Access Logic
MAL......... Mercury Arc Lamp
MAL......... Meta Assembly Language
MAL......... Methacrolein [*Also, MACR*] [*Organic chemistry*]
MAL......... Microfabrication Applications Laboratory [*University of Illinois at Chicago*] (RCD)
MAL......... Midaxillary Line [*Medicine*]
MAL......... Middle Assyrian Laws (BJA)
MAL......... Mobile Airlock (MCD)
MAL......... Modern American Law [*A publication*] (DLA)
MAL......... Multiairline [*Type of British pole line construction*]

MAL .... Multiple Address Letter (NOAA)
MALA........ Malaguti [*NCIC motorcycle make code*]
MALA........ Malarial Parasites [*Infectious diseases Laboratory and respiratory*] (DAVI)
MALA........ Manpower and Logistics Analysis (MCD)
MALA........ Master of Arts in Liberal Arts (PGP)
MALA........ Master of Arts in Liturgical Arts (PGP)
MALA........ Mississippi Association of Legal Assistants (EARSL)
MAL-AAACE... Media and Adult Learning Section of the American Association for Adult and Continuing Education (EA)
MALAC ...... Malacology
MALAD...... Maladjusted Child [*Social Work*] [*British*] (DSUE)
MALAGOC... Mutual Assistance of the Latin American Government Oil Companies G2 [*See also ARPEL*] (EA)
Malag Rep... Malagasy Republic
MalanR ..... Malan Realty Investors [*Associated Press*] (SAG)
MALAR...... Malaria [*Infectious diseases*] (DAVI)
MALAS ...... Master of Arts in Latin American Studies (PGP)
MALAS ...... Midwestern Association for Latin American Studies
Malay .... Malaysia (VRA)
Malayan J Trop Geogr... Malayan Journal of Topical Geography (SAUO)
Malayan Nat J... Malayan Nature Journal (SAUO)
Malayan Nat J... Malayan Nature Journal, The (SAUS)
Malaysa..... Malaysia Fund, Inc. [*Associated Press*] (SAG)
Malays For... Malaysian Forester (SAUO)
Mal-BSA .... Maleated Bovine Serum Albumin [*Medicine*] (DMAA)
MALC........ Madison Area Library Council [*Library network*]
MALC........ Mallard Coach Company, Inc. [*NASDAQ symbol*] (COMM)
MALC........ Management of Acquisition Logistics Course (AAGC)
MALC........ Midwest Academic Librarians Conference (SAUO)
MALC........ Model Aircraft League of Canada (SAUO)
MALCAP .... Maryland Academic Library Center for Automated Processing (NITA)
MALCAP .... Maryland Library Center for Automated Processing [*Library network*]
MALCD...... Matrix-Addressed Liquid Crystal Display
MALCM ..... Mercantile Adjuster and the Lawyer and Credit Man [*A publication*] (DLA)
Malcolm Ethics... Malcolm's Legal and Judicial Ethics [*A publication*] (DLA)
MALCS ...... Mujeres Activas en Letras y Cambio Social (EA)
MALD........ Master of Arts in Law and Diplomacy
MA(LD)...... Master of Arts (Landscape Design), University of Manchester [*British*] (DBQ)
MALD........ Modular Analysis of Learning Difficulties (OICC)
MALDEF...... Mexican American Legal Defense and Educational Fund (EA)
MALDI....... Matrix-Assisted LASER Desorption Ionization [*Spectroscopy*]
Mald Isls ... Maldive Islands
MALDMS..... Matrix-Assisted LASER Desorption Mass Spectrometry
MALDT ...... Mean Administrative and Logistics Downtime [*Quality control*] (MCD)
MALE........ Military Airlift Estimator (SAUO)
MALE........ Multiaperture Logic Element
MALER...... Master of Arts in Labor and Employment Relations (PGP)
Malerei u Zeichn... Malerei und Zeichnung [*A publication*] (OCD)
Malev .... Hungarian Airlines (BUAC)
MALF........ Malfunction (KSC)
MALF........ Mobile Aerobee Launch Facility
MALFIRM... Maximum Allowable Level of Fishing Related Mortality (SAUS)
MALG........ Minnesota Antilymphoblast Globulin [*Medicine*] (DMAA)
Malg Rep... Malagasy Republic (SAUO)
MALH........ Malheur Mobile Homes [*NCIC trailer make code*]
MALI......... Malibu Campers [*NCIC trailer make code*]
MALI......... Material Annex Line Item [*Military*]
MALI......... Matrix-Assisted Laser Ionizaion [*Spectrometry*]
MALI......... Michigan Accident Location Index [*Michigan State Police*] [*Information service or system*] (IID)
MALIB ...... Math Analysis Library (MCD)
MA(LibSc)... Master of Arts (Library Science)
malig........ Malignant [*Medicine*]
MALIMET... Master List of Medical Indexing Terms
Malinc....... Mallinckrodt Group [*Formerly, IMCERA Group*] [*Associated Press*] (SAG)
Malinckr .... Mallinckrodt Group [*Formerly, IMCERA Group*] [*Associated Press*] (SAG)
MALIPR ..... Material Annex Line Item Progress Report [*Military*] (NG)
MALIS .... Master of Arts in Library and Information Science (PGP)
Mal Isl ...... Maldive Islands (SAUO)
MALL........ Creative Computers [*NASDAQ symbol*] (TTSB)
MALL........ Creative Computers, Inc. [*NASDAQ symbol*] (SAG)
MALL........ Mall [*Postal Service standard*] (OPSA)
MALL........ Mallard Coach Corporation [*NCIC trailer make code*]
MALL........ Malleable
MALL........ Master of Arts in Liberal Learning (PGP)
MALL........ Minnesota Association of Law Libraries [*Library network*]
MALL........ Multi-Function Alarm, Locks, and Lighting [*Automotive electronics*]
MALL........ PC Mall [*Company symbol*]
MALLAR .... Manned Lunar Landing and Return [*NASA*]
Mal Law M... Malynes' Ancient Law Merchant [*A publication*] (DLA)
Mall Ent... Mallory's Modern Entries [*A publication*] (DLA)
Mal Lex Merc... Malynes' Lex Mercatoria [*3 eds.*] [*1622-36*] [*A publication*] (DLA)
Mallon ...... Mallon Resources Corp. [*Associated Press*] (SAG)
Mallory..... Mallory's Irish Chancery Reports [*A publication*] (DLA)
Mal L Rev... Malaya Law Review [*A publication*] (DLA)
MALLS ...... Multiangle LASER Light-Scattering [*Instrumentation*]
MALM .... Maryknoll Associate Lay Missioners (EA)
MALM .... Maryknoll Mission Association of the Faithful (EA)
MALM .... Master Air Loadmaster (SAUO)
MALMARC... Malaysian MARC (NITA)
MAL MISCH... Malicious Mischief [*Legal term*] (DLA)
MALN........ Malanca [*NCIC motorcycle make code*]
MALN........ Mallon Minerals Corp. [*NASDAQ symbol*] (COMM)
MALN........ Minimum Air Low Noise (PDAA)
MALN........ Mouvement Africain de Liberation Nationale [*African Movement for National Liberation*]
MALO........ Malro USA [*NCIC trailer make code*]
MALODES... Modern Army Logistics Data Exchange System
MALOF ...... Minimum Accepted Level of Fill [*Military*]
Malone...... Editor, 6, 9, and 10, Heiskell's Tennessee Reports [*A publication*] (DLA)
MALOR...... Mortar and Artillery Location RADAR (RDA)
MALOS ...... Maintenance and Logistics Space [*System*]
MALOS ...... Miniature Laser Optical Sight [*Police and security equipment*]
MALOS ...... Miniature Optical Laser Sight (SAUS)
MALP........ Major Assembly Labor and Performance (MCD)
MALP........ Master Alarm Light Panel [*NASA*] (SPST)
MALPAS..... Malvern Program Analysis System (NITA)
MALPH...... Michigan Association for Local Public Health (EARSL)
MAL PROS... Malicious Prosecution [*Legal term*] (DLA)
MALR........ Malrite Communications Group, Inc. [*NASDAQ symbol*] (COMM)
MALR........ Mortar/Artillery Locating RADAR (PDAA)
MALRA ...... Malaysian Leprosy Relief Association (SAUO)
MALRY ...... Malaysian Leprosy Relief Association (BUAC)
MALS........ Master of Arts in Liberal Studies
MALS........ Master of Arts in Library Science
MALS........ Master of Arts in Library Service (NADA)
MALS........ Median Arcuate Ligament Syndrome [*Medicine*] (MELL)
MALS........ Medium-Intensity Approach Lighting System [*Aviation*]
MALS........ Members of an Amalgamated Society [*Slang*] [*British*] (DSUE)
MALS........ Miniature Air Launcher System (ACAE)
MALS........ Multiangle Light Scattering
MALSCE..... Massachusetts Association of Land Surveyors and Civil Engineers (SRA)
MALSF ...... Medium-Intensity Approach Lighting System with Sequenced Flashers [*Aviation*]
MALSF ...... Medium Intensity Approach Light System with Sequenced Flashing Lights [*FAA*] (TAG)
MALSP ...... Marine Aviation Logistics Support Program
MALSR ...... Medium-Intensity Approach Lighting System with Runway Alignment Indicator Lights [*Aviation*]
MALSR ...... Medium Intensity Approach Light System with Rail [*FAA*] (TAG)
MALS/RAIL... Minimum-Approach Lighting System with Runway Alignment Indicator Lights [*Aviation*] (DNAB)
Mal St....... Malay States (SAUO)
MALT........ Lion Brewery [*NASDAQ symbol*] (TTSB)
MALT........ Lion Brewery, Inc. (The) [*NASDAQ symbol*] (SAG)
MALT........ Macosa-Associated Lymphoid Tissue [*Medicine*]
MALT........ Male, Altered Animal (DMAA)
MALT........ Maltese (DSUE)
MALT........ Master of Arts in Language Teaching (GAGS)
MALT........ Military Administration of Liberated Territory (SAUO)
MALT........ Military Adviser's Language Text
MALT........ Military Assistance Language Training
MALT........ Mnemonic Assembly Language Translator [*Computer science*] (IEEE)
MALT........ Monetary Allowance in Lieu of Transportation [*DoD*]
MALT........ Mucosa-Associated Lymphoid Tissue [*Anatomy*]
MALT........ Munich Alcoholism Test [*Medicine*] (DMAA)
MALTA....... Middle Atlantic Lawn Tennis Association
MALTA SE... Malta Stock Exchange
Malt CM .... Maltby on Courts-Martial [*A publication*] (DLA)
MALTL....... Mucosa-Associated Lymphoid Tissue Lymphoma [*Medicine*] (MELL)
MALT lymphoma... Mucosa-Associated Lymphoid Tissue Lymphoma [*Medicine*] (PALA)
MALTS....... Marine Layer Thickness Study (SAUO)
MALTT....... Massachusetts Adult Literacy and Technology Team
MALU........ Maine Association of Life Underwriters (SRA)
MALU........ Massachusetts Association of Life Underwriters (SRA)
MALU........ Messer Greisheim [*Intermodal shipping container symbol*] (TVRC)
MALU........ Michigan Association of Life Underwriters (SRA)
MALU........ Minnesota State Association of Life Underwriters (SRA)
MALU........ Mississippi Association of Life Underwriters (SRA)
MALU........ Missouri Association of Life Underwriters (SRA)
MALU........ Mode Annunciator and Logic Unit (PDAA)
MALV........ Malva [*Mallow*] [*Pharmacy*] (ROG)
MALVINE.... Manuscripts and Letters via Integrated Networks in Europe (TELE)
MALY........ Malyette [*NCIC motorcycle make code*]
Malynes..... Malynes' Lex Mercatoria [*3 eds.*] [*1622-36*] [*A publication*] (DLA)
MALZ........ American President Lines [*Intermodal trailer symbol*]
MAm......... Amesbury Public Library, Amesbury, MA [*Library symbol*] [*Library of Congress*] (LCLS)
M + Am ..... Compound Myopic Astigmatism [*Ophthalmology*]
MAM......... Joint II March-May Study [*Coastal Upwelling Ecosystems Analysis*] (MSC)
MAM......... Madam (DSUE)
MaM......... Mailman [*U.S. Navy enlisted rating*] (AUER)
MAM......... Maintenance Assist Module
MAM......... Maintenance Assumes Monitor [*Aviation*] (FAAC)
MAM......... Mambajao [*Philippines*] [*Seismograph station code, US Geological Survey*] [*Closed*] (SEIS)
MAM......... Mammoth [*Telegraphy*] (PCTE)
Mam......... Mammoth
MAM......... Management Analysis Memorandum [*DoD*] (MCD)

MAM......... Management Analysis Model (SAUO)
MAM......... Management and Administration Manual (NRCH)
MAM......... Marquis Academic Media [*Publisher*]
MAM......... Mars Aeronomy Mission (MCD)
MAM......... Master Model (MCD)
MAM......... Master of Agriculture and Management (PGP)
MAM......... Master of Animal Medicine (GAGS)
MAM......... Master of Applied Mechanics (PGP)
MAM......... Master of Arts in Management
MAM......... Master of Arts Management (PGP)
MAM......... Master of Arts - Ministry (PGP)
MAM......... Master of Association Management (PGP)
MAM......... Master of Avian Medicine (PGP)
MAM......... Master of Aviation Management (GAGS)
MAM......... Matamoros [*Mexico*] [*Airport symbol*] (OAG)
MAM......... Material Acquisition Manager [*Army*] (AAGC)
MAM......... Materiel Acquisition Management Program [*Army*] (RDA)
MAM......... Matter-Anti-Matter (PDAA)
MAM......... Maxxim Medical [*NYSE symbol*] (TTSB)
MAM......... Maxxim Medical, Inc. [*NYSE symbol*] (SPSG)
MAM......... Medical Association of Malta (BUAC)
MAM......... Medium-Altitude Missile (MCD)
MAM......... Medium Automotive Maintenance
MAM......... Memory Access Multiplexer (NITA)
MAM......... Memory Allocation Manager
MAM......... Mercury Asset Management [*Commercial firm*] [*British*]
MAM......... Message Access Method [*Honeywell, Inc.*]
MAM......... Meta Aviotransport-Macedonia [*Yugoslavia*] [*ICAO designator*] (FAAC)
MAM......... Methylazoxymethanol (STED)
MAM......... Methylazoxymethanol Acetate [*Organic chemistry*]
MAM......... Microwave Attenuator Monitor (IAA)
MAM......... Mid-America Industries, Inc. [*AMEX symbol*] (COMM)
MAM......... Military Air Movement
MAM......... Military Assistance Manual (AFM)
MAM......... Milliammeter
mam......... Milliampere-Minute (STED)
MAM......... Milliampere Minutes
MAM......... Missile Alarm Monitor
MAM......... Missile Assembly and Maintenance [*NASA*] (IAA)
MAM......... Mission Air Ministries [*Defunct*] (EA)
MAM......... Mission Area Manager [*Army*]
MAM......... Monoacetylmorphine [*Organic chemistry*]
MAM......... Montclair Art Museum (SAUO)
MAM......... Mot a Mot [*Word for Word*] [*French*]
MAM......... Multiapplication Monitor
MAM......... Multiple Access to Memory [*Computer science*] (IEEE)
MAM......... Munitions Assessment Model (SAUO)
M+Am....... Myopic Astigmatism [*Ophthalmology*] (DAVI)
MAM......... Society of Automotive Engineers, Inc. (AAGC)
MAMA....... Maintenance and Malfunction Analysis (ACAE)
MAMA....... Mammacom [*NASDAQ symbol*]
MAMA....... Management Accounting Maintenance Advertising, Inc.
MAMA....... Manual-Automatic Multipoint Apparatus (MCD)
MAMA....... Material Acquisition Management Application [*Suggested name for the Library of Congress computer system*]
MAMA....... Meet-a-Mum Association [*British*] (DI)
MAMA....... Michigan Association of Municipal Attorneys (EARSL)
MAMA....... Midarm Muscle Area (STED)
MAMA....... Middletown Air Materiel Area [*Air Force*]
MAMA....... Mobile Air Materiel Area (SAUO)
MAMA....... Mobile Automated Metabolic Analyzer [*Aerospace*]
MAMA....... Monoammonium Methanearsonate
MAMA....... Monoclonal Antimalignant Antibody [*Immunochemistry*]
MAMA....... Mothers Against Munchausen Syndrome by Proxy Allegations (SAUO)
MAMA....... Movement for All-Macedonian Action [*Political party*]
MAMA....... Multi-Anode Microchannel Array (PDAA)
MAMAA..... Mothers Against Murder and Aggression [*An association*] (BUAC)
MAM Ac..... Methylazoxymethanol Acetate [*Organic chemistry*] (DMAA)
MAMB....... Master of Applied Molecular Biology (PGP)
MAMB....... Military Acquisition Management Branch [*Army*] (RDA)
MAMB....... Military Advisory Mission, Brazil
MAMB....... Missile Assembly and Maintenance Building [*NASA*] (IAA)
MAMB....... Mission Avionics Multiplex Bus (ACAE)
MAMBA..... Marconi Artillery & Mortar Ballistic Aide (SAUS)
MAMBO..... Maryland Association of Mountain Bike Operators (EARSL)
MAMBO..... Mediterranean Association for Marine Biology and Oceanology [*ICSU*] (EAIO)
MAMBO..... Mediterranean Association of Marine Biological Oceanography (SAUO)
MAMBO..... Minuteman Assembly-Maintenance Building, Ogden (SAA)
MAMC....... Altona Medical Centre Library, Manitoba [*Library symbol*] [*National Library of Canada*] (NLC)
MAMC....... Madigan Army Medical Center (AABC)
MAMC....... Master of Arts in Mass Communication (PGP)
MAMC....... Mean Arm Muscle Circumference (STED)
MAMC....... Midarm Muscle Circumference [*Myology*]
MAMDC..... Multipurpose Arthritis and Musculoskeletal Diseases Center [*University of Alabama, Birmingham*] [*Research center*] (RCD)
MAME....... Master of Arts in Missions/Evangelism (PGP)
MAME....... Michigan Association for Media in Education
MAME....... Michigan Association of Media Educators
MAME....... Missile and Munitions Evaluation (MCD)
MAME....... Mobile America [*NASDAQ symbol*] (TTSB)
MAME....... Mobile America Corp. [*NASDAQ symbol*] (NQ)
MAME....... Multiple Arcade Machine Emulator (SAUS)
MA Mech... Master of Applied Mechanics
MAMEE..... Meyer Ammunition Module - Emerson Electric
MAMEME... Member of the Association of Mining, Electrical and Mechanical Engineers (SAUO)
MAMF....... Michigan Association of Metal Finishers (EARSL)
MAMFC..... Master of Arts in Marriage and Family Counseling (GAGS)
MAMFCC.... Master of Arts in Marriage, Family, and Child Counseling (PGP)
MAMFT...... Master of Arts in Marriage and Family Therapy (PGP)
MAmg....... Medial Amygdaloid [*Nucleus*] (STED)
MAMGRAPHY... Mammography
MA Mgt..... Master of Arts in Management (PGP)
MaMHCA.... Massachusetts Mental Health Counselors Association (SEAT)
MAmHi...... Amesbury Historical Society, Amesbury, MA [*Library symbol*] [*Library of Congress*] (LCLS)
MAMI........ Machine-Aided Manufacturing Information [*Computer science*]
MAMI........ Modified Alternate Mark Inversion [*Telecommunications*] (TEL)
MAMI........ Multicultural Association of Medical Interpreters of Central New York (SAUO)
MAMI........ Multiple Association Management Institute [*Later, IAMC*] (EA)
MAMIE...... Magnetic Amplification of Microwave Integrated Emissions (IEEE)
MAMIE...... Minimum Automatic Machine for Interpolation and Extrapolation
M Am IMME........ Member of the American Institute of Mining and Metallurgical Engineers
MA Min..... Master of Arts in Ministry (PGP)
MA min..... Milli-Ampere-Minute (STED)
Ma-Min..... Milliampere-Minute
MAMIS...... Mandatory Modification and Inspection Summary [*Aviation*] (DA)
MA Missions... Master of Arts in Missions (PGP)
MAML....... Master of Arts in School Media Librarianship (PGP)
MA/ML...... Missile Active/Missile Launch (SAUS)
MAMM....... Master of Arts in Ministry Management (PGP)
MAMMA..... Men Against the Maxi-Midi Atrocity [*Klosters, Switzerland, group opposing below-the-knee fashions introduced in 1970*]
MAMMAX... Machine-Made and Machine-Assisted Index [*Computer science*] (IAA)
mammo..... Mammography [*Gynecology*] (DAVI)
Mamm Rev... Mammal Review (SAUS)
MAM Number... Military Air Movement Number (SAUO)
MAMO....... Advanced Mammography Sys [*NASDAQ symbol*] (TTSB)
MAMO....... Advanced Mammography Systems [*NASDAQ symbol*] (SAG)
MAMOE..... Medical Administration and Miscellaneous Operating Expenses [*Veterans Administration*]
MAMOS..... Marine Automatic Meteorological Observing Station [*Automatic system*]
MAMOS..... Missouri Associated Migrant Opportunities Services (EA)
MaMP....... Maine State Planning Office, Augusta, ME [*Library symbol*] [*Library of Congress*] (LCLS)
MAMP....... Mainz Army Maintenance Plant (MCD)
MAMP....... Materiel Acquisition Management Plan
MAMP....... Michigan Army Missile Plant (MCD)
MAMP....... Millampere [*or Milliamperage*] (IAA)
MAMP....... Mission Area Materiel Plan [*Army*]
MAMRC..... Military Aerospace Maintenance and Regeneration Center (MUSM)
MAMRD..... Master of Agricultural Management and Resource Development (GAGS)
MAMRON... Marine Aircraft Maintenance Squadron
MAMS....... Maintenance Activity Management System [*Military*]
MAMS....... Maintenance Assist Modules (MCD)
MAMS....... Marine Meteorological Services [*Marine science*] (MSC)
MAMS....... Master of Applied Mathematical Sciences (PGP)
MAMS....... Master of Associated Medical Sciences (PGP)
MAMS....... Materiel Acquisition Management System
MAMS....... Medical Administration Management System (SAUO)
MAMS....... Medical Administrative Management System
MAMS....... Member of the Association of Medical Secretaries, Practice Administrators, and Receptionists [*British*] (DBQ)
MAMS....... Microgravity Acceleration Measurement System (SAUS)
MAMS....... Mid Atlantic Medical Services (EFIS)
MAMS....... Military Aircraft Marshaling System
MAMS....... Military Airspace Management System (SAUS)
MAMS....... MIRCOM [*Missile Material Readiness Command*] Automated Microfilm System [*Army*] (IID)
MAMS....... Missile Altitude Measurement System
MAMS....... Missile Assembly and Maintenance Shop [*NASA*]
MAMS....... Missile Assistance Maintenance Structure (IAA)
MAMS....... Mobile Air Movement Squadron (SAUO)
MAMS....... Modern Army Maintenance System
MAMS....... Multiple Access to Memory System [*Computer science*]
MAMS....... Multispectral Atmospheric Mapping Sensor
m-AMSA.... Acridinyl Ansidide [*Antineoplastic drug*] (DAVI)
m-AMSA.... Amsacrine [*Antineoplastic drug*] [*Also, AMSA*] (CDI)
MAMSA..... Managing and Marketing Sales Association [*British*] (DBA)
MAM Sc..... Master of Applied Mathematical Science (PGP)
MAMSER.... Mass Mobilisation for Self Reliance, Social Justice, and Economic Recovery [*Nigeria*] (BUAC)
MAMSI...... Mid Atlantic Medical Services (MHID)
MAMS-II.... Maintenance Activity Management System II (SAUO)
M Am Soc CE... Member of the American Society of Civil Engineers
MAmSocHRAE... Member of the American Society of Heating, Refrigeration and Air Conditioning Engineers (SAUO)
MAmSocMechE... Member of the American Society of Mechanical Engineers (SAUO)

MAMSPAR... Member of the Association of Medical Secretaries, Practice Administrators, and Receptionists [*British*] (DI)
MAMS-R.... Medical Administrative Management System-Revision (SAUO)
MAMSS..... Machine Augmented Manual Scheduling System (MCD)
MAMT....... Mean Active Maintenance Time (MCD)
MAMT....... Mobile Air Movements Team (SAUO)
MAMTC..... Main Administration for Military-Technical Co-operation (SAUO)
MAMTF..... Mobile Automated Microwave Test Facility (PDAA)
MAMTR..... Milliammeter
MA (Mus)... Master of Arts in Music
MAMV....... Maclura Mosaic Virus [*Plant pathology*]
MAmW...... Whittier Home Association, Amesbury, MA [*Library symbol*] [*Library of Congress*] (LCLS)
MAN......... Magnetic Automatic Navigation [*System*] (RDA)
MAN......... Magnocellular Nucleus [*of anterior neostriatum*] [*Neurology*] (DAVI)
MAN......... Mailorder Association of Nurserymen [*Defunct*] (EA)
MAN......... Mainly about Nature [*A publication*]
MAN......... Maintenance Alert Network [*RCA*]
MAN......... Management (WDAA)
MAN......... Manager [*or Managing*] (EY)
man.......... Managing (DD)
Man.......... Mancando [*Dying Away*] [*Music*]
MAN......... Manchester [*England*] [*Airport symbol*] (OAG)
MAN......... Manchester Regiment (SAUO)
MAN......... Mandato de Accion y Unidad Nacional [*Mandate of Action and National Unity*] [*Bolivia*] [*Political party*] (PPW)
man.......... Mandingo [*MARC language code*] [*Library of Congress*] (LCCP)
man.......... Mandolin
MAN......... Mane [*Morning*] [*Pharmacy*]
MAN......... Manege [*Horsemanship*] [*French*]
MAN......... Manhattan
MAN......... Manhattan (automobile) [*NCIC car model code*]
MAN......... Manifest (AABC)
MAN......... Manila [*Philippines*] [*Seismograph station code, US Geological Survey*] (SEIS)
Man.......... Manila (WDAA)
MAN......... Manilla (ADA)
man.......... Manipulate [*Medicine*] (MAE)
MAN......... Manipulus [*A Handful*] [*Pharmacy*]
Man.......... Manitoba [*Canada*] (DD)
MAN......... Manitoba [*Canadian province*]
Man.......... Manitoba Law Reports [*Canada*] [*A publication*] (DLA)
Man.......... Manning's Reports [*1 Michigan*] [*A publication*] (DLA)
Man.......... Manning's Reports, English Revision Court [*1832-35*] [*A publication*] (DLA)
MAN......... Mannion Air Charter, Inc. [*ICAO designator*] (FAAC)
MAN......... Mann Oil Resources, Inc. [*Vancouver Stock Exchange symbol*]
MAN......... Mannose (STED)
Man.......... Mannose [*A sugar*]
MAN......... Manpower, Inc. [*NYSE symbol*] (SPSG)
MAN......... Mansfield State College, Mansfield, PA [*OCLC symbol*] (OCLC)
Man.......... Manson's English Bankruptcy Cases [*A publication*] (DLA)
MAN......... Manta [*NCIC car model code*]
Man.......... Mantra [*Medicine*] (EDAA)
MAN......... Manual (KSC)
man.......... Manual [*A handbook*] (WDMC)
MAN......... Manuel Antonio Noriega [*Military commander and de facto ruler of Panama*]
MAN......... Manufacture
Man.......... Manufacturer (SAUO)
MAN......... Manufacturer (WDAA)
MAN......... Manufacturers Association of Nigeria (BUAC)
MAN......... Maschinenfabrik Augsburg-Nuernburg [*Manufacturer of diesel engines*]
MAN......... Meaningful Assistance in the Neighborhood [*of Legal Aid Bureau of George Washington University Law School*] (EA)
MAN......... Medical Articular Nerve [*Medicine*] (EDAA)
MAN......... Medic Alert Newsletter [*Medicine*] (EDAA)
MAN......... Methacrylonitrile (EDCT)
MAN......... Methylammonium Nitrate (EDCT)
MAN......... Metropolitan Area Network [*Telecommunications*]
MAN......... Microwave Aerospace Navigation
MAN......... Military Aviation Notice [*Air Force*]
MAN......... Molecular Anatomy
MAN......... Molesters Anonymous (EA)
MAN......... Motorcyclists Against Noise (SAUO)
MAN......... Mouvement pour une Alternative Non-Violente [*Movement for a Nonviolent Alternative*] [*France*] [*Political party*] (PPE)
MAN......... Movementu Antiyas Nobo [*New Antilles Movement*] [*Netherlands*] [*Political party*] (EAIO)
MAN......... Movimentu Antiyas Nobo [*New Antilles Movement*] [*Political party*] (EY)
MAN......... Movimiento de Accion Nacionalista [*National Action Movement*] [*Uruguay*] [*Political party*] (EY)
MAN......... Muslim Association of Nigeria (SAUO)
MAN......... University of Manitoba Library [*UTLAS symbol*]
Man.......... Victoria University of Manchester (SAUO)
MAN-6-P.... Mannose-6-Phosphate [*Chemistry*] (DAVI)
MANA....... Major and National Account (TIMI)
MANA....... Malawi News Agency (BUAC)
MANA....... Manac [*NCIC trailer make code*]
MANA....... Manassas National Battlefield Park
MANA....... Manatron, Inc. [*NASDAQ symbol*] (NQ)
MANA....... Mannosidase Alpha (DMAA)
MANA....... Manufacturers Agents National Association (EA)
MANA....... Mazda North America [*Automotive industry*]
MANA....... Mexican American Women's National Association (EA)
MANA....... Michigan Association of Nurse Anesthetists (SAUO)
MANA....... Midwives Alliance of North America (EA)
MANA....... Music Advisers' National Association [*British*]
MANA....... Musicians Against Nuclear Arms [*Defunct*] (EA)
MAN-AEDS... Manitoba Association for Educational Data Systems [*Canada*] (EDAC)
MAnaes..... Master of Anaesthesiology (SAUO)
MANAG...... Manage
Manage Acc... Management Accounting [*A publication*] (JLIT)
Managem... Management (SAUO)
Manage Train Rev... Management Training Review [*A publication*] (JLIT)
MANAM...... Manual Amendment
Man & G.... Manning and Granger's English Common Pleas Reports [*A publication*] (DLA)
Man & R.... Manning and Ryland's English King's Bench Reports [*1827-30*] [*A publication*] (DLA)
Man & R.... Manning and Ryland's English Magistrates' Cases [*1827-30*] [*A publication*] (DLA)
Man & Ry... Manning and Ryland's English King's Bench Reports [*1827-30*] [*A publication*] (DLA)
Man & Ry... Manning and Ryland's English Magistrates' Cases [*1827-30*] [*A publication*] (DLA)
Man & Ry KB... Manning and Ryland's English King's Bench Reports [*1827-30*] [*A publication*] (ILCA)
Man & Ry Mag... Manning and Ryland's English Magistrates' Cases [*1827-30*] [*A publication*] (DLA)
Man & Ry Mag Cas... Manning and Ryland's English Magistrates' Cases [*1827-30*] [*A publication*] (DLA)
Man & Ry MC... Manning and Ryland's English Magistrates' Cases [*1827-30*] [*A publication*] (DLA)
Man & S.... Manning and Scott's English Common Bench Reports, Old Series [*IX*] [*A publication*] (DLA)
Man & Sask Tax Rep (CCH)... Manitoba and Saskatchewan Tax Reporter (Commerce Clearing House) [*A publication*] (DLA)
Man & Sc... Manning and Scott's English Common Bench Reports, Old Series [*IX*] [*A publication*] (DLA)
MANAV...... Maneuvering and Navigation System [*Military*] (IAA)
MANB....... Mannosidase Beta (DMAA)
ManBagel... Manhattan Bagel Co., Inc. [*Associated Press*] (SAG)
Manb Coke... Manby's Abridgement of Coke's Reports [*A publication*] (DLA)
Manb Fines... Manby on Fines [*A publication*] (DLA)
Man B News... Manitoba Bar News [*A publication*] (ILCA)
MANC....... Mancando [*Decreasing in Loudness*] [*Music*]
MANC....... Manchester Equipment Co., Inc. [*NASDAQ symbol*] (NASQ)
MANC....... Mozambique African National Congress (SAUO)
Manc........ Victoria University of Manchester (SAUO)
MANCAN.... Man-Carried Automatic Navigator (MCD)
Man Cas.... Manumission Cases in New Jersey, by Bloomfield [*A publication*] (DLA)
MANCH...... Manchester [*England*]
Manch....... Manchuria
MANCLOS... Manual Command to Line-Of-Sight (SAUS)
MANCO...... Mancando [*Decreasing in Loudness*] [*Music*]
MANCOVA... Multivariate Analysis of Covariance
MANCPEC... Malaysia National Committee for Pacific Economic Cooperation
MANCUN.... Mancunium [*Signature of the Bishops of Manchester*] (ROG)
Mand........ Mandaic (BJA)
MAND....... Mandamus [*We Command*] [*Latin*] (ADA)
MAND....... Mandatory (AABC)
Mand........ Mandatory (TBD)
mand........ Mandibar [*Dentistry*] (DAVI)
mand........ Mandible [*Therapy term*] (CTAA)
MAND....... Mandible
mand........ Mandolin (WDAA)
MAND....... Mandolin [*Music*]
MAND....... McCarron Assessment of Neuromuscular Development [*Psychology*] (DHP)
M&A......... Maintenance and Administration (CIST)
M & A....... Maintenance and Assembly (MCD)
M & A....... Management and Administration
M&A......... Mergers and Acquisitions (TDOB)
M & A....... Mergers & Acquisitions Data Base [*MLR Publishing Co.*] [*Information service or system*] (CRD)
M & A....... Mississippi & Alabama Railroad (IIA)
M & A....... Missouri & Arkansas Railway Co.
M & A....... Money and Advice
M & A....... Montagu and Ayrton's English Bankruptcy Reports [*1833-38*] [*A publication*] (DLA)
M & ABL.... Montagu and Ayrton's Bankrupt Laws [*A publication*] (DLA)
M&AS....... Music and Art School (SAUO)
MANDATE... MCCIS Austere Northwood Database & Terminal Equipment (SAUS)
MANDATE... Multiline Automatic Network Diagnostic and Transmission Equipment [*Computer science*] (CIST)
M & AW..... Mountain and Arctic Warfare [*British military*] (DMA)
M & Ayr..... Montagu and Ayrton's English Bankruptcy Reports [*1833-38*] [*A publication*] (DLA)
M & B....... Marianna & Blountstown [*Railroad*] (MHDB)
M & B....... Marianna & Blountstown Railroad Co. (IIA)
M & B....... Matched and Beaded
M&B......... May & Baker (WDAA)
M&B......... May & Baker Ltd. (SAUO)
M & B....... Mild and Bitter [*Beer*]
M & B....... Mills and Boon (ODA)

M&B .... Mitchells and Butlers Ltd. (SAUO)
M & B .... Montagu and Bligh's English Bankruptcy Reports [*1832-33*] [*A publication*] (DLA)
M & BR ..... Meridian & Bigbee River Railroad Co. (IIA)
M&BU .... Mother & Baby Unit (WDAA)
M & C .... Maintenance and Checkout (NASA)
M & C .... Maintenance and Cure [*Legal shorthand*] (LWAP)
M&C .... Management & Control (SAUS)
M & C .... Manufacturers and Contractors
M&C .... Measurement and Control [*The Journal of InstMC*] (ACII)
M & C .... Monitor and Control Panel [*Computer science*] (NASA)
M & C .... Montagu and Chitty's English Bankruptcy Reports [*1838-40*] [*A publication*] (DLA)
M&C .... Morphine and Cocaine [*Medicine*] (DMAA)
M & C .... Mylne and Craig's English Chancery Reports [*A publication*] (DLA)
M&CA .... Materials & Chemical Applications (SAUO)
M & C Bills... Miller and Collier on Bills of Sale [*A publication*] (DLA)
M&CD .... Metals and Ceramics Division (SAUO)
M & Chit Bankr... Montagu and Chitty's English Bankruptcy Reports [*1838-40*] [*A publication*] (DLA)
M & Cht Bankr... Montagu and Chitty's English Bankruptcy Reports [*1838-40*] [*A publication*] (DLA)
M & C Partidas... Moreau-Lislet and Carleton's Laws of Las Siete Partidas in Force in Louisiana [*A publication*] (DLA)
M&CS .... Materials & Chemical Sciences Center (SAUO)
M & CSq .... Mapping and Charting Squadron [*Air Force*]
M & CU ..... Monitor and Control Unit [*Aerospace*] (AAG)
M and CW... Maternity and Child Welfare [*Medicine*] [*British*]
M & D .... Maidstone & District Motor Services Ltd. [*British*] (DCTA)
M&D .... Maintenance and Diagnostics (SAUO)
M & D .... McCormack & Dodge (NITA)
M & D .... Medicine and Duty [*Marked on a medical report and implying a suspicion of malingering*] [*Military*] [*British*]
M & D .... Mergers and Divestures
M&DOD ..... Mision and Data Operations Directorate (ACAE)
M & DV ..... Map and Data Viewer [*NASA*] (KSC)
M&E .... Machinery and Equipment (ACAE)
M & E .... Maintenance and Equipment (NATG)
M & E .... Maneuvers and Exercises (NATG)
M & E .... Material and Equipment [*Nuclear energy*] (NRCH)
M & E .... Mechanical and Electrical Room (AAG)
M&E .... Metcalf & Eddy Companies (EFIS)
M&E .... Monitoring and Enforcement (SAUS)
M & E .... Monitoring and Evaluation (ECON)
M&E .... Monitoring and Evaluation (SAUS)
M & E .... Morning and Evening (WDMC)
M & E .... Music and Effects [*Television*]
M & E .... Music and Sound Effects (WDMC)
MANDEC .... Maneuvering Decoy (MCD)
Man Dem ... Mansel on Demurrer [*1828*] [*A publication*] (DLA)
M & ER ..... Mechanical and Electrical Room (AAG)
M&ES .... Magnetic & Electromagnetic Silencing (SAUS)
M & F .... Male and Female [*Components, as of connecting devices*]
M & F .... Materials and Facilities (MCD)
M & F .... Mother and Father
M&FCS ...... Management and Financial Control System (SAUO)
MANDFHAB... Male and Female Homosexual Association of Great Britain
M & G .... Macnaghten and Gordon's English Chancery Reports [*A publication*] (DLA)
M & G .... Maddock and Geldart's English Chancery Reports [*1815-22*] [*A publication*] (DLA)
M & G .... Manning and Granger's English Common Pleas Reports [*A publication*] (DLA)
M & G .... Mapping and Geodesy [*Army*] (AABC)
M&G .... Mercantile & General Reinsurance Co. Ltd. (SAUO)
M&G .... Mobile & Gulf (SAUO)
M & Gel .... Maddock and Geldart's English Chancery Reports [*1815-22*] [*A publication*] (DLA)
M & GN ..... Midland and Great Northern Joint Line [*Railway*] [*British*] (ROG)
M&GN ...... Midland and Great Northern Joint Railway (SAUO)
M&GNR ..... Midland and Great Northern Railway (SAUO)
M & Gord... Macnaghten and Gordon's English Chancery Reports [*A publication*] (DLA)
M&GWR .... Midland and Great Western Railway (SAUO)
M&H .... Malone & Hyde, Inc. (EFIS)
M&H .... Mason and Hangar (SAUO)
M & H .... Murphy and Hurlstone's English Exchequer Reports [*1836-37*] [*A publication*] (DLA)
M & HDA ... Medical and Hospital Department, Army
M&HDA ..... Medical and Hospital Department, U.S. Army (SAUO)
M&I .... Management and Integration (SAUO)
M & I .... Manpower and Immigration [*Canada*]
M & I .... Marine & Industrial
M & I .... Marshall & Ilsley Bank
M & I .... Minnesota & International Railway
M & I .... Modernization and Improvement (AABC)
M & I .... Modification and Installation (KSC)
M & I .... Moisture and Impurities [*In fats*]
M & I .... Movements and Identification [*Military*] (AFM)
M & I .... Municipal and Industrial [*Users of water*]
M&IE .... Meals and Incidental Expenses (EAGT)
M&IP .... Management and Integration Plan (SAUO)
Man Dir ..... Managing Director (SAUO)
Man Dir ..... Managing Directress (SAUO)
M & IR ...... Manufacturing and Inspection Record (KSC)
M & K .... Mylne and Keen's English Chancery Reports [*A publication*] (DLA)
M and L .... Management and Logistics [*NATO*] (NATG)
mandl .... Mandorla (VRA)
M&L .... Matched and Lost [*Investment term*] (DFIT)
M & LA ..... Manpower and Logistics Analysis
M&LC .... Mission and Launch Control (ACAE)
M&LS .... Manistique & Lake Superior (SAUO)
M&M .... Maintenance Management Committee (SAUO)
M & M ...... Make and Mend
M & M ...... Manchester & Milford Railway [*Wales*]
M & M ...... Martha and the Muffins [*Musical group*]
M & M ...... Materials and Maintenance (NASA)
M & M ...... Merchants and Manufacturers Association (EA)
M&M .... Mess and Maintenance [*Marine Corps*] (MUSM)
M & M ...... Metals and Minerals Research Services [*British*]
M & M ...... Milk and Molasses [*Enema*] [*Medicine*]
M&M .... Mining & Metallurgy Divisions (ACII)
M & M ...... Montagu and MacArthur's English Bankruptcy Reports [*A publication*] (DLA)
M & M ...... Moody and Malkin's English Nisi Prius Reports [*A publication*] (DLA)
M&M .... Morbidity and Mortality [*Medicine*] (DMAA)
M & M'A.... Montagu and MacArthur's English Bankruptcy Reports [*A publication*] (DLA)
M & McA ... Montagu and MacArthur's English Bankruptcy Reports [*A publication*] (DLA)
M & M's .... Mass and Meals [*Refers to nuns who appear only at these activities*]
M & N .... May and November [*Denotes semiannual payments of interest or dividends in these months*] [*Business term*]
M & N .... Medical and Nursing [*Red Cross Disaster Services*]
M & N .... Morning and Night [*Medicine*]
M&N .... Mydriacyl and Neosynephrine [*Medicine*] (MELL)
M & NA ..... Missouri & North Arkansas Railroad [*Nickname: May Never Arrive*]
M & NE ..... Manistee & Northeastern Railroad (IIA)
M&NE .... Manistee and North-Eastern Railway Co. (SAUO)
M & NW .... Minnesota & Northwestern Railroad
M & O .... Machinery and Optics
M & O .... Maintenance and Operation (MCD)
m & o .... Maintenance and Overhaul (AD)
M & O .... Maintenance and Overhaul
M&O .... Management and Operating (AUEG)
M&O .... Management and Operations (ABAC)
m & o .... Management and Organization (AD)
M & O .... Management and Organization
M&O .... Management and Oversight (SAUO)
MANDO ..... Mancando [*Decreasing in Loudness*] [*Music*] (ROG)
M & O .... Manpower and Organization [*Military*]
M & O .... Materials and Others
M & O .... Mobile & Ohio Railroad
M & O .... Muscat and Oran (AD)
M & OB ..... Maintenance and Operations Branch [*BUPERS*]
M & OC ..... Monitor and Operations Control System [*Space Flight Operations Facility, NASA*]
M&P .... Maintenance and Process Engineering (SAUO)
M&P .... Managerial and Professional (DMAA)
M & P .... Maryland & Pennsylvania Railroad Co. (IIA)
M & P .... Material and Process
m & p .... Materials and Processes (AD)
M&P .... Materials and Processing (SAUO)
M&P .... Materials and Producibility (SAUO)
M&P .... Melphenal and Prednisone [*Medicine*] (MELL)
M & P .... Moore and Payne's English Common Pleas Reports [*A publication*] (DLA)
M & PE ..... Materials and Process Engineering (MCD)
M&PL .... Materials and Processes List (ACAE)
M & PP ..... Manitou & Pike's Peak Railway
M & PP ..... Materials and Plant Protection [*Nuclear energy*] (NRCH)
M & P Sh... Maude and Pollock's Law of Merchant Shipping [*A publication*] (DLA)
M&Q .... Mines and Quarries (AD)
M & R .... Maclean and Robinson's Scotch Appeal Cases [*1839*] [*A publication*] (DLA)
m & r .... Maintainability and Reliability (AD)
m & r .... Maintainability and Repairs (AD)
M & R .... Maintenance and Refurbishment (NASA)
M & R .... Maintenance and Repair
M & R .... Manning and Ryland's English King's Bench Reports [*1827-30*] [*A publication*] (DLA)
M&R .... Martini & Rossi
M & R .... Measure and Record
M & R .... Moody and Robinson's English Nisi Prius Reports [*1830-44*] [*A publication*] (DLA)
M & RA ..... Manpower and Reserve Affairs
MANDRA.... Mid-Atlantic Nostalgia Drag Racing Association
M & RDET.. Maintenance and Repair Detachment
M & RE ..... Money and Real Estate [*Newspaper section*] (ADA)
M&RF .... Maintenance and Refurbishing Facility [*Aerospace*] (NAKS)
M & R I & O... Measure and Record Intake and Output [*Fluid measurement*] [*Medicine*] (CPH)
M & RMC... Manning and Ryland's English Magistrates' Cases [*1827-30*] [*A publication*] (DLA)
M&RO .... Maintenance and Refurbishment Operations (SAUS)
MANDRO.... Mechanically-Alterable Nondestructive Read Out [*Computer science*] (IAA)
M & Rob.... Maclean and Robinson's Scotch Appeal Cases [*1839*] [*A publication*] (DLA)

M & Rob.... Moody and Robinson's English Nisi Prius Reports [*A publication*] (DLA)
M & S....... Bureau of Medicine and Surgery [*Navy*]
M&S......... Maintainability and Supportability (ACAE)
M & S....... Maintenance and Supply
MANDS...... Maintenance and Supply
M & S....... Manning and Scott's English Common Bench Reports [*IX*] [*A publication*] (DLA)
M & S....... March and September [*Denotes semiannual payments of interest or dividends in these months*] [*Business term*]
M&S......... Marketing & Sales Division (ACII)
M & S....... Marks & Spencer [*English department store chain*]
M&S......... Marred & Scarred (SAUS)
M & S....... Marshall and Swift Cost Index (DICI)
M & S....... Materials and Services [*NASA*] (KSC)
M & S....... Materials and Structures (SDI)
M&S......... Maternity and Surgical (AD)
M & S....... Maule and Selwyn's English King's Bench Reports [*A publication*] (DLA)
M & S....... McClelland & Stewart [*Canadian publisher*]
M & S....... Media and Status [*Code*] [*DoD*]
M&S......... Medical and Surgical (AD)
M & S....... Medicine and Surgery (AD)
M & S....... Methods and Standards
M & S....... Microculture and Sensitivity [*Laboratory*] (DAVI)
M & S....... Milwaukee & Superior Railroad
M & S....... Model and Series (AAG)
m & s....... Model and Series (AD)
M & S....... Modeling and Simulation
M & S....... Moore and Scott's English Common Pleas Reports [*1831-34*] [*A publication*] (DLA)
m & s....... Mud and Snow (AD)
M & S....... Mud and Snow Tire [*Automotive engineering*]
M & SC..... Missile and Space Council [*Defunct*] (EA)
M & Sc...... Moore and Scott's English Common Pleas Reports [*1831-34*] [*A publication*] (DLA)
M & Scott... Moore and Scott's English Common Pleas Reports [*1831-34*] [*A publication*] (DLA)
MANDSD.... Mean and Standard Deviation
M&SRG..... Messengers and Signalling Research Group [*King's College London*] [*United Kingdom*] (RCD)
M & SS..... Mapping and Survey System (KSC)
M & SSq.... Maintenance and Supply Squadron [*Air Force*]
M & StP.... Milwaukee & St. Paul Railway
M&T......... Main and Trim (COE)
M & T....... Maintenance and Test (AAG)
M&T......... Manufacturers & Traders Trust Company (EFIS)
M&T......... Monitor and Test (ACAE)
M and T..... Movements and Transports (NATG)
M&T......... Muscles and Tendons (MELL)
M & T BANK PAC... Manufacturers and Traders Trust Company PAC [*Buffalo, NY*] (PACS)
M&TC....... Mission and Traffic Control (ACAE)
M & TE...... Measurement and Test Equipment (KSC)
M & TP..... Manufacturing and Testing Process (KSC)
M & U....... Middletown & Unionville Railroad [*Nickname: Miserable and Useless*]
M&V......... Magmatism & Volcanoes (SAUS)
M and V.... Meat-and-Vegetable [*A canned ration*] [*Military*]
M&W........ Marine and War Risks [*Insurance*] (MARI)
M & W...... Meeson and Welsby's English Exchequer Reports [*A publication*] (DLA)
M&W........ Moore & Wright (WDAA)
M&W........ Morecambe & Wise [*Comedians*] (WDAA)
M & WAA... Movers' and Warehousemen's Association of America [*Defunct*]
M & W Abr... Marshall and Wood's Abridgment [*A publication*] (DLA)
M & W Cas... Mining and Water Cases, Annotated [*United States*] [*A publication*] (DLA)
M & WH..... Missile and Warhead Magazines
M & W Law Dic... Mozley and Whiteley's Law Dictionary [*A publication*] (ILCA)
M & X....... Microscope and X-Ray Inspection
M & Y....... Martin and Yerger's Tennessee Reports [*8 Tennessee*] [*1825-28*] [*A publication*] (DLA)
M and Yerger's Rep... Martin and Yerger's Tennessee Reports [*8 Tennessee*] [*1825-28*] [*A publication*] (DLA)
M & YR..... Martin and Yerger's Tennessee Reports [*8 Tennessee*] [*1825-28*] [*A publication*] (DLA)
MANE........ Manet [*NCIC motorcycle make code*]
MAN ED..... Managing Editor (DGA)
Man El Cas... Manning's English Election Cases (Court of Revision) [*A publication*] (DLA)
M Anesth Ed... Master of Anesthesiology Education (PGP)
MANEX...... Management Experten-Nachweis [*Management Experts Data Base*] [*Society for Business Information*] [*Information service or system*] (IID)
Man Exch Pr... Manning's English Exchequer Practice [*A publication*] (DLA)
MANF........ Manifold (KSC)
MANF........ Manufacturer (WGA)
MANF........ May, August, November, and February [*Denotes quarterly payments of interest or dividends in these months*] [*Business term*]
MANFED.... Manufacturers Federation (SAUO)
MANFG...... Manufacturing (ROG)
MANFIST.... Maneuver and Fire Support Team (MCD)
Man For..... Management Forum [*A publication*]
MANFOR.... Manpower Force Packaging [*Military*]
MANFOR.... Manpower Force Packaging System (SAUO)
MANFORCE... Manpower for a Clean Environment [*Water Pollution Control Federation*]
MANFR...... Manufacturer
MANFRD.... Manufactured
MANFRG.... Manufacturing
MANFST.... Manifest
MANG........ Management
MANG........ Mangar Company [*NCIC trailer make code*]
Man G & S... Manning, Granger, and Scott's English Common Bench Reports, Old Series [*I-VIII*] [*A publication*] (DLA)
Man Gaz.... Manitoba Gazette [*A publication*] (DLA)
MANGR...... Manager
Man Gr & S... Manning, Granger, and Scott's English Common Bench Reports, Old Series [*I-VIII*] [*A publication*] (DLA)
MANGRSS... Manageress (ROG)
MANGT...... Management (ROG)
MANH....... Manhattan Associates [*NASDAQ symbol*]
MANH....... Manhattan Associates, Inc. [*NASDAQ symbol*] (NASQ)
MANHA...... Manhattan, KS [*American Association of Railroads railroad junction routing code*]
Manhattan C... Manhattan College (GAGS)
Manhattan Sch Music... Manhattan School of Music (GAGS)
Manhattanville C... Manhattanville College (GAGS)
MANHC...... Madras Army Native Hospital Corps [*British military*] (DMA)
MAnHi....... Andover Historical Society, Andover, MA [*Library symbol*] [*Library of Congress*] (LCLS)
ManhLfe.... Manhattan Life Insurance Co. [*Associated Press*] (SAG)
MA-NHP..... Massachusetts Natural Heritage Program [*Massachusetts State Division of Fisheries and Wildlife*] [*Information service or system*] (IID)
MANI........ Manifold [*Automotive engineering*]
MANI........ Manitoulin Transport [*Common carrier symbol*]
MANI........ Midwest Alliance for Nursing Informatics (SAUO)
MANI........ Minister of Agriculture for Northern Ireland (SAUO)
MANIAC..... Mathematical Analyzer, Numerical Integrator and Computer
MANIAC..... Mechanical and Numerical Integrator and Computer (IEEE)
MANICOM... Manned Information and Communications Facility (SAA)
MANIET..... Manifest Update (SAUO)
MANIF...... Manifest
manif........ Manifesto (VRA)
manifest.... Manifestation [*Medicine*]
MAnimSc.... Master of Animal Science, University of Liverpool [*British*] (DBQ)
Man Int Law... Manning's Commentaries on the Law of Nations [*A publication*] (DLA)
Manip....... All India Reporter, Manipur [*A publication*] (DLA)
manip....... Manipulation [*Medicine*]
Manip....... Manipulus [*A Handful*] [*Pharmacy*]
MANIP....... Manual Input [*Computer science*]
MANIS....... Modified Atlantic Naval Intelligence Summary
MANIT....... Manitoba [*Canadian province*]
MANIT....... Manitowoc, WI [*American Association of Railroads railroad junction routing code*]
Manit........ University of Manitoba (SAUO)
ManitDns.... Manitoba Dragoons (SAUO)
Manitoba... Armour. Queen's Bench and County Court Reports Tempore Wood [*Manitoba*] [*A publication*] (DLA)
Manitoba... Manitoba Law Reports [*Canada*] [*A publication*] (DLA)
Manitoba L (Can)... Manitoba Law Reports [*Canada*] [*A publication*] (DLA)
Manitw...... [*The*] Manitowoc Co., Inc. [*Associated Press*] (SAG)
MANIX....... Machine Aids to Nike-X [*Army*] (AABC)
MANK........ Mankato Mobile Homes [*NCIC trailer make code*]
Mankato St U... Mankato State University (GAGS)
M-ANL........ Argonne National Laboratory (SAUO)
MANL......... M and N Truck Line [*Common carrier symbol*]
MANL......... Manual (IAA)
MANLA...... Malawi National Liberation Army (BUAC)
ManLaw..... Managerial Law (SAFN)
Man Lim.... Mansel on Limitations [*1839*] [*A publication*] (DLA)
MANLOS.... Manportable Non-Line-Of-Sight (SAUS)
Man LR..... Manitoba Law Reports [*Canada*] [*A publication*] (DLA)
Man LS Chron... Manchester Law Students' Chronicle [*A publication*] (DLA)
Man LSJ.... Manchester Law Students' Journal [*A publication*] (DLA)
MANLY...... Manly, IA [*American Association of Railroads railroad junction routing code*]
MANM....... Methylated Albumin-Nitrocelluse Membrane [*Analytical biochemistry*]
MANMAM... Manufacturing Management (PDAA)
MANMAN... Manufacturing Management (MHDI)
MANMED... Manual of the Medical Department [*Navy*]
MANMEDDEPT... Manual of the Medical Department [*Navy*]
MANN....... Manna [*Pharmacy*] (ROG)
Mann......... Manning's Digest of the Nisi Prius Reports [*England*] [*A publication*] (DLA)
Mann......... Manning's English Court of Revision Reports [*A publication*] (DLA)
Mann......... Manning's Reports [*1 Michigan*] [*A publication*] (DLA)
MANN........ Mannlicher Rifle
MANN........ Richard Manning [*NCIC trailer make code*]
ManNac...... N-Acetylmannosamine [*Biochemistry*]
Mann & G (Eng)... Manning and Granger's English Common Pleas Reports [*A publication*] (DLA)
Mann & R... Manning and Ryland's English King's Bench Reports [*1827-30*] [*A publication*] (DLA)
Mann & R... Manning and Ryland's English Magistrates' Cases [*1827-30*] [*A publication*] (DLA)

Mann & R (Eng)... Manning and Ryland's English King's Bench Reports [*1827-30*] [*A publication*] (DLA)
Mann Bills... Manning on Bills and Notes [*A publication*] (DLA)
Mann Com... Manning's Commentaries on the Law of Nations [*A publication*] (DLA)
Mann EC.... Manning's Revision Cases [*1832-35*] [*A publication*] (DLA)
Mann Ex Pr... Manning's English Exchequer Practice [*A publication*] (DLA)
Mann G & S... Manning, Granger, and Scott's English Common Bench Reports [*135-39 English Reprint*] [*1845-56*] [*A publication*] (DLA)
Mann G & S (Eng)... Manning, Granger, and Scott's English Common Bench Reports, Old Series [*I-VIII*] [*A publication*] (DLA)
Manning.... Manning's Reports [*1 Michigan*] [*A publication*] (DLA)
Manning.... Manning's Unreported Cases [*Louisiana*] [*A publication*] (DLA)
Manning LA... Manning's Unreported Cases [*Louisiana*] [*A publication*] (DLA)
Manning's UC... Manning's Unreported Cases [*Louisiana*] [*A publication*] (DLA)
Manning's Unrep Cases... Manning's Unreported Cases [*Louisiana*] [*A publication*] (DLA)
Mann Nat... Manning's Commentaries on the Law of Nations [*A publication*] (DLA)
Mann Unrep Cas... Manning's Unreported Cases [*Louisiana*] [*A publication*] (DLA)
MANO....... Manometer
MANO....... Manor Homes [*NCIC trailer make code*]
MANO....... Mexican-American Neighborhood Association (SAUO)
MANOP...... Manganese Nodule Program [*For sampling on ocean floor*]
MANOP...... Manual of Operations
MANOPA.... Manufacture Normande de Papeterie (EFIS)
MANOR..... Manor [*Commonly used*] (OPSA)
ManorCr.... Manor Care, Inc. [*Associated Press*] (SAG)
MANORS.... Manors [*Commonly used*] (OPSA)
MANOVA.... Multivariate Analysis of Variance [*Statistics*]
MANOVA.... Multiway Analysis of Variance (MCD)
MANP....... Masai Amboseli National Park (SAUO)
MANP....... Mount Apo National Park (SAUO)
MANP....... Mount Arayat National Park (SAUO)
MAnP........ Phillips Academy, Andover, MA [*Library symbol*] [*Library of Congress*] (LCLS)
MANPAD.... Man-Portable Air Defense (AABC)
MANPADS... Man-Portable Air Defense System (MCD)
MANPER.... Manpower/Personnel Module (SAUO)
MANPER-B... Manpower and Personnel Module-Base Level (SAUO)
MANPER-M... Manpower and Personnel Module-Major Command Level (SAUO)
MANPLAWS... Manportable Assault Laser Weapons System (ACAE)
MAN PR..... Mane Primo [*Early in the Morning*] [*Pharmacy*]
MANPRINT... Manpower and Personnel Integration [*Military*] (RDA)
MANPRINT... Manpower, Personnel and Training Integration (SAUO)
Manpwl..... Manpower, Inc. [*Associated Press*] (SAG)
MANPWR... Manpower (KSC)
MANR....... Manager (ROG)
Man R....... Manitoba Reports [*Maritime Law Book Co. Ltd.*] [*Information service or system*] [*A publication*] [*A publication*] (DLA)
MANR....... Ministry of Agriculture and Natural Resources [*Nigeria*] (BUAC)
MANR....... Ministry of Agriculture, Northern Region (SAUO)
Man Ray.... Emmanuel Radnitsky [*American artist, 1890-1976*]
MANREQ.... Manpower Requirements System (SAUO)
Man Rev Stat... Manitoba Revised Statutes [*Canada*] [*A publication*] (DLA)
MANRRDC... Manpower Resources Research and Development Center [*Army*] (RDA)
Man RT Wood... Manitoba Reports Tempore Wood [*Canada*] [*A publication*] (DLA)
MANS....... M and S Transport [*Common carrier symbol*]
Mans........ Mansfield College, Oxford (SAUO)
Mans........ Mansfield's Reports [*49-52 Arkansas*] [*A publication*] (DLA)
MANS....... Mansiones
MANS....... Mansions
Mans........ Manson's English Bankruptcy and Winding-Up Cases [*A publication*] (DLA)
MANS....... Map Analysis System [*Computer science*]
MANS....... Mathematics Applied to novel Situations Test (EDAC)
MANS....... Michigan Association of Non-Public Schools
MANS....... Microcosm Autonomous Navigation System (ADWA)
MANS....... Missile and Nudet Surveillance (SAUS)
MANS....... Mission Analysis for Missile and NUDET Surveillance (SAUO)
MANSA...... Man-Made Soling Association Ltd. [*British*] (BI)
ManSA...... Manufacturing Society of Australia (SAUO)
MANSA...... Marine Aquarium Societies of North America [*Association*] (EA)
MAN/SAFE... Manual/Automatic Separation and Flotation Equipment (DNAB)
MANSAT.... Manned Satellite
Mans Dem.. Mansel on Demurrer [*1828*] [*A publication*] (DLA)
Mansf....... Mansfield College, Oxford (SAUO)
MANSF...... Mansfield, IL [*American Association of Railroads railroad junction routing code*]
Mansf Coll... Mansfield College, Oxford (SAUO)
Mansf Dig... Mansfield's Digest of Statutes [*Arkansas*] [*A publication*] (DLA)
Mansfield U... Mansfield University of Pennsylvania (GAGS)
MANSH...... Manshead [*England*]
MANSL 1... Manslaughter, First Degree [*Conviction term used in state of Oregon*] (MVRD)
MANSL 2... Manslaughter, Second Degree [*Conviction term used in state of Oregon*] (MVRD)
Mans Lim... Mansel on Limitations [*1839*] [*A publication*] (DLA)
Manson..... Manson's English Bankruptcy and Winding-Up Cases [*A publication*] (DLA)
Manson Bankr Cas... Manson's English Bankruptcy and Winding-Up Cases [*A publication*] (DLA)
Mans on C... Mansel on Costs [*A publication*] (DLA)
Manson (Eng)... Manson's English Bankruptcy Cases [*A publication*] (DLA)
Man Stat.... Manitoba Statutes [*Canada*] [*A publication*] (DLA)
MAN SWBD... Manual Switchboard [*Communications term*] (DCT)
MANSWG... Manpower Systems Work Group
MANT........ Manatee Homes [*NCIC trailer make code*]
MANT........ Manitowoc Company, Inc. [*NASDAQ symbol*] (COMM)
M Ant........ Marcus Antoninus [*of Scriptores Historiae Augustae*] [*Classical studies*] (OCD)
MANT........ Master of Arts in New Testament (PGP)
MANT........ Monoamine Neurotransmission/Mitter [*Medicine*] (EDAA)
MANTA...... Middle Atlantic Neutron Therapy Association [*Medicine*] (EDAA)
MANTAPS... Maneuver Arms Tactical Protective System [*Army*] (RDA)
MANTECH... Manufacturing Technology
MANTIS..... Man-in-the-loop Target Interdiction System (SAUS)
MANTIS..... Manpack Tactical Intelligence System
MANTIS..... Manual, Alternative, and Natural Therapy Index System (ADWA)
MANTIS..... Manufacturing Team Information Systems (SAUO)
MANTIS..... Multi-Adaptable Night Tactical Imaging System [*Police and security equipment*]
MANTRA.... Middle Atmosphere Nitrogen Trend Assessment
MANTRAC... Manual Angle Tracking Capability
MANTRAP... Management Training Program [*of Center for Research in Business and Economics, University of Houston*]
MANTRAPERS... Manpower, Training, and Personnel (MCD)
Mantrn...... Manatron, Inc. [*Associated Press*] (SAG)
MANTW..... Manitouwadge, ON [*American Association of Railroads railroad junction routing code*]
Man T Wood... Manitoba Reports Tempore Wood [*Canada*] [*A publication*] (DLA)
MANU....... Manual Estimate [*Electric utility company*]
manu........ Manufacture (DAVI)
MANU....... Manugistics Group [*NASDAQ symbol*] (TTSB)
MANU....... Manugistics Group, Inc. [*NASDAQ symbol*] (SAG)
MANU....... Mozambique African National Union [*Later, FRELIMO*]
manuf....... Manufactured (SHCU)
MANUF...... Manufacturer [*or Manufacturing*] (ROG)
Manuf....... Manufactures (DIAR)
Manuf....... Manufacturing (SAUO)
Manufacturing Mgmt... Manufacturing and Management [*A publication*]
MANUFD.... Manufactured (ROG)
MANUFG.... Manufacturing (ADA)
ManufHm... Manufactured Home Communities, Inc. [*Associated Press*] (SAG)
Manugist.... Manugistics Group, Inc. [*Associated Press*] (SAG)
MANULIFE... Manufacturers Life Insurance Company (EFIS)
Manum Cas... Bloomfield's Manumission (or Negro) Cases [*New Jersey*] [*A publication*] (DLA)
Manum Cases... Bloomfield's Manumission (or Negro) Cases [*New Jersey*] [*A publication*] (DLA)
Man Unr Cases... Manning's Unreported Cases [*Louisiana*] [*A publication*] (DLA)
Man Unrep Cas... Manning's Unreported Cases [*Louisiana*] [*A publication*] (DLA)
Man Unrep Cas (LA)... Manning's Unreported Cases [*Louisiana*] [*A publication*] (DLA)
MANUPACS... Manufacturing Planning and Control System (PDAA)
MANUV...... Maneuvering (KSC)
MANVE...... Manver, PA [*American Association of Railroads railroad junction routing code*]
Manvl....... Manville Corp. [*Associated Press*] (SAG)
Manvlle..... Manville Corp. [*Associated Press*] (SAG)
MANVOS.... Manual Visas for Overseas System [*Australia*]
Manw........ Manwood's Forest Laws [*1592, 1598, 1615*] [*A publication*] (DLA)
MANWEB... Merseyside and North Wales Electricity Board (SAUO)
Manw For Law... Manwood's Forest Laws [*1592, 1598, 1615*] [*A publication*] (DLA)
Manwood... Manwood's Forest Laws [*1592, 1598, 1615*] [*A publication*] (DLA)
MANX....... Energy North Natural Gas [*Private rail car owner code*]
MANX....... Mannion Air Charter, Inc. [*Air carrier designation symbol*]
MANZ........ Manchester Terminal [*Federal Railroad Administration identification code*]
MANZ........ Medical Association of New Zealand (BUAC)
MANZ........ Montreal, Australia and New Zealand Shipping Co. Ltd. (SAUO)
MANZ........ Montreal-Australia New Zealand (SAUO)
MANZ........ Motel Association of New Zealand (SAUO)
MANZCP.... Member, Australian & New Zealand College of Psychiatry (CMD)
MAO......... MAC Aviation SL [*Spain*] [*ICAO designator*] (FAAC)
MAO......... Magnetic Amplifier Output
MAO......... Mailing Address Only [*Military*] (AABC)
MAO......... Maintenance and Operation [*Army*] (AFIT)
MAO......... Major Attack Option [*Military*] (MCD)
MAO......... Manaus [*Brazil*] [*Airport symbol*] (OAG)
MAO......... Manned Apollo Operations [*NASA*] (KSC)
mao.......... Maori [*MARC language code*] [*Library of Congress*] (LCCP)
MAO......... Marion, SC [*Location identifier*] [*FAA*] (FAAL)
MAO......... Mars Aeronomy Orbiter (MCD)
MAO......... Massive Attack Option (MCD)
MAO......... Master of Art of Oratory
MAO......... Master of the Art of Obstetrics
MAO......... Matair Ltd. [*British*] [*ICAO designator*] (FAAC)
MAO......... Material Adjustment Order (MCD)
MAO......... Maximum [*or Minimum*] Acid Output [*Clinical chemistry*]
MAO......... Mechanization of Algebraic Operations (PDAA)
MAO......... Medial Ankle Orthosis [*Orthopedics*] (DAVI)
MAO......... Medical Assistance Only (GFGA)
MAO......... Methylaluminoxane [*Organic chemistry*]
MAO......... Methyl Aluminoxane Cocatalyst
MAO......... Military Assistance Officer [*Army*]

MAO .... Minneapolis Age and Opportunity (Center) [*Medicine*] (EDAA)
MAO .... Monoamine Oxidase [*An enzyme*]
MAO .... Monoamin Oxidase Inhibitors [*An antidepressant*]
MAO .... Movement to Arrest Oppressors (EA)
MAO .... Muhammadan Anglo-Oriental
MAOA .... Meteorological Aspects of Ocean Affairs [*Marine science*] (MSC)
MAOA .... Methaqualone [*Medicine*] (EDAA)
MAOA .... Meyers Aircraft Owners Association (EA)
MAOA .... Mid-America Orthopaedic Association (SAUO)
MAOA .... Monoamine Oxidase A [*An enzyme*]
MAOA .... Panel of Meteorological Aspects of Ocean Affairs [*Marine science*] (OSRA)
MAOB .... Monoamine Oxidase B [*Medicine*] (EDAA)
MAO-B ...... Monoamine Oxidase B [*An enzyme*]
MAODP...... Medic Alert Organ Donor Program (EA)
MAOE........ Manchester Association of Engineers (SAUO)
MAOE........ Master of Adult and Occupational Education (PGP)
MAOF........ Mexican-American Opportunity Foundation (EA)
MA of A..... Motel Association of America (SAUO)
MAOGP...... Middle Atlantic Neutron Therapy Association [*Medicine*] (EDAA)
MAOI .... Monoamine Oxidase Inhibitor [*Biochemistry*]
MAOM....... Master of Aerospace Operations Management (GAGS)
MAOP .... Maximum Allowable Operating Pressure [*In pipelines*]
MAOPS...... Missouri Association of Osteopathic Physicians and Surgeons (EARSL)
MAOS .... Magnetic Amplifier Output Stage
MAOS .... Metal Alumina Dielectric Oxide Semiconductor (CIST)
MAOS .... Metal-Alumina-Oxide Semiconductor [*Computer science*] (IAA)
MAOS .... Metal-Aluminum-Oxide Silicon (MSA)
MAOS .... Minimum Aircraft Operating Strips (SAUO)
MAOS .... Minimum Airfield Operating Surface [*Military*]
MAOSco..... Multiple Application Operating System Consortium [*Formed in 1997*] (GART)
MAOT........ Master of Arts in Occupational Therapy
MAOT........ Master of Arts in Old Testament (PGP)
MAOT........ Maximum Allowable Operating Time (NASA)
MAOT........ Medium Aperture Optical Telescope (PDAA)
MAOT........ Member, Association of Occupational Therapists [*British*]
MAOT........ Member of the Association of Occupational Therapists (SAUO)
MAOT........ Military Assistance Observer Team
MAOT........ Missile Auxiliary Output Tester
MAOT........ Mobile Air Operations Team [*Military*]
MAOTS...... Missile Auxiliary Output Testers (ACAE)
MAOU .... Member of the American Ornithologists' Union
MAOV .... Mid-America Overseas [*Common carrier symbol*]
MAOV .... Mobile Artillery Observation Vehicle (SAUS)
MAP .... Aeronautical Maps and charts (SAUS)
MAP .... Down Syndrome Clinic [*Rainbow Babies and Children's Hospital*] (MHID)
MAP .... Machine Analyzer Package (PDAA)
MAP .... Machinist Apprentice Program (SAUO)
MAP .... Macro Arithmetic Processor [*Computer science*] (MDG)
MAP .... Macroassembly Program [*Computer science*]
MAP .... Madeira Abyssal Plain [*Geology*]
MAP .... Maghreb-Arabe Presse [*Maghreb Arab Press Agency*] [*Morocco*]
MAP .... Magnetic-Acoustic-Pressure (NVT)
MAP .... Main Arithmetic Processor (IAA)
MAP .... Maine Public Service [*AMEX symbol*] (TTSB)
MAP .... Maine Public Service Co. [*AMEX symbol*] (SPSG)
MAP .... Mainly about People [*A publication*]
MAP .... Main Memory, Arithmetic Unit, and Post Processor (ACAE)
MAP .... Maintenance Administration Panel (ACRL)
MAP .... Maintenance Analysis Procedure [*Computer science*]
MAP .... Maintenance Analysis Program [*NASA*] (KSC)
MAP .... Maintenance and Administration Position (SAUO)
MAP .... Maitre en Administration Publique [*Master of Public Administration*]
MAP .... Major Air Pollutant (ODA)
MAP .... Major Point (VLIE)
MAP .... Major Sync Point [*Open Systems Interconnection*] (ODAA)
map.......... Malayo-Polynesian [*MARC language code*] [*Library of Congress*] (LCCP)
MAP .... Malaysian Alliance Party (SAUO)
MAP .... Mamai [*Papua New Guinea*] [*Airport symbol*] (OAG)
MAP .... Management Action Program (ACAE)
MAP .... Management Analysis and Projection (VLIE)
MAP .... Management Analysis [*or Assessment*] Program
MAP .... Management and Planning Committee [*Library of Congress*]
MAP .... Management and Programming (IAA)
MAP .... Management Application Protocol (ACRL)
MAP .... Management Assessment Program (SAUO)
MAP .... Management Assistance for Profits
MAP .... Management Assistance Program (SAUO)
MAP .... Management Association of the Philippines (BUAC)
MAP .... Management of an Accounting Practice (SAUO)
MAP .... Manifold Absolute Pressure
MAP .... Manifold Air Pressure
MAP .... Manpower [*A publication*]
MAP .... Manpower Absorption Plan [*Department of Labor*]
MAP .... Manpower Analysis Paper
MAP .... Manpower Analysis Procedure (VLIE)
MAP .... Manpower Assistance Project [*Department of Labor*]
MAP .... Manufacturers' Assistance Program [*Michigan State Department of Commerce*] [*Lansing, MI*] [*Information service or system*] (IID)
MAP .... Manufacturing Activity Projection
MAP .... Manufacturing Automation Protocol [*Data communications standards*]
MAP .... Map Analysis Package (SAUO)
MAP .... MAP [*Medical Assistance Programs*] International (EA)
MAP .... Maples, MO [*Location identifier*] [*FAA*] (FAAL)
MAP .... Mapping (MSA)
MAP .... Mapping Alliance Program (SAUO)
MAP .... Map section of AIP (SAUS)
MAP .... Marine Advisory Program [*Marine science*] (MSC)
MAP .... Market Area Planner (SAUO)
MAP .... Marketing Action Planner [*National Association of Printers and Lithographers*] [*A publication*]
MAP .... Marketing Assistance Program [*Department of Agriculture*]
MAP .... Mars Atmosphere Probe
MAP .... Master Activity Programming
MAP .... Master Air Pilot
MAP .... Master Attack Plan [*Military*] (DOMA)
MAP .... Master Automation Plan (ACAE)
MAP .... Master of Applied Psychology (PGP)
MAP .... Master of Arts in Planning (PGP)
MAP .... Material Acquisition Process [*or Program*] (MCD)
MAP .... Material Archive Program
MAP .... Materiel Acquisition Plan [*Army*]
MAP .... Mathematical Analysis without Programming [*Computer science*]
MAP .... Maxilla Alveolar Process [*Medicine*] (MELL)
MAP .... Maximal Aerobic Power [*Laboratory*] (DAVI)
MAP .... Maximum A Posteriori [*Statistics*]
MAP .... Maximum Average Pressure
MAP .... Maximum Average Price
MAP .... Mean Airway Pressure [*Medicine*] (DMAA)
MAP .... Mean Aortic Pressure [*Medicine*]
MAP .... Mean Arterial Pressure [*Medicine*]
MAP .... Measurement Analysis Program (VLIE)
MAP .... Measurement Assurance Program [*National Institute of Standards and Technology*]
MAP .... Measure of Academic Progress [*Educational test*]
MAP .... Mechanized Assignment Processing (VLIE)
MAP .... Mecury All Position (IAA)
MAP .... Media Access Project (EA)
MAP .... Media Analysis Project (EA)
MAP .... Media and People [*Information service or system*] (IID)
MAP .... Medical Aid for the Palestinians (BUAC)
MAP .... Medical Aid Post
MAP .... Medical Assistace Program [*Public human service program*] (PHSD)
MAP .... Medical Audit Program [*Computerized system of abstracted medical record information*]
MAP .... Medicare Advocacy Project
MAP .... Mediterranean Action Plan (BUAC)
MAP .... Megaloblastic Anemia of Pregnancy [*Obstetrics*] (MAE)
MAP .... Melanesian Alliance Party (SAUO)
MAP .... Melphalan, Adriamycin, Prednisone [*Antineoplastic drug regimen*]
MAP .... Memory Allocation and Protection
MAP .... Memory Allocation Map (VLIE)
MAP .... Memory Allocation Processor (NITA)
MAP .... Mercapturic Acid Pathway [*Biochemistry*]
MAP .... Mesenterial Arterial Pressure [*Medicine*]
MAP .... Message Acceptance Pulse [*Aerospace communications*]
MAP .... Meta-Aminophenol [*Organic chemistry*]
MAP .... Meta-Aminopyrimethamine [*Biochemistry*]
MAP .... Methionyl Aminopeptidase [*An enzyme*]
MAP .... Methyl Acceptor Protein [*Biochemistry*] (DAVI)
MAP .... Methylacetoxyprogesterone [*Also, MPA*] [*Endocrinology*]
MAP .... Methylacetylene Propadiene [*Organic chemistry*]
MAP .... Methyl(acetylenyl)putrescine [*Biochemistry*]
MAP .... Methyl Alcohol Poisoning [*Medicine*] (MELL)
MAP .... Methyl(amino)propanediol [*Organic chemistry*]
MAP .... Methylaminopurine (MAE)
MAP .... Michigan Anthropometric Processor (LDOE)
MAP .... Microelectronics Application Programme (AIE)
MAP .... Microelectronics Application Project [*British*] (DCTA)
MAP .... Microlithiasis Alveolarum Pulmonum (DB)
MAP .... Microprocessor Application Project [*In manufacturing industry*] [*Department of the Interior*]
MAP .... Microprogrammed Array Processor
MAP .... Microtubule-Associated Protein [*Cytology*]
MAP .... Microwave Anisotropy Probe [*NASA*]
MAP .... Microwave Anistropy Probe
MAP .... Mid-America Partnership [*Emergency Management*] (EMA)
MAP .... Middle Atmosphere Programme [*International Council of Scientific Unions*]
MAP .... Migrant Action Program (OICC)
MAP .... Milestone Analysis Procedure
MAP .... Military Airport Plan [*FAA*] (TAG)
MAP .... Military Assistance Program [*DoD*]
MAP .... Military Assistant Program (SAUO)
MAP .... Military Association of Podiatrists [*Later, FSPMA*] (EA)
MAP .... Military Audit Project
MAP .... Military Awards Profile [*Information service or system*] (IID)
MAP .... Millennium Access Plus
MAP .... Miller Assessment for Preschoolers
MAP .... Million Annual Passengers (SAUO)
MAP .... MILSTAR Advanced Processor (SAUS)
MAP .... Minimal Audible Pressure (DIPS)
MAP .... Minimum Acceptable Performance [*Telecommunications*] (TEL)

MAP .... Minimum Annual Premium (MHDW)
MAP .... Minimum Association Price (WDAA)
MAP .... Minimum Attack Parameter [*Military*]
MAP .... Minimum Audible Pressure
MAP .... Ministry of Aircraft Production [*British*]
MAP .... Ministry of Aviation Technology (SAUO)
MAP .... Minorities Advancement Plan
MAP .... Missed Approach Point [*Aviation*] (AFM)
MAP .... Missed Approach Procedure [*Aviation*]
MAP .... Missile and Package Tester
MAP .... Missile Application Propulsion
MAP .... Missile Assignment Program (SAA)
MAP .... Mission Activity Plan (ACAE)
MAP .... Mission Application Program (NASA)
MAP .... Mission Area Plans (ACAE)
MAP .... Mission Automation Plan (SAUO)
MAP .... Missouri Assessment Program
MAP .... Mitigation Action Plans (COE)
MAP .... Mitogen-Activated Protein [*Biochemistry*]
MAP .... Mixed Aniline Point
MAP .... Mobile Access Part (CGWS)
MAP .... Model Accreditation Plan (AUEG)
MAP .... Model and Program [*Computer science*]
MAP .... Modeling and Analysis Package [*Computer science*] (HODG)
MAP .... Modern Aids to Planning (SAUO)
MAP .... Modification Application Plan [*Army*]
MAP .... Modified American Plan [*Travel*]
MAP .... Modified Atmosphere Packaging (SAUS)
MAP .... Modified Atmospheric Packaging [*Food industry*]
MAP .... Modular Acoustic Panel
MAP .... Modular Analysis Processor [*Applied Data Research, Inc.*]
MAP .... Modular Application Program (VLIE)
MAP .... Modular Application System [*Computer science*]
MAP .... Modular Array Processor; Hughes Aircraft Co. (SAUO)
MAP .... Modular Assembly Prosthesis [*Medicine*]
MAP .... Monitoring Attitudes of the Public [*ACLI*]
MAP .... Monitoring the AIDS Pandemic (SAUO)
MAP .... Monoammonium Phosphate [*Inorganic chemistry*]
MAP .... Monophasic Action Potential [*Electrophysiology*] (AAMN)
MAP .... Mood and Anxiety Disorders Program [*National Institute of Mental Health*] (RCD)
MAP .... Mothers of AIDS [*Acquired Immune Deficiency Syndrome*] Patients (EA)
MAP .... Mouse Antibody Production [*Test for virus*]
MAP .... Movement of the Assemblies of People [*Grenada*]
MAP .... Multi-Access Pointer (PCM)
MAP .... Multibus Accounting Package (PDAA)
MAP .... Multichannel Astrometric Photometer [*Astronomy*]
MAP .... Multicoverage Account Program [*Insurance*]
MAP .... Multicultural Australia Papers [*A publication*]
MAP .... Multifunction Adaptive Processor (NITA)
MAP .... Multiple Address Processing
MAP .... Multiple Aim Point [*ICBM*]
MAP .... Multiple Allocation Procedure [*PERT*]
MAP .... Multiple Antigen Peptide [*Medicine*] (MELL)
MAP .... Multiple Array Processor
MAP .... Municipal Airport (MCD)
MAP .... Muscle Action Potential
MAP .... Museum Assessment Program [*National Foundation on the Arts and the Humanities*]
MAP .... Musical Aptitude Profile
MAP .... Mutamycin, Adriamycin, Platinol [*Antineoplastic drug*] (CDI)
MAP .... Mutual African Press Agency
MAP .... Mutual Assistance Pact
MAP .... Mutual Assistance Plan (NATG)
MAP .... Mutual Assistance Program
MAP .... National Oceanic and Atmospheric Administration [*ICAO designator*] (FAAC)
MAP3S ...... Multistate Atmospheric Power Production Pollution Study [*Department of Energy*]
MAP3S/PCN... Multistate Atmospheric Power Production Pollution Study/ Precipitation Chemistry Network (SAUO)
MAP27 ...... Mobile Access Protocol (SAUS)
MAPA........ Malayan Agricultural Producers Association (SAUO)
MAPA........ Malaysian Airlines Pilots Association (SAUO)
MAPA........ Master of Arts in Public Administration (GAGS)
MAPA........ Master of Arts in Public Affairs (GAGS)
MAPA........ Materials and Product Assurance (TIMI)
MAPA........ Mexican-American Political Association
MAPA........ Mine Action Programme for Afghanistan [*United Nations*]
MAPA........ Minnesota Academy of Physician Assistants (EARSL)
MAPA........ Mooney Aircraft Pilots Association (EA)
MAPA........ Multi Addictions Processing Agency (MHID)
MAPA........ Muscle Adenosine Phosphoric Acid [*Biochemistry*] (DB)
MAPAC ...... Marine Pollution Advisory Committee (SAUO)
MAPAC ...... Military Assistance Program Address Code (ACAE)
MAPAD ...... Military Assistance Program Address Directory
MAPAF ...... Military Assistance Program Address File
MAPAG ...... Military Assistance Program Advisory Group
MAPAG ...... Multi-Association Policy Advisory Group [*An association*]
MAPAI .... Mifleget Po'alei Eretz-Yisrael (BJA)
MAPAM ..... Mifleget Po'alim Me'uhedet (BJA)
MAPAM ..... United Workers Party (Israel) [*Political party*] (PSAP)
MAPAR...... Materials and Processes Acceptance Requirement
MAPAS ...... Master of Arts in Public Administration in Spanish (PGP)
MAPASE..... Mobile Application Part-Application Service Elements (SAUS)
MAPBIN..... Mauritian Action for Promotion of Breast-Feeding and Infant Nutrition (BUAC)
MAPC........ Manpower Model for Control Agencies (SAUO)
MAPC........ Master of Arts in Pastoral Counseling (PGP)
MAPC........ Maximum Allowable Pevailing Charge [*Medicine*]
MAPC........ Migrating Action Potential Complex [*Electrophysiology*]
MAPC........ Minnesota Association of Private Colleges (SAUO)
MAPCC ...... Master of Arts in Pastoral Care and Counseling (PGP)
MAPCC ...... Military Assistance Program Country Code (AFM)
MAPCHE .... Mobile Automatic Programmed Checkout Equipment
MAP/CIO .... Military Assistance Program/Common Item Order
MAPCO...... Malaysian Association of Private Colleges
MAPCO...... Map Code (SAUS)
MAPCO...... MAPCO, Inc. [*Associated Press*] (SAG)
MAPCO...... Mid-American Pipeline Co.
MAPCON .... Microprocessor Applications Consultancy (NITA)
MAPD .... Master Part Dimensioned (MCD)
MAPD .... Maximum Allowable Percent Defective (PDAA)
MAPDA...... Mid-America Periodical Distributors Association
MAPDFA .... Media-Advertising Partnership for a Drug-Free America [*Later, DFA*] (EA)
MAPDU...... Management Application Protocol Data Unit [*Telecommunications*] (OSI)
MAPE........ Master of Arts in Physical Education (GAGS)
MAPE........ Master of Arts in Political Economy (PGP)
MAPE........ Maximum Absolute Percentage Error [*Statistics*]
MAPE........ Mean Absolute Percentage Error [*Statistics*]
MAPE........ Microcomputers and Primary Education
MAPES ...... Management of Personnel Records (SAUO)
MAPESS .... Ministry of Public Administration, Employment and Social Security (SAUO)
MAP estimate... Maximum a Posteriori Estimate
MAPETT..... Military Assistance Program Evaluation Team, Thailand (CINC)
MAPEX ...... Map Exercise [*Military*] (INF)
MAPEX ...... Mid-America Payment Exchange
MAPEX ...... Military Articles Pacific Excesses (AFIT)
MAPF........ Microatomized Protein Food (MAE)
MAPF........ Mobile Aerial Port Flight [*Air Force*]
MAPG .... Maximum Available Power Gain (MSA)
MAPG .... Monograph Advisory Planning Group (ACAE)
MAP-GA..... Military Assistance Program - Grant Aid
MAPGEN .... Map Generator (MHDI)
MAPGR...... Maple Grove, OH [*American Association of Railroads railroad junction routing code*]
MAPHI....... Member of the Association of Public Health Inspectors (SAUO)
MAPHILINDO... Malaysia, Philippines, Indonesia (SAUO)
MAPI .... Machinery and Allied Products Institute (MHDI)
MAPI .... Mail Application Programming Interface [*Computer science*] (PCM)
MAPI .... Mail Applications Program Interface [*Microsoft Corp.*]
MAPI .... Manufacturers Alliance (NTPA)
MAPI .... Manufacturers Alliance for Productivity and Innovation (EA)
MAPI .... Messaging API [*Application Programming Interface*] [*Computer science*]
MAPI .... Messaging Application Interface [*Communications*]
MAPI .... Messaging Application Programming Interface [*Computer science*] (NETL)
MAPI .... Microbial Alkaline Protease Inhibitor (DB)
MAPI .... Millon Adolescent Personality Inventory [*Personality development test*] [*Psychology*]
MAPI .... Mitsubishi Atomic Power Industries (IAA)
MAPICS ..... Manufacturing, Accounting and Product Information Central System (NITA)
MAPICS ..... Manufacturing, Accounting, and Production Information Control System [*IBM Corp.*]
MAPICS/XA... Manufacturing and Accounting Production Information Control System/Extended Advantage [*Computer science*] (HODG)
MAPID....... Machine-Aided Program for Preparation of Instruction Data
MapInfo ..... Mapinfo Corp. [*Associated Press*] (SAG)
MAPIS....... Map Products Information System (SAUO)
MAPK........ Mitogen Activated Protein Kinase [*An enzyme*]
MaPKBS .... Map Projection Knowledge-based System (SAUO)
MAPL........ Manufacturing Assembly Parts List
MAPL........ Maple Leaf [*NCIC trailer make code*]
MAPL........ Master Allowance Parts List [*Military*] (CAAL)
MAPL........ Military Acquisition Position List (RDA)
MAPLA ...... Military Assistance Program Logistics Agency [*Merged with Defense Supply Agency*]
MAPLE ...... Marketing and Product Line Evaluation (PDAA)
MAPLE ...... Minor Atomic Prolonged Life Equipment (PDAA)
Maple Flag... Exercise held in Canada (SAUS)
Maple Tech Newsl... Maple Technical Newsletter (SAUO)
MAPLHGN... Maximum Average Planar Linear Heat-Generator [*Nuclear energy*] (IAA)
MAPLHGR... Maximum Average Planar Linear Heat-Generation Rate [*Nuclear energy*] (NRCH)
MAPM....... Master of Arts in Pastoral Ministry (PGP)
MAPM....... Master of Arts in Pastoral Music (PGP)
M Ap Ma.... Master of Applied Mathematics (PGP)
MAP Min.... Master of Arts in Pastoral Ministry (PGP)
MAPMIS .... Manpower and Personnel Management Information System [*Navy*]

MAPMISMAN... Manpower and Personnel Management Information System Manual [*Navy*] (DNAB)
MAPMOPP... Marine Pollution [*or Petroleum*] Monitoring Pilot Project [*Marine science*] (MSC)
MAPNY...... Maritime Association of the Port of New York [*Later, MAPONY/NJ*] (EA)
MAPOLE.... Magnetic Dipole Spark Transmitter (NASA)
MAPOM..... Military Assistance Program Owned Materiel (AFM)
MAP/One.... Manufacturing Automation Protocol/One [*Local area network*] [*Industrial Networking, Inc.*]
MAPONY.... Maritime Association of the Port of New York
MAPONY/NJ... Maritime Association of the Port of New York/New Jersey (EA)
MAPORD.... Methodology Approach to Planning and Programming Air Force Operational Requirements, Research and Development (IEEE)
MAP/OSP... Military Assistance Program Offshore Procurement (DNAB)
MAPP........ Major Accident Prevention Policy (HEAS)
MAPP........ Manpower and Personnel Plan [*Army*] (AABC)
MAPP........ Manpower and Production Projections [*LIMRA*]
MAPP........ Masking Parameter Printout [*Computer science*]
MAPP........ MasterCard Automated Point-of-Sale Program
MAPP........ Master of Arts in Public Policy (GAGS)
MAPP........ Mathematical Analysis of a Perception and Preference
MAPP........ Methyl Acetyl Propadrine and Propane (MCD)
MAPP........ Mid-Continent Area Power Pool [*Electric power*]
MAPP........ Midwest AIDS Prevention Project (EARSL)
MAPP........ Mission Analysis and Performance Program
MAPP........ Modern Aids to Planning Program [*Military*] (GFGA)
MApp........ Musical Appreciation [*Record label*]
MAppEpidem... Master of Applied Epidemiology
MAPPER.... Maintaining, Preparing, and Processing Executive Reports [*Computer science*] (CDE)
MAPPER.... Maintaining, Preparing and Producing Executive Reports (NITA)
MAPPEX.... Magazine and Periodical Publishers Exhibition (NITA)
MAPPLE..... Macro-Associative Processor Programming Language [*Computer science*] (PDAA)
MAppLing... Master of Applied Linguistics
MApplLit.... Master of Applied Literature (GAGS)
MApplM.... Master of Applied Mathematics (GAGS)
M Appl Stat... Master of Applied Statistics (PGP)
MAppPsych... Master of Applied Psychology
MAPPS...... Legislative Council for Photogrammetry (SAUO)
MAPPS...... Management Association of Private Photogrammetric Surveyors (EA)
MAppSc..... Master of Applied Science
MAppSc-BltEnvir... Master of Applied Science - Built Environment
MAppSci.... Master of Applied Science
MAppSc-MedPhys... Master of Applied Science - Medical Physics
MAppSc(SocEcol)... Master of Applied Science in Social Ecology
MAPPS PAC... Management Association for Private Photogrammetric Surveyors PAC [*Reston, VA*] (PACS)
MAPR....... Arm Multiple Antenna Profiler (SAUS)
MAPR....... Manufacturing Aids Program Requirements (AAG)
MAPR....... Miniature Autonomous Plume Recorder [*Oceanography*]
MAPR....... Miniaturization and Automation of Personnel Record (SAUO)
MAPR....... Multiple Antenna Profiler Radar (ARMP)
MAPRAT.... Maximum Power Ratio (IEEE)
MAPRC..... Mediterranean Allied Photographic Reconnaissance Command
MAPRES.... Mini Air Passenger Reservation System
MAPRIAL... Mezhdunarodnaja Assotsiatsija Professorov Russkogo Jazyka i Literatury [*International Association of Teachers of Russian Language and Literature*] (EAIO)
MAPROS.... Maintain Production Schedules
MAPRP...... Mesoscale Atmospheric Processes Research Program [*National Oceanic and Atmospheric Administration*]
MAPRS...... Master of Arts in Pacific Rim Studies (GAGS)
MAPS........ Machine Automated Parts System (MCD)
MAPS........ Mail Abuse Prevention System
MAPS........ Maintenance Analysis and Procedures System [*Computer science*]
MAPS........ Major Assembly Performance System (MCD)
MAPS........ Make-a-Picture Story [*Psychological testing*]
MAPS........ Management Accounting and Payroll System (NITA)
MAPS........ Management Accounting and Performance System
MAPS........ Management Analysis and Planning System
MAPS........ Management and Planning System (SAUO)
MAPS........ Managerial Administrative Problem Solving (ACAE)
MAPS........ Manifold Air Pressure Sensor [*Automotive engineering*]
MAPS........ Manpower Analysis and Planning Society (EA)
MAPS........ Manpower and Personnel System (SAUO)
MAPS........ Manpower and Production Survey [*LIMRA*]
MAPS........ Manpower Area Planning System [*Under CAMPS*]
MAPS........ Manual of Administrative Procedures and Standards (SAUO)
MAPS........ Manual of ADP Policies and Procedures (SAUO)
MAPS........ Manufacturing and Production System (CIST)
MAPS........ Map Analysis Package System (SAUO)
MAPS........ Mapinfo Corp. [*NASDAQ symbol*] (SAG)
MAPS........ Map Plotting System (SAUS)
MAPS........ Maritime Asset Planning System (SAUS)
MAPS........ Market-Auction Preferred Stock
MAPS........ Marketing, Advertising, and Promotions Solutions Exhibition [*British*] (ITD)
MAPS........ Master Activation Phasing Schedule (IAA)
MAPS........ Master Antiretroviral Protocol Strategy [*Medicine*] (HVTR)
MAPS........ Master of Arts in Pastoral Studies (PGP)
MA Ps....... Master of Arts in Psychology (PGP)
MAPS........ Master of Arts in Public Service
MAPS........ McGill Action Planning System
MAPS........ Measurement of Air Pollution from Satellites
MAPS........ Measurement of Atmospheric Pollutants from Space (ACAE)
MAPS........ Measurement of Atmospheric Pollution from Satellites (EOSA)
MAPS........ Measuring Air Pollution from Space [*Marine science*] (OSRA)
MAPS........ Memory-Archives-Programmes-TV (SAUO)
MAPS........ Mesoscale Analysis and Prediction System [*Marine science*] (OSRA)
MAPS........ Mesoscale Atmospheric Prediction System (SAUO)
MAPS........ Meteorological and Aeronautical Presentation System (CTAS)
MAPS........ Meteorological Applied Problem Solving
MAPS........ Methyl(deazaisoalloxazine)propanesulfonic Acid [*Organic chemistry*]
MAPS........ Metropolitan Air Post Society (EA)
MAPS........ Microprogramable Arithmetic Processor System (PDAA)
MAPS........ Microsoft Authorized Premier Support (GART)
MAPS........ MidAmerica Automated Payments Systems [*Banking*] (TBD)
MAPS........ Middle Atlantic Planetarium Society (EA)
MAPS........ Migratory Animal Pathological Survey (PDAA)
MAPS........ Military Academy Preparatory School (SAUO)
MAPS........ Military Airlift Command Automated Planning System (SAUO)
MAPS........ Military Applications of Photovoltaic Systems
MAPS........ Military Aviation Preservation Society (EA)
MAPS........ Miller Assessment for Preschoolers (DIPS)
MAPS........ Million Adds per Second
MAPS........ Millions of Actions per Second (SAUS)
MAPS........ Miniature Air Pilot System
MAPS........ Minnesota Analysis and Planning System [*University of Minnesota*] [*Research center*] (RCD)
MAPS........ Missile Application Propulsion Study
MAPS........ Mission Analysis and Planning System (MCD)
MAPS........ Mississippi Association of Professional Surveyors (SAUO)
MAPS........ Mobile Aerial Port Squadron [*Air Force*]
MAPS........ Mobile Applicaitons Pilot Scheme (EURO)
MAPS........ Mobility Analysis and Planning System (SAUO)
MAPS........ Mobility Analysis Planning System (MCD)
MAPS........ Mobilization Asset Planning System [*Army*]
MAPS........ Modern Accounts Payable System (MHDW)
MAPS........ Modern American Poetry Site
MAPS........ Modular Acoustic Processing System (MCD)
MAPS........ Modular Automated Parking System [*Developed by Robotic Parking*] (IDAI)
MAPS........ Modular Azimuth Positioning System (SAUS)
MAPS........ Modular Azimuth Position System [*Army*] (RDA)
MAPS........ Monetary and Payments System [*Committee*] [*American Bankers Association*]
MAPS........ Monitoring of Air Pollution by Satellites (KSC)
MAPS........ Monoclonal Antibody Purification System
MAPS........ Monopropellant Accessory Power Supply [*Aerospace*] (AAG)
MAPS........ Muhammad Ali Professional Sports [*Commercial firm*]
MAPS........ Multicolor Automatic Projection System (IEEE)
MAPS........ Multidimensional Affect and Pain Survey [*Medicine*] (DMAA)
MAPS........ Multidisciplinary Association for Psychedelic Studies (EA)
MAPS........ Multi-jurisdictional Automated Pre-clearance System
MAPS........ Multiple Address Processing System
MAPS........ Multiple Agency Processing System
MAPS........ Multiple Aim-Point System
MAPS........ Multiple Application Phototypesetting System (DGA)
MAPS........ Multiple Application Pro-Fan Studies (ACAE)
MAPS........ Multiple Assessment Programs and Services
MAPS........ Multiple Automated Printing Systems (MCD)
MAPS........ Multisatellite Attitude Program System [*NASA*]
MAPS........ Multispectral Active Passive Scanner (ACAE)
MAPS........ Multistate Atmospheric Power Production Pollution Study (EEVL)
MAPS........ Multitarget Automatic Plotting System
MAPS........ Multivariate Analysis and Prediction of Schedules
MAPS........ Multivariate Analysis, Participation, and Structure
MAPS........ Region 2 Environmental Map Catalog System (SAUS)
MAPSAC.... Machine-Aided Planning, Scheduling, and Control
MAPSAD.... Military Assistance Property Sales and Disposal (AFM)
MAPS/ALPS... Multiple Aim Point System / Alternate Launch Point System (PDAA)
MAP/SAMSR... Joint Army-Air Force Master Plan for the Satisfaction of Army Meteorological Support Requirements (MCD)
MAPSAS.... Member of APSAS [*Association of Public Service Administrative Staff*] [*British*]
MApSc...... Master of Applied Science (GAGS)
MAPSE...... Minimal APSE [*Ada Program Support Environment*] [*Computer science*]
MAPSE...... Minimum Implementation ADA Programming Support Environment (NITA)
MAPSEP.... Mission Analysis Program for Solar Electric Propulsion [*Computer science*] [*NASA*]
MAPSIM.... Mesoscale Air Pollution Simulation Model [*Environmental Protection Agency*] (GFGA)
MAPSP...... Map Supply Point (SAUS)
MAPSq...... Mobile Aerial Port Squadron [*Air Force*]
M Ap Stat... Master of Applied Statistics (PGP)
MAPsych.... Master of Arts in Psychology (GAGS)
MAPT........ Military Assistance Program Training (AFM)
MAPT........ Military Assistance Program Transfer (AFM)
MAPT........ Missed Approach Point [*Aviation*] (FAAC)
MAPT........ More Advanced Petrol Tractors [*Germany*]
MAPT........ Mothers Are People Too [*Defunct*] (EA)
MAPTA...... Metropolitan Association of Professional Travel Agents (TRID)
MAPTAC.... Methacrylamidopropyltrimethylammonium Chloride [*Organic chemistry*]

MAPTEL..... Maplin Telecommunications (NITA)
MAPTIP..... Marine Aerosol Properties & Thermal Imager Performance (SAUS)
MAPTIS..... Manpower Personnel and Training Information System [*Navy*]
MAPTIS..... Materials and Processes Technical Information Services (SAUO)
MAP-TOE... Management Practices in TOE Units [*Military*] (GFGA)
MAP/TOP... Manufacturing Automation Protocol / Technical Office Protocol (BTTJ)
MAPTOP.... Manufacturing Automation Protocol/Technical Office Protocol (SAUS)
MAP/TOP... MAP Technical Office Protocol (SAUO)
MAP-TV..... Methods of Assessing the Radiological Impact of Accidents (SAUO)
MAPU....... Memory Allocation and Protection Unit (MSA)
MAPU....... Movimiento de Accion Popular Unida [*Unified Popular Action Movement*] [*Chile*] [*Political party*] (PD)
MAPU....... Multiple Address Processing Unit [*Military*] (AABC)
MAPU....... Puchov Leasing [*Intermodal shipping container symbol*] (TVRC)
MAPUC...... Member of the Association for Promoting the Unity of Christendom [*British*]
MAPUC...... Modified Area Production Urgency Committee [*World War II*]
MAPVL...... Maplesville, AL [*American Association of Railroads railroad junction routing code*]
MAPW....... Master of Arts in Professional Writing (PGP)
MAPW....... Medical Association for the Prevention of War [*British*] (DBA)
MAPX........ MAPICS [*NASDAQ symbol*]
MAPX........ MAPICS, Inc. [*NASDAQ symbol*] (NASQ)
MAQ......... MAC Aviation, S.L. [*Spain*] [*FAA designator*] (FAAC)
MAQ......... Macquarie Island (SAUO)
maq......... Maquette (VRA)
M Aq........ Master of Aquaculture (PGP)
MAq......... Master of Aquacultures (GAGS)
MAQ......... Maximizing Access and Quality (SAUO)
MAQ......... Maximum Acceptance Quantity
MAQ......... Measures for Air Quality [*Program*] [*National Institute of Standards and Technology*]
MAQ......... Monetary Allowance in Lieu of Quarters
MAQ......... Monmouthshire Associated Quarries (SAUO)
MAQ......... Sena Madureira [*Brazil*] [*Airport symbol*] (AD)
MAQI........ Marque, Incorporated [*NCIC truck make code*]
MAQ Program... Measures for Air Quality Program (SAUO)
MAR......... Macroaddress Register
MAR......... Magnetic Amplifier Relay
MAR......... Main Admitting Room (STED)
MAR......... Maine Association of Retirees (EARSL)
MAR......... Maintainability Action Request (MCD)
MAR......... Maintenance Action Request
MAR......... Maintenance Analysis Report (MCD)
MAR......... Maintenance and Refurbishment (MCD)
MAR......... Maintenance and Repair
MAR......... Major Acquisition Review (CTAS)
MAR......... Major Aircraft Review [*Navy*]
MAR......... Major Area of Responsibility
MAR......... Major Assembly Release [*Military*] (AABC)
MAR......... Malfunction Array RADAR
MAR......... Managed Approach Reservoir [*FAA*] (TAG)
MAR......... Management Analysis Report [*DoD*] (MCD)
MAR......... Management and Administration Regulations (HEAS)
MAR......... Management Assessment Report (MCD)
MAR......... Management Assessment Review (MCD)
MAR......... Management Assistance Review (SAUO)
MAR......... Management Attainment Report [*USDA Forest Service*] (ALAC)
MAR......... Manistee & Repton R. R. [*AAR code*]
MAR......... Manufacturing Action Request (MCD)
MAR......... Manufacturing Assembly Report (IAA)
MAR......... Maracaibo [*Venezuela*] [*Airport symbol*] (OAG)
MAR......... Maranello [*NCIC car model code*]
MAR......... Marasmus (STED)
mar......... Marathi [*MARC language code*] [*Library of Congress*] (LCCP)
MAR......... Marcade Group, Inc. [*NYSE symbol*] (COMM)
MAR......... March (AFM)
Mar......... March (BEE)
MAR......... March Helicopters Ltd. [*British*] [*ICAO designator*] (FAAC)
Mar......... March's English King's Bench Reports [*1639-42*] [*A publication*] (DLA)
MAR......... Marcia [*NCIC car model code*]
MAR......... Maremont Corporation (SAUO)
MAR......... Margin (DAVI)
mar......... Margin (STED)
MAR......... Mar-Gold Resources [*Vancouver Stock Exchange symbol*]
MAR......... Marian Minerals [*Vancouver Stock Exchange symbol*]
mar......... Marimba (WDAA)
MAR......... Marimba [*Music*]
MAR......... Marina (automobile) [*NCIC car model code*]
Mar......... Marine (DIAR)
MAR......... Marine (MSA)
Mar......... Marion Laboratories, Inc.
mar......... Maritime (SHCU)
MAR......... Maritime
MAR......... Maritime Administration Report [*Department of Commerce*]
MAR......... Maritime Central Airways
Mar......... Marius [*of Plutarch*] [*Classical studies*] (OCD)
mar......... Marker [*Chromosome*] (STED)
MAR......... Market
MAR......... Marlin [*NCIC car model code*]
mar......... Maroon [*Philately*]
MAR......... Marquette [*Diocesan abbreviation*] [*Michigan*] (TOCD)
MAR......... Marquis [*NCIC car model code*]
MAR......... Married
MAR......... Marriott International [*NYSE symbol*] (SPSG)
MAR......... Marrow (STED)
MAR......... Marseilles [*France*] [*Seismograph station code, US Geological Survey*] [*Closed*] (SEIS)
MAR......... Marshal (ROG)
Mar......... Marshall and Sevestre's Appeals [*1862-64*] [*Bengal, India*] [*A publication*] (DLA)
MAR......... Marshall Field Site (SAUO)
Mar......... Marshall's Circuit Court Reports [*United States*] [*A publication*] (DLA)
Mar......... Marshall's Reports [*Kentucky*] [*A publication*] (DLA)
Mar......... Marshall's Reports [*Ceylon*] [*A publication*] (DLA)
Mar......... Marshall's Reports [*Bengal*] [*A publication*] (DLA)
MAR......... Martial [*Roman poet of the first century AD*] (ROG)
Mar......... Martin's Louisiana Reports [*A publication*] (DLA)
Mar......... Martin's North Carolina Reports [*1 North Carolina*] [*A publication*] (DLA)
Mar......... Marvel's Reports [*Delaware*] [*A publication*] (DLA)
Mar......... Mary (Queen of England) (DLA)
MAR......... Mass Accumulation Rate [*Geology*]
MAR......... Massachusetts College of Art, Boston, MA [*OCLC symbol*] (OCLC)
M-Ar........ Massachusetts Secretary of State, Archives Division, Boston, MA [*Library symbol*] [*Library of Congress*] (LCLS)
MAR......... Master Angular Reference (IAA)
M Ar........ Master of Architecture
MAR......... Master of Arts in Religion
MAR......... Master of Arts in Research (GAGS)
MA(R)....... Master of Arts (Research) (PGP)
MAR......... Material Availability Report [*NASA*] (KSC)
MAR......... Material Availability Request
MAR......... Matrix Attachment Region [*Genetics*]
MAR......... Maximal Aggregation Ratio (STED)
MAR......... Medication Administration Record [*Medicine*]
MAR......... Memory-Address Register [*Computer science*]
MAR......... Mercury Arc Rectifier (IAA)
MAR......... Michigan Association of Realtors (EARSL)
MAR......... Microanalytical Reagent
MAR......... Microprogram Address Register
MAR......... Mid-Air Retrieval (MCD)
MAR......... Mid-Atlantic Ridge [*of sea floor*]
MAR......... Middeck Accommodations Rack (SAUS)
MAR......... Minimal Angle Resolution
MAR......... Minimally Attended RADAR (MCD)
MAR......... Minimum Acceptable Rate of Return (MHDW)
MAR......... Minimum Acceptable Reliability
MAR......... Minimum Angle of Resolution (MCD)
MAR......... Miscellaneous Apparatus Rack (IAA)
MAR......... Missing at Random (IDAI)
MAR......... Mission Analysis Report (SAUO)
MAR......... Mission Analysis Representative
MAR......... Mississippi-Atchafalaya River [*System*] (USDC)
MAR......... Mixed Antiglobulin Reaction (STED)
MAR......... Modernization and Associated Restructing (SAUO)
MAR......... Monoclonal Antibody Resistant [*Immunochemistry*]
MAR......... Monoclonal Antibody to Rat (DB)
MAR......... Montana Administrative Register [*A publication*] (AAGC)
MAR......... Montana Association of Realtors (EARSL)
MAR......... Morocco [*ANSI three-letter standard code*] (CNC)
MAR......... Movimento di Azione Rivoluzionaria [*Revolutionary Action Movement*] [*Italian*] (PD)
MAR......... Movimiento de Accion Revolucionaria [*Revolutionary Action Movement*] [*Mexico*] (PD)
MAR......... Multi-Adversity Resistance [*to root rot*] [*Plant pathology*]
MAR......... Multifunction Array RADAR
MAR......... Multiple Aberration Region [*Genetics*]
MAR......... Multiple Access Receiver (ACAE)
MAR......... Multiple Access Relay
MAR......... Multiple Access Return (SSD)
MAR......... Multiple Array RADAR (IAA)
MAR......... Municipal Association Record [*A publication*]
MAR......... Muscarinic Acetylcholine Receptor [*Biochemistry*]
MaR......... Myth and Ritual. Essays on the Myth and Ritual of the Hebrews in Relation to theCulture Pattern of the Ancient East [*A publication*] (BJA)
MAR......... Mythology of All Races [*A publication*]
MAr......... Robbins Public Library, Arlington, MA [*Library symbol*] [*Library of Congress*] (LCLS)
MAR......... Superior Court Mandatory Arbitration Rules (SAUO)
MAR......... Tacoma, WA [*Location identifier*] [*FAA*] (FAAL)
MARA....... Majority Rule Association (EA)
MARA....... Margaret Anne Rogers & Associates, Inc. (EFIS)
MARA....... Mark Twain Manufacturing [*NCIC trailer make code*]
MARA....... Mexican-American Research Association (SAUO)
MARA....... Midget Auto Racing Association [*Sanctioning organization*]
MARA....... Modular Architecture for Real-time Applications (SAUS)
MARAAWEX... Marine Antiair Warfare Exercise (NVT)
MARAC...... Marine Athletic Conference (PSS)
MARAC...... Member of the Australasian Register of Agricultural Consultants (ODA)
MARAD...... Maritime Administration [*Also, MA, MARITADMIN*] [*Department of Transportation*]
MArAd...... Master of Archive Administration, University of Liverpool [*British*] (DBQ)
MARAD Program... Maritime Administration Program (SAUO)
MARADVU... Marine Advisory Unit

MARAIRMED... Maritime Air Forces Mediterranean [*NATO*] (NATG)
MARAIRWING... Marine Aircraft Wing
MARAL FEDERAL PAC... MARAL [*Michigan Abortion & Reproductive Rights Action League*] [*Lansing, MI*] (PACS)
MARALLWEAFITRARON... Marine All Weather Fighter Training Squadron
MarAMA.... Marianas Air Materiel Area (SAUO)
MARAMA... Mid-Atlantic Regional Air Management Association
Mar & Yer... Martin and Yerger's Tennessee Reports [*8 Tennessee*] [*1825-28*] [*A publication*] (DLA)
MARAS...... Middle Airspace RADAR Advisory Service [*Military*] (DA)
Mar Av...... Marvin on General Average [*A publication*] (DLA)
MARB....... Marathon Bancorp [*NASDAQ symbol*] (QUAN)
marb......... Marble (VRA)
MARB....... Marbled [*Edges or sides of cover*] [*Bookbinding*] (ROG)
MARB....... Marbrough Boat Trailer [*NCIC trailer make code*]
MARB....... Marine Assistance Request Broadcast [*Coast Guard*]
MARB....... Materiel Acquisition Review Board [*Army*]
MARBA...... Mid-America Regional Bargaining Association
MARBARGE... Maritime Maintenance Barge
Marbascol... Marine Corps Basic School (SAUO)
MARBASSCOL... Marine Corps Basic School
MarbFn...... Marble Financial Corp. [*Associated Press*] (SAG)
MARBG...... Martinsburg, WV [*American Association of Railroads railroad junction routing code*]
MARBI....... Machine-Readable Bibliographic Information (AL)
MARBI....... Machine-Readable Bibliographic Information Committee (SAUO)
MARBI....... Machine-Readable Form of Bibliographic Information [*American Library Association*]
MARBID..... Marine Biodiversity Database (SAUO)
Mar Bills.... Marius on Bills of Exchange [*A publication*] (DLA)
MarBiol..... Marine Biology (SAUO)
MARBKS.... Marine Barracks
MARBO..... Marianas-Bonins Command
Mar Br...... March's Brooke's New Cases [*1651*] [*England*] [*A publication*] (DLA)
MARBRIG... Marine Brigade
MARC....... Genesis Multiple Addictions Recovery Center (MHID)
MARC....... Hruska Meat Animal Research Center [*Department of Agriculture*] (GRD)
MARC....... Maastricht Referendum Campaign [*British*] (ECON)
MARC....... MAC Airlift Reaction Communications (SAUS)
MARC....... Machine Readable card Catalog (SAUO)
MARC....... Machine-Readable Cards
MARC....... Machine-Readable Catalog (NITA)
MARC....... Machine-Readable Cataloging [*Library of Congress*]
MARC....... Machine-Readable Code (IAA)
MARC....... Magnetic Abrasion Resistant Coating (IAA)
MARC....... Management & Applied Research Consultants (SAUO)
MARC....... Manpower Allocation Requirement Criteria [*Military*] (RDA)
MARC....... Manpower Authorization Request for Change [*Air Force*]
MARC....... Manpower Requirements Criteria [*Army*]
MARC....... Manual Recharge [*Electric utility company*]
MARC....... Manufacturers Association of Radiators and Convectors (SAUO)
MARC....... Manufacturing Resource Control System [*Deritend Computer Bureau Ltd.*] [*Software package*] (NCC)
MARC....... Marcato [*Emphasized*] [*Music*]
Marc......... Marcellus [*of Plutarch*] [*Classical studies*] (OCD)
MARC....... MARC, Inc. [*NASDAQ symbol*] (SAG)
MARC....... Marcos [*NCIC car make code*]
Marc......... Marcus [*of Scriptores Historiae Augustae*] [*Classical studies*] (OCD)
M/A/R/C..... Marketing And Research Counselors Inc. [*Irving, TX*] (WDMC)
MARC....... Marquette Cement [*Federal Railroad Administration identification code*]
MARC....... Maryland Automotive Reclamation Corp. [*Automotive materials recycling project*]
MARC....... Master of Arts in Religious Communication (PGP)
MARC....... Matador Automatic RADAR Command
MARC....... Material Accountability Recoverability Code
MARC....... Materiel Acquisition Resource Committee [*Military*]
MARC....... Meat Animal Research Center (SAUO)
MARC....... Media Action Research Center (EA)
MARC....... Medical Automation Research Center
MARC....... Methodist Archives and Research Centre [*John Rylands University Library of Manchester*] [*British*] (CB)
MARC....... Methodology for Assessing Radiological Consequences (PDAA)
MARC....... Metropolitan Administration for Review and Comment [*Program using regional councils of government to serve as clearinghouses for Federal grants*]
MARC....... Metropolitan Applied Research Center (BARN)
MARC....... Michigan Aeronautical Research Center (SAUO)
MARC....... Micronesian Area Research Center [*University of Guam*] [*Research center*] (RCD)
MARC....... Mid-America Regional Council [*Information service or system*] (IID)
MARC....... Mid-America Remote Sensing Center (SAUO)
MARC....... Midland Association for Citizens with Retardation (EARSL)
MARC....... Midwest Alcoholism Research Center (RCD)
MARC....... Military Airlift Command ALCE Reactions Communications (SAUO)
MARC....... Mining and Reclamation Council of America (EA)
MARC....... Minority Access to Research Careers [*Program*] [*Public Health Service*] [*Bethesda, MD*]
MARC....... Missile Annex Review Committee (SAUO)
MARC....... Missions Advanced Research and Communication Center (EA)
MARC....... Mobile Area Repair Calibration (ACAE)
MARC....... Model "A" Restorers Club (EA)
MARC....... Modified Azimuth RADAR Correlator
MARC....... Monitor and Results Computer (IAA)
MARC....... Monitoring and Assessment Research Centre [*Marine science*] (MSC)
MARC....... Monitoring and Risk Assessment Centre [*British*]
MARC....... Montcalm Adult Reading Council (EARSL)
MARC....... Moore Automatic Remote Control
MARC....... Mortgage Account Report Compiler (IAA)
MARC....... Mouvement d'Action pour la Resurrection du Congo [*Action Movement for the Resurrection of the Congo*] [*Zaire*] (PD)
MARC....... Movimiento Agrario Revolucionario del Campesinado Boliviano [*Revolutionary Movement of Bolivian Indian Peasants*] [*Political party*] (PPW)
MARC....... Multiaxial Radial Circuit (IAA)
MARC....... Multifocal and Recurrent Choroidopathy [*Medicine*] (DMAA)
MARC....... Multi-Technology Automated Reader Card (SAUO)
MARC....... Munich American Reinsurance Company (EFIS)
MARC....... Mutliple Access Remote Computing (PDAA)
MA(RCA).... Master of Arts, Royal College of Art (Photography) [*British*] (DBQ)
MARCA..... Mid-Continent Area Reliability Coordinating Agreement (SAUO)
MARCA..... Mid-Continent Area Reliability Coordination Agreement [*Regional power council*]
Mar Cad.... Marine Cadet (SAUO)
MARCAD.... Marine Corps Aviation Cadet
Marcam..... Marcam Corp. [*Associated Press*] (SAG)
MARCAMP.. Marine Corps Accrued Military Pay System (NG)
MARCAN.... Maneuvering Reentry Control and Ablation Studies
MarCap.... Marion Capital Holdings, Inc. [*Associated Press*] (SAG)
MARCAS.... Maneuvering Reentry Control and Ablation Studies (MCD)
Mar Cas..... Maritime Cases, by Crockford and Cox [*1860-71*] [*A publication*] (DLA)
MARCCO.... Master Real-Time Circulation Controller (PDAA)
MARCE...... Materiel Asset Redistribution Center Europe [*Military*]
Marcell...... Pro Marcello [*of Cicero*] [*Classical studies*] (OCD)
MARCENT... Marine Corps, Central Command (SAUO)
MARCEP... Maintainability and Reliability Cost-Effectiveness Program (IEEE)
MARCH...... Marchioness
March....... March's English King's Bench and Common Pleas Reports [*A publication*] (DLA)
March....... March's Translation of Brooke's New Cases, English King's Bench [*82 English Reprint*] [*A publication*] (DLA)
MArch....... Master of Architectural Engineering (GAGS)
M Arch..... Master of Architecture
MARCH...... Melt-Down Accident Response Characteristics [*Nuclear energy*] (NRCH)
MARCH...... Mothers Alone Raising Children (EARSL)
MARCHA.... Methodists Associated Representing the Cause of Hispanic Americans [*An association*]
M Arch Des... Master of Architectural Design
M Arch E.... Master of Architectural Engineering
Mar Chem... Marine Chemistry [*A publication*] (PABS)
M Arch Eng... Master of Architectural Engineering
MArchH..... Master of Architectural History (GAGS)
M Arch H... Master of Architectural History (PGP)
M Arch in CP... Master of Architecture in City Planning
MArchivAdmin... Master of Archives Administration (ADA)
March N.... March's New Cases, English King's Bench and Common Pleas Reports [*A publication*] (DLA)
March NC... March's New Cases, English King's Bench [*1639-42*] [*A publication*] (DLA)
March NC... Translation of Brook's New Cases [*1515-58*] [*A publication*] (DLA)
March NR... March's New Cases, English King's Bench [*1639-42*] [*A publication*] (DLA)
M Arch Studies... Master of Architectural Studies (PGP)
MArchUD... Master of Architecture in Urban Design (GAGS)
M Arch UD... Master of Architecture in Urban Design (PGP)
MARCIA..... Mathematical Analysis of Requirements for Career Information Appraisal
MARC II..... Machine-Readable Catalogue (SAUO)
MARC IS.... MARC Israel (NITA)
MARCIVE... MARC Five (NITA)
MARCKS.... Myristoylated Alanine-Rich C-Kinase Substrate [*Biochemistry*]
MARC(LC).. MARC Library of Congress (NITA)
MARCLIP... Maritime Commands Long-Term Infrastructure Plan (SAUO)
Marc Mant.. Marcus Mantua Benavidius [*Deceased, 1582*] [*Authority cited in pre-1607 legal work*] (DSA)
MarcNG..... Marcum Natural Gas Services, Inc. [*Associated Press*] (SAG)
MARCO...... Machine Referenced and Coordinated Outline
MARCO...... Marine Bancorporation (EFIS)
MARCO...... Marine Construction and Design Company (SAUO)
MARCO...... Microelectronics Advanced Research Corporation (SAUO)
MARCO...... Mid-American Research Corp.
MARCOGAZ... Union of the Gas Industries of the Common Market Countries [*Defunct*] (EAIO)
MARCOM... Maritime Command [*Canada, since 1964*]
MARCOM... Microwave Airborne Communications Relay (IEEE)
MARCOMM. Maritime Commission (DNAB)
MARCOMMDET... Marine Communications Detachment (DNAB)
MARCOMNAVADGRU... Marine Corps Component Navy Advisory Group (CINC)
MARCON.... Marine Construction Ltd. (SAUO)
MARCON.... Mars Consortium
MARCON.... Micro Archives and Records Online [*Developed by AirS, Inc.*]
MARCONFOR... Maritime Contingency Force [*NATO*] (NATG)
MARCONFORLANT... Maritime Contingency Forces, Atlantic [*NATO*] (NATG)
MARCONP.. Maritime Contingency Plans (NATG)
Mar Conv... Marcy's Epitome of Conveyancing [*1881*] [*A publication*] (DLA)

Mar Conv St... Marcy's Conveyancing Statutes [*5th ed.*] [*1893*] [*A publication*] (DLA)
MARCOR.... Marine Corps
MARCORABSCOLLUNIT... Marine Corps Absentee Collection Unit (DNAB)
MARCORADMINDET... Marine Corps Administrative Detachment (DNAB)
MARCORASBCOLLUNITDET... Marine Corps Absentee Collection Unit Detachment (DNAB)
MARCORDISBOF... Marine Corps Disbursing Office
MARCOREP... Marine Corps Representative (DNAB)
MARCORESTRACEN... Marine Corps Reserve Training Center
MARCORHISTCEN... Marine Corps Historical Center (DNAB)
MARCORMAN... Marine Corps Manual
MARCORMEMO... Marine Corps Memorandum (SAUO)
MARCORPERSMAN... Marine Corps Personnel Manual
MARCORPS... Marine Corps
MarCorps... Marine Corps
MARCORPS... US Marine Corps (SAUS)
MARCORSUPDEP... Marine Corps Supply Depot
MARCORSYSCOM... Marine Corps Systems Command
MARCOT.... Maritime Command Operational Team Training [*Canadian Navy*]
Mar Crp G.. Marine Corps Gazette [*A publication*] (BRI)
MARCS...... MAC Airlift Return Communications System (SAUS)
MARC-S...... Machine-Readable Cataloguing - Serials (ADA)
MARC(S)...... MARC Serials (NITA)
MARCS...... Marine Computer System (PDAA)
MARCS...... Melcom All Round Adaptive Consolidated Software [*Japan*]
MARC(UK).. MARC (United Kingdom) (NITA)
Marcus...... [*The*] Marcus Corp. [*Associated Press*] (SAG)
Marcus An.. Marcus Antonius Blancus [*Deceased, 1548*] [*Authority cited in pre-1607 legal work*] (DSA)
Marcus Anto... Marcus Antonius Blancus [*Deceased, 1548*] [*Authority cited in pre-1607 legal work*] (DSA)
MARCY...... Marcy, FL [*American Association of Railroads railroad junction routing code*]
MARD....... Marine Assessment Research Division [*Marine science*] (OSRA)
MA-RD...... Maritime Administration Office of Research and Development [*Washington, DC*]
MARD....... Military Aeronautical Research and Development (PDAA)
MARDAC.... Manpower Research and Data Analysis Center [*DoD*] (NVT)
MARDAN.... Marine Differential Analyzer
MARDATA... Maritime Data Network [*Lloyd's Maritime Data Network Ltd.*] [*Stamford, CT*] [*Database*]
MARDB...... Mountain Agricultural Resources Development Bureau [*Taiwan*] (BUAC)
MARDEC.... Malaysian Rubber Development Corp. (BUAC)
Mar de Lau... Martinus Caratti de Laude [*Flourished, 1438-45*] [*Authority cited in pre-1607 legal work*] (DSA)
MARDET.... Marine Detachment
MARDEZ.... Maritime Defense Zone [*Navy*] [*Coast Guard*] (DOMA)
MARDI...... Malaysian Agricultural Research and Development Institute (BUAC)
MARDI...... Mobile Advanced Robotic Defence Initiative (SAUS)
MARDIS..... Modernized Army Research and Development Information System
MARDIV..... Marine Division
MARDO..... Months after Receipt of Delivery Order (MCD)
MARDOS.... Sources of Radioactivity in the Marine Environment and their Relative Contributors to Overall Dose Assessment from Marine Radioactivity (SAUO)
MarDrl...... Marine Drilling Co. [*Associated Press*] (SAG)
MARDS...... Medium Artillery Delivered Sensor [*Army*]
MARE........ Major Accident Response Exercise (MCD)
MARE........ Major Account Response Evaluation (MCD)
MARE........ Mare Island Naval Shipyard Island (SAUO)
MARE........ Maritime Engineering [*Canadian Navy*]
MARE........ Master of Arts in Religious Education (PGP)
MARE........ Miniature Analogue Recording Electronics (SAUS)
MARE........ Months after Receipt of Equipment [*Navy*]
MAREA...... Member of the American Railway Engineering Association
MAREA...... Middle Leaf Area [*Botany*]
MAREAC.... Mallee Agricultural Research and Extension Advisory Committee (SAUO)
MAREC...... Maritime Reconnaissance radar (SAUS)
MARECEBO... Manned Research on Celestial Bodies Committee [*International Academy of Astronautics*]
MARECO.... Marine Radioecology Working Group (SAUO)
Mar Ecol.... Marine Ecology [*A publication*] (PABS)
Mar Ecol Prog Ser... Marine Ecology Progress Series [*A publication*] (PABS)
MARECS.... Marine Communications Satellites (NITA)
MARECS.... Maritime Communications Satellite
MARECS.... Maritime European Communications Satellite (ACAE)
MARED...... Materiel Acquisition and Readiness Executive Development [*Program*] [*Army*] (RDA)
MAREE...... Multiple Access Radio Frequency Equipment (ACAE)
Ma Reg..... Massachusetts Register [*A publication*] (AAGC)
MAREGSQ.. Marine Air Regulating Squadron
MAREMIC... Maintenance Repair and Minor Construction [*Program*] [*Air Force*]
MAREMICS... Maintenance, Repair and Minor Construction (SAUO)
Mar Eng..... Marine Engineer (PGP)
MARENGRLAB... Marine Engineering Laboratory (SAUO)
MARENTS... Modified Advanced Research Environmental Test Satellite [*Air Force*]
Mar Environ Res... Marine Environmental Research [*A publication*] (PABS)
MAREP...... Marine Environmental Prediction Task Group [*US government*] [*Terminated, 1969*]
MAREP...... Maritime Reporting System (SAUO)
MAREQ...... Military Assistance Requirement (SAUS)
MARES...... Marine Corps Automated Readiness Evaluation System
MARES...... Massachusetts Association for Recreation and Employee Services [*Massachusetts and New England*] (EARSL)
MARES/FORSTAT... Marine Corps Automated Readiness Evaluation System/Status of Forces
MARESTNG... Marine Corps Reserve Training (NVT)
MAREX...... Marine Array Experiment (SAUS)
MARF........ Mark Fore Vatco [*NCIC trailer make code*]
MARF........ Master Area Reference File [*Bureau of the Census*] (GFGA)
MARF........ Master Availability Reference File [*Army Electronics Command*]
MARF........ Medical Acupuncture Research Foundation (SAUO)
MARF........ Medical and Actuarial Research Foundation (SAUO)
MARF........ Metadata Archive Retrieval Facility (SAUO)
Mar Fa...... Martinus de Fano [*Deceased circa 1275*] [*Authority cited in pre-1607 legal work*] (DSA)
MARFAIR... Marine Fleet Air
MARFAIRWEST... Marine Fleet Air, West Coast
Mar Fan..... Martinus de Fano [*Deceased circa 1275*] [*Authority cited in pre-1607 legal work*] (DSA)
MARFE...... Martins Ferry, OH [*American Association of Railroads railroad junction routing code*]
MARFINCEN... Marine Corps Finance Center (DNAB)
MARFIREX... Marine Firing Exercise (NVT)
Mar Fish Rev... Marine Fisheries Review [*A publication*] (PABS)
MARFOR.... Marine Forces [*Element of a Joint Task Force*]
Mar Freshwat Res... Marine & Freshwater Research [*A publication*] (PABS)
MARFS...... Multienvironment Active RF [*Radio Frequency*] Seeker
MARFY...... Maryland Association of Resources for Families and Youth (EARSL)
MARG....... Margarine
Marg......... Margin (EBF)
marg......... Margin (WDMC)
MARG....... Margin [*or Marginal*]
MARG....... Marine Amphibious Ready Group (MCD)
MARG....... Market Analysis Report Generator [*Computer science*]
MARG....... Mediterranean Amphibious Ready Group (MCD)
MARG....... Modern Architectural Research Group (SAUO)
MARGARFOR... Marine Garrison Force
Margate..... Margate Ventures [*Associated Press*] (SAG)
MARGE...... Margarine (ADA)
MARGEN.... Management Report Generator [*Randolph Data Services, Inc.*] [*Software package*] [*Computer science*] (IEEE)
MARGEN.... Mask and Record Generator (TIMI)
Mar Geol.... Marine Geology [*A publication*] (PABS)
MARGI...... Methodology for Analysing Reliability & maintainability Goals (SAUS)
MARGIE..... Memory Analysis, Response Generation, and Interference in English
MARGILSAREA... Marshalls-Gilberts Area
MARGL...... Marginal (ROG)
Margo....... Margo Nursery Farms [*Associated Press*] (SAG)
MARH....... Marietta Homes [*NCIC trailer make code*]
MARHELILEX... Marine Helicopter Landing Exercise (NVT)
MARHGN.... Mid-Atlantic Regional Human Genetics Network (SAUO)
MARI........ Marijuana Cigarette [*Slang*] (DSUE)
MARI........ Marine Camper Trailer [*NCIC trailer make code*]
Mari......... Marinus de Caramanico [*Flourished, 1269-85*] [*Authority cited in pre-1607 legal work*] (DSA)
MARI........ Maros Agricultural Research Institute (SAUO)
MARI........ Medicare Administrative Reform Initiative [*Health Care Financing Administration*]
MARI........ Mercantile Atlantic Routing Instructions
MARI........ Mexico City Air Quality Research Initiative (SAUO)
MARI........ Microelectronics Applications Research Institute [*Newcastle-Upon-Tyne, England*]
MARI........ Middle America Research Institute (SAUO)
MARI........ Mortgage Asset Research Institute Inc.
MARI........ Motivator and Response Indicator
MARIA....... Macroaggregated Radioiodinated Albumin [*Radiology*] [*Pharmacy*] (DAVI)
MARIA....... Methods for Assessing the Radiological Impact of Accidents (SAUO)
MARIAL..... Emory Center for Myth and Ritual in American Life [*Emory University*] (RCD)
Marianists... Society of Mary (SAUO)
MARIARC... Magnetic Resonance and Image Analysis Research Centre [*Liverpool University*] [*United Kingdom*] (RCD)
Maria Soci... Marianus Socinus [*Authority cited in pre-1607 legal work*] (DSA)
MARIC....... Marine Resources Information Center [*Massachusetts Institute of Technology*] (NOAA)
MARID...... Mica-Amphibole-Rutile-Ilmenite-Diopside [*Geology*]
MARIDAS... Maritime Data System (IAA)
MARIE....... Mobile Autonomous Robot in an Industrial Environment (SAUO)
Mariet....... Marietta Corp. [*Associated Press*] (SAG)
MARIF....... Malang Research Institute for Food Crops [*Indonesia*] (BUAC)
Marijuana Rev... Marijuana Review [*A publication*] (DLA)
MARIN...... Marine Industry Application of Broadband Communications (SAUO)
MARIN...... Maritime Research Institute Netherlands (SAUO)
MARINALG International... World Association of Seaweed Processors (SAUO)
MARINCO... Marketing International Consultants (BUAC)
MARINE..... Management Analysis Reporting Information on the Naval Environment System (NG)
Marine Ct R... Marine Court Reporter (McAdam's) [*New York*] [*A publication*] (DLA)
MarinerH... Mariner Health Group, Inc. [*Associated Press*] (SAG)
MARINE System... Management Analysis Reporting Information on the Naval Environment System (SAUO)
MARINEX... Marine Express (AABC)

Marin Frecc... Marinus Freccia [*Flourished, 16th century*] [*Authority cited in pre-1607 legal work*] (DSA)
mar insce... Marine Insurance (ODA)
MARINTRARON... Marine Instrument Training Squadron
MARINTSUM... Maritime Intelligence Summary (SAUS)
MARIO ...... Marion, OH [*American Association of Railroads railroad junction routing code*]
MARIP....... Maintenance And Repair Inspection Program [*Military*] (DNAB)
MARIS....... Marine Information Service (SAUO)
MARIS....... Maritime Research Information Service (SAUO)
MARIS....... Materials and Resources Information Service (NITA)
MARIS....... Mississippi Automated Resource Information System (SAUO)
MarisaC..... Marisa Christina, Inc. [*Associated Press*] (SAG)
MARISAT.... Maritime Satellite System [*COMSAT*]
MARISAT.... Maritime Satellite, United States Maritime Administration (SAUO)
MARISP..... Maritime Strike Plan
Marist Brothers... Little Brothers of Mary (SAUO)
MARIT....... Marinette, WI [*American Association of Railroads railroad junction routing code*]
MARIT....... Maritime
MARITA ..... Maritime Airfield (NATG)
MARITADMIN... Maritime Administration [*Also, MA, MARAD*] [*Department of Transportation*] (MUGU)
MARITCOM... Maritime Commission
MARITIME... Maritime-Niddesc Cooperation (SAUO)
MARITIME... Modelling and Reuse of Information over Time (SAUO)
Maritimes L Rep (CCH)... Maritimes Law Reporter (Commerce Clearing House) [*A publication*] (DLA)
Marit Policy Manage... Maritime Policy & Management [*A publication*] (PABS)
Maritrn...... Maritrans, Inc. [*Associated Press*] (SAG)
MARITZ ..... Maritzburg (ROG)
Marius ...... Marius. Concerning Bills of Exchange [*4 eds.*] [*1651-84*] [*A publication*] (DLA)
MARJO...... Marjorie, TX [*American Association of Railroads railroad junction routing code*]
MARK .... Maintenance and Reliability Kit [*Military*] (NVT)
mark......... Market (VRA)
Mark......... Market
MARK .... Marking Manufacturing [*NCIC trailer make code*]
MARK .... MarkitStar, Inc. [*NASDAQ symbol*] (COMM)
MARK .... Material Accountability & Robotic Kitting (SAUS)
MARK .... Mechanized Assignment and Record Keeping [*Database management system*]
MARK .... Mid-Atlantic Ridge Kane
MARKAR.... Mapping and Reconnaissance Ku-Band Airborne RADAR
MarkCtr ..... Mark Centers Trust [*Associated Press*] (SAG)
MARK ED... Marketing Educational Consortium (SAUO)
Mark El ..... Markby's Elements of Law [*6th ed.*] [*1905*] [*A publication*] (DLA)
Markel ...... Markel Corp. [*Associated Press*] (SAG)
Markerl ..... Marker International [*Associated Press*] (SAG)
Marketing Sci... Marketing Science [*A publication*] (JLIT)
MARKFED... Punjab State Co-operative Supply and Marketing Federation (SAUO)
MARKH...... Markham, IL [*American Association of Railroads railroad junction routing code*]
MarkIV ...... Mark IV Industries, Inc. [*Associated Press*] (SAG)
MARK PAC.. Minnesota Alliance of Republican Kennedys PAC [*St.Paul, MN*] (PACS)
MarkR....... Markham Review [*A publication*] (ANEX)
MARKS...... Modern Army Record Keeping System (INF)
Marks & Sayre... Marks and Sayre's Reports [*108 Alabama*] [*A publication*] (DLA)
Marks & Sayre's... Marks' and Sayre's Reports [*108 Alabama*] [*A publication*] (DLA)
MarksBr..... Marks Bros. Jewelers, Inc. [*Associated Press*] (SAG)
MARKSIM... [*A*] Marketing Decision Simulation [*Game*]
MarkSol..... Mark Solutions, Inc. [*Associated Press*] (SAG)
MARKSTRAT... Marketing Strategy [*Simulation package developed by Professors Jean-Claude Larreche and Hubert Gatignon*]
Markup...... Formatierungsmerkmal (SAUS)
MarkVII ..... Mark VII, Inc. [*Associated Press*] (SAG)
MarkWst ..... MarkWest Hydrocarbon, Inc. [*Associated Press*] (SAG)
MARL........ Marlboro [*Vermont*] [*Seismograph station code, US Geological Survey*] (SEIS)
MARL........ Marshall [*NCIC trailer make code*]
MARL........ Master of Arts and Letters
MARL........ Master of Arts in Religious Leadership (PGP)
MARL........ Mobile Acoustics Research Laboratory (MCD)
Marl .... Statute of Marlborough [*A publication*] (DSA)
Mar LA...... Martin's Louisiana Reports [*A publication*] (DLA)
MARLAB .... Mobile Air Research Laboratory (PDAA)
MARLAGS... Marine Life and Geochemical Studies [*Marine science*] (MSC)
MARLB ...... Marlborough (ROG)
Mar LC...... Maritime Law Cases, by Crockford [*1860-71*] [*A publication*] (DLA)
Mar L Cas (NS)... Maritime Law Cases (New Series), by Aspinall [*1870-1940*] [*A publication*] (DLA)
Mar LC NS... Maritime Law Cases, New Series, by Aspinall [*1870-1940*] [*England*] [*A publication*] (DLA)
Mar Leg Bib... Marvin's Legal Bibliography [*A publication*] (DLA)
MARLENNAN... Marsh & McLennan (EFIS)
MARLEX .... Marine Corps Reserve Landing Exercise (NVT)
MARLF ...... Middle Atlantic Regional Library Federation (SAUO)
MARLIB ..... An information service based on the Institute of Marine Engineers Library (SAUO)
MAR LIC .... Marriage License (WDAA)
Mar Life .... Marine Life [*A publication*] (PABS)
MarLIN...... Marine Life Information Network for Britain & Ireland
MARLIN..... Middle Atlantic Regional Information Network
MARLIS ..... Multi-Agent Relevance Linkage Information System (NITA)
MARLIS ..... Multiaspect Relevance Linkage Information System
Mar LJ ...... Maryland Law Journal and Real Estate Record [*A publication*] (DLA)
MARLNO.... Marine Liaison Office (DNAB)
MARLO...... Marine Liaison Officer (DOMA)
MARLOG.... Marine Logistical Command (VNW)
Mar LR...... Maritime Law Cases, First Series, by Crockford [*1860-71*] [*A publication*] (DLA)
Mar LR...... Maritime Law Cases, New Series, by Aspinall [*1870-1940*] [*A publication*] (DLA)
Mar L Rec... Maryland Law Record [*A publication*] (DLA)
MARLS ...... Missouri Association of Registered Land Surveyors (SAUO)
MARLS ...... Montana Association of Registered Land Surveyors (SAUO)
MARLSR .... Manufacturers Association of Robes, Leisurewear, Shirts, and Rainwear [*Defunct*] (EA)
Marlton ..... Marlton Technologies, Inc. [*Associated Press*] (SAG)
MarM........ Marine Midland Banks, Inc. [*Associated Press*] (SAG)
MARM....... Marmon [*NCIC car make code*]
MARM....... Mensa Animal Rights Movement (BUAC)
MARM....... Microprocessor Arithmetic Model
MARM....... Middle Atlantic Regional Meeting [*of American Chemical Society*]
MARM....... Moving Average Rating Method [*Insurance*]
Mar Mant... Marcus Mantua Benavidius [*Deceased, 1582*] [*Authority cited in pre-1607 legal work*] (DSA)
MARMAP ... Marine Resources Monitoring, Assessment, and Prediction [*National Oceanic and Atmospheric Administration*]
MARMAP Program... Marine Resources Monitoring, Assessment and Prediction Program (SAUO)
Mar Mech E... Marine Mechanical Engineer
MARMETS... Marine Meteorological Service
MARMIC .... Command Level Maintenance Repair and Minor Construction Program Reporting System (SAUO)
MARMID .... Marine Midland Banks, Inc. (EFIS)
MARMOSET... Marconi Mobile Satellite Earth Terminal (SAUS)
MARMOT ... Colorado libraries electronic system (SAUO)
Marm Par... Marmor Parium [*Classical studies*] (OCD)
MAR/MSR... Multifunction Array RADAR / Missile Site RADAR (SAA)
MARN....... Manitoba Association of Registered Nurses (SAUO)
MARN .... Marion Capital Holdings [*NASDAQ symbol*] (NQ)
MARN .... Marion, IN [*American Association of Railroads railroad junction routing code*]
MARN .... Marion Metal Products Company [*NCIC trailer make code*]
MARNA...... Marine Navigation (NITA)
MARNAF.... Marquardt Navair Fuel [*A boron slurry propellant for spacecraft*]
Mar N & Q... Maritime Notes and Queries [*1873-1900*] [*A publication*] (DLA)
MARNAVCOR... Marine Navy Corps (SAUO)
MarNB....... Marine National Bank (California) [*Associated Press*] (SAG)
MarNBk ..... Marine National Bank (California) [*Associated Press*] (SAG)
Mar NC...... March's New Cases, English King's Bench [*1639-42*] [*A publication*] (DLA)
Mar NC...... Martin's North Carolina Reports [*1 North Carolina*] [*A publication*] (DLA)
MarnLP ..... Marine Ltd. [*Associated Press*] (SAG)
MarnLP ..... Marine Ltd. Partnership [*Associated Press*] (SAG)
Mar NR ...... March's New Cases [*1639-42*] [*A publication*] (DLA)
Mar NS...... Martin's Louisiana Reports, New Series [*A publication*] (DLA)
MARO .... Maritime Air Radio Organization [*NATO*] (NATG)
MARO .... Marlette Homes [*NCIC trailer make code*]
MAROA...... Maroa, IL [*American Association of Railroads railroad junction routing code*]
MARON ..... Marion, IL [*American Association of Railroads railroad junction routing code*]
MAROPS.... Maritime Operations
MAROPT .... Marine Optical Recording System (SAUO)
MAROTS.... Maritime Orbital Test Satellite
MARP .... Manpower Allocation/Requirements Plan [*Navy*]
MARP .... Manpower Requirements Plan (SAUO)
MARP .... Marathon Homes Corporation [*NCIC trailer make code*]
MARP .... Marine Petroleum Trust [*NASDAQ symbol*] (NQ)
MARP .... Mating and Ranging Program (SAUO)
MARP .... Maximum Authorized for Repair Parts (DNAB)
MARP .... Microtubule-Associated Repetitive Protein [*Biochemistry*] (QSUL)
MARP .... Minnesota Association of Rehabilitation Providers (EARSL)
MARP .... Mobilization Augmentee Revitalization Program [*Military*]
MARP .... Months after Receipt of Problem [*Navy*] (NG)
MARPA...... Mini Automatic Radar Plotting Aid (SAUS)
MARPAC .... Headquarters, Department of the Pacific [*Marine Corps*]
MARPAC .... Maritime Command Pacific [*Canada, since 1964*]
MARPAC .... Maritime Forces, Pacific (SAUO)
MARPAC/ORT... Maritime Forces Pacific Operational Research Team [*Canada*]
MARPDA.... Mid-America Periodical Distributors Association (EA)
MARPE...... Multi-Atom Resonant Photoemission [*Physics*]
MARPEP .... Marine Physical Environmental Prediction
MarPet ...... Marine Petroleum Trust [*Associated Press*] (SAG)
Mar Pet Geol... Marine and Petroleum Geology [*A publication*] (PABS)
MARPEX .... Management of Repair Parts Expenditure [*Army*] (PDAA)
MARPIC..... Marine Pollution Information Centre [*Marine Biological Association of the United Kingdom*] (IID)
Marpie ...... Middle-Aged Rural Professional [*Lifestyle classification*]
MARPOL .... Convention for the Prevention of Marine Pollution from Ships (SAUS)
MARPOL .... International Convention for the Prevention of Pollution from Ships [*1973*]

MARPOL .... Marine Pollution [*Fuels and lubricants*]
MARPOL .... Maritime Pollution Convention [*1978*] (DS)
Mar Policy... Marine Policy [*A publication*] (PABS)
MarPollutBull... Marine Pollution Bulletin (SAUO)
MARPOLMON... Marine Pollution Monitoring System (SAUO)
MARPOLMON... Sub-Group of Experts on Marine Pollution Monitoring [*Marine science*] (MSC)
MARPRO .... Country Marine Profile Database (SAUS)
MARPRO .... Marine Profile Data Base (GNE)
Mar Prov .... Maritime Provinces Reports [*Canada*] [*A publication*] (DLA)
MARPS ...... Marine Petrol Tr. [*NASDAQ symbol*] (SG)
MARPS ...... Mechanized Accounting Reserve Pay System
marq .... Marquetry (VRA)
MARQ .... Marquette Custom Boat Trailer [*NCIC trailer make code*]
MARQ .... Marquette Electronics, Inc. [*NASDAQ symbol*] (SPSG)
MARQ .... Marquette Medical Systems, Inc. [*NASDAQ symbol*] (SAG)
MARQ .... Marquis [*or Marquess*]
MARQ .... MO Air International [*Common carrier symbol*]
MARQA ...... Marquette Electronics'A' [*NASDAQ symbol*] (TTSB)
MARQA ...... Marquette Medical System [*NASDAQ symbol*] [*Formerly, Marquette Electronics*] (SG)
MarqEl ...... Marquette Electronics, Inc. [*Associated Press*] (SAG)
MarqG .... Marquee Group, Inc. (The) [*Associated Press*] (SAG)
MarqGrp .... Marquee Group, Inc. (The) [*Associated Press*] (SAG)
MarqMed ... Marquette Medical Systems, Inc. [*Associated Press*] (SAG)
Marqst ...... Marquest Medical Products, Inc. [*Associated Press*] (SAG)
MARQU ..... Marquette, MI [*American Association of Railroads railroad junction routing code*]
MARQUES... Association of European Trade Mark Owners [*United Kingdom*] (EAIO)
Marquette Bus Rev... Marquette Business Review [*A publication*] (DLA)
Marquette U... Marquette University (GAGS)
MARQUIS... Master Remote Query Interface System [*Computer science*]
Marr .... Hay and Marriott's English Admiralty Reports [*A publication*] (DLA)
MARR .... Manpower Authorization Requirement Review (SAUO)
MARR .... Marine Accidents Requiring Rescue (OA)
Mar R .... Maritime Law Reports [*A publication*] (DLA)
MARR .... Marlin Manufacturing [*NCIC trailer make code*]
Marr .... Marrack's European Assurance Cases [*England*] [*A publication*] (DLA)
Marr .... Marriage (DLA)
MARR .... Maximum Annual Rate of Return [*Finance*]
MARR .... Minimum Attractive Rate of Return [*Economics*]
Marr Adm... Marriott's English Admiralty Reports [*A publication*] (DLA)
MARRC ...... Multi-Channel Automatic Remote Recording
MARRCS .... Manpower Requirements and Resources Control System [*Navy*] (NVT)
MARRD ..... Married (ROG)
MARRE ...... Manual RADAR Reconnaissance Exploitation (MCD)
MARRE ...... Marriage (ROG)
Mar Rec B.. Martin's Recital Book [*A publication*] (DLA)
Mar Reg .... Mitchell's Maritime Register [*England*] [*A publication*] (DLA)
MARREP .... Maritime Report (SAUS)
MARRES .... Manual RADAR Reconnaissance Exploitation System [*Air Force*]
Marr Form.. Marriott's Formulare Instrumentorum [*Admiralty Court*] [*1802*] [*A publication*] (DLA)
MarriotI ..... Marriott International [*Associated Press*] (SAG)
MARRS ...... Mechanized Ammunition Recording and Reporting System
MARRS ...... Modular Armoured Repair & Recovery System (SAUS)
MARR SETTL... Marriage Settlement [*Legal term*] (DLA)
MARRTC .... Missouri Arthritis Rehabilitation Research and Training Center [*University of Missouri--Columbia*] (RCD)
MARS .... Machine-Activated Recovery System (TIMI)
MARS .... Machine-Aided Realization System
MARS .... Machine-Assisted Reference Section [*American Library Association*] [*Information service or system*] (IID)
MARS .... Machine-Assisted Reference Service [*St. Paul Public Library*] (OLDSS)
MARS .... Machine Automated Realty Service
MARS .... Machine Retrieval System
MARS .... Magnetic Airborne Recording System
MARS .... Magnetic Array Sensor System (SAUS)
MARS .... Maintenance Activities and Resources Simulation [*Computer science*]
MARS .... Maintenance Analysis and Recording Systems
MARS .... Maintenance Analysis Repair Set
MARS .... Maintenance and Recovery Services, Inc. (MHID)
MARS .... Maintenance and Repair System (ACAE)
MARS .... Maintenance Assistance and Repair System [*Military*]
MARS .... Major Accident Reporting System [*Engineering*]
MARS .... Management Accounting Reporting System (SAUO)
MARS .... Management Action Reporting System (MCD)
MARS .... Management Analysis Reporting System [*Computer science*]
MARS .... Management and Administrative Reporting Subsystem [*Department of Health and Human Services*] (GFGA)
MARS .... Management Reports and Statistics
MARS .... Man-Hour Accounting and Reporting System [*Military*] (MCD)
MARS .... Manned Aerodynamic Reusable Spaceship
MARS .... Manned Astronautical Research Station [*Space laboratory*]
MARS .... Marconi Automatic Relay System (IEEE)
MARS .... Marine Account Reconciliation Service
MARS .... Marine Aircraft Repair Squadron
MARS .... Marine Corps Ammunition Reporting System (SAUO)
MARS .... Marine Reporting Station [*National Weather Service*]
MARS .... Marine Research Stations network (SAUO)
MARS .... Maritime Mobile Access and Retrieval System (SAUO)
MARS .... Maritime Surface and Subsurface [*Canadian Navy*]
MARS .... Market Analysis and Reference System [*Vancouver stock exchange computer system*] [*Canada*]
MARS .... Marketing and Advertising Reference Service (NITA)
MARS .... Mars Camper Company [*NCIC trailer make code*]
Mars .... Marsden's Select Pleas in the Court of Admiralty [*Selden Society Publications, Vols. 6, 11*] [*A publication*] (DLA)
MARS .... Marsh Supermarkets, Inc. [*NASDAQ symbol*] (NQ)
MARS .... Martin Automatic Reporting System
MARS .... Master Attitude Reference System
MARS .... Master of Arts in Religious Studies (PGP)
MARS .... Material Action Reporting System (MCD)
MARS .... Material Response Study
MARS .... Materials at Risk Survey (SAUO)
MARS .... Materiel Acquisition Resource System [*Military*]
MARS .... Mathematics Anxiety Rating Scale [*Psychology*]
MARS .... Matrix Analysis of Redundant/Routine Structure (ACAE)
MARS .... Maximum Asset Return Strategy [*Allingham, Anderson, Roll & Ross*] [*British*] (ECON)
MARS .... McGill Arctic Research Station [*McGill University*] [*Canada*] (RCD)
MARS .... Measuring Accuracy and Repeatability Study
MARS .... Mechanical Accessory Repair Shop (MCD)
MARS .... Media Alert and Response System [*Public relations project devised by Pharmaceutical Manufacturers Association*]
MARS .... Memory-Address Register Storage [*Computer science*]
MARS .... Message Archiving and Retrieval Service (SAUO)
MARS .... Meteorological Airborne Radar Data System (SAUO)
MARS .... Meteorological Automatic Reporting Station [*Canada*]
MARS .... Meteorological Automatic Reporting System (SAUO)
MARS .... Mevinolin Atherosclerosis Regression Study (MEDA)
MARS .... Microprogrammable Accelerator for Rapid Simulations (ACAE)
MARS .... Midair Recovery [*or Retrieval*] System [*Rescue by helicopter*] [*Military*]
MARS .... Mid-Air Retrieval System (SAUO)
MARS .... Migration Agents' Registration Scheme [*Australia*]
MARS .... Military Affiliated Radio System [*or Stations*] [*Amateur-operated radio stations*]
MARS .... Military Airborne RADAR System [*Air Force*] (IAA)
MARS .... Military Amateur Radio Service (SAUO)
MARS .... Military Amateur Radio System (IAA)
MARS .... Military Amphibious Reconnaissance System (RDA)
MARS .... Military Archive & Research Services (SAUO)
MARS .... Millimeter Wave Amplification by Resonance Saturation (IAA)
MARS .... Miniature Attitude Reference System
MARS .... Minimally Attended Radar Station (SAUO)
MARS .... Minimum-Altitude Release and Strafe (MCD)
MARS .... Minolta Automatic Retrieval System (NITA)
MARS .... Mirror Advanced Reactor Study (MCD)
MARS .... Mission Maintenance and Reliability Simulation (MCD)
MARS .... Mitigation and Adaption Research Strategies (SAUO)
MARS .... Mobile Air Defense Radar System (ACAE)
MARS .... Mobile Atlantic Range Stations [*Tracking stations*] (MUGU)
MARS .... Mobile Augmented Reality System
MARS .... Mobile Automatic Reporting Station (SAUO)
MARS .... Mobile Automatic Reporting System (MCD)
MARS .... Mobile Autonomous Robot Software Program [*Defense Advanced Research Projects Agency*] (RCD)
MARS .... Model Annotation Search and Retrieval System [*Geological program*]
MARS .... Modern Architectural Research Society (SAUO)
MARS .... Modular Access Random Storage [*Computer science*] (VLIE)
MARS .... Modular Adaptable Radar Simulator (SAUS)
MARS .... Modular Airborne Recorder System (MCD)
MARS .... Modular Airborne Recording System (SAUS)
MARS .... Modular Attack RADAR System (MCD)
MARS .... Monitor and Replenisher System
MARS .... Monitoring Accounting Reporting and Statistical System [*Aviation*]
MARS .... Monitoring Agriculture with Remote Sensing (EURO)
MARS .... Monograph Acquisitions and Record System [*Library science*] (TELE)
MARS .... Monthly Aerial Reconnaissance Summary (MCD)
MARS .... Motorola Aerial Remote Sensing [*Flying laboratory*]
MARS .... Mouse Antirat Serum (DB)
MARS .... Multi-Access Reservations System [*Travel industry*] (TRID)
MARS .... Multi-Access Reservation System [*Travel industry*] (TVEL)
MARS .... Multiaperture Reluctance Switch [*Data storage unit*]
MARS .... Multicast Address Resolution Server (MLOA)
MARS .... Multicast Address Resolution Service [*Computer science*]
MARS .... Multiple Access Retrieval System [*Control Data Corp.*]
MARS .... Multiple Action Raid Simulation [*France*]
MARS .... Multiple Aerial Refueling System (PDAA)
MARS .... Multiple-Angle Reference System
MARS .... Multiple Aperture Reluctance Switch (VLIE)
MARS .... Multiple Artillery Rocket System [*Army*]
MARS .... Multiuser Archival and Retrieval System [*Computer science*]
MARS .... Multivariate Adaptive Regression Spline (IDAI)
MARS .... Multivariate Adaptive Regression Splines
MARS .... Multivariate Analysis, Retrieval, and Storage [*System*] [*NASA*]
MARS .... PTS Marketing and Advertising Reference Service [*Predicasts, Inc.*] [*Cleveland, OH*] [*Information service or system*] (IID)
MARSA ...... Marsh Supermarkets [*NASDAQ symbol*]
MARSA ...... Marsh Supermkts'A' [*NASDAQ symbol*] (TTSB)
MARS-A ..... Mathematics Anxiety Rating Scale-Adolescents (STED)
MARSA ...... Microfilm Association of the Republic of South Africa (BUAC)
MARSA ...... Military Accepts Responsibility for Separation of Aircraft (AFM)

Mars Adm .. Marsden's English Admiralty [*A publication*] (DLA)
Mar Sal ..... Marius Salomonius [*Deceased, 1557*] [*Authority cited in pre-1607 legal work*] (DSA)
MARSAM ... Multiple Airborne Reconnaissance Sensors Assessment Model (MCD)
MARSAP .... Mutual Assistance Rescue and Salvage Plan (SAUO)
MARSAS .... Marine Search and Attack System (PDAA)
MARSAT .... Maritime Satellite [*COMSAT*]
MARSATS... Maritime Satellite System [*COMSAT*]
MARSB...... Marsh Supermkts'B' [*NASDAQ symbol*] (TTSB)
M Ar Sc..... Master of Arts and Sciences
MArSci ...... Master of Arts and Sciences (NADA)
Mars Coll... Marsden's Collisions at Sea [*11th ed.*] [*1961*] [*A publication*] (DLA)
MARSD...... Minimal Attended RADAR Station Display (DWSG)
MARSEN .... Marine Remote Sensing Experiment (SAUO)
MARSEN .... Maritime Remote Sensing (MCD)
Marsh .... Marshall and Sevestre's Appeals [*1862-64*] [*Bengal, India*] [*A publication*] (DLA)
Marsh .... Marshall's Circuit Court Decisions [*United States*] [*A publication*] (DLA)
Marsh .... Marshall's English Common Pleas Reports [*1814-16*] [*A publication*] (DLA)
Marsh .... Marshall's High Court Reports [*Bengal*] [*A publication*] (DLA)
Marsh .... Marshall's Reports [*Kentucky*] [*A publication*] (DLA)
Marsh .... Marshall's Reports [*4 Utah*] [*A publication*] (DLA)
Marsh .... Marshall's Reports [*Ceylon*] [*A publication*] (DLA)
MARSH...... Matching Aid to Restore States Habitat (GNE)
Marshall .... Marshall's Reports [*Bengal*] [*A publication*] (DLA)
Marshall .... Reports of Cases on Appeal [*Calcutta*] [*A publication*] (DLA)
Marshall U... Marshall University (GAGS)
Marsh Beng... Marshall's Reports [*Bengal*] [*A publication*] (DLA)
Marsh Calc... Marshall's Reports [*Calcutta*] [*A publication*] (DLA)
Marsh Car... Marshall on Railways as Carriers [*A publication*] (DLA)
Marsh Ceylon... Marshall's Ceylon Reports [*A publication*] (DLA)
Marsh Costs... Marshall on the Law of Costs [*A publication*] (DLA)
Marsh CP ... Marshall's English Common Pleas Reports [*A publication*] (DLA)
Marsh Dec... Marshall on the Federal Constitution [*A publication*] (DLA)
Marsh Dec... Marshall's Circuit Court Decisions, by Brockenbrough [*United States*] [*A publication*] (DLA)
Marsh (Eng)... Marshall's English Common Pleas Reports [*A publication*] (DLA)
MarshFn .... Marshalltown Financial Corp. [*Associated Press*] (SAG)
Marshl ...... Marshall & Isley Corp. [*Associated Press*] (SAG)
Marshlls .... Marshall & Isley Corp. [*Associated Press*] (SAG)
Marsh Ins... Marshall on Marine Insurance [*A publication*] (DLA)
Marsh (KY)... Marshall's Reports [*Kentucky*] [*A publication*] (DLA)
MARSHL .... Marshal (ROG)
Marsh Op ... Marshall's Constitutional Opinions [*A publication*] (DLA)
Marsh Ry ... Marshall on Railways as Carriers [*A publication*] (DLA)
Marsh Ry ... Marshall's Duties and Obligations of Railway Companies [*A publication*] (DLA)
Mar Sill ..... Martinus Sillimanus [*Flourished, 13th century*] [*Authority cited in pre-1607 legal work*] (DSA)
MARSIM .... International Conference on Marine Simulation (PDAA)
MARSIS ..... Marine Remote Sensing Information System for Regional European Seas (SAUO)
MARSL...... Machine-Readable Shelf List [*Carleton University*] [*Canada*] (NITA)
Mars Microprobe... Mars Microprobe Project (SAUS)
MARSO...... Marine Corps Shipping Order (NG)
MA/RSO..... Mobilization Augmentee/Reserve Supplement Officer [*Air Force*] (AFM)
MARSPTBN... Marine Support Battalion (DNAB)
MARSREPSYS... Military Affiliate Radio System Repeater System (DNAB)
MARSS...... Meteorological and Range Safety Support (ACAE)
MARSTA .... Marital Status [*Army*] (AABC)
MARSTELSYS... Military Affiliate Radio System Teletypewriter Relay System (DNAB)
MARSTSIC... Marst on Sicca [*England*]
MARSYAS... Marshall System for Aerospace Simulation [*Programming language*] [*1966-68*] (CSR)
MArt......... Magazine of Art (SAUO)
MART........ Maintenance Analysis and Review Technique (VLIE)
MART........ Maintenance Analysis Review Technique
Mart .... Martial [*Roman poet, 40-104AD*] [*Classical studies*] (OCD)
Mart .... Martinique (SHCU)
MART........ Martinique [*West Indies*] (WDAA)
Mart .... Martin's Louisiana Term Reports [*1809-30*] [*A publication*] (DLA)
Mart .... Martin's North Carolina Reports [*1 North Carolina*] [*A publication*] (DLA)
MART........ Martin Trailers [*NCIC trailer make code*]
Mart .... Martinus Gosia [*Authority cited in pre-1607 legal work*] (DSA)
MART........ Martius [*March*] [*Latin*]
MART........ Martyr
MART........ Mask X-ray Telescope [*Spectrum-X-Gamma*] (HCJD)
MART........ Master of Arts in Religion and Theology (PGP)
MART........ Mathematical Modeling and Reliability Transducer (MCD)
MART........ Maximising the Market for Telecommunications-Based Rehabilitation Technology (SAUO)
MART........ Mean Active Repair Time (IEEE)
MART........ Metropolitan Area Rapid Transit (SAUO)
MART........ Missile Automation Radiation Test (IAA)
MART........ Mobile Automatic Radiation Tester
MART........ Multiplicative Algebraic Reconstruction Technique (DMAA)
MARTA ...... Metropolitan Atlanta Rapid Transit Authority [*FTA*] (TAG)
MARTA ...... Metropolitan Regional Transit Authority
MARTAC..... Martin Automatic Rapid Test and Control
Mart & Y.... Martin and Yerger's Tennessee Reports [*8 Tennessee*] [*1825-28*] [*A publication*] (DLA)
Mart & Yer... Martin and Yerger's Tennessee Reports [*8 Tennessee*] [*1825-28*] [*A publication*] (DLA)
Mart & Yerg... Martin and Yerger's Tennessee Reports [*8 Tennessee*] [*1825-28*] [*A publication*] (DLA)
Mart & Y (Tenn)... Martin and Yerger's Tennessee Reports [*8 Tennessee*] [*1825-28*] [*A publication*] (DLA)
Mart Ark .... Martin's Decisions in Equity [*Arkansas*] [*A publication*] (DLA)
MARTC ...... Marine Air Reserve Training Command
MartCol ..... Martin Color-Fi, Inc. [*Associated Press*] (SAG)
MARTCOM.. Marine Air Reserve Training Command
Mart Cond LA... Martin's Condensed Louisiana Reports [*A publication*] (DLA)
Mart Conv... Martin's Practice of Conveyancing [*A publication*] (DLA)
MARTD ...... Marine Air Reserve Training Detachment
MARTD ...... Marine Corps Aviation Reserve Training Depot (SAUO)
Mart Dec.... United States Decisions in Martin's North Carolina Reports [*A publication*] (DLA)
MARTEC..... Martin Thin-Film Electronic Circuit
Mar Technol Soc J... Marine Technology Society Journal (SAUO)
Martek ...... Martek Biosciences, Inc. [*Associated Press*] (SAG)
MARTEL..... Missile Antiradiation Television [*Military*] (CAAL)
MARTELO... Maritime Air Telecommunications Organisation (SAUO)
Marten ...... Marten Transport Ltd. [*Associated Press*] (SAG)
Mart Ex ..... Martin on Executors [*A publication*] (DLA)
Mart GA..... Martin's Reports [*21-30 Georgia*] [*A publication*] (DLA)
MARTHA .... Mobile Autonomous Robots for Transportation and Handling Applications (SAUO)
Marth W Ca... Martha Washington Cases [*A publication*] (DLA)
MARTI .... Maneuverable Reentry Technology Investigation
MARTI .... Mobile Advanced Realtime Image (STED)
Martin .... Martin's Louisiana Reports [*A publication*] (DLA)
Martin .... Martin's North Carolina Reports [*1 North Carolina*] [*A publication*] (DLA)
Martin .... Martin's Reports [*21-30, 54-70 Georgia*] [*A publication*] (DLA)
Mart Ind .... Martin's Reports [*54-70 Indiana*] [*A publication*] (DLA)
MARTINI .... Massive Analog Recording Technical Instrument for Nebulous Indications
Martin Index... Martin's Index to Virginia Reports [*A publication*] (DLA)
Martin (Lou) NS... Martin's Louisiana Reports, New Series [*A publication*] (DLA)
Martin's Chy... Martin's Chancery Decisions [*Arkansas*] [*A publication*] (DLA)
Martin's LA Rep... Martin's Louisiana Reports [*A publication*] (DLA)
Martin's LA Rep NS... Martin's Louisiana Reports, New Series [*A publication*] (DLA)
Martin's Louisiana R... Martin's Louisiana Reports [*A publication*] (DLA)
Martin's NS... Martin's Louisiana Reports, New Series [*A publication*] (DLA)
Martin's R NS... Martin's Louisiana Reports, New Series [*A publication*] (DLA)
Martls .... Martyrdom of Isaiah [*Pseudepigrapha*] (BJA)
Martlsa...... Martyrdom of Isaiah [*Pseudepigrapha*] (BJA)
Mart LA ..... Martin's Louisiana Reports, Old and New Series [*A publication*] (DLA)
Mart Laud... Martinus Caratti de Laude [*Flourished, 1438-45*] [*Authority cited in pre-1607 legal work*] (DSA)
Mart Law Nat... Martens' Law of Nations [*A publication*] (DLA)
Mart MC .... Martin's Mining Cases [*Canada*] [*A publication*] (DLA)
MartMM..... Martin Marietta Materials [*Associated Press*] (SAG)
Mart NC..... Martin's North Carolina Reports [*1 North Carolina*] [*A publication*] (DLA)
Martnln ..... Martin Industries, Inc. [*Associated Press*] (SAG)
MartnL ...... Martin Lawrence Ltd. [*Associated Press*] (SAG)
Mart NS..... Martin's Louisiana Reports, New Series [*A publication*] (DLA)
Mart NS (LA)... Martin's Louisiana Reports, New Series [*A publication*] (DLA)
MARTOS .... Multiaccess Real-Time Operating System [*AEG Telefunken*] [*Germany*]
Mart OS (LA)... Martin's Louisiana Reports, Old Series [*A publication*] (DLA)
MARTRA & REPLCOMS... Marine Training and Replacement Commands
MArt RCA ... Master of Art of the Royal College of Art (SAUO)
M Art (RCA)... Master of Art, Royal College of Art
Mart Rep ... Martin's Louisiana Reports [*A publication*] (DLA)
Mart Rep NS... Martin's Louisiana Reports, New Series [*A publication*] (DLA)
MARTS ...... Advance Monthly Retail Trade Survey (SAUO)
MARTS ...... Master RADAR Tracking Station
MARTS ...... Master RADAR Training System
MARTS ...... Mobile Automatic Radio Telephone System (MCD)
MARTS ...... Monthly Advance Retail Trade Survey [*Bureau of the Census*] (GFGA)
MARTS ...... MSFC Accounting and Resources Tracking System (SAUS)
Mart USCC... Martin's Circuit Court Reports [*1 North Carolina*] [*A publication*] (DLA)
MARU .... Marcon Line [*Intermodal shipping container symbol*] (TVRC)
MARU .... Marusho [*NCIC motorcycle make code*]
MARU .... Medical Architecture Research Unit [*Polytechnic of North London*] [*British*] (IRC)
MARU .... Middle America Research Unit
MARU .... Mobile Aircraft Repair Unit (SAUO)
MARUNET... Maruzen Online Network [*Maruzen Co. Ltd.*] [*Japan*] [*Telecommunications*]
MARUNITNG... Marine Unit Training (NVT)
Maruwhenua... Maori policy section of the Ministry of the Environment (SAUO)
MARV .... Maneuverable AntiRADAR Vehicle (MCD)
MARV .... Maneuverable Reentry Vehicle (AABC)
MaRV........ Maneuvering Reentry Vehicle
MARV .... Mar-Val Industries [*NCIC trailer make code*]
MARV .... Marvelous (DSUE)

Marv......... Marvel's Reports [*15-16 Delaware*] [*A publication*] (DLA)
Marv......... Marvetol [*medicine*] (WDAA)
MARV....... Micro Autonomous Robotic Vehicle
MARV....... Mobile Acoustic Recording Vehicle (MCD)
MARV....... Mobile Armored Reconnaissance/Operational Vehicle (MCD)
MARV....... Mobile Armoured Reconnaissance Vehicle (SAUS)
MARV....... Multi-Element Articulated Research Vehicle [*Engineering*] (OA)
MARVAC.... Michigan Association of Recreational Vehicles and Campgrounds (EARSL)
Marv Av..... Marvin on General Average [*A publication*] (DLA)
Marv (Del)... Marvel's Reports [*15-16 Delaware*] [*A publication*] (DLA)
MARVEL.... Machine-Assisted Realization of the Virtual Electronic Library [*Information service or system*] [*Library of Congress*]
Marvel...... Marvel Entertainment Corp. [*Associated Press*] (SAG)
Marvel...... Marvel's Reports [*15-16 Delaware*] [*A publication*] (DLA)
MARVEL.... Mississippi Aerophysics Research Vehicle with Extended Latitude
MARVIN..... Mobile Autonomous Robot with Video-Based Navigation (VLIE)
MARVL...... Marysville, CA [*American Association of Railroads railroad junction routing code*]
Marv Leg Bib... Marvin's Legal Bibliography [*A publication*] (DLA)
MARVLS.... MARC Video Disc Library System (NITA)
MARVOR.... French Subsurface Float (SAUO)
MARVS...... Material Acquisition Requirements Validation System (SAUO)
Marv Wr & S... Marvin on Wreck and Salvage [*A publication*] (DLA)
MARW....... Marshfield Homes [*NCIC trailer make code*]
Mar Wr & S... Marvin on Wreck and Salvage [*A publication*] (DLA)
MARX....... Mark Aero [*Air carrier designation symbol*]
MARX....... Mississippi Alabama Railroad Authority [*Federal Railroad Administration identification code*]
Mary......... Maryland Reports [*A publication*] (DLA)
MARY........ Saint Mary Land & Exploration [*NASDAQ symbol*] (SAG)
Marygrove C... Marygrove College (GAGS)
Maryknoll Fathers... Catholic Foreign Missionary Society of America (SAUO)
Maryland... Maryland Reports [*A publication*] (DLA)
Maryland Ch Dec... Maryland Chancery Decisions [*A publication*] (DLA)
Maryville U... Maryville University of St. Louis (GAGS)
Marywood C... Marywood College (GAGS)
MAS......... Astronomical Observatory of Cordoba (SAUS)
MAS......... Lithuanian Catholic Youth Association Ateitis (EA)
MAS......... MacDonald Agricultural Services Ltd. [*British*]
MAS......... Machine Accounting School
MAS......... Macintosh Application System [*Computer science*] (CDE)
MAS......... Macroassembler
MAS......... Madang Air Services [*Australia*]
MAS......... Madras, OR [*Amtrak Busline code*]
MAS......... Magazine Article Summaries
MAS......... Magic Angle Spinning [*Spectroscopy*]
MAS......... Magnesia-Alumina-Silicate [*Inorganic chemistry*]
MAS......... Main Store (VLIE)
MAS......... Maintenance Alert System [*Truck operations*]
MAS......... Maintenance and Services (AFIT)
MAS......... Maintenance and Supply (AFIT)
MAS......... Malabsorption Syndrome (MELL)
MAS......... Malaysian Airline System [*ICAO designator*] (FAAC)
MAS......... Managed Airspace (SAUO)
MAS......... Managed Application System (VLIE)
MAS......... Management Accounting System
MAS......... Management Advisory Services
MAS......... Management and Administrative Statistics (OICC)
MAS......... Management Appraisal Survey [*Test*]
MAS......... Manchester Astronomical Society [*England*] (BUAC)
MAS......... Man-day Account System (SAUO)
MAS......... Maneuvering Attack System (MCD)
MAS......... Manifest Anxiety Scale [*Psychology*]
MAS......... Manned Aerial Surveillance
MAS......... Manual A1 Simplex [*Aviation*]
MAS......... Manufacturing Advisory Service (DCTA)
MAS......... Manufacturing Agility Server (VLIE)
MAS......... Manufacturing Assembly Specification
MAS......... Manufacturing Automation and Support (TIMI)
MAS......... Manus [*Papua New Guinea*] [*Airport symbol*] (OAG)
MAS......... Manus Island [*Bismarck Archipelago*] [*Airport symbol*] (AD)
MAS......... MAP [*Manufacturing Automation Protocol*]/One Applications Services [*Software*] [*Automotive engineering*]
MAS......... Marine Acoustical Services
MAS......... Marine Advisory Service [*See also NMAS*] [*National Oceanic and Atmospheric Administration*] [*Information service or system*] (IID)
MAS......... Maritime Air Superiority (NVT)
MAS......... Marker Assisted Selection (SAUO)
MAS......... Market Advisory Service [*British Overseas Trade Board*] (DS)
MAS......... Mars Approach Sensor
MAS......... Martin Shaffer [*Federal Railroad Administration identification code*]
MAS......... Maryland Academy of Sciences (SAUO)
mas......... Masai [*MARC language code*] [*Library of Congress*] (LCCP)
MAS......... Masco Corp. [*NYSE symbol*] (SPSG)
MAS......... Masculine
MAS......... Mason [*or Masonry*] (ROG)
MAS......... Mason Butte [*Idaho*] [*Seismograph station code, US Geological Survey*] [*Closed*] (SEIS)
mas......... Masonry (VRA)
Mas......... Mason's United States Circuit Court Reports [*A publication*] (DLA)
Mas......... Masorah (BJA)
MAS......... Massachusetts [*Telegraphy*] (PCTE)
MAS......... Massachusetts Audubon Society, Incorporated (SAUO)
Mas......... Massachusetts Reports [*A publication*] (DLA)
MAS......... Massachusetts State Library, Boston, MA [*OCLC symbol*] (OCLC)
Mas......... Masseketh (BJA)
MAS......... Master (DSUE)
MAS......... Master Activation Schedule (AAG)
MAS......... Master Analysis Scheme [*Monitoring technique*]
MAS......... Master Assembly Schedule (SAUO)
MAS......... Master of Accounting Science
MAS......... Master of Actuarial Science
MAS......... Master of Administrative Science (PGP)
MAS......... Master of Administrative Studies (ADA)
MAS......... Master of Aeronautical Science (GAGS)
MAS......... Master of Applied Science
MAS......... Master of Applied Spirituality (PGP)
MAS......... Master of Applied Statistics (GAGS)
MAS......... Master of Archival Studies (GAGS)
MAS......... Material Activity Schedule
MAS......... Material Application Service [*NASA*] (IAA)
MAS......... Material Availability Schedule
MAS......... Mathematics Attitude Scale (EDAC)
MAS......... Mature Age Student (ADA)
MAS......... Maximum Aerobic Speed [*Biology*]
MAS......... Maximum Amount Subject (MARI)
MAS......... McCune-Albright Syndrome [*Medicine*] (EDAA)
MAS......... McMaster University Library [*UTLAS symbol*]
MAS......... Meconium Aspiration Syndrome [*Medicine*]
MAS......... Media Advisory Service [*British*]
MAS......... Medical Administrative Service (DAVI)
MAS......... Medical Advisory Service [*British*]
MAS......... Medical Audit Statistics (PDAA)
MAS......... Medical Audit Study (HCT)
MAS......... Meiosis-Activating Sterol [*Cytology*]
MAS......... Member of the Arundel Society [*British*]
MAS......... Memory and Auxiliary Storage Subsystem [*Space Flight Operations Facility, NASA*]
MAS......... Mercury Analyzer System [*Perkin-Elmer Co. instrument designation*]
MAS......... Merged Area Schools (OICC)
MAS......... Merseyside Archaeological Society (SAUO)
MAS......... Merseyside Aviation Society [*British*] (DBA)
MAS......... Mesoatrial Shunt [*Medicine*] (DMAA)
MAS......... Metal-Alumina Semiconductor (IAA)
MAS......... Metal-Alumina-Silicon (IEEE)
MAS......... Metal Anchor Slots [*Technical drawings*]
MAS......... Metals/Alloy Solidification (SAUS)
MAS......... Metastable Atomic State
MAS......... Methods and Standards (MCD)
MAS......... Methods of Air Sampling and Analysis [*Air Pollution Control Association*]
MAS......... Methods of Analysis Sub-committee (SAUO)
MAS......... Mezhdunarodnaya Assotsiatsiya Sudovladeltsev [*International Shipowners' Association*] [*Poland*] (EAIO)
MAS......... Michigan Academy of Science (SAUO)
MAS......... Michigan Adaptive Sports (EARSL)
MAS......... Michigan Audubon Society (SAUO)
MAS......... Microage Solutions, Inc. (EFIS)
MAS......... Micro-Alloyed Steel [*Metallurgical engineering*]
MAS......... Micro-Assembly System (VLIE)
MAS......... Micro Automation System
MAS......... Microbeam Analysis Society (EA)
MAS......... Microprogram Automation System [*Computer science*] (IAA)
MAS......... Midcourse Active System (MCD)
MAS......... Middle Air Space (PDAA)
MAS......... Military Agency for Standardization [*Brussels, Belgium*] [*NATO*]
MAS......... Military Airlift Squadron [*Air Force*] (CINC)
MAS......... Military Antiquarian Society (SAUO)
MAS......... Military Area Services (SAUO)
MAS......... Military Assistance Sales (MCD)
MAS......... Milk-Alkali Syndrome [*Medicine*] (DMAA)
mAs......... Milliampere-Second
MAS......... Millimeterwave Atmospheric Sounder (SAUO)
MAS......... Milwaukee Astronomical Society (SAUO)
MAS......... Mine Avoidance Sonar (SAUS)
MAS......... Minimal Access Surgery (SAUO)
MAS......... Ministry of Aviation Supply [*British*]
MAS......... Minnesota Academy of Science
MAS......... Missile Alignment Set
MAS......... Missile Assembly Site (NATG)
MAS......... Missile Assigned Switch
MAS......... Missile Auxiliaries System
MAS......... Mission Area Summary (ACAE)
MAS......... Mission Auxiliary Subsystem (ACAE)
MAS......... Mississippi Academy of Sciences (BUAC)
MAS......... Mississippi Association of Supervisors (EARSL)
MAS......... Missouri Academy of Science (SAUO)
MAS......... Mobile Access Structure [*Space launch term*] (ISAK)
MAS......... Mobile Arm Support [*Orthopedics*] (DAVI)
MAS......... Mobile Atmospheric Spectrometer [*Marine science*] (OSRA)
MAS......... Model Abattoir Society (SAUO)
MAS......... Model Assignment Sheet (MCD)
MAS......... Modern Army Supply
MAS......... Modern Army System
MAS......... Modular Accounting System [*Computer science*] (IAA)
MAS......... Modular Application Systems [*Martin Marietta Data Systems*]
MAS......... Monaco Group, Inc. [*Toronto Stock Exchange symbol*]

MAS .... Monetary Allowance in Lieu of Subsistence
MAS .... Monetary Authority of Singapore (NUMA)
MAS .... Money Advice Scotland (BUAC)
MAS .... Monitor and Alarm System (MCD)
MAS .... Monmouth Antiquarian Society (EA)
MAS .... Monoacetoxylscirpenol [*Organic toxin*]
MAS .... Morgagni-Adam-Stokes (DB)
MAS .... Morphing Aircraft Structures Program [*Defense Advanced Research Projects Agency*] (RCD)
MAS .... Mortgage Analysis System (FOTI)
MAs.......... Mothers Anonymous (SAUO)
MAS .... Mount Alvernia Seminary (SAUO)
MAS .... Mount Angel Seminary [*Oregon*]
MAS .... Movement Alarm System [*Gynecology*]
MAS .... Movimiento al Socialismo [*Movement towards Socialism*] [*Argentina*] [*Political party*] (PPW)
MAS .... Movimiento al Socialismo [*Movement towards Socialism*] [*Venezuela*] [*Political party*] (PPW)
MAS .... Movimiento de Accion Socialista [*Peru*] [*Political party*] (EY)
MAS .... Movimiento para Accion y Solidaridad [*Guatemala*] [*Political party*] (EY)
MAS .... Muerte a los Secuestradores [*Death to Kidnappers*] [*Colombia*] (PD)
MAS .... Mujeres en Accion Sindical [*Organizes national and international conferences on women in the economy*] [*Mexico*] (CROSS)
MAS .... Multi-Agent System (IDAI)
MAS .... Multiaspect Signaling (IEEE)
MAS .... Multiple Address System [*Telecommunications*] (CDE)
MAS .... Multiple Aim Structure (MCD)
MAS .... Multiple Award Schedule [*Government contracting*]
MAS .... Municipal Analysis Services, Inc. [*Information service or system*] (IID)
MAS .... Municipal Art Society (SAUO)
MAS .... Mutually Assured Survival
MAS .... Myanmar Agricultural Service (SAUO)
MAS .... Society of African Missions (SAUO)
MASA........ Mail Advertising Service Association International [*Bethesda, MD*]
MASA........ Malaysian Shipowners Association (SAUO)
MASA........ Marine Accessories and Services Association [*Later, NAMPS*] (EA)
MASA........ Master of Advanced Studies in Architecture (PGP)
MASA........ Mathematical Association of South Australia
MASA........ Medical Acronyms, Symbols & Abbreviations [*A publication*]
MASA........ Medical Association of South Africa (DMAA)
MASA........ Medical Association of the State of Alabama (SAUO)
MASA........ Member of the Acoustical Society of America (SAUO)
MASA........ Men Against Sexual Assault [*Australia*]
MASA........ Mental Retardation-Aphasia-Shuffling Gait-Adducted Thumbs [*Syndrome*] [*Medicine*] (DMAA)
MASA........ Merged Area Schools Administrators Association (OICC)
MASA........ Metals and Alloys Solidification Apparatus (SAUS)
MASA........ Michigan Association of School Administrators (SAUO)
MASA........ Military Accessories Service Association (EA)
MASA........ Military Automotive Supply Agency
MASA........ Minnesota Association of School Administrators (SAUO)
MASA........ Mission Analysis for reconnaissance-Spanning & Attack (SAUS)
MASA........ Mississippi Association of School Administrators (SAUO)
MASA........ Missouri Association of School Administrators (EARSL)
MASA........ Modular Avionics Systems Architecture (MCD)
MASA........ Montana Association of School Administrators (SAUO)
MASA........ Multimedia Services Affiliate Forum (SAUO)
MASA........ Multiple Anodic Stripping Analyzer (PDAA)
MASA........ Music and Arts Society of America (EA)
MASAAV .... Mid-Atlantic States Association of Avian Veterinarians (EA)
MASAC ...... Master of Arts in Substance Abuse Counseling (PGP)
MASACA .... Michigan Association of Substance Abuse Coordinating Agencies (EARSL)
MASAD...... Mission Analysis and Systems Acquisition Division (AAGC)
MASAE ...... Member of the American Society of Agricultural Engineering
MASAF...... Mediterranean Allied Strategic Air Force
MASAI...... Mail Advertising Service Association International (EA)
MASAL...... Michigan Academy of Science, Arts, and Letters
MASANYC .. Mail Advertising Service Association of New York City (SAUO)
MASAP...... Michigan Association of Single Adoptive Parents (EA)
MASAQUE .. Major Action Significantly Affecting the Quality of the Human Environment (DNAB)
MASAR...... Management Assurance of Safety, Adequacy, and Reliability (MHDB)
MASAR...... Microwave Accurate Surface Antenna Reflector (PDAA)
MASAR...... Multimode Airborne Solid-State Array RADAR System [*Military*] (PDAA)
MASB........ Main Array Signal Band
MASB........ MASSBANK Corp. [*NASDAQ symbol*] (NQ)
MASB........ Michigan Association of School Boards (SAUO)
MA/SB....... Motor Antisubmarine Boat [*Obsolete*] [*British*]
MASBAL .... RCRA Mass Balance System (SAUS)
MASBO...... Minnesota Association of School Business Officials (SAUO)
MASC........ Magazine Advertising Sales Club (EA)
MASC........ Magnetic Attitude Spin Coil
MASC........ MAGTF [*Marine Air-Ground Task Force*] Automated Services Center (GFGA)
MASC........ Maintenance Support Concept Model (MCD)
MASC........ Managed Audio Sound Compression [*Electronics*]
MASC........ Management Systems Concept (PDAA)
MASC........ Manpower Authorization Standards and Criteria (SAUO)
MASC........ Maori Affairs Select Committee (SAUO)
MASC........ Mascot Homes [*NCIC trailer make code*]
masc .... Masculine (SHCU)
MASC........ Masculine
MASC........ Massachusetts Association of School Committees (SAUO)
masc .... Mass Concentration [*Medicine*] (MAE)
MASc........ Master of Agricultural Science (DD)
MA Sc....... Master of Applied Science
MASC........ Medical Academic Staff Committee (SAUO)
MASC........ Medical Advisers Support Centre (SAUO)
MASC........ Methylaluminum Sesquichloride [*Organic chemistry*]
MASC........ Microsoft Access Script Command [*Computer language*]
MASC........ Middletown Air Service Command [*Air Force*]
MASC........ Military Automotive Supply Center (MCD)
MASC........ Model to Evaluate Maintenance Support Concepts (MCD)
MASC........ Mountain Administration Support Center (SAUO)
MASC........ Mountain Administrative Support Center [*Marine science*] (OSRA)
MASC........ Multilayer Aluminium Oxide-Silicon-Dioxide Combination (IAA)
MASC........ Multiple Award Schedule Contract [*Government contracting*]
MASCA...... Middle Atlantic States Correctional Association (SAUO)
MASCA...... Museum Applied Science Center for Archeology [*University of Pennsylvania*]
MASCAC .... Middle Atlantic States Collegiate Athletic Conference (PSS)
MASCAJ..... MASCA Journal. Museum Applied Science Center for Archaeology, University Museum, University of Pennsylvania [*A publication*] (ABAR)
MASCAL .... Mass Casualty [*Military*]
MASCD...... Maine Association for Supervision and Curriculum Development (EARSL)
MASCD...... Maryland Association of Soil Conservation Districts (EARSL)
MASCD...... Missouri Association for Supervision and Curriculum Development (EARSL)
MASCDC .... Military Aircraft Storage and Disposition Center (SAUO)
MASCDCS .. Madison Avenue Sports Car Driving and Chowder Society (EA)
MASCE ...... Member of the American Society of Civil Engineers
MASCE ...... Member of the Australian Society of Civil Engineers (SAUO)
MASCO...... Maintenance Schedule Code (PDAA)
Masco....... Masco Corp. [*Associated Press*] (SAG)
MASCO...... Mead Access Systems Co.
MASCO...... Microprogrammed and Simulated Computer Organization
MASCOM ... Master Communications (PDAA)
MASCON.... Mass Concentration [*of gravitational pull*]
MASCOT .... Management Advisory System using Computerized Optimization Techniques (PDAA)
MASCOT .... Manned Shuttle Comprehensive Optimization and Targeting [*NASA*]
Mascot...... Mascotech [*Commercial firm*] [*Associated Press*] (SAG)
MASCOT .... Meteorological Auxiliary Sea Current Observation Transmitter
MASCOT .... Military Air-Transportable Satellite Communications Terminal
MASCOT .... Mobile Air-Transportable Satellite Communications Terminal [*Military*] (IAA)
MASCOT .... Modern Approach to Software Construction, Operation and Test [*Ministry of Defence*] [*British*]
MASCOT .... Modular Approach to Software Construction Operation and Test (NITA)
MASCOT .... Modular Approach to System Construction Operation and Test (MCD)
MASCOT .... Motorola Automatic Sequential Computer Operated Tester
Mascotch ... Mascotech [*Commercial firm*] [*Associated Press*] (SAG)
MasCp....... MassMutual Corporate Investors, Inc. [*Associated Press*] (SAG)
MASCP...... Multicultural and Cross-Cultural Supplementation Program [*Australia*]
MASCP&T... Member, American Society for Clinical Pharmacology & Therapeutics (CMD)
MASCS .... Marriage Adjustment Sentence Completion Survey [*Psychology*]
MASCU...... Marine Air Support Control Unit
MASCY...... Mason City, IA [*American Association of Railroads railroad junction routing code*]
MASD .... Mach Aids to Surface-to-Air Missile Development (IAA)
MASD .... Master of Arts in Spiritual Direction (PGP)
MASD .... Menstrual-Associatied Sleep Disorder [*Medicine*] (MELL)
MASD .... Mobile Air and Space Defense [*Air Force*]
MASD .... Motion Analysis Systems Division [*Automotive engineering*]
MASDC...... Military Aircraft Storage and Disposition Center
MASDCMIS... MASDC Management Information System (SAUO)
MASDR...... Measurement and Signature Data Requirements (MCD)
MasdSec.... Masada Security Holdings, Inc. [*Associated Press*] (SAG)
MASE........ Maserati [*NCIC car make code*]
MASE........ McDonnell Airborne Sidewinder Evaluator [*McDonnell Douglas Corp.*] (MCD)
MASE........ Medical and Scientific Equipment
MASE........ Message Administration Service Element [*Open Systems Interconnection*] (ODAA)
MASE........ Military Assistance Service Fund (AAGC)
MASE........ Mission and Systems Engineering (ACAE)
MASE........ Moore School Air Space Simulation Effort (MCD)
MASE........ Multi-Axis Seat Ejection (SAUS)
MASEA ...... Midwest Association of Student Employment Administrators [*Formerly, MAUSED*] (EA)
MASEAN .... Medical Association of South East Asian Nations (BUAC)
MASEC ...... Mid-America Solar Energy Conference (SAUO)
MASEC ...... Multi-Access Systems Control Terminal (PDAA)
MASECA .... Maderas Secas C.A. (EFIS)
MASEE ...... Member of the Association of Supervisory and Executive Engineers [*British*] (DBQ)
MASEFI ..... Mass Air Sequential Electronic Fuel Injection [*Automotive engineering*]
MASEG ...... Microwave Antenna Systems Engineering Group (SAUO)
MASER ...... Microwave [*or Molecular*] Amplification by Stimulated Emission of Radiation
maser .... Microwave Amplification by Stimulated Emission of Radiation (WDMC)

MASER ...... Molecular Application by Stimulated Emission of Radiation [*Organic chemistry*] (DAVI)
MASES ...... Microcomputer Advice and Selection Expert System (PDAA)
MASEX ...... Maritime Air Superiority Exercise (NVT)
MASF .... Maintenance and Storage Facility (SAUO)
MASF .... Marconi Advanced Sample Facility (NITA)
MASF .... Military Assistance Service Fund (SAUO)
MASF .... Military Assistance Service Funded
MASF .... Mobile Aeromedical Staging Facility
MASF .... Mobile Aeromedical Staging Flights (SAUS)
MASF .... Multiracial American Scholarship Fund
MASFA ...... Middle Atlantic States Fencing Association (PSS)
MASFC ...... MAGTF All Source Fusion Center (SAUO)
MASFET ..... Metal-Alumina-Silicon Field Effect Transistor (IAA)
MASFLEX ... Marginal Sea Flux Experiment (SAUO)
MASFLEX ... Marginal Sea Flux Experiment in the West Pacific (SAUO)
MASFM ..... Maintenance and Supply Facility Management (AFIT)
MAS/FS ..... Mohawk Aerial Surveillance/Flight Simulator (MCD)
MASG .... Marine Air Support Group
MASG .... Master Liner Manufacturing [*NCIC trailer make code*]
MASG .... Military Airlift Support Group [*Air Force*]
MASG .... Missile Auxiliary Signal Generator
MASG .... Monitor and Alarm Subsystem Group (MCD)
MASGC ...... Mississippi-Alabama Sea Grant Consortium [*Sea Grant College*] [*Research center*] (RCD)
MASGP ...... Military Airlift Support Group [*Air Force*]
MASH .... Male Anglo-Saxon Heterosexual [*Medicine*] (EDAA)
MASH .... Manned Antisubmarine Helicopter
MASH .... Medical Aid for Sick Hippies [*Volunteer medical group*]
MASH .... Melting-Assimilation-Storage-Homogenization [*Geology*]
MASH .... Members of Arthritics for Self-Help [*Medicine*] (EDAA)
MASH .... Memphians Against Social Harassment (SAUO)
MASH .... Michigan Area Serial Holdings Consortium [*Library network*]
MASH .... Micro-Analytic Simulation of Households (PDAA)
MASH .... Mobile Army Surgical Hospital [*Acronym also used as title of a satirical film, 1970, and a TV series*]
MASH .... Mobilization for Adolescent Student Health [*Medicine*] (EDAA)
MASH .... Multiple Accelerated Summary Hearing [*Deportation of illegal aliens*] [*Immigration and Naturalization Service*]
MASH .... Multiple Automated Sample Harvester [*for culture systems*]
MASH .... Municipalities, Academia, Schools, and Hospitals (FOTI)
MASH .... Mutual Aid Self-Help Group
MASHAE .... Member of the American Society of Heating and Air-conditioning Engineers (SAUO)
MASHONLD... Mashonaland (ROG)
MASHRAG .. Egypt, Jordan, Lebanon & Syria (SAUS)
MASHVE .... Member of the American Society of Heating and Ventilating Engineers (SAUO)
M/ASI .... Mach/Airspeed Indicator (GAVI)
MASI .... Media Association of the Solomon Islands (BUAC)
MASI .... Member of the Architects' and Surveyors' Institute (ODA)
MASI .... Middle Atmosphere Science Initiative (SAUO)
MASI .... Multilevel Academic Skills Inventory [*Educational test*]
MASI .... Multinational Agribusiness Systems, Inc. (SAUO)
MASID .... Marine Science Division [*Instrument Society of America*] (MSC)
MASIIS ...... Maintenance Analysis Structural Integrity Information System (SAUO)
MASINT ..... Measurement and Signature Intelligence (MCD)
MASINT ..... Measuring & Signature Intelligence (SAUS)
MASIS .... Management and Scientific Information Service (SAUO)
MASIS .... Management and Scientific Information System [*Air Force*]
MASIS .... Maruzen Scientific Information Service Center [*Maruzen Co. Ltd.*] [*Japan*] [*Telecommunications*]
MASIS .... Mercury Abort Sensing Instrumentation System [*NASA*] (AAG)
MASK .... Align-Rite International, Inc. [*NASDAQ symbol*] (SAG)
MASK .... Align-Rite Intl. [*NASDAQ symbol*] (TTSB)
MASK .... Maneuvering and Seakeeping
MASK .... Medical Anatomy Segmentation Kit (DMAA)
MASK .... Mobile Armored Strike Kommand [*Game*]
MASK .... Mothers and Fathers Aligned Saving Kids [*Association*] (EA)
MASK .... Multilevel Amplitude Shift Keying
maskon ..... Mass Concentration (BARN)
MAsl .... Ashland Public Library, Ashland, MA [*Library symbol*] [*Library of Congress*] (LCLS)
MASL .... MA [*Military Assistance*] Articles and Services List [*DoD*]
MASL .... Masterbilt Trailers [*NCIC trailer make code*]
masl .... Meters above Sea Level
Masl .... Metres above sea level (SAUS)
MASL .... Military Articles and Services List
MASL .... Military Assistance Article and Service List (MCD)
MASL .... Missouri Association of School Librarian
MASL .... Missouri Association of School Librarians
Masland .... Masland Corp. [*Associated Press*] (SAG)
MASLIG ..... Association of Management Analysts in State and Local Government (EA)
MASLPI ..... Mexican American State Legislators Policy Institute (CROSS)
MASM .... Macro Assembler [*Computer language*] (PCM)
MASM .... Master of Arts in Sacred Music (BJA)
MASM .... Meta-Assembler (NITA)
MASM .... Meta-Assembler Language [*Sperry UNIVAC computer language*]
MASM .... Microsoft Assembler (SAUS)
MASM .... Military Assistance and Sales Manual (AFIT)
MASM .... Motorized Antenna Switching Matrix
MASME ..... Member of the American Society of Mechanical Engineers
MASME ..... Member of the Australian Society of Mechanical Engineers (SAUO)
MAS/MILS... Minerals Availability System/Minerals Industry Location Subsystem [*Bureau of Mines*] [*Database*]
MASMOD ... Mass Model [*Computer program*]
MASMR ..... Multidimensional Attitude Scale on Mental Retardation (EDAC)
MASN .... Machine Accountant, Seaman [*Navy*]
masn .... Masonite (VRA)
MASN .... Masson's Welding [*NCIC trailer make code*]
MASN .... Maximum Aggregate Student Number [*Higher Education Funding Council*] (AIE)
MASNC ...... Minerals Availability System [*Bureau of Mines*] [*Information service or system*] (IID)
Mas NE Pr... Mason's New England Civil Practice [*A publication*] (DLA)
MASnet ..... Mainframe and Server network (SAUS)
MASNET .... Management Support Network (SAUO)
MASNMR ... Magic Angle Spinning Nuclear Magnetic Resonance [*Spectroscopy*]
Masnte ...... Maisonette
MASO .... Military Assistance Sales Order (CINC)
MASO .... Munition Accountable Supply Officer [*Air Force*] (AFM)
MASOA ...... Master and Slave Oscillator Array (PDAA)
MA (Social Studies)... Master of Arts (Social Studies)
MA(SocSci)... Master of Arts (Social Sciences), University of Glasgow [*British*] (DBQ)
MASocStud... Master of Arts in Social Studies (NADA)
MASON ...... Masonry
Mason .... Mason's United States Circuit Court Reports [*A publication*] (DLA)
Mason CCR. Mason's United States Circuit Court Reports [*A publication*] (DLA)
Mason Circt Ct R... Mason's United States Circuit Court Reports [*A publication*] (DLA)
MasonDix... Mason-Dixon Bancshares, Inc. [*Associated Press*] (SAG)
Mason R .... Mason's United States Circuit Court Reports [*A publication*] (DLA)
Mason's Code... Mason's United States Code, Annotated [*A publication*] (DLA)
Mason's R... Mason's United States Circuit Court Reports [*A publication*] (DLA)
Mason's Rep... Mason's United States Circuit Court Reports [*A publication*] (DLA)
Mason US... Mason's United States Circuit Court Reports [*A publication*] (DLA)
Mason US Circ Ct Rep... Mason's United States Circuit Court Reports [*A publication*] (DLA)
Mason USR .... Mason's United States Circuit Court Reports [*A publication*] (DLA)
MASP .... Medical Application Service Provider (SAUO)
MASP .... Microaerophilus Stationary Phase [*Biochemistry*] (DAVI)
MASP .... Modular Atmosphere Simulation Program [*NASA*] (KSC)
MASP .... Multiple Access Signal Processor (ACAE)
MASPAC .... Microfilm Advisory Service of the Public Archives of Canada (PDAA)
MAS PIL .... Massa Pilularum [*A Pill Mass*] [*Pharmacy*]
MasPrt ...... MassMutual Participation Investors [*Associated Press*] (SAG)
MASPS ...... Minimum Aviation System Performance Standards [*FAA*] (TAG)
MASPSq .... Military Airlift Special Squadron [*Air Force*]
MASPTSq ... Military Airlift Support Squadron [*Air Force*]
MASq .... Military Airlift Squadron [*Air Force*] (AFM)
MASQUES... Medical Application Software Quality Enhancement by Standards (SAUO)
Mas R .... Massachusetts Reports [*A publication*] (DLA)
MASR .... Mastercraft [*NCIC trailer make code*]
MASR .... Memory-Address Select Register [*Computer science*] (IAA)
MASR .... Microwave Atmosphere Sounding Radiometer (PDAA)
MASR .... Miniature Airborne/Spaceborne Reconnaissance (ACAE)
MASR .... Multiple-Antenna Moving-Target Surveillance RADAR
MASR .... Multiple Antenna Surveillance Radar (SAUS)
MASRC ...... Major Automated System Review Council [*Military*]
MASRC ...... Mexican American Studies and Research Center [*University of Arizona*] [*Research center*] (RCD)
Mas Rep .... Massachusetts Reports [*A publication*] (DLA)
MASRO ...... Mid-Atlantic Society of Radiation Oncologists (SAUO)
MASRT ...... Marine Air Support RADAR Teams (IEEE)
MASRU ...... Marine Air Support RADAR Unit [*DoD*]
MASS .... Magic Angle Sample Spinning [*Spectroscopy*]
MASS .... Manned Activity Scheduling System [*NASA*]
MASS .... Manned Aircraft Surface to Surface (ACAE)
MASS .... Manned Aircraft Versus Surface to Surface (ACAE)
MASS .... MARC [*Machine-Readable Cataloging*] Automated Serials System (PDAA)
MASS .... MARC-Based Automated Serials System (NITA)
MASS .... Marine Air Support Squadron
MASS .... Maritime Air Surveillance Sortie (SAUS)
MASS .... Maritime Anti-Standing SONAR System (DNAB)
MASS .... Massa [*A Mass*] [*Pharmacy*]
MASS .... Massachusetts (AFM)
Mass .... Massachusetts (BEE)
MASS .... Massachusetts Association of School Superintendents (SAUO)
MASS .... Massachusetts Bay (GAAI)
Mass .... Massachusetts Supreme Judicial Court Reports [*A publication*] (DLA)
mass .... Massage (DMAA)
MASS .... Massage
MASS .... Massey-Ferguson [*NCIC truck make code*]
MASS .... Massey-Ferguson [*NCIC trailer make code*]
MASS .... Massive (SAUS)
MA(SS) ...... Master of Arts in Social Science (ADA)
MASS .... Master of Arts in Special Studies (PGP)
M As S ...... Master of Association Science
MASS .... Material Accountability and Safeguards System (SAUO)
MASS .... Materials Acquisition Sub-System [*Computer science*]
MASS .... Matrix Analysis Subsystem (MCD)
MASS .... Maximum Availability and Support Subsystem (VLIE)
MAS/S .... Mechanical Arm Sub-System (ACAE)

MASS........ Mechanically Accelerated Sabot System [*Generation of high-density molecular beams*]
MASS........ Medicine, Angioplasty, or Surgery Study (DMAA)
MASS........ Membrane Affinity Separation System
MASS........ Memorandum Accounts Statement System (DCTA)
MASS........ MICAP [*Mission Critical Parts*] Asset Sourcing System (DOMA)
MASS........ Michigan Aging Services System (SAUO)
MASS........ Michigan Automatic Scanning System (IEEE)
MASS........ Microsystem Analysis and Simulation System (SAUO)
MAss........ Middle Assyrian [*Language, etc.*] (BJA)
MASS........ Military Agency for Supply and Service (SAUO)
MASS........ Military Airlift Support Squadron [*Air Force*]
MASS........ Military Airlift Survivability Study (ACAE)
MASS........ Military Approach and Surveillance System (SAUO)
MASS........ Missile and Space Summary (MCD)
MASS........ Missiles/Ammunition System Study
MASS........ Mission Avionics Sensor Synergism (SAUS)
MASS........ Mobility Analysis Support System [*Air Force*]
MASS........ Mobilization Automated Support System (SAUO)
MASS........ Modern Army Supply System
MASS........ Modular Adaptive Signal Sorter
MASS........ Modular Aircrew Simulation System (SAUS)
MASS........ Money Advice Support Services (BUAC)
MASS........ Monitor and Assembly System [*or Subsystem*] [*Computer science*] (BUR)
MASS........ Multiple Access Sequential Selection [*Computer science*] (BUR)
MASS........ Multiple Access Switching System (NITA)
MASS........ Multiple Array Serial Scan (ACAE)
MASS........ Multi-role Aid & Support Ship (SAUS)
Mass Acts... Acts and Resolves of Massachusetts [*A publication*] (DLA)
Mass AD.... Massachusetts Appellate Decisions [*A publication*] (DLA)
Mass Admin Code... Code of Massachusetts Regulations [*A publication*] (DLA)
Mass Admin Reg... Massachusetts Register [*A publication*] (DLA)
Mass ADR... Massachusetts Appellate Division Reports [*A publication*] (DLA)
Mass Adv Legis Serv... Massachusetts Advance Legislative Service [*Lawyers Co-Operative Publishing Co.*] [*A publication*] (DLA)
Mass Adv Sh... Massachusetts Advance Sheets [*A publication*] (DLA)
Mass Adv Sheets... Massachusetts Advance Sheets [*A publication*] (DLA)
MASS-ALFA... Massachusetts Assisted Living Facilities Association (EARSL)
Mass Ann Laws... Annotated Laws of Massachusetts [*A publication*] (DLA)
Mass Ann Laws... Annotated Laws of Massachusetts (journ.) (SAUS)
Mass App Ct... Massachusetts Appeals Court Reports [*A publication*] (DLA)
Mass App Ct Adv Sh... Massachusetts Appeals Court Advance Sheets [*A publication*] (DLA)
Mass App Dec... Massachusetts Appellate Decisions [*A publication*] (DLA)
Mass App Div... Massachusetts Appellate Division Reports [*A publication*] (DLA)
Mass App Rep... Massachusetts Appeals Court Reports [*A publication*] (DLA)
MASSAR.... Multimode Airborne Solid State Array RADAR
Mass BC & A... Massachusetts Board of Conciliation and Arbitration Reports [*A publication*] (DLA)
Massbnk.... Massbank Corp. [*Associated Press*] (SAG)
MASSBUS... Memory Bus [*Digital Equipment Corp.*]
massc....... Mass Concentration (DMAA)
M As Sc..... Master of Association Science
MASSCAL... Mass Casualties [*Military*] (AABC)
Mass C Art... Massachusetts College of Art (GAGS)
MASSCOMP... Massachusetts Computer Corp. (SAUO)
Mass Cont Election Cushing S & J... Massachusetts Controverted Election Cases [*A publication*] (DLA)
Mass C Pharmacy... Massachusetts College of Pharmacy (GAGS)
MASSDAR... Modular Analysis, Speedup, Sampling, and Data Reduction
MASSDATA... Mark Sense Source Data Automation Test and Analysis (MCD)
Mass Dent Soc J... Massachusetts Dental Society Journal (SAUO)
MASSDET... Marine Air Support Squadron Detachment (DNAB)
Mass DIA... Massachusetts. Department of Industrial Accidents. Bulletin [*A publication*] (DLA)
Mass Dr Com... Masse. Le Droit Commercial [*A publication*] (DLA)
MASSE...... Massena, NY [*American Association of Railroads railroad junction routing code*]
Mass EC L & R... Loring and Russell's Election Cases in Massachusetts [*A publication*] (DLA)
Mass Elec Ca... Massachusetts Election Cases [*A publication*] (DLA)
Mass Elec Cas... Massachusetts Election Cases [*A publication*] (DLA)
Mass Election Cases... Loring and Russell's Election Cases in Massachusetts [*A publication*] (DLA)
Mass Election Cases... Russell's Contested Election Cases [*Massachusetts*] [*A publication*] (DLA)
Mass Gen L... General Laws of the Commonwealth of Massachusetts (journ.) (SAUS)
Mass Gen Laws... Massachusetts General Laws [*A publication*] (DLA)
Mass Gen Laws Ann (West)... Massachusetts General Laws, Annotated (West) [*A publication*] (DLA)
MassHe..... Massachusetts Health & Education Tax Exempt Trust [*Associated Press*] (SAG)
MASS HFD... Multi-Additional SCSI [*Small Computer System Interface*] Subsystem Hot Fix Device [*Computer science*]
MASSI....... Massillon, OH [*American Association of Railroads railroad junction routing code*]
Mass IAB... Massachusetts Industrial Accident Board Reports of Cases [*A publication*] (DLA)
MASSIIS.... Maintenance Analysis and Structural Integration Information System
MassINC.... Massachusetts Institute for a New Commonwealth (RCD)
Mass LRC Dec... Massachusetts Labor Relations Commission Decisions [*A publication*] (DLA)
MASSMUTUAL... Massachusetts Mutual Life Insurance Co. (EFIS)
MASSOP.... Multi-Automatic System for Simulation and Operational Planning (PDAA)
MASSP...... Michigan Association of Secondary School Principals (SAUO)
MASSP...... Minnesota Association of Secondary School Principals (SAUO)
MASSP...... Missouri Association of Secondary School Principals (SAUO)
MASSP...... Montana Association of Secondary School Principals (SAUO)
Mass Pil.... Massa Pilularum [*A Pill Mass*] [*Pharmacy*]
MassPIRG... Massachusetts Public Interest Research Group (SAUO)
MASSPO.... Manned Space Flight Support Project Office [*NASA*] (IAA)
MASSq...... Military Airlift Support Squadron [*Air Force*] (AFM)
Mass R...... Massachusetts Reports [*A publication*] (DLA)
MASSR...... Mordovian Autonomous Soviet Socialist Republic (SAUO)
Mass Rep... Massachusetts Reports [*A publication*] (DLA)
MASS SPEC... Mass Spectrometry (GOBB)
Mass St BC & A... Massachusetts State Board of Conciliation and Arbitration Reports [*A publication*] (DLA)**Mass Supp**... Massachusetts Reports Supplement [*A publication*] (AAGC)
MASST...... Major Shipboard SATCOM Terminal (MCD)
MASST...... Major Ship Satellite Terminal
MASSTER... Mobile Army Sensor System Test, Evaluation, and Review
MASSTER... Modern Army Selected System Test, Evaluation, and Review
Mass UCC Op... Massachusetts Unemployment Compensation Commission Opinions [*A publication*] (DLA)
Mass UC Dig... Massachusetts Division of Unemployment Compensation Digest of Board of Review Decisions [*A publication*] (DLA)
Mass UC Ops... Massachusetts Division of Unemployment Compensation Opinions [*A publication*] (DLA)
Mass WCC... Massachusetts Workmen's Compensation Cases [*A publication*] (DLA)
MAST........ Arousal Seeking Tendency Scale [*Test*] (TMMY)
MAST........ Machine Automated Speech Transcription (PDAA)
MAST........ Magnetic Annular Shock Tube
MaST........ Management and Skills Training (BUAC)
MAST........ Marine Science and Technology
MAST........ Marine Science and Technology Programme (SAUO)
MAST........ Marine Stable Element
MAST........ Market Structures and Trends on Italy [*Databank Ltd.*] [*British*] (ECON)
MAST........ Mastech Corp. [*NASDAQ symbol*] (SAG)
MAST........ Mastectomy [*Medicine*] (AAMN)
MAST........ Master (ROG)
MAST........ Masterline Company [*NCIC trailer make code*]
Mast......... Master's Supreme Court Reports [*25-28 Canada*] [*A publication*] (DLA)
MAST........ Mastoid [*Medicine*]
MAST........ Measurement and Stimuli System (SSD)
MAST........ Medical Antishock Trausers (MELL)
MAST........ Medical Anti-Shock Trousers [*Military*]
MAST........ Membrane Applied Science and Technology Center [*University of Colorado at Boulder*] (RCD)
MAST........ Meteorological Automated Sensor and Transceiver [*Military*]
MAST........ Metro Arson Strike Team (SAUO)
MAST........ Metropolitan Arson Strike Team (SAUO)
MAST........ Michelin Americas Small Tires
MAST........ Michigan Alcoholism Screening Test
MAST........ Midlevel Positions in Administrative, Staff, and Technical Services [*Civil Service Commission*]
MAST........ Midwest Agents Selling Travel (TVEL)
MAST........ Military Antishock Trousers [*Medicine*]
MAST........ Military Assistance to Safety and Traffic [*Project*] [*Army*] (RDA)
MAST........ Minimum Abbreviations of Serial Titles [*A publication*]
MAST........ Missile Automatic Supply Technique
MAST........ Mobile Aircrew Sustainment Trainer (SAUS)
MAST........ Mobile Assembly Sterilizer for Testing
MAST........ Model Assembly Sterilizer for Testing [*NASA*]
MAST........ Monterey Area Ship Experiment (SAUO)
MAST........ Monterey Area Ship Track experiment (SAUO)
MAST........ Multi-Axis Simulation Table [*Automotive engineering*]
MAST........ Multilevel Academic Survey Test [*Educational test*]
MAST........ Multimission Airborne Surveillance Technology programme (SAUS)
MAST........ Multiple-Aircraft Simulation Terminal (DA)
MAST........ Multiple Applications Storage Tube
MAST........ Multivalued Advanced Simulation Techniques (VLIE)
MAST........ Munitions Assistance and Standardization Team (MCD)
MASTA...... American String Teachers Association, Michigan Chapter (EARSL)
MASTA...... Medical Advisory Services for Travellers Abroad [*London School of Hygiene andTropical Medicine*] [*Information service or system*] (IID)
MastAcftCrmnBad... Master Aircraft Crewman Badge [*Military decoration*] (AABC)
MASTACS... Maneuverability Augmentation System for Tactical Air Combat Simulation (PDAA)
MASTA Ltd.... Medical Advisory Services for Travellers Abroad Ltd. (IID)
MASTAP..... Master System Tape (IAA)
MASTAP..... Master Tape (VLIE)
MASTARAV... Master Army Aviator (AABC)
Mast AR Av Bad... Master Army Aviator Badge [*Military decoration*]
MASTARS... Mechanical and Structural Testing and Referral Service [*National Institute of Standards and Technology*]
MAStat...... Master of Applied Statistics
Mast Div Bad... Master Diver Badge [*Military decoration*]
MAST-E..... Multicenter Acute Stroke Trial-Europe [*Neurology*]

Mastec...... Mastec, Inc. [*Associated Press*] (SAG)
Mastech..... Mastech Corp. [*Associated Press*] (SAG)
Mast El...... Masterman's Parliamentary Elections [*1880*] [*A publication*] (DLA)
MASTER .... Manuscript Access through Standards for Electronic Records [*Library science*] (TELE)
MASTER .... Matching Available Student Time to Educational Resources [*Computer science*]
MASTER .... Military Aircraft Satcoms Terminal (SAUS)
MASTER .... Miniaturized Sink-Rate Telemetering RADAR
MASTER .... Modular Acoustic Stimulator/Emulator (SAUS)
MASTER .... Multiple Access Shared Time Executive Routine [*Control Data Corp.*] [*Computer science*]
MASTER KEY... Managership of Soldier Training, Education, and Readiness with Knowledge and Excellence Year-Round [*Army*] (INF)
MASTEX..... Mediterranean Aircraft and Ship Transmission Experiment (SAUO)
MASTICH ... Mastiche [*Mastic*] [*Pharmacy*] (ROG)
MASTIF ..... Multi-Axis Spin Test Inertia Facility [*Training device for astronauts*]
MASTIFF.... Modular Automated System to Identify Friend from Foe [*Military*] (PDAA)
Mastin Art... Masters in Art (SAUO)
Mastin Music... Masters in Music (SAUO)
MASTIR ..... Handbook on Marine Scientific and Technological Information Resources (SAUS)
MASTIR ..... Microfilmed Abstract System for Technical Information Retrieval [*Illinois Institute of Technology*] (IID)
MASTOR .... Main Storage (VLIE)
MastPrchtBad... Master Parachutist Badge [*Military decoration*] (AABC)
MASTS ...... Marine Associated Services Technology Systems Exposition [*Canada*] (ITD)
MaSTS ...... Marine Strategy for the Torres Strait (SAUO)
MAstS ...... Member of the Astronomical Society
MASTT ...... MPS Action Speed Tactical Trainer (SAUS)
MASTU...... Mobile Antisubmarine Training Unit [*British*]
MASU .... Machined Surface
MASU .... MAT Transport [*Intermodal shipping container symbol*] (TVRC)
MASU .... Mediterranean and African Society for Ultrasound (SAUO)
MASU .... Mediterranean and African Society of Ultrasound [*France*] (BUAC)
MASU .... Mesoamerican Archaeology Study Unit [*American Topical Association*] (EA)
MASU .... Metal Alloy Separation Unit
MASU .... Mid-Atlantic State University
MASU .... Mobile Army Surgical Unit
MASU .... Multiple Acceleration Sensor Unit (PDAA)
MASUA...... Mid-America State Universities Association [*Defunct*] (EA)
MASURCA... Marine Surface Contre Avions (SAA)
MASV........ Master View [*NCIC trailer make code*]
MASW....... Master of Arts in Social Work
MASW....... Master Switch (IAA)
MASW....... Military Airlift Support Wing [*Air Force*]
MASW....... Mission Application Software (SAUO)
MASW....... Missouri Association for Social Welfare (EARSL)
MASWEP.... Medium Active Solid Waste Encapsulation Plant [*Nuclear energy*] (NUCP)
MASWg ..... Military Airlift Support Wing [*Air Force*] (AFM)
MASWSP ... Manager, Antisubmarine Warfare Systems Project [*Navy*]
MASWSPO... Manager, Antisubmarine Warfare Systems Project Office [*Navy*]
MASWT ..... Mobile Antisubmarine Warfare Target (MCD)
MASWT ..... MPS Anti-Submarine Warfare Trainer (SAUS)
MASX........ Masco Corporation (EFIS)
MASX........ Masco Industries, Inc. (EFIS)
MASX........ Mastec, Inc. [*NASDAQ symbol*] (SAG)
MASY........ Marketing Systems of America [*NASDAQ symbol*]
MASY........ Massey [*NCIC motorcycle make code*]
MASZ........ Maersk Shipping [*Federal Railroad Administration identification code*]
MAT.......... Machine-Aided Translation (NITA)
MAT.......... Machine Analysis Table (IAA)
MAT.......... Machine-Assisted Translation
MAT.......... Machine Available Time [*Computer science*]
MAT.......... Macro-Alloy Transistor (VLIE)
MAT.......... Maine Air Transport, Inc. (SAUO)
MAT.......... Maine Aviation Corp. [*ICAO designator*] (FAAC)
MAT.......... Maintainability of Software Analysis Tool (MCD)
MAT.......... Maintenance Access Terminal [*Aviation*]
MAT.......... Maintenance Appraisal Team (MCD)
MAT.......... Mammary Ascites Tumor [*Oncology*]
MAT.......... Management Advisory Team (NRCH)
MAT.......... Manifold Air Temperature [*Automotive engineering*]
MAT.......... Manual Arts Therapist
MAT.......... Manufacture and Test (SAUO)
MAT.......... Marine Air Temperature [*Meteorology*]
MAT.......... Maritime, Aviation, and Transport Insurance (DLA)
MAT.......... Marketing Assistance Test
MAT.......... Marksman Advanced Trainer (SAUS)
MAT.......... Master Account Title [*Office of Management and Budget*]
MA(T) .... Master of Arts in Teaching (PGP)
MAT.......... Master of Arts in Theology (PGP)
MAT.......... Master Operational Recording Tape Address Table (IAA)
MAT.......... Matachewan Consolidated Mines Ltd. [*Toronto Stock Exchange symbol*]
MAT.......... Matadi [*Zaire*] [*Airport symbol*] [*Obsolete*] (OAG)
MAT.......... Matador [*NCIC car model code*]
MAT.......... Matching Abacus Test [*Parapsychology*]
MAT.......... Material (AFM)
Mat .... Material (DIAR)
mat .... Material (VRA)
MAT.......... Materials Department [*David W. Taylor Naval Ship Research and Development Center*] [*Annapolis, MD*]
MAT.......... Materiel [*Military*] (AFM)
mat .... Maternal (GEAB)
Mat .... Maternal (STED)
Mat .... Maternity (STED)
MAT.......... Maternity
MAT.......... Mathematical Automata Theory
mat .... Matinee (WDAA)
MAT.......... Matinee
MAT.......... Matins (ROG)
MAT.......... Matrix (MSA)
mat .... Matrix (WDAA)
MAT.......... Matrix Analogies Test [*Intelligence test*]
MAT.......... Matsushiro [*Japan*] [*Seismograph station code, US Geological Survey*] (SEIS)
MAT.......... Mattel, Inc. [*NYSE symbol*] (SPSG)
Mat .... Mattheus de Mathesillanis [*Flourished, 1381-1402*] [*Authority cited in pre-1607 legal work*] (DSA)
MAT.......... Matthew [*New Testament book*]
MAT.......... Mattoon, IL [*Amtrak rail station code*]
Mat .... Mature (STED)
MAT.......... Matured
Mat .... Maturity (EBF)
MAT.......... Maturity
MAT.......... Matutinal (ADA)
MAT.......... Mean Absorption Time [*Medicine*] (MELL)
MAT.......... Mean Annual Temperature [*Climatology*]
MAT.......... Measurement of Atmospheric Turbulence
MAT.......... Mechanical Aptitude Test
MAT.......... Mechanical Assembly Technique (IAA)
MAT.......... Mechanically Agitated Tank [*Engineering*]
MAT.......... Medial Axes Transformation (MHDI)
MAT.......... Medial Axis Transformation (MHDB)
MAT.......... Medical Assessment Tribunal [*Queensland, Australia*]
MAT.......... Medical Assistance (Emergency) Team [*Medicine*] (EDAA)
MAT.......... Medication Administration Team [*Medicine*] (EDAA)
MAT.......... Medium Artillery Tractor [*British military*] (DMA)
MAT.......... Medium Assault Transport (MCD)
MAT.......... Memory Access Table [*Computer science*]
MAT.......... Memory-Address Test
MAT.......... Memory Address Translator (NITA)
MAT.......... Mercury Amalgamation Trap [*Analytical chemistry*]
MAT.......... Meridian Administration Tools [*Telecommunications*] (ITD)
MAT.......... Meteorological Atmospheric Turbulence (MCD)
MAT.......... Methionine Adenosyltransferase [*An enzyme*]
MAT.......... Metropolitan Achievement Test
MAT.......... Metropolitan Area Trunk [*Telecommunications*] (TEL)
MAT.......... Microactivity Testing [*Catalysis technology*]
MAT.......... Microagglutination Test [*Medicine*] (MELL)
MAT.......... Microalloy Transistor
MAT.......... Microtray Agglutination Test [*Clinical chemistry*]
MAT.......... Microwave Anisotropy Telescope (SAUS)
MAT.......... Microwave Antenna Tower
MAT.......... Military Aircraft Types
MAT.......... Military Air Transport
MAT.......... Miller-Abbott Tube [*Surgery*] [*Medicine*] (DAVI)
MAT.......... Miller Analogies Test [*Psychology*]
MAT.......... Mine Action Team (SAUO)
MAT.......... Mine Assembly Team [*Navy*] (NVT)
MAT.......... Minimal Aversion Threshold [*to noise*]
MAT.......... Minimum Allowable Threshold [*Chemistry*]
MAT.......... Minnesota Association of Townships (EARSL)
MAT.......... Missile Acceptance Team (AAG)
MAT.......... Missile Acceptance Test
MAT.......... Missile Acquisition and Track
MAT.......... Missile Adapter Tester
MAT.......... Missile Airframe Technology (MCD)
MAT.......... Missile Antitank
MAT.......... Mobile Advisor Team [*Vietnamese team trained by US Army advisors*] (VNW)
MAT.......... Mobile Aerial Target (AAG)
MAT.......... Mobile Arming Tower (KSC)
MAT.......... Mobile Assistance Team [*Federal disaster planning*]
MAT.......... Mobile Mine Assembly Team
MAT.......... Mobilization Assistance Team (SAUO)
MAT.......... Models and Assimilation Team [*National Oceanic and Atmospheric Administration*] (RCD)
MAT.......... Modular Advanced Test (SAUS)
MAT.......... Modular Allocation Technique (PDAA)
MAT.......... Modular Assembly Technique (IAA)
MAT.......... Molecular Analysis Team
MAT.......... Monoamine Transporter [*Biochemistry*]
MAT.......... Monocyto-Angiotropin [*Biochemistry*]
MAT.......... Monopulse Angle Tracker (ACAE)
MAT.......... Motivation Analysis Test [*Psychology*]
MAT.......... Motor Ambulance Trolley [*British*]
MAT.......... Moving Annual Total [*Statistics*] (DCTA)
MAT.......... Multiallelic Mating-Type Regulatory Gene
MAT.......... Multifocal Atrial Tachycardia [*Cardiology*]
MAT.......... Multimedia Access Terminals [*Philips*] [*Electronics*]
MAT.......... Multiple Access Test
MAT.......... Multiple Access Time [*Telecommunications*] (ECII)

MAT.......... Multiple Actuator Test (MCD)
MAT.......... Multiple Address Telegrams
MAT.......... Multiple-Agent Chemotherapy [*Medicine*] (DB)
MAT.......... Multiple Aptitude Test [*Education*] (AEBS)
MATA........ Matra [*NCIC car make code*]
MATA........ Michigan Aviation Trades Association (SAUO)
MATA........ Military Air Transport Association (SAUO)
MATA........ Military Assistance Training Advisor
MATA........ Missouri Association of Trial Attorneys (EARSL)
MATA........ Motorcycle and Allied Trades Association [*Later, MIC*] (EA)
MATA........ Multiple Answering Teaching Aid (PDAA)
MATA........ Museums Association of Tropical Africa (BUAC)
MATA........ Musical Arena Theatres Association [*Later, PAMI*] (EA)
MATABE..... Multiple-Weapon Automatic Target and Battery Evaluator (SAA)
MATAC...... Money Advice Trust Advisory Committee (BUAC)
MAT ACCAT... Mobile Access Terminal Advanced Command & Control Architectural Test-bed (SAUS)
MATACQ..... Material Acquisition (NG)
MATADOR... Mobile and Three-Dimensional Air Defense Operations RADAR [*Military*] (PDAA)
MATADOR... Multi-role Adaptive Tactical Auto-programmable Dynamic Radio System (SAUS)
MATAF....... Mediterranean Allied Tactical Air Force
Mataph...... Metaphysics (SAUO)
Mata Soc... Mattachine Society (SAUO)
MATB........ Military Air Transport Board
MATB........ Missile Auxiliary Test Bench
MATC........ Maximum Acceptable Tolerance Concentration (GNE)
MATC........ Maximum Acceptable Toxicant Concentration
MATC........ Maximum Allowable Toxicant Concentration (EEVL)
MATC........ Mid-America Transportation Center [*University of Nebraska--Lincoln*] (RCD)
MATC........ Middle Atlantic Conference (PSS)
MATC........ Military Air Transport Command (MUGU)
MATC........ Milwaukee Area Technical College (PCM)
MATC........ Missile Auxiliaries Test Console
MATC........ Mobilization Army Training Center
MATC........ Mountain Artillery Training Centre [*British military*] (DMA)
MATCALS... Marine Air Traffic and Landing Systems (SAUO)
MATCALS... Marine Air Traffic Control and Landing System [*Navy*]
MATCALS... Mobile Air Traffic Control and All-Weather Landing System (MCD)
MATCAT..... Material Category
MATCD...... Marine Air Traffic Control Detachment
MATCen..... Military Air Traffic Center (SAUO)
MATCH...... Manned Anti-submarine Troop-Carrying Helicopter (SAUS)
MATCH...... Manned Attack Torpedo Carrying Helicopter (PDAA)
MATCH...... Manpower and Talent Clearinghouse
MATCH...... Matching Alcoholism Treatments to Client Heterogeneity
MATCH...... Materials and Activities for Teachers and Children
MATCH...... Medium-Range Antisubmarine Torpedo Carrying Helicopter (NATG)
MATCH...... Model for Atmospheric Chemistry and Transport (SAUO)
MATCH...... Mothers Apart from Their Children [*British*] (DI)
MATCH...... MTMC [*Military Traffic Management Command*] Automated Transportation Scheduler (GFGA)
MATCH...... Multielement Assured Tracking Chopper
MATCH...... Multimedia Authoring Environments for Children (SAUO)
MATCH...... Research Program in Managing Technological Change [*Carleton University*] [*Canada*] (RCD)
MATCM...... Master of Acupuncture and Traditional Chinese Medicine (PGP)
MATCO...... Materials Analysis, Tracking, and Control [*Johnson Space Center data system*] [*NASA*] (NASA)
MATCO...... Military Air Traffic Coordinating Office [*or Officer*] [*Air Force*] (AFM)
MATCOM.... Material and Techniques for Cooperative Management Training (SAUO)
MATCOM.... Materiel Command [*Army*] (AABC)
MATCOMEUR... Materiel Command, Europe
MATCON.... Microwave Aerospace Terminal Control [*Air Force*]
MATCon..... Military Air Traffic Control (SAUO)
MATCONOFF... Material Control Officer (MCD)
MatCo-Ord(N)... Material Co-Ordination Division (Naval) [*British*]
MATCS...... Marine Air Traffic Control Squadron (DNAB)
MATCSDET... Marine Air Traffic Control Squadron Detachment (DNAB)
MATCU...... Marine Air Tactical [*later, Traffic*] Control Unit [*Marine Corps*]
MATCU...... Military Air Traffic Coordinating Unit [*MTMC*] (TAG)
MATCV...... Mobile Air Traffic Control Vehicle [*Military*]
MATD........ Maximum Acceptable Transit Delay [*Open Systems Interconnection*] (ODAA)
MATD........ Mine and Torpedo Detector [*SONAR*] [*Navy*]
MATDA...... Methylene-bis-(aminothiadiazole) [*Pesticide*]
MATDEV..... Materiel Developer
MATE........ Machine-Aided Translation Editing (PDAA)
MATE........ Manual Adaptive TMA [*Target Motion Analysis*] Estimator [*Navy*] (ANA)
MATE........ Manually Aided Tracking Enhancement (MCD)
MATE........ Marital Attitude Evaluation [*Psychology*]
MATE........ Master of Arts in the Teaching of English
MATE........ Mate [*NCIC trailer make code*]
Mat E........ Materials Engineer
MATE........ Materials for Advanced Turbine Engines (SAUS)
MATE........ Maternal Attitudes Evaluation (STED)
MATE........ Matewan BancShares [*NASDAQ symbol*] (TTSB)
MATE........ Matewan BancShares, Inc. [*NASDAQ symbol*] (SAG)
MATE........ Matrix Automation through EMATS [*Military*] (MCD)
MATE........ McDonnell Airborne Trainer and Evaluator [*McDonnell Douglas Corp.*] (MCD)
MATE........ Measuring and Test Equipment (IEEE)
MATE........ Memory-Assisted Terminal Equipment (PDAA)
MATE........ Meteorological Analog Test and Evaluation (PDAA)
MATE........ MICOM [*Missile Command*] Automated Test Equipment
MATE........ Microprocessor Automatic Testing [*ASMAP Electronics Ltd.*] [*Software package*] (NCC)
MATE........ Missile/Aircraft Test Equipment
MATE........ Mission Analysis Technique for Experiments
MATE........ Mobilization and Training Equipment (MCD)
MATE........ Modular AUTODIN Terminal Equipment (SAUO)
MATE........ Modular Automated Test Equipment (SAUO)
MATE........ Modular Automatic Test Equipment
MATE........ Modular Avionics Test Equipment (ACAE)
MATE........ Modulated Automatic Test Equipment (SAUS)
MATE........ Montana Agri-Trade Exposition [*Jerry Hanson and Associates, Inc.*] (TSPED)
MATE........ Multiband Automatic Test Equipment
MATE........ Multiple-Access Time-Division Experiment (IEEE)
MATE........ Multiple Advanced Technique Evaluation [*Military*] (CAAL)
MATE........ Multipurpose Automatic Test Equipment
MATE........ Multisystem Automatic Test Equipment [*British*]
MATE........ Scientific Society of Measurement and Automation (SAUO)
MATEAM.... Manufacturing Process Applications Team (ACAE)
MATEC...... Maintenance Technician (NOAA)
Matec........ MATEC Corp. [*Associated Press*] (SAG)
MA (T Ed)... Master of Arts in Teacher Education
MAT-EF...... Matrix Analogies Test - Expanded Form [*Intelligence test*]
MATEL....... Multiplexed Automatic Telephone Equipment (SAUS)
MATELO..... Maritime Air-Radio Telegraph Organization (BUAC)
MATELO..... Maritime Air Telecommunications Organization [*NATO*] (NATG)
MATEM...... Manual Templating Model (MCD)
MATEP...... Matewan Bancshrs 7.5% Cv'A'Pfd [*NASDAQ symbol*] (TTSB)
MATER...... Magnetic Tape Event Recorder (ACAE)
MATER...... Material
MATERN.... Maternal (WDAA)
MATERN.... Maternity (WDAA)
Mater Note Aust Aeronaut Res Lab... Australia. Aeronautical Research Laboratories. Materials Note (journ.) (SAUS)
Mater Rep Aust Aeronaut Res lb... Australia. Aeronautical Research Laboratories. Materials Report (journ.) (SAUS)
MATES...... Medium Attack Tactical Employment School [*Military*] (CAAL)
MATES...... Mobilization and Training Equipment Site [*Military*] (AABC)
MATES...... Multi-band Anti-ship Tactical Electronic warfare System (SAUS)
MATES...... Multimedia Assisted distributed Tele-Engineering Services (SAUO)
MATESL..... Master of Arts in Teaching English as a Second Language (PGP)
MA(TESOL)... Master of Arts in Teaching English to Speakers of Other Languages
Matewan.... Matewan BancShares, Inc. [*Associated Press*] (SAG)
MATEX...... Macrotext Editor (MHDB)
MATEX...... Massive Air Tracer Experiment (SAUO)
MATEX...... Master of Arts in Textiles (PGP)
MATEX...... Material Expediting [*Program*] (DNAB)
MATFA...... Meat and Allied Trades Federation of Australia (BUAC)
MATFL...... Master of Arts in Teaching Foreign Language (PGP)
Math......... Adversus Mathematicos [*of Sextus Empiricus*] [*Classical studies*] (OCD)
MATH........ Astronomy/Mathematic/Statistics Library (SAUS)
MA(Th)...... Master of Arts in Theology
MATH........ Master of Arts in Therapy (PGP)
Math......... Mathematical (SAUO)
Math......... Mathematics (AL)
math......... Mathematics (ELAL)
MATH........ Mathematics (EY)
MATH........ Mathematics Abstracts [*Fachinformationszentrum Karlsruhe GmbH*] [*Information service or system*]
Math......... Matheus de Mathesillanis [*Flourished, 1381-1402*] [*Authority cited in pre-1607 legal work*] (DSA)
Math......... Mathieu's Quebec Reports [*A publication*] (DLA)
MATH........ Mathsoft, Inc. [*NASDAQ symbol*] (SAG)
MATH........ Mobile, Air-Transportable Hospital [*Military*]
MATH........ Modern Approach to Treatment of Hypertension [*Medicine*] (DMAA)
MathBiosci... Mathematical Biosciences (SAUO)
MathComput... Mathematics of Computation (SAUO)
Math Comput Model... Mathematical and Computer Modelling [*A publication*] (PABS)
Math D...... Doctor of Mathematics
MATHDI..... Mathematical Didactics [*Fachinformationszentrum Energie, Physik, Mathematik GmbH*] [*Database*]
Mathe de Afflcti... Matthaeus de Afflictis [*Deceased, 1528*] [*Authority cited in pre-1607 legal work*] (DSA)
MA Theol... Master of Arts in Theology
Math Finance... Mathematical Finance [*A publication*] (JLIT)
MATHL...... Mathematical
MATHLAB... Mathematical Laboratory [*Programming language*] (CSR)
MathML..... Mathematical Markup Language [*Computer science*] (GART)
MathMo..... Mathematical Monthly (SAUO)
MATHN...... Mathematician (AFM)
Math N...... Matthaeus Nerutius [*Flourished, 16th century*] [*Authority cited in pre-1607 legal work*] (DSA)
MathNotes.. Mathematical Notes (SAUO)
MATHP...... Medium Artillery Terminal Homing Projectile
MATHPAC... Mathematical Package (IAA)
Math Pres Ev... Mathews on Presumptive Evidence [*A publication*] (DLA)
MathR....... Mathematical Reviews (SAUO)

MATHS ...... Mathematical Access for Technology and Science for visually disabled users (SAUO)
MATHS ...... Mathematics
Mathsft ...... Mathsoft, Inc. [*Associated Press*] (SAG)
MathSystTheory... Mathematical Systems Theory (SAUO)
Math T ...... Mathematics Teacher [*A publication*] (BRI)
MathUSSR-Izv... Mathematics of the USSR-Izvestiya (SAUO)
MathUSSR-Sb... Mathematics of the USSR-Sbornik (SAUO)
MATI .... Maldives Association of the Tourism Industry (EY)
MATI .... Moscow Aviation Technology Institute (SAUO)
MATIC .... Multiple Area Technical Information Center
MATIC .... Multi-Strategy Authoring Toolkit for Intelligent Courseware (SAUO)
MATICO ..... Machine Applications to Technical Information Center Operations
MATICO ..... Mastic Tile Corporation of America (SAUO)
MATIF .... Marche a Terme des Instruments Financiere [*French stock exchange*]
MATIF .... Marche a Terme des Instruments Financiers [*French Financial Futures Market*]
MATILDA.... Microwave Analysis Threat Indication and Launch Direction Apparatus [*Military*]
MATINSP.... Material Inspection [*Navy*] (NVT)
MATK .... Martek Biosciences, Inc. [*NASDAQ symbol*] (SAG)
MATL .... Master of Arts in Teaching of Languages (PGP)
MATL .... Material (KSC)
matl .... Material (MIST)
MATL .... Materiel
MATL .... Matlock Trailer Corporation [*NCIC trailer make code*]
MATL .... Middle Atlantic
Mat Lab..... Material Laboratory (SAUO)
MATLAB..... Matrix Laboratory [*Computer science*]
Matlack ..... Matlack Systems, Inc. [*Associated Press*] (SAG)
MATLAN..... Matrix Language [*Computer science*] (IEEE)
Mat L & T... Mathews on Landlord and Tenant [*A publication*] (DLA)
MATLC ...... Mid-Atlantic Conference (PSS)
MATL REQ... Material Requisition
MATL RR ... Material Receiving Report
MATM .... Master of Arts in Teaching of Mathematics (PGP)
MATMO ..... Medical Advanced Technology Management Office
MATMO ..... Military Advanced Technology Management Office (RDA)
MATMOP.... Materiel Management Optimization Program [*DoD*]
MATMS...... Marine Aviation Training Management System (SAUO)
MATMU ..... Mobile Aircraft Torpedo Maintenance Unit
MATNET..... Mobile Access Terminal Advanced Command & Control Architectural test-bed (SAUS)
MATNO...... Material Requested Is Not Available
MATO........ Military Air Traffic Operations [*British military*] (DMA)
MATOC...... Mobility Air Terminal Operations Center (SAUO)
MATP........ Masking Template [*Tool*] (AAG)
MATP........ Military Assistance Training Program (AABC)
MATP........ Missile Auxiliary Test Position
MATP........ Mobilization Assignment Training Plan (SAUO)
Mat Par..... Matthew Paris. Historia Minor [*A publication*] (DLA)
Mat Paris... Matthew Paris. Historia Minor [*A publication*] (DLA)
Mat Part.... Mathews on the Law of Partnership [*A publication*] (DLA)
MA-TPM .... Maritime Administration Transport Planning Mobilization [*Federal emergency order*]
Mat Por..... Mathews on the Law of Portions [*A publication*] (DLA)
MATPS ...... Machine-Aided Technical Processing System [*Yale University Library*] [*New Haven, CT*] [*Computer science*]
MATR........ Management Access to Records
MATR........ Matrette [*NCIC motorcycle make code*]
MATR........ Matriculate (ROG)
MATR........ Matron
MATR........ Maynard Transportation [*Common carrier symbol*]
MATRAC .... Military Air Traffic Control Radar Center (SAUO)
MATRAC .... Military Air Traffic Control System
MATRACS... Military Air Traffic Control System (ACAE)
MATRAS .... Manufacturing Technology for Complex Geometries based on Rational Splines (SAUO)
MatrCap..... Matrix Capital Corp. [*Associated Press*] (SAG)
MATRD ...... Materiel Release Denial [*Army*] (AABC)
MATRE ...... Material Requested
MATRED .... Material Redistribution [*Program*] (DNAB)
matric .... matriculated (SAUO)
MATRIC ..... Matriculation
MATRIC ..... Midwest Agribusiness Trade Research and Information Center [*Iowa State University of Science and Technology*] [*Research center*] (RCD)
MATRIS ..... Manpower and Training Research Information System [*DoD*] [*Information service or system*] (IID)
MATRIS ..... Medical Manpower and Training Information Service [*British*] (DAVI)
Matritch..... Matritech, Inc. [*Associated Press*] (SAG)
MATRIX ..... Management Trial Exercise [*Career orientation simulation*]
MATRIX ..... Market Trend Index [*Associated Equipment Distributors program*]
Matrl .... Material
MATRL ...... Matrimonial (ROG)
MATRS ...... Mattress
MATRS ...... Military Airlift Training Squadron [*Air Force*]
MATRS ...... Miniature Airborne Telemetry Receiving Station
Matrtc ...... Matritech, Inc. [*Associated Press*] (SAG)
MATRW ..... Military Airlift Training Wing [*Air Force*]
MatrxPh..... Matrix Pharmaceutical, Inc. [*Associated Press*] (SAG)
MatrxSv..... Matrix Service Co. [*Associated Press*] (SAG)
MATS........ Maintenance Analysis Task Sheet
MATS........ Maintenance Analysis Test Set
MATS........ Management Action Tracking System (SAUO)
MATS........ Managers Action Tracking System (SAUO)
MATS........ Manual Versus Automatic Transmission Study (MCD)
MATS........ Marconi Acoustic Training System (SAUS)
MATS........ Master of Arts in Teaching of Science (PGP)
MATS........ Master of Arts in Theological Studies (PGP)
MATS........ Material and Toxicology System
MATS........ Material Transport Segment (AAEL)
MATS........ Materiel Squadron
MATS........ Matrimonial Matters [*Slang*] (DSUE)
MATS........ Matson Navigation Company [*Common carrier symbol*]
Mats......... Matson's Reports [*22-24 Connecticut*] [*A publication*] (DLA)
MATS........ Mechanical Accounting for Telephone Service (IAA)
MATS........ Mechanical Anti-Theft System [*Automotive engineering*]
MATS........ Mediterranean Air Transport Service
MATS........ Mesoscale Atmospheric Transport Studies (SAUO)
MATS........ Midcourse Airborne Target Signature [*Military*] (PDAA)
MATS........ Military Aircraft Target System (SAUS)
MATS........ Military Air Transportation Service [*Nautical term*] (NTA)
MATS........ Military Air Transport Service [*Later, Military Airlift Command*]
MATS........ Miniature Addressable Transceiver (ACAE)
MATS........ Missile Adapter Test Set (ACAE)
MATS........ Missile Auxiliaries Test Set
MATS........ Mission Analysis and Trajectory Simulation (MCD)
MATS........ Mobile Automatic Telephone System [*Telecommunications*]
MATS........ Mobile Automatic Test Set (MCD)
MATS........ Model Aircraft Target System [*British military*] (DMA)
MATS........ Model Aircrew Training System (SAUS)
MATS........ Monitoring and Test Subsystem
MATS........ Multiparticipant Airbattle Training System (ACAE)
MATS........ Multiple-Access Time Sharing [*Computer science*] (IAA)
MATS........ Multiple Array Test Set (SAUS)
MATS........ Multipurpose Automatic Test System (IAA)
MATSA ...... Managerial, Administrative, Technical, and Supervisory Association [*British*] (DCTA)
MATSA ...... Managerial Administrative Technical Trajectory System (ODA)
MATSA ...... Marek-Associated Tumor-Specific Antigen [*Medicine*] (DMAA)
MATSA ...... Marek Associated Tumor-Specified Antigen [*Medicine*] (STED)
MATSB ...... Mobile Advance Tactical Support Base [*Navy*] (VNW)
MATSC ...... Middletown Air Technical Service Command [*Air Force*]
MatSci ...... Material Sciences Corp. [*Associated Press*] (SAG)
MATSCO .... Management and Technical Services Company (AAGC)
MATSE ...... Military Air Transport Service in Europe (SAUO)
MAT-SF...... Matrix Analogies Test - Short Form [*Intelligence test*]
MATSG ...... Marine Aviation Training Support Group (DNAB)
MATSO ...... Material Requested Being Supplied [*Military*]
Mat Soc..... Mattachine Society (SAUO)
MATSOL..... Massachusetts Association of Teachers of English to Speakers of Other Languages
Matson...... Matson's Reports [*22-24 Connecticut*] [*A publication*] (DLA)
MATSR ...... Military Air Transport Service [*later, Military Airlift Command*] Regulation
MATSS ...... Marine Aviation Training Support Squadron (DNAB)
MATSS ...... Midwest Automated Technical Services Systems [*Information service or system*] (IID)
MATSTAT.... Materiel Status [*Military*]
MaTSU ...... Marine Technology Support Unit (HEAS)
Matsu .... Matsushita Electric Industrial Co. Ltd. [*Associated Press*] (SAG)
MAtt .... Attleboro Public Library, Attleboro, MA [*Library symbol*] [*Library of Congress*] (LCLS)
Matt .... Matthew [*New Testament book*]
MATT .... Matthews Studio Equipment Group [*NASDAQ symbol*] (NQ)
Matt .... Mess Attendant [*U.S. Navy enlisted rating*] (AUER)
MATT .... Missile ASW [*Antisubmarine Warfare*] Torpedo Target (MCD)
MATT .... Mobile Acoustic Torpedo Target (NG)
MATT .... Multimission Advanced Tactical Terminal (DWSG)
MATTA....... Mattawamkeag, ME [*American Association of Railroads railroad junction routing code*]
MATTE....... Matteson, IL [*American Association of Railroads railroad junction routing code*]
Mattel .... Mattel, Inc. [*Associated Press*] (SAG)**Matth Com**... Matthews' Guide to Commissioner in Chancery [*A publication*] (DLA)
Matth Cr L... Matthews' Digest of Criminal Law [*A publication*] (DLA)
Matthe de Affli... Matthaeus de Afflictis [*Deceased, 1528*] [*Authority cited in pre-1607 legal work*] (DSA)
Matthews ... Matthews' Reports [*75 Virginia*] [*A publication*] (DLA)
Matthews ... Matthews' Reports [*6-9 West Virginia*] [*A publication*] (DLA)
Matth Exe... Matthews' Executors and Administrators [*2nd ed.*] [*1839*] [*A publication*] (DLA)
Matth Gribal... Matthaeus Gribaldus [*Deceased, 1564*] [*Authority cited in pre-1607 legal work*] (DSA)
Matth Part... Matthews on Partnership [*A publication*] (DLA)
Matth Pr Ev... Matthews on Presumptive Evidence [*A publication*] (DLA)
MatthwInt... Matthews International Corp. [*Associated Press*] (SAG)
MatthwSt ... Matthews Studio Equipment Group [*Associated Press*] (SAG)
MATTS ...... Mobile Air Transportable Telecommunications System (SAUO)
MATTS ...... Multiple Airborne Target Trajectory System
Mattson ..... Mattson Technology, Inc. [*Associated Press*] (SAG)
MATU .... Marine Air Traffic Unit
MATU........ Matson Navigation [*Intermodal shipping container symbol*] (TVRC)
matut .... Matutinus [*In the Morning*] [*Latin*] (STED)
MATUT ...... Matutinus [*In the Morning*] [*Pharmacy*]
MATV........ Master Antenna Television

MATV........ Matav-Cable Systems Media Ltd. [*NASDAQ symbol*] (SAG)
MatvCab.... Matav-Cable Systems Media Ltd. [*Associated Press*] (SAG)
MATVY....... Matav-Cable Sys ADS [*NASDAQ symbol*] (SG)
MATW....... Matthews International Corp. [*NASDAQ symbol*] (SAG)
MATW....... Matthews Intl. 'A' [*NASDAQ symbol*] (TTSB)
MATW....... Metal Awning Type Window
MATWAS.... Marine Automatic Telephone Weather Answering Service [*Marine science*] (MSC)
MATWING... Medium Attack Wing (NVT)
MATX........ Maryland Transit Administration [*Federal Railroad Administration identification code*]
MATX........ Matrix Pharmaceutical [*NASDAQ symbol*] (TTSB)
MATX........ Matrix Pharmaceutical, Inc. [*NASDAQ symbol*] (SAG)
MATX........ Mid-American Car and Equipment [*Private rail car owner code*]
MATZ........ Matson Navigation [*Intermodal trailer symbol*]
MATZ........ Military Aerodrome Traffic Zone
MATZ........ Military Air Traffic Zone (SAUO)
MAU......... Air Mauritius Ltd. [*ICAO designator*] (FAAC)
MAU......... Maghreb Arab Union (SAUO)
MAU......... Maintenance Analysis Unit
MAU......... Maintenance Augmenting Unit (NG)
MAU......... Marauder [*NCIC car model code*]
MAU......... Marine Advisory Unit [*Marine Corps*]
MAU......... Marine Amphibious Unit (NVT)
mau.......... Massachusetts [*MARC country of publication code*] [*Library of Congress*] (LCCP)
MAU......... Master Augmentation Unit [*Navy*] (DOMA)
MAU......... Mastung [*Pakistan*] [*Airport symbol*] (AD)
MAU......... Math Acceleration Unit (NITA)
MAU......... Mathematical Advisory Unit [*Ministry of Transport*] [*British*]
MAU......... Matua [*Former USSR*] [*Seismograph station code, US Geological Survey*] (SEIS)
MAU......... Maupiti [*French Polynesia*] [*Airport symbol*] (OAG)
Mau.......... Mauricius [*Authority cited in pre-1607 legal work*] (DSA)
MAU......... Mauritius (ROG)
MAU......... Media Access Unit [*Telecommunications*]
MAU......... Medical Assistance Unit [*HEW*]
MAU......... Medium Access Unit [*Computer science*] (BYTE)
MAU......... Medium Attachment Unit [*Computer science*] (TNIG)
MAU......... Memory Access Unit
MAU......... Meyenburg-Altherr-Uehlinger [*Syndrome*] [*Medicine*] (STED)
MAU......... Microalbuminuria [*Medicine*] (MELL)
mAU......... Milliabsorbance Unit [*Spectroscopy*]
MAU......... Million Accounting Units (NASA)
MAU......... Miscellaneous Armament Unit
MAU......... Missile Auxiliary Unit (ACAE)
MAU......... Modern American Usage [*A publication*]
MAU......... Modular Avionics Unit (HLLA)
MAU......... Mount Allison University [*New Brunswick, Canada*]
MAU......... Movement African Union (SAUO)
MAU......... Multiattribute Utility (IEEE)
MAU......... Multiple Access Unit
MAU......... Multiple Aircraft Universal (ACAE)
MAU......... Multistation Access Unit [*Telecommunications*] (PCM)
MAUA....... Master of Arts in Urban Affairs (GAGS)
Mau & Pol Sh... Maude and Pollock's Law of Merchant Shipping [*A publication*] (DLA)
Mau & Sel... Maule and Selwyn's English King's Bench Reports [*A publication*] (DLA)
MAU/ATU... Marine Amphibious Unit/Amphibious Task Unit (SAUO)
MAUC....... Middle Atlantic Underwater Council (SAUO)
MAUD....... Manually-Assisted Universal Deviator
MAUD....... Master of Arts in Urban Design (GAGS)
MAud........ Master of Audiology
MAUD....... Ministry of Aircraft Uranium Development [*British*] [*World War II*]
MAUD....... Movimento Academico pela Uniao Democrata [*Academic Movement for Democratic Union*] [*Portugal*] [*Political party*] (PPE)
MAUDE...... Manufacturer and User Facility Device Experience [*Database*] (GDD)
MAUDE...... Morse Automatic Decoder
Maude & P... Maude and Pollock's Law of Merchant Shipping [*A publication*] (DLA)
Maude & P Mer Shipp... Maude and Pollock's Law of Merchant Shipping [*A publication*] (DLA)
Maude & P Shipp... Maude and Pollock's Law of Merchant Shipping [*A publication*] (DLA)
MAUDEP.... Metropolitan Association of Urban Designers and Environmental Planners (EA)
MAUDER.... Metropolitan Association of Urban Designers and Environmental Planners (SAUO)
Maud Ment Res... Maudsley on Mental Responsibility [*A publication*] (DLA)
MAUDR..... Angolan Democratic Unity Movement for Reconstruction [*Political party*] (PSAP)
M Au E...... Master of Automobile Engineering
M Au Eng... Master of Automobile Engineering
MAUF........ Multiattribute Utility Function
MAUFS...... Municipal Arborists and Urban Foresters Society (EA)
MAUG....... MicroNet Apple User's Group [*CompuServe*] [*Database*]
Maug Att.... Maugham's Attorneys, Solicitors, and Agents [*1825*] [*A publication*] (DLA)
Maug Att.... Maugham's Statutes Relating to Attorneys, Etc. [*1839*] [*A publication*] (DLA)
Maug Cr L.. Maugham's Outlines of Criminal Law [*2nd ed.*] [*1842*] [*A publication*] (DLA)
Maugh Lit Pr... Maugham's Literary Property [*1828*] [*A publication*] (DLA)
Maugh RP... Maugham's Outlines of Real Property Law [*1842*] [*A publication*] (DLA)
Maug Jur... Maugham's Outlines of the Jurisdiction [*1838*] [*A publication*] (DLA)
Maug Law... Maugham's Outlines of Law [*1837*] [*A publication*] (DLA)
MAUK....... Mining Association of the United Kingdom (BUAC)
Maul & Sel... Maule and Selwyn's English King's Bench Reports [*A publication*] (DLA)
Maule & S.. Maule and Selwyn's English King's Bench Reports [*A publication*] (DLA)
MAULEX.... Marine Amphibious Unit Landing Exercise (NVT)
MauLoa..... Mauna Loa Macadamia Partners Ltd. [*Associated Press*] (SAG)
MAULT...... Manual or Automatic Ultrasonic Laboratory Test
MAUM....... Movement Against Uranium Mining (SAUO)
MAUP....... Port of Manatee [*Federal Railroad Administration identification code*]
MAUR....... Maurell Trailer [*NCIC trailer make code*]
Maur......... Mauritania
Maur......... Mauritius
MA Urb Plan... Master of Arts in Urban Planning (SAUO)
MAUR Coy... Maintenance Area Universal Repair Company (SAUO)
Maur Dec... Mauritius Decisions [*A publication*] (DLA)
Maurit....... Mauritania
MAURP...... Master of Arts in Urban and Regional Planning (GAGS)
Maurti....... Mauritania (VRA)
MAUS....... Mammography Attitudes and Usage Study [*Medicine*] (DMAA)
MAUS....... Mauser Rifle
MAUS....... Messensch Afteliche Autonome Experiment Unter Schewerelosigkeit
MAUS....... Metric Association of the United States (SAUO)
MAUS....... Mobile Automated Scanner
MAUS....... Movimiento de Accion y Unidad Socialista [*Socialist Movement for Action and Unity*] [*Mexico*] [*Political party*] (PPW)
MAUS....... Muensters Apple User Service (SAUO)
MAUSED.... Midwest Association of University Student Employment Directors [*Later, MASEA*] (EA)
MAusIMM... Member of the Australasian Institute of Mining and Metallurgy (SAUO)
mauso....... Mausoleum (VRA)
MAUTEL..... Microminiaturized Autonetics Telemetry
MAUU....... Massachusetts Alliance of Utility Unions (SAUO)
MauU........ University of Mauritius, Reduit, Mauritius [*Library symbol*] [*Library of Congress*] (LCLS)
MAUV....... Multiple Autonomous Vehicle
MAUVL...... Mauriceville, TX [*American Association of Railroads railroad junction routing code*]
MAUW...... Modified Advanced Underwater Weapons (MCD)
MAV......... Macrosiphum avenae Virus
MAV......... Magyar Allamvasutak [*Hungarian State Railways*]
MAV......... Maintenance Assistance Vehicle (MCD)
MAV......... Maintenance Assist Vehicle (SAUS)
MAV......... Maloelap [*Marshall Islands*] [*Airport symbol*] (OAG)
MAV......... Manpower Authorization Voucher
MAV......... Mars Ascent Vehicle [*NASA*]
MAV......... Massive Resources Ltd. [*Vancouver Stock Exchange symbol*]
MAV......... Maverick [*NCIC car model code*]
MAV......... Maverick (motorcycle) [*NCIC motorcycle make code*]
MAV......... Mavesa SA ADS [*NYSE symbol*] (SAG)
MAV......... Max-Aviation [*Canada*] [*ICAO designator*] (FAAC)
MAV......... Maximum Allowable Variation [*Net weight labeling*]
MAV......... McLaren Advanced Vehicles [*Automobile manufacturer*]
MAV......... Mean Absolute Value [*Statistics*]
MAV......... MeCCNU [*Semustine*], Adriamycin, Vincristine [*Antineoplastic drug regimen*]
MAV......... Mechanical Auxiliary Ventricle (PDAA)
MAV......... Micro Air Vehicle [*Remote controlled device*]
MAV......... Military Aerospace Vehicle
mA/V........ Milliamperes per Volt (DEN)
MAV......... Minimal Apparent Viscosity (STED)
MAV......... Minimum Acceptable Value (MCD)
MAV......... Minimum Apparent Viscosity (DB)
MAV......... Minute Alveolar Volume [*Medicine*] (DAVI)
MAV......... Moscavia [*Former USSR*] [*FAA designator*] (FAAC)
MAV......... Motor Ambulance Van [*British*]
MA(V)....... Motorcycling Australia (Victoria) [*Australia*] [*An association*]
MAV......... Movement Arm Vector (STED)
MAV......... Multi-Appeal Vehicle
MAV......... Multinucleated Atypia of the Vulva [*Medicine*] (PALA)
MAV......... Myeloblastosis-Associated Virus
MAV......... Satere-Mawe [*Language symbol*] (ETLW)
MAV......... Transmembrane Activation Voltage [*Biochemistry*] (DAVI)
MAVA........ Moored Acoustic Vertical Array
MAVA........ Multiple Abstract Variance Analysis (STED)
MAVAR...... Microwave Amplification by Variable Reactance (IAA)
MAVAR...... Mixer Amplification by Variable Reactance (IAA)
MAVAR...... Modulating Amplifier Using Variable Resistance
MAVCC...... Mid-America Vocational Curriculum Consortium (OICC)
MAVCC...... Munich Audio-Visual Communication Center (SAUO)
MAVCS...... Multi Axis Vibration Control System (ACAE)
MAVDM..... Multiple Application VDM (SAUO)
MAVE........ Maverick Mobile Home [*NCIC trailer make code*]
MAVE........ Model for Articulated Vocational Education (EDAC)
MAVE........ Multiple Aerial Vehicle Expert [*Army*]
MAV Ed..... Master of Administration in Vocational Education (PGP)
MAVERICK... Manufacturers Assistance in Verifying, Identification in Cataloging
MAVES...... Manned Mars and Venus Exploration Studies
Mavesa..... Mavesa SA ADS [*Associated Press*] (SAG)

MAVI......... Microwave Automatic Vehicle Identification (MCD)
MAVIBEI..... Maatschappij Voor Internationale Beleggingen (EFIS)
MAVICA..... Magnetic Video Camera [*Sony Corp.*]
MAVICA..... Magnetic Video Card (NITA)
MAVID....... Modular Architecture for Video & Image Distribution system (SAUS)
MAVIN....... Machine-Assisted Vendor Information Network
MAVIN....... Multiple Angle, Variable Interval, Nonorthogonal [*Magnetic resonance imaging*]
MAVIS....... Master Vision Screener (PDAA)
MAVIS....... McDonnell Douglas Automated Voice Information System (MCD)
MAVIS....... Microprocessor-Based Audio Visual Information System (PDAA)
MAVIS....... Mobile Armored Vehicle Indigo System [*Radio-controlled tank*]
MAVIS....... Mobile Artery and Vein Imaging System [*Medicine*] (STED)
MAVK........ Maverick Tube [*NASDAQ symbol*] (TTSB)
MAVK........ Maverick Tube Corp. [*NASDAQ symbol*] (SAG)
MAVL........ Marvell [*NCIC truck make code*]
MAVMA..... Massachusetts Veterinary Medical Association (GVA)
MAVMS..... MACOM Automated Vehicle Management System (SAUO)
MAVOAD.... Massachusetts Active in Disaster [*Emergency Management*] (EMA)
MAVOGA.... Malaysian Vocational Guidance Association (SAUO)
MAVPE...... Metal Alkyl Vapor-Phase Epitaxy [*Semiconductor technology*]
MAVR........ Maverick Restaurant Corp. [*NASDAQ symbol*] (COMM)
MAVR........ Mitral and Aortic Valve Replacement [*Medicine*] (DMAA)
MAVS........ Manned Aerial Vehicle for Surveillance (MCD)
MAVS........ Manned Airborne Vehicle Surveillance (ACAE)
MAVS........ Modular Advanced Vision System (TIMI)
MavTube.... Maverick Tube Corp. [*Associated Press*] (SAG)
MAVU........ Maritima Argua Line [*Intermodal shipping container symbol*] (TVRC)
MAVU........ Modular Audio Visual Unit (PDAA)
MAVUS...... Maritime VTOL UAV System (SAUS)
MAVWC..... Military Aircraft Voice Weather Code (NATG)
MAW......... Machinists and Aerospace Workers (DICI)
MAW......... Magdeburger Armaturenwerke AG (EFIS)
MAW......... Malden, MO [*Location identifier*] [*FAA*] (FAAL)
MAW......... Management Action Workshop (ACAE)
MAW......... Management Application Workshop (SAUO)
MAW......... Marine Aircraft Wing (SAUO)
MAW......... Marine Air Wing (ACAE)
mAw......... Maritime Arctic Warm [*Air Mass*] [*Meteorology*] (BARN)
MAW......... Master of Arts in Worship (PGP)
MAW......... Master of Arts in Writing (GAGS)
MAW......... Maumee & Western Railroad [*Federal Railroad Administration identification code*]
MAW......... Mauritius Alliance of Women (BUAC)
MAW......... Maverick Alternate Warhead (SAUS)
MAW......... Mawson [*Antarctica*] [*Seismograph station code, US Geological Survey*] (SEIS)
MAW......... Maximum Allowable Weight [*Military*] (INF)
MAW......... Mechanically Armed Warhead (ACAE)
MAW......... Medium Active Waste [*Nuclear energy*]
MAW......... Medium Antiarmor Weapon (INF)
MAW......... Medium Antitank Weapon
MAW......... Medium Assault Weapon
MAW......... Microsoft At Work [*Computer software*] (PCM)
MAW......... Mid-American Waste Sys [*NYSE symbol*] (TTSB)
MAW......... Mid-American Waste Systems, Inc. [*NYSE symbol*] (SPSG)
MAW......... Military Airlift Wing [*Air Force*] (MCD)
MAW......... Ministry of Agriculture and Water (SAUO)
MAW......... Minor Assist Work
MAW......... Missile Approach Warning system (SAUS)
MAW......... Mission Adaptive Wing (MCD)
MAW......... Mobile Approach Warner (SAUS)
MAW......... Mothers for Adequate Welfare (SAUO)
MAW......... Mountain & Arctic Warfare (SAUS)
MAW......... Multipurpose Assault Weapon (ACAE)
MAW......... Mustique Airways [*Barbados*] [*ICAO designator*] (FAAC)
MAWA....... Maltese Australian Women's Association
MAWA....... Matehematical Association of Western Australia
MAWA....... Missile Attack Warning and Assessment [*Military*] (PDAA)
MAWB....... Master Air Waybill [*Shipping*] (DS)
MAWC....... Marine Air West Coast
MAWCS..... Mobile Air Weapons Control System [*ESD*]
MAWD....... Mars Atmospheric Water Detection [*NASA*]
MA/WD...... Material Annex/Weapons Dictionary [*Military*]
MAWEC..... Maritime Aircraft Weather Code (NATG)
MAWFA..... Make-a-Wish Foundation of America (EA)
MAWG....... Message Attachment Work Group (SAUO)
MAWg....... Military Airlift Wing [*Air Force*] (AFM)
MAWG....... Mission Analysis Working Group (ACAE)
MAWIA...... Mexican American Workers Importation Act
MAWL....... Magnetic Aircraft Weapons Link
MAWLOGS... Models of the [*US*] Army Worldwide Logistics System (AABC)
MAWP....... Marine Air Wing Pacific
MAWP....... Maximum Allowable Working Pressure (PDAA)
MAWPS..... Mechanically Attached Wear Plate System
MAWR....... Ministry of Agriculture Western Region (SAUO)
MAWS....... Marine Air Warning Squadron
MAWS....... Minimum Additive Waste Stabilization System [*Department of Energy*]
MAWS....... Missile Approach Warning System (DOMA)
MAWS....... Mobile Aircraft Weighing System (OA)
MAWS....... Modular Automated Weather System
MAWste..... Mid-American Waste Systems, Inc. [*Associated Press*] (SAG)
MAWTS..... Marine Aviation Weapons and Tactics Squadron
MAWTS-1... Marine Aviation Weapons and Tactics Squadron 1
MAWTU..... Marine Air Weapons Training Unit (MCD)
MAWU....... Montserrat Allied Workers Union (SAUO)
MAWVA..... Make-a-Wish Foundation of Eastern Virginia (EARSL)
MAWX....... Olin Mathieson Chemical [*Private rail car owner code*]
MAX......... Cinemax [*Cable television channel*]
MAX......... Madrid, Spain [*Spaceflight Tracking and Data Network*] [*NASA*]
MAX......... Magic Answer Extractor [*Database*]
max......... Manx [*MARC language code*] [*Library of Congress*] (LCCP)
MAX......... Matam [*Senegal*] [*Airport symbol*] (OAG)
MAX......... Matrix Corp. [*AMEX symbol*] (COMM)
MAX......... Max-Aviation [*Canada*] [*FAA designator*] (FAAC)
MAX......... Maxilla [*Jawbone*]
MAX......... Maxim (ROG)
MAX......... Maxima (WDAA)
MAX......... Maxima [*NCIC car model code*]
MAX......... Maximal (SAUS)
MAX......... Maximilian Numismatic and Historical Society (EA)
Max......... Maximinus [*of Scriptores Historiae Augustae*] [*Classical studies*] (OCD)
max......... Maximum (WDMC)
MAX......... Maximum
MAX......... Maxi-Taxi [*NCIC car model code*]
MAX......... Maxwell [*Unit of Magnetic Flux*] [*Electronics*] (IAA)
MAX......... Media Access Exchange (SAUS)
MAX......... Mediterranean Airlines SA [*Greece*] [*ICAO designator*] (FAAC)
MAX......... Mercury Air Group [*AMEX symbol*] (TTSB)
MAX......... Mercury Air Group, Inc. [*AMEX symbol*] (SPSG)
MAX......... Message Automatic Exchange (SAUO)
MAX......... Metropolitan Area Communication System (SAUO)
MAX......... Metropolitan Area Express [*Railway*] [*Portland, OR*] (ECON)
MAX......... Mid-Atlantic Crossroads
MAX......... Minerex Resources Ltd. [*Vancouver Stock Exchange symbol*] [*Toronto Stock Exchange symbol*]
MAX......... Mobile Automatic Exchange [*Telecommunications*] (NITA)
MAX......... Mobile Automatic X-Ray (PDAA)
MAX......... Modular Applications Executive [*Modular Computer Systems*]
Maxam...... Maxxam Corp. [*Associated Press*] (SAG)
max asst.... Maximum Assistance [*Medicine*] (BCRP)
MAXAT...... Maximum Aperture Telescope (SAUS)
MAXC........ Maxco, Inc. [*NASDAQ symbol*] (NQ)
MAXC........ Maxcraft Trailer Manufacturing [*NCIC trailer make code*]
MAXC........ Multiple Access Xerox Computer (NITA)
MAX CLB... Maximum Engine Thrust for Two-Engine Climb (GAVI)
Maxco....... Maxco, Inc. [*Associated Press*] (SAG)
MAXCO...... Maximum Dynamic Pressure (NASA)
MAXCOL.... Maximum Column [*Computer science*] (PCM)
MAXCOM... Modular Applications Executive for Communications [*Modular Computer Systems*]
MaxcrHlt.... Maxicare Health Plans, Inc. [*Associated Press*] (SAG)
MAX CRZ... Maximum Engine Thrust for Two-Engine Cruise (GAVI)
Max Dig..... Maxwell's Nebraska Digest [*A publication*] (DLA)
MAXDOSE... Maximum Individual Dose (EAGT)
MAXE........ Max & Erma's Restaurants [*NASDAQ symbol*] (TTSB)
MAXE........ Max & Erma's Restaurants, Inc. [*NASDAQ symbol*] (NQ)
MAXE........ Maxey Manufacturing [*NCIC trailer make code*]
Max EP...... Maximal Esophageal Pressure [*Medicine*] (MAE)
MaxEr....... Max & Erma's Restaurants, Inc. [*Associated Press*] (SAG)
MAXF........ Maxcor Financial Group [*NASDAQ symbol*]
MAXG........ Maximum Girth [*Pisciculture*]
MAXI......... Maxicare Health Plans [*NASDAQ symbol*] (TTSB)
MAXI......... Maxicare Health Plans, Inc. [*NASDAQ symbol*] (NQ)
MAXI......... Maxim [*NCIC truck make code*]
MAXI......... Maximum Potential Licence Period (WDAA)
MAXI......... Modular Architecture for the Exchange of Intelligence (SAUO)
MAXID....... Maximize Indefinite Delivery Contracts (AFM)
Maxim....... Maxim Integrated Products, Inc. [*Associated Press*] (SAG)
MAXIM....... Micro Arcsecond X-ray Imaging Mission (SAUS)
MaximGp... Maxim Group [*Associated Press*] (SAG)
MaximPh... Maxim Pharmaceuticals, Inc. [*Associated Press*] (SAG)
Max Int Stat... Maxwell on the Interpretation of Statutes [*A publication*] (DLA)
MAXIQ....... Maxicare Health Plans [*OTCBB symbol*]
Maxis........ Maxis, Inc. [*Associated Press*] (SAG)
MAXIT....... Maximum Interference Threshold [*Telecommunications*] (TEL)
MAX/IT...... Modular, Adaptable, Expandable, Intelligent Terminal [*Link Technologies, Inc.*] (PCM)
MAXL........ Maxwell [*NCIC car make code*]
Max LD..... Maxwell's Law Dictionary [*A publication*] (DLA)
MAXM....... Maxim Group [*NASDAQ symbol*] (SAG)
MAXM....... Maxim Pharmaceuticals [*NASDAQ symbol*]
MAXMAR... Maximum Mobile Army
Max Mar L... Maxwell's Marine Law [*A publication*] (DLA)
MAX/MIN... Maximum Disclosure / Minimum Delay (DNAB)
MaxmP...... Maxim Pharmaceuticals, Inc. [*Associated Press*] (SAG)
MAXNET.... Modular Application Executive for Computer Networks (PDAA)
MAXNET.... Modular Applications Executive Network (NITA)
MAXNOR.... Maximum Number of Runs (MCD)
MAXO........ Maxon [*NCIC truck make code*]
MAXPAC.... Maximus Inc. PAC [*Reston, VA*] (PACS)
MAX-PAC... Maxxam Inc. Federal PAC [*Houston, TX*] (PACS)
MAXPAR.... Maximum Pain Relief [*Medicine*]
MAXPAX.... Maxwell House Coffee Package [*Vendor-machine system for Maxwell House coffee*]
MAXPEN.... Maximum Penalty

MAXPID ..... Maximum Pain Intensity Difference [*Medicine*]
MAX-Q .... Maximum Dynamic Pressure (SAUS)
MAXR .... Maximum Rate (TVEL)
MAXS........ Maxwell Shoe'A' [*NASDAQ symbol*] (TTSB)
MAXS........ Maxwell Shoe Company, Inc. [*NASDAQ symbol*] (SAG)
MAXSECOM... Maximum Security Communications (IAA)
MAXSECON... Maximum Security Communications
Maxserv..... Maxserv, Inc. [*Associated Press*] (SAG)
MAX SOCIETY... Maximilian Numismatic and Historical Society (EA)
MAXTOP .... Maximum Total Duration Penalty
Maxtor ...... Maxtor Corp. [*Associated Press*] (SAG)
MAXTTR .... Maximum Time to Repair [*Navy*] (CAAL)
MAXTWK.... Maximum Total Work Content
MAXU .... Maxu Containers [*Intermodal shipping container symbol*] (TVRC)
Maxu .... Maxus Energy Corp. [*Associated Press*] (SAG)
MAXUPO.... Maximum Undistorted Power Output (IAA)
Maxus....... Maxus Energy [*Associated Press*] (SAG)
Maxw Cr Proc... Maxwell's Treatise on Criminal Procedure [*A publication*] (DLA)
Maxwel ...... Maxwell Laboratories, Inc. [*Associated Press*] (SAG)
Maxwell...... Irish Land Purchase Cases [*1904-11*] [*A publication*] (DLA)
Maxwell...... Maxwell on the Interpretation of Statutes [*A publication*] (DLA)
Maxw Interp St... Maxwell on the Interpretation of Statutes [*A publication*] (DLA)
MaxwlISh... Maxwell Shoe Co., Inc. [*Associated Press*] (SAG)
MaxwlIT..... Maxwell Technologies, Inc. [*Associated Press*] (SAG)
MAXX........ Maximum Access to Diagnosis and Therapy (SAUO)
MAXX........ Maximum Access to Diagnosis and Therapy: The Electronic Library of Medicine (MHID)
MAXX........ Mid-American Energy [*Private rail car owner code*]
Maxxim ..... Maxxim Medical, Inc. [*Associated Press*] (SAG)
may.......... Malay [*MARC language code*] [*Library of Congress*] (LCCP)
MAY .... Malye Karmakuly [*Former USSR*] [*Geomagnetic observatory code*]
MAY .... Mangrove Cay [*Bahamas*] [*Airport symbol*] (OAG)
MAY .... Maya Airways Ltd. [*Belize*] [*ICAO designator*] (FAAC)
MAY .... Maybelline, Inc. [*NYSE symbol*] (SPSG)
MAY .... May Department Stores Co., Corporate Information Center, St. Louis, MO [*OCLC symbol*] (OCLC)
MAY .... Mayfield [*Washington*] [*Seismograph station code, US Geological Survey*] [*Closed*] (SEIS)
MAY .... Maynard Energy, Inc. [*Toronto Stock Exchange symbol*]
MAY .... Mayor (ROG)
MAY .... Mayor's Court [*Court type found in state of Virginia*] (MVRD)
MAY .... Maysville, KY [*Amtrak rail station code*]
MAYA........ Mayfair Mobile Home [*NCIC trailer make code*]
MAYA........ Mexican-American Youth Association (SAUO)
MAYA........ Most Advanced, Yet Acceptable [*Industrial design*]
MAYA........ Muslim Arab Youth Association
May Act..... Mayhew's Action at Law [*1828*] [*A publication*] (DLA)
MAYB........ Mad About You, Baby (SAUS)
Maybel...... Maybelline, Inc. [*Associated Press*] (SAG)
MAYC........ Mayco Trailer [*NCIC trailer make code*]
MAYC........ Mayflower Conference (PSS)
MAYC........ Methodist Association of Youth Clubs [*British*] (BI)
May Const Hist... May's Constitutional History of England [*A publication*] (DLA)
MAYCOR .... Maytag Corp. (EFIS)
May Crim Law... May's Criminal Law [*A publication*] (DLA)
May Dam ... Mayne on the Law of Damages [*A publication*] (DLA)
MAYDAY .... International Distress Signal [*Aviation*] (PIPO)
MayDS ...... May Department Stores Co. [*Associated Press*] (SAG)
MAYER ELECTRIC PAC... Mayer Electric Supply Company Inc. PAC [*Birmingham, AL*] (PACS)
MAYF........ Mayflower Trailers [*NCIC trailer make code*]
MayflCo ..... Mayflower Co-Operative Bank [*Associated Press*] (SAG)
May Fr Conv... May's Fraudulent Conveyances [*3rd ed.*] [*1908*] [*A publication*] (DLA)
May Ins ...... May on Insurance [*A publication*] (DLA)
May Just.... Mayo's Justice [*A publication*] (DLA)
May LR ..... Mayurbhani Law Report [*India*] [*A publication*] (DLA)
May Merg... Mayhew on Merger [*1861*] [*A publication*] (DLA)
Mayn .... Maynard's English Reports, Exchequer Memoranda of Edward I, and Year Books of Edward II [*A publication*] (DLA)
MaynOl...... Maynard Oil Co. [*Associated Press*] (SAG)
MAYNY...... Mayne Group Ltd. [*OTCBB symbol*]
MAYO........ Mexican-American Youth Organization (SAUO)
Mayo & Moul... Mayo and Moulton's Pension Laws [*A publication*] (DLA)
Mayo Just .. Mayo's Justice [*A publication*] (DLA)
Mayo Med Sch... Mayo Medicine School (GAGS)
MAYPAC..... May Department Stores Company PAC [*St. Louis, MO*] (PACS)
May Parl.... May's Parliamentary Practice [*A publication*] (ILCA)
May Parl Law... May's Parliamentary Law [*A publication*] (DLA)
May Parl Pr... May's Parliamentary Practice [*A publication*] (DLA)
May PL...... May's Parliamentary Practice [*A publication*] (DLA)
MAYPOLE... May Polarization Experiment [*RADAR storm sensing*]
MAYS........ Mays [*J. W.*], Inc. [*NASDAQ symbol*] (NQ)
MAYS........ Mays (JW) [*NASDAQ symbol*] (TTSB)
MaysJ....... Mays [*J. W.*], Inc. [*Associated Press*] (SAG)
MaySpeh... May & Speh, Inc. [*Associated Press*] (SAG)
MAYT........ May Trucking Company [*Common carrier symbol*]
Maytag...... Maytag Corp. [*Associated Press*] (SAG)
MAYVL ...... Maysville, KY [*American Association of Railroads railroad junction routing code*]
MAYW....... Maywood & Sugar Creek [*AAR code*]
MAZ .... Mayaguez [*Puerto Rico*] [*Airport symbol*] (OAG)
MAZ .... Mazatlan [*Mexico*] [*Seismograph station code, US Geological Survey*] (SEIS)
MAZ .... Mazzite [*A zeolite*]
MAZ .... Mines Air Service Zambia Ltd. [*ICAO designator*] (FAAC)
MAZ .... Missed Approach Azimuth [*Aviation*]
MAZ .... Mounting Azimuth [*Weaponry*] (INF)
MAZD........ Mazda [*NCIC truck make code*]
MAZD........ Mazda [*NCIC car make code*]
MazelSt ..... Mazel Stores, Inc. [*Associated Press*] (SAG)
MAZH........ Missile Azimuth Heading [*Air Force*]
MAZI......... Movement for the Advancement of the Zionist Idea [*Israel*] [*Political party*] (EY)
MAZL........ Mazel Stores, Inc. [*NASDAQ symbol*] (SAG)
MAZO........ Missile Azimuth Orientation [*Air Force*] (IAA)
MAZZ........ Mazer Chemical [*Federal Railroad Administration identification code*]
MB........... All India Reporter, Madhya Bharat [*1950-57*] [*A publication*] (DLA)
MB........... Bachelor of Medicine [*Other than from Oxford*]
MB........... Bachelor of Music (WDAA)
mb---........ Black Sea and Area [*MARC geographic area code*] [*Library of Congress*] (LCCP)
Mb........... Body Wave Magnitude (COE)
MB........... Boston Public Library and Eastern Massachusetts Regional Public Library System, Boston, MA [*Library symbol*] [*Library of Congress*] (LCLS)
MB........... Countrywide [*ICAO designator*] (AD)
MB........... Current Motorized Bicycle Permit [*Motor vehicle violation driver status code in state of North Dakota*] (MVRD)
MB........... Machine Batch (AAEL)
MB........... Machine Bolt [*Technical drawings*]
MB........... MacMillan Bloedel Ltd. [*Associated Press*] (SAG)
MB........... Magnetic Bearing [*Navigation*]
MB........... Magnetic Belt (VLIE)
MB........... Magnetic Brake [*Industrial control*] (IEEE)
MB........... Magnetron Branch [*Electronics*] (OA)
MB........... Mailbox (AAG)
MB........... Main Ballast
MB........... Main Base [*Air Force*] (AFM)
MB........... Main Battery [*Guns*]
MB........... Main Bus (MCD)
MB........... Maintenance Busy [*Telecommunications*] (TEL)
M-B.......... Make-Break
MB........... Mallory Body [*Medicine*]
MB........... Mamillary Body [*Medicine*] (DB)
MB........... Management Baseline (NASA)
MB........... Management Board (ACII)
MB........... Manitoba [*Canadian province*] [*Postal code*]
MB........... Manned Base (SAUO)
MB........... March-Bender Factor [*Physiology*]
MB........... Margin Buccal [*Medicine*] (MAE)
MB........... Marie-Bamberger [*Disease*] [*Medicine*] (DB)
MB........... Marine Barracks
MB........... Marine Base
MB........... Marine Board (EA)
MB........... Maritime Board (SAUO)
MB........... Marker Beacon (PIPO)
MB........... Market Bare [*Telegraphy*] (PCTE)
MB........... Marketing Board (SAUO)
MB........... Mark of the Beast [*Disparaging term for 19th century Protestant clerical waistcoats that had Catholic influences*]
MB........... Marks Banco (ROG)
MB........... Marsh-Bender [*Factor*] [*Muscle tissue*]
MB........... Mass Balance
MB........... Master Block (VLIE)
MB........... Matchbox [*Mattel*]
MB........... Material Balance
MB........... May & Baker Ltd. [*Great Britain*] [*Research code symbol*]
MB........... MBB-UV, MBB-UD [*Messerschmitt-Boelkow-Blohm*], und Pneuma-Technik [*Germany*] [*ICAO aircraft manufacturer identifier*] (ICAO)
MB........... Measurement Base [*Military*]
MB........... Mechanized Battalion [*Army*]
MB........... Medal of Bravery
MB........... Medial Bilateral (Neuron) [*Neuroanatomy*]
MB........... Median Bundle [*Botany*]
MB........... Medical Board
MB........... Medical Branch (SAUO)
MB........... Medical Bulletin
MB........... Medicare Bureau [*Health Care Financing Administration - Social Security Administration*] (OICC)
MB........... Medicinae Baccalaureus [*Bachelor of Medicine*] [*Latin*]
MB........... Medium Bomber
MB........... Medium Bronze [*Numismatics*]
MB........... Megabar
Mb........... Megabase [*A unit of molecular size*]
Mb........... Megabit [*Computer science*] (WDMC)
MB........... Megabit [*Binary Digit*] [*Computer science*]
MB........... Megabuck [*Defense industry colloquialism for one million dollars*] (AAG)
mb........... Megabyte (ELAL)
MB........... Megabyte [*Data storage capacity*] [*Computer science*]
Mb........... Megabyte
MB........... Melt Back
MB........... Memorandum Book (ROG)
MB........... Memory Bank
MB........... Memory Buffer [*Computer science*]
MB........... Memory Bus
MB........... Memoryless Behaviour (VLIE)
MB........... Mercedes-Benz [*Automobile*]

MB .... Merchant Bank
MB .... Merchant Broker (RIMS)
MB .... Meridian & Bigbee Railroad Co. [*Later, MBRR*] [*AAR code*]
MB .... Mesiobuccal [*Dentistry*]
MB .... Message Buffer (ACRL)
MB .... Message Business
MB .... Messages of the Bible [*A publication*]
MB .... Metabisulfite [*Inorganic chemistry*]
MB .... Metal Box [*Commercial firm*] [*British*]
MB .... Metal Box Co. Ltd. (SAUO)
MB .... Methyl Bromide [*Organic chemistry*]
MB .... Methylene Blue [*Organic chemistry*]
MB .... Metrication Board [*British*]
MB .... Metric Board (OICC)
MB .... Microbeam [*Physics*]
MB .... Microbiological Assay [*Biochemistry*] (DAVI)
MB .... Microbody
MB .... Microelectronics Bibliography [*A publication*]
MB .... Midbody
MB .... Mid Byte (ACAE)
MB .... Middle Babylonian [*Language, etc.*] (BJA)
MB .... Middle Berth [*Indian Railway*] (TIR)
MB .... Middle Bronze Age (BJA)
MB .... Middle Button (VLIE)
MB .... Middle of Bow [*Music*] (ROG)
MB .... Miesbach [*German license plate city code*]
MB .... Militia Bureau [*Superseded in 1933 by National Guard Bureau*]
MB .... Millibar
mb .... Millibar [*Unit of pressure*]
mb .... Millibarn [*Area of nuclear cross-section*]
mb .... Millibyte [*Computer science*]
MB .... Million Bytes [*Computer science*] (BUR)
MB .... Milton Bradley Co. (SAUO)
MB .... Milton Bradley Ltd. [*British*]
MB .... Milwaukee Brace [*Medicine*] (MELL)
MB .... Minimum Bid [*Philately*]
MB .... Ministry of Blockade (SAUO)
MB .... Misce Bene [*Mix Well*] [*Pharmacy*]
MB .... Miscellaneous Branch, Internal Revenue Bureau [*United States*] (DLA)
MB .... Missed Byte [*Computer science*] (ECII)
MB .... Missile Base [*Military*]
MB .... Missile Body
MB .... Missile Bomber
MB .... Mixed Bed [*Nuclear energy*] (NRCH)
MB .... Mixing Box (OA)
MB .... Mobile Base (DEN)
MB .... Model Block (MSA)
MB .... Module Balance [*Computer science*]
MB .... Mohelbuch (BJA)
MB .... Moisture Balance
MB .... Molecular Biosystems [*NYSE symbol*] (TTSB)
MB .... Molecular Biosystems, Inc. [*NYSE symbol*] (SPSG)
MB .... Molybdenum [*Chemical element*] (ROG)
MB .... Momentum Bias (ACAE)
MB .... Monthly Breakdown [*Used in atmospheric studies*]
MB .... Monthly Bulletin of Decisions of the High Court of Uganda [*A publication*] (DLA)
MB .... Months Before
MB .... Montpelier & Barre Railroad Co. [*AAR code*]
MB .... Mooring Buoy
MB .... Morale Branch [*Military*]
MB .... Morrell's English Bankruptcy Reports [*A publication*] (DLA)
MB .... Mortar Board (EA)
M/B .... Mother Board (AGLO)
MB .... Motor Barge (ADA)
MB .... Motor Boat
MB .... Mountain Battery [*British military*] (DMA)
MB .... Mucosal Barrier [*Medicine*] (MELL)
MB .... Mucosal Bleeding [*Medicine*] (MELL)
MB .... Multiband (DEN)
MB .... Municipal Bond
MB .... Municipal Borough
MB .... Munitions Board [*Abolished 1953, functions transferred to Department of Defense*]
MB .... Muscle Balance (SAUS)
MB .... Museum of Broadcasting
MB .... Mushroom Body [*Nerve center in insects*]
MB .... Musicae Baccalaureus [*Bachelor of Music*]
MB .... Music for the Blind [*Defunct*] (EA)
MB .... Muslim Brotherhood [*Jordan*] (BUAC)
MB .... Must Be [*Sold*] [*Classified advertising*]
MB .... Myocardial Band [*Cardiology*]
Mb .... Myoglobin [*Biochemistry, medicine*]
Mb .... Myoglobin Tritium [*Hematology*] (DAVI)
MB .... Optical Fiber Mounting Bracket [*Communications term*] (DCT)
MB .... Western Airlines [*ICAO designator*] (AD)
MB-2 .... Model Boiler-Two [*Nuclear energy*] (GFGA)
MBA .... American Academy of Arts and Sciences, Boston, MA [*Library symbol*] [*Library of Congress*] (LCLS)
MBA .... Automobilvertriebs Aktiengesellschaft [*Austria*] [*ICAO designator*] (FAAC)
MBA .... Main Battle Area (AABC)
MBA .... Main-Belt Asteroid [*Astronomy*]
MBA .... Mainhardt-Biehl Associates (SAUO)
MBA .... Make-or-Buy Authorization (AAG)
MBA .... Makers of British Art [*A publication*]
MBA .... Male Bonding Alert [*Screenwriter's lexicon*]
MBA .... Male Bowhunter Aided [*International Bowhunting Organization*] [*Class equipment*]
MBA .... Malta Broadcasting Authority (BUAC)
MBA .... Management Buy-Out Association (BUAC)
MBA .... Mantle Bouguer Anomaly [*Geology*]
MBA .... Manufactured Buildings Association [*Defunct*] (EA)
MBA .... Many-Body Alloy [*Metallurgy*]
MBA .... Marching Bands of America (EA)
mba .... Marimba
MBA .... Marine Biological Association [*British*]
MBA .... Marine Biological Association of the United Kingdom (BUAC)
MBA .... Maschhoff, Barr & Associates (ALAC)
MBA .... Massachusetts Bar Association (EARSL)
MBA .... Mass Balance Area (NUCP)
MBA .... Master Bakers' Association [*Australia*]
MBA .... Master Builders' Association [*South Africa*] (BUAC)
MBA .... Master Business Administration (SAUO)
MBA .... Master of Business Administration
MBA .... Master of the British Arts Association (DBQ)
MBA .... Material Balance Accounting (SAUO)
MBA .... Material Balance Area [*Nuclear energy*]
MBA .... Maximum Benefit Amount [*Unemployment insurance*]
MBA .... MB Associates (SAUO)
MBA .... Mechlorethamine [*War gas*] [*Medicine*] (EDAA)
MBA .... Meier Burnout Assessment [*Psychology*] (DHP)
MBA .... Merion Bluegrass Association [*Defunct*] (EA)
MBA .... Methods of Biochemical Analysis [*Journal*] [*Medicine*] (EDAA)
MBA .... Methyl Benzyl Alcohol [*Organic chemistry*]
MBA .... Methylbis(beta-chloroethyl)amine [*Nitrogen mustard*] [*Also, HN, NM*] [*Antineoplastic; war-gas base*]
MBA .... Methylbovine Albumin (DMAA)
MBA .... Methylenebisacrylamide [*Organic chemistry*]
MBA .... Metropolitan Boxing Alliance (SAUO)
MBA .... Microbiological Associates, Inc.
MBA .... Migratory Bird Act
MBA .... Military Base Agreement (CINC)
MBA .... Military Benefit Association (EA)
MBA .... Milk Bars Association of Great Britain and Ireland Ltd. (BI)
MBa .... Miniature Ball [*Horticulture*]
MBA .... Minimum Burst Altitude (AABC)
MBA .... Minor Basic Allergens [*Immunology*]
MBA .... Missouri Broadcasters Association (EARSL)
MBA .... Model Based Autonomy Group [*Ames Research Center*] (RCD)
MBA .... Mombasa [*Kenya*] [*Airport symbol*] (OAG)
MBA .... Monument Builders of America [*Later, MBNA*]
MBA .... Mortar Box Assembly
MBA .... Mortgage Bankers Association of America [*Washington, DC*] (EA)
MBA .... Mortgage Brokers Association (SAUO)
MBA .... Motor Bearing Assembly (ACAE)
MBA .... Motorized Bicycle Association [*Later, MAA*] (EA)
MBA .... Mount Bingar [*Australia*] [*Seismograph station code, US Geological Survey*] [*Closed*] (SEIS)
MBA .... Multibeam Antenna
MBA .... Multiple Berthing Adaptor (SSD)
MBA .... Multiple Birth Association [*Australia*]
MBA .... Rural Municipality of Argyle Public Library, Baldur, Manitoba [*Library symbol*] [*National Library of Canada*] (NLC)
MBA .... Woodcock-McGrew-Werder Mini-Battery of Achievement [*Test*] (TMMY)
MBA .... Yacht and Motor Boat Association (SAUO)
MBAA .... Master Brewers Association of the Americas (EA)
MBAA .... Master of Business Administration in Aviation (PGP)
MBAA .... Messinian Benevolent Association "Aristomenis" (EA)
MBAA .... Methylene Bisacrylamide (PDAA)
MBAA .... Mini Bike Association of America (EA)
MBAA .... Mortgage Bankers Association of America (SAUO)
MBAA .... Mortgage Brokers' Association of Australia
MBAA .... Motel Brokers Association of America [*Later, AHMB*] (EA)
MBAA .... Mountain Bike Association of Arizona (EARSL)
MBAAS .... Master of Business Administration in Actuarial Science
MBab .... Middle Babylonian [*Language, etc.*] (BJA)
MBABS .... Synod Office, Diocese of Brandon, Anglican Church of Canada, Manitoba [*Library symbol*] [*National Library of Canada*] (NLC)
MBAC .... Assiniboine Community College, Brandon, Manitoba [*Library symbol*] [*National Library of Canada*] (NLC)
MBAC .... Marshall Booster Assembly Contractor (MCD)
MBAC .... Member of the British Association of Chemists (DAS)
MBACFM .... American Board of Commissioners for Foreign Missions, Boston, MA [*Library symbol*] [*Library of Congress*] (LCLS)
M-BACOD .... Methotrexate (High-Dose) (with Citrovorum Factor Rescue), Bleomycin, Adriamycin,Cyclophosphamide, Oncovin [*Vincristine*], Dexamethasone [*Antineoplastic drug regimen*]
M-BACOP .... Myelosuppressive Bleomycin, Adriamycin, Cyclophosphamide, Oncovin [*Vincristine*], Prednisone [*Antineoplastic drug regimen*]
M-BACOS .... Bleomycin, Adriamycin, Cytoxan, Oncovin, Methotrexate with Leucovorin Rescue [*Antineoplastic drug*] (CDI)
MBACT .... Medical Board of the Australian Capital Territory
MBAD .... Medical Badge
MB Adm .... Master of Business Administration
MBAE .... Master of Biological and Agricultural Engineering (PGP)
MBAE .... Master of Biosystems and Agricultural Engineering (PGP)

MBAE........ Member of the British Association of Electrolysis (DI)
MBA-EP..... Master of Business Administration - Experienced Professionals (PGP)
MBAF........ Mortgage Bankers Association of Florida (EARSL)
MBAG....... Modulated Bayard-Alpert Gauge
MBAG....... Research Station, Agriculture Canada [*Station de Recherches, Agriculture Canada*] Brandon, Manitoba [*Library symbol*] [*National Library of Canada*] (NLC)
MBAI........ Massachusetts Independent Bankers Association, Inc. (TBD)
MBAI........ Mosquito Biting Activity Index [*Canada*]
MBAIB....... Master of Business Administration in International Business (GAGS)
MBAIT....... Master of Business Administration in International Trade (PGP)
MBAJ........ Magna Bibliotheca Anglo-Judaica (BJA)
MBALs...... Minimum Biological Acceptable Levels (SAUO)
MBAM....... Main Beam Avoidance Maneuver
MBAM....... Mortgage Bankers Association of Missouri (EARSL)
MBA/MPP... Master of Business Administration/Master of Public Policy
MBAMT..... Methyl(benzylideneamino)mercaptotriazole [*Reagent*]
MBAMTG.... Mortgage Delinquency Rates [*Database*] (GDD)
M-band..... Central Region of A-band in Striated Muscle Sarcomere [*Cell biology*] (QSUL)
MBANSW... Master Butchers' Association of New South Wales [*Australia*]
MBANSW... Medical Benevolent Association of New South Wales [*Australia*]
MBAOT...... Member of the British Association of Occupational Therapists (DI)
MBA-PE..... Master of Business Administration - Physician's Executive (PGP)
MBA Prep... Master of Business Administration Preparatory
mbar......... Millibar [*Unit of pressure*]
MBAR....... Multibeam Acquisition RADAR (MCD)
MBAR....... Myocardial Beta Adrenergic Receptor [*Cardiology*] (DMAA)
MBARI....... Monterey Bay Aquarium Research Institute [*California*]
MBarL....... Barnstable Law Library, Barnstable, MA [*Library symbol*] [*Library of Congress*] (LCLS)
MBAS........ Methylene Blue Active Substance [*Organic chemistry*]
MBAS........ Mutual Benefit and Aid Society [*Later, WBF*] (EA)
MBASA...... Medical Benevolent Association of South Australia
MBASW..... Member of the British Association of Social Workers
MBAt........ Boston Athenaeum, Boston, MA [*Library symbol*] [*Library of Congress*] (LCLS)
MBAT........ Multi-Beam Array Transmitter (SAUS)
MBATM...... Master of Business in Telecommunication Management (PGP)
MBAUK...... Marine Biological Association of the United Kingdom (ARC)
MBAV........ Main Battle Air Vehicle [*Military*] (PDAA)
MBAV........ Multi-purpose Base Armoured Vehicle (SAUS)
MBAWS..... Marine Base Air Warning System
MBAY........ MediaBay [*NASDAQ symbol*]
MBB.......... Brandeis University, Waltham, MA [*OCLC symbol*] (OCLC)
MBB.......... Make-before-Break
MBB.......... Marble Bar [*Australia*] [*Airport symbol*] (OAG)
MBB.......... Maurer, B. B., Chicago IL [*STAC*]
MBB.......... Messerschmitt-Boelkow-Blohm GmbH [*West German aircraft company*]
MBB.......... Messerschmitt-Boklow-Blahn (NAKS)
MBB.......... Miniature Brushless Blower
MBB.......... Modified Barbiturate Buffer (DMAA)
MBB.......... Modular Building Block (ACAE)
MBB.......... Mortgage-Backed Bonds
MBB.......... MSB Bancorp, Inc. [*AMEX symbol*] (SAG)
MBB.......... Museum of the Borough of Brooklyn (SAUO)
MBBA........ Boston Bar Association, Boston, MA [*Library symbol*] [*Library of Congress*] (LCLS)
MBBA........ Methoxybenzylidene Butylaniline [*Organic chemistry*]
MBBA........ (Methozybenzylidene)butylaniline [*Organic chemistry*]
MBBA........ Military Benefit Base Amounts
MBBAQ...... Master Boat Builders' Association of Queensland [*Australia*]
MBBC........ Monterey Bay Bancorp [*NASDAQ symbol*] (TTSB)
MBBC........ Monterey Bay Bancorp, Inc. [*NASDAQ symbol*] (SAG)
MBBC........ Monterey Bay Bancorporation [*NASDAQ symbol*]
MBBI........ Babson College, Babson Park, MA [*Library symbol*] [*Library of Congress*] (LCLS)
MBBI........ Multiple-Bit Binary Input
MBBL........ Massachusetts Bureau of Library Extension, Boston, MA [*Library symbol*] [*Library of Congress*] (LCLS)
MBBL........ Thousand Barrels (EG)
MBBLS...... Thousands of Barrels (MCD)
MBbM....... Massachusetts Maritime Academy, Buzzards Bay, MA [*Library symbol*] [*Library of Congress*] (LCLS)
MBBO....... Multiple-Bit Binary Output
MBBR....... Brokenhead River Regional Library, Beausejour, Manitoba [*Library symbol*] [*National Library of Canada*] (NLC)
MBBS........ Bostonian Society, Boston, MA [*Library symbol*] [*Library of Congress*] (LCLS)
MBBS........ Managed Broad-Band Services (VLIE)
MBBSC...... Bachelor of Medicine and Bachelor of Science [*British*] (ROG)
MBC.......... American Congregational Association, Boston, MA [*Library symbol*] [*Library of Congress*] (LCLS)
MBC.......... Brandon University, Manitoba [*Library symbol*] [*National Library of Canada*] (NLC)
MBC.......... Machine Bath Collection
MBC.......... Magnetic Bias Coil (IIA)
MBC.......... Magnetic Bias Control (DNAB)
MBC.......... Mailbox Club [*Later, MCI*] (EA)
MBC.......... Main Beam Clutter
MBC.......... Male Breast Cancer [*Medicine*] (DB)
MBC.......... Malwa Bhil Corps [*British military*] (DMA)
MBC.......... Manhattan Bible College [*Kansas*]
MBC.......... Manhattan Bowery Corp. (EA)
mbc.......... Manitoba [*MARC country of publication code*] [*Library of Congress*] (LCCP)
MBC.......... Manual Battery Control (AAG)
MBC.......... Marine Biomedical Center [*Duke University*] [*Research center*] (RCD)
MBC.......... Marine Broadcasting Company (SAUO)
MBC.......... Marine/Freshwater Biomedical Center [*Duke University*] (RCD)
MBC.......... Mary Baldwin College [*Virginia*]
MBC.......... Massachusetts Biotechnology Council (SAUO)
MBC.......... Mass Bias Correction (ABAC)
MBC.......... Master Bus Controller [*Computer science*]
MBC.......... Master of Beauty Culture
MBC.......... Master of Building Construction (PGP)
MBC.......... Maximum Bladder Capacity [*Medicine*] (DB)
MBC.......... Maximum Breathing Capacity
MBC.......... M'Bigou [*Gabon*] [*Airport symbol*] (OAG)
MBC.......... McLaughlin-Buick Club of Canada (EAIO)
MBC.......... Mean Bacterial Concentration [*Therapy term*] (CTAA)
MBC.......... Media Briefing Center (COE)
MBC.......... Mediterranean Bombardment Code
MBC.......... Mediterranean Burns Club (SAUO)
MBC.......... Megabar Diamond Cell [*For high-pressure measurements*]
MBC.......... Memory Bus Controller
MBC.......... Mercantile Bank of Canada [*Toronto Stock Exchange symbol*] [*Vancouver Stock Exchange symbol*]
MBC.......... Mercantile Bankshares Corp. (EFIS)
MBC.......... Merchant Banking Company (SAUO)
MBC.......... Message Broadcast Controller [*Computer science*] (CIST)
MBC.......... Metastatic Breast Cancer [*Medicine*]
MBC.......... Meteor Burst Communications [*Military*]
MBC.......... Methotrexate, Bleomycin, Cisplatin [*Antineoplastic drug*] (CDI)
MBC.......... Methyl Benzimidazole Carbamate (ODA)
MBC.......... Methyl Benzimidazolecarbamate [*Organic chemistry*]
MBC.......... Methylthymol Blue Complex (BABM)
MBC.......... Metropolitan Borough Council [*British*]
MBC.......... Mewar Bhil Corps [*British military*] (DMA)
MBC.......... Mickelberry Corp. (EFIS)
MBC.......... Microcrystalline Bovine Collagen (DB)
MBC.......... Middle East Broadcasting Centre (BUAC)
MBC.......... Military Budget Committee [*NATO*] (NATG)
MBC.......... Military Budget Council (SAUO)
MBC.......... Miname Nihon Broadcasting (SAUO)
MBC.......... Miniature Bayonet Cap
MBC.......... Miniaturized Ballistic Computer
MBC.......... Minimum Bactericidal Concentration
MBC.......... Minnesota Bible College [*Rochester*]
MBC.......... Missile Boresight Correlator (ACAE)
MBC.......... Mitsubishi Bank of California (SAUO)
MBC.......... Modified Brequet Cruise [*SST*]
MBC.......... Monkees Buttonmania Club [*Defunct*] (EA)
MBC.......... Mononuclear Blood Cell [*Hematology*]
MBC.......... Morris Brown College [*Atlanta, GA*]
MBC.......... Morris Brown College, Atlanta, GA [*OCLC symbol*] (OCLC)
MBC.......... Morrow Bulk Commodities, Inc. (EFIS)
MBC.......... Mortar Ballistic Computer [*Formerly, MFCC*] [*Army*] (INF)
MBC.......... Mother and Baby Care [*Red Cross Nursing Services*]
MBC.......... Motorboat Crew [*British military*] (DMA)
MBC.......... Mould Bay [*Northwest Territories*] [*Seismograph station code, US Geological Survey*] (SEIS)
MBC.......... Mountain Bike Club [*British*] (DBA)
MBC.......... Multiple Base Channel (VLIE)
MBC.......... Multiple Basic Channel
MBC.......... Multiple Board Computer (IAA)
MBC.......... Multiple Burst Correcting
MBC.......... Munhwa Broadcasting Corp. [*Republic of Korea*] (BUAC)
MBC.......... Municipal Borough Council (SAUO)
MBC.......... Mutual Broadcasting Company (SAUO)
MBC.......... Muzzle/Brake Compensator (SAUS)
MBCA........ Archives, Brandon University, Manitoba [*Library symbol*] [*National Library of Canada*] (BIB)
MBCA........ Mechanical Bank Collectors of America (EA)
MBCA........ Mercedes-Benz Club of America (EA)
MBCA........ Merchant Bank of Central Africa Ltd.
MBCA........ Migratory Bird Conservation Act of 1929 (COE)
MBCA........ Motor Boat Club of America (SAUO)
MBCA........ Munitions Board Cataloging Agency
MBCAM..... Commonwealth Air Training Plan Museum, Inc., Brandon, Manitoba [*Library symbol*] [*National Library of Canada*] (NLC)
MBCC........ Mail Boxes Coast to Coast, Inc. [*NASDAQ symbol*] (COMM)
MBCC........ Massachusetts Bay Community College [*Wellesley*]
MBCC........ Matchbox Challenge Cars [*Toy collection*]
MBCC........ McBurnie Coach Craft [*NCIC car make code*]
MBCC........ McLaughlin-Buick Club of Canada (EA)
MBCC........ Medical Benefits Consultative Committee
MBCC........ Migratory Bird Conservation Commission [*A federal government body*]
MBCD....... Modified Binary-Coded Decimal
MBCG....... Department of Geography, Brandon University, Manitoba [*Library symbol*] [*National Library of Canada*] (NLC)
MBCI........ Medical Books for China International (SAUO)
MBCI........ Member of the Business Continuity Institute [*Emergency Management*] (EMA)
MBCK........ Mallory Body Cytokeratin [*Medicine*]
MBCL........ Monocytoid B-Cell Lymphoma [*Medicine*] (EDAA)

MBCM .... Baccalaureus Medicinae, Chirurgiae Magister [*Bachelor of Medicine, Master of Surgery*]
MBCM .... New England Conservatory of Music, Boston, MA [*Library symbol*] [*Library of Congress*] (LCLS)
MBCMA ...... Metal Building Component Manufacturers' Association (EA)
MBCMC ..... Milk Bottle Crate Manufacturers Council [*Defunct*] (EA)
MBCMS ..... Michael Barber Centre for Mass Spectrometry [*United Kingdom*] (RCD)
MBCNT ...... Multilingual Broadcasting Council of the Northern Territory [*Australia*]
MBCo .... Countway Library of Medicine, Boston, MA [*Library symbol*] [*Library of Congress*] (LCLS)
MBCO .... Member of the British College of Ophthalmic Opticians [*British*] (DBQ)
MbCO .... Myoglobin, Carboxy [*Biochemistry, medicine*]
MBCP .... Master Business Continuity Professional [*Emergency Management*] (EMA)
MBCP .... Mauler Battery Command Post (ACAE)
MBCP .... Missile Base Communications Processor (SAUO)
MBC PAC ... Mercantile Bankshares Corporation PAC [*Baltimore, MD*] (PACS)
MBCS .... Managed Business Consultancy Service (SAUO)
MBCS .... Medium Bandwidth Compression System
MBCS .... Member of the British Computer Society (DCTA)
MBCS .... Meteor Burst Communication System
MBCS .... Motion Base Crew Station [*NASA*] (NASA)
MBCS .... Multi-Byte Character Set [*Computer science*] (VLIE)
MBCU .... Business Centre Mangistau [*Intermodal shipping container symbol*] (TVRC)
MBCU .... Mobile Bombardment Communications Unit [*Military*] (IAA)
MBCX .... Material Brokage [*Private rail car owner code*]
MBd .... Bedford Free Public Library, Bedford, MA [*Library symbol*] [*Library of Congress*] (LCLS)
MBD .... Episcopal Diocese of Massachusetts, Boston, MA [*Library symbol*] [*Library of Congress*] (LCLS)
MBD .... Machinery Breakdown (MARI)
MBD .... Macroblock Design
MBD .... Magnetic-Bubble Domain Device [*Computer science*] (IEEE)
MBD .... Manual Board [*Telecommunications*] (NITA)
MBD .... Manual Burst Disable (AABC)
MBD .... Maple Bark Disease [*Medicine*] (MELL)
MBD .... Marble Bone Disease [*Medicine*] (MELL)
MBD .... Marchiafava-Bignami Disease [*Medicine*] (MELL)
MBD .... Marie-Bamberger Disease [*Medicine*] (MELL)
MBD .... Materials-by-Design [*Chemical engineering*]
MBD .... Meander Belt Deposit [*Geology*]
MBD .... Mental Deterioration Battery [*Medicine*] (EDAA)
MBD .... Metabolic Bone Disease [*Medicine*] (MELL)
MBD .... Methotrexate, Bleomycin, Diamminedichloroplatinum [*Cisplatin*] [*Antineoplastic drug regimen*]
MBD .... Methoxybenzylaminonitrobenzoxadiazole [*Fluorescent probe*] [*Biochemistry*]
MBD .... Methylbutenedial [*Organic chemistry*]
MBD .... Methylene Blue Dye [*Organic chemistry*] (MAE)
MBD .... Meyer-Betz Disease [*Medicine*] (MELL)
MBD .... Million Barrels Daily
MBD .... Minimal Brain Damage [*or Dysfunction*]
MBD .... Minimal Brain Dysfunction [*Neurology*] (DAVI)
MBD .... Minority Business Development Agency (EBF)
MBD .... Mission Baseline Description [*NASA*] (KSC)
MBD .... Moeller-Barlow Disease [*Medicine*] (MELL)
MBD .... Morquio-Brailsford Disease [*Medicine*] (DMAA)
MBD .... Motor Belt Drive (MSA)
M Bd .... Munitions Board (SAUO)
MBD .... Muzzle Boresight Device [*Army*] (INF)
MBDA .... Metal Building Dealers Association [*Later, Systems Builders Association*] (EA)
MBDA .... Minority Business Development Agency [*Formerly, OMBE*] [*Department of Commerce*]
MBDAACC ... Milling and Baking Division of American Association of Cereal Chemists (EA)
MBdAF ...... United States Air Force, Cambridge Research Center, Bedford, MA [*Library symbol*] [*Library of Congress*] (LCLS)
MBDAP ...... Malt Beverage Distributors Association of Pennsylvania (EARSL)
MBDC .... Minority Business Development Center [*Minority Business Development Administration*]
MBdD .... Document Research Center, Bedford, MA [*Library symbol*] [*Library of Congress*] (LCLS)
MBDE .... Market and Business Development Ltd. (IID)
MBDET ...... Mobile Boarding Detachment [*Coast Guard*]
MBDF .... Medicare Beneficiaries Defense Fund (EA)
MBDG .... Marine Base Defense Group
MBDG .... Mesiobuccal Developmental Groove [*Medicine*] (DMAA)
MBDG .... Mesiobuccal Development Groove (STED)
MBdgSc ..... Master of Building Science
MBDI .... Major Business Development Initiative
MBDio .... Diocesan Library, Boston, MA [*Library symbol*] [*Library of Congress*] (LCLS)
MBDL .... Missile Battery Data Link (MCD)
MBdM .... Middlesex Community College, Bedford, MA [*Library symbol*] [*Library of Congress*] (LCLS)
MBdMi ...... Mitre Corps., Bedford, MA [*Library symbol*] [*Library of Congress*] (LCLS)
MBDOE ...... Million Barrels per Day Oil Equivalent (MHDB)
MBDP .... Minority Bank Deposit Program [*Treasury Department*]
MB(DP)AC ... Medical Benefits (Dental Practitioners) Advisory Committee
MBDR .... Make-or-Buy Data Record (KSC)
MBdR .... Raytheon Co., Missile Systems Division Library, Bedford, MA [*Library symbol*] [*Library of Congress*] (LCLS)
MBDS .... Modular Building Distribution System [*Telecommunications*] (TEL)
MBdV .... United States Veterans Administration Hospital, Bedford, MA [*Library symbol*] [*Library of Congress*] (LCLS)
MBE .... Bethany Lutheran College, Mankato, MN [*OCLC symbol*] (OCLC)
MBE .... Emerson College, Boston, MA [*Library symbol*] [*Library of Congress*] (LCLS)
MBE .... Mail Boxes Etc. USA [*San Diego, CA*] [*Telecommunications*] (TSSD)
MBE .... Malibu Entertainment Worldwide, Inc. [*AMEX symbol*] (NASQ)
MBE .... Malibu Entmt Intl. [*AMEX symbol*] (SG)
MBE .... Management by Exception
MBE .... Martin-Baker Ltd. [*British*] [*ICAO designator*] (FAAC)
MBE .... Mary Baker Eddy [*Founder of Christian Science*]
MBE .... Master of Bilingual Education (PGP)
MBE .... Master of Business Economics
MBE .... Master of Business Education (GAGS)
MBE .... May Be Elevated [*Medicine*] (DAVI)
MBE .... Medical and Biological Engineering [*Medicine*] (EDAA)
MBE .... Medium Below-Elbow [*Cast*] (STED)
MBE .... Member of the [*Order of the*] British Empire [*Facetious translation: "My Bloody Efforts"*]
MBE .... Mennonite Board of Education (EA)
MBE .... Metals-Based Engineering
MBE .... Minority Business Enterprise (MCD)
MBE .... Missile-Borne Equipment
MBE .... Molecular Beam Epitaxy [*Crystallography*]
MBE .... Monbetsu [*Japan*] [*Airport symbol*] (OAG)
MBE .... Monumenta Biblica et Ecclesiastica [*Rome*] [*A publication*] (BJA)
MBE .... Mountasia Entertainment Intl., Inc. [*AMEX symbol*] (SAG)
MBE .... Moving Boundary Electrophoresis [*Analytical biochemistry*]
MBE .... Multiple-Beam Experiment [*In MBE-4, a heavy-ion accelerator at the Lawrence Berkeley Laboratory*]
MBE .... Multistate Bar Examination
MBEA .... Missouri Business Education Association (EDAC)
MBE-ARMS ... Multiple Business Entity - Accounts Receivable Management System (MHDB)
MBED .... Episcopal Diocese of Massachusetts, Diocesan Library and Archives, Boston, MA [*Library symbol*] [*Library of Congress*] (LCLS)
MB Ed .... Master of Business Education
MBEE .... Motobee [*NCIC motorcycle make code*]
MBEH .... Monobenzyl Ether of Hydroquinone [*Ointment prepared by the Royal Free Hospital, London and used locally as a depigmenting agent in Addison's disease and pregnancy*] [*Medicine*] (EDAA)
MBehaviouralSc ... Master of Behavioural Sciences (ADA)
MBEI .... Member of the Institute of Body Engineers [*British*] (DBQ)
MBEI .... Minnesota Business Educators, Inc (EDAC)
MBELAB ..... Molecular Beam Epitaxy Laboratory [*University of British Columbia*] [*Canada*] (RCD)
MBELDEF ... Minority Business Enterprise Legal Defense and Education Fund (EA)
MBelm ...... Belmont Memorial Library, Belmont, MA [*Library symbol*] [*Library of Congress*] (LCLS)
MBelmM .... McLean Hospital, Belmont, MA [*Library symbol*] [*Library of Congress*] (LCLS)
MBEmm ..... Emmanuel College, Boston, MA [*Library symbol*] [*Library of Congress*] (LCLS)
MBEN .... Benjamin Moore and Co. [*OTCBB symbol*]
MBEnv .... Master of the Built Environment (ADA)
MBEP .... Metals-Based Engineering Program
MBEP .... Minority Business Enterprise Program (SAUO)
MBEP .... Minority Business Tracking (SAUO)
MBEP .... Region 4 Minority Business Tracking (SAUS)
MBEPA ...... United States Environmental Protection Agency, Region I Library, Boston, MA [*Library symbol*] [*Library of Congress*] (LCLS)
MBER .... Member
MBER .... Minority Business Enterprise Representative (COE)
MBER .... Molecular Beam Electric Resonance [*Physics*]
MBES .... Member of the Bureau of Engineer Surveyors [*British*] (DBQ)
MBES .... Mezhdunarodnyi Bank Ekonomicheskovo Sotrudnichestva [*International Bank for Economic Co-Operation - IBEC*] [*Moscow, USSR*] (EAIO)
MBES .... Multi-Beam Echo Sounder [*Mapping*]
MBEST ...... Modulus Blipped Echo-Planar Single-Pulse Technique (STED)
MBev .... Beverly Public Library, Beverly, MA [*Library symbol*] [*Library of Congress*] (LCLS)
MBev-F ...... Beverly Farms Public Library, Beverly, MA [*Library symbol*] [*Library of Congress*] (LCLS)
MBevHi ..... Beverly Historical Society, Beverly, MA [*Library symbol*] [*Library of Congress*] (LCLS)
MBevN ...... North Shore Community College, Beverly, MA [*Library symbol*] [*Library of Congress*] (LCLS)
MBevT .... Beverly Times, Beverly, MA [*Library symbol*] [*Library of Congress*] (LCLS)
MBE/WBE ... Certification Questionnaire-Minority/ Women Business Enterprise (SAUS)
MBE/WBE ... Certification Questionnaire-Minority/Women Business Enterprise (SAUO)
MBF .... MAI Basic Four, Inc. [*NASDAQ symbol*] (COMM)
MBF .... Main Boundary Fault [*Geophysics*]
MBF .... Management by Fear (SAUO)
MBF .... Marsh-Bender Factor [*Medicine*] (EDAA)
MBF .... Master Bibliographic File (ADA)
MBF .... Master Builders Federation [*British*] (BI)

MBF .... Materials Business File [*American Society for Metals, The Institute for Metals*] [*Information service or system*] (IID)
MBF .... MBF USA, Inc. [*Associated Press*] (SAG)
MBF .... Meat Base Formula [*Medicine*] (MEDA)
MBF .... Medical Benefits Fund (SAUO)
MBF .... Medical Benevolence Foundation [*Association*] (EA)
MBF .... Medullary Blood Flow [*Medicine*] (DMAA)
MBF .... Military Banking Facility
MBF .... Milk Bottlers Federation
MBF .... Missile Beacon Filter
MBF .... Modulator Band Filter (IAA)
MBF .... Molecular Beam Facility [*NASA*]
MBF .... Moving-Bed Filter [*Waste*] (DICI)
MBF .... Multiple Births Foundation (BUAC)
MBF .... Muscle Blood Flow [*Medicine*] (DMAA)
MBF .... Musicians Benevolent Fund [*British*] (BI)
MBF .... Myocardial Blood Flow [*Cardiology*]
MBF .... Thousand Board Feet [*Lumber*]
MBFA .... Fellowes Athenaeum, Boston, MA [*Library symbol*] [*Library of Congress*] (LCLS)
MBFA .... MBF USA, Inc. [*NASDAQ symbol*] (SAG)
MBFC .... Magic of Bewitched Fan Club (EA)
MBFC .... Medial Brachial Fascial Compartment [*Medicine*] (DMAA)
MBFC .... Medical Branch Fascial Compartment [*Medicine*] (EDAA)
MBFC .... Mega Bank Financial Corp. [*NASDAQ symbol*] (NASQ)
MBFC .... Moe Bandy Fan Club (EA)
MBFL .... Mid-Bergen Federation of Public Libraries [*Library network*]
MBFLB .... Monaural Bifrequency Loudness Balance [*Audiology*] (MAE)
MBFM .... Massachusetts Grand Lodge, F & AM, Boston, MA [*Library symbol*] [*Library of Congress*] (LCLS)
MBFN .... Multiple Beam Forming Network [*Military*] (LAIN)
MBFo .... Forsyth Dental Center, Boston, MA [*Library symbol*] [*Library of Congress*] (LCLS)
MBFP .... Manufacturing, Build, and Flow Plan (NASA)
MBFR .... Federal Reserve Bank of Boston, Boston, MA [*Library symbol*] [*Library of Congress*] (LCLS)
MBFR .... More Better for Russia [*Facetious translation of MBFR - Mutual and Balanced Force Reduction*]
MBFR .... Mutual and Balanced Force Reduction [*Proposed reduction of forces in central Europe by NATO and Warsaw Pact nations*]
MBFRT .... Mutual Balanced Force Reduction Talks (CARL)
MBFT .... Multi Band Frequency Translator (ACAE)
MBFUSA ...... MBF USA, Inc. [*Associated Press*] (SAG)
MBG .... Gardner Museum, Boston, MA [*Library symbol*] [*Library of Congress*] (LCLS)
MBG .... Mandalay Resort Group [*NYSE symbol*]
MBG .... Marburg [*Disease*] [*Medicine*] (DMAA)
MBG .... Mean Blood Glucose [*Medicine*] (STED)
MBG .... Medicine Book Guide [*Journal*] [*Medicine*] (EDAA)
MBG .... Message Buffer Group (SAUO)
MBG .... Midland Bank Group (SAUO)
MBG .... Missouri Botanical Garden
MBG .... Mobridge, SD [*Location identifier*] [*FAA*] (FAAL)
MBG .... Money-Back Guarantee
MBG .... Morphine-Benzedrine Group [*Scale*] [*Medicine*] (DMAA)
MBG .... Northern Nambikuara [*Language symbol*] (ETLW)
MBG & H ... Magna Brittannia, Gallia, et Hibernia [*Great Britain, France, and Ireland*] [*Latin*] (ROG)
MBGE .... Missile-Borne Guidance Equipment (AFM)
MBGH .... Library Services, Brandon General Hospital, Manitoba [*Library symbol*] [*National Library of Canada*] (NLC)
MBGi .... Gillette Co., Boston R and D Laboratory, Boston, MA [*Library symbol*] [*Library of Congress*] (LCLS)
MBGil .... Gillette Co., Boston R and D Laboratory, Boston, MA [*Library symbol*] [*Library of Congress*] (LCLS)
MBGS .... Missile-Borne Guidance Set (MCD)
MBGS .... Morphine-Benzedrine Group Scale (STED)
MBGT .... General Theological Library, Boston, MA [*Library symbol*] [*Library of Congress*] (LCLS)
MBGT .... Grand Turk [*Turks and Caicos Islands*] [*ICAO location identifier*] (ICLI)
MBGTS .... Missile-Borne Guidance Test Set (AABC)
MBH .... Manual Bomb Hoist
MBH .... Maryborough [*Australia*] [*Airport symbol*] (OAG)
MBH .... Massachusetts Horticultural Society, Boston, MA [*Library symbol*] [*Library of Congress*] (LCLS)
MBH .... Massive Black Hole [*Galactic science*]
MBH .... Maximal Benefit from Hospitalization (STED)
MBH .... Maximum Benefit from Hospitalization (SAUS)
MBH .... Medial Basal Hypothalamus [*Medicine*] (STED)
MBH .... Mediobasal Hypothalamus [*Brain anatomy*]
MBH .... Minard, Bryant H., Pennsauken NJ [*STAC*]
mbH .... Mit Beschraenkter Haftung [*With Limited Liability*] [*German*] (EG)
MBH .... Movimiento de Bases Hayistas [*Movement of Hayista Bases*] [*Peru*] [*Political party*] (PPW)
MBH .... Thousands of BTU per Hour
MBH2 .... Reduced Methylene Blue [*Medicine*] (DMAA)
MBHA .... Member of the British Hypnotherapy Association (DBQ)
MBHC .... Boissevain Health Centre, Manitoba [*Library symbol*] [*National Library of Canada*] (NLC)
MBHCM ...... Master of Behavioral Health Care Management (PGP)
MBHE .... Ministries to Blacks in Higher Education (EA)
MBHH .... Handel and Haydn Society, Boston, MA [*Library symbol*] [*Library of Congress*] (LCLS)
MBHI .... Member of the British Horological Institute (DBQ)
MBHI .... Midwest Banc Holdings, Inc. [*NASDAQ symbol*] (NASQ)
MBHI .... Millon Behavioral Health Inventory [*Personality development test*] [*Psychology*]
MBHINST ... Member of the British Horological Institute (ROG)
MBHM .... Harvard Musical Association, Boston, MA [*Library symbol*] [*Library of Congress*] (LCLS)
MBHO .... Managed Behavioral Healthcare Organization (DMAA)
MBHoM ..... Houghton Mifflin Co., Boston, MA [*Library symbol*] [*Library of Congress*] (LCLS)
MBHPFC .... [*The*] Monkees, Boyce and Hart Photo Fan Club (EA)
MBI .... 2-Mercaptobenzimidazol (SAUS)
MBI .... Insurance Library Association of Boston, Boston, MA [*Library symbol*] [*Library of Congress*] (LCLS)
MBI .... Major Budget Issue (COE)
MBI .... Management by Initiative [*Management technique*]
MBI .... Marine Biomedical Institute [*University of Texas*] [*Research center*] (RCD)
MBI .... Maritime Bank of Israel (BJA)
MBI .... Maslach Burnout Inventory
MBI .... Masonic Benevolent Institution (SAUO)
MBI .... Master of Biological Illustration (GAGS)
MBI .... Maximal Blink Index [*Medicine*] (MELL)
MBI .... May Be Issued
MBI .... Mbeya [*Tanzania*] [*Airport symbol*] [*Obsolete*] (OAG)
MBI .... MBIA, Inc. [*NYSE symbol*] (SPSG)
MBI .... Memory Bank Interface
MBI .... Menan Buttes [*Idaho*] [*Seismograph station code, US Geological Survey*] [*Closed*] (SEIS)
MBI .... Metal Belt Institute [*Defunct*] (EA)
MBI .... Methylene Bisphenyl Isocyanate [*Medicine*] (MELL)
MBI .... Methylene Blue Installation [*Medicine*] (DAVI)
MBI .... Michigan Biotechnology Institute [*Michigan State University*] [*Research center*] (RCD)
MBI .... Middle Bronze I [*Age*]
MBI .... Military Board Instruction
MBI .... Minimal Baryonic Isocurvature [*Galactic science*]
MBI .... Miscellaneous Babylonian Inscriptions [*A publication*] (BJA)
MBI .... Modular Building Institute (NTPA)
MBI .... Molecular Biosystems, Inc.
MBI .... Multi Beam Imaging (ACAE)
MBI .... Multibus Interface [*Computer science*] (MCD)
MBI .... Mycobacterial Infection [*Medicine*] (MELL)
MBIA .... Malting Barley Improvement Association (EA)
MBIA .... MBIA, Inc. [*Associated Press*] (SAG)
MBIA .... Merchants Bancorp [*NASDAQ symbol*] (SAG)
MBIA .... Merchants Bancorporation [*NASDAQ symbol*]
MBIA .... Municipal Bond Insurance Association (EA)
MBIA .... Municipal Bond Investors Assurance Corp. (EFIS)
MBIAC .... Missouri Basin Inter-Agency Committee
MBIBTC ..... Malting and Brewing Industry Barley Technical Committee [*Australia*]
MBIC .... Michigan Bigfoot Information Center [*Later, MCBIC*] (EA)
MBIC .... Monmouth Biomedical Information Consortium [*Library network*]
M Bi Ch ..... Master of Biological Chemistry
MBiChem ... Master of Biological Chemistry (NADA)
MBID .... Member of the British Institute of Interior Design (DBQ)
M Bi E .... Master of Biological Engineering
MBIE .... Member of the British Institute of Embalmers (DBQ)
MBIE .... Mobile International [*NCIC trailer make code*]
MBiEng ...... Master of Biological Engineering (NADA)
MBIFCT ..... Mgahinga and Bwindi Inpenetrable Forest Conservation Trust (ECON)
MBII .... Masonic Benevolent Institution Ireland (SAUO)
MBII .... Minority Business Information Institute [*Defunct*] (EA)
MBIITR ...... Multi-Band Inter-Intra Team Radio [*Police and security equipment*]
MBIL .... Mobile Traveler [*NCIC trailer make code*]
MBilC .... Cabot Corp., Technical Information Center, Billerica, MA [*Library symbol*] [*Library of Congress*] (LCLS)
MBilHi .... Billerica Historical Society, Billerica, MA [*Library symbol*] [*Library of Congress*] (LCLS)
MBIM .... Member of the British Institute of Management [*Formerly, MIIA*]
MBIO .... Microprogrammable Block Input/Output
MBIO .... Moleculon, Inc. [*NASDAQ symbol*] (COMM)
M Bio E ..... Master of Bioengineering (PGP)
MBioEth .... Master of Bioethics
M Biomath ... Master of Biomathematics (PGP)
MBiomedE ... Master of Biomedical Engineering (ADA)
M Biorad .... Master of Bioradiology
MBiotech ... Master of Biotechnology
M Bi Phy .... Master of Biological Physics
MBIS .... Mackenzie Basin Impact Study (SAUO)
M Bi S .... Master of Biological Sciences
MBIS .... Master of Business Information Systems
M-BIT .... 1 024 000 bits [*Communications term*] (DCT)
MB (IT) ...... Master of Business (Information Technology)
MBIT .... MegaBIT [*Binary Digit*] [*Computer science*] (MDG)
M-bit .... More Data Bit [*Open Systems Interconnection*] (ODAA)
Mbits/sec ... Megabits per Second [*Computer science*] (IGQR)
MBIU .... Maintenance Bus Interface Unit (ACAE)
MBIU .... Multiplex Bus Interface Unit (MCD)
MBJ .... Montego Bay [*Jamaica*] [*Airport symbol*] (OAG)
MBJ .... Multiple Blinking Jammer (MCD)
MBJI .... Marks Bros Jewelers [*NASDAQ symbol*] (TTSB)
MBJI .... Marks Bros. Jewelers, Inc. [*NASDAQ symbol*] (SAG)
MBJT .... Grand Turk [*Turks and Caicos Islands*] [*ICAO location identifier*] (ICLI)
MBK .... Bank of Mitsubishi Ltd. [*NYSE symbol*] (SAG)

MBK .... Bank of Tokyo-MitsubishiADS [*NYSE symbol*] (TTSB)
MBK .... Madchen-Bibel-Kreise [*Bible Reading Circles*] [*German*]
MBK .... Make-Break Keying (IAA)
MBK .... Medications and Bandage kit (NAKS)
MBK .... Methyl Butyl Ketone [*Organic chemistry*]
MBK .... Methyl-n-Butyl Ketone [*Industrial Poison*] [*Medicine*] (EDAA)
MBK .... Missing, Believed Killed (ADA)
MBK .... Mitsubishi Bank Ltd. ADS [*NYSE symbol*] (SPSG)
MBK .... Multibanc Financial Corp. [*Toronto Stock Exchange symbol*]
MBK .... Multiple Beam Klystron
MBKS......... Multibutton Key Service [*Communications term*] (DCT)
MBKU .... Mitsui Lines [*Intermodal shipping container symbol*] (TVRC)
MBL .... Main Battle Line [*Military*] (IAA)
MBL .... Manistee [*Michigan*] [*Airport symbol*] (OAG)
MBL .... Mannan-Binding Lectin [*Immunology*]
MBL .... Marble Bar [*Australia*] [*Seismograph station code, US Geological Survey*] (SEIS)
MBL .... Marine Biological Laboratory
MBL .... Marine Boundary Layer [*Oceanography*]
MBL .... Master Bidders List (NG)
MBL .... Maximum Benefit Level [*Health insurance*] (GHCT)
MBL .... Measured Blood Loss [*Physiology*]
MBL .... Mechanical Boundary Layer [*Geology*]
MBL .... Medium Brightness Laser (ACAE)
MBL .... Medium Brown Loose [*Stool*] [*Gastroenterology*] (DAVI)
MBL .... Menstrual Blood Loss [*Medicine*]
MBL .... Metropolitan Business League (EARSL)
MBL .... Miniature Button Light
MBL .... Minimal Bactericidal Level
MBL .... Missile Baseline
MBL .... Mitsubishi Brasileira de Industria Pesada (EFIS)
MBL .... Mobile (AFM)
MBL .... Mobile Unit (SAUS)
MBL .... Model Breakdown List
MBL .... Modern Business Law (SAFN)
MBL .... Monterey Bay Area Cooperative Library System, Salinas, CA [*OCLC symbol*] (OCLC)
MBL .... Movimiento Bolivia Libre [*Political party*] (EY)
MBL .... Multiples of Background Level [*Of environmental contaminants*]
MBL .... Mutual Benefit Life Insurance Co. (EFIS)
MBLA........ MBLA Financial Corp. [*Associated Press*] (SAG)
MBLA........ Methylbenzyllinoleic Acid [*Organic chemistry*]
MBLA........ Mouse Specific Bone-Marrow-Derived Lymphocyte Antigen [*Immunology*]
MBLA........ National Mercantile Bancorp [*NASDAQ symbol*] (NQ)
MBLC........ Lahey Clinic Foundation, Boston, MA [*Library symbol*] [*Library of Congress*] (LCLS)
MBLC........ Massachusetts Board of Library Commissioners
MBLC........ Microbore Liquid Chromatography
MBldg .... Master of Building (ADA)
MBldgSc .... Master of Building Science (ADA)
MBldSc...... Master of Building Science
MBLE........ Mobile Gas Service [*NASDAQ symbol*] (TTSB)
MBLE........ Mobile Gas Service Corp. [*NASDAQ symbol*] (NQ)
MBLF........ MBLA Financial [*NASDAQ symbol*] (TTSB)
MBLF........ MBLA Financial Corp. [*NASDAQ symbol*] (SAG)
MBLIC....... Mutual Benefit Life Insurance Company (SAUO)
MBLM .... MobileMedia Corp. [*NASDAQ symbol*] (SAG)
MBLR........ Madhya Bharat Law Reports [*India*] [*A publication*] (DLA)
MblTel....... Mobile Telecommunications & Technology Corp. [*Associated Press*] (SAG)
MBLX........ Municipal Belt Line [*Federal Railroad Administration identification code*]
MBLY........ Mobley Environmental Services [*NASDAQ symbol*] (SPSG)
MBLYA....... Mobley Environmental Services [*OTCBB symbol*]
MBM......... Centre for the Study of Metals in Biology and Medicine [*King's College London*] [*United Kingdom*] (RCD)
MBM......... Mac Bride Museum (SAUO)
MBM......... Magnetic Bubble Memory [*Computer science*]
MBM......... Mambone [*Mozambique*] [*Airport symbol*] (AD)
MBM......... Manual Berthing Mechanism [*NASA*] (SPST)
MBM......... Market Buy Market [*Information service or system*] (IID)
MBM......... Market-by-Market Allocation [*Business term*] (DOAD)
MBM......... Master of Brand Management (GAGS)
MBM......... Master of Building Management (ADA)
MBM......... Master of Business Management
MBM......... MBM [*NCIC car make code*]
MBM......... Meat and Bone Meal
MBM......... Mennonite Board of Missions (SAUO)
MBM......... Metal-Barrier-Metal (IEEE)
MBM......... Mineral Basal Medium [*Microbiology*]
MBM......... Modern Black Men [*Johnson Publishing Co., Inc.*] [*A publication*]
MBM......... Mother's Breast Milk [*Neonatology*] (DAVI)
MBM......... Multibuoy Mooring [*Oil platform*]
Mbm......... Thousand Board (Feet) Measure (WPI)
MBM......... Thousand Feet Board Measure [*Lumber*] (GPO)
MBM......... University of Massachusetts, Joseph P. Healy Library, Boston, MA [*Library symbol*] [*Library of Congress*] (LCLS)
MBMA....... Manuel G. Mancebo [*Common carrier symbol*]
MBMA....... Master Boiler Makers' Association (BUAC)
MBMA....... Metal Building Manufacturers Association (EA)
MBMA....... Military Boot Manufacturers Association (EA)
MBMC....... Middle Caicos [*Turks and Caicos Islands*] [*ICAO location identifier*] (ICLI)
MBMCC ..... Mercedes-Benz Model Car Club
MBMetE..... Metcalf & Eddy, Inc., Boston, MA [*Library symbol*] [*Library of Congress*] (LCLS)
MBMF .... Multibeam Multifrequency (CAAL)
MBMG....... Montana Bureau of Mines and Geology [*Montana College of Mineral Science and Technology*] [*Research center*] (RCD)
MBMGH-T... Massachusetts General Hospital, Treadwell Library, Boston, MA [*Library symbol*] [*Library of Congress*] (LCLS)
MBMH....... Brandon Mental Health Centre, Manitoba [*Library symbol*] [*National Library of Canada*] (NLC)
MBMHC ..... Malcolm Bliss Mental Health Center (SAUO)
MBMI........ Mean Body Mass Index
MBMI........ Micro Bio-Medics [*NASDAQ symbol*] (TTSB)
MBMI........ Micro Bio-Medics, Inc. [*NASDAQ symbol*] (NQ)
MBMI........ Mind/Body Medical Institute
MBMR....... MacArthur Bridge-Saint Louis [*Federal Railroad Administration identification code*]
MBMS....... Bachelor of Medicine, Master of Surgery
MBMS....... Model Base Management Software [*Computer science*] (IAA)
MBMS....... Molecular Beam Mass Spectrometry (AAEL)
MBMSA ..... Massachusetts College of Art, Boston, MA [*Library symbol*] [*Library of Congress*] (LCLS)
MBMSE ..... Master of Business Management and Software Engineering (PGP)
MBMU....... Mobile Base Maintenance Unit
MBMu .... Museum of Fine Arts, Boston, MA [*Library symbol*] [*Library of Congress*] (LCLS)
MBMU....... University of Massachusetts, Boston, MA [*Library symbol*] [*Library of Congress*] (LCLS)
MBN .... Boston Museum of Science, Boston, MA [*Library symbol*] [*Library of Congress*] (LCLS)
MBN .... Medical Benefits Notice [*Medicare*] [*Medicine*] (EDAA)
MBN .... Metal Building News [*A publication*] (APTA)
MBN .... Methylbenzylnitrosamine [*Organic chemistry*]
MBN .... Metrobank NA [*AMEX symbol*] (SPSG)
MBN .... Mixed Base Notation
MBN .... Mombo [*Tanzania*] [*Airport symbol*] (AD)
MBN .... Mutual Black Network (NTCM)
MBNA .... MBNA Corp. [*Associated Press*] (SAG)
MBNA .... Mercedes Benz of North America
MBNA .... Methyl(butyl)nitrosamine [*Organic chemistry*]
MBNA .... Monument Builders of North America (EA)
MBNAD...... Marine Barracks, Naval Ammunition Depot
MBNAS...... Marine Barracks, Naval Air Station
MBNBR...... Mount Bruce Native Bird Reserve (SAUO)
MBNC .... North Caicos [*Turks and Caicos Islands*] [*ICAO location identifier*] (ICLI)
MBNECO .... New England College of Optometry, Boston MA [*Library symbol*] [*Library of Congress*] (LCLS)
MBNEH...... New England Historic Genealogical Society, Boston, MA [*Library symbol*] [*Library of Congress*] (LCLS)
MBNEL ...... New England School of Law, Boston, MA [*Library symbol*] [*Library of Congress*] (LCLS)
MBNEN...... New England Nuclear Corp., Boston, MA [*Library symbol*] [*Library of Congress*] (LCLS)
MBnet .... [*The*] Manitoba Network [*Canada*] [*Computer science*] (TNIG)
MBNK .... Main Street Bancorp, Inc. [*NASDAQ symbol*] (NASQ)
MBNMD..... Marine Barracks, Naval Mine Depot
MBNMHi .... New England Methodist Historical Society, Inc., Boston, MA [*Library symbol*] [*Library of Congress*] (LCLS)
MBNMS ..... Monterey Bay National Marine Sanctuary [*National Oceanic and Atmospheric Administration*] (RCD)
MBNOA...... Member of the British Naturopathic and Osteopathic Association
MBNOB...... Marine Barracks, Naval Operating Base
MBNQA...... Malcolm Baldrige National Quality Award [*Department of Commerce*]
MBNS .... Marine Barracks, Naval Station
MBNU .... Northeastern University, Boston, MA [*Library symbol*] [*Library of Congress*] (LCLS)
MBNU-L..... Northeastern University, Law School, Boston, MA [*Library symbol*] [*Library of Congress*] (LCLS)
MBNW....... Multiple-Breath Nitrogen Washout [*Medicine*] (EDAA)
MBNY .... Merchants Bank of New York [*NASDAQ symbol*] (NQ)
MBNY .... Merchants New York Bancorp [*NASDAQ symbol*] (SAG)
MBNY .... Merchants NY Bancorp [*NASDAQ symbol*] (TTSB)
MBNYD...... Marine Barracks, Navy Yard
MBO .... Liberal Bosnian Organization (BUAC)
MBO .... Madison, MS [*Location identifier*] [*FAA*] (FAAL)
MBO .... Mamburao [*Philippines*] [*Airport symbol*] (OAG)
MBO .... Management and Budget Office (MCD)
MBO .... Management Buy-Out
MBO .... Management by Objectives [*Management technique*] [*Facetious translations: "Management by Oblivion," and "Management by Others"*]
MBO .... M'Bour [*Senegal*] [*Seismograph station code, US Geological Survey*] (SEIS)
MBO .... Meacham Bridge Oscillator [*Electronics*]
MBO .... Mesiobucco-Occlusal [*Dentistry*]
MBO .... Million Barrels of Oil (ABAC)
MBO .... Mobil Oil Ltd. [*Canada*] [*ICAO designator*] (FAAC)
MBO .... Moist Burn Ointment [*Medicine*]
MBO .... Monostable Blocking Oscillator [*Electronics*]
MBO .... Motor Burnout (AABC)
MBO .... Moving Base Operator
MBO .... Muslim Bosnian Organization (BUAC)
MBO .... Mutual Benefit Organization (SAUO)
MBO .... Secondary Vocational Education (SAUS)
MbO_2......... Myoglobin, Oxy [*Biochemistry, medicine*]
MBOA .... Methoxybenzoxazolinone [*Biochemistry*]

MBOA .... Motor Barge Owners Association (BUAC)
MBOC .... Middle Bay Oil [*NASDAQ symbol*] (TTSB)
MBOC .... Middle Bay Oil Co. [*NASDAQ symbol*]
MBOC .... Middle Bay Oil Co., Inc. [*NASDAQ symbol*] (SAG)
MBOC .... Minority Business Opportunity Committee [*Federal interagency group*]
MbOCA ...... Methylene-bis-Orthochloro Aniline (SAUS)
MBOCA ...... Methylenebis(ortho-chloroaniline) [*Also, MOCA*] [*Organic chemistry*]
MBOH .... Minimum Break-Off Height
MBOL .... Motor Burnout Locking (AABC)
MBOM .... Boissevain and Morton Regional Library, Boissevain, Manitoba [*Library symbol*] [*National Library of Canada*] (NLC)
Mbone .... Multicast Backbone [*Computer science*] (NETL)
MBONE ...... Multicast Backbone on the Internet [*Communications term*] (DCT)
MBOR .... Management by Objectives and Results [*Management technique*] (MCD)
MBOS .... Missile Base Operations Supervisor [*Air Force*] (IAA)
MBOS .... Multi-User Business Operating System (NITA)
MBou .... Jonathan Bourne Public Library, Bourne, MA [*Library symbol*] [*Library of Congress*] (LCLS)
MBOU .... Member of the British Ornithologists Union (EY)
MBOU .... Mobilbox [*Intermodal shipping container symbol*] (TVRC)
MBP .... Magneto-Dynamic Positioning
MBP .... Major Basic Protein
MBP .... Malignant Bone Pain (MELL)
MBP .... Maltose-Binding Protein [*Biochemistry*]
MBP .... Management by Planning (ACAE)
MBP .... Manhattan Bowery Project (EA)
MBP .... Manpack Battery Pack
MBP .... Market-Based Pricing (GART)
MBP .... Massachusetts College of Pharmacy, Boston, MA [*Library symbol*] [*Library of Congress*] (LCLS)
MBP .... Master Buy Plan (AAGC)
MBP .... Maternal Blood Pressure [*Medicine*] (EDAA)
MBP .... Maximum Boiling Point
MBP .... MB Brand Present [*Cardiology*] (DAVI)
MBP .... Mean Blood Pressure [*Medicine*]
MBP .... Mean Brachial Artery Pressure [*Medicine*]
MBP .... Mechanical Balance Package (OA)
MBP .... Mechanical Booster Pump
MBP .... Melitensis, Bovine, Porcine [*Antigen*] (AAMN)
MBP .... Mesiobuccopulpal [*Dentistry*]
MBP .... Mid-Boiling Point
MBP .... Mid Penn Bancorp [*AMEX symbol*] (SG)
MBP .... Minnesota Business Partnership (SAUO)
MBP .... Modified Bagshawe Protocol [*Medicine*] (MELL)
MBP .... Monodibutyl Phosphate [*Organic chemistry*] (NUCP)
MBP .... Myelin Basic Protein [*Neurology*]
MBPA .... Master of Business and Public Administration
MBPA .... Metropolitan Bicycle Polo Association (SAUO)
MBPA .... Michigan Business and Professional Association (EARSL)
MBPA .... Military Blood Program Agency (AABC)
MBPAS ...... Monthly Bulk Petroleum Accounting Summary [*Army*] (AABC)
MBP-C ...... Mannose-Binding Protein C [*Biochemistry*]
MBPC .... Model-Based Process Control (AAEL)
MBPC .... Munitions Board Petroleum Committee
MBPCX ...... Merrill Lynch: Pacific Fund Cl.B [*Mutual fund ticker symbol*] (SG)
MBPD .... Medical and Biological Physics Division [*CAP - Canadian Association of Physicists*] [*Medicine*] (EDAA)
MBPD .... Million Barrels per Day
MBPDA ...... Metropolitan Bag and Paper Distribution Association (SAUO)
MBPDA ...... Metropolitan Bag and Paper Distributors Association (EA)
MBPI .... Pine Cay [*Turks and Caicos Islands*] [*ICAO location identifier*] (ICLI)
MBPICS ..... Member of the British Production and Inventory Control Society (ODA)
MBPKN ...... Perry Normal School, Boston, MA [*Library symbol*] [*Library of Congress*] (LCLS)
MBPM .... Master of Business and Public Management
MBPM .... Maurice Bishop Patriotic Movement [*Grenada*] (BUAC)
MBPO .... Military Blood Program Office (AABC)
MBPP .... Movimiento Blanco Popular y Progresista [*National Action Movement*] [*Uruguay*] [*Political party*] (EY)
MBPRE ...... Multitype Branching Process in a Random Environment [*Computer science*]
MBPS .... Mechanical Booster Pump System
MBPS .... MegaBITS [*Binary Digits*] per Second [*Transmission rate*] [*Computer science*]
Mbps .... Megabits per Second (NAKS)
MBps .... Megabytes Per Second [*Communications term*] (DCT)
Mbps .... Megabytes per Second [*Computer science*] (IGQR)
MBPS .... Million BITs [*Binary Digits*] per Second [*Data transmission speed*] [*Computer science*] (NASA)
Mbps .... Millions of Bits Per Second (bps) [*Communications term*] (DCT)
MBPS .... Multigated Blood Pool Scanning [*Medicine*] (DMAA)
MBPS .... Munchausen-by-Proxy Syndrome [*Medicine*] (MELL)
MBPT .... Many-Body Perturbation Theory [*Physics*]
MBPV .... Providenciales [*Turks and Caicos Islands*] [*ICAO location identifier*] (ICLI)
MBPXL ...... MBPXL Corp. [*Formerly, Missouri Beef Packers - Kansas Beef Industries*]
MBPXL ...... Missouri Beef Packers (EFIS)
MBPXL ...... Missouri Beef Packers Express Line (SAUO)
MBQ .... Marine Board of Queensland [*Australia*]
MBQ .... Mbarara [*Uganda*] [*Airport symbol*] (OAG)
MBQ .... Medical Board of Queensland [*Australia*]
mBq .... Millibecquerel, 1 E-3 Bq [*Industrial hygiene term*] (OHS)
MBQ .... Modified Biquinary Code [*Computer science*]
MBR .... Maladapted Behavior Record [*Personality development test*] [*Psychology*]
MBR .... Management by Results [*Management technique*]
MBR .... Marker Beacon Receiver
MBR .... Mars Balloon Relay (ACAE)
MBR .... Master Bedroom [*Real estate*]
MBR .... Master Beneficiary Record [*Social Security Administration*]
MBR .... Master Boot Record [*Computer science*] (PCM)
MBR .... Material Balance Report [*Nuclear energy*]
MBR .... Maximum Base Rent
MBR .... Mbout [*Mauritania*] [*Airport symbol*] (AD)
MBR .... Mechanical Bag Retriever [*Garbage collector*]
MBR .... Mechanical Buffer Register [*Computer science*]
MBR .... Member (AFM)
Mbr .... Member (AL)
mbr .... Member (DD)
MBR .... Membrane Bioreactor [*Chemical engineering*]
MBR .... Membrane-Bound Ribosomes [*Cytology*]
MBR .... Memory Base Register
MBR .... Memory Buffer Register [*Computer science*]
MBR .... Metal Bulletin Research [*Commercial firm*] [*British*] (ECON)
MBR .... Methylene Blue Reduced
MBR .... Microwave Background Radiation [*Physics*]
MBR .... Mini Badge Reader (IAA)
MBR .... Mission Briefing Room [*NASA*] (KSC)
MBR .... Modern Business Reports (SAUO)
MBR .... Modified Bitumen, Reinforced
MBR .... Montebello Resources Ltd. [*Vancouver Stock Exchange symbol*]
MBR .... Motivation by Rotation
MBR .... Moving Belt Radiator
MBR .... Multibomb Rack
MBR .... Nukak Maku [*Language symbol*] (ETLW)
MBr .... Public Library of Brookline, Brookline, MA [*Library symbol*] [*Library of Congress*] (LCLS)
MBRA .... Marathon Boat Racers Association
MBRA .... Multibeam Radiometer Antenna
MBradJ ...... Bradford Junior College [*Later, BC*], Bradford, MA [*Library symbol*] [*Library of Congress*] (LCLS)
MBRBA ...... Motor Body Repairers and Builders Association (SAUO)
MBRC .... Marine Biology Research Centre [*University of Moncton*] [*Canada*] (IRC)
MBRDC ...... Medical Bioengineering Research and Development Command [*Army*] (PDAA)
MBRDL ...... Medical Bioengineering Research and Development Laboratory [*Army*] (MCD)
MBre .... Brewster Ladies Library, Brewster, MA [*Library symbol*] [*Library of Congress*] (LCLS)
MBRE .... Memory Buffer Register, Even [*Computer science*]
MBreC .... Cape Cod Museum of Natural History, Brewster, MA [*Library symbol*] [*Library of Congress*] (LCLS)
MBRET ...... Middle Breton [*Language, etc.*]
MBRF .... Midbrain Reticular Formation [*Anatomy*]
MBRF .... Mission Bay Research Foundation (SAUO)
MBRG .... Ropes & Gray, Boston, MA [*Library symbol*] [*Library of Congress*] (LCLS)
MBrH .... Hebrew College, Brookline, MA [*Library symbol*] [*Library of Congress*] (LCLS)
MBrHC ...... Hellenic College of Arts and Sciences and Holy Cross Greek Orthodox Theological School, Brookline, MA [*Library symbol*] [*Library of Congress*] (LCLS)
MBridT ...... Bridgewater State College, Bridgewater, MA [*Library symbol*] [*Library of Congress*] (LCLS)
M Brit IRE... Member of the British Institution of Radio Engineers [*Later, MIERE*]
M/BRK .... Manual Brake [*Automotive engineering*]
MBRK .... Meadowbrook Rehab Grp'A' [*NASDAQ symbol*] (TTSB)
MBRK .... Meadowbrook Rehabilitation Group [*NASDAQ symbol*] (SAG)
MBRL .... Multiple Ballistic Rocket Launcher
MBRLS ...... Multi-Barrel Rocket Launching System (SAUS)
MBRM .... McCambridge Brothers Material Supplies [*Common carrier symbol*]
MBRM .... Membrane
MBRO .... Memory Buffer Register, Odd [*Computer science*]
MBrock ...... Brockton Public Library, Brockton, MA [*Library symbol*] [*Library of Congress*] (LCLS)
MBrockV .... United States Veterans Administration Hospital, Brockton, MA [*Library symbol*] [*Library of Congress*] (LCLS)
MBRR .... Meridian & Bigbee Railroad Co. [*Formerly, MB*] [*AAR code*]
MBRS .... Meanook Biological Research Station [*University of Alberta*] [*Canada*] (RCD)
MBRS .... MemberWorks, Inc. [*NASDAQ symbol*] (SAG)
MBRS .... Minority Biomedical Research Support Program [*Bethesda, MD*] [*National Institutes of Health*] (GRD)
MBRS .... Mount Barker Research Station (SAUO)
MBRSHP .... Membership
MBRT .... Methylene Blue Reduction Time
MBRUU ..... May Be Retained until Unserviceable
MBRV .... Maneuverable Ballistic Reentry Vehicle
MBRW .... Matchbox Regular Wheels [*Toy collection*]
MBRW .... Minnesota Brewing [*NASDAQ symbol*] (TTSB)
MBRW .... Minnesota Brewing Co. [*NASDAQ symbol*] (SAG)
MBRWQ ..... MBC Holding Co. [*OTCBB symbol*]
MBRX .... Milford-Bennington Railroad [*Federal Railroad Administration identification code*]
MBrZ .... Zion Research Library, Brookline, Boston, MA [*Library symbol*] [*Library of Congress*] (LCLS)

MBS .... Bay City-Midland-Saginaw [*Michigan*] [*Airport symbol*] (AD)
MBS .... Bethany Lutheran Theological Seminary, Mankato, MN [*OCLC symbol*] (OCLC)
MBS .... Macquarie Broadcasting Service (SAUO)
MBS .... Magnetron Beam Switching
MBS .... Main "Bang" Suppressor
MBS .... Main Buffer Storage (IAA)
MBS .... Mainichi Broadcasting System (SAUO)
MBS .... Maleimidobenzoyl N-Hydroxysuccinimide [*Organic chemistry*]
MBS .... Malta Board of Standards (BUAC)
MBS .... Managed Bandwidth Service
MBS .... Management by System [*Management technique*] (IAA)
MBS .... Manchester Business School [*England*]
MBS .... Marker Board Supplies Limited (SAUO)
MBS .... Market Basket Survey [*Business term*]
MBS .... Martin-Bell Syndrome [*Medicine*] (DMAA)
MBS .... Master Bibliographic System (ADA)
MBS .... Master Boot Sector (SAUS)
MBS .... Master of Basic Science
MBS .... Master of Behavioral Science (GAGS)
MBS .... Master of Building Science (GAGS)
MBS .... Master of Business Science (SAUO)
MBS .... Maximum Burst Size (MLOA)
MBS .... Medborgerlig Samling [*Citizens Rally*] [*Sweden*] [*Political party*] (PPE)
MBS .... Mediterranean Base Section [*Army*] [*World War II*]
MBS .... Medium Bomber Strike (NATG)
MBS .... MedQuist, Inc. [*AMEX symbol*] (SAG)
MBS .... Megabits Per Second (NITA)
mbs .... Megabits per Second (COE)
Mbs .... Megabits per Second [*Computer science*] (IGQR)
M B/S .... Megabits per Second (NAKS)
Mb/s .... Megabits per Second (VLIE)
MB/s .... Megabytes per Second (VLIE)
MBS .... Member of the Bibliographical Society (ROG)
MBS .... Menorah Book Service (BJA)
MBS .... Methacrylate Butadiene Styrene [*Plastics technology*]
MBS .... Methionyl Bovine Somatotropin [*Biochemistry*]
MBS .... Methodist Boys' School
MBS .... Miami Beach Symphony (SAUO)
MBS .... Micro Business Systems (NITA)
MBS .... Miniature Book Society (EA)
MBS .... Minimum Basis Sets [*Chemistry*] (MEC)
MBS .... Mission Bit Stream (SAUO)
MBS .... Mission Budget Statement [*Army*]
MBS .... Mobile-Base Simulator (PDAA)
MBS .... Mobile Broadband System (SAUO)
MBS .... Modular Banking System (PDAA)
MBS .... Modular Barrier System [*Police and security equipment*]
MBS .... Molecular Beam Scattering (SAUS)
MBS .... Monobromo-Salicylanilide [*Medicine*] (EDAA)
MBS .... Monobutyl Sulfate [*Organic chemistry*]
MBS .... Monumental Brass Society (EA)
MBS .... Morpholine-Based Sulfenamide [*Chemistry*]
MBS .... Mortgage-Backed Securities Information Services [*The Bond Buyer, Inc.*] [*New York, NY*] [*Information service or system*] (IID)
MBS .... Mortgage-Backed Security (DFIT)
MBS .... Mortgage-Backed Security Program [*Government National Mortgage Association*]
MBS .... Motion Base Simulator (MCD)
MBS .... Motor Bus Society (EA)
MBS .... Multibit Shifter (IAA)
MBS .... Multiblade Slurry Saw [*Semiconductor technology*]
MBS .... Multiblock Synchronization Signal Unit [*Telecommunications*] (TEL)
MBS .... Multicore Bar Solder
MBS .... Multilingual Biblioservice of Alberta, Alberta Culture [*UTLAS symbol*]
MBS .... Multiple Batch Station [*Computer science*]
MBS .... Multiple Business System
MBS .... Municipal Broadcasting System (SAUO)
MBS .... Music Broadcasting Society (NADA)
MBS .... Mutual Broadcasting System
MBS .... Muzzle Bore Sight [*British military*] (DMA)
MBS .... Myrtle Beach, SC [*Amtrak Busline code*]
MBS .... Saginaw [*Michigan*] [*Airport symbol*] (OAG)
MBS .... Saginaw, MI [*Location identifier*] [*FAA*] (FAAL)
MBS .... Social Law Library, Boston, MA [*Library symbol*] [*Library of Congress*] (LCLS)
MBSA .... Main Bus-Switching Assembly (SSD)
MBSA .... Maleylated Bovine Serum Albumin [*Biochemistry*]
MBSA .... Manual Business Systems Association [*British*] (DBA)
MBSA .... Medical Board of South Australia
MBSA .... Methylated Bovine Serum Albumin
MBSA .... Model-Based System Analysis (PDAA)
MBSA .... Modular Building Standards Association (EA)
MBSA .... Municipal Board Standards Association (NADA)
MBSA .... Munitions Board Standards Agency
MBSA .... Museum Board of South Australia
MBSB .... Marine Barracks, Submarine Base
MBSC .... Boston State College, Boston, MA [*Library symbol*] [*Library of Congress*] (LCLS)
MBSc .... Master of Behavioural Science
MB Sc .... Master of Business Science
MBSC .... Modular Building Systems Council (EA)
MBSC .... South Caicos [*Turks and Caicos Islands*] [*ICAO location identifier*] (ICLI)
MBSCC .... Mortgage-Backed Securities Clearing Corp. (EMRF)
MBSCSDD .. Master of Back Stabbin', Cork Screwin', and Dirty Dealin' [*Self-conferred degree held by Mordecai Jones in 1967 movie "The Flim-Flam Man"*]
MBSD .... Model Based System Design Laboratory [*University of Arizona*] (RCD)
MBSD .... Multi-Barrel Smoke Discharger [*Military*] (PDAA)
MBS Division... Moore Business Systems Division (SAUO)
MBSE .... Member of Belgian Society of Engineers (SAUO)
MBSF .... Matchbox Superfast [*Toy collection*]
MBSG .... Missouri Basin Systems Group (SAUO)
MBSGM ...... Multi-Base Sortie Generation Model (SAUO)
MBSHC ...... Mediterranean and Black Seas Hydrographic Commission (SAUO)
MBSI .... Master of Business Information Science (PGP)
MBSI .... Member of the Boot and Shoe Industry [*British*] (DAS)
MBSI .... Member of the British Boot and Shoe Institution (SAUO)
MBSI .... Missile Battery Status Indicator
MBSI .... Musical Box Society, International (EA)
MBSi .... Simmons College, Boston, MA [*Library symbol*] [*Library of Congress*] (LCLS)
MBSJC .... Metropolitan Boroughs Standing Joint Committee (SAUO)
MB-SL .... British Museum - Sloan Herbarium [*London*]
MBSL .... Mobile Surgery Laboratory (SAUO)
MBSL .... Mouse Biochemical Specific Locus [*Test for mutagenesis*]
MBSL .... Multiple-Bubble Sonoluminescence [*Physics*]
MBSM .... Maize Bushy Stunt Mycoplasm [*Plant pathology*]
MBSM .... Mexican Border Service Medal
MBSOGB .... Musical Box Society of Great Britain
MBSP .... Main Bang Synchronization Pulse (IAA)
MBSP .... Mitchell Bancorp, Inc. [*NASDAQ symbol*] (SAG)
MBSpnea ... Society for the Preservation of New England Antiquities, Boston, MA [*Library symbol*] [*Library of Congress*] (LCLS)
MBSP-R ..... Monitoring Basic Skills Progress-Reading (TES)
MBSQ .... Music Broadcasting Society of Queensland [*Australia*]
MBSS .... Main Beach Signal Station (IAA)
MBSS .... Mercedes-Benz Vehicle Security System
MBSS .... Multi-Band Staring Sensor (ACAE)
MBSS .... Multi-Bank Staring System Sensor (SAUS)
MBSSM ...... Maxfield-Buchholz Scale of Social Maturity [*Psychology*]
MBST .... Miller Building Systems, Inc. [*NASDAQ symbol*] (NASQ)
MBST .... Motor Behavior Screening Test [*Physical education*]
MBST .... Multiple Beam Switching Tube
MBSTA .... Mobilization Station (SAUO)
MBSU .... Multi Bus Switching Unit
MBSuf .... Suffolk University, Boston, MA [*Library symbol*] [*Library of Congress*] (LCLS)
MBSufC ..... Suffolk County Court House, Boston, MA [*Library symbol*] [*Library of Congress*] (LCLS)
MBSX .... MBS Textbook Exchange, Inc. [*NASDAQ symbol*] (COMM)
MBSY .... Salt Cay [*Turks and Caicos Islands*] [*ICAO location identifier*] (ICLI)
MBT .... Main Ballast Tank
MBT .... Main Battle Tank
MBT .... Main Boundary Thrust [*Geology*]
MBT .... Many-Body Theory [*Physics*] (BARN)
MBT .... Marble Bar - Town [*Australia*] [*Seismograph station code, US Geological Survey*] [*Closed*] (SEIS)
MBT .... Marianna & Blountstown Railroad Co. [*AAR code*]
MBT .... Masbate [*Philippines*] [*Airport symbol*] (OAG)
MBT .... Massive Blood Transfusion [*Medicine*] (MELL)
MBT .... Master of Business and Technology
MBT .... Master of Business Taxation (GAGS)
MBT .... Mean Body Temperature (WDAA)
MBT .... Mechanical Bathythermograph
MBT .... Memory Block Table [*Computer science*] (HGAA)
MBT .... Mercaptobenzothiazole [*Organic chemistry*]
MBT .... Mercury Bombardment Thrustor
MBT .... Metal-Base Transistor [*Electronics*] (IEEE)
MBT .... Metal Bond Tape
MBT .... Methylenebisthiocyanate [*Antimicrobial agent*]
MBT .... Methylene Blue Test [*Analytical chemistry*]
MBT .... Metropolitan Ballet Theatre [*Detroit*]
MBT .... Midblastula Stage [*Embryology*]
MBT .... Mid-Blastula Transition [*Developmental biology*]
MBT .... Minimum Best Torque
MBT .... Mixed Bacterial Toxin
MBT .... Mobile Boarding Team
MBT .... Mobile Telesystems OJSC ADS [*NYSE symbol*]
MBT .... Modified Boiling Test (PDAA)
MBT .... Mother's Blood Type (ADWA)
MBT .... Motion Base Technologies
MBT .... Motor Burning Time
MBT .... Multimedia-Based Training
MBT .... Murfreesboro, TN [*Location identifier*] [*FAA*] (FAAL)
MBT .... Vias Aereas Manabitas CIA Ltds. [*Ecuador*] [*FAA designator*] (FAAC)
MBTA .... Malaysia Baggage Transport Agency (SAUO)
MBTA .... Massachusetts Bay Transit Authority [*Federal Railroad Administration identification code*]
MBTA .... Massachusetts Bay Transportation Authority [*Formerly, MTA*]
MBTA .... Metropolitan Boston Transit Authority (BARN)
MBTA .... Midwest Book Travelers Association (SAUO)
MBTA .... Migratory Bird Treaty Act (GNE)
MBTA .... Migratory Bird Treaty Act of 1918 (COE)
MBTA .... Multiple Beam Tows Antenna [*Communications term*] (DCT)
MBTC .... Mercedes-Benz Truck Co.
MBTC .... Model-Based Temperature Control (AAEL)

MBTCA ...... Miniature Bull Terrier Club of America (EA)
MBTD/RP ... Main Battle Tank Distribution/Redistribution Plan (MCD)
MBTFA ...... Methylbistrifluoroacetamide [*Organic chemistry*]
MBTG .... Millennium Biotechnologies Group [*OTCBB symbol*]
MBTH .... Methylbenzothiazolinone Hydrazone [*Organic chemistry*]
MbThSt ...... Marburger Theologische Studien (BJA)
MBTI .... Boston Theological Institute, Learning Development Program, Boston, MA [*Library symbol*] [*Library of Congress*] (LCLS)
MBTI .... Manpower Business Training Institute
MBTI .... Myers-Briggs Type Indicator [*Psychology*]
MBTI:AV ..... Myers-Briggs Type Indicator: Abbreviated Version [*Personality development test*] [*Psychology*]
MBTR .... Mobile Traveler [*NCIC truck make code*]
MBTS .... Mercaptobenzothiazole Disulfide [*Organic chemistry*]
MBTS .... Meteorological Balloon Tracking System
MBTS .... Michelin Bead Tension Structure [*Tire design*]
MBTS .... Missile Battery Test Set [*Military*] (IAA)
MBtS .... Saint John's Seminary, Brighton, MA [*Library symbol*] [*Library of Congress*] (LCLS)
MBTT .... Marine Builders Training Trust (AIE)
MBTTE ...... MB Tech [*OTCBB symbol*]
MBtu .... Million British Thermal Units
MBTWK ..... Multiple Beam Traveling Wave Klystron
MBU .... Boston University, Boston, MA [*Library symbol*] [*Library of Congress*] (LCLS)
MBU .... Boston University, School of Medicine, Boston, MA [*OCLC symbol*] (OCLC)
MBU .... Hayward Map, CA [*Location identifier*] [*FAA*] (FAAL)
MBU .... Magnetic Bubble Unit (NITA)
MBU .... Mbambanakira [*Solomon Islands*] [*Airport symbol*] (OAG)
MBU .... Memory Buffer Unit [*Computer science*]
MBU .... MIRA [*Multifunctional Inertial Reference Assembly*] Basic Unit [*Air Force*] (MCD)
MBU .... Mission Briefing Unit
MBU .... Modern Burner Unit [*Military*] (STAH)
MBUC .... Mind Bogglingly Unlikely Coincidence (SAUS)
MBU-E .... Boston University, School of Education, Boston, MA [*Library symbol*] [*Library of Congress*] (LCLS)
MBUF .... United Fruit Co., Boston, MA [*Library symbol*] [*Library of Congress*] (LCLS)
MBuild ...... Master of Building (ADA)
MBUK .... Mercedes-Benz (United Kingdom)
MBU-L .... Boston University, School of Law, Boston, MA [*Library symbol*] [*Library of Congress*] (LCLS)
MBU-M ...... Boston University, School of Medicine, Boston, MA [*Library symbol*] [*Library of Congress*] (LCLS)
MBUMA ..... Mean Time between Unscheduled Maintenance Actions
MBUMR ..... MIRA [*Multifunctional Inertial Reference Assembly*] Basic Unit Mounting Rack [*Air Force*] (MCD)
MBurPRM ... P. R. Mallory & Co., Burlington, MA [*Library symbol*] [*Library of Congress*] (LCLS)
MBus .... Master of Business (ADA)
MBUS .... Memory Bus (TIMI)
MBUS .... Module BUS (SAUS)
MBus-Accy ... Master of Business - Accountancy
MBusAd ..... Master of Business Administration (ADA)
MBus-Comn .... Master of Business - Communication
M Bus Ed ... Master of Business Education
MBUSI .... Mercedes-Benz United States International [*Manufacturing operations*]
MBus-Mgt ... Master of Business - Management
MBU-T .... Boston University, School of Theology, Boston, MA [*Library symbol*] [*Library of Congress*] (LCLS)
MBUUC ...... Minnesota Business Utility Users Council [*An association*] (TSSD)
MBV .... Main Base Visit (NASA)
MBV .... Marine Board of Victoria [*Australia*]
MBV .... Medical Board of Victoria [*Australia*]
MBV .... Mexican Border Veterans (EA)
MBV .... Minimum Breakdown Voltage
MBV .... Model-Based Vision (ADWA)
MBV .... United States Veterans Administration Hospital, Boston, MA [*Library symbol*] [*Library of Congress*] (LCLS)
MBV-O .... United States Veterans Administration, Outpatients Clinic, Boston, MA [*Library symbol*] [*Library of Congress*] (LCLS)
MBVP .... Mechanical Booster Vacuum Pump
MBVPS ...... Mechanical Booster Vacuum Pump System
MBVT .... Merchants Banchares, Inc. [*NASDAQ symbol*] (NQ)
MBVT .... Merchants Bancshares [*NASDAQ symbol*] (SAG)
MBVT .... Merchants Bancshares (VT) [*NASDAQ symbol*] (TTSB)
MBW .... Mean Body Weight
MBW .... Medicine Bow, WY [*Location identifier*] [*FAA*] (FAAL)
MBW .... Medium Black and White [*Film*] (KSC)
MBW .... Metropolitan Board of Works [*British*]
MBW .... Microbiological Warfare
MBW .... Moorabbin [*Airport symbol*]
MBW .... Mount Baker [*Washington*] [*Seismograph station code, US Geological Survey*] (SEIS)
MBW .... Movement for a Better World (EA)
MBW .... Munitions Assignment Board (Washington) [*World War II*]
MBW .... Western Manitoba Regional Library, Brandon, Manitoba [*Library symbol*] [*National Library of Canada*] (NLC)
MBWA .... Management by Walking About [*or Wandering Around*] [*Facetious translation of MBO - Management by Objectives*]
MBWA .... Management by Walking Around (SAUO)
MBWA .... Management by Wandering Around (SAUO)
MBWA .... Minnesota Beer Wholesalers Association (EARSL)
MBWI .... Wentworth Institute of Technical, Boston, MA [*Library symbol*] [*Library of Congress*] (LCLS)
MBWO .... Microwave Backward Wave Oscillator
MBWS .... Wheelock College, Boston, MA [*Library symbol*] [*Library of Congress*] (LCLS)
MBX .... Electronic mailbox (SAUS)
MBX .... Mailbox (ROAS)
MBX .... Management by Exception [*Management technique*] (IAA)
MBX .... Maribor [*Former Yugoslavia*] [*Airport symbol*] (OAG)
MBX .... Matchbox [*Toy collection*]
MBX .... Message Bus Exchange (AAEL)
MBY .... Make Busy (IAA)
MBY .... Middleby Corp. [*AMEX symbol*] (SPSG)
MBY .... Miller Brewery [*Federal Railroad Administration identification code*]
MBY .... Moberly, MO [*Location identifier*] [*FAA*] (FAAL)
MBY & D ... Maintenance, Bureau of Yards and Docks [*Budget category*] [*Obsolete; see FEC*] [*Navy*]
MBYC .... Manhasset Bay Yacht Club (SAUO)
Mbyte .... Megabyte
Mbyte .... Million Bytes [*Computer science*]
MBYY .... Matchbox Models of Yesteryear [*Toy collection*]
MBZ .... Magnesia-Buffered Zinc Oxide (PDAA)
MBZ .... Mandatory Broadcast Zone [*Telecommunications*] (DA)
MBZ .... Maues [*Brazil*] [*Airport symbol*] (AD)
MBZ .... Menxel Bouzelfa [*Tunisia*] [*Seismograph station code, US Geological Survey*] (SEIS)
MBZ .... Middle Border Zone [*Geology*]
MBZ .... Mobilize [*Telegraphy*] (PCTE)
MBZ .... Must Be Zero (IAA)
MBZN .... Mobilization [*Telegraphy*] (PCTE)
MBZS .... Maximum Bandwidth Zero Suppression (VLIE)
MC .... Aermacchi SpA [*Italy*] [*ICAO aircraft manufacturer identifier*] (ICAO)
MC .... CAA Flying Unit [*British*] [*ICAO designator*] (ICDA)
MC .... Cambridge Public Library, Cambridge, MA [*Library symbol*] [*Library of Congress*] (LCLS)
MC .... Chemists' Club [*Formerly, Mining Club*] (EA)
MC .... Consolata Missionary Sisters [*Roman Catholic religious order*]
MC .... Department of Mass Communication (SAUO)
MC .... Macalester College (SAUO)
Mc .... Maccabees [*Old Testament book*] [*Roman Catholic canon*]
M-C .... MacDonald-Cartier Highway [*Canada*]
M/C .... Machine (ROG)
MC .... Machine Cancellation [*Philately*]
MC .... Machine Check [*Computer science*] (IAA)
MC .... Machine Code (IAA)
MC .... Machine Console
MC .... Machine Cycle (IAA)
MC .... Machinery Certificate [*Shipping*]
MC .... Macula Coloboma [*Medicine*] (MELL)
MC .... Madison College (SAUO)
MC .... Madonna College (SAUO)
MC .... Magic Circle [*An association*] (EA)
MC .... Magister Chirurgiae [*Master of Surgery*]
MC .... Magistrates Cases [*Legal term*] [*British*]
MC .... Magistrates Court (SAUO)
MC .... Magnesium Chlorate [*Inorganic chemistry*]
MC .... Magnetic Card [*Word processing*]
MC .... Magnetic Clutch
MC .... Magnetic Core
MC .... Magnetic Course [*Navigation*]
M-C .... Magovern-Cromie [*Prosthesis*] (AAMN)
MC .... Mail Chute (DAC)
MC .... Mailet College (SAUO)
MC .... Main Cabin
M/C .... Main Chamber [*NASA*] (KSC)
MC .... Main Channel
MC .... Main Chute (KSC)
MC .... Main Cock
MC .... Main Color [*Crocheting*]
MC .... Main Condenser [*Nuclear energy*] (NRCH)
MC .... Main Coolant (MSA)
MC .... Maine Central (SAUO)
MC .... Maine Coast Railroad [*Federal Railroad Administration identification code*]
M/C .... Maintenance and Calibration
MC .... Maintenance Center (MCD)
MC .... Maintenance Command [*Obsolete*] [*Air Force*] [*British*]
MC .... Maintenance Console
MC .... Maintenance Cycle (MCD)
MC .... Major Component
MC .... Major Critical (ACAE)
MC .... Major Cycle
MC .... Makers of Canada [*A publication*]
MC .... Making Capacity (IAA)
MC .... Malayan Cases [*1908-58*] [*A publication*] (DLA)
M/C .... Male, Castrated Animal (DMAA)
MC .... Malignant Carcinoid [*Medicine*] (MELL)
MC .... Malone College (SAUO)
MC .... Managed Care [*Insurance*] (WYGK)
MC .... Managed Competition
MC .... Management Center (VLIE)
MC .... Management Code (ALAC)
MC .... Management Committee (IAA)

MC .... Management Contents [*Information Access Co.*] [*Information service or system*] (IID)
MC .... Management Council (SAUO)
MC .... Manatee College (SAUO)
M/C .... Manchester (ROG)
Mc .... Manchester, Chetham Library (SAUO)
MC .... Manchester College (SAUO)
Mc .... Mandible Coronoid (STED)
MC .... Manganese Centre (EA)
MC .... Manhattan College (SAUO)
MC .... Manhattanville College (SAUO)
MC .... Manhole Cover
MC .... Manned Core (SSD)
MC .... Manpower Commission (NADA)
MC .... Manpower Council [*Northern Ireland*] (BUAC)
MC .... Mantle Cavity
MC .... Mantle Collar
MC .... Manual Code (NITA)
MC .... Manual Control
MC .... Manufacturing Center (TIMI)
MC .... Manufacturing Change (IAA)
MC .... Mapping Camera
MC .... Mapping Center (SAUO)
MC .... Maps and Charts [*Interservice*] [*NATO*]
MC .... Mare Crisium [*Sea of Crises*] [*Lunar area*]
MC .... Marginal Check [*Computer*]
MC .... Marginal Checking (NITA)
MC .... Marginal Cost [*Business term*]
M/C .... Marginal Credit [*Business term*]
MC .... Margin Call [*Banking, investments*]
MC .... Maria College (SAUO)
MC .... Marian College (SAUO)
MC .... Marietta College (SAUO)
MC .... Marine Corps
MC .... Marine Craft [*British military*] (DMA)
MC .... Marion College (SAUO)
MC .... Marist College (SAUO)
MC .... Maritime Commission [*of Department of Commerce*] [*Merged with Federal Maritime Commission*]
MC .... Mark Cross [*Initials often used as pattern on Mark Cross leather goods*]
MC .... Marked Capacity [*Freight cars*]
MC .... Market Capacity (ADA)
MC .... Marketing Center [*Veterans Administration*]
MC .... Mark of the Craft [*Freemasonry*]
MC .... Marlboro College (SAUO)
MC .... Marmon Club (EA)
MC .... Marque de Commerce [*Trademark*]
MC .... Marriage Certificate
MC .... Married Couple (ADA)
MC .... Marshall College (SAUO)
MC .... Martin Co. (MCD)
MC .... Martin College (SAUO)
MC .... Mary College (SAUO)
MC .... Marycrest College (SAUO)
MC .... Maryglade College (SAUO)
MC .... Marygrove College (SAUO)
MC .... Maryheart Crusaders (EA)
MC .... Marylhurst College (SAUO)
MC .... Marymount College (SAUO)
MC .... Maryville College (SAUO)
MC .... Marywood College (SAUO)
MC .... Mass Communication (NTCM)
MC .... Mast Cell
MC .... Mast Controller (DNAB)
MC .... MasterCard [*Credit card*]
MC .... Mastercard International [*New York, NY*] (EA)
MC .... Master Change (IAA)
MC .... Master Clock (IAA)
MC .... Master Commandant
MC .... Master Commander [*Navy*] [*British*] (ROG)
MC .... Master Control
MC .... Master Controller (SAUS)
M/C .... Master Copy
MC .... Master of Ceremonies
MC .... Master of Chemistry
MC .... Master of Classics
MC .... Master of Commerce (GAGS)
MC .... Master of Communication (GAGS)
MC .... Master of Congress [*British*] (DAS)
MC .... Master of Counseling (GAGS)
MC .... Master of Criminology (SAUO)
MC .... Master of Surgery (SAUO)
MC .... Matara Cases [*Ceylon*] [*A publication*] (DLA)
MC .... Material Center (SAUO)
MC .... Material Code (MCD)
MC .... Material Control (AAG)
MC .... Materials Committee (MCD)
MC .... Materiel Center (SAUO)
MC .... Materiel Change [*Military*]
MC .... Materiel Command [*Air Force*]
MC .... Materiel Concept [*Army*]
MC .... Mathematical Center (IAA)
MC .... Matsushita Electric Industrial (SAUO)
MC .... Matsushita Electric Industrial Co. Ltd. [*NYSE symbol*] (SPSG)
MC .... Matsushita Electric Industrial Company Ltd. [*NYSE symbol*]
MC .... Matsushita El Ind ADR [*NYSE symbol*] (TTSB)
MC .... Mature Cataract (MELL)
MC .... Maunaolu College (SAUO)
MC .... Maury Center for Ocean Science [*Washington, DC*]
MC .... Maximum Concentration
MC .... Maximum Count Output (IAA)
MC .... Mayor's Court (DLA)
MC .... Mazda Club (EA)
MC .... Measure Code (NITA)
MC .... Measuring Core (HAWK)
MC .... Mechanical Council (EA)
MC .... Media Coalition [*Later, MC/ACF*] (EA)
MC .... Medial Canthus (MELL)
MC .... Medical Cabinet (SAUO)
MC .... Medical Care, Civilian Source (DNAB)
MC .... Medical Center
MC .... Medical Certificate (ADA)
MC .... Medical College (SAUO)
MC .... Medical Consultant [*Social Security Administration*] (OICC)
MC .... Medical Corps [*Navy*]
MC .... Medicine Cabinet [*Technical drawings*] (NFPA)
MC .... Medicines Commission (SAUO)
M-C .... Medico-Chirurgical [*Medicine*] (EDAA)
MC .... Medium Capacity [*or Charge*] [*Bomb*]
MC .... Medium Case bomb (SAUS)
MC .... Medium-Chain [*Triglycerides*] [*Biochemistry*] (MAE)
MC .... Medium Curing [*Asphalt grade*]
MC .... Medugorje Center (EA)
MC .... Medullary Cavity [*Medicine*] (MELL)
MC .... Medullary Cystic Disease [*Medicine*] (AAMN)
Mc .... Megacurie
mc .... Megacycle (IDOE)
Mc .... Megacycle
MC .... Megacycles (VLIE)
MC .... Megacycles per Second (IAA)
MC .... Megalocornea (MELL)
MC .... Melamine Council [*Defunct*] (EA)
MC .... Melter Cell (ABAC)
MC .... Member of Congress
MC .... Member of Council
MC .... Memorandum Club [*Defunct*] (EA)
MC .... Memorandum of Conditions
MC .... Memorial Commission [*Federal body*]
MC .... Memory Cell [*Immunology*] (QSUL)
MC .... Memory Channel [*Computer science*] (GART)
MC .... Memory Charts
MC .... Memory Clear [*Computer science*] (PCM)
MC .... Memory Configuration [*Computer science*] (MCD)
mc .... Memory Configuration (NAKS)
MC .... Memory-Constrained [*Computer science*]
MC .... Memory Control [*Unit*] [*Computer science*]
MC .... Memphis College (SAUO)
MC .... Menlo College (SAUO)
MC .... Mennonite Church (SAUO)
MC .... Mercury Club [*Defunct*] (EA)
MC .... Mercury Contact (IAA)
MC .... Meredith Corp. (EFIS)
MC .... Merkel Cell [*Anatomy*]
MC .... Mesa College (SAUO)
MC .... Mesenteric Collateral [*Cardiology*] (DAVI)
MC .... Mesiocervical [*Dentistry*]
MC .... Message Center
MC .... Message Change (MCD)
MC .... Message$_{C}$heck (EA)
MC .... Message Composer [*Communications, data processing*]
MC .... Mess Call [*Military*]
MC .... Metacarpal [*or Metacarpus*] [*Anatomy*]
MC .... Metal Carbide
MC .... Metal Case [*Bullet*] (DICI)
MC .... Metal Clad (IAA)
MC .... Metaling Clause [*Marine insurance*]
M/C .... Metallic Currency (ROG)
MC .... Metatarsocuneiform [*Orthopedics*] (DAVI)
MC .... Meteorological Codes (SAUO)
mc .... Meter-Candle (IDOE)
M-C .... Meter-Candle
MC .... Methacholine Challenge [*Medicine*]
MC .... Methodist Chaplain
MC .... Methodist Church (WDAA)
MC .... Methyl Carbamate [*Organic chemistry*]
MC .... Methylcellulose [*Organic chemistry*]
MC .... Methylchloroform [*Organic chemistry*]
MC .... Methylcholanthrene [*Also, MCA*] [*Organic chemistry*]
MC .... Methylcystyosine [*Biochemistry*]
MC .... Methylene Chloride [*Organic chemistry*]
MC .... Metric Carat [*200 milligrams*]
MC .... Metrology Center (SAUO)
MC .... Metropolitan Counties [*British*]
MC .... Michigan Central (SAUO)
MC .... Michigan Central Railroad [*Absorbed into Consolidated Rail Corp.*] [*AAR code*]
MC .... Michigan Central Railroad Co. (SAUO)

MC .... Michigan Chemical Corp.
mc .... Micro (SHCU)
MC .... Microcarrier [*Cell culture technology*]
MC .... Microcell (SAUS)
MC .... Microcephaly [*Medicine*] (AAMN)
MC .... Microchromatographic
MC .... Micro Compact Car AG (EFIS)
MC .... Micro Composer (SAUS)
MC .... Microcomputer (IAA)
MC .... Microcontrol
MC .... Microcrystalline Cellulose (DB)
MC .... Microfilm Corporation (SAUO)
MC .... Microminiature Circuit (IAA)
MC .... Micronesia Coalition [*Defunct*] (EA)
MC .... Microphase Corporation (SAUO)
MC .... Microstat Corporation (SAUO)
MC .... Midcourse
MC .... Midcourse Correction (SAA)
MC .... Middle Chamber [*Freemasonry*]
MC .... Middle Creek Railroad (IIA)
MC .... Midland College (SAUO)
MC .... Miles College (SAUO)
MC .... Miles on Course
MC .... Military Characteristics
MC .... Military College [*British*] (ROG)
MC .... Military Committee [*NATO*]
MC .... Military Community (COE)
MC .... Military Computer (IEEE)
MC .... Military Construction (AFM)
MC .... Military Coordination [*British*]
MC .... Military Cross [*World War I nickname: Maconochie Cross*] [*British*]
MC .... Mill Cutter [*Tool*] (MCD)
mC .... Millicoulomb (MAE)
mc .... Millicurie (IDOE)
mC .... Millicurie [*Also, mCi*]
MC .... Millicycle [*Also, as millihertz*] (WGA)
MC .... Milligan College (SAUO)
MC .... Millipore Corp. [*Bedford, MA*]
MC .... Millipore Corporation (SAUO)
MC .... Mills College (SAUO)
MC .... Milsaps College (SAUO)
MC .... Milton College (SAUO)
MC .... Mine Clearance [*British military*] (DMA)
MC .... Mineralocortcoid (LDT)
M-C .... Mineralo-Corticoid [*Endocrinology*]
m/c .... Minha Carta [*My Respects*] [*Correspondence*] [*Portuguese*]
m/c .... Minha Conta [*My Regards*] [*Correspondence*] [*Portuguese*]
MC .... Mini-Cartridge (SAUS)
MC .... Minimum Call [*Television studio on standby*]
MC .... Mining Club (EA)
MC .... Ministry of Commerce (SAUO)
MC .... Minkowski-Chauffard [*Syndrome*] [*Medicine*] (DB)
MC .... Minor Construction (AFIT)
MC .... Minorities in Cable [*Defunct*] (EA)
MC .... Mirror Coil (MCD)
MC .... Miscarriage [*Obstetrics*] (DAVI)
MC .... Miserriocordia College (SAUO)
MC .... Misionaras Clarisas [*Poor Clare Missionary Sisters*] [*Roman Catholic religious order*]
MC .... Missile Car (SAA)
MC .... Missile Checkout
MC .... Missile Code (MUGU)
MC .... Missile Command [*Army*]
MC .... Missile Compartment
MC .... Missile Container
MC .... Missile Control
MC .... Missile Controller (SAUS)
MC .... Missionaries of Charity [*Roman Catholic women's religious order*]
MC .... Missionary Catechists of the Sacred Hearts of Jesus and Mary [*Violetas*] [*Roman Catholic women's religious order*]
MC .... Missionary Church (EA)
mc .... Mission Capability [*NASA*] (NAKS)
MC .... Mission Capability [*NASA*] (NASA)
MC .... Mission Capable (SAUO)
MC .... Mission Completion (MCD)
mc .... Mission Completion/Continuation [*NASA*] (NAKS)
MC .... Mission Computer (MCD)
MC .... Mission Continuation (MCD)
MC .... Mission Control [*NASA*]
MC .... Mission Critical (SAUO)
MC .... Mississippi Central [*Railroad*] (MHDB)
MC .... Mississippi Central Railroad (IIA)
MC .... Mitchell College (SAUO)
MC .... Mitchell Cotts Group Ltd. (SAUO)
MC .... Mitochondrial Complementation
MC .... Mitomycin [*Also, M, MT*] [*Antineoplastic drug*]
MC .... Mitotic Cycle [*Biochemistry*] (DAVI)
MC .... Mitoxantrone, Cytarabine [*Antineoplastic drug*] (CDI)
MC .... Mitral Valve Closure [*Cardiology*]
MC .... Mitsubishi Corporation (SAUO)
MC .... Mixed Cell [*Lymphoma classification*]
MC .... Mixed Cellularity [*Biochemistry*] (DAVI)
MC .... Mixed Condition [*Deltiology*]
MC .... Mixed Cryoglobulinemia [*Medicine*]
MC .... Mixing Chamber
M/C .... Mixture Control [*Automobile fuel technology*]
MC .... Mixture Control [*Automotive engineering*]
MC .... Mnemonic Code (AAG)
MC .... Mobile Control (DEN)
MC .... Mobile Crane (DCTA)
MC .... Mobility Control Center (SAUO)
MC .... Mobilization Center (SAUO)
MC .... Mode Change (CET)
MC .... Mode Code
MC .... Mode Control (IAA)
MC .... Mode Counter
MC .... Model Cities (OICC)
MC .... Modem Controller [*Telecommunications*] (IAA)
MC .... Modification Center (SAUO)
MC .... Modular Computer
MC .... Moisture Content
MC .... Molded Components (IEEE)
MC .... Molecular Contamination [*of Clean rooms*]
MC .... Momentary Contact [*Electronics*]
MC .... Monaco [*ANSI two-letter standard code*] (CNC)
mc .... Monaco [*MARC country of publication code*] [*Library of Congress*] (LCCP)
MC .... Moneda Corriente [*Current Money*] [*Spanish*]
MC .... Monetary Committee
MC .... Monetary Contact
MC .... Monitor and Control [*Computer science*] (BUR)
MC .... Monitor Call [*Computer science*] (IBMDP)
MC .... Monitoring Center (SAUO)
MC .... Monkey Cells
MC .... Monkey Complement [*Immunology*]
MC .... Monmouth College (SAUO)
MC .... Monocomponent Highly Purified Port Insulin [*Endocrinology*] [*Pharmacology*] (DAVI)
MC .... Monocoupe Club (EA)
MC .... Mononuclear Cell [*Clinical chemistry*] [*Also, MNC*]
MC .... Monopolies Commission [*British*] (DCTA)
MC .... Monotype Caster (DGA)
MC .... Monte Carlo [*Calculation technique*] [*Nuclear energy*] (NUCP)
MC .... Montecatini Mining & Chemical Co. (SAUO)
MC .... Montessori Center [*Education*]
MC .... Monticello College (SAUO)
MC .... Moravian College (SAUO)
MC .... Morehouse College (SAUO)
MC .... Morgan Crucible Co. Ltd. (SAUO)
MC .... Morris College (SAUO)
MC .... Morse Code
MC .... Morse Code - Barry Morse Fan Club (EA)
MC .... Mortar Carrier [*British*]
MC .... Mortgage Constant (DICI)
MC .... Mortgage Credit Condition (EMRF)
MC .... Mothercraft Certificate [*British*] (ADA)
MC .... Motor Car (IAA)
MC .... Motor Carrier
MC .... Motor Chain
MC .... Motor Coaches [*Public-performance tariff class*] [*British*]
MC .... Motor Contact (WGA)
MC .... Motor Converter (IAA)
MC .... Motor Cortex [*Neuroanatomy*]
M/C .... Motorcycle [*Motor vehicle term used in state of Washington*] (MVRD)
MC .... Motorcycle
MC .... Motorcycle Driver [*British military*] (DMA)
MC .... Mount Carmel Fraternity (SAUO)
MC .... Movement Control [*of troops*]
MC .... Moving Coil [*Electronics*] (DEN)
MC .... Muan Chon [*Mass Party*] [*Political party*]
MC .... Mucous Cell
MC .... Muhlenberg College (SAUO)
MC .... Multi Carrier (SAUS)
MC .... Multi Cast (SAUS)
MC .... Multichip [*Circuit*] [*Electronics*]
MC .... Multichromatic
MC .... Multicomputing (IAA)
MC .... Multiconfiguration [*Quantum mechanics*]
MC .... Multipartisan Coalition (EA)
MC .... Multiple Choice
MC .... Multiple Contact
MC .... Multiple Cyclones (EEVL)
MC .... Multiplex Channel (IAA)
MC .... Multiply-Convolve (SAUS)
MC .... Multnomah College (SAUO)
MC .... Mundelein College (SAUO)
MC .... Munitions Command [*Later, Armaments Command*] [*Army*]
MC .... Mushroom Caucus (EA)
MC .... Muskingum College (SAUO)
MC .... Muskogee College (SAUO)
MC .... Mycelial [*of fungi*] (AAMN)
MC .... Myelocytomatosis [*Avian disease*]
MC .... Myocarditis [*Medicine*]
MC .... Myotonia Congenita [*Medicine*]
MC .... Poor Clare Missionary Sisters (TOCD)
MC .... Rapidair [*ICAO designator*] (AD)
MC .... Royal Military College (SAUO)
MC .... Saugus Marine Corporation (SAUO)

MC .... Submarine Chaser [*Navy symbol*]
MC2 .... Maximized Conservation Concept [*Tires*]
MC3 .... Multi-channel Crypto Controller (SAUS)
MC4 .... Medical Communications for Combat Casualty Care [*Army*]
MC4-R .... Melanocortin-4 Receptor (DIPS)
MC5 .... Motor City Five [*Rock music group*]
MC-130 ..... Combat Talon (SAUS)
MCA .... Arthur D. Little, Inc., Cambridge, MA [*Library symbol*] [*Library of Congress*] (LCLS)
MCA .... Macenta [*Guinea*] [*Airport symbol*] (AD)
MCA .... Magic Collectors' Association (EA)
MCA .... Magnetocrystalline Anisotropy [*Physics*]
MCA .... Mail Control Authority (AFM)
MCA .... Main Console Assembly [*NASA*] (KSC)
MCA .... Main Coronary Artery [*Cardiology*] (DAVI)
MCA .... Maintenance Capability Audit [*Military*] (CAAL)
MCA .... Major Coronary Arteries [*Cardiology*]
MCA .... Malacca Consumers Association (SAUO)
MCA .... Malaysian Chinese Association [*Political party*] (PPW)
MCA .... Malaysian Commercial Association (BUAC)
MCA .... Management and Command Ashore (NVT)
MCA .... Management Consultancies Association (SAUO)
MCA .... Management Consultants Association [*British*] (DCTA)
MCA .... Management Control Activity
MCA .... Management Control Authority (NVT)
MCA .... Maneuvering at Critically Slow Airspeed [*Aviation*] (PIPO)
MCA .... Manning Control Authority (MCD)
MCA .... Mannlicher Collectors Association (EA)
MCA .... Manufacturers' Consumer Advertising
MCA .... Manufacturing Change Analysis (MCD)
MCA .... Manufacturing Chemists Association [*Later, CMA*] (EA)
MCA .... Marine Coastguard Agency (SAUO)
MCA .... Marine Corps Association (EA)
MCA .... Marine Cranking Amperes [*Battery*] [*Automotive engineering*]
MCA .... Maritime and Coastguard Agency [*Emergency Management*] (EMA)
MCA .... Maritime Central Airways (SAUO)
MCA .... Maritime Central Airways, Ltd. (SAUO)
MCA .... Maritime Control Area
MCA .... Market Research Corp. of America
MCA .... Marky Cattle Association (EA)
MCA .... Marquee Contractors Association (BUAC)
MCA .... Mars-Crossing Asteroid [*Cosmology*]
MCA .... Maserati Club of America (EA)
MCA .... Massachusetts Correctional Association (SAUO)
MCA .... Master Carvers Association [*British*] (DBA)
MCA .... Master Clock Assembly
MCA .... Master Community Antenna
MCA .... Master Control Assembly [*NASA*] (NASA)
MCA .... Master Craftsmen's Association [*British*] (DBA)
MCA .... Master of Commercial Arts
MCA .... Master of Commercial Aviation (PGP)
MCA .... Master of Communication Arts (PGP)
MCA .... Master of Creative Arts
MCA .... Mastiff Club of America (EA)
MCA .... Material Condition and Aging (SAUO)
MCA .... Material Control Adjustment
MCA .... Material Control and Accountability (NRCH)
MCA .... Material Control Area (AAG)
MCA .... Material Coordinating Agency
MCA .... Maternity Center Association (EA)
MCA .... Matrix Case Arrangement (DGA)
MCA .... Maximal Credible Accident [*Nuclear technology*]
MCA .... Maximum Ceiling Absolute [*Aerospace*] (AAG)
MCA .... Maximum Credible Accident [*Nuclear energy*] (NRCH)
MCA .... Maximum Crossing Altitude (MCD)
MCA .... McCall, ID [*Amtrak Busline code*]
MCA .... McDonnell Douglas Automation Co., McAuto Campus Library, St. Louis, MO [*OCLC symbol*] (OCLC)
MCA .... Measurement Capability Analysis (AAEL)
MCA .... Mechanical Contractors Association of America
MCA .... Mechanization Control Area (AAG)
MCA .... Media Communications Association (SAUO)
MCA .... Media Credit Association (EA)
MCA .... Medical Care Administration (STED)
MCA .... Medical Control Agency (SAUO)
MCA .... Medical Correctional Association [*Defunct*] (EA)
MCA .... Medical Council of Australia (SAUO)
MCA .... Medical Council on Alcoholism [*British*]
MCA .... Medicines Control Agency [*British*] (ECON)
MCA .... Megestrol, Cyclophosphamide, and Adriamycin (Doxorubicin) (STED)
MCA .... Merchandising Corp. of America, Inc. (EFIS)
MCA .... Metal Construction Association (EA)
MCA .... Methyl Cation Affinity [*Physical chemistry*]
MCA .... Methylcholanthrene [*Also, MC*] [*Biochemistry*]
MCA .... Methyl Cyanoacrylate [*Organic chemistry*]
MCA .... Metropolitan Club of America (EA)
MCA .... Metropolitan Cycle Association (SAUO)
MCA .... Michigan Counseling Association (EARSL)
MCA .... Microcentrifugal Analyzer [*Instrumentation*]
MCA .... Micro Channel [*Computer science*] (CDE)
MCA .... Microchannel Analyzer [*Instrumentation*]
MCA .... Micro Channel Architecture [*Computer hardware*]
MCA .... Microfilm Corporation of America (NITA)
MCA .... Microfilming Corp. of America [*Information service or system*] (IID)
McA .... Microfilming Corp. of America, Glen Rock, NJ [*Library symbol*] [*Library of Congress*] (LCLS)
MCA .... Microwave Communications Association (EA)
MCA .... Microwave Control Assembly
MCA .... Mid-Continent Airlines (SAUO)
MCA .... Midcontinent Airlines, Inc. [*ICAO designator*] (FAAC)
MCA .... Mid-Continental Airlines
MCA .... Middle Cerebral Aneurysm [*Cardiology*] [*Neurology*] (DAVI)
MCA .... Middle Cerebral Artery [*Anatomy*]
MCA .... Midwest Commuter Airlines (SAUO)
MCA .... Mid-West Compensation Association [*Superseded by ACA*] (EA)
MCA .... Midwest Curling Association [*Defunct*] (EA)
MCA .... Military Chaplains Association (SAUO)
MCA .... Military Chaplains Association of the USA (EA)
MCA .... Military Civic Action (DOMA)
MCA .... Military Construction Appropriation [*or Authorization*] (AFM)
MCA .... Military Construction Army (AFIT)
MCA .... Military Coordinating Activity (MCD)
MCA .... Miller Crichton & Associates (SAUO)
MCA .... Millinery Credit Association [*Defunct*] (EA)
MCA .... Minerals Council of Australia (SAUO)
MCA .... Minimum Crossing Altitude [*Aviation*]
MCA .... Ministry of Civil Aviation [*Later, MTCA*] [*British*]
MCA .... Minnesota Correctional Authority (SAUO)
MCA .... Minnesota Corrections Association (SAUO)
MCA .... Minor Consuming Alcohol [*Law enforcement*] (ALAC)
MCA .... Missile Command Amplifier (ACAE)
MCA .... Missing Children of America (EA)
MCA .... Mission Critical Applications (SAUO)
MCA .... Mississippi Code, Annotated [*A publication*] (DLA)
MCA .... Missouri Corrections Association (SAUO)
MCA .... Mistral Class Association (EA)
MCA .... Mitsubishi Clean Air [*Automotive engineering*]
MCA .... Mobilisation Combat Aircraft (SAUS)
MCA .... Model Cities Administration [*HUD*]
MCA .... Modified Cost Approach Document [*Department of Housing and Urban Development*]
MCA .... Mohair Council of America (EA)
MCA .... Moist Convective Adjustment (SAUS)
MCA .... Monetary Compensation Amount [*European Community*]
MCA .... Monetary Compensation Amounts (SAUO)
MCA .... Monetary Control Act
MCA .... Monitoring and Control Assembly [*NASA*] (NASA)
MCA .... Monocarboxylic Acid (STED)
MCA .... Monochloroacetic Acid [*Also, MCAA*] [*Organic chemistry*]
MCA .... Monoclonal Antibodies [*Microbiology*] (DAVI)
MCA .... Montana Code, Annotated [*A publication*] (DLA)
MCA .... Montreat College Alumni Association (EA)
MCA .... Motion Capture and Analysis (SAUS)
MCA .... Motor Carriers Traffic Association Inc., Greensboro NC [*STAC*]
MCA .... Motor Control Assembly (MCD)
MCA .... Motorcycle Accident (DAVI)
MCA .... Motor Cycle Industry Association of Great Britain (EAIO)
MCA .... Movement Control Agency [*Army*]
MCA .... Movers Conference of America
MCA .... Multichannel Analyzer
MCA .... Multi-Criteria Analysis (SAUO)
MCA .... Multiple Classification Analysis [*Aviation*]
MCA .... Multiple Communications Adapter (DGA)
MCA .... Multiple Congenital Abnormalities [*Medicine*] (STED)
MCA .... Multiple Congenital Anomaly [*Syndrome*] [*Medicine*]
MCA .... Multiplexing Channel Adapter [*Telecommunications*] (IAA)
MCA .... Multiprocessor (SAUO)
MCA .... Multiprocessor Communications Adapter
MCA .... MuniYield CA Insured Fund II [*NYSE symbol*] (TTSB)
MCA .... MuniYield California Insured Fund II [*NYSE symbol*] (SPSG)
MCA .... Muscat Control Agency (SAUO)
MCA .... Musical Corp. of America (NADA)
MCA .... Music Corporation of America (EFIS)
MCA .... Music Critics Association (EA)
MCA .... Musicians Club of America (EA)
MCA .... Mustang Club of America (EA)
MCAA .... Maine College Admissions Association (SEAT)
MCAA .... Marine Corps Aviation Association (EA)
MCAA .... Mason Contractors Association of America (EA)
MCAA .... Measurement, Control, and Automation Association (NTPA)
MCAA .... Mechanical Contractors Association of America (EA)
MCAA .... Mechanical Contractors Association of Arkansas (EARSL)
MCAA .... Member, Canadian Academy of Allergy (CMD)
MCAA .... Messenger Courier Association of America (EA)
MCAA .... Military Civil Affairs Administration (NADA)
MCAA .... Military Construction Appropriations Act (AAGC)
MCAA .... Monochloroacetic Acid [*Also, MCA*] [*Organic chemistry*]
MCAAA .... Midland Counties Amateur Athletic Association (SAUO)
MCAAAC .... Medium Caliber Antiarmor Automatic Cannon
MCAAC ...... Medium Caliber Advanced Automatic Cannon (TIMI)
MCAAC ...... Medium Caliber Antiarmor Automatic Cannon (MCD)
MCAAF ...... Marine Corps Auxiliary Air Facility
MCAAP ...... McAlester Army Ammunition Plant [*Oklahoma*] (AABC)
MCAAP ...... Medical College Admissions Assessment Program [*AAMC*] [*Medicine*] (EDAA)
MCAAPAC ... Mason Contractors Association of America PAC [*Lombard, IL*] (PACS)
MCAAS ...... Manpower Central Address & AIG System (SAUS)

MCAAS...... Marine Corps Auxiliary Air Station
MCAB........ Marine Corps Air Base
MCAB........ Monoclonal Antibody [*Immunochemistry*]
MCABM..... Manner Common among Business Men
MCAC........ Machine Accessory [*Tool*] (AAG)
MCAC........ Measurement, Control and Automation Conference (SAUO)
MCAC........ Mechanical Contractors Association of Canada
MCAC........ Mechanical Contractors Association of Connecticut (EARSL)
MCAC........ Meet the Composer/Arizona (EARSL)
MCAC........ Midlands Collegiate Athletic Conference (PSS)
MCAC........ Military Common Area Control
MCACE...... Measurement Characterization and Control of Ambulatory Care in Europe (SAUO)
MC/ACF..... Media Coalition/Americans for Constitutional Freedom (EA)
MCACO...... Mechanical Contractors Association of Central Ohio (EARSL)
MCACS...... Marine Centralized Automatic Control System (PDAA)
MCAD....... Marine Corps Air Depot
MCAD....... Massachusetts Commission Against Discrimination (SAUO)
MCAD....... Mast Cell Activation Disorder [*Medicine*] (EDAA)
MCAD....... Mechanical Computer-Aided Design
MCAD....... Medium Chain Acyl-CoA Dehydrogenase (DMAA)
MCAD....... Medium Chain Acyl-Coenzyme A Dehydrogenase (DB)
MCAD....... Military Contracts Administration Department
MCAD....... Minneapolis College of Art and Design
McAdam Landl & T... McAdam on Landlord and Tenant [*A publication*] (DLA)
MCADO...... Micronesian Community Action Development Organization (SAUO)
MCADSV.... Michigan Coalition Against Domestic and Sexual Violence (EARSL)
MCAE........ Massachusetts Coalition for Adult Education
MCAE........ Mechanical Computer-Aided Engineering
MCAE........ Mining, Construction, and Agricultural Equipment
MCAEP...... Mechanical Contractors Association of Eastern Pennsylvania (EARSL)
MCAF........ Macrophage Chemotactic, and Activating Factor (LDT)
MCAF........ Marine Corps Air Facility
MCAF........ Marine Corps Air Field
MCAF........ McAfee Associates [*NASDAQ symbol*] (SAG)
MCAF........ McAfeecom Corp. [*NASDAQ symbol*]
MCAF........ Mediterranean Coastal Air Force Headquarters
MCAF........ Military Construction, Air Force
MCAF........ Monocyte Chemotaxis-Activating Factor [*Immunology*] (QSUL)
MCAFB...... McConnell Air Force Base [*Kansas*]
McAfee...... McAfee Associates [*Associated Press*] (SAG)
MCA/FYP.... Military Construction, Army / Five Year Plan
MCAG........ Mapping, Charting, and Geodesy [*Activity*] (MCD)
MCAGCC.... Marine Corps Air-Ground Combat Center [*Twenty-nine Palms, Calif.*] (DOMA)
MCAGCTC... Marine Corps Air Ground Combat Training Center (MCD)
MCAG/MGI.. Mapping, Charting, and Geodesy/Military Geography Information [*DoD*] (MCD)
MCAI........ Maximum Calling Area Indicator (DNAB)
MCA-I....... Media Communications Association - International [*An association*]
MCAI........ Microcomputer-Assisted Instruction (NITA)
MCAIR....... McDonnell Aircraft Co. [*Later, McDonnell Douglas Corp.*]
MCAL........ Arthur D. Little, Inc., Cambridge, MA [*Library symbol*] [*Library of Congress*] (LCLS)
McAl......... McAllister's United States Circuit Court Reports [*A publication*] (DLA)
McA L & Ten... McAdam on Landlord and Tenant [*A publication*] (DLA)
MCALF...... Marine Corps Auxiliary Landing Field
MCALL...... McAllen, TX [*American Association of Railroads railroad junction routing code*]
McAll........ McAllister's United States Circuit Court Reports [*A publication*] (DLA)
McAll (Cal)... McAllister's United States Circuit Court Reports [*California*] [*A publication*] (DLA)
McAllister US Circ Court R... McAllister's United States Circuit Court Reports [*A publication*] (DLA)
MCALS...... Minnesota Computer-Aided Library System [*University of Minnesota*]
MCAM....... Marcam Corp. [*NASDAQ symbol*]
MCAM....... Marine Corps Achievement Medal [*Military decoration*]
MCAM....... Member of the Communication, Advertising, and Marketing Education Foundation [*British*] (DBQ)
McA Mar Ct... McAdam's Marine Court Practice [*A publication*] (DLA)
MCA/MR.... Multiple Congenital Anomalies/Mental Retardation Syndrome [*Medicine*] (DMAA)
MCA/MR.... Multiple Congenital Anomaly/Mental Retardation (SAUO)
Mcan........ J. S. Canner & Co., Boston, MA [*Library symbol*] [*Library of Congress*] (LCLS)
MC&A....... Material Control and Accountability
MC & A..... Material Control and Accounting [*Nuclear energy*] (NRCH)
MC & B..... Michigan Contractor & Builder [*A publication*]
MC & C..... Measurement, Command, and Control (NASA)
MC&C....... Measurement, Command, and Control (SAUS)
MC & G..... Mapping, Charting, and Geodesy [*Air Force*] (AFM)
MC & G/MGI... Mapping, Charting, and Geodesy/Military Geography Information [*DoD*]
MC & R..... Manufacturing Controls and Requirements
MC&S....... Microscopy Culture & Sensitivity [*Medicine*] (WDAA)
MC & W.... Master Caution and Warning [*NASA*] (KSC)
M Can L.... Master of Canon Law
MCANSW... Medical Consumers' Association of New South Wales [*Australia*]
MCANW..... Medical Campaign against Nuclear Weapons (PDAA)
MCAO....... Middle Cerebral Artery Occlusion [*Medicine*] (EDAA)
MCAP........ Major Command ADP Plan (SAUO)
MCAP........ Managed Care Appropriateness Protocol (GART)
MCAP........ Material Control and Accountability Plan (SAUO)
MCAP........ Maximum Calling Area Procedure (SAUO)
MCAP........ Medical Commission on Accident Prevention (PDAA)
MCAP........ [*The*] MicroCap Fund [*NASDAQ symbol*] (SAG)
MCAP........ Microwave Circuit Analysis Package (PDAA)
MCAP........ Military Construction Authorized Program
MCAP........ Mine Clearance & Armour Protection (SAUS)
MCAP........ Ministry of Civil Aviation Publication (SAUO)
MCAP........ Minority Contractors Assistance Project [*Jamaica, NY*] (EA)
MCAP........ Mobile Consolidated Aerial Port Subsystem (SAUO)
MCAP........ Multiple Channel Analysis Program
MCA-PAC... Mechanical Contractors Association of America PAC [*Rockville, MD*] (PACS)
MCAPD...... Medical Committee against the Abuse of Prisoners by Drugging (SAUO)
MCAPI....... Mid-Continent Association of the Pet Industry
MCAR....... Machine Check Analysis and Recording (BUR)
MCAR....... Machining Arbor [*Tool*] (AAG)
McAr......... McArthur's District of Columbia Reports [*A publication*] (DLA)
MCAR....... Military Construction, Army Reserve (AABC)
MCAR....... Minnesota Code of Agency Rules [*A publication*]
MCAR....... Missing Completely at Random (IDAI)
MCAR....... Mixed Cell Agglutination Reaction [*Immunology*]
MCAR....... Multichannel Acoustic Relay [*Navy*] (ANA)
MCARNG.... Military Construction, Army National Guard (AABC)
MCARQUALS... Marine Carrier Qualifications (NVT)
McArth & M... MacArthur and Mackey's District of Columbia Reports [*A publication*] (DLA)
MCAS........ Machinery Control and Surveillance (SAUS)
MCAS........ Marine Corps Air Station
MCAS........ Massachusetts Comprehensive Assessment System [*Education*]
MCAS........ Master Component Analysis System (TIMI)
MCAS........ Material Control Accounting System (SAUO)
MCAS........ Medical College Application Service [*Medicine*] (EDAA)
MCAS........ Middle Cerebral Artery Syndrome [*Medicine*] (DMAA)
MCAS........ Minuteman Configuration Accountability System [*Air Force*] (IAA)
MCAS........ Modular Component Assembly System (ACAE)
MCAs........ Monetary Compensation Amounts (SAUO)
MCASA...... Master Cleaners' Association of South Australia [*Australia*]
MCASE...... Mechanical Computer-Aided Engineering
MCAS(H).... Marine Corps Air Station (Helicopter) (FAAC)
MCASP...... Multiple Constraint Alternative Selector Program [*Bell System*]
MCASTRO... McDonnell Douglas Astronautics Company (SAUO)
MCAT........ Maritime Central Analysis Team [*NATO*] (NATG)
MCAT........ Master of Creative Arts in Therapy (PGP)
MCAT........ Mean Corpuscular Average Thickness [*Medicine*] (EDAA)
MCAT........ Medical College Admissions Test (GAGS)
MCAT........ Medical College Admission [*or Aptitude*] Test
MCAT........ Middle Cerebral Artery Thrombosis [*Medicine*] (DMAA)
MCAT........ Midwest Council on Airborne Television
MCAT........ Military Committee Atlantic (SAUO)
MCAT........ Monoclonal Antibody Therapy (MELL)
MCATA...... Management Council of the American Trucking Association [*Defunct*] (EA)
MCATF...... Mechanized Combined Arms Task Force (SAUO)
MCATS...... Maneuver Control Automated Test System (SAUO)
MCATS...... Marine Corps Automated Test System (DWSG)
MCATS...... Marine Corps Aviation Technical School (SAUO)
MCATS...... Medium Capacity Automated Telecommunications System (SAUO)
M-CATS..... Municipal Certificates of Accrual on Tax-Exempt Securities [*Investment term*] (DFIT)
M-cats....... Municipal Certificates of Accumulation on Tax-Exempt Securities (EBF)
MCATT...... Multi-weapon Combined Arms Tactical Trainer (SAUS)
MCAU....... Main Carrier Acquisition Unit (MCD)
MCAU....... Marconi Communications [*Intermodal shipping container symbol*] (TVRC)
M CAUTE... Misce Caute [*Mix Cautiously*] [*Pharmacy*]
MCAUTO.... McDonnell Douglas Automation Co. [*Robotics*]
MCAUTO Company... McDonnell Douglas Automation Company (SAUO)
MCAV........ Modified Constant Angular Velocity (TELE)
MCAVO...... McAvoy, CA [*American Association of Railroads railroad junction routing code*]
MCAVRET... Marine Corps Aviation Refresher Training
MCAWA..... McCaw Cellular Communications, Inc. [*NASDAQ symbol*] (COMM)
MCAWW.... Methods for Chemical Analysis of Water and Wastes [*Environmental Protection Agency*]
MCB......... Boyne Regional Library, Carman, Manitoba [*Library symbol*] [*National Library of Canada*] (NLC)
MCB......... Machine Coated Board (DGA)
MCB......... Macrochromatin Body [*Genetics*]
MCB......... Main Circuit Breaker (SAUS)
MCB......... Main Control Board (NRCH)
MCB......... Malaysian Cocoa Butter
MCB......... Managing Civilians to Budget [*Army*]
MCB......... Manually Controlled Barrier (HEAS)
MCB......... Marine Construction Battalion
MCB......... Marine Corps Base
MCB......... Markings Center Brief (MCD)
MCB......... Mason/Menninger Clinic Bulletin [*Medicine*] (EDAA)
MCB......... Master Car Builder
MCB......... Master Cell Bank [*Cell line*]
MCB......... Master Circuit Breaker [*Indian Railway*] (TIR)
MCB......... Master of Clinical Biochemistry
MCB......... Material Certification Board (SAUO)
MCB......... Material Classification Board (DNAB)

MCB .... Matheson, Coleman & Bell [*Commercial firm*]
MCB .... MC Beverages [*Vancouver Stock Exchange symbol*]
McB .... McBurney's [*Point*] [*Medicine*]
MCB .... McComb, MS [*Location identifier*] [*FAA*] (FAAL)
MCB .... Mechanically Controllable Break [*Junction*] [*In microstructures*]
MCB .... Medical Consultative Board (SAUO)
MCB .... Membranous Cytoplasmic Body
MCB .... Memory Control Block (ROAS)
MCB .... Message Control Block [*Computer science*] (CET)
MCB .... Metal Corner Bead [*Technical drawings*]
MCB .... Methodist College, Belfast [*Northern Ireland*]
MCB .... Methylamino(chloro)benzophenone [*Organic chemistry*]
MCB .... Metric Conversion Board (NADA)
MCB .... Metric Conversion Bureau (NADA)
MCB .... Metropolitan Cemeteries Board [*Western Australia*]
MCB .... Miami City Ballet
MCB .... Microbus [*NCIC car model code*]
MCB .... Microcomputer Board
MCB .... Microwave Circuit Board (TIMI)
MCB .... Millwork Cost Bureau [*Later, AWI*]
MCB .... Miniature Circuit Breaker
MCB .... Miscellaneous Change Board (SAUO)
MCB .... Miscellaneous Charges Book (SAUO)
MCB .... Missouri Concert Ballet
MCB .... Missouri Council of the Blind (EARSL)
MCB .... Mobile Construction Battalion [*Navy*]
MCB .... Modular Controllable Booster (MCD)
MCB .... Module Control Block (KSC)
MCB .... Molecular and Cellular Biochemistry [*Journal*] [*Medicine*] (EDAA)
MCB .... Monochlorinated Biphenyl [*Organic chemistry*]
MCB .... Monochlorobenzene [*Organic chemistry*]
MCB .... Moose Creek [*Alaska*] [*Seismograph station code, US Geological Survey*] [*Closed*] (SEIS)
MCB .... Mortgage Collateralized Bond
MCB .... Moscow Classical Ballet
MCB .... Motor Cargo Boat
MCB .... Motor Carriers Tariff Bureau Inc., Cleveland OH [*STAC*]
MCB .... Motor Company of Botswana
MCB .... Multilateral Control Board (SSD)
MCB .... Mutant Cell Bank [*Medicine*] (EDAA)
MCB .... Myocardial Bridging [*Cardiology*]
MCBA .... Magnesite and Chrome Brickmakers Association [*British*] (DBA)
MCBA .... Master Car Builders' Association [*Later, CDOA*]
MCBA .... Mean Cycles Between Assists (AAEL)
MCBA .... Member of the Certified Bailiffs Association [*British*] (DI)
MCBC .... Metropolitan Chicago/Michigan Community Blood Center [*Medicine*] (EDAA)
MCBD .... Multi Purpose Chemical Biological Decontaminant (ACAE)
MCBETH .... Military Computer Basic Environment for Test Handling
MCBF .... Mast Cell Burst Factor (SAUS)
MCBF .... Mean Countdown Between Failures
MCBF .... Mean Cycles between Failures [*Quality control*]
MCBF .... Microwave Component Business Function (TIMI)
MCBH .... Multiple Cloud Base Height (ARMP)
MCBI .... Mean Cycles Between Interrupts (AAEL)
MCBIC .... Michigan/Canadian Bigfoot Information Center (EA)
MCBKA ...... Merchants Capital Corp. (Class A) [*NASDAQ symbol*] (COMM)
MCBKB ...... Merchants Capital Corp. (Class B) [*NASDAQ symbol*] (COMM)
MCBL .... Motor Cargo Boat (Large) [*Coast Guard*] (DNAB)
MCBM .... Marine Corps Brevet Medal
MCBM .... Muscle Capillary Basement Membrane [*Medicine*]
MCBN .... Mid-Coast Bancorp [*NASDAQ symbol*] (TTSB)
MCBN .... Mid-Coast Bancorp, Inc. [*NASDAQ symbol*] (NQ)
MCBO .... Mid-Continent Base Oil [*Fuels and lubricants*]
MCBOMF .... Mean Cycles between Operational Mission Failures [*Quality control*]
MCBP .... Mean Cycles between Premature Removals [*Quality control*] (MCD)
MCBP .... Melphalan, Cyclophosphamide, BCNU [*Carmustine*], Prednisone [*Antineoplastic drug regimen*]
MCBP .... Methylchlorobiphenyl [*Organic chemistry*]
MCBP .... Muscle Calcium Binding Parvalbumin [*Biochemistry*]
McB Pt ...... McBurney's Point [*Medicine*] (CPH)
MCBR .... Master Car Builders' Rules
MCBR .... Minimum Concentration of Bilirubin [*Medicine*] (MAE)
McBride ...... McBride's Reports [*1 Missouri*] [*A publication*] (DLA)
MCBs .... Metacarpal Bone [*Medicine*] (MELL)
MCBS .... Micro Computer Business Services
MCBS .... Mid Continent Bancshares [*NASDAQ symbol*] (TTSB)
MCBS .... Mid Continent Bancshares, Inc. [*NASDAQ symbol*] (SAG)
MCBS .... Mine-Clearing Blade System [*Military*] (INF)
MCBS .... Missionary Congregation of the Blessed Sacrament (TOCD)
mcbs .... Missionary Congregation of the Blessed Sacrament (TOCD)
MCBS .... Multicomponent Boot System [*Army*] (INF)
MCBSE .... Mean Cycles Between Scrap Event (AAEL)
MCBSI .... Member of the Chartered Building Societies Institute (ODA)
MCBSP ...... Multi Channel Buffered Serial Port (SAUS)
MCBU .... Microconfined Bed Unit [*Chemical engineering*]
MCBU .... Murmansk Cargo Bureau [*Intermodal shipping container symbol*] (TVRC)
MCBW .... Amalgamated Meat Cutters and Butcher Workmen of North America [*Later, UFCWIU*]
MCC .... Canada-US Military Co-operation Community (SAUO)
MCC .... MacGillivray's Copyright Cases [*1901-49*] [*A publication*] (DLA)
MCC .... Machine Control Computer (TIMI)
MCC .... Magdalene College, Cambridge University [*England*] (ROG)
MCC .... Magnetic Card Code (ELAL)
MCC .... Magnetometer Calibration Coil (ACAE)
MCC .... Mail Classification Center (DNAB)
mcc .... Main Combustion Chamber [*NASA*] (NAKS)
MCC .... Main Combustion Chamber (NASA)
MCC .... Main Communications Center
MCC .... Main Control Circuit (IAA)
MCC .... Main Control Console [*Diving apparatus*]
MCC .... Maintenance Control Center [*Telecommunications*] (AFM)
MCC .... Maintenance Control Circuit (IAA)
MCC .... Maintenance of Close Contact
MCC .... Major Category Code (MCD)
MCC .... Major City Code [*IRS*]
MCC .... Majority Congress Committee [*Defunct*] (EA)
MCC .... Management, Command & Control (SAUO)
MCC .... Management Communication Consultants, Inc. [*Cincinnati, OH*] (TSSD)
MCC .... Management Control Center [*Computer science*] (BUR)
MCC .... Management Controls Corporation, Inc. (SAUO)
MCC .... Manchester Computing Centre (SAUO)
MCC .... Mandarin Capital Corp. [*Vancouver Stock Exchange symbol*]
MCC .... Manhattan Chess Club (EA)
MCC .... Manipulative Communications Cover [*Military*] (ADDR)
MCC .... Manned Control Car [*Nuclear energy*]
MCC .... Manoeuvre Camber Control (SAUS)
MCC .... Manual Combat Center [*Air Force*]
MCC .... Manual Control & Counter (SAUO)
MCC .... Manual Control Center [*Air Force*]
MCC .... Map Collectors' Circle [*Defunct*] (EA)
MCC .... Marine Corps Commandant
MCC .... Marine Corps Commander (SAUO)
MCC .... Maritime Coordination Center
MCC .... Mark Controls Corp. (EFIS)
MCC .... Marked Cocontraction [*Medicine*]
MCC .... Martin's Mining Cases [*British Columbia*] [*A publication*] (DLA)
MCC .... Maryland Committee for Children (EDAC)
MCC .... Marylebone Cricket Club [*Governing body for cricket*]
MCC .... Massachusetts Council of Churches (SAUO)
MCC .... Master Change Committee
MCC .... Master Control Card [*IRS*]
MCC .... Master Control Center (NATG)
MCC .... Master Control Code (ELAL)
MCC .... Master Control Console
MCC .... Matchbox Collectors Club [*Defunct*] (EA)
MCC .... Material Category Code (MCD)
MCC .... Material Characterization Center [*For nuclear wastes*]
MCC .... Material Control Code
MCC .... Material Control Coordinator (MCD)
MCC .... Materials Characterization Center (SAUO)
MCC .... Materials Control Center (SAUO)
MCC .... Matrimonial Causes Committee (SAUO)
MCC .... Maui Community College [*Hawaii*]
MCC .... Maximized Conservation Concept [*Tires*]
MCC .... Maxwell Communication Corp. [*Formerly, BPCC*] [*British*]
McC .... McCarthy [*Panendoscope*] [*Medicine*] (BABM)
McC .... McCoy [*Antibodies*] [*Immunology*]
MCC .... Mean Cell [*or Corpuscular*] Hemoglobin Concentration [*Hematology*]
MCC .... Mechanical Chemical Codes
MCC .... Mechanically Compensated Crystal
MCC .... Media Center for Children (EA)
MCC .... Media Club of Canada [*Formerly, Canadian Women's Press Club*]
MCC .... Media Commentary Council [*Defunct*] (EA)
MCC .... Media Conversion Center [*Space Flight Operations Facility, NASA*]
MCC .... Medial Cell Column [*Medicine*] (EDAA)
MCC .... Medical Control Center [*Military*]
MCC .... Medical Council of Canada
MCC .... Melbourne Cricket Club (SAUO)
MCC .... Member of the County Council [*British*]
MCC .... Memory Cache Controller (SAUO)
MCC .... Memory Control Circuit [*Computer science*] (IAA)
MCC .... Mennonite Central Committee (EA)
MCC .... Mercury Control Center
MCC .... Mesenchymal Cell Concentration [*Medicine*] (MELL)
MCC .... Mesoscale Convective Complex [*Meteorology*]
MCC .... Message Class Code (ACAE)
MCC .... Mesta Machine Company (SAUO)
MCC .... Mestek, Inc. [*NYSE symbol*] (SPSG)
MCC .... Metacentric Chromosome [*Medicine*] (MELL)
MCC .... Metacerebral Cell [*Neurobiology*]
MCC .... Metamorphic Core Complex [*Geology*]
MCC .... Metastatic Cord Compression [*Medicine*] (EDAA)
MCC .... Meteor Communications Corporation (SAUO)
MCC .... Meteorological Communications Center (SAUO)
MCC .... Metrology and Calibration Center [*Army*] (MCD)
MCC .... Metropolitan Correctional Center (SAUO)
MCC .... Metropolitan County Council [*British*]
MCC .... Mica Creek [*British Columbia*] [*Seismograph station code, US Geological Survey*] [*Closed*] (SEIS)
MCC .... Michigan Chemical Council (EARSL)
MCC .... Microclimatic Conditioning
MCC .... Microclimatic Cooling System [*Army*]
MCC .... Micro-Computer Chip (VLIE)
MCC .... Micro Concept Car
MCC .... Microcrystalline Cellulose [*Organic chemistry*]

MCC .... Microcrystalline Chitin
MCC .... Microcrystalline Collagen (DB)
MCC .... Microelectronics & Computer Cooperative (SAUO)
MCC .... Microelectronics and Computer Technology Corp.
MCC .... Microfilm Card Catalog (GEAB)
McC......... Micro Library Canisianum, Maastricht, Holland [*Library symbol*] [*Library of Congress*] (LCLS)
MCC .... Midcourse Correction
MCC .... Middlesex Community College [*Bedford, MA*]
MCC .... Middlesex County Council (SAUO)
MCC .... Middlesex Cricket Club (SAUO)
MCC .... Midstream Cleancatch [*Urine Sample*] [*Medicine*] (EDAA)
MCC .... Midwest Climate Center [*Marine science*] (OSRA)
MCC .... Midwestern Collegiate Conference (PSS)
MCC .... Migrating Combustion Chamber [*Increases fuel efficiency*]
MCC .... Military Climb Corridor [*Aviation*]
MCC .... Military Code of Conduct (VNW)
MCC .... Military Colonization Company [*British ranch in the Calgary area of Canada*]
MCC .... Military Committee (SAUO)
MCC .... Military Communications Center, Inc. [*Minneapolis, MN*] (TSSD)
MCC .... Military Complements Committee (SAUO)
MCC .... Military Comptrollership Course (MCD)
MCC .... Military Control Center (SAUO)
MCC .... Military Cooperation Committee [*US-Canada*]
MCC .... Military Co-operation Community (SAUS)
MCC .... Military Coordinating Committee
MCC .... Military Co-ordination Centre (SAUO)
MCC .... Military Coordination Committee (SAUO)
MCC .... Mine Countermeasures Command and Support Ship [*Navy*]
MCC .... Miniature Center Cap
MCC .... Miniaturized Cassegranian Concentration [*Instrumentation*]
MCC .... Mini Car Club (SAUO)
MCC .... Mini Car Club, USA (EA)
MCC .... Mini-Channel Communications Control (NITA)
MCC .... Mini-Cylinder Core (SAUS)
MCC .... Minimum Circumscribed Circle [*Manufacturing term*]
MCC .... Minimum Complete-Killing Concentration (MAE)
MCC .... Mining Commissioner's Cases [*Canada*] [*A publication*] (DLA)
MCC .... Ministerial Collecting Center (SAUO)
MCC .... Ministerial Committee on Military Coordination [*British*] [*World War II*]
MCC .... Ministerial Council for Corporations [*Australia*]
MCC .... Minuteman Change Committee [*Air Force*] (IAA)
MCC .... Miscellaneous Common Carrier
MCC .... Missile Capability Console (MCD)
MCC .... Missile Change Committed (SAA)
MCC .... Missile Checkout Console (SAA)
MCC .... Missile Combat Crew (AAG)
MCC .... Missile Command Coder (AAG)
MCC .... Missile Compensating Control
MCC .... Missile Control Center [*Air Force*]
MCC .... Missile Control Console
MCC .... Missing in Colon Cancer [*Genetics*]
MCC .... Mission Control Center [*NASA*] (MCD)
mcc......... Mission Control Center [*NASA*] (NAKS)
MCC .... Mission Control Complex [*Air Force*]
MCC .... Mission Crew Commander (SAUO)
MCC .... Mississippi Chemical Corporation (SAUO)
MCC .... Mississippi College, Law Library, Clinton, MS [*OCLC symbol*] (OCLC)
MCC .... Mixing Cross-Bar Connector [*Telecommunications*] (OA)
MCC .... Mobile Command Center
MCC .... Mobile Communications Center (SAUO)
MCC .... Mobile Country Code (CGWS)
MCC .... Mobility Control Center (SAUO)
MCC .... Modem Controller Chip (VLIE)
MCC .... Modern Cereal Chemistry (OA)
MCC .... Modified Close Control [*Air Force*]
MCC .... Modified Continuous Cooking [*Pulp and paper technology*]
MCC .... Modulation Coding and Compression (CCCA)
MCC .... Modulation with Constant Control
MCC .... Monier Construction Company Ltd. (SAUO)
MCC .... Monitor Control Console (CAAL)
MCC .... Monitored Command Code [*Marine Corps*]
MCC .... Monroe Community College (SAUO)
MCC .... Monthly Calibration Check [*Automotive emissions*]
MCC .... Moody's English Crown Cases Reserved [*1824-44*] [*A publication*] (DLA)
MCC .... Morgan Car Club (EA)
MCC .... Morris County Central [*Federal Railroad Administration identification code*]
MCC .... Morrison Commemorative Stamp Committee (EA)
MCC .... Mortgage Credit Certificate (EMRF)
MCC .... Motor Carrier Cases [*ICC*]
mcc......... Motor Control Center [*NASA*] (NAKS)
MCC .... Motor Control Center [*NASA*]
MCC .... Motor Cycle Club [*British*]
MCC .... Motorcycle Combination [*British*]
MCC .... Mount Carmel Confraternity (SAUO)
MCC .... Movement Control Center [*Army*]
MCC .... Movement Coordination Center (SAUO)
MCC .... Mucocutaneous Candidiasis [*Medicine*] (EDAA)
MCC .... Multicell Compound Tire [*Automotive engineering*]
MCC .... Multichannel Cochlear Implant [*Medicine*] (MELL)
MCC .... Multichannel Communications Controller
MCC .... Multicomponent Circuits
MCC .... Multiple-Chip Carrier [*Computer technology*]
MCC .... Multiple Column Control [*Computer science*] (VLIE)
MCC .... Multiple Communications Control (BUR)
MCC .... Multiple Computer Complex
MCC .... Municipal Corporation's Chronicle [*Privately Printed*] [*A publication*] (DLA)
MCC .... Munitions Carriers Conference (EA)
MCC .... Music Critics Circle (SAUO)
MCC .... Muskegon Community College [*Michigan*]
MCC .... Mutated in Colorectal Cancer [*Genetics*]
MCC .... Mutual Capital Certificate
MCC .... Mutum [*Language symbol*] (ETLW)
MCC .... Ontario Ministry of Culture and Communications (TSSD)
MCC .... Royal Military College Certificate (Senior Department) [*British*] (ROG)
MCC .... Sacramento, CA [*Location identifier*] [*FAA*] (FAAL)
MCCA........ Conference of the Methodist Church in the Caribbean and the Americas (EAIO)
MCCA........ Maine Clinical Counselors Association (SEAT)
MCCA........ Manufacturers Council on Color and Appearance [*Defunct*] (EA)
MCCA........ McCain Industries [*NCIC trailer make code*]
MCCA........ Media Conversion Computer Assembly [*Space Flight Operations Facility, NASA*]
MCCA........ Medicare Catastrophic Coverage Act [*1988*]
MCCA........ Michigan Community College Association (SAUO)
MCCA........ Minor Counties Cricket Association [*British*] (DBA)
MCCA........ Model Car Collectors Association (EA)
MCCA........ Motor Car Collectors of America (EA)
MCCAA...... Michigan Community College Athletic Association (PSS)
MCCAC...... Massachusetts Community College Athletic Conference (PSS)
McCah....... McCahon's Kansas Reports [*1858-68*] [*A publication*] (DLA)
McCahon.... McCahon's Kansas Reports [*1858-68*] [*A publication*] (DLA)
McCall Nee... McCall's Needlework [*A publication*] (BRI)
McCall Pr... McCall's Precedents [*A publication*] (DLA)
MC-CAM .... Mitsubishi Chemical Center for Advanced Materials [*University of California, Santa Barbara*] (RCD)
McCanless.. McCanless' Tennessee Reports [*A publication*] (DLA)
McCar .... McCarter's New Jersey Equity Reports [*A publication*] (DLA)
McCart ...... McCarter's New Jersey Equity Reports [*A publication*] (DLA)
McCart ...... McCarty's New York Civil Procedure Reports [*A publication*] (DLA)
McCarter.... McCarter's New Jersey Chancery Reports [*A publication*] (DLA)
McCartney... McCarty's New York Civil Procedure Reports [*A publication*] (DLA)
McCarty..... McCarty's New York Civil Procedure Reports [*A publication*] (DLA)
McCarty Civ Proc... McCarty's New York Civil Procedure Reports [*A publication*] (DLA)
MC Cas ..... Municipal Corporation Cases, Annotated [*11 vols.*] [*A publication*] (DLA)
MCCB........ McCabe-Powers Body [*NCIC trailer make code*]
MCCB........ Minuteman Change Commitment Board (SAUO)
MCCB........ Multinational Configuration Control Board (ACAE)
MCCC........ Macomb County Community College [*Michigan*]
MCCC........ Marie Curie Cancer Care [*United Kingdom*] (EAIO)
MCCC........ Marine Corps Command Center (SAUO)
MCCC........ Mediacom Communic. 'A' [*NASDAQ symbol*] (SG)
MCCC........ Metropolitan Correctional Center (SAUO)
MCCC........ Middlesex County Cricket Club (SAUO)
MCCC........ Ministerial Consultative Committee on Curriculum [*Queensland, Australia*]
MCCC........ Minnesota Community College Conference (PSS)
MCCC........ Missile Combat Crew Commander
mccc........ Mission Control and Computing Center [*NASA*] (NAKS)
MCCC........ Mission Control and Computing Center [*NASA*] (NASA)
MCCC........ Motor Carrier Claims Commission (SAUO)
MCCC........ Muskegon County Community College (SAUO)
MCCCA...... Marine Corps Combat Correspondents Association (EA)
McC Cl Ass... McCall's Clerk's Assistant [*A publication*] (DLA)
MCCD .... Marine Corps Clothing Depot
MCCD .... Maryland Center for Community Development (EARSL)
MCCD .... McCarthy Draying Company [*Common carrier symbol*]
MCCD .... Mechanical Compatibility Control Drawing (MCD)
MCCD .... Message Cryptographic Check Digits
MCCD .... Michigan Council on Crime and Delinquency (EARSL)
MCCD .... Minimal Cumulative Cardiotoxic Dose [*Medicine*] (STED)
MCCD .... Minimum Cumulative Cardiotoxic Dose [*Medicine*] (DMAA)
MCCD .... Mission Control Console Display (ACAE)
MCCD .... Multispectral Close Combat Decoy (DWSG)
MCCDC...... Marine Corps Combat Development Command [*Quantico, VA*] (GRD)
MCC-DoD... Mission Control Center - Department of Defense [*NASA*] (NASA)
MCC-DOD... Mission Control Center-DOD (SAUS)
MCCDPA .... Marine Corps Central Design and Programming Activity (DNAB)
MCCDS...... Modified Central Computer Display Set (DNAB)
MCCE........ Modulation, Coding, Compression and Encryption (CCCA)
MCCE........ Montana Council for Computers in Education (EDAC)
MCCEd ...... Member of the College of Craft Education [*British*] (DI)
MCCEM ..... Multi-Chamber Concentration and Exposure Model [*Environmental Protection Agency*] (AEPA)
MCCES ...... Marine Corps Communications Electronics School (DNAB)
MCCF........ Master Class Code File (MCD)
McC F........ McCall's Forms [*A publication*] (DLA)
MCCF........ Michigan Coalition for Clean Forests
MCCF........ Mission Control Centre France (SAUO)
M/CCFLS.... Manitowoc Calumet Counties Library System [*Library network*]
MCC-H ...... Mission Control Center - Houston [*NASA*] (MCD)

McCl......... Micro-Copy, Inc., Rochester, NY [*Library symbol*] [*Library of Congress*] (LCLS)
MCCI......... MIDCOM Communications [*NASDAQ symbol*] (TTSB)
MCCI......... Midcom Communications, Inc. [*NASDAQ symbol*] (SAG)
MCCI......... Mucocutaneous Candidiasis [*Medicine*] (MELL)
MCCIS........ Maritime Command, Control & Information System (SAUO)
MCCISWG.. Military Command, Control, and Information Systems Working Group (NATG)
mccj......... Comboni Missionaries of the Heart of Jesus (TOCD)
MCCJ......... Comboni Missionaries of the Heart of Jesus (Verona) (TOCD)
McC Just.... McCall's New York Justice [*A publication*] (DLA)
MCCK......... McCook Manufacturing Company [*NCIC trailer make code*]
MCC-K........ Mission Control Center - Cape Kennedy [*NASA*] (KSC)
MCC-K........ Mission Control Center-Kennedy (SAUS)
MCCL......... Mason City & Clear Lake R. R. [*AAR code*]
McCL......... McCabe Library (SAUO)
MCCL......... McClain Industries [*NASDAQ symbol*] (TTSB)
MCCL......... McClain Industries, Inc. [*NASDAQ symbol*] (NQ)
MCCL......... McClain Trailer [*NCIC trailer make code*]
McCl......... McClelland's English Exchequer Reports [*A publication*] (DLA)
McClain Cr Law... McClain's Criminal Law [*A publication*] (DLA)
McClain's Code... McClain's Annotated Code and Statutes [*Iowa*] [*A publication*] (DLA)
McCl & Y... McClelland and Younge's English Exchequer Reports [*1824-25*] [*A publication*] (DLA)
McClat...... McClatchy Newspapers, Inc. [*Associated Press*] (SAG)
McClatN..... McClatchy Newspapers [*Associated Press*] (SAG)
McCl Dig.... McClellan's Florida Digest [*A publication*] (DLA)
McCle....... McClelland's English Exchequer Reports [*A publication*] (DLA)
McCle & Yo... McClelland and Younge's English Exchequer Reports [*1824-25*] [*A publication*] (DLA)
McClel...... McClelland's English Exchequer Reports [*A publication*] (DLA)
McClel Dig... McClellan's Digest of Laws [*Florida*] [*A publication*] (DLA)
McClell...... McClelland's English Exchequer Reports [*A publication*] (DLA)
McClell & Y... McClelland and Younge's English Exchequer Reports [*1824-25*] [*A publication*] (DLA)
McCl Ex..... McClellan's Manual for Executors [*A publication*] (DLA)
McCl IA Co... McClain's Iowa Code [*A publication*] (DLA)
MC CLING... Motorcyclist Clinging to Another Vehicle [*Conviction term used in state of Oregon*] (MVRD)
McCl Mal... McClelland on Civil Malpractice [*A publication*] (DLA)
McCln....... McClain Industries, Inc. [*Associated Press*] (SAG)
MCCLPHEI... Mass Conference of Chief Librarians of Public Higher Educational Institutions [*Library network*]
McCl Pr.... McClellan's Probate Practice [*A publication*] (DLA)
MCCM........ McCrabb Manufacturing [*NCIC trailer make code*]
MCCM........ Mexican Chamber of Commerce of US
MCCM........ Military Council of Catholic Men (SAUO)
MCC-M....... Mission Control Center-Moscow (SAUO)
MCCM........ Modular Crowd Control Munition [*Military*]
MCCN........ Marine and Coastal Community Network (SAUO)
MCCN........ Midwest Curriculum Coordination Network (OICC)
MCC-NASA... Mission Control Center-NASA (SAUS)
MCC-NASA... Mission Control Center - National Aeronautics and Space Administration (NASA)
MCCNSW... Mini Car Club of New South Wales [*Australia*]
MCCNU...... Methylchlorethylcyclakexylinitrosourea (Semustine) [*Medicine*] (STED)
MCCNU...... Methyl-(Chloroethyl)-Cyclohexyl-Nitrosourea [*Antineoplastic drug regimen*] (DAVI)
MCCO........ McCoy Manufacturing & Sales Company [*NCIC trailer make code*]
MCCO........ Mobile Chemical [*Federal Railroad Administration identification code*]
MCCO........ Monaco Coach [*NASDAQ symbol*] (TTSB)
MCCO........ Monaco Coach Corp. [*NASDAQ symbol*] (SAG)
MC Co....... Motor Car Company (SAUO)
MCCOEES.... Michigan Community College Occupational Education Evaluation System (EDAC)
MCCOI....... Multimedia Communications Community of Interest (SAUO)
MCCOL...... McCool, IN [*American Association of Railroads railroad junction routing code*]
MCCOO...... McCook, IL [*American Association of Railroads railroad junction routing code*]
McCook..... McCook's Reports [*1 Ohio*] [*A publication*] (DLA)
MCCOPO.... Mennonite Central Committee Overseas Peace Office (EA)
McCor....... McCormick & Co., Inc. [*Associated Press*] (SAG)
MCCOR...... Motion Compensation - Coherent on Receive
McCord...... McCord's South Carolina Law Reports [*1821-28*] [*A publication*] (DLA)
McCord Ch. McCord's South Carolina Equity Reports [*1825-27*] [*A publication*] (DLA)
McCord Eq.. McCord's South Carolina Chancery Reports [*1825-27*] [*A publication*] (DLA)
McCork...... McCorkle's Reports [*65 North Carolina*] [*A publication*] (DLA)
McCorkle... McCorkle's Reports [*65 North Carolina*] [*A publication*] (DLA)
MCCP........ Main Communications Control Panel (SAUS)
MCCP........ Maintenance Console Control Panel
MCCP........ Manufacturing Cost Control Program [*DoD*]
MCCP........ Marine Corps Capabilities Plan (DOMA)
MCCP........ Meta-Chlorophenylpiperazine [*Biochemistry*]
MCCP........ Microwave Circuit Control Program [*Computer science*]
MCCP........ Military Consolidated Command Post (SAUO)
MCCP........ Mission Control Computer Program [*NASA*]
MCCP........ Mountain Cloud Chemistry Project (SAUO)
MCCP........ Movement Control Check Point (SAUO)
MCCP........ Muskogee City-County Port Authority [*Federal Railroad Administration identification code*]
MCC/PS..... Microclimate Conditioning / Power Subsystem [*Army*] (RDA)
MCCQE...... Medical Council of Canada's Qualifying Examination
MCCR........ Master Change Compliance Record
MCCR........ McCarthy Trailers [*NCIC trailer make code*]
McCr......... McCrary's United States Circuit Court Reports [*A publication*] (DLA)
MCCR........ Medical Committee for Civil Rights [*Defunct*] (EA)
MCCR........ Memory Data Capture Cash and Credit Register [*Datacap Systems, Inc.*]
MCCR........ Mission-Critical Computer Resource [*Computer science*]
MCCR........ Molded Case Circuit Breaker
MCCRA...... Medicare Catastrophic Coverage Repeal Act of 1989 (WYGK)
McCrary..... McCrary's United States Circuit Court Reports [*A publication*] (DLA)
McCrary Elect... McCrary's American Law of Elections [*A publication*] (DLA)
McCrary's Rep... McCrary's United States Circuit Court Reports [*A publication*] (DLA)
McCr Elect... McCrary's American Law of Elections [*A publication*] (DLA)
MCCRES.... Marine Corps Combat Readiness Evaluation System
MCCRK...... McCormick & Co. [*NASDAQ symbol*] (TTSB)
MCCRK...... McCormick & Co., Inc. [*NASDAQ symbol*] (NQ)
MCCRTG.... Marine Corps Combat Readiness Training Group
MCCS........ Machine Centralized Control System (DWSG)
MCCS........ Manual Closed-Loop Control System (VLIE)
MCCS........ Marconi Command & Control Systems (SAUS)
MCCS........ Master Calendar Control System [*New York City courts' speedup system*]
MCCS........ Master Control Communication Station (ACAE)
MCCS........ Mechanized Calling Card Service [*Formerly, ABC*] [*Telecommunications*]
MCCS........ Medco Containment Services, Inc. [*NASDAQ symbol*] (COMM)
MCCs........ Metropolitan Correctional Centers (SAUO)
MCCs........ Microclimate Cooling System (HEAS)
MCCS........ Military Committee in Chiefs of Staff Session [*NATO*] (NATG)
MCCS........ Mine Countermeasures Control System (SAUS)
MCCS........ Missile Critical Circuit Simulator
mccs......... Mission Control Center Simulation [*NASA*] (NAKS)
MCCS........ Mission Control Center Simulation [*NASA*] (NASA)
MCCS........ Mission Control Center System (SAUO)
MCCS........ Mission Critical Computer System (DOMA)
MCCS........ Mobile Command and Control System (MCD)
MCCSD...... Charles Stark Draper Laboratory, Inc., Technical Information Center, Cambridge, MA [*Library symbol*] [*Library of Congress*] (LCLS)
MCCSL...... Marconi Command and Control Systems Ltd. (NITA)
MCCSP...... Ministerial Council on Common Services Provision [*Australia*]
MCCSS...... Mobile Command Center Strategic System (SAUO)
MCCT........ Multistrip Cesium Contact Thrustor
MCCTA...... Manufacturing Confectioners' Commercial Travellers Association [*British*] (BI)
MCCTP...... Manpower and Community College Counselor Training Program (OICC)
MCCU........ Micro-Climate Cooling Unit (SAUS)
MCCU........ Mobile Coronary Care Unit [*Medicine*]
MCCU........ Multiple Channel Control Unit
MCCU........ Multiple Communications Control Unit [*Computer science*]
MCCU........ Multisystem Channel Communication Unit (SAUS)
McCul Dict... McCullough's Commercial Dictionary [*A publication*] (DLA)
McCul Pol Econ... McCulloch's Political Economy [*A publication*] (DLA)
MCCUS...... Mexican Chamber of Commerce of the United States (SAUO)
MCCUSCUSRPG... Military Coordinating Committee, United States Element, Canada-United States Regional Planning Group (AABC)
MCCW....... Miami Citizens Crime Watch (SAUO)
MCCW....... Military Council of Catholic Women (SAUO)
MCCX........ Multimedia Communications Exchange (VLIE)
MCCY........ McClenny Machine Company [*NCIC trailer make code*]
MCCZ........ Morton Chemical [*Federal Railroad Administration identification code*]
MCD......... Air Medical Ltd. [*British*] [*ICAO designator*] (FAAC)
MCD......... Doctor of Comparative Medicine
MCD......... Dynatech Research/Development Co., Cambridge, MA [*Library symbol*] [*Library of Congress*] (LCLS)
MCD......... Mad Cow Disease [*Medicine*] (MELL)
MCD......... Magistrates' Court Decisions [*New Zealand*] [*A publication*] (DLA)
MCD......... Magna Carta Dames, National Society (EA)
MCD......... Magnetic Circular Dichroism
MCD......... Magnetic Crack Definer [*Aviation*]
MCD......... Maintenance Control Department [*Military*] (DNAB)
MCD......... Malaria Control Detachment [*Army*] [*World War II*]
MCD......... Manipulative Communications Deception [*Military*] (NVT)
MCD......... Manual Control Device
MCD......... Manufacturing and Construction Division (SAUO)
MCD......... Manufacturing Construction Document (SAA)
MCD......... Marginal Checking and Distribution
MCD......... Margin Crease Distance (STED)
MCD......... Marine Corps District (DNAB)
MCD......... Marine Craft Detachment (SAUS)
MCD......... Maritime Commission Decisions
MCD......... Marr, Cahalan & Dunn [*Law firm*]
MCD......... Mast Cell Degranulating [*or Destroying*] Peptide [*Biochemistry*]
MCD......... Mast-Cell Degranulation (STED)
MCD......... Master Clerical Data [*Management system*]
MCD......... Master of Civic Design
MCD......... Master of Communication Disorders (GAGS)
MCD......... Mathematics and Computer Division [*Supreme Headquarters Allied Powers Europe*] (NATG)

MCD .... McDonald's Corp. [*NYSE symbol*] [*Toronto Stock Exchange symbol*] (SPSG)
MCD .... McDonnell Douglas Corp.
MCD .... Mean Cell [*or Corpuscular*] Diameter [*Hematology*]
MCD .... Mean Character Difference (EES)
MCD .... Mean of Consecutive Differences (MAE)
MCD .... Median Control Death
MCD .... Medical Care Development, Inc. [*Augusta, ME*] (TSSD)
MCD .... Medical Crew Director
MCD .... Medium Corpuscular Density [*Cardiology*] (DAVI)
MCD .... Medullary Collecting Duct (DB)
MCD .... Medullary Cystic Disease [*Medicine*] (MAE)
MCD .... Megawatt Cassegrain Diplexer
MCD .... Member of the College of Dentists [*British*]
MCD .... Memory Control Data
MCD .... Merced, CA [*Amtrak rail station code*]
MCD .... Mercy College of Detroit [*Michigan*]
MCD .... Metabolic Coronary Dilation [*Medicine*] (AAMN)
MCD .... Metacarpal Cortical Density [*Anatomy*]
MCD .... Metal-Covered Door [*Technical drawings*]
MCD .... Metals and Ceramics Division [*Air Force*]
MCD .... Metaphyseal Chondrodysplasia [*Medicine*]
MCD .... Microbial Coal Desulfurization
MCD .... Microelectronic Circuits Division (AAGC)
MCD .... Mid-Central District [*ATSC*]
MCD .... Military Contracts Department
MCD .... Military Coordination Detachment (NATG)
MCD .... Millicandela
mcD .... Millicurie-Destroyed
MCD .... Mines, Countermines, and Demolitions [*Military*] (RDA)
MCD .... Mine Warfare and Clearance Diving [*Navy*] [*British*]
MCD .... Mini-Client Driver [*Computer science*] (MWOL)
MCD .... Minimal Cerebral Dysfunction
MCD .... Minimal Change Disease [*Nephrology*]
MCD .... Minimum Cost Design (MCD)
MCD .... Minister for Coordination of Defence (SAUO)
MCD .... Minor Civil Division [*Bureau of Census*]
MCD .... Missile Countermeasure Device (DWSG)
MCD .... Mission Communication Display (MCD)
MCD .... Mission Control Directorate [*NASA*]
MCD .... Mobile Communications Device
MCD .... Mobile Communications Division (SAUO)
MCD .... Modification of Contract Documents (AAGC)
MCD .... Modular Capabilities Document (SAUS)
MCD .... Monitor Criteria Data [*Space Flight Operations Facility, NASA*]
MCD .... Months for Cyclical Dominance [*Economics*]
MCD .... Mouse Cytogenetic Database (HGEN)
MCD .... Movement for Christian Democracy [*Political party*] (WDAA)
MCD .... Movimiento por el Cambio Democratico [*Mexico*] [*Political party*] (EY)
MCD .... Multicystic Disease [*Medicine*] (STED)
MCD .... Multimedia Cartridge Drive (SAUS)
MCD .... Multiple Carboxylase Deficiency [*Medicine*]
MCD .... Multiple Concrete Duct [*Telecommunications*] (TEL)
MCD .... Multiple Cropping Department (SAUO)
MCD .... Municipal Civil District (GEAB)
MCD .... Municipal Construction Division [*Environmental Protection Agency*] (GFGA)
MCD .... Muscle Carnitine Deficiency [*Medicine*] (STED)
MCD .... Music Cataloging Decisions [*Library of Congress*]
MCDA .... Magna Carta Day Association (SAUO)
MCDA .... Maine Career Development Association (SEAT)
MCDA .... Manpower and Career Development Agency
McDA .... McDonnell Aircraft Corporation (SAUO)
MCDA .... Micro Channel Developers Association (NTPA)
MCDA .... Motor Car Dealers Association (SAUO)
McDAC .... McDonnell Aircraft Corporation (SAUO)
MCDARS .... Mechanized Cost Distribution and Reporting System (MCD)
MCDAS ...... Metropolitan Cities Drug Association Secretaries (EA)
MC-DAS ..... Multiple Channel Data Acquisition System (NITA)
MCDB .... Master Code Database (MCD)
MCDB .... Minimum Cost Design Booster (KSC)
MCDB .... Molecular Cellular, and Developmental Biology [*A discipline division*]
MCDBSU .... Master Control and Data Buffer Storage Unit
MCDC .... Manitoba Crop Diversification Centre [*Agriculture and Agri-Food Canada*] [*Canada*] (RCD)
MCDC .... Marine Corps Development Center (SAUO)
MCDC .... McDonnell Douglas Corp.
MCDC .... Mobilization Concepts Development Center [*Washington, DC*] [*DoD*] (MCD)
MCDC .... Montgomery County Detention Center (SAUO)
MCDD .... Marine and Coastal Data Directory (SAUO)
MCDD .... Monochlorodioxin [*Organic chemistry*]
MCDD .... Multichannel Demux/Demod (ACAE)
MCDDI ...... Congolese Movement for Democracy and Comprehensive Development (Rep. of Congo) [*Political party*] (PSAP)
MCDE .... Microcide Pharmaceuticals [*NASDAQ symbol*] (TTSB)
MCDE .... Microcide Pharmaceuticals, Inc. [*NASDAQ symbol*] (SAG)
MCDE .... Monochlorodimethyl Ether [*Organic chemistry*]
MCDEC ...... Marine Corps Development and Education Command
MCDEC ...... Marine Corps School (SAUO)
MCDEMA .... Mississippi Civil Defense Emergency Management Association [*Emergency Management*] (EMA)
McDerl ...... McDermott International, Inc. [*Associated Press*] (SAG)
McDerJ ...... McDermott [*J. Ray*] SA [*Associated Press*] (SAG)
McDer Land L ... McDermot's Irish Land Laws [*A publication*] (DLA)
MC Det ...... Malaria Control Detachment (SAUO)
McDevitt .... McDevitt's Irish Land Commissioner's Reports [*A publication*] (DLA)
MCDF .... Master Code Descriptor File (EAGT)
MCDF .... Methyltrichlorodibenzofuran [*Organic chemistry*]
MCDF .... Missile Defense [*or Alert*] System Control and Display Facility [*Air Force*] (IAA)
MCDF .... Mobile Combustion Diagnostic Fixture (MCD)
MCDG .... Monitor Criteria Data Set Generation Processor Assembly [*Space Flight Operations Facility, NASA*]
MCDH .... Master of Community Dental Health, University of Birmingham [*British*] (DBQ)
MCDI .... Magneto Capacitor Discharge Ignition
MCDI .... Minnesota Child Development Inventory [*Child development test*] [*Psychology*]
McDInv ...... McDonald & Co. Investment, Inc. [*Associated Press*] (SAG)
MCDK .... Multicystic Dysplastic Kidney [*Medicine*] (DMAA)
MCDM .... Modern College for Distressed Merchants (SAUO)
MCDM .... Multiple Criteria Decision Making
MCDN .... Marine Corps Data Network [*Marine Corps*] (CIST)
McDn .... McDonald's Corp. [*Associated Press*] (SAG)
MCDN .... Multi-cellular Data Network [*Metricom*]
McDn25 .... McDonalds Corp. [*Associated Press*] (SAG)
McDn36 .... McDonalds Corp. [*Associated Press*] (SAG)
McDnD ...... McDonnell Douglas Corp. [*Associated Press*] (SAG)
McDnlds .... McDonald's Corp. [*Associated Press*] (SAG)
McDO .... McDonald Observatory (SAUO)
MCDOA ...... Minewarfare & Clearance Diving Officers' Association (WDAA)
McD Obs .... McDonald Observatory (SAUO)
MCDON ..... McDonald, PA [*American Association of Railroads railroad junction routing code*]
McDon Jus ... McDonald's Justice [*A publication*] (DLA)
McDonnell ... McDonnell's Sierra Leone Reports [*A publication*] (DLA)
McDow Inst ... McDowall's Institutes of the Law of Scotland [*A publication*] (DLA)
MCDP .... Marine Conservation and Development Program (SAUO)
MCDP .... Memphis Chronic/Methadone Chest Disease Program [*Medicine*] (EDAA)
MCDP .... Microprogrammed Communication Data Processor (MCD)
MCDP .... Missionary Catechists of Divine Providence [*Roman Catholic women's religious order*]
MCDP .... Missionary Catechists of Divine Providence, San Antonio, TX (TOCD)
MCDPrE ..... McDonald's Corp. 7.72% Dep Pfd [*NYSE symbol*] (TTSB)
McDr .... McDermott, Inc. [*Associated Press*] (SAG)
MCDR .... Multichannel DIFAR [*Directional Frequency Analysis and Recording System*] Relay (NVT)
MCDS .... Maintenance Control and Display System [*NASA*] (NASA)
MCDS .... Management Communications and Data System (SSD)
MCDS .... Management Control Data System [*Computer science*] (IAA)
MCDS .... Mission Control & Display Subsystem (SAUS)
MCDS .... Mission-Critical Defense System [*Army*]
MCDS .... Modular Cargo Delivery System [*MARAD*] (TAG)
MCDS .... Multicommand Data System
MCDS .... Multifunction CRT [*Cathode-Ray Tube*] Display System (NASA)
MCDSH ...... Management Communications and Data System Hardware (SSD)
MCD/SLV .... Minimum Cost Design/Space Launch Vehicle [*NASA*] (KSC)
MCDSP ...... Master Combat Data System Plan [*Military*] (CAAL)
MCDT .... Mast Cell Degranulation Test [*Medicine*] (DAVI)
MCDT .... Mean Corrective Downtime [*Computer science*]
MCDT .... Michigan Department of Transportation [*Federal Railroad Administration identification code*]
MCDU .... Military and Civil Defense Unit [*Emergency Management*] [*United Nations*] (EMA)
MCDU .... Multifunction Control & Display Unit (SAUS)
MCDU .... Multifunction CRT [*Cathode-Ray Tube*] Display Unit (NASA)
MCDU .... Multipurpose Control Display Unit (GAVI)
MCDV .... Maize Chlorotic Dwarf Virus [*Plant pathology*]
MCDV .... Maritime Coastal Defense Vessel (MILB)
MCDV .... Maximum Cell Delay Variation (SAUS)
MCDVL ...... McDonoghville, LA [*American Association of Railroads railroad junction routing code*]
MCDW .... Monthly Climate Data for the World (SAUO)
MCDX .... Cementos Mexicanos [*Private rail car owner code*]
MCDY .... Microdyne Corp. [*NASDAQ symbol*] (NQ)
MCE .... Episcopal Divinity School, Cambridge, MA [*Library symbol*] [*Library of Congress*] (LCLS)
MCE .... MacNeill Industrial, Inc. [*Vancouver Stock Exchange symbol*]
MCE .... Main Component Elements (EURO)
MCE .... Maintenance Cleaning Equipment (MCD)
MCE .... Management Centre Europe (SAUO)
MCE .... Management Communication Engine (SAUS)
MCE .... Mandatory Continuing Education
MCE .... Manual Core Endarteretomy [*Medicine*] (EDAA)
MCE .... Manually Coded English [*Medicine*] (EDAA)
MCE .... Manufacturing Cycle Effectiveness
MCE .... Marginal Cost Efficiency [*Marketing*]
MCE .... Maritime Commission, Emergency Ship
MCE .... Marshall of Cambridge (Engineering) Ltd. [*British*] [*ICAO designator*] (FAAC)
MCE .... Master of Chemical Engineering (GAGS)
MCE .... Master of Christian Education
MCE .... Master of Civil Engineering
MCE .... Maximum Capability Envelope
MCE .... MCN Corp. [*NYSE symbol*] (SAG)
MCE .... MCN Corp. 8.75%'PRIDE' [*NYSE symbol*] (TTSB)
MCE .... Mean Chance Expectation [*Parapsychology*]
MCE .... Mechanism Control Electronics (SAUS)

MCE .... Media Conversion Equipment [*Space Flight Operations Facility, NASA*]
MCE .... Medical Care Evaluation
MCE .... Medicare Code Editor (MEDA)
MCE .... Melbourne Corn Exchange [*Australia*]
MCE .... Member of Civil Engineering [*Canada*] (ASC)
MCE .... Membrane Chlorine Expansion [*Plastics*]
MCE .... Memphis Cotton Exchange (EA)
MCE .... Merced [*California*] [*Airport symbol*] (AD)
MCE .... Merced, CA [*Location identifier*] [*FAA*] (FAAL)
MCE .... Metabolism, Clinical and Experimental [*Medicine*] (EDAA)
McE.......... Microcard Editions, Inc., Englewood, CO [*Library symbol*] [*Library of Congress*] (LCLS)
MCE .... Micro Circuit Engineering Ltd. (SAUO)
MCE .... Microscopically Controlled Excision [*Medicine*]
MCE .... Microwave Communications Equipment
MCE .... Mid Course Early (ACAE)
MCE .... Mid Cretaceous Events (SAUO)
MCE .... Military Characteristics Equipment
MCE .... Military Clinical Engineering (DMAA)
MCE .... Military Corrective Establishment
MCE .... Missile Command Electronics (ACAE)
MCE .... Missile Compensating Equipment
MCE .... Mission Control Element (SAUO)
MCE .... Mission Control Equipment [*NASA*]
MCE .... Mixed Cellulose Esters Membrane Filters
MCE .... Mobile Command Element (NATG)
MCE .... Modular Communications Engine (AGLO)
MCE .... Modular Control Element (MCD)
MCE .... Modular Control Equipment [*DoD*]
MCE .... Montgomery Cotton Exchange [*Defunct*] (EA)
MCE .... Moscow Commodity Exchange [*Russian Federation*] (EY)
MCE .... Multicystic Encephalopathy [*Medicine*] (DMAA)
MCE .... Multiple Cartilaginous Exostosis [*Medicine*] (DMAA)
MCE .... Myocardial Contrast Echocardiography [*Medicine*] (DMAA)
MCE .... Myocardial Embolism [*Medicine*] (MELL)
MCE .... National Council of Churches, Ministries in Christian Education (EA)
MCEA........ Madison Center for Educational Affairs (EA)
MCEA........ Maryland Classified Employees Association
MCEAC ...... Marine Corps Emergency Actions Center
MCEAMS.... Marine Corps Expeditionary Aircraft Maintenance Shelter (SAUO)
MCEARD .... National Exposure Research Laboratory [*Environmental Protection Agency*] (RCD)
MCEB........ Marine Corps Equipment Board
MCEB........ Military Communications-Electronics Board [*DoD*] [*Washington, DC*]
MCEC........ Marine Corps Education Center
MCED........ Episcopal Divinity School, Cambridge, MA [*Library symbol*] [*Library of Congress*] (LCLS)
MC Ed....... Master of Commercial Education
MCED........ Master of Community Economic Development (PGP)
MC Ed....... Master of Continuing Education (PGP)
MC/EDS..... Mission Control/Electronic Display System (MCD)
M Ce Eng... Master of Cement Engineering
MCEER...... Multidisciplinary Center for Earthquake Engineering Research [*Emergency Management*] (EMA)
MCEF........ Mixed Cellulose Ester Filter (GNE)
MCEG........ Management Co. Entertainment Group, Inc. [*NASDAQ symbol*] (COMM)
MCEGGS.... Melbourne Church of England Girls Grammar School (SAUO)
MCEI......... Marketing Communications Executives International [*Dallas, TX*] (EA)
MCEI......... Minnesota Committee for Environmental Information [*Medicine*] (EDAA)
MCEL........ Machine Check Extended Logout
McEM .... Microfilming Executors & Methods Organization Ltd., Dublin, Ireland [*Library symbol*] [*Library of Congress*] (LCLS)
MCEM....... Military Committee Emergency Memorandum (SAUO)
MCEM....... Mississippi Certified Emergency Manager [*Emergency Management*] (EMA)
MCE(Melb)... Master of Civil Engineering (Melbourne University)
MCEMS ..... Marine Corps Environmentally Controlled Medical System (MCD)
MCen........ Centerville Public Library, Centerville, MA [*Library symbol*] [*Library of Congress*] (LCLS)
MCEN........ Magic Circle Energy (EFIS)
MCEN........ Modified Current Expendable Launch Vehicle [*NASA*] (KSC)
MCENC...... Mid-Central Conference (PSS)
MC Eng ..... Master of Civil Engineering
MCEO........ Malayan Council of Employers Organization (SAUO)
MCEP........ Maneuver Criteria Evaluation Program [*Army*]
MCEPEN .... Midwest Continuing Education Professional Nurses (DHSM)
MCER........ Massachusetts Central [*AAR code*]
M Cer E..... Master of Ceramic Engineering
MCES........ Main Condenser Evacuation System [*Nuclear energy*] (NRCH)
MCES........ Major City Earth Stations [*Telecommunications*] (TSSD)
MCES........ Marine Corps Exchange System (SAUO)
MCES........ Medical Care Evaluation Study (HCT)
MCES........ Modular Command and Control Evaluation Structure (SAUO)
MCES........ Multiple Cholesterol Emboli Syndrome [*Medicine*]
MCESS...... Marine Corps Expeditionary Shelter System (MCD)
MCET........ Massachusetts Corporation for Educational Telecommunications
MCET........ Mercer Transportation Company [*Common carrier symbol*]
MCET........ Mississippi Center for Educational Television (SAUO)
MCEU........ Massachusetts Central Railroad [*Intermodal shipping container symbol*] (TVRC)
MCEU........ Mobile Civil Emergency Unit
MCEWG..... Multinational Communication-Electronics Working Group [*Formerly, SGCEC*] [*NATO*] (NATG)
MCEZ........ Massachusetts Central Railroad [*Intermodal trailer symbol*]
MCEZ........ Merna Co-Operative Elevator [*Federal Railroad Administration identification code*]
MCF .... Macrophage Chemotactic Factor [*Immunochemistry*] (MAE)
MCF .... Magic Chef, Inc. (SAUO)
MCF .... Magnetic Confinement Fusion [*Physics*]
MCF .... Magyar Communion of Friends (EA)
MCF .... Maintenance and Checkout Facility [*NASA*] (KSC)
MCF .... Maintenance Condemnation Factor (MCD)
MCF .... Maintenance Control Facility (SAUO)
MCF .... Major Component Fail (SAUS)
MCF .... Manual Cervical Fraction [*Medicine*] (DMAA)
MCF .... Marine Commando Force (SAUO)
MCF .... Master Code File
MCF .... Master Control Facility (ACAE)
MCF .... Master Control File
MCF .... Matched Crystal Filters
MCF .... Maximal Contraction Force [*Myology*]
MCF .... McFinley Red Lake Mines Ltd. [*Toronto Stock Exchange symbol*]
MCF .... Mean Carrier Frequency [*Radio*] (IAA)
MCF .... Measurement Compensation Factor (PDAA)
MCF .... Median Cleft Face [*Medicine*] (EDAA)
MCF .... Medical Care Foundation [*Medicine*] (EDAA)
MCF .... Medical Cybernetics Foundation (EA)
MCF .... Medium Corpuscular Fragility [*Hematology*]
MCF .... Merced County Free Library, Merced, CA [*OCLC symbol*] (OCLC)
MCF .... Meta Content File [*Netscape*] [*Computer science*]
MCF .... Meta Content Format [*Computer science*]
MCF .... Meta Content Framework [*Computer science*] (GART)
MCF .... Metroplex Control Facility [*FAA*] (TAG)
MCF .... Michigan Colleges Foundation (SAUO)
MCF .... Microcomplement Fixation [*Immunochemistry*]
MCF .... Middle Cranial Fossa [*Medicine*] (MELL)
MCF .... Migrant Children's Fund [*Absorbed by NCEMC*]
MCF .... Military Christian Fellowship of Canada (SAUO)
MCF .... Military Computer Family (MCD)
MCF .... Milled Carbon Fiber
MCF .... Million Cubic Feet
MCF .... Mine-Clearing Force (SAUO)
MCF .... Mink Cell Focus-Inducing [*Virus*]
MCF .... Mission Control Facility (MCD)
MCF .... Mission Control Forecast (SAUO)
MCF .... Mission-Critical Function (PDAA)
MCF .... Missouri Colleges Fund (SAUO)
MCF .... Mobile Calibration Facility
MCF .... Mode Change Flag
MCF .... Modular Combustion Facility (SSD)
MCF .... Monolithic Crystal Filter
MCF .... Mononuclear Cell Factor [*Cytology*]
MCF .... Most Comfortable Frequency [*Medicine*] (EDAA)
MCF .... Multichannel Fixed
MCF .... Multilateral Clearing Facility [*Caribbean Community and Common Market*] (EY)
MCF .... Multiple Cassegrain Feed [*Deep Space Instrumentation Facility, NASA*]
MCF .... Multiple Cost Factor
MCF .... Museum Communication Format (NITA)
MCF .... Mutual Coherence Function
MCF .... Myocardial Contractile Force [*Cardiology*]
MCF .... Myocardial Fascicles [*Medicine*] (MELL)
MCF .... Tampa, FL [*Location identifier*] [*FAA*] (FAAL)
MCF .... Taurus MuniCalif Hldgs [*NYSE symbol*] (TTSB)
MCF .... Taurus Municipal California Holdings [*NYSE symbol*] (SPSG)
McF.......... Thousand Cubic Feet [*Industrial hygiene term*] (OHS)
MCF .... Thousand Cubic Feet
MCF-7....... Michigan Cancer Foundation - Seventh Sample [*Strain of rapid-growing breast cancer cells used world-wide in cancer research*]
MCFA........ McFarlane Manufacturing Company [*NCIC trailer make code*]
MCFA........ Medium-Chain Fatty Acids [*Organic chemistry*]
MCFA........ Miniature Centrifugal Fast Analyzer (DMAA)
MCFA........ Mitsubishi Caterpillar Forklift America
MCFA........ Monosegmented Continuous Flow Analysis [*Analytical chemistry*]
MCFA........ Royal Ministry for Consumer and Family Affairs (SAUO)
McFar .... McFarlane's Jury Court Reports [*Scotland*] [*A publication*] (DLA)
McFarl ...... McFarland Energy, Inc. [*Associated Press*] (SAG)
MCFC........ Mary Jo Cattlett Fan Club (EA)
MCFC........ Molten Carbonate Fuel Cell [*Energy source*]
MCFC........ Motley Crue Fan Club (EA)
MCFD........ Malta College of Family Doctors (SAUO)
MCFD........ Modular Chaff/Flare Dispenser (PDAA)
MCFD........ Thousand Cubic Feet per Day
MCFE........ McFarland Energy [*NASDAQ symbol*] (TTSB)
MCFE........ McFarland Energy, Inc. [*NASDAQ symbol*] (NQ)
MCFF........ Moving Call for Fire [*Military*]
MCFFA ...... Ministerial Council of/on Forestry, Fisheries and Aquaculture (SAUO)
MCFH........ Thousand Cubic Feet per Hour
MCFI......... Malaysian Chamber of Film Industries (SAUO)
MCFIM ...... Microfilm
MCFIX....... Ivy Bond Fund Cl.A [*Mutual fund ticker symbol*] (SG)
MCFL........ Master Civilian Facilities Listing [*DoD*]
MCFLM...... Microfilm (AAG)
MCFMIS..... Marine Corps Food Management Information System (SAUO)

MCFO........ Marine Corps Freight Office
MCFOS...... Military Computer Family Operating System (ACAE)
MCFP........ Mean Circulating Filling Pressure (DMAA)
MCFP........ Medical Center for Federal Prisoners (SAUO)
MCFP........ Member of the College of Family Physicians [*British*]
MCFP(EM)... Member, College of Family Physicians (Emergency Medicine) (CMD)
MCFR........ Microframe, Inc. [*NASDAQ symbol*] (SAG)
MCFS........ Maneuver Control Functional Segment [*Army*] (RDA)
MCFS........ Master Container Freight [*MARAD*] (TAG)
MCFS........ Median Cleft Face Syndrome [*Medicine*] (MELL)
MCFS........ Middle Cranial Fossa Syndrome [*Medicine*] (MELL)
MCFS........ MPS Coastal Fortress Simulator (SAUS)
MCFSA...... Minority Caucus of Family Service America (EA)
MCFSAA.... Minorities Caucus of Family Service Association of America [*Later, MCFSA*] (EA)
MCFSHE.... Microfische
MCFTU...... Mauritius Confederation of Free Trade Unions (SAUO)
MCFV........ Mink Cell Focus-Forming Virus [*Virology*] (QSUL)
McFx........ Microfax, Universal Information System, Paramus, NJ [*Library symbol*] [*Library of Congress*] (LCLS)
MCG......... Macquarie Communications Infrastructure Group [*Australian Stock Exchange symbol*]
MCG......... Magazine Cartoonists Guild [*Later, CG*] (EA)
MCG......... Magnetic Compensator Group
MCG......... Magnetocardiogram
MCG......... Magnetocardiograph (IDOE)
MCG......... Magneto Cumulative Generator (MCD)
MCG......... Mains Cable Group [*British*] (DBA)
MCG......... Man Computer Graphics [*Computer science*] (MCD)
MCG......... Mandalay Coral Gardens (SAUO)
MCG......... Marine Corps Gazette [*A publication*] (DOMA)
MCG......... Master Control Gauge (IAA)
MCG......... Master Control Group (SAUO)
MCG......... Master of Clinical Gerontology (PGP)
McG......... McGill University (SAUO)
MCG......... McGill University, Graduate School of Library Science, Montreal, PQ, Canada [*OCLC symbol*] (OCLC)
McG......... McGloin's Louisiana Court of Appeal Reports [*A publication*] (DLA)
MCG......... McGrath [*Alaska*] [*Airport symbol*] (OAG)
MCG......... McGrath, AK [*Location identifier*] [*FAA*] (FAAL)
MCG......... McGregor, TX [*Amtrak rail station code*]
MCG......... Medical College of Georgia [*Augusta*]
MCG......... Membrane Coating Granule (DB)
MCG......... Memory Character Generator
MCG......... Memory Controller Group (DWSG)
MCG......... Mesangiocapillary Glomerulonephritis (DB)
MCG......... Mesencephalic Central Grey (DB)
MCG......... Metric Coordinating Group (MCD)
MCG......... Michigan Energy Resources Co. [*NYSE symbol*] (COMM)
MCG......... Michigan Gas Utilities Company (SAUO)
mcg.......... Microgram (LDT)
MCG......... Microgram [*One millionth of a gram*]
MCG......... Microwave Command Guidance
MCG......... Midbrain Central Gray [*Brain anatomy*]
MCG......... Mid-Canada Gold & Copper [*Vancouver Stock Exchange symbol*]
MCG......... Midcourse Guidance [*Navy*] (CAAL)
MCG......... Millimeter Wave Contrast Guidance [*Munitions*] (MCD)
MCG......... Minimally-Cleaned, Coal-Derived Gas
MCG......... Minkowski-Chauffard-Gaeusslen [*Syndrome*] [*Medicine*] (DB)
MCG......... Mobile Civilian Group (SAUO)
MCG......... Mobile Command Guidance
MCG......... Mobile Communications Group [*Air Force*] (MCD)
mCG......... Monkey Chorionic Gonadotrophin [*Endocrinology*]
MCG......... Monoclonal Gammopathy [*Immunochemistry*] (DMAA)
MCG......... Morgan Crucible Company (EFIS)
MCG......... Mount Cook Group (SAUO)
MCG......... Mount Cook Group of companies (SAUO)
MCG......... Movement Control Group (SAUO)
MCG......... Moving Coil Galvanometer [*Electronics*]
MCGA....... Memory Controller Gate Array [*Computer science*]
MCGA....... Multicolor Graphics Adapter [*Computer technology*]
MCGA....... Multicolor /Graphics Array [*Computer science*]
McGAP...... Mesoscale Climate Model Garmisch-Partenkirchen (SAUO)
MCGC....... Metacerebral Giant Cell (DMAA)
MCGC....... Michigan Consolidated Gas Co. [*Associated Press*] (SAG)
McGC....... Micro Graphic Corp., Garfield, NJ [*Library symbol*] [*Library of Congress*] (LCLS)
MCGCIS..... Marine Corps Ground-Controlled Interceptor Squadron (IAA)
MCGCM..... Marine Corps Good Conduct Medal
MCGF........ Mast Cell Growth Factor (DB)
MCGF........ Myeloma Cell Growth Factor [*Biochemistry*]
MCGFP...... Maraschino Cherry and Glace Fruit Processors (EA)
MCGGR..... McGregor, TX [*American Association of Railroads railroad junction routing code*]
MCGH....... Marine Corps Gun Howitzer (MCD)
McG-H....... McGraw-Hill (SAUO)
MCGH....... Milwaukee County General Hospital [*Medicine*] (EDAA)
MCGI........ Morse Construction Group Incorporated (SAUO)
McGI......... TIGR [*The Institute of Genomic Research*] Mesembryanthemum crystallinum Gene Index [*Database*] (GDD)
McGill....... McGill's Manuscript Decisions, Scotch Court of Session [*A publication*] (DLA)
McGl......... McGloin's Louisiana Courts of Appeal Reports [*A publication*] (DLA)
McGl Al..... McGlashan. Aliment [*Scotland*] [*A publication*] (DLA)
McGl (LA)... McGloin's Louisiana Courts of Appeal Reports [*A publication*] (DLA)
McGloin..... McGloin's Louisiana Courts of Appeal Reports [*A publication*] (DLA)
McGloin Rep (LA)... McGloin's Louisiana Courts of Appeal Reports [*A publication*] (DLA)
McGl Sh.... McGlashan's Sheriff Court Practice [*Scotland*] [*A publication*] (DLA)
MCGLX...... Ivy Global Fund Cl.A [*Mutual fund ticker symbol*] (SG)
mcgm....... Microgram [*Medicine*] (BCRP)
MCGN....... Mesangiocapillary Glomerulonephritis [*Medicine*] (AAMN)
MCGN....... Minimal-Change Glomerular Nephritis [*Minimal-change glomerulonephritis*] [*Nephrology*] (DAVI)
MCGN....... Mixed Cryoglobulinemia-Associated Glomerulonephritis [*Medicine*]
MCGP....... Magnavox Code Generation Package (SAUO)
MCGP....... Member of the College of General Practitioners [*British*]
MCGp....... Mobile Communications Group [*Air Force*] (AFM)
MCGPPC.... Manual on the Control of Government Property in the Possession of Contractors
McGrath..... McGrath's Mandamus Cases [*Michigan*] [*A publication*] (DLA)
MCGRE...... McGregor, MN [*American Association of Railroads railroad junction routing code*]
McGrH....... McGraw-Hill, Inc. [*Associated Press*] (SAG)
McGrth...... McGrath Rent Corp. [*Associated Press*] (SAG)
MCGS....... Manual Cover Gas System (SAUO)
MCGS....... Microwave Command Guidance System [*RADC*]
mcgtts....... Microdrops [*Medicine*] (BCRP)
McGU........ McGill University (SAUO)
McGUL...... McGill University Library (SAUO)
MCGW....... Maximum Certificated Gross Weight (MCD)
MCGW....... Millimeter Wave Contrast Guidance Weapon (ACAE)
MCH......... Churchill Public Library, Manitoba [*Library symbol*] [*National Library of Canada*] (NLC)
MCH......... Greater Manchester (SAUS)
MCH......... Machala [*Ecuador*] [*Airport symbol*] (OAG)
MCH......... Machine [*Telegraphy*] (PCTE)
MCH......... Machine Channel Handler (ECII)
MCH......... Machine Check Handle (NITA)
MCH......... Machine-Check Handler [*Computer science*] (MCD)
MCH......... Machynlleth [*Welsh depot code*]
M Ch........ Magister Chirurgiae [*Master of Surgery*] [*Latin*]
MCH......... Mail Chute (AAG)
MCH......... March
MCH......... Masachapa [*Nicaragua*] [*Seismograph station code, US Geological Survey*] (SEIS)
MCH......... Massachusetts Council for the Humanities [*Defunct*] (EA)
MCH......... Master of Community Health (GAGS)
MCH......... Master of Surgery (SAUO)
MCH......... Maternal and Child Health (STED)
MCH......... Maternal and Child Health Services [*Generic term*] (DHSM)
MCH......... McAlpine Helicopters Ltd. [*British*] [*ICAO designator*] (FAAC)
MCH......... Mean Cell [*or Corpuscular*] Hemoglobin [*Hematology*]
MCH......... Mean Corpuscular Hemoglobin [*Medicine*] (ADWA)
MCH......... Mean Corpuscular Hemoglobin and Red Cell Indices [*Hematology*] (DAVI)
MCH......... MedChem Products, Inc. [*AMEX symbol*] (COMM)
mch.......... Megacharacter (ELAL)
MCH......... Melanin-Concentrating Hormone [*Endocrinology*]
M-Ch........ Memory Channel
MCH......... Memory Controller Hub
MCH......... Methacholine [*A cholinergic*]
MCH......... Methylcyclohexane [*Organic chemistry*]
MCH......... Methylcyclohexanol [*Organic chemistry*]
MCH......... Methylcyclohexenone [*Organic chemistry*]
MCH......... Methylenecyclohexadiene [*Organic chemistry*]
MCH......... Micham Explorations, Inc. [*Vancouver Stock Exchange symbol*]
Mch.......... Michigan Reports [*A publication*] (DLA)
McH......... Microeditions Hachette, Paris, France [*Library symbol*] [*Library of Congress*] (LCLS)
MCH......... Microfibrillar Collagen Hemostat [*Medicine*] (MEDA)
MCH......... Millenium Chemicals, Inc. [*NYSE symbol*] (SAG)
mc-h......... Millicurie-Hour (STED)
MCH......... Milwaukee County Hospital [*Medicine*] (EDAA)
MCH......... Mission Chapel [*Church of England*]
MCH......... Moravian Church House (SAUO)
MCH......... Mother-Child Health
MCH......... Moveable Cultural Heritage (SAUO)
MCH......... Muscle Contraction Headache [*Medicine*] (CPH)
MCha........ Eldredge Public Library, Chatham, MA [*Library symbol*] [*Library of Congress*] (LCLS)
MCHA....... Moveable Cultural Heritage Act (SAUO)
MCHAN...... Multichannel (AABC)
MChB........ Boston College, Chestnut Hill, MA [*Library symbol*] [*Library of Congress*] (LCLS)
MChB........ Magneto-Chiral Birefringence [*Optics*]
MCHB....... Maternal and Child Health Bureau (MELL)
MCHb........ Mean Corpuscular Hemoglobin [*Hematology*] (DAVI)
MCHbC...... Mean Cell Hemoglobin Concentration [*Medicine*] (STED)
MCHbC...... Mean Corpuscular Hemoglobin Concentration [*Hematology*] (DAVI)
MCHbC...... Mean Corpuscular Hemoglobin Count [*Hematology*] (DAVI)
MCHBG...... Maternal and Child Health Block Grant [*Department of Health and Human Services*] (GFGA)
MChB-WO... Boston College, Weston Observatory, Weston, MA [*Library symbol*] [*Library of Congress*] (LCLS)
MCHC....... Marine Corps Historical Center (SAUO)
MCHC....... Maternal and Child Health Care (STED)
MCHC....... Mean Cell [*or Corpuscular*] Hemoglobin Concentration [*Hematology*]
MCHC....... Mean Corpuscular Hemoglobin Concentration [*Medicine*] (STED)

MCHC .... Mean Corpuscular Hemoglobin Concentration and Red Cell Indices [*Hematology*] (DAVI)
MCHC .... Mean Corpuscular Hemoglobin Count [*Hematology*] (DAVI)
MCHC .... Mean Corpusculsar Hemoglobin Concentration [*Physiology*]
MCHC .... Metropolitan Collegiate Hockey Conference (PSS)
MCHC .... Missing Children...Help Center (EA)
MCHCC ...... Midwest Christian College Conference (PSS)
MCHCL ...... Mechanically Cooled
M Ch D ...... Magister Chirurgiae Dentalis [*Master of Dental Surgery*]
MChD .... Magneto-Chiral Dichroism [*Optics*]
MChD .... Master of Dental Surgery (SAUO)
MCHE .... Eskimo Museum, Churchill, Manitoba [*Library symbol*] [*National Library of Canada*] (NLC)
M Ch E ...... Master of Chemical Engineering
MChE .... Member of Chemical Engineering (ASC)
MCHEL ...... Michigan Community Health Electronic Library (SAUO)
MChelm ..... Adams Library (Chelmsford Public Library), Chelmsford, MA [*Library symbol*] [*Library of Congress*] (LCLS)
MChels ...... Chelsea Public Library, Chelsea, MA [*Library symbol*] [*Library of Congress*] (LCLS)
MChem ...... Master of Chemistry (ADA)
MChemA ..... Master in Chemical Analysis
M Chem E ... Master of Chemical Engineering
MCHF .... Marine Corps Historical Foundation (EA)
MCHFR ...... Minimum Critical Heat Flux Rates [*Nuclear energy*] (NRCH)
MCHFR ...... Minimum Critical Heat Flux Ratio [*Nuclear energy*] (NRCH)
MCHg .... Mean Corpuscular Hemoglobin [*Hematology*] (DAVI)
MCHgb ...... Mean Corpuscular Hemogobin [*Hematology*] (DAVI)
MCHGD ..... Mott Center for Human Growth and Development (EA)
MChi .... Chicopee Public Library, Chicopee, MA [*Library symbol*] [*Library of Congress*] (LCLS)
MCHI .... Mobile Communications Holdings, Inc.
MChiD .... Dow Jones & Co., Inc., Chicopee, MA [*Library symbol*] [*Library of Congress*] (LCLS)
MChiL .... College of Our Lady of the Elms, Chicopee, MA [*Library symbol*] [*Library of Congress*] (LCLS)
M Chir .... Magister Chirurgiae [*Master of Surgery*]
MCHJ .... Maternal and Child Health Journal (SAUO)
MCHL .... Mayo Clinic Health Letter [*A publication*]
MCHL .... Mean Corpuscular Hemoglobin [*Count*] [*Hematology*] (DAVI)
MCHLL ...... Mitchell, IN [*American Association of Railroads railroad junction routing code*]
MCHM .... MacroChem Corp. [*NASDAQ symbol*] (NQ)
MCHMAS ... Michaelmas [*Feast of St. Michael the Archangel, September 29*] (ROG)
MCHML ...... Macrochem Corp. Wrrt'A' [*NASDAQ symbol*] (TTSB)
MCHMM .... Macrochem Corp. Wrrt'AA' [*NASDAQ symbol*] (TTSB)
MCHMN ..... Macrochem Corp. Wrrt'X' [*NASDAQ symbol*] (TTSB)
MCHN .... Machine
MCHN .... Merchants National Corp. [*NASDAQ symbol*] (COMM)
MCHND ..... Machined
M Ch Orth ... Master of Orthopaedic Surgery
M Ch Otol ... Master of Oto-Rhino-Laryngological Surgery
MCHP .... (Methylcinnamylhydrazono)propionate [*Biochemistry*]
MCHP .... Microchip Technology [*NASDAQ symbol*] (TTSB)
MCHP .... Microchip Technology, Inc. [*NASDAQ symbol*] (SAG)
MCHP .... Micro-Combined Heat and Power [*Motor generators*]
MChP .... Pine Manor College, Chestnut Hill, MA [*Library symbol*] [*Library of Congress*] (LCLS)
MCHPE ...... Manitoba Centre for Health Policy & Evaluation (SAUO)
MCHPRC .... Maternal and Child Health Policy Research Center (ADWA)
MCHQ .... Marine Corps Headquarters (SAUO)
MCHQ .... McHenry Truck Line [*Common carrier symbol*]
M'CHR ...... Manchester [*County in England*] (ROG)
MCHR .... Medical Committee for Human Rights [*Defunct*]
mchr .... Millicurie Hour (MAE)
M Chr Ed ... Master of Christian Education
MCHRF ...... Mechanically Refrigerated
MChrLit ..... Magazine of Christian Literature (SAUO)
MChrom .... Master of Chromatics [*British*]
MCHRY ...... Machinery (MSA)
MCHS .... Maternal and Child Health Service (EA)
MChS .... Member of the Society of Chiropodists
MCHS .... Microclimate Cooling/Heating System (ACAE)
M chs .... Thousands (10^3) of Characters (NITA)
MCHSM ..... Mechanism
MCHST ...... Machinist (MSA)
MCHT .... Merchant
MCHTR ...... Maintenance Channel Transmit Receiver Register (MHDI)
M'CHTR ..... Manchester [*County in England*] (ROG)
MCHX .... Trinity Rail Management [*Private rail car owner code*]
MCHY .... Machinery (ROG)
Mchy fwd ... Machinery Forward (DS)
MCHZ .... Merckens Chocolate [*Federal Railroad Administration identification code*]
MCI .... Data-Media Communications Co. (SAUO)
MCI .... Kansas City [*Missouri*] [*Airport symbol*] (OAG)
MCI .... Kansas City, MO [*Location identifier*] [*FAA*] (FAAL)
MCI .... Machine Check Interrupt (NITA)
MCI .... Machine Check Interruption [*Computer science*] (BUR)
MCI .... Major Capital Improvement [*Justification for rent increase*]
MCI .... Malicious Call Identification [*Telecommunications*] (TEL)
mci .... Malleable Cast Iron (ODA)
MCI .... Malleable Cast Iron
MCI .... Managed Cost Improvement (NRCH)
MCI .... Management Charter Initiative (SAUO)
MCI .... Management Consultants International, Inc. [*Information service or system*] (IID)
MCI .... Management Cost Improvement (SAUO)
MCI .... Management Counselors International Ltd. (SAUO)
MCI .... Mandatory Customer Inspection (ACAE)
MCI .... Manual of Clinical Immunology [*A publication*]
MCI .... Marine Corps Institute
MCI .... Marketing Concepts, Inc. [*New York, NY*] [*Telecommunications*] (TSSD)
MCI .... Massachusetts Correctional Institution (SAUO)
MCI .... Mass Casualty Incident [*Emergency Management*] (EMA)
MCI .... MassMutual Corp. Inv [*NYSE symbol*] (TTSB)
MCI .... MassMutual Corporate Investors [*NYSE symbol*] (SPSG)
MCI .... Master Configuration Index (MCD)
MCI .... Material Concept Investigation (MCD)
MCI .... Materials Cost Index
MCI .... Matsushita Communication Industrial [*Japan*]
MCI .... Maya Carga Internacional SA de CV [*Mexico*] [*ICAO designator*] (FAAC)
MCI .... MCI Communications Corp. [*Associated Press*] (SAG)
MCI .... MCI Communications, Incorporated (SAUO)
MCI .... Mead Carney International Company (SAUO)
MCI .... Meal, Combat, Individual [*Military*] (AABC)
MCI .... Mean Cardiac Index
MCI .... Media Control Interface
MCi .... Megacurie
MCI .... Member Canadian Credit Institute (SAUO)
MCI .... Member of the Concrete Institute (SAUO)
MCI .... Member of the Credit Institute
MCI .... Member of the Institute of Commerce [*British*] (DBQ)
MCI .... Meridian Control Integrator
MCI .... Methicillin [*Medicine*] (DMAA)
MCI .... Metropolitan Convalescent Institution (SAUO)
MCI .... Mexican Coffee Institute (EA)
MCI .... Michigan City, IN [*Amtrak rail station code*]
MCi .... Microcurie [*Emergency Management*] (EMA)
MCI .... Microelectronics Computer Corp. (SAUO)
McI .... Microfilm Center, Incorporated, Dallas, Texas [*Library symbol*] [*Library of Congress*] (LCLS)
McI .... Microplex, Inc., Dallas, TX [*Library symbol*] [*Library of Congress*] (LCLS)
MCI .... Microwave Communications Inc. (NITA)
MCI .... Microwave Communications of America, Inc.
MCI .... MIDAS Component Index (SAUO)
MCI .... Midland Cooperatives, Inc. (EFIS)
MCI .... Midland Counties Institution of Engineers (SAUO)
MCI .... Mild Cognitive Impairments [*Medical term*]
MCI .... Milk Can Institute [*Defunct*]
mCi .... Millicurie [*Also, mC*]
MCI .... Ministry of Commerce and Industry [*Korea*]
MCI .... Minnesota Counseling Inventory [*Psychology*]
MCI .... Mission Capability Inspection (SAUO)
MCI .... Mission Change Indicator [*Air Force*] (AFIT)
MCI .... Monetary Conditions Index
MCI .... Monitor Call Instruction (ELAL)
MCI .... Monte Cassino [*Italy*] [*Seismograph station code, US Geological Survey*] [*Closed*] (SEIS)
MCI .... Mother and Child International [*Switzerland*] (EAIO)
MCI .... Motor Coach Industries (SAUO)
MCI .... Motor Coach Industries International, Inc. (EFIS)
MCI .... Motor Coach Institute (SAUO)
MCI .... Motorcycle Industry Association of Great Britain (EAIO)
MCI .... Mottled Cast Iron
MCI .... Mucociliary Insufficiency [*Medicine*] (DMAA)
MCI .... Multichip Integration [*Computer science*] (PDAA)
MCI .... Muscle Contraction Interference [*Medicine*] (DMAA)
MCIA .... Methyl Chloride Industry Alliance (SAUO)
MCIA .... Methyl Chloride Industry Association (EA)
MCIA .... MicroComputer Investors Association [*Database producer*] (EA)
MCIA .... Mirror Class International Association (SAUO)
MCIA .... Mississippi Concrete Industries Association (EARSL)
MCIAS .... Multi-Channel Intelligent/Intercept Announcement System [*Telecommunications*]
MCIBS .... Member of the Chartered Institution of Building Services [*British*] (DBQ)
MCIC .... Machine Check Interruption Code [*Computer science*]
MCIC .... Managed Care Information Center (ADWA)
MCIC .... Management Control Information Center (SAUO)
MCIC .... Marine Corps Intelligence Center (DOMA)
MCIC .... MCI Communications [*NASDAQ symbol*] (TTSB)
MCIC .... MCI Communications Corp. [*NASDAQ symbol*] (NQ)
MCIC .... Medical Care Insurance Commission [*Canada*]
MCIC .... Member of the Chemical Institute of Canada
MCIC .... Metals and Ceramics Information Center [*Battelle Memorial Institute*] [*DoD*] [*Information service or system*] (IID)
MCIC .... Micro-Computer Information Center (ACAE)
McIC .... Micro Industrial Corp., Bayville, NJ [*Library symbol*] [*Library of Congress*] (LCLS)
MCICU .... Medical Coronary Intensive Care Unit (DMAA)
MCID .... Malicious Call Identification [*Telecommunications*] (DOM)
MCID .... Minimum Clinically Important Difference [*Medicine*] (DMAA)
MCID .... Multipurpose Concealed Intrusion Detector [*Army*] (RDA)
McIDAS ..... Man computer Interactive Data Access System (SAUO)
McIDAS ..... Man-Computer Interactive Data Access System

MCIDAS ..... Man-Computer Interactive Data Acquisition System (SAUO)
McIDAS ..... Mancomputer Interactive Data Analysis System (SAUO)
MCIE .... Midland Counties Institute of Engineers (SAUO)
MCIE .... Multi-Cultural Institute for Excellence
MCIF .... Marketing Customer Information File (GART)
MCIF .... MC Informatics [*OTCBB symbol*]
MCIF .... Member of the Canadian Institute of Forestry
mCihr .... Millicurie Hour (MAE)
MCIM .... Member Canadian Institute of Mining and Metallurgy (DD)
MCIM .... Member of the Canadian Institute of Mining
MCIM .... Member of the Chartered Institute of Marketing (ODA)
MCIMM ..... Member of the Canadian Institute of Mining and Metallurgy
MCIN .... Motor Coach Industries [*NCIC truck make code*]
McIn & E Jud Pr... McIntyre and Evans' Judicature Practice [*A publication*] (DLA)
McInc .... MAICO Micrographics, Inc., Wormleysburg, PA [*Library symbol*] [*Library of Congress*] (LCLS)
McInc .... Microcomfax, Incorporated, Camp Hill, PA [*Library symbol*] [*Library of Congress*] (LCLS)
McINP .... McIwaine National Park (SAUO)
MCINS .... Minimal Change Idiopathic Nephrotic Syndrome [*Medicine*] (DMAA)
MCInstM .... Member of the Canadian Institute of Marketing (ASC)
McInt .... McIntosh Music [*Record label*]
MCINTOSH... Julian & Vera McIntosh Theatre, School of Music (SAUS)
MCIOB .... Member of the Chartered Institute of Building [*British*] (DBQ)
MCIP .... Mated Cast Iron Pair
MCIP .... MCI [*NASDAQ symbol*]
MCIRA .... Microelectronic Replacement Assembly (NG)
M CIRP ...... Member of the International Institution for Production Engineering Research (ODA)
MCIS .... Maintenance Control Information System (IEEE)
MCIS .... Management Consultancy Information Service (SAUO)
MCIS .... Management Controlled Information System (VLIE)
MCIS .... Map and Chart Information System (MHDB)
MCIS .... Maps and Chart Information System (SAUO)
MCIS .... Master of Computer and Information Science (PGP)
MCIS .... Master of Computer Information Systems (GAGS)
MCIS .... Materials Compatibility in Sodium [*Nuclear energy*] (NRCH)
MCIS .... Materials Control Information System (MHDB)
MCIS .... Member of the Institute of Chartered Secretaries and Administrators (ODA)
MCIS .... Microsoft Commercial Internet System [*Computer science*]
MCIS .... Multichannel Initial System (MCD)
MCIS .... Multiple Corridor Identification System [*Air Force*]
MCISc .... Master of Clinical Science (CMD)
MCIT .... Institute of Traditional Science, Cambridge, MA [*Library symbol*] [*Library of Congress*] (LCLS)
MCIT .... Member of the Chartered Institute of Transport [*British*] (DCTA)
MCIU .... Manipulator Controller Interface Unit (NASA)
MCIU .... Maryland Council for International Understanding (SAUO)
MCIU .... Master Control and Interface Unit [*NASA*] (NASA)
MCIU .... Milano Containers Service [*Intermodal shipping container symbol*] (TVRC)
MCIU .... Mission Control and Interface Unit [*NASA*] (NASA)
M Civil E .... Master of Civil Engineering (PGP)
MCIZ .... Midwest Carbide [*Federal Railroad Administration identification code*]
MCJ .... Maicao [*Colombia*] [*Airport symbol*] (OAG)
MCJ .... Master of Comparative Jurisprudence
MCJ .... Master of Criminal Justice (GAGS)
MCJ .... Memory Control J Bus
MCJ .... Michigan Civil Jurisprudence [*A publication*] (DLA)
MCJ .... Model Car Journal Association [*Publishing company*] (EA)
MCJA .... Master of Criminal Justice Administration (GAGS)
MCJC .... Maryknoll Center for Justice Concerns (EA)
MCJC .... Mason City Junior College [*Iowa*]
MCJR .... Multichannel Jezebel [*Sonobuoy System*] Relay [*Military*] (NG)
MCJZ .... McJunkyard [*Federal Railroad Administration identification code*]
MCK .... Maintenance Check (FAAC)
MCK .... Manson Creek Resources Ltd. [*Vancouver Stock Exchange symbol*]
MCK .... Marital Check-Up Kit [*Test*] (TMMY)
MCK .... Master Cook [*Navy*]
MCK .... McCook [*Nebraska*] [*Airport symbol*] (OAG)
MCK .... McCook, NE [*Location identifier*] [*FAA*] (FAAL)
MCK .... McKesson & Robins, Inc. (SAUO)
MCK .... McKesson Corp. [*Formerly, SP Ventures*] [*NYSE symbol*] (SPSG)
MCK .... McKinley [*Alaska*] [*Seismograph station code, US Geological Survey*] (SEIS)
MCK .... Mechanic [*Telegraphy*] (PCTE)
MCK .... Mission/Communication Keyboard (MCD)
MCK .... Modification Change Kit
MCK .... M-Type Creatine Kinase (DB)
MCK .... Multicystic Kidney [*Medicine*] (DMAA)
MCK .... Muscle Creatine Kinase [*An enzyme*]
MCKA .... John A. McKay [*NCIC trailer make code*]
MCKA .... Metal Cutting Knife Association (EA)
McK Consol Laws... McKinney's Consolidated Laws of New York [*A publication*] (DLA)
MCKD .... Multicystic Kidney Disease [*Medicine*]
MCKEES ..... Marine Corps Key Experiences Evaluation System (MCD)
McKelvey Ev... McKelvey on Evidence [*A publication*] (DLA)
McKesson... McKesson Corp. [*Associated Press*] (SAG)
McKin Jus... McKinney's Justice [*A publication*] (DLA)
McKin Phil Ev... McKinnon's Philosophy of Evidence [*A publication*] (DLA)
MCKPT ...... McKeesport, PA [*American Association of Railroads railroad junction routing code*]
MCKRO ...... McKees Rocks, PA [*American Association of Railroads railroad junction routing code*]
McKS .... McKenzie Sanctuary (SAUO)
MCKT .... Mack Trailer Manufacturing [*NCIC trailer make code*]
MCKT .... McKinlay Transport [*Common carrier symbol*]
McKVHS .... McKee Vocational High School (SAUO)
MCKZ .... McKesson Chemical [*Federal Railroad Administration identification code*]
MCL .... Intervega - Movement for Compassionate Living the Vegan Way (EAIO)
MCL .... Lesley College, Cambridge, MA [*Library symbol*] [*Library of Congress*] (LCLS)
MCL .... Machine Change Levels (SAUS)
MCL .... Maintenance Checkoff List
M-CL .... Managment List - Consolidated (IID)
MCL .... Manchester Central Library (SAUO)
MCL .... Manufacturing Control Language [*Computer science*] (MCD)
MCL .... Manufacturing Cost Level (ACAE)
MCL .... Marine Corps League (EA)
MCL .... Marine Cylinder Lubricant [*Fuels and lubricants*]
MCL .... Mass Change Log (MCD)
MCL .... Master Change Log
MCL .... Master Clear Line (IAA)
MCL .... Master Component List (MCD)
MCL .... Master Configuration List
MCL .... Master Control List
MCL .... Master of Canon Law (PGP)
MCL .... Master of Civil Law
MCL .... Master of Comparative Law
MCL .... Mathematics Computation Laboratory [*General Services Administration*]
MCL .... Mature Corpus Luteum [*Medicine*] (MELL)
MCL .... Mauritius Congress of Labour (SAUO)
MCL .... Maximum Contaminant Level
MCL .... Maximum Contaminant Levels
MCL .... McClellan Central Laboratory (MCD)
M'Cl .... McClelland's English Exchequer Reports [*A publication*] (DLA)
McL .... McLaren Micropublishing, Toronto, ON, Canada [*Library symbol*] [*Library of Congress*] (LCLS)
Mc L .... McLean's United States Circuit Court Reports [*A publication*] (DLA)
MCL .... McNeil River [*Alaska*] [*Seismograph station code, US Geological Survey*] (SEIS)
MCL .... Mechanical [*Telegraphy*] (PCTE)
MCL .... Media Communication Lab (SAUS)
MCL .... Media Communication Laboratory (SAUO)
MCL .... Medial Collateral Ligament [*Anatomy*]
MCL .... Medial Cruciate Ligament [*Anatomy*]
MCL .... Medical Aviation Services Ltd. [*British*] [*ICAO designator*] (FAAC)
MCL .... Medical College of Ohio at Toledo, Toledo, OH [*OCLC symbol*] (OCLC)
MCL .... Memory Control and Logging [*Hewlett-Packard Co.*]
MCL .... Memory Core Loader (VLIE)
MCL .... Mercury Communications Limited (SAUO)
MCL .... Message Control Language [*Computer science*]
MCL .... Metal Control Laboratories (SAUO)
MCL .... Metal Crystal Lattice
MCL .... Metropolitan Central Library (SAUO)
MCL .... Michigan Compiled Laws (AAGC)
MCL .... Micro-Code Language (VLIE)
MCL .... Microcomputer Center and Library [*Wisconsin State Department of Public Instruction*] [*Information service or system*] (IID)
MCL .... Microcomputer Center/Library (SAUO)
MCL .... Microcomputer Language [*Computer science*] (ECII)
MCL .... Microprogram Control Logic [*Computer science*] (MDG)
MCL .... Microsoft Compatibility Laboratories (VLIE)
MCL .... Microwave Cavity Laboratories (SAUO)
MCL .... Microwave Cavity Laboratory (IAA)
MCL .... Mid-Canada Line [*RADAR warning chain of fence across Canada; sometimes called the McGill Fence*]
MCL .... Midclavicular Line [*Medicine*]
MCL .... Midcostal Line [*Medicine*]
MCL .... Mid Course Late (ACAE)
MCL .... Mineral Constitution Laboratories [*Pennsylvania State University*] [*Research center*] (RCD)
MCL .... Miniature Cartridge Light
MCL .... Mini Circuits Laboratory (IAA)
MCL .... Minimal Computer Load
MCL .... Minimum Clear Length (ACAE)
MCL .... Ministering Children's League [*Australia*]
MCL .... Minority Carrier Lifetime [*Solar cell technology*]
MCL .... Missile Continuity Loop (MCD)
MCL .... Mobilization Cross-Leveling (SAUO)
MCL .... Modified Chest Lead [*Medicine*]
MCL .... Molten-Caustic-Leaching [*Coal technology*]
MCL .... Monitor Control Language [*Computer science*] (ELAL)
MCL .... Moore & McCormack Lines, Inc. (SAUO)
MCL .... Moore Corp. Ltd. [*NYSE symbol*] [*Toronto Stock Exchange symbol*] (SPSG)
MCL .... Moore McCormack Resources, Inc. (SAUO)
MCL .... Most Comfortable Level [*Referring to sound level*] [*Otorhinolaryngology*] (DAVI)
MCL .... Most Comfortable Loudness Test [*Audiometry*]
MCL .... Moving Coil Loudspeaker [*Electronics*]
MCL .... Mucocutaneous Leishmaniasis [*Medicine*]

MCL .... Multicolor LASER
MCL .... Multifunctional Composites Laboratory [*University of California, Los Angeles*] (RCD)
MCL .... Mushroom Canners League (EA)
MCLA........ Marine Corps League Auxiliary (EA)
MCLA........ Medical Contact Lens Association [*British*]
MCLA........ Michigan Compiled Laws, Annotated [*A publication*] (DLA)
MCLA........ Microcoded Communications Line Adapter
MCLA........ Micro-Coded Communications Link Adaptor (NITA)
MCLA........ Monetary Centre for Latin America (SAUO)
MCLA........ Motor Carrier Lawyers Association (EA)
MCLAA...... Minnesota Computer Literacy and Awareness Assessment (EDAC)
MCLAMS.... Measurement, Control, LEID [*Limit of Error of the Inventory Difference*], and MUF Inventory Difference Simulation [*Material Unaccounted For*] [*Nuclear energy*] (NRCH)
McL & R.... McLean and Robinson's Scotch Appeal Cases [*1839*] [*A publication*] (DLA)
M'Cl & Y.... McClelland and Younge's English Exchequer Reports [*1824-25*] [*A publication*] (DLA)
M'Cl & Yo... M'Clelland and Younge's English Exchequer Reports [*148 English Reprint*] [*A publication*] (DLA)
McLar Tr.... McLaren's Trusts in Scotland [*A publication*] (DLA)
McLar W.... McLaren's Law of Wills [*Scotland*] [*A publication*] (DLA)
M-CLASS ... Mobile CLASS [*Cross-Chain Long-Range Navigation Atmospheric Sounding System*] (USDC)
MCLB........ Marine Corps Logistics Base (DOMA)
MCLBA...... Marine Corps Logistics Base Albany (SAUO)
MClBiochem... Master of Clinical Biochemistry
MCLC........ Lesley College, Cambridge, MA [*Library symbol*] [*Library of Congress*] (LCLS)
MCLC........ Main Catalog of the Library of Congress (SAUO)
MCLC........ Mine Clearing Line Charge [*Army*]
MCLC........ Modern Chinese Literature and Culture [*Internet resource*]
M Cl D ...... Master of Clinical Dentistry (PGP)
MCLD........ McLeodUSA, Inc. [*NASDAQ symbol*] [*Formerly, McLeod, Inc.*] (SG)
MCLD........ Multicolor LASER Display
MCLE........ Mandatory Continuing Legal Education [*Australia*] [*A publication*]
M'Cle........ M'Clelland's English Exchequer Reports [*148 English Reprint*] [*A publication*] (DLA)
McLean ..... McLean's United States Circuit Court Reports [*A publication*] (DLA)
M'Cle & Yo... M'Clelland and Younge's English Exchequer Reports [*148 English Reprint*] [*A publication*] (DLA)
McLean's CCR... McLean's United States Circuit Court Reports [*A publication*] (DLA)
McLean's Rep... McLean's United States Circuit Court Reports [*A publication*] (DLA)
M'Clel....... M'Clelland's English Exchequer Reports [*148 English Reprint*] [*A publication*] (DLA)
M'Clel & Y... M'Clelland and Younge's English Exchequer Reports [*148 English Reprint*] [*A publication*] (DLA)
M'Clel & Y (Eng)... M'Clelland and Younge's English Exchequer Reports [*148 English Reprint*] [*A publication*] (DLA)
M'Clel (Eng)... McClelland's English Exchequer Reports [*A publication*] (DLA)
MCLFDC .... Marine Corps Landing Force Development Center
MCLG........ Major Caliber Lightweight Gun [*Navy*] (MCD)
MCLG........ Maximum Contaminant Level [*Environment term*] (EGA)
MCLG........ Maximum Contaminant Level Goal [*Environmental Protection Agency*]
MCLI......... Meiklejohn Civil Liberties Institute (EA)
MCLI5........ Manual of Clinical Laboratory Immunology, Fifth Edition (SAUO)
MClinPsych... Master of Clinical Psychology
MClinPsychol... Master of Clinical Psychology (ADA)
MClinSc..... Master of Clinical Science (ADA)
MCLJ........ Mifflin County Legal Journal [*Pennsylvania*] [*A publication*] (DLA)
MCLK........ Master Clock
MCLL........ Metrocall, Inc. [*NASDAQ symbol*] (SAG)
MCLL........ Missile Compartment, Lower Level
MCLL........ Most Comfortable Loudness Level [*On audiometry*] [*Otorhinolaryngology*] (DAVI)
MCLN........ MacLeod Trucking [*Common carrier symbol*]
MCLN........ McLaren Performance Technologies [*OTCBB symbol*]
MCLN........ Mouvement Centrafricain de Liberation Nationale [*Central African Movement for National Liberation*] (PD)
MCLNS...... Mucocutaneous Lymph Node Synrome [*Kawasaki's disease*] (DAVI)
MCLO........ Marine Corps Liaison Office (ACAE)
MCLO........ Medical Construction Liaison Office [*or Officer*] [*Air Force*] (AFM)
MCLOF...... Market Center Limit Order File [*Investment term*] (DICI)
MCLong..... Longfellow House, Longfellow National Historic Site, Cambridge, MA [*Library symbol*] [*Library of Congress*] (LCLS)
MCLORA.... Marine Corps Level of Repair Analysis
MCLOS...... Manual Command-to-Line-of-Sight [*Missile guidance system*] (INF)
MCLOSA.... Member of the Continental Law Office Society of America (SAUO)
MCLP........ Military Committee Representative Liaison Paper to the International Staff [*North Atlantic Council*] (NATG)
MCLR........ Maximum Cell Loss Ratio (SAUS)
MCLR........ McLaughlin Line Railroad [*Federal Railroad Administration identification code*]
MCLR........ Midwest Center for Labor Research (EA)
MCLR........ Minimum Critical Leaching Rate
MCLS........ Maintenance Contractor Logistic Support [*Army*]
MCLS........ Metropolitan Cooperative Library System [*Library network*]
MCLS........ Monroe County Library System [*Library network*]
MCLS........ Mucocutaneous Lymph Node Syndrome [*Medicine*]
MCLSBLANT... Marine Corps Logistic Support Base, Atlantic (MCD)
MCLSBPAC... Marine Corps Logistic Support Base, Pacific (MCD)
MClSc....... Master of Clinical Science (ADA)
MClSci...... Master Clinical Science (DAVI)
MCLT........ Maximum Cruise Level Thrust (MCD)
MCLU........ Maritime Container Leasing [*Intermodal shipping container symbol*] (TVRC)
MCLUB...... Mothers Club (SAUO)
MCLV........ Missile Control & Launch Vehicle (SAUS)
MCLV........ Modified Constant Linear Velocity (ODA)
MCLWG..... Major Caliber Lightweight Gun [*Navy*] (NG)
MCLX........ MacLeod Metals [*Private rail car owner code*]
MCLY........ McCauley Trucking Company [*Common carrier symbol*]
MCM......... Circular Mils, Thousands
MCM......... Controladora Comercial Mexicana SA de CV [*NYSE symbol*] (SAG)
MCM......... Controladora Comer'l Mex GDS [*NYSE symbol*] (SG)
MCM......... Cordi-Marian Missionary Sisters [*Roman Catholic religious order*]
MCM......... Cordi Marian Sisters (TOCD)
MCM......... Heli-Air-Monaco [*ICAO designator*] (FAAC)
MCM......... Mac-Am Resources Corp. [*Vancouver Stock Exchange symbol*]
MCM......... Machine Control Medium (MCD)
MCM......... Machines for Coordinated Multiprocessing
MCM......... Macon, MO [*Location identifier*] [*FAA*] (FAAL)
MCM......... MADS Control Module (SAUS)
MCM......... Magnetic Card Memory [*Computer science*] (IAA)
MCM......... Magnetic Core Memory [*Computer science*]
MCM......... Maintenance Control Manual [*Canadian Airlines International*]
MCM......... Maintenance Control Module [*Telecommunications*] (TEL)
MCM......... Management Control Model (VLIE)
MCM......... Manned Circumlunar Mission
MCM......... Mannes College of Music [*New York, NY*]
MCM......... Manual Communication Module [*Telecommunication device for the deaf*]
MCM......... Manual Computer Makeready (DGA)
MCM......... Manual for Courts-Martial
MCM......... Manual of Clinical Microbiology [*A publication*]
MCM......... Manufacturing Cycle Management (AAEL)
MCM......... Marine Corps Manual
MCM......... Marketing Content Management (GART)
MCM......... Massachusetts Institute of Technology, Cambridge, MA [*Library symbol*] [*Library of Congress*] (LCLS)
MCM......... Mass Casualty Management [*Emergency Management*] (EMA)
MCM......... Mass Control Module
MCM......... Master Control Module
MCM......... Master of Christian Ministry (PGP)
MCM......... Master of Church Management (PGP)
MCM......... Master of Church Music
MCM......... Master of Clinical Microbiology (PGP)
MCM......... Master of Construction Management (PGP)
MCM......... Materiel Change Management
MCM......... McCarthy, Crisanti and Maffei (IID)
MCM......... McCarthy, Crisanti & Maffei, Inc. [*Information service or system*] (IID)
McM......... McMaster University (SAUO)
MCM......... McMurdo Sound [*Antarctica*] [*Seismograph station code, US Geological Survey*] [*Closed*] (SEIS)
MCM......... Mechanical Current Meter [*Marine science*] (OSRA)
MCM......... Media and Communication Management (SAUO)
MCM......... Medical Corps, Merchant Marine [*USNR officer designation*]
MCM......... Mega Cisterna Magna [*Medicine*]
MCM......... Megawatt Cassegrain Monopulse
MCM......... Melt Compression Molding [*Plastics*]
MCM......... Member of the College of Musicians [*British*]
MCM......... Memory Control Module
MCM......... Meningococcal Meningitis [*Medicine*] (MELL)
MCM......... Merged Charge Memory [*Computer science*] (IAA)
MCM......... Message Center Module [*Automotive engineering*]
MCM......... Message Control Module
MCM......... Metastatic Carcinomatous Meningitis [*Medicine*] (MELL)
MCM......... Microchip Module
MCM......... Microcircuit Module
MCM......... Microcomputer Machine (IAA)
McM......... Micromedia Ltd., Toronto, ON, Canada [*Library symbol*] [*Library of Congress*] (LCLS)
MCM......... Microwave Circuit Module [*Computer science*] (IAA)
MCM......... Mid-continent Mapping Center (SAUO)
MCM......... Mid Course Maneuver (ACAE)
MCM......... Military Characteristics Motor Vehicles
MCM......... Military Committee Memoranda (SAUO)
MCM......... Military Committee Memorandum [*NATO*] (NATG)
MCM......... Milli Circular Mil (IAA)
MCM......... Million Centimeters (MCD)
Mcm......... Million cubic metre (SAUS)
MCM......... Mine Countermeasures (NG)
MCM......... Mine Countermeasures Ship (SAUO)
MCM......... Minichromosome Maintenance [*Cytology*]
MCM......... Ministerial Council Meeting (SAUO)
MCM......... Minneapolis College of Music
MCM......... Miscellaneous Contract Material
MCM......... Missile Carrying Missile (AAG)
MCM......... Missile Control Module (NVT)
MCM......... Missile Coordination Meeting (SAUO)
MCM......... Mission Communications Manager (SSD)
MCM......... Mission Control Module
MCM......... Mississippi College, Clinton, MS [*OCLC symbol*] (OCLC)
MCM......... Mitsubishi Common Modules (SAUS)
MCM......... Mobile Cinetheodolite Mounts (SAA)
MCM......... Mode Control Message (MCD)

MCM......... Modular Auxiliary Data System Control Module [*Aerospace*] (NAKS)
MCM......... Monolithic Circuit Mask
MCM......... Monte Carlo [*Monaco*] [*Airport symbol*] (OAG)
MCM......... Monte Carlo Method [*Computer science*]
MCM......... Moving Coil Microphone [*Electronics*]
MCM......... Moving Coil Motor [*Electronics*] (IAA)
MCM......... Multi-Channel Multiplex (VLIE)
MCM......... Multichipmodul (SAUO)
MCM......... Multichip Module [*Computer science*]
MCM......... Multi-Command Manual (SAUS)
MCM......... Multilayer Ceramic Multichip [*Electronics*]
MCM......... Multinational Computer Models, Inc. [*Information service or system*] (IID)
MCM......... Multiple Connected Motor
MCM......... Multiple Constant Multiplication (VLIE)
MCM......... Multiple Contact Miscible [*Physical chemistry*]
MCM......... Multiply-Convolve-Multiply (SAUS)
MCM......... Multistage Conventional Munition (ODA)
MCM......... Municipal Court of Montreal (DLA)
MCM......... Thousand Circular Mils
MCM6........ Manual of Clinical Microbiology, 6th Edition (SAUO)
MCMA........ Machine Chain Manufacturers Association (EA)
MCMA........ Marine Corps Mustang Association (EA)
MCMA........ Metal Cookware Manufacturers Association [*Later, CMA*] (EA)
MCMA........ Mexico City Metropolitan Area (SAUO)
MCMAI....... Milton Clinical Multi-Axial Inventory [*Psychology*] (DAVI)
MC Mask... Mary Caterall Mask [*For oxygen administration*] [*Medicine*] (EDAA)
McMas RR... McMaster's New York Railroad Laws [*A publication*] (DLA)
MCMB........ Multiple Conductor, Marker Buoy (IAA)
MCMC........ Marine Corps Memorial Commission
MCMC........ Markov Chain Monte Carlo (IDAI)
MCMC........ Markov Chain Monte Carlo Method
MCM-C....... MCM-Ceramic (SAUS)
MCMC........ MCM Corp. [*NASDAQ symbol*] (NQ)
MCMC........ Medicine Cabinet Manufacturers Council (EA)
MCMC........ Midwest Committee for Military Counseling (EA)
MCMC........ Military Construction, Marine Corps (DNAB)
MCMCAT.... Mine Countermeasures Catamaran [*Military*]
MCMCC..... Marine Corps Manpower Control Center (SAUO)
MCMCC..... Marine Corps Movement Coordination Center (DNAB)
MCMCC..... Mid-Century Mercury Car Club (EA)
McM Com Cas... McMaster's United States Commercial Cases [*A publication*] (DLA)
McM Com Dec... McMaster's Commercial Decisions [*A publication*] (DLA)
MCM Cp.... MCM Corp. [*Associated Press*] (SAG)
MCM/CS.... Mine Countermeasures/Command and Support Ship (MILB)
MCM-D...... MCM-Dielectric (SAUS)
McMdL...... Micromedia Ltd., Toronto, ON, Canada [*Library symbol*] [*Library of Congress*] (LCLS)
MCMES..... Member of the Civil and Mechanical Engineering Society
MCMF........ Marie Curie Memorial Foundation (SAUO)
MCM-F...... Massachusetts Institute of Technology, University Film Study Center, Cambridge, MA [*Library symbol*] [*Library of Congress*] (LCLS)
MCMF........ Motor City Music Foundation
MCMFA...... Meeting of Consultation of Ministers of Foreign Affairs
MCMFE...... Membrane-Covered Mercury Film Electrode [*Electrochemistry*]
MCMG........ Man-Carrying Motion Generator [*Space-flight simulation*]
MCMG........ Marine Corps Meteorological Group (COE)
MCMG........ Military Committee Meteorological Group [*NATO*] (NATG)
MCM-H...... Massachusetts Institute of Technology, Francis Russell Hart Nautical Museum, Cambridge, MA [*Library symbol*] [*Library of Congress*] (LCLS)
MCMH........ Mine Counter-Measures Hovercraft [*Military*] (PDAA)
MCMHA..... Metropolitan College Mental Health Association (EA)
MCMHC..... Mine Countermeasures Helicopter Controller (MCD)
MCMI......... Malleable Chain Manufacturers Institute [*Later, American Chain Association*]
MCMI......... Millon Clinical Multiaxial Inventory [*Psychology*]
MCMI......... Minneapolis Center for Microbiological Investigations [*Public Health Service*] (GRD)
MCMI-III.... Millon Clinical Multiaxial Inventory-III (DIPS)
MCMIS...... Motor Carrier Management Information System [*BTS*] [*MM*] (TAG)
MCM-L...... Massachusetts Institute of Technology, Lincoln Laboratory, Lexington, MA [*Library symbol*] [*Library of Congress*] (LCLS)
MCML........ Mathematical-Computational Modeling Laboratory [*University of Virginia*] (RCD)
MCML........ Missile Compartment, Middle Level
MCMLA..... Midcontinental Chapter of the Medical Library Association (SAUO)
MCMM...... Management Control - Material Management (IEEE)
MCMOPS... Mine Countermeasures Operations [*Military*] (NVT)
McMoRn.... McMoRan Oil and Gas Co. [*Associated Press*] (SAG)
MCMOS..... Motorola Complementary Metal-Oxide Semi-Conductor [*Electronics*] (IAA)
MCMOV..... Maize Chlorotic Mottle Virus [*Plant pathology*]
MCMP........ Marina Cartage Company [*Common carrier symbol*]
MCM-P...... MCM-Plastic (SAUS)
MCMP........ Middle Constrictor Muscle of Pharynx [*Medicine*] (MELL)
MCMP........ Multi-Channel Multi-Port [*Telecommunications*]
MCMQ........ McCauley Moving and Storage of Fayetteville [*Common carrier symbol*]
MCMR........ Medical Corps, Merchant Marine, General Service [*USNR officer designation*]
MC/MR...... Minimum Change/Minimum Risk [*Mask design concept*] [*Army*] (INF)
MCMS........ Marin County Medical Society (SAUO)
MCMS........ Medical Corps, Merchant Marine, Special Service [*USNR officer designation*]
MCMS........ Midwest Center for Mass Spectrometry [*University of Nebraska - Lincoln*] [*Research center*] (RCD)
M-CM-S..... Mobility, Countermobility, and Survivability
MCMS........ Multichannel Memory System [*Computer science*] (AAG)
MCMS........ Multiple Countermeasure System
MCMS........ Multnomah County Medical Society [*Medicine*] (EDAA)
MCMST..... Montana College of Mineral Science and Technology (SAUO)
MCMTA...... MCM Tasking Authority (SAUS)
MCMU........ Management Control and Maintenance [*Intermodal shipping container symbol*] (TVRC)
MCMU........ Mass Core Memory Unit (MCD)
McMU........ McMaster University (SAUO)
McMUL....... McMaster University Library (SAUO)
McMul....... McMullan's South Carolina Law Reports [*A publication*] (DLA)
McMul Eq... McMullan's South Carolina Equity Reports [*A publication*] (DLA)
McMull Eq (SC)... McMullan's South Carolina Equity Reports [*A publication*] (DLA)
McMull L (SC)... McMullan's South Carolina Law Reports [*A publication*] (DLA)
McMUMC... McMaster University Medical Center (SAUO)
MCMUS..... Manual of Courts-Martial, United States
MCMV........ Maize Chlorotic Mottle Virus [*Plant pathology*]
MCMV........ Mine Countermeasures Vessel [*or Vehicle*] (NATG)
MCMV........ Mine Counter-Measure Vessel
MCMV........ Murine Cytomegalovirus
MCMWTC... Marine Corps Mountain Warfare Training Center [*Bridgeport, CA*]
MCMZ........ McLaughlin Metals [*Federal Railroad Administration identification code*]
MCN......... American Journal of Maternal/Child Health Nursing (SAUS)
MCN......... American Journal of Maternal/Child Nursing (SAUO)
MCN......... Mac Dan Aviation Corp. [*ICAO designator*] (FAAC)
MCN......... MACIMS Communication Network (SAUO)
MCN......... Macon [*Georgia*] [*Airport symbol*] (OAG)
MCN......... Macon, GA [*Amtrak Busline code*]
MCN......... Maintenance Communications Net (MCD)
MCN......... Maintenance Control Number
MCN......... Malignant Cystic Neoplasm [*Medicine*] (MELL)
MCN......... Management Change Notice (MCD)
MCN......... Management Control Number [*Army*] (AABC)
MCN......... Manual Control Number
MCN......... Manufacturing Change Notice
MCN......... Manufacturing Control Number
MCN......... Mapping Cylinder Neighborhood
MCN......... Masana [*Language symbol*] (ETLW)
MCN......... Master Change Notice (KSC)
MCN......... Master Control Number
MCN......... Master of Clinical Nutrition
MCN......... Material Change Notice (MCD)
MCN......... Material Complaint Notice
MCN......... MCN Corp. [*Formerly, Michigan Consolidated Gas Co.*] [*Associated Press*] (SAG)
McN......... McNeil Laboratories, Inc. [*Research code symbol*]
MCN......... McNeil Mantha, Inc. [*Toronto Stock Exchange symbol*]
MCN......... MCN Financing [*NYSE symbol*] (SAG)
MCN......... MCN Michigan LP [*NYSE symbol*] (SAG)
MCN......... Mechanician [*Telegraphy*] (PCTE)
MCN......... Mercury [*Nevada*] [*Seismograph station code, US Geological Survey*] [*Closed*] (SEIS)
MCN......... Metropolitan Campus Network (SAUO)
MCN......... MichCon (EFIS)
MCN......... Micro Cellular Network [*Computer science*]
MCN......... Micrococcal Nuclease [*Also, MN*] [*An enzyme*]
MCN......... Midcourse Navigation [*Navy*] (IAA)
MCN......... Military Construction, Navy
MCN......... Minimal Change Nephropathy [*Medicine*] (DMAA)
MCN......... Missing Children Network [*Defunct*] (EA)
MC-N........ Mixed Cell Nodular [*Lymphoma*] [*Medicine*] (STED)
MCN......... Molecular and Cellular Neuroscience [*A publication*]
MCN......... Mouvement Congolais National [*Zaire*] [*Political party*] (EY)
MCN......... Movimiento de Conciliacion Nacional [*National Conciliation Movement*] [*Dominican Republic*] [*Political party*] (PPW)
MCN......... Musculocutaneous Nerve [*Medicine*] (MELL)
MCN......... Museum Computer Network (NITA)
MCN......... Museum Computer Network, Inc. [*American Association of Museums*] [*Research center*] (RCD)
MCNA....... McNamee Coach Corporation [*NCIC trailer make code*]
MCNA....... The Medical Clinics of North America [*Journal*] [*Medicine*] (EDAA)
McNagh..... Macnaghten's Select Cases in Chancery Tempore King [*A publication*] (DLA)
McNal Ev... Macnally's Rules of Evidence [*A publication*] (DLA)
MCNC....... Carberry/North Cypress Library, Carberry, Manitoba [*Library symbol*] [*National Library of Canada*] (NLC)
MCNC....... Microcomputer Numerical Control (IAA)
MCNC....... Microelectronics Center of North Carolina [*Research center*] (RCD)
MCNC....... Micromachining Center of North Carolina (SAUO)
MCNE....... Master Certified Netware Engineer (SAUO)
MCNE....... Master Certified Novell Engineer (SAUO)
McNeese St U... McNeese State University (GAGS)
MCNEI....... McNeil, AR [*American Association of Railroads railroad junction routing code*]
MCN F....... MCN Financing [*Associated Press*] (SAG)
MCNG....... Military Construction, National Guard
McN-JR..... McNeil Laboratories, Inc. [*Research code symbol*]
McN-JR 3345... Dipiperon [*Tranquilizing drug*] [*Medicine*] (EDAA)

McN-JR 8299... Tetramisole Hydrochloride [*Medicine*] (EDAA)
MCNL........ Military Committee of National Liberation [*Mali*] [*Political party*] (PPW)
MCNLL...... McNeil, TX [*American Association of Railroads railroad junction routing code*]
MCNM....... MCN Mobile Homes [*NCIC trailer make code*]
MCNMI...... MCN Michigan Ltd. [*Associated Press*] (SAG)
MCNP....... Mammoth Cave National Park (SAUO)
MCNP....... Massachusetts Coalition of Nurse Practitioners (SAUO)
MCNP....... Mobile Network Computing Protocol (AEBE)
MCNP....... Monitoring Completed Navigation Projects [*Army*]
MCNP....... Mount Cook National Park (SAUO)
MCNPB...... Marine Corps - Navy Publicity Bureau (SAA)
MCNPrT..... MCN Mich L.P.9.375% Pfd [*NYSE symbol*] (TTSB)
MCNR....... Military Construction, Naval Reserves
MCNRF...... Military Construction, Naval Reserve Facilities
MCNRS...... Meal Card Number Recording System (MCD)
MCNS....... Mediconsult.com, Inc. [*NASDAQ symbol*] (NASQ)
MCNS....... Member, Congress of Neurological Surgeons (CMD)
MCNS....... Minimal Change Nephrotic Syndrome [*Medicine*] (DMAA)
MCNS....... Multimedia Cable Networking Systems (AEBE)
MCNY....... Museum of the City of New York
MCNZ........ Medical Council of New Zealand (SAUO)
MCO......... Aerolineas Marcos SA de CV [*Mexico*] [*ICAO designator*] (FAAC)
MCo......... Concord Free Public Library, Concord, MA [*Library symbol*] [*Library of Congress*] (LCLS)
MCO......... Magnetron Cutoff
MCO......... Main Civilian Occupation
MCO......... Maintenance Checkoff
MCO......... Manged Care Organization
MCO......... Manual Change Order (MSA)
MCO......... Marine Corps Officer
MCO......... Marine Corps Order
MCO......... Mars Climate Orbiter [*NASA*]
MCO......... Massachusetts College of Optometry
M Co........ Master of Cosmology
MCO......... Materials Characterization Organization (SAUO)
MCO......... MCO Holdings, Inc. [*AMEX symbol*] (COMM)
MCO......... Medical Care Organization (STED)
MCO......... Medicare Carve-Out [*Insurance*] (WYGK)
MCO......... Merrill Lyn 6.00%'STRYPES' [*NYSE symbol*] (TTSB)
MCO......... Merrill Lynch & Co. [*NYSE symbol*] (SAG)
MCO......... Metal Catalyzed Oxidation [*Chemistry*]
MCO......... Methodist Conference Office (SAUO)
MCO......... Michigan Corrections Organization (SAUO)
MCO......... Military City Online [*Computer program*]
MCO......... Military Control Office [*Indian Railway*] (TIR)
MCO......... Mill Culls Out [*Lumber*]
MCO......... Mill Cuts Out [*Forest industry*] (WPI)
MCO......... Minneapolis Community College, Minneapolis, MN [*OCLC symbol*] (OCLC)
MCO......... Miscellaneous Charges Order [*Business term*]
MCO......... Missile Checkout (NG)
MCO......... Missile Control Officer
MCO......... Mission Control Operation [*NASA*]
mco......... Mission Control Operations [*NASA*] (NAKS)
MCO......... Monaco [*ANSI three-letter standard code*] (CNC)
MCO......... Moody's [*Company symbol*]
MCO......... Moody's Investors Service [*NYSE symbol*]
MCO......... Morocco Leather [*Bookbinding*] (DGA)
MCO......... Movement Control Officer [*Army*]
MCO......... Multi Column Option (DGA)
MCO......... Multicystic Ovary [*Medicine*] (MELL)
MCO......... Multiple Channel Oscilloscope
MCO......... Orlando, FL [*Location identifier*] [*FAA*] (FAAL)
MCO......... Orlando [*Florida*] International [*Airport symbol*] (OAG)
MCOA....... Mastiff Club of America (EA)
MCOA....... Music Center Opera Association [*Los Angeles*]
MCOAG...... Marine Corps Operations Analysis Group
MCOAM..... Material Control Order Additional Material
MCOA/P.... Multi-Company Accounts Payable (MHDB)
MCOD....... Multiple Cause of Death [*Highway safety*]
MCODA..... Motor Cab Owner Drivers' Association [*British*] (BI)
M-COFT..... Mobile Conduct of Fire Trainer [*Combat simulator*]
MCOG....... Member of the British College of Obstetricians and Gynaecologists (DAS)
MCOGA...... Mid-Continent Oil and Gas Association (EA)
MCogSc..... Master of Cognitive Science
MCOHM..... Military Community Oral Health Managers [*Army*]
MCOI........ Minority Centers of Influence (DNAB)
MCOL........ Manner of Collision [*National Highway Traffic Safety Administration Fatal Accident Recording System code*]
MCOL........ McCollough Corporation [*NCIC trailer make code*]
MCOLF...... Marine Corps Outlying Landing Field
MCollH..... Member of the College of Handcrafts (SAUO)
MCollP..... Member of the College of Preceptors [*British*] (DBQ)
MCOM....... Marketing Communications (SAUO)
M Com...... Master of Commerce
MCOM....... Mathematics of Computation (IEEE)
MCOM....... McCombs Freight Line [*Common carrier symbol*]
MCOM....... Metricom, Inc. [*NASDAQ symbol*] (SAG)
MCOM....... Michigan College of Osteopathic Medicine [*Medicine*] (EDAA)
MCom....... Minister of Commerce (SAUO)
MCOM....... Missile Command [*Army*] (MCD)
MCOM....... Mobility Command (SAUO)
M Com Adm......... Master of Commercial Administration
MComm..... Master of Commerce (ADA)
M Comm.... Master of Commerce and Administration (ROG)
MCOMM.... Minimize Communications
MComm..... Minister of Commerce (SAUO)
M Comm A... Master of Commerce and Administration (SAUO)
m-command... Maximal Command [*Linguistics*] (IEL)
m-commerce... Mobile Commerce [*E-commerce*] (NETL)
M Comm H... Master of Community Health
MCommSc... Master in Commercial Science (DD)
MCommun... Master in Communication (DD)
M Comp..... Master of Computing
M Comp E... Master of Computer Engineering (PGP)
M Comp L... Master of Comparative Law
MCompLaw... Master of Comparative Law (NADA)
MCOMQ..... Metricom [*OTCBB symbol*]
M Com Sc... Master of Commercial Science
MComSc.... Master of Computer Science
MCON....... EMCON [*NASDAQ symbol*] (TTSB)
MCON....... EMCON Associates [*NASDAQ symbol*] (NQ)
MCON....... Military Construction
MCON....... Military Construction-Navy (SAUO)
MCON....... Moment Connections [*Computer Services Consultants Ltd.*] [*Software package*] (NCC)
MConsE..... Member of the Association of Consulting Engineers [*British*] (EY)
MCOO....... Monte Carlo Opera Orchestra (SAUO)
MCOP....... Major Command Orientation Program [*Air Force*] (AFM)
MCOP....... Managed Care Outcomes Project [*Medicine*] (EDAA)
MCOP....... Marine Corps Ordnance Publication
mCOP....... Measured Colloidal Osmotic Pressure [*Clinical chemistry*]
MCOP....... Mission Control Operations Panel [*NASA*] (KSC)
MCOP....... Multiple Conductor, Oil-Resistant, Portable [*Cable*]
MCOphth.... Member of the College of Ophthalmologists (SAUO)
MCOPR...... Major Command of Primary Responsibility [*Air Force*] (AFM)
MCOPS...... Millions of Complex Operations Per Second (SAUS)
MCOQ....... Multiple Choice Objective Question (DA)
MCOR....... Marine Corp. (EFIS)
MCOR....... Methodist Committee for Overseas Relief [*Later, UMCOR*] (EA)
MC/ORB..... Maritime Command Operational Research Branch [*Canada*]
MC/ORD..... Maritime Command Operational Research Division [*Canada*]
MC/ORD..... Military Command Operational Research Division (SAUO)
M'Cord Eq (SC)... M'Cord's South Carolina Equity Reports [*A publication*] (DLA)
M'Cord L (SC)... M'Cord's South Carolina Law Reports [*A publication*] (DLA)
MCOS....... Microprogrammable Computer Operating System
MCoS........ Military College of Science [*British military*] (DMA)
MCOS....... Mission Control Operations Section (SAUO)
MCot........ Cotuit Library, Cotuit, MA [*Library symbol*] [*Library of Congress*] (LCLS)
MCOT........ Matco Transportation [*Common carrier symbol*]
MCOT........ Missile Checkout Trailer
MCOT........ Missile Control Officer, Trainer (NG)
MCOTEA.... Marine Corps Operational Test and Evaluation Activity (CAAL)
MCOTT...... Mobile Outreach Teams (MHID)
MCOU....... Montcocol [*Intermodal shipping container symbol*] (TVRC)
mcoul....... Millicoulomb (STED)
Mcoul....... Millicoulomb
M Coun..... Master of Counseling (PGP)
MCouns(Ed)... Master of Counselling (Education) (ADA)
MCOV....... Main Chamber Oxidizer Valve [*NASA*] (KSC)
MCOV....... Modified Covariance (DMAA)
MCOW....... Medical College of Wisconsin
MCoW....... Wayside [*Minute Man National Historical Park*], Concord, MA [*Library symbol*] [*Library of Congress*] (LCLS)
MCOwi...... Moody's Corp. [*NYSE symbol*]
MCOY....... McCoy-Taylor [*NCIC trailer make code*]
MCOY....... Military Citizen of the Year (DNAB)
MCP......... Bear Stearns Companies, Inc. [*AMEX symbol*] (SAG)
MCP......... Bear Sterns 5.50%MRK'CHIPS' [*AMEX symbol*] (TTSB)
MCP......... Macapa [*Brazil*] [*Airport symbol*] (OAG)
MCP......... Macrophage-Capping Protein [*Biochemistry*]
MCP......... Main Call Process [*Telecommunications*] (TEL)
MCP......... Main Condensate Pump [*Navy*] (CAAL)
MCP......... Main Coolant Pump (NVT)
MCP......... Maintenance Control Panel [*Navy*] (CAAL)
MCP......... Maintenance Control Point (NG)
MCP......... Malawi Congress Party [*Nyasaland*] [*Political party*] (PPW)
MCP......... Malayan Communist Party [*Political party*]
MCP......... Malaysian Communist Party (SAUO)
MCP......... Male Chauvinist Pig [*Feminist term*]
MCP......... Managed Care Program (MELL)
MCP......... Management and Control of Provisioning (SAUO)
MCP......... Management Control Plan
MCP......... Manhattan Cyber Project [*Emergency Management*] (EMA)
MCP......... Manual Control Panel
MCP......... Manufacturing Change Point
MCP......... Marcana Petroleum Ltd. [*Vancouver Stock Exchange symbol*]
MCP......... Marine Corps Capabilities Plan (MCD)
MCP......... Maritime Company of Philadelphia (SAUO)
MCP......... Maritime Company of the Philippines (SAUO)
MCP......... Martinique Communist Party [*Political party*]
MCP......... Mary Cheney Library, Manchester, CT [*OCLC symbol*] (OCLC)
MCP......... Massachusetts College of Pharmacy [*Boston*]

MCP .... Master Change Proposal (KSC)
MCP .... Master Computer Program [*NASA*] (KSC)
MCP .... Master COMSEC Plan (SAUO)
MCP .... Master Control Program [*Burroughs Corp.*]
M Cp .... Master of Chiropody
MCP .... Master of City Planning
MCP .... Master of Community Planning (GAGS)
MCP .... Master of Community Psychology (PGP)
MCP .... Master of Counseling Psychology (GAGS)
MCP .... Materials Control Plan (NASA)
MCP .... Materiel Command Procedure [*Military*]
MCP .... Maximal Closure Pressure (STED)
MCP .... Maximal Coverage Problem [*Mathematical modelling*]
MCP .... Maximum Continuous Power
MCP .... Maximum Contraction Pattern [*Medicine*] (EDAA)
MCP .... Mayo Clinic Proceedings [*Medicine*] (EDAA)
MCP .... Measure and Control Panel (ACAE)
MCP .... Measurements Control Procedure (KSC)
MCP .... Medical Care Program [*Medicine*] (EDAA)
MCP .... Medical College of Pennsylvania
MCP .... Medical Continuation Pay [*Military*] (AABC)
MCP .... MEECN [*Minimum Essential Emergency Communications Network*] Communication Plan (MCD)
MCP .... Melanosis Circumscripta Precancerosa (STED)
MCP .... Melphalan, Cyclophosphamide, Prednisone [*Antineoplastic drug regimen*]
MCP .... Member of the College of Preceptors [*British*]
MCP .... Member of the Colonial Parliament [*British*]
MCP .... Membrane Cofactor Protein [*Biochemistry*]
MCP .... Memory-Centered Processing [*or Processor*] [*System*] [*Computer science*]
MCP .... Message Control Program [*Computer science*]
MCP .... Metacarpal (STED)
MCP .... Metacarpophalangeal [*Anatomy*]
MCP .... Metaclopramide (STED)
MCP .... Meta-Cresol Purple [*Organic chemistry*]
MCP .... Metal Case Profile [*Ammunition*]
MCP .... Metal Casting Pattern (MSA)
MCP .... Meteacarpophalangeal [*Joint*] [*Anatomy*] (DAVI)
MCP .... Meteorological Communications Package (EOSA)
MCP .... Methyl-Accepting Chemotaxis Proteins [*Biochemistry*]
MCP .... Methylchlorophenoxyacetic Acid [*Also, MCPA*] [*Herbicide*]
MCP .... Methylcyclopentane [*Organic chemistry*]
MCP .... Metropolitan and City Police (SAUO)
MCP .... Microchannel Plate [*Computer science*]
MCP .... Microcrystalline Polymer [*Plastics technology*]
McP .... Micro Photo Division, Bell & Howell Co., Wooster, OH [*Library symbol*] [*Library of Congress*] (LCLS)
MCP .... Microsoft Certified Professional (SAUO)
MCP .... Microwave Coupled Plasma [*Spectroscopy*]
MCP .... Midclavicular Plane [*Medicine*] (MELL)
MCP .... Military Construction Plan
MCP .... Military Construction Program (AFIT)
MCP .... Military Construction Project (SAUO)
MCP .... Militia Career Program [*DoD*]
MCP .... Minimum Convex Polygon
MCP .... Missile Control Panel
MCP .... Missile Control Point (NATG)
MCP .... Mission Concept Paper (MCD)
MCP .... Mission Control Processor (ACAE)
MCP .... Mission Control Programmer [*NASA*] (NAKS)
MCP .... Missioneras Catequestas de los Pobres (TOCD)
MCP .... Mitotic-Control Protein [*Cytology*] (MAE)
MCP .... Moca [*Puerto Rico*] [*Seismograph station code, US Geological Survey*] (SEIS)
MCP .... Mode Control Panel
MCP .... Model Cities Program
MCP .... Modified Citrus Pectin
MCP .... Monitoring and Control Panel (NASA)
MCP .... Monitoring Control Panel (SAUS)
MCP .... Monocalcium Phosphate [*Inorganic chemistry*] [*Food additive*]
MCP .... Monocyte Chemotactic Protein [*Biochemistry*]
MCP .... Monte Capellino [*Italy*] [*Later, ROB*] [*Geomagnetic observatory code*]
MCP .... Morganite Consumer Products (EFIS)
MCP .... Mouvement Chretien pour la Paix [*Christian Movement for Peace - CMP*] [*Brussels, Belgium*] (EAIO)
MCP .... Movimiento Civico Popular [*Panama*] [*Political party*] (EY)
MCP .... Mucin Clot-Prevention [*Test*] [*Medicine*] (STED)
MCP .... Mullet-Channel Plate [*Spectrometry*]
MCP .... Multibeam Communication Package (SAUS)
MCP .... Multicatalytic Proteinase [*An enzyme*]
MCP .... Multichannel Communications Program (IEEE)
MCP .... Multichip Package (AAEL)
MCP .... Multicomponent Plasma
MCP .... Multi-Location Calling Plan [*Communications term*] (DCT)
MCP .... Multiple-Chip Package
MCP .... Multiple Comparison Procedure [*Statistics*]
MCP .... Multiple Control Program [*Computer science*]
MCP .... Municipal Compliance Plan [*Environmental Protection Agency*] (GFGA)
MCP .... Mutation as Cellular Process
MCP .... Polaroid Corp., Cambridge, MA [*Library symbol*] [*Library of Congress*] (LCLS)
MCP-1 .... Monocyte Chemoattractant Protein-1 [*Medicine*] (PALA)
MCPA .... Manatee County Port Authority [*Federal Railroad Administration identification code*]
MCPA .... Mansfield Center for Pacific Affairs (RCD)
MCPA .... Member of the Canadian Psychological Association
MCPA .... Member of the College of Pathologists Australasia
MCPA .... Member of the College of Pathologists of Australia (SAUO)
MCPA .... Memory Clock Pulse Amplifier
MCPA .... Methylchlorophenoxyacetic Acid [*Also, MCP*] [*Herbicide*]
MCPA .... Methylenecyclopropylacetic Acid [*Organic chemistry*]
MCPA .... Michigan Concrete Paving Association (SAUO)
McPA .... Microfilm Corp. of Pennsylvania, Pittsburgh, PA [*Library symbol*] [*Library of Congress*] (LCLS)
MCPA .... Midwest College Placement Association
MCPA .... Mine Clearance Planning Agency (SAUO)
MCPAC .... Military Construction Programs Advisory Committee (AFM)
MCP/AS ...... Master Control Program / Advanced System (HGAA)
MC Path ..... Member of the College of Pathologists [*British*]
MCPBA .... Meta-Chloroperoxybenzoic Acid [*Organic chemistry*]
MCPC .... Central African People's Liberation Movement [*Political party*] (PSAP)
MCPC .... Manipulator Controller Power Conditioner (MCD)
MCPC .... Multiple Channel per Carrier (ACAE)
MCPC .... Musee Canadien de la Photographie Contemporaine [*Canadian Museum of Contemporary Photography - CMCP*]
MCPC .... Parks Canada [*Parcs Canada*] Churchill, Manitoba [*Library symbol*] [*National Library of Canada*] (NLC)
MCPC .... Polaroid Corp. Library, Cambridge, MA [*Library symbol*] [*Library of Congress*] (LCLS)
MCPD .... Marine Corps Procurement District
MCPDM .... Marine Corps Program Decision Meeting (DOMA)
MCPDP .... Meander Channels Plasma Display Panel (IAA)
MCPE .... Modular Collective Protection Equipment (RDA)
MCPER .... Multiple Critical-Pole Equal-Ripple Rational (MCD)
MCPESCF ..... Multiconfiguration Paired Excitation Self-Consistent Field [*Physics*]
MCPF .... Modular Containerless Processing Facility (SSD)
MCPF .... Multichannel Peak Factor (IAA)
MCPG .... Media Conversion Program Generator
MCPG .... Methycarboxyphenglycine [*Biochemistry*]
MCPH .... Metacarpophalangeal [*Anatomy*]
MCPH .... Ministry of Concern for Public Health (EA)
MCPHE .... McPherson, KS [*American Association of Railroads railroad junction routing code*]
McPherson ... McPherson, Lee, and Bell's Scotch Session Cases [*A publication*] (DLA)
MCPI .... Materiel Command Procurement Inspection (SAUO)
MCPI .... Medical Consumer Price Index (DHSM)
MCPJ .... Metacarpal Phalangeal [*Medicine*] (STED)
MCPL .... Magnetic Circularly Polarized Luminescence [*Spectroscopy*]
MCPL .... Mandatory Components Parts List (ACAE)
MCPL .... Members of Congress for Peace through Law [*An association*]
MCPL .... Middle Country Public Library [*New York*]
MCPL .... Multiple-Cue Probability Learning [*Psychology*]
MCPM .... Marine Corps Personnel Manual (SAA)
MCPM .... Member of the Confederation of Professional Management [*British*] (DBQ)
MCPM .... Moncalcium Phosphate Monohydrate [*Inorganic chemistry*]
MCPN .... Metro Community Provider Network (MHID)
MCPO .... Master Chief Petty Officer [*Navy*]
MCPO .... Military Committee Representative Communication to the Private Office of the NATO Secretary General (NATG)
MCPOC .... Master Chief Petty Officer of Command [*Navy*]
MCPOF .... Master Chief Petty Officer of the Fleet [*or Force*] (DNAB)
MCPOF .... Metropolitan and City Police Orphan Fund (SAUO)
MCPON .... Master Chief Petty Officer of the Navy
mCPP .... M-Chlorophenylpiperazine [*Organic chemistry*]
MCPP .... Mecoprop [*Herbicide*]
MCPPR .... Marine Corps Program Progress Report
MCPQ .... Municipal Code of the Province of Quebec [*A publication*] (DLA)
MCPR .... Maximum Critical Power Ratio [*Nuclear energy*] (NRCH)
MCPR .... Minimum Critical Power Ratio [*Nuclear energy*] (NRCH)
MC/PRI ...... Major Claimant/Priority Rating Indicator (MCD)
MCPS .... Major Cost Proposal System (MCD)
MCPS .... Mechanical Copyright Protection Society [*British*]
MCPS .... Megachips per Second (MCD)
mcps .... Megacycles per Second (STED)
MCPS .... Megacycles per Second [*Megahertz*] [*See also MC/S, MCS, MH, MHz*]
MCPS .... Member of the Cambridge Philosophical Society (ROG)
MCPS .... Member of the College of Physicians and Surgeons [*British*]
MCPS .... Microsoft Certified Product Specialist (SAUO)
MCPS .... Military Committee in Permanent Session [*NATO*] (NATG)
MCPS .... Mini Core Processing Subsystem (TEL)
MCPS .... Missouri Children's Picture Series [*Child development test*] [*Psychology*]
MCPS .... Montgomery County Public Schools [*Maryland*]
MCPT .... Maritime Central Planning Team [*NATO*] (NATG)
MCPT .... Maryland Congress of Parents and Teachers (EARSL)
MCPTM .... Monte Carlo Particle Trajectory Model [*Physics*]
MCPU .... Master Controller Processor Unit (MCD)
MCPU .... Militzer and Munch [*Intermodal shipping container symbol*] (TVRC)
MCPU .... Mine Clearance and Policy Unit (SAUO)
MCPU .... Multiple Central Processing Unit
MCPX .... Solutia [*Private rail car owner code*]
MCPZ .... Minnesota Corn Processors [*Federal Railroad Administration identification code*]

MCQ .... Macquarie Island [*Australia*] [*Seismograph station code, US Geological Survey*] (SEIS)
Mcq .... Macqueen's Scotch Appeal Cases, House of Lords [*A publication*] (DLA)
MCQ .... Memory Call Queue [*Computer science*] (IAA)
MCQ .... Multiple Choice Questions (ADA)
MCQC .... Musicassette Quality Committee (NTCM)
MCQF .... WC McQuaide [*Common carrier symbol*]
MCQP .... Milk Carton Quality Performing Council (EA)
MCQS .... Member of the Chapter of Quantity Surveyors of the South African Institute of Architects (SAUO)
MCQU .... McQuerry-Tan [*NCIC trailer make code*]
McQuillin Mun Corp ... McQuillin on Municipal Corporations [*A publication*] (DLA)
MCQV .... McQuerry Trailer [*NCIC trailer make code*]
MCR .... Magistrates' Court Reports [*New Zealand*] [*A publication*] (DLA)
MCR .... Magnetic Card Reader [*Computer science*]
MCR .... Magnetic Character Reader [*Computer science*] (IEEE)
MCR .... Magnetic Character Recognition [*Computer science*] (BUR)
MCR .... Magnetic Confinement Reactor
MCR .... Main Control Room (IEEE)
MCR .... Maintenance Control Report
MCR .... Management Coaching Relations Test
MCR .... Management Consulting & Research Inc. (SAUO)
MCR .... Management Control Review (AAGC)
MCR .... Manpower Change Request (SAUO)
MCR .... Manpower Control Report
MCR .... Manual Change Request (MSA)
MCR .... Manufacturing Change Request
MCR .... Marine Corps Representative (SAA)
MCR .... Marine Corps Reserve
MCR .... Maryport & Carlisle Railway (SAUO)
MCR .... Massachusetts Communications Research (SAUO)
MCR .... Master Change Record
MCR .... Master Clock Receiver
MCR .... Master Control Record System (AABC)
MCR .... Master Control Register
MCR .... Master Control Relay [*Manufacturing term*]
MCR .... Master Control Room (MCD)
MCR .... Master Control Routine
MCR .... Master of Comparative Religion [*Education*] (FOTI)
M Cr .... Master of Criminology
MCR .... Matrimonial Causes Rules [*A publication*] (DLA)
MCR .... Maximum Combat Readiness [*Military*]
MCR .... Maximum Continuous Rating [*Also, MC(S)R*] [*Mechanical engineering*]
MCR .... McCloud Railway [*Federal Railroad Administration identification code*]
MCR .... McCloud River Railroad Co. [*AAR code*]
MCR .... McCord Corp. (SAUO)
MCR .... MCO Resources, Inc. [*AMEX symbol*] (COMM)
MCR .... Medical Corps, General Service [*USNR officer designation*]
MCR .... Medical Corps Reserve [*Military*] (DAVI)
MCR .... Medical Cost Ratio (MHCS)
MCR .... Mediterranean Communications Region [*Air Force*] (MCD)
MCR .... Melanocortin Receptor [*Biochemistry*]
MCR .... Memory Control Register
MCR .... Mercer [*Alaska*] [*Seismograph station code, US Geological Survey*] [*Closed*] (SEIS)
MCR .... Message Competition Ratio (MAE)
MCR .... Metabolic Clearance Rate
MCR .... Methodists for Church Renewal
MCR .... Metronome-Conditioned Relaxation
MCR .... MFS Charter Income Tr [*NYSE symbol*] (TTSB)
MCR .... MFS Charter Income Trust [*NYSE symbol*] (SPSG)
McR .... Micrecord Sales Corp., Chicago, IL [*Library symbol*] [*Library of Congress*] (LCLS)
MCR .... Micro
MCR .... Microcarbon Residue [*Petroleum analysis*]
MCR .... Micro Copier-Reproducer (VLIE)
MCR .... Micrographic Catalog Retrieval
MCR .... Micron Industries Ltd. [*Vancouver Stock Exchange symbol*]
MCR .... Microwave Cloud Radiometer (ACAE)
MCR .... Middle Common Room (SAUO)
MCR .... Military Census Report (SAUO)
MCR .... Military Characteristics Requirement (MCD)
MCR .... Military Command Region (MCD)
MCR .... Military Communications Representative (SAUO)
MCR .... Military Compact Reactor
MCR .... Mine Clearing Roller [*Military*] (INF)
MCR .... Minimum Cell Rate [*Telecommunications*] (ACRL)
MCR .... Minuteman Change Request [*Air Force*] (IAA)
MCR .... Missed Contact Rate (CAAL)
MCR .... Missile Clock Receiver
MCR .... Missile Computer Room
MCR .... Mission Control Room [*Space Flight Operations Facility, NASA*]
MCR .... Mission Control Routine [*NASA*]
MCR .... Mobile Communication Radio (SAUO)
MCR .... Mobile Control Room (DEN)
MCR .... Mobilization Contracting Requirement (AFIT)
MCR .... Modified Community Rating
MCR .... Monacair-Agusta [*Monaco*] [*ICAO designator*] (FAAC)
MCR .... Monitor Console Routine (VLIE)
MCR .... Montreal Condensed Reports [*A publication*] (DLA)
MCR .... Mother-Child Relationship [*Psychology*]
MCR .... Motor Conduction Velocity (DB)
MCR .... Multichannel Cloud Radiometer (SAUS)
MCR .... Multichannel Receiver
MCR .... Multi-Contact Relay (IAA)
MCR .... Multispectral Cloud Radiometer (MCD)
MCR .... Mutual Climatic Range (QUAC)
MCR .... Myotonia Congenita, Recessive Type [*Medicine*] (DMAA)
MCR .... Radcliffe College, Cambridge, MA [*Library symbol*] [*Library of Congress*] (LCLS)
MCR .... University of Minnesota Technical College, Crookston, MN [*OCLC symbol*] (OCLC)
MCRA .... Member of the College of Radiologists Australasia
MCRA .... Member of the College of Radiologists of Australia (SAUO)
MCRA .... Mitomycin C Resistance Protein A
McRae ...... McRae Industries, Inc. [*Associated Press*] (SAG)
MCR-Ar ..... Radcliffe College, Archives, Cambridge, MA [*Library symbol*] [*Library of Congress*] (LCLS)
MCRB .... Magnetic Compass Record Book
MCRB .... Market Compilation and Research Bureau, Inc. [*North Hollywood, CA*] [*Information service or system*] (IID)
MCRB .... Military Cost Review Board (MCD)
MCRB .... Motor Carrier Rate Bureau
MCRBBS ..... Marine Corps Reserve Bulletin Board System (DOMA)
MCRBIO ..... Microbiology
MCRBLGY ... Microbiology
M Cr C ...... Madras Criminal Cases [*A publication*] (DLA)
MCRC .... Marine Corps Recruiting Command
MCRC .... Marketing Communications Research Center [*Later, CMC*]
MCRC .... Mass Communications Research Center (SAUO)
MCRC .... Master Component Rework Capability (MCD)
MCRC .... Master Control and Reporting Center (SAUO)
McRC .... Microfilm Recording Co., Weston, ON, Canada [*Library symbol*] [*Library of Congress*] (LCLS)
MCRC .... Mobile Control & Reporting Centre (SAUO)
MCRC .... Molecular Cardiology Research Center [*Tufts University*] (RCD)
MCRCB ...... Motor Cycle Racing Control Board [*Motorsports*]
MCRD .... Marine Corps Recruit Depot
MCRD .... Marine Corps Requirements Document (MCD)
MCRD .... McCord Manufacturing [*NCIC trailer make code*]
MCRD .... Medullary Cystic Renal Disease [*Medicine*] (MELL)
MCRDAC .... Marine Corps Research, Development, and Acquisition Command [*Quantico, VA*] (GRD)
MCRDEP .... Marine Corps Recruit Depot
MCRDT ...... Microdata
MCRE .... MetaCreations Corp. [*NASDAQ symbol*] (SG)
McRe .... Micrecord Sales Corp., Lombard, IL [*Library symbol*] [*Library of Congress*] (LCLS)
MCRE .... Mother-Child Relationship Evaluation [*Psychology*]
MCREGIS ... Motor Carrier Regulation Information System [*BTS*] (TAG)
MCREL ...... Mid-Continent Regional Educational Laboratory [*Aurora, CO*] [*Department of Education*]
McREL ...... Mid-Continent Research for Education and Learning
MCRELCTRNC ... Microelectronic
MCREP ...... Military Committee Representative [*to the North Atlantic Council*] (AABC)
MCRep ...... Military Committee Representative to the North Atlantic Council (SAUO)
MCRF .... Master Cross-Reference File
MCRFCH .... Microfiche
MCRFP ...... Monitoring of Chemical Residues in Food Products (SAUO)
MCRG .... Medical Career Research Group (SAUO)
MCRG .... Music Copyright Reform Group
MCRH .... Main Control Room Habitability [*Nuclear energy*] (NRCH)
MCRHS ...... Main Control Room Habitability System [*Nuclear energy*] (NRCH)
MCRHS ...... Mid-Continent Railway Historical Society (EA)
MCRI .... Cambridge Research Institute, Inc., Cambridge, MA [*Library symbol*] [*Library of Congress*] (LCLS)
MCRI .... Marine Craft Radio Installation
McRI .... McCrone Research Institute (RCD)
MCRI .... Microcirculation Research Institute [*Texas A & M University*] [*Research center*] (RCD)
MCRI .... Monarch Casino & Resort [*NASDAQ symbol*] (SAG)
MCRI .... Multifactorial Cardiac Risk Index [*Cardiology*] (DMAA)
MCRIB .... Naval Communications Improvement Review Board (DNAB)
MCrim .... Master of Criminology (GAGS)
MCRL .... Mapping and Charting Research Laboratory [*Ohio State University*] (MCD)
MCRL .... Marine Corrosion Research Laboratory [*Navy*] (PDAA)
MCRL .... Master Component Repair List
MCRL .... Master Cross Reference Library (SAUO)
MCRL .... Master Cross-Reference List
MCRL .... Material Cross-Reference List (MCD)
MCRL .... Micrel, Inc. [*NASDAQ symbol*] (SAG)
MCRL .... Micrel Semiconductor [*NASDAQ symbol*]
MCRM .... Mid-Continent Museum [*Federal Railroad Administration identification code*]
MCRML ..... Midcontinental Regional Medical Library (SAUO)
MCRML ..... Midcontinental Regional Medical Library Program [*University of Nebraska*] [*Library network*] (IID)
MCRMLP .... Midcontinental Regional Medical Library Program [*McGoogan Library of Medicine*] [*Information service or system*] (IID)
MCRN .... Macaroni
MCRN .... Micronics Computers [*NASDAQ symbol*] (SPSG)
MCRN .... Moscow City Relay Network
MCR (NZ) ... Magistrates' Court Reports (New Zealand) [*A publication*] (ILCA)

MCRO .... Medical Council and Registration Office (SAUO)
MCRO .... Micro Mask, Inc. [*NASDAQ symbol*] (COMM)
MCROA...... Marine Corps Reserve Officers Association (EA)
MCROC...... Marine Corps Recruit Option Center
MCROSCPY... Microscopy
MCRP .... Maritime Coal, Railway & Power Co. Ltd. [*AAR code*]
MCRP .... Master of City and Regional Planning (GAGS)
MCRR .... Machine Check Recognition and Recording (VLIE)
MCRR .... Machine Check Recording and Recovery [*Computer science*]
MCRR .... Maine Central Railroad Co. (SAUO)
MCRR .... Maine Central Road Railroad (MHDB)
MCRR .... Marine Corps Reserve Ribbon
MCRR .... McKee Roughrider [*NCIC truck make code*]
MCRR .... Medical Care Research and Review (SAUO)
MCRR .... Michigan Central Railroad (SAUO)
MCRR .... [*The*] Monongahela Connecting Railroad Co. [*AAR code*]
MCRRCMPTR... Microcomputer
MCRRD ..... Marine Corps Reserve/Recruitment District
MCRS .... Maintenance Computing and Recording System
MCRS .... Marine Corps Recruiting Station
MCRS .... Material Condition Reporting System
MCRS .... Micrographic Catalog Retrieval System
MCRS .... Micros Systems, Inc. [*NASDAQ symbol*] (NQ)
MCR-S ...... Radcliffe College, Schlesinger Library, Cambridge, MA [*Library symbol*] [*Library of Congress*] (LCLS)
MCRSC...... Marine Corps Reserve Support Center
MCRSCMS... Marine Corps Reserve Support Center Management System (SAUO)
MCRSS...... Marine Corps Recruiting Substation
MCRT........ Mean Cell Retention Time (GNE)
MCRT........ Multichannel Rotary Transformer [*Electronics*]
MCRU .... Maritime Container Lines [*Intermodal shipping container symbol*] (TVRC)
MCRU .... Medical Care Research Unit [*University of Sheffield*] [*British*] (ECON)
MCRU .... Mobile Control and Reporting Unit (IAA)
MCRUD ..... Michigan Coalition to Reduce Underage Drinking (SAUO)
MCRV .... Manned Command/Reconnaissance Vehicle
MCRV .... Mechanised Combat Repair Vehicle (SAUS)
Mcrvsn ...... Microvision, Inc. [*Associated Press*] (SAG)
MCRWV..... Microwave (AAG)
MCRX .... Marcus [*Private rail car owner code*]
MCRX .... Morrison Cove Railroad [*Federal Railroad Administration identification code*]
MCRY........ Mid-Continent Railway [*Federal Railroad Administration identification code*]
MCS .... esoscale convective system (SAUS)
MCS .... Harvard University, Monographic Cataloging Support Service, Cambridge, MA [*OCLC symbol*] (OCLC)
MCS .... MacCartney Clan Society (EA)
MCS .... Machine Cancel Society (EA)
MCS .... Machine Control System (VLIE)
MCS .... Machinery Control System (SAUS)
MCS .... Macmillan's Commercial Series [*A publication*]
MCS .... Madras Civil Service [*British*]
MCS .... Magnetic Card Selecting (DNAB)
MCS .... Magnetic Card Store [*Computer science*] (VLIE)
MCS .... Magnetic Character Sensing [*Computer science*] (VLIE)
MCS .... Magnetic Coupling System (MCD)
MCS .... Main Compution System
MCS .... Main Control Station [*Nuclear energy*] (IAA)
mcs .... Maintenance and Checkout Station (NAKS)
MCS .... Maintenance and Checkout Station [*NASA*] (NASA)
MCS .... Maintenance Control Section [*DCE*]
MCS .... Maintenance Control Subsystem [*Computer science*] (VLIE)
MCS .... Maintenance Control System [*NASA*] (IAA)
MCS .... Maintenance Cost System (MCD)
MCS .... Major Component Schedule (AAG)
MCS .... Malayan Civil Service
MCS .... Malignant Carcinoid Syndrome [*Medicine*] (MELL)
MCS .... Management Computing Services (SAUO)
MCS .... Management Consulting Services (SAUO)
MCS .... Management Control System (MCD)
MCS .... Maneuver Control System [*Computer science*]
MCS .... Mannesmann Cylinder Systems GmbH (EFIS)
MCS .... Manpower Consultative Service [*Canada*] (PDAA)
MCS .... Manufacturing and Consulting Services (PCM)
MCS .... Manufacturing Control System
MCS .... Mapping Camera System
MCS .... [*The*] Marcus Corp. [*NYSE symbol*] (SPSG)
MCS .... Marcus Island [*Japan*] [*Seismograph station code, US Geological Survey*] (SEIS)
MCS .... Marine Casualty Statistics (OA)
MCS .... Marine Conservation Society [*British*]
MCS .... Marine Cooks and Stewards (SAUO)
MCS .... Marine Cooks and Stewards Union
MCS .... Marine Corps School [*Quantico, VA*]
MCS .... Marine Corps Schools (SAUO)
MCS .... Marine Corps Station
MCS .... Marine Corps Supply Activity [*Obsolete*]
MCS .... Maritime Communications System (SAUO)
MCS .... Maritime Communication Subsystem [*INTELSAT/INMARSAT*]
MCS .... Massachusetts Chiropractic Society (EARSL)
MCS .... Mass Casualty Supplement [*Military*]
MCS .... Mast Check System
MCS .... Mast Connection System (SAA)
MCS .... Master Circuit System
MCS .... Master Composite Specification (MCD)
MCS .... Master Control Set (IAA)
MCS .... Master Control Station (NRCH)
MCS .... Master Control System [*or Subsystem*]
MCS .... Master of Clinical Science (PGP)
MCS .... Master of Commercial Science
MCS .... Master of Communication Studies (PGP)
MCS .... Master of Computer Science (WGA)
MCS .... Material Control Station (SAUO)
MCS .... Material Control System (AAEL)
MCS .... Mathematical Code System
MCS .... Maximal Compatible Set (PDAA)
MCS .... McChip Resources, Inc. [*Toronto Stock Exchange symbol*]
MCS .... Mean Crew Size (MCD)
MCS .... Measurements Calibration System (KSC)
mcs .... Measurements Calibration System (NAKS)
MCS .... Mechanical Control System [*Aviation*]
MCS .... Mechanized Characteristics Screening
MCS .... Media and Communication Studies Site [*Internet resource*]
MCS .... Medical Computer Services (IEEE)
MCS .... Medical Consultant Staff [*Social Security Administration*] (OICC)
MCS .... Medical Corps, Special Service [*USNR officer designation*]
MCS .... Medico-Chirurgical Society (SAUO)
MCS .... Medium Close Shot [*Photography*] (ADA)
MCS .... Meeting Communications Service (VLIE)
MC/s......... Megacycles per Second (VLIE)
MCS .... Megacycles per Second [*Megahertz*] [*See also MCPS, MH, MHz*]
MCS .... Meridian Control Signal
MCS .... Merritt-Chapman & Scott Corp. (SAUO)
MCS .... Merseyside Civic Society (SAUO)
MCS .... Mesocaval Shunt [*Medicine*] (DMAA)
MCS .... Mesoscale Cloud System (SAUO)
MCS .... Mesoscale Convective System [*Meteorology*]
MCS .... Message Control Supervisor [*Computer science*] (MHDI)
MCS .... Message Control System [*Burroughs Corp.*] [*Computer science*] (BUR)
MCS .... Message Conversion System (SAUO)
MCS .... Metachronous Seeding [*Medicine*] (MELL)
MCS .... Meter-Candle Second
MCS .... Method of Constant Stimuli [*Psychophysics*]
MCS .... Methylcholanthrene[*Induced*] Sarcoma [*Medicine*] (DB)
MCS .... Metropolitan Communications Squadron [*British military*] (DMA)
MCS .... Microcirculatory Society (EA)
MCS .... MIcrocirculatory Society of America (NTPA)
MCS .... Microclimatic Cooling System [*Army*] (DWSG)
MCS .... Microcode Control Storage [*Computer science*] (VLIE)
MCS .... Microcomputer System
MCS .... Microculture and Sensitivity [*Microbiology*] (DAVI)
McS......... Micromation Systems, Inc., Feasterville, PA [*Library symbol*] [*Library of Congress*] (LCLS)
MCS .... Microprocessor Communications System (MCD)
MCS .... Microprogram Certification System (MHDB)
MCS .... Microsoft Cluster Service
MCS .... Microsoft Consulting Services (CDE)
MCS .... Microwave Carrier Supply
MCS .... Microwave Communication System
MCS .... Midget Car Series [*Motorsports*]
MCS .... Mildly Context-Sensitive [*Linguistics*] (IEL)
MCS .... Milestone Car Society (EA)
MC's......... Military Characteristics [*Technical specification document for nuclear bombs and warheads*]
MCS .... Military Communications Stations
MCS .... Military Communications Systems (SAUO)
MCS .... Miller Communications Systems Ltd. [*Telecommunications service*] (TSSD)
MCS .... Millimeter Wave Contrast Seekers (ACAE)
MCS .... Mine Countermeasures command, control & support Ship (SAUS)
MCS .... Mine Countermeasures Ship [*Navy symbol*]
MCS .... Mine Countermeasure Support [*Obsolete*] [*Military*]
MCS .... Mini-Computer Systems Inc. (NITA)
MCS .... Mini Conference System (PDAA)
MCS .... Minimal Cut Set [*Engineering*]
MCS .... Minimum Chi-Square
MCS .... Mining Certification Service (HEAS)
MCS .... Missile Calibration Station
MCS .... Missile Checkout Set (AAG)
MCS .... Missile Checkout Station
MCS .... Missile Commit Sequence (AAG)
MCS .... Missile Compensating System
MCS .... Missile Controller Set
MCS .... Missile Control System
MCS .... Missionary Sisters of the Sacred Side (TOCD)
MCS .... Mission Control Segment (SSD)
MCS .... Mission Critical Server (SAUS)
MCS .... Mitochondrial Capsule Selenoprotein [*Biochemistry*]
MCS .... Mixture Control Solenoid [*Automotive engineering*]
MCS .... Mobile Calibration Station (IAA)
MCS .... Mobile Checkout Station (AAG)
MC/S .... Mobile Client/Server [*Computer science*] (GART)
MCS .... Mobile Coastal Service (SAUO)
MCS .... Mobile Communications System (MCD)
MCS .... Mobile Computer System

MCS .... Mobile Control Station (SAUO)
MCS .... Model-Controlled System [*NASA*]
MCS .... Modular Charge System (SAUS)
MCS .... Modular Composition System [*Diskettes*]
MCS .... Modular Computer System (IEEE)
MCS .... Modulation-Controlled Synchronization (IAA)
MCS .... Module Control Station (ACAE)
MCS .... Moisture Control System (DB)
MCS .... Monitor and Control Software [*FAA*] (TAG)
MCS .... Monitor and Control Subsystem
MCS .... Monitor and Control System [*Deep Space Instrumentation Facility, NASA*]
MCS .... Monitoring Control System (SAUO)
MCS .... Monte Carlo Simulation [*Computer science*] (IAA)
MCS .... Monte Caseros [*Argentina*] [*Airport symbol*] (AD)
MCS .... Monthly Cost Summary (ACAE)
MCS .... Motion Compensation System (ACAE)
MCS .... Motor Circuit Switch
MCS .... Motorized Compact Spindle [*Metal fabricating*]
MCS .... Movements Control Section [*British military*] (DMA)
MCS .... Multicast Server (MLOA)
MCS .... Multi-Channel Communications Software (NITA)
MCS .... Multichannel Communication System (IAA)
MCS .... Multichannel Scaling [*Mode*]
MCS .... Multi Channel Seismics (SAUO)
MCS .... Multichannel Seismology [*Geophysics*]
MCS .... Multichannel Switch (IAA)
MCS .... Multichannel System (IAA)
MCS .... Multi-Chemical Sensitivity [*Medicine*] (MELL)
MCS .... Multi-Console System (NITA)
MCS .... Multidirectional Category System
MCS .... Multi-media Communications Station (SAUO)
MCS .... Multimedia Conference Service [*Telecommunications*] (CDE)
MCS .... Multiple Character Set (CMD)
MCS .... Multiple Chemical Sensitivities [*Medicine*]
MCS .... Multiple Chemical Sensitivity (SAUO)
MCS .... Multiple Column Selector (IAA)
MCS .... Multiple Combined Sclerosis [*Medicine*] (DB)
MCS .... Multiple Compression Shear (OA)
MCS .... Multiple Computer System
MCS .... Multiple Console Support [*Fujitsu Ltd.*] [*Computer science*] (MCD)
MCS .... Multiplexer Computer Systems (MCD)
MCS .... Multipoint Communication Services (SAUO)
MCS .... Multiprogrammed Computer System (IEEE)
MCS .... Multipurpose Communications and Signaling
MCS .... Multivender Customer Services (SAUO)
MCS .... Multivendor Customer Service [*Computer science*] (CDE)
MCs .... Municipal Councils (Sri Lanka) [*Political party*] (PSAP)
MCS .... Music Construction Set [*Computer program designed by Will Harvey and published by Electronic Arts*]
MCS .... Myocardial Contractile State [*Cardiology*] (MAE)
MCS .... Residential Model Conservation Standard [*Pacific Northwest Electric Power and Conservation Planning Council*] [*Portland, OR*] (EGAO)
MCSA .... Malta Civil Service Association (SAUO)
MCSA .... Marble Collectors Society of America (EA)
MCSA .... Marine Corps Supply Activity [*Obsolete*] (NVT)
MCSA .... Medical Computer Services Administration (SAUO)
MCSA .... Meritorious Civilian Service Award
MCSA .... Methuen's Commercial Series [*A publication*]
MCSA .... Metropolitan Church Schoolmasters' Association [*A union*] [*British*]
MCSA .... Michigan Council for the Study of Abortion (SAUO)
MCSA .... Microcomputer Software Association - of ADAPSO [*Association of Data Processing Service Organizations*] (EA)
MCSA .... Midwest Collegiate Sailing Association
MCSA .... Military Construction Supply Agency [*Later, Defense Construction Supply Center*]
MCSA .... Minimal Cross-Sectional Area [*Radiology*] (DAVI)
MCSA .... Moloney Cell Surface Antigen [*Medicine*] (DMAA)
MCSA .... Moscow, Camden & San Augustine Railroad [*AAR code*]
MCSA .... Motor Carrier Safety Act of 1984 [*FHWA*] (TAG)
MCSA .... Multichannel Spectrum Analyzer [*Instrumentation*]
MCS-A .... Multi-Functional Communications System - Asynchronous (HGAA)
MCSA .... Smithsonian Institution, Astrophysical Observatory, Cambridge, MA [*Library symbol*] [*Library of Congress*] (LCLS)
MCS&T ...... Manchester College of Science and Technology (SAUO)
MCSAP ...... Motor Carrier Safety Assistance Program [*Department of Transportation*]
MCSB .... Milk Cap Statistical Bureau (SAUO)
MCSB .... Motor Carriers Service Bureau
MCSC .... Magdalen College School Cadets [*British military*] (DMA)
MCSC .... Marine Corps Supply Center
MC Sc .... Master of Commercial Science
MC Sc .... Master of Computer Science (PGP)
MCSC .... Materiel Category Structure Code [*Military*]
MCSC .... Medical College of South Carolina
MCSC .... Metropolitan Collegiate Swimming Conference (PSS)
MCSC .... Miami Computer Supply Corp. [*NASDAQ symbol*] (SAG)
MCSC .... Microsoft Certified Support Centers (GART)
MCSC .... Military College of South Carolina (SAUO)
MCSC .... Model Codes Standardization Council [*Defunct*]
MCSC .... Movement Control Sub-Committee [*IATA*] (DS)
MCSCF ...... Multiconfigurational Self-Consistent Field [*Chemical physics*]
MCSCF ...... Multiconfiguration Self-Consistent Field [*Physical chemistry*]
MCS/CHS ... Maneuver Control System / Common Hardware System [*Computer science*]
MCSD .... Marine Corps Supply Depot (MUGU)
MCSD .... Mediterranean Commission on Sustainable Development (SAUO)
MCSD .... Microsoft Certified Software Developer (GART)
MCSD .... Microsoft Certified Solution Developer (SAUS)
MCSD .... Microsoft Certified Systems Developer (SAUO)
MCSDS ...... Marlowe-Crowne Social Desirability Scale [*Medicine*] (DMAA)
MCSE .... Massachusetts Citizens for Safe Energy (EARSL)
MC Se .... Master of Commercial Service
MCSE .... Master of Computer Science and Engineering (GAGS)
MCSE .... Microsoft Certified Systems Engineer [*Information technology*]
MCSE .... Minimum Critical Size of Ecosystem [*Project*]
MCSEE ...... Member of the Canadian Society of Electrical Engineers (DI)
M-CSF ...... Macrophage-Colony Stimulating Factor [*Biochemistry*]
MCSF .... Marine Corps Security Force (DNAB)
MCSF .... Mobile Cryptologic Support Facility (DOMA)
MCSFE ...... Member of the Canadian Society of Forest Engineers (SAUO)
MCSG .... Mathematical and Computational Sciences Group (SAUO)
MCSG .... Mildly Context-Sensitive Grammar [*Artificial intelligence*]
MCSGX ...... Mainstay Government Fund [*Mutual fund ticker symbol*] (SG)
MCSH .... Manhattanville College of the Sacred Heart (SAUO)
MCSH .... Maryville College of the Sacred Heart [*Missouri*]
MC Shp ..... MC Shipping, Inc. [*Associated Press*] (SAG)
MCSI .... Macsi Lines [*Common carrier symbol*]
MCSI .... Mark Solutions [*NASDAQ symbol*] (TTSB)
MCSI .... Mark Solutions, Inc. [*NASDAQ symbol*] (SAG)
MCSI .... Member of the Construction Surveyors' Institute [*British*] (DBQ)
MCSI .... Miami Computer Supply Corporation (EFIS)
MCSI .... Morgan Stanley Capital International [*Database*] (GDD)
MCSIQ ...... MCSi [*OTCBB symbol*]
MCSJM ...... Congregation of Missionary Catechists of the Sacred Heart of Jesus and Mary (TOCD)
MCSK .... Mine Clearance System Kit (SAUS)
MCSK .... Multiple-Code-Shift Keying (CCCA)
MCSKR ...... Member of the Council, Secretary and Keeper of Records (SAUO)
MCSL .... Management Control Systems List [*DoD*]
MCSL .... Marconi Communications Systems Limited (SAUO)
MCSL .... Marine Corps Stock [*or Supply*] Lists
MCSM .... Master of Construction Science/Management (PGP)
MCSMAW ... Marine Corps Shoulder-Launched Multipurpose Assault Weapon (MCD)
MCSME ..... Member of the Canadian Society of Mechanical Engineers (SAUO)
MCSMP ..... Message Conversion System Message Processor (SAUS)
MCSO .... Marine Corps Special Orders (SAA)
MCSOII ...... Multiple-Cause, Systems-Oriented Incident Investigation [*Engineering*]
MCSP .... Maintenance Control and Statistics Process [*Telecommunications*] (TEL)
MCSP .... Member of the Chartered Society of Physiotherapists [*British*]
MCSP .... Member of the Chartered Society of Physiotherapy (SAUO)
MCSP .... Mission Completion Success Probability (MCD)
MCSP .... Multiple Conductor, Shielded, Pressure-Resistant [*Cable*]
McSPI .... Multicenter Study of Perioperative Ischemia
MCSR .... Material Condition Status Report [*Military*]
MCSR .... Materiel Condition Status Reporting System (SAUO)
MC(S)R ..... Maximum Continuous (Service) Rating [*Also, MCR*] [*Mechanical engineering*]
MCSR .... Mission Completion Success Rate (SAUS)
MCSR .... Motor Carrier Safety Regulations [*Department of Transportation*]
MCSRP ...... Management Control Systems Research Project (SAA)
MCSS .... Magnetron Compensator Signal Simulator (ACAE)
MCSS .... Marine Climatological Summaries Scheme [*World Meteorological Organization*] [*United Nations*] (DUND)
MCSS .... Massachusetts Council for the Social Studies (EARSL)
MCSS .... MATE Control & Support Software (SAUS)
MCSS .... Mathematics of Control, Signals, and Systems [*Database*] [*United Kingdom*] (GDD)
MCSS .... MCS Cargo Systems [*Common carrier symbol*]
MCSS .... Mechanical Circulatory Support System
MCSS .... Microscopic Camera Subsystem (KSC)
MCSS .... Mid Course Surveillance System (ACAE)
MCSS .... Military Clothing Sales Store
MCSS .... Military Communications Satellite System
MCSS .... Mine Countermeasure Support Ship [*Military*] (PDAA)
MCSS .... Missile Checkout System Selector
MCSS .... Missile Control Sub System (ACAE)
MCSS .... Mitac Computer Security System (SAUO)
MCSS .... Monitor and Control Subsystem [*Deep Space Instrumentation Facility, NASA*]
MCSSB ...... Manufacturers Council of Small School Buses (NTPA)
MCSSC ...... Multi-Color Spin-Scan Camera (ACAE)
MCSSCCJM ... Missionary Catechists of the Sacred Hearts of Jesus and Mary (TOCD)
MCSSD ...... Mobile Combat Service Support Detachment (DOMA)
MCSSG ...... Military Committee Special Study Group [*NATO*] (NATG)
MCSSQT .... Modified Combat System Ship Qualification Trial [*Navy*] (CAAL)
MCSST ...... Multichannel Sea Surface Temperature [*Algorithms for oceanography*]
MCSST ...... Multi-Channel SST [*Sea Surface Temperature*] (USDC)
MCST .... Magnetic Card "Selectric" Typewriter [*IBM Corp.*]
MCST .... Member of the College of Speech Therapists [*British*]
MCST .... Ministerial Committee on Science and Technology [*South Africa*]
MCSTB ...... Motor Carriers Service Tariff Bureau

MCSTSC .... Military Communications System Technical Standards Committee [*Army*] (AABC)
MCSU .... China Ocean Shipping [*Intermodal shipping container symbol*] (TVRC)
MCSU .... Management Consultation Services Unit [*LIMRA*]
MCSU .... Maximum Card Study Unit (EA)
MCSW .... Mining Club of the Southwest (EA)
MCSW .... Motor Circuit Switch (MSA)
MCSWG ..... Multinational Command Systems Working Group (NATG)
MCSX .... Managed Care Solutions [*NQS*] (TTSB)
MCSX .... Managed Care Solutions, Inc. [*NASDAQ symbol*] (SAG)
MCSY .... Medic Computer Systems [*NASDAQ symbol*] (TTSB)
MCSY .... Medic Computer Systems, Inc. [*NASDAQ symbol*] (SAG)
MCSYSCOM ... Marine Corps System Command (DOMA)
MCT .... Magnetically-Coupled Transformer (IAA)
MCT .... Magnetic Card and Tape Unit (IAA)
MCT .... Magnetic Character Typewriter (PDAA)
MCT .... Magnetic Compass Table (DNAB)
MCT .... Magnetic Core Tape
MCT .... Magnetic Core Tester
MCT .... Main Central Thrust [*Geophysics*]
MCT .... Main Control Tank (MSA)
MCT .... Mainstream Corporation Tax
MCT .... Managed Change Technique [*Management*]
MCT .... Manchester College of Technology (SAUO)
MCT .... Manifold Charge Temperature [*Automotive engineering*]
MCT .... MANPRINT [*Manpower and Personnel Integration*] Coordination Team [*Army*]
MCT .... Manual Cervical Traction [*Medicine*] (MELL)
MCT .... Maritime Crew Trainer (SAUO)
MCT .... Mark Centers Trust [*NYSE symbol*] (SPSG)
MCT .... Mass Culturing Technique [*Microbiology*]
MCT .... Master Cycle Trader (SAUO)
MCT .... Master of Christian Training
MCT .... Mathematical Cuneiform Texts [*A publication*] (BJA)
MCT .... Mature Cystic Teratoma [*Medicine*] (MELL)
MCT .... Maximum Climb Thrust (NASA)
MCT .... Maximum Continuous Thrust [*Aviation*]
MCT .... Maximum Corrective Time (SAUO)
MCT .... Maxwell Color Triangle
MCT .... Mean Cell [*or Corpuscular*] Thickness [*Hematology*]
MCT .... Mean Cell [*or Corpuscular*] Threshold [*Hematology*] (MAE)
MCT .... Mean Circulation Time [*Medicine*]
MCT .... Mean Corpuscular Thickness [*Hematology*] (CPH)
MCT .... Mean Corrective-Maintenance Time (MCD)
MCT .... Mean Corrective Time (SAUO)
MCT .... Mean Corrective Times (SAUO)
MCT .... Mean Correct Time
MCT .... Mechanical Comprehension Test
MCT .... Medial Canthal Tendon [*Medicine*] (DMAA)
MCT .... Medium-Chain Triglyceride [*Biochemistry*]
MCT .... Medium Combat Truck (SAUS)
MCT .... Medullary Cancer of the Thyroid [*Medicine*]
MCT .... Medullary Carcinoma of the Thyroid [*Medicine*] (AAMN)
MCT .... Medullary Collecting Tubules [*Anatomy*]
MCT .... Member of College of Technology (SAUO)
MCT .... Member of the College of Technologists (SAUO)
MCT .... Memory Cycle Time [*Computer science*] (MCD)
MCT .... Mercury Cadmium Telluride [*Photodetector*]
MCT .... Message Control Task [*Computer science*]
MCT .... Metabolic Control Test (SAUS)
MCT .... Metabolic Control Theory [*Biochemistry*]
MCT .... Meta-Chlorotoluene [*Organic chemistry*]
MCT .... Metal-Oxide-Controlled Thyristor (CIST)
MCT .... Metric Color Tag [*Computer science*] (PCM)
MCT .... Metrizamide Computed Tomography
MCT .... Micro Component Technology Inc. (NITA)
MCT .... Microsoft Certified Trainer (SAUS)
MCT .... Microstat Development Corp. [*Vancouver Stock Exchange symbol*]
MCT .... Microtoxicity Test [*Medicine*] (DB)
MCT .... Microwave Ceramic Triode
MCT .... Mid-Cycle Test [*Army training*] (INF)
MCT .... Midline Cerebellar Tumor [*Medicine*] (EDAA)
MCT .... MILAN Compact Turret (SAUS)
MCT .... Military Combat Thrust (SAUS)
MCT .... Military Command Technology (AAG)
MCT .... Minimum Competency Test [*Education*]
MCT .... Minimum Connecting Time [*Travel industry*]
MCT .... Minnesota Clerical Test
MCT .... Missile Compensating Tank
MCT .... Mission Control Table (MCD)
MCT .... Mobile Communication Terminal
MCT .... Mobile Contact Teams [*Military*] (AABC)
MCT .... Mode Coupling Theory [*Physics*]
MCT .... Modem Compatibility Test [*Computer science*] (MWOL)
MCT .... Modified Clinical Technique [*Medicine*]
MCT .... Module and Cell Tester (ACAE)
MCT .... Moment to Change Trim (DS)
MCT .... Monochlorotriazine [*Organic chemistry*]
MCT .... Mouse Colon Tumor [*Pathology*]
MCT .... Movable Core Transformer [*Nuclear energy*]
MCT .... Movement Control Team [*Air Force*] (AFM)
MCT .... Moving Coil Transducer (SAUS)
MCT .... Mucociliary Transport [*Physiology*]
MCT .... Multicell Test (MCD)
MCT .... Multiple Compressed Tablet [*Pharmacy*]
MCT .... Multistrip Cesium Thrustor
MCT .... Muscat [*Oman*] [*Airport symbol*] (OAG)
MCT .... United States Department of Transportation, Technical Information Center, Cambridge, MA [*Library symbol*] [*Library of Congress*] (LCLS)
MCTA .... Metropolitan Commuter Transportation Authority [*Greater New York City*] [*Later, Metropolitan Transportation Authority*]
MCTA .... Minnesota Central Railroad [*Federal Railroad Administration identification code*]
MCTA .... Motor Carriers Tariff Association
MCTA .... Motor Carriers Traffic Association
MCTA .... Motor Carriers Traffic Association Inc. (SAUO)
MCTA .... Multiple-Cycle Transient Analysis [*Chemistry*]
MCTAS ...... Military/Commercial Transport Aircraft Simulation (PDAA)
MCTB .... Motor Carriers Tariff Bureau (EA)
MCTC .... Golda Meir Mount Carmel International Training Centre (SAUO)
MCTC .... Maritime Cargo Transportation Conference [*of MTRB*]
MCTC .... Metrizamide Computed Tomography Cisternography [*Medicine*] (DMAA)
MCTC .... Metropolitan Collegiate Tennis Conference (PSS)
MCTC .... Microelectronics and Computer Technology Corporation (SAUO)
MCTC .... Military Corrective Training Centre (SAUO)
MCTC .... Movimiento Campesino Tupaj Catari [*Bolivia*] [*Political party*] (PPW)
MCTC .... Museum Center Transportation & Commerce [*Federal Railroad Administration identification code*]
MCTD .... Maximum Cell Transfer Delay (SAUS)
MCTD .... Medium Capacity Bomb with Temporary Delay Fuse [*British military*] (DMA)
MCTD .... Mixed Connective Tissue Disease [*Medicine*]
MCTE .... Michigan Council of Teachers of English (SAUO)
MCTEX ...... Marine Continent Thunderstorm Experiment (SAUO)
MCTEX ...... Maritime Continent Thunderstorm Experiment (SAUO)
MCTF .... Monouclear Cell Tissue Factor [*Medicine*] (DB)
MCTFIST .... Marine Corps Tank Full-Crew Interactive Simulator Trainer
MCTFL ...... Minnesota Council on the Teaching of Foreign Languages (EDAC)
MCTG .... Model Change Training Guide
MCTH .... MedCath, Inc. [*NASDAQ symbol*] (SAG)
MCTI .... Metal Cutting Tool Institute (EA)
MCTI .... Micro Component Tech [*NASDAQ symbol*] (TTSB)
MCTI .... Micro Component Technology, Inc. [*NASDAQ symbol*] (SAG)
MCTI .... Motion Compensated Target Identification (ACAE)
MCTL .... Mediterranean Contingency Target List (MCD)
MCTL .... Microtel Franchise&Development [*NASDAQ symbol*] (TTSB)
MCTL .... Microtel Franchise & Development Corp. [*NASDAQ symbol*] (NQ)
MCTL .... Microtel International, Inc. [*NASDAQ symbol*] (SAG)
MCTL .... Militarily Critical Technology List [*DoD*]
MCTLA ...... Motor Car Traders' Licensing Authority [*Victoria, Australia*]
MCTNS ...... Manportable Cannon Thermal Night Sight (MCD)
MCTP .... Missile Control Test Panel
MCTR .... Mackinac Transportation Co. [*AAR code*]
MCTR .... Maryland Center for Telecommunications Research [*University of Maryland, Baltimore County*] (RCD)
MCTR .... Message Center
MCTR .... Military CTR (SAUS)
MCTRAP .... Mechanized Customer Trouble Report Analysis Plan [*Telecommunications*] (TEL)
MCTRF ...... Manitoba Cancer Treatment and Research Foundation (SAUO)
MCTS .... Master Central Timing System [*NASA*]
MCT/S .... MILAN Combat Turret on Spartan (SAUS)
MCTS .... Ministerial Correspondence Tracking System [*Australia*]
MCTS .... Moravian College and Theological Seminary (SAUO)
MCTS .... Motor Carriers Tariff Service (EA)
MCTSA ...... Military Clothing and Textile Supply Agency [*Merged with Defense Supply Agency*] [*Army*]
MCTSE ...... Marine Corps Test Support Element (MCD)
MCTSSA .... Marine Corps Tactical Systems and Support Activity [*Camp Pendleton, CA*] (GRD)
MCTT .... Metal-Ceramic Transmitting Tube
MCTU .... Maintainer [*Intermodal shipping container symbol*] (TVRC)
MCTV .... Man-Carrying Test Vehicle (MCD)
MCTV .... Manhattan Cable TV, Inc. [*New York, NY*] [*Telecommunications*] (TSSD)
MCTX .... Modern Continental Construction [*Private rail car owner code*]
MCTZ .... Mountain Cement [*Federal Railroad Administration identification code*]
MCU .... Machine Control Unit
MCU .... Machine Tool Control Unit (IAA)
MCU .... Magma Copper Co. [*NYSE symbol*] (SPSG)
MCU .... Magnetic Card Unit [*Computer science*] (IAA)
MCU .... Main Control Unit (IAA)
MCU .... Maintenance Communications Unit [*Environmental science*] (COE)
MCU .... Maintenance Control Unit [*Computer science*]
MCU .... Major Crime Unit [*Elite police squad on television series "Crime Story"*]
MCU .... Malaria Control Unit [*Army*] [*World War II*]
MCU .... Management & Cascade Unit (SAUS)
MCU .... Management Control Unit (PDAA)
MCU .... Manual Control Unit
MCU .... Marangoni Convection Unit (SAUS)
MCU .... Marble Collectors Unlimited (EA)
MCU .... Marine Corps University
MCU .... Marine Craft Unit (SAUS)
MCU .... Master Clock Unit

mcu .... Master Control Unit [*NASA*] (NAKS)
MCU .... Master Control Unit
MCU .... Maximum Care Unit [*Medicine*]
MCU .... Measurement Control Unit (IAA)
MCU .... Mechanism Control Unit (SPST)
MCU .... Median Control Unit (WDAA)
MCU .... Mediterranean Coordination Unit (GNE)
MCU .... Medium Close Up [*A photograph or motion picture sequence taken from a relatively short distance*]
MCU .... Memory Controller Unit (SAUO)
MCU .... Memory Control Unit
MCU .... Message Construction Unit
MCU .... Microcomputer Control Unit
MCU .... Microcontroller Unit (CDE)
MCU .... Micro-Control Unit (NITA)
MCU .... Microprocessor Control Unit
MCU .... Microprogram Control Unit (NITA)
MCU .... Microprogrammed Control Unit [*Navy*]
mcU .... Microunit
MCU .... Micturating Cystourethrography [*Medicine*] (DMAA)
MCU .... Millicurie [*Also, mC, mCi*] (IAA)
MCU .... Miniature Command Unit
MCU .... Minicomputer Unit (IAA)
MCU .... Missile Control Unit (SAUS)
MCU .... Mission Control Unit (MCD)
mcu .... Mission Control Unit [*NASA*] (NAKS)
MCU .... Mobile Calibration Unit
MCU .... Mobile Care Unit [*Emergency medicine*] (DAVI)
MCU .... Modern Churchmen's Union [*British*]
MCU .... Modern Churchpeople's Union [*United Kingdom*] (EAIO)
MCU .... Modular Concept Unit (DA)
MCU .... Moment Control Unit
MCU .... Monitor and Control Unit [*Communications term*] (DCT)
MCU .... Monte Cristo Peak [*Utah*] [*Seismograph station code, US Geological Survey*] (SEIS)
MCU .... Mosquito Conversion Unit [*British military*] (DMA)
MCU .... Motor Cortex Unit [*Medicine*] (EDAA)
MCU .... Motor Cycle Union (SAUO)
MCU .... Mountain Commando Units (CINC)
MCU .... Multi-Chip Unit (SAUO)
MCU .... Multicoupler Unit [*Antenna*] [*Telecommunications*] (TEL)
MCU .... Multiplexer Control Unit
MCU .... Multipoint Conferencing Unit [*Communications term*] (DCT)
MCU .... Multipoint Control Unit [*Telecommunications*]
MCU .... Multiprocessor Communications Unit
MCU .... Multi-System Communications Unit (NITA)
MCU .... Rochester, NY [*Location identifier*] [*FAA*] (FAAL)
MCUAF ...... Multi-Corp. [*NASDAQ symbol*] (TTSB)
MCUAF ...... Multi-Corp, Inc. [*NASDAQ symbol*] (SAG)
MCUB .... Marine Corps Uniform Board [*Washington, DC*] (EGAO)
MCUG .... Micturating Cystourethrogram/Graph [*Medicine*] (EDAA)
MCUG .... Military Computers Users Group
MCUIS ...... Master Control and User Interface Software Subsystem [*Space Flight Operations Facility, NASA*]
MCUL .... Missile Compartment, Upper Level
MCUMP ..... Multidisciplinary Center for Urban and Minority Problems [*Florida State University*] [*Research center*] [*Defunct*] (RCD)
MCUPA ...... Medical Committee Under the Poisons Act [*Australia*]
MCurrSt ..... Master of Curriculum Studies
MCurrStud ... Master of Curriculum Studies
MCUSR ...... Memory Control Unit Special Register [*Computer science*] (MHDB)
MCV .... Magnetic Cushion Vehicle (IEEE)
MCV .... Manifold Control Valve [*Automotive engineering*]
MCV .... Manufacturing Council of Victoria [*Australia*]
MCV .... Maritime Commission, Victory Ship
MCV .... Mean Cell [*or Corpuscular*] Volume [*Hematology*]
MCV .... Mean Clinical Value (AAMN)
MCV .... Mean Corpuscular Volume [*Physiology*]
MCV .... Measles-Containing Vaccine
MCV .... Mechanicville, NY [*American Association of Railroads railroad junction routing code*]
MCV .... Mechanised Combat Vehicle [*British military*] (DMA)
MCV .... Median Cell Volume (DB)
MCV .... Medical Center of Virginia [*University of Virginia*]
MCV .... Medical College of Virginia (SAUO)
MCV .... Meningococcus Vaccine [*Medicine*] (MELL)
MCV .... Mercury [*Nevada*] [*Seismograph station code, US Geological Survey*] (SEIS)
MCV .... Mesabi Community College, Virginia, MN [*OCLC symbol*] (OCLC)
MCV .... Mesoscale Convectively-Generated Vortices [*Marine science*] (OSRA)
MCV .... Method of Composition Velocity [*Physical chemistry*]
MCV .... Microbial Check Valve (PDAA)
MCV .... Middle Cardiac Vein [*Medicine*] (MELL)
MCV .... Missile Corvette (SAUS)
MCV .... Mixture Control Valve [*Automotive engineering*]
MCV .... Modular Chemical Vessel (TIMI)
MCV .... Molluscum Contagiosum Virus
MCV .... Motor Conduction Velocity (DMAA)
MCV .... Movable Closure Valve (NRCH)
MCV .... Muerto Canyon Virus [*Hantavirus strain*]
MCVD .... Metal Chemical Vapor Deposition (AAEL)
MCVD .... Modified Chemical Vapor Deposition [*Telecommunications*]
McVey Dig ... McVey's Ohio Digest [*A publication*] (DLA)
MCVF .... Multichannel Voice Frequency [*Telecommunications*]
MCVFT ...... Multichannel Voice Frequency Telegraphy [*Telecommunications*] (TEL)
MC-V(G) .... Medical Officers (Qualified for General Detail) [*USNR designation*]
MCVG .... Memory Character Vector Generator
MCVP .... Materials Control and Verification Program [*NASA*] (NASA)
MCVr .... Reticulocyte Mean Corpuscular Volume [*Medicine*] (PALA)
MCVS .... Management and Cost Visibility System (SSD)
MC-V(S) ..... Medical Officers (Qualified for Specialist Duties) [*USNR designation*]
MCVS .... Multi-Crew Visual System (ACAE)
MCVT .... Multi-Channel Voice Terminal (SAUS)
MCW .... Central Missouri State University, Warrensburg, MO [*OCLC symbol*] (OCLC)
MCW .... Clarence W. Mills, Laurel MD (SAUO)
MCW .... Mallinckrodt Chemical Works [*Later, Mallinckrodt, Inc.*]
MCW .... Mason City [*Iowa*] [*Airport symbol*] (OAG)
MCW .... Mason City, IA [*Location identifier*] [*FAA*] (FAAL)
MCW .... Maternal and Child Welfare (SAUO)
MCW .... Maternity and Child Welfare (SAUO)
MCW .... McDonalds Corp. [*NYSE symbol*] (SAG)
MCW .... Medical College of Wisconsin [*Medicine*] (EDAA)
MCW .... Medical Corps, Women's Reserve [*USNR officer designation*]
MCW .... Memory Card Writer [*Telecommunications*] (TEL)
MCW .... Metal Casement Window [*Technical drawings*]
MCW .... Metro-Cammell Weymaua Ltd. [*British*] (DCTA)
MCW .... Mills, Clarence W., Laurel MD [*STAC*]
MCW .... Minimum Clear Width (ACAE)
MCW .... Modified Continuous Wave [*Telecommunications*] (IAA)
MCW .... Modulated Carrier Wave [*Telecommunications*] (IAA)
mcw .... Modulated Continuous Wave (NAKS)
MCW .... Modulated Continuous Wave [*Radio signal transmission*]
MCW .... Mount Constitution [*Washington*] [*Seismograph station code, US Geological Survey*] (SEIS)
MCW .... Weston School of Theology, Cambridge, MA [*Library symbol*] [*Library of Congress*] (LCLS)
MCWA .... Malaria Control in War Areas [*Later, Centers for Disease Control*]
MCWA .... Massey College Wool Association (SAUO)
MCWA .... Mid Continent Wildcatters Association [*Defunct*] (EA)
MCWC .... Maternity and Child Welfare Centre (SAUO)
MCWC .... World Conservation Monitoring Centre (SAUO)
MCWCS ..... Ministerial Conference of West and Central African States on Maritime Transportation [*See also CMEAOC*] [*Abidjan, Ivory Coast*] (EAIO)
MCWCS ..... Ministerial Conference of Western and Central African States on Sea Transport (SAUO)
MCWG .... Marine Chemistry Working Group (SAUO)
MCWG .... Materiel Center Work Group (SAUO)
McWhrtr .... McWhorter Technologies, Inc. [*Associated Press*] (SAG)
McWillie .... McWillie's Reports [*73-76 Mississippi*] [*A publication*] (DLA)
MCWK .... Miller's Custom Work [*Common carrier symbol*]
MCWL .... Marine Corps Warfighting Lab
MCW/LRP ... Meal, Cold Weather/Food Packet, Long Range Patrol
MCWM .... Military Committee Working Memorandum (NATG)
MCWR .... Marine Corps Women's Reserve
MCWR .... Ministry of Communications and Works of the Republic of Cyprus (SAUO)
MCWS .... Minor Caliber Weapon Station (SAUO)
MCWU .... Military Committee of Western European Union (NATG)
MCWX .... Morton International [*Private rail car owner code*]
MCX .... Marine Corps Exchange
MCX .... MC Shipping [*AMEX symbol*] (TTSB)
MCX .... MC Shipping, Inc. [*AMEX symbol*] (SPSG)
MCX .... Michelin Capital Ltd. [*Toronto Stock Exchange symbol*]
MCX .... Minimum-Cost Expediting
MCX .... Monticello, IN [*Location identifier*] [*FAA*] (FAAL)
MCXD .... Magnetic Circular X-Ray Dichroism [*Light polarization*]
MCXM .... Marine Corps Exchange Manual (SAA)
MCXO .... Master Crystal Oscillator [*Electronics*]
MCXO .... Microprocessor-Controlled Crystal Oscillator [*Hughes Aircraft Co.*] (ECON)
MCXSERV ... Marine Corps Exchange Service Branch (DNAB)
MCY .... Machinery (IAA)
MCY .... Maroochydore [*Australia*] [*Airport symbol*] (OAG)
MCY .... Mercury General [*NYSE symbol*] (SAG)
MCY .... Mercury, NV [*Location identifier*] [*FAA*] (FAAL)
MCY .... Mount Calvery Resources Ltd. [*Vancouver Stock Exchange symbol*]
M/CYL .... Master Cylinder [*Automotive engineering*]
MCZ .... Maceio [*Brazil*] [*Airport symbol*] (OAG)
MCZ .... Magnetic Czochralski Process [*Crystallization*]
MCZ .... Mawan [*Language symbol*] (ETLW)
MCZ .... McDonald' Corp. 8.35% 'QUIDS' [*NYSE symbol*] (TTSB)
MCZ .... McDonalds Corp. [*NYSE symbol*] (SAG)
mcz .... Mechanized (ELAL)
MCZ .... Mesoscale Compressible Community Model (SAUO)
MCZ .... Monsanto [*Federal Railroad Administration identification code*]
MCZ .... Museum of Comparative Zoology [*Harvard University*] [*Research center*]
MCZ .... Williamston, NC [*Location identifier*] [*FAA*] (FAAL)
MCZDO ...... Multicenter Zero Differential Overlap [*Physics*]
MCZNE ...... Minimum When Control Zone Effective (FAAC)
MD .... Air Madagascar [*ICAO designator*] (AD)
MD .... Application for Writ of Mandamus Dismissed for Want of Jurisdiction [*Legal term*] (DLA)
MD .... Biomedical Office [*Kennedy Space Center Directorate*] (NAKS)
MD .... Delalande [*France*] [*Research code symbol*]

MD.......... Doctor of Medicine (PGP)
MD.......... Fissile Materials Disposition, Office of (SAUS)
MD.......... La Maison-Dieu [*Paris*] [*A publication*] (BJA)
MD.......... Machine Dried Paper (DGA)
MD.......... Macro Data (IAA)
MD.......... Macro Directory [*Computer science*] (IAA)
MD.......... Macular Degeneration [*Ophthalmology*]
MD.......... Made [*Telegraphy*] (PCTE)
Md.......... Madinhae (BJA)
MD.......... Madres de los Desamparados [*Mothers of the Helpless*] [*Roman Catholic religious order*]
MD.......... Magdeburg [*German license plate city code*]
MD.......... Magnesium Deficiency [*Medicine*] (DMAA)
MD.......... Magnetic Deflection [*Cathode-ray tube*] (DEN)
MD.......... Magnetic Disk [*Computer science*] (BUR)
MD.......... Magnetic Drum
MD.......... Mail Drop (COE)
MD.......... Main Deck [*Naval engineering*]
MD.......... Main Droite [*With the Right Hand*] [*Music*]
MD.......... Main Drum (CET)
MD.......... Main Duct
MD.......... Maintainability Demonstration (MCD)
M/D.......... Maintenance/Development [*Effort ratio*]
MD.......... Maintenance Documentation [*Bell System*] (IAA)
MD.......... Maintenance Dose [*Medicine*]
M-D.......... Maiz Dulce [*Race of maize*]
MD.......... Major/Mental Depression [*Medicine*] (EDAA)
MD.......... Make Directory [*Computer science*]
MD.......... Malate Dehydrogenase [*Also, MDH*] [*An enzyme*]
MD.......... Male Treated with DOC [*Deoxycorticosterone*]
MD.......... Malfunction Detection (NASA)
MD.......... Malic Dehydrogenase [*An enzyme*] (MAE)
MD.......... Malicious Damage (MARI)
MD.......... Malrotation of Duodenum [*Medicine*] (EDAA)
MD.......... Management Data (MCD)
MD.......... Management Directive
MD.......... Management Division [*Environmental Protection Agency*] (GFGA)
MD.......... Managing Director
MD.......... Managment Domain [*Telecommunications*] (OSI)
M/D.......... Man Day
M-D.......... Manic Depression
MD.......... Manic-Depressive
MD.......... Manning Department (SAUO)
MD.......... Mano Destra [*With the Right Hand*] [*Music*]
MD.......... Mantoux Diameter [*Medicine*] (EDAA)
MD.......... Manual Damper (OA)
MD.......... Manual Data
MD.......... Manual Direct (NASA)
MD.......... Manual Disconnect (MCD)
MD.......... Manu Dextra [*With the Right Hand*] [*Latin*]
MD.......... Manufacturer Defect
MD.......... Manufacturing Development (SAUO)
MD.......... Manufacturing Division (ACAE)
MD.......... Map Distance (ADA)
MD.......... Marchand [*Merchant, Trader*] [*French*]
MD.......... March of Dimes [*Medicine*] (EDAA)
MD.......... Marek's Disease [*Avian pathology*]
MD.......... Marine Detachment
MD.......... Maritime Defense (SAUO)
MD.......... Market Day [*British*]
MD.......... Marque Deposee [*Trademark*]
MD.......... Married
MD.......... Marshaled Deployability Posture (SAUO)
Md.......... Maryland (BEE)
MD.......... Maryland [*Postal code*]
MD.......... Maryland Reports [*A publication*] (DLA)
Md.......... Maryland State Library, Annapolis, MD [*Library symbol*] [*Library of Congress*] (LCLS)
MD.......... Master Diagram (MCD)
MD.......... Master Dimension (NASA)
MD.......... Master Directory [*NASA*] [*Information service or system*] (IID)
MD.......... Master's Decisions (Patents) [*A publication*] (DLA)
MD.......... Match Dissolve [*Cinematography*] (WDMC)
MD.......... Material Developer (SAUO)
MD.......... Material Division (SAUO)
MD.......... Materiel Developer [*Army*]
MD.......... Materiels Directorate (SAUO)
MD.......... Maternal Deprivation (MAE)
MD.......... Matrimonio Duxit [*Led into Matrimony*] [*Latin*] (ROG)
MD.......... Maturity Date [*Banking*]
MD.......... Maximum Degree Allowed to Fit
MD.......... Maximum Demand (IAA)
MD.......... Maximum Design Meter
MD.......... McDonnell Douglas [*NYSE symbol*] (TTSB)
MD.......... McDonnell Douglas Corp. [*NYSE symbol*] (SPSG)
MD.......... McDonnell Douglas Corporation (SAUO)
MD.......... Mean Deviation
MD.......... Measured Depth [*Diamonds*]
MD.......... Measured Discard [*Nuclear energy*] (NRCH)
MD.......... Measured Drilling [*Diamonds*]
MD.......... Mechanical Diode [*Mechanical power transmission*]
MD.......... Meckel's Diverticulum [*Medicine*] (EDAA)
MD.......... Medial Dorsal Cutaneous [*Nerve*] [*Medicine*] (EDAA)
Md.......... Median
MD.......... Mediastinal Disease [*Medicine*] (DB)
MD.......... Mediation Device (VLIE)
MD.......... Medical Department [*Army*]
MD.......... Medical Discharge [*from military service*]
MD.......... Medical Doctor (AMHC)
MD.......... Medicinae Doctor [*Doctor of Medicine*] [*Latin*]
M/D.......... Medicines/Drugs
MD.......... Mediodorsal [*Anatomy*]
MD.......... Medium Dosage [*Pharmacology*] (MAE)
MD.......... Medium Duty
MD.......... Megadalton
MD.......... Memorandum of Deposit [*Business term*]
MD.......... Memory Data Register (DNAB)
MD.......... Memory Decrement (MHDB)
Md.......... Mendelevium [*Preferred form, but also see Mv*] [*Chemical element*]
MD.......... Meniere's Disease [*Medicine*] (DMAA)
MD.......... Mental Deficiency (DIPS)
MD.......... Mental Development Center [*Medicine*] (EDAA)
MD.......... Mentally Deficient
MD.......... Mentally Depressed [*Psychology*] (DB)
MD.......... Mentally Disabled (OICC)
md.......... Mercedarious Descalzos (TOCD)
MD.......... Mesiodistal [*Dentistry*]
Md.......... Mesoderm [*Botany*]
MD.......... Message Data
MD.......... Message Digest (ACRL)
MD.......... Message-Dropping [*Military*]
MD.......... Messages per Day
MD.......... Mess Deck [*Naval*]
MD.......... Metal Deactivator
MD.......... Metal Dome [*Watchmaking*] (ROG)
MD.......... Metals Disintegrating
MD.......... Metaphors Dictionary [*A publication*]
MD.......... Meteorological Department (SAUO)
MD.......... Meteorology Department [*Navy*]
MD.......... Meter Dispute [*Electric utility company*]
M/D.......... Meters per Day
MD.......... Methyldichloroarsine [*Poison gas*]
MD.......... Methyldopa [*Also, AMD*] [*Antihypertensive compound*]
MD.......... Metropolitan District [*British*]
MD.......... Microalloy Diffused
MD.......... Micro Diagnostics (VLIE)
MD.......... Microdot (KSC)
MD.......... Micrometeoroid Detector (ACAE)
MD.......... Microsoft DoubleSpace [*Computer science*] (PCM)
MD.......... Microwave Desorber [*Instrumentation*]
MD.......... Middeck (SAUS)
MD.......... Middle Deltoid [*Myology*]
MD.......... Middle Distillate [*Fuel technology*]
MD.......... Middle District (DLA)
MD.......... Middle Door [*Theater*]
MD.......... Middle Dutch [*Language, etc.*]
MD.......... Midnight Dumping (MHDW)
MD.......... Migrant with English Language Difficulty
MD.......... Mildly Diabetic
MD.......... Military District [*Former USSR*] (NATG)
mD.......... Millidarcy
MD.......... Millwall Dock [*British*]
MD.......... Mine Depot [*Naval*]
MD.......... Mine Disposal
MD.......... Mini Disk [*Audio/video technology*]
MD.......... Minimum Dosage [*Medicine*]
MD.......... Ministry of Defence (SAUO)
MD.......... Minute Difference
MD.......... Miscellaneous Direct (MCD)
MD.......... Miscellaneous Document
MD.......... Misfire Detection [*Automotive engineering*]
MD.......... Miss Distance [*Military*]
MD.......... Missile Defense (SAUO)
MD.......... Missile Division (AAG)
MD.......... Missile Driver
MD.......... Missionary Dentists [*An association*] (EA)
MD.......... Mission Day
MD.......... Mission Dependent
MD.......... Mission Deviation (MCD)
MD.......... Mission Director [*NASA*] (KSC)
MD.......... Mitral Disease [*Medicine*]
MD.......... Mix Design
MD.......... Mixed Diet (DMAA)
MD.......... Mobile Decontamination
MD.......... Mobile Depot [*Air Force*] (MCD)
MD.......... Mobilization Department (SAUO)
MD.......... Mode [*Grammar*] (ROG)
MD.......... Moderate Dose [*Medicine*]
MD.......... Moderately Differentiated
MD.......... Modernization Division (SAUO)
MD.......... Modification Document (MCD)
MD.......... Modified Design [*Cordite*] [*British military*] (DMA)
MD.......... Modify (VLIE)
MD.......... Modular Design
MD.......... Modulated Displacement [*Automotive engineering*]
M-D.......... Modulation-Demodulation (HGAA)
M/D.......... Modulator-Demodulator [*Telecommunications*] (CET)
MD.......... Modulators [*JETDS nomenclature*] [*Military*] (CET)

MD.......... Moldova [*Internet country code*]
MD.......... Molecular Diameter
MD.......... Molecular Dynamics
MD.......... Money Down
MD.......... Monitor Displays [*Computer science*] (BUR)
MD.......... Monochrome Display (VLIE)
MD.......... Monocular Deprivation [*Optics*]
MD.......... Monocyte-Depleted Mononuclear Cell [*Medicine*] (EDAA)
MD.......... Monroe Doctrine
MD.......... Monsanto Research Co. (SAUO)
md.......... Months after Date (EBF)
MD.......... Months after Date [*or Month's Date*] [*Business term*]
md.......... Months' Date (EBF)
MD.......... Mood [*Grammar*] (ROG)
MD.......... More Dicto [*As Directed*] [*Pharmacy*]
MD.......... More Dirt (SAUS)
M/D.......... Mother/Daughter [*Apartment*] (BARN)
MD.......... Mothers of the Helpless (TOCD)
MD.......... Motion-Defined (SAUS)
MD.......... Motor Direct
MD.......... Motor Drive
MD.......... Mound Laboratory (SAUO)
MD.......... Movement Directive
MD.......... Movement Disorder (MAE)
MD.......... Movement Distance (SAUO)
MD.......... Multidimensional
MD.......... Multidomain [*Grains in rocks*] [*Geophysics*]
MD.......... Multinomial Distribution [*Statistics*]
MD.......... Multiple Deficiency [*Syndrome*] [*Medicine*] (DB)
MD.......... Multiple Dialyzer [*Chemical analysis*]
MD.......... Multiple Dissemination
MD.......... Multiply-Divide (IAA)
MD.......... Multipurpose Display (MCD)
MD.......... Municipal Docks Railway of the Jacksonville Port Authority [*AAR code*]
MD.......... Muscular Dystrophy [*Medicine*]
MD.......... Musicae Doctor [*Doctor of Music*] (ROG)
MD.......... Musical Director
MD.......... Music Director (NTCM)
MD.......... Myocardial Damage [*Cardiology*] (MAE)
MD.......... Myocardial Disease [*Cardiology*]
MD.......... Myotonic Dystrophy [*See also MyMD*] [*Medicine*]
MD5.......... Message Digent 5 [*Communications term*] (DCT)
MDA.......... Macdonald, Dettwiler & Association Ltd. (SAUO)
MDA.......... Magen David Adom [*Israel's Red Cross Service*]
MDA.......... Magic Dealers Association [*Later, IMDA*]
MDA.......... Magnetic Deflection Amplifier
MDA.......... Main Distribution Assembly (NASA)
MDA.......... Maintainability Design Approach
MDA.......... Maintenance Data Analysis (MCD)
MDA.......... Maintenance Depot Assistance [*Air Force*] (AFM)
MDA.......... Maintenance Design Approach
MDA.......... Malfunction Detector Analyzer (PDAA)
MDA.......... Malondialdehyde [*Biochemistry*]
MDA.......... Management Development Adviser (AIE)
MDA.......... Mandarian Airlines [*ICAO designator*] (FAAC)
MDA.......... Manic-Depressive Association (EA)
MDA.......... Manual Dilation of the Anus (AAMN)
MDA.......... Manufacturing Defect Analyzer [*Automotive engineering*]
MDA.......... MAPCO, Inc. [*NYSE symbol*] (SPSG)
MDA.......... Marking Device Association (EA)
MD A.......... Maryland Appellate Reports [*A publication*] (DLA)
MDA.......... Maryland Independent Truckers and Drivers Association (SAUO)
MDA.......... Master Design Award
MDA.......... Master Diversion Airfield (AIA)
MDA.......... Master Drawings Association (EA)
MDA.......... Master Dyers Association (EA)
MDA.......... Master of Development Adminstration (PGP)
MDA.......... Master of Dramatic Art
MDA.......... Material Data Administrator (DNAB)
MDA.......... Material Disposal Area (SAUO)
MDA.......... Material Disposal Authority
MDA.......... Maximum Deficit Amount [*Office of Management and Budget*] (GFGA)
MDA.......... Maximum Demographic Appeal [*Objective of commercial television programming*]
MDA.......... Maximum Detachable Activity [*Nuclear energy*] (NUCP)
MDA.......... McDonald, Dettwiley and Associates (ACAE)
MDA.......... McDonnell-Designed Assembly
MDA.......... McDonnell-Douglas Aerospace (GAVI)
MDA.......... Measurement, Decision, and Actuation [*Computer science*]
MDA.......... Mechanical Design Automation (TIMI)
MDA.......... Mechanically Despun Antenna (KSC)
MDA.......... Mechanized Directory Assistance [*Telecommunications*] (TEL)
MDA.......... Media Arts Group [*Stock market symbol*]
MDA.......... Media Dependent Adapter (SAUS)
MDA.......... Media Device Adapter (SAUS)
MDA.......... Medical Devices Agency (SAUO)
MDa.......... Megadalton (DMAA)
MDA.......... Menthanediamine [*Organic chemistry*]
MDA.......... Mento-Dextra Anterior [*A fetal position*] [*Obstetrics*]
MDA.......... Mentodextroanterior [*Medicine*] (DB)
MDA.......... Mesocyclone Detection Algorithm [*Marine science*] (OSRA)
MDA.......... Message Delivery Agent (RALS)
MDA.......... Metal Deactivator [*Fuel technology*]
MDA.......... Meteoroid Detector-Analyzer
MDA.......... Methyl Diamphetamine
MDA.......... Methyldopamine [*Biochemistry*]
MDA.......... Methylenedianiline [*Also, DAPM, DDM*] [*Organic chemistry*]
MDA.......... Methylenedioxyamphetamine [*Biochemistry*]
MDA.......... Michigan Dental Association (SAUO)
MDA.......... Microprocessor Development Aid
MDA.......... Middeck Assembly (MCD)
MDA.......... Milestone Decision Authority
MDA.......... Military Damage Assessment
MDA.......... Millinery Distributors Association [*British*] (BI)
MDA.......... Mine Danger Area (SAUS)
MDA.......... Minimum Decision Altitude (SAA)
MDA.......... Minimum Descent Altitude [*Aviation*]
MDA.......... Minimum Detectable Activity [*Nuclear energy*] (NRCH)
MDA.......... Minimum Detectable Amount [*of radiation*] [*Analytical chemistry*]
MDA.......... Minnesota Department of Agriculture, St. Paul, MN [*OCLC symbol*] (OCLC)
MDA.......... Miscellaneous Defense Activities (AAGC)
MDA.......... Miss Distance Analyser (SAUS)
MDA.......... Missile Defense Act (SAUO)
MDA.......... Missilized Driver Assembly (MCD)
MDA.......... Mission Data Assurance (ACAE)
MDA.......... Mission Doctors Association (EA)
MDA.......... Mixed Distribution Analysis [*Mathematics*]
MDA.......... Mobile Data Association (SAUO)
MDA.......... Mobile Depot Activities [*Air Force*]
MDA.......... Modified Diffusion Approximation (PDAA)
MDA.......... Modulation-Domain Analysis [*Computer science*] (CIST)
MDA.......... Monday [*Telegraphy*] (PCTE)
MDA.......... Monoalythic Design Automation (IAA)
MDA.......... Monochrome Display Adapter [*Computer technology*]
MDA.......... Monodehydroascorbate [*Biochemistry*]
MDA.......... Mothers for Decency in Action [*Group opposing sex education in schools*]
MDA.......... Motorcycling Doctors Association (EA)
MDA.......... Motor Discriminative Acuity [*Psychology*]
MDA.......... Motor Drive Amplifier
MDA.......... Motorized Door Assembly (SAUS)
MDA.......... Mouvement pour la Democratie en Algerie [*Algeria*] [*Political party*] (MENA)
MDA.......... Multidimensional Access
MDA.......... Multidimensional Analysis (IEEE)
MDA.......... Multidimensional Array
MDA.......... Multidocking Adapter (IAA)
MDA.......... Multiple Digit Absorbing [*Telecommunications*] (TEL)
MDA.......... Multiple Discriminant Analysis [*Statistics*]
MDA.......... Multiple Docking Adapter [*Apollo*] [*NASA*]
MDA.......... Multivariant Discriminant Analysis [*Medicine*] (DMAA)
MDA.......... Mural Decorators Association (SAUO)
MDA.......... Murray-Darling Association (SAUO)
MDA.......... Muscular Dystrophy Association (EA)
MDA.......... Museum Documentation Association [*British*] (DBA)
MDA.......... Music Distributors Association (EA)
MDA.......... Mutual Defense Agency (NADA)
MDA.......... Mutual Defense Assistance
MDA.......... San Antonio, TX [*Location identifier*] [*FAA*] (FAAL)
MdAA.......... Hall of Records Commission, Annapolis, MD [*Library symbol*] [*Library of Congress*] (LCLS)
MDAA.......... Michigan Dental Assistants Association (EARSL)
MDAA.......... Mon-Dak Athletic Association (PSS)
MDAA.......... Muscular Dystrophy Associations of America (EA)
MDAA.......... Mutual Defense Assistance Act
MdAAC.......... Public Library of Annapolis and Anne Arundel County, Annapolis, MD [*Library symbol*] [*Library of Congress*] (LCLS)
MDAAQS.......... Miscellaneous Data Analysis and Air Quality Simulation Studies (SAUO)
MDaAr.......... Danvers Archival Center, Peabody Institute, Danvers, MA [*Library symbol*] [*Library of Congress*] (LCLS)
MDAC.......... MacDonnell Douglas Aerospace Corp. (SAUS)
MDAC.......... McDonnell Douglas Aircraft Corp.
MDAC.......... McDonnell Douglas Astronautics Co. (NAKS)
MDAC.......... Medical Data Acquisition System
MDAC.......... Methyl(ciethylamino)coumarin [*Organic chemistry*]
MDAC.......... Microsoft Data Access Component (SAUS)
MDAC.......... Multi-Channel Digital Audio Codec [*Intraplex, Inc.*]
MDAC.......... Multiplying Digital-to-Analog Converter [*Computer science*] (IEEE)
MDAC.......... Muscular Dystrophy Association of Canada
MDAC.......... Mutual Defense Assistance-China area (SAUO)
MDAC.......... Mutual Defense Assistance Committee (SAUO)
MDAC.......... Mutual Defense Assistance, General Area of China
MDACA.......... Medical Defense Against Chemical Agents (ACAE)
MDAC/ACDM.......... Muscular Dystrophy Association of Canada/Association Canadienne de la Dystrophie Musculaire (SAUO)
MdaCad.......... ModaCad, Inc. [*Associated Press*] (SAG)
MDACC.......... Management of Defense Acquisition Contracts Course [*DoD*] (RDA)
MDACC.......... M. D. Anderson Cancer Center (SAUO)
MdaCd.......... ModaCad, Inc. [*Associated Press*] (SAG)
MDAC/E.......... McDonnell Douglas Astronautics Company/East (SAUO)
MDAC/W.......... McDonnell Douglas Astronautics Company/West (SAUO)
MDAD.......... Mineral Dust Airway Disease [*Medicine*] (DMAA)
MDAD.......... Monitoring and Data Analysis Division [*Environmental Protection Agency*] (GFGA)
MD Admin Code... Code of Maryland Regulations [*A publication*] (DLA)

MdAEPA..... United States Environmental Protection Agency, Annapolis Field Office, AnnapolisScience Center, Annapolis, MD [*Library symbol*] [*Library of Congress*] (LCLS)
MDAERP.... Medical Devices Adverse Experience Reporting Project
MDAF........ Memoires. Delegation Archeologique Francaise [*A publication*] (BJA)
MDAFWP... Motor-Driven Auxiliary Feedwater Pump (IEEE)
MDAGT...... Mutual Defense Assistance, Greece and Turkey
MDAH....... M. D. Anderson Hospital and Tumor Institute [*Houston, TX*]
MDAI........ Marking Device Association International (NTPA)
MDAI........ Multidisciplinary Accident Investigation [*National Accident Sampling System*]
MDAIKP..... Mutual Defense Assistance, Iran, Republic of Korea, and Philippines
MDAIR...... Multi-Disciplinary Accident Investigation Report [*Traffic safety*]
MDAIS....... McDonnell Douglas Aerospace Information Services [*Formerly, MCATO*] (MCD)
MD Ala...... United States District Court for the Middle District of Alabama (DLA)
MDAN....... Angelina, Cotui [*Dominican Republic*] [*ICAO location identifier*] (ICLI)
MdAN........ United States Naval Academy, Annapolis, MD [*Library symbol*] [*Library of Congress*] (LCLS)
MDANAA.... Mutual Defense Assistance, North Atlantic Area
MD & D..... Montagu, Deacon, and De Gex's English Bankruptcy Reports [*1840-44*] [*A publication*] (DLA)
MD & DeG... Montagu, Deacon, and De Gex's English Bankruptcy Reports [*1840-44*] [*A publication*] (DLA)
MD & S..... Macon, Dublin & Savannah Railroad (IIA)
MdANE...... United States Navy, Naval Ship Research and Development Laboratory, Annapolis, MD [*Library symbol*] [*Library of Congress*] (LCLS)
MD Ann Code... Annotated Code of Maryland [*A publication*] (DLA)
MDANSW... Muscular Dystrophy Association of New South Wales [*Australia*]
MDAO....... Mutual Defense Assistance Office (DOMA)
MDA-OSP... Mutual Defense Assistance - Offshore Procurement (SAUO)
MDA-OSP Program... Mutual Defense Assistance-Offshore Procurement Program (SAUO)
MDAP....... Machine and Display Application Program (SAUO)
MDAP....... Machover Draw-A-Person Test [*Psychology*]
MDAP....... Major Defense Acquisition Program (AAGC)
MDAP....... Materiel Deployment/Acceptance Plan (MCD)
MDAP....... Military Defense Aid Program (SAUO)
MDAP....... Military Defense Assistance Program (SAUO)
MDAP....... Military Department Aid Program (ACAE)
MDAP....... Morphological Dictionary Adaptor Program (PDAA)
MDAP....... Mutual Defense Assistance Pact [*or Program*]
MDaP........ Peabody Institute, Danvers, MA [*Library symbol*] [*Library of Congress*] (LCLS)
MdApg...... United States Army, Technical Library, Aberdeen Proving Ground, Aberdeen, MD [*Library symbol*] [*Library of Congress*] (LCLS)
MdApgC..... United States Army, Chemical Systems Laboratory, Aberdeen Proving Ground, Aberdeen, MD [*Library symbol*] [*Library of Congress*] (LCLS)
MdApgO..... United States Army, Ordnance School, Aberdeen Proving Ground, Aberdeen, MD [*Library symbol*] [*Library of Congress*] (LCLS)
MdApgOB... United States Army, Ordnance Board, Aberdeen Proving Ground, Aberdeen, MD [*Library symbol*] [*Library of Congress*] (LCLS)
MdApgP..... United States Army, Post Library, Aberdeen Proving Ground, Aberdeen, MD [*Library symbol*] [*Library of Congress*] (LCLS)
MD App..... Maryland Appellate Reports [*A publication*] (DLA)
MDAR....... Malfunction Detection Analysis and Recording [*NASA*] (KSC)
MDAR....... Minimum Daily Adult Requirement
MDAR....... Mobile Detection Assessment Response System [*USA*]
MDar 1...... Dartmouth Public Library, Darmouth, MA [*Library symbol*] [*Library of Congress*] (LCLS)
MDarHi...... Old Dartmouth Historical Society, Dartmouth, MA [*Library symbol*] [*Library of Congress*] (LCLS)
MDARS...... Military Damage Assessment Reporting System (MCD)
MDARS...... Mobile Detection, Assessment, and Response System
MDAS....... Manpower Data Automated System (DNAB)
MDAS....... Medical Data Acquisition System (KSC)
MDAS....... Meteorological Data Acquisition System [*NASA*] (KSC)
MDAS....... Midas Express [*Common carrier symbol*]
MDAS....... Miniature Data Acquisition System
MDAS....... Mission Data Acquisition System [*NASA*] (NASA)
MDAS....... Modular Data Acquisition System (NITA)
MDAS....... Multispectral Data Analysis System (ACAE)
MdAS........ Saint John's College, Annapolis, MD [*Library symbol*] [*Library of Congress*] (LCLS)
MDASA...... Muscular Dystrophy Association of South Australia
MDA-TR..... Mutual Defense Assistance - Training Program (SAUO)
MDAU....... Maintenance Data Acquisition Unit (HLLA)
MDAU....... Med-Africa Line [*Intermodal shipping container symbol*] (TVRC)
MDAV........ Medical Defence Association of Victoria (SAUO)
MDAVG...... Mission Duration, Average (MCD)
M (Day)..... Mobilization Day [*Military*] (AFM)
M (Days).... Metrication Days [*Sponsored by the Metrication Board to educate merchants and public on metric system*] [*British*]
MDAZ........ Meridian Aggregates [*Federal Railroad Administration identification code*]
MDB......... Brazilian Democratic Movement [*Political party*] (PSAP)
MDB......... Bren Del Win Centennial Library, Deloraine, Manitoba [*Library symbol*] [*National Library of Canada*] (NLC)
MDB......... Enoch Pratt Free Library, Baltimore, MD [*OCLC symbol*] (OCLC)
MDB......... Maintenance Data Bank
MDB......... Management Database (ACRL)
MDB......... Master Database (MCD)
MDB......... Master Distribution Box [*Missile system*] [*Army*]
MDB......... Material Distribution Board (DNAB)
MDB......... MDI Mobile Data International, Inc. [*Toronto Stock Exchange symbol*] [*Vancouver Stock Exchange symbol*]
MDB......... Medulloblastoma [*Medicine*] (DMAA)
MDB......... Memory-Data Bank
MDB......... Mersey Dock Board [*British*] (DAS)
MDB......... Message Database (MCD)
MDB......... Metalloprotein Database Browser (GDD)
MDB......... Methylenedioxybenzene [*Organic chemistry*]
MDB......... Metrology Data Bank [*GIDEP*]
MDB......... Microelectronic Data Bank (ACAE)
MDB......... Minimally Distinct Border [*Color perception*]
MDB......... Mission Data Book [*NASA*] (NASA)
MDB......... Mission Display Board Assembly [*Space Flight Operations Facility, NASA*]
MDB......... Mitglied des Deutschen Bundestages [*Member of the German Federal Parliament*]
MDB......... Mojave Desert Block [*Geology*]
MDB......... Movable Deformable Barrier [*Automotive safety*]
MDB......... Movimento Democratico Brasileiro [*Brazilian Democratic Movement*] [*Political party*] (PPW)
MDB......... Moving Deformable Barrier [*Automotive engineering*]
MDB......... Multichannel Distributed Bridge (CCCA)
MDB......... Multilateral Development Bank
MDB......... Multiple Drive Block
MDB......... Multiplex Data Bus [*Computer science*] (MCD)
MDB......... Mutual Defense Board [*US-Philippines*] (CINC)
MDB......... Professional Bancorp [*AMEX symbol*] (SPSG)
MDB......... Professional Bancorporation [*AMEX symbol*]
MDBA....... Mariner Distributing Company [*Common carrier symbol*]
MDBA....... Murray-Darling Basin Agreement (SAUO)
MdBAE...... United States Army, Corps of Engineers, Baltimore, MD [*Library symbol*] [*Library of Congress*] (LCLS)
MdBaH...... Harford Community College, Bel Air, MD [*Library symbol*] [*Library of Congress*] (LCLS)
MdBaHC.... Harford County Library, Bel Air, MD [*Library symbol*] [*Library of Congress*] (LCLS)
MdBAS...... Armco, Inc., Advanced Materials Division, Research Library, Baltimore, MD [*Library symbol*] [*Library of Congress*] (LCLS)
MdBASI..... Allied Signal, Inc., Baltimore, MD [*Library symbol*] [*Library of Congress*] (LCLS)
MdBASI-C... Allied Signal, Inc., Communications Diviaion, Baltimore, MD [*Library symbol*] [*Library of Congress*] (LCLS)
MdBB........ Baltimore Bar Library, Baltimore, MD [*Library symbol*] [*Library of Congress*] (LCLS)
MdBb........ United States Naval Training Center, Bainbridge, MD [*Library symbol*] [*Library of Congress*] (LCLS)
MdBBC...... Baltimore Conference, Inc., United Methodist Historical Society, Baltimore, MD [*Library symbol*] [*Library of Congress*] (LCLS)
MdBBH...... Harford Community College, Bel Air (SAUS)
MdBBJC..... Community College of Baltimore, Baltimore, MD [*Library symbol*] [*Library of Congress*] (LCLS)
MdBbN...... US Naval Training Center, Bainbridge, MD [*Library symbol*] [*Library of Congress*] (LCLS)
MdBBO...... [*The*] Baltimore & Ohio Railroad Co., Employees' Library, Baltimore, MD [*Library symbol*] [*Library of Congress*] [*Obsolete*] (LCLS)
MdBBR...... Bendix Corp., Baltimore, MD [*Library symbol*] [*Library of Congress*] (LCLS)
MdBBS...... Bon Secours Medical Library, Baltimore, MD [*Library symbol*] [*Library of Congress*] (LCLS)
MDBC....... Murray-Darling Basin Commission (SAUO)
MdBCC...... Catonsville Community College, Learning Resources Division, Baltimore, MD [*Library symbol*] [*Library of Congress*] (LCLS)
MdBCH...... Baltimore City Court House, Baltimore, MD [*Library symbol*] [*Library of Congress*] (LCLS)
MdBCIC..... Counter Intelligence Center Corps School, Fort Holabird, Baltimore, MD [*Library symbol*] [*Library of Congress*] (LCLS)
MdBCIC..... Counter Intelligence Center Corps School, Fort Holabird, Baltimore (SAUS)
MdBCP...... Baltimore County Public Library, Towson, MD [*Library symbol*] [*Library of Congress*] (LCLS)
MdBCPM.... Chemical Pigment Co., Metals Division, Baltimore, MD [*Library symbol*] [*Library of Congress*] (LCLS)
MdBCS...... Coppin State College, Baltimore, MD [*Library symbol*] [*Library of Congress*] (LCLS)
MD-BD...... Major Depression and Bipolar Disorder [*Medicine*] (MELL)
MDBDF...... March of Dimes Birth Defects Foundation (EA)
MDBDFTC... March of Dimes Birth Defects Foundation, Central Texas Area Chapter (EARSL)
MdBDH...... United States Department of Health and Human Services, Health Care Financing Administration, Office of Research Demonstrations and Statistics, Baltimore, MD [*Library symbol*] [*Library of Congress*] (LCLS)
MdBE........ Enoch Pratt Free Library, Baltimore, MD [*Library symbol*] [*Library of Congress*] (LCLS)
MdBeCA..... Concepts Analysis Agency, Bethesda, MD [*Library symbol*] [*Library of Congress*] (LCLS)
MdBeCI..... Congressional Information Service, Bethesda, MD [*Library symbol*] [*Library of Congress*] (LCLS)
MdBEs....... Essex Community College, Baltimore, MD [*Library symbol*] [*Library of Congress*] (LCLS)
MdBeU...... Uniform Services University of the Health Sciences, Bethesda, MD [*Library symbol*] [*Library of Congress*] (LCLS)
MDBF........ Mean Distance between Failures [*Quality control*] (MCD)
MdBFamP... Family Planning Training Institute, Baltimore, MD [*Library symbol*] [*Library of Congress*] (LCLS)
MdBFH...... Fort Holabird Post Library, Baltimore, MD [*Library symbol*] [*Library of Congress*] (LCLS)

MdBFM...... Grand Lodge of Ancient Free and Accepted Masons of Maryland, Masonic Library, Baltimore, MD [*Library symbol*] [*Library of Congress*] (LCLS)
MdBFr....... Friends Meeting, Stony Run, Baltimore, MD [*Library symbol*] [*Library of Congress*] (LCLS)
MdBG........ Goucher College, Baltimore, MD [*Library symbol*] [*Library of Congress*] (LCLS)
MdBGM-E... Manin Marietta Corp., Science and Technology Library, Baltimore (SAUO)
MdBGM-E... Martin Marietta Corp., Science and Technology Library, Baltimore, MD [*Library symbol*] [*Library of Congress*] (LCLS)
MdBGM-N... Martin Marietta Corp., RIAS Library, Baltimore, MD [*Library symbol*] [*Library of Congress*] (LCLS)
MdBH........ Baltimore City Hospitals, Doctors' Library, Baltimore, MD [*Library symbol*] [*Library of Congress*] (LCLS)
MDBH....... Barahona [*Dominican Republic*] [*ICAO location identifier*] (ICLI)
MdBHC...... Baltimore Hebrew College, Baltimore, MD [*Library symbol*] [*Library of Congress*] (LCLS)
MdBHC...... Harford County Library, Bel Air (SAUS)
MDBI........ Mean Days between Injuries
MDBI........ Murray Darling Basin Initiative [*Australia*]
MdBJ........ Johns Hopkins University, Baltimore, MD [*Library symbol*] [*Library of Congress*] (LCLS)
MdBJ-A..... Johns Hopkins University, Applied Physics Laboratory, Baltimore (SAUO)
MdBJ-A..... Johns Hopkins University, Applied Physics Laboratory, Silver Spring, MD [*Library symbol*] [*Library of Congress*] (LCLS)
MdBJ-AIS... Johns Hopkins University, School of Advanced International Studies, Washington, DC [*Library symbol*] [*Library of Congress*] (LCLS)
MdBJ-C..... Johns Hopkins university, Alan Chesney Medical Archives, Baltimore, MD [*Library symbol*] [*Library of Congress*] (LCLS)
MdBJ-G..... Johns Hopkins University, John Work Garrett Library, Baltimore, MD [*Library symbol*] [*Library of Congress*] (LCLS)
MdBJ-H..... Johns Hopkins University, School of Hygiene and Public Health, Maternal and Child Health-Population Dynamics Library, Baltimore, MD [*Library symbol*] [*Library of Congress*] (LCLS)
MdBJ-P..... Johns Hopkins University, George Peabody Library, Baltimore, MD [*Library symbol*] [*Library of Congress*] (LCLS)
MdBJ-W..... Johns Hopkins University, William H. Welch Medical Library, Baltimore, MD [*Library symbol*] [*Library of Congress*] (LCLS)
MDBK....... Madin-Darby Bovine Kidney [*Cell line*]
MDBK....... Medford Bancorp [*NASDAQ symbol*] [*Formerly, Medford Savings Bank*] (SG)
MDBK....... Medford Savings Bank [*NASDAQ symbol*] (SAG)
MdbkIns.... Meadowbrook Insurance Group [*Associated Press*] (SAG)
MDBL........ Maintainability Data Baseline (MCD)
MDBL........ Maintainability Design Baseline (MCD)
MdBLH...... Lutheran Hospital of Maryland, Baltimore, MD [*Library symbol*] [*Library of Congress*] (LCLS)
MdBLN...... Loyola - Notre Dame Library, Inc., Baltimore, MD [*Library symbol*] [*Library of Congress*] (LCLS)
MdBM....... Medical and Chirurgical Faculty of the State of Maryland, Baltimore, MD [*Library symbol*] [*Library of Congress*] (LCLS)
MDBM....... MULTICS Data Base Manager
MdBMA..... Baltimore Museum of Art, Baltimore, MD [*Library symbol*] [*Library of Congress*] (LCLS)
MdBMC..... Morgan State College [*Later, Morgan State University*] Baltimore, MD [*Library symbol*] [*Library of Congress*] (LCLS)
MDBMC..... Murray-Darling Basin Ministerial Council [*Australia*]
MdBMH..... Mercy Hospital, McGlannan Memorial Library, Baltimore, MD [*Library symbol*] [*Library of Congress*] (LCLS)
MdBMH-N... Mercy Hospital, School of Nursing, Baltimore, MD [*Library symbol*] [*Library of Congress*] (LCLS)
MdBMI...... Maryland Institute, School of Fine and Applied Arts, Baltimore, MD [*Library symbol*] [*Library of Congress*] (LCLS)
MDBMS..... Medical Data Base Management System (SSD)
MDBMS..... Megadatabase Management System (SAUS)
MDBMS..... Multidimensional DataBase Management System (SAUS)
MdBMStA... Mount Saint Agnes College, Baltimore, MD [*Library symbol*] [*Library of Congress*] (LCLS)
MdBNA...... National Institute on Aging, Gerontology Research Center, Baltimore, MD [*Library symbol*] [*Library of Congress*] (LCLS)
MdBo........ Bowie State College, Bowie, MD [*Library symbol*] [*Library of Congress*] (LCLS)
MdBOAS.... United States Social Security Administration, Baltimore, MD [*Library symbol*] [*Library of Congress*] (LCLS)
MdBP........ Enoch Pratt Free Library, George Peabody Branch, Baltimore, MD [*Library symbol*] [*Library of Congress*] (LCLS)
MDBP....... Mechanically Deboned Broiler Product [*Food technology*]
MDBPB...... Microsoft DoubleSpace BIOS [*Basic Input-Output System*] Parameter Block [*Computer science*] (PCM)
MdBPC...... Peabody Conservatory of Music, Baltimore, MD [*Library symbol*] [*Library of Congress*] (LCLS)
MdBPH...... United States Public Health Service Hospital, Baltimore, MD [*Library symbol*] [*Library of Congress*] (LCLS)
MdBPM..... Peale Museum, Baltimore, MD [*Library symbol*] [*Library of Congress*] (LCLS)
MdBR........ Research Institute for Advanced Study, Baltimore, MD [*Library symbol*] [*Library of Congress*] (LCLS)
MdBREC.... Engineering Society of Baltimore, Baltimore, MD [*Library symbol*] [*Library of Congress*] (LCLS)
MdbrkRe.... Meadowbrook Rehabilitation Group [*Associated Press*] (SAG)
MDBS....... Micro Data Base Systems (NITA)
MDBS....... Micro Data Base Systems, Inc. (SAUO)
MDBS....... Mobile Data Base Station (SAUO)
MDBS....... Mobile Database Station [*Telecommunications*] (ACRL)
MDBs........ Multilateral Development Banks (SAUO)
MdBS........ Saint Mary's Seminary and University, Baltimore, MD [*Library symbol*] [*Library of Congress*] (LCLS)
MdBSAr..... Sulpician Archives Baltimore, Baltimore, MD [*Library symbol*] [*Library of Congress*] (LCLS)
MdBSet..... Seton Psychiatric Institute, Baltimore, MD [*Library symbol*] [*Library of Congress*] (LCLS)
MdBSH...... Sinai Hospital, Staff Library, Baltimore, MD [*Library symbol*] [*Library of Congress*] (LCLS)
MdBS-P..... Saint Mary's Seminary and University, Philosophy Library, Baltimore, MD [*Library symbol*] [*Library of Congress*] (LCLS)
MdBSP...... Sheppard-Pratt Hospital, Baltimore, MD [*Library symbol*] [*Library of Congress*] (LCLS)
MdBSp...... Sunpapers Library, Baltimore, MD [*Library symbol*] [*Library of Congress*] (LCLS)
MDBSS...... Mischell-Dutton Balanced Salt Solution (STED)
MdBSt....... Saint Agnes Hospital, Baltimore, MD [*Library symbol*] [*Library of Congress*] (LCLS)
MdBSTS..... Space Telescope Science Institute, Baltimore, MD [*Library symbol*] [*Library of Congress*] (LCLS)
MdBSup..... Sunpapers Library, Baltimore, MD [*Library symbol*] [*Library of Congress*] (LCLS)
MdBT........ Towson State University, Baltimore, MD [*Library symbol*] [*Library of Congress*] (LCLS)
MdBU........ University of Baltimore, Baltimore, MD [*Library symbol*] [*Library of Congress*] (LCLS)
MdBU-L..... University of Baltimore, Law Library, Baltimore, MD [*Library symbol*] [*Library of Congress*] (LCLS)
MdBUM..... Union Memorial Hospital, Finney Medical Library, Baltimore, MD [*Library symbol*] [*Library of Congress*] (LCLS)
MdBV........ United States Veterans Administration Hospital, Baltimore, MD [*Library symbol*] [*Library of Congress*] (LCLS)
MDBVHS.... Mabel D. Bacon Vocational High School (SAUO)
MdBWA..... Walters Art Gallery, Baltimore, MD [*Library symbol*] [*Library of Congress*] (LCLS)
MdBWe...... Westinghouse Defense and Space Center, Baltimore, MD [*Library symbol*] [*Library of Congress*] (LCLS)
MdBWesE... Western Electric Co., Inc., Baltimore, MD [*Library symbol*] [*Library of Congress*] (LCLS)
MdBwiNA... National Aeronautics and Space Administration, Scientific and Technical Information Facility, Baltimore/Washington International Airport, MD [*Library symbol*] [*Library of Congress*] (LCLS)
MDC......... Atlantic Aero, Inc. [*ICAO designator*] (FAAC)
MDC......... Boston, MA [*Location identifier*] [*FAA*] (FAAL)
MDC......... Citizen's Movement (France) [*Political party*] (PSAP)
MDC......... Dow Chemical Co., Library, Midland, MI [*OCLC symbol*] (OCLC)
MDC......... Machinability Data Center [*Computerized search service*] [*Metcut Research Associates, Inc.*] (IID)
MDC......... Machinery Diagnostic Consultant [*Software program*]
MDC......... Machining Xcellence Division [*Institute of Advanced Manufacturing Sciences/Tech Solve*] (IID)
MDC......... Macrophage-Derived Chemokine [*Immunology*]
MDC......... Macular Degeneration Center [*Medicine*] (EDAA)
MDC......... Magnetic Drum Calculator (RALS)
MDC......... Main Display Console
MDC......... Mainframe Data Center [*Computer science*] (GART)
MDC......... Maintenance Data Center (MCD)
MDC......... Maintenance Data Collection [*Military*] (AFM)
MDC......... Maintenance Dependency Chart (IEEE)
MDC......... Major Diagnostic Categories [*Medicine*]
MDC......... Major Distribution Centre (SAUO)
MDC......... Malawi Development Corporation [*Political party*] (PSAP)
MDC......... Management Data Corporation (SAUO)
MDC......... Management Development Course (MCD)
MDC......... Manhattan Drug Co.
MDC......... Manhattan Drug Corporation (SAUO)
MDC......... Manitoba Development Corporation (SAUO)
MDC......... Manual Direction Center [*Air Force*] (AFM)
MDC......... Manufacturer Declaration of Conformity (SAUO)
MDC......... Manufacturing Development Center (SAUO)
MDC......... Manufacturing Development Council (SAUO)
MDC......... Marshal of the Diplomatic Corps (SAUO)
MDC......... Mason-Dixon Conference (PSS)
MDC......... Master Data Center, Inc. [*Information service or system*] (IID)
MDC......... Master Direction Center [*Air Force*]
MDC......... Master Document Control (ACAE)
MDC......... Materials Dissemination Center [*Institute for Development of Educational Activities*]
MDC......... Max-Delbrueck-Center [*Berlin, Germany*]
MDC......... Maximum Deductible Contribution [*Superannuation*]
MDC......... Maximum Dependable Capacity [*Nuclear energy*] (NRCH)
MDC......... Maximum Depth of Colonization [*Botany*]
MDC......... McAfee Development Center (SAUO)
MDC......... McDonnell Douglas Corp. (MCD)
MDC......... MDC Corp. [*Associated Press*] (SAG)
MDC......... M.D.C Hldgs [*NYSE symbol*] (TTSB)
MDC......... MDC Holdings, Inc. [*NYSE symbol*] (SPSG)
MDC......... MD of Canada [*Journal*] [*Medicine*] (EDAA)
MDC......... Mead Data Central, Inc. [*Dayton, OH*]
MDC......... Mead Data Control (NITA)
MDC......... Mechanical Development Committee (SAUO)
MDC......... Mechanically Deboned Chicken [*Food technology*]
MDC......... Medial Dorsal Cutaneous [*Nerve*] [*Medicine*] (STED)
Md C........ Medical Corps (SAUO)
MDC......... Mediterranean Development Corporation Fund S.A. (SAUO)
MDC......... Medullary Collecting Duct [*Medicine*] (STED)

MDC Memory Disk Controller
MDC Menado [*Indonesia*] [*Airport symbol*] (OAG)
MDC Message conversion system directory Component (SAUS)
MDC Message Display Console (MCD)
MDC Message Distribution Center (NATG)
MDC Metadata Coalition [*Computer science*] (GART)
MDC Meteorological Data Collection
MDC Metropolitan District Commission
MDC Metropolitan District Council [*British*]
MDC Microcomputer Development Center (SAUO)
MDC Micro-Dome Camera [*Police and security equipment*]
MDC Microprocessor Development Center [*American Microsystems Inc. US*] (NITA)
MDC Mild Detonating Cord (MCD)
MDC Military Discipline Code (SAFN)
MDC Military District Commander
MDC Military District Court (SAUO)
MDC Milk Development Council (GVA)
MDC Million Dollar Contract [*File*] [*Military*]
MDC Milwaukee-Downer College [*Later, Lawrence University*] [*Wisconsin*]
MDC Mine Data Centre (SAUO)
MDC Mine Dispatch Control
MDC Minerals Development Corporation (SAUO)
MDC Miniature Detonating Cord (MCD)
MDC Minimal Detectable Concentration (STED)
MDC Minimobile Data Center [*Military*]
MDC Minimum Detectable Concentration [*Analytical chemistry*]
MDC Ministere des Communications [*Department of Communications*] [*Canada*]
MDC Minnesota Department of Corrections (SAUO)
MDC Missile Development Center [*Air Force*]
MDC Missile Direction Center
MDC Missile Display Conference (SAUO)
MDC Mission Director Center [*NASA*] (KSC)
MDC Mission Duty Cycle [*NASA*] (KSC)
MDC Mobile Data Center (ACAE)
MDC Mobile Defence Corps [*British military*] (DMA)
MDC Mobile Distress Call
MDC Modification Detection Code (HGAA)
MDC Modified Direct Costs (SAUO)
MDC Mongoloid Development Council [*Later, NADS*] (EA)
MDC Montreal Diocesan College [*Quebec*]
MDC Montreux Development [*Vancouver Stock Exchange symbol*]
MDC More Developed Country
MDC Mother's Day Council (EA)
MDC Motor Dealers' Council [*New South Wales, Australia*]
MDC Motor Direct-Connected
MDC Mount Diablo [*California*] [*Seismograph station code, US Geological Survey*] (SEIS)
MDC Movement Designator Code
MDC Movement for Democratic Change [*Political party*]
MDC Muller Data Corp. [*Information service or system*] (IID)
MDC Mullerian Duct Cyst [*Medicine*] (MELL)
MDC Multidimensional Concept [*Combines robotic combat vehicles with other unmanned systems*] [*Army*] (RDA)
MDC Multilayer Dielectric Coating
MDC Multiple Delay Code (AFIT)
MDC Multiple Device Controller
MDC Multiple Drone Control (MCD)
MDC Multistage Depressed Collector (IAA)
MDC Radio set control group (SAUO)
MDCA Main Distribution Control Assembly (MCD)
MDCA Manufacturing Design Change Analysis
MDCA Master Diamond Cutters Association (SAUO)
MDCA MDC Corp. Cl'A' [*NASDAQ symbol*] (SG)
MDCA MDC Partners [*NASDAQ symbol*]
MDCA Midwest Decoy Collectors Association (EARSL)
MDCA Mind Development and Control Association (EA)
MDCAC Manufacturing Department Change Analysis Commitment (SAA)
MdCam Dorchester County Public Library, Cambridge, MD [*Library symbol*] [*Library of Congress*] (LCLS)
MdCatSG Spring Grove State Hospital, Catonsville, MD [*Library symbol*] [*Library of Congress*] (LCLS)
MDCB Moisture Detector Control Box
MDCC Master Data Control Console
MDCC Molecular Devices [*NASDAQ symbol*] (TTSB)
MDCC Molecular Devices Corp. [*NASDAQ symbol*] (SAG)
MDCC Monaural Detection with Contralateral Cue (PDAA)
MDCD Meridian Data [*NASDAQ symbol*] (TTSB)
MDCD Meridian Data, Inc. [*NASDAQ symbol*] (SAG)
MDCD Michigan Department of Career Development (IID)
MdCe Queen Anne's County Free Library, Centreville, MD [*Library symbol*] [*Library of Congress*] (LCLS)
MDCEF Medical-Dental Committee on Evaluation of Fluoridation [*Defunct*] (EA)
MDCGC Multidimensional Capillary Gas Chromatography
MD Ch Maryland Chancery Reports, by Johnson [*4 vols.*] [*A publication*] (DLA)
MDCH MDC Holdings, Inc. (MCD)
MDCH Michigan Department of Community Health (SAUO)
MDCH Middlesex, Duke of Cambridge's Hussars [*Military unit*] [*British*]
MD Chan Maryland Chancery Decisions [*A publication*] (DLA)
MD Chan Dec Maryland Chancery Decisions [*A publication*] (DLA)
MD Ch D Maryland Chancery Decisions [*A publication*] (DLA)
MD Ch Dec Maryland Chancery Decisions [*A publication*] (DLA)
MdChW Washington College, Chestertown, MD [*Library symbol*] [*Library of Congress*] (LCLS)
MDCI Medical Action Industries [*NASDAQ symbol*] (TTSB)
MDCI Medical Action Industries, Inc. [*NASDAQ symbol*] (NQ)
MDCI Multidisciplinary Counterintelligence (MCD)
MDCK Madin-Darby Canine Kidney [*Cell line*]
MDCL Medical Control [*NASDAQ symbol*] (SAG)
MDCL MedicalControl Inc [*NASDAQ symbol*] (TTSB)
MDCLC Medical Control, Inc. [*NASDAQ symbol*] (SG)
MDCLW MedicalControl Wrrt [*NASDAQ symbol*] (TTSB)
MDCM Doctor of Medicine and Master of Surgery (DD)
MDCM Medicinae Doctor Chirurgia Magister [*Doctor of Medicine and Master of Surgery*]
MDCMA Melvil Dui Chowder and Marching Association [*Later, MDMCA*] (EA)
MDCO Consuelo, San Pedro De Macoris [*Dominican Republic*] [*ICAO location identifier*] (ICLI)
MDCO Marine Drilling [*NASDAQ symbol*] (TTSB)
MDCO Marine Drilling Co. [*NASDAQ symbol*] (NQ)
MDCO Medicines Co. [*NASDAQ National Market symbol*]
MDCO The Medicines Co. [*NASDAQ symbol*]
MdCoA Arctec, Inc., Columbia, MD [*Library symbol*] [*Library of Congress*] (LCLS)
MD Code Ann Annotated Code of Maryland [*A publication*] (DLA)
MdCoG W. R. Grace & Co., Research Library, Columbia, MD [*Library symbol*] [*Library of Congress*] (LCLS)
MdCoH Hittman Associates, Inc., Columbia, MD [*Library symbol*] [*Library of Congress*] (LCLS)
MdConn Mid-Conn Bank [*Associated Press*] (SAG)
MD Const Maryland Constitution [*A publication*] (DLA)
Mdcore Medicore, Inc. [*Associated Press*] (SAG)
MdCpM United States Bureau of Mines, College Park Research Center, College Park, MD [*Library symbol*] [*Library of Congress*] (LCLS)
MDCPZ Monodesmethylchlorpromazine [*Biochemistry*]
MDCR Cabo Rojo [*Dominican Republic*] [*ICAO location identifier*] (ICLI)
MDCR Maintenance Data Collection Report (MCD)
MDCR Medcross, Inc. [*NASDAQ symbol*] (NQ)
MDCR Michigan Department of Civil Rights
MDCR Midland Courier Services [*Common carrier symbol*]
MDCR Miller-Dieker Chromosomal Region [*Genetics*]
MDCR Mini Digital Cassette Recorder (VLIE)
MDCRS Meteorological Data Collection and Reporting System [*FAA*] (TAG)
MDCS Maintenance Data Collection System [*or Subsystem*] [*Navy*]
MDCS Malfunction Display and Control System (MCD)
MDCS Manufacturing and Distribution Control System
MDCS Master Data Control System [*Computer science*] (IAA)
MDCS Master Digital Command System
MDCS Material Data Collection System [*NASA*] (KSC)
MDCS Metering and Directional Control System
MDCS Mission Data Collection Sheets (CINC)
MDCS Mutual Defense Control Staff [*Department of State*]
MDCS Santo Domingo [*Dominican Republic*] [*ICAO location identifier*] (ICLI)
MDCSC McDonnell Douglas Computer Systems Co. [*Formerly, MICRODATA*] (MCD)
MDC/SS Multiple Drone Control Strike System (MCD)
MD/CSU Motor Drive Cassette Support Unit
MDCSW Mitchell Development Corp. of the Southwest (EFIS)
MDCT Mechanical Draft Cooling Tower [*Nuclear energy*] (NRCH)
MDCT Median Corrective Maintenance Time (MCD)
MDCT Multidimensional Compensatory Task
MdCtr Medical Control [*Associated Press*] (SAG)
MdCu Allegany County Library, Cumberland, MD [*Library symbol*] [*Library of Congress*] (LCLS)
MDCU Magnetic Disk Control Unit
MDCU Mobile Dynamic Checkout Unit (AAG)
MDCU Multi-Display Control Unit (VLIE)
MdCuAC Allegany Community College, Cumberland, MD [*Library symbol*] [*Library of Congress*] (LCLS)
MdCvH Crownsville State Hospital, Crownsville, MD [*Library symbol*] [*Library of Congress*] (LCLS)
MDC-W McDonnell Douglas Corporation-West (SAUO)
MDCX Mexicana de Acido Sulfurico [*Private rail car owner code*]
MDCZ Constanza [*Dominican Republic*] [*ICAO location identifier*] (ICLI)
MdD Caroline County Public Library, Denton, MD [*Library symbol*] [*Library of Congress*] (LCLS)
MDD Doctor of Dental Medicine
MDD Machine Dependent Data (OA)
MDD Madrid [*Spain*] [*Seismograph station code, US Geological Survey*] [*Closed*] (SEIS)
MDD Magnetic Disk Drive
MDD Maintenance Design Disclosure
MDD Maintenance Due Date (NVT)
MDD Major Depressive Disorder [*Psychiatry*]
MDD Male Development Disorder (MELL)
MDD Management Division Director (SAUO)
MdD Mandaic Dictionary [*Oxford*] [*A publication*] (BJA)
MDD Manic-Depressive Disorder [*Medicine*] (STED)
MDD Marijuana Detection Dog (DNAB)
MDD Mate/Demate Device [*Aerospace*] (NAKS)
MDD Maximum Daily Dose (SAUO)
MDD McDonald & Co. Invest [*NYSE symbol*] (TTSB)
MDD McDonald & Co. Investments, Inc. [*NYSE symbol*] (SPSG)
MDD Mean Daily Difference [*Medicine*]
MDD Mean Daily Dose
MdD Median Deviation [*Statistics*]
MDD Median Droplet Diameter

MDD .... Medical Device Directive (SAUO)
MDD .... Medical Device Directorate (SAUO)
MDD .... Meteorological Data Distribution
MDD .... Midland, TX [*Location identifier*] [*FAA*] (FAAL)
MDD .... Milligrams per Square Decimeter per Day
MDD .... Million-Dollar Deal
MDD .... Million Dollar Directory [*Dun's Marketing Services*] [*Parsippany, NJ*] [*Database*]
MDD .... Mineral Deposits Division, Geological Association of Canada (SAUO)
MDD .... Mission Data Display
MDD .... Mission Description Document (SSD)
MDD .... Mixed Depressive Disorder [*Medicine*] (EDAA)
MDD .... Modern Drug Discovery [*Database*] (GDD)
MDD .... Mouvement Democratique Dahomeen [*Dahomean Democratic Movement*] [*Political party*]
MDD .... Multichannel Demultiplexer and Distributor
MDD .... Multidimensional Database
MDD .... Multiple Disk Drive [*Computer science*] (VLIE)
MDD .... Puerto Maldonado [*Peru*] [*Airport symbol*] (AD)
MDDA .... Manic Depressive and Depressive Association [*Later, NDMDA*] (EA)
MDDA .... Mechanicsburg Defense Depot Activity [*AEC*]
MDDA .... Minnesota Differential Diagnosis of Aphasia (STED)
MDDB .... Multi-Dimensional Data Base [*Computer science*] (VLIE)
MDDB .... Multidimensional Database (IDAI)
MDDBMS ... Multi-Dimensional Data Base Management System [*Computer science*] (VLIE)
MDDBMS ... Multidimensional Database Management System (GART)
MDDC .... Management Decisions Development Corporation [*Canada*] (NITA)
MDDC .... Manhattan District Declassified Code [*AEC*]
MDDC .... Military Dependents Dental Clinic (SAUO)
MDDC .... Motor Dealers' Disputes Council [*Australia*]
MDDCS...... Memorial Dose Distribution Computation Service [*Memorial Sloan-Kettering Cancer Center*] [*Information service or system*] (IID)
MDDD .... Merrill-Demos DD Scale [*Drug abuse and delinquent behavior test*]
MDDE .... Maryland & Delaware Railroad Co. [*AAR code*]
MDDF .... Minimum Delay Data Format (MCD)
MDDI .... Medical Devices, Diagnostics, & Instrumentation [*Center for Devices and Radiological Health*] [*Also known as The Gray Sheet*] [*A publication*]
MDDJ........ Dajabon [*Dominican Republic*] [*ICAO location identifier*] (ICLI)
MDDK .... Roger Maddock Transportation [*Common carrier symbol*]
MDDL .... Market Data Definition Language
MDDO .... Maintenance Department (SAUO)
MDDPC...... Methyl Dimethyldihydropyrancarboxylate [*Organic chemistry*]
MDDPM ..... Magnetic Drum Data Processing Machine (IAA)
MDDQP ..... MEDIQ [*OTCBB symbol*]
MDDR .... Maintenance Design Data Report (ACAE)
MDDR .... MDL Drug Data Report [*Database*] (GDD)
MDDR .... Mimimum Distance Decoding Rule (IAA)
MDDS .... Maintainability Design Data Sheets (MCD)
MDDS .... Material Directory Data Sheet (MCD)
MDDS .... Media Documentation Distribution Set (VLIE)
MDDS .... Monarch Dental Corp. [*NASDAQ symbol*] (NASQ)
MDDT .... Master Digital Data Tape (PDAA)
MDDU .... Manual Data Display Unit [*Computer science*] (VLIE)
MDDUS ..... Medical and Dental Defence Union of Scotland (SAUO)
MDDX .... Middlesex [*Region of London*]
MDE .... Cincinnati, OH [*Location identifier*] [*FAA*] (FAAL)
MDE .... Madame (ROG)
MDE .... Magnetic Decision Element [*Computer science*] (BUR)
MDE .... Main Distribution Equipment (IAA)
MDE .... Major Defense Equipment (MCD)
MDE .... Major Depressive Episode [*Medicine*] (DMAA)
MDE .... Manufacturing Development Engineering (SAUO)
MDE .... Master of Developmental Economics (PGP)
MDE .... Master of Distance Education (PGP)
MDE .... Master of Domestic Economy (NADA)
MDE .... Matrix Difference Equation
MDE .... McDermott, Inc. [*Formerly, Offshore Pipelines*] [*NYSE symbol*] (SAG)
MDE .... Mechanical Design Environment
MDE .... Medeea Ltd. [*Romania*] [*FAA designator*] (FAAC)
MDE .... Medellin [*Colombia*] [*Airport symbol*] (OAG)
MDE .... Message Distribution Element (SAUO)
MDE .... Meteoroid Detection Experiment (KSC)
MDE .... Metina Development [*Vancouver Stock Exchange symbol*]
MDE .... Middle East (CARB)
MDE .... Midland Diving Equipment Ltd. (SAUO)
MDE .... Military Damage Expectancy
MDE .... Mindy Explorations Ltd. [*Vancouver Stock Exchange symbol*]
MDE .... Minnesota State Department of Education, Professional Library, St. Paul, MN [*OCLC symbol*] (OCLC)
MDE .... Missile Display Equipment
MDE .... Mission Defendent Experiment
MDE .... Mission Dependent Elements [*NASA*] (KSC)
MDE .... Mission Dependent Equipment [*NASA*] (KSC)
MDE .... Mission Dependent Experiment [*NASA*] (NASA)
MDE .... Mission Display Equipment
MDE .... Mobile District Engineer (AAG)
MDE .... Mobile Telemetering Station [*ITU designation*] (DEN)
MDE .... Modern Drug Encyclopedia [*A publication*]
MDE .... Modular Design of Electronics (MCD)
MDE .... Modular Display Electronics (MCD)
MDE .... Mooring Dynamics Experiment [*Marine science*] (MSC)
MDE .... Motor Drive Electronics (ACAE)
MdE.......... Mount St. Mary's College, Emmitsburg, MD [*Library symbol*] [*Library of Congress*] (LCLS)
MDE .... Multidisciplinary Evaluation
MDE .... National Library of Medicine [*Source file*] [*UTLAS symbol*]
MDEA........ Marketing and Distributive Education Association [*Later, MEA*] (EA)
MDEA........ Media 100
MDEA........ Methyldiethanolamine [*Organic chemistry*]
MDEA........ Methylenedioxyethamphetamine [*Biochemistry*]
MdEa .... Talbot County Free Library, Easton, MD [*Library symbol*] [*Library of Congress*] (LCLS)
MDEBP...... Mean Daily Erect Blood Pressure (STED)
MDEC........ Marine Corps Development and Education Command (SAUO)
MDEC........ McDonnell Douglas Electronics Company (SAUO)
MDEC........ Motion Decoder (SAUS)
M-DECA..... Michigan DECA (EARSL)
M Dec S .... Master of Decision Sciences (PGP)
MdEdgA..... United States Army, Technical Library, Army Chemical Center, Edgewood, MD [*Library symbol*] [*Library of Congress*] (LCLS)
MDedHi ..... Dedham Historical Society, Dedham, MA [*Library symbol*] [*Library of Congress*] (LCLS)
MDee........ Dickinson Library, Deerfield, MA [*Library symbol*] [*Library of Congress*] (LCLS)
MDeeD ...... Deerfield Academy, Deerfield, MA [*Library symbol*] [*Library of Congress*] (LCLS)
MDeeH...... Historic Deerfield, Inc., Deerfield, MA [*Library symbol*] [*Library of Congress*] (LCLS)
MDeeP ...... Pocumtuck Valley Memorial Association, Deerfield, MA [*Library symbol*] [*Library of Congress*] (LCLS)
MDefStudies... Master of Defence Studies
MDEFWP.... Motor-Driven Emergency Feedwater Pump [*Nuclear energy*] (NRCH)
MDEL........ Major Defense Equipment List
M-DEMO .... Maintenance Demonstration [*DoD*]
MDEN .... Enriquillo [*Dominican Republic*] [*ICAO location identifier*] (ICLI)
MDEN .... Males, Density Of [*Ecology*]
MDENDET... Mobile Dental Detachment [*Coast Guard*]
M Dent Sc... Master of Dental Science [*British*]
MDEP........ Maine Department of Environmental Protection
MDEP........ Management Decision Package [*DoD*]
MDEP........ Modernization Development Plan (SAUS)
MDEPrA ..... McDermott Inc $2.20 cm Cv A Pfd [*NYSE symbol*] (TTSB)
MDEPrB ..... McDermott Inc. $2.60 cm Pfd [*NYSE symbol*] (TTSB)
MDEQ .... Massachusetts Department of Environmental Quality (SAUO)
MDERDA.... Maximum Degree of Emissions Reduction Deemed Achievable [*Environmental Protection Agency*]
M Des....... Master of Design
MDes........ Mercedarios Descalzos (TOCD)
MDES........ Multi-Data Entry System [*Computer science*] (VLIE)
MDES........ Multiple Data Entry System
M Des (RCA)... Master of Design, Royal College of Art
MDesS ...... Master of Design Studies (GAGS)
MDesSt ..... Master of Design Studies
MDET........ Militarized Digital Element Tester (MCD)
MDEU .... Material Delivery Expeditor Unit (DNAB)
MDEX........ Medex, Inc. [*NASDAQ symbol*] (NQ)
MDF .... Macrodefect Free [*Materials science*]
MDF .... Macular Degeneration Foundation (SAUO)
MDF .... Magnetic Direction Finding [*Meteorology*]
MDF .... Magyar Demokrata Forum [*Hungarian Democratic Forum*] [*Political party*] (EY)
MDF .... Main Distributing Frame [*Bell System*]
MDF .... Main Distribution Frame (NITA)
MDF .... Maine Development Foundation (EARSL)
MDF .... Maintenance Data Form (ACAE)
MDF .... Maintenance Depot Fabrication
MDF .... Manipulator Deployment Facility (MCD)
MDF .... Manipulator Development Facility [*NASA*] (NASA)
MDF .... Manitoba Development Fund (SAUO)
MDF .... Manpower Data File (SAUO)
MDF .... Manual Direction Finder [*Radio*]
MDF .... Manufacturer's Designated Fuel [*Automotive engineering*]
MDF .... Map-Dot-Fingerprint Dystrophy (SAUS)
MDF .... Marine Diesel Fuel [*Fuels and lubricants*]
MDF .... Maritime Defence Force (SAUO)
MDF .... Market Development Funds [*Business term*]
MDF .... Master Data File (AFIT)
MDF .... Master Directory File [*Computer science*]
MDF .... Master Distribution Frame [*Electronics*] (ECII)
MDF .... Master Document File [*Computer science*]
MDF .... Mate/Demate Facility [*NASA*] (NASA)
MDF .... Mating/Demating Facilities (SAUS)
MDF .... Mean Dominant Frequency (MAE)
MDF .... Median Demagnetizing Field [*Geophysics*]
MDF .... Medium Density Fiberboard
MDF .... Medium-Frequency Direction Finder [*or Finding*]
MDF .... Menu Definition File (SAUS)
MDF .... Message Development Framework (GART)
MDF .... Metals Datafile [*Materials Information*] [*Information service or system*] (IID)
MDF .... Methlene Diphosphate/Sphonate [*Medicine*] (EDAA)
MDF .... Metric Data Facility (MCD)
MDF .... Microcomputer Development Facilities (IEEE)
MDF .... Micro Defect Free
MDF .... Micro-Dose-Focusing [*Electron microscopy*]
MDF .... Midland Doherty Financial Corp. [*Toronto Stock Exchange symbol*]
MDF .... Midtfly Aps [*Denmark*] [*ICAO designator*] (FAAC)

MDF .... Midwest Democratic Front (SAUO)
MDF .... Mild Detonating Fuse
MDF .... Minimum Detectable Flux
MDF .... Mission Data File (SAUS)
MDF .... Mission Degradation Factor (SAUS)
MDF .... Mixed Dipterocarp Forest
MDF .... Modify
MDF .... Monopulse Direction Finding (SAUS)
MDF .... Mooreland, OK [*Location identifier*] [*FAA*] (FAAL)
MDF .... Multiband Direction Finder
MDF .... Multiple Domain Facility [*Computer science*] (GART)
MDF .... Multiple Domain Feature [*Computer science*] (GART)
MDF .... Myocardial Depressant Factor
MDF/1 .... Metals Data File/1 (NITA)
MDFA .... Magnet Distributors and Fabricators Association (NTPA)
MDFA .... Mitochondrial Disorders Foundation of America (SAUO)
MDFAT ...... Microsoft DoubleSpace File Allocation Table (PCM)
MDFC .... Mason Dixon International Fan Club (EA)
MDFC .... Matt Dillon Fan Club (EA)
MDFC .... McDonnel Douglas Finance Corporation (SAUO)
MDFC .... McDonnell Douglas Finance Corp. Ltd. [*British*]
MDFCTA ..... Metropolitan Drinking Fountain and Cattle Trough Association (SAUO)
MDFD .... Map-Dot-Fingerprint Dystrophy [*Medicine*] (DMAA)
MdFdBc ..... Maryland Federal Bancorp, Inc. [*Associated Press*] (SAG)
MdFdM ...... United States Army Medical Intelligence and Information Agency, Fort Detrick, MD [*Library symbol*] [*Library of Congress*] (LCLS)
MdFhV ...... United States Veterans Administration Hospital, Fort Howard, MD [*Library symbol*] [*Library of Congress*] (LCLS)
MD Fla ...... United States District Court for the Middle District of Florida (DLA)
MDFLT ...... Multi-Directional Forklift Truck (MCD)
MdFmA ...... United States Army, Fort George G. Meade Post Recreation Services Library, Fort George G. Meade, MD [*Library symbol*] [*Library of Congress*] (LCLS)
MdFmN ..... National Security Agency, Fort George G. Meade, MD [*Library symbol*] [*Library of Congress*] (LCLS)
MDFMR ..... M-Day Force Materiel Requirement
MDFN .... Modification [*Telegraphy*] (PCTE)
MDFNA ...... Maximum Density Fuming Nitric Acid
MDFP .... Mission Data Formats Project [*NASA*] (SSD)
MDFPAC .... Minn-Dak Farmers Cooperative PAC [*Wahpeton, ND*] (PACS)
MDFR .... Make Descent From [*Aviation*] (FAAC)
MDFR .... Master Data File Record (ACAE)
MDFRC ...... Murray-Darling Freshwater Research Centre (SAUO)
MdFre .... Frederick County Public Library, Frederick, MD [*Library symbol*] [*Library of Congress*] (LCLS)
MdFreCR .... Frederick Cancer Research Center, Frederick, MD [*Library symbol*] [*Library of Congress*] (LCLS)
MdFreD ..... Fort Detrick Technical Library, Frederick, MD [*Library symbol*] [*Library of Congress*] (LCLS)
MdFreFC .... Frederick Community College, Frederick, MD [*Library symbol*] [*Library of Congress*] (LCLS)
MdFreH ..... Hood College, Frederick, MD [*Library symbol*] [*Library of Congress*] (LCLS)
MdFreHi .... [*The*] Historical Society of Frederick County, Inc., Frederick, MD [*Library symbol*] [*Library of Congress*] (LCLS)
MdFreSD .... Maryland School for the Deaf, Frederick, MD [*Library symbol*] [*Library of Congress*] (LCLS)
MdFroS ..... Frostburg State College, Frostburg, MD [*Library symbol*] [*Library of Congress*] (LCLS)
MDFRR ...... Mission Directors Flight Readiness Review [*NASA*] (KSC)
MDFT .... Medifast, Inc. [*NASDAQ symbol*] (QUAN)
MDFU .... Navigazione San Paulo [*Intermodal shipping container symbol*] (TVRC)
MDG .... Air Madagascar, Societe Nationale Malgache de Transports Aeriens [*ICAO designator*] (FAAC)
MDG .... Machinery Defective, Government-Furnished (DNAB)
MDG .... Machining-Intensive Durable Goods [*Manufacturing*]
MDG .... Madagascar [*ANSI three-letter standard code*] (CNC)
Mdg .... Madagascar (MILB)
MDG .... Madang [*Papua New Guinea*] [*Seismograph station code, US Geological Survey*] (SEIS)
MDG .... Major Donors Group (SAUO)
MDG .... Marina Development Group [*Commercial firm*] [*British*]
MDG .... Marine Data Group (SAUO)
MDG .... Mean Diastolic Gradient [*Medicine*] (DMAA)
MDG .... Medical Director-General [*Navy*] [*British*]
MDG .... Meridian Gold [*NYSE symbol*] [*Formerly, FMC Gold*] (SG)
MDG .... Message Design Guidelines Group (SAUO)
MDG .... Metal Density Gauge
MDG .... Metasystems Design Group, Inc. [*Arlington, VA*] [*Telecommunications service*] (TSSD)
MDG .... Methyladenine Deoxyribonucleic Acid Glycosylase [*Medicine*] (DMAA)
MDG .... Middling [*Telegraphy*] (PCTE)
MDG .... Mission Data Generation (ACAE)
MDG .... Mission Data Generator (SAUO)
MDG .... Mission Definition Group (SAUO)
MDG .... Molecular Drag Gauge [*Instrumentation*]
MDG .... Mono/Diglycerides
MDG .... Multi-Disciplinary Group (SAUO)
MDG .... Multimedia Development Group (DDC)
MDG .... Multiple Diffraction Gratings (ACAE)
MDG .... Multiplier Decoder Gate [*Computer science*]
MDG .... Multipurpose Display Group (MCD)
MDG .... Valdosta, GA [*Location identifier*] [*FAA*] (FAAL)
MDGA .... Guerra [*Dominican Republic*] [*ICAO location identifier*] (ICLI)
MD GA ...... United States District Court for the Middle District of Georgia (DLA)
MDGC .... Multidimensional Gas Chromatography
MDGD .... Mercury Doped Germanium Detector
MDGF .... Macrophage Derived Growth Factor [*Biochemistry*]
MDGGB ...... Muscular Dystrophy Group of Great Britain (SAUO)
MDGLS ...... Missouri Division of Geology and Land Survey (SAUO)
MDGN .... Med Gen [*OTCBB symbol*]
MDG(N) ..... Medical Director-General (Navy) [*British*]
MDGP .... Medgroup Inc. Calif [*NASDAQ symbol*] (TTSB)
MDGP .... Monash Division of General Practice (SAUO)
MDGR .... Multi-Differential GPS Receiver
MDG RCN ... Medical Director General of the Royal Canadian Navy (SAUO)
MDGT .... Midget (MSA)
MDGWS ..... Modular Digital Guided Weapon System (ACAE)
MDH .... Carbondale [*Illinois*] [*Airport symbol*] (OAG)
MDH .... Carbondale/Murphysboro, IL [*Location identifier*] [*FAA*] (FAAL)
MDH .... Madison Holdings Ltd. [*Vancouver Stock Exchange symbol*]
MDH .... Magnetic Drum Head
MDH .... Major Damage History [*Aviation*] (PIPO)
MDH .... Malate Dehydrogenase [*Also, MD*] [*An enzyme*]
MDH .... Malate/Malic Dehydrogenase [*Medicine*] (EDAA)
MDH .... Maneuver Director Headquarters [*Military*]
MDH .... Maximum Diameter Heat [*Nuclear science*] (OA)
MDH .... Mean Dominant Height
MDH .... Medullary Dorsal Horn [*Anatomy*]
MDH .... Minimum Descent Height [*Aviation*] (FAAC)
MDH .... Minnesota Department of Health (SAUO)
MDH .... Month-Day-Hour [*Automotive manufacturing*]
MDH .... Multidirectional Harassment (PDAA)
MDHA .... Masters Deerhounds Association [*British*] (DBA)
MdHag ...... Washington County Free Library, Hagerstown, MD [*Library symbol*] [*Library of Congress*] (LCLS)
MDHBA ...... Medical-Dental-Hospital Bureaus of America (EA)
MDHBA ...... Medical Dental Hospital Business Associates [*Association*] (EA)
MDHC .... McDonnell Douglas Helicopter Co. [*Formerly, HHI*] (MCD)
MDHC .... Mersey Docks and Harbour Co. [*British*]
MDHE .... Herrera [*Dominican Republic*] [*ICAO location identifier*] (ICLI)
MdHeH ...... Henryton State Hospital, Henryton, MD [*Library symbol*] [*Library of Congress*] (LCLS)
MdHi .... Maryland Historical Society, Baltimore, MD [*Library symbol*] [*Library of Congress*] (LCLS)
Md Hist ..... Maryland Historical Society (SAUO)
MDHJ .... Methyl Dihydrojasmonate [*Organic chemistry*]
MDHL .... Modified Hodges-Lehmann Estimator [*Statistics*]
MDHR .... Maximum Determined Heart Rate (STED)
MDHR .... Methyl Dihydroretinoate [*Biochemistry*]
MDHR .... Mini-Decay Heat Removal [*Nuclear energy*] (NRCH)
MDHS .... Malate Dehydrogenase, Soluble (STED)
MDHS .... McDonnell Douglas Helicopter Systems
MDHTSNAGEJTR... Movement of Dependents and Household Goods to Temporary Station[*s*] Not Authorized at Government Expense, Except as Prescribed in Joint Travel Regulations [*Army*] (AABC)
MDHV .... Marek's Disease Herpesvirus [*Medicine*] (DMAA)
MDHY .... Higuey [*Dominican Republic*] [*ICAO location identifier*] (ICLI)
MdHyD ...... De Sales Hall School of Theology, Hyattsville, MD [*Library symbol*] [*Library of Congress*] (LCLS)
MdHyP ...... Prince George's County Memorial Library, Hyattsville, MD [*Library symbol*] [*Library of Congress*] (LCLS)
MDI .... Bemidji, MN [*Location identifier*] [*FAA*] (FAAL)
MDI .... C-Methylene-Bisphenol-Isocyanate (SAUS)
MDI .... Magnetic Detection Indicator (IAA)
MDI .... Magnetic Direction Indicator
MDI .... Makurdi [*Nigeria*] [*Airport symbol*] (OAG)
MDI .... Management Development Institute (MCD)
MDI .... Manic Depression Interval [*Course*]
MDI .... Manic Depressive Illness
MDI .... Manual Data Input [*SAGE*]
MDI .... Manufacturing Development Initiative (SAUO)
MDI .... Manufacturing Division Instructions (ACAE)
MDI .... Market Decisions, Inc. [*Information service or system*] (IID)
MDI .... Market Development Index [*Business term*] (DOAD)
MDI .... Master Dimension Information
MDI .... Master Direction Indicator
MDI .... Master of Didactics
MDI .... Material Departmental Instruction
MDI .... Mechanical Dynamics Inc. (NITA)
MDI .... Media Directions, Inc.
MDI .... Media Directors, Incorporated (SAUO)
MDI .... Media (or Medium) Dependant (or Dependent) Interface (SAUS)
MDI .... Medium Dependent Interface [*Computer science*] (CDE)
MDI .... Memotec Data, Inc. [*Toronto Stock Exchange symbol*]
MDI .... Mental Deterioration Index [*Medicine*] (EDAA)
MDI .... Mental Development Index [*Bayley Scales of Infant Development*] [*Psychometrics*]
MDI .... Meridian Diagnostics, Inc.
MDI .... Metered Dose Inhaler [*Medicine*]
MDI .... Methylendiphenyldiisocyanat (SAUS)
MDI .... Methylenebis (Phenylisocyanate) (GNE)
MDI .... Methylene Diisocyanate [*Organic chemistry*]
MDI .... Methylene Diphenyl Diisocyanate [*Organic chemistry*]
MDI .... Methylene Diphenylene Diisocyanate (SAUS)
MDI .... Methylenediphenyl Isocyanate [*Organic chemistry*]
MDI .... Michelson Doppler Imager [*Instrumentation*]
MDI .... Michigan Disposal, Inc. (EFIS)

MDI.......... Micro Design International
MDI.......... Microdosimetric Instrumentation
MDI.......... Mid America Realty, Inc. [*Formerly, Dial REIT*] [*NYSE symbol*] (SAG)
MDI.......... Mid-America Realty Inv [*NYSE symbol*] (TTSB)
MDI.......... Mild/Moderate Depressive Illness [*Medicine*] (EDAA)
MDI.......... Military Decision Items (AFIT)
MDI.......... Mineral Deposit Inventory Database [*Ontario Geological Survey*] [*Information service or system*] [*Canada*] (CRD)
MDI.......... Minimum Discrimination Information [*Statistics*]
MDI.......... Miss-Distance Indicator [*Missiles*] (MUGU)
MDI.......... Mission Dependent Interface
MDI.......... Mission to the Deaf, International (EA)
MDI.......... Mobile Data Initiative (SAUO)
MDI.......... Mobilization Day Increment [*Military*]
MDI.......... Mobilization Day Index [*Military*] (NG)
MDI.......... Modular Devices Inc. (SAUS)
MDI.......... Monopulse Display Improvement (IAA)
MDI.......... Monthly Debit Industrial [*Insurance*]
MDI.......... Motor Development International [*Automotive supplier*]
MDI.......... Mouvement pour la Democratie et l'Independance [*Movement for Democracy and Independence*] [*Central Africa*] (PD)
MDI.......... Multidocument Interface [*Computer science*] (GART)
MDI.......... Multiple Daily Injection [*Medicine*] (MELL)
MDI.......... Multiple Design Interface
MDI.......... Multiple Display Indicator
MDI.......... Multiple Document Interface [*Computer science*] (PCM)
MDI.......... Multiple Dosage Insulin [*Medicine*] (STED)
MDI.......... Multipurpose Display Indicator (ACAE)
MDI.......... Multiscore Depression Inventory [*Medicine*] (STED)
MDI.......... Muscular Dystrophy Ireland (NRGU)
MDIA........ Mental Development Index, Adjusted (STED)
MDIA........ Multidimensional Intraction Analysis (DMAA)
MDIB........ Minimum Distribution Incidental Benefit [*Finance*]
MDIBL....... Mount Desert Island Biological Laboratory [*Salsbury Cove, ME*] [*Research center*]
MDIC........ Malaysian Defence Industries Council (SAUO)
MDIC........ Manchester Decoder and Interface Chip (SAUO)
MDIC........ Microwave Dielectric Integrated Circuit (IEEE)
MDIC........ Multi-Disciplinary Counter Intelligence
MDIC........ Multilateral Disarmament Information Centre [*British*]
MDICP....... McDonnell Douglas Industrial Control Products (MCD)
M DICT...... More Dicto [*As Directed*] [*Pharmacy*]
M Dict...... Morison's Dictionary of Decisions, Scotch Court of Session [*1540-1808*] [*A publication*] (DLA)
M Dict...... Morrison's Dictionary of Decisions, Scotch Court of Session [*A publication*] (DLA)
M Did....... Master of Didactics
M Di E...... Master of Diesel Engineering
MDIE........ Mother-Daughter Ionosphere Experiment
M Di Eng... Master of Diesel Engineering
MDIF........ Manual Data Input Function [*Computer science*]
MDIF & W... Maine Department of Inland Fisheries and Wildlife, Fishery Research Management Division [*Research center*] (RCD)
MDIG........ Multiple Display Indicator Group (SAUO)
MDIG........ Multipurpose Display Indicator Group (SAUO)
MDII........ Management Development II (SAUO)
MDII........ Mechanical Dynamics [*NASDAQ symbol*] (TTSB)
MDII........ Mechanical Dynamics, Inc. [*NASDAQ symbol*] (SAG)
MDII........ Multiple Daily Insulin Injection (STED)
MDIII....... Management Development III (SAUO)
MDIN........ Medalist Indus [*NASDAQ symbol*] (TTSB)
MDIN........ Medalist Industries, Inc. [*NASDAQ symbol*] (NQ)
Md Inst C Art... Maryland Institute College of Art (GAGS)
MDIO........ Maine Debris Information Office [*National Oceanic and Atmospheric Administration*]
M Dip....... Master of Diplomacy
MD IPA...... MD Individual Practice Association (MHID)
MDIR........ Merchants Distribution Service [*Common carrier symbol*]
M-DIRT...... Miss-Distance-Indicator Radioactive Tests [*Missiles*] (MUGU)
MDIS........ Maintenance and Diagnostic Information System (ACAE)
MDIS........ Manual Data Input Section [*Computer science*]
MDIS........ Manual Data Input System [*Computer science*]
M Dis....... Marriage Dissolved
MDIS........ McDonnell Douglas Information Services
MDIS........ McDonnell Information Systems Group (SAUO)
MDIS........ Medical Diagnostics Imagery System (SAUS)
MDIS........ Medical Digital Imaging Support (RDA)
MDIS........ Metadata Interchange Specification [*Computer science*]
MDISC....... McDonnell Douglas International Sales Corp. (MCD)
MDISE....... Merchandise
MDISI....... McDonnell Douglas Information Systems International (SAUO)
MDIT........ Madera International [*NASDAQ symbol*]
MDIT........ Mean Disintegration Time (STED)
MDIU........ Manned Data Insertion Unit (KSC)
MDIU........ Manual Data Input Unit [*Computer science*]
M Div....... Master of Divinity
MDIX........ Media Dependant Interface Crossed (SAUS)
MDIX........ Medium Dependant Interface Crossed (SAUS)
MDJ......... Jaro International SA [*Romania*] [*ICAO designator*] (FAAC)
MDJAPAN... McDonnell Douglas Japan Ltd. (SAUO)
MdJC........ Maryland House of Corrections, Jessup, MD [*Library symbol*] [*Library of Congress*] (LCLS)
MDJC........ Miami-Dade Junior College (SAUO)
MDJC........ Mississippi Delta Junior College (SAUO)
MDJCS...... Memorandum by the Director, Joint Staff for the Joint Chiefs of Staff (MCD)
Md J Int'l L & Trade... Maryland Journal of International Law and Trade [*A publication*] (DLA)
MDJL........ McDonnell Douglas Japan Ltd. (SAUO)
MDJM........ Jainamosa [*Dominican Republic*] [*ICAO location identifier*] (ICLI)
MDK......... Mangbutu [*Language symbol*] (ETLW)
MDK......... Mbandaka [*Zaire*] [*Airport symbol*] (OAG)
MDK......... Mechanical Disconnect Kit
MDK......... Medicore, Inc. [*AMEX symbol*] (SPSG)
MDK......... Modem Developers Kit [*Computer science*] (MWOL)
MDK......... Montana-Dakota Utilities Company (SAUO)
MDK......... Multimedia Developers Kit (SAUO)
MDK......... Multimedia Development Kit [*Microsoft Corp.*] [*Computer science*]
MDKI........ Medicore, Inc. [*NASDAQ symbol*] (NASQ)
MDKI........ Michigan District of Kiwanis International (EARSL)
MDL......... Macro Description Language [*Computer science*] (BUR)
MDL......... Madill [*S.*] Ltd. [*Vancouver Stock Exchange symbol*]
MDL......... Magnetic Delay Line
MDL......... Magnetic Double Layer
MDL......... Main Defense Line (IAA)
MDL......... Maintenance and Diagnostic Logic Display [*Burroughs*] (NITA)
MDL......... Maintenance Diagnostic Logic [*Computer science*] (BUR)
MDL......... Management Data List (AABC)
MDL......... Manager's Discretionary Limit (DCTA)
MDL......... Mandala Airlines PT [*Indonesia*] [*ICAO designator*] (FAAC)
MDL......... Mandalay [*Burma*] [*Airport symbol*] (AD)
MDL......... Mandalay [*Myanmar*] [*Airport symbol*] (OAG)
MDL......... Man Days Lost (NUCP)
MDL......... Master Data Library [*NASA*]
MDL......... Master Deliverables List (AAEL)
MDL......... Master Drawing List
MDL......... Master Drug List (STED)
MDL......... Master of Divine Literature
MDL......... Material Deviation List [*Military*]
MDL......... Maximum Doping Limit
MDL......... Measurement Devices Limited (SAUO)
MDL......... Medical Data Limited (SAUO)
MDL......... Medical DeviceLink Directory of North American Suppliers [*Database*] (GDD)
MDL......... Medulloblastoma [*A type of brain cancer*] (CDI)
MDL......... Memory Descriptor List [*Computer science*] (MWOL)
MDL......... Mercury Delay Line
MDL......... Method Detection Limit [*Analytical chemistry*]
MDL......... Microprocessor Development Lab (MHDI)
MDL......... MicroStation Development Language [*Intergraph Corp.*] (PCM)
MDL......... Microwave Delay Line
MDL......... Microwave Development Laboratories
MDL......... Middle (MSA)
MDL......... Military Demarcation Line (CINC)
MDL......... Mine Defense Laboratory [*Panama City, Florida*] [*Navy*]
MDL......... Miniature Display Light
MDL......... Minimum Detectable Level
MDL......... Minimum Detection Limit [*Chemistry*]
MDL......... Mission Data Load [*Space launch term*] (ISAK)
MDL......... Model (ADA)
MDL......... Modular Design Language [*Computer science*] (CSR)
MDL......... Modular Dummy Load
MDL......... Module (MSA)
MDL......... Morris Dam Laboratory
MDL......... Motor Distal Latency [*Medicine*]
MDL......... Muddle [*A computer language*]
MDL......... Multi-Disciplinary Laboratory (SAUO)
MDL......... Multipurpose Data Link (GAVI)
MDL......... S Madill Ltd. [*Vancouver Stock Exchange symbol*]
MDL......... University of Baltimore, Law Library, Baltimore, MD [*OCLC symbol*] (OCLC)
MdLA........ Maryland Library Association
MD LA....... United States District Court for the Middle District of Louisiana (DLA)
MdLaD...... Divine Saviour Seminary, Lanham, MD [*Library symbol*] [*Library of Congress*] (LCLS)
MdLapC..... Charles County Community College, La Plata, MD [*Library symbol*] [*Library of Congress*] (LCLS)
MD Laws... Laws of Maryland [*A publication*] (DLA)
MDLB........ Municipal Development and Loan Board [*Canada*]
MDLC........ Material Development and Logistic Command (SAUO)
MDLC........ Materiel Development and Logistic Command [*Army - replaced Ordnance, Engineer, Signal, Chemical and Quartermaster Overall Commands*]
MDLC........ Mutliple Data Link Controller
MDLD........ Midland Financial Group [*NASDAQ symbol*] (SAG)
MDLD........ Midland Transport [*Common carrier symbol*]
MDLF........ Mobile Drydock Launch Facility
MDLI........ MDL Information Sys [*NASDAQ symbol*] (TTSB)
MDLI........ MDL Information Systems, Inc. [*NASDAQ symbol*] (SAG)
MDL Info.... MDL Information Systems, Inc. [*Associated Press*] (SAG)
Md-LL....... Maryland State Law Library, Annapolis, MD [*Library symbol*] [*Library of Congress*] (LCLS)
MDLLE...... Mademoiselle
MDLLS...... Mediastinal Diffuse Large-Cell Lymphoma with Sclerosis [*Oncology*]
MDLND...... Midland
MDLND...... Midland, MI [*American Association of Railroads railroad junction routing code*]
MDLP........ Minimum Description Length Principle (IDAI)

MDLP........ Mobile Dryer Loan Program
MDLP........ Module Data Link Protocol [*Computer science*] (VLIE)
MdLP........ United States Department of the Interior, Patuxent Wildlife Research Center, Laurel, MD [*Library symbol*] [*Library of Congress*] (LCLS)
MDLR........ La Romana [*Dominican Republic*] [*ICAO location identifier*] (ICLI)
Md-LR........ Maryland Department of Legislative Reference, Baltimore, MD [*Library symbol*] [*Library of Congress*] (LCLS)
MDLR........ Midland Terminal [*Federal Railroad Administration identification code*]
MDLRC...... Mental Disability Legal Resource Center [*Later, MPDLRSDB*] (EA)
MD L Rec... Maryland Law Record [*Baltimore*] [*A publication*] (DLA)
MD L Rep... Maryland Law Reporter [*Baltimore*] [*A publication*] (DLA)
MDLS........ Marine Data Logger System
MDLS........ Middles [*Telegraphy*] (PCTE)
MDLT........ Mobile Data Link Terminal (SAUS)
MDLTN...... Middletown, NY [*American Association of Railroads railroad junction routing code*]
MdLuW...... Maryland College for Women, Lutherville, MD [*Library symbol*] [*Library of Congress*] (LCLS)
MDLV........ Martin's Freight Systems [*Common carrier symbol*]
MDLX........ Military Demarkation Line Extended (MCD)
MdLxp....... Lexington Park Library, Lexington Park, MD [*Library symbol*] [*Library of Congress*] (LCLS)
Mdm......... Madam (WGA)
MDM......... Magnetic Disc Memory
MDM......... Magnetic Drum Memorex [*Computer science*] (IAA)
MDM......... Magneto-Optical Display Memory
MDM......... Main Data Memory [*Computer science*] (VLIE)
MDM......... Maintenance Depot Material Control
MDM......... Maize Dwarf Mosaic Virus [*Plant pathology*]
MDM......... Manipulator Deployment Mechanism (MCD)
MDM......... Manpower Determination Model [*Military*]
MDM......... Manufacturing Data Management (VLIE)
MDM......... Maps Distribution Management (SAUO)
MDM......... Marketing Data Management (VLIE)
MDM......... Marketing Data Mart (GART)
MDM......... Marking Diagram Master (MCD)
MDM......... Marshall Drummond McCall, Inc. [*Toronto Stock Exchange symbol*]
MDM......... Mass Democratic Movement [*Political coalition*] [*South Africa*]
MDM......... Master of Development Management
MDM......... Maternal Diabetes Mellitus [*Medicine*]
MDM......... Maximum Design Meter (MSA)
MDM......... Mechanically Deboned Meat [*Food technology*]
MDM......... Medical Decision Making (DMAA)
MDM......... Medical Monitor (MCD)
MDM......... Medium (AABC)
MDM......... Medium-Depth Mine (MCD)
MDM......... MedPartners/Mullikin [*NYSE symbol*] (TTSB)
MDM......... Message Distribution Module (CCCA)
MDM......... Metal-Dielectric-Metal [*Filter*]
MDM......... Metal Disintegration Machining [*Nuclear energy*] (NRCH)
MDM......... Methylenedioxymethamphetamine [*A hallucinogenic drug, also known as "Ecstasy," banned in 1985*] [*Also, MDMA*]
MDM......... Michigan-Dartmouth-Massachusetts Institute of Technology [*Observatory*]
MDM......... Microdensitometer (IAA)
MDM......... Midas Minerals, Inc. [*Toronto Stock Exchange symbol*]
MDM......... Mid-Diastolic Murmur [*Medicine*]
MDM......... Minor Determinant Mix [*Penicillin*] [*Medicine*] (STED)
MDM......... Minor Determinant Mixture [*Medicine*]
MDM......... Mission Data Message (SAUO)
MDM......... Mission Data Module (ACAE)
MDM......... Mixed Dark Matter [*Cosmology*]
MDM......... Mobile Depot Maintenance [*Air Force*] (AFM)
MDM......... Modified Diffusion Method (NRCH)
MDM......... Modular Data Module (HGAA)
MDM......... Monolithic Diode Matrix
MDM......... Monomethylol Dimethyl (ACAE)
MDM......... Movement for a Democratic Military (EA)
MDM......... Movimento Democratico de Mocambique [*Democratic Movement of Mozambique*] (AF)
MDM......... Multiplexer/Demultiplexer (NASA)
MDM......... Multiprocessor Diagnostic Monitor (IAA)
MDM......... Working Group on Marine Data Management (SAUO)
MDMA........ M-Day Materiel Assets (AFIT)
MDMA........ Medical Device Manufacturers Association (NTPA)
MDMA........ Methylenedioxymethamphetamine [*A hallucinogenic drug, also known as "Ecstasy," banned in 1985*] [*Also, MDM*]
MDMAA...... Mess Deck Master-at-Arms (DNAB)
MDMAF...... Mekong Delta Mobile Afloat Force [*Vietnam*]
Mdmarco... Medmarco, Inc. [*Associated Press*] (SAG)
MDMC........ Medmarco, Inc. [*NASDAQ symbol*] (SAG)
MDMC........ Monte Cristy [*Dominican Republic*] [*ICAO location identifier*] (ICLI)
MDMCA...... Melvil Dui Marching and Chowder Association (EA)
MdMC-G..... Montgomery College, Germantown Campus, Germantown, MD [*Library symbol*] [*Library of Congress*] (LCLS)
MdMC-R..... Montgomery College, Rockville Campus, Rockville, MD [*Library symbol*] [*Library of Congress*] (LCLS)
MdMC-T..... Montgomery College, Takoma Park Campus, Takoma Park, MD [*Library symbol*] [*Library of Congress*] (LCLS)
MDMCW...... Medmarco Inc. Wrrt'A' [*NASDAQ symbol*] (TTSB)
MDMCZ...... Medmarco Inc. Wrrt'B' [*NASDAQ symbol*] (TTSB)
MDMD........ Medirisk, Inc. [*NASDAQ symbol*] (NASQ)
mDMD........ Mouse Duchenne Muscular Dystrophy [*Medicine*]
MDME........ Madame
MDMFM...... Miniature Digital Matched Filter Module [*Computer science*] (VLIE)
Md-MH....... Maryland Department of Mental Hygiene, Baltimore, MD [*Library symbol*] [*Library of Congress*] (LCLS)
MDMH........ Methylol Dimethylhydantoin [*Organic chemistry*]
MdMHCA.... Maryland Mental Health Counselors Association (SEAT)
MDML........ Modified Maximum Likelihood [*Statistics*]
MDMLG...... Metropolitan Detroit Medical Library Group (SAUO)
MDMMS..... Multidimensional Microscopes and Maize Structures Research Group (SAUO)
MDMN........ Modified Posterior Mean [*Statistics*]
MD-MOS.... Multi-Drain Metal-Oxide Semiconductor (AAEL)
MDMR........ M-Day Materiel Requirement (AFIT)
MDMR........ M-Day Mobilization Requirement
MDMS........ Maintenance Data Management Schedule
MDMS........ Maintenance Data Management System (SAUO)
MDMS........ Marketing Data Management System [*British*]
MDMS........ Microbiology Data Management System
MDMS........ Miss-Distance Measuring System
MDMS........ Moore Data Management Services [*Information service or system*] (IID)
MDMS........ Moore North American (IID)
MDMS........ Multiple Database Management System (NITA)
MDMS........ Multiple Delivery Mine System (SAUS)
MDMSC...... McDonnell Douglas Missile Systems Co. (SAUO)
MDMU........ Midmac Contracting International [*Intermodal shipping container symbol*] (TVRC)
MDMV........ Maize Dwarf Mosaic Virus [*Plant pathology*]
MdMwH...... Mount Wilson State Hospital, Mount Wilson, MD [*Library symbol*] [*Library of Congress*] (LCLS)
MDN......... Madison, IN [*Location identifier*] [*FAA*] (FAAL)
MDN......... Maiden Race [*Horse racing*]
MDN......... Managed Data Network
MDN......... Managed Data Networks (SAUO)
MdN......... Mandibular Nerve [*Anatomy*]
MDN......... Manufacturing Day Number (MCD)
MDN......... Mark der Deutschen Notenbank [*Mark of the German Bank of Issue*] [*Later, M*] (EG)
Mdn......... Median (DIPS)
MDN......... Median (STED)
MDN......... Mercury Deposition Network
MDN......... Meridian Industrial Trust [*NYSE symbol*] (TTSB)
MDN......... Meridian Industrial Trust, Inc. [*AMEX symbol*] (SAG)
MDN......... Meta Data Navigator (SAUO)
MDN......... Ministere de la Defense Nationale [*Department of National Defense*] [*Canada*]
MDN......... Mobilisation pour le Developpement National [*Haiti*] [*Political party*] (EY)
MDN......... Moderation [*Telegraphy*] (PCTE)
MDN......... Movimiento Democratico Nacionalista [*Nationalist Democratic Movement*] [*Guatemala*] [*Political party*]
MDN......... Movimiento Democratico Nicaraguense [*Nicaraguan Democratic Movement*] [*Political party*] (PPW)
MDN......... Northern Mining Explorations Ltd. [*Toronto Stock Exchange symbol*] [*Canada*]
MDN......... Universair [*Spain*] [*ICAO designator*] (FAAC)
MDN.WS.... Meridian Indl Tr Wrrt [*AMEX symbol*] (TTSB)
MDNA........ Machinery Dealers National Association (EA)
MDNA........ Maximum Density Nitric Acid
MDNA........ Mobilehome Dealers National Association (EA)
MDNA........ Modena [*NCIC car make code*]
MDNB........ Mean Daily Nitrogen Balance [*Medicine*]
MDNB........ Meta-Dinitrobenzene [*Organic chemistry*]
MD/NC...... Mechanical Drafting/Numerical Control (IEEE)
MDNC........ United States District Court for the Middle District of North Carolina (DLA)
MDNCF...... Monocyte-Derived Neutrophil Chemotactic Factor [*Medicine*] (PALA)
MDNF........ Minimal Disjunctive Normal Form (MHDB)
MDNIS....... Machinery Dealers' National Information System
MDNMNA... Moorish Divine and National Movement in North America (EA)
MDNP........ Methyl Dinitropentanoate [*An explosive*]
Md-NR....... Maryland State Department of Natural Resources, Annapolis, MD [*Library symbol*] [*Library of Congress*] (LCLS)
MDNR........ Michigan Department of Natural Resources
MDNR........ Minnesota Department of Natural Resources
MDNR........ Missouri Department of Natural Resources (DOGT)
MDNS........ Managed Data Network Service (SAUO)
MDNS........ Managed Data Network Services (NITA)
MDNT........ Midnight
MDNT........ MNC Financial, Inc. [*NASDAQ symbol*] (COMM)
MDNX........ Medinex Systems, Inc. [*NASDAQ symbol*] (QUAN)
MDNX........ Modern Air Transport [*Air carrier designation symbol*]
MDO......... Macedonia AS [*Yugoslavia*] [*ICAO designator*] (FAAC)
MDO......... Madison, FL [*Amtrak rail station code*]
MDO......... Maintenance Development Officer (MCD)
MDO......... MARC Development Office (NITA)
MDO......... Marine Diesel Oil
MdO......... Masoreten des Ostens (BJA)
MDO......... Massive Dark Object [*Galactic science*]
MDO......... Mechanized Desert Operations [*Military*] (MCD)
MDO......... Medium Density Overlay [*Plywood*]
MDO......... Membrane-Derived Oligosaccharide [*Biochemistry*]
MDO......... Methylenedioxyphenyl [*Organic chemistry*]
MDO......... Middleton Island, AK [*Location identifier*] [*FAA*] (FAAL)
MDO......... Mobile District Office [*Army Corps of Engineers*]
MDO......... Monthly Debit Ordinary [*Insurance*]

MDO .... Moora District Office (SAUO)
MdO .... Ruth Enlow Library of Garrett County, Oakland, MD [*Library symbol*] [*Library of Congress*] (LCLS)
MDOA .... Material Date of Arrival (DNAB)
MDOC .... Missouri Department of Conservation
MdOdN ...... National Plastics Products Co., Odenton, MD [*Library symbol*] [*Library of Congress*] [*Obsolete*] (LCLS)
MdOdS ...... Saran Yarn Co., Odenton, MD [*Library symbol*] [*Library of Congress*] [*Obsolete*] (LCLS)
MDOF .... Multiple Degree of Freedom [*Acoustics*]
MdOmR ..... Rosewood Center, Owing Mills, MD [*Library symbol*] [*Library of Congress*] (LCLS)
MDOP .... Malicious Destruction of Property
MDOP .... Maximum Design Operating Pressure [*NASA*]
MDOPA...... Methyldopamine [*Biochemistry*]
MDOS .... Motorola Disk Operating System
MDOS .... Multiprocessor Disk Operating System [*Computer science*] (VLIE)
MDOSIS..... Management Data Online Status/Inquiry System (MCD)
MDOT .... Department of Transportation (SAUS)
MDOT .... Michigan Department of Transportation
MDOT .... Modular Digital Output Timer
MDovC ...... Chickering House, Dover, MA [*Library symbol*] [*Library of Congress*] (LCLS)
MDovS ...... Saint Stephen's College, Dover, MA [*Library symbol*] [*Library of Congress*] (LCLS)
MDP .... Coppin State College, Parlett L. Moore Library, Baltimore, MD [*OCLC symbol*] (OCLC)
MDP .... Ferrocarril Mexicano del Pacifico [*Mexican Pacific Railroad Co., Inc.*] [*AAR code*]
MDP .... Madagascar-Press (SAUO)
MDP .... Magyar Dolgozok Partja [*Hungarian Workers' Party*] [*Political party*] (PPE)
MDP .... Main Data Path
MDP .... Main Display Panel (SAA)
MDP .... Maintainability Demonstration Plan (MCD)
MDP .... Maintenance Data Panel (SAUS)
MDP .... Maintenance Data Program (MCD)
MDP .... Maintenance Depot Production
MDP .... Maintenance Diagnostic Processor (NITA)
MDP .... Maintenance Diagnostic Program [*Computer science*] (IAA)
MDP .... Maintenance Display Panel (MCD)
MDP .... Malfunction Detection Package
MDP .... Malicious Destruction of Property
MDP .... Management Development Program (SAUS)
MDP .... Management Development Programme [*British*] (DCTA)
MDP .... Managing Director Posts [*British*] (DCTA)
MDP .... Mandibular Dysostosis and Peromelia (DB)
MDP .... Manic Depressive Psychosis
MDP .... Manifold Differential Pressure [*Automotive term*] (HAWK)
MDP .... Manpower Development Program [*Department of Labor*]
MDP .... Markov Decision Problem (IDAI)
MDP .... Master Data Processing (ACAE)
MDP .... Master Decommissioning Plan [*Nuclear energy*] (NRCH)
MDP .... Master Design Plan (MCD)
MDP .... Master Display Panel (KSC)
MDP .... Maximum Diastolic Potential [*Physiology*]
MDP .... Mean Datum Plane
MDP .... Mean Designation Point (CAAL)
MDP .... Mechanically Deboned Poultry [*Food technology*]
MDP .... Menthyldiphenyphosphine [*Organic chemistry*]
MDP .... Mento-Dextra Posterior [*A fetal position*] [*Obstetrics*]
MDP .... Meredith Corp. [*NYSE symbol*] (SPSG)
MDP .... Message Discrimination Process [*Telecommunications*] (TEL)
MDP .... Meteorological Datum Plane
MDP .... Methyldichlorophosphine [*Organic chemistry*]
MDP .... Methylene Diphosphonate [*Organic chemistry*]
MDP .... Methylenediphosphonic Acid [*Organic chemistry*]
MDP .... Microprocessor Debugging Program [*Computer science*] (IAA)
MDP .... Midpines, CA [*Amtrak Busline code*]
MDP .... Millennium Democratic Party [*Political party*] [*South Korea*]
MDP .... Milliyetci Demokrasi Partisi [*Nationalist Democracy Party*] [*Turkey*] [*Political party*] (EY)
MDP .... Mindiptana [*Indonesia*] [*Airport symbol*] (OAG)
MDP .... Minimal Distance Principle [*Linguistics*] (IEL)
MDP .... Minimum Discernible Pulse (MCD)
MDP .... Minimum Distance Probability
MDP .... Ministry of Defence Police (SAUS)
MDP .... Missile Data Processor (OA)
MDP .... Mode Products, Inc. [*Vancouver Stock Exchange symbol*]
MDP .... Modular Display Processor (SAUS)
MDP .... Mongolian Democratic Party (ODA)
MDP .... Moslem Democratic Party [*Philippines*] [*Political party*] (PPW)
MDP .... Most Dispensable Program [*Television*]
MDP .... Motorola Data Processor [*Computer science*] (IAA)
MDP .... Mouvement Democratique et Populaire [*Popular Democratic Movement*] [*Senegal*] [*Political party*] (PPW)
MDP .... Mouvement Democratique Populaire [*Popular Democratic Party*] [*The Comoros*] [*Political party*] (EY)
MDP .... Mouvement des Democrates Progressistes [*Burkina Faso*] [*Political party*] (EY)
MDP .... Movement for Democracy and Progress (Cameroon) [*Political party*] (PSAP)
MDP .... Movement for the Defense of the Republic (Cameroon) [*Political party*] (PSAP)
MDP .... Movimento Democratico Portugues [*Portuguese Democratic Movement*] [*Political party*] (PPE)
MDP .... Movimiento Democratico del Pueblo [*Paraguay*] [*Political party*] (EY)
MDP .... Movimiento Democratico Peruano [*Peruvian Democratic Movement*] [*Political party*]
MDP .... Movimiento Democratico Popular [*Popular Democratic Movement*] [*Chile*] [*Political party*] (PPW)
MDP .... Movimiento Democratico Popular [*Popular Democratic Movement*] [*Ecuador*] [*Political party*] (PPW)
MDP .... Moving Deformable Barrier [*NHTSA*] (TAG)
MDP .... Multi-Designation Protocol (SAUS)
MDP .... Multi-Disciplinary Practice
MDP .... Multi-Divisional Program (SAUO)
MDP .... Multidomain Polymer [*Biology*]
MDP .... Muramyl Dipeptide [*Immunochemistry*]
MDP .... Parkland Regional Library, Dauphin, Manitoba [*Library symbol*] [*National Library of Canada*] (NLC)
MDPA........ Master Data Processing Authorization (ACAE)
MDPA........ Metropolitan Health Networks [*OTCBB symbol*]
MDPA........ Mutual Defense Procurement Authority (SAUO)
MD PA....... United States District Court for the Middle District of Pennsylvania (DLA)
MdPa .... United States Naval Air Station, Patuxent River, MD [*Library symbol*] [*Library of Congress*] (LCLS)
MDPB .... Maine Dairy Promotion Board (EARSL)
MDPC .... Mount Diablo Peace Center (EA)
MDPC .... Punta Cana [*Dominican Republic*] [*ICAO location identifier*] (ICLI)
MDPD .... Medical Director
MDPE........ Medium-Density Polyethylene (EDCT)
MDPE........ Med-Pacific Express [*Common carrier symbol*]
MDPF........ Metal Diesel Particulate Filter
MDPF........ Methoxy(diphenyl)furanone [*Organic chemistry*]
MDPG .... Magnetic Digital-Pulse Generator
MDPH .... Massachusetts Department of Public Health (SAUO)
MDPHI ...... Media Development Project for the Hearing Impaired (NITA)
MDPI .... David P. McCarthy [*Common carrier symbol*]
MDPI .... Mathematics Diagnostic/Prescriptive Inventory (EDAC)
MDPI .... Media Products, Inc. [*NASDAQ symbol*] (COMM)
MDPI .... Molecular Diversity Preservation International (SAUO)
MDPL........ Madera Pallets and Transports [*Common carrier symbol*]
MDPL........ Movement for Disarmament, Peace and Liberty (SAUO)
MDPM....... Maintenance Douglas Process Manual
MDPM....... Mechanically Deboned Poultry Meat [*Food technology*]
MdPM .... University of Maryland, Eastern Shore, Princess Anne, MD [*Library symbol*] [*Library of Congress*] (LCLS)
MDPMA ..... Member of the Data Processing Managers Association (SAUO)
MDPN .... Midshipman
MDPNE...... Ministry of the Protection of Nature and the Environment (SAUO)
MDPO .... Medina Transport [*Common carrier symbol*]
MDPP .... Puerto Plata/La Union [*Dominican Republic*] [*ICAO location identifier*] (ICLI)
MDPPQ...... Mouvement pour la Defense des Prisonniers Politiques du Quebec [*Movement for the Defense of Political Prisoners of Quebec*]
MdPpV ...... United States Veterans Administration Hospital, Perry Point, MD [*Library symbol*] [*Library of Congress*] (LCLS)
MDPR .... Madrid Predict [*Orbit identification*]
MDPR .... Manufacturing Development and Process Request (AAG)
MDPS .... Metric Data Processing System [*Air Force*]
MDPS .... Mission Data Planning System (SAUS)
MDPS .... Mission Data Preparations Systems (SAUO)
MDPS .... Mission Data Preparation System [*Military*] (CAAL)
MDPS .... Mission Data Processing System (SAUS)
MDPS .... Mobilization and Deployment Planning System [*Army*]
MDPS .... Mouvement pour la Democratie et le Progres Social [*Benin*] [*Political party*] (EY)
MDPSK...... Multilevel Differential Phase Shift Keying [*Computer science*] (CIST)
MDPT........ Median Preventive Maintenance Time (MCD)
MDPV .... Medium-Duty Passenger Vehicle
MDPVM ..... Missionary Daughters of the Most Pure Virgin Mary (TOCD)
MDQ .... Mar Del Plata [*Argentina*] [*Airport symbol*] (OAG)
MDQ .... Market Driven Quality (AAEL)
MDQ .... MDC Communication Cl [*AMEX symbol*] [*Formerly, MDC Corp. Cl*] (SG)
MDQ .... MDC Communication Cl'A' [*AMEX symbol*] (TTSB)
MDQ .... MDC Corp. [*AMEX symbol*] (SAG)
MDQ .... MDE Explorations [*Vancouver Stock Exchange symbol*]
MDQ .... Memory Deviation Quotient (DMAA)
MDQ .... Menstrual Distress Questionnaire [*Medicine*] (DMAA)
MDQ .... Minimum Detectable Quantity
MDQL .... Multidimensional Query Language [*Computer science*]
MDQS .... Management Data Query System [*Computer science*]
MDQW ...... Modulation Dope Quantum Well (AAEL)
MDR .... Compania Mexicana de Aeroplanos SA [*Mexico*] [*ICAO designator*] (FAAC)
MDR .... Democratic Republican Movement (Rwanda) [*Political party*] (PSAP)
MDR .... Madera, CA [*Amtrak rail station code*]
MDR .... Madras [*India*] [*Seismograph station code, US Geological Survey*] (SEIS)
MDR .... Magnetic Dipole Radiation
MDR .... Magnetic Disc Recorder (NTCM)
MDR .... Magnetic Document Reader (IAA)
MDR .... Magnetic Drum Recorder
MDR .... Magnetic Field Dependent Resistor (IAA)
MDR .... Maintainability Demonstration Report (MCD)
MDR .... Maintenance Data Recorder (ACAE)
MDR .... Maintenance Data Report [*Army*] (AABC)
MDR .... Maintenance Demand Rate (NASA)

MDR........ Maintenance Design Requirement
MDR........ Major Design Review (KSC)
MDR........ Mandatory Device Reporting [*Program*]
MDR........ Manual Data Room
MDR........ Manually Digitized Radar (SAUS)
MDR........ Mark Document Reader [*Trademark*] [*Bell & Howell*]
MDR........ Market Data Retrieval [*Westport, CT*] [*Information service or system*] (IID)
MDR........ Market Data Retrieval Division (IID)
MD R........ Maryland Reports [*A publication*] (DLA)
MDR........ Master Data Record (NG)
MDR........ Master Discrepancy Report (AAG)
MDR........ Master of Dispute Resolution (PGP)
MDR........ Material Deficiency Reports [*Program*]
MDR........ Materiel Deficiency Report (SAUO)
MDR........ Maximum Desired Result (SAUO)
MDR........ McDermott International, Inc. [*NYSE symbol*] (SPSG)
MDR........ McDermott Intl. [*NYSE symbol*] (TTSB)
MDR........ MD Review [*Social Security Administration*] (OICC)
MDR........ Mechanical Development Report (MCD)
MDR........ Medfra, AK [*Location identifier*] [*FAA*] (FAAL)
MDR........ Median Detection Range (NVT)
MDR........ Medical Department Representative (SAUO)
MDR........ Medical Device Register, Inc. (IID)
MDR........ Medical Device Reporting (MHID)
MDR........ Medical Device Reporting System
MDR........ Medium Data Rate (DOMA)
MDR........ Medium Deep Recess [*Automotive engineering*]
MDR........ Memory-Data Register
MDR........ Message Detail Recording [*Later, SMDR*] [*Telecommunications*]
MDR........ Metropolitan District Railway [*London*]
MDR........ MicroDesign Resources
MDR........ Microwave Device Reliability (MCD)
MDR........ Mid-Louisiana Rail [*Federal Railroad Administration identification code*]
MDR........ Milestone Decision Review (MCD)
MDR........ Military Defense Readiness (SAA)
MDR........ Minimum Daily Requirement [*of a vitamin, etc.*] [*Later, Recommended Daily Requirement*] [*FDA*]
MDR........ Minimum Design Requirement (SAUO)
mdr........ Minimum Detectable Radiance (ARMP)
MDR........ Minimum Detectable Radiance (CARB)
MDR........ Minor Discrepancy Repair [*NASA*] (KSC)
MDR........ Minor Discrepancy Review [*NASA*] (GFGA)
MDR........ Miscellaneous Data Record [*Communications term*] (DCT)
MDR........ Missile Deviation Report (AAG)
MDR........ Missing Data Report (NASA)
MDR........ Mission Data Reduction
MDR........ Mock-Up Discrepancy Report [*Aerospace*] (AAG)
MDR........ Monthly Director's Review [*NASA*] (NASA)
MDR........ Morphine-Dependent Rate
MDR........ Morphology Dependent Resonance [*Physics*]
MDR........ Motion Detection Radar [*Hughes Electronics*]
MDR........ Motor-Driven Relay [*or Roter*]
MDR........ Multichannel Data Recorder
MDR........ Multi Disc Reader [*Computer science*] (DGA)
MDR........ Multidrug Resistance [*Medicine*]
MDR........ Multidrug-Resistant
MDR........ Multiple Drug Resistance [*Medicine*] (PALA)
MDR........ Munition Data Requirement
MDRA....... Material Deficiency Report Analysis (SAUO)
MDRA....... Multidrug-Resistance Associated [*Genetics*]
MDRA....... Muscular Dystrophy Research Association (SAUO)
MDRAF...... Mekong Delta Riverine Assault Force [*Vietnam*]
MDRAM..... Multibank DRAM [*Computer science*]
MDRAM..... Multibank Dynamic Random Access Memory [*Computer science*]
MDRC....... Manpower Demonstration Research Corporation (SAUO)
MDRC....... Manual Data Relay Center (MCD)
MDRC....... Materiel Development and Readiness Command [*Formerly, AMC*] [*See also DARCOM*] [*Army*]
MDRCBB.... Minnesota Dental Research Center for Biomaterials and Biomechanics (SAUO)
MDRD....... Mission Data Requirements Document [*NASA*] (KSC)
MDRE....... Mass Driver Reaction Engine [*Aerospace*]
MDREC...... Movement for Democracy, Renaissance and Revolution in Central Africa [*Political party*] (PSAP)
MD Rep..... Maryland Reports [*A publication*] (DLA)
MDRF....... Materials Dosimetry Reference Facility
MdRFD...... United States Food and Drug Administration, Rockville, MD [*Library symbol*] [*Library of Congress*] (LCLS)
MDRI........ Multidrug-Resistant Infection (MELL)
MDRI........ Multi-purpose Display Repeater Indicator (SAUS)
MDRL....... Mandrel [*Mechanical engineering*]
MDRL....... McDonnell Douglas Research Laboratories (SAUO)
MDRM...... Mouvement Democratique de Renovation Malgache [*Democratic Movement Malagasy Restoration*]
MdRMC..... Montgomery County Department of Public Libraries, Rockville, MD [*Library symbol*] [*Library of Congress*] (LCLS)
MdRNIO.... National Institute for Occupational Safety and Health, Rockville, MD [*Library symbol*] [*Library of Congress*] (LCLS)
MDRO....... Mission Disaster Relief Officer
MDROC..... Mission Design Requirements, Objectives, and Constraints
MDROF..... Managing Director of Royal Ordnance Factories [*British*] (RDA)
MDRP....... Migrant Dropout Reconnection Program [*Board of Cooperative Educational Services Geneseo Migrant Center*] (EA)
MDRP....... Movimiento Democratico Reformista Peruano [*Peruvian Democratic Reformist Movement*] [*Political party*] (PPW)
MDRS....... Management Data Reporting System (MCD)
MDRS....... Manpower Data Relay Station (IAA)
MDRS....... Manufacturing Data Retrieval System (NASA)
MDRS....... Mattis Dementia Rating Scale [*Medicine*] (DMAA)
MDRS....... Mission Data Retrieval System [*NASA*]
MDRS....... Mobilization Designation Reserve Section
MDRS....... Mobilization Designation Reserve Station (SAUO)
MDRS....... Mylar Diaphragm Rupture System
MDRSF...... Multi-Dimensional Random Sea Facility [*Hydraulics Research Station*] (PDAA)
MDRSV..... Maize Dwarf Ringspot Virus [*Plant pathology*]
MDRT....... Million Dollar Round Table [*Des Plaines, IL*] (EA)
MDRT....... Multidrug-Resistant Tuberculosis (MELL)
MDRTB..... Multidrug-Resistant Tuberculosis [*Medicine*]
MDRTC..... Diabetes Research and Training Center [*University of Michigan*] [*Research center*] (RCD)
MDRUS..... Miniature Donkey Registry of the United States (EA)
MDRX....... Allscripts, Inc. [*NASDAQ symbol*] (SG)
MDRX....... Medicis Pharmaceutical Corp. [*NASDAQ symbol*] (SAG)
MDRX....... Medicis Pharmaceutical 'A' [*NASDAQ symbol*] (TTSB)
MDRY....... Madison Railway Co., Inc. [*AAR code*]
MDRY....... Midlands Railway [*Federal Railroad Administration identification code*]
MDS........ Democratic and Social Movement (Morocco) [*Political party*] (PSAP)
MDS........ Macintosh Development System [*Computer science*]
MDS........ Madison [*Wisconsin*] [*Seismograph station code, US Geological Survey*] [*Closed*] (SEIS)
MDS........ Madison Flying Service, Inc. (SAUO)
MDS........ Madison, SD [*Location identifier*] [*FAA*] (FAAL)
Mds......... Madrepores [*Quality of the bottom*] [*Nautical charts*]
MDS........ Madrona Resources, Inc. [*Vancouver Stock Exchange symbol*]
MDS........ Magnetic Detection of Submarines [*British military*] (DMA)
MDS........ Magnetic Disk Storage [*Computer science*] (IAA)
MDS........ Magnetic Drum Storage [*Computer science*] (IAA)
MDS........ Magnetic Drum System
MDS........ Mail Distribution Schedule [*Air Force*] (AFM)
MDS........ Mail Distribution Scheme [*Army*]
MDS........ Main Device Scheduler (IAA)
MDS........ Main Dressing Station
MDS........ Maintenance Data System (MCD)
MDS........ Maintenance Diagnostic System (MCD)
MDS........ Maintenance Distribution Services Ltd. (EFIS)
MDS........ Maintenance Documentation System [*Bell System*]
MDS........ Malfunction Detection System [*Gemini*] [*NASA*]
MDS........ Management Data System (NASA)
MDS........ Management Decision System (TIMI)
MDS........ Manned Destruct SEAD (SAUS)
MDS........ Mannesmann Demag Sack (EFIS)
MDS........ Manpower Data System (SAUO)
MDS........ Manual Data Supervisor [*Computer science*] (IAA)
MDS........ Manufacturing Design System (SAUO)
MDS........ Marine Distress Signal (IAA)
MDS........ Market Data System [*NYSE*]
MDS........ Market Decision System (HGAA)
MDS........ Marketing Database System (GART)
MDS........ Massachusetts Dental Society (SAUO)
MDS........ Mass Digital Storage
MDS........ Master Delivery Schedule (AAG)
MDS........ Master Development Schedule (KSC)
MDS........ Master Dimension Specification (MSA)
MDS........ Master Drum Sender
MDS........ Master of Decision Sciences (GAGS)
MDS........ Master of Dental Science (GAGS)
MDS........ Master of Dental Surgery
MDS........ Materiel Deployment Schedule
MDS........ Maternal Deprivation Syndrome [*Medicine*] (DMAA)
MDS........ Mccarron-Dial System (TES)
MDS........ Mechanized Documentation System
MDS........ Medical Dental Service (SAUO)
MDS........ Medical Documentation Service [*College of Physicians of Philadelphia*] [*Information service or system*] (IID)
MDS........ Medical Dressing Station
MDS........ Megawatt Demand Setter (NRCH)
MDS........ Memory Disk System [*Computer science*] (IEEE)
MDS........ Mennonite Disaster Service (EA)
MDS........ Mercedes Development System [*Automotive engineering*]
MDS........ Message Distribution Systems
MDS........ Message-Dropping Station [*Military*] (IAA)
MDS........ Metacomputing Directory Service [*Computer science*]
MDS........ Meta Data System (SAUO)
MDS........ Metal-Dielectric Semiconductor [*Electronics*] (PDAA)
MDS........ Metastable-Atom De-excitation Spectroscopy
MDS........ Meteoroid Detection Satellite [*NASA*]
MDS........ Meteorological Data System
MDS........ Meteorological Distribution System (SAUO)
MDS........ Methods Development Survey [*Bureau of the Census*] (GFGA)
MDS........ Metrofiber Multi-Megabit Data Service [*Metropolitan Fiber Systems, Inc.*]
MDS........ Metropolitan Dairymen's Society [*British*] (BI)
MDS........ Metropolitan Disposal Services, Inc. (EFIS)
MDS........ "Micky the D" Show [*Later, MDS/MMFC*] [*An association*] (EA)
MDS........ Microcomputer Development System (IAA)

MDS Microphonic Detection System [*Police and security equipment*]
MDS Microprocessor Development System [*Motorola, Inc.*]
MDS Microsurgery Drill System (DAVI)
MDS Microwave Doppler Speed [*Electronic engineering*]
MDS Microwave Multipoint Distribution Systems (EDAC)
MDS Midas, Inc. [*NYSE symbol*] (SG)
MDS Middle Caicos [*British West Indies*] [*Airport symbol*] (OAG)
MDS Middle Distance Swimmer
MDS Middle Distillate Synthesis [*Petroleum engineering*]
MDS Milestone Description Sheet (ABAC)
MDS Milford Docks Air Services Ltd. [*British*] [*ICAO designator*] (FAAC)
MDS Milk Drinker's Syndrome [*Medicine*] (DMAA)
MDS Miller-Dieker Lissencephaly Syndrome [*Medicine*]
MDS Miller-Dieker Syndrome [*Medicine*] (DMAA)
MDS Mine Detection Set
MDS Minerals Data System [*Database*]
MDS Miniature Doll Show
MDS Minimal Data Set (SAUS)
MDS Minimum Data Set [*Computer science*]
MDS Minimum Detectable Signal
MDS Minimum Discernable System
MDS Minimum Discernible Signal [*Radio*]
MDS Minimum Discernible System (NASA)
MDS Minnesota Dermatological Society (SAUO)
MDS Minuteman Defense Study [*DoD*]
MDS Minuteman Defense System [*DoD*]
MDS Miss Distance Sensor (ACAE)
MDS Missile Detection System (ACAE)
MDS Mission Design and Series [*Military*] (AFM)
MDS Mission Development Simulator [*NASA*] (NASA)
MDS Mission Display System [*Navy*] (DOMA)
MDS Mobile Data Service (DA)
MDS Mobile Dental Section (SAUO)
MDS Mobile Dental Services
MDS Mobile Distribution System (AFM)
MDS Mobilization, Deployment and Sustainment (SAUO)
MDS Model Designation and Series [*Military*] (AFIT)
MDS Model Design Series (SAUO)
MDS Modern Data Systems (IEEE)
MDS Modify Device Status (AAEL)
MDS Modular Data System
MDS Modular Decontamination System (DWSG)
MDS Modular Disc Storage (NITA)
MDS Modular Dispenser System (SAUS)
MDS Modular Display System (ACAE)
MDS Modular Distribution System
MDS Modulate-Demodulate Subsystem
MDS Mohawk Data Sciences [*Computer science*] (IAA)
MDS Mohawk Data Sciences Corp. (SAUO)
MDS Mohawk Data Systems Corporation (NITA)
MDS Molybdenum Disulfide [*Inorganic chemistry*]
MDS Monitor Distribution System [*Television*]
MDS Montant de Soutien [*Amount of Support*] [*A trade negotiating plan*] [*EC*]
MDS Motion Detection System (SAUS)
MDS Mouvement Democrate Socialiste [*Democratic Socialist Movement*] [*France*] [*Political party*] (PPW)
MDS Mouvement des Democrates Socialistes [*Movement of Socialist Democrats*] [*Tunisia*] [*Political party*] (PPW)
MDS Mouvement pour la Democratie Sociale [*Burkina Faso*] [*Political party*] (EY)
MDS Movement Disorder Society [*Association*] (EA)
MDS Movement for a Democratic Slovakia [*Former Czechoslovakia*] [*Political party*] (EY)
MDS Multidimensional Scaling [*Statistics*]
MDS Multiple Dataset System
MDS Multiple Deficiency Syndrome [*Medicine*] (DB)
MDS Multiple Deployment System [*Military*] (IAA)
MDS Multipoint Distribution Service [*Educational television*]
MDS Multipoint Distribution Services (ACRL)
MDS Multipoint Distribution System [*Line-of-sight relay system for electronic signals*]
MDS Multipoint Microwave Distribution System (WDAA)
MDS Multiprocessor Distributed System [*Raytheon*] (NITA)
MDS Municipal Data Service [*International City Management Association*] [*Information service or system*] (IID)
MDS Myelodysplasia [*Medicine*]
MDS Myelodysplastic Syndrome [*Medicine*]
MDS Myocardial Depressant Substance [*Cardiology*] (DAVI)
MDS Myocardial-Dysplasia Syndrome [*Medicine*] (MELL)
MDS St. Mary's College of Maryland, St. Mary's City, MD [*OCLC symbol*] (OCLC)
MdSalS Salisbury State College, Salisbury, MD [*Library symbol*] [*Library of Congress*] (LCLS)
MdSalW Wicomico County Free Library, Salisbury, MD [*Library symbol*] [*Library of Congress*] (LCLS)
MDSB Medical Devices Standards Board (AG)
MDSB Message Digest Signature Block (HGAA)
MDSBP Mean Daily Supine Blood Pressure [*Medicine*] (EDAA)
MDSC Management Data Service Center
MD Sc Master of Dental Science [*British*]
MDSC Mediscience Technology Corp. [*NASDAQ symbol*] (QUAN)
MDSC Modular Digital Scan Converter (MCD)
MDSC Mohawk Data Sciences Corporation (SAUO)
MDSCB Model Data Set Control Block (NITA)
MDSCC Madrid Deep Space Communications Complex
MDS Corporation Mohawk Data Sciences Corporation (SAUO)
MDSD Magnetic Disk Storage Device [*Computer science*]
MDSD Mate/Demate Stiff Leg Derrick (MCD)
MDSD Monitoring and Data Support Division [*Environmental Protection Agency*] (GFGA)
MDSD Santo Domingo/De las Americas Internacional [*Dominican Republic*] [*ICAO location identifier*] (ICLI)
MDSE Merchandise (AFM)
Mdse Merchandise (EBF)
mdse Merchandise (WDAA)
MDSE Message Delivery Service Element [*Open Systems Interconnection*] (ODAA)
MDSEAD Manned Destruct SEAD (SAUS)
MDSEF Madison Enterprises Corp. [*OTCBB symbol*]
MDSF Manipulator Development and Simulation Facility (SAUS)
MDSF Mass Data Storage Facility
MDSF Mission for Deep Sea Fishermen [*British*] (DI)
MDSF Mission to Deep Sea Fishermen (SAUO)
MDSF Mouvement Democrate Socialiste de France [*Democratic Socialist Movement of France*] [*Political party*] (PPE)
mdsg Merchandising (DD)
MDSG Merchandising
MDSG Mobilisation Deployment Steering Group (SAUO)
MDSHPMN Midshipman
MDSI Manufacturing Data Systems Inc. (NITA)
MDSI Manufacturing Data Systems International (SAUO)
MDSI Modular Display Systems, Incorporated (ACAE)
MDSI Multiprotection Design Summer Institute [*Emergency Management*] (EMA)
MDSI San Isidro [*Dominican Republic*] [*ICAO location identifier*] (ICLI)
MDSIA MDS [*Multipoint Distribution System*] Industry Association [*Telecommunications*] (EA)
MDSIC Metal-Dielectric-Semiconductor Integrated Circuit [*Electronics*] (PDAA)
MdSim Howard County Library, Simpsonville, MD [*Library symbol*] [*Library of Congress*] (LCLS)
MDSJ San Juan [*Dominican Republic*] [*ICAO location identifier*] (ICLI)
MDSL Marconi Defence Systems Ltd. (SAUO)
MDSL Medis E Ltd. [*NASDAQ symbol*] (SAG)
MDSL Moderate Speed Digital Subscriber Line [*Telecommunications*] (ACRL)
MDSL Multi-Rate Digital Subscriber Line (AEBE)
MDSL Multirate DSL (SAUS)
MDSLD Mate/Demate Stiff Leg Derrick
MDSLF Medis El Ltd [*NASDAQ symbol*] (TTSB)
MDS/MMFC "Micky the D" Show/Metal Micky Fan Club (EA)
MDS-MPOLL Mail Distribution Scheme / Military Post Office Location List (DNAB)
MDSN Madisn Gas & Elec [*NASDAQ symbol*] (TTSB)
MDSN Madison Gas & Electric Co. [*NASDAQ symbol*] (NQ)
MDSN Maximum Dissolved Solids Nebulizer [*Product of Applied Research Laboratories*]
MDSNG Merchandising
MdSnW Worcester County Public Library, Snow Hill, MD [*Library symbol*] [*Library of Congress*] (LCLS)
MDSO Medical and Dental Supply Office [*Military*]
MDSO Mentally Disordered Sex Offender
MDSOR Monthly Depot Space and Operating Report
Md-SP Maryland State Planning Commission, Baltimore, MD [*Library symbol*] [*Library of Congress*] (LCLS)
MDSP San Pedro De Macoris [*Dominican Republic*] [*ICAO location identifier*] (ICLI)
MDSPR Mode Suppressor (KSC)
MDSR Malaya District Signal Regiment (SAUO)
MDSRS Morphology-Dependent Stimulated Raman Scattering (CARB)
MDSS Magnetic Drum Storage System
MDSS MAGTF [*Marine Air-Ground Task Force*] Decision-Support System (DOMA)
MDSS Maintenance Decision Support System
MDSS Maritime Pre-Positioned Ships Decision Support System (SAUO)
MDSS Mass Digital Storage System
MDSS McDonnell Douglas Support Services (MCD)
MDSS Medical Decision Support System (DMAA)
MDSS Meteorological Data Sounding System (IEEE)
MDSS Microprocessor Development Support System
MDSS Mission Data Support System [*NASA*] (KSC)
MDSS Multidimensional Switching System [*Instrumentation*]
MDSS Multiple Distribution Switching Subsystem (SAUO)
MDSSC McDonnell Douglas Space Systems Company (SAUO)
MDSSC McDonnell Douglas Space Systems Corporation (SAUO)
MdSsD Library of Dianetics and Scientology, Silver Spring, MD [*Library symbol*] [*Library of Congress*] (LCLS)
MdSsFD United States Food and Drug Administration, Bureau of Medical Services, Silver Spring, MD [*Library symbol*] [*Library of Congress*] (LCLS)
MdSsGS Church of Jesus Christ of Latter-Day Saints, Genealogical Society Library, Silver Spring Branch, Silver Spring, MD [*Library symbol*] [*Library of Congress*] (LCLS)
MDSS-PCT Multidimensional Switching System - Packed Column Trap [*Instrumentation*]
MdSsV Vitro Laboratories, Silver Spring Laboratory Library, Silver Spring, MD [*Library symbol*] [*Library of Congress*] (LCLS)
MdSsW Washington Theological Coalition, Silver Spring, MD [*Library symbol*] [*Library of Congress*] (LCLS)

MdSsX ...... Xaverian College, Silver Spring, MD [*Library symbol*] [*Library of Congress*] (LCLS)
MDST .... Medstat Systems, Inc. [*NASDAQ symbol*] (COMM)
MDST .... Mid-State Bancshares [*NASDAQ symbol*] (NASQ)
MDST .... Mid-States Camping Trailer [*NCIC trailer make code*]
MDST .... Mountain Daylight Saving Time (SSD)
MDST .... Santiago [*Dominican Republic*] [*ICAO location identifier*] (ICLI)
MdStm ...... St. Mary's College of Maryland, St. Mary's City, MD [*Library symbol*] [*Library of Congress*] (LCLS)
MDSU .... Mobile Diving and Salvage Unit (COE)
MdSuFR ..... Washington National Records Center, General Services Administration, Suitland, MD [*Library symbol*] [*Library of Congress*] (LCLS)
MDSV .... Manned Deep Space Vehicle
MdsxWat .... Middlesex Water Co. [*Associated Press*] (SAG)
MdSyH ...... Springfield State Hospital, Sykesville, MD [*Library symbol*] [*Library of Congress*] (LCLS)
MDSZ .... Medspan Shipping Service [*Intermodal trailer symbol*]
MDT .... Compagnie Air Mediterrannee [*France*] [*ICAO designator*] (FAAC)
MDT .... Harrisburg [*Pennsylvania*] [*Airport symbol*] (OAG)
MDT .... Machine Data Transducer
MDT .... Macro Definition Trailer (VLIE)
MDT .... Maintainability Development Test [*Army*]
MDT .... Maintenance Demand Time (MCD)
MDT .... Maintenance Downtime (MCD)
MDT .... Mandatory Date of Transportation [*Military*]
MDT .... Mandatory Drugs Testing (WDAA)
MDT .... Manual Data Technician [*Computer science*] (IAA)
MDT .... Manufacturers Delegated Testing (NITA)
MDT .... Maryland Department of Transportation [*Federal Railroad Administration identification code*]
MDT .... Mass Cell Degeneration Test [*Medicine*] (DB)
MDT .... Master Data Tape (ACAE)
MDT .... Maximum Dive Time
MDT .... Mean Death Time
MDT .... Mean Delay Time (CAAL)
MDT .... Mean Detonating Time (NASA)
MDT .... Mean Dissolution Time [*Medicine*] (EDAA)
MDT .... Mean Downtime [*Computer science*]
MDT .... Measurement Descriptor Table (NASA)
MDT .... Mechanical Desktop (VLIE)
MDT .... Mechanically Deboned Turkey [*Food technology*]
MDT .... Median Detection Threshold (MAE)
MDT .... Median Dorsal Tract [*Anatomy*]
MDT .... Medium Data Technique [*Computer science*] (IAA)
MDT .... Medium-Duty Truck [*Automotive engineering*]
MDT .... Med-Tech Systems, Inc. [*Vancouver Stock Exchange symbol*]
MDT .... Medtronic, Inc. [*NYSE symbol*] (SPSG)
MDT .... Mendota, IL [*Amtrak rail station code*]
MDT .... Mento-Dextra Transversa [*A fetal position*] [*Obstetrics*]
MDT .... Merchant Deposit Transmittal
MDT .... Mercury Dynamic Test
MDT .... Message Direction Table (MCD)
MDT .... Message Display Terminal (MCD)
MDT .... Message Distribution Terminal (SAUS)
MDT .... Micro Debugging Tool (VLIE)
MDT .... Middletown, PA [*Location identifier*] [*FAA*] (FAAL)
MDT .... Mini Disc Terminal [*Computer science*] (DGA)
MDT .... Minnesota Dance Theatre
MDT .... Mission Data Table (SAUS)
MDT .... Mission Design Team (ACAE)
MDT .... Mobile Data Terminal (MCD)
MDT .... Mobile Display Terminal [*Vehicle navigation systems*]
MDT .... Moderate (AFM)
MDT .... Modified Data Tag [*Computer science*] (IAA)
MDT .... Modular Display Tactical
MDT .... Most Demands to Be Traded [*Baseball*]
MDT .... Mountain Daylight Time
MDT .... Moviment de Defensa de la Terra [*Spain*] [*Political party*] (EY)
MDT .... Multidimensional Tasking [*Honeywell, Inc.*]
MDT .... Multidisciplinary Team
MDT .... Munitions Disposal Technician (SAA)
MDT .... Mutual Defense Treaty
MDT2 .... Martin Marietta, Diehl, Thorn-EMI, Thomson [*Army*]
MDTA .... Manpower Development and Training Act [*1962*] [*Later, CETA*] [*Department of Labor*]
MDTA .... McDonald Deep Test of Articulation [*Speech and language therapy*] (DAVI)
MDTA .... Midland Transportation Company [*Common carrier symbol*]
MDTA .... Modulation, Demodulation, Terminal, and Associated Equipment
MDTB .... Milk Distribution Trade Board [*British*] (DAS)
MDTC .... MDT Corp. [*NASDAQ symbol*] (NQ)
MDT Cp ..... MDT Corp. [*Associated Press*] (SAG)
MDTD .... Minimum Detectable Temperature Difference (ACAE)
MD Tenn .... United States District Court for the Middle District of Tennessee (DLA)
MDTERP .... Maryland Terrestrial Radiation Package (SAUO)
MDTF .... Macular Degeneration Task Force [*Medicine*]
MDTH .... MedCath, Inc. (MHID)
MDTI .... Missile Director Train Indicator
MDTI .... Multiple Director Train Indicator (MCD)
MDTL .... Modified Diode Transistor Logic [*Electronics*] (IAA)
MDTM .... Mechanically Deboned Turkey Meat [*Food technology*]
MDTM .... Medium-Duty Tank Target Mechanism (SAUS)
MDTM .... Multidisciplinary Team Meeting [*Medicine*] (EDAA)
MDTP .... Materiel Developer's Test Program [*Military*]
MDTP .... Multidisciplinary Diagnostics and Training Program [*University of Florida*] (RCD)
MDTP .... Multidisciplinary Treatment Plan [*Medicine*] (DAVI)
MDTR .... M-D Trailer [*NCIC trailer make code*]
MDTR .... Mean Diameter-Thickness Ratio (MAE)
MDTS .... McDonnell Douglas Training Systems (SAUO)
MDTS .... MegaBIT [*Binary Digit*] Digital Troposcatter Subsystem [*Communications*] (MCD)
MDTS .... Mission Data Transfer System (SAUO)
MDTS .... Mobile Doppler Tracking Station
MDTS .... Modem Diagnostic and Test System (VLIE)
MDTS .... Modular Data Transaction System
MDTS .... Multiple Dealer Trading System [*Investment term*] (DICI)
MDTSA ...... Methods for the Detection of Toxic Substances in Air (HEAS)
MDTSCO .... McDonnell Douglas Technical Services Co. (NAKS)
MDTT .... Maine Department of Transportation [*Federal Railroad Administration identification code*]
MDTU .... Mobile Dockside Transfer Unit
MdTW .... Washington Missionary College, Tacoma Park, MD [*Library symbol*] [*Library of Congress*] [*Obsolete*] (LCLS)
MDTWN ..... Middletown, OH [*American Association of Railroads railroad junction routing code*]
MDTWN ..... Midtown
MDTX .... Mount Dora, Tavares, & Eustis Railroad [*Federal Railroad Administration identification code*]
MDTZ .... Midtec [*Federal Railroad Administration identification code*]
MDU .... Maintenance Data Unit (MCD)
MDU .... Maintenance Diagnostic Unit
MDU .... Malawi Democratic Union [*Political party*] (PSAP)
MDU .... Marker Decoder Unit (VLIE)
mdu .... Maryland [*MARC country of publication code*] [*Library of Congress*] (LCCP)
MDU .... Master Data Unit [*Space launch term*] (ISAK)
MDU .... Master Driver Unit
MDU .... MDU Resources Group [*NYSE symbol*] (TTSB)
MDU .... MDU Resources Group, Inc. [*NYSE symbol*] (SPSG)
MDU .... Medical Defence (or Defense) Union (SAUO)
MDU .... Medical Defence Union (SAUO)
MDU .... Medical Defence Union Ltd. [*British*] (BI)
MDU .... MEK/T (Methyl-Ethyl Ketone/Toluene) Dewaxing Unit [*Petroleum engineering*]
MDU .... Memory Drum Unit (ACAE)
MDU .... Mendi [*Papua New Guinea*] [*Airport symbol*] (OAG)
MDU .... Message Decoder Unit
MDU .... Message Display Unit [*Computer science*] (VLIE)
MDu .... Middle Dutch (BEE)
MDU .... Middle Dutch [*Language, etc.*]
MDU .... Mid-North Resources [*Vancouver Stock Exchange symbol*]
MDU .... Mine Disposal Unit
MDU .... Mine Distributing Unit (SAUS)
MDU .... Missile Design Unit (SAA)
MDU .... Mobile Demonstration Unit
MDU .... Mobile Development Unit [*Military*] (GFGA)
MDU .... Mobile Dynamic Unit (AAG)
MDU .... Modular Dispensing Unit (AAEL)
MDU .... Montana-Dakota Utilities Co. (SAUO)
MDU .... Moral Development Unit [*Prisoner reform program*]
mdu .... More Dicto Utendus [*To Be Used as Directed*] [*Latin*] (WDAA)
MDU .... Motion Detection Unit [*Nuclear energy*] (NRCH)
MDU .... Multidimensional Unfolding [*Model*] [*Statistics*]
MDU .... To Be Used as Directed [*Medicine*] (EDAA)
MDU .... University of Maryland, Baltimore, Health Sciences Library, Baltimore, MD [*OCLC symbol*] (OCLC)
MdU .... University of Maryland, College Park, MD [*Library symbol*] [*Library of Congress*] (LCLS)
MDUA .... Mission Defined Unit Assemblage [*Army*]
MdU-A .... University of Maryland, Art Library, College Park, MD [*Library symbol*] [*Library of Congress*] (LCLS)
MdU-Ar ...... University of Maryland, Architecture Library, College Park, MD [*Library symbol*] [*Library of Congress*] (LCLS)
MdU-BC ..... University of Maryland, Baltimore County Campus, Baltimore, MD [*Library symbol*] [*Library of Congress*] (LCLS)
MduC .... Canada Medal (FOTI)
MDUC .... Meteorological Data Utilization Center (SAUO)
MdU-C .... University of Maryland, Chemistry Library, College Park, MD [*Library symbol*] [*Library of Congress*] (LCLS)
MdU-E .... University of Maryland, Engineering and Physical Sciences Library, College Park,MD [*Library symbol*] [*Library of Congress*] (LCLS)
MdU-H .... University of Maryland, Health Sciences Library, Baltimore, MD [*Library symbol*] [*Library of Congress*] (LCLS)
MDuHi .... Duxbury Rural and Historical Society, Duxbury, MA [*Library symbol*] [*Library of Congress*] (LCLS)
MdU-I .... International Piano Archives at Maryland, University of Maryland, College Park, MD [*Library symbol*] [*Library of Congress*] (LCLS)
MdU-L .... University of Maryland, School of Law, Baltimore, MD [*Library symbol*] [*Library of Congress*] (LCLS)
MDUO .... Myocardial Disease of Unknown Origin [*Cardiology*]
MDUS .... Medium Data Utilization Station (ACAE)
MDUS .... Meteorological Data Utilization Station (SAUO)
MdU-U .... University of Maryland, Undergraduate Library, College Park, MD [*Library symbol*] [*Library of Congress*] (LCLS)
MDV .... Baltimore, MD [*Location identifier*] [*FAA*] (FAAL)
MDV .... Doctor of Veterinary Medicine
MDV .... Maldives [*ANSI three-letter standard code*] (CNC)
MDV .... Map and Data Viewer [*NASA*] (KSC)
MDV .... Marek's Disease Virus [*Avian pathology*]

MDV .... Master of Veterinary Medicine
MDV .... Maxim Development Ltd. [*Vancouver Stock Exchange symbol*]
MDV .... Mean Dye Velocity [*Medicine*] (EDAA)
MDV .... Medeva [*AMEX symbol*] (SPSG)
MDV .... Medeva ADR [*AMEX symbol*] (TTSB)
MDV .... Medium-Dollar Value
MDV .... Medium-Duty Vehicle [*Automotive engineering*]
MDV .... Medouneu [*Gabon*] [*Airport symbol*] (OAG)
MDV .... Merrieux Diploid Vaccine [*Used for immunization in rabies*] [*Medicine*] (EDAA)
MDV .... Metropolitan District Valuer (SAUO)
MDV .... Middlebury [*Vermont*] [*Seismograph station code, US Geological Survey*] (SEIS)
MDV .... Midivariant [*Genetics*]
MDV .... Mine Destruction Vehicle (SAUS)
MDV .... Mine Detection Vehicle (SAUS)
MDV .... Mine-Dispensing Vehicle [*Army*]
MDV .... Minimum Detectable Velocity [*Physics*]
MDV .... Minimum Domian Velocity (IAA)
MDV .... Mission Development Co. (SAUO)
MDV .... Mobile Directional Valve [*Hydraulics*]
MDV .... Moldavian Airlines [*Macedonia*] [*FAA designator*] (FAAC)
MDV .... Mouvement Democratique Voltaique [*Upper Volta Democratic Movement*]
MDV .... Mucosal Disease Virus
MDV .... Multiple Dose Vial [*Pharmacy*]
MDV .... Santa Lucia Monteverde Mixteco [*Language symbol*] (ETLW)
MDVA .... Michigan Distributors and Vendors Association (EARSL)
M-DVD .... Magnetic Digital Versatile Disc
MDVL .... Medeva plc [*LO, exchange symbol*] (TTSB)
mdvl .... Medieval (VRA)
MDVMA .... Maryland Veterinary Medical Association (GVA)
MDW .... Chicago [*Illinois*] Midway [*Airport symbol*] (OAG)
MDW .... Delta Waterfowl Research Station, Manitoba [*Library symbol*] [*National Library of Canada*] (NLC)
MDW .... Fort Myer Library System and Fort McNair Post Library, Fort Myer, VA [*OCLC symbol*] (OCLC)
MDW .... Mars Departure Window [*Aerospace*]
MdW .... Masoreten des Westens (BJA)
MDW .... Mass Destruction Weapons
MDW .... Meadow [*Postal Service standard*] (OPSA)
MDW .... Meadow Mountain [*Vancouver Stock Exchange symbol*]
MDW .... Measured Daywork [*Payment system*]
MDW .... Midway [*Washington*] [*Seismograph station code, US Geological Survey*] (SEIS)
MDW .... Midway Airlines, Inc. [*FAA designator*] (FAAC)
MDW .... Midway Aviation, Inc. [*ICAO designator*] (FAAC)
MDW .... Military Defence Works [*British*]
MDW .... Military District of Washington [*DC*]
MDW .... Mine Disposal Weapon (NATG)
MDW .... Minnesota, Dakota & Western Railway Co. [*AAR code*]
MDW .... Multidimensional Warfare [*Military*] (CAAL)
MDW .... Multipair Distribution Wire
MDW .... Multiple Drop Wire [*Telecommunications*] (TEL)
MDWAC ..... Midwest Athletic Conference (PSS)
MD WCC .... Maryland Workmen's Compensation Cases [*A publication*] (DLA)
MdWem ..... Carroll County Public Library, Westminster, MD [*Library symbol*] [*Library of Congress*] (LCLS)
MdWemC ... Western Maryland College, Westminster, MD [*Library symbol*] [*Library of Congress*] (LCLS)
MdWemHi ... Carroll County Historical Society, Westminister, MD [*Library symbol*] [*Library of Congress*] (LCLS)
MdwEx ...... Midwest Exprss Holding [*Associated Press*] (SAG)
MDWF .... Midwife
MdwFdl ..... Midwest Federal Financial [*Associated Press*] (SAG)
MDWFY ..... Midwifery
MDWP ...... Mutual Defense Weapons Program (SAUS)
MDWR ...... Mule Deer Winter Ranges (SAUO)
MDWS ...... Meadows (MCD)
MDWS ...... Missile Detection & Warning System (SAUO)
MdWst ..... Med Waste [*Associated Press*] (SAG)
MDWST ..... Midwest
MDWSTRN ... Midwestern
MD/WT ...... Marine Division/Wing Team (SAUO)
MDWT ...... Metric Deadweight Tons (RIMS)
MDWU ...... Minnesota, Dakota, and Western Railway [*Intermodal shipping container symbol*] (TVRC)
MDWV ...... Medwave, Inc. [*NASDAQ symbol*] (SAG)
MDWY ...... Midway
MDWY ...... Midway Airlines Corp. [*NASDAQ symbol*] (NASQ)
MDWY ...... Midway Motor Freight Lines [*Common carrier symbol*]
MDWZ ...... Minnesota, Dakota and Western Railway [*Intermodal trailer symbol*]
MDX .... Medical Data Exchange (IID)
MDX .... Medical Data Exchange [*Los Altos, CA*] [*Commercial firm*]
MDX .... Mercedes [*Argentina*] [*Airport symbol*] (OAG)
MDX .... Merritech Development [*Vancouver Stock Exchange symbol*]
MDX .... Middlesex [*County in England*]
MDX .... Middlesex Regiment (SAUO)
MDX .... Multi-Indexing [*Computer science*] (CIST)
MDX .... University of Maryland, College of Library and Information Services, College Park, MD [*OCLC symbol*] (OCLC)
MDXDCR .... Mode Transducer (KSC)
MDXP .... Midas Express [*Common carrier symbol*]
MDXR .... Medar, Inc. [*NASDAQ symbol*] (NQ)
MDY .... Magnetic Deflection Yoke
MDY .... MidCap SPDRs [*AMEX symbol*] (NASQ)
MDY .... Middlebury College, Middlebury, VT [*OCLC symbol*] (OCLC)
MDY .... Midland Gold Corp. [*Formerly, Midland Energy Corp.*] [*Vancouver Stock Exchange symbol*]
MDY .... Midway [*Midway Islands*] [*Seismograph station code, US Geological Survey*] [*Closed*] (SEIS)
MDY .... Moderately [*Telegraphy*] (PCTE)
MDY .... Month, Date, Year
MDY .... Standard & Poor's MidCap 400 Depository Receipts [*AMEX symbol*] (SAG)
MDY .... Standard & Poor's MidCap Dep Rc [*AMEX symbol*] (TTSB)
MDYAC ...... Moderately Active [*Telegraphy*] (PCTE)
MDYN .... Molecular Dynamics, Inc. [*NASDAQ symbol*] (SAG)
MDYR .... Model Year
MDZ .... Maritime Defense Zone [*Program for drug interdiction*]
MDZ .... MDC Corp. [*Toronto Stock Exchange symbol*]
MDZ .... MDZ, Inc. [*NYSE symbol*] (SG)
MDZ .... Medford, WI [*Location identifier*] [*FAA*] (FAAL)
MDZ .... Mendoza [*Argentina*] [*Seismograph station code, US Geological Survey*] (SEIS)
MDZ .... Merchandise [*Telegraphy*] (PCTE)
MDZ .... Middle Zero (IAA)
MDZ .... Missile Danger Zone (NVT)
MDZ.A .... MDC Partners [*Toronto Stock Exchange symbol*] [*Canada*]
MDZL .... Maritime Defense Zone Atlantic (SAUO)
MDZP .... Maritime Defense Zone Pacific (SAUO)
Me .... C. H. Boehringer Sohn, Ingelheim [*Germany*] [*Research code symbol*]
me--- .... Eurasia [*MARC geographic area code*] [*Library of Congress*] (LCCP)
ME .... Mache Einkeit (STED)
M/E .... Machine (ROG)
M/E .... Macrocytic/Normochromic [*Anemia*] [*Hematology*] (DAVI)
ME .... Macular Edema [*Ophthalmology*] (DAVI)
ME .... Magic Eye (DEN)
ME .... Magnetic Estimation (OA)
ME .... Magnetoelastic
ME .... Magneto-Electronic (PDAA)
ME .... Magnitude Estimation
M/E .... Mail/Express [*Indian Railway*] (TIR)
Me .... Maine (SHCU)
ME .... Maine [*Postal code*]
ME .... Main Engine (KSC)
ME .... Main Entry [*Library Science*] [*Online database field identifier*]
Me .... Maine Reports (AAGC)
Me .... Maine State Library, Augusta, ME [*Library symbol*] [*Library of Congress*] (LCLS)
ME .... Maine Supreme Judicial Court Reports [*A publication*] (DLA)
ME .... Maintenance Engineering (ACAE)
ME .... Maintenance Equipment
ME .... Maintenance Error (SAUS)
ME .... Maintenance Evaluation (MCD)
ME .... Maitre [*Barrister, Advocate*] [*French*] (ROG)
ME .... Majestic Eagles (EA)
Me .... Male (Entire) (SPVS)
ME .... Male Equivalents [*Entomology*]
ME .... Male Escutcheon [*Medicine*] (MELL)
ME .... "Malic" Enzyme
ME .... Malt Extract [*Microbiology*]
ME .... Management Engineering (KSC)
ME .... Management Evaluation [*Food Stamp Program*] [*Department of Agriculture*] (GFGA)
ME .... Managing Editor
ME .... Man-Hours Earned
ME .... Manic Episode [*Medicine*] (MELL)
ME .... Manoeuvre Enhancement mode (SAUS)
ME .... Manpower Estimate (AAG)
ME .... Manson Evaluation [*Psychology*]
ME .... Manufacturing Engineering (MCD)
me .... Marbled Edges (MIST)
ME .... Marbled Edges [*Bookbinding*]
ME .... Marche de l'Europe [*March of Europe*] (EAIO)
ME .... March of Europe (SAUO)
ME .... Marine Engine
ME .... Marine Engineer
ME .... Marine Engineering [*Repairs*] [*Nautical term*] (NTA)
ME .... Marketing Education
ME .... Marriage Encounter
ME .... Marriage Evaluation [*Marital relations test*]
M-E .... Martini-Enfield [*Rifle*]
ME .... Mass Effectiveness (SAUS)
ME .... Master Equatorial
ME .... Master of Education
ME .... Master of Elements
ME .... Master of Engineering
ME .... Master of Mechanical Engineering [*Canada*] (ASC)
ME .... Materials Evaluation (PDAA)
ME .... Math Error [*IRS*]
ME .... Mature Equivalent (OA)
ME .... Maximal Efficacy [*Medicine*] (MELL)
ME .... Maximum Effort
ME .... Maximum Energy
ME .... Meal
ME .... Measurement Engine (IAA)
ME .... Measuring Element

ME .... Mechanical Efficiency
M/E .... Mechanical/Electrical (AAG)
ME .... Mechanical Engineer [*or Engineering*]
ME .... Mechanical Equipment
ME .... Medial Eminence (DB)
ME .... Medial Epicondyle [*Medicine*]
Me .... Median
ME .... Median Eminence [*of hypothalamus*] [*Anatomy*]
ME .... Medical Economics [*Journal*] [*Medicine*] (EDAA)
ME .... Medical Education (MAE)
ME .... Medical Examiner
ME .... Medication Error [*Medicine*] (MELL)
ME .... Medication Evaluation (DHP)
ME .... Mediterranean
ME .... Medium Electroendosmosis [*Analytical biochemistry*]
ME .... Medium Energy
ME .... Megacycle (IAA)
Me .... Me'ilah (BJA)
Me .... Melendus [*Flourished, 1188-1209*] [*Authority cited in pre-1607 legal work*] (DSA)
ME .... Memory Element [*Computer science*]
ME .... Memory Error (WDAA)
ME .... Meningoencephalitis [*Medicine*] (DB)
ME .... Mercaptoethanol [*Biochemistry*]
ME .... Mesic [*Soil biology*] [*Soil temperature regime*] (QSUL)
ME .... Message Element [*Telecommunications*] (TEL)
ME .... Messerschmitt AG [*Germany*] [*ICAO aircraft manufacturer identifier*] (ICAO)
ME .... Metabolic and Electrolyte Disorders [*Medicine*] (MEDA)
ME .... Metabolism (STED)
ME .... Metabolizable Energy
ME .... Metairie Site Office (SAUO)
ME .... Metal Evaporated [*Videotape*]
ME .... Metalsmith [*Navy*]
ME .... Metamyelocyte (STED)
ME .... Meters [*JETDS nomenclature*] [*Military*] (CET)
ME .... Methionine Enkephalin [*Biochemistry*]
ME .... Methodist
ME .... Methodist Episcopal
ME .... Methods Engineering (NG)
ME .... Methods in Enzymology [*Journal*] [*Medicine*] (EDAA)
ME .... Methoxyethanol [*Organic chemistry*]
Me .... Methyl [*Organic chemistry*]
ME .... Methyleugenol (STED)
ME .... Mettmann [*German license plate city code*]
ME .... Mexican Stock Exchange
Me .... Mexico (SAUO)
ME .... Microelectronic
ME .... Microemboli [*Medicine*] (MELL)
ME .... Microembolization (STED)
M-E .... Microencapsulated
ME .... Micrometeoroid Explorer [*Satellite*]
ME .... Microsoft Editor [*Computer program*] (PCM)
ME .... Middle Ear
ME .... Middle East [*or Middle Eastern*]
ME .... Middle East Airlines [*ICAO designator*] (AD)
ME .... Middle East Airlines/Air Liban (SAUO)
ME .... Middle English [*Language, etc.*]
ME .... Mid-Engine [*Automotive engineering*]
ME .... Military Electronics (MCD)
ME .... Military Engineer
ME .... Mill Edge (ADA)
ME .... Milliequivalent [*or Milligram Equivalent*] [*Also, MEQ*]
ME .... Mining Engineer
ME .... Ministry of Education (SAUO)
ME .... Minneapolis Eastern Railway
ME .... Miscellaneous Equipment (KSC)
ME .... Missile Electrician
ME .... Missionary Ecumenical (Rome) (TOCD)
ME .... Mission Capital Ltd. [*NYSE symbol*] (SAG)
ME .... Mission Envelope (AAG)
ME .... Mistress of English
ME .... Miter End [*Technical drawings*]
ME .... Mixture-of-Experts (IDAI)
ME .... Mobile Equipment (CGWS)
ME .... Mobility Equipment [*Military*] (AFM)
ME .... Modular Electronics (IAA)
ME .... Modulation Efficiency
ME .... Moessbauer Effect (OA)
ME .... Molecular Electronics
ME .... Molecular Emission (SARE)
ME .... Moment Estimator (PDAA)
ME .... Moneta Porcupine Mines, Inc. [*Toronto Stock Exchange symbol*]
M/E .... Month Ending (SAUO)
ME .... Montreal Exchange [*Canada*] (NUMA)
ME .... Morristown & Erie Railroad Co. [*AAR code*]
ME .... Most Eminent [*Freemasonry*] (ROG)
ME .... Most Excellent [*In titles*]
ME .... Motion Estimation (TIMI)
ME .... Mottled Edges [*Bookbinding*] (DGA)
ME .... Mouse Embryo [*Medicine*] (DMAA)
ME .... Mouse Encephalitis
ME .... Mouse Epithelial [*Cells*] [*Hematology*] (DAVI)
ME .... Mouvement Europeen [*European Movement*]
ME .... Movie Editor
ME .... Muhammadan Era
ME .... Multiengine
ME .... Multiple Embolisms [*Medicine*] (MELL)
ME .... Multiple Exostoses [*Medicine*] (MELL)
ME .... Municipal Engineering (SAUO)
ME .... Municipal Engineering and Environmental Technology [*A publication*] [*British*]
ME .... Munitions Effectiveness
ME .... Muscle Examination (STED)
ME .... Mutation Engine (SAUO)
ME .... Muzzle Energy
ME .... Myalgic Encephalomyelitis [*Medicine*]
ME .... Mycobacterial Extracts [*Biochemistry*]
M:E .... Myeloid:Erythroid [*Ratio*] [*Hematology*]
ME .... Myoepithelium [*Cytology*]
ME3 .... Minority Engineering Education Effort [*Later, NACME*]
MEa .... Eastham Public Library, Eastham, MA [*Library symbol*] [*Library of Congress*] (LCLS)
MEA .... Macae [*Brazil*] [*Airport symbol*] (OAG)
MEA .... Magnetic Engineering Associates, Inc.
MEA .... Main Electronics Assembly (MCD)
MEA .... Maine State Library, Augusta, ME [*OCLC symbol*] (OCLC)
MEA .... Maintenance Engineering Analysis
MEA .... Major Emergency Actions (SAUO)
MEA .... Malaysian Economics Association (SAUO)
MEA .... Male-Enhanced Antigen [*Medicine*] (DMAA)
MEA .... Malic Enzyme A (DB)
MEA .... Malt Extract Agar [*Culture media*]
MEA .... Manufacturing Engineering Analysis
MEA .... Marine Engineering Artificer [*Navy rating*] [*British*]
MEA .... Marine Engineers' Association [*A union*] [*British*]
MEA .... Marine Environmental Activities [*Marine science*] (MSC)
MEA .... Maritime Employers Association (NADA)
MEA .... Marketing Education Association (EA)
MEA .... Master of Engineering Administration
MEA .... Master of Engineering Architecture (GAGS)
MEA .... Material Experiment Analysis
MEA .... Materials Experiment Assembly (ACAE)
MEA .... [*The*] Mead Corp. [*NYSE symbol*] (SPSG)
MEA .... Meadowbrook [*NCIC car model code*]
MEA .... Meanook [*Canada*] [*Geomagnetic observatory code*]
MEA .... Measurements (NATG)
MEA .... Meat Extract Agar [*Microbiology*]
MEA .... Meath [*County in Ireland*] (ROG)
MEA .... Medical Equestrian Association [*British*] (DBA)
MEA .... Medical Exhibitors Association [*Later, HCEA*] (EA)
MEA .... Member of the European Assembly (ODA)
MEA .... Membrane and Electrode Assembly [*Automotive engineering*]
MEA .... Membrane Electrode Assembly [*Fuel cells*]
MEA .... Memory Inspection Ending Address (MHDB)
MEA .... Mercaptoethylamine [*Pharmacology*]
MEA .... Metal Edge Amplifier (MCD)
MEA .... Metopon Ethnikis Adadimiourgias [*National Regeneration Front*] [*Greece*] [*Political party*] (PPE)
MEA .... Metropolitan Economic Area
MEA .... Metropolitan Entertainers' Association [*British*] (BI)
MEA .... Michigan Education Association (SAUO)
MEA .... Mid Atlantic Employers' Association (EARSL)
MEA .... Middle East Airlines - Air Liban [*Lebanon*]
MEA .... Middle East Association [*British*] (EAIO)
MEA .... Migrant Education Agency (SAUO)
MEA .... Minimum Energy Absorbed
MEA .... Minimum Enroute Altitude
MEA .... Minimum en Route IFR Altitude [*FAA*] (TAG)
MEA .... Minister, External Affairs (CINC)
MEA .... Ministry of External Affairs, Library Services Division [*UTLAS symbol*]
MEA .... Minnesota Education Association (SAUO)
MEA .... Missionary Evangelical Alliance [*See also AME*] [*Switzerland*] (EAIO)
MEA .... Mission Engagement Area [*Military*]
MEA .... Mission of Economic Affairs (SAUO)
MEA .... Modular Engine Analyzer [*Automotive engineering*]
MEA .... Moisture Evaluation Analysis (PDAA)
MEA .... Monoethanolamine [*Organic chemistry*]
MEA .... Monoethylamine [*Organic chemistry*]
MEA .... Montana Education Association (SAUO)
MEA .... Monteagle [*Australia*] [*Seismograph station code, US Geological Survey*] [*Closed*] (SEIS)
MEA .... Motorcycle Events Association (EA)
MEA .... Multimode Error Analysis
MEA .... Multiple Endocrine Abnormalities [*Medicine*]
MEA .... Multiple Endocrine Adenomas [*Oncology*]
MEA .... Multiple Endocrine Adenomatosis [*Medicine*] (DMAA)
MEA .... Multiple Endocrine Adenopathy [*Endocrinology*] (DAVI)
MEA .... Municipal Employees Association (NADA)
MEA .... Munitions Effectiveness Assessment (DOMA)
MEA .... Musical Educators Association (NADA)
MEA .... Music Editors Association (EA)
MEA .... Music Education Association (SAUO)
MEA .... Myalgic Encephalomyelitis Association [*British*] (DBA)
MEAA .... Mitsubishi Electric Automotive America [*Automotive supplier*]
MEAB .... Maintenance Engineering Analysis Board

MEAC........ Manufacturing Engineering Applications Center [*Worchester Polytechnic Institute*] [*Research center*] (RCD)
MEAC........ Mid-Eastern Athletic Conference
MEAC........ Mutual Economic Assistance Council (SAUO)
MEACC...... Marine Engineering Artificer Candidate Course (SAUO)
MEACE...... Military Engineering Applications of Commercial Explosives [*Army*] (PDAA)
MEACN...... Maintenance Engineering Analyses Control Number [*DoD*]
MEACON.... Masking Beacon (IAA)
MEACONING... Measuring and Confusing (DNAB)
ME Acts..... Acts, Resolves, and Constitutional Resolutions of the State of Maine [*A publication*] (DLA)
MEAD........ Maintenance Engineering Analysis Data
MEAD........ Maintenance Engineering Analysis Division (SAUO)
Mead........ [*The*] Mead Corp. [*Associated Press*] (SAG)
MEAD........ Meade [*NCIC trailer make code*]
MEAD........ Memphis Army Depot (AABC)
MEAD........ Microbial Evaluation Analysis Device (PDAA)
Mead-J....... Mead Johnson [*Commercial firm*] [*Pharmacology*] (DAVI)
MEADOW... Meadow [*Commonly used*] (OPSA)
MEADOWS... Meadows [*Commonly used*] (OPSA)
MEADS...... Maintenance Engineering Analysis Data System
MEADS...... Medium Extended Air Defence System (SAUO)
MEADS...... Medium [*Range*] Extended Air Defense System [*USA-Europe*]
ME/AEROSPACE... Department of Mechanical and Aerospace Engineering (SAUO)
MEAF........ Middle East Air Force [*British*]
MEAF........ Middle Eastern Air Forces (SAUO)
MEAFSA..... Middle East/Southern Asia and Africa South of the Sahara [*Military*]
MeAIB....... (Methylamino)isobutyric Acid [*Biochemistry*]
MEAL........ Master Equipment Allowance [*or Authorization*] List [*Military*]
MEAL........ Media Expenditure Analysis Ltd. [*Database producer*]
MEAL........ Mission for Economic Affairs in London (SAUO)
MEA(L)....... Mission of Economic Affairs in London [*World War II*]
MEAL........ Mobile Equipment Allowance List (MCD)
MEAM....... Advisory Committee for Mechanical Engineering and Applied Mechanics [*Washington, DC*] [*Terminated, 1985*] [*National Science Foundation*] (EGAO)
MeAM....... Augusta Mental Health Institute, Augusta, ME [*Library symbol*] [*Library of Congress*] (LCLS)
MEAM....... Department of Mechanical Engineering and Applied Mechanics (SAUO)
MEAM....... Municipal Electric Association of Massachusetts (SAUO)
MEA-MFT... Montana Education Association - Montana Federation of Teachers (EARSL)
MeAMH..... Maine State Department of Human Services, Augusta, ME [*Library symbol*] [*Library of Congress*] (LCLS)
MeAMM..... Maine State Museum, Augusta, ME [*Library symbol*] [*Library of Congress*] (LCLS)
MeAMP..... Maine State Planning Office, Augusta, ME [*Library symbol*] [*Library of Congress*] (LCLS)
MEAN........ Manganese-Enhanced Austenitic Nitrogen Steel
MEAN........ Microcomputer Education Application Network [*Commercial firm*] (EA)
ME&ES...... Maintenance Environmental and Engineering Services (SAUO)
ME&S....... Management Evaluation & Support (SAUO)
MEANG...... Maine Air National Guard (ACAE)
MEANINGEX... Meaning Extraction [*Programming language*] [*1971*] (CSR)
Means....... Mean's Kansas Reports [*A publication*] (DLA)
MEANT...... Meat Exporters' Association of the Northern Territory [*Australia*]
MEAP........ Maintenance Engineering Analysis Process (SAUO)
MEAP........ Maintenance Engineering Analysis Program
MEAP........ Michigan Educational Assessment Program
MEAP........ Military Economic Advisory Panel (MCD)
MEAP........ Multiphasic Environmental Assessment Procedure (DMAA)
MEAPL...... Manufacturing and Engineering Assembly Parts List [*File*]
MEAPO...... Middle East/Africa Projects Office (SAUO)
MEAPS...... Method of Ensemble Average of Periodic Systems
MEAR........ Maintenance Engineering Analysis Record [*or Report*]
MEAR........ Maintenance Engineering Analysis Request [*NASA*] (NASA)
MEARS...... Maintenance Engineering Analysis Records (SAUO)
MEARS...... Multi-User Engineering Change Proposal Automated Review System (RDA)
Mears Just... Mears' Edition of Justinian and Gaius [*A publication*] (DLA)
MEAS........ Marconi-Elliot Avionic Systems (SAUO)
MEAS........ Measure (AABC)
meas........ Measure (ELAL)
meas........ Measurement (REAL)
MEAS........ Measurement (ROG)
MEAS........ Measuring
MEAS........ Mechanical Engineering Aircraft Squadron (SAUO)
MEAS........ Middle East Air Staff (SAUO)
MEAs........ Multilateral Environmental Agreements (SAUO)
MEASAT..... Malaysia East Asia Satellite
MEASCAL... Measure Calibrate (IAA)
Meas Control (1962-64)... Measurement and Control (1962-64) [*A publication*]
ME Association... Myalgic Encephalomyelitis Association (NRGU)
Meas Spcl.. Measurement Specialities, Inc. [*Associated Press*] (SAG)
MEAST...... Multi-Echelon Automatic Shop Tester (ACAE)
MeasTech... Measurement Techniques (SAUO)
MEASURE... Metrology Automated System for Uniform Recall and Reporting [*Navy*]
MEASURE... Monitoring and Evaluation to Assess and Use Results [*US Agency for International Development*] (RCD)
MEAT........ Manpower Employment Assistance Training [*Act*] [*Pennsylvania*]
MEAT........ Meat Exporters' Association of Tasmania [*Australia*]
MEAT........ Multiedge Adaptive Tracker (MCD)
MEATR...... Materials, Engineering, and Advanced Test Reactor (SAA)
MeAu........ Auburn Public Library, Auburn, ME [*Library symbol*] [*Library of Congress*] (LCLS)
MeAU........ University of Maine at Augusta, Augusta, ME [*Library symbol*] [*Library of Congress*] (LCLS)
MeAub...... Auburn Public Library, Auburn, ME [*Library symbol*] [*Library of Congress*] (LCLS)
ME Auto..... Master of Automobile Engineering (SAUO)
ME Auto..... Master of Automotive Engineering (SAUO)
MEAV........ Meat Exporters' Association of Victoria [*Australia*]
MeaVlly..... Meadow Valley Corp. [*Associated Press*] (SAG)
MeaVly...... Meadow Valley Corp. [*Associated Press*] (SAG)
MEAWS..... Maintenance Engineering Analysis Work Sheet (DNAB)
Me B........ Bachelor of Metaphysics
MEB......... Bangor Mental Health Institute, Bangor, ME [*OCLC symbol*] (OCLC)
MeB......... Bowdoin College, Brunswick, ME [*Library symbol*] [*Library of Congress*] (LCLS)
MEB......... Main Electronics Box (NASA)
MEB......... Maine Motor Rate Bureau, Portland ME [*STAC*]
MEB......... Maintenance Evaluation Branch (SAUO)
MEB......... Malic Enzyme B (DB)
MEB......... Manufacturing Evaluation Board (MCD)
MEB......... Marine Expeditionary Brigade
MEB......... Master Electronics Board
MEB......... Maxton, NC [*Location identifier*] [*FAA*] (FAAL)
MEB......... Mechanical Engineering Bulletin [*A publication*] (GFGA)
MEB......... Medial Efferent Bundle [*Neuroanatomy*]
MEB......... Medical Board
MEB......... Medical Evaluation Board [*Military*] (DAVI)
MEB......... Medical Examining Board (SAUO)
MEB......... Melbourne [*Australia*] [*Airport symbol*] (OAG)
MEB......... Memory Expansion Board (SAUO)
MEB......... Mercury Electron Bombardment
MEB......... Metalsmith (Blacksmith) [*U.S. Navy enlisted rating*] (AUER)
MeB......... Methylene Blue [*Organic chemistry*]
MEB......... Microelectronics Bulletin (SAUO)
MEB......... Midlands Electricity Board [*British*]
MEB......... Military Early Bird
MEB......... Modem Evaluation Board (NITA)
MEB......... Moderate Environment Buoy [*Marine science*] (MSC)
MEB......... Muscle-Eye-Brain [*Disease*] [*Medicine*] (DMAA)
MeBa........ Bangor Public Library, Bangor, ME [*Library symbol*] [*Library of Congress*] (LCLS)
MEBA........ Marine Engineers' Beneficial Association
MEBA........ Michigan Elk Breeders Association (GVA)
MeBaH...... Husson College, Bangor, ME [*Library symbol*] [*Library of Congress*] (LCLS)
MeBaHi..... Bangor Historical Society, Bangor, ME [*Library symbol*] [*Library of Congress*] (LCLS)
MEBA/NMU... Marine Engineers' Beneficial Association/National Maritime Union (EA)
MEBA-PAF... District No. 1-PCD MEBA Political Action Fund [*Washington, DC*] (PACS)
MEBA RETIREES GROUP FUND... Marine Engineers Beneficial Association Retirees Group Fund [*Washington, DC*] (PACS)
MeBarhJ.... Jackson Laboratory, Bar Harbor, ME [*Library symbol*] [*Library of Congress*] (LCLS)
MeBaT...... Bangor Theological Seminary, Bangor, ME [*Library symbol*] [*Library of Congress*] (LCLS)
MeBath...... Patten Free Library, Bath, ME [*Library symbol*] [*Library of Congress*] (LCLS)
MeBathM... Maine Maritime Museum, Bath, ME [*Library symbol*] [*Library of Congress*] (LCLS)
MEBBAS.... Mission Essential Bare Base Augmentation Sets [*Air Force*]
MeBC........ Captain John Curtis Memorial Library, Brunswick, ME [*Library symbol*] [*Library of Congress*] (LCLS)
MEBD........ Medical Evaluation Board [*Military*] (GFGA)
MEBE........ Middle East Basic Encyclopedia [*A publication*] (MCD)
MEBES...... Manufacturing Electron Beam Exposure System (IAA)
MEBFEX..... Marine Expeditionary Brigade Field Exercise (NVT)
ME-BH....... Medial Eminence-Basal Hypothalamus (DB)
MEBLEX..... Marine Expeditionary Brigade Landing Exercise
MEBO........ Main Engine Burnout (NASA)
MeBP........ Pejepscot Historical Society, Brunswick, ME [*Library symbol*] [*Library of Congress*] (LCLS)
Me-BPH..... Maine State Library Service for the Blind and Physically Handicapped, Augusta, ME [*Library symbol*] [*Library of Congress*] (LCLS)
MEBS........ Management Evaluation Guides (SAUO)
MEBS........ Marketing, Engineering, and Business Services [*Telecommunications*] (TEL)
MEBS........ Medium Energy Backscattering Spectrometry (AAEL)
MEBS........ Multicore Extruded Bar Solder
MeBSA...... Methylated Bovine Serum Albumin [*Biochemistry*]
MEBSS...... Materials/Energy Balance Statistical System (SAUO)
MEBTC...... Midwest Eye Banks and Transplantation Center (MHID)
MEBU........ Maschinengewehr-Eisenbeton-Unterstand [*Machine-Gun-Iron-Concrete-Emplacement*] [*German "pill box," battlefield redoubts*] [*World War I*]
MEBU........ Minimum Essential Back Up (CCCA)
MEBU........ Mission Essential Backup (MCD)
MEC......... Committee of Ministers on Energy Conservation (SAUO)
MEC......... International Microbiological Education Committee (SAUO)
MEC......... Maine Central (SAUO)

MEC .... Maine Central Railroad Co. [*AAR code*]
MEC .... Main Engine Console (AAG)
MEC .... Main Engine Controller [*NASA*] (NASA)
MEC .... Main Engine Cutoff [*Aerospace*] (AAG)
MEC .... Main Evaluation Center (NVT)
MEC .... Major Events Committee [*Victoria, Australia*]
MEC .... Management Education for Clinicians (SAUO)
MEC .... Manta [*Ecuador*] [*Airport symbol*] (OAG)
MEC .... Manual Emergency Controls [*Aerospace*] (KSC)
MEC .... Manufacturing Engineering Council (EA)
MEC .... Manufacturing Equipment Committee (SAUO)
MEC .... Map Editing Console
MEC .... Marginal Efficiency of Capital [*Economics*]
MEC .... Marine Expeditionary Corps (NVT)
MEC .... Maritime Electric Co. Ltd. [*Toronto Stock Exchange symbol*]
MEC .... Market Economy Country
MEC .... Master Evaluation Center (MCD)
MEC .... Master Event Controller [*NASA*] (NASA)
MEC .... Master Executive Control (ACAE)
MEC .... Master Executive Council (SAUO)
M Ec .... Master of Economics
MEC .... Master of Engineering Chemistry
MEC .... Materials Engineering Code
MEC .... Materials Experiment Carrier (SAUS)
MEC .... Maximum Endurable Concentration (NATG)
MEC .... Mechanical Engineers & Contractors (EFIS)
MEC .... Mechanical Fabrication Division (SAUO)
MEC .... Mechernich [*Federal Republic of Germany*] [*Seismograph station code, US Geological Survey*] [*Closed*] (SEIS)
MEC .... Meconium [*Gynecology*]
MEC .... Median Effective Concentration (DMAA)
MEC .... Medical Economics Co.
MEC .... Medical Examination Centre [*British*] [*World War II*]
MEC .... Medicines Evaluation Committee [*Australia*]
MEC .... Member of Executive Council [*British*]
MEC .... Member of the Executive Committee (SAUO)
MEC .... Member of the Executive Council (SAUO)
MEC .... Members of the Executive Council (SAUO)
MEC .... Memphis Environmental Center, Inc. (EFIS)
MEC .... Mercado Comune Europeo [*European Common Market*] [*Spanish*] (DLA)
MEC .... Mercury Aircourier Service [*ICAO designator*] (FAAC)
MEC .... Merrimack Education Center [*Chelmsford, MA*] [*Information service or system*]
MEC .... Meteorological Equipment Change (MCD)
MEC .... Meteorology Engineering Center [*Navy*] (MCD)
MEC .... Methodist Episcopal Church
MEC .... Methods Engineering Council (SAUO)
MEC .... Metrolina Educational Consortium [*North Carolina*] (EDAC)
MEC .... Metrology Engineering Center (SAUO)
MEC .... Metropolitan East Coast [*Emergency Management*] (EMA)
MEC .... Microelectronics Center
MEC .... Microencapsulation [*Chemical engineering*]
MEC .... Microsystems Engineering Corporation (ACAE)
MEC .... Microwave Electronics Corp.
MEC .... Microwave Electronics Corporation (SAUO)
MEC .... MidAmerican Energy [*NYSE symbol*] (TTSB)
MEC .... Mid American Energy Co. [*NYSE symbol*] (SAG)
MEC .... MidAmerican Energy Holdings Co. [*NASDAQ symbol*]
MEC .... Middle Ear Canal (DMAA)
MEC .... Middle Ear Cell (BABM)
MEC .... Middle East Centre [*University of Cambridge*] [*British*] (CB)
MEC .... Middle East Command [*Military*]
MEC .... Milgo Electronics Corporation (SAUO)
MEC .... Military Equipment Code (DNAB)
MEC .... Military Essentiality Class [*or Code*]
MEC .... Millennium Eco-Communities [*Canada*]
MEC .... Mineral Exploration Company (SAUO)
MEC .... Minimum Effective Concentration [*Medicine*]
MEC .... Minimum Energy Curve (IAA)
MEC .... Minimum Essential Criteria (MCD)
MEC .... Minimum Explosive Concentration [*Safety*]
MEC .... Minnesota Electronic Corporation (SAUO)
MEC .... Missile Engagement Console [*Military*] (CAAL)
MEC .... Missile Engagement Controller [*Military*] (CAAL)
MEC .... Missile Equipment Code
MEC .... Missile Event Conference (SAUO)
MEC .... Mission Events Controller [*NASA*] (MCD)
MEC .... Mitchell Energy Corp. (EFIS)
MEC .... Mitsubishi Estate Company, Ltd (EFIS)
MEC .... Mobile Examination Center [*Department of Health and Human Services*] (GFGA)
MEC .... Mobility Equipment Center (SAUO)
MEC .... Mobility Equipment Command [*Later, TROSCOM*] [*Army*]
MEC .... Model Energy Code [*Environmental Protection Agency*] (EPAT)
MEC .... Modular Electronics Concept (SAUS)
MEC .... Molecular Exclusion Chromatography
MEC .... Monetary and Economic Council (NADA)
MEC .... Monethylcholine [*Biochemistry*]
MEC .... Monolithic Elastic Convolver (TIMI)
MEC .... Most Excellent Companion [*Freemasonry*] (ROG)
MEC .... Movimiento Emergente de Concordia [*Emerging Movement for Harmony*] [*Guatemala*] [*Political party*] (PPW)
MEC .... Multimedia European Center
MEC .... Multiple Element Correlation (ACAE)
MECA .... Macedonian Educational and Cultural Association [*Australia*]
MeCA .... Maine Counseling Association (SEAT)
MECA .... Main Engine Controller Assembly [*NASA*] (NASA)
MECA .... Maintainable Electronics Component Assembly
MECA .... Malfunctioned Equipment Corrective Action
MECA .... Manufacturers of Emission Controls Association (EA)
MECA .... Map Exercise Computer Assistance (MCD)
MECA .... Mars: Evolution of Its Climate and Atmosphere [*Planetary science project*]
MECA .... Matsushita Electric Corp. of America (IAA)
MECA .... Measure of Elementary Communication Apprehension (EDAC)
MECA .... Mecca and Son Trucking Corporation [*Common carrier symbol*]
MECA .... Medical Emergency Calling Aid (MCD)
MECA .... Mercury Evaporation and Condensation Analysis [*NASA*]
MECA .... Micro Education Corp. of America
MECA .... Military Educators and Counselors Association (EA)
MECA .... Missile Electronics and Computer Assembly [*Military*] (PDAA)
MECA .... Molecular Emission Cavity Analysis [*Flame spectrophotometry*]
MECA .... Multielement Centrifugal Aerowindow
MECA .... Multielement Component Array
MECA .... Multivalue Electronic Circuit Analysis (IAA)
MECAB ...... Regional Bureau of the Middle East Committee for the Affairs of the Blind [*Saudi Arabia*] (EAIO)
MECACON ... Middle East Civil Aviation Conference (PDAA)
MECANO .... Mechanism of automatic Comparison of Answers with OPACs (SAUO)
Mecano ..... Mechanotherapy [*Physical therapy*] (DAVI)
MECAP ...... Medical Examiners and Coroners Alert Program [*Consumer Product Safety Commission*]
MECAP ...... Medical Examiners and Coroners Alert Project (SAUO)
MECAR ...... Metropolitan Engineers Council on Air Resources
MECAS ...... Middle East Center for Arab Studies
MECAS ...... Middle Eastern Center for Arab Studies (SAUO)
MECAS ...... Middle Eastern College for Arabic Studies (SAUO)
MECAS ...... Multienergy Californium Assay System [*Nuclear energy*] (NRCH)
MeCasM .... Maine Maritime Academy, Castine, ME [*Library symbol*] [*Library of Congress*] (LCLS)
MECAssn .... Medical Eye Centre Association [*British*] (DBA)
MECC .... Ecumenical Training Center (SAUO)
MECC .... Master Engineering Control Center (SAUO)
MECC .... Micellar Electrokinetic Capillary Chromatography
MECC .... Middle East Council of Churches (EA)
MECC .... Minnesota Educational Computing Consortium (SAUO)
MECC .... Minnesota Educational Computing Corp. [*NASDAQ symbol*] (SAG)
MECC .... Muslim Education Co-Ordinating Council (AIE)
MECCA ...... Management Enlisted Central Career Administration (SAUO)
MECCA ...... Manufacturing Engineering and Cost Control Applications (NITA)
MECCA ...... Master Electrical Common Connector Assembly (MCD)
MECCA ...... Mechanized Catalog (IEEE)
MECCA ...... Mesoscale Experiment Center for Control and Analysis (SAUO)
MECCA ...... Mid Eastern Council on Chemical Abuse (MHID)
MECCA ...... Milwaukee Exposition and Convention Center and Arena
MECCA ...... Minnesota Environmental Control Citizens Association (SAUO)
MECCA ...... Missile Environment Computer Control Analysis (MCD)
MECCA ...... Missionary and Ecumenical Council of the Church Assembly [*Church of England*]
MECCA ...... Model Evaluation Consortium for Climate Assessment
MECCA ...... Modular Electron Column Control and Automation
MECCAS .... Microbial Exchanges and Coupling in Coastal Atlantic Systems
MeCCNU .... Methyl(chloroethyl)cyclohexylnitrosourea [*Semustine*] [*Antineoplastic drug*]
MECD .... Military Equipment Characteristics Document (RDA)
MEcDev ..... Master of Economics of Development
MECDL ...... Mission Equipment Control Data Link (SAUS)
MECE .... Master of Electrical and Computer Engineering (PGP)
MECE .... Master of Electrochemical Engineering
MECE .... Micellar Electrokinetic Capillary Electrophoresis [*Analytical chemistry*]
MECE .... Movement, Ethyl Chloride, and Elevation [*Medicine*]
MECEA .... Mutual Educational and Cultural Exchange Act of 1961
MEC-ECR ... Management Engineering Steering Committee for Embedded Computer Resources (MCD)
MECEd ...... Master of Early Childhood Education
MECEP ...... Maine Center for Economic Policy (RCD)
MECEP ...... Marine Corps Enlisted Commissioning Education Program (DNAB)
MECF .... Main Engine Computational Facilities [*NASA*] (NASA)
MECF .... Micks External Compression Fixator [*Instrumentation*]
MECG .... Material Electrocardiogram (MCD)
MECG .... Maternal Electrocardiogram [*Cardiology*] [*Obstetrics*] (DAVI)
MECH .... Mechanic [*or Mechanics*] (AFM)
Mech .... Mechanica [*of Aristotle*] [*Classical studies*] (OCD)
Mech .... Mechanical (AL)
mech .... Mechanical (DD)
MECH .... Mechanical (NAKS)
Mech .... Mechanics (BEE)
mech .... Mechanics (SHCU)
MECH .... Mechanics Savings Bank [*NASDAQ symbol*] (SAG)
MECH .... Mechanism [*Automotive engineering*]
MECH .... Mechanized (DOMA)
Mech .... Mechanized (VNW)
mech .... Mechanized (MILB)
MECH .... MECH Financial [*NASDAQ symbol*] (SG)
MECH .... Mech Handling Company [*NCIC trailer make code*]
MECH .... Methodist Episcopal Church

MECH........ Motor End Cap and Housing
MECHBAD... Mechanic Badge
MECHBAT... Mechanized Battalion [*Army*]
MechDy..... Mechanical Dynamics, Inc. [*Associated Press*] (SAG)
ME Ch E.... Master of Electrochemical Engineering
Mech E...... Mechanical Engineer (PGP)
ME(Chem).. Master of Engineering (Chemical) (ADA)
Mechem.... Mechem on Agency [*A publication*] (DLA)
Mechem.... Mechem on Partnership [*A publication*] (DLA)
Mechem Ag... Mechem on Agency [*A publication*] (DLA)
Mechem Pub Off... Mechem on Public Offices and Officers [*A publication*] (DLA)
MECHEN.... Mechanical Engineering (NITA)
Mech Eng... Mechanical Engineer
MECHENGR... Mechanical Engineer
MECH/HYD... Mechanical/Hydraulic
MECH I/C... Mechanic in Charge (DCTA)
MECHINF... Mechanized Infantry [*Army*]
MECHL...... Mechanical
MECH L...... Mechanic's Lien [*Legal term*] (DLA)
MECHM..... MedChem Products, Inc. (SAUO)
MECHN...... Mechanician [*Navy*] [*British*]
MECHNL..... Mechanical
MECHRIC... Middle East Christian Committee
MECHSFIL... Mechanized Sandbag Filler and Sealer (MCD)
MECHSIM... Mechanical Simulation [*of a computer-based directory assistance system*]
MECHSM... Mechanism
MechSv..... Mechanics Savings Bank [*Associated Press*] (SAG)
MECHTRAM... Mechanization of Selected Transportation Movement
MECI......... Member of the Institute of Employment Consultants [*British*] (DBQ)
MECI......... Midwest Enviro-Control, Inc. (EFIS)
MECI......... Mission Essential Contingency Item [*Military*]
MECIF....... Monocyte-Derived Endothelial Cell Inhibitory Factor (DB)
MECK........ Mecklermedia Corp. [*NASDAQ symbol*] (SAG)
Mecklm..... Mecklermedia Corp. [*Associated Press*] (SAG)
MECL........ Families of ECL logic (SAUS)
MECL........ Minimum Essential Circuit List (SAUO)
MECL........ Mistress of English and Classical Literature (SAUO)
MECL........ Motorola Emitter-Coupled Logic (IEEE)
MECL........ Multiemitter-Coupled Logic (IAA)
MECM........ Meridional Elementary Circulation Mechanism
MECM........ Methodist Episcopal Church Mission (SAUO)
MECN........ Mecon Inc. [*NASDAQ symbol*] (TTSB)
MECN........ Mobile Extended Corporate Network (SAUO)
MECNY....... Municipal Engineers of the City of New York (SAUO)
MECO........ Main Engine Cutoff [*Aerospace*]
MECO........ Manual Equipment Checkout (NG)
MECo........ Massachusetts Electric Company (SAUO)
Meco........ Mechanical Corporation (SAUO)
MECO........ Mechanical Equipment Co. Inc. (SAUS)
MECO........ Metropolitan Edison Company (SAUO)
MECOBO.... Military Export Cargo Offering and Booking Office
MECOD...... Member of the College of Dentists (SAUO)
MECOG...... Mechatronics Coordination Group (SAUO)
MECOM..... Marine Engine Condition Monitor (PDAA)
MECOM..... Middle East Command [*Military*]
MECOM..... Middle East Electronic Communications Exhibition (SAUO)
MECOM..... Middle East Electronic Communications Show and Conference [*Arabian Exhibition Management WLL*] [*Manama, Bahrain*]
MECOM..... Mobility Equipment Command [*Later, TROSCOM*] [*Army*]
M-E COMPANIES PAC... M-E Companies, Inc. [*Westerville, OH*] (PACS)
MECOMSAG... Mobility Equipment Command Scientific Advisory Group (MCD)
M Econ...... Master of Economics (PGP)
MECON...... Metallurgical and Engineering Consultants (SAUO)
MEconS..... Master of Economic Science (ADA)
MEconSt.... Master of Economic Studies (ADA)
ME Coy...... Mechanical Equipment Company (SAUO)
MeCP........ Methyl-CCNU, Cytoxan, Prednisone [*Antineoplastic drug*] (CDI)
MECP........ Multielliptical Cavity Pump
MECPr....... MidAmer Energy $1.7375 Pfd [*NYSE symbol*] (TTSB)
MECR........ Maintenance Engineering Change Request (MCD)
MEc(Reg Plan)... Master of Economics in Regional Planning (ADA)
MECS........ Manufacturing Energy Consumption Survey [*Department of Energy*] (GFGA)
MECS........ Maximal Electroconvulsive Seizure [*Neurophysiology*]
MECS........ Mazda Electronic Control System (HAWK)
MECS........ Medicus Systems Corp. [*NASDAQ symbol*] (SAG)
MECS........ Medicus Systems Softwr [*NASDAQ symbol*] (TTSB)
MECS........ Middle East Container Service (SAUO)
MECS........ Mining Equipment Certification Service (HEAS)
MECS........ Mobile Emergency Communication System (CCCA)
MECSIP..... Mechanical Subsystems and Equipment Integrity Program (ACAE)
MECSIP..... Mechanical Subsystems & equipment Structural Integrity Program (SAUS)
MECSLSI.... Mission Equipment Cargo Support Launch Site Installation [*NASA*] (SPST)
MECT........ Mellon Educational and Charitable Trust (SAUO)
MECT........ Mission Endurance Cycle Test
MECTAT..... Middle East Center for the Transfer of Appropriate Technology (SAUO)
MECTS...... Modular Electronic Combat Training System (SAUS)
MECU........ Main Engine Control Unit (SAUS)
MECU........ Master Engine Control Unit
MECU........ Melfi Marine [*Intermodal shipping container symbol*] (TVRC)
MECU........ Member of the English Church Union
MECU........ Municipal Employees Credit Union (NADA)
MECV........ Murine Encephalomyocarditis Virus [*Virology*] (QSUL)
MECWB..... Middle East Committee for the Welfare of the Blind (EA)
MECX........ Trinity Rail Management [*Private rail car owner code*]
MECY........ Methotrexate, Cyclophosphamide [*Antineoplastic drug regimen*]
MECZ........ Mechanize (AAG)
MED......... Chicago, IL [*Location identifier*] [*FAA*] (FAAL)
MED......... e-MedSoft.com [*AMEX symbol*] (SG)
MED......... Macro Editor/Debugger [*Personics Corp.*] [*Computer science*] (PCM)
MED......... Maine Department of Transportation, Augusta, ME [*OCLC symbol*] (OCLC)
MED......... Manhattan Energy District (SAUO)
MED......... Manhattan Engineer District [*Developed atomic bomb; dissolved, 1946*]
MED......... Manipulative Electronic Deception (SAUO)
MED......... Manipulative Electronics Deception (MCD)
MED......... Manual Electron Device
MED......... Manual Entry Device
MED......... Manufacturing Engineering Document (SAA)
MEd......... Master of Education [*British*] (DET)
M Ed......... Master of Education
MED......... Master of Education of the Deaf (GAGS)
MED......... Master of Elementary Didactics
MED......... Master of English Divinity
MED......... Master of Environmental Design (GAGS)
MED......... Maximum Equivalent Dose (ODA)
MED......... Mechanical Equipment Design
MED......... Meckeren-Ehlers-Danlos [*Syndrome*] [*Medicine*] (DB)
med......... Medal (VRA)
MED......... Medal [*Numismatics*]
MED......... Medalist (automobile) [*NCIC car model code*]
MED......... Medallion (automobile) [*NCIC car model code*]
MED......... Medallion Explorations Ltd. [*Vancouver Stock Exchange symbol*]
MED......... Medallist [*British*] (ROG)
MED......... Medan [*Sumatra*] [*Seismograph station code, US Geological Survey*] [*Closed*] (SEIS)
Med......... Medea [*of Euripides*] [*Classical studies*] (OCD)
MED......... Media
med......... Medial [*Medicine*]
MED......... Median (AFM)
med......... Median (DMAA)
MED......... Median Effective Dose [*Medicine*]
MED......... Median Erythrocyte Diameter [*Medicine*]
Med......... Mediator [*Legal term*] (DLA)
MED......... Medical (AFM)
med......... Medical (SHCU)
Med......... Medical (PHSD)
MED......... Medical Department (SAUO)
MED......... Medical Engineering Development (IIA)
MED......... Medicamenta [*Medicaments*] [*Pharmacy*] (ROG)
med......... Medication (DMAA)
MED......... Medication
MED......... Medicine (AABC)
med......... Medicine (WDAA)
Med......... Medicine (AL)
Med......... Medicinical (SAUO)
med......... Medieval (BEE)
MED......... Medieval
MED......... Medina [*Saudi Arabia*] [*Airport symbol*] (OAG)
MED......... MEDIQ, Inc. [*AMEX symbol*] (SPSG)
MED......... Meditation (ROG)
MED......... Mediterranean (AFM)
Med......... Mediterranean (SHCU)
MED......... Mediterranean Engineer Division [*Army Engineers*]
MED......... Medium (AFM)
med......... Medium (DMAA)
MED......... Message Element Dictionary (SAUO)
MED......... Message Entry Device
MED......... Message Exchange Device (SAUS)
MED......... Metalworking Equipment Division (SAUO)
MED......... Microelectronic Device
MED......... Micro-Enterprise Development (FOTI)
MED......... Microwave Emission Detector [*Instrumentation*]
MED......... Mid-Continent Ecology Division [*Duluth*] [*Environmental Protection Agency*] (AEPA)
MED......... Military Electronics Division (SAUO)
MED......... Military Energy Depot (SAA)
MED......... Minimal Effective Dose [*Medicine*]
MED......... Minimal Erythema Dose [*Medicine*]
MED......... Minimum Effective Dose [*Medicine*] (LDT)
MED......... Minimum Engineering Development (MCD)
MED......... Ministry of Education (SAUO)
MED......... Minority Enterprise Development
MED......... Mobile Energy Depot
MED......... Modeling for Equipment Design (AAEL)
MED......... Modem Equivalent Device (ACRL)
MED......... Modular Evolutionary Development (MCD)
MED......... Molecular Electronic Device
MED......... Monitor Execution Dump [*Computer science*]
MED......... Multieffect Distillation [*Chemical engineering*]
MED......... Multiformat Electroluminescent Display (PDAA)
MED......... Multiple Endocrin Deficiency [*Medicine*] (MELL)
MED......... Multiple Epiphyseal Dysplasia [*Medicine*] (CPH)

MED .... Municipal Electricity Department [*New Zealand*] (WDAA)
MED .... Office of Medical Services (SAUS)
MEDA........ Maintenance Error Detection Aid
MEDA........ Medallion Mobile Homes [*NCIC trailer make code*]
MEDA........ Medaphis Corp. [*NASDAQ symbol*] (SPSG)
MEDA........ Mennonite Economic Development Associates (EA)
MEDA........ (Mercaptoethyl)dimethylammonium Chloride [*Organic chemistry*]
MEDA........ Midwest Equipment Dealers Association (EA)
MEDA........ Military Emergency Diversion Aerodrome (DA)
MEDA........ Military Emergency Diversion Airfield (PIAV)
MEDA........ Multiplex Electronic Doppler Analyzer (ACAE)
MEDAAC .... Medical Data System for Analysis of Clinical Information (SAUO)
MEDAB ...... Middle East Database (IID)
MEDAC ...... Medical Accounting [*and Billing Process*]
MEDAC ...... Medical Electronic Data Aquisition and Control
MEDAC ...... Medical Equipment Display and Conference (IAA)
MEDAC ...... Military Electronic Data Advisory Committee [*NATO*] (NATG)
MEDAC ...... Mouvement de l'Evolution Democratique de l'Afrique Centrale [*Central African Democratic Evolution Movement*]
MEDAC ...... Multiple, Endocrine Deficiency - Addison's Disease - Candidiasis [*Syndrome*] [*Endocrinology*] (DAVI)
MEDAC ...... Multiple Endocrine Deficiency, Autoimmune-Candidiasis [*Syndrome*] [*Medicine*]
MEDACS .... Medical Administrative Control System (IAA)
MedAct...... Medical Action Industries, Inc. [*Associated Press*] (SAG)
MEdAd ...... Master of Educational Administration (ADA)
MEdAdm .... Master of Educational Administration (ADA)
Med Adm C... Medical Administrative Corps [*Army*] [*World War II*]
MEdAdmin.. Master of Educational Administration
MEDAIR..... Medical Environmental Development with Air Assistance (SAUO)
MEDAL ...... Medallion [*Automotive engineering*]
MEDAL ...... Micromechanized Engineering Data for Automated Logistics
MEDAL ...... Mine warfare Environmental Decision Air Library (SAUO)
MEDALPEX... Mediterranean Alpine Experiment (SAUO)
MEDALS .... Military Engineering Data Asset Locator (SAUO)
MEDALS .... Modular Engineering Drafting and Library System (IAA)
MEDALSA... Mediterranean Algeria-Sahara Zone [*NATO*] (NATG)
Medalst ..... Medalist Industries, Inc. [*Associated Press*] (SAG)
Medamic.... Medamicus, Inc. [*Associated Press*] (SAG)
Medaph ..... Medaphis Corp. [*Associated Press*] (SAG)
Medar .... Medar, Inc. [*Associated Press*] (SAG)
MedArch .... Medieval Archaeology (SAUO)
Medarex .... Medarex, Inc. [*Associated Press*] (SAG)
MEDARS .... Medical Access and Retrieval System (SAUO)
MED-ART ... Medical Automated Records Technology (STED)
Medarx...... Medarex, Inc. [*Associated Press*] (SAG)
MEDAS ...... Medical Emergency Decisions Assistance System (MCD)
MEDAS ...... Meteorological Data Acquisition System [*NASA*] (KSC)
MEDAS ...... Microfilm Enhanced Data System (PDAA)
MEDASSET... Mediterranean Association to Save the Turtles (SAUO)
MEDAT ...... Multi-Element Discrete Angle Tracker (ACAE)
MedAu ...... Medicine Australia-The Online Journal of Medicine (SAUO)
MEDAUG .... Medical Augmentation (MCD)
MEDAX ...... Message Data Exchange Terminal (MCD)
MEDBAD .... Medical Badge
MedBiolEng... Medical and Biological Engineering (SAUO)
MEDBLD .... Medical and Blood Products Management (SAUO)
MEDBN ...... Medical Battalion [*Marine Corps*]
MEDBO ...... Mediterranean Shipping Board [*World War II*]
MEDBR ...... Medical Branch
Med Bull Exxon Corp Affil Co... Medical Bulletin. Exxon Corporation and Affliated Companies (SAUO)
MEDC........ [*The*] Med-Design Corp. [*NASDAQ symbol*] (SAG)
MEDC........ Medical Care International, Inc. (SAUO)
Med C .... Medical Corps (SAUO)
MEDC........ Michigan Economic Development Corp. (IID)
MEDC........ Microelectronics Educational Development Centre [*Paisley College*] [*British*] (CB)
MEDC........ Moessbauer Effect Data Center [*University of North Carolina*] [*Information service or system*] (IID)
MEdCA ...... Master of Education in Creative Arts
MED-CAMPUS... A project for cooperation between higher education institutes around the Mediterranean (SAUO)
MEDCAP .... Medical Civic Action Program (SAUO)
MEDCAP .... Patrol [*or Assistance*] [*or Program*] [*Military*]
MEDCASE... Medical Care Support Equipment (AABC)
MEDCAT..... Medical Civic Action Teams
MEDCAT..... Medium Altitude Clear-Air Turbulence (MCD)
MEDCAT..... Medium-Altitude Critical Atmospheric Turbulence (MCD)
MEDCATE ... Medical College Admissions Test [*Medicine*] (EDAA)
MedCath .... MedCath, Inc. [*Associated Press*] (SAG)
MEDCEN .... Medical Center [*Army*] (AABC)
MEDCEN .... United States Army Medical Center (SAUO)
MEDCENT... Allied Forces, Central Mediterranean (SAUO)
MEDCENT... Central Mediterranean Area [*NATO*]
Med C Georgia... Medical College of Georgia (GAGS)
MedChi...... Medical and Chirurgical Faculty of Maryland (MHID)
MEDCL ...... Medical
MedClinNAmer... Medical Clinics of North America (SAUO)
MEDCMNT... Medicament
MedCmp .... Medic Computer Systems, Inc. [*Associated Press*] (SAG)
MEDCN...... Medicine
MEDCO...... Meat Export Development Company (SAUO)
Med Co ..... Medical Company (SAUO)
MEDCOAST... International Conference on the Mediterranean Coastal Environment (SAUS)
MEDCO HEALTH PAC... MEDCO Health Solutions Inc [*Franklin Lakes, NJ*] (PACS)
Med C Ohio... Medical College of Ohio at Toledo (GAGS)
MEDCOM ... Medical Command (MCD)
MEDCOM ... Mediterranean Communications [*Military*] (AFM)
MEDCOM ... Mediterranean Communication System (SAUO)
MEDCOM ... Mediterranean Planning Committee (SAUO)
MEDCOM ... Mediterranean Regional Committee for START (SAUO)
MEDCOMP... International Conference on Medical Computer Science (SAUS)
MEDCOMP... International Congress on Computing in Medicine (SAUO)
MEDCOMP... Medical Early Direct Commissioning Program (MCD)
MEDCOMPLAN... Mediterranean Communications Plans [*NATO*] (NATG)
Medcom System... Mediterranean Communications System (SAUO)
MEDCON.... Medical Contingency Report [*Air Force*]
MEDCOOP... Medical Continuity of Operations Plan [*Army*] (AABC)
MEDCORE... Medical Resources Consortium of Central New Jersey [*Library network*]
MEDCORPS... Medical Corps [*Air Force*]
MEDCOS .... Mediterranean Chiefs of Staff [*British*] [*World War II*]
Med C Penn... Medicine College of Pennsylvania (GAGS)
MedcR ...... Medco Research, Inc. [*Associated Press*] (SAG)
Medcross ... Medcross, Inc. [*Associated Press*] (SAG)
MedCtr ...... Medical Center (SAUO)
MedCtrl ..... Medical Contol [*Associated Press*] (SAG)
Med C Wis... Medicine College of Wisconsin (GAGS)
Medd .... Meddaugh's Reports [*13 Michigan*] [*A publication*] (DLA)
MEDD .... Medical Device Technol [*NASDAQ symbol*] (TTSB)
MEDD .... Medical Device Technologies, Inc. [*NASDAQ symbol*] (SAG)
MEDDA....... Mechanized Defense Decision Anticipation [*AFSC*]
MEDDAC .... Medical Department Activity [*Army*] (AABC)
MEDDARS... Medical Display Analysis and Recording System
Meddaugh... Meddaugh's Reports [*13 Michigan*] [*A publication*] (DLA)
MED-DENT... Medical Dental Division [*Air Force*]
Med Dep Co... Medical Depot Company (SAUO)
Med Devices Rep (CCH)... Medical Devices Reports (Commerce Clearing House) [*A publication*] (DLA)
MedDevT ... Medical Device Technologies, Inc. [*Associated Press*] (SAG)
MEDDF...... Master Engineering Drawing Data File System
MEdDHi ..... Dukes County Historical Society, Edgartown (SAUO)
MEdDHi ..... Dukes County Historical Society, Edgartown, MA [*Library symbol*] [*Library of Congress*] (LCLS)
MEDDIC ..... Medical Evidence Disaggregated Direct Input of Costs Database [*Social Security Administration*] (GFGA)
MEDDOC .... Medical Documentation Systems [*Eli Lilly & Co.*] [*Information service or system*] (IID)
MEDDPERSA... Medical Department Personnel Support Agency [*Army*] (MCD)
MEDDS...... Mechem Explosives & Drug Detection System (SAUS)
MEDDS...... Medical Data Specialist (AABC)
MedDsg ..... [*The*] Med-Design Corp. [*Associated Press*] (SAG)
MedDv ...... Medical Device Technologies, Inc. [*Associated Press*] (SAG)
MedDvt...... Medical Device Technologies, Inc. [*Associated Press*] (SAG)
MEDDY...... Mediterranean Eddy [*Oceanography*]
MedDyn ..... Medical Dynamics, Inc. [*Associated Press*] (SAG)
MEDE........ Message Entry & Distribution Equipment (SAUS)
MEDE........ Military Electronics Defense Exhibition (SAUO)
MEDEA ...... International Medical Engineering and Automation Exhibition (SAUO)
MEDEA ...... Masters Degree in Energy and Environmental Management and Economics (ECON)
MEDEA ...... Material Science Experiment Double Rack for Experiment (SAUS)
MEDEA ...... Measurements of Earth Data for Environmental Analysis [*Marine science*] (OSRA)
MEDEA ...... Micro-Electronics Development for European Applications (SAUO)
MEDEA ...... Modules and Apparatus (SAUS)
MEDEA ...... Multidiscipline Engineering Design, Evaluation, and Analysis (RDA)
MEDEAST... Allied Forces, Southern Europe, Mediterranean East (SAUO)
MEDEAST... Eastern Mediterranean Area [*NATO*] (NATG)
MEd(Ed/Psych)... Master of Education (Educational Psychology), University of Birmingham [*British*] (DBQ)
MEDEF ...... Middle East Defence & Security Exhibition (SAUO)
MEDEFLUX... Mediterranean Flux Measurement Network (SAUO)
MEDEMG.... Medical Emergencies [*Computerized management course*]
MEDENCO... Myers Dental Laboratories (EFIS)
Med Eng Phys... Medical Engineering and Physics (SAUS)
MEDes ...... Master of Environmental Design (DD)
Medeva ..... Medeva Ltd. [*Associated Press*] (SAG)
MEDEVAC... Medical Evacuation Team [*Army*]
MEDEVAL... Medical Evaluation [*Military*] (AABC)
MEDEX ...... Medecin Extension [*Doctors' Aides, or Medics*] [*French*]
Medex........ Medex, Inc. [*Associated Press*] (SAG)
MEDF........ Maximum Energy Distribution Function
MEDF........ Medford Industries [*NCIC trailer make code*]
MEDF........ Midexpiratory Dynamic Flow Rate [*Medicine*] (DAVI)
MEDFAD .... Medical Field Assistance Branch (SAUO)
MedfdSv .... Medford Savings Bank [*Associated Press*] (SAG)
medfly....... Mediterranean Fruit Fly (SHCU)
MEDFLY..... Mediterranean Fruit Fly
MEDGP...... Medical Group [*Air Force*]
MedGr....... Medical Graphics Corp. [*Associated Press*] (SAG)
MEd(Guid&Coun)... Master of Education in Guidance and Counselling
MEDH .... Maintainability Engineering Design Handbook
MEDHOC.... Macro-Economic Databank House of Commons (SAUO)

MEDI .... Marine Environmental Data Information Referral System [*UNESCO*] [*Paris, France*]
medi .... Media (VRA)
MEDI .... Medical Coaches [*NCIC trailer make code*]
Medi .... Medicare [*Medicine*] (EDAA)
MEDI .... Medicine (DSUE)
MEDI .... MedImmune, Inc. [*NASDAQ symbol*] (SPSG)
MEDI .... Missile Error Data Integration [*Military*] (IAA)
MEDI .... Moessbauer Effect Data Index
MEDIA .... Magnavox Electronic Data Image Apparatus
MEDIA .... Man's Environments - Display Implication and Applications (PDAA)
MEDIA .... Manufacturers Educational Drug Information Association
MEDIA .... Measures for Encouraging the Development of the Audiovisual Production Industry [*EC*] (ECED)
Media .... Media General, Inc. [*Associated Press*] (SAG)
MEDIA .... Missile Era Data Integration Analysis
MEDIA .... Modular Electronic Digital Instrumentation Assemblies (PDAA)
MEDIA .... Move to End Deception in Advertising [*Student legal action organization*]
MediaArt .... Media Arts Group, Inc. [*Associated Press*] (SAG)
MEDIACULT ... International Institute for Audio-visual Communication and Cultural Development (SAUO)
Media L & P ... Media Law and Practice [*A publication*] (DLA)
MediaLog ... Media Logic, Inc. [*Associated Press*] (SAG)
Media M .... Media and Methods [*A publication*] (BRI)
MEDIA/M .... Media/Medicine (NITA)
MEDIAN .... Medical Information Access Network [*Medicine*] (EDAA)
MEDIAS ..... Mediterranean and Subtropical Africa (SAUO)
MEDIAS ..... Mediterranean Basin and Sub-tropical Africa (SAUO)
MEDIAS ..... Regional Research Network for the Mediterranean Basin and Subtropical Africa (SAUS)
MEDIC .... Mechanized Design and Integrated Control
MEDIC .... Medical Education Development in Communities [*Medicine*] (EDAA)
MEDIC .... Medical Electronic Data Interpretation and Correlation (IAA)
MEDIC .... Medical Emergency Development International Committee (SAUO)
Medic .... Medicamina Faciei [*of Ovid*] [*Classical studies*] (OCD)
Medic .... Military Medical Corpsman [*Medicine*] [*L. medicus*] (EDAA)
MEDIC .... Monthly Ethical Drug Indexed Compilation [*Medicine*] (EDAA)
MEDICA ...... Multimedial Medical Diagnostic Assistant (SAUO)
Medicaid .... Medical Aid (SHCU)
MEDICAID ... Medical Aid [*Federal program providing financial assistance for medical expenses of individual needy citizens*]
MEDI-CAL ... Medical Aid of California (SAUO)
Medicare ... Medical Care (SHCU)
MEDICARE ... Medical Care [*Federal program providing financial assistance for medical expenses of individual senior citizens*]
MEDICC ..... Medical Education Cooperation with Cuba (SAUO)
MEDICEF .... International Center for Medical Environmental Sciences and Future Research (SAUO)
MEDICI ...... Melodic Dictation Computerized Instruction (EDAC)
Medicinal Chem ... Medicinal Chemistry (MEC)
Medicis ..... Medicis Pharmaceutical Corp. [*Associated Press*] (SAG)
MEDICO ..... Medical Information Cooperation (DAVI)
MEDICO ..... Medical International Cooperation
MEDICO ..... Model Experiment in Drug Indexing by Computer [*Rutgers University*]
MEDICOM ... Medical Communications
MEDICOM ... Medical Image Communication standard components (AG)
MEDICOR ... Centre for Offshore and Remote Medicine [*Memorial University of Newfoundland*] [*Research center*] (RCD)
Medicorp ... American Medicorp, Inc. (SAUO)
MEDICOS ... Mediterranean Instructions to Convoys [*World War II*]
MEDICS ..... Majors Electronic Data Interchange Communications System [*Computer science*]
MEDICS ..... Medical Information and Career Service [*British*] (DAVI)
MEDICS ..... Medical Information and Communications System (NITA)
MEDICS ..... Medical Information Computer System (NASA)
MEDICS ..... Michael E. DeBakey International Cardiovascular Society [*Later, MEDISS*] (EA)
Medicus ..... Medicus Systems Corp. [*Associated Press*] (SAG)
MEDIEV ..... Medieval
MEDIF .... Medical Information Form [*British*]
Medigap .... Medicare Supplement Insurance
medi gen ... Media Generated (VRA)
MEDIGEN ... Medical Energy Generation (EFIS)
MEDIHC ..... Military Experience Directed into Health Careers [*DoD/HEW project*]
MedImun ... MedImmune, Inc. [*Associated Press*] (SAG)
MEDIN .... Medina, OH [*American Association of Railroads railroad junction routing code*]
MedInd ...... Medical Industries of America [*Associated Press*] (SAG)
MedIndA .... Medical Industries of America [*Associated Press*] (SAG)
MEDINET .... Medical Information Network [*GTE Telenet Communications Corp.*] [*Telecommunications*]
MEDINFO ... Medical Informatics
MedInn ...... Medical Innovations, Inc. [*Associated Press*] (SAG)
MEDINSP ... Medical Inspection [*Military*] (NVT)
MEDINT ..... Medical Intelligence (MCD)
MEDIOC ..... Mediocris [*Middling*] [*Pharmacy*] (ROG)
MEDIOL ..... Mediolanum [*Milan*] [*Imprint*] (ROG)
MEDIPHOR ... Monitoring and Evaluation of Drug Interactions in a Pharmacy-Oriented Reporting System [*National Center for Health Services Research*] (DHSM)
MEDIPP ..... Medical District Initiated Program Planning [*Veterans Administration*]
MEDIPRO ... Medical District Initiated Peer Review Organization [*Veterans Administration*] (GFGA)
Mediq .... Mediq, Inc. [*Associated Press*] (SAG)
MEDIS .... International Symposium on Medical Information Systems (SAUO)
MEDIS .... Medical Dietary Information System (SAUO)
MEDIS .... Message Diversion Relay System (IAA)
MedisE ...... Medis E Ltd. [*Associated Press*] (SAG)
MediSens ... MediSense, Inc. [*Associated Press*] (SAG)
MEDI-SOTA LIBR ... Medi-Sota Library Consortium [*Library network*]
MEDISPA .... Medical Sterile Products Association (SAUO)
MEDISS ..... Michael E. DeBakey International Surgical Society (EA)
MEDISTAT ... Banque de Donnees Socio-Economiques des Pays Mediterraneens [*Socioeconomic Data Bank on the Mediterranean Countries*] [*International Center for Advanced Mediterranean Agronomic Studies*] [*Information service or system*] (IID)
Medit .... Mediterranean (DIAR)
MEDIT .... Mediterranean
MeditArch ... Mediterranean Archaeology [*A publication*] (ABAR)
MEDITEC .... Dodumentation Medizinische Technik [*Medical Technology Documentation*] [*TechnicalInformation Center*] [*Germany*] [*Information service or system*] (IID)
MEDITECH ... Medical Information Technology (IID)
Meditr .... Meditrust [*Associated Press*] (SAG)
MEDIUM .... Missile Era Data Integration - Ultimate Method
Mediwre .... Mediware Information Systems, Inc. [*Associated Press*] (SAG)
MEDIX .... Medical Data Interchange (RALS)
M Ed J ...... Music Educators Journal [*A publication*] (BRI)
MEDJC ...... Medfield Junction, MA [*American Association of Railroads railroad junction routing code*]
Med J Osaka Univ ... Medical Journal of Osaka University (SAUO)
MED JUR ... Medical Jurisprudence (ADA)
MEDL .... Marconi Electronic Devices Ltd. [*British*] (IRUK)
MEDL .... Materials Evaluation and Development Laboratory [*General Services Administration*]
MEDL .... Medical
medL .... medieval Latin (SAUO)
MEDL .... Mission Equipment Development Laboratory (SAUO)
MEDLA ...... Molecular Electron Density Lego Assembler [*Modeling technique*] [*Organic chemistry*]
Med L & P ... Media Law and Practice [*1980*] [*A publication*] (DLA)
Med L & Pub Pol ... Medicine, Law, and Public Policy [*A publication*] (DLA)
MEDLARS ... Medical Literature Analysis and Retrieval System [*National Library of Medicine*] [*Bethesda, MD*] [*Database*]
Med Lat ..... Medieval Latin [*Language*]
Med-Legal J ... Medico-Legal Journal [*A publication*] (DLA)
Med-Legal Soc'y Trans ... Medico-Legal Society. Transactions [*A publication*] (DLA)
Med Leg Pap ... Medico-Legal Papers [*A publication*] (DLA)
Med Leg Soc Trans ... Transactions. Medico-Legal Society [*A publication*] (ILCA)
Med Leg Vic Proc ... Medico-Legal Society of Victoria. Proceedings [*A publication*]
MEDLI .... Motoring Experience for the Disabled by Lions International [*British*]
MEDLINE .... CD-ROM database equivalent of Index Medicus (SAUS)
MEDLINE .... Medical Information Online (NITA)
MEDLINE .... Medical literature analysis and retrieval system (SAUO)
MEDLINE .... MEDLARS [*Medical Literature Analysis and Retrieval System*] On-Line [*National Library of Medicine*] [*Bibliographic database*]
MEDList ..... Master Enumeration District List [*Bureau of Census*]
MEDLL ...... Multi-path Estimating Delay Lock Loop [*Communications*]
medln .... Medallion (VRA)
Med LN ..... Medico-Legal News [*A publication*] (DLA)
MEDLOC .... Mediterranean Lines of Communication [*Military*] (IAA)
MEDLOC .... Mediterranean Location [*Navy*]
MEDLOG .... Medical Logistics (SAUO)
Med LP ..... Medico-Legal Papers [*A publication*] (DLA)
Med L Rptr ... Media Law Reporter [*A publication*] (NTCM)
M Ed LS .... Master of Education in Library Science
M ED L SC ... Master of Education in Library Science (WDAA)
MEDM .... Medamicus, Inc. [*NASDAQ symbol*] (SAG)
MEDM .... Medium
Medm .... Medmarco, Inc. [*Associated Press*] (SAG)
MEDM .... Med-Mobile, Inc. (SAUO)
MEDMAF .... Mekong Delta Mobile Afloat Force [*Vietnam*] [*Military*] (VNW)
MEDMAILCOORD ... Mediterranean Mail Coordinating Office (DNAB)
MEDMAL .... Medical Malpractice Lawsuit Filings [*Medical Malpractice Verdicts, Settlements & Experts*] [*Information service or system*] (CRD)
MEd(Maths) ... Master of Education (Mathematics)
MEDMATS ... Medical Materiel Management System [*Army*]
med men ... Medial Meniscectomy [*orthopedics*] (DAVI)
med men ... Medial Meniscus [*Orthopedics*] (DAVI)
MEDMER .... Medical Emergency Report [*Air Force*]
MedMgt ..... Medical Management, Inc. [*Associated Press*] (SAG)
MEDMIS .... Medical Management Information System [*Army*]
Med Moor ... Mediterranean Moor (MUSM)
MEDNET .... Medical Systems Network (SAUO)
Mednet ...... Mednet MPC Corp. [*Associated Press*] (SAG)
MEDNOREAST ... Allied Forces, Southern Europe, Mediterranean North East (SAUO)
MEDNOREAST ... Northeast Mediterranean Area [*NATO*] (NATG)
MEDNTPS ... Mediterranean Near-Term Prepositioned Ship
MEDO .... Middle East Defense Organization (NATG)
MEDO .... Multipole Expansion of Diatomic Overlap [*Physics*]
MEDOC ...... Allied Forces, Southern Europe, Mediterranean West (SAUO)
MEDOC ...... Medical Documents [*Eccles Health Sciences Library - University of Utah*] [*Salt Lake City, UT*] [*Bibliographic database*]
MEDOC ...... Mediterranean Oceanographic Project [*1969*]

MEDOC...... Western Mediterranean Area [*NATO*] (NATG)
MEDOCHAN... Mary Ellen, Dorothy, Chuck, Ann [*Famous Canadian resort, named for the owners' children*]
MEDOFCOM... Medical Officer-in-Command [*Military*]
MEDOL...... Medically Oriented Language
MEDOR...... Medora, KS [*American Association of Railroads railroad junction routing code*]
MEDOWS... Meadows [*Commonly used*] (OPSA)
MEDP........ Medium Port
MEDP........ MedPlus, Inc. [*NASDAQ symbol*] (SAG)
MEDP........ Mission Essential Data Processing (SAUO)
MedPAC..... Medicare Payment Advisory Commission
MedPAC..... Medicare Payment Assessment Commission
MEDPAR.... Medical Patient Accounting and Reporting (SAUO)
MEDPAR.... Medicare Provider Analysis and Review (GFGA)
MedPart..... MedPartners, Inc. [*Associated Press*] (SAG)
MEDPED.... Make Early Diagnosis to Prevent Early Death [*Association*] (EA)
MED-PED-FH... Making Early Diagnosis to Prevent Early Deaths (in Medical Pedigrees) with Familial Hypercholesterolemia [*Medicine*] (EDAA)
MEDPERFAC... Medical and Personnel Planning Factors Report (SAUO)
MEDPES.... Medical Planning and Execution System (COE)
M EdPh..... Master of Physical Education (SAUO)
MedPlus.... MedPlus, Inc. [*Associated Press*] (SAG)
MEDPOL.... Coordinated Mediterranean Pollution Monitoring and Research Programme (SAUS)
MEDPOL.... Mediterranean Action Plan Pollution Monitoring and Research Program (SAUO)
MED POL... Mediterranean Pollution Monitoring and Research Programme (SAUO)
MEDPr....... MEDIQ Inc. Cv Pfd [*AMEX symbol*] (TTSB)
MEDPRO.... Medical Education Resources Program (MEDA)
MEDPRP.... Medical Properties, Inc. (SAUO)
MEdPsych.. Master of Educational Psychology (ADA)
MEDQ....... MedQuist Inc. [*NASDAQ symbol*] (TTSB)
MedQst...... MedQuist, Inc. [*Associated Press*] (SAG)
MEDR....... Medco Research, Inc. (SAUO)
MedRA...... Medical Resource Companies of America [*Associated Press*] (SAG)
MEDRAMS... Medical Readiness Assemblage Medical System [*Air Force*] (GFGA)
MEDRC...... Medical Reserve Corps [*Military*] (WDAA)
MEDRECO.. Mediterranean Refining Company (SAUO)
MEDRED.... Medical Readiness Report Capability (SAUO)
MEDRED.... Medical Unit Readiness Report [*Air Force*]
MEDREG.... Medical Regulating (SAUS)
MEDREG.... Medical Regulating (or Regulation) (SAUO)
MEDREGREP... Medical Regulating Report (COE)
MEDREQ.... Medical Requirements Model (SAUO)
Med Res Bull Rept Dept... Repatriation Department. Medical Research Bulletin (SAUS)
Med Res C... Medical Reserve Corps (SAUO)
MedResc..... Medical Resources, Inc. [*Associated Press*] (SAG)
MEDRESCO... Medical Research Council (NADA)
Me-dResEng.... Medical Research Engineering (SAUO)
MEDRETES... Medical Readiness Training Exercises [*Army*]
MEDREX.... Medical Readiness Exercise (MCD)
medRNA.... Ribonucleic Acid, Mini-Exon-Derived [*Biochemistry, genetics*]
MEDRTS.... Medical Requirements Model (SAUO)
MEDRU...... Medical Design Research Unit [*University of Central England*] [*United Kingdom*] (RCD)
MEd(RuralEd)... Master of Education in Rural Education
MEDS........ Maintenance Engineering Data System (SAUO)
MEDS........ Management Engineering Data System (SAUO)
MEDS........ Marine Ecological Database System [*Marine science*] (OSRA)
MEDS........ Marine Embarkation Data System (SAUO)
MEDS........ Marine Environmental Data Service [*Canada*] (NOAA)
MEDS........ Master of Environmental Design Studies [*Canada*] (ASC)
MEDS........ Mechanized Embarkation Data System [*Military*] (NVT)
MEDS........ Medical Electronics and Data Society [*Later, MES*] (EA)
MEDS........ Medical Evaluation Data System (IEEE)
Meds........ Medications [*or Medicines*]
MEDS........ Medstone International, Inc. [*NASDAQ symbol*] (SAG)
MEDS........ Medstone Intl. [*NASDAQ symbol*] (TTSB)
MEDS........ Meteorological and Environmental Data Services (USDC)
MEDS........ Meteorological Data Systems (SAUO)
MEDS........ Meteorological Environmental Data Services [*Marine science*] (OSRA)
MEDS........ Monitoring, Evaluation and Design Support Activity (SAUO)
MEDS........ Multifunction Electronic Display System [*NASA*]
MEDSAC.... Medical Service Activity [*Army*] (AABC)
MEDSARS... Maintenance Engineering Data Storage and Retrieval System (NG)
Med Sc D... Doctor of Medical Science [*or the Science of Medicine*]
MEDSCH.... Medical School (ADA)
MedSch(N)... Institute of Naval Medicine [*British*]
Med Sci Sports and Exercise... Medicine and Science in Sports and Exercise (MEC)
MEDSERV... Medical Service Corps [*Military*] (MCD)
MEDSERVC... Medical Service Corps [*Military*]
MEDSERWRNT... Medical Service Warrant
MEDSOM... Medical Supply, Optical, and Maintenance [*Army*] (RDA)
MEDSOUEAST... Southeast Mediterranean Area [*NATO*] (NATG)
MEDSOUTHEAST... Allied Forces, Southern Europe, Mediterranean South East (SAUO)
MEDSPA.... Mediterranean Special Programme of Action (SAUO)
MEDSPECC... Medical Specialist Corps [*Military*]
MEd(SpecEd)... Master of Education (Special Education)
MEd(SpEd)... Master of Education in Special Education (ADA)
MEDSS...... Multiple Echelon Direct Support System (MCD)
MEdSt....... Master of Educational Studies (ADA)
MEDSTAR... Medical Staffing and Training to Augment Readiness (MCD)
MEDSTAT... Medicaid Statistical Reporting and Analysis System (GFGA)
MEDSTATS... Medical Statistics Expert System (DMAA)
med stern... Median Sternotomy (CPH)
MEDSTOC... Medical Stock Control System [*Army*]
MEDSTOCK... Medical Stock Control System (SAUO)
Medstone... Medstone International, Inc. [*Associated Press*] (SAG)
MEdStud.... Master of Educational Studies
MEDSUPDEP... Medical Supply Depot
Medsupp.... Medicare Supplement Insurance
Med Supt... Medical Superintendent (SAUO)
Med/Surg... Medical Surgical Unit or Section [*Therapy term*] (CTAA)
MedSurg.... Medicine and Surgery (DAVI)
M Ed T...... Master of Education in Teaching (PGP)
MEDT....... Mean Elapsed Downtime [*Computer science*] (MCD)
MedT........ Medical Technology Systems, Inc. [*Associated Press*] (SAG)
MEDT........ Military Equipment Delivery Team
MEDTC...... Military Equipment Delivery Team Cambodia (VNW)
med tech... Medical Technician [*or Technologist*] (AAMN)
Med Tech... Medical Technologist (SAUO)
Med Tech... Medical Technology (DAVI)
MedTech.... Medical Technology Systems, Inc. [*Associated Press*] (SAG)
Med Tox..... Medical Toxicology and Adverse Drug Experience (MEC)
MEDTRAIN... Medical Literature Training File (NITA)
Medtrnc..... Medtronic, Inc. [*Associated Press*] (SAG)
MEDU....... Co-ordinating Unit for the MAP (SAUO)
MEDU....... US-Mediterranean Line [*Intermodal shipping container symbol*] (TVRC)
MEDUNSA... Medical University of Southern Africa (SAUO)
Medusa..... Medusa Corp. [*Associated Press*] (SAG)
MEDUSA.... Multiple Element Directional Universally Steerable Antenna
Med U So Car... Medical University of South Carolina (GAGS)
MedVat...... MediVators, Inc. [*Associated Press*] (SAG)
MEDW....... Mediware Information Sys [*NASDAQ symbol*] (TTSB)
MEDW....... Mediware Information Systems, Inc. [*NASDAQ symbol*] (SAG)
MedWorld News... Medical World News (SAUO)
MED-WRAP... Medical War Reserve Automated Process (SAUO)
Medwve..... Medwave, Inc. [*Associated Press*] (SAG)
MEDX........ Medarex, Inc. [*NASDAQ symbol*] (SPSG)
MEDXW..... Medarex Inc. Wrrt [*NASDAQ symbol*] (TTSB)
MEDY........ Medial Dynamics [*NASDAQ symbol*] (TTSB)
MEDYN...... Medical Dynamics, Inc. [*NASDAQ symbol*] (NQ)
MEE.......... Maine Office of Energy Resources Library, Augusta, ME [*OCLC symbol*] (OCLC)
MEE.......... Maintenance Engineering Evaluation (MCD)
MEE.......... Mare [*Loyalty Islands*] [*Airport symbol*] (OAG)
MEE.......... Mass Energy Equivalent
MEE.......... Massey Energy [*NYSE symbol*]
MEE.......... Master of Electrical Engineering
MEE.......... Measured Energy Expenditure (DMAA)
MEE.......... Mechanical, Electrical, and Electronic (MCD)
MEE.......... Mechanical Evaluation Equipment
MEE.......... Meerut [*India*] [*Seismograph station code, US Geological Survey*] [*Closed*] (SEIS)
MEE.......... Merrill Lynch & Co., Inc. [*NYSE symbol*] (SAG)
MEE.......... Methyl Ethyl Ether [*Organic chemistry*]
MEE.......... Middle Ear Effusion [*Medicine*]
MEE.......... Middle East Enterprises, Beirut (SAUO)
MEE.......... Migration Enhanced Epitaxy (AAEL)
MEE.......... Military Engineering Establishment (SAUO)
MEE.......... Military Essential Equipment (CINC)
MEE.......... Minimum Essential Equipment
MEE.......... Mission Essential Equipment [*NASA*] (KSC)
MEE.......... Multilocus Enzyme Electrophoresis (DMAA)
MEE.......... Muskogee, OK [*Location identifier*] [*FAA*] (FAAL)
MEEC........ Massachusetts Energy Efficiency Council (SAUO)
MEEC........ Membrane Enclosed Enzymatic Catalysis
MEEC........ Middle East Economic Committee (SAUO)
MEECES..... Multi-Experimental Event-Controlled Entry System [*Computer science*] (VLIE)
MEECN...... Minimal Essential Emergency Communications Network (SAUO)
MEECN...... Minimum Essential Emergency Communications Network [*Military*]
MEECO...... Metallurgical Equipment Export Company (SAUO)
MEED........ Mechanical and Electrical Engineering Division (SAUO)
MEED........ Medium-Energy Electron Diffraction
MEED........ Microbial Ecology Evaluation Device [*NASA*] (KSC)
MEED........ Middle East Economic Digest [*A publication*]
MEED Conferences... Middle East Economic Digest Conferences (SAUO)
ME-EE....... Mechanical Engineer and Electrical Engineer [*Academic degree*]
MEEF........ Manufacturing Engineering Education Foundation
MEEF........ Mobile Equipment Employment File [*Air Force*] (AFM)
MEEG........ Morale-Effect Explosive Grenade [*Police and security equipment*]
MEEI......... Manufacturing Engineering Equipment Instruction (SAUO)
MEEL........ Mission Equipment Essentiality List
MeEl......... William Fogg Memorial Library, Eliot, ME [*Library symbol*] [*Library of Congress*] (LCLS)
ME(Elec).... Master of Engineering (Electrical) (ADA)
MEEM....... Master of Environmental Engineering and Management (PGP)

MEEM .... Metastable Electron Emission Microscopy
ME Eng...... Master of Electrical Engineering
MEEP .... Management and Equipment Evaluation Program
MEER .... Mechanical/Electrical Equipment Room (MCD)
MEEREC..... Middle East Environmental Research and Education Committee (SAUO)
MEERS ...... Maximum Effective Echo Ranging Speed (NVT)
MEES .... Marine-Estuarine-Environmental Sciences (PDAA)
MEES .... Medical Element Engineering and Simulation (DMAA)
MEES .... Middle East Economic Survey [*A publication*]
MEES .... Missile End Game Evaluation System (ACAE)
MEES .... Multipurpose Electromagnetic Environment Simulator (MCD)
Mees & Ros... Meeson and Roscoe's English Exchequer Reports [*A publication*] (DLA)
Mees & W... Meeson and Welsby's English Exchequer Reports [*A publication*] (DLA)
Mees & Wels... Meeson and Welsby's English Exchequer Reports [*A publication*] (DLA)
MEET .... Minimum Essential Equipment for Training
MEETA....... Maximum Improvement in Electronics Effectiveness through Advanced Techniques
MEETAT ..... Maximum Improvement in Electronics Effectiveness through Advanced Techniques
MEETS ...... Minimum Engine Tracking System (SAUO)
MEEU........ Mediterranean Reefer [*Intermodal shipping container symbol*] (TVRC)
MEEV........ Maintenance and Electricity Equipment Vault (MCD)
MEF.......... Emerging Mexico Fund [*NYSE symbol*] (SPSG)
MEF.......... Maintenance Efficiency Factor
MEF.......... Major Emitting Facility [*Environmental Protection Agency*]
MEF.......... Major Equipment File (MCD)
MEF.......... Management Engineering Flight [*Air Force*]
MEF.......... Marine Expeditionary Force
MEF.......... Master Edit File [*Computer science*] (VLIE)
MEF.......... Maximal Expiratory Flow [*Medicine*]
MEF.......... Maximum Elevation Figure [*Aviation*] (PIPO)
MEF.......... Meal Export Federation (SAUO)
MEF.......... Mechanized Engineering File
MEF.......... Median Energy of Fission (NRCH)
MEF.......... Mediterranean Expeditionary Force [*World War I*] [*British*]
MEF.......... Melfi [*Chad*] [*Airport symbol*] (AD)
MEF.......... Mesopotamian Expeditionary Force [*British*]
MEF.......... Microsoft Easy Fulfillment (VLIE)
MEF.......... Middle Ear Fluid
MEF.......... Middle East Forces [*British*]
MEF.......... Middle East Forum [*Lebanon*] (BJA)
MEF.......... Mideast File [*Tel-Aviv University*] [*Israel*] [*Information service or system*] (IID)
MEF.......... Midexpiratory Flow [*Medicine*] (DMAA)
MEF.......... Migration Enhancement Factor [*Biochemistry*]
MEF.......... Minimum Essential Facilities (SAUO)
MEF.......... Minimum Essential Force (CINC)
MEF.......... Minimum Essential Functions (SAUO)
MEF.......... Ministry for Environment and Forests [*India*]
MEF.......... Ministry of Economy & Finance (SAUO)
MEF.......... Mission Equipment Facility (MCD)
MEF.......... Mortality Enhancing Factors [*Chemical and biological warfare*]
MEF.......... Mouse Embryo Fibroblast
MEF.......... Multiple Effect Flash [*Evaporator*] [*Seawater conversion system*]
MEF.......... Multi-Purpose Electric Furnace (PDAA)
MEF.......... Munitions Equipment Facility (SAUO)
MEF.......... Muscle Enhancer Factor [*Genetics*]
MEF.......... Musicians Emergency Fund (EA)
MEF.......... Myocyte Enhancing Factor [*Genetics*]
MEFA .... Metal Etching and Fabricating Association [*Later, National Association of Name Plate Manufacturers*] (EA)
MEFA .... Methyl-CCNU 5-Fluorouracil, Adriamycin [*Antineoplastic drug regimen*] (DAVI)
MeFarGS.... Church of Jesus Christ of Latter-Day Saints, Genealogical Society Library, Augusta Branch, Farmingdale, ME [*Library symbol*] [*Library of Congress*] (LCLS)
MeFarU ..... University of Maine at Farmington, Farmington, ME [*Library symbol*] [*Library of Congress*] (LCLS)
MEF/B/U .... Marine Expeditionary Force/Brigade/Unit (MILB)
MEFC .... Maximum Economic Finding Cost
MEFC .... Mister Ed Fan Club (EA)
MEFENET ... Department of Energy Network (SAUS)
MEFEX ...... Middle East Food and Equipment Exhibition [*Arabian Exhibition Management*]
M-EFF .... Myocardial Efficiency [*Cardiology*]
MEFFEX.... Marine Expeditionary Force Field Exercise (NVT)
MEFF Renta Fija... derivatives exchange in Barcelona, Spain (SAUS)
MEFF Renta Variable... derivatives exchange in Madrid, Spain (SAUS)
MEFLEX..... Marine Expeditionary Force Landing Exercise (NVT)
MEFPAK..... Manpower and Equipment Force Packaging [*Military*]
MEFPAK..... Manpower and Equipment Force Packaging System (SAUO)
MEFPMRS... Marine Expeditionary Force Primary Multi-channel Radio System (SAUS)
MEFR........ Maximum Expiratory Flow Rate [*Medicine*]
MEFR........ Maximum Midexpiratory Flow Rate [*Medicine*] (DAVI)
MEFS .... Midterm Energy Forecasting System [*Department of Energy*] (GFGA)
ME/FS .... Missing/Embryo Fetus Syndrome
MEFSR ...... Maximal Expiratory Flow Static Recoil Curve [*Medicine*] (MAE)
MEFT .... Minimum Essential Functional Task (SAUO)
MEFTA....... Metalworking Industries in the European Free Trade Association (SAUO)
MeFtkU...... University of Maine at Fort Kent, Fort Kent, ME [*Library symbol*] [*Library of Congress*] (LCLS)
MEFTL....... Middle East Force Target List (MCD)
MEFV........ Maintenance Equipment Floor Valve (NRCH)
MEFV........ Maximal Expiratory Flow Volume [*Medicine*] (AAMN)
MEFV........ Maximum Expiratory Flow Volume (EEVL)
MEG .... Madly Enthusiastic about Grapes
MEG .... Magnetoencephalogram [*Medicine*]
MEG .... Magnetoencephalography [*Medicine*] (ECON)
MEG .... Malange [*Angola*] [*Airport symbol*] (OAG)
MEG .... Management Evaluation Group [*Department of State*]
MEG .... Marketing Executives Group (SAUO)
MEG .... Mea [*Language symbol*] (ETLW)
MEG .... Media General Advertising, Inc. (EFIS)
MEG .... Media General, Inc. [*AMEX symbol*] (SPSG)
MEG .... Mega [*A prefix meaning multiplied by one million*] (AAG)
Meg.......... Megabyte (COE)
MEG .... Megabyte [*Computer science*] (DDC)
meg.......... Megabyte
MEG .... Megacycle (NTCM)
MEG .... Megakaryocyte [*Medicine*] (EDAA)
Meg.......... Megakaryocyte [*Hematology*]
meg.......... Megaloblastic [*Cytology*] (AAMN)
meg.......... Megaron (VRA)
MEG .... Megaton (WDAA)
MEG .... Megawatt (WDAA)
Meg.......... Megiddo (BJA)
MEG .... Megillah (BJA)
Meg.......... Megillah [*Religion*] [*Judaism*]
MEG .... Meglumine (SAUS)
MEG .... Megohm (AAG)
meg.......... Megohm (IDOE)
Meg.......... Megone's Companies Acts Cases [*1888-90*] [*England*] [*A publication*] (DLA)
MEG .... Mercaptoethylguanidine [*Biochemistry*] (AAMN)
MEG .... Message Entry Generator (NVT)
MEG .... Message Expediting Group (IEEE)
MEG .... Metalsmith (Shipboard) [*U.S. Navy enlisted rating*] (AUER)
MEG .... Methyl(ethyl)glycine [*Biochemistry*]
MEG .... Midlands Examining Group [*British*] (AIE)
MEG .... Miniature Electronic Group (SAUO)
MEG .... Miniature Electrostatic Gyro
MEG .... Mitsubishi Electric Europe (SAUO)
MEG .... Mobilization Employment Group (SAUO)
MEG .... Monoethylene Glycol [*Chemicals*]
MEG .... Multifocal Eosinophilic Granuloma [*Medicine*] (DMAA)
MEG .... Multimedia Environmental Goals [*Environmental Protection Agency*]
MEG .... NRA [*National Restaurant Association*] Marketing Executives Group [*Chicago, IL*] (EA)
MEGA........ Manoeuvre Enhancement/Gust Alleviation (SAUS)
MEGA........ Media General Advertising, Inc. (EFIS)
MEGA........ Megaampere (IAA)
MEGA........ Megakaryocyte [*Hematology*] (DAVI)
MEGA........ Michigan Electric and Gas Association (EARSL)
MEGA........ Middle East Genetics Association (EA)
MEGA........ Military Evaluation of Geographic Areas
mega- .... Millions (10^6) (IDOE)
MEGA........ Molecular Evolutionary Genetics Analysis [*Computer software*]
MEGACE .... Megestrol Acetate [*Antineoplastic drug*]
MEGAFLOPS... Millions of Floating Point Operations per Second (PDAA)
Me-GAG..... Methylglyoxalbis(guanylhydrazone) [*Mitoguazone*] [*Also, MGBG*] [*Antineoplastic drug*]
MEGAN...... Megantic, PQ [*American Association of Railroads railroad junction routing code*]
MeGar....... Gardiner Public Library, Gardiner, ME [*Library symbol*] [*Library of Congress*] (LCLS)
Megarry..... Megarry's The Rent Acts [*A publication*] (DLA)
MEGAS ...... Multienergy Gamma Assay System [*Nuclear energy*] (NRCH)
MEGASTAR... Meaning of Energy Growth: An Assessment of Systems, Technologies, and Requirements [*NASA*]
Megatest.... Megatest Corp. [*Associated Press*] (SAG)
MEGC........ Megacycle (IAA)
MEGC........ Megacycle per Second [*Megahertz*] (IAA)
MEGD .... Minimal Euthyroid Graves' Disease [*Medicine*] (EDAA)
mEGF........ Mouse Epidermal Growth Factor
mEGF-URO... Mouse Epidermal Growth Factor - Urogastrone [*Endocrinology*]
MEGG .... Merging (FAAC)
Megg Ass... Meggison's Assets in Equity [*1832*] [*A publication*] (DLA)
Meg-GPA.... Megakaryocyte Growth-Promoting Activity [*Hematology*]
MEGHP...... Most Excellent Grand High Priest [*Freemasonry*]
MEGI .... Missile Exhaust Gas Ingestion (MCD)
MEGJR ...... Middle European Good Templar Youth (SAUO)
MEGLUMINE... N-Methylglucamine [*USAN*] [*Organic chemistry*]
MEGM....... Most Eminent Grand Master [*Freemasonry*] (ROG)
MEGO .... Mego Financial [*NASDAQ symbol*] (TTSB)
MEGO .... Mego Financial Corp. [*NASDAQ symbol*] (SAG)
MEGO .... Megohm (MSA)
MEGO .... My Eyes Glaze Over [*An article, written about an important subject, that resists reader interest and has a soporific effect*] [*Journalistic slang*]
MegoFin .... Mego Financial Corp. [*Associated Press*] (SAG)
MegoFinl ... Mego Financial [*Associated Press*] (SAG)
MegoMrt.... Mego Mortgage Corp. [*Associated Press*] (SAG)

Megone ..... Megone's Companies Acts Cases [*1888-90*] [*England*] [*A publication*] (DLA)
Me Gov't Reg ... Maine Government Register [*A publication*] (AAGC)
MEGQ .... Menini Cartage [*Common carrier symbol*]
MEGS .... Male Electronic Genital Stimulator [*Developed by Biosonics, Inc.*]
MEGS .... Market Entry Guarantee Scheme [*Board of Trade*] [*British*] (DI)
MEGS .... Meeting of European Geological Societies (SAUO)
MEGS .... Megasecond (AAG)
MEGS .... Missile End-Game Scoring (SAUS)
MEGS .... Missile End-Game Scoring System (DWSG)
MEGSSS .... Mathematics Education for Gifted Secondary School Students Project (EDAC)
MEGT .... Megatest Corp. [*NASDAQ symbol*] (SAG)
MEGT .... Megaton [*Nuclear equivalent of one million tons of high explosive*] (AAG)
MegTa'an ... Megillat Ta'anit (BJA)
MEGU .... Messer Griesheim [*Intermodal shipping container symbol*] (TVRC)
MEGV .... Megavolt (AAG)
MEGW .... Megawatt [*Also, MW*]
MEGWH ...... Megawatt-Hour
MEGX .... Megacards Inc. [*NASDAQ symbol*] (TTSB)
MEGX .... Monoethylglycine Xylidide [*Biochemistry*]
MEH .... Maine State Department of Human Services, Augusta, ME [*OCLC symbol*] (OCLC)
MEH .... Meacham, OR [*Location identifier*] [*FAA*] (FAAL)
MEH .... Medical Eye History (SAUS)
MEH .... Mehamn [*Norway*] [*Airport symbol*] (OAG)
MEH .... Microsomal Epoxide Hydrolase
MEH .... Midwest Express Holdings [*NYSE symbol*] (SAG)
MEH .... Moorfields Eye Hospital (SAUO)
MEH .... Multi-Engined Helicopter (MCD)
Meharry Med C ... Meharry Medicine College (GAGS)
MEHDHQ .... Medical Embarkment and Hospital Distribution Headquarters [*World War II*]
MeHi .... Maine Historical Society, Portland, ME [*Library symbol*] [*Library of Congress*] (LCLS)
MEHL .... Mehl Biophile International Corp. [*NASDAQ symbol*] (SAG)
MehlBio ..... Mehl Biophile International Corp. [*Associated Press*] (SAG)
MEHP .... Mean Effective Horsepower (IAA)
MEHP .... Monoethylhexyl Phthalate [*Organic chemistry*]
MEHQ .... Monomethyl Ether of Hydroquinone [*Organic chemistry*]
MEHT .... Minimum Eye Height over Threshold [*Aviation*] (FAAC)
MEI .... Independent Ecology Movement (France) [*Political party*] (PSAP)
MEI .... Machine Efficiency Index (LDOE)
MEI .... Main Economic Indicators (NITA)
MEI .... Maine Electronics, Incorporated (ACAE)
MEI .... Main Engine Ignition [*Aerospace*]
MEI .... Maintenance and Engineering Inspection
MEI .... Maintenance Effectiveness Inspection (MCD)
MEI .... Maintenance Engineering Investigation [*DoD*]
MEI .... Maintenance Evaluation Inspection (MCD)
MEI .... Major End Item
MEI .... Management Education Institute [*Arthur D. Little, Inc.*]
MEI .... Management Effectiveness Inspection
MEI .... Management Efficiency Inspection (ACAE)
MEI .... Manpower Education Institute (EA)
MEI .... Manual of Engineering Instructions
MEI .... Manufacturing Engineering Instructions (ACAE)
MEI .... Maps Etc. Incorporated (SAUO)
MEI .... Marginal Efficiency of Investment
MEI .... Marine Ecological Institute (SAUO)
MEI .... Marketing Economics Institute (SAUO)
MEI .... Marketing Economics Institute Ltd. [*New York, NY*]
MEI .... Master Enterprise Identifier (GART)
MEI .... Master Inspection Item [*NASA*] (NAKS)
MEI .... Master of English Literature (SAUO)
MEI .... Mathematics in Education and Industry (SAUO)
MEI .... Matsushita Electronics Incorporated (SAUO)
MEI .... Maximally Exposed Individual
MEI .... Maximum Exposed Individual [*Health risk assessment*] [*Environmental Protection Agency*]
MeI .... Meconium Ileus [*Medicine*]
MEI .... Medicare Economic Index
MEI .... MEI Corporation (SAUO)
Mei .... Meiji Seika Kaisha Ltd. [*Japan*]
MEI .... Meissen-Radebeul [*German license plate city code*]
MEI .... Meres et Enfants Internationale [*Switzerland*] (EAIO)
MEI .... Meridian [*Mississippi*] [*Airport symbol*] (OAG)
MEI .... Meridian, MS [*Location identifier*] [*FAA*] (FAAL)
MEI .... Metals Engineering Institute (EA)
MEI .... Metastatic Efficiency Index [*Medicine*] (MELL)
MEI .... Middle-Ear Infection (MELL)
MEI .... Middle East Information Service (BJA)
MEI .... Middle East Institute (EA)
MEI .... Military Engineering Item (MCD)
MEI .... Military Environment Inventory [*Rudolf H. Moos*] (TES)
MEI .... [*The*] Ministry of Electronics Industry [*China*]
MEI .... Minnesota Enterprises, Inc. (EFIS)
MEI .... Minnesota Enterprises, Incorporated (SAUO)
MEI .... Minority Educational Institution
MEI .... Mission Essential Item [*Army*]
MEI .... Module Execution Interval [*Computer science*] (VLIE)
MEI .... Montreal Economic Institute [*Canada*] (RCD)
MEI .... Morpholinoethylisocyanide [*Organic chemistry*]
MEI .... Most Exposed Individual [*Environmental science*] (FFDE)
MEI .... Multi-Engine Instrument (PIPO)
MEI .... Multivariate ENSO Index (SAUO)
MEI .... Myocardial Efficiency Index [*Cardiology*]
MEIA .... Member of the Institution of Engineers Australia
MEIA .... Microparticle Enzyme Immunoassay
MEIAW ...... Marine Athletic Intercollegiate Association for Women (PSS)
MEIC .... Member of the Engineering Institute of Canada
MEIC .... Middle East Intelligence Center [*World War II*]
Meid .... Against Meidias [*of Demosthenes*] [*Classical studies*] (OCD)
MEIDL .... Manually Entered Identification Library (CAAL)
MEIDS .... Military [*or Miniaturized*] Electronic Information Delivery System (MCD)
MEIDS .... Miniaturized Electronic Information Delivery System (SAUO)
MEIE .... Meier Trucking Company [*Common carrier symbol*]
MEIE .... Microcomputer Electronic Information Exchange [*Institute for Computer Science and Technology*]
MEIEA .... Music and Entertainment Industry Educators Association (NTPA)
MEIEC .... Metropolitan Electronic Industry Education Council (SAUO)
MEIEng ...... Master of Electrical Engineering [*Education*] (FOTI)
MEIF .... Mobile Equipment Information File [*Air Force*] (AFM)
MEIG .... Main Engine Ignition [*Aerospace*] (KSC)
MEIGN .... Main Engine Ignition [*Aerospace*]
Meigs .... Meigs' Tennessee Supreme Court Reports [*1838-39*] [*A publication*] (DLA)
Meigs Dig ... Meigs' Digest of Decisions of the Courts of Tennessee [*A publication*] (DLA)
Meigs' R .... Meigs' Tennessee Reports [*A publication*] (DLA)
Me'il .... Me'ilah (BJA)
MEIM .... Minuteman Engineering Instruction Manual (SAA)
MEIMN .... Multiend Item Modification Notice [*NASA*] (KSC)
MEIN .... Medium-Energy Intense Neutron
MEIP .... Marine Engineering Improvement Programme (SAUS)
MEIP .... Market Economy Investor Principle (EURO)
MEIP .... Mean Effective Injection Pressure [*Diesel engines*]
MEIR .... Mideast Information Resource (BJA)
MEIR .... Minimum Essential Information Requirement (SAUO)
MEIR .... Ministere Federal de l'Expansion Industrielle Regionale [*Department of Regional Industrial Expansion - DRIE*] [*Canada*]
MEIS .... Medium Energy Ion Scattering (MCD)
MEIS .... Middle East Information Service (BJA)
MEIS .... Military Entomology Information Service
MEISER ..... Minimum Essential Improvement in System Reliability (ACAE)
Meison ...... All-Ethiopia Socialist League (SAUS)
MEISONE ... All Ethiopia Socialist Union
MEISR .... Minimum Essential Improvement in System Reliability (MCD)
meiss .... Melodramma Semiserio [*Music*] (GROV)
MEIT .... Momentum/Energy Integral Technique (MCD)
MEITS .... Mission Effective Information Transmission System
MEITS .... Mission Essential/Effective Information Transmission System (SAUO)
MEIU .... Main Engine Interface Unit (MCD)
MEIU .... Management Education Information Unit, Spastics Society (SAUO)
MEIU .... Middle East Interpretation Unit [*British*]
MEIU .... Mobile Explosives Investigation Unit
MEIVA .... Men's Intercollegiate Volleyball Association (PSS)
MEJ .... Maine Criminal Justice Academy, Waterville, ME [*OCLC symbol*] (OCLC)
MEJ .... Marman Expansion Joint
MEJ .... Maximum Economic Justification
MEJ .... Meade, KS [*Location identifier*] [*FAA*] (FAAL)
MEJ .... Medjet International, Inc. [*ICAO designator*] (FAAC)
MEJ .... Middle East Journal [*A publication*] (BRI)
MEJ .... Movement for Economic Justice (EA)
MEJC .... Miniature Excitatory Junction Potential [*Neurophysiology*]
MEK .... Maine State Library, Bookmobiles, Augusta, ME [*OCLC symbol*] (OCLC)
MEK .... Med-Trans of Florida, Inc. [*ICAO designator*] (FAAC)
MEK .... Meekatharra [*Australia*] [*Seismograph station code, US Geological Survey*] (SEIS)
Mek .... Mekhilta (BJA)
MEK .... Meknes [*Morocco*] [*Airport symbol*] (AD)
MEK .... Methyl Ethyl Ketone [*Organic chemistry*]
MEK .... Mittlerer Erzgebirgskreis [*German license plate city code*]
MEK .... Mujahedin-e-Khalq [*Government term*] (GA)
MEK .... Mujahedin-e Khalq Organization [*Militant organization*] (EMA)
MEK .... Salomon, Inc. [*AMEX symbol*] (SPSG)
MEK .... Salomon Inc. 5% MSFI'ELKA' [*AMEX symbol*] (TTSB)
MEKC .... Melmark Cartage Company [*Common carrier symbol*]
MEKC .... Micellar Electrokinetic Chromatography
MEKFO ...... Mary Ellen Kinney Family Organization [*Association*] (EA)
MeKh .... Mekhilta (BJA)
MEKO .... Methyl Ethyl Ketoxime [*Organic chemistry*]
MEKP .... Methyl Ethyl Ketone Peroxide [*Organic chemistry*]
MEKTS ...... Modular Electronic Kay Telephone System (IAA)
MeL .... Lewiston Public Library, Lewiston, ME [*Library symbol*] [*Library of Congress*] (LCLS)
MEL .... Magnesium Elektron Ltd. [*British*] (IRUK)
MEL .... Maintenance Expenditure Limit (MCD)
MEL .... Maneuvering Element [*Military*] (AABC)
MEL .... Many-Element LASER
MEL .... Marchwood Engineering Laboratories [*Research center*] [*British*] (IRUK)
MEL .... Marine Engineering Laboratory [*Navy*]
MEL .... Master Equipment List [*Military*] (NG)
M El .... Master of Elements

MEL Master of English Language (PGP)
MEL Master of English Literature
MEL Material Engineering Laboratory
MEL Materials Evaluation Laboratory (MCD)
MEL Maximum Engagement Line [*Military*] (INF)
MEL Maximum Excess Loss
MEL Maximum Expenditure Limit (MCD)
MEL Maximum Exposure Level [*Hazardous materials*]
MEL Maximum Exposure Limit [*Hazardous material control*]
MEL Maya Embedded Language (SAUS)
MEL Mean Ear Location [*Automotive engineering*]
MEL Medium Energy Laser (SAUO)
MEL Melamine
MEL Melanoma [*Oncology*]
MEL Melbourne [*Australia*] [*Airport symbol*] (OAG)
MEL Melbourne [*Later, TOO*] [*Australia*] [*Geomagnetic observatory code*]
mel Melena [*Gastroenterology*] (DAVI)
Mel Melendus [*Flourished, 1188-1209*] [*Authority cited in pre-1607 legal work*] (DSA)
MEL Mellis [*Of Honey*] [*Pharmacy*] (ROG)
MEL Mellon Bank Corp. [*NYSE symbol*] (SPSG)
MEL Mellon Financial [*Company symbol*]
MEL Mellon Financial Corp. [*NYSE symbol*]
mel Melodramma [*Music*] (GROV)
MEL Melody
Mel Melphalan [*Antineoplastic drug*] (DAVI)
MEL Melrose Resources Ltd. [*Vancouver Stock Exchange symbol*]
MEL Metabolic Equivalent Level [*Medicine*]
MEL Michigan Electronic Library
MeL Michigan eLibrary (IID)
MEL Microenergy Logic (IAA)
MEL Military Education Level (INF)
MEL Minimum Earnings Level
MEL Minimum Equipment List
MEL Misappropriation of the English Language (SAUO)
MEL Missile Ejector Launcher (SAUS)
MEL Mistress of English Literature
MEL Mobile Erector Launcher [*Military*]
MEL Modular Electromagnetic Levitator (SAUS)
MEL Moslem Electoral Lobby [*Australia*]
MEL Most Efficient Level [*Fire budget term*] [*USDA Forest Service*] (ALAC)
MEL Mouse Erythroleukemia
MEL Multiengine Land [*Pilot rating*] (AIA)
MEL Multi/Entry Layout [*USDA Forest Service*] (ALAC)
MEL Multos Executable Language [*Computer science*] (GART)
MEL Murine Erythroleukemia [*Oncology*]
MEL Music Education League [*Defunct*] (EA)
MEL Musika Esperanta Ligo (SAUO)
MEL Muzika Esperanto Ligo [*Esperantist Music League*] (EAIO)
MEL National Herbarium of Victoria (SAUO)
ME L University of Maine. Law Review [*A publication*] (DLA)
MEL 1 Military Education Level One [*Army*]
MEL-A Marine Engineering Laboratory - Annapolis [*Navy*] (DNAB)
MELA Melmar [*NCIC truck make code*]
MELA Middle East Librarians' Association (EA)
MELAB Mechanical Engineering Laboratory [*NASA*] (KSC)
MELAB Michigan English Language Assessment Battery (GAGS)
MELABS Microwave Engineering Laboratories, Inc. (MCD)
Melami Melamine Chemicals, Inc. [*Associated Press*] (SAG)
MELAN Melanesia (ROG)
MELAN Melanin [*Pigmentation*] (DAVI)
Melanges d'Arch Melanges d'Archeologie et d'Histoire. Ecole Francaise de Rome [*A publication*] (OCD)
MELAS Mitochondrial Myopathy, Encephalopathy, Lactic Acidosis, and Stroke-Like Episod es [*Medicine*]
MELAS Mitochrondrial Encephalomyopathy with Acidosis and Stroke [*Medicine*] (MELL)
MeLB Bates College, Lewiston, ME [*Library symbol*] [*Library of Congress*] (LCLS)
MELB Mission Enhancement-Little Bird [*Military*] (RDA)
Melb University of Melbourne (SAUO)
MELBA Multipurpose Extended Lift Blanket Assembly (IEEE)
Melbonrne Univ Dep Civ Eng Transp Bull University of Melbourne. Depament of Civil Engineering. Transport Section. Bulletin (SAUS)
Melb Rpt Melbourne Report [*A publication*]
Melb Stud Ed Melbourne Studies in Education [*A publication*]
MELC Melcombe [*England*]
MELC Melrose Transport Systems [*Common carrier symbol*]
MELC Mouse Erythroleukemia Cell
MELC Murine Erythroleukemia Cell [*Medicine*] (STED)
MELCO Melville Shoe Corp. (EFIS)
MELCO Mitsubishi Electric Company (SAUO)
MELCO Mitsubishi Electric Corp. [*Japan*]
MELCOM Middle East Libraries Committee
Melcom Mitsubishi Electric Company (SAUO)
MELCU Multiple External Line Control Unit
MELD Minnesota Early Learning Design [*Medicine*] (EDAA)
MELD Multilingual Enhanced Learning for Diversity
MELDI Master Equipment List Drawing Index (SAUO)
MeLDL Methylated Low-Density Lipoprotein [*Biochemistry*]
MELDOS Melioidosis [*Dermatology*] (DAVI)
MELEC Microelectronics (IEEE)
M Elec E Master of Electrical Engineering (PGP)
ME Legis Serv Maine Legislative Service [*A publication*] (DLA)
MELEM Microelement (IEEE)
MELEO Material Exposure in Low Earth Orbit (SAUS)
MELETA Mechanical Endurance Load on Environment Test Apparatus (SAUO)
MELF Metal Electrode Face Bonding (IAA)
MELF Middle East Land Forces [*British*] (NATG)
MELFO Melfort, SK [*American Association of Railroads railroad junction routing code*]
MELG Melges Boat Works [*NCIC trailer make code*]
MELG Middle East Liaison Group [*Military*] (AABC)
MELH Missile Elevation Heading (IAA)
MELI Master Equipment List Identification [*Military*] (IAA)
MELI Master Equipment List Index [*Military*] (KSC)
MELI Melita International Corp. [*NASDAQ symbol*] (NASQ)
MELI Met-Enkaphalin-Like Immunoreactivity [*Medicine*] (STED)
MELI Minimum Equipment List Index (NASA)
MELIOS Miniature Eyesafe LASER Infrared Observation Set [*A rangefinder*]
MELISR National Herbarium of Victoria Specimen Information Register (SAUO)
MELISS Mitsubishi Electric Corp. Literature and Information Search Service
MELISS Mitsubishi Electric Corporation Literature and Information Search Service (SAUO)
MELISSA Meta-Linguistic Syntax Specification Analyzer (VLIE)
MELISSA Micro Ecological Life Support Alternative [*European Space Agency*]
Melitco Melanesia International Trust Company Limited (SAUO)
MELKONG Mechanical Electric Kong [*Robot*]
MELL Mellis [*Of Honey*] [*Pharmacy*] (ROG)
MellonBk Mellon Bank Corp. [*Associated Press*] (SAG)
MellonP Mellon Participating Mortgage Trust Commercial Property Series [*Associated Press*] (SAG)
Mell Parl Pr Mell's Parliamentary Practice [*A publication*] (DLA)
MELM Melmak [*NCIC truck make code*]
MELM Middle East Lutheran Ministry [*Lebanon*] (EAIO)
MELM Minimum Equipment List Manual
Mel Masp Melanges Maspero [*A publication*] (OCD)
Meln Mellon Bank Corp. [*Associated Press*] (SAG)
MELN Metropolitan Electrical League of New Jersey
M Elo Master of Elocution
MELO Melody Home Manufacturing [*NCIC trailer make code*]
MELO Minimum Expected Loss [*Statistics*]
Melon Mellon Bank Corp. [*Associated Press*] (SAG)
MELP Master English Language Program (ACAE)
MELP Measure of Language Proficiency (EDAC)
MELP Microsoft Enterprise License Pak (GART)
MELP Mid-European Law Project
MELP Ministry of Environment, Lands and Parks (SAUO)
MELP Multi-Entry Layout Plan [*USDA Forest Service*] (ALAC)
MELPrJ Mellon Bk 8.50% 'J'Pfd [*NYSE symbol*] (TTSB)
MELPrK Mellon Bk 8.20% 'K' Pfd [*NYSE symbol*] (TTSB)
MELPrI Mellon Bk 9.60% 'I' Pfd [*NYSE symbol*] (TTSB)
Me-LR Law and Legislative Reference Library, Augusta, ME [*Library symbol*] [*Library of Congress*] (LCLS)
mels Melodramma Serio [*Music*] (GROV)
MELS Microwave and Electronic System (IAA)
MELS Molecularly Engineered Layered Structure
MELSA Metropolitan Library Service Agency [*Library network*]
MELSOR Marx, Engels, Lenin, Stalin, October Revolution [*Given name popular in Russia after the Bolshevik Revolution*]
MELT Mantle Electromagnetic and Tomography [*Geology*]
MELT Minimum Equipment Level for Training (MCD)
MELTER Mesosphere/Lower Thermosphere Explorer (SAUS)
MELU Messer Industries [*Intermodal shipping container symbol*] (TVRC)
MELUS Society for the Study of Multi-Ethnic Literature of the United States (BARN)
MELV Medium Expendable Launch Vehicle (CARB)
MELV Melilotus Latent Virus [*Plant pathology*]
MELVA Military Electronic Light Valve
Melvile Melville Corp. [*Formerly, Melville Shoe Corp.*] [*Associated Press*] (SAG)
Melv Tr Melvill's Trial (Impeachment) [*London*] [*A publication*] (DLA)
MELVYL Melvil Dewey [*Public access online catalog, University of California*] (NITA)
MELX Sunbelt Cement [*Private rail car owner code*]
MELZ Milligan Elevator [*Federal Railroad Administration identification code*]
Mem De Memoria [*of Aristotle*] [*Classical studies*] (OCD)
MEM Macrophage Electrophoretic Migration [*Clinical chemistry*] (AAMN)
MEM Macrophage Electrophoretic Mobility [*Medicine*] (EDAA)
MEM Macrophage Electrophoretic Mobility Test (MAE)
MEM Magnetic Electron Multiplier (PDAA)
MEM Magyar Elet Mozgalma [*Movement of Hungarian Life*] [*Political party*] (PPE)
MEM Maine State Museum, Augusta, ME [*OCLC symbol*] (OCLC)
MEM Malic Enzyme, Mitochondrial (STED)
MEM Manufacturing Enterprise Model
MEM Marine Engineering Mechanic [*Navy rating*] [*British*]
MEM Mars Excursion Mission [*NASA*] (IAA)
MEM Mars Excursion Module
MEM Master of Ecosystem Management (PGP)
MEM Master of Educational Ministry (PGP)
MEM Master of Engineering Management
MEM Master of Environmental Management (PGP)
Me M Master of Metaphysics
MEM Materials Experimentation Module (SAUS)
MEM Maximum Entropy Method [*Geomagnetism*] [*Computer science*]
MEM Mediterranean Air Ambulance, SL [*Spain*] [*FAA designator*] (FAAC)

MEM........ Membach [*Belgium*] [*Seismograph station code, US Geological Survey*] (SEIS)
MEM........ Member (EY)
mem........ Member (WDMC)
mem........ Membership (NTIO)
MEM........ MEM Co. [*AMEX symbol*] (TTSB)
MEM........ MEM Co., Inc. [*AMEX symbol*] (SPSG)
MEM........ Memento
mem........ Memoir (WDMC)
MEM........ Memoir
Mem........ Memorabilia [*of Xenophon*] [*Classical studies*] (OCD)
mem........ Memorandum (WDMC)
MEM........ Memorandum
mem........ Memorial (WDMC)
MEM........ Memorial
mem........ Memory (ELAL)
MEM........ Memory (MSA)
MEM........ Memphis [*Tennessee*] [*Airport symbol*] (OAG)
MEM........ Memphis, TN [*Amtrak rail station code*]
MEM........ Meteoroid Exposure Module (MCD)
MEM........ Methoxyethoxymethyl [*Organic chemistry*]
MEM........ Micro Electro Mechanical (AAEL)
MEM........ Middeck Electronics Module (SAUS)
MEM........ Middle-Ear Muscle [*Anatomy*]
MEM........ Midland Electric Manufacturing Co. (SAUO)
MEM........ Minimal Essential Medium (STED)
MEM........ Minimum Essential Medium [*Culture medium*]
MEM........ Ministry for Energy and Mines (SAUO)
MEM........ Mirror Electron Microscope (PDAA)
MEM........ Missile Engagement Mechanism (MCD)
MEM........ Mission Effectiveness Model (ACAE)
MEM........ Modal Emission Model (EEVL)
MEM........ Model Emission Model [*Environmental Protection Agency*] (GFGA)
MEM........ Module Exchange Mechanism [*NASA*] (NASA)
MEM........ Molecular Exciton Microscopy
MEM........ Mondpaca Esperantista Movada (SAUO)
MEM........ Mondpaca Esperantista Movado [*Esperantist Movement for World Peace - EMWP*] [*Tours, France*] (EAIO)
MEM........ Morpholinyl-Ethyl-Morphine [*Medicine*] (EDAA)
MEM........ Most Efficient/Effective Method [*DoD*]
MEM........ Most Excellent Master [*Freemasonry*]
MEM........ Mount Emily Exploration Ltd. [*Vancouver Stock Exchange symbol*]
MEM........ Multienvironmental Electron Microscope
MEM........ Myxedema(tous) Madness [*Medicine*] [*in severe hypothyroidism*] (EDAA)
MEMA....... Marine Engine Manufacturers Association [*Formerly, OMMA*] (EA)
MEMA....... Methyl Methacrylate (STED)
MEMA....... Microelectronic Modular Assembly
MEMa....... Micro-Membranes, Inc. (SAUO)
MEMA....... Middle-Ear Muscle Activity
MEMA....... Motor and Equipment Manufacturers Association (EA)
MEMAC..... Machinery and Equipment Manufacturers Association of Canada (SAUO)
MEMAC..... Middle East Medical Advisory Committee [*World War II*]
MeMacU.... University of Maine at Machias, Machias, ME [*Library symbol*] [*Library of Congress*] (LCLS)
MemAIEE... Member of the American Institute of Electrical Engineers (SAUO)
MemAmAnthrAssoc... Memoirs of the American Anthropological Association (SAUO)
MemAmerAcadRome... Memoirs of the American Academy in Rome (SAUO)
MemASME... Member of the American Society of Mechanical Engineers (SAUO)
MEMA/TTC... Motor and Equipment Manufacturers Association's Technical Training Council
memb....... Member (MIST)
Memb....... Member (TBD)
MEMB....... Member
Memb....... Membership (AL)
MEMB....... Membranaceous Vellum [*Manuscripts*] (ROG)
MEMB....... Membrane (MSA)
memb....... Membrane (STED)
MEMB....... Micro Membranes, Inc. [*NASDAQ symbol*] (COMM)
MEMBERS.. Microprogrammed Experimental Machine with a Basic Executive for Real-Time Systems (PDAA)
MEMBIS..... Member Budget Information System [*for House of Representatives*]
MEMBLE.... Memorable (ROG)
MEMBR..... Middle East Marketing Research Bureau (SAUO)
MEMC....... Marathon Electric Manufacturers Corporation (SAUO)
MEMC....... MEMC Electronic Materials, Inc. [*Associated Press*] (SAG)
MEMC....... Memco Software Ltd. [*NASDAQ symbol*] (SAG)
MEMC....... Methoxyethylmercuric Chloride
MEMC....... Monsanto Electronic Materials Company (SAUO)
MEMC....... Munich Maintenance Equipment Center (SAUO)
MEMCAL.... Memory Calibration (HAWK)
MEMCO..... Miller Electric Manufacturing Company (SAUO)
Mem Comm Solar Observ Aust... Memoirs. Commonwealth Solar Observatory. Australia [*A publication*]
MEMCON... Memorandum of Conversation
MemcoSf... Memco Software Ltd. [*Associated Press*] (SAG)
MEMDA..... Memoranda (ROG)
MEMDB..... Medieval and Early Modern Data Bank [*Information service or system*] (IID)
MEMDT..... Message Execution Matrix Display Task (SAUO)
MEMDUM... Memorandum (ROG)
MEME....... Magnetic Environment Measuring Equipment (CAAL)
MEME....... Multiple Entry Multiple Exit
MEME....... Multitasking Extensible Messaging Environment
MEMEC...... Memory and Electronic Components [*Commercial firm*] [*British*]
ME(Mech)... Master of Engineering (Mechanical) (ADA)
MEM ERR... Memory Error [*Information retrieval*]
Mem Fac Ed Shiga Univ Natur Sci... Shiga University. Faculty of Education Memoirs. Natural Science (SAUS)
Mem Geol Survey Vic... Memoirs. Geological Survey of Victoria [*Australia*] [*A publication*]
MEMI....... Master Equipment Management Index [*Air Force*] (AFM)
MeMi....... Millinocket Memorial Library, Millinocket, ME [*Library symbol*] [*Library of Congress*] (LCLS)
MEMIC...... Medical Microbiology Interdisciplinary Committee [*International Council of Scientific Unions*]
MEMIC...... Mobile Eletromagnetic Incompatibility (PDAA)
MemIMD.... Memoirs of the India Meteorological Department (SAUO)
MEMIS...... Maintenance and Engineering Management Information System (SAUO)
MEMISTOR... Memory Resistor (DEN)
MEML....... Master Equipment Management List [*Air Force*] (AFM)
Meml....... Memorial (PROS)
MEML....... Memorial
MEML....... Molecular Engineering and Materials Laboratory [*MIT*] (MCD)
MEMLACTV... Memorial Activities [*Military*] (AABC)
Mem LJ..... Memphis Law Journal [*Tennessee*] [*A publication*] (DLA)
MEMLZ...... Memorialize (ABBR)
MEMLZD.... Memorialized (ABBR)
MEMLZG.... Memorializing (ABBR)
MEMLZN.... Memorialization (ABBR)
MEMLZR.... Memorializer (ABBR)
MEMMA..... Mining Electromechanical Maintenance Association (IAA)
MEMMDLE... Memory Module (IAA)
MEMO....... Marine Environmental Management Office [*Marine science*] (MSC)
MEMO....... Maryland Educational Media Organization
MEMO....... Medical Equipment Management Office [*Air Force*] (AFM)
memo....... Memorandum (WDMC)
MEMO....... Memorandum
MEMO....... Middle East Money [*London-Beirut*] (BJA)
MEMO....... Minnesota Educational Media Organization (EDAC)
MEMO....... Mission Essential Maintenance Only (MCD)
MEMO....... Mission Essential Maintenance Operation (MCD)
MEMO....... Model for Evaluating Missile Observation
MEMO....... More Education - More Opportunities (DNAB)
MEMO....... Voice It Worldwide [*NASDAQ symbol*] (TTSB)
MEMO....... Voice It Worldwide, Inc. [*NASDAQ symbol*] (SAG)
MEMOCS.... Mitsubishi Electric Corp. Multiterm Out-of-Context System
MEMO/MAINT... Medical Equipment Management Office/Maintenance (SAUO)
Memo Mgmt... Memo to Management [*Australian Institute of Management, Queensland Division*] [*A publication*]
Memorex... Memorex Telex NV [*Associated Press*] (SAG)
MEMOREX... Memory Excellence [*Brand name*]
MEMOS....... Manufacturing Engineering Management Operations System (MCD)
MEMP....... Maximization of Expected Maximum Profit [*Econometrics*]
MEMP....... Mechanical Engineering and Motive Power (SAUO)
MEMPH..... Memphis, TN [*American Association of Railroads railroad junction routing code*]
Memphis LJ... Memphis Law Journal [*Tennessee*] [*A publication*] (DLA)
Memphis St U... Memphis State University (GAGS)
Memp LJ..... Memphis Law Journal [*Tennessee*] [*A publication*] (DLA)
MEMPP..... Morpholinoethylmethylphenylpyridazone [*An analgesic*]
MEMPR..... Ministry of Energy, Mines and Petroleum Resources (SAUO)
MEMPT...... Memory Point
MEMQ....... Married Enlisted Men's Quarters
ME (MR).... Medical Evidence (Medical Report or Record) (OICC)
MEMR....... Memory Read [*Computer science*] (VLIE)
MEMR....... Multiple Exostoses-Mental Retardation Syndrome [*Medicine*] (DMAA)
MEMR....... Ramtron Australia Ltd. (SAUO)
MEMRA..... Mechanical Equipment Manufacturers Representatives Association (EA)
MEMRAC.... Mission Essential Material Readiness and Condition (MCD)
MEMRB..... Middle East Marketing Research Bureau (SAUO)
memrl....... Memorial (VRA)
MEMS....... Master of Emergency Medical Service (PGP)
MEMS....... Master of Engineering in Manufacturing Systems (GAGS)
MEMS....... Michelin Earthmover Management System [*Tire design*]
MEMS....... Microbial Ecological Monitoring System [*Apollo*] [*NASA*]
MEMS....... Microelectromechanical System [*Materials science and technology*]
MEMS....... Micro Electro Mechanical Systems
MEMS....... Mineral Economics and Management Society
MEMS....... Missile Equipment Maintenance Sets (MUGU)
MEMS....... Modular Engine Management System [*Automotive engineering*]
MEMS....... Multieffect, Multistage
MEMSEL.... Memory Select [*Computer science*] (MHDI)
MEMSIC..... Micro Electro-Mechanical Systems and Integrated Circuits [*Automotive industry*]
MEMS INS... Micro-Electromechanical Sensor Inertial Navigation System [*Defense Advanced Research Projects Agency*] (RCD)
Mem Soc Assn... Memorial Society Association (SAUO)
MEMSPO.... Michigan Elementary and Middle School Principals Organization (SAUO)
Mem St UL Rev... Memphis State University. Law Review [*A publication*] (DLA)
MEMTC...... Memphis TOFC, TN [*American Association of Railroads railroad junction routing code*]

Memtec Memtec Ltd. [*Associated Press*] (SAG)
MEMTRB Mechanical Engineering and Machine Tools Requirements Board (SAUO)
MEMU Main-Line Electric Multiple Unit [*Indian Railway*] (TIR)
MEMU Manned Extravehicular Manipulating Unit (MCD)
MEMU Melkweg Muller Combinatie [*Intermodal shipping container symbol*] (TVRC)
MEMW Memory Write [*Computer science*] (MHDB)
MemWks MemberWorks, Inc. [*Associated Press*] (SAG)
MEMX Memorex Telex NV [*NASDAQ symbol*] (SAG)
MEMX Memory Sciences Corp. [*NASDAQ symbol*] (COMM)
MEMXY Memorex Telex ADS [*NASDAQ symbol*] (TTSB)
MEMY Memory (ROG)
MEMY Memory Pharmaceuticals Corp. [*NASDAQ symbol*]
MEMZ Meridian Minerals [*Federal Railroad Administration identification code*]
MEN Master Equipment Number [*Military*] (NG)
M En Master of English
MEN McAllen, TX [*Amtrak Busline code*]
Men Menaechmi [*of Plautus*] [*Classical studies*] (OCD)
Men Menahot (BJA)
Men Menander [*Fourth century BC*] [*Classical studies*] (OCD)
MEN Menasco Manufacturing Co. (SAUO)
men Mende [*MARC language code*] [*Library of Congress*] (LCCP)
MEN Mendoza [*Argentina*] [*Seismograph station code, US Geological Survey*] [*Closed*] (SEIS)
men Meningeal (STED)
MEN Meningitis [*Medicine*] (MELL)
MEN Mennonite (ABBR)
MEN Meno [*Slower*] [*Music*]
MEN Menology
Men Menorah: Australian Journal of Jewish Studies [*A publication*] (APTA)
Men Mensa [*Constellation*]
MEN Mense [*or Menses*] (ABBR)
MEN Men's Equality Now International (EA)
MEN Menstruation (ABBR)
MEN Mensuration (ABBR)
MEN Mention
Men Menzies' Cape Of Good Hope Reports [*1828-49*] [*A publication*] (DLA)
MEN Methylethylnitrosamine (STED)
MEN Middle-East News Agency (SAUO)
MEN Mistozen Electronic Nebulizer
MEN Multiple Earthed Neutral (IAA)
MEN Multiple Endocrine Neoplasia [*Medicine*]
MEN Multiple Endocrine Neoplasia/Neoplasms (STED)
MEN Multiple Event Network
MEN MuniEnhanced Fund [*NYSE symbol*] (SPSG)
MEN-1 Multiple Endocrine Neoplasia/sm-Type 1 [*Medicine*] (EDAA)
MEN-2 Multiple Endocrine Neoplasia/sm-Type 2 [*Medicine*] (EDAA)
MENA Middle East and North Africa [*A publication*]
MENA Middle East News Agency
MENA Mission Element Need Analysis (MCD)
MENA Mitsubishi Engine North America
MENA Mitsubishi Engine North America, Inc.
MENA Mitsubishi Engines North America [*Automotive engineering*]
MENAS Menasha, WI [*American Association of Railroads railroad junction routing code*]
MENC Music Educators National Conference (EA)
MENCAP Royal Society for Mentally Handicapped Children & Adults [*England*]
Mence Lib Mence's Law of Libel [*1824*] [*A publication*] (DLA)
MEND Massive Economic Neighborhood Development [*New York City*]
MEND Maximum Entropy Noise Deconvolution [*Statistics*]
MEND Medical Education for National Defense
MEND Mendelism
MEND Mothers Embracing Nuclear Disarmament [*An association*] (EA)
MENDAP Melbourne Network Dimensioning and Analysis Programmes (SAUO)
Mendl Lib Mendelssohn Library (SAUO)
MENDO Mendota, IL [*American Association of Railroads railroad junction routing code*]
MENEV Menevensis [*Signature of the Bishops of St. David's*] [*British*] (ROG)
MENEX Maintenance Engineering Exchange
Menex Menexemus [*of Plato*] [*Classical studies*] (OCD)
M Eng Master of Engineering
M Eng Master of English
MENG Meaning (ABBR)
M Eng Mechanical Engineer
MEng Member of Environmental Sciences/Studies [*Canada*] (ASC)
MEng Mining Engineer (SAUO)
M-ENG Multiengined
M Eng&PA Master in Engineering and Public Administration (SAUO)
M Eng & PA Master in Engineering and Public Administration
MENGF Meaningful (ABBR)
MENGFY Meaningfully (ABBR)
MENGLS Meaningless (ABBR)
MENGLSY Meaninglessly (ABBR)
M Eng Mgt Master of Engineering Management (PGP)
MEngPA Master of Engineering and Public Administration (NADA)
M Engr Master of Engineering (PGP)
MEngrg Master of Engineering (SAUO)
MEngS Master of Engineering Science
M Eng Sc Master of Engineering Science
MEngSt Master of Engineering Studies (ADA)
MENI Ministry of Education in Northern Ireland (SAUO)
ME(NI) Ministry of Education (Northern Ireland)
MENI Multiple Endocrine Neoplasia Type I [*Medicine*] (DMAA)
MENIC Middle East Network Information Center [*Internet resource*]
MENIT Mennonite
MENJ Menley & James, Inc. [*NASDAQ symbol*] (SPSG)
Menken Menken's Civil Procedure Reports [*30 New York*] [*A publication*] (DLA)
MenleyJ Menley & James, Inc. [*Associated Press*] (SAG)
Menn Menninger [*Karl Augustus*] [*American psychiatrist*] (DAVI)
MENNON Mennonite (ABBR)
MENNS Meanness (ABBR)
MENO Menopause (DSUE)
MENO Menorrhoea (ABBR)
MENOM Menominee, MI [*American Association of Railroads railroad junction routing code*]
MENP Menasha Transport [*Common carrier symbol*]
MENP Menopause (ABBR)
MENP Mount Elgon National Park (SAUO)
MENPL Menopausal (ABBR)
Men Rel Menandri Reliquiae [*A publication*] (OCD)
MENRIS Mountain Environment and Natural Resources Information System (SAUO)
MENS K&G Men's Center [*NQS*] (TTSB)
MENS K & G Mens Center, Inc. [*NASDAQ symbol*] (SAG)
M En S Master of Environmental Science (PGP)
MENS Mecanismos Ensamblados [*NCIC trailer make code*]
Mens Mensa [*Constellation*]
MENS Mensis [*Month*] [*Latin*]
MENS Mensura [*By Measure*] [*Pharmacy*]
MENS Microamperage Electrical Nerve Stimulation [*Medicine*] (MELL)
MENS Middle East Neurosurgical Society (EAIO)
MENS Missile Element Need Statement
MENS Mission Element Needs Statement (MCD)
MENS Mission Essential Needs Statement (SAUO)
MENS IIB Multiple Endocrine Neoplasia Syndrome IIB (SAUS)
Men's J Men's Journal [*A publication*] (BRI)
menst Menstrual [*or Menstruate*] (AAMN)
MENSTD Menstruated (ABBR)
MENSTG Menstruating (ABBR)
MENSTL Menstrual (ABBR)
MENSTN Menstruation (ABBR)
MENSUR Mensuration (ROG)
M Ent Master of Entomology
MENT Mental
MENT Mentalis (ABBR)
MENT Mentioned
MENT Mentor Graphics [*NASDAQ symbol*] (TTSB)
MENT Mentor Graphics Corp. [*NASDAQ symbol*] (NQ)
Mental & Physical Disab L Rep Mental and Physical Disability Law Reporter [*A publication*] (DLA)
MENTD Mentioned
MentGr Mentor Graphics Corp. [*Associated Press*] (SAG)
MENTH Mentha [*Mint*] [*Pharmacy*] (ROG)
MENTH Menthol (SAUS)
Ment Hlth Aust Mental Health in Australia [*A publication*]
MentInc Mentor Income Fund [*Associated Press*] (SAG)
MENTL Mental
MentlHlt Mental Health Management, Inc. [*Associated Press*] (SAG)
MENTLY Mentally
MENTN Mention (ROG)
MENTNB Mentionable (ABBR)
MENTND Mentioned (ABBR)
MENTNG Mentioning (ABBR)
MENTNR Mentioner (ABBR)
Mentor Mentor Corp. [*Associated Press*] (SAG)
MENTOR Mobile Electrical Network Testing, Observation, and Recording (PDAA)
MENTOR [*A*] Programming Language [*1963*] (CSR)
MENTT Mentality (ABBR)
MENTY Mentally (ABBR)
M Env Master of Environment (PGP)
MEnv Master of Environmental Studies (DD)
M Env Des Master of Environmental Design (PGP)
M Env E Master of Environmental Engineering (PGP)
MENVEGR Master of Environmental Engineering (PGP)
M Envir E Master of Environmental Engineering (PGP)
MEnvPlan Master of Environmental Planning
MEnvS Master of Environmental Science (GAGS)
MEnvS Master of Environmental Studies
MEnvSc Master of Environmental Science (ADA)
M Env Sc Master of Environmental Science (PGP)
MEnvSt Master of Environmental Studies (ADA)
MEnvStud Master of Environmental Studies (ADA)
MEnvStudies Master of Environmental Studies
MenWre Mens Warehouse [*Associated Press*] (SAG)
MeNwS Saint Joseph's College, North Windham, ME [*Library symbol*] [*Library of Congress*] (LCLS)
MENY Mates [*Common carrier symbol*]
Menz Menzies' Cape Of Good Hope Reports [*1828-49*] [*A publication*] (DLA)
Menz Conv Menzies' Conveyancing [*A publication*] (DLA)
Menzies Menzies' Cape Of Good Hope Reports [*1828-49*] [*A publication*] (DLA)
Menzingen Sisters Sisters of the Holy Cross (SAUO)

MEO .... Jefferson City, MO [*Location identifier*] [*FAA*] (FAAL)
MEO .... Maintenance Engineering Order [*NASA*] (KSC)
MEO .... Major Engine Overhaul
MEO .... Malignant External Otitis [*Medicine*] (EDAA)
MEO .... Management Engineering Office (SAUO)
MEO .... Managing Emergency Operations [*Emergency Management*] (EMA)
MEO .... Manned Earth Orbit
MEO .... Manned Extravehicular Operation
MEO .... Marine Engineer Officer [*British*]
MEO .... Mass in Earth Orbit [*NASA*]
MEO .... Medical Education Online (SAUO)
MEO .... Medical Emergency Officer (DAVI)
MEO .... Medium Earth Orbit (SSD)
MEO .... Message Exchange Occurrence (SAUO)
MEO .... Middle Earth Orbit
MEO .... Military Electronics Office (SAUO)
MEO .... Military Equal Opportunity (MCD)
MEO .... Mining Engineering Officer [*British military*] (DMA)
MEO .... Montello Resources Ltd. [*Vancouver Stock Exchange symbol*]
MEO .... Most Efficient/Effective Organization [*DoD*]
MEO .... Scandinavian Aviation Center AS [*Denmark*] [*ICAO designator*] (FAAC)
MEOC........ Marine Emergency Operations Center [*Western Australia*]
MEOC........ Marine Environmental Quality Committee [*Marine science*] (OSRA)
MEOC........ Medium Earth Orbit, Circular (ACAE)
MEOC........ Mountain Empire Older Citizens [*Virginia*] (EARSL)
MEOD .... Maximum Extended Operating Domain (SAUO)
MEOER...... Member of the European Osteopathic Register
MEOF........ Marine Environmental Observation and Forecasting (NOAA)
MEOH .... Methanex Corp. [*NASDAQ symbol*] (SAG)
MEOH .... Methyl Alcohol
MEOHF...... Methanex Corp. [*NASDAQ symbol*] (TTSB)
MEOL........ Manned Earth Orbit Laboratory (IAA)
MEOM....... Manned Earth Orbit Mission
MEOM....... Medium Earth Orbit, Molniya (ACAE)
MEOOW..... Marine Engineer Officer of the Watch [*British*]
MEOP........ Maximum Engine Operating Pressure
MEOP........ Maximum Expected Operating Pressure
MEOPT...... Multi-Engine Operations & Procedures Trainer (SAUS)
MEOR .... Microbial Enhanced Oil Recovery [*Petroleum technology*]
MEOs........ Mass Education Officers (SAUO)
MEOS........ Medium Earth Orbit Satellites (ACRL)
MEOS........ Microsomal Ethanol Oxidizing System [*Medicine*] (EDAA)
MEOS........ Microsomal Ethanol-Oxidizing System [*Biochemistry*]
MEOS........ Mode/Energy Offset
MEOSAB .... Missile Explosive Ordnance Safety Advisory Board [*Pacific Missile Range*] (MUGU)
MEOSP...... Multi-mission Electro-Optic Stabilized Payload [*Police and security equipment*]
MEOSS...... Mobile Electro-Optical Surveillance System (SAUS)
MEOTBF.... Mean Engine Operating Time between Failures [*Quality control*]
MEOV........ Maximum Expected Operating Value [*FCC*]
MEOW....... Marine Engineer Officer's Writer [*British military*] (DMA)
MEOW....... Maximum Envelope of Wind/Water [*Emergency Management*] (EMA)
MEOW....... Mono-Extraction Orthophoto Workstation (SAUO)
MEOW....... [*The*] Moral Equivalent of War [*Phrase used by President Jimmy Carter to describe his energy bill*]
MEOW....... Multiple Engineering Order Wire (SAUS)
MEOWS..... Multimode Electro-Optical Weapon System
MEP .... Magnetic Energy Product
MEP .... Magyar Elet Partja [*Party of Hungarian Life*] [*Political party*] (PPE)
MEP .... Mahajana Eksath Peramuna [*People's United Front*] [*Sri Lanka*] [*Political party*] (PPW)
MEP .... Main Enable Plug (ACAE)
MEP .... Main Engine Propellant (MCD)
MEP .... Main Entry Point (NASA)
MEP .... Main European Port (SAUO)
MEP .... Maintainability Evaluation Process (MCD)
MEP .... Maintenance Engineering Program (SAUO)
MEP .... Major Electronics Procurement
MEP .... Major Extinction Position [*Polarizer-Analyzer*]
MEP .... Management Engineering Plan (CCCA)
MEP .... Management Engineering Program [*Air Force*] (AFM)
MEP .... Management Evaluation Program (AAG)
MEP .... Manual Entry Panel [*Military*] (CAAL)
MEP .... Manuals of Engineering Practice [*ASCE*]
MEP .... Manufacturing Engineering Plan
MEP .... Manufacturing Extension Partnership [*National Institute for Science and Technology*]
MEP .... Mars Entry Probe
MEP .... Master Environmental Plan (BCP)
MEP .... Master Evaluation Plan [*Army*]
MEP .... Master of Engineering Physics
MEP .... Master of Environmental Planning (GAGS)
MEP .... Maximal Expiratory Pressure [*Medicine*] (DB)
MEP .... Maximum Economic Potential
MEP .... Maximum Entropy Principle (PDAA)
MEP .... Maximum Escape Performance [*Ejection seat*] (MCD)
MEP .... Maximum Expiratory Pressure [*Medicine*] (DMAA)
MEP .... Maxwell Electronic Publishing [*Information service or system*] (IID)
mep.......... Mean Effective Pressure (MIST)
MEP .... Mean Effective Pressure
Mep.......... Mean Effective Pressure
MEP .... Medical Education Program [*Air Force*]
MEP .... Medium External Pintle (SAUS)
MEP .... Member of the European Parliament
MEP .... Meperidine [*Also, M*] [*An analgesic*]
MEP .... Meprobamate [*Medicine*] [*Tranquilizer*] (EDAA)
MEP .... Mersing [*Malaysia*] [*Airport symbol*] (OAG)
MEP .... Methanol Environmental Performance [*Automotive engineering*]
MEP .... Methods Engineering Program [*Navy*] (NVT)
MEP .... Methyl(ethyl)pyridine [*Organic chemistry*]
MEP .... Methyl Parathion [*Also, MP, MPN*] [*Pesticide*]
MEP .... Microcircuit Emulation Program
MEP .... Micro-Electronics Education Programme (NITA)
MEP .... Microelectronics Package (SAUS)
MEP .... Microelectronics Programme [*British*]
MEP .... Microfile Enlarger Printer (NITA)
MEP .... Middle East Policy [*A publication*] (BRI)
MEP .... Midwest Express Airlines, Inc. [*ICAO designator*] (FAAC)
MEP .... Migrant Education Projects
MEP .... Miniature Endplate Potential [*Medicine*] (QSUL)
MEP .... Minimum Energy Path [*Physical chemistry*]
MEP .... Minimum Entry Point (MCD)
MEP .... Minority Engineering Program (SAUO)
MEP .... Minority Entrepreneurship Program [*Small Business Administration*]
MEP .... Minuteman Education Program [*Air Force*] (AFM)
MEP .... Mission Effects Projector [*Lunar exploration*]
MEP .... Mission Equipment Package
MEP .... Mitochondrial Encephalopathy [*Medicine*] (DMAA)
MEP .... Mobile Electric Power (NG)
MEP .... Mobil Exploration & Producing Services, Inc., Dallas, TX [*OCLC symbol*] (OCLC)
MEP .... Mogul End Prong [*Lamp base*] (NTCM)
MEP .... Molecular Electrostatic Potentials [*Physical chemistry*]
MEP .... Monitoring Environmental Progress (SAUO)
MEP .... Moon-Earth-Plane (SAA)
MEP .... Motor End Plate
MEP .... Motor-Evoked Potential (OA)
MEP .... Motor Evoked Potentials (SAUS)
MEP .... Mouvement d'Ecologie Politique [*Ecology Political Movement*] [*France*] [*Political party*] (PPW)
MEP .... Movimiento Electoral del Pueblo [*People's Electoral Movement*] [*Venezuela*] [*Political party*] (PPW)
MEP .... Movimiento Electoral del Pueblo [*People's Electoral Movement*] [*Netherlands Antilles*] [*Political party*] (PPW)
MEP .... Mucoid Exopolysaccharide [*Biochemistry*]
MEP .... Multielliptical Pump
MEP .... Multimodality Evoked Potential [*Neurophysiology*]
MEP .... Multiple Equipment Package (SAUS)
MEP .... Multiple-Exposure Photography
MEP .... Multiple Extraction Procedure (GNE)
MEP .... Paris Foreign Mission Society (TOCD)
mep.......... Paris Foreign Mission Society (TOCD)
MeP .... Portland Public Library, Portland, ME [*Library symbol*] [*Library of Congress*] (LCLS)
MEP .... Societas Parisiensis Missionum ad Exteros [*Paris Foreign Missions Society*] [*Roman Catholic men's religious order*]
MEP-91 ..... Mesoscale Evolution Project-1991 [*Marine science*] (OSRA)
MEPA........ Marine and Estuarine Protected Area
MEPA........ Master in Engineering and Public Administration
MEPA........ Master of Engineering and Public Administration (SAUO)
MEPA........ Masters Electro-Plating Association (SAUO)
MEPA........ Meteorology and Environmental Protection Administration (SAUO)
MEPA........ Meterological and Environmental Protection Administration (SAUO)
MEPAC ...... Marathon Oil Company Employees PAC [*Findlay, OH*] (PACS)
MEPARC .... Middle East Policy and Research Center (EA)
MEPAS ...... Multimedia Environmental Pollutant Assessment System (SAUO)
MEPAV ...... Municipal Electric Power Association of Virginia (EARSL)
MEPC........ Marine Environment Protection Committee [*IMCO*] (MSC)
MEPC........ Maritime Environment Protection Committee (NADA)
MEPC........ Master of Environmental Pollution Control (GAGS)
MEPC........ MEPC International Capital LP [*Associated Press*] (SAG)
MEPC........ Metropolitan Estate and Property Corporation Munich Ltd. (SAUO)
MEPC........ Metropolitan Estate and Property International N.V. (SAUO)
MEPC........ Miniature End Plate Current
MEPC BMCM....... Marine Environment Protection Committee Baltic Maritime Coordinating Meeting (SAUO)
MEPCOM.... Military Enlistment Processing Command [*DoD*]
MEPCOM.... Military Entrance Processing Command (SAUO)
MEPD........ Master of Education - Professional Development (PGP)
MEPDP...... Meander Electrodes Plasma Display Panel (IAA)
MEPED ...... Medium-Energy Proton and Electron Detector
MEPES ...... Medical Planning and Execution System (DOMA)
MEPES ...... Medical Planning and Execution System (Model)
MEPEX ...... Middle East Ports Exhibition (SAUO)
MEPF........ Multiple Experiment Processing Furnace
MEPF-GCF... Multiple Experiment Processing Facility-Crystal Growth Furnace (SAUS)
MEPF-MAS... Multiple Experiment Processing Facility-Metal Alloy Solidification (SAUS)
MEPGS ...... Mobile Electric Power Generator Set (MCD)
MEPH........ Master of Public Health Engineering (NADA)
MEPH........ Mephobarital [*A sedative and anticonvulsant*] [*Pharmacology*] (DAVI)
MEPHISTO... Mephistopheles [*Foreman*] [*Slang*] [*British*] (DSUE)
ME Phy....... Master of Engineering Physics
MEPIS....... Management Engineering Program Information System (SAUO)
MEPL........ Master Engineering Parts Library (TIMI)

MePM .... Maine Charitable Mechanic Association, Portland, ME [*Library symbol*] [*Library of Congress*] (LCLS)
MEPM .... Medium-Term Energy Policy Model
MePMC ..... Maine Medical Center, Portland, ME [*Library symbol*] [*Library of Congress*] (LCLS)
MEPOL ...... Metropolitan Police Officers [*British*]
MePosS ..... United Society of Shakers, Shaker Library, Poland Spring, ME [*Library symbol*] [*Library of Congress*] (LCLS)
MEPP .... Marine Electric Power Plant (PDAA)
MEPP .... Middle East Peace Process (SAUO)
MEPP .... Middle East Peace Project (EA)
MEPP .... Miniature End Plate Potential
MEPP .... Mobile Electric Power Plant (NG)
MEPR .... Medical Expense and Performance Report (SAUO)
MEPrA .... Mission Capital 9.875%'MIPS' [*NYSE symbol*] (TTSB)
MEPrB .... Mission Capital 8.50% 'MIPS' [*NYSE symbol*] (TTSB)
MEPRD ...... Ministry of Environmental Protection and Regional Development (SAUO)
MePriU ...... University of Maine at Presque Isle, Presque Isle, ME [*Library symbol*] [*Library of Congress*] (LCLS)
MEPROB .... Meprobamate [*Mythyl propyltrimethylene carbamate*] [*Tranquilizer*] (DAVI)
MEPROBAMATE ... Methyl Propyltrimethylene Carbamate [*Tranquilizer*]
MEPRS ...... Medical Expense and Performance Reporting System (SAUO)
MEPRS ...... Military Entrant-Processing and Reporting System (GFGA)
MEPRS/DDS .... Medical Expense and Performance Reporting System/Dental Data System [*Air Force*] (GFGA)
MePS .... Maine Public Service Co. [*Associated Press*] (SAG)
MEPS .... Means-End Problem-Solving Procedure [*or Test*] [*Psychology*]
MEPS .... Medical Expenditure Panel Survey [*Database*] (GDD)
MEPS .... Medium-Energy Particle Spectrometer (MCD)
MEPS .... Member of the Emergency Planning Society [*Emergency Management*] (EMA)
MEPS .... Members of the European Parliament (ECON)
MEPS .... Message Editing and Preparation Service (SAUO)
MEPS .... Message Editing and Processing Station (SAUO)
MEPS .... Message Editing and Processing System (MCD)
MEPS .... Military Entrance and Processing Station
MEPS .... Military Entrance Processing Stations (SAUO)
MEPS .... Military Express and Passenger Bus Service (SAUO)
MEPS .... Modular Electrical Power Station
MEPS .... Monochrome Electronic Prepress Systems (DGA)
MEPS .... Multimedia Environmental Pollutant Assessment System (COE)
MEPSA ...... Middle East Peace and Stability Act [*1957*]
mEPSC ...... Miniature Excitory Postsynaptic Currents [*Neurobiology*]
MEPSCAT ... Military Entrance Physical Strength Capacity Test (INF)
MEPSDU .... Module Experimental Process System Development Unit [*Photovoltaic energy systems*]
MEPSI .... Mexico-Elmhurst Philatelic Society, International (EA)
MEPSP ...... Miniature Excitatory Postsynaptic Potential [*Neurophysiology*]
MEPU .... McAlister Engineering [*Intermodal shipping container symbol*] (TVRC)
MEPU .... Ministry of Pre-University Education (SAUO)
MEPU .... Monofuel Emergency Power Unit
MEPW .... Ministry of Economic Planning Western Region (SAUO)
MEPX .... Mead Paper [*Federal Railroad Administration identification code*]
MEQ .... Marine Environmental Quality [*Marine science*] (MSC)
MEQ .... Married Enlisted Quarters
MEQ .... Middle East Quarterly [*A publication*] (BRI)
mEq .... Milliequavalent (ADWA)
meq .... Milliequivalent [*Gram equivalent weight*] (DOG)
MEQ .... Milliequivalent [*or Milligram Equivalent*] [*Also, ME*]
MEQ .... Mission Equities Corporation (SAUO)
MEQ .... Modified Examination Question (SAUO)
MEQA .... Mechanized Equipment Assignment [*AT & T*]
MEQC .... Marine Environmental Quality Committee (SAUO)
MEQC .... Medicaid Eligibility Quality Control (GFGA)
MEQ/L .... Milliequivalent per Liter
MEQPT ...... Major Equipment (COE)
MEQPT ...... Major Equipment ID Code (SAUO)
MEQT .... Mattos Equipment Transport [*Common carrier symbol*]
MER .... Ethamoxytriphetol [*An antiestrogen*] (DAVI)
MER .... Madras European Regiment [*British military*] (DMA)
MER .... Magneto-Elastic Resonance (PDAA)
MER .... Main Engine Room [*Navy*] (CAAL)
MER .... Maine State Department of Environmental Protection and Department of Conservation, Augusta, ME [*OCLC symbol*] (OCLC)
MER .... Maintenance Engineering Report (MCD)
MER .... Maintenance Evaluation Report (SAUO)
MER .... Management Expense Ratio
MER .... Manager, External Relations (SAUO)
MER .... Mandatory Experience Regulation (DB)
MER .... Manned Earth Reconnaissance [*Naval Air Electronic Systems Command project*]
MER .... Manpower Estimate Report (AAGC)
MER .... Manpower Estimating Relationships (MCD)
MER .... Manpower Evaluation Report [*Military*]
MER .... Marine Environmental Response [*USCG*] (TAG)
MER .... Market Exchange Rates [*Monetary conversion rate*] (ECON)
MER .... Mass Energy Relationship
MER .... Master Employee Record [*DoD*]
MER .... Master of Energy Resources (GAGS)
MER .... Maximum Effective Range
MER .... Maximum Efficient Rate [*Oil*]
MER .... Maximum Energy Recovery [*Chemical engineering*]
MER .... Mean Ejection Rate [*Medicine*]
MER .... Mechanical Equipment Room (DAC)
MER .... Mechanics, Electrical, and Radio (MCD)
MER .... Medical Emergency Room (DMAA)
MER .... Medical Error Reduction (MELL)
MER .... Medication Errors Reporting
MER .... Merak [*NCIC car model code*]
MER .... Mercantile
MER .... Merced, CA [*Location identifier*] [*FAA*] (FAAL)
MER .... Merchandise (ADA)
MER .... Merchant (AFM)
MER .... Merchant Ship (SAUO)
MER .... Mercurial (WDAA)
MER .... Mercury (ADA)
Mer .... Mercury [*Record label*]
MER .... Merida [*Mexico*] [*Seismograph station code, US Geological Survey*] (SEIS)
MER .... Meridian (KSC)
mer .... Meridian (SHCU)
MER .... Meridional [*Geology*]
Mer .... Merionethshire (ODA)
Mer .... Merivale's English Chancery Reports [*A publication*] (DLA)
MER .... Merlinoite [*A zeolite*]
MER .... Merrell-National Laboratories [*Research code symbol*]
MER .... Merrill Lynch [*NYSE symbol*] (TTSB)
MER .... Merrill Lynch & Co. [*NYSE symbol*] (SAG)
MER .... Merrill Lynch & Co. Preferred Capital Trust I [*NYSE symbol*] (SAG)
MER .... Meru [*Language symbol*] (ETLW)
MER .... Message Error Rate (SAUO)
MER .... Metal Etch Resist
MER .... Metal Evaporated Resistor
MER .... Methanol Extraction [*or Extruded*] Residue [*Immunology*]
MER .... Methow Aviation, Inc. [*ICAO designator*] (FAAC)
MER .... Metropolitan Elevated Railroad (SAUO)
MER .... Middle East Record [*A publication*] (BJA)
MER .... Minimum Energy Requirements
MER .... Ministry of Energy Resources (SAUO)
MER .... Mission Evaluation Room [*NASA*] (NASA)
MER .... Mitteleuropaeisches Reisebuero [*Middle European Travel Bureau*] [*German*]
MER .... Monthly Energy Review [*Department of Energy*] [*Database*]
MER .... Most Economical Rating
MER .... Multielement RADAR
MER .... Multiple Ejection Rack (SAUO)
MER .... Multiple Ejector Rack (NG)
MER .... Murmur/Energy Ratio (DMAA)
MER .... Museum Education Roundtable (EA)
MER .... Myeloid-Erythrocyte [*or Erythroid*] [*Hematology*] (DAVI)
MER-29 ..... Triparanol [*Pharmacology*] [*A cholesterol biosynthesis inhibitor removed from market due to side effects*] (DAVI)
MERA .... Maeventec Employers Rated Almanac [*Maeventec*] [*Information service or system*] (CRD)
MERA .... Michigan Educational Research Association (SAUO)
MERA .... Microelectronic Radar (ACAE)
MERA .... Microelectronics for RADAR Application (MCD)
MERA .... Molecular Electronics for RADAR Applications (IEEE)
MERA .... Mormons for ERA (EA)
MERADCOM ... Mobility Equipment Research and Development Command [*Army*]
MERADO .... Mechanical Engineering Research and Development Organisation
MERAG ...... Middle-East Research and Action Group (SAUO)
MERALCO ... Manila Electric Railroad & Light Company [*Still known by acronym, although official name now Manila Electric Company*]
MERALT ..... Meridian Altitude [*Navigation*]
Mer & St Corp ... Merewether and Stephen's Municipal Corporations [*A publication*] (DLA)
MERASEX ... Mesoscale Rain and Snowfall Experiment (SAUO)
MERB .... Mechanical Engineering Research Board (SAUO)
MERB .... Medical Examiniation and Review Board [*DoD*] (DAVI)
MERB .... Mercury Boat Company [*NCIC trailer make code*]
MERB .... Merrill Merchants Bancshares, Inc. [*NASDAQ symbol*] (NASQ)
MERB .... Molecular Ecology Research Branch [*Environmental Protection Agency*] (RCD)
MerBkNY .... Merchants New York Bancorp [*Associated Press*] (SAG)
MerBNY ..... Merchants New York Bancorp [*Associated Press*] (SAG)
MERC .... Chicago Mercantile Exchange (EBF)
MERC .... Meat Export Research Center [*Iowa State University*] [*Research center*] (RCD)
MERC .... Medical Education Resource Center [*Medicine*] (EDAA)
MERC .... Medical Equipment Repair Center (SAUO)
MERC .... Mercantile (ROG)
Merc .... Mercator [*of Plautus*] [*Classical studies*] (OCD)
MERC .... Mercedes [*Automobile*] (DSUE)
MERC .... [*A*] Mercenary
MERC .... Mercer International, Inc. [*NASDAQ symbol*] (NASQ)
MERC .... Mercurial (ABBR)
MERC .... Mercury
MERC .... Mercury [*NCIC car make code*]
MERC .... Mercury Project [*NASA*] (KSC)
MERC .... Mercury (trucks) [*NCIC truck make code*]
MERC .... Metropolitan Educational Research Consortium [*Virginia Commonwealth University*] (RCD)
MERC .... MetroWest Economic Research Center [*Framingham State College*] (RCD)
MERC .... Middle-Atlantic Educational and Research Center
MERC .... Middle East Regional Cooperation [*U.S. Agency for International Development*]

MERC........ Middle East Regional Cooperation Program (SAUO)
MERC........ Middle East Resource Center [*Defunct*] (EA)
MERC........ Midwest Energy Research Center (RCD)
MERC........ Mineral Exploration Research Centre [*Laurentian University*] [*Canada*] (RCD)
MERC........ Minimum Electrical Resistance Condition (PDAA)
MERC........ Minority Economic Resource Center [*Howard University, Washington, DC*]
MERC........ Mobile Equipment Replacement Cask [*Nuclear energy*] (NUCP)
MERC........ Morgantown Energy Research Center (SAUO)
MERC........ Multi-Racial Education Resources Centre [*British*] (AIE)
MERC........ Music Education Research Council (EA)
Merc Ad & Law & Credit Man... Mercantile Adjuster and Lawyer and Credit Man [*A publication*] (DLA)
MercAir ..... Mercury Air Group, Inc. [*Associated Press*] (SAG)
MERCASREP... Merchant Ship Casualty Report [*Navy*] (NVT)
MERCAST... Merchant Ship Broadcast [*Navy*]
MERCAST... Merchant Shop Broadcast System (SAUO)
MERCASUM... Merchant Ship Casualty Summary [*Navy*] (NVT)
MercBcp .... Mercantile Bancorp [*Associated Press*] (SAG)
Merc Cas ... Mercantile Cases [*A publication*] (DLA)
MERCE...... Mercedes [*Automobile*] (DSUE)
Mercedarians... Order of Our Lady of Mercy (SAUO)
Mercer ...... Mercer County Law Journal [*Pennsylvania*] [*A publication*] (DLA)
Mercer ...... Mercer International [*Associated Press*] (SAG)
Mercer Beasley L Rev... Mercer Beasley Law Review [*A publication*] (DLA)
Mercer BL Rev... Mercer Beasley Law Review [*A publication*] (DLA)
Mercer U ... Mercer University (GAGS)
MercFn ..... Mercury Finance Co. [*Associated Press*] (SAG)
MercGn ..... Mercury General Corp. [*Associated Press*] (SAG)
Merch ...... Merchant (TBD)
MERCH...... Merchantable
MERCHANT... Methods in Electronic Retail Cash Handling (SAUO)
Merch Dict... Merchants' Dictionary [*A publication*] (DLA)
Merc (Hob)... Mercury (Hobart) [*A publication*]
MERCHT .... Merchant
Merch V..... [*The*] Merchant of Venice [*Shakespearean work*] (BARN)
MERCI...... Multimedia European Research Conferencing Integration (SAUO)
MercInt...... Mercury Interactive Corp. [*Associated Press*] (SAG)
Merck .... Merck & Co., Inc. [*Associated Press*] (SAG)
MERCK
PAC.......... The PAC for Merck & Company Inc. [*Washington, DC*] (PACS)
Merc LJ ..... Mercantile Law Journal [*New York or Madras*] [*A publication*] (DLA)
MERCM ..... Mercantilism (ABBR)
MERCO...... Mercantile Communications [*Shipping*]
MERCO...... Merchant Ship Control [*Navy*]
MERCOFORM... Merchant Ship Communications Formatted (MCD)
MERCOMMS... Merchant Marine Communications System (DNAB)
MERComP .. New England Regional Computing Program (SAUO)
MERCON.... Universal Transversal Mercator Converter [*Computer program*]
MERCOS.... Merchant Codes [*Shipping*]
MERCOSUR... Common Market of the South
MERCPAC... Mercury Enthusiast Restorer Custom Performance Auto Club (EA)
MERCRy .... Mercury [*Chemistry*] (DAVI)
MERCS...... Mercer International [*NASDAQ symbol*]
MERCS...... Mercer International SBI [*NASDAQ symbol*] (SPSG)
MERCS...... Mercer Intl. SBI [*NASDAQ symbol*] (TTSB)
MercSt ...... Mercantile Stores Co., Inc. [*Associated Press*] (SAG)
MERCT ...... Mercantilist (ABBR)
MERCTL...... Mercantile
MerctlBk ... Mercantile Bankshares Corp. [*Associated Press*] (SAG)
MERCY...... Medical Emergency Relief Care for Youth
MERDC...... Mobility Equipment Research and Development Center [*Army*] (MCD)
MERDI....... Montana Energy and Magneto-Hydrodynamics Research Institute [*Later, Montana Energy Research and Development Institute*] [*Research center*]
MERDIFF.... Meridian Difference
MerdIns..... Meridian Insurance Group, Inc. [*Associated Press*] (SAG)
MERDL...... Medical Equipment Research and Development Laboratory [*Army*]
MerdrNt.... Meridian National Corp. [*Associated Press*] (SAG)
Merdth ...... Meredith Corp. [*Associated Press*] (SAG)
MERE....... Mortar Elevation & Ranging Equipment (SAUS)
MEREA...... Member of the American Electrical Railway Engineering Association
MEREC ...... Meridith Real Estate Corporation (EFIS)
MERECEN... Movimiento Estable Republicano Centrista [*El Salvador*] [*Political party*] (EY)
MEREP ...... Merchant Ship Arrival and/or Departure Report (NATG)
MEREP ...... Merchant Ship Report [*Navy*]
MERERCAC... Middle Eastern Regional Radioisotope Centre for the Arab Countries (SAUO)
ME(Res) .... Master of Engineering (Research)
MERES ...... Matrix of Environmental Residuals for Energy Systems [*Computerized information system*]
ME Rev Stat... Maine Revised Statutes [*A publication*] (DLA)
ME Rev Stat Ann... Maine Revised Statutes, Annotated [*A publication*] (DLA)
MERF........ Medical Education Research Foundation [*San Diego*]
MERG .... Macular Electroretinogram (DB)
MERGE...... Mechanized Retrieval for Greater Efficiency [*Computer science*]
MERGE...... Model for Evaluating Regional and Global Effects of GHG reduction policies (SAUO)
MERGV...... Martian Exploratory Rocket Glide Vehicle
MERH .... Mercury Coach Corporation [*NCIC trailer make code*]
MERI .... Marine Environmental Research Institute (RCD)
MERI .... Meadowlands Environmental Research Institute [*Rutgers University*] (RCD)
MERI .... Medical Education Research and Information Database
MERI .... Medical Research Institute (SAUO)
MERI .... Meritrust Federal Savings Bank [*NASDAQ symbol*] (SAG)
MERI .... Meritrust Fed Svg Bk Morgan [*NASDAQ symbol*] (TTSB)
MERI .... Merritt Equipment Company [*NCIC trailer make code*]
MERI .... Mineral Exploration Research Institute [*See also IREM*] [*Canada*] [*Research center*] (RCD)
MERI .... Mining and Excavation Research Institute [*Research center*] (RCD)
MERI .... Moderate Resolution Imaging Spectrometer (ACAE)
MERIC....... Michigan Education Resources Information Center [*Michigan State Library*] [*Information service or system*] [*Defunct*] (IID)
MERID....... Meridian (ABBR)
MERID....... Meridian, MS [*American Association of Railroads railroad junction routing code*]
MeridDia.... Meridian Diagnostics, Inc. [*Associated Press*] (SAG)
MeridDta.... Meridian Data, Inc. [*Associated Press*] (SAG)
MeridI...... Meridian Industrial Trust, Inc. [*Associated Press*] (SAG)
Meridn ...... Meridian [*A publication*]
MeridSpt.... Meridian Sports, Inc. [*Associated Press*] (SAG)
MERIE....... Magnetically Enhanced Reactive Ion Etching [*By plasmas*]
MeriFdl ..... Meritrust Federal Savings Bank [*Associated Press*] (SAG)
MerilCp ..... Merrill Corp. [*Associated Press*] (SAG)
MERINT ..... Merchant Intelligence Report [*Navy*]
MERINT ..... Merchant Ship Intelligence (NVT)
MERINTREP... Merchant Ship Arrival and/or Departure Intermediate Report (NATG)
MERINTREP... Merchant Shipping Intelligence Report (SAUO)
Merions ..... Merionethshire (DIAR)
MERIONS ... Merionethshire [*County in Wales*]
MERIP....... Middle East Research and Information Project (EA)
MERIS....... European Medium Resolution Imaging Spectrometer (SAUO)
MERIS....... Medium Resolution Imaging Spectrometer (SSD)
Merisel...... Merisel, Inc. [*Associated Press*] (SAG)
MerisL ...... Meris Laboratories, Inc. [*Associated Press*] (SAG)
MERIT....... Maastricht Economic Research Institute on Innovation and Technology
MERIT....... Maintenance and Reliability [*Petroleum engineering*]
MERIT....... Mechanical Engineers Reading Improvement Techniques (SAUO)
MERIT....... Medical Relief International (SAUO)
MERIT....... Method to Extend Research in Time [*National Institutes of Health*]
MERIT....... Military Exploitation of Reconnaissance and Intelligence Technology (SAUO)
MERIT....... Monitor the Earth Rotation and Intercompare Techniques [*by means of radio telescope measurements*]
MERIT....... Multiple RADAR-Integrated Tracking [*Military*] (PDAA)
MERIT....... [*The*] The Michigan Educational Research Network [*Computer science*] (TNIG)
MeritH....... Merit Holding Corp. [*Associated Press*] (SAG)
MERITOC ... Meritocracy (ABBR)
MERITOC ... Meritocrat (ABBR)
Meriv........ Merivale's English Chancery Reports [*A publication*] (DLA)
Meriv (Eng)... Merivale's English Chancery Reports [*A publication*] (DLA)
Merix Cp.... Merix Corp. [*Associated Press*] (SAG)
MERK........ Merkert American [*NASDAQ symbol*] (SG)
MERK........ Merkur [*NCIC car make code*]
MERL........ Marine Ecosystem Research Laboratory [*University of Rhode Island*] [*Research center*]
MERL........ Massachusetts Institute of Technology Electronic Research Laboratory (SAUO)
MERL........ Materials Engineering Research Laboratory [*NASA*] (NASA)
MERL........ Materials Engineering Research Laboratory Ltd. [*British*] (IRC)
MERL........ Materials Equipment Requirements List (NASA)
MERL........ Mechanical Engineering Research Laboratory (SAUO)
MerL......... Merrill Lynch & Co., Inc. [*Associated Press*] (SAG)
MerL......... Merrill Lynch & Co. Preferred Capital Trust I [*Associated Press*] (SAG)
MERL........ Mobile Emergency Radiological Laboratory (DEMM)
MERL........ Municipal Environmental Research Laboratory [*Environmental Protection Agency*] (GRD)
MerLEur.... Merrill Lynch & Co., Inc. [*Associated Press*] (SAG)
MERLIN ..... Machine Readable Library Information [*British Library*] [*Information service or system*] (IID)
MERLIN ..... Management of Expenditure and Resident-Linked Information Network [*Computer science*]
MERLIN ..... Medical Emergency Relief International (MELL)
MERLIN ..... Medium-Energy Reactor Light-Water Industrial Neutron [*British*] (DEN)
MERLIN ..... Modular Ejection-Rated Low-profile Imaging for Night (SAUS)
MERLIN ..... Multielement Radio-Linked Interferometer Network [*Astronomy*]
MERLin ..... Multimedia Ethnographic Research Laboratory [*University of British Columbia*] [*Canada*] (RCD)
Mer LJ ...... Mercantile Law Journal [*Madras, India*] [*A publication*] (DLA)
MERLOT .... Multimedia Educational Resources for Learning and Online Teaching
MERM....... Masters of Earth Resources Management (PGP)
MERM....... Material Evaluation Rocket Motor
MERM....... Merrimac Corporation [*NCIC trailer make code*]
MERM....... Multilateral Exchange Rate Model (ADA)
MERMAID... Marine Environment Remote-Controlled Measuring and Integrated Detection (SAUO)
MERMAID... Metrication and Resource Modelling Aid (SAUO)
MERMAIDS... Mediterranean Eddy Resolving Modelling and Interdisc Studies (SAUO)
Mermic...... Merrimac Industries, Inc. [*Associated Press*] (SAG)
MERMLS.... Mid-Eastern Regional Medical Library Service [*Library network*]

MERMUT.... Mobile Electronic Robot Manipulator and Underwater Television (IEEE)
MERN .... Medical Ethics Resource Network of Michigan (SAUO)
MEROD...... Message Entry & Read Out Device (SAUS)
MERP........ Marine Ecosystem Response Project (SAUO)
MERP........ Maximum Effective Radiated Power [*Telecommunications*] (OTD)
MERP........ Miniature Electronic Repair Program (DNAB)
MerP6....... Meridian Point Realty Trust VI Co. [*Associated Press*] (SAG)
MERPASS... Meridian Passage [*Navigation*]
MERPL ...... Mission Essential Repair Parts List (MCD)
MerPnt 8.... Meridian Point Realty Trust VIII [*Associated Press*] (SAG)
MERPrA..... Merrill Lynch 9% Sr'A'Dep Pfd [*NYSE symbol*] (TTSB)
MERPS...... Multiple Event Record and Playback System (NTCM)
MerPt4...... Meridian Point Realty Trust IV [*Associated Press*] (SAG)
MerPt6...... Meridian Point Realty Trust VI [*Associated Press*] (SAG)
MerPt7...... Meridian Point Realty Trust VII [*Associated Press*] (SAG)
MerPt 8..... Meridian Point Realty Trust VIII Co. [*Associated Press*] (SAG)
MerPt83.... Meridian Point Realty Trust 1983 [*Associated Press*] (SAG)
MERQ .... Mercury Interactive [*NASDAQ symbol*] (TTSB)
MERQ .... Mercury Interactive Corp. [*NASDAQ symbol*] (SAG)
MerR .... Mercuric Ion Receptor [*Biochemistry*]
MERR .... Mercury Trailer Industries [*NCIC trailer make code*]
MERR .... Minor Equipment Relocations, Replacements (DNAB)
MERRA...... Michigan Energy and Resources Research Association (SAUO)
MERRA...... Middle East Relief and Rehabilitation Administration [*World War II*]
Merr Att..... Merrifield on Attorneys [*1830*] [*A publication*] (DLA)
MERRC...... Middle Eastern Regional Radioisotope Centre for the Arab Countries [*Cairo, Egypt*] (WND)
Merr Costs... Merrifield's Law of Costs [*A publication*] (DLA)
MERRECT... Mercury Rectifier (IAA)
MERRF...... Myoclonic Epilepsy Associated with Ragged Red Fibres [*Medicine*]
MERRI....... Merrillan, WI [*American Association of Railroads railroad junction routing code*]
Merrimack... Smith's New Hampshire Reports [*A publication*] (DLA)
MerrLyn..... Merrill Lynch & Co., Inc. [*Associated Press*] (SAG)
MERRT....... Medical Emergency Radiological Response Team (SAUO)
Merry W .... [*The*] Merry Wives of Windsor [*Shakespearean work*] (BARN)
MERS........ Marine Ecotoxicology Research Station [*US Geological Survey*] (RCD)
MERS........ Mechanical Engineering in Radar Symposium (SAUO)
MERS........ Medical Equipment Reporting System [*Veterans Administration*]
MERS........ Medium Resolution Imaging Spectrometer (CARB)
MERS........ Meris Laboratories [*NASDAQ symbol*] (SPSG)
MERS........ Mobile Emergency Response Support
MERS........ Mobile Emergency Response System (DEMM)
MERS........ Mobility Environmental Research Studies
MERS........ Mobility Environmental Research Study (SAUO)
MERS........ Most Economical Route Selection [*Also, ARS*] [*Bell System*] [*Telecommunications*]
MERS........ Movimiento de Estudiantes Revolucionarios Salvadorenos [*Revolutionary Movement of Salvadoran Students*] (PD)
MERS........ Multielement Radiometer System
MERS........ Mysore Engineering Research Station (SAUO)
MERSAP .... Merchant Ship Auxiliary Program (DNAB)
MERSAR .... Merchant Ship Search and Rescue (PDAA)
MERSAR .... Merchant Ship Search and Rescue Manual (SAUO)
MERSAT..... Meteorology and Earth Observation Satellite (NASA)
MERSEX..... Merchant Ship Code Systems [*NATO*] (NATG)
Mersey...... Merseyside [*County in England*] (WGA)
MERSHIP ... Merchant Ship [*Navy*] (NVT)
MERSHIP ... Merchant Shipping system (SAUO)
MERSIGS ... Merchant Signals [*Shipping*]
MERSSAR .. Merchant Ship Search and Rescue (SAUO)
MERSY...... Mercedes Recycling System [*Automotive manufacturing*]
MERT........ Maintenance Engineering Review Team [*Navy*] (NG)
MERT........ Merit Tank & Body [*NCIC trailer make code*]
Mert .... Merten's Law of Federal Income Taxation [*A publication*] (DLA)
MERT........ Merton College [*Oxford University*] (ROG)
Mert .... Merton College, Oxford (SAUO)
MERT........ Milwaukee Electric Railway & Transport Co. [*AAR code*]
MERT........ Modified Effective-Range Theory (PDAA)
Mert Coll ... Merton College (SAUO)
MER/TER.... Multiple Ejection Rack/Triple Ejection Rack (MCD)
MertMd ..... Merit Medical Systems, Inc. [*Associated Press*] (SAG)
MERTS ...... Micropound Extended Range Thrust Stand [*NASA*]
MERTU ...... Medical Entomology Research and Training Unit, University de Valle (SAUO)
MERTU/G ... Medical Entomology Research and Training Unit/Guatemala
MERU .... Andrea Merzario [*Intermodal shipping container symbol*] (TVRC)
MERU .... Merzario Line [*Common carrier symbol*]
MERU .... Milliearth Rate Unit [*NASA*] (KSC)
MERVS...... Mobile Emergency Response Vehicles [*Emergency Management*] (EMA)
MERW....... Mercerburg Railway [*Federal Railroad Administration identification code*]
MERW....... Merhow Industries [*NCIC trailer make code*]
MERX........ Mercer Enterprises [*Air carrier designation symbol*]
MERX........ Merix Corp. [*NASDAQ symbol*] (SAG)
MERY........ Merry Land & Investment Company, Inc. [*NASDAQ symbol*] (COMM)
MeryL .... Merry Land & Investment Co., Inc. [*Associated Press*] (SAG)
MeryLd ...... Merry Land & Investment Co., Inc. [*Associated Press*] (SAG)
MERZ........ Mercedes-Benz [*NCIC car make code*]
MERZ........ Mercedes-Benz (trucks) [*NCIC truck make code*]
MERZ........ Meridian [*Federal Railroad Administration identification code*]
MERZONE... Merchant Shipping Control Zone [*NATO*] (NATG)
MERZONES... Merchant shipping Zones (SAUS)
MES .... Maharashtra Ekikaran Samithi [*India*] [*Political party*] (PPW)
MES .... Main Engine Start [*NASA*] (KSC)
MES .... Main Equipment Supplier (NATG)
MES .... Maine State Planning Office, Augusta, ME [*OCLC symbol*] (OCLC)
MES .... Mainly English-Speaking
MES .... Maintenance Electrolyte Solution [*Physiology*]
MES .... Major Equipment Supplier (ACAE)
MES .... Malaysian Economic Society (SAUO)
MES .... Management Engineering Squadron [*Air Force*]
MES .... Managing Editor Software, Inc. (SAUO)
MES .... Manned Exploration Site (MCD)
MES .... Manual Entry System [*or Subsystem*] (IEEE)
MES .... Manuals of Elementary Science [*A publication*]
MES .... Manufaturing Execution System [*Engineering*]
MES .... Mapping and Earth Science (ELAL)
MES .... Marine Environmental Services (SAUO)
MES .... Marine Evacuation System (SAUO)
MES .... Marketable Equity Securities [*Investment term*] (DICI)
MES .... Marketing Encyclopedia System (GART)
MES .... Mass Expulsion System (MCD)
MES .... Master, Environmental Studies (CMD)
MES .... Master Erection Schedule (DNAB)
MES .... Master of Engineering Science (SAUO)
MES .... Master of Engineering Sciences
MES .... Master of Engineering Studies
MES .... Master of Environmental Science (DD)
MES .... Master of Environmental Studies (PGP)
MES .... Master of Special Education (PGP)
MES .... Mated Elements [*or Events*] Simulator [*NASA*] (MCD)
MES .... Mated Events Simulator
MES .... Maximal Electroshock [*Physiology*]
MES .... Maximum Electroshock Seizure [*Medicine*]
MES .... Mechanical Engineering Society (SAUO)
MES .... Medan [*Indonesia*] [*Airport symbol*] (OAG)
MES .... Medical Electronics Society [*Defunct*] (EA)
MES .... Medical Emergency Service [*Medicine*] (EDAA)
MES .... Medical Equipment Set [*Army*]
MES .... Medium Energy Source (SAUS)
MES .... Medium Energy Source Program [*Air Force*]
MES .... Medsource Systems, Inc. [*Vancouver Stock Exchange symbol*]
MES .... Melville Corp. [*Formerly, Melville Shoe Corp.*] [*NYSE symbol*] (SPSG)
MES .... Mesaba Aviation [*ICAO designator*] (FAAC)
Mes.......... Mesencephalic (DB)
MES .... Mesozoic [*Period, era, or system*] [*Geology*]
MES .... Message Entry Subsystem (SAUO)
MES .... Message Entry System (MCD)
MES .... Messina [*Italy*] [*Seismograph station code, US Geological Survey*] (SEIS)
MES .... Mesylate [*Organic chemistry*]
MES .... Metalsmith (Sheet Metal Worker) [*U.S. Navy enlisted rating*] (AUER)
ME(S) .... Methodist Episcopal, South
MES .... Mexican Epigraphic Society (EA)
MES .... Michigan Engineering Society (SAUO)
MES .... Midwest Electronic Society (SAUO)
MES .... Military Engineer Services [*British*]
MES .... Minerals Engineering Society [*British*]
MES .... Miniature Edison Screw
MES .... Minimum Efficiency Scale
MES .... Minor Earth Stations (ACAE)
MES .... Miscellaneous Equipment Specification (HGAA)
MES .... Missile Electrical Simulator
MES .... Missile Engineering Station
MES .... Mission Events Sequence (MCD)
MES .... Mobile Earth Station (DA)
M-ES .... Mobile End System (ACRL)
MES .... Modal Emission Model (SAUO)
MES .... Moessbauer Emission Spectroscopy
MES .... MOL [*Manned Orbiting Laboratory*] Environmental Shelter
MES .... Monitoring Energy Systems
MES .... More Effective Schools [*Program*] [*Defunct*]
MES .... Morpholinoethanesulfonic Acid [*A buffer*]
MES .... Motor End Support
MES .... Movimento de Esquerda Socialista [*Movement of the Socialist Left*] [*Portugal*] [*Political party*] (PPE)
MES .... Moving Earth Simulator (MCD)
MES .... Multiengine Sea [*Pilot rating*] (AIA)
MES .... Multilinear Events Sequencing [*Engineering*]
MES .... Multiple Earning Statement [*Banking*] (MHDW)
MES .... Multiple Endocrine Syndrome [*Endocrinology*]
MES .... Myoelectric Signal
MES .... South Methodist Episcopal Church (SAUO)
MESA........ Maintenance Engineering Support Analysis [*Military*] (CAAL)
MesA........ Maitre es Arts [*Master of Arts*] [*French*]
MESA........ Malaria Eradication Special Account
MESA........ Manned Environmental Systems Assessment [*NASA*]
MESA........ Marine Ecosystems Analysis [*Pollution-monitoring project*]
MESA........ Marine Education Society of Australia (SAUO)
MESA........ Marshall Engineers and Scientists Association (SAUO)
MESA........ Mathematics, Engineering, and Science Achievement (ABAC)
MESA........ Maximum Entropy Spectrum Analysis
MESA........ Mechanics Educational Society of America (EA)
MESA........ Medical Emergency Service Associates (SAUO)
MESA........ Medium Power-Switching Application (IAA)

MESA........ Men to End Spouse Abuse (EA)
MESA........ Mesa Air Group [*NASDAQ symbol*] (TTSB)
MESA........ Mesa Air Group, Inc. [*NASDAQ symbol*] (SAG)
MESA........ Mesa Airlines, Inc. [*NASDAQ symbol*] (NQ)
MESA........ Mesa III Travel Trailer [*NCIC trailer make code*]
MESA........ Meta Email Search Agent [*Computer science*]
MESA........ Microsurgical Epididymal Sperm Aspiration
ME/SA........ Middle East/Southern Asia
MESA........ Middle East Studies Association of North America (EA)
M ESA....... Miniature Electrostatic Accelerometer (NAKS)
MESA........ Miniature Electrostatically Suspended Accelerometer (MCD)
MESA........ Minimum Essential Support Analysis (MCD)
MESA........ Mining Enforcement and Safety Administration [*Terminated, 1978; functions transferred to Mine Safety and Health Administration, Department of Labor*]
MESA........ Mobile Entertainments, Southern Area [*British military*] (DMA)
MESA........ Model Experimental Systems Analysis [*In-depth study of sewage outfall in the New York Bight*] [*Inactive*] (OSRA)
M ESA....... Modular Equipment Stowage Assembly [*Aerospace*] (NAKS)
MESA........ Modularized Equipment Storage [*or Stowage*] Area [*or Assembly*] [*Apollo*] [*NASA*]
MESA........ Module Tool Set Evaluation Strategic Achitectures (ACAE)
MESA........ Moving to End Sexual Assault (MHID)
MESA........ MSFC Engineering Support Area (SAUS)
MESA........ Multi-Ethnic Study of Atherosclerosis
MESA........ Multiple Engagement Simulation Analyzer [*Military*]
MESA........ Multiplexed Electronic Synthetic Array (ACAE)
MESA........ Multi-role Electronically Scanned Array (SAUS)
MESA........ Music Editor, Scorer, and Arranger [*Computer program*] (PCM)
MESA........ Myoepithelial Sialadenitis [*Medicine*] (DMAA)
MesaAir..... Mesa Air Group, Inc. [*Associated Press*] (SAG)
MesaAr...... Mesa Airlines, Inc. [*Associated Press*] (SAG)
MESAB....... Medical Education for South African Blacks [*An association*] (EA)
Mesab....... Mesabi Trust [*Associated Press*] (SAG)
Mesaba...... Mesaba Holdings, Inc. [*Associated Press*] (SAG)
MesabaH..... Mesaba Holdings, Inc. [*Associated Press*] (SAG)
MeSaco...... Dyer Library, Saco, ME [*Library symbol*] [*Library of Congress*] (LCLS)
MeSacoT..... Thornton Academy, Saco, ME [*Library symbol*] [*Library of Congress*] (LCLS)
MesaInc..... Mesa, Inc. [*Associated Press*] (SAG)
MesaLb...... Mesa Laboratories, Inc. [*Associated Press*] (SAG)
MESAMAC... Engine Status Accounting System (SAUO)
MESAN...... Mouvement de l'Evolution Sociale de l'Afrique Noire [*Black African Social Evolution Movement*]
MESANA.... Middle East Studies Association of North America (SAUO)
MesaR...... Mesa Royalty Trust [*Associated Press*] (SAG)
MESAR...... Minimum-Essential Security Assistance Requirements (COE)
MESAR...... Multifunction Electric Scan Adaptive RADAR [*Military*] [*British*]
MESAR...... Multi-function Electronically Scanned Adaptive Radar (SAUS)
MESB........ Mechanical Standards Board (SAUO)
MESB........ Michigan Environmental Science Board
MESBIC..... Minority Enterprise Small Business Investment Company
MESC........ Marine Environmental Sciences Consortium [*Library network*]
MESC........ Master Event Sequence Controller (KSC)
ME Sc....... Master of Engineering Science
MESC........ Mescaline
MESC........ Middle East Service Command [*Army*] [*World War II*]
MESC........ Middle East Supercomputer Centre [*Bahrain Centre for Studies and Research*] (ECON)
MESC........ Middle East Supply Center [*World War II*]
MESC........ Middle East Supply Centre (SAUO)
MESC........ Middle East Supply Council [*World War II*]
MESC........ Miniature Excitatory Synaptic Current [*Neurophysiology*]
MESC........ Mission Events Sequence Controller [*NASA*] (KSC)
MESC........ Modular Equipment Standards Committee (AAEL)
MESC........ Modular Equipment Sub-Committee for Communications (SAUO)
MESCA...... Maine School Counselor Association (SEAT)
MESCAL..... United States Biological Cruise of Baja California (SAUS)
MESCH...... Multi-Environment Scheme [*Medicine*] (DMAA)
MESCH...... Multi-WAIS Engine for Searching Commercial Hosts (SAUS)
MESCO...... Message Electronic Switching Computer (IAA)
MESCO...... Michigan Environmental Services Co. (EFIS)
MESCO...... Middle East Science Cooperation Office (SAUO)
MESCPL..... Mess Corporal [*Marine Corps*]
MESC(W)... Middle East Supply Committee (Washington) [*World War II*]
MESD........ Mesdames [*Plural of Mrs.*] [*France*]
MESDIS..... Message Distribution System (SAUO)
MESEC...... Multi-Cultural Environmental Science Education Centers (ABAC)
MESEEC..... Methodologies to Estimate Social, Environmental and Economic Consequences (SAUO)
MeSepPM... Penobscot Marine Museum, Searsport, ME [*Library symbol*] [*Library of Congress*] (LCLS)
MESF........ Minimum Engineered Safety Features (NRCH)
MESF........ Mobile Earth Station Facility
MESFET..... Metal-Semiconductor Field-Effect Transistor
MESFET..... Metal Silicon Field-Effect Transistor (VLIE)
MESG........ Maximum Experimental Safe Gap (IEEE)
MESG........ Mediterranean Shipping Group [*NATO*] (NATG)
mesg........ Message (ELAL)
MESG........ Message Media, Inc. [*NASDAQ symbol*] (NASQ)
MESG........ Microelectrostatic Gyro
MESGA...... Microelectrostatic Gyro-Accelerometer
MESGE...... Message (ABBR)
MESGER.... Messenger (ABBR)
MESH........ Macintosh Enhanced SCSI Hardware (SAUS)
MESH........ Marine Aspects of Earth System History [*Research programs*]
MESH........ Media Source, Inc. [*NASDAQ symbol*] (QUAN)
MeSH........ Medical Subject Headings (ADWA)
MESH........ Medical Subject Headings (NITA)
MeSH........ Medical Subject Headings Vocabulary File [*National Library of Medicine*] [*Information service or system*] (CRD)
MESH........ Multiple Electronically Synopsing Hierarchy (RDA)
MESH........ Museum Exchange for System's Help [*National Museum of Natural History*] (IID)
MESI........ Modified, Exclusive, Shared, and Invalid Data (PCM)
MESIM...... Mission Essential Subsystem Inoperative Maintenance
MeSk........ Skowhegan Free Public Library, Skowhegan, ME [*Library symbol*] [*Library of Congress*] (LCLS)
MeSkS...... Margaret Chase Smith Library Center, Skowhegan, ME [*Library symbol*] [*Library of Congress*] (LCLS)
MESL........ Marine Environment Studies Laboratory [*Marine science*] (OSRA)
MESL........ Membrane-Enveloped Soil Layer
MESL........ Merchants' Exchange of St. Louis (EA)
MESL........ Mesa Airlines, Inc. [*NASDAQ symbol*] (COMM)
MESL........ Microwave Electronic Systems Ltd.
MESL........ Minimum Essential Subsystem List (SAUO)
MESL........ Mission Essential Subsystems List (NVT)
MESL........ Multimedia Environmental Simulations Laboratory [*Georgia Institute of Technology*] (RCD)
MESM........ Master of Environmental Science (PGP)
MESM........ Mission Essential Subsystem Matrix [*Navy*] (ANA)
MESM........ Multiechelon Supply Model (AABC)
MESN........ Media Event Status Notification (MWOL)
MesoAm..... Meso American (VRA)
MESOL...... Management Education Scheme by Open Learning (SAUO)
Mesol....... Mesolithic (VRA)
MesoNet.... Mesoscale Network (SAUS)
Mesop....... Mesopotamia (VRA)
MESOP...... Mesopotamia
MESOPAC... Mesoscale Meteorological Preprocessor Program (COE)
MESOPLUME... Mesoscale Bent Plume Model (EAGT)
MESOPUFF... Mesoscale Puff Model (EEVL)
MESOSOFT... Mesoscale Data Management Facility (SAUO)
MESP........ Management Engineering Scheduling Program (SAUO)
MESP........ Minuteman Extended Survivable Power (DWSG)
MESPA...... Minnesota Elementary School Principals Association (SAUO)
MESPF...... Malayan Estates Staff Provident Fund (SAUO)
MesPGN..... Mesangial Proliferative Glomerulonephritis [*Nephrology*] (DMAA)
MESPOT.... Mesopotamia (DSUE)
MESPREP... Message Preparation (SAUO)
MeSprN..... Nasson College, Springvale, ME [*Library symbol*] [*Library of Congress*] (LCLS)
MESQ........ Amarillo Mesquite Grill [*OTCBB symbol*]
MESq........ Management Engineering Squadron [*Air Force*]
MESRF...... Middle East Special Requirement Fund
MESROM... Materials-Evaluation Subcaliber Rocket Motor (SAA)
Mesrx........ Measurex Corp. [*Associated Press*] (SAG)
MESS........ Magnetic Emulsion Spectrometer
MESS........ Mangled Extremity Severity Score [*Medicine*] (MELL)
MESS........ Master of Exercise and Sport Sciences (PGP)
MESS........ Maximum Effective SONAR Speed (NVT)
MESS........ Maximum Efficiency Structural System (IAA)
MESS........ Mechanical Electronic Subassembly Simulator
MESS........ Messenger (MSA)
MESS........ Messerschmitt [*German fighter aircraft*] (DSUE)
MESS........ Messerschmitt [*NCIC car make code*]
MESS........ Military Equipment Support Subsystem (SAUO)
MESS........ Misalignment Estimation Software System (MCD)
MESS........ Mixed Evolutionarily Stable Strategy [*Breeding selection*]
MESS........ Model Evaluation Support System (COE)
MESS........ Monitor Event Simulation System (IEEE)
MESSAGE... Modular Electronic Solid-State Aerospace Ground Equipment
MESSCPL... Mess Corporal [*Marine Corps*]
MESSE...... Messuage (ROG)
MESSENGER... Mercury Surface, Space Environment, Geochemistry and Ranging Mission [*NASA launch date proposed for March 2004*]
MESSER.... Messerschmitt [*German fighter aircraft*] (DSUE)
MESSR...... Multispectrum Electronic Self-Scanning Radiometer (MCD)
MESSRS.... Messieurs [*Plural of Mister*] [*French*]
Messrs...... Monsieurs (SHCU)
MESSSGT... Mess Sergeant [*Marine Corps*]
MESST...... Eucharistic Missionaries of the Most Holy Trinity (TOCD)
MEST........ Eucharistic Missionaries of St. Theresa (Mexico) (TOCD)
MEST........ Maintenance Engineering Support Team (MCD)
MEST........ Matter, Energy, Space and Time (SAUO)
MEST........ Mestizo (ABBR)
MEST........ Ministere d'Etat, Sciences et Technologie [*Ministry of State for Science and Technology - MOSST*] [*Canada*]
MEST........ Missile Electrical System Test (NG)
MEST........ Mouse Ear Swelling Test [*Analytical biochemistry*]
MESTA...... Marine Ecosystem Study in Tropical Areas [*Marine science*] (MSC)
Mestek...... Mestek, Inc. [*Associated Press*] (SAG)
MESTIND... Measurement Standards Instrumentation Division (SAUO)
MESTS...... Missile Electric System Test Set [*Military*] (PDAA)
MESU........ Mediterranean Shipping [*Intermodal shipping container symbol*] (TVRC)
MESU........ Microelectronics Support Unit [*for the Microelectronics Education Programme*] [*British*]

MESUCORA... International Exhibition of Measurement, Control, Regulation and Automation (SAUO)
MESUCORA... Measurement, Control, Regulation, and Automation (IEEE)
MESUR...... Mars Environmental Survey [*NASA*]
MESW...... Meta-Software [*NASDAQ symbol*] (TTSB)
MESW...... Meta-Software, Inc. [*NASDAQ symbol*] (SAG)
ME/SWA.... Middle East/Southwest Asia (SAUO)
MESYLATE... Methansulfonate (ACAE)
MESZ........ Mehan Service [*Federal Railroad Administration identification code*]
MET.......... East Tennessee State University, Medical Library, Johnson City, TN [*OCLC symbol*] (OCLC)
MET.......... Magic Eye Tube
MET.......... Maintenance Engineering Technique
MET.......... Maintenance Evaluation Team
MET.......... Management Engineering Team [*Air Force*] (AFM)
MET.......... Manufacturer's Excise Tax
MET.......... Marksmanship Expert Trainer (SAUS)
MET.......... Maryland Electrical Testing Co. (EFIS)
MET.......... Master Events Timer (MCD)
MET.......... Master of Education in Teaching (GAGS)
MET.......... Materials-Energy-Toxics [*Recycling*]
MET.......... Maximal Exercise Test (DMAA)
MET.......... Mean Elapsed Time (MCD)
met.......... Measurement (DS)
MET.......... Mechanical Engineering Technician
MET.......... Medical Emergency Technician [*Medicine*] (EDAA)
MET.......... Medium Energy Telescope
MET.......... Medium Equipment Transporter (MCD)
MET.......... Memphis [*Tennessee*] [*Seismograph station code, US Geological Survey*] (SEIS)
MET.......... Metabolic Equivalent [*Medicine*]
MET.......... Metabolic Equivalent of the Task (DMAA)
MET.......... Metal [*or Metallic*] (AAG)
met.......... Metallic [*Referring to breath sounds*] [*Medicine*] (DAVI)
MET.......... Metallic [*Automotive advertising*]
met.......... Metallophone
MET.......... Metallurgical
met.......... Metallurgy (MIST)
MET.......... Metalore Resources Ltd. [*Toronto Stock Exchange symbol*]
Met.......... Metamorphoses [*of Ovid*] [*Classical studies*] (OCD)
Met.......... Metamorphoses [*of Apuleius*] [*Classical studies*] (OCD)
MET.......... Metaphor
MET.......... Metaphysics
Met.......... Metastasis [*Medicine*] (AMHC)
met.......... Metastasis [*Medicine*] (BCRP)
MET.......... Metastasis [*Medicine*] (EDAA)
MET.......... Metatarsus [*Flamenco dance term*]
Met.......... Metcalfe's Reports [*58-61 Kentucky*] [*A publication*] (DLA)
Met.......... Metcalf's Reports [*Rhode Island*] [*A publication*] (DLA)
Met.......... Metcalf's Reports [*Massachusetts*] [*A publication*] (DLA)
MET.......... MET Electrical Testing Co [*Medicine*] (EDAA)
MET.......... Meteorological (NAKS)
MET.......... Meteorological Broadcast (IAA)
MET.......... Meteorological Committee (SAUO)
MET.......... Meteorological Office [*British*] (DSUE)
MET.......... Meteorological Research Flight [*British*] [*ICAO designator*] (FAAC)
MET.......... Meteorologist [*Emergency Management*] (EMA)
MET.......... Meteorology (AFM)
MET.......... Methionine (DB)
met.......... Methionine [*An amino acid*] (DOG)
Met.......... Methionine [*Also, M*] [*An amino acid*]
MET.......... MetLife [*NYSE symbol*]
MET.......... Metro (automobile) [*NCIC car model code*]
MET.......... Metronome [*Music*]
MET.......... Metropark, NJ [*Amtrak rail station code*]
MET.......... Metropolis (ROG)
MET.......... Metropolitan (AAG)
Met.......... Metropolitan (DIAR)
met.......... Metropolitan (ELAL)
MET.......... Metropolitan (automobile) [*NCIC car model code*]
Met.......... Metropolitan Correction Center (SAUO)
MET.......... Metropolitan Electric Tramways [*British*] (ROG)
Met.......... Metropolitan Museum of Art (SAUO)
MET.......... Metropolitan Music Hall [*London*] [*British*] (DSUE)
Met.......... Metropolitan Opera (SAUO)
Met.......... [*New York*] Metropolitan Opera House
Met.......... Metropolitan Police [*British*] (WDAA)
MET.......... [*The*] Metropolitan Railway [*British*] (ROG)
MET.......... Metropolitan Realty [*AMEX symbol*] (TTSB)
MET.......... Metropolitan Realty Corp. [*AMEX symbol*] (CTT)
MET.......... Metropolitan Transport Authority (SAUO)
MET.......... Metuchen [*Diocesan abbreviation*] [*New Jersey*] (TOCD)
MET.......... Micro-Electronic Technology (ADA)
MET.......... Middle European Time (SAUO)
MET.......... Mid-European Time (SAUO)
MET.......... Midexpiratory Time [*Medicine*]
MET.......... Midshipman Embarkation Team [*Navy*]
MET.......... Minimum Energy Trajectory
MET.......... Minimum Essentials Test [*Educational test*]
MET.......... Minimum Exposure Time
MET.......... Minor Expendable Tool (MCD)
MET.......... Missile Electrical Technician [*Aerospace*] (IAA)
MET.......... Missile Escort Team [*Air Force*] (AFM)
MET.......... Mission Elapsed Time [*NASA*] (NAKS)
MET.......... Mission Entry Time
MET.......... Mission Environment Tape
MET.......... Mission Equipment Team (ACAE)
MET.......... Mission Event Timer [*NASA*] (KSC)
MET.......... Mobile Engineering Team [*Navy*]
MET.......... Mobile Environmental Teams (SAUO)
MET.......... Mobile Equipment Transporter [*NASA*]
MET.......... Mobile Examining Team (SAUO)
MET.......... Modality Examination Terminal (DMAA)
MET.......... Modesto & Empire Traction Co. [*Formerly, METC*] [*AAR code*]
MET.......... Modified Expansion Tube (IEEE)
MET.......... Modular Equipment Transporter [*NASA*]
MET.......... Molecular Electronic Technique
MET.......... Mond Excavation at Thebes [*London*] [*A publication*] (BJA)
MET.......... Monitoring & Enforcement Teams (SAUO)
MET.......... Motorola Environmental Telemetry
MET.......... Multibutton Electronic Telephone (NITA)
MET.......... Multi-Element Tracker (ACAE)
MET.......... Multiemitter Transistor
MET.......... Multi-Environment Trainer (MCD)
MET.......... Multiple Employer Trust [*Insurance*]
MET.......... Multistage Exercise Test (DMAA)
MET.......... Multistage Exercise Testing (DB)
MET.......... Sensor Meteorological Satellite Sensor (SAUS)
META........ Computer series [*Digital Scientific*]
META........ Maintenance Engineering Training Agency (SAUO)
META........ Management Engineering Training Agency (SAUO)
META........ Maritime Education and Training Act of 1980
META........ Maryland Electronics Technicians Association (SAUO)
META........ Megachannel Extraterrestrial Array [*For receiving possible radio signals from non-earth civilizations*]
META........ Megachannel Extra-Terrestrial Assay
meta........ Metacarpal [*Anatomy*] (DAVI)
META........ Metal Craft Manufacturing [*NCIC trailer make code*]
META........ metamyelocyte [*Hematology*] (DAVI)
meta........ Metatarsal [*Anatomy*] (DAVI)
META........ Metatec Corp. [*NASDAQ symbol*] (SAG)
META........ Metatec International, Inc. [*NASDAQ symbol*] (NASQ)
META........ Methods of Extracting Text Automatically [*Programming language*] [*General Electric Co.*] [*Computer science*] (IEEE)
META........ Metropolitan Educational Television Association [*Canada*]
META........ Model Engineering Trade Association [*British*] (BI)
META 1...... Metabolic Profile 1 [*Biochemistry*] (DAVI)
METAB...... Metabolism
METABC..... Metabolic (ABBR)
Metabol..... Metabolism: Clinical and Experimental (MEC)
METABZ..... Metabolize (ABBR)
METABZD... Metabolized (ABBR)
METABZG... Metabolizing (ABBR)
METAC...... Medium Tactical Transport Aircraft [*Military*]
METAC...... Methacryloyloxyethyltrimethylammonium Chloride [*Organic chemistry*]
METADEX... Metal Abstracts Index Data Base [*Bibliographic database*] [*British*] (IID)
METADEX... Metals Abstracts Inex (NITA)
METADS..... Meteorological Acquisition and Display System (PDAA)
METAF...... Meteorological Terminal Aviation Weather Forecast [*FAA*] (TAG)
METAG...... Meteorological Advisory Group [*ICAO*] (DA)
MetaGp..... Meta Group, Inc. [*Associated Press*] (SAG)
META II..... Megachannel Extra Terrestrial Array II (SAUS)
METAL...... Machine Evaluation & Translation Language (SAUO)
METAL...... Meta-Language (VLIE)
Metal........ Metallurgy (DIAR)
METAL...... Metallurgy
METAL...... Militarily Significant Emergent Technologies Awareness List [*Proposed*] [*DoD*]
Metalcld.... Metaclad Corp. [*Associated Press*] (SAG)
Metalcld.... Metalclad Corp. [*Associated Press*] (SAG)
METALESCAUT... Societe Metallurgique de l'Escaut (EFIS)
Metall....... Metallurgy (BEE)
METALL..... Metallurgy
METALLOG... Metallography (DGA)
Metall Rep Aeronaut Res Lab Aust... Australia. Aeronautical Research Laboratories. Metallurgy Report (journ.) (SAUS)
Metall Tech Memo Aust Aeronaut Res Lab... Australia. Aeronautical Research Laboratories Metallurgy Technical Memorandum (journ.) (SAUS)
MetalR...... Metallica Resources, Inc. [*Associated Press*] (SAG)
META M..... Metaphysical Magazine [*A publication*] (ROG)
Metamin.... Metals and Minerals Investment Corp. Ltd. (SAUO)
MET & E.... Medical Equipment Test and Evaluation [*Army Medical Material Agency*] (PDAA)
MET&E...... Medical Equipment Test and Evaluation Division (SAUO)
METAPH..... Metaphorical (ROG)
Metaph...... Metaphysica [*of Aristotle*] [*Classical studies*] (OCD)
METAPH..... Metaphysical [*or Metaphysics*] (ROG)
METAPH..... Metaphysician (ABBR)
metaph...... Metaphysics [*Parapsychology*] (DAVI)
METAPHYS... Metaphysic (ABBR)
METAPLAN... Methods of Extracting Text Automatically Programming - Language [*General Electric Co.*] [*Computer science*] (IEEE)
METAR...... Aviation Route Weather Report (SAUO)
METAR...... Aviation Routine Weather Report [*ICAO*] (FAAC)
METAR...... Meteorological Actual Report (WEAT)
METAR...... Meteorological Aviation Report (SAUO)

METAR ...... Meteorological Terminal Aviation Routine Weather Report [*FAA*] (TAG)
METAS ...... Metastasize [*Medicine*]
MetaSft ..... Meta-Software, Inc. [*Associated Press*] (SAG)
METASYMBOL... Metalanguage Symbol
Metatec ..... Metatec Corp. [*Associated Press*] (SAG)
METATH ..... Metathesis
METB .... Metal Base
METB .... MetroBanCorp [*NASDAQ symbol*] (SAG)
METB .... Metropolitan Borough
METBX ...... Mgn. Stanley D. Witter Precious Metals & Min. [*Mutual fund ticker symbol*] (SG)
METC .... Medesto & Empire Traction Co. (MHDB)
METC .... Metal Curb (AAG)
METC .... Metallic (VLIE)
Metc .... Metcalfe's Reports [*58-61 Kentucky*] [*A publication*] (DLA)
Metc .... Metcalf's Reports [*Massachusetts*] [*A publication*] (DLA)
Metc .... Metcalf's Reports [*Rhode Island*] [*A publication*] (DLA)
METC .... Metropolitan Conference (PSS)
METC .... Military Equipment Test Center (CAAL)
METC .... Modesto & Empire Traction Co. [*Later, MET*] [*AAR code*]
METC .... Monthly Estimate to Completion (MCD)
METC .... Morgantown Energy Technology Center [*Morgantown, WV*] [*Department of Energy*] (GRD)
METC .... Mouse Embryo Tissue Culture
METCA ...... Merchant Token Collectors Association (EA)
METCA ...... Metcalf, IL [*American Association of Railroads railroad junction routing code*]
METCAL..... Metrology and Calibration [*Air Force*] (AFIT)
METCAN .... Metal Matrix Composite Analyzer [*Organic chemistry*]
MET-CAR.... Metallo-Carbohedrene [*Organic chemistry*]
Metc Cont... Metcalf on the Law of Contracts [*A publication*] (DLA)
METCHEM... Metals/Materials, Fabricating and Testing Conference and Show for the Petrochemical Industry (SAUO)
METCIR ..... Metropolitan Circuits, Inc. (SAUO)
Metc KY.... Metcalfe's Reports [*58-61 Kentucky*] [*A publication*] (DLA)
Metc Mass... Metcalf's Reports [*Massachusetts*] [*A publication*] (DLA)
Met Co ...... Meteorological Company (SAUO)
METCO ...... Meteorological Coordinating Committee (SAUO)
METCO ...... Meteorological Coordination Office (SAUO)
METCO ...... Meteorological Coordination Officer (MUGU)
METCO ...... Metropolitan Council for Educational Opportunity (EA)
METCO ...... Mobile Engine Tester, Computer-Operated (DNAB)
METCO ...... Mullins Environmental Testing Co., Inc. (EFIS)
MetCoil ..... Met Coil Systems Corp. [*Associated Press*] (SAG)
METCOM.... Mechanical and Metal Trades Confederation [*United Kingdom*] (EAIO)
METCON .... Metropolitan Consortium for Minorities in Science and Engineering (USDC)
Metc Yelv... Metcalf's Edition of Yelverton [*A publication*] (DLA)
METD........ Management Education Training and Development (AIE)
METD........ Mean Effective Temperature Difference [*Refrigeration*]
METD........ Metal Door
METD........ Metastatic Disease [*Oncology*]
METDLGY... Methodology
MetDR....... Metropolitan District Railway (SAUO)
METDST..... Middle European Time Daylight Saving Time (SAUO)
METE........ Hungarian Scientific Society for the Food Industry (SAUO)
Met E........ Metallurgical Engineer
METE........ Meteor [*NCIC car make code*]
Mete......... Meteorologica [*of Aristotle*] [*Classical studies*] (OCD)
METE........ Multiple ECM [*Electronic Countermeasures*] Threat Environment [*Military*] (CAAL)
METE........ Multiple Engagement Test Environment [*Military*] (PDAA)
METE........ Multiple Environment Threat Emitter (MCD)
METEC ...... Meteoroid Technology [*Satellite*] [*NASA*]
METEC ...... Meteorologist Technician (NOAA)
MetEC....... Metropolitan Edison Capital Ltd. [*Associated Press*] (SAG)
METEI .... Medical Expedition to Eastern Island (SAUO)
MetEng...... Metallurgical Engineering (DD)
METEOR .... Manned Earth-Satellite Terminal Evolving from Earth-to-Orbit Ferry Rockets (SAA)
METEOR .... Marine Environmental Testing and Electro-Optical Radiation (MCD)
METEOR .... Meteorological Event Oriented Reporting System (SAUO)
METEOR .... Meteorological Satellite [*Former USSR*]
METEOR .... Meteorology
Meteor ...... Meteorology
METEOR .... Multiple Experiment Transporter into Earth Orbit and Return (SAUS)
METEOR .... Operational Weather Satellite (SAUO)
METEORIT... Meteoritical
Meteorol .... Meteorological (SAUO)
meteorol .... Meteorology (ADWA)
Meteorol .... Meteorology (BEE)
METEOROL... Meteorology
Meteorol Appl... Meteorological Applications [*A publication*] (PABS)
Meteorol Atmos Phys... Meteorology and Atmospheric Physics (SAUO)
Meteorol Mag... Meteorological Magazine [*A publication*] (PABS)
METEOROLO... Meteorology (ABBR)
METEOSAT... ESA Geostationary Meteorological Satellite (SAUS)
METEOSAT... European earth resources and meteorological satellite of the ESA program (SAUS)
METEOSAT... European Geostationary Meteorological Satellite (SAUO)
Meteosat.... European Geostationary Meteorological Satellite operated by EUMETSAT (SAUS)
METEOSAT... European Space Agency Meteorological Satellite (SAUS)
METEOSAT... Geosynchronous Meteorology Satellite (EOSA)
METEOSAT... Meteorological Satellite [*European Space Agency*]
METEOSAT... Meteorology Satellite (SAUO)
METEOSAT-3... European Space Agency geostationary meteorological satellite (SAUS)
METEOSTAT... European Meteorological Satellite (SAUO)
METEPA..... Tris(methylethylene)phosphoric Triamide [*Organic chemistry*]
METER ...... Machine Examination Teaching, Evaluation, and Re-education (PDAA)
METF .... Metal Flashing
MetFACS.... Metropolitan Life Insurance Co. Financial and Administrative Customer Services System (HGAA)
METG........ META Group [*NASDAQ symbol*] (TTSB)
METG........ Meta Group, Inc. [*NASDAQ symbol*] (SAG)
METG........ Metal Grill
METG........ Middle East Task Group (DNAB)
METG........ Military Effects Test Group (SAUO)
METGG ...... Medium-Emission Tear Gas Grenade [*Police and security equipment*]
METGL ...... Meteorological (WGA)
MetGlob.... Metro Global Media, Inc. [*Associated Press*] (SAG)
Meth......... Mercaptoethanol [*Organic chemistry*]
METH........ Methadone (ABBR)
METH........ Methamphetamine (ABBR)
meth......... Methamphetamine (ADWA)
METH........ Methane (AAG)
Meth......... Methaphetamine Hydrochloride [*An amphetamine, commonly known as speed*] (VNW)
Meth......... Methedrine [*Stimulant*]
METH........ Methicillin [*An antibiotic*]
METH........ Method (ROG)
METH........ Methode Electronics, Inc. [*NASDAQ symbol*] (NQ)
Meth......... Methodist (WDAA)
METH........ Methodist
meth......... Methyl [*Organic chemistry*] (DAVI)
METH........ Methylated (ADA)
METH........ Methylated Spirit (DSUE)
METH........ Methylmeth (ABBR)
METH........ Methyprylon (ABBR)
METHA ...... Methode Electronics [*NASDAQ symbol*]
METHA ...... Methode Electronics'A' [*NASDAQ symbol*] (TTSB)
METHALC... Method of Alcohol-Determination [*National Highway Traffic Safety Administration Fatal Accident Recording System code*]
Methanx .... Methanex Corp. [*Associated Press*] (SAG)
MetHb....... Methemoglobin [*Biochemistry, medicine*]
METHB ...... Methode Electronics [*NASDAQ symbol*]
METHB ...... Methode Electronics'B' [*NASDAQ symbol*] (TTSB)
METH BL.... Methylene Blue (SAUS)
METHC ...... Methodic (ABBR)
MethCh..... Methodist Chaplain [*Navy*] [*British*]
MeThCh..... Methylthiocholine [*Biochemistry*]
Meth Ch Ca... Report of Methodist Church Cases [*A publication*] (DLA)
Methd .... Methode Electronics, Inc. [*Associated Press*] (SAG)
METHDST... Methodist
METHEN .... Methenamine (SAUS)
METHEN MAN... Methenamine Mandelate (SAUS)
METHEN SULF... Methenamine Sulfate (SAUS)
METHEN SULFOSAL... Methenamine Sulfosalicylate (SAUS)
Meth Epis... Methodist Episcopal (SAUO)
MeTHF ...... Methyltetrahydrofolic Acid [*Biochemistry*]
met hgh..... Methemoglobin [*Biochemistry*] (DAVI)
METHIMAZOLE... Methylmercaptoimidazole [*Also, MMI*] [*Thyroid inhibitor*]
METHO ...... Methodology (ABBR)
METHOG .... Methodology (ABBR)
METHOGL... Methodological (ABBR)
METHS ...... Methylated Spirits (ADA)
METH SAL.. Methyl Salicylate (SAUS)
methyl-CCNU... Methyl-1-(2-chloroethyl)-3-cyclohexyl-1 Nitrosourea [*Antineoplastic drug regimen*] (DAVI)
Methyl-GAG... Methylglyoxal-bis-guanylhydrazone [*Antineoplastic drug*] (CDI)
METHYLPRED ACE... Methylprednisolone Acetate (SAUS)
METHYL TEST... Methyltestosterone (SAUS)
METHZ ...... Methodize (ABBR)
METHZD .... Methodized (ABBR)
METI......... Major Engineering Test Item (AAG)
METI......... Medical Education Technologies, Inc.
METIC .... Meticulous (ABBR)
METIMP..... Meteorological Equipment Improvement Program (NG)
METIS .... Meteorological Information System (SAUO)
METJ .... Metal Jalousie
METJC....... Methven Junction, MB [*American Association of Railroads railroad junction routing code*]
METJET ..... Meteorological Sounding Rocket, Ramjet-Powered [*NASA*] (SAA)
METK........ Memtek, Inc. [*NASDAQ symbol*] (COMM)
METKIT...... Metrics Education Toolkit (SAUO)
METL........ Materials and Ecological Testing Laboratory [*Research center*] (RCD)
METL........ Metal
METL........ Metallica Resources, Inc. [*NASDAQ symbol*] (SAG)
METL........ Metallurgy (VLIE)
METL........ Mission Essential Task List [*Army*] (INF)
METL........ Multielement Two-Layer (AAEL)
METL........ Region 4 Metals System (SAUS)
METLA ...... Finnish Forest Research Institute (SAUO)

METLAB..... Media and Entertainment Technologies Laboratory [*Michigan State University*] (RCD)
Met Lab..... Metabolic Laboratory [*Colorado State University*] (RCD)
MET LAB.... Metallurgical Laboratory (SAUO)
METLAND... Metropolitan Landscape Planning Model (SAUO)
METLC........ Metallic
METLIFE.... Metropolitan Life Insurance Co. (EFIS)
METLIFE.... Metropolitan Life Insurance Company Employees' Political Participation Fund [*New York, NY*] (PACS)
Met Lith Assn... Metropolitan Lithographers Association (SAUO)
METLLRGCL... Metallurgical
METLLRGST... Metallurgist
METLO...... Metrological Equipment and Technical Liaison Officer [*Navy*] (NG)
METM....... Master of Engineering and Technology Management (PGP)
METM....... Metal Mold
MET/M...... Missile Engine Technician/Mechanic (AAG)
Metmail..... Metromail Corp. [*Associated Press*] (SAG)
Met Man.... Metro Manila (SAUO)
metMb....... Metmyoglobin [*Medicine*] (MEDA)
METMF...... Marine Corps Meteorological Mobile Facility (SAUO)
m et n....... Mane et Nocte [*Morning and night*] [*Latin*] [*Pharmacy*] (DAVI)
M et N...... Mane et Nocte [*Morning and Night*] [*Pharmacy*]
METNF...... MetroNet Communications Corp. [*Toronto Stock Exchange symbol*] [*Canada*]
METNO...... Advance telegraphic notification relating to the operation of WWW (SAUS)
METO........ Maximum Engine Takeoff [*Power*] [*Air Force*]
METO........ Maximum Except during Takeoff
METO........ Maximum Except Take-Off (SAUS)
METO........ Mediterranean Treaty Organization (SAUO)
METO........ Meteorological Office [*or Officer*] [*Air Force*]
METO........ Meteorological Officer (SAUO)
METO........ Metoo Travel Trailer [*NCIC trailer make code*]
METO........ Metro Capital Corp. [*NASDAQ symbol*] (SAG)
METO........ Middle East Treaty Organization
METOB....... Meteorologist Observation (NOAA)
METOC...... Bureau of Meteorology and Oceanographic Services (SAUS)
METOC...... Meteorological and Oceanographic (SAUO)
METOF...... Meteorological Office
Met Off...... Meteorological Office [*British*] (AIA)
METOFOR... Methodology for Total Force Concept [*Military*]
METON...... Measured Tons Discharged or Loaded [*Shipping*]
meton....... metonymice (SAUS)
METON...... Metonymy
METOP...... Maximum Expected Takeoff Power (AFM)
METOP...... Meteorological Operation (SAUO)
METOP...... Meteorological Operational Satellite (SAUS)
METOP...... Meteorological Orbiting Platform (SAUS)
Metopera... Metropolitan Opera Association (EA)
MeToV....... United States Veterans Administration Center, Togus, ME [*Library symbol*] [*Library of Congress*] (LCLS)
METOXI..... Military Effectiveness in a Toxin Environment (AABC)
METP........ Metal Partition
METP........ Metal Portion
MET P&C... Metropolitan Property & Casualty Insurance Co. (EFIS)
MetPro...... Met-Pro Corp. [*Associated Press*] (SAG)
metpt........ Metalpoint (VRA)
METR........ Metal Roof
METR........ Meteorology (NG)
Metr......... Metropolitan (RION)
METR........ Metropolitan
METR........ Metropolitan [*NCIC car make code*]
MetR......... Metropolitan Railway [*British*]
METR........ Minimum Essential Training Requirements
METRA...... Media Education Training (SAUO)
METRA...... Metal RADAR
METRA...... Multiple-Event Time Recording Apparatus (PDAA)
MetraB...... Metra Biosystems [*Associated Press*] (SAG)
MetrBcp..... MetroBancorp [*Associated Press*] (SAG)
Metrbk...... Metrobank North America [*Associated Press*] (SAG)
MetrCap..... Metro Capital Corp. [*Associated Press*] (SAG)
Metrcm...... Metricom, Inc. [*Associated Press*] (SAG)
METREX..... Metropolitan Centrex [*Telephone network*]
METRG...... Metering (VLIE)
METRI....... Military Essentiality through Readiness Indices
METRIA..... Metropolitan Tree Improvement Alliance (EA)
METRIC..... Multiechelon Technique for Recoverable Item Control (MCD)
MetrisCo.... Metris Companies, Inc. [*Associated Press*] (SAG)
METRL...... Meteorology (NG)
METRL...... Metrology Requirements List [*DoD*]
METRLGST... Meteorologist
MetRlt....... Metropolitan Realty Corp. [*Associated Press*] (SAG)
MetrNet..... Metro Networks, Inc. [*Associated Press*] (SAG)
METRO...... Materiel Essential to Reconstitution Operations [*Air Force*] (AFM)
METRO...... Messenger Transport Organizer [*Developmental biology*]
METRO...... Meteorological (SAUO)
METRO...... Meteorological Equipment Terminal and Representative Observation (MCD)
METRO...... Meteorology
METRO...... Metering and Traffic Recording with Offline Processing (PDAA)
Metro........ Metro-Goldwyn-Mayer (WDMC)
METRO...... Metropolis, IL [*American Association of Railroads railroad junction routing code*]
Metro........ Metropolitan (AL)
metro........ Metropolitan (SHCU)
METRO...... Metropolitan
METRO...... Metropolitan Collegiate Athletic Conference (EA)
METRO...... Metropolitan Reference and Research Library Organization (SAUO)
METRO...... Michigan Effectuation, Training, and Research Organization [*Computer-programmed simulation game*]
METRO...... New York Metropolitan Reference and Research Library Agency [*Brooklyn, NY*] [*Library network*]
MetroBcp... Metropolitan Bancorp [*Associated Press*] (SAG)
METROC... Meteorological Rocket
Metrocall... Metrocall, Inc. [*Associated Press*] (SAG)
MetroFn..... Metro Financial Corp. [*Associated Press*] (SAG)
Metrogs..... Metrogas SA [*Associated Press*] (SAG)
METROL... Metrology
Metrolog.... Metrologic Instruments, Inc. [*Associated Press*] (SAG)
Metromda... Metromedia International Group [*Associated Press*] (SAG)
METROMEX... Metropolitan Meteorological Experiment
METROP.... Metropol (WDAA)
METROP.... Metropolis (ADA)
METROP.... Metropolitan
METROPOL... Metropolis [*or Metropolitan*] (ABBR)
Metropolis... World Association of the Major Metropolises (SAUO)
Metrotrn.... Metrotrans Corp. [*Associated Press*] (SAG)
MetroV...... MetroVision of North America, Inc. [*Associated Press*] (SAG)
METRRA..... Metal Re-Radiation RADAR [*Mine detection system*] [*Army*] (RDA)
MetRS........ Methionyl-Transfer Ribonucleic Acid Synthetase [*An enzyme*]
MetrTl........ Metro-Tel Corp. [*Associated Press*] (SAG)
MetrV......... MetroVision of North America, Inc. [*Associated Press*] (SAG)
METS........ Maintainability Evaluation and Tracking System (MCD)
METS........ Maintenance Equipment Transport System (SAUO)
METS........ Masters Exercise Tests [*Medicine*] (EDAA)
METS........ Materials and Equipment Trading Service (AAEL)
METS........ Mechanized Export Traffic System [*Army*] (AABC)
METS........ Metabolic Equivalents [*Medicine*] [*of oxygen consumption*] (EDAA)
METS........ Metadata Encoding and Transmission Standard
METS........ Metal Strip
mets......... metastases (SAUS)
Mets......... Metastasis [*Oncology*] (MAE)
METS........ Met-Coil Systems [*NASDAQ symbol*] (TTSB)
METS........ Met-Coil Systems Corp. [*NASDAQ symbol*] (NQ)
METS........ Metropolitan Emergency Telephone System (COE)
METS........ Microwave Engine Timing System [*Automotive engineering*]
METS........ Mineral and Energy Technology Sector (FOTI)
METS........ Mining and Earthmoving Technology System
METS........ Missile Electrical Technician Specialist (SAUO)
MET/S....... Missile Electrical Technician/Specialist (AAG)
METS........ Missile Environmental Testing Study
METS........ Mobile Electronic Test Set (MCD)
METS........ Mobile Engine Test Stand
METS........ Modified Engineered Time Standards
METS........ Modular Engine Test System (MCD)
METS........ Modularized Equipment Transport System [*NASA*]
METS........ Multiple Exposure Testing System [*Advertising analysis*]
METSAAT... Meteorological Satellite (USDC)
metsat....... Meteorological Satellite (ODA)
MET/SAT.... Meteorological Satellite
METSATS... Multi-Echelon Tester Standard Analog Test Set (ACAE)
METSATT... Meteorological Satellite [*Marine science*] (OSRA)
Met Serv.... Meteorological Service (SAUO)
m et sig..... Misce et Signa [*Mix and write a label*] [*Latin*] [*Pharmacy*] (DAVI)
M et Sig..... Misce et Signa [*Mix and Label*] [*Pharmacy*]
m et sign... Misce et Signa [*Mix and Label*] [*Latin*] (WDAA)
METSII/ACI... Military Export Traffic System II-Enhanced/Automated Carrier Interface (SAUO)
METT........ Manned, Evasive Target Tank [*Army*]
METT........ Maximum Exercise Tolerance Test (DMAA)
METT........ Microwave Energy Transmission Test (SSD)
METT........ Mission, Enemy, Terrain and Troops (SAUO)
METT........ Mission, Enemy, Terrain and Weather, Troops and Firepower Available
METTAG..... Medical Emergency Triage Tag [*Emergency Management*] (EMA)
Met Tec..... Meteorologist Technician (SAUO)
METTL...... Microelectronics and Emerging Technologies Thermal Laboratory [*Georgia Institute of Technology*] (RCD)
METTM...... Mission, Enemy, Terrain and Weather, Troops and Firepower Available, and Maneuver Space (MCD)
Met Tr J..... Metal Trades Journal [*A publication*]
METT-T...... Mission, Enemy, Terrain and Weather, Troops and Firepower Available and Time (INF)
METT-T...... Mission, Enemy, Terrain, Troops, and Time [*Military*]
METTW...... Mission, Enemy, Terrain, Tactics, Weather [*Criteria for establishing military strategy*] [*Army*] (VNW)
METU........ Enichem Polimeri [*Intermodal shipping container symbol*] (TVRC)
METU........ Marine Electronic Technical Unit (MUGU)
METU........ Mobile Electronics Technical Unit
METU........ Mobile Electronics Training Unit
METVC...... Main Engine Thrust Vector [*Aerospace*] (NAKS)
METVC...... Main Engine Thrust Vector Control (MCD)
METW....... Military Emergency Travel Warrant [*MTMC*] (TAG)
METW....... Municipality of East Troy, Wisconsin [*AAR code*]
MET Watch... Meteorological Watch (SAUO)
metwk....... Metalwork (VRA)
METX........ Illinois Regional Commuter Railroad [*Private rail car owner code*]
Metz......... Metzenbaum [*Instruments*] [*Surgery*] (DAVI)

METZ .... Metzendorf Trailer Manufacturing [*NCIC trailer make code*]
METZ .... Metzler Group, Inc. [*NASDAQ symbol*] (NASQ)
meu.......... Maine [*MARC country of publication code*] [*Library of Congress*] (LCCP)
MEU .... Main Electronics Unit (SAUS)
MEU .... Main Electronic Unit (INF)
MEU .... Marine Expeditionary Unit
MEU .... Marromeu [*Mozambique*] [*Airport symbol*] (AD)
MEU .... Maximum Expected Utility (DMAA)
MEU .... Memory Expansion Unit
MEU .... Message Encoder Unit
MEU .... Methylumbelliferone [*Biochemistry*]
MEU .... Mind Extension University [*Cable television channel*]
MEU .... Mission Essential Unit (SAUO)
MEU .... Modern English Usage (WDAA)
MEU .... Multiplexer Encoder Unit
MEU .... Municipal Electricity Undertaking
MeU .... University of Maine, Orono, ME [*Library symbol*] [*Library of Congress*] (LCLS)
MEUA........ Million European Units of Account (PDAA)
MEUF........ Micellar-Enhanced Ultrafiltration [*Chemical engineering*]
MEUG .... Major Energy Users' Group [*British*]
MeU-G ...... University of Maine at Portland/Gorham, Gorham, ME [*Library symbol*] [*Library of Congress*] (LCLS)
MEUI .... Machine Effective Utilization Index (LDOE)
MeU-L....... University of Maine, Law Library, Portland, ME [*Library symbol*] [*Library of Congress*] (LCLS)
MEULEX..... Marine Expeditionary Unit Landing Exercise (NVT)
MeUmb ..... Methylumbelliferyl [*Biochemistry*]
MeU-P....... University of Maine at Portland/Gorham, Portland, ME [*Library symbol*] [*Library of Congress*] (LCLS)
MEU/SOC ... Marine Expeditionary Unit/Special Opperations Capable (MUSM)
MEV .... Manned Entry Vehicle
MEV .... Mars Excursion Vehicle (SAUO)
MEV .... Maximal Exercise Ventilation (MELL)
MEV .... Medical Evacuation Vehicle (MCD)
MeV .... Mega-Electronvolt (ODBW)
MEV .... Mega [*or Million*] Electron Volts
MEV .... Middle Ear Ventilation (MELL)
meV .... Millielectron Volt(s), 1 E-3 eV [*Industrial hygiene term*] (OHS)
MEV .... Million Electron Volts (MCD)
MeV .... Million Electronvolts (COE)
MEV .... Minden, NV [*Location identifier*] [*FAA*] (FAAL)
MEV .... Murine Erythroblastosis Virus [*Medicine*] (DB)
MEV .... Myalgic Encephalomyelitis Virus [*Medicine*] (EDAA)
MEvA .... Avco-Everett Research Laboratory, Everett, MA [*Library symbol*] [*Library of Congress*] (LCLS)
MEVE........ Mesa Verde National Park
MeVEMsJ... Mercury, Venus, Earth, Mars, Jupiter (PDAA)
MEVMA ..... Maine Veterinary Medical Association (GVA)
MEvP .... Parlin Memorial Library, Everett, MA [*Library symbol*] [*Library of Congress*] (LCLS)
MEVU........ Morcon [*Intermodal shipping container symbol*] (TVRC)
MEW......... Maintenance Equipment Wing (SAUO)
MEW......... Manitoba Department of Environment, Workplace Safety, and Health [*UTLAS symbol*]
MEW......... Manufactures Empty Weight (MCD)
MEW......... Marine Early Warning
MEW......... Mean Equivalent Wind [*Meteorology*] (DA)
MEW......... Measure of Economic Welfare
MEW......... Metalsmith (Welder) [*U.S. Navy enlisted rating*] (AUER)
MEW......... Microwave Early Warning [*Radio*] [*Air Force*]
MEW......... Microwave Early Warning Radar (SAUO)
MEW......... Middle East Watch [*An association*] (EA)
MEW......... Minimum Envelope Weight (MCD)
MEW......... Ministry of Economic Warfare [*British*]
MEW......... Missionaries of the Eternal Word [*Formerly, CFMA*] (EA)
MEW......... Mobile Early Warning
MEW......... Modern English Writers [*A publication*]
MEW......... Monroe, WA [*Amtrak Busline code*]
MeW......... Waterville Public Library, Waterville, ME [*Library symbol*] [*Library of Congress*] (LCLS)
MEWA....... Ministry of Education, Western Australia
MEWA....... Missile Electronics Warfare Area (ACAE)
MEWA....... Motor and Equipment Wholesalers Association [*Later, ASIA*]
MEWA....... Multiple Employer Welfare Arrangement
MEWA....... Multiple-Employer Welfare Association (WYGK)
MEWAC ..... Mediterranean Europe, West Africa Conference (SAUO)
MeWC....... Colby College, Waterville, ME [*Library symbol*] [*Library of Congress*] (LCLS)
MEWC....... Middle East Section of the War Cabinet [*British*] [*World War II*]
MEWC....... Middle East War Council [*British military*] (DMA)
MEWD....... Missile Electronic Warfare Division [*White Sands Missile Range*] (AAG)
MEWDS ..... Multifocal Evanescent White Dot Syndrome (SAUS)
MeWe .... Wells Public Library, Wells, ME [*Library symbol*] [*Library of Congress*] (LCLS)
MeWebr..... Walker Memorial Library, Westbrook, ME [*Library symbol*] [*Library of Congress*] (LCLS)
MEWES ..... Mobile Electronic Warfare Environment Simulator (ACAE)
MEWETS.... Multiple Electronic Warfare Emitter Target System (ACAE)
MEWG....... Maintenance Engineering Working Group [*NASA*] (NASA)
MEWO....... Manufacturing Engineering Work Order (MCD)
MEWP....... Matthews Transportation Service [*Common carrier symbol*]
MEWPP ..... Modular Electronic Warfare Pre-Processor (SAUS)
MEWS....... Mews [*Postal Service standard*] (OPSA)
Mews....... Mews' Digest of English Case Law [*A publication*] (DLA)
MEWS....... Microwave Electronic Warfare System
MEWS....... Missile Early Warning Station (AFM)
MEWS....... Missile Early Warning System (ACAE)
MEWS....... Missile Electronic Warfare System [*Army*]
MEWS....... Mission Essential Weapon System [*Military*] (CAAL)
MEWS....... Mobile Electronic Warfare Simulator (MCD)
MEWS....... Modular Electronic Warfare Simulator [*Navy*]
MEWS....... Modular Electronic Warfare System (ACAE)
MEWS....... Modular EW Simulator (SAUS)
MEWS....... Mono-Extraction Workstation (SAUO)
Mews....... [*The*] Reports [*1893-95*] [*England*] [*A publication*] (DLA)
Mews Dig... Mews' Digest of English Case Law [*A publication*] (DLA)
MEWSG..... Maritime Electronic Warfare Support Group (SAUO)
MEWSG..... Multinational Electronic Warfare Support Group (SAUO)
MEWSG..... Multiservice Electronic Warfare Support Group [*Originally Maritime Electronic Warfare Support Group*] [*NATO*] (DOMA)
MEWSS ..... Mobile Electronic Warfare Support System [*Military*] (LAIN)
MEWT .... Matrix Electrostatic Writing Technique
MEWT .... Microelectronic Weld Tester
MEWTA...... Missile Electronic Warfare Technical Area [*White Sands Missile Range*] (AABC)
MEWU....... Metal and Engineering Workers Union (SAUO)
MEWU....... Qatar Ministry of Electricity and Water [*Intermodal shipping container symbol*] (TVRC)
MEWUSA ... Metal and Electrical Workers Union of South Africa (SAUO)
MEX .... Mariner Explorations [*Vancouver Stock Exchange symbol*]
M Ex......... Master of Expression
MEx.......... Mekhilta Exodus (BJA)
MEX .... Memorex Corp., Memorex Technical Information Library, Santa Clara, CA [*OCLC symbol*] (OCLC)
MEX .... Metro Express II, Inc. [*ICAO designator*] (FAAC)
Mex.......... Mexican (DIAR)
MEX .... Mexican (ROG)
MEX .... Mexico [*ANSI three-letter standard code*] (CNC)
Mex.......... Mexico (VRA)
MEX .... Mexico (automobile) [*NCIC car model code*]
MEX .... Mexico City [*Mexico*] [*Airport symbol*] (OAG)
MEX .... Microcell Extender (SAUS)
MEX .... Microelectronics (SAUS)
MEX .... Military Engineering Experimental Establishment [*British*]
MEX .... Military Exchange
MEX .... Mississippi Export Railroad (IIA)
MEX .... Mobile Exercise
MEX .... MODEM Executive [*Computer telecommunications program*]
MEX .... Temporary Rank [*Army slang*]
MEXA........ Mexicana Airlines [*Common carrier symbol*]
MEXA........ Motor Exhaust Analyzer
Mexamerican... Mexican-American (SHCU)
MEXAMS.... Metals Exposure Analysis Modeling System (EEVL)
MExB .... Motor Explosive Boat [*British military*] (DMA)
MEXE........ Military Engineering Experimental Establishment [*British*]
MexEqt...... Mexico Equity & Income Fund [*Associated Press*] (SAG)
MexFd....... [*The*] Mexico Fund, Inc. [*Associated Press*] (SAG)
MexG........ Gulf of Mexico (SAUS)
MEXH........ Multi-Energy X-Ray Holography [*Physics*]
MEXIC....... Mexico, MO [*American Association of Railroads railroad junction routing code*]
MEXIS....... Multi-Energy X-ray Inspection System [*Police and security equipment*]
MEXnet..... Mexico Network
MexP .... Mexican Pharmacopoeia [*A publication*]
MEXP........ Miller Exploration Co. [*NASDAQ symbol*] (NASQ)
MExSt .... Master of Experimental Statistics (GAGS)
MEXT .... Maximal Exercise Testing
MExtEd...... Master of Extension Education (GAGS)
MEXU........ Mad Express Lines [*Intermodal shipping container symbol*] (TVRC)
MEY .... Mapleton, IA [*Location identifier*] [*FAA*] (FAAL)
MEY .... Maximum Economic Yield [*Fishery management*] (MSC)
MEY .... Meghauli [*Nepal*] [*Airport symbol*] (OAG)
Meyer Des Inst Judiciares... Meyer's Des Institutiones Judiciares [*A publication*] (DLA)
MeYoO ...... Old York Historical Society, York, ME [*Library symbol*] [*Library of Congress*] (LCLS)
MEYT........ Meyers Transport [*Common carrier symbol*]
MEZ.......... Augusta Mental Health Institute, Augusta, ME [*OCLC symbol*] (OCLC)
MEZ.......... Maritime Exclusion Zone (SAUO)
MEZ.......... Mena, AR [*Location identifier*] [*FAA*] (FAAL)
MEZ.......... Merces [*Brazil*] [*Airport symbol*] (AD)
Mez.......... Mezuzah (BJA)
MEZ.......... Mezzo [*Moderate*] [*Music*]
Mez.......... Mezzo-Soprano (GROV)
mez.......... Mezzotint (VRA)
MEZ.......... Mezzotinto [*Medium Tint, Half Tone*] [*Engraving*] (ROG)
MEZ.......... Minnesota Explosives [*Federal Railroad Administration identification code*]
MEZ.......... Missile Engagement Zone (NVT)
MEZ.......... Mittel Europaeische Zeit [*Central European Time*] [*German*]
MEZN........ Mezzanine (ABBR)
mezn .... Mezzanine (VRA)
Mezrabpom... International Workers Aid (SAUO)
Mezsovprof... International Council of Trade and Industrial Unions (SAUO)

MEZT .... Mezzotint [*Printing*] (ABBR)
MEZZ .... Mezzanine (KSC)
mezz .... Mezzanine (MIST)
MEZZ .... Mezzotint [*Printing*] (ABBR)
MEZZO ...... Mezzosoprano (ABBR)
MEZZO ...... Mezzotint [*Printing*] (ROG)
MF .... 5-Methyltetrahydrofolate [*Biochemistry*] (DAVI)
MF .... Fall River Public Library, Fall River, MA [*Library symbol*] [*Library of Congress*] (LCLS)
MF .... Le Maitre Phonetique [*A publication*] (BJA)
MF .... MacAndrews & Forbes Co., Inc. (EFIS)
MF .... Machine Finish [*Paper*]
mf .... Machine-Finish Paper (WDMC)
MF .... Magazines for Friendship [*An association*] (EA)
MF .... Magnetic Field
MF .... Magnetic Fluid [*Physics*]
MF .... Magnetic Focus [*of cathode-ray tube*] (DEN)
MF .... Magneto [*or Magnetic*] Field Generators [*JETDS Nomenclature*] [*Military*] (CET)
MF .... Magnetomotive Force (KSC)
MF .... Main Feed [*Technical drawings*]
MF .... Main Force [*Military*]
MF .... Mainframe (TIMI)
MF .... Maintenance Facility (ACAE)
MF .... Maintenance Factor
MF .... Maintenance Float [*Military*]
MF .... Maintenance Fuel
M/F .... Maintenance to Flight [*Ratio*]
MF .... Maisonneuve Fracture [*Medicine*] (MELL)
MF .... Major Facilitator [*Biochemistry*]
MF .... Major Function (MCD)
M/F .... Make From (SAA)
MF .... Malassezia Furfur [*Medicine*] (EDAA)
MF .... Malaysia Fund [*NYSE symbol*] (TTSB)
MF .... Malaysia Fund, Inc. [*NYSE symbol*] (SPSG)
M/F .... Male or Female
MF .... Male to Female [*Ratio*]
MF .... Mali Franc [*Monetary unit*]
MF .... Mallet Finger (MELL)
MF .... Mallet Fracture [*Medicine*] (MELL)
MF .... MAM Aviation Ltd. [*British*] [*ICAO designator*] (ICDA)
MF .... Management Finding (SAUO)
MF .... Mandatory Frequency (DA)
MF .... Mandibular Foramen [*Medicine*] (MELL)
MF .... Mantle Floor
MF .... Manufacture (WGA)
MF .... March Fracture [*Medicine*] (MELL)
MF .... Mare Feccunditatis [*Sea of Fertility*] [*Lunar area*]
M/F .... Marked For
MF .... Mark Forward [*Papers*] [*British*]
MF .... Marshall Field & Co. (SAUO)
MF .... Martinus de Fano [*Deceased circa 1275*] [*Authority cited in pre-1607 legal work*] (DSA)
MF .... Masculinity-Femininity (AEBS)
M-F .... Massey-Ferguson (SAUO)
MF .... Massey-Ferguson GmbH (SAUO)
MF .... Massey-Ferguson, Inc. (EFIS)
M$_f$ .... Mass Flow of Fuel [*Aviation*] (DA)
MF .... Mass Fraction (ACAE)
MF .... Mass Fragmentography [*Medicine*] (EDAA)
MF .... Massora Finalis (BJA)
M/F .... Master File
MF .... Master Frame
MF .... Master of Finance
MF .... Master of Forestry
MF .... Master of Hounds [*Equine term*] (TED)
MF .... Mastic Floor [*Technical drawings*]
MF .... Matching Funds (OICC)
MF .... Mate and Ferry [*NASA*] (NASA)
MF .... Material Factor
MF .... Maurice-Farman [*British military*] (DMA)
mf .... Mauritius [*MARC country of publication code*] [*Library of Congress*] (LCCP)
MF .... Maximum Flowering Day [*Botany*]
MF .... Mayo Foundation [*Medicine*] (EDAA)
MF .... Measurement Facility [*Computer science*] (IBMDP)
MF .... Meat Free [*Diet*]
MF .... Mechanical Flap [*Aviation*]
MF .... Meclofenamate [*Organic chemistry*]
MF .... Medal of Freedom [*Military decoration*]
MF .... Media Filter (ACRL)
MF .... Media Forum (EA)
MF .... Mediation Function [*Open Systems Interconnection*] (ODAA)
MF .... Medical Foundation [*Australia*]
MF .... Mediterranean Fleet (SAUO)
mf .... Medium Frequency (WDMC)
MF .... Medium Frequency [*Radio electronics*]
MF .... Megafarad [*Medicine*] (EDAA)
MF .... Melamine-Formaldehyde [*Plastics technology*]
MF .... Melomanes Francais [*Record label*] [*France*]
MF .... Membrane Filter
MF .... Menninger Foundation [*Medicine*] (EDAA)
MF .... Merck Frosst Laboratories [*Canada*]
MF .... Merthiolate-Formaldehyde [*Solution*]
MF .... Message Format (ECII)
MF .... Metal Factor [*Geophysical measurement*]
MF .... Metallic Film
MF .... Meter Fix (CTAS)
MF .... Methotrexate, Fluorourcil, Calcium Leucovorin Rescue [*Antineoplastic drug*] (CDI)
MF .... Methoxyflurane [*Medicine*] (EDAA)
MF .... Methyl Farnesoate [*Organic chemistry*]
MF .... Methylformamide (ACAE)
MF .... Methyl Formate [*Organic chemistry*]
MF .... Methylfuran [*Organic chemistry*]
mf .... Mezzo Forte (NTIO)
MF .... Mezzo Forte [*Moderately Loud*] [*Music*] (ROG)
MF .... Microfarad
MF .... Microfibril [*Medicine*] (EDAA)
MF .... Microfiche [*Sheet microfilm*]
MF .... Microfilament (MELL)
mf .... Microfilaria (STED)
Mf .... Microfilariae
MF .... Microfilm
MF .... Microfiltration
MF .... Microflocculation [*Biochemistry*] (DAVI)
MF .... Microform
MF .... Microscopic Factor
MF .... Midcavity Forcep [*Medicine*] (DMAA)
MF .... Middeck Forward (MCD)
MF .... Middle Fork [*AAR code*]
MF .... Middle French [*Language, etc.*]
MF .... Middling Fair (IAA)
mf .... Mid-Frequency (IDOE)
MF .... Mid Fuselage
MF .... Midfuselage (SAUS)
MF .... Mi Favor [*My Favor*] [*Spanish*]
MF .... Mike Force [*Indigenous personnel trained and commanded jointly by US and Vietnamese forces, and used as a reaction and/or reinforcing unit*]
MF .... Milk Foundation [*National Dairy Council*] (EA)
MF .... Millard Filmore [*US president, 1800-1874*]
MF .... Miller-Fischer [*Syndrome*] [*Medicine*] (DB)
mf .... Mill Finish [*Construction term*] (MIST)
MF .... Mill Finish
MF .... Mill Fixture (MCD)
MF .... Millifarad (GPO)
mF .... Millifarad (IDOE)
MF .... Millipore Filter [*Intravenous therapy*] (CPH)
MF .... Mind Freedom
MF .... Minister [*or Ministry*] of Food [*British*]
MF .... Ministry of Food (SAUO)
M/F .... Minorities/Females
MF .... Missile Failure (AAG)
MF .... Mitogenic Factor [*Cytology*]
MF .... Mitomycin, Fluorouracil [*Antineoplastic drug regimen*]
MF .... Mitotic Figure [*Genetics*]
MF .... Mixed Flow (AAG)
MF .... Mobile Facility (MCD)
MF .... Modern Fiction
MF .... Modifying Factor [*Toxicology*]
MF .... Modulated Frequency (SAUS)
MF .... Modulation Factor
MF .... Molecular Formula (NITA)
MF .... Mole Fraction [*Chemistry*]
M-F .... Monday through Friday (CDAI)
MF .... More Follows [*Newspaper copy*] (DGA)
mf .... More Follows [*Copyediting*] (WDMC)
MF .... More Fragments (ACRL)
MF .... Morningstar Foundation (EA)
MF .... Morphogenetic Furrow [*Cell differentiation*]
MF .... Morris Foundation [*British*] (DBA)
MF .... Mossy Fiber [*Neuroanatomy*]
MF .... Mother Fooler [*Bowdlerized version*]
MF .... Motor Field
MF .... Motor Freight
MF .... Mound Facility (SAUO)
MF .... Mucosal Fluid (DB)
MF .... Multifactorial (DIPS)
MF .... Multifamily (PA)
MF .... Multifrequency [*Telecommunications*]
MF .... Multi-Function (SAUO)
MF .... Multifunctional (MCD)
MF .... Multiple Feedback (MED)
MF .... Multiplying Factor [*Microscopy*]
MF .... Munitions Facility (ACAE)
MF .... Muscle Feedback [*Medicine*] (EDAA)
MF .... Muscle Fiber
MF .... Musicians Foundation (EA)
MF .... Mutation Frequency [*Medicine*] (DMAA)
MF .... Mutual Fund [*Business term*]
MF .... Mycosis Fungoides [*Dermatology*]
MF .... Myelinated Fiber [*Neuroanatomy*]
MF .... Myelin Figure [*Medicine*]
MF .... Myelofibrosis [*Medicine*] (DB)
M/F .... My Favor (ADA)
MF .... Myocardial Fibrosis [*Cardiology*]
MF .... Myofibrillar [*Anatomy*]

MF .... Red Carpet Flying Service [*ICAO designator*] (AD)
MF .... Royal Munster Fusiliers [*Military unit*] (DMA)
MF .... SAAB-Scania AB [*Sweden*] [*ICAO aircraft manufacturer identifier*] (ICAO)
MF .... Spofa Ltd. [*Czechoslovakia*] [*Research code symbol*]
MF/1 .... Measurement Frequency/1 [*IBM*] (NITA)
MF²K .... Medical Force 2000 [*Army*] (DOMA)
MFA .... America First Mtg Investments [*NYSE symbol*] (SG)
MFA .... Armed Forces Movement (Portugal) [*Political party*] (PSAP)
MFA .... Macrofollicular Adenoma [*Medicine*] (MELL)
MFA .... Mafia Islands [*Tanzania*] [*Airport symbol*] (OAG)
MFA .... Magny Families Association (EA)
MFA .... Malfunction Alert [*Computer science*] (BUR)
MFA .... Malicious False Alarm [*Firefighting*]
MFA .... Malta Fencible Artillery [*British*]
MFA .... Managed Funds Association (EA)
MFA .... Managed Futures Association (NTPA)
MFA .... Manned Flight Awareness [*NASA*] (NASA)
MFA .... Marconi-Franklin Antenna
MFA .... Marine Fabricators Association (NTPA)
M Fa .... Martinus de Fano [*Deceased circa 1275*] [*Authority cited in pre-1607 legal work*] (DSA)
MFA .... Master Fencers Association (NADA)
MFA .... Master File Activities [*Computer science*]
MFA .... Master Fine Arts (SAUO)
MFA .... Master of Fine Arts
MFA .... Material Fielding Agreement [*Army*]
MFA .... Materiel Fielding Agreement (SAUO)
MFA .... Mauritius Freeport Authority
MFA .... McAlpin(e) Family Association (EA)
MFA .... McCune Family Association (EA)
MFA .... McGregor Family Association (EA)
MFA .... Meader Family Association (EA)
MFA .... Meningitis Foundation of America (NRGU)
MFA .... Menningar- og Fraedslusamband Althydu [*Workers' Educational Association*] [*Iceland*] (EY)
MFA .... Men's Fashion Association of America (EA)
MFA .... Mercantile Fleet Auxiliary [*British*]
MFA .... Metal Finishing Association [*British*] (DBA)
MFA .... Methyl Fluoracetate [*Organic chemistry*]
MFA .... MFA Mortgage Investments [*Stock exchange symbol*] [*Formerly America First Mtg Investments*]
MFA .... Miami, FL [*Location identifier*] [*FAA*] (FAAL)
MFA .... Michigan Forest Association (EARSL)
MFA .... Microelectronics for All Kit (NITA)
MFA .... Military Flying Area [*Canadian*]
MFA .... Military Functions Appropriation (AABC)
MFA .... Minimum Flight Altitude [*Aviation*] (DA)
MFA .... Minister for Foreign Affairs [*British*]
MFA .... Miscellaneous Federal Agencies (SAUO)
MFA .... Misr Freight Agencies (EFIS)
MFA .... Mississippi Forestry Association (WPI)
MFA .... Missouri Farmers Association (EFIS)
MFA .... Mitchell Field [*Alaska*] [*Seismograph station code, US Geological Survey*] [*Closed*] (SEIS)
MFA .... Mobilization for Animals (EA)
MFA .... Modify Field Attribute [*Computer science*] (DCDG)
MFA .... Monofluoroacetate [*Organic chemistry*]
MFA .... Moody Family Association (EA)
MFA .... Motor Factors Association [*British*] (BI)
MFA .... Movement for Federation of the Americas (EA)
MFA .... Movimento das Forcas Armadas [*Armed Forces Movement*] [*Portugal*] [*Political party*] (PPE)
MFA .... Multi-Fiber Arrangement [*International trade*]
MFA .... Multi-Fibre Agreement (SAUO)
MFA .... Multifocal Functional Autonomy [*Medicine*] (DMAA)
MFA .... Multifunctional Acrylate [*Organic chemistry*]
MFA .... Multifunction Antenna
MFA .... Multiple Factor Analysis (DB)
MFA .... Multiple Filer Audit Program
MFA .... Mumford Family Association (EA)
MFA .... Mumpower Family Association (EA)
MFA .... Museum of Fine Arts [*Boston*] (BJA)
MFAA .... Masters of Foxhounds Association of America [*Later, American Master of Foxhounds Association*] (EA)
MFAA .... Monuments, Fine Arts and Archives Section (SAUO)
MFA & A .... Monuments, Fine Arts, and Archives [*SHAEF*] [*World War II*]
MFA Art and Arch ... Master of Fine Arts in Art and Archaeology (SAUO)
MFAB .... Metal Fabrication [*NCIC trailer make code*]
MFAB .... Museum of Fine Arts, Boston
MFAB-F ..... Mobile Floating Assault Bridge-Ferry [*Military*]
MFABI .... Metal Fixing Association for Building Insulation (SAUO)
MFAC .... Magnetic Fusion Advisory Committee [*Department of Energy*] [*Washington, DC*]
MFAC .... Market Facts [*NASDAQ symbol*] (TTSB)
MFAC .... Market Facts, Inc. [*NASDAQ symbol*] (NQ)
M Fac Hom ... Member of the Faculty of Homeopathy (SAUO)
MFAD .... Maneuver Force Air Defense
MFAF .... Matheson Fast Freight [*Common carrier symbol*]
MFAG .... Medical First Aid Guide for use in Accidents Involving Dangerous Goods (SAUO)
MFAH .... Museum of Fine Arts of Houston (SAUO)
MFai .... Millicent Library, Fairhaven, MA [*Library symbol*] [*Library of Congress*] (LCLS)
MFAIRWEST ... Marine Fleet Air, West Coast
MFal .... Falmouth Public Library, Falmouth, MA [*Library symbol*] [*Library of Congress*] (LCLS)
MFALDA ..... Marginal Farmers and Agricultural Labourers Development Agency (SAUO)
MFalHi ...... Falmouth Historical Society, Falmouth, MA [*Library symbol*] [*Library of Congress*] (LCLS)
MFAMUS .... Master of Fine Arts in Music (WDAA)
MFAMW ..... Modern Free and Accepted Masons of the World (EA)
MF&A .... Monuments, Fine Arts and Archives (SAUO)
MF & P ..... Materials Finishes and Processes (MCD)
MF & R ..... Manpower Forces and Readiness [*Military*]
MF & S ..... Magazine Flooding and Sprinkling
MFANSW .... Master Farriers' Association of New South Wales [*Australia*]
MFAP .... Manned Flight Awareness Program [*NASA*] (KSC)
MFA PAC .... Managed Funds Association PAC [*Formerly known as Managed Futures Association PAC*] [*Washington, DC*] (PACS)
MFAR .... Meter Fix Acceptance Rate (CTAS)
MFAR .... Michigan Foundation for Advanced Research (SAUO)
MFAR .... Modernized Fleet Accounting and Reporting
MFAR .... Multi-Function Array RADAR (MCD)
MFARCS .... Member of the Faculty of Anaesthetists of the Royal College of Surgeons (SAUO)
MFARS ...... Defense Mapping Agency Federal Acquisition Regulation Supplement [*A publication*] (AAGC)
MFAS .... Master of Fisheries and Aquatic Science (PGP)
MFASMR .... Multifrequency Aperture Synthesis Microwave Radiometer (ACAE)
MFAST ...... Mwave Folded Array Signal Transform (SAUS)
MFAT .... Multifocal Atrial Tachycardia [*Cardiology*] (DAVI)
MFAW .... Master of Fine Arts in Writing (PGP)
MFAZ .... MFA Industries [*Federal Railroad Administration identification code*]
MFB .... Bristol Community College, Fall River, MA [*Library symbol*] [*Library of Congress*] (LCLS)
MFB .... Mammal Fibroblast (DB)
MFB .... Mass Fraction Burn [*Automotive engine combustion analysis*]
MFB .... Master of Finance and Banking (PGP)
MFB .... Medial Forebrain Bundle [*Medicine*]
MFB .... Message from Base
MFB .... Metallic Foreign Body
MFB .... Metropolitan Fire Brigade [*British*]
MFB .... MFB Mutual Insurance Co. [*from Manufacturers Mutual Fire Insurance Co., Firemen's Mutual Insurance Co., Blackstone Mutual Insurance Co.*]
MFB .... Michigan Farm Bureau (EARSL)
MFB .... Mill Fixture Base (MCD)
MFB .... Mixed Functional Block (IEEE)
MFB .... Moisture Free Basis
MFB .... Motional Feedback
MFB .... Motor Freight Tariff Bureau, Springfield IL [*STAC*]
MFBAR ...... Multifunction Band Airborne Radio
MFBARS .... Multifunction-Multiband Airborne Radio System (ACAE)
MFBB .... Mexican Food and Beverage Board (EA)
MFBC .... MFB Corp. [*NASDAQ symbol*] (SAG)
MFB Cp ..... MFB Corp. [*Associated Press*] (SAG)
MFBE .... Minority/Female Business Enterprise
MFBF .... Mean Flights between Failures [*Military*] (CAAL)
MFBF .... Minimum Film Boiling Flux
MFBF .... Multi-Function Bomb Fuze (SAUS)
MFBI .... Major Fuel Burning Installation (GFGA)
MFBI .... Major Industrial Fuel-Burning Installations (SAUO)
MFBM .... Thousand Feet Board Measure [*Lumber*]
MFBMP ..... Project Manager, Fleet Ballistic Missile [*Navy*]
MFBP .... Main Feed Booster Pump (NVT)
MFBP .... Manufacturing Flow and Building Plan (NASA)
MFBS .... Marine and Freshwater Biomedical Science (GNE)
MFBS .... McKinney Functional Board Shop (TIMI)
MFBTE ...... Midland Federation of Building Trades Employees (SAUO)
MFC .... Madison Financial Corporation (EFIS)
MFC .... Magnesium Flat Cell
MFC .... Magnetic Film Counter
MFC .... Magnetic Tape Field Scan [*Computer science*]
MFC .... Main Fuel Control (MCD)
MFC .... Manual Frequency Control
MFC .... Manulife Financial Corp. [*Toronto Stock Exchange symbol*] [*Canada*]
MFC .... Manulife Financial Corp. [*NYSE symbol*]
MFC .... Maritime Fruit Carriers [*Steamship*] (MHDW)
MFC .... Maritime Fruit Carriers Company (SAUO)
MFC .... Mass Flow Controller [*Engineering*]
MFC .... Master File Copy [*Computer science*] (KSC)
MFC .... Master Flow Controller [*Nuclear energy*] (NRCH)
MFC .... Master of Forest Conservation (PGP)
MFC .... Mastership in Food Control [*British*] (DBQ)
MFC .... MB Capital I [*AMEX symbol*] (NASQ)
MFC .... Mean Frequency of Compensation (STED)
MFC .... Median Femoral Condyle [*Anatomy*]
MFC .... Medicated Face Conditioner [*Brand manufactured by Mennen*]
MFC .... Membrane Fecal Coliform (PDAA)
m-FC .... Membrane Focal Coli [*Broth*] (STED)
MFC .... Merrell's Fan Club (EA)
MFC .... Message Formatting Committee (SAUO)
MFC .... Metal-Finishing Category (GNE)
MFC .... Meteorological and Oceanographic Forecast Center (COE)
MFC .... Metropolitan Financial (EFIS)
MFC .... Microfibrillated Cellulose (DB)
MFC .... Microfilm Frame Card
MFC .... MicroFluidics Center [*University of Illinois at Chicago*] (RCD)

MFC .... Microfunctional Circuit
MFC .... Microsoft Foundation Classes [*Computer science*] (PCM)
MFC .... Microsoft Foundation Class Library [*Computer science*] (PCM)
MFC .... Military Forces of the Crown (SAUO)
MFC .... Military Frequency Changer
MFC .... Minimal Flight Forecasting Charts [*Air Force*]
MFC .... Minimal Fungicidal Concentration [*Medicine*] (DMAA)
MFC .... Minnesota Family Council [*Minnesota Family Institute*] (RCD)
MFC .... Mirinda's Friendship Club (EA)
MFC .... Missile Fire Control (MCD)
MFC .... Mission Football Conference (PSS)
MFC .... Mississippi Flyway Council
MFC .... Modern Foods Council [*Defunct*] (EA)
MFC .... Modular Feature Construction [*Communications term*] (DCT)
MFC .... Moncton Flying Club [*Canada*] [*ICAO designator*] (FAAC)
MFC .... Morrison Fresh Cooking [*NYSE symbol*] (TTSB)
MFC .... Morrison Fresh Cooking, Inc. [*NYSE symbol*] (SAG)
MFC .... Mortar Fire Controller [*British*]
MFC .... Mortgage Funding Corp. [*British*]
MFC .... Most-Favored Customer (AAGC)
MFC .... Motor Freight Controller [*National Accounting and Finance Council*] [*A publication*]
MFC .... Motorized Flow Control
MFC .... Movimiento Familiar Cristiano (EA)
MFC .... Multi-Frequency Code [*Telecommunications*] (DA)
MFC .... Multifrequency Signaling, Compelled [*Telecommunications*] (TEL)
MFC .... Multifunctional Chipcard (SAUO)
MFC .... Multifunctional Concentrate (EDCT)
MFC .... Multi-Function Console (SAUS)
MFC .... Multiple File Concept (DNAB)
MFC .... Multiple Flight Computer (NASA)
MFC .... Multiple Flight Controller (NASA)
MFC .... Municipal Financial Corp. [*Toronto Stock Exchange symbol*]
MFC .... Music Feature Card (SAUS)
MFCA .... Master File Change Activity [*Computer science*] (MCD)
MFCA .... Master Fruit Carriers Association (SAUO)
MFCA .... Methanol Fuel Cell Alliance [*Automotive industry*]
MFCA .... Miniature Figure Collectors of America (EA)
MFCA .... Multi-Function Communications Adaptor (NITA)
MFCA .... Mutlifunction Communications Adapter
MFCAE ...... Masters of Foxhounds Club of America and England [*Defunct*] (EA)
MFCB .... Michigan Financial Corp. [*NASDAQ symbol*] (SAG)
MFCB .... Michigan Finl Corp. [*NASDAQ symbol*] (TTSB)
MFCC .... Marriage and Family Counseling Certificate (PGP)
MFCC .... Marriage, Family, and Child Counseling (PGP)
MFCC .... Marriage, Family, and Child Counselor [*Psychology*] (DAVI)
MFCC .... Maximum Free Carrier Concentration (AAEL)
MFCC .... McFarland Cascade Company (SAUO)
MFCC .... Minimum Functional Combat Capability
MFCC .... Missile Fire Control Computer [*Military*] (CAAL)
MFCC .... Missile Flight Caution Corridor (AFM)
MFCC .... Mission Flight Control Center (SAUO)
MFCC .... Mortar Fire Control Calculator [*Later, MBC*] [*Military*] (INF)
MFCC .... Mortar Fire Direction Center Data Calculator [*Army*]
MFCC .... Multi-Function Common Console (SAUS)
MFCCA ...... Master Floorcovering Contractors Association (SAUO)
MFCD .... Microgravity Fluids and Combustion Diagnostics (SAUS)
MFCD .... Modular Flare Chaff Dispenser [*Military*] (PDAA)
MFCD .... Multifunction Colour Display (SAUS)
MFCDU ...... Multi-Function Control and Display Unit
MFCF .... Multinational Fuel Cycle Facility
MFCI .... Molten Fuel Coolant Interaction [*Nuclear energy*] (NRCH)
MFCL .... Master Fund Control List [*Air Force*] (AFM)
MFC/LB ..... Multi-Frequency / Local Battery [*Telecommunications*] (DA)
MFCM .... Member of the Faculty of Community Medicine [*British*]
MFCM .... Multifunction Card Machine (BUR)
MFCMA ..... Magnuson Fishery Conservation and Management Act [*1976*] [*Also, FCMA*]
MFCO .... Manual Fuel Cutoff (AAG)
MFCO .... Microwave Filter [*NASDAQ symbol*] (TTSB)
MFCO .... Microwave Filter Co., Inc. [*NASDAQ symbol*] (NQ)
MFCP .... Midwest Free Community Papers [*Association*] (EA)
MFCP .... Multifunction Control/Panel (MCD)
MFCRS ...... Multifunction Flight Control Reference System (ACAE)
MFCS .... Magnetic Field Calibration System
MFCS .... Manual Flight Control System [*NASA*]
MFCS .... Mason Fracture Classification System [*Medicine*] (MELL)
MFCS .... Master of Family and Consumer Sciences (PGP)
MFCS .... Mathematical Foundation of Computer Science (PDAA)
MFCS .... Maximum Flat Control System
MFCS .... Medical Function Control System (PDAA)
MFCS .... Microprocessor Flight Control System (DOMA)
MFCS .... Missile Fire Control System (NG)
MFCS .... Modified Fire Control System (SAUS)
MFCS .... Mortar Fire Control System [*Military*] (INF)
MFC's .... Multi-Function Center Models
MFCSB ...... Missile Fire Control Status Board (SAUO)
MFCT .... Major Fraction Thereof
MFCT .... Modular Furnace Component Technology (SAUS)
MFCU .... Multifunction Card Unit
MFCV .... Modulating Flow Control Valve (MCD)
MFCV .... Muscle Fibre Conduction Velocity (DMAA)
MFCX .... First Union Rail [*Private rail car owner code*]
MFCX .... Marshalltown Financial [*NASDAQ symbol*] (TTSB)
MFCX .... Marshalltown Financial Corp. [*NASDAQ symbol*] (SAG)
MFD .... Canadian Department of Fisheries and Oceans, Marine Fish Division [*Research center*] (RCD)
MFD .... Magic Foods, Inc. [*Vancouver Stock Exchange symbol*]
MFD .... Magnetic Frequency Detector
MFD .... Magnetofluiddynamic
MFD .... Main Feed (MCD)
MFD .... Malfunction Detection (NASA)
MFD .... Malfunctioning Display (DA)
MFD .... Mandibulofacial Dysostosis (STED)
MFD .... Manifold [*Paper*] (DGA)
MFD .... Mansfield [*Ohio*] [*Airport symbol*] (OAG)
MFD .... Mansfield, OH [*Location identifier*] [*FAA*] (FAAL)
mfd .... Manufactured (WDAA)
MFD .... Manufactured
MFD .... Massachusetts Financial Development Fund, Inc. (SAUO)
MFD .... Master File Directory [*Computer science*]
MFD .... Maximum Frequency Difference [*Statistics*]
MFD .... Mechanical-Front-Drive [*Tractor*]
MFD .... Memory-for-Designs [*Test*] [*Psychology*]
MFD .... Mendankwe [*Language symbol*] (ETLW)
MFD .... Mesa Fire Department [*Emergency Management*] (EMA)
MFD .... Message Format Designator
MFD .... Metal Floor Deck [*Technical drawings*]
MFD .... Microfarad
MFD .... Microfinance Development (FOTI)
MFD .... Midflight Deck (SAUS)
MFD .... Midforceps Delivery [*Obstetrics*]
MFD .... Military First Destination (SAUO)
MFD .... Military Forwarding Depot [*British military*] (DMA)
MFD .... Milk-Free Diet (STED)
MFD .... Millifarad (MCD)
MFD .... Minimal Fatal Dose [*Medicine*] (STED)
MFD .... Minimum Fatal Dose
MFD .... Minimum Focusing Distance [*Optics*]
MFD .... Monteggia Fracture-Dislocation [*Medicine*] (MELL)
MFD .... Multifunctional Device [*Computer science*] (FOTI)
MFD .... Multi-Function Device (NETL)
MFD .... Multifunction Display (MCD)
MFD .... Multiple Family Dwelling [*Real estate*]
MFD .... Multistage Flash Distillation (PDAA)
MFD .... Multivariable Frequency Domain
MFD .... Munford, Inc. [*NYSE symbol*] (COMM)
MFD .... Municipal Facilities Division [*Environmental Protection Agency*] (GFGA)
MFDA .... Minnesota Funeral Directors Association (EARSL)
MFDA .... Montana Food Distributors Association (EARSL)
MFDB .... Manufacturing Data Base (TIMI)
MFDC .... Main Facility Device Controller [*Telecommunications*] (CIST)
MFDC .... Marshfield Drayage Company [*Common carrier symbol*]
MFDC .... Mortar Fire Data Computer (SAUS)
MFDC .... Morzen Mortar Fire Data Computer [*Military*] [*British*] (INF)
MFDC .... Mouvement des Forces Democratiques de la Casamance [*Senegal*] [*Political party*]
MFDC .... Movement of Democratic Forces of Casamance (Sengal) [*Political party*] (PSAP)
MFDCC ...... Marine Fire Detection Control Center
MFDE .... Midflight Deck Experiment (SAUS)
MF/DF .... Medium-Frequency Direction Finder [*or Finding*] (NVT)
MFDO .... Member of the Faculty of Dispensing Opticians [*British*] (DBQ)
MFDP .... Maintenance Float Distribution Point [*Computer science*] (NATG)
MFDP .... Mississippi Freedom Democratic Party
MFDS .... Modular Fuel Delivery Station [*Shipboard installation*] [*Navy*] (DOMA)
MFDSG ...... Multifunction Display Symbol Generator (MCD)
MFDSUL .... Multifunction Data Set Utility Language
MFDT .... Memory-for-Designs Test [*Psychology*]
MFDT .... Multiple False Doppler Target
MFDU .... Multifunction Display Unit [*Aviation*]
MFE .... Machinery and Fixed Equipment [*British*]
MFE .... Magnetic Field Energy
MFE .... Magnetic Field Experiment (SAUO)
MFE .... Magnetic Field Explorer [*NASA*]
MFE .... Maison de la Fondation Europeenne (EAIO)
MFE .... Major Fleet Escort
MFE .... Manpower Force Element (SAUO)
MFE .... Manual of Field Engineering [*British military*] (DMA)
MFE .... Master of Financial Economics (PGP)
MFE .... Master of Forest Engineering
MFE .... McAllen [*Texas*] [*Airport symbol*] (OAG)
MFE .... McAllen, TX [*Location identifier*] [*FAA*] (FAAL)
MFE .... Mean Fibre Extent (PDAA)
MFE .... Mercury Film Electrode [*Electrochemistry*]
MFE .... Microabrasion Foil Experiment [*For cosmic dust retrieval*]
MFE .... Mid-Frequency Execution
MFE .... Mid-Frequency Executive (NASA)
MFE .... Military Forwarding Establishment (SAUO)
MFE .... Ministry for the Environment (SAUO)
MFE .... Mischief Enterprises Ltd. [*Vancouver Stock Exchange symbol*]
MFE .... Moire Fringe Effect (PDAA)
MFE .... Mouvement Federaliste Europeen [*European Federalist Movement*] [*France*]
MFEA .... Magnetic Fusion Engineering Act
MFEA .... Mutual Fund Education Alliance (NTPA)
MFECC ...... Magnetic Fusion Energy Computing Center (ACAE)

MFECS ...... Mediterranean Far East Container Service (SAUO)
MFED .... Manned Flight Engineering Division [*NASA*]
MFED .... Maximum Flat Envelope Delay
MFed .... Miners' Federation of Great Britain (DAS)
MFED .... Multifunctional Exercise Device (SPST)
MFEIP .... Ministry of Food Education and Information Practice [*British*]
MFEL .... Manpower Force Element Listing (SAUO)
MFEL .... Medical Free Electron LASER
MFEM .... Magnetic Field Explorer Mission (SAUO)
MFEM .... Maximal Forced Expiratory Maneuver [*Medicine*] (DAVI)
MFE/MAGNOLIA... MFE /Magnetic Field Experiment (SAUO)
MFEnet .... Magnetic Fusion Energy Network
MFENET ..... Magnetic Fusion Energy Research Network [*Department of Energy*]
MFENET ..... National Magnetic Fusion Energy Network (SAUO)
MF Eng ...... Master of Forest Engineering
MFEQ .... Mechanical Facilities and Equipment (SAA)
MFER .... Ministry of Foreign Economic Relations (SAUO)
MFES .... Main Fixed Earth Station [*NASA*] (PDAA)
MFES .... Major Fleet Escort Study [*Navy*] (CAAL)
MFF .... Flin Flon Public Library, Manitoba [*Library symbol*] [*National Library of Canada*] (NLC)
MFF .... MacFadden Foundation (SAUO)
MFF .... Macrophage Fusion Factor [*Immunology*] (QSUL)
MFF .... Magnetic Flip-Flop [*Computer science*]
MFF .... Mariposa Folk Foundation (EAIO)
MFF .... Master Freight File
MFF .... Match Flip Flop [*Computer science*] (MHDI)
MFF .... Matching Familiar Figures [*Psychology*]
MFF .... MDM [*Manipulator Deployment Mechanism*] Flight Forward [*NASA*] (GFGA)
MFF .... Melbourne Film Festival [*Australia*]
MFF .... Mezzo Fortissimo [*Rather Loud*] [*Music*] (ADA)
MFF .... Military Free Fall [*Parachute jump*] (MCD)
MFF .... Mixed Fighter Force (SAUO)
MFF .... Moanda [*Gabon*] [*Airport symbol*] (OAG)
MFF .... Munitions Filling Factory (ADA)
MFF .... St. Martin Du Fouilloux [*France*] [*Seismograph station code, US Geological Survey*] (SEIS)
MFFC .... Mayflower Financial Corp. [*NASDAQ symbol*] (COMM)
MFFC .... Milton Federal Financial [*NASDAQ symbol*] (TTSB)
MFFC .... Milton Federal Financial Corp. [*NASDAQ symbol*] (SAG)
MFFC .... Mixed Fighter Force Concept (SAUS)
MFFGH ...... Flin Flon General Hospital, Manitoba [*Library symbol*] [*National Library of Canada*] (NLC)
MFF/HALO... Military Free Fall / High Altitude Low Opening Parachute
MFFHB ...... Hudson Bay Mining & Smelting Co. Ltd., Flin Flon, Manitoba [*Library symbol*] [*National Library of Canada*] (NLC)
MFFLR ...... Muffler [*Automotive advertising*]
MFFO .... Mixed Force Fighter Operations (SAUO)
MFFR .... Modified Field Fire Range (MCD)
MFFS .... Microsoft Flash File System (VLIE)
MFFT .... Matching Familiar Figures Test [*Education*]
MFFT .... Minimum Film Formation Temperature [*Coating technology*]
MFFV .... MRS Freight Forwarding Services [*Common carrier symbol*]
MFG .... Magnetic Field Gradient (MELL)
MFG .... Major Functional Group [*NASA*] (KSC)
mfg .... Manufactured (MIST)
MFG .... Manufacturer [*Motor vehicle violation code used in state of Maryland*] (MVRD)
Mfg .... Manufacturer (SAUO)
mfg .... Manufacturing (DD)
MFG .... Manufacturing [*Telegraphy*] (PCTE)
Mfg .... Manufacturing (PROS)
MFG .... Manufacturing [*United States Postal Service last word addressing abbreviation*]
MFG .... McQuay-Norris Manufacturing Co. (SAUO)
MFG .... Message Flow Graph
MFG .... Metropolitan Fire Brigade (SAUO)
MFG .... Milk Fat Globule
MfG .... Mit Freundlichen Gruessen [*E-mail salutation meaning "with friendly greetings"*] [*German*] (NETL)
MFG .... Modified Heat-Degraded Gelatin [*Medicine*] (MEDA)
MFG .... Molded Fiberglass
MFG .... More Friendly Garbage (VLIE)
MFG .... Multi-Function Gateway (SAUS)
MFG .... Multi-Function Generator (NITA)
MFG .... Multi-Function Grip [*Automotive engineering*]
MFG .... Munitions Family Group
MFGA .... Master Furriers Guild of America (EA)
MFGDP ...... Manual of Federal Geographic Data Products (SAUO)
MfgDTF ..... Manufacturing Domain Task Force (SAUO)
MFGM .... Milk Fat Globule Membrane
MFGNG ...... Manufacturing [*United States Postal Service last word addressing abbreviation*]
MFGR .... Manufacturer
MFGRS ...... Manufacturers [*United States Postal Service last word addressing abbreviation*]
MFH .... Magnetic Film Handler (CMD)
MFH .... Malignant Fibrous Histiocytoma [*Oncology*]
MFH .... Markel Financial Holdings Ltd. [*Toronto Stock Exchange symbol*]
MFH .... Master of Fox Hounds
MFH .... Master of Foxhounds (SAUO)
MFH .... Master of the Fox Hunt (DD)
MFH .... Membrane-Free Hemolystate [*Hematology*] (DAVI)
MFH .... Military Family Housing (AFM)
M/F/H .... Minorities, Females, Handicapped
MFH .... Mobile Field Hospital
MFHA .... Master of Foxhounds Association (SAUO)
MFHA .... Masters of Foxhounds Association [*British*] (BI)
MFHA .... Medal for Humane Action [*Berlin Airlift, 1948-9*] [*Military decoration*]
MFHA .... MultiCultural Foodservice and Hospitality Alliance [*Association*] (EA)
MFHBF ...... Mean Flight Hours between Failures [*Quality control*] (MCD)
MFHBMA.... Mean Flight Hours between Maintenance Actions [*Quality control*] (NVT)
MFHBUMA... Mean Flight Hour between Unscheduled Maintenance Actions [*Quality control*] (MCD)
MFHC .... Missile Flight Hazard Corridor (AFM)
MFHD .... Multi-Function Head-down Display (SAUS)
MFHD .... My First Hard Drive [*Computer science*]
MFHF .... Mobile Fuel Handling Flight (SAUS)
MFHFS ...... Multifunction High-Frequency SONAR (MCD)
MFHom ..... Member of the Faculty of Homeopathy (SAUO)
MF Hom .... Member of the Faculty of Homoeopathy [*British*]
MFHR .... Media Fund for Human Rights (EA)
MFHS .... Mobile Fuel Handling Squadron (SAUO)
MFHSEP .... Mohn Family History Society of Eastern Pennsylvania [*Association*] (EA)
m/f/h/v ...... Male, Female, Handicapped, Veteran (BARN)
MFi .... Fitchburg Public Library and Regional Center for Central Massachusetts, RegionalLibrary System, Fitchburg, MA [*Library symbol*] [*Library of Congress*] (LCLS)
MFI .... MacFrugal's Bargains [*Formerly, Pic'n'Save Corp.*] [*NYSE symbol*] (SPSG)
MFI .... MacFrugals Bargains Closeouts [*NYSE symbol*] (TTSB)
MFI .... Magazines for Industry [*An association*]
MFI .... Magnetic Field Indicator
MFI .... Magnetic Field Intensity
MFI .... Major Force Issues [*Army*] (AABC)
MFI .... Marketfax Infoservices Ltd. [*Vancouver Stock Exchange symbol*]
MFI .... Marketing Freedom Index [*OPEC*] [*Business term*]
MFI .... Marshfield [*Wisconsin*] [*Airport symbol*] (OAG)
MFI .... Marshfield, WI [*Location identifier*] [*FAA*] (FAAL)
MFI .... Master Facility Inventory [*Department of Health and Human Services*] (GFGA)
MFI .... Mean Flourescence Intensity [*Biochemistry*]
MFI .... Melt-Flow Index [*of plastics*]
MFI .... Metal Fabricating Institute (EA)
MFI .... Metal-Finishing Industy
MFI .... Microfinance Institution (FOTI)
MFI .... MicroFinancial, Inc. [*NYSE symbol*] (SG)
MFI .... Military Financial Instruction
MFI .... Mobile Fuel Irradiator (IEEE)
MFI .... Multifunction Interpreter (SAUS)
MFI .... Multipoint Flexible Injection [*Automotive fuel systems*]
MFI .... Multi-point Fuel Injection
MFI .... Multiport Fuel Injection [*Automotive technology*]
MFI .... Musicians Foundation Incorporated (SAUO)
MFI .... Myofibril Fragmentation Index [*Food technology*]
MFIA .... Member, Fundraising Institute-Australia, Inc. (NFD)
MFIA .... Municipal Finance Industry Association (NTPA)
MFIANE ..... Mutual Fire Insurance Association of New England (SAUO)
MFIBNE ..... Mutual Fire Inspection Bureau of New England (SAUO)
MFIC .... MFIC Corp. [*OTCBB symbol*]
MFIC .... Microfluidics International [*NASDAQ symbol*] (TTSB)
MFIC .... Microfluidics International Corp. [*NASDAQ symbol*] (SAG)
MFIC .... Military Flight Information Center
MFIC .... Missile Flight Information Center (SAUO)
MFIC .... Mutual Federation of Independent Cooperatives [*Later, Northeast Dairy Cooperative Federation*] (EA)
MFID .... Multiple-Electrode Flame Ionization Detector
MFIE .... Magnetic Field Integral Equation (PDAA)
MF-IFGR .... Michael Fund (International Foundation for Genetic Research) (EA)
MFin .... Master of Finance
MFIN .... Metro Financial Corp. [*NASDAQ symbol*] (SAG)
MFinStud ... Master of Financial Studies
MFIOP .... Multifunction I/O Processor (SAUS)
MFIP .... Microforms in Print [*Database*]
MFIP .... Multi-Function Interoperability Processor (SAUS)
MFIS .... Magnetic Field-Induced Superconductivity
MFisc .... Maitrise en Fiscalite (DD)
MFish .... Ministry of Fisheries (SAUO)
MFISH .... Multiplex Fluorescence in Situ Hybridization
MFIST DMD .... Modified FIST DMD (SAUS)
MFiT .... Fitchburg State College, Fitchburg, MA [*Library symbol*] [*Library of Congress*] (LCLS)
MFIT .... Manual Fault Isolation Test
MFIT .... Modified Flight Intersection Tape (SAA)
MFIV .... Mainwater Feed Isolation Valve [*Nuclear energy*] (NRCH)
MFJ .... Minister for Justice (SAUO)
MFJ .... Moala [*Fiji*] [*Airport symbol*] (OAG)
MFJ .... Modified Final Judgment [*Telecommunications*]
MFJ .... Movement for Freedom and Justice [*Ghana*] [*Political party*] (EY)
MFJC .... Memorial Foundation for Jewish Culture (EA)
MFJSA ...... Mass Finishing Job Shops Association (EA)
MFK .... Mafeking [*South Africa*] [*Airport symbol*] (OAG)
MFK .... Mill Fixture Key [*Tool*]
MFKP .... Multifrequency Key Pulsing
MFKT .... Mobile Field Kitchen Trailer (MCD)

MFKY........ Maxey Flats, Kentucky [*Commercial waste site*] (GAAI)
MFL.......... Magnetic Field Line
MFL.......... Main Feedwater Line [*Nuclear energy*] (NRCH)
MFL.......... Maintain Flight Level [*Aviation*]
MFL.......... Maintenance Fault List (ACAE)
MFL.......... Maintenance-Free Lifetime (PDAA)
MFL.......... Master Force List [*DoD*]
MFL.......... Master of Family Life
MFL.......... Matrimonial and Family Law [*New York, NY*] [*A publication*]
MFL.......... Matrimonial and Family Life [*A publication*]
MFL.......... Maximum Foreseeable Loss [*Insurance*]
MFL.......... Methodists for Life [*Defunct*] (EA)
MFL.......... MicroFabrication Laboratory [*Northeastern University*] (RCD)
MfL.......... Microfile (Pty.) Ltd., Johannesburg, South Africa [*Library symbol*] [*Library of Congress*] (LCLS)
MFL.......... Midland Forensic Laboratory (SAUO)
MFL.......... Million Fibers per Liter (EEVL)
MFL.......... Missile Firing Laboratory (KSC)
MFL.......... Mobile Field Laboratory
MFL.......... Mobile Field Laundry [*Military*]
MFL.......... Modern Foreign Language
MFL.......... Motor Freight Line
MFL.......... Multiple Fragment Laceration [*Shrapnel wound*] [*Military*] (VNW)
MFL.......... Mutual Funds Limited (SAUO)
MFLA........ Midwest Federation of Library Associations
m flac....... Membrana Flaccida [*Flaccid Membrane*] [*Latin*] [*Medicine*] (MAE)
MFLB........ Motor Fuel Licensing Board [*Australia*]
MFLC........ Mid-Florida Conference (PSS)
MFLD........ Male-Female Longevity Difference
MFLD........ Manifold (KSC)
MFLD........ Message Field [*Computer science*]
MFLDA...... Malaysian Federal Land Development Authority (SAUO)
MFlem...... Middle Flemish [*Language*] (BARN)
MFLFd....... MuniVest Florida Fund [*Associated Press*] (SAG)
MFLIC....... Modified Fluid in Cell [*Automotive engine combustion analysis*]
MFLJC....... Mifflin Junction, PA [*American Association of Railroads railroad junction routing code*]
MFLOP...... Mega-Floating Point Operation
MFLOP...... Mega Floating-Point Operations per Second [*Computer science*]
MFLOP...... Megaflop (DCOM)
MFLOP...... Million Floating Point Operations (SAUO)
MFLOPS.... Million Floating Point Instructions per Second (AAEL)
Mflops....... Million Floating-Point Operations per Second [*Computer science*] (ODBW)
MFLOPS.... Million Floating-Point Operations per Second [*Processing power units*] [*Computer science*]
MFLOPS.... Millions of Floating Point Operations Per Second [*Telecommunications*] (ACRL)
MFLP........ Mattel Family Learning Program
MFLP........ Multifile Linear Programming
MFLR........ Mayflower Co-Operative Bank [*NASDAQ symbol*] (NQ)
MFLT........ Mathematics Functional Literacy Test (EDAC)
MFLT........ Mean Fault Location Time (DNAB)
MFLT........ Mean First Lesions Time [*Immunochemistry*]
MFLU........ Mainfreight Transport [*Intermodal shipping container symbol*] (TVRC)
MFLZ........ Mejdunarodna Fondatzia Lyudmila Zhivkova [*Lyudmila Zhivkova International Foundation*] (EAIO)
MFm......... Framingham Town Library, Framingham, MA [*Library symbol*] [*Library of Congress*] (LCLS)
MFM......... Glenair [*British*] [*FAA designator*] (FAAC)
MFM......... Magnetic-Field Modulation [*Computer science*] (PCM)
MFM......... Magnetic Field Monitor [*NASA*]
MFM......... Magnetic Force Microscope
MFM......... Magnetic Forming Machine
MFM......... Magnetofluid Mechanic
MFM......... Mass Flow Meter (AAEL)
MFM......... Master File Maintenance [*Computer science*]
MFM......... Master of Financial Management (ADA)
MFM......... Materials Flow Management [*Manufacturing*]
MFM......... Maternal-Fetal Medicine (MELL)
MFM......... Maximally Flat Magnitude
MFM......... Meals for Millions Foundation [*Later, MFM/FFH*] (EA)
MFM......... MFC Mining Finance Corp. [*Toronto Stock Exchange symbol*] [*Vancouver Stock Exchange symbol*]
MFM......... MFS Municipal Income Trust [*NYSE symbol*] (SPSG)
MFM......... MFS Municipal Inc. Tr [*NYSE symbol*] (TTSB)
MFM......... Micrometer Frequency Meter
MFM......... Minced Fish Meat [*Food technology*]
MFM......... Mine Firing Mechanism
MFM......... Miniature Fluxgate Magnetometer
MFM......... Minneapolis-St. Paul [*Minnesota*] [*Seismograph station code, US Geological Survey*] (SEIS)
MFM......... Missile Farm Monitor [*Army*] (AABC)
MFM......... Missile Fatigue Monitor
MFM......... Mississippi State University, Mississippi State, MS [*OCLC symbol*] (OCLC)
MFM......... Modified Frequency Modulation [*Electronics*]
MFM......... Morrissey, Fernie & Michel Railway [*AAR code*]
MFM......... Mouvement pour le Pouvoir Proletarien [*or aux Petits*] [*Movement for Proletarian Power*] [*Malagasy*] [*Political party*] (PPW)
MFM......... Movable Fine Mesh
MFM......... Multi-Faith Meal [*Army*] (INF)
MFM......... Multifunctional Monomer [*Organic chemistry*]
MFM......... Multistage Frequency Multiplexer
MFM......... Municipal Finance and Management (SAUO)
MFMA....... Maple Flooring Manufacturers Association (EA)
MFMA....... Master Fish Merchants Association (SAUO)
MFMA....... Metal Farming Manufacturers Association (SAUO)
MFMA....... Metal Findings Manufacturers Association (EA)
MFMA....... Metal Framing Manufacturers Association (EA)
MFMA....... Midwest Feed Manufacturers Association [*Later, AFMA*] (EA)
MFMA....... Monolithic Ferrite Memory Array
MFMA....... Multi-Function Microwave Aperture (SAUS)
MF/MAGNOLIA... Magnetic Field Experiment (SAUO)
MFMANSW... Master Fish Merchants' Association of New South Wales [*Australia*]
MFMBARS... Multi-Function, Multi-Band Airborne Radio System (PDAA)
MFmcM..... Marist College and Seminary, Framingham Center, MA [*Library symbol*] [*Library of Congress*] (LCLS)
MFMD....... MonofluoromethylDOPA (DB)
MFM/FFH... Meals for Millions/Freedom from Hunger Foundation (EA)
MFMH....... Monofluoromethylhistidine [*Antineoplastic drug*]
MFmHi...... Framingham Historical society, Framingham, MA [*Library symbol*] [*Library of Congress*] (LCLS)
MFMI........ Men for Missions International (EA)
MFMIS....... Metal Ferroelectric Metal Insulator Semiconductor
MFML....... Merchants Fast Motor Lines [*Common carrier symbol*]
MFMM...... Microwave Frequency Measurement Module
MFMMA..... Metal Forming Machinery Makers' Association (HEAS)
MFMR....... Multifrequency Microwave Radiometer (MCD)
MFMS....... Military Flight Management System (SAUS)
MFMS....... Mobile Flight Mission Simulator [*Army*]
MFmT....... Framingham State College, Framingham, MA [*Library symbol*] [*Library of Congress*] (LCLS)
MFMT....... Maryland Functional Mathematics Test (EDAC)
MFMT....... Microwave Frequency Modulation Transmitter
MFMT....... National Federation of Meat Traders (SAUO)
MF/MWS.... Male/Female - Married/Widow [*or Widower*]/Single
MFN......... MDC Financial, Inc. [*Vancouver Stock Exchange symbol*]
MFN......... Mercury Finance [*NYSE symbol*] (TTSB)
MFN......... Mercury Finance Co. [*NYSE symbol*] (SPSG)
MFN......... Metabolic Fecal Nitrogen (PDAA)
MFN......... Milford Sound [*New Zealand*] [*Airport symbol*] (OAG)
MFN......... Most-Favored-Nation [*Trading status*]
MFN......... Muffin (ABBR)
MFNG....... Motion for a Finding of Not Guilty
MFNM....... Misty Fiords National Monument [*Alaska*] (ALAC)
MFNO....... Midland Federation of Newspaper Owners (SAUO)
MFNP........ Mount Field National Park (SAUO)
MFNP........ Murchison Falls National Park (SAUO)
MFNS........ Millard Fillmore National Society [*Defunct*] (EA)
MFNX........ Metromedia Fiber Network'A' [*NASDAQ symbol*] (SG)
MFNX........ Metromedia Fiber Network, Inc. [*NASDAQ symbol*] (NASQ)
MFNZ........ Music Federation of New Zealand (SAUO)
MFO......... Mafco Consolidated Group [*NYSE symbol*] (SAG)
MFO......... Major Function Overlay (MCD)
MFO......... Marine Fuel Oil
MFO......... Master Frequency Oscillator (NG)
MFO......... Material Fielding Operations (MCD)
MFO......... Maxfield Family Organization [*Association*] (EA)
MFO......... Mbe [*Language symbol*] (ETLW)
MFO......... Medium Frequency Oscillator (DMAA)
MFO......... Member of the Faculty of Ophthalmologists (SAUO)
MFO......... MFS Income & Opportunity Trust [*NYSE symbol*] (COMM)
MFO......... Military Forwarding Officer
MFO......... Military Forwarding Organization
MFO......... Missile Field Office (AAG)
MFO......... Missile Firing Order
MFO......... Missile Flight Office (SAUO)
MFO......... Mixed-Function Oxidase [*Biochemistry*]
MFO......... Multi-Functional Optimization
MFO......... Multinational Force and Observers [*Eleven-nation peace-keeping force for the Sinai*]
MFO......... Multinational Forces and Observer [*Army*]
MFO......... Multiple Facility Organization
MFOA........ Municipal Finance Officers Association (SAUS)
MFOA........ Municipal Finance Officers Association of US and Canada [*Later, GFOA*] (EA)
MFOC........ Military and Government Fiber Optics and Communications [*Conference*] (TSSD)
MFOccM..... Member of the Faculty of Occupational Medicine (SAUO)
MFOD....... Manned Flight Operations Directive [*NASA*] (KSC)
MFOE........ Mixed-Function Oxidase Enzyme System
MFOI........ Major Force Oriented Issue [*Military*] (AFM)
MFOM....... Master, Faculty of Occupational Medicine (DAVI)
MFOM....... Member, Faculty of Occupational Medicine (CMD)
MFOM....... MLRS Family of Munitions (SAUS)
MFON....... Missile Firing Order Normal [*Military*] (CAAL)
MFOPP...... Missile Firing Order Patch Panel
MFOPSS.... Marine Fiber-Optic Perimeter Security System [*Police and security equipment*]
MFor......... Master of Forestry
MForSc...... Master of Forest Science (ADA)
MFOS........ MultiFunction Operations System [*Communications term*] (DCT)
MFOT........ Mean Forced Outage Time (PDAA)
MFOV........ Medium Field-Of-View (SAUS)
MFOW....... Pacific Coast Marine Firemen, Oilers, Watertenders, and Wipers Association
MFOWW.... Marine Firemen, Oilers, Watertenders and Wipers (SAUO)
MFOX........ Multipurpose Fiber Optic Transceiver (ACAE)

MFP .... Franciscan Missionaries Our Lady of Peace (TOCD)
MFP .... Magnetic Field Perturbation
MFP .... Main Feed Power [*Nuclear energy*] (NRCH)
MFP .... Main Feed Pump (NVT)
MFP .... Main Feedwater Pump [*Nuclear energy*] (NRCH)
MFP .... Main Force Patrol [*In movie "Mad Max"*]
MFP .... Main Fuel Pump (SAUS)
MFP .... Major Force Program [*Air Force*] (AFIT)
MFP .... Management Framework Plan
MFP .... Marematlou Freedom Party (Lesotho) [*Political party*] (PSAP)
MFP .... Maryland Psychiatric Society (EARSL)
MFP .... Master File Program [*Computer science*]
MFP .... Master Personnel File (SAUO)
MFP .... Matched Filter Performance
MFP .... Materiel Fielding Plan
MFP .... Maximum Fluoride Protection [*Colgate-Palmolive Co.*]
MFP .... Maximum Freezing Point
MFP .... Mean Free Path
MFP .... Meat, Fish and Poultry
MFP .... Medium Floor Pintle (SAUS)
MFP .... Melphalan, Fluorouracil, Farlutal (Medroxyprogesterone acetate) [*Antineoplastic drug regimen*]
MF(P) .... Microfiche (Positive)
MFP .... Middle Free Path
MFP .... Military Foot Police (SAUO)
MFP .... Minimal Flight Path
MFP .... Minimum Facility Plan (ACAE)
MFP .... Minister of Fuel and Power (SAUO)
MFP .... Ministry of Fuel and Power [*British*]
MFP .... Mixed Fission Products [*Nuclear energy*]
MFP .... Mobile Flux Platform (USDC)
MFP .... Moca [*Fernando Poo*] [*Equatorial Guinea*] [*Seismograph station code, US Geological Survey*] (SEIS)
MFP .... Molecular Free Path
MFP .... Monofluorophosphate [*Inorganic chemistry*]
MFP .... Movement for a Free Philippines (EA)
MFP .... Multi-Factor Productivity
MFP .... Multiform Printer
MFP .... Multifrequency Pulsing (MSA)
MFP .... Multifunction Peripheral [*Chip*] [*Computer science*]
MFP .... Multifunction Polis
MFP .... Multifunction Printers (PS)
MFP .... Multifunction Product (GART)
MFP .... Multi-Purpose Facility (SAUO)
MFP .... Myofascial Pain [*Medicine*]
MFPA .... Massachusetts Forest and Park Association (SAUO)
MFPA .... Michigan Forest and Park Association (SAUO)
MFPA .... Missouri Forest Products Association (EARSL)
MFPA .... Monolithic Focal Plane Array (PDAA)
MFPA .... Mosaic Focal Plane Array (ACAE)
MFPA .... Mouth and Foot Painting Artists (ODA)
MFPA .... Multi-Function Peripheral Association (SAUO)
MFPB .... Mineral Fiber Products Bureau
MFPC .... Maine Forest Products Council (EARSL)
MFPC .... Man-Made Fibres Producers Committee [*British*] (DBA)
MFPC .... Multifunction Protocol Converter
mfpcf .... Million Fibers Per Cubic Foot [*Industrial hygiene term*] (OHS)
MFPCFA ..... Michigan Federation of Private Child and Family Agencies (EARSL)
MFPD .... Modern Federal Practice Digest [*A publication*] (DLA)
MFPE .... Minimum Final Prediction Error (MHDI)
MFPE .... Minimum Foundation Program for Education (SAUO)
MFPE .... Misson From Planet Earth (SAUO)
MFPF .... Minefield Planning Folder [*Navy*] (DOMA)
MFPG .... Mechanical Failures Prevention Group
MFPG .... Mixed Fission Products Generator [*Nuclear energy*]
MFPh .... Member of the Faculty of Physiotherapists [*British*]
MFPharmM ... Member of the Faculty of Pharmaceutical Medicine (SAUO)
MFPHM ..... Member, Faculty of Public Health Medicine (CMD)
MFPhys ..... Member of the Faculty of Physiatrists [*British*]
MFPK .... Multifunction Program Keyboard (MCD)
mfpm .... Made from Purchased Materials [*Manufacturing*]
MFP/MTP ... Materiel Fielding Plan/Materiel Transfer Plan [*Army*] (RDA)
MFPS .... Materiel Fielding Plans (ACAE)
MFPS .... Member of the Faculty of Physicians and Surgeons [*Glasgow*]
MFPS .... Mobile Field Photographic Section (NATG)
MFPS .... Modular Force Planning System (MCD)
MFPT .... Machinery Failure Prevention Technology (RDA)
MFPT .... Main Feedwater Pump Turbine [*Nuclear energy*] (NRCH)
MFPT .... Mean First-Passage Time [*Biochemistry*]
MFPTC ..... Main Feed Pump Turbine Condenser [*Nuclear energy*] (NRCH)
MFPU .... Mobile Field Photographic Unit (SAUS)
MFP-UK ..... Mothers for Peace - UK (EAIO)
MFPUL ..... Mississippi Forest Products Utilization Laboratory [*Mississippi State University*] [*Research center*] (RCD)
MFPVC ..... Multifocal Premature Ventricular Contractions [*Medicine*] (MEDA)
MFPZ .... McFarland Pole [*Federal Railroad Administration identification code*]
MFQ .... Maradi [*Niger*] [*Airport symbol*] (OAG)
M'F R .... MacFarlane's Scotch Jury Court Reports [*1838-39*] [*A publication*] (DLA)
MFR .... Macfie Resources [*Vancouver Stock Exchange symbol*]
MFR .... Machine Feature Recognition
MFR .... Mail File Requirement [*Code*] [*Computer science*]
MFR .... Malfunctional Review
MFR .... Malfunction Rate
MFR .... Malfunction Receiver
MFR .... Manipulator Foot Restraint (NASA)
MFR .... Manufacture [*or Manufacturer*] (AFM)
mfr .... Manufacture (DD)
mfr .... Manufacturer (ELAL)
Mfr .... Manufacturer (PROS)
MFR .... Manufacturer
MFr .... Mare Frigoris [*Sea of Cold*] [*Lunar area*]
MFR .... Marine Fishery Reserve
MFR .... Master Facility Register [*Nuclear energy*]
MFR .... Master Frame Recognize (MCD)
MFR .... Master Frequency Record [*FCC list*] (NTCM)
MFR .... Master of Forest Resources (GAGS)
M Fr .... Master of French (PGP)
MFR .... Maximum Flight Rate (NASA)
MFR .... Mean Firing Rate [*Neurophysiology*]
MFR .... Mean Flow Rate [*Medicine*] (EDAA)
MFR .... Medford [*Oregon*] [*Airport symbol*] (OAG)
MFR .... Medford, OR [*Location identifier*] [*FAA*] (FAAL)
MFr .... Melomanes Francais [*Record label*] [*France*]
MFR .... Melt-Flow Rate [*of plastics*]
MFR .... Memorandum for Record [*Military*]
MFR .... Memorandum for the Record (SAUO)
MFR .... Methanofuran (QSUL)
MfR .... Microform Review, Inc., Weston, CT [*Library symbol*] [*Library of Congress*] (LCLS)
MFR .... Middle French [*Language, etc.*]
MFR .... Mid-Forceps Rotation [*Obstetrics*] (DAVI)
MFR .... Military Field Representative (SAA)
MFR .... Minimum Funding Requirement
MFR .... Missile Firing Range (AAG)
MFR .... Mission Fired Report (SAUO)
MFR .... Model Form and Record
MFR .... Mucus Flow Rate [*Medicine*] (EDAA)
MFR .... Multifilter Radiometer (ARMP)
MFR .... Multifrequency Receiver [*Telecommunications*]
MFR .... Multifunctional Receiver (NASA)
MFR .... Multifunctional Review (NASA)
MFR .... Multifunction RADAR
MFR .... Mutual Force Reductions
MFR .... Myofascial Release [*Medicine*] (IDYL)
MFran ...... Ray Memorial Library, Franklin, MA [*Library symbol*] [*Library of Congress*] (LCLS)
MFRC .... Manufacturer Code [*Automotive emissions*]
MFRC .... Maritimes Forest Research Centre [*Research center*] (RCD)
MFRC .... Master of Forest Resources and Conservation (PGP)
MFRD .... Manufactured (ABBR)
MFRE .... Manufacture (ADA)
MFREA ...... Multiple Food Retailers Employers' Association [*British*]
MFRF .... Mean-Family Replacement Factor
MFRG .... Manufacturing
MFRG .... Medical Functional Requirements Group (MCD)
MFRI .... MFRI, Inc. [*NASDAQ symbol*] (SPSG)
MFRI .... Midwesco Filter Resources (EFIS)
MFRI .... Migratory Fish Research Institute [*University of Maine*] [*Research center*] (RCD)
MFRI .... Military Family Research Institute [*Purdue University*] (RCD)
MFRL .... Merchants Freight Line [*Common carrier symbol*]
MFRN .... Manufacturer Name [*Automotive emissions*]
MFRN .... Manufacturers Number
MFRP .... Midwest Fuel Recovery Plant [*AEC*]
MFRP .... Multigrade Functional Rehabilitation Platform [*Medicine*]
MFRPA ...... Maxey Flats Radioactive Protective Association (EA)
MFRR .... Manufacturer (ABBR)
MFRS .... Maritime Force Requirements Study (SAUO)
MFRS .... Master File Replacement System [*Computer science*]
MFRS .... Multifunction Receiver System
MFRSR ...... Multifilter Rotating Shadowband Radiometer (CARB)
MFRT .... Maryland Functional Reading Test (EDAC)
MFRT .... Mercury Freight [*Common carrier symbol*]
MFRT .... Modulated Frequency Radio Telephone (PDAA)
MFRU .... Marfret [*Intermodal shipping container symbol*] (TVRC)
MFRY .... Manufactory (ABBR)
MFS .... Fleet Minesweeper (Steel-Hulled) [*Navy symbol*]
MFS .... Frostburg State College, Library, Frostburg, MD [*OCLC symbol*] (OCLC)
MFS .... Macintosh File Structure [*Apple Computer, Inc.*] [*Computer science*] (CIST)
MFS .... Macintosh File System [*Computer science*]
MFS .... Magnetic Field Strength
MFS .... Magnetic Tape Field Search [*Computer science*]
MFS .... Maine Forest Service (SAUO)
MFS .... Major Frame Synchronization (ACAE)
MFS .... Malleable Founders' Society [*Later, Iron Castings Society - ICS*]
MFS .... Maltese Falcon Society [*Defunct*] (EA)
MFS .... Manned Flying System (MCD)
MFS .... Manufactures
MFS .... Marble Falls, TX [*Location identifier*] [*FAA*] (FAAL)
MFS .... Marfan Syndrome [*Medicine*]
MFS .... Marine-Finish Slate (MSA)
MFS .... Massachusetts Financial Services
MFS .... Master Fabrication Schedule (DNAB)
MFS .... Master of Family Studies (GAGS)
MFS .... Master of Food Science

MFS .... Master of Foreign Service
MFS .... Master of Foreign Study
MFS .... Master of Forensic Science (GAGS)
MFS .... Master of Forest Science (GAGS)
MFS .... Master of Forest Studies (PGP)
MFS .... Master of French Studies (PGP)
MFS .... Material False Statement [*Nuclear energy*] (NUCP)
MFS .... Maxillofacial Surgery [*Medical specialty*] (DHSM)
MFS .... McCloud Flat South [*California*] [*Seismograph station code, US Geological Survey*] (SEIS)
MFS .... Medal Field Service [*Canada*]
MFS .... Medicare Fee Schedule
MFS .... Medicated Feeding Stuff (GVA)
MFS .... Member of the Faraday Society (SAUO)
MFS .... Mercury Feed System
MFS .... Message Format Service
MFS .... Metropolitan Fiber Systems, Inc.
MfS .... Microfilm Systems, Colorado Springs, CO [*Library symbol*] [*Library of Congress*] (LCLS)
MFS .... Microfuel Systems [*Vancouver Stock Exchange symbol*]
MFS .... Military Flight Service
MFS .... Miller Fisher Syndrome [*Medicine*] (EDAA)
MFS .... Miller Flying Services, Inc. [*ICAO designator*] (FAAC)
MfS .... Ministerium fuer Staatssicherheit [*Ministry for State Security*] [*See also MISTAI, MSS*] [*Germany*] (EG)
MFS .... Minnesota Follow-Up Study Rehabilitation Rating Scale
MFS .... Miraflores [*Colombia*] [*Airport symbol*] (OAG)
MFS .... Missile Firing Simulator (NATG)
MFS .... Missile Firing Station [*Army*]
MFS .... Missile Fuse Set Servo
MFS .... Missing from Shelf (ADA)
MFS .... Missouri Followback Survey [*Department of Health and Human Services*] (GFGA)
MFS .... Mitral First Sound [*Cardiology*] (CPH)
MFS .... Mobile File Sync (SAUS)
MFS .... Mobilization for Survival (SAUO)
MFS .... Modern Fiction Studies [*A publication*] (BRI)
MFS .... Modified Filing System [*Computer science*] (PCM)
MFS .... Modified Full Spray
MFS .... Modular Flexible Scheduling [*Education*]
MFS .... Mountain Fuel Supply Co. (SAUO)
MFS .... Multi-Frequency Signalling [*Telecommunications*] (NITA)
MFS .... Multifunction Sensor (MCD)
MFS .... Multi-Function Switch [*Automotive engineering*]
MFS .... Multiple-Frequency Synthesizer
MFS .... Multiple Sclerosis Foundation (EA)
MFS .... Municipal Ferrous Scrap
MFS .... Museum of Fisheries and Shipping (SAUO)
MFS .... National Mobilization for Survival (EA)
MFSA .... Master Floor Sanders Association (NADA)
MFSA .... Metal Finishing Suppliers' Association (EA)
MFSA .... Methodist Federation for Social Action (EA)
MFSA .... Missile Flight Safety Approval (ACAE)
MFSA .... Missouri Financial Services Association (EARSL)
MFSB .... Mother, Father, Sister, Brother [*Musical group*]
MFSB .... Mutual Bancompany [*NASDAQ symbol*] (TTSB)
MFSB .... Mutual Bancompany, Inc. [*NASDAQ symbol*] (SAG)
MFSc .... Master of Fisheries Science
MFS C .... MFS Communication Co. [*Associated Press*] (SAG)
MFSC .... Missile Flight Safety Center [*Pacific Missile Range*] (MUGU)
MFS Cm .... MFS Communication Co. [*Associated Press*] (SAG)
MFSD .... Maritime Fire Support Demonstrator
MFSE .... Main Fire Support Element (AABC)
MFSF .... Magazine of Fantasy and Science Fiction [*A publication*] (BRI)
MFSFU ...... Matt-Finish Structural Facing Units [*Technical drawings*]
MFSG .... Microbiological Food Surveillance Group (SAUO)
MFSG .... Missile Firing Safety Group (MUGU)
MFSK .... Multiple-Frequency Shift Keying
MFSL .... Maryland Fed Bancorp [*NASDAQ symbol*] (TTSB)
MFSL .... Maryland Federal Bancorp, Inc. [*NASDAQ symbol*] (NQ)
MFSL .... Mathematical and Functional Subroutine Library (MHDB)
MFSO .... Missile Flight Safety Officer
MFSOA ...... Missile Flight Safety Officer Assistant (MUGU)
MFSOC ...... Missile Flight Safety Officer Console (MUGU)
MF SOL ...... Merthiolate-Formaldehyde [*Stock*] Solution (BABM)
MFSOP ...... Missile Flight Safety Operations Plan
MFSP .... Macro Function Signal Processor (SAUS)
MFS PAC .... Massachusetts Financial Services Company PAC [*Boston, MA*] (PACS)
MFSR .... Magnetic Film Strip Recorder
MFSS .... Medical Field Service School [*Army*]
MFSS .... Missile Flight Safety System (AAG)
MFSS .... Multi-Frequency Signalling System [*Telecommunications*] (EECA)
Mfst .... Manifest (EBF)
mfst .... Manifest (ELAL)
MFST .... Manifest
MFST .... Medical Field Service Technician (BABM)
MFST .... MFS Communiations [*NASDAQ symbol*] (TTSB)
MFST .... MFS Communication Co. [*NASDAQ symbol*] (SAG)
MFST .... Mobile Fire Safety Team
MFSTB ...... Manifestable (ABBR)
MFSTD ...... Manifested (ABBR)
MFSTG ...... Manifesting (ABBR)
MFSTN ...... Manifestation (ABBR)
MFSTO ...... Manifesto (ABBR)
MFSTP ...... MFS Commun 8% Cv Dep'A'Pfd [*NASDAQ symbol*] (TTSB)
MFSU .... Mobile Field Service Unit
MFSW .... Madison Freight Systems [*Common carrier symbol*]
MFSW .... Membrane-Filtered Sea Water
MFSW .... Mining Foundation of the Southwest (EARSL)
MFT .... Drury Military Extension, Springfield, MO [*OCLC symbol*] (OCLC)
MFT .... Magnetic Flow Transmitter
MFT .... Mail for Tots (EA)
MFT .... Mainframe Termination [*Telecommunications*] (TEL)
MFT .... Major Fraction Thereof
MFT .... Manson Finance Trust Ltd. (SAUO)
MFT .... Manufacturing (SAUO)
MFT .... Manufacturing Fit Test
MFT .... Marconi Fast Tuning (MCD)
MFT .... Marriage and Family Therapist [*Psychology*]
MFT .... Maryland Functional Test
MFT .... Master File Table
MFT .... Master File Tax [*Code*] [*IRS*]
MFT .... Master Fitness Trainer [*Army*] (INF)
MFT .... Master of Family Therapy (GAGS)
MFT .... Master of Foreign Trade
MFT .... Materiel Fielding Team [*Army*] (RDA)
MFT .... Materiel Field Test (MCD)
MFT .... Mean Flight Time (KSC)
MFT .... Mean Free Time
MFT .... Mechanized Flame Thrower
MFT .... Medical Field Service Technician [*Navy*]
MFT .... Melter Feed Tank (ABAC)
MFT .... Meson Field Theory
MFT .... Metal Film Resistor
MFT .... Metallic Facility Terminal [*Telecommunications*] (TEL)
MFT .... Meter Fix Crossing Time (CTAS)
MFT .... Meter Fix Time/Slot Time [*FAA*] (TAG)
MFT .... MFS Multimarket Total Return Trust [*NYSE symbol*] (COMM)
MFT .... Mine Fuse Train
MFT .... Minimum Film-Forming Temperature [*Wax polishes*]
MFT .... Minimum Flexible Targeting (SAUO)
MFT .... Minuteman Flexible Targeting (ACAE)
MFT .... Missile Flight Time
MFT .... Mission Flight Trainer [*Navy*]
M FT .... Mistura Fiat [*Let a Mixture Be Made*] [*Pharmacy*]
MFT .... Mobile Foot Restraint (SSD)
MFT .... Molecular Field Theory [*Physical chemistry*]
MFT .... Monolayer Formation Time [*Physical chemistry*] (OA)
MFT .... Morgan Financial Corp. [*Toronto Stock Exchange symbol*]
MFT .... Most-Favorable Term (MHDW)
MFT .... Motor Freight Tariff [*Business term*] (ADA)
MFT .... Motor Freight Terminal
MFT .... Multifocal Atrial Tachycardia [*Cardiology*] (DMAA)
MFT .... Multilingual Forestry Terminology
MFT .... Multiple Family Therapy (DHP)
MFT .... Multiposition Frequency Telegraphy [*Telecommunications*] (OA)
MFT .... Multiprogramming (NITA)
MFT .... Multiprogramming with a Finite Amount of Trouble [*Computer science*]
MFT .... Multiprogramming with Fixed Number of Tasks [*Computer science*] (BUR)
MFT .... MuniYield FL Insured Fund [*NYSE symbol*] (TTSB)
MFT .... MuniYield Florida Insured Fund [*NYSE symbol*] (SPSG)
MFT .... Muscle Function Test
MFTA .... Managed Futures Trade Association (EA)
MFTA .... Multiduct Fuel Test Assembly [*Nuclear energy*] (NRCH)
MFTA .... Multi-Function Towed Array
MFTAD ...... Master Flight Test Assignment Document (NASA)
MFTAD ...... Master Flight Test Assignments Document [*NASA*]
MFTB .... Motor Freight Tariff Bureau
MFTC .... Metalworking Fair Trade Coalition [*Later, MTC*] (EA)
MFTCom .... Member of the Faculty of Teachers in Commerce [*British*] (DBQ)
MFTD .... Mobile Field Training Detachment [*Military*] (AFM)
MF-TDA ..... Multiple-Feedback, Time-Division Multiple Access (MED)
MFTDMA .... Multiple Frequency Time Division Multiple Access (LAIN)
MFTF .... Mirror Fusion Test Facility [*For study of new energy source*]
MFTF .... Missionary Flight Training Foundation [*Defunct*]
MFTGS ...... Midcourse Fix and Terminal Guidance System (MCD)
MFTHBA .... Missouri Fox Trotting Horse Breed Association (EA)
MFT L .... Millifoot Lamberts (DEN)
MFTL .... Modular Field Test Laser (ACAE)
MFTL .... My Favorite Toy Language [*Computer hacker terminology*] (NHD)
M FT M ...... Misce Fiat Mistura [*Mix to Make a Mixture*] [*Pharmacy*]
m ft mist .... Misce Flat Mistura [*Mix and Let a Mixture be Made*] [*Latin*] (WDAA)
MFTP .... Modified Federal Test Procedure [*EPA engine test*]
MFTRS ...... Magnetic Flight Test Recording System
MFTS .... Medial Femorotibial Space [*Anatomy*]
MFT/S .... Missile Facilities Technician/Specialist (AAG)
MFTT .... Multi-Function Tanker Transport (SAUS)
MFTT .... Multi-Function Telephone Terminal [*Telecommunications*] (VLIE)
MFTU .... Macao Federation of Trade Unions
MFTU .... Macau Federation of Trade Unions (SAUO)
MFTU .... Marfret [*Intermodal shipping container symbol*] (TVRC)
MFTU .... Multi-Function Tape Unit (VLIE)
MFTV .... Mechanical Fit Test Vehicle
MFTVP ...... Motor-Free Test of Visual Perception [*Psychology*] (DAVI)
MFU .... Magnetic Force Upset [*Metals*]

MFU .... Marine Forecast Unit [*National Weather Service*]
MFU .... Medical Follow up (SAUS)
MFU .... Mfuwe [*Zambia*] [*Airport symbol*] (OAG)
MFU .... Military Foul-Up [*Bowdlerized version*] (DSUE)
MFU .... MIRA [*Multifunctional Inertial Reference Assembly*] Fighter Unit [*Air Force*] (MCD)
MFU .... Myoclonus Families United (EA)
MFU .... Pacific Coast Marine Firemen, Oilers, Watertenders, and Wipers Association [*Also known as Marine Firemen's Union*] (EA)
MFUA........ Medical Follow-Up Agency [*National Research Council*]
MFUI .... Mechanics Friendly Union Institution [*British*]
MFUMR ..... MIRA [*Multifunctional Inertial Reference Assembly*] Fighter Unit Mounting Rack [*Air Force*] (MCD)
MFUN .... Morgan Funshares [*NASDAQ symbol*] (TTSB)
MFUN .... Morgan Funshares, Inc. [*NASDAQ symbol*] (SAG)
MFURB...... Maryland Fire Underwriters Rating Bureau (SAUO)
Mfurers Mon... Manufacturers' Monthly [*A publication*]
MFUS........ Marfret [*Common carrier symbol*]
MFUSYS .... Microfiche File Update System [*Computer science*] (PDAA)
MFUW....... Magnetic Force Upset Welding [*Metals*]
MFV .... Forward Visibility More than ___ Miles [*Aviation*] (FAAC)
MFV .... Magnetic Field Vector
MFV .... Main Feedwater Valve [*Nuclear energy*] (NRCH)
MFV .... Main Fuel Valve [*Aerospace*] (NAKS)
MFV .... Maintenance Floor Valve (NRCH)
MFV .... Mars Flyby Vehicle [*Aerospace*]
MF V .... Materiel Division, Western Military Region Command (SAUO)
MFV .... Melfa, VA [*Location identifier*] [*FAA*] (FAAL)
MFV .... Methanol-Fueled Vehicle [*Automotive engineering*]
MFV .... MFS Special Value Trust [*NYSE symbol*] (SPSG)
MFV .... Microfilm Viewer
MFV .... Military Flight Vehicles
MFV .... Motor Fishing Vessel [*British military*] (DMA)
MFV .... Motor Fleet Vesel (ODA)
MFVA........ Main Fuel Valve Actuator (SAUS)
MFVD........ Maximum Forward Voltage Drop
MFVP........ Mauler Feasibility Validation Program
MFVPT ...... Motor-Free Visual Perception Test
mfVSG....... Membrane Form of Variant Surface Glycoprotein [*Biochemistry*]
MFVT........ Mixed-Flow Vectored Thrust (SAUS)
MFVT........ Motor Free Visual Perception Test [*Therapy term*] (CTAA)
MFW......... Main Feedwater [*Nuclear energy*] (NRCH)
MFW......... M&F Worldwide [*NYSE symbol*] (SG)
MFW......... Maritime Federation of the World (NADA)
MFW......... Metres of Fresh Water
MFW......... Migrant Farm Worker (OICC)
MFW......... Milton-Freewater [*Oregon*] [*Seismograph station code, US Geological Survey*] (SEIS)
MFW......... Ms. Foundation for Women (EA)
MFW......... Multi-Function Wheel [*Automotive classified advertising*]
MFW......... Multi-Function Workstation (SAUO)
MFW......... Multiple Fragment Wound (MAE)
MFW......... Multiple Fragment Wounds (SAUS)
MFWC....... Marine Fleet Air, West Coast
MFWCS ..... Main Feedwater and Condensate System [*Environmental science*] (COE)
MFWD....... Mechanical Four-Wheel Drive [*Off-Highway equipment*]
MFWD....... Mechanical Front Wheel Drive [*Off-highway equipment*]
MFWG....... Mechanical Failures Working Group (SAUO)
MFWLB ..... Main Feedwater Line Break [*Nuclear energy*] (NRCH)
MFWP....... Maryland Functional Writing Program (EDAC)
MFWV....... Main Feedwater Valve [*Nuclear energy*] (NRCH)
MFX .... Mirror Fusion Experiment [*Nuclear energy*]
MFXT .... Meter Fix Time [*Aviation*] (FAAC)
MFY .... Manufactory (ABBR)
MFY .... Mobilization for Youth
MFY .... Music for Youth
MFZ.......... Mabaan [*Language symbol*] (ETLW)
MFZ.......... Mezzo Forzando [*Music*]
MFZ.......... Missile Firing Zone
MFZ.......... Mofaz Air [*Malawi*] [*FAA designator*] (FAAC)
MG........... Geometric Mean [*Psychology*]
MG........... Groundswell, Inc. of Minnesota (EA)
mg .... Guadalupe Missioners (TOCD)
MG........... Gudalupe Missioners (TOCD)
MG........... Machine-Glazed [*Poster paper*]
MG........... Machine Group (SAUO)
MG........... Machine Gun (MUGU)
MG........... Machine Gunner [*British military*] (DMA)
MG........... Machinery of Government [*British*]
MG........... Madagascar [*ANSI two-letter standard code*] (CNC)
mg .... Mafic Granulite [*Geology*]
MG........... Magenta (ROG)
MG........... Maggioni & C. [*Italy*] [*Research code symbol*]
Mg .... Maghemite [*A mineral*]
MG........... Magna International, Inc. [*Toronto Stock Exchange symbol*]
Mg .... Magnesium [*Chemical element*]
MG........... Magnetic Armature (MSA)
MG........... Maharashtrawadi Gomantak [*India*] [*Political party*] (PPW)
MG........... Main Gauche [*With the Left Hand*] [*Music*]
MG........... Main Generator (IAA)
MG........... Main Group (SAUO)
MG........... Maintainability Group (SAUO)
MG........... Major General
Mg .... Major General
MG........... Make Good
MG........... Malachite Green [*A dye*]
mg .... Malagasy Republic [*Madagascar*] [*MARC country of publication code*] [*Library of Congress*] (LCCP)
MG........... Mammary Gland [*Anatomy*]
MG........... Manage [*Telegraphy*] (PCTE)
MG........... Management Group (SAUO)
MG........... Management Guide (SAUO)
MG........... Managerial Grid
MG........... Manager's Guide
Mg .... Mangrove [*Maps and charts*]
MG........... Manual Group (NRCH)
MG........... Manufactured Goods (AAEL)
MG........... Manufacturing
MG........... Maof Airlines [*Israel*] [*ICAO designator*] (ICDA)
MG........... Marcus Gunn (Pupil) [*Ophthalmology*]
MG........... Margin (DAVI)
MG........... Marginal (AAG)
MG........... Margun Music [*Publisher*]
MG........... Marine Gunner
MG........... Martinus Gosia [*Authority cited in pre-1607 legal work*] (DSA)
MG........... Master-General [*Military*] [*British*]
MG........... Master Generator [*Telecommunications*] (OA)
MG........... Master Group (VLIE)
mg .... Master-Group (SAUO)
MG........... Matrix Glass [*Geology*]
MG........... Meaning (ROG)
MG........... Measurements Group (SAUO)
MG........... Medal for Gallantry
MG........... Media General Financial Services [*Information retrieval*]
MG........... Media Guide
MG........... Medial Gastrocnemius [*Anatomy*]
MG........... Medium Grain [*Lumber*]
MG........... Mega-Gauss
Mg .... Megagram (COE)
MG........... Megagram
MG........... Membranous Glomerulonephritis [*Medicine*] (EDAA)
MG........... Membranous Glomerulopathy [*Nephrology*]
MG........... Menopausal Gonadotropin [*Endocrinology*]
MG........... Mentor Graphics Corporation (EFIS)
MG........... Mesiogingival [*Dentistry*]
MG........... Message Generator
MG........... Metal Glass (IAA)
MG........... Metal Goods [*Department of Employment*] [*British*]
MG........... Metallgesellschaft [*German commodities and futures contractor*] (ECON)
MG........... Metallurgical Grade
MG........... Meteorological Group [*Range Commanders Council*] [*White Sands Missile Range, NM*]
MG........... Meter Gauge [*Indian Railway*] (TIR)
MG........... Methylene Glutamine
MG........... Methylglucoside [*Organic chemistry*]
MG........... Methylglyoxal [*Also, MGLY*] [*Organic chemistry*]
MG........... Methyl Green [*A dye*]
MG........... MG [*NCIC car make code*]
MG........... MG Car Club (EA)
MG........... MGM Grand Air [*ICAO designator*] (AD)
MG........... Michaelis-Gutmann Bodies (MAE)
MG........... Michigan State Grange (EARSL)
mg .... Microgram (DAVI)
MG........... Microwave Generator
MG........... Middle Gimbal [*Yaw*]
M/G.......... Miles per Gallon
MG........... Military Government [*or Governor*]
MG........... Millard-Gubler [*Syndrome*] [*Medicine*] (DB)
MG........... Millennium Guild (EA)
MG........... Mill Glazed [*Paper*]
MG........... Milligauss (ABBR)
mG........... Milligauss, 1 E-3 G [*Industrial hygiene term*] (OHS)
MG........... Milli Gram (ACAE)
Mg .... Milligram (DIPS)
mg .... Milligram
mg%......... Milligram per 100 ml (SAUS)
MG........... Millwright Group (EA)
MG........... Minister General (SAUO)
MG........... Minister of the Gospel (GEAB)
MG........... Minnesota Groundswell (EA)
MG........... Minority Group
MG........... Miracle of Grace [*Pseudonym used by William Smith*]
MG........... Mirage Group [*Association*] (EA)
MG........... Misioneros de Guadalupe [*Missionaries of Guadelupe*] [*Mexico*] (EAIO)
MG........... Missile Gas
MG........... Missile Guidance
MG........... Mixed Grain
MG........... [*The*] Mobile & Gulf Railroad Co. [*Formerly, MGU*] [*AAR code*]
MG........... Mobile Generator (KSC)
MG........... Modified Guaranteed [*Securities trading*]
MG........... Moenchengladbach [*German license plate city code*]
MG........... Moeso-Gothic [*Language, etc.*] (ROG)
MG........... Monoclonal Gammopathy [*Medicine*] (EDAA)
MG........... Monoglyceride [*An enzyme*] (MAE)
MG........... Monogram Industries, Inc. (SAUO)

MG ... Montague Grammar [*Linguistics*] (IEL)
MG ... Morgan Group [*AMEX symbol*] (TTSB)
MG ... [*The*] Morgan Group, Inc. [*AMEX symbol*] (SAG)
MG ... Morning
MG ... Morris Garages [*British automobile manufacturer; initialism used as name of sports car it produces*]
MG ... Motion for Mandamus Granted [*Legal term*] (ILCA)
MG ... Motor Generator
MG ... Mucus Granule [*Medicine*] (EDAA)
MG ... Mug (ABBR)
MG ... Multigauge
MG ... Multi-Grade [*Fuels and lubricants*]
MG ... Muncie-Getrag [*Refers to an automotive transmission designed by Getrag, a West German company, and built by General Motors in Muncie, IN*]
MG ... Muscle Group (MAE)
MG ... Myasthenia Gravis [*Medicine*]
MG ... Myasthenia Gravis Foundation (EA)
MG ... Mycoplasma Gallisepticum (DB)
MG ... Myoglobin [*Medicine*] (DMAA)
MG ... Myriagram [*Ten Thousand Grams*] (ROG)
MG ... Pompano Airways [*ICAO designator*] (AD)
Mg/l ... Milligrams per Liter (GNE)
MGA ... Macroglobulinaemia [*Medicine*] (EDAA)
MGA ... Madras Geographical Association (SAUO)
MGA ... Magna International, Inc. [*NYSE symbol*] (SPSG)
MGA ... Mailorder Gardening Association (EA)
MGA ... Major-General i/c Administration (SAUO)
MGA ... Major-General in Charge of Administration [*British*]
MGA ... Mammary Gland Adenoma [*Medicine*] (MELL)
MGA ... Managing General Agency [*Insurance*]
MGA ... Managing General Agent [*Insurance*]
MGA ... Managua [*Nicaragua*] [*Airport symbol*] (OAG)
MGA ... Marble and Granite Association [*British*] (BI)
MGA ... Martin Goffman Associates (IID)
MGA ... Massachusetts Golf Association (EARSL)
MGA ... Master Gemology Association (EA)
MGA ... Master of General Administration (DMAA)
MGA ... Master of Government Administration (GAGS)
MGA ... Matrox Graphics Architecture [*Matrox Eletronics Systems Ltd.*] (PCM)
MGA ... Medical Gas Analyzer [*Medicine*] (EDAA)
MGA ... Medium-Gain Antenna
MGA ... Megaline Resources [*Vancouver Stock Exchange symbol*]
MGA ... Melengestrol Acetate [*Endocrinology*]
MGA ... Member of the General Assembly (SAUO)
MGA ... Mercantile Gold [*Vancouver Stock Exchange symbol*]
MGA ... Meteorological and Geoastrophysical Abstracts [*Database*] (GDD)
MGA ... Middle Gimbal Angle (NASA)
MGA ... Middle Gimbal Assembly (KSC)
MGA ... Middle Gimbal Axis (KSC)
MGA ... Milagra Ridge [*California*] [*Seismograph station code, US Geological Survey*] (SEIS)
MGA ... Military Government Association
MGA ... Minnesota Geophysical Associates, Inc. (EFIS)
MGA ... Minnesota Golf Association (EARSL)
MGA ... Module Generator Assembly (DWSG)
MGA ... Monochrome Graphics Adapter [*Hercules*] [*Computer science*] (PCM)
MGA ... [*The*] Monongahela Railway Co. [*AAR code*]
MGA ... Monongahela Railway Company (SAUO)
MGA ... Mother Guardian Allowance
MGA ... Multimedia Graphics Architecture [*Computer science*] (PCM)
MGA ... Multiple Gas Analyzer
MGA ... Mushroom Growers Association [*Commercial firm*] (EA)
MGA ... Mushroom Growers Cooperative Association [*Defunct*] (EA)
MGAA ... Major-General, Anti-Aircraft Artillery (SAUO)
MGAA ... Medium-Gain Autotrack Antenna
MGAA ... Miniature Golf Association of America (EA)
MGAB ... Maintenance Ground Abort [*Air Force*] (AFIT)
MGAB ... Mucous Gland Adenoma of Bronchus [*Medicine*] (PALA)
MGABR ... Maintenance Ground Abort Rate [*Air Force*] (AFIT)
MGAC ... Monongahela Connecting Railroad (SAUO)
MGACG ... Missile Guidance Alignment Checkout Group (SAUO)
MGAD ... Machine-Gun Artillery Division [*Former USSR*]
mgal ... Milligal [*Unit of acceleration*]
MGAL ... Thousand Gallons (EG)
MGAL/D ... Million Gallons per Day
mgallon ... Million Gallons (COE)
MGALS ... Milligals (ABBR)
MGAM ... Member Get a Member [*Prodigy Services Co.*]
MGAM ... Morgan Grenfell Asset Management [*Investment management firm*] [*British*]
MGAM ... Multimedia Games [*NASDAQ symbol*] (TTSB)
MGAM ... Multimedia Games, Inc. [*NASDAQ symbol*] (SAG)
MGAMS/CDTR ... Microgravity Accelerometer Measurement System/Cassette Data Tape Recorder (SAUS)
MGaMW ... Mount Wachusett Community College, Gardner, MA [*Library symbol*] [*Library of Congress*] (LCLS)
MG&E ... Madison Gas & Electric Co. (EFIS)
MG&E ... Michigan Gas and Electric Co. (SAUO)
MG & L ... Measurement of Gains and Losses (DICI)
MG & S ... Manning, Granger, and Scott's English Common Pleas Reports [*1845-56*] [*A publication*] (DLA)
MGAO ... Minority Graphic Arts Organization (EA)
MGAP ... Magnetic Attitude Prediction
MGAP ... Micro-Grain Array Processor [*Electronics*]
MGARJS ... Mobile Ground-to-Air RADAR Jamming System
MGAS ... Marcum Natural Gas Service, Inc. [*NASDAQ symbol*] (SAG)
MGAS ... Marcum Natural Gas Svcs [*NASDAQ symbol*] (TTSB)
MGAS ... Morgan Southern [*Common carrier symbol*]
MGAS ... Motor Gasoline [*Military*]
MGAT ... Manchester General Ability Test [*Education*] (AEBS)
MGAWA ... Market Gardeners' Association of Western Australia
MGAWD ... Make Good All Works Distributed [*Legal term*] (BARN)
MGB ... Main Gear Box (MCD)
MGB ... Manageable (ABBR)
MGB ... Medial Geniculate Body (DIPS)
MGB ... Medium-Girder Bridge (RDA)
MGB ... Medizinische Gerate GmbH Berlin (EFIS)
MGB ... Ministerstvo Gosudarstvennoy Bezopasnosti [*Ministry of State Security*] [*Former USSR*] (LAIN)
MGB ... Missile Gunboat (SAUS)
MGB ... Mississippi Bureau of Geology (SAUO)
MGB ... Mobile Garbage Bin
MGB ... Morgan Stan Global Opt Bd Fd [*NYSE symbol*] (TTSB)
MGB ... Morgan Stanley Global Opportunities Bond Fund, Inc. [*NYSE symbol*] (SAG)
MGB ... Motor Gunboat [*British*]
MGB ... Mount Gambier [*Australia*] [*Airport symbol*] (OAG)
MGBC ... Maranatha Gospel Bottle Crusade [*Later, CEM*] (EA)
MGBC ... Modelling Global Biogeochemical Cycles (SAUO)
MGBCS ... Murray Grey Beef Cattle Society [*Australia*]
MGBG ... Methylglyoxalbis(guanylhydrazone) [*Mitoguazone*] [*Also, Me-GAG*] [*Antineoplastic drug*]
MGBG ... Methylglyoxal-Bis[*guanylhydrazone*] (DB)
MGBN ... Bananera [*Guatemala*] [*ICAO location identifier*] (ICLI)
MGBNVCP ... Murray Geological Basin Native Vegetation Clearance Policy (SAUO)
MGBT ... Manageability (ABBR)
MGBY ... Manageably (ABBR)
MGC ... Machine-Gun Car [*or Carrier*] [*British*]
MGC ... Machine-Gun Co. [*or Corps*]
MGC ... Machine-Gun Combination [*British*]
MGC ... Machine Gun Corps (SAUO)
MGC ... Magec Aviation Ltd. [*British*] [*ICAO designator*] (FAAC)
MGC ... Magic (ABBR)
MgC ... Magnocellular Neuroendocrine Cell [*Medicine*] (DMAA)
MGC ... Major Gain Control
MGC ... Major General Commandant [*Marine Corps*]
MGC ... Management Group Codes (MCD)
MGC ... Manual Gain Control
MGC ... Manufactured Goods Collection (AAEL)
MGC ... Marriage Guidance Council [*British*]
MGC ... Marriage Guidance Counsellor (SAUO)
MGC ... Metacerebral Giant Cell [*Cytology*]
MGC ... Metallized Glass Coil
MGC ... Michigan City [*Indiana*] [*Airport symbol*] (OAG)
MGC ... Michigan City, IN [*Location identifier*] [*FAA*] (FAAL)
MGC ... Midcourse Guidance and Control
MGC ... Middle Georgia College [*Cochran*]
MGC ... Minimal Glomerular Change [*Nephrology*]
MGC ... Minimum Gelling Concentration [*Hematology*]
MGC ... Missile Guidance and Control
MGC ... Missile Guidance Computer (MCD)
MGC ... Montgomery County Community College, Blue Bell, PA [*OCLC symbol*] (OCLC)
MGC ... Morgan Grenfell Smallcap [*NYSE symbol*] (TTSB)
MGC ... Morgan Grenfell Smallcap Fund, Inc. [*NYSE symbol*] (SPSG)
MGC ... Mouse Genome Conference (HGEN)
MGC ... Movers Association of Greater Chicago, Chicago, IL [*STAC*]
MGC ... Museums and Galleries Commission [*Government body*] [*British*]
MGCA ... Men's Garden Clubs of America (EA)
MGCA ... Mobile Ground-Controlled Approach [*Aviation*]
MGCA ... Mushroom Growers Cooperative Association [*Defunct*]
MG CARB ... Magnesium Carbonate (SAUS)
MGCAX ... Managers Capital Appreciation Fund
MGCB ... Coban [*Guatemala*] [*ICAO location identifier*] (ICLI)
MGCB ... Master Gate Control Block [*Computer science*] (VLIE)
MGCC ... Medical Graphics [*NASDAQ symbol*] (TTSB)
MGCC ... Medical Graphics Corp. [*NASDAQ symbol*] (NQ)
MGCC ... MG [*Morris Garage*]Car Club
MGCC ... Missile Guidance and Control Computer
MGCD ... Maximum Gapless Coverage Distance (NG)
MGCE ... Multifocal Giant Cell Encephalitis [*Medicine*] (MELL)
MGCI ... Master Ground-Controller Interception RADAR (NATG)
MGCI ... Most General Common Instance (IDAI)
MGCL ... Magical (ABBR)
MGCLY ... Magically (ABBR)
mg/cm ... Milligram per Centimeter (COE)
MGCN ... Magician (ABBR)
MGCO ... Mars Geoscience/Climatology Orbiter
MGCOA ... National Golf Course Owners Association (NTPA)
MGCP ... Media Gateway Control Protocol [*Computer science*] (VLIE)
MGCP ... Media-Gateway Control Protocol [*Computer science*] (AGLO)
MGCR ... Carmelita [*Guatemala*] [*ICAO location identifier*] (ICLI)
MGCR ... Maritime Gas-Cooled Reactor
MGCRB ... Medicare Geographic Classification Review Board
MGCR-CX ... Maritime Gas-Cooled Reactor Critical Experiment
MGCS ... Manual Gas Control Station (SAUO)
MGCS ... Meteosat Ground Computer System [*Aviation*] (DA)

MGCS .... Meteosat Ground Computing Station (SAUO)
MGCS .... Missile Guidance and Control System (MCD)
MGCS .... Missile Guidance Cooling System (DWSG)
MGCS .... Mobile Ground Control Station (SAUO)
MGCT........ Coatepeque [*Guatemala*] [*ICAO location identifier*] (ICLI)
MGCT........ Mixed Germ Cell Tumor [*Medicine*] (MELL)
MGCX .... MGC Communications [*NASDAQ symbol*]
MGCYL...... Megacycle (ABBR)
MGD......... Machine Gaming Division [*Queensland, Australia*]
MGD......... Magadan [*Later, FUR*] [*Former USSR*] [*Geomagnetic observatory code*]
MGD......... Magadan 1 [*Former USSR*] [*Seismograph station code, US Geological Survey*] (SEIS)
MGD......... Magnetogasdynamic
MGD......... Managed
MGD......... Master of Graphic Design (PGP)
MGD......... Maternal Genetic Disease (MELL)
MGD......... Maximal Glucose Disposal [*Medicine*] (DMAA)
MGD......... McGregor-Doniger, Inc. (SAUO)
MGD......... Mean Gain Deviation (IEEE)
MG/D........ Megagrams per Day
MGD......... Mercury Germanium Detector
MGD......... Microbial Germplasm Database (GDD)
MGD......... Miehle-Goss-Dexter [*Rockwell International Corp.*]
MGD......... Military Geographic Documentation (AABC)
mg/d......... Milligrams per Deciliter
MGD......... Million Gallons per Day
MGD......... Millions of Gallons per Day (COE)
MGD......... Minority Group Designator [*Office of Personnel Management*] (GFGA)
MGD......... Mixed Gonadal Dysgenesis [*Medicine*]
MGD......... Molybdopterin Guanine Dinucleotide [*Biochemistry*]
MGD......... Mouse Genome Database
MGD......... Mugged (ABBR)
MGD......... Murgold Resources, Inc. [*Toronto Stock Exchange symbol*]
MGD......... North-East Cargo Airlines [*Russian Federation*] [*ICAO designator*] (FAAC)
MGD.V ...... Mandorin Goldfields [*Toronto Stock Exchange symbol*] [*Canada*]
MGDB .... Microbial Genome Database (MHID)
MGDC .... Morgan Grenfell Development Capital (WDAA)
MgdCare.... Managed Care Solutions, Inc. [*Associated Press*] (SAG)
MGDF .... Megakaryocyte Growth and Development Factor [*Cytology*]
MGDF .... Modified Granular Diffusion Flame [*Propellant*]
MgdHi....... Managed High-Income Income Portfolio [*Associated Press*] (SAG)
mg/dl........ milligrams per 100 milliliters (SAUS)
MgdMun.... Managed Municipals Portfolio [*Associated Press*] (SAG)
MgdMun2... Managed Municipals Portfolio II [*Associated Press*] (SAG)
MGDS .... Member in General Dental Surgery (DMAA)
MGDS .... Mines Geologic Disposal System (SAUO)
MGDSRCS Eng... Membership in General Dental Surgery, Royal College of Surgeons of England [*British*] (DBQ)
MGDVF...... Murgold Resources, Inc. [*NASDAQ symbol*] (COMM)
MGE......... Evergreen Regional Library, Gimli, Manitoba [*Library symbol*] [*National Library of Canada*] (NLC)
MGE......... Maintenance Ground Equipment [*Formerly, GSF*]
MGE......... Manage (ABBR)
MGE......... Marge Enterprises [*Vancouver Stock Exchange symbol*]
MGE......... Marietta, GA [*Location identifier*] [*FAA*] (FAAL)
MGE......... Master of Geological Engineering (NADA)
MGE......... Megaloblastic Erythropoiesis [*Medicine*] (MELL)
MGE......... Message (ADA)
MGE......... Micro-Station Foundation and Modular GIS Environment (SAUO)
MGE......... Milwaukee Grain Exchange [*Defunct*]
MGE......... Minneapolis Grain Exchange (EA)
MGE......... Missile Guidance Element
MGE......... Modular Geographic Environment
MGE......... Modular Gis Environment (SAUO)
MGE......... Modular GIS (Geographic Information System) Environment [*Navigation systems*]
MGEB........ Manageable (ABBR)
MGEBT...... Manageability (ABBR)
MGEBY...... Manageably (ABBR)
MGED........ Managed (ABBR)
M Ge E...... Master of Geological Engineering
MGEE........ MGE Energy [*Stock exchange symbol*] [*Formerly Madison Gas & Electric*]
M Ge Eng... Master of Geological Engineering
MGEG .... Managing (ABBR)
mg-el........ Milligram-Element (MAE)
MGEM....... Modern Gun Effectiveness Model (MCD)
M GEN ...... Major General
MGEN .... Micro General [*NASDAQ symbol*] (TTSB)
MGEN .... Micro General Corp. [*NASDAQ symbol*] (NQ)
M Gen E.... Master of General Engineering (PGP)
MGenStud... Master of General Studies (ADA)
MGENT...... Management (ABBR)
M Geo E.... Master of Geological Engineering (PGP)
M Geol E... Master of Geological Engineering
MGeolEng... Master of Geological Engineering (NADA)
MGER .... Manager (ABBR)
MGERL...... Managerial (ABBR)
MGES........ Esquipulas [*Guatemala*] [*ICAO location identifier*] (ICLI)
MGES........ Maintenance Ground Equipment Section
MGES........ Multiple-Gated Equilibrium Scintigraphy (DB)
MGEUS...... Maintenance Ground Equipment Utilization Sheets
Mgf........... Free Magnesium
MGF......... Macrophage Growth Factor (PDAA)
MGF......... Magnify (MSA)
MGF......... Maringa [*Brazil*] [*Airport symbol*] (OAG)
MGF......... Mast-Cell Growth Factor [*Cytology*]
MGF......... Maternal Grandfather (AAMN)
MGF......... Metallised Glass-Fibre chaff (SAUS)
MGF......... MFS Government Markets Income Trust [*NYSE symbol*] (SPSG)
MGF......... MFS Gvt Mkts Income Tr [*NYSE symbol*] (TTSB)
MGF......... Missionary Gospel Fellowship (EA)
MGF......... Mobile Guerrilla Force [*Vietnam*]
MGF......... Moment-Generating Function [*Mathematics*]
MGF......... Motor-Generator Flywheel (MCD)
MGF......... Multipotent Growth Factor [*Medicine*] (MELL)
MGF......... Myasthenia Gravis Foundation
MGF......... Myoblast Growth Factor [*Biochemistry*]
MGF......... Myxoma Growth Factor [*Biochemistry*]
MGFA........ Myasthenia Gravis Foundation of America (SAUO)
MGFC........ Mickey Gilley Fan Club [*Defunct*] (EA)
MGFE........ Moment-Generating Function Estimator
MGFEL ...... Master Government-Furnished Equipment List (NVT)
MGFG .... Magnifying
MGFL........ Flores [*Guatemala*] [*ICAO location identifier*] (ICLI)
MGFN .... Myasthenia Gravis Foundation Newsletter [*Medicine*] (EDAA)
MGFS........ Media General Financial Services, Inc. [*Information service or system*] (IID)
MGFY........ Magnify (VLIE)
MGFZB ...... Mein Gott, Fueg Es zum Besten [*My God, Order It for the Best*] [*Motto of Sophie, consort of Georg Friedrich, Margrave of Brandenburg-Anspach (1563-1639)*] [*German*]
MGG......... Machine Gun Guards [*British military*] (DMA)
MGG......... Managing (ABBR)
MGG......... Marine Geology and Geophysics (SAUO)
MGG......... Marine Geology and Geophysics Report (SAUO)
MGG......... May-Gruenwald-Giemsa [*A stain*] [*Hematology*]
MGG......... Mega Gold Resources Ltd. [*Vancouver Stock Exchange symbol*]
MGG......... Memory Gate Generator [*Computer science*]
MGG......... Metropolitan Greetings, Incorporated (SAUO)
MGG......... MGB GT [*NCIC car model code*]
MGG......... MGM Grand [*NYSE symbol*] (TTSB)
MGG......... MGM Grand, Inc. [*NYSE symbol*] (SPSG)
MGG......... MGM Mirage [*Company symbol*]
MGG......... Military Government for Germany (SAUO)
MGG......... Missile Guidance Group
MGG......... Molecular and General Genetics (SAUO)
MGG......... Monopropellant Gas Generator (PDAA)
MGG......... Mouse Gamma-Globulin
MGG......... Mugging (ABBR)
MGG......... Musik in Geschichte und Gegenwart [*A publication*]
MGGB .... Modular Guided Glide Bomb (MCD)
MGGH .... Methylglyoxal Guanylhydrazone [*Antineoplastic drug*] (MAE)
MgGI .... TIGR [*The Institute of Genomic Research*] Magnaporthe grisea Gene Index [*Database*] (GDD)
MGGM....... Mars General Circulation Model [*For planetary weather study*]
MGGM....... Maternal Great Grandfather (SAUS)
MGGS .... Major General, General Staff
MGGT .... Guatemala/La Aurora [*Guatemala*] [*ICAO location identifier*] (ICLI)
MGGU .... Marcevaggi [*Intermodal shipping container symbol*] (TVRC)
MGH......... Madigan General Hospital (SAUO)
MGH......... Mammogenic Hormone [*Medicine*] (MELL)
MGH......... Margate [*South Africa*] [*Airport symbol*] (OAG)
MGH......... Massachusetts General Hospital (DAVI)
MGH......... Massachusetts General Hospital, Treadwell Library, Boston, MA [*OCLC symbol*] (OCLC)
mgh.......... Milligram Hour [*Pharmacy*]
MGH......... Monoglyceride Hydrolase [*An enzyme*] (MAE)
MGH......... Monosodium Glutamate Headache [*Medicine*] (MELL)
MGH......... Monumenta Germaniae Historica [*A publication*] (ODCC)
MGH......... Morden & Helwig Group, Inc. [*Toronto Stock Exchange symbol*]
MGH......... Museum of Garden History [*British*]
MgHiYld .... Managed High Yield Fund [*Associated Press*] (SAG)
MGHT .... Huehuetenango [*Guatemala*] [*ICAO location identifier*] (ICLI)
MG HYDROX... Magnesium Hydroxide (SAUS)
MGI.......... Gillam Municipal Library, Manitoba [*Library symbol*] [*National Library of Canada*] (NLC)
MGI.......... Macrophage and Granulocyte Inducer [*Biochemistry*]
MgI........... Magazine Index
MGI.......... Magnetics International Ltd. [*Toronto Stock Exchange symbol*]
MGI.......... Management Games Institute [*Raytheon Co.*]
MGI.......... Mapping and Geography Institute (SAUO)
MGI.......... Marine Geological Institute [*Indonesia*] [*Marine science*] (OSRA)
MGI.......... Matagorda Island, TX [*Location identifier*] [*FAA*] (FAAL)
MGI.......... Mavtech Holdings, Inc. [*Toronto Stock Exchange symbol*]
MGI.......... Media Group Inc. (SAUO)
MGI.......... Medial Giant Interneuron [*Neurobiology*]
MGI.......... Member of the Gas Institute [*British*]
MGI.......... Member of the Institute of Certificated Grocers [*British*]
MGI.......... Member of the Institute of Certified Grocers (SAUO)
MGI.......... Metal Grating Institute [*Defunct*]
MGI.......... MGIC Investment Corp. (SAUO)
MGI.......... MGI Properties [*NYSE symbol*] (SPSG)
MGI.......... Microbial Genome Initiative (HGEN)
MGI.......... Military Geographic Information [*or Intelligence*] (MCD)

MGI .... Mobile Gamma Irradiator [*Nuclear energy*]
MGI .... Multi-Function Interpreter (SAUS)
MGI .... Multigraphic Interface [*XOR Systems*]
MGI .... TIGR [*The Institute of Genomic Research*] Mouse Gene Index [*Database*] (GDD)
MGIB .... Management and Graduate Item Bank [*Reasoning skills test*]
MGIB .... Montgomery GI Bill (INF)
MGIC .... Magic Software Enterprises, Inc. [*NASDAQ symbol*] (SAG)
MGIC .... Magic Software Enterprises Ltd. [*NASDAQ symbol*] (NASQ)
MGIC .... MGIC Investment Co. [*Associated Press*] (SAG)
MGIC .... Mortgage Guaranty Insurance Corp. [*Subsidiary of MGIC Investment Corp.*]
MGICA .... Mortgage Guaranteed Insurance Corporation of Australia (SAUO)
MGICF .... Magic Software Enterprises [*NASDAQ symbol*] (TTSB)
MGID .... Military Geographic Information and Documentation (AABC)
MGIKQ ...... Magic Restaurants [*NASDAQ symbol*] (TTSB)
MGIN .... Margin (ROG)
MGINS ...... Mugginess (ABBR)
MGI Phr ..... MGI PHARMA, Inc. [*Associated Press*] (SAG)
MGI Prp ..... MGI Properties [*Associated Press*] (SAG)
MGIR .... Motor Glider Instructor Rating [*Aviation*] (DA)
MGIS .... Micro Geographic Information System (SAUO)
MGIS .... Military Geographic Information System (SAUO)
MGIU .... Chameleon Containers [*Intermodal shipping container symbol*] (TVRC)
MGIWQ ...... Magic Restaurants Wrrt [*NASDAQ symbol*] (TTSB)
MGJ .... Montgomery, NY [*Location identifier*] [*FAA*] (FAAL)
MGK .... Mawes [*Language symbol*] (ETLW)
MGk .... Medieval Greek (ODA)
MGK .... Michele Gold Mountain Ltd. [*Vancouver Stock Exchange symbol*]
MGk .... Middle Greek [*Language*] (BARN)
MGK .... Modern Greek [*Language, etc.*]
mg/kg .... Milligrams per Kilogram (AAMN)
mg/kg/day ... milligram per kilogram per day (SAUS)
mg/kg/hr .... milligram per kilogram per hour (SAUS)
MGKN .... Morgan's Trucking [*Common carrier symbol*]
MGl .... Gloucester Lyceum and Sawyer Free Public Library, Gloucester, MA [*Library symbol*] [*Library of Congress*] (LCLS)
MGL .... Machine Group Listing (SAUO)
MGL .... Machine Gun LASER (MCD)
MGL .... Magalia [*California*] [*Seismograph station code, US Geological Survey*] (SEIS)
MGL .... Magellan Health Svcs [*AMEX symbol*] (TTSB)
MGL .... Magnanimous Green Leprechaun
MGL .... Malachite Green Leucocyanite (OA)
MGL .... Management Guidance Letter (SAUO)
MGL .... Marginal (MSA)
MGL .... Matrix Generator Language [*Computer science*] (BUR)
MGL .... Michigan General Corporation (SAUO)
mg/l .... Milligram per Liter (COE)
mg/L .... Milligrams per Liter (MEC)
MG/L .... Milligrams per Liter
MGL .... Mingle (ABBR)
MGL .... Missouri Gravity Low [*Geology*]
MGL .... Mogul
Mgl .... Mongolia (MILB)
MGL .... Mongolian Airlines [*ICAO designator*] (FAAC)
MGL .... Mongrel (ABBR)
MGL .... Mono Gold Mines, Inc. [*Vancouver Stock Exchange symbol*]
MGL .... Monteagle, TN [*Location identifier*] [*FAA*] (FAAL)
MGL .... Morris Geneological Library (SAUO)
MGL .... Move-Grow-Learn [*Program for visual perception development*]
MGLA .... Massachusetts General Laws Annotated [*A publication*]
M GLAM .... Mid Glamorgan [*County in Wales*]
MGLC .... Misty Mountain Gold Ltd. [*NASDAQ symbol*] (SAG)
MGLD .... Mild General Learning Disability
MGLD .... Mingled (ABBR)
MGLG .... Mingling (ABBR)
MGlHi .... Cape Ann Historical Association, Gloucester, MA [*Library symbol*] [*Library of Congress*] (LCLS)
MGLL .... La Libertad [*Guatemala*] [*ICAO location identifier*] (ICLI)
MGLMNA ... Megalomania (ABBR)
MGLMNAC ... Megalomaniac (ABBR)
MGLP .... Methylglucose Lipopolysaccharide [*Biochemistry*]
MGLPS ...... Megalopolis (ABBR)
MGLY .... Methylglyoxal [*Also, MG*] [*Organic chemistry*]
MGM .... Mailgram
MGM .... Management [*Telegraphy*] (PCTE)
MGM .... Master Group Multiplexer
MGM .... Maternal Grandmother (AAMN)
MGM .... Mayer's Ganz Mispocheh [*Mayer's Whole Family*] [*A Yiddish nickname for Metro-Goldwyn-Mayer, it reflects the tendency of early studio chiefs to hire their relatives and friends*]
MGM .... Mechanics of Granular Materials
MGM .... Medical Group Management Journal (SAUO)
MGM .... Medical Group Missions of the Christian Medical and Dental Society (EA)
MGM .... Member-Get-a-Member [*Marketing*] (WDMC)
MGM .... Memory Grant Manager (SAUS)
MGM .... Metro-Goldwyn-Mayer [*Record label*] [*USA, Great Britain, etc.*]
MGM .... MGM [*NCIC trailer make code*]
MGM .... MGM Grand Air, Inc. [*ICAO designator*] (FAAC)
MGM .... MGM/UA Communications Co. [*NYSE symbol*] (COMM)
MGM .... Milligram (DFIT)
mgm .... Milligram
MGM .... Mobile-Launched Ground-Attack Missile
MGM .... Molecular and Genetic Medicine
MGM .... Monadnock Gay Men [*New Hampshire, Vermont, and Massachusetts*] (EARSL)
MGM .... Montgomery [*Alabama*] [*Airport symbol*] (OAG)
MGM .... Morgain Minerals, Inc. [*Vancouver Stock Exchange symbol*]
MGM .... Mother's Grandmother (MAE)
MG/M^2 .... Megagrams per Square Meter
MG/M^3 .... Megagrams per Cubic Meter
mg/m$_3$ .... Milligrams of Material per Cubic Meter of Air (GNE)
MGM-31 .... Pershing II [*Military*] [*Surface-to-surface nuclear battlefield missile*] (POLM)
MGM-51 .... Shillelagh [*Military*] [*Guided missile fired from 152-mm gun fitted in the Sheridan M551 armored vehicle*] (POLM)
MGM-52 .... Lance [*Military*] [*Surface-to-surface battlefield attack missile*] (POLM)
MGMA .... Magma (ABBR)
MGMA .... Medical Group Management Association (EA)
MGMA .... Metro Global Media [*NASDAQ symbol*] (TTSB)
MGMA .... Metro Global Media, Inc. [*NASDAQ symbol*] (SAG)
MG-MA ...... Motor Generator-Motor Alternator (COE)
MGMC .... Multiple Gun Motor Carriage
MGMD .... Ministerial Group on the Misuse of Drugs [*British*]
MGMG .... MGM Grand, Inc. [*Associated Press*] (SAG)
MG/MGI ..... Mapping, Geodesy and Military Geographic Intelligence (SAUO)
MGMGMG ... Milwaukee and Greatlakes MG [*Morris Garage*] Motorcar Group
MGMI .... Metallgezellschaft Metals Index [*British*] (NUMA)
mg/min ...... milligrams per minute (SAUS)
MGMIS ...... Medical Group Management Information Service [*Medical Group Management Association*] (DHSM)
MGML .... Malacatan [*Guatemala*] [*ICAO location identifier*] (ICLI)
MGML .... Minimal Generalized Markup Language (SAUS)
MGMM ...... Melchor De Mencos [*Guatemala*] [*ICAO location identifier*] (ICLI)
MGM MIRAGE PAC ... MGM Mirage PAC [*Mill Valley, CA*] (PACS)
MGMNT ..... Management
MGMR .... Ministry of Geology and Mineral Resources [*China*]
MGMS .... Manchester Geological and Mining Society (SAUO)
MGMT .... Make Good a Magnetic Track of (Degrees) [*Aviation*] (FAAC)
mgmt .... Management (DD)
Mgmt .... Management (TBD)
MGMT .... Management
Mgmt Forum ... Management Forum [*A publication*]
MGMX .... J and J Partnership [*Private rail car owner code*]
MGN .... Magangue [*Colombia*] [*Airport symbol*] (AD)
MGN .... Magazine (ABBR)
MGN .... Magneto [*Generator*]
MGN .... Margin [*Accounting*]
MGN .... Marine Guidance Note (SAUO)
MGN .... Medial Geniculate Nucleus [*Medicine*]
MGN .... Membranous Glomerulonephritis [*Nephrology*]
MGN .... Mendial Geniculate Nucleus (PDAA)
MGN .... Mengen [*Turkey*] [*Seismograph station code, US Geological Survey*] (SEIS)
MGN .... Micrograin (ABBR)
MGN .... Mirror Group Newspapers [*British*]
MGN .... Morgan Aviation Services Ltd. [*Nigeria*] [*ICAO designator*] (FAAC)
MGN .... Morgan Products Ltd. [*NYSE symbol*] (SPSG)
MGN .... Multigrounded Neutral [*Telecommunications*] (TEL)
Mgna .... Magna-Lab, Inc. [*Associated Press*] (SAG)
MGNAN ..... Margination (ABBR)
MGNB .... Mahoning National Bancorp, Inc. [*NASDAQ symbol*] (NASQ)
MGNES ...... Metal Goods Not Elsewhere Specified [*Department of Employment*] [*British*]
MGNETC .... Magnetic (ABBR)
MGNETCY ... Magnetically (ABBR)
MGNETMTR ... Magnetometer (ABBR)
MGNETSM ... Magnetism (ABBR)
MGNETZ .... Magnetization (ABBR)
MGNETZ .... Magnetize [*or Magnetized*] (ABBR)
MGNFI .... Magnify (ABBR)
MGNFIB ..... Magnifiable (ABBR)
MGNFID ..... Magnified (ABBR)
MGNFIG ..... Magnifying (ABBR)
MGNFIN ..... Magnification (ABBR)
MGNFIR ..... Magnifier (ABBR)
MGNFNC .... Magnificence (ABBR)
MGNFNT .... Magnificent (ABBR)
MGNFTY .... Magnificently (ABBR)
MGNIA ...... Marginalia (ABBR)
MGNL .... Magna Bancorp [*NASDAQ symbol*] (SAG)
MGNLT ...... Marginality (ABBR)
MGNLY ...... Marginally (ABBR)
MGNM .... Magnum Manufacturing [*NCIC truck make code*]
MGNMT ..... Magnanimity (ABBR)
MGNMU ..... Magnanimous (ABBR)
MGNO .... Mgnol Tandem Boat Trailer [*NCIC trailer make code*]
MGNSM ..... Magnesium [*Chemical symbol is Mg*]
MGNT .... Magnate (ABBR)
MGNT .... Magnet (ABBR)
MGNTC ...... Magnetic
MGNTO ...... Magneto
MGNTUD .... Magnitude (ABBR)
MGNTZD .... Magnetized
MGO .... Machine Gun Officer [*British military*] (DMA)

MGO .... Main Geophysical Observatory [*Russia*] (CARB)
MGO .... Management by Goals and Objectives (MCD)
MGO .... Marine Gas Oil (SAUS)
MGO .... Master General of the Ordnance [*Army*] [*British*]
MGO .... Master of Gynaecology and Obstetrics (ADA)
MGO .... Mato Grosso [*Brazil*] [*Airport symbol*] (AD)
MGO .... Megagauss-Oersted [*Magnetic field strength*]
MGO .... Military Government Officer
MGO .... Million Gauss Oersted [*Unit of energy density*]
MGO .... Montego (automobile) [*NCIC car model code*]
MGO .... Mortgage Insurance Co. of Canada [*Toronto Stock Exchange symbol*]
MGOCC ...... Morris Garage Octagon Car Club [*British*] (EAIO)
MGOe .... Megagauss-Oersted [*Also, MGO*] [*Magnetic field strength*]
MGOS .... Metal-Glass-Oxide-Silicon (PDAA)
MGOT .... Maggot (ABBR)
M GOTH ..... Moeso-Gothic [*Language, etc.*] (ROG)
MGovt ...... Military Government (SAUO)
MGP .... Application for Mandamus Granted in Part [*Legal term*] (DLA)
MGP .... Macarthur Gruen Party [*Political party*] [*Australia*]
MG(P) ...... Machinery of Government, Parliamentary Procedure [*British*]
MGP .... Maguayo [*Puerto Rico*] [*Seismograph station code, US Geological Survey*] (SEIS)
MGP .... Maharastrawadi Gomantak Party (SAUO)
MGP .... Maintenance Ground Point
MGP .... Manga [*Papua New Guinea*] [*Airport symbol*] (OAG)
MGP .... Manufactured Gas Plant [*Environmental biotechnology*]
MGP .... Marcus Garvey Park (SAUO)
MGP .... Marginal Granulocyte Pool [*Hematology*]
MGP .... Mary Glawgow Publications [*Publisher*] [*British*]
MGP .... Membranous Glomerulopathy [*Medicine*] (DB)
MGP .... Merchants Group [*AMEX symbol*] (TTSB)
MGP .... Merchants Group, Inc. [*AMEX symbol*] (SPSG)
MGP .... Meteorology/Geophysics Package (ACAE)
MGP .... Methylglucose Polysaccharide [*Biochemistry*]
MGP .... Methyl Green Pyronine [*A stain*]
MGP .... Micro-G Physics and Chemistry Experiments Group [*NASA*] (SSD)
MGP .... Monochrome Graphics Printer [*Computer science*] (CDE)
MGP .... Morrison-Grey Enterprises [*Vancouver Stock Exchange symbol*]
MGP .... Mountain Gorilla Project (EA)
MGP .... Mouvement Gaulliste Populaire [*Popular Gaullist Movement*] [*France*] [*Political party*] (PPW)
MGP .... Mucous Glycoproteins [*Biochemistry*]
MGP .... Multiple Goal Programming
MGP .... Museum of the Great Plains [*Lawton, OK*]
MGPB .... Puerto Barrios [*Guatemala*] [*ICAO location identifier*] (ICLI)
MGPC .... Grandview Personal Care Home, Manitoba [*Library symbol*] [*National Library of Canada*] (NLC)
MGPC .... Medical Group Practice Council (SAUO)
MGPCU ...... Missile Ground Power Control Unit (AAG)
M-GPD ...... Million US Gallons per Day [*AEC, OSW*]
MGPF .... Multiprogram General-Purpose Facilities [*Oak Ridge National Laboratory*]
MGPGP ...... Master of Group Process and Group Psychotherapy (PGP)
MGPHN ...... Megaphone (ABBR)
MGPL .... Marine Gene Probe Laboratory [*Dalhousie University*] [*Canada*]
MGPP .... Poptun [*Guatemala*] [*ICAO location identifier*] (ICLI)
MGPPL ...... Motor Glider Private Pilot's Licence [*British*] (AIA)
MGPR .... M.G. Products [*NASDAQ symbol*] (TTSB)
MGPR .... MG Products, Inc. [*NASDAQ symbol*] (SAG)
MG Prod .... MG Products, Inc. [*Associated Press*] (SAG)
MGQ .... Maximum Guarantee Quality (SAUO)
MGQ .... Mogadishu [*Somalia*] [*Airport symbol*] (OAG)
MGQC .... Quiche [*Guatemala*] [*ICAO location identifier*] (ICLI)
MGQZ .... Quezaltenango [*Guatemala*] [*ICAO location identifier*] (ICLI)
MGR .... Machine Gun Regiment [*British military*] (DMA)
mgr .... Magister [*Master*] [*Latin*]
MGR .... Manager (AFM)
Mgr .... Manager (ODBW)
mgr .... Manager (NTIO)
MGR .... Marrow Graft Rejection [*Medicine*] (MELL)
MGR .... Marrow Granulocyte Reserves [*Hematology*]
MGR .... Mars Geologic Rover
MGR .... Matusadona Game Reserve (SAUO)
MGR .... McGraw-Edison Co. (SAUO)
MGr .... Medieval Greek (ODA)
MGR .... Medieval Greek [*Language, etc.*]
MGR .... Merry-Go-Round Entertainment (EFIS)
MGR .... Metal Glaze Resistor
MGR .... Method of Generated Responses [*Psychology*]
MGR .... M.G. Ramachaudran (India) [*Political party*] (PSAP)
MGR .... Micro-Graphic Reporting (PDAA)
MGR .... Middlegate Resources, Inc. [*Vancouver Stock Exchange symbol*]
M GR .... Middle Greek [*Language, etc.*] (ROG)
MGR .... Minimum Government Requirements (SAUO)
MGR .... Mixed Gas Rebreather
MGR .... Mobile-Launched Ground-Attack Rocket
MGR .... Modified Gain Ratio [*Medicine*] (MAE)
MGR .... Modular Gas-Cooled Reactor [*Developed by MIT*] [*Nuclear energy*]
Mgr .... Monsignor (ODBW)
MGR .... Monsignor
MGR .... Moraga Resources Ltd. [*Vancouver Stock Exchange symbol*]
MGR .... Moultrie, GA [*Location identifier*] [*FAA*] (FAAL)
MGR .... Moultrie/Thomasville [*Georgia*] [*Airport symbol*] (OAG)
MGR .... Mouvement de la Gauche Reformatrice [*Movement of the Reformist Left*] [*France*] [*Political party*] (PPW)
MGR .... Mugger (ABBR)
MGR .... Multiple Gas Rebreathing [*Medicine*] (DMAA)
MGR .... Murmurs, Gallops, or Rubs [*Cardiology*] (DAVI)
MGRA .... Magra [*Common carrier symbol*]
MGRA .... Major-General, Royal Artillery [*Army*] [*British*]
MGRA .... Master Geographical Reference Area (SAUO)
MGRA .... Migrate (ABBR)
MGRAD ...... Migrated (ABBR)
MGRAD ...... Minimum Guidelines and Requirements for Accessible Design (IDYL)
MGRAG ...... Migrating (ABBR)
MGRAN ...... Migration (ABBR)
MGranbyS ... Saint Hyacinth College and Seminary, Granby, MA [*Library symbol*] [*Library of Congress*] (LCLS)
MGRATR ..... Migrator (ABBR)
MGRATRY .... Migratory (ABBR)
MGRC .... McGrath RentCorp [*NASDAQ symbol*] (NQ)
MGRC .... Melbourne Greyhound Racing Club [*Australia*]
mgrd .... Middleground (VRA)
MGRE .... Merry-Go-Round Enterprises, Inc. [*NASDAQ symbol*] (COMM)
MGREC ...... Magnetic Recorder [*or Recording*] (IAA)
MGrefC ..... Greenfield Community College, Greenfield, MA [*Library symbol*] [*Library of Congress*] (LCLS)
MGRESS ..... Manageress (ROG)
MGRFO ...... Merier-Gourley-Roark Family Organization [*Association*] (EA)
MGRGT ...... Modular Gas-Cooled Reactor Gas Turbine [*Developed by MIT*] [*Nuclear energy*]
MGRHS ...... May God Rest His Soul
MGRI .... MG Rail [*Federal Railroad Administration identification code*]
MGRI .... Mobile Ground Radio Installation
MGRL .... Managerial (ABBR)
MGRM .... Major-General, Royal Marines [*British military*] (DMA)
MGRM .... Metallgesellschaft Refining & Marketing [*American subsidiary of the German commodities and futures contractor*] (ECON)
MGRM .... Milligram (ROG)
MGRMTRSF ... MGRM Training, Reserve & Special Forces (SAUO)
MGRN .... Migration (ABBR)
MGRNL ...... Migrational (ABBR)
MGRP .... Minimum-Gradient Reaction Path [*Chemical kinetics*]
MGRP .... Morton Industrial Group [*NASDAQ symbol*]
MGRS .... Ferrocarriles Nacionales de Mexico [*AAR code*]
MGrS .... Groton School, Groton, MA [*Library symbol*] [*Library of Congress*] (LCLS)
MGRS .... Meter Gauge Rolling-Stock [*British*]
MGRs .... Microbial Genetic Resources (SAUS)
MGRS .... Military Grid Reference System (AABC)
MGRT .... Migrant (ABBR)
MGRT .... Retalhuleu [*Guatemala*] [*ICAO location identifier*] (ICLI)
MGRTY ...... Migratory (ABBR)
MGRW .... Matrix Generator and Report Writer [*Computer science*]
MGRY .... Milgray Electronics [*NASDAQ symbol*] (TTSB)
MGRY .... Milgray Electronics, Inc. [*NASDAQ symbol*] (NQ)
MGRZ .... Merchant's Grain Rail [*Federal Railroad Administration identification code*]
MGS .... MacGregor Sporting Goods, Inc. [*AMEX symbol*] (COMM)
MGS .... Machine Gun School [*British military*] (DMA)
MGS .... Magellan Resources Corp. [*Vancouver Stock Exchange symbol*]
MGS .... Maine Geological Survey (SAUO)
MGS .... Manages [*Telegraphy*] (PCTE)
MGS .... Manchester Geographical Society (SAUO)
MGS .... Mangaia [*Cook Islands*] [*Airport symbol*] (OAG)
MGS .... Marine Geophysical Survey [*NOO*]
MGS .... Mars Global Surveyor [*NASA*]
MGS .... Maryland Geological Survey (SAUO)
MGS .... Master Gemology Society [*Defunct*] (EA)
MGS .... Master of General Studies (GAGS)
MGS .... Master of Gerontological Studies (GAGS)
MGS .... Memoirs of the Geological Survey (SAUO)
MG's .... Memphis Group [*In name of singing group "Booker T and the MG's"*]
MGS .... Metal Gravel Stop
MGS .... Metre-Gram-Second
MGS .... Metrogas SA [*NYSE symbol*] (SAG)
MGS .... MetroGas S.A. Cl'B'ADS [*NYSE symbol*] (TTSB)
MGS .... MGS [*NCIC trailer make code*]
MGS .... Microcomputer Graphic System
MGS .... Middleton Gardens [*South Carolina*] [*Seismograph station code, US Geological Survey*] (SEIS)
MGS .... Midwestern Gilbert and Sullivan Society (EA)
MGS .... Military Government Section [*World War II*]
MGS .... Minnesota Geological Survey (SAUO)
MGS .... Missile Guidance Section [*or Set, or System*]
MGS .... Mission Ground Station (MCD)
MGS .... Mobile Gas Service Corp. (EFIS)
MGS .... Mobile Ground Station (SAUO)
MGS .... Mobile Ground System
MGS .... Moment Gyro System
MGS .... Motor Generator Set (CAAL)
MGS .... Moveable Ground Station (ACAE)
MgS04 ...... Magnesium Sulfate (SAUS)
MGSA .... Marriage Guidance South Australia
MGSA .... Melanoma Growth Stimulatory Activity [*Biochemistry*]
MGSA .... Memoirs of the Geological Society of America (SAUO)

MGSA .... Military General Supply Agency [*Merged with Defense General Supply Center*]
MGSA .... Modern Greek Studies Association (EA)
MG SAL ..... Magnesium Salicylate (SAUS)
MGSC .... Missile Guidance Set Control
MGSCD ...... Martha Graham School of Contemporary Dance [*New York, NY*]
MGSch ...... Machine Gun School (SAUO)
MGSD .... Michigan Geological Survey Division (SAUO)
MGSE .... Maintenance Ground Support Equipment
MGSE .... Mechanical Ground Support Equipment
MGSE .... Missile Ground Support Equipment
MGSE .... Mobile Ground Support Equipment
MGSE-ECM ... Maintenance Ground Support Equipment-Environmental Controls and Mechanisms (SAA)
MGSGT ...... Master Gunnery Sergeant [*Marine Corps*] (DNAB)
MGSI .... Memoirs of the Geological Survey of India (SAUO)
MGSIUF ..... Marquis Giuseppe Scicluna International University Foundation (EA)
MGSJ .... San Jose [*Guatemala*] [*ICAO location identifier*] (ICLI)
MGSL .... Memoirs of the Geological Society of London (SAUO)
MGSM .... Medium Ground Station Module (SAUS)
MGSM .... San Marcos [*Guatemala*] [*ICAO location identifier*] (ICLI)
MGSMTC .... Mid-Gulf Seaports Marine Terminal Conference (SAUO)
MgSO .... Magnesium Sulfate (IDYL)
MGSpS ...... Guadalupan Missionaries of the Holy Spirit (TOCD)
MGSS .... Manned Geosynchronous Spacecraft Servicer (SSD)
MGST .... Miles [*Multiple Integrated Laser Engagement System*] Gunnery Skills Test [*USA*]
MGST .... Military Geography Specialist Team
MGSTL ...... Magisterial (ABBR)
MGSTRA .... Magistrate (ABBR)
MGT .... Magenta Development Corp. [*Vancouver Stock Exchange symbol*]
MGT .... Major Ground Test (NASA)
MGT .... Management (AFM)
mgt .... Management (ELAL)
Mgt .... Management (AL)
MGT .... Margate Air Services [*South Africa*] [*ICAO designator*] (FAAC)
MGT .... Master-Group Translator [*Telecommunications*] (TEL)
MGT .... Master of Gas Technology (GAGS)
MGT .... Megaton [*Nuclear equivalent of one million tons of high explosive*] (AAG)
MGT .... Meteorological and Geoastrophysical Titles
MGT .... MGC GT [*NCIC car model code*]
MGT .... Millingimbi [*Airport symbol*]
MGT .... Mobile [*Truck-Mounted*] Ground Terminal
MGT .... Movie Going Time
MGT .... Multiple Glomus Tumor [*Medicine*] (MELL)
MGT .... Multiplex Genetic Testing [*Medicine*] (MELL)
MG/TA .... Map Graphic and Terrain Anaiysis (SAUO)
MG/TA .... Map Graphic and Terrain Analysis (SAUS)
MGTANALYSO ... Management Analysis Officer [*Air Force*]
MGTAV ...... Modern Greek Teachers' Association of Victoria [*Australia*]
MGTB .... Mexican Government Tourist Bureau (SAUO)
MGTC .... Megatech Corp. [*OTCBB symbol*]
MGTC .... Morgan Guaranty Trust Company (SAUO)
MGTD .... Mexican Government Tourist Delegation (SAUO)
MGTENGR ... Management Engineer [*Air Force*]
MGTG .... Moving Ground Target Detection
MGTI .... Member of the Gymnastic Teachers' Institute [*British*] (ROG)
MGTIR .... Mightier (ABBR)
mgtis .... Meningitis [*Medicine*] (MAE)
MGTIST ..... Mightiest (ABBR)
MGTMTR .... Magnetometer
MGTNS ...... Mightiness (ABBR)
MGTO .... Mexican Government Tourism Office (EA)
MGTO .... Mexican Government Tourist Office (SAUO)
MG TRISIL ... Magnesium Trisilicate (SAUS)
MgtTch ...... Management Technologies, Inc. [*Associated Press*] (SAG)
MGTY .... Mighty (ABBR)
MGU .... Main-Group Ureilite [*Meteorite component*]
MGU .... MGM Resources Corp. [*Vancouver Stock Exchange symbol*]
MGU .... Michigan Gas Utilities Company (EFIS)
MGU .... Midcourse Guidance Unit [*Navy*] (CAAL)
MGU .... Military Government Unit
MGU .... [*The*] Mobile & Gulf Railroad Co. [*Later, MG*] [*AAR code*]
MGU .... Moscow State University (SAUO)
MGU .... Moskovskiy Gosudarstvenniy Universitet [*Moscow State University*] [*Former USSR*] (MSC)
MGU .... Most General Unifier (IDAI)
MGUL .... Magnum LTL [*Common carrier symbol*]
MGUN .... Marine Gunner
M Gun Sgt ... Master Gunnery Sergeant (SAUO)
MGUS .... Monoclonal Gammopathies of Undetermined Significance [*Medicine*] (DMAA)
MGV .... Matengo [*Language symbol*] (ETLW)
MGV .... Mechanically-Guided Vehicle
MGV .... Miniature Gate Valve
MGV .... Monogram Oil & Gas, Inc. [*Vancouver Stock Exchange symbol*]
MGVC .... Manual Governing Valve Control [*Nuclear energy*] (NRCH)
MGVC .... Mendenhall Glacier Visitor Center (ALAC)
MGVT .... Mated Ground Vibration Test (NASA)
MGVT .... Montgomery [*Vermont*] [*Seismograph station code, US Geological Survey*] (SEIS)
MGW .... G. W. Murphy Industries, Inc. (SAUO)
MGW .... Magnesium Sulfate, Glycerine, and Water (Enema) [*Medicine*]
MGW .... Maximum Gross Weight (WDAA)
MGW .... Midland Great Western (SAUO)
MGW .... Mission Gross Weight
MGW .... Morgantown [*West Virginia*] [*Airport symbol*] (OAG)
MGW .... Morgantown, WV [*Location identifier*] [*FAA*] (FAAL)
MGWA .... Marriage Guidance Western Australia
MGWR ...... Midland Great Western Railway [*British*] (ROG)
MGWS .... Modular Guided Weapon System (MCD)
MGWU ...... Malta General Workers Union, Valetta (SAUO)
MGX .... Moabi [*Gabon*] [*Airport symbol*] (OAG)
MGX .... Mossimo, Inc. [*NYSE symbol*] (SAG)
MGXI .... Micrografx, Inc. [*NASDAQ symbol*] (SAG)
M-GXT .... Multistage Graded Exercise Test [*Cardiology*] (DAVI)
MGY .... Dayton, OH [*Location identifier*] [*FAA*] (FAAL)
MGY .... Mega-Dyne Industrial Corp. [*Vancouver Stock Exchange symbol*]
mGy .... Milligray [*Emergency Management*] (EMA)
mGy .... Milligray(s), 1 E-3 Gy [*Industrial hygiene term*] (OHS)
MGY .... Muggy (ABBR)
MGyn and Obs ... Master of Gynaecology and Obstetrics (SAUO)
Mgy Sgt ..... Master Gunnery Sergeant [*Military*] (POLM)
MGYSGT .... Master Gunnery Sergeant [*Marine Corps*]
MGZ .... Maschinengewehr-Zieleinrichtung [*Machine-Gun Sighting Mechanism*] [*German military - World War II*]
MGZ .... Mayaguez [*Diocesan abbreviation*] [*Puerto Rico*] (TOCD)
MGZ .... Mergui [*Myanmar*] [*Airport symbol*] (OAG)
MGZF .... Maschinengewehr-Zielfernrohr [*Machine-Gun Telescopic Sight*] [*German military - World War II*]
MH .... Air-Cushion Vehicle built by Mitsubishi [*Japan*] [*Usually used in combination with numerals*]
MH .... Fe3O4-Fe2O3 buffer (SAUS)
MH .... [*A*] Grammar of Masoretic Hebrew [*A publication*] (BJA)
MH .... Ha-Mo'atsah ha-Hakla'it (BJA)
MH .... Harvard University, Cambridge, MA [*Library symbol*] [*Library of Congress*] (LCLS)
mh .... Macao [*MARC country of publication code*] [*Library of Congress*] (LCCP)
MH .... Maclean Hunter Publishing Company (EFIS)
MH .... Magdalen Hospital (SAUO)
MH .... Magnetic Head [*or Heading*]
MH .... Magnetite-Hematite [*Geology*]
MH .... Mail Handler [*Computer science*]
MH .... Main Hatch
MH .... Maintenance Handbook
MH .... Maintenance Hemodialysis [*Nephrology*] (CPH)
MH .... Major Hangover [*Internet lingo*] (NETL)
MH .... Makkabi Hazair (BJA)
MH .... Malaysia Airlines [*Airline flight code*] (ODBW)
MH .... Malaysian Airline System [*ICAO designator*] (AD)
MH .... Malden Hospital [*Malden, MA*]
MH .... Maleic Hydrazide [*Plant growth regulator*]
MH .... Malignant Histiocytosis [*Medicine*]
MH .... Malignant Hyperpyrexia [*Medicine*]
MH .... Malignant Hypertension [*Medicine*] (DMAA)
MH .... Malignant Hyperthermia [*Medicine*]
MH .... Malt House
MH .... Mammotropic Hormone [*Endocrinology*]
MH .... Manhole (AAG)
MH .... Man-Hour (MCD)
MH .... Man Hours (EAGT)
MH .... Mannoheptulose (DB)
MH .... Manual Hold [*Telecommunications*]
MH .... Manufactured Housing (PA)
MH .... Manufacturers Hanover Corp. (EFIS)
MH .... Manufacturers Hanover Trust Co. (SAUO)
MH .... Mare Humorum [*Sea of Moisture*] [*Lunar area*]
MH .... Marital History
MH .... Marshall Islands [*ANSI two-letter standard code*] (CNC)
M-H .... Martini-Henry [*Rifle*]
MH .... Masonic Hall (ROG)
MH .... Mass Hysteria [*Medicine*] (EDAA)
MH .... Master Herbalist
MH .... Master Hosts [*An association*] [*Defunct*] (EA)
MH .... Master of Hamburgerology [*McDonald's Corp. Hamburger University*]
MH .... Master of Harriers [*British*] (WDAA)
MH .... Master of Health (GAGS)
MH .... Master of Horticulture
MH .... Master of Hounds [*British*]
MH .... Master of Humanics
MH .... Master of Humanities (GAGS)
MH .... Master of Hygiene
MH .... Master of the Horse [*British*] (ROG)
MH .... Master of the Hunt
MH .... Materials Handling (NATG)
MH .... Maximum Height [*Ballistics*]
M-H .... McGraw-Hill (NITA)
MH .... Mechanical Handling [*Describes type of produce; for example, MH-1 refers to a kind of tomato*]
MH .... Medal of Honor [*Often erroneously called Congressional Medal of Honor*] [*Military decoration*]
MH .... Medal of Honour (SAUO)
MH .... Medial Hypothalamus [*Medicine*] (DMAA)
MH .... Medical History
MH .... Medium Power Homing (PIPO)

MH Megahertz [*Megacycles per second*] [*See also MCPS, MCS, MC/S, MHZ*] (NATG)
Mh Mehri (BJA)
MH Melanophore Hormone [*Also, MSH*] [*Endocrinology*]
MH Melanophore-Stimulating Hormone [*Medicine*] (DMAA)
MH Mended Hearts (EA)
MH Menstrual History [*Medicine*]
MH Mental Health
MH Mental Hygiene (DMAA)
MH Mentally Handicapped (AIE)
MH Merchants Haulage (DS)
MH Mercurihematoporphyrin [*Pharmacology*]
MH Meristem Height [*Botany*]
MH Merphyrin [*Medicine*] (EDAA)
MH MeSH Heading [*Online database field identifier*]
MH Message Handler [*Computer science*]
MH Metal Halide (MCD)
M/H Meters per Hour
M/H Microcytic/Hypochromic [*Anemia*] [*Hematology*] (DAVI)
MH Microhematuria [*Medicine*]
mH Microhenry
MH Middle Hebrew [*Linguistics*] (IEL)
MH Middlesex Hussars (Duke of Cambridge's) [*British military*] (DMA)
MH Migraine Headache (MELL)
M/H Miles per Hour [*Also, MPH*]
MH Military History (AABC)
MH Military Hospital (ADA)
mh Millihenry (AEBE)
mH Millihenry (GPO)
mH Millihour [*One-thousandth of an hour*] (AAG)
MH Minehunter (SAUS)
MH Ministry of Health [*British*]
MH Ministry of Housing (SAUO)
M-H Minneapolis-Honeywell Regulator Co. [*Later, HON*]
MH Miscellaneous Hardware
MH Mishnaic Hebrew [*Linguistics*] (IEL)
MH Mitsubishi Heavy Industries Ltd. [*Japan*] [*ICAO aircraft manufacturer identifier*] (ICAO)
MH Mobile High-Power [*Reactor*] [*Proposed*] (NRCH)
MH Mobile Home (WGA)
MH Mobile Host (SAUS)
MH Mobility Haiti (EA)
MH Modern Healthcare [*Medicine*] [*Journal*] (EDAA)
MH Modified Huffman (SAUO)
MH Moist Heat (STED)
MH Molting Hormone [*Endocrinology, entomology*]
MH Monosymptomatic Hypochondriasis [*Medicine*] (DMAA)
MH Morgagni Hernia [*Medicine*] (MELL)
MH Most High [*Freemasonry*]
MH Most Honorable
MH Mostly Harmless (SAUS)
MH Mount Hood Railway Co. [*AAR code*]
MH Much [*Telegraphy*] (PCTE)
MH Muelheim [*Ruhr*] [*German license plate city code*]
M-H Mueller-Hinton [*Agar*] [*Microbiology*]
MH Mulberry Heart (OA)
MH Multihandicapped
MH Multiple Handicapped (STED)
MH Murine Hepatitis
MH Music Hall [*Record label*]
MH Mutant Hybrid [*Medicine*] (DMAA)
MH Muzzle Hatch
MH Myocardial Hypertrophy [*Medicine*] (MELL)
MH Myohyoid [*Medicine*] (DMAA)
MH2 Mary Hartman, Mary Hartman [*Initialism is shortened form of television program title*] [*Also,* M^{2H2}]
MHA Canadian Malignant Hyperthermia Association (SAUO)
MHA Hamline University, St. Paul, MN [*OCLC symbol*] (OCLC)
MH-A Harvard University, Arnold Arboretum, Cambridge, MA [*Library symbol*] [*Library of Congress*] (LCLS)
MHa Haverhill Public Library, Haverhill, MA [*Library symbol*] [*Library of Congress*] (LCLS)
MHA Machinery Haulers Association (SAUO)
MHA Machinery Haulers Association Agent, Saint Paul MN [*STAC*]
MHA Madonna House Apostolate [*Combermere, ON*] (EAIO)
MHA Mahdia [*Guyana*] [*Airport symbol*] (OAG)
MHA Maine Hospital Association (EARSL)
MHA Maintenance Hazard Analysis (MCD)
MHA Major Histocompatibility Antigen [*Medicine*] (EDAA)
MHA Malignant Hyperthermia Association [*Canada*] (EAIO)
MHA Man-Hour Accounting (NVT)
MHA Manila Hemp Association [*British*] (DBA)
MHA Mansion House Association on Transport (SAUO)
MHA Mansion House Association on Transport, Inc. [*British*] (BI)
MHA Marine Historical Association [*Later, MSM*] (EA)
MHA Masonry Heather Association of North America (NTPA)
MHA Master in Health Care Administration (CPGU)
MHA Master of Health Administration
MHA Master of Hospital Administration
MHA Material Handling Area
MHA Maximum Hypothetical Accident [*Nuclear energy*] (IEEE)
MHA Mean Horizontal Acceleration
MHA Meat Hygiene Authority [*Australia*]
MHA Medal for Humane Action [*Berlin Airlift, 1948-9*] [*Military decoration*]
MHA Medical Hospitals Association (SAUO)
MHA Member of House of Assembly [*British*]
MHA Mennonite Health Assembly (SAUO)
MHA Mennonite Health Association (EA)
MHA Mental Health Abstracts [*Database*] [*IFI/Plenum Data Co.*] [*Information service or system*] (CRD)
MHA Mental Health Administration [*Later, ADAMHA*]
MHA Mental Health Analysis [*Psychology*] (AEBS)
MHA Mental Health Association [*Later, NMHA*] (EA)
MHA Mental Health Authority (NADA)
MHA Mental Hospitals Association (SAUO)
MHA Mervyn Hughes Associates Ltd. (SAUO)
MHA Methemalbumin [*Medicine*] (MAE)
MHA Methionine Hydroxy Analog [*Poultry feed*]
MHA Methodist Homes for the Aged [*British*] (BI)
MHA Metlakatla Housing Authority (SAUO)
MHA Michigan Health & Hospital Association (SAUO)
MHA Microangiopathic Hemolytic Anemia [*Medicine*]
MHA Microhemagglutination [*Test for Syphilis*] [*Immunochemistry*] (DAVI)
MHA Middle Hepatic Artery [*Medicine*] (EDAA)
MHA Military Health Affairs (DOMA)
MHA Minehunter, Auxiliary [*Navy symbol*] [*Obsolete*]
MHA Minimum Holding Altitude [*Aviation*]
MHA Ministry of Home Affairs (SAUO)
MHA Minnesota Heart Association [*Medicine*] (EDAA)
MHA Mixed Hemadsorption Assay [*Clinical chemistry*]
MHA Modified Handling Authorized [*Air Force*]
MHA Montana Hospital Association (EARSL)
MHA Mormon History Association (EA)
MHA Mountain High Aviation [*ICAO designator*] (FAAC)
MHA Mueller Hinton Agar [*Microbiology*] (OA)
MHA Multiple Handicapped Association (NADA)
MHA Multiple Hazard Analysis [*Department of Emergency Management*] (DEMM)
MHA Multiple Headset Adapter [*Aerospace*] (NAKS)
MHA Mutual Households Associations Ltd. [*British*] (BI)
MH-AA Harvard University, Afro-American Studies, Lamont Undergraduate Library, Cambridge, MA [*Library symbol*] [*Library of Congress*] (LCLS)
MHAC Man-Hour Accounting Card
MHAC Mental Health Act Commission (SAUO)
MHAC Midwest Hispanic AIDS Coalition (SAUO)
MHAC Multifrequency High-Gain Antenna Configuration (SSD)
MHadP Porter-Phelps-Hunting Foundation, Hadley, MA [*Library symbol*] [*Library of Congress*] (LCLS)
MH-AH Harvard University, Andover-Harvard Theological Library, Cambridge, MA [*Library symbol*] [*Library of Congress*] (LCLS)
MHAH Mental Health Association in Hawaii (EARSL)
MHAM Amapala [*Honduras*] [*ICAO location identifier*] (ICLI)
MHAM Multiple Hamartoma [*Medicine*] (DMAA)
MHAMS Master of Historical Administration and Museum Studies (GAGS)
MHAND Mental Health Association in North Dakota (EARSL)
MH&M Medical, Health, and Mortuary [*Emergency Management*] (EMA)
MHaNE Northern Essex Community College, Haverhill, MA [*Library symbol*] [*Library of Congress*] (LCLS)
MHansAF United States Air Force Research Library, Hanscom Air Force Base, Hanscom, MA [*Library symbol*] [*Library of Congress*] (LCLS)
MH-AO Harvard University, Oakes Ames Orchid Library, Cambridge, MA [*Library symbol*] [*Library of Congress*] (LCLS)
MHAO Mental Health Association of Oregon (SAUO)
MHAQ Material Handling Association of Quebec (AC)
MHar Brooks Free Library, Harwich, MA [*Library symbol*] [*Library of Congress*] (LCLS)
MH-Ar Harvard University Archives, Cambridge, MA [*Library symbol*] [*Library of Congress*] (LCLS)
MHARCT Mansion House Association on Railway and Canal Traffic (SAUO)
MH-AS Harvard University, George R. Agassiz Station, Cambridge, MA [*Library symbol*] [*Library of Congress*] (LCLS)
MHAS Man-Hour Accounting System (DNAB)
MHathD Danvers State Hospital, Hathorne, MA [*Library symbol*] [*Library of Congress*] (LCLS)
MHA-TP Microhemagglutination Assay Treponema Pallidum [*Immunochemistry*]
MHA-TP Micro-Hemagglutination-Treponema pallidum (SAUS)
MHAU Major Hazards Assessment Unit (HEAS)
MHAUS Malignant Hyperthermia Association of the United States (EA)
MHAWA Master Hairdressers' Association of Western Australia
MHB Hungarian Credit Bank
MHB Maintenance Handbook
MHB Mary Hardin-Baylor College, Belton, TX [*OCLC symbol*] (OCLC)
MHB Master Horizontal Bomber
MHB Material Handling Bureau (SAUO)
MHB Maximum Hospital Benefit [*Medicine*] (DMAA)
MHb Medial Habenular [*Neuroanatomy*]
MHB Mental Health Branch (SAUO)
MHB Methemoglobin [*Immunochemistry*] (DAVI)
MHb Methemoglobin [*Biochemistry, medicine*]
MHB Military History Branch [*USMACV*]
MHB Mine-Hauling Bogie [*Mining engineering*]
MHB Mueller-Hinton Base (DMAA)
MHB Mueller-Hinton Broth [*Cell growth medium*]
MHb Myohemoglobin [*Hematology*]
MH-BA Harvard University, Graduate School of Business Administration, Boston, MA [*Library symbol*] [*Library of Congress*] (LCLS)
MHBA Maryland Horse Breeders Association (EARSL)

MHBA .... Medical-Dental-Hospital Bureaus of America (SAUO)
MHBA .... Morgan Horse Breeders Association [*Defunct*] (EA)
MHBC .... Michigan Heritage Bancorp, Inc. [*NASDAQ symbol*] (QUAN)
MH-BH ...... Harvard University, Blue Hill Meteorological Observatory, Cambridge, MA [*Library symbol*] [*Library of Congress*] (LCLS)
MH-BL ...... Harvard University, Biological Laboratories, Cambridge, MA [*Library symbol*] [*Library of Congress*] (LCLS)
MH-BM ...... Harvard University, George David Birkhoff Mathematics Library, Cambridge, MA [*Library symbol*] [*Library of Congress*] (LCLS)
MHBM .... Modern Heavy Ballistic Missile (ADA)
MHBN .... Mothers' Home Business Network (EA)
MHBNL ...... Mt. Hope Bay Natural Laboratory [*University of Massachusetts Dartmouth*] (RCD)
MH-BR ...... Harvard University, Busch-Reisinger Museum of Germanic Culture, Cambridge, MA [*Library symbol*] [*Library of Congress*] (LCLS)
MHBR .... McHugh Brothers [*Federal Railroad Administration identification code*]
MH-BS ...... Harvard University, Biochemical Sciences Tutorial Library, Cambridge, MA [*Library symbol*] [*Library of Congress*] (LCLS)
MHBSS ...... Modified Hank's Balanced Salt Solution [*Cell culture*]
MHC .... Coastal Minehunter (SAUS)
MH-C .... Harvard University, Chemistry Library, Cambridge, MA [*Library symbol*] [*Library of Congress*] (LCLS)
MHC .... Historical Committee of the Mennonite Church (EA)
MHC .... MAD [*Magnetic Anomaly Detector*] Hunting Circle (NVT)
MHC .... Madras High Court Reports [*India*] [*A publication*] (DLA)
MHC .... Major Histocompatibility Complex [*Immunology*]
MHC .... Managed Health Care (SAUO)
MHC .... Manipulator Hand Controller [*Aerospace*] (NAKS)
MHC .... Manipulator Handset Controller (MCD)
MHC .... Manufactured Home Communities [*NYSE symbol*] (SPSG)
MHC .... Manufacturers Hanover Corp. (EFIS)
MHC .... Mars Hill College [*North Carolina*]
MHC .... Mary Holmes College, West Point, MS [*OCLC symbol*] (OCLC)
MHC .... Mason & Hanger Corp.
MHC .... Material Handling Crane [*Autocrane*] (MCD)
MHC .... Materials Handling Crane (SAUS)
MHC .... Mauritian Housing Corporation (SAUO)
MHC .... Meadowbrook Healthcare, Inc. (MHID)
MHC .... Mean Horizontal Candle [*Aerospace*]
MHC .... Mechanical-Hydraulic Control [*Nuclear energy*] (NRCH)
MHC .... Mediterranean Committee for Thalassemia (SAUO)
MHC .... Mental Health Care [*British*] (DAVI)
MHC .... Mental Health Center (MEDA)
MHC .... Mental Health Clinic (DAVI)
MHC .... Mental Health Commission (SAUO)
MHC .... Mental Health Course [*British*]
MHC .... Mental Hygiene Clinic (IDYL)
MHC .... Mild Hydrocracking [*Petroleum technology*]
MHC .... Minehunter, Coastal [*Navy symbol*]
MHC .... Mobile Housing Carriers Conference Inc., Arlington VA [*STAC*]
MHC .... Modified Huffman Coding (NITA)
MHC .... Moisture Holding Capacity
MHC .... Morgan Horse Club [*Later, American Morgan Horse Association*] (EA)
MHC .... Morris Harvey College [*West Virginia*]
MHC .... Mount Hamilton [*Lick Observatory*] [*California*] [*Seismograph station code, US Geological Survey*] (SEIS)
MHC .... Mount Holyoke College [*South Hadley, MA*]
MHC .... Multiphasic Health Checkup [*Medicine*] (AAMN)
MHC .... Myosin Heavy Chain [*Muscle biology*]
MHCA .... Catacamas [*Honduras*] [*ICAO location identifier*] (ICLI)
MHCA .... Employers' Managed Health Care Association (EA)
MHCA .... Mariner Health Care, Inc. [*NASDAQ symbol*] (QUAN)
MHCA .... Master of Health Care Administration (GAGS)
MHCA .... Mental Health Corporations of America [*Association*] (EA)
MHCA .... Tumor Histocompatibility Antigen [*Medicine*] (MELL)
MHC & W ... Mississippi, Hill City & Western Railroad
MHCAT ...... Minehunter Catamaran [*Military*]
MHCC .... Mobile Housing Carriers Conference [*Defunct*] (EA)
MHCC .... Multipak Heliax Coaxial Cable
MHCD .... CD Matthes [*Common carrier symbol*]
MH/CD ...... Mental Health/Chemical Dependency
MH-CE ...... Harvard University, Commission on Extension Courses, Cambridge, MA [*Library symbol*] [*Library of Congress*] (LCLS)
MH-CE ...... Materials Handling and Construction Equipment (DNAB)
MHCG .... Comayagua [*Honduras*] [*ICAO location identifier*] (ICLI)
MHCH .... Choluteca [*Honduras*] [*ICAO location identifier*] (ICLI)
MH-CI .... Harvard University, Center for International Affairs, Semitic Museum, Cambridge,MA [*Library symbol*] [*Library of Congress*] (LCLS)
MHCI .... Master of Human-Computer Interaction (PGP)
MHCI .... Member of the Hotel and Catering Institute (SAUO)
MHCIMA .... Member of the Hotel, Catering, and Institutional Management Association [*British*] (DBQ)
MHC/I/O .... Minehunter, Coastal/Inshore/Offshore (MILB)
MH-CL ...... Harvard University, Career Reference Library, Cambridge, MA [*Library symbol*] [*Library of Congress*] (LCLS)
MH-CM ...... Harvard University, Child Memorial and English Tutorial Library, Cambridge, MA [*Library symbol*] [*Library of Congress*] (LCLS)
MHCO .... Marquette & Huron Mountain Railroad Co., Inc. [*AAR code*]
MHCO .... Mine-Hunting Control Officer (NATG)
MHCO .... Moore-Handley, Inc. [*Birmingham, AL*] [*NASDAQ symbol*] (NQ)
MHCOA ...... Motor, Hearse, and Car Owners Association (EA)
MH-CP ...... Harvard University, Center for Population Studies, Boston, MA [*Library symbol*] [*Library of Congress*] (LCLS)
MHCP .... Mean Horizontal Candlepower
MHCR .... Madras High Court Reports [*India*] [*A publication*] (DLA)
MH-CS ...... Harvard University, Godfrey Lowell Cabot Science Library, Cambridge, MA [*Library symbol*] [*Library of Congress*] (LCLS)
MHCS .... Mental Hygiene Consultation Service
MHCS .... Multicultural Health Communication Service (SAUO)
M/hct .... Microhematocrit [*Clinical chemistry*]
MHCT .... Modified Human Calcitonin (DB)
MHCT .... Puerto Castilla [*Honduras*] [*ICAO location identifier*] (ICLI)
MHCU .... Intermodal Container Equipment Leasing [*Intermodal shipping container symbol*] (TVRC)
MHCU .... Mental Health Care Unit [*Medicine*]
MHD .... Magnethydrodynamics (EAGT)
MHD .... Magnetohydrodynamic [*Simulation*] [*Marine science*] (OSRA)
MHD .... Magnetohydrodynamics [*Electric power*]
MHD .... Maintenance Hemodialysis [*Medicine*] (DMAA)
MHD .... Mashhad [*Iran*] [*Airport symbol*] (OAG)
MHD .... Master of Human Development (PGP)
MHD .... Masthead (MSA)
MHD .... Mean Hemolytic Dose [*Pharmacology*] (MAE)
MHD .... Mechanized Hebrew Dictionary [*A publication*] (BJA)
MHD .... Medical and Health Department (SAUO)
MHD .... Medical Holding Detachment
MHD .... Medium Hard Drawn (MSA)
MHD .... Mental Health Department [*Medicine*]
MHD .... Mental Health Digest
MHD .... Meshed [*Iran*] [*Airport symbol*] (AD)
MHD .... Meter Heading Differential
MHD .... Military History Detachment
MHD .... Minimal Hemolytic Dose [*Medicine*] (LDT)
MHD .... Minimum Hamming Distance [*Computer science*]
MHD .... Minimum Hemolytic Dilution [*Medicine*] (DMAA)
MHD .... Minimum Hemolytic Dose
MHD .... Movable Head Disc (NITA)
MHD .... Moving Head Disk [*Computer science*] (TEL)
MHD .... Multihead Disk (NASA)
MHD .... Multiple Head Disc (NITA)
MHDA .... Modified High-Density Acid (MCD)
MHDA .... Multiplex Heteroduplex Analysis [*Medicine*] (MELL)
MHDC .... Magnetohydrodynamic Conversion [*Nuclear energy*] (NRCH)
MHDDE ...... Medium Heavy-Duty Diesel Engine [*Motor vehicle specifications*]
MHDDV ...... Medium Heavy-Duty Diesel Vehicle (EPAT)
MHDF .... Medium- and High-Frequency Direction-Finding Station
MHDG .... Magnetohydrodynamic Generator (PDAA)
MHDI .... Morgan Horse Development Institute [*Defunct*] (EA)
MH-DJ ...... Harvard University, Documentation Center on Contemporary Japan, Cambridge, MA [*Library symbol*] [*Library of Congress*] (LCLS)
MHDL .... Magnetohydrodynamic LASER (PDAA)
MHDL .... Microwave Hardware Design Language
MHDNA ...... Mobile Home Dealers National Association [*Defunct*]
MH-DO ...... Harvard University, Harvard University Development Office, Cambridge, MA [*Library symbol*] [*Library of Congress*] (LCLS)
MHDPA ...... Monohexadecylphosphoric Acid [*Organic chemistry*]
MHDSRIP ... May His Departed Soul Rest in Peace (BJA)
MHDU .... Medical Hemodialysis Unit [*Nephrology*] (DAVI)
MHE .... Maintenance and Handling Equipment
MHE .... Manufactured Home Estates
MHE .... Mass Health & Education Tax-Exempt [*AMEX symbol*] (SPSG)
MHE .... Mass Hlth & Edu Tax-Exempt Tr [*AMEX symbol*] (TTSB)
MHE .... Master of Health Education (GAGS)
MHE .... Master of Higher Education (GAGS)
MHE .... Master of Highway Engineering (NADA)
MHE .... Master of Home Economics (GAGS)
MHE .... Master of Home Economics Engineering (NADA)
MHE .... Master of Human Ecology (PGP)
MHE .... Materials Handling Equipment [*Military*] (AFM)
MHE .... Materiel Handling Equipment [*Army*] (INF)
MHE .... Mean Hook Extent (PDAA)
MHE .... Mechanical Handling Equipment (MCD)
MHE .... Mental Health Enquiry [*Medical/computing registers*] [*British*]
MHE .... Message Handling Element (SAUO)
MHE .... Ministry of Higher Education (SAUO)
MHE .... Missile Handling Equipment
MHE .... Mitchell [*South Dakota*] [*Airport symbol*] (OAG)
MHE .... Mitchell, SD [*Location identifier*] [*FAA*] (FAAL)
MHE .... Multiple Headspace Extraction [*Analytical chemistry*]
MHE .... Munitions Handling Equipment (MCD)
MHE .... Muzzle Hatch Electrical
MHE .... Myddleton Hotels & Estates Limited (SAUO)
MH-EA ...... Harvard University, East Asian Research Center, Cambridge, MA [*Library symbol*] [*Library of Congress*] (LCLS)
MHEA .... Material Handling Engineers Association (SAUO)
MHEA .... Mechanical Handling Engineers' Association [*British*] (BI)
MHealthAdmin ... Master of Health Administration (ADA)
MHEANA .... Masonic Homes Executives' Association of North America (EA)
MH-EB ...... Harvard University, Oakes Ames Library of Economic Botany, Cambridge, MA [*Library symbol*] [*Library of Congress*] (LCLS)
MHEB .... MH Eby [*NCIC trailer make code*]
MHeb .... Middle Hebrew [*Language, etc.*] (BJA)
MH Ec ...... Master of Home Economics (PGP)
MHEC .... Midwestern Higher Education Commission
MHEC .... Muzzle Hatch Electrical Control
MH-Ed ...... Harvard University, Graduate School of Education, Cambridge, MA [*Library symbol*] [*Library of Congress*] (LCLS)

MHEd .... Master of Health Education (GAGS)
MHEd .... Master of Higher Education
MHEDA ...... Material Handling Equipment Distributors Association (EA)
MHEE .... Master of Home Economics Education (NADA)
MHEEd ...... Master of Home Economics Education (NADA)
MHEF .... Milton H. Erickson Foundation (EA)
MHEG .... Multimedia and Hypermedia Expert Group (TELE)
MHEO .... Migrant Health Education Officer [*Australia*]
MHEOWS ... Multicolored High Energy Outgoing Wavefront Sampling (ACAE)
MH-ER ...... Harvard University, East Asian Studies Reading Room, Cambridge, MA [*Library symbol*] [*Library of Congress*] (LCLS)
MH-ES .... Harvard University, Center for European Studies, Cambridge, MA [*Library symbol*] [*Library of Congress*] (LCLS)
MHET .... Monolithic Hot Electron Transistor (NITA)
MHEVENT ... Most Harmful Event [*National Highway Traffic Safety Administration Fatal Accident Recording System code*]
MHEX .... Methohexital [*An anesthetic*]
MH-F .... Harvard University, Farlow Reference Library, Cambridge, MA [*Library symbol*] [*Library of Congress*] (LCLS)
M-H-F .... Massey-Harris-Ferguson (SAUO)
MHF .... Master History File
MHF .... Medium-High Frequency
MHF .... Mental Health Foundation (SAUO)
MHF .... Meridian House Foundation [*Later, MHI*]
MHF .... Message Handling Facility (SAUO)
MHF .... Microsillon et Haute-Fidelite [*Record label*] [*France*]
MHF .... Mirror Furnace (SAUS)
MHF .... Mixed Hydrazine Fuel
MHF .... Municipal High Care [*NYSE symbol*] (TTSB)
MHF .... Municipal High Income Fund, Inc. [*NYSE symbol*] (CTT)
MHF .... Muni High Income Fund (EFIS)
MHF .... Myosin Head Fragment [*Biochemistry*]
MHF .... Smith Point, TX [*Location identifier*] [*FAA*] (FAAL)
MH-FA .... Harvard University, Fine Arts Library, Cambridge, MA [*Library symbol*] [*Library of Congress*] (LCLS)
MHFA .... Multiple Conductor, Heat and Flame Resistant, Armor [*Cable*]
MHFB .... Mental Health Film Board (EA)
MHFC .... Merle Haggard Fan Club (EA)
MHFES ...... Materials Handbook for Fusion Energy Systems (SAUO)
MHFF .... Mile-Hi Frozen Foods Company [*Common carrier symbol*]
MH/FH .... Man-Hours per Flying Hour [*Air Force*] (DNAB)
MHFNZ ...... Mental Health Foundation of New Zealand (SAUO)
MHFPR ...... Maximum Hypothetical Fission Product Release [*Nuclear energy*] (NRCH)
MHFR .... Maximum Hypothetical Fission Product Release [*Nuclear energy*] (NRCH)
MHF(V) ...... Mental Health Foundation (Victoria) [*Australia*]
MHFWPR ... Mental Health Fieldwork Performance Report [*Occupational therapy*]
MHFX .... MHF Logistical Solutions [*Private rail car owner code*]
MH-G .... Harvard University, Gray Herbarium, Cambridge, MA [*Library symbol*] [*Library of Congress*] (LCLS)
MHG .... Mahogany (WGA)
MHG .... Malartic Hygrade Gold Mines Ltd. (MHDW)
MHG .... Mannheim [*Germany*] [*Airport symbol*] (OAG)
MHG .... Margu [*Language symbol*] (ETLW)
MHG .... MDS Health Group Ltd. [*Toronto Stock Exchange symbol*]
MHG .... Message Header Generator (PDAA)
MHG .... Metropolitan Health Group (DMAA)
MHG .... Middle High German [*Language, etc.*]
MHG .... Midrash ha-Gadol (BJA)
mHg .... Millimeters of Mercury [*A measurement of pressure*] (MAE)
MHG .... Miniature Hydrogen Generator
MHG .... Modern High German [*Language, etc.*] (ROG)
MH-GG ...... Harvard University, Committee on Experimental Geology and Geophysics, Hoffman Laboratory, Cambridge, MA [*Library symbol*] [*Library of Congress*] (LCLS)
MH-GI .... Harvard University, Hamilton A. R. Gibb Islamic Seminar, Cambridge, MA [*Library symbol*] [*Library of Congress*] (LCLS)
MH-GM ...... Harvard University, Gordon McKay Library, Cambridge, MA [*Library symbol*] [*Library of Congress*] (LCLS)
MH-GS ...... Harvard University, Geological Sciences Library, Cambridge, MA [*Library symbol*] [*Library of Congress*] (LCLS)
MH-H .... Harvard University, Houghton Library, Cambridge, MA [*Library symbol*] [*Library of Congress*] (LCLS)
MHH .... Mandala Holistic Health [*Defunct*] (EA)
MH-H .... Mare Humorum-Helmet [*Lunar area*]
MHH .... Marsh Harbour [*Bahamas*] [*Airport symbol*] (OAG)
MH-HD ...... Harvard University, History Department Library, Cambridge, MA [*Library symbol*] [*Library of Congress*] (LCLS)
MH-HF ...... Harvard University, Harvard Forest Library, Petersham, MA [*Library symbol*] [*Library of Congress*] (LCLS)
MHHFC ...... Machine and Hull History File Card (DNAB)
MH-Hi .... Harvard University, Hilles Library of Radcliffe College, Cambridge, MA [*Library symbol*] [*Library of Congress*] (LCLS)
MHHI .... Multihandicapped Hearing-Impaired
MH-HJ .... Harvard University, Arnold Arboretum, Horticultural Library, Jamaica Plain, MA [*Library symbol*] [*Library of Congress*] (LCLS)
MH-HO ...... Harvard University, Lucien Howe Library of Ophthalmology, Boston, MA [*Library symbol*] [*Library of Congress*] (LCLS)
MH-HP ...... Harvard University, Center for Analysis of Health Practices, Cambridge, MA [*Library symbol*] [*Library of Congress*] (LCLS)
MHHPA ...... Methylhexahydrophthalic Anhydride [*Organic chemistry*]
MH-HS ...... Harvard University, History of Science Library, Cambridge, MA [*Library symbol*] [*Library of Congress*] (LCLS)
MHHS .... Medal of Honor Historical Society (EA)
MHHW ...... Mean Higher High Water [*Tides and currents*]
MHHWS ..... Mean Higher High-Water Springs [*Tides and currents*]
MH-HY ...... Harvard University, Harvard-Yenching Library, Cambridge, MA [*Library symbol*] [*Library of Congress*] (LCLS)
MHHZO ...... Move High-to-High Zone (VLIE)
MHI .... Malignant Histiocytosis of Intestine [*Medicine*] (DMAA)
MHI .... Malone & Hyde, Incorporated (SAUO)
MHI .... Manual Hit Indicator (SAUS)
MHI .... Manufactured Housing Insitute (WPI)
MHI .... Manufactured Housing Institute (EA)
MHI .... Marine Hydrophysical Institute
MHI .... Mashhad [*Iran*] [*Seismograph station code, US Geological Survey*] (SEIS)
MHi .... Massachusetts Historical Society, Boston, MA [*Library symbol*] [*Library of Congress*] (LCLS)
MHI .... Material Handling Institute (EA)
MHI .... Material Hazard Index (AAEL)
MHI .... Materials Handling Institute, Inc.
MHI .... Meat Hygiene Inspector (GVA)
MHI .... Mended Hearts, Inc. [*Affiliated with the American Heart Association*] (NRGU)
MHI .... Mental Health Index (DMAA)
MHI .... Mental Health Institute (OICC)
MHI .... Mental Health Inventory (DMAA)
MHI .... Meridian House International (EA)
MHI .... Meridian International Center [*Washington, D.C.*] (EA)
MHI .... Metal Hydrides Incorporated (SAUO)
MHI .... Military Health Institute
MHI .... Military History Institute [*Army*] (MCD)
MHI .... Ministry of Health Inspectorate (SAUO)
MHI .... Minor Head Injury (MELL)
MHI .... Minority Health Initiative (SAUO)
mhi .... misc.health.infertility newsgroup (SAUO)
MHI .... Mitsubishi Heavy Industries
MHI .... Mitsubishi Heavy Industries Ltd.
MHI .... Mobile Home Industries, Inc. (EFIS)
MHI .... Morgan Hydrocarbons, Inc. [*Toronto Stock Exchange symbol*]
MHI .... Morrison Health Care, Inc. [*NYSE symbol*] (SAG)
MHI .... Morrison Management Specialists [*NYSE symbol*] (SG)
MHIA .... Material Handling Industry Association (NTPA)
MHIA .... Mitsubishi Heavy Industries America, Inc.
MHIA .... Mitsubishi Heavy Industries Ltd (EFIS)
MHIBL .... Mile High Intercollegiate Baseball League (PSS)
MH-IC .... Harvard University, Collection of Historic Scientific Instruments Collection, Cambridge, MA [*Library symbol*] [*Library of Congress*] (LCLS)
MHIC .... Islas Del Cisne O Santanilla [*Honduras*] [*ICAO location identifier*] (ICLI)
MH-ID .... Harvard University, Harvard Institute for International Development, Cambridge, MA [*Library symbol*] [*Library of Congress*] (LCLS)
MHID .... Medical and Health Information Directory [*A publication*]
MHIDAS ..... Major Hazard Incident Data Service [*Atomic Energy Authority*] [*British*] [*Information service or system*] (IID)
MHIDAS ..... Modular High Integration Distributed Architecture databus System (SAUS)
M Hi E ...... Master of Highway Engineering
MHIE .... Mitsubishi Heavy Industries Europe, Ltd (EFIS)
M Hi Eng ... Master of Highway Engineering
MHIFC ...... Michael Harding International Fan Club (EA)
MHIFM ...... Milton Helpern Institute of Forensic Medicine (EA)
MHII .... Material Handling Institute Incorporated (SAUO)
MHILC .... Hampshire Inter-Library Center, Inc., Amherst, MA [*Library symbol*] [*Library of Congress*] [*Obsolete*] (LCLS)
MHIMA ...... Michigan Health Information Management Association (EARSL)
MHingM ..... Hingham Marine Museum, Hingham, MA [*Library symbol*] [*Library of Congress*] (LCLS)
MHIP .... Missile Homing Improvement Program (DWSG)
MHI PAC .... Manufactured Housing Institute PAC [*Arlington, VA*] (PACS)
MHISC .... Manufactured Housing Institute of South Carolina Federal PAC [*Columbia, SC*] (PACS)
MHISL .... Mile High Intercollegiate Softball League (PSS)
MHJ .... Microwave Hybrid Junction
MHJC .... Mary Holmes Junior College (SAUO)
MHJU .... Juticalpa [*Honduras*] [*ICAO location identifier*] (ICLI)
MHK .... Manhattan [*Kansas*] [*Airport symbol*] (OAG)
MHK .... Manhattan, KS [*Location identifier*] [*FAA*] (FAAL)
MHK .... Master of Human Kinetics (GAGS)
MHK .... Member of the House of Keys [*Isle Of Man*] [*British*]
MHK .... Military History of Korea
MH/K .... Mine Hunter/Killer [*Military*]
MHK .... Mohawk Industries [*NYSE symbol*] (SG)
MHK .... Morgan Stanley Group, Inc. [*AMEX symbol*] (SAG)
MH-KG ...... Harvard University, Kennedy School of Government, Cambridge, MA [*Library symbol*] [*Library of Congress*] (LCLS)
MH-KM ...... Harvard University, Kennedy Inter-Faculty Program in Medical Ethics, Cambridge, MA [*Library symbol*] [*Library of Congress*] (LCLS)
MHKVLY .... Mohawk Valley (FAAC)
MHL .... Hamline University, School of Law, St. Paul, MN [*OCLC symbol*] (OCLC)
MH-L .... Harvard University, Law School, Cambridge, MA [*Library symbol*] [*Library of Congress*] (LCLS)
M (HL) ...... House of Lords' Appeals, in Macpherson's Court of Sessions Cases, Third Series [*1862-73*] [*Scotland*] [*A publication*] (DLA)
MHL .... Manaus Harbour Limited (SAUO)
MHL .... March Resources [*Vancouver Stock Exchange symbol*]
MHL .... Marshall Islands [*ANSI three-letter standard code*] (CNC)

MHL .... Marshall, MO [*Location identifier*] [*FAA*] (FAAL)
MHL .... Marshall, TX [*Amtrak rail station code*]
MHL .... Master of Hebrew Letters (BJA)
MHL .... Master of Hebrew Literature
MHL .... Master of Humane Letters
MHL .... Mast Hull Loop
MHL .... Medial Hypothalamic Lesion [*Medicine*] (EDAA)
MHL .... Metastable Helium Level
MHL .... Microprocessor Host Loader (TIMI)
MHL .... Minimum Helium Loss [*System*]
MHL .... Mission Hills Library (SAUO)
MHI .... Morrison Health Care [*NYSE symbol*] (TTSB)
MHLA........ McGraw-Hill Learning Architecture
MHLB........ Ministry of Health, Legal Branch (SAUO)
MHLC........ La Ceiba/Goloson Internacional [*Honduras*] [*ICAO location identifier*] (ICLI)
MHLC........ Multidimensional Health Locus of Control [*Diagnostic scale*]
MHLE........ La Esperanza [*Honduras*] [*ICAO location identifier*] (ICLI)
MHLF........ Mutual Home Loan Funds (SAUO)
MHLG .... Ministry of Housing and Local Government (SAUO)
MHLH .... Myogenic Helix-Loop-Helix [*Genetics*]
MH-Li .... Harvard University, Linguistics Library, Cambridge, MA [*Library symbol*] [*Library of Congress*] (LCLS)
MHLL........ McGraw-Hill Lifetime Learning
MHLLDA .... Mobile Home Landscapers and Landscape Designers Association (EA)
MH-Lm...... Harvard University, Lamont Undergraduate Library, Cambridge, MA [*Library symbol*] [*Library of Congress*] (LCLS)
MHLM....... San Pedro Sula/La Mesa Internacional [*Honduras*] [*ICAO location identifier*] (ICLI)
MHLN .... McGraw-Hill Learning Network
MHLOS...... Mega High Level Language Operations per Second (CCCA)
MHLP........ Mental Health Law Project (EA)
MHLP........ Mesa Holding Limited Partnership (EFIS)
MHLS........ Metabolic Heat Load Simulator
MHLS........ Mid-Hudson Library System [*Library network*]
MHLTA....... Men's Hat Linings and Trimmings Association [*Defunct*] (EA)
MHLW .... Major Hazards Legislation Working Party (HEAS)
MHLW .... Mean Higher Low Water [*Tides and currents*]
MHLZO...... Move High-to-Low Zone (VLIE)
MHM .... Master of Hotel Management (PGP)
MHM .... Mental Health Management [*AMEX symbol*] (SPSG)
MHM .... Metal-Hydrogen-Metal [*Chemical bond*]
MHM .... MHM Services [*AMEX symbol*] (SAG)
mhm......... Mill Hill Missionaries (TOCD)
MHM .... Mill Hill Missionaries [*Roman Catholic men's religious order*]
MHM .... Minchumina, AK [*Location identifier*] [*FAA*] (FAAL)
MHM .... Minimum Hardware Modification [*Aircraft landing*]
MHM .... Mount Hope Mineral Railroad Co. [*Absorbed into Consolidated Rail Corp.*] [*AAR code*]
MHM .... Muzzle Hatch Mechanical
MH/MA...... Manhours/Maintenance Action (ACAE)
MHMA....... Marcala [*Honduras*] [*ICAO location identifier*] (ICLI)
MHMA....... Master House Movers' Association [*Australia*]
MHMA....... Mobile Home Manufacturers Association [*Later, Manufactured Housing Institute*]
MHMB....... Ministry of Health, Medical Branch (SAUO)
MHMC....... Manufactured Housing Management Corporation [*NCIC trailer make code*]
MHMC....... Mental Health Materials Center (EA)
MHMC....... Mercy Hospital and Medical Center (SAUO)
MHMC....... Montefiore Hospital and Medical Center (SAUO)
MH-ME...... Harvard University, Center for Middle Eastern Studies, Cambridge, MA [*Library symbol*] [*Library of Congress*] (LCLS)
MHME....... More Heart More Edge [*Screenwriter's lexicon*]
MHMey...... Meyerson [*M.H.*] & Co. [*Associated Press*] (SAG)
MHMeyer ... Meyerson [*M.H.*] & Co. [*Associated Press*] (SAG)
MH-MH...... Harvard University, John Peabody Monks Library, Cambridge, MA [*Library symbol*] [*Library of Congress*] (LCLS)
MH-ML....... Harvard University, Ticknor Library of Modern Languages, Cambridge, MA [*Library symbol*] [*Library of Congress*] (LCLS)
MHMP....... Moving Head Multiple Platter (RALS)
MH/MR...... Mental Health and Mental Retardation (DAVI)
MHMS....... Master of Health Management Systems (PGP)
MHMS....... Master of Human Movement Studies (ADA)
MHMS....... Material Handling and Management Society (EAIO)
MHMS....... Middlesex Hospital Medical School (SAUO)
MHMS....... Modular Hydrologic Modeling System [*Marine science*] (OSRA)
MHM Serv... MHM Services [*Associated Press*] (SAG)
MH-Mu...... Harvard University, Music Library, Cambridge, MA [*Library symbol*] [*Library of Congress*] (LCLS)
MHMX....... Miner-Hillard Milling [*Private rail car owner code*]
MHMY....... Meyerson [*M.H.*] & Co. [*NASDAQ symbol*] (SAG)
MHMY....... M.H. Meyerson & Co. [*NASDAQ symbol*] (TTSB)
MHMYW .... M H Meyerson & Co. Wrtt [*NASDAQ symbol*] (TTSB)
MHN......... Managed HealthCare Northwest (MHID)
MHN......... Managed Health Network (SEAT)
MHN......... Manhattan Mineral [*Vancouver Stock Exchange symbol*]
MHN......... Mannitol Hexanitrate [*Organic chemistry*]
MHN......... Massive Hepatic Necrosis [*Medicine*] (MAE)
MHN......... McGraw-Hill News [*Database*] (IT)
MHN......... Mental Health Net (SAUO)
MHN......... Morbus Hemolyticus Neonatorum [*Medicine*] (MELL)
MHN......... Moving Haven (SAUS)
MHN......... Mullen, NE [*Location identifier*] [*FAA*] (FAAL)
MHN......... Musical Heritage Network [*Internet resource*]
MHN......... Mylohyoid Nerve [*Medicine*] (MELL)
MHNAMT ... Methyl(hydroxylnaphthalamino)mercaptotriazole [*Organic chemistry*]
MHNC....... Merchants of California [*Common carrier symbol*]
MH-NE ...... Harvard University, Near Eastern Languages and Literatures Library, Cambridge, MA [*Library symbol*] [*Library of Congress*] (LCLS)
MHNGS ..... Marble Hill Nuclear Generating Station (NRCH)
MHNJ........ Guanaja [*Honduras*] [*ICAO location identifier*] (ICLI)
MH-NJ....... Harvard University, Nieman Collection of Contemporary Journalism, Cambridge, MA [*Library symbol*] [*Library of Congress*] (LCLS)
MHNPS...... Marble Hill Nuclear Power Station (NRCH)
MHNV .... Nuevo Ocotepeque [*Honduras*] [*ICAO location identifier*] (ICLI)
MH-O .... Harvard University, Harvard College Observatory, Cambridge, MA [*Library symbol*] [*Library of Congress*] (LCLS)
MHO......... Manchester Resources Corp. [*Vancouver Stock Exchange symbol*]
MHO......... Medical House Officer (MELL)
MHO......... Metallurgie Hoboken-Overpelt (EFIS)
MHO......... Microsomal Heme Oxygenase (DB)
MHO......... Millhouse Developments Ltd. [*British*] [*ICAO designator*] (FAAC)
MHO......... Minehunter Ocean [*Navy*] (ANA)
MHO......... M/I Schottenstein Homes, Inc. [*NYSE symbol*] (SPSG)
MHO......... Modern Human Origins
MHO......... Mohanbari [*India*] [*Airport symbol*] (AD)
MHO......... Mount Hopkins Observatory [*Later, FLWO*] [*Smithsonian Institution*] (GRD)
mho.......... Reciprocal Ohm [*Unit of conductance*]
MHOA .... McDonald's Hispanic Operators Association (EA)
MHOA .... Mutual Help and Occupancy Agreement [*Department of Housing and Urban Development*] (GFGA)
MHOA .... Olanchito [*Honduras*] [*ICAO location identifier*] (ICLI)
M Ho Ec .... Master of Household Economy
MHOF .... Mobile Home Owners Federation [*NFMHO*] [*Superseded by*] (EA)
MH/OH ...... Man Hours per Operating Hour [*Maintenance*] (RDA)
MHoly .... Holyoke Public Library, Holyoke, MA [*Library symbol*] [*Library of Congress*] (LCLS)
MHolyC ..... Holyoke Community College, Holyoke, MA [*Library symbol*] [*Library of Congress*] (LCLS)
M Hor .... Master of Horticulture
MHort(RHS)... National Diploma in Horticulture (Royal Horticultural Society) [*British*] (DBQ)
MHortSc .... Master of Horticultural Science
M Ho Sc .... Master of Household Science
MHOTY...... My Hat's Off To You (VLIE)
MH-P .... Harvard University, Peabody Museum, Cambridge, MA [*Library symbol*] [*Library of Congress*] (LCLS)
MHp .... Harwich Port Library Association, Harwich Port, MA [*Library symbol*] [*Library of Congress*] (LCLS)
MHP......... Maclean Hunter Ltd. [*Toronto Stock Exchange symbol*]
MHP......... Malignant Hyperpyrexia [*Medicine*] (EDAA)
MHP......... Master of Health Planning (ADA)
MHP......... Master of Health Professions (PGP)
MHP......... Master of Heritage Preservation (GAGS)
MHP......... Master of Historical Preservation (GAGS)
MHP......... Master of Humanities in Philosophy (PGP)
MHP......... Maximum House Price (FOTI)
MHP......... McGraw-Hill Companies [*NYSE symbol*] (TTSB)
MHP......... McGraw-Hill, Inc. [*NYSE symbol*] (SPSG)
MHP......... Medium-High Pressure (MSA)
MHP......... Mental Health Project
MHP......... Mercurihydroxypropane [*Clinical chemistry*]
MHP......... Message Handling Processor
MHP......... Metabolic Heat Production [*Physiology*]
MHP......... Military Health Plan [*DoD*]
MHP......... Milli Hedef Partisi [*National Goal Party*] [*Turkish Cyprus*] [*Political party*] (PPE)
MHP......... Mississippi Highway Patrol (SAUO)
MHP......... Missouri Highway Patrol (SAUO)
MHP......... Mobile Host Protocol (SAUS)
MHP......... Monosymptomatic Hypochondriacal Psychosis [*Medicine*] (EDAA)
MH-PA....... Harvard University, Littauer Library of the Kennedy School of Government, Cambridge, MA [*Library symbol*] [*Library of Congress*] (LCLS)
MHPA........ Palmerola [*Honduras*] [*ICAO location identifier*] (ICLI)
MH-PC ...... Harvard University, Palaeography Library, Cambridge, MA [*Library symbol*] [*Library of Congress*] (LCLS)
MHPCC...... Maui High Performance Computer Center (SAUO)
MHPCC...... Maui High Performance Computing Center (SAUO)
MHPD .... Masonite Hydropress Die (MSA)
MHPE........ Master of Health Professions Education (PGP)
MHPE........ Methoxy-Hydroxyphenylethanol [*Organic chemistry*] (MAH)
MHPE........ Progreso [*Honduras*] [*ICAO location identifier*] (ICLI)
MH PE & R... Master of Health, Physical Education, and Recreation
MHPE Conj... Methoxy-Hydroxyphenylethanol Conjugate [*Organic chemistry*] (DAVI)
MHPEd ...... Master of Health Personnel Education (ADA)
MHPF........ Minority Health Professions Foundation [*Association*] (EA)
MHPG .... (Methoxyhydroxyphenyl)ethyleneglycol [*Also, MOPEG*] [*Organic chemistry*]
MHPG Conj... Methoxyhydropheny Gylcol Conjugate [*Organic chemistry*] (DAVI)
MHPH .... Man-Hours per Flying Hour [*Air Force*] (AFIT)
MHPI .... Military Housing Privatization Initiative [*1996*]
MH-PL....... Harvard University, Milman Parry Collection of Oral Literature, Cambridge, MA [*Library symbol*] [*Library of Congress*] (LCLS)
MHPL........ Puerto Lempira [*Honduras*] [*ICAO location identifier*] (ICLI)

MH-PO ...... Harvard University, Personnel Office Library, Cambridge, MA [*Library symbol*] [*Library of Congress*] (LCLS)
MH-PP ...... Harvard University, Public Policy Program, Cambridge, MA [*Library symbol*] [*Library of Congress*] (LCLS)
MH-PR ...... Harvard University, Physics Research Library, Cambridge, MA [*Library symbol*] [*Library of Congress*] (LCLS)
MH-Ps...... Harvard University, Psychology Research Library, Cambridge, MA [*Library symbol*] [*Library of Congress*] (LCLS)
MHPT........ Methyl-Hydroxy-P-Toluidine [*Plastics*]
MHPU .... Puerto Cortes [*Honduras*] [*ICAO location identifier*] (ICLI)
MH-Pv...... Harvard University, Preservation Center, Cambridge, MA [*Library symbol*] [*Library of Congress*] (LCLS)
MHQ......... Mariehamn [*Finland*] [*Airport symbol*] (OAG)
MHQ......... Maritime Headquarters (NVT)
MHQ......... Mediterranean Headquarters (SAUO)
MHQU .... United States Military Sealift Command [*Intermodal shipping container symbol*] (TVRC)
MHQV .... Mobile Headquarters Van [*Police and security equipment*]
MHQZ .... United States Military Sealift Command [*Intermodal trailer symbol*]
MH-R .... Harvard University, Russian Research Center, Cambridge, MA [*Library symbol*] [*Library of Congress*] (LCLS)
MHR......... Magnum Hunter Resources [*AMEX symbol*] (SG)
MHR......... Major Histocompatibility Region [*Immunology*]
MHR......... Major Homology Region [*Biochemistry*]
MHR......... Malignant Hyperthermia Resistance [*Medicine*] (DMAA)
MHR......... Man-Hour
MHR......... Master of Human Resources (GAGS)
MHR......... Maternal Heart Rate (MELL)
MHR......... Maximal Heart Rate (SAUS)
MHR......... Maximum Heart Rate
MHR......... McGraw-Hill Ryerson Ltd. [*Toronto Stock Exchange symbol*]
MHR......... Measurement Handicap Rule [*Sailing*]
MHR......... Medical Humanities Review [*A publication*] (BRI)
MHR......... Mehri [*Language symbol*] (ETLW)
MHR......... Member of the House of Representatives
MHR......... Methemoglobin Reductase [*Hematology and laboratory*] (DAVI)
MHR......... Microwave Hologram RADAR
MHR......... Mile High Radar (SAUS)
MHR......... Miniature Helium Refrigerator
MHR......... Missile Hazard Report (AFM)
MHR......... Mount Hamilton Road [*California*] [*Seismograph station code, US Geological Survey*] (SEIS)
MHr......... Myohemerythrin [*Biochemistry*]
MHR......... Sacramento, CA [*Location identifier*] [*FAA*] (FAAL)
MHR......... United States Army Military History Institute, Carlisle Barracks, PA [*OCLC symbol*] (OCLC)
MH-RA ...... Harvard University, Harvard Radio Astronomy Center, Fort Davis, TX [*Library symbol*] [*Library of Congress*] (LCLS)
MHRA .... Manufactured Housing Research Alliance [*Association*] (EA)
MHRA .... Mauritanian Human Rights Association [*Political party*] (PSAP)
MHRA .... Medical and Health Research Association of New York City (SAUO)
MHRA .... Modern Humanities Research Association [*United Kingdom*] (RCD)
MHRA .... Modern Humanities Research Association, American Branch [*Defunct*] (EA)
MHRA .... Morab Horse Registry of America (EA)
MHRAC...... Mine Health Research Advisory Committee [*National Institute for Occupational Safety and Health*] [*Morgantown, WV*] (EGAO)
MH-RB ...... Harvard University, Rubel Asiatic Research Bureau, Fogg Art Museum, Cambridge, MA [*Library symbol*] [*Library of Congress*] [*Obsolete*] (LCLS)
MHRB .... Mental Health Review Board [*Victoria, Australia*]
MH-RC ...... Harvard University, Fred N. Robinson Celtic Seminar, Cambridge, MA [*Library symbol*] [*Library of Congress*] (LCLS)
MHRC .... Manitoba Health Research Council [*Canada*]
MHRD .... Master in Human Resource Department (PGP)
MHRF .... Mental Health Research Fund (SAUO)
MH-RI .... Harvard University, RISM-US Project Center, Cambridge, MA [*Library symbol*] [*Library of Congress*] (LCLS)
MHRI .... Mental Health Research Institute [*University of Michigan*] [*Research center*]
MHRI .... Miami Heart Research Institute (SAUO)
MHRIM...... Master of Hotel, Restaurant, and Institutional Management (PGP)
MHRIR ...... Master of Human Resources and Industrial Relations (PGP)
MHRM....... Master of Human Resources Management (PGP)
MHRM....... Microcomputers in Human Resource Management [*Advanced Personnel Systems*] [*Information service or system*] (CRD)
MHROD ..... Master of Human Resources and Organization Development (PGP)
MH-RP ...... Harvard University, Robbins Library of Philosophy, Cambridge, MA [*Library symbol*] [*Library of Congress*] (LCLS)
MHRR .... MSAD Hardware Reflight Review (SAUS)
MHRS .... Magnetic Heading Reference System
MHRS .... Million Hours (SAUO)
MHRS .... Modified Hazard Ranking System (ABAC)
MHRST...... Medical and Health Related Sciences Thesaurus [*A publication*] (IEEE)
MHRT........ Mental Health Review Tribunal [*British*]
MHRTA...... Masters in Hotel, Restaurant, Tourism, and Administration (PGP)
MHRU .... Ruinas De Copan [*Honduras*] [*ICAO location identifier*] (ICLI)
MHRV .... Movement for Human Rights in Vietnam [*Defunct*] (EA)
MH-S .... Harvard University, Statistics Library, Cambridge, MA [*Library symbol*] [*Library of Congress*] (LCLS)
MHS .... Machined Hemispherical Shell
MHS .... Magnetic Hand Scanner [*Computer science*] (ELAL)
MHS .... Magnetic Heading System (AAG)
MHS .... Magnetomotive Hammer System
MHS .... Maher, Inc. [*Toronto Stock Exchange symbol*]
MHS .... Mail Handling Service (SAUO)
MHS .... Mail Handling System [*Computer science*]
MHS .... Maine Historical Society (EARSL)
MHS .... Major Histocompatibility System [*Immunology*]
MHS .... Malignant Hyperthermia Susceptible [*Medicine*]
MHS .... Malignant Hypothermia Susceptible [*Patients*] [*Emergency medicine*] (DAVI)
MHS .... Mammoth Hot Springs [*Wyoming*] [*Seismograph station code, US Geological Survey*] (SEIS)
MHS .... Man-Hours per Sortie [*Air Force*] (AFIT)
MHS .... Marine Hospital Service [*Public Health Service*]
MHS .... Marriott Corp. [*NYSE symbol*] (COMM)
MHS .... Massachusetts Historical Society (SAUO)
MHS .... Massachusetts Horticultural Society (SAUO)
MHS .... Master Hotel Supplier [*Educational Institute of the American Hotel and M otel Association*] [*Designation awarded by*]
MHS .... Master of Health Sciences (PGP)
MHS .... Master of Health Services (GAGS)
MHS .... Master of Hispanic Studies (PGP)
MHS .... Master of Humane Studies (PGP)
MHS .... Master of Human Services (GAGS)
MHS .... Maximum Histalog Stimulation [*Gastroenterology*] (DAVI)
MHS .... McMaster University Health Sciences Library [*UTLAS symbol*]
MHS .... Measurement Handicapping System [*Yacht racing*]
MHS .... Meat Hygiene Service (GVA)
MHS .... Mechanical Handling System
MHS .... Medco Health Solutions [*NYSE symbol*]
MHS .... Member of the Historical Society
MHS .... Mental Health Specialist [*Therapy term*] (CTAA)
MHS .... Message Handling Service [*Telecommunications*] (PCM)
MHS .... Message Handling System [*Computer science*]
MHS .... Methylhydrazine Sulfate [*Organic chemistry*]
MHS .... Michigan Humane Society (EARSL)
MHS .... Microwave Humidity Sounder (EOSA)
M/H/S .... Miles per Hour per Second
MHS .... Military Health System (SAUO)
MHS .... Military Heraldry Society (SAUO)
MHS .... Military Historical Society [*Defunct*] (EA)
MHS .... Ministry of Home Security [*British*]
MHS .... Minnesota Historical Society, St. Paul, MN [*OCLC symbol*] (OCLC)
MHS .... Missile Hazard Space (AFM)
MHS .... Modular Hardware System [*Computer science*] (VLIE)
MHS .... Modulated Hybrid System [*Electric vehicles*]
MHS .... Moravian Historical Society (EA)
MHS .... Morris High School (SAUO)
MHS .... Mount Shasta, CA [*Location identifier*] [*FAA*] (FAAL)
MHS .... Multiple Hospital System
MHS .... Multiple Host Support
MHS .... Musical Heritage Society [*Commercial firm*] (EA)
MHS .... Sisters of the Most Holy Sacrament [*Roman Catholic religious order*]
MHSA .... Master of Health Services Administration (GAGS)
MHSA .... Master of Human Services Administration (PGP)
MH/SA...... Mental Health/Substance Abuse
MHSA .... Microaggregated Human Serum Albumin [*Medicine*] (EDAA)
MHSA .... Montana High School Association (EARSL)
MH-SC ...... Harvard University, Herbert Weir Smyth Classical Library, Cambridge, MA [*Library symbol*] [*Library of Congress*] (LCLS)
MHSC .... Manipulator Handset Controller (MCD)
MHSc........ Master of Health Sciences (CMD)
MH Sc....... Master of Home Science (SAUO)
MHSc........ Master of Household Science (SAUO)
MHSC .... Mental Health Study Center [*National Institute of Mental Health*] (GRD)
MHSCA...... Michigan High School Coaches Association (EARSL)
MHSCP...... Mean Hemispherical Candlepower
MH-SD ...... Harvard University, Graduate School of Design, Cambridge, MA [*Library symbol*] [*Library of Congress*] (LCLS)
MHSDC...... Multiple High-Speed Data Channel
MHSE........ Master of Health Science Education (PGP)
MH-SF....... Harvard University, Schering Foundation Library, Boston, MA [*Library symbol*] [*Library of Congress*] (LCLS)
MHSF........ Metropolitan Hospital Sunday Fund (SAUO)
MHSH .... Mental Health Services for the Homeless [*Department of Health and Human Services*] (GFGA)
MHSH .... Mission Helpers of the Sacred Heart [*Roman Catholic women's religious order*]
MH-SI .... Harvard University, Program for Science and International Affairs Library, Cambridge, MA [*Library symbol*] [*Library of Congress*] (LCLS)
MHSIP....... Mental Health Statistics Improvement Program [*Department of Health and Human Services*] (GFGA)
MH-SL....... Harvard University, Sanskrit Library, Cambridge, MA [*Library symbol*] [*Library of Congress*] (LCLS)
MHSLA...... Michigan Health Sciences Libraries Association (SAUO)
MHSLN...... Midwest Health Science Library Network [*Library network*]
MHSM....... Mason & Hanger-Silas Mason Co., Inc. (RDA)
MHSM....... Mental Hygiene Society of Maryland (SAUO)
MHSO .... Masada, the Holocaust Survivors Organization (EA)
MHSO .... Minehunter Sweeper Ocean [*Navy*] (ANA)
MH-SP ...... Harvard University, Science and Public Police Program Library, Cambridge, MA [*Library symbol*] [*Library of Congress*] (LCLS)
MHSP .... Moving Head Single Platter (RALS)
MHSP .... Municipal Health Services Program [*Department of Health and Human Services*] (GFGA)
MHSP .... San Pedro Sula [*Honduras*] [*ICAO location identifier*] (ICLI)

MH-SR ...... Harvard University, Social Relations Library, Cambridge, MA [*Library symbol*] [*Library of Congress*] (LCLS)
MHSR .... Santa Rosa De Copan [*Honduras*] [*ICAO location identifier*] (ICLI)
MHSRC...... Midwest Hazardous Substance Research Center [*Purdue University*] (RCD)
MHSS .... Materials Handling Support System [*Military*] (AFM)
MHSS .... Mental Health Special Interest Section [*American Occupational Therapy Association*]
MHSS .... Message Handling System Service (NITA)
MHSS .... Military Health Service System
MHSS .... Ministry of Home Security Schools (SAUO)
MHSS(NI)... Ministry of Health and Social Services (Northern Ireland)
MHSSRI..... Michigan Health and Social Security Research Institute [*Detroit, MI*] [*Research center*] (RCD)
MHST........ Multiphasic Health Screen Test (DAVI)
MHSTB...... Mental Handicap Staff Training Board [*British*]
MHSU .... Marsh Harbour Shipping [*Intermodal shipping container symbol*] (TVRC)
MHSV .... Multipurpose High-Speed Vehicle (MCD)
MHSX .... Midvale-Heppenstall [*Private rail car owner code*]
MHSZ........ Santa Barbara [*Honduras*] [*ICAO location identifier*] (ICLI)
MHT .... Maghemite, Inc. [*Vancouver Stock Exchange symbol*]
MHT .... Main Himalayan Thrust [*Geology*]
MHT .... Manchester [*New Hampshire*] [*Airport symbol*] (OAG)
MHT .... Manchester, NH [*Location identifier*] [*FAA*] (FAAL)
MHT .... Manhattan [*Kansas*] [*Seismograph station code, US Geological Survey*] [*Closed*] (SEIS)
MHT .... Manhattan Industries, Inc. (SAUO)
MHT .... Manufacturers Hanover Trust Co. [*of Manufacturers Hanover Corp.*] [*Nickname: "Manny Hanny"*]
MHT .... Mean High Tide [*Tides and currents*]
MHT .... Mental Health Technician [*Therapy term*] (CTAA)
MHT .... Methyl(hydroxyethyl)thiazole [*Organic chemistry*]
MHT .... Meyer Hydraulic Theory
MHT .... Mild Heat Treatment (IEEE)
MHT .... Missile Handling Trailer (AAG)
MHT .... Missile Height Target [*Military*]
MHT .... Mixed Hemagglutination Test [*Medicine*] (EDAA)
MHT .... Multiphase Health Testing [*Medicine*] (EDAA)
MHT .... Museum of History and Technology [*Smithsonian Institution*]
MHTA........ Molten High-Temperature Alloy
MHTC........ Manufacturers Hanover Trust Company (SAUO)
MHTD .... Missouri Highway and Transportation Department (SAUO)
MHTE........ Tela [*Honduras*] [*ICAO location identifier*] (ICLI)
MHTF........ Manhattan Homicide Task Force (SAUO)
MHTF........ Manufactured Housing Task Force [*Defunct*] (EA)
MHTG .... Marine Helicopter Training Group (NVT)
MHTG .... Tegucigalpa/Toncontin Internacional [*Honduras*] [*ICAO location identifier*] (ICLI)
MHTGR...... Modular High-Temperature Gas Reactor [*Nuclear energy*]
MHTJ........ Trujillo [*Honduras*] [*ICAO location identifier*] (ICLI)
MHTL........ Motorola High-Threshold Logic
MHTML ..... Messaging Hypertext Markup Language [*Computer science*] (GART)
MHTS........ Main Heat Transport System [*Nuclear energy*] (NRCH)
MH/TS...... Manhours/Troubleshooting Action (ACAE)
MHTS........ Message Handling Test System [*Computer science*] (VLIE)
MHTS........ Multiphasic Health Testing Services (DMAA)
MHTTA ...... Member of the Highway and Traffic Technicians Association [*British*] (DBQ)
MHTV........ Manned Hypersonic Test Vehicle (MCD)
M Hu .... Master of Humanities
MHU......... Material Handling Unit (AFIT)
MHU......... MIIX Group [*NYSE symbol*] (SG)
MHUC .... Mid-Hudson Conference (PSS)
MHUD .... Monocular Heads-Up Display [*Aviation*]
MHuGH...... John H. Glenn High School, Huntington, NY [*Library symbol*] [*Library of Congress*] (LCLS)
M Hum ...... Master of Humanities
M Hum Svcs... Master of Human Services (PGP)
MH-UR ...... Harvard University, Ukrainian Research Institute Reference Library, Cambridge, MA [*Library symbol*] [*Library of Congress*] (LCLS)
MHV .... Magnetic Heart Vector [*Cardiology*]
MHV .... Manned Hypersonic Vehicle
MHV .... Mean Horizontal Velocity
MHV .... Mill Hill Virus [*Medicine*] (DB)
MHV .... Mill Hill Vocabulary Scale [*Test*] (TMMY)
MHV .... Mine Hunting Vessel (SAUS)
MHV .... Miniature Homing Vehicle [*Missile*]
MHV .... Mojave, CA [*Location identifier*] [*FAA*] (FAAL)
MHV .... Mouse Hepatitis Virus
MHV .... Murine Hepatitis Virus
MHVCN...... Midwife, Health Visitor and Community Nurse [*Medicine*] [*United Kingdom*] [*Journal*] (EDAA)
MHVD .... Marek's Herpesvirus Disease [*Avian pathology*] (MAE)
MHVDF...... Medium-, High-, and Very-High-Frequency Direction-Finding Station
MHVPS...... Manual High-Voltage Power Supply
MHW .... H. W. Morgan, Los Angeles (SAUO)
MHW .... Mean High Water [*Tides and currents*]
MHW .... Medial Heel Wedge [*Orthopedics*] (DAVI)
MHW .... Mental Health Worker (SAUO)
MHW .... Merrill Lynch & Co. [*AMEX symbol*] (SAG)
MHW .... Ministry of Health and Welfare [*Japan*] (ECON)
MHW .... Morgan, H. W., Los Angeles CA [*STAC*]
MHW .... Multihundred Watt
MH-WA...... Harvard University, Charles Warren Center for Studies in American History, Cambridge, MA [*Library symbol*] [*Library of Congress*] (LCLS)
MHWA....... Mohawk, Adirondack & Northern Railroad [*Federal Railroad Administration identification code*]
MHWI .... Mean High-Water Lunitidal Interval [*Tides and currents*]
MHWL....... Mean High Water Level (QUAC)
MHWLR..... Mobile Hostile Weapon Locating RADAR (NATG)
MHWN ...... Mean High-Water Neap [*Tides and currents*]
MHW-RTG... Multi-Hundred-Watt Radioisotope Thermoelectric Generator (PDAA)
MHWS....... Mean High-Water Springs [*Tides and currents*]
MHx .... Medical History [*Medicine*] (EDAA)
M Hx .... Medical History (MAE)
MHX .... MeriStar Hospitality [*Formerly, CapStar Hotel*] [*NYSE symbol*]
MHX .... MeriStar Hospitality Corp. [*NYSE symbol*]
MHX .... Mine Hunter Experimental
MHy .... Hyannis Public Library, Hyannis, MA [*Library symbol*] [*Library of Congress*] (LCLS)
MHY .... Managed High Income Portfolio [*NYSE symbol*] (SPSG)
MHY .... Managed High Inc. Portfolio [*NYSE symbol*] (TTSB)
M Hy .... Master of Hygiene
MHY .... Morehead [*Papua New Guinea*] [*Airport symbol*] (OAG)
M Hyg....... Master of Hygiene
MHyT........ State Teachers' College, Hyannis, MA [*Library symbol*] [*Library of Congress*] [*Obsolete*] (LCLS)
MH-Z .... Harvard University, Museum of Comparative Zoology, Cambridge, MA [*Library symbol*] [*Library of Congress*] (LCLS)
MHz.......... Megahertz [*Megacycles per Second*] [*See also MCPS, MCS, MC/S, MH*]
MHZ .... Millihertz (WDAA)
MI............ Lab. Miquel [*Spain*] [*Research code symbol*]
MI............ Mach Indicated
MI............ Machine Independent
MI............ Machine Intelligence (RDA)
MI............ Mackey International Airlines [*ICAO designator*] (AD)
MI............ Mackey International, Inc. [*USA*] [*ICAO designator*] (OAG)
MI............ Madras Infantry [*British*]
MI............ Magazine Index [*Information Access Corp.*] [*Information service or system*] (IID)
MI............ Magnetic Instability (ELAL)
MI............ Maintenance Indicator (SAUO)
MI............ Maintenance Instruction (AAG)
MI............ Major Issue (MCD)
MI............ Major Item [*Military*]
MI............ Malachi [*Old Testament book*] (BJA)
MI............ Malleable Iron
MI............ Management Indicator (SAUO)
MI............ Management Information (CAAL)
mi............ Management Information (NAKS)
MI............ Management Interface [*Computer science*] (MWOL)
MI............ Management Intern
MI............ Management International Review (SAUO)
MI............ Mandatory Investigation (HEAS)
MI............ Manhattan Industries, Inc. (EFIS)
MI............ Manual Individual [*Nuclear energy*] (NRCH)
MI............ Manual Input [*Computer science*]
MI............ Manufacturer Inquiry
MI............ Manufacturing Index (MCD)
MI............ Manufacturing Industries [*Department of Employment*] [*British*]
MI............ Manufacturing Inspector (FAAC)
MI............ Manufacturing Instruction (MSA)
MI............ Marconi Industries [*General Electric Co.*] [*British*]
MI............ Marconi Instruments Ltd. (SAUO)
MI............ Mare Imbrium [*Sea of Showers*] [*Lunar area*]
MI............ Mare Island, California [*Site of naval base*]
MI............ Marginal Income [*Economics*]
MI............ Mariana Islands (ACAE)
MI............ Marine Insurance
MI............ Marine Investigation (LAIN)
MI............ Maritime Interdiction (SAUS)
MI............ Market Identifiers [*Dun's Marketing Services*] [*Database*]
MI............ Marketing Improvements Ltd. (SAUO)
MI............ Market Investigation [*Army*]
MI............ Marshall & Ilsley [*Company symbol*]
MI............ Marshall and Ilsley Corp. [*NYSE symbol*]
MI............ Marshall Indus [*NYSE symbol*] (TTSB)
MI............ Marshall Industries [*NYSE symbol*] (SPSG)
MI............ Marshall Islands
MI............ Massa Intermedia (DB)
MI............ Master Index
MI............ Master Item (MSA)
MI............ Master of Instruction (PGP)
MI............ Master of Insurance (GAGS)
MI............ Match Institute [*Defunct*] (EA)
MI............ Material Inspection [*Navy*]
MI............ Maturation Index (MAE)
MI............ Mauritius Institute (SAUO)
MI............ Measurement Incorporated (SAUO)
MI............ Meat Inspection (SAUO)
MI............ Meat Inspection Division [*of ARS, Department of Agriculture*]
MI............ Mechanical Impedance
M/I........... Mechanical Impulse (KSC)
MI............ Mechanical Incontinence [*Medicine*] (MELL)
MI............ Meconium Ileus [*Medicine*]

MI .... Medical Illustrator
MI .... Medical Improvement [*Social Security Administration*]
MI .... Medical Inspection
MI .... Medium Intensity (MSA)
MI .... Melanophore Index [*Biology*]
MI .... Mellon Institute [*Carnegie-Mellon University*] [*Research center*] (RCD)
MI .... Meloidogyne incognita [*A nematode*]
MI .... Melt Inclusions [*Geology*]
MI .... Member of the Institute (SAUO)
MI .... Member of the Institution (SAUO)
MI .... Memorial Inscription
MI .... Memory Interface [*Computer science*] (ELAL)
MI .... Mensa International [*British*] (EAIO)
MI .... Menstrual Induction [*Medicine*]
MI .... Mental Illness
MI .... (Mercaptoethyl)trimethylammonium Iodide [*Pharmacology*]
MI .... Mercaptoimidazole [*Organic chemistry*] (MAE)
MI .... Merit Increase (MHDW)
MI .... Merritt Island [*Florida*] [*NASA*] (KSC)
MI .... Mesha Inscription (BJA)
MI .... Mesioincisal [*Dentistry*]
MI .... Meso-Inositol [*or Myoinositol*] [*Organic chemistry*]
MI .... Metabolic Index
MI .... Metal Industries (SAUO)
MI .... Metal-to-Insulator [*Transition*]
MI .... Metastases below the Head and Neck [*Oncology*]
MI .... Methanol Institute [*Association*] (EA)
MI .... Method Index [*British police term*]
MI .... Methods Instruction (DNAB)
MI .... Methylindole [*Organic chemistry*]
M-I .... Metro-International Program Services of New York (EA)
MI .... Mexican Isthmus [*Crude oil*]
MI .... Mica [*A mineral*]
Mi .... Micah [*Old Testament book*]
MI .... Michelin [*Tire casing code*]
MI .... Michelson Interferometer (PDAA)
MI .... Michigan [*Postal code*]
MI .... Michigan Reports [*A publication*] (DLA)
Mi .... Michigan State Library, Lansing, MI [*Library symbol*] [*Library of Congress*] (LCLS)
MI .... Microbiological Inputs [*Canning*] (DICI)
MI .... Microinch (IAA)
MI .... Microinstruction [*Computer science*]
MI .... Microwave Imager (ACAE)
MI .... Micru International (EA)
MI .... Middle Initial
MI .... Middle Iron Age (BJA)
MI .... Middlesex Regiment (SAUO)
MI .... Migration Index [*Immunology*]
MI .... Migration Inhibition [*Cytology*]
MI .... Mil [*Former USSR*] [*ICAO aircraft manufacturer identifier*] (ICAO)
MI .... Mile
mi .... Mile
mi .... Miles (SHCU)
MI .... Military Institute
MI .... Military Intelligence [*Army*]
MI .... Military Internee
MI .... Military Item
MI .... Militia Mariae Immaculatae [*Militia of the Immaculate*] (EAIO)
MI .... Mill
MI .... Miller Integrator
MI .... Millet [*Soil biology*] [*Human-introduced crops*] (QSUL)
MI .... Minden-Luebbecke [*German license plate city code*]
MI .... Mineral Insulated [*Cable*] (NRCH)
MI .... Miniaturized Instrumentation (MCD)
M/I .... Minimum Impulse (KSC)
MI .... Mining Inspectorate (HEAS)
MI .... Ministry of Information [*British*] [*World War II*]
MI .... Minor (ROG)
MI .... Minority Institution
MI .... Minority Interest [*Business term*]
MI .... Minute (ADA)
MI .... Miscellaneous Income (MHDW)
Mi .... Mishnah [*Basis of the Talmud*] (BJA)
MI .... Missed Interception [*Military*]
MI .... Missile (CINC)
MI .... Missile Industry (AAG)
MI .... Missionary Internship [*An association*] (EA)
MI .... Mission Independent [*NASA*]
MI .... Mississippi [*Obsolete*] (ROG)
M-I .... Missouri-Illinois Railroad (SAUO)
MI .... Missouri-Illinois Railroad Co. [*AAR code*]
Mi .... Mitomycin C [*Also, MMC, MTC*] [*Antineoplastic drug*]
MI .... Mitosis Index [*Medicine*] (MELL)
MI .... Mitotic Indices [*Cytology*]
MI .... Mitral Incompetence [*Cardiology*]
MI .... Mitral Insufficiency [*Cardiology*]
MI .... Mixed Income
MI .... Mobility Impairment (NVT)
MI .... Mobility International (EA)
MI .... Mode Indicator (HGAA)
MI .... Moderately Included [*Colored gemstone grade*]
MI .... Modification Instructions (KSC)
MI .... Moment of Inertia
MI .... Monetary Incentive
MI .... Money Stock [*British*] (DCTA)
MI .... Monitoring Information (NITA)
MI .... Monitor Inspection (AFM)
MI .... Monitor International (ASF)
MI .... Mononucleosis Infectiosa [*Medicine*] (DB)
MI .... Monument Inscription [*Genealogy*]
MI .... Mooseheart, International
MI .... Moose, International (EAIO)
MI .... Morphologic Index [*Volume of trunk divided by length of limbs*]
MI .... [*The*] Mortgage Index [*Hale Systems, Inc.*] [*Information service or system*] (CRD)
MI .... Mortgage Insurance (EMRF)
MI .... Motility Index [*Of intestine*] [*Gastroenterology*]
MI .... Motion Imagery
MI .... Motorola Interconnect [*Electronics*]
MI .... Mounted Infantry
MI .... Move In (WDMC)
MI .... Movement Instruction [*British military*] (DMA)
MI .... Multi-Industry Interest
MI .... Multiple Instruction (HGAA)
MI .... Multiple-Intelligences
MI .... Murphy International Transport [*Commercial firm*] [*British*]
MI .... Muskies, Inc. (EA)
MI .... Mutual Inductance
MI .... Mutual Interference
MI .... Myocardial Infarction [*Cardiology*]
MI .... Myo-Inositol [*Chemistry*] [*Dietetics*] (DAVI)
MI .... Office of Minority Economic Impact (SAUO)
MI .... Shallow [*Weather codes - aviation*] [*Minimal*] (PIPO)
MI .... Writ of Mandamus Will Issue [*Legal term*] (DLA)
mi^2 .... Square Mile (CDAI)
MI^3MS .... Minolta Integrated Information and Image Management System [*Optical disc*] (IT)
MI5 .... Military Intelligence [*State security*] [*British*] (ODBW)
MI6 .... Military Intelligence [*Espionage*] [*British*] (ODBW)
MiA .... Alma Public Library, Alma, MI [*Library symbol*] [*Library of Congress*] (LCLS)
MIA .... AMI (Air Mercury International) [*Belgium*] [*ICAO designator*] (FAAC)
MIA .... [*An*] Introduction to the Apocrypha [*B. Metzger*] [*A publication*] (BJA)
MIA .... Malaysian Institute of Art (SAUO)
MIA .... Management Information Analysis (SAUO)
MIA .... Manager, Internal Audit (SAUO)
MIA .... Manchester International Airport [*British*] (DS)
MIA .... Manila International Airport
MIA .... Manitoba Institute of Agrologists (SAUO)
MIA .... Marble Institute of America (EA)
MIA .... Marine Industries Association (SAUO)
MIA .... Marine Insurance Act (MARI)
MIA .... Maritime Information Association [*British*] (EAIO)
MIA .... Master of Industrial Arts
MIA .... Master of Intercultural Administration (PGP)
MIA .... Master of Internal Affairs (NADA)
MIA .... Master of International Administration (PGP)
MIA .... Master of International Affairs
MIA .... Meat Industry Authority (SAUO)
MIA .... Medical Indemnity of America, Inc. (DHSM)
MIA .... Medically Indigent Adult (MEDA)
MIA .... Meetings Industry Association (COBU)
MIA .... Member Insurance Association (EA)
MIA .... Member of the Institute of Arbitrators [*British*]
MIA .... Member of the South African Institute of Architects (SAUO)
MIA .... Metal Interface Amplifier
MIA .... Methylisatoic Anhydride [*Organic chemistry*]
MIA .... Metropolitan Intercollegiate Association (PSS)
MIA .... Miami [*Florida*] [*Seismograph station code, US Geological Survey*] [*Closed*] (SEIS)
Mia .... Miami Dolphins [*National Football League*] [*1966-present*] (NFLA)
MIA .... Miami International Airport (SAUO)
MIA .... Miami University, Oxford, OH [*OCLC symbol*] (OCLC)
MIA .... Miata [*NCIC car model code*]
MIA .... Mica Industry Association [*Defunct*] (EA)
MIA .... Middle Indo-Aryan [*Linguistics*] (IEL)
MIA .... Military Inspection Agency (NATG)
MIA .... Military Intelligence Agency (MCD)
MIA .... Millinery Institute of America [*Later, MIB*] (EA)
MIA .... Minimum IFR Altitude [*FAA*] (TAG)
MIA .... Minimum Instrument Altitude [*Aviation*] (AFM)
MIA .... Minor Acknowledgment (VLIE)
MIA .... Missile Intelligence Agency (AABC)
MIA .... Missing in Action [*Military*]
MIA .... Mission Implementation Agreement (SAUO)
MIA .... Mission-Independent Area [*NASA*]
MIA .... Monoiodoacetic Acid [*Organic chemistry*]
MIA .... Montgomery Improvement Association (SAUO)
MIA .... Moore's Indian Appeals [*A publication*] (DLA)
MIA .... Mouse in Able (SAUO)
MIA .... "Mouse in Able" Program
MIA .... Multiflex Interface Adapter
MIA .... Multiplexer Interface Adapter (NASA)
MIA .... Multiplex Interface Adapter (NASA)
MIA .... Murrumbidgee Irrigation Area [*Australia*] (BARN)
MIA .... Music Industries Association [*British*] (DBA)

MIA .... Music Industry Association of Newfoundland and Labrador [*An association*] [*Canada*]
MIA .... Mutual Improvement Association [*Mormon Youth Movement*] (BARN)
MIA .... Mythmaking in America [*A publication*]
MiAa .... Ann Arbor Public Library, Ann Arbor, MI [*Library symbol*] [*Library of Congress*] (LCLS)
MIAA .... Maine Insurance Agents Association (EARSL)
MIAA .... Medical Industry Association of Australia
MIAA .... Meetings Industry Association of Australia
MIAA .... Member of the Incorporated Association of Architects and Surveyors [*British*] (DBQ)
MIAA .... Member of the Institute of Affiliate Accountants (ADA)
MIAA .... Member of the Institute of Automobile Assessors [*British*]
MIAA .... Michigan Intercollegiate Athletics Association (PSS)
MIAA .... Miniatures Industry Association of America (EA)
MIAA .... Mutual Insurance Advisory Association [*Defunct*] (EA)
MIAAA .... Michigan Interscholastic Athletic Administrators Association (EARSL)
MIAA&S ..... Member of the Incorporated Association of Architects and Surveyors (ODA)
MiAaC .... Concordia Lutheran College, Ann Arbor, MI [*Library symbol*] [*Library of Congress*] (LCLS)
MiAaE .... Environmental Research Institute of Michigan, Ann Arbor, MI [*Library symbol*] [*Library of Congress*] (LCLS)
MiAaF .... Gerald R. Ford Library, Ann Arbor, MI [*Library symbol*] [*Library of Congress*] (LCLS)
MiAaFL ...... Great Lakes Fisheries Laboratory, Ann Arbor, MI [*Library symbol*] [*Library of Congress*] (LCLS)
MIAAHC ..... Michigan Alliance Against Hate Crimes
MiAaI .... Inter-University Consortium for Political and Social Research, Ann Arbor, MI [*Library symbol*] [*Library of Congress*] (LCLS)
MiAaK .... KMS Fusion, Inc., Ann Arbor, MI [*Library symbol*] [*Library of Congress*] (LCLS)
MiAaP .... Parke, Davis & Co., Research Library, Ann Arbor, MI [*Library symbol*] [*Library of Congress*] (LCLS)
MIA(APS) ... Meat Inspectors' Association (Australian Public Service)
MIAASM .... Member, International Academy of Aviation & Space Medicine (CMD)
MiAaW ...... Washtenaw County Library, Ann Arbor, MI [*Library symbol*] [*Library of Congress*] (LCLS)
MiAaWC .... Washtenaw Community College, Ann Arbor, MI [*Library symbol*] [*Library of Congress*] (LCLS)
MIAB .... Magnetically Impelled Arc Butt [*Welding*] (MCD)
MIAB .... Modular Interchangeable Ambulance Body [*Military*] [*British*]
MiAC .... Alma College, Alma, MI [*Library symbol*] [*Library of Congress*] (LCLS)
MIAC .... Maintenance Information and Control [*Environmental science*] (COE)
MIAC .... Manufacturing Industries Advisory Council (NADA)
MIAC .... Material Identification Accounting Code
MIAC .... Metals Information Analysis Center (IID)
MIAC .... Minimum Automatic Computer (IEEE)
MIAC .... Minnesota Intercollegiate Athletic Conference (PSS)
MIAC .... Multipoint Interactive Audio-Visual Communication (NITA)
MIACC .... Major Industrial Accidents Council of Canada [*Emergency Management*] (EMA)
MIACF .... Meander Inverted Autocorrelated Function
MIA-CHI ..... Miami-Chicago (SAUO)
MIACS .... Manufacturing Information and Control System
MiAd .... Adrian Public Library, Adrian, MI [*Library symbol*] [*Library of Congress*] (LCLS)
MiAdC .... Adrian College, Adrian, MI [*Library symbol*] [*Library of Congress*] (LCLS)
MiAdL .... Lenawee County Library, Adrian, MI [*Library symbol*] [*Library of Congress*] (LCLS)
MIADMB .... Murrumbidgee Irrigation Area and Districts Management Board (SAUO)
MIADS .... Map Information Assembly and Display System
MIADS .... Minot Air Defense Sector [*ADC*]
MiAdS .... Siena Heights College, Adrian, MI [*Library symbol*] [*Library of Congress*] (LCLS)
MIAE .... Member of the Institute (or Institution) of Automobile Engineers (SAUO)
MIAE .... Member of the Institution of Agricultural Engineers (SAUO)
MIAE .... Member of the Institution of Automobile Engineers [*British*]
MIAEA .... Member of the Institute of Automotive Engineer Assessors [*British*] (DBQ)
MIAEA .... Member of the Institute of Automotive Engineers of America (SAUO)
MI Ae E ..... Member of the Institute of Aeronautical Engineers [*British*]
MIAEF .... Missed Interception Due to Airborne Equipment Failure [*Air Force*]
MIAeS .... Member of the Institute of Aeronautical Science (SAUO)
MIAeS .... Member of the Institute of Aeronautical Sciences
MIAESR ..... Melbourne Institute of Applied Economic and Social Research [*Australia*]
MIAEYC ..... Michigan Association for the Education of Young Children (EARSL)
MIAFTR ..... Motor Insurance Anti-Fraud and Theft Register [*Database*] [*British*]
MIAG .... Management Information and Analysis Group (MCD)
MIAgrE ...... Member of the Institution of Agricultural Engineers [*British*]
MiAhO .... Oakland Community College, Auburn Heights, MI [*Library symbol*] [*Library of Congress*] (LCLS)
MIAIF .... Meteorological Information for Aircraft in Flight
MIAK .... Methyl Isoamyl Ketone [*Organic chemistry*]
MIAL .... Maine Image Analysis Laboratory (SAUO)
MiAlb .... Albion Public Library, Albion, MI [*Library symbol*] [*Library of Congress*] (LCLS)
MiAlbC ...... Albion College, Albion, MI [*Library symbol*] [*Library of Congress*] (LCLS)
MiAlbW ..... Woodlands Library Cooperative, Albion, MI [*Library symbol*] [*Library of Congress*] (LCLS)
MiAld .... Helena Township Public Library, Alden, MI [*Library symbol*] [*Library of Congress*] (LCLS)
MiAll .... Allendale Township Library, Allendale, MI [*Library symbol*] [*Library of Congress*] (LCLS)
MiAlle .... Allegan Public Library, Allegan, MI [*Library symbol*] [*Library of Congress*] (LCLS)
MiAllG ...... Grand Valley State College, Allendale, MI [*Library symbol*] [*Library of Congress*] (LCLS)
MiAlmo ..... Henry Stephens Memorial Library, Almont, MI [*Library symbol*] [*Library of Congress*] (LCLS)
MiAln .... Alanson Public Library, Alanson, MI [*Library symbol*] [*Library of Congress*] (LCLS)
MiAlp .... Alpena County Library, Alpena, MI [*Library symbol*] [*Library of Congress*] (LCLS)
MiAlpC ...... Alpena Community College, Alpena, MI [*Library symbol*] [*Library of Congress*] (LCLS)
MIALS .... Medium Intensity Approach Light System [*Aviation*] (DA)
MIAM .... Major Items Automated Management (AAGC)
MIAM .... Member of the Institute of Administrative Management (ODA)
MIAM .... Mid-Am, Inc. [*NASDAQ symbol*] (NQ)
MIAMA ...... Member of the Incorporated Advertising Managers' Association [*British*] (DAS)
MIAME ...... Member of the Institute of Automotive Mechanical Engineers (ADA)
MIAMI .... Metoprolol in Acute Myocardial Infarction [*Cardiology study*]
MIAMI .... Miami, FL [*American Association of Railroads railroad junction routing code*]
MIAMI .... Microwave Ice Accretion Measurement Instrument (MCD)
MiamiCm ... Miami Computer Supply Corp. [*Associated Press*] (SAG)
Miami LQ ... Miami Law Quarterly [*A publication*] (DLA)
Miami L Rev ... Miami Law Review [*Florida*] [*A publication*] (DLA)
Miami U (Ohio) ... Miami University (Ohio) (GAGS)
MIAMP ...... Mid Am $1.8125 Cv'A'Pfd [*NASDAQ symbol*] (TTSB)
MiamSb ..... Miami Subs Corp. [*Associated Press*] (SAG)
MIAMSI ..... Mouvement International d'Apostolat des Milieux Sociaux Independants [*International Movement of Apostolate in the Independent Social Milieux*] [*Vatican City*] (EAIO)
MI & RR .... Material Inspection and Receiving Report [*Military*] (KSC)
MI and SInst ... Member of the Iron and Steel Institute (SAUO)
MIANG ...... Michigan Air National Guard (MUSM)
MIANS .... Music Industry Association of Nova Scotia [*An association*] [*Canada*]
MIA-NY ..... Miami-New York (SAUO)
MIAO .... Master Index Assembly Outline [*Paper*]
MiAp .... Allen Park Public Library, Allen Park, MI [*Library symbol*] [*Library of Congress*] (LCLS)
MIAP .... International Movement for Peace Action (SAUO)
MIAP .... Member of the Institution of Analysts and Programmers [*British*] (DBQ)
MIAP .... Miami International Airport (SAUO)
MIAP .... Military Incentive Analysis Program (MCD)
MIAP .... Modified Innervated Antral Pouch [*Medicine*] (EDAA)
MIAPD .... Mid-Central Air Procurement District
MiApDB ..... Detroit Baptist Divinity School, Allen Park, MI [*Library symbol*] [*Library of Congress*] (LCLS)
MIAPL .... Master Index of Allowable Parts Lists [*Navy*]
MiApV .... United States Veterans Administration Hospital, Allen Park, MI [*Library symbol*] [*Library of Congress*] (LCLS)
MIAQ .... Music Industry Association of Queensland [*Australia*]
MIAR .... Microaddress Register [*Computer science*] (MHDI)
MI Arch ..... Master of Interior Architecture (PGP)
M I Arch Eng ... Master of Interior Architectural Engineering
MiArm .... Armada Free Public Library, Armada, MI [*Library symbol*] [*Library of Congress*] (LCLS)
MIARS .... Maintenance Information Automated Retrieval System [*DoD*]
MIARS .... Microfilm Information and Retrieval System (DNAB)
MIAS .... Maintenance Information Authorizing System (MCD)
MIAS .... Major Item Automated System [*Army Materiel Command*] (AABC)
MIAS .... Marine Information and Advisory Service [*Institute of Oceanographic Sciences*] [*Databank*] [*British*] (IID)
MIAS .... Member of the Incorporated Association of Architects and Surveyors [*British*] (DBQ)
MIAS .... Member of the Institute of Accounting Staff (ODA)
MIAS .... Member of the Institute of Aeronautical Science [*Later, MAIAA*]
MIAS .... Mobile Intelligence Analysis Center (ACAE)
MIAS .... Monroe Institute of Applied Sciences [*Later, TMI*] (EA)
MIAS .... Muhyiddin Ibn Arabi Society
MIAS .... Multipoint Interactive Audiovisual System (EURO)
MIASA .... Motorcycle Industry Association of South Australia
MIA-SFO .... Miami-San Francisco (SAUO)
MIASI .... Moore Institute of Art, Science and Industry (SAUO)
MIAT .... Mean Interarrival Time (MHDB)
MIAT .... Member of the Institute of Asphalt Technology [*British*] (DBQ)
MiAt .... Montmorency County Public Library, Atlanta, MI [*Library symbol*] [*Library of Congress*] (LCLS)
MIAT .... Music Industry Association of Tasmania [*Australia*]
MIATA .... Murrumbidgee Irrigation Area Tourist Association [*Australia*]
MIATCO ..... Mid-America International Agri-Trade Council
MiAth .... Athens Township Library, Athens, MI [*Library symbol*] [*Library of Congress*] (LCLS)
MIA-TOR .... Miami-Toronto (SAUO)
MiAu .... Augusta-Ross Township District Library (McKay Library), Augusta, MI [*Library symbol*] [*Library of Congress*] (LCLS)
MIAW .... Movie in a Window (SAUS)
MIAWA ...... Member of the International Association of Wood Anatomists (SAUO)
MIAX .... McCulloch International Airlines [*Air carrier designation symbol*]
MIB .... Management Improvement Board (AAG)
MIB .... Management Information Base

MIB .... Management Information Block [*Computer science*]
MIB .... Management Information Database (CGWS)
MIB .... Manual Input Buffer [*Computer science*]
MIB .... Marine Index Bureau
MIB .... Maritime Index Bureau (NADA)
MIB .... Marketing of Investments Board [*Finance*] [*British*]
MIB .... Master Instruction Book
MIB .... Master Interconnect Board (MCD)
MIB .... Master of International Business (GAGS)
MIB .... Meat Inspection Branch (SAUO)
MIB .... Mechanized Infantry Battalion (MCD)
MIB .... Medical Impairment Bureau [*Insurance*]
MIB .... Medical Information Bureau [*Databank*]
MIB .... Medical Information Bus (RALS)
MIB .... Medical Information Bus Standard (AG)
MIB .... Medium Industry Bank [*South Korea*] (IMH)
MIB .... Member Information Bank [*Computer science*] (ELAL)
MIB .... Member of the Institute of Bankers in Scotland (ODA)
MIB .... Men in Black [*UFO mythology*]
MiB .... Men in Black [*UFO mythology*]
MIB .... Mental Information Bureau (SAUO)
MIB .... Metal Information Bureau (SAUO)
MIB .... Mexican Investment Board [*Public relations and investor assistance*] [*Mexico*] (CROSS)
MIB .... Mezhdunarodnyi Investitsionnyi Bank [*International Investment Bank - IIB*] [*Moscow, USSR*] (EAIO)
MIB .... Michigan Inspection Bureau (SAUO)
MIB .... Michigan Intra-State Motor Tariff Bureau Inc., Lansing MI [*STAC*]
MIB .... Microinstruction Bus [*Computer science*]
MIB .... Midland Bancorp [*NYSE symbol*] (SPSG)
MIB .... Midland Bank PLC [*NYSE symbol*] (SAG)
MIB .... Military Intelligence Battalion (MCD)
MIB .... Military Intelligence Board (MCD)
MIB .... Military Intelligence Branch (SAUO)
MIB .... Military Intelligence Bureau (SAUO)
MIB .... Millinery Information Bureau (EA)
MIB .... Minimum Impulse BIT [*Binary Digit*] [*Computer science*] (MCD)
MIB .... Minot, ND [*Location identifier*] [*FAA*] (FAAL)
MIB .... Mint in the Box [*Doll collecting*]
MIB .... Missile Interceptor Base (SAUO)
MIB .... Missionary Information Bureau
MIB .... Missouri Inspection Bureau (SAUO)
MIB .... Montana Independent Bankers (TBD)
MIB .... Motor Inspection Building
MIB .... Motor Insurers' Bureau Ltd. [*British*] (ILCA)
MIB .... Mouvement d'Insoumission Bretonne [*Breton Insubordination Movement*] [*France*] (PD)
MIB .... Multibanc NT Financial Corp. [*Toronto Stock Exchange symbol*]
MIB .... Multilayer Interconnection Board
MIB .... Mustard Information Bureau (EA)
MIB .... Mutual Inductance Bridge
MiBa .... Bad Axe Public Library, Bad Axe, MI [*Library symbol*] [*Library of Congress*] (LCLS)
MIBA .... Malta International Business Authority (EY)
MIBA .... Master of International Business Administration (GAGS)
MIBA .... Member of the Institute of British Architects (ROG)
MIBA .... Metropolitan Intercollegiate Basketball Association (EA)
MIBA .... Miniere de Bakwanga [*Zaire*]
MIBA .... Missouri Independent Bankers Association (TBD)
MiBaC .... Battle Creek College (SAUS)
MiBal .... Pathfinder Community Library, Baldwin, MI [*Library symbol*] [*Library of Congress*] (LCLS)
MIBANKPAC- FEDERAL... Michigan Bankers Association [*Lansing, MI*] (PACS)
MiBar .... Barryton Public Library, Barryton, MI [*Library symbol*] [*Library of Congress*] (LCLS)
MiBar .... Burr Oak Township Library, Burr Oak, MI [*Library symbol*] [*Library of Congress*] (LCLS)
MIBAR .... Multi-Channel In-Band Airborne Relay (PDAA)
MIBARS ..... Mechanized Infantry Battalion Air Reconnaissance Support (ACAE)
MIBARS ..... Military Intelligence Battalion (SAUO)
MIBARS ..... Military Intelligence Battalion Aerial Reconnaissance and Support [*Army*] (AFM)
MiBat .... Battle Creek Public School, Battle Creek, MI [*Library symbol*] [*Library of Congress*] (LCLS)
MiBatC ...... Battle Creek College, Battle Creek, MI [*Library symbol*] [*Library of Congress*] [*Obsolete*] (LCLS)
MiBatK ...... Kellogg Community College, Battle Creek, MI [*Library symbol*] [*Library of Congress*] (LCLS)
MiBatV ...... United States Veterans Administration Hospital, Battle Creek, MI [*Library symbol*] [*Library of Congress*] (LCLS)
MiBatW ..... Willard Public Library, Battle Creek, MI [*Library symbol*] [*Library of Congress*] (LCLS)
MiBay .... Bay City Public Library, Bay City, MI [*Library symbol*] [*Library of Congress*] (LCLS)
MiBayM ..... Bay Medical Center, Bay City, MI [*Library symbol*] [*Library of Congress*] (LCLS)
MiBayS ...... Bay County Library System, Bay City, MI [*Library symbol*] [*Library of Congress*] (LCLS)
MiBay-S..... Bay County Library System, Sage Branch Library (SAUS)
MiBayS-A ... Bay County Library System, Auburn Branch Library, Auburn, MI [*Library symbol*] [*Library of Congress*] (LCLS)
MiBayS-B ... Bay County Library System, Broadway Branch Library, Bay City, MI [*Library symbol*] [*Library of Congress*] (LCLS)
MiBayS-L ... Bay County Library System, Linwood Branch Library, Linwood, MI [*Library symbol*] [*Library of Congress*] (LCLS)
MiBayS-P ... Bay County Library System, Pinconning Branch Library, Pinconning, MI [*Library symbol*] [*Library of Congress*] (LCLS)
MiBayS-S ... Bay County Library System, Sage Branch Library, Bay City, MI [*Library symbol*] [*Library of Congress*] (LCLS)
MIBB .... Missouri & Illinois Bridge & Belt Railroad [*AAR code*] [*Terminated*]
MIBC .... Methyl Cap. Isobutyl Carbinol [*Also, MIC*] [*Organic chemistry*]
MIBCO....... Member of the Institution of Building Control Officers [*British*] (DBQ)
MIBE......... Member of the Institution of British Engineers (SAUO)
MiBeiM ..... Beaver Island Mormon Colony Library, St. James, Beaver Island, MI [*Library symbol*] [*Library of Congress*] [*Obsolete*] (LCLS)
MiBel........ Bellevue Township Library, Bellevue, MI [*Library symbol*] [*Library of Congress*] (LCLS)
MiBela ...... Bellaire Public Library, Bellaire, MI [*Library symbol*] [*Library of Congress*] (LCLS)
MiBen .... Benzonia Public Library, Benzonia, MI [*Library symbol*] [*Library of Congress*] (LCLS)
MiBes .... Bessemer Public Library, Bessemer, MI [*Library symbol*] [*Library of Congress*] (LCLS)
MiBeu .... Beulah Public Library, Beulah, MI [*Library symbol*] [*Library of Congress*] (LCLS)
MIBF......... Member of the Institute of British Foundrymen
MIBF......... Member of the Institution of British Foundrymen (SAUO)
MIBF......... Montreal International Book Fair
MIBG .... Meta-Iodobenzylguanidine [*Biochemistry*]
MiBh......... Benton Harbor Public Library, Benton Harbor, MI [*Library symbol*] [*Library of Congress*] (LCLS)
MiBhL .... Lake Michigan College, Benton Harbor, MI [*Library symbol*] [*Library of Congress*] (LCLS)
MiBhW ...... Whirlpool Corp., Technical Information Center, Benton Harbor, MI [*Library symbol*] [*Library of Congress*] (LCLS)
MiBicr....... Thomas Fleschner Memorial Library, Birch Run, MI [*Library symbol*] [*Library of Congress*] (LCLS)
Mibid........ Madrid Interbank Bid Rate [*Spain*] (NUMA)
MI Biol ...... Member of the Institute of Biology [*British*] (EY)
MiBir .... Baldwin Public Library, Birmingham, MI [*Library symbol*] [*Library of Congress*] (LCLS)
MIBK .... Methyl Isobutyl Ketone [*Also, MIK*] [*Organic chemistry*]
MIBL......... Molecular Imaging and Bioinformatics Laboratory (SAUO)
MiBla........ Rolland Township Library, Blanchard, MI [*Library symbol*] [*Library of Congress*] (LCLS)
MiBloA ...... Cranbrook Academy of Art, Bloomfield Hills, MI [*Library symbol*] [*Library of Congress*] (LCLS)
MiBloC ...... Cranbrook Institute of Science, Bloomfield Hills, MI [*Library symbol*] [*Library of Congress*] (LCLS)
MiBloCAr ... Cranbrook Edcutional Community, Archives and Historical Collections, Bloomfield Hills, MI [*Library symbol*] [*Library of Congress*] (LCLS)
MiBloGS .... Church of Jesus Christ of Latter-Day Saints, Genealogical Society Library, Bloomfield Hills Branch, Bloomfield Hills, MI [*Library symbol*] [*Library of Congress*] (LCLS)
MIBNAU..... Instituut voor Toegepast Biologisch Onderzoek in de Natuur. Mededeling (journ.) (SAUS)
MIBOC....... Marketing of Investments Board Organising Committee [*British*]
MIBOC....... Marketing of Investments Board Organizing Committee (SAUO)
MIBOR ...... Madrid Interbank Offered Rate (MHDW)
MIBOR ...... Metropolitan Indianapolis Board of Realtors (EARSL)
MIBOS....... Measurement of Ingratiatory Behaviours in Organisational Settings (WDAA)
MiBoy .... Boyne City Public Library (SAUS)
MiBoy .... Boyne City Public Library, Boyne City, MI [*Library symbol*] [*Library of Congress*] (LCLS)
MiBoyf ...... Boyne Falls Public Library (SAUS)
MiBoyf ...... Boyne Falls Public Library, Boyne Falls, MI [*Library symbol*] [*Library of Congress*] (LCLS)
MIBPA....... Methyliminobispropylamine [*Organic chemistry*]
Mi-BPH...... Michigan Department of Education, State Library Services, Blind and Physically Handicapped Library, Lansing, MI [*Library symbol*] [*Library of Congress*] (LCLS)
MIBPrA...... Midland Bank A1/A2 Unit ADS [*NYSE symbol*] (TTSB)
MIBPrB...... Midland Bank B1/B2 Unit ADS (TTSB)
MIBPrC...... Midland Bank C1/C2 Unit ADS [*NYSE symbol*] (TTSB)
MiBr .... Big Rapids Community Library, Big Rapids, MI [*Library symbol*] [*Library of Congress*] (LCLS)
MIBR .... Miller Brothers [*Common carrier symbol*]
MIBRAG..... Mitteldeutschen Brunkohle (ECON)
MiBrc........ Brown City Public Library, Brown City, MI [*Library symbol*] [*Library of Congress*] (LCLS)
MiBre........ Howe Memorial Library, Breckenridge, MI [*Library symbol*] [*Library of Congress*] (LCLS)
MiBrF........ Ferris State College, Big Rapids, MI [*Library symbol*] [*Library of Congress*] (LCLS)
MiBrid....... Bridgeport Public Library, Bridgeport, MI [*Library symbol*] [*Library of Congress*] (LCLS)
MiBridm .... Bridgman Public Library, Bridgman, MI [*Library symbol*] [*Library of Congress*] (LCLS)
MiBrig....... Brighton City Library, Brighton, MI [*Library symbol*] [*Library of Congress*] (LCLS)
MIBritE...... Member of the Institute of British Engineers (EY)
MIBritE...... Member of the Institution of British Engineers (SAUO)
MIBritishE... Member of the Institute of British Engineers
MI British E... Member of the Institution of British Engineers (SAUO)
MIBs......... Management Information Bases [*Compaq*] [*Computer science*]
MIBS .... Master of International Business Studies
MIBS .... Miami International Boat Show and Sailboat Show (ITD)
MiBs......... Sparks Memorial Library, Berrien Springs, MI [*Library symbol*] [*Library of Congress*] (LCLS)

MiBsA .... Andrews University, Berrien Springs, MI [*Library symbol*] [*Library of Congress*] (LCLS)
MIBT .... Methyl Isatin-beta-thiosemicarbazone
MiBu .... Taymouth Township Library, Burt, MI [*Library symbol*] [*Library of Congress*] (LCLS)
MiBur .... Burr Oak Township Library, Burr Oak, MI [*Library symbol*] [*Library of Congress*] (LCLS)
MiBurl .... Burlington Township Library, Burlington, MI [*Library symbol*] [*Library of Congress*] (LCLS)
MIBURN ..... Mississippi Burning [*Code name of FBI investigation*]
MIBWG ...... Military Intelligence Board Working Group
MIC .... Aerolineas de Michoacan [*Mexico*] [*ICAO designator*] (FAAC)
MIC .... Congregatio Clericorum Regularium Marianorum sub titulo Immaculatae ConceptionisBeatae Mariae Virginis [*Marian Fathers*] [*Roman Catholic religious order*]
MIC .... Congregation of Marians of the Immaculate Conception (TOCD)
mic .... Congregation of Marians of the Immaculate Conception (TOCD)
MIC .... IEEE Medical Imaging Committee (EA)
MIC .... Itasca Community College, Grand Rapids, MN [*OCLC symbol*] (OCLC)
MIC .... Machine Intelligence Corporation (SAUO)
MIC .... Machinery Installation Certificate
MIC .... Made in Canada [*Business term*]
MIC .... Magnesium Industry Council [*British*] (BI)
MIC .... Magnetic Ink Character [*Computer science*] (HGAA)
MIC .... Maintenance Identification Code [*Military*] (CAAL)
MIC .... Maintenance Index Code (DNAB)
MIC .... Maintenance Information Center [*Navy*] (NG)
MIC .... Maintenance Information Chart [*DoD*]
MIC .... Maintenance Inventory Center [*Air Force*] (AFIT)
MIC .... Major Immunogene Complex [*Genetics*] (DOG)
MIC .... Malayan Indian Congress (SAUO)
MIC .... Malaysian Indian Congress [*Political party*] (PPW)
MIC .... Management & Industrial Consultants
MIC .... Management Indicator Code (MCD)
mic .... Management Information Center (NAKS)
MIC .... Management Information Center
MIC .... Management Information Corp. [*Cherry Hill, NJ*] [*Information service or system*] (IID)
MIC .... Management Integration Consortium
MIC .... Manchester Information Committee (SAUO)
MIC .... Manufacturer Identification Code (LDOE)
MIC .... Manufacturers Identification Code [*Nautical term*] (NTA)
MIC .... Marine Information Centre [*Information service or system*] (IID)
MIC .... Market Impact Clearance
MIC .... Marketing Intelligence Corp. [*Information service or system*] (IID)
MIC .... Marketing International Corp. [*Washington, DC*] (TSSD)
MIC .... Marshall Islands Congress (SAUO)
MIC .... Martinello Importing Co. Ltd. (SAUS)
MIC .... Maruman Integrated Circuits (NITA)
MIC .... Maruzen International Co., Inc. [*Information service or system*] (IID)
MIC .... Masonry Industry Committee (EA)
MIC .... Master Interrupt Control [*Computer science*] (OA)
MIC .... Master Item Code (EAGT)
MIC .... Match Indicator Code (MCD)
MIC .... Material Identification and Control (DNAB)
MIC .... Material Inventory Control
MIC .... Materials Irradiation Chamber
MIC .... Maternal and Infant Care [*Medicine*]
MiC .... Mathematics in Context
MIC .... Maximum Inscribed Circle [*Manufacturing term*]
MIC .... Meat Importers' Council [*Later, MICA*] (EA)
MIC .... Meat Industry Council [*Australia*]
MIC .... Mechanical Instrument Cluster (HAWK)
MIC .... Mechanized Information Center [*Information service or system*]
MIC .... Media Information Control (SAUO)
MIC .... Media Interface Connector (SAUO)
MIC .... Medical Imaging Committee (NTPA)
MIC .... Medical Industrial Complex
MIC .... Medical Information Centre (NITA)
MIC .... Medical Intensive Care
MIC .... Medical Interfraternity Conference (EA)
MIC .... Medium-Intensity Conflict [*Military*]
MIC .... Medium Interface Cable [*Open Systems Interconnection*] (ODAA)
MIC .... Medium Interface Connector [*Optics*] (CDE)
MIC .... Medugorje Information Center (EA)
MIC .... Mellonics Information Center [*Information service or system*] (IID)
MIC .... Mellon InvestData Corp. [*New York, NY*] [*Information service or system*] (IID)
MIC .... Memory in Cassette
MIC .... Memory Interface Connection [*Computer science*]
MIC .... Merseyside Innovation Centre Ltd. [*Research center*] [*British*] (CB)
MIC .... Message Identification Code [*Computer science*] (BUR)
MIC .... Message Integrity Code
MIC .... Meteorological Information Committee [*NATO*] (NATG)
MIC .... Meteorologist-In-Charge [*Marine science*] (OSRA)
MIC .... Methylisobutyl Carbinol [*Also, MIBC*] [*Organic chemistry*]
MIC .... Methyl Isocyanate [*Organic chemistry*]
MIC .... Metro Industrial [*Vancouver Stock Exchange symbol*]
Mic .... Micah [*Old Testament book*]
MIC .... Michigan Information Center [*Michigan State Department of Management and Budget*] [*Information service or system*] (IID)
MIC .... Michigan Instructional Computer
MIC .... Michilla [*Chile*] [*Seismograph station code, US Geological Survey*] (SEIS)
MIC .... Micmac [*Language symbol*] (ETLW)
mic .... Micmac [*MARC language code*] [*Library of Congress*] (LCCP)
MIC .... Microbiologically-Influenced Corrosion [*Metallurgical engineering*]
MIC .... Microcomputer Index [*Information service or system*] (IID)
MIC .... Microcytosis [*Biochemistry*] (DAVI)
MIC .... Microelectronic Integrated Circuit (MCD)
mic .... Micrometer (WDMC)
MIC .... Micrometer [*A "mike"*]
MIC .... Microphone (AABC)
mic .... Microphone (WDMC)
MIC .... Microscopic (DAVI)
MIC .... Microscopic Findings in Centrifugal Urinary Sediment [*Biochemistry*] (DAVI)
Mic .... Microscopium [*Constellation*]
MIC .... Microscopy
MIC .... Microsoft Internet Chat (SAUS)
MIC .... Microwave Integrated Circuitry
MIC .... Microwave Integrated Circuits (NITA)
MIC .... Microwave Interference Coordination
MIC .... Microwave International Corporation (SAUO)
MIC .... Middle-in-Chain (ELAL)
MIC .... Middle Income Country [*Category of developing country*]
MIC .... Mid-Intensity Conflict [*Military*] (INF)
MIC .... Midwest Intercollegiate Conference (PSS)
MIC .... Milgo Electronics Corporation (SAUO)
MIC .... Military Indoctrination Center
MIC .... Military-Industrial Complex (ADWA)
MIC .... Military Information Center [*Defunct*] (EA)
MIC .... Military Intelligence Corps (SAUO)
MIC .... Military Introductory Letter
MIC .... Millicm International Cellular S.A. [*Commercial firm*] [*Luxembourg*]
MIC .... Mineral Industries Census
MIC .... Mini Cooper [*NCIC car model code*]
MIC .... Minimal [*or Minimum*] Inhibitory Concentration
MIC .... Minimal Isorrheic Concentration [*Medicine*]
MIC .... Minimum Ignition Current (IEEE)
MIC .... Minimum Inhibitory Concentration [*Bactericidal characteristic*]
MIC .... Minneapolis, MN [*Location identifier*] [*FAA*] (FAAL)
MiC .... Minocycline [*Antibiotic compound*] (AAMN)
MIC .... Minor Care Clinic [*Medicine*]
MIC .... Missile Identification Code [*Military*] (CAAL)
MIC .... Missing Interruption Character (NITA)
MIC .... Missing Interruption Checker (MCD)
MIC .... Missionary Sisters of the Immaculate Conception [*Roman Catholic religious order*]
MIC .... Missionary Sisters of the Immaculate Conception (Canada) (TOCD)
MIC .... Mississippi Industrial College [*Holly Springs*]
MIC .... Mitsubishi International Corporation (SAUO)
MIC .... MLRS International Corp. (SAUS)
MIC .... Mobile Incident Center (WDAA)
MIC .... Mobile Information Center [*An association*]
MIC .... Mobile Intelligence Center (SAUO)
MIC .... Mobile Intensive Care [*Medicine*] (DHSM)
MIC .... Model Immune Complex [*Medicine*] (DMAA)
MIC .... Molded-In Color [*Plastics*]
MIC .... Monaco Information Centre (SAUO)
MIC .... Monitoring, Identification, and Correlation
MIC .... Monolithic Integrated Circuit
MIC .... Mononuclear Inflammatory Cell (DMAA)
MIC .... Morphology-Immunology-Cytogenetics [*Classification of Leukemias*]
MIC .... Mortgage Insurance Certificate (EMRF)
MIC .... Mortgage Insurance Co.
MIC .... Mortgage Investment Corporation (FOTI)
MIC .... Motorcycle Industrial Council (SAUO)
MIC .... Motorcycle Industry Council (EA)
MIC .... Motors Insurance Corporation (SAUO)
MIC .... Mountain Instructor's Certificate [*British*] (DI)
MIC .... Movimiento de Integracion Colorada [*Paraguay*] [*Political party*] (EY)
MIC .... Multichip Integrated Circuit (NITA)
MIC .... Multifield Identification Chip (ACAE)
MIC .... Multimedia Interactive Control
MIC .... Multinational Intelligence Cell (MCD)
MIC .... Multiperil Insurance Conference
MIC .... Multiple Input Change (VLIE)
MIC .... Multiple Interface Connection (SAUS)
MIC .... MuniYield CA Insured Fund [*NYSE symbol*] (TTSB)
MIC .... MuniYield California Insured Fund [*NYSE symbol*] (SPSG)
MIC .... Music Industry Conference (EA)
MIC .... Music Industry Council [*Later, Music Industry Conference*] (EA)
MIC .... Music Information Center (TELE)
MIC .... Mutual Improvement Class [*British railroad term*]
MIC .... Mutual Interference Chart (IEEE)
MiCa .... Indianfields Public Library, Caro, MI [*Library symbol*] [*Library of Congress*] (LCLS)
MICA .... Macroinstruction Compiler Assembler [*Computer science*]
MICA .... Major Incidents Computer Application (PDAA)
MICA .... Management Improvement Corporation of America (SAUO)
MICA .... Maryland Improvement Contractors Association (EARSL)
MICA .... Maternity and Infant Care Association (SAUO)
MICA .... Meat Importers' Council of America (EA)
MICA .... Mentally Ill Chemical Abuser
MICA .... Michalke Manufacturing Corporation [*NCIC trailer make code*]
MICA .... MicroAge, Inc. [*NASDAQ symbol*] (COMM)
MICA .... Midwest Insulation Contractors Association

MICA .... Mobile Industrial Caterers' Association (EA)
MICA .... Mortgage Insurance Companies of America (EA)
MICA .... Moscow Institute for Complex Automation (SAUO)
MiCac .... Rawson Memorial Library, Cass City, MI [*Library symbol*] [*Library of Congress*] (LCLS)
MiCad .... Cadillac-Wexford Public Library, Cadillac, MI [*Library symbol*] [*Library of Congress*] (LCLS)
MICAD....... Micro-Installation, Inc. (SAUO)
MICAD....... Multipurpose Integrated Chemical Agent Alarm [*Army*] (DOMA)
MiCadCS.... Cadillac Public School, Cadillac, MI [*Library symbol*] [*Library of Congress*] (LCLS)
MiCadM..... Mid-Michigan Library League, Cadillac, MI [*Library symbol*] [*Library of Congress*] (LCLS)
MiCadPS.... Wexford Public Schools, Cadillac, MI [*Library symbol*] [*Library of Congress*] (LCLS)
MICAF....... Measuring Improved Capabilities of Army Forces (SAUO)
MICAF....... Measuring Improved Capability of Army Forces
MiCal........ Calumet Public-School Library, Calumet, MI [*Library symbol*] [*Library of Congress*] (LCLS)
MICALL ..... Microprocedure Call [*Computer science*] (MHDB)
MiCam ...... Camden Township Library, Camden, MI [*Library symbol*] [*Library of Congress*] (LCLS)
MICAM ...... Microammeter [*Electronics*]
MICAM ...... Micro Camera (NITA)
MICAM ...... Micro-Connection Assembly Method
MICAM ...... Mid-Function Integral Control Alarm Module [*Electronics systems*] [*Automotive engineering*]
MICAM ...... Module Integrated Connection and Assembly Method (ACAE)
MICAP....... Measuring Improved Capability [*Army*]
MICAP....... Mission Capability
MICAP....... Mission Capability Analysis System (SAUO)
MICAP....... Mission Capable (SAUS)
MICAP....... Mission Impaired Capability Awaiting Parts (SAUO)
MICAP....... Mission Incapable, Awaiting Parts (MCD)
MICAP....... Multi-National Investigations Cooperative on Aerial Phenomena
MICAPS ..... Mine/Countermine Casualty Assessment Producing System (MCD)
MICAS....... Military Intelligence Co., Aerial Surveillance (MCD)
MICAS....... Military Intelligence Company (SAUO)
MiCassC .... Cass County Library, Cassopolis, MI [*Library symbol*] [*Library of Congress*] (LCLS)
MICB .... Meck Island Control Building [*Army*] (AABC)
MICB .... Military Mechanized Infantry Combat Vehicle (ODA)
MICBM ...... Mobile Intercontinental Ballistic Missile
MiCc......... Carson City Public Library, Carson City, MI [*Library symbol*] [*Library of Congress*] (LCLS)
MICC .... Malaysian International Chambers of Commerce (SAUO)
MICC .... Maritime International Cooperation Centre (SAUO)
MICC .... Metal Interconnect Cascade Cell [*Photovoltaic energy systems*]
MICC .... Micro Concept Cars [*NCIC car make code*]
MICC .... Military Information Control Committee (CINC)
MICC .... Millicom International Cellular [*NASDAQ symbol*] (SAG)
MICC .... Mineral Insulated Conductor Cable (VLIE)
MICC .... Mineral Insulated, Copper Covered [*Cable*]
MICC .... Mitogen-Induced Cellular Cytotoxicity [*Medicine*] (DB)
MICC .... Mortgage Insurance Co. of Canada
MICCF....... Millicom Intl Cellular S.A. [*NASDAQ symbol*] (TTSB)
MICCI........ Malaysia International Chamber of Commerce and Industry (EAIO)
MICCLE ..... Michigan Interorganizational Committee on Continuing Library Education (EDAC)
MICCO....... Model Inner City Community Organization [*Washington, DC*]
MICCS....... Management Information and Commitment Control System (SAUO)
MICCS....... Minuteman Integrated Command and Control System [*Missiles*]
MICCY....... Michigan City, IN [*American Association of Railroads railroad junction routing code*]
Mic D........ Doctor of Microbiology
MICD .... Mechanical, Thermal, and Optical Interface Control Document (MCD)
MICDS....... Movable In-Core Detector System [*Nuclear energy*] (NRCH)
MICE......... Management Information Capability for Enforcement [*Environmental Protection Agency*] (GFGA)
MICE......... Man's Impact on Coastal and Estuarine Ecosystems [*Marine science*] [*United Nations*] (OSRA)
MICE......... Material Transfer, Information Transfer, Control Transfer, Energy Transfer
MICE......... Member of the Institute of Civil Engineers (SAUO)
MICE......... Member of the Institution of Chemical Engineers (SAUO)
MICE......... Member of the Institution of Civil Engineers [*Formerly, AMICE*] [*British*]
MICE......... Methods Information Communication Exchange Service (AEPA)
MICE......... Methods Information Communications Exchange (SAUO)
MICE......... Microelectronic Integrated Checkout Equipment
MICE......... Missile Intercept Computer Evaluation (ACAE)
MICE......... Modular Integrated Communications Environment (VLIE)
MICE......... Money, Ideology, Compromise, Ego [*CIA acronym for possible explanations for spy defections*]
MICE......... Morphological Image Complexity Evaluation (ACAE)
MICE......... Multi-Interface Computer Equipment (SAUS)
MICE......... Multi-Media, Information, Communication, and Entertainment [*Automotive electronics*]
MICE......... Multimedia Information Communications and Entertainment [*Automotive engineering*]
MICE......... Multimedia Integrated Conferencing for Europe (SAUO)
MICE......... Multimedia Integrated Conferencing for European Researchers (SAUO)
MICE......... Mutual Insurance Council of Editors [*Later, PICA*] (EA)
MiCe......... Nottawa Township Library, Centerville, MI [*Library symbol*] [*Library of Congress*] (LCLS)
MiCeG....... Glen Oaks Community College, Centreville, MI [*Library symbol*] [*Library of Congress*] (LCLS)
MICEI........ Member of the Institution of Civil Engineers India (SAUO)
MICEI........ Member of the Institution of Civil Engineers Ireland (SAUO)
MICEI........ Member of the Institution of Civil Engineers of Ireland
MICELEM ... Microphone Element (IEEE)
MiCen .... Leslie R. Foss Public Library, Center Line, MI [*Library symbol*] [*Library of Congress*] (LCLS)
MiCenl ...... Central Lake Township Library, Central Lake, MI [*Library symbol*] [*Library of Congress*] (LCLS)
MICES....... Microcomputer-Controlled Electroanalysis System [*Interactive Microwave*]
MiCf .... Crystal Falls Community Library, Crystal Falls, MI [*Library symbol*] [*Library of Congress*] (LCLS)
MicFocu..... Micro Focus Group PLC [*Associated Press*] (SAG)
Micfrm ...... Microframe, Inc. [*Associated Press*] (SAG)
MICG .... Macromolecular Insoluble Cold Globulin (DMAA)
MICG .... Management Information Coordinating Group [*Navy*]
MICG .... Mercury Iodide Crystal Growth
MICG .... Michigan Central Airlines [*NCIC trailer make code*]
MICG .... Microfield Graphics [*NASDAQ symbol*] (TTSB)
MICG .... Microfield Graphics, Inc. [*NASDAQ symbol*] (SAG)
MICH .... Michaelmas [*Feast of St. Michael the Archangel, September 29*]
Mich .... Michaelmas Term [*British*] [*Legal term*] (DLA)
MICH .... Michaels [J.], Inc. [*NASDAQ symbol*] (NQ)
MICH .... Michaels J [*NASDAQ symbol*] (TTSB)
MICH .... Micheas [*Old Testament book*] [*Douay version*]
Mich......... Michigan (ODBW)
MICH .... Michigan
Mich......... Michigan Supreme Court Reports [*A publication*] (DLA)
MiCha .... Chase Public Library, Chase, MI [*Library symbol*] [*Library of Congress*] (LCLS)
Mich Acad... Michigan Academician [*A publication*] (PABS)
Mich Academician... Michigan Academician [*A publication*] (JLIT)
Mich Admin Code... Michigan Administrative Code [*A publication*] (DLA)
Mich Adv ... Michigan Reports Advanced Sheets [*A publication*] (DLA)
MICHAMBER FED PAC... Michigan Chamber of Commerce Federal PAC [*Lansing, MI*] (PACS)
MICHANT ... Michael Anthony Jewelers, Inc. (SAUO)
MichAnt..... Michael Anthony Jewelers, Inc. [*Associated Press*] (SAG)
Mich App ... Michigan Court of Appeals Reports [*A publication*] (DLA)
MiChar ...... Charlotte Public Library, Charlotte, MI [*Library symbol*] [*Library of Congress*] (LCLS)
Mich AS..... Michigan Audubon Society (SAUO)
Mich Att'y Gen Biennial Rep... Biennial Report of the Attorney General of the State of Michigan [*A publication*] (DLA)
MichBr ...... Michigan Brewery, Inc. [*Associated Press*] (SAG)
MichBrw .... Michigan Brewery, Inc. [*Associated Press*] (SAG)
Mich Calidon... Michael Calidonius [*Flourished, 16th century*] [*Authority cited in pre-1607 legal work*] (DSA)
Mich CCR... Michigan Circuit Court Reporter [*A publication*] (DLA)
Mich Comp L Ann... Michigan Compiled Laws, Annotated [*A publication*] (DLA)
Mich Comp Laws... Michigan Compiled Laws [*A publication*] (DLA)
Mich Comp Laws... Michigan Compiled Laws Annotated [*West*] [*A publication*] (AAGC)
Mich Comp Laws Ann... Michigan Compiled Laws, Annotated [*A publication*] (DLA)
Mich Cr Ct Rep... Michigan Circuit Court Reporter [*A publication*] (DLA)
Mich Ct Cl... Michigan Court of Claims (AAGC)
Mich Ct Cl... Michigan Court of Claims Reports [*A publication*] (DLA)
MiChe .... Cheboygan Area Public Library, Cheboygan, MI [*Library symbol*] [*Library of Congress*] (LCLS)
MiChel ...... McKune Memorial Library, Chelsea, MI [*Library symbol*] [*Library of Congress*] (LCLS)
MIChemE ... Member of the Institution of Chemical Engineers [*British*] (EY)
MiChes...... Chesaning Public Library, Chesaning, MI [*Library symbol*] [*Library of Congress*] (LCLS)
MichFncl.... Michigan Financial Corp. [*Associated Press*] (SAG)
Michie's GA Repts Ann... Georgia Reports, Annotated [*A publication*] (DLA)
Michie's Jur... Michie's Jurisprudence of Virginia and West Virginia [*A publication*] (DLA)
Michigan LRC... Michigan Law Review Commission (SAFN)
MichJ........ Michaels [*J.*], Inc. [*Associated Press*] (SAG)
MichJInt'LL... Michigan Journal of International Law [*A publication*] (SAFN)
Mich Jur.... Michigan Jurisprudence [*A publication*] (DLA)
Mich L ...... Michigan Lawyer [*A publication*] (DLA)
Mich Legis Serv... Michigan Legislative Service [*A publication*] (DLA)
Mich Leg News... Michigan Legal News [*A publication*] (DLA)
MichIF....... Michael Foods, Inc. [*Associated Press*] (SAG)
Mich LJ..... Michigan Law Journal [*A publication*] (DLA)
MichLR...... Michigan Law Review (SAFN)
MichLRev... Michigan Law Review (SAUO)
Mich Nisi Prius... Brown's Michigan Nisi Prius Reports [*A publication*] (DLA)
Mich NP .... Brown's Michigan Nisi Prius Reports [*A publication*] (DLA)
Mich Pub Acts... Public and Local Acts of the Legislature of the State of Michigan [*A publication*] (DLA)
Mich PUC Ops... Michigan Public Utilities Commission Orders and Opinions [*A publication*] (DLA)
Mich R ...... Michigan Reports [*A publication*] (DLA)
Mich RC Dec... Michigan Railroad Commission Decisions [*A publication*] (DLA)
MICHS....... Michaelmas [*Feast of St. Michael the Archangel, September 29*]
Mich SBA Jo... Michigan State Bar Association. Journal [*A publication*] (DLA)
Mich Stat Ann... Michigan Statutes, Annotated [*A publication*] (DLA)
MichStr ..... Michael Stores [*Associated Press*] (SAG)

Mich St U... Michigan State University (GAGS)
Mich Supr Ct Rep... Michigan Reports [*A publication*] (DLA)
Mich T...... Michaelmas Term [*British*] [*Legal term*] (DLA)
Mich Tech U... Michigan Technological University (GAGS)
MiChv....... Charlevoix Public Library, Charlevoix, MI [*Library symbol*] [*Library of Congress*] (LCLS)
Mich Vac.... Michaelmas Vacation [*British*] [*Legal term*] (DLA)
Mich WCC.. Michigan Industrial Accident Board, Workmen's Compensation Cases [*A publication*] (DLA)
MICI........ Metadata Information Clearinghouse Interactive
MICIM....... Methodology for the Introduction of CIM (SAUO)
MICIS....... Material Information Control and Information System (MCD)
MiCiS....... Material Information Control and Information System (NAKS)
MICIS....... Material Inventory Control and Inventory System (NASA)
MICIS....... Microbial Culture Information Service [*Department of Trade and Industry*] [*British*] [*Information service or system*]
MICIS....... Midwestern Climate Information System [*Marine science*] (OSRA)
MICK........ Manufacturers Item Correlation Key
Mickey Finn... Chloral Hydrate [*Medicine*] (EDAA)
MICL......... Mid Infrared Chemical Laser (ACAE)
MICL......... Missile In-Commission Level
MiCla........ Garfield Memorial Public Library, Clare, MI [*Library symbol*] [*Library of Congress*] (LCLS)
MICLE....... Institute of Continuing Legal Education, University of Michigan (DLA)
MICLE....... Michigan Institute of Continuing Legal Education (SAUO)
MICLIC...... Mine Clearing Line Charge [*Army*] (INF)
MiClin....... Clinton Public Library, Clinton, MI [*Library symbol*] [*Library of Congress*] (LCLS)
MICLO....... Management Information Control Liaison Officers (MCD)
MICLP....... Medical Informatics Cultural Literacy Project (ADWA)
MICM........ Associate Member of the Institute of Credit Management [*British*] (DBQ)
MICM........ Member of the Institute of Credit Management (SAUO)
MICM........ MICOM Communications [*NASDAQ symbol*] (TTSB)
MICM........ Micom Communications Corp. [*NASDAQ symbol*] (SAG)
MICM........ Monolithic Integrated Circuit Mask
MICMD...... Milwaukee Contract Management District (SAA)
MICMPTR... Microcomputer (MSA)
MICN........ Medical Intensive Care Nurse (DAVI)
MICN........ Micrion Corp. [*NASDAQ symbol*] (SAG)
MICN........ Mobile Intensive Care Nurse [*Emergency Medicine*] (DAVI)
MICNIA...... Modular Integrated Communication, Navigation & Identification Avionics (SAUS)
MICNS....... Modular Integrated Communications and Navigation System (RDA)
MICO........ Management Information Systems Control Officer (MCD)
MICO........ Mankato Industrial Corp. [*Automotive industry supplier*]
MICO........ Member of the Institute of Careers Officers [*British*] (DBQ)
MICO........ Michael & Company (EFIS)
MICO........ Midland Continental R. R. [*AAR code*] [*Obsolete*]
MICo......... Military Intelligence Company (SAUO)
MICO........ MLV Integration and Checkout (MCD)
MICOFT..... Mutual Insurance Committee on Federal Taxation (EA)
MiCol........ Coloma Public Library, Coloma, MI [*Library symbol*] [*Library of Congress*] (LCLS)
MiCole...... Coleman Area Library, Coleman, MI [*Library symbol*] [*Library of Congress*] (LCLS)
MiCole...... Coleman Art Library (SAUS)
MiColo...... Colon Township Library, Colon, MI [*Library symbol*] [*Library of Congress*] (LCLS)
MiCom...... Comstock Township Library, Comstock, MI [*Library symbol*] [*Library of Congress*] (LCLS)
Micom....... Microwave Communications of America Inc. (SAUO)
MICOM...... Missile Command [*Redstone Arsenal, AL*] [*Army*]
MICOM...... Mission Command (SAUO)
MICOM...... US Army Missile Command (AAGC)
MicomC..... Micom Communications Corp. [*Associated Press*] (SAG)
MICOM-RDEC... Missile Command Research, Development, and Engineering Center [*Army*] (RDA)
MICOMS.... Maintenance Information Concerning [*the repair and operation of*] Missile Systems
MiCon....... Constatine Township Library, Constatine, MI [*Library symbol*] [*Library of Congress*] (LCLS)
MICON...... Military Construction Program (MUGU)
micon....... Motion Icon [*Computer science*] (WDMC)
MICONEX... Multinational Instrumentation Conference and Exposition [*China Instrument Society*]
MiCoop...... Coopersville District Library, Coopersville, MI [*Library symbol*] [*Library of Congress*] (LCLS)
MI-COPICS... Management Information for COPICS [*Communications Oriented Production Information and Control System*] Users [*IBM Corp.*]
MICORE..... Management Improvement/Cost Reduction Program (SAUO)
MICorrST... Member of the Institute of Corrosion Science and Technology [*British*] (DBQ)
MICOS....... Mini Computer Systems (NITA)
MICOS....... Multifunctional Infra-red Coherent Optical Scanner (SAUS)
MICOS....... Multi Functional Infrared Coherent Optical Sensor (ACAE)
MICOT....... Minimum Completion Time (VLIE)
MICOTOWS... Minister in Charge of Treaty of Waitangi Settlements (SAUO)
MICP........ Management and Investment Companies Program
MICP........ Maternity and Infant Care Project [*Medicine*] (EDAA)
MICP........ Military Inventory Control Point (MCD)
MICPAC..... Microelectronic Integrated Circuit Package (MCD)
MICPAK..... Modular Integrated Circuit Package
MIC PAN.... Mica Panis [*Crumb of Bread*] [*Pharmacy*]
MicPwr...... Microwave Power Devices, Inc. [*Associated Press*] (SAG)
MICR........ Magnetic Ink Character Recognition [*Banking*] [*Computer science*]
MICR........ Management Improvement and Cost Reduction Project Reporting System
MIC/R....... Media Interface Connector/Receptacle [*Computer science*] (AGLO)
MICR........ Michigan Central Railroad [*Federal Railroad Administration identification code*]
MICR........ Microenergy, Inc. [*NASDAQ symbol*] (SAG)
MICR........ Microscope (MSA)
Micr......... Microscopium [*Constellation*]
MICRA....... Medical Injury Compensation Reform Act
MICRA....... Microelectronic Integrated Circuit Replaceable (ACAE)
MICRA....... Miniature Insulated Contact Range (PDAA)
MICRAD..... Microwave Radiometry (MCD)
MICRADS... Microwave Radiation System (PDAA)
MICRAM.... Microminiature Individual Components Reliable Assembled Modules
MicrBi....... Micro Bio-Medics, Inc. [*Associated Press*] (SAG)
Micrdy....... Microdyne Corp. [*Associated Press*] (SAG)
Micrel....... Micrel, Inc. [*Associated Press*] (SAG)
Micrenr..... Microenergy, Inc. [*Associated Press*] (SAG)
MicrFlt...... Microwave Filter Co., Inc. [*Associated Press*] (SAG)
Micrgfx...... Micrografx, Inc. [*Associated Press*] (SAG)
MicrGn...... Micro General Corp. [*Associated Press*] (SAG)
Micrion...... Micrion Corp. [*Associated Press*] (SAG)
Micrl......... Microleague Multimedia, Inc. [*Associated Press*] (SAG)
Micrleag.... Microleague Multimedia, Inc. [*Associated Press*] (SAG)
MICR/ MIMR........ Magnetic Ink Character Recognition / Magnetic Ink Mark Recognition (BTTJ)
MIC-RN..... Mobile Intensive Care Registered Nurse [*Emergency medicine*] (DAVI)
Micrnics.... Micronics Computers, Inc. [*Associated Press*] (SAG)
MicrnT...... Micron Technology [*Associated Press*] (SAG)
micro....... Extremely Small (IDOE)
MICRO...... Microcomputer
MICRO...... Microelectronics Innovation and Computer Science Research Program [*University of California*] [*Research center*] (RCD)
micro........ Microphone [*Therapy term*] (CTAA)
MICRO...... Microprocessor
micro........ Microscopic
MICRO...... Multiple Indexing and Console Retrieval Operations (NITA)
MICRO...... Multiple Indexing and Console Retrieval Options [*Information retrieval*] [*Computer science*]
MICROACE... Microminiature Automatic Checkout Equipment
MicroAge... MicroAge, Inc., [*Associated Press*] (SAG)
Micro-AIDS... Micro-Aircraft Integrated Data System (SAUS)
Microb Ecol... Microbial Ecology [*A publication*] (PABS)
MICROBIOL... Microbiological [*or Microbiology*]
MicroCap... [*The*] MicroCap Fund [*Associated Press*] (SAG)
MICROCAT... Micro-Catalogue (NITA)
Microchip... Microchip Technology, Inc. [*Associated Press*] (SAG)
Microcm.... Microcom, Inc. [*Associated Press*] (SAG)
MICROCON... Microcomputer Based Services for Retrospective Conversions (NITA)
microcryst... Microcrystalline (BARN)
MicroCSI.... MicroStation Customer Support Library [*Intergraph Corp.*] (PCM)
MicroCT..... Micro Component Technology, Inc. [*Associated Press*] (SAG)
MICROD..... Council for Microphotography and Document Reproduction (SAUO)
MICRODIS... Microform Document of Information System (MCD)
MICRO-DISC... Microcomputer-Videodisc
MICRODOC... Council for Microphotography and Document Reproduction [*British*]
Microelectron Eng... Microelectronic Engineering [*A publication*] (CABS)
Microelectron J... Microelectronic Journal [*A publication*] (CABS)
Microelectron Reliab... Microelectronics and Reliability [*A publication*] (CABS)
Microfd...... Microfield Graphics, Inc. [*Associated Press*] (SAG)
MicrofdG..... Microfield Graphics, Inc. [*Associated Press*] (SAG)
Microflu..... Microfluidics International Corp. [*Associated Press*] (SAG)
MICROFX.... Intelligence Data Processing Set (SAUO)
MICROG..... Microgram [*One millionth of a gram*]
MicroIntg... Micro-Integration Corp. [*Associated Press*] (SAG)
MICROLAB... Microfabrication Laboratory [*University of California, Berkeley*] [*Research center*] (RCD)
Microlg...... Microlog Corp. [*Associated Press*] (SAG)
MicroLin.... Micro Linear Corp. [*Associated Press*] (SAG)
MICROM.... Microinstruction Read-Only Memory [*Computer science*]
MICROMET... Micro Metallics Corporation (EFIS)
MICROMIN... Microminiature (IEEE)
MICRON..... Micronavigator [*Air Force*]
MICRON..... Micron Products, Inc. (SAUO)
MicronEl..... Micron Electronics, Inc. [*Associated Press*] (SAG)
Micrones.... Micronesian (DIAR)
MICRONET... Microcomputer Network (NITA)
Micront...... Micronetics, Inc. [*Associated Press*] (SAG)
Microp....... Micropolis Corp. [*Associated Press*] (SAG)
MICROPAC... Micromodule Data Processor and Computer (IEEE)
MicroPh..... Microcide Pharmaceuticals, Inc. [*Associated Press*] (SAG)
Microporous Mater... Microporous Materials [*A publication*] (CABS)
MICROPOWER SOURCES... Design, Study and Construction of Micropower Sources and Their Use in Microelectronics and Communication Technologies (SAUO)
Micro Proc Ann Workshop Microprogram... Micro Proceedings. Annual Workshop on Microprogramming (SAUO)
MICROPSI... Microcomputer Printed Subject Indexes (NITA)
MICROS..... Microscopy
Micros....... Micros Systems, Inc. [*Associated Press*] (SAG)

MICROSECS... Microfilm Sequential Coding System [*Bell System*]
Microsft..... Microsoft Corp. [*Associated Press*] (SAG)
MICROSID... Small Seismic Intrusion Detector (PDAA)
MicroSIFT... Microcomputer Software and Information for Teachers [*Northwest Regional Educational Laboratory*] [*Information service or system*] (IID)
MICROSIM... Microinstruction Simulator [*Computer science*] (MHDI)
Microsoft ... Microsoft Corp. [*Associated Press*] (SAG)
microSQUID... Microscopy, Microscopic Superconducting Quantum Interference Devices
MicrosTo.... Micros-To Mainframe, Inc. [*Associated Press*] (SAG)
MICROTEL... Microsoft/Intel (SAUS)
Microtel..... Microtel International, Inc. [*Associated Press*] (SAG)
Microtl ..... Microtel Franchise & Development Corp. [*Associated Press*] (SAG)
MicroTo ..... Micros-To Mainframe, Inc. [*Associated Press*] (SAG)
MICRO TR... Microwave Tower [*Nautical charts*]
MICRO-VERS... Microcomputer Vocational Education Reporting System (EDAC)
Microwave Opt Technol Lett... Microwave and Optical Technology Letters [*A publication*] (CABS)
MicroWre ... Micro Warehouse, Inc. [*Associated Press*] (SAG)
MicrPck ..... Microelectronic Packaging, Inc. [*Associated Press*] (SAG)
MICRS....... Main Instrument Console and Readout Stations (NATG)
MicrtcRs .... Microtec Research, Inc. [*Associated Press*] (SAG)
Micrtek...... Microtek Medical, Inc. [*Associated Press*] (SAG)
Micrtest..... Microtest, Inc. [*Associated Press*] (SAG)
MICRU ...... MICRU International (EA)
Micrvisn .... Microvision, Inc. [*Associated Press*] (SAG)
MICS .... Machine Inventory Control System [*Computer science*] (VLIE)
MICS .... Macro Interpretive Commands [*Computer science*] (VLIE)
MICS .... Macro Interpretive Command System (SAUO)
MICS .... Maintenance Inventory Control System [*Bell System*]
MICS .... Management Information and Control System [*Navy*]
MICS .... Management Information Conformance Statement [*Open Systems Interconnection*] (ODAA)
MICS .... Management Integrated Control System
MICS .... Manned Interactive Control Stations (MCD)
MICS .... Manufacturing Information and Control System (OA)
MICS .... Material Inventory Control System [*NASA*] (SSD)
MICS .... Materiel Intransit Control System (SAUO)
MICS .... Medical Instrument Calibration System (PDAA)
MICS .... Micom Systems, Inc. [*NASDAQ symbol*] (COMM)
MICS .... Microprocessor Inertia and Communication System
MICS .... Military Integrated Communications System (CINC)
MICS .... Mineral-Insulated Copper-Sheathed [*Cable*] (IEEE)
MICS .... Mingan Island Cetacean Study [*Canada*] (RCD)
Mics .... Miscellaneous (SAUO)
MICS .... Missile Inspection Completion Sheet (MCD)
MICS .... Mitsubishi Intelligent Cockpit System [*Automotive engineering*]
MICS .... Mobile Integrated Communications System (SAUS)
MICS .... Multiman Intermittent Cooling System (SAUS)
MICS .... Multiplex Interior Communications (NG)
MICS .... Museum of the International College of Surgeons (NADA)
MICS .... MVS Integrated Control System (NITA)
MICSA....... Maine Indian Claims Settlement Act [*1980*]
MicSem..... Microsemi Corp. [*Associated Press*] (SAG)
Micsft .... Microsoft Corp. [*Associated Press*] (SAG)
MICSLP ..... Maintenance Inventory Control Stock Levels Projection (SAUO)
MICTAR ..... Minnesota Center for Twin and Adoption Research (ECON)
MictchS ..... Microtouch Systems, Inc. [*Associated Press*] (SAG)
MictchSy.... Microtouch Systems, Inc. [*Associated Press*] (SAG)
MICTF .... Microcell Telecommunications, Inc. [*NASDAQ symbol*] (QUAN)
MICU .... Medical Intensive Care Unit [*Medicine*] (EDAA)
MICU .... Mobile Intensive Care Unit [*Medicine*] (EDAA)
MICU(N) .... Mobile Intensive Care Unit [*or Nurse*] (GNE)
MIC UNESCO-IOC/MIC... Marine Information Centre (SAUO)
MICV .... Mechanized Infantry Combat Vehicle [*Army*]
MICV-FPW... Mechanized Infantry Combat Vehicle - Firing Port Weapon (MCD)
MICVS....... Mechanized Infantry Combat Vehicle Systems [*Army*] (RDA)
MiCw .... Coldwater Public Library, Coldwater, MI [*Library symbol*] [*Library of Congress*] (LCLS)
MICW........ Member of the Institute of Clerks of Works of Great Britain, Inc. (DBQ)
Micware .... Microware Systems Corp. [*Associated Press*] (SAG)
MiCwB ...... Branch County Library, Coldwater, MI [*Library symbol*] [*Library of Congress*] (LCLS)
MICWU...... Motor Industry Combined Workers Union (SAUO)
MICX .... Mississippi Chemical [*Private rail car owner code*]
MICZ......... Mid-Iowa Co-Operative [*Federal Railroad Administration identification code*]
MiD......... Detroit Public Library, Detroit, MI [*Library symbol*] [*Library of Congress*] (LCLS)
MID .... Magnetically Insulated Diode [*Physics*]
MID .... Maintenace Index Page (DNAB)
MID .... Manpower Information Division [*Navy*]
MID .... Mare Island Division [*San Francisco Bay Naval Shipyard, Vallejo, CA*]
MID .... Marginally Indigent Defendant
MID .... Master of Industrial Design
MID .... Master of Interior Design (GAGS)
MID .... Material Identification (AAEL)
MID .... Maximum Inhibiting Dilution [*Medicine*] (MAE)
MID .... Maximum Inhibiting Duration [*Medicine*] (DAVI)
MID .... Measure of Intellectual Development (EDAC)
MID .... Meat Inspection Division [*of ARS, Department of Agriculture*]
MID .... Mechanical Inertia Dynamometer [*Automotive emissions*]
MID .... Median Incisal Diastema [*Medicine*] (MELL)
MID .... Median Infective Dose [*Bacteriology*]
MID .... Mentioned in Dispatches (ADA)
MID .... Merida [*Mexico*] [*Airport symbol*] (OAG)
MID .... Mesioincisodistal [*Dentistry*]
MID .... Message Identification [*Computer science*]
MID .... Message Identifier (ACRL)
MID .... Message Input Description
MID .... Message Input Device (AABC)
MID .... Mid Airways [*France*] [*FAA designator*] (FAAC)
MID .... Midbody
MID .... Midcon Oil & Gas Ltd. [*Toronto Stock Exchange symbol*]
MID .... Mid-Continent Telephone Corp. (SAUO)
MID .... Middle (AFM)
mid .... Middle (VRA)
MID .... Middleton Island [*Alaska*] [*Seismograph station code, US Geological Survey*] (SEIS)
MID .... Middling Space [*Typesetting*] (DGA)
Mid .... Middoth (BJA)
MID .... Midget [*NCIC car model code*]
MID .... Midland [*Topography*] (ROG)
MID .... MIDLNET [*Midwest Regional Library Network*], St. Louis, MO [*OCLC symbol*] (OCLC)
MID .... Midnight
Mid .... Midrash [*Interpretation of Old Testament writings*] (BJA)
Mid .... Midshipman (WDAA)
MID .... Midshipman [*Navy*]
MID .... Midway Railroad Co. [*AAR code*]
MID .... Midwest Stock Exchange [*Chicago, IL*] (CDAI)
MID .... Midwifery (ROG)
MID .... Military Information Division (SAUO)
MID .... Military Intelligence Department (SAUO)
MID .... Military Intelligence Detachment (AABC)
MID .... Military Intelligence Division [*War Department*] [*World War II*]
MID .... Mines Inspection Department (SAUO)
MID .... Minimal Infecting Dose [*Medicine*] (MELL)
MID .... Minimal Inhibiting Dose [*Medicine*]
MID .... Minimal Irradiation Dose [*Medicine*] (MELL)
MID .... Minimum Infective Dose [*Bacteriology*]
MID .... Ministerstvo Inostrannykh Del [*Ministry of Foreign Affairs*] [*Former USSR*]
MID .... Missile Intelligence Directorate [*Army*] (AABC)
MID .... Missile Intelligence Directory
MID .... Missing Insects Department
MID .... Modified Ionization Detector (MCD)
MID .... Mortgage Interest Differential
MID .... Movimiento de Integracion Democratica [*Democratic Integration Movement*] [*Dominican Republic*] [*Political party*] (PPW)
MID .... Movimiento Independiente Democratico [*Independent Democratic Movement*] [*Panama*] [*Political party*] (PPW)
MID .... Multi-Information Display [*Automotive engineering*]
MID .... Multinfarct Dementia (DIPS)
MID .... Multiple Individually Designated (ACAE)
MID .... Multiple Infant Dementia [*Neurology*] (CPH)
MID .... Multiple Infarct Dementia [*Neurology*]
MID .... Multiple Ion Detection
MID .... Multiplex Identification (SAUS)
MID .... Multiplexing Identifier [*Telecommunications*] (ACRL)
MID .... Munitions Inventions Department [*British military*] (DMA)
MID .... Musically Intelligent Device [*Electronic musical instruments*]
MiDA .... Detroit Institute of Arts, Detroit, MI [*Library symbol*] [*Library of Congress*] (LCLS)
MIDA .... Major Item Data Agency (SAUO)
MIDA .... Major Items Data Agency [*Military*]
Mida......... Malaysian Industrial Development Authority (SAUO)
MIDA .... Message Interchange Distributed Application [*Telecommunications*] (OSI)
MIDA .... Mid-American International Development Association [*Nigeria*]
MIDA .... Mid-Atlantic Homes Company [*NCIC trailer make code*]
MIDA .... Moviemiento de Integracion Democratica [*The Dominican Republic*] [*Political party*] (EY)
MIDA .... Myocardial Ischemia Dynamic Analysis [*Medicine*] (DMAA)
MiDAA....... Catholic Archdiocese of Detroit, Archives, Detroit, MI [*Library symbol*] [*Library of Congress*] (LCLS)
MidAApt..... Mid America Apartment Communities, Inc. [*Associated Press*] (SAG)
MidABc..... Mid-America Bancorp [*Associated Press*] (SAG)
MIDAC....... Management Information for Decision and Control
MIDAC....... Michigan [*University of*] Digital Automatic Computer
MiDACI...... American Concrete Institute, Detroit, MI [*Library symbol*] [*Library of Congress*] (LCLS)
MIDADE..... Mouvement International d'Apostolat des Enfants [*International Movement of Apostolate of Children*] [*France*]
MidAE .... Mid American Energy Co. [*Associated Press*] (SAG)
MidAg .... Midrash Aggadah (BJA)
Mid-Am ..... Mid-America: An Historical Review [*A publication*] (BRI)
MIDAM ...... Midamerica Commodity Exchange (EA)
MidAm ...... Mid-Am, Inc. [*Associated Press*] (SAG)
MiDAMA .... Automobile Manufacturers Association, Inc., Detroit (SAUS)
MiDAMA .... Automobile Manufacturers' Association, Inc., Detroit, MI [*Library symbol*] [*Library of Congress*] (LCLS)
MidAmEn ... Mid American Energy Co. [*Associated Press*] (SAG)
MidAmIn.... Mid-Am, Inc. [*Associated Press*] (SAG)
MidAmR .... Mid America Realty, Inc. [*Formerly, Dial REIT*] [*Associated Press*] (SAG)

MIDAN ...... Microprocessor Data Analyzer [*Instrumentation*]
MIDANET ... Mortgage Information Direct Access Network [*FHLMC*] (EMRF)
MidAp .... Mid America Apartment Communities [*Associated Press*] (SAG)
MIDAR ...... Microwave Detection and Ranging
MIDAR ...... Motion Indicating RADAR (MCD)
MID-ARK.... Mid-Arkansas Regional Library [*Library network*]
MIDARM .... Microdynamic Angle and Rate Monitoring System
MIDAS....... Mainline Information Display and Automation System [*Salford Electrical Instruments*] (NITA)
MIDAS....... Maintenance Integrated Data Access System (MCD)
MIDAS....... Management Information and Development Aids System (SSD)
MIDAS....... Management Information, Data & Accounting System (SAUS)
MIDAS....... Management Information Dissemination Administrative System (SAUO)
MIDAS....... Management Integrated Data Accumulating System
MIDAS....... Management Interactive Data Accounting System [*Computer science*] (CIST)
MIDAS....... Man-Machine Integration Design and Analysis System (GAVI)
MIDAS....... Manufacturing Information Distribution and Acquisition System (ACAE)
MIDAS....... Marine Inclination Differential Alignment System (SAUS)
MIDAS....... Maritime Industrial Development Area [*Navy*]
MIDAS....... Materiel Inventory Data Acquisition System
MIDAS....... Measurement Information Data Analysis System [*or Subsystem*] (IEEE)
MIDAS....... Mechanism Integration Design and Analysis System [*Computer-assisted engineering*]
MIDAS....... Medical Information Dissemination Using ASSASSIN (NITA)
MIDAS....... Memory Implemented Data Acquisition Systems
MIDAS....... Meteorological Information and Dose Acquisition System [*Nuclear energy*] (NRCH)
MIDAS....... Meteorological Integrating Data Acquisition System [*Marine science*] (MSC)
MIDAS....... Microcomputer-Interfaced Data Acquisition System [*Computer science*]
MIDAS....... Micro-Diagnostics for Analysis and Repair (NITA)
MIDAS....... Microimaged Data Addition System [*CAPS Equipment Ltd.*]
MIDAS....... Microprogrammable Integrated Data Acquisition System
MIDAS....... Microprogramming Design Aided System [*RCA*]
MIDAS....... Microscopic Image Digital Acquisition System (PDAA)
MIDAS....... Mine & Ice Detection/Avoidance System (SAUS)
MIDAS....... Mine Detection and Avoidance System (MCD)
MIDAS....... Miniature Data Acquisition System
MIDAS....... Missile Defense Alarm [*or Alert*] System [*Air Force*]
MIDAS....... Missile Detection and Alarm System [*Army*] (AABC)
MIDAS....... Missile Detection and Surveillance (CAAL)
MIDAS....... Missile Intercept Data Acquisition System
MIDAS....... Mobile Integrated Digital Automatic System (SAUS)
MIDAS....... Model for Interheater Deployment by Air and Sea [*DoD*]
MIDAS....... Model for Intertheater Deployment and Scheduling (SAUO)
MIDAS....... Modified Integration Digital Analog Simulator [*Computer science*] (MCD)
MIDAS....... Modular Integrated Design Automated System
MIDAS....... Modular Interactive Data Acquisition System [*National Institute of Standards and Technology*]
MIDAS....... Modular International Dealing and Accounting System (NITA)
MIDAS....... Modulator Isolation Diagnostic Analysis System (IEEE)
MIDAS....... Monopoly Information and Data Analysis System
MIDAS....... Multicenter Isradipine Diuretic Atherosclerosis Study
MIDAS....... Multi-Discipline Data Analysis System (GAVI)
MIDAS....... Multi-Mode International Data Acquisition Service (NITA)
MIDAS....... Multioptional Interactive Display and Analytic System (MCD)
MIDAS....... Multiple Index Data Access System [*Prime Computer, Inc.*]
MIDAS....... Multiple Input Data Acquisition System [*Bell System*]
MIDAS....... Multiple Integrated Document Assembly System [*Computer science*] (BYTE)
MIDAS....... Multitier Distributed Application Services [*Computer science*]
MIDAS....... Munich Image Data Analysis System
MID/ASIA ... Middle East/Asia Region [*USTTA*] (TAG)
MIDATA ..... Marconi Integrated Design and Test Automation [*Marconi Industries*] [*Telecommunications*] [*British*]
MIDATL ..... Mid-Atlantic (DNAB)
MidAtlan.... Mid-Atlantic Medical Services, Inc. [*Associated Press*] (SAG)
MidatRty.... Midatlantic Realty Trust [*Associated Press*] (SAG)
MIDATS ..... Modular Intermediate Depot Automatic Test System (ACAE)
MiDb .... Dearborn Public [*Henry Ford Centennial*] Library, Dearborn, MI [*Library symbol*] [*Library of Congress*] (LCLS)
MiDB .... Detroit Bar Association, Detroit, MI [*Library symbol*] [*Library of Congress*] (LCLS)
MiD-B .... Detroit Public Library, Burton Historical Collection, Detroit, MI [*Library symbol*] [*Library of Congress*] (LCLS)
MIDB .... Major Item Data Base (SAUO)
MIDB .... Misr Iran Development Bank
MiDBA....... Detroit Bar Association, Detroit, MI [*Library symbol*] [*Library of Congress*] (LCLS)
MidBay...... Middle Bay Oil Co., Inc. [*Associated Press*] (SAG)
MiDbEI ...... Edison Institute [*Henry Ford Museum and Greenfield Village*] Library, Dearborn, MI [*Library symbol*] [*Library of Congress*] (LCLS)
MiDbF....... Ford Motor Co., Dearborn, MI [*Library symbol*] [*Library of Congress*] (LCLS)
MiDbGS..... Church of Jesus Christ of Latter-Day Saints, Genealogical Society Library, Dearborn Stake Branch, LDS Chapel, Dearborn, MI [*Library symbol*] [*Library of Congress*] (LCLS)
MiDbHi...... Dearborn Historical Museum, Dearborn, MI [*Library symbol*] [*Library of Congress*] (LCLS)
MidBk....... Midland Bank PLC [*Associated Press*] (SAG)
MiDbME..... Society of Manufacturing Engineers, Dearborn, MI [*Library symbol*] [*Library of Congress*] (LCLS)
MIDBO ..... Middleboro, MA [*American Association of Railroads railroad junction routing code*]
MidbO....... Oakwood Hospital, Dearborn, MI [*Library symbol*] [*Library of Congress*] (LCLS)
MiDbU....... University of Michigan, Dearborn Campus, Dearborn, MI [*Library symbol*] [*Library of Congress*] (LCLS)
MIDBX....... Mgn. Stanley D. Witter Mid-Cap Growth Cl.B [*Mutual fund ticker symbol*] (SG)
MiDC .... Detroit Chancery [*Catholic Church*] Archives, Detroit, MI [*Library symbol*] [*Library of Congress*] (LCLS)
MIDC .... MidConn Bank [*NASDAQ symbol*] (NQ)
MIDC .... Mid-Counties Delivery Service [*Common carrier symbol*]
MIDC .... Midland Continental Railroad [*Federal Railroad Administration identification code*]
MIDC .... Movement for an Independent and Democratic Cuba (EA)
MIDC .... Municipal and Industrial Disposal Co. (EFIS)
MIDCAB..... Minimally Invasive Direct Coronary Artery Bypass [*Medicine*] (MELL)
MiDCh....... Children's Hospital of Michigan, Detroit, MI [*Library symbol*] [*Library of Congress*] (LCLS)
MiDChryE... Chrysler Corp., Engineering Division, Detroit, MI [*Library symbol*] [*Library of Congress*] (LCLS)
MiDCL....... Detroit College of Law, Detroit, ME [*Library symbol*] [*Library of Congress*] (LCLS)
Midcom..... Midcom Communications, Inc. [*Associated Press*] (SAG)
MidContB... Mid Continent Bancshares, Inc. [*Associated Press*] (SAG)
MIDCRU.... Midshipman Cruise [*Navy*] (NVT)
MidCst...... Mid-Coast Bancorp, Inc. [*Associated Press*] (SAG)
MidcstE..... Midcoast Energy Resources, Inc. [*Associated Press*] (SAG)
MIDD........ Middleby Corp. [*NASDAQ symbol*] (TTSB)
MIDD........ Middlesex Equipment Company [*NCIC trailer make code*]
MIDDB ...... Middlesboro, KY [*American Association of Railroads railroad junction routing code*]
MIDDL....... Middleton, NS [*American Association of Railroads railroad junction routing code*]
MIDDLE..... Microprogram Design Description Language [*1977*] [*Computer science*] (CSR)
Middlebury C... Middlebury College (GAGS)
MiDDS ...... Duns Scotus College, Detroit, MI [*Library symbol*] [*Library of Congress*] (LCLS)
MIDDS ...... Meteorological Interactive Data Display System (ACAE)
MIDDS/MEIDAS... Meteorological Interactive Display Data System/Man Computer Interactive Data Access System (SAUS)
Middx .... Middlesex [*County in England*] (ODBW)
MIDDX ...... Middlesex [*County in England*]
Middx Sit... Sittings for Middlesex at Nisi Prius [*A publication*] (DLA)
MIDE......... Midway Engineering Company [*NCIC trailer make code*]
MIDEASTFOR... Middle East Force [*Military*] (AABC)
Mid East L Rev... Middle East Law Review [*A publication*] (DLA)
MIDEAST MI LIB... Mideastern Michigan Library Cooperative [*Library network*]
MiDec....... Van Buren County Library, Decatur, MI [*Library symbol*] [*Library of Congress*] (LCLS)
MiDecD ..... Decatur Township Library, Webster Memorial Library Building, Decatur, MI [*Library symbol*] [*Library of Congress*] (LCLS)
MiDeck..... Deckerville Public Library, Deckerville, MI [*Library symbol*] [*Library of Congress*] (LCLS)
MiDecV ..... Van Buren County Library, Webster Memorial Library Building, Decatur, MI [*Library symbol*] [*Library of Congress*] (LCLS)
MiDEd....... Detroit Edison Co., Detroit, MI [*Library symbol*] [*Library of Congress*] (LCLS)
MIDEF....... Microprocedure Definition
MIDEFO..... Mission Debrief Forms (CINC)
MIDEH....... Indigenous Humanist Democratic Movement (SAUO)
MiDelD...... Delton District Library, Delton, MI [*Library symbol*] [*Library of Congress*] (LCLS)
MIDELEC.... Midlands Electricity Board (SAUO)
MIDES....... Missile Detection System
MiDet........ De Tour Area School and Public Library, De Tour Village, MI [*Library symbol*] [*Library of Congress*] (LCLS)
MIDET....... Military Intelligence Detachment (ACAE)
MiDew ...... De Witt Public Library, De Witt, MI [*Library symbol*] [*Library of Congress*] (LCLS)
MiDex....... Dexter District Library, Dexter, MI [*Library symbol*] [*Library of Congress*] (LCLS)
MIDEX....... Medium-Class Explorer
MIDF .... Major Item Data File (AABC)
MIDF .... Malaysian Industrial Development Finance Co. (SAUO)
MIDF .... Multiple Input Describing Function (PDAA)
MIDFC....... Malaysian Industrial Development Finance Company (SAUO)
MiDG .... Gale Research Co., Detroit, MI [*Library symbol*] [*Library of Congress*] (LCLS)
Mid G .... Graduate Midwife
MIDGET..... Modular Integrated Digital Equipment Tester (ACAE)
MiDGH ...... Detroit General Hospital, Medical Library, Detroit, MI [*Library symbol*] [*Library of Congress*] (LCLS)
MiDGM-L ... General Motors World Headquarters, General Motors Law Library, Detroit, MI [*Library symbol*] [*Library of Congress*] (LCLS)
MiDGrH ..... Grace Hospital, Detroit, MI [*Library symbol*] [*Library of Congress*] (LCLS)
MIDH .... Middletown & Hummelstown Railroad Co. [*AAR code*]
MIDH .... Mouvement pour l'Instauration de la Democratie en Haiti [*Political party*] (EY)
MidHag ..... Midrash ha-Gadol (BJA)
MiDHF....... Henry Ford Hospital, Detroit, MI [*Library symbol*] [*Library of Congress*] (LCLS)

MiDHH ...... Harper Hospital, Department of Libraries, Detroit, MI [*Library symbol*] [*Library of Congress*] (LCLS)
MiDHi .... Detroit Historical Society, Detroit, MI [*Library symbol*] [*Library of Congress*] (LCLS)
MIDI .... Manufacturer Association (SAUO)
Mid I .... Middle Insomnia [*Medicine*] (EDAA)
MIDI .... Midisoft Corp. [*NASDAQ symbol*] (SAG)
MIDI .... Midwest Industries [*NCIC trailer make code*]
MIDI .... Minnesota Infant Development Inventory [*Child development test*] [*Psychology*]
MIDI .... Miss Distance Indicator (MCD)
MIDI .... Musical Instrument Digital Interface [*Port*] [*Socket on an electronic synthesizer that permits a direct computer connection*]
MIDI .... Record Lab Corp. [*OTCBB symbol*]
MiDi .... Windsor Township Library, Dimondale, MI [*Library symbol*] [*Library of Congress*] (LCLS)
MIDIRS ...... Midwives Information and Resource Service [*British*] (EAIO)
Midisoft ..... Midisoft Corp. [*Associated Press*] (SAG)
MIDIST ...... Mission Interministerielle de l'Information Scientifique et Technique [*Interministerial Mission for Scientific and Technical Information*] [*France*] [*Information service or system*] (IID)
MiDIT .... Detroit Institute of Technology, Detroit, MI [*Library symbol*] [*Library of Congress*] (LCLS)
MidIwa ...... Mid Iowa Financial Corp. [*Associated Press*] (SAG)
MIDIZ .... Mid-Canada Identification Zone
MidJob ...... Midrash Job (BJA)
MidJonah ... Midrash Jonah (BJA)
MiDL .... Michigan Library Consortium, Wayne State University, Detroit, MI [*Library symbol*] [*Library of Congress*] (LCLS)
MIDL .... Midland [*English dialect*] (ROG)
MIDL .... Midland Industries [*NCIC trailer make code*]
MIDL .... Midlantic Corp. [*NASDAQ symbol*] (NQ)
MIDL .... Miniature Interoperable Data Link (ACAE)
MIDL .... Modular Interoperable Data Link (ACAE)
MIDLA .... Midland, IN [*American Association of Railroads railroad junction routing code*]
MIDLAT ..... Middle Latitude [*Navigation*]
MidlBk ...... Midland Bank PLC [*Associated Press*] (SAG)
Midlby .... Middleby Corp. [*Associated Press*] (SAG)
MidlCp ...... Midlantic Corp. [*Associated Press*] (SAG)
MIDLD .... Midland, ON [*American Association of Railroads railroad junction routing code*]
MidLekTov ... Midrash Lekah Tov (BJA)
MidlFn ...... Midland Financial Group [*Associated Press*] (SAG)
MIDLIS ...... Multifamily Insurance and Direct Loan Information System [*Department of Housing and Urban Development*] (GFGA)
MIDLN .... Midland, PA [*American Association of Railroads railroad junction routing code*]
Midlnd ...... Midland Co. [*Associated Press*] (SAG)
MIDLNET .... Midwest Regional Library Network
MidlRs ...... Midland Resources, Inc. [*Associated Press*] (SAG)
MiDM .... Marygrove College, Detroit, MI [*Library symbol*] [*Library of Congress*] (LCLS)
MiDMC ...... Mercy College of Detroit, Detroit, MI [*Library symbol*] [*Library of Congress*] (LCLS)
MiDMch ...... Mariners' Church, Detroit, MI [*Library symbol*] [*Library of Congress*] (LCLS)
MID-MO ..... Mid-Month [*Amount of pay to be received by payee on the 15th day of the month*] (AABC)
MiDMP ...... Merrill-Palmer Institute, Detroit, MI [*Library symbol*] [*Library of Congress*] (LCLS)
MIDMS ...... Machine Independent Data Management System [*Defense Intelligence Agency*] (MCD)
MiDMtC ..... Mount Carmel Mercy Hospital, Medical Library, Detroit, MI [*Library symbol*] [*Library of Congress*] (LCLS)
MIDN .... Midshipman [*Navy*]
MIDNET ..... Midland Network (NITA)
MIDnet ...... [*The*] Midwest Network [*Computer science*] (TNIG)
midnoc ...... Midnight (DAVI)
MiDo .... Dorr Township Library, Dorr, MI [*Library symbol*] [*Library of Congress*] (LCLS)
MIDOC ...... Mildew-Induced Defacement of Organic Coatings
MidOcn ...... Mid Ocean Ltd. [*Associated Press*] (SAG)
MiDolb ...... Osceola Township Public and School Library, Dollar Bay, MI [*Library symbol*] [*Library of Congress*] (LCLS)
MIDOP ...... Missile Doppler
MIDOR ...... Miss Distance Optical Recorder [*Military*] (PDAA)
MIDORI ..... Modern Information and Documentation Organizing and Rearrangement, Incorporated (SAUO)
MIDOT .... Multiple Interferometer Determination of Trajectories
MiDow ...... Dowagiac Public Library, Dowagiac, MI [*Library symbol*] [*Library of Congress*] (LCLS)
MIDP .... Major Item Distribution Plan (AABC)
MIDP .... Microbiology and Infectious Diseases Program [*Bethesda, MD*] [*National Institute of Allergy and Infectious Diseases*] [*Department of Health and Human Services*] (GRD)
MIDP .... Microwave Induced Delayed Phosphorescence (AAEL)
MIDP .... Motor Industry Development Program
MiDP .... Providence Hospital, School of Nursing, Detroit, MI [*Library symbol*] [*Library of Congress*] (LCLS)
MIDPA .... Middletown, PA [*American Association of Railroads railroad junction routing code*]
MID PAC .... Mid-Continent Oil and Gas Association PAC [*Washington, DC*] (PACS)
MID PAC .... Mid Manhattan PAC [*New York, NY*] (PACS)
MIDPAC ..... Mid-Pacific
MIDPAC ..... US Army Forces, Middle Pacific [*Name commonly used for AFMIDPAC*] [*World War II*]
MiDPD ...... Parke, Davis & Co., Detroit, MI [*Library symbol*] [*Library of Congress*] (LCLS)
MIDPM ...... Member of the Institute of Data Processing Management [*British*] (DCTA)
MidProv ..... Midrash Proverbs (BJA)
MidPs .... Midrash Tehillim [*or The Midrash on Psalms*] (BJA)
MIDPT .... Midpoint (FAAC)
MIDQ .... Mid-Equipment Corporation [*NCIC trailer make code*]
MidQ .... Midwest Quarterly: A Journal of Contemporary Thought [*A publication*] (ANEX)
MIDR .... Mandatory Incident and Defect Reporting (NATG)
MidR .... Midland Resources, Inc. [*Associated Press*] (SAG)
Midr .... Midrash [*Interpretation of Old Testament writings*] (BJA)
MIDR .... Mosaicked Image Data Record (SAUS)
MID-RATS ... Midnight Rations [*Navy*]
MiDRI .... Rehabilitiation Institute, Detroit, MI [*Library symbol*] [*Library of Congress*] (LCLS)
MidrR .... Midrash Rabbah (BJA)
MidrSong ... Midrash to the Song of Songs (BJA)
MiDry .... Dryden Township Library, Dryden, MI [*Library symbol*] [*Library of Congress*] (LCLS)
MIDS .... Management Information and Data Systems (NVT)
MIDS .... Management Information and Decision System (VLIE)
MIDS .... Management Information Decision Support [*Computer science*] (CIST)
MIDS .... Management Information Decision System [*Computer science*] (CIST)
MIDS .... Management Information Display System (MCD)
MIDS .... Marketing Information Data Systems, Inc. [*Information service or system*] (IID)
MIDS .... Matrix Information and Directory Services
MIDS .... Matrix Information and Directory Services, Inc.
MIDS .... Midas [*NCIC truck make code*]
MIDS .... Midas International [*NCIC trailer make code*]
MIDS .... Mid-South Insurance Co. [*NASDAQ symbol*] (NQ)
MIDS .... Miniature Integrated Data System (MCD)
MIDS .... Miscarriage Infant Death Stillbirth Support Group
MIDS .... Missile Ignition and Destruct Simulator
MIDS .... Mission Information Dispensing System (VLIE)
MIDS .... Movable Instrument Drive System [*Nuclear energy*] (NRCH)
MIDS .... Movement Information Distribution Station
MIDS .... MPAC Information Data System (SAUO)
MIDS .... Multifunctional Information Distribution System [*NATO*] (MCD)
MIDS .... Multimode Information Distribution System
Midsag ...... Midsagittal [*Medicine*]
MidSam ..... Midrash Samuel (BJA)
MIDSD ...... Management Information and Data Systems Division [*Environmental Protection Agency*] (GFGA)
MiDSH ...... Sacred Heart Seminary, Detroit, MI [*Library symbol*] [*Library of Congress*] (LCLS)
MIDSIM ..... Maxwell International Development Simulation
MIDSIM ..... Midcourse Simulation (ACAE)
MiDSn .... Sinai Hospital, Detroit, MI [*Library symbol*] [*Library of Congress*] (LCLS)
Mids ND .... [*A*] Midsummer Night's Dream [*Shakespearean work*] (BARN)
MidSou ...... Mid-South Insurance Co. [*Associated Press*] (SAG)
MIDSR ...... Midsummer (ROG)
MidStat ..... Mid-States PLC [*Associated Press*] (SAG)
Midsth .... Midsouth Bancorp, Inc. [*Associated Press*] (SAG)
MidsthB ..... Midsouth Bancorp, Inc. [*Associated Press*] (SAG)
MIDT .... Midwest Mini-Tote Company [*NCIC trailer make code*]
MIDTA .... Member of the International Dance Teachers' Association [*British*] (DBQ)
MidTan ...... Midrash Tanna'im on Deuteronomy (BJA)
Mid'Tehil .... Midrash Tehillim [*or The Midrash on Psalms*] (BJA)
Mid Tenn St U ... Middle Tennessee State University (GAGS)
MIDTRARON ... Midshipman Training Squadron [*Navy*] (NVT)
MIDU .... Deugro Transports [*Intermodal shipping container symbol*] (TVRC)
MIDU .... Malfunction Insertion and Display Unit [*Aviation*]
MIDU .... Missile Ignition Delay Unit (SAUS)
MiDU .... University of Detroit, Detroit, MI [*Library symbol*] [*Library of Congress*] (LCLS)
MiDU-C ..... University of Detroit, Colombiere Campus, Clarkston, MI [*Library symbol*] [*Library of Congress*] (LCLS)
MiDU-D ..... University of Detroit, Dental Library, Detroit, MI [*Library symbol*] [*Library of Congress*] (LCLS)
MiDU-L ...... University of Detroit, Law Library, Detroit, MI [*Library symbol*] [*Library of Congress*] (LCLS)
MIDVA .... Midvale, UT [*American Association of Railroads railroad junction routing code*]
MIDW .... Midwestern (AFM)
MIDW .... Midwest Mobile Homes & Trailer [*NCIC trailer make code*]
MIDW .... Midwest Motor Express [*Common carrier symbol*]
MiDW .... Wayne State University, Detroit, MI [*Library symbol*] [*Library of Congress*] (LCLS)
MIDWA ...... Midway, IL [*American Association of Railroads railroad junction routing code*]
MiDW-AL ... Wayne State University, Walter P. Reuther Library of Labor and Urban Affairs, Archivesof Labor History and Urban Affairs, Detroit, MI [*Library symbol*] [*Library of Congress*] (LCLS)
MidwBn ..... Midwest Bancshares [*Associated Press*] (SAG)
MiDWc ...... Wayne County Records, Court House, Wayne County, Detroit, MI [*Library symbol*] [*Library of Congress*] (LCLS)

MiDWcC .... Wayne County Community College, Detroit, MI [*Library symbol*] [*Library of Congress*] (LCLS)
MIDWEEK... Manager Integrated Dictionary Week [*Manager Software Products*] (EA)
MIDWEST... Midwest Automated Clearing House Association (TBD)
MIDWESTNAVFACENGCOM... Midwest Division Naval Facilities Engineering Command
Midwest S U... Midwestern State University (GAGS)
MidwGm .... Midway Games, Inc. [*Associated Press*] (SAG)
MidwGr ..... Midwest Grain Products, Inc. [*Associated Press*] (SAG)
MiDW-L..... Wayne State University, Law Library, Detroit, MI [*Library symbol*] [*Library of Congress*] (LCLS)
MiDW-M .... Wayne State University, Medical Library, Detroit, MI [*Library symbol*] [*Library of Congress*] (LCLS)
MiDW-Mi ... Wayne State University, Miles Manuscript Collection, Detroit, MI [*Library symbol*] [*Library of Congress*] [*Obsolete*] (LCLS)
MiDW-P..... Wayne State University, School of Pharmacy, Detroit, MI [*Library symbol*] [*Library of Congress*] (LCLS)
MidwRE..... Midwest Real Estate Shopping Centers Ltd. [*Associated Press*] (SAG)
MiDW-S..... Wayne State University, Kresge-Hooker Science Library, Detroit, MI [*Library symbol*] [*Library of Congress*] (LCLS)
MIDX .... Midwest Energy Services [*Private rail car owner code*]
MIE .... Aero Premier de Mexico, SA de CV [*Mexico*] [*FAA designator*] (FAAC)
MiE .... East Lansing Public Library, East Lansing, MI [*Library symbol*] [*Library of Congress*] (LCLS)
MIE .... European Federation for Medical Informatics [*Sweden*] (EAIO)
MIE .... Hungarian Association for the Protection of Industrial Property (SAUO)
MIE .... Magnetic Isotope Effect [*Physics*]
MIE .... Magnetron Ion Etching [*Semiconductor technology*]
MIE .... Major Items of Equipment
MIE .... Management Improvement and Evaluation
MIE .... Management Information Element [*Telecommunications*] (OSI)
MIE .... Maserati Information Exchange (EA)
MIE .... Mass Inertia Excitation
MIE .... Master of Industrial Engineering
MIE .... Master of Irrigation Engineering
MIE .... Medical Improvement Expectation (MELL)
MIE .... Member of the Institute of Engineers (SAUO)
MIE .... Member of the Institution of Mechanical Engineers (SAUO)
MIE .... Merrill Lynch & Co. "MITTS" 98 [*NYSE symbol*] (SPSG)
MIE .... Meteor Ionizing Efficiency
Mi-E .... Michigan State Library, Escanaba Branch, Escanaba, MI [*Library symbol*] [*Library of Congress*] (LCLS)
MiE .... Minimum Effect [*Pharmacology*]
MIE .... Minimum Ignition Energy
MIE .... Mission-Independent Equipment [*NASA*]
MIE .... Mobile Inspection Equipment (SAA)
MIE .... Modal Identification Experiment [*NASA*] (SPST)
MIE .... Monitor Inertial Electronics (ACAE)
MIE .... Muncie [*Indiana*] [*Airport symbol*] (OAG)
MIE .... Muncie, IN [*Location identifier*] [*FAA*] (FAAL)
MIEA......... Master Information Exchange Agreement (SAUS)
MIEA......... Member of the Institution of Engineers, Australia (SAUO)
MIEA......... Music Industry Educators Association (EA)
MiEad .... East Detroit Memorial Library, East Detroit, MI [*Library symbol*] [*Library of Congress*] (LCLS)
MiEat........ Eaton Rapids Public Library, Eaton Rapids, MI [*Library symbol*] [*Library of Congress*] (LCLS)
MIEAWA..... Meat Industries Employers' Association of Western Australia
MIEC......... Branche Africaine du Mouvement International des Etudiants Catholiques [*African International Movement of Catholic Students - AIMCS*] (EAIO)
MiEc......... Eau Claire District Library, Eau Claire, MI [*Library symbol*] [*Library of Congress*] (LCLS)
MIEC......... Medical Insurance Exchange of California [*Medicine*] (EDAA)
MIEC......... Meteorological Information Extraction Center
MIEC......... Military Intelligence Exchange Center (CINC)
MIEC......... Mixed Ionic and Electronic Conducting [*Polymers*]
MIEC......... [*Meteorological Information Extraction Center*] Operator Guide
MIEC......... Pax Romana, Mouvement International des Etudiants Catholiques [*Pax Romana, International Movement of Catholic Students - IMCS*] [*Paris, France*] (EAIO)
MIECI........ Muslim Educational and Cultural Institute [*University of Cincinnati*] (EARSL)
MIECO....... Marshall Islands Import-Export Company (SAUO)
MIED .... Member of the Institution of Engineering Designers [*British*] (DBQ)
MIEE......... Mechanical, Instrument, and Electrical Engineering [*Department of Employment*] [*British*]
MIEE......... Member of the Institution of Electrical Engineers [*Formerly, AMIEE*] [*British*] (EY)
MIEEE .... Member of the Institute of Electrical and Electronic Engineers
MIEETAT .... Major Improvements in Electronic Effectiveness through Advanced Technology (MCD)
MIEF......... Master Imagery Exchange Format (MCD)
MIEI .... Member of the Institution of Engineering Inspection [*British*]
MIE(Ind) .... Member of the Institution of Engineers, India
MiElb........ Elberta Public Library, Elberta, MI [*Library symbol*] [*Library of Congress*] (LCLS)
MIElecIE .... Corporate Member of the Institution of Electrical and Electronics Incorporated Engineers [*British*] (DBQ)
MiElk........ Elk Rapids District Library, Elk Rapids, MI [*Library symbol*] [*Library of Congress*] (LCLS)
MiEm........ Glen Lake Community Library, Empire, MI [*Library symbol*] [*Library of Congress*] (LCLS)
MIEM........ Master in International Economics and Management (ECON)
MIEM........ Master Member of the Institute of Executives and Managers [*British*] (DBQ)
MIEM........ Masters Degree in International Economics and Management (ECON)
MiEM........ Michigan State University, East Lansing, MI [*Library symbol*] [*Library of Congress*] (LCLS)
MIE Mgmt.. Master of Industrial Engineering Management (PGP)
MiEmp ...... Glen Lake Community Library, Empire, MI [*Library symbol*] [*Library of Congress*] (LCLS)
MI Eng ...... Master of Industrial Engineering
MIER .... Management-Initiated Early Retirement (ADA)
MIER .... Military Intelligence Enlisted Reserve (SAUO)
MIERE....... Member of the British Institute of Electronic and Radio Engineers (SAUO)
MIERE....... Member of the Institution of Electronic and Radio Engineers [*Formerly, M Brit IRE*] [*British*]
MIERS....... Modernized Imagery Exploitation and Reporting System (MCD)
MIES......... Member of the Institution of Engineers and Shipbuilders, Scotland
MIES......... Metastable Impact Electron Spectroscopy (SAUS)
MIES......... Modernised-Imagery Exploitation System (SAUS)
MIES......... Multi-Imagery Exploitation System
MiEsc........ Escanaba Public Library, Escanaba, MI [*Library symbol*] [*Library of Congress*] (LCLS)
MiEscB...... Bay De Noc Community College, Escanaba, MI [*Library symbol*] [*Library of Congress*] (LCLS)
MIESR....... Matrix Isolation and Electron Spin Resonance [*Analytical chemistry*]
MIESS....... Member of the Institution of Engineers and Shipbuilders, Scotland (SAUO)
MIEU .... Mi Engineering [*Intermodal shipping container symbol*] (TVRC)
MiEv......... Evart Public Library, Evart, MI [*Library symbol*] [*Library of Congress*] (LCLS)
MiEw .... McMillan Township Library, Ewen, MI [*Library symbol*] [*Library of Congress*] (LCLS)
MI Ex........ Member of the Institute of Export [*British*]
MIExE .... Member of the Institute of Executive Engineers and Officers [*British*] (DBQ)
MIEx(Grad)... Member of the Institute of Export [*British*] (DBQ)
MIExpE....... Member of the Institute of Explosives Engineers [*British*] (DBQ)
MIEZ......... Midwest Energy [*Federal Railroad Administration identification code*]
MIF .... International Falcon Movement (SAUO)
MIF .... Macrophage Inhibition Factor [*Immunology*] (QSUL)
MIF .... Macrophage Inhibitory Factor [*Immunology*]
MIF .... Maker Interchange Format [*Computer science*] (CDE)
MIF .... Malfunction Investigations File (MCD)
MIF .... Management Information File [*Computer science*] (PCM)
MIF .... Management Information Format [*Computer science*]
MIF .... Manual Intervention Facility
MIF .... MARC [*Machine-Readable Cataloging*] International Format
MIF .... Maritime Industries Forum (EURO)
MIF .... Maritime Interception Force (DOMA)
MIF .... Maritime Interdiction Force (SAUO)
MIF .... Marker Interchange Format (SAUO)
MIF .... Mass-Independent Fractionation [*Chemistry*]
MIF .... Master Index File
MIF .... Master Inventory File (AFIT)
MIF .... Master Item File (MCD)
MIF .... Maximal Inspiratory Flow [*Medicine*]
MIF .... Maximum Inspiratory Force [*Medicine*] (MELL)
MIF .... Medina, OH [*Location identifier*] [*FAA*] (FAAL)
MIF .... Melanocyte-Inhibiting Factor [*Endocrinology*]
MIF .... Melanocyte-Stimulating-Hormone Release Inhibiting Factor [*Also, MRIF*] [*Endocrinology*]
MIF .... Melanotropin Inhibiting Factor [*Biochemistry*]
MIF .... Melbourne International Festival [*Australia*]
MIF .... Member of the Institute of Fuel (SAUO)
MIF .... Membrane Immunofluorescence [*Analytical biochemistry*]
MIF .... Merthiolate-Iodine-Formaldehyde [*Technique*]
MIF .... Mesoderm-Inducing Factor [*Embryology*]
MIF .... Michigan Insurance Federation (EARSL)
MIF .... Midinspiratory Flow [*Medicine*] (DMAA)
MIF .... Mid-inspiratory Flow Rate [*Medicine*] (EDAA)
MIF .... Migration Inhibition [*or Inhibitory*] Factor [*Cytology*]
MIF .... Milk Industry Foundation (EA)
MIF .... Milk in First [*Tea-pouring procedure*]
MIF .... Miners' International Federation [*See also FIM*] [*Brussels, Belgium*] (EAIO)
MIF .... Minimum Internetworking Functionality (VLIE)
MIF .... Missile-in-Flight
MIF .... Mixed Immunofluorescence [*Medicine*] (MAE)
MIF .... Mobile Instrument Facility
MIF .... Modernization and Implementation Facility (SAUO)
MIF .... Module Integration Facility (SSD)
MIF .... Monopulse Interference Filter
MIF .... Mortgage Indemnity Fund [*Veterans Administration*]
MIF .... Mortgage Insurance Fund (FOTI)
MIF .... Multisource Intelligence File (MCD)
MIF .... MuniInsured Fund Inc. [*AMEX symbol*] (SPSG)
MIF .... MuniInsred Fund [*AMEX symbol*] (TTSB)
MIF .... Myocardial Infarction [*Cardiology*] (DHSM)
MIFA......... Member of the Institute of Foresters of Australia (SAUO)
MIFA......... Michigan Interscholastic Forensic Association (EARSL)
MIFA......... Mitomycin C, Fluorouracil, Adriamycin [*Antineoplastic drug regimen*]
MIFACS ..... Medical Institutions' Financial Accounting System

MI-FA-MI.... Misery, Famine, Misery [*Said to be "earth's song," in theory that all planets emit musical sounds governed by their paths around the sun*]
MIFAS .... Mechanized Integrated Financial Accounting System [*Department of State*]
MIFASS ..... Marine Integral (or Integrated) Fire and Air Support System (SAUO)
MIFASS ..... Marine Integrated Fire and Air Support System
MiFaw....... Farwell Public Library, Farwell, MI [*Library symbol*] [*Library of Congress*] (LCLS)
MIFC......... Madonna International Fan Club [*Defunct*] (EA)
MIFC......... Merthiolate-Iodine Formalin Concentration
MIFC......... Mid Iowa Financial Corp. [*NASDAQ symbol*] (SAG)
MIFC......... Mid-Iowa Finl [*NASDAQ symbol*] (TTSB)
MIFCT .... Moscow Institute of Fine Chemical Technology (SAUO)
MIFD .... Material Information Flow Device [*Military*] (AFM)
MIFE......... Manila International Futures Exchange [*Philippines*] (NUMA)
MIFE......... Minimum Independent Failure Element
MIFERSO ... Eastern Senegal Iron Ore Mining Co. (SAUO)
MIFERSO ... Eastern Senegal Iron Ore Mining Company (SAUS)
MIFF......... Management Information Format File [*Computer science*]
MIFF......... Member of the Institute of Freight Forwarders [*British*] (ODBW)
MiFg......... Fairgrove Township Library, Fairgrove, MI [*Library symbol*] [*Library of Congress*] (LCLS)
MIFG .... Micro Focus Group Ltd. [*NASDAQ symbol*] (SAG)
MIFG .... Patches of Shallow Fog not Deeper Than Two Meters [*NWS*] (FAAC)
MIFGY....... Micro Focus Grp ADS [*NASDAQ symbol*] (TTSB)
MIFI .... Missile In-Flight Indicator
MiFil......... Fife Lake Public Library, Fife Lake, MI [*Library symbol*] [*Library of Congress*] (LCLS)
MIFIR........ Microwave Instantaneous Frequency Indication Receiver (MCD)
MIFirE....... Member of the Institution of Fire Engineers [*British*] (DCTA)
MIFireE ..... Member of the Institution of Fire Engineers [*British*] (EY)
MIFL......... Master International Frequency List
MiFli......... Flint Public Library, Flint, MI [*Library symbol*] [*Library of Congress*] (LCLS)
MiFliACS.... AC Spark Plug Co., General Motors Corp., Flint, MI [*Library symbol*] [*Library of Congress*] (LCLS)
MiFliC .... University of Michigan at Flint, and Charles Stewart Mott Community College, Flint, MI [*Library symbol*] [*Library of Congress*] (LCLS)
MiFliG....... GMI Engineering and Management Institute, Flint, MI [*Library symbol*] [*Library of Congress*] (LCLS)
MiFos .... Watertown Township Library, Fostoria, MI [*Library symbol*] [*Library of Congress*] (LCLS)
MiFow....... Fowlerville Public Library, Fowlerville, MI [*Library symbol*] [*Library of Congress*] (LCLS)
MIFR .... Master International Frequency Register
MIFR .... Maximal Inspiratory Flow Rate [*Medicine*]
MIFR .... Minor Frame (ACAE)
MIFR .... Monitored International Frequency Register (NITA)
MIFR .... Mullerian Inhibiting Factor [*Medicine*] (MELL)
MIFR .... Multiband Infrared Filter Radiometer
MiFra........ Frankfort City Library, Frankfort, MI [*Library symbol*] [*Library of Congress*] (LCLS)
MiFram ..... James E. Wickson Memorial Library, Frankenmuth, MI [*Library symbol*] [*Library of Congress*] (LCLS)
MiFras ...... Fraser Public Library, Fraser, MI [*Library symbol*] [*Library of Congress*] (LCLS)
MiFrem ..... Fremont Public Library, Fremont, MI [*Library symbol*] [*Library of Congress*] (LCLS)
MIFS......... Material Information Flow System [*Military*] (AFM)
MIFS......... Multiplex Interferometric Fourier Spectroscopy
MIFS......... Myanmar-IRRI Farming Systems (SAUO)
M/IFS........ VM/Interactive File Snaring (SAUS)
MIFSA........ Missile In-Flight Safety Approval (MUGU)
MIFT......... Manchester International Freight Terminal [*British*] (DS)
MIFU .... Mitsubishi Fuso [*NCIC truck make code*]
MIFV......... Mechanised Infantry Fighting Vehicle (SAUS)
Mig .... De Migratione Abrahami [*Philo*] (BJA)
MIG......... Mach Interface Generator (SAUS)
MIG......... Magnetic Injection Gun (IEEE)
MIG......... Magnetized Ionized Gas
MIG......... Malaria Immune Globulin
MIG......... Management Information Guide [*Reference series*]
MIG......... Marine Industry Group (SAUO)
MIG......... Mars Investigation Group [*Defunct*] (EA)
MIG......... MCE Interface Group (SAUO)
MIG......... Meadowbrook Insurance Group [*NYSE symbol*] (SAG)
MIG......... Meadowbrook Insurance Grp [*NYSE symbol*] (TTSB)
MIG......... Measles Immune Globulin [*Immunology*]
MIG......... Meat Innovation Grant
MIG......... Medial Inferior Geniculate Artery [*Anatomy*]
MIG......... Medical Information Group (SAUO)
MIG......... Medicare Insured Group (HCT)
M-Ig .... Membrane Immunoglobulin [*Immunology*]
MIG......... Message Identification Group (SAUO)
MIG......... Metal-Inert-Gas [*Underwater welding*]
MIG......... Metallic Inert Gas (SAUS)
MIG......... Methane Inert Gas (MCD)
MIG......... Migi [*NCIC car model code*]
Mig .... Mignon [*Horticulture*]
MIG......... Migration (SAUO)
MIG......... Mikoyan and Gurevich [*Acronym used as designation for a Russian aircraft and is formed from the names of the aircraft's designers*]
MIG......... Military Intelligence Group (MCD)
MIG......... Military Intelligence Guide (MCD)
MIG......... Millington, TN [*Location identifier*] [*FAA*] (FAAL)
MIG......... Ming Mines Ltd. [*Vancouver Stock Exchange symbol*]
MIG......... Miniature Integrating Gyroscope
MIG......... Minimum Income Guarantee
MIG......... Moody's Investment Grade
MIG......... Mortgage Indemnity Guarantee (WDAA)
MIG......... Multilevel Interconnect Generator
MIG-1 .... Moody's Investment Grade (DFIT)
MIGA .... Multilateral Investment Guarantee Agency [*World Bank*]
MIGA .... Multinational Investment Guarantee Agency (SAUO)
MiGal........ Galesburg Memorial Library, Galesburg, MI [*Library symbol*] [*Library of Congress*] (LCLS)
MI/GAL...... Miles per Gallon (WDAA)
MiGali....... Galien Township Public Library, Galien, MI [*Library symbol*] [*Library of Congress*] (LCLS)
MIGasE...... Member of the Institution of Gas Engineers [*British*]
MiGay .... Gaylord-Otsego County Public Library, Gaylord, MI [*Library symbol*] [*Library of Congress*] (LCLS)
MIGB .... Millinery Institute of Great Britain (BI)
MiGc......... Garden City Public Library, Garden City, MI [*Library symbol*] [*Library of Congress*] (LCLS)
MIGCAP..... MIG [*Mikoyan and Gurevich*] Combat Air Patrol (DNAB)
MIGD......... Member of the Institute of Grocery Distribution [*British*] (DBQ)
MIGE .... Missile Impact and Gaseous Explosions (HEAS)
MIGeol ...... Member of the Institution of Geologists [*British*] (DBQ)
MIGET....... Miniature Interface General-Purpose Economy Terminal [*Computer science*] (MHDB)
MIgG .... Monkey Immunoglobulin G [*Immunology*]
MIGG......... MRA Implementation Guide Group (SAUO)
MiGh .... Loutit Library, Grand Haven, MI [*Library symbol*] [*Library of Congress*] (LCLS)
MIGI......... Meridian Insrance Gp [*NASDAQ symbol*] (TTSB)
MIGI......... Meridian Insurance Group, Inc. [*NASDAQ symbol*] (NQ)
MIGITS...... Miniature Integrated GPS/INS Tactical System (SAUS)
MiGl......... Gladstone Public Library, Gladstone, MI [*Library symbol*] [*Library of Congress*] (LCLS)
MiGlad ...... Gladwin County Library, Gladwin, MI [*Library symbol*] [*Library of Congress*] (LCLS)
MiGlad-B ... Gladwin County Library, Beaverton Branch Library, Beaverton, MI [*Library symbol*] [*Library of Congress*] (LCLS)
MIGN......... Michigan Northern Railway Co., Inc. [*AAR code*]
MiGp .... Grosse Pointe Public Library, Grosse Pointe, MI [*Library symbol*] [*Library of Congress*] (LCLS)
MiGr......... Grand Rapids Public Library, Grand Rapids, MI [*Library symbol*] [*Library of Congress*] (LCLS)
MiGrA .... Aquinas College, Grand Rapids, MI [*Library symbol*] [*Library of Congress*] (LCLS)
MiGran...... Grant Public Library, Grant, MI [*Library symbol*] [*Library of Congress*] (LCLS)
MiGray...... Crawford County Library, Grayling, MI [*Library symbol*] [*Library of Congress*] (LCLS)
MiGrB .... Grand Rapids Baptist College, Grand Rapids, MI [*Library symbol*] [*Library of Congress*] (LCLS)
MiGrC .... Calvin College and Seminary, Grand Rapids, MI [*Library symbol*] [*Library of Congress*] (LCLS)
MiGre .... Greenville Public Library, Greenville, MI [*Library symbol*] [*Library of Congress*] (LCLS)
MiGrJC...... Grand Rapids Junior College, Grand Rapids, MI [*Library symbol*] [*Library of Congress*] (LCLS)
MiGrl........ Grand Ledge Public Library, Grand Ledge, MI [*Library symbol*] [*Library of Congress*] (LCLS)
MiGrL .... Grand Rapids Law Library, Grand Rapids, MI [*Library symbol*] [*Library of Congress*] (LCLS)
MiGrlP ...... Grand Ledge Public Library, Grand Ledge, MI [*Library symbol*] [*Library of Congress*] (LCLS)
MiGrMtM ... Mount Mercy Academy, Grand Rapids, MI [*Library symbol*] [*Library of Congress*] (LCLS)
MiGrW ...... Western Michigan Genealogical Society, Grand Rapids, MI [*Library symbol*] [*Library of Congress*] (LCLS)
MIGS .... MASnet Internet Gateway Server (SAUS)
MIGS .... Metal-Induced Gap States (AAEL)
MIGS .... Miniature Infrared Guidance Sensor (ACAE)
MIGS .... Montreal Institute for Genocide and Human Rights Studies [*Concordia University (Montreal, QC, Canada)*] [*Canada*] (RCD)
MIGS .... Music Industries Golfing Society [*British*] (BI)
MIGT .... Multiple Inert Gas (elimination) Technique [*Medicine*] (EDAA)
MiGw........ Forsythe Township Public Library, Gwinn, MI [*Library symbol*] [*Library of Congress*] (LCLS)
MIH......... Brownsville, TX [*Location identifier*] [*FAA*] (FAAL)
MIH......... Master of Industrial Health
MIH......... Melanocyte-Stimulating Hormone-Inhibitory Hormone [*Endocrinology*] (DAVI)
MIH......... Melanotropin Release Inhibiting Hormone (SAUS)
MIH......... Member of the Institute of Housing [*British*] (DBQ)
MIH......... Member of the Institute of Hygiene [*British*]
MIH......... Migraine with Interparoxysmal Headache [*Neurology*] (DAVI)
MIH......... Migraine with Interval Headache (MELL)
MIH......... Miles in the Hour [*Rate of military march*]
MIH......... Minimal Intermittent [*Dosage of*] Heparin [*Pharmacology*] (DAVI)
MIH......... Missing Interruption Handler [*Computer science*] (IBMDP)
MIH......... Molecule-Induced Homolysis [*Chemistry*]
MIH......... Molt Inhibitory Hormone
MIH......... Multiplex Interface Handler
MiHa .... Hart Public Library, Hart, MI [*Library symbol*] [*Library of Congress*] (LCLS)
MIHA .... Minor Histocompatibility Antigen [*Medicine*] (EDAA)

MIHA .... Move-In Housing Allowance
MiHaf........ Hartford Public Library, Hartford, MI [*Library symbol*] [*Library of Congress*] (LCLS)
MiHal........ Cromaine Library, Hartland, MI [*Library symbol*] [*Library of Congress*] (LCLS)
MiHam ...... Hamtramck Public Library, Hamtramck, MI [*Library symbol*] [*Library of Congress*] (LCLS)
MiHamb..... Hamburg Township Library, Hamburg, MI [*Library symbol*] [*Library of Congress*] (LCLS)
MiHan .... Hancock Public-School Library, Hancock, MI [*Library symbol*] [*Library of Congress*] (LCLS)
MiHanS ..... Suomi College, Hancock, MI [*Library symbol*] [*Library of Congress*] (LCLS)
MiHars ...... Harrison Public Library, Harrison, MI [*Library symbol*] [*Library of Congress*] (LCLS)
MiHarsM.... Mid-Michigan Community College, Harrison, MI [*Library symbol*] [*Library of Congress*] (LCLS)
MiHarv ...... Alcona County Library, Harrisville, MI [*Library symbol*] [*Library of Congress*] (LCLS)
MiHas .... Hastings Public Library, Hastings, MI [*Library symbol*] [*Library of Congress*] (LCLS)
MiHb .... Harbor Beach Public Library, Harbor Beach, MI [*Library symbol*] [*Library of Congress*] (LCLS)
Mi-HC .... Michigan Historical Commission, State Archives Library, Lansing, MI [*Library symbol*] [*Library of Congress*] (LCLS)
MIHC .... M. I. Hummel Club (EA)
MiHe .... Hesperia Public Library, Hesperia, MI [*Library symbol*] [*Library of Congress*] (LCLS)
MIHE .... Member of the Institute of Health Education [*British*]
MIHE .... Member of the Institution of Highway Engineers (SAUO)
MIHEc .... Member of the Institute of Home Economics [*British*] (DBQ)
MiHem ...... Mary C. Rauchholz Memorial Library, Hemlock, MI [*Library symbol*] [*Library of Congress*] (LCLS)
MIHIC .... Mile High Conference (PSS)
MiHil .... Mitchell Public Library, Hillsdale, MI [*Library symbol*] [*Library of Congress*] (LCLS)
MiHilC....... Hillsdale College, Hillsdale, MI [*Library symbol*] [*Library of Congress*] (LCLS)
MiHilm ...... Hillman Public Library, Hillman, MI [*Library symbol*] [*Library of Congress*] (LCLS)
MiHl .... Houghton Lake Public Library, Houghton Lake, MI [*Library symbol*] [*Library of Congress*] (LCLS)
MIHL .... MIH Limited'A' [*NASDAQ symbol*] (SG)
MIHM........ Master of International Health Management (PGP)
MiHM........ Michigan Technological University, Houghton, MI [*Library symbol*] [*Library of Congress*] (LCLS)
MIHO .... Miles Homes [*NASDAQ symbol*] (TTSB)
MIHO .... Miles Homes, Inc. [*NASDAQ symbol*] (SAG)
MiHol........ Herrick Public Library, Holland, MI [*Library symbol*] [*Library of Congress*] (LCLS)
MiHolH...... Hope College, Holland, MI [*Library symbol*] [*Library of Congress*] (LCLS)
MiHolW ..... Western Theological Seminary, Holland, MI [*Library symbol*] [*Library of Congress*] (LCLS)
MiHom ...... Homer Public Library, Homer, MI [*Library symbol*] [*Library of Congress*] (LCLS)
MiHow ...... Howell Carnegie Library, Howell, MI [*Library symbol*] [*Library of Congress*] (LCLS)
MiHp .... McGregor Public Library, Highland Park, MI [*Library symbol*] [*Library of Congress*] (LCLS)
MiHP .... Portage Lake District Library, Houghton, MI [*Library symbol*] [*Library of Congress*] (LCLS)
MiHpDH..... Detroit Osteopathic Hospital, Highland Park, MI [*Library symbol*] [*Library of Congress*] (LCLS)
MIHPED..... Microwave-Induced Helium Plasma Emission Detection (NATG)
MiHPL....... Portage Lake District Library, Houghton, MI [*Library symbol*] [*Library of Congress*] (LCLS)
MIHS .... Marshall Islands High School (SAUO)
MIHS .... Mercy International Health Services [*Association*] (EA)
MIHT .... Member of the Institution of Highways and Transportation [*British*] (DBQ)
MIHT .... Moscow Institute of Heat Technology (IGSL)
MiHu .... Hudson Public Library, Hudson, MI [*Library symbol*] [*Library of Congress*] (LCLS)
MiHudv...... Hudsonville Public Library, Hudsonville, MI [*Library symbol*] [*Library of Congress*] (LCLS)
MIHVE....... Member of the Institution of Heating and Ventilating Engineers [*British*]
MII........... Caddo Mills, TX [*Location identifier*] [*FAA*] (FAAL)
MII........... Management Interest Inventory [*Test*]
MII........... Manufacturing Impact Item (MCD)
MII........... Marilia [*Brazil*] [*Airport symbol*] (OAG)
MII........... Mark II [*NCIC car model code*]
MII........... Masonry Institute of Iowa (EARSL)
MII........... Medical Imaging Informatics (RALS)
MII........... Miami International Airport, FL [*Amtrak Busline code*]
MI/I.......... Microinches per Inch (KSC)
MII........... Microsoft, IBM, Intel (SAUO)
MII........... Military Intelligence Interpreter
MII........... Military Intelligence Interrogation
MII........... Mineral Information Institute (EA)
MII........... Mini [*NCIC car model code*]
MII........... Ministry of Industry Information (SAUO)
MII........... Minnesota Interlibrary Telecommunications Exchange, Minneapolis, MN [*OCLC symbol*] (OCLC)
MII........... Modular Image Interpretation (ACAE)
MII........... Morton International [*NYSE symbol*] (TTSB)
MII........... Morton International, Inc. [*NYSE symbol*] (SPSG)
MII........... Motorists Information, Inc. [*Defunct*] (EA)
MII........... Mustang II [*Automotive industry*]
MIIA .... Medical Information and Intelligence Agency (SAUO)
MIIA .... Medical Intelligence and Information Agency [*Formerly, MIO*] [*DoD*]
MIIA .... Member of the Institute of Industrial Administration [*Later, MBIM*] [*British*]
MIIA .... Merritt Island Industrial Area [*NASA*] (KSC)
MIIA .... Mine Inspectors' Institute of America (EA)
MIIB .... Molecular Immunology and Inflammation Branch [*National Institute of Arthritis and Musculoskeletal and Skin Diseases*] (RCD)
MIIC .... International Catholic Movement for Intellectual and Cultural Affairs (SAUO)
MIIC .... Pax Romana, Mouvement International des Intellectuels Catholiques [*Pax Romana, International Catholic Movement for Intellectual and Cultural Affairs - ICMICA*] [*Geneva, Switzerland*] (EAIO)
MIICS........ Master Item Identification Control System
MiId .... Idlewild Public Library, Idlewild, MI [*Library symbol*] [*Library of Congress*] (LCLS)
MIID .... Media Institutes for Institute Directors
MIIDS .... Military Intelligence Integrated Data System (SAUO)
MIIDS .... Missile Interior Intrusion Detection System (DWSG)
MIIDS/IDB... Military Intelligence Integrated Data System/Integrated Database (SAUS)
MIIE .... Member of the Institution of Industrial Engineers (SAUO)
MIIF .... Maintenance of Inactive Industrial Facilities
MIIF .... Master Item Intelligence File
MIIFC........ Michigan Intercollegiate Football Conference (PSS)
MIIL .... Master Item Identification List
MIIM......... Master of International and Intercultural Management (PGP)
MIIM......... Member of the Institution of Industrial Managers [*British*] (DCTA)
MI Inf Sc.... Member of the Institute of Information Scientists [*British*]
MiInr .... Indian River Public Library, Indian River, MI [*Library symbol*] [*Library of Congress*] (LCLS)
MI insuf..... Mitral Insufficiency [*Cardiology*] (DAVI)
MiInt......... Interlovhen Public Library, Interlochen, MI [*Library symbol*] [*Library of Congress*] (LCLS)
MIIR .... Mellon Institute of Industrial Research (SAUO)
MiIrmD....... Dickinson County Library, Iron Mountain, MI [*Library symbol*] [*Library of Congress*] (LCLS)
MiIrmD-N... Dickinson County Library, Norway Branch, Norway, MI [*Library symbol*] [*Library of Congress*] (LCLS)
MiIrmM ..... Mid-Peninsula Library Federation Headquarters, Iron Mountain, MI [*Library symbol*] [*Library of Congress*] (LCLS)
MiIrmV...... United States Veterans Administration Hospital, Iron Mountain, MI [*Library symbol*] [*Library of Congress*] (LCLS)
MiIrr......... West Iron District Library, Iron River, MI [*Library symbol*] [*Library of Congress*] (LCLS)
MIIRS .... Modular Imagery Interpretation & Reporting System (SAUS)
MiIrw........ Ironwood Carnegie Library, Ironwood, MI [*Library symbol*] [*Library of Congress*] (LCLS)
MiIs.......... Ishpeming Carnegie Library, Ishpeming, MI [*Library symbol*] [*Library of Congress*] (LCLS)
MIIS .... Marshall Islands Intermediate School (SAUO)
MIIS .... Member of the Institute of Industrial Supervisors (SAUO)
MIIS .... Miscellaneous Inputs Information Subsystem [*Computer science*]
MIIS .... Modular Imagery Interpretation System
MIIS .... Monterey Institute of International Studies (ECON)
MIISA........ Management Information and Instructional Systems Activity (DNAB)
MIISADET... Management Information and Instructional Systems Activity Detachment (DNAB)
MIISAU...... Management Information and Instructional Systems Activity Unit (DNAB)
MIISE........ Member of the International Institute of Social Economics [*British*] (DBQ)
MIISE........ MicroIslet, Inc. [*NASDAQ symbol*] (QUAN)
MIISec ...... Member of the Institute of Industrial Security [*British*] (DBQ)
MIIT .... Manned Interceptor Integration Team (SAA)
MiIt.......... Thompson Home Library, Ithaca, MI [*Library symbol*] [*Library of Congress*] (LCLS)
MIIU .... Marine Incident Investigation Unit (SAUO)
MIJ .... Dugway/Tooele, UT [*Location identifier*] [*FAA*] (FAAL)
MIJ .... Maatschappij [*Joint Stock Company*] [*Netherlands*]
MIJ .... Master of International Journalism (PGP)
MIJ .... Member of the Institution of Journalists
MIJ .... Metal Insulator Junction
MIJ .... Mili [*Marshall Islands*] [*Airport symbol*] (OAG)
MiJa......... Jackson Public Library, Jackson, MI [*Library symbol*] [*Library of Congress*] (LCLS)
MiJaC .... Jackson County Library, Jackson, MI [*Library symbol*] [*Library of Congress*] (LCLS)
MiJaCc...... Jackson Community College, Jackson, MI [*Library symbol*] [*Library of Congress*] (LCLS)
MiJaCP...... Consumers Power Co., Parnall Technical Library, Jackson, MI [*Library symbol*] [*Library of Congress*] (LCLS)
MIJAL .... Memoirs, International Journal of American Linguists (SAUO)
MiJam....... Jamestown Township Library, Jamestown, MI [*Library symbol*] [*Library of Congress*] (LCLS)
MIJARC ..... Mouvement International de la Jeunesse Agricole et Rurale Catholique [*International Movement of Catholic Agricultural and Rural Youth - IMCARY*] [*Louvain, Belgium*] (EAIO)
MIJC......... Mouvement International des Juristes Catholiques, Pax Romana [*France*]
MIJCT .... Milton Junction, WI [*American Association of Railroads railroad junction routing code*]

MiJen .... Georgetown Township Library, Jenison, MI [*Library symbol*] [*Library of Congress*] (LCLS)
MIJI .... Meaconing, Interference, Jamming and Intrusion (SAUO)
MIJI .... Meaconing, Intrusion, Jamming, Interference [*Military*] (NVT)
MIJO .... Missile Joint Optimization
MiK .... Kalamazoo Public Library, Kalamazoo, MI [*Library symbol*] [*Library of Congress*] (LCLS)
MIK .... Meerblick, SA [*Spain*] [*FAA designator*] (FAAC)
MIK .... Methyl Isobutyl Ketone [*Also, MIBK*] [*Organic chemistry*]
MIK .... Michaels Stores [*Company symbol*]
MIK .... Mikkeli [*Finland*] [*Airport symbol*] (OAG)
Mik .... Mikva'ot (BJA)
MIK .... Minitrack [*Alaska*] [*Seismograph station code, US Geological Survey*] [*Closed*] (SEIS)
MIK .... Missile Installation Kit (ACAE)
MIK .... More in the Kitchen [*Family dinner-table expression*]
MiKa .... Kalkaska County Library, Kalkaska, MI [*Library symbol*] [*Library of Congress*] (LCLS)
MIKA .... Medical Imaging Centers of America (EFIS)
MIKA .... Mikasa [*NCIC car make code*]
MIKA .... Minor Karyotypic Abnormalities [*Medicine*]
MIKADOS ... Mini Instant Keyboard Assembler, Debug, and Operating System [*Computer science*] (MHDI)
Mikasa ...... Mikasa, Inc. [*Associated Press*] (SAG)
MiKB .... Borgess Hospital, Medical Library, Kalamazoo, MI [*Library symbol*] [*Library of Congress*] (LCLS)
MiKC .... Kalamazoo College, Kalamazoo, MI [*Library symbol*] [*Library of Congress*] (LCLS)
MiKCS .... Institute of Cistercian Studies, Western Michigan University, Kalamazoo, MI [*Library symbol*] [*Library of Congress*] (LCLS)
MIKE .... Manipulator Interactive Kinematics Evaluator (SSD)
MIKE .... Mass-Analyzed Ion Kinetic Energy
MIKE .... Measurement of Instantaneous Kinetic Energy (IEEE)
MIKE .... Michael Stores [*NASDAQ symbol*] (SAG)
MIKE .... Micro Interpreter for Knowledge Engineering [*Computer science*]
MIKE .... Microphone (CET)
mike .... Microphone (IDOE)
MIKE .... Multiwave Italian Key System (NITA)
MIKE PAC ... MIKE PAC [*Washington, DC*] (PACS)
MIKER .... Microbalance Inverted Knudsen Effusion Recoil
MIKES .... Mass-Analyzed Ion Kinetic Energy Spectrometry
MikGed ...... Mikra'ot Gedolot (BJA)
MIKID .... Mentally Ill Kids in Distress - Support Groups (EARSL)
MiKin .... Kingston Community Public Library, Kingston, MI [*Library symbol*] [*Library of Congress*] (LCLS)
MiKins ...... Kingsley Public Library, Kingsley, MI [*Library symbol*] [*Library of Congress*] (LCLS)
MIKK .... Medjunarodni Institut za Kucnu Knjizevnost [*International Institute for Home Literature - IIHL*] [*Belgrade, Yugoslavia*] (EAIO)
MiKL .... Kalamazoo Library System, Kalamazoo, MI [*Library symbol*] [*Library of Congress*] (LCLS)
MIKL .... Michael Foods [*NASDAQ symbol*] (TTSB)
MIKL .... Michael Foods, Inc. [*NASDAQ symbol*] (NQ)
MIKN .... Mikohn Gaming [*NASDAQ symbol*] (TTSB)
MIKN .... Mikohn Gaming Corp. [*NASDAQ symbol*] (SAG)
Mikohn ...... Mikohn Gaming Corp. [*Associated Press*] (SAG)
MiKPSc ..... Kalamazoo Public School District, Kalamazoo, MI [*Library symbol*] [*Library of Congress*] (LCLS)
MIKR .... Mikron Instr [*NASDAQ symbol*] (TTSB)
MIKR .... Mikron Instrument Co., Inc. [*NASDAQ symbol*] (NQ)
MIKR .... Mikrus [*NCIC car make code*]
Mikron ...... Mikron Instrument Co., Inc. [*Associated Press*] (SAG)
MiKUp .... Upjohn Co., Kalamazoo, MI [*Library symbol*] [*Library of Congress*] (LCLS)
MiKUp_B .... Upjohn Co., Business Library, Kalamazoo, MI [*Library symbol*] [*Library of Congress*] (LCLS)
MiKV .... Kalamazoo Valley Community College, Kalamazoo, MI [*Library symbol*] [*Library of Congress*] (LCLS)
Mikv .... Mikva'ot (BJA)
MiKW .... Western Michigan University, Kalamazoo, MI [*Library symbol*] [*Library of Congress*] (LCLS)
MiKWUp .... W. E. Upjohn Institute for Employment Research, Kalamazoo, MI [*Library symbol*] [*Library of Congress*] (LCLS)
miky .... Milky [*Philately*]
MiL .... Lansing Public Library, Lansing, MI [*Library symbol*] [*Library of Congress*] (LCLS)
MIL .... Machine Independent Language (VLIE)
MIL .... Machine Interface Layer [*Computer science*] (VLIE)
MIL .... Macro-Instruction Link [*Computer science*] (VLIE)
MIL .... Magnetic Indicator Loop (NVT)
MIL .... Malaya Indonesia Line (SAUO)
MIL .... Malfunction Indicator Lamp [*Automotive diagnosis*]
MIL .... Malfunction Indicator Light [*Automotive engineering*]
MIL .... Malfunction Investigation Laboratory
MIL .... Management Information Library [*Open Systems Interconnection*] (ODAA)
MIL .... Map and Imagery Laboratory (SAUO)
MIL .... Marine Instrumentation Laboratory [*Marine science*] (OSRA)
MIL .... Market Investigations Limited (SAUO)
MIL .... Master Index List (MCD)
MIL .... Master Instrumentation List
MIL .... Master Item Identification List (AABC)
MIL .... Material
MIL .... Matrox Imaging Library (SAUS)
MIL .... Meat Import Law (SAUO)
MIL .... Member of the Institute of Linguists [*British*]
MIL .... Mensa International [*British*] (EAIO)
MIL .... Merrit Island (SAUO)
MIL .... Merritt Island Tracking Station [*Florida*]
MIL .... Microimplementation Language [*Burroughs Corp.*]
MIL .... Microsystems International Limited (SAUO)
MIL .... Milan [*Italy*] [*Seismograph station code, US Geological Survey*] [*Closed*] (SEIS)
MIL .... Milano [*NCIC car model code*]
MIL .... Mileage
MIL .... Miles Laboratories, Inc. (SAUO)
Mil .... Miles' Pennsylvania Reports [*A publication*] (DLA)
mil .... Military (BEE)
Mil .... Military (CMD)
MIL .... Military (EY)
MIL .... Military Instrumentation List
MIL .... Military in the Loop (ACAE)
MIL .... Military Specification [*Followed by a single capital letter and numbers*] (IEEE)
mil .... Militia (WDAA)
MIL .... Militia
MIL .... Millenia (automobile) [*NCIC car model code*]
MIL .... Miller Electric Manufacturing Company [*NCIC trailer make code*]
Mil .... Miller's Reports [*1-5 Louisiana*] [*A publication*] (DLA)
Mil .... Miller's Reports [*3-18 Maryland*] [*A publication*] (DLA)
MIL .... Millieme [*Monetary unit*] [*Egypt, Sudan*]
mil .... Milli-Inch
MIL .... Milliliter
MIL .... Milling
MIL .... Million
MIL .... Millipore Corp. [*NYSE symbol*] (SPSG)
Mil .... Mills' New York Surrogate's Court Reports [*A publication*] (DLA)
Mil .... Mill's South Carolina Constitutional Reports [*A publication*] (DLA)
MIL .... Miltenberg [*German license plate city code*]
MIL .... Milwaukee [*Wisconsin*]
MIL .... Minnesota Instructional Language [*Computer science*] (CSR)
MIL .... Missile Industry Liaison (SAA)
MIL .... Module Interconnection Language
MIL .... Mother-in-law (EDAA)
MIL .... Mothers-in-Law Club International (EA)
MIL .... Movimiento Iberico Libertario [*Spain*] [*Political party*]
MIL .... Moving Inspection Lot
MIL .... Office of Public Library and Interlibrary Cooperation, St. Paul, MN [*OCLC symbol*] (OCLC)
Mil .... Pro Milone [*of Cicero*] [*Classical studies*] (OCD)
mil .... Unit of Length Equal to One-Thousandth of an Inch, 1 E-3 in [*Industrial hygiene term*] (OHS)
MILA .... Merritt Island Launch Area [*NASA*]
Mila .... Militia [*British military*] (DMA)
MILA .... Millan Flatdeck [*NCIC trailer make code*]
MILAA ...... Milastar Corp. [*NASDAQ symbol*] (NQ)
MiLac .... Missaukee County Library, Lake City, MI [*Library symbol*] [*Library of Congress*] (LCLS)
MiLacES .... Lake City Elementary School, Lake City, MI [*Library symbol*] [*Library of Congress*] (LCLS)
MiLacHS .... Lake City High School, Lake City, MI [*Library symbol*] [*Library of Congress*] (LCLS)
MILAD .... Military Advisor [*SEATO or ANZUS Council*] (CINC)
MILADGOVT ... Military Advisory Government
MILADGRU ... Military Advisory Group
MILADREP ... Military Advisors Representative (CINC)
MiLai .... Laingsburg Public Library, Laingsburg, MI [*Library symbol*] [*Library of Congress*] (LCLS)
MiLakv ...... Cato Township Public Library, Lakeview, MI [*Library symbol*] [*Library of Congress*] (LCLS)
MiLal .... Lake Linden-Hubbell Public School Library, Lake Linden, MI [*Library symbol*] [*Library of Congress*] (LCLS)
MiLan .... L'Anse Township School and Public Library, L'Anse, MI [*Library symbol*] [*Library of Congress*] (LCLS)
MILAN .... Milan, MI [*American Association of Railroads railroad junction routing code*]
MILAN .... Missile d'Infanterie Leger Antichar
MILAN .... Missile, Infantry Light Antiarmor [*Antitank system*] (INF)
Mil & Vet C ... Military and Veterans Code [*A publication*] (DLA)
MILAP .... Maintenance Information Logically Analyzed and Presented (SAUO)
MILAP .... Modified Industry and Labour Adjustment Program (SAUO)
MILAS .... Micrometer Low-Approach System
MilATCC .... Military Air Traffic Control Centre (SAUO)
Mil Av .... Military Aviator [*Army*]
MiLaw .... Lawton Public Library, Lawton, MI [*Library symbol*] [*Library of Congress*] (LCLS)
MILBA .... Milbank, SD [*American Association of Railroads railroad junction routing code*]
MILBA .... Military Base Agreement (CINC)
MiLC .... Lansing Community College, Lansing, MI [*Library symbol*] [*Library of Congress*] (LCLS)
MILC .... Metal Ion Liquid Chromatography
MILC .... Midwest Interlibrary Center [*Later, CRL*]
MILC .... Milco Tank & Boat Company [*NCIC trailer make code*]
MILC .... Military Characteristics
MILC .... Modified Intermediate Low Cycle (SAUS)
MILCAP ..... Military Civic Action Program
MILCAP ..... Military Standard Contract Administration Procedures [*DoD*]
MILCAPSYS ... Measuring Military Capability & Constraints Information System (SAUS)
MILCEST .... Military Communications Electronic Systems Technology (MCD)

MilcmIn..... Millicom International Cellular [*Associated Press*] (SAG)
MilColl...... Military College (SAUO)
MILCOM.... Military Command (DNAB)
MILCOM.... Military Committee Communication [*NATO*]
MILCOMP... Military Computer
MILCOMSAT... Military Communications Satellite
MILCON..... Military Construction
MILCON-DA... Military Construction, Defense Agencies
MILCONF... Military Confinement
MILCS....... Metropolitan Interlibrary Cooperative System [*New York Public Library*] [*Information service or system*]
MILD........ Magnetic-Intrusion Line Detector (SAUS)
MILDAT..... Military Damage Assessment Team (AABC)
MILDDU..... Military-Industry Logistics Data Development Unit
MILDEC..... Military Decision (NATG)
MILDEP..... Army's Military Deputy
MILDEP..... Military Department (COE)
MILDEPS.... Military Departments (AABC)
MILDEPT.... Military Department
MILDET..... Military Detachment
MILDIP...... Military-Industry Logistics Data Interchange Procedures
MILDIS...... Military-Industry Logistics Data Interchange System
MILDOC..... Military Document (AAGC)
MiLe......... Leland Township Public Library, Leland, MI [*Library symbol*] [*Library of Congress*] (LCLS)
MILE......... Member of the Institution of Locomotive Engineers (SAUO)
MiLE......... Michigan Library Exchange
MILE......... Micro Investment Lending Enterprise
MILE......... Miller & Smith [*NCIC trailer make code*]
MILE......... Minuteman Integrated Life Extension [*Telecommunications*] (LAIN)
MIL-E-CON... Military Electronic Conference
MileH........ Miles Homes, Inc. [*Associated Press*] (SAG)
MileHme.... Miles Homes, Inc. [*Associated Press*] (SAG)
MilePr....... Milestone Properties [*Associated Press*] (SAG)
MiLer........ LeRoy Public Library, LeRoy, MI [*Library symbol*] [*Library of Congress*] (LCLS)
MILES....... Magnetic Intrusion Line Sensor (PDAA)
Miles........ Miles' District Court Reports [*1825-41*] [*Philadelphia, PA*] [*A publication*] (DLA)
MILES....... Military Implications of LASER Employment by the Soviets
MILES....... Multiple Integrated LASER Engagement Simulation [*or System*] [*Army*]
MILES....... Multiple Integrated LASER Engagement System (COE)
MILES/AGES... Multiple-Integrated LASER Engagement Simulation / Air Ground Engagement Simulator
Miles (PA)... Miles' Pennsylvania Reports [*A publication*] (DLA)
Miles R..... Miles' Pennsylvania Reports [*A publication*] (DLA)
Miles R & O... Miles' Rules and Orders [*A publication*] (DLA)
Miles Rep... Miles' Pennsylvania Reports [*A publication*] (DLA)
MilestnSci... Milestone Scientific, Inc. [*Associated Press*] (SAG)
MiLew....... Lewiston Public Library, Lewiston, MI [*Library symbol*] [*Library of Congress*] (LCLS)
MiLex....... Moore Public Library, Lexington, MI [*Library symbol*] [*Library of Congress*] (LCLS)
MILF......... Moro Islamic Liberation Front [*Philippines*] [*Political party*]
MILFO....... Milford, MA [*American Association of Railroads railroad junction routing code*]
MILFR....... Milton-Freewater, OR [*American Association of Railroads railroad junction routing code*]
MILFS....... Millers Falls, MA [*American Association of Railroads railroad junction routing code*]
MiLG........ Great Lakes Bible College, Lansing, MI [*Library symbol*] [*Library of Congress*] (LCLS)
MILGA....... Member of the Institute of Local Government Administrators [*British*] (ODBW)
MiLGH....... Lansing General Hospital Library, Lansing, MI [*Library symbol*] [*Library of Congress*] (LCLS)
MILGOV..... Military Government (SAUO)
Mil Govt.... Military Government (SAUO)
MILGP...... Military Group
Milgray...... Milgray Electronics, Inc. [*Associated Press*] (SAG)
MILGRP..... Military Group (DNAB)
MILGRU..... Military Group (DNAB)
MiLGS....... Church of Jesus Christ of Latter-Day Saints, Genealogical Society Library, Lansing Branch, Stake Center, Lansing, MI [*Library symbol*] [*Library of Congress*] (LCLS)
MIL GSFC... Spaceflight Tracking and Data Network Station (SAUO)
MIL-HDBK... Military Handbook
MIL-I........ Military Instruction (AAGC)
MIL-I........ Military Specification on Interference (IEEE)
MILI......... Multilevel Informal Language Inventory [*Test*]
MILIC........ Microwave Insular Line Integrated Circuit (IEEE)
MILIC........ Millimeter Insular Line Integrated Circuit (PDAA)
MILIC........ Ministerial Libraries and Information Centers
MiLIM....... Ingham Medical Center, John W. Chi Memorial Library, Lansing, MI [*Library symbol*] [*Library of Congress*] (LCLS)
MILIMETS... Military Meteorological System (SAUO)
MILINREP... Military Incident Report (MCD)
MILIRAD.... Millimeter RADAR (MCD)
MILIRAD.... Millimeter Wave RADAR Fuze (MCD)
MILIS........ Multicenter Investigation of the Limitation of Infarct Size (MEDA)
MiLit......... Litchfield District Library, Litchfield, MI [*Library symbol*] [*Library of Congress*] (LCLS)
milit......... Military (WDAA)
MILIT........ Military
MILIT........ Military, KS [*American Association of Railroads railroad junction routing code*]
Military LJ... Military Law Journal [*A publication*] (DLA)
MILITRAN... Military in Transition Database [*Information service or system*] (IID)
MiLivM...... Madonna College, Livonia, MI [*Library symbol*] [*Library of Congress*] (LCLS)
MiLivPS..... Livonia Public Schools, Livonia, MI [*Library symbol*] [*Library of Congress*] (LCLS)
MILJC....... Milford Junction, IN [*American Association of Railroads railroad junction routing code*]
Mil Jur Cas & Mat... Military Jurisprudence, Cases and Materials [*A publication*] (DLA)
MILJUSDOCFILE... Military Justice Docket File (DNAB)
MILK......... Broughton Foods Co. [*NASDAQ symbol*] (NASQ)
MILK......... Moments of Intimacy, Laughter and Kinship
Mill.......... Millenium (DIAR)
MILL......... Miller Industries, Inc. [*NASDAQ symbol*] (SAG)
Mill.......... Miller's Reports [*3-18 Maryland*] [*A publication*] (DLA)
Mill.......... Miller's Reports [*1-5 Louisiana*] [*A publication*] (DLA)
MILL......... Miller Trailers [*NCIC trailer make code*]
MILL......... Million
Mill.......... Mills' New York Surrogate's Court Reports [*A publication*] (DLA)
Mill.......... Mill's South Carolina Constitutional Reports [*A publication*] (DLA)
Mill & C Bills... Miller and Collier on Bills of Sale [*A publication*] (DLA)
Mill & F Pr... Miller and Field's Federal Practice [*A publication*] (DLA)
Mill & V Code... Milliken and Vertrees' Tennessee Code [*A publication*] (DLA)
Mill Civ L... Miller's Civil Law of England [*1825*] [*A publication*] (DLA)
Mill Code... Miller's Iowa Code [*A publication*] (DLA)
Mill Const... Mill's South Carolina Constitutional Reports [*A publication*] (DLA)
Mill Const (SC)... Mill's South Carolina Constitutional Reports [*A publication*] (DLA)
Mill Dec.... Miller's Circuit Court Decisions (Woolworth) [*United States*] [*A publication*] (DLA)
Mill Dec.... Miller's United States Supreme Court Decisions [*Condensed, Continuation of Curtis*] [*A publication*] (DLA)
MILLE....... Miller, IN [*American Association of Railroads railroad junction routing code*]
Mill El...... Miller's Elements of the Law of Insurances [*A publication*] (DLA)
MillenCh.... Millenium Chemicals, Inc. [*Associated Press*] (SAG)
Millenia..... Millenia, Inc. [*Associated Press*] (SAG)
Mill Eq M... Miller's Equitable Mortgages [*1844*] [*A publication*] (DLA)
Miller........ Miller's Reports [*3-18 Maryland*] [*A publication*] (DLA)
Miller........ Miller's Reports [*1-5 Louisiana*] [*A publication*] (DLA)
Miller Const... Miller on the Constitution of the United States [*A publication*] (DLA)
MillerIn..... Miller Indusries, Inc. [*Associated Press*] (SAG)
Miller's Code... Miller's Revised and Annotated Code [*Iowa*] [*A publication*] (DLA)
Millersville U... Millersville University of Pennsylvania (GAGS)
MILLI........ Milliken, CO [*American Association of Railroads railroad junction routing code*]
MILLIE...... Maximum Interchange of the Latest Logistic Information Is Essential
milli IU/ml... Milli-International Unit per Milliliter (DAVI)
Millin........ Petty Sessions Cases [*1875-98*] [*Ireland*] [*A publication*] (DLA)
Mill Ins..... Miller's Elements of the Law of Insurances [*A publication*] (DLA)
Millipore.... Millipore Corp. [*Associated Press*] (SAG)
Millipre..... Millipore Corp. [*Associated Press*] (SAG)
millisec..... Millisecond
Mill LA...... Miller's Reports [*1-5 Louisiana*] [*A publication*] (DLA)
Mill Log..... Mill's Logic [*A publication*] (DLA)
Mill MD..... Miller's Reports [*3-18 Maryland*] [*A publication*] (DLA)
Mill Op...... Miller's Circuit Court Decisions (Woolworth) [*United States*] [*A publication*] (DLA)
Mill Part.... Miller on Partition [*A publication*] (DLA)
MillPhar.... Millennium Pharmaceuticals, Inc. [*Associated Press*] (SAG)
Mill Pl & Pr... Miller's Iowa Pleading and Practice [*A publication*] (DLA)
MillrHr...... Miller [*Herman*], Inc. [*Associated Press*] (SAG)
MILLS....... Mills [*Commonly used*] (OPSA)
Mills......... Mills' New York Surrogate's Court Reports [*A publication*] (DLA)
Mills Ann St... Mills' Annotated Statutes [*Colorado*] [*A publication*] (DLA)
Mills C...... Mills College (GAGS)
MillsCp...... Mills Corp. [*Associated Press*] (SAG)
Mills Em D... Mills on Eminent Domain [*A publication*] (DLA)
Mills Em Dom... Mills on Eminent Domain [*A publication*] (DLA)
Mills (NY)... Mills' New York Surrogate's Court Reports [*A publication*] (DLA)
Mills' Surr Ct... Mills' New York Surrogate's Court Reports [*A publication*] (DLA)
MILLT........ Milltown, NB [*American Association of Railroads railroad junction routing code*]
MIllumES... Member of the Illuminating Engineers Society (SAUO)
MILLV....... Millvale, PA [*American Association of Railroads railroad junction routing code*]
MIL-M....... Military Manual (MCD)
MILMO...... Military Motorcycle [*Army*] (INF)
MILNET..... Military Network
MILNRY..... Millinery
MILO........ Magnetically Insulated Line Oscillator (ADWA)
MILO........ Mainframe Interface to Libraries Online [*Illinois Library Computer Systems Office online union catalog*]
MILO........ Maryland Interlibrary Loan (NITA)
MILO........ Maryland Interlibrary Organization [*Information service or system*] (IID)
MILO........ Miami Valley Library Organization [*Library network*]
MILO........ Microphone Locator (ACAE)
MILO........ Military Intelligence Liaison Officer (SAUO)
MILO........ Most Input for the Least Output [*Business term*]
MILOC....... Military Oceanography (PDAA)

MILocoE .... Member of the Institution of Locomotive Engineers [*British*] (EY)
MILOGS ..... Marine Integrated Logistic System (SAUO)
MIL OPS .... Military Operations [*USCG*] (TAG)
MIL/OS ...... Military/Ordnance Specification (MCD)
MILOX .... Mid-Latitude Ecosystems and Photochemical Oxidants (SAUO)
MIL P .... Military Police (SAUO)
Mil P .... Military Post
MILP .... Mitogen-induced Lymphocyte Proliferation [*Medicine*] (EDAA)
MILP .... Mixed Integer Linear Program [*Statistics*]
MIL PAC .... MIL Corporation PAC [*Bowie, MD*] (PACS)
MILPAC ..... Military Personnel Accounting Activity [*Army*] (AABC)
MILPAS ..... Miscellaneous Information Listing Program Apollo Spacecraft [*NASA*] (KSC)
MILPAY ...... Military Pay (SAUO)
MILPER ..... Military Personnel
MILPERCEN ... Military Personnel Center [*Alexandria, VA*] [*Army*] (AABC)
MILPERS .... Military Personnel
MILPERSINS ... Military Personnel Information System
MILPERSINST ... Military Personnel Instructions (MCD)
MILPERSIS ... Military Personnel Information Subsystem (MCD)
MILPHAP ... Military Provincial Health Assistance Program (AABC)
MILPINS .... Military Police Information System (DNAB)
MILPO .... Military Personnel Office (AABC)
MILPOD ..... Mixed Integer and Linear Programming Open Deck (PDAA)
MilPr .... Milestone Properties [*Associated Press*] (SAG)
MILR .... Maintenance Incident Log Report [*Navy*] (CAAL)
MILR .... Master of Industrial and Labor Relations
MilrBld ...... Miller Building Systems, Inc. [*Associated Press*] (SAG)
MILREP ..... Military Representative (NATG)
Mil Rep ..... Militia Reporter [*Boston*] [*A publication*] (DLA)
MILREPC .... Military Representatives Committee (SAUO)
Mil Rev ..... Military Review [*A publication*] (BRI)
MILRIS .... Military Routing Identifier System
MILS .... Marine Integrated Logistics System
MILS .... Master of Information and Library Science (GAGS)
MILS .... Medication Information Leaflet for Seniors [*Medicine*] (DMAA)
MILS .... Member of the Incorporated Law Society [*British*]
MILS .... Microcomputer Integrated Library System
MILS .... Microwave Instrument Landing System
MILS .... Military Standard Logistics System (MCD)
MILS .... Milliradians (KSC)
MILS .... Mills Transfer [*Common carrier symbol*]
MILS .... Mineral Industry Location System [*Bureau of Mines*] [*Information service or system*] (IID)
MILS .... Missile Impact Locating [*or Location*] System
MiLS .... Sparrow (E.W.) Hospital Library, Lansing, MI [*Library symbol*] [*Library of Congress*] (LCLS)
MILSAT ...... Military Satellite
MILSATCOM ... Military Satellite Communications [*Systems*]
MILSBILLS ... Military Standard Billing System
MILSCAP .... Military Standard Administrative Procedure (ACAE)
MILSCAP .... Military Standard Contract Administration Procedures [*DoD*]
MILSICCS ... Military Standard Item Characteristics Coding Structure (SAA)
MILSIMDS ... Military Standard Item Management Data System
MILSIMS .... Military Standard Inventory Management System
MILSO .... Military Standard Logistics Systems Office [*DoD*] (MCD)
MILSOLV .... Milwaukee Solvents & Chemicals Corp. (EFIS)
MILS/PAC ... Missile Impact Location System, Pacific (SAA)
MILSPEC .... Military Specification
MILSPEC .... Military Specifications (GAVI)
Mil-Specs ... Military Specifications (WDAA)
MILSPETS ... Military Standard Petroleum System (MCD)
MIL SPOT ... Military Standard Procurement Operations Technique
MILSPOT .... Military Standard Purchase Operating Technique
MILSPRED ... Military Standard for Providing Research and Exploratory Development Data
MILSTAAD ... Military Standard Activity Address Directory
MILSTAC .... Military Staff Communication (NATG)
MILSTAG .... Military Standardization Agreement (CINC)
MILSTAM ... International Military Staff Memorandum [*NATO*] (NATG)
MILSTAMP ... Military Standard Movement Procedures (SAUO)
MILSTAMP ... Military Standard Requisitioning and Issue Procedure (SAUO)
MILSTAMP ... Military Standard Transportation and Movement Procedure
MILSTAN .... Military Agency for Standardization [*NATO*]
MILSTAN .... Military Standard (SAUO)
MILSTAR .... Military Satellite Tracking and Reconnaissance (ACAE)
MILSTAR .... Military Strategic and Tactical Relay Satellite (SAUO)
MILSTAR .... Military Strategic and Tactical Relay System [*Satellite communications*]
MILSTAR .... Military Strategic Tactical (SAUO)
MILSTARAP ... Military Standard Transportation Action Report and Accounting Procedures (MCD)
MIL STD .... Military Standard
MILSTD ..... Military Standard
MILSTEP .... Military Standard Evaluation Procedure
MILSTEP .... Military Supply and Transportation Evaluation Procedures (AFM)
MILSTICC ... Military Standard Item Characteristics Coding
MILSTICCS ... Military Standard Item Characteristics Coding Structure
MILSTIICS ... Military Standard Item Identification Coding System
MiLStL ...... Saint Lawrence Hospital Medical Library, Lansing, MI [*Library symbol*] [*Library of Congress*] (LCLS)
MILSTRAMP ... Military Standard Transportation and Movement Procedure
MILSTRAP ... Military Standard Requisition and Accounting Procedures (MCD)
MILSTRAP ... Military Standard Transaction Reporting and Accounting Procedures
MILSTRAP ... Military Standard Transaction Reports and Accounting Procedures (SAUO)
MILSTRIP ... Military Standard Requisitioning and Issue Procedure
MILSTRIP ... Military Standard Transportation and Movement Procedure (SAUO)
MILSVC ..... Military Services
Mil Sym ..... Milwaukee Symphony (SAUO)
MILT .... Military Language Tutor
MILT .... Miller Tilt-Top Trailer [*NCIC trailer make code*]
MILT .... Milton [*England*]
MILT .... Miltope Group [*NASDAQ symbol*] (TTSB)
MILT .... Miltope Group, Inc. [*NASDAQ symbol*] (NQ)
MILTAG ...... Military Technical Assistance Group
MILTAM ..... Misrad Isre'eli Li-tevi'ot Mi-Germanyah (BJA)
MiLTC .... Thomas M. Cooley Law School, Lansing, MI [*Library symbol*] [*Library of Congress*] (LCLS)
MILTELCOMM ... Military Telecommunications
MILTO .... Milton, ON [*American Association of Railroads railroad junction routing code*]
MiltonF ...... Milton Federal Financial Corp. [*Associated Press*] (SAG)
MILTOP ...... Man-in-the-Loop Trajectory Optimization Program [*NASA*]
Miltope ...... Miltope Group, Inc. [*Associated Press*] (SAG)
MILTOSS .... Military Transportation of Small Shipments (NVT)
MIL TRA .... Military Training [*USCG*] (TAG)
MILTRACS ... Military Air Traffic Control System (SAUO)
Mil Trib ..... Military Tribunal (SAUO)
MILU .... Chicago, Milwaukee, Saint Paul, and Pacific Railroad [*Intermodal shipping container symbol*] (TVRC)
MILU .... Missile Interface & Logic Unit (SAUS)
MiLud .... Ludington Public Library, Ludington, MI [*Library symbol*] [*Library of Congress*] (LCLS)
MiLut .... Luther Public Library, Luther, MI [*Library symbol*] [*Library of Congress*] (LCLS)
MiLv .... Mink Endogenous Virus (DB)
MILVAN ..... Military Van (MCD)
MIL VIG ..... Military Vigilance (SAUO)
MILVL .... Milledgeville, GA [*American Association of Railroads railroad junction routing code*]
MILW .... Chicago, Milwaukee, St. Paul & Pacific Railroad Co. [*AAR code*]
Milw .... Milward's Irish Ecclesiastical Reports [*1819-43*] [*A publication*] (DLA)
Milw .... Milwaukee [*Wisconsin*]
MILW .... Milwaukee, WI [*American Association of Railroads railroad junction routing code*]
Milwaukee Law ... Milwaukee Lawyer [*A publication*] (DLA)
Milwau Sch Eng ... Milwaukee School of Engineering (GAGS)
MILWD ...... Millwood, WA [*American Association of Railroads railroad junction routing code*]
Milw Ir Ecc Rep ... Milward's Irish Ecclesiastical Reports [*1819-43*] [*A publication*] (DLA)
MilwLnd .... Milwaukee Land Co. [*Associated Press*] (SAG)
MILX .... Milpark Drilling Fluids [*Private rail car owner code*]
MiLy .... Lyons Public Library, Lyons, MI [*Library symbol*] [*Library of Congress*] (LCLS)
MILY .... Miley Trailer Company [*NCIC trailer make code*]
MILYA .... Miller Yard, VA [*American Association of Railroads railroad junction routing code*]
MILZ .... Soo Line Railroad [*Intermodal trailer symbol*]
MIM .... Magnetic Interaction Mechanism
MIM .... Maintenance Instructions Manual [*DoD*]
MIM .... Maintenance Interface Machine (NITA)
MIM .... Management Information Model [*Open Systems Interconnection*] (ODAA)
MIM .... Manufacturing Information Memorandum
MIM .... Maoist Internationalist Movement [*Association*] (EA)
MIM .... Map Image Metafile (SAUS)
MIM .... Marine Information Management [*Marine science*] (MSC)
MIM .... Marine Information Management and Metadata (SAUO)
MIM .... Master of Industrial Management
MIM .... Master of International Management
MIM .... Member of the Institute of Management (DD)
MIM .... Member of the Institution of Metallurgists [*British*] (DBQ)
MIM .... Memory-Intensive Modules (TIMI)
MIM .... Mendelian Inheritance in Man [*Genetics*]
MIM .... Merimbula [*Australia*] [*Airport symbol*] (OAG)
MIM .... Message Input Module [*Telecommunications*] (TEL)
MIM .... Metal Injection Molding [*Metal fabrication*]
MIM .... Metal Insulator Metal [*Light detector*]
MIM .... Methods and Information in Medicine [*Medicine*] [*Journal*] (EDAA)
MIM .... Microion Mill
MIM .... Micro Isolation Mount (SAUS)
MIM .... Microwave Interface Module
MIM .... Mid Mountain Mining [*Vancouver Stock Exchange symbol*]
MIM .... Military Iranian Mission [*World War II*]
MIM .... Milo [*Maine*] [*Seismograph station code, US Geological Survey*] (SEIS)
Mim .... Mimeograph (AAGC)
MIM .... Mimeographed (ADA)
MIM .... Mimino [*Former USSR*] [*FAA designator*] (FAAC)
MIM .... Mindanao Independence Movement [*Philippines*] [*Political party*]
MIM .... Minimum (DA)
MIM .... Minorities in Media (EA)
MIM .... Minorities in Medicine [*Eastern Michigan University Macy Scholarship*]
MIM .... Misappropriation, Interference and Misrepresentation
MIM .... Missile Identification Module [*Military*] (CAAL)
MIM .... Mobile-Launched Interceptor Missile

MIM .... Mobile-launched surface-to-air Missile (SAUS)

MIM .... MODEM Interface Modules [*Computer science*]

MIM .... Modified Index Method (IEEE)

MIM .... Montagu Investments Management [*Commercial firm*] [*British*]

MIM .... Morality in Media (EA)

MIM .... Mouvement Independantiste Martiniquais [*Martinique Independence Movement*] [*Political party*] (PD)

MIM .... Multilateral Initiative in Malaria

MIM .... Multilateral Initiative on Malaria [*International coordination effort*]

MIM .... Multilayer Interference Mirror [*Optical instrumentation*]

MIM .... Multiple Ion Monitoring [*Mass spectrometry*]

MIM .... Multiplex Interface Module (ACAE)

Mim .... United States Internal Revenue Bureau, Commissioner's Mimeographed Published Opinions [*A publication*] (DLA)

MIM-23 ..... Hawk [*Military*] [*Medium-range, mobile surface-to-air missile*] (POLM)

MIM-43 ..... Redeye [*Military*] [*Man-portable, short-range, surface-to-air missile*] (POLM)

MIM-72 ..... Chaparral [*Military*] [*Short-range, surface-to-air missile*] (POLM)

MIM-115 ..... Roland [*Military*] [*Short-range, surface-to-air missile*] (POLM)

MIMA .... Member, Industrial Medical Association (CMD)

MIMA .... Metal Injection Molding Association (NTPA)

MIMA .... Mineral Insulation Manufacturers Association (EA)

MIMA .... Minor Machine Accessory (MCD)

MIMA .... Minute Man National Historical Park

MIMA .... Music Industry Manufacturers Association [*Defunct*] (EA)

MIMAA ...... Motor Inn, Motel and Accommodation Association [*Australia*]

MIMAC ...... Measurement and Improvement of Manufacturing Capacity

MiMaci ...... Mackinac Island Public Library, Mackinac Island, MI [*Library symbol*] [*Library of Congress*] (LCLS)

MiMack ..... Mackinaw City Public Library, Mackinaw City, MI [*Library symbol*] [*Library of Congress*] (LCLS)

MIMAF ...... Musicians International Mutual Aid Fund

MiMan ...... Manchester Township Library, Manchester, MI [*Library symbol*] [*Library of Congress*] (LCLS)

MiManc ..... Mancelona Township Library, Mancelona, MI [*Library symbol*] [*Library of Congress*] (LCLS)

MIM&GE .... Member of the Institute of Mechanical & General Engineers (SAUO)

MIManf ...... Member of the Institute of Manufacturing [*British*] (DBQ)

MiMani ...... Manistee County Library, Manistee, MI [*Library symbol*] [*Library of Congress*] (LCLS)

MiMant ...... Manton Public Library, Manton, MI [*Library symbol*] [*Library of Congress*] (LCLS)

MiMar .... M. Alice Chapin Memorial Library, Marion, MI [*Library symbol*] [*Library of Congress*] (LCLS)

MiMarc ...... Marcellus Township Library, Marcellus, MI [*Library symbol*] [*Library of Congress*] (LCLS)

MIMarE ..... Member of the Institute of Marine Engineers [*British*] (EY)

MI Mar E ... Member of the Institute (or Institution) of Marine Engineers (SAUO)

MiMarl ...... Marlette Township Library, Marlette, MI [*Library symbol*] [*Library of Congress*] (LCLS)

MiMaRP .... Maple Rapids Public Library, Maple Rapids, MI [*Library symbol*] [*Library of Congress*] (LCLS)

MiMarq ..... Peter White Public Library, Marquette, MI [*Library symbol*] [*Library of Congress*] (LCLS)

MiMarqAS ... Marquette-Alger Intermediate School District, Learning Materials Center, Marquette, MI [*Library symbol*] [*Library of Congress*] (LCLS)

MiMarqHi ... Marquette County Historical Society, John M. Longyear Memorial Library, Marquette, MI [*Library symbol*] [*Library of Congress*] (LCLS)

MiMarqN .... Northern Michigan University, Marquette, MI [*Library symbol*] [*Library of Congress*] (LCLS)

MiMarqNA ... Northern Michigan University, University Archives and Historical Collections, Marquette, MI [*Library symbol*] [*Library of Congress*] (LCLS)

MiMarqS .... Superiorland Library Cooperative System, Marquette, MI [*Library symbol*] [*Library of Congress*] (LCLS)

MiMars ...... Marshall Public Library, Marshall, MI [*Library symbol*] [*Library of Congress*] (LCLS)

MiMary ...... Marysville Public Library, Marysville, MI [*Library symbol*] [*Library of Congress*] (LCLS)

MiMas ...... Ingham County Library, Mason, MI [*Library symbol*] [*Library of Congress*] (LCLS)

MIMAS ...... Magnetically Insulated Macroparticle Accelerator System

MIMAS ...... Multifield Integrated Meltdown Analysis System (SAUO)

MiMay .... Mayville District Public Library, Mayville, MI [*Library symbol*] [*Library of Congress*] (LCLS)

MIMB .... Malaysia International Merchant Bankers (SAUO)

MIMB .... Mint in a Mint Box [*Collectibles*]

MIMBD ...... Meeting on the Interconnection of Molecular Biological (or Biology) Databases (SAUO)

MIMBD ...... Meeting on the Interconnection of Mology Biology Databases (SAUS)

MIMBM ..... Member of the Institute of Municipal Building Management [*British*] (DBQ)

MIMC .... Management Inventory on Managing Change [*Test*]

MIMC .... Marconi International Marine Communication Company (SAUO)

MIMC .... Massachusetts Interactive Media Council

MimC .... Maxwell International Microforms Corporation, Fairview Park, Elmsford, NY [*Library symbol*] [*Library of Congress*] (LCLS)

MIMC .... Maxwell International Microforms Corporation Incorporated (SAUO)

MIMC .... Member of the Institute of Management Consultants

MIMC .... Microforms International Marketing Corp. [*Pergamon*]

MIMC .... Multivariable Internal Model Control [*Control engineering*]

MIM-CD ..... MIM CD: Mendelian Inheritance in Man (MHID)

MIMCO ...... McGraw-Hill Information Management Co. [*Database producer*] (IID)

MiMD .... Dorsch Memorial Public Library, Monroe, MI [*Library symbol*] [*Library of Congress*] (LCLS)

MIMD .... Management Information of Metrology Data (AAEL)

MIMD .... Multiple Instruction/Multiple Data (NITA)

MIMD .... Multiple Instruction, Multiple Data Processor [*Computer science*] (CIST)

MIMD .... Multiple Instruction Stream, Multiple Data Stream (MCD)

MIME .... Member of the Institute of Mining Engineers

MIME .... Member of the Institution of Mechanical Engineers [*Formerly, AMIMechE*] [*British*]

MIME .... Member of the Institution of Mining Engineers (SAUO)

MIME .... Microcomputers in Mathematics Education (AIE)

MIME .... Ministry of Information Middle East [*British*] [*World War II*]

MIME .... Minor Machine Equipment (MCD)

MIME .... Multimedia Internet Mail Extension

MIME .... Multipurpose Internet Mail Extension [*Computer science*]

MIME .... Multipurpose Internet Mail Extensions [*Computer science*] (ACRL)

MIME .... Multipurpose Internet Messaging Extensions (GART)

MiMe .... Spies Public Library, Menominee, MI [*Library symbol*] [*Library of Congress*] (LCLS)

MiMec .... Morton Township Library, Mecosta, MI [*Library symbol*] [*Library of Congress*] (LCLS)

MIMechE .... Member of the Institution of Mechanical Engineers [*Formerly, AMIMechE*] [*British*] (EY)

MiMen ...... Mendon Township Library, Mendon, MI [*Library symbol*] [*Library of Congress*] (LCLS)

MIMEO ...... Mimeographed (ADA)

MIMEO ...... Multiple Input Memo Engineering Order (MCD)

MiMer .... Merrill District Library, Merrill, MI [*Library symbol*] [*Library of Congress*] (LCLS)

MiMes .... Mesick Public Library, Mesick, MI [*Library symbol*] [*Library of Congress*] (LCLS)

MIMEX ...... Major Item Material Excess [*Air Force*] (AFIT)

MIMF .... Member of the Institute of Metal Finishing [*British*] (DBQ)

MIMG .... Mission Motor Lines [*Common carrier symbol*]

MIMGTechE ... Member of the Institution of Mechanical Engineers and General Technician Engineers [*British*] (DBQ)

MIMH .... Member of the Institute of Materials Handling [*British*] (DBQ)

MIMHP ...... Mim Health Plans Inc. PAC [*Elmsford, NY*] (PACS)

MIMI .... Magnetospheric Imaging Instrument (ACAE)

MIMI .... Market Incentives for Mitigation Investment [*Emergency Management*] (EMA)

MIMI .... Medical Workstations for Intelligent Interactive Acquisition and Analysis of Digital Medical Images (SAUO)

MIMI .... Member of the Institute of Motor Industry [*British*]

MIMI .... Member of the Institute of the Motor Industry (SAUO)

MIMI .... Micro Miniature Compact Harness (MCD)

MIMI .... Multipurpose Internet Mail Extension [*Communications term*] (DCT)

MIMIC .... Measure and Inspection Masks for Integrated Circuits (MCD)

MIMIC .... Method of Micromolding in Capillaries [*Materials science*]

MIMIC .... Microfilm Information Master Image Converter (PDAA)

MIMIC .... Micromoulding in Capillaries [*Plastics technology*]

MIMIC .... Microwave and Millimeter-Wave Monolithic Integrated Circuits Project [*DoD*]

MIMIC .... Microwave Monolithic Integrated Circuit [*Used in wireless communication*]

MIMIC .... Millimetric Wave Monolithic Integrated Circuit (SAUS)

MIMIC/CUS ... Michigan Metropolitan Information Center [*Wayne State University*] [*Center for Urban Studies*] (IID)

MIMIC/CUS ... Michigan Metropolitan Information Center/Center for Urban Studies [*Wayne State University*] [*Information service or system*] (IID)

MIMIC model ... Multiple Indicator Multiple Cause Model

MIMICS ..... Micromodule Microprogrammed Computer System (PDAA)

MiMid .... Grace A. Dow Memorial [*Public*] Library, Midland, MI [*Library symbol*] [*Library of Congress*] (LCLS)

MiMidD ..... Dow Chemical Co., Midland, MI [*Library symbol*] [*Library of Congress*] (LCLS)

MiMidDC .... Dow Corning Corp., Midland, MI [*Library symbol*] [*Library of Congress*] (LCLS)

MiMidDG ... Dow Gardens, Midland, MI [*Library symbol*] [*Library of Congress*] (LCLS)

MiMidGS .... Church of Jesus Christ of Latter-Day Saints, Genealogical Society Library, Midland Stake Branch, Midland, MI [*Library symbol*] [*Library of Congress*] (LCLS)

MiMidN ..... Northwood Institute, Midland, MI [*Library symbol*] [*Library of Congress*] (LCLS)

MiMil .... Milan Public Library, Milan, MI [*Library symbol*] [*Library of Congress*] (LCLS)

MiMill .... Millington Township Library, Millington, MI [*Library symbol*] [*Library of Congress*] (LCLS)

MI MIN ...... Miles per Minute (WDAA)

MIMinE ...... Member of the Institution of Mining Engineers [*British*] (EY)

MiMio .... Oscoda County Public Library, Mio, MI [*Library symbol*] [*Library of Congress*] (LCLS)

MIMIS .... Major Item Management Information System (SAUO)

MIMIS .... Municipal Improvement Management Information System (ACAE)

MIMIT .... Member of the Institute of Musical Instrument Technology [*British*] (DBQ)

MIMJ .... Metal Insulator - Metal Junction

MIMLIC ..... Minnesota Mutual Life Insurance Company (EFIS)

MIMM .... Management Inventory on Modern Management [*Test*]

MIMM .... Master of Mining and Metallurgy (DD)

MIMM .... Member of the Institute of Mining and Metallurgy [*British*] (EY)

MIMM .... Member of the Institution of Mining and Metallurgy (SAUO)

MIMM .... Mexican Institution of Mining and Metallurgy (SAUO)

MIMMIS..... Marine Corps Integrated Manpower Management Information System
MIMMS..... Marine Corps Integrated Maintenance Management System
MIMO........ Man In, Machine Out [*Computer science*]
MIMO........ Modified Input - Modified Output [*Computer science*]
MiMo........ Monroe County Library System, Monroe, MI [*Library symbol*] [*Library of Congress*] (LCLS)
MIMO........ Multi-Input, Multi-Output [*Electronics*] (AAEL)
MIMO........ Multiple-Input/Multiple-Output [*Computer science*]
MiMoHi..... Monroe County Historical Museum, Archives, Monroe, MI [*Library symbol*] [*Library of Congress*] (LCLS)
MIMOLA.... Machine Independent Microprogramming Language
MiMor........ Stair Public Library, Morenci, MI [*Library symbol*] [*Library of Congress*] (LCLS)
MiMory...... Morley-Stanwood Community Library, Morley, MI [*Library symbol*] [*Library of Congress*] (LCLS)
MIMOS...... Malaysian Institute of Microelectronic Systems (SAUO)
MIMOSA.... Mission Modes and Space Analysis (NASA)
MIMOSA.... Mission Modes and Systems Analysis (ACAE)
MIMOT...... Master of International Management of Technology (PGP)
MIMP........ Magazine Industry Market Place [*A publication*]
MIMP........ Mint in Manufacturer's Packaging [*Collectibles*]
MIMP........ Mint in Mint Package [*Collectibles*]
MIMR........ Magnetic Ink Mark Recognition
MIMR........ May Institute of Medical Research
MIMR........ Minimal Inhibitor Mole Ratio [*Biochemistry*]
MIMR........ Multi-Frequency Imaging Microwave Radiometer (EOSA)
MIMS........ Major Item Management System (AABC)
MIMS........ Manifest Information Management System (GAAI)
MIMS........ Master of Integrated Manufacturing Systems (PGP)
MIMS........ Material Information Management System (MCD)
MiMS........ Medical Information Management System (NAKS)
MIMS........ Medical Inventory Management System
MIMS........ Member of the Institute of Management Specialists [*British*] (DBQ)
MIMS........ Metal Impact Monitoring System [*Nuclear energy*] (NRCH)
MIMS........ MIM Corp. [*NASDAQ symbol*] (SG)
MIMS........ Mincom Information Management System (SAUS)
MIMS........ Mineral Insulated, Metal Sheathed [*Cable*]
MIMS........ Minnesota Incident Management System [*Emergency Management*] (EMA)
MIMS........ Missile Maintenance Squadron [*Air Force*]
MIMS........ Mitrol Industrial Management System [*Mitrol, Inc.*] [*Information service or system*] (IID)
MIMS........ Mobile Information System (SAUO)
MIMS........ Modular Isodrive Memory Series
MIMS........ Moment of Inertia Measuring System [*Automotive engineering*]
MIMS........ Monthly Index of Medical Specialties [*A publication*] (DB)
MIMS........ Multi-Item Multisource (IEEE)
MIMS........ Multiple Independently Maneuvering Submunitions (MCD)
MIMS........ Multiple Independent Maneuvering Submissile (ACAE)
MIMSA...... Minority Institutions in Marine Sciences Association (SAUO)
MIMSE...... Microwave-Infrared Mesopheric-Stratospheric Experiment (SAUO)
MIMSO...... Military Indoctrination for Medical Service Officers (SAUO)
MIMSq...... Missile Maintenance Squadron [*Air Force*] (AFM)
MIMT........ Member of the Institute of Music Teachers (ADA)
MIMT........ Member of the Institute of the Motor Trade (SAUO)
MiMtc........ Mount Clemens Public Library, Mount Clemens, MI [*Library symbol*] [*Library of Congress*] (LCLS)
MiMtcM..... Macomb County Library, Mount Clemens, MI [*Library symbol*] [*Library of Congress*] (LCLS)
MiMtp........ Mount Pleasant Public Library, Mount Pleasant, MI [*Library symbol*] [*Library of Congress*] (LCLS)
MiMtpC..... Chippewa Library League, Mt. Pleasant, MI [*Library symbol*] [*Library of Congress*] (LCLS)
MiMtpT...... Central Michigan University, Mount Pleasant, MI [*Library symbol*] [*Library of Congress*] (LCLS)
MiMu........ Hackley Public Library, Muskegon, MI [*Library symbol*] [*Library of Congress*] (LCLS)
MIMU........ Miniature Inertial Measurement Unit
MIMU........ Miniaturization Inertial Measurement Unit (TIMI)
MiMuB...... Muskegon Business College, Muskegon, MI [*Library symbol*] [*Library of Congress*] (LCLS)
MIMUG...... Meetings Industry Microcomputer Users Group [*Defunct*] (EA)
MiMul....... Mulliken District Library, Mulliken, MI [*Library symbol*] [*Library of Congress*] (LCLS)
MiMuM...... Muskegon County Library, Muskegon, MI [*Library symbol*] [*Library of Congress*] (LCLS)
MIMUN...... Marine Institute of Memorial University (SAUO)
MiMun...... Munising Public Library, Munising, MI [*Library symbol*] [*Library of Congress*] (LCLS)
MIMunE..... Member of the Institute of Municipal Engineers [*British*] (EY)
MIMUSA.... Matrix Iteration Method of Unfolding Spectra [*Computer science*]
MIMV........ Mirabilis Mosaic Virus [*Plant pathology*]
MIMZ........ Minnesota Mining [*Federal Railroad Administration identification code*]
MIN.......... Business European Airways Ltd. [*British*] [*FAA designator*] (FAAC)
MIN.......... Marketing Information Network [*Information service or system*] (IID)
MIN.......... Master of Insurance
MIN.......... Media Industry Newsletter [*A publication*]
MIN.......... Medial Interlaminar Nucleus (DMAA)
MIN.......... Meeting Individual Needs [*Educational publishing*]
MIN.......... Member Information Network [*for House of Representatives*]
MIN.......... Member of the Institute of Navigation [*British*]
MIN.......... Metabolic Information Network [*Founded in 1989*] (NRGU)
MIN.......... MFS Intermediate Income SBI [*NYSE symbol*] (SPSG)
MIN.......... MFS Intermediate Income Trust [*Associated Press*] (SAG)
MIN.......... MFS Interm Incme SBI [*NYSE symbol*] (TTSB)
min.......... Microinch (BARN)
MIN.......... Milikin [*Language symbol*] (ETLW)
Min.......... Minaean [*or Minean*] (BJA)
MIN.......... Mine [*or Minecraft*] [*Navy*]
MIN.......... Mine Identification and Neutralization (PDAA)
MIN.......... Mineola, TX [*Amtrak rail station code*]
MIN.......... Mineral [*California*] [*Seismograph station code, US Geological Survey*] (SEIS)
Min.......... Mineralogical (SAUO)
MIN.......... Mineralogy
MIN.......... Mini [*NCIC car model code*]
MIN.......... Miniature
MIN.......... Minica [*NCIC car model code*]
MIN.......... Minim
MIN.......... Minimal (SAUS)
MIN.......... Mini-Mark [*NCIC car model code*]
MIN.......... Minimum (AFM)
min.......... Minimum [*A minim measurement*] (DAVI)
Min.......... Minimum (DFIT)
min.......... Mining (DD)
MIN.......... Mining
MIN.......... Minion [*Typography*] (DGA)
MIN.......... Minister [*or Ministry*]
Min.......... Minister [*or Ministry*] (ODBW)
MIN.......... Ministry (SAUO)
Min.......... Minnesota Reports [*A publication*] (DLA)
Min.......... Minnesota Vikings [*National Football League*] [*1961-present*] (NFLA)
min.......... Minor (SHCU)
MIN.......... Minor
MIN.......... Minor [*NCIC car model code*]
MIN.......... Minority
Min.......... Minor's Alabama Reports [*A publication*] (DLA)
MIN.......... Minto Resources [*Vancouver Stock Exchange symbol*]
MIN.......... Minute (AFM)
min.......... Minute (IDOE)
Min.......... Minutes (DIAR)
MIN.......... Minx [*NCIC car model code*]
MIN.......... Mobile Identification Number (ACRL)
MIN.......... Mobile Intelligent Network (SAUO)
MIN.......... Mobilization Identification Number [*Military*]
MIN.......... Molasses Information Network (EA)
MIN.......... Most in Need Population
MIN.......... Motor Interneuron (MELL)
MIN.......... Movimiento de Integracion Nacional [*National Integration Movement*] [*Venezuela*] [*Political party*] (PPW)
MIN.......... Movimiento de Integracion Nacional [*National Integration Movement*] [*Ecuador*] [*Political party*] (PPW)
MIN.......... Movimiento de Izquierda Nacional [*National Left-Wing Movement*] [*Bolivia*] [*Political party*] (PPW)
M-IN......... Multimedia Intelligent Networking (SAUO)
MIN.......... Multipath Interconnection Network (VLIE)
MIN.......... Multistage Interconnection Network (RALS)
MINA........ Member of the Institution of Naval Architects [*British*]
MINA........ Monoisonitrosoacetone [*Biochemistry*]
MINA........ Multiplexed Input NHRE [*National Hail Research Experiment*] Averager
MINABB..... Minimum Abbreviations [*of MAST*]
MINAC....... Miniature Navigation Airborne Computer
MINAC....... Minuteman Action Committee (SAA)
MINAGE..... Minimum Seed-Bearing Age [*Botany*]
MinAgric.... Ministry of Agriculture, Fisheries and Food (SAUO)
MiNas....... Putnam Public Library, Nashville, MI [*Library symbol*] [*Library of Congress*] (LCLS)
minat........ Miniature (VRA)
MINAT....... Miniature
MINATOM... Ministry for Atomic Energy Issues (SAUO)
MiNazC...... Nazareth College, Nazareth, MI [*Library symbol*] [*Library of Congress*] (LCLS)
MiNb........ New Buffalo Public Library, New Buffalo, MI [*Library symbol*] [*Library of Congress*] (LCLS)
MINBATFOR... Minecraft Battle Force, Pacific Fleet
MINBL........ Minimum Balance (VLIE)
Min B/L..... Minimum Bill of Lading (DS)
M-in-C....... Matron-in-Chief [*Navy*] [*British*]
MINC........ Minicomputer
MINC........ Modular Instrumentation Computer (VLIE)
MINC........ Module Interconnect (SAUS)
MINCOM.... Miniaturized Communications [*Navy*] (DNAB)
MINCOMS... Multiple Interior Communications System (MCD)
MINCONMAR... Ministerial Conference of West and Central African States on Maritime Transport [*Ivory Coast*] (EAIO)
MINCOS..... Modular Inventory Control System [*Computer science*] (VLIE)
MIND........ Magnetic Integrator Neuron Duplicator
MIND........ Management Institute for National Development
MIND........ Management of Information through Natural Discourse (SAUO)
MIND........ Method in Natural Development [*Mental diet plan*]
MIND........ Methods of Intellectual Development [*National Association of Manufacturers*]
MIND........ Microsoft Internet Developer (SAUO)
MIND........ Mining Item Name Directory [*A publication*]
MIND........ Mitcham Indus [*NASDAQ symbol*] (TTSB)
MIND........ Mitcham Industries [*NASDAQ symbol*] (SAG)
MIND........ Modular Interactive Network Designer

MIND .... Multidisciplinary Institute for Neuropsychological Development (EA)
MIND .... Multiple Infrared Naval Decoy
MIND .... National Association for Mental Health [*Medicine*] [*United Kingdom*] (EDAA)
MINDAC ..... Marine Inertial Navigation Data Assimilation Computer (IEEE)
MIndAdm ... Master of Industrial Administration (GAGS)
MINDAL ..... Meat Importers National Defence Association (SAUO)
MINDAP ..... Microwave-Induced Nitrogen Discharge at Atmospheric Pressure [*Spectrometry*]
MINDAT ..... Minerals Data Base [*of the Law of the Sea*] (GNE)
MINDD ...... Minimum Due Date per Order
MIndE .... Master of Industrial Engineering (SAUO)
MIndEd ...... Master of Industrial Education
Min Def ..... Ministry of Defence (SAUO)
MIN-DEF .... Ministry of Defence [*British*]
MINDER ..... Miniature Detection Radar [*Police and security equipment*]
Min Dig ..... Minot's Digest [*Massachusetts*] [*A publication*] (DLA)
MIND/INDUS... Automation of Proofs by Mathematical Induction (SAUO)
MinDirig .... Ministerialdirigent (SAUO)
MINDIV ...... Mine Division [*Navy*]
MINDO ...... Modified Intermediate Neglect of Diatomic Overlap (AAEL)
MINDO ...... Modified Intermediate Neglect of Differential Overlap [*Quantum mechanics*]
MIndR .... Master of Industrial Relations (CPGU)
MINDS ...... Mental Illness Nervous Disorders Society [*Australia*]
MindSpr ..... MindSpring Enterprises, Inc. [*Associated Press*] (SAG)
MINE .... Medical Improvement not Expected (DHP)
MINE .... Mesna, Ifosfamide, Mitoxantrone, Etoposide [*Antineoplastic drug*] (CDI)
MINE .... Microbial Information Network Europe [*EEC*]
Min E .... Mineral Engineer
Min E .... Mining Engineer
MINE .... Minneapolis Eastern Railway Co. [*AAR code*]
MINE .... Minnesota Information Network for Educators (SAUO)
MINE .... Montana Information Network Exchange [*Library network*]
MINE .... Multi-Indenture NORS [*Not Operationally Ready Status*] Evaluator (MCD)
MINEAC ..... Miniature Electronic Auto-Collimator
MINEASYFAC... Mine Assembly Facilities
MINEC .... Military Necessity
MINECTRMEASSTA... Mine Countermeasure Station [*Military*]
MINECTRMEASTA... Mine Countermeasures Station [*Military*] (DNAB)
M In Ed ..... Master of Industrial Education (PGP)
MINEDAF ... Conference of Ministers of Education and Those Responsible for Economic Planing in African Member States (SAUO)
MINEDAP ... Regional Conference of Ministers of Education and Those Responsible for Economic Planning in Asia and the Pacific (SAUO)
MINEDARAB... Conference of Ministers of Education and Those Responsible for Economic Planning in Arab States (SAUO)
MINEDEFLAB... Mine Defense Laboratory [*Navy*]
MINEDEUROPE... Conference of Ministers of Education of Member States of the Europe Region (SAUO)
MINEDLAC... Conference of Ministers of Education and those Responsible for Economic Planning in Latin America and Caribbean (SAUO)
MiNeg .... Negaunee Public Library, Negaunee, MI [*Library symbol*] [*Library of Congress*] (LCLS)
MINELCO ... Miniature Electronic Component (WDAA)
Min Eng ..... Minerals Engineering [*A publication*] (CABS)
MINEPACSUPPGRU... Mine Force, Pacific Fleet, Support Group Unit (DNAB)
miner .... Minerology (DD)
MINER .... Minerva, OH [*American Association of Railroads railroad junction routing code*]
Mineral ..... Mineralogical (SAUO)
Mineral ..... Mineralogy (BEE)
MINERAL ... Mineralogy
MINERALOG... Mineralogical
Mineralog Mag... Mineralogical Magazine (SAUS)
Mineral Soc... Mineralogical Society (SAUO)
MINERVA ... Minimization of Earthworks for Vertical Alignment (PDAA)
MineSf ...... Mine Safety Appliances Co. [*Associated Press*] (SAG)
MINESLA.... Conference of Ministers of Education and those Responsible for the Promotion of Science and Technology in Relation to Development in Latin American and the Caribbean (SAUO)
MINET .... Medical Information Network [*GTE Telenet Communications Corp.*] [*Reston, VA*] [*Telecommunications*]
MINET .... Metropolitan Information Network
MINET .... Movement Information Network (SAUO)
MIN EV ...... Minutes of Evidence [*Legal term*] (DLA)
MINEVDET... Mine Warfare Evaluation Detachment
MiNew ...... Newaygo Carnegie Public Library, Newaygo, MI [*Library symbol*] [*Library of Congress*] (LCLS)
MINEWARCOM... Mine Warfare Command [*Navy*]
MiNew-C.... Croton Public Library, Newaygo, MI [*Library symbol*] [*Library of Congress*] (LCLS)
MINEX .... Minelaying, Minesweeping, and Mine-Hunting Exercise [*NATO*] (NATG)
MINEX .... Mine Warfare Exercise (NVT)
MINFLOT.... Mine Flotilla [*Navy*]
MInfoTech... Master of Information Technology and Communication
MInfSys ..... Master of Information Systems
Min Fuel .... Ministry of Fuel and Power (SAUO)
MING .... Magnetic Induction Nuclear Gyroscope
MIng .... Maitre en Ingenierie [*Master of Engineering*] [*French*]
Ming .... Maitrise en Ingenierie [*Master of Engineering*] (DD)
MING .... Middle Class, Intelligent, Nice Girl [*Lifestyle classification*]
MINGSE ..... Minimum Ground Support Equipment Concept (MCD)
MiNhL .... Lenox Township Library, New Haven, MI [*Library symbol*] [*Library of Congress*] (LCLS)
MinHous .... Ministry of Housing and Local Government (SAUO)
MINI .... Method of Implicit Nonstationary Iteration (PDAA)
MINI .... Miniature (KSC)
MINI .... Minicomputer (VLIE)
MINI .... Minicomputer Industry National Interchange [*An association*] (EA)
MINI .... Minimize Individually Negotiated Instruments (AFM)
MINI .... Minimum (DSUE)
MINI .... Miniscooter [*NCIC motorcycle make code*]
MINI .... Mobile Mini [*NASDAQ symbol*] (TTSB)
MINI .... Mobile Mini, Inc. [*NASDAQ symbol*] (SAG)
MiNi .... Niles Community Library, Niles, MI [*Library symbol*] [*Library of Congress*] (LCLS)
MINIA .... Monkey Intranuclear Inclusion Agent (MAE)
MINIAC ...... Minimal Automatic Computer (VLIE)
MINIACT .... Minimum Acquisition Tracking System (MUGU)
MINIAPS .... Miniature Accessory Power Supply
MINIBIB ..... Danish government libraries catalogue (SAUS)
MINIBIB ..... Government libraries catalogue (SAUO)
MINICATS... Miniaturization of Federal Catalog System Publications
MINICOM ... Minimum Communications
MINI COMP... Miniature Compact (MCD)
MINICS ...... Minimal-Input Cataloguing System [*Loughborough University of Technology*]
MINICS/PDS... MINICS Periodicals Data System (NITA)
MINIDAU.... Miniature Data Acquisition Unit
MINIDOS.... Mini Disk Operating System (IDOE)
MINI-ELS ... Mini-Emitter Location System (MCD)
MINIEX ...... Modeling and Simulation [*Training term*] (LPT)
MINI-IR ..... Minimum Incident Report (VLIE)
Miniluv ...... Ministry of Love [*From George Orwell's novel, "1984"*]
Mini-MADS... Minimodular Auxiliary Data System (SAUS)
MiniMd ...... MiniMed, Inc. [*Associated Press*] (SAG)
MINI-MEG... Mini Message Entry Generator (ACAE)
MINI MUX... Miniaturized Multiplexes (MCD)
MiNiN .... National Standard Information Resources, Niles, MI [*Library symbol*] [*Library of Congress*] (LCLS)
Mining Chem Engng Rev... Mining and Chemical Engineering Review [*A publication*]
Mining Engng Rev... Mining and Engineering Review [*A publication*]
MiningS ..... Mining Services International Corp. [*Associated Press*] (SAG)
Min Inst ..... Minor's Institutes of Common and Statute Law [*A publication*] (DLA)
MIN INVEST... Minimum Investment [*Finance*]
Minipax ..... Ministry of Peace [*From George Orwell's novel, "1984"*]
MINIPERT... Mini Program Evaluation and Review Technique (VLIE)
Miniplenty... Ministry of Plenty [*From George Orwell's novel, "1984"*]
Mini-POPs... Mini Points of Presence
MINIRAD .... Minimum Radiation (CAAL)
MINIRAR .... Minimum Radiation Requirements [*Missiles*] (IEEE)
MINIS .... Mini Intraport Network Information System (SAUO)
MINISID ..... Miniature Seismic Intrusion Detector [*DoD*]
MINISINS... Miniature Ship Inertial Navigation System (MCD)
MINI-STE ... Mini-Special Test Equipment (ACAE)
MiniSTEP ... Mini Satellite Test of the Equivalence Principle (SAUS)
MINISTREL... Models for Information Storage and Retrieval (SAUO)
MINI-SUBLAB... Miniature Submarine Laboratory
MINIT .... Minimum Interference Threshold [*Telecommunications*] (TEL)
MINITAS .... Miniature True Airspeed Computer
MINITECH... Ministry of Technology (SAUO)
MINITEX .... Minnesota Interlibrary Telecommunications Exchange [*Library cooperative*] [*Minnesota Higher Education Coordinating Board*] [*Minneapolis, MN*]
MINITEX .... Minnesota Interlibrary Teletex Experiment (SAUO)
MINITRACK... Minimum-Weight Tracking [*System*] (MUGU)
Minitrue ..... Ministry of Truth [*From George Orwell's novel, "1984"*]
MINIVAR .... Minimum Variance Orbit Determination (MCD)
MINIW .... Mobile Mini Wrrt [*NASDAQ symbol*] (TTSB)
MINJC .... Minnesota Junction, WI [*American Association of Railroads railroad junction routing code*]
MINK .... Missouri-Iowa-Nebraska-Kansas (SAUO)
MINK .... Missouri-Iowa-Nebraska-Kansas League [*Old baseball league*]
MINL .... Minimum Licence Period (WDAA)
MINL .... Minnetonka Corp. (SAUO)
MINLANT ... Mine Warfare Forces, Atlantic [*Navy*]
Minl E .... Mineral Engineer (PGP)
MINLP .... Mixed-Integer Nonlinear Program [*Computer science*]
minm .... Minimum [*Medicine*] (BCRP)
MINMAC-PC... Mini-Macroeconomic Personal Computer Model [*Department of Energy*] (GFGA)
minm asst... Minimal Assistance [*Medicine*] (BCRP)
MIN/MAX ... Minimum/Maximum (RIMS)
MINMB ...... Mint in a Near Mint Box [*Collectibles*]
MIN MC ...... Minimum Material Condition [*Computer science*]
MINMP ...... Mint in Near Mint Package [*Collectibles*]
MINN .... Minelli [*NCIC motorcycle make code*]
MINN .... Minnesota (AFM)
Minn .... Minnesota (ODBW)
Minn .... Minnesota Supreme Court Reports [*A publication*] (DLA)
Minn Admin Reg... Minnesota State Register [*A publication*] (DLA)
MinNauki ... Ministry of Science and Technical Policy (SAUO)

MinnBrw .... Minnesota Brewing Co. [*Associated Press*] (SAG)
Minn Code Agency... Minnesota Code of Agency Rules [*A publication*] (DLA)
Minn Code Ann... Minnesota Code, Annotated [*A publication*] (DLA)
Minn Ct Rep... Minnesota Court Reporter [*A publication*] (DLA)
Minn DL & I Comp... Minnesota Department of Labor and Industries. Compilation of Court Decisions [*A publication*] (DLA)
MINN DPW LIB... Minnesota Department of Public Welfare Library Consortium [*Library network*]
MINNE....... Minneapolis, KS [*American Association of Railroads railroad junction routing code*]
MinnEd...... Minnesota Educational Computing Corp. [*Associated Press*] (SAG)
MINNEMAST... Minnesota School Mathematics and Science Teaching Project [*University of Minnesota*] (AEE)
Minn Gen Laws... Minnesota General Laws [*A publication*] (DLA)
Minn (Gil)... Minnesota Reports (Gilfillan Edition) [*A publication*] (DLA)
Minn (Gill)... Minnesota Reports (Gilfillan Edition) [*A publication*] (DLA)
Minn Hist Soc... Minnesota Historical Society (SAUO)
Minn Law J... Minnesota Law Journal [*A publication*] (DLA)
Minn Laws... Laws of Minnesota [*A publication*] (DLA)
Minn LJ..... Minnesota Law Journal [*St. Paul*] [*A publication*] (DLA)
MINNLP..... Minnesota Linear Programming (SAUO)
MinnMul .... Minnesota Municipal Income Trust [*Associated Press*] (SAG)
MinnMuT ... Minnesota Municipal Term Trust [*Associated Press*] (SAG)
Minn Orch... Minnesota Orchestra (SAUO)
MinnPL...... Minnesota Power & Light Co. [*Associated Press*] (SAG)
Minn R & WCAT Div... Minnesota Railroad and Warehouse Commission. Auto Transportation Co. Division Reports [*A publication*] (DLA)
Minn Reg... Minnesota Register [*A publication*] (AAGC)
Minn Rep... Minnesota Reports [*A publication*] (DLA)
Minn Reps... Minnesota Reports [*A publication*] (DLA)
Minn Sess Law Serv (West)... Minnesota Session Law Service (West) [*A publication*] (DLA)
Minn Stat... Minnesota Statutes [*A publication*] (AAGC)
Minn Stat Ann... Minnesota Statutes, Annotated [*A publication*] (DLA)
Minn Stat Ann (West)... West's Minnesota Statutes, Annotated [*A publication*] (DLA)
Minntc....... Minntech Corp. [*Associated Press*] (SAG)
MinnTr2..... Minnesota Term Trust, Inc. II [*Associated Press*] (SAG)
Minn WCD... Minnesota Workmen's Compensation Decisions [*A publication*] (DLA)
MINOD ...... Miniaturized Infrared Night Observation Device (ACAE)
MIN OIL..... Mineral Oil (SAUS)
MINON ...... Minonk, IL [*American Association of Railroads railroad junction routing code*]
MiNop....... Leelanau Township Library, Northport, MI [*Library symbol*] [*Library of Congress*] (LCLS)
Minor........ Minor's Alabama Supreme Court Reports [*1820-26*] [*A publication*] (DLA)
Minor........ Minor's Institutes [*A publication*] (DLA)
Minor (Ala)... Minor's Alabama Reports [*A publication*] (DLA)
Minor (Ala)... Minor's Institutes [*Alabama*] [*A publication*] (DLA)
Minorc ...... Minorco [*Formerly, Minerals & Resources Corp. Ltd.*] [*Associated Press*] (SAG)
MINORCO... Minerals & Resources Corporation (SAUO)
Minor Inst... Minor's Institutes of Common and Statute Law [*A publication*] (DLA)
Minor's Alabama Rep... Minor's Alabama Reports [*A publication*] (DLA)
Minor's Ala R... Minor's Alabama Reports [*A publication*] (DLA)
Minor's Ala Rep... Minor's Alabama Reports [*A publication*] (DLA)
Minor's R... Minor's Alabama Reports [*A publication*] (DLA)
Minor's Rep... Minor's Alabama Reports [*A publication*] (DLA)
MINOS ...... Main Injector Neutrino Oscillation Search [*Particle Physics*]
MINOS ...... Manual Intervention and Observation Simulator (AAG)
MINOS ...... Marconi Integrated Naval Operations System (SAUS)
MINOS ...... Mine Operating System (PDAA)
MINOS ...... Mixed Integer Operational Scheduling (PDAA)
MINOS ...... Modular Input/Output System
MINOT....... Minot, ND [*American Association of Railroads railroad junction routing code*]
Minot St U... Minot State University (GAGS)
MINOX ...... Minimum Oxidizer (KSC)
MINP .... Mallacoota Inlet National Park (SAUO)
MinP......... Minnesota Power & Light Co. [*Associated Press*] (SAG)
MINPAC..... Mine Warfare Forces, Pacific [*Navy*]
MinPBW .... Ministry of Public Building and Works (SAUO)
MIN PLEN... Minister Plenipotentiary (WDAA)
Min Plenit... Minister Plenipotentiary (SAUO)
MINPOREN... National Association of Commercial Broadcasters in Japan (EY)
MinPres..... Minister President
MINPRIRODI... Ministry of Protection of the Environment and Natural Resources of the Russian Federation (SAUO)
MINPROC... Mineral Processing Technology [*Canada Department of Energy, Mines, and Resources*] [*Information service or system*] (CRD)
MINPRT..... Minimum Processing Time per Operation
Min PW..... Ministry of Public Works (SAUO)
MINQA ...... Minnequa, CO [*American Association of Railroads railroad junction routing code*]
MINQU ...... Minimum Norm Quadratic Unbiased [*Statistics*]
MINQUE..... Minimum Norm Quadratic Unbiased Estimation [*Statistics*] (PDAA)
MINR .... Minimum Rate [*Travel industry*] (TRID)
MINR .... Minimum R Factor [*Spectrometry*]
Min R .... Minnesota Reports [*A publication*] (DLA)
MINRA ...... Miniature International Racing Association
MINRAD..... Minimum Radiation (MCD)
Min Rep .... Minnesota Reports [*A publication*] (DLA)
Min Res..... Minister Resident (ODA)
MINRL....... Mineral
MINRON .... Mine Squadron [*Navy*]
MINRTY..... Minority
MINS .... Mare Island Naval Shipyard [*Also, MINSY*] [*Later, MID*]
MINS .... Marine Integrated Navigation System (SAUS)
MINS .... Miniature Inertial Navigation System
MINS .... Minors in Need of Supervision [*Classification for delinquent children*]
MINSA....... Ministry of Health (SAUO)
MINSAT ..... Minimum Safe Air Travel (SAA)
MINSD ...... Minimum Planned Start Date per Operation
Minsec ...... Mineral Securities Australia Ltd. (SAUO)
MINSK....... [*A*] Russian digital computer [*Moscow University*]
MINSOP..... Minimum Slack Time per Operation
MINSQ ...... Minimum Squares [*Mathematical statistics*]
MInstAEA ... Member of the Institute of Automotive Engineer Assessors [*British*] (DBQ)
M Inst AM... Member of the Institute of Administrative Management [*British*] (DCTA)
MInstBB..... Member of the Institute of British Bakers (DBQ)
MInstBCA ... Member of the Institute of Burial and Cremation Administration [*British*] (DBQ)
MInstBE...... Member of the Institution of British Engineers
MInstBRM... Member of the Institute of Baths and Recreation Management [*British*] (DBQ)
MInstBRMDip... Diploma Member of the Institute of Baths and Recreation Management [*British*] (DBQ)
MInstBTM... Member of the Institute of Business and Technical Management [*British*] (DBQ)
MInstCE..... Member of the Institution of Civil Engineers [*Later, MICE*] [*British*] (EY)
M Inst CM... Member of the Institute of Commercial Management [*British*] (DCTA)
MInstD ...... Member of the Institute of Directors [*British*] (DI)
MInstE....... Member of the Institute of Energy [*British*] (DBQ)
MInstE....... Member of the Institution of Engineers [*British*] (EY)
MInstF....... Member of the Institute of Fuel [*British*]
MInstFF ..... Member of the Institute of Freight Forwarders [*British*] (DBQ)
MInstGasE... Member of the Institution of Gas Engineers [*British*] (EY)
MInstHE..... Member of the Institution of Highway Engineers [*British*]
M INST J ... Member of the Institute of Journalists [*British*] (DGA)
M Inst Jour... Member of the Institute of Journalists [*British*] (ROG)
MInstM...... Member of the Institute of Marketing [*British*]
MInstM...... Member of the Institute of Metals (SAUO)
MInstMC .... Member of the Institute of Measurement and Control [*British*] (DBQ)
MInstME .... Member of the Institution of Mining Engineers [*British*]
MInstMet ... Member of the Institute of Metals [*British*]
MInstMM ... Member of the Institute of Mining and Metallurgy (SAUO)
MInstMM ... Member of the Institution of Mining and Metallurgy [*British*]
MInstMO .... Member of the Institute of Market Officers [*British*] (DI)
MInstMSM... Member of the Institute of Marketing and Sales Management (SAUO)
MInstNA..... Member of the Institution of Naval Architects [*British*] (EY)
MInstNDT... Member of the British Institute of Non-Destructive Testing (DBQ)
MInstP ...... Member of the Institute of Physics (ADA)
MInstPC..... Member of the Institute of Public Cleansing (SAUO)
MInstPE..... Member of the Institute of Petroleum Engineers (ADA)
MInstPet .... Member of the Institute of Petroleum [*British*] (EY)
MInstPI...... Member of the Institute of Patentees and Inventors [*British*] (EY)
MInstPI...... Member of the Institute of Patentees Inc. (SAUO)
MInstPkg.... Member of the Institute of Packaging [*British*] (DI)
M Inst PS... Member of the Institute of Purchasing and Supply [*British*] (DCTA)
MInstPT ..... Member of the Institute of Petroleum Technologists (SAUO)
MInstR ...... Member of the Institute of Refrigeration [*British*] (DBQ)
MINSTR..... Minister
MInstRA..... Member of the Institute of Registered Architects [*British*]
MInstRadE... Member of Institute of Radio-Engineers (SAUO)
M Inst RE... Member of the Institute of Radio Engineers (SAUO)
MINSTREL... Management Information Software Tool-Research in Libraries (SAUO)
MInstSM .... Member of the Institute of Sales Management (SAUO)
MInstSMM... Member of the Institute of Sales and Marketing Management [*British*] (DBQ)
MInstSP..... Member Institution of Sewage Purification [*Ecology*] (DAVI)
MInstSP..... Member of the Institution of Sewage Purification (SAUO)
MInstStructE... Member of the Institution of Structural Engineers (ADA)
MInstSWM... Member of the Institute of Solid Waste Management [*British*] (DI)
MInstT....... Member of the Institute of Technology [*British*] (EY)
MInstT....... Member of the Institute of Transport [*British*]
M Inst TA... Member of the Institute of Transport Administration [*British*] (DCTA)
MInstTM .... Member of the Institute of Travel Managers in Industry and Commerce [*British*] (ODBW)
MInstW...... Member of the Institute of Welding [*British*]
MInstWE .... Member of the Institution of Water Engineers [*British*]
MInstWHS... Member of the Institute of Works and Highways Superintendents [*British*] (DI)
MInstWM ... Member of the Institute of Wastes Management (ODA)
MInstWPC... Member of the Institution of Water Pollution Control [*British*] (DI)
MINSY....... Mare Island Naval Shipyard [*Also, MINS*] [*Later, MID*]
MINT .... Bank of Montreal, Canadian Imperial Bank of Commerce, Bank of Nova Scotia, and Toronto-Dominion Bank
MINT .... Center for Micromagnetics and Information Technologies [*University of Minnesota*] (RCD)

MINT .... Major International Narcotics Traffickers [*Register*] [*Drug Enforcement Administration*]
MINT .... Management Information Network for Training (SAUO)
MINT .... Management of Innovation and New Technology Research Centre [*McMaster University*] [*Canada*] (RCD)
MINT .... Managing the Integration of New Technology (SAUO)
MINT .... Materiel Identification and New Item Control Technique [*AFLC*]
MINT .... Media Integration [*Computer science*]
MINT .... Micro-Integration [*NASDAQ symbol*] (TTSB)
MINT .... Micro-Integration Corp. [*NASDAQ symbol*] (SAG)
MINT .... Minorities International Network for Trade (EA)
MINT .... Municipal Insured National Trust
MINT .... Mutual Interference (SAUS)
MinTch ...... Minerals Technologies, Inc. [*Associated Press*] (SAG)
MINTEC ..... Mining Technology Abstracts [*Canada Centre for Mineral and Energy Technology*] [*Information service or system*] (CRD)
MINTECH ... Ministry of Technology [*British*]
Min Technol... Mining Technology [*A publication*] (CABS)
MINTEK ..... Council for Mineral Technology (SAUO)
MINTEL ..... Market Intelligence Report
MINTEQ ..... Geochemical Model (SAUS)
MINTER ..... Ministerio do Interior [*Ministry of the Interior*] [*Information service or system*] (IID)
MINTERM... Miniature Terminal (SAUS)
MINTEX ..... Mineral Textile [*Automotive parts*]
MINTEX ..... M International Inc. (SAUO)
MINTIE ...... Minimum Test Instrumentation Equipment
MIntLaw .... Master of International Law
M Int Med... Master of Internal Medicine (SAUO)
MIntMed .... Master of International Medicine (NADA)
MinTopEnergo... Ministry of Fuel and Energy (SAUO)
MINTR....... Miniature (MSA)
MINTR....... Minnesota Transfer, MN [*American Association of Railroads railroad junction routing code*]
MINTS....... Mutual Institutions National Transfer System, Inc. [*Banking*]
MINTS....... Mutual Insurance National Transfer System, Inc.
MINTSS ..... Military Airlift Command Intelligence Support System (SAUO)
MINTWK .... Minimum Total Work Content
MINU .... China Ocean Shipping [*Intermodal shipping container symbol*] (TVRC)
MINU .... Mobile Instrument Investigation Unit
MINucE...... Member of the Institution of Nuclear Engineers [*British*]
MI Nucl E... Member of the Institution of Nuclear Engineers [*British*]
MINUET ..... Minimum Energy Trajectory Model [*Army*] (AABC)
MINUET ..... Minnesota Internet User's Essential Tool (VLIE)
MINUGUA... United Nations Verification Mission for/in Guatemala (SAUO)
MiNun....... Crockery Township Library, Nunica, MI [*Library symbol*] [*Library of Congress*] (LCLS)
MINUS ...... Modular Integrated Utility Systems (MCD)
MinutInt..... Minuteman International [*Associated Press*] (SAG)
MINW .... Master Interface Network (MCD)
MINWARA... Mine Warfare Association (EA)
MINWARCOM... Mine Warfare Command (SAUO)
MINWARTECH... Mine Warfare Technician [*Navy*] (DNAB)
MINWR...... Merritt Island National Wildlife Refuge (SAUO)
MINWR...... Minimum Weapon Radius (SAA)
MIN WT..... Minimum Weight (WDAA)
MINX .... Mines in the New Century programme (SAUS)
MINX .... Minnesota Mining and Manufacturing [*Private rail car owner code*]
MINX .... Multimedia Information Network Exchange [*Computer science*]
MINY .... Mineralogy (ROG)
MINY .... Minority (ROG)
MinZdravMedProm... Ministry of Public Health and Medical Industry (SAUO)
MIO .... Management Improvement and Operating Plan [*Department of Housing and Urban Development*] (GFGA)
MIO .... Management Information Office [*or Officer*] [*Air Force*] (AFM)
mio .... Management Integration Office (NAKS)
MIO .... Management Integration Office [*NASA*] (NASA)
MIO .... Map Information Office [*US Geological Survey*]
MIO .... Marine Inspection Office [*Coast Guard*]
MIO .... Marine Inspection Operations [*USCG*] (TAG)
MIO .... Marion, WI [*Amtrak Busline code*]
MIO .... Maritime Interception Operations [*Coast Guard*] (DOMA)
MIO .... Maritime Interdiction Operations
MIO .... Medical Intelligence Office [*Later, MIIA*] [*DoD*]
MIO .... Meteoritic Impact Origin (AAG)
MIO .... Metric Information Office [*National Institute of Standards and Technology*]
MIO .... Miami, OK [*Location identifier*] [*FAA*] (FAAL)
MIO .... Midas Commuter Airlines CA [*Venezuela*] [*ICAO designator*] (FAAC)
MIO .... Military Industrial Organization (ACAE)
MIO .... Military Intelligence Officer [*British military*] (DMA)
MIO .... Military Interviewing Officer (SAUO)
MIO .... Minimal Identifiable Odor
MIO .... Mobile Ionospheric Observatory [*Boston University*]
MIO .... Mobile Issuing Office [*Navy*]
MIO .... Modular Input/Output [*Telecommunications*]
MIO .... Motility Indol Ornithine [*Medium*] [*Medicine*] (BABM)
MIO .... Movements Identification Officer [*Air Force*]
MIO .... Movements Identification Order (SAUO)
MIO .... Movements Integration Office
MIO .... Multi-Institutional Organization [*Generic term*] (DHSM)
MIO .... Multiple Input/Output (NITA)
MIO .... Multiple Input/Output Stream [*Computer science*]
MIOA .... Medical Industries of America [*NASDAQ symbol*] (SAG)
MIOAC....... Military Intelligence Officer Advanced Course (DOMA)
MIOB .... Member of the Institute of Building [*British*]
MIOB .... Member of the Institute (or Institution) of Builders (or Building) (SAUO)
MiOC .... Olivet College, Olivet, MI [*Library symbol*] [*Library of Congress*] (LCLS)
MIOCA....... Monolithic Integrated Optics for Customer Access Applications (SAUO)
MIOD .... Message Input-Output Devices (MCD)
MIOG .... Manual of Investigative and Operational Guidelines [*FBI*]
MIOK .... Magyar Izraelitak Orszagos Kepviselete (BJA)
MiOlA .... Alumni Memorial Library, Orchard Lake, MI [*Library symbol*] [*Library of Congress*] (LCLS)
MIOM........ Member, Institute of Office Management (SAUO)
MIoM........ Member of the Institute of Metals (SAUO)
MIONP ...... Microwave-Induced Optical Nuclear Polarization [*Physics*]
MiOnt........ Ontonagon Township Library, Ontonagon, MI [*Library symbol*] [*Library of Congress*] (LCLS)
MIOP .... Magnetic Iron Oxide Particle (DMAA)
MIOP .... Master Input/Output Processor (NITA)
MIOP .... Member of the Institute of Osteopathy and Physiotherapy [*British*]
MIOP .... Member of the Institute of Printing [*British*] (DBQ)
MIOP .... Multiplexing Input-Output Processor [*Computer science*] (BUR)
MIOS .... Modular Input-Output System [*Telecommunications*] (TEL)
MIOS .... Multi-IMU [*Internal Measuring Unit*] Operation System [*NASA*]
MIOSH ...... Member of the Institution of Occupational Safety and Health [*British*] (DCTA)
MIOSHA..... Michigan Occupational Safety and Health Act (SAUO)
MIOSHA..... Michigan Occupational Safety and Health Administration [*Michigan Department of Labor and Economic Growth*] (MHID)
MIOT .... Member of the Institute of Operating Theatre Technicians [*British*]
MIOT .... Municipal Income Opportunities Trust [*Associated Press*] (SAG)
MiOt.......... Otsego District Public Library, Otsego, MI [*Library symbol*] [*Library of Congress*] (LCLS)
MIOT2....... Municipal Income Opportunities Trust II [*Associated Press*] (SAG)
MIOT3....... Municipal Income Opportunities Trust III [*Associated Press*] (SAG)
MiOv.......... Ovid Public Library, Ovid, MI [*Library symbol*] [*Library of Congress*] (LCLS)
MIOW .... Member of the Institute of Welding (SAUO)
MiOw......... Owosso Public Library, Owosso, MI [*Library symbol*] [*Library of Congress*] (LCLS)
MiOwJW .... John Wesley College, Owosso, MI [*Library symbol*] [*Library of Congress*] (LCLS)
MIP .... Machine Independent Package (DGA)
MIP .... Machine Instruction Processor [*Computer science*] (BUR)
MIP .... Macrophage-Induced Protein [*Biochemistry*]
MIP .... Macrophage Inflammatory Protein [*Biochemistry*]
MIP .... Magnetic Index Pulse (ACAE)
MIP .... Mainframe Internetting Project (SAUO)
MIP .... Main Instrument Panel (MCD)
MIP .... Maintainer Instructional Package (MCD)
MIP .... Maintenance Implementation Plan [*FAA*] (TAG)
MIP .... Maintenance Improvement Program
MIP .... Maintenance Index Page
MIP .... Major Intrinsic Protein [*Biochemistry*]
MIP .... Malleable Iron Pipe
MIP .... Management Implementation Plan (MCD)
MIP .... Management Improvement Plan
MIP .... Management Improvement Program [*Military*]
MIP .... Management Incentive Program
MIP .... Management Information Protocol [*Telecommunications*] (OSI)
MIP .... Management Intern Program
MIP .... Mandatory Inspection Point (KSC)
MIP .... Manual Index Page [*SNMMMS*]
MIP .... Manual Input Processing [*or Program*] [*Computer science*]
MIP .... Manufacturers of Illumination Products (EA)
MIP .... Marche International des Programmes de Television International [*International Marketplace for Buyers and Sellers of Television Programs*] (NTCM)
MIP .... Marine Insurance Policy
MIP .... Master Improvement Program (AFIT)
MIP .... Master Index Pulse (ACAE)
MIP .... Master Information Paper [*Military*] (CAAL)
MIP .... Master Insurance Program
MIP .... Master of Intellectual Property (PGP)
MIP .... Material Improvement Plan [*or Program*] [*Aviation*]
MIP .... Material in Process [*Computer science*] (CIST)
MIP .... Materiel Improvement Project [*Military*]
MIP .... Matrix Inversion Program [*Computer science*] (BUR)
MIP .... Maximum Inspiratory Pressure [*Medicine*]
MIP .... Maximum Integration Phone (SAUO)
MIP .... Maximum Investment Plan (WDAA)
MIP .... Mean Incubation Perios (MELL)
MIP .... Mean Indicated Pressure
MIP .... Mean Intravascular Pressure [*Cardiology*] (MAE)
MIP .... Measuring Instruments Pullin Ltd. (SAUO)
MIP .... Mechanized Infantry Program [*United States Army, Europe*] (MCD)
MIP .... Medicaid Interim Payments
MIP .... Member of the Institute of Petroleum (SAUO)
MIP .... Member of the Institute of Plumbing [*British*] (DBQ)
MIP .... Membrane-Intercalated Particles [*Cytology*]
MIP .... Membrane Isolation Process [*Food technology*]
MIP .... Merfin Hygienic [*Vancouver Stock Exchange symbol*]
MIP .... Message Input Processor

MIP .... Methodology Investigation Proposal (MCD)
MIP .... Methods Improvement Program [*IBM Corp.*]
MIP .... Microelectronic Integrated Processing [*Symposium*]
MIP .... Microwave-Induced Plasma [*Spectrometry*]
MIP .... Microwave Interference Protection
MIP .... Middle Interphalangeal Joint [*Anatomy*] (DAVI)
MIP .... Military Improvement Program
MIP .... Military Information Program
MIP .... Military Interdepartmental Purchase
MIP .... Military International Police (SAUO)
MIP .... Million Instructions per Second
MIP .... Milton, PA [*Location identifier*] [*FAA*] (FAAL)
MIP .... Minimal Inspiratory Pressure [*Medicine*] (DB)
MIP .... Minimum Import Prices [*Economics*]
MIP .... Minimum Impulse Pulse
MIP .... Ministry of Irrigation and Power (SAUO)
MIP .... Minor Sync Point [*Open Systems Interconnection*] (ODAA)
MIP .... Mint in Package [*Doll collecting*]
MIP .... Missile Impact Prediction (SAUO)
MIP .... Missile Impact Predictor [*Air Force*]
MIP .... Missile Instrumentation Package [*Military*] (CAAL)
MIP .... Mission Integration Panel [*NASA*] (SSD)
MIP .... Missouri Institute of Psychiatry (SAUO)
MIP .... Missouri Institute of Psychiatry Library, St. Louis, MO [*OCLC symbol*] (OCLC)
MIP .... Mixed Integer Programming [*Computer science*]
MIP .... Mixture Inlet Pressure [*Automotive engineering*]
MIP .... MMU [*Manned Maneuvering Unit*] Integration Plan [*NASA*] (GFGA)
MIP .... Mobilization Improvement Program [*MTMC*] (TAG)
MIP .... Model Implementation Plan
MIP .... Model Improvements Program [*TRADOC*] (MCD)
MIP .... Model Installation Program (AAGC)
MIP .... Modern Irish Printer [*A publication*] [*British*] (DGA)
MIP .... Modest Improvement Program [*Military*] (NVT)
MIP .... Modification Instruction Package (KSC)
MIP .... Modulated Interframe Plan
MIP .... Molded-in-Place [*Automotive engineering*]
MIP .... Molecularly Imprinted Polymer [*Biotechnology*]
MIP .... Monthly Intelligence Production (MCD)
MIP .... Monthly Investment Plan [*Stock exchange term*] (SPSG)
MIP .... Mortgage Insurance Premium
MIP .... Mortgage Investments Plus, Inc. (MHDW)
MIP .... Most Important Person
MIP .... Motivation Indoctrination Program [*Military*]
MIP .... Mouvement Independent Populaire [*Popular Independent Movement*] [*Luxembourg*] [*Political party*] (PPE)
MIP .... Mouvement Islamique Progressiste [*Islamic Progressive Movement*] [*Tunisia*] [*Political party*] (PD)
MIP .... Movimiento Independiente Peruano [*Peruvian Independent Movement*] [*Political party*]
MIP .... Multi-Island Programme (SAUO)
MIP .... Multimission Interactive Picture (MWOL)
MIP .... Multipurpose Information Processor [*Computer science*] (MHDB)
MIP .... Museums Informatics Project (SAUO)
MIP .... Mycorrhiza Inoculum Potential [*Soil science*]
MIP .... Myo-inositolphosphate [*Biochemistry*]
MIPA .... Macrophage Inflammatory Protein Alpha (DMAA)
MIPA .... Master of International Public Administration (GAGS)
MIPA .... Member of the Institute of Practitioners in Advertising [*British*]
MIPA .... Member of the Institute of Public Administration (ADA)
MIPA .... Methylisopropylaniline [*Organic chemistry*]
MIPA .... Missile Procurement, Army (AABC)
MIPA .... Monoisopropylamine [*Organic chemistry*]
MiPa .... Port Austin Township Library, Port Austin, MI [*Library symbol*] [*Library of Congress*] (LCLS)
MIPAC .... Motamar International Peace Advancement Campaign (SAUO)
Mipad .... Multimodal, Interactive Note Pad
MIP-AES .... Microwave-Induced Plasma-Atomic Emission Spectroscopy
MiPal .... Richmond Township Public Library, Palmer, MI [*Library symbol*] [*Library of Congress*] (LCLS)
MIPAR .... Maryland Institute for Policy Analysis and Research [*University of Maryland, Baltimore County*] (RCD)
MiPar .... Parchment Community Library, Parchment, MI [*Library symbol*] [*Library of Congress*] (LCLS)
MIPAS .... Management Information Planning and Accountancy Service (MHDI)
MIPAS .... Michelson Interferometric Passive Atmosphere Sounder (EOSA)
MiPaw .... Paw Paw Public Library, Paw Paw, MI [*Library symbol*] [*Library of Congress*] (LCLS)
MIPB .... Macrophage Inflammatory Protein Beta (DMAA)
MIPB .... Material Improvement Project Board (SAUO)
MIPB .... Monoisopropylbiphenyl (PDAA)
MIPC .... Manifold Ignition Primary Charge
MIPC .... Master Index Pulse Corrected (ACAE)
MIPC .... Member of the Institute of Production Control [*British*] (DBQ)
MIPC .... Metropolitan Information Processing Conference (MCD)
MIPCC .... Mass Injected Pre-Compressor Cooled
MIPD .... Manpower Intelligence and Planning Division (AIE)
MIPD .... Manufacturing Industry Products Division (MCD)
MIPDS .... Minuteman Instrumented Payload Delivery System (ACAE)
MIPE .... Magnetic Induction Plasma Engine
MIPE .... Member of the Institution of Production Engineers [*British*] (DAS)
MIPE .... Men's International Peace Exchange (EA)
MIPE .... Mobile Intelligence Processing Element (DOMA)
MIPE .... Modular Information Processing Equipment
MIPE .... Moscow Institute of Power Engineering (SAUO)
MiPec .... Elk Township Library, Peck, MI [*Library symbol*] [*Library of Congress*] (LCLS)
MiPel .... Pellston Public Library, Pellston, MI [*Library symbol*] [*Library of Congress*] (LCLS)
MiPen .... Pentwater Township Library, Pentwater, MI [*Library symbol*] [*Library of Congress*] (LCLS)
MIPet .... Member of the Institute of Petroleum (SAUO)
MiPet .... Petoskey Public Library, Petoskey, MI [*Library symbol*] [*Library of Congress*] (LCLS)
MiPetN ...... North Central Michigan College, Petoskey, MI [*Library symbol*] [*Library of Congress*] (LCLS)
MIPEX .... Model Improvement Experiment (MCD)
MIPG .... Master Index Pulse Generator
MiPh .... Saint Clair County Library System, Port Huron, MI [*Library symbol*] [*Library of Congress*] (LCLS)
MIPHE .... Member of the Institute of Public Health Engineers [*British*] (DBQ)
MIPHE .... Member of the Institution of Public Health Engineers (SAUO)
MiPhM ...... Saint Clair County Community Mental Health Services, Port Huron, MI [*Library symbol*] [*Library of Congress*] (LCLS)
MiPHS .... Michigan Photographic Historical Society (EARSL)
MiPhS .... Saint Clair Community College, Port Huron, MI [*Library symbol*] [*Library of Congress*] (LCLS)
MIPI .... Medicine in the Public Interest (EA)
MIPI .... Member of the Institute of Professional Investigators [*British*] (DBQ)
MiPi .... Pigeon District Library, Pigeon, MI [*Library symbol*] [*Library of Congress*] (LCLS)
MIPIE .... Michigan Products Information Exchange [*Interchange Plus, Inc.*] [*Information service or system*] (IID)
MiPin .... Pinckney Community Public Library, Pinckney, MI [*Library symbol*] [*Library of Congress*] (LCLS)
MIPIR .... Missile Precision Instrumentation RADAR
MIPIR .... Multimission Imagery Photographic Interpretation Report (MCD)
MiPit .... Pittsford Township Library, Pittsford, MI [*Library symbol*] [*Library of Congress*] (LCLS)
MIPK .... Methyl Isopropyl Ketone [*Organic chemistry*]
MiPl .... Charles A. Ransom Public Library, Plainwell, MI [*Library symbol*] [*Library of Congress*] (LCLS)
MIPL .... Master Indentured Parts List
MIPL .... Mauritius Institute Public Library (SAUO)
MIPL .... Monthly Intelligence Production Listing (MCD)
MIPL .... Multidimensional Image Processing Laboratory [*University of Arizona*] (RCD)
MIPL .... Multimission Image Processing Laboratory (SAUO)
MIPlantE .... Member of the Institution of Plant Engineers [*British*]
MIPLOGS ... Marine Integrated Personnel and Logistics Subsystem
MiPIS .... State Technical Institute and Rehabilitation Center, Plainwell, MI [*Library symbol*] [*Library of Congress*] (LCLS)
MiPlySJ ..... Saint John's Provincial Seminary, Plymouth, MI [*Library symbol*] [*Library of Congress*] (LCLS)
MIPM .... Member of the Institute of Personnel Management [*British*]
MIP/MA ..... Missile in Place/Missile Away
MIPMS ...... Microwave-Induced Plasma Mass Spectrometry
MIPO .... Multiple Item Purchase Order (AAG)
MiPon .... Pontiac Public Libraries, Pontiac, MI [*Library symbol*] [*Library of Congress*] (LCLS)
MiPonO ..... Oakland County Law Library, Clark J. Adams-Philip Pratt Library, Pontiac, MI [*Library symbol*] [*Library of Congress*] (LCLS)
MiPonSJ .... Saint Joseph Mercy Hospital, General Medical Library, Pontiac, MI [*Library symbol*] [*Library of Congress*] (LCLS)
MiPor .... Portage Public Library, Portage, MI [*Library symbol*] [*Library of Congress*] (LCLS)
MIPORN ..... Miami Pornography [*FBI undercover investigation, 1977-80*]
MiPorPS .... Portage Public Schools, Portage, MI [*Library symbol*] [*Library of Congress*] (LCLS)
MiPorS ...... Seventh Day Adventists Junior Academy, Portage, MI [*Library symbol*] [*Library of Congress*] (LCLS)
MiPot .... Benton Township - Potterville District Library, Potterville, MI [*Library symbol*] [*Library of Congress*] (LCLS)
MIPP .... Maintainability Index Prediction Procedure
MIPP .... Master of International Public Policy (GAGS)
MIPP .... Milk Indemnity Payment Program
MiPPT .... McMaster Institute for Polymer Production Technology [*McMaster University*] [*Canada*] (IRC)
MIPR .... Manhattan Institute for Policy Research (EA)
MIPR .... Master Index Pulse Reference (ACAE)
MIPR .... Medical Intelligence Production Requirements (MCD)
MIPR .... Member of the Institute of Public Relations [*British*]
MIPR .... Military Interagency Procurement Requisition (SAUO)
MIPR .... Military Interagency Purchase Request (SAUO)
MIPR .... Military Interdepartmental Procurement [*or Purchase*] Request
MIPR .... Military Intergovernmental Purchase Request (NASA)
MIPR .... Monthly Interim Progress Report
MIPRCS ..... Microprocessor (MSA)
MIPRG ...... Master Index Pulse Reference Generator (ACAE)
Mipro .... Manufactures Import Promotion Organization (SAUO)
MIProdE .... Member of the Institution of Production Engineers [*British*] (EY)
MIPS .... Maintenance Index Pages (ACAE)
MIPS .... Management Information Progress Sheets (MCD)
MIPS .... Marine Integrated Personnel System (MCD)
MIPS .... Martinsried Institute for Protein Sequences [*Database producer*]
MIPS .... Master Installment Purchase System (ACAE)
MIPS .... Meaningless Information per Second (SAUS)
MIPS .... Medium Integrated Propulsion System (SAUS)
MIPS .... Member of the Phonographic Society [*British*] (ROG)
MIPS .... Membership Information Processing System [*AARP*]
MIPS .... Merritt Island Press Site [*NASA*] (NASA)

MIPS .... Microprocessor with Interlocked Pipeline Stages (RALS)
MIPS .... Microprocessor Without Interlocked Pipeline Stages (NITA)
MIPS .... Microwave-Induced Plasma Spectroscopy (MEC)
MIPS .... Microwave Pulse Storage System [*or Subsystem*] (MCD)
MIPS .... Military Information Processing System
mips .... Million Instructions Per Second [*Computer science*] (WDMC)
MIPS .... Million Instructions per Second (ACAE)
mips .... Millions of Instructions per Second [*Computer processing speed*] (NETL)
MIPS .... Millon Index of Personality Styles [*Test*] (TMMY)
MIPS .... Miniature Implantable Power System
MIPS .... MIPS Technologies, Inc. [*NASDAQ symbol*] (NASQ)
MIPS .... Missile Impact Prediction System
MIPS .... Missile Information Processing System (MCD)
MIPS .... Mission and Information Planning System (ACAE)
MIPS .... Modular Instrumentation Package System (MCD)
MIPS .... Modular Integrated Pallet System [*Tank monitoring*] [*Army*] (RDA)
MIPS .... Multi Instruction Processing System (SAUO)
MIPS .... Multimission Image Processing Subsystem (SAUS)
MIPS .... Multiple Index Processing System (MCD)
MIPS .... Munich Information Center for Protein Sequences (SAUO)
MIPS .... Myocardial Isotopic Perfusion Scan [*Cardiology*] (DAVI)
MiPs .... Sanilac Township Library, Port Sanilac, MI [*Library symbol*] [*Library of Congress*] (LCLS)
MIPsiMed ... Member of the Institute of Psionic Medicine [*British*]
MIPSL .... Manufacturing Indentured Parts Summary List (ACAE)
MIPSM ...... Member of the Institute of Purchasing and Supply Management (ADA)
MIPSNY ..... Metro-International Program Services of New York (EA)
MIPT .... Memorial Institute for the Prevention of Terrorism [*Emergency Management*] [*Oklahoma City, OK*] (EMA)
MIPTC .... Men's International Professional Tennis Council [*Defunct*] (EA)
MI PTG M ... Member of the Institute of Printing Management [*British*] (DGA)
MiPtl .... Portland District Library, Portland, MI [*Library symbol*] [*Library of Congress*] (LCLS)
MIPTV .... Marche International des Programmes de Television [*Cannes Film Festival*] [*France*]
MIPVCE ..... Multiple-Input Phase-Variable Canonical Form (PDAA)
MIPX .... Millennium Petrochemicals [*Private rail car owner code*]
MIQ .... Maiquetia [*Venezuela*] [*Airport symbol*] (AD)
MIQ .... Maniwaki [*Quebec*] [*Seismograph station code, US Geological Survey*] (SEIS)
MIQ .... Member of the Institute of Quarrying [*British*] (DBQ)
MIQ .... Minimum Identifiable Quantity [*Analytical chemistry*]
MIQ .... Minnesota Importance Questionnaire [*Vocational test*]
Miq .... Miqva'ot [*or Miqwa'ot*] (BJA)
MIQA .... Member of the Institute of Quality Assurance [*British*] (DBQ)
MIQE/F ..... Master of Arts in Quantitative Economics and Finance [*Educational term*]
MIQPS ...... Member of the Institute of Qualified Private Secretaries [*British*] (DI)
Mir .... Horne's Mirror of Justice [*A publication*] (DLA)
MIR .... Magnetic Ink Read
MIR .... Main Immunogenic Region [*Immunology*]
MIR .... Maintenance Infusion Rate [*Medicine*]
MIR .... Maintenance Inspection Report
MIR .... Major Impact Report (SAUO)
MIR .... Malfunction Investigation Report [*NASA*] (KSC)
MIR .... Management Information Report
MIR .... Management Information Repository [*Computer science*] (CIST)
MIR .... Management Information Requirement [*Production management*]
MIR .... Manager, Iwi Relationships (SAUO)
MIR .... Mandatory Inspection Report (MCD)
MIR .... Manual Input Room (SAA)
MIR .... Master Index of Repairables (MCD)
MIR .... Master Inventory Record
MIR .... Master of Industrial Relations
MIR .... Material Inspection Report [*Navy*]
MIR .... Material Investigators Reactor [*NASA*]
MIR .... Maverick Interim Report
MIR .... Maximum Incremental Reactivity [*Exhaust emissions*] [*Automotive engineering*]
MIR .... Maximum Individual Risk [*Environmental science*] (FFDE)
MIR .... Maximum Information Rate (SAUO)
MIR .... M.D.C. Asset Investors, Inc. [*NYSE symbol*] (COMM)
MIR .... Medical Incident Report
MIR .... Medium Infrared (MWOL)
MIR .... Member of the Institute of Population Registration [*British*] (DBQ)
MIR .... Memory-Information Register [*Computer science*]
MIR .... Memory Input Register [*Computer science*]
MIR .... Method Improvement Request (MCD)
MIR .... Method of Integral Relations
MIR .... Microinstruction Register
MIR .... Micropower Impulse RADAR [*For fluid level sensing*]
MIR .... Midday Intelligence Report (SAUO)
MIr .... Middle Irish (ADWA)
MIR .... Middle Irish [*Language, etc.*]
MIR .... Mid Infrared (ACAE)
MIR .... Mid-Infrared Spectrum [*Spectroscopy*]
MIR .... Military Intelligence, Research [*World War II*]
MIR .... Millimeter-Wave Imaging Radiometer (ARMP)
MIR .... Mineta Resources Ltd. [*Vancouver Stock Exchange symbol*]
MIR .... Minimum Income Requirements (OICC)
MIR .... Minister [*Telegraphy*] (PCTE)
MIR .... Minneapolis Industrial Railway Co. [*AAR code*]
MIR .... Mirada [*NCIC car model code*]
MIR .... Mirage [*NCIC car model code*]
MIR .... Mirage Resorts [*NYSE symbol*] (SPSG)
MIR .... Miramichi Air Services Ltd. [*Canada*] [*ICAO designator*] (FAAC)
MIR .... MIRLYN [*Michigan Research Library Network*]
MIR .... Mirny [*Antarctica*] [*Seismograph station code, US Geological Survey*] (SEIS)
MIR .... Mirror (KSC)
MIR .... Mishap Investigation Report (MCD)
MIR .... Missile Identification Record
MIR .... Missile Intelligence Report
MIR .... Mission Inherent Reliability
MIR .... Mitochondrial Import Receptor [*Biochemistry*]
MIR .... Model Incident Report [*Telecommunications*] (TEL)
MIR .... Modular Integrated Rack (MCD)
MIR .... Moisture Insulation Resistance [*Electronics*] (AAEL)
MIR .... Molded-In Electronics [*Automotive engineering*]
MIR .... Monastir [*Tunisia*] [*Airport symbol*] (OAG)
MIR .... Mouvement International de la Reconciliation [*International Fellowship of Reconciliation*]
MIR .... Mouvement pour l'Independance de la Reunion [*Movement for the Independence of Reunion*] [*Political party*] (PD)
MIR .... Movement for International Reconciliation (SAUO)
MIR .... Movimiento de Izquierda Revolucionario [*Movement of the Revolutionary Left*] [*Bolivia*] [*Political party*] (PPW)
MIR .... Movimiento de Izquierda Revolucionario [*Movement of the Revolutionary Left*] [*Chile*] [*Political party*]
MIR .... Movimiento de Izquierda Revolucionario [*Movement of the Revolutionary Left*] [*Venezuela*] [*Political party*]
MIR .... Multiband Infrared Radiometer
MIR .... Multiple Instrumentation RADAR (MCD)
MIR .... Multiple Internal Reflectance (EDCT)
MIR .... Multiple Internal Reflection [*Spectroscopy*]
MIR .... Multiple Isomorphous Replacement [*Crystallography*]
MIR .... Multiple-target Instrumentation Radar (SAUS)
MIR .... Multiplex Intensity Rules
MIR .... Multitarget Instrumentation RADAR [*Military*] (CAAL)
MIR .... Music Information Retrieval [*Computer science*]
MIR .... Mutual Interference Report (MCD)
MIR .... Orbital System (SAUS)
MIR .... Russian Space Station (SAUO)
MIRA .... Management Information Research Associates (SAUO)
MIRA .... Massachusetts Immigrant and Refugee Advocacy Coalition
MIRA .... Member of the Institute of Registered Architects (SAUO)
MIRA .... Merchants Instant Response Authorization (SAA)
MIRA .... MILAN Infra-Red Attachment (SAUS)
MIRA .... Miniature Infrared Alarm
MIRA .... Mirage [*NCIC truck make code*]
MIRA .... MIRA-Motor Industry Research [*Database*] [*United Kingdom*] (GDD)
MIRA .... Monterey Institute for Research in Astronomy
MIRA .... Monthly Index of Russian Accessions [*Library of Congress*]
MIRA .... Motor Industry Research Association [*British*] (DCTA)
MIRA .... Movimiento de Independencia Revolutionaria en Armas [*Puerto Rican independence group*] [*Political party*]
MIRA .... Movimiento Independentista Armado [*Armed Pro-Independence Movement*] [*Puerto Rico*] [*Political party*] (PD)
MIRA .... Multifunctional Inertial Reference Assembly [*Air Force*] (MCD)
MIRAC .... Management Information Research Assistance Center (AABC)
MIRAC .... Master Index Remote Access Capability (MHDI)
MIRAC .... Microfilmed Reports and Accounts (PDAA)
MIRACL ..... Management Information Report Access without Computer Languages [*Computer science*] (IEEE)
MIRACL ..... Mid-Infrared Advanced Chemical LASER
MIRACLE .... Mokum Industrial Research Automatic Calculator for Laboratory and Engineering
MIRACLE .... Multidisciplinary Integrated Research Activities in Complex Laboratory Environments [*National Science Foundation*]
MIRACLE .... Music and Image Resources Assisted Computer Library Exchange (TELE)
MIRACL/SLBD ... MIRACL/Sea Lite Beam Director (SAUS)
MIRACODE ... Microfilm Information Retrieval Access Code
MIRAD ...... Monostatic Infrared Intrusion Detector (WDAA)
MIRADCOM ... Missile Research and Development Command [*Army*]
MIRADOR ... Minefield Reconnaissance and Detector System [*Army*]
MIRADS ..... Management Information and Display System [*NASA*]
MIRADS ..... Marshall [*Space Flight Center*] Information Retrieval and Display System [*NASA*] (PDAA)
MIRAGE ..... Megacity Impact on Regional and Global Environments (SAUO)
MIRAGE ..... Microelectronic Indicator for RADAR Ground Equipment (MCD)
MIRAGE ..... Migration of Radioisotopes in the Geosphere (SAUO)
MIRAGE ..... Moessbauer Isotopic Resonant Absorption of Gamma Emission [*Physics*]
MIRAGE ..... Multi-disciplinary Interest in Rural and General Health Education (SAUO)
MIRAID ...... Maintenance Information Retrieval Aid
MIRAID ...... Maritime Institute for Research and Industrial Development [*Washington, DC*] (EA)
MIRAMO .... Missionary Radio Monitors (SAUO)
Miramr ...... Miramar Mining Corp. [*Associated Press*] (SAG)
MIRAN ...... Miniature Infrared Analyzer [*Spectrometer*]
MIRAN ...... Missile Ranging
MIRANT PAC ... Mirant Corporation PAC Inc. [*Atlanta, GA*] (PACS)
MIRAS .... Mortgage Interest Relief at Source [*British*] (DCTA)
MIRAS .... Multiple Isomorphous Replacement with Anomalous Scattering [*Crystallography*]
MIRAT .... MILPERCEN Initial Recruiting and Training Plan (MCD)

MIRB .... Mutual Insurance Rating Bureau [*Defunct*] (EA)
MIRBM ...... Medium Intermediate-Range Ballistic Missile (MCD)
MIRC .... Market Intelligence Research Co. [*Palo Alto, CA*] (TSSD)
MIRC .... Member of the Idle Rich Class (SAUO)
MIRC .... Michael-Initiated Ring Closure [*Organic chemistry*]
MIRC .... Microtubuloreticular Complex (DMAA)
MIRC .... Missile-in-Range Computer (MCD)
MiRc .... Reed City Public Library, Reed City, MI [*Library symbol*] [*Library of Congress*] (LCLS)
MIRCA .... Michigan Roofing Contractors Association (EARSL)
MIRCEN ..... Microbial Resources Centres Network (SAUO)
MIRCEN ..... Microbiological Resource Center [*UNESCO*]
Mirch D & S ... Mirchall's Doctor and Student [*A publication*] (DLA)
MIRCLE ..... Mid-Infrared Chemical Laser (ACAE)
MIRCOM .... Missile Materiel Readiness Command [*Army*]
MIRCOM .... Missile Research Command (SAUO)
MIRCS .... Mechanical Instrument Repair and Calibration Shop (DNAB)
MIRD .... Medical Internal Radiation Dose [*Committee*] [*Society of Nuclear Medicine*]
MIRD .... Medium Internal Radiation Dose (WDAA)
MIRD .... Minor Irregularities and Deficiencies
MiRd .... Seville Township Library, Riverdale, MI [*Library symbol*] [*Library of Congress*] (LCLS)
MIRE .... Media Information Research Exchange (SAUO)
MIRE .... Member of the Institution of Radio Engineers [*British*] (EY)
MIRE .... Mine Identification, Recovery & Exploitation (SAUS)
MiRea .... Reading Community Library, Reading, MI [*Library symbol*] [*Library of Congress*] (LCLS)
MIRECC ..... Mental Illness Research, Education, and Clinical Center [*Department of Veterans Affairs*]
MIRED ...... Microreciprocal Degrees
Mireh Advow ... Mirehouse on Advowsons [*1824*] [*A publication*] (DLA)
Mireh Ti ..... Mirehouse on Tithes [*2nd ed.*] [*1822*] [*A publication*] (DLA)
MiRem ...... Wheatland Township Library, Remus, MI [*Library symbol*] [*Library of Congress*] (LCLS)
MiRep .... Republic-Michigamme Public Library, Republic, MI [*Library symbol*] [*Library of Congress*] (LCLS)
MIREQ .... Minimum Requirements (FOTI)
MIREQ .... Minimum Requirements Specified
MiRes .... Reading Community Library, Reading, MI [*Library symbol*] [*Library of Congress*] (LCLS)
MIRF .... Major Item Removal Frequency [*Army Aviation Systems Command*]
MIRF .... Multiple Instantaneous Response File
MIRF .... Myopia International Research Foundation (EA)
MIRFAC ..... Mathematics in Recognizable Form Automatically Compiled [*Computer science*]
MIRIAM ..... Major Incident Room Index and Action Management [*Police computer*] [*British*]
MIRIAM ..... Model Scheme for Information on Rural Development Initiatives and Agree Markets (SAUO)
MiRic .... Richmond Public Library, Richmond, MI [*Library symbol*] [*Library of Congress*] (LCLS)
MiRicl .... Richland Community Library, Richland, MI [*Library symbol*] [*Library of Congress*] (LCLS)
MIRICLE .... Mirrored Ions Closed-Loop Electrons (MCD)
MIRID .... Miniature RADAR Illumination Detector (MCD)
MIRID .... Mobile Infrared Inspection and Diagnostic (ACAE)
MIRID .... Monostatic Infrared Intrusion Detector (PDAA)
MIRINZ ...... Meat Industry Research Institute of New Zealand
MIR-IR ...... Multiple Internal Reflectance Infrared Spectroscopy (MCD)
MIRIS .... Michigan Inventory and Resource Information System (SAUO)
MIRIS .... Modified Infrared Interferometer Spectrometer
Mir Just ..... Horne's Mirror of Justice [*A publication*] (DLA)
MIRL .... Macrophage Ia Recruiting Factor (SAUS)
MIRL .... Medium Intensity Runway Edge Lights [*Aviation*] (FAAC)
MIRL .... Mineral Industry Research Laboratory
MIRLS .... Miniature Infra-Red Linescan (SAUS)
MIRLTD ..... Mid-Infrared Laser Target Designator (ACAE)
MIRLYN ..... Michigan Research Library Network
MIRM .... McGowan Institute for Regenerative Medicine [*University of Pittsburgh*] (RCD)
MIRN .... Movimento Independente da Reconstrucao Nacional [*Independent Movement of National Reconstruction*] [*Portugal*] (PPE)
MIRN-PDP ... Movimento Independente de Reconstrucao Nacional - Partido da Derecha Portuguesa [*Independent Movement for National Reconstruction - Party of the Portuguese Right*] [*Political party*] (PPW)
MIRO .... Malaysia Inter-Religious Organization (SAUO)
MIRO .... Mineral Industry Research Organisation [*British*] (DBA)
MIRO .... Mining Industry Research Organisation [*British*]
MiRochOU ... Oakland University, Rochester, MI [*Library symbol*] [*Library of Congress*] (LCLS)
MiRog .... Presque Isle County Library, Rogers City, MI [*Library symbol*] [*Library of Congress*] (LCLS)
MiRom ...... Romeo District Library, Romeo, MI [*Library symbol*] [*Library of Congress*] (LCLS)
MIROS ...... Modulation Inducing Retrodirective Optical System [*NASA*]
MiRos .... Roseville Public Library, Roseville, MI [*Library symbol*] [*Library of Congress*] (LCLS)
MiRosc ...... Gerrish-Higgins School District Public Library, Roscommon, MI [*Library symbol*] [*Library of Congress*] (LCLS)
MiRoscK .... Kirtland Community College, Roscommon, MI [*Library symbol*] [*Library of Congress*] (LCLS)
MiRoy .... Royal Oak Public Library, Royal Oak, MI [*Library symbol*] [*Library of Congress*] (LCLS)
MiRoyWB ... William Beaumont Hospital, Royal Oak, MI [*Library symbol*] [*Library of Congress*] (LCLS)
MIRP .... Manipulated Information Rate Processor
MIRP .... Myocardial Infarction Rehabilitation Program [*Cardiology*] (DAVI)
Mir Parl ..... Mirror of Parliament, London [*A publication*] (DLA)
Mir Pat Off ... Mirror of the Patent Office [*Washington, DC*] [*A publication*] (DLA)
MIR-Peru ... Movimiento de Izquierda Revolucionaria [*Movement of the Revolutionary Left of Peru*] [*Political party*] (PPW)
MIRPF .... Micro Image Relative Position Formula [*Computer science*]
MIRPL .... Major Item Repair Parts List (NATG)
MIRPS .... Multiple Information Retrieval by Parallel Selection
Mirr .... Horne's Mirror of Justice [*A publication*] (DLA)
MIRR .... Material Inspection and Receiving Report [*Military*]
MIRR .... Materiel Inspection and Receiving Report (SAUO)
MIRR .... Michigan Interstate Railroad [*Federal Railroad Administration identification code*]
mirr .... Mirror (VRA)
MIRR .... Mitsubishi Research Reactor [*Japan*]
MIRRC ...... Motor Industry Repair Research Center
MIRRC ...... Motor Insurance Repair Research Centre [*British*] (CB)
MIRRER ..... Microwave Identification Railroad Encoding Reflector (DNAB)
MIRROR .... Management Information Reporting and Review of Operational Resources System
MIRROS ..... Modulation Inducing Reactive Retrodirective Optical System [*NASA*]
MirRsrt ...... Mirage Resorts [*Associated Press*] (SAG)
MIRS .... Management Information and Reporting System (VLIE)
MIRS .... Management Information Retrieval System (TIMI)
MIRS .... Mandibular Inclined Repositioning Splint [*Medicine*]
MIRS .... Manpower Information Retrieval System (IEEE)
MIRS .... Marketing Information Retrieval System (SAUO)
MIRS .... Medical Information Retrieval Service (NITA)
MIRS .... Micro-Interactive Retrieval System (DNAB)
MIRS .... Mid-America Interventional Radiological Society (SAUO)
MIRS .... Mid-Infrared Source (ACAE)
MIRS .... Military Intelligence Research Section [*Navy*]
MIRS .... Military Intelligence Research Service (SAUO)
MIRS .... Military Intelligence Reserve Society (SAUO)
MIRS .... Millimeter Wave Instrumentation Radar Station (ACAE)
MIRS .... Miniaturized Imagery Receive System (SAUS)
MIRS .... Modular Integrated Radar System (ACAE)
MIRS .... MOTS [*Module Test Set*] Information Retrieval System
MIRS .... Multimedia Information Retrieval Services (SAUO)
MIRS .... Multiple Internal Reflection Spectroscopy
MIRS .... Multi-purpose Infrared Sight (PDAA)
MIRS .... Musical Information Retrieval System (TELE)
MiRsc .... Ogemaw District Library, Rose City, MI [*Library symbol*] [*Library of Congress*] (LCLS)
MIRSE .... Member of the Institution of Railway Signal Engineers [*British*] (DBQ)
MIRSE .... Multipurpose Imaging Radiometer Spectrometer Equipment
MIRSI .... Monthly Inventory Report of Special Items
MIRSIM ..... Mineral Resource Simulation Model (PDAA)
MirSIP .... Mirage System Improvement Programme (SAUS)
MIRSL .... Microwave Remote Sensing Laboratory (CARB)
MIRST .... Multiple Infrared Scattered Light Recorder
MIRT .... Member, Institute of Reprographic Technicians (SAUO)
MIRT .... Molecular Infrared Track (IEEE)
MIRT .... Movement for the Islamic Revival of Tajikistan [*Political party*] (PSAP)
MIRTAK ..... Martin Infrared Tracker
MIRTE .... Member of the Institute of Road Transport Engineering [*British*] (DBQ)
MIRTE .... Member of the Institute of Road Transport Engineers (SAUO)
MIRTOS ..... Minimum Real Time Operating System (NITA)
MIRTRAC ... Missile Infrared Tracking System (DNAB)
MIRTRAK ... Martin Infrared Tracker (SAA)
MIRTS .... Modular Infra-Red Transmitting System (SAUS)
MIRU .... Missile Inertial Reference Unit (ACAE)
MIRU .... Mother and Infant Research Unit [*University of Leeds*] [*United Kingdom*] (RCD)
MIRU .... Myocardial Infarction Research Unit [*Cardiology*] (DAVI)
MIRU .... Roland [*Intermodal shipping container symbol*] (TVRC)
MiRud .... Rudyard School Public Library, Rudyard, MI [*Library symbol*] [*Library of Congress*] (LCLS)
MIRV .... Multiple Independently-Guided Re-entry Vehicle [*NASA*] (PDAA)
MIRV .... Multiple Independently-Targetable Reentry Vehicle [*Military*]
MIS .... Machine Instruction Set (VLIE)
MIS .... Magnetic Isolation System (SAUS)
MIS .... Maintenance Indicator System [*TACOM*] [*Army*] (RDA)
MIS .... Maintenance Information System (SAUO)
MIS .... Managed Internet Service [*Computer science*]
MIS .... Management Indicator Species (SAUO)
MIS .... Management Information Science
MIS .... Management Information Service
MIS .... Management Information Services (SAUO)
MIS .... Management Information Specialist
MIS .... Management Information Strategy
mis .... Management Information System [*NASA*] (NAKS)
MIS .... Management Information System [*Generic term*]
MIS .... Management Information Systems [*Corporation for Public Broadcasting*] [*Information service or system*] (IID)
MIS .... Management Integrated System (TEL)
MIS .... Manager of Information Services [*Computer science*] (NETL)
MIS .... Manifold Interest Schedule
MIS .... Man in Space
MIS .... Manpower Information System (MCD)
MIS .... Manson Impact Structure [*Iowa*] [*Geology*]

MIS .... Manufacturing Information System [*Computer science*] (BUR)
MIS .... Map Information System (SAUO)
MIS .... Marine Information System (NITA)
MIS .... Marine Isotope Stage [*Climatology*]
MIS .... Market Impact Study
MIS .... Marketing Information System
MIS .... Mary Immaculate Seminary [*Pennsylvania*]
MIS .... Master Implementation Schedule [*NATO Air Defense Ground Environment*] (NATG)
MIS .... Master Integrated Schedule (AAG)
MIS .... Master of Individualized Studies (GAGS)
MIS .... Master of Industrial Safety (SARE)
MIS .... Master of Information Science (PGP)
MIS .... Master of Information Services (GAGS)
MIS .... Master of Information Systems (PGP)
MIS .... Master of Interdisciplinary Studies (GAGS)
MIS .... Master of International Service
MIS .... Master of International Studies (PGP)
MIS .... Material Inspection Service [*Navy*]
MIS .... Maturation-Inducing Substance [*Endocrinology*]
MIS .... Mechanical Impact System [*Aerospace*]
MIS .... Mechanical Inertia Simulation [*Automotive emissions*]
MIS .... Mechanical Insulation Services, Inc. (EFIS)
MIS .... Mechanical Interruption Summary [*FAA*]
MIS .... Mechanically Induced Stress [*Agriculture*]
MIS .... Media and Information Services [*Queensland, Australia*]
MIS .... Median Iris Society (EA)
MIS .... Medical Information Science
MIS .... Medical Information System (COE)
MIS .... Medical Information Systems (SAUO)
MIS .... Medical Inspector of Seamen (SAUO)
MIS .... Meiosis-Inducing Substance (DB)
MIS .... Member of the Institute of Statisticians [*Formerly, AIS*] [*British*]
MIS .... Member of the Institute of Surveyors (ADA)
MIS .... Merchandise Information System (PDAA)
MIS .... Message Input Segment (SAUS)
MIS .... Metal Insulated Semiconductor (VLIE)
MIS .... Metal Insulated Structure
MIS .... Metal-Insulator-Semiconductor (MCD)
MIS .... Metal Insulator Silicon (AAEL)
MIS .... Meteorological Impact Statement [*FAA*] (TAG)
MIS .... Metering Information System [*Telecommunications*] (OA)
MIS .... Metrology Information Service [*GIDEP*]
MIS .... MICOM [*Missile Command*] Specification [*Army*]
MIS .... MicroServe Information Systems
MIS .... Microwave Imager and Sounder (ACAE)
MIS .... Midstate Airlines, Inc. [*ICAO designator*] (FAAC)
MIS .... Migrant Information Service (SAUO)
MIS .... Milieu Information Service (EA)
MIS .... Military Information System (SAUO)
MIS .... Military Intelligence Section [*South Africa*]
MIS .... Military Intelligence Services [*Army*]
MIS .... Military Intelligence Summary [*Defense Intelligence Agency*]
MIS .... Military Interim Specification [*Army*] (MCD)
MIS .... Military Interpreter Service (SAUO)
MIS .... Mine Issuing Ship
MIS .... Mineral Industry Survey [*Department of Commerce*] (GFGA)
MIS .... Mineral Industry Surveys (SAUO)
MIS .... Mineral Information Section [*Natural Environment Research Council*] (IID)
MIS .... Minicube System, Inc., Carlisle PA [*STAC*]
MIS .... Minority Institutions (COE)
MIS .... Minstrel Instruction Service (NADA)
MIS .... Minstrel Instruction Society (SAUO)
MIS .... Miscarriage (DSUE)
mis .... Miscellaneous [*MARC language code*] [*Library of Congress*] (LCCP)
MIS .... Miscellaneous (NATG)
MIS .... Miserable (DSUE)
MIS .... Miser (automobile) [*NCIC car model code*]
MIS .... Mishima [*Japan*] [*Seismograph station code, US Geological Survey*] (SEIS)
MIS .... Misima [*Papua New Guinea*] [*Airport symbol*] (OAG)
Mis .... Misopogon [*of Julian*] [*Classical studies*] (OCD)
MIS .... Missile
MIS .... Missile Interim Specification [*Army*]
MIS .... Missile Specification
MIS .... Missile Squadron (SAUO)
MIS .... Missing (AABC)
MIS .... Mission College, Santa Clara, CA [*OCLC symbol*] (OCLC)
mis .... Mission Information Subsystem [*NASA*] (NAKS)
MIS .... Mission Information System [*or Subsystem*]
Mis .... Mississippi Reports [*A publication*] (DLA)
MIS .... Mississippi River Corporation (SAUO)
MIS .... Missouri
Mis .... Missouri Reports [*A publication*] (DLA)
MIS .... Mistico [*Ship's rigging*] (ROG)
MIS .... Mistral [*NCIC car model code*]
MIS .... Mobile Telephone Service (SAUO)
MIS .... Mobility Information Service [*British*]
MIS .... Modified in Situ [*Experimental technique for converting shale into oil*]
MIS .... Modular Injection System [*Plastics*]
MIS .... Monte-Carlo Inelastic Scattering [*Code*] [*Computer science*] (NRCH)
MIS .... Month-in-Sample [*Bureau of the Census*] (GFGA)
MIS .... Months in Service
MIS .... Moody Institute of Science (EA)
MIS .... Moody's Investor Service [*A publication*] (MHDW)
MIS .... Motor Inert Storage
MIS .... Muellerian Inhibiting Substance [*Embryology*] [*Biochemistry*]
MIS .... Multicultural Information Strategy
MIS .... Multicurrency Intervention System (FOTI)
MIS .... Multilingual Information System (SAUO)
MIS .... Multimedia Information Sources (VLIE)
MIS .... Multistage Information System [*Computer science*] (ELAL)
Mis .... New York Miscellaneous Reports [*A publication*] (DLA)
MIS .... NRA [*National Restaurant Association*] Management Information Services [*Defunct*] (EA)
MiS .... Saginaw Public Libraries, Saginaw, MI [*Library symbol*] [*Library of Congress*] (LCLS)
MISA .... Maritime Industry Seagoing Award (SAUO)
MISA .... Maxwell International Subscription Agency
MISA .... Meat Industry Suppliers Association (EA)
MISA .... Military Impacted Schools Association (NTPA)
MISA .... Military-Industrial Supply Agency
MISA .... Motorists Information Services Association (EA)
MISA .... Municipal and Industry Strategy for Abatement
MISAA .... Middle Income Student Assistance Act [*1978*]
MISAC .... Member of the Incorporated Society of Advertisement Consultants [*British*] (DAS)
MiSal .... Saline Public Library, Saline, MI [*Library symbol*] [*Library of Congress*] (LCLS)
MISAM ...... Multiple Index Sequential Access Method
MiSan .... Sandusky Public Library, Sandusky, MI [*Library symbol*] [*Library of Congress*] (LCLS)
MISAR .... Microfilm Information Storage and Retrieval (MCD)
MISAR .... Microprocessed Sensing and Automatic Regulation [*Engine control system*] [*Automotive industry*]
MISAR .... Miniature Information Storage and Retrieval (PDAA)
MiSaS .... Spring Arbor College, Spring Arbor, MI [*Library symbol*] [*Library of Congress*] (LCLS)
Mis Astig ... Mixed Astigmatism [*Ophthalmology*] (DAVI)
MiSb .... Bingham Township Library, Suttons Bay, MI [*Library symbol*] [*Library of Congress*] (LCLS)
MiS-B .... Saginaw Public Libraries, Butman-Fish Library, Saginaw, MI [*Library symbol*] [*Library of Congress*] (LCLS)
MISC .... Malaysian International Shipping Corp. (DS)
MISC .... Malaysian International Shipping Corporation (SAUO)
MiSc .... Mason County Library, Scottville, MI [*Library symbol*] [*Library of Congress*] (LCLS)
MISC .... Military Intelligence Service Center (SAUO)
MISC .... Minimum Instruction Set Computer (CIST)
MISC .... Minimum Instruction Set Computing (SAUO)
MISC .... Miscarriage [*Medicine*]
MISC .... Miscellaneous (AFM)
Misc .... Miscellaneous (DFIT)
misc .... Miscellaneous (WDMC)
MISC .... Miscellaneous and Other Operations [*USCG*] (TAG)
Misc .... Miscellaneous Reports [*New York*] [*A publication*] (DLA)
MISC .... Movement for an Independent Socialist Canada
MiS-C .... Saginaw Public Libraries, Claytor Branch Library, Saginaw, MI [*Library symbol*] [*Library of Congress*] (LCLS)
Misc 2d ..... Miscellaneous Reports, Second Series [*New York*] [*A publication*] (DLA)
MisCa .... Mission Capital Ltd. [*Associated Press*] (SAG)
MISCAP ..... Mission Capability (COE)
MISCAP ..... Mission Capability Statement (MCD)
Misc Dec ... Ohio Miscellaneous Decisions (Gottschall) [*1865-73*] [*A publication*] (DLA)
Misc Doc ... Miscellaneous Document [*US. House of Representatives of Senate*] (BARN)
Miscel .... Miscellaneous Reports [*New York*] [*A publication*] (DLA)
MISCEND ... Miscendus [*To Be Mixed*] [*Pharmacy*]
MISCEX ..... Miscellaneous Exercise [*Military*] (NVT)
MISchott .... Schottenstein [*M. I.*] Homes, Inc. [*Associated Press*] (SAG)
MISCL .... Miscellaneous
Misc New York... Miscellaneous New York Reports [*A publication*] (AAGC)
Misc (NY)... Miscellaneous Reports [*New York*] [*A publication*] (DLA)
MISCO .... McCall Information Systems Co.
MISCO .... Microchemical Specialties Company (SAUO)
MISCON ..... Misconduct
Misc Publ Univ KY Co-Op Ext Serv Agr Home Econ HE... Miscellaneous Publication. University of Kentucky. Cooperative Extension Service. Agriculture and Home Economics HE (SAUO)
Misc Rep ... Miscellaneous Reports [*New York*] [*A publication*] (DLA)
Misc Reports... New York Miscellaneous Reports [*A publication*] (DLA)
Misc Repts... New York Miscellaneous Reports [*A publication*] (DLA)
MiScW ...... West Shore Community College, Scottville, MI [*Library symbol*] [*Library of Congress*] (LCLS)
MISD .... Management Information Systems Directorate [*Army Missile Command*] [*Redstone Arsenal, AL*]
MISD .... Misdemeanor [*FBI standardized term*]
MISD .... Multiple Instruction, Single Data [*Processor configuration*] (IEEE)
MISDAS ..... Mechanical Impact System Design for Advanced Spacecraft (IEEE)
MISDM ...... Misdemeanor [*Legal shorthand*] (LWAP)
MISDM ...... Misdemeanor and Cure [*Legal shorthand*] (LWAP)
MISDMR .... Misdemeanor (ROG)
MISDO ...... Management Information System Development Office (DNAB)
MISE .... Integrated Management of Emergency Supplies [*Emergency Management*] (EMA)
MISE .... Mechanized Infantry in a Smoke Environment (MCD)
MISE .... Member of the Institution of Structural Engineers (SAUO)

MISE......... Miniature Sample (AAG)
MiSe......... Sebewaing Township Library, Sebewaing, MI [*Library symbol*] [*Library of Congress*] (LCLS)
MISEA....... Management Information Systems Economic Analysis
MISEA....... Meat Industry Supply and Equipment Association [*Later, MISA*] (EA)
MISED....... Machine Independent Systems Effectiveness Data System (MCD)
MISEG....... Management Information System Executive Group (DNAB)
MISEP....... Mutual Information System on Employment Policies (SAUO)
MISEP....... Mutual Information System on Employment Policies in Europe (IID)
MISER....... Management Information System for Expenditure Reporting (PDAA)
MISER....... Manned Interceptor SAGE Evaluation Routine (MCD)
MISER....... Massachusetts Institute for Social and Economic Research [*University of Massachusetts, Amherst*] (IID)
MISER....... Mean Integral Square Error (PDAA)
MISER....... Media Insertion Schedule Evaluation Report [*Advertising*]
MISER....... Microwave Space Electronics Relay
MISER....... Militant Society for the Eradication of Rounds [*British*] (DI)
MISER....... Miniature, Indicating and Sampling Electronic Respirometer (PDAA)
MISER....... Minimum Size Executive Routines
MISES....... Merchandises (ROG)
MiSf......... Southfield Public Library, Southfield, MI [*Library symbol*] [*Library of Congress*] (LCLS)
MiSfB........ Bendix Corp., Engineering Development Center, Bendix Center, Southfield, MI [*Library symbol*] [*Library of Congress*] (LCLS)
MiSfE........ Eaton Corp. Engineering Research Center, Southfield, MI [*Library symbol*] [*Library of Congress*] (LCLS)
MISFET...... Metal-Insulator-Semiconductor Field-Effect Transistor
MiSfL........ Lawrence Institute of Technology, Southfield, MI [*Library symbol*] [*Library of Congress*] (LCLS)
MiSfM....... Midrasha College of Jewish Studies, Southfield, MI [*Library symbol*] [*Library of Congress*] (LCLS)
MiSfP........ Providence Hospital Library, Southfield, MI [*Library symbol*] [*Library of Congress*] (LCLS)
MISFROR... Multiple Investment Sinking Fund Rate of Return (ADA)
MISG........ Management Information Systems Group [*Association*] (EA)
MISG........ Mental Illness Specific Grant (SAUO)
MISG........ Missing (VLIE)
MISG........ Modified Immune Serum Globulin [*Medicine*] (MELL)
MISG-C...... Maintenance Interservice Support Group Center (MCD)
Mish......... Mishnah [*Basis of the Talmud*] (BJA)
MiSh......... Shelby Public Library, Shelby, MI [*Library symbol*] [*Library of Congress*] (LCLS)
MISHAP..... Missiles High-Speed Assembly Program
MISHAP..... Much Increased Salary, Hardly Any Pension [*Lifestyle classification*]
MiShep...... Coe Township Library, Shepherd, MI [*Library symbol*] [*Library of Congress*] (LCLS)
MiSHS....... Saginaw Health Sciences Library, Saginaw, MI [*Library symbol*] [*Library of Congress*] (LCLS)
MISI......... Member of the Iron and Steel Institute [*British*]
MISI......... Metro Information Services [*Stock market symbol*]
MISI......... Metro Information Services, Inc. [*NASDAQ symbol*] (NASQ)
MISI......... Metro Information Svcs. [*NASDAQ symbol*] (SG)
MISI......... Micro Imaging Systems, Incorporated (SAUO)
MISI......... Micro Information Systems, Incorporated (SAUO)
MISI......... Multipath Intersymbol Interference (PDAA)
MISIAS...... Management Information Systems Inventory and Analysis System [*Navy*]
MISICC...... Management Information System Input to Command and Control (SAUO)
MIS/IL....... Metal-Insulator-Semiconductor Inversion Layer [*Photovoltaic energy systems*]
MISIM....... Metal-Insulator-Semiconductor Insulator Metal (MCD)
MIS/INAS... MIS for Industrial Naval Air Stations (SAUO)
MIS(India)... Member of the Institution of Surveyors of India
MISIP........ Management Information System Improvement Plan
MISIP........ Merck Infrared Spectral Interpretation Package [*For minicomputers*] [*Analytical chemistry*]
MISIP........ Minority Institutions Science Improvement Program [*National Science Foundation*]
MISIS........ Micro Integrated Storm Information System [*Marine science*] (OSRA)
MISJ......... Medical Instrument Society of Japan (SAUO)
MISJC....... Star City Junction, MI [*American Association of Railroads railroad junction routing code*]
MISK........ Confederation of Nationalist Labor Unions (Turkey) [*Political party*] (PSAP)
MISL......... Major Indoor Soccer League [*Defunct*] (EA)
MISL......... Malfunction Investigation Support Laboratory [*NASA*] (KSC)
MISL......... Management Information System Laboratory
MISL......... Missile
MiSl......... South Lyon Public Library, South Lyon, MI [*Library symbol*] [*Library of Congress*] (LCLS)
MIS LABS... Midwest Integrated Systems Laboratories, Inc. [*Watertown, WI*] (TSSD)
MISLIC...... Mid- and South Staffordshire Libraries in Cooperation (NITA)
MISLIC...... Mid-Staffordshire Libraries in Co-operation (SAUO)
MISLPA..... Major Indoor Soccer League Players Association (EA)
MISM........ MAJCOM Information System Manager (SAUO)
MISM........ Member of the Institute of Supervisory Management [*British*] (DBQ)
MISM........ Metal-Insulator-Semiconductor Metal (MCD)
MiSM........ Michigan Lutheran Seminary, Saginaw, MI [*Library symbol*] [*Library of Congress*] (LCLS)
MISMA...... Major Item Supply Management Agency
MISMA...... Member of the Incorporated Sales Managers Association [*British*] (DAS)
MISMA...... Model Improvement and Study Management [*Army*]
MISMAC.... Missile and Munitions Materiel Center (MCD)
MISMD...... Medical Illustration Service for Museum Design [*Armed Forces Institute of Pathology*] (RDA)
MISMDS.... Multiple Instruction Streams Multiple Data Steams
MISMO...... Maintenance Interservice [*or Intersupport*] Management Office [*DARCOM*] (AFIT)
MISMO...... MAJCOM Information Systems Management Office (SAUO)
MISMR...... Michigan Society for Medical Research (GVA)
Mis Mus.... Mistress of Music
MISN........ Misnumbered (WGA)
MISO........ Maintenance Interservice Office [*Air Force*] (AFIT)
MISO........ Management Information Systems Office (AABC)
MISO........ Military Intelligence Service Organization (NADA)
MISO........ Misonidazole [*Azomycin*] [*Oncology, Radiosensitizer*]
MiSod....... Sodus Township Library, Sodus, MI [*Library symbol*] [*Library of Congress*] (LCLS)
Misonix..... Misonix, Inc. [*Associated Press*] (SAG)
Misonx...... Misonix, Inc. [*Associated Press*] (SAG)
MISP........ Maintenance Integrated Support Plan (SAUO)
MISP........ MAJCOM Information Systems Plan (SAUO)
MISP........ Management Information System Plan
MISP........ Manned Interceptor Simulation Program
MISP........ Mathematics in Society Project (AIE)
MISP........ Medical Information Systems Program [*Computer science*] (BUR)
MISP........ Member of the Institute of Sales Promotion [*British*] (DI)
MISP........ Member of the Institution of Sewage Purification (SAUO)
MISP........ Microelectronics Industry Support Programme (NITA)
MISP........ Microprocessor Industry Support Programme [*British*] (DCTA)
MISPAY..... Misc. Payments (ALAC)
MISPC...... Mechanized Infantry Squad Proficiency Course [*Army*]
MISPE...... Monopulse Information Signal Processing Element (ACAE)
MiSpl........ Warner Baird Library, Spring Lake (SAUS)
MiSpl........ Warner Baird Library, Spring Lake, MI [*Library symbol*] [*Library of Congress*] (LCLS)
MIS-Q....... Maintenance Information System for Quality (MCD)
MISR........ Machine Supply Requisition (VLIE)
MISR........ Major Item Status Report
MISR........ Makerere Institute of Social Research (SAUO)
MISR........ Mars In-situ-utilization Sample Return [*Computer science*]
MISR........ Matrix Ion Species Ratio [*Spectroscopy*]
MISR........ Minimum Industrial Sustaining Role (NG)
Mis R........ Missouri Reports [*A publication*] (DLA)
MISR........ Modular Industrial Solar Retrofit Program [*Department of Energy*]
MISR........ Mosler Information Storage and Retrieval System (MCD)
MISR........ Multi-Angle Imaging Spectrometer [*Marine science*] (OSRA)
MISR........ Multi-Angle Imaging Spectroradiometer (EOSA)
MISR........ Multi-Impact Signature Register (PDAA)
MISR........ Multiple Input Signal Register (NITA)
MISRAN..... Missile Range
MISRC....... Management Information Systems Research Center [*University of Minnesota*] [*Research center*] (RCD)
MISRE....... Microwave Space Relay [*Electronics*]
MISREP..... Joint Tactical Air Reconnaissance/Surveillance Mission Report (SAUO)
MISREP..... Misrepresentation [*Legal shorthand*] (LWAP)
MISREP..... Mission Report [*Air Force*] (AFM)
Mis Rep..... Missouri Reports [*A publication*] (DLA)
MISS........ Major Item Special Study [*Army Aviation Systems Command*]
MISS........ Management and Information System Staff [*United Nations Development Program*]
MISS........ Man in Space Simulator
MISS........ Man in Space Soonest
MISS........ Manpower Information Systems Support (SAUO)
MISS........ Mechanical Interruption Statistical Summary (IEEE)
MISS........ Mecklenburg Internet Service System (SAUO)
MISS........ Medical Information Science Section [*National Institutes of Health*] [*Information service or system*] (IID)
MISS........ Microwave Imager Sensor Study (MCD)
MISS........ Mid-Course Surveillance System (MCD)
MISS........ Miniature SOFAR [*Sound Fixing and Ranging*] System
MISS........ Minicomputer Interfacing Support System [*Computer science*]
MISS........ Missile Intercept Scoring System (SAUS)
MISS........ Missile Intercept Simulation System
Miss......... Mission (DIAR)
MISS........ Mission
miss......... Missionary
MISS........ Mississippi (AFM)
Miss......... Mississippi (ODBW)
MISS........ Mississippian [*Period, era, or system*] [*Geology*]
MISS........ Mississippian [*Railway*] [*AAR code*]
MISS........ Mississippi Chemical [*NASDAQ symbol*] (TTSB)
MISS........ Mississippi Chemical Corp. [*NASDAQ symbol*] (SAG)
Miss......... Mississippi Supreme Court Reports [*A publication*] (DLA)
MISS........ Mobile Instrumentation Support System
MISS........ Mobile Integrated Support System (MCD)
MISS........ Modified Injury Severity Scale [*Medicine*] (EDAA)
MISS........ Modified Injury Severity Score [*Medicine*] (EDAA)
MISS........ Modular Infrared Sensor System (ACAE)
MISS........ Multiband Image Scanning System
MISS........ Multi-Input-Safety-Shutdown (PDAA)
MISS........ Multi-Item Single Source (IEEE)
MiS-S....... Saginaw Public Libraries, South Jefferson Branch, Saginaw, MI [*Library symbol*] [*Library of Congress*] (LCLS)
MiSs......... Sault Ste. Marie Carnegie Public Library, Sault Ste. Marie, MI [*Library symbol*] [*Library of Congress*] (LCLS)
MISSA....... Management Information System Support Agency (SAUO)

MiSsB .... Baylis Public Library, Sault Ste. Marie, MI [*Library symbol*] [*Library of Congress*] (LCLS)
Miss C ...... Mississippi College (GAGS)
MissChm.... Mississippi Chemical Corp. [*Associated Press*] (SAG)
Miss Code Ann... Mississippi Code, Annotated [*A publication*] (DLA)
MISS-D...... Minuteman Integrated Schedules Status and Data Systems [*Missiles*]
Miss Dec ... Mississippi Decisions [*A publication*] (DLA)
MIS-SDS.... Multiple Instruction Streams - Single Data Streams [*Computer science*] (MHDB)
MISSI........ Mission, TX [*American Association of Railroads railroad junction routing code*]
MISSI........ Multilevel Information System Security [*Communications term*] (DCT)
MISSI........ Multilevel Information System Security Initiative (SAUO)
MISS-IDA... Meteorology Interactive Software System for Image Data Analysis (ACAE)
MISSIL ...... Management Information System Symbolic Interpretive Language [*Computer science*] (MCD)
MISSILEX... Missile Firing Exercise (NVT)
MISSIO...... Internationales Katholisches Missionswerk [*Pontifical Mission Society*] [*Aachen, Federal Republic of Germany*] (EAIO)
MISSION.... Manufacturing Information System Support Integrated Online [*Computer science*] (MHDI)
MISSION.... Mission [*Commonly used*] (OPSA)
MISSIS...... Mississippi Student Information System (EDAC)
MiSsL .... Lake Superior State College, Sault Ste. Marie, MI [*Library symbol*] [*Library of Congress*] (LCLS)
Miss Law ... Mississippi Lawyer [*A publication*] (DLA)
Miss Law Rev... Mississippi Law Review [*A publication*] (DLA)
Miss Laws... General Laws of Mississippi [*A publication*] (DLA)
Miss Laws... General Laws of Mississippi (journ.) (SAUS)
Miss Lawyer... Mississippi Lawyer [*A publication*] (DLA)
Miss L Rev... Mississippi Law Review [*A publication*] (DLA)
MISSN....... Mission [*Commonly used*] (OPSA)
MissnW ...... Mission West Properties [*Associated Press*] (SAG)
Misso........ Missouri Reports [*A publication*] (DLA)
MISSOPH ... Man in Space Sophisticated (MUGU)
Misso R..... Missouri Reports [*A publication*] (DLA)
Misso Rep... Missouri Reports [*A publication*] (DLA)
Missouri .... Missouri Reports [*A publication*] (DLA)
Missouri R... Missouri Reports [*A publication*] (DLA)
Missouri Rep... Missouri Reports [*A publication*] (DLA)
Missour Rep... Missouri Reports [*A publication*] (DLA)
MissPw ..... Mississippi Power Co. [*Associated Press*] (SAG)
MissQ .... Mississippi Quarterly [*A publication*] (ANEX)
MISSR....... Missioner (ROG)
Miss R ...... Mississippi Reports [*A publication*] (DLA)
Miss RC..... Mississippi Railroad Commission Reports [*A publication*] (DLA)
Miss Reg ... Mississippi Register [*A publication*] (AAGC)
Miss Rep ... Mississippi Reports [*A publication*] (DLA)
Miss Serv W... Missionary Service With
Miss St Ca... Morris' Mississippi State Cases [*1818-72*] [*A publication*] (DLA)
Miss St Cas... Morris' Mississippi State Cases [*1818-72*] [*A publication*] (DLA)
Miss St U... Mississippi State University (GAGS)
Miss St U Women... Mississippi State University for Women (GAGS)
MISST....... Missile-Supersonic Transport
MIS Sulf U... End Uses of Sulfur and Sulfuric Acid. Mineral Industry Survey (journ.) (SAUS)
MissVly ..... Mississippi Valley Bancshares, Inc. [*Associated Press*] (SAG)
MissVw ..... Mississippi View Holding Co. [*Associated Press*] (SAG)
MISSY....... Missionary
MIST......... Avalon Capital [*NASDAQ symbol*] (TTSB)
MIST......... Avalon Capital, Inc. [*NASDAQ symbol*] (SAG)
MIST......... Magnetosphere, Ionosphere and Solar Terrestrial (SAUO)
MIST......... Manchester Institute of Science and Technology (SAUO)
MI St .... Master of Information Studies (PGP)
MIST......... Maximum Isothermal System Temperature [*Nuclear energy*] (NRCH)
MIST......... Medical Information Service by Telephone [*Medicine*] [*Alabama*] (EDAA)
MIST......... Medical Information System via Telephone [*University of Alabama*]
MIST......... Member of the Institute of Science Technology [*British*] (DBQ)
MIST......... Metal-Insulator-Semiconductor Transistor (CCCA)
MIST......... Metal Insulator Silicon Field-Effect Transistor [*Also, MISFET*] (EECA)
MIST......... Microburst and Severe Thunderstorm Experiment (or Project) (SAUO)
MIST......... Microburst and Severe Thunderstorm Project (SAUS)
MIST......... Microbursts in Severe Thunderstorms
MIST+....... Microcomputer Information Support Tools [*2B Enterprises*] [*Washington, DC*] (TSSD)
MIST......... Minimum Structure Module
MIST......... Minor Isotopes Safeguards Techniques [*Nuclear energy*]
MIST......... Mistral [*NCIC car make code*]
MIST......... Mistura [*Mixture*] [*Pharmacy*]
MIST......... MIUS [*Modular Integrated Utility Systems*] Integration and Subsystems Test (MCD)
mist.......... Mixture [*Medicine*] (BCRP)
MIST......... Modular Interoperable Surface Terminal (SAUS)
MIST......... Mosaic Infrared Sensor Technology (ACAE)
MIST......... Multi-Input Standard Tape
MIST......... Multiloop Integral System Test [*Nuclear energy*] (NRCH)
MIST......... Multipurpose In-Space Throttleable Engine (MCD)
MIST......... Music Information System for Theorists (PDAA)
MISTAF...... Management Information Systems Task Force (SAA)
MiStan ...... Stanton Public Library, Stanton, MI [*Library symbol*] [*Library of Congress*] (LCLS)
MISTC....... Member of the Institute of Scientific and Technical Communicators [*British*] (DBQ)
MISTC....... Men's International Squash Tournament Council [*Cardiff, Wales*] (EAIO)
MISTC....... Multiple Information Set Tracking Correlator System (SAUO)
MiStc........ Saint Clair Shores Public Library, Saint Clair Shores, MI [*Library symbol*] [*Library of Congress*] (LCLS)
MiStch ...... Saint Charles Public Library, Saint Charles, MI [*Library symbol*] [*Library of Congress*] (LCLS)
MiSte........ Lincoln Township Public Library, Stevensville, MI [*Library symbol*] [*Library of Congress*] (LCLS)
MISTE....... Military Intelligence Special Training Element (DOMA)
MISTEL...... Delft Monograph Document Delivery And Catalogue (SAUS)
MiStep ...... Menominee County Library, Stephenson, MI [*Library symbol*] [*Library of Congress*] (LCLS)
MISTER ..... Mobile Integrated System Trainer, Evaluator, and Recorder [*Navy*]
MIST-FOAL... Multi-Stage Force Allocation (SAA)
MiSth........ Sterling Heights Public Library, Sterling Heights, MI [*Library symbol*] [*Library of Congress*] (LCLS)
MiSthe ...... Richfield Township Public Library, St. Helen, MI [*Library symbol*] [*Library of Congress*] (LCLS)
MISTI........ Multipurpose International Securities Trading Information (MHDW)
MiSti .... St. Ignace Public Library, St. Ignace, MI [*Library symbol*] [*Library of Congress*] (LCLS)
MISTIC ...... Michigan State Integral Computer
MISTIC ...... Missile System Target Illuminator Controlled (MCD)
MISTIC ...... Model Interstate Scientific and Technical Information Clearinghouse
MISTIC ...... Multiple Information Set Tracking Correlation (ACAE)
MISTIGRI... Mobile Integrated Surveillance of Tactical Information Gathered (SAUS)
MISTIR...... Multifunction Imaging Search/Track Infrared
MiStjo....... Bement Public Library, St. Johns (SAUS)
MiStjo....... Bement Public Library, St. Johns, MI [*Library symbol*] [*Library of Congress*] (LCLS)
MiStjW...... Whirlpool Corp., Research Library, St. Joseph, MI [*Library symbol*] [*Library of Congress*] (LCLS)
MiStlo....... Theodore Austin Cutler Memorial Library, St. Louis, MI [*Library symbol*] [*Library of Congress*] (LCLS)
MISTM ...... Member of the Institute of Sales Technology and Management [*British*] (DBQ)
MISTR....... Management of Items Subject to Repair [*Air Force*] (AFM)
MISTRA..... Minnesota Study of Twins Reared Apart
MISTRAM... Missile Trajectory Measurement [*Air Force*]
MISTRANS... Mistranslation (ADA)
MISTRAULANT... Missile Weapons System Training Unit, Atlantic (DNAB)
MISTRAUPAC... Missile Weapons System Training Unit, Pacific (DNAB)
MistrJay .... Mister Jay Fashions International, Inc. [*Associated Press*] (SAG)
MIStructE... Member of the Institution of Structural Engineers [*British*] (EY)
MISTT .... Midwest Interstate Sulfur Transformation and Transport [*Meteorology*]
MiStu........ Sturgis Public Library, Sturgis, MI [*Library symbol*] [*Library of Congress*] (LCLS)
MISTY....... Missile System for Tactical Telephony (ACAE)
MistyM...... Misty Mountain Gold Ltd. [*Associated Press*] (SAG)
MISU .... Malaysian International Shipping [*Intermodal shipping container symbol*] (TVRC)
MISU .... Meteorological Institute Stockholm University (SAUO)
MiSun .... Sunfield District Library, Sunfield, MI [*Library symbol*] [*Library of Congress*] (LCLS)
MISURA..... Miskito, Sumo, and Rama [*Nicaraguan Indian coalition*]
MISURASATA... Miskito, Sumo, and Rama [*Nicaraguan Indian coalition*]
MiSV .... United States Veterans Administration Hospital, Saginaw, MI [*Library symbol*] [*Library of Congress*] (LCLS)
MISVAL ..... Missile Evaluation (ACAE)
MISVE....... Management Information Systems for Vocational Education (OICC)
MISW........ Member of the Institute of Shorthand Writers, practising in High Court of Justice (SAUO)
MISW........ Member of the Institute of Social Welfare [*British*] (DBQ)
MiSW........ White Pine Library System, Saginaw, MI [*Library symbol*] [*Library of Congress*] (LCLS)
M-ISWS..... Illinois State Water Survey (SAUO)
MISX .... Metered Services Information Exchange (SAUO)
MiS-Z........ Saginaw Public Libraries, Zauel Memorial Library, Saginaw, MI [*Library symbol*] [*Library of Congress*] (LCLS)
MIT .... Advanced Magnetics, Inc. (SAUO)
MIT .... Machine Interface Terminal [*Tangram Computer Aided Engineering*] [*Software package*] (NCC)
MIT .... Macrotrends International [*Vancouver Stock Exchange symbol*]
MIT .... Made in Taiwan (SAUO)
MIT .... Madras Institute of Technology (SAUO)
MIT .... Makari Intradermal Test [*Medicine*] (DB)
MIT .... Male Impotence Test [*Medicine*] (DMAA)
MIT .... Management Information Tree [*Telecommunications*] (OSI)
MIT .... Mandatory Independent Taxation [*British*] (DI)
MIT .... Manual Inputs-Tracks (SAA)
MIT .... Mara Institute of Technology (SAUO)
MIT .... Maritime Institute of Technology (SAUO)
MIT .... Marked If Touched (VLIE)
MIT .... Market if Touched [*Stock exchange term*]
MIT .... Market if Touched order (SAUO)
MIT .... Marrow Iron Turnover [*Medicine*] (DMAA)
MIT .... Massachusetts Institute of Technology (GAGS)
MIT .... Massachusetts Investors Trust
MIT .... Master Instruction Tape [*Computer science*]
MIT .... Master in Teaching (PGP)
MIT .... Master of Industrial Technology (PGP)

MIT .... Master of Initial Teaching (PGP)
MIT .... Material Improvement Team (MCD)
MIT .... Material in Transit (MCD)
MIT .... Material Introduction Team
MIT .... Materials Interaction Test (ABAC)
MIT .... Medium Intertheater Transport (MCD)
MIT .... Melodic Intonation Therapy (DMAA)
MIT .... Mercury Integrated Test
MIT .... Mercury Ion Thruster
MIT .... Merrill Lynch & Co., Inc. [*NYSE symbol*] (SPSG)
MIT .... Merrill Lynch & Co'MITTS' 2001 [*NASDAQ symbol*] (TTSB)
MIT .... Metabolism Inhibition Test [*Medicine*] (DMAA)
MIT .... Metal Insulator Transition [*Electronics*] (AAEL)
MIT .... Middle Italian [*Language, etc.*]
MIT .... Might [*Telegraphy*] (PCTE)
MIT .... Miles in-Trail [*FAA*] (TAG)
MIT .... Military Intelligence Translator
MIT .... Milled in Transit [*Commodities*]
MIT .... Miller Air Transporters [*ICAO designator*] (FAAC)
MIT .... Milwaukee Institute of Technology [*Wisconsin*]
MIT .... Minimum Individual Training
MIT .... Ministry of Industry and Trade [*Israel*]
MIT .... Minnesota Institute of Technology (SAUO)
MIT .... MIPS Technologies Inc. (SAUO)
MIT .... Miracidal Immobilization Test [*Parasitology*]
MIT .... Miscellaneous Tool (SAA)
MIT .... Mission West Properties (EFIS)
MIT .... Missouri-Illinois Traffic Service, East Saint Louis IL [*STAC*]
Mit .... Mitannian (BJA)
MIT .... Mitchell Camper Trailer [*NCIC trailer make code*]
MIT .... Miter
MIT .... Mitigate
MIT .... Mito [*Japan*] [*Seismograph station code, US Geological Survey*] (SEIS)
MIT .... Mitomycin [*Medicine*] (DMAA)
MIT .... Mitsubishi Electric Corporation (NITA)
MIT .... Mitte [*Send*] [*Latin*]
MIT .... Mobile Instructor Team (MCD)
MIT .... Mobile Instructor Training [*Army*]
MIT .... Modern Investment Theory [*Finance*] (MHDB)
MIT .... Modular Industrial Terminal
MIT .... Modular Intelligent Terminal
MIT .... Monoiodotyrosine [*Biochemistry*]
MIT .... Motorist Inclusive Tour [*British*] (DCTA)
MIT .... Movements Identification Technican (SAA)
MIT .... Multiple Incidence Technique [*Structure testing*]
MIT .... Multiple Insert Tooling
MIT .... Municipal Investment Trust
MIT .... Myocardial Infarction Triage [*Medicine*] (MELL)
MIT .... Shafter, CA [*Location identifier*] [*FAA*] (FAAL)
MIT .... Society of Management Information Technology [*British*]
MiT .... Traverse City Public Library, Traverse City, MI [*Library symbol*] [*Library of Congress*] (LCLS)
MITA .... Maine Island Trail Association
MITA .... Member of the Industrial Transport Association [*British*]
MITA .... MetLife's Intelligent Text Analyzer [*Textual analysis of life insurance applications*] (IDAI)
MITA .... Microcomputer Industry Trade Association
MITA .... Minority Information Trade Annual [*A publication*]
MITAC .... Medical Informatics and Technology Applications Consortium [*Virginia Commonwealth University*] (RCD)
MITACS ..... Mathematics of Information Technology and Complex Systems [*Canada*] (RCD)
MITAG .... Minority Affairs Task Group (DNAB)
MITAGS ..... Maritime Institute of Technology and Graduate Studies (SAUO)
MITAN .... Microwave Technology as Applied to Air Navigation (ADA)
MITAS .... Missile Threat Analysis Simulator (ACAE)
MITAS .... Multi-sensor Imaging Technology for Airborne Surveillance (SAUS)
MITASK ..... Mission Tasking (COE)
MITB .... Missile Interface Test Bench
MiTc .... Iosco-Arenac Regional Library, Tawas City, MI [*Library symbol*] [*Library of Congress*] (LCLS)
MITC .... Magdalen Island Transportation Company (SAUO)
MITC .... Manufacturing Information Technology Center [*University of Alabama*] (RCD)
MITC .... Methylisothiocyanate [*Pesticide*]
MITC .... Microfilm and Information Technology Center
MITC .... Mitchell Industrial Tire Company [*NCIC trailer make code*]
MiTc-A .... Iosco-Arenac Regional Library, AuGres Branch Library, AuGres, MI [*Library symbol*] [*Library of Congress*] (LCLS)
MiTc-E .... Iosco-Arenac Regional Library, East Tawas Branch Library, East Tawas, MI [*Library symbol*] [*Library of Congress*] (LCLS)
Mitch .... Mitcham Industries [*Associated Press*] (SAG)
MITCH .... Mitchell, IL [*American Association of Railroads railroad junction routing code*]
Mitcham .... Mitcham Industries [*Associated Press*] (SAG)
Mitch B & N... Mitchell on Bills, Notes, Etc. [*1829*] [*A publication*] (DLA)
Mitchell's Mar Reg... Mitchell's Maritime Register [*England*] [*A publication*] (DLA)
Mitch Mod Geog... Mitchell's Modern Geography [*A publication*] (DLA)
Mitch MR ... Mitchell's Maritime Register [*England*] [*A publication*] (DLA)
Mit Ch Pl ... Mitford on Equity Pleading [*A publication*] (DLA)
MiTc-O ...... Iosco-Arenac Regional Library, Oscoda Township Branch Library, Oscoda, MI [*Library symbol*] [*Library of Congress*] (LCLS)
MITCO .... Mitchell Energy & Development Corp. (EFIS)
MiTc-P .... Iosco-Arenac Regional Library, Plainfield Township Branch Library, Hale, MI [*Library symbol*] [*Library of Congress*] (LCLS)
MiTc-S .... Iosco-Arenac Regional Library, Standish Branch Library, Standish, MI [*Library symbol*] [*Library of Congress*] (LCLS)
MiTc-T .... Iosco-Arenac Regional Library, Tawas City Branch Library, Tawas City, MI [*Library symbol*] [*Library of Congress*] (LCLS)
MiTc-W ...... Iosco-Arenac Regional Library, Whittemore Branch Library, Whittemore, MI [*Library symbol*] [*Library of Congress*] (LCLS)
MITD .... Member of the Institute of Training and Development [*British*] (DBQ)
MITDA .... Maryland Independent Truckers and Drivers Association [*Later, ITDA*] (EA)
MIT DIC ..... Massachusetts Institute of Technology, Division of Industrial Cooperation (SAUO)
Mit Drunk ... Mittermaier's Effect of Drunkenness on Criminal Responsibilty [*A publication*] (DLA)
MITE .... Magnetic Insulation Test Experiment
MITE .... Master Instrumentation Timing Equipment (CET)
MITE .... Mathematics Institute for Teacher Enhancement (SAUO)
MITE .... Meetings and Incentive Travel Exposition [*Trade show*]
MITE .... Metals in the Environment (FOTI)
MITE .... Microelectronic Integrated Test Equipment
MITE .... Microelectronics Test and Evaluation [*Raytheon Co.*]
MITE .... Microprocessor Industrial Terminal [*Computer science*] (MHDB)
MITE .... Miniaturized Integrated Telephone Equipment
MITE .... Missile Integration Terminal Equipment [*Computer science*]
MITE .... Mission Training and Evaluation (ACAE)
MITE .... Multiple Input Terminal Equipment
MiTe .... Tecumseh Public Library, Tecumseh, MI [*Library symbol*] [*Library of Congress*] (LCLS)
MITEC .... Machine Intelligent Technical Controller (SAUO)
MITECS ..... MIT (Massachusetts Institute of Technology) Encyclopedia of Cognitive Sciences
MITECS ..... Multi-International Teacher Education Cooperatives (EDAC)
MiTek .... Tekonsha Public Library, Tekonsha, MI [*Library symbol*] [*Library of Congress*] (LCLS)
MitekS ...... Mitek Systems, Inc. [*Associated Press*] (SAG)
MITEL .... Mike and Terry's Lawnmowers [*Commercial firm*] [*canada*]
Mitel .... Mitel Corp. [*Associated Press*] (SAG)
MITER .... Modular Installation of Telecommunications Equipment Racks (TEL)
MITF .... Municipal Investment Trust Fund
MITF .... Musser International Turfgrass Foundation (EA)
MITFA .... Metropolitan Intercollegiate Track & Field Association (PSS)
Mitf & Ty Eq Pl... Tyler's Edition of Mitford's Equity Pleading [*A publication*] (DLA)
Mitf Eq Pl... Mitford on Equity Pleading [*A publication*] (DLA)
MIT-FMP .... Minimal Impact Technologies for Forest Materials Processing (FOTI)
MITGS .... Marine Institute of Technology and Graduate Studies [*Baltimore*]
MITH .... Marble-in-the-Hole [*Game used in psychometrics*]
MITH .... Mithracin [*Antineoplastic drug*] (CDI)
Mith .... Mithramycin [*Antineoplastic drug*] (DAVI)
MiTho .... Betsie Valley District Library, Thompsonville, MI [*Library symbol*] [*Library of Congress*] (LCLS)
MiThr .... Three Rivers Public Library, Three Rivers, MI [*Library symbol*] [*Library of Congress*] (LCLS)
MITI .... Ministry of International Trade and Industry [*Japan*]
MITI .... Ministry of International Trade and Investment (SAUO)
MITI .... Moms in Touch International (EA)
MITI .... Multilingual Intelligence Interface (SAUO)
MITI .... Myocardial Infarction, Triage, and Intervention Project [*or Trial*] [*Cardiology study*]
MITIC .... Myanmar International Trust and Investment Co. (ECON)
MITIL .... Massachusetts Institute of Technology Instrumentation Laboratory (SAA)
MITILAC ..... Massachusetts Institute of Technology Information Laboratory Automatic Coding
Mit Insuf .... Mitral Insufficiency [*Cardiology*]
MITJ .... Member of the Institute of Technical Journalists [*British*] (DGA)
MITK .... Mitek Systems [*NASDAQ symbol*] (TTSB)
MITK .... Mitek Systems Inc. [*NASDAQ symbol*] (SAG)
MITKA .... Movimiento Indio Tupaj Katari [*Tupaj Katari Indian Movement*] [*Bolivia*] [*Political party*] (PPW)
MITL .... Magnetically Insulated Transmission Line (ODA)
MITL .... Man-in-the-Loop [*Army*]
MITLA .... Microcircuit Technology in Logistics Applications [*Defense Logistics Agency*]
MIT/LIN ..... Massachusetts Institute of Technology, Lincoln Laboratory (SAUO)
MIT/LL ...... Massachusetts Institute of Technology/Lincoln Laboratory (AAG)
MITLS .... Man-in-the-Loop Simulator [*Military*]
MITM .... Management Inventory on Time Management [*Test*]
MITM .... Michigan Transit Museum [*Federal Railroad Administration identification code*]
MITM .... Military-Industry Technical Manual
MITMA ...... Man in the Middle Attack (SAUS)
MITMA ...... Member, Institute of Trade Mark Agents (SAUO)
MITMA ...... Member of the Institute of Trade Mark Agents [*British*]
MITMA ...... Military Traffic Management Agency [*Later, DTMS*]
MIT/MAT ... Missile Interface Test/Missile Auxiliary Test (ACAE)
Mit MR ..... Mitchell's Maritime Register [*England*] [*A publication*] (ILCA)
MITMS ...... Military-Industry Technical Manual Specifications
MITN .... Michigan Information Technology Network
MiTN .... Northwestern Michigan College, Traverse City, MI [*Library symbol*] [*Library of Congress*] (LCLS)
MITNJ .... Member of the Industrial Team of New Jersey (SAUO)
MIT/NSL .... Massachusetts Institute of Technology/Naval Supersonic Laboratory (AAG)
MITO .... Meat Industry Training Organisation (AIE)

MITO .... Member of the Institute of Training Officers [*International Institute of Social Economics*] [*British*] (DI)
MITO .... Minimum Interval Takeoff
mito .... mitochondria (SAUS)
Mito .... Mitomycin-C [*Antineoplastic drug*] (DAVI)
MITO-C ...... Mitomycin-C [*Antineoplastic drug*] (DAVI)
MITOC .... Multiple Intercommunications Technical Operations Communications [*NASA*] (KSC)
MITOCS ..... Missile Technical Operations Communications System (MCD)
MITOL .... Machine-Independent Telemetry-Oriented Language [*Computer science*] (IEEE)
MiTop .... Topinabee Public Library, Topinabee, MI [*Library symbol*] [*Library of Congress*] (LCLS)
MITP .... Master Intern Training Plan [*Military*]
MITP .... Measurement and Instrumentation Technology Panel (ACII)
MITP .... Miniature Template [*Tool*]
MiTP .... Peninsula Community Library, Traverse City, MI [*Library symbol*] [*Library of Congress*] (LCLS)
MITR .... Massachusetts Institute of Technology Reactor
MITR .... Mortgage Interest Tax Relief [*British*]
MiTr .... Troy Public Library, Troy, MI [*Library symbol*] [*Library of Congress*] (LCLS)
MITRA .... Management Institute for Training and Research in Asia (SAUO)
MitrArd ...... Mitropolia Ardealului [*Sibiu, Rumania*] (BJA)
MitrBan ..... Mitropolia Banatului [*Timisoara, Rumania*] (BJA)
MITRE .... Massachusetts Institute of Technology, Research and Engineering (SAUO)
MIT-RE ...... Massachusetts Institute of Technology, Research and Engineering Group (SAUO)
MITRE .... Massachusetts Institute of Technology Research Establishment (NATG)
MITRE .... Miniature Individual Transmitter-Receiver Equipment (MCD)
MITRE .... MITRE Corp. (SAUO)
MitrMoldSuc ... Mitropolia Moldovei si Sucevei [*Jassy, Rumania*] (BJA)
MiTrWB ..... William Beaumont Hospital, Troy, MI [*Library symbol*] [*Library of Congress*] (LCLS)
MITS .... Management Information and Text System
MITS .... Management Information Tracking System (COE)
MITS .... Man-in-the-Sea Program [*Navy*]
MITS .... Man in the Street [*The average man*] [*Usually "Mr. Mits"*] [*See also T C MITS*]
MITS .... Mariposa in the Schools [*Canada*] (EAIO)
MITS .... Marshall Integrated Telecommunications System (SAUO)
MITS .... Master's Intelligent Terminal System [*Software package*] [*Nippon Kokan*]
MITS .... Michigan Information Transfer Source [*University of Michigan*] (IID)
MITS .... Michigan Travel System
MITS .... Microfiche Image Transmission System (MCD)
MITS .... Micro Instrumentation and Telemetry Systems (NITA)
MITS .... Military Air Lift Command Imagery Transmission System (ACAE)
MITS .... Military Airlift Command Intra-Theater Transmission System (SAUO)
MITS .... Missile Ignition Test Simulator
MITS .... Missile Interface Test Set
MITS .... Mission Integrated Transparency System (ACAE)
MITS .... Missouri-Illinois Traffic Service
MITS .... Mitsubishi [*NCIC truck make code*]
MITS .... Mitsubishi [*NCIC car make code*]
MITS .... Mitsui & Co. Ltd. [*NASDAQ symbol*] (NQ)
MITS .... Mobile Independent Target System (INF)
MITS .... Model Instrumentation Telemetry Systems (SAUO)
MITS .... Monthly International Terrorist Summary (MCD)
MITS .... Multiple Inward-Turning Scoop (MCD)
MITS .... Multiplex Information Transfer System (PDAA)
MITSA .... Member of the Institute of Trading Standards Administration [*British*] (DBQ)
mit sang .... Mitte Sanguinem [*Take Away Blood*] [*Latin*] (MAE)
MitsbBk ..... Mitsubishi Bank Ltd. [*Associated Press*] (SAG)
mitse .... Made in the Same Establihment [*Manufacturing*]
MITSG .... Massachusetts Institute of Technology Sea Grant Program (NOAA)
MIT/SL ...... Massachusetts Institute of Technology/Sloan Laboratory (AAG)
MIT/SmL .... Massachusetts Institute of Technology/Servomechanisms Laboratory (AAG)
MIT/SpL ..... Massachusetts Institute of Technology/Spectroscopy Laboratory (AAG)
Mitsui .... Mitsui & Co. Ltd. [*Associated Press*] (SAG)
MITSY .... Memory Interface Test System (ACAE)
MITSY .... Mitsui & Co ADR [*NASDAQ symbol*] (TTSB)
MITT .... Member of the Institute of Travel and Tourism [*British*] (ODBW)
MITT .... Mitte [*Send*] [*Latin*]
MITT .... Mitts & Merill [*NCIC trailer make code*]
MITT .... Mobile Imagery Transmission Terminal (DOMA)
MITT .... Mobile Integrated Tactical Terminal (DOMA)
MITTAT ...... Mittatur [*Let Be Sent*] [*Pharmacy*] (ROG)
Mitte Sang ... Mitte Sanguinem [*Bleed*] [*Pharmacy*] (BABM)
mitte sang ... Mitte Sanguineum [*Bleed*] [*Latin*] (DAVI)
MITTINS .... Michigan Travel Trade Information Service
MITTS .... Minutes of Telecommunications Traffic [*Measure of voice, fax, and data transmission*]
MITTS .... Mobile IGOR [*Intercept Ground Optical Recorder*] Tracking Telescope System [*Air Force*]
MITT SANG ad UNC SALTEM ... Mitte Sanguinem ad Uncias ___ Saltem [*Take Away ___ Ounces of Blood at Least*] [*Pharmacy*] (ROG)
MITT TAL ... Mitte Tales [*Send Such*] [*Pharmacy*]
MITU .... Force V [*Intermodal shipping container symbol*] (TVRC)
MITU .... Mobile Inflatable Treatment Unit [*Medicine*] (EDAA)
MiTu .... Tustin Public Library, Tustin, MI [*Library symbol*] [*Library of Congress*] (LCLS)
MITY .... Mity Lite, Inc. [*NASDAQ symbol*] (SAG)
MityLite ..... Mity Lite, Inc. [*Associated Press*] (SAG)
MIU .... Machine Interface Unit (HGAA)
MIU .... Maharishi International University, Fairfield, IA [*OCLC symbol*] (OCLC)
MIU .... Maiduguri [*Nigeria*] [*Airport symbol*] (OAG)
MIU .... Malfunction Insertion Unit [*Aviation*]
MIU .... Message Interface Unit (CAAL)
MIU .... Methylisourea [*Organic chemistry*]
miu .... Michigan [*MARC country of publication code*] [*Library of Congress*] (LCCP)
MIU .... Microalgae International Union (EA)
MIU .... Micronesian Insurance Underwriters (SAUO)
mIU .... Milli-International Unit
MIU .... Missile Interface Unit
MIU .... Miura [*NCIC car model code*]
MIU .... Mobile Inspection Unit [*Military*] (AFM)
MIU .... Model Interface Unit (NITA)
MIU .... Modem Interface Unit [*Computer science*] (ELAL)
MIU .... Moisture, Insolubles, and Unsaponifiables [*Fat analysis*]
MIU .... Motor Impeller Unit
MIU .... Multi-Input Unit [*Testing equipment*]
miu .... Multiplex Interface Unit (NAKS)
MIU .... Multiplex Interface Unit (NASA)
MIU .... Multistation Interface Unit [*Computer science*]
MIU .... Myocardial Infarction Unit [*Medicine*] (EDAA)
MiU .... University of Michigan, Ann Arbor, MI [*Library symbol*] [*Library of Congress*] (LCLS)
MiU .... University of Michigan, Physics-Astronomy Library (SAUO)
MiU-A .... University of Michigan, Asia Library, Ann Arbor, MI [*Library symbol*] [*Library of Congress*] (LCLS)
MiUb .... Sleeper Public Library, Ubly, MI [*Library symbol*] [*Library of Congress*] (LCLS)
MiU-BA ...... University of Michigan, Graduate School of Business Administration, Ann Arbor, MI [*Library symbol*] [*Library of Congress*] (LCLS)
MiU-C .... University of Michigan, William L. Clements Library, Ann Arbor, MI [*Library symbol*] [*Library of Congress*] (LCLS)
MiUcD .... Delta College, University Center, MI [*Library symbol*] [*Library of Congress*] (LCLS)
MiUcS .... Saginaw Valley College, University Center, MI [*Library symbol*] [*Library of Congress*] (LCLS)
MIU/FCO .... Mobile Inspection Unit / Functional Checkout (SAA)
MiU-G .... University of Michigan, Bureau of Government Library, Ann Arbor, MI [*Library symbol*] [*Library of Congress*] (LCLS)
MiU-H .... University of Michigan, Michigan Historical Collection, Ann Arbor, MI [*Library symbol*] [*Library of Congress*] (LCLS)
MiU-Ho ...... University of Michigan, Avery and Julie Hopwood Room, Ann Arbor, MI [*Library symbol*] [*Library of Congress*] (LCLS)
MIUL .... M and I Truck Line [*Common carrier symbol*]
MiU-L .... University of Michigan, Law Library, Ann Arbor, MI [*Library symbol*] [*Library of Congress*] (LCLS)
MiU-M .... University of Michigan, Medical Center, Ann Arbor, MI [*Library symbol*] [*Library of Congress*] (LCLS)
MiUnv .... Columbia Township Library, Unionville, MI [*Library symbol*] [*Library of Congress*] (LCLS)
MiU-RE ...... University of Michigan, Center for Research on Economic Development, Ann Arbor, MI [*Library symbol*] [*Library of Congress*] (LCLS)
MIUS .... Modular Integrated Utility System [*HUD*]
MIUSA .... Mobility International USA (EA)
MIUT .... Mobile Information Unit Time
MiU-T .... University of Michigan, Transportation Library, Ann Arbor, MI [*Library symbol*] [*Library of Congress*] (LCLS)
MiUt .... Utica Public Library, Utica, MI [*Library symbol*] [*Library of Congress*] (LCLS)
MIUTC .... Military Intelligence Unit Training Center (AABC)
MiUtS .... Shelby Township Library, Utica, MI [*Library symbol*] [*Library of Congress*] (LCLS)
MIUU .... Meteorological Institute of the University of Uppsala [*Sweden*] (USDC)
MIUU .... Meterorological Institute of the University of Uppsala, Sweden [*Marine science*] (OSRA)
MIUW .... Mobile Inshore Undersea Warfare [*Navy*] (NG)
MIUWG ...... Mobile Inshore Undersea War Group [*Navy*] (VNW)
MIUWS ...... Mobile Inshore Undersea Warfare Surveillance [*Navy*] (NVT)
MIUWSU .... Mobile Inshore Undersea Warfare Surveillance Unit [*Navy*] (CINC)
MIV .... Main Instrumentation Van [*NASA*]
MIV .... Mi-Avia [*Russian Federation*] [*ICAO designator*] (FAAC)
MIV .... MICC Investments Ltd. [*Toronto Stock Exchange symbol*]
MIV .... Millville, NJ [*Location identifier*] [*FAA*] (FAAL)
MIV .... Mobile Instrumentation Van (KSC)
MIV .... Moving Ion Voltmeter
MiVa .... Bullard-Sanford Public Library, Vassar, MI [*Library symbol*] [*Library of Congress*] (LCLS)
MIVA .... Midwestern Intercollegiate Volleyball Association (PSS)
MIVA .... Missionary Vehicle Association (EA)
MIVA-America ... Missionary Vehicle Association of America (EA)
MIVAC .... Microwave Vacuum [*Dryer*] (MCD)
MIVC .... Magnetically Induced Velocity Charge [*Southwest Research Institute*]
MIVEC .... Mitsubishi Innovative Valve Timing and Lift Electronic Control System [*Automotive engineering*] (PS)
MiVer .... Vermontville Public Library, Vermontville, MI [*Library symbol*] [*Library of Congress*] (LCLS)

MiVes .... Vestaburg Public Library, Vestaburg, MI [*Library symbol*] [*Library of Congress*] (LCLS)
MIVI .... Mississippi View Holding [*NASDAQ symbol*] (TTSB)
MIVI .... Mississippi View Holding Co. [*NASDAQ symbol*] (SAG)
MiVi .... Vicksburg Community Library, Vicksburg, MI [*Library symbol*] [*Library of Congress*] (LCLS)
MIVPO....... Modified Inside Vapor Phase Oxidation (EECA)
MIW .... Airborne of Sweden AB [*ICAO designator*] (FAAC)
MIW .... Marshalltown, IA [*Location identifier*] [*FAA*] (FAAL)
MiW .... Med in Web (SAUO)
MIW .... Microinstruction Word
MIW .... Milk Ingredient Water (OA)
MIW .... Mine Warfare (NVT)
MiWaC ...... Wayne County Federated Library System, Wayne, MI [*Library symbol*] [*Library of Congress*] (LCLS)
MiWaC-B.... Wayne County Federated Library System, Department for the Blind and Physically Handicapped, Wayne, MI [*Library symbol*] [*Library of Congress*] (LCLS)
MIWACS .... Modular Integrated Weapon Aiming & Control System (SAUS)
MiWak....... Wakefield Public Library, Wakefield, MI [*Library symbol*] [*Library of Congress*] (LCLS)
MiWal .... Melrose Township Public Library, Walloon Lake, MI [*Library symbol*] [*Library of Congress*] (LCLS)
MiWald...... Waldron District Library, Waldron, MI [*Library symbol*] [*Library of Congress*] (LCLS)
MiWalv...... Walkerville Public Library, Walkerville, MI [*Library symbol*] [*Library of Congress*] (LCLS)
MiWar....... Warren Public Library, Warren, MI [*Library symbol*] [*Library of Congress*] (LCLS)
MiWarBH ... Bi-County Community Hospital, Warren, MI [*Library symbol*] [*Library of Congress*] (LCLS)
MiWarGME... General Motors Corp., Engineering Library and Information Services, Warren, MI [*Library symbol*] [*Library of Congress*] (LCLS)
MiWarGMR... General Motors Corp., Research Laboratories Division, Warren, MI [*Library symbol*] [*Library of Congress*] (LCLS)
MiWarGMR-E... General Motors Corp., Engineering Staff Library, Warren, MI [*Library symbol*] [*Library of Congress*] (LCLS)
MiWarM..... Macomb County Community College, Warren, MI [*Library symbol*] [*Library of Congress*] (LCLS)
MiWatv...... Watervliet Public Library, Watervliet, MI [*Library symbol*] [*Library of Congress*] (LCLS)
MiWbH ...... Holocaust Memorial Center, West Bloomfield, MI [*Library symbol*] [*Library of Congress*] (LCLS)
MIWE........ Member of the Institution of Water Engineers [*British*] (EY)
MiWe........ West Branch Public Library, West Branch, MI [*Library symbol*] [*Library of Congress*] (LCLS)
MiWeld...... Gladys MacArthur Memorial Library, Weidman, MI [*Library symbol*] [*Library of Congress*] (LCLS)
MIWES ...... Member of the Institution of Water Engineers and Scientists [*British*] (DI)
MIWG .... Military Airlift Command Interoperability Working Group (SAUO)
MiWh........ White Pigeon Township Library, White Pigeon, MI [*Library symbol*] [*Library of Congress*] (LCLS)
MiWhc ...... E. Jack Sharpe Public Library, White Cloud, MI [*Library symbol*] [*Library of Congress*] (LCLS)
MIWHR...... Melpomene Institute for Women's Health Research (EA)
MIWHTE .... Member of the Institution of Works and Highways Technician Engineers [*British*] (DBQ)
MiWin....... Fremont Township Library, Winn, MI [*Library symbol*] [*Library of Congress*] (LCLS)
MIWM....... Member of the Institution of Works Managers [*British*]
MIWMA ..... Member of the Institute of Weights and Measures Administration [*British*]
MiWol .... Wolverine Community Library, Wolverine, MI [*Library symbol*] [*Library of Congress*] (LCLS)
MiWp........ Carp Lake Township Library, White Pine, MI [*Library symbol*] [*Library of Congress*] (LCLS)
MIWPC...... Member of the Institute of Water Pollution Control [*British*]
MIWS........ Multipurpose Individual Weapon System (MCD)
MIWSP...... Member of the Institute of Work Study Practitioners [*British*]
MIWT........ Member of the Institute of Wireless Technology [*British*]
MiWy........ Bacon Memorial Public Library, Wyandotte, MI [*Library symbol*] [*Library of Congress*] (LCLS)
MIX.......... Magnetic Ionization Experiment
MIX.......... McGraw-Hill Information Exchange for Educators
MIX.......... Mediation of Information Using XML [*Computer science*] (HODG)
MIX.......... Member Information Exchange [*American Society for Training and Development - ASTD*] [*Alexandria, VA*] [*Information service or system*] (IID)
MIX.......... Merrill Lynch & Co. [*NYSE symbol*] (SAG)
MIX.......... Merrill Lynch & Co'MITTS' 2001 [*NYSE symbol*] (TTSB)
MIX.......... Methylisobutylxanthine [*Also, IBMX*] [*Biochemistry*]
MIX.......... Metropolis, IL [*Location identifier*] [*FAA*] (FAAL)
MIX.......... Microprogram Index Register [*Computer science*] (CIST)
MIX.......... Mix Canyon Road [*California*] [*Seismograph station code, US Geological Survey*] (SEIS)
MIX.......... Mixed Schedule of Reinforcement (DIPS)
MIX.......... Mixing
MIX.......... Mixture (KSC)
mix.......... Mixture (MEC)
MIX.......... Mores Island [*Bahamas*] [*Airport symbol*] (AD)
mix mon.... Mixed Monitor [*Obstetrics*] (DAVI)
MIXT......... Mixtura [*Mixture*] [*Pharmacy*]
mixt.......... Mixture (MIST)
MIXX........ Medical Innovations [*NASDAQ symbol*] (TTSB)
MIXX........ Medical Innovations, Inc. [*NASDAQ symbol*] (NQ)
MIY.......... Ayutla Mixteco [*Language symbol*] (ETLW)
MIY.......... Miyako [*Japan*] [*Seismograph station code, US Geological Survey*] (SEIS)
MIY.......... Montgomeryshire Imperial Yeomanry [*British military*] (DMA)
MIY.......... MuniYield Michigan Insured Fund [*NYSE symbol*] (SPSG)
MiY.......... Ypsilanti Area Public Library, Ypsilanti, MI [*Library symbol*] [*Library of Congress*] (LCLS)
MiYCC....... Cleary College, Ypsilanti, MI [*Library symbol*] [*Library of Congress*] (LCLS)
MiYEM...... Eastern Michigan University, Ypsilanti, MI [*Library symbol*] [*Library of Congress*] (LCLS)
MIZ.......... Marginal Ice Zone [*Oceanography*]
MIZ.......... Menderhall [*Federal Railroad Administration identification code*]
MIZ.......... Missile Interception Zone [*Military*]
Miz........... Mizrachi [*or Mizrahi*] (BJA)
MIZ.......... Mizusawa [*Japan*] [*Seismograph station code, US Geological Survey*] (SEIS)
MiZ.......... Zeeland Public Library, Zeeland, MI [*Library symbol*] [*Library of Congress*] (LCLS)
Mizar........ Mizar, Inc. [*Associated Press*] (SAG)
MIZEX....... Marginal Ice Zone Experiment [*Oceanography*]
MIZPAC..... Marginal Sea Ice Zone Pacific [*Marine science*] (MSC)
MIZR........ Mizar, Inc. [*NASDAQ symbol*] (SAG)
MJ........... Lineas Aereas Privadas Argentinas [*ICAO designator*] (AD)
MJ........... Madras Jurist [*India*] [*A publication*] (DLA)
MJ........... Main Jet [*Automotive engineering*]
MJ........... Major Subject Descriptor [*Online database field identifier*]
MJ........... Manual Jack (VLIE)
MJ........... Manufacturers' Junction Railway Co. [*AAR code*]
MJ........... Marijuana
MJ........... Marine Jet
MJ........... Master of Journalism
MJ........... Master of Jurisprudence
MJ........... Mastic Joint [*Technical drawings*]
MJ........... Mead Johnson & Co. [*Research code symbol*]
MJ........... Mechanical Joint (NASA)
MJ........... Megajoule
MJ........... Michael Joseph [*Commercial firm*] [*British*]
MJ........... Microturbo [*France*] [*ICAO aircraft manufacturer identifier*] (ICAO)
MJ........... Military Judge (AFM)
MJ........... Military Justice Reporter (West) [*A publication*] (DLA)
MJ........... Milwaukee Journal [*A newspaper*]
MJ........... Mineralogical Journal [*A publication*] (STAH)
MJ........... Minerva Jacket [*Medicine*] (MELL)
MJ........... Ministry of Justice (SAUO)
mj............ Missionaries of St. Joseph (TOCD)
MJ........... Missionaries of St. Joseph (Mexico) (TOCD)
MJ........... Missionary Sisters of Jesus (TOCD)
MJ........... Modular Jack (VLIE)
mj............ Montserrat [*MARC country of publication code*] [*Library of Congress*] (LCCP)
MJA.......... Manja [*Madagascar*] [*Airport symbol*] (OAG)
MJA.......... Master of Justice Administration (PGP)
MJA.......... Mechanical Joint Apparatus [*Medicine*] (EDAA)
MJA.......... Medical Journalists Association [*British*] (DBA)
MJA.......... Medical Journal of Australia [*Medicine*] (EDAA)
MJA.......... Merchant Jewellers' Association Ltd. [*British*] (BI)
MJA.......... Midstates Jeepster Association (EA)
MJAA........ Messianic Jewish Alliance of America (EA)
MJAC........ MJA Cartage [*Common carrier symbol*]
MJAD........ Machado-Joseph Azorean Disease [*Medicine*] (EDAA)
MJAJ......... Maanpuolustuksen ja Turvallisuuden Ammattijaerjestoet [*Defence and Security Employees Union*] [*Finalnd*] (EY)
MJAO........ Mediterranean Joint Air Orders
MJB.......... Master Jet Base [*Navy*] (NVT)
MJB.......... Mejit [*Marshall Islands*] [*Airport symbol*] (OAG)
MJB.......... Missile Junction Box
MJB.......... Moore Jig Borer
MJBF........ MJB Freight Systems [*Common carrier symbol*]
MJC.......... Junior College District, Kansas City, MO [*OCLC symbol*] (OCLC)
MJC.......... Majestic Contractors Ltd. [*Toronto Stock Exchange symbol*]
MJC.......... Man [*Ivory Coast*] [*Airport symbol*] (OAG)
MJC.......... Manatee Junior College (SAUO)
MJC.......... Manitoba Journal of Counselling [*A publication*]
MJC.......... Marshalltown Junior College [*Iowa*]
MJC.......... Marymount Junior College (SAUO)
MJC.......... Massachusetts Job Council
MJC.......... Masters and Johnson Center (SAUO)
MJC.......... Medieval Jewish Chronicles [*A publication*] (BJA)
MJC.......... Mercy Junior College [*Missouri*] [*Closed, 1971*]
MJC.......... Metropolitan Junior College (SAUO)
MJC.......... Miami-Jacobs College [*Ohio*]
MJC.......... Midway Junior College [*Kentucky*]
MJC.......... Military Junior College (AABC)
MJC.......... Moberly Junior College [*Missouri*]
MJC.......... Modesto Junior College [*California*]
MJC.......... Montgomery Junior College [*Maryland*]
MJC.......... Morse Junior College [*Connecticut*]
MJC.......... Morton Junior College [*Later, Morton College*] [*Cicero, IL*]
MJC.......... Muscatine Junior College [*Iowa*]
MJC.......... Muslim Judicial Council (SAUO)
MJCA........ Midbody Jettison Control Assembly (NASA)
MJCA........ Mississippi Junior College Association (SAUO)
MJCAA...... Mississippi Junior College Athletic Association (PSS)

MJCAC ...... Midwest Junior College Athletic Conference (PSS)
MJCC .... Maryland Junior College Athletic Conference (PSS)
MJCC .... Melbourne Junior Chamber of Commerce [*Australia*]
MJCOM ..... Major Command (SAUO)
MJCS .... Joint Chiefs of Staff Memorandum (SAUO)
MJCS .... Memorandum for the Joint Chiefs of Staff (MCD)
MJD .... Doctor of Medical Jurisprudence
MJD .... Machado-Joseph Disease [*Medicine*] (EDAA)
MJD .... Management Job Description (PDAA)
MJD .... Modified Julian Date [*Astronomy*] (TEL)
MJD .... Mohenjo Daro [*Pakistan*] [*Airport symbol*] (OAG)
MJD .... Mouvement de la Jeunesse Djiboutienne [*Political party*] (EY)
MJD .... Mseleni Joint Disease [*Medicine*] (EDAA)
MJDQ........ Minnesota Job Description Questionnaire [*Research test*]
MJ Ed .... Master of Jewish Education (PGP)
MJEMS....... Modular Jet Engine Management Simulator (SAUO)
MJF.......... Greenville, TX [*Location identifier*] [*FAA*] (FAAL)
MJF.......... Medical Journal Finder (SAUO)
MJF.......... Multiple Juxtapositional Fixedness [*Tongue-in-cheek description of unusually strong bonding between metal ions and some ligands*]
MJF.......... Muslim Janbaz Force (SAUO)
MJG .... Mayajigua [*Cuba*] [*Airport symbol*] (AD)
MJG .... Moore Jig Grinder
MJGA........ Manufacturing Jewelers Golf Association (EA)
MJGA........ Midwest Job Galvanizers Association [*Defunct*] (EA)
MJH .... Majma [*Saudi Arabia*] [*Airport symbol*] (AD)
MJI .... Maji [*Ethiopia*] [*Airport symbol*] (AD)
MJI .... Masters and Johnson Institute [*St. Louis, MO*] [*Formerly, Reproductive Biology Research Foundation*] [*Research center*]
MJI .... Member of the Journalists Institute
MJI .... MuniYield New Jersey Insured Fund [*NYSE symbol*] (SPSG)
MJI .... MuniYield NJ Insured Fund [*NYSE symbol*] (TTSB)
MJIE......... Member of the Junior Institute of Engineers [*British*]
MJInstE ..... Member of the Junior Institution of Engineers (SAUO)
MJJ.......... Mawak [*Language symbol*] (ETLW)
MJKN........ MRJ Trucking [*Common carrier symbol*]
MJL.......... Medial Joint Line [*Orthopedics*] (DAVI)
MJL.......... Meyer, Jr., L. Agnew, Washington DC [*STAC*]
MJL.......... Mouila [*Gabon*] [*Airport symbol*] (OAG)
MJL.......... Murray's Jat Lancers [*British military*] (DMA)
MJLT......... Joseph Martin Logging and Trucking [*Common carrier symbol*]
MJM......... Man-Job Match [*Military*]
MJM......... Mbuji-Mayi [*Zaire*] [*Airport symbol*] (OAG)
MJMA .... Mechanical Jack Manufacturers Association [*Defunct*] (EA)
MJMI .... Messianic Jewish Movement International (EA)
MJMJ........ Missionaries of Jesus, Mary, and Joseph [*Roman Catholic women's religious order*]
MJMT .... Mean Job Mill Time [*Quality control*] (MHDB)
MJMT .... MJM Trailer Manufacturing [*NCIC trailer make code*]
MJN .... Majunga [*Madagascar*] [*Airport symbol*] (OAG)
MJN .... Royal Air Force of Oman (Air Transport) [*ICAO designator*] (FAAC)
MJNB........ J and B Marathon [*Common carrier symbol*]
MJNMM..... Master of Journalism in New Media Management (GAGS)
MJNPE ...... Mobile Joint Nuclear Planning Element (SAUO)
MJO .... Madden-Julian Oscillation (SAUO)
MJO .... Mariner Jupiter Orbit [*NASA*]
MJO .... Owens Technical College, Learning Resource Media Center, Toledo, OH [*OCLC symbol*] (OCLC)
MJOC........ Maritime Joint Operations Centre (SAUO)
MJP.......... Jackson Metropolitan Library System, Jackson, MS [*OCLC symbol*] (OCLC)
MJP.......... Master of Jewish Pedagogy
MJP.......... Mastuj [*Pakistan*] [*Airport symbol*] (AD)
MJP.......... Military Justice Procedure (SAUO)
MJP.......... Mount John Pukaki [*New Zealand*] [*Seismograph station code, US Geological Survey*] (SEIS)
MJP.......... Movement for Justice and Peace [*Political group*] [*Africa*]
mjp .... Mudded Joint Packing [*Industrial hygiene term*] (OHS)
MJP.......... Multiple Job Processing [*Computer science*] (VLIE)
M-JPEG ..... Motion-Joint Photographic Expert Group [*Computer science*] (DCDG)
MJPM .... Master of Justice Policy and Management (PGP)
MJPS .... Mouvement des Jeunesses Progressistes Soudanaises [*Sudanese Progressive Youth Movement*] [*Mali*]
MJQ .... Jackson, MN [*Location identifier*] [*FAA*] (FAAL)
MJQ .... Modern Jazz Quartet [*Musical group*]
MJR .... Maintenance Job Request
MJR .... Major
Mjr.......... Major [*Record label*]
MJR .... Management Job Review [*LIMRA*]
MJRT .... Maximum Junctional Recovery Time [*Medicine*] (EDAA)
MJS.......... Maintenance Jettison System [*NASA*]
MJS.......... Manipulator Jettison System [*or Subsystem*] (MCD)
MJS.......... Mariner Jupiter-Saturn [*NASA*]
MJS.......... Master of Japanese Studies (ADA)
MJS.......... Master of Judaic Studies (PGP)
MJS.......... Master of Juridical Science (DLA)
MJS.......... Member of the Japan Society
MJS.......... Movimiento Juvenil Salesiano [*Salesian Youth Movement - SYM*] (EAIO)
MJSA........ Manufacturing Jewelers and Silversmiths of America (EA)
MJSA........ Manufacturing Jewelers Sales Association
MJSA........ Mouvement des Jeunesses Socialistes Africaines [*African Socialist Youth Movement*]
MJSD........ March, June, September, and December [*Denotes quarterly payments of interest or dividends in these months*] [*Business term*]
MJSG........ Medem Jewish Socialist Group [*Defunct*] (EA)
MJSTC ...... Majestic
MJT.......... Magic Johnson Theaters
MJT.......... Magistrate [*Telegraphy*] (PCTE)
MJT.......... Maintenance Job Tracking (ACAE)
MJT.......... Maintenance Job Tracking System (SAUO)
MJT.......... Majorteck Industries [*Vancouver Stock Exchange symbol*]
MJT.......... Materials Joining Tool
MJT.......... Mead Johnson Tube [*Medicine*] (DMAA)
MJT.......... Multijet Transport
MJT.......... Multi-Job Terminal [*Computer science*] (VLIE)
MJT.......... Museum of Jurassic Technology
MJT.......... Mytilene [*Greece*] [*Airport symbol*] (OAG)
MJTG........ Mitigation Joint Test Group (SAUO)
MJTS........ Marjon Transportation [*Common carrier symbol*]
MJU .... Jackson State University, Jackson, MS [*OCLC symbol*] (OCLC)
MJU .... Mamuju [*Indonesia*] [*Airport symbol*] (OAG)
MJU .... Manna-Dora [*Language symbol*] (ETLW)
MJU .... Mariner Jupiter-Uranus [*Mission*] [*NASA*]
MJu.......... Medica Judaica [*A publication*] (BJA)
MJU .... Multijunction Unit [*Computer science*] (BUR)
MJU .... Multipoint Junction Unit [*Communications term*] (DCT)
MJUO........ Mount John University Observatory [*New Zealand*]
MJUPG...... Movimiento da Juventude da Uniao Popular da Guine [*Youth Movement of Guinean People's Union*]
MJUPS ...... Mouvement des Jeunes de l'Union Progressiste Senegalaise [*Youth Movement of the Senegalese Progressive Movement*]
MJur......... Master of Jurisprudence
MJV.......... Mojud Hosiery Company (SAUO)
MJV.......... Murcia [*Spain*] [*Airport symbol*] (OAG)
MJVU........ Merco [*Intermodal shipping container symbol*] (TVRC)
MJW......... J. W. Mays, Inc. (SAUO)
MJW......... Madison Junction [*Wyoming*] [*Seismograph station code, US Geological Survey*] [*Closed*] (SEIS)
MJWG....... MANPRINT [*Manpower and Personnel Integration*] Joint Working Group [*Army*]
MJX.......... Masjed Soleyman [*Iran*] [*Airport symbol*] (AD)
MJX.......... Toms River, NJ [*Location identifier*] [*FAA*] (FAAL)
MJY.......... Majesty Resources [*Vancouver Stock Exchange symbol*]
MJY.......... Majority [*Telegraphy*] (PCTE)
MJZ.......... Mahfid [*South Arabia*] [*Airport symbol*] (AD)
MJZ.......... Mount John [*New Zealand*] [*Seismograph station code, US Geological Survey*] (SEIS)
MK........... Air Mauritius [*ICAO designator*] (AD)
MK........... Macedonia [*Internet country code*]
MK........... Machinery Technician [*Military*] (POLM)
MK........... Maerkischer Kreis [*German license plate city code*]
MK........... Magic Kingdom [*Walt Disney World*]
MK........... Make [*Telegraphy*] (PCTE)
MK........... Malawi Kwacha [*Monetary unit*]
MK........... Manual Clock [*Computer science*] (MDG)
MK........... Mark [*Ammunition*] (NATG)
mk .... Mark (WDMC)
Mk .... Mark [*New Testament book*]
MK........... Markka [*Monetary unit*] [*Finland*] (GPO)
MK........... Marschkolonne [*March Column*] [*German military - World War II*]
MK........... Mask [*Computer science*]
MK........... Master Key [*Locks*] (ADA)
MK........... Mebyon Kernow [*Sons of Cornwall*] [*National liberation party*] [*Political party*]
MK........... Megakaryocyte (DMAA)
MK........... Member of Knesset (BJA)
M/K.......... Member of the Knesset (SAUO)
MK........... Menaquinone [*Vitamin K*] [*Also, MQ*] [*Biochemistry*]
MK........... Merck & Co., Inc. [*Research code symbol*]
MK........... Metarrithmistikon Komma [*Reformist Party*] [*Greece*] [*Political party*] (PPE)
MK........... Microphone (MDG)
MK........... Middle Kingdom [*Egyptology*] (ROG)
mK........... Millikelvin
MK........... Milton Keynes [*Russian city*]
MK........... Miscellaneous Kits [*JETDS nomenclature*] [*Military*] (CET)
MK........... Mit Kappe [*With Cap*] [*German military - World War II*]
MK........... Mit Kern [*With Core*] [*German military - World War II*]
MK........... Modification Kit (AAG)
MK........... Mo'ed Katan (BJA)
MK........... Monk
MK........... Monkey Kidney
MK........... Mon-Khmer [*Linguistics*] (IEL)
MK........... More-Kraepelin [*Disease*] [*Medicine*] (DB)
MK........... Morgan Keenan [*System*] [*Astronomy*]
MK........... Morrison Knudsen [*NYSE symbol*]
M-K.......... Morrison-Knudsen Co., Inc. [*Boise, ID*] (TSSD)
MK........... Morrison Knudsen Corp. (SAUO)
MK........... Morse Key (DEN)
MK........... Mounier-Kuhn [*Syndrome*] [*Medicine*] (DB)
MK........... Multiple Kill [*Aerospace*]
mk .... Muscat and Oman [*Oman*] [*MARC country of publication code*] [*Library of Congress*] (LCCP)
MK........... Myokinase (DMAA)
MKA .... Machine Knife Association (EA)
MKA .... Makaopuhi [*Hawaii*] [*Seismograph station code, US Geological Survey*] (SEIS)
MKA .... Marine-Kuestenartillerie [*Naval Coast Artillery*] [*German military - World War II*]

MKA .... Master Kennel Association [*Commercial firm*] (EA)
MKA .... Metrika Systems [*AMEX symbol*] (SG)
MKA .... Miller, SD [*Location identifier*] [*FAA*] (FAAL)
MKA .... MK Aircargo [*British*] [*ICAO designator*] (FAAC)
MKAB .... May Keep at Bedside [*Medicine*] (EDAA)
MKAI .... Molokai Ranch Ltd. [*NASDAQ symbol*] (COMM)
MKAS .... Meyer-Kendall Assessment Survey [*Interpersonal skills and attitudes test*]
MKATA ...... Machine Knife and Allied Trades Association (SAUO)
MKAU .... MK Gold [*NASDAQ symbol*] (TTSB)
MKAU .... MK Gold Co. [*NASDAQ symbol*] (SAG)
MKB .... Foreign Trade Bank
MKB .... Mary Kathryn Bonk [*Editor*]
MKB .... Mary K. Bonk [*Editor*]
MKB .... Megakaryoblast [*Hematology*]
MKB .... Mekambo [*Gabon*] [*Airport symbol*] (OAG)
MKBF .... Mean Kilometers between Failures
MKBWU ..... Machine Knife and Bayonet Workers' Union [*British*]
MKC .... Kansas City [*Missouri*] [*Airport symbol*] (OAG)
MKC .... Magic Kingdom Club [*Walt Disney Productions*]
MKC .... Mammal Kidney Cell (DB)
MKC .... Marion Laboratories, Inc. (SAUO)
MKC .... Mark Resources, Inc. [*Toronto Stock Exchange symbol*]
MKC .... McCormick & Co. [*NYSE symbol*] (SG)
MKC .... McKeesport Connecting Railroad Co. [*AAR code*]
MKC .... Megakaryocyte [*Medicine*] (MELL)
MKC .... Moncks Corner [*South Carolina*] [*Seismograph station code, US Geological Survey*] [*Closed*] (SEIS)
MKC .... Monkey Kidney Cell (DMAA)
MKC .... University of Health Sciences, Kansas City, MO [*OCLC symbol*] (OCLC)
MKCO .... M. Kamenstein Inc. (EFIS)
MKCO .... Morrison-Knudsen [*Federal Railroad Administration identification code*]
MKCS .... Milwaukee-Kansas City Southern Joint Agency [*Federal Railroad Administration identification code*]
MKD .... Marked (MSA)
MKDH .... Hungarian Christian Democratic Movement (Slovakia) [*Political party*] (PSAP)
MKDIR ...... Make Directory [*Computer science*]
MKDS .... Master Key Data Set [*Computer science*] (VLIE)
MKE .... Arthur G. McKee & Co. (SAUO)
MKE .... Association of the Hungarian Librarians (SAUO)
MKE .... General Mitchell International Airport [*FAA*] (TAG)
MKE .... Hungarian Chemical Society (SAUO)
MKE .... Michaels Stores, Inc. [*AMEX symbol*] (COMM)
MKE .... Milwaukee [*Wisconsin*] [*Airport symbol*] (OAG)
MKE .... Molecular Kinetic Energy
MKET .... Market Transport [*Common carrier symbol*]
MKF .... Mackenzie Financial Corp. [*Toronto Stock Exchange symbol*]
MKF .... Miya [*Language symbol*] (ETLW)
MKFC .... Mackenzie Financial Corp. [*NASDAQ symbol*] (SAG)
MKFCF ...... Mackenzie Financial [*NASDAQ symbol*] (TTSB)
MKG .... K.G. Munson (SAUO)
MKG .... Magnetocardiogram
MKG .... Making
MKG .... Mallinckrodt Group [*Formerly, IMCERA Group*] [*NYSE symbol*] (SAG)
MKG .... Marking
MKG .... Maurer Kunst Geselle [*Fellowcraft*] [*Freemasonry*] [*German*]
M-KG .... Meteor-Kilogram
M-KG .... Meter-Kilogram (KSC)
MKG .... Munson, K. G., Weyers Cave VA [*STAC*]
MKG .... Muskegon [*Michigan*] [*Airport symbol*] (OAG)
MK Gold .... MK Gold Co. [*Associated Press*] (SAG)
MKgP .... Posse School, Inc., Kendal Green, MA [*Library symbol*] [*Library of Congress*] [*Obsolete*] (LCLS)
MKGPr ...... Mallincrodt Group 4% Pfd [*NYSE symbol*] (TTSB)
MKGS .... Markings
MKH .... Mackintosh-Hemphill Co. (SAUO)
MKH .... Mauna Kea [*Hawaii*] [*Seismograph station code, US Geological Survey*] (SEIS)
MKH .... Million of Kilowatt Hours (MCD)
MKH .... Mokhotlong [*Lesotho*] [*Airport symbol*] (OAG)
MKH .... Multiple Key Hashing
MKHS .... Menkes' Kinky Hair Syndrome [*Medicine*] (DMAA)
MKI .... Max Kade German-American Research Institute [*Pennsylvania State University*] (RCD)
MKI .... M-Corp Inc. [*Formerly, Mike's Submarines*] [*Toronto Stock Exchange symbol*]
MKI .... Midas Kapiti International (IID)
MKI .... Mitosis-Karyorrhexis Index [*Medicine*] (PALA)
MKIE .... Mackie Designs [*NASDAQ symbol*] (TTSB)
MKIE .... Mackie Designs, Inc. [*NASDAQ symbol*] (SAG)
M Kin .... Master of Kinesiology (PGP)
MkIS .... Marketing Information System
MKJ .... Makoua [*Congo*] [*Airport symbol*] (OAG)
MKJK .... Kingston [*Jamaica*] [*ICAO location identifier*] (ICLI)
MKJM .... Montego Bay [*Jamaica*] [*ICAO location identifier*] (ICLI)
MKJP .... Kingston/Norman Manley International [*Jamaica*] [*ICAO location identifier*] (ICLI)
MKJS .... Montego Bay/Sangster International [*Jamaica*] [*ICAO location identifier*] (ICLI)
MKK .... Kaunakakai, HI [*Location identifier*] [*FAA*] (FAAL)
Mkk .... Markka [*Monetary unit*] [*Finland*]
MKK .... Molokai/Kaunakakai [*Hawaii*] [*Airport symbol*] (OAG)
MkK .... Monkey Kidney [*Medicine*] (DMAA)
MKK .... Morgan, Keenan, Kellman [*System*] [*Astronomy*]
MKL .... Jackson [*Tennessee*] [*Airport symbol*] (OAG)
MKL .... Jackson, TN [*Location identifier*] [*FAA*] (FAAL)
MKL .... Lakeland Regional Library, Killarney, Manitoba [*Library symbol*] [*National Library of Canada*] (NLC)
MKL .... Markel Corp. [*NYSE symbol*] (SG)
MKL .... Maskali [*Djibouti*] [*Seismograph station code, US Geological Survey*] (SEIS)
MKL .... Megakaryocytic Leukemia [*Hematology*]
MKLC .... Monkey Kidney Lung Culture [*Medicine*] (EDAA)
MKLD .... Markland Technologies, Inc. [*NASDAQ symbol*] (QUAN)
MKLP .... Mitotic Kinesin-Like Protein [*Biochemistry*]
MKM .... Kansas City, MO [*Location identifier*] [*FAA*] (FAAL)
MKM .... Manawatu Knitting Mills (SAUO)
MKM .... Marksman [*Marine Corps*]
MKM .... Mink Minerals Resources, Inc. [*Vancouver Stock Exchange symbol*]
MKM .... Mukah [*Malaysia*] [*Airport symbol*] (OAG)
MKM .... Myopic Keratomileusis [*Ophthalmology*]
MKMA .... Machine Knife Manufacturers Association (EA)
MkmQualBad ... Marksman Qualification Badge [*Military decoration*] (AABC)
MKN .... Malekolon [*Papua New Guinea*] [*Airport symbol*] (OAG)
MKN .... Mouvement Cooperatif National [*Haiti*] [*Political party*] (EY)
MKN .... Northeast Missouri State University, Kirksville, MO [*OCLC symbol*] (OCLC)
MKNG .... Macchia Trucking [*Common carrier symbol*]
MKNLA ...... Multnomah Kennel Club (Class A) [*NASDAQ symbol*] (COMM)
MKNP .... Malawi Kasungu National Park (SAUO)
MKNP .... Mount Kenya National Park (SAUO)
MKNW .... Mount Kisco-New York Express Company [*Common carrier symbol*]
MKO .... Makung Airlines [*Taiwan*] [*ICAO designator*] (FAAC)
MKO .... Mauna Kea Observatory [*Hawaii*] (BARN)
MKO .... Mikado Resources Ltd. [*Vancouver Stock Exchange symbol*]
MKO .... Modification Kit Order
MKO .... Mujahedin-e Khalq Organization [*Militant organization*] (EMA)
MKO .... Munafiqeen Khalq Organization (SAUO)
MKO .... Muskogee, OK [*Location identifier*] [*FAA*] (FAAL)
MKOF .... Meiko Freight Service [*Common carrier symbol*]
MKOPSC .... Mary Kay O'Connor Process Safety Center [*Texas A&M University*] (RCD)
MKOU .... Metin Akdurak [*Intermodal shipping container symbol*] (TVRC)
MKP .... Magyar Kommunista Part [*Hungarian Communist Party*] [*Political party*] (PPE)
MKP .... Makemo [*French Polynesia*] [*Airport symbol*] (OAG)
MKP .... McKeesport, PA [*Location identifier*] [*FAA*] (FAAL)
MkP .... Mikropress GmbH, Bonn, Germany [*Library symbol*] [*Library of Congress*] (LCLS)
mkp .... misc.kids.pregnancy newsgroup (SAUO)
MKP .... Monobasic Potassium Phosphate [*Medicine*] (EDAA)
MKP .... Myokinetic Psychodiagnosis [*Psychology*] (AEBS)
MKPL .... Computer Marketplace [*NASDAQ symbol*] (TTSB)
MKPL .... Computer Marketplace, Inc. [*NASDAQ symbol*] (SAG)
MKPLW ...... Computer Marketplace Wrrt'A' [*NASDAQ symbol*] (TTSB)
MKPLZ ...... Computer Marketplace Wrrt'B' [*NASDAQ symbol*] (TTSB)
MKQ .... Bay Miwok [*Language symbol*] (ETLW)
MKQ .... Merauke [*Indonesia*] [*Airport symbol*] (OAG)
MKQCP ...... Member of the King's and Queen's College of Physicians [*Ireland*]
MKQT .... Mark's Trucking Company [*Common carrier symbol*]
MKR .... Glasgow, MT [*Location identifier*] [*FAA*] (FAAL)
mkr .... Maker (VRA)
MKR .... Maker
MKR .... Marker [*Beacon*]
MKR .... Meekatharra [*Australia*] [*Airport symbol*] (OAG)
MKR .... Mkuzi Game Reserve (SAUO)
MKRADC .... Middle Kentucky River Area Development Council (SAUO)
MK Rail ..... MK Rail Corp. [*Associated Press*] (SAG)
mKRB .... Modified Krebs-Ringer Bicarbonate [*Solution*]
MKRF .... Malcolm Knapp Research Forest [*University of British Columbia*] [*Canada*] (RCD)
MKRL .... MK Rail [*NASDAQ symbol*] (TTSB)
MKRL .... MK Rail Corp. [*NASDAQ symbol*] (SAG)
MKRS .... Mikros Systems Corp. [*OTCBB symbol*]
MKRX .... MK Rail [*Federal Railroad Administration identification code*]
MKS .... Makassar [*Celebes*] [*Seismograph station code, US Geological Survey*] (SEIS)
MKS .... Makes [*Telegraphy*] (PCTE)
MKS .... Marks & Spencer Canada, Inc. [*Toronto Stock Exchange symbol*]
MKS .... Marksman [*Marine Corps*]
MKS .... Mekane [*Ethiopia*] [*Airport symbol*] (OAG)
mks .... Meter-Kilogram-Second (IDOE)
MKS .... Meter-Kilogram-Second [*System of units*]
MKS .... Microwave Keying Switch
MKS .... Mikasa, Inc. [*NYSE symbol*] (SAG)
MKS .... Moncks Corner, SC [*Location identifier*] [*FAA*] (FAAL)
MKS .... Mortice Kern Systems, Inc. [*Waterloo, ON Canada*] [*Commercial firm*] (CDE)
MKS .... Pimichikamac Air Ltd. [*Canada*] [*FAA designator*] (FAAC)
MKSA .... Absolute MKS (SAUS)
mksa .... Meter, Kilogram, Second, Ampere (VLIE)
MKSA .... Meter-Kilogram-Second-Ampere [*System of units*]
MKSAP ...... Medical Knowledge Self-Assessment Program (SAUO)
MKSI .... MKS Instruments [*NASDAQ symbol*] (SG)
MKSS .... Microwave Keying Switching Station
MKSTNG .... Marksmanship Training (NVT)
MKSU .... Martin Kroll [*Intermodal shipping container symbol*] (TVRC)

MKT .... Advanced Marketing Services [*Company symbol*]
MKT .... Mankato, MN [*Location identifier*] [*FAA*] (FAAL)
Mkt .... Market (EBF)
MKT .... Market
mkt .... Market (WDMC)
MKT .... Market order (SAUO)
MKT .... Mark II [*NCIC car model code*]
MKT .... Missouri-Kansas-Texas Railroad Co. [*AAR code*]
MKT .... Mobile Kitchen Trailer [*Military*] (INF)
MKT .... Mu Kappa Tau (EA)
MKTA .... Makita Corp. [*NASDAQ symbol*] (SAG)
MKTAY .... Makita Corp. [*NASDAQ symbol*] (TTSB)
MKTC .... Monkey Kidney Tissue Culture (DB)
MktFct .... Market Facts, Inc. [*Associated Press*] (SAG)
Mktg .... Marketing (TBD)
mktg .... Marketing (WDMC)
MKTG .... Marketing
MKTI .... Mission Kit Technical Instruction
MKTI .... Morrison-Knudsen Technologies, Inc. [*Boise, ID*] [*Telecommunications*] (TSSD)
MKTK .... Manke Trucking [*Common carrier symbol*]
MKTL .... MarketLink, Inc. [*NASDAQ symbol*] (SAG)
MKTLH .... Tri-Lake Health Centre, Killarney, Manitoba [*Library symbol*] [*National Library of Canada*] (NLC)
MktLink .... MarketLink, Inc. [*Associated Press*] (SAG)
Mkt Mgr .... Marketing Manager (SAUO)
MKTNG .... Marketing
MKTP .... Market Planning (SAUO)
MKTP .... Mark Template [*Tool*]
MKTT .... Missouri-Kansas-Texas Railroad Co. (of Texas) [*AAR code*]
MKTT .... Modification Kit Tank Telephone (SAUS)
MKTU .... Marksmanship Training Unit (AABC)
MKTW .... MarketWatch.com [*NYSE symbol*] (SG)
MkTwain .... Mark Twain Bancshares, Inc. [*Associated Press*] (SAG)
MKTZ .... Missouri Pacific Railroad [*Intermodal trailer symbol*]
MKU .... Makokou [*Gabon*] [*Airport symbol*] (OAG)
MKU .... Mary Kathleen Uranium (SAUO)
MKU .... Mock-Up
MKUP .... Makeup
MKV .... Killed-Measles Vaccine [*Immunology*] (MAE)
MKV .... Marksville, LA [*Location identifier*] [*FAA*] (FAAL)
MKV .... McKinleyville, CA [*Amtrak Busline code*]
MKV .... Miniature Kill Vehicle [*Military*] (SDI)
MKV .... Multiple Kill Vehicle
MKVNV .... Muskmelon Vein Necrosis Virus [*Plant pathology*]
MKW .... Magnetokinetic Wave
MKW .... Manokwari [*Indonesia*] [*Airport symbol*] (OAG)
MKW .... Mikawa [*Japan*] [*Seismograph station code, US Geological Survey*] (SEIS)
MKW .... Military Knight of Windsor [*British*]
MKW .... Munitionskraftwagen [*Ammunition Truck*] [*German military - World War II*]
MKX .... Mukalla [*South Arabia*] [*Airport symbol*] (AD)
MKXR .... Market Express Transportation [*Common carrier symbol*]
MKY .... Mackay [*Australia*] [*Airport symbol*] (OAG)
MKY .... Makeyevka [*Former USSR*] [*Seismograph station code, US Geological Survey*] [*Closed*] (SEIS)
MKY .... Marco Island, FL [*Location identifier*] [*FAA*] (FAAL)
MKY .... Monky Aerotaxis SA [*Mexico*] [*ICAO designator*] (FAAC)
MKYFC .... Mike and Kathy Yager Fan Club [*Later, MYFC*] (EA)
MKZ .... Los Angeles, CA [*Location identifier*] [*FAA*] (FAAL)
MKZ .... Malacca [*Malaysia*] [*Airport symbol*] (OAG)
ML .... Aviation Services [*ICAO designator*] (AD)
ML .... Holder of a Major Licence (SAUO)
ML .... Land Mobile Station [*ITU designation*] (NATG)
ML .... Liberty Movement (Peru) [*Political party*] (PSAP)
ML .... Licentiate in Medicine
ML .... Licentiate in Midwifery
ML .... Machine Language [*Computer science*]
ML .... Macro Library (VLIE)
ML .... Macula Lutea (MELL)
ML .... Madras Lancers [*British military*] (DMA)
ML .... Magic Lantern Society of the United States and Canada (EA)
ML .... Magnetic Latching [*Electronics*] (OA)
ML .... Magnetogasdynamics Laboratory [*MIT*] (MCD)
ML .... Magnitude Local (COE)
ML .... Mail
ML .... Mail Label
ML .... Mail List (SAUS)
ML .... Mainland (MUGU)
ML .... Main Line [*Business term*]
ML .... Main Lobe
ML .... Maintained Load (WDAA)
ML .... Maintenance Laboratory (MUGU)
ML .... Maintenance Level (VLIE)
M/L .... Maintenance Loop (MCD)
ML .... Major League [*Baseball*]
ML .... Major Lobe (MSA)
ML .... Malachi [*Old Testament book*]
Ml .... Malaysia (SAUO)
ML .... Mali [*ANSI two-letter standard code*] (CNC)
ml .... Mali [*MARC country of publication code*] [*Library of Congress*] (LCCP)
ML .... Malignant Lymphoma [*Oncology*]
M:L .... maltase-to-Lactase [*Ratio*] [*Biochemistry*] (DAVI)
ML .... Management Level
ML .... Management List
ML .... Mandibular Line [*Jaw anatomy*]
ML .... Manipulation Language (NITA)
ML .... Manipulator Language [*Computer science*]
ML .... Mansfelder Land [*German license plate city code*]
ML .... Mantle Length
ML .... Mantle Lip
ML .... Manual Loader (AAG)
ML .... Manual Local (IAA)
ML .... Manually-Calculated Late-Fee [*Electric utility company*]
ML .... Manufacturing License (NRCH)
ML .... Maple Leaf Gardens Ltd. [*Toronto Stock Exchange symbol*]
ML .... March for Life (EA)
ML .... Marie-Leri [*Syndrome*] [*Medicine*] (DB)
ML .... Marine Limit (QUAC)
ML .... Mark-Up Language [*Computer science*]
Ml .... Marl [*Quality of the bottom*] [*Nautical charts*]
M-L .... Martin-Lewis [*Medium*] [*Microbiology*]
M/L .... Mass to Luminosity [*Ratio*] [*Astronomy*]
ML .... Master of Laws
ML .... Master of Letters
ML .... Master of Librarianship (GAGS)
ML .... Master of Literature
ml .... Material List (MIST)
ML .... Material List (MSA)
ML .... Materials Laboratory (SAUO)
ML .... Mater Lectionis (BJA)
ML .... Maule Aircraft Corp. [*ICAO aircraft manufacturer identifier*] (ICAO)
ML .... Mauna Loa (EFIS)
ML .... Mauna Loa Macadamia Partners (EFIS)
ML .... Maurice Lacroix
ML .... Maximum Likelihood [*Statistics*]
ML .... Maximum to Left (SAUS)
ML .... Mean Level
ML .... Medial Lemniscus [*Neuroanatomy*]
ML .... Medical Laboratory (SAUO)
ML .... Medical Letter (EA)
ML .... Medical Logistics (SAUO)
ML .... Medieval Latin [*Language, etc.*]
ML .... Medium Lorry [*British*]
ML .... Megaliter
ML .... Member Library [*OCLC or RLIN*]
ML .... Member's Liability [*Health insurance*] (GHCT)
ML .... Memory Layout [*Computer science*] (ELAL)
ML .... Memory Location [*Computer science*]
ML .... Memory Loss (MELL)
ML .... Merrill Lynch & Co., Inc. (EFIS)
ML .... Mesa Laboratory (SAUO)
ML .... Mesiolingual [*Dentistry*]
ML .... Metabolic Loss [*Physiology*]
M-L .... Metallic-Longitudinal (IEEE)
ML .... Meteorological Devices [*JETDS nomenclature*] [*Military*] (CET)
ML .... Meteorology Laboratory (GNE)
ML .... Methods of Limits (IEEE)
ML .... Metromail Corp. [*NYSE symbol*] (SAG)
ML .... Mexican League [*Baseball*]
ML .... Microprogramming Language
ML .... Microwave Laboratory [*Stanford University*] (MCD)
ML .... Middeck Left (MCD)
ML .... Middle Compass Locator (PIPO)
ML .... Middle Latin [*Language, etc.*]
ML .... Middle Left (WDAA)
ML .... Middle Lobe [*Of lung*]
ML .... Midlife (DAVI)
ML .... Midline
ML .... Migne Series [*Latina*] [*A publication*] (BJA)
ML .... Milan Stock Exchange (SG)
ml .... Mile (IDOE)
ML .... Milieu
ML .... Military Law
ML .... Military Leave (GFGA)
ML .... Military Liaison
ML .... Military Payroll Money List
ML .... Milk Letdown (MELL)
ML .... Mill
ml .... Millilambert (DIPS)
mL .... Millilambert
ml .... Milliliter (AEBE)
ML .... Milliliter (GOBB)
mL .... Milliliter
ML .... Mine Layer (WDAA)
ML .... Mineral Lease (ADA)
ML .... Minerva Library [*A publication*]
ML .... Minilab
ML .... Minimum Level (EEVL)
ML .... Mining and Logging [*Tires*]
ML .... Ministry of Labour (SAUO)
ML .... Missile Launcher
ML .... Missile Layout
ML .... Missile Lethality [*Military*]
M/L .... Missile-Lift [*Aerospace*] (AAG)
ML .... Missile Liner

ML .... Mission Life [*Aerospace*]
ML .... Mission Load (AABC)
ML .... Mixed Lengths
ML .... Mobile Launcher [*NASA*] (KSC)
ML .... Mobile Low-Power [*Reactor*] (NRCH)
ML .... Mode-Locked [*Laser technology*]
ML .... Moderate Load service [*Automotive engineering*]
ML .... Moderately Long [*Botany*]
ML .... Modern Languages (AIE)
ML .... Modern Lithographer [*A publication*] (DGA)
ML .... Modified License [*FCC*] (NTCM)
ML .... Molder [*Navy rating*]
ML .... Mold Line [*Technical drawings*]
ML .... Molecular Layer [*of the hippocampus*] [*Neurology*]
ML .... Monarchist League [*Defunct*] (EA)
ML .... Moneda Legal [*Legal Tender*] [*Spanish*] [*Business term*]
ML .... Money List
M/L .... Monocyte-Lymphocyte [*Ratio*] [*Clinical chemistry*]
ML .... Monolayer [*Physical chemistry*]
ML .... Monolithic
ML .... More Later (SAUS)
ML .... Morocco Lined [*Covers*] [*Bookbinding*] (ROG)
ML .... Motherwell [*Postcode*] (ODBW)
ML .... Motor Launch
ML .... Mountain Leader [*British military*] (DMA)
ML .... Mouse Laminin
ML .... Mouse Lysozyme [*Biochemistry*]
ML .... Mucolipidosis [*Medicine*]
ML .... Mucrones Length [*Of Crustacea*]
ML .... Multilayer [*Pharmacy*]
ML .... Multiple-Line [*Insurance*]
ML .... Multiple Location [*Insurance*]
ML .... Multiple-Locus [*Light flashes*]
ML .... Munitions List
ML .... Music Library Records [*Record label*]
ML .... Muslim League [*Bangladesh*] [*Political party*] (FEA)
ML .... Mutual Inductance [*Symbol*] (DEN)
ML .... Muzzle-Loading
ML .... Myelogenous Leukemia [*Oncology*]
ML .... Myeloid Leukemia [*Medicine*] (DB)
ML .... Myrialiter [*Unit of measurement*] (ROG)
ML .... Small Minesweeper [*Navy symbol*]
ML1 .... Molder, First Class [*Navy rating*]
ML2 .... Molder, Second Class [*Navy rating*]
ML3 .... Molder, Third Class [*Navy rating*]
MLa .... Acute Monocytic Leukemia [*Medicine*] (PALA)
MLA .... Auxiliary Motor Launches (NATG)
MLA .... Forty-Mile Air [*ICAO designator*] (FAAC)
MLA .... Macedonian Literary Association [*Australia*]
MLA .... Magic Lantern Adaption (SAUS)
MLA .... Magnetic Lens Assembly
MLA .... Mail List Agent (SAUS)
MLA .... Maine Library Association (SAUO)
MLA .... Maine Lobstermen's Association (EA)
mla .... Malagasy [*MARC language code*] [*Library of Congress*] (LCCP)
MLA .... Malaspina [*Alaska*] [*Seismograph station code, US Geological Survey*] (SEIS)
MLA .... Malta [*Airport symbol*] (OAG)
MLA .... Mandatory Liquid Assets [*Finance*]
MLA .... Maneuver Limited Altitude (GAVI)
MLA .... Maneuver Load Alleviation [*Aviation*]
MLA .... Manitoba Library Association (SAUO)
MLA .... Manpack Loop Antenna
MLA .... Manufacturing License Agreement
MLA .... Marine Librarians Association (EA)
MLA .... Maritime Law Association of the US (EA)
MLA .... Marker-Labelled Antigen (DB)
MLA .... Marlat Resources Ltd. [*Vancouver Stock Exchange symbol*]
MLA .... Martial Law Administrator (Pakistan) [*Political party*] (PSAP)
MLA .... Martin Landau Aficionados [*An association*]
MLA .... Maryland Library Association (SAUO)
MLA .... Massachusetts Library Association (SAUO)
MLA .... Master License Agreement [*Novell*] (GART)
MLA .... Master Locksmiths Association [*British*] (BI)
MLA .... Master of Landscape Architecture
MLA .... Master of Liberal Arts (GAGS)
MLA .... Matching Logic and Adder
MLA .... MDM [*Manipulator Deployment Mechanism*] Launch Aft [*NASA*]
MLA .... Mean Line of Advance [*Military*] (NVT)
MLA .... Mechanical Lubricator Association
MLA .... Medial Left Abdomen [*Injection site*]
MLA .... Medical Laboratory Automation, Inc. [*Medicine*] (EDAA)
MLA .... Medical Library Association (EA)
MLA .... Member of Legislative Assembly (SAUO)
MLA .... Member of the Legislative Assembly
MLA .... Member of the Library Association [*British*] (ROG)
MLA .... Mento-Laeval Anterior [*A fetal position*] [*Obstetrics*]
MLA .... Mercantile Library Association (SAUO)
MLA .... Merritt Island Tracking Station [*Florida*]
MLA .... Mesiolabial [*Dentistry*]
MLA .... Metal Lath Association [*Later, ML/SFA*] (EA)
MLA .... Metrolina Library Association [*Library network*]
MLA .... Michigan Library Association (SAUO)
MLA .... Microprocessor Language Assembler [*Computer science*]
MLA .... Microwave Linear Accelerator
MLA .... Microwave Link Analyzer (ACAE)
MLA .... Midland Co. [*AMEX symbol*] (SPSG)
MLA .... Midwest Lacrosse Association (PSS)
MLA .... Military Liaison Assistant (DOMA)
MLA .... Minimal Lactose-Arabinose [*Culture medium*]
MLA .... Mining Lease Application
MLA .... Minnesota Lakes Association (EARSL)
MLA .... Minnesota Library Association
MLA .... Mississippi Library Association (SAUO)
MLA .... Missouri Library Association (SAUO)
MLA .... Mistress of Liberal Arts
MLA .... Mixed Lead Alkalis (EDCT)
MLA .... Mixed Lead Alkyl [*Organic chemistry*]
MLA .... MLA International Biography of Books & Articles on the Modern Languages and Lit.
MLA .... Modern Language Association (NADA)
MLA .... Modern Language Association of America (EA)
MLA .... Modern Languages Association (SAUO)
MLA .... Modern Learning Aids [*Medicine*] (EDAA)
MLA .... Monochrome Lens Assembly (MCD)
MLA .... Monocytic Leukemia, Acute (MAE)
MLA .... Monophosphoryl Lipid A [*Medicine*] (MELL)
MLA .... Montana Library Association (SAUO)
MLA .... Motor Launch, Auxiliary [*NATO*]
MLA .... Multi-Housing Laundry Association (EA)
MLA .... Multi Letter Acronym (ACAE)
MLA .... Multilinear Array [*In earth scanning*]
MLA .... MultiLink Advanced [*Local area network*] [*The Software Link, Inc.*]
MLA .... Multiple Letter Acronym
MLA .... Multiple Line Adaptor (NITA)
MLA .... Multiplex Line Adapter
MLA .... Multispectral Linear Array (SSD)
MLA .... Music Library Association (EA)
MLA .... Muzzle Loaders' Association of Great Britain
MLA .... Valetta [*Malta*] [*Airport symbol*] (AD)
MLAA .... Medical Library Assistance Act [*1965*]
MLAA .... Modern Language Association of America (SAUO)
MLA/ATG .... Modern Language Association/ Association of Teachers of German (SAUO)
MLAB .... Medical Library Association Bulletin [*Medicine*] (EDAA)
MLAB .... Mesa Laboratories [*NASDAQ symbol*] (TTSB)
MLAB .... Mesa Laboratories, Inc. [*NASDAQ symbol*] (SAG)
MLAB .... Modeling Laboratory [*Programming language*] [*1970*] (CSR)
MLAB .... Monitor Technologies, Inc. [*NASDAQ symbol*] (COMM)
MLAB .... Multilingual Aphasia Battery [*Medicine*] (DMAA)
M Lab R .... Monthly Labor Review [*A publication*] (BRI)
MLAF .... Missile Loading Alignment Fixture
MLAGB ...... Muzzle Loaders Association of Great Britain (BI)
MLAI .... Mesiolabioincisal [*Dentistry*]
M La L ...... Master of Latin Letters
MLaI .... Mesiolabioincisal [*Medicine*] (MEDA)
MLAMH ..... Mona Lisas and Mad Hatters [*Defunct*] (EA)
MLAN .... Midland Co. [*NASDAQ symbol*] (SG)
MLANA .... Melkite Laymen's Association of North America (EA)
MLanc .... Lancaster Town Library, Lancaster, MA [*Library symbol*] [*Library of Congress*] (LCLS)
MLandArch ... Master of Landscape Architecture [*Canada*] (DD)
MLandEc .... Master in Land Economy
ML&T .... Master of Law and Taxation (GAGS)
MLANO ...... Milano, TX [*American Association of Railroads railroad junction routing code*]
MLAP .... Mean Left Atrial Pressure [*Cardiology*]
MLaP .... Mesiolabiopulpal [*Dentistry*]
MLAP .... Migrant Legal Action Program (EA)
MLAP .... Muslim League Assembly Party [*Pakistan*] [*Political party*] (FEA)
MLAPU ...... Marxist-Leninist Armed Propaganda Unit [*Turkey*]
MLAR .... Mill Arbor
MLAR .... Multilayer Antireflection [*Coating*]
ML Arch ..... Master of Landscape Architecture
MLARE ...... Micro Laboratories, Inc. [*NASDAQ symbol*] (QUAN)
MLAS .... Master of Laboratory Animal Science (PGP)
MLASES ..... Molasses [*Freight*]
MLA-SMHL ... Medical Library Association, Section on Mental Health Libraries (EA)
MLA/SWIR ... Multispectral Linear Array Short Wave Infrared (ACAE)
MLAT .... Mean Latitude
MLAT .... Modern Language Aptitude Test [*Military*] (AFM)
MLATD ...... Mediterranean League Against Thromboembolic Diseases (SAUO)
MLAUD ...... Master of Landscape Architecture in Urban Development (GAGS)
MLAUK ...... Member of the Library Association, United Kingdom (ROG)
M'Laur ...... M'Laurin's Scotch Judiciary Cases [*1774*] [*A publication*] (DLA)
MLAUS ...... Maritime Law Association of the United States (SAUO)
MLaw .... Lawrence Free Public Library, Lawrence, MA [*Library symbol*] [*Library of Congress*] (LCLS)
MLb .... Macrolymphoblast (DB)
MLB .... Magnetic Linear Birefringence (MCD)
MLB .... Major League Baseball
MLB .... Malabar [*Java*] [*Seismograph station code, US Geological Survey*] [*Closed*] (SEIS)
MLB .... Manufacturing Load Boards (MCD)
MLB .... Marginal Lands Board (SAUO)
MLB .... Maritime Labor Board [*Terminated, 1942*]

MLB .... Maritime Law Book Key Number Data Base [*Maritime Law Book Co. Ltd.*] [*Canada*] [*Information service or system*] (CRD)
MLB .... Mbule [*Language symbol*] (ETLW)
MLB .... Medallion Books Ltd. [*Vancouver Stock Exchange symbol*]
MLB .... Melbourne [*Florida*] [*Airport symbol*] (OAG)
MLB .... Merrill Lynch & Co. [*NYSE symbol*] (SAG)
MLB .... Metallic Link Belt (AABC)
MLB .... Metropolitan Toronto Library Board, Systems Unit [*UTLAS symbol*]
MLB .... Micro-Laryngobronchoscopy [*Medicine*] (DMAA)
MLB .... Middle Linebacker [*Football*]
MLB .... Millbrae, CA [*Amtrak Busline code*]
MLB .... Mini Landbridge [*MARAD*] (TAG)
MLB .... Mobile Logistics Support Base (NVT)
MLB .... Monaural Loudness Balance [*Audiology*]
MLB .... Motor Lifeboat
MLB .... Multilayer Board
MLB .... Multiple Listing Board (BARN)
MLB .... Multiple Listing Bureau (SAUO)
MLBA .... Minnesota Licensed Beverage Association (EARSL)
MLBC .... ML Bancorp. [*NASDAQ symbol*] [*Formerly, MLF Bancorp.*] (SG)
MLBC .... ML Bancorp, Inc. [*NASDAQ symbol*] (SAG)
MLBL .... MLBLT [*NCIC trailer make code*]
MLBM .... Modern Large Ballistic Missile
MLBMA ...... Michigan Lumber and Building Materials Association (EARSL)
ML Bncp .... ML Bancorp, Inc. [*Associated Press*] (SAG)
MLBP .... Major League Baseball Properties (NDBD)
MLBP .... Mechanical Low Back Pain (MELL)
MLBPA ...... Mailing List Brokers Professional Association [*Defunct*] (EA)
MLBPA ...... Major League Baseball Players Association (EA)
MLBPAA ..... Major League Baseball Players Alumni Association (NDBD)
MLBR .... Medium Low-BIT [*Binary Digit*] Rate [*Computer science*]
MLBS .... Multi Layer Boards (ACAE)
MLBU .... Mobile Laundry and Bath Unit [*Military*] [*British*]
MLBW .... Moderately Low Birth Weight (MELL)
MLC .... Machine Cornering Limit [*Equipment design*]
MLC .... Machine Level Control [*Computer science*]
MLC .... Madras Light Cavalry [*British military*] (DMA)
MLC .... Magnetic Ledger Card (CMD)
MLC .... Main Lobe Cancellation (ACAE)
MLC .... Main Lobe Clutter
MLC .... Major Landing Craft
MLC .... Major Legislation of Congress [*Data processing system*] [*Congressional Research Service*]
MLC .... Major Line Component [*of NOAA*] (NOAA)
MLC .... Management Level Chart [*Military*] (AFIT)
MLC .... Management Level Code [*Military*] (AFIT)
ML-C .... Management List - Consolidated
MLC .... Maneuver Load Control [*Aviation*]
MLC .... Manhattan National Corp. [*NYSE symbol*] (SPSG)
MLC .... Mansfield Law Club (SAUO)
MLC .... Manufacturers Life Capital Corp., Inc. [*Toronto Stock Exchange symbol*]
MLC .... Manzanita Lake [*California*] [*Seismograph station code, US Geological Survey*] (SEIS)
MLC .... Maori Land Court (SAUO)
MLC .... Maple Leaf Club (EA)
MLC .... Master Labor Contract (AABC)
MLC .... McAlester, OK [*Location identifier*] [*FAA*] (FAAL)
MLC .... Meat and Livestock Commission [*British*] (ARC)
MLC .... Median Lethal Concentration [*Toxiclogy*] (LDT)
MLC .... Medical Liability Commission [*Defunct*] (EA)
MLC .... Medical Library Center (DIT)
MLC .... Medium Level Center (ELAL)
MLC .... Member of the Legislative Council
MLC .... Memphis Library Council [*Library network*]
MLC .... Mergenthaler Linotype Company, Brooklyn (SAUO)
MLC .... Merrill Lynch & Co., Inc. [*NYSE symbol*] (SAG)
MLC .... Merrill Lyn GI'MITTS'98 [*NYSE symbol*] (TTSB)
MLC .... Mesh Level Control
MLC .... Metropolitan Toronto Library Board, Cataloguing Department [*UTLAS symbol*]
MLC .... Micellar Liquid Chromatography
MLC .... Michigan Library Consortium [*Lansing, MI*] [*Library network*]
MLC .... Michigan Limestone & Chemical [*Federal Railroad Administration identification code*]
MLC .... Microelectric Logic Circuit
MLC .... Microprogram Location Counter
MLC .... Midlife Conversion
MLC .... Miles College, Birmingham, AL [*OCLC symbol*] (OCLC)
MLC .... Military Landing Craft
MLC .... Military Liaison Committee [*Energy Research and Development Administration*]
MLC .... Military Load Class (RDA)
MLC .... Minimum Lethal Concentration
MLC .... Mining Life-Cycle Center [*University of Nevada, Reno*] (RCD)
MLC .... Missile Launch Car (SAUS)
MLC .... Missile Logistics Center [*Army*]
MLC .... Mississippi Library Commission (IID)
MLC .... Mississippi-Louisiana Conference (PSS)
MLC .... Mississippi State Library Commission [*Information service or system*] (IID)
MLC .... Mixed Leukocyte Culture [*Hematology*]
MLC .... Mixed Ligand Chelate (DB)
MLC .... Mixed Lymphocyte Culture [*Hematology*]
MLC .... Mobile Launch Center
MLC .... Mobile Launcher Computer [*NASA*] (NASA)
MLC .... Modern Language Caucus [*of New University Conference*]
MLC .... Modern Language Centre [*Ontario Institute for Studies in Education*] [*Canada*] (IRC)
MLC .... Modular Load Carrier (SAUS)
MLC .... Molder, Chief [*Navy rating*]
MLC .... MOL [*Manned Orbiting Laboratory*] Launch Complex (MCD)
MLC .... Monarchist League of Canada (EAIO)
MLC .... Money Laundering Control Act (GOBB)
MLC .... Monthly License Charge [*For software*] (GART)
MLC .... Morphine-Like Compound [*Immunology*]
MLC .... Motor Launch, Cabin
MLC .... Motor Load Control
MLC .... Mountain Leadership Certificate [*British*] (DI)
MLC .... Multilamellar Cytosome [*Biochemistry*] (MAE)
MLC .... Multilayer Capacitor [*Electronics*]
MLC .... Multilayer Ceramic [*Materials technology*]
MLC .... Multilayer Ceramic Capacitor (NITA)
MLC .... Multilayer Circuit
MLC .... Multilens Camera
MLC .... Multi-Level Cell (AAEL)
MLC .... Multiline Communications Controller (SAUO)
MLC .... Multiline Control (BUR)
MLC .... Multilink Control Field [*Telecommunications*] (ACRL)
MLC .... Multilumen Catheter [*Medicine*] (MELL)
MLC .... Multiplanar Link Chain
MLC .... Municipal Leasing Corp.
MLC .... Myelomonocytic Leukemia, Chronic (MAE)
MLC .... Myosin Light Chain [*Muscle biology*]
MLC .... Myth, Legend, Custom in the Old Testament [*A publication*] (BJA)
MLCA .... Modified Life Cycle Assessment [*Recycling*]
MLCAD ...... Maintenance and Logistics Factors in Computer Aided Design (SAUO)
MLCAEC ..... Military Liaison Committee to the Atomic Energy Commission (IEEE)
MLCB .... Missile Launch Control Blockhouse
MLCB .... Moored Limited Capability Buoy [*Marine science*] (MSC)
MLCB .... Multilayer Circuit Board
ML/CB-CC... Malignant Lymphoma/Centroblastic-Centrocytic [*Oncology*]
ML/CC .... Malignant Lymphoma/Centrocytic [*Oncology*]
MLCC .... Mined Land Conservation Conference [*Later, BCR*]
MLCC .... Modular Life Cycle Cost (ACAE)
MLCC .... Multilayer Ceramic Capacitor [*Electronics*]
MLCD .... Multi-Line Call Detail (ROAS)
MLCG .... Missile Launcher Control Group
MLCH .... Major Logistical Control Headquarters (MCD)
MLCH .... MLC Holdings, Inc. [*NASDAQ symbol*] (SAG)
MLC Hld .... MLC Holdings, Inc. [*Associated Press*] (SAG)
MLCI .... Multi-Link Channel Interface [*Computer science*] (VLIE)
MLCIM ...... Marquette League for Catholic Indian Missions [*Defunct*] (EA)
MLCK .... Myosin Light Chain Kinase [*An enzyme*]
MLCM .... Molder, Master Chief [*Navy rating*]
MLCN .... Multilocular Cystic Nephroma (DMAA)
MLCNY ...... Medical Library Center of New York [*Information service or system*] (IID)
MLCO .... Member of the London College of Osteopathy [*British*] (DI)
MLCOM ..... Member of the London College of Osteopathic Medicine [*British*] (DBQ)
MLCox99n... Merrill Lynch & Co. [*Associated Press*] (SAG)
MLCP .... Machine Level Control Program (VLIE)
MLCP .... Mobile Land Command Post (AABC)
MLCP .... Multilayer Ceramic Package [*Electronics*]
MLCP .... Multiline Communications Processor
MLCP .... Myosin Light-Chain Phosphatase (DB)
MLCPX ...... Merrill Lynch: Capital Fund Cl.A [*Mutual fund ticker symbol*] (SG)
MLCR .... Medical Laboratories Army Chemical Center [*Maryland*]
MLCR .... Medical Laboratory Contract Reports [*Army*] (MCD)
MLCR .... Mixed Lymphocyte Culture Reaction [*Hematology*] (AAMN)
MLCRO ...... Ministry of Labour Claims and Records Office (SAUO)
MLCS .... Molder, Senior Chief [*Navy rating*]
MLCS .... Multilayer Ceramic Substrates [*Electronic circuit boards*]
MLCSP ...... Multi-Level Continuous Sampling Plan (VLIE)
MLCT .... Metal-to-Ligand Charge Transfer [*Physical chemistry*]
MLCU .... Magnetic Ledger Card Unit [*Computer science*] (MHDB)
MLCU .... Matson Leasing [*Intermodal shipping container symbol*] (TVRC)
MLCU .... Mill Cutter [*Tool*]
MLCur .... Merrill Lynch & Co. [*Associated Press*] (SAG)
MLD .... Air Moldova [*ICAO designator*] (FAAC)
MLD .... Legislative Reference Library - Minnesota Document Collection, St. Paul, MN [*OCLC symbol*] (OCLC)
MLD .... Machine Language Debugger [*National Computer Sharing Service*]
MLD .... Mailed [*Telegraphy*] (PCTE)
MLD .... Main Line of Defense
MLD .... MAJCOM Level Data (SAUO)
MLD .... Malad City, ID [*Location identifier*] [*FAA*] (FAAL)
MLD .... Malden [*Missouri*] [*Seismograph station code, US Geological Survey*] [*Closed*] (SEIS)
MLD .... Marginally Learning Disabled
MLD .... Masking Level Difference [*Hearing*]
MLD .... Master Layout Duplicate (MSA)
MLD .... Master of Landscape Design
MLD .... Maximum Lateral Damage (PDAA)
MLD .... Maximum Likelihood Detection (MCD)
MLD .... Mean Level Detector (ACAE)
MLD .... Mean Low-Water Datum [*Nuclear energy*] (NRCH)

MLD .... Medial Lethal Dose [*Genetics*] (DOG)
MLD .... Median Lethal Dose [*Also, LD_{50}*] [*Lethal for 50%*] [*Medicine*]
MLD .... Mesencephalicus Lateralis Dorsalis (DB)
MLD .... Metachromatic Leukodystrophy [*Medicine*]
MLD .... Middle Landing
MLD .... Midland [*AAR code*]
MLD .... Mild (WGA)
MLD .... Military Liaison Department (SAUO)
MLD .... Minimal Lesion Disease
MLD .... Minimum Lethal Dose
MLD .... Minimum Line of Detection [*Air Force*]
MLD .... Missile Launch Detector (MCD)
MLD .... Mixed Layer Depth (MCD)
MLD .... Mixed Liaison Detachment (SAUO)
MLD .... Moderate Learning Difficulties (AIE)
mld .... Mold (VRA)
MLD .... Molded (KSC)
MLD .... Molding [*Technical drawings*]
MLD .... Mouvement pour la Liberation de Djibouti [*Movement for the Liberation of Djibouti*] (PD)
MLD .... Ocean Mixed Layer Depth (SAUS)
MLDAS ...... Meteorological and Lighting Data Acquisition System [*NASA*] (KSC)
MLDB .... Regional Library, Lac Du Bonnet, Manitoba [*Library symbol*] [*National Library of Canada*] (NLC)
MLDC .... Miner's Legal Defense Committee [*Defunct*] (EA)
MLDD .... Moderately Lightly Doped Drains (NITA)
MLDD .... Mooring Leg Deployment Device (PDAA)
ML Des ..... Master of Landscape Design
MLDG .... Molding (KSC)
mldg .... Molding (MIST)
mldg .... Moulding (ODA)
MLDI .... Meter List Display Interval [*FAA*] (TAG)
ML Dig & R... Monthly Law Digest and Reporter [*Canada*] [*A publication*] (DLA)
ML Dirct .... ML Direct, Inc. [*Associated Press*] (SAG)
MLDL .... Mooring Line Data Line [*Environmental buoy cable*]
MLDLP ...... Mailing Label and Directory Lookup Package (PDAA)
MLDNG ...... Moulding
MLDR .... ML Direct, Inc. [*NASDAQ symbol*] (SAG)
MLDR .... Molder (ADA)
Mldr(A) ...... Molder (Aviation) [*U.S. Navy enlisted rating*] (AUER)
MLDS .... Motor Launch, Double Shelter
MLD/S ...... Multi-Legend Display Switch (MCD)
MLDT .... Mean Logistic Delay Time [*Military*] (CAAL)
MLDT .... Mean Logistic Down Time
MLDT .... Medical Letter on Drugs and Therapeutics [*Medicine*] (EDAA)
MLDU .... Marriage Law Defence Union [*British*]
MLDW .... Mobil Luboil Dewaxing [*Petroleum engineering*]
MLE .... Magazine Lee-Enfield [*British military*] (DMA)
MLE .... Male [*Maldives*] [*Airport symbol*] (OAG)
MLE .... Manned Lunar Exploration [*NASA*] (AAG)
MLE .... Mariner-Like Elements [*Genetics*]
MLE .... Martin Lawrence Limited Editions [*NYSE symbol*] (SAG)
MLE .... Maryland Law Encyclopedia [*A publication*] (DLA)
MLE .... Master of Applied Linguistics and Exegesis (PGP)
MLE .... Master of Land Economy
MLE .... Maximum Likelihood Estimate [*or Estimator*] [*Statistics*]
MLE .... Maximum Loss Expectancy [*Insurance*]
MLE .... Medium Local Exchange [*Telecommunications*] (TEL)
MLE .... Merrill Lynch Economics (NITA)
MLE .... Mesoscale Lightning Experiment (ACAE)
MLE .... Meta-Language Extension (VLIE)
MLE .... Microprocessor Language Editor [*Computer science*]
MLE .... Mid-Latitude Ecosystem (SAUO)
MLE .... Midline Episiotomy [*Obstetrics*] (DAVI)
MLE .... Mile
MLE .... Mileto [*Italy*] [*Seismograph station code, US Geological Survey*] [*Closed*] (SEIS)
MLE .... Millenium Language Extension (SAUS)
MLE .... Missile Launch Envelope
MLE .... Mobile Launcher Equipment [*NASA*] (SAA)
MLE .... Module Resources, Inc. [*Vancouver Stock Exchange symbol*]
MLE .... Molecular Layer Epitaxy [*Coating technology*]
MLE .... Muconate Lactonizing Enzyme
MLE .... Multi-Line Editor (SAUS)
MLE .... Myocardial Lactate Extraction [*Clinical chemistry*]
MLE .... Omaha, NE [*Location identifier*] [*FAA*] (FAAL)
MLEA .... Metal Lath Export Association (SAUO)
MLEA .... Multiple-Line Exclusive Agent [*Insurance*]
M'Lean's R... McLean's United States Circuit Court Reports [*A publication*] (DLA)
MLED .... Maximum Likelihood Estimator Deconvolution [*Statistics*]
MLEE .... Multi-Locus Enzyme Electrophoresis [*Biophysics*] [*Biochemistry*] (QSUL)
MLegS ...... Master of Legal Studies
MLEL .... Malignant Lymphoepithelial Lesion [*Medicine*] (DMAA)
MLEM .... Multi-Language Environment (VLIE)
MLenB ...... Berkshire Christian College, Lenox, MA [*Library symbol*] [*Library of Congress*] (LCLS)
ML Eng ..... Master of Landscape Engineering
MLeo .... Leominster Public Library, Leominster, MA [*Library symbol*] [*Library of Congress*] (LCLS)
MLeoHi ..... Leominster Historical Society, Inc., Leominster, MA [*Library symbol*] [*Library of Congress*] (LCLS)
MLEP .... Manned Lunar Exploration Program [*NASA*] (KSC)
MLEP .... Minority Legislative Education Program
MLEP .... Multipurpose Long Endurance Plane
MLEQ .... LC MacDonald [*Common carrier symbol*]
MLES .... Microsomal Liver Enzyme System [*Medicine*] (EDAA)
MLES .... Multiple-Line Encryption System (AABC)
MLEV .... Manned Lifting Entry Vehicle (MCD)
MLex .... Cary Memorial Library, Lexington, MA [*Library symbol*] [*Library of Congress*] (LCLS)
MLexHi ...... Lexington Historical Society, Lexington, MA [*Library symbol*] [*Library of Congress*] (LCLS)
MLexK .... Kennecott Copper Corp., Ledgemont Laboratory, Lexington, MA [*Library symbol*] [*Library of Congress*] (LCLS)
MLexM ...... Museum of Our National Heritage, Lexington, MA [*Library symbol*] [*Library of Congress*] (LCLS)
MLexSC ..... Scottish Rite of Freemasonry, Northern Jurisdiction USA, Supreme Council Library, Lexington, MA [*Library symbol*] [*Library of Congress*] (LCLS)
MLF .... Fast Motor Launches (NATG)
MLF .... Maintenance Level Function
MLF .... Male Liberation Foundation (EA)
MLF .... Malolactic Fermentation
MLF .... Maple Leaf Foods [*Toronto Stock Exchange symbol*] (SPSG)
MLF .... Maximum Load Factor
MLF .... MDM [*Manipulator Deployment Mechanism*] Launch Forward [*NASA*]
MLF .... Media Language and Format (CET)
MLF .... Medial Longitudinal Fasciculus [*Medicine*]
MLF .... Medical Liberation Front (EA)
M/LF .... Medium/Low Frequency (NATG)
MLF .... Micro Louver Film [*Adhesives*]
MLF .... Milford [*Ohio*] [*Seismograph station code, US Geological Survey*] (SEIS)
MLF .... Milford, UT [*Location identifier*] [*FAA*] (FAAL)
MLF .... Mobile Land Force (NATG)
MLF .... Mobile Launcher Facility [*NASA*] (KSC)
MLF .... Modelling Language and Formalism (VLIE)
MLF .... MOL [*Manned Orbiting Laboratory*] Launch Facilities (MCD)
MLF .... Morphine-Like Factor [*Medicine*] (DB)
MLF .... Motor Launch, Fast [*NATO*]
MLF .... Multilaminar Film (SAUS)
MLF .... Multi-Lateral Fleet (SAUO)
MLF .... Multilateral Force [*NATO*]
MLFA .... Fireman Apprentice, Molder, Striker [*Navy rating*]
MLFA .... Machine-Learned Fragment Analysis (AGLO)
MLFA .... Maine Lobster Fishermen's Association (EA)
MLFA .... Merrill Lynch Financial Advantage
MLFAT .... MOL [*Manned Orbiting Laboratory*] Launch Facilities Acceptance Team (MCD)
MLFB .... MLF Bancorp [*NASDAQ symbol*] (TTSB)
MLFB .... MLF Bancorp, Inc. [*NASDAQ symbol*] (SAG)
MLF Bc ...... MLF Bancorp, Inc. [*Associated Press*] (SAG)
MLFC .... Michele Lee Fan Club (EA)
MLFC .... Michigan Library Film Circuit [*Library network*]
MLFC .... Mike Lunsford Fan Club (EA)
MLFC .... Moses Lake Flight Center [*Washington*] (SAA)
MLFI .... Missouri League of Financial Institutions (EARSL)
MLFN .... Fireman, Molder, Striker [*Navy rating*]
MLFN .... Malfunction (VLIE)
MLFS .... Magic Lantern Film Society [*An association*]
MLFS .... Master Library File System (VLIE)
MLFS .... Modular Lightweight FLIR System (SAUS)
MLFU .... Saudi Arabia Ministry of Defence Military Factories [*Intermodal shipping container symbol*] (TVRC)
MLFX .... Mill Fixture [*Tool*]
MLG .... Mailing
MLG .... Main Landing Gear [*Aerospace*] (NAKS)
MLG .... Malang [*Indonesia*] [*Airport symbol*] (OAG)
mlg .... malignant (SAUS)
MLG .... Mesiolingual Groove [*Medicine*] (EDAA)
MLG .... Metalgesellschaft Canada Investment [*Toronto Stock Exchange symbol*]
MLG .... Middle Low German [*Language, etc.*]
MLG .... Milling [*Freight*]
MLG .... Mission Liaison Group [*Military*]
MLG .... Mitochondria Lipid Glucogen [*Cytology*] (AAMN)
MLG .... Moulage
MLG .... Multiple Line Group [*Radiation*]
MLG .... Musicland Stores [*NYSE symbol*] (SAG)
MLGCV ...... Movement for the Liberation of Portuguese Guinea and the Cape Verde Islands
MLGN .... Minimal Lesion Glomerulonephritis [*Medicine*] (DMAA)
MLGP .... Movimento de Libertacao da Guine Portuguesa [*Movement for the Liberation of Portuguese Guinea*]
MLGS .... Microwave Landing Guidance System [*FAA*]
MLGSCA .... Medical Library Group of Southern California and Arizona (SAUO)
MLGT98 ..... Merrill Lynch & Co., Inc. [*Associated Press*] (SAG)
MLGW .... Maximum Landing Gross Weight
ML-H .... Malignant Lymphoma, Histiocytic [*Medicine*] (DB)
MLH .... Mauna Loa [*Hawaii*] [*Seismograph station code, US Geological Survey*] (SEIS)
MLH .... Medium Lift Helicopter (MCD)
MLH .... Merlin Resources Ltd. [*Vancouver Stock Exchange symbol*]
MLH .... Merrill Lynch & Co., Inc. [*AMEX symbol*] (NASQ)
MLH .... Minimum List Heading [*Standard Industrial Classification*] (PDAA)
MLH .... Mulhouse/Basel [*France*] [*Airport symbol*] (OAG)
MLHA .... Master Ladies Hairdressers Association (SAUO)

MLHC........ Main Line [*Common carrier symbol*]
MLHCP...... Mean Lower Hemispherical Candlepower (IAA)
MLHGR...... Maximum Linear Heat Generation Ratio (NRCH)
MLHIX....... Merrill Lynch: Corp. Bond: Hi Inc. CL.A [*Mutual fund ticker symbol*] (SG)
MLHK........ Merrill Lynch & Co. [*Associated Press*] (SAG)
MLHR........ Herman Miller [*NASDAQ symbol*]
MLHR........ Master of Labor and Human Resources (PGP)
MLHR........ Miller (Herman) [*NASDAQ symbol*] (TTSB)
MLHR........ Miller [*Herman*], Inc. [*NASDAQ symbol*] (NQ)
MLHRC...... Midwest Latino Health, Research, Training, and Policy Center [*University of Illinois at Chicago*] (RCD)
MLHW....... Mean Lower High Water [*Tides and currents*]
MLHYX...... Merrill Lynch: Muni Bond National Cl.A [*Mutual fund ticker symbol*] (SG)
MLHZO...... Move Low-to-High Zone (VLIE)
MLI........... Machine Language Instruction
MLI........... Magnetic Level Indicator
MLI........... Maislin Industries Ltd. [*Toronto Stock Exchange symbol*]
MLI........... Malad Range [*Idaho*] [*Seismograph station code, US Geological Survey*] (SEIS)
MLI........... Mali [*ANSI three-letter standard code*] (CNC)
MLI........... Maltese Light Infantry [*British military*] (DMA)
MLI........... Marine Light Infantry [*Navy*] [*British*] (ROG)
MLI........... Marker Light Indicator
MLI........... Master Listing Index
MLI........... Master of Literary Interpretation
MLI........... Mean Linear Intercept
MLI........... Measurement Layer Interface (SAUS)
MLI........... Mesiolinguoincisal [*Dentistry*]
MLI........... Message Level Interface (NITA)
MLI........... Michigan Literacy (EARSL)
MLI........... Mid-Life Improvement (SAUS)
MLI........... Minimum Line of Interception [*Air Force*]
MLI........... Mintel Leisure Intelligence [*Database*] [*United Kingdom*] (GDD)
MLI........... Mixed Lymphocyte Interaction [*Immunology*]
MLI........... Moline, IL [*Location identifier*] [*FAA*] (FAAL)
MLI........... Mollie Gibson Mines [*Vancouver Stock Exchange symbol*]
MLI........... Mueller Industries [*NYSE symbol*] (SPSG)
MLI........... Muller Industries [*NYSE symbol*] (SAG)
MLI........... Multilayer Insulation
MLI........... Multi-Leaving Interface [*Computer science*] (VLIE)
MLI........... Multiple Link Interface [*Computer science*]
MLI........... Munitions List Item (MCD)
MLIA......... Multiplex Loop Interface Adapter
MLib......... Master of Librarianship
M Libr....... Master of Librarianship (PGP)
M Lib Sc.... Master of Library Science (BARN)
MLibSci..... Master of Library Science (NADA)
MLIC......... Manhattan Life Insurance [*NASDAQ symbol*] (TTSB)
MLIC......... Manhattan Life Insurance Co. [*NASDAQ symbol*] (SAG)
MLIC......... Mello [*Common carrier symbol*]
MLID......... Multiple Link Interface Drive [*Telecommunications*] (PCM)
MLID......... Multiple Link Interface Driver [*Telecommunications*] (ACRL)
MLIFC....... Mark Lindsay International Fan Club [*Defunct*] (EA)
MLIFC....... Michelle Lynn International Fan Club (EA)
MLIGL01.... Merrill Lynch & Co. [*Associated Press*] (SAG)
MLIH......... Irish Malone Trucking [*Common carrier symbol*]
MLIM......... Matrix Log-In Memory
MLIN......... Micro Linear [*NASDAQ symbol*] (TTSB)
MLIN......... Micro Linear Corp. [*NASDAQ symbol*] (SAG)
MLing....... Master of Languages [*British*] (DBQ)
MLIP......... Message Level Interface Port (NITA)
MLIR......... Master of Labor and Industrial Relations (GAGS)
MLIRB....... Multi-Line Insurance Rating Bureau [*Later, ISO*]
MLIS......... Master of Library and Information Science
MLIS......... Measurement Laboratory Information Service [*Battelle Memorial Institute*]
MLIS......... Metal-Liquid-Insulator Semiconductor [*Electronics*] (PDAA)
MLIS......... Micropolis Corp. [*NASDAQ symbol*] (NQ)
MLIS......... Molecular LASER Isotope Separation
MLIS......... Multilingual Information Society (SAUO)
MLIS......... Multiple Level Indexing Scheme [*Computer science*]
MLISP....... Meta LISP [*List Processor*] [*Programming language*] [*Computer science*] (CSR)
M Lit......... Master of Letters
M Lit......... Master of Literature
MLitl......... Inforonics Inc., Littleton, MA [*Library symbol*] [*Library of Congress*] (LCLS)
MLitM....... Master of Liturgical Music (GAGS)
MLitSt...... Master of Literary Studies (ADA)
M Litt....... Master of Letters
MLitt........ Master of Literature
MLIU......... Associated International Finance [*Intermodal shipping container symbol*] (TVRC)
ML IV........ Mucolipidosis IV [*A genetic disease*]
MLJ........... Medico-Legal Journal [*Medicine*] (EDAA)
MLJ........... Memphis Law Journal [*A publication*] (DLA)
MLJ........... Milledgeville, GA [*Location identifier*] [*FAA*] (FAAL)
MLJ........... Modern Language Journal [*A publication*] (BRI)
MLK.......... 3 Series of X-ray Lines [*Medicine*] (EDAA)
MLK.......... Malta, MT [*Location identifier*] [*FAA*] (FAAL)
MLK.......... Martin Luther King, Jr.
MLK.......... Matlack Systems [*NYSE symbol*] (TTSB)
MLK.......... Matlack Systems, Inc. [*NYSE symbol*] (CTT)
MLK.......... Michael Lenhart Kaiserslautern [*Automotive parts*]
MLK.......... Milford [*Kansas*] [*Seismograph station code, US Geological Survey*] (SEIS)
MLK.......... Moses Lake, WA [*Amtrak Busline code*]
MLKCNSC... Martin Luther King, Jr., Center for Nonviolent Social Change (EA)
MLKCSC..... Martin Luther King, Jr., Center for Social Change [*Later, MLKCNSC*] (EA)
MLKD........ MLK Delivery Service [*Common carrier symbol*]
MLKIII........ Martin Luther King III
MLKJRFC.... Martin Luther King, Jr. Family Clinic (MHID)
MLL........... Manchester Lines Ltd. (SAUO)
MLL........... Mandella Resources Ltd. [*Vancouver Stock Exchange symbol*]
MLL........... Manned Lunar Landing [*NASA*]
MLL........... Marshall [*Alaska*] [*Airport symbol*] (OAG)
MLL........... Marshall, AK [*Location identifier*] [*FAA*] (FAAL)
MLL........... Master Lines Layout (MSA)
MLL........... Master of Latin Literature
MLL........... Master of Law Librarianship (ILCA)
MLL........... Maynard Listener Library [*Defunct*] (EA)
MLL........... MDM [*Manipulator Deployment Mechanism*] Launch Left [*NASA*]
MLL........... Mean Lesion Length [*Pathology*]
MLL........... Middle Lobe of Lung (MELL)
mL/L......... Milliliters per Liter (EEVL)
ML/L......... Milliliters per Liter (EG)
MLL........... Minimum Level of Living (SAUO)
MLL........... Mistress of Liberal Learning
MLL........... Mixed Lineage Leukemia [*Medicine*] (DMAA)
MLL........... Modify Lot Location (AAEL)
MLL........... Music Lovers League (NADA)
MLL........... University of Minnesota, Law Library, Minneapolis, MN [*OCLC symbol*] (OCLC)
MLLA......... Mineral Lands Leasing Act of 1920 (COE)
MLLAA....... Modern Language Association of America (NADA)
ML/LB....... Malignant Lymphoma/Lymphoblastic [*Oncology*]
MLLDI....... Multi-Level Laser Designator Illuminator (ACAE)
MLLE......... Mademoiselle [*Miss*] [*French*] (EY)
Mlle.......... Mademoiselle [*Miss*] [*French*] (WA)
MLLE......... Medium Large Local Exchange [*Telecommunications*] (TEL)
Mlles......... Mesdemoiselles [*Misses*] [*French*]
MLLFT....... Modified Lensless Fourier Transform (PDAA)
ML Libr..... Master of Law Librarianship
MLLM........ Microminiature Low Level Multicoders (ACAE)
MLLO......... Mello's Trucking [*Common carrier symbol*]
MLLP......... Manned Lunar Landing Program [*NASA*]
ML/LPC..... Malignant Lymphoma/Lymphoplasmacytoid [*Oncology*]
MLLR......... Miller [*NCIC trailer make code*]
MLLR......... Roy Miller Freight Lines [*Common carrier symbol*]
MLLU......... Hamburg Sudamerkanische Dampfschiffahrts [*Intermodal shipping container symbol*] (TVRC)
MLLV......... Medium-Lift Launch Vehicle (SAUS)
MLLW........ Mean Lower Low Water [*Tides and currents*]
MLLW........ Medium Level Liquid Waste [*Nuclear energy*] (NUCP)
MLLW........ Mixed Low-Level Waste (GAAI)
MLLWK...... Millwork
MLLWL...... Mean Lower Low Water Line [*Tides and currents*] (PDAA)
MLLWS...... Mean Lower Low-Water Springs [*Tides and currents*]
MLLX......... Montell USA [*Private rail car owner code*]
MLM.......... Magazine Lee-Metford [*British military*] (DMA)
MLM.......... Mailing-List Manager [*Type of database*]
MLM.......... Martin Marietta Materials [*NYSE symbol*] (SAG)
MLM.......... Massive Liver Metastasis [*Oncology*]
MLM.......... Master of Landscape Management
MLM.......... Master of Library Media (PGP)
MLM.......... Maximum Likelihood Method [*Statistics*]
MLM.......... Medical Logic Module (IDYL)
MLM.......... Membrane Light Modulator (PDAA)
MLM.......... Mesa Lucera [*New Mexico*] [*Seismograph station code, US Geological Survey*] (SEIS)
MLM.......... Metall Mining Corp. [*Toronto Stock Exchange symbol*]
MLM.......... Microbial Load Monitor (MCD)
MLM.......... Middle Limiting Membrane (SAUS)
MLM.......... Military Liaison Mission [*Germany*]
MLM.......... Minesweeper, River [*Navy symbol*] (VNW)
MLM.......... Mixed Level Matrix
MLM.......... Modern Labelling Methods Ltd. (SAUO)
MLM.......... Moody Literature Ministries (EA)
MLM.......... Morelia [*Mexico*] [*Airport symbol*] (OAG)
MLM.......... Mound Laboratory, Miamisburg [*AEC*] (MCD)
MLM.......... Mulam [*Language symbol*] (ETLW)
MLM.......... Multilayer Metalization (IEEE)
MLM.......... Multilevel Marketing
MLM.......... Multilevel Metal (AAEL)
MLM.......... Multi-Longitudinal Mode (ACRL)
MLM.......... Multipurpose Lightweight Missile
MLM.......... Multnomah Literature Ministries [*Publisher*] [*Portland, OR*]
MLM.......... Muslim League of Malaya, Kuala Lumpur (SAUO)
MLMA........ Metal Ladder Manufacturers Association (EA)
MLMA........ Metal Lath Manufacturers Association [*Later, ML/SFA*]
MLMA........ Miners' Lamp Manufacturers' Association [*British*] (BI)
MLMA........ Moss Litter Manufacturers Association (SAUO)
MLMA........ Multilevel Multiaccess
MLMBX..... Merrill Lynch: Muni Bond: Insured Cl.A [*Mutual fund ticker symbol*] (SG)
MLMGIC98... Merrill Lynch & Co. [*Associated Press*] (SAG)

MLMI........ Microleague Multimedia [*NASDAQ symbol*] (TTSB)
MLMI........ Microleague Multimedia, Inc. [*NASDAQ symbol*] (SAG)
MLMIA...... Multi-Level Marketing International Association [*Irvine, CA*] (EA)
MLMIC...... Medical Liability Mutual Insurance Company [*Medicine*] [*New York*] (EDAA)
MLMIC...... Minnesota Land Management Information Center (SAUO)
ml/min/m^2... Milliliters per Minute per Square Meter (CPH)
MLMIS...... Minnesota Land Management Information System (SAUO)
MLMIW..... Microleague Multimedia Wrrt [*NASDAQ symbol*] (TTSB)
MLML....... Moss Landing Marine Laboratories [*San Jose State University*] [*Research center*] (RCD)
MLMR....... Multi-Level Message Release (SAUS)
MLMS....... Member of the London Mathematical Society
MLMS....... Multipurpose Lightweight Missile System
MLMTT...... Marxism-Leninism-Mao Tse-Tung Thought [*Ideologies guiding the New People's Army, a guerrilla movement in the Philippines*]
MLN......... Management List - Navy (NVT)
MLN......... Mancelona, MI [*Amtrak Busline code*]
MLN......... Manifest Latent Nystagmus [*Medicine*] (EDAA)
MLN......... Mediastinal Lymph Node [*Medicine*] (MELL)
MLN......... Melilla [*Spain*] [*Airport symbol*] (OAG)
MLN......... Membranous Lupus Nephropathy [*Medicine*] (MELL)
MLN......... Mesenteric Lymph Node [*Medicine*] (STED)
MLN......... Message Ledger Number (SAUO)
MLN......... Metropolitan Library Network [*Library network*]
MLN......... Michigan League for Nursing (EARSL)
MLN......... Mid-Lateral Nerve
MLN......... Milan Resources & Development [*Vancouver Stock Exchange symbol*]
MLN......... Minuteman Library Network [*Information service or system*] (IT)
MLN......... MLN (Modern Language Notes) [*A publication*] (BRI)
MLN......... Mobile Large Node (SAUS)
MLN......... Mouvement de Liberation Nationale [*National Liberation Movement*] [*Burkina Faso*] [*Banned, 1974*] [*Political party*]
MLN......... Movimiento de Liberacion Nacional [*National Liberation Movement*] [*Guatemala*] [*Political party*] (PPW)
MLN......... Movimiento de Liberacion Nacional [*National Liberation Movement*] [*Uruguay*] [*Political party*]
MLN......... Multiple Length Number
MLN......... Mulungwishi [*Zaire*] [*Seismograph station code, US Geological Survey*] (SEIS)
MLN......... Museum Loan Network
MLNAC...... Mesa Laboratory Network Access Completion (SAUO)
MLNC........ Missouri Library Network Corp. [*Information service or system*] (IID)
Mlnd........ Maximum Landing Weight [*Aviation*] (DA)
MLNG....... Melange
MLNHA...... Missouri League of Nursing Home Administrators (EARSL)
MLNik 97... Merrill Lynch & Co. [*Associated Press*] (SAG)
MLNIS...... Modified Atlantic Naval Intelligence Summary (MCD)
MLNM....... Millennium Pharmaceuticals [*NASDAQ symbol*] (TTSB)
MLNM....... Millennium Pharmaceuticals, Inc. [*NASDAQ symbol*] (SAG)
MLNP....... Malawi Lengwe National Park (SAUO)
MLNR....... Milliner (WGA)
MLNR....... Ministry of Land and Natural Resources (SAUO)
mLNRc...... Mouse Lymph Node Homing Receptor
MLNS....... Minimal Lesion Nephrotic Syndrome [*Medicine*] (EDAA)
MLNS....... Ministry of Labour and National Service [*British*] [*World War II*]
MLNS....... Mucocutaneous Lymph Node Syndrome [*Medicine*] (STED)
MLNSC...... Manual Lujan Jr. Neutron Scattering Center (SAUO)
MLNWR..... Medicine Lake National Wildlife Refuge (SAUO)
MLNY....... JJ Maloney [*Common carrier symbol*]
MLNYX..... Merrill Lynch: N.Y. Muni Bond Cl.B [*Mutual fund ticker symbol*] (SG)
MLO......... Main Lube Oil [*System*] (NRCH)
MLO......... Manipulative Learning Operation [*in laboratory work*]
MLO......... Manned Lunar Orbiter [*NASA*]
MLO......... Marxisten-Leninisten Oesterreichs [*Marxists-Leninists of Austria*] [*Political party*] (PPE)
MLO......... Master Layout Original (MSA)
MLO......... Mauna Loa Observatory [*Hawaii*] [*National Weather Service*]
MLO......... Mechanized Letter Office (DCTA)
MLO......... Media Liaison Officer
MLO......... Medical Laboratory Observer [*Medicine*] [*Journal*] (EDAA)
MLO......... Medio-Lateral Oblique [*Medicine*] (AMHC)
MLO......... Mesiolinguo-Occlusal [*Dentistry*]
MLO......... Midland Light Orchestra (SAUO)
MLO......... Military Landing Officer
MLO......... Milos [*Greece*] [*Airport symbol*] (OAG)
MLO......... Mine-Like Objects (SAUS)
MLO......... Missile Launch Officer (AAG)
MLO......... Missile Lift-Off (AAG)
MLO......... M. L. Cass Petroleum [*Vancouver Stock Exchange symbol*]
MLO......... Mortgage Loan Officer [*Banking*] (TBD)
MLO......... Movement Liaison Officer (NATG)
MLO......... Mycoplasma-Like Organisms [*Microbiology*]
MLOC........ Million Lines of Code (ACAE)
MLOG....... Microlog Corp. [*NASDAQ symbol*] (NQ)
MLOI........ Master List of Outstanding Items [*Military*] (DNAB)
MLon........ Richard Salter Storrs Library, Longmeadow, MA [*Library symbol*] [*Library of Congress*] (LCLS)
MLonHi..... Longmeadow Historical Society, Longmeadow, MA [*Library symbol*] [*Library of Congress*] (LCLS)
MLOP........ Median Lethal Overpressure [*Emergency Management*] (EMA)
MLOPEX.... Mauna Loa Observatory Photochemical Experiment (SAUO)
MLOPEX.... Mauna Loa Observatory Photochemistry Experiment (SAUO)
MLOPEX II... Mauna Loa Observatory Photochemical Experiment II (SAUO)
MLOR....... Maintenance/Logistics Observer Report
MLow........ Lowell City Library, Lowell, MA [*Library symbol*] [*Library of Congress*] (LCLS)
MLowT...... Lowell Technological Institute, Lowell, MA [*Library symbol*] [*Library of Congress*] [*Obsolete*] (LCLS)
MLowTC.... Lowell State College, Lowell, MA [*Library symbol*] [*Library of Congress*] [*Obsolete*] (LCLS)
MLowU...... University of Lowell, Lowell, MA [*Library symbol*] [*Library of Congress*] (LCLS)
MLowU-N... University of Lowell - North Campus, Alumni/Lydon Memorial Library, Lowell, MA [*Library symbol*] [*Library of Congress*] (LCLS)
MLP......... Machine Language Program [*Computer science*]
MLP......... Major Late Promoter [*Genetics*]
MLP......... Major Late Promotor [*Biochemistry*]
MLP......... Malabang [*Philippines*] [*Airport symbol*] (OAG)
MLP......... Malaspina [*Alaska*] [*Seismograph station code, US Geological Survey*] (SEIS)
MLP......... Malfunction-Linked People
MLP......... Malta Labor Party [*Political party*] (PPW)
MLP......... Manual Lever Position (HAWK)
MLP......... Master Limited Partnership
MLP......... Master Logistics Plan (AABC)
MLP......... Maui Land & Pineapple [*AMEX symbol*] (SG)
MLP......... Maui Land and Pineapple Co. [*AMEX symbol*]
MLP......... Mauritius Labor Party [*Political party*] (PPW)
MLP......... Maximum Likelihood Program
MLP......... Mentoleva Posterior [*A fetal position*] [*Obstetrics*]
MLP......... Mesa Limited Partnership (EFIS)
MLP......... Mesiolinguopulpal [*Dentistry*]
MLP......... Message Link Protocol (SAUO)
MLP......... Metal Lath and Plaster [*Technical drawings*]
MLP......... Michigan Law and Practice [*A publication*] (DLA)
MLP......... Microsomal Lipoprotein [*Immunochemistry*]
MLP......... Millipore Corp., Bedford, MA [*OCLC symbol*] (OCLC)
MLP......... Minimum Latency Programming
MLP......... Mirror Landing Procedures (MCD)
MLP......... Mobile Launcher Platform [*NASA*] (NASA)
MLP......... Modified Longest Path
MLP......... Monitored Line Program (SPST)
MLP......... Mortgage Loan Partnership [*Investment term*]
MLP......... Movimiento de Liberacion del Pueblo [*People's Liberation Movement*] [*El Salvador*] [*Political party*] (PD)
MLP......... Movimiento de Liberacion Proletaria [*Proletarian Liberation Movement*] [*Mexico*] [*Political party*]
MLP......... Mullan Pass, ID [*Location identifier*] [*FAA*] (FAAL)
MLP......... Multi-Layered Packaging (PDAA)
MLP......... Multilayer Link Protocol (SAUS)
MLP......... Multi-Layer Perceptron (AAEL)
MLP......... Multilevel Precedence
MLP......... Multilevel Procedure (MCD)
MLP......... Multilevel Programmer
MLP......... Multilink Point-to-Point protocol (SAUS)
MLP......... Multilink Procedure [*Computer science*] (TNIG)
MLP......... Multilink Protocol [*Telecommunications*] (ACRL)
MLP......... Multiple Layer Perceptron (IDAI)
MLP......... Multiple Line Printing (CMD)
MLP......... Multi-Step Products [*Toronto Stock Exchange symbol*]
MLPA........ Modified Link Pack Area (MCD)
MLPC........ Management-Labor Policy Committee
MLPC........ Mouvement de Liberation du Peuple Centrafricain [*Movement for the Liberation of the Central African People*] (PD)
MLPC........ Multilayer Printed Circuit
MLPCB...... Machine Language Printed Circuit Boards [*Computer science*] (IEEE)
MLPD........ Maximum Likelihood Predictive Density [*Statistics*]
ML-PDL..... Malignant Lymphoma, Poorly Differentiated Lymphocytic [*Medicine*] (STED)
MLPED...... Mobile Launcher Pedestal [*NASA*] (NASA)
MLPF........ Miniature Low Pass Filter
MLPFS...... Merrill Lynch, Pierce, Fenner & Smith [*of Merrill Lynch & Co., Inc.*] [*Stockbrokers*] [*Wall Street slang name: "Thundering Herd"*]
MLPI......... Maximum Likelihood Parameter Identification (ACAE)
MLPN........ Maintenance Planning (SAUS)
MLPNA...... Michigan Licensed Practical Nurses Association (EARSL)
MLPNPP.... Mobile Low-Power Nuclear Power Plant
MLPP........ Multilevel Precedence and Preemption [*Telecommunications*] (TEL)
ML-PPP..... Multilink Point-to-Point Protocol [*Telecommunications*] (ACRL)
MLPRF...... Modular Low Power Radio Frequency (SAUS)
MLPS........ Manchester Literary and Philosophical Society (SAUO)
MLPS........ Multilingual Publishing Software
MLPS........ Multilink Processing System (SAUS)
MLPS........ Myxoid Liposarcoma [*Genetics*]
MLP USA... Marxist-Leninist Party of the United States of America (SAUO)
MLP USA... Marxist-Leninist Party of the USA (EA)
MLPWB..... Multilayer Printed-Wiring Board (IEEE)
MLQ......... Malabar Law Quarterly [*A publication*] (DLA)
MLQ......... Malalaua [*Papua New Guinea*] [*Airport symbol*] (OAG)
MLQ......... Modern Language Quarterly [*A publication*] (ANEX)
MLR......... Leaf Rapids Public Library, Manitoba [*Library symbol*] [*National Library of Canada*] (NLC)
MLR......... Machine Location Report (VLIE)
MLR......... Magnetic Latching Relay (MCD)
MLR......... Mailer
MLR......... Main Line of Resistance
M/LR........ Maintenance Loop Recorder (MCD)
MLR......... Malayan Law Reports [*1950-54*] [*A publication*] (DLA)

MLR .... Manitoba Law Reports [*Canada*] [*A publication*] (DLA)
MLR .... Marginal Lending Rate [*Finance*]
MLR .... Marine Life Resources [*Program*]
MLR .... Maryland Law Record [*A publication*] (DLA)
MLR .... Master-Locating RADAR (AABC)
MLR .... Matched Logistic Regression [*Statistics*]
MLR .... Matheran Light Railway [*Indian Railway*] (TIR)
MLR .... Mauritius Law Reporter [*A publication*] (DLA)
MLR .... Maximum Logical Records [*Computer science*] (VLIE)
MLR .... MDM [*Manipulator Deployment Mechanism*] Launch Right [*NASA*]
MLR .... Mean Length Response (DMAA)
MLR .... Mean Lethal Radius
MLR .... Mechanized Line Records [*Later, LMOS*] [*Bell System*]
MLR .... Medium Lift Replacement programme (SAUS)
MLR .... Medium-Lift Requirement [*Helicopter/VSTOL*] [*Marine Corps*] (DOMA)
MLR .... Memory Lockout Register [*Computer science*]
MLR .... Message Log Report (AAEL)
MLR .... Meston Lake Resources, Inc. [*Toronto Stock Exchange symbol*] [*Vancouver Stock Exchange symbol*]
MLR .... Middle Latency Response [*Medicine*]
MLR .... Miller Industries [*NYSE symbol*] (TTSB)
MLR .... Millersburg, OH [*Location identifier*] [*FAA*] (FAAL)
MLR .... Minimum Latency Routine
MLR .... Minimum Lending Rate
MLR .... Minnesota Legislative Reference Library, St. Paul, MN [*OCLC symbol*] (OCLC)
MLR .... Missile Launch Response [*Navy*] (CAAL)
MLR .... Mixed Leukocyte Reaction [*Analytical biochemistry*]
MLR .... Mixed Lymphocyte [*or Leukocyte*] Reaction [*or Response*] [*Immunology*]
MLR .... Modern Language Review [*A publication*] (BRI)
MLR .... Modern Law Review [*A publication*] (SAFN)
MLR .... Modular Laser Rangefinder (ACAE)
MLR .... Monodisperse Latex Reactor
MLR .... Monotone Likelihood Ratio [*Statistics*]
MLR .... Monthly Letter Report
MLR .... Montreal Law Reports [*A publication*] (DLA)
MLR .... Mortar Locating RADAR (MCD)
MLR .... Multichannel Linear Recording (GART)
MLR .... Multi-Disperse Latex Reactor
MLR .... Multilayer Resist [*Lithography*]
MLR .... Multilevel Resist [*For microlithography*]
MLR .... Multiple Linear Regression [*Mathematics*]
MLR .... Multiple Linear Regression Analysis (SAUO)
MLR .... Multiple Line Reading [*Computer science*] (ELAL)
MLR .... Multiple Location Risk [*Insurance*]
MLR .... Multiple Logistic Regression [*Medicine*] (EDAA)
MLR .... Multiply and Round
MLR .... Muntele Rosu [*Romania*] [*Seismograph station code, US Geological Survey*] (SEIS)
MLR .... Muzzle-Loading Rifle
MLRA........ Major Land Resource Area [*USDA topographic characterization*]
MLRA........ Marriage Law Reform Association [*British*]
MLRA........ Multivariate Linear Regression Analysis [*Advertising marketing*]
MLRB........ Master Logistics Review Board (AAG)
MLRB........ Mutual Loss Research Bureau [*Later, Property Loss Research Bureau*] (EA)
MLRC........ Mallon Resources [*NASDAQ symbol*] (TTSB)
MLRC........ Mallon Resources Corp. [*NASDAQ symbol*] (CTT)
MLRC........ Master Logistics Review Committee (AAG)
MLRC........ Mickey Leland National Urban Air Toxics Research Center (COE)
MLRC........ Minor League Research Committee (EA)
MLRC........ Multilevel Rail Car
MLRCA...... Mini Lop Rabbit Club of America (EA)
MLR CS..... Montreal Law Reports, Superior Court [*Canada*] [*A publication*] (DLA)
MLRF........ Mini Laser Range Finder (ACAE)
MLRG .... Marine Life Research Group [*Scripps Institution of Oceanography*]
MLRG .... Muzzle-Loading Rifled Gun
MLRHR...... Master of Labor Relations and Human Resources (PGP)
MLRI .... Multi-Lamp Route Indicator [*Indian Railway*] (TIR)
MLRO .... Melroe [*NCIC truck make code*]
MLRP........ Marine Corps Long-Range Plans
MLRP........ Marine Life Research Program
MLRP........ Minuteman Long Range Plan [*Telecommunications*] (LAIN)
MLRQB...... Montreal Law Reports, Queen's Bench [*A publication*] (DLA)
MLRS........ Manual Launch - RADAR Search
MLRS........ McDonald Laser Ranging System [*For observations*]
MLRS........ Monodisperse Latex Reactor System
MLRS........ Multiple Launch Rocket System [*DoD*] (MCD)
MLRSC...... Montreal Law Reports, Superior Court [*Canada*] [*A publication*] (DLA)
MLRS ER ... Multiple Launch Rocket System Extended Range Rocket [*Military*]
MLRS FDS... Mobile Launch Rocket System Fire Direction System (SAUO)
MLRS-PGM... Multiple Launch Rocket System Precision Guided Munitions (RDA)
MLRS-TGW... Multiple Launch Rocket System Terminally Guided Warhead
MLRTP ...... Multileaving Remote Terminal Processor [*Computer science*] (MHDI)
MLRus98 ... Merrill Lynch & Co. [*Associated Press*] (SAG)
MLRV........ Manned Lunar Roving Vehicle [*NASA*] (PDAA)
MLRV........ Myrobalan Latent Ringspot Virus [*Plant pathology*]
MLS .... Machine Literature Searching [*Computer science*] (DIT)
MLS .... Mac Library System [*Computer Advanced Software Products - CASPR*] [*Cupertino, CA*] [*Information service or system*] (IID)
MLS .... Macrolide/Lincosamide/Streptogramine (DB)
MLS .... Magnetically-Linked Solenoid (MCD)
MLS .... Mails [*Telegraphy*] (PCTE)
MLS .... Main-Line Station (ODA)
MLS .... Maintenance Loading Sheet (MCD)
MLS .... Major League Soccer
MLS .... Mall Airways, Inc. [*ICAO designator*] (FAAC)
MLS .... Managed Learning System
MLS .... Manistique & Lake Superior R. R. [*AAR code*]
MLS .... Manned Lunar Surface [*NASA*]
MLS .... Marketing Library Services
MLS .... Master Laboratory Station
MLS .... Master of Legal Studies (GAGS)
MLS .... Master of Liberal Studies (GAGS)
MLS .... Master of Librarianship
MLS .... Master of Library Science
MLS .... Master of Library Services (PGP)
MLS .... Master of Library Studies
MLS .... Master of Life Science (GAGS)
MLS .... Maximized LOD [*Logarithm of the Odds*] Score [*Statistics*]
MLS .... Maximum Life-Span
MLS .... Maxwell Library Systems [*Information service or system*] (IID)
MLS .... Mean Lifespan (AAMN)
MLS .... Mechanical Limit Stop
MLS .... Mechanical Limit Switch
MLS .... Median Life Span [*Oncology*] (DAVI)
MLS .... Median Longitudinal Section
MLS .... Medico-Legal Society (SAUO)
MLS .... Medium Life Span
MLS .... Medium Long Shot [*A photograph or motion picture sequence taken from a relatively great distance*]
MLS .... Member of the Linnean Society (SAUO)
MLS .... Metal Slitting
MLS .... Metropolitan Libraries Section [*Public Library Association*]
MLS .... Microprocessor Line Set (VLIE)
MLS .... Microwave Landing System [*Aviation*]
MLS .... Microwave Limb Sounder
MLS .... Microwave Line Stretcher
MLS .... Middle Lobe Syndrome [*Medicine*] (STED)
MLS .... Midget Lights Series [*Motorsports*]
MLS .... Miles City [*Montana*] [*Airport symbol*] (OAG)
MLS .... Miles City, MT [*Location identifier*] [*FAA*] (FAAL)
MLS .... Military Labor Service
MLS .... Military Labour Service (SAUO)
MLS .... Military Sealift Command
ML/S........ Milliliters per Second
MLS .... Mills (MCD)
MLS .... Mills Corp. [*NYSE symbol*] (SAG)
MLS .... Miniature Linguistic Systems
MLS .... Minimum Launch Speed [*British military*] (DMA)
MLS .... Minimum Legal Size [*Pisciculture*]
MLS .... Minor Lymphocyte Stimulating [*Genetics*]
MLS .... Missile-Launching System (NG)
MLS .... Missile Lift System (AAG)
MLS .... Missile Location System (IEEE)
MLS .... Mississippi County Library System, Blytheville, AR [*Inactive*] [*OCLC symbol*] (OCLC)
MLS .... Mixed Language System (PDAA)
MLS .... Mobile Library Service [*British*]
MLS .... Mobile Logistic Support (CINC)
MLS .... Modern Language Studies [*A publication*] (ANEX)
MLS .... MOL [*Manned Orbiting Laboratory*] Launch Site (MCD)
MLS .... Moulis [*France*] [*Seismograph station code, US Geological Survey*] (SEIS)
MLS .... Movement for the Liberation of the Sanwi (SAUO)
MLS .... Movimento per le Liberta Statuarie [*Movement for Statutory Liberty*] [*Sanmarinese*] (PPE)
MLS .... Movimiento de Liberacion Sebta [*Ceuta Liberation Movement*] [*Spain*] (PD)
MLS .... Multifrequency LASER Sounding (MCD)
MLS .... Multilanguage System [*Computer science*] (IEEE)
MLS .... Multilan Switch [*Communications term*] (DCT)
MLS .... Multilayered Structure [*Botany*]
MLS .... Multi-Layer Steel [*Engine gaskets*] [*Automotive engineering*]
MLS .... Multilevel Security (MCD)
MLS .... Multiline Selection [*Asahi Glass of Japan*]
MLS .... Multiparameter Light Scattering [*Physics*]
MLS .... Multiple Level Security (CCCA)
MLS .... Multiple Link Support (SAUO)
MLS .... Multiple Listing Service [*Real estate*]
MLS .... Music Learning System [*Trademark*]
MLS .... Myelomonocytic Leukemia, Subacute (MAE)
MLS .... Subacute Myelomonocytic Leukemia [*Medicine*] (PALA)
MLSA........ Ministry of Labour Staff Association [*British*]
MLSA........ Modified Launch Services Agreement (ACAE)
MLSAA ...... Middle Level Student Activities Association
ML SAI99... Merrill Lynch & Co. [*Associated Press*] (SAG)
MLSB........ Major League Scouting Bureau [*Baseball*]
MLSB........ Member of the London School Board
MLSB........ Migrating Long Spike Burst (DMAA)
ML Sc .... Master of Library Science
MLSC........ Measured Logistics Support Cost (SAUS)
MLSC........ Member of the London Society of Compositors
MLSC........ Micronesian Legal Services Corp. (EA)
MLSC........ Multiple Loop Sidelobe Canceller (CCCA)
MLS/CP ..... Microwave Landing System / Curved Path [*Aviation*]
MLS DDN... Multi-Level Secure Defense Data Network (SAUO)

MLSE........ Malformed Low-Set Ears (MELL)
MLSE........ Maximum Likelihood Sequence Estimation (VLIE)
MLSE........ Mechanical Launch Support Equipment [*NASA*] (KSC)
MLSF........ Mobile Laboratory Storage Facility (SAUO)
MLSF........ Mobile Logistic Support Forces (MCD)
ML/SFA...... Metal Lath/Steel Framing Association Division of National Association of Architectural Metal Manufacturers (EA)
MLSG........ Mobile Logistics Support Group (NVT)
MLSI........ Mulitple Line Scan Imaging (DMAA)
MLSI........ Multilevel Large-Scale Integration
MLSIDS..... Moving LASER Speed and Image Detection System [*Traffic operations*]
MLSIS....... Major License Silviculture Information System (SAUO)
MLSIT....... Master of Library Science and International Technology (PGP)
MLSJ........ Macquarie Law Students Journal [*A publication*]
MLSK........ Master Lock, Skeleton Key
MLSO........ Mauna Loa Solar Observatory (SAUO)
MLSO........ Medical Laboratory Scientific Officer (SAUO)
MLSO........ Mode-Locked Surface-Acoustic Wave Oscillator [*Telecommunications*] (TEL)
ML Society... Magic Latern Society of the United States and Canada (EA)
MLSOP...... Movement for the Liberation of Soa Tome and Principe [*Political party*]
MLSP........ Master of Law and Social Policy (GAGS)
MLSP........ Multiple-Link Satellite Program
MLSP97..... Merrill Lynch & Co., Inc. [*Associated Press*] (SAG)
MLSP98..... Merrill Lynch & Co., Inc. [*Associated Press*] (SAG)
M-L-S-R..... Missing, Lost, Stolen, or Recovered [*Government property*] (DNAB)
MLSR........ Molder, Ship Repair [*Navy rating*]
MLSRC...... Molder, Ship Repair, Cupola Tender [*Navy rating*]
MLSRF...... Molder, Ship Repair, Foundryman [*Navy rating*]
MLSRM..... Molder, Ship Repair, Molder [*Navy rating*]
MLSS........ Mechanized Letter Sorting System [*Hong Kong Post Office*]
MLSS........ Military and Federal Specifications and Standards [*Information Handling Services*] [*Information service or system*] (CRD)
MLSS........ Mixed-Liquor Suspended Solid [*Water pollution*]
MLST........ Medico-Legal Society of Tasmania [*Australia*]
MLST........ Merrill Language Screening Test [*Educational test*]
MLST........ Milstead [*AAR code*]
MLSTP...... Movimento de Libertacao de Sao Tome e Principe [*Movement for the Liberation of Sao Tome and Principe*] [*Portugal*] (PPW)
MLSU........ Miller Intermodal Logistics Services [*Intermodal shipping container symbol*] (TVRC)
MLSU........ Moscow Lomonosov State University (SAUO)
MLSU........ Multiple Listening Station Unit (VLIE)
MLSW/SSNCC... Ministry of Labour and Social Welfare/Social Services National Coordination Council (SAUO)
MLSW/SSNCC... Molsw/Social Services National Coordination Council (SAUO)
MLSW/SWC........ Ministry of Labour and Social Welfare/Social Welfare Council (SAUO)
MLSW/SWC........ Molsw/Social Welfare Council (SAUS)
MLSX........ Solutia [*Private rail car owner code*]
ML SYP98... Merrill Lynch & Co. [*Associated Press*] (SAG)
MLS-ZKD... Mehr Lagen Stahl-Zylinderkopfdichtung [*Automotive engines*]
MLT.......... Machine Learning Toolbox (EURO)
MLT.......... Madras Law Times [*India*] [*A publication*] (DLA)
MLT.......... Magnetic Levitation Transportation
MLT.......... Magnetic Local Time
MLT.......... Malta [*ANSI three-letter standard code*] (CNC)
mlt.......... Maltese [*MARC language code*] [*Library of Congress*] (LCCP)
MLT.......... Manned Lunar Test [*NASA*] (KSC)
MLT.......... Manufacturing Lead Time
MLT.......... Mass Loaded Transducer
MLT.......... Master Library Tape [*Computer science*]
MLT.......... Master Lower Tester (SAUS)
MLT.......... Master of Law and Taxation
MLT.......... Maximum Lethal Time [*of radiation exposure*] (DEN)
MLT.......... Mean Latency Time (DB)
MLT.......... Mean Length per Turn
MLT.......... Mean Level Tracker (ACAE)
MLT.......... Mean Life Time (NATG)
MLT.......... Mean Logistical Time (IEEE)
MLT.......... Mean Low Tide [*Tides and currents*]
MLT.......... Mechanized Line Testing [*Telecommunications*] (TEL)
MLT.......... Mechanized Loop Testing (MCD)
MLT.......... Median Lethal Time (DB)
MLT.......... Medical Laboratory Technician [*or Technologist*]
MLT.......... Medium Level Tripod [*British military*] (DMA)
MLT.......... Melatonin
MLT.......... Mentolaeva Transverse [*A fetal position*] [*Obstetrics*] (AAMN)
MLT.......... Microlayer Transistor
MLT.......... Millinocket, ME [*Location identifier*] [*FAA*] (FAAL)
MLT.......... Misallat [*Egypt*] [*Geomagnetic observatory code*]
MLT.......... Missile Loader Transport (SAUS)
MLT.......... Mitel Corp. [*NYSE symbol*] [*Toronto Stock Exchange symbol*] (SPSG)
MLT.......... Mixing-Length Theory [*Physics of convection*] [*Chemical engineering*]
MLT.......... Mobile Laboratory Table
MLT.......... Mobile Launch Tower
MLT.......... Modulated Lapped Transform [*Telecommunications*]
MLT.......... Monolithic Logic Technology (ELAL)
MLT.......... Muexins-Length Theory
MLT.......... Multi-Level Transition (SAUO)
MLT.......... Multiple Logical Terminal (SAUS)
MLT.......... Munitions Lift Trailer (SAUS)
MLTA........ Maine Land Title Association (SAUO)
MLTA........ Modern Languages Teachers Association (SAUO)
MLTA........ Multiple Line Terminal Adapter [*Computer science*] (BUR)
MLT-AD...... Medical Laboratory Technology-Associate Degree
MLT (AMT)... Medical Laboratory Technician (American Medical Technologists) (DAVI)
MLT(ASCP)... Medical Laboratory Technician (American Society of Clinical Pathologists) (DMAA)
MLTC........ Mixed Leukocyte-trophoblast Culture [*Medicine*] (EDAA)
MLTC........ Mixed Lymphocyte Tumor Cell [*Medicine*] (EDAA)
MLTC........ Mixed Lymphocyte-Tumor Culture [*Immunology*]
MLTC........ Mortgage Lending Training Centre (FOTI)
MltcPrt...... Multicanal Participacoes [*Associated Press*] (SAG)
ML Tech01... Merrill Lynch & Co. [*Associated Press*] (SAG)
MLTF........ Major Late Transcription Factor [*Genetics*]
MLTF........ Military Law Task Force (EA)
MLTG........ Melting
MLTG........ Missile Launch Tube Group
MLTG........ Multi-Link Transmission Group (SAUO)
MLTI........ Mixed Lymphocyte Target Interaction (DMAA)
MLTI........ Mixed Lymphocyte-Tumor [*Cell*] Interaction [*Immunology*]
MLTI........ Multition [*NCIC truck make code*]
ML/TL....... Mucrones Length to Total Body Length Ratio [*Of Crustacea*]
MLTLVL..... Melting Level [*NWS*] (FAAC)
MltmdG..... Multimedia Games, Inc. [*Associated Press*] (SAG)
MLTMS...... Multileg Tanker Mooring System (MCD)
MLTN........ Molten Metal Technology [*NASDAQ symbol*] (TTSB)
MLTN........ Molten Metal Technology, Inc. [*NASDAQ symbol*] (SAG)
MLTP........ Ministers Leadership Training Program [*Defunct*] (EA)
MLTPL....... Multiplane
MLTRY...... Military
MLTS........ Medium and Long-Term Translation Service (EURO)
MLTS........ Military Land Transportation Service (SAUO)
MLTSL....... Multiple Sail [*Navy*] (NVT)
MLTU........ CP Rail Intermodal Freight Services [*Intermodal shipping container symbol*] (TVRC)
MLTU........ Missile Loop Test Unit
MLTX........ Multex.com, Inc. [*NASDAQ symbol*] (NASQ)
MLTY........ Military (MDG)
MLU......... Major League Umpires Association
MLU......... Malka Resources Ltd. [*Vancouver Stock Exchange symbol*]
MLU......... Mean Length of Utterance [*Linguistics*]
MLU......... Memory Loading Unit [*of FADAC*] [*Military*]
MLU......... Memory Logic Unit [*Computer science*]
MLU......... Mid-Life Update
MLU......... Miscellaneous Live Unit [*Military*] (AFM)
MLU......... Mobile Laundry Unit
MLU......... Mobile Living Unit [*Mobile home*]
MLU......... Monitor & Logic Unit (SAUS)
MLU......... Monroe [*Louisiana*] [*Airport symbol*] (OAG)
MLU......... Monroe, LA [*Location identifier*] [*FAA*] (FAAL)
MLU......... Montlucon Air Service [*France*] [*ICAO designator*] (FAAC)
MLU......... Multiple Logical Unit
MLUA........ Major League Umpires Association (EA)
MLUG........ William G. McCullough [*Common carrier symbol*]
MLURI....... Macaulay Land Use Research Institute, Aberdeen [*British*] (IRUK)
MLUS........ Merrill Lynch & Co. [*Associated Press*] (SAG)
MLUS........ Modulated Lock-Up Solenoid [*Automotive engineering*]
ML/USA..... Mailing List User and Supplier Association [*Defunct*] (EA)
MLUX........ Solutia [*Private rail car owner code*]
MLV.......... Air Moldova International, SA [*FAA designator*] (FAAC)
MLV.......... Magnetic Levitation Vehicle (BARN)
MLV.......... Main LOX [*Liquid Oxygen*] Valve [*NASA*] (KSC)
MLV.......... Maloney Leukemia Virus [*Virology*] (QSUL)
MLV.......... Malvaux [*France*] [*Seismograph station code, US Geological Survey*] (SEIS)
MLV.......... Matrix Light Valve
MLV.......... Maximum Lung Volume [*Physiology*]
MLV.......... McDonnell Launch Vehicle [*McDonnell Douglas Corp.*] (MCD)
MLV.......... Medium Launch Vehicle
MLV.......... Medium Lift Vehicle (ACAE)
MLV.......... Membrane Light Valve [*Optics*]
MLV.......... Memory Loader Verifier (DWSG)
MLV.......... Mobile Launch Vehicle [*Air Force*]
MLV.......... Modify Logging Versions (AAEL)
MLV.......... Moloney Leukemia Virus [*Medicine*] (DMAA)
MLV.......... Mouse Leukemia Virus (MAE)
MLV.......... Mulberry Latent Virus [*Plant pathology*]
MLV.......... Multilamellar Large Vesicle [*Pharmacy*] [*Biochemistry*]
MLV.......... Multilamellar Lipid Vesicle (DB)
MLV.......... Multilaminar Phospholipid Vesicle [*Immunology*]
MLV.......... Multilaminar Vesicle [*Medicine*] (DMAA)
MLV.......... Munchener Leben Vermogensanlageund Vermittlungs (EFIS)
MLV.......... Murine Leukemia Virus [*Also, MuLV*]
MLV(A)...... Murine Leukemia Virus (Abelson)
MLVDP...... Maximum Left Ventricular Developed Pressure [*Cardiology*] (DMAA)
MLV(M)..... Murine Leukemia Virus (Moloney)
MLVP........ Manned Lunar Vehicle Program [*NASA*] (AAG)
MLVPS...... Manual Low-Voltage Power Supply
MLV(R)...... Murine Leukemia Virus (Rauscher)
MLVS........ Mill Vise
MLVS........ Multilevel Voltage Select (MCD)

MLVSS ...... Mixed-Liquor Volatile Suspended Solids [*Chemical engineering*]
MLVT .... Mobile Launch Vehicle Transporter [*Air Force*]
MLVW .... Maximum Loaded Vehicle Weight
MLVW .... Medium Logistic Vehicle, Wheeled (SAUS)
MLW .... Madras Law Weekly [*India*] [*A publication*] (DLA)
Mlw .... Malawi (MILB)
MLW .... Master of Labour Welfare (SAUO)
MLW .... Master Warning Light (IAA)
MLW .... Maximum Landing Weight [*Aviation*]
MLW .... Mean Low Water [*Tides and currents*]
MLW .... Medium-Level Radioactive Waste (NUCP)
MLW .... Military Land Warrant (GEAB)
MLW .... Milwaukee [*Wisconsin*] [*Seismograph station code, US Geological Survey*] [*Closed*] (SEIS)
MLW .... Monrovia [*Liberia*] [*Airport symbol*] (OAG)
MLW .... Montreal Locomotive Works [*Indian Railway*] (TIR)
MLW .... Multiple Logical Windowing [*Computer science*]
MLWA .... Maximum Landing Weight Authorized [*Aviation*] (DA)
MLWG .... Modern Languages Working Group (AIE)
MLWI .... Mean Low-Water Lunitidal Interval [*Tides and currents*]
MLWL .... Mail-Well, Inc. [*NASDAQ symbol*] (SAG)
MLWL .... Mean Low Water Level (QUAC)
MLWMS ..... Miscellaneous Liquid Waste Management System (NRCH)
MLWN .... Mean Low-Water Neap [*Tides and currents*]
MLWS .... Mean Low-Water Spring [*Tides and currents*]
MLWS .... Miniature LASER Weapon Simulator (MCD)
MLWS .... Minimum Level Water Stand (NATG)
MLX .... Malatya [*Turkey*] [*Airport symbol*] (OAG)
MLX .... Malfaxal [*Language symbol*] (ETLW)
MLX .... Malicious [*Telegraphy*] (PCTE)
MLX .... Mauna Loa 2 [*Hawaii*] [*Seismograph station code, US Geological Survey*] (SEIS)
MLX .... Merritt Island, Florida [*Spaceflight Tracking and Data Network*] [*NASA*]
MLX .... MLX Corp. [*Associated Press*] (SAG)
MLX01 ...... Magnetically-levitated Linear Motor Vehicle
MLXC .... Mobilux [*NCIC truck make code*]
MLXP .... Milan Express Company [*Common carrier symbol*]
MLXR .... MLX Corp. [*NASDAQ symbol*] (SAG)
MLXU .... Latvijas Jurniecibas Savieniba [*Intermodal shipping container symbol*] (TVRC)
MLXX .... MLX Corp. [*NASDAQ symbol*] (COMM)
MLXY .... Maliciously [*Telegraphy*] (PCTE)
MLy .... Lynn Public Library, Lynn, MA [*Library symbol*] [*Library of Congress*] (LCLS)
MLY .... Manley Hot Springs [*Alaska*] [*Airport symbol*] (OAG)
MLY .... Manley Hot Springs, AK [*Location identifier*] [*FAA*] (FAAL)
MLY .... Moly Mite Resources [*Vancouver Stock Exchange symbol*]
MLY .... Multiply (MDG)
Mly .... National Library of Malaysia, Kuala Lumpur, Malaysia [*Library symbol*] [*Library of Congress*] (LCLS)
MLYC .... Moosehead Lake Yacht Club (SAUO)
MlyKA .... Arkib Negara [*National Archives of Malaysia*], Federal Government Building,Kuala Lumpur, Malaysia [*Library symbol*] [*Library of Congress*] (LCLS)
MlyKgM ..... Sarawak Museum, Kuching, Malaysia [*Library symbol*] [*Library of Congress*] (LCLS)
MlyKU .... University of Malaya, Kuala Lumpur, Malaysia [*Library symbol*] [*Library of Congress*] (LCLS)
MLyL .... Lynn Public Library, Lynn, MA [*Library symbol*] [*Library of Congress*] (LCLS)
MlyPS .... Universiti Sains Malaysia (University of Science, Malaysia), Minden, Penang, Malaysia [*Library symbol*] [*Library of Congress*] (LCLS)
MLZ .... Melo [*Uruguay*] [*Airport symbol*] (OAG)
MLZ .... Montana Limestone [*Federal Railroad Administration identification code*]
MM .... Machine Made Paper (DGA)
MM .... Machine-Made Snow [*Skiing*]
MM .... Machinery
MM .... Machinist's Mate [*Navy rating*]
M/m .... Made Merchandise (EBF)
MM .... Made Merchantable
MM .... Maelzel's Metronome [*Music*]
MM .... Magister Melendus [*Flourished, 1188-1209*] [*Authority cited in pre-1607 legal work*] (DSA)
mm .... Main Memory (NAKS)
MM .... Main Memory
mm .... Main Module (NAKS)
MM .... Main Module (NASA)
MM .... Maintenance Manual
MM .... Maintenance Monitor
MM .... Majesties
MM .... Major Medical [*Insurance*]
MM .... Major Mode (KSC)
mm .... Major Mode (NAKS)
MM .... Malignant Melanoma [*Oncology*]
mm .... Malta [*MARC country of publication code*] [*Library of Congress*] (LCCP)
MM .... Management Manual (KSC)
MM .... Management Trainee (FOTI)
MM .... Man Machine (CGWS)
M/M .... Man/Machine
MM .... Manmade [*Diamonds*]
MM .... Man-Month (AFM)
mm .... Man-Month (NAKS)
MM .... Manual Maximal Displacement [*Sports medicine*]
MM .... Manual Morse (MCD)
MM .... Manual Muscle (IDYL)
MM .... Manual of Movement (SAUO)
MM .... Manufacturing Management
MM .... Manufacturing Manual (AAG)
MM .... Manufacturing Methods (AAEL)
MM .... Marilyn Monroe [*American motion picture star, 1926-1962*]
MM .... Mariner Mars Project [*NASA*]
MM .... Maritime Mobile
MM .... Mark Mason (ROG)
MM .... Mark Master [*Freemasonry*]
MM .... Marshall Manual (SSD)
MM .... Marshall-Marchetti Procedure [*Medicine*] (MAE)
MM .... Martha Movement (EA)
M-M .... Martin Marietta Corp.
MM .... Martyres [*Martyrs*]
mm .... Maryknoll Fathers, Catholic Foreign Mission Society of America (TOCD)
MM .... Maryknoll Missionary (SAUO)
MM .... Maryknoll Missioners [*Catholic Foreign Mission Society*] [*Roman Catholic religious order*]
MM .... Maryknoll Sisters of St. Dominic (TOCD)
mm .... Mass Memory (NAKS)
MM .... Mass Memory (NASA)
MM .... Massorah Magna [*or Massora Magna*] (BJA)
MM .... Master Mason [*Freemasonry*]
MM .... Master Mechanic
MM .... Master Monitor
MM .... Master of Management
MM .... Master of Mathematics (GAGS)
MM .... Master of Medicine
MM .... Master of Ministry (PGP)
MM .... Master of Modern Studies (PGP)
MM .... Master of Music (GAGS)
MM .... Masters
MM .... Master's Mate [*Civil War term*]
MM .... Material Manufacturer (SAUO)
MM .... Materials Management [*Nuclear energy*]
MM .... Materials Measurement (IEEE)
MM .... Materia Medica (ROG)
MM .... Mathematics Model
MM .... Math Model (KSC)
mm .... Math Model (NAKS)
MM .... Matrimonium [*Matrimony*] [*Latin*]
M/M .... Maximum and Minimum (KSC)
MM .... Measure for Measure [*Shakespearean work*]
MM .... Mechanical Maintenance
MM .... Medal for Merit [*Military decoration*]
MM .... Medial Malleolus [*Anatomy*] (AAMN)
MM .... Medial Meniscus [*Anatomy*]
MM .... Media Manager (SAUO)
MM .... Median Method [*Mathematics*]
MM .... Medical Man (ROG)
MM .... Medical Management (GART)
MM .... Medical Monitor (HVTR)
mm--- .... Mediterranean Sea and Area [*MARC geographic area code*] [*Library of Congress*] (LCCP)
MM .... Medium Maintenance
MM .... Med Mera [*And So Forth*] [*Latin*] (ILCA)
MM .... Megamega [*A prefix meaning multiplied by one trillion*] (DEN)
MM .... Megameter
MM .... Melanotic Melanoma [*Medicine*] (DB)
MM .... Melaveh Malka (BJA)
MM .... Melbourne Marathon [*Australia*]
MM .... Melody Maker [*A publication*] (WDAA)
MM .... Membranes [*Leaves of parchment*] (ROG)
MM .... Memmingen [*German license plate city code*]
MM .... Memory Module (MCD)
MM .... Memory Multiplexer [*Computer science*] (MDG)
MM .... Mercantile Marine (SAUO)
MM .... Merchant Marine
MM .... Mesoscale Model [*Marine science*] (OSRA)
MM .... Messageries Maritimes [*Forwarding agents*] [*French*]
MM .... Messieurs [*Plural of Mister*] [*French*]
MM .... Metal Manufacture [*Department of Employment*] [*British*]
MM .... Metered Market Service [*A. C. Nielsen Co.*] (NTCM)
MM .... Methadone Maintenance [*Medicine*] (DHP)
MM .... Methylmalonyl-CoA Mutase [*An enzyme*]
MM .... Methyl Mercaptan [*Organic chemistry*]
MM .... Methyl Methacrylate [*Also, MMA*] [*Organic chemistry*]
MM .... Metronome Mark (ROG)
MM .... Metropolitana Milanese (EFIS)
MM .... Metropolitan Museum (SAUO)
MM .... Microfilm
MM .... Micromanipulator [*Instrumentation*]
MM .... Micro-Marketplace (GART)
MM .... Micromodule (AAG)
MM .... Micro Mole (ACAE)
MM .... Midcourse Mode [*Navy*] (CAAL)
MM .... Middle Manager
MM .... Middle Marker [*in an instrument landing system*]
MM .... Middle Minoan [*Archaeology*] (BJA)
MM .... Middle Mongolian [*Linguistics*] (IEL)

MM .... Mid-Meridian [*Telegraphy*] (PCTE)
MM .... Military Macaw [*Bird*]
MM .... Military Medal [*World War I nickname: Maconochie Medal*] [*British*]
MM .... Military Medicine
MM .... Military Message (SAUO)
MM .... Military Mission (SAUO)
MM .... Milla Wa-Milla (BJA)
MM .... Millimeter (DFIT)
mm .... Millimeter [*Metric*]
mM .... Millimole [*Mass*]
mm .... Million (WDMC)
MM .... Minelayer Fleet [*Navy symbol*] [*Obsolete*]
MM .... Mineralogical Magazine [*A publication*] (STAH)
MM .... Minimal Medium [*Microbiology*]
M/M .... Minimum/Maximum
MM .... Minister of Munitions [*British*] [*World War II*]
MM .... Ministry of Mines [*British*] (DAS)
MM .... Ministry of Munitions (SAUO)
MM .... Mint Mark [*Numismatics*]
MM .... Minuteman [*Missile*] (AABC)
Mm .... Misch Metal [*A commercial mixture of rare earth metals*]
MM .... Mismated [*Merchandising slang*]
MM .... Missile Master [*Fire direction and coordination system*]
MM .... Missile Minder (MCD)
MM .... Missile Motion
MM .... Missionary of Maryknoll (SAUO)
mm .... Mission Manager [*NASA*] (NAKS)
MM .... Mission Manager [*NASA/USAF*]
MM .... Mission Module
MM .... Mission Monitor (MCD)
M/M .... Mister or Mrs. [*In addresses*] [*Correspondence*]
MM .... Mistress of Music
MM .... Mitochondrial Myopathy [*Medicine*]
MM .... Mitral Murmur [*Medicine*] (MELL)
mm .... Mixed Media (VRA)
MM .... Mixed Monitor [*External Tocotransducer and internal scalp electrode*] [*Neonatology*] [*Obstetrics*] (DAVI)
MM .... Mobile Management (SAUO)
MM .... Mobility Management (SAUO)
MM .... Moderation Management
MM .... Modern Motor [*A publication*]
MM .... Modification or Maintenance [*Aircraft*]
MM .... Modified Mercalli [*Scale measuring earthquake intensity*] [*Seismology*]
MM .... Modigliani-Miller Propositions [*Corporate finance*] (ECON)
MM .... Mois Maconnique [*Masonic Month*] [*Freemasonry*] [*French*]
MM .... Molecular Mechanics [*Physical chemistry*]
MM .... Money Market [*Investment term*]
MM .... Monmouthshire Regiment (SAUO)
MM .... Mononeuritis Multiplex [*Inflammation of nerves*] [*Medicine*] (TAD)
MM .... Monostable Multivibrator [*Electronics*] (OA)
MM .... Monthly Meetings [*Quakers*]
MM .... Morality in Media (EA)
MM .... Moral Majority [*An association*] (EA)
MM .... Morbidity and Mortality [*Medicine*] (DMAA)
MM .... Morel-Morgagni [*Syndrome*] [*Medicine*] (DB)
MM .... More Moderate Service [*Automotive engineering*]
MM .... Morrison-Maierle, Inc. (EFIS)
MM .... Moslem Mosque (EA)
MM .... Mothers Matter [*Commercial firm*] (EA)
MM .... Motor Magnet
MM .... Motor Maintenance [*Army*]
MM .... Motor Maintenance Aptitude Area [*Army*]
MM .... Motor Meal [*Medicine*] (MEDA)
MM .... Motor Mechanic [*British military*] (DMA)
MM .... Motor Movement (SAUO)
MM .... Mould Made Paper (DGA)
MM .... Mouse Myoblast [*Cell line*]
MM .... Moving Magnet [*Stereo equipment*]
MM .... Mozambique Metical [*Monetary unit*] (IMH)
M/M .... Mr. & Mrs. (VRA)
MM .... Much Married [*Slang*]
MM .... Mucous Membrane
MM .... Multi-Media (OICC)
MM .... Multimeter
MM .... Multi Mission Surveillance System (ACAE)
MM .... Multimode
MM .... Multiple Master [*Computer science*] (CDE)
MM .... Multiple Myeloma [*Medicine*]
MM .... Multipolar Magnetic [*Sun*] (DICI)
MM .... Munitions Maintenance (MCD)
mm .... Murmur [*Cardiology*] (DAVI)
MM .... Muscles [*Medicine*]
MM .... Muscularis Mucosa [*Medicine*] (MAE)
MM .... Museum Media [*A publication*]
MM .... Musical Majority [*Defunct*] (EA)
MM .... Mutatis Mutandis [*With the Necessary Changes*] [*Latin*]
MM .... Mutual Risk Management [*NYSE symbol*] (SPSG)
MM .... Myanmar [*Internet country code*]
MM .... Myeloid Metaplasia [*Medicine*]
MM .... Myelomeningocele [*Medicine*]
MM .... Myriameters [*Metric system*] (ROG)
MM .... Program Maintenance Manual (SAUO)
MM .... SAM Colombia [*Airline flight code*] (ODBW)
MM .... Sociedad Aeronautica Medellin [*ICAO designator*] (AD)
MM .... Xaverian Missionary Society of Mary, Inc. [*Roman Catholic women's religious order*]
MM1 .... Machinist's Mate, First Class [*Navy rating*]
MM2 .... Machinist's Mate, Second Class [*Navy rating*]
MM^2 .... Square Millimeter
mm2 .... Square Millimeters [*Industrial hygiene term*] (OHS)
MM^3 .... Cubic Millimeter
mm3 .... Cubic Millimeter (or Millimetre) (SAUS)
MM3 .... Machinist's Mate, Third Class [*Navy rating*]
MM4 .... Mesoscale Meteorological Model-Version 4 [*Marine science*] (OSRA)
MM5 .... Fifth Generation of Penn State/NCAR Mesoscale Model (SAUS)
MM5 .... Mesoscale Model Version 5 [*Marine science*] [*Pennsylvania State University*] (OSRA)
MMA .... Average Male Mass
MMA .... Caltech Millimeter Array (SAUS)
MM(A) .... Machinist's Mate (Aviation) [*U.S. Navy enlisted rating*] (AUER)
MMA .... MacRobertson Miller Airline Services [*Australia*]
MMA .... Magnetotactic Multicellular Aggregate [*Microbiology*]
MMA .... Maine Maritime Academy (SAUO)
MMA .... Maine Medical Association (SAUO)
MMA .... Main Mission Antennas
MMA .... Major Machine Accessory (MCD)
MMA .... Major Maintenance Availability (MHDB)
MMA .... Malmo [*Sweden*] [*Airport symbol*] (OAG)
MMA .... Management and Marketing Abstracts [*PIRA*] [*Bibliographic database*] [*British*]
MMA .... Manchester Mathematics Association (SAUO)
MMA .... Maneuver Motor Array (MCD)
MMA .... Manitoba Medical Association (SAUO)
MMA .... Manual Metal Arc [*Welding*]
MMA .... Maria Mitchell Association (EA)
MMA .... Marine Machinery Association (EA)
MMA .... Marine Mammal Act [*1972*] (MSC)
MMA .... Marine Maritime Academy
MMA .... Marine Motor Association (ROG)
MMA .... Married Man's Allowance [*Taxes*] [*British*]
MMA .... Martin Marietta Aerospace (ACAE)
MMA .... Massachusetts Maritime Academy [*Buzzards Bay*]
MMA .... Massachusetts Maritime Academy, Captain C. H. Hurley Library, Buzzards Bay, MA [*OCLC symbol*] (OCLC)
MMA .... Massachusetts Military Academy
MMA .... Mass Memory Assembly (SAUS)
MMA .... Master of Management and Administration, Cranfield Institute of Technology [*British*] (DBQ)
MMA .... Master of Manpower Administration (GAGS)
MMA .... Master of Marine Affairs (GAGS)
MMA .... Master of Media Arts (PGP)
MMA .... Master of Medical Art (GAGS)
MMA .... Master of Municipal Administration
MMA .... Master of Musical Art (GAGS)
MMA .... Master of Musical Arts
MMA .... Masters of Medicine [*A publication*]
MMA .... Mastitis-Metritis-Agalactia Syndrome [*Medicine*] (DMAA)
MMA .... Material Management Activity (SAUO)
MMA .... Material Manufacturing Authorization (AAG)
MMA .... Materials Marketing Associates [*Hartford, CT*] (EA)
MMA .... Maymac Petroleum Corp. [*Vancouver Stock Exchange symbol*]
MMA .... Mazda Motors of America
MMA .... McLoughlin Memorial Association [*Oregon*] (EARSL)
MMA .... Media in Ministry Association (EA)
MMA .... Medical Management Analysis System (HCT)
MMA .... Medical Marketing Association (NTPA)
MMA .... Medical Materiel Account [*Military*] (AABC)
MMA .... Medical Mutual Aid (GNE)
MMA .... Memory-to-Memory Adapter [*Computer science*]
MMA .... Merchandise Marks Act (ROG)
MMA .... Merchant Marine Academy (SAUO)
MMA .... Merchants and Manufacturers Association
MMA .... Mercy Medical Airlift (EA)
MMA .... Merrill's Marauders Association (EA)
MMA .... Meter Manufacturers' Association (IAA)
MMA .... Methylmalonic Acid [*Organic chemistry*]
MMA .... Methylmalonic Acidemia [*Medicine*]
MMA .... Methyl Methacrylate [*Also, MM*] [*Organic chemistry*]
MMA .... Metro Manila Airways International, Inc. [*Philippines*] [*ICAO designator*] (FAAC)
MMA .... Metropolitan Magazine Association [*Later, Magazine Publishers Association*] (EA)
MMA .... Metropolitan Museum of Art [*New York*] (BJA)
MMA .... Michigan Manufacturers Association (EARSL)
MMA .... Michigan Midwives Association (EARSL)
MMA .... Microcomputer Managers Association (HGAA)
MMA .... Micro Manager's Association (AGLO)
MMA .... Microminiature Mixer Amplifier
MMA .... Microtome Manufacturers Association [*British*] (DBA)
MMA .... Middle Meningeal Artery [*Neuroanatomy*]
MMA .... MIDI Manufacturers Association (EA)
MMA .... Military Medical Academy [*Armed forces medical college*]
MMA .... Millimeter Array [*Astronomy*]
MMA .... Minelayer Auxiliary Ship [*Navy symbol*] [*Obsolete*]
MMA .... Minor Morphologic Aberration [*Medicine*] (EDAA)
MMA .... Minor Motor Aphasia [*Medicine*] (MELL)
MMA .... Mirror Manufacturers Association

MMA .... Missile Maintenance Area (AAG)
MMA .... Mitomycin A [*Antineoplastic drug*]
MMA .... Modified Motorcycle Association
MMA .... Momentum Management Assembly (ACAE)
MMA .... Monomer Methyl Methacrylate [*Medicine*] [*Liquid*] (EDAA)
MMA .... Monomethyl Adenosine [*Medicine*] (EDAA)
MMA .... Monomethylamine [*Organic chemistry*]
MMA .... Monomethyl Arsonic Acid [*Organic chemistry*]
MMA .... Monorail Manufacturers Association (EA)
MMA .... Monosil Manufacturers Association
MMA .... Monovalent Metal Azide [*Inorganic chemistry*]
MMA .... Montana Medical Association [*Medicine*] (EDAA)
MMA .... Mothers and Midwives Action [*Australia*] [*An association*]
MMA .... Motoring in Miniature Association (EA)
MMA .... Motorsports Marketing Association [*Langhorne, PA*] [*Defunct*] (EA)
MMA .... MSFC Management Association (SAUO)
MMA .... Multifunction Microwave Aperture
MMA .... Multi-Megabit-Anpassung (SAUS)
MMA .... Multimission Aircraft (SAUS)
MMA .... Multiple Module Access
MMA .... Multiplexed Matrix Array
MMA .... Mummy Mountain [*Arizona*] [*Seismograph station code, US Geological Survey*] [*Closed*] (SEIS)
MMA .... Municipal Mortgage & Equity LLC [*AMEX symbol*] (SAG)
MMA .... Municipal Mortgage and Equity LLC [*NYSE symbol*]
MMA .... Museum of Modern Art (SAUO)
MMA .... Music Masters' Association [*British*]
MMA .... Music of Modern Art (NADA)
MMA .... Muttahida Majlis-i-Amal [*Political group*] [*Islamic group*] [*Pakistan*]
MMAA .... Acapulco/General Juan N. Alvarez Internacional [*Mexico*] [*ICAO location identifier*] (ICLI)
MMAA .... Man/Machine Assembly Analysis (MCD)
MMAA .... Merchandise Mart Apparel Association [*Defunct*]
MMAA .... Mini-Microaggregates of Albumin (DMAA)
MMAA .... Monomethylarsonic Acid [*Organic chemistry*]
MMAA .... Mono-N-methylacetoacetamide [*Organic chemistry*]
MMAB .... Made Me a Believer [*Internet lingo*] (NETL)
MMAC .... Material Management Aggregation Code (MCD)
MMAC .... Medical Materiel Advice Code [*Military*] (AFM)
MMAC .... Multi-Media Access Center [*Cabletron Systems, Inc.*]
MMAC .... Multimedia Mobile Access Communications (SAUO)
MMAC .... Multiple Model Adaptive Control [*Flight control*]
MMAC-FNB ... Multi-Media Access Center with Flexible Network Bus [*Cabletron Systems, Inc.*]
MMACS ..... Maintenance Management and Control System (MCD)
MMACS ..... Maintenance, Mechanical Arm, and Crew System Engineer (SAUS)
MMACS ..... Medicaid/Medicare Automated Certification System (GFGA)
mmad .... Mass Media Aerodynamic Diameter [*Industrial hygiene term*] (OHS)
MMAD .... Mass-Median Aerodynamic Diameter [*of particles*]
MMAD .... Millimeter Wave Active Decoy (ACAE)
MM Adm .... Master of Municipal Administration
M Ma E ..... Master of Marine Engineering
MMAE .... Master of Mechanical and Aerospace Engineering (PGP)
M Ma Eng ... Master of Marine Engineering
MMAG .... Martin Marietta Astronautics Group (SAUO)
MMAJ .... Metropolitan Museum of Art Journal [*A publication*] (ABAR)
MMal .... Malden Public Library, Malden, MA [*Library symbol*] [*Library of Congress*] (LCLS)
MMAL .... Mitsubishi Motors Australia, Limited (SAUO)
M-MALS .... Multimode Aircraft Landing System (MCD)
MMam ...... Marstons Mills Public Library, Marstons Mills, MA [*Library symbol*] [*Library of Congress*] (LCLS)
MMAN .... Aeropuerto del Norte [*Mexico*] [*ICAO location identifier*] (ICLI)
MMAN .... Minuteman International [*NASDAQ symbol*] (SAG)
MMAN .... Minuteman Int'l [*NASDAQ symbol*] (TTSB)
MM & F ..... Merchant Marine and Fisheries Committee [*Congressional committee*] (MSC)
MM&M ...... Manning, Maxwell & Moore, Incorporated (SAUO)
MM & M .... Material Manual and Memorandum (AAG)
MM & M .... Minerals, Mining, and Metallurgy
MM & M Soc of Am ... Member of the Mining and Metallurgical Society of America
MM&P .... Masters, Mates and Pilots (SAUO)
MM & SC ... Major Mission and Support Category
MM & T ..... Manufacturing Methods and Technology [*Program*] [*Army Materiel Command*] (RDA)
MManHi ..... Manchester Historical Society, Manchester, MA [*Library symbol*] [*Library of Congress*] (LCLS)
MMAO .... Monomethylamine Oxidase (DB)
MMAP .... Marine Mammal Action Plan (SAUO)
MMAP .... Microgravity Measurement and Analysis Project (SAUS)
MMAP .... Microwave Multi-Application Payload [*NASA*] (PDAA)
MMAP .... Multi Media Access Profile (SAUS)
MMAR .... Main Memory Address Register
MMar .... Marlborough Public Library, Marlborough, MA [*Library symbol*] [*Library of Congress*] (LCLS)
MMAR .... Money Management Analytical Research Group
M-MARP .... Mobilization Manpower Allocations/Requirements Plan [*Military*]
MMARS ..... Military Middle Airspace Radar Service (PIAV)
MMarsW .... Historic Winslow House, Marshfield, MA [*Library symbol*] [*Library of Congress*] (LCLS)
MMART ..... Mobile Medical Augmentation Readiness Team (DNAB)
MMAS .... Aguascalientes [*Mexico*] [*ICAO location identifier*] (ICLI)
MMAS .... Manufacturing Management Accounting System (PDAA)
MMAS .... Master of Military Art and Science (MCD)
MMAS .... Material Management Accountability System (NASA)
MMAS .... Material Management and Accounting System (AAGC)
MMAS .... Medical Materiel Accounting System (SAUO)
MmAS .... Minerva Mikrofilm A/S, Hellerup, Denmark [*Library symbol*] [*Library of Congress*] (LCLS)
MMAS .... Mini-Manned Aircraft System (PDAA)
MMASC ..... Major Mission and Support Category
MMat .... Free Public Library, Mattapoisett, MA [*Library symbol*] [*Library of Congress*] (LCLS)
MMAT .... Mobile Mine Assembly Team (NG)
MMath ...... Master of Mathematics
MMATP ..... Methadone Maintenance and Aftercare Treatment Program [*Medicine*] (DMAA)
M Mat SE ... Master of Material Science and Engineering (PGP)
MMAU .... Master Multiattribute Utility (IEEE)
MMAU .... Millimass Unit (IAA)
MMAXc ..... Maximum Corrective Maintenance Down-Time (SAUO)
MMAXCT .... Maximum Corrective Time (SAUO)
MMAZ .... Martin Marietta Aggregates [*Federal Railroad Administration identification code*]
MMB .... Marine Midland Banks, Inc. [*NYSE symbol*] (SPSG)
MMB .... Master Menu Board [*Military*]
MMB .... Master of Medical Biochemistry (GAGS)
MMB .... Mast Mounting Bracket (SAUS)
MMB .... Memanbetsu [*Japan*] [*Geomagnetic observatory code*]
MMB .... Membrane [*Medicine*]
MMB .... Memorable [*Telegraphy*] (PCTE)
MMB .... Mercedarian Missionaries of Berriz [*Also, OMerc*] [*Roman Catholic women's religious order*]
MMB .... Method of Mass Balance [*Physical chemistry*]
MMB .... Methylmercury Bromide [*Organic chemistry*]
MMB .... Metropolitan Milk Board [*South Australia*]
MMB .... Midwest Motor Carriers Bureau, Inc., Oklahoma City OK [*STAC*]
MMB .... Milk Marketing Board (SAUO)
MMB .... Milk Marketing Board for England and Wales
MMB .... Million Barrels
MMB .... Minimum Monthly Balance [*Finance*]
MMB .... Mitsui Manufacturers Bank (SAUO)
MMB .... Mixer Manufacturers Bureau [*Defunct*] (EA)
MMB .... Mouth-to-Mouth Breathing (MELL)
Mmb .... Mucous Membranes (SPVS)
MMB .... Multi-Mission Bus (ACAE)
MMB .... Multiport Memory Bank [*Computer science*] (MHDB)
MMB .... Sisters Mercederian Missionaries of Berriz (SAUO)
MMBA .... Mississippi Malt Beverage Association (EARSL)
MMBA .... Money Market Deposit Account (EBF)
MMBAT ..... Main Missile Battery
MMBB .... Molecular Marine Biology and Biotechnology [*A publication*]
MMBC .... Maryland Motor Boat Club (SAUO)
MMB/D ..... Million Barrels per Day
MMBDC ..... Michigan Minority Business Development Council (EARSL)
MMBEMD ... Mean Miles between Essential Maintenance Demand [*Quality control*]
MMBF .... Mean Miles between Failures [*Quality control*]
MMBF .... Million Board Feet (WPI)
MMBI KNC RAN ... Murmansk Marine Biological Institute, Kola Scientific Centre Academy of Sciences (SAUS)
MMBI KNC RAN ... Murmansk Marine Biological Institute, Kola Scientific Centre, Russian Academy of Sciences (SAUO)
MMBL .... MacMillan Bloedel Ltd. [*NASDAQ symbol*] (NQ)
MMBLF ..... MacMillan-Bloedel [*NASDAQ symbol*] (TTSB)
MMBM .... Mammalian Meat and Bone Meal (SAUS)
MMBMF ..... Mean Miles between Mission Failures [*Quality control*] (MCD)
MMBOMF ... Mean Miles between Operational Mission Failures [*Quality control*] (MCD)
MMBP .... Military Medical Benefits Property (AABC)
MMBR .... Mean Miles between Removals [*Quality control*] (MCD)
MMBR .... Microbiology and Molecular Biology Reviews [*A publication*]
MMBR .... Multipurpose Supersonic Beamrider (ACAE)
MMBSF ..... Mean Miles between System Failures [*Quality control*] (MCD)
MMBTU ..... Million British Thermal Units (MENA)
MMBUMA ... Mean Miles between Unscheduled Maintenance Actions [*Quality control*] (MCD)
MMC .... Ciudad Mante [*Mexico*] [*Airport symbol*] (AD)
MMC .... Machinist's Mate, Chief [*Navy rating*]
MMC .... Magical Mystery Chip (VLIE)
MMC .... Magnesium Methyl Carbonate [*Organic chemistry*]
MMC .... Main Memory Controller [*Computer science*] (CIST)
MMC .... Maintenance Management Center
MMC .... Maintenance Management Course [*Army*]
MMC .... Maintenance Monitor Console (CTAS)
MMC .... Malaya Military College (SAUO)
MMC .... Malaysian Marketing Corporation (SAUO)
MMC .... Malaysian Mining Corporation (SAUO)
MMC .... Manifold-Mounted Converter [*Automotive emissions*]
MMC .... Man Machine Communication (SAUO)
MMC .... Man-Machine Communication [*Computer science*]
MMC .... Man Marketing Council [*New York City*]
MMC .... Manufacturing Methods Committee
MMC .... Manufacturing Methods Council (AAEL)
MMC .... Marine Mammal Commission [*Marine science*] (MSC)
MMC .... Marsh & McLennan Companies, Inc. [*NYSE symbol*] (SPSG)
MMC .... Martin Marietta Composites [*Automotive industry*]
MMC .... Martin Marietta Corp. (KSC)

mmc .... Martin Marietta Corp. (NAKS)
MMC .... Martin's Reports of Mining Cases [*Canada*] [*A publication*] (DLA)
MMC .... Mary Morstan's Companions [*An association*]
MMC .... Marymount Manhattan College [*New York, NY*]
MMC .... Massachusetts Microelectronics Center [*Research center*] (RCD)
MMC .... Master of Mass Communication (GAGS)
MMC .... Matched Memory Cycle [*Computer science*]
MMC .... Materiel Management Center [*Military*] (AABC)
MMC .... Materiel Management Code [*Military*] (AFM)
MMC .... Maximum Material Condition
MMC .... Maximum Metal Concept
MMC .... Maximum Metal Condition (IEEE)
MMC .... Maximum Miscibility Composition [*Physical chemistry*]
MMC .... Mazda Motor Corp.
MMC .... Mean Meridional Circulation [*Climatology*]
MMC .... Medecine Moderne du Canada [*Medicine*] [*Journal*] (EDAA)
MMC .... Medical Milk Commission (SAUO)
MMC .... Meet Me Conference [*Telecommunications*] (DOM)
MMC .... Meharry Medical College (SAUO)
MMC .... Melbourne Magistrates Court [*Australia*]
MMC .... Memory Management Controller (IEEE)
MMC .... Meningomyelocele [*Medicine*] (MELL)
MMC .... Merchant Marine Council [*Coast Guard*]
MMC .... Metabolic Measurement Cart [*Beckman Instruments, Inc.*]
MMC .... Metal-Matrix Composite
MMC .... Metropolitan Medical Center [*Medicine*] [*New York, NY*] (EDAA)
MMC .... Metropolitan Motor Carriers Conference Inc., Dover NJ [*STAC*]
MMC .... Microcar and Minicar Club (EA)
MMC .... Microcomputer Marketing Council [*Direct Marketing Association*] (PCM)
MMC .... Micrometeoroid Capsule (OA)
MMC .... Micronesian Minerals [*Vancouver Stock Exchange symbol*]
MMC .... Microsoft Management Console
MMC .... Microsoft Management Control
MMC .... Midcourse Measurement Correction
MMC .... Middle Cape [*Alaska*] [*Seismograph station code, US Geological Survey*] (SEIS)
MMC .... Middle Management Council (SAUO)
MMC .... Mid Motor Controller [*Aerospace*] (NAKS)
MMC .... Migrating Myoelectric Complexes [*Electrophysiology*]
MMC .... Military Microwave Components (TIMI)
MMC .... Millsaps College, Jackson, MS [*OCLC symbol*] (OCLC)
MMC .... Minelayer, Coastal [*Navy symbol*] [*Obsolete*]
MMC .... Minerals Marketing Corporation (SAUO)
MMC .... Minicar and Microcar Club (EA)
MMC .... Minicomputer Maintenance Center (VLIE)
MMC .... Minimal Medullary Concentration [*Medicine*] (MAE)
MMC .... Missile Maintenance Crew (AFM)
MMC .... Missile Measurements Center
MMC .... Missile Motion Computer
mmc .... Mission Management Center [*NASA*] (NAKS)
MMC .... Mission Management Center [*NASA*] (NASA)
MMC .... Mission Management Computer (SAUS)
MMC .... Mission Monitoring Center [*Army*]
MMC .... Mitomycin C [*Mutamycin*] [*Also, Mi, MTC*] [*Antineoplastic drug*]
MMC .... Mitsubishi Materials Corporation (EFIS)
MMC .... Mitsubishi Motors Corp.
MMC .... Mixed Medical Commission (SAUO)
MMC .... Modern Medicine of Canada [*Medicine*] [*Journal*] (EDAA)
MMC .... Modular Mission Computer (SAUS)
MMC .... Money Management Council [*British*]
MMC .... Money Market Certificate [*Investment term*]
MMC .... Money Market Certificate of Deposit
MMC .... Monopolies and Mergers Commission [*British*]
MMC .... Monthly Maintenance Charge (VLIE)
MMC .... Mortar Motor Carrier
MMC .... Mount Marty College [*South Dakota*]
MMC .... Mount Mary College [*Wisconsin*]
MMC .... Mount Mercy College [*Iowa; Pennsylvania*]
MMC .... Movements Monitoring Center (SAUO)
MMC .... Mucosal Mast Cell [*Medicine*]
MMC .... Multihazard Mitigation Council [*Emergency Management*] (EMA)
MMC .... Multimedia Marketing Council (DOM)
MMC .... Multipart Memory Controller (NITA)
MMC .... Multiport Memory Controller
MMCA .... Cananea [*Mexico*] [*ICAO location identifier*] (ICLI)
MMCA .... M and M Cartage [*Common carrier symbol*]
MMCA .... Methyl Monochloroacetate [*Organic chemistry*]
MMCA .... Midbody Motor Control Assembly (NASA)
MMCA .... Mid Motor Controller Assembly [*Aerospace*] (NAKS)
MMCA .... Minor Military Construction, Army
M McA ...... Montague and McArthur's English Bankruptcy Reports [*A publication*] (DLA)
MMCAA ..... Mt. Marty College Alumni Association (EA)
MM Cas ..... Martin's Reports of Mining Cases [*Canada*] [*A publication*] (DLA)
MMCB .... Cuernavaca [*Mexico*] [*ICAO location identifier*] (ICLI)
MMCB .... Methods in Molecular and Cellular Biology [*A publication*]
MMCB .... Midwest Motor Carriers Bureau, Inc.
MMCBE ..... Machinist's Mate, Construction Battalion, Equipment Operator [*Navy rating*]
MMCC .... Ciudad Acuna [*Mexico*] [*ICAO location identifier*] (ICLI)
MMCC .... Manhattan Miniature Camera Club (EA)
MMCC .... Medicare Managed Care Contract (SAUO)
MMCC .... Mid-Century Mercury Car Club (EA)
MMCC .... Military Manpower Claimant Code (DNAB)
MMCC .... Mission Management and Control Centre (SAUO)
MMCC .... Moscow Mission Control Center (SAUO)
MMCC .... Multimini Computer Compiler (MHDI)
MMCCS ..... MILSTAR [*Military Strategic and Tactical Relay System*] Mobile Consolidation and Control Station (DWSG)
MMCD .... Master Monitor Criteria Data File
MMCD .... Multimedia CD [*Computer science*]
MMCD .... Multimedia Compact Disc
MMCE .... Ciudad Del Carmen [*Mexico*] [*ICAO location identifier*] (ICLI)
mmcf .... Million Cubic Feet [*Industrial hygiene term*] (OHS)
MMCF .... Million Cubic Feet
MMCF .... Multimedia Communications Forum (DDC)
MMCFD ..... Million Cubic Feet a Day
MMCG .... Mid-Murray Citrus Growers [*Australia*]
MMCG .... Nuevo Casas Grandes [*Mexico*] [*ICAO location identifier*] (ICLI)
MMCH .... Chilpancingo [*Mexico*] [*ICAO location identifier*] (ICLI)
MMCI .... Money, Meaning & Choices Institute
MMCI .... Mopar Muscle Club International (EA)
MMCI .... MultiMedia Concepts International, Inc. [*NASDAQ symbol*] (SAG)
MMCI .... MultiMedia Concepts Intl. [*NASDAQ symbol*] (TTSB)
MMCIAC .... Metal Matrix Composites Information Analysis Center [*DoD*] [*Information service or system*] (IID)
MMCIL ...... Majhuee Multipurpose Cooperative Institution Limited (SAUO)
MMCIL ...... Majhuee Multipurpose Cooperative Institution Ltd. (SAUS)
MMCIW ..... MultiMeda Concepts Intl-Wrrt [*NASDAQ symbol*] (TTSB)
MMCIW ..... MultiMedia Concepts International, Inc. [*NASDAQ symbol*] (SAG)
MMcKNP .... Mount McKinley National Park (SAUO)
MMCL .... Culiacan [*Mexico*] [*ICAO location identifier*] (ICLI)
MMCL .... Magneti-Marelli Climatizzione [*Automotive parts*]
MMCL .... Major Missile Component List
MMCL .... Master Measurement and Control List (MCD)
MMCL .... Mini-Marcellino [*NCIC motorcycle make code*]
MMCM ...... Chetumal [*Mexico*] [*ICAO location identifier*] (ICLI)
MMCM ...... Machinist's Mate, Master Chief [*Navy rating*]
MMCM ...... Master of Music in Church Music (PGP)
MMCMP ..... Mobilization, Military and Civilian Manpower Program (AABC)
MMCN .... Ciudad Obregon [*Mexico*] [*ICAO location identifier*] (ICLI)
MMCN .... MMC Networks [*NASDAQ symbol*] (SG)
MMCNA ..... Moto Morini Club of North America (EA)
MMCNE ..... Maryknoll Mission Center of New England [*Catholic Foreign Mission Society of America*] (EARSL)
MMCNY ..... Marine Museum of the City of New York (SAUO)
MMCO .... Maintenance Material Control Officer (DNAB)
MMCOI ...... Multimedia Communications Community of Interest (SAUO)
MMCP .... Campeche [*Mexico*] [*ICAO location identifier*] (ICLI)
MMCP .... Medicaid Managed Care Program (SAUO)
MMCP .... Micro-Master Control Processor (NITA)
M/MCRP .... AUTODIN Memory/Memory Control Replacement Program (MCD)
MMCS .... Ciudad Juarez/Abraham Gonzalez Internacional [*Mexico*] [*ICAO location identifier*] (ICLI)
MMCS .... Machinist's Mate, Senior Chief [*Navy rating*]
MMCS .... Manufacturing Management Control System (VLIE)
MMCS .... Mass Memory Control Subsystem (TEL)
MMCS .... Mauritius Marine Conservation Society (SAUO)
MMCS .... McCullough/McCulloch Clan Society (EA)
MMCS .... Minimum Modified Chi-Squared [*Statistics*]
MMCS .... Missile and Munitions Center and School [*Army*] (RDA)
MMCS .... Mitsubishi Multi-Communication System [*Driver information system*]
MMCS .... Modernization Management and Control System [*Social Security Administration*]
MMCS .... Multidimensional-Multiattributional Causality Scale (EDAC)
MMCS .... Multiple-Mission Command System [*NASA*]
MMCSA ..... Microwave Microminiature Communications System for Aircraft (DNAB)
MMCSEER ... Marjorie Mayrock Center for CIS [*Commonwealth of Independent States*] and East European Research [*Israel*] (EAIO)
MMCSRS ... MACOM Materiel Condition Status Reporting System (SAUO)
MM/CSSA ... Morrison-Majerle/CSSA, Inc. (EFIS)
MMCT .... Maritime Mobile Coastal Telegraphy
MMCT .... Metal-to-Metal Charge Transfer [*Physical chemistry*]
MMCT .... Metro Mobile CTS, Inc. [*NASDAQ symbol*] (COMM)
MMCT .... Microcell-Mediated Chromosome Transfer [*Genetics*]
MMCT .... Mobile Maintenance Contact Team (MCD)
MMCTS ..... Material Management Center Theater Supply [*Army*]
MMCU .... Chihuahua/Internacional [*Mexico*] [*ICAO location identifier*] (ICLI)
MMCU .... Societe des Messageries Maritimes [*Intermodal shipping container symbol*] (TVRC)
MMCV .... Ciudad Victoria [*Mexico*] [*ICAO location identifier*] (ICLI)
MMCX .... Multimedia Communication Exchange (SAUO)
MMCY .... Celaya [*Mexico*] [*ICAO location identifier*] (ICLI)
MMCZ .... Cozumel/Internacional [*Mexico*] [*ICAO location identifier*] (ICLI)
MMCZ .... M & M [*Federal Railroad Administration identification code*]
MMD .... Magical Mystery Disease (WDAA)
MMD .... Magnetic Mirror Device
MMD .... Maintenance Management Division [*Army*] (INF)
MMD .... Manual of the Medical Department [*Navy*]
MMD .... Mass Median Diameter
MMD .... Master Makeup and Display
MMD .... Master Monitor Display
MMD .... Material, Maintenance, and Distribution (MCD)
MMD .... Materiel Management Decision [*Military*]
MMD .... Materiel Management Division [*Army*]

MMD .... Maximum Mixing Depths [*Meteorology*]
MMD .... Mean Mass Density
MMD .... Mean Mass Diameter
MMD .... Mean Measure of Divergence [*Statistics*]
MMD .... Mean Missile [*or Mission*] Duration (KSC)
MMD .... Medical Management of Disasters [*Emergency Management*] (EMA)
MMD .... Menstrual Mood Disorder [*Medicine*] (EDAA)
MMD .... Mercantile Marine Department (SAUO)
MMD .... Merchang Mariner's Document [*Navy*]
MMD .... Merchant Marine Detail
MMD .... Methyl-mercury Dicyanimide [*Medicine*] (EDAA)
MMD .... Microlithographic Mask Development [*Program*] (AAEL)
MMD .... Microwave Mixer Diode
MMD .... Middle Management Development
MMD .... Milkmaid's Dislocation [*Medicine*] (MELL)
MMD .... Minami Daito Jima [*Volcano Islands*] [*Airport symbol*] (OAG)
MMD .... Minelayer, Fast [*Navy symbol*]
MMD .... Minimal Morbidostatic Dose [*Medicine*] (MAE)
MMD .... Mini-Module Drive (PDAA)
MMD .... Missile Miss Distance [*Military*] (CAAL)
MMD .... Mission Management and Dissemination (MCD)
MMD .... Mobile Multi-function Device (SAUS)
MMD .... Mobile Servicing Center, Maintenance Department [*Canada*]
MMD .... Molecular Mass Distribution [*Organic chemistry*]
MMD .... Money Market Directories, Inc. [*Also, an information service or system*] (IID)
MMD .... Moore Medical Corp. [*AMEX symbol*] (SPSG)
MMD .... Movement for Multi-Party Democracy [*Zambia*] [*Political party*]
MMD .... Moving Map Display
MMD .... Moyamoya Disease [*Medicine*] (DMAA)
MMD .... MSC [*Mobile Servicing Center*] Maintenance Depot (SSD)
MMD .... MSFC [*Marshall Space Flight Center*] Management Directive [*NASA*]
MMD .... Multi-Effect Multistage Distillation (PDAA)
MMD .... Multimedia Document [*Open Systems Interconnection*] (ODAA)
MMD .... Multimode Display
MMD .... Municipal Market Data (IID)
MMD .... Myotonic Muscular Dystrophy [*Medicine*] [*Medicine*] (DMAA)
MMD .... Servite Missionary Sisters of the Sorrowful Mother (TOCD)
MMD .... Standard and Poors Money Market Directories (IID)
MMDA....... Martin Marietta Denver Aerospace (ACAE)
MMDA....... Mass Merchandising Distributors' Association (EA)
MMDA....... (Methoxy)methylenedioxyamphetamine [*A hallucinogen*]
MMDA....... Money Market Deposit Account [*Investment term*]
MMDA....... Myristicin [*or glyceryl trimyristate*] [*Chemical dependency*] (DAVI)
MMDB....... Mass Memory Database (NASA)
MMDB....... Master Measurement Database (NASA)
MMDB....... Molecular Modeling DataBase (GDD)
MMDB....... Molecular Modelling Database (SAUO)
MMDC....... Manual Master Direction Center
MMDC....... Master Message Display Console (MCD)
MMDC....... Mount Misalignment Data Collection Routine
MMDDS...... Mucous Membrane Drug Delivery System [*Medicine*] (DB)
mmddyy..... Month, Day, Year (HGAA)
MMDF....... Mission Mode Data File
MMDF....... Mission Model Data File [*NASA*] (NASA)
MMDF....... Multichannel Memorandum Distribution Facility (SAUO)
MMDG....... Mark Morris Dance Group
MMDH....... Mitochondrial Malate Dehydrogenase [*Medicine*] (EDAA)
MMDI....... Metropolitan Model Deployment Initiative [*Highway engineering*]
MMDI....... Middle Management Development Initiative
MMDI....... Momentum Distribution (EFIS)
MMDL....... Microminiature Delay Line
MMDM...... Ciudad Mante [*Mexico*] [*ICAO location identifier*] (ICLI)
MMDM...... Mobile Mixed Deployment Minuteman (SAA)
MMDMTI.... Multi Mode Display Moving Target Indicator (ACAE)
MMDO....... Durango [*Mexico*] [*ICAO location identifier*] (ICLI)
MMDO....... Magnetic Modulation Direct Overwrite (SAUS)
MMDOC..... Merchant Mariners Documentation [*BTS*] (TAG)
MMDP....... Middle Management Development Program
MMDR....... Microcircuit Module, Driver/Receiver
MMDS....... Maintenance Management Data System [*Military*] (CAAL)
MMDS....... Marketing Management Data System
MMDS....... Martin Marietta Data Systems
MMDS....... Moving Map Display Equipment (SAUS)
MMDS....... Multichannel Memorandum Distribution Facility (SAUO)
MMDS....... Multichannel Multipoint Distribution Service [*Broadcasting term*]
MMDS....... Multichannel, Multipoint Distribution System [*Telecommunications*] (ACRL)
MMDS....... Multi-Mode Seeker Demonstration project (SAUS)
MMDS....... Multipoint Microwave Distribution System (WDAA)
MMDS....... Multipoint Multichannel Distribution Service (SAUS)
MMDT....... Multimodal Transportation Corporation [*Common carrier symbol*]
MMDU....... Creamery [*Intermodal shipping container symbol*] (TVRC)
MME......... Machinist's Mate, Engineman [*Navy rating*]
Mme......... Madame (WA)
MME......... Major Machine Equipment (MCD)
MME......... Major Movable Equipment (MEDA)
MME......... Man Month Equivalents (SPST)
MME......... Manned Mars Expedition (SAUO)
MME......... Manufacturing Machines and Equipment [*National Science Foundation*] (RCD)
MME......... Master of Manufacturing Engineering (PGP)
MME......... Master of Material Engineering (GAGS)
MME......... Master of Mathematics for Educators (PGP)
MME......... Master of Mechanical Engineering (GAGS)
M Me........ Master of Metaphysics
MME......... Master of Mineral Engineering (GAGS)
MME......... Master of Mining Engineering
MME......... Master of Music Education
MME......... Material Military Establishment [*Formerly, OSRD*] (MCD)
MME......... Maximum Maintenance Effort [*Military*] (AFM)
MMe......... Medford Public Library, Medford, MA [*Library symbol*] [*Library of Congress*] (LCLS)
MME......... Mediterranean Medical Entente (EAIO)
MME......... Methylmethacrylate [*Organic chemistry*]
MME......... Micrometeoric Erosion (AAG)
MME......... Mid-Atlantic Medical Services, Inc. [*NYSE symbol*] (SAG)
MME......... Middlesborough [*England*] [*Airport symbol*] (AD)
MME......... Military Message Experiment (SAUO)
MME......... Milkmaid's Elbow [*Medicine*] (MELL)
MME......... Million Market Edition [*US News and World Report*]
MME......... Minimum Mean Estimate
MME......... Missile Maintenance Equipment (AABC)
MME......... M-Mode Echocardiography [*Medicine*] (DB)
MME......... Mobile Meteorological Equipment (SAUO)
MME......... Montessori Method of Education (WDAA)
MME......... Multimedia Extensions [*Computer science*] (DCOM)
MME......... Tees-Side [*England*] [*Airport symbol*] (OAG)
MMEA....... Maryland Music Educators Association (SAUO)
MMEA....... Massachusetts Music Educators Association (SAUO)
MMEA....... Michigan Music Educators Association (SAUO)
MMEA....... Minnesota Music Educators Association (SAUO)
MMEA....... Mississippi Music Educators Association (SAUO)
MMEA....... Montana Music Educators Association (SAUO)
MMEC....... Machinery Maintenance Engineering Center (AFIT)
MMEC....... Machinery-Metals Export Club [*Later, International Industrial Marketing Club*] (EA)
MMEC....... Migrating Myoelectric Complex [*Physiology*]
M Mech E... Master of Mechanical Engineering
MMechEng... Master of Mechanical Engineering (NADA)
MMECT...... Multimonitored Electroconvulsive Treatment (DIPS)
MMECT...... Multiple-Monitored Electroconvulsive Therapy [*Schizophrenia*]
MMED....... Mass Median Equivalent Diameter [*of airborne particles*]
M Med....... Master of Medicine
MM Ed...... Master of Music Education
MMed....... Moore Medical Corp. [*Associated Press*] (SAG)
MMED....... Multimedia, Inc. [*NASDAQ symbol*] (SAG)
MMedAnaes... Master of Medicine (Anaesthesia)
MMEDC..... Multimedia, Inc. (MHDW)
MMedCardiol... Master of Medicine (Cardiology)
MMed(CM)... Master of Medicine (Community Medicine)
MMedEd.... Master of Medical Education
MMedPaed... Master of Medicine (Paediatrics)
MMedPath... Master of Medicine (Pathology)
MMedRadD... Master of Medicine (Diagnostic Radiology)
M Med Sc... Master of Medical Science
MMedVen... Master of Medicine (Venereology)
MMEE....... Medicare, Medicaid, Education and the Environment [*President Clinton political agenda*]
MMEF....... Maximal Midexpiratory Flow [*Also, MMF*] [*Medicine*]
MMEFR..... Maximal Midexpiratory Flow Rate [*Medicine*]
MMEI........ Mass Media Exposure Index (SAUO)
MMEI........ Military Medicine Education Institute [*DoD*] (DOMA)
MMEI........ Minute-Man Express [*Common carrier symbol*]
MMEL....... Master Minimum Equipment List (DA)
MMel........ Melrose Public Library, Melrose, MA [*Library symbol*] [*Library of Congress*] (LCLS)
MM Eng..... Master of Mechanical Engineering
MMEP....... Marine Mammal Events Program (EA)
MMEP....... Minuteman Education Program [*Air Force*] (AFM)
MMEP....... Missouri Mathematics Effectiveness Project (EDAC)
MMEP....... Multiple Modality Evoked Potential [*Neurophysiology*]
MMEP....... Tepic [*Mexico*] [*ICAO location identifier*] (ICLI)
MMER....... Marine Models Electronic Record (SAUO)
MMES....... Ensenada [*Mexico*] [*ICAO location identifier*] (ICLI)
MMES....... Maritime Mobile Earth Station (ACAE)
MMES....... Martin Marietta Energy Systems, Inc. (SAUO)
MMES....... Master Material Erection Schedule [*Shipbuilding*] (NG)
Mmes....... Mesdames [*Ladies*] [*French*]
MMES....... MSFC [*Marshall Space Flight Center*] Mated Element Systems [*NASA*] (NASA)
MMES....... Southwestern Manitoba Regional Library, Melita, Manitoba [*Library symbol*] [*National Library of Canada*] (NLC)
MMET....... Maintenance Management Engineering Team [*Military*]
M Met....... Master of Metallurgy
MMeT....... Tufts University, Medford, MA [*Library symbol*] [*Library of Congress*] (LCLS)
M Met E.... Master of Metallurgical Engineering
MMetEng... Master of Metallurgy and Engineering, University of Sheffield [*British*] (DBQ)
MMeT-EP... Tufts University, Eliot Pearson Department of Child Study, Medford, MA [*Library symbol*] [*Library of Congress*] (LCLS)
MMeT-F.... Tufts University, Fletcher School of Law and Diplomacy, Medford, MA [*Library symbol*] [*Library of Congress*] (LCLS)
MMeT-Hi.... Tufts University, Universalist Historical Society, Medford, MA [*Library symbol*] [*Library of Congress*] (LCLS)

MMeT-M .... Tufts University, Medical and Dental School, Boston, MA [*Library symbol*] [*Library of Congress*] (LCLS)
MMEX .... Map Maneuver Exercise (MCD)
MMEX .... Mexico [*Mexico*] [*ICAO location identifier*] (ICLI)
MMF .... Fleet Minelayer [*Navy symbol*]
MMF .... Machine Master File (ACAE)
MMF .... Magnetomotive Force (MIST)
mmf .... Magnetomotive Force
MMF .... Make Money Fast (SAUS)
MMF .... Mamfe [*Cameroon*] [*Airport symbol*] (OAG)
MMF .... Maritime Life Assurance Co. [*Toronto Stock Exchange symbol*]
MMF .... Maximum Midexpiratory Flow [*Also, MMEF*] [*Medicine*]
MMF .... Meals for Millions Foundation (SAUO)
MMF .... Mean Maximum Flow [*Medicine*]
MMF .... Mechanical Machine-Finished Paper (DGA)
MMF .... Member of the Medical Faculty
MMF .... Memory Mapped File (SAUS)
MMF .... Microelectronics Manufacturing Facility [*Philco-Ford Corp.*] (MCD)
MMF .... Micromation Microfilm
MMF .... Micromembrane Filter
mmf .... Micromicrofarad (IDOE)
MMF .... Micromicrofarad (MUGU)
MMF .... Milbank Memorial Fund (SAUO)
MMF .... Minelayer, Fleet [*Navy symbol*] [*Obsolete*]
MMF .... Missile Maintenance Facility (ACAE)
MMF .... Mobile Magnetic Field
MMF .... Mobile Missile Facility (MCD)
MMF .... Mobility Maintenance Facility (NVT)
mmf .... Modern Maid Food Products, Inc. (SAUO)
MMF .... Module Maintenance Facility
MMF .... Money Market Fund [*Investment term*]
MMF .... Moravian Music Foundation (EA)
MMF .... Moving Magnetic Feature [*Astronomy*] (OA)
MMF .... Multimode Fiber (ACRL)
MMF .... MultiMode Fiberoptic Cable [*Telecommunications*] (DDC)
MMF .... Music Managers Forum [*United Kingdom*] (EAIO)
MMF .... Mutual Musicians Foundation (EA)
MMF .... National Association of Master Mechanics and Foremen of Naval Shore Establishments
MMFA .... Fireman Apprentice, Machinist's Mate, Striker [*Navy rating*]
MMFA .... Montreal Museum of Fine Arts (SAUO)
MMFA .... Movius, Mevius, Mobius Family Association (EA)
MMFAB ..... Metals and Machine Fabricators (SAUO)
MMFC .... Michael Murphy Fan Club (EA)
MMFCC ..... Master of Marriage, Family and Child Counseling (GAGS)
MMFCG ..... Maintenance Management Functional Coordinating Group [*Army*]
MMFC-MF... Marilyn Monroe Fan Club - Marilyn Forever (EA)
MMFCS ..... Multi-Missile Fire Control System [*Military*]
MMFD .... Micromicrofarad (GPO)
MMFF .... Modular Multizone Furnace Facility (SAUS)
MMFF .... Multimode Fire & Forget (SAUS)
MMFFS ..... Multi-Modular Fluid Filtration System
MMFI .... Moravian Music Foundation, Incorporated (SAUO)
MMFITB ..... Man-Made Fibres Producing Industry Training Board [*British*] (BI)
MMFIY ...... Mitsui Marine and Fire Insurance Co. Ltd. [*OTCBB symbol*]
MMFL .... Mobile Maintenance Facility Liaison (ACAE)
MMFM ...... Modified Modified Frequency Modulation (NITA)
MMFN ...... Fireman, Machinist's Mate, Striker [*Navy rating*]
MMFO ...... Maintenance Management Field Office [*Military*] (MCD)
MMFO ...... Material Management Field Office
MMFPA ..... Man-Made Fiber Producers Association [*Later, MMFPAI*] (EA)
MMFPAI ..... Man-Made Fiber Producers Association, Inc. (EA)
MMFPB ..... Mill Mutual Fire Prevention Bureau [*Defunct*] (EA)
MMFPI ...... Man-Made Fiber Producers Institute (SAUO)
MMFR ...... Maximal Midflow Rate [*Medicine*] (MAE)
MMFR ...... Maximum Midexpiratory Flow Rate [*Physiology*]
MMFS ...... Manufacturing Message Format Service (NITA)
MMFS ...... Manufacturing Message Format Specification [*Communications term*] (DCT)
MMFS ...... Manufacturing Messaging Format Standards [*Automotive engineering*]
MMFT ...... Master of Marriage and Family Therapy (GAGS)
MMFV ...... Manned Mars Flyby Vehicle [*Aerospace*]
MMG .... Machinist's Mate, Industrial Gas Generating Mechanic [*Navy rating*]
MMG .... MacMillan Gold [*Vancouver Stock Exchange symbol*]
MMG .... Magdalena Milpas Altas [*Guatemala*] [*Seismograph station code, US Geological Survey*] (SEIS)
MMG .... Magnetomyogramm (SAUS)
MMG .... Mean Maternal Glucose [*Clinical chemistry*]
MMG .... Mechanomyography [*Medicine*]
MMG .... Medium Machine Gun
MMG .... Metromedia International Group [*AMEX symbol*] (SAG)
MMG .... Motor Machine Gun Corps [*British military*] (DMA)
MMG .... Motor-Motor Generator [*Nuclear energy*] (NRCH)
MMG .... Mount Magnet [*Australia*] [*Airport symbol*] (OAG)
MMG .... Movie Makers Guild (EA)
MMG .... Multimedia Management Group (SAUO)
MMG .... Multimode Guidance (MCD)
MMGA ...... Mannequin and Models' Guild of Australia
MMGB ...... Motor Machine Gun Battalion [*British military*] (DMA)
MMGC ...... Mego Mortgage Corp. [*NASDAQ symbol*] (SAG)
MMGI .... Medical Marketing Group (EFIS)
MMGI .... Member of the Mining, Geological, and Metallurgical Institute of India
MMGL .... Guadalajara/Miguel Hidalgo Y Costilla Internacional [*Mexico*] [*ICAO location identifier*] (ICLI)
MMGM ...... Guaymas/General Jose Maria Yanez Internacional [*Mexico*] [*ICAO location identifier*] (ICLI)
M Mgmt ..... Master of Management (PGP)
MMGR ...... Masai Mara Game Reserve (SAUO)
MMGR ...... Medical Manager Corp. [*NASDAQ symbol*] (NASQ)
MMGS ...... Motor Machine Gun Service [*British military*] (DMA)
MMGS ...... Mount Muhavura Gorilla Sanctuary (SAUO)
MMGT ...... Guanajuato [*Mexico*] [*ICAO location identifier*] (ICLI)
MMgt .... Master of Management
MMGT ...... Medical Management, Inc. [*NASDAQ symbol*] (SAG)
MMGT ...... Microwave Magneto-Transconductance (ACAE)
MMGT ...... Multimastergroup Translator (SAUO)
MMgtE ...... Master of Management Engineering [*Education*] (FOTI)
MMgtEng ... Master of Management Engineering (NADA)
MMGZ ...... Merchants Management [*Federal Railroad Administration identification code*]
MMh .... Abbot Public Library Marblehead, Ma [*Library symbol*] [*Library of Congress*] (LCLS)
MMH .... Macromicromodular Hyperplasia [*Medicine*]
MMH .... Maintenance Man-Hours (NG)
MMH .... Mammoth Lakes [*California*] [*Airport symbol*] (OAG)
MMH .... Mammoth Lakes, CA [*Location identifier*] [*FAA*] (FAAL)
MMH .... Maplex Management & Holdings Ltd. [*Toronto Stock Exchange symbol*]
MMH .... Master of Management in Hospitality (PGP)
MMH .... Master of Medical Humanities (PGP)
MMH .... Meristar Hotels & Resorts [*NYSE symbol*] (SG)
MMH .... Methylmercuric Hydroxide [*Organic chemistry*]
MMH .... Mikromatika Air Cargo Ltd. [*Hungary*] [*ICAO designator*] (FAAC)
MM/H ...... Millimeters per Hour
MMH .... Mismatched Hand Holes [*Tire maintenance*]
MMH .... Monomethylhydrazine [*Organic chemistry*]
MMH .... Multimode Hydrophone [*Military*] (CAAL)
MMHA ...... Maryland Multi-Housing Association (EARSL)
MMHA ...... Metropolitan Mutual Housing Association [*Defunct*] (EA)
MMHA ...... Michigan Manufactured Housing Association (EARSL)
MMHC ...... Tehuacan [*Mexico*] [*ICAO location identifier*] (ICLI)
MMH/FH .... Maintenance Man-Hours per Flight Hours
mmHg ...... Millimeters of Mercury [*A measurement of pressure*] (KSC)
MMhHi ..... Marblehead Historical Society, Marblehead, MA [*Library symbol*] [*Library of Congress*] (LCLS)
MMHi .... Milton Historical Society, Milton, MA [*Library symbol*] [*Library of Congress*] (LCLS)
MMHID ..... Multimedia Human Interface Device (MWOL)
MMHIO ..... Midwest Migrant Health Information Office (EA)
MMH/MA ... Mean Manhours per Maintenance Action
MMHO ...... Hermosillo/Internacional [*Mexico*] [*ICAO location identifier*] (ICLI)
MMH/OH ... Maintenance Man-Hours per Operating Hours (MCD)
MMHQ ...... Meta-Methoxyhydroquinone [*Organic chemistry*]
MMHR ...... Maintenance Man-Hours
MMHR/FH ... Maintenance Man-Hours per Flight Hours (MCD)
MMH/S ..... Maintenance Man-Hours per Sortie [*Aerospace*] (MCD)
MMHS ...... Mechanized Materials Handling System [*Air Force*]
MMHS ...... Military Message Handling System (SAUO)
MMHSRA ... Marine Mammal Health and Stranding Response Act
MMHT ...... Michael H. Mitchell Trucking [*Common carrier symbol*]
MMH/UH .... Maintenance Man-Hours per Utilization Hour (ACAE)
MMI .... Athens, TN [*Location identifier*] [*FAA*] (FAAL)
MMI .... Macrophage Migration Inhibition [*Cytology*]
MMI .... Main Memory Interface (NITA)
MMI .... Major Market Index
MMI .... Malaysian Marine Industries (SAUO)
MMI .... Management and Maintenance Inspection (NVT)
MMI .... Management of Motives Index [*Test*]
MMI .... Man-Machine Interaction (NITA)
MMI .... Man-Machine Interface
MMI .... Manpower Management Information
MMI .... Manufacturing Message Interface [*Data communications standards*]
MMI .... Marshall Management Instruction (SAUO)
MMI .... Martin Marietta International
MMI .... Materials Management Institute
MMI .... Materials Management International (SAUO)
MMI .... Mature Market Institute [*An association*] [*Defunct*] (EA)
MMI .... Mean Motility Index [*For intestine*]
MMI .... Mechanized Manufacturing Information
MMI .... Medicus Mundi Internationalis [*International Organization for Cooperation in Health Care - IOCHC*] [*Nijmegen, Netherlands*] (EAIO)
MMI .... Methylmercaptoimidazole [*Also, METHIMAZOLE*] [*Thyroid inhibitor*]
MMI .... Michigan Molecular Institute, Inc. [*Formerly, Midland Macromolecular Institute*] [*Research center*] (RCD)
MMI .... Micromagnetic Industries
MMI .... Middle Management Institute [*Special Libraries Association*]
MMI .... Midland Macromolecular Institute [*Midland, MI*]
MMI .... Mild [*or Minimal*] Memory Impairment [*Medicine*]
MMI .... Minnesota Mining & Manufacturing Co., St. Paul, MN [*OCLC symbol*] (OCLC)
MMI .... Mintel Market Intelligence [*Database*] [*United Kingdom*] (GDD)
MMI .... MMI Companies [*NYSE symbol*] (SPSG)
MMI .... Mode-Media Interaction (MCD)
MMI .... Mode-Medium Instability (SAUS)
MMI .... Modified Mercalli Intensity [*Earthquake magnitude*] [*Seismology*]
MMI .... Money Management Institute [*Commercial firm*] (EA)

MMI .... Money Management International [*Association*] (EA)
MMI .... Monolithic Memories, Inc. [*Computer science*]
MMI .... Montana Myotis Leukoencephalitis [*Virus*]
MMI .... Monthly Management Information Report (SAUO)
MMI .... Moslem Mosque Incorporated (SAUO)
MMI .... MSFC [*Marshall Space Flight Center*] Management Instruction [*NASA*]
MMI .... Multi-Media Integration (AGLO)
MMI .... Multi-Message Interface (NITA)
MMI .... Multiport Memory Interface [*Computer science*] (MHDB)
MMI .... Mutual Mortgage Insurance Fund [*FHA*] (EMRF)
MMIA .... Colima [*Mexico*] [*ICAO location identifier*] (ICLI)
MMIA .... Medical Malpractice Insurance Association
MMIA .... Military Mission to the Italian Army [*World War II*]
MMI&CS .... Martin Marietta Information and Communication System (ACAE)
MMIB .... Man-Machine Integration Branch [*Ames Research Center*] [*NASA*]
MMIC .... Maintenance Management Information and Control (MCD)
MMIC .... Marinduque Mining and Industrial Corporation (SAUO)
M Mic .... Master of Microbiology
MMIC .... Millimeter/Microwave Integrated Circuit
MMIC .... Miniature Microwave Integrated Circuit
MMIC .... Monolithic Microwave Integrated Circuit
MMI CoS .... MMI Companies [*Associated Press*] (SAG)
MMICRO-LANGUAGE ARTS... Microcomputer Managed Information for Criterion Referenced Objectives-Language Arts [*Educational Development Corp.*] (TES)
MMICRO-MATH... Microcomputer Managed Information for Criterion Referenced Objectives-Math [*R. Hambleton*] (TES)
MMICS ...... Maintenance Management Information and Control System
MMID .... Maryland Midland Railway [*Federal Railroad Administration identification code*]
MMID .... Merida [*Mexico*] [*ICAO location identifier*] (ICLI)
MMidwif .... Master of Midwifery
M Mi E ...... Master of Mining Engineering
MMiEng ..... Master of Mining Engineering (NADA)
MMIF .... Macrophage Migration Inhibitory Factor (DMAA)
MMIF .... Mutual Mortgage Insurance Fund [*Federal Housing Administration*]
MMIFC ...... Marilyn Monroe International Fan Club (EA)
MMI/HMI .... Man-Machine Interface/Human-Machine Interface (GART)
MMIHS ...... Megacystis-Microcolon-Intestinal Hypoperistalsis Syndrome [*Medicine*] (DMAA)
MMII .... Mass Marketing Insurance Institute (EA)
MMII .... Matrix Medica, Inc. [*NASDAQ symbol*] (COMM)
MMII .... Multimedia Individualized Instruction [*Army*]
MMIIL .... Multi-Input Multi-Output Integrated Injection Logic (IAA)
MMIIP .... Multimedia Individualized Instructional Package [*Army*]
MMIIS .... Material Management Integrated Information System (ACAE)
MMIJ .... Mining and Materials Processing Institute of Japan
MMIJ .... Mining and Metallurgical Institute of Japan (SAUO)
M Mil .... Master of Military Science (SAUO)
MMilt .... Milton Public Library, Milton, MA [*Library symbol*] [*Library of Congress*] (LCLS)
MMiltC ...... Curry College, Milton, MA [*Library symbol*] [*Library of Congress*] (LCLS)
MMIM .... Isla Mujeres [*Mexico*] [*ICAO location identifier*] (ICLI)
MMIM .... MMI Medical, Inc. [*NASDAQ symbol*] (COMM)
MMIMS ..... Modular Multi-Influence Minesweeping System (SAUS)
M Min .... Master of Ministries (PGP)
MMinMgt ... Master of Mining Management
MMINTERFACE... Multimedia Assisted Teleoperation (SAUO)
MMIO .... Saltillo [*Mexico*] [*ICAO location identifier*] (ICLI)
MMIP .... Maintenance Management Improvement Program (MCD)
MMIP .... Manual of Meat Inspection Procedures [*of the USDA*]
MMIPS ...... Man-Machine Interactive Processing System (PDAA)
MMIPS ...... Multiple Mode Integrated Propulsion System (PDAA)
MMIR .... Multispectral Microwave Imaging Radiometer (ACAE)
MMIRA ...... Multi-Mission Intermeshing Rotor Aircraft (SAUS)
MMIRC ...... Mind-Machine Interaction Research Center [*University of Florida*] [*Research center*] (RCD)
MMIS .... Maintenance Management Information System [*Military*] (AFM)
MMIS .... Manpower Management Information System (SAUS)
MMIS .... Master of Management Information Systems (GAGS)
MMIS .... Material Management Information System [*Management information systems*]
MMIS .... Materials Management Information System (SAUO)
MMIS .... Materials Manager Information System (SAUO)
MMIS .... Medicaid Management and Information System [*Medicine*] [*HEW*] (EDAA)
MMIS .... Medicaid Management Information System [*HEW*]
MMIS .... Medical Management Information System (MHCS)
MMIS .... Member of the Mining Institute of Scotland (SAUO)
MMIS .... Mortgage Market Information Service
MMIS .... Multinational Meetings Information Services BV [*Netherlands*] [*Information service or system*] (IID)
MMIS .... Municipal Management Information System [*Civil Defense*]
M Miss ...... Master of Missiology (PGP)
MMIT .... Iztepec [*Mexico*] [*ICAO location identifier*] (ICLI)
MMIT .... Man-Machine Interrogation Technique
MMIT .... Microsoft Mobile Internet Toolkit
MMITI .... Martin Marietta Information Technology Institute (ACAE)
MMITS ...... Modular Multifunction Information Transfer System (SAUO)
MMIU .... Multi-Part Memory Interface Unit (NITA)
MMIU .... Multiport Memory Interface Unit
MMIZ .... Montana Merchandising Industries [*Federal Railroad Administration identification code*]
MMJ .... Main Metering Jet [*Automotive engineering*]
MMJ .... Majhwar [*Language symbol*] (ETLW)
MMJ .... Matsumoto [*Japan*] [*Airport symbol*] (OAG)
MMJ .... Modified Modular Jack (SAUO)
MMJ .... Pittsburgh, PA [*Location identifier*] [*FAA*] (FAAL)
MMJA .... Jalapa [*Mexico*] [*ICAO location identifier*] (ICLI)
MMJC .... Meridian Municipal Junior College [*Mississippi*]
MMJP .... Main Metering Jet-Primary [*Automotive engineering*]
MMJS .... Main Metering Jet-Secondary [*Automotive engineering*]
MMK .... Loparskaya [*Formerly, Murmansk*] [*Former USSR*] [*Geomagnetic observatory code*]
MMK .... Maison Master Keyed [*Locks*] (ADA)
MMK .... Marshall-Marchetti-Krantz [*Procedure*] [*Medicine*] (MEDA)
MMK .... Material Mark
MMK .... Meriden, CT [*Location identifier*] [*FAA*] (FAAL)
MMK .... Murmansk [*Former USSR*] [*Airport symbol*] (OAG)
MMKA .... Management & Marketing Abstracts [*Database*] [*United Kingdom*] (GDD)
MMKR .... Middle Marker [*in an instrument landing system*]
MML .... Machinist's Mate (General) [*U.S. Navy enlisted rating*] (AUER)
MML .... Maintenance Management Level [*Military*]
MML .... Maker Markup Language [*Computer science*] (AGLO)
MML .... Managing the Modern Laboratory [*A publication*]
MML .... Man-Machine Language [*Computer science*] (TEL)
MML .... Manual of Military Law [*British*]
MML .... Marshall [*Minnesota*] [*Airport symbol*] (OAG)
MML .... Marshall, MN [*Location identifier*] [*FAA*] (FAAL)
MML .... Marx Memorial Library (SAUO)
MML .... Maryland MEMS Laboratory [*University of Maryland at College Park*] (RCD)
MML .... Massachusetts Mutual Life Insurance Co. (EFIS)
MML .... Mass Mutual Mortgage and Realty Investors (SAUO)
MML .... Master Measurements List (NASA)
MML .... Master of Modern Languages
MML .... Mathematics Markup Language (SAUS)
MML .... McKinley Memorial Library, Niles, OH [*OCLC symbol*] (OCLC)
MML .... Memorial [*Telegraphy*] (PCTE)
MML .... Menika Mining Ltd. [*Vancouver Stock Exchange symbol*]
MML .... Merrill Lyn 6.50%'STRYPES' [*NYSE symbol*] (TTSB)
MML .... Merrill Lynch & Co. [*NYSE symbol*] (SAG)
MML .... Metal-Metal Laminate
MML .... Michigan Municipal League (EARSL)
MML .... Micromedia Ltd. [*ACCORD*] [*UTLAS symbol*]
mM/L .... Millimole/Liter [*Chemistry*]
MML .... Minimum Message Length (IDAI)
MML .... Missouri Municipal League (SAUO)
MML .... Mobile Media Line
MML .... Moloney Murine Leukemia [*Medicine*] (DMAA)
MML .... Monomethyllysine (DB)
MML .... Mote Marine Laboratory (NOAA)
MML .... Motor Movement Latency
MML .... Multimaterial Laminate
MML .... Myelomonocytic Leukemia [*Medicine*] (DMAA)
MMLA .... Midwest Modern Language Association (BARN)
MMLA .... Military Mission of Liaison Administration [*World War II*]
MMLAN ..... Multi Media Local Area Network (ACAE)
MMLC .... Lazaro Cardenas [*Mexico*] [*ICAO location identifier*] (ICLI)
MMLC .... Medium Mobility Load Carrier (SAUS)
MMLD .... Merchant Mariners Licensing and Documentation [*BTS*] (TAG)
MMLE .... Modified Maximum Likelihood Estimates [*Statistics*]
MMLEC ...... Munitions Management and Labour Efficiency Committee [*British*] [*World War II*]
MMLES ...... Map-Matching Location - Estimation System [*Aviation*]
mmlhg ...... Millimeters of Mercury [*Medicine*] (BCRP)
MMLL .... Michigan Regional Libraries Film Program at Cadillac [*Library network*]
MMLM ...... Los Mochis [*Mexico*] [*ICAO location identifier*] (ICLI)
MMLME ..... Mediterranean, Mediterranean Littoral, and/or Middle East
MMLO .... Leon [*Mexico*] [*ICAO location identifier*] (ICLI)
MMLP .... La Paz/General Manuel Marquez de Leon Internacional [*Mexico*] [*ICAO location identifier*] (ICLI)
MMLP .... Mesa Midcontinent Limited Partnership (EFIS)
MMLRF ..... Micro Modular Laser Range Finder (ACAE)
MMLS .... Martin Motor Lines [*Common carrier symbol*]
MMLS .... Measuring for Medicine and the Life Sciences [*Medicine*] [*Journal*] (EDAA)
MMLS .... Military Microwave Landing System (MCD)
MMLS .... Mobile Microwave Landing System (SAUO)
M-M-L-S .... Model-Modes-Loads-Stresses [*Aerospace*] (NAKS)
MMLSA ..... Military Microwave Landing System, Avionics (DWSG)
MMLT .... Loreto [*Mexico*] [*ICAO location identifier*] (ICLI)
MMLV .... Moloney Murine Leukaemia Virus [*Medicine*] (BABM)
MMLV .... Moloney Murine Leukemia Virus [*of mice*] [*Veterinary medicine*] (DAVI)
MMM .... 3M [*Company symbol*]
MMM .... Aviation Co. Meridian [*Former USSR*] [*FAA designator*] (FAAC)
MMM .... International Association of Margaret Morris Method (SAUO)
MMM .... Magnetism and Magnetic Materials
MMM .... Maine Maritime Academy, Castine, ME [*OCLC symbol*] (OCLC)
MMM .... Maintenance and Material Management [*Navy*]
MMM .... Maintenance Management Manual
MMM .... Maintenance Man-Minute
MMM .... Manned Maneuvering Module [*Aerospace*] (IIA)
MMM .... Manned Mars Mission [*NASA*]
MMM .... Margaret Morris Movement [*British*] (BI)

MMM........ Marine & Aviation Management International [*British*] [*ICAO designator*] (FAAC)
MMM........ Marine Multipurpose Missile (DNAB)
MMM........ Mariner Mission to Mars (ACAE)
MMM........ Mark Master Mason [*Freemasonry*]
MMM........ Mars Mission Module
MMM........ Mass Media Ministries [*An association*]
MMM........ Master in Media Management
MMM........ Master of Management in Manufacturing (PGP)
MMM........ Master of Medical Management (PGP)
MMM........ Master of Ministry Management (PGP)
MMM........ Material Maintenance Management (MCD)
MMM........ Material Movement Management (AAEL)
MMM........ Materials Management Manual (SAUO)
MMM........ Mauritian Militant Movement (SAUO)
MMM........ McAdam Resources, Inc. [*Toronto Stock Exchange symbol*]
MMM........ Meaningful Measures of Merit (SAUO)
MMM........ Measuring Monitoring Module (KSC)
MMM........ Medical Materiel Manager [*Military*] (AABC)
MMM........ Medical Missionaries of Mary [*Roman Catholic women's religious order*]
MMM........ Member of the Order of Military Merit [*Canada*] (DD)
MMM........ Memory Mapper Modul (SAUO)
MMM........ Mesocale and Microscale Meteorology (GNE)
MMM........ Micro Macro Magician (SAUS)
mmm........ Micromillimeter (WGA)
MMM........ Microsome-Mediated Mutagenesis (DB)
MMM........ Middle Management Module
MMM........ Middlemount [*Australia*] [*Airport symbol*] (OAG)
MMM........ Militia Mea Multiplex [*Pseudonym used by William Tooke*]
mmm........ Millimicron [*Microscopy*] (CPH)
MMM........ Minnesota Mining & Manufacturing Co. [*Also known as 3M Co.*] [*Associated Press*] (SAG)
MMM........ Minnesota Mining and Manufacturing Co. [*NYSE symbol*]
M:MM....... Mission: Moving Mountains [*Association*] (EA)
MMM........ Mobile Media Mode (SAUS)
MMM........ Mode Management Module (SAUO)
MMM........ Modern Music Management (SAUO)
MMM........ Modern Music Masters Society
MMM........ Money Market Monitor [*Financial Products Group*] [*Information service or system*] (IID)
MMM........ Monomethylmetoxuron [*Organic chemistry*]
MMM........ Montana Myotis Meningoencephalitis [*Medicine*] (DB)
MMM........ Mormon Mesa, NV [*Location identifier*] [*FAA*] (FAAL)
MMM........ Mouvement Militant Mauricien [*Mauritian Militant Movement*] [*Political party*] (PPW)
MMM........ Mouvement Mondial des Meres [*World Movement of Mothers - WMM*] [*Paris, France*] (EAIO)
MMM........ Multigrid Modulator Multiplier
MMM........ Multi-Mission Missile (ACAE)
MMM........ Multimission Module [*Aerospace*]
MMM........ Multimode Mode Matrix (MCD)
MMM........ Myelofibrosis and Myeloid Metaplasia [*Hematology*]
MMM........ Myelosclerosis with Myeloid Metaplasia [*Medicine*] (MAE)
MMM........ Mysteria Mystica Maxima (SAUO)
MMMA...... Maine Merchant Marine Academy (SAUO)
MMMA...... Matamoros Internacional [*Mexico*] [*ICAO location identifier*] (ICLI)
MMMA...... Metalforming Machinery Makers Association [*British*] (DBA)
MMMA...... Milking Machine Manufacturers Association [*British*] (DBA)
MMMA...... Music Masters and Mistresses Association (AIE)
MMM&SA... Master Monumental Masons and Sculptors Association (SAUO)
MM(MB).... Machinist's Mate (Motor Boat) [*U.S. Navy enlisted rating*] (AUER)
MMMC...... Machine Material Movement Component (AAEL)
MMMC...... M & M Manufacturing Company [*NCIC trailer make code*]
MMMC...... Medical Materiel Management Center [*Military*] (AABC)
MMMC...... Milking Machine Manufacturers Council (EA)
MMMC...... Minimum Monthly Maintenance Charge (MHDW)
MMMD...... Merida/Lic. Manuel Crecencio Rejon Internacional [*Mexico*] [*ICAO location identifier*] (ICLI)
MMMDCS... Multi-National Maintenance Management Data Collection System (SAUO)
MMME...... Martin Marietta Missile Electronics Division [*Military*]
MMME...... Master of Metallurgical and Materials Engineering (PGP)
MMMEP..... Military Manpower Management Evaluation Project (NG)
MMMF...... Man-Made Mineral Fiber
MMMF...... Money Market Mutual Fund [*Investment term*]
MMMF...... Multinational Mixed Manned Force (NATG)
MMMFS..... Money Market Mutual Fund Shares [*Investment term*]
MMMFTP... Matched Maturity Marginal Fund Transfer Pricing (EBF)
MMMI...... Meat Machinery Manufacturers Institute (EA)
MMMIS..... Maintenance and Material Management Information System
MMML...... Mexicali/General Rodolfo Sanchez Taboada Internacional [*Mexico*] [*ICAO location identifier*] (ICLI)
MMMLTG... Mixed Media Multi-Link Transmission Group (SAUO)
MMMM..... Man, Material, Machinery, Methods [*Statistical process control*]
MMMM..... Morelia [*Mexico*] [*ICAO location identifier*] (ICLI)
MMMN..... [*The*] Memorial of Moses on Mount Nebo [*A publication*] (BJA)
MMMOS.... Mobile Micrometeorological Observation System
MMMPC.... Maintenance and Material Management Project Center [*Navy*]
MMMR...... Medical Material Mission Reserve [*Military*] (AABC)
MMMS...... Maintenance and Material Management System (KSC)
MMMS...... Martin Marietta Manned Space System (SAUO)
MMMS...... Martin Marietta Missile System [*Military*]
MMMS...... Material Movement Management Standard (AAEL)
MMMS...... Medical Materiel Management System (SAUO)
MMMS...... Merck Molecular Modelling System (DB)
MMMS...... Militarized Multimission Modular Spacecraft (SAUS)
MMMS...... Minerals, Metals, and Materials Society (EA)
MMMS...... Modern Music Masters Society (SAUO)
MMMS...... Multi-Mission Management System (SAUS)
MMMS-OL... Medical Materiel Management System-On Line [*Air Force*] (GFGA)
MMMSP..... Mouvement Militant Mauricien Socialiste Progressiste [*Mauritius Militant Socialist Progressive Movement*] (PPW)
MMMT...... Malignant Mixed Mesodermal Tumor [*Medicine*] (MELL)
MMMT...... Malignant Mixed Muellerian Tumor [*Oncology*]
MMMT...... Metastatic Mixed Mullerian Tumor [*Medicine*] (MELL)
MMMT...... Minatitlan [*Mexico*] [*ICAO location identifier*] (ICLI)
MMMTF..... Mobilization Materiel Management Task Force
MMMU...... Morcontainer Sovinfolt [*Intermodal shipping container symbol*] (TVRC)
MMM/UH... Maintenance Man-Minutes per Utilization Hour (ACAE)
MMMV...... Monclova [*Mexico*] [*ICAO location identifier*] (ICLI)
MMMX...... Mexico/Lic. Benito Juarez Internacional [*Mexico*] [*ICAO location identifier*] (ICLI)
MMMX...... Minnesota Mining and Manufacturing [*Private rail car owner code*]
MMMY...... Monterrey/General Mariano Escobedo Internacional [*Mexico*] [*ICAO location identifier*] (ICLI)
MMMZ...... Mazatlan/General Rafael Buelna [*Mexico*] [*ICAO location identifier*] (ICLI)
MMn......... Elizabth Taber Library, Marion, MA [*Library symbol*] [*Library of Congress*] (LCLS)
MMN........ Maintenance Module Node (ACAE)
MMN........ Marathon Minerals [*Vancouver Stock Exchange symbol*]
MMN........ Medial Muscle Motoneuron [*Neuroanatomy*]
MMN........ Medical Moral Newsletter [*Medicine*] [*Formerly MNR*] (EDAA)
MMN........ Miami, FL [*Location identifier*] [*FAA*] (FAAL)
MMN........ Mismatch Negativity [*Neurophysiology*]
MMN........ Modified Melin-Norkram's Agar [*Microbiology*]
MMN........ Morbus Maculosus Neonatorum [*Medicine*] (DMAA)
MMN........ Multiple Mucosal Neuroma [*Medicine*] (EDAA)
MMN........ Museum of Man and Nature (SAUO)
MMNA....... Moto Morini Club of North America (EA)
MMNAFWB... Master's Men of the National Association of Free Will Baptists (EA)
MMNC....... Marrow Mononuclear Cell (DMAA)
MMNG....... Nogales/Internacional [*Mexico*] [*ICAO location identifier*] (ICLI)
MMNIC...... Main Mediterranean Naval Intelligence Center [*Navy*]
MMNL....... Nuevo Laredo [*Mexico*] [*ICAO location identifier*] (ICLI)
MMNOM.... Monmouths Nominal [*Software engineering cost model*]
MMNP....... Mount McKinley National Park (SAUO)
MM(NSW)... Milk Marketing (New South Wales) [*Australia*]
MMNU....... Nautla [*Mexico*] [*ICAO location identifier*] (ICLI)
MMNZ....... Modern Medicine of New Zealand [*Medicine*] [*Journal*] (EDAA)
MMO........ Intel Mobile Module [*Computer science*]
MM(O)...... Machinist's Mate (Optician) [*U.S. Navy enlisted rating*] (AUER)
MMO........ Mach Max Operating (GAVI)
MMO........ Main Meteorological Office
MMO........ Maintenance Management Office (SAUO)
MMO........ Maio [*Cape Verde Islands*] [*Airport symbol*] (OAG)
MMO........ Marseilles, IL [*Location identifier*] [*FAA*] (FAAL)
Mmo......... Maximum operating (SAUS)
M_{mo}......... Maximum Operating Mach Number [*Aviation*] (DA)
MMO........ Medio Mundo [*Nicaragua*] [*Seismograph station code, US Geological Survey*] (SEIS)
MMO........ Medium Machine Oil (BARN)
MMO........ Mercantile Marine Office [*or Officer*] [*British*]
MMO........ Methane Monooxygenase [*An enzyme*]
MMO........ Micrographics Management Officer (MCD)
MMO........ Minuteman Ordnance (SAA)
MMO........ MIPR [*Military Interdepartmental Purchase Request*] Management Office (AFIT)
MMO........ Mismatched Outer Diameter [*Tire maintenance*]
MMO........ Mission Management Office (ACAE)
MMO........ Mission Management Office Meeting (SAUO)
MMO........ MMT Resources [*Vancouver Stock Exchange symbol*]
MMO........ Mobile Module [*Computer science*]
MMO........ Monarch Machine Tool Co. [*NYSE symbol*] (SPSG)
MMO........ Multimodel Optimization (AAEL)
MMO........ Music Minus One [*Recording label*]
MMOA....... Martin Marietta Orlando Aerospace (ACAE)
MMOA....... Maxillary Mandibular Odentectomy Alveolectomy [*Dentistry*] (DAVI)
MMOA....... Mobile Modular Office Association (EA)
MMOAG..... Research Station, Agriculture Canada [*Station de Recherches, Agriculture Canada*] Morden, Manitoba [*Library symbol*] [*National Library of Canada*] (NLC)
MMOB....... Military Money Order Branch (AFM)
MMOBCD... Millions of Octane-Barrels per Calendar Day [*Petroleum industry*]
MMOC....... Modified Method of Characteristics [*Environmental Protection Agency*] (AEPA)
MMOC....... Multimissions Operations Center (ACAE)
MMOD....... Micromodule (IEEE)
M Mod A.... Museum of Modern Art (SAUO)
MMODE..... Mirror Mode (MCD)
MMODS..... Master Material Ordering and Delivery Schedule (DNAB)
MMOECB... Maintenance Mode Operational Equipment Checkout Box (MCD)
MMOF....... Merchants Motor Freight [*Common carrier symbol*]
MMOG....... Massively Multiplayer Online Games
MMOG....... Merchant Marine Officers Guild [*Defunct*] (EA)
MMOL....... Manned Orbital Laboratory (SAUO)
mmol........ micromole (SAUS)

mmol........ Millimole [*Mass*]
MMoL........ Myelomonoblastic Leukemia [*Medicine*] (DMAA)
mmol/l........ Millimole per Liter [*Measurement*] (DAVI)
MMONS........ Methyl-methoxy-nitrostilbene [*Organic chemistry*]
MMOR........ McM Corp. [*OTCBB symbol*]
MMORPGS... Massively Multiplayer Online Role-Playing Games [*Multiplayer Internet games*] (NETL)
MMOS........ Message Multiplexer Operating System
MMOS........ Mobile Micrometeorological Observation System (KSC)
MMOS........ Modified Metal-Oxide Semiconductor (AAEL)
MMOS........ Multicomputing Multitasking Operating System (NITA)
MMOS........ Multi-Modal Organ Modeling System (SAUO)
mmos........ Multimode Optical Sensor (NAKS)
MMOS........ Multimode Optical Sensor (NASA)
MMOU........ Multilateral Memorandum of Understanding
MMOW........ Morden-Winkler Regional Library, Morden, Manitoba [*Library symbol*] [*National Library of Canada*] (NLC)
MMOW........ South Central Regional Library, Morden, Manitoba [*Library symbol*] [*National Library of Canada*] (NLC)
MMOX........ Oaxaca [*Mexico*] [*ICAO location identifier*] (ICLI)
MMP........ AMP, Inc. [*FAA designator*] (FAAC)
MMP........ International Organization of Masters, Mates, and Pilots (EA)
MMP........ Machined Metal Part
MMP........ Machine Main Performance (VLIE)
MMP........ Magnetospheric Multiprobe (SSD)
MMP........ Magnetotactic, Many-Celled Prokaryote [*Biology*]
MMP........ Magyar Megujulas Partja [*Party of Hungarian Renewal*] [*Political party*] (PPE)
MMP........ Main Micro-Processor (VLIE)
MMP........ Maintenance and Modernization Program (ACAE)
MMP........ Maintenance Management Plan
MMP........ Maintenance Management Program (SAUO)
MMP........ Maintenance Message Process [*Telecommunications*] (TEL)
MMP........ Maintenance Monitor Panel (MCD)
MMP........ M & M Porcupine Gold Mines [*Vancouver Stock Exchange symbol*]
MMP........ Manufacturing Methods Procedure (MCD)
MMP........ Marian Movement of Priests (EA)
MMP........ Marilyn Monroe Productions, Inc. (SAUO)
MMP........ Maritime Mobile Phone
MMP........ Mashonaland Mounted Police [*British military*] (DMA)
MMP........ Massively Multi-Processing [*Computer science*] (VLIE)
MMP........ Master Mobilization Plan [*DoD*]
MMP........ Master Music Printers and Engravers Association (DGA)
MMP........ Master of Marine Policy (GAGS)
MMP........ Master of Museum Practice (GAGS)
MMP........ Master of Music Performance (PGP)
MMP........ Masters in Management Program (SAUO)
MMP........ Matabeleland Mounted Police [*British military*] (DMA)
MMP........ Materials Management Plan (ABAC)
MMP........ Matrix Metalloproteinase [*An enzyme*]
MMP........ Maxim Pharmaceuticals, Inc. [*AMEX symbol*] (SAG)
MMP........ Mean Maximum Pressure (SAUS)
MMP........ Medical Mission Planner (SAUO)
MMP........ Merchant Marine Personnel Division [*Coast Guard*]
MMP........ Meteorological Monitoring Plan (SAUO)
MMP........ Methadone Maintenance Program
MMP........ Methyl-D-Mannopyranoside [*Organic chemistry*]
MMP........ Microprogrammable Multiprocessor (MCD)
MMP........ Microsatellite Mutator Phenotype [*Cytology*]
MMP........ Military Microprocessor (ACAE)
MMP........ Military Mounted Police
MMP........ Minimum Miscibility Pressure [*Physical chemistry*]
MMP........ Missile Mode Panel (MCD)
mmp........ Mixed Melting Point [*Chemistry*]
MMP........ Mixed-Member Proportion (New Zealand) [*Political party*] (PSAP)
MMP........ Modernization Management Plan
MMP........ Modes in Math Project [*National Science Foundation*]
MMP........ Modular Midcourse Package [*DoD*]
MMP........ Modular Mission Payload (SAUS)
MMP........ Module Message Processor [*Communications term*] (DCT)
MMP........ Momentum Management Program [*NASA*] (KSC)
MMP........ Mompos [*Colombia*] [*Airport symbol*] (OAG)
MMP........ Money Market Preferred Stock [*Investment term*]
MMP........ Money Market Premium (AGLO)
MMP........ Monitoring/Metering Panel [*Telecommunications*] (OA)
MMP........ Mortar Master Plan [*Military*] (INF)
MMP........ Mount Mary [*New Zealand*] [*Seismograph station code, US Geological Survey*] (SEIS)
MMP........ Multiplexed Message Processor
MMP........ Munich Military Post (SAUO)
MMPA........ Magnetic Materials Producers Association (EA)
MMPA........ Magnetic Materials Products Association (AAGC)
MMPA........ Marine Mammals Protection Act [*1972*]
MMPA........ Mining and Mineral Policy Act of 1970 (COE)
MMPA........ Mississippi Meat Packers Association (EARSL)
MMPA........ Poza Rica [*Mexico*] [*ICAO location identifier*] (ICLI)
MMPAC........ Mississippi Medical PAC [*Ridgeland, MS*] (PACS)
MMPAS........ Mobilization Manpower Policy Analysis [*Military*]
MMPB........ Manpower Management Planning Board
MMPB........ Michigan Medical Practice Board [*Medicine*] (EDAA)
MMPB........ Puebla [*Mexico*] [*ICAO location identifier*] (ICLI)
MMPC........ Maritime Mobile Phone Coastal
MMPC........ Market Milk Producers' Council [*Australia*]
MMPC........ Mobilization Material Procurement Capability
MMPC........ Multi Message Package Chaffing (SAUS)
MMPC........ Pachuca [*Mexico*] [*ICAO location identifier*] (ICLI)
MMPD........ Material Movement Priority Designator (DNAB)
MMPD........ Methoxy-Meta-Phenylenediamine [*Organic chemistry*]
MMPD........ Money Manager Profile Diskettes [*Investment Management Institute*] [*Information service or system*] (IID)
MMPDABC... Medical Materiel Program for Defense Against Biological and Chemical Agents [*Army*] (AABC)
MMPDABC... Prepositioned Materiel Program for Defense Against Biological and Chemical Agents (SAUO)
MMPDC........ Maritime Mobile Phone Distress and Calling
MMPDS........ Methoxy-Meta-Phenylenediamine Sulfate [*Organic chemistry*]
MMPE........ Punta Penasco [*Mexico*] [*ICAO location identifier*] (ICLI)
MMPF........ Master Military Pay File (AABC)
MMPF........ Microgravity and Materials Processing Facility
MMPG........ Piedras Negras [*Mexico*] [*ICAO location identifier*] (ICLI)
MMPGS........ Massively Multi-Player Games
MMPI........ Marquest Medical Products, Inc. [*NASDAQ symbol*] (NQ)
MMPI........ McGill-Melzack Pain Index [*Questionnaire and Home Life Change Index*] (DAVI)
MMPI........ Minnesota Multiphasic Personality Inventory [*Psychology*]
MMPI........ Montgomery Medical and Psychological Institute (EA)
MMPI-2........ Minnesota Multiphasic Personality Inventory-2 (DIPS)
MMPI-A........ Minnesota Multiphasic Personality Inventory-Adolescent (DIPS)
MMPI-D........ Depression scale of the Minnesota Multiphasic Personality Inventory (SAUS)
MMPI-Ds........ Minnesota Multiphasic Personality Inventory - Depression Scale [*Medicine*] (EDAA)
MMPM........ Marine Management Programming Model (SAUO)
MMPM........ Multimedia Presentation Manager [*IBM Corp.*] (PCM)
MMPN........ Uruapan [*Mexico*] [*ICAO location identifier*] (ICLI)
MMPNC........ Medical Materiel Program for Nuclear Casualties [*Army*] (AABC)
MMPO........ Mission Management and Planning Office (SAUO)
MMPP........ Mechanized Market Programming Procedures [*Computer science*] (TEL)
mmpp........ Millimeters Partial Pressure
MMPP........ Moose Mountain Provincial Park (SAUO)
MMPPPA........ Medicare and Medicaid Patient and Program Protection Act
MMPR........ Methylmercaptopurine Ribose [*Biochemistry*]
MMPR........ Missile Manufacturer's Planning Report
MMPR........ Puerto Vallarta/Lic. Gustavo Dias Ordaz Internacional [*Mexico*] [*ICAO location identifier*] (ICLI)
MMPS........ Manpower Mobilization Planning System (SAUO)
MMPS........ Manufacturing Material Planning System (MHDB)
MMPS........ Manufacturing Message Format System
MMPS........ Medical Media Production Service [*Commercial firm*] (DAVI)
MMPS........ Money Market Preferred Stock (EBF)
MMPS........ Puerto Escondido [*Mexico*] [*ICAO location identifier*] (ICLI)
MMPSE........ Multiuse Mission Payload Support Equipment (MCD)
MMPT........ Man-Machine Partnership Translation [*Telecommunications*] (IEEE)
MMPT........ Modem Media.Poppe Tyson'A' [*NASDAQ symbol*] (SG)
MMPT........ Monitored and Modulated Periodontal Therapeutics [*Dentistry*]
mm-PTH........ Mid-Molecule Parathyroid Hormone [*Endocrinology*] (DAVI)
MMPU........ Memory Manager and Protect Unit (IEEE)
MMPVS........ Modified Military Pay Voucher System (AABC)
MMPW........ Matched Mean Percentage Weight [*Medicine*] (EDAA)
MMQ........ Market Milk Quota (SAUO)
MMQ........ Minimum Manufacturing Quality
MMQ........ Moos Menstrual Questionnaire [*Medicine*] (EDAA)
MMQT........ Queretaro [*Mexico*] [*ICAO location identifier*] (ICLI)
MMR........ Austin, TX [*Location identifier*] [*FAA*] (FAAL)
MMR........ Machinist's Mate, Refrigeration [*Navy rating*]
MMR........ Mach Meter Reading (MCD)
MMR........ Magnetically-Modulated Microwave Reflection [*Spectrometer*]
MMR........ Magnetic Memory Record (NITA)
MMR........ Maine State Department of Marine Resources, West Boothbay Harbor, ME [*OCLC symbol*] (OCLC)
MMR........ Main Memory Register
MMR........ Maintenance Management Report (SAUO)
MMR........ Maintenance Management Review (ACAE)
MMR........ Management Milestone Records [*Navy*] (NG)
MMR........ Mass Migration Response (DEMM)
MMR........ Mass Miniature Radiography
MMR........ Master Microfiche Record
MMR........ Master of Marketing Research (GAGS)
MMR........ Materiel Management Review [*DoD*]
MMR........ Maternal Mortality Rate [*Gynecology*]
MMR........ Maternal Mortality Ratio (SAUO)
MMR........ McMoRan Exploration [*NYSE symbol*] (SG)
MMR........ McMoran Exploration Co. [*NYSE symbol*]
MMR........ Mean Motion Resonance [*Astrophysics*]
MMR........ Measles-Mumps-Rubella [*Immunology*]
MMR........ Merchant Marine Reserve (DNAB)
MMR........ Method of Mixed Ranges (PDAA)
MMR........ Methyl-Directed Mismatch Repair
MMR........ Midland Medical Review [*Medicine*] [*United Kingdom*] [*Journal*] (EDAA)
MMR........ Midline Malignant Reticulosis [*Hematology*] (DAVI)
MMR........ Mild Mental Retardation (MELL)
MMR........ Military Media Review [*A publication*] (DNAB)
MMR........ Miniature Micropower Resistor
MMR........ Minimum Marginal Return
MMR........ Minimum Military Requirement (SAUS)
MMR........ Minnedosa Regional Library, Minnedosa, Manitoba [*Library symbol*] [*National Library of Canada*] (NLC)

MMR .... Minnesota & Manitoba Railroad [*Federal Railroad Administration identification code*]
MMR .... Mismatch Repair [*Genetics*]
MMR .... Missed Message Rate (CAAL)
MMR .... Mitchell's Maritime Register [*England*] [*A publication*] (DLA)
MMR .... Mixed Municipal Refuse
MMR .... Mobile Mass Radiography [*Medicine*] (EDAA)
MMR .... Mobile Mass X-Ray (MAE)
MMR .... Mobilization Materiel Requirement [*Military*]
MMR .... Moderate Mental Retardation (DIPS)
MMR .... Modular Multiband Radiometer
MMR .... Monomethylolrutin [*Organic chemistry*]
MMR .... Monroe Mendelsohn Research, Inc. [*Information service or system*] (IID)
MMR .... Monthly Management Review (ACAE)
MMR .... Monthly Meteorological Records (DNAB)
MMR .... Monthly Musical Record (SAUO)
MMR .... Monumental Maintenance Requirements (MCD)
MMR .... Morris Minor Registry (EA)
MMR .... Motorized Microfilm Reader
MMR .... Mouth-to-Mouth Resucitation (MELL)
MMR .... Multi-Market Radio
MMR .... Multi Mission Radar (ACAE)
MMR .... Multimode RADAR
MMR .... Multimode Radiometer (MCD)
MMR .... Multi-Mode Receiver [*Navigation systems*]
MMR .... Multiple Match Resolver
MMR .... Mustang Motorcycle Registry [*Defunct*] (EA)
MMR .... Myocardial Metabolic Rate [*Cardiology*] (MAE)
MMRA....... Maritime Marshland Rehabilitation Administration (SAUO)
MMRA....... Maritime Marshland Rehabilitation Association (SAUO)
MMRA....... Metallurgique et Miniere de Rodange-Athus (EFIS)
MMRA....... Mobilization Materiel Requirement Adjustment [*Military*] (NG)
MMR & S... Military Medical Research and Services Program (CINC)
MMRB....... Maintenance Management Review Board (MCD)
MMRB....... Master Material Review Board (NADA)
MMRB....... Materiel Management Review Board (AFIT)
MMRB....... MOS [*Military Occupational Specialty*] Medical Retention Board [*Army*]
MMRBM .... Mobile Medium-Range Ballistic Missile [*Air Force*]
MMRC....... Materials and Mechanics Research Center [*Army*] (MCD)
MMRC....... Materiel Management Review Committee (SAUO)
MMRC....... Mature Market Resource Center (EA)
MMRC....... Mental Retardation Research Center
MMRC....... Mountain Meadow Research Center [*Colorado State University*] [*Research center*] (RCD)
M-MRCP.... Multi-Management Resolution Control Processor
MMRD....... Materials and Molecular Research Division [*Lawrence Berkeley Laboratory*] [*Research center*] (RCD)
MMRD....... Miniature Multipurpose RADIAC Device (MCD)
MMRD....... Multi Mode Radar Display (ACAE)
MMRDDP... Multi Mode Radar Digital Doppler Processor (ACAE)
MMRE....... Materials Methods Research and Engineering (MCD)
MMRF....... Marshfield Medical Research Foundation (HGEN)
MMRFS..... Multi Mode Radar Feasibility Study (ACAE)
MMRH....... MMR Holding Corp. [*NASDAQ symbol*] (COMM)
MMRI........ Macheezmo Mouse Restaurants, Inc. [*NASDAQ symbol*] (SAG)
MMRI........ Metallurgy and Materials Science Research Institute [*Thailand*] (BUAC)
MMRI........ Mississippi Mineral Resources Institute [*University of Mississippi*] [*Research center*] (RCD)
MMRIM..... Mat Molding Reaction Injection Molding [*Plastics technology*]
MMRI........ Macheezmo Mouse Restaurants [*NASDAQ symbol*] (TTSB)
MMRP....... Marine Corps Midrange Objectives Plan (MCD)
MMRP....... Minerals and Materials Research Programs [*North Carolina State University*] [*Research center*] (RCD)
MMRP....... Missile Master Replacement Program
MMRPOG... Massively Multiplayer Role-playing Online Game [*Computer gaming*]
MMRPV..... Multi Mission Remotely Piloted Vehicle (ACAE)
MMRPV..... Multimission RPV (SAUS)
MMRR....... Mid-Michigan Railroad [*Federal Railroad Administration identification code*]
MMRR....... Military Manpower Requirements Report (MCD)
MMRRI...... Mining and Minerals Resources Research Institute (SAUO)
MMRRI...... Utah Mining and Minerals Resources Research Institute [*University of Utah*] [*Research center*] (RCD)
MMRS....... Manned Military Recovery System (SAA)
MMRS....... Metal and Minerals Research Service (BUAC)
MMRS....... Metropolitan Medical Response System [*Emergency Management*] (EMA)
MMRU....... Abou Merhi Linienagentur [*Intermodal shipping container symbol*] (TVRC)
MMRX....... Mecdet MPC Corp. [*NASDAQ symbol*] (SAG)
MMRX....... Mednet MPC [*NASDAQ symbol*] (TTSB)
MMRX....... Mednet MPC Corp. [*NASDAQ symbol*] (SAG)
MMRX....... Reynosa/General Lucio Blanco Internacional [*Mexico*] [*ICAO location identifier*] (ICLI)
MMS......... Macbride Museum Society (EA)
MMS......... Machinist's Mate, Shop Mechanic [*Navy rating*]
MMS......... Macmillan's Manuals for Students [*A publication*]
MMS......... Magnetic Minesweeping (MSA)
MMS......... Maintenance Management Software
MMS......... Maintenance Management System
MMS......... Manager, Ministerial Services (SAUO)
MMS......... Man-Machine System (MCD)
MMS......... Manpower Management Staff [*NATO*] (NATG)
MMS......... Manpower Management System [*Marine Corps*]
MMS......... Manufacturing Management Sciences, Inc. (SAUO)
MMS......... Manufacturing Message Service (GART)
MMS......... Manufacturing Message [*or Messaging*] Specification [*or Standard*] [*Computer science*]
MMS......... Manufacturing Monitoring System [*Computer science*] (IBMDP)
MMS......... Marist Missionary Sisters (BUAC)
MMS......... Marks, MS [*Location identifier*] [*FAA*] (FAAL)
MMS......... Massachusetts Medical Society (BUAC)
MMS......... Mass Mammographic Screening [*Medicine*] (DMAA)
MMS......... Mass Memory Store [*Computer science*] (IEEE)
MMS......... Mass Memory Subsystem [*Aviation*]
MMS......... Master of Management Science (GAGS)
MMS......... Master of Management Studies
MMS......... Master of Marine Science (GAGS)
MMS......... Master of Marketing Science (PGP)
MMS......... Master of Materials Science (GAGS)
MMS......... Master of Mechanical Science
MMS......... Master of Medical Science
MMS......... Master of Modern Studies (PGP)
MMS......... Mast Mounted Sight
MMS......... Mast-Mounted Sight
MMS......... Mast Mounted Signal (MCD)
MMS......... Matam [*Senegal*] [*Seismograph station code, US Geological Survey*] [*Closed*] (SEIS)
MMS......... Maternity and Maternity Services [*British*]
MMS......... MAXIMUS, Inc. [*NYSE symbol*] (SG)
MMS......... Measurement of Materials Systems [*Mechanical engineering*]
MMS......... Media Messaging Services
MMS......... Medical Mission Sisters (EA)
MMS......... Medicus Mundi Switzerland (SAUO)
MMS......... Meetings Management Society (NTPA)
MMS......... Megacystis-Megaureter Syndrome [*Medicine*] (MELL)
MMS......... Member of the Institute of Management Services [*British*] (DBQ)
MMS......... Memory Management System
MMS......... Merchant Marine Safety
MMS......... Message Management System [*Computer science*] (CIST)
MMS......... Metabolic Monitoring System
MMS......... Metacaine Methanesulfonate [*Local anesthetic*]
MMS......... Metastable Metal Surface [*Catalyst science*]
MMS......... Meteorological Measuring System
MMS......... Methodist Missionary Society [*British*]
MMS......... Methyl Methanesulfonate [*Experimental mutagen*]
MMS......... Metropolitan Map Series [*Bureau of the Census*] (GFGA)
MMS......... Metropolitan Museum Studies [*A publication*] (ABAR)
MMS......... Mexican Mathematical Society (BUAC)
MMS......... Mexican Meteorological Service
MMS......... Michigan Multispectral Scanner
MMS......... Microfiche Management System
MMS......... Micro Measurement System [*3D Digital Design & Development Ltd.*] [*Software package*] (NCC)
MMS......... Micromembrane Suppressor [*Ion chromatography*]
MMS......... Micro Memory Systems (NITA)
MMS......... Microscale Meteorology Section (SAUO)
MMS......... Microsoft Metadirectory Services [*Computer science*] (HODG)
MMS......... Middle Meningeal System [*Neuroanatomy*]
MMS......... Mid Maine Savings Bank (EFIS)
MMS......... Military Message Service [*British military*] (DMA)
MMS......... Milkman's Syndrome [*Medicine*] (MELL)
MM/S........ Millimeters per Second
MMS......... Minerals Management Service [*Department of the Interior*] [*Washington, DC*]
MMS......... Mini-Mental State [*Psychometric testing*]
MMS......... Minimum Manned Satellite (ACAE)
MMS......... Minimum Mean Square (PDAA)
MMS......... Minimum Methadone Service [*Medicine*] (MELL)
MMS......... Missile Maintenance Squadron (SAA)
MMS......... Missile Management System (SAUS)
MMS......... Missile Mix Study [*NAVAIR*] (NG)
MMS......... Missile Monitor System [*Army*]
MMS......... Mission Modular Spacecraft (MCD)
mms......... Mission Modular Spacecraft [*NASA*] (NAKS)
MMS......... Mississippi County Community College Library, Blytheville, AR [*OCLC symbol*] (OCLC)
MMS......... Mitigation Management Series [*Emergency Management*] (EMA)
MMS......... Mobile Monitoring Station
MMS......... Modular Measuring System
MMS......... Modular Message Sign
MMS......... Modular Modeling System
MMS......... Modular Multiband Scanner (MCD)
mms......... Modular Multiband Scanner (NAKS)
MMS......... Modular Multimission Spacecraft [*NASA*]
MMS......... Modular Multispectral Scanner
MMS......... Module Making System (SAUS)
MMS......... Module Management System [*Computer science*] (CIST)
MMS......... Mohs' Micrographic Surgery
MMS......... Momentum Management System [*NASA*] (SSD)
MMS......... Money Management System
MMS......... Money Market Services, Inc. [*Belmont, CA*] [*Database producer*]
MMS......... Moravian Missionary Society
MMS......... Motor Minesweeper
MMS......... Movement Monitoring System (SAUO)
MMS......... Multilevel Mail Server (SAUS)

MMS .... Multimedia Messaging Service (SAUO)
MMS .... Multimedia System
mms .... Multimission Modular Spacecraft [*NASA*] (NAKS)
MMS .... Multimission Modular Spacecraft [*NASA*] (NASA)
MMS .... Multimission Ship [*DoD*]
MMS .... Multi-Mission Spaceccraft
MMS .... Multimode Seeker (MCD)
MMS .... Multimodular Mission Spacecraft (ACAE)
MMS .... Multi-Part Memory System [*Perkin-Elmer*] (NITA)
MMS .... Multiple Microprocessor System (ACAE)
MMS .... Multiplex Modulation System
MMS .... Municipal Management System (HGAA)
MMS .... Munitions Maintenance and Storage
MMS .... Munitions Maintenance Squadron [*Air Force*]
MMS .... Musical Masterpiece Society [*Record label*] [*USA, Europe*]
MMS .... Mycon Marketing Services Ltd. (SAUO)
MMS .... Myeloma Morphology Score [*Oncology*]
MMS .... US Minerals Management Services (SAUS)
MMS1 ...... Mobile Mast Spectrometer 1 (SAUS)
MMSA ...... Man-Machine System Analysis [*Engineering*]
MMSA ...... Manual Molder Shielded Arc
MMSA ...... Master of Midwifery, Society of Apothecaries
MMSA ...... Materials and Methods Standards Association (EA)
MMSA ...... Medical Mycological Society of the Americas (EA)
MMSA ...... Member, Medical Specialists' Association (CMD)
MMSA ...... Mercantile Marine Service Association [*British*]
MMSA ...... Methods and Materials Standards Association (EA)
MMSA ...... Military Medical Supply Agency [*Later, Defense Medical Supply Center*]
MMSA ...... Mining and Metallurgical Society of America (EA)
MMSA ...... Mistress of Midwifery, Society of Apothecaries (SAUO)
MMSA ...... Mitsubishi Motor Sales of America, Inc.
MMSA ...... Multiple-Mission Support Area [*Space Flight Operations Facility, NASA*]
MMSAA .... Metals and Minerals Shippers Association of Australia
MMSAC .... Medical Manpower Standing Advisory Committee (SAUO)
MMSB ...... Methyl(methionine)sulfonium Bromide [*Organic chemistry*]
MMSBC .... Master, Medical Science in Biomedical Communication (CMD)
MMSc ...... Master of Management Science (GAGS)
MMSc ...... Master of Marine Science (GAGS)
MM Sc ..... Master of Mechanical Science
MMSc ...... Master of Medical Science (GAGS)
MMSC ...... Mediterranean Marine Sorting Center
MMSC ...... Minnesota Metropolitan State College
MMSC ...... Multimode SONAR Console
MMSCFD.... Million Standard Cubic Feet per Day
MMSCR/W... Motorized Magnetic Stripe Card Reader/Writer [*Police and security equipment*]
MMSCV .... Manned Military System Capability Vehicle
MMSD ...... Mass Memory Storage Device (DWSG)
MMSD ...... Mixed Motor and Sensory Deficits [*Neurology*]
MMSD ...... Multimode Seeker Deduction (DWSG)
MMSD ...... Multiple Minor Symptoms Day [*Environmental medicine*]
MMSD ...... San Jose Del Cabo [*Mexico*] [*ICAO location identifier*] (ICLI)
MMSE ...... Master of Manufacturing Systems Engineering (PGP)
MMSE ...... Mini-Mental State Examination [*Psychometrics*]
MMSE ...... Mini Mental Status Examination [*Medicine*]
MMSE ...... Minimum Mean Squared Error
MMSE ...... Minimum Mean Square Error
MMSE ...... Mission Module Simulation Equipment (MCD)
MMSE ...... Molecular Monitor Shuttle Experiment (ACAE)
MMSE ...... Multiple-Mission Support Equipment [*NASA*]
MMSE ...... Multiuse Mission Support Equipment [*NASA*] (NAKS)
MMSG ...... Molecular Manufacturing Shortcut Group (BUAC)
MMSI ...... Maritime Mobile Service Identity (SAUO)
MMSI ...... Merit Medical Systems, Inc. [*NASDAQ symbol*] (SAG)
MMSI ...... Multi-Medium Scale Integration (SAA)
MMSIP .... Maintenance Management Systems Improvement Project [*Air Force*] (DOMA)
MMSJ ...... Medical Mobilization for Soviet Jewry (EA)
MMSI ...... Merit Medical Systems [*NASDAQ symbol*] (TTSB)
MMSL ...... Microgravity Materials Science Laboratory [*NASA*]
MMSL ...... Mining and Mineral Sciences Laboratories [*Natural Resources Canada*] (RCD)
MMSM ...... Santa Lucia [*Mexico*] [*ICAO location identifier*] (ICLI)
MMSP ...... Malignant Melanoma of Soft Parts [*Medicine*] (DMAA)
MMSP ...... San Luis Potosi [*Mexico*] [*ICAO location identifier*] (ICLI)
MMSPA .... Minnesota Maple Syrup Producers (EARSL)
MMSQ ...... Munitions Maintenance Squadron [*Air Force*]
MMSR ...... Machinist's Mate, Ship Repair [*Navy rating*]
MMSR ...... Master Materiel Support Record
MMSR ...... Monthly Materiel Status Report
MMSR ...... Multiple-Mission Support Recording [*NASA*]
MMSRC .... Mediterranean Maritime Surveillance and Reconnaissance Center (DNAB)
MMSRE .... Machinist's Mate, Ship Repair, Engine Operator [*Navy rating*]
MMSRI ..... Machinist's Mate, Ship Repair, Instrument Maker [*Navy rating*]
MMSRO .... Machinist's Mate, Ship Repair, Outside Machinist [*Navy rating*]
MMSRS .... Machinist's Mate, Ship Repair, Inside Machinist [*Navy rating*]
MMSS ...... Manned Maneuverable Space System
MMSS ...... Manual Mode Space Simulator
MMSS ...... Marine Meteorological Services System [*WMO*] (MSC)
MMSS ...... Maritime Mobile Satellite Service (ACAE)
MMSS ...... Massachusettensis Medicinae Societatis Socius [*Fellow of the Massachusetts Medical Society*]
MMSS ...... Mast Mounted Sight System (MCD)
M/MSS ..... Medicare and Medicaid Statistical Systems (GFGA)
MMSS ...... Missile Motion Subsystem
MMSS ...... Multi Mission System Study (ACAE)
MMSS ...... Multimodule Space Station [*NASA*] (KSC)
MMSSF .... Man Machine System Simulation Facility (ACAE)
MM St ...... Master of Museum Studies (PGP)
MMST ...... Metropolitan Medical Strike Team [*Emergency Management*] (EMA)
MMST ...... Microelectronics Manufacturing Science and Technology (AAEL)
MMST ...... Mini-Mental State Test (SAUS)
MMST ...... Multimode Storage Tube
MM ST ..... Muscle Strength (BABM)
mm st ...... Muscle Strength [*Neurology*] (DAVI)
MMSTP .... Master Missile System Training Program (SAA)
MMSU ...... Marco Mare Shipping [*Intermodal shipping container symbol*] (TVRC)
MMSU ...... Mariano Marcos State University (SAUO)
MMSU ...... Modular Metallic Service Unit [*Communications term*] (DCT)
MMSV ...... Mouse Moloney Sarcoma and Leukemia Virus [*Medicine*] (DB)
MMSW ...... International Union of Mine, Mill, and Smelter Workers [*Later, USWA*]
MMSZ ...... Martin Marietta Systems [*Federal Railroad Administration identification code*]
MMT .... Alpha-Methyl-m-tyrosine [*Pharmacology*]
MMT .... Columbia, SC [*Location identifier*] [*FAA*] (FAAL)
MMT .... Macmillan's Manuals for Teachers [*A publication*]
MMT .... Main Mantle Thrust [*Geology*]
MMT .... Malignant Mixed Tumor [*Medicine*] (MELL)
MMT .... Manportable MILSTAR [*Military Strategic and Tactical Relay*] Terminal [*Army*]
MMT .... Manual Muscle Test
MMT .... Manufacturing Methods Technology (AAGC)
MMT .... Marine Minerals Technology [*National Oceanic and Atmospheric Administration*]
MMT .... Maritime Mobile Telegraph
MMT .... Mass Memory Test (NASA)
MMT .... Master of Medical Technology
MMT .... Master of Movement Therapy (GAGS)
MMT .... Master of Music Teaching (GAGS)
MMT .... Math Model Test (MCD)
MMT .... Medial Meniscus Tear [*Medicine*] (MELL)
MMT .... Merchant Marine Technical Division [*Coast Guard*]
MMT .... Metal Mount
MMT .... Methadone Mainetnance Treatment [*Medicine*] (MELL)
MMT .... Methylcyclopentadienyl Manganese Tricarbonyl [*Organic chemistry*]
MMT .... MFS Multimarket Income [*NYSE symbol*] (SPSG)
MMT .... MFS Multimarket Income Trust [*Associated Press*] (SAG)
MMT .... Midland Mortgage Investors Trust (SAUO)
MMT .... Military Mail Terminal (AFM)
MMT .... Military Maintenance Technician
MMT .... Million Metric Tons (IMH)
MMT .... Miniature Mobile Target (SAUS)
MMT .... Miniature Moving Target (MCD)
MMT .... Miniaturized Munitions Technology
MMT .... Mini Mobile Target [*Military*] (CAAL)
MMT .... Missile Maintenance Technician (AABC)
MMT .... Missile Mate Test
MMT .... Mobile Maintenance Team (MCD)
MMT .... Model-Mapping Tables [*Computer science*] (GART)
MMT .... Modernization Management Team [*Military*] (CAAL)
MMT .... Molten Metal Technology [*Waste management*] (ECON)
MMT .... Monolithic Mirror Telescope
mmt .... Monomethoxytrityl [*As substituent on nucleoside*] [*Biochemistry*]
MMT .... Monthly Mean Temperature [*Meteorology*]
MMT .... Monument Resources [*Vancouver Stock Exchange symbol*]
MMT .... Morse Mission Trainer
mMT .... Mouse Metallothionein [*Biochemistry*]
MMT .... Muenchner Mode-Tage [*Germany*]
MMT .... Multimodal Therapy [*Arnold Lazarus*] (DIPS)
MMT .... Multimode Tonotron
MMT .... Multi Mode Transponder (ACAE)
MMT .... Multiple Mirror Observatory
MMT .... Multiple-Mirror Telescope [*Mount Hopkins, AZ*] [*Jointly operated by Smithsonian Institution and the University of Arizona*] [*Astronomy*]
MMT .... Multiple-Mission Telemetry [*NASA*]
MMT .... Murine Metallothionein [*Biochemistry*]
MMTA ...... Mercantile Marine Trawlermen's Association [*A union*] [*British*]
MMTA ...... Methylmetatyramine (DB)
MMTA ...... Minor Metals Traders' Association [*British*]
MMTA ...... MultiMedia Telecommunications Association (DDC)
MMTA ...... Tlaxcala [*Mexico*] [*ICAO location identifier*] (ICLI)
MMTB ...... Tuxtla Gutierrez [*Mexico*] [*ICAO location identifier*] (ICLI)
MMTC ...... Marine Minerals Technology Center [*National Oceanic and Atmospheric Administration*]
MMTC ...... Maritime Mobile Telegraphy Calling
MMTC ...... Materiel Management Training Center [*Military*]
MMTC ...... Memtec Ltd. [*NASDAQ symbol*] (SAG)
MMTC ...... Midwest Manufacturing Technology Council (SAUO)
MMTC ...... Minerals and Metals Trading Corp. (BUAC)
MMTC ...... Mouvement Mondial des Travailleurs Chretiens [*World Movement of Christian Workers - WMCW*] [*Brussels, Belgium*] (EAIO)
MMTC ...... Torreon [*Mexico*] [*ICAO location identifier*] (ICLI)
MMTCY .... Memtec Ltd ADS [*NASDAQ symbol*] (TTSB)

MMTD .... Multimode Tonotron Display
MMTDC ..... Maritime Mobile Telegraph Distress and Calling
MMTE .... Manufacturing Methods Technology Engineering (ACAE)
MMTF .... Military Manpower Task Force
MMTG .... Tuxtla Gutierrez [*Mexico*] [*ICAO location identifier*] (ICLI)
MMTI .... Member of the Metal Treating Institute (SAUO)
MMTIC ...... Murphy-Meisgeier Type Indicator for Children [*Test*] (TES)
MMTIF ...... Micromem Technologies, Inc. [*NASDAQ symbol*] (QUAN)
MMTJ .... Tijuana/General Abelardo L. Rodriguez Internacional [*Mexico*] [*ICAO location identifier*] (ICLI)
MMTL .... Tulancingo [*Mexico*] [*ICAO location identifier*] (ICLI)
M Mtl E ..... Master of Materials Engineering (PGP)
M Mtl E ..... Master of Metal Engineering (PGP)
MMTLN ...... Map Margin Top Line (SAA)
MMT/M ...... Missile Maintenance Technician/Mechanic (AAG)
MMTM ...... Momentum Business Applications, Inc. [*NASDAQ symbol*] (NASQ)
MMTM ...... Multimedia Training Material
MMTM ...... Tampico/General Francisco Javier Mina Internacional [*Mexico*] [*ICAO location identifier*] (ICLI)
MMTN .... Tamuin [*Mexico*] [*ICAO location identifier*] (ICLI)
MMTO .... Missiles Made to Order [*Military*] (RDA)
MMTO .... Multiple Mirror Telescope Observatory [*Research center*] (RCD)
MMTO .... Toluca [*Mexico*] [*ICAO location identifier*] (ICLI)
MMTP .... Methadone Maintenance Treatment Program (AAMN)
MMTP .... Methyl(methylthio)phenol [*Organic chemistry*]
MMTP .... Microwave Temperature Profiler (SAUS)
MMTP .... Tapachula [*Mexico*] [*ICAO location identifier*] (ICLI)
MMTPS ..... Maintenance Materiel Transaction Processing System (SAUO)
MMTQ .... Tequesquitengo [*Mexico*] [*ICAO location identifier*] (ICLI)
MMTR .... Mean-Maintenance-Man-Hours to Repair (MCD)
MMTR .... Military Manpower Training Report (MCD)
M/MTRG .... Main Metering [*Automotive engineering*]
MMTRS ..... Mills Music Trust [*NASDAQ symbol*] (QUAN)
MMTS .... Maximum Minimum Temperature System
MMTS .... Methyl Methanethiolsulfonate [*Organic chemistry*]
MMTS .... MILAN Moving Target System (SAUS)
MMTS .... Multi-Media Tutorial Services, Inc. [*NASDAQ symbol*] (SAG)
MMTS .... Multiple-Mission Telemetry System [*NASA*]
MMTSF ...... Million Metric Tons of Standard Fuel
MMTSW ..... Multi-Media Tutorial Wrrt [*NASDAQ symbol*] (TTSB)
MMTT .... Mechanised Moving Target Trainer (SAUS)
MMTT .... Mobile Minuteman Train Test (SAA)
MMTT .... Multimechanical Thermal Treatment
MMTTU ..... Modular Magnetic Tape Transport Units (MCD)
MMTU .... Multi-Modal Transport Equipment [*Intermodal shipping container symbol*] (TVRC)
MMTV .... Mouse Mammary Tumor Virus
MMTX .... Tuxpan [*Mexico*] [*ICAO location identifier*] (ICLI)
MMTY .... Monterrey [*Mexico*] [*ICAO location identifier*] (ICLI)
MMU .... Main Memory Unit
MMU .... Managed Municipal Portfolio [*NYSE symbol*] (SPSG)
MMU .... Manchester Metropolitan University [*British*] (AIE)
mmu .... Manned Maneuvering Unit [*NASA*] (NAKS)
MMU .... Manned Maneuvering Unit [*Aerospace*]
mmu .... Mass Memory Unit (NAKS)
MMU .... Mass Memory Unit
MMu .... Master of Music (GAGS)
MMU .... McMaster University (SAUO)
MMU .... Medical Maintenance Unit [*Army*] [*World War II*]
MMU .... Memory Management Unit [*Computer chip*]
MMU .... Memory Mapping Unit (NITA)
MMU .... Mercaptomethyl Uracil [*Pharmacology*] (MAE)
MMU .... Metered Message Unit [*Telecommunications*] (TEL)
MMU .... Midcourse Maneuvering Unit [*Aerospace*] (MCD)
MMU .... Midcourse Measurement Unit [*Aerospace*] (KSC)
MMU .... Millimass Unit (DEN)
MMU .... Million Monetary Units (PDAA)
MMU .... Missile Motion Unit
MMU .... Mmaala [*Language symbol*] (ETLW)
MMU .... Mobile Monitoring Unit
MMU .... Modular Maneuvering Unit [*Aerospace*]
MMU .... Monolithic Memory Unit
MMU .... Morristown, NJ [*Location identifier*] [*FAA*] (FAAL)
MMU .... Multimessage Unit [*Telecommunications*] (TEL)
MMU .... University of Missouri, Columbia, Health Sciences Library, Columbia, MO [*OCLC symbol*] (OCLC)
MMUA .... Major Mail Users of Australia
MMUAV ..... Multi-Mission Unmanned Aerial Vehicle
MMUC .... Mazda Manufacturing USA Corporation [*Automotive industry*]
MMUC .... Mazda Motor Manufacturing USA Corp.
MMUC .... Midwest Medical Union Catalog
MMUD .... Monolithic Memory Unit Diagnostic
M Mu Ed .... Master of Music Education (PGP)
MMUFX ..... MFS Utilities
M'Mul Ch SC ... M'Mullan's South Carolina Equity Reports [*1840-42*] [*A publication*] (DLA)
M'Mul LSC ... M'Mullan's South Carolina Law Reports [*1840-42*] [*A publication*] (DLA)
MMuLV ...... Moloney Murine Leukemia Virus [*Medicine*] (DMAA)
MMUN .... Cancun [*Mexico*] [*ICAO location identifier*] (ICLI)
MMus .... Master of Music (GAGS)
M Mus Ed .. Master of Music Education
M Mus (Mus Ed) ... Master of Music in Music Education
M Mus (Mus Lit) ... Master of Music in Music Literature
M Mus (PSM) ... Master of Music in Public School Music
MMusRCM ... Master of Music of the Royal College of Music (SAUO)
M Mus (RCM) ... Master of Music, Royal College of Music
M Mus (W Inst) ... Master of Music in Wind Instruments
MMUU .... United Kingdom Ministry of Defence [*Intermodal shipping container symbol*] (TVRC)
MMV .... Eaton Vance Massachusetts Municipal Income Trust [*AMEX symbol*] (NASQ)
MMV .... Maize Mosaic Virus [*Plant pathology*]
MMV .... Mandatory Minute Ventilation (DMAA)
MMV .... Mandatory Minute Volume (DMAA)
MMV .... Mast Mount Visionics (MCD)
MMV .... Maubois, Mocquot, and Vassal [*Cheesemaking*]
MMV .... McMinnville, OR [*Location identifier*] [*FAA*] (FAAL)
MMV .... Medal of Military Valour [*Canada*] (FOTI)
MMV .... Minimale Mandatory Ventilation (SAUS)
MMV .... Modular Military Vehicle (SAUS)
mmv .... Monostable Multivibrator (IDOE)
MMV .... Monostable Multivibrator
MMV .... Multi-Mission Vehicle (SAUS)
MMVA .... Villahermosa [*Mexico*] [*ICAO location identifier*] (ICLI)
MMVD .... Mixed Mitral Valve Disease [*Medicine*] (DMAA)
MMVF .... Man-Made Vitreous Fiber (LDOE)
MMVF .... Multimedia Video File [*Computer science*]
MMVR .... Veracruz/General Heriberto Jara [*Mexico*] [*ICAO location identifier*] (ICLI)
MMVS .... Mast Mount Visionics System (MCD)
MMVU .... Multi-Modal International [*Intermodal shipping container symbol*] (TVRC)
MM(W) ...... Machinist's Mate (Watchmaker) [*U.S. Navy enlisted rating*] (AUER)
MMW .... Main Magnetization Winding [*Telecommunications*] (OA)
MMW .... Mean Maximum Weight
MMW .... Medium Multi-purpose Wheeled (SAUS)
MMW .... Miami, OK [*Location identifier*] [*FAA*] (FAAL)
MMW .... Multimegawatt (SDI)
mmwave .... Millimeter Wave (AAEL)
MMWCS .... Multimission Weapons Control System
MMWE ...... Millimeter Wave Experiment
MMWEC ..... Massachusetts Municipal Wholesale Electric Company (SAUO)
MMWG ...... Military Mobilization Working Group
MMWM ..... Multimedia Window Manager (SAUS)
MMWR ...... Millimetric Wave Radar (SAUS)
MMWR ...... Morbidity and Mortality Weekly Report [*A publication*] (DMAA)
MMWW ..... Metamor Worldwide [*NASDAQ symbol*] [*Formerly, COREstaff, Inc.*]
MMX .... Magma Copper Co. (SAUO)
MMX .... Mastergroup Multiplex [*AT & T*]
MMX .... Matrix Math Extensions (PCM)
MMX .... Maxx Petroleum Ltd. [*AMEX symbol*] (NASQ)
MMX .... Memory Multiplexer [*Computer science*]
MMX .... Micron's Millenia XKU [*Computer science*]
MMX .... Miracema do Norte [*Brazil*] [*Airport symbol*] (AD)
MMX .... Multi-Media Extensions [*Computer chip*] (NETL)
MMXI .... Media Metrix [*NASDAQ symbol*] (SG)
MMXU .... Mobile Mini Storage Systems [*Intermodal shipping container symbol*] (TVRC)
MMXZ .... Murphy Motor Express [*Intermodal trailer symbol*]
MMY .... Many, LA [*Location identifier*] [*FAA*] (FAAL)
MMY .... Memory [*Telegraphy*] (PCTE)
MMY .... Mental Measurements Yearbook [*Psychology*] [*A publication*]
MMY .... Military Man-Years (AABC)
MMY .... Miyakojima [*Japan*] [*Airport symbol*] (OAG)
MMY .... Money Market Yield
MMYD .... Mental Measurements Yearbook Database [*University of Nebraska, Lincoln*] [*Database*]
MMZ .... Maimana [*Afghanistan*] [*Airport symbol*] [*Obsolete*] (OAG)
MMZ .... Martin Marietta [*Federal Railroad Administration identification code*]
MMZ .... Memorize [*Telegraphy*] (PCTE)
MMZ .... Metro Mobile Centers (EFIS)
MMZC .... Zacatecas [*Mexico*] [*ICAO location identifier*] (ICLI)
MMZH .... Zihuatanejo [*Mexico*] [*ICAO location identifier*] (ICLI)
MMZM ...... Zamora [*Mexico*] [*ICAO location identifier*] (ICLI)
MMZO .... Manzanillo [*Mexico*] [*ICAO location identifier*] (ICLI)
MMZP .... Zapopan [*Mexico*] [*ICAO location identifier*] (ICLI)
MMZT .... Mazatlan [*Mexico*] [*ICAO location identifier*] (ICLI)
MN .... Machinery Numeral [*Marine insurance*] (DS)
MN .... Madeleine Mines Ltd. [*Toronto Stock Exchange symbol*]
MN .... Magnetic North
MN .... Main (AAG)
MN .... Main Network [*Telecommunications*] (TEL)
MN .... Making of the Nations [*A publication*]
Mn .... Male (neutered) (SPVS)
MN .... Malignant Nephrosclerosis [*Medicine*] (DB)
MN .... Management Network (MCD)
Mn .... Manganese [*Chemical element*]
MN .... Mansion
MN .... Mantle Nerve
MN .... Manual
MN .... Manufacturer's Name (NITA)
MN .... Manufacturing [*Automotive engineering*]
MN .... Manx Airlines Ltd.
MN .... Mare Nectaris [*Sea of Nectar*] [*Lunar area*]
MN .... Marketspan Corp. [*NYSE symbol*] [*Formerly, Long Island Lighting*]
MN .... Master Degree in Nursing (SEAT)
MN .... Master Navigator [*Air Force*]

MN.......... Master of Nursing
MN.......... Material Number
MN.......... Materiel Needs [*Army*]
MN.......... Maxim Nordenfelt Gun
Mn.......... Mean Range [*Difference in height between mean high water and mean low water*] [*Tides and currents*]
MN.......... Measurement Name (NITA)
MN.......... Mecanorma [*Graphic artist products*] [*British*]
MN.......... Medial Interlaminar Nucleus [*Neurology*] (DAVI)
MN.......... Media Network (EA)
MN.......... Median Nerve [*Anatomy*]
MN.......... Meeting Number (NITA)
MN.......... Meetings Name (NITA)
MN.......... Meganewton
MN.......... Melanocytic Nevus [*Medicine*] (MELL)
MN.......... Melena Neonatorum (DB)
MN.......... Membranous Nephropathy [*Medicine*] (MELL)
MN.......... Meniere's Network [*An association*] (EA)
MN.......... Meningopneumonitis [*Medicine*]
Mn.......... Merchant Navy (WDAA)
MN.......... Merchant Navy
M-N.......... Merrell-National [*Commercial firm*] (DAVI)
MN.......... Message Number [*Computer science*] (ELAL)
MN.......... Metanephrine [*Medicine*] (DMAA)
MN.......... Meter-Handling Non-Residential [*Electric utility company*]
m-N.......... Meter-Newton
MN.......... Michigan [*Obsolete*] (ROG)
MN.......... Micrococcal Nuclease [*Also, MCN*] [*An enzyme*]
M/N.......... Microcytic/Normochromic [*Anemia*] [*Hematology*] (DAVI)
MN.......... Microneutralization [*Chemistry*]
mn.......... Midnight [*Therapy term*] (CTAA)
MN.......... Midnight
MN.......... Migrating Neuron [*Neuroanatomy*]
mN.......... Millinormal [*One one-thousandth of normal*]
MN.......... Mindelheim [*German license plate city code*]
MN.......... Mineman [*Navy rating*]
MN.......... Minnesota [*Postal code*]
Mn.......... Minnesota State Law Library, St. Paul, MN [*Library symbol*] [*Library of Congress*] (LCLS)
MN.......... Minor Descriptor (SAUS)
MN.......... Minor Subject Descriptor [*Online database field identifier*]
MN.......... Minus (VLIE)
MN.......... Mission Need
MN.......... Mnemonic
Mn.......... Modern [*Linguistics*]
M/N.......... Moneda Nacional [*National Money*] [*Spanish*]
MN.......... Mongolia [*ANSI two-letter standard code*] (CNC)
MN.......... Mononuclear [*Hematology*]
MN.......... Mononuclear Lymphocytes (SAUS)
MN.......... Monthly Notices of the Royal Astronomical Society (SAUO)
MN.......... Month Name (BJA)
MN.......... Montpelier & Barre Railroad [*Federal Railroad Administration identification code*]
MN.......... Moon (ROG)
MN.......... Moreh Nebukhim [*Maimonides*] (BJA)
M-N.......... Motility Nitrate [*Medium*] [*Microbiology*] (DAVI)
MN.......... Moto Nave [*Motor ship*] [*Latin*] (IIA)
MN.......... Motor Neuron [*Anatomy*]
MN.......... Mouvement National [*Morocco*] [*Political party*] (EY)
MN.......... Movimiento Nacional [*Costa Rica*] [*Political party*] (EY)
MN.......... Multinodular [*or Multinodulate*] [*Medicine*]
MN.......... Municipal Notice (SAFN)
MN.......... Mutato Nomine [*The Name Being Changed*] [*Latin*]
MN.......... Myoneural [*Medicine*]
MN1.......... Mineman, First Class [*Navy rating*]
MN2.......... Mineman, Second Class [*Navy rating*]
MN3.......... Mineman, Third Class [*Navy rating*]
MnA.......... Aitken Public Library, Aitken, MN [*Library symbol*] [*Library of Congress*] (LCLS)
MNA.......... Augsburg College, Minneapolis, MN [*OCLC symbol*] (OCLC)
MNA.......... Management Network Architecture (SAUO)
MNA.......... Mangusta [*NCIC car model code*]
MNA.......... Massachusetts Nurses Association (SAUO)
MNA.......... Master Negative Assembly [*Monophoto*] (DGA)
M Na.......... Master of Navigation
MNA.......... Master of Nonprofit Administration (GAGS)
MNA.......... Master of Nurse Anesthesia (PGP)
MNA.......... Master of Nursing Administration
MN(A).......... Material Need (Abbreviated) (MCD)
MNA.......... Maximum Noise Area
MNA.......... Medical Nurse Associate [*Medicine*] (EDAA)
MNA.......... Melanguane [*Indonesia*] [*Airport symbol*] (OAG)
MNA.......... Melinga Resources Ltd. [*Vancouver Stock Exchange symbol*]
MNA.......... Member of the National Assembly [*British*]
MNA.......... Merpati Nusantara Airlines PT [*Indonesia*] [*ICAO designator*] (FAAC)
MNA.......... Meta-Nitroaniline [*Organic chemistry*]
MNA.......... Methoxynaphthylamine [*Organic chemistry*]
MNA.......... Methylnadic Anhydride [*Organic chemistry*]
MNA.......... Methylnitroaniline [*Organic chemistry*]
MNA.......... Michigan Nurses Association (SAUO)
MNA.......... Mina [*Nevada*] [*Seismograph station code, US Geological Survey*] (SEIS)
MNA.......... Minnesota Municipal Term Trust [*NYSE symbol*] (SPSG)
MNA.......... Minnesota Newspaper Association (EARSL)
MNA.......... Minnesota Nurses Association (SAUO)
MNA.......... Missing, Not Enemy Action
MNA.......... Mississippi Nurses Association (SAUO)
MNA.......... Missouri & Northern Arkansas Railroad [*Federal Railroad Administration identification code*]
MNA.......... Molybdenum-Nickel-Alumina (ODA)
MNA.......... Mouvement d'Action Politique et Sociale [*Political and Social Action Movement*] [*Switzerland*] [*Political party*] (PPW)
MNA.......... Mouvement National Algerien [*National Algerian Movement*]
MNA.......... Multinetwork Area [*Term used in TV ratings*]
MNA.......... Multiple Newsagents Association [*British*] (DBA)
MNA.......... Multishare Network Architecture [*Mitsubishi Corp.*] (BUR)
MNA.......... Myanmar News Agency (EY)
MNAA.......... Molecular Neutron Activation Analysis
MnAbnE.......... Alborn Elementary School, Alborn, MN [*Library symbol*] [*Library of Congress*] (LCLS)
MNAC.......... Michigan Natural Areas Council (EARSL)
MNAC.......... Monaco Motor Home [*NCIC truck make code*]
MnAd.......... Annandale Public Library, Annandale, MN [*Library symbol*] [*Library of Congress*] (LCLS)
Mn-Ad.......... Minnesota State Department of Administration, Budget Library, St. Paul, MN [*Library symbol*] [*Library of Congress*] (LCLS)
MNAD.......... Multi-National Airmobile Division (SAUO)
MnAda.......... Ada Public Library, Ada, MN [*Library symbol*] [*Library of Congress*] (LCLS)
MNAdaE.......... Ada Elementary School, Ada, MN [*Library symbol*] [*Library of Congress*] (LCLS)
MnAdaH.......... Ada High School, Ada, MN [*Library symbol*] [*Library of Congress*] (LCLS)
MnAdBE.......... Bendix Elementary School Annandale, MN [*Library symbol*] [*Library of Congress*] (LCLS)
MnAdH.......... Annandale High School, Annandale, MN [*Library symbol*] [*Library of Congress*] (LCLS)
MnADM.......... Depot Museum, Aitken, MN [*Library symbol*] [*Library of Congress*] (LCLS)
MnAdMS.......... Annandale Middle School, Annandale, MN [*Library symbol*] [*Library of Congress*] (LCLS)
MNAEA.......... Member of the National Association of Estate Agents [*British*] (DBQ)
Mn-Ag.......... Minnesota Department of Agriculture, St. Paul, MN [*Library symbol*] [*Library of Congress*] (LCLS)
MnAJ.......... Aitken Jr.-Sr. High School Media Center, Aitken, MN [*Library symbol*] [*Library of Congress*] (LCLS)
MnAkE.......... Akeley Elementary School, Akeley, MN [*Library symbol*] [*Library of Congress*] (LCLS)
MnAkH.......... Akeley High School, Akeley, MN [*Library symbol*] [*Library of Congress*] (LCLS)
MnAl.......... Albany Public Library, Alabany, MN [*Library symbol*] [*Library of Congress*] (LCLS)
MnAlb.......... Albert Lea Public Library, Albert Lea, MN [*Library symbol*] [*Library of Congress*] (LCLS)
MnAlbeCH.......... Chokio-Alberta High School, Alberta, MN [*Library symbol*] [*Library of Congress*] (LCLS)
MnAle.......... Alexandria Public Library, Alexandria, MN [*Library symbol*] [*Library of Congress*] (LCLS)
MnAleCJ.......... Central Junior High School, Alexandria, MN [*Library symbol*] [*Library of Congress*] (LCLS)
MnAleDH.......... Douglas County Hospital, Health Science Library, Alexandria, MN [*Library symbol*] [*Library of Congress*] (LCLS)
MnAleJH.......... Jefferson High School, Alexandria, MN [*Library symbol*] [*Library of Congress*] (LCLS)
MnAleLE.......... Lincoln Elementary School, Alexandria, MN [*Library symbol*] [*Library of Congress*] (LCLS)
MnAleR.......... Alexandria Runestone Museum, Alexandria, MN [*Library symbol*] [*Library of Congress*] (LCLS)
MnAleSM.......... St. Mary's School, Alexandria, MN [*Library symbol*] [*Library of Congress*] (LCLS)
MnAleTI.......... Alexandria Technical Institute, Alexandria, MN [*Library symbol*] [*Library of Congress*] (LCLS)
MnAleWE.......... Washington Elementary School, Alexandria, MN [*Library symbol*] [*Library of Congress*] (LCLS)
MnAlFE.......... Farming Elementary School, Albany, MN [*Library symbol*] [*Library of Congress*] (LCLS)
MnAlH.......... Holy Family School, Albany, MN [*Library symbol*] [*Library of Congress*] (LCLS)
MnAlJ.......... Albany Jr. H.S./Elementary Library, Albany, MN [*Library symbol*] [*Library of Congress*] (LCLS)
MnAlmA.......... Amador Heritage Center, Almelund, MN [*Library symbol*] [*Library of Congress*] (LCLS)
MnAlS.......... Albany Senior High School, Albany, MN [*Library symbol*] [*Library of Congress*] (LCLS)
MnAlSP.......... St. Pius V School, Albany, MN [*Library symbol*] [*Library of Congress*] (LCLS)
MnAlvE.......... Albertville Elementary School, Albertville, MN [*Library symbol*] [*Library of Congress*] (LCLS)
MNAM.......... Military North African Mission [*World War II*]
MNam.......... Nantucket Athenaeum, Nantucket, MA [*Library symbol*] [*Library of Congress*] (LCLS)
MnAnA.......... Anoka-Ramsey Community College, Anoka, MN [*Library symbol*] [*Library of Congress*] (LCLS)
MN & ALOA.......... Merchant Navy and Air Line Officers' Association [*A union*] [*British*] (DS)
MNANG.......... Minnesota Air National Guard (MUSM)
MnAnGS.......... Anoka County Genealogical Society, Anoka, MN [*Library symbol*] [*Library of Congress*] (LCLS)
MnAnHi.......... Anoka County Historical Society, Anoka, MN [*Library symbol*] [*Library of Congress*] (LCLS)
MNanHi.......... Nantucket Historical Association, Nantucket, MA [*Library symbol*] [*Library of Congress*] (LCLS)

MNanMM ... Nantucket Maria Mitchell Association, Nantucket, MA [*Library symbol*] [*Library of Congress*] (LCLS)
MnAnVT ..... Anoka Area Vocational Technical Institute, Anoka, MN [*Library symbol*] [*Library of Congress*] (LCLS)
MNanW ..... Nantucket Whaling Museum, Nantucket, MA [*Library symbol*] [*Library of Congress*] (LCLS)
MNAO .... Mazda North American Operations [*Automotive industry*]
MNAO .... Mobile Naval Airfield Organization
MNAOA ...... Merchant Navy and Air Line Officers' Association [*A union*] [*British*] (DCTA)
MnAp .... Appleton Public Library, Appleton, MN [*Library symbol*] [*Library of Congress*] (LCLS)
MNAP .... Manager of National Antarctic Programme (SAUO)
MNAP .... Mixed Nerve Action Potential [*Medicine*] (DMAA)
MnApH ...... Appleton Municipal Hospital, Appleton, MN [*Library symbol*] [*Library of Congress*] (LCLS)
MnApPS ..... Appleton Public Schools, Appleton, MN [*Library symbol*] [*Library of Congress*] (LCLS)
MNAPTA ..... American Physical Therapy Association, Minnesota Chapter (EARSL)
MNAR .... Monarch [*NCIC motorcycle make code*]
MN Arch .... Master of Naval Architecture
MnARE ...... Rippleside Elementary School, Rippleside Elementary IMC, Aitken, Mn [*Library symbol*] [*Library of Congress*] (LCLS)
MnArS .... Argyle School, Argyle, MN [*Library symbol*] [*Library of Congress*] (LCLS)
MNAS .... Member of the National Academy of Sciences
MNAs .... Members of the National Assembly (SAUO)
MNASc ...... Memoirs of the National Academy of Sciences (SAUO)
MnAsHi ..... Pine County Historical Reference Library, Askov, MN [*Library symbol*] [*Library of Congress*] (LCLS)
MnAshS ..... Ashby Public School, Ashby, MN [*Library symbol*] [*Library of Congress*] (LCLS)
MNASSA .... Monthly Notes. Astronomical Society of Southern Africa [*A publication*]
MNASTD .... Multicultural Network of the American Society for Training and Development (EA)
MnAt .... Atwater Public Library, Atwater, MN [*Library symbol*] [*Library of Congress*] (LCLS)
MNAT .... Marquette National Corp. [*NASDAQ symbol*] (QUAN)
MnAtPS ..... Atwater-Grove City Public Schools, Atwater, MN [*Library symbol*] [*Library of Congress*] (LCLS)
MNatQ .... United States Quartermaster Research and Development Center, Natick, MA [*Library symbol*] [*Library of Congress*] (LCLS)
MNatRes .... Master of Natural Resources (ADA)
MNatSci ..... Master of Natural Science (GAGS)
MnAtSJS .... St. John's Lutheran School, Atwater, MN [*Library symbol*] [*Library of Congress*] (LCLS)
MnAu .... Austin Public Library, Austin, MN [*Library symbol*] [*Library of Congress*] (LCLS)
MNAU .... Mobile Naval Airfield Unit
MnAudS ..... Audubon Public School, Audubon, MN [*Library symbol*] [*Library of Congress*] (LCLS)
MnAuH ...... Hormel Institute, University of Minnesota, Austin, MN [*Library symbol*] [*Library of Congress*] (LCLS)
MnAuPS ..... Austin Public Schools Media, Austin, MN [*Library symbol*] [*Library of Congress*] (LCLS)
MnAur .... Aurora Public Library, Aurora, MN [*Library symbol*] [*Library of Congress*] (LCLS)
MnAurH ..... Mesabi East High School, Aurora,MN [*Library symbol*] [*Library of Congress*] (LCLS)
MnAuS ...... Austin State Junior College, Austin, MN [*Library symbol*] [*Library of Congress*] (LCLS)
MnAuV ...... Austin Vocational Technical Institute, Austin, MN [*Library symbol*] [*Library of Congress*] (LCLS)
MnAvoE ..... Avon Elementary School, Avon, MN [*Library symbol*] [*Library of Congress*] (LCLS)
MnAvZ .... Minnesota Zoological Garden, Apple Valley, MN [*Library symbol*] [*Library of Congress*] (LCLS)
MnB .... Becker Public Library, Becker Elementary School, Becker, MN [*Library symbol*] [*Library of Congress*] (LCLS)
MNB .... Bemidji State University, Bemidji, MN [*OCLC symbol*] (OCLC)
MNB .... Maldives News Bureau (EY)
MNB .... Mandibular Nerve Block [*Medicine*] (MELL)
MNB .... Mannosidase Beta (DMAA)
MNB .... Maverick Naturalite Beef Corp. [*Vancouver Stock Exchange symbol*]
MNB .... Median Neuroblast [*Cytology*]
MNB .... Medical Negligence Board (WDAA)
MNB .... Minnesota Muni Term Tr-II [*AMEX symbol*] (TTSB)
MNB .... Minnesota Term Trust, Inc. II [*AMEX symbol*] (SAG)
MNB .... Mint No Box [*Doll collecting*]
MNB .... Moanda [*Zaire*] [*Airport symbol*] (OAG)
MNB .... Mobile Naval Base [*British military*] (DMA)
MNB .... Moscow Narodny Bank Ltd. [*Former USSR*]
MNB .... Multinozzle Base
MNB .... Murine Neuroblastoma (DB)
MNB .... Texte de Louvre [*Paris*]: Monuments de Ninive et de Babylone [*A publication*] (BJA)
MnBa .... Balaton Public Library, Balaton, MN [*Library symbol*] [*Library of Congress*] (LCLS)
MNBA .... Minimum Normal Burst Altitude
MNBA .... Mono-normal-butylamine [*Organic chemistry*]
MNBA .... Multinational Business Association (BUAC)
MnBab ...... Babbitt Public Library, Babbitt, MN [*Library symbol*] [*Library of Congress*] (LCLS)
MnBabE ..... J.F. Kennedy Elementary School, Babbit, MN [*Library symbol*] [*Library of Congress*] (LCLS)
MnBabH ..... J.F. Kennedy High School, Babbitt, MN [*Library symbol*] [*Library of Congress*] (LCLS)
MnBacS ..... Backus School, Backus, MN [*Library symbol*] [*Library of Congress*] (LCLS)
MnBadS ..... Badger School, Badger, MN [*Library symbol*] [*Library of Congress*] (LCLS)
MnBag ...... Bagley Public Library, Bagley, MN [*Library symbol*] [*Library of Congress*] (LCLS)
MnBagE ..... Bagley Elementary School, Bagley, MN [*Library symbol*] [*Library of Congress*] (LCLS)
MnBaPS ..... Balaton Public Schools, Balaton, MN [*Library symbol*] [*Library of Congress*] (LCLS)
MnBar .... Barnesville Public Library, Barnesville, MN [*Library symbol*] [*Library of Congress*] (LCLS)
MnBarFe .... Florence Atkinson Elementary School, Barnesville, MN [*Library symbol*] [*Library of Congress*] (LCLS)
MnBarH ..... Barnesville High School, Barnesville, MN [*Library symbol*] [*Library of Congress*] (LCLS)
MnBaSPL ... St. Peter's Lutheran School, Balaton, MN [*Library symbol*] [*Library of Congress*] (LCLS)
MnBatS ..... Battle Lake Public School, Battle Lake, MN [*Library symbol*] [*Library of Congress*] (LCLS)
MnBau ...... Baudette Public Library, Baudette, MN [*Library symbol*] [*Library of Congress*] (LCLS)
MnBauLH ... Lake of the Woods High School, Baudette, MN [*Library symbol*] [*Library of Congress*] (LCLS)
MnBaxE ..... Baxter Elementary School, Baxter, MN [*Library symbol*] [*Library of Congress*] (LCLS)
MNBB .... MNB Bancshares [*NASDAQ symbol*] (SAG)
MNB Bn ..... MNB Bancshares [*Associated Press*] (SAG)
MNBCCS .... Multi-Nevoid Basal-Cell Carcinoma Syndrome [*Medicine*] (MELL)
MNBDF ...... Meta-Nitrobenzenediazonium Tetrafluoroborate [*Organic chemistry*]
MNBDO ..... Mobile Naval Base Defence Organization [*British*] [*World War II*]
MnBE .... Becker Elementary School, Becker, MN [*Library symbol*] [*Library of Congress*] (LCLS)
MnBeaPS ... Beardlsey-Brown Valley Public Schools, Beardlsey, MN [*Library symbol*] [*Library of Congress*] (LCLS)
MnBeB ...... Bertha-Hweitt School, Bertha, MN [*Library symbol*] [*Library of Congress*] (LCLS)
MNBedf ..... New Bedford Free Public Library, New Bedford, MA [*Library symbol*] [*Library of Congress*] (LCLS)
MNBedfHi ... Old Dartmouth Historical Society, New Bedford Whaling Museum, New Bedford, MA [*Library symbol*] [*Library of Congress*] (LCLS)
MnBelPS .... Bellingham Public Schools, Bellingham, MN [*Library symbol*] [*Library of Congress*] (LCLS)
MnBem ...... Bemidji Public Library, Bemidji, MN [*Library symbol*] [*Library of Congress*] (LCLS)
MnBemCE ... Central Elementary School, Bemidji, MN [*Library symbol*] [*Library of Congress*] (LCLS)
MnBemDE ... Deer Lake Elementary School, Bemidji, MN [*Library symbol*] [*Library of Congress*] (LCLS)
MnBemH .... Bemidji High School, Bemidji, MN [*Library symbol*] [*Library of Congress*] (LCLS)
MnBemHE ... Horace May Elementary School, Bemidji, MN [*Library symbol*] [*Library of Congress*] (LCLS)
MnBemJE ... J.W. Smith Elementary School, Bemidji, MN [*Library symbol*] [*Library of Congress*] (LCLS)
MnBemLE ... Lincoln Elementary School, Bemidji, MN [*Library symbol*] [*Library of Congress*] (LCLS)
MnBemMS ... Benidji Middle School, Bemidji, MN [*Library symbol*] [*Library of Congress*] (LCLS)
MnBemNE ... Northern Elementary School, Bemidji, MN [*Library symbol*] [*Library of Congress*] (LCLS)
MnBemOH ... Oak Hills Bible College, Bemidji, MN [*Library symbol*] [*Library of Congress*] (LCLS)
MnBemPE ... Paul Bunyan Elementary School, Bemidji, MN [*Library symbol*] [*Library of Congress*] (LCLS)
MnBemS .... Bemidji State College [*Later, Bemidji State University*], Bemidji, MN [*Library symbol*] [*Library of Congress*] (LCLS)
MnBemSE ... Solway Elementary School, Bemidji, MN [*Library symbol*] [*Library of Congress*] (LCLS)
MnBemSP ... St. Philips School, Bemidji, MN [*Library symbol*] [*Library of Congress*] (LCLS)
MnBenPS ... Benson Public Schools, Benson, MN [*Library symbol*] [*Library of Congress*] (LCLS)
MnBenSF ... St. Francis Xavier School, Benson, MN [*Library symbol*] [*Library of Congress*] (LCLS)
MnBevPS ... Belview Public School, Bleview, MN [*Library symbol*] [*Library of Congress*] (LCLS)
MnBf .... Buffalo Public Library, Buffalo, MN [*Library symbol*] [*Library of Congress*] (LCLS)
MnBfaE ...... Big Falls Elementary School, Big Falls, MN [*Library symbol*] [*Library of Congress*] (LCLS)
MnBfH .... Buffalo Memorial Hospital, Medical Library, Buffalo, MN [*Library symbol*] [*Library of Congress*] (LCLS)
MnBfHi ...... Wright County Historical Society, Buffalo, MN [*Library symbol*] [*Library of Congress*] (LCLS)
MnBfI .... Buffalo Intermediate School, Buffalo, MN [*Library symbol*] [*Library of Congress*] (LCLS)
MnBfJ .... Buffalo Junior High School, Buffalo, MN [*Library symbol*] [*Library of Congress*] (LCLS)
MnBfoS ..... Bigfork School, Bigford, MN [*Library symbol*] [*Library of Congress*] (LCLS)
MnBfP .... Buffalo Primary Library, Buffalo, MN [*Library symbol*] [*Library of Congress*] (LCLS)

MnBfS .... Buffalo Senior High School, Buffalo, MN [*Library symbol*] [*Library of Congress*] (LCLS)
MnBfSF ..... St. Francis Xavier School, Buffalo, MN [*Library symbol*] [*Library of Congress*] (LCLS)
MnBfW ...... Wright Vocational Coop Center, Buffalo, MN [*Library symbol*] [*Library of Congress*] (LCLS)
MnBg .... Myrtle Mabee Library, Belgrade, MN [*Library symbol*] [*Library of Congress*] (LCLS)
MnBgE ...... Belgrade Elementary School, Belgrade, MN [*Library symbol*] [*Library of Congress*] (LCLS)
MnBgH ...... Belgrade High School, Media Center, Belgrade, MN [*Library symbol*] [*Library of Congress*] (LCLS)
MnBH .... Becker High School, Becker, MN [*Library symbol*] [*Library of Congress*] (LCLS)
MnBHi .... Sherbourne County Historical Society, Becker, MN [*Library symbol*] [*Library of Congress*] (LCLS)
MnBhM ...... Braham Middle School, Braham, MN [*Library symbol*] [*Library of Congress*] (LCLS)
MnBhSE ..... Southview Elementary School, Braham, MN [*Library symbol*] [*Library of Congress*] (LCLS)
MnBhWH .... Westview High School, Media Center, Braham, MN [*Library symbol*] [*Library of Congress*] (LCLS)
MnBi .... Bird Island Public Library, Bird Island, MN [*Library symbol*] [*Library of Congress*] (LCLS)
MnBirIS ..... Indus School, Birchdale, MN [*Library symbol*] [*Library of Congress*] (LCLS)
MnBiSM ..... St. Mary's School, Bird Island, MN [*Library symbol*] [*Library of Congress*] (LCLS)
MnBiwE ..... Bray Elementary School, Biwabik, MN [*Library symbol*] [*Library of Congress*] (LCLS)
MnBiwH ..... V.L. Reishus High School, Biwabik, MN [*Library symbol*] [*Library of Congress*] (LCLS)
MNBK .... Marine National Bank (California) [*NASDAQ symbol*] (SAG)
MNBK .... Marine Nat'l Bank [*NASDAQ symbol*] (TTSB)
MnBkES ..... Blomkest Elementary School, Blomkest, MN [*Library symbol*] [*Library of Congress*] (LCLS)
MNBKW ..... Marine Natl Bk Irvine CA Wrrt [*NASDAQ symbol*] (TTSB)
MnBl .... Big Lake Public Library, Big Lake, MN [*Library symbol*] [*Library of Congress*] (LCLS)
MNBL .... Bluefields [*Nicaragua*] [*ICAO location identifier*] (ICLI)
MnBla .... Blackduck Public Library, Blackduck, MN [*Library symbol*] [*Library of Congress*] (LCLS)
MnBlaE ...... Blackduck Elementary School, Blackduck, MN [*Library symbol*] [*Library of Congress*] (LCLS)
MnBlaH ..... Blackduck High School, Blackduck, MN [*Library symbol*] [*Library of Congress*] (LCLS)
MnBlE .... Big Lake Elementary School, Big Lake, MN [*Library symbol*] [*Library of Congress*] (LCLS)
MNBLE ...... Modified Nearly Best Linear Estimator [*Statistics*]
MnBlH .... Big Lake High School, Big Lake, MN [*Library symbol*] [*Library of Congress*] (LCLS)
MnBloPS .... Bloomington Public Schools, Bloomington, MN [*Library symbol*] [*Library of Congress*] (LCLS)
MnBmE ...... Barnum Elementary School, Barnum, MN [*Library symbol*] [*Library of Congress*] (LCLS)
MnBmH ..... Barnum High School, Barnum, MN [*Library symbol*] [*Library of Congress*] (LCLS)
MNBO .... Management Buy-Out
MnBov .... Bovey Public Library, Bovey, MN [*Library symbol*] [*Library of Congress*] (LCLS)
MnBovM .... Connor-Jasper Middle School, Bovey, MN [*Library symbol*] [*Library of Congress*] (LCLS)
MnBovS ..... Balsam School, Bovey, MN [*Library symbol*] [*Library of Congress*] (LCLS)
MnBr .... Brainerd Public Library, Brainerd, MN [*Library symbol*] [*Library of Congress*] (LCLS)
MNBR .... Los Brasiles/Carlos Ulloa [*Nicaragua*] [*ICAO location identifier*] (ICLI)
MNBR .... M & B Railroad [*Federal Railroad Administration identification code*]
MnBraS ..... Brandon Public School, Brandon, MN [*Library symbol*] [*Library of Congress*] (LCLS)
MnBrC .... Brainerd Community College, Brainerd, MN [*Library symbol*] [*Library of Congress*] (LCLS)
MnBre .... Breckenridge Public Library, Breckenridge, MN [*Library symbol*] [*Library of Congress*] (LCLS)
MnBreE ..... Breckenridge Elementary School, Breckenridge, MN [*Library symbol*] [*Library of Congress*] (LCLS)
MnBreH ..... Breckenridge High School, Breckenridge, MN [*Library symbol*] [*Library of Congress*] (LCLS)
MnBrFJ ...... Franklin Junior High School, Brainerd, MN [*Library symbol*] [*Library of Congress*] (LCLS)
MnBrGE ..... Garfield Elementary School, Brainerd, MN [*Library symbol*] [*Library of Congress*] (LCLS)
MnBrHE ..... Harrison Elementary School, Brainerd, MN [*Library symbol*] [*Library of Congress*] (LCLS)
MnBrHS ..... Brainerd High School, Brainerd, MN [*Library symbol*] [*Library of Congress*] (LCLS)
MnBrLE ..... Lincoln Elementary School, Brainerd, MN [*Library symbol*] [*Library of Congress*] (LCLS)
MnBrLoE .... Lowell Elementary School, Brainerd, MN [*Library symbol*] [*Library of Congress*] (LCLS)
MnBro .... Browntown Public Library, Browntown, MN [*Library symbol*] [*Library of Congress*] (LCLS)
MnBroPS .... Brownton Public Schools, Brownton, MN [*Library symbol*] [*Library of Congress*] (LCLS)
MnBrRE ..... Riverside Elementary School, Brainerd, MN [*Library symbol*] [*Library of Congress*] (LCLS)
MnBruE ..... Bruno Elementary School, Bruno, MN [*Library symbol*] [*Library of Congress*] (LCLS)
MnBrv .... Carnegie Public Library, Browns Valley, MN [*Library symbol*] [*Library of Congress*] (LCLS)
MnBrvPS .... Beardsley-Browns Valley Public Schools, Browns Valley, MN [*Library symbol*] [*Library of Congress*] (LCLS)
MnBrWE .... Whittier Elementary School, Brainerd,MN [*Library symbol*] [*Library of Congress*] (LCLS)
MnBrwES ... Brewster Elementary School, Brewster, MN [*Library symbol*] [*Library of Congress*] (LCLS)
MnBrWM .... Washington Middle School, Brainerd, MN [*Library symbol*] [*Library of Congress*] (LCLS)
MnBtH .... Brooten High School, Brooten, MN [*Library symbol*] [*Library of Congress*] (LCLS)
MnBul .... Buhl Public Library, Buhl, MN [*Library symbol*] [*Library of Congress*] (LCLS)
MnBulR ..... Range Geneaological Society, Buhl, MN [*Library symbol*] [*Library of Congress*] (LCLS)
MnBuS ...... St. Michael School, Buckman, MN [*Library symbol*] [*Library of Congress*] (LCLS)
MnBvC ...... Christ the King School, Browerville, MN [*Library symbol*] [*Library of Congress*] (LCLS)
MnBvP ...... Browerville Public School, Browerville, MN [*Library symbol*] [*Library of Congress*] (LCLS)
MNBWS ..... Miami Nature Biotechnology Winter Symposium (HGEN)
MNBZ .... Bonanza [*Nicaragua*] [*ICAO location identifier*] (ICLI)
MNC .... Concordia College, St. Paul, MN [*OCLC symbol*] (OCLC)
MNC .... Magnocellular Neurosecretory Cells
MNC .... Major NATO Command [*or Commander*] (NATG)
MNC .... Manager, National Clients (SAUO)
MNC .... Maryland National Affiliates Corporation (EFIS)
MNC .... Masonite Corporation (SAUO)
MNC .... Media News Corporation (SAUO)
MNC .... Mental Nurses' Cooperation (ROG)
MNC .... Michigan National Corporation (EFIS)
MNC .... Microcomputer Numerical Control (MCD)
MNC .... Mineman, Chief [*Navy rating*]
MNC .... Ministerial Nomination Committee [*Australia*]
Mn-C .... Minnesota State Department of Corrections, St. Paul, MN [*Library symbol*] [*Library of Congress*] (LCLS)
MNC .... MIT Airlines Ltd. [*ICAO designator*] (FAAC)
MNC .... Mobile Network Code (CGWS)
MNC .... Mobile Network Computer (GART)
MNC .... Monaco Coach [*NYSE symbol*] (SG)
MNC .... Moncalieri [*Italy*] [*Seismograph station code, US Geological Survey*] [*Closed*] (SEIS)
MNC .... Monica Resources [*Vancouver Stock Exchange symbol*]
MNC .... Mononuclear Cell (DB)
MNC .... Mononucleated Cell [*Clinical chemistry*] [*Also, MC*]
MNC .... Motornuclear Cell [*Medicine*] (EDAA)
MNC .... Mouvement National Congolais [*Congolese National Movement*]
MNC .... Mouvement National du Congo-Lumumba [*Congo National Movement-Lumumba*] [*Zaire*] (PD)
MNC .... Movement for a New Congress (SAUO)
MNC .... Movimiento Nacional Conservador [*National Conservative Movement*] [*Colombia*] [*Political party*] (EY)
MNC .... Multinational Company [*Business term*]
MNC .... Multinational Corp.
MNC .... Multi-National Corporation
MNC .... Multinucleated Cell [*Medicine*] (MELL)
MNC .... Multiplicative Noise Compensator [*Telecommunications*] (TEL)
MNC .... Nacala [*Mozambique*] [*Airport symbol*] (AD)
MNC .... Shelton, WA [*Location identifier*] [*FAA*] (FAAL)
MnCaCC .... Cambridge Community College, Cambridge, MN [*Library symbol*] [*Library of Congress*] (LCLS)
MnCaE ...... East Central Regional Library, Cambridge, MN [*Library symbol*] [*Library of Congress*] (LCLS)
MnCaES ..... Cambridge Elementary School, Media Center, Cambridge, MN [*Library symbol*] [*Library of Congress*] (LCLS)
MnCaH ...... Cambridge Memorial Hospital, Health Sciences Library, Cambridge, MN [*Library symbol*] [*Library of Congress*] (LCLS)
MnCaHi ..... Isanti County Historical Society, Cambridge, MN [*Library symbol*] [*Library of Congress*] (LCLS)
MnCaHS .... Cambridge High School, Media Center, Cambridge, MN [*Library symbol*] [*Library of Congress*] (LCLS)
MnCalE ...... Callaway Elementary School, Callaway, MN [*Library symbol*] [*Library of Congress*] (LCLS)
MnCaM ...... Cambridge Middle School, Media Center, Cambridge, MN [*Library symbol*] [*Library of Congress*] (LCLS)
MnCamE .... Campbell-Tintah Elementary School, Campbell, MN [*Library symbol*] [*Library of Congress*] (LCLS)
MnCamH .... Campbell-Tintah High School, Campbell, MN [*Library symbol*] [*Library of Congress*] (LCLS)
MnCan ...... Canby Public Library, Canby, MN [*Library symbol*] [*Library of Congress*] (LCLS)
MnCanH ..... Canby Community Hospital, Canby, MN [*Library symbol*] [*Library of Congress*] (LCLS)
MnCanHS ... Canby High School, Canby, MN [*Library symbol*] [*Library of Congress*] (LCLS)
MnCarE ..... Carlos Elementary School, Carlos, MN [*Library symbol*] [*Library of Congress*] (LCLS)
MnCas .... Cass Lake Community Library, Lake, MN [*Library symbol*] [*Library of Congress*] (LCLS)
MnCasCB ... Chief Bug-O-Nay-Ge-Shig Library, Cass Lake, MN [*Library symbol*] [*Library of Congress*] (LCLS)
MnCaSD .... Cambridge Seventh Day Adventist Library, Cambridge, MN [*Library symbol*] [*Library of Congress*] (LCLS)
MnCasE ..... Cass Lake Elementary School, Cass Lake, MN [*Library symbol*] [*Library of Congress*] (LCLS)

MnCaSH .... Cambridge State Hospital, Staff Library, Cambridge, MN [*Library symbol*] [*Library of Congress*] (LCLS)
MnCasHS ... Cass Lake High School, Cass Lake, MN [*Library symbol*] [*Library of Congress*] (LCLS)
MNCC .... Multinational Coordination Center [*NATO*]
MnCcH ...... Hazelden Foundation, Staff library, Center City, MN [*Library symbol*] [*Library of Congress*] (LCLS)
MNCF........ Merchant Navy Comforts Fund (SAUO)
MnCgL ...... Lakeside Intermediate Media Center, Chisago City, MN [*Library symbol*] [*Library of Congress*] (LCLS)
MnCgP ...... Chisago Lakes Primary School, Chisago City, MN [*Library symbol*] [*Library of Congress*] (LCLS)
MnCh........ Carver County Library, Chaska, MN [*Library symbol*] [*Library of Congress*] (LCLS)
MNCH .... Chinandega/German Pomares [*Nicaragua*] [*ICAO location identifier*] (ICLI)
MnChaHS ... Chandler-Lake Wilson High School, Chandler, MN [*Library symbol*] [*Library of Congress*] (LCLS)
MnChi....... Chisholm Public Library, Chisholm, MN [*Library symbol*] [*Library of Congress*] (LCLS)
MnChiE...... Vaughan-Steffensrud Elementary School, Chisholm, MN [*Library symbol*] [*Library of Congress*] (LCLS)
MnChiJ...... Chisholm Junior High School, Chisholm, MN [*Library symbol*] [*Library of Congress*] (LCLS)
MnChil ...... Iron Range Research Library, Chisholm, MN [*Library symbol*] [*Library of Congress*] (LCLS)
MnChiSH.... Chisholm Senior High School, Chisholm, MN [*Library symbol*] [*Library of Congress*] (LCLS)
MnChoE..... Chokio-Alberto Elementary School, Chokio, MN [*Library symbol*] [*Library of Congress*] (LCLS)
MNCI .... Corn Island [*Nicaragua*] [*ICAO location identifier*] (ICLI)
MNCI .... Neepawa Collegiate Institute, Manitoba [*Library symbol*] [*National Library of Canada*] (NLC)
MNCIS....... Management Numerical Control Information System (MCD)
MNC-K ...... Mouvement National Congolais - Kalonji [*Congolese National Movement*] [*Kalonji Wing*]
MnCl......... Cloquet Public Library, Cloquet, MN [*Library symbol*] [*Library of Congress*] (LCLS)
MNCL........ Monoclonal Gammopathy Identified [*Immunology*] (DAVI)
MNC-L....... Mouvement National Congolais - Lumumba [*Congolese National Movement*] [*Lumumba Wing*]
MnClaE...... Clarissa Elementary School, Clarissa, MN [*Library symbol*] [*Library of Congress*] (LCLS)
MnCLaH..... Clarissa High School, Clarissa, MN [*Library symbol*] [*Library of Congress*] (LCLS)
MnClc .... Clara City Public Library, Clara City, MN [*Library symbol*] [*Library of Congress*] (LCLS)
MnClCE ..... Churchill Elementary School, Cloquet, MN [*Library symbol*] [*Library of Congress*] (LCLS)
MnClcPS.... Clara City Public Schools, Clara City, MN [*Library symbol*] [*Library of Congress*] (LCLS)
MnCleS ..... Clearbrook Public School, Clearbrook, MN [*Library symbol*] [*Library of Congress*] (LCLS)
MnClHi...... Carlton County Historical Society, Cloquet, MN [*Library symbol*] [*Library of Congress*] (LCLS)
MnClim ..... Climax Public Library, Climax, MN [*Library symbol*] [*Library of Congress*] (LCLS)
MnClimS.... Climax-Shelly School, Climax, MN [*Library symbol*] [*Library of Congress*] (LCLS)
MnClkE...... Clearview Elementary School, Clear lake, MN [*Library symbol*] [*Library of Congress*] (LCLS)
MnClM ...... Cloquet Middle School, Cloquet, MN [*Library symbol*] [*Library of Congress*] (LCLS)
MnClOS ..... Fond du Lac Ojibway School, Cloquet, MN [*Library symbol*] [*Library of Congress*] (LCLS)
MnCls .... Cold Spring Community Library, Cold Spring, MN [*Library symbol*] [*Library of Congress*] (LCLS)
MnClsE...... Cold Spring Elementary/Rocori Junior School, Cold Spring, MN [*Library symbol*] [*Library of Congress*] (LCLS)
MnClSH ..... Cloquet Senior High School, Cloquet, MN [*Library symbol*] [*Library of Congress*] (LCLS)
MnClsR ..... Rocori High School, Cold Spring, MN [*Library symbol*] [*Library of Congress*] (LCLS)
MnClsS...... St. Boniface Elementary School, Cold Spring, MN [*Library symbol*] [*Library of Congress*] (LCLS)
MnClWE..... Washington Elementary School, Cloquet, MN [*Library symbol*] [*Library of Congress*] (LCLS)
MnCm .... Calumet Public Library, Calumet, MN [*Library symbol*] [*Library of Congress*] (LCLS)
MNCM....... Mineman, Master Chief [*Navy rating*]
MNCMPTR... Minicomputer (MSA)
MnCo........ Cokato Public Library, Cokato, MN [*Library symbol*] [*Library of Congress*] (LCLS)
MNCO .... Michigan National Corp. [*NASDAQ symbol*] (COMM)
MnCoD ...... Dassel-Cokato Jr./Sr. High School, Cakoto, MN [*Library symbol*] [*Library of Congress*] (LCLS)
MnCoE ...... Cokato Elementary School, Media Center, Cokato, MN [*Library symbol*] [*Library of Congress*] (LCLS)
MnCohS..... Cohasset School, Cohasset, MN [*Library symbol*] [*Library of Congress*] (LCLS)
MnCol .... Coleraine Public Library, Coleraine, MN [*Library symbol*] [*Library of Congress*] (LCLS)
MnColH ..... Greenway High School, Coleraine, MN [*Library symbol*] [*Library of Congress*] (LCLS)
MnCoM...... Cokato Museum, Cokato, MN [*Library symbol*] [*Library of Congress*] (LCLS)
MN-COMPAC... Minn League of Savings & Community Bankers Community Campaign Committee [*Eden Prairie, MN*] (PACS)
MnCoo ...... Cook Public Library, Cook, MN [*Library symbol*] [*Library of Congress*] (LCLS)
MnCooS..... Cook Public School, Cook, MN [*Library symbol*] [*Library of Congress*] (LCLS)
MnCosPS ... Cosmos Public School, Cosmos, MN [*Library symbol*] [*Library of Congress*] (LCLS)
MnCotS ..... Cotton Public School, Cotton, MN [*Library symbol*] [*Library of Congress*] (LCLS)
MNCP .... Math Network Curriculum Project (EDAC)
MNCP .... Mbandzeni National Convention Party [*Swaziland*] (BUAC)
MNCP .... Motient Corp. [*OTCBB symbol*]
MNCPE...... Motient Corp. [*NASDAQ symbol*] (QUAN)
MNCPL...... Municipal
MNCPPC.... Maryland-National Capital Park and Planning Commission
MNCPPLTY... Municipality
MnCr .... Crookston Public Library, Crookston, MN [*Library symbol*] [*Library of Congress*] (LCLS)
MNCR .... Material Nonconformance Report (COE)
MnCr .... Polk County Library, Crookston, MN [*Library symbol*] [*Library of Congress*] (LCLS)
MnCrCH..... Central High School, Crookston,MN [*Library symbol*] [*Library of Congress*] (LCLS)
MnCrHE ..... Highland Elementary School, Crookston, MN [*Library symbol*] [*Library of Congress*] (LCLS)
MnCrLE ..... Lincoln Elementary School, Crookston, MN [*Library symbol*] [*Library of Congress*] (LCLS)
MnCrMS .... Mount St. Benedict, Crookston, MN [*Library symbol*] [*Library of Congress*] (LCLS)
MnCroE ..... Crosby-Ironton Elementary School, Crosby, MN [*Library symbol*] [*Library of Congress*] (LCLS)
MnCroH ..... Crosby-Ironton High School, Crosby, MN [*Library symbol*] [*Library of Congress*] (LCLS)
MnCrpM..... Mercy Medical Center, Coon Rapids, MN [*Library symbol*] [*Library of Congress*] (LCLS)
MNCRR ..... Metro-North Commuter Railroad (SAUO)
MNCRS...... Mobile Network Computing Reference Specification (GART)
MnCrU....... University of Minnesota Technical College, Crookston, MN [*Library symbol*] [*Library of Congress*] (LCLS)
MnCrWE .... Washington Elementary School, Crookston, MN [*Library symbol*] [*Library of Congress*] (LCLS)
MnCrwHS... Cromwell High School, Cromwell, MN [*Library symbol*] [*Library of Congress*] (LCLS)
MNCS .... Master Net Control Station (SAUO)
MNCS .... Merchant Navy Comforts Service (SAUO)
MNCS .... Mineman, Senior Chief [*Navy rating*]
MNCS .... Multipoint Network-Control System
MnCS........ St. John's University, Collegeville, MN [*Library symbol*] [*Library of Congress*] (LCLS)
MnCt......... Carlton Public Library, Carlton, MN [*Library symbol*] [*Library of Congress*] (LCLS)
MnCtE....... South Terrace Elementary School, Carlton, MN [*Library symbol*] [*Library of Congress*] (LCLS)
MnCtH....... Carlotn High School, Carlton, MN [*Library symbol*] [*Library of Congress*] (LCLS)
MnCtwPS ... Cottonwood Public School, Cottonwood, MN [*Library symbol*] [*Library of Congress*] (LCLS)
MNCV .... Motor Nerve Conduction Velocity [*Medicine*]
MNCW....... Metro North Commuter Railroad [*Federal Railroad Administration identification code*]
MNCY .... Marion County Railway [*Federal Railroad Administration identification code*]
MnCyS ...... Cyrus Public School, Cyrus, MN [*Library symbol*] [*Library of Congress*] (LCLS)
MNCZ........ Northshore Mining [*Federal Railroad Administration identification code*]
MND......... Mandalay [*Burma*] [*Seismograph station code, US Geological Survey*] [*Closed*] (SEIS)
MND......... Marlin Developments [*Vancouver Stock Exchange symbol*]
MND......... Martin Nuclear Division [*AEC*] (MCD)
MND......... Material Need Document [*DoD*]
MND......... Mean Narrow Dose [*Radiation therapy*] (DAVI)
MND......... Medial Nuclear Division [*Cytology*]
MND......... Mendenhall, AK [*Location identifier*] [*FAA*] (FAAL)
MND......... Midsummer Night's Dream [*Shakespearean work*]
MND......... Minimum Necrosing Dose
MND......... Minister of National Defence [*Canada*]
MND......... Ministry of National Defence [*British*] (MCD)
MND......... Minor Neurological Dysfunction
MND......... Mission Need Determination (DOMA)
MND......... Mission Need Document [*DoD*]
MND......... Mission Non-Delivery (MCD)
MND......... Mitchell Energy & Development Corp. [*NYSE symbol*] (SAG)
MND......... Modified Neck Dissection [*Medicine*] (DMAA)
MND......... Motor Neuron Disease [*Medicine*]
MND......... Mound
MND......... Movimento Nacional Democratico [*National Democratic Movement*] [*Portugal*] [*Political party*] (PPE)
MND......... Multi-National Division (SAUO)
MND......... University of Minnesota-Duluth, Duluth, MN [*OCLC symbol*] (OCLC)
MNDA .... Missionary Sisters of Notre Dame des Anges [*Roman Catholic religious order*]
MNDA .... Missionary Sisters of Our Lady of the Angels (BUAC)
MND A ...... Mitchell Energy/Dev'A' [*NYSE symbol*] (TTSB)
MNDA .... Motor Neurone Disease Association [*British*] (DBA)
MND/ALS ... Motor Neurone Disease/Amyotrophic Lateral Sclerosis [*Medicine*] [*Lou Gehrig's Disease*] (EDAA)
MND Association... Motor Neurone Disease Association (NRGU)

MnDaw ...... Carnegie Library, Dawson, MN [*Library symbol*] [*Library of Congress*] (LCLS)
MNDAWA ... Motor Neurone Disease Association of Western Australia
MnDawJH... Johnson Memorial Hospital and Nursing School, Dawson, MN [*Library symbol*] [*Library of Congress*] (LCLS)
MnDawPS... Dawson-Boyd Public Library, Dawson, MN [*Library symbol*] [*Library of Congress*] (LCLS)
MNDAX...... MFS New Discovery
MND B ...... Mitchell Energy/Dev'B' [*NYSE symbol*] (TTSB)
MND-C ...... Multi-National Division, Centre (SAUO)
MND-C ...... Multi-National Division, Centre. To be formed between October (SAUS)
MNDD .... Mouvement National pour la Democratie et le Developpement [*Benin*] [*Political party*] (EY)
MnDe........ Delano Public Library, Delano, MN [*Library symbol*] [*Library of Congress*] (LCLS)
MnDeE ...... Delano Elementary School, Delano, MN [*Library symbol*] [*Library of Congress*] (LCLS)
MnDeH...... Delano High School, Delano, MN [*Library symbol*] [*Library of Congress*] (LCLS)
MnDeM ..... Delano Middle School, Delano, MN [*Library symbol*] [*Library of Congress*] (LCLS)
MNDEP...... Mineral Deposits Data Base (SAUO)
MnDerE ..... King Elementary School, Deer River, MN [*Library symbol*] [*Library of Congress*] (LCLS)
MnDerH..... Deer River High School, Deer River, MN [*Library symbol*] [*Library of Congress*] (LCLS)
MnDES ...... Dassel Elementary School, Media Center, Dassel, MN [*Library symbol*] [*Library of Congress*] (LCLS)
MnDeSP ..... St. Peter's School, Delano, MN [*Library symbol*] [*Library of Congress*] (LCLS)
MnDl .... Detroit Lakes Public Library, Detroit Lakes, MN [*Library symbol*] [*Library of Congress*] (LCLS)
MnDlH....... Community High School, Detroit Lakes, MN [*Library symbol*] [*Library of Congress*] (LCLS)
MnDlHi...... Becker County Historical Society, Detroit Lakes, MN [*Library symbol*] [*Library of Congress*] (LCLS)
MnDlJ .... Community Junior High School, Detroit Lakes, MN [*Library symbol*] [*Library of Congress*] (LCLS)
MnDlLe ..... Lincoln Elementary School, Detroit Lakes, MN [*Library symbol*] [*Library of Congress*] (LCLS)
MnDlRE..... Rossman Elementary School, Detroit Lakes, MN [*Library symbol*] [*Library of Congress*] (LCLS)
MnDlTI ...... Detroit Lakes Technical Institute, Detroit Lakes, MN [*Library symbol*] [*Library of Congress*] (LCLS)
MnDlWE .... Washington Elementary School, Detroit Lakes, MN [*Library symbol*] [*Library of Congress*] (LCLS)
MNDO .... Merchant Navy Discipline Organisation [*British*] (DS)
MNDO .... Modified Neglect of Diatomic Overlap (AAEL)
MNDO .... Modified Neglect of Differential Overlap [*Quantum mechanics*]
MNDP .... Bibliotheque Pere Champagne [*Pere Champagne Library*], Notre-Dame-De-Lourdes, Manitoba [*Library symbol*] [*National Library of Canada*] (BIB)
MNDP .... Malawi National Democratic Party [*Political party*] (PSAP)
MNDP .... Multinational Data Processing (MHDB)
MND-S ...... Multi-National Division, South (SAUO)
MND-S ...... Multi-National Division, South. Due to become operational in (SAUS)
MNDTH...... Minimum Depth (NOAA)
MNDTS...... Member of the Non-Destructive Testing Society of Great Britain
MnDu........ Duluth Public Library, Duluth, MN [*Library symbol*] [*Library of Congress*] (LCLS)
MnDuBE..... Birchwood Elementary School, Duluth, MN [*Library symbol*] [*Library of Congress*] (LCLS)
MnDuBVE... Bay View Elementary School, Duluth, MN [*Library symbol*] [*Library of Congress*] (LCLS)
MnDuCE..... Cobb Elementary Library, Duluth, MN [*Library symbol*] [*Library of Congress*] (LCLS)
MnDuCH .... Central High School, Duluth, MN [*Library symbol*] [*Library of Congress*] (LCLS)
MnDuCOE... Congdon Park Elementary School, Duluth, MN [*Library symbol*] [*Library of Congress*] (LCLS)
MnDuCPE... Chester Park Elementary School, Duluth, MN [*Library symbol*] [*Library of Congress*] (LCLS)
MnDuDH .... Denfeld High School, Duluth, MN [*Library symbol*] [*Library of Congress*] (LCLS)
MnDuEH .... East High School, Duluth, MN [*Library symbol*] [*Library of Congress*] (LCLS)
MnDuEPA... United States Environmental Protection Agency, National Water Quality Laboratory, Duluth, MN [*Library symbol*] [*Library of Congress*] (LCLS)
MnDuGE .... Grant Elementary School, Duluth, MN [*Library symbol*] [*Library of Congress*] (LCLS)
MnDuHE .... Homcroft Elementary School, Duluth, MN [*Library symbol*] [*Library of Congress*] (LCLS)
MnDuHi ..... Northeast Minnesota Historical Center Library, Duluth, MN [*Library symbol*] [*Library of Congress*] (LCLS)
MnDuHS .... Hermantown High School, Duluth, MN [*Library symbol*] [*Library of Congress*] (LCLS)
MnDuLE..... Lincoln Elementary School, Duluth, MN [*Library symbol*] [*Library of Congress*] (LCLS)
MnDuLOE... Lowell Elementary School, Duluth, MN [*Library symbol*] [*Library of Congress*] (LCLS)
MnDuLPE... Lester Park Elementary School, Duluth, MN [*Library symbol*] [*Library of Congress*] (LCLS)
MnDuLWE... Lakewood Elementary School, Duluth, MN [*Library symbol*] [*Library of Congress*] (LCLS)
MnDuM ..... Miller-Dawn Hospital and Medical Center, Duluth, MN [*Library symbol*] [*Library of Congress*] (LCLS)
MnDuME.... Merritt Elementary School, Duluth, MN [*Library symbol*] [*Library of Congress*] (LCLS)
MnDuMPJ... Morgan Park Junior High School, Duluth, MN [*Library symbol*] [*Library of Congress*] (LCLS)
MnDuMS.... Marshall School, Duluth, MN [*Library symbol*] [*Library of Congress*] (LCLS)
MnDuMWE... MacArthue/West Elementary School, Duluth MN [*Library symbol*] [*Library of Congress*] (LCLS)
MnDuNE .... Nettleton Elementary School, Duluth, MN [*Library symbol*] [*Library of Congress*] (LCLS)
MnDuNR .... Natural Resources Research Institute, Duluth, MN [*Library symbol*] [*Library of Congress*] (LCLS)
MnDuNSE... North Shore Elementary School, Duluth, MN [*Library symbol*] [*Library of Congress*] (LCLS)
MnDuOJ..... Ordean Junior High School, Duluth, MN [*Library symbol*] [*Library of Congress*] (LCLS)
MnDuPC .... Duluth Prison Camp, Duluth, MN [*Library symbol*] [*Library of Congress*] (LCLS)
MnDuPE..... Piedmont Elementary School, Duluth, MN [*Library symbol*] [*Library of Congress*] (LCLS)
MnDuSE..... Stowe Elementary School, Duluth, MN [*Library symbol*] [*Library of Congress*] (LCLS)
MnDuSLH... St. Louis County Helth Dept., Duluth, MN [*Library symbol*] [*Library of Congress*] (LCLS)
MnDuStL.... Saint Luke's Hospital, Duluth, MN [*Library symbol*] [*Library of Congress*] (LCLS)
MnDuStM... Saint Mary's Hospital, Duluth, MN [*Library symbol*] [*Library of Congress*] (LCLS)
MnDuStS.... College of Saint Scholastica, Duluth, MN [*Library symbol*] [*Library of Congress*] (LCLS)
MnDuTI ..... Duluth Technical Institute, Duluth, MN [*Library symbol*] [*Library of Congress*] (LCLS)
MnDuTRC... Teachers' Resource Center, Duluth, MN [*Library symbol*] [*Library of Congress*] (LCLS)
MnDuU ..... University of Minnesota, Duluth, MN [*Library symbol*] [*Library of Congress*] (LCLS)
MnDuWE.... Washburn Elementary School, Duluth, MN [*Library symbol*] [*Library of Congress*] (LCLS)
MnDuWJ .... Washington Junior High School, Duluth, MN [*Library symbol*] [*Library of Congress*] (LCLS)
MnDuWJH... Woodland Junior High School, Duluth, MN [*Library symbol*] [*Library of Congress*] (LCLS)
MNDX .... Mobile Non-Director Exchange [*Telecommunications*] (NITA)
MNE .... College of St. Catherine, St. Paul, MN [*OCLC symbol*] (OCLC)
Mne.......... Marine [*British military*] (DMA)
MNE .... Master of Naval Engineering
MNE .... Master of Nuclear Engineering
MNE .... Mentone [*France*] [*Airport symbol*] (AD)
MNE .... Merchant Navy Establishment [*British*] (DS)
MNE .... Methylallyl Nitrophenyl Ether [*Organic chemistry*]
MNE .... Methylnorepinephrine [*Also, Normetanephrine*] [*Biochemistry*]
MNE .... Minden, LA [*Location identifier*] [*FAA*] (FAAL)
MNE .... Mineo [*Sicily*] [*Seismograph station code, US Geological Survey*] [*Closed*] (SEIS)
MNE .... Minimum Number of Elements
Mn-E......... Minnesota State Department of Education, St. Paul, MN [*Library symbol*] [*Library of Congress*] (LCLS)
MNE .... Modern English [*Language, etc.*]
MNE .... Moneygram Payment Systems [*NYSE symbol*] (SAG)
MNE.......... Multinational Enterprise
MNe .... Newburyport Public Library, Newburyport, MA [*Library symbol*] [*Library of Congress*] (LCLS)
MNEA........ Merchant Navy Establishment Administration [*British*] (DS)
MNEAF ...... Minera Andes, Inc. [*NASDAQ symbol*] (QUAN)
MnEb .... Eagle Bend Public Library, Eagle Bend, MN [*Library symbol*] [*Library of Congress*] (LCLS)
MnEbS ...... Eagle Bend School, Eagle Bend, MN [*Library symbol*] [*Library of Congress*] (LCLS)
MNEC........ Midnight Express Trucking Company [*Common carrier symbol*]
MnEcES ..... Echo-Wood Lake Elementary School, Echo, MN [*Library symbol*] [*Library of Congress*] (LCLS)
MNECInst of E&S... Member of North East Coast Institution of Engineers & Shipbuilders (SAUO)
MNECP...... Mobile National Emergency Command Post [*Air Force*]
MN Ed....... Master of Nursing Education
MN ED ...... Material Need Engineering Development (MCD)
MnEdS ...... Southdale-Hennepin Area Library, Edina, MN [*Library symbol*] [*Library of Congress*] (LCLS)
MNEE........ Mission Nonessential Equipment [*NASA*] (KSC)
MNeeS ...... GTE-Sylvania, Electric Systems Group, Needham, MA [*Library symbol*] [*Library of Congress*] (LCLS)
MnEfAE...... Adams Elementary School, Fergus Falls, MN [*Library symbol*] [*Library of Congress*] (LCLS)
MNEFF ...... Minefinders Corp. Ltd [*NASDAQ symbol*] (QUAN)
MnEfS .... Effie School, Effie, MN [*Library symbol*] [*Library of Congress*] (LCLS)
MnEgfCE .... Crestwood Elementary School, East Grand Forks, MN [*Library symbol*] [*Library of Congress*] (LCLS)
MnEgfH ..... East Grand Forks High School, East Grand Forks, MN [*Library symbol*] [*Library of Congress*] (LCLS)
MnEgfJ ..... Central Junior High School, Grand Forks, MN [*Library symbol*] [*Library of Congress*] (LCLS)
MnEgfRE.... River Heights Elementary School, East Grand Forks, MN [*Library symbol*] [*Library of Congress*] (LCLS)
MnEgfTI..... East Grand Forks Technical Institute, East Grand Forks, MN [*Library symbol*] [*Library of Congress*] (LCLS)

MnEgfVE .... Valley Elementary School, East Grand Forks, MN [*Library symbol*] [*Library of Congress*] (LCLS)
MNeHi .... Newburyport Historical Society, Newburyport, MA [*Library symbol*] [*Library of Congress*] (LCLS)
MNEIMME ... Member of the North of England Institute of Mining and Mechanical Engineers (SAUO)
MnElb .... Thorsen Memorial Public Library, Elbow Lake, MN [*Library symbol*] [*Library of Congress*] (LCLS)
MnElbE ...... West Central Elementary School, Elbow Lake, MN [*Library symbol*] [*Library of Congress*] (LCLS)
MnElbH ..... West Central High School, Elbow Lake, MN [*Library symbol*] [*Library of Congress*] (LCLS)
MnEly .... Ely Public Library, Ely, MN [*Library symbol*] [*Library of Congress*] (LCLS)
MnElyJS .... Memorial Junior/Senior High School, Ely, MN [*Library symbol*] [*Library of Congress*] (LCLS)
MnElyV ...... Vermillion Community College, Ely, MN [*Library symbol*] [*Library of Congress*] (LCLS)
MnElyWE ... Washington Elementary School, Ely, MN [*Library symbol*] [*Library of Congress*] (LCLS)
Mnemos .... Mnemosyne [*A publication*] (OCD)
MN Eng .... Master of Naval Engineering
MnEr .... Elk River Public Library, Elk River, MN [*Library symbol*] [*Library of Congress*] (LCLS)
MNERAM ... Members of New England Regional Art Museum
MnErHE ..... Handke Elementary School, Elk River, MN [*Library symbol*] [*Library of Congress*] (LCLS)
MnErPE ..... K.G. Parker Elementary School, Elk River, MN [*Library symbol*] [*Library of Congress*] (LCLS)
MnErS .... Elk River Senior High School, Elk River, MN [*Library symbol*] [*Library of Congress*] (LCLS)
MnErSA ..... St. Andrew's School, Elk River, MN [*Library symbol*] [*Library of Congress*] (LCLS)
MnErSJ ...... Salk Junior High School, Elk River, MN [*Library symbol*] [*Library of Congress*] (LCLS)
MnErSJL .... St. John's Lutheran School, Elk River, MN [*Library symbol*] [*Library of Congress*] (LCLS)
MnErsS ...... Erksine Public School, Erkskine, MN [*Library symbol*] [*Library of Congress*] (LCLS)
MnErVJ ...... Vandenberge Junior High School, Elk River, MN [*Library symbol*] [*Library of Congress*] (LCLS)
MNES .... Median Nerve Entrapment Syndrome [*Medicine*] (MELL)
MNES .... Mine Safety Appl [*NASDAQ symbol*] (TTSB)
MNES .... Mine Safety Appliances Co. [*NASDAQ symbol*] (NQ)
MnEskH ..... Esko High School, Esko, MN [*Library symbol*] [*Library of Congress*] (LCLS)
MnEskWE ... Winterquist Elementary School, Esko, MN [*Library symbol*] [*Library of Congress*] (LCLS)
MNet .... Media Awareness Network
MNET .... Mission and Data Operations Directorate Network (MCD)
MNET .... Multicom Publishing [*NASDAQ symbol*] (SAG)
MNEV .... Musica Nostra et Vostra, National Corp. of America (EA)
MnEvaE ..... Evansville Elementary School, Evansville, MN [*Library symbol*] [*Library of Congress*] (LCLS)
MnEvaH ..... Evansville High School, Evansville, MN [*Library symbol*] [*Library of Congress*] (LCLS)
MnEvH ...... Eden Valley-Watkins High School, Eden Valley, MN [*Library symbol*] [*Library of Congress*] (LCLS)
MnEvI .... Eveleth Public Library, Eveleth, MN [*Library symbol*] [*Library of Congress*] (LCLS)
MnEvIFE .... Franklin Elementary School, Eveleth, MN [*Library symbol*] [*Library of Congress*] (LCLS)
MnEvISH .... Eveleth-Gilbert Senior High School, Eveleth, MN [*Library symbol*] [*Library of Congress*] (LCLS)
MnF .... Buckham Memorial Library, Faribault, MN [*Library symbol*] [*Library of Congress*] (LCLS)
MNF .... College of St. Benedict, St. Joseph, MN [*OCLC symbol*] (OCLC)
MNF .... Forbes Library, Northampton, MA [*Library symbol*] [*Library of Congress*] (LCLS)
MNF .... Mana [*Fiji*] [*Airport symbol*] (OAG)
MNF .... Manager, National Finance (SAUO)
MNF .... Manifest [*Telegraphy*] (PCTE)
MNF .... Manitou Reef Resources [*Vancouver Stock Exchange symbol*]
MNF .... Maritime Nuclear Forces (SAUO)
MNF .... Menagasha National Forest (SAUO)
MNF .... Millers' National Federation (EA)
MNF .... Mizo National Front [*India*] (PD)
MNF .... Morehead & North Fork R. R. [*AAR code*]
MNF .... Motor Neurone Function [*Medicine*] (EDAA)
MNF .... Mountain View, MO [*Location identifier*] [*FAA*] (FAAL)
MNF .... Multilateral Nuclear Force
MNF .... Multinational Force [*Eleven-nation peace-keeping force for the Sinai*]
MNF .... Multinational Peace-Keeping Force (SAUO)
MNF .... Multisystem Networking Facility
MNF .... Myelinated Nerve Fiber [*Medicine*] (MELL)
MNF .... Umbundu [*Language symbol*] (ETLW)
MnFa .... Martin County Library, Fairmont, MN [*Library symbol*] [*Library of Congress*] (LCLS)
MNFD .... Manifested [*Telegraphy*] (PCTE)
MNFD .... Manifold (ECII)
MNFE .... M and S Transfer [*Common carrier symbol*]
MNFE .... Missile Not Fully Equipped (AAG)
MnFer .... Fertile Public Library, Fertile, MN [*Library symbol*] [*Library of Congress*] (LCLS)
MnFerS ..... Fertile-Betrami School, Fertile, MN [*Library symbol*] [*Library of Congress*] (LCLS)
MnFf .... Fergus Falls Public Library, Fergus Falls, MN [*Library symbol*] [*Library of Congress*] (LCLS)
MNFF .... Magyar Nemzeti Fueggetlensegi Front [*Hungarian National Independence Front*] [*Political party*]
MNFF .... Modern Traffic Services [*Common carrier symbol*]
MnFfC .... Fergus Falls Community College, Fergus Falls, MN [*Library symbol*] [*Library of Congress*] (LCLS)
MnFfCE ...... Cleveland Elementary School, Fergus Falls, MN [*Library symbol*] [*Library of Congress*] (LCLS)
MnFfEC ...... West Central Educational Cooperative Service Unit, Fergus Falls, MN [*Library symbol*] [*Library of Congress*] (LCLS)
MnFfH .... Lake Region Hospital, Fergus Falls, MN [*Library symbol*] [*Library of Congress*] (LCLS)
MnFfHA ..... Hillcrest Academy, Fergus Falls, MN [*Library symbol*] [*Library of Congress*] (LCLS)
MnFfHi ...... Otter Tail County Historical Society, Fergus Falls, MN [*Library symbol*] [*Library of Congress*] (LCLS)
MnFfL .... Lutheran Brethren Schools, Fergus Falls, MN [*Library symbol*] [*Library of Congress*] (LCLS)
MnFfM ...... Fergus Falls Middle School, Fergus Falls, MN [*Library symbol*] [*Library of Congress*] (LCLS)
MnFfME ..... McKinley Elementary School, Fergus Falls, MN [*Library symbol*] [*Library of Congress*] (LCLS)
MnFfO .... Otter Tail Power Co., Fergus Falls, MN [*Library symbol*] [*Library of Congress*] (LCLS)
MnFfRT ...... Fergus Falls Regional Treatment Center, Fergus Falls, MN [*Library symbol*] [*Library of Congress*] (LCLS)
MnFfSH ..... Fergus Falls Senior High School, Fergus Falls, MN [*Library symbol*] [*Library of Congress*] (LCLS)
MnFfV .... Viking Library System, Fergus Falls, MN [*Library symbol*] [*Library of Congress*] (LCLS)
MNFG .... Manator Freight [*Common carrier symbol*]
MNFG .... Manifesting [*Telegraphy*] (PCTE)
MNFI .... Michigan Natural Features Inventory [*Michigan State Department of Natural Resources*] [*Information service or system*] (IID)
MnFiE .... Finlayson Elementary School, Finlayson, MN [*Library symbol*] [*Library of Congress*] (LCLS)
MnFiH .... Finlayson High School, Finlayson, MN [*Library symbol*] [*Library of Congress*] (LCLS)
MnFisS ...... Fisher Public School, Fisher, MN [*Library symbol*] [*Library of Congress*] (LCLS)
MNFLD ...... Manifold (KSC)
MnFlLS ...... Lincoln School, Floodwood, MN [*Library symbol*] [*Library of Congress*] (LCLS)
MNFN .... Manifestation [*Telegraphy*] (PCTE)
MnFo .... Foley Community Library, Foley, MN [*Library symbol*] [*Library of Congress*] (LCLS)
MnFoE .... Foley Elementary School, Foley, MN [*Library symbol*] [*Library of Congress*] (LCLS)
MnFoH ...... Foley High School, Foley, MN [*Library symbol*] [*Library of Congress*] (LCLS)
MnFoS ...... St. John's School, Foley, MN [*Library symbol*] [*Library of Congress*] (LCLS)
MNFP .... Magyar Nemzeti Fueggetlensegi Part [*Hungarian National Independence Party*] [*Political party*] (PPE)
MNFP .... Multinational Fighter Program [*Air Force*]
MNFP .... Multiple Number of Faults per Pass (PDAA)
MnFpS ...... Sacred Heart School, Freeport MN [*Library symbol*] [*Library of Congress*] (LCLS)
MnFraE ...... Frazee Elementary School, Frazee, MN [*Library symbol*] [*Library of Congress*] (LCLS)
MnFraHS .... Frazee-Vergas High School, Frazee, MN [*Library symbol*] [*Library of Congress*] (LCLS)
MNFRM ..... Main Frame
MnFrnCES ... Cedar Mt. Elementary School, Franklin, MN [*Library symbol*] [*Library of Congress*] (LCLS)
MnFrUH ..... Unity Hospital, Fridley, MN [*Library symbol*] [*Library of Congress*] (LCLS)
MNFS .... Minor Frame Synchronization (ACAE)
MnFS .... Seabury Divinity School, Faribault, MN [*Library symbol*] [*Library of Congress*] (LCLS)
MnFt .... Fosston Public Library, Fosston,MN [*Library symbol*] [*Library of Congress*] (LCLS)
MnFtH .... Fosston High School, Fosston, MN [*Library symbol*] [*Library of Congress*] (LCLS)
MnFtME ..... Magelssen Elementary School, Fosston, MN [*Library symbol*] [*Library of Congress*] (LCLS)
MnFu .... Fulda Public Library, Fulda, MN [*Library symbol*] [*Library of Congress*] (LCLS)
MNFU .... Manx National Farmers Union [*British*] (DBA)
MNFU .... Monfer [*Intermodal shipping container symbol*] (TVRC)
MnFuES ..... Fulda Elementary School, Fulda, MN [*Library symbol*] [*Library of Congress*] (LCLS)
MnFuJSH ... Fulda Junior-Senior High School, Fulda, MN [*Library symbol*] [*Library of Congress*] (LCLS)
MnFuStP .... St. Paul's Lutheran School, Fulda, MN [*Library symbol*] [*Library of Congress*] (LCLS)
MNFZ .... Monfort [*Federal Railroad Administration identification code*]
MNG .... Gustavus Adolphus College, St. Peter, MN [*OCLC symbol*] (OCLC)
MNG .... Managing (MSA)
Mng .... Managing (TBD)
MNG .... Mangahao [*New Zealand*] [*Seismograph station code, US Geological Survey*] (SEIS)
MNG .... Maningrida [*Australia*] [*Airport symbol*] [*Obsolete*] (OAG)
mng .... Meaning
MNG .... MediaNews Group (IID)
MNG .... Microwave Negative Grid
MNG .... Minimal No-Good (SAUS)

MNG......... Miramar Mining [*Stock exchange symbol*]
MNG......... Modulated Noise Generator (PDAA)
MNG......... Mongolia [*ANSI three-letter standard code*] (CNC)
MNG......... Montgomery, WV [*Amtrak rail station code*]
MNG......... Morning
MNG......... Mourning (ROG)
MNG......... Multinodular Goiter [*Endocrinology*] (DAVI)
MnGarE..... Garfield Elementary School, Garfield, MN [*Library symbol*] [*Library of Congress*] (LCLS)
MnGBES.... Helen Baker Elementary School, Glencoe, MN [*Library symbol*] [*Library of Congress*] (LCLS)
MnGc........ Grove City Public Library, Grove City, MN [*Library symbol*] [*Library of Congress*] (LCLS)
MnGcJH..... Atwater-Grove City Junior High School, Grove City, MN [*Library symbol*] [*Library of Congress*] (LCLS)
MnGeH...... Grey Eagle High School, Grey Eagle, MN [*Library symbol*] [*Library of Congress*] (LCLS)
MnGf........ Granite Falls Public Library, Granite Falls, MN [*Library symbol*] [*Library of Congress*] (LCLS)
MnGfH....... Granite Falls Municipal Hospital, Granite Falls, MN [*Library symbol*] [*Library of Congress*] (LCLS)
MnGfODS... Open Door Bible School, Granite Falls, MN [*Library symbol*] [*Library of Congress*] (LCLS)
MnGfPS..... Granite Falls Public School, Granite Falls, MN [*Library symbol*] [*Library of Congress*] (LCLS)
MnGfTC..... Southwest Technical College, Granite Falls, MN [*Library symbol*] [*Library of Congress*] (LCLS)
MnGGH...... Glencoe Hospital, Glencoe, MN [*Library symbol*] [*Library of Congress*] (LCLS)
MnGHS...... Glencoe Public High School, Glencoe, MN [*Library symbol*] [*Library of Congress*] (LCLS)
MnGi........ Gilbert Public Library, Gilbert, MN [*Library symbol*] [*Library of Congress*] (LCLS)
MNGIE....... Mitochrondrial Neurogastrointestinal Encephalomyopathy
MNGIE....... Nyo-, Neuro-, Gastrointestinal Encephalopathy [*Medicine*] (EDAA)
MnGiHi...... Iron Range Historical Society, Gilbert MN [*Library symbol*] [*Library of Congress*] (LCLS)
MnGiJH..... Gilbert-Eveleth Junior High School, Gilbert, MN [*Library symbol*] [*Library of Congress*] (LCLS)
MnGiNSE... Nelle Shean Elementary School, Gilbert, MN [*Library symbol*] [*Library of Congress*] (LCLS)
MnGle....... Glenwood Public Library, Glenwood, MN [*Library symbol*] [*Library of Congress*] (LCLS)
MnGLES..... Lincoln Elementary School, Glencoe, MN [*Library symbol*] [*Library of Congress*] (LCLS)
MnGleSH... Glenwood Senior High School, Glenwood, MN [*Library symbol*] [*Library of Congress*] (LCLS)
MNGLX...... Montgomery Global Long-Short Fund [*Investment term*]
MnGlyE...... Glyndon Elementary School, Glyndon, MN [*Library symbol*] [*Library of Congress*] (LCLS)
MnGlyHS.... Glyndon-Felton High School, Glyndon, MN [*Library symbol*] [*Library of Congress*] (LCLS)
MnGm....... Grand Marais Public Library, Grand Marais, MN [*Library symbol*] [*Library of Congress*] (LCLS)
MnGmFT.... United States National Park Service, Grand Portage Northern Minnesota Fur Trade Library, Grand Marais, MN [*Library symbol*] [*Library of Congress*] (LCLS)
MnGmH..... Cook County High School, Grand Marais, MN [*Library symbol*] [*Library of Congress*] (LCLS)
MnGMS..... Glencoe Middle School, Glencoe, MN [*Library symbol*] [*Library of Congress*] (LCLS)
MnGmSE.... Sawtooth Elementary School, Grand Marais, MN [*Library symbol*] [*Library of Congress*] (LCLS)
MNGMT..... Management (ADA)
MNGNG..... Managing
MnGonS..... Gonvick-Trail Community School, Gonvick, MN [*Library symbol*] [*Library of Congress*] (LCLS)
MnGoos..... Goodridge Public School, Goodridge, MN [*Library symbol*] [*Library of Congress*] (LCLS)
MNGP....... Monticello Nuclear Generating Plant (NRCH)
MnGpE...... Grand Portage Elementary School, Grand Portage, MN [*Library symbol*] [*Library of Congress*] (LCLS)
MnGr........ Grand Rapids Public Library, Grand Rapids, MN [*Library symbol*] [*Library of Congress*] (LCLS)
mngr......... Manager (SHCU)
MNGR....... Manager
MNGR....... Monsignor
MnGra....... Graceville Public Library, Graceville, MN [*Library symbol*] [*Library of Congress*] (LCLS)
MnGraBS... Big Stone Hutterite Colony School, Graceville, MN [*Library symbol*] [*Library of Congress*] (LCLS)
MnGraCHS... Clinton-Graceville High School, Graceville, MN [*Library symbol*] [*Library of Congress*] (LCLS)
MnGraH..... Holy Trinity Hospital, Graceville, MN [*Library symbol*] [*Library of Congress*] (LCLS)
MnGre....... Greenbush Public Library, Greenbush, MN [*Library symbol*] [*Library of Congress*] (LCLS)
MnGrEMS... Edna I. Murphy School, Grand Rapids, MN [*Library symbol*] [*Library of Congress*] (LCLS)
MnGreS..... Greenbush Public School, Greenbush, MN [*Library symbol*] [*Library of Congress*] (LCLS)
MnGrFLS.... Forrest Lake School, Grand Rapids, MN [*Library symbol*] [*Library of Congress*] (LCLS)
MnGrFW.... Forest Wildlife Population and Research Group, Grand Rapids, MN [*Library symbol*] [*Library of Congress*] (LCLS)
MnGrI....... Itasca Community College, Grand Rapids, MN [*Library symbol*] [*Library of Congress*] (LCLS)
MnGrM...... Grand Rapids Middle School, Grand Rapids, MN [*Library symbol*] [*Library of Congress*] (LCLS)
MNGRM..... Monogram
MnGrRS..... Riverview School, Grand Rapids, MN [*Library symbol*] [*Library of Congress*] (LCLS)
MnGrSH..... Grand Rapids Senior HighSchool, Grand Rapids, MN [*Library symbol*] [*Library of Congress*] (LCLS)
MnGrSS..... Southwest School, Grand Rapids, MN [*Library symbol*] [*Library of Congress*] (LCLS)
MnGryS..... Grygla Public School, Grygla, MN [*Library symbol*] [*Library of Congress*] (LCLS)
Mngt......... Management
MnGvH..... Golden Valley Health Center, Golden Valley, MN [*Library symbol*] [*Library of Congress*] (LCLS)
MNH......... Magnum Resources [*Vancouver Stock Exchange symbol*]
MNH......... Makers of National History [*A publication*]
MNH......... Maternal and Neonatal Health (SAUO)
Mn-H........ Minnesota State Department of Health, St. Paul, MN [*Library symbol*] [*Library of Congress*] (LCLS)
MNH......... Mint Never Hinged [*Philately*]
MNH......... Monarch [*NCIC car model code*]
MNH......... Monarch Airlines [*ICAO designator*] (FAAC)
MNH......... Munich [*Germany*] [*Seismograph station code, US Geological Survey*] [*Closed*] (SEIS)
MNH......... Museum of National History (SAUO)
MNH......... Museum of Natural History [*Smithsonian Institution*]
MNH......... University of Minnesota-Duluth, Health Science Library, Duluth, MN [*OCLC symbol*] (OCLC)
MnHaH...... Norman County West High School, Halstad, MN [*Library symbol*] [*Library of Congress*] (LCLS)
MnHal....... Hallock Public Library, Hallock, MN [*Library symbol*] [*Library of Congress*] (LCLS)
MnHalH..... Hallock High School, Hallock, MN [*Library symbol*] [*Library of Congress*] (LCLS)
MnHan...... Hancock Community Library, Hancock, MN [*Library symbol*] [*Library of Congress*] (LCLS)
MnHanE..... Hancock Elementary School, Hancock, MN [*Library symbol*] [*Library of Congress*] (LCLS)
MnHanH.... Hancock High School, Hancock, MN [*Library symbol*] [*Library of Congress*] (LCLS)
MnHaw...... Hawley Public Library, Hawley, MN [*Library symbol*] [*Library of Congress*] (LCLS)
MnHawE.... Hawley Elementary School, Hawley, MN [*Library symbol*] [*Library of Congress*] (LCLS)
MnHawH.... Hawley High School, Hawley, MN [*Library symbol*] [*Library of Congress*] (LCLS)
MnHcS...... Hill City School, Hill City, MN [*Library symbol*] [*Library of Congress*] (LCLS)
MnHe........ Hector Public Library, Hector, MN [*Library symbol*] [*Library of Congress*] (LCLS)
MnHE........ Hinckley Elementary School, Hinckley, MN [*Library symbol*] [*Library of Congress*] (LCLS)
MnHel....... Heron Lake Public Library, Heron Lake, MN [*Library symbol*] [*Library of Congress*] (LCLS)
MnHelES.... Heron Lake Elementary School, Heron Lake, MN [*Library symbol*] [*Library of Congress*] (LCLS)
MnHendH... Hendricks Community Hospital, Hendricks, MN [*Library symbol*] [*Library of Congress*] (LCLS)
MnHendPS... Hendircks Public School, Hendricks, MN [*Library symbol*] [*Library of Congress*] (LCLS)
MnHenE..... West Elementary School, Hendrum, MN [*Library symbol*] [*Library of Congress*] (LCLS)
MnHennS... Henning Public School, Henning, MN [*Library symbol*] [*Library of Congress*] (LCLS)
MnHePS.... Hector Public School, Hector, MN [*Library symbol*] [*Library of Congress*] (LCLS)
MnHH....... Hinckley High School, Hinckley, MN [*Library symbol*] [*Library of Congress*] (LCLS)
MnHi........ Minnesota Historical Society, St. Paul, MN [*Library symbol*] [*Library of Congress*] (LCLS)
MnHi-Ar..... minnesota Historical Society, Division of Archives and Manuscripts, St. Paul, MN [*Library symbol*] [*Library of Congress*] (LCLS)
MnHib....... Hibbing Public Library, Hibbing, MN [*Library symbol*] [*Library of Congress*] (LCLS)
MnHibC..... Hibbing Community College, Hibbing, MN [*Library symbol*] [*Library of Congress*] (LCLS)
MnHibM..... Central Mesabi Medical Center, Hibbing, MN [*Library symbol*] [*Library of Congress*] (LCLS)
MnHiICS.... Hills Christian School, Hills, MN [*Library symbol*] [*Library of Congress*] (LCLS)
MnHiIES.... Hills-Beaver Creek Elementary School, Hills, MN [*Library symbol*] [*Library of Congress*] (LCLS)
MnHiIHS.... Hills-Beaver Creek High School, Hills, MN [*Library symbol*] [*Library of Congress*] (LCLS)
MnHitE...... Ulen-Hitterdal Elementary School, Hitterdal, MN [*Library symbol*] [*Library of Congress*] (LCLS)
MnHI........ Howard Lake Public Library, Howard Lake, MN [*Library symbol*] [*Library of Congress*] (LCLS)
MNHLA...... Musicians National Hot Line Association (EA)
MnHldSDS... Seventh Day Adventist School, Holland, MN [*Library symbol*] [*Library of Congress*] (LCLS)
MnHIE....... Howard Lake-Waverly Elementary School, Howard Lake, MN [*Library symbol*] [*Library of Congress*] (LCLS)
MnHIH....... Howard Lake-Waverly High School, Howard Lake, MN [*Library symbol*] [*Library of Congress*] (LCLS)
MnHIS....... St. James Lutheran School, Howard Lake, MN [*Library symbol*] [*Library of Congress*] (LCLS)

MnHoE ...... Holdingford Elementary School, Holdingford, MN [*Library symbol*] [*Library of Congress*] (LCLS)
MnHofS ..... Hoffman Public School, Hoffman, MN [*Library symbol*] [*Library of Congress*] (LCLS)
MnHoH ...... Holdingford Jr./Sr. High School, Holdingford, MN [*Library symbol*] [*Library of Congress*] (LCLS)
MnHol .... Hoyt Lakes Public Library, Hoyt Lakes, MN [*Library symbol*] [*Library of Congress*] (LCLS)
M-NHSS ..... Modified New Haven Schizophrenic Scale
MnHu .... Hutchinson Public Library, Hutchinson, MN [*Library symbol*] [*Library of Congress*] (LCLS)
MnHuHMS ... Hutchinson Middle School, Hutchinson, MN [*Library symbol*] [*Library of Congress*] (LCLS)
MnHumS .... Humbolt School, Humbolt, MN [*Library symbol*] [*Library of Congress*] (LCLS)
MnHuPES ... Park Elementary School, Hutchinson, MN [*Library symbol*] [*Library of Congress*] (LCLS)
MnHuSH .... Hutchinson Senior High School, Hutchinson, MN [*Library symbol*] [*Library of Congress*] (LCLS)
MnHuStA .... St. Anastasis School, Hutchinson, MN [*Library symbol*] [*Library of Congress*] (LCLS)
Mn-Hw ...... Minnesota State Department of Transportation, St. Paul, MN [*Library symbol*] [*Library of Congress*] (LCLS)
MNI .... Mach Number Indicated (MCD)
MNI .... Madras Native Infantry [*British*]
MNI .... Maina Air Ltd. [*Nigeria*] [*FAA designator*] (FAAC)
MNI .... Malaysian National Insurance (SAUO)
MNI .... Manado [*Celebes*] [*Seismograph station code, US Geological Survey*] (SEIS)
MNI .... Manning, OR [*Amtrak Busline code*]
MNI .... Manning, SC [*Location identifier*] [*FAA*] (FAAL)
MNI .... Many [*Amanteur radio shorthand*] (WDAA)
MNI .... Masoneilan International (SAUO)
MNI .... McClatchy Newspapers, Inc. [*NYSE symbol*] (SPSG)
MNI .... Media Networks, Inc.
MNI .... Member of the Nautical Institute [*British*]
MNI .... Meridian Technologies, Inc. [*Toronto Stock Exchange symbol*]
MnI .... Mille lacs Lake Community Library, Isle, MN [*Library symbol*] [*Library of Congress*] (LCLS)
MNI .... Minimum Number of Individuals [*Statistics*]
MNI .... Ministry of National Insurance [*British*]
MNI .... Modified Non-Interlocked [*Indian Railway*] (TIR)
MNI .... Montreal Neurological Institute [*Medicine*] (EDAA)
MNI .... Montserrat [*West Indies*] [*Airport symbol*] (OAG)
MNI .... Movimiento Nacionalista de Izquierda [*Bolivia*] (PPW)
MNI .... Winona State University, Winona, MN [*OCLC symbol*] (OCLC)
MNIA .... Member of the National Institute of Accountants [*Australia*]
MNIA .... Multinational Nuclear Incident Agreement (SAUO)
MNIC .... Mnemonic Instruction Code (VLIE)
MnIf .... International Falls Public Library, International Falls, MN [*Library symbol*] [*Library of Congress*] (LCLS)
MnIfBC ...... Boise Cascade Corp., Research Library, International Falls, MN [*Library symbol*] [*Library of Congress*] (LCLS)
MnIfE .... International Falls Elementary School, International Falls, MN [*Library symbol*] [*Library of Congress*] (LCLS)
MnIfH .... International Falls High School, International Falls, MN [*Library symbol*] [*Library of Congress*] (LCLS)
MnIfM .... A.B. Middle School, International Falls, MN [*Library symbol*] [*Library of Congress*] (LCLS)
MnIfRC ...... Rainy River Community College, International Falls, MN [*Library symbol*] [*Library of Congress*] (LCLS)
MnIgS .... Inver Hills State Junior College, Inver Grove Heights, MN [*Library symbol*] [*Library of Congress*] (LCLS)
MnIH .... Isle High School/Elementary School, Isle, MN [*Library symbol*] [*Library of Congress*] (LCLS)
MNIH .... Member of the National Institute of Hardware [*British*] (DBQ)
MNIMH ...... Member of the National Institute of Medical Herbalists [*British*]
MNIND ...... Mineral Industry Data Base (SAUO)
MnIrCS ...... Cherry Public School, Iron, MN [*Library symbol*] [*Library of Congress*] (LCLS)
MNIS .... Manning & Napier Information Services
MnIsE .... Isanti Elementary School, Isanti, MN [*Library symbol*] [*Library of Congress*] (LCLS)
MnIsM .... Isnati Middle School, Isanti, MN [*Library symbol*] [*Library of Congress*] (LCLS)
MNIT .... Mobile Networks Integration Technology (SAUO)
MnIv .... Ivanhoe Public Library, Ivanhoe, MN [*Library symbol*] [*Library of Congress*] (LCLS)
MnIvEHS .... Lincoln Elementary-High School, Ivanhoe, MN [*Library symbol*] [*Library of Congress*] (LCLS)
MnJ .... Jackson County Library System, Jackson, MN [*Library symbol*] [*Library of Congress*] (LCLS)
MNJ .... Mananjary [*Madagascar*] [*Airport symbol*] (OAG)
MNJ .... Microelectronic Noise Jammer
MNJ .... Middletown & New Jersey Railway Co., Inc. [*AAR code*]
MNJ .... Movimiento Nacionalista Justicialista [*Justicialist Nationalist Movement - JNM*] [*Argentina*] (PPW)
MNJ .... Myoneural Junction [*Medicine*]
MNJ .... St. John's University, Collegeville, MN [*OCLC symbol*] (OCLC)
MnJaPS ..... Jasper Public Schools, Jasper, MN [*Library symbol*] [*Library of Congress*] (LCLS)
MnJeJSH ... Storden-Jeffers Junior Senior High School, Jeffers, MN [*Library symbol*] [*Library of Congress*] (LCLS)
MnJES .... Jackson Elementary School, Jackson, MN [*Library symbol*] [*Library of Congress*] (LCLS)
MnJoTS ..... Trinity Lutheran School, Johnson, MN [*Library symbol*] [*Library of Congress*] (LCLS)
MnJPS ...... Jackson Public Schools, Jackson, MN [*Library symbol*] [*Library of Congress*] (LCLS)
MNJTS ...... Mouvement National des Jeunes Travailleurs du Senegal [*National Movement of Young Workers of Senegal*]
MNK .... Bethel College, Learning Resources Center, St. Paul, MN [*OCLC symbol*] (OCLC)
MnK .... Kimball Public Library, Kimball, MN [*Library symbol*] [*Library of Congress*] (LCLS)
MNK .... Maiana [*Kiribati*] [*Airport symbol*] (OAG)
MNK .... Mankoya [*Zambia*] [*Airport symbol*] (AD)
MNK .... Pleshenitzi [*Formerly, Minsk*] [*Former USSR*] [*Geomagnetic observatory code*]
MNK .... Rochester, MN [*Location identifier*] [*FAA*] (FAAL)
MNKA .... Minimum Number of Animals Known Alive [*Ecology*]
MnKaES ..... Kandiyohi Elementary School, Kandiyohi, MN [*Library symbol*] [*Library of Congress*] (LCLS)
MnKarE ..... Karlstad Elementary School, Karlstad, MN [*Library symbol*] [*Library of Congress*] (LCLS)
MnKarH ..... Tri-County High School, Karlstad, MN [*Library symbol*] [*Library of Congress*] (LCLS)
MnKE .... Kimball Elementary School, Kimball, MN [*Library symbol*] [*Library of Congress*] (LCLS)
MnKee ...... Keewatin Public Library, Keewatin, MN [*Library symbol*] [*Library of Congress*] (LCLS)
MnKeEs ..... Kerkhoven-Murdoch-Sunberg Elementary School, Kerkhoven, MN [*Library symbol*] [*Library of Congress*] (LCLS)
MnKeHS .... Kerkhoven-Murdoch-Sunberg High School, Kerkhoven, MN [*Library symbol*] [*Library of Congress*] (LCLS)
MnKenS ..... Kensington Public School, Kensington, MN [*Library symbol*] [*Library of Congress*] (LCLS)
MnKeP ...... Kerkoven Public Library, Kerkoven, MN [*Library symbol*] [*Library of Congress*] (LCLS)
MnKH .... Kimball High School, Kimball, MN [*Library symbol*] [*Library of Congress*] (LCLS)
MnKHC ...... Holy Cross School, Kimball, MN [*Library symbol*] [*Library of Congress*] (LCLS)
MnKin .... Kinney Public Library, City Hall, Kinney, MN [*Library symbol*] [*Library of Congress*] (LCLS)
MNL .... Mangla [*New Mirpur*] [*Pakistan*] [*Seismograph station code, US Geological Survey*] (SEIS)
MNL .... Manila [*Philippines*] [*Airport symbol*] (OAG)
MNL .... Manual (MSA)
MNL .... Marine Navigating Light
MNL .... Marine Navigation Levy (SAUO)
MNL .... Marked Neutrophilic Leukocytosis [*Medicine*] (DMAA)
MNL .... Maximum Number of Lamellae (DMAA)
MNI .... McClatchy Newspapers'A' [*NYSE symbol*] (TTSB)
MNL .... McConnell Peel Resources [*Vancouver Stock Exchange symbol*]
MNL .... Medical Nutrition Laboratory [*Army*]
MNL .... Mesenteric Node Lymphocyte
MNL .... Minerals Officer [*Foreign service*]
MNL .... Miniliner SRL [*Italy*] [*ICAO designator*] (FAAC)
MNL .... Minnesota National Laboratory
MNL .... Molecular Neurobiology Laboratory [*Salk Institute for Biological Studies*]
MNL .... Mononuclear Leukocyte [*Hematology*]
MNL .... Montgomery County-Norristown Public Library, Norristown, PA [*OCLC symbol*] (OCLC)
MNL .... Mountain Laurel Railroad [*Federal Railroad Administration identification code*]
MNL .... Movement for National Liberation [*Barbados*] [*Political party*] (PPW)
MNL .... Multinomial Logit [*Statistics*]
MNL .... National Liberation Movement [*Guatemala*] [*Political party*] (PD)
MNL .... Valdez, AK [*Location identifier*] [*FAA*] (FAAL)
MNLA .... Malayan National Liberation Army (SAUO)
MNLA .... Minnesota Nursery and Landscape Association (EARSL)
MNLA .... Mon National Liberation Army [*Myanmar*] [*Political party*] (EY)
MnLaiL ...... Lake Itasca Forestry and Biological Station, Lake Itasca, MN [*Library symbol*] [*Library of Congress*] (LCLS)
MnLam ...... Lamberton Public Library, Lamberton, MN [*Library symbol*] [*Library of Congress*] (LCLS)
MnLamS ..... Lamberton School, Lamberton, MN [*Library symbol*] [*Library of Congress*] (LCLS)
MnLanS ..... Lancaster Public School, Lancaster, MN [*Library symbol*] [*Library of Congress*] (LCLS)
MnLapS ..... Laporte Public School, Laporte, MN [*Library symbol*] [*Library of Congress*] (LCLS)
MnLb .... Lake Benton Public Library, Lake Benton, MN [*Library symbol*] [*Library of Congress*] (LCLS)
MnLbBa ..... Buffalo Ridge Baptist Academy, Lake Benton, MN [*Library symbol*] [*Library of Congress*] (LCLS)
MnLbPS ..... Lake Benton Public Schools, Lake Benton, MN [*Library symbol*] [*Library of Congress*] (LCLS)
MNLCA ...... Methylnorlaudanosolinecarboxylic Acid [*Biochemistry*]
MNLD .... Mainland (FAAC)
Mn-Leg ...... Minnesota State Legislative Library, St. Paul, MN [*Library symbol*] [*Library of Congress*] (LCLS)
MnLeoCS ... Leota Christian School, Leota, MN [*Library symbol*] [*Library of Congress*] (LCLS)
MnLepPS ... Lester Prairie Public School, Lester Prairie, MN [*Library symbol*] [*Library of Congress*] (LCLS)
MnLeW ...... Washington County Library, Lake Elmo, MN [*Library symbol*] [*Library of Congress*] (LCLS)
MnLf .... Carnegie City Library, Little Falls, MN [*Library symbol*] [*Library of Congress*] (LCLS)
MNLF .... Malayan National Liberation Front [*Singapore*] [*Political party*] (PD)
MNLF .... Moro National Liberation Front [*Philippines*] [*Political party*] (PD)

MnLfCL...... Charles Lindbergh Elementary School, Little Falls, MN [*Library symbol*] [*Library of Congress*] (LCLS)
MnLfH....... Little Falls Community High School, Little Falls, MN [*Library symbol*] [*Library of Congress*] (LCLS)
MnLfLE...... Lincoln Elementary School, Little Falls, MN [*Library symbol*] [*Library of Congress*] (LCLS)
MnLfM...... Little Falls Community Middle School, Little Falls, MN [*Library symbol*] [*Library of Congress*] (LCLS)
MnLfMS..... Mid-State Educational Cooperative, Little Falls, MN [*Library symbol*] [*Library of Congress*] (LCLS)
MnLfN....... North Star Christian Academy, Little Falls, MN [*Library symbol*] [*Library of Congress*] (LCLS)
MnLfO....... Our Lady of Lourdes School, Little Falls, MN [*Library symbol*] [*Library of Congress*] (LCLS)
MnLfoE...... Littlefork Elementary School, Littlefork, MN [*Library symbol*] [*Library of Congress*] (LCLS)
MnLfoH..... Littlefork High School, Littlefork, MN [*Library symbol*] [*Library of Congress*] (LCLS)
MnLfS....... St. Francis Convent, Little Falls, MN [*Library symbol*] [*Library of Congress*] (LCLS)
MnLfSG..... St. Gabriel's Hospital, Little Falls, MN [*Library symbol*] [*Library of Congress*] (LCLS)
MnLfSM..... St. Mary's School, Little Falls, MN [*Library symbol*] [*Library of Congress*] (LCLS)
MnLfW...... Weyerhauser Memorial Museum, Little Falls, MN [*Library symbol*] [*Library of Congress*] (LCLS)
MnLi......... Lindstrom Public Library, Lindstrom, MN [*Library symbol*] [*Library of Congress*] (LCLS)
MnLiJ....... Chisago Lakes Area Junior High School, Lindstrom, MN [*Library symbol*] [*Library of Congress*] (LCLS)
MnLiS....... Chisago Lakes Senior High School, Lindstrom, MN [*Library symbol*] [*Library of Congress*] (LCLS)
MnLit........ Litchfield Public Library, Litchfield, MN [*Library symbol*] [*Library of Congress*] (LCLS)
MnLitSH.... Litchfield Senior High School, Litchfield, MN [*Library symbol*] [*Library of Congress*] (LCLS)
MnLitSP..... St. Philip's School, Litchfield, MN [*Library symbol*] [*Library of Congress*] (LCLS)
MnLitWES... Wagner Elementary School, Litchfield, MN [*Library symbol*] [*Library of Congress*] (LCLS)
MnLkpE..... Lake Park Elementary School, Lake Park, MN [*Library symbol*] [*Library of Congress*] (LCLS)
MnLkpH..... Lake Park High School, Lake Park, MN [*Library symbol*] [*Library of Congress*] (LCLS)
MnLl......... Lake Lillian Public Library, Lake Lillian, MN [*Library symbol*] [*Library of Congress*] (LCLS)
MNLL........ Malaysian National Liberation League (NADA)
MNLN....... Leon/Fanor Urroz [*Nicaragua*] [*ICAO location identifier*] (ICLI)
MNLO....... Merchant Navy Liaison Officer (SAUO)
MnLon....... Margaret Welch Memorial Library, Longville, MN [*Library symbol*] [*Library of Congress*] (LCLS)
MnLp........ Long Prairie Public Library, Long Prairie, MN [*Library symbol*] [*Library of Congress*] (LCLS)
MnLpCHi.... Christie Home Historical Society, Long Prairie, MN [*Library symbol*] [*Library of Congress*] (LCLS)
MnLpE....... Long Prairie Elementary School, Long Prairie, MN [*Library symbol*] [*Library of Congress*] (LCLS)
MnLpH...... Long Prairie High School, Long Prairie, MN [*Library symbol*] [*Library of Congress*] (LCLS)
MnLpHi..... Todd County Historical Society, Long Prairie, MN [*Library symbol*] [*Library of Congress*] (LCLS)
MnLpM...... Meadowview School, Long Prairie, MN [*Library symbol*] [*Library of Congress*] (LCLS)
MnLpS...... St. Mary of Mt. Carmel, Long Prairie, MN [*Library symbol*] [*Library of Congress*] (LCLS)
MnLpT....... Trinity Lutheran School, Long Prairie, MN [*Library symbol*] [*Library of Congress*] (LCLS)
MNLS........ Marine Navigating Light System
MNLS........ Modified New Least Square (PDAA)
MnLS........ St. John Nepomuk School, Lastrup, MN [*Library symbol*] [*Library of Congress*] (LCLS)
MnLsG...... Green Giant Corp., Le Sueur, MN [*Library symbol*] [*Library of Congress*] (LCLS)
MNLU....... Malaysian International Shipping [*Intermodal shipping container symbol*] (TVRC)
MnLucOLS... Our Lady of Victory School, Lucan, MN [*Library symbol*] [*Library of Congress*] (LCLS)
MNLY........ Mainly (FAAC)
MnLyPS..... Lynd Public Library, Lynd, MN [*Library symbol*] [*Library of Congress*] (LCLS)
MNM........ Mankato State University, Mankato, MN [*OCLC symbol*] (OCLC)
MNM........ Master of Nonprofit Management (PGP)
MNM........ Menominee [*Michigan*] [*Airport symbol*] (OAG)
MNM........ Metal Nonmetal [*Materials science*]
MNM........ Military Necessity Modification
mnm......... Minimum (AD)
MNM........ Minimum
MNM........ Minneapolis [*Minnesota*] [*Seismograph station code, US Geological Survey*] (SEIS)
MnM......... Minneapolis Public Library and Information Center, Minneapolis, MN [*Library symbol*] [*Library of Congress*] (LCLS)
mnm......... Mnemonic (AD)
MNM........ Motile with Normal Morphology [*Medicine*] (MELL)
MNM........ Museum of New Mexico [*Research center*] (RCD)
MnMA....... Augsburg College and Seminary, Minneapolis, MN [*Library symbol*] [*Library of Congress*] (LCLS)
MnMAb...... Abbott-Northwestern Hospitals, Inc., Minneapolis, MN [*Library symbol*] [*Library of Congress*] (LCLS)
MnMAC..... Anoka County Library, Minneapolis, MN [*Library symbol*] [*Library of Congress*] (LCLS)
MnMaE...... Mahnomen Elementary School, Mahnomen, MN [*Library symbol*] [*Library of Congress*] (LCLS)
MnMah...... Mahnomen High School, Mahnomen, MN [*Library symbol*] [*Library of Congress*] (LCLS)
MnMAM..... American Medical Systems, Inc., Minneapolis, MN [*Library symbol*] [*Library of Congress*] (LCLS)
MnManBC... Bethany Lutheran College, Mankato, MN [*Library symbol*] [*Library of Congress*] (LCLS)
MnManBS... Bethany Lutheran Theological Seminary, Mankato, MN [*Library symbol*] [*Library of Congress*] (LCLS)
MnManM... Minnesota Valley Regional Library, Mankato, MN [*Library symbol*] [*Library of Congress*] (LCLS)
MnManS.... Mankato State College [*Later, Mankato State University*], Mankato, MN [*Library symbol*] [*Library of Congress*] (LCLS)
MnManTD... Traverse des Sioux Library System, Mankato, MN [*Library symbol*] [*Library of Congress*] (LCLS)
MNMANY... Men's Neckwear Manufacturers Association of New York [*Defunct*] (EA)
MnMAR..... American Rehabilitation Foundation Minneapolis, MN [*Library symbol*] [*Library of Congress*] (LCLS)
MnMar...... Marshall-Lyon County Library, Marshall, MN [*Library symbol*] [*Library of Congress*] (LCLS)
MnMarb..... Marble Public Library, Marble, MN [*Library symbol*] [*Library of Congress*] (LCLS)
MnMarC..... Marshall-Lyon County Library, Marshall, MN [*Library symbol*] [*Library of Congress*] (LCLS)
MnMarH.... Weiner Memorial Hospital, Marshall, MN [*Library symbol*] [*Library of Congress*] (LCLS)
MnMarLS... Samuel Lutheran School, Marshall, MN [*Library symbol*] [*Library of Congress*] (LCLS)
MnMarPE... Parkside Elementary School, Marshall, MN [*Library symbol*] [*Library of Congress*] (LCLS)
MnMarS..... Southwest Minnesota State College, Marshall, MN [*Library symbol*] [*Library of Congress*] (LCLS)
MnMarWES. West Side Elementary School, Marshall, MN [*Library symbol*] [*Library of Congress*] (LCLS)
MnMay...... Maynard Public Library, Maynard, MN [*Library symbol*] [*Library of Congress*] (LCLS)
MnMayPS... Maynard Public Schools, Maynard, MN [*Library symbol*] [*Library of Congress*] (LCLS)
MnMBL...... Bakken Library of Electricity in Life, Minneapolis, MN [*Library symbol*] [*Library of Congress*] (LCLS)
MNMC....... Medical Network for Missing Children (EA)
MNMC....... Miller-Morrell Trucking [*Common carrier symbol*]
MnMc....... Monticello Public Library, Monticello, MN [*Library symbol*] [*Library of Congress*] (LCLS)
MnMCA..... Minneapolis College of Art and Design, Minneapolis, MN [*Library symbol*] [*Library of Congress*] (LCLS)
MnMCC..... Minneapolis Community College, Minneapolis, MN [*Library symbol*] [*Library of Congress*] (LCLS)
MnMcgE.... McGrath Elementary School, McGrath, MN [*Library symbol*] [*Library of Congress*] (LCLS)
MnMcgr..... McGregor Public Library, McGregor, MN [*Library symbol*] [*Library of Congress*] (LCLS)
MnMcgrS... McGregor School, McGregor, MN [*Library symbol*] [*Library of Congress*] (LCLS)
MnMcgrSL... Sandy Lake Visitor Center, McGregor, MN [*Library symbol*] [*Library of Congress*] (LCLS)
MnMcH...... Monticello-Big Lake Community Hospital Library, Monticello, MN [*Library symbol*] [*Library of Congress*] (LCLS)
MnMci....... McInotosh Public Library, McIntosh, MN [*Library symbol*] [*Library of Congress*] (LCLS)
MnMciE..... McIntosh Elementary School, McIntosh, MN [*Library symbol*] [*Library of Congress*] (LCLS)
MnMciH..... McIntosh-Winger High School, McIntosh, MN [*Library symbol*] [*Library of Congress*] (LCLS)
MnMcJ...... Monticello Junior High School, Monticello, MN [*Library symbol*] [*Library of Congress*] (LCLS)
MnMck...... McKinley Public Library, McKinley, MN [*Library symbol*] [*Library of Congress*] (LCLS)
MnMcPE.... Pinewood East Elementary School, Monticello, MN [*Library symbol*] [*Library of Congress*] (LCLS)
MnMcPW... Pinewood West Elementary School, Monticello, MN [*Library symbol*] [*Library of Congress*] (LCLS)
MnMcR...... Rivercrest Christian School, Monticello, MN [*Library symbol*] [*Library of Congress*] (LCLS)
MnMcS...... Monticello Senior High School, Monticello, MN [*Library symbol*] [*Library of Congress*] (LCLS)
MnMcSR.... St. Henry Catholic Church, School of Religion Library, Monticello, MN [*Library symbol*] [*Library of Congress*] (LCLS)
MNMD....... MiniMed, Inc. [*NASDAQ symbol*] (SAG)
MnMe....... Melrose Public Library, Melrose, MN [*Library symbol*] [*Library of Congress*] (LCLS)
MnMeaS.... Toivola-Meadowlands School, Meadowlands, MN [*Library symbol*] [*Library of Congress*] (LCLS)
MnMeE...... Melrose, New Munich, Spring Hill Elementary School, Melrose, MN [*Library symbol*] [*Library of Congress*] (LCLS)
MnMeH..... Melrose High School, Melrose, MN [*Library symbol*] [*Library of Congress*] (LCLS)
MnMeJ...... Melrose Junior High School, Melrose, MN [*Library symbol*] [*Library of Congress*] (LCLS)
MnMenE.... Menahga Elementary School, Menagha, MN [*Library symbol*] [*Library of Congress*] (LCLS)

MnMenH.... Menagha High School, Menagha, MN [*Library symbol*] [*Library of Congress*] (LCLS)
MnMeS...... St. John-St. Andrew School, Melrose, MN [*Library symbol*] [*Library of Congress*] (LCLS)
MnMeSM... St. Mary's Elementary School, Melrose, MN [*Library symbol*] [*Library of Congress*] (LCLS)
MnMF....... Fairview Hospital, Minneapolis, MN [*Library symbol*] [*Library of Congress*] (LCLS)
MnMFL...... Association of Free Lutheran Congregation and Seminary Headquarters, Minneapolis, MN [*Library symbol*] [*Library of Congress*] (LCLS)
MnMFR..... Federation Reserve Bank of Minneapolis, Minneapolis, MN [*Library symbol*] [*Library of Congress*] (LCLS)
MnMG....... Golden Valley Lutheran College, Minneapolis, MN [*Library symbol*] [*Library of Congress*] (LCLS)
MNMG....... Managua/Augusto Cesar Sandino [*Nicaragua*] [*ICAO location identifier*] (ICLI)
MnMGM..... General Mills, Inc., Minneapolis, MN [*Library symbol*] [*Library of Congress*] (LCLS)
MnMGS..... Church of Jesus Christ of Latter-Day Saints, Genealogical Society Library, Minneapolis Branch, Minneapolis, MN [*Library symbol*] [*Library of Congress*] (LCLS)
MnMH....... Hennepin County Medical Society, Minneapolis, MN [*Library symbol*] [*Library of Congress*] (LCLS)
MnMHCL.... Hennepin County Library, Minneapolis, MN [*Library symbol*] [*Library of Congress*] (LCLS)
MnMHen.... Henkel Corp., Minneapolis, MN [*Library symbol*] [*Library of Congress*] (LCLS)
MnMHH..... Hennepin County General Hospital, Minneapolis, MN [*Library symbol*] [*Library of Congress*] (LCLS)
MnMHLL.... Hennepin County Law Library, Minneapolis, MN [*Library symbol*] [*Library of Congress*] (LCLS)
MnMI........ Interlutheran Theological Seminary and Bible School, Minneapolis, MN [*Library symbol*] [*Library of Congress*] (LCLS)
MNMIA...... Men's Neckwear Manufacturers Institute of America (EA)
MNMIC...... Modernized National Military Intelligence Center
MNMIC...... Modernized NMIC [*National Military Intelligence Center*] (MCD)
MnMiE...... Milaca Elementary School, Milaca, MN [*Library symbol*] [*Library of Congress*] (LCLS)
MnMiH...... Milaca High School, Milaca, MN [*Library symbol*] [*Library of Congress*] (LCLS)
MnMilE...... Miltona Elementary School, Miltona, MN [*Library symbol*] [*Library of Congress*] (LCLS)
MnMiM...... Milaca Middle School, Milaca, MN [*Library symbol*] [*Library of Congress*] (LCLS)
MnMIn...... Interstudy, Minneapolis, MN [*Library symbol*] [*Library of Congress*] (LCLS)
MnMinPS... Minneota Public Schools, Minneota, MN [*Library symbol*] [*Library of Congress*] (LCLS)
MnMinSE... St. Edward School, Minneota, MN [*Library symbol*] [*Library of Congress*] (LCLS)
MnMirS..... Middle River School, Middle River, MN [*Library symbol*] [*Library of Congress*] (LCLS)
MnMK....... Kenny Rehabilitation Institute, Minneapolis, MN [*Library symbol*] [*Library of Congress*] (LCLS)
MNMKT..... Money Market (NITA)
MnMLD..... Lutheran Deaconess Hospital, Minneapolis, MN [*Library symbol*] [*Library of Congress*] (LCLS)
MNMlE...... Maple Lake Elementary School, Maple Lake, MN [*Library symbol*] [*Library of Congress*] (LCLS)
MnMlH...... Maple Lake High, Maple Lake, MN [*Library symbol*] [*Library of Congress*] (LCLS)
MnMln...... Milan Public Library, Milan, MN [*Library symbol*] [*Library of Congress*] (LCLS)
MnMlnES... Milan Elementary School, Milan, MN [*Library symbol*] [*Library of Congress*] (LCLS)
MnMlS...... St. Timothy School, Maple Lake, MN [*Library symbol*] [*Library of Congress*] (LCLS)
MnMlyPS... Milroy Public Schools, Milan, MN [*Library symbol*] [*Library of Congress*] (LCLS)
MNMM...... Mines Management, Inc. [*NASDAQ symbol*] (QUAN)
MnMMC..... Metropolitan State Community College, Minneapolis, MN [*Library symbol*] [*Library of Congress*] (LCLS)
MnMMe..... Medtronic, Inc., Minneapolis, MN [*Library symbol*] [*Library of Congress*] (LCLS)
MnMMeH... Methodist Hospital, Minneapolis, MN [*Library symbol*] [*Library of Congress*] (LCLS)
MnMMet.... Metropolitan Medical Center, Medical Library, Minneapolis, MN [*Library symbol*] [*Library of Congress*] (LCLS)
MnMMet-H... Metropolitan Medical Center, Hospital Services Library, Minneapolis, MN [*Library symbol*] [*Library of Congress*] (LCLS)
MnMMetS... Metropolitan State Junior College, Minneapolis, MN [*Library symbol*] [*Library of Congress*] (LCLS)
MnMMH..... Minneapolis-Honeywell Regulator Co., Minneapolis, MN [*Library symbol*] [*Library of Congress*] (LCLS)
MnMMSC... MTS Systems Corporation, Minneapolis, MN [*Library symbol*] [*Library of Congress*] (LCLS)
MnMMSP... Minnesota School of Professional Psychology, Minneapolis, MN [*Library symbol*] [*Library of Congress*] (LCLS)
MnMMtS.... Mount Sinai Hospital, Minneapolis, MN [*Library symbol*] [*Library of Congress*] (LCLS)
MnMN....... Normandale Community College, Minneapolis, MN [*Library symbol*] [*Library of Congress*] (LCLS)
MnMNC..... North Central Bible College, Minneapolis, MN [*Library symbol*] [*Library of Congress*] (LCLS)
MnMnCMS... Cedar Mountain School, Morgan, MN [*Library symbol*] [*Library of Congress*] (LCLS)
MnMNH..... North Memorial Hospital, Minneapolis, MN [*Library symbol*] [*Library of Congress*] (LCLS)
MnMNHe.... North Hennepin Community College, Minneapolis, MN [*Library symbol*] [*Library of Congress*] (LCLS)
MnMnl...... Mountain Lake Public Library, Mountain Lake, MN [*Library symbol*] [*Library of Congress*] (LCLS)
MnMnlCS... Mountain Lake Christian School, Mountain Lake, MN [*Library symbol*] [*Library of Congress*] (LCLS)
MnMnlHS... Mountain Lake Public High School, Mountain Lake, MN [*Library symbol*] [*Library of Congress*] (LCLS)
MnMnlMB... Mt. Bethany Christian School, Mountain Lake, MN [*Library symbol*] [*Library of Congress*] (LCLS)
MnMnP...... Morgan Pubic Library, Morgan, MN [*Library symbol*] [*Library of Congress*] (LCLS)
MnMo....... Morris Public Library, Morris, MN [*Library symbol*] [*Library of Congress*] (LCLS)
MnMoE...... Morris Elementary School, Morris, MN [*Library symbol*] [*Library of Congress*] (LCLS)
MnMoh...... Moorhead Public Library, Moorhead, MN [*Library symbol*] [*Library of Congress*] (LCLS)
MnMohC.... Concordia College, Moorhead, MN [*Library symbol*] [*Library of Congress*] (LCLS)
MnMohEE... Edison Elementary School, Moorhead, MN [*Library symbol*] [*Library of Congress*] (LCLS)
MnMohHi... Clay County Historical Society, Library and Archives, Moorhead, MN [*Library symbol*] [*Library of Congress*] (LCLS)
MnMohJ.... Moorhead Junior High School, Moorhead, MN [*Library symbol*] [*Library of Congress*] (LCLS)
MnMohL.... Lake Agassiz Regional Library, Moorhead, MN [*Library symbol*] [*Library of Congress*] (LCLS)
MnMohPS... Moorhead Public Schools System, Moorhead, MN [*Library symbol*] [*Library of Congress*] (LCLS)
MnMohS.... Moorhead State College, Moorhead, MN [*Library symbol*] [*Library of Congress*] (LCLS)
MnMohSA... St. Ansgar Hospital, Health Science Library, Moorhead, MN [*Library symbol*] [*Library of Congress*] (LCLS)
MnMohSH... Moorhead Senior High School, Moorhead, MN [*Library symbol*] [*Library of Congress*] (LCLS)
MnMohSJ... St. Joseph School, Moorhead, MN [*Library symbol*] [*Library of Congress*] (LCLS)
MnMohWE... Washington Elementary School, Moorhead, MN [*Library symbol*] [*Library of Congress*] (LCLS)
MnMol...... Moose Lake Public Lake, Moose Lake, MN [*Library symbol*] [*Library of Congress*] (LCLS)
MnMolS..... Moose Lake Public School, Moose Lake, MN [*Library symbol*] [*Library of Congress*] (LCLS)
MnMoM..... Morris Middle School, Morris, MN [*Library symbol*] [*Library of Congress*] (LCLS)
MnMoMHS... Morris High School, Morris, MN [*Library symbol*] [*Library of Congress*] (LCLS)
MnMotS..... Motley School, Motley, MN [*Library symbol*] [*Library of Congress*] (LCLS)
MnMoU..... University of Minnesota, Morris, MN [*Library symbol*] [*Library of Congress*] (LCLS)
MnMov...... Chippewa County Library System, Montevideo, MN [*Library symbol*] [*Library of Congress*] (LCLS)
MnMovCH... Chippewa County-Montevideo Hospital, Montevideo, MN [*Library symbol*] [*Library of Congress*] (LCLS)
MnMovMS... Montevideo Middle School, Montevideo, MN [*Library symbol*] [*Library of Congress*] (LCLS)
MnMovRE... Ramsey Elementary School, Montevideo, MN [*Library symbol*] [*Library of Congress*] (LCLS)
MnMovSE... Sanford Elementary School, Montevideo, MN [*Library symbol*] [*Library of Congress*] (LCLS)
MnMovSEC... Southwest-West Central Educational Cooperative Service Unit, Montevideo, MN [*Library symbol*] [*Library of Congress*] (LCLS)
MnMovSH... Montevideo Senior High School, Montevideo, MN [*Library symbol*] [*Library of Congress*] (LCLS)
MnMP....... Pillsbury Co., Minneapolis, MN [*Library symbol*] [*Library of Congress*] (LCLS)
MnMrFE..... Fairview Elementary Library, Mora, MN [*Library symbol*] [*Library of Congress*] (LCLS)
MnMrH...... Mora High School, Mora, MN [*Library symbol*] [*Library of Congress*] (LCLS)
MnMrHi..... Kanabec County Historical Society, Mora, MN [*Library symbol*] [*Library of Congress*] (LCLS)
MnMrMS.... Mora Fairview Central Middle School, Mora, MN [*Library symbol*] [*Library of Congress*] (LCLS)
MnMrR...... Rum River Vocational Center, Mora, MN [*Library symbol*] [*Library of Congress*] (LCLS)
MNMS....... Myonephropathic Metabolic Syndrome [*Medicine*] (EDAA)
MnMS....... Saint Louis Park Medical Center, Minneapolis, MN [*Library symbol*] [*Library of Congress*] (LCLS)
MnMSMC... Saint Mary's Junior College, Minneapolis, MN [*Library symbol*] [*Library of Congress*] (LCLS)
MnMSMH... Saint Mary's Hospital, Minneapolis, MN [*Library symbol*] [*Library of Congress*] (LCLS)
MNMT....... Monument
MnMtE...... Montrose Elementary School, Montrose, MN [*Library symbol*] [*Library of Congress*] (LCLS)
MnMti....... Mountain Iron Public Library, Mt. Iron, MN [*Library symbol*] [*Library of Congress*] (LCLS)
MnMtiE...... Merritt Elementary School, Mt. Iron, MN [*Library symbol*] [*Library of Congress*] (LCLS)
MnMtiHS.... Mt. Iron High School, Mt. Iron, MN [*Library symbol*] [*Library of Congress*] (LCLS)

Mnmtl .... Monumental (DIAR)
MnMuKS .... Kerkhover-Murdock-Sunberg School, Murdock, MN [*Library symbol*] [*Library of Congress*] (LCLS)
MnMULS .... University of Minnesota Union List of Serials, Minneapolis, MN [*Library symbol*] [*Library of Congress*] (LCLS)
MnMVA ...... United States Veterans Administration Hospital, Minneapolis, MN [*Library symbol*] [*Library of Congress*] (LCLS)
MnMW ...... Walker Art Center, Minneapolis, MN [*Library symbol*] [*Library of Congress*] (LCLS)
MNN .... Carleton College, Northfield, MN [*OCLC symbol*] (OCLC)
MNN .... Madness Network News (EA)
MNN .... Main Network Node [*Computer science*] (CIST)
MNN .... Marion, OH [*Location identifier*] [*FAA*] (FAAL)
MNN .... Median Nerve Neuropathy [*Medicine*] (MELL)
MNN .... Minneapolis [*Minnesota*] [*Seismograph station code, US Geological Survey*] (SEIS)
MNN .... Minnesota Northern Railroad [*Federal Railroad Administration identification code*]
Mn-N .... Minnesota State Department of Natural Resources, St. Paul, MN [*Library symbol*] [*Library of Congress*] (LCLS)
MNN .... Monenco Ltd. [*Toronto Stock Exchange symbol*]
MnNaSH .... Nashwauk-Keewatin Senior High School, Nashwauk, MN [*Library symbol*] [*Library of Congress*] (LCLS)
MnNbU ...... United Theological Seminary of the Twin Cities, New Brighton, MN [*Library symbol*] [*Library of Congress*] (LCLS)
MnNC .... Carleton College, Northfield, MN [*Library symbol*] [*Library of Congress*] (LCLS)
MnNeS ...... Nevis Public School, Nevis, MN [*Library symbol*] [*Library of Congress*] (LCLS)
MnNeuL ..... Doctor Martin Luther College, New Ulm, MN [*Library symbol*] [*Library of Congress*] (LCLS)
MNNG .... Methylnitronitrosoguanidine [*Biochemistry*]
MNNG .... N-methyl N'-nitro-N-nitrosoguanidine [*Medicine*] (EDAA)
MnNHi .... Norwegian-American Historical Association, Northfield, MN [*Library symbol*] [*Library of Congress*] (LCLS)
MnNisE ...... Nisswa Elementary School, Nisswa, MN [*Library symbol*] [*Library of Congress*] (LCLS)
MnNl .... New London Public Library, New London, MN [*Library symbol*] [*Library of Congress*] (LCLS)
MnNlES ..... New London Elementary School, New London, MN [*Library symbol*] [*Library of Congress*] (LCLS)
MnNlJSH .... New London-Spicer Junior Senior High School, New London, MN [*Library symbol*] [*Library of Congress*] (LCLS)
MnNlPES .... Prairie Woods Elementary School, New London, MN [*Library symbol*] [*Library of Congress*] (LCLS)
MnNmT ..... Mankato Area Vocational-Technical Institute, North Mankato, MN [*Library symbol*] [*Library of Congress*] (LCLS)
MNNO .... Minnesota Express [*Common carrier symbol*]
MnNob .... North Branch Area Library, North Branch, MN [*Library symbol*] [*Library of Congress*] (LCLS)
MnNobH .... North Branch High School, North Branch, MN [*Library symbol*] [*Library of Congress*] (LCLS)
MnNobM .... North Branch Middle School, North Branch, MN [*Library symbol*] [*Library of Congress*] (LCLS)
MnNoS ...... Northome School, Northome, MN [*Library symbol*] [*Library of Congress*] (LCLS)
MNNP .... Malawi Nyika National Park (AD)
MNNR .... Marine National Nature Reserve (SAUO)
MNNR .... Minnesota Commercial Railway [*Federal Railroad Administration identification code*]
MnNS .... Saint Olaf College, Northfield, MN [*Library symbol*] [*Library of Congress*] (LCLS)
MnNS-K ..... Saint Olaf College, Kierkegaard Library, Northfield, MN [*Library symbol*] [*Library of Congress*] (LCLS)
MnNym ...... New York Mills Public Library, New York Mills, MN [*Library symbol*] [*Library of Congress*] (LCLS)
MnNymH .... New York Mills High School, New York Mills, MN [*Library symbol*] [*Library of Congress*] (LCLS)
MNO .... Maddona Resources Corp. [*Vancouver Stock Exchange symbol*]
mno .... Manobo [*MARC language code*] [*Library of Congress*] (LCCP)
MNO .... Manono [*Zaire*] [*Airport symbol*] (OAG)
MNO .... Master of Nonprofit Organization (PGP)
MNO .... Mauritanian Nationalist Organisation (BUAC)
MNO .... Mobile Network Operators (SAUO)
MnO .... Owatonna Free Public Library, Owatonna, MN [*Library symbol*] [*Library of Congress*] (LCLS)
MNO .... Refugio, TX [*Location identifier*] [*FAA*] (FAAL)
MNO .... Saint Olaf College, Northfield, MN [*OCLC symbol*] (OCLC)
MNoadT ..... North Adams State College, North Adams, MA [*Library symbol*] [*Library of Congress*] (LCLS)
MNoanM .... Merrimack College, North Andover, MA [*Library symbol*] [*Library of Congress*] (LCLS)
MNoanMV ... Merrimack Valley Textile Museum, North Andover, MA [*Library symbol*] [*Library of Congress*] (LCLS)
MNO complex ... Contraction of Sinus Venosus [*Medicine*] (EDAA)
MNOD .... Marine Night Observation Device [*Police and security equipment*]
MNodS ...... Southeastern Massachusetts University, North Dartmouth, MA [*Library symbol*] [*Library of Congress*] (LCLS)
MNoeS ...... Stonehill College, North Easton, MA [*Library symbol*] [*Library of Congress*] (LCLS)
MnOgS ...... Ogilvie Public School, Ogilvie, MN [*Library symbol*] [*Library of Congress*] (LCLS)
MnOkaHJH ... Huron Lake-Okabena-Lakefield Junior High School, Okabena, MN [*Library symbol*] [*Library of Congress*] (LCLS)
MnOkS ...... Oklee Public School, Oklee, MN [*Library symbol*] [*Library of Congress*] (LCLS)
MnOl .... Olivia Public Library, Olivia, MN [*Library symbol*] [*Library of Congress*] (LCLS)
MnOlES ..... Olivia Elementary School, Olivia, MN [*Library symbol*] [*Library of Congress*] (LCLS)
MnOlStA .... St. Aloysious School, Olivia, MN [*Library symbol*] [*Library of Congress*] (LCLS)
MNOMU ..... Mobile Nuclear Ordnance Maintenance Unit (MCD)
MnOnC ...... Crosier Seminary Library, Onamia, MN [*Library symbol*] [*Library of Congress*] (LCLS)
MnOnE ...... Onamia Elementary School, Onamia, MN [*Library symbol*] [*Library of Congress*] (LCLS)
MnOnG ...... Galloway Boy's Ranch School, Onamia, MN [*Library symbol*] [*Library of Congress*] (LCLS)
MnOnH ...... Onamia High School, Onamia, MN [*Library symbol*] [*Library of Congress*] (LCLS)
MNOPF ...... Merchant Navy Officers' Pension Fund [*British*] (DS)
MNOR .... Missile Not Operationally Ready [*Air Force*] (SAA)
MNORM ..... Missile Not Operationally Ready - Maintenance [*Air Force*]
MNORP ..... Missile Not Operationally Ready - Parts [*Air Force*]
MnOrS .... Orr Public School, Orr, MN [*Library symbol*] [*Library of Congress*] (LCLS)
MnOrv .... Ortonville Public Library, Ortonville, MN [*Library symbol*] [*Library of Congress*] (LCLS)
MnOrvH ..... Ortonville Hospital, Ortonville, MN [*Library symbol*] [*Library of Congress*] (LCLS)
MnOrvPS .... Ortonville Public School, Ortonville, MN [*Library symbol*] [*Library of Congress*] (LCLS)
mnos .... Metallic Nitrogen-Oxide Semiconductor (AD)
MNOS .... Metal Nitride Oxide Semiconductor (SAUO)
MNOS .... Metal-Nitride-Oxide Silicon [*or Semiconductor*]
MNOSFET ... Metal-Nitride-Oxide-Semiconductor Field-Effect Transistor
MnOsS ...... Osakis School, Osakis, MN [*Library symbol*] [*Library of Congress*] (LCLS)
MNOS/SOS ... Metal-Nitride Oxide Semiconductor / Silicon-on-Sapphire
MNot .... Cobb Memorial Library, North Truro,MA [*Library symbol*] [*Library of Congress*] (LCLS)
MNoW .... Wheaton College, Norton, MA [*Library symbol*] [*Library of Congress*] (LCLS)
MNP .... Malay National Party [*Political party*] (AD)
MNP .... Marsabit National Park [*Kenya*] (AD)
MNP .... Master Navigation Plan
MNP .... Maximum Negative Pressure [*Nuclear energy*] (NRCH)
MNP .... Median Nerve Palsy [*Medicine*] (MELL)
MNP .... Medical Nurse Practitioner [*Medicine*] (EDAA)
MNP .... Meru National Park [*Equatorial Kenya*] (AD)
MNP .... Meta-Nitrophenol [*Organic chemistry*]
MNP .... Microcom Networking Protocol [*Telecommunications*] (ACRL)
MNP .... Microcom Network Protocol (ADWA)
MNP .... Microcomputer Networking Protocol
MNP .... Microcone Networking Protocol
MNP .... Midnapore (1979) Resources, Inc. [*Vancouver Stock Exchange symbol*]
MNP .... Mikumi National Park [*Tanzania*] (AD)
Mn-P .... Minnesota State Department of Planning, St. Paul, MN [*Library symbol*] [*Library of Congress*] (LCLS)
MNP .... Mobile Number Portability
MNP .... Mononeuropathy [*Medicine*] (EDAA)
MNP .... Mononuclear Phagocyte (DMAA)
MNP .... Moravian National Party [*Czech Republic*] [*Political party*] (BUAC)
MNP .... More Nearly Perfect [*Microsoft Corp.*] [*Computer science*]
MNP .... Morton-Norwich Products, Inc. (SAUO)
MNP .... Mouvement Nationale Patriotique [*Haiti*] [*Political party*] (EY)
MNP .... Movimiento Nacionalista Popular [*Popular Nationalist Movement*] [*Chile*] [*Political party*] (PD)
MNP .... Movimiento Nacional y Popular [*Paraguay*] [*Political party*] (EY)
MNP .... Movimiento No Partidarizado [*Peru*] [*Political party*] (EY)
MNP .... Multinomial Probit [*Statistics*]
MNP .... Multiple Networking Protocol (SAUO)
MNP .... Municipal Partners Fund [*NYSE symbol*] (SPSG)
MNP .... Mushandike National Park [*Rhodesia*] (AD)
MNP .... Northern Mariana Islands [*ANSI three-letter standard code*] (CNC)
MnP .... Princeton Community Library, Princeton, MN [*Library symbol*] [*Library of Congress*] (LCLS)
MNP .... University of Minnesota, St. Paul, MN [*OCLC symbol*] (OCLC)
MNP-4 .... Microcon Network Protocol-4 [*Computer science*] (DDC)
MNP5 .... Microcon Networking Protocol, Class Five [*Computer science*]
MNP-5 .... Microcon Network Protocol-5 [*Computer science*] (DDC)
MNPA .... Malaysian Newspaper Publishers Association (EAIO)
MNPA .... Mono-normal-propylamine [*Organic chemistry*]
MnPapH ..... Parkers Prairie High School, Parkers Prairie, MN [*Library symbol*] [*Library of Congress*] (LCLS)
MnParFE .... Frank White Elementary School, Park Rapids, MN [*Library symbol*] [*Library of Congress*] (LCLS)
MnParH ..... Park Rapids Area High School, Park Rapids, MN [*Library symbol*] [*Library of Congress*] (LCLS)
MnParM ..... Park Rapids Middle School, Park Rapids, MN [*Library symbol*] [*Library of Congress*] (LCLS)
MnPc .... Pine City Pubic Library, Pine City, MN [*Library symbol*] [*Library of Congress*] (LCLS)
MNPC .... Puerto Cabezas [*Nicaragua*] [*ICAO location identifier*] (ICLI)
MnPcE .... Pine City Elementary School, Pine City, MN [*Library symbol*] [*Library of Congress*] (LCLS)
MnPcH ...... Pine City High School, Pine City, MN [*Library symbol*] [*Library of Congress*] (LCLS)
MnPcS ...... St. Mary's School, Pine City, MN [*Library symbol*] [*Library of Congress*] (LCLS)

MnPcT....... Pine Technical Institute Learning Resource Center, Pine City, MN [*Library symbol*] [*Library of Congress*] (LCLS)
MNPD....... Missile and Nuclear Programming Data (AABC)
MnPeC...... Pease Community Christian School, Pease, MN [*Library symbol*] [*Library of Congress*] (LCLS)
MnPelE...... Pequot Lakes Elementary School, Pequot Lakes, MN [*Library symbol*] [*Library of Congress*] (LCLS)
MnPelH..... Pequot Lakes High School, Pequot Lakes MN [*Library symbol*] [*Library of Congress*] (LCLS)
MnPerH..... Pelican Rapids High School, Pelican Rapids, MN [*Library symbol*] [*Library of Congress*] (LCLS)
MnPerVE.... Viking Elementary School, Pelican Rapids, MN [*Library symbol*] [*Library of Congress*] (LCLS)
MnPH........ Princeton High School, Princeton, MN [*Library symbol*] [*Library of Congress*] (LCLS)
MnPhE...... Perham Elementary School, Perham, MN [*Library symbol*] [*Library of Congress*] (LCLS)
MnPhP...... Perham Public Library, Perham, MN [*Library symbol*] [*Library of Congress*] (LCLS)
MNPI........ Microcom, Inc. [*NASDAQ symbol*] (NQ)
MnPi......... Pierz Public Library, Pierz, MN [*Library symbol*] [*Library of Congress*] (LCLS)
MnPiH....... Healy High School, Pierz, MN [*Library symbol*] [*Library of Congress*] (LCLS)
MnPiHE..... Harding Elementary School, Pierz, MN [*Library symbol*] [*Library of Congress*] (LCLS)
MnPilS...... Pillager Public School, Pillager, MN [*Library symbol*] [*Library of Congress*] (LCLS)
MnPiS....... St. Joseph's Elementary School, Pierz, MN [*Library symbol*] [*Library of Congress*] (LCLS)
MnPJ........ Princeton Junior High School, Princeton, MN [*Library symbol*] [*Library of Congress*] (LCLS)
MNPL........ Machinists Non-Partisan Political League (EA)
MnPluS..... Pershing Public School, Plummer, MN [*Library symbol*] [*Library of Congress*] (LCLS)
MnPNE...... Princeton North Elementary School, Princeton, MN [*Library symbol*] [*Library of Congress*] (LCLS)
mnpo........ Main Port (AD)
MnPO........ Median Preoptic Area (DB)
MNPO....... Median Preoptic Area [*Brain anatomy*]
MNPO....... Mobile Navy Post Office
MNPO....... Multi National Program Office (ACAE)
MNPP....... Midland Nuclear Power Plant (NRCH)
MNPP....... New Country Movement (Ecuador) [*Political party*] (PSAP)
MnPpBES... Dr. Brown Elementary School, Pipestone, MN [*Library symbol*] [*Library of Congress*] (LCLS)
MnPpHES... Hill Elementary School, Pipestone, MN [*Library symbol*] [*Library of Congress*] (LCLS)
MnPpHS.... Pipestone Cental High School, Pipestone, MN [*Library symbol*] [*Library of Congress*] (LCLS)
MN-PPL..... Machinists Non-Partisan Political League (EA)
MnPpTC..... Southwest Technical College, Pipestone, MN [*Library symbol*] [*Library of Congress*] (LCLS)
MnPr........ Kitchigami Regional Library, Pine River, MN [*Library symbol*] [*Library of Congress*] (LCLS)
MnPrbMCS. Central Minnesota Christian School, Prinsburg, MN [*Library symbol*] [*Library of Congress*] (LCLS)
MnPrbPS.... Prinsburg Public Schools, Prinsburg, MN [*Library symbol*] [*Library of Congress*] (LCLS)
MnPrE....... Pine River Elementary School, Pine River, MN [*Library symbol*] [*Library of Congress*] (LCLS)
MnPrH....... Pine River High School, Pine River, MN [*Library symbol*] [*Library of Congress*] (LCLS)
MnProJ...... Jedlicka Junior High School, Proctor, MN [*Library symbol*] [*Library of Congress*] (LCLS)
MnProSH... Proctor Senior High School, Proctor, MN [*Library symbol*] [*Library of Congress*] (LCLS)
MnPrP....... Pine River Public Library, Pine River, MN [*Library symbol*] [*Library of Congress*] (LCLS)
MNPS....... Millstone Nuclear Power Station (NRCH)
MNPS....... Minimum Navigation Performance Specification [*Aviation*] (FAAC)
MNPS....... Minimum Navigation Performance Specification Airspace (PIPO)
MNPS....... Movimiento Nazionale Pan-Somalo [*Pan-Somali National Movement*] [*Political party*]
MNPSA...... Minimum Navigation Performance Specification Airspace [*Aviation*] (FAAC)
MnPSE...... Princeton South Elementary School, Princeton, MN [*Library symbol*] [*Library of Congress*] (LCLS)
MNPT........ Meta-Nitro-para-toluidine [*Organic chemistry*]
MnPv........ Paynesville Public Library, Paynesville, MN [*Library symbol*] [*Library of Congress*] (LCLS)
MnPvEM.... Paynesville Elementary & Middle School, Paynesville, MN [*Library symbol*] [*Library of Congress*] (LCLS)
MnPvH...... Paynesville Hospital, Medical Staff Library, Paynesville, MN [*Library symbol*] [*Library of Congress*] (LCLS)
MnPvHi..... Paynesville Historical Society, Paynesville, MN [*Library symbol*] [*Library of Congress*] (LCLS)
MnPvHS..... Paynesville, High School, Paynesville, MN [*Library symbol*] [*Library of Congress*] (LCLS)
MNPWR..... Manpower (AFM)
MNPZ........ Mononitrosopiperazine [*Biochemistry*]
mnpz........ Monopolize (AD)
mnpzd....... Monopolized (AD)
mnpzg....... Monopolizing (AD)
mnpzn....... Monopolization (AD)
MNQ......... Manicouagan [*Quebec*] [*Seismograph station code, US Geological Survey*] (SEIS)
MNQ......... Manifest Needs Questionnaire (EDAC)
MNQ......... Methylnaphthoquinone [*Organic chemistry*]
MNQ......... Minriq [*Language symbol*] (ETLW)
MNQ......... Monto [*Australia*] [*Airport symbol*] (OAG)
MNQ......... Montoro Resources [*Vancouver Stock Exchange symbol*]
MNQ......... University of Minnesota, Waseca, Waseca, MN [*OCLC symbol*] (OCLC)
MNR......... James J. Hill Reference Library, St. Paul, MN [*OCLC symbol*] (OCLC)
MNR......... Maintenance/Nonconformance Record (MCD)
MNR......... Manner [*Telegraphy*] (PCTE)
MNR......... Manor (MCD)
MNR......... Manor Care, Inc. [*NYSE symbol*] (SPSG)
MNR......... Marrow Neutrophil Reserve [*Medicine*]
MNR......... Massive Nuclear Retaliation (AAG)
mnr.......... Massive Nuclear Retaliation (AD)
MNR......... Maximum Number of Records (MHDB)
MNR......... McMaster Nuclear Reactor [*Canada*]
MNR......... McNellen Resources, Inc. [*Vancouver Stock Exchange symbol*] [*Toronto Stock Exchange symbol*]
MNR......... Mean Neap [*Tide*] Rise [*Tides and currents*]
mnr.......... Mean Neap Rise (AD)
MNR......... Michigan Northern Railroad [*Federal Railroad Administration identification code*]
Mnr.......... Mijnherr [*Mr.*] [*Dutch*] (AD)
MNR......... Mines Road [*California*] [*Seismograph station code, US Geological Survey*] (SEIS)
MNR......... Minimum Noise Routes
MNR......... Ministry of Natural Resources (SAUO)
MNR......... Monair SA [*Switzerland*] [*ICAO designator*] (FAAC)
MNR......... Mongu [*Zambia*] [*Airport symbol*] (OAG)
MNR......... Morphine-Naive Rats
MNr.......... Morrill Memorial Library, Norwood, MA [*Library symbol*] [*Library of Congress*] (LCLS)
MNR......... Mouvement Nationaliste Revolutionnaire [*Revolutionary Nationalist Movement*] [*France*] [*Political party*] (PD)
MNR......... Movimiento Nacionalista Revolucionario [*National Revolutionary Movement*] [*Bolivia*] [*Political party*] (PPW)
MNR......... Movimiento Nacional Reformista [*National Reformist Movement*] [*Honduras*] [*Political party*]
MNR......... Movimiento Nacional Revolucionario [*National Revolutionary Movement*] [*El Salvador*] [*Political party*] (PPW)
MNR......... Mozambique National Resistance [*Political party*] (AD)
MNR......... Mozambique National Resistance Movement
MNR......... National Movement of Revolution (Republic of Congo) [*Political party*] (PSAP)
MnR.......... Rochester Public Library, Rochester, MN [*Library symbol*] [*Library of Congress*] (LCLS)
MnRa........ Raymond Public Library, Raymond, MN [*Library symbol*] [*Library of Congress*] (LCLS)
MnRaKE..... Knight Elementary School, Randall, MN [*Library symbol*] [*Library of Congress*] (LCLS)
MNRAS...... Monthly Notices of the Royal Astronomical Society (SAUO)
MNRC....... Minorco [*Formerly, Minerals & Resources Corp. Ltd.*] [*NASDAQ symbol*] (NQ)
MNRC....... Monarc [*NCIC trailer make code*]
MnRc........ Rush City Public Library, Rush City, MN [*Library symbol*] [*Library of Congress*] (LCLS)
MnRcE...... Rush City Elementary School, Rush City, MN [*Library symbol*] [*Library of Congress*] (LCLS)
MnRcH...... Rush City High School, Rush City, MN [*Library symbol*] [*Library of Congress*] (LCLS)
MNRCS...... Median Normalized RADAR Cross Section
MNRCY...... Minorco ADR [*NASDAQ symbol*] (TTSB)
MNRCY...... Monorco S.A. [*NASDAQ symbol*] (COMM)
MnRelE..... Redlake Elementary School, Redlake, MN [*Library symbol*] [*Library of Congress*] (LCLS)
MnRelH..... Redlake High School, Redlake, MN [*Library symbol*] [*Library of Congress*] (LCLS)
MnRemE.... Remer Elementary School, Remer, MN [*Library symbol*] [*Library of Congress*] (LCLS)
MnRemH.... Northland High School, Remer, MN [*Library symbol*] [*Library of Congress*] (LCLS)
MnRen...... Renville City Library, Renville, MN [*Library symbol*] [*Library of Congress*] (LCLS)
MnRenBPS... Bird Island-Danube-Renville-Sacred Heart (BDRSH) Public Schools, Renville, MN [*Library symbol*] [*Library of Congress*] (LCLS)
MNRF....... Moonroof [*Automotive advertising*]
MnRfE....... Rockford Elementary School, Rockford, MN [*Library symbol*] [*Library of Congress*] (LCLS)
MnRfH....... Rockford High School, Rockford, MN [*Library symbol*] [*Library of Congress*] (LCLS)
MnRfM...... Rockford Middle School, Rockford, MN [*Library symbol*] [*Library of Congress*] (LCLS)
MnRgE...... Rogers Elementary School, Rogers, MN [*Library symbol*] [*Library of Congress*] (LCLS)
MnRgS...... St. Martin's School, Rogers, MN [*Library symbol*] [*Library of Congress*] (LCLS)
MNRH....... Movimiento Nacionalista Revolucionario Historico [*Historic Revolutionary Nationalist Movement*] [*Bolivia*] [*Political party*] (PPW)
MnRiE....... Rice Elementary School, Rice, MN [*Library symbol*] [*Library of Congress*] (LCLS)
MNRJ........ Museo Nacional de Rio de Janeiro [*National Museum of Rio de Janeiro*] [*Portugal*] (AD)
MNRK....... Monark [*NCIC motorcycle make code*]

MNRL .... Mineral (MSA)
mnrl .... Mineral (VRA)
MNrL .... Morrill Memorial Library, Norwood, MA [*Library symbol*] [*Library of Congress*] (LCLS)
MnRlF .... Red Lake Falls Public Library, Red Lake Falls, MN [*Library symbol*] [*Library of Congress*] (LCLS)
MnRlfHE .... J.A. Hughes Elementary School, Red Lake Falls, MN [*Library symbol*] [*Library of Congress*] (LCLS)
MnRlPS ..... Sioux Valley-Round Lake-Brewster Public School, Round Lake, MN [*Library symbol*] [*Library of Congress*] (LCLS)
MNRM....... Master of Natural Resource Management (PGP)
MnRM .... Mayo Clinic, Rochester, MN [*Library symbol*] [*Library of Congress*] (LCLS)
MnRmE ..... Richmond Elementary School, Richmond, MN [*Library symbol*] [*Library of Congress*] (LCLS)
MnRMeH.... Rochester Methodist Hospital, Rochester, MN [*Library symbol*] [*Library of Congress*] (LCLS)
MnRmP ..... Richmond Public Library, Richmond, MN [*Library symbol*] [*Library of Congress*] (LCLS)
MnRmS ..... Sts. Peter and Paul Elementary School Library, Richmond, MN [*Library symbol*] [*Library of Congress*] (LCLS)
MNRO .... Monroe Motors [*NCIC trailer make code*]
MNRO .... Monroe Muffler Brake [*NASDAQ symbol*] (SPSG)
MNRO .... Monro Muffler Brake, Inc. [*NASDAQ symbol*] (SAG)
MNROE...... Monroe, MI [*American Association of Railroads railroad junction routing code*]
MnRoN...... Northwestern College, Roseville, MN [*Library symbol*] [*Library of Congress*] (LCLS)
MnRoP ...... Minnesota State Pollution Control Agency, Roseville, MN [*Library symbol*] [*Library of Congress*] (LCLS)
MnRos ...... Roseau Public Library, Roseau, MN [*Library symbol*] [*Library of Congress*] (LCLS)
MnRosE..... Roseau Elementary School, Roseau, MN [*Library symbol*] [*Library of Congress*] (LCLS)
MnRosH..... Roseau High School, Roseau, MN [*Library symbol*] [*Library of Congress*] (LCLS)
MnRosMS... Malung School, Roseau, MN [*Library symbol*] [*Library of Congress*] (LCLS)
MnRothS.... Rothsay Public School, Rothsay, MN [*Library symbol*] [*Library of Congress*] (LCLS)
MnRoy ...... Royalton Public Library, Royalton, MN [*Library symbol*] [*Library of Congress*] (LCLS)
MnRoyS..... Royalton School, Royalton, MN [*Library symbol*] [*Library of Congress*] (LCLS)
MNRP .... Movimiento Nacionalista Revolucionario del Pueblo [*Nationalist Revolutionary People's Movement*] [*Bolivia*] [*Political party*] (PPW)
MNRPM..... Malay Nationalist Revolutionary Party of Malaya [*Partai Kebangsaan Melayu Revolusioner Malaya*] [*Political party*] (PPW)
MnRPS...... Rochester Public Schools, Rochester, MN [*Library symbol*] [*Library of Congress*] (LCLS)
MnRR .... Rochester State Junior College, Rochester, MN [*Library symbol*] [*Library of Congress*] (LCLS)
MNR/Renamo... Mozambique National Resistance [*Political party*] (PSAP)
MNRS .... Manors [*Postal Service standard*] (OPSA)
MNRS .... Midwest Nursing Research Society (SAUO)
MNRS .... Mobile Neutron Radiographic System
MnRS........ Southeastern Libraries Cooperating [*SELCO*], Rochester Public Library, Rochester, MN [*Library symbol*] [*Library of Congress*] (LCLS)
Mnrsm ...... Mannerism (VRA)
MnRStM .... Saint Mary's Hospital, Rochester, MN [*Library symbol*] [*Library of Congress*] (LCLS)
mnrt .... Minaret (VRA)
MNRT........ Minister of State for Research and Technology (SAUO)
MNRT........ Monmouth Real Estate Investment Corp. [*NASDAQ symbol*] (NASQ)
MNRT........ Monmouth Real Estate Investment Trust [*NASDAQ symbol*] (NQ)
MNRTA...... Monmouth Real Estate Investment Corp. [*NASDAQ symbol*]
MNRTA...... Monmouth R.E. Inv CL'A' [*NASDAQ symbol*] (TTSB)
MNRU .... Medical Neuropsychiatric Research Unit (AD)
MNRU .... Modulated Noise Reference Unit [*Telecommunications*] (TEL)
MnRuPS .... Ruthton Public Schools, Ruthton, MN [*Library symbol*] [*Library of Congress*] (LCLS)
MnRusPS ... Russell Public Schools, Russell, MN [*Library symbol*] [*Library of Congress*] (LCLS)
MNRV .... Movimiento Nacionalista Revolucionario - Vanguardia Revolucionaria 9 de Abril [*Bolivia*] [*Political party*] (EY)
MnRvJ....... John Clark Elementary School, Rockville, MN [*Library symbol*] [*Library of Congress*] (LCLS)
MnRw .... Red Wing Public Library, Red Wing, MN [*Library symbol*] [*Library of Congress*] (LCLS)
MnRwf ...... Redwood Falls Public Library, Redwood Falls, MN [*Library symbol*] [*Library of Congress*] (LCLS)
MnRwfGES... Reede Gray Elementary School, Redwood Falls, MN [*Library symbol*] [*Library of Congress*] (LCLS)
MnRwfH..... Redwood Falls Hospital, Redwood Falls, MN [*Library symbol*] [*Library of Congress*] (LCLS)
MnRwfJSH... Redwood Falls-Morton Junior Senior High School, Redwood Falls, MN [*Library symbol*] [*Library of Congress*] (LCLS)
MnRwfSJL... St. John's Lutheran School, Redwood Falls, MN [*Library symbol*] [*Library of Congress*] (LCLS)
MNS .... College of Saint Scholastica Library, Duluth, MN [*OCLC symbol*] (OCLC)
MNS .... MacNeal-Schwendler [*AMEX symbol*] (TTSB)
MNS .... Malayan Nature Society (BUAC)
MNS .... Managed Network Services (SAUS)
MNS .... Management Need Statement (AAGC)
Mns.......... Manaus (AD)
MNS .... Manitoba Naturalists Society [*Canada*] (BUAC)
MNS .... Mansa [*Zambia*] [*Airport symbol*] (OAG)
MNS .... Martin's Louisiana Reports, New Series [*A publication*] (DLA)
MNS .... Master of Natural Sciences (GAGS)
MNS .... Master of Nuclear Science (GAGS)
MNS .... Master of Nursing Science
MNS .... Master of Nutritional Science
MNS .... Materiel Need Statement [*Army*]
MNS .... Maturity News Service
MNS .... McGuire Nuclear Station (NRCH)
MNS .... Mechanical Neutral Start [*Automotive engineering*]
MNS .... Medial Nuclear Stratum (DB)
MNS .... Member of the Numismatical Society [*British*]
mns.......... Metal-Nitride-Semiconductor (AD)
MNS .... Meta-Nitride Semiconductor (MCD)
MNS .... Microband National System, Inc. [*New York, NY*] [*Telecommunications*] (TSSD)
MNS .... Microneurography Society (EA)
MNS .... Mine Neutralization System [*Military*] (CAAL)
Mns.......... Mines (AD)
MNS .... Mines
MNS .... Ministic Air [*Canada*] [*ICAO designator*] (FAAC)
MNS .... Ministry of National Service [*World War I*] [*British*]
MNS .... Minneapolis, Northfield & Southern Railway [*AAR code*]
MNS .... Minneapolis, Northfield & Southern Railway Co. (SAUO)
MNS .... Minutes [*International telex abbreviation*] (WDMC)
MNS .... Mission Needs Statement [*Army*] (RDA)
MNS .... Molded Nylon Screw
MNS .... Money Show
MNS .... Moravian National Party [*Political party*] (BUAC)
MNS .... Movement for a New Society [*Defunct*] (EA)
MNS .... Movimiento Nacional de Salvacion [*National Movement of Salvation*] [*Dominican Republic*] [*Political party*] (PPW)
MNS .... MSCSoftware Corp. [*NYSE symbol*]
MNS .... Smith College, Northampton, MA [*Library symbol*] [*Library of Congress*] (LCLS)
MnS .... St. Paul Public Library, St. Paul, MN [*Library symbol*] [*Library of Congress*] (LCLS)
MnSa........ Sandstone Public Library, Sandstone, MN [*Library symbol*] [*Library of Congress*] (LCLS)
MNSA .... Seaman Apprentice, Mineman, Striker [*Navy rating*]
MnSaE ...... Sandstone Elementary School, Sandstone, MN [*Library symbol*] [*Library of Congress*] (LCLS)
MnSaF ...... Federal Correctional Institute Library, Sandstone, MN [*Library symbol*] [*Library of Congress*] (LCLS)
MnSAG...... Minnesota Attorney General's Office, St. Paul, MN [*Library symbol*] [*Library of Congress*] (LCLS)
MnSagHS... Albrook High School, Saginaw, MN [*Library symbol*] [*Library of Congress*] (LCLS)
MnSaH ...... Sandstone Area Hospital/Nursing Home, Sandstone, MN [*Library symbol*] [*Library of Congress*] (LCLS)
MnSaJS..... Sandstone Junior/Senior High School, Sandstone, MN [*Library symbol*] [*Library of Congress*] (LCLS)
MnSanLS ... Zion Lutheran School, Sanborn, MN [*Library symbol*] [*Library of Congress*] (LCLS)
MnSanPS ... Sanborn Public School, Sanborn, MN [*Library symbol*] [*Library of Congress*] (LCLS)
MnSarH ..... Sartell High School, Sartell, MN [*Library symbol*] [*Library of Congress*] (LCLS)
MnSarM..... Sartell Middle School, Sartell, MN [*Library symbol*] [*Library of Congress*] (LCLS)
MnSarS ..... St. Francis Xavier School, Sartell, MN [*Library symbol*] [*Library of Congress*] (LCLS)
MNSaS...... Swift River Valley Historical Society, New Salem, MA [*Library symbol*] [*Library of Congress*] (LCLS)
MnSB........ Bethel College, St. Paul, MN [*Library symbol*] [*Library of Congress*] (LCLS)
MNSBC...... Minnesota North Stars Booster Club (EA)
MnSBH...... Bethesda Lutheran Hospital, St. Paul, MN [*Library symbol*] [*Library of Congress*] (LCLS)
MNSC .... Main Network Switching Center [*Telecommunications*] (TEL)
MN Sc....... Master of Nursing Science
MNSC .... San Carlos/San Juan [*Nicaragua*] [*ICAO location identifier*] (ICLI)
MnSc .... Sauk Centre Public Library, Sauk Centre, MN [*Library symbol*] [*Library of Congress*] (LCLS)
MnSCC ...... Concordia College, St. Paul, MN [*Library symbol*] [*Library of Congress*] (LCLS)
MnSCH ...... Children's Hospital, St. Paul, MN [*Library symbol*] [*Library of Congress*] (LCLS)
MnScHF..... Holy Family School, Sauk Center, MN [*Library symbol*] [*Library of Congress*] (LCLS)
MNSCL...... Miniscule
MnScL...... Sinclair Lewis Foundation, Sauk Centre, MN [*Library symbol*] [*Library of Congress*] (LCLS)
MnScM..... Meadow View School, Sauk Centre, MN [*Library symbol*] [*Library of Congress*] (LCLS)
MnScML .... Mary Lyon School, Minnesota Correctional Facility, Sauk Centre, MN [*Library symbol*] [*Library of Congress*] (LCLS)
MnScP ...... Sauk Centre Public Schools, Sauk Centre, MN [*Library symbol*] [*Library of Congress*] (LCLS)
MnScSM .... St. Michael's Hospital and Convalescent and Nursing Center, Sauk Centre, MN [*Library symbol*] [*Library of Congress*] (LCLS)
MnSCU...... Minnesota State Colleges and Universities
MNSCU/PALS... Minnesota State University System (IID)
MNSD .... Mouvement National pour une Societe de Developpement [*Niger*] [*Political party*] (EY)

MNSD .... National Movement for Solidarity and Democracy (Cameroon) [*Political party*] (PSAP)
MnSEA ...... Minnesota Energy Agency, St. Paul, MN [*Library symbol*] [*Library of Congress*] (LCLS)
MnSebS ..... Sebeka School, Sebeka, MN [*Library symbol*] [*Library of Congress*] (LCLS)
MNSER ...... Mean Normalized Systolic Ejection Rate [*Cardiology*]
MNSF .... Monoclonal-Nonspecific Suppressor Factor [*Immunology*]
MNSFD ...... Mansfield, OH [*American Association of Railroads railroad junction routing code*]
MnSG .... Gillette State Hospital for Crippled Children, St. Paul, MN [*Library symbol*] [*Library of Congress*] (LCLS)
MnSGC ...... Minnesota Governor's Commission on Crime Prevention and Control, St. Paul, MN [*Library symbol*] [*Library of Congress*] (LCLS)
MnSGC ...... Minnesota Space Grant Consortium (RCD)
MnSGH ...... Group Health, Inc., St. Paul, MN [*Library symbol*] [*Library of Congress*] (LCLS)
MnSH .... Hamline University, St. Paul, MN [*Library symbol*] [*Library of Congress*] (LCLS)
MnSheS ..... Shelly School, Shelly, MN [*Library symbol*] [*Library of Congress*] (LCLS)
MnSH-L ...... Hamline University, School of Law, St. Paul, MN [*Library symbol*] [*Library of Congress*] (LCLS)
MnShS ...... Scott County Library, Shakopee, MN [*Library symbol*] [*Library of Congress*] (LCLS)
MNSI .... Siuna [*Nicaragua*] [*ICAO location identifier*] (ICLI)
MnSib .... Silver Bay Public Library, Silver Bay, MN [*Library symbol*] [*Library of Congress*] (LCLS)
MnSibHS .... Wm. Kelley High School, Silver Bay, MN [*Library symbol*] [*Library of Congress*] (LCLS)
MnSibME ... Mary MacDonald Elementary School, Silver Bay, MN [*Library symbol*] [*Library of Congress*] (LCLS)
MnSifE ...... Holler Elementary School, South International Falls, MN [*Library symbol*] [*Library of Congress*] (LCLS)
MnSJ .... James J. Hill Reference Library, St. Paul, MN [*Library symbol*] [*Library of Congress*] (LCLS)
MnSL .... Luther Theological Seminary, St. Paul, MN [*Library symbol*] [*Library of Congress*] [*Obsolete*] (LCLS)
MNSL .... Mainsail
MNSL .... Maintenance Non-Significant Lists (ACAE)
MnSLBF ..... Lutheran Brotherhood Foundation Reformation Library, St. Paul, MN [*Library symbol*] [*Library of Congress*] (LCLS)
MnSLN ...... Luther-Northwestern Seminary, St. Paul, MN [*Library symbol*] [*Library of Congress*] (LCLS)
MnSly .... Slayton Public Library, Slayton, MN [*Library symbol*] [*Library of Congress*] (LCLS)
MnSlyES .... Slayton Elementary School, Slayton, MN [*Library symbol*] [*Library of Congress*] (LCLS)
MnSlyJSH ... Slayton Junior-Senior High School, Slayton, MN [*Library symbol*] [*Library of Congress*] (LCLS)
MnSM .... Macalester College, St. Paul, MN [*Library symbol*] [*Library of Congress*] (LCLS)
MnSmH ...... St. Michael-Albertville High School, St. Michael, MN [*Library symbol*] [*Library of Congress*] (LCLS)
MnSmM ..... St. Michael-Albertville Middle School, St. Michael, MN [*Library symbol*] [*Library of Congress*] (LCLS)
MnSMMfg .. Minnesota Mining & Manufacturing Co., Technical Library, St. Paul, MN [*Library symbol*] [*Library of Congress*] [*Obsolete*] (LCLS)
MnSMN ..... Mounds-Midway School of Nursing, St. Paul, MN [*Library symbol*] [*Library of Congress*] (LCLS)
MnSmP ..... St. Michael Parish School, St. Michael, MN [*Library symbol*] [*Library of Congress*] (LCLS)
MnSN .... Northwestern Lutheran Theological Seminary, St. Paul, MN [*Library symbol*] [*Library of Congress*] [*Obsolete*] (LCLS)
MNSN .... Seaman, Mineman, Striker [*Navy rating*]
MnSOD ...... Manganese Superoxide Dismutase
MnSOEO .... Minnesota Office of Economic Opportunity, St. Paul, MN [*Library symbol*] [*Library of Congress*] (LCLS)
MnSP .... Saint Paul Public Library, St. Paul, MN [*Library symbol*] [*Library of Congress*] (LCLS)
MNSPE ...... Member of the National Society of Physical Education (SAUO)
MnSpES ..... Spicer Elementary School, Spicer, MN [*Library symbol*] [*Library of Congress*] (LCLS)
MnSpP ...... Spicer Public Library, Spicer, MN [*Library symbol*] [*Library of Congress*] (LCLS)
MNSQ .... Motor Neurone Society of Queensland [*Australia*]
MnSqlS ..... Squaw Lake School, Squaw Lake, MN [*Library symbol*] [*Library of Congress*] (LCLS)
MnSrB ...... Benton County Historical Museum, Sauk Rapids, MN [*Library symbol*] [*Library of Congress*] (LCLS)
MnSRC ...... Ramsey County Public Library, St. Paul, MN [*Library symbol*] [*Library of Congress*] (LCLS)
MnSrH .... Sauk Rapids High School, Sauk Rapids, MN [*Library symbol*] [*Library of Congress*] (LCLS)
MnSrHJ ..... Hillside Junior High School, Sauk Rapids, MN [*Library symbol*] [*Library of Congress*] (LCLS)
MnSRM ..... Ramsey County Medical Society, St. Paul, MN [*Library symbol*] [*Library of Congress*] (LCLS)
MnSrPE ..... Pleasantview Elementary School, Sauk Rapids, MN [*Library symbol*] [*Library of Congress*] (LCLS)
MnSrS .... Sacred Heart School, Sauk Rapids, MN [*Library symbol*] [*Library of Congress*] (LCLS)
MnSrT .... Trinity Lutheran School, Sauk Rapids, MN [*Library symbol*] [*Library of Congress*] (LCLS)
MNSS .... Modified Need Satisfaction Schedule
MNS-S ...... Smith College, Sophia Smith Collection, Northampton, MA [*Library symbol*] [*Library of Congress*] (LCLS)
MnSS .... St. Paul Seminary, St. Paul, MN [*Library symbol*] [*Library of Congress*] (LCLS)
MNSSA ...... Motor Neurone Society of South Australia
MnSSC ...... College of St. Catherine, St. Paul, MN [*Library symbol*] [*Library of Congress*] (LCLS)
MnSSEP ..... Median Nerve Somatosensory Evoked Potential [*Neurology*] (DAVI)
MnSSJ ...... St. John's Hospital, St. Paul, MN [*Library symbol*] [*Library of Congress*] (LCLS)
MnSSJos .... St. Joseph's Hospital, St. Paul, MN [*Library symbol*] [*Library of Congress*] (LCLS)
MnSSM ..... Science Museum of Minnesota, Louis S. Headley Memorial Library, St. Paul, MN [*Library symbol*] [*Library of Congress*] (LCLS)
MnSSP ...... St. Paul Ramsey Hospital, St. Paul, MN [*Library symbol*] [*Library of Congress*] (LCLS)
MnSSpU .... Sperry UNIVAC, St. Paul, MN [*Library symbol*] [*Library of Congress*] (LCLS)
MnSST ...... College of St. Thomas, St. Paul, MN [*Library symbol*] [*Library of Congress*] (LCLS)
MNST .... Minstar, Inc. [*NASDAQ symbol*] (COMM)
MNST .... Motor Neurone Society of Tasmania [*Australia*]
MnSt .... Staples Public Library, Staples, MN [*Library symbol*] [*Library of Congress*] (LCLS)
MNSTB ...... Monostable (MSA)
MNSTBMV ... Monostable Multivibrator (MSA)
MnStbSP .... Saint Paul Bible College, Saint Bonifacius, MN [*Library symbol*] [*Library of Congress*] (LCLS)
MnStclA ..... Appollo High School, St. Cloud, MN [*Library symbol*] [*Library of Congress*] (LCLS)
MnStclBS ... Benton/Stearns Special Education Professional Library, St. Cloud, MN [*Library symbol*] [*Library of Congress*] (LCLS)
MnStclCF ... Minnesota Corrections Facility Library, St. Cloud, MN [*Library symbol*] [*Library of Congress*] (LCLS)
MnStclCH ... St. Cloud Cathedral High School, St. Cloud, MN [*Library symbol*] [*Library of Congress*] (LCLS)
MnStclD ..... Diocese of St. Cloud, St. Cloud, MN [*Library symbol*] [*Library of Congress*] (LCLS)
MnStclEC ... Central Minnesota Educational Cooperative Service Unit, St. Cloud, MN [*Library symbol*] [*Library of Congress*] (LCLS)
MnStclER ... Central Minnesota Educational Research and Development Council, Film Library, St. Cloud, MN [*Library symbol*] [*Library of Congress*] (LCLS)
MnStclG ..... Great River Regional Library, St. Cloud, MN [*Library symbol*] [*Library of Congress*] (LCLS)
MnStclGP ... Green Pastures Christian School, St. Cloud, MN [*Library symbol*] [*Library of Congress*] (LCLS)
MnStclH ..... St. Cloud Hospital, Health Sciences Library, St. Cloud, MN [*Library symbol*] [*Library of Congress*] (LCLS)
MnStclHi .... Stearns County Historical Society, St. Cloud, MN [*Library symbol*] [*Library of Congress*] (LCLS)
MnStclHS ... Holy Spirit School, St. Cloud, MN [*Library symbol*] [*Library of Congress*] (LCLS)
MnStclJ ..... Jefferson Elementary School, St. Cloud, MN [*Library symbol*] [*Library of Congress*] (LCLS)
MnStclL ..... Lincoln Elementary School, St. Cloud, MN [*Library symbol*] [*Library of Congress*] (LCLS)
MnStclM .... Madison Elementary School, St. Cloud, MN [*Library symbol*] [*Library of Congress*] (LCLS)
MnStclMc ... McKinley Elementary School, St. Cloud, MN [*Library symbol*] [*Library of Congress*] (LCLS)
MnStclMS .. St. Cloud Media Services, St. Cloud, MN [*Library symbol*] [*Library of Congress*] (LCLS)
MnStclN ..... St. Cloud School of Nursing Library, St. Cloud, MN [*Library symbol*] [*Library of Congress*] (LCLS)
MnStclP ..... Sts. Peter & Paul Primary School, St. Cloud, MN [*Library symbol*] [*Library of Congress*] (LCLS)
MnStclR ..... Roosevelt Elementary School, St. Cloud, MN [*Library symbol*] [*Library of Congress*] (LCLS)
MnStclS ..... St. Cloud State University, St. Cloud, MN [*Library symbol*] [*Library of Congress*] (LCLS)
MnStclSA ... St. Anthony School, St. Cloud, MN [*Library symbol*] [*Library of Congress*] (LCLS)
MnStclSC ... Stearns/Benton Counties Law Library, St. Cloud, MN [*Library symbol*] [*Library of Congress*] (LCLS)
MnStclSE ... St. Cloud South Elementary School, St. Cloud, MN [*Library symbol*] [*Library of Congress*] (LCLS)
MnStclSM ... St. Mary Help of Christians School, St. Cloud, MN [*Library symbol*] [*Library of Congress*] (LCLS)
MnStclSP ... Sts. Peter & Paul Middle Schol, St. Cloud, MN [*Library symbol*] [*Library of Congress*] (LCLS)
MnStclSt .... St. Augustine School, St. Cloud, MN [*Library symbol*] [*Library of Congress*] (LCLS)
MnStclV ..... United States Veterans Administration Hospital, St. Cloud, MN [*Library symbol*] [*Library of Congress*] (LCLS)
MnStclVT ... St. Cloud Area Vo-Tech Institute, St. Cloud, MN [*Library symbol*] [*Library of Congress*] (LCLS)
MnStclW .... Westwood Elementary School, St. Cloud, MN [*Library symbol*] [*Library of Congress*] (LCLS)
MnSteE ...... Stephen Elementary School, Stpehen, MN [*Library symbol*] [*Library of Congress*] (LCLS)
MnSteH ..... Stephen High School, Stephen, MN [*Library symbol*] [*Library of Congress*] (LCLS)
MnStH .... United District Hospital, Staples, MN [*Library symbol*] [*Library of Congress*] (LCLS)
MnStHS ..... Staples High School, Staples, MN [*Library symbol*] [*Library of Congress*] (LCLS)
MnStj .... Watonwan County Library, St. James, MN [*Library symbol*] [*Library of Congress*] (LCLS)

MnStjoKE ... Kennedy Elementary School, St. Joseph, MN [*Library symbol*] [*Library of Congress*] (LCLS)
MnStjoL ..... St. Joseph Lab School, St. Joseph, MN [*Library symbol*] [*Library of Congress*] (LCLS)
MnStjoS ..... College of St. Benedict, St. Joseph, MN [*Library symbol*] [*Library of Congress*] (LCLS)
MnStLE ...... Lincoln Model Elementary School, Staples, MN [*Library symbol*] [*Library of Congress*] (LCLS)
MnSTM ...... Three M (3M) Co., St. Paul, MN [*Library symbol*] [*Library of Congress*] (LCLS)
MnSTM-A ... Three M (3M) Co., St. Paul, MN [*Library symbol*] [*Library of Congress*] (LCLS)
MnSTM-B ... Three M (3M) Co., Business Information Service, St. Paul, MN [*Library symbol*] [*Library of Congress*] (LCLS)
MnSTM-E ... Three M (3M) Co., Engineering Information Services, St. Paul, MN [*Library symbol*] [*Library of Congress*] (LCLS)
MnSTM-G ... Three M (3M) Co., St. Paul, MN [*Library symbol*] [*Library of Congress*] (LCLS)
MnSTM-H ... Three M (3M) Co., Health Care Library, St. Paul, MN [*Library symbol*] [*Library of Congress*] (LCLS)
MnSTM-M ... Three M (3M) Co., St. Paul, MN [*Library symbol*] [*Library of Congress*] (LCLS)
MnSTM-P ... Three M (3M) Co., St. Paul, MN [*Library symbol*] [*Library of Congress*] (LCLS)
MnSTM-T ... Three M (3M) Co., St. Paul, MN [*Library symbol*] [*Library of Congress*] (LCLS)
MnStNE ..... North Elementary School, Staples, MN [*Library symbol*] [*Library of Congress*] (LCLS)
MnStoES .... Storden-Jeffers Elementary School, Storden, MN [*Library symbol*] [*Library of Congress*] (LCLS)
MnStpeG .... Gustavus Adolphus College, St. Peter, MN [*Library symbol*] [*Library of Congress*] (LCLS)
Mnstr .... Munster (AD)
MNSTRY .... Ministry
MnStS .... Sacred Heart School, Staples, MN [*Library symbol*] [*Library of Congress*] (LCLS)
MnStT .... Staples Technical Institute, Staples, MN [*Library symbol*] [*Library of Congress*] (LCLS)
MnStwPS ... Stewart Public Schools, Stewart, MN [*Library symbol*] [*Library of Congress*] (LCLS)
MnSU .... University of Minnesota, St. Paul, MN [*Library symbol*] [*Library of Congress*] (LCLS)
MnSU-Bc .... University of Minnesota, Biochemistry Library, St. Paul, MN [*Library symbol*] [*Library of Congress*] (LCLS)
MnSuES ..... Sunberg Elementary School, Sunberg, MN [*Library symbol*] [*Library of Congress*] (LCLS)
MnSU-Et .... University of Minnesota, Entomology Library, St. Paul, MN [*Library symbol*] [*Library of Congress*] (LCLS)
MnSU-F ..... University of Minnesota, Forestry Library, St. Paul, MN [*Library symbol*] [*Library of Congress*] (LCLS)
MnSUH ...... United Hospitals, Inc., St. Paul, MN [*Library symbol*] [*Library of Congress*] (LCLS)
MnSU-PP ... University of Minnesota, Plant Pathology Library, St. Paul, MN [*Library symbol*] [*Library of Congress*] (LCLS)
MnSUSF .... United States Forest Service, North Central Forest Experiment Station, St. Paul,MN [*Library symbol*] [*Library of Congress*] (LCLS)
MnSU-V ..... University of Minnesota, Veterinary Medicine Library, St. Paul, MN [*Library symbol*] [*Library of Congress*] (LCLS)
MNSV .... Motor Neurone Society of Victoria [*Australia*]
MnSw .... Swanville Public Library, Swanville, MN [*Library symbol*] [*Library of Congress*] (LCLS)
MnSwE ...... Swanville Elementary School, Swanville, MN [*Library symbol*] [*Library of Congress*] (LCLS)
MnSwH ...... Swanville High School, Swanville, MN [*Library symbol*] [*Library of Congress*] (LCLS)
MnSWM ..... William Mitchell College of Law, St. Paul, MN [*Library symbol*] [*Library of Congress*] (LCLS)
MNT .... College of St. Thomas, St. Paul, MN [*OCLC symbol*] (OCLC)
M/N/T .... Main/Satellite/Tributary Network [*Telecommunications*] (ACRL)
MNT .... Maintained [*Automotive advertising*]
MNT .... Maternal and Neonatal Tetanus [*Medicine*]
mnt .... Mean Neap Tide (AD)
MNT .... Medical Nutrition Therapy (ADWA)
MNT .... Minnesota and Ontario Paper [*Stock exchange symbol*] (AD)
Mn-T .... Minnesota State Department of Taxation, St. Paul, MN [*Library symbol*] [*Library of Congress*] (LCLS)
MNT .... Minto [*Alaska*] [*Airport symbol*] (OAG)
MNT .... Minute [*Angle*]
MNT .... Modern Network Theory [*Electrical engineering computer*]
MNT .... Moffatt New Testament Commentary [*A publication*] (BJA)
MNT .... Monitor
MNT .... Mononitrotoluene [*Organic chemistry*]
MNT .... Montedison SpA [*NYSE symbol*] (SPSG)
MNT .... Montoro Gold, Inc. [*Vancouver Stock Exchange symbol*]
MNT .... Montreal [*Quebec*] [*Seismograph station code, US Geological Survey*] (SEIS)
MNT .... Montserrat Airways Ltd. [*Antigua and Barbuda*] [*ICAO designator*] (FAAC)
MNT .... Morton's Neuroma of Toe [*Medicine*] (MELL)
MNT .... Mount (KSC)
MNT .... Mountain
MNT .... Mouse Infection Neutralization Test [*Medicine*] (MELL)
MNT .... NewsChoice Online Newspaper Network [*MediaNews Group*] (IID)
MNt .... Newton Free Library, Newton, MA [*Library symbol*] [*Library of Congress*] (LCLS)
MNTA .... Minnesota Telephone Association (CGWS)
MNTAIN ..... Mountain [*Commonly used*] (OPSA)
MnTaIE ...... North Elementary School, Talmoon, MN [*Library symbol*] [*Library of Congress*] (LCLS)
MnTAP ...... Minnesota Technical Assistance Program [*University of Minnesota*] (RCD)
MntasiaE .... Mountasia Entertainment International, Inc. [*Associated Press*] (SAG)
MNTB .... Medial Nucleus of Trapezoid Body [*Neuroanatomy*]
MNTB .... Merchant Navy Training Board [*British*] (DS)
MNTC .... Mexican National Tourist Council (EA)
MNTC .... Moffatt New Testament Commentary [*A publication*] (BJA)
MNtcA .... Andover Newton Theological School, Newton Center, MA [*Library symbol*] [*Library of Congress*] (LCLS)
MnTcFW ..... United States Fish and Wildlife Service, Science Reference Library, Twin Cities,MN [*Library symbol*] [*Library of Congress*] (LCLS)
MnTcM ...... United States Bureau of Mines, Twin Cities, MN [*Library symbol*] [*Library of Congress*] (LCLS)
MNTD .... Maximum Non-Toxic Dose [*Toxicology*] (LDT)
MNTE .... Montebello Mobile Home Trailer [*NCIC trailer make code*]
MnTEC ...... Northwest Education Cooperative Service Unit, Thief River Falls, MN [*Library symbol*] [*Library of Congress*] (LCLS)
MnTf .... Taylor Falls Public Library, Taylor Falls, MN [*Library symbol*] [*Library of Congress*] (LCLS)
MnTFM ...... Franklin Middle School, Thief River Falls, MN [*Library symbol*] [*Library of Congress*] (LCLS)
MnTfS .... Taylor Falls School, Taylor Falls, MN [*Library symbol*] [*Library of Congress*] (LCLS)
MNTG .... Bill Montgomery [*NCIC trailer make code*]
MNTG .... Mounting
MNTG .... MTR Gaming Group
MnTh .... Two Harbors Public Library, Two Harbors, MN [*Library symbol*] [*Library of Congress*] (LCLS)
MnThE .... John A. Johnson Elementary School, Two Harbors, MN [*Library symbol*] [*Library of Congress*] (LCLS)
MnThHS ..... Two Harbors High School, Two Harbors, MN [*Library symbol*] [*Library of Congress*] (LCLS)
MNTHLY ..... Monthly
MnThM ...... Minnehaha Middle School, Two Harbors, MN [*Library symbol*] [*Library of Congress*] (LCLS)
MNTHZ ...... Methylnitrosothiazolidine [*Organic chemistry*]
MNTK .... Mezhotraslevoi Naucho-Tekhni-Cheskii Kompleks [*Interdisciplinary Scientific-Technological Complex*] [*Russian*]
MNTK .... Movimiento Nacional Tupaj Katari [*Bolivia*] [*Political party*] (PPW)
MnTKS ...... Knox School, Thief River Falls, MN [*Library symbol*] [*Library of Congress*] (LCLS)
MNTL .... Manufacturers National (EFIS)
MNTL .... Mental
MnTLH ...... Lincoln High School, Thief River Falls, MN [*Library symbol*] [*Library of Congress*] (LCLS)
MNTM .... Minnesota Transportation Museum [*Federal Railroad Administration identification code*]
mntmp ...... Minimum Temperature (AD)
MNTMP ..... Minimum Temperature (NOAA)
MnTMT ...... Mark Twain School, Thief River Falls, MN [*Library symbol*] [*Library of Congress*] (LCLS)
mntn .... Maintain (AD)
MNTN .... Maintain
MNTN .... Mountain
MnTN .... Northland State Junior College, Thief River Falls, MN [*Library symbol*] [*Library of Congress*] (LCLS)
mntnc .... Maintenance (AD)
MNTNC ..... Maintenance
mntnd .... Maintained (AD)
mntng .... Maintaining (AD)
MnTNo ...... Northrop Resource Room, Thief River Falls, MN [*Library symbol*] [*Library of Congress*] (LCLS)
MnTNR ...... Northwest Regional Library, Thief River Falls, MN [*Library symbol*] [*Library of Congress*] (LCLS)
MNTNS ...... Mountains [*Commonly used*] (OPSA)
MNTO .... Moroccan National Tourist Office (AD)
MnToS .... Togo School, Togo, MN [*Library symbol*] [*Library of Congress*] (LCLS)
MnTP .... Thief River Falls Public Library, Thief River Falls, MN [*Library symbol*] [*Library of Congress*] (LCLS)
MnTPC ...... Pennington County Extension Office, Thief River Falls, MN [*Library symbol*] [*Library of Congress*] (LCLS)
MnTPPS ..... Manganese Tetraphenylporphine Sulfonate [*Organic chemistry*]
MNTPr .... Montedison Bearer Svg Pfd ADS [*NYSE symbol*] (TTSB)
MNTR .... Mentor Corp. [*NASDAQ symbol*] (NQ)
mntr .... Monitor (AD)
MNTR .... Monitor (MDG)
MnTrES ..... Tracy Elementary School, Tracy, MN [*Library symbol*] [*Library of Congress*] (LCLS)
MnTrJSH .... Trace Junior-Senior High School, Tracy, MN [*Library symbol*] [*Library of Congress*] (LCLS)
MNTRNG .... Monitoring
MnTrStM .... St. Mary's School, Tracy, MN [*Library symbol*] [*Library of Congress*] (LCLS)
MNTS .... Medial Nucleus Tractus Solitarius [*Neuroanatomy*]
MNTS .... Methyl(Nitroso) Toluenesulphonamide [*Organic chemistry*]
MNTS .... Mountains
MNtS .... Swedenborg School of Religion, Newton, MA [*Library symbol*] [*Library of Congress*] (LCLS)
MnTSB ...... St. Bernard's School, Thief River Falls, MN [*Library symbol*] [*Library of Congress*] (LCLS)
MNtSH ...... Newton College of the Sacred Heart [*Later, Newton College*], Newton, MA [*Library symbol*] [*Library of Congress*] (LCLS)
MNTV .... Mercury Network Test Vehicle (MUGU)
MNTVC ...... Movable Nozzle Thrust-Vector Control [*Space launch term*] (ISAK)

MNTVN...... Mount Vernon, OH [*American Association of Railroads railroad junction routing code*]
MnTW....... Washington School, Thief River Falls, MN [*Library symbol*] [*Library of Congress*] (LCLS)
MnTwvE..... Twin Valley Elementary School, Twin Valley, MN [*Library symbol*] [*Library of Congress*] (LCLS)
MnTwvH..... Twin Valley High School, Twin Valley, MN [*Library symbol*] [*Library of Congress*] (LCLS)
MNTX........ Minntech Corp. [*NASDAQ symbol*] (NQ)
MnTy........ Tyler Public Library, Tyler, MN [*Library symbol*] [*Library of Congress*] (LCLS)
MnTyHS..... Russell-Tyler-Ruthon High School, Tyler, MN [*Library symbol*] [*Library of Congress*] (LCLS)
MNU......... Maniti Sugar [*Stock exchange symbol*] (AD)
MNu......... Mare Nubium [*Sea of Clouds*] [*Lunar area*]
MNU......... Methylnitrosourea [*Also, NMU*] [*Organic chemistry*]
MNU......... Middle Name Unknown (MCD)
MNU......... Milford North [*Utah*] [*Seismograph station code, US Geological Survey*] (SEIS)
MNU......... Minimum Number of Units [*Chemical engineering*]
mnu......... Minnesota [*MARC country of publication code*] [*Library of Congress*] (LCCP)
MNU......... Moulmein [*Myanmar*] [*Airport symbol*] (OAG)
MNU......... Movement for National Unity [*St. Vincent*] (BUAC)
MNU......... Mundee Mines Ltd. [*Vancouver Stock Exchange symbol*]
MnU......... University of Minnesota, Minneapolis, MN [*Library symbol*] [*Library of Congress*] (LCLS)
MNU......... University of Minnesota, Minneapolis, MN [*OCLC symbol*] (OCLC)
MnU-Ar...... University of Minnesota, Archives, Minneapolis, MN [*Library symbol*] [*Library of Congress*] (LCLS)
MnU-B....... University of Minnesota, Biomedical Library, Minneapolis, MN [*Library symbol*] [*Library of Congress*] (LCLS)
MNucSc..... Master of Nuclear Science (GAGS)
MnU-Fb..... University of Minnesota, Freshwater Biological Institute, Navarre, MN [*Library symbol*] [*Library of Congress*] (LCLS)
MnU-IA...... University of Minnesota, Immigration History Research Center, St. Paul, MN [*Library symbol*] [*Library of Congress*] (LCLS)
MnU-K....... University of Minnesota, Kerlan Children's Books Collection, Minneapolis, MN [*Library symbol*] [*Library of Congress*] (LCLS)
MnU-L....... University of Minnesota, Law Library, Minneapolis, MN [*Library symbol*] [*Library of Congress*] (LCLS)
MnUIH....... Ulen-Hitteral High School, Ulen, MN [*Library symbol*] [*Library of Congress*] (LCLS)
MnU-MS.... University of Minnesota, Manuscript Collection, Minneapolis, MN [*Library symbol*] [*Library of Congress*] (LCLS)
MnUnS...... Underwood Public School, Underwood, MN [*Library symbol*] [*Library of Congress*] (LCLS)
MnUpE...... Upsala Elementary School, Upsala, MN [*Library symbol*] [*Library of Congress*] (LCLS)
MnU-Ph..... University of Minnesota, Pharmacy Library, Minneapolis, MN [*Library symbol*] [*Library of Congress*] (LCLS)
MnUpH...... Upsala High School, Upsala, MN [*Library symbol*] [*Library of Congress*] (LCLS)
MNUR....... Mouvement National pour l'Union et la Reconciliation au Zaire [*National Movement for Union and Reconciliation in Zaire*] [*Political party*] (PD)
MnU-Rb..... University of Minnesota, Rare Book Division, Minneapolis, MN [*Library symbol*] [*Library of Congress*] (LCLS)
MNurs....... Master of Nursing (NADA)
MNursing... Master of Nursing
MNUSS...... Map Needs Update Support System [*Emergency Management*] (EMA)
MnU-SW.... University of Minnesota, Social Welfare History Archives Center, St. Paul, MN [*Library symbol*] [*Library of Congress*] (LCLS)
MNUT....... Methylnitrosourethane [*Organic chemistry*]
MNutrSc.... Master of Nutritional Science
MNV......... Madisonville, TN [*Location identifier*] [*FAA*] (FAAL)
MNV......... Maneuver [*Telegraphy*] (PCTE)
MNV......... Marginal Net Value
MNV......... Marion Power Shovel [*Stock exchange symbol*] (AD)
MNV......... Mina [*Nevada*] [*Seismograph station code, US Geological Survey*] (SEIS)
MNV......... Mine-Neutralization Vehicle [*Military*] (MCD)
Mn-V........ Minnesota State Vocational Rehabilitation Library, St. Paul, MN [*Library symbol*] [*Library of Congress*] (LCLS)
MNV......... Modular Nuclear Vehicle
MNV......... Southwest State University, Marshall, MN [*OCLC symbol*] (OCLC)
MNV......... United States Veterans Administration Hospital, Northampton, MA [*Library symbol*] [*Library of Congress*] (LCLS)
MnV......... Virginia Public Library, Virginia, MN [*Library symbol*] [*Library of Congress*] (LCLS)
MnVA........ Arrowhead Library System, Virginia, MN [*Library symbol*] [*Library of Congress*] (LCLS)
MNVA........ MNVA Railroad [*Federal Railroad Administration identification code*]
MnVePS..... Verdi Public School, Verdi, MN [*Library symbol*] [*Library of Congress*] (LCLS)
MnVerS..... Verndale Public School, Verndale, MN [*Library symbol*] [*Library of Congress*] (LCLS)
MnVHS...... Virginia Junior-Senior High School, Virginia, MN [*Library symbol*] [*Library of Congress*] (LCLS)
MnViIS...... Villard Public School, Villard, MN [*Library symbol*] [*Library of Congress*] (LCLS)
MnVM........ Mesabi Community College, Virginia, MN [*Library symbol*] [*Library of Congress*] (LCLS)
MNVM........ Million Nighttime Vehicle Mile
MnVME...... James Madison Elementary School, Virginia, MN [*Library symbol*] [*Library of Congress*] (LCLS)
MNVR....... Maneuver
MnVRE...... Roosevelt Elementary School, Virginia, MN [*Library symbol*] [*Library of Congress*] (LCLS)
MnVRM..... Virginia Regional Medical Center, Virginia, MN [*Library symbol*] [*Library of Congress*] (LCLS)
MNVS........ Modular Night Vision System [*Police and security equipment*]
MNW......... Chicago, Missouri & Western Railway [*Federal Railroad Administration identification code*]
Mn-W........ Minnesota State Department of Public Welfare, St. Paul, MN [*Library symbol*] [*Library of Congress*] (LCLS)
MNW......... Moneywise Resources [*Vancouver Stock Exchange symbol*]
MNW......... Monowai [*New Zealand*] [*Seismograph station code, US Geological Survey*] (SEIS)
MNW......... Northwest Missouri State University, Maryville, MO [*OCLC symbol*] (OCLC)
MnWa........ Wabasso Public Library, Wabasso, MN [*Library symbol*] [*Library of Congress*] (LCLS)
MnWad...... Wadena City Library, Wadena, MN [*Library symbol*] [*Library of Congress*] (LCLS)
MnWadE.... Wadena Elementary School, Wadena, MN [*Library symbol*] [*Library of Congress*] (LCLS)
MnWadH.... Wadena High School, Wadena, MN [*Library symbol*] [*Library of Congress*] (LCLS)
MnWadJ.... Wadena Junior High School, Wadena, MN [*Library symbol*] [*Library of Congress*] (LCLS)
MnWaES.... Wabasso Elementary School, Wabasso, MN [*Library symbol*] [*Library of Congress*] (LCLS)
MnWaHS.... Wabasso High School, Wabasso, MN [*Library symbol*] [*Library of Congress*] (LCLS)
MnWal....... Walker Public Library, Walker, MN [*Library symbol*] [*Library of Congress*] (LCLS)
MnWalC..... Cass County Extension Office, Walker, MN [*Library symbol*] [*Library of Congress*] (LCLS)
MnWalH..... Walker-Hackensack High School, Walker, MN [*Library symbol*] [*Library of Congress*] (LCLS)
MnWalHi.... Cass County Historical Society, Walker, MN [*Library symbol*] [*Library of Congress*] (LCLS)
MnWanS.... Wannaska School, Wannaska, MN [*Library symbol*] [*Library of Congress*] (LCLS)
MnWar...... Godell Memorial Library, Warren, MN [*Library symbol*] [*Library of Congress*] (LCLS)
MnWarE..... Warren Elementary School, Warren, MN [*Library symbol*] [*Library of Congress*] (LCLS)
MnWarJS... Warren Junior/Senior High School, Warren, MN [*Library symbol*] [*Library of Congress*] (LCLS)
MnWarr..... Warroad Public Library, Warroad, MN [*Library symbol*] [*Library of Congress*] (LCLS)
MnWarrE.... Warroad Elementary School, Warroad, MN [*Library symbol*] [*Library of Congress*] (LCLS)
MnWarrH... Warroad High School, Warroad, MN [*Library symbol*] [*Library of Congress*] (LCLS)
MnWas...... Le Sueur-Waseca Regional Library, Waseca, MN [*Library symbol*] [*Library of Congress*] (LCLS)
MnWaStA... St. Anne School, Wabasso, MN [*Library symbol*] [*Library of Congress*] (LCLS)
MnWasU.... University of Minnesota Technical College, Waseca, MN [*Library symbol*] [*Library of Congress*] (LCLS)
MnWatSA... St. Anthony School, Watkins, MN [*Library symbol*] [*Library of Congress*] (LCLS)
MnWauWE.. Waubon-Ogema-White Earth School, Waubon, MN [*Library symbol*] [*Library of Congress*] (LCLS)
MnWayC.... Cargill Instructional Center, Wayzata, MN [*Library symbol*] [*Library of Congress*] (LCLS)
MnWbIL..... Lakewood Community College, White Bear Lake, MN [*Library symbol*] [*Library of Congress*] (LCLS)
MnWbS..... Warba School, Warba, MN [*Library symbol*] [*Library of Congress*] (LCLS)
MnWE....... Isle-Wahkon Elementary School, Wahkon, MN [*Library symbol*] [*Library of Congress*] (LCLS)
MNWEB..... Merseyside and North Wales Electricity Board [*British*] (AD)
MNWEB..... Midlands & North Western Electricity Board (SAUO)
MnWeCS.... Westbrook Christian School, Westbrook, MN [*Library symbol*] [*Library of Congress*] (LCLS)
MnWeP...... Westbrook Public Library, Westbrook, MN [*Library symbol*] [*Library of Congress*] (LCLS)
MnWePS.... Westbrook Public School, Westbrook, MN [*Library symbol*] [*Library of Congress*] (LCLS)
MnWgMS... Westbrook-Walnut Grove Middle School, Walnut Grove, MN [*Library symbol*] [*Library of Congress*] (LCLS)
MNWH...... Mojo Nixon World Headquarters (EA)
MnWhe...... Wheaton Community Library, Wheaton, MN [*Library symbol*] [*Library of Congress*] (LCLS)
MnWheH.... Wheaton Community Hospital, Wheaton, MN [*Library symbol*] [*Library of Congress*] (LCLS)
MnWheHS... Wheaton-Dumont High School, Wheaton, MN [*Library symbol*] [*Library of Congress*] (LCLS)
MnWhePE... J.E. Pearson Elementary School, Wheaton, MN [*Library symbol*] [*Library of Congress*] (LCLS)
MnWil....... Lawson Memorial Library, Willmar, MN [*Library symbol*] [*Library of Congress*] (LCLS)
MnWiICS.... Christian Community School, Willmar, MN [*Library symbol*] [*Library of Congress*] (LCLS)
MNWiLES... Lafayette Elementary School, Willmar, MN [*Library symbol*] [*Library of Congress*] (LCLS)
MnWiIGES... Garfield Elementary School, Willmar, MN [*Library symbol*] [*Library of Congress*] (LCLS)
MnWiIH..... Rice Memorial Hospital, Willmar, MN [*Library symbol*] [*Library of Congress*] (LCLS)

MnWilIL..... Immanuel Lutheran School, Willmar, MN [*Library symbol*] [*Library of Congress*] (LCLS)
MnWilJES... Jefferson Elementary School, Willmar, MN [*Library symbol*] [*Library of Congress*] (LCLS)
MnWilJS.... Willmar Junior High School, Willmar, MN [*Library symbol*] [*Library of Congress*] (LCLS)
MnWilLiS... Lincoln Elementary School, Willmar, MN [*Library symbol*] [*Library of Congress*] (LCLS)
MnWilPS.... Willmar Public Schools, Willmar, MN [*Library symbol*] [*Library of Congress*] (LCLS)
MnWilRC ... Willmar Regional Treatment Center, Staff Library, Willmar, MN [*Library symbol*] [*Library of Congress*] (LCLS)
MnWilRE.... Roosevelt Elementary School, Willmar, MN [*Library symbol*] [*Library of Congress*] (LCLS)
MnWilRL.... Crow River Regional Library, Willmar, MN [*Library symbol*] [*Library of Congress*] (LCLS)
MnWilS ..... Willmar State Junior College, Willmar, MN [*Library symbol*] [*Library of Congress*] (LCLS)
MnWilSH ... Willmar Senior High School, Willmar, MN [*Library symbol*] [*Library of Congress*] (LCLS)
MnWilTC.... Willmar Technical Center, Willmar, MN [*Library symbol*] [*Library of Congress*] (LCLS)
MnWilWES... Washington Elementary School, Willmar, MN [*Library symbol*] [*Library of Congress*] (LCLS)
MnWin ...... Windom Public Library, Windom, MN [*Library symbol*] [*Library of Congress*] (LCLS)
MnWinH .... Windom Area Hospital, Windom, MN [*Library symbol*] [*Library of Congress*] (LCLS)
MnWinHS... Windom Area High School, Windom, MN [*Library symbol*] [*Library of Congress*] (LCLS)
MnWino..... Winona Public Library, Winona, MN [*Library symbol*] [*Library of Congress*] (LCLS)**MnWinoCT**... College of Saint Teresa, Winona, MN [*Library symbol*] [*Library of Congress*] (LCLS)
MnWinoS... Winona State College [*Later, Winona State University*], Winona, MN [*Library symbol*] [*Library of Congress*] (LCLS)
MnWinoSM... Saint Mary's College, Winona, MN [*Library symbol*] [*Library of Congress*] (LCLS)
MnWinWES... Winfair Elementary School, Windom, MN [*Library symbol*] [*Library of Congress*] (LCLS)
MnWlHS .... Echo-Wood Lake High School, Wood Lake, MN [*Library symbol*] [*Library of Congress*] (LCLS)
MnWlSJ..... St. John's School, Wood Lake, MN [*Library symbol*] [*Library of Congress*] (LCLS)
MnWnSJL... St. John's Lutheran School, Winsted, MN [*Library symbol*] [*Library of Congress*] (LCLS)
MnWoCCS... Calvary Christian School, Worthington, MN [*Library symbol*] [*Library of Congress*] (LCLS)
MnWoCES... Central Elementary School, Worthington, MN [*Library symbol*] [*Library of Congress*] (LCLS)
MnWoH ..... Worthington Regional Hospital, Worthington, MN [*Library symbol*] [*Library of Congress*] (LCLS)
MnWoJH.... Worthington Junior High, Worthington, MN [*Library symbol*] [*Library of Congress*] (LCLS)
MnWoLS.... Lakeview School, Worthington, MN [*Library symbol*] [*Library of Congress*] (LCLS)
MnWoN ..... Nobles County Library, Worthington, MN [*Library symbol*] [*Library of Congress*] (LCLS)
MnWoP...... Plum Creek Library System, Worthington, MN [*Library symbol*] [*Library of Congress*] (LCLS)
MnWoS...... Worthington State Junior College [*Later, Worthington Community College*], Worthington, MN [*Library symbol*] [*Library of Congress*] (LCLS)
MnWoSH.... Worthington Senior High School, Worthington, MN [*Library symbol*] [*Library of Congress*] (LCLS)
MnWoSMS... St. Mary's School, Worthington, MN [*Library symbol*] [*Library of Congress*] (LCLS)
MnWoWCS... Worthington Christian School, Worthington, MN [*Library symbol*] [*Library of Congress*] (LCLS)
MnWoWES... West Elementary School, Worthington, MN [*Library symbol*] [*Library of Congress*] (LCLS)
MnWp .... Waite Park Public Library, Waite Park, MN [*Library symbol*] [*Library of Congress*] (LCLS)
MnWpS ..... St. Joseph's School, Waite Park, MN [*Library symbol*] [*Library of Congress*] (LCLS)
MNWR ...... Malheur National Wildlife Refuge [*Oregon*] (AD)
MNWR ...... Mattamuskeet National Wildlife Refuge [*North Carolina*] (AD)
MNWR ...... Merced National Wildlife Refuge [*California*] (AD)
MNWR ...... Mingo National Wildlife Refuge [*Missouri*] (AD)
MNWR ...... Minidoka National Wildlife Refuge [*Idaho*] (AD)
MNWR ...... Mississiquoi National Wildlife Refuge [*Vermont*] (AD)
MNWR ...... Modoc National Wildlife Refuge [*California*] (AD)
MNWR ...... Montezuma National Wildlife Refuge [*New York*] (AD)
MNWR ...... Moosehorn National Wildlife Refuge [*Maine*] (AD)
MnWrC...... Willow River Camp Library, Willow River, MN [*Library symbol*] [*Library of Congress*] (LCLS)
MnWreS .... Wrenshall Public School, Wrenshall, MN [*Library symbol*] [*Library of Congress*] (LCLS)
MnWriLE.... Lincoln Elementary School, Wright, MN [*Library symbol*] [*Library of Congress*] (LCLS)
MnWrS...... Willow River School, Willow River, MN [*Library symbol*] [*Library of Congress*] (LCLS)
MnWs .... Winsted Public Library, Winsted, MN [*Library symbol*] [*Library of Congress*] (LCLS)
MnWsHT.... Holy Trinity School, Winsted, MN [*Library symbol*] [*Library of Congress*] (LCLS)
MNWSL..... Merchant Navy War Service League [*Australia*]
MnWspD.... Dakota County Library, West St. Paul, MN [*Library symbol*] [*Library of Congress*] (LCLS)
MnWsPS.... Winsted Public School, Winsted, MN [*Library symbol*] [*Library of Congress*] (LCLS)
MNX......... Manx Airlines Ltd. [*British*] [*ICAO designator*] (FAAC)
Mnx.......... Manx Gaelic (AD)
MNX......... Merrill Lynch & Co., Inc. [*AMEX symbol*] (NASQ)
MNX......... Missouri-Nebraska Express, Inc. (EFIS)
MNX......... Monotonous [*Telegraphy*] (PCTE)
MNX......... University of Minnesota, Morris, Morris, MN [*OCLC symbol*] (OCLC)
MNXI........ MNX, Inc. [*NASDAQ symbol*] (COMM)
MNY......... Many [*Telegraphy*] (PCTE)
MNY......... Money
MNY......... Mono Island [*Solomon Islands*] [*Airport symbol*] (OAG)
MNY......... Monteynard [*France*] [*Seismograph station code, US Geological Survey*] (SEIS)
MNY......... MONY Group [*NYSE symbol*] (SG)
MNY......... Saint Mary's College, Winona, MN [*OCLC symbol*] (OCLC)
MNY......... Taurus Municipal New York Holdings [*NYSE symbol*] (SPSG)
MNY......... Taurus MuniNewYork Hldgs [*NYSE symbol*] (TTSB)
MNYRC..... Metropolitan New York Rugby Conference (PSS)
MNZ......... College of Saint Teresa, Winona, MN [*OCLC symbol*] (OCLC)
MNZ......... Manassas [*Virginia*] [*Airport symbol*] (OAG)
MNZ......... Manzanillo [*Mexico*] [*Seismograph station code, US Geological Survey*] (SEIS)
MnZE........ Zimmerman Elementary School, Zimmerman, MN [*Library symbol*] [*Library of Congress*] (LCLS)
MNZIE....... Member of the New Zealand Institution of Engineers (SAUO)
Mnzlo....... Manzanillo (AD)
MO.......... Abbott Laboratories [*Research code symbol*]
MO.......... Calm Air International [*ICAO designator*] (AD)
MO.......... Macau [*ANSI two-letter standard code*] (CNC)
MO.......... Machine Operation (AFM)
Mo.......... Maestro GG1MasterGG2 [*Italian*] (AD)
MO.......... Magneto-Optic [*Computer science*]
MO.......... Magneto-Optical [*Physics*]
mo.......... Mail Order (AD)
MO.......... Mail Order [*Business term*]
MO.......... Maintenance and Operating [*Factor*] (NG)
MO.......... Maintenance Officer (MCD)
M/O......... Maintenance/Organization (MCD)
M/O......... Maintenance to Operation [*Ratio*]
m/o......... Maintenance-to-Operation (AD)
MO.......... Maize Oil (PDAA)
MO.......... Major Objective (KSC)
mo.......... Major Objective (NAKS)
MO.......... Make Offer
MO.......... Making Objects [*Research test*] [*Psychology*]
MO.......... Malaoxon (LDT)
m/O......... Male Oriental (AD)
MO.......... Managed Object [*Telecommunications*] (OSI)
MO.......... Management Object (SAUO)
MO.......... Management Office
MO.......... Management Operations (SPST)
MO.......... Management Order (NOAA)
MO.......... Managing Owner (RIMS)
M/O......... Manned and Operational (MUGU)
MO.......... Manned Orbiter (MCD)
mo.......... Manned Orbiter [*NASA*] (NAKS)
MO.......... Manually Operated
mo.......... Manual Operation (AD)
MO.......... Manual Orientation (MCD)
mo.......... Manual Orientation (NAKS)
MO.......... Manual Output
MO.......... Manufacturer's Output
mo.......... Manufacturing Order (NAKS)
MO.......... Manufacturing Order (NASA)
MO.......... Manufacturing Outline
MO.......... March Order [*Military*]
MO.......... Marketing Organization (AD)
MO.......... Mark Off
MO.......... Mars Observer [*Astronomy term*]
MO.......... Mars Observer Mission (MCD)
MO.......... Mars Orbiter [*NASA*] (KSC)
mo.......... Masonry Opening (AD)
MO.......... Masonry Opening [*Technical drawings*]
mo.......... Mass Observation (AD)
MO.......... Mass Observation
MO.......... Master of Obstetrics
MO.......... Master of Oratory
MO.......... Master of Osteopathy
mo.......... Master Oscillator (AD)
MO.......... Master Oscillator [*Radio*]
MO.......... Mature Outlook (EA)
MO.......... Mechanical Obstruction (MELL)
MO.......... Medial Oblique [*View*] [*Radiology*] (DAVI)
MO.......... Medical Officer [*Military*]
MO.......... Medical Orderly (WDAA)
MO.......... Medium Oocyte
MO.......... Medulla Oblongata [*Medicine*] (MELL)
MO.......... Member Organisation (ACII)
MO.......... Memory Operation
MO.......... Memory Output [*Computer science*]
MO.......... Mesio-Occlusal [*Dentistry*]

MO.......... Mesityl Oxide [*Also, MSO*] [*Organic chemistry*]
MO.......... Metal-Organic (AAEL)
MO.......... Meteorological Office [*British*]
MO.......... Meteorology Officer (MUGU)
mo.......... Method of Operation (AD)
MO.......... Method of Operation
MO.......... Methoxime [*Organic chemistry*]
MO.......... Methyl Orange [*Organic chemistry*]
MO.......... Micro-Opaque
mo.......... Microoperation (MHDB)
MO.......... Micro-Osmometer
MO.......... Microwave Oven (PDAA)
MO.......... Middeck Overhead (MCD)
mo.......... Middeck Overhead (NAKS)
mO.......... Mid-Oxygen [*Beta-alumina crystallography*]
MO.......... Military Observer (WDAA)
MO.......... Military Operations [*British military*] (DMA)
MO.......... Military Orders Issued by the President as Commander in Chief of the Armed Forces [*A publication*] (DLA)
MO.......... Military Services [*Diocesan abbreviation*] [*Maryland*] (TOCD)
Mo.......... Mineral Oil (DB)
MO.......... Mineral Oil
MO.......... Mineral Order [*Defense Minerals Exploration Administration*] [*Department of the Interior*] [*A publication*] (DLA)
MO.......... Ministerstvo Oborony [*Ministry of Defense*] [*Former USSR*]
MO.......... Ministry Outstanding (SAUO)
MO.......... Minor-Oppenheim [*Syndrome*] [*Medicine*] (DB)
MO.......... Minute Output [*Of heart*]
m/o.......... Mi Orden [*My Order*] [*Spanish*] (AD)
MO.......... Miscellaneous Operation (MUGU)
MO.......... Missile Officer (AAG)
mo.......... Mission Operations [*NASA*] (NAKS)
MO.......... Mission Operations [*NASA*]
MO.......... Mission Oriented
MO.......... Missouri [*Postal code*] (AFM)
Mo.......... Missouri (BEE)
Mo.......... Missourian (AD)
Mo.......... Missouri Reports [*A publication*] (AAGC)
Mo.......... Missouri State Library, Jefferson City, MO [*Library symbol*] [*Library of Congress*] (LCLS)
MO.......... Missouri Supreme Court Reports [*1821-1956*] [*A publication*] (DLA)
MO.......... Mitral Valve Opening [*Cardiology*]
MO.......... Mixed Oxide (NRCH)
MO.......... Mobile Object [*Telecommunications*] (OA)
MO.......... Mobile Station [*Air Force*]
MO.......... Mobil Oil [*Federal Railroad Administration identification code*]
Mo.......... Mode [*Statistics*]
MO.......... Moderato [*Moderate Speed*] [*Music*] (ADA)
MO.......... Moderator
MO.......... Modern Orthodox (BJA)
Mo.......... Modern Reports [*England*] [*A publication*] (DLA)
MO.......... Modification Order (AFIT)
MO.......... Modulate Open [*Nuclear energy*] (NRCH)
MO.......... Modus Operandi [*Police term for distinctive techniques used by criminals*]
MO.......... Mohawk [*Tire retread brand*]
MO.......... Mohawk Airlines, Inc. [*Obsolete*]
MO.......... Molded [*Construction*]
mo.......... Molecular Orbital (AD)
MO.......... Molecular Orbital [*Atomic physics*]
Mo.......... Moloney [*Strain*] [*Medicine*] (DB)
Mo.......... Molybdenum [*Chemical element*]
mo.......... Moment (AD)
MO.......... Moment (DSUE)
MO.......... Monaco [*IYRU nationality code*] (IYR)
Mo.......... Monaldus [*Flourished, 13th century*] [*Authority cited in pre-1607 legal work*] (DSA)
Mo.......... Monday (CDAI)
MO.......... Money Order
MO.......... Monitor Output
MO.......... Monooxygenase [*An enzyme*]
MO.......... Month (AFM)
mo.......... Month (WDMC)
MO.......... Monthly Order [*Navy*]
mo.......... Month Old [*Therapy term*] (CTAA)
m-o.......... Months Old (AD)
MO.......... Months Old (MEDA)
Mo.......... Montreal Stock Exchange [*Canada*]
MO.......... Mooney Aircraft, Inc. [*ICAO aircraft manufacturer identifier*] (ICAO)
Mo.......... Moore's English Privy Council Reports [*1836-62*] [*A publication*] (DLA)
Mo.......... Moore's Indian Appeals [*A publication*] (DLA)
MO.......... Morale Operations (CARL)
MO.......... Moral Obligation (MHDW)
MO.......... Moravian
MO.......... Morning
MO.......... Morphin (SAUS)
Mo.......... Morphine [*Medicine*] (WDAA)
M-O.......... Morris-Oxford (AD)
Mo.......... Morse [*Nautical term*] (NTA)
MO.......... Morse Code Light [*or Fog Signal*] [*Navigation signal*]
mo.......... Moth Eaten (AD)
mo.......... Mother (GEAB)
MO.......... Mother
M/O.......... Mother of (SAUS)
MO.......... Motion for Mandamus Overruled [*Legal term*] (DLA)
mo.......... Motor Operated (AD)
MO.......... Motor Operated (MSA)
MO.......... Motorscooter [*Motor vehicle violation code used in state of Maryland*] (MVRD)
MO.......... Moustache (DSUE)
MO.......... Mouth
mo.......... Move (NAKS)
MO.......... Move (NASA)
MO.......... Movement Orders
MO.......... Move Out (WDMC)
MO.......... Multi-Option (MCD)
MO.......... Mumps Orchitis [*Medicine*] (MELL)
MO.......... Municipal Offices (ROG)
MO.......... Murphy Oil Co. Ltd. [*Toronto Stock Exchange symbol*]
mo.......... Mustered Out (AD)
MO.......... Mustered Out [*of military service*]
MO.......... No Evidence of Distal Metastasis [*Oncology*] (DAVI)
MO.......... Philip Morris Companies, Inc. [*NYSE symbol*] (SPSG)
MO_2.......... Mixed Oxides
MO_2.......... Myocardial Oxygen Consumption [*Cardiology*] (MAE)
MO7.......... Magneto-Optic 7 (IGQR)
MOA.......... Made on Assembly
MOA.......... Magnetic Optical Activity
MOA.......... Mail Order Association of America (NTPA)
MOA.......... Make on Arrival (NASA)
MOA.......... Management Operations Audit [*Navy*] (NG)
MOA.......... Manual-Off-Automatic (KSC)
MOA.......... Marine Office of America (AD)
MOA.......... Marine Officer's Attendant [*British military*] (DMA)
MOA.......... Massachusetts Orthopaedic Association (SAUO)
MOA.......... Matrix Output Amplifier
MOA.......... McDonald's Operators' Association (EA)
MOA.......... Mechanism of Action [*Medicine*] (DAVI)
MOA.......... Medical Outreach for Armenians (EA)
moa.......... Medium Observation Aircraft (AD)
MOA.......... Medium Observation Aircraft
M o A.......... Memorandum of Agreement (AD)
MOA.......... Memorandum of Agreement
MOA.......... Memorandum of Assistance
MoA.......... Memorandum of Association (WDAA)
MOA.......... Method of Accomplishment (AFIT)
MOA.......... Method of Adjustment [*Aviation*]
MOA.......... Methods of Administration [*Department of Education*] (OICC)
MOA.......... Metropolitan Opera Association (AD)
MOA.......... Metropolitan Opera Auditions (AD)
MOA.......... Michigan Optometric Association (SAUO)
MOA.......... Michigan Osteopathic Association (EARSL)
MOA.......... Microlensing Observations in Astrophysics (SAUS)
MOA.......... Microwave Oven Association (BUAC)
MOA.......... Military Assistance Program Order Amendment (AFM)
MOA.......... Military Operations Area [*FAA*] (TAG)
MoA.......... Ministry of Agriculture [*British*] (AD)
MOA.......... Ministry of Aviation [*British*]
MOA.......... Minnesota Orchestral Association (AD)
moa.......... Minute of Angle (AD)
MOA.......... Minute of Angle
MOA.......... Misr Overseas Airways [*Egypt*]
moa.......... Missile Optical Alignment (AD)
MOA.......... Missile Optical Alignment
MOA.......... Missouri Botanical Garden, St. Louis, MO [*OCLC symbol*] (OCLC)
MOA.......... Moa [*Cuba*] [*Airport symbol*] (OAG)
MOA.......... Model A [*NCIC car model code*]
MOA.......... Modern Operating Agreement [*Labor negotiations*]
MOA.......... Molln [*Austria*] [*Seismograph station code, US Geological Survey*] (SEIS)
MOA.......... Monoamine Oxidase (MELL)
MOA.......... Mountain Lake Resources, Inc. [*Vancouver Stock Exchange symbol*]
moa.......... Mud on Airstrip (AD)
MOA.......... Municipality of Anchorage (SAUO)
MOA.......... Municipal Officers' Association (ROG)
MoA.......... Museum of Australia (BUAC)
MOA.......... Music Operators of America [*Later, AMOA*] (EA)
MOAA.......... Mail Order Association of America (EA)
MOAA.......... Marina Operators Association of America (NTPA)
MOAA.......... Municipal Officers' Association of Australia
MOA/ACD.......... Ministry of Agriculture/ Agriculture Communication Division (SAUO)
MOA/AIC.......... Ministry of Agriculture/ Agricultural Inputs Corp. (SAUS)
MOA/AIC.......... Ministry of Agriculture/ Agricultural Inputs Corporation (SAUO)
MOA/APROSC... Ministry of Agriculture/ Agricultural Projects Service Centre (SAUO)
MOAB.......... Massive Ordnance Air Blast [*Military*]
MoAB.......... Monoclonal Antibody [*Immunochemistry*]
MOAB.......... Mother of All Bombs [*Military*]
MOABWEPO... Members of Anything Bill [*Clinton*] Was Ever Part Of [*Pronounced "Mo-ab-wee-po"*]
MOAC.......... Message Origin Authentication Check [*Open Systems Interconnection*] (ODAA)
MOAC.......... Ministry of Agriculture and Cooperatives [*Thailand*] (BUAC)
MOACA.......... Ministry of Aviation Cataloguing Authority (SAUO)
MOA/CDB.......... Ministry of Agriculture/Cotton Development Board (SAUO)
MOAD.......... Methotrexate, Oncovin [*Vincristine*] L-asparaginase, Dexamethasone [*Antineoplastic drug regimen*] (DAVI)

MOA/DDC ... Ministry of Agriculture/Dairy Development Corp. (SAUO)
MOA/DFAMS... Ministry of Agriculture/ Department of Food and Agricultural Marketing Services (SAUO)
MOA/DLDAH... Ministry of Agriculture/ Department of Livestock Development & Animal Health (SAUO)
MO Admin Code... Missouri Code of State Regulations [*A publication*] (DLA)
MO Admin Reg... Missouri Register [*A publication*] (DLA)
MOA/DOA... Ministry of Agriculture/ Department of Agriculture (SAUO)
MOA/DOAD... DEPARTMENT OF AGRICULTURE DEVELOPMENT (SAUS)
MOA/DOAD... Ministry of Agriculture/ Department of Agriculture Development (SAUO)
MOA/DOF... Ministry of Agriculture/ Department of Fisheries (SAUO)
MOA/DOH... Ministry of Agriculture/ Department of Horticulture (SAUO)
MOA/DOI.... Ministry of Agriculture/ Department of Irrigation (SAUO)
MOA/DOL... Ministry of Agriculture/ Department of Livestock (SAUO)
MOADS...... Maneuver Oriented Ammunition Distribution System (SAUS)
MOADS...... Montgomery Air Defense Sector [*of SAGE*] (MUGU)
MOAE........ AE Morris [*Common carrier symbol*]
MOAE........ Mitigation of Adverse Effect [*Environmental science*] (COE)
MOAF........ Meteorological and Oceanographic Analyst/Forecaster [*Course*] (DNAB)
MOAF........ Ministry of Agriculture and Forests [*Republic of Korea*] (BUAC)
MOA/JDTC... Ministry of Agriculture/Jute Development and Trading Corp. (SAUS)
MOA/JDTC... Ministry of Agriculture/Jute Development and Trading Corporation (SAUO)
Moak........ Moak's English Reports [*A publication*] (DLA)
Moak (Eng)... Moak's English Reports [*A publication*] (DLA)
Moak Eng Rep... Moak's English Reports [*A publication*] (DLA)
Moak Und... Moak's Edition of Underhill on Torts [*A publication*] (DLA)
Moak Underh Torts... Moak's Edition of Underhill on Torts [*A publication*] (DLA)
Moak Van S Pl... Moak's Edition of Van Santvoord's Equity Pleading [*A publication*] (DLA)
MOAL........ Mail-Order Action Line [*Direct marketing association*] (WDMC)
MOAL........ Monte Dump Trailer [*NCIC trailer make code*]
MOALC...... Mobile Air Logistics Center [*Air Force*]
MOAMA..... Mobile Air Materiel Area
MOA/NARC... Ministry of Agriculture/ National Agricultural Research Centre (SAUO)
MO&DA..... Mission Operations and Data Analysis (ACAE)
MO&DS..... Mission Operations and Data System (SAUO)
MO & DSD. Mission Operations and Data Systems Directorate (SSD)
MO & G..... Master of Obstetrics and Gynaecology
MO & O..... Memorandum Opinion and Order (NTCM)
Mo & P..... Moore and Payne's English Common Pleas Reports [*A publication*] (DLA)
Mo & R..... Moody and Robinson's English Nisi Prius Reports [*A publication*] (DLA)
Mo & S..... Moore and Scott's English Common Pleas Reports [*1831-34*] [*A publication*] (DLA)
Mo & Sc.... Moore and Scott's English Common Pleas Reports [*1831-34*] [*A publication*] (DLA)
MOANG..... Missouri Air National Guard (MUSM)
MO Ann Stat (Vernon)... Vernon's Annotated Missouri Statutes [*A publication*] (DLA)
MOA/NTDC... Ministry of Agriculture/Nepal Tea Development Corp. (SAUS)
MOA/NTDC... Ministry of Agriculture/ Nepal Tea Development Corporation (SAUO)
MOAP....... Management Observation Assessment Program (SAUO)
MO Ap....... Missouri Appeal Reports [*A publication*] (DLA)
MOAP....... Moapa Valley Freight and Passenger Service [*Common carrier symbol*]
MO App..... Missouri Appeal Reports [*A publication*] (DLA)
MO Appeals... Missouri Appeal Reports [*A publication*] (DLA)
MO App (KC)... Missouri Appeal Reports [*Kansas City*] [*A publication*] (DLA)
MO App Rep... Missouri Appeal Reports [*A publication*] (DLA)
MO Apps.... Missouri Appeal Reports [*A publication*] (DLA)
MO App (St L)... Missouri Appeal Reports [*St. Louis*] [*A publication*] (DLA)
MO AR...... Missouri Appellate Reporter [*A publication*] (DLA)
MOARS...... Mobilization Assignment Reserve Section [*Military*]
moAt......... Mainstream of American Thought (AD)
MOAT........ Methods of Appraisal and Test (MHDB)
MOAT........ Minewarfare Operational Analysis Tool (SAUS)
MOAT........ Missile on Aircraft Test
moat......... Missile-on-Aircraft Testing [*Military*] (AD)
MOAT........ Mission Opportunities for Airship Technology (ACAE)
MOATL...... Modal Acoustic Transmission Loss (MCD)
MOATRS.... MAJCOM On-Line Aerospace Vehicle Training Report System (SAUO)
MOATS...... Message Originating and Terminating Station (ACAE)
MOB......... Mail Order Buyer (WDMC)
MOB......... Main Olfactory Bulb [*Anatomy*]
MOB......... Main Operating Base
MOB......... Main Operations Base (SAUO)
mob.......... Make or Buy (AD)
MOB......... Make or Buy [*Economics*]
MOB......... Man-Overboard
MOB......... Master of Organizational Behavior (GAGS)
MOB......... Medical Office Building (DAVI)
MOB......... Menlo Park [*California*] [*Seismograph station code, US Geological Survey*] (SEIS)
MOB......... Methane-Oxidizing Bacteria
MOB......... Military Order of Battle (SAUO)
MOB......... Missile Order of Battle (AFM)
MOB......... Mobil Corp. [*NYSE symbol*] [*Toronto Stock Exchange symbol*] (SPSG)
mob.......... Mobile (AD)
MOB......... Mobile [*Alabama*] [*Airport symbol*]
Mob.......... Mobile, Alabama [*Maritime abbreviation*] (AD)
MOB......... Mobile Operating Base (ACAE)
mob.......... Mobile Vulgus [*Disorderly Group of People*] [*Latin*] (AD)
MOB......... Mobility [*MTMC*] (TAG)
MOB......... Mobility Status (SAUO)
MOB......... Mobilization [*or Mobilize*] (AFM)
Mob.......... Mobley's Contested Election Cases, United States House of Representatives [*1882-89*] [*A publication*] (DLA)
MOB......... Mock-Up Board [*Navy*] (AFIT)
MOB......... Modification of Benefits [*Health insurance*] (GHCT)
MOB......... Moinba [*Language symbol*] (ETLW)
MOB......... Money-Order Business
MOB......... Montreux-Oberland-Bernois [*Railway*] [*Canada*] (AD)
MOB......... Movable Object Block (ODA)
MOB......... Municipals over Bonds [*Investment term*]
MOB......... Mustargen [*Nitrogen mustard*], Oncovin , Bleomycin [*Vincristine*] [*Antineoplastic drug regimen*]
Mob.......... National Mobilization Committee to end the War in Viet-Nam (SAUO)
MOB......... Southwest Baptist College, Bolivar, MO [*OCLC symbol*] (OCLC)
MOBA....... Military Operations in Built-Up Areas
MOBA....... Museum of Bad Art (ADWA)
MOBAC...... Monterey Bay Area Cooperative Library System [*Library network*]
MOBAS...... Model Basin
MOBAT...... Mobile Battalion Antitank Gun [*British military*] (DMA)
Mo' Bay..... Mobile Bay, Alabama [*Montego Bay, Jamaica*] (AD)
MOBB....... Mobilaire Mobile Homes [*NCIC trailer make code*]
MOBC....... Mobile Chapel Trailer [*NCIC trailer make code*]
MOBC2...... Mobilization Command and Control (SAUO)
MOBCOM... Mobile Command [*Canada*] (AD)
mobcom.... Mobile Communications (AD)
MOBCOM... Mobile Communications
Mob Con.... Mobilising Control (WDAA)
MOBCON.... Mobilization Construction Plan [*Military*] (NVT)
MOBCON.... Mobilization Movement Control [*MTMC*] (TAG)
MOBCONBAT... Mobile Construction Battalion [*Navy*] (DNAB)
MOBCTR.... Mobilization Center (DNAB)
MOBD....... Mediterranean Oceanic Data Base (SAUO)
MOBDES.... Mobilization Designation [*or Designee*]
MOBDET.... Mobility Deployment Planning System (SAUO)
MOBDIC.... Mobile Digital Computer
MOBE....... Moto Beta [*NCIC motorcycle make code*]
MOBED...... Mobile Education Demonstration
MoBeHi..... Scott County Historical Society, Benton, MO [*Library symbol*] [*Library of Congress*] (LCLS)
MOBERS.... Mobilization Equipment Redistribution System
mobeu....... Mobile Emergency Unit (AD)
MOBEU...... Mobile Emergency Unit (NOAA)
MOBEX...... Mobile Excursion (MCD)
MOBEX...... Mobile Exploration [*NASA*]
MOBEX...... Mobility Test Exercise [*Military*]
MOBF........ Mobile Freeze [*NCIC trailer make code*]
MOBG....... Mobile Engineering Company [*NCIC trailer make code*]
MOBH....... Mobile Facility Engineering Company [*NCIC trailer make code*]
MOBI........ Mobius Management Systems, Inc. [*NASDAQ symbol*] (NASQ)
MOBI........ Motobic [*NCIC motorcycle make code*]
MOBIC....... Mobility of Blind and elderly people Interacting with Computers (SAUO)
MOBIDA..... Mobile Data Acquisition System (MCD)
MOBIDAC... Mobile Data Acquisition System
MOBIDACS... Mobile Data Acquisition System (AD)
mobidic..... Mobile Digital Computer (AD)
MOBIDIC... Mobile Digital Computer [*Sylvania Electric Products Co.*]
MOBIDICK... Multivariable On-Line Bilingual Dictionary Kit (SAUO)
MOB-III...... Methotrexate, Oncovin [*Vineristine*], Bleomycin [*Antineoplastic drug regimen*] (DAVI)
MOB-III...... Mitomycin C, Oncovin [*Vincristine*], Bleomycin, Cisplatin [*Antineoplastic drug regimen*]
Mobil........ Mobil Corp. [*Associated Press*] (SAG)
MOBIL....... Mobile, AL [*American Association of Railroads railroad junction routing code*]
mobil........ Mobility (AD)
MOBIL....... Mobility
MOBILAB... Mobile Rapid Photo Processing Laboratory (ACAE)
Mobilarian... Mobile Branch Librarian (AD)
mobilary.... Mobile Library (AD)
MOBILE..... Mobile Source Emissions Model (SAUO)
MOBILE5A... Mobile Source Emission Factor Model (SAUO)
MOBILESAT... Mobile Satellite Corp. [*King Of Prussia, PA*] [*Telecommunications*] (TSSD)
MOBILHY... Hydrological Atmospheric Pilot Experiment (SAUO)
MOBIS....... Management-Oriented Budget Information System
MOBJ........ Mobile Garage Manufacturing Company [*NCIC trailer make code*]
MOBK....... Mobile Holding Corporation [*NCIC trailer make code*]
mobl......... Macro-Oriented Business Language [*Computer science*] (AD)
MOBL........ Macro-Oriented Business Language [*Computer science*]
MOBL........ Main Operating Base LASER
MOBL........ Mobile Home Company [*NCIC trailer make code*]
Mobl......... Mobley's Contested Election Cases, United States House of Representatives [*1882-89*] [*A publication*] (DLA)
mobl......... Mopliert [*Furnished*] [*German*] (AD)

MoblAm..... Mobile America Corp. [*Associated Press*] (SAG)
MOBLAS.... Mobile Laser (ACAE)
moblas...... Mobile LASER Satellite Tracking Station (AD)
Mobley...... Mobley Environmental Services [*Associated Press*] (SAG)
MoblGs...... Mobile Gas Service Corp. [*Associated Press*] (SAG)
mob lib..... Mobile Librarian (AD)
MoblM...... Mobile Mini, Inc. [*Associated Press*] (SAG)
MoblMin.... Mobile Mini, Inc. [*Associated Press*] (SAG)
mob lt....... Man Overboard and Breakdown Light (AD)
MOBMAN... Mobilization Manpower Planning System [*DoD*]
MobMda.... MobileMedia Corp. [*Associated Press*] (SAG)
MOBMDR... Mobilization Master Data Record [*Army*]
MOBN....... Mobile Home Service [*NCIC trailer make code*]
MOBO....... Mobile Manufacturing Corporation [*NCIC trailer make code*]
Mob O....... Mobilising Officer (WDAA)
MOBO....... Mother Board (VLIE)
MOBOL...... Mohawk Business-Oriented Language [*Mohawk Data Systems*]
MoBolS..... Southwest Baptist College, Bolivar, MO [*Library symbol*] [*Library of Congress*] (LCLS)
MOBOT...... Mobile Remote-Controlled Robot
mobot....... Mobile Robot (AD)
MOBOT...... Mobile Robot (VLIE)
MOBOT...... Modular Robot
MOBP....... Mobile of Marysville [*NCIC trailer make code*]
MOBPERS... Mobilization Personnel Processing System (SAUO)
MOBPERSACS... Mobilization Personnel Structure and Composition System [*DoD*]
MOBPLANS... Mobility Plans (SAUO)
MoBr........ Brentwood Public Library, Brentwood, MO [*Library symbol*] [*Library of Congress*] (LCLS)
MOBR....... Mobile Office [*NCIC trailer make code*]
MOBRA...... Monsanto Do Brasil Ltd (EFIS)
MOBRASOP... Mobilization Requirements in Support of the Army Strategic Objectives Plan
MOBREM... Mobilization Base Requirements Model (SAUO)
MOBS....... Mobile Hospitals [*Military slang*]
MOBS....... Mobile Ocean Basing System (PDAA)
MOBS....... Mobile Products [*NCIC trailer make code*]
MOBS....... Moebius Syndrome [*Medicine*] (DMAA)
MOBS....... Multiple-Orbit Bombardment System
MOBSCOPE... Mobilization Shipments Configured for Operation Planning and Execution [*MTMC*] (TAG)
MOBSF...... Mobility Support Flight [*Military*]
MOBSS...... Mobility Support Squadron [*Air Force*]
MOBSS...... Mobilization Support System [*MTMC*] (TAG)
MOBSSL-UAF... Merritt and Miller's Own Block Structured Simulation Language, Unpronounceable Acronym For [*1969*] [*Computer science*] (CSR)
MOBSSq.... Mobility Support Squadron [*Air Force*]
MOBSUPPGRU... Mobile Support Group [*Military*] (DNAB)
MOBT........ Mobile Scout [*NCIC trailer make code*]
MOBTA...... Mobilization Table of Distribution and Allowances (AD)
MOBTB...... Mobilization Troop Basis [*Army*] (AABC)
MOBTDA.... Mobilization Table of Distribution and Allowances [*Military*] (AABC)
MOBTR...... Mobile Trainer
MOBTRAN... Mobilization and Deployment Transportability (SAUO)
MOBU....... Mobile Structures [*NCIC trailer make code*]
MOBU....... Mobilization Base Units
MOBULA.... Model Building Language [*Programming language*] (IEEE)
mobula...... Model-Building Language (AD)
MOBV....... Mobile Tops [*NCIC trailer make code*]
MOBW....... Mobile Unit Manufacturing [*NCIC trailer make code*]
Mob Wkshp... Mobile Workshop (SAUO)
MOBX....... Mobilemanor [*NCIC trailer make code*]
MOBX....... Mobil Oil [*Private rail car owner code*]
MOBY....... Marine Optical Buoy (ROAS)
MOBYC...... My Own Bloody Yacht Club [*Founded in England; registered with Lloyds of London*]
MOC......... Magnetic Optic Converter
MOC......... Maintenance Operational Check
MOC......... Maintenance Operations Center [*Military*]
MOC......... Maintenance Operations Control [*Canadian Airlines International*]
MOC......... Makapuu Oceanic Center [*Hawaii*] (AD)
MOC......... Management and Operating Contractor (ODBW)
MOC......... Management of Change
MOC......... Management-Oriented Computing (MHDB)
MOC......... Manual Operations Control
moc.......... Manufacturing Other Charges (AD)
MOC......... Manufacturing Outreach Center
MOC......... Marcos Owners Club [*Formerly, Marcos Club*] (EA)
MOC......... Margin of Control [*Environmental science*] (COE)
MOC......... Margin of Criticality [*Environmental science*] (COE)
moc.......... Marine Operation Center (NAKS)
MOC......... Marine Operation Center [*NASA*] (NASA)
MOC......... Market on Close [*Investment term*] (NUMA)
MOC......... Marlin Owners' Club (EA)
MOC......... Mars Observer Camera
MOC......... Mars Orbiter Camera
MOC......... Massachusetts Oilheat Council (SAUO)
MOC......... Master Operational Computer [*or Controller*]
moc.......... Master Operation Control (AD)
MOC......... Master Operations Center
MOC......... Master Operations Console
MOC......... Master Operations Control
MOC......... Master Ordnance Configuration File [*Navy*]
MOC......... Materials Operations Center (SAUO)
MOC......... Materiel Obligation Code (ACAE)
MOC......... Mathematical Operations Computer
MOC......... Mauna Olu College [*Maui*] (AD)
MOC......... Maximum Operational Capacity [*Chemical engineering*]
MOC......... Maximum Oxygen Consumption
MOC......... Mechanical Off-Machine Coated Paper (DGA)
MOC......... Memorandum of Conditions
MOC......... Memorandum of Cooperation (SAUO)
MOC......... Memory Operating Characteristic [*Computer science*] (IEEE)
MOC......... Meridional Overturning Cell (SAUS)
MOC......... Meridional Overturning Circulation
MOC......... Merland Explorations Ltd. [*Toronto Stock Exchange symbol*]
MOC......... Messerschmitt Owners Club (EA)
MOC......... Method of Characteristics [*Equilibrium flow*]
MOC......... Metropolitan Owners' Club [*Woking, Surrey, England*] (EAIO)
MOC......... Microelectronics and Computer (SAUO)
MOC......... Microwave Oven Control (TIMI)
MOC......... Mid Ocean Limited [*NYSE symbol*] (SAG)
MOC......... Mid Ocean Ltd [*NYSE symbol*] (TTSB)
MOC......... Mid-Ohio Conference (PSS)
MOC......... Military Occupation Code (MCD)
MOC......... Military Order of the Carabao (EA)
MOC......... Minimal Oxygen Consumption
MOC......... Minimum Obstacle Clearance [*Aviation*] (FAAC)
MOC......... Minimum Operating Capability (SAUO)
MOC......... Minimum Operational Characteristics
MOC......... Minister of Conservation (SAUO)
MOC......... Ministry of Communications (CINC)
MOC......... Ministry of Construction [*Republic of Korea*] (BUAC)
MOC......... Missile Operation Center [*Air Force*]
MOC......... Missionaries of Charity [*Australia*]
MOC......... Mission Operation Computer
MOC......... Mission Operations Complex [*NASA*] (KSC)
moc.......... Mission Operations Computer (AD)
MOC......... Missions Operations Center (or Centre) (SAUO)
MOC......... Mobile Emergency Response Support Operations Center [*Emergency Management*] (EMA)
MOC......... Mobile Oil Cooler
MOC......... Mobile Operations Center [*Air Force*] (DOMA)
MOC......... Mobile-Originated Call (CGWS)
moc.......... Mocassin (AD)
MOC......... Moccasin
MOC......... Modern Operating Contract [*Automibile industry labor relations*]
MOC......... Modular Operations Centre (SAUS)
MOC......... Modular Organization Charting (PDAA)
MOC......... Monte Carlo [*NCIC car model code*]
MOC......... Montes Claros [*Brazil*] [*Airport symbol*] (OAG)
MOC......... Morris College, Sumter, SC [*Inactive*] [*OCLC symbol*] (OCLC)
MOC......... Moscow, ID [*Amtrak Busline code*]
MOC......... Mother of the Chapel [*Unions*] [*British*] (DI)
MOC......... Multifunction Operator Console (SAUS)
MOC......... Multiple Ocular Coloboma [*Medicine*] (DMAA)
MoC......... Museum of the Confederacy (SAUO)
MOC......... Mustang Owners Club (EA)
MOC......... Myanma Oil Corporation (SAUO)
MOC......... Supreme Pup Tent, Military Order of the Cootie (EA)
MOCA....... Merisel Open Computing Alliance (SAUO)
MOCA....... Methotrexate, Oncovin [*Vincristine*], Cyclophosphamide, Adriamycin [*Antineoplastic drug regimen*]
MOCA....... Methylenebis(ortho-chloroaniline) [*Also, MBOCA*] [*Organic chemistry*]
moca........ Minimum Obstruction Clearance Altitude (AD)
MOCA....... Minimum Obstruction Clearance Altitude [*Aviation*]
MOCA....... Missouri Classical Association (SAUO)
MOCA....... Mitsubishi Owner's Club of America
MOCA....... Mixed Object Document Content Architecture [*Computer science*] (CIST)
MOCA....... Monte Carlo Mobile Homes [*NCIC trailer make code*]
MOCA....... Montezuma Castle National Monument
MOCA....... Museum of Contemporary Art [*Los Angeles*]
MoCAD...... Museum of Contemporary African Diasporian Arts
MOCAM..... Mobile Checkout and Maintenance (AAG)
mocamp.... Motor Camp (AD)
MOCAN...... Motor Can
MoCanC..... Culver-Stockton College, Canton, MO [*Library symbol*] [*Library of Congress*] (LCLS)
MOCAPT.... Missouri Center for Agricultural Products Technology (BUAC)
MOCAS...... Mechanization of Contract Administration Service (MCD)
MOCAT...... Measurement and Observation of Clear Air Turbulence (ACAE)
MOCC....... Master Operations Control Center (SAA)
MOCC....... Memory-Operating Characteristic Curve (DIPS)
MOCC....... Metal-Oxygen Cluster Compounds [*Chemistry*]
MOCC....... MG Octagon Car Club [*Formerly, Octagon Car Club*] (EA)
MOCC....... Miniature Operations Control Center (SAUO)
MOCC....... Mission Operations Control Center (SSD)
MOCC....... Mobile Operations Command Center (DOMA)
MOCC....... Mobile Operations Control Centre (SAUO)
MOCC....... Mobley Metal Works [*NCIC trailer make code*]
MOCCA...... , Cyclophosphamide, Alkeran [*Lomustine*] [*Melphalan*] [*Antineoplastic drug regimen*]
MOCCA...... Mobile Computing & Communication Appliance [*Digital Equipment Corp.*]
MoCCA...... Mobile Computing and Communication Appliance [*Digital Equipment Corp.*]

MOCCA...... Mobile Operations Center for Communication and Analysis (SAUO)
MOCCAC.... Missouri Community College Athletic Conference (PSS)
MOCCC...... Massachusetts Organized Crime Control Council (AD)
MOccThy.... Master of Occupational Therapy (ADA)
MOcE........ Master of Oceanographic Engineering (GAGS)
MOCEM..... Meteorological and Oceanographic Equipment Maintenance Course (DNAB)
MOCERT.... Motorcycle Certification Data (SAUO)
MOCF........ Maintenance Operations Control File (MCD)
MOCF........ Manchester Open College Federation [*British*] (AIE)
MOCF........ Mission Operations Computational Facilities [*NASA*] (NASA)
MoCg........ Cape Girardeau Public Library, Cape Girardeau, MO [*Library symbol*] [*Library of Congress*] (LCLS)
MoCgS...... Southeast Missouri State University, Cape Girardeau, MO [*Library symbol*] [*Library of Congress*] (LCLS)
MoCheL..... Logan College of Chiropractic, Chesterfield, MO [*Library symbol*] [*Library of Congress*] (LCLS)
mochwr..... Mochaware (VRA)
MOCI........ Ministry of Commerce and Industry [*British*] (AD)
MOCI........ Ministry of Commerce and Industry [*Republic of Korea*] (BUAC)
MOCI........ Mound City Group National Monument
MOCI........ Mustang Owners Club International (EA)
MOCIC....... Molecular Orbital Constraint of Interaction Coordinates [*Atomic physics*]
MOCL........ Metz Owners Club Library (EA)
MoCli........ Henry County Library, Clinton, MO [*Library symbol*] [*Library of Congress*] (LCLS)
MoCIS....... Saint Louis Junior College, Clayton, MO [*Library symbol*] [*Library of Congress*] [*Obsolete*] (LCLS)
MOCM....... Missile Out of Commission for Maintenance (MUGU)
MOCN....... Mid Ocean Ltd. [*NASDAQ symbol*] (SAG)
MOCN....... Modern Controls, Inc. [*Associated Press*] (SAG)
MOCNA...... Maserati Owners Club of North America (EAIO)
MOCNA...... Metropolitan Owners Club of North America (EA)
MOCNESS... Multiple Opening-Closing Net and Environmental Sensing System [*For collecting marine samples*]
MOCO....... Machinery Overhaul Co.
MOCO....... Missile Operations Control Officer (AAG)
MOCO....... MOCON, Inc. [*NASDAQ symbol*] (SG)
MOCO....... Modern Controls [*NASDAQ symbol*] (TTSB)
MOCO....... Modern Controls, Inc. [*NASDAQ symbol*] (NQ)
MoCoC...... Christian College, Columbia, MO [*Library symbol*] [*Library of Congress*] (LCLS)
MOCOCO.... Movement Coordinating Committee (SAUO)
Mo Code Regs... State of Missouri Code of State Regulations Annotated [*A publication*] (AAGC)
MOCODES... Mobile Coastal Defense System (MCD)
MoCoGS.... Church of Jesus Christ of Latter-Day Saints, Genealogical Society Library, Columbia Missouri Branch, Columbia, MO [*Library symbol*] [*Library of Congress*] (LCLS)
MoCoJ....... Joint Collection, Western Historical Manuscript Collection and State Historical,Columbia, MO [*Library symbol*] [*Library of Congress*] (LCLS)
MoCom...... Mobile Command (AD)
MOCOM..... Mobility Command [*AMC*]
MOCOMMDOPS... DEPARTMENT OF POSTAL SERVICES (SAUS)
MOCOMMDOPS... Ministry of Communications Department of Postal Services (SAUO)
MOCOMMDOPS... Ministry of Communications/Department of Postal Services (SAUS)
MOCOMM/NTC... Ministry of Communications/Nepal Telecommunications Corp. (SAUS)
MOCON..... Mobile Repair Parts Container
MOCON..... Modern Controls, Inc. (EFIS)
MoConA..... Conception Abbey and Seminary, Conception, MO [*Library symbol*] [*Library of Congress*] (LCLS)
MoCoS...... Stephens College, Columbia, MO [*Library symbol*] [*Library of Congress*] (LCLS)
MoCoV...... Harry S Truman Memorial Veterans Hospital, Columbia, MO [*Library symbol*] [*Library of Congress*] (LCLS)
mocp........ Missile Out of Commission for Parts [*Military*] (AD)
MOCP....... Missile Out of Commission for Parts (AFM)
MOCP....... Mission Operational Computer Program (SAUO)
MOCR....... Metz Owners Club Register (EA)
mocr......... Mission Operation Control Room (AD)
MOCR....... Mission Operations Control Room
MOCR....... Moores Creek National Military Park
MOCR....... Motocicletas Carabela [*NCIC motorcycle make code*]
MOCS....... MacPhail Operant Chambers (SAUO)
MOCS....... Managed Object Conformance Statement [*Telecommunications*] (OSI)
MOCS....... Master Operations Control System (KSC)
MOCS....... Microsoft Official Curriculum Seminar (SAUO)
MOCS....... Military Order of Columbia's Shield (EA)
MOCS....... Missile Operational Communications Systems (ACAE)
MOCS....... Mission Operation and Control Subsystem (ACAE)
MOCS....... Mons Officer Cadet School (SAUO)
MOCS....... Multichannel Ocean Color Scanner (ACAE)
mocs........ Multichannel Ocean Color Sensor (NAKS)
MOCS....... Multichannel Ocean Color Sensor [*NASA*]
MOCS....... Multiple Output Control System (ECII)
MoCStP..... Saint Paul's College, Concordia, MO [*Library symbol*] [*Library of Congress*] (LCLS)
MOCSW..... Monitor and Operations Control Software Subsystem [*Space Flight Operations Facility, NASA*]
MOCT........ Mean Overhaul Cycle Time [*Quality control*] (MCD)
MOC/TPC... Ministry of Commerce/Trade Promotion Centre (SAUO)
MOCU....... Maritime Carrier Shipping [*Intermodal shipping container symbol*] (TVRC)
MOCV....... Manual Oxygen Control Valve (NASA)
MO-CVD.... Metal-Organic Chemical Vapor Deposition [*Also, MO-VPE, OM-CVD, OM-VPE*] [*Semiconductor technology*]
MOCX....... Missouri Portland Cement [*Private rail car owner code*]
MOCZ....... Murphy Oil [*Federal Railroad Administration identification code*]
MOD......... Drury College, Springfield, MO [*OCLC symbol*] (OCLC)
Mod.......... Made Over Democrat [*Facetious translation referring to Mods - Moderate Republicans*]
MOD......... Magnetic Optical Display
MOD......... Magneto-Optical Disc [*Digital audio technology*]
MOD......... Magneto-Optic Disk [*Computer science*] (CIST)
MOD......... Mail-Order Delivery
MOD......... Mail Order Department [*Business term*]
MOD......... Maintenance of Deception
MOD......... Maintenance of Defense (ACAE)
MOD......... Management and Organization Division [*Environmental Protection Agency*] (GFGA)
MOD......... Manager on Duty
MOD......... Manned Orbital Development Station [*See also MODS, MOSS, MTSS*] [*Air Force/NASA*]
MOD......... Manpower and Organization Division [*Air Force*]
MOD......... Manual Overdrive [*Automotive engineering*]
MOD......... Manufacturers Operations Division [*Environmental Protection Agency*] (GFGA)
MOD......... Mapping of Disease
MOD......... March of Dimes (HGEN)
MOD......... March on Drugs [*An association*]
MOD......... Marine Operations Division [*Environmental Protection Agency*] (GFGA)
Mod.......... Marxist on Drugs [*Mods - Facetious translation referring to Moderate Republicians*]
MOD......... Master of Organizational Development (GAGS)
MoD......... Masters of Deception (SAUS)
MOD......... Masters of Disaster [*Computer hacker gang*]
MOD......... Masters of Downloading [*Computer science*] (VLIE)
MOD......... Maturity Onset Diabetes [*Medicine*]
MOD......... Maximum Operating Depth (SAUO)
MOD......... Medical Officer of the Day [*Military*]
MOD......... Medical Officer on Duty (DAVI)
MOD......... Medicine, Osteopathy, and Dentistry [*HEW program*]
MOD......... Memorandum of Decision (COE)
MOD......... Mesial, Occlusal, and Distal [*Describes location of openings in a carious tooth*] [*Dentistry*]
m-o-d........ Mesial-Occlusal-Distal [*Dentistry*] (AD)
MOD......... Message Output Description [*Computer science*]
MOD......... Message Output Descriptor [*Computer science*] (CIST)
MOD......... Metallo-Organic Deposition [*Materials technology*]
MOD......... Method of Delivery
MOD......... Microfilm-Output Device
MOD......... Microsoft Office 2000 Developer [*Microsoft*]
MOD......... Microwave Oscillating Diode (MCD)
MOD......... Military Airlift Command Operational Directive (SAUO)
MOD......... Military Obligation Designator
MOD......... Military Orbital Development System [*See also MODS, MOSS, MTSS*] [*Air Force/NASA*]
Mod.......... Mindless Operative of the Devil [*Mods - Facetious translation referring to Moderate Republicans*]
MOD......... Ministry of Defence [*British*]
MOD......... Ministry of Overseas Development [*British*] (ILCA)
MOD......... Minuteman Operating Directive (SAA)
MOD......... Miscellaneous Obligation Document
MOD......... Mission Objectives Document (MCD)
MOD......... Mission Operating Directive (SAUO)
MOD......... Mission Operations Director [*NASA*] (KSC)
MOD......... Mission Operations Directorate (SAUO)
MOD......... Mobile Obstacle Detachment (MCD)
MOD......... Mobility Opportunity and Development
mod.......... modality [*Physical therapy*] (DAVI)
MOD......... Modal (Verb) [*Linguistics*]
MOD......... Modatech Systems, Inc. [*Vancouver Stock Exchange symbol*]
mod.......... Model (AD)
MOD......... Model (KSC)
MOD......... Modem (SAUO)
MOD......... Moderate [*or Moderator*] (AABC)
mod.......... Moderate (AD)
MOD......... Moderate Room [*Travel industry*] (TRID)
mod.......... Moderato (SHCU)
MOD......... Moderato [*Moderate Speed*] [*Music*]
Mod.......... Modern (AD)
mod.......... Modern (AD)
MOD......... Modern
MOD......... Modernism Show
Mod.......... Modernist (DIAR)
Mod.......... Modern Reports [*England*] [*A publication*] (DLA)
MOD......... Modesto [*California*] [*Airport symbol*] (OAG)
mod.......... Modification (AD)
MOD......... Modification [*or Modify*] (AFM)
MOD......... Modifier [*Linguistics*]
MOD......... Modiim [*Israel*] [*Later, AMT*] [*Geomagnetic observatory code*]
mod.......... Modular (AD)
MOD......... Modular Observation Device (RDA)
MOD......... Modulation [*Telecommunications*] (KSC)

MOD......... Modulator (CET)
mod......... Modulator (IDOE)
MOD......... Modulator-Demodulator [*Telecommunications*] (MCD)
mod......... Modulo [*Mathematics*] (CDE)
mod......... Modulus (IDOE)
MOD......... Modulus
MOD......... Money-Order Department
MOD......... Month of Detachment
MOD......... Motor-Operated Disconnect [*Nuclear energy*] (NRCH)
MOD......... Moving Domain Memories [*Computer science*] (MDG)
Mod......... Style's English King's Bench Reports [*1646-55*] [*A publication*] (DLA)
MOD......... Supreme Industries [*AMEX symbol*] (SAG)
MOD10...... Modulus 10 Check Digit [*Computer science*]
MODA....... Ministry of Defense and Aviation (MCD)
MODA....... ModaCad, Inc. [*NASDAQ symbol*] (SAG)
Mod A....... Moderate Assist (IDYL)
MODA....... Motion Detector and Alarm [*Army*]
MODABUND... Mosquito Data Bank of the University of Notre Dame
MODAC...... Meteorological Observation and Data Assimilation Center (SAUO)
MODAC...... Mountain System Digital Automatic Computer
MODACOM... Mobile Data Communication (SAUO)
MODACS.... Modular Data Acquisition and Control System [*or Subsystem*] [*Modular Computing Systems, Inc.*]
MOD(AD)... Ministry of Defence (Army Department) [*British*]
Mod Am Law... Modern American Law [*A publication*] (DLA)
MODAP...... Modified Apollo [*NASA*] (MCD)
MODAP...... Multiple Operational Data Acquisition Program [*Computer science*]
MODAPS.... Maintenance and Operational Data Presentation Study (AAG)
MODAPS.... Modal Data Acquisition and Processing System
MODAPTS... Modular Arrangement of Predetermined Time Standards
Modarco.... Modern Art Collection S.A. (SAUO)
MODARI..... Methods of Defeating Advanced RADAR Threats [*NASA*] (NAKS)
MODART.... Methods of Defeating Advanced RADAR Threats (NASA)
MODAS...... Maintenance and Operational Data Access Subsystem (SAUO)
MODAS...... Maintenance and Operational Data Access System (ACAE)
MODAS...... Model for Intertheater Deployment by Air & Sea (SAUO)
MODAS...... Modular Data Acquisition System (SAUS)
MODAS...... Multidirectional Osmotic Drug Absorption System [*Medicine*]
modasm.... Modular Air-to-Surface Missile [*Military*] (AD)
MODASM... Modular Air-to-Surface Missile (MCD)
mod asst.... Moderate Assistance [*Medicine*] (BCRP)
MODATS.... Mohawk Data Transmission System (MCD)
MODAW..... ModaCAD Inc. Wrrt [*NASDAQ symbol*] (TTSB)
MODB....... Master Object Data Base (SAUS)
m-o-d-b..... Mesial-Occlusal-Distal-Buccal [*Dentistry*] (AD)
MODB....... Military Occupational Data Bank [*Later, AOSP*] (AABC)
MODBSC.... Modular Boresight Computer (ACAE)
MODCA...... Mixed Object Document Content Architecture [*Computer science*] (BTTJ)
MO:DCA..... Mixed Object: Document Content Architecure [*Computer science*] (CDE)
MODCAR.... Modified Owners and Drivers Corp. for the Advancement of Racing (EA)
Mod Cas.... Modern Cases [*6 Modern Reports*] [*1702-45*] [*A publication*] (DLA)
Mod Cas L & Eq... Modern Cases at Law and Equity [*8, 9 Modern Reports*] [*1721-55*] [*A publication*] (DLA)
Mod Cas per Far... Modern Cases Tempore Holt, by Farresley [*7 Modern Reports*] [*A publication*] (DLA)
Mod Cas T Holt... Modern Cases Tempore Holt, by Farresley [*7 Modern Reports*] [*A publication*] (DLA)
MOD CIS.... Ministry of Defence Communication Information System (SAUO)
MOD CIS.... Ministry of Defense Communication Information System (SAUS)
modcom.... Modernity Commercialized (AD)
MODCOM... Modular Computer System
MODCOMP... Modular Computer Systems Inc. (NITA)
MODCON.... Man Machine System for the Optimum Design and Construction of Buildings (PDAA)
MOD CON... Modern Convenience (DSUE)
mod-cons... Modern-Construction Houses (AD)
mod cons... Modern Conveniences (AD)
MODCPS.... Multiple Output Direct Current Power Supply
MODC-USA... United States Army Modification Center (SAUO)
MODD....... Meteorological and Omega Data Digitizer (SAUS)
MODD....... Military Order of Devil Dogs (EA)
Modd........ Modern Medical Modalities Corp. [*Associated Press*] (SAG)
moddem.... Modulator-Demodulator (AD)
mod/demod... Modulate-Demodulate (AD)
MODDF...... Military Order, Devil Dog Fleas (EA)
MOD DICT... In the Manner Directed [*Abbreviation from the Latin*] [*Pharmacy*] (ROG)
MOD DIG... Modular Digital Image Generator (SAUS)
MODE....... Management of Objectives with Dollars through Employees [*Department of Agriculture*]
MODE....... Merchant Oriented Data Entry
MODE....... Methoxy(O-desmethyl)encainide [*Biochemistry*]
MODE....... Middeck Zero-Gravity Dynamics Experiment (SAUO)
MODE....... Mid-Ocean Dynamics Experiment [*National Science Foundation*]
MODE....... Model A and Model T Motor Car [*NCIC car make code*]
ModE........ Modern English (AD)
MODE....... Modesti Brothers [*Common carrier symbol*]
MODE....... Monitor Data Equipment
MODE....... Monitoring Overseas Direct Employment (DNAB)
MODE....... Music on Demand (TELE)
MODE 4..... Refueling (SAUS)
MODE C..... Altitude Reporting Mode of Secondary Radar [*FAA*] (TAG)
MODE C..... Automatic Altitude Reporting [*Aviation*] (PIPO)
MO Dec..... Missouri Decisions [*A publication*] (DLA)
MODEC...... Motor Optimization Design Evaluation Code (MCD)
Model Bus Corp Act Anno 2d... American Bar Association Model Business Corporation Act, Annotated, Second Series [*A publication*] (DLA)
Model Business Corp Act... American Bar Association Model Business Corporation Act, Annotated [*A publication*] (DLA)
MODELH/PRDH... Mouvement pour la Liberation d'Haiti/Parti Revolutionnaire d'Haiti [*Political party*] (EY)
ModelImp... Model Imperial, Inc. [*Associated Press*] (SAG)
Model Land Dev Code... American Law Institute Model Land Development Code [*A publication*] (DLA)
Model R.... Model Railroader [*A publication*]
MODELS.... Modernization of the Defense Logistics Standard System (SAUO)
MODELYR... Model Year [*National Highway Traffic Safety Administration Fatal Accident Recording System code*]
MODEM..... Modelling of Emission and Consumption in Urban Areas (SAUO)
MODEM..... Modulate/Demodulate [*or Modulation/Demodulation or Modulator-Demodulator*] [*Computer science*]
modem...... Modulating-Demodulating (AD)
modem...... Modulator, Demodulator [*Computer hardware*] (NETL)
MODEN...... Modena, PA [*American Association of Railroads railroad junction routing code*]
Mod (Eng)... English King's Bench Modern Reports [*86-88 English Reprint*] [*A publication*] (DLA)
MOD ENT... Modern Entries [*Legal term*] (DLA)
Modern Lib... Modern Library (AD)
MODES...... Mode Optimization and Delivery Estimation System (SAUO)
MODES...... Modesto, CA [*American Association of Railroads railroad junction routing code*]
MODEST.... Missile Optical Destruction Technique
MODESTI... Mould Design and Manufacturing Optimization (SAUO)
Modest Pistor... Modestinus Pistoris [*Deceased, 1565*] [*Authority cited in pre-1607 legal work*] (DSA)
MODET...... Mortar Detection
MODEX...... Mobilization Deployment Exercise (MCD)
modf......... Modification (AD)
MODF....... Modify (AAG)
MODFET.... Modulation-Doped Field-Effect Transistor [*Solid-state physics*]
MODFLIR... Modular Forward-Looking Infrared Seeker
MODFN...... Modification (AAG)
MODFR...... Modifier (AAG)
Mod'g....... Modifying [*Legal term*] (DLA)
ModGr....... Modern Greek [*Language*]
MODH....... Modern Mobile Homes [*NCIC trailer make code*]
MODHATR... Modified Hatrack [*Cyclone forecasting*] [*Navy*]
ModHeb..... Modern Hebrew (AD)
MODHIWAY... Modified Highway Program (SAUO)
MODI........ Major Oversea Depot and Installation Method [*Army*]
Mod I........ Moderate Independence (IDYL)
MODI........ Modernistic Industries [*NCIC trailer make code*]
MODI........ Modified [*Motor vehicle violation code used in state of Maryland*] (MVRD)
MODI........ Modified Distribution
MODI........ Modine Manufacturing Co. [*NASDAQ symbol*] (NQ)
MODI........ Modine Mfg [*NASDAQ symbol*] (TTSB)
MODI........ Modular Optical Digital Interface
MODIA...... Method of Designing Instructional Alternatives (PDAA)
MODICON... Modular-Dispersed-Control
MODIF....... Modification (KSC)
modif........ Modification (MIST)
MODIG...... Modular Digital Image Generation [*Computer science*]
MODIGSI... Modular Digital Simulation (MCD)
MODIL....... Manufacturing Operations Development and Integration Laboratory
MODILS..... Modular Instrument Landing System
MODIM...... MOTS [*Module Test Set*] Design Information Memorandum
MODIMS.... Modular Order Entry and Inventory Management System [*Computer science*] (HODG)
Modin....... Movement for Dignity and National Independence (Argentina) [*Political party*] (PSAP)
Modine...... Modine Manufacturing Co. [*Associated Press*] (SAG)
Mod Int..... Brown's Modus Intrandi [*A publication*] (DLA)
Modio....... MODEM and Radio [*Telecommunications*]
MODIR...... Modulated Infra-Red jammer (SAUS)
mod/iran... Modification, Inspection, and Repair as Necessary (AD)
MOD/IRAN... Modification/Inspection and Repair as Necessary
MODIS...... Moderate Resolution Imaging Spectroradiometer (EOSA)
MODIS...... Mode Shape Display [*Module*]
MODISCO... Mechanization of Defense Industrial Security Clearance Office [*DoD*]
MODIS-N... Moderate Resolution Imaging Spectrometer-Nadir (EOSA)
MODIS-T... Moderate Resolution Imaging Spectrometer-Tilt (EOSA)
MODL....... Model [*Automotive emissions*]
MODL....... Model Imperial, Inc. [*NASDAQ symbol*] (SAG)
ModL........ Modern Latin [*Language*]
MODL....... Moduline International [*NCIC trailer make code*]
ModLA...... Modern Language Association, New York, NY [*Library symbol*] [*Library of Congress*] (LCLS)
MODLAN.... Mission Operations Division Local Area Network (SAUO)
Mod L & Soc'y... Modern Law and Society [*A publication*] (DLA)
ModLA-R.... Modern Language Association Research in Progress Program, New York NY [*Library symbol*] [*Library of Congress*] (LCLS)
MOD LITH... Modern Lithographer [*A publication*] (DGA)

MODLOC.... Miscellaneous Operational Details, Local Operations [*Marine Corps*] (POLM)
MODLOC.... Modified Location
MODLOG 77... Modernization of Logistics 1977 [*Army*]
ModLRev... Modern Law Review [*A publication*] (SAFN)
MODM....... Magneto-Optical Display Memory
MODM....... Major Oversea Depot Method [*Army*]
MODM....... Manned One-Day Mission [*NASA*]
MODM....... Mature-Onset Diabetes Mellitus (MAE)
MODM....... Moderate Demand [*Telegraphy*] (PCTE)
MODM....... Modern Medical Modalities Corp. [*NASDAQ symbol*] (SAG)
MODM....... Modern Medl Modalities [*NASDAQ symbol*] (TTSB)
MODMATS... Modified Missile Auxiliary Test Set (ACAE)
ModMd....... Modern Medical Modalities Corp. [*Associated Press*] (SAG)
ModMed.... Modern Medical Modalities Corp. [*Associated Press*] (SAG)
Mod Med Aust... Modern Medicine of Australia [*A publication*]
MODMW.... Modern Med Modalities Wrrt'A' [*NASDAQ symbol*] (TTSB)
MODMZ..... Modern Med Modalities Wrr'B' [*NASDAQ symbol*] (TTSB)
MOD(N)..... Ministry of Defence (Navy) [*British*]
MODN...... Modern [*NCIC trailer make code*]
MODNA..... Mid Ohio District Nurses Association (EARSL)
MODNET.... Mission Operations Directorate Network (SAUO)
MoDNM..... Morpholinodaunomycin [*Also, MRD*] [*Antineoplastic drug*]
MODO...... Moderato [*Moderate Speed*] [*Music*] (ROG)
modo........ Moderato [*Moderately*] [*Italian*] (AD)
MODO....... Mo och Domsjo (EFIS)
MODOCELL... Mo och Domsjo (EFIS)
Mod Off Dat Man... Modern Office and Data Management [*A publication*]
Mod Office Data Mgmt... Modern Office and Data Management [*A publication*]
MOD/OP..... Maintenance of Deception/Operation
MODOP..... Mobil Oil Direct Oxidation Process [*Gas desulfurization process*]
MODOR..... Molecularized Doppler RADAR
MODP....... Modern Programming Practice
MODPAC.... Modular Restraint, Recovery, and Survival Package
MOD(PE).... Ministry of Defence (Procurement Executive) [*British*]
MODPLAN... Model Planning (TIMI)
MODPOT.... Model Potential [*Physics*]
Mod Pract Comm... Modern Practice Commentator [*A publication*] (DLA)
mod praes... Modo Praescripto [*In the manner prescribed*] [*Latin*] [*Pharmacy*] (BARN)
MOD PRAESC... Modo Praescripto [*In the Manner Prescribed*] [*Latin*] [*Pharmacy*] (MAH)
MOD PRAESCRIPT... Modo Praescripto [*In the Manner Prescribed*] [*Pharmacy*]
mod pres... Modo Prescripto [*In the Manner Prescribed*] [*Latin*] (AD)
MOD PRESCR... Modo Praescripto [*In the Manner Prescribed*] [*Pharmacy*] (ROG)
mod pst..... Modeling Paste (VRA)
MODR....... Microwave Optical Double Resonance (PDAA)
MODR....... Moderate Rate [*Travel industry*] (TRID)
modr........ Moderate Room Rate Desired (AD)
MODR....... Monodetail Drawing (MSA)
MODREFTRA... Modified Refresher Training [*Navy*] (NVT)
Mod Rep.... Modern Reports [*England*] [*A publication*] (DLA)
Mod Rep.... Style's English King's Bench Reports [*1646-55*] [*A publication*] (DLA)
MODS....... Major Operations Data System (NVT)
MODS....... Manned Orbital Development Station [*See also MOD, MOSS, MTSS*] [*Air Force/NASA*]
MODS....... Manpower Operations Data System [*Employment and Training Administration*] [*Department of Labor*]
MODS....... Material Ordering and Delivery Schedule (DNAB)
MODS....... Medically Oriented Data System (MCD)
MODS....... Medium Ocean Data Station
mods........ Mesial-Occlusal-Distal [*Dentistry*] (AD)
MODS....... Metadata Object Description Schema [*Computer term*]
MODS....... Military Orbital Development System [*See also MOD, MOSS, MTSS*] [*Air Force/NASA*]
MODS....... Missile Offense/Defense System
MODS....... Mission Operations and Data System (SAUO)
MODS....... Mission Operations Design Support
MODS....... Mobility-Planning Data System [*Military*] (GFGA)
MODS....... Mobilization Planning Data System (SAUO)
MODS....... Models (MCD)
MODS....... Models for Organizational Design and Staffing (DNAB)
Mods........ Moderates [*Reference to political philosophy of some members of the Republican party*]
MODS....... Moderations [*First public Oxford examination*] (ROG)
MODS....... Modifications
MODS....... Modular Oriented Direct Support (MCD)
MODS....... Multiple Organ Dysfunction Syndrome [*Medicine*]
MODSA...... Ministry of Defence Staff Association (BUAC)
ModSAF..... Modular Semi-Automated Forces (SAUS)
MODSAF.... Modular Semi-Automatic Forces
MODSC...... Magnetooptically Detected Spin Conversion [*Physics*]
ModStealth... Modular Stealth (SAUS)
MODT....... Mean Operational Delay Time
MODT....... Modtech Holdings, Inc. [*NASDAQ symbol*] (NASQ)
MODT....... Modtech, Inc. [*NASDAQ symbol*] (SAG)
Modtec...... Modtech, Inc. [*Associated Press*] (SAG)
MODTEPS... Modular Toxic Environment Protective Suit [*NASA*]
MODTLE.... Mobilization on Development, Trade, Labor, and Environment [*An association*]
MODTO...... Moderato [*Moderate Speed*] [*Music*]
modto....... Moderato [*Moderately*] [*Italian*] (AD)
MODU....... Mobile Offshore Drilling Unit
MODU....... Module [*NCIC trailer make code*]
MODU Code... Code for the Construction and Equipment of Mobile Offshore Drilling Units (SAUO)
MODUK..... Ministry of Defence UK (SAUS)
MODUK..... Ministry of Defence United Kingdom (SAUO)
MODULA.... Modular Programming Language (CSR)
Modula-2... Modular Language-2 [*Computer science*]
MODULAB... Modular Clinical Laboratory [*Military*] (CAAL)
MOD/UM.... Modulated/Unmodulated (SSD)
Mod Un..... Modern Unionist [*A publication*]
Mod Unionist... Modern Unionist [*A publication*]
MODUS..... Modular One Dynamic User System [*Computer science*] (MHDI)
MODUSSE... Manufacturers of Domestic Unvented Supply Systems Equipment [*British*] (DBA)
MODWORS... Modification Work Order Report Status
MODWT..... Maximal Overlap Discrete Wavelet Transform (SAUS)
MODY....... Maturity Onset Diabetes of the Young [*Medicine*] (DMAA)
MOE......... Evangel College, Springfield, MO [*OCLC symbol*] (OCLC)
MOE......... MAD Operational Effectiveness (DNAB)
MOE......... Maintenance of Effort [*Medicare Act*]
MOE......... Major Organizational Entity (MCD)
MOE......... Margin of Exposure [*Toxicology*]
MOE......... Mars Orbit Ejection (MCD)
MOE......... Master of Ocean Engineering (GAGS)
MOE......... Master of Oral English
MOE......... Maximum Output Entropy (PDAA)
moe......... Measure of Effectiveness (AD)
MOE......... Measure of Effectiveness
MoE......... Ministry of Education [*British*] (AD)
MOE......... Ministry of Education [*British*] (DAS)
M o E........ Ministry of Energy [*British*] (AD)
MOE......... Ministry of Environment [*Canada*]
MOE......... Ministry of the Environment [*Bulgaria*] (BUAC)
MOE......... Mission-Oriented Equipment
MOE......... Mobile, AL [*Amtrak rail station code*]
MOE......... Model Operational Environment (SAA)
MOE......... Modulus of Elasticity [*Mechanics*]
MOE......... Moli Energy Ltd. [*Toronto Stock Exchange symbol*] [*Vancouver Stock Exchange symbol*]
MOE......... Momeik [*Myanmar*] [*Airport symbol*] (OAG)
MOE......... Mu Phi Epsilon [*An association*] (NTPA)
MOE......... Mythical Operational Environment (SAA)
MOE......... Ontario Ministry of Education, Information Centre, Research Branch [*UTLAS symbol*]
MOE......... Telemetering Mobile Station [*ITU designation*]
MOEA........ Ministry of Economic Affairs [*British*] (AD)
MOEC........ Ministry of Education and Culture (SAUO)
MOEC/AES... Ministry of Education and Culture/Adult Education Section (SAUO)
MOEC/CTSDC... Ministry of Education and Culture/Curriculum, Textbook, Supervision Development Centre (SAUO)
MOEC/DOA... Ministry of Education and Culture/Department of Archaeology (SAUO)
MOEC/LDT... Ministry of Education and Culture/Lumbini Development Trust (SAUO)
MOECSW... Ministry of Education, Culture and Social Welfare (SAUO)
MOECSW/SWC... Ministry of Education, Culture and Social Welfare/Social Welfare Council (SAUO)
MOED....... Molecular Orbital Energy Diagram
MOED....... Morristown-Edison National Park Service Group
MOEDA...... Measures of Effectiveness, Development, and Application (MCD)
MOEH....... Medical Officer for Environmental Health (WDAA)
MOEK....... Ezekiel Morris Transportation [*Common carrier symbol*]
MOELP...... Ministry of Environment, Lands and Parks (SAUO)
MOEP........ Meteorological and Oceanographic Equipment Program (NG)
MOER....... MACOM [*Major Command*] Outstanding Excess Report
MOERO...... Medium Orbiting Earth Resources Observatory (IEEE)
MOES........ Mathematics Olympiads for Elementary Schools (EDAC)
MOET........ Multiple Ovulation and Embryo Transfer (SAUO)
MOETLO.... Meteorological and Oceanographic Equipment Technical Liaison Officer
MOEX........ Morgan Engineering [*Private rail car owner code*]
MoExGS..... Excelsior Springs Genealogical Society, Excelsior Springs, MO [*Library symbol*] [*Library of Congress*] (LCLS)
MOF......... Fontbonne College, St. Louis, MO [*OCLC symbol*] (OCLC)
MOF......... Mal-Union of Fracture [*Medicine*] (MELL)
MOF......... Managed Object Format [*Computer science*] (MWOL)
MOF......... Manned Orbital Flight [*NASA*] (NASA)
MOF......... Marine Oxidation/Fermentation
MOF......... Matter of Fact [*Telegraphy*] (PCTE)
MOF......... Mature Ovarian Folicle [*Medicine*] (MELL)
MOF......... Maumere [*Indonesia*] [*Airport symbol*] (OAG)
mof......... Maximum Observed Frequency (AD)
MOF......... Maximum Observed Frequency [*Radio*]
MOF......... Maximum Operating Frequency
MOF......... MeCCNU [*Semustine*], Oncovin , Fluorouracil [*Vincristine*] [*Antineoplastic drug regimen*]
MOF......... Meilleur Ouvrier de France
MOF......... Member of the Force (LAIN)
mof......... Member of the Police Force (AD)
mof......... Metal Oxide Film (AD)
MOF......... Metal-Oxide Film
MOF......... Meta Object Facility [*Computer science*] (GART)
MOF......... Methotrexate, Oncovin [*Vincristine*] 5-Fluorouracil [*Antineoplastic drug regimen*] (DAVI)
MOF......... Methoxyflurane [*Anesthetic*] (AAMN)

MOF .... Methylo-CCNU, Vineristine, Fluorouracil [*Antineoplastic drug regimen*] (DAVI)
MOF .... Michoud Operations Facility [*NASA*] (AAG)
MoF .... Ministry of Finance [*British*] (AD)
MOF .... Ministry of Finance [*Japan*] (ECON)
MOF .... Ministry of Food [*British*]
MOF .... Ministry of Forests (SAUO)
MOF .... Mission Operations Facility [*NASA*] (KSC)
MOF .... Modified Olefin Film [*Plastics*]
MOF .... Moffat Communications Ltd. [*Toronto Stock Exchange symbol*]
MOF .... Months of Operational Flying (DNAB)
MOF .... Multi-Option Facility
MOF .... Multioption Fuze (MCD)
MOF .... Multiple Organ Failure [*Medicine*]
M of A .... Ministry of Agriculture, Fisheries and Food (SAUO)
MOFA .... Multi-Option Fuze, Artillery
M of A&F ... Ministry of Agriculture and Fisheries (SAUO)
MOFAB .... Mobile Floating Assault Bridge-Ferry [*Military*] (MCD)
MOFACS .... Multiorder Feedback and Compensation Synthesis
MOF/ADBN ... Ministry of Finance/ Agriculture Development Bank of Nepal (SAUO)
M of AP ..... Ministry of Aircraft Production (SAUO)
MOFAP ...... Ministry of Fuel and Power [*British*]
M of Arch ... Master of Architecture
MOFARS .... Maintenance Overload Factor Reporting System
MOFAST ..... Mechanization of Freight and Shipping Terminal [*DoD*]
MOFAT ...... Multi Phase Flow and Transport (SAUO)
MoFC .... Central Methodist College, Fayette, MO [*Library symbol*] [*Library of Congress*] (LCLS)
M of C .... Master of Commerce
MOFC .... Michael O'Leary Fan Club [*Defunct*] (EA)
M of D .... Ministry of Defence [*British*]
M of E .... Ministry of Education [*British*]
M of E .... Minutes of Evidence
MOFE/DNPWC ... Ministry of Forests and Environment/Department of National Parks & Wildlife Conservation (SAUO)
MOFE/DOF ... Ministry of Forests and Environment/Department of Forests (SAUO)
MOFE/DOMP ... Ministry of Forests and Environment/Department of Medicinal Plants (SAUO)
MOFE/DOSC ... Ministry of Forests and Environment/Department of Soil Conservation (SAUO)
MOFE/FPDB ... Ministry of Forests and Environment/Forest Products Development Board (SAUO)
Mofert .... Ministry of Foreign Economic Relations and Trade [*China*] (BUAC)
MOFERT ..... Ministry of Foreign Economic Relations and Trade [*China*]
MOFE/TCN ... Ministry of Forests and Environment/Timber Corporation of Nepal (SAUO)
M of F .... Ministry of Food (SAUO)
MOFF .... Multiple Options Funding Facility [*Euronotes*]
M of F&P ... Ministry of Fuel and Power (SAUO)
MOFFS ...... Multi-Megabit Operation Flexible Frame Synchronizer (ACAE)
M of HA ..... Matrons of Hospitals Association (ROG)
M of Hist ... Magazine of History [*A publication*] (BRI)
M of I .... Ministry of Information (SAUO)
M of I .... Moment of Inertia
MoFIM ...... Mark Twain Shrine, Mark Twain State Park, Florida, MO [*Library symbol*] [*Library of Congress*] (LCLS)
MoFloSS .... Saint Stanislaus Seminary, Florissant, MO [*Library symbol*] [*Library of Congress*] (LCLS)
M of M ...... Maintenance of Membership [*Labor unions*]
M of M ...... Museum of Man (SAUO)
MOFN .... AOL MovieFone [*NASDAQ symbol*]
MOFN .... MovieFone Cl'A' [*NASDAQ symbol*] (TTSB)
MOFN .... MovieFone, Inc. [*NASDAQ symbol*] (SAG)
M of P .... Ministry of Pensions and National Insurance (SAUO)
M of P .... Ministry of Power (SAUO)
MOFR .... Marine, Oceanographic & Freshwater Resources [*Database*] (GDD)
M of R ...... Minister of Reconstruction [*British*] (AD)
M of R ...... Ministry of Reconstruction (SAUO)
MOF/RATC ... Ministry of Finance/Revenue Administration Training Centre (SAUO)
MOFS .... Maintenance of Flying Skills (ACAE)
M of S .... Ministry of Supply (SAUO)
MOFS .... Multiple Organ Failure Syndrome [*Medicine*] (DMAA)
MOF-STREP ... MeCCNU [*Semustine*], Oncovin , Fluorouracil, Streptozotocin [*Vincristine*] [*Antineoplastic drug regimen*]
MOFTEC ..... Ministry of Foreign Trade & Economic Cooperation [*China*]
Moftec .... Ministry of Foreign Trade and Economic Co-Operation [*China*] (BUAC)
MOFTU ...... MIG Operational Fighter Training Unit [*India*] [*Air Force*]
MoFuWC .... Westminster College, Fulton, MO [*Library symbol*] [*Library of Congress*] (LCLS)
M of V .... [*The*] Merchant of Venice [*Shakespearean work*]
M of W ...... Maintenance of Way [*Railroading*]
MOFW .... Military Order of Foreign Wars of the United States (EA)
MofX .... Maxton Oil and Fertilizer [*Private rail car owner code*]
MOFZ .... Mohasco Furniture [*Federal Railroad Administration identification code*]
MOG .... Assemblies of God Graduate School, Springfield, MO [*OCLC symbol*] (OCLC)
MOG .... Machinery of Government
MOG .... Managed Object Group (SAUO)
MOG .... Mannville Oil & Gas Ltd. [*Toronto Stock Exchange symbol*]
Mog .... Margaret (AD)
MOG .... Master of Obstetrics and Gynecology (AD)
MOG .... Material Ordering Guide [*Shipbuilding*]
MOG .... Material Other than Grape [*Wine making*]
MOG .... Medical Oncology Group
MOG .... Metropolitan Opera Guild (EA)
MOG .... Micro-Optic Gyroscope
MOG .... Mid-On Generator [*Car*] [*Indian Railway*] (TIR)
MOG .... Milicias Obreras Guatemaltecas [*Guatemalan Workers' Militia*] (PD)
MOG .... Minicomputer Operations Group (SAUO)
MOG .... Mogadishu [*Somalia*] [*Seismograph station code, US Geological Survey*] [*Closed*] (SEIS)
MOG .... Molded Gasket [*Automotive engineering*]
MOG .... Monghsat [*Myanmar*] [*Airport symbol*] (OAG)
MOG .... Montague, CA [*Location identifier*] [*FAA*] (FAAL)
MOG .... Moog, Inc. [*AMEX symbol*] (SPSG)
MOG .... Morgan [*Automobile*]
MOG .... Municipal Officers' Guild (ROG)
MOG .... Myelin Oligodendrocyte Glycoprotein [*Biochemistry*]
MOGA .... Management of Officer Grade Authorization (MCD)
MOGA .... Microwave and Optical Generation and Amplification (MCD)
MOGA .... Mid-Continent Oil and Gas Association (SAUO)
MOGA .... Ministry of General Administration (SAUO)
MOGA .... Montana Outfitters and Guides Association (EA)
MOGA/NASC ... Ministry of General Administration/Nepal Administrative Staff College (SAUO)
MOGAS ...... Auto Gas Used for Aircraft [*Aviation*] (PIPO)
mogas .... Motor Gasoline (AD)
MOGAS ...... Motor Gasoline [*Military*]
MOGN .... MGI PHARMA, Inc. [*NASDAQ symbol*] (NQ)
MOGN .... Molecular Genetics, Inc. (MHDW)
MOGR .... Moderate or Greater [*Weather codes - aviation*] (PIPO)
MOGU .... Moto Guzzi [*NCIC motorcycle make code*]
MOGUL ...... Modular Gun Laying System (SAUS)
MOGUNTIA ... Model of the Global Universal Tracer Transport in the Atmosphere [*Marine science*] (OSRA)
Moguyde .... Mouvement Guyanais de Decolonisation [*Guiana Decolonization Movement*] [*France*] [*Political party*] (PPW)
MoGvS ...... Grain Valley Associated School District, Grain Valley, MO [*Library symbol*] [*Library of Congress*] (LCLS)
MoH .... Hannibal Free Public Library, Hannibal, MO [*Library symbol*] [*Library of Congress*] (LCLS)
MOH .... Hydrological and Meteorological Mobile Station [*ITU designation*]
MOH .... Master, Occupational Health (CMD)
MOH .... Master of Occupational Health (PGP)
MOH .... Master of Otter Hounds
MOH .... Master of Otter-hounds (SAUO)
moh .... Material Overhead (AD)
moh .... Maximum Operating Hours (AD)
MOH .... Maximum Operating Hours (MCD)
MOH .... Medal of Honor [*Often erroneously called Congressional Medal of Honor*] [*Military decoration*]
MOH .... Medical Officer of Health [*British*]
MOH .... Metropolitan Opera House (SAUO)
MOH .... Ministry of Health [*British*]
MoH .... Ministry of Housing and Local Government (SAUO)
MOH .... Moche Resources, Inc. [*Vancouver Stock Exchange symbol*]
MOH .... Mohasco Corp. (SAUO)
moh .... Mohawk [*MARC language code*] [*Library of Congress*] (LCCP)
MOH .... Mohawk Airlines, Inc. [*Obsolete*]
MOH .... Museum of Holography [*New York City*]
MOH .... Music on Hold (ITD)
MOH .... New York, NY [*Location identifier*] [*FAA*] (FAAL)
MOH .... St. Louis Priory School, St. Louis, MO [*OCLC symbol*] (OCLC)
MOH .... Tigerfly [*British*] [*ICAO designator*] (FAAC)
MOHA .... Mohawk [*NCIC trailer make code*]
MoHam ..... Hamilton Public Library, Hamilton, MO [*Library symbol*] [*Library of Congress*] (LCLS)
Moham ...... Mohammedan (AD)
MOHAM ..... Mohammedan (ROG)
MoHarC ..... Cass County Public Library, Harrisonville, MO [*Library symbol*] [*Library of Congress*] (LCLS)
MOHAT ...... Modular Handling and Transport
MOHATS .... Mobile Overland Hauling and Transport System [*Air Force*]
MOHAVE .... Measurement of Haze and Visual Effects [*Study*] [*Marine science*] (OSRA)
MOHAVE .... Measurement of Haze and Visusal Effects [*Study*] (USDC)
MOHAWC ... Models of Human Actions in Work Context (EURO)
Mohawk ..... Mohawk Industries, Inc. [*Associated Press*] (SAG)
MOHE .... Ministry of Health (SAUO)
MOHE/APH ... Ministry of Health/Amp Pipal Hospital (SAUO)
MOHEC ...... Maintenance of Hercules Capability (SAA)
MOHE/CHL ... Ministry of Health/Central Health Laboratory (SAUO)
MOHE/DAU ... Ministry of Health/ Department of Ayurveda (SAUO)
MOHE/DWSS ... DEPARTMENT OF WATER SUPPLY AND SANITATION (SAUS)
MOHE/DWSS ... Ministry of Health/ Department of Water Supply and Sanitation (SAUO)
MOHE/HICC ... Ministry of Health/Health Education, Information and Communication (SAUS)
MOHE/HICC ... Ministry of Health/National Health Education, Information and Communication (SAUO)
MOHE/NCAID ... Ministry of Health/ National Centre For Aid & Standard Control (SAUS)
MOHE/NCAID ... Ministry of Health/ National Centre For Aid & Std Control (SAUO)
MOHE/NFPMC ... Ministry of Health/ Nutritious Food Programme Management Committee (SAUO)

MOHE/OH ... Ministry of Health/ Okhaldhunga Hospital (SAUO)
MOHE/PA ... Ministry of Health/Patan Hospital (SAUO)
MOHE/PHD... Ministry of Health/Public Health Division (SAUS)
MOHE/RDRL... Ministry of Health/Royal Drugs Research Laboratory (SAUO)
MOHE/TS ... Ministry of Health/Tansen Hospital (SAUO)
MOHE/WRH... Ministry of Health/Western Regional Hospital (SAUO)
MoHi .... Missouri State Historical Society, Columbia, MO [*Library symbol*] [*Library of Congress*] (LCLS)
MoHig .... Robertson Memorial Library, Higginsville, MO [*Library symbol*] [*Library of Congress*] (LCLS)
MoHigH ..... Habilitation Center, Higginsville, MO [*Library symbol*] [*Library of Congress*] (LCLS)
MOHILL ..... Machine-Oriented High-Level Language [*Computer science*] (HGAA)
MOHK .... Mohawk Industries [*NASDAQ symbol*] (SAG)
MOHLG...... Ministry of Housing and Local Government [*British*] (AD)
MOH(LHA).. Medical Officer of Health (Local Health Authority) [*British*]
MOHLL ...... Machine Oriented High Level Language (SAUS)
MoHM .... Mark Twain Museum, Hannibal, MO [*Library symbol*] [*Library of Congress*] (LCLS)
mohms ...... Milliohms (AD)
MOHMS ..... Milliohms (WDAA)
MOHO .... Mobile Home Industries [*NCIC trailer make code*]
moho .... Mohorovicic Discontinuity [*Geology*] (AD)
Moho .... Mohorovicic Discontinuity (ADWA)
MOHO .... Mohorovicic Discontinuity [*Geology*]
MOHOL...... Machine-Oriented Higher Order Language [*Computer science*] (MHDI)
MOHOME ... Ministry of Home (SAUO)
MOH/PHD ... Ministry of Health/public Health Division (SAUO)
MOHPP/DHM... Ministry of Housing and Physical Planning/Department of Hydrology and Meteorology (SAUO)
MOHPP/DHUD... Ministry of Housing and Physical Planning/Department of Housing and Urban Development (SAUO)
MOHPP/DOA... Ministry of Housing and Physical Planning/Department of Archaeology (SAUO)
MOHPP/DOB... Ministry of Housing and Physical Planning/Department of Buildings (SAUO)
MOHPP/DWSS... Ministry of Housing and Physical Planning/Department of Water Supply and Sewerage (SAUO)
MOHPP/NWSC... Ministry of Housing and Physical Planning/Nepal Water Supply Corp. (SAUS)
MOHPP/NWSC... Ministry of Housing and Physical Planning/Nepal Water Supply Corporation (SAUO)
MOHS .... Master of Occupational Health and Safety
mohs .... Mud, Oil, Hooks, Slings [*Insurance*] (AD)
MOHSA...... Ministry of Health and Social Affairs [*Medicine*] [*United Kingdom*] (EDAA)
MOHSLG.... Health Sciences Library [*Library network*]
MOHU .... Corinth Refineries [*Intermodal shipping container symbol*] (TVRC)
MoHu........ Huntsville Public Library, Huntsville, MO [*Library symbol*] [*Library of Congress*] (LCLS)
MOHX .... Solutia [*Private rail car owner code*]
MOI.......... Main-d'Oeuvre Indigene [*Indigenous Manpower*] [*Congo - Leopoldville*]
MOI.......... Maintenance Operating Instruction [*Air Force Logistics Command*]
MOI.......... Make on Installation (SAA)
MOI.......... Marine Officer Instructor (DOMA)
MOI.......... Mars Orbit [*or Orbital*] Insertion [*Aerospace*]
moi .... Maximum Obtainable Irradiance (AD)
MOI.......... Maximum Obtainable Irradiance
MOI.......... Maximum Oxygen Intake [*Medicine*] (DB)
MOI.......... Mechanism of Injury (SAUO)
MOI.......... Memorandum of Information (SAUO)
MOI.......... Memorandum of Instruction (INF)
MOI.......... Memorandum of Intent (COE)
MOI.......... Memorandum of Interest (MCD)
MOI.......... Message of Operational Intent (NVT)
MOI.......... Methods of Instruction
MOI.......... Military Occupational Information (AABC)
moi .... Military Occupational Information (AD)
MOI.......... Military Operations and Intelligence
MOI.......... Minimum Operating Inventory [*Business term*]
MOI.......... Ministry of Information [*British*] [*World War II*]
MoI .... Ministry of the Interior [*British*] (AD)
MOI.......... Mission Oriented Items (SAUO)
MOI.......... Mitiaro [*Cook Islands*] [*Airport symbol*] (OAG)
MOI.......... Molco Industries [*Vancouver Stock Exchange symbol*]
MOI.......... Moment of Inertia
MOI.......... Monaco Oceanographic Institute
MOI.......... Mouvement Ouvrier International (BJA)
moi .... Multiplicity of Infection (AD)
MOI.......... Multiplicity of Infection
MOI.......... William Jewell College, Liberty, MO [*OCLC symbol*] (OCLC)
MOIA .... Mission Oriented Item Activity (SAUO)
Mo IA........ Moore's Indian Appeals [*A publication*] (DLA)
MOIAA....... Missouri Intercollegiate Athletic Association (PSS)
MOI/BLSF... Ministry of Industry/Bansbari Leather and Shoe Factory (SAUO)
MOIC .... Medical Officer-in-Charge [*Military*]
MOIC .... Medical Officer in Command (AD)
MOIC .... Military Oceanographic Information Center (NATG)
MOIC .... Missile Ordnance Inhibit Circuit (ACAE)
MOI/CIDB... Ministry of Industry/Cottage Industry Development Board (SAUO)
MOI/CIDB... Ministry of Information and Communication/Cottage Industry Development Board (SAUS)
MOIC/NTC... Ministry of Information and Communication/Nepal Telecommunication Corp. (SAUS)
MOIC/NTC... Ministry of Information and Communication/Nepal Telecommunication Corporation (SAUO)
MOI/DCVSSI... Ministry of Industry/ Department of Cottage, Village & Small Scale Industries (SAUO)
MOI/DCVSSI... Ministry of Information and Communication/Department of Cottage, Village & Small Scale Industries (SAUS)
MOIDE....... Military Occupational Information Data Bank
MOI/DMG... Ministry of Industry/ Department of Mines and Geology (SAUO)
MOI/DMG... Ministry of Information and Communication/Department of Mines and Geology (SAUS)
MOI/FIPD... Ministry of Industry/Foreign Investment Promotion Division (SAUO)
MOI/FIPD... Ministry of Information and Communication/Foreign Investment Promotion Division (SAUS)
MOIG .... Master of Occupational Information and Guidance
MOI/HCC.... Ministry of Industry/Himal Cement Company (SAUO)
MOI/HCC.... Ministry of Information and Communication/Himal Cement Company (SAUS)
MOI/HCI..... Ministry of Industries/Hetauda Cement Industries Ltd. (SAUO)
MOIL .... Marine Operations and Instrumentation Laboratory [*Marine science*] (OSRA)
MOIL .... Maynard Oil [*NASDAQ symbol*] (TTSB)
MOIL .... Maynard Oil Co. [*NASDAQ symbol*] (NQ)
MOIL .... Motor Oil
MOI/LICC... Ministry of Industry/Leather Industries Coordination Cell (SAUO)
MOI/LICC... Ministry of Information and Communication/Leather Industries Coordination Cell (SAUS)
MoIM........ Mid-Continent Public Library Service, Independence, MO [*Library symbol*] [*Library of Congress*] (LCLS)
MoIMC ...... Independence Medical Center, Independence, MO [*Library symbol*] [*Library of Congress*] (LCLS)
MOI/NBR.... Ministry of Industry/Nepal Bureau of Standards (SAUO)
MOI/NIDC... Ministry of Industry/Nepal Industrial Development Corporation (SAUO)
MOI/NIDC... Ministry of Information and Communication/Nepal Industrial Development Corp. (SAUS)
MOI/NTDC... Ministry of Industry/Nepal Tea Development Corporation (SAUO)
MOI/NTDC... Ministry of Information and Communication/Nepal Tea Development Corp. (SAUS)
MOIP .... Mandatory Oil Import Program
moip......... Missile on Internal Power [*Military*] (AD)
MOIP .... Missile on Internal Power
MOIPI .... Multi-Purpose Offshore Industrial Port Islands (NOAA)
MoIPS....... Independence Public School District, Independence, MO [*Library symbol*] [*Library of Congress*] (LCLS)
MOIR .... Maximum Ozone Incremental Reactivity [*Environmental science*]
MOIR .... Movimiento Obrero Independiente Revolucionario [*Independent Revolutionary Workers' Movement*] [*Colombia*] [*Political party*] (PPW)
MOIR .... Movimiento Obrero Izquierdista Revolucionario [*Colombia*] [*Political party*] (PPW)
MOIRA ...... Model of International Relations in Agriculture (PDAA)
MoIRC....... Reorganized Church of Jesus Christ of Latter-Day Saints, Independence, MO [*Library symbol*] [*Library of Congress*] (LCLS)
Moir Cap Pun... Moir on Capital Punishment [*A publication*] (DLA)
MoIS......... Independence Sanitarium and Hospital, Independence, MO [*Library symbol*] [*Library of Congress*] (LCLS)
MOIS .... Maritime Operational Intelligence Summary
MOIS .... Michigan Occupational Information System [*Michigan State Department of Education*] [*Lansing*] [*Information service or system*] (IID)
MOIS .... Ministry of Intelligence and Security [*Government term*] (GA)
MOIS .... Mission Operations Intercommunication System [*NASA*]
Moish .... Moishe (AD)
MOIST....... Macro Output System [*NASA*] (KSC)
MOISTR..... Moisture
MoIT......... Harry S Truman Library, Independence, MO [*Library symbol*] [*Library of Congress*] (LCLS)
moiv......... Mechanically Operated Inlet Valve (AD)
MOIV .... Mechanically Operated Inlet Valve (ADA)
MOIVC....... Membranous Obstruction of the Inferior Vena Cava [*Medicine*] (EDAA)
MOJ .... Material on Job Date [*Telecommunications*] (TEL)
MOJ .... Metering over Junction [*Network administration*] [*Telecommunications*] (TEL)
MOJ .... Ministry of Jute [*Bangladesh*]
MOJ .... Mojave, CA [*Amtrak Busline code*]
MOJ .... Muong Sing [*Laos*] [*Airport symbol*] (AD)
MOJA........ Mojave (motorcycle) [*NCIC motorcycle make code*]
MOJA........ Mojave Transportation Company [*Common carrier symbol*]
MOJA........ Movement for Justice in Africa [*Liberia*] [*Political party*] (PPW)
MOJAC ...... Mood, Orientation, Judgment, Affect, Content (AAMN)
MOJA-G..... Movement for Justice in Africa-Gambia [*Political party*]
MOJAV ...... Mojave, CA [*American Association of Railroads railroad junction routing code*]
MoJc .... Thomas Jefferson Library System, Jefferson City, MO [*Library symbol*] [*Library of Congress*] (LCLS)
MoJcL....... Lincoln University, Jefferson City, MO [*Library symbol*] [*Library of Congress*] (LCLS)
MOJMRP.... Meteorological Office, Joint Meteorological Radio Propagation Sub-Committee (BUAC)

MoJo .... Joplin Public Library, Joplin, MO [*Library symbol*] [*Library of Congress*] (LCLS)
Mojo .... Morphine, Heroin or Cocaine [*Medicine*] (EDAA)
MoJoM ...... Missouri Southern State College, Joplin, MO [*Library symbol*] [*Library of Congress*] (LCLS)
MOJT .... Managed On-the-Job Training (DNAB)
Mo Jur ...... Monthly Jurist [*A publication*] (DLA)
MoK .... Kansas City Public Library, Kansas City, MO [*Library symbol*] [*Library of Congress*] (LCLS)
MOK .... Mohawk Carpet Mills [*Stock exchange symbol*] (AD)
MOK .... Mokapu [*Hawaii*] [*Seismograph station code, US Geological Survey*] (SEIS)
Mok .... Mokpo (AD)
MoKA .... American Nurses' Association, Kansas City, MO [*Library symbol*] [*Library of Congress*] (LCLS)
MOKA .... Coffee People, Inc. [*NASDAQ symbol*] (SAG)
MoKAI .... Kansas City Arts Institute, Kansas City, MO [*Library symbol*] [*Library of Congress*] (LCLS)
MoKAr .... Avila College, Kansas City (SAUS)
MoKAv .... Avila College, Kansas City, MO [*Library symbol*] [*Library of Congress*] (LCLS)
MoKB .... Bar Library Association of Kansas City, Kansas City, MO [*Library symbol*] [*Library of Congress*] (LCLS)
MoKBa ...... Barstow School, Kansas City, MO [*Library symbol*] [*Library of Congress*] (LCLS)
MoKBen ..... Bendix Corp., Technical Information Center, Kansas City, MO [*Library symbol*] [*Library of Congress*] (LCLS)
MoKBH ...... Baptist Memorial Hospital, Kansas City, MO [*Library symbol*] [*Library of Congress*] (LCLS)
MoKBM ..... Burns and McDonnell Engineering Co., Kansas City, MO [*Library symbol*] [*Library of Congress*] (LCLS)
MoKBV ...... Black & Veatch Consulting Engineers, Central Library, Kansas City, MO [*Library symbol*] [*Library of Congress*] (LCLS)
MoKCH ...... Children's Mercy Hospital, Kansas City, MO [*Library symbol*] [*Library of Congress*] (LCLS)
MoKChe ..... Chemagro, Kansas City, MO [*Library symbol*] [*Library of Congress*] (LCLS)
MoKCO ...... Kansas City College of Osteopathic Medicine, Kansas City, MO [*Library symbol*] [*Library of Congress*] (LCLS)
MoKCoH .... Jackson County Public Hospital, Kansas City, MO [*Library symbol*] [*Library of Congress*] (LCLS)
MOKE .... Magneto-Optic Kerr Effect
MoKEP ...... United States Environmental Protection Agency, Kansas City, MO [*Library symbol*] [*Library of Congress*] (LCLS)
MoKF .... Farmland Industries Inc., Communications Services, Kansas City, MO [*Library symbol*] [*Library of Congress*] (LCLS)
MoKFR ...... Federal Reserve Bank of Kansas City, Kansas City, MO [*Library symbol*] [*Library of Congress*] (LCLS)
MOKG .... Morgan, Olmstead, Kennedy & Gardner Corp. (SAUO)
MoKGH ...... Kansas City General Hospital, Kansas City, MO [*Library symbol*] [*Library of Congress*] (LCLS)
MoKGS ...... Church of Jesus Christ of Latter-Day Saints, Genealogical Society Library, Kansas City Branch, Kansas City, MO [*Library symbol*] [*Library of Congress*] (LCLS)
MoKHA ...... Kansas City Area Hospital Association, Kansas City, MO [*Library symbol*] [*Library of Congress*] (LCLS)
MoKHC ...... Hallmark Cards, Inc., Kansas City, MO [*Library symbol*] [*Library of Congress*] (LCLS)
MoKiCO ..... Kirksville College of Osteopathy and Surgery, Kirksville, MO [*Library symbol*] [*Library of Congress*] (LCLS)
MoKiU .... Northeast Missouri State University, Kirksville, MO [*Library symbol*] [*Library of Congress*] (LCLS)
MoKJ .... Jackson County Medical Society, Kansas City, MO [*Library symbol*] [*Library of Congress*] (LCLS)
MoKKM ..... Martin Luther King Memorial Hospital, Kansas City, MO [*Library symbol*] [*Library of Congress*] (LCLS)
MoKL .... Linda Hall Library, Kansas City, MO [*Library symbol*] [*Library of Congress*] (LCLS)
MoKLH ...... Lakeside Hospital, Kansas City, MO [*Library symbol*] [*Library of Congress*] (LCLS)
MoKLo ...... Loretto in Kansas City, Kansas City, MO [*Library symbol*] [*Library of Congress*] (LCLS)
MoKMB ..... Midwestern Baptist Theological Seminary, Kansas City, MO [*Library symbol*] [*Library of Congress*] (LCLS)
MoKMC ..... Midwest College of Medical Assistants, Kansas City, MO [*Library symbol*] [*Library of Congress*] (LCLS)
MoKMI ...... Missouri Institute of Technology, Kansas City, MO [*Library symbol*] [*Library of Congress*] (LCLS)
MoKML ...... Marion Laboratories, Inc., Kansas City, MO [*Library symbol*] [*Library of Congress*] (LCLS)
MoKMM ..... Menorah Medical Center, Kansas City, MO [*Library symbol*] [*Library of Congress*] (LCLS)
MoKMoC .... Mobay Chemical Corp., Kansas City, MO [*Library symbol*] [*Library of Congress*] (LCLS)
MoKMR ..... Midwest Research Institute, Kansas City, MO [*Library symbol*] [*Library of Congress*] (LCLS)
MoKMW ..... Maple Woods Community College, Kansas City, MO [*Library symbol*] [*Library of Congress*] (LCLS)
MOKN .... Mo-Kan Distribution Service [*Common carrier symbol*]
MoKN .... Nazarene Theological Seminary, Kansas City, MO [*Library symbol*] [*Library of Congress*] (LCLS)
MoKNA ..... Nelson-Atkins Museum of Art, Spencer Art Reference Library, Kansas City, MO [*Library symbol*] [*Library of Congress*] (LCLS)
MoKNE ...... Newman Ecumenical Seminary, Kansas City, MO [*Library symbol*] [*Library of Congress*] (LCLS)
MoKNG ...... Nelson Art Gallery, Art Reference Library, Kansas City, MO [*Library symbol*] [*Library of Congress*] (LCLS)
MoKNT ...... Saint Paul School of Theology, Kansas City, MO [*Library symbol*] [*Library of Congress*] (LCLS)
MoKP .... Penn Valley Junior College, Kansas City, MO [*Library symbol*] [*Library of Congress*] (LCLS)
MoKPC ...... Pembroke County Day School, Kansas City, MO [*Library symbol*] [*Library of Congress*] (LCLS)
MoKPh ...... Park Hill North Junior High School, Kansas City, MO [*Library symbol*] [*Library of Congress*] (LCLS)
MoKphJH ... Park Hill North Junior High School, Kansas City, MO [*Library symbol*] [*Library of Congress*] (LCLS)
MoKPHS .... Pembroke Hill School, Kansas City, MO [*Library symbol*] [*Library of Congress*] (LCLS)
MoKPhSD ... Park Hill School District, Kansas City, MO [*Library symbol*] [*Library of Congress*] (LCLS)
MoKPi .... Pioneer Community College Library, Kansas City, MO [*Library symbol*] [*Library of Congress*] (LCLS)
MoKR .... Rockhurst College, Kansas City, MO [*Library symbol*] [*Library of Congress*] (LCLS)
MoKRes ..... Research Hospital and Medical Center, Kansas City, MO [*Library symbol*] [*Library of Congress*] (LCLS)
MoKRh ...... Rockhurst High School, Kansas City, MO [*Library symbol*] [*Library of Congress*] (LCLS)
MoKSH ...... Sunset Hill School, Kansas City, MO [*Library symbol*] [*Library of Congress*] (LCLS)
MoKStJ ..... Saint Joseph's Hospital, Kansas City, MO [*Library symbol*] [*Library of Congress*] (LCLS)
MoKStL ..... Saint Luke's Hospital of Kansas City, Kansas City, MO [*Library symbol*] [*Library of Congress*] (LCLS)
MoKStM ..... Saint Mary's Hospital, Kansas City, MO [*Library symbol*] [*Library of Congress*] (LCLS)
MoKStP ..... Saint Paul Theological Seminary, Kansas City, MO [*Library symbol*] [*Library of Congress*] (LCLS)
MoKStT ..... Saint Theresa's Academy, Kansas City, MO [*Library symbol*] [*Library of Congress*] (LCLS)
MoKT .... Teachers College of Kansas City, Kansas City, MO [*Library symbol*] [*Library of Congress*] [*Obsolete*] (LCLS)
MoKTrL ...... Trinity Lutheran Hospital, Kansas City, MO [*Library symbol*] [*Library of Congress*] (LCLS)
MoKU .... University of Missouri at Kansas City, Kansas City, MO [*Library symbol*] [*Library of Congress*] (LCLS)
MoKU-D ..... University of Missouri at Kansas City, Dental School, Kansas City, MO [*Library symbol*] [*Library of Congress*] (LCLS)
MoKU-I ...... University of Missouri at Kansas City, Instructional Materials Center, Kansas City, MO [*Library symbol*] [*Library of Congress*] (LCLS)
MoKu-L ..... University of Missouri at Kansas City, Law Library, Kansas City, MO [*Library symbol*] [*Library of Congress*] (LCLS)
MoKU-M ..... University of Missouri at Kansas City, Medical Library, Kansas City, MO [*Library symbol*] [*Library of Congress*] (LCLS)
MoKU-Mus . University of Missouri at Kansas City, Music Conservatory, Kansas City, MO [*Library symbol*] [*Library of Congress*] (LCLS)
MoKVA ...... United States Veterans Administration Hospital, Kansas City, MO [*Library symbol*] [*Library of Congress*] (LCLS)
MoKW .... Western Missouri Mental Health Center, Kansas City, MO [*Library symbol*] [*Library of Congress*] (LCLS)
MOL .... John Morrell & Co. (SAUO)
mol .... Machine-Oriented Language (AD)
MOL .... Machine-Oriented Language [*Programming language*]
MOL .... Maerkisch-Oderland [*German license plate city code*]
MOL .... Manned Orbital Laboratory (SAUO)
MOL .... Manned Orbiting Laboratory [*NASA*]
MOL .... Master of Organizational Leadership (PGP)
MOL .... Master of Oriental Languages
MOL .... Master of Oriental Learning
MOL .... Maximum Operating Level
MOL .... Maximum Order Limitation (AAGC)
mol .... Maximum Output Level (AD)
MOL .... Maximum Output Level
MOL .... Maximum Overall Length (DAC)
MOL .... Metallo-Organic LASER
MOL .... Method of Lines [*Mathematics*]
MOL .... Microsoft Open License (SAUS)
MOL .... Microtel International, Inc. [*AMEX symbol*] (SAG)
MOL .... Middle of Life (ACAE)
MOL .... Minimum Oxygen Concentration [*at which ignition occurs*]
MOL .... Ministry of Labour [*Later, DE*] [*British*]
MOL .... Missouri State Library, Jefferson City, MO [*OCLC symbol*] (OCLC)
MOL .... Molasses [*Telegraphy*] (PCTE)
mol .... Moldavian [*MARC language code*] [*Library of Congress*] (LCCP)
MOL .... Molde [*Norway*] [*Airport symbol*] (OAG)
Mol .... Moldova (MILB)
mol .... Mole [*Amount of substance*] [*SI unit*]
mol .... Molecular (AD)
MOL .... Molecular (DMAA)
MOL .... Molecular Layer
MOL .... Molecule [*or Molecular*] (AAG)
mol .... Molecule (SHCU)
MOL .... Molesting [*FBI standardized term*]
MOL .... Moliere [*Pseudonym of French actor and dramatist Jean Baptiste Poquelin, 1622-1673*] (ROG)
Mol .... Mollendo (AD)
mol .... Mollis [*Soft*] [*Latin*] (AD)
Mol .... Molloy's De Jure Maritimo [*A publication*] (DLA)
Mol .... Molloy's Irish Chancery Reports [*1827-31*] [*A publication*] (DLA)
MOL .... Molodezhnaya [*Former USSR*] [*Geomagnetic observatory code*]
MOL .... Molson Companies Ltd. [*Toronto Stock Exchange symbol*] [*Vancouver Stock Exchange symbol*]
MOL .... Montebello, VA [*Location identifier*] [*FAA*] (FAAL)

MOL .... More or Less [*Telegraphy*] (PCTE)
MOL .... Multiple On-Line Programming [*Computer science*] (EECA)
M-O-L .... My Old Lady [*Wife*] [*Slang*]
MOL .... Universite de Moncton, Law Library [*UTLAS symbol*]
MOLA........ Major Orchestra Librarians' Association (EA)
MOLA........ Mars Observer Laser Altimeter
MOLA........ Mars Orbiter LASER Alitmeter
MOLA........ Mars Orbiter LASER Altimeter
MOLA........ Midwest Open Land Association (EA)
molab .... Mobile Laboratory (AD)
MOLAB ...... Mobile Laboratory [*NASA*]
MOLAB ...... Mobile Lunar Laboratory (AD)
MOL/ACTS... Manned Orbiting Laboratory / Altitude Control and Transmission System (DNAB)
MOLAP ...... Multidimensional Online Analytical Processing (RALS)
MOLAR ...... Mortar/Artillery Locating Radar (SAUS)
MOLARA .... Motoring Organisations Land Access and Rights Association [*British*] (DBA)
MOLARS .... Meteorological Office Library Accessions and Retrieval System (NITA)
MOLAS ...... Mono Lake APIPS Study (SAUO)
Mo Law Rep... Monthly Law Reporter [*A publication*] (DLA)
MO Laws ... Laws of Missouri [*A publication*] (DLA)
MOLB........ Majestic Circle, Military Order of Lady Bugs of USA (EA)
MolBio ...... Molecular Biosystems, Inc. [*Associated Press*] (SAG)
molc .... Molar Concentration [*Chemistry*] (MAE)
MOLC........ Multiple Operational Launch Complex (MUGU)
MOLCAB .... Mobile Landing Craft Advanced Base
MOLCHOP... More or Less Charterer's Option (RIMS)
Mol Crys Liq Crys... Molecular Crystals and Liquid Crystals (AD)
MOLD .... Model of Light Diode
Moldav...... Moldavian (DIAR)
Mol De Jure Mar... Molloy's De Jure Maritimo et Navali [*A publication*] (DLA)
Moldov...... Moldovan (DIAR)
MOLD/RADC... Ministry of Local Development/Remote Area Development Committee (SAUO)
MOLDS...... Institute for Modernization of Land Data Systems (SAUO)
MOLDS...... Management On-Line Data System [*University of Syracuse*]
MOLDS...... Modernization of Land Data Systems [*North American Institute for the Modernization of Land Data Systems*] [*Falls Church, VA*]
MOLDS...... Multiple Online Debugging System [*Computer science*] (IEEE)
Moldv .... Moldavia (AD)
MOLD/WDD... Ministry of Local Development/Women Development Division (SAUO)
MOLE........ Flow Mole Corp. [*NASDAQ symbol*] (COMM)
MOLE........ Market Odd-Lot Execution System [*Computer science*] (MHDI)
MOLE........ Material and Ordnance Locator and Eliminator [*Police and security equipment*]
MOLE........ Mentoring Online for Excellence
MOLE........ Military Overlay Editor [*Mapping*]
mole......... Molecular (AD)
MOLE........ Molecular Ecology (SAUO)
MOLE........ Molecular Optics LASER Examiner [*Spectrometry*]
MOLEC ...... Molecular
MolecDev... Molecular Devices Corp. [*Associated Press*] (SAG)
MolecDy .... Molecular Dynamics, Inc. [*Associated Press*] (SAG)
Mol Ecol .... Molecular Ecology (SAUO)
molecom.... Molecularized Computer (AD)
MOLECOM... Molecularized Digital Computer
MOLED ...... Molecule Organic Light Emitting Display (SAUS)
MoLeeH..... Lee's Summit Hospital, Lee's Summit, MO [*Library symbol*] [*Library of Congress*] (LCLS)
MoLeeL ..... Longview Community College, Lee's Summit, MO [*Library symbol*] [*Library of Congress*] (LCLS)
MoLeeS ..... Lees Summit Public School District, Lees Summit, MO [*Library symbol*] [*Library of Congress*] (LCLS)
MoLeeU..... Unity School Library, Lee's Summit, MO [*Library symbol*] [*Library of Congress*] (LCLS)
Mo Leg Exam... Monthly Legal Examiner [*New York*] [*A publication*] (DLA)
MO Legis Serv (Vernon)... Missouri Legislative Service (Vernon) [*A publication*] (DLA)
MOLEM ..... Mobile Lunar Excursion Module [*NASA*] (PDAA)
MOLETRONICS... Molecular Electronics
MOLEVATOR... Motor Elevator [*Mechanical lifting stand for arc lamps*]
MOLEX ...... Molecular Executive [*Graphic substructure chemical search system*]
Molex .... Molex, Inc. [*Associated Press*] (SAG)
MOLF........ Modular Laser Fire Control (SAUS)
molfr .... Mole Fraction [*Chemistry*] (DMAA)
MOLGEN .... Molecular Genetics [*Program*] [*Computer science*]
MOLI .... Microsoft Online Institute (SAUO)
MOLIDER... Movimiento Liberal Democratico Revolucionario [*Revolutionary Democratic Liberal Movement*] [*Honduras*] [*Political party*]
MOLIN....... Moline, IL [*American Association of Railroads railroad junction routing code*]
Molink....... Moscow Link (AD)
MOLINK..... Moscow-Washington Direct Communications Link (SAUO)
MOLINK..... Moscow/Washington Emergency Communications Link (MCD)
MoLiPS ..... Liberty Public Schools District, Liberty, MO [*Library symbol*] [*Library of Congress*] (LCLS)
Molirena.... Movimiento Liberal Republicano Nacionalista [*Nationalist Liberal Republican Movement*] [*Panama*] [*Political party*] (PPW)
MOLIS....... Minority On-Line Information Service
MOLISV ..... Movement for Liberation and Development [*Italy*] Political party] (EAIO)
MoLiWJ..... William Jewell College, Liberty, MO [*Library symbol*] [*Library of Congress*] (LCLS)
Mol JM...... Molloy's De Jure Maritimo et Navali [*A publication*] (DLA)
moll .... Metallo-Organic Liquid LASER (AD)
MOLL........ Metallo-Organic Liquid LASER
mol/l......... Molecules per Liter [*Measurement*] (DAVI)
Moll .... Moller Organ Co. [*Record label*]
MOLL........ Mollis [*Soft*] [*Pharmacy*]
MOLL........ Molloy Mobile Crafts [*NCIC trailer make code*]
Moll .... Molloy's De Jure Maritimo [*A publication*] (DLA)
Moll .... Molloy's Irish Chancery Reports [*1827-31*] [*A publication*] (DLA)
moll .... Soft [*Medicine*] (BCRP)
MOLLE ...... Modular Light-Weight Load-Carrying Equipment [*Army*]
MOLLI....... Micro OnLine Library Information [*Nichols Advanced Technologies, Inc.*]
mollie....... Mollienisia (AD)
MOLLUS .... Military Order of the Loyal Legion of the United States (EA)
Mollus....... Mollusca (AD)
MOLLUSA... Military Order of the Loyal Legion of the USA (AD)
MOL/M^3.... Moles per Cubic Meter
Mo L Mag .. Monthly Law Magazine [*London*] [*A publication*] (DLA)
MOLNS...... Ministry of Labour and National Service [*World War II*] [*British*] (DAS)
MOLO .... Mideastern Ohio Library Organization [*Library network*]
MOLOC...... Ministry of Labour Occupational Classification [*Later, CODOT*] [*British*]
MOLOO...... More or Less Owner's Option (RIMS)
MOLP........ Mesa Operating Limited Partnership (EFIS)
MOLP........ Microsoft Open License Pak (SAUO)
MOLP........ Multiple Objective Linear Programming [*Computer science*] (PDAA)
Mol Pharmacol... Molecular Pharmacology (MEC)
Mol Phys ... Molecular Physics (AD)
Mol Plant-Microbe Interact... Molecular Plant-Microbe Interactions (SAUO)
MOLR/DOS... Ministry of Land Reforms/ Department of Survey (SAUS)
MOLR/DOS... Ministry of Land Reforms/Department of Survey (SAUO)
MOLS........ Magnetic-Operated Limit Switch
MOLS........ Mirror Optional Landing System [*Aviation*] (NG)
MOLS........ Mobile Object Location System
MOLS........ Multiple Object Location System [*Army*]
MOLS........ Mutually Orthogonal Latin Square
Mol Screen News... Molecular Screening News (SAUO)
MOLSINK... Molecular Sink of Outer Space [*Vacuum testing chamber for spacecraft systems*]
MOLSW/DOL... Ministry of Labour and Social Welfare/Department of Labour (SAUO)
MolT......... Hany S Truman Library, Independence (SAUS)
MOLT .... Manually-Operated Lift Truck (DWSG)
molt .... Molten (AD)
MOLT........ Molten
MoltenM .... Molten Metal Technology, Inc. [*Associated Press*] (SAG)
MOLTOL..... Manned Orbiting Laboratory Test-Oriented Language [*NASA*] (MCD)
MOLTS ...... Model Output Location Time Series (SAUO)
MOLU .... Mitsui Osaka Shosen Kaisha Lines [*Intermodal shipping container symbol*] (TVRC)
MOLU .... Mitsui OSK Lines [*Common carrier symbol*]
mol wt ...... Molecular Weight (AD)
Mol wt ...... Molecular Weight (DB)
MOL WT .... Molecular Weight [*Also, M, MW*]
MOLX........ International Molasses [*Private rail car owner code*]
MOLX........ Molex, Inc. [*NASDAQ symbol*] (NQ)
MOLXA...... Molex Inc'A' [*NASDAQ symbol*] (TTSB)
MOLY........ Molecular Analysis [*by a computer graphics system*] [*Chemistry*]
moly......... Molybdenum (AD)
Moly......... Molyneaux's Reports. English Courts, Tempore Car. I [*A publication*] (DLA)
MOLY........ Mouse Lymphoma Cells [*Oncology*]
MOLZ........ Molasses Industry [*Federal Railroad Administration identification code*]
MOM .... Macro Observation Module [*Microscopy*]
MOM .... Main Outcome Measure [*Medicine*] (MELL)
MOM .... Maintenance Operations Management (MCD)
MOM .... Management of Migration [*of wastewaters*]
MOM .... Manager of Managers (SAUO)
MOM .... Manned Orbiting Mission [*NASA*]
MOM .... Man-on-the-Move [*Military slang*] (DNAB)
MOM .... Man Overboard Module [*Boating*]
MOM .... Manufacturing Operations Management (SAUO)
MOM .... Many on Many (ACAE)
MoM......... Map oriented Machine (SAUO)
MOM .... Mark XII Output and Monitoring System (SAA)
m/ o m/..... Mas o Menos [*More or Less*] [*Spanish*] (AD)
MOM .... Master of Manufacturing (PGP)
MOM .... Maximum of the Maximums [*Emergency Management*] (EMA)
MOM .... Measure of Merit (MCD)
MOM .... Medical Opportunities in Michigan (SAUO)
MOM .... Men Our Masters (SAUO)
MOM .... Message-Oriented Middleware [*Computer science*]
MOM .... Message Output Module [*Telecommunications*] (TEL)
MOM .... Metal-Oxide Metal (MCD)
MOM .... Method of Moments (SAUS)
MOM .... Methods of Moderation [*An association*] (EA)
MOM .... Methoxymethyl [*Organic chemistry*]
mom......... Micromation Online Microfilmer [*Computer science*] (AD)
MOM .... Micromation Online Microfilmer
MOM .... Microsoft Office Manager [*Microsoft Corp. computer program*] (PCM)

m-o-m .... Middle of Month (AD)
MOM .... Middle of the Month
MOM .... Military Official Mail (AABC)
MOM .... Military Ordinary Mail (AABC)
mom .... Military Ordinary Mail (AD)
MOM .... Military Overseas Mail [*An association*] (EA)
mom .... Milk of Magnesia (AD)
MOM .... Milk of Magnesia
MOM .... Ministry of Munitions (SAUO)
MOM .... Minutes of Meeting
MOM .... Missile Operations Manager (MUGU)
MOM .... Missionary Sisters of Our Lady of Mercy [*Roman Catholic religious order*]
MOM .... Mission Operations Manager (EOSA)
MOM .... Mitochondrial Outer-Membrane [*Biochemistry*]
MOM .... Modified Operational Missile
MOM .... Modular Ocean Model (USDC)
mom .... Moment (NAKS)
MOM .... Moment
MOM .... Momentary (MSA)
MOM .... Momentum
Mom .... Momma (AD)
MOM .... Momote [*Admiralty Islands*] [*Seismograph station code, US Geological Survey*] (SEIS)
MOM .... Mongo-Nkundu [*Language symbol*] (ETLW)
MOM .... Mother's Restaurants Ltd. [*Toronto Stock Exchange symbol*]
MOM .... Mucoid Otitis Media [*Medicine*] (DMAA)
MOM .... Multipurpose Office Machine (VLIE)
MOM .... Multirole OTO Munition (SAUS)
MOM .... Musee Oceanographique Monaco [*Monaco Oceanographic Museum*] [*France*] (AD)
M-O-M ...... My Old Man [*Husband*] [*Slang*]
MOM .... Myxoedema(tous) Madness [*Medicine*] (EDAA)
MOMA .... Madagasikara Otronin'ny Malagasy [*Formerly, MONIMA*] [*Madagascar Led by Malagasy*]
MOMA .... Message-Oriented Middleware Association (SAUO)
MOMA .... Methoxyhydroxymandelic Acid [*Organic chemistry*]
MoMA .... Museum of Modern Art [*New York*] (AD)
MOMA .... Museum of Modern Art [*New York*]
MOMAC ..... Monkey Mountain Advisory Center [*Military*] (CINC)
MOMAG ..... Mobile Mine Assembly Group [*Military*] (CAAL)
MOMAGDET... Mobile Mine Assembly Group Detachment (DNAB)
MOMAGU ... Mobile Mine Assembly Group Unit (DNAB)
MoManW ... Laura Ingalls Wilder - Rose Wilder Lane Home and Museum, Mansfield, MO [*Library symbol*] [*Library of Congress*] (LCLS)
momar ...... Modern Mobile Army (AD)
MOMAR ..... Modern Mobile Army [*Military*]
MoMaryU ... Northwest Missouri State University, Maryville, MO [*Library symbol*] [*Library of Congress*] (LCLS)
MOMAT ..... Mobile Mine Assembly Team
MOMATLANT... Mobile Mine Assembly Team, Atlantic (DNAB)
MOMATPAC... Mobile Mine Assembly Team, Pacific (DNAB)
momau ...... Mobile Mine Assembly Unit (AD)
MOMAU ..... Mobile Mine Assembly Unit (NVT)
MOMAULANT... Mobile Mine Assembly Unit, Atlantic (DNAB)
MOMAULANTDETKEF... Mobile Mine Assembly Unit, Atlantic, Keflavik Detachment (DNAB)
MOMAUPAC... Mobile Mine Assembly Unit, Pacific (DNAB)
MO-MB ...... Mail-out/Mail-back (SAUS)
MOMB ...... Mombasa [*Island near Kenya*] (ROG)
MOMBE ..... Metallo-Organic Molecular Beam Epitaxy [*Solid state physics*]
MOMC ...... Mint on a Mint Card [*Collectibles*]
MOMC ...... Mint on Mint Card [*Toy collection*]
MOMC ...... Mount McKinley National Park
MOMCC ..... Midwest Open Air Museums Coordinating Council [*An association*]
MOMCOMS... Man-On-the-Move Communications System (SAUS)
MOMCOMS... Mobile Mine Countermeasures Command (DNAB)
MOMEN ..... Momence, IL [*American Association of Railroads railroad junction routing code*]
MoMex ...... Mexico-Audrain County Library, Mexico, MO [*Library symbol*] [*Library of Congress*] (LCLS)
MOMI .... Museum of the Moving Image [*London*] (ECON)
MOMIMTS... Military and Orchestral Musical Instrument Makers' Trade Society [*A union*] [*British*] (DCTA)
m-o-m in am if no bm by pm... Milk-of-Magnesia in the Morning if No Bowel Movement by Evening [*Medicine*] (AD)
MOMISMAINTU... Mobile, Missile Maintenance Unit (DNAB)
MomI .... Moslem Meal (AD)
MOML .... Moslem Meal [*Airline notation*] (ADA)
MoMLV ...... Moloney Murine Luekemia Virus [*Used for gene transfer protocols*] (DOG)
MoMM ...... Missouri Valley College, Marshall, MO [*Library symbol*] [*Library of Congress*] (LCLS)
MOMM ...... Motor Machinist's Mate [*Navy rating*]
MOMMSR... Motor Machinist's Mate, Ship Repair [*Navy rating*]
MOMO .... Macrosomia-Obesity-Macrocephaly-Ocular Abnormalities [*Syndrome*] [*Medicine*] (DMAA)
MOMO .... Moto Morini [*NCIC motorcycle make code*]
MOMP .... Major Outer Membrane Protein [*Biochemistry*]
MOMP .... Michigan Ordnance Missile Plant [*Army*]
MOMP .... Mid-Ocean Meeting Place
MOMP .... Mustargen [*Nitrogen mustard*], Oncovin , Methotrexate, Prednisone [*Vincristine*] [*Antineoplastic drug regimen*]
MOMR .... Mayor's Office of Manpower Resources (AD)
MOMS .... Manganese Oxide Mesoporous Structure [*Inorganic Chemistry*]
MOMS .... Measure of Mission Success [*Military*] (CAAL)
MOMS .... Member of the Organisation and Methods Society [*British*] (DI)
moms .... Mervaerdiomsaetningsskat [*Value-Added Tax*] [*Danish*] (AD)
MOMS .... Meteorological and Oceanographic Measurements System [*Chevron Oil Co.*]
MOMS .... Meteorological Optic Measuring System (MCD)
MOMS .... Michigan-University Own Mathematical System (SAUO)
MOMS .... Micro-Opto-Mechanical Systems
moms .... Missile Operate Mode Simulator (AD)
MOMS .... Missile Operate Mode Simulator
MOMS .... Modified Operational Missile System (DNAB)
MOMS .... Modular Optoelectronic Multispectral Scanner (MCD)
MOMS .... Modular Optoelectronic Stereo Scanner (SAUS)
MOMS .... Mothers for Moral Stability [*Group opposing sex education in schools*]
MOMS .... Mothers Offering Maternal Support [*An association*] (MELL)
MOMS .... Mothers of Men in Service [*World War II*]
MOMS .... Multimegabit Operation Multiplexer System
MOMS .... Multiple Orbit - Multiple Satellite
MOMS .... Multiple Organ Malrotation Syndrome [*Medicine*] (DMAA)
MOM's ...... Multiples over the Median [*Statistics*]
MOMSCIS... Missouri Model Spinal Cord Injury System [*University of Missouri--Columbia*] (RCD)
MoMSV ..... Moloney Mouse Sarcoma Virus
MOMTD ..... Metal on Metal Tunnel Diode (ACAE)
MOMU ...... Montemar [*Common carrier symbol*]
MoMuLV .... Moloney Murine Leukemia Virus [*Also, MLV*]
MOMV ...... Manned Orbital Maneuvering Vehicle
MOM/WOW... Men Our Masters/Women Our Wonders [*Antifeminist group*] (EA)
MOMX .... Momentous [*Telegraphy*] (PCTE)
MOMY .... Mothers of Murdered Youth [*Association*] (EA)
MOMZ .... Monterey Mine [*Federal Railroad Administration identification code*]
MON .... Above Mountains [*ICAO*] (FAAC)
mon .... Maison [*House*] [*French*] (AD)
MON .... Malton, Ontario, Canada [*Amtrak rail station code*]
MON .... Member of the Order of the Niger [*Nigeria*]
MON .... Memorandum of Need
MON .... Memorandum of Negotiation (MCD)
MON .... Missouri Valley College, Marshall, MO [*Inactive*] [*OCLC symbol*] (OCLC)
MON .... Mixed Oxides of Nitrogen
Mon .... Monaco (AD)
MON .... Monaco [*Monaco*] [*Seismograph station code, US Geological Survey*] (SEIS)
MON .... Monaco [*NCIC car model code*]
MON .... Monaghan [*County in Republic of Ireland*] (ROG)
Mon .... Monaghan's Unreported Cases (Pennsylvania Superior Court) [*A publication*] (DLA)
Mon .... Monarch [*Record label*] [*British*]
MON .... Monarch Airlines Ltd. [*British*] [*ICAO designator*] (FAAC)
MON .... Monarch Capital Corp. [*NYSE symbol*] (COMM)
MON .... Monarch Investments Ltd. [*Toronto Stock Exchange symbol*]
mon .... Monastery (SHCU)
MON .... Monastery
Mon .... Monday (AD)
MON .... Monday (AFM)
MON .... Mondial [*NCIC car model code*]
Mon .... Monegasque (AD)
mon .... Monetary (AD)
MON .... Monetary (AFM)
MON .... Money [*Telegraphy*] (PCTE)
Mon .... Mongol [*One affected with Down's syndrome*] [*Medicine*] (DAVI)
mon .... Mongol [*MARC language code*] [*Library of Congress*] (LCCP)
MON .... Mongolian (AABC)
Mon .... Moniteur Belge [*A publication*] (ILCA)
Mon .... Monitor (AD)
mon .... Monitor (WDMC)
MON .... Monitor [*Navy ship symbol*]
mon .... Monitor/Contractor [*MARC relator code*] [*Library of Congress*] (LCCP)
Mon .... Monmouthshire (AD)
MON .... Monmouthshire [*County in Wales*]
Mon .... Monoceros [*Constellation*]
MON .... Monoclinic [*Crystallography*]
Mon .... Monoclonal Antibodies, Inc.
MON .... Monocyte [*Hematology*]
MON .... Monogram [*Numismatics*]
mon .... Monograph (BJA)
MON .... Monomoy Surfboat [*Coast Guard*] (DNAB)
MON .... Monon [*Railroad*] (MHDW)
Mon .... Monongahela (AD)
MON .... Monsanto Co. [*NYSE symbol*]
Mon .... Monsieur [*Mister*] [*French*]
Mon .... Monsignor (WGA)
mon .... Monsoon (AD)
Mon .... Montag [*Monday*] [*German*] (AD)
MON .... Montana
Mon .... Montana Reports [*A publication*] (DLA)
Mon .... Montana Supreme Court Reports [*A publication*] (DLA)
MON .... Montcalm [*NCIC car model code*]
MON .... Monterey [*NCIC car model code*]
MON .... Montero [*NCIC car model code*]
MON .... Month
MON .... Monticello, AR [*Location identifier*] [*FAA*] (FAAL)
MON .... Monument (AAG)

Mon.......... Monument (AD)
mon.......... Monument (AD)
MON.......... Monument Still Exists [*Genealogy*] (ROG)
MON.......... Monza [*NCIC car model code*]
mon.......... Motor Octane Number (AD)
MON.......... Motor Octane Number [*Fuel technology*]
MoN.......... Mountain Name (BJA)
MON.......... Mount Cook [*New Zealand*] [*Airport symbol*] (OAG)
MoN.......... North Kansas City Public Library, North Kansas City, MO [*Library symbol*] [*Library of Congress*] (LCLS)
MON.......... Universite de Moncton, Bibliotheque [*UTLAS symbol*]
Mona........ Madonna [*Our Lady*] [*Italian*] (AD)
MONA........ Marche des Options Negociables sur Actions [*Options exchange*] [*France*] (EY)
MONA........ Missouri Nurses Association (SAUO)
MONA........ Modular Navigation [*Aviation*]
Mona........ Monaco (VRA)
Mona........ Monaghan's Reports [*147-165 Pennsylvania*] [*A publication*] (DLA)
MONA........ Monarch [*NCIC car make code*]
MONA........ Monitor Assembly [*Ground Communications Facility, NASA*]
MONAB...... Mobile Naval Advanced Base [*British military*] (DMA)
MONAB...... Mobile Noise Analysis Barge
MONAB...... Mobile Operating Naval Air Base
Monac....... Monaco Finance [*Associated Press*] (SAG)
MonacoC.... Monaco Coach Corp. [*Associated Press*] (SAG)
MonacoF.... Monaco Finance [*Associated Press*] (SAG)
Monag....... Monaghan (AD)
Monag....... Monaghan's Reports [*147-165 Pennsylvania*] [*A publication*] (DLA)
MONAGH.... Monaghan [*County in Republic of Ireland*] (ROG)
Monaghan... Monaghan's Reports [*147-165 Pennsylvania*] [*A publication*] (DLA)
Monaghan (PA)... Monaghan's Reports [*147-165 Pennsylvania*] [*A publication*] (DLA)
MONAGN.... Monaghan [*County in Republic of Ireland*]
MONAL...... Mobile Nondestructive Assay Laboratory [*AEC*]
MONALISA... Modelling Natural Images for Synthesis and Animation (SAUS)
Mon Anc.... Monumentum Ancyranum [*Classical studies*] (OCD)
Mon Angl... Monasticon Anglicanum [*A publication*] (DLA)
MO NARAL... Missouri National Abortion and Reproductive Rights Action League (EARSL)
MONARC.... Master Office Network Adaptive Real-time Control [*Communications*]
Monare...... Movement for National Redemption (SAUO)
Monas...... Monastic (AD)
Monash U... Monash University (SAUO)
Monash Univ Law Rev... Monash University. Law Review [*A publication*]
MON (automobile)... Montreal [*NCIC car model code*]
MonAvl...... Monarch Avalon, Inc. [*Associated Press*] (SAG)
MONB........ Monarch Boat Company [*NCIC trailer make code*]
monbas...... Monobasic (AD)
MONBUSHO... Ministry of Education, Science and Culture Japan (SAUO)
MONC........ Metropolitan Opera National Council
MONC........ Monarch Industries [*NCIC trailer make code*]
MONC........ Monroe Transportation Services [*Common carrier symbol*]
MonCap..... Monmouth Capital Corp. [*Associated Press*] (SAG)
MonCasn.... Monarch Casino & Resort [*Associated Press*] (SAG)
monch....... Monochrome (VRA)
Monc Inn... Moncrieff's Liability of Innkeepers [*1874*] [*A publication*] (DLA)
MOND........ Modified Newtonian Dynamics
MOND........ Mondavi [*Robert*] [*NASDAQ symbol*] (SAG)
MOND........ Monday (ROG)
MOND........ Mondial [*NCIC motorcycle make code*]
MOND........ Robert Mondavi 'A' [*NASDAQ symbol*] (TTSB)
Mondavi.... Mondavi [*Robert*] [*Associated Press*] (SAG)
MON/DIR.... Mission Monitoring Direction
mon/dir..... Monitoring Direction (AD)
MONE........ MatrixOne, Inc. [*NASDAQ symbol*] (SG)
MONE........ Money Store [*NASDAQ symbol*] (TTSB)
MONE........ [*The*] Money Store, Inc. [*NASDAQ symbol*] (SAG)
MONECA.... Motor Network Calculator
MONEG...... Monsoon Numerical Experimental Group (SAUO)
MONEG...... Monsoon Numerical Experimentation Group (SAUO)
MONEP...... Marche des Options Negotiables de Paris [*French Traded Options Market*] (ODBW)
MONES...... Molecular Nonthermal Excitation Spectrometry
MONET...... High Data Rate Mobile Internet (SAUS)
MONET...... Managing Open Networks (AGLO)
MONET...... Mobile Networks Integration [*Telecommunications*]
MONET...... Monetary
MONET...... Multi-Wavelength Optical Network (AAEL)
MONEVAL... Monthly Evaluation Report [*Military*]
monex....... Monsoon Experiment (AD)
MONEX...... Monsoon Experiment [*Also, MONSOONEX*]
Moneygr.... Moneygram Payment Systems [*Associated Press*] (SAG)
MoneySt.... [*The*] Money Store, Inc. [*Associated Press*] (SAG)
MONF........ Monaco Finance [*NASDAQ symbol*] (SAG)
MONFA...... Monaco Finance'A' [*NASDAQ symbol*] (TTSB)
Mong........ Mongol (AD)
Mong........ Mongolia (SHCU)
MONG........ Mongolian [*Language, etc.*]
mong........ Mongolisch [*Mongolian*] [*German*] (AD)
MONG........ Mongrel (DSUE)
MONG........ Moning [*Tea trade*] (ROG)
Mongo....... Mongolia (VRA)
Mongol...... Mongolian (DIAR)
MONG SOCK... Mongolia Society (SAUO)
MONH........ Monarch Mobile Homes [*NCIC trailer make code*]
MONH........ Monarch Motor Home [*NCIC truck make code*]
mon-H....... Monohydrogen (AD)
MoNHI....... Missouri Natural Heritage Inventory [*Missouri State Department of Conservation*] [*Information service or system*] (IID)
MONI........ Monitor Coach Company [*NCIC trailer make code*]
MONICA..... Monitoring of Trends and Determinants in Cardiovascular Disease
MONICA..... Multilateral Monitoring of Trends and Determinants in Cardiovascular Disease (SAUO)
monik........ Moniker (AD)
MONIL....... Mobile Non-Destructive Inspection Laboratory (DNAB)
MONIMA.... Mouvement National pour l'Independance de Madagascar [*National Movement for the Independence of Madagascar*] [*Political party*] (PPW)
MONITOR... Strategic Analysis, Forecasting and Evaluation in Research and Technology (SAUO)
MONJC...... Montpelier Junction, VT [*American Association of Railroads railroad junction routing code*]
Mon Lab Rev... Monthly Labor Review [*A publication*] (JLIT)
Mon Law Mag... Monthly Law Magazine [*London*] [*A publication*] (DLA)
Mon Law Rep... Monthly Law Reporter [*A publication*] (DLA)
Mon Leg R (PA)... Monroe Legal Reporter [*Pennsylvania*] [*A publication*] (DLA)
Mon LR..... Monash University Law Review (SAUO)
MONM....... Monmouth Capital [*NASDAQ symbol*] (TTSB)
MONM....... Monmouth Capital Corp. [*NASDAQ symbol*] (SAG)
MONMC..... Mint on Near Mint Card [*Collectibles*]
Mon Meth... Monahan's Method of the Law [*1878*] [*A publication*] (DLA)
MoNMH..... North Kansas City Memorial Hospital, North Kansas City, MO [*Library symbol*] [*Library of Congress*] (LCLS)
Monmouth C... Monmouth College (GAGS)
MONMS..... Monmouthshire [*County in Wales*]
MONN....... Monon Trailer [*NCIC trailer make code*]
Mon Not Roy Soc Tas... Monthly Notices. Royal Society of Tasmania [*A publication*]
MONO....... Monaural (KSC)
MONO....... Mono [*NCIC trailer make code*]
Mono........ Monoceros [*Constellation*]
MONO....... Monochrome (DSUE)
Mono........ Monocyte [*Immunology*] (QSUL)
mono........ Monocyte [*Hematology*]
Mono........ Monogram [*Record label*]
mono........ Mononucleosis [*Medicine*] (AD)
MONO....... Mononucleosis [*Medicine*]
mono........ Monophonic (AD)
MONO....... Monophonic
mono........ Monopoly (AD)
mono........ Monopropellant (AD)
mono........ Monorail (AD)
MONO....... Monorail (WDAA)
MONO....... Monotone (DOAD)
mono........ Monotype (AD)
MONO....... Monotype (ADA)
monob....... Mobile Noise Barge (AD)
MONOB..... Mobile Noise Barge
MONOC..... Monocoque (MSA)
monocl..... Monoclinic (AD)
MONOCL.... Monoclinic
monocot.... Monocotyledon [*Biology*] (BARN)
Monod....... Monon Railroad (AD)
monog....... Monogram (AD)
monog....... Monograph (AD)
MONOG..... Monograph
Monogr Soc Res Child Dev... Monographs of the Society for Research in Child Development (SAUO)
MONOHUD... Monocular Head-Up Display (SAUS)
MONOK..... Monitor Resumed Normal Operation [*Aviation communications*]
MONOLIN... Mobile Node Logistics and Industrial Network (SAUO)
MONOP..... Monopoly [*Legal shorthand*] (LWAP)
monos....... Monitor Out of Service (AD)
MONOS..... Monitor Out of Service [*Aviation communications*]
monot....... Monotonous (AD)
monot....... Monotype (AD)
MonP........ Monongahela Power Co. [*Associated Press*] (SAG)
MonP25..... Monongahela Power Co. [*Associated Press*] (SAG)
MONPA...... Montandon, PA [*American Association of Railroads railroad junction routing code*]
monpl....... Monopoly (AD)
monpr....... Monoprint (VRA)
MonPw...... Montana Power Co. [*Associated Press*] (SAG)
MONR........ Montana Central Railroad [*Federal Railroad Administration identification code*]
Monrch...... Monarch Machine Tool Co. [*Associated Press*] (SAG)
MoNRDEP... Ministry of Natural Resources Development and Environmental Protection [*Ethiopia*] (ECON)
MonRE....... Monmouth Real Estate Investment Corp. [*Associated Press*] (SAG)
Mon River... Monongahela River (AD)
Monro....... Acta Cancellariae [*England*] [*A publication*] (DLA)
MONRO..... Monroe, LA [*American Association of Railroads railroad junction routing code*]
Monro AC... Monro's Acta Cancellariae [*1545-1625*] [*A publication*] (DLA)
Monroc...... Monroc, Inc. [*Associated Press*] (SAG)
Monroe...... Monroe Legal Reporter [*Pennsylvania*] [*A publication*] (DLA)
Monroe LR... Monroe Legal Reporter [*Pennsylvania*] [*A publication*] (DLA)

MonroM..... Monro Muffler Brake, Inc. [*Associated Press*] (SAG)
MONS....... Monastery
Mons....... Monmouthshire (DIAR)
MONS....... Monmouthshire [*County in Wales*]
MONS....... Monsieur [*In France this form is considered contemptuous*] [*Preferred form is M*]
Mons....... Monsieur [*Mister*] [*French*] (AD)
MONS....... Monson & Sons Trailer [*NCIC trailer make code*]
Monsan..... Monsanto Co. [*Associated Press*] (SAG)
Monsanto Res Corp Mound Lab Res Dev Rep... Monsanto Research Corporation. Mound Laboratory. Research and Development Report (SAUO)
Mons Cur... Monsoon Current (AD)
MONSE...... Modified Navier-Stokes Equations for Numerical Investigation of 3D Unsteady Viscous Flows (SAUO)
MONSEE.... Monitoring of the Sun Earth Environment [*International Council of Scientific Unions*] (MCD)
Monsig...... Monseigneur [*My Lord*] [*French*] (AD)
MONSIG...... Monsignor [*Lord, Sir*] [*French*]
MONSOONEX... Monsoon Experiment [*Also, MONEX*]
MonSt....... Montgomery Street Income Securities, Inc. [*Associated Press*] (SAG)
monstro..... Monstrosity (AD)
MONSTRY... Monastery
MONSU..... Movement for National Student Union (SAUO)
Mont......... Montagu's English Bankruptcy Reports [*A publication*] (DLA)
Mont......... Montana (AD)
MONT....... Montana (AFM)
Mont......... Montana Supreme Court Reports [*A publication*] (DLA)
MONT....... Monte [*NCIC motorcycle make code*]
Mont......... Monterrey (AD)
Mont......... Montevideo (AD)
Mont......... Montgomery (AD)
MONT....... Montgomeryshire [*County in Wales*]
Mont......... Montilla [*Record label*] [*USA, Spain, etc.*]
MONT....... Montmorillonite [*Mineralogy*]
Mont......... Montpelier (AD)
Mont......... Montreal (AD)
Mont......... Montriou's Bengal Reports [*A publication*] (DLA)
MONT....... Montrose District Office (SAUO)
mont......... Monument (VRA)
MONTA...... Montague, CA [*American Association of Railroads railroad junction routing code*]
Mont Admin R... Administrative Rules of Montana [*A publication*] (DLA)
Mont Admin Reg... Montana Administrative Register [*A publication*] (DLA)
MonTal...... Monumenta Talmudica (BJA)
MONTANA CUPAC... Montana Credit Unions League PAC [*Helena, MT*] (PACS)
Mont & A... Montagu and Ayrton's English Bankruptcy Reports [*1833-38*] [*A publication*] (DLA)
Mont & Ayr... Montagu and Ayrton's English Bankruptcy Reports [*1833-38*] [*A publication*] (DLA)
Mont & Ayr Bankr... Montagu and Ayrton's English Bankruptcy Reports [*1833-38*] [*A publication*] (DLA)
Mont & Ayr Bankr (Eng)... Montagu and Ayrton's English Bankruptcy Reports [*1833-38*] [*A publication*] (DLA)
Mont & Ayr BL... Montagu and Ayrton's Bankrupt Laws [*A publication*] (DLA)
Mont & B... Montagu and Bligh's English Bankruptcy Reports [*1832-33*] [*A publication*] (DLA)
Mont & B Bankr... Montagu and Bligh's English Bankruptcy Reports [*1832-33*] [*A publication*] (DLA)
Mont & B Bankr (Eng)... Montagu and Bligh's English Bankruptcy Reports [*1832-33*] [*A publication*] (DLA)
Mont & Bl... Montagu and Bligh's English Bankruptcy Reports [*1832-33*] [*A publication*] (DLA)
Mont & C... Montagu and Chitty's English Bankruptcy Reports [*1838-40*] [*A publication*] (DLA)
Mont & C Bankr... Montagu and Chitty's English Bankruptcy Reports [*1838-40*] [*A publication*] (DLA)
Mont & C Bankr (Eng)... Montagu and Chitty's English Bankruptcy Reports [*1838-40*] [*A publication*] (DLA)
Mont & Ch... Montagu and Chitty's English Bankruptcy Reports [*1838-40*] [*A publication*] (DLA)
Mont & Chitt... Montagu and Chitty's English Bankruptcy Reports [*1838-40*] [*A publication*] (DLA)
Mont & M... Montagu and MacArthur's English Bankruptcy Reports [*A publication*] (DLA)
Mont & MacA... Montagu and MacArthur's English Bankruptcy Reports [*A publication*] (DLA)
Mont & M Bankr (Eng)... Mantagu and MacArthur's English Bankruptcy Reports [*1826-30*] [*A publication*] (DLA)
Mon T B.... T. B. Monroe's Kentucky Reports [*17-23 Kentucky*] [*A publication*] (DLA)
Mont Bankr (Eng)... Montagu's English Bankruptcy Reports [*A publication*] (DLA)
Mont Bank Rep... Montagu's English Bankruptcy Reports [*A publication*] (DLA)
MontBB..... Monterey Bay Bancorp, Inc. [*Associated Press*] (SAG)
Mont BC.... Montagu's English Bankruptcy Reports [*A publication*] (DLA)
Mont Bk L... Montagu's Bankrupt Law [*4th ed.*] [*1827*] [*A publication*] (DLA)
MONTBLEX... Monsoon Trough Boundary Layer Experiment (SAUO)
Mont Cas... Montriou's Cases in Hindoo Law [*A publication*] (DLA)
Montclair St C... Montclair State College (GAGS)
Mont CMS&T... Montana College of Mineral Science and Technology (GAGS)
Mont Code Ann... Montana Code, Annotated [*A publication*] (DLA)
Mont Comp... Montagu on Composition [*1823*] [*A publication*] (DLA)
Mont Cond Rep... Montreal Condensed Reports [*A publication*] (DLA)
Mont D & DeG... Montagu, Deacon, and De Gex's English Bankruptcy Reports [*1840-44*] [*A publication*] (DLA)
Mont Dig.... Montagu's Digest of Pleadings in Equity [*A publication*] (DLA)
Monte....... Montebianco (AD)
Monte....... Monte Carlo (AD)
Monte....... Montefiore (AD)
Monte....... Montevideo (AD)
Monte....... Montgomery (AD)
Monted...... Montedison SpA [*Associated Press*] (SAG)
Monten...... Montenegro
Mont Eq Pl... Montagu's Digest of Pleadings in Equity [*A publication*] (DLA)
Monterey Inst... Monterey Institute of Foreign Studies (GAGS)
Montfort Fathers... Missionaries of the Company of Mary (SAUO)
montg....... Montage (VRA)
MONTG...... Montgomery, AL [*American Association of Railroads railroad junction routing code*]
MONTG...... Montgomeryshire [*County in Wales*]
Montgom... Montgomeryshire [*England*] (AD)
MONTGOM... Montgomeryshire [*County in Wales*]
Montgoms.. Montgomeryshire (DIAR)
Month Dig Tax Articles... Monthly Digest of Tax Articles [*A publication*] (DLA)
Month JL... Monthly Journal of Law [*A publication*] (DLA)
Month Jur... Monthly Jurist [*Bloomington, IL*] [*A publication*] (DLA)
Month Law Bul... Monthly Law Bulletin [*New York*] [*A publication*] (DLA)
Month Law Rep... Law Reporter [*Boston*] [*A publication*] (DLA)
Month L Bull (NY)... Monthly Law Bulletin (New York) [*A publication*] (DLA)
Month Leg Ex... Monthly Legal Examiner [*New York*] [*A publication*] (DLA)
Month Leg Exam... Monthly Legal Examiner [*New York*] [*A publication*] (DLA)
Month Leg Exam (NY)... Monthly Legal Examiner (New York) [*A publication*] (DLA)
Month LJ... Monthly Journal of Law [*Washington*] [*A publication*] (DLA)
Month LM... Monthly Law Magazine [*London*] [*A publication*] (DLA)
Month L Rep... Monthly Law Reporter [*Boston*] [*A publication*] (DLA)
Month L Rep... Monthly Law Reports [*Canada*] [*A publication*] (DLA)
Month L Rev... Monthly Law Review [*A publication*] (DLA)
Monthly Lab Rev... Monthly Labor Review [*A publication*] (DLA)
Monthly L Bul... New York Monthly Law Bulletin [*A publication*] (DLA)
Month West Jur... Monthly Western Jurist [*A publication*] (DLA)
MONTI....... Monticello, AR [*American Association of Railroads railroad junction routing code*]
Mont Ind.... Monthly Index to Reporters [*A publication*] (DLA)
Mont Inst... Montriou's Institutes of Jurisprudence [*A publication*] (DLA)
Mont Law... Montana Lawyer [*A publication*] (DLA)
Mont Laws... Laws of Montana [*A publication*] (DLA)
Mont Leg News... Montreal Legal News [*A publication*] (DLA)
Mont Liens... Montagu on Liens [*A publication*] (DLA)
Mont LR.... Montreal Law Reports, Queen's Bench [*A publication*] (DLA)
Mont LR.... Montreal Law Reports, Superior Court [*A publication*] (DLA)
Mont LRQB... Montreal Law Reports, Queen's Bench [*A publication*] (DLA)
Mont LRSC... Montreal Law Reports, Superior Court [*A publication*] (DLA)
Mont Merc Law... Montefiore's Synopsis of Mercantile Law [*A publication*] (DLA)
montp....... Monotype (VRA)
Montparno... Montparnasse (AD)
Mont Part... Montagu's Digest of the Law of Partnership [*A publication*] (DLA)
MontPas.... Monterey Pasta [*Associated Press*] (SAG)
MONT-PEA... Montana Public Employees Association
Montpellier MAI... Mediterranean Agronomic Institute of Montpellier (SAUO)
Montr........ Montreal [*Canada*] (AD)
MONTR...... Montreal [*Canada*]
Montr........ Montriou's Bengal Reports [*A publication*] (DLA)
Montr........ Montriou's Supplement to Morton's Reports [*A publication*] (DLA)
Montr Cond Rep... Montreal Condensed Reports [*A publication*] (DLA)
Montreal LQB (Can)... Montreal Law Reports, Queen's Bench [*Canada*] [*A publication*] (DLA)
Montreal LRQB... Montreal Law Reports, Queen's Bench [*Canada*] [*A publication*] (DLA)
Montreal LRSC... Montreal Law Reports, Superior Court [*Canada*] [*A publication*] (DLA)
Montreal LSC (Can)... Montreal Law Reports, Superior Court [*Canada*] [*A publication*] (DLA)
Mont Rep... Montriou's Reports, Supreme Court [*1846*] [*Bengal, India*] [*A publication*] (DLA)
Mont Rev Code Ann... Montana Revised Code, Annotated [*A publication*] (DLA)
MONTRG.... Monitoring (AABC)
montrg...... Monitoring (AD)
Montr Leg N... Montreal Legal News [*A publication*] (DLA)
Montr QB... Montreal Law Reports, Queen's Bench [*A publication*] (DLA)
Montr Super... Montreal Law Reports, Superior Court [*A publication*] (DLA)
MontryH..... Monterey Homes Corp. [*Associated Press*] (SAG)
MontryR..... Monterey Resources, Inc. [*Associated Press*] (SAG)
Mont S....... Montreal Star [*A publication*] (AD)
MONTSAME... Mongolyn Tsahilgaan Medeeniy Agentlag [*Press agency*] [*Mongolia*]
Mont SO.... Montagu. Set-Off [*2nd ed.*] [*1828*] [*A publication*] (DLA)
Mont Sp L... Montesquieu's Spirit of Laws [*A publication*] (DLA)
Mont St U... Montana State University (GAGS)
Mont Super... Montreal Law Reports, Superior Court [*A publication*] (DLA)
MONT TER... Montana Territory
Monty....... Montgomery (AD)
Monty....... Montmorency (AD)
MONU....... Montgomery Manufacturing Company [*NCIC trailer make code*]
MONUA..... United Nations Angola Observation Mission (SAUO)
MONUC..... United Nations Organization Mission in the Democratic Republic of the Congo (SAUO)
Mon ULR... Monash University. Law Review [*A publication*]

MONV .... Monticlaire Mobile Homes [*NCIC trailer make code*]
MoNvC ...... Cottey College, Nevada, MO [*Library symbol*] [*Library of Congress*] (LCLS)
MONW .... Montone Manufacturing Company [*NCIC trailer make code*]
Mon Weather Rev... Monthly Weather Review (SAUO)
Mon WJ..... Monthly Western Jurist [*A publication*] (DLA)
MONX .... Monsanto [*Private rail car owner code*]
Mony .... Monastery (AD)
MONY .... Music Operators of New York (AD)
MONY .... Mutual Life Insurance Co. of New York (EFIS)
MONY .... Mutual of New York [*Insurance company*]
MONZ .... Montgomery County [*Federal Railroad Administration identification code*]
MONZ .... Museum of New Zealand (SAUO)
MOO .... Management Operations Officer [*Social Security Administration*]
MOO .... Matter of Opinion [*Internet lingo*] (NETL)
MOO .... Milkbottles Only Organization (EA)
MOO .... Missile Operations Officer [*NASA*] (KSC)
MOO .... Money-Order Office
Moo.......... Moody's English Crown Cases [*168, 169 English Reprint*] [*A publication*] (DLA)
MOO .... Moomba [*Australia*] [*Airport symbol*] [*Obsolete*] (OAG)
MOO .... Moongold Resources [*Vancouver Stock Exchange symbol*]
MOO .... Moorlands [*Tasmania*] [*Seismograph station code, US Geological Survey*] (SEIS)
MOO .... MUD [*Multi-User Dungeon*] Object-Oriented [*Computer science*] (DOM)
MOO .... Multiple-User Dimension Object Oriented [*Computer technology*]
MOO .... School of the Ozarks, Point Lookout, MO [*OCLC symbol*] (OCLC)
Moo A....... Moore's Reports [*Bosanquet and Puller*] [*England*] [*A publication*] (DLA)
Moo & M ... Moody and Malkin's English Nisi Prius Reports [*A publication*] (DLA)
Moo & Mal... Moody and Malkin's English Nisi Prius Reports [*A publication*] (DLA)
Moo & P.... Moore and Payne's English Common Pleas Reports [*A publication*] (DLA)
Moo & Pay... Moore and Payne's English Common Pleas Reports [*A publication*] (DLA)
Moo & R.... Moody and Robinson's English Nisi Prius Reports [*A publication*] (DLA)
Moo & Rob... Moody and Robinson's English Nisi Prius Reports [*A publication*] (DLA)
Moo & S.... Moore and Scott's English Common Pleas Reports [*1831-34*] [*A publication*] (DLA)
Moo & Sc... Moore and Scott's English Common Pleas Reports [*1831-34*] [*A publication*] (DLA)
Moo CC ..... Moody's English Crown Cases Reserved [*1824-44*] [*A publication*] (DLA)
MOO C of S... Management Office, Office, Chief of Staff
Moo CP ..... Moore's English Common Pleas Reports [*A publication*] (DLA)
Moo Cr C ... Moody's English Crown Cases Reserved [*1824-44*] [*A publication*] (DLA)
MOOD .... Moodus Savings Bank [*NASDAQ symbol*] (COMM)
MOOD .... Moody Manufacturing Company [*NCIC trailer make code*]
Mood .... Moody's English Crown Cases Reserved [*1824-44*] [*A publication*] (DLA)
Mood & M... Moody and Malkin's English Nisi Prius Reports [*A publication*] (DLA)
Mood & Malk... Moody and Malkin's English Nisi Prius Reports [*A publication*] (DLA)
Mood & R... Moody and Robinson's English Nisi Prius Reports [*A publication*] (DLA)
Mood & Rob... Moody and Robinson's English Nisi Prius Reports [*A publication*] (DLA)
Mood CC.... Moody's English Crown Cases Reserved [*1824-44*] [*A publication*] (DLA)
MOODS ..... Multimedia Object-Oriented Database Schema [*Computer science*] (HODG)
MOODS ..... Music Object-Oriented Distributed System
Moody....... Moody's English Crown Cases [*168, 169 English Reprint*] [*A publication*] (DLA)
Moody & M... Moody and Malkin's English Nisi Prius Reports [*A publication*] (DLA)
Moody & M (Eng)... Moody and Malkin's English Nisi Prius Reports [*A publication*] (DLA)
Moody & R... Moody and Robinson's English Nisi Prius Reports [*A publication*] (DLA)
Moody & R (Eng)... Moody and Robinson's English Nisi Prius Reports [*A publication*] (DLA)
Moody CC (Eng)... Moody's English Crown Cases [*168, 169 English Reprint*] [*A publication*] (DLA)
Moody Cr C... Moody's English Crown Cases [*168, 169 English Reprint*] [*A publication*] (DLA)
Moody Cr Cas... Moody's English Crown Cases [*168, 169 English Reprint*] [*A publication*] (DLA)
Moog .... Moog, Inc. [*Associated Press*] (SAG)
Moo GC ..... Moore's Gorham Case, English Privy Council [*A publication*] (DLA)
Moo Ind App... Moore's Reports, Privy Council, Indian Appeals [*1836-72*] [*A publication*] (DLA)
MOOJA ...... Moose Jaw, SK [*American Association of Railroads railroad junction routing code*]
MOON .... Management of Optical Networks (SAUO)
MOON .... Meeting Our Operational Needs
Moon .... Moon's Reports [*133-144 Indiana*] [*6-14 Indiana Appeals*] [*A publication*] (DLA)
moop .... Mechlorethamine, Vincristine, Procarbazine, Prednisone [*Medicine*] (AD)
MOOP .... Ministerstvo Okhrany Obshchestvennogo Poryadka [*Ministry for Maintenance of Public Order*] [*Former USSR*] (LAIN)
MOOP .... Missile Out of Order for Parts (MCD)
Moo PC ..... Moore's English Privy Council Cases, Old and New Series [*A publication*] (DLA)
Moo PCC.... Moore's English Privy Council Cases [*A publication*] (DLA)
Moo PC Cas NS... Moore's English Privy Council Cases, New Series [*A publication*] (DLA)
Moo PCC NS... Moore's English Privy Council Cases, New Series [*A publication*] (DLA)
Moo PC (NS)... Moore's English Privy Council Cases, New Series [*A publication*] (DLA)
MOOQ .... Moore Truck Lines [*Common carrier symbol*]
MOOR .... Chadmoore Wireless Group [*OTCBB symbol*]
Moor......... Dartmoor Prison [*Devon, England*] (AD)
Moor......... English King's Bench Reports, by Sir Francis Moore [*1512-1621*] [*A publication*] (DLA)
Moore .... Moore Corp. Ltd. [*Associated Press*] (SAG)
Moore .... Moore's English Common Pleas Reports [*A publication*] (DLA)
Moore .... Moore's English Privy Council Reports [*A publication*] (DLA)
Moore .... Moore's Reports [*Texas*] [*A publication*] (DLA)
Moore .... Moore's Reports [*Alabama*] [*A publication*] (DLA)
Moore .... Moore's Reports [*Arkansas*] [*A publication*] (DLA)
Moore A .... Moore's Reports [*Bosanquet and Puller*] [*England*] [*A publication*] (DLA)
Moore Abs... Moore's Abstracts of Title [*6th ed.*] [*1925*] [*A publication*] (DLA)
Moore & P... Moore and Payne's English Common Pleas Reports [*A publication*] (DLA)
Moore & P (Eng)... Moore and Payne's English Common Pleas Reports [*A publication*] (DLA)
Moore & S... Moore and Scott's English Common Pleas Reports [*1831-34*] [*A publication*] (DLA)
Moore & S (Eng)... Moore and Scott's English Common Pleas Reports [*1831-34*] [*A publication*] (DLA)
Moore & W... Moore and Walker's Reports [*22-24 Texas*] [*A publication*] (DLA)
Moore & Walker... Moore and Walker's Reports [*22-24 Texas*] [*A publication*] (DLA)
Moore CP... Moore's English Common Pleas Reports [*A publication*] (DLA)
Moore Cr Law... Moore's Criminal Law and Procedure [*A publication*] (DLA)
Moore EI.... Moore's East Indian Appeals [*A publication*] (DLA)
Moore Fed Practice... Moore's Federal Practice [*A publication*] (DLA)
Moore GC... Moore's Gorham Case, English Privy Council [*A publication*] (DLA)
MooreHd.... Moore-Handley, Inc. [*Associated Press*] (SAG)
Moore Ind App... Moore's Indian Appeals [*A publication*] (DLA)
Moore Ind App (Eng)... Moore's Indian Appeals [*England*] [*A publication*] (DLA)
Moore Indian App... Moore's Indian Appeals [*England*] [*A publication*] (DLA)
Moore Int L... Moore's Digest of International Law [*A publication*] (DLA)
MooreP ..... Moore Products Corp. [*Associated Press*] (SAG)
Moore PC... Moore's English Privy Council Reports [*A publication*] (DLA)
Moore PCC... Moore's English Privy Council Cases [*A publication*] (DLA)
Moore PCC (Eng)... Moore's English Privy Council Cases [*A publication*] (DLA)
Moore PCC NS... Moore's English Privy Council Cases, New Series [*A publication*] (DLA)
Moore PCC NS (Eng)... Moore's English Privy Council Cases, New Series [*A publication*] (DLA)
Moore PC NS... Moore's English Privy Council Reports, New Series [*A publication*] (DLA)
Moore Presby Dig... Moore's Presbyterian Digest [*A publication*] (DLA)
Moore QB... Moore's English Queen's Bench Reports [*A publication*] (DLA)
Moore's Adj... Moore's International Adjudications [*Legal term*] (AD)
Moore's Arb... Moore's International Arbitrations [*Legal term*] (AD)
Moore's Dig... Moore's Digest [*Legal term*] (AD)
Moorhead St U... Moorhead State University (GAGS)
MOORNG ... Mooring [*Freight*]
MOOS .... Modular Ocean Observation System [*Marine science*] (MSC)
MoOs........ Saint Clair County Library, Osceola, MO [*Library symbol*] [*Library of Congress*] (LCLS)
MOOSE...... Man [*or Manual*] Orbital Operations Safety Equipment [*Space life raft*] [*NASA*]
MOOSE...... Man Out of Space Easiest
MOOSE...... Method for Object-Oriented Software Engineering [*Computer science*] (VLIE)
MOOSE...... Move Out of Saigon Expeditiously [*or Earliest*] [*Army project, Vietnam*]
MOOSEMUSS... Maneuver, Objective, Offensive, Surprise, Economy of Force, Mass, Unity of Command, Simplicity, Security [*Basic principles of war*] [*See also MOSS MOUSE*]
Moo Sep Rep... Moore's Separate Report of Westerton Versus Liddell [*A publication*] (DLA)
MOOSSE.... Manned Orbital Oceanographic Survey System Experiment
moot......... Moved Out of Town (AD)
MOOT .... Move Out of Town [*Reduction of troop concentrations in cities*] [*Military*]
Moot Ct Bull... University of Illinois. Moot Court Bulletin [*A publication*] (DLA)
Moo Tr ...... Moore's Divorce Trials [*A publication*] (DLA)
MOOTW..... Military Operations Other than War (RDA)
MOOV .... Moovies, Inc. [*NASDAQ symbol*] (SAG)
Moovie ...... Moovies, Inc. [*Associated Press*] (SAG)
MOOW ...... Medical Officer of the Watch
MOOZ .... Minnesota Oil Operation [*Federal Railroad Administration identification code*]
MOP .... Machine Operating Processing (ACAE)
MOP .... Magnetized Orange Pipe [*Minesweeping device*] [*Navy*]
MOP .... Maintenance of Property
MOP .... Maintenance Operating Procedure (MCD)

MOP .... Maintenance Operations Protocol (ACRL)
MOP .... Maintenance Outline Procedure [*Nuclear energy*] (NRCH)
MOP .... Major Organ Profile [*Medicine*] (DMAA)
MOP .... Major Overhaul Program [*Navy*]
MOP .... Make or Purchase [*Engineering design*]
MOP .... Management Oversight Practices (SAUO)
MOP .... Management Overview Program (SAUO)
MOP .... Manned Orbital Platform
MOP .... Manner of Performance [*Officer rating*]
MOP .... Manual of Operations (HVTR)
MOP .... Manual of Practice (GNE)
MOP .... Manual Operations Panel
MOP .... Manual Override Panel (AAG)
MOP .... Manufacturers Output Policy [*Insurance*]
MOP .... Manufacturing Order Processing [*Computer science*] (HODG)
MOP .... Manuscript on Paper
MOP .... Margin of Profit [*Accounting*]
MOP .... Master Operating Panel (CAAL)
MOP .... Matrix Operations Programming
MOP .... Maximal Onset Principle [*Linguistics*] (IEL)
MOP .... Measures of Performance (MCD)
mop .... Medical Outpatient (AD)
MOP .... Medical Outpatient
MoP .... Meeting of the Parties to the Kyoto Protocol (SAUO)
M o P ...... Member of Parliament [*British*] (AD)
MOP .... Member of Parliament [*British*]
MOP .... Memorandum of Participation (ARMP)
MOP .... Memorandum of Policy
MOP .... Memory Organization Packet [*Artificial intelligence*]
MOP .... Message Output Processing
MOP .... Meta Object Protocol (SAUS)
MOP .... Meteorological Operational Programme (SAUO)
MOP .... Methallyloxyphenol
MOP .... Method of Procedure [*Telecommunications*] (ITD)
MOP .... Methoxypsoralen [*Also, MP*] [*Pharmacology*]
MOP .... Migrant Opportunity Program [*Department of Labor*]
MOP .... Military Operation (GFGA)
MOP .... Minimum Ordered Partition
MOP .... Ministerio de Obras Publicas [*Ministry of Public Works*] [*Spanish*] (AD)
M o P ...... Minister of Pensions [*British*] (AD)
M o P ...... Minister of Power [*British*] (AD)
M o P ...... Minister of Production [*British*] (AD)
MOP .... Ministry of Pensions [*British*]
MOP .... Ministry of Pensions and Social Insurance (SAUO)
MOP .... Ministry of Power [*British*]
MOP .... Ministry of Production [*British*]
MOP .... Minute of Program [*Broadcasting*] (NTCM)
MOP .... Mission Operations Plan (MCD)
MOP .... Mobile Offshore Production (SAUS)
MOP .... Mobility Operating Procedure [*Military*] (AFM)
MOP .... Model Office Project
MOP .... Model Operational Plan
MOP .... Mode of Operation
MOP .... Modify Operating Procedures (AAEL)
MOP .... Modular Operating Procedure (MUGU)
MOP .... Modulation on the Pulse (NG)
MOP .... Monarch Peak [*California*] [*Seismograph station code, US Geological Survey*] (SEIS)
MOP .... Monthly Obligation Plan (SAUO)
mop .... Mother of Pearl (AD)
MOP .... Mother-of-Pearl
MOP .... Mount Pleasant, MI [*Location identifier*] [*FAA*] (FAAL)
MOP .... Mouvement d'Organisation du Pays [*Haiti*] [*Political party*] (EY)
MOP .... Mouvement Ouvriers-Paysans [*Workers' and Peasants' Movement*] [*Haiti*] (PD)
MOP .... Mouvement pour l'Ordre et la Paix [*Movement for Order and Peace*] [*New Caledonia*] [*Political party*] (PD)
MOP .... Multiple Online Processing (NITA)
MOP .... Multiple Online Programming [*Computer science*] (DIT)
MOP .... Multiple Oocytes per Disk [*Medicine*] (MELL)
MOP .... Multiple Output Program (MCD)
MOP .... Muriate of Potash [*Fertilizer*]
MOP .... Mustard, Onions, Pickles [*Restaurant slang*]
MOP .... Mustargen [*Nitrogen mustard*], Oncovin , Prednisone [*Vincristine*] [*Antineoplastic drug regimen*]
mop .... Mustering-Out Pay (AD)
MOP .... Mustering-Out Pay [*Military*]
MOP .... Myositis Ossificans Progressiva [*Medicine*] (MELL)
MOP .... , Procarbazine [*Vincristine*] [*Antineoplastic drug regimen*]
MOP .... St. Louis College of Pharmacy, St. Louis, MO [*OCLC symbol*] (OCLC)
MOPA .... Mail Order Publisher Authority (PDAA)
mopa .... Master Oscilator Power Amplifier (AD)
MOPA .... Master Oscillator Power Amplifier [*Radio*]
MOPA .... Method of Physical Action [*Acting technique*] (WDAA)
MOPA .... Methoxyphenylacetic Acid [*Herbicide*]
MOPA .... Methoxypropylamine [*Organic chemistry*]
MOPA .... Modus Operandi - Personal Appearance [*FBI computer procedure*]
MOPA .... Museum of Photographic Arts [*San Diego*] (AD)
MOPAC ...... Methoxyhydroxyphenylacetic Acid [*Organic chemistry*]
MOPAC ...... Missouri Pacific Railroad Co.
Mo-Pac ..... Missouri-Pacific Railroad Company (SAUO)
MoPac ...... Missouri Pacific - Texas & Pacific (AD)
MOPAC ...... Mixed Oligonucleotide Primed Amplification of cDNA [*Biochemistry*]
MOPAC ...... MOPAC [*Bloomfield Hills, MI*] (PACS)
MoPacRR .... Missouri-Pacific Railroad Company (SAUO)
MOPALI ..... Movimiento Paraguayo de Liberacion [*Political party*] (EY)
MOPAR ...... Management of Post Attack Resources (ACAE)
MOPAR ...... Master Oscillator Power Amplifier RADAR
mopar ...... Master Oscillator-Power Amplifier RADAR (AD)
MOPAR ...... Motor Parts [*Chrysler Corp.*]
MoParkC .... Park College, Parkville, MO [*Library symbol*] [*Library of Congress*] (LCLS)
mopb .... Manually Operated Plotting Board (AD)
MOPB .... Manually Operated Plotting Board
MOPB .... Metallo-Organic Petroleum-Based Coating [*Materials science*]
MOP-BAP .... Mustargen [*Nitrogen mustard*], Oncovin , Procarbazine, Bleomycin, Adriamycin, Prednisone [*Vincristine*] [*Antineoplastic drug regimen*]
Mo PC ...... Moore's English Privy Council Reports [*A publication*] (DLA)
MOPC .... Mouse Plasmocytoma [*Cell line*]
MOPCOM ..... Matrix Operations Programming Combination of Estimates
MOPD .... Maximum Operating Pressure Differential (ECII)
MOPE .... Method of Personnel Evaluation
MOPE .... Multiple Object Parameter Estimation
MOPED ...... Ministry of Planning and Economic Development [*Ethiopia*] (ECON)
MOPED ...... Motor/Pedal [*Motorized bicycle*]
mopeds ..... Motorized Pedals (AD)
MOPEG ...... (Methoxyhydroxyphenyl)ethyleneglycol [*Also, MHPG*] [*Organic chemistry*]
MoPeS ...... Saint Mary's Seminary, Perryville, MO [*Library symbol*] [*Library of Congress*] (LCLS)
MOPET ...... Methoxyhydroxyphenylethanol [*Organic chemistry*]
mopf .... Missile Onloading Prism Fixture (AD)
MOPF .... Missile Onloading Prism Fixture
MOPF .... Mobile Optical Propagation Facility
MOPFAC ..... Market Opened Firmer, but Fell At Close [*Telegraphy*] (PCTE)
MOPH .... Military Order of the Purple Heart of the United States of America (EA)
MOPH .... Ministry of Public Health (SAUO)
MOPI .... Maximum Rate Output Initiator (NASA)
MOPIC ...... Motion Picture [*Army*] (AABC)
mopic ...... Motion Picture [*Military*] (WDMC)
MOPIMS ..... Mathematical, Optical, and Philosophical Instrument Makers' Society [*A union*] [*British*]
MOPITT ..... Measurement of Pollution in the Troposphere
MOPITT ..... Measurements of Pollution in the Troposphere
MOPIX ...... Motion Pictures
MoPL .... Map oriented Programming Language (SAUO)
MOPLN ...... Mission Orbit Planning (ACAE)
MoPIS ...... School of the Ozarks, Point Lookout, MO [*Library symbol*] [*Library of Congress*] (LCLS)
MOPMS ...... Modular Pack Mine System (RDA)
MOPN .... Methoxypropionitrile [*Organic chemistry*]
MoPobT ..... Three Rivers Community College, Poplar Bluff, MO [*Library symbol*] [*Library of Congress*] (LCLS)
MoPobV ..... United States Veterans Administration Hospital, Medical Library, Poplar Bluff, MO [*Library symbol*] [*Library of Congress*] (LCLS)
MOPOCO ..... Movimiento Popular Colorado [*Colorado Popular Movement*] [*Paraguay*] [*Political party*] (PD)
MOPP .... Material Operations and Parts Procurement (ACAE)
MOPP .... Mechlorethamine, Oncovin, Procarbazine, Prednisone [*Medicine*] (MEDA)
MOPP .... Methotrexate, Oncomycin, Prednisone, Procarbazine [*Antineoplastic drug regimen*] (DAVI)
MOPP .... Military Operational Protective Posture [*Chemical warfare*] (RDA)
MOPP .... Military-Oriented Protective Posture
MOPP .... Mission Objective Protective Posture (SAUO)
MOPP .... Mission-Oriented Protection Posture [*Army*] (AABC)
MOPP .... Mission Oriented Protective Posture [*Chemical warfare*]
MOPP .... Modular Operating Procedure (MUGU)
MOPP .... Mustargen hydrochloride, Oncovin [*Vincristine*], Procarbazine, Prednisone [*Antineoplastic drug regimen*]
MOPP .... Mustargen [*Nitrogen mustard*], Oncovin , Procarbazine, Prednisone [*Vincristine*] [*Antineoplastic drug regimen*]
MOPP .... Mustine, Oncovin [*Vincristine*] Procarbazine, Prednisone [*Antineoplastic drug regimen*] (DAVI)
MOPP .... nitrogen Mustard, Oncovin, Prednisone, Procarbazine (SAUS)
MOPP/ABV ... Mustargen [*Nitrogen mustard*], Oncovin , Procarbazine, Prednisone, Adriamycin, Bleomycin, Vinblastine [*Vincristine*] [*Antineoplastic drug regimen*]
MOPP/ABVD ... Mechlorethamine, Oncovin [*Vincristine*] Procarbazine, Prednisone, Doxo rubicin, Bleomycin, Vinblastine, Dacarbazine [*Antineoplastic drug regimen*] (DAVI)
MOPP-BLEO ... Mustargen [*Nitrogen mustard*], Oncovin , Procarbazine, Prednisone, Bleomycin [*Vincristine*] [*Antineoplastic drug regimen*]
MOPPCPF ... Mustargen [*Nitrogen mustard*], Oncovin , Procarbazine, Prednisone (for Patients with Compromised Pulmonary Function) [*Vincristine*] [*Antineoplastic drug regimen*]
MOPPE ...... Modified Operational Propulsion Plan Examination [*Navy*] (NVT)
MOPPHDB ... Mustargen [*Nitrogen mustard*], Oncovin , Procarbazine, Prednisone, High-Dose Bleomycin [*Vincristine*] [*Antineoplastic drug regimen*]
MOPPLDB ... Mustargen [*Nitrogen mustard*], Oncovin , Procarbazine, Prednisone, Low-DoseBleomycin [*Vincristine*] [*Antineoplastic drug regimen*]
MOPP-LO BLEO ... Mechlorethamine [*Vincristine*] Procarbazine, Prednisone, Bleomycin [*Antineoplastic drug regimen*] (DAVI)
MOPPS ...... Mixing Operations in Pulp and Paper Systems
MOPPS ...... Modelling and Prototyping of a Clinical Support System (SAUO)

MOPPS...... Multiple Opportunistic Pathogens Prophylaxis [*Medicine*] (HVTR)
mopr......... Manner of Performance Rating (AD)
MOPR....... Manner of Performing Rating
MOPR....... Mission Operations Planning Review [*NASA*] (NASA)
MOPR....... Mission Operations Planning Room (MCD)
mopr......... Mop Rack (AD)
MOPR....... Mop Rack
MOPr........ Mustargen [*Nitrogen mustard*], Oncovin , Procarbazine [*Vincristine*] [*Antineoplastic drug regimen*]
MOPr........ , Prednisone [*Vincristine*] [*Antineoplastic drug regimen*]
Mo Prec..... Moile's Precedents [*A publication*] (DLA)
moprl......... Mother-of-Pearl (VRA)
MoPrP....... Mouse Prion Protein
MOPS....... Mail-Order Protection Scheme [*British*]
MOPS....... Maneuver Operations Program System [*NASA*]
MOPS....... Man-Operated Propulsion System
MOPS....... Marine Oil Pickup Service [*Marine science*] (MSC)
MOPS....... Maritime Officer Production Study [*Canadian Navy*]
MOPS....... Measures of Performance System
MOPS....... Mechanization Outside Plant Scheduling System (MHDB)
MOPS....... Mechanized Outdoor Planning System
MOPS....... Merchandise Ordering Processing System (AD)
MOPS....... Message Output Processing System (SAUO)
MOPS....... Microwave Optical-Photoselection Microscopy
MOPS....... Military Operation Phone System
MOPS....... Million Operations per Second [*Processing power units*] [*Computer science*]
MOPS....... Minimum Operational Performance Standard [*Aviation*] (DA)
MOPS....... Missile Operations
MOPS....... Missile Operations Paging [*or Phone*] System [*NASA*]
MOPS....... Missile Operations System (AD)
MOPS....... Mission Operations Planning System [*NASA*] (KSC)
MOPS....... Morpholinopropanesulfonic Acid [*A buffer*]
MOPS....... Mothers of Preschoolers International (PAZ)
MOPS....... Multispectral Opium Poppy Sensor System
MO PSC..... Missouri Public Service Commission Reports [*A publication*] (DLA)
MO PSC (NS)... Missouri Public Service Commission Reports (New Series) [*A publication*] (DLA)
MO PSCR... Missouri Public Service Commission Reports [*A publication*] (DLA)
MOPSS...... Management & Operation of Public Services Section [*Reference and User Services Association*] [*American Library Association*]
MOPSS...... Multispectral Opium Poppy Sensor System (AD)
MOPSY...... Multi-Programming Operating System [*Computer science*] (PDAA)
MOpt........ Master of Optometry (GAGS)
MOPT........ Mean One Way Propagation Time [*Telecommunications*] (TEL)
MOPTAR.... Multiobject Phase Tracking and Ranging [*FAA*]
MOPTARS... Multi-Object Phase-Tracking and Ranging System [*FAA*] (PDAA)
MOPTE...... Measure of Potential Training Effectiveness [*Army*]
MOptom..... Master of Optometry (ADA)
MOPTS...... Mobile Photographic Tracking Station (IEEE)
MO PUR.... Missouri Public Utility Reports [*A publication*] (DLA)
MOPV....... Monovalent Oral Polio Vaccine [*Immunology*]
MOPW....... Ministry of Population Welfare [*Pakistan*] (ECON)
MOQ......... Fort Stewart (Hinesville), GA [*Location identifier*] [*FAA*] (FAAL)
MOQ......... Lindenwood College, St. Charles, MO [*OCLC symbol*] (OCLC)
MOQ......... Married Officer Quarters
MOQ......... Minimum Order Quantity (MCD)
MOQ......... Morocco Explorations [*Vancouver Stock Exchange symbol*]
MOQ......... Morondava [*Madagascar*] [*Airport symbol*] (OAG)
MOQU....... AP Moller [*Intermodal shipping container symbol*] (TVRC)
MOR......... AS Morefly [*Norway*] [*ICAO designator*] (FAAC)
MOR......... Magneto-Optical Rotation
MOR......... Main Operating Room (MELL)
MOR......... Management Operating Ratios (NG)
MOR......... Mandatory Occurrence Reporting
MOR......... Manually Operated Rifle (GOBB)
MOR......... Manufacturing Operation Record (NASA)
MOR......... Marital Opportunity Ratio (DIPS)
MOR......... Market Opinion Research, Inc. [*Information service or system*] (IID)
MOR......... Mars Orbital Rendezvous
MOR......... Master of Operations Research (PGP)
M Or......... Master of Oratory
MOR......... Maximum Ozone Reactivity [*Exhaust emissions*] [*Automotive engineering*]
MOR......... Medical Officer Report [*Navy*] (NG)
MOR......... Memorandum of Record (COE)
MOR......... Memory Output Register [*Computer science*]
MOR......... Merchandising and Operating Results
MOR......... Meteorological Optical Range (PDAA)
mor.......... Middle of the Road (AD)
MOR......... Middle of the Road [*Broadcasting*]
MOR......... Mid-Oceanic Ridge
MOR......... Military Operational Requirement (SAUO)
MOR......... Military Operations Research
M o R....... Ministry of Reconstruction [*British*] (AD)
MOR......... Missile Operationally Ready [*Air Force*]
MOR......... Mission Operations Room (MCD)
MOR......... Missions Operations Report [*NASA*] (KSC)
MO R........ Missouri Reports [*A publication*] (DLA)
MOR......... Modulus of Rupture [*Mechanics*]
MOR......... Monthly Operating Report (IEEE)
MOR......... Monthly Operating Review (USDC)
Mor.......... Moral (DIAR)
MOR......... Moral (ROG)
Mor.......... Moralia [*of Plutarch*] [*Classical studies*] (OCD)
MOR......... Moravian College, Bethlehem, PA [*OCLC symbol*] (OCLC)
MOR......... Moray [*County in Scotland*] (ROG)
MOR......... Mordenite [*A zeolite*]
Mor.......... Morelia (AD)
Mor.......... Morelos (AD)
MOR......... Morendo [*Gradually Softer*] [*Music*]
mor.......... Morendo [*Dying Away*] [*Italian*] (AD)
MOR......... Morgan Keegan & Co., Inc. [*NYSE symbol*] (SPSG)
MOR......... Morgan Keegan Inc. [*NYSE symbol*] (TTSB)
MOR......... Morgan Owners Register (EA)
MOR......... Mori [*Japan*] [*Seismograph station code, US Geological Survey*] [*Closed*] (SEIS)
Mor.......... Morisco (AD)
Mor.......... Morison's Dictionary of Decisions, Scotch Court of Session [*1540-1808*] [*A publication*] (DLA)
MOR......... Morning Star Resources [*Vancouver Stock Exchange symbol*]
Mor.......... Moroccan (AD)
mor.......... Morocco (AD)
Mor.......... Morocco (SHCU)
MOR......... Morocco
MOR......... Morocco Leather [*Bookbinding*] (ROG)
MOR......... Morphine [*A narcotic*]
MOR......... Morpholine [*Organic chemistry*]
MOR......... Morphology (MELL)
Mor.......... Morris' Reports [*Jamaica*] [*A publication*] (ILCA)
MOR......... Morristown, TN [*Location identifier*] [*FAA*] (FAAL)
MOR......... Mortality Odds Ratio
mor.......... Mortar (AD)
MOR......... Mortar
MOR......... Movimiento Obrero Revolucionario Salvado Cayetano Carpio [*El Salvador*] [*Political party*] (EY)
MOR......... Museum of the Rockies [*Montana, USA*]
MORA....... Mandibular Orthopedic Repositioning Appliance [*Dentistry*]
MORA....... Mimimum Off-Route Altitude [*Aviation*] (DA)
MORA....... Mount Rainier National Park
MORAB...... Morgan and Arabian [*Type of horse developed from these two breeds*] [*Acronym is also said to stand for "Muscular, Outstanding, Refined, Athletic, Beautiful," the horse's distinguishing characteristics*]
MORAL...... Massachusetts Organization for the Repeal of Abortion Laws
MORAN..... Management of Resources, Accesses & Network (SAUO)
Mor & Carl... Moreau-Lislet and Carleton's Laws of Las Siete Partidas in Force in Louisiana [*A publication*] (DLA)
MoRAP...... Missouri Resource Assessment Partnership (SAUO)
MORASS.... Modern Ramjet System Synthesis (MCD)
Morav....... Moravia (AD)
MORB....... Mid-Ocean Ridge Basalt [*Geology*]
Morb......... Morbihan (AD)
MORBREPT... Morbidity Report
MORBTGREPT... Morbidity Telegraphic Report
MORC....... Medical Officers' Reserve Corps
MORC....... Midget Ocean Racing Class [*or Club*]
MORC....... Monroe Contractors Equipment [*Common carrier symbol*]
Mor Chy Acts... Morgan's Chancery Acts and Orders [*6th ed.*] [*1885*] [*A publication*] (DLA)
MORCO..... Morrison, Inc. (EFIS)
Mor Comp... Morris on Compensations [*A publication*] (DLA)
Mor Corp... Morawetz on Private Corporations [*A publication*] (DLA)
MORCOS..... Mortar Computer System (SAUS)
MORCY...... Morehead City, NC [*American Association of Railroads railroad junction routing code*]
MORD....... Magneto-Optic Rotary Dispersion (PDAA)
MORD....... Medical Operations Requirements Document (MCD)
MORD....... Military Operations Research Department
MORD....... Ministry of Revolutionary Development [*Vietnam*]
MORD....... Mission Operations Requirements Document [*NASA*] (NASA)
Mord......... Mordehai (AD)
Mordhy...... Mordehai (AD)
Mor Dic..... Morison's Dictionary of Decisions, Scotch Court of Session [*1540-1808*] [*A publication*] (DLA)
mor dict..... More Dicto [*As Directed*] [*Latin*] (AD)
Mor Dict.... Morison's Dictionary of Decisions, Scotch Court of Session [*1540-1808*] [*A publication*] (DLA)
MOR DICT... Moro Dicto [*As Directed*] [*Pharmacy*]
Mor Dig.... Morley's Digest of the Indian Reports [*A publication*] (DLA)
Mor Dig.... Morrison's New Hampshire Digest [*A publication*] (DLA)
Mor Dil..... Morris on Dilapidations [*2nd ed.*] [*1871*] [*A publication*] (DLA)
MORDS..... Manned Orbital Research and Development System
MORDT...... Mobilization Operational Readiness Deployment Test [*DoD*]
Mordy....... Mordechai (AD)
MORE....... Management of Radiographic Environments [*Radiology*] (DAVI)
MORE....... Meal, Ordered Ready-to-Eat [*Army*] (RDA)
MORE....... Microbial Oil Recovery Enhancement [*Petroleum technology*]
MORE....... Mid-Atlantic Off-Road Enthusiasts (EARSL)
MORE....... Midwest Organization for Research in Education (AEBS)
MORE....... Military Officer Record Examination
MORE....... Minority Officer Recruitment Effort
MORE....... Minority Outreach Research and Education (SAUO)
MORE....... Mission for Outreach, Renewal, and Evangelism (AD)
MORE....... Money, Opportunity, Responsibility, and Equality [*Of organization "MORE for Women"*]
MORE....... Moretti [*NCIC car make code*]
MORE....... Multioptical Reconnaissance Equipment [*Military*] (CAAL)

Mor E & RD Law... Morice's English and Roman Dutch Law [*A publication*] (DLA)
Mor Eas..... Morris on the Law of Easements [*A publication*] (DLA)
Moreau & Carleton's Partidas... Moreau-Lislet and Carleton's Laws of Las Siete Partidas in Force in Louisiana [*A publication*] (DLA)
MORE DICT... More Dicto [*As Directed*] [*Pharmacy*] (ROG)
Morehead St U... Morehead State University (GAGS)
Morehouse Sch of Med... Morehouse School of Medicine (GAGS)
MOREL...... Michigan-Ohio Regional Educational Laboratory
More Lect... More's Lectures on the Law of Scotland [*A publication*] (DLA)
MORENA.... Mouvement de Redressement National [*Gabon*] [*Political party*] (EY)
MORENA.... Movimiento de Renovacion Nacional [*National Renewal Movement*] [*Venezuela*] [*Political party*] (PPW)
MORENA.... Movimiento de Restauracion Nacional [*National Restoration Movement*] [*Colombia*] [*Political party*] (EY)
MORENA.... National Renovation Movement (Panama) [*Political party*] (PSAP)
MORENA-B... Movement for National Regeneration-Woodcutters (Gabon) [*Political party*] (PSAP)
MORENET... Missouri Research and Education Network
MO Rep..... Missouri Reports [*A publication*] (DLA)
MOREP...... Monthly Report
moreps...... Monitor Station Reports (AD)
MOREPS.... Monitor Station Reports
MORES...... Minerals, Oils, and Resources Shares Fund [*British*]
MORE SOL... More Solito [*In the Usual Way*] [*Pharmacy*] (ROG)
MOREST.... Mobile Arresting Gear [*Navy*]
More St..... More's Notes on Stair's Institutes of Scotland [*A publication*] (DLA)
MORET...... Moreton [*England*]
MO Rev Stat... Missouri Revised Statutes [*A publication*] (DLA)
Morey Out Rom Law... Morey's Outlines of Roman Law [*A publication*] (DLA)
MORF....... Male or Female (NHD)
MorF......... Male or Female
MORF....... Manned Orbital Research Facility [*NASA*] (MCD)
MORF....... Midget Ocean Racing Fleet [*Nautical term*] (NTA)
MORF....... Mor-Flo Industries (EFIS)
mor fib...... Moral Fiber (AD)
MORFLOT... Ministry of the Merchant Marine of the Soviet Union (SAUO)
MORG....... Morgan [*NCIC car make code*]
MORG....... Morgan Financial Corp. [*NASDAQ symbol*] (SAG)
MORG....... Morgan Finl (Del) [*NASDAQ symbol*] (TTSB)
Morg......... Morgan's Chancery Acts and Orders [*6th ed.*] [*1885*] [*A publication*] (DLA)
MORG....... Movements Reports Generator (DNAB)
MORG....... Museo Oceanografico de Rio Grande [*Oceanographic Museum of Rio Grande*] [*Brazil*] (AD)
MORGA..... Municipal Organization Act (DICI)
Morgan...... Morgan [*J. P.*] & Co., Inc. [*Associated Press*] (SAG)
Morgan...... Morgan's Digest [*Ceylon*] [*A publication*] (DLA)
Morg & Ch Jud Acts... Morgan and Chute on the Judicature Acts [*A publication*] (DLA)
Morg & WLJ... Morgan and Williams' Law Journal [*London*] [*A publication*] (DLA)
Morgan LM... Morgan's Legal Miscellany [*Ceylon*] [*A publication*] (DLA)
MORGANPAC... J P Morgan Chase & Company Federal PAC [*New York, NY*] (PACS)
Morgan St U... Morgan State University (GAGS)
Morg Ch.... Morgan's Chancery Acts and Orders [*6th ed.*] [*1885*] [*A publication*] (DLA)
MorgFn...... Morgan Financial Corp. [*Associated Press*] (SAG)
MorgFun.... Morgan Funshares, Inc. [*Associated Press*] (SAG)
MorgGr...... Morgan Grenfell Smallcap Fund, Inc. [*Associated Press*] (SAG)
MorgK....... Morgan Keegan [*Associated Press*] (SAG)
MorgKeg.... Morgan Keegan & Co., Inc. [*Associated Press*] (SAG)
Morg Lit.... Morgan on the Law of Literature [*A publication*] (DLA)
morg mar... Morganatic Marriage (AD)
Morgn....... Morgan [*J. P.*] & Co., Inc. [*Associated Press*] (SAG)
MorgnF..... Morgan's Foods, Inc. [*Associated Press*] (SAG)
MorgnP..... Morgan Products Ltd. [*Associated Press*] (SAG)
MorgSt...... Morgan Stanley Group, Inc. [*Associated Press*] (SAG)
Morg Tar.... Morgan on the United States Tariff [*A publication*] (DLA)
Mor Hors... Morrell on the Law of Horses [*A publication*] (DLA)
MORI........ F. Maros Research Institute for Food Crops (SAUO)
Mori......... Market and Opinion Research International [*Polling organization*] (ODBW)
MORI........ Market and Opinion Research International [*Polling organization*]
MORI........ Morris Brothers [*NCIC trailer make code*]
Mor IA....... Morris' Iowa Reports [*1839-46*] [*A publication*] (DLA)
MORIE....... Metalorganic Reactive Ion Etching (AAEL)
MORIF....... Microprogram Optimization Technique Considering Resource Occupancy and Instruction Formats (MHDB)
MoRih....... Richmond Heights Memorial Library, Richmond Heights, MO [*Library symbol*] [*Library of Congress*] (LCLS)
moritzer..... Mortar Howitzer (AD)
MORITZER... Mortar Howitzer (NATG)
MorKnd..... Morrison-Knudsen Co., Inc. [*Associated Press*] (SAG)
MORL....... Manned Orbital [*or Orbiting*] Research Laboratory [*NASA*]
MORL....... Medium-Sized Orbital Research Laboratory (SAA)
Morl Dig.... Morley's East Indian Digest [*A publication*] (DLA)
Mor Lib..... Morgan Library (AD)
Mor M....... Master Mortician
MORM....... Morgan Mobile [*NCIC trailer make code*]
Morm........ Mormon (AD)
MORM....... Mormon (WDAA)
MoRM....... University of Missouri at Rolla, Rolla, MO [*Library symbol*] [*Library of Congress*] (LCLS)
Mor Maj.... Moral Majority (AD)
Mor Min Rep... Morrison's Mining Reports [*A publication*] (DLA)
Mor Miss... Morris' Reports [*Mississippi*] [*A publication*] (DLA)
MORN....... Morgan Trailer Manufacturing Company [*NCIC trailer make code*]
morn......... Morning (AD)
MORN....... Morning
MornGp..... Morningstar Group [*Associated Press*] (SAG)
Morningside C... Morningside College (GAGS)
Moro......... Book of Moroni (AD)
MORO....... Moon Orbiting Observatory (SAUS)
Moro......... Morocco (VRA)
MORO....... Morocco Leather [*Bookbinding*] (ROG)
Moroc........ Moroccan (AD)
MOROCLANT... Maritime Forces Morocco (SAUO)
MORP....... Medical and Occupational Radiation Program [*HEW*]
MORP....... Meteorite Observation and Recovery Project [*Canada*]
MORP....... Mid-Ocean Ridge Peridotite [*Geology*]
MORP....... Moore Products [*NASDAQ symbol*] (TTSB)
MORP....... Moore Products Co. [*NASDAQ symbol*] (NQ)
MORPAC.... Mortgage Bankers Association of America PAC [*Washington, DC*] (PACS)
morph....... Morphine (AD)
MORPH...... Morphine (WDAA)
morph....... Morphology (AD)
MORPH..... Morphology
Morphing... Metamorphosizing [*Video technology*]
MORPHOL... Morphology
morphophysio... Morphophysiological (AD)
MORPHS.... Minicomputer-Operated Retrieval (Partially Heuristic) System [*Computer science*]
Mor Pr...... Morehead's Practice [*A publication*] (DLA)
Mor Priv Corp... Morawetz on Private Corporations [*A publication*] (DLA)
MORPS...... Maritime Other Ranks Production Study [*Canadian Navy*]
MorR........ Bibliotheque Generale et Archives, Rabat, Morocco [*Library symbol*] [*Library of Congress*] (LCLS)
Morr......... Morrell's English Bankruptcy Reports [*A publication*] (DLA)
MORR....... Morrell Transfer [*Common carrier symbol*]
MORR....... Morris [*NCIC car make code*]
Morr......... Morris' Iowa Reports [*1839-46*] [*A publication*] (DLA)
Morr......... Morris' Jamaica Reports [*A publication*] (DLA)
Morr......... Morris' Reports [*Bombay, India*] [*A publication*] (DLA)
Morr......... Morris' Reports [*Oregon*] [*A publication*] (DLA)
Morr......... Morris' Reports [*California*] [*A publication*] (DLA)
MORR....... Morristown National Historical Park
Morr Bankr Cas... Morrell's English Bankruptcy Cases [*A publication*] (DLA)
Morr BC..... Morrell's English Bankruptcy Reports [*A publication*] (DLA)
Morr Bomb... Morris' Reports [*Bombay, India*] [*A publication*] (DLA)
Morr Cal.... Morris' Reports [*California*] [*A publication*] (DLA)
Morr Dict... Morrison's Dictionary of Decisions, Scotch Court of Session [*A publication*] (DLA)
Morr Dig.... Morrison's Digest of Mining Decisions [*A publication*] (DLA)
Morr Dig.... Morrison's New Hampshire Digest [*A publication*] (DLA)
Morrell Bankr Cas... Morrell's English Bankruptcy Cases [*A publication*] (DLA)
Morrell BC... Morrell's English Bankruptcy Cases [*A publication*] (DLA)
Morrell (Eng)... Morrell's English Bankruptcy Cases [*A publication*] (DLA)
Mor Rep.... Morris' Law of Replevin [*A publication*] (DLA)
Morris....... Morris' Iowa Reports [*1839-46*] [*A publication*] (DLA)
Morris....... Morris' Jamaica Reports [*A publication*] (DLA)
Morris....... Morris' Reports [*California*] [*A publication*] (DLA)
Morris....... Morris' Reports [*Oregon*] [*A publication*] (DLA)
Morris....... Morris' Reports [*Bombay, India*] [*A publication*] (DLA)
Morris....... Morris' Reports [*Mississippi*] [*A publication*] (DLA)
Morris....... Morrissett's Reports [*80, 98 Alabama*] [*A publication*] (DLA)
Morris & Har... Morris and Harrington's Reports [*Bombay, India*] [*A publication*] (DLA)
Morris (IA)... Morris' Iowa Reports [*1839-46*] [*A publication*] (DLA)
Morris (Iowa)... Morris' Iowa Reports [*1839-46*] [*A publication*] (DLA)
Morrison.... Morrison Restaurants, Inc. [*Associated Press*] (SAG)
Morrison Min Rep... Morrison's Mining Reports [*United States*] [*A publication*] (DLA)
Morris R.... Morris' Jamaica Reports [*A publication*] (DLA)
Morris Repl... Morris on Replevin [*A publication*] (DLA)
Morris St Cas... Morris' Mississippi State Cases [*1818-72*] [*A publication*] (DLA)
Morr Jam... Morris' Jamaica Reports [*A publication*] (DLA)
MorrKn...... Morrison Knudsen Corp. [*Associated Press*] (SAG)
MorrKnud... Morrison Knudsen Corp. [*Associated Press*] (SAG)
Morr Mines... Morrison's Digest of Mining Decisions [*A publication*] (DLA)
Morr Min R... Morrison's Mining Reports [*United States*] [*A publication*] (DLA)
Morr Min Rep... Morrison's Mining Reports [*A publication*] (DLA)
Morr Miss... Morris' Reports [*Mississippi*] [*A publication*] (DLA)
Morr MR.... Morrison's Mining Reports [*United States*] [*A publication*] (DLA)
MorrowSn... Morrow Snowboards, Inc. [*Associated Press*] (SAG)
Morr Repl... Morris' Law of Replevin [*A publication*] (DLA)
Morr St Cas... Morris' Mississippi State Cases [*1818-72*] [*A publication*] (DLA)
Morr Trans... Morrison's Transcript of United States Supreme Court Decisions [*A publication*] (DLA)
Mor Ry Com... Morris on Railway Compensations [*A publication*] (DLA)
MORS....... Group of Experts Monitoring of Radioactive Substances in the Baltic Sea (SAUO)
MORS....... Midland Operational Research Society (AD)
MORS....... Military Operations Research Society (EA)
MORS....... Military Operations Research Symposia (MCD)
MORS....... Military Operations Research Symposium (SAUO)
MORS....... Minefield & Ordnance Recovery Management System (SAUS)
MORS....... Morse Horse Trailer [*NCIC trailer make code*]

MORS .... Multi-Outlet Reservoir Study [*Department of the Interior*] (GRD)
MORSA...... Movement Requirements for Staff Planning and Special Studies Applications (SAUO)
mor sal ..... More Solito [*In the Usual Manner*] [*Latin*] (AD)
M Or Sc..... Master of the Science of Oratory
MORSEAFRON... Moroccan Sea Frontier [*Navy*] [*World War II*]
Morse Arb... Morse on the Law of Arbitration and Award [*A publication*] (DLA)
Morse Banks... Morse on the Law of Banks and Banking [*A publication*] (DLA)
Morse Bk ... Morse on the Law of Banks and Banking [*A publication*] (DLA)
Morse Exch Rep... Morse's Exchequer Reports [*Canada*] [*A publication*] (DLA)
MorSEm..... Morgan Stanley Emerging Markets [*Associated Press*] (SAG)
Morse Tr.... Morse's Famous Trials [*A publication*] (DLA)
MORSL...... Mobilization Reserve Stockage List [*Army*] (AABC)
MorsnFr..... Morrison Fresh Cooking, Inc. [*Associated Press*] (SAG)
MorsnHl..... Morrison Health Care, Inc. [*Associated Press*] (SAG)
mor sol ..... More Solito [*In the usual manner*] [*Latin*] [*Pharmacy*] (DAVI)
MOR SOL.... More Solito [*In the Usual Way*] [*Pharmacy*]
MORST...... Ministry of Research, Science and Technology (SAUO)
Mor St Ca... Morris' Mississippi State Cases [*1818-72*] [*A publication*] (DLA)
Mor St Cas... Morris' Mississippi State Cases [*1818-72*] [*A publication*] (DLA)
Mor Supp... Morison's Dictionary of Decisions, Scotch Court of Session, Supplement [*1620-1768*] [*A publication*] (DLA)
Mor Syn..... Morison's Synopsis, Scotch Session Cases [*1808-16*] [*A publication*] (DLA)
moRt .... Mainstream of Republican Thought (AD)
MORT........ Management Oversight and Risk Tree (NASA)
MORT........ Master Operational Recording Tape [*SAGE*]
MORT........ Ministry of Research and Technology (SAUO)
MORT........ Ministry of Roads and Trees (SAUO)
MORT........ Missile Operation [*or Ordnance*] Readiness Test [*or Testing*]
MORT........ Moritz [*NCIC trailer make code*]
mor t .... Morse Taper (AD)
MORT........ Morse Taper
mort .... Mortal (AD)
mort .... Mortality
MORT........ Mortar (AABC)
mort .... Mortar (AD)
Mort .... Mortemart (AD)
mort .... Mortgage (AD)
MORT........ Mortgage (ADA)
mort .... Mortician (AD)
MORT........ Mortician
Mort .... Mortimer (AD)
Mort .... Morton (AD)
MORT........ Mortuary (ADA)
MORTAL..... Mortality (BABM)
mortal .... Mortality [*Statistics*] (DAVI)
MORTG...... Mortgage
MORTI....... Mortimer, IL [*American Association of Railroads railroad junction routing code*]
MORTN...... Morristown, NJ [*American Association of Railroads railroad junction routing code*]
MortnRst.... Mortons Restaurant Group [*Associated Press*] (SAG)
MORTO...... Morton, IL [*American Association of Railroads railroad junction routing code*]
Morton ...... Morton's Reports, Calcutta Superior Court [*India*] [*A publication*] (DLA)
Morton Int... Morton International, Inc. [*Associated Press*] (SAG)
Mor Tran.... Morrison's Transcript of United States Supreme Court Decisions [*A publication*] (DLA)
MORTREP... Mortar Bombing Report
Mort Vend... Morton's Vendors and Purchasers [*1837*] [*A publication*] (DLA)
MORU .... Moto Rumi [*NCIC motorcycle make code*]
MORU .... Mount Rushmore National Memorial
MORV .... Mobile Overpass Roadway-Repair Vehicle
Mor Wills... Morrell on the Law of Wills [*A publication*] (DLA)
MORZ .... Mitsui Osaka Shosen Kaisha Lines [*Intermodal trailer symbol*]
Mos.......... Book of Mosiah (AD)
Mos.......... De Vita Mosis [*Philo*] (BJA)
MOS .... Machinery and Occupational Safety Act [*Environmental science*]
MOS .... Macula of Saccule [*Medicine*] (MELL)
MOS .... Magneto-Optical System (AD)
MOS .... Mail-Order Sales (WDAA)
MOS .... Maintenance Operations Section [*Marine Corps*] (DOMA)
MOS .... Major Operating System [*Army*] (AABC)
MOS .... Malta Ornithological Society (SAUO)
MOS .... Management Operating System
MOS .... Management Operations Staff [*Environmental Protection Agency*] (GFGA)
MOS .... Management Orientation School [*LIMRA*]
MOS .... Manned Orbital Station (AAG)
MOS .... Man on the Street (WDMC)
MOS .... Man-on-the-Street Interview [*Journalism*]
MOS .... Manual Override Switch
MOS .... Manufacturing Operating System [*IBM Corp.*]
MOS .... Manufacturing Operations Survey (MCD)
MOS .... Margin of Safety [*Business term*]
MOS .... Marine Observation Satellite [*Japan*]
MOS .... Marine Occupational Standard (DNAB)
MOS .... Maritime Operational Intelligence Summary (MCD)
MOS .... Marking of Overseas Shipments
MOS .... Martian Operation System [*Computer science*] (HODG)
MOS .... Mass On-Line Storage (SAUO)
MOS .... Master Operating System [*Sperry UNIVAC*]
MOS .... Material Ordering Schedule
MOS .... Mathematical Off-Print Service [*American Mathematical Society*]
MOS .... Mean Opinion Score
MOS .... Measurement of Skill (AEBS)
MOS .... Measure of Suitability (CAAL)
MOS .... Mechanical Oblique Sketcher
MOS .... Medial Orbital Sulcus (DB)
MOS .... Medical Outcomes Study (DMAA)
MOS .... Member of the Opposite Sex (SAUS)
MOS .... Memorandum of Support (SAUO)
MOS .... Memory Operating Software [*Computer science*]
MOS .... Memory-Oriented System
MOS .... Mercantile Open Stock
MOS .... Meridian Ocean Systems (SAUS)
MOS .... Mesa Offshore Trust (EFIS)
MOS .... Metal Oxide on a Substrate (MCD)
mos.......... Metal-Oxide Semiconductor (AD)
MOS .... Metal-Oxide Semiconductor
MOS .... Metal Oxide Sensor [*Industrial hygiene term*] (OHS)
mos.......... Metal-Oxide Silicon (AD)
MOS .... Metal-Oxide-Silicon [*Integrated circuit*] [*Electronics*]
MOS .... Metal Oxide Software Similarity (AGLO)
MOS .... Michigan Ophthalmological Society (EARSL)
MOS .... Microprogram Operating System
MOS .... Microsomal Ethanol-Oxidizing System (DMAA)
MOS .... Military Occupational Skill (SAUO)
mos.......... Military Occupational Specialty (AD)
MOS .... Military Occupational Specialty [*Army*]
MOS .... Military Occupational Specification Serial Number [*British*] [*World War II*]
MOS .... Military Oceanography Subcommittee [*National Security Industrial Association*] (USDC)
MOS .... Military Overseas Supply [*British*]
mOs .... Milliosmole [*or Milliosmolar*] (AAMN)
MOS .... Minimum Operating Strip (SAUO)
MOS .... Minimum Operating System [*Sperry Univac*] (NITA)
MOS .... Ministry of Sound (SAUO)
MOS .... Ministry of State [*British*]
MOS .... Ministry of Supply [*Also, MS*] [*British*]
MOS .... Minus Optical Sound [*Film industry*]
MOS .... Mirror Optical System [*Medicine*] (EDAA)
mos.......... Missile On Stand (AD)
MOS .... Missile on Stand
MOS .... Missile Operations Station
MOS .... Mission Operations Software (ACAE)
MOS .... Mission Operations Strategy [*NASA*]
MOS .... Mission Operations System [*NASA*]
MOS .... Mit Out Sound [*i.e., "without sound"*] [*Film industry*]
mos.......... Mit-Out Sound (AD)
MOS .... Mitral Opening Sound [*Cardiology*]
MOS .... Model Output Statistics [*Meteorology*]
MOS .... Mode of Shipment (ACAE)
MOS .... Modular Operating System (BUR)
MOS .... Moloney Murine Sarcoma [*Medicine*] (DMAA)
MOS .... Monitor Only crew Station (SAUS)
MOS .... Monolithic Oxide Silicon (SAUO)
mos.......... Months (AD)
MOS .... Months
MOS .... Morton Air Services Ltd.
mos.......... Mosaic (VRA)
MOS .... Mosaic
MOS .... Mosbach [*German license plate city code*]
Mos.......... Moscow (AD)
MOS .... Moscow [*Russia*] [*Seismograph station code, US Geological Survey*] (SEIS)
Mos.......... Moseley's English Chancery Reports [*25 English Reprint*] [*A publication*] (DLA)
Mos.......... Mosella [*of Ausonius*] [*Classical studies*] (OCD)
MOS .... Moses Point, AK [*Location identifier*] [*FAA*] (FAAL)
Mos.......... Moshe (AD)
Mos.......... Moslem (AD)
MOS .... Mosport Park Corp. [*Vancouver Stock Exchange symbol*]
mos.......... Mossi [*MARC language code*] [*Library of Congress*] (LCCP)
MOS .... Multiple Object Spectroscopy (PDAA)
MOS .... Multiprogramming Operating System
MoS .... Museum of Sydney [*Australia*]
MOS .... Myelofibrosis Osteosclerosis [*Medicine*] (DMAA)
MOS .... Myocardial Oxygen Supply [*Medicine*] (MELL)
MOS .... Springfield-Greene County Library, Springfield, MO [*OCLC symbol*] (OCLC)
MoS .... St. Louis Public Library, St. Louis, MO [*Library symbol*] [*Library of Congress*] (LCLS)
MOS-1....... Marine Observations Satellite-1 (SAUO)
MOSA .... Medical Officers of Schools Association (SAUO)
MOSA .... Medical Officers of Schools Associations [*British*]
MOSA .... Method of Standard Addition [*Statistics*]
MOSA .... Michigan Optometric Student Association (SAUO)
MOSA .... Minimum Operational Safe Altitude (DOMA)
MOSA .... Ministry of Science and Arts [*US and Israel*]
MOSA .... Moderate Sales [*Telegraphy*] (PCTE)
MoSAB ...... Anheuser-Busch, Inc., St. Louis, MO [*Library symbol*] [*Library of Congress*] (LCLS)
MOSAIC..... Macro Operation Symbolic Assembler and Information Compiler [*Computer science*] (IEEE)

MOSAIC ..... Metal-Oxide-Semiconductor Advanced Integrated Circuit [*Electronics*] (IEEE)
MOSAIC ..... Method of Scenic Alternative Impacts by Computer (PDAA)
MOSAIC ..... Ministry of Supply Automatic Integrator and Computer [*British*] (DEN)
MOSAIC ..... Mobile SONAR Automatic Information Classifier (TIMI)
MOSAIC ..... Mobile System for Accurate ICBM Control (MCD)
MOSAIC ..... Modular Open System Architecture for Industrial Motion Control (SAUO)
MOSAIC ..... Molecular Observation, Spectroscopy and Imaging using Cantilevers [*Defense Advanced Research Projects Agency*] (RCD)
MOSAIC ..... Multifunctional on-the-Move Secure Adaptive Integrated Communications [*Military*]
MOSAIC ..... Multi-User, On-Line System for Automated Information Communication (SAUO)
MOSAICC ... Micro-organisms Sustainable Use and Access Regulation (SAUO)
MOSAICC ... Micro-organisms Sustainable Use and Access Regulation, an International Code of Conduct (SAUS)
MOSAICS ... Melcom Optical Software Applications for Integrated Commercial Systems (PDAA)
MOSAP ...... Marine Oil Spills Action Plan (SAUO)
MOSAR ...... Modulation Scan Array RADAR [*or Receiver*]
MOSART .... Monolithic Signal Processor and Detector Array (ACAE)
MOSASR .... Metal Oxide Semiconductor Analogue Shift Register [*Electronics*] (PDAA)
MoSavHi .... Andrew County Historical Society, Savannah, MO [*Library symbol*] [*Library of Congress*] (LCLS)
MOSAW ..... Medium Operating Speed Automatic Weapon [*Military*]
MOSB .... Military Order of the Stars and Bars (EA)
MoSB .... Missouri Botanical Garden, St. Louis, MO [*Library symbol*] [*Library of Congress*] (LCLS)
Mosbas ..... Moscow Basin (AD)
MOSBY ...... More Sellers than Buyers [*Telegraphy*] (PCTE)
MOSC .... Management Orientation Study Course [*LIMRA*]
mosc .... Manned Orbital Systems Concept (AD)
MOSC .... Manned Orbital Systems Concepts [*NASA*]
MOSC .... Marine Oil Spills Committee (SAUO)
MOSC .... Maritime Operations Support Center (SAUO)
MOS-C .... Metal-Oxide Semiconductor Capacitor (AAEL)
MOSC .... Midland-Odessa Symphony and Chorale (AD)
MOSC .... Military Occupational Specialty Code (AABC)
MOSC .... Military Oil Subcommittee [*of North African Economic Board*] [*World War II*]
MOSC .... Mission Operations System Center (ACAE)
MOSC .... Mosaic
MOSCA ...... McNamara-O'Hara Service Contract Act of 1965 (WYGK)
MOSCAP .... Modified Service Contract and Procedures [*DoD*]
MoSCC ...... St. Louis Community College, Instructional Resource Technical Services, St. Louis, MO [*Library symbol*] [*Library of Congress*] (LCLS)
MoSCEx ..... Christ Seminary-Seminex, St. Louis, MO [*Library symbol*] [*Library of Congress*] (LCLS)
MoSCH ...... Concordia Historical Institute, St. Louis, MO [*Library symbol*] [*Library of Congress*] (LCLS)
MOSCH ...... Moschus [*Musk*] [*Pharmacology*] (ROG)
MOSCO ...... Moscow, ID [*American Association of Railroads railroad junction routing code*]
MoSCo ...... St. Louis County Library, St. Louis, MO [*Library symbol*] [*Library of Congress*] (LCLS)
Moscom ..... Moscom Corp. [*Associated Press*] (SAG)
Mos Cont ... Moseley's Contraband of War [*1861*] [*A publication*] (DLA)
MOSCOW ... Museum of Soviet Calculators on the Web [*Computer science*]
MoSCP ...... St. Louis College of Pharmacy, St. Louis, MO [*Library symbol*] [*Library of Congress*] (LCLS)
MoSCRR .... Center for Reformation Research, St. Louis, MO [*Library symbol*] [*Library of Congress*] (LCLS)
MoSCS ...... Concordia Seminary, St. Louis, MO [*Library symbol*] [*Library of Congress*] (LCLS)
MoSCT ...... Covenant Theological Seminary, St. Louis, MO [*Library symbol*] [*Library of Congress*] (LCLS)
MOSD .... Military Occupational Specialty Division (SAUO)
MoSDM ..... United States Air Force, Defense Mapping Agency Aerospace Center, St. Louis, MO [*Library symbol*] [*Library of Congress*] (LCLS)
Mose .... Moises (AD)
Mose .... Moseley (AD)
Mose .... Mosen (AD)
MOSE .... Moser [*NCIC trailer make code*]
Mose .... Moses (AD)
MoSe .... Sedalia Public Library, Sedalia, MO [*Library symbol*] [*Library of Congress*] (LCLS)
MoSE .... United States Army, Corps of Engineers, District Library St. Louis, St. Louis, MO [*Library symbol*] [*Library of Congress*] (LCLS)
MoSed ...... Sedalia Public Library, Sedalia, MO [*Library symbol*] [*Library of Congress*] (LCLS)
MOSEL ...... Molten-Salt Epithermal Reactor
Moseley ..... Moseley's English Chancery Reports [*25 English Reprint*] [*A publication*] (DLA)
Mos El L .... Moseley's Elementary Law [*2nd ed.*] [*1878*] [*A publication*] (DLA)
Mosely (Eng) ... Moseley's English Chancery Reports [*25 English Reprint*] [*A publication*] (DLA)
MOSES ...... Major Open Systems Environment Standards (SAUO)
MOSES ...... Manned Open Sea Experiment Station (NOAA)
MOSES ...... Manufacturing Operations Short Event Scheduling
MOSES ...... Massive Open Systems Environment Standard [*Computer science*]
MOSES ...... Meteorological Observing Station (SAUO)
MOSES ...... Methodology for Object-Oriented Software Engineering [*Computer science*] (HODG)
MOSES ...... Mobile Station for Environmental Services (SAUO)
MOSES ...... Molecular Orbital Self-Consistent Energy System (PDAA)
MOSES ...... Mothers Organized to Stop Environmental Sins [*Texas*] (EARSL)
MOSES ...... Motor-Operated Sled Ejection System (MCD)
MOSES ...... Movable Search System (MCD)
MOSES ...... Multioccupant Sealed Environment Simulator
MoSF .... Fontbonne College, St. Louis, MO [*Library symbol*] [*Library of Congress*] (LCLS)
MOSF .... Multiple Organ System Failure [*Medicine*] (MELL)
MOSFET ..... Metal Oxide Semiconductor Field Effect Transformer (NITA)
mosfet .... Metal-Oxide Semiconductor Field-Effect Transistor (AD)
MOSFET ..... Metal-Oxide-Semiconductor [*or Silicon*] Field-Effect Transistor
MOSFETS ... Metal Oxide Substrate Field Effect Transistor
MoSFi .... Eugene Field House, St. Louis, MO [*Library symbol*] [*Library of Congress*] (LCLS)
MoSFRR .... Foundation for Reformation Research, St. Louis, MO [*Library symbol*] [*Library of Congress*] [*Obsolete*] (LCLS)
MoSGS ...... Church of Jesus Christ of Latter-Day Saints, Genealogical Society Library, St. Louis Branch, St. Louis, MO [*Library symbol*] [*Library of Congress*] (LCLS)
MOsH .... Medical Officers of Health (SAUO)
Mosh .... Moshav [*or Moshava*] (BJA)
MoSHi .... Missouri Historical Society, St. Louis, MO [*Library symbol*] [*Library of Congress*] (LCLS)
MoSHS ...... Harris-Stowe State College Library, St. Louis, MO [*Library symbol*] [*Library of Congress*] (LCLS)
MoSHT ...... Harris Teachers College, St. Louis, MO [*Library symbol*] [*Library of Congress*] (LCLS)
MOSI .... Mosinee Paper [*NASDAQ symbol*] (TTSB)
MOSI .... Mosinee Paper Corp. [*NASDAQ symbol*] (NQ)
mosic .... Metal-Oxide-Semiconductor Integrated Circuit (AD)
MOSID ...... Ministry of Supply Inspection Department [*British*] (AD)
MoSIG .... International Graduate School, St. Louis, MO [*Library symbol*] [*Library of Congress*] (LCLS)
Mosine ...... Mosinee Paper Co. [*Associated Press*] (SAG)
MoSIO .... International Library, Archives, and Museum of Optometry, St. Louis, MO [*Library symbol*] [*Library of Congress*] (LCLS)
MoSIP .... Missouri Institute of Psychiatry, St. Louis, MO [*Library symbol*] [*Library of Congress*] (LCLS)
MOSIS .... Monolithic Silicon Detector (ACAE)
MOSIS .... MOS Implementation Service (NITA)
MOSIX .... Multicomputer Operating System for UNIX (SAUO)
Mosk .... Moscovici (AD)
Mosk .... Moscowitz (AD)
MOSK .... Moskovitch [*NCIC car make code*]
Mosk .... Moskowitz (AD)
MOSK .... Moskowitz Motor Transportation [*Common carrier symbol*]
MOSK .... Multimode Operation Support Services (ACAE)
MoSL .... Law Library Association of St. Louis, St. Louis, MO [*Library symbol*] [*Library of Congress*] (LCLS)
MOSLS ...... Military Occupational Specialty Level System
MOS/LSI .... Metal Oxide Silicon/Large Scale Integration [*Electronics*]
MOSM .... Metal-Oxide Semimetal (IEEE)
mosm .... Milliosmol (AD)
mOsm .... Milliosmol [*or Milliosmole*] [*Chemistry*]
MOSM .... Mission Operations System Manager [*NASA*]
MoSM .... St. Louis Mercantile Library Association, St. Louis, MO [*Library symbol*] [*Library of Congress*] (LCLS)
MoSMa ...... Maryville College, St. Louis, MO [*Library symbol*] [*Library of Congress*] (LCLS)
MoSMal ..... Mallinckrodt Chemical Works [*Later, Mallinckrodt, Inc.*], St. Louis, MO [*Library symbol*] [*Library of Congress*] (LCLS)
Mos Man ... Moses on the Law of Mandamus [*A publication*] (DLA)
MoSMc ...... McDonnell Douglas Corp., Corporate Library, St. Louis, MO [*Library symbol*] [*Library of Congress*] (LCLS)
MoSMcA .... McDonnell Douglas Automation Co., St. Louis, MO [*Library symbol*] [*Library of Congress*] (LCLS)
MoSMed .... St. Louis Medical Society, St. Louis, MO [*Library symbol*] [*Library of Congress*] (LCLS)
mOsmol ..... Milliosmole [*Measurement*] (DAVI)
MoSMon .... Monsanto Chemical Co., St. Louis, MO [*Library symbol*] [*Library of Congress*] (LCLS)
MOSNAG .... Mossine Nagant Rifle
MOS/NFC ... Ministry of Supplies/Nepal Food Corp. (SAUS)
MOS/NFC ... Ministry of Supplies/Nepal Food Corporation (SAUO)
MOS/NOC ... Ministry Of Supplies/Nepal Oil Corp. (SAUS)
MOS/NOC ... Ministry Of Supplies/Nepal Oil Corporation (SAUO)
MOSOP ...... Missouri Sexual Offender Program (AD)
MOSOP ...... Movement for the Survival of Ogoni People
MOSOP ...... Movement for the Survival of the Ogoni People
MO SOYPAC ... Missouri Soybean Association PAC [*Jefferson City, MO*] (PACS)
MOSP .... Master Ordnance Systems Pattern File [*Navy*]
MOSP .... Medical and Osteopathic Scholarship Program (DNAB)
MOSP .... Microsoft Online Services Partnership (SAUO)
MOSP .... Multicultural Organization Strategic Plan [*USDA Forest Service*] (ALAC)
MOSP .... Multi-mission Optronic Stabilised Payload (SAUS)
MoSp .... Public Libraries of Springfield and Greene County, Springfield, MO [*Library symbol*] [*Library of Congress*] (LCLS)
MoSpA ...... Assemblies of God Graduate School, Springfield, MO [*Library symbol*] [*Library of Congress*] (LCLS)
MoSpBB ..... Baptist Bible College, Springfield, MO [*Library symbol*] [*Library of Congress*] (LCLS)
MoSpCB ..... Central Bible College, Springfield, MO [*Library symbol*] [*Library of Congress*] (LCLS)

MoSpD ...... Drury College, Springfield, MO [*Library symbol*] [*Library of Congress*] (LCLS)
MoSPD ...... St. Louis Post-Dispatch, St. Louis, MO [*Library symbol*] [*Library of Congress*] (LCLS)
MoSpDC .... Drury College, Springfield, MO [*Library symbol*] [*Library of Congress*] (LCLS)
MoSpE ...... Evangel College, Springfield, MO [*Library symbol*] [*Library of Congress*] (LCLS)
MOSPF ...... Multicast Open Shortest Path First (SAUS)
MoSPI .... Pet, Inc., St. Louis, MO [*Library symbol*] [*Library of Congress*] (LCLS)
MOSPO ...... Mobile Satellite Photometric Observatory [*NASA*] (NASA)
MOS Poland... Ministerstwo Opieki Spotecznes [*Ministry of Social Welfare*] [*Poland*] (AD)
MOSPOR.... Movement for the Struggle for Political Rights [*Uganda*] (PD)
MoSpS ...... Southwest Missouri State College, Springfield, MO [*Library symbol*] [*Library of Congress*] (LCLS)
MoSPS ...... St. Louis Priory School, St. Louis, MO [*Library symbol*] [*Library of Congress*] (LCLS)
MoSPSc..... Saint Louis Priory School, St. Louis, MO [*Library symbol*] [*Library of Congress*] (LCLS)
MoSR........ City Art Museum of St. Louis, St. Louis, MO [*Library symbol*] [*Library of Congress*] (LCLS)
MoSR........ Saint Louis Art Museum, Richardson Memorial Library, St. Louis, MO [*Library symbol*] [*Library of Congress*] (LCLS)
MOSRAM ... Metal-Oxide Semiconductor Random-Access Memory (EECA)
MOSRD ..... Motor Machinist's Mate, Ship Repair, Diesel Engineering Mechanic [*Navy rating*]
MOSRG ..... Motor Machinist's Mate, Ship Repair, Gasoline Engine Mechanic [*Navy rating*]
MOSROM ... Metal-Oxide Semiconductor Read-Only Memory [*Computer science*] (CIST)
MOSROM ... Metal-Oxide-Silicon Read-Only Memory (IDOE)
MOSS .... Maintenance and Operator SubSystem [*IBM's VTAM*] [*Communications term*] (DCT)
moss .... Maintenance-Operations Support Set (AD)
MOSS .... Maintenance-Operations Support Set (AFM)
MOSS .... Management and Organisation in Secondary Schools (AIE)
MOSS .... Manned Orbital Space Station [*or System*] [*See also MOD, MODS, MTSS*] [*Air Force/NASA*]
MOSS .... Map Overlay Statistical System (SAUO)
MOSS .... Market Opening Sector Specific (AD)
MOSS .... Market-Oriented, Sector-Selective [*or Specific*] [*Trade negotiations between United States and Japan*]
MOSS .... Market Oversight Surveillance System
MOSS .... Mathematical Optimization Subroutine System (VLIE)
MOSS .... Measure of Semiconductor (AGLO)
MOSS .... Middle-Aged, Overstressed, Semiaffluent Suburbanite [*Lifestyle classification*]
MOSS .... Military Orbital Space System [*See also MOD, MODS, MTSS*] [*Air Force/NASA*]
MOSS .... Military Overseas Shelter Survey [*Civil Defense*]
MOSS .... Mission Operations Support Satellites (ACAE)
MOSS .... Mission Operation Support Services (ACAE)
MOSS .... Mobile Oceanography Support System (SAUO)
MOSS .... Mobile Submarine Simulator (NVT)
MOSS .... Mobility Support Set [*or System*] [*for aircraft*] (MCD)
MOSS .... Modelling Systems [*Moss Systems Ltd.*] [*Software package*] (NCC)
MOSS .... Monitor Output Signal Strength
MOSS .... Mossimo [*NASDAQ symbol*]
MOSS .... Mothers of Sons in Service [*World War II*]
MOSS .... Mutually Owned Society for Songwriters
MOSS .... Myelofibrosis-osteosclerosis Syndrome [*Medicine*] (EDAA)
MOSSA...... Mine Officials and Salaried Staff Association (SAUO)
MOSSA...... Northern Rhodesia Mine Officials and Salaried Staff Association
Mossies..... Middle-Aged, Overstressed Semiaffluent Suburbanites [*Lifestyle Classification*]
Mossimo.... Mossimo, Inc. [*Associated Press*] (SAG)
MoSSJ ...... St. John Cantius Seminary, St. Louis, MO [*Library symbol*] [*Library of Congress*] (LCLS)
MOSS MOUSE... Maneuver, Objective, Security, Surprise, Mass, Offensive, Unity of Command, Simplicity, Economy of Force [*Basic principles of war*] [*See also MOOSEMUSS*] (MCD)
MOSSRS.... Management Order Ship Status Reporting System (MCD)
MOSST...... Ministry of State for Science and Technology [*Canada*]
MOST........ Management Operation System Technique
MOST........ Manned Orbital Solar Telescope
MOST........ Mass Optical Storage Technologies [*Computer science*]
MOST........ Maynard Operation Sequence Technique (LDOE)
MOST........ Mediterranean Oak Forest (SAUS)
most......... Metal-Oxide Semiconductor Transistor (AD)
MOST........ Metal-Oxide-Semiconductor Transistor
MOST........ Metal-Oxide-Silicon Transistor (IDOE)
MOST........ Michigan Opportunities and Skills Training (AD)
MOST........ Ministry of Science and Technology (SAUO)
MOST........ Missile on Shipboard Test (ACAE)
MOST........ Mission-Orientated Simulator Training (SAUS)
MOST........ Mission Oriented System Tape [*Military*] (CAAL)
MOST........ Mobile Open Systems Technologies (SAUO)
MOST........ Mobile Optical Surveillance Tracker
MOST........ Mobile Oversnow Transport
MOST........ Mobile SONAR Technology [*Marine science*] (MSC)
MOST........ Modified OECD [*Organization for Economic Cooperation and Development*] Screening Test [*Biodegradability Test*]
MOST........ Modular Office System Terminal [*Computer science*] (VLIE)
MOST........ Molonglo Observatory Synthesis Telescope
MOST........ Mothers of Super Twins [*Military*]
MOST........ Motorcycle Operator Skill Test
MOST........ Multidisciplinary Optical Switching Technology Center [*University of California, Santa Barbara*] (RCD)
MOST........ Multipulse Observation Sizing Technique [*Southwest Research Institute*]
MOSTA ...... Midwest Old Settlers and Threshers Association (EA)
MOSTAB .... Modular Stability [*Derivative program*]
MO St Ann... Missouri Statutes, Annotated [*A publication*] (DLA)
MoStc .... St. Charles City-County Library, St. Charles, MO [*Library symbol*] [*Library of Congress*] (LCLS)
MoStcL...... Lindenwood College, St. Charles, MO [*Library symbol*] [*Library of Congress*] (LCLS)
MOSTE ...... Ministry of Science, Technology and Environment (SAUO)
Mostell...... Mostellaria [*of Plautus*] [*Classical studies*] (OCD)
MoStgA ..... Sainte Genevieve Archives, Sainte Genevieve County Court, Ste. Genevieve, MO [*Library symbol*] [*Library of Congress*] (LCLS)
MoStj........ St. Joseph Public Library, St. Joseph, MO [*Library symbol*] [*Library of Congress*] (LCLS)
MoStjM ..... Methodist Medical Center, St. Joseph, MO [*Library symbol*] [*Library of Congress*] (LCLS)
MoStjMW... Missouri Western State College, St. Joseph, MO [*Library symbol*] [*Library of Congress*] (LCLS)
MoStjS ...... St. Joseph State Hospital, St. Joseph, MO [*Library symbol*] [*Library of Congress*] (LCLS)
mostl .... Metal-Oxide Semiconductor Transistor Logic (AD)
MOSTL ...... Metal-Oxide-Semiconductor Transistor Logic (CET)
MOSTT ...... Mosaic Optical Sensor Technology Testbed (ACAE)
MOST/TDIS... Mobile SONAR Technology/Technical Document Information System [*Marine science*] (MSC)
MOSU .... Mobile Ordnance Service Unit
MoSU........ St. Louis University, St. Louis, MO [*Library symbol*] [*Library of Congress*] (LCLS)
MoSU-C ..... St. Louis University, School of Commerce and Finance, St. Louis, MO [*Library symbol*] [*Library of Congress*] (LCLS)
MoSU-D..... St. Louis University, School of Divinity, St. Louis, MO [*Library symbol*] [*Library of Congress*] (LCLS)
MoSUE ...... Union Electric Co., St. Louis, MO [*Library symbol*] [*Library of Congress*] (LCLS)
MoSU-L ..... St. Louis University, School of Law, St. Louis, MO [*Library symbol*] [*Library of Congress*] (LCLS)
MoSU-M .... St. Louis University, School of Medicine, St. Louis, MO [*Library symbol*] [*Library of Congress*] (LCLS)
MoSU-P..... St. Louis University, School of Philosophy, St. Louis, MO [*Library symbol*] [*Library of Congress*] (LCLS)
MOSUPPU... Mobile Support Unit (DNAB)
MoSV........ Catholic Central Union of America, St. Louis, MO [*Library symbol*] [*Library of Congress*] (LCLS)
MoSVA ...... United States Veterans Administration Hospital, St. Louis, MO [*Library symbol*] [*Library of Congress*] (LCLS)
MoSW....... Washington University, St. Louis, MO [*Library symbol*] [*Library of Congress*] (LCLS)
MoSW-D .... Washington University, School of Dentistry, St. Louis, MO [*Library symbol*] [*Library of Congress*] (LCLS)
MoSW-F..... Washington University, School of Fine Arts, St. Louis, MO [*Library symbol*] [*Library of Congress*] (LCLS)
MoSW-L..... Washington University, School of Law, St. Louis, MO [*Library symbol*] [*Library of Congress*] (LCLS)
MoSW-M.... Washington University, Medical School, St. Louis, MO [*Library symbol*] [*Library of Congress*] (LCLS)
MoSX........ Martin Oil Service [*Private rail car owner code*]
MOSX .... Mosaix, Inc. [*NASDAQ symbol*] (NASQ)
MOSZ........ Massive Offshore Surf Zone
MOSZ........ Mitsui Osaka Shosen Kaisha Lines [*Intermodal trailer symbol*]
MOSZK ...... Central Union of Hungarian Cooperative Societies (SAUO)
MOT .... Aeromonterrey SA [*Mexico*] [*ICAO designator*] (FAAC)
MOT .... Magneto-Optical Trap [*Physics*]
MOT .... Managed Object to Test [*Open Systems Interconnection*] (ODAA)
MOT .... Management of Technology
MOT .... Manned Orbital Telescope [*NASA*]
MOT .... Manufacturing Operation and Tooling
MOT .... [*The*] March of Time [*Radio and motion picture series*]
MOT .... Marine Oil Transportation [*AAR code*]
MOT .... Mark on Top (NVT)
MOT .... Marquette, MI [*Amtrak Busline code*]
MOT .... Master of Occupational Therapy (GAGS)
MOT .... Master Operability Test (CAAL)
MOT .... Maximum Operating Time (NG)
MOT .... Maximum Overhaul Time (SAUS)
MOT .... McDonald Observatory [*Texas*] [*Seismograph station code, US Geological Survey*] (SEIS)
mot .... Mean Operating Time (AD)
MOT .... Mean Operating Time
MOT .... Means of Testing [*Telecommunications*] (OSI)
mot .... Mechanical Operability Test (AD)
MOT .... Mechanical Operability Test
MOT .... Medial Olfactory Tract [*Anatomy*]
mot .... Member of Our Tribe (AD)
MOT .... Member of Our Tribe [*Jewish slang*]
MOT .... Men of the Trees [*Australia*] [*An association*]
MOT .... Method of Testing (MCD)
mot .... Middle of Target (AD)
MOT .... Military Ocean Terminal (AABC)
MOT .... Mineral-Oil Tolerance [*of resin solutions*]
M o T........ Minister of Transport [*British*] (AD)
MOT .... Ministry of Tourism [*Philippines*] (DS)
MOT .... Ministry of Trade (SAUO)

MOT .... Ministry of Transport [*British or Canadian*]
MOT .... Ministry of Transportation (SAUO)
MOT .... Minot [*North Dakota*] [*Airport symbol*] (OAG)
MOT .... Missile Operability Test (MCD)
MOT .... Model T [*NCIC car model code*]
MOT .... Molecular-Orbital Theory [*Physical chemistry*]
MOT .... Monalta Resources, Inc. [*Vancouver Stock Exchange symbol*]
MOT .... Montclair [*NCIC car model code*]
MOT .... Monthly Overtime (RIMS)
MOT .... Month of Travel [*Military*]
MOT .... Morphous Object Technology [*Computer science*] (HODG)
MOT .... Motion
MOT .... Motor (AAG)
mot .... Motor (AD)
MOT .... Motoring [*Indian Railway*] (TIR)
MOT .... Motorized
MOT .... Motorola, Inc. [*NYSE symbol*] (SPSG)
MOT .... Motor Operating Time
MOT .... Mouse Operating Table [*Research instrumentation*]
MOT .... Mouse Ovarian Tumor [*Veterinary science*] (DB)
MOT .... Murine Ovarian Teratocarcinoma [*Animal pathology*]
MOT .... Tarkio College, Tarkio, MO [*OCLC symbol*] (OCLC)
MOTA .... Mail Order Traders Association (MHDB)
MOTA .... Manitoba Oculo-Tricho-Anal [*Syndrome*] [*Medicine*] (DMAA)
MOTA .... Materials Open-Test Assembly [*Nuclear energy*] (NRCH)
MOTA .... Michigan Occupational Therapy Association (EARSL)
MOTA .... Michigan Ohio Telecommunications Association (TSSD)
MOTA .... Mid-Ocean Target Array (AAG)
MOTA .... Motoc Semi-Flatbed Trailer [*NCIC trailer make code*]
MOTA .... Museum of Temporary Art [*Washington, DC*]
MoTaC .... Tarkio College, Tarkio, MO [*Library symbol*] [*Library of Congress*] (LCLS)
MOTACC .... Manufacturers of Telescoping and Articulating Cranes Council (EA)
MOTA-IC ... Alloy Test (SAUS)
MOTAM ..... Moving Target Attack Missile (ACAE)
MOT & E.... Multinational Operational Test and Evaluation
MOTAR...... Modular Thermal Analyzer Routine [*Computer science*]
MOTARDES... Moving Target Detection System (IEEE)
MOTARDIV... Mobile Target Division [*Mine Force*] [*Navy*]
MOTARDS... Moving Target Detection System
MOTAS ...... Member of the Appropriate Sex (NHD)
MOTAT ...... Museum of Transport and Technology (AD)
MOTBA ...... Military Ocean Terminal, Bay Area [*Oakland, CA*] (AABC)
MOTBY ...... Military Ocean Terminal, Bayonne (AABC)
MOTC .... Ministry of Transit and Communications [*Philippines*] (AD)
MOTC .... Montreal Tramways [*AAR code*]
Motcc .... Motility with correction (SAUS)
MotClb ...... Motor Club of America [*Associated Press*] (SAG)
M o TCP .... Ministry of Town and Country Planning [*British*] (AD)
MOTD .... Maintenance and Operating Technical Data (ACAE)
MOTD .... Message of the Day (SAUS)
MOT/DCA ... Ministry of Tourism/ Department of Civil Aviation (SAUO)
MOTE .... Measure of Training Effectiveness [*Military*]
MOTE .... Motel Mobile Corporation of America [*NCIC trailer make code*]
MOTEC ...... Maritime Operations Tactical Evaluation Centre (SAUO)
MOTECS .... Mobile Tactical Exercise Control System (DNAB)
MOTEL ...... Motor Hotel
MOTESZ..... Magyar Orvostudomanyi Tarsasagok Szovetsege [*Federation of Hungarian Medical Societies*] (EAIO)
MOTET ...... Mother Tongue and English Teaching (AIE)
MOTF .... Manganese Oxide Thin Film
MOTG .... Marine Operational Training Group
MOTG .... Morally Obliged to Go [*British*] [*Slang*]
moth .... Mother (AD)
moth-in-law... Mother-in-Law (AD)
Moth Jones... Mother Jones [*A publication*] (BRI)
MothrWk.... Mothers Work, Inc. [*Associated Press*] (SAG)
MOTI .... Message Oriented Text Interchange [*Telecommunications*] (OSI)
MOTIF .... Main Optical Tracking and Identification Facility (CARL)
MOTIF .... Maui Optical Tracking and Identification Facility [*Hawaii*] [*Air Force*]
MOTION..... Model for Transforming, Identifying and Optimising Core Processes (SAUO)
MOTION..... Movement for Social Transformation (Trinidad & Tobago) [*Political party*] (PSAP)
MOTIS....... Message-Oriented Text Interchange Standard [*Communications term*] (DCT)
MOTIS....... Message Oriented Text Interchange System [*Telecommunications*] (OSI)
MOTIS....... Missile on Stand Timing Simulator (MCD)
MOTIS....... MOS Timing Simulator Software (NITA)
MOT-key .... Modified One-Time key (SAUS)
MOTKI....... Military Ocean Terminal, King's Bay (AABC)
MOTM .... Member of the Month (SAUO)
MOTM .... Motom [*NCIC motorcycle make code*]
MOTN .... Motion
MOTN .... Motron [*NCIC motorcycle make code*]
MOTNAC .... Manual of Tumor Nomenclature [*Medicine*] (DHSM)
MOTNE...... Meteorological Operational Telecommunications Network Europe
MOTNEG .... Meteorological Operational Telecommunication Network in Europe, Regional Planning Group [*ICAO*] (PDAA)
MO/TO....... Mail Order/Telephone Order (GART)
MOTO .... Moto Photo [*NQS*] (TTSB)
MOTO .... Moto Photo, Inc. [*NASDAQ symbol*] (NQ)
MOTO .... Motoroam [*NCIC truck make code*]
motoboard... Motorized Skateboard (AD)
motocross... Motorcycle Cross Country Race (AD)
MOTOGAS... Motor Gasoline [*Military*]
mot op ...... Motor Operated (AD)
MotoPh...... Moto Photo, Inc. [*Associated Press*] (SAG)
MOTOR...... Mobile Oriented Triangulation of Reentry
MOTOR...... Monthly Throughput Observation Report (DNAB)
motorcade... Motorized-Vehicle Parade (AD)
motorcross... Motorcycle Cross (AD)
MOTOREDE... Movement to Restore Decency [*Group opposing sex education in schools*]
MOTORISTS INSURANCE CIVIC FUND... Motorists Mutual Insurance Company Civic Fund [*Columbus, OH*] (PACS)
MOTORWAY... Motorway [*Commonly used*] (OPSA)
MOTOS...... Member of the Opposite Sex [*Electronic mail language*]
MOTOS...... Members of the Opposite Sex [*Internet lingo*] (NETL)
MOTOUR/DCA... Ministry of Tourism/ Department of Civil Aviation (SAUO)
MOTOUR/DCA... Ministry of Tourism/Department of Civil Aviation (SAUS)
MOTOUR/HMT... Ministry of Tourism/ Hotel Management and Tourism Training Centre (SAUO)
MOTP........ Manufacturing or Testing Process (KSC)
MOTP........ Medical Officer Training Plan [*Canada*]
MOTP........ Minuteman Operational Targeting Program (ACAE)
MOTPICT... Motion Picture
MOTPT ...... Ministry of Transport (SAUO)
MoTr......... Grundy County-Jewett Norris Library, Trenton, MO [*Library symbol*] [*Library of Congress*] (LCLS)
MOTR .... Motor Club of America [*NASDAQ symbol*] (NQ)
MOTR .... Mo Trailer Corporation [*NCIC trailer make code*]
MOTR .... Multiple Object-Tracking RADAR (MCD)
MotrPrt...... Motorcar Parts & Accessories, Inc. [*Associated Press*] (SAG)
MOTS........ Mend Our Tongues Society (EA)
MOTS........ Metal Oxide Threshold Switches (MCD)
MOTS........ Military off the Shelf (ACAE)
MOTS........ Minitrack Optical Tracking Station [*or System*] [*NASA*]
mots......... Minitrack Optical Tracking System (AD)
MOTS........ Missile Operability Test Station (MCD)
MOTS........ Mobile Optical Tracking System
MOTS........ Module Test Set
MOTS........ Montesa [*NCIC motorcycle make code*]
Motsc........ Motility without correction (SAUS)
MOTSS ...... Member of the Same Sex [*Electronic mail language*]
MOTSS ...... More of the Sameold Sameold (SAUS)
MOTSU ...... Military Ocean Terminal, Sunny Point (AABC)
MOTT........ Men of the Trees (SAUO)
MOTT........ Mycobacteria Other Than Tubercle Bacilli
MOTU .... Mobile Operating Technical Unit (SAUO)
MOTU .... Mobile Operational Training Unit (MCD)
MOTU .... Mobile Optical Tracking Unit (MCD)
MOTU .... Mobile Ordnance Technical Unit [*Military*] (CAAL)
MOTU .... Mobile Technical Unit (NG)
MOTU .... Monsanto [*Intermodal shipping container symbol*] (TVRC)
MOTUDET... Mobile Ordnance Technical Unit Detachment (DNAB)
MOTV........ Manned Orbit Transfer Vehicle (MCD)
MotV......... Motor Nucleus of the Trigeminal Nerve [*Medicine*] (DB)
MOTX........ Military Ocean Terminal Railroad [*Federal Railroad Administration identification code*]
MOTX........ Saint Louis Museum of Transportation [*Private rail car owner code*]
MOTZ........ Mitsui Osaka Shosen Kaisha Lines [*Intermodal trailer symbol*]
MOU......... Macula of Utricle [*Medicine*] (MELL)
MOU......... Maximum Oxygen Uptake
MOU......... Memo of Understanding (HVTR)
MoU......... Memorandum of Understanding (AD)
mou......... Memorandum of Understanding (AD)
MOU......... Memorandum of Understanding
mou......... Missouri [*MARC country of publication code*] [*Library of Congress*] (LCCP)
MOU......... Mountain States Telephone & Telegraph Co. (SAUO)
MOU......... Mountain Village [*Alaska*] [*Airport symbol*] (OAG)
Mou......... Mouse [*Computer science*] (PCM)
MOU......... Southwest Missouri State University, Springfield, MO [*OCLC symbol*] (OCLC)
MoU .... University of Missouri, Columbia, MO [*Library symbol*] [*Library of Congress*] (LCLS)
MOUA .... Mount Vernon Mobile Home [*NCIC trailer make code*]
MoU-D ...... University of Missouri, School of Dentistry, Kansas City, MO [*Library symbol*] [*Library of Congress*] (LCLS)
MOUE .... Mountain Valley Enterprises [*NCIC trailer make code*]
MOUG .... Map Online Users Group (EA)
MOUG .... Maryland Online User Group (NITA)
MOULT ...... Moultrie, GA [*American Association of Railroads railroad junction routing code*]
Moult Ch.... Moulton's New York Chancery Practice [*A publication*] (DLA)
Moult Ch P... Moulton's New York Chancery Practice [*A publication*] (DLA)
MOUM....... Mountain View Campers [*NCIC trailer make code*]
MoU-M ...... University of Missouri, Medical Library, Kansas City, MO [*Library symbol*] [*Library of Congress*] (LCLS)
MOUN .... Mountaineer Manufacturing Company [*NCIC trailer make code*]
MOUND ..... Mound Plant [*Department of Energy*] [*Miamisburg, OH*] (GAAI)
MOUNT...... Mount [*Commonly used*] (OPSA)
MOUNTAIN... Mountain [*Commonly used*] (OPSA)
MOUNTAINS... Mountains [*Commonly used*] (OPSA)
Mountbtn ... Mountbatten, Inc. [*Associated Press*] (SAG)
MOUNTIN... Mountain [*Commonly used*] (OPSA)

MountPr..... Mountain Province Mining, Inc. [*Associated Press*] (SAG)
Mounty...... Member of the Royal Canadian Mounted Police (SAUO)
MOURAD.... Mouvement pour la Renovation et l'Action Democratique [*The Comoros*] [*Political party*] (EY)
MOUS....... Microsoft Office User Specialist
MOUS....... Multiple Occurrences of Unexplained Symptoms [*Medicine*]
MOUSE...... Manager Owner User Systems Engineer (OA)
MOUSE...... Minimum Orbital Unmanned Satellite (AD)
MOUSE...... Minimum Orbital Unmanned Satellite of the Earth
MOUSS...... Management and Operation of User Services Section
MOUSS...... Management and Operations of User Services Section [*American Library Association*]
MoU-St...... University of Missouri at St. Louis, St. Louis, MO [*Library symbol*] [*Library of Congress*] (LCLS)
MOUT....... Military Operations in Urbanized Terrain (POLM)
MOUT....... Mobile Operation in Urban Terrain (SAUS)
MOUTH...... Modular Output Unit for Talking to Humans
MOUTRE.... Mission Oriented Unit Training by Echelon [*Military*] (INF)
MoU-V....... University of Missouri, Veterinary Medicine Library, Columbia, MO [*Library symbol*] [*Library of Congress*] (LCLS)
mov.......... Apple QuickTime [*Computer science*]
MOV......... Main Oxidizer Valve (KSC)
mov.......... Main Oxidizer Valve (NAKS)
MOV......... Manned Orbiting Vehicle [*NASA*]
MOV......... Manuscript on Vellum
MOV......... Margin of Victory [*Automobile racing*]
MOV......... Mass of Vehicle
MOV......... Materiel Obligation Validation (AFIT)
MOV......... Metal-Oxide Varistor
MOV......... Method of Validation
MOV......... Military-Owned Vehicle
MOV......... Minimal Occlusive Volume (DMAA)
MOV......... Monclova, MX [*Location identifier*] [*FAA*] (FAAL)
MOV......... Monument Valley, UT [*Location identifier*] [*FAA*] (FAAL)
MOV......... Moranbah [*Australia*] [*Airport symbol*] (OAG)
MOV......... Moreno Valley, CA [*Amtrak Busline code*]
MOV......... Morovis [*Puerto Rico*] [*Seismograph station code, US Geological Survey*] (SEIS)
MOV......... Moshassuck Valley Railroad Co. [*AAR code*]
MOV......... Motor Oil Volatility
MOV......... Motor-Operated Valve (NRCH)
mov.......... Movable (AD)
MOV......... Movable [*Technical drawings*]
mov.......... Moved (GEAB)
MOV......... Movement (AABC)
MOV......... Movie
mov.......... Movimento [*Movement*] [*Italian*] (AD)
MOV......... Multiple Oral Vitamins [*Medicine*] (EDAA)
mov.......... Multiple-Orifice Valve (AD)
MOV......... Stephens College, Columbia, MO [*OCLC symbol*] (OCLC)
MOVA........ Main Oxidizer Valve Actuator (SAUS)
MOVA........ Microprocessor Optimized Vehicle Actuation
MOVA........ Movado Group, Inc. [*NASDAQ symbol*] (SAG)
MOVAD...... Movement Adaptability (SAUO)
MOVAD...... Movement and Delivery (SAUO)
Movado...... Movado Group, Inc. [*Associated Press*] (SAG)
M-OVAL..... Macrovalocytes [*Microbiology*] (DAVI)
MOVC........ Membranous Obstruction (of the Inferior) Vena Cava [*Medicine*] (EDAA)
MOVCO...... Movement Control Organisation [*British military*] (DMA)
MOVCORD... Movement Coordinator
MOVDHHG... Movement of Dependents and Household Goods in Advance of Permanent Change of Station Orders is Authorized [*Army*] (AABC)
MOVE........ Cinema Ride Inc. [*NASDAQ symbol*] (TTSB)
MOVE........ Management of Value Engineering
MOVE........ Manage Old Vehicles Easily [*Performance Data Services, Inc.*] [*Software*]
MOVE........ Men Over Violence (ODA)
MOVE........ Microprocessor Open Vision Environment (SAUO)
MOVE........ Microsoft Overlay Virtual Environment (SAUS)
MOVE........ Mobility Opportunities Via Education (SAUO)
move........ Movement (WDAA)
MOVE........ Moving
MOVE........ Multiple Occupancy Vehicles (DICI)
MOVE........ Peregrine Entertainment Ltd. [*NASDAQ symbol*] (COMM)
MOVECAP... Movement Capabilities [*Military*] (CINC)
MOVEET..... Ministers of Vocational Education, Employment and Training (SAUO)
MOVEM..... Movement Overseas Verification of Enlisted Members [*Army*] (AABC)
movem...... Movement Overseas Verification of Enlisted Members (AD)
moverep.... Movement Report (AD)
MOVEREP... Movement Report [*Military*] (NATG)
MOVERS.... Movement for Responsible Public Service (Philippines) [*Political party*] (PSAP)
Move Short Soc... Movement Shorthand Society (AD)
MOVEW..... Cinema Ride Wrrt [*NASDAQ symbol*] (TTSB)
movi......... Movie (AD)
MOVI........ Movie Gallery [*NASDAQ symbol*] (TTSB)
MOVI........ Movie Gallery, Inc. [*NASDAQ symbol*] (SAG)
MOVIEBYU... Colored Movie Software produced by Brigham Young University (SAUO)
MovieFn.... MovieFone, Inc. [*Associated Press*] (SAG)
MovieGal... Move Gallery, Inc. [*Associated Press*] (SAG)
MovieGal... Movie Gallery, Inc. [*Associated Press*] (SAG)
MovieStr.... Movie Star, Inc. [*Associated Press*] (SAG)
MOVIMS.... Motor Vehicle Information Management System [*Bell System*]
MOVL........ Moving Left (VLIE)
MOVLAS.... Manually Operated Visual Landing Aid System (NG)
MOVMT..... Movement
MOVOAD.... Missouri Voluntary Organizations Active in Disaster [*Emergency Management*] (EMA)
movord...... Movement Order (AD)
MOVORD.... Movement Order [*Military*] (NVT)
MOVP....... Military-Owned Vehicle Plan (AFM)
MO-VPE..... Metal-Organic Vapor Phase Epitaxy [*Also, MO-CVD, OM-CVD, OM-VPE*] [*Semiconductor technology*]
MOVPE...... Metal Oxide Vapour Phase Epitaxy (SAUS)
MOVPER.... Supreme Council, Mystic Order Veiled Prophets of Enchanted Realm (EA)
MOVR....... Moving Right (VLIE)
MOVREP.... Movement Report [*Military*] (NVT)
MOVREP.... Movement Reporting (SAUO)
MOVREP System... Movement Reports System (SAUO)
MOVS....... Manual Overseas Visa System
MOVS....... Military-Owned Vehicle Service (AABC)
MOVSUM... Movement Summary (SAUO)
MOVT........ Miller Object Visualization Test [*Medicine*] (EDAA)
Movt........ Movement (DIAR)
movt........ Movement (GROV)
MOVT........ Movement [*Music*] (ROG)
MOVTAS.... Modified Visual Target Acquisition System (ACAE)
MOVU....... Movaline International [*Intermodal shipping container symbol*] (TVRC)
MOW........ Catskill Airways, Inc. [*FAA designator*] (FAAC)
MOW........ Maintenance of Way [*Indian Railway*] (TIR)
MoW......... Meals on Wheels [*Medicine*] (EDAA)
MOW........ Meals on Wheels
M o W....... Minister of Works [*British*] (AD)
MOW........ Ministry of Works [*British*] (MCD)
MoW......... Ministry of Works (SAUO)
mow......... Mission Operations Wing [*NASA*] (NAKS)
MOW........ Mission Operation Wing [*NASA*] (KSC)
MOW........ Mohawk Airlines [*ICAO designator*] (FAAC)
MOW........ Montana Western Railway [*AAR code*]
MOW........ Moscow [*Former USSR*] [*Airport symbol*] (OAG)
MOW........ Movement for the Ordination of Women [*British lobbying group*] (ECON)
MOW........ Movie of the Week [*Television programming*]
MOW........ Westminster College, Fulton, MO [*OCLC symbol*] (OCLC)
MOWA....... Meals-on-Wheels America [*An association*]
MOWA....... Michigan Outdoor Writers Association
MOWAM.... Mobile Water Mine (MCD)
MoWarbT... Central Missouri State University, Warrensburg, MO [*Library symbol*] [*Library of Congress*] (LCLS)
MoWarbTR... Trails Regional Library, Johnson County-Lafayette County Library, Warrensburg, MO [*Library symbol*] [*Library of Congress*] (LCLS)
MOWASP... Mechanization of Warehousing and Shipment Procedures [*or Processing*] [*Defense Supply Agency*]
mowasp..... Mechanization of Warehousing and Shipment Processing (AD)
MOWB....... Ministry of Works and Buildings [*British*]
MOWBC..... Winnipeg Bible College, Otterburne, Manitoba [*Library symbol*] [*National Library of Canada*] (NLC)
MoWD....... Ministry of Works and Development [*British*] (AD)
MOWG....... Mission Operations Working Group (SAUO)
MoWgK..... Saint Louis Roman Catholic Theological [*Kenrick*] Seminary, Webster Groves,MO [*Library symbol*] [*Library of Congress*] (LCLS)
MoWgT...... Eden Theological Seminary, Webster Groves, MO [*Library symbol*] [*Library of Congress*] (LCLS)
MoWgW..... Webster College, Webster Groves, MO [*Library symbol*] [*Library of Congress*] (LCLS)
MoWhAF.... United States Air Force, Whiteman Air Force Base Library, Whiteman AFB, MO [*Library symbol*] [*Library of Congress*] (LCLS)
MoWitt...... Mobile Window Thermal Test Facility [*Berkeley, CA*] [*Lawrence Berkeley Laboratory*] [*Department of Energy*] (GRD)
Mo W Jur... Monthly Western Jurist [*A publication*] (DLA)
MOWOG..... Morris Wolseley Group [*Automobile manufacturing organization*]
MOWOS..... Meteorological Office Weather Observing System (PDAA)
MOWR/DOI... Ministry of Water Resources/ Department of Irrigation (SAUO)
MOWR/DOI... Ministry of Water Resources/Department of Irrigation (SAUS)
MOWR/DOMH... Ministry of Water Resources/Department of Meteorology and Hydrology (SAUO)
MOWR/GROUND... Ministry of Water Resources/Water Resources Development Board (SAUS)
MOWR/GWRDB... Ministry of Water Resources/Ground Water Resources Development Board (SAUO)
MOWR/MHDB... Ministry of Water Resources/Marsyangdi Hydroelectric Development Board (SAUO)
MOWR/NEA... Ministry of Water Resources/Nepal Electricity Authority (SAUO)
MOWR/SHDP... Ministry of Water Resources/Small Hydro Power Department (SAUO)
MOWS....... Manned Orbital Weapon Station [*or System*]
MOWS....... Motor West [*Common carrier symbol*]
Mow St...... Mowbray's Styles of Deeds [*A publication*] (DLA)
M o WT..... Minister of War Transport [*British*] (AD)
MOWT....... Ministry of War Transport [*Terminated, 1956*] [*British*]
MOWT/DOR... Ministry of Works and Transport/Department of Roads (SAUO)
MOWT/NTRC... Ministry of Works and Transport/Nepal Transport Corp. (SAUS)
MOWT/NTRC... Ministry of Works and Transport/Nepal Transport Corporation (SAUO)
MOWT/SBC... Ministry of Works and Transport/Sajha Bus Corp. (SAUS)

MOWT/SBC... Ministry of Works and Transport/Sajha Bus Corporation (SAUO)
MOWW...... Military Order of the World Wars (EA)
MOWY....... Molerway Freight Lines [*Common carrier symbol*]
MOWZ....... Motor Wheel [*Federal Railroad Administration identification code*]
MOX......... Manually-Operated Changeover [*Computer science*]
MOX......... Mars Oxident Experiment [*NASA*]
MOX......... Mixed Oxide [*Fuel*]
mox.......... Mixed Oxides (AD)
MOX......... Mixed Uranium Plutonium Oxide
MOX......... Molima [*Language symbol*] (ETLW)
MOX......... Morris, MN [*Location identifier*] [*FAA*] (FAAL)
MOX......... Moxa [*German Democratic Republic*] [*Seismograph station code, US Geological Survey*] (SEIS)
MOX......... Moxalactam [*An antibiotic*]
mox.......... Oxidized Metal Explosive (AD)
MOXB....... Moxham Bank [*NASDAQ symbol*] (TTSB)
MOXB....... Moxham Bank Corp. [*NASDAQ symbol*] (SAG)
MOXE........ All sky monitor on Spectrum-X-Gamma (SAUS)
Moxham.... Moxham Bank Corp. [*Associated Press*] (SAG)
MOXIE....... Men Organized to X-press Indignant Exasperation [*Seattle group opposing below-the-knee fashions introduced in 1970*]
MOXV....... Moxahala Valley Railway [*Federal Railroad Administration identification code*]
MOXY....... McMoRan Oil & Gas [*NASDAQ symbol*] (TTSB)
MOXY....... McMoRan Oil and Gas Co. [*NASDAQ symbol*] (SAG)
MOXY....... Model X-Y [*AEC computer code*]
MOY......... Mahogany Minerals [*Vancouver Stock Exchange symbol*]
MOY......... Matchbox Models of Yesteryear [*Toy collection*]
MOY......... Mondy [*Former USSR*] [*Seismograph station code, US Geological Survey*] (SEIS)
moy.......... Money (AD)
MOY......... Money
MOY......... Monterrey [*Colombia*] [*Airport symbol*] (AD)
MOY......... Monthly [*Telegraphy*] (PCTE)
MOY......... Moya [*NCIC car model code*]
MOY......... Salt Lake City, UT [*Location identifier*] [*FAA*] (FAAL)
MOYA........ Ministry of Youth Affairs (SAUO)
MOYC....... Moyco Technologies [*NASDAQ symbol*] (TTSB)
MOYC....... Moyco Technologies, Inc. [*NASDAQ symbol*] (SAG)
MoycoT..... Moyco Technologies, Inc. [*Associated Press*] (SAG)
Moyle....... Moyle's Criminal Circulars [*India*] [*A publication*] (DLA)
Moyle....... Moyle's Entries [*1658*] [*England*] [*A publication*] (DLA)
MOZ......... Aerocharter GmbH [*Austria*] [*ICAO designator*] (FAAC)
MOZ......... Mezhdunarodnaya Organizacia Zhurnalistov [*International Organization of Journalists*] [*Russian*] (AD)
MOZ......... Missouri Southern State College, Library, Joplin, MO [*OCLC symbol*] (OCLC)
MOZ......... Mittlere Ortszeit (SAUO)
MOZ......... Moorea Island [*French Polynesia*] [*Airport symbol*] (OAG)
Moz.......... Mozambique (AD)
MOZ......... Mozambique [*ANSI three-letter standard code*] (CNC)
MOZAIC..... Measurement of Ozone by Airbus-in-Service Aircraft
Mozam...... Mozambique (AD)
Moz & W... Mozley and Whiteley's Law Dictionary [*A publication*] (DLA)
Moz Cur..... Mozambique Current (AD)
MOZL....... Military Order of the Zouave Legion of the United States (EA)
Mozley & W... Mozley and Whiteley's Law Dictionary [*A publication*] (DLA)
Mozley & Whiteley... Mozley and Whiteley's Law Dictionary [*A publication*] (DLA)
MOZLUS.... Military Order of the Zouave Legion of the US (EA)
MOZMVUS... Military Order of Zouaves, Militia and Volunteers of the United States (EA)
mozza....... Mozzarella (AD)
MP........... All India Reporter, Madhya Pradesh [*A publication*] (DLA)
MP........... Atlantis Airlines [*ICAO designator*] (AD)
MP........... Ecology Party (Sweden) [*Political party*] (PSAP)
Mp........... Import [*Economics*]
MP........... Machine Pistol [*Military*] (IIA)
MP........... Machine Pressed
MP........... Machine Processable [*Open Systems Interconnection*] (ODAA)
MP........... Macrophage (MELL)
MP........... Macroprocessor
MP........... Madhya Pradesh [*Indian Railway*] (TIR)
MP........... Madonna Plan (EA)
MP........... Magic Packet (SAUS)
MP........... Magnetic Particle
MP........... Magnetic Pressure (NVT)
MP........... Magnetopause [*In a magnetic field*]
MP........... Magnifying Power (IIA)
mp........... Mail Payment (AD)
MP........... Mail Payment (EBF)
MP........... Maine Preservation (EARSL)
M/P.......... Main Parachute (MCD)
MP........... Main Phase (IEEE)
MP........... Main Propulsion (DNAB)
MP........... Mains Propres [*Personal Delivery*] [*French*]
MP........... Maintainability Plan
MP........... Maintenance Panel (AAG)
mp........... Maintenance Part (AD)
MP........... Maintenance Period
MP........... Maintenance Plan
MP........... Maintenance Planning (SAUO)
MP........... Maintenance Point
MP........... Maintenance Prints
MP........... Maintenance Procedure (MCD)
MP........... Maintenance Program
MP........... Major Path [*Communications term*] (DCT)
MP........... Major Payload (SAUS)
MP........... Major Program (CAAL)
MP........... Major Project (SAUO)
MP........... Malayo-Polynesian [*Linguistics*] (IEL)
MP........... Mallinckrodt, Inc. [*Research code symbol*]
MP........... Malpractice (MELL)
MP........... Management Package (NASA)
MP........... Management Plan
MP........... Management Policy (SAUO)
MP........... Management Process (SAUO)
MP........... Managing Printer [*A publication*] (DGA)
MP........... Managing Process [*Open Systems Interconnection*] (ODAA)
MP........... Manganese Poisoning [*Medicine*] (MELL)
mp........... Manifold Pressure (AD)
MP........... Manifold Pressure
MP........... Manoeuvre Programmer (SAUO)
MP........... Manpower
MP........... Manpower and Personnel (MCD)
MP........... Manpower Plan (SAUO)
MP........... Mansfield Park [*Novel by Jane Austen*]
MP........... Manual Proportional [*Attitude control system of Mercury spacecraft*]
MP........... Manual Pulser
MP........... Manufacturing Process
MP........... Manufacturing-Use Product (EEVL)
MP........... Manu Propria [*In documents, after king's signature*] [*Italian*]
MP........... Marbled Paper (DGA)
MP........... Marching Pack (DNAB)
MP........... Marginal Physical Product [*Economics*]
MP........... Marginal Product
MP........... Marine Police
MP........... Marine Pollution
MP........... Marine Provost [*British military*] (DMA)
MP........... Maritime Patrol (NATG)
MP........... Maritime Polar Air Mass
MP........... Maritime Policy [*British*] (ROG)
MP........... Market Price [*Business term*]
MP........... Marshall's Posse (EA)
MP........... Maschinenpistole [*Submachine Gun*] [*German*] (AD)
MP........... Massa Pilularum [*A Pill Mass*] [*Pharmacy*] (ROG)
MP........... Massively Parallel (AAEL)
MP........... Massorah Parva [*or Massora Parva*] (BJA)
MP........... Mass Properties (MCD)
MP........... Master of Painting
MP........... Master of Pharmacy (GAGS)
MP........... Master of Planning (GAGS)
MP........... Master Pointer [*Computer science*] (BYTE)
MP........... Master Printer (DGA)
MP........... Master Printers Annual [*A publication*] (DGA)
MP........... Mastoid Process [*Medicine*] (MELL)
MP........... Match Problems [*Research test*] [*Psychology*]
MP........... Material Pass (AAG)
MP........... Material Professional [*Army*]
MP........... Mathematical Programming [*Computer science*]
MP........... Matrix Protein (DB)
MP........... Matthew Pelosi [*Designer's mark when appearing on US coins*]
MP........... Maturity Phase
MP........... Maxillary Process
MP........... Maximum Flowering Period [*Botany*]
M/P.......... Maximum Performance [*Automotive engineering*]
MP........... McIntyre Porcupine Mines, Ltd. (SAUO)
MP........... Mean Pressure (MAE)
MP........... Measurement Pipette
MP........... Measurement Pragmatic [*Computer science*] (OA)
MP........... Measuring Point (NASA)
MP........... Mechanical Paper
MP........... Mechanical Part
MP........... Mechanical Printer
MP........... Medial Pallium [*Neuroanatomy*]
MP........... Media Processor [*Computer science*] (BUR)
MP........... Media Project (EA)
MP........... Medical Payment [*Insurance*]
MP........... Medical Physics [*Medicine*] [*AAPM*] [*Journal*] (EDAA)
MP........... Medium Energy Physics Division (SAUO)
mp........... Medium Pressure (AD)
MP........... Medium Pressure
MP........... Meeting Point [*Military*]
MP........... Melchor Developments Ltd. [*Toronto Stock Exchange symbol*]
MP........... Melphalan, Prednisone [*Antineoplastic drug regimen*]
MP........... Melrose Place [*Television program title*]
mp........... Melting Point [*Industrial hygiene term*] (OHS)
MP........... Melting Point
MP........... Melting Pot
MP........... Member of Parliament [*British*]
MP........... Member of Police
MP........... Membrane Production (SSD)
M/P.......... Memorandum of Partnership [*Business term*]
MP........... Menstrual Period [*Medicine*]
MP........... Mental Process [*Work-factor system*]
MP........... Mentum Posterior [*In reference to the chin*]
MP........... Meralgia Paraesthetica [*Medicine*] [*Numbness on the thigh*] (EDAA)
MP........... Mercaptopurine [*Purinethol*] [*Also, M, P*] [*Antineoplastic drug*]
MP........... Mercator's Projection (BARN)

MP .... Mercury Poisoning [*Medicine*] (MELL)
MP .... Meridian Point Realty (EFIS)
MP .... Meridional Part [*Navigation*]
MP .... Merzbacher-Pelizaeus [*Disease*] [*Medicine*] (DB)
MP .... Mesial Pit [*Medicine*] (EDAA)
MP .... Mesiopulpal [*Dentistry*]
MP .... Message Processing (SAUO)
MP .... Message Processor
MP .... Metacarpophalangeal [*Anatomy*]
M-P .... Metal or Plastic (AAG)
MP .... Metal Particle
MP .... Metal-Piercing (SAUS)
m-p .... Metal-Point (AD)
MP .... Metal-Powder [*Videotape*]
MP .... MetaProcessor Platform [*Computer term*]
MP .... Metatarsophalangeal [*Anatomy*]
MP .... Meteorology Panel (MCD)
MP .... Methodist Protestant
MP .... Methoxypsoralen [*Also, MOP*] [*Pharmacology*]
MP .... Methyl Palmoxirate [*Organic chemistry*]
MP .... Methyl Parathion [*Also, MEP, MPN*] [*Pesticide*]
MP .... Methylphenidate [*Central Nervous system stimulant*]
MP .... Methylprednisolone [*Endocrinology*]
MP .... Methylprednisolone Sodium Succinate [*Medicine*] (DAVI)
MP .... Methylpurine [*Organic chemistry*]
MP .... Metra Potential (NITA)
MP .... Metropolitan Police
MP .... Mexican Peso [*Monetary unit*]
MP .... Mezzo Piano [*Moderately Soft*] [*Music*]
mp .... Mezzo-Piano [*Moderately Soft*] [*Italian*] (AD)
MP .... Michoud Plant [*NASA*] (MCD)
M(P) .... Microfilm (Positive)
MP .... Micronized Progesterone
MP .... Microprint
mp .... Microprocessor (ELAL)
MP .... Microprocessor [*Instrumentation*]
MP .... Microprogram
MP .... Middle Persian [*Linguistics*] (IEL)
MP .... Middle phalanx [*Anatomy*] (DAVI)
MP .... Middle Point
MP .... Midland Plant [*Nuclear energy*] (NRCH)
MP .... Midline Precursor [*Cytology*]
MP .... Mid-Phase
MP .... Midpoint (DIPS)
MP .... Mile-Post
mp .... Milepost (AD)
MP .... Military Pay (AFM)
MP .... Military Police [*Army*]
MP .... Military Post (SAUO)
MP .... Military Prohibitionist [*Slang*]
MP .... Military Property (MCD)
M/P .... Milk/Plasma [*Ratio*] [*Physiology*]
m/p .... Milk Powder (AD)
MP .... Minimum Phase (IEEE)
MP .... Minimum Premium [*Insurance*]
MP .... Mining Permit (AD)
MP .... [*The*] Mini Page [*A newspaper supplement*]
MP .... Minister Plenipotentiary
MP .... Minister Provincial (AD)
MP .... Minuteman Platform
MP .... Minutes Played [*Hockey*]
MP .... Miscellaneous Paper [*or Publication*]
MP .... Miscellaneous Proposal (AD)
MP .... Missile Platform
MP .... Missile Positioning
MP .... Missile Possessed (SAA)
M/P .... Missing Parts
MP .... Missing Perforation [*Philately*]
MP .... Missing Person
MP .... Mission Payload (MCD)
MP .... Mission Planner (MCD)
MP .... Mission Profile (MCD)
MP .... Mississippi Power Co. [*NYSE symbol*] (SPSG)
MP .... Missouri Pacific Corporation (EFIS)
MP .... Missouri Pacific Railroad Co. [*AAR code*]
MP .... Mistress of Philosophy
MP .... Mitsubishi Plastics [*Japan*] (PDAA)
MP .... Mixed Pattern
MP .... Mixed Population
MP .... Mobilization Plan
MP .... Modem Port [*Communications term*] (DCT)
MP .... Modern Philology [*A publication*] (BRI)
MP .... Modification Package
MP .... Modified Construction Permit [*FCC*] (NTCM)
MP .... Modo Praescripto [*In the Manner Prescribed*] [*Pharmacy*]
MP .... Mod Package (SAUS)
MP .... Modus Ponens [*Rule of inference*] [*Logic*] [*Latin*]
MP .... Molecular Pair [*Physical Chemistry*]
MP .... Molecular Pathology (SAUO)
MP .... Monetary Policy
mp .... Mongolia [*MARC country of publication code*] [*Library of Congress*] (LCCP)
MP .... Monitor Panel
MP .... Monitor Printer (CET)
MP .... Monophosphate [*Chemistry*] (MAE)
MP .... [*The*] Month in Parliament [*A publication*] [*British*]
MP .... Months after Payment (EBF)
MP .... Montreal Protocol (SAUO)
MP .... Monumentum Posuit [*Erected a Monument*] [*Latin*]
MP .... Mooring Pipe [*or Post*] (ADA)
M/P .... Morjumiid-Pterocephalid Boundary [*Paleogeologic boundary*]
MP .... Morning Prayer (WGA)
MP .... Mortgage-Participation Certificate [*Investment term*]
MP .... Mortgage Payment in Full
MP .... Motherland Party [*Anatavan Partisi*] [*Turkey*] [*Political party*] (PPW)
MP .... Motherland Party (Turkey) [*Political party*] (PSAP)
mp .... Motion Picture (AD)
MP .... Motion Picture Production [*Navy*]
MP .... Motor Potential
MP .... Mounted Police
mp .... Mouthpiece [*Medicine*] (BCRP)
MP .... Mouth Pressure [*Dentistry*] (DAVI)
MP .... Mouvement Populaire [*Popular Movement*] [*Morocco*] [*Political party*] (PPW)
MP .... Mouvement Progressif [*Cameroon*] [*Political party*] (EY)
MP .... Movement Protein [*Cytology*]
MP .... Mucopeptide [*Biochemistry*]
MP .... Mucopolysaccharide [*Also, MPS*] [*Clinical chemistry*]
MP .... Mucopurulent [*Biochemistry*] (DAVI)
MP .... Multilink PPP [*Point-to-Point Protocol*] (PCM)
MP .... Multiparous [*Obstetrics*]
MP .... Multiperil [*Insurance*]
MP .... Multiphase [*Physics*]
MP .... Multi Phonon (AAEL)
MP .... Multiple Processor [*or Multiprocessing*] [*Computer science*] (BUR)
MP .... Multiple Punch (DNAB)
MP .... Multiplex (VLIE)
MP .... Multiplier Phototube
MP .... Multipoint (VLIE)
mp .... Multipole (AD)
MP .... Multipole
MP .... Multiprocessing [*Computer science*] (CDE)
mp .... Multipurpose (AD)
MP .... Multipurpose
MP .... Municipal Police
M/P .... Muscle Plasma [*Ratio*]
MP .... Mycoplasma Pneumonia [*Medicine*]
MP .... Mycoplasma Pulmonis [*A bacterium*]
mp .... Myeloma Protein [*Oncology*] (DAVI)
MP .... My Pal [*Slang*]
MP .... Northern Mariana Islands [*ANSI two-letter standard code*] (CNC)
MP .... Pinawa Public Library, Manitoba [*Library symbol*] [*National Library of Canada*] (NLC)
MP2D .... Multipart, Two Dimensional
MP3 .... MPEG-1, Audio Layer 3 [*Digital music storage and transmission medium*] (NETL)
MP3 .... MPEG Audio Layer 3 (SAUS)
MPA .... Magazine Publisher's Association (NTCM)
MPA .... Magazine Publishers of America [*New York, NY*] [*Database producer*] (IID)
MPA .... Maine Pharmaceutical Association (SAUO)
MPA .... Main Political Administration [*of the Army and Navy*] [*Russian*] (DOMA)
MPA .... Main Propulsion Assistant
MPA .... Main Pulmonary Artery [*Anatomy*]
MPA .... Maintenance Planning Analysis (MCD)
MPA .... Major Projects Association [*British*] (DBA)
MPA .... Management Professionals Association [*Madras, India*] (EA)
MPA .... Manager, Public Awareness (SAUO)
MPA .... Maneuver Propulsion Assembly (MCD)
MPA .... Manpower and Personnel Administration [*Military*] [*British*]
MPA .... Man-Powered Aircraft
MPA .... Marine Physician Assistant (AD)
MPA .... Marine Preservation Association
MPA .... Marine Protected Area
mpa .... Maritime Patrol Aircraft (AD)
MPA .... Maritime Patrol Aircraft (NATG)
MPA .... Marketing and Promotion Association [*British*]
MPA .... Maryland & Pennsylvania Railroad Co. [*AAR code*]
MPA .... Maryland Pharmaceutical Association (SAUO)
mpa .... Maryland Port Authority (AD)
MPA .... Maryland Psychological Association (EARSL)
MPA .... Massachusetts Police Association (EARSL)
MPA .... Mass Processing Analysis (SAUS)
MPA .... Master Degree in Public Administration (SEAT)
M Pa .... Master of Painting
MPA .... Master of Physician Assistant (PGP)
MPA .... Master of Professional Accountancy [*or Accounting*]
MPA .... Master of Professional Accounting (NADA)
MPA .... Master of Professional Arts
MPA .... Master of Public Accounting (SAUO)
MPA .... Master of Public Administration
MPA .... Master of Public Affairs
MPA .... Master Pastrycooks' Association [*Australia*]
MPA .... Master Personnel Administration
MPA .... Master Photographers Association (AD)
MPA .... Master Photographers Association of Great Britain (BI)
MPA .... Master Printers of America (EA)

MPA .... Master Project Assignment (MCD)
MPA .... Materiel Project Administration (ACAE)
MPA .... Mechanical Packing Association [*Later, Fluid Sealing Association*] (EA)
MPA .... Medical Prescibing Adviser (SAUO)
MPA .... Medical Procurement Agency
MPA .... Medium Performance Amplifier (ACAE)
MPA .... Medroxyprogesterone [*Medicine*] (AD)
MPA .... Medroxyprogesterone Acetate [*Also, MAP*] [*Endocrinology*]
mpa .... Megapascal (AD)
MPa .... Megapascal
MPA .... Member of Parliamentary Assembly (SAUO)
MPA .... Member of the Parliamentary Assembly of Northern Ireland (ODA)
MPA .... Mercaptopropionic Acid [*Organic chemistry*]
MPA .... Metal Powder Association [*Later, MPIF*]
MPA .... Methacrylate Producers Association (EA)
MPA .... Methoxypropylamine [*Organic chemistry*]
MPA .... Methylphosphoric Acid [*Organic chemistry*]
MPA .... Methylprednisolone Acetate [*A glucocorticoid*] (MAE)
MPA .... Metropolitan Pensions Association (SAUO)
MPA .... Metropolitan Pensions Associations (AD)
MPA .... Michigan Paraoptometric Association (SAUO)
MPA .... Michigan Petroleum Association (EARSL)
MPA .... Michigan Prevention Association (SAUO)
MPA .... Micropattern Analyzer (DB)
MPA .... Microwave Power Absorption (AAEL)
MPA .... Microwave Power Amplifier
MPA .... Mid Pacific Air Corp. [*ICAO designator*] (FAAC)
MPA .... Midwestern Psychological Association (MCD)
MPA .... Military Pay Account
MPA .... Military Pay and Allowance
MPA .... Military Pay Area (AFM)
MPA .... Military Personnel Appropriation (AFM)
MPA .... Military Personnel, Army
MPA .... Military Police Association [*Defunct*] (EA)
MPA .... Military Proposal and Analysis
mPa .... Millipascal [*Unit of pressure*]
MPA .... Mines Police Association (SAUO)
MPA .... Miniature Pendulum Accelerometer (SAA)
MPA .... Miniature Photocell Activator
MPA .... Miniature Piston Actuator (MCD)
MPA .... Minnesota Psychological Association (EARSL)
MPA .... Missile Procurement, Army (AABC)
MPA .... Missionary Pilots Association [*Defunct*] (EA)
MPA .... Mission Payload Assessment [*Air Force*] (DOMA)
MPA .... Mission Performance Assessment [*NASA*] (KSC)
MPA .... Mission Phase Analysis
MPA .... Mission Profile Analysis
MPA .... Missouri Pharmaceutical Association (SAUO)
MPA .... Mixer/Power Amplifier [*Telecommunications*]
MPA .... Mobile Press Association (EA)
MPA .... Models and Photographers of America (EA)
MPA .... Modern Poetry Association (EA)
MPA .... Modern Professional Army (SAUO)
MPA .... Modification Proposal and Analysis (MCD)
MPA .... Modulated Pulse Amplifier [*Telecommunications*] (IAA)
MPA .... Molybdeophosphoric Acid [*Inorganic chemistry*]
MPA .... Monthly Product Announcement [*Bureau of the Census*] (GFGA)
MPA .... Moose Pass [*Alaska*] [*Seismograph station code, US Geological Survey*] (SEIS)
MPA .... Mortar Package Assembly
MPA .... Mortar Producers Association [*British*] (DBA)
MPA .... Motion Picture Alliance
MPA .... Motion Picture Association (NTPA)
MPA .... Motion Picture Association of America (SAUO)
MPA .... Motivation Problem Analysis [*Training term*] (LPT)
MPA .... Motoring Press Association
MPA .... Multimode Processing Array (ACAE)
MPA .... Multiplant Action [*Nuclear energy*] (NRCH)
MPA .... Multiple Parameter Analysis
MPA .... Multiple Payload Adapter [*Space launch term*] (ISAK)
MPA .... Multiple Peptide Analysis [*Biochemistry*]
MPA .... Multiple-Period Average (IEEE)
MPA .... Multiple Peripheral Adapter
mpa .... Multiple Product Announcement (AD)
MPA .... Multiple Product Announcement (NTCM)
MPA .... Multiple Project Assurance
MPA .... Multiple Project Insurance [*Medicine*] (HVTR)
MPA .... Multiple Protocol Architecture [*Computer science*] (PCM)
MPA .... Multiple-Use Planning Area
MPA .... Multi-Point Asynchronous (NITA)
MPA .... Multiprecision Arithmetic
MPA .... Multipurpose Additive (EDCT)
MPA .... Multi-Purpose Aircraft (SAUS)
MPA .... MuniYield Pennsylvania Fund [*NYSE symbol*] (SPSG)
MPA .... Museum Publications of America
MPA .... Music Publishers Association (NADA)
MPA .... Music Publishers' Association of the United States (EA)
MPA .... Mycophenolic Acid [*Biochemistry*]
MPA .... Nampa, ID [*Location identifier*] [*FAA*] (FAAL)
MPA .... Premenstrual Asthma [*Medicine*] (DAVI)
MPAA .... Motion Picture Association of America (EA)
MPAA .... Motorcar Parts & Accesories, Inc. [*NASDAQ symbol*] (SAG)
MPAA .... Multi-beam Phased-Array Antenna (SAUS)
MPAA .... Multifunctional Phased-Array Antenna (SAUS)
MPAA .... Musical Performing Arts Association (NTCM)
MPAB .... Military Petroleum Advisory Board
MPAC .... Impact Systems, Inc. [*NASDAQ symbol*] (NQ)
MPAC .... Mallinckrodt Inc. PAC [*St. Louis, MO*] (PACS)
MPAC .... Master Plan for Academic Computing (AD)
MPAC .... Materials and Parts Availability Control (SAUO)
MPAC .... Military Pay and Allowance Committee (AFM)
M-PAC ...... M-PAC [*Washington, DC*] (PACS)
MPAC .... Multipurpose Application Console (SSD)
MP Acc ..... Master of Professional Accountancy (PGP)
MP Acc ..... Master of Professional Accounting (PGP)
MPAcc ...... Master of Public Accounting (GAGS)
MP Acct .... Master of Professional Accounting (PGP)
MPACS ...... Management Planning and Control System [*IBM Corp.*]
MPACT ...... Microprocessor Application to Control-Firmware Translator [*Computer science*] (MHDI)
MPAD .... Manpower Personnel Assignment Document (AFM)
MPAD .... Maryland Port Authority [*Federal Railroad Administration identification code*]
MPAD .... Maximum Permissible Accumulated Dose [*of radiation*] (ADA)
mpad .... Maximum Permissible Annual Dose (AD)
MPAD .... Menlo Park Applications Development [*IBM Corp.*]
MPAD .... Mission Planning and Analysis Division [*NASA*]
MP Adm .... Master of Public Administration
MPAE .... Max-Planck-Institut fur Aeronomie [*An association*]
MPAEA ...... Mountain Plains Adult Education Association (AEBS)
MPaed ...... Master of Paediatrics
MPAFD ...... Multiple Pulse Arm Fire Device (MCD)
MP Aff ..... Master of Public Affairs (PGP)
MPAG .... Maxwell Pensioners' Action Group (WDAA)
MPAGB ...... Modern Pentathlon Association of Great Britain (DBA)
MPAI .... Master Plan for Army Intelligence (SAUO)
mpai .... Maximum Permissible Annual Intake (AD)
MPAI .... Maximum Permissible Annual Intake [*Radiation*] (NRCH)
MPAIAC ..... Movimiento para la Autodeterminacion y Independencia del Archipielago Canario [*Movement for the Self-Determination and Independence of the Canary Archipelago*] [*Canary Islands*] [*Spanish*] (PD)
MPAJA ...... Malayan People's Anti-Japanese Army [*World War II*]
MPAJU ...... Malayan People's Anti-Japanese Union [*World War II*]
MPAK .... Middeck Payload Accommodation Kit (SAUS)
mpam .... Maritime Polar Air Mass (AD)
MPAM .... Maritime Polar Air Mass (MSA)
MPAMA ...... Milk Products Advertising-Merchandising Association (EA)
MPAN .... Macrosopic Polyarteritis Nodosa [*Medicine*] (MELL)
MPAN .... Mariner Post Acute Network (MHID)
MP&C .... Maintenance Planning and Control
MP & CS .... Management Planning and Control System
MP & IS .... Material Process and Inspection Specification (AAG)
MP&L .... Minnesota Power and Light Co. (SAUO)
MP&L .... Mississippi Power and Light Co. (SAUO)
MP&L Company ... Minnesota Power & Light Company (SAUO)
MP & MAC ... Marine Petroleum and Minerals Advisory Committee [*Terminated, 1976*] [*National Oceanic and Atmospheric Administration*] (NOAA)
MP&MTD ... Motion Picture & Medical Television Department (SAUO)
MP&QA ..... Manufacturing, Production, and Quality Assurance
mp & rs .... Motive Power and Rolling Stock (AD)
MP & TF .... Motion Picture and Television Fund
MPANE ...... Mariner Post Acute Network [*OTCBB symbol*]
MPANSW ... Master Patternmakers' Association of New South Wales [*Australia*]
MPANSW ... Master Poulterers' Association of New South Wales [*Australia*]
MPAP .... Mean Pulmonary Artery Pressure [*Cardiology*]
MPAPS ...... Motivation and Potential for Adoptive Parenthood Scale [*Psychology*]
MPAQ .... McGill Pain Assessment Questionnaire (MELL)
MPAR .... Maintenance Program Analysis Report
MPAR .... Microprogram Address Register
MPAR .... Multicanal Participacoes [*NASDAQ symbol*] (SAG)
m part ...... Movable Partition (AD)
MPAS .... Maritime Patrol Airship Study
MPAS .... Maryland Parent Attitude Survey [*Psychology*]
MPAS .... Master of Physical Activity Studies (PGP)
MPAS .... Master of Physician Assistant Studies (PGP)
MPAS .... Mild Perioxic Acid Schiff [*Reaction*] [*Medicine*] (DMAA)
mpas .... Millipascal Second (AD)
MPASK ...... Multi-Phase and Amplitude-Shift-Keying [*Computer science*] (PDAA)
MPASS ...... Modular Processing and Support System
MPASS ...... Multi-Purpose Amphibious Support Ship (SAUS)
MPast .... Master in Pastoral Studies
MPAT .... Management Postition Analysis Test [*William J. Reddin*] (TES)
MPAT .... Multipurpose All-Terrain Vehicle
MPAT .... Multi-Purpose Anti-Tank (SAUS)
MPATI ...... Midwest Program for Airborne Television Instruction [*Defunct*]
MPAU .... Mahatma Phule Agricultural University (SAUO)
MPA-URP ... Master of Public Affairs and Urban and Regional Planning (PGP)
MPAUS ...... Music Publishers' Association of the United States (DGA)
m payl ...... Maximum Payload (AD)
MPB .... Berkshire Athenaeum, Pittsfield, MA [*Library symbol*] [*Library of Congress*] (LCLS)
MPB .... Machine-Pressed Bales
MPB .... Magnetic Particle Brake
MPB .... Maine Potato Board (EA)
MPB .... Maintenance Parts Breakdown (KSC)
mpb .... Male Pattern Baldness (AD)

MPB .... Male-Pattern Baldness
MPB .... Master of Physical Biology
MPB .... Material Performance Branch [*Air Force*]
MPB .... Materials Properties Branch [*Army*] (RDA)
MPB .... Matrix Program Board
MPB .... Maximum Participation Base (IIA)
MPB .... Mechanically Processed Beef [*Food technology*]
MPB .... Mephobarbital [*Antiepileptic drug*]
MPB .... Meprobamate (DMAA)
MPB .... Merit Promotion Bulletin [*Military*]
MPB .... Miami [*Florida*] Public Seaplane Base [*Airport symbol*] (OAG)
MPB .... Military Personnel Branch (SAUO)
MPB .... Miniature Precision Bearing, Inc.
MPB .... Missing Persons Bureau
MPB .... Montpelier & Barre Railroad Co. [*Later, MB*] [*AAR code*]
MPB .... Motorized Pontoon Bridge (MCD)
MPB .... Mouvement Progressiste de Burundi [*Progressive Movement of Burundi*]
MPB .... Mucopurulent Bronchitis [*Medicine*] (MELL)
MPB .... Multilayer Printed Board
MPB .... Munitions Packaging Branch [*Picatinny Arsenal*] [*Army*] (RDA)
MPB .... Musica Popular Brasileira [*Pop music*]
MPBA......... Machine Printers' Beneficial Association [*Later, MPEA*]
MPBA......... Model Power Boat Association [*British*] (DBA)
MPBA......... Mountains and Plains Booksellers Association (EA)
MPBA......... Multiple Practice Bomb Adapter (SAUS)
MPB and W... Ministry of Public Buildings and Works (SAUO)
MPBB......... Maximum Permissible Body Burden [*Radiation*]
mpbb......... Maximum Permissible Body Burden [*of Radiation*] (AD)
MPBB......... Methyl(phenyl)(butyl)barbituric (Acid) [*Biochemistry*]
MPBC......... Berkshire Community College, Pittsfield, MA [*Library symbol*] [*Library of Congress*] (LCLS)
MPBC......... Memphis Power Boat Club [*Tennessee*] (AD)
MPBDS...... Material Properties Bibliographic Data System [*Purdue University*] [*Database*]
MPBE......... Molten Plutonium Burn-Up Experiment [*Nuclear energy*] (IEEE)
MPBEA...... Mountain Plains Business Education Association (AEBS)
MPBI......... Multiple Post Boost Intercept Study (ACAE)
MPBL......... Berkshire Law Library Association, Pittsfield, MA [*Library symbol*] [*Library of Congress*] (LCLS)
MPBMA..... Munitions Production Base Modernization Agency (SAUO)
MPBME..... Munitions Production Base Modernization, Expansion (RDA)
MPBN....... Military Police Battalion
MPBO....... Bocas Del Toro [*Panama*] [*ICAO location identifier*] (ICLI)
MPBP......... Mechanically Processed Beef Product [*Food technology*]
MPBP......... Metal Polishers, Buffers, Platers, and Allied Workers International Union (EA)
mp br......... Multipunch Bar (AD)
MPBR......... Multipunch Bar
MPBRS....... Maintenance Production/Backlog Reporting System (SAUO)
MPBS......... Medical Pocket-Book Series [*A publication*]
MPBS......... Multipurpose Bayonet System [*Army*] (INF)
MPBS......... Mutual Permanent Building Society (AD)
MPBW......... Ministry of Public Building and Works [*Later, DOE*] [*British*]
MPC .... Machine Punch Card
MPC .... Magellan Petroleum [*Exchange Symbol*] (TTSB)
MPC .... Magnetic Particle Clutch
MPC .... Maharashtra Prajatantra Congress [*India*] [*Political party*] (PPW)
MPC .... Maharashtra Progressive Congress [*India*] [*Political party*] (PPW)
MPC .... Maidstone Paper Converters [*Commercial firm*] [*British*]
MPC .... Maine Potato Council [*Later, MPB*] (EA)
MPC .... Maintenance Parts Catalog
MPC .... Maintenance Policy Council [*DoD*] [*Washington, DC*]
MPC .... Maintenance Priority Code
MPC .... Maintenance Procedure Chart
MPC .... Mandatory Product Control
MPC .... Manpower and Personnel Center (SAUO)
MPC .... Manpower & Personnel Centre (SAUO)
MPC .... Manpower and Personnel Council [*DoD*]
MPC .... Manpower Planning Council
MPC .... Manpower Policy Committee (SAUO)
MPC .... Manpower Priorities Committee
MPC .... Manual Pointing Controller (MCD)
MPC .... Manufacturing Plan Change
MPC .... Manufacturing, Planning, and Control
MPC .... Marco Polo Club (EA)
MPC .... Marginal Producers Cost [*Engineering economics*]
mpc......... Marginal Propensity to Consume (AD)
MPC .... Marginal Propensity to Consume [*Economics*]
MPC .... Marine Policy Center (GNE)
MPC .... Marine Pollution Control, Inc. (EFIS)
mpc......... Marine Protein Concentrate (AD)
MPC .... Marine Protein Concentrate [*See also FPC*] (MSC)
MPC .... Marker Pulse Conversion [*Telecommunications*] (TEL)
MPC .... Market Performance Committee [*of NYSE*]
MPC .... Massively Parallel Computer (GART)
MPC .... Master Control Program [*Computer science*] (ECII)
MPC .... Master of Pastoral Counseling (PGP)
MPC .... Master of Personnel Counseling (GAGS)
MPC .... Master of Professional Counseling (PGP)
MPC .... Master of Public Communication (PGP)
MPC .... Master Parts Card
MPC .... Master Phasing Chart (MCD)
MPC .... Master Program Chart (MCD)
MPC .... Materials Policy Commission (SAUO)
MPC .... Materials Preparation Center [*Ames, IA*] [*Ames Laboratory*] [*Department of Energy*] (GRD)
MPC .... Materials Processing Center [*Massachusetts Institute of Technology*] [*Research center*] (RCD)
mpc......... Materials Program Code (AD)
MPC .... Materials Properties Council (EA)
MPC .... Materiel Program Code [*Air Force*] (AFM)
MPC .... Materiel Program Costs (ACAE)
mpc......... Mathematics, Physics, Chemistry (AD)
mpc......... Maximum Permissible Concentration (AD)
MPC .... Maximum Permissible Concentration [*Later, RCG*] [*Radiation*]
MPC .... McAfee Parental Controls [*Computer science*] [*Internet security software*]
MPC .... McKechnie (EFIS)
MPC .... Mean Plasma Concentration [*Medicine*] (MELL)
MPC .... Mechanical Positioning Control
MPC .... Mechanized Production Control
MPC .... Medical Policy Committee [*Medicine*] [*UMS*] (EDAA)
MPC .... Medical Practices' Committee (WDAA)
MPC .... Medium Processing Channel [*Carbon*] (DICI)
MPC .... Megaparsec
MPC .... Member of Parliament of Canada
MPC .... Member of Provincial Council (SAUO)
MPC .... Member Pickwick Club [*From "The Pickwick Papers" by Charles Dickens*]
MPC .... Membrane Protein Complex [*Cytology*]
MPC .... Memory Protection Check (MCD)
MPC .... Meningococcal Protein Conjugate [*Medicine*] (MELL)
MPC .... Meperidine, Promethazine, and Chlorpromazine [*Drug regime*]
MPC .... Merleau-Ponty Circle (EA)
MPC .... Message Processing Center
MPc......... Metallophthalocyanine [*Organic chemistry*]
MPC .... Metal Properties Council (SAUO)
MPC .... Meteorological Prediction Center (KSC)
MPC .... Metromedia Producers Corp.
MPC .... Metropolitan Police College (AD)
MPC .... Metropolitan Police Commissioner (AD)
MPC .... Microcircuit Power Converter
MPC .... Microparticle Concentration [*Analytical chemistry*]
MPC .... Microprocessor [*Computer science*] [*Unit*] (ECII)
MPC .... Micro-Processor Controller [*Computer science*] (AGLO)
MPC .... Microprogram Control
MPC .... Micropurulent Cervicitis [*Medicine*]
MPC .... Midbody Pyro Controller (NASA)
MPC .... Midpalmar Crease [*Medicine*] (MELL)
MPC .... Mid Power Controller [*Aerospace*] (NAKS)
MPC .... Midwest Parentcraft Center (EA)
mpc......... Military Payment Certificate (AD)
MPC .... Military Payment Certificate
MPC .... Military Personnel Center (AFM)
MPC .... Military Pioneer Corps [*British*]
MPC .... Military Police Corps
MPC .... Military Police Force (AD)
MPC .... Military Postal Clerk (AFM)
MPC .... Military Property Custodian (AFIT)
Mpc......... Million Parsecs [*Interstellar space measure*]
MPC .... Mineral Policy Center (EA)
MPC .... Miniature Protector Connector [*Telecommunications*] (TEL)
MPC .... Minimal Flight Planning Charts [*Air Force*]
MPC .... Minimum Mycoplasmacidal Concentration [*Medicine*] (MAE)
mpc......... Minimum Planning Chart (AD)
MPC .... Minimum Protozoacidal Concentration
MPC .... Ministry Partnership Committee (SAUO)
MPC .... Minnesota Population Center [*University of Minnesota*] (RCD)
MPC .... Minor Planet Center [*Smithsonian Institution*]
MPC .... Minor Planets Circular [*Astronomy term*]
MPC .... Missile Practice Camp (SAUO)
MPC .... Mission Planning Center (MCD)
MPC .... Mission Profile Course (MCD)
MPC .... Mississippi Library Commission, Jackson, MS [*OCLC symbol*] (OCLC)
MPC .... Mitsubishi Petrochemical Co. Ltd. (SAUO)
MPC .... Mobile Processing Center (MCD)
MPC .... Mobile Productivity Center
MPC .... Mode and Power Control [*Aviation*]
MPC .... Model Penal Code (AD)
MPC .... Model Predictive Control [*Chemical engineering*]
MPC .... Model Procurement Code [*for State and Local Governments*] (AAGC)
MPC .... Modular Peripheral Interface Converter
MPC .... Monagas Pipeline Crude [*Petrochemical engineering*]
MPC .... Monetary Policy Committee [*France*] (ECON)
MPC .... Monetary Policy Committee [*Bank of England*]
MPC .... Monitor Proportional Counter (MCD)
MPC .... Monolayer-Protected Metal Cluster [*Materials science*]
MPC .... Monopolistic [*Telegraphy*] (PCTE)
MPC .... Montana Power Company (SAUO)
MPC .... Monterey Peninsula College [*California*]
MPC .... Montreal Presbyterian College
MPC .... Moore's English Privy Council Cases [*A publication*] (DLA)
MPC .... Morphine Positive Control [*Epidemiology*]
MPC .... Mortgage-Participation Certificate [*Investment term*] (GFGA)
MPC .... Most Probable Cost (AAGC)
MPC .... Mother-of-Pearl Clouds [*Meteorology*] (PDAA)

MPL .... Mandatory Parts List [*DoD*]
MPL .... Manipulation Positioning Latches [*Aerospace*] (NAKS)
MPL .... Manipulator Positioning Latches (MCD)
MPL .... Man Position Locator
MPL .... Manufacturing Parts List (AAG)
mpl .... Maple (DAC)
MPL .... Maple
MPL .... Maple Technology Ltd. [*Vancouver Stock Exchange symbol*]
MPL .... Marine Physical Laboratory [*Research center*] (RCD)
MPL .... Marine Physics Laboratory [*Scripps*]
MPL .... Mars Poplar Lander [*Astronomy term*]
MPL .... Mars Probe Lander [*Aerospace*]
MPL .... Master of Patent Law
MPl .... Master of Planning
MPL .... Master of Polite Literature
MPL .... Master of Public Law
MPL .... Master Parts List
MPL .... Master Planner, Inc. [*ICAO designator*] (FAAC)
MPL .... Material Processing Laboratory (SSD)
mpl .... Mathematical Programming Language [*Computer science*] (AD)
MPL .... Mathematical Programming Language [*Computer science*] (PDAA)
MPL .... Mavis, Paul A., South Bend IN [*STAC*]
MPL .... Maxillofacial Prosthesis Laboratory [*WRAMC*] (RDA)
mpl .... Maximum Payload (AD)
MPL .... Maximum Penalized-Likelihood [*Statistics*]
mpl .... Maximum Permissible Language (AD)
mpl .... Maximum Permissible Level (AD)
MPL .... Maximum Permissible Level [*Radiation*] (DEN)
MPL .... Maximum Permissible Limit (LDOE)
MPL .... Maximum Possible Loss (COE)
MPL .... Maximum Probable Loss [*Insurance*]
MPL .... Maximum Procurement Level (AFIT)
MPL .... Mechanical Parts List (NASA)
MPL .... Mechanical Properties Loop [*Nuclear energy*] (NRCH)
MPL .... Megneto Photo Luminescence (AAEL)
MPL .... Melphalan [*Also, A, L-PAM, M, MPH*] [*Antineoplastic drug*]
MPL .... Memphis Public Library (AD)
MPL .... Mesiopulpolingual [*Dentistry*] (MAE)
mpl .... Message Processing Language [*Computer science*] (AD)
MPL .... Message Processing Language [*Burroughs Corp.*]
MPL .... Metals Processing Laboratory [*MIT*] (MCD)
MPL .... Metering Pumps Limited
MPL .... Metropolitan Police Laboratory (AD)
MPL .... Metropolitan Property & Liability Insurance Co. (EFIS)
MPL .... Miami Public Library (AD)
MPL .... Micro Power Light [*Automotive lighting*]
MPL .... Microprocessor [*or Motorola's*] Programming Language [*1975*] [*Computer science*] (CSR)
MPL .... Microprogramming Language (NITA)
MPL .... Milwaukee Public Library (AD)
MPL .... Mine Planter (NATG)
MPL .... Minimum Power Level [*Aerospace*] (NAKS)
MPL .... Minnesota Power [*NYSE symbol*] [*Formerly, Minnesota Power & Light*]
MPL .... Minnesota Power & Light Co. [*NYSE symbol*] (SPSG)
MPL .... Mission Planning Laboratory [*NASA*] (KSC)
MPL .... Mississippi Power and Light (SAUO)
MPL .... Missouri Pacific Lines (AD)
MPL .... Mistress of Patent Law (SAUO)
MPL .... Mistress of Polite Literature
MPL .... Mixer/Preamplifier/Local Oscillator (ACAE)
MP/L .... Modified Construction Permit and License [*FCC*] (NTCM)
MPL .... Monessen Public Library, Monessen, PA [*OCLC symbol*] (OCLC)
MPL .... Monkey Placental Lactogen
MPL .... Monophosphoryl Lipid [*Biochemistry*]
MPL .... Montoneros Patria Libre [*Guerrila group*] [*Ecuador*] (EY)
MPL .... Montpellier [*France*] [*Airport symbol*] (OAG)
MPL .... Montreal Public Library [*Canada*] (AD)
MPL .... Motion Picture Laboratories [*Commercial firm*]
MPL .... Motivated Productivity Level [*Quality control*]
MPL .... Mouvement Politique Lulua [*Lulua Political Movement*] [*Political party*]
MPL .... Movimento Politica dei Lavoratori [*Workers' Political Movement*] [*Italy*] [*Political party*] (PPE)
MPL .... Movimiento Popular de Liberacion "Cinchoneros" [*"Cinchoneros" Popular Liberation Movement*] [*Honduras*] [*Political party*]
MPL .... Mozilla Public License (SAUO)
MPL .... Multilevel Pass transistor Logic (SAUS)
MPL .... Multi-Platform Launcher (SAUS)
MPL .... Multiple Payload Launcher
mpl .... Multiple-Position Lock (AD)
MPL .... Multiple-Pulsed Laser (ACAE)
MPL .... Multipurpose Limousine
MPL .... Multischedule Private Line
MPL .... Multi-Services, Inc. [*FAA designator*] (FAAC)
MPL .... Patrologia Latina [*J. P. Migne*] [*Paris*] [*A publication*] (BJA)
MPl .... Plymouth Public Library, Plymouth, MA [*Library symbol*] [*Library of Congress*] (LCLS)
MPlA .... Antiquarian House, Plymouth, MA [*Library symbol*] [*Library of Congress*] (LCLS)
MPLA .... Malayan People's Liberation Army
MPLA .... Mask Programmable Logic Array (NITA)
MPLa .... Mesiopulpolabial [*Dentistry*] (MAE)
MPLA .... Metropolitan Public Libraries Association [*New South Wales, Australia*]
MPLA .... Monophosphoryl Lipid A [*Biochemistry*]
MPLA .... Mountain Plains Library Association (AEBS)
MPLA .... Movimento Popular de Libertacao de Angola [*Popular Movement for the Liberation of Angola*] [*Political party*]
MPLA .... Multiport Link Aggregation (GART)
MPLA .... Popular Movement for the Liberation of Angola (SAUO)
MPlan .... Master of Planning
MPlanStud ... Master of Planning Studies
MPlanStudies ... Master of Planning Studies
MPLA-PT ... Movimento Popular de Libertacao de Angola - Partido do Trabalho [*Popular Movement for the Liberation of Angola - Party of Labor*] [*Political party*] (PPW)
MPLAW ..... Melamine Paper Laminate (PDAA)
MPLAW ..... Modified Programmers Language [*Computer science*] (PDAA)
MPLAW ..... Moving Part Logic (PDAA)
MPLAW ..... Multipulse Scaling-Law Code using Data Base Interpolation (PDAA)
MPLB .... Balboa/Albrook [*Panama*] [*ICAO location identifier*] (ICLI)
MPLB .... Maximum Permissible Lung Burden [*Industrial hygiene*]
MPLC .... Medium-Pressure Liquid Chromatography
MPLC .... Mid-Peninsula Library Cooperative [*Library network*]
MPLC .... Movimento Popular de Libertacao de Cabinda [*Popular Movement for the Liberation of Cabinda*] [*Angola*] [*Political party*] (PD)
MPLC .... Movimiento Popular de Liberacion Cinchonero [*Guerrilla forces*] [*Honduras*] (EY)
MPLC .... Multi-Platform Launch Controller
MPLCC ...... Most Probable Life Cycle Cost (ACAE)
MPLCC ...... Most-Probable Life Cycle Cost
MPLD .... Mouvement Populaire pour la Liberation de Djibouti [*Political party*] (EY)
MPLE .... Multipurpose Long Endurance [*Aircraft*]
MPLEJ .... Military Police Law Enforcement Journal (SAUO)
MPLG .... Materials Processing in Low Gravity (SAUS)
MPLG .... Multi-Purpose Lithium Grease
MPLH .... Multipurpose Light Helicopter (DOMA)
MPLI .... Michigan Picture Language Inventory (EDAC)
MPLL .... Malayan People's Liberation League
MPLM .... Machine-Prepared List of Materials (ACAE)
MPLM .... Mini-Pressurized Logistic Modules [*Space technology*]
MPLN .... Maintenance Planning [*Database*] (NASA)
MPLO .... Military Postal Liaison Office
MPLP .... La Palma [*Panama*] [*ICAO location identifier*] (ICLI)
MPLP .... Marxist Progressive Labor Party [*Political party*] (AD)
MPLP .... Mental Patients Liberation Projects
MPlP .... Plimoth Plantation, Inc., Plymouth, MA [*Library symbol*] [*Library of Congress*] (LCLS)
MPLP .... Portage Plains Regional Library, Portage La Prairie, Manitoba [*Library symbol*] [*National Library of Canada*] (NLC)
MPLPC ...... Multipulse Linear Productive Coding (PDAA)
MPLPDC ... MDC Library, Manitoba Developmental Centre, Portage La Prairie [*Library symbol*] [*National Library of Canada*] (BIB)
MPLPM ..... Manitoba School, Portage La Prairie, Manitoba [*Library symbol*] [*National Library of Canada*] (NLC)
MPLPr .... MP&L Cap I 8.05% 'QUIPS' [*NYSE symbol*] (TTSB)
MPLPrA ...... Minn Pwr & Lt 5% cm Pfd [*AMEX symbol*] (TTSB)
MPL + PRED ... Melphalan and Prednisone [*Antineoplastic drug regimen*] (DAVI)
MPL + PRED(MP) ... Melphalan and Prednisone [*Antineoplastic drug regimen*] (DAVI)
MPlPS .... Pilgrim Society, Plymouth, MA [*Library symbol*] [*Library of Congress*] (LCLS)
MPLR .... Medium Power Loop Range
MPLR .... Movement for the Liberation of Reunion (SAUO)
MPLS .... Maximal Principle Least Squares
Mpls .... Minneapolis (AD)
MPLS .... Minneapolis, MN [*American Association of Railroads railroad junction routing code*]
MPLS .... Multi-Protocol Label Switching (MLOA)
MPLSM ..... Multiple Position Letter Sorting Machine (PDAA)
MPLSM ..... Multiple Position Letter Sort Machine
MPLSS ...... Marketing of Public Library Services Section [*Public Library Association*]
MPLU .... Most Probable Library User
MPLX .... Multiplexer
MPLXR ...... Multiplexer
MPLZ .... Minnesota Power & Light [*Federal Railroad Administration identification code*]
MPM .... Magnetic Phase Modulator
MPM .... Magnum Petroleum [*AMEX symbol*] (SAG)
MPM .... Mahorais Peoples Movement (SAUO)
MPM .... Main Propulsion Motor
MPM .... Maintenance and Peripheral Module (SAUS)
MPM .... Maintenance Planning Manual (NG)
MPM .... Maintenance Program Management [*Military*] (AABC)
MPM .... Major Program Memorandum [*Military*]
MPM .... Major Project Manager
MPM .... Malignant Papillary Mesothelioma [*Medicine*]
MPM .... Malignant Pleural Mesothelioma (ADWA)
MPM .... Manipulator Positioning Mechanism [*Aerospace*] (NAKS)
MPM .... Manpower Planning Model
MPM .... Manufacture Procedure Manual (KSC)
MPM .... Maputo [*Mozambique*] [*Airport symbol*] (OAG)
MPM .... Marginal Propensity to Import [*Economics*]
MPM .... Marshall Plan of the Mind [*BBC radio program*] (ECON)
MPM .... Master of Personnel Management (GAGS)
MPM .... Master of Pest Management (DD)
MPM .... Master of Professional Management (PGP)

MPM........ Master of Project Management (PGP)
MPM........ Master of Psychological Management
MPM........ Master of Psychological Medicine (ADA)
MPM........ Master of Public Management
MPM........ Materials Properties Manual (SAUO)
MPM........ Mauritian Patriotic Movement (SAUO)
MPM........ Maximum Permitted Mileage [*Airlines*]
MPM........ Maximum Pionization Method (OA)
MPM........ Medical Planning Module (DOMA)
MPM........ Message Processing Modules (MCD)
MPM........ Metal-Plastic Metal [*Automotive engineering*]
MPM........ Metal-Plastic-Metal [*Automotive engineering*]
mpm........ Meters Per Minute (AD)
MPM........ Meters per Minute
MPM........ Metra-Potential Method [*Graph theory*]
MPM........ Microprogram Memory
MPM........ Microscope-Photometer
MPM........ Microwave Power Meter
MPM........ Microwave Power Module (SAUS)
MPM........ Mid-Pacific Mountains [*Geology*]
MPM........ Miles per Minute
MPM........ Milestone Planning Meeting (MCD)
MPM........ Milk Plant Monthly (SAUO)
MPM........ Milwaukee Public Museum (AD)
MPM........ Miniaturized Pointing Mount [*Spacelab*] [*NASA*]
MPM........ Missile Power Monitor (AAG)
mpm........ Missile Power Monitor (AD)
MPM........ Modest Petrovich Mussorgsky [*1839-1881*] (AD)
mpm........ Mole-Percent Metal (AD)
MPM........ Monoclonal Paratopic Molecule (DB)
MPM........ Monocycle Position Modulation
MPM........ Mortality Probability Models [*Medicine*]
MPM........ Mouse Peritoneal Macrophages
MPM........ Mouvement Populaire Mahorais [*Mayotte People's Movement*] [*Comoros*] [*Political party*] (PPW)
MPM........ Movement Planning Module (SAUO)
MPM........ Moving Presentation Mode
MP/M........ Multiprocessing Monitor Control Program [*Computer science*]
MP/M........ Multiprogramming Control Program for Microcomputers
MP/M........ Multiprogramming Control Program for Microprocessors (NITA)
MPM........ Multiprogramming Monitor
mpm........ Multipurpose Meal (AD)
MPM........ Multipurpose Meal
MPM........ Multipurpose Missile (MCD)
MP-M........ Museum Plantin Moretus [*Belgium*] (AD)
MPM2........ Multimedia Presentation Manager/2 (SAUS)
MPMA....... Master of Public Management and Administration
MPMA....... Metal Packaging Manufacturers Association [*British*] (DBA)
MPMA....... Methylphorbol Myristate Acetate [*Organic chemistry*]
MPMA....... Montford Point Marine Association (EA)
MPMA....... Motion Picture Museum Association [*British*] (BI)
MPM&PH... Master of Preventive Medicine and Public Health (GAGS)
MPMA PAC... Michigan Podiatric Medical Association PAC [*Lansing, MI*] (PACS)
MPMC....... Microprogram Memory Control (NITA)
MPMC....... Military Personnel, Marine Corps
MPMCANSW... Master Plumbers and Mechanical Contractors Association of New South Wales [*Australia*]
MPMCAV....... Master Plumbers and Mechanical Contractors' Association of Victoria [*Australia*]
MPMCAWA... Master Plumbers and Mechanical Contractors' Association of Western Australia
MPMD....... Methylpentemethylenediamine [*Plastics*]
MPMD....... Multiple Processor Multiple Data Architecture (RALS)
MPMG....... Marine Pollution Management Group [*British*]
MPMG....... Melt-Powder Melt-Growth [*Materials Science*]
MPMG....... Multi-Purpose Molybdenum Grease
MPMG....... Panama/Paitilla, Marco A. Gelabert [*Panama*] [*ICAO location identifier*] (ICLI)
MPMH....... Mean Preventive Maintenance Hours
MPMI....... Magazine and Paperback Marketing Institute (EA)
MPMIC...... Mechanical Properties of Materials Information Center (MCD)
MPMIS...... Military Personnel Management Information System (SAUO)
MPMIS...... Military Police Management Information System
MPML....... Main Profile-Main Level (SAUS)
MPML....... Mid-Pacific Marine Laboratory (MSC)
MP/ML...... Modified Construction Permit and Modified License [*FCC*] (NTCM)
MPML....... MPM Technologies, Inc. [*NASDAQ symbol*] (SAG)
MPMLE....... MPM Technologies [*NASDAQ symbol*] (TTSB)
MPMLQ...... Multipulse Maximum Likelihood Quantization (SAUS)
MPMM...... Monthly Project Management Meetings (SAUO)
MPMMG.... Marine Pollution Monitoring Management Group (ASF)
MPMO....... Motion Picture Machine Operator [*A union*] (NTCM)
MPMP....... Mass Properties Management Plan (NASA)
MPMP....... Master Program Management Plan (SAUO)
MPMP....... (Methylpiperidyl)methylphenothiazine [*Sedative*]
MPMP....... Modification Program Management Plan (MCD)
MPMPR...... Metropolitan Police Missing Persons Register [*British*]
MPMPrEC... Magnum Pete $1.10 Cv'C'Pfd [*AMEX symbol*] (TTSB)
MPMR....... Movimiento Patriotica Manuel Rodriguez [*Manuel Rodriguez Patriotic Movement*] [*Chile*] [*Political party*] (EY)
MPMRP..... Master Petroleum Material Requirements Plan (MCD)
MPMS....... Mattress and Palliasse Makers' Society [*A union*] [*British*]
MPMS....... Missile Performance Measurement System (SAUO)
MPMS....... Missile Performance Measuring System (MCD)
MPMS....... Multiple-Pressure Measuring System
MPMSE..... Multiuse Payload and Mission Support Equipment (MCD)
MPMT....... Mean Preventive Maintenance Time (MCD)
MPMT....... Mellon Participating Mortgage Trust Commercial Properties Series [*NASDAQ symbol*] (NQ)
MPMT....... Multiple Primary Malignant Tumor [*Oncology*]
MPMT....... Murphy Punch Maneuver Test [*Medicine*] (EDAA)
MPM Tch.... MPM Technologies, Inc. [*Associated Press*] (SAG)
MPMTS..... Mellon Ptc Mortgage Trust (EFIS)
MPMUL..... Military Production Master Urgency List
MPMV..... Mason-Pfizer Monkey Virus
MPN......... Manipulation [*Telegraphy*] (PCTE)
MPN......... Manpower Personnel, Navy (DOMA)
MPN......... Manufacturers Part Number (MCD)
MPN......... Manufacturer's Productivity Network [*Hewlett-Packard Co.*]
MPN......... Mariner Post-Acute Network [*Formerly, Paragon Health Network*] [*NYSE symbol*]
MPN......... Master in Psychiatric Nursing (GAGS)
MPN......... Master Part Number (MCD)
MPN......... Maximum Possible Number (EPAT)
MPN......... Maximum Probable Number (EEVL)
MPN......... Mean Probable Number (MCD)
MPN......... Medial Preoptic Nucleus [*Brain anatomy*]
MPN......... Methyl Parathion [*Also, MEP, MP*] [*Pesticide*]
MPN......... Microwave Product News (SAUO)
MPN......... Military Pay, Navy [*An appropriation*]
MPN......... Military Personnel, Navy
MPN......... Military Procurement, Navy (MCD)
MPN......... Missing Pet Network [*Emergency Management*] (EMA)
MPN......... Mobility Position Number (SAUO)
MPN......... Monongahela Power Co. [*AMEX symbol*] (SPSG)
mpn......... Most Probable Number (AD)
MPN......... Most Probable Number
MPN......... Multiprotocol Network (GART)
MPNA....... Midwest Professional Needlework Association [*Later, APNRA*] (EA)
MPNA....... Working Group on Pollution Baseline and Monitoring Studies in the North Atlantic (SAUO)
MPNC....... Mouvement pour le Progres National Congolais [*Movement for National Congolese Progress*]
MPNDS...... Material Properties Numerical Data System [*Purdue University*] [*Database*]
MPNE........ Manpower Needs [*Military*]
MPNF........ Manpower-Needs Forecasting (MCD)
MPNI........ Ministry of Pensions and National Insurance [*Later, MSS*] [*British*]
MPNPrA..... Monogahela Pwr 4.4% Pfd [*AMEX symbol*] (TTSB)
MPNPrC..... Monongah Power 4/50%cm C Pfd [*AMEX symbol*] (TTSB)
MPNST...... Malignant Peripheral Nerve Sheath Tumor
MPNVS...... Multi-Purpose Night Vision Sight [*Police and security equipment*]
MPN-XX..... Next Generation Mobile Ground Radar (SAUS)
MPO......... Macedonian Patriotic Organization of US and Canada (EA)
MPO......... Main Production Order (SAUO)
MPO......... Major Program Objective (MCD)
MPO......... Management and Personnel Office (ODBW)
MPO......... Managerial & Professional Officers (WDAA)
MPO......... Managers, Proprietors, and Officials
MPO......... Manual Purchase Orders (SAUO)
MPO......... Manufacturer's Point of Origin (TIMI)
MPO......... Manufacturing Production Order (NRCH)
MPO......... Maputo [*Mozambique*] [*Geomagnetic observatory code*]
MPO......... Material Project Office (ACAE)
MPO......... Maximum Power Output
MPO......... Medial Preoptic [*Brain anatomy*]
MPO......... Medical and Pediatric Oncology [*Medicine*] [*Journal*] (EDAA)
MPO......... Member of the Post Office [*British*]
MPO......... Memorandum Purchase Order (AD)
mpo......... Memory Printout (AD)
MPO......... Memory Printout [*Computer science*]
MPO......... Memory Protect Override
MPO......... Mercury Project Office [*NASA*] (SAA)
MPO......... Metropolitan Planning Organization
MPO......... Metropolitan Police Office [*Familiarly called "Scotland Yard' from its site at New Scotland Yard*] [*British*]
MPO......... Miami Philharmonic Orchestra (AD)
MPO......... Military Pay Order
MPO......... Military Permit Office [*or Officer*]
MPO......... Military Personnel Office
MPO......... Military Planning Office [*SEATO*] (CINC)
MPO......... Military Post Office
MPO......... Minimal Perceptible Odor (MELL)
MPO......... Misconduct Policy Officer [*National Institutes of Health*]
MPO......... Missile Processing Operation (MCD)
MPO......... Mission Planning Officer (SAUO)
MPO......... Mobile Post Office
MPO......... Mobile Printing Office (AD)
MPO......... Modular Personnel Office (SSD)
MPO......... Motion Picture Operator
MPO......... MotivePower Indus. [*NYSE symbol*] (SG)
MPO......... Mount Pocono, PA [*Location identifier*] [*FAA*] (FAAL)
MPO......... Mustering Petty Officer
MPO......... Myeloperoxidase [*An enzyme*]
MPOA....... Medial Preoptic Area [*Medicine*]
MPOA....... Medical Power of Attorney (MELL)
MPOA....... Multiprotocol over Asynchronous Transfer Mode [*Computer science*] (IGQR)

MPOA .... Puerto Obaldia [*Panama*] [*ICAO location identifier*] (ICLI)
MPOAH...... Medial Preoptic-Anterior Hypothalamic [*Brain anatomy*]
MPOC .... Mini-Pilot Open Chamber [*Automotive engineering*]
MPOC .... Multipurpose Operators Console (SAUS)
MPOD .... Mean Planned Outage Duration [*Electronics*] (IEEE)
MPOD .... Myeloperoxidase Deficiency [*Medicine*] (EDAA)
MPOE........ Minimum Point of Entry [*Communications term*] (DCT)
MP-OES..... Multi-Point Optical Emission Spectroscopy (AAEL)
MPOI .... Master Program of Instruction [*Army*] (AABC)
MPOIS....... Military Police Operations and Information System [*Army*] (MCD)
M-POL....... Maritime Policy Division (SAUO)
MPol......... Master of Policy
M Pol........ Master of Political Science (PGP)
MPolAdmin... Master of Policy and Administration
MPolEcon... Master of Political Economy [*British*] (ADA)
MPol Econ... Mistress of Political Economy (SAUO)
MPOLL ...... Military Post Office Location List (AFM)
MPolLaw.... Master of Policy and Law
M Pol Sc.... Master of Political Science
MPOM....... Maintenance Program Operations Management [*Military*] (AABC)
MPON .... Metropolitan [*Telegraphy*] (PCTE)
MPOP .... Minimum Point of Penetration [*Communications term*] (DCT)
MPOR .... Maintenance Plant at Ober Ramstadt [*Army*] (MCD)
MPOS .... Manportable Office System [*Army*] (RDA)
MPOS .... Message-Passing Operating System [*Computer science*] (GART)
MPOS .... Military Plans and Operations Staff
MPOS .... Mobile Post Office Society (EA)
MPOS .... Movie Projector Operator's School (DNAB)
MPOS .... Multipurpose Optimization System [*Computer science*]
MPOSC...... Master of Polar and Ocean Science
MPOT........ Master in Psychiatric Occupational Therapy (GAGS)
M-POTS..... Mobile Psychological Operations Transmitter (DOMA)
MPOW....... Multiple Purpose Operator Workstation (SAUO)
MPP .... General Cigar Holdings [*NYSE symbol*]
MPP .... Mailer's Postmark Permit
MPP .... Maintainability Program Plan
MPP .... Major Program Proposal (AAG)
MPP .... Malleable Penile Prosthesis [*Medicine*] (MELL)
MPP .... Manipur People's Party [*India*] [*Political party*] (PPW)
MPP .... Manitou & Pike's Peak Railroad [*Federal Railroad Administration identification code*]
mpp.......... Marginal Physical Product (AD)
MPP .... Marginal Physical Product [*Agriculture*]
MPP .... Marine Power Plant (PDAA)
MPP .... Market Promotion Program (WPI)
MPP .... Martens Polarization Photometer [*Physics*]
MPP .... Massively Parallel Processor [*Image processing*]
MPP .... Massive Periretinal Proliferation [*Ophthalmology*] (DAVI)
MPP .... Master in Public Policy [*National University of Singapore*]
MPP .... Master of Physical Planning (NADA)
MPP .... Master of Public Policy
MPP .... Master Patch Panel [*Air Force*] (MCD)
MPP .... Master Program Plan (NG)
MPP .... Master's Degree in Public Policy
MPP .... Material Processing Platform (SPST)
MPP .... Material Processing Procedure (NASA)
MPP .... Materials Preparation Program (SAA)
MPP .... Materiel Performance Package [*Military*] (AFM)
MPP .... Matrix Processing Peptidase [*An enzyme*]
MPP .... Maximum Performance Penalty (ACAE)
MPP .... Maximum Perfusion Pressure [*Cardiology*] (DAVI)
MPP .... Maximum Positive Pressure [*Nuclear energy*] (NRCH)
MPP .... Medial Pterygoid Plate [*Medicine*] (MELL)
MPP .... Medical Personnel Pool
MPP .... Medical Planning Program (SAUO)
MPP .... Medical Properties (EFIS)
MPP .... Medical Provisioning Point (SAUS)
MPP .... Melanesian Progressive Parti [*Vanuatu*] [*Political party*] (EY)
MPP .... Melphalan, Prednisone, Procarbazine [*Antineoplastic drug regimen*]
MPP .... Member of Provincial Parliament [*British*]
MPP .... Memory Parity and Protect (NITA)
MPP .... Mercaptopyrazidopyrimidine [*Antineoplastic drug*] (MAE)
MPP .... Mercury Policy Project [*Association*] (EA)
MPP .... Merit Promotion Plan [*or Program*] [*NASA*] (NASA)
MPP .... Message Posting Protocol (SAUO)
MPP .... Message Processing Program [*Computer science*]
MPP .... Metacarpophalangeal Profile [*Medicine*] (EDAA)
MPP .... Meta Postprocessor [*Software program*] [*Symbolic Control, Inc.*]
MPP .... Methyl(phenyl)pyridine [*Biochemistry*]
MPP .... Methylpiperazine [*Organic chemistry*]
MPP .... Microfilm Printer/Plotter
MPP .... Microprogrammable Processor (MCD)
MPP .... Miles per Pound [*NASA*] (KSC)
MPP .... Military Pay Procedures
MPP .... Minimum Premium Plans [*Insurance*]
MPP .... Minority Procurement Policy (AAGC)
MPP .... Miscellaneous Personal Property [*Legal term*] (DLA)
MPP .... Missile Power Panel (AAG)
MPP .... Mission Payload Package (ACAE)
MPP .... Mission-Planning Program [*Gerospace*] (BARN)
MPP .... Mistress of Physical Planning (SAUO)
MPP .... Mitochondrial Processing Peptidase [*Biochemistry*]
MPP .... Modern Programming Practice
MPP .... Molypermalloy Powder [*Metallurgy*] (EECA)
MPP .... Mongol People's Party [*Mongolia*] [*Political party*] (FEA)
MPP .... Monodisperse Polymer Particle
MPP .... Mono Power Pack (HGAA)
mpp.......... Most Probable Position (AD)
MPP .... Most Probable Position [*Navigation*]
MPP .... Mothers in Prison Projects (EA)
MPP .... Motion Picture Pioneers (EA)
MPP .... Motion Picture Projector (MSA)
MPP .... Mount Pasian [*Philippines*] [*Seismograph station code, US Geological Survey*] (SEIS)
MPP .... Mulatupo [*Panama*] [*Airport symbol*] (OAG)
MPP .... Multichannel Point-to-Point Protocol (GART)
MPP .... Multiphase Printing (AAEL)
MPP .... Multiple Particle Plasma
MPP .... Multiple Payload Program [*Military*]
MPP .... Multiple-Product Pricing [*Business term*] (MHDB)
MPP .... Multi-Programmable Processor (VLIE)
MPP .... Multiprogrammable Processor Port (VLIE)
MPP .... Multi-Purpose Platform (SAUS)
MPP .... Programme of Mass Privatisation [*Poland*] (ECON)
MPPA........ Management Plans for Protected Areas (SAUO)
MPPA........ Master of Public Policy Administration (GAGS)
MPPA........ Metal Powder Producers Association (EA)
MPPA........ Metro Professional Photographers Association (EARSL)
MPPA........ Michigan Press Photographers Association (SAUO)
MPPA........ Motion Picture Producers Association (SAUO)
MPPA........ Music Publishers' Protective Association [*Later, NMPA*] (EA)
MPPAA ...... Multiemployer Pension Plan Amendments Act [*1980*] (GFGA)
MPPAR ...... Mouse Peroxisome Proliferator-Activated Receptor [*Biochemistry*]
MPPAV ...... Master Poultry Processors' Association of Victoria [*Australia*]
MPPB........ Meeting of Presidents of Professional Bodies (SAUO)
MPPB........ Methyl(phenyl)(propyl)barbituric (Acid) [*Biochemistry*]
MPPC........ Mailer's Postmark Permit Club (EA)
MPPC........ Master Program Phasing Chart (MCD)
MPPC........ Mean Peak Plasma Concentration [*Medicine*] (EDAA)
MPPC........ Medical Personnel (Priority) Committee [*World War II*]
MPPC........ Microsoft Point to Point Compression [*Microsoft Corp.*] [*Computer science*] (PCM)
MPPC........ Military Pay Procedure Committee
MPPC........ Multipotent Hematopoietic Progenitor Cell [*Biochemistry*]
MPPC........ Multipurpose Parallel Computing (GART)
MPPC........ Panama [*Panama*] [*ICAO location identifier*] (ICLI)
MPPCA ...... Maryland Probation, Patrol and Corrections Association (AD)
MPPCF ...... Million Particles per Cubic Foot [*in air*]
mppcf .... Millions of Particles per Cubic Foot of Air (AD)
MPPCS ...... Manpower and Personnel Contingency Support System (SAUO)
MPPD .... Machine, Process, and Product Design Center [*University of Alabama*] (RCD)
MPPD .... Maximum Probable Property Damage [*Hazard analysis*]
MPPD .... Military Personnel Procurement Division (SAUO)
MPPD .... Multi-Purpose Peripheral Device (VLIE)
MPPDA...... Medicine-Pediatrics Program Directors Association (SAUO)
MPPE........ Microsoft Point-to-Point Encryption (MWOL)
MPPEAS .... GEF/UNDP/IMO Regional Programme for the Prevention and Management of Marine Pollution in the East Asian Seas (SAUO)
MPPEAS .... Regional Programme for the Prevention and Management of Marine Pollution in the East Asian Seas (SAUS)
MPPEC ...... Mean Peak Plasma Ethanol Concentration [*Medicine*] (DMAA)
MPPF........ Malayan Planters Provident Fund (SAUO)
MPPG .... Magnesium Pyridoxal Phosphate Glutamate [*Biochemistry*]
MPPG .... Microphotoelectric Plethysmography [*Medicine*] (EDAA)
MPPH .... (Methylphenyl)phenylhydantoin [*Organic chemistry*]
MPPH .... Motion Picture Phonographic Unit
MPPHA...... Multiparameter Pulse Height Analyzer
MPPhS...... Member of the Royal Pharmaceutical Society [*Canada*] (DD)
MPPL........ Mobilization Procurement Planning List (SAUO)
mp pl........ Multipunch Plate (AD)
MPPL........ Multipunch Plate
MPPL........ Multipurpose Processing Language [*Computer science*] (IEEE)
MPPL........ Multipurpose Programming Language
MPPLT....... Military Police Platoon (DNAB)
MPPM........ Master of Public and Private Management
MPPM........ Materials-Process-Product Model (PDAA)
MPPM........ Military Personnel Procurement Manual
MPPM........ Mission Prediction and Performance Module [*Aerospace*]
MPP MEDICAL MARIJUANNA PAC... Marijuanna Policy Project Medical Marijuanna PAC [*Washington, DC*] (PACS)
MPPN .... Malignant Persistent Positional Nystagmus [*Medicine*] (DMAA)
MPPO .... Modified Polyphenylene Oxide [*Plastics technology*]
MPPP........ Mechanically Processed Pork Product [*Food technology*]
MPPP........ Methyl(phenyl)(propionoxy)piperidine [*Organic chemistry*]
MPPP........ Money-Purchase Pension Plan [*Human resources*] (WYGK)
MPPP........ MP3.com, Inc. [*NASDAQ symbol*] (SG)
MPPP........ Multilink Point-to-Point Protocol (SAUS)
MPPPM ..... Master of Plant Protection and Pest Management (GAGS)
MPPR .... Mobilization Production Planning Requirements [*Military*]
MPPR .... Modification Program Progress Report (AFIT)
MPPR .... Monthly Production Progress Reports (MCD)
MPPrA....... Mississippi Pwr 7.25% Dep Pfd [*NYSE symbol*] (TTSB)
MPPRB...... Materiel Procurement Priorities Review Board [*Army*] (AABC)
MPPrB....... Mississippi Pwr 6.65% Dep Pfd [*NYSE symbol*] (TTSB)
MPPRC...... Materiel Procurement Priorities Review Committee [*Army*] (RDA)
MPPrC....... Mississippi Pwr 6.32% Dep Pfd [*NYSE symbol*] (TTSB)
MPPRCA.... Marine Plastic Pollution Research and Control Act

MPPS........ Mammary Gland Physiology and Pathology Society (GVA)
MPPS........ Master Production Planning Schedule [*Air Force*] (AFIT)
MPPS........ Master Program Planning Schedule
MPPS........ Medicare Prospective Payment System
MPPS........ Military Personnel Procurement Service (SAUO)
mpps........ Million Pulses per Second (AD)
MPPS........ Moroccan Party of Progress and Socialism [*Political party*]
MPPS........ Multipurpose (AABC)
MPPSE...... Multipurpose Payload Support Equipment (NASA)
MPPT........ Maximum Power Point Tracking [*Power system*]
MPPT........ Message Preparation Processing Task (SAUO)
MPPT........ Methylprednisolone Pulse Therapy [*Medicine*]
MPPT........ Moller-Plesset Perturbation Theory [*Physical chemistry*]
MPPU........ Multi-Purpose Processor Unit (SAUS)
MPPUP...... Master of Public Policy and Urban Planning (PGP)
MPPV........ Mechanical Positive Pressure Ventilation [*Medicine*] (EDAA)
MPPWCOM... Military Police Prisoner of War Command (AABC)
MPPZ........ Moba Power Plant [*Federal Railroad Administration identification code*]
MPQ......... Manchester Personality Questionnaire [*Test*] (TMMY)
MPQ......... Manpower Planning Quota (PDAA)
mpq......... Manpower-Planning Quota (AD)
MPQ......... McGill Pain Questionnaire [*Dentistry*]
MPQ......... Minnesota Personality Questionnaire [*Psychology*] (QSUL)
MPQ......... Morgan Stanley Group [*AMEX symbol*] (SAG)
MPQ......... Multidimensional Personality Questionnaire [*Personality development test*] [*Psychology*]
MPQA....... Minuteman Production Quality Assurance (MCD)
MPQP....... Multi-Protocol Quad Port [*Computer science*] (VLIE)
MPQ/T....... Mean Personnel Quantity per Task (MCD)
MPQT........ Missile Performance Qualification Test (TIMI)
MPR......... Machined Part Requisition (MCD)
MPR......... Maculopapular Rash [*Medicine*]
MPR......... Madjelis Permusiawaratan Rakat [*People's Deliberative Assembly*] [*Indonesia*] (AD)
MPR......... Maintainability Problem Report (NASA)
MPR......... Maintainability Program Requirements (AD)
MPR......... Maintenance Personnel Roster
MPR......... Major Project Report (SAUS)
MPR......... Make Pages Resident (VLIE)
MPR......... Management Policies and Requirements (SAUO)
MPR......... Management Program Review [*NASA*] (NASA)
MPR......... Manager Profile Record [*Test*] [*Richardson, Bellows, Henry, and Co. Inc.*] (TES)
MPR......... Mane Primo [*Early in the Morning*] [*Pharmacy*] (ROG)
MPR......... Mannose Phosphate Receptor [*Biochemistry*]
MPR......... Manpack Radio (SAUS)
MPR......... Manpower (AABC)
MPR......... Manpower Policy and Requirements Branch [*Department of Defence*] [*Australia*]
MPR......... Manufacturing Parts Record (KSC)
MPR......... Manufacturing Planning Review (MCD)
MPR......... Mariposa Resources, Inc. [*Vancouver Stock Exchange symbol*]
MPR......... Maritime Provinces Reports [*Canada*] [*A publication*] (DLA)
MPR......... Marked Page Reader (VLIE)
MPR......... Marrow Production Rate [*Hematology*]
MPR......... Massive Preretinal Retraction [*Medicine*] (EDAA)
MPR......... Master Personnel Records (ACAE)
MPR......... Master Power Regulator
MPR......... Material Purchase Requisition
MPR......... Materials and Process Requirement [*Navy*]
MPR......... Mathematica Policy Research
MPR......... Mauritanian Party for Renewal [*Political party*] (EY)
MPR......... Maximal Pulse Rate [*Medicine*] (MELL)
MPR......... Maximum Performance Reward (ACAE)
MPR......... Maximum Potential Representation (MUGU)
MPR......... Maximum Practical Rate [*Aviation*]
MPR......... Mayaguez [*Puerto Rico*] [*Seismograph station code, US Geological Survey*] (SEIS)
MPR......... McPherson, KS [*Location identifier*] [*FAA*] (FAAL)
MPR......... Mechanical Pressure Regulator (NRCH)
MPR......... Medium Power RADAR (NATG)
mpr......... Medium-Power RADAR (AD)
MPR......... Melt-Processible Rubber
MPR......... Mercaptopurine Ribonucleoside [*Antineoplastic drug*]
MPR......... Mercury Plunger Relay
MPR......... Message Processing Region [*IBM Corp.*]
MPR......... Met-Pro Corp. [*AMEX symbol*] (SPSG)
MPR......... Microperipheral (GART)
MPR......... Microprogram Register (MHDI)
MPR......... Milepost Review (ACAE)
MPR......... Military Pay Record
MPR......... Military Personnel Record (AFM)
MPR......... Military Photo-Reconnaissance (PDAA)
MPR......... Military Power Reserve (SAUO)
MPR......... Mine Production Report
MPR......... Minimum Processing Requirement
MPR......... Mission Planning Room (SAUS)
MPR......... Mock-Up Purchase Request [*NASA*] (NASA)
MPR......... Model Parts Release (VLIE)
MPR......... Mongolian Peoples Republic
MPR......... Monoclonal Antibody Production Rate
MPR......... Monopulse RADAR (MSA)
MPR......... Monthly Program Review (USDC)
MPR......... Monthly Progress Report
MPR......... Monthly Project Report
MPR......... Montpelier, VT [*Amtrak rail station code*]
MPR......... Morphophonological Rule [*Linguistics*] (IEL)
MPR......... Mouvement Populaire de la Revolution [*Popular Revolutionary Movement*] [*Zaire*] [*Political party*] (PD)
MPR......... Mouvement Populaire Revolutionnaire [*Popular Revolutionary Movement*] [*Tunisia*] [*Political party*] (PD)
MPR......... Movimento Popolare Rivoluzionario [*Popular Revolutionary Movement*] [*Italy*] [*Political party*] (PD)
MPR......... Multi-band Pulsed Radar (SAUS)
MPR......... Multi-Part Repeater (VLIE)
MPR......... Multiple-Pass Radiator [*Automotive engineering*]
MPR......... Multiple Provider Router [*Computer science*] (ACRL)
MPR......... Multi-Port Repeater [*Computer science*] (CIST)
MPR......... MultiProtocol Router [*Novell, Inc.*] (PCM)
MPR......... Multipurpose Recorder
MPR......... Music Power Rating
MPR......... Myeloproliferative Reaction [*Medicine*] (MELL)
MPR......... Patriotic Movement for Renewal (Mali) [*Political party*] (PSAP)
MPR......... Popular Movement of the Revolution (D. Rep. Congo) [*Political party*] (PSAP)
M Pr A...... Master of Professional Accountancy (PGP)
MPRA....... Military Police Regimental Association (EA)
MPRC....... Maryland & Pennsylvania Railroad [*Federal Railroad Administration identification code*]
MPRC....... Maryland Psychiatric Research Center [*University of Maryland*] [*Research center*] (RCD)
MPRC....... Mayday Pain Resource Center (SAUO)
MPRC....... Medical Program Review Committee [*DoD*] [*Washington, DC*] (EGAO)
MPRC....... Military Personnel Records Center (MCD)
MPRC....... Motion Picture Research Council
MPRC....... Multipurpose Range Complex [*Army*] (INF)
MPRC-H..... Multipurpose Range Complex - Heavy [*Army*]
MPRC-L..... Multipurpose Range Complex - Light [*Army*]
MPRE........ Medium Power Reactor Experiment
MPRE........ Minimum Pure Radium Equivalent (MCD)
MPRES...... Modular Plasma Reactor Simulator (AAEL)
mpress...... Medium Pressure (AD)
MPRESS.... Medium Pressure
MPRF........ Master Parts Record File (VLIE)
mPRF........ Median Pontine Reticular Formation [*Neurophysiology*]
MPRF........ Medium Pulse Recurrence Frequency (MCD)
MPRF........ Motion Picture Relief Fund [*Later, MPTF*] (EA)
MPRG........ Multi-Purpose Riot Gun [*Police and security equipment*]
M Pr Gph... Master in Professional Geophysics
MPRH........ Rio Hato [*Panama*] [*ICAO location identifier*] (ICLI)
MPRI........ Member of the Plastics and Rubber Institute [*British*] (DBQ)
MPRI........ Merchant Pacific Routing Instructions [*Shipping*]
MPRI........ Mount Prat [*Italy*] [*Seismograph station code, US Geological Survey*] (SEIS)
MPRI........ Multiphoton Resonance Ionization [*Spectrometry*]
MPRJ........ Military Personnel Records Jacket [*Army*] (AABC)
MPRL........ Manpower and Personnel Research Laboratory [*Army Research Institute for the Behavioral and Social Sciences*] (RDA)
MPRL........ Master Parts Reference List
MPRL........ Military Physics Research Laboratory [*University of Texas*] (MCD)
MPRM....... Marine Pollution Research and Monitoring (SAUO)
M Pr M...... Master of Preventive Medicine
MPRMAC... Military Participation Ratio of the Military Age Cohorts
MPrMet..... Master of Professional Meteorology (GAGS)
MPRO....... Machine Processing Section [*National Security Agency*]
M Prob S... Master of Probability and Statistics (PGP)
MProcEng... Master of Process Engineering, University of Sheffield [*British*] (DBQ)
M Prof Acc... Master of Professional Accountancy
MProfAcc... Master of Professional Accounting (GAGS)
M Prof Past... Master of Professional Pastoral (PGP)
MPROM..... Mask Programmed Read-Only Memory [*Computer science*]
MPRP....... Mean Prioritized Replacement Position (SAUO)
MPRP....... Mercaptopurine Ribonucleotide [*Antineoplastic drug*]
MPRP....... Milestone Properties [*OTCBB symbol*]
MPRP....... Mongolian People's Revolutionary Party [*Mongol Ardyn Khuv'sgalt Nam*] [*Political party*] (PPW)
MPRP....... Muslim Peoples Republican Party [*Political party*] (AD)
MPRR....... Management Program Review Report [*NASA*] (MCD)
MPRR....... Missouri-Pacific Railroad Company (SAUO)
MPRR....... Mobility Personnel Resource Roster (SAUO)
MPRS....... Management Planning and Reporting System (COE)
MPRS....... Marine Pollution Retrieval System [*BTS*] (TAG)
MPRS....... Microform Personnel Records System (NVT)
MPRS....... MicroProse Inc. (EFIS)
MPRSA...... Marine Protection, Research, and Sanctuaries Act [*1972*]
MPRST...... Maximum Probability Ratio Sequential Test (PDAA)
MPRT........ Multipurpose Rail Transport (NRCH)
MPRTM..... Master of Park, Recreation, and Tourism Management (GAGS)
MPRT/R..... Missile Pneudraulic Repair Technician/Repairman (AAG)
MPRU....... Mediterranean-Puerto Rican Conference [*Intermodal shipping container symbol*] (TVRC)
MPS......... Macular Photocoagulation Study (SAUS)
MPS......... Magazine Printers Section (EA)
MPS......... Magnetic Pole Strength
MPS......... Mail Preference Service [*Direct Mail Advertising Association*]
MPS......... Main Power Switch
MPS......... Main Propulsion System [*or Subsystem*] [*NASA*] (KSC)

MPS .... Maintenance Performance System [*DoD*]
MPS .... Maintenance Problem Summary
MPS .... Maitrise en Psychologie Industrielle [*French*] (CPGU)
MPS .... Management of Parts Shortages (SAUO)
MPS .... Management Planning System [*Medicine*] (EDAA)
MPS .... Management Policy Statement
MPS .... Managerial Philosophies Scale [*Test*]
MPS .... Manpower Planning System (SAUO)
MPS .... Manpower System (NRCH)
MPS .... Manual Phase Shifter
MPS .... Manufacturer's Part Specification (ODA)
MPS .... Manufacturing Process Specification (AAG)
mps .... Marbled Paper Sides (AD)
MPS .... Marbled Paper Sides [*Bookbinding*]
MPS .... Marginal Propensity to Save [*Economics*]
MPS .... Marine Polymetalic Sulfide
MPS .... Marine Prepositioned Ships Program
MPS .... Maritime Postmark Society [*Later, USCS*] (EA)
MPS .... Maritime Prepositioning Ship (MCD)
MPS .... Maritime Prepositioning Squadron (DOMA)
MPS .... Marriage Prediction Schedule [*Psychology*]
MPS .... Massachusetts Psychiatric Society (EARSL)
MPs .... Master in/of Psychology (SAUO)
MPS .... Master of Pastoral Studies (PGP)
MPS .... Master of Personnel Service (GAGS)
MPS .... Master of Policy Sciences (PGP)
MPS .... Master of Political Science (GAGS)
MPS .... Master of Professional Studies (PGP)
MPS .... Master of Professional Studies in Human Relations
M Ps .... Master of Psychology
MPS .... Master of Public Service (GAGS)
MPS .... Master Performance System
MPS .... Master Phasing Schedule (ACAE)
MPS .... Master Planning Schedule (MCD)
MPS .... Master Production Schedule
MPS .... Master Program Schedule (NASA)
MPS .... Master Project Summary [*Civil Defense*]
MPS .... Material Planning Study
MPS .... Material Planning System [*Manufacturing management*]
MPS .... Material Processing Specification (NASA)
MPS .... Material Processing System
MPS .... Materials Processing in Space [*NASA*]
MPS .... Materiel Planning Study [*Army*]
MPS .... Mathematical Programming Society [*Voorburg, Netherlands*] (EAIO)
MPS .... Mathematical Programming System [*Computer science*]
MPS .... Maximum Performance Escape System (MCD)
MPS .... Max Planck Society [*Germany*]
MPS .... Mazda Performance Series [*Automotive marketing*]
MPS .... Mean Prognostic Score [*Medicine*] (MELL)
MPS .... Mechanical Phase Shifter
MPS .... Mechanical Power Systems
MPS .... Meconium Plug Syndrome [*Medicine*] (EDAA)
MPS .... Median Period of Survival
MPS .... Medical Practice Study
MPS .... Medical Products Sales (SAUO)
MPS .... Medical Products Salesman [*Medicine*] [*A publication*] (EDAA)
MPS .... Medical Protection Society [*British*] (DBA)
MPS .... Medical Provider Survey [*Department of Health and Human Services*] (GFGA)
MPS .... Medical Publishing Standard (DB)
MPS .... MegaBITS [*Binary Digits*] per Second [*Transmission rate*] [*Computer science*] (MCD)
mps .... Megacycles per Second (AD)
MPS .... Meiosis-Preventing Substance [*Cytology*]
MPS .... Member of the Pharmaceutical Society [*British*]
MPS .... Member of the Philogical Society (SAUO)
MPS .... Member of the Philological Society [*British*]
MPS .... Member of the Physical Society [*British*]
MPs .... Members of Parliament (SAUO)
MPS .... Memory Processor Switch
MPS .... Mercury Procedures Simulator [*NASA*]
MPS .... Merit Pay System (MCD)
MPS .... Merrill-Palmer School (SAUO)
MPS .... Mervyn Peake Society (EA)
MPS .... Mesoscale Prediction Section (SAUO)
MPS .... Message Processing Service (SAUS)
MPS .... Message Processing Subsystem (SAUO)
MPS .... Message Processing System (NVT)
mps .... Meters per Second (AD)
MPS .... Meters per Second
MPS .... Methodist Philatelic Society (EA)
MPS .... Methyl Phenyl Sulfide [*Organic chemistry*]
MPS .... Michigan Picture Stories [*Psychology*] (DAVI)
MPS .... Microbial Profile System [*Microbiology*]
MPS .... Microlensing Planet Search (SAUS)
MPS .... Microphone Power Supply
MPS .... Microprocessor Series [*or System*] (MDG)
MPS .... Micro Processor Systems A/S (SAUO)
MPS .... Microwave Phase Shifter
MPS .... Microwave Pressure Sounder (MCD)
MPS .... Microwave Protection System [*Police and security equipment*]
MPS .... Microwave Pulse Source
mps .... Miles per Second (IDOE)
MPS .... Miles per Second
MPS .... Military Planning Staff (CINC)
MPS .... Military Postal Service (AFM)
MPS .... Military Postal System (SAUO)
MPS .... Military Production Specifications
MPS .... Milwaukee Public Museum (AD)
MPS .... Minimum Performance Specification (DA)
MPS .... Minimum Piecework Standard [*British*]
MPS .... Minimum Property Standards [*FHA*]
MPS .... Minister of Public Security [*British*]
MPS .... Ministry of Posts and Telecommunications (SAUO)
MPS .... Ministry of Public Security (SAUO)
MPS .... Minnesota Pathological Society (SAUO)
MPS .... Misioneras del Perpetual Socorro (TOCD)
MPS .... Missionary Sisters of Our Lady of Perpetual Help (TOCD)
MPS .... Mission Parcels Society [*British*]
MPS .... Mission Payload Subsystem (SAUS)
MPS .... Mission Planning System (SAUO)
MPS .... Mission Preparation Sheet
MPS .... Mission-Processing Subsystem (MCD)
MPS .... Mission Profile Simulator [*NASA*]
MPS .... Miss Porter's School [*Farmington, CT*]
MPS .... Mixed Potential System (PDAA)
MPS .... Mixed-Propellant System (SAUS)
MPS .... Mobile Pointing Station (ACAE)
MPS .... Mobile Positioning Ship (DNAB)
MPS .... Modis Professional Svcs. [*NYSE symbol*] (SG)
MPS .... Modular Power Subsystem
MPS .... Modular Power System (MCD)
MPS .... Modular Processor System [*Computer science*] (PCM)
MPS .... Molecular Photoemission Spectroscopy
MPS .... Monocyte-Phagocyte System [*Immunology*] (QSUL)
MPS .... Mononuclear Phagocyte System [*Hematology*]
MPS .... Mont Pelerin Society (EA)
MPS .... Montreal Platelet Syndrome [*Medicine*] (DMAA)
MPS .... Motion Picture Service [*Department of Agriculture*]
mps .... Motor Parts Stock (AD)
MPS .... Motor Products Corporation (SAUO)
MPS .... Motor Pump Set (SAUS)
MPS .... Motor Pump System (MCD)
MPS .... Mount Pleasant [*Texas*] [*Airport symbol*] [*Obsolete*] (OAG)
MPS .... Mouvement Patriotique du Salut [*Chad*] [*Political party*] (EY)
MPS .... Mouvement Populaire Senegalais [*Senegalese Popular Movement*] [*Political party*]
MPS .... Movement-Produced Stimuli
MPS .... Movimiento de Patria Socialista [*Venezuela*] [*Political party*] (EY)
MPS .... MPS Group [*Company symbol*]
MPS .... Mucopolysaccharide [*Also, MP*] [*Clinical chemistry*]
MPS .... Mucopolysaccharidoses [*Medical term*]
MPS .... Mucopolysaccharidosis [*Medicine*]
MPS .... Multi-Format Photointerpretation System (SAA)
MPS .... Multiparticle Spectrometer [*Brookhaven National Laboratory*]
MPS .... Multiphasic Screening [*Medicine*]
MPS .... Multi-Plane Programming System (NITA)
MPS .... Multiple Peptide Synthesis [*Biochemistry*]
MPS .... Multiple Personality Syndrome [*Medicine*] (EDAA)
MPS .... Multiple Protective Shelter (SAUS)
MPS .... Multiple Protective Structure [*Missile bases*]
MPS .... Multiple Vertical Protective Shelter [*for missiles*]
MPS .... Multiprocessing System [*Computer science*]
MPS .... Multiprocessor Specification (MWOL)
MPS .... Multiprogramming Periodic Tasking System (NITA)
MPS .... Multiprogramming System [*Computer science*]
MPS .... Multi-Protocol Support [*Computer science*] (AGLO)
MPS .... Multipurpose Ship (AABC)
MPS .... Musclepain-spasm (Syndrome) [*Medicine*] (EDAA)
MPS .... Muzzle Position Sensor (MCD)
MPS .... Myeloma Progression Score [*Oncology*]
MPS .... Myocardial Perfusion Scintigraphy [*Medicine*] (DB)
MPS .... Society for Mucopolysaccharide Diseases (EA)
MPS2 .... Region 2 Merit Pay System (SAUS)
MPSA .... Master of Public School Art
MPSA .... Metropolitan Pharmaceutical Secretaries Association (EA)
MPSA .... Military Petroleum Supply Agency [*Later, Defense Petroleum Supply Center*]
MPSA .... Military Postal Service Agency
MPSA .... Military Production Supply Agency (SAUO)
MPSA .... Mississippi Private School Association (EARSL)
MPSA .... Santiago [*Panama*] [*ICAO location identifier*] (ICLI)
MPSB .... Military Production and Supply Board (SAUO)
MPSB-PWS ... Permanent Working Staff of the Military Production and Supply Board (SAUO)
MPSC .... Marianas Political Status Commission
MPSC .... Material Planning Schedule and Control [*Division of Inspection Offices, Navy*]
MPSC .... Michigan Public Services Commission (SAUO)
MPSC .... Military Personnel Security Committee
MPSC .... Military Provost Staff Corps [*British*]
MPSC .... Missouri Public Service [*Federal Railroad Administration identification code*]
MPSC .... Movimiento Popular Socialcristiano [*Christian Social Popular Movement*] [*El Salvador*] [*Political party*] (PD)
MPSCL ...... Mathematical Programming System Control Language [*1974*] [*Computer science*] (CSR)
MP/SCM .... Multiport Semiconductor Memory (MHDI)

MPSCOA .... Military Pay Service Center Overseas Areas (SAUO)
MPSE .... Moreless Payload Specialist Experiment (SAUS)
MPSE .... Motion Picture Sound Editors (EA)
MPSE .... Multipurpose Payload Support Equipment (MCD)
MPSF .... Mountain Pacific Sports Federation (PSS)
MPSF .... Multi-Purpose Special Fund [*Asian Development Bank*] [*United Nations*] (EY)
MPSG .... Marketing Programs and Services Group, Inc. [*Gaithersburg, MD*] [*Information service or system*] [*Telecommunications*] (TSSD)
MPSG .... MPSI System, Inc. [*NASDAQ symbol*] (COMM)
MPSG .... Multi-Band Portable Signal Generator (PDAA)
MPSGB ...... Member of the Pharmaceutical Society of Great Britain (SAUO)
MPSH .... Mean Pressure Suction Head (AAG)
mpsh .... Mean Pressure Suction Head (AD)
MPS-HHSA ... Master of Professional Studies-Hospital and Health Services Administration
MPSI .... Message Processing Systems, Inc. [*Charlotte, NC*] [*Telecommunications service*] (TSSD)
MPSI .... Meyers Parking System, Inc. [*NASDAQ symbol*] (COMM)
MPSI .... MPSI Systems, Inc. [*NASDAQ symbol*] (SAG)
MPS I .... Mucopolysaccharidoses [*Hurler Syndrome*] [*Also, Scheie Syndrome and Hurler/Scheie Syndrome*] (PAZ)
MPSIG .... Monty Python Special Interest Group (EA)
MPS II .... Mucopolysaccharidoses [*Hunter Syndrome*] (PAZ)
MPS IV ...... Mucopolysaccaridoses [*Morquio Syndrome*] (PAZ)
MPSK .... Multiple Phase Shift Keying [*Computer science*] (TEL)
MPSL .... Materials and Process Specification List (SAUS)
MPSM .... Master of Public School Music
MPSM .... Master Problem Status Manual
MPSM .... MODEM Pooling Service Module [*Telecommunications*]
MPSM .... Multipurpose Submunition (RDA)
MPSMT ..... Merrill-Palmer Scale of Mental Tests [*Psychology*] (DAVI)
MPSN .... Microwave Pulse Shaping Network
MPSNY ...... Montserrat Progressive Society of New York (EA)
MPsO .... Master of Psychology Orientation (NADA)
MPsO .... Master of Psychology-Orientation (SAUO)
MPsO .... Mistress of Psychology Orientation (SAUO)
MPSOC ...... Multi Purpose Satellite Operations Center (ACAE)
MP SOV GR COM ... Most Puissant Sovereign Grand Commander [*United States*] [*Freemasonry*] (ROG)
MPSP .... Mathematical Problem-Solving Project [*National Science Foundation*]
MP(S)P ...... Mechanically Processed (Species) Product (DICI)
MPSP .... Micro Programmable Scene Processor (ACAE)
MPSP .... Military Personnel Security Program
MPSP .... Modular Programmable Scene Processor (ACAE)
MPSR .... Military Petroleum Stocks Report (SAUO)
MPSR .... Mission Profile Storage and Retrieval [*NASA*] (NASA)
MPSR .... Multipurpose Support Room (MCD)
MPSRE ...... Master of Professional Studies in Real Estate (PGP)
MPSRON ..... Maritime Prepositioning Ship Squadron (DOMA)
MPSRT ...... Matched-Pairs Signed-Rank Test [*Statistics*]
MPSS .... Main Parachute Support Structure (NASA)
MPSS .... Maryland Preschool Self-Concept Scale (EDAC)
MPSS .... Master Production Scheduling System (TIMI)
MPSS .... Message Processing Subsystem (ACAE)
MPSS .... Mission Payload System Segment
MPSS .... Mission Planning and Scheduling System (SAUS)
MPSS .... Multiple Payload Support Structure (SAUS)
MPSS .... Multiple Protective Structure System (AD)
MPSS .... Multipurpose Sampling System
M Ps Sc ..... Master of Physic Sciences
MPsSc .... Master of Psychological Science (GAGS)
MPST .... Minimum Performance Standard Test [*Military*] (CAAL)
MPST .... Multipurpose Support Team [*NASA*] (NAKS)
M Ps Th ..... Master of Psycho-Therapy
MPSTWG ... Mission Planning System Test Working Group [*Military*] (CAAL)
MPSU .... Missile Pressure Status Unit (AAG)
MPSV .... Myeloproliferative Sarcoma Virus
MPSW .... Master of Psychiatric Social Work (NADA)
MP SWAT ... Military Police Special Weapons and Tactics Team (VNW)
MPSX .... Mathematical Linear Programming Extended [*Computer science*] (HODG)
MPSX .... Mathematical Programming System Extended [*IBM Corp.*] [*Computer science*]
MPSX .... Missouri Public Service [*Federal Railroad Administration identification code*]
MPsych ..... Master of Psychology
MPsych ..... Mistress of Psychology (SAUO)
MPsychApp ... Master of Applied Psychology (ADA)
MPsych(Clin) ... Master of Psychology (Clinical)
MPsych(Ed) ... Master of Psychology (Education)
MPsychMed ... Master of Psychological Medicine, University of Liverpool [*British*] (DBQ)
MPsychol ... Master of Psychology
MPsychTh ... Master of Psychotherapy
M Psy Med ... Master of Psychological Medicine
MPSZ .... Missouri Public Service [*Federal Railroad Administration identification code*]
MPT .... Alpha-Methyl-p-tyrosine [*Also, AMPT*] [*Pharmacology*]
MPT .... Magnetic Particle Testing [*Nuclear energy*] (NRCH)
MPT .... Main Propulsion Test [*NASA*] (NASA)
mpt .... Male Pipe Thread (AD)
MPT .... Male Pipe Thread (MSA)
MPT .... Maneuver Planning Table [*NASA*]
MPT .... Manpower and Training (DOMA)
MPT .... Manpower, Personnel, and Training
MPT .... Manpower Target (SAUS)
MPT .... Marginal Propensity to Tax [*Economics*]
MPT .... Marquis Public Theater (SAUO)
MPT .... Maryland Public Television [*Owings Mills*] [*Information service or system*] [*Telecommunications*] (TSSD)
Mpt .... Maryport (AD)
MPT .... Master of Pastoral Theology (PGP)
MPT .... Master of Physical Therapy (GAGS)
MPT .... Matupit Island [*New Britain*] [*Seismograph station code, US Geological Survey*] (SEIS)
MPT .... Maximum Part Time (SAUO)
MPT .... Maximum Power Transfer (IDOE)
MPT .... Mean Preventive Maintenance Time (MCD)
MPT .... Mean Pulse Time
MPT .... Mechanical Power Transmission
MPT .... Medical Proficiency Training (SAUO)
mpt .... Melting Point (AD)
M PT .... Melting Point (ROG)
MPT .... Memory Point Track (SAUS)
MPT .... Memory Processing Time
MPT .... Mercury Procedures Trainer
MPT .... Message Processing Task [*Computer science*] (ECII)
MPT .... Message Processing Time (SAUO)
MPT .... Metal-Phthalocyanine Tetramine [*Organic chemistry*]
MPT .... Methyl-para-Tyrosine [*Biochemistry*]
MPT .... Mian [*Language symbol*] (ETLW)
MPT .... Michigan Picture Test [*Psychology*]
mpt .... Microprocessing Programmable Terminal [*Computer science*] (AD)
MPT .... Microprogramming Technique
mpt .... Midpoint (AD)
MPT .... Miles per Tankful (AD)
mpt .... Miles per Tankful (AD)
MPT .... Military Potential Test (AABC)
MPT .... Milk Pasteurization Tribunal [*Australia*]
MPT .... Minimum Pressurization Temperature [*Nuclear energy*] (NRCH)
MPT .... Minimum Process Time
MPT .... Ministry of Post and Telegraph (SAUO)
MPT .... Ministry of Posts and Telecommunications [*People's Republic of China*] (ECON)
MPT .... Missile Preflight Tester
MPT .... Missile Procedure Trainer
MPT .... Mission Planning Table [*NASA*] (KSC)
MPT .... Mission Planning Terminal (MCD)
MPT .... Mixed Parotid Gland Tumor [*Oncology*]
MPT .... Modern Poetry in Translation [*A publication*] (WDAA)
MPT .... Modern Portfolio Theory [*Finance*]
MPT .... Molydopterin [*Biochemistry*]
MPT .... Morphine Provocative Test [*Gastroenterology*] (DAVI)
MPT .... MOS [*Military Occupational Specialty*] Proficiency Training [*DoD*]
MPT .... Motional Pickup Transducer (MCD)
MPT .... Mouvement Populaire Tchadien [*Chadian Popular Movement*] [*Political party*]
MPT .... Mouvement Populaire Togolais [*Togolese Popular Movement*] [*Political party*]
MPT .... Mouvement pour le Progres et la Tolerance [*Burkina Faso*] [*Political party*] (EY)
MPT .... Multilateral Preparatory Talks (NATG)
mpt .... Multiple Pure Tone (AD)
MPT .... Multiple Pure Tone [*Sound*]
MPT .... Multiple-Purpose Telescope
mpt .... Multipower Transmission (AD)
MPT .... Multi-Purpose Tracer (SAUS)
MPT .... Mumbai Port Trust [*Indian Railway*] (TIR)
MPT .... Municipal Partners Fund II [*NYSE symbol*] (TTSB)
MPT 1327 ... European hybrid digital trunked radio (SAUS)
MPTA .... Machine Power Transmission Association (AD)
mpta .... Main Propulsion Test Article (AD)
MPTA .... Main Propulsion Test Article [*Aerospace*] (NAKS)
MPTA .... Manpower, Personnel, and Training Analysis
MPTA .... Mechanical Power Transmission Association (EA)
MPTA .... Michigan Public Transit Association (EARSL)
MPTA .... Missouri Public Transit Association (EARSL)
MPTA .... Municipal Passenger Transport Association, Inc. [*British*] (BI)
MPTAC ...... Motion Picture Theatre Associations of Canada (EAIO)
MPTAO ...... Military Personnel and Transportation Assistance Office (MCD)
MPTB .... Meridian Point Realty Trust [*NASDAQ symbol*] (SAG)
MPTB .... Monophosphate Tungsten Bronze [*Metallurgy*]
MPTB .... Multisolid Pneumatic Transport Bed [*Chemical engineering*]
MPTBS ...... Meridian Point Rity Tr 83 [*NASDAQ symbol*] (TTSB)
MPTC .... Mount Pleasant Transfer [*Common carrier symbol*]
MPTCA ...... Motion Picture and Television Credit Association (EA)
MPTCC ...... Most Probable Total Contract Cost (AAGC)
MPTCMA .... Motion Picture and Television Credit Managers Association [*Later, MPTCA*] (EA)
MPTD .... Metropolitan Police, Thames Division (SAUO)
MPTDS ...... Multi-Purpose Tactical Display Set (ACAE)
MPTE .... Manual Peculiar Test Equipment (ACAE)
MPTE .... Multipurpose Test Equipment
MPTEDA .... Mechanical Power Transmission Equipment Distributors Association [*Later, Power Transmission Distributors Association*] (EA)

MPTER ...... Multiple Point Source Model with Terrain [*Environmental Protection Agency*] (GFGA)
MPTF .... Main Propulsion Test Facility [*NASA*] (NASA)
MPTF .... Mission Planning Task Force (KSC)
MPTF .... Motion Picture and Television Fund (EA)
MPTF .... Multiple Protocol Transport Feature (SAUO)
MPTF .... Music Performance Trust Funds (EA)
MPTH .... Methylphenothiazine [*Organic chemistry*]
MPTH .... Mpath Interactive [*NASDAQ symbol*] (SG)
MPTIS .... Manpower, Personnel and Training Integration System (ACAE)
MPTL .... Materials Processing Technology Laboratory (SSD)
MPTM .... Multiparty Test Method [*Open Systems Interconnection*] (ODAA)
MPTMH ..... Major Peace Treaties of Modern History, 1648-1967 [*A publication*] (DLA)
MPTN .... Multiprotocol Transport Network [*Telecommunications*] (ACRL)
MPTO .... Methods and Procedures Technical Orders
MPTO .... Tocumen/General Omar Torrijos H. [*Panama*] [*ICAO location identifier*] (ICLI)
MPTP .... 1-Methyl-4-Phenyl-1,2,3,6-Tetrahydropyridin (SAUS)
MPTP .... Main Propulsion Test Program (MCD)
MPTP .... Methyl(phenyl)tetrahydropyridine [*Organic chemistry*]
MPTP .... Music Preference Test of Personality [*Psychology*]
MPTR .... MedPartners, Inc. [*NASDAQ symbol*] (SAG)
MPTR .... Mobile Position Tracking RADAR
MPTR .... Motor, Pain, Touch, Reflex [*Neurology*] (DAVI)
MPTR .... Multipurpose Training Range [*Army*]
MPTR .... Murphy Hauling Service [*Common carrier symbol*]
MPTS .... Manpower, Personnel, and Training Support [*Military*] (CAAL)
MPTS .... Manpower, Personnel, Training, and Safety [*Army*]
MPTS .... Metal Parts (AABC)
MPTS .... Metropolitan Police Training School (SAUO)
MPTS .... Mobile Photographic Tracking Station
MPTS .... Multi-Protocol Transport Service [*Telecommunications*]
MPTS .... Multipurpose Test Set (DWSG)
MPTS .... Multipurpose Tool Set (MCD)
MP-T-SD .... Multi-Purpose Tracer, Self-Destroying (SAUS)
MPT-SD ..... Multipurpose, Tracer, Self-Destruct [*Army*]
MP(TSWG)... Military Police Tripartite Standing Working Group (AABC)
MPTT .... Maintenance Part Task Trainer [*Army*]
MPTU .... C-Cam International [*Intermodal shipping container symbol*] (TVRC)
MPTUS ...... Marble Polishers' Trade Union Society [*British*]
MPTUSU .... Malayan Postal and Telecommunications Uniformed Staff Union (SAUO)
MPTV .... MPTV, Inc. [*NASDAQ symbol*] (SAG)
MPTWT ..... Medium Power Traveling Wave Tube
MPU .... Computing Microprocessor Unit (ODA)
MPU .... Magnetic Pickup [*Electronics*]
MPU .... Main Power Unit
MPU .... Main Propulsion Unit
MPU .... Maintenance Processor Unit (VLIE)
MPU .... Malayan Planning Unit [*World War II*]
MPU .... Malposition of Uterus [*Medicine*] (MELL)
MPU .... Manipulate [*Telegraphy*] (PCTE)
MPU .... Manpack Unit (MCD)
MPU .... Mapua [*Papua New Guinea*] [*Airport symbol*] [*Obsolete*] (OAG)
MPU .... Maximum Pressure Units
MPU .... Medical Practitioners' Union [*Later, Medical Practitioners' Section - MPS*] [*British*] (DCTA)
MPU .... Memory Protection Unit
MPU .... Mental Parents Union (AD)
MPU .... Message Picking-Up
MPU .... Microphone Preamplifier Unit (ACAE)
mpu .... Microprocessor Unit (AD)
MPU .... Microprocessor Unit [*CPU of microcomputer*] [*Computer science*]
MPU .... MIDI [*Musical Instrument Digital Interface*] Processing Unit [*Computer technology*]
MPU .... Miniature Portable Unit
MPU .... Minutes per Unit
MPU .... Missile Power Unit (DNAB)
MPU .... Missing Persons Unit (AD)
MPU .... Mission Programming Unit (SAUS)
MPU .... Missouri Pacific Railroad [*Intermodal shipping container symbol*] (TVRC)
MPU .... Mixing and Pumping Unit [*Bulk explosives*] (MCD)
MPU .... Mobile Production Unit [*On-site television recording*] (NTCM)
mpu .... Monitor Printing Unit (AD)
MPU .... Monitor Printing Unit [*Computer science*]
MPU .... Motorola Processor Unit
MPU .... Motor Pressurization Unit
MPU .... Multi-Processor Unit (VLIE)
MPU401 ..... MIDI Processing Unit 401 (SAUS)
MPUA .... Military and Police Uniform Association (EA)
M Pub .... Master of Publishing (PGP)
M Pub Adm... Master of Public Administration
MPubAdmin... Master of Public Administration
MPubLaw ... Master of Public Law
MPubPol .... Master of Public Policy
MPUL .... Military Production Urgencies List (NG)
MPUS .... Military Production Urgencies System
MPU/VPU ... Modem Processor Unit/Voice Processor Unit (SAUS)
MPV .... Magistrae Piae Venerini [*Religious Venerini Sisters*] [*Roman Catholic religious order*]
MPV .... Magnetic Polarization Vector
MPV .... Main Portal Vein [*Medicine*] (DMAA)
MPV .... Man-Powered Vehicle
M-P v .... Mason-Pfizer Virus [*Medicine*] (AD)
MPV .... Mass Mutual Participating Investors [*NYSE symbol*] (CTT)
MPV .... MassMutual Participation Investors [*NYSE symbol*] (SAG)
MPV .... MassMutual Partnership Inv. (EFIS)
MPV .... Mean Platelet Volume [*Hematology*]
MPV .... Meerwein-Ponndorf-Verley [*Organic chemistry*]
MPV .... Metatarsus Primus Varus [*Orthopedics*] (DAVI)
MPV .... Methane-Powered Vehicle
MPV .... Military Pay Voucher
MPV .... Missouri Public Service Company (SAUO)
MPV .... Mitral Valve Prolapse [*Medicine*] (DMAA)
MPV .... Montpelier [*Vermont*] [*Airport symbol*] (OAG)
MPV .... Mountain Province [*Vancouver Stock Exchange symbol*]
MPV .... Mountain Province Diamonds [*Toronto Stock Exchange symbol*] [*Canada*]
MPV .... Multipurpose Passenger Vehicle
MPV .... Multi-Purpose Variant (SAUS)
mpv .... Multipurpose Vehicle (AD)
MPV .... Multipurpose Vehicle [*Automotive engineering*]
MPVA .... Main Propellant Valve Actuator (MCD)
MP/VAP ..... Maritime Patrol/Reconnaissance Attack Aircraft (NATG)
MPVI .... Mountain Province Mining, Inc. [*NASDAQ symbol*] (SAG)
MPVIF .... Mountain Province Mining [*NASDAQ symbol*] (TTSB)
MPVM .... Master of Preventive Veterinary Medicine (GAGS)
MPVO .... Local Anti-Air Defense [*Emergency Management*] (EMA)
MPVP .... Mean Pulmonary Venous Pressure [*Cardiology*]
MPVPC ...... Montreal Paint and Varnish Production Club (SAUO)
MPVR .... El Porvenir [*Panama*] [*ICAO location identifier*] (ICLI)
MPVSCS .... Military Pay Voucher Summary and Certification Sheet
MPVT .... Montpelier [*Vermont*] [*Seismograph station code, US Geological Survey*] (SEIS)
MPVU .... Multi-Plot Variable Updating (SAUS)
MPW .... Macintosh Programmers Workbench (SAUO)
MPW .... Macintosh Programmer's Workshop [*Computer science*] (BTTJ)
MPW .... Magnetic Pulse Welding [*Automotive engineering*]
mPw .... Maritime Polar [*Air Mass*] Warm [*Meteorology*] (BARN)
MPW .... Master of Public Works (PGP)
MPW .... Minneapolis-Moline [*Stock exchange symbol*] (AD)
MPW .... Modified Plane Wave (IEEE)
MPW .... Multi-Product Wafer (AAEL)
MPW .... Whiteshell Nuclear Research Establishment, Atomic Energy of Canada [*Etablissement de Recherche Nucleaire Whiteshell, L'Energie Atomique du Canada*] Pinawa,Manitoba [*Library symbol*] [*National Library of Canada*] (NLC)
MPWB .... Multilayer Printed-Wiring Board
MPWBS ..... Master Plan Works Breakdown Structure (AD)
MPWC .... Michigan Pure Water Council (EA)
MPWC .... Multiprocess Wet Cleaning (EPAT)
MPWD .... Machine-Prepared Wiring Data [*Telecommunications*] (TEL)
MPWG .... Mechanical Properties Working Group (SAUO)
MPWG .... Minuteman Parts Working Group [*Missiles*]
MPWG .... MPW Industrial Services Group, Inc. [*NASDAQ symbol*] (NASQ)
MPWG .... MPW Industrial Svcs. [*NASDAQ symbol*] (SG)
MPWP .... Maximum Permissible Working Pressure (HEAS)
MPWQ .... Metro Park Warehouses [*Common carrier symbol*]
MPWS .... Mobile Protected Weapon System (RDA)
MPWU .... Movement for Political World Union [*Blommenslyst, Fyn, Denmark*] (EA)
MPWUPH ... Ministry of Public Works, Urban Planning and Housing (SAUO)
MPX .... Aeromexpress, SA de CV [*Mexico*] [*FAA designator*] (FAAC)
MPX .... Magazine Page Exposure [*Publishing*] (WDMC)
MPX .... Mapped Programming Executive [*Systems Engineering Laboratories U.S.*] (NITA)
MPX .... Microprocessor Exchange [*Computer science*]
MPX .... Mid-America Payment Exchange [*Banking*] (TBD)
mpx .... Multiplex (AD)
MPX .... Multiplex [*or Multiplexer*] [*Telecommunications*]
MPX .... Multiprocessor Extension (PCM)
MPX .... Multiprogramming Executive [*Computer science*]
MPXE .... MAT Parcel Express [*Common carrier symbol*]
MPXR .... Multiplexer
mpxr .... Multiplexor (AD)
Mpy .... Maatschappij [*Company*] [*Dutch*] (AD)
MPY .... Milli-Inches per Year [*Corrosion technology*]
mpy .... Mils per Year (ABAC)
MPY .... Monopoly [*Telegraphy*] (PCTE)
MPY .... Multiple Problem Youth
mpy .... Multiply (AD)
MPY .... Multiply (MDG)
MPY .... Multiprobe Yield (TIMI)
MPYH .... John A. Murphy [*Common carrier symbol*]
MPZ .... Mid-Continent Petroleum [*Stock exchange symbol*] (AD)
MPZ .... Missouri Pacific Railroad [*Intermodal trailer symbol*]
MPZ .... Modified Protamine Zinc [*Insulin*]
MPZ .... Monopolize [*Telegraphy*] (PCTE)
MPZ .... Mount Pleasant, IA [*Location identifier*] [*FAA*] (FAAL)
MPZ .... Myelin Protein, Zero (DMAA)
MPZL .... Panama [*Panama*] [*ICAO location identifier*] (ICLI)
MQ .... Mack Trucks, Inc. (SAUO)
MQ .... Magnum Airlines [*ICAO designator*] (AD)
MQ .... Management Quarterly Magazine [*A publication*] (EAAP)
MQ .... MARC [*Machine-Readable Cataloging*] Quebecois [*Source file*] [*UTLAS symbol*]

MQ .... Marketing Quota
MQ .... Market Quiet [*Telegraphy*] (PCTE)
MQ .... Martinique [*ANSI two-letter standard code*] (CNC)
mq .... Martinique [*MARC country of publication code*] [*Library of Congress*] (LCCP)
MQ .... Mayflower Quarterly [*A publication*] (GEAB)
mq .... Memory Quotient (AD)
MQ .... Memory Quotient
MQ .... Menaquinone [*Vitamin K*] [*Also, MK*] [*Biochemistry*]
MQ .... Merit Quotient
MQ .... Merseburg-Querfurt [*German license plate city code*]
MQ .... Message Queue [*Computer science*] (VLIE)
mq .... Metol-Quinol [*Medicine*] (AD)
MQ .... Metol-Quinol [*Developer*] [*Photography*] (ROG)
MQ .... Metol-Quinone [*Medicine*] (AD)
mq .... Metol-Quinone [*Medicine*] (AD)
MQ .... Mining and Quarrying [*Department of Employment*] [*British*]
MQ .... Modular Queueing [*Communications term*] (DCT)
MQ .... Mo'ed Qatan [*or Qattan*] (BJA)
Mq .... Mosque (AD)
mq .... Mosque (BARN)
MQ .... Mothering Quotient
mq .... Multiple Quotient (AD)
MQ .... Multiplier Quotient [*Computer science*]
MQ .... Musical Quarterly [*A publication*] (BRI)
MQ .... Simmons Airlines [*ICAO designator*] (AD)
MQ .... Thomas Crane Public Library, Quincy, MA [*Library symbol*] [*Library of Congress*] (LCLS)
MQA .... Adams Mansion, Quincy, MA [*Library symbol*] [*Library of Congress*] (LCLS)
MQA .... Manual of Qualification for Advancement
MQA .... Manufacturing Quality Assurance
MQA .... Manufacturing Quality Audit
MQA .... Measurement Quality Assurance
MQA .... Medical Quality Assurance (AD)
MQA .... Multiple Queue Assignment [*Computer science*] (ITD)
MQA .... Murrayaquinone-A [*Biochemistry*]
MQAB .... Medical Quality Assurance Board (AD)
MQAD .... Materials Quality Assurance Directorate [*Ministry of Defence*] [*British*]
MQB .... Macomb, IL [*Location identifier*] [*FAA*] (FAAL)
MQB .... Mining Qualifications Board [*British*] (BI)
MQC .... Macroscopic Quantum Coherence [*Physics*]
MQC .... Mammography Quality Control
MQC .... Manufacturing Quality Control (MCD)
MQC .... Marquette Company (SAUO)
MQC .... Microbiologic Quality Control (DMAA)
MQCD .... DSR-MCCS [*Common carrier symbol*]
MQCL .... Master Quality Characteristic List (MCD)
MQD .... Manhattan, KS [*Location identifier*] [*FAA*] (FAAL)
MQD .... Metallurgical Quenching Dilatometry
MQD .... Milner. Questions de Droit [*A publication*] (DLA)
MQD .... Monolithic Quad Device
MQDT .... Multichannel Quantum Defect Theory [*Physics*]
MQE .... Managed Query Environment [*Computer science*] (ITCA)
Mqe .... Martinique (AD)
MQE .... Martinique [*West Indies*] (WDAA)
MQE .... Matepi [*Language symbol*] (ETLW)
MQE .... Message Queue Element [*Computer science*]
MQEM .... Michigan Quarterly Economic Model (NITA)
mqf .... Mobile Quarantine Facility (AD)
MQF .... Mobile Quarantine Facility [*NASA*]
MQG .... General Dynamics, Quincy Shipbuilding Division, Quincy, MA [*Library symbol*] [*Library of Congress*] (LCLS)
MQG .... Milgarra [*Queensland*] [*Airport symbol*] (AD)
MQHi .... Quincy Historical Society, Quincy, MA [*Library symbol*] [*Library of Congress*] (LCLS)
MQI .... Macquarie Island [*Australia*] [*Seismograph station code, US Geological Survey*] [*Closed*] (SEIS)
MQI .... Maiquetia [*Venezuelan airport*] (AD)
MQI .... Manteo, NC [*Location identifier*] [*FAA*] (FAAL)
MQI .... Message Queuing Interface [*Computer science*] (VLIE)
MQID .... Message Queue Identification [*Computer science*] (VLIE)
MQIFX .... Mutual Qualified Fund [*Mutual fund ticker symbol*] (SG)
mqil .... Miniature Quartz Incandescent Lamp (AD)
MQIL .... Miniature Quartz Incandescent Lamp
MQJ .... Indianapolis, IN [*Location identifier*] [*FAA*] (FAAL)
MQK .... Youngstown, OH [*Location identifier*] [*FAA*] (FAAL)
MQL .... Mean Queue Length [*Computer science*] (VLIE)
MQL .... Method Quantification Limits (COE)
MQL .... Mildura [*Australia*] [*Airport symbol*] (OAG)
mql .... Miniature Quartz Lamp (AD)
MQL .... Miniature Quartz Lamp
MQLF .... Mobile Quick-Look Facility (SAUS)
MQM .... Master of Quality Management (PGP)
MQM .... Master of the Queen's Music [*British*] (AD)
MQM .... Message Queue Manager [*Computer science*] (MCD)
MQM .... Message-Queuing Middleware [*Computer science*] (GART)
MQM .... Mohajir Qami Movement [*Pakistan*] [*Political party*]
MQM .... Monida, MT [*Location identifier*] [*FAA*] (FAAL)
MQM .... Muhajir Qaumi Movement [*Pakistan*] [*Political party*] (ECON)
MQM .... University of New Mexico, Medical Center Library, Albuquerque, NM [*OCLC symbol*] (OCLC)
MQM-A ...... Mutahida Qaumi Movement (Altaf) (Pakistan) [*Political party*] (PSAP)
MQM-H ...... Mutahida Qaumi Movement (Haqiqi) (Pakistan) [*Political party*] (PSAP)
MQN .... Magnetic Quantum Number [*Atomic physics*]
MQN .... Message Queue Name [*Computer science*] (VLIE)
MQ-NMR .... Multiple Quantum Nuclear Magnetic Resonance (AAEL)
MQO .... Marksmanship Qualification Order [*Marine Corps*]
MQO .... Mosquito Creek Gold Mining [*Vancouver Stock Exchange symbol*]
MQP .... Mandatory Quote Period (NUMA)
MQP .... Manipa [*Language symbol*] (ETLW)
MQP .... Military Qualification Program (NG)
MQP .... Mineral Wells, TX [*Location identifier*] [*FAA*] (FAAL)
MQP .... Motor Qualification Program (NG)
MQQ .... Moundou [*Chad*] [*Airport symbol*] (AD)
MQR .... Michigan Quarterly Review [*A publication*] (BRI)
MQR .... Miscellaneous Quote Request (MCD)
MQR .... Multiplier Quotient Register [*Computer science*]
MQRNS ..... Modified Quadratic Residue Number System (MCD)
MQS .... Coatesville, PA [*Location identifier*] [*FAA*] (FAAL)
MQS .... Maintenance Quality Specialist (MCD)
MQS .... Manufacturing Quality System (TIMI)
MQS .... Master of Quantitative Systems
MQS .... Message Queuing Series [*Computer science*] (GART)
MQS .... Military Qualification Standard
MQS .... Mobile Quality Services (AD)
MQS .... Modified Q-Switching (ODA)
MQS .... Motion to Quash Subpoena (NRCH)
MQS .... Multiprogrammed Queued Tasking System (NITA)
MQS .... Mustique [*Windward Islands*] [*Airport symbol*] (OAG)
MQSA .... Mammography Quality Standards Act
MQSA .... Mammography Quality Standards Act of 1992
MQSS .... Mary Queen of Scots Society (EAIO)
MQST .... MapQuest.com, Inc. [*NASDAQ symbol*] (SG)
MQT .... Macquest Resources Ltd. [*Toronto Stock Exchange symbol*]
MQT .... Macroscopic Quantum Tunneling [*Quantum mechanics*]
MQT .... Marquette [*Michigan*] [*Airport symbol*] (OAG)
MQT .... Military Qualification Test (NG)
MQT .... Mission Qualification Training
MQT .... Model Qualification Test
MQT .... Motor Qualification Test (NG)
MQT .... MuniYield Quality Fund II [*NYSE symbol*] (SPSG)
MQU .... Beckley, WV [*Location identifier*] [*FAA*] (FAAL)
MQU .... Makus Resources, Inc. [*Vancouver Stock Exchange symbol*]
MQU .... Mariquita [*Colombia*] [*Airport symbol*] (OAG)
MQU .... Media Quality Unit [*Communications*]
MQU .... Multiplier Quotient Unit [*Computer science*]
MQUAD ..... Metal Quad
MQUIPS .... Million Quality Improvements Per Second (SAUS)
MQV .... Ministere de la Qualite de la Vie [*Ministry of the Quality of Life*] [*France*] (AD)
MQW .... McRae, GA [*Location identifier*] [*FAA*] (FAAL)
MQW .... Multiple Quantum Well [*Switch for an optical computer*]
MQW .... Multiquantum Well (NITA)
MQWL .... Multiquantum Well Lasers (NITA)
MQX .... Makale [*Ethiopia*] [*Airport symbol*] (OAG)
MQY .... MuniYield Quality Fund [*NYSE symbol*] (SPSG)
MQY .... Smyrna, TN [*Location identifier*] [*FAA*] (FAAL)
mqyco .... Minimum Quantity Yards per Color (AD)
mqyds .... Minimum Quantity Yards per Design (AD)
MR .... Air Mauritanie [*Mauritania*] [*ICAO designator*] (ICDA)
MR .... Application for Writ of Mandamus Refused [*Legal term*] (DLA)
M/R .... Machine Receipt
mr. .... Machine Record (AD)
MR .... Machine Records
mr. .... Machine Rifle (AD)
MR .... Machine Rifle
MR .... Machinery Repairman [*Navy rating*]
MR .... Macrophage Rich
MR .... Madras Railway [*Indian Railway*] (TIR)
MR .... Magister [*Master*] [*Latin*] (ROG)
MR .... Magnetic Recorder (DEN)
MR .... Magnetic Resonance
MR .... Magnetic Resonating (AD)
MR .... Magnetoresistive [*Computer science*] (FOTI)
MR .... Magnitude of Rotation
MR .... Mail and Records Group (SAUO)
MR .... Maine Rail [*Federal Railroad Administration identification code*]
MR .... Main Ring (SAUS)
MR .... Maintainability Report
M+R .... Maintenance and Refurbishment
M+R .... Maintenance and Repair
MR .... Maintenance Ratio (MCD)
MR .... Maintenance Request (TIMI)
MR .... Maintenance Review
MR .... Management Requirements (MCD)
MR .... Management Reserve (MCD)
MR .... Management Review (SAUO)
MR .... Mandatory Reporting (HEAS)
MR .... Mandelate Racemase [*An enzyme*]
MR .... Maneuver Radius (ACAE)
MR .... Manifest Refraction (SAUS)
MR .... Manitoba Law Reports [*Canada*] [*A publication*] (DLA)
MR .... Mannose Resistant [*Biochemistry*]
MR .... Manpower Requirements
MR .... Manual Removal [*Medicine*]

MR.......... Manufacturer's Representative
MR.......... Manufacturing Requisition
m/r.......... Map Reading (AD)
MR.......... Map Reading
mr.......... Map Reference (AD)
MR.......... Map Reference
MR.......... Marble (AAG)
MR.......... Marburg [*Lahn*] [*German license plate city code*]
MR.......... Marca Registrada [*Registered Trademark*] [*Spanish*]
Mr.......... March (RION)
MR.......... March
MR.......... Marginal Return [*Army*] (AABC)
mr.......... Marginal Revenue (AD)
MR.......... Marginal Revenue [*Economics*]
MR.......... Marianist Sisters (TOCD)
MR.......... Mariner (ACAE)
MR.......... Maritime Reconnaissance (NATG)
MR.......... Maritime Regiment
MR.......... Marker Ranger (SAUS)
MR.......... Marketing Research Division [*of AMS, Department of Agriculture*]
MR.......... Market Rate (SAUO)
MR.......... Mark Russell (AD)
MR.......... Marston Radiators Ltd. (SAUO)
MR.......... Mask Register
MR.......... Massachusetts Review: A Quarterly of Literature, the Arts and Public Affairs [*A publication*] (ANEX)
Mr.......... Master (AD)
MR.......... Master [*British military*] (DMA)
MR.......... Master of the Rolls
MR.......... Master Relay [*Electrical*] (DICI)
MR.......... Master Reset (MCD)
MR.......... Master Routing (SAA)
MR.......... Material Request [*or Requisition*] (MCD)
MR.......... Material Review [*Aviation*] (AAG)
MR.......... Materiel Readiness [*Army*]
MR.......... Mate's Receipt
m/r.......... Mates' Receipt (RIMS)
MR.......... Mathematical Review (SAUO)
MR.......... Matted Rib [*Gunnery*]
MR.......... Mauritania [*ANSI two-letter standard code*] (CNC)
MR.......... Mauritius Decisions [*A publication*] (DLA)
MR.......... Mauritius Reports [*A publication*] (DLA)
MR.......... Maximal Response
MR.......... Maximum Range (IAA)
MR.......... Maximum to Right (SAUS)
MR.......... May Repeat [*Medicine*]
MR.......... McCloud River [*Railroad*] (MHDW)
MR.......... McCloud River Railroad Co. (SAUO)
MR.......... Mean Radius (MCD)
MR.......... Mean Rate (SAUS)
MR.......... Measles, Rubella [*Immunology*]
MR.......... Measured Rating [*IOR*] [*Yacht racing*]
MR.......... Mechanical Restraint [*for mental patients*] [*British*]
MR.......... Medial Rectus [*Eye anatomy*]
MR.......... [*The*] Media Report [*A publication*] (NTCM)
MR.......... Medical Record
MR.......... Medical Rectus [*Muscle*] [*Anatomy*]
MR.......... Medical Report
mr.......... Medium Range (AD)
MR.......... Medium Range
MR.......... Medium-Range Planes [*Navy*]
MR.......... Medium Reduction (NITA)
MR.......... Medium Release (WDAA)
MR.......... Medium Resolution
MR.......... Medium-Riser [*Automotive engines*]
MR.......... Medullary Ray [*Botany*] (BARN)
mr.......... Meester [*Master*] [*Dutch*] (AD)
MR.......... Megarayleigh [*Optics*]
MR.......... Melkersson-Rosenthal [*Syndrome*] [*Medicine*] (DB)
MR.......... Memorandum for Record [*Military*] (AFM)
MR.......... Memorandum Receipt [*Military*] (MUGU)
MR.......... Memory Read [*Computer science*]
MR.......... Memory Recall [*Computer science*] (PCM)
MR.......... Memory Reclaimer
MR.......... Memory Register [*Computer science*]
mr.......... Mentally Retarded (AD)
MR.......... Mental Retardation
MR.......... Mental Retardation Program [*Public human service program*] (PHSD)
MR.......... Mercury-Redstone [*NASA*]
MR.......... Message Register (AAG)
MR.......... Message Repeat
MR.......... Message Retrieval [*Open Systems Interconnection*] (ODAA)
mr.......... Metabolic Rate (AD)
MR.......... Metabolic Rate
MR.......... Metallica Resources [*Toronto Stock Exchange symbol*] [*Canada*]
MR.......... Metal Removing Co. (SAUO)
MR.......... Meter
MR.......... Meter-Handling Residential [*Electric utility company*]
MR.......... Methacholine Response [*Medicine*]
MR.......... Methane Recovery (CARB)
MR.......... Methane Response [*Automotive emissions*]
MR.......... Methodist Review (SAUO)
mr.......... Methyl Red (AD)
MR.......... Methyl Red [*A dye*]
MR.......... Methyl Reductase [*An enzyme*]
MR.......... Metropolitan Railway [*British*]
MR.......... Metropolitan Railway Co. (SAUO)
MR.......... Michael Resources Ltd. [*Vancouver Stock Exchange symbol*]
MR.......... Michigan Reformatory (AD)
MR.......... Microfilm Review (SAUO)
MR.......... Microminiature Relay
MR.......... Microplate Reader [*Computer science*]
MR.......... Microwave Radiometer (ACAE)
MR.......... Middle Repetitive [*Genetics*]
m/r.......... Middle Right (AD)
MR.......... [*The*] Middlesex Regiment [*British*]
MR.......... Mid-Engine, Rear-Drive [*Automotive engineering*]
MR.......... Midland Railway [*British*]
MR.......... Midland Railway Co. (SAUO)
MR.......... Midland Red Bus Co. (SAUO)
MR.......... Midrib [*Botany*]
MR.......... Migration Ratio (DNAB)
MR.......... Military Railroad (AD)
MR.......... Military Readiness
MR.......... Military Region [*Viet Cong term*]
MR.......... Military Regulation
MR.......... Military Representative (NATG)
MR.......... Military Requirement
M/R.......... Military Reserve (CINC)
MR.......... Military Review (MCD)
MR.......... Militia Reserve [*British military*] (DMA)
MR.......... Milk-Ring [*Test*] [*Medicine*] (MEDA)
MR.......... Milliradian (DEN)
MR.......... Millirem (DEN)
mr.......... Millirem [*Emergency Management*] (EMA)
mR.......... Milliroentgen (AD)
mr.......... Milliroentgen
mr.......... Mill Run (AD)
MR.......... Mill Run [*Unselected lot of a manufactured product*]
MR.......... Milrinone [*Biochemistry*]
MR.......... Mine Rake (DWSG)
MR.......... Mineralo-Corticoid Receptor [*Endocrinology*]
MR.......... Mineralogical Record [*A publication*] (STAH)
MR.......... Mineral Range Railroad (IIA)
mr.......... Mineral Rubber (AD)
MR.......... Mineral Rubber
mr.......... Mine Run (AD)
MR.......... Mine-Run
MR.......... Miniatures Rules (VLIE)
MR.......... Minimum Required
MR.......... Mining Reports, Edited by R. S. Morrison [*Chicago*] [*A publication*] (DLA)
MR.......... Mining Review [*A publication*]
MR.......... Mini Registry (EA)
MR.......... Minister of Reconstruction (SAUO)
MR.......... Minister-Residentiary [*Diplomacy*]
MR.......... Ministry of Reconstruction [*World War I*] [*British*]
MR.......... Minnesota Review [*A publication*] (BRI)
MR.......... Minor Repair (MCD)
MR.......... Mi Remesa [*My Remittance*] [*Spanish*] [*Business term*]
MR.......... Miscellaneous Report
MR.......... Missed Recognition (SAA)
MR.......... Missile RADAR [*Military*] (CAAL)
MR.......... Missile Receiver
MR.......... Missile Reference
MR.......... Missile Rounds (MCD)
M/R.......... Missiles and Rockets [*A publication*]
MR.......... Missionarius Rector [*Missionary Rector*] [*Latin*]
MR.......... Mission Radius (MCD)
MR.......... Mission Ready [*Aircraft*]
MR.......... Mission Reliability
MR.......... Mission Report [*NASA*]
MR.......... Mission Requirements (ACAE)
Mr.......... Mister (WDAA)
Mr.......... Mister
MR.......... Mistura [*Mixture*] [*Pharmacy*] (ROG)
MR.......... Mitochondriarich [*Cytology*]
MR.......... Mitral Reflux [*Cardiology*] (MAE)
MR.......... Mitral Regurgitation [*Cardiology*]
MR.......... Mittleres Reich in Aegypten [*A publication*] (BJA)
M/R.......... Mixture Radio (SAUS)
MR.......... Mixture Ratio (KSC)
Mr.......... Mobile Revertant [*Bacteriology*]
MR.......... Mobility Required [*Civil Service*]
MR.......... Mobilizacion Republicana [*Republican Mobilization*] [*Nicaragua*] [*Political party*] (AD)
MR.......... Mobilization Regulation [*Army*]
MR.......... MODEM Ready [*Computer science*]
MR.......... Moderately Resistant [*Plant pathology*]
MR.......... [*The*] Modern Reader's Bible (1907) [*A publication*] (BJA)
M-R.......... Modification and Restriction [*of DNA*] [*Biochemistry, genetics*]
MR.......... Modification Request [*or Requirement*]
MR.......... Modified Road (SAUO)
MR.......... Modular Redundancy
MR.......... Modulation Rate (DB)
MR.......... Modulation Response
MR.......... Moisture Resistant (IEEE)
mr.......... Moisture Resistant (MIST)

MR.......... Molar Refraction
MR.......... Molecular Replacement [*Crystallography*]
MR.......... Moment of Resistance
MR.......... Mondcivitan Republic [*Defunct*] (EAIO)
MR.......... Monitor Recorder
MR.......... Monon Railroad (AD)
MR.......... Monthly Rental (VLIE)
MR.......... Monthly Report
MR.......... Monthly Review
MR.......... Moon Rise (DNAB)
MR.......... Morgan Refractories Limited (SAUO)
MR.......... Morgan's Foods, Inc. [*AMEX symbol*] (SPSG)
MR.......... Morning Report [*Army*]
mr.......... Morocco [*MARC country of publication code*] [*Library of Congress*] (LCCP)
MR.......... Moro's Reflex [*Medicine*] (MELL)
MR.......... Morris Register [*An association*] (EAIO)
MR.......... Mortality Rates
MR.......... Mortality Ratio (MAE)
Mr.......... Mother (AD)
mr.......... Motivational Research (AD)
MR.......... Motivation Research
MR.......... Motormannes Riksforbund [*Motorists' Association*] [*Swedish*] (AD)
MR.......... Motor Reduction
MR.......... Motor Rifle (CCCA)
MR.......... Mounted Rifles (SAUO)
MR.......... Mounted Route (TBD)
MR.......... Movement Region (SAUO)
MR.......... Multifamily Residential Zone (AD)
MR.......... Multi-Mirror Reflector [*Lamp*]
MR.......... Multiple Requesting [*IBM Corp.*]
MR.......... Multiplier Register
MR.......... Multi-Reflecton [*Lighting*]
MR.......... Multi-Role (SAUS)
MR.......... Municipal Reform [*or Reformer*]
MR.......... Municipal Reform Party (SAUO)
MR.......... Muscle Receptor [*Medicine*] (DMAA)
MR.......... Muscle Relaxant [*Medicine*] (DMAA)
MR.......... Music Records [*Record label*]
MR.......... Muster Report
MR.......... Mutual Recognition
MR.......... Mutual Responsibility [*Movement within Anglican Communion to make its mission more efficacious*]
MR.......... Mycorrhizal Roots [*Botany*]
MR.......... Radiolocation Mobile Station [*ITU designation*]
MR.......... Reading Public Library, Reading, MA [*Library symbol*] [*Library of Congress*] (LCLS)
mr---.......... Red Sea and Area [*MARC geographic area code*] [*Library of Congress*] (LCCP)
Mr.......... Relative Molecular Mass (DOG)
MR1.......... Machinery Repairman, First Class [*Navy rating*]
MR2.......... Machinery Repairman, Second Class [*Navy rating*]
MR2.......... Mid-engine, Rear-drive, 2-seater [*Automotive model designation*]
MR3.......... Machinery Repairman, Third Class [*Navy rating*]
MR-13.......... Movimiento Revolucionario 13 de Noviembre [*November 13 Revolutionary Movement*] [*Guatemala*]
MR-13 Movement of 13 NoGuatemala... Movimiento Revolucionario de 13 de Noviembre [*Revolutionary Movement of 13 November*] [*Guatemala*] [*Political party*] (AD)
MRA.......... Golden Myra Resources, Inc. [*Toronto Stock Exchange symbol*]
MRA.......... Machine Readable Archives Division [*Public Archives of Canada*] [*Information service or system*] (IID)
MRA.......... Machine Records Activity
MRA.......... Magnetic Reaction Analyzer (PDAA)
MRA.......... Magnetic Resonance Angiography [*Medicine*] (DMAA)
MRA.......... Main Renal Artery [*Medicine*] (DB)
MRA.......... Main Ring Assembly (SAUS)
MRA.......... Maneuver Right Area [*Army*]
MRA.......... Manufacturers Representatives of America (EA)
MRA.......... Marine Reserves Act (SAUO)
MRA.......... Maritime Royal Artillery [*British military*] (DMA)
MRA.......... Marketing Research Association [*Chicago, IL*] (EA)
MRA.......... Marrow Repopulating Activity [*Medicine*] (DB)
MRA.......... Martinaire [*ICAO designator*] (FAAC)
MRA.......... Masonic Relief Association of USA and Canada (EA)
MRA.......... Master of Recreation Administration (GAGS)
MRA.......... Master of Rehabilitation Administration (GAGS)
MRA.......... Master of Resource Administration (GAGS)
MRA.......... Master Retailers Association (AD)
MRA.......... Material Review Activity
MRA.......... Materials Requirement Analysis (PDAA)
MRA.......... Materials Review Area (AAG)
MRA.......... Matrix Reducibility Algorithm (PDAA)
MRA.......... Maximum Rendezvous Altitude
MRA.......... Mazda Research & Development of North America
MRA.......... Mean Reference Axis (MCD)
MRA.......... Mean Right Atrial [*Cardiology*]
MRA.......... Mechanical Readiness Assessment (NASA)
MRA.......... Medial Right Abdomen [*Injection site*]
MRA.......... Medical Record Administrator
MRA.......... Medical Record Analyst (HCT)
MRA.......... Medical Resource Co. of America [*AMEX symbol*] (SPSG)
mra.......... Medium-Powered Radio Range (AD)
MRA.......... Medium-Powered Radio Range (Adcock)
MRA.......... Membrane Reactive Antibody [*Medicine*] (EDAA)
MRA.......... Men's Rights Association (EA)
MRA.......... Menswear Retailers of America (EA)
MRA.......... Mental Retardation Abstracts [*Medicine*] [*Journal*] (EDAA)
MRA.......... Messtechnik, Regelungstechnik, Automatik [*Hoppenstedt Wirtschaftsdatenbank GmbH*] [*Germany*] [*Information service or system*] (CRD)
mra.......... Metro Rating Area (AD)
MRA.......... Metro Rating Area [*Arbitron television ratings*] (NTCM)
MRA.......... Michigan Retailers Association (EARSL)
MRA.......... Microgravity Research Associates
MRA.......... Mid-right Atrium [*Medicine*] (EDAA)
MRA.......... Midwest Resources Association [*Defunct*]
mra.......... Minimum Reception Altitude (AD)
MRA.......... Minimum Reception Altitude [*Aviation*]
MRA.......... Minimum Reserve Authorization
MRA.......... Minimum Resolvable Angle
MRA.......... Minimum Retirement Age (GFGA)
MRA.......... Ministry for Rural Affairs [*British*] (WDAA)
MRA.......... Missile RADAR Altimeter (MCD)
MRA.......... Mission Ready and Available (ACAE)
MRA.......... Misurata [*Libya*] [*Airport symbol*] (OAG)
MRA.......... Mixed Refrigerant Autocascade [*Cryogenic system*]
MRA.......... Mlabri [*Language symbol*] (ETLW)
MRA.......... Model Reporting Area [*for Blindness Statistics*] [*HEW*]
MRA.......... Module Rack Assembly
MRA.......... Moral Re-Armament (EA)
MRA.......... Motorcycle Retailers of America [*Later, NMRA*] (EA)
MRA.......... Mountain Rescue Association (EA)
MRA.......... Moving Right Along [*Internet lingo*] (NETL)
MRA.......... Multiple Recording Accelerometer
MRA.......... Multiple Regression Analysis
MRA.......... Multiple Resource Area Nomination [*National Register of Historic Places*]
MRA.......... Multi Resolutions Analysis (SAUS)
MRA.......... Multivariate Regression Analysis [*Medicine*] (DMAA)
MRA.......... Mutual Recognition Agreement (SAUO)
MRA.......... Mycelium Radius Atrovirens [*A fungus*]
MRA.......... Rapid City Regional Library, Manitoba [*Library symbol*] [*National Library of Canada*] (NLC)
MRAA.......... Marine Retailers Association of America (EA)
MRAA.......... Mental Retardation Association of America (EA)
MRAALS.......... Marine Corps Remote Area Approach and Landing System (MCD)
mraam.......... Medium-Range Air-to-Air Missile [*Military*] (AD)
MRAAM.......... Medium-Range Air-to-Air Missile (MCD)
MRA&L.......... Manpower Accounting System (SAUO)
MRA & L.......... Manpower, Reserve Affairs and Logistics (MCD)
mrac.......... Manifold-Regulator Accumulator Charging (AD)
MRAC.......... Manifold-Regulator Accumulator Charging [*Formerly, NCP*] (AAG)
MRAC.......... Member of the Royal Agricultural College [*British*]
MRAC.......... Meter-Reading Access Circuit [*Bell Laboratories*]
MRAC.......... Model Reference Adaptive Control (VLIE)
MRAC.......... Moore and Son Company [*Common carrier symbol*]
MRACGP.......... Member of the Royal Australasian College of General Practice (BABM)
MRACO.......... Member of the Royal Australasian College of Ophthalmologists [*British*] (BABM)
MRACP.......... Member of Royal Australasian College of Physicians
MRACR.......... Member of the Royal Australasian College of Radiologists [*British*] (BABM)
MRACS.......... Model Reference Adaptive Control System (VLIE)
MRAD.......... Mass Random Access Disk [*Computer science*]
M Rad.......... Master of Radiology
mrad.......... Megarad (AD)
MRAD.......... Microwave Radiometer (ACAE)
mrad.......... Millirad [*Medicine*] (EDAA)
mrad.......... Milliradian (IDOE)
MRAD.......... Milliradians (KSC)
MRAD.......... Minor Restricted Activity Day [*Environmental medicine*]
MRAD.......... Multiple Range Alignment Device [*Army*] (INF)
MRadA.......... Member of the Radionic Association [*British*]
M Rad (D).......... Master of Radiology (Radiodiagnosis)
MRAD/IN.......... Milliradians per Inch
MRADS.......... Mass Random Access Data Storage [*Computer science*]
M Rad (T).......... Master of Radiology (Radiotherapy)
MRAE.......... Bill McRae Trucking [*Common carrier symbol*]
M Ra E.......... Master of Radio Engineering
M Ra Eng.......... Master of Radio Engineering
MRAeS.......... Member of the Royal Aeronautical Society [*British*] (ADA)
MRAF.......... Marshal of the Royal Air Force [*British*]
MRAF.......... Missile Round Assembly Facility
M-RAG.......... Moderately Repressive Authoritarian Government
MRAIC.......... Member of the Royal Architectural Institute of Canada
MRAJ.......... Aranjuez [*Costa Rica*] [*ICAO location identifier*] (ICLI)
MRaK.......... Myth, Ritual, and Kingship. Essays on the Theory and Practice of Kingship in theAncient Near East and in Israel [*A publication*] (BJA)
MRAL.......... Alajuela [*Costa Rica*] [*ICAO location identifier*] (ICLI)
MRAL.......... Mandatory Retirement Age Law of 1978 (WYGK)
MRAL.......... Materiel Readiness Authorization List [*Military*]
MRAL.......... Mobile Radionuclide Analysis Laboratory (SAUO)
MRAM.......... Amubri [*Costa Rica*] [*ICAO location identifier*] (ICLI)
MRAM.......... MacPhail Radial Arm Maze (EAGT)
MRAM.......... Magnetic Random-Access Memory [*Computer science*] (PS)
MRAM.......... Member of the Royal Academy of Music [*British*]

MRAM .... Multi-Mission Redeye Air-Launched Missile [*Military*] (PDAA)
MRAN .... Medical Resident Admitting Note (MEDA)
MR & A ..... Market Research and Analysis
MR & D ..... Material Redistribution and Disposal
MR & DA ... Material Redistribution and Disposal Administration
MR & DC ... Medical Research and Development Command [*Army*] (AD)
MR&DF ..... Malleable Research and Development Foundation (AD)
MR&E .... Mobile Reclamation & Repair (SAUS)
MR & S ...... Materials Research and Standards (AD)
MR & T ..... Mississippi River and Tributaries [*Flood-control project*]
MRANZCP... Member of the Royal Australian and New Zealand College of Psychiatrists [*British*] (BABM)
MRAO .... Mobilization Reserve Acquisition Objective [*Military*]
MRAO .... Mullard Radio Astronomy Observatory (USDC)
MRAP .... JA Miara Transport [*Common carrier symbol*]
MRAP .... Management Review and Analysis Program (AD)
MRAP .... Marginal Revenue/Average Physical Product [*Economics*]
MRAP .... Maximal Resting Anal Pressure [*Medicine*] (EDAA)
MRAP .... Mean Right Atrial Pressure [*Cardiology*]
MRAP .... Mortgage and Rental Assistance Program [*Australia*]
MRAP .... Mouvement Contre le Racisme et pour l'Amitie Entre les Peuples [*Movement Against Racism and for Friendship between People*] (EAIO)
MRAP .... Movement Against Racism and for Friendship between Peoples (SAUO)
MRAP .... Movimiento de Resistencia Armada Puertorriquena [*Puerto Rican Armed Resistance Movement*] [*Political party*] (PD)
MRAPCON... Mobile RADAR Approach Control (AFM)
MRAPM ..... Materials Research and Protection Methods (SAA)
MRAR .... Atirro [*Costa Rica*] [*ICAO location identifier*] (ICLI)
MRAR .... Manpower Requirements Analysis Report [*Military*]
MRAS .... Main Renal Artery Stenosis [*Medicine*] (DMAA)
MRAS .... Management Resources Accounting System
MRAS .... Manpower Resources Accounting System [*Air Force*]
MRAS .... Member of the Royal Academy of Science [*British*]
MRAS .... Member of the Royal Asiatic Society [*British*]
MRAS .... Member of the Royal Astronomical Society [*British*] (DI)
MRAS .... Model Reference Adaptive System (PDAA)
MRASB ...... Member of the Royal Asiatic Society of Bengal
MRASE ...... Member of the Royal Agricultural Society of England
mrasm .... Medium-Range Air-to-Surface Missile [*Military*] (AD)
MRASM ...... Medium-Range Air-to-Surface Missile (MCD)
MRASTU .... Marine Reserve Aviation Supply Training Unit (DNAB)
MRAT .... Altamira De San Carlos [*Costa Rica*] [*ICAO location identifier*] (ICLI)
mrat .... Medium-Range Applied Technology (AD)
MRAT .... Mobile Radiation Tester (IAA)
MRATE ...... Money Market Rates [*I. P. Sharp Associates*] [*Canada*] [*Information service or system*] (CRD)
MRATGW ... Medium Range ATGW (SAUS)
MR ATOMIC... Multiple Rapid Automatic Test of Monolithic Integrated Circuits (PDAA)
MRAU .... Marauder Travelers [*NCIC trailer make code*]
MRAUSCAN... Masonic Relief Association of the United States and Canada (AD)
MRB .... Magnetic Recording Boresight [*or Borescope*]
MRB .... Magnetospheric Radio Burst
MRB .... Maintenance Review Board (MCD)
MRB .... Malaysian Rubber Bureau (EA)
MRB .... Management Reserve Budget (SAUO)
MRB .... Management Review Board (SAUO)
MRB .... Marble [*Technical drawings*]
MRB .... Marble Base (AAG)
mrb .... Marble Base (AD)
MRB .... Martinsburg, WV [*Location identifier*] [*FAA*] (FAAL)
MRB .... Master Reference Buoy [*Navy*] (NVT)
MRB .... Material Review Board [*Aviation*] (MCD)
MRB .... Medical Research Bulletin [*Medicine*] [*Australia*] (EDAA)
MRB .... Medium Range Blast (SAUS)
MRB .... Mersey River Board (SAUO)
MRB .... Metallica Resources [*AMEX symbol*]
MRB .... Metals Reserve Board [*of the Reconstruction Finance Corp.*]
MRB .... Method Request Broker (SAUO)
MRB .... Microcircuit Reliability Bibliography (NITA)
MRB .... Mileage Rationing Board [*World War II*]
MRB .... Missile Review Board (SAUO)
MRB .... Mission Review Board [*NASA*]
MRB .... Mister Build Industry, Inc. [*Vancouver Stock Exchange symbol*]
MRB .... Mobile Radio Broadcasting (SAUO)
MRB .... Mobile Riverine Base [*Navy*]
MRB .... Modification Requirements Board [*NASA*] (KSC)
MRB .... Modification Review Board (AFM)
MRB .... Mortgage Revenue Bond
MRB .... Mortgage Review Board (SAUO)
MRB .... Motorized Rifle Battalion [*Former USSR*]
MRB .... Motor Rescue Boat
MRB .... Motor Surfboat [*Coast Guard*] (DNAB)
MRB .... Motor Truck Rate Bureau Inc., Columbia SC [*STAC*]
MRB .... Multi-Role Boat (SAUS)
MRB .... Multi-Role Bomber [*Program*] [*DoD*]
MRB .... Mutual Reinsurance Bureau (EA)
MRBA .... Buenos Aires [*Costa Rica*] [*ICAO location identifier*] (ICLI)
MRBA .... Marimba, Inc. [*NASDAQ symbol*] (SG)
MRBA .... Mississippi River Bridge Authority (AD)
MRBB .... Babilonia [*Costa Rica*] [*ICAO location identifier*] (ICLI)
MRBC .... Barra Del Colorado [*Costa Rica*] [*ICAO location identifier*] (ICLI)
MRBC .... Missouri River Basin Commission
MRBC .... Molded Rubber Blended Cover
MRBC .... Monkey Red Blood Cells
MRBC .... Mouse Red Blood Cell [*Medicine*] (DMAA)
MRBC .... Multiple Resolution Bitmap Compiler (SAUS)
MRBCMA ... Mean Rounds between Corrective Maintenance Actions [*Quality control*] (MCD)
MR-BD ...... Mercury-Redstone Booster Development [*Spacecraft*] [*NASA*]
MRBF .... Mean Renal Blood Flow [*Nephrology*]
MRBF .... Mean Rounds between Failures [*Military*] (CAAL)
MRBI .... Market Research Bureau Ireland (SAUO)
MRBIR ...... Municipal Registered Bond Interest Record [*Standard & Poor's Corp.*] [*Information service or system*] (CRD)
MRBK .... Mercantile Bankshares [*NASDAQ symbol*] (TTSB)
MRBK .... Mercantile Bankshares Corp. [*NASDAQ symbol*] (NQ)
MRBL .... Marble
MRBL .... Marble Financial Corp. [*NASDAQ symbol*] (NQ)
MRBM .... Bremen [*Costa Rica*] [*ICAO location identifier*] (ICLI)
MRBM .... Medium [*or Mid*]-Range Ballistic Missile
mrbm .... Medium-Range Ballistic Missile [*Military*] (AD)
MRBN .... Bataan [*Costa Rica*] [*ICAO location identifier*] (ICLI)
MRBNA ...... Member of the Royal British Nursing Association (ROG)
MRBO .... Boca Naranjo [*Costa Rica*] [*ICAO location identifier*] (ICLI)
MRBOMF ... Mean Rounds between Operational Mission Failures [*Quality control*] (MCD)
MRBP .... Barra De Parismina [*Costa Rica*] [*ICAO location identifier*] (ICLI)
MRBP .... Missouri River Basin Project
MRBS .... Mean Rounds between Stoppages [*Quality control*] (MCD)
MRBS .... Medium Range Bit Synchronizer (ACAE)
MRBS .... Modified Road Brigade Slice (MCD)
MRBT .... Barra De Tortuguero [*Costa Rica*] [*ICAO location identifier*] (ICLI)
MRBT .... Multirod Burst Test [*Nuclear energy*] (NRCH)
MRBU .... Deutsche Forschungs und Versuchsanstalt fuer Luft und Raumfahrt [*Intermodal shipping container symbol*] (TVRC)
MRC .... Columbia/Mt. Pleasant, TN [*Location identifier*] [*FAA*] (FAAL)
MRC .... Graduate Center for Materials Research [*University of Missouri - Rolla*] [*Research center*] (RCD)
MRC .... Interdepartmental Committee on Manpower Requirements [*British*] [*World War II*]
MRC .... Machine-Readable Code
MRC .... Machinery Repairman, Chief [*Navy rating*]
mrc .... Magnetic Rectifier Control (AD)
MRC .... Magnetic Rectifier Control
MRC .... Magnetic Research Corp. (MCD)
MRC .... Magneto-Resistive Cluster (SAUS)
MRC .... Mail Reminder Card (SAUS)
MRC .... Maintenance and Reliability Center [*University of Tennessee, Knoxville*] (RCD)
MRC .... Maintenance and Repair Craft [*Military*]
MRC .... Maintenance and Repair Cycle
MRC .... Maintenance Requirement Card
MRC .... Major Readiness Command (MCD)
MRC .... Major Reality Corp. (EFIS)
MRC .... Major Regional Conflict (SAUO)
MRC .... Major Regional Contingency (DOMA)
MRC .... Major Renal Calix [*Medicine*] (MELL)
MRC .... Major Retail Center
MRC .... Malaria Research Centre [*India*]
MRC .... Management Research Center [*University of Wisconsin - Milwaukee*] [*Research center*] (RCD)
MRC .... Management Research Corp. [*Shelbyville, IN*] [*Information service or system*] (IID)
MRC .... Manitoba Research Council [*Research center*] (RCD)
MRC .... Manpower Requirements Change [*Military*] (GFGA)
MRC .... Manufacturing Research Center [*Florida International University*] (RCD)
MRC .... Manufacturing Resource Control [*Kongsberg Vaapenfabrikk*] [*Software package*] (NCC)
MRC .... Manufacturing Rules Checker (TIMI)
MRC .... Maracas
MRC .... Maricopa, AZ [*Amtrak rail station code*]
MRC .... Marietta College, Marietta, OH [*OCLC symbol*] (OCLC)
MRC .... Marine Research Committee
MRC .... Marine Research Corp. [*Marine science*] (OSRA)
MRC .... Marine Resources Council
MRC .... Marketing Research Council (NTPA)
MRC .... Market Research Council
MRC .... Marlin-Rockwell Corp. (AD)
MRC .... Massachusetts Rehabilitation Commission (SAUO)
MRC .... Master of Rehabilitation Counseling
MRC .... Master Requirements Code
MRC .... Master Routing Control (SAA)
MRC .... Material Redistribution Center
MRC .... Materials Research Center [*Lehigh University*] (RCD)
MRC .... Materials Research Center [*Northwestern University*] (RCD)
MRC .... Materials Research Corp.
MRC .... Materials Review Crib (AAG)
MRC .... Materiel Readiness Command [*Military*]
MRC .... Materiel Release Confirmation [*Army*] (AABC)
MRC .... Mathematics Research Center (MCD)
Mrc .... Mauricio [*Mauritius*] [*Spanish*] (AD)
MRC .... Maximum Recycling Capacity (DMAA)
MRC .... Maximum Reverse Current
MRC .... Measurement Requirements Committee [*NASA*] (NASA)
MRC .... Measurement Research Center [*University of Iowa*]

MRC .... Media Resource Center [*Adelaide, Australia*]
MRC .... Media Resource Controller (ACAE)
MRC .... Medical Registration Council [*British*] (DAVI)
MRC .... Medical Research Center (SAUO)
MRC .... Medical Research Committee
MRC .... Medical Research Council [*Research center*] [*British*] (IRC)
MRC .... Medical Research Council of South Africa (SAUO)
MRC .... Medical Reserve Corps
MRC .... Mekong River Commission [*Thailand*]
MRC .... Memorial Research Center [*University of Tennessee*] [*Research center*] (RCD)
MRC .... Memory Request Controller
MRC .... Men's Republican Club (NADA)
MRC .... Men's Resource Center (EA)
MRC .... Men's Resource Connection [*An association*] (EA)
MRC .... Message-based Reliable Channel (SAUS)
MRC .... Metabolic Clearance Rate (DB)
MRC .... Metals Reserve Co. [*World War II*]
MRC .... Metals Reserve Company (SAUO)
MRC .... Meteorological Research Committee [*British*]
MRC .... Methods Research Corp. (AD)
MRC .... Methylrosaniline Chloride [*Also, GV*] [*A dye*]
MRC .... Metrics Research Corp. [*Information service or system*] (IID)
MRC .... Microelectronics Research Centre [*University of Cambridge*] [*United Kingdom*] (RCD)
MRC .... Microwave Radio Corp. (SAUS)
MRC .... Mid-Roll Change Capability
MRC .... Mid-Roll Interchange [*Advanced photo system*]
MRC .... Midwestern Relay Co. [*Milwaukee, WI*] [*Telecommunications*] (TSSD)
MRC .... Military Reform Caucus (EA)
MRC .... Military Region Command (MCD)
MRC .... Military Representatives Committee [*NATO*] (NATG)
MRC .... Military Reunions Council (EA)
MRC .... Military Revolutionary Council (CINC)
MRC .... Miniature Rifle Club (SAUO)
MRC .... Minnesota Restitution Center (AD)
MRC .... Minorco Canada Ltd. [*Toronto Stock Exchange symbol*]
MRC .... Minor Renal Calix [*Medicine*] (MELL)
MRC .... Missile Research Corp.
MRC .... Mission Requirements Change [*NASA*] (KSC)
MRC .... Mission Research Corporation (SAUO)
MRC .... Mission Resources Center [*Sydney, Australia*]
MRC .... Mississippi River Commission [*Vicksburg, MS*] [*Army*]
MRC .... Mobile Radio Communications
MRC .... Model Railway Club [*British*]
MRC .... Modern Railroad Club (AD)
MRC .... Modern Records Centre [*University of Warwick*] [*United Kingdom*] (RCD)
MRC .... Modified River Compatible Alteration (SAUO)
MRC .... Monroe Railroad [*Federal Railroad Administration identification code*]
MRC .... Monterey Resources, Inc. [*NYSE symbol*] (SAG)
MRC .... Monthly Recurring Charge (SAUO)
MRC .... Montrose [*Colorado*] [*Seismograph station code, US Geological Survey*] [*Closed*] (SEIS)
MRC .... Moon's RADAR Coordinates
MRC .... Morning Readiness Check
MRC .... Motorized Rifle Co. (INF)
MRC .... Motor Racing Club (AD)
MRC .... Mouvement des Renovateurs Communistes [*France*] [*Political party*] (EY)
MRC .... Movement Report Center [*Military*]
MRC .... Mueller-Ribbing-Clement [*Syndrome*] [*Medicine*] (DB)
MRC .... Multiple Register Counter (IEEE)
MRC .... Multiple Regression/Correlation [*Statistical analysis*]
MRC .... Museum Reference Center [*Smithsonian Institution*]
MRCA .... Canas [*Costa Rica*] [*ICAO location identifier*] (ICLI)
MRCA .... Market Research Corp. of America (AD)
MRCA .... Member of the Royal College of Anaesthetists (SAUO)
MRCA .... Midwest Roofing Contractors Association (EARSL)
MRCA .... Most Recent Common Ancestor
mrca .... Multirole Combat Aircraft (AD)
MRCA .... Multirole Combat Aircraft
MRCAS ...... Monetary Ration Credit Allowance System [*Military*] (AFM)
MRCAT ...... Miniature Radio-Controlled Aerial Target (MCD)
MrcBnc ...... Merchants Bancshares [*Associated Press*] (SAG)
MRCC .... Coto 47 [*Costa Rica*] [*ICAO location identifier*] (ICLI)
MRCC .... Marine Rescue Coordination Centre [*Nautical term*] (NTA)
MRCC .... Maritime Rescue Coordination Center [*Australia*]
MRCC .... Material Review Central Control [*Aviation*] (MCD)
MRCC .... Medical Research Council of Canada (BARN)
MRCC .... Medical Resource Control Center [*Emergency Management*] (EMA)
MRCC .... Member of the Royal College of Chemistry [*British*]
MRCC .... Mercury Recovery Control Center
MRCC .... Molded Rubber Coupling Cushion
MRCC .... Movement Report Control Center [*Military*]
MRCC .... Multibus Remote Channel Controller (TIMI)
MRCCC ...... Medical Research Council, Collaborative Centre [*British*] (CB)
MRCCV ...... Mark Controls Corp. [*NASDAQ symbol*] (COMM)
MRCD .... Caledonia [*Costa Rica*] [*ICAO location identifier*] (ICLI)
MRCD .... Memory Raster Colour Display (PDAA)
MRCD .... Merchants Delivery [*Common carrier symbol*]
MRCD .... Movement for Responsible Coastal Development (SAUO)
MRCE .... Carate [*Costa Rica*] [*ICAO location identifier*] (ICLI)
MRCE .... Marginal Relative Certainty Effect [*Statistics*]
MRCF .... Martin Color-Fi, Inc. [*NASDAQ symbol*] (SAG)
MRCF .... Mayo Biotechnology Research Computer Facility [*Mayo Clinic*] [*Research center*] (RCD)
MRCF .... Microsoft Real-Time Compression Format [*Microsoft Corp.*] (PCM)
MRCF .... Missile Recycle Facility (SAA)
MRCF .... Module Repair Calibration Facility
MRCGP ...... Member of the Royal College of General Practitioners [*British*]
MRCGP ...... Member, Royal College of General Practice [*British*] (CMD)
MRCH .... Chacarita [*Costa Rica*] [*ICAO location identifier*] (ICLI)
MrchBcp .... Merchants Bcp. [*Associated Press*] (SAG)
MrchBnc .... Merchants Bancshares, Inc. [*Associated Press*] (SAG)
MrchGp ..... Merchants Group, Inc. [*Associated Press*] (SAG)
MRCHNT .... Merchant
MRCI .... Ciruelas [*Costa Rica*] [*ICAO location identifier*] (ICLI)
MRCI .... Marci International Imports, Inc. [*NASDAQ symbol*] (COMM)
MRCI .... Maximum Rescue Coverage Intercept [*Environmental science*] (COE)
MRCI .... Medical Registration Council of Ireland (AD)
MRCI .... Medical Research Council of Ireland (SLS)
MRCI .... Microelectronics Research and Communications Institute [*University of Idaho*] (RCD)
MRCI .... Microsoft Real-Time Compression Interface [*Microsoft Corp.*] (PCM)
MRCI .... Mine Readiness/Certification Inspection (MCD)
MRCI .... Modular Re-configurable C4I Interface (SAUS)
MRCI .... Multireference Configuration Interaction [*Quantum chemistry*] (MCD)
MRCIY ...... Marconi Corporation PLC [*NASDAQ symbol*]
MRCL .... Master Cross-Reference List
MRCL .... Medical Research Council Laboratories (SAUO)
MRCL .... Mercurial
MRCLOS .... Missile Reference Command-to-Line-Of-Sight (SAUS)
MRCM .... Machinery Repairman, Master Chief [*Navy rating*]
MRCM .... Marcam Solutions, Inc. [*NASDAQ symbol*] (NASQ)
MRCMC ..... Murrumbidgee Regional Catchment Management Committee (SAUO)
MRCMCCR... Medical Responsibility Center Manager Cost Center Report (SAUO)
MRCN .... Medical Research Council Newsletter [*Medicine*] [*Canada*] (EDAA)
MRCN .... Minuteman Requirement Control Number (SAA)
MRCNP ...... Medical Research Council Neuroimmunology Project [*Medicine*] [*United Kingdom*] (EDAA)
MRCO .... Madison Railway [*Federal Railroad Administration identification code*]
MRCo .... Malaysian Refrigerator Co. (AD)
MRCO .... Manufacturing Research Corp. of Ontario [*Research center*] [*Canada*] (RCD)
MRCO .... Marco [*NCIC motorcycle make code*]
MRCO .... Member of the Royal College of Ophthalmologists (SAUO)
MRCO .... Member of the Royal College of Organists [*British*]
MRCO .... Meridian National Corp. [*NASDAQ symbol*] (NQ)
MRCOA ...... Medical Research Council Trial in Older Adults
MRCOG ..... Member of the Royal College of Obstetricians and Gynaecologists [*British*]
MRCOL ...... Meridian Natl Wrrt'A' [*NASDAQ symbol*] (TTSB)
MRCOP ...... Meridan Natl $3.75 Cv'B'Pfd [*NASDAQ symbol*] (TTSB)
MRCOZ ...... Meridian Natl Wrrt [*NASDAQ symbol*] (TTSB)
MRCP .... Maoist Revolutionary Communist Party [*Political party*] (AD)
MRCP .... Master of Regional and City Planning (PGP)
MRCP .... Master of Regional and Community Planning (GAGS)
MRCP .... Member of the Royal College of Physicians [*British*]
MRCP .... Member of the Royal College of Preceptors [*British*]
MRCP .... Microfilm Research Centers Project [*Defunct*] (EA)
MRCP .... Mobile RADAR Control Post
MRCPA ...... Mobilization Reserve Components Program of the Army (AABC)
MRC Path... Member of the Royal College of Pathologists [*British*]
MRCPCH .... Member of the Royal College of Paediatrics and Child Health (SAUO)
MRCPE ...... Member of the Royal College of Physicians, Edinburgh
MRCPEd .... Member of the Royal College of Physicians of Edinburgh
MRCP Edin... Member of the Royal College of Physicians of Edinburgh
MRCPGlas... Member of the Royal College of Physicians of Glasgow
MRCP (Glasg)... Member of the Royal College of Physicians and Surgeons of Glasgow (AAMN)
MRCP Glasg... Member of the Royal College of Physicians of Glasgow
MRCPI .... Member of the Royal College of Physicians of Ireland
MRCP Ire ... Member of the Royal College of Physicians of Ireland (SAUO)
MRCP Irel... Member of the Royal College of Physicians of Ireland
MRCPOWH... McMaster Research Centre for the Promotion of Women's Health [*McMaster University*] [*Canada*] (RCD)
MRC Psych... Member of the Royal College of Psychiatrists [*British*]
MRCPUK .... Member of the Royal College of Physicians of the United Kingdom [*British*] (AD)
MRCP UK... Member of the Royal Colleges of Physicians of the United Kingdom
MRCR .... Carrillo [*Costa Rica*] [*ICAO location identifier*] (ICLI)
MRCR .... Measurement Requirement Change Request [*NASA*] (KSC)
MRCR .... Member of the Royal College of Radiologists (SAUO)
MRCRR ..... Machine-Readable Collections Reading Room [*Library of Congress*] (IT)
MRCS .... Machinery Repairman, Senior Chief [*Navy rating*]
MRCS .... Marcus Corp. [*NASDAQ symbol*] (COMM)
MRCS .... Mechanoreceptor Cueing Subsystem (MCD)
MRCS .... Medium Resolution Camera System (MCD)
MRCS .... Member of the Royal College of Surgeons [*British*]
MRCS .... Missile Range Calibration Satellite
MRCS .... Mobile Reporting & Control System (SAUS)
MRCS .... Morrison Rail Car Service [*Federal Railroad Administration identification code*]
MRCS .... Multiple Report Creation System
MRCS .... Multiple RPV [*Remotely Piloted Vehicle*] Control System (PDAA)

MRCSA ...... Migrant Resource Center of South Australia
MRCSE ...... Member of the Royal College of Surgeons, Edinburgh
MRCSI ...... Member of the Royal College of Surgeons, Ireland (ROG)
MRCTS ...... Missile Round Cable Test System
MRCU ...... Mercantile Shipping [*Intermodal shipping container symbol*] (TVRC)
MRCU ...... Mercator Shipping [*Common carrier symbol*]
MRCU ...... Mini-Remote Control Unit (MHDI)
MRCV ...... Cabo Velas [*Costa Rica*] [*ICAO location identifier*] (ICLI)
MRCV ...... Mixture Ratio Control Valve (KSC)
MRCV ...... Multi-Role Combat Vehicle (SAUS)
MRCVS ...... Member of the Royal College of Veterinary Surgeons [*British*] (EY)
MRCWA ...... Midland Railway Company of Western Australia (AD)
MRCX ...... Miner Rail Car Service [*Federal Railroad Administration identification code*]
MRCY ...... Mercury Computer Systems [*NASDAQ symbol*] (NASQ)
MRCY ...... Mercury General [*NASDAQ symbol*] (TTSB)
MRCY ...... Mercury General Corp. [*NASDAQ symbol*] (NQ)
MRCZ ...... Carrizal [*Costa Rica*] [*ICAO location identifier*] (ICLI)
MRCZ ...... Medical Research Council of Zimbabwe (SAUO)
MRCZ ...... Moorman [*Federal Railroad Administration identification code*]
MRD ...... MacDermid, Inc. [*NYSE symbol*] (SG)
MRD ...... Main Roads Department (SAUO)
MRD ...... Maintenance Requirements Documents (CTAS)
MRD ...... Management Review Division (SAUO)
MRD ...... Mandatory Retirement Date [*Army*] (AABC)
MRD ...... Manual Ringdown [*Telecommunications*] (TEL)
MRD ...... Margin-Reflex Distance (SAUS)
MRD ...... Maritime Research Department [*An association*] [*Inactive*] (EA)
MRD ...... Marketing Requirement Document
MRD ...... Married [*Telegraphy*] (PCTE)
MRD ...... Master Requirements Directory [*Military*] (AFM)
MRD ...... Material Required Date
MRD ...... Material Requirement Document (SAUO)
MRD ...... Material Requirements Deck (AAG)
MRD ...... Material Requirements Drawing (MCD)
MRD ...... Material Review Disposition [*Aviation*]
MRD ...... Materials Required Data (SAUO)
MRD ...... Materiel Redistribution Division [*Army*] (AFIT)
MRD ...... Materiel Release Denial [*Military*] (AABC)
MRD ...... Materiel Requirements Document [*Army*]
MRD ...... McCloud Ranger District (SAUO)
MRD ...... Measuring & Reference Device (SAUS)
MRD ...... Media Review Digest
MRD ...... Medical Records Department (DAVI)
MRD ...... Medical Reference Department (AD)
MRD ...... Medical Research Division
MRD ...... Medium Rate Demodulator (ACAE)
MRD ...... Melcor Developments Ltd. [*Toronto Stock Exchange symbol*]
MRD ...... Memorandum for Regional Directors (AAGC)
MRD ...... Memory Raster Display [*Computer science*]
MRD ...... Memory Read [*Computer science*] (MHDI)
MRD ...... Merida [*Venezuela*] [*Airport symbol*] (OAG)
MRD ...... Meridian Air Cargo, Inc. [*ICAO designator*] (FAAC)
MRD ...... Mesoscale Research Division [*National Severe Storms Laboratory*] (USDC)
MRD ...... Metabolic Renal Disease [*Medicine*] (MELL)
mrd ...... Metal Rolling Door (AD)
MRD ...... Metal Rolling Door [*Technical drawings*]
mrd ...... Metal Roof Deck (AD)
MRD ...... Metal Roof Deck [*Technical drawings*]
MRD ...... Methane Response Definition [*Automotive emissions*]
MRD ...... Microbiological Research Department (AD)
MRD ...... Milestone Review Documentation [*Army*]
MRD ...... Military Reference Data
MRD ...... Military Requirements Determination
mrd ...... Millirutherford
MRD ...... Minimal Renal Disease [*Medicine*] (MELL)
MRD ...... Minimal Residual Disease [*Medicine*]
mrd ...... Minimum Reacting Dose (AD)
MRD ...... Minimum Reacting Dose
MRD ...... Mission Rehearsal Device (SAUS)
MRD ...... Mission Requirements Document [*NASA*] (KSC)
MRD ...... Mississippi River Division [*Army Corps of Engineers*]
MRD ...... Missouri River Division [*Army Corps of Engineers*]
MRD ...... Mobil Research & Development Corp., Engineering Information Center, Princeton, NJ [*OCLC symbol*] (OCLC)
MRD ...... Monostable Relay Driver
MRD ...... Morpholinodaunorubicin [*Also, MoDNM*] [*Antineoplastic drug*]
MRD ...... Mortality Rate to Double
MRD ...... Motorized Rifle Division [*Military*] (AD)
MRD ...... Motor Racing Developments
MRD ...... Motor Receiving Dolly
MRD ...... Movement for the Restoration of Democracy [*Pakistan*] [*Political party*] (PD)
MRD ...... Movement for the Restoration of Democracy [*Nepal*] [*Political party*]
MRD ...... Multireference Double Excitation [*Physics*]
MRD ...... Russell and District Regional Library, Russell, Manitoba [*Library symbol*] [*National Library of Canada*] (NLC)
MRDA ...... Maintenance Requirement Development Activity [*Military*] (CAAL)
MRDA ...... Media Research Directors Association (EA)
MRDA ...... Mission Requirements Definition and Analysis (SAUO)
MRDA ...... Mitsubishi Research and Development of America [*Automotive industry*]
MRDA ...... Mundri Relief and Development International Committee (SAUO)
MRDAC ...... Manpower Research and Data Analysis Center [*DoD*] (DNAB)
MRDB ...... Materiel Returns Data Base (SAUO)
MRDB ...... Mission Requirements Data Base [*NASA*] (SSD)
MRDC ...... Medical Research and Development Command [*Frederick, MD*] [*Army*]
MRDC ...... Microelectronic Research and Development Center (SAUO)
MRDC ...... Military Requirement and Development Committee (NATG)
MRDC ...... Military Research and Development Center [*US-Thailand*]
MRDC ...... Missile Research and Development Command [*Army*] (MCD)
MRDC ...... Module RADAR Display Console
MRDCC ...... Metropolitan Refuse Disposal Consultative Committee [*Melbourne, Australia*]
MRDD ...... Don Diego [*Costa Rica*] [*ICAO location identifier*] (ICLI)
MR/DD ...... Mentally Retarded and Developmentally Disabled
MRDD ...... Mental Retardation and Developmental Disabilities [*National Institutes of Health*]
MRDE ...... Mining Research and Development Establishment [*National Coal Board*] [*British*]
MRDEC ...... Missile Research Development and Engineering Center [*Formerly, Army Missile Laboratory*] (RDA)
mrdf ...... Machine-Readable Data Files [*Computer science*] (AD)
MRDF ...... Machine-Readable Data Files
MRDF ...... Marine Resources Development Foundation
MRDF ...... Maritime Radio Direction Finding
MRDF ...... Metals Research and Development Foundation [*Defunct*] (EA)
MRDFS ...... Manpack Radio Direction Finding System (SAUO)
MRDFS ...... Man-Portable Radio Direction-Finding System
MRDG ...... Manufacturing Research and Design Group [*McMaster University*] [*Canada*] [*Research center*] (RCD)
MRDGP ...... Mackay Region Division of General Practice (SAUO)
mrdhd ...... Maximum Recommended Daily Human Dose (AD)
MRDI ...... Merchants Delivery Systems [*Common carrier symbol*]
MRDIS ...... Message Reproduction and Distribution System [*Military*] (CAAL)
MRDL ...... Mean Reciprocal Detection Latency
MRDL ...... Mineral Respurces Development Laboratory [*Australia*]
MRDL ...... Missouri River Division Laboratory [*Army Corps of Engineers*]
MRDM ...... Malnutrition Related Diabetes Mellitus (SAUS)
MRDN ...... Material Receipt Discrepancy Notice (AD)
MRDN ...... Meridian Bancorp, Inc. [*NASDAQ symbol*] (NQ)
MrdN ...... Meridian National Corp. [*Associated Press*] (SAG)
MRDN ...... Mouvement Revolutionnaire pour la Democratie Nouvelle [*Revolutionary Movement for New Democracy*] [*Senegal*] (PD)
MrdN 99 ...... Meridian National Corp. [*Associated Press*] (SAG)
MrdnBc ...... Meridian Bancorp, Inc. [*Associated Press*] (SAG)
MRDNL ...... Meridional
MRDO ...... Dieciocho [*Costa Rica*] [*ICAO location identifier*] (ICLI)
MRDOS ...... Mapped Real-Time Disk Operating System [*Computer science*] (MDG)
MRDR ...... Material Receipt Discrepancy Record
MRDR ...... Material Review Disposition Record (NASA)
MRDS ...... Maintenance Ratio at Direct Support level (SAUO)
MRDS ...... Maintenance Requirements Data Systems (SAUO)
MRDS ...... Malfunction Rate Detection System (DNAB)
MRDS ...... MARC [*Machine-Readable Cataloging*] Records Distribution Service [*National Library of Canada*] (IID)
MRDS ...... Member of the Royal Drawing Society [*British*] (ROG)
MRDS ...... Message Reproduction and Distribution System [*Military*] (MCD)
MRDS ...... Mineral Resources Data System [*US Geological Survey*] [*Information service or system*] (IID)
MRDS ...... Mission Recorder Display Set (MCD)
MRDS ...... Modular Responsive Defense System
MRDS ...... Molded Rubber Duct System
MRDS ...... Multics Relational Data Store [*Computer science*] (HODG)
MRDT ...... Mortality Rate Doubling Time
MRDTI ...... Metal Roof Deck Technical Institute [*Later, Steel Deck Institute*] (EA)
MRDV ...... Maize Rough Dwarf Virus [*Plant pathology*]
MRDY ...... Message Ready [*Computer science*] (MHDI)
MRE ...... Magnitude of Relative Error
MRE ...... Major Research Equipment
MRE ...... Malayan Royal Engineers (SAUO)
MRE ...... Managed Reporting Environment [*Knowledge management*]
MRE ...... Manicore [*Brazil*] [*Airport symbol*] (AD)
MRE ...... Mara Lodges [*Kenya*] [*Airport symbol*] (OAG)
MRE ...... Maritime Radio Executive [*British*]
MRE ...... Market Research Extracts Report (JAGO)
M Re ...... Master of Religion
MRE ...... Master of Religious Education
MRE ...... Material Requirement External
MRE ...... Materiel Readiness Expediter [*Army*]
MRE ...... Matter (ROG)
MRE ...... Maximal Relative Error [*Mathematical statistics*]
MRE ...... Maximal Resistive Exercise (DMAA)
MRE ...... Maximal Respiratory Effectiveness (DMAA)
MRE ...... Mazda Research of Europe [*Automobile manufacturer operations*]
mre ...... Meal Ready to Eat (AD)
MRE ...... Meal Ready to Eat [*Military*]
MRE ...... Meal, Ready-to-Eat [*Army rations designation, replaces C-rations*]
MRE ...... Meals Rejected by Everyone
mre ...... Mean Radial Error (AD)
MRE ...... Mean Radial Error
MRE ...... Medco Research, Inc. [*AMEX symbol*] (SAG)
MRE ...... Melissa Resources, Inc. [*Vancouver Stock Exchange symbol*]
MRE ...... Memory Register Exponent [*Computer science*] (MHDI)
MRE ...... Message Reference File
MRE ...... Metal Regulatory Element [*Genetics*]

MRE .... Metal-Responsive Element [*Genetics*]
MR-E .... Methemoglobin Reductase [*An enzyme*] (MAE)
MRE .... Microbiological Research Establishment [*British*]
MRE .... Microrocket Engine
MRE .... Mid-Range Estimate
MRE .... Military Records Envelope
MRE .... Military Rules of Evidence
MRE .... Militia Royal Engineers [*British military*] (DMA)
MRE .... Mining Research Establishment (ODA)
MRE .... Missile Recertification Equipment
MRE .... Missile Recycle Equipment (SAA)
MRE .... Mission Readiness Exercise
MRE .... Mission Rehearsal Exercise
MRE .... Mobil Research & Development Corp., Paulsboro, NJ [*OCLC symbol*] (OCLC)
MRE .... Modern Ramjet Engine (MCD)
MRE .... Monopropellant Rocket Engine (SAUS)
MRE .... Morally Repugnant Elite [*Lifestyle classification*] (ECON)
MRE .... Motor Requirement Evaluation (SAUS)
MRE .... Movimiento Revolucionario Espartaco [*Bolivia*] [*Political party*] (PPW)
MRE .... Movimiento Revolucionario Estudantil [*Colombia*] [*Political party*] (EY)
MRE .... Multifunction RADIAC Equipment
MRE .... Multiple Representation Environment
MRE .... Multiple-Response Enable (IEEE)
MREA .... Estero Azul [*Costa Rica*] [*ICAO location identifier*] (ICLI)
MREA .... Midwest Renewable Energy Association (EARSL)
MREAC ...... Mon Repos Est au Ciel [*My Rest Is in Heaven*] [*Motto of Ludwig Philipp, Count of the Palatinate of Simmern (1602-1654)*] [*French*]
MREAC ...... Murmansk Regional Environmental Affairs Committee (SAUO)
MREC .... El Carmen [*Costa Rica*] [*ICAO location identifier*] (ICLI)
MREC .... Materials Research and Education Center [*Auburn University*] (RCD)
MREC .... Medical Research Ethics Committee
MREC .... Multicentre Research Ethics Committee (SAUO)
MRECM ..... Master of Real Estate and Construction Management (GAGS)
MRED .... Master of Real Estate Development (GAGS)
MREd .... Master of Recreation Education (GAGS)
MR Ed .... Master of Religious Education
MRED .... Mister Ed Boat Trailer [*NCIC trailer make code*]
MREDA ...... Marine Resources and Engineering Development Act [*1966*] (MSC)
M Re E ...... Master of Refrigeration Engineering
M Re Eng ... Master of Refrigeration Engineering
MREF .... Medical Research Endowment Fund
MRefEng .... Master of Refrigeration Engineering (NADA)
MREGAD .... Multiplexer Regenerator Address [*Computer science*] (MHDI)
MRegSc ..... Master of Regional Science (ADA)
MReh .... Blanding Free Public Library, Rehoboth, MA [*Library symbol*] [*Library of Congress*] (LCLS)
MREHIS ..... Member of the Royal Environmental Health Institute of Scotland (DBQ)
MREI .... Marriage Role Expectation Inventory [*Psychology*]
M-REIT ..... Mutual Real Estate Investment Trust
M Rel .... Master of Religion (PGP)
MREL .... Mining Resource Engineering Ltd. (SAUO)
MRELB ...... Malaysian Rubber Exchange and Licensing Board (AD)
MRelEd ..... Master of Religious Education (GAGS)
mrem .... Millirem
mrem .... Milliroentgen Equivalent Man (AD)
MREM .... Milliroentgen Equivalent Man [*Radiation measurement*]
mrem/h ...... Millirem per Hour (DS)
MREmpS .... Member of the Royal Empire Society [*British*]
MREM/YR ... Millirems per Year (SAUO)
MREP .... Maneuvering Room Equipment Panel (DNAB)
MREP .... Medical Remedial Enlistment Program (DNAB)
mrep .... Milliroentgen Equivalent Physical (MAE)
MRER .... El Ron Ron [*Costa Rica*] [*ICAO location identifier*] (ICLI)
MRERF ...... Manufacturers Representatives Educational Research Foundation [*Rolling Meadows, IL*] (EA)
MRES .... Material Requirements Estimation System [*Navy*]
MRES .... Member of the Royal Entomological Society [*British*] (ROG)
MRES .... Military Requirements Estimation System
MRES .... Missing Research and Enquiry Service (SAUO)
MResEnvS ... Master of Resource and Environmental Studies
MResEnvSt ... Master of Resource and Environmental Studies
MRESS ...... Marine Recreational Fishing Statistics Survey [*Marine science*] (OSRA)
MResSc ..... Master of Resource Science
MREST ...... Main Restraint [*National Highway Traffic Safety Administration Fatal Accident Recording System code*]
MRET .... Esterillos [*Costa Rica*] [*ICAO location identifier*] (ICLI)
M Ret .... Master of Retailing
MRET .... Merit Holding [*NASDAQ symbol*] (TTSB)
MRET .... Merit Holding Corp. [*NASDAQ symbol*] (SAG)
M REV .... Most Reverend
MRev .... Revere Public Library, Revere, MA [*Library symbol*] [*Library of Congress*] (LCLS)
MREX .... Monad Railway Equipment [*Private rail car owner code*]
MREZ .... Milk River Elevator [*Federal Railroad Administration identification code*]
MRF .... Magnetorheological Finishing [*Optics manufacturing*] (RDA)
MRF .... Maintenance and Refurbishment Facility [*NASA*] (KSC)
MRF .... Maintenance Repair Facility
MRF .... Maintenance Repair Frequency
mrf .... Maintenance Replacement Factor (AD)
MRF .... Maintenance Replacement Factor (NG)
MRF .... Maintenance Responsibility File (MCD)
MRF .... Mankind Research Foundation (EA)
MRF .... Marble Floor (AAG)
mrf .... Marble Floor (AD)
MRF .... Marfa, TX [*Location identifier*] [*FAA*] (FAAL)
MRF .... MariFarms, Inc. [*Later, Marine Harvest International*] [*AMEX symbol*] (SPSG)
MRF .... Marine Recreational Fishing [*Marine science*] (MSC)
MRF .... Markov Random Field [*Mathematics*]
MRF .... Materials Recovery Facility [*for recycling of glass, plastics, etc.*]
MRF .... Maternal Resistance Factor (BARN)
MRF .... Maximum Retarding Force (NASA)
MRF .... Mayo Research Foundation (AD)
MRF .... Measurements/Stimuli Request Form [*NASA*] (NASA)
MRF .... Medical Record File (DMAA)
MRF .... Medical Red Flag (SAUS)
MRF .... Medical Research Foundation [*Medicine*] [*Palo Alto, CA*] (EDAA)
MRF .... Medium-Range Forecast [*Model*] [*Marine science*] (OSRA)
MRF .... Megawatt Receiver Filter
MRF .... Melanocyte-Stimulating Hormone Releasing Factor [*Endocrinology*]
MRF .... Melanotropin Releasing Factor [*Biochemistry*]
MRF .... Mental Retardation Facility
MRF .... Mentor Income Fund [*Formerly, RAC Income Fund*] [*NYSE symbol*] (SPSG)
MRF .... Merfin Resources Ltd. [*Vancouver Stock Exchange symbol*]
MRF .... Mesencephalic [*or Midbrain*] Reticular Formation [*Anatomy*]
MRF .... Message Refusal [*Telecommunications*] (TEL)
MRF .... Metal Regulatory Factor [*Genetics*]
MRF .... Meteorological Radar Facility (ACAE)
MRF .... Meteorological Research Flight
MRF .... Meteorological Rocket Facility
MRF .... Metering Research Facility [*Research center*] (RCD)
MRF .... Methodist Relief Fund [*British*]
MRF .... Midbrain Reticular Formation [*Brain anatomy*]
MRF .... Milestone Reference File [*Military*] (CAAL)
MRF .... Military Reconnaissance Force [*British military*] (DMA)
MRF .... Miraflores [*Peru*] [*Seismograph station code, US Geological Survey*] (SEIS)
MRF .... Missile Reconstitution Force [*Air Force*] (DOMA)
MRF .... Mission Readiness Flying
MRF .... Mission Reliability Factor [*Military*] (AABC)
MRF .... Mitral Regurgitant Flow [*Medicine*]
MRF .... Mobile Reaction Force (SAUO)
MRF .... Mobile Riverine Force [*Navy*] (NVT)
MRF .... Moderate Renal Failure [*Medicine*] (DMAA)
MRF .... Modular Rigid Frame (PDAA)
MRF .... Module Release Form (ACAE)
MRF .... Module Repair Facility (DNAB)
MRF .... Monoclonal Rheumatoid Factor [*Medicine*] (DB)
mRF .... Monoclonal Rheumatoid Factor [*Medicine*] (MELL)
MRF .... Motorcycle Riders Foundation (SAUO)
MRF .... Movement for Rights and Freedoms [*Bulgaria*] [*Political party*]
MRF .... MSH [*Melanophore-Stimulating Hormone*] Releasing Factor [*Medicine*] (DAVI)
MRF .... Muellerian Regression Factor [*Embryology*] (DAVI)
MRF .... Muellerian Repressor Factor [*Embryology*]
MRF .... Multipath Reduction Factor [*Electronics*]
MRF .... Multiple Risk Factor [*Medicine*] [*MR factor*] (EDAA)
MRF .... Multirole Fighter [*Replacement for the F-16*] [*Air Force*] (DOMA)
MRF .... Multi-Role Fuze (SAUS)
MRF .... Muscle Regulatory Factor [*Physiology*]
MRF .... Music Research Foundation
MRF .... Myopia Research Foundation [*Later, MIRF*]
MRFA .... Fireman Apprentice, Machinery Repairman, Striker [*Navy rating*]
MRFAC ...... Manufacturers Radio Frequency Advisory Committee (EA)
MRFB .... Malayan Rubber Fund Board (AD)
MRFC .... Malawi Rural Finance Co. Ltd.
MRFC .... Mouse Rosette-Forming Cell (DMAA)
MRFCA ...... Mental Residual Functional Capacity Assessment [*Social Security Administration*]
MRFD .... Finca Delicias [*Costa Rica*] [*ICAO location identifier*] (ICLI)
MRFDK ...... Mechanical Remote Fuze Disassembly Kit [*Military*] (CAAL)
MRFI .... Finca 10 (Nuevo Palmar Sur) [*Costa Rica*] [*ICAO location identifier*] (ICLI)
MRFI .... Mutually Responsible Facilitation Inventory [*Personality development test*] [*Psychology*]
MRFIT .... Multiple Risk Factor Intervention Trial [*Cardiology*]
MRFL .... Flamengo [*Costa Rica*] [*ICAO location identifier*] (ICLI)
MRFL .... Master Radio Frequency List (NATG)
mr flight .... Meteorological Research Flight (AD)
MRFN .... Fireman, Machinery Repairman, Striker [*Navy rating*]
MRFP .... Finca La Promesa [*Costa Rica*] [*ICAO location identifier*] (ICLI)
MRFR .... Mobilization Reserve for Retention [*Military*]
MRFS .... Finca 63 [*Costa Rica*] [*ICAO location identifier*] (ICLI)
MRFS .... Mid-Range Force Study [*DoD*]
MRFSS ...... Marine Recreational Fishing Statistics Survey (USDC)
MRFT .... Missile Ready for Test (MCD)
MRFT .... Modified Rapid Fermentation Test
MRFU .... Multiple Rocket Firing Unit
MRFV .... Maize Rayado Fino Virus [*Plant pathology*]
mrg .... Magnetic Radiation Generator (AD)
MRG .... Magnetic Radiation Generator
MRG .... Magnetic Resonance Gyro (MCD)
MRG .... Main Repair Group [*British military*] (DMA)

MRG .... Maintainability Requirements Group (AD)
MRG .... Maintenance Requirements General (MCD)
MRG .... Management Requirement General (ACAE)
MRG .... Management Research Group (SAUO)
MRG .... Management Research Groups [*British*]
MRG .... Management Review Group (SAUO)
MRG .... Mandatory Resource Group (MCD)
MRG .... Manridge Explorations Ltd. [*Toronto Stock Exchange symbol*]
mrg .... Margin (AD)
mrg .... Marginalia (AD)
MRG .... Master of Religious Guidance
MRG .... Master Reference Gyro (PDAA)
MRG .... Material Review Group [*Aviation*]
MRG .... Medium Range
MRG .... Merge [*Computer science*]
MRG .... Mesters Vig [*Greenland*] [*Airport symbol*] (AD)
MRG .... Metabolic Research Group [*University of Kentucky*] (RCD)
MRG .... Methane Rich Gas
mrg .... Methane-Rich Gas (AD)
MRG .... Military Research Group (SAUO)
MRG .... Minimum Revenue Guarantee (SAUO)
MRG .... Minorities Research Group (AD)
MRG .... Minority Rights Group (EAIO)
MRG .... Mission Rules Guidelines [*NASA*] (KSC)
MRG .... Mobile River Group [*Navy*] (VNW)
MRG .... Modelling Research Group [*University of Southern California*] [*Research center*] (RCD)
MRG .... Modern Rythmic Gynmastics (EDAC)
MRG .... Mooring (MSA)
MRG .... Morgantown [*West Virginia*] [*Seismograph station code, US Geological Survey*] (SEIS)
MRG .... Mortgage [*Telegraphy*] (PCTE)
MRG .... Mortons Restaurant Group [*NYSE symbol*] (SAG)
MRG .... Mouvement des Radicaux de Gauche [*Left Radical Movement*] [*Wallis and Futuna Islands*] [*Political party*] (EY)
MRG .... Mouvement des Radicaux de Gauche [*Left Radical Movement*] [*France*] [*Political party*] (PPE)
MRG .... Movement Requirements Generator
MRG .... Multinational Recruitment Group (SAUO)
MRG .... Municipal Reform Group [*Tasmania, Australia*]
MRG .... Murmurs, Rubs, and Gallops [*Cardiology*] (DAVI)
MRGA .... Garza [*Costa Rica*] [*ICAO location identifier*] (ICLI)
MRGA .... Manhattan Ryegrass Growers Association (EA)
MRGF .... Golfito [*Costa Rica*] [*ICAO location identifier*] (ICLI)
MRGI .... MGI of Chicago [*Common carrier symbol*]
MRGI .... Minority Rights Group International [*British*] (EAIO)
MRGITF ..... Machine-Readable Government Information Task Force [*Government Documents Round Table*] [*American Library Association*]
MRGO .... Margo Nursery Farms [*NASDAQ symbol*] (TTSB)
MRGO .... Margo Nursery Farms, Inc. [*NASDAQ symbol*] (NQ)
MRGO .... Mississippi River Gulf Outflow (AD)
MR-GO ...... Mississippi River-Gulf Outlet
MRGP .... Guapiles [*Costa Rica*] [*ICAO location identifier*] (ICLI)
MRGQ .... Mergenthaler Transfer and Storage Company [*Common carrier symbol*]
MRGR .... Mean Relative Growth Rate [*Physiology*]
MRGS .... Member of the Royal Geographical Society [*British*]
MrgS .... Morgan Stanley Group, Inc. [*Associated Press*] (SAG)
MrgSHY ..... MorgaN Stanley High Yield Fund [*Associated Press*] (SAG)
MRGT .... Guatuso [*Costa Rica*] [*ICAO location identifier*] (ICLI)
MRGU .... Guanacaste [*Costa Rica*] [*ICAO location identifier*] (ICLI)
MRGU .... Margalo [*Intermodal shipping container symbol*] (TVRC)
MRGV .... Marine Research Group of Victoria [*Australia*]
MRGX .... Margaux, Inc. [*NASDAQ symbol*] (COMM)
MRH .... Beaufort, NC [*Location identifier*] [*FAA*] (FAAL)
MRH .... Hinds Junior College, Raymond, MS [*OCLC symbol*] (OCLC)
MRH .... Maddox Rod Hyperphoria [*Medicine*] (EDAA)
MRH .... Magnetic Recording Head
MRH .... Mango Resources [*Vancouver Stock Exchange symbol*]
MRH .... Master of Russian History
MRH .... Mechanical Recording Head
MRH .... Melanocyte-Releasing Hormone [*Endocrinology*]
MRH .... Member of the Royal Household [*British*] (AD)
mr/h .... Microroentgon per Hour (COE)
MRH .... Midwest Railway Historical Foundation [*Federal Railroad Administration identification code*]
MRH .... Mild Resid Hydrocracking [*M. W. Kellogg Co. process*]
mr/h .... Milliroentgens per Hour (DS)
MRH .... Mission-Related Hardware
MRH .... Mobile Remote Handler
MRH .... Monitoring River Health (SAUO)
MRH .... MSH [*Melanophore-Stimulating Hormone*] Releasing Hormone [*Laboratory Science*] (DAVI)
MRH .... Rossburn District Hospital, Rossburn, Manitoba [*Library symbol*] [*National Library of Canada*] (NLC)
MRHA .... Mannose-Resistant Hemagglutination
MRHD .... Maximum Recommended Human Dose [*Medicine*] (EDAA)
MRHD .... Mounted Ration Heating Device [*Army*] (INF)
MR head .... Magneto-Resistive Head [*Computer science*] (DDC)
MRHG .... Hacienda Rancho Grande [*Costa Rica*] [*ICAO location identifier*] (ICLI)
MRHI .... Monitoring River Health Initiative (SAUO)
MRHIB ...... Multiantimicrobial Resistant Hemophilus Influenza B
MRHJ .... Hacienda Jaco (Harbor Land) [*Costa Rica*] [*ICAO location identifier*] (ICLI)
mrhm .... Milliroentgens per Hour at One Meter
MRHMC ...... Michael Reese Hospital and Medical Center (AD)
MRHO .... Hacienda Rio Cuarto [*Costa Rica*] [*ICAO location identifier*] (ICLI)
MRHP .... Hacienda Platanar [*Costa Rica*] [*ICAO location identifier*] (ICLI)
mr/hr ...... Milliroentgens per Hour
MRHRC ...... Maine Rural Health Research Center [*University of Southern Maine*] (RCD)
MRHS .... Hacienda La Suerte [*Costa Rica*] [*ICAO location identifier*] (ICLI)
MRHS .... Materiel Request History and Status
MRHS .... Member of the Royal Historical Society [*British*] (ROG)
MRHS .... Midwest Railway Historical Society (EA)
MRHSF ...... Materiel Request History and Storage File
MRHT .... Modified Rhyme Hearing Test [*Medicine*] (EDAA)
MRI .... Anchorage, AK [*Location identifier*] [*FAA*] (FAAL)
MRI .... Information Dynamics Corp., Reading, MA [*Library symbol*] [*Library of Congress*] (LCLS)
MRI .... Machine Records Installation [*Military*]
MRI .... Magazine Research, Inc. (AD)
mri .... Magnetic-Resonance Imager (AD)
MRI .... Magnetic Resonance Imagery (SHCU)
MRI .... Magnetic Resonance Imaging [*Medicine*] (AMHC)
mri .... Magnetic Rubber Inspection (AD)
MRI .... Malt Research Institute [*Later, NMRI*]
MRI .... Management Recruiters International (HGAA)
MRI .... Management Resources International (SAUO)
MRI .... Manufacturing Run-In
MRI .... Marine Research Institute
MRI .... Marital Roles Inventory [*Psychology*]
MRI .... Mass Retailing Institute [*Formerly, Mass Merchandising Research Institute*] [*Later, NMRI*]
MRI .... Material Receiving Instruction [*Bechtel*] [*Nuclear energy*] (NRCH)
MRI .... Material Review Item [*Aviation*]
MRI .... Materials Research Institute [*Pennsylvania State University*] (RCD)
MRI .... Materials Research Institute [*Sheffield Hallam University*] [*United Kingdom*] (RCD)
MRI .... Materials Research Laboratory [*Lawrence Livermore National Laboratory*] (RCD)
MRI .... Mauritius Island [*Mascarene Islands*] [*Seismograph station code, US Geological Survey*] [*Closed*] (SEIS)
MRI .... McRae Industries, Inc. [*AMEX symbol*] (SPSG)
mri .... Mean Rise Interval (AD)
MRI .... Mean Rise Interval [*Tides and currents*]
MRI .... Measurement Requirements and Interface (MCD)
MRI .... Meat Research Institute [*British*]
MRI .... Mediamark Research, Inc. [*Database producer and database*] [*Information service or system*] (IID)
MRI .... Mediator Release Inhibitor [*Biochemistry*]
MRI .... Medical Records Index (AD)
MRI .... Medical Research Institute [*Florida Institute of Technology*] [*Research center*] (RCD)
mri .... Medium-Range Interceptor (AD)
MRI .... Medium-Range Interceptor
MRI .... Member of the Royal Institution [*British*]
MRI .... Memory Reference Instruction
MRI .... Mental Research Institute (EA)
MRI .... Mesoscale Research Initiative (SAUO)
MRI .... Message Routing Indicator (COE)
MRI .... Meteorological Research, Incorporated (SAUO)
MRI .... Meteorological Research Institute (AD)
MRI .... Microwave Research Institute [*Polytechnic Institute of Brooklyn*] (MCD)
MRI .... Midwest Research Institute
MRI .... Military Reform Institute (AD)
mri .... Milstrip Routing Identifier (AD)
MRI .... Mineral Resources Institute [*University of Alabama*] [*Research center*] (RCD)
MRI .... Mineral Resources International Ltd. [*Toronto Stock Exchange symbol*]
MRI .... Minimum Release Interval (DNAB)
MRI .... Ministry of Radio Industry (SAUO)
MRI .... Minority Research Initiation (SAUS)
MRI .... Minority Research Institution [*Program*] [*National Science Foundation*]
MRI .... Mintel Retail Intelligence [*Database*] [*United Kingdom*] (GDD)
MRI .... Miscellaneous RADAR Input
MRI .... Missile Range Index
MRI .... Modeling, Rendering, and Interaction (RALS)
MRI .... Moderate Renal Insufficiency [*Medicine*]
MRI .... Moderate Resolution Imager (SAUS)
MRI .... Modified River Incompatible Alteration (SAUO)
mri .... Monopulse Resolution Improvement (AD)
MRI .... Monopulse Resolution Improvement
MRI .... Morganite Refractory Industries (EFIS)
MRI .... Motor Repair Insurance (AD)
MRI .... Multiple RADAR Interrogator (MUGU)
MRI.A ...... McRae Indus'A' [*AMEX symbol*] (TTSB)
MRI.B ...... McRae Indus Cv 'B' [*AMEX symbol*] (TTSB)
MRIA .... Magnetic Recording Industry Association [*Later, Electronic Industries Association*] (EA)
MRIA .... Member of the Royal Irish Academy (EY)
MRIA .... Model Railroad Industry Association (EA)
MRIAI ...... Member of the Royal Institute of the Architects of Ireland
MRIAS ...... Manchester Region Industrial Archaeology Society (SAUO)
MRIBA ...... Member of the Royal Institute of British Architects (ROG)
MRIC .... Mandatory Recovery Items Code (MCD)

M-RIC .... Manpower Resource Identification Code [*Military*]
MRIC .... Member of the Royal Institute of Chemistry [*British*]
MRIC .... Morning Report Indicator Code [*Army*] (AABC)
MRIC .... Revolutionary Movement of the Christian Left [*Ecuador*] [*Political party*] (PPW)
MRICC .... Missile and Rockets Inventory Control Center [*Army*]
MRICD .... Medical Research Institute of Chemical Defense (RDA)
MRICS .... Member of the Royal Institution of Chartered Surveyors [*British*]
MRID .... Master Record Identification Number (EPAT)
MRIF .... Maintenance Ratio Intermediate Forward
MRIF .... Melanocyte-Stimulating-Hormone Release Inhibiting Factor [*Also, MIF*] [*Endocrinology*]
MRIF .... MSH [*Melanophore-Stimulating Hormone*] Release Inhibiting Factor [*Laboratory science*] (DAVI)
MRIH .... Melanocyte-Stimulating Hormone-Release-Inhibiting Hormone [*Endocrinology*] (MAE)
MRII .... Medical Resources [*NASDAQ symbol*] (TTSB)
MRII .... Medical Resources, Inc. [*NASDAQ symbol*] (SAG)
MRIID .... Medical Research Institute of Infectious Diseases [*Army*] (RDA)
MRIL .... Mandatory Recovery Items List (MCD)
MRIL .... Master Repairable Item List
MRIN .... Marion Homes [*NCIC trailer make code*]
MRIN .... Member of the Royal Institute of Navigation [*British*] (DBQ)
MRINA .... Member of the Royal Institution of Naval Architects [*British*]
MR INC .... Men's Rights, Inc. (EA)
MRINDO .... Modified Rydberg Intermediate Neglect of Differential Overlap [*Physics*]
MRINZ .... Meat Research Institute of New Zealand (AD)
MRIO .... Marion Trailer Sales [*NCIC trailer make code*]
MRIO .... Multiregional Input-Output
MRION .... Marion, NC [*American Association of Railroads railroad junction routing code*]
MRIP .... Imperio [*Costa Rica*] [*ICAO location identifier*] (ICLI)
MRIP .... Management Review and Improvement Program [*Department of Labor*]
MRIP .... Prairie Crocus Regional Library, Rivers, Manitoba [*Library symbol*] [*National Library of Canada*] (NLC)
MRIPA .... Member of the Royal Institute of Public Administration (ADA)
MRIPHH .... Member of the Royal Institute of Public Health and Hygiene [*British*]
MRIPS .... Multi-modality Radiological Image Processing System (SAUO)
MRIPWC .... Member of the Royal Institute of Painters in Water Colours [*British*] (ROG)
mrir .... Medium Resolution Infrared (AD)
MRIR .... Medium-Resolution Infrared Radiometer [*NASA*]
MRIR .... Modification and Retrofit Installation Report (ACAE)
MRIRBM .... Medium-Range and Intermediate-Range Ballistic Missile (MCD)
MRIS .... Maritime Research Information Service [*National Academy of Sciences*]
MRIS .... Market Research Information System [*Bell System*]
MRIS .... Marshall & Isley Corp. [*NASDAQ symbol*] (NQ)
MRIS .... Material Readiness Index System [*Military*]
MRIS .... Media Relations & Information Services (SAUO)
MRIS .... Medical Research Information System [*Veterans Administration*]
MRIS .... Mobile Range Instrumentation System
MRIS .... Modernization Resource Information Submission [*Army*] (RDA)
MRISAN .... Maintenance Requirement Interim Support Asset Notice (MCD)
MRIT .... Marine RADAR Interrogator-Transponder (PDAA)
MRIT .... Mean Re-Initialization Time
MRIT .... Merit Software, Inc. [*NASDAQ symbol*] (SAG)
MRIT .... Mobile Remote Intelligence Terminal (ACAE)
MRITC .... Methylrhodamine Isothiocyanate [*Organic chemistry*]
MRIU .... Missile Round Interface Unit
MRIU .... Mjolkurfelag Reykjavikur [*Intermodal shipping container symbol*] (TVRC)
MRIW .... Medical Research Institute of Worcester (SAUO)
MRIX .... Meadow River Mine [*Federal Railroad Administration identification code*]
MRIX .... Midland Resources [*NASDAQ symbol*] (SPSG)
MRIXZ .... Midland Res Inc. Wrrt [*NASDAQ symbol*] (TTSB)
MRJ .... Marriage [*Telegraphy*] (PCTE)
MRJ .... Microwave Rotary Joint
MRJ .... Mineral Point, WI [*Location identifier*] [*FAA*] (FAAL)
MRJ .... Miniature Revolving Joint
MRJE .... Multileaving Remote Job Entry [*IBM Corp.*]
MRJE .... Multiple Remote Job Entry (NITA)
MRJSDK .... Macintosh Runtime for Java Software Developer Kit (SAUS)
MRJX .... Museum & Rollo Jamison [*Federal Railroad Administration identification code*]
MRJY .... Mister Jay Fashions International, Inc. [*NASDAQ symbol*] (SAG)
MRJY .... Mr Jay Fashions Intl [*NASDAQ symbol*] (TTSB)
MRK .... Marco Island [*Florida*] [*Airport symbol*] (OAG)
mrk .... Mark (VRA)
MRK .... Mark
MRK .... Markair, Inc. [*ICAO designator*] (FAAC)
MRK .... Merck & Co. [*NYSE symbol*] (TTSB)
MRK .... Merck & Co., Inc. [*NYSE symbol*] (SPSG)
MRK .... Merrimack College, McQuade Library, North Andover, MA [*OCLC symbol*] (OCLC)
MRK .... Millrock Development Corp. [*Vancouver Stock Exchange symbol*]
MRK .... Modified Redlich-Kwong [*Chemical equation*]
MRK .... Morioka [*Japan*] [*Seismograph station code, US Geological Survey*] (SEIS)
MRK .... Myth, Ritual, and Kingship [*A publication*] (BJA)
MRK .... Rayville, LA [*Location identifier*] [*FAA*] (FAAL)
mrkd .... Marked (AD)
MRKD .... Marked [*Computer science*] (MDG)
mrkg .... Marking (AD)
MRKHS .... Mayer-Rokitansky-Kuester-Hauser Syndrome [*Medicine*] (MELL)
mrkr .... Marker (AD)
MRKR .... Marker (WGA)
MRKR .... Marker International [*NASDAQ symbol*] (SAG)
MRKR .... Marker Intl. [*NASDAQ symbol*] (TTSB)
MRKTPLC .... Marketplace
MRKTR .... Marketer
Mrkts .... Markets (AD)
MRKU .... Marc Shipping and Trading [*Intermodal shipping container symbol*] (TVRC)
MRL .... Aeromorelos SA de CV [*Mexico*] [*ICAO designator*] (FAAC)
MRL .... Machine Representation Language
MRL .... Magnetic Resonance Laboratory [*Medicine*] (EDAA)
MRL .... Magnovox Research Laboratories (CCCA)
MRL .... Main Rail Launcher (DWSG)
MRL .... Maintenance Repair Level (MCD)
MRL .... Maintenance Requirements List (MCD)
MRL .... Manipulator Retention Latch [*or Lock*] (NASA)
MRL .... Manipulator Retention Lock (SAUS)
MRL .... Manufacturing Reference Line
MRL .... Manufacturing Research Laboratory
MRL .... Marine Drilling [*NYSE symbol*]
MRL .... Marine Drilling Cos. [*NYSE symbol*]
MRL .... Marine Research Laboratory (SAUO)
MRL .... Maritime Rear Link (MCD)
MRL .... Marketing Research Library
MRL .... Marshal [*Telegraphy*] (PCTE)
MRL .... Martel Oil & Gas [*Vancouver Stock Exchange symbol*]
MRL .... Master Repair List (AFIT)
MRL .... Master Report List
MRL .... Master Requirements List (SAUO)
MRL .... Material Requirements Lists
MRL .... Materials Research Laboratories [*National Science Foundation*] [*Research center*]
MRL .... Materiel Requirements List [*Military*]
MRL .... Maximized Relative Likelihood (PDAA)
MRL .... Maximum Recording Level
MRL .... Maximum Residue Level (SAUO)
MRL .... Maximum Residue Limit (PDAA)
MRL .... Meaning-Representation Language [*Computer science*]
MRL .... Medical Record Librarian
MRL .... Medical Records Library (AD)
MRL .... Medical Research Laboratory [*Navy and Air Force*] (MCD)
MRL .... Merrell-National Laboratories [*Research code symbol*]
MRL .... Minerals Research Laboratory (MCD)
MRL .... Minimal Response Level [*Audiometry*]
MRL .... Minimum Residue Level
MRL .... Minimum Residues Limit (SAUO)
MRL .... Minimum-Risk Level [*Environmental science*] (COE)
MRL .... Ministers Referral Letters (SAUO)
MRL .... Missionary Research Library (EA)
MRL .... Mobile Replenishment List (AFIT)
MRL .... Modular Rocket Launcher (SAUS)
MRL .... Montana Rail Link [*Federal Railroad Administration identification code*]
MRL .... Mortlockese [*Language symbol*] (ETLW)
MRL .... Motor Refrigeration Lighter (ADA)
mrl .... Motor Refrigerator Lighter (AD)
mrl .... Multiple Rocket Launcher (AD)
MRL .... Multiple Rocket Launcher
MRL .... Multiple Ruby LASER
MRL .... Multipoint Recorder/Logger
MRLA .... La Paquita [*Costa Rica*] [*ICAO location identifier*] (ICLI)
MRLA .... Malayan Races Liberation Army
MRLB .... Liberia/Tomas Guardia Internacional [*Costa Rica*] [*ICAO location identifier*] (ICLI)
MRLC .... Los Chiles [*Costa Rica*] [*ICAO location identifier*] (ICLI)
MRLC .... Maintenance Repair Level Code (ACAE)
MRLC .... Multi-Resolution Land Cover Characterization (SAUS)
MRLDC .... Milton Roy Laboratory Data Control (SAUO)
MRLE .... Laurel [*Costa Rica*] [*ICAO location identifier*] (ICLI)
MRLF .... La Flor [*Costa Rica*] [*ICAO location identifier*] (ICLI)
MRLF .... Monthly Report on the Labor Force (OICC)
MRLG .... La Garroba [*Costa Rica*] [*ICAO location identifier*] (ICLI)
MRLI .... La Ligia [*Costa Rica*] [*ICAO location identifier*] (ICLI)
MRLL .... Las Lomas [*Costa Rica*] [*ICAO location identifier*] (ICLI)
MRLL .... Merrill Corp. [*NASDAQ symbol*] (NQ)
MRLM .... Limon/Limon Internacional [*Costa Rica*] [*ICAO location identifier*] (ICLI)
MRLOGAEUR ... Minimum Required Logistics Augmentation Europe (MCD)
MRLP .... Monster Raving Loony Party (WDAA)
MRLPC .... Mouvement de Regroupement et de Liberation du Peuple Congolais [*Movement for the Regroupment and Liberation of the Congolese People*]
MRLR .... La Roca [*Costa Rica*] [*ICAO location identifier*] (ICLI)
MRLS .... Mini Raman Lidar System
MRLS .... Multiple Rocket Launcher System (SAUS)
MRLT .... Las Trancas [*Costa Rica*] [*ICAO location identifier*] (ICLI)
MRLU .... La Maruca [*Costa Rica*] [*ICAO location identifier*] (ICLI)
MRLV .... La Cueva [*Costa Rica*] [*ICAO location identifier*] (ICLI)
MRLV .... Mobile Raman Lidar Van
MRLY .... La Yolanda [*Costa Rica*] [*ICAO location identifier*] (ICLI)

MRLZ........ Meadow River Lumber [*Federal Railroad Administration identification code*]
MRM........ Aerocharter, Inc. [*Canada*] [*ICAO designator*] (FAAC)
MRM........ Assembly of Combatant Clerics (Iran) [*Political party*] (PSAP)
MRM........ Magnetic Resonance Microscopy
mrm........ Mail Readership Measurement (AD)
MRM........ Mail Readership Measurement
MRM........ Maintenance, Reporting, and Management [*Military*] (MCD)
MRM........ Management Responsibility Matrix
MRM........ Management Review Meeting (AFIT)
MRM........ Manari [*Papua New Guinea*] [*Airport symbol*] (OAG)
MRM........ Master of Resource Management (GAGS)
MRM........ Materiel Readiness and Modernization (SAUO)
mrm........ Mechanically Recovered Meat (AD)
MRM........ Mechanically Removed Meat (ODA)
MRM........ Medical Record Manager
MRM........ Medical Repair Technician [*Navy*]
MRM........ Medium-Range Missile (MCD)
MRM........ Merrimac Industries, Inc. [*AMEX symbol*] (SPSG)
MRM........ Metabolic Rate Monitor [*Trademark*]
MRM........ Metastable Reaction Monitoring [*Analytical chemistry*]
MRM........ Michelson Rotating Mirror
MRM........ Midland Railway of Manitoba [*Federal Railroad Administration identification code*]
MRM........ Mid-Range Munition [*Military*] [*Army*]
mrm........ Miles of Relative Movement (AD)
MRM........ Miles of Relative Movement [*Navigation*]
MRM........ Miscellaneous Radioactive Material (GAAI)
MRM........ Modified Radical Mastectomy [*Medicine*] (MELL)
MRM........ Most Recently Used Master [*Computer science*]
MRM........ Motif Resource Manager [*Computer science*] (AGLO)
MRM........ Movement for the Redemption of Liberian Muslims [*Political party*] (EY)
MRM........ Movimento da Resistencia de Mozambique [*Mozambique Resistance Movement*]
MRM........ Multiple Reaction Monitoring [*Chemistry*]
MRM........ Multiple Residue Method [*Medicine*] (MELL)
MRM........ Music for the Rights of Man (EA)
MRMA....... Montealto [*Costa Rica*] [*ICAO location identifier*] (ICLI)
MRMC....... Medical Research and Materiel Command [*Army*]
MRMC....... Medical Research Modernization Committee (EA)
MRMC....... Michael Reese Medical Center [*Medicine*] (EDAA)
MRMC....... Murcielago [*Costa Rica*] [*ICAO location identifier*] (ICLI)
MRMDF...... Multi-Use Remote Manipulator Development Facility [*NASA*] (SPST)
MRMJ....... Mojica [*Costa Rica*] [*ICAO location identifier*] (ICLI)
MRMK....... Merrimack Bancorp, Inc. [*NASDAQ symbol*] (COMM)
MRML....... Medium-Range Missile Launcher
MRML....... Montelimar O Los Sitios [*Costa Rica*] [*ICAO location identifier*] (ICLI)
MRMO....... Mobilization Reserve Materiel Objective [*Army*]
MRMO-A..... Mobilization Reserve Materiel Objective - Acquisition [*Army*] (AFIT)
MRMP....... Marginal Revenue/Marginal Physical Product [*Economics*]
MRMPO...... Mobilization Reserve Materiel Procurement Objective [*Army*]
MRMR....... Mining Rock-Mass Rating [*Mining technology*]
MRMR....... Mobilization Reserve Materiel Requirement [*Army*]
MRMS....... MARC [*Machine-Readable Cataloging*] Record Management System
MRMS....... Maritime Resources Management Service (SAUO)
MRMS....... Metabolic Rate Measuring System
MRMS....... Mobile/Tracked Remote Manipulator System (SSD)
MRMS....... Monetary Ration Management System [*Military*] (AFM)
MRMS....... Mount Rushmore Memorial Society (EA)
MRMU....... Mermaid Containers [*Intermodal shipping container symbol*] (TVRC)
MRMU....... Mobile Radiological Measuring Unit
MRMU....... Mobile Remote Manipulating Unit [*Air Force*]
MRMVA...... Master Retail Milk Vendors Association (AD)
MRMW....... Memory Write [*Computer science*] (MHDI)
MRMZ....... Monticello Railway Museum [*Federal Railroad Administration identification code*]
MRN........ Malignant Renal Neoplasm [*Medicine*] (MELL)
MRN........ Marion [*South Africa*] [*Geomagnetic observatory code*]
MRN........ Maritime Radionavigation
MRN........ Material Recorder Notice (AD)
MRN........ Median Raphe Nucleus [*Medicine*]
MRN........ Medical Record News [*Medicine*] [*AMRA*] [*Journal*] (EDAA)
MRN........ Medical Staffing Network Holdings [*NYSE symbol*]
MRN........ Medium-Round Nose [*Diamond drilling*]
MRN........ Meteorological Rocket Network [*NASA*]
MRN........ Minimum Rejection Number
MRN........ Missions Gouvernementales Francaises [*France*] [*ICAO designator*] (FAAC)
MRN........ Modified Random Network [*Crystallography*]
MRN........ Moran Resources Corp. [*Vancouver Stock Exchange symbol*]
MRN........ Morganton, NC [*Location identifier*] [*FAA*] (FAAL)
MRN........ Morning (ROG)
MRN........ Morrison Knudsen [*NYSE symbol*] (TTSB)
MRN........ Morrison-Knudsen Co., Inc. [*NYSE symbol*] (SPSG)
MRN........ Motor Racing Network
MRN........ Mouvement pour la Reconstruction Nationale [*Haiti*] [*Political party*] (EY)
MRN........ Movimiento de Renovacion Nacional [*Movement for National Renovation*] [*Colombia*] [*Political party*] (PPW)
MRNA....... Marina
mRNA....... Ribonucleic Acid, Messenger [*Biochemistry, genetics*]
MRNC....... Marine Ltd. Partnership [*NASDAQ symbol*] (SAG)
MRNC....... Meteorological Rocket Network Committee [*NASA*] (SAA)
MRNC....... Nicoya [*Costa Rica*] [*ICAO location identifier*] (ICLI)
MRNCZ...... Marina LP [*NASDAQ symbol*]
MRNCZ...... Marina Ltd Partnership [*NASDAQ symbol*] (TTSB)
MRND....... Maintenance Required Not Developed (MSA)
MRND....... Mouvement Revolutionnaire National pour le Developpement [*National Revolutionary Movement for Development*] [*Rwanda*] [*Political party*] (PPW)
MRNDD...... National Republican Movement for Democracy and Development (Rwanda) [*Political party*] (PSAP)
MRNE....... Marine
MRNet...... [*The*] Minnesota Regional Network [*Computer science*] (TNIG)
mrng....... Mooring (AD)
mrng....... Morning (AD)
MRNG....... Morning
MRNJ....... Naranjo (Seveers) [*Costa Rica*] [*ICAO location identifier*] (ICLI)
MRNL....... Medical Research and Nutrition Laboratory [*Army*] (MCD)
MRNP....... Mount Rainier National Park [*Washington*] (AD)
MRNP....... Mount Revelstoke National Park [*British Columbia*] (AD)
mRNP....... Ribonucleoprotein, Messenger [*Biochemistry*]
MRNPF...... Member, Royal Nurses Pension Fund [*British*] (ROG)
MRNR....... Mariner Health Group [*NASDAQ symbol*] (TTSB)
MRNR....... Mariner Health Group, Inc. [*NASDAQ symbol*] (SAG)
MRNS....... Marine Radar & Navigation Simulator (SAUS)
MRNS....... Modular Reusable Nuclear Shuttle
MRNS....... Nosara [*Costa Rica*] [*ICAO location identifier*] (ICLI)
MRNT....... MERANT PLC [*NASDAQ symbol*] (NASQ)
Mro........ Maestro (AD)
mro........ Maintenance, Repair, and Operating (AD)
MRO........ Maintenance, Repair, and Operation
MRO........ Maintenance, Repair, and Overhaul
MRO........ Maintenance Report Order (SAA)
MRO........ Management and Resources Office (SAUO)
MRO........ Management Review Officer
MRO........ Mandatory Requirements Office (SAUO)
MRO........ Mandatory Router Option (SAUS)
MRO........ Manufacturing Rework Order
MRO........ Marathon Oil [*Company symbol*]
MRO........ Marathon Oil Corp. [*NYSE symbol*]
MRO........ Master Reference Oscillator (DMAA)
MRO........ Masterton [*New Zealand*] [*Airport symbol*] (OAG)
MRO........ Materiel Readiness Officer (MCD)
MRO........ Materiel Release Order [*Air Force*]
MRO........ Mechanized RADAR Observer
MRO........ Media Resources Officer (AIE)
MRO........ Medical Regulating Office [*or Officer*] [*Army*] (AABC)
MRO........ Medical Research Organization [*Generic term*]
MRO........ Medical Review Officer (GFGA)
MRO........ Member of the Register of Osteopaths [*British*]
MRO........ Meridor Resources Ltd. [*Vancouver Stock Exchange symbol*]
MRO........ Message Releasing Officer
MRO........ Message Review Officer (MCD)
MRO........ Mid-Range Objectives
MRO........ Military Release Orders
MRO........ Mine Radiographic Outfit [*Military*] (PDAA)
MRO........ Minimal Recognizable Odor [*Medicine*] (DMAA)
MRO........ Minority Recruiting Officer (DNAB)
MRO........ Morrison Flying Service, Inc. [*ICAO designator*] (FAAC)
MRO........ Motor Routing Order
MRO........ Movement Report Office [*Military*]
MRO........ Multi-Region Operation (SAUO)
MRO........ Multi-Region Option (HGAA)
MRO........ Muscle Receptor Organ [*Neurophysiology*]
MRO........ Rossburn Regional Library, Manitoba [*Library symbol*] [*National Library of Canada*] (NLC)
MRO........ USX-Marathon Group [*NYSE symbol*] (SPSG)
MROA....... Magnetic Raman Optical Activity [*Spectrometry*]
MROAR...... Modification and Repair Order and Acceptance Record (AD)
MROC....... Marine Requirements Oversight Council
MROC....... Mobile Range Operation Center (NVT)
MROC....... Monroc, Inc. [*NASDAQ symbol*] (SAG)
MROC....... Multi-Command Required Operational Capability (ACAE)
MROC....... Multiple-Command Required Operational Capability (SAUO)
MROC....... Multi-Role Operations Cabin (SAUS)
MROC....... San Jose/Juan Santamaria Internacional [*Costa Rica*] [*ICAO location identifier*] (ICLI)
MROCC...... Medical Review Officer Certification Council (SAUO)
MROD....... Medical Research and Operations Directorate [*NASA*] (KSC)
MROF....... Maintenance, Repair, and Operation of Facility (KSC)
MROFIE..... Mission Requirements on Facilities/Instruments/Experiments (SAUS)
MROL....... Minimum Resolvable Object Length
MROM....... Macro Read-Only Memory [*Computer science*]
MROM....... Masked Read Only Memory [*Automotive engineering*]
MROM....... Masked Read-Only Memory [*Computer science*]
MROP....... Major Reconstruction of Obsolete Public Housing (SAUO)
MRORG...... Maintenance Ratio at Organizational Level (SAUO)
MROS....... Material Requirements and Operating Standards (SAUO)
MROS....... Multirole Operations Cabin (SAUS)
MROV....... Miniature Remotely Operated Vehicle [*Police and security equipment*]
mrov....... Moreover (AD)
M-ROVER.... Michigan's Remote Operated Vehicle for Education and Research
MROW....... Manufacture, Repair & Overhaul Wing (SAUS)
MRoxH...... Hebrew Teachers College, Roxbury, MA [*Library symbol*] [*Library of Congress*] (LCLS)
MRP........ Application for Writ of Mandamus Refused in Part [*Legal term*] (DLA)

MRp .... Carnegie Library, Rockport, MA [*Library symbol*] [*Library of Congress*] (LCLS)
mrp .... Machine-Readable Passport (AD)
MRP .... Machine-Readable Passport (DA)
MRP .... Magnum Rifle Powder (DICI)
MRP .... Maintenance Rally Point [*Military*] (INF)
MRP .... Maintenance Real Property (NVT)
MRP .... Maintenance Repair Part (ACAE)
MRP .... Malfunction Reporting Program [*Navy*]
MRP .... Management Readiness Profile [*London House, Inc.*] (TES)
MRP .... Management Requirements and Practices (SAUO)
MRP .... Management Requirements & Procedures (SAUO)
mrp .... Manned Reusable Payload (AD)
MRP .... Manned Reusable Payload
mrp .... Manned Reusable Product (AD)
MRP .... Manned Rotating Platform
MRP .... Manpower Requirements & Personnel (SAUO)
MRP .... Manual Repair Point (SAUS)
MRP .... Manual Reporting Post (NATG)
MRP .... Manufacturer's Recommended Price (ODBW)
MRP .... Manufacturing Requirements Planning [*Purchasing computer program*] (PCM)
MRP .... Manufacturing Resource Planning [*Computer science*]
mrp .... Marginal Revenue Product (AD)
MRP .... Marginal Revenue Product [*Economics*]
MRP .... Mariposa, CA [*Amtrak Busline code*]
MRP .... Marketing and Regulatory Programs
MRP .... Marketing Resources Plus (IIDC)
MRP .... Markov Renewal Program
MRP .... Marla [*Australia*] [*Airport symbol*] (OAG)
MRP .... Mass Resolving Power [*Physics*]
MRP .... Master in Regional Planning (DD)
MRP .... Master of Regional Planning
MRP .... Master Restationing Plan [*DoD*]
MRP .... Material Reliability Program [*Military*] (AFIT)
MRP .... Material Requirements Planning [*Pronounced "merp"*]
MRP .... Material Reserve Planning
MRP .... Material Resource Planning (ACII)
MRP .... Materiel Returns Program [*Military*] (AFIT)
MRP .... Mathematics Resources Project [*National Science Foundation*]
MRP .... Maximum Rated Power
mrp .... Maximum Resolving Power (AD)
MRP .... Maximum Resolving Power
mrp .... Maximum Retail Price (AD)
MRP .... Maximum Retail Price [*British*]
MRP .... Mechanical Repair Protection [*Automotive service*]
MRP .... Medical Record Practitioner [*Medicare*] (DHSM)
MRP .... Medical Reimbursement Plan
MRP .... Medical Removal Protection (SARE)
MRP .... Members Retirement Plan [*of the American Medical Association*] (DAVI)
MRP .... Merapi [*Java*] [*Seismograph station code, US Geological Survey*] [*Closed*] (SEIS)
MRP .... Message Routing Process [*Telecommunications*] (TEL)
MRP .... Mid-Range Plan [*1969-70*] [*Military*]
MRP .... Militarism Resource Project (EA)
MRP .... Military Rated Power (NG)
MRP .... Military Representatives of Associated Pacific Powers [*World War II*]
MRP .... Military Requirements Plan (NATG)
MRP .... Minimum Reaction Posture (NVT)
MRP .... Miscellaneous Relay Panel (MCD)
MRP .... Mississippi River Plume [*Marine science*] (OSRA)
MRP .... Mitochondrial RNA [*Ribonucleic Acid*] Processing [*Cytology*]
MRP .... Mobile RADAR Post
MRP .... Mobile Repair Party (MCD)
MRP .... Mobile Reporting Post (SAUS)
MRP .... Modern Religious Problems [*A publication*]
MRP .... Molybdate-Reactive Phosphorus [*Analytical chemistry*]
MRP .... Monthly Report of Progress
MRP .... Morley Library, Painesville, OH [*OCLC symbol*] (OCLC)
MRP .... Morrison Petroleums Ltd. [*Toronto Stock Exchange symbol*]
MRP .... Motor Racing Publications [*Publisher*] [*British*]
MRP .... Mouvement Republicain Populaire [*Popular Republican Movement*] [*France*] [*Political party*] (PPE)
MRP .... Mouvement Revolutionnaire du Peuple [*Chad*] [*Political party*] (EY)
MRP .... Movimiento Republicano Progresista [*Progressive Republican Movement*] [*Venezuela*] [*Political party*]
MRP .... Movimiento Revolucionario del Pueblo - Ixim [*People's Revolutionary Movement - Ixim*] [*Guatemala*] [*Political party*] (PD)
MRP .... Movimiento Revolucionario Popular [*Venezuela*] [*Political party*] (EY)
MRP .... Multimode Radar Processor (ACAE)
MRP .... Multiple-Rate Processor (CCCA)
MRP .... Multiplex Recording Photography
MRP .... Multi-Racial Party [*Zambia*] [*Political party*] (EY)
MRP .... Multi-Roller Press (EEVL)
MRP .... Reston and District Regional Library, Reston, Manitoba [*Library symbol*] [*National Library of Canada*] (NLC)
MR/PA .... Make Ready / Put Away (DNAB)
MRPA .... Master of Recreation and Parks Administration (GAGS)
MRPA .... Metropolitan Region Planning Authority (AD)
MRPA .... Michigan Recreation and Park Association (EARSL)
MRPA .... Minnesota Recreation and Park Association (EARSL)
MRPA .... Modified Random Phase Approximation
MRPA .... Punta Burica [*Costa Rica*] [*ICAO location identifier*] (ICLI)
MRPARABAD ... Master Parachutist Badge [*Military decoration*]
MRPB .... Playa Blanca [*Costa Rica*] [*ICAO location identifier*] (ICLI)
MRPC .... Mercury Rankine Power Conversion [*Nuclear energy*]
MRPC .... Mouvement de Regroupement des Populations Congolaises [*Movement for the Regroupment of the Congolese People*] [*Political party*]
MRPC .... Paso Canoas [*Costa Rica*] [*ICAO location identifier*] (ICLI)
MRPD .... Medium Repetition-Rate Pulsed Doppler (ACAE)
MRPD .... Pandora [*Costa Rica*] [*ICAO location identifier*] (ICLI)
MRPE .... Palo Verde [*Costa Rica*] [*ICAO location identifier*] (ICLI)
MRPF .... Maintenance of Real Property Facilities (AABC)
MRPG .... Potrero Grande [*Costa Rica*] [*ICAO location identifier*] (ICLI)
MRPH .... CW Murphy [*Common carrier symbol*]
MRPhS .... Member of the Royal Pharmaceutical Society [*Canada*] (DD)
MRPI .... Paissa [*Costa Rica*] [*ICAO location identifier*] (ICLI)
MRP II ...... Manufacturing Resource Planning (SAUO)
MRPJ .... Puerto Jimenez [*Costa Rica*] [*ICAO location identifier*] (ICLI)
MRPL .... Main Ring Path Length (SAUO)
MRPL .... Material Requirements Planning List [*Navy*]
MRPL .... Portalon [*Costa Rica*] [*ICAO location identifier*] (ICLI)
MRPM .... Material Research and Production Methods (MCD)
MRPM .... Palmar Sur [*Costa Rica*] [*ICAO location identifier*] (ICLI)
MRPN .... Pelon Nuevo [*Costa Rica*] [*ICAO location identifier*] (ICLI)
MRPP .... Maoist Reorganization Movement of the Party of the Proletariat [*Political party*] (AD)
MRPP .... Mortgage Rate Protection Program [*Canada*]
MRPR .... Parrita [*Costa Rica*] [*ICAO location identifier*] (ICLI)
MRPRA .... Malaysian Rubber Producers' Research Association [*Research center*] [*British*] (IRC)
MRPS .... Manufacturing and Resource Planning System [*Cincom Systems Ltd.*] [*Software package*] (NCC)
MRPS .... Marine Petrol Tr [*NASDAQ symbol*] (TTSB)
MRPS .... Materials Requirement Planning System (HGAA)
M rps .... Maurituis Rupee [*Monetary unit*] (AD)
MRPS .... Midline Retroperitoneal Syndrome [*Medicine*] (MELL)
MRPS .... Paissa [*Costa Rica*] [*ICAO location identifier*] (ICLI)
MRPU .... Maropol [*Intermodal shipping container symbol*] (TVRC)
MRPV .... Mini-Remotely Piloted Vehicle (PDAA)
MRPV .... San Jose/Tobias Bolanos Internacional [*Costa Rica*] [*ICAO location identifier*] (ICLI)
MRQ .... Marinduque [*Philippines*] [*Airport symbol*] (OAG)
MRQ .... Marquardt Corp. [*Stock exchange symbol*] (AD)
MRQ .... Maximum Release Quantity [*DoD*]
MRQE .... Marquee Group, Inc. (The) [*NASDAQ symbol*] (SAG)
MRQM .... Marquez Manufacturing [*NCIC trailer make code*]
MRQP .... Quepos (La Managua) [*Costa Rica*] [*ICAO location identifier*] (ICLI)
MRR .... Macara [*Ecuador*] [*Airport symbol*] (OAG)
MRR .... Machine-Readable Record (MCD)
MRR .... [*The*] Magistrates of the Roman Republic [*A publication*] (OCD)
MRR .... Mail Return Rate (SAUS)
MRR .... Maintenance, Repairs, and Replacements [*Military*]
MRR .... Maintenance, Replacement, Removal (AFIT)
MRR .... Mandatory Removal Roster [*Army*]
MRR .... Manila Railroad (SAUO)
MRR .... Manistee Railroad
MRR .... Manufacturing Readiness Review (ACAE)
MRR .... Marrow Release Rate [*Hematology*]
MRR .... Master Record Repository (MCD)
MRR .... Material Readiness Report (MCD)
MRR .... Material Receiving [*Inspection*] Report [*Nuclear energy*] (NRCH)
MRR .... Material Rejection Report
MRR .... Material Release Point (SAUO)
MRR .... Material Reliability Report (MCD)
MRR .... Material Removal Rate (MCD)
MRR .... Material Review Record [*or Reports*] [*Aviation*] (MCD)
MRR .... Material Review Request
MRR .... Materiel Readiness Report [*Army*] (AABC)
MRR .... Maximal Relaxation Rate [*Medicine*]
MRR .... Maximum Rate of Rise [*Biometrics*]
MRR .... Mechanical Reliability Report [*FAA*]
MRR .... Mechanical Research Report
mrr .... Medical Research Reactor (AD)
MRR .... Medical Research Reactor
MRR .... Medium-Range RADAR (NG)
MRR .... Medium-Range Recovery
MRR .... Metal Removal Rate
MRR .... Microelectronic Radio Receiver
MRR .... Microfilm Reader Recorder
MRR .... Mid-Atlantic Railroad [*Federal Railroad Administration identification code*]
MRR .... Mid-Atlantic Realty Trust [*AMEX symbol*] (SPSG)
MRR .... Middlesborough & Redcar Railway (SAUO)
MRR .... Milestone Readiness Review [*NASA*] (KSC)
MRR .... Military Renegotiation Regulation
MRR .... Miniature Reed Relay
MRR .... Minimum Rediscount Rate
MRR .... Minimum Reporting Requirement [*NASA*] (KSC)
MRR .... Minimum Residual Radiation (SAUS)
MRR .... Minimum Risk Route (MCD)
MRR .... Missile Reliability Restoration (SAUS)
MRR .... Missile Restraint Release
MRR .... Mission Readiness Review (SAUS)
MRR .... Mission Reconfiguration Request (MCD)
MRR .... Mission Requirements Review (ACAE)
MRR .... Molecular Rotational Resonance

MRR......... Monomer Reactivity Ratio (PDAA)
MRR......... Monthly Review Report
MRR......... Motorized Rifle Regiment [*Former USSR*]
MRR......... Movement for the Recovery of the Revolution (CARL)
MRR......... Multiple Response Resolver
MRR......... Multi-Role Radar (ACAE)
MRR......... Muroran [*Japan*] [*Seismograph station code, US Geological Survey*] (SEIS)
MRRA....... Master of Recreation Resources (F6) Administration (PGP)
MRRA....... Military Retirement Reform Act
MRRA....... Murray Marine Corporation [*NCIC trailer make code*]
MRRAS...... Murder Release Risk Assessment Scale (AD)
MRRB....... Maintenance Requirements Review Board [*Military*] (AFIT)
MRRB....... Manual Remote Rebroadcast Box (SAUS)
MRRB....... Materiel Release Review Board [*Military*]
MRRB....... Materiel Requirements Review Board [*Military*] (AFIT)
MRRC....... Materiel Requirements Review Committee [*Military*]
MRRC....... Mechanical Reliability Research Center
MRRC....... Mental Retardation Research Center [*University of California, Los Angeles*] [*Research center*] (RCD)
MRRC....... Mental Retardation Research Center [*University of Alabama at Birmingham*] (RCD)
MRRC....... North Carolina Mental Retardation Research Center [*University of North Carolina at Chapel Hill*] (RCD)
MRRC....... Ralph L. Smith Mental Retardation Research Center [*University of Kansas*] [*Research center*] (RCD)
MRRD....... Marine Resources Research Division [*Now Ocean Environment Research Division*] (USDC)
MRRDB..... Malaysian Rubber Research and Development Board (AD)
MRRF....... Monitor Research and Recovery Foundation
MRRF....... Rio Frio O Progreso [*Costa Rica*] [*ICAO location identifier*] (ICLI)
MRRI........ Marine Resources Research Institute [*South Carolina Wildlife and Marine Resources Department*] [*Research center*] (RCD)
MRRL....... Materiel Repair Requirement List [*Military*] (AFIT)
MRRL....... Metabolism and Radiation Research Laboratory [*North Dakota State University*] [*Research center*] (RCD)
MRRM....... Rancho Del Mar [*Costa Rica*] [*ICAO location identifier*] (ICLI)
MRRN....... Rancho Nuevo [*Costa Rica*] [*ICAO location identifier*] (ICLI)
MRRP....... Maintenance and Repair of Real Property [*Military*]
MRRP....... Medical Radioisotopes Research Program (SAUO)
MRRP....... Motorways, Roads, and Road Programmes [*British*]
MR-RPV.... Mid Range Remotely Piloted Vehicle (ACAE)
MRRS....... Magnetic Reed Rotary Switch
MRRS....... Materiel Readiness Reporting System [*Army*]
MRRS....... Military Route Reconnaissance Staff (SAUO)
MRRS....... Mobile Rail Repair Shop (MCD)
MRRS....... Multiple Railroad System
MRRS....... Multi-Rail Rocket System (PDAA)
MRRT....... Maintenance Requirements Review Team (MUGU)
MRRTC..... Maligaya Rice Research and Training Center (SAUO)
MRRV....... Manoeuvring Re-entry Research Vehicle (SAUS)
MRRW....... Morrow Snowboards [*NASDAQ symbol*] (TTSB)
MRRW....... Morrow Snowboards, Inc. [*NASDAQ symbol*] (SAG)
MRRX....... Roxana Farms [*Costa Rica*] [*ICAO location identifier*] (ICLI)
MRS......... Airline of the Marshall Islands [*ICAO designator*] (FAAC)
MRS......... Maars [*Alaska*] [*Seismograph station code, US Geological Survey*] (SEIS)
MRS......... Mado Robin Society [*Defunct*] (EA)
MRS......... Magnetic Reed Switch
MRS......... Magnetic-Resonance Spectroscopy [*Biochemistry*] (ECON)
MRS......... Magnetic Resonance Spectrum
MRS......... Maintenance Repair and Service (ACAE)
MRS......... Maintenance Reporting System [*Army*]
MRS......... Maintenance Requirement Substantiated (MSA)
MRS......... Malfunction Reporting System [*Boeing*]
MRS......... Management Relations Survey [*Test*]
MRS......... Management Reporting System
MRS......... Management Review System (NASA)
MRS......... Manipulator Repair Shop (NRCH)
MRS......... Manned Reconnaissance Satellite [*Air Force*]
MRS......... Manned Repeater Station [*Telecommunications*] (OA)
MRS......... Manufacturers Railway Co. [*AAR code*]
MRS......... Marches (ROG)
mrs.......... Marginal Rate of Substitution (AD)
MRS......... Marginal Rate of Substitution [*Economics*]
MRS......... Mariah Resources Ltd. [*Vancouver Stock Exchange symbol*]
MRS......... Market Research Society [*British*]
MRS......... Marseille [*France*] [*Airport symbol*] (OAG)
MRS......... Master Radar Station (SAUO)
MRS......... Master Repair Schedule [*Air Force*] (AFM)
MRS......... Material Request [*or Requirement*] Summary
MRS......... Material Research Society Meeting (SAUO)
MRS......... Material Returned to Store [*NASA*] (KSC)
MRS......... Material Routing Slip
MRS......... Materials Research Society (EA)
MRS......... Materiel Repair System [*Air Force*] (AFM)
MRS......... Media Recognition System [*Computer science*] (PCM)
MRS......... Media Report Service (NITA)
MRS......... Media Resource Service [*Scientists' Institute for Public Information*] [*Information service or system*] (IID)
MRS......... Medical Readiness System (SAUO)
MRS......... Medical Receiving Station
MRS......... Medical Reception Station [*Military*]
MRS......... Medical Research Society [*British*]
MRS......... Medical Resupply Set Model (SAUO)
MRS......... Medium Range Search
MRS......... Medium-Range SONAR (NVT)
MRS......... Medium Range Surveillance (SAUS)
MRS......... Melkersson-Rosenthal Syndrome [*Medicine*] (DMAA)
MRS......... Memo Routing Slip
MRS......... Meritor Automotive [*NYSE symbol*] (SG)
MRS......... Mesoscale Research Section (SAUO)
MRS......... Metals Removal System [*Petroleum refining*]
MRS......... Metastasis Research Society (SAUO)
MRS......... Methicillin-Resistant Staphylococcus [*Qureus*] [*Medicine*] (DAVI)
MRS......... Methicillin-Resistant Staphylococcus Aureus [*Antimicrobial therapy*] (MEDA)
MRS......... Metro Recovery Systems (EFIS)
MRS......... Michigan Radiological Society (SAUO)
MrS.......... Microfilm Records System, Inc., Mamaroneck, NY [*Library symbol*] [*Library of Congress*] (LCLS)
MRS......... Microfilm Replacement System [*Computer science*]
MRS......... Micro Reflective Structure [*Computer science*]
MRS......... Midcoast Energy Resources, Inc. [*AMEX symbol*] (SAG)
MRS......... Midlands Research Station [*British Gas*] (WDAA)
MRS......... Migration and Refugee Services (EA)
MRS......... Military Radar Stations (ACAE)
MRS......... Military Railway Service [*Army*]
MRS......... Military Requirements Study (AAGC)
MRS......... Military Retirement System
MRS......... Minimum Radial Separation [*Manufacturing term*]
MRS......... Minimum Reporting Standard [*Broadcasting*] (NTCM)
MRS......... Minimum Residual Shutdown [*Space launch term*] (ISAK)
MRS......... Mini-Reconstruction System (MCD)
MRS......... Ministry of Recreation and Sport [*British*] (AD)
MRS......... Missile Reentry Systems (AFIT)
MRS......... Missile Round Simulator
MRS......... Mission de Ras Shamra [*A publication*] (BJA)
MRS......... Mission Radio System (SAUO)
MRS......... Mission Rehearsal System (SAUS)
MRS......... Mission-Related Software
Mrs.......... Missus (AD)
Mrs.......... Mistress (AD)
MRS......... Mistress (DAVI)
MRS......... Mitochondria Research Society [*Association*] (EA)
MRS......... Mixed Reproductive Strategy [*Avian biology*]
MRS......... Mobile Radio Service (DA)
MRS......... Mobile Reception System (SAUS)
MRS......... Mobile Remote Servicer (SSD)
MRS......... Mobility Requirements Study [*DoD*]
MRS......... Mobilization Requirement Study
MRS......... Mobilization Reserve Stocks [*Army*]
MRS......... Moderator Recovery System (COE)
MRS......... Modification Record Sheet [*NASA*] (KSC)
MRS......... Monitored Retrievable Storage [*of nuclear waste*]
MRS......... Monitored Retrievable Storage Facility [*Environmental science*] (COE)
MRS......... Monorail System
MRS......... Moore-Rott-Sears [*Theory*]
MRS......... Mortgage-Related Security (EMRF)
MRS......... Mothers Return to School
MRS......... Motor Rotation Stand
MRS......... Mountain Rescue Service (AD)
MRS......... Mouvement Republicain Senegalais [*Senegalese Republican Movement*] [*Political party*] (PPW)
MRS......... Movement and Reinforcement Study (MCD)
MRS......... Movement Report Sheet [*Military*]
MRS......... Movement Report System [*Military*]
MRS......... Multilateral RADAR Strike System [*Air Force*] (MCD)
MRS......... Multilateral RADAR Surveillance System [*Air Force*] (MCD)
MRS......... Multiple Representative Sections [*Pathology*] (DAVI)
MRS......... Multiple Rocket System (SAUS)
MrS.......... Multipurpose Research System
MRS......... Multipurpose Reusable Spacecraft (IIA)
MRS......... Multirole System (SAUS)
MRS......... Multispectral Resource Scanner (ACAE)
MRS......... Music Reading Software (PCM)
MRS......... Muzzle Reference System (MCD)
MRS......... Sandinista Renovation Movement (Nicaragua) [*Political party*] (PSAP)
MRS3....... Multilateral RADAR Surveillance/Strike System [*Air Force*]
MRSA....... Machinery Repairman, Seaman Apprentice [*Navy rating*]
MRSA....... Maine Revised Statutes, Annotated [*A publication*] (DLA)
MRSA....... Mandatory RADAR Service Area
MRSA....... Marisa Christina, Inc. [*NASDAQ symbol*] (SAG)
MRSA....... Materiel Readiness Support Activity [*Army*] (RDA)
MRSA....... Materiel Readiness Support Agency [*Navy*]
MRSA....... Medium Range Surveillance Aircraft [*Military*] (PDAA)
mrsa........ Medium-Range Surveillance Aircraft (AD)
MRSA....... Member of the Royal Society of Arts [*British*]
MRSA....... Merrimack River Study Act of 1990 (COE)
MRSA....... Metal Roofing Systems Association (NTPA)
MRSA....... Methicillin-Resistant Staphylococcus Aureus [*Antimicrobial therapy*]
MRSA....... Microwave Radiometer, Scatterometer, and Altimeter (MCD)
MRSA....... Military RADAR Service Area [*Aviation*] (AIA)
MRSA....... San Alberto [*Costa Rica*] [*ICAO location identifier*] (ICLI)
MRSAM..... Medium-Range Surface-to-Air Missile (SAUS)
MR San A... Member of the Royal Sanitary Association of Scotland
MRSanAS... Member of the Royal Sanitary Association of Scotland (SAUO)
MR San Asn... Member of the Royal Sanitary Association [*British*] (AD)

MRSB .... Material Requirements for Stock Balance
MRSB .... San Cristobal [*Costa Rica*] [*ICAO location identifier*] (ICLI)
Mr SBA...... Maryland State Bar Association, Report [*A publication*] (DLA)
MRSC .... Magnetic Resonance Science Center [*University of California, San Francisco*] (RCD)
MRSC .... Marine Rescue Sub-Centre [*Nautical term*] (NTA)
MRSC .... Maritime Rescue Sub-Center [*Canada*]
MRSc........ Master of Rural Science [*British*] (ADA)
MRSC .... Member of the Royal Society of Canada
MRSC .... Member of the Royal Society of Chemistry [*British*] (DBQ)
MRSC .... Mississippi Remote Sensing Center [*Mississippi State University*] [*Research center*] (RCD)
MRSC .... Missouri Republican State Committee (EARSL)
MRSC .... Municipal Research & Services Center of Washington (SAUO)
MRSC .... Santa Cruz [*Costa Rica*] [*ICAO location identifier*] (ICLI)
MRSD .... Maximum Rated Standard Deviation [*Statistics*]
MRSD .... Mission Requirements on System Design [*NASA*]
MRSE........ Message Retrieval Service Element [*Open Systems Interconnection*] (ODAA)
MRSE........ Microwave Remote Sensing Experiment (ACAE)
MRSEC...... Materials Research Science and Engineering Center [*Johns Hopkins University*] (RCD)
MRSEC...... Materials Research Science and Engineering Center [*University of Minnesota*] (RCD)
MRSEC...... Materials Research Science and Engineering Center [*Columbia University*] (RCD)
MRSEC...... Materials Research Science and Engineering Center [*University of Wisconsin--Madison*] (RCD)
MRSEC...... Materials Research Science and Engineering Center [*University of Maryland at College Park*] (RCD)
MRSG .... Santa Clara De Guapiles [*Costa Rica*] [*ICAO location identifier*] (ICLI)
MRSGB...... Member of the Radio Society of Great Britain (SAUO)
MRSH .... Marsh (ADA)
MRSH .... Member of the Royal Society of Health [*British*]
MRSh........ Modern Red Schoolhouse
MRSH .... Shiroles [*Costa Rica*] [*ICAO location identifier*] (ICLI)
MRSHL...... Marshall, MO [*American Association of Railroads railroad junction routing code*]
MRSHLL .... Marshall
MrshllInd... Marshall Industries [*Associated Press*] (SAG)
MrshMc..... Marsh & McLennan Companies, Inc. [*Associated Press*] (SAG)
MrshS....... Marsh Supermarkets, Inc. [*Associated Press*] (SAG)
MrshSu..... Marsh Supermarkets, Inc. [*Associated Press*] (SAG)
MRSI .... Maintenance and Repair Support Items
MRSI .... Maintenance Repair Spares Instruction (MCD)
MRSI .... Medium-Range SOF [*Special Operations Forces*] Insertion (DOMA)
MRSI .... Member of the Royal Sanitary Institute [*British*] (ROG)
MRSI .... Michigan Recovery Systems, Inc. (EFIS)
MRSI .... Mobilization Requirements, Secondary Items
MRSI .... MRS Technology, Inc. [*NASDAQ symbol*] (SAG)
MRSI .... Multi-Round Simultaneous Impact (SAUS)
MRSI .... San Isidro De El General [*Costa Rica*] [*ICAO location identifier*] (ICLI)
MRSID ...... Multi-Resolution Seamless Image Database
MRSJ........ Commission for Racial Justice (EA)
MRSJ........ San Jose [*Costa Rica*] [*ICAO location identifier*] (ICLI)
MRSJ........ United Church of Christ Ministers for Racial and Social Justice (EA)
MRSL........ Member of the Royal Society of Literature [*British*]
MRSM....... Maintenance and Reliability Simulation Model (PDAA)
MRSM....... Member of the Royal Society of Medicine [*British*] (DI)
MRSM....... Member of the Royal Society of Musicians [*British*] (DI)
MRSM....... Mississippi River Suspended Matter
MRSM....... Santa Marta [*Costa Rica*] [*ICAO location identifier*] (ICLI)
MRSMA ..... Member of the Royal Society of Marine Artists [*British*] (DI)
MRSMGB ... Member of the Royal Society of Musicians of Great Britain (SAUO)
MRSMP ..... Member of the Royal Society of Miniature Painters [*British*] (DI)
MRSN .... Machinery Repairman, Seaman [*Navy rating*]
MRSN .... Sirena [*Costa Rica*] [*ICAO location identifier*] (ICLI)
MRSO .... Mobilization Reserve Stockage Objective [*Army*]
MRSO .... Santa Maria De Guacimo [*Costa Rica*] [*ICAO location identifier*] (ICLI)
MRSP .... Model Railway Society of Pune [*Indian Railway*] (TIR)
MRSP .... Multifunction RADAR Signal Processor (MCD)
MRSP .... Myakka River State Park [*Florida*] (AD)
MRSP .... San Pedro [*Costa Rica*] [*ICAO location identifier*] (ICLI)
MRSPE...... Member of the Royal Society of Painters and Etchers [*British*] (DI)
MRSPH...... Member of the Royal Society for the Promotion of Health (SAUO)
MRSPP...... Member of the Royal Society of Portrait Painters (SAUO)
MRSPWC ... Member of the Royal Society of Painters in Water Colours [*British*]
MRSR .... Magazine Ready Service Rings (SAUS)
MRSR .... Mars Rover Sample Return (ACAE)
MR-SR ...... Material Review - Ships Record (MCD)
MRSR .... Mount Rainier Scenic Railroad [*Federal Railroad Administration identification code*]
MRSR .... Multi-Role Survivable Radar [*Army*] (DOMA)
MRSR .... Samara [*Costa Rica*] [*ICAO location identifier*] (ICLI)
MRSRM...... Mars Rover and Sample Return Mission (SAUO)
MRSS .... Main and Reheat Steam System [*Nuclear energy*] (NRCH)
MRSS .... Manned Rovolving Simulated Space Station (SAA)
MRSS .... Master Remote Slave Station (MCD)
MRSS .... Missile Response Simulation Software
MRSS .... San Joaquin de Abangares [*Costa Rica*] [*ICAO location identifier*] (ICLI)
mrsss........ Manned Revolving Space Systems Simulator (AD)
MRST........ Member of the Royal Society of Teachers [*British*]
MRST........ Minimum Remaining Slack Time (PDAA)
MRST........ San Agustin [*Costa Rica*] [*ICAO location identifier*] (ICLI)
MRS Tch.... MRS Technology, Inc. [*Associated Press*] (SAG)
MRSU .... Marine Repair Service [*Intermodal shipping container symbol*] (TVRC)
MRSV .... Maneuverable Recoverable Space Vehicle
MRSV .... Military Railway Service Veterans (EA)
MRSV .... San Vito De Jaba [*Costa Rica*] [*ICAO location identifier*] (ICLI)
MRSW....... Member of the Royal Society of Scottish Painters and Watercolours [*British*] (DAS)
MRSX .... Military Ocean Terminal Railroad-Sunny Point [*Federal Railroad Administration identification code*]
MRSX .... Sixaola [*Costa Rica*] [*ICAO location identifier*] (ICLI)
MRSZ........ Midwest Rail Switching Services [*Federal Railroad Administration identification code*]
MRT .... Air Mauritanie [*Mauritania*] [*ICAO designator*] (FAAC)
MRT .... Machine-Readable Tapes [*Computer science*]
MRT .... Magnetic Resonance Tomography (ODA)
MRT .... Maintainability Review Team [*Navy*] (NG)
MRT .... Maintenance Readiness Training (DNAB)
MRT .... Maintenance Recovery Team (SAUO)
MRT .... Maintenance Response Team (SAUO)
MRT .... Major Role Therapy [*Schizophrenia*]
MRT .... Malignant Rhabdoid Tumor [*Oncology*]
MRT .... Manpack Radio Telephone (SAUO)
MRT .... Marble Threshold (AAG)
MRT .... Marietta Resources [*Vancouver Stock Exchange symbol*]
Mrt........... Martinique (AD)
MRT .... Marysville, OH [*Location identifier*] [*FAA*] (FAAL)
MRT .... Mass Rapid Transit (AD)
MRT .... Mass Rapid Transport [*British*]
MRT .... Material Review Tag [*Aviation*] (MCD)
MRT .... Mauritania [*ANSI three-letter standard code*] (CNC)
MRT .... Mauritius Radio Telescope (SAUO)
MRT .... Maximum Rated Thrust (MCD)
MRT .... Maximum Repair Time (PDAA)
MRT .... Maze-Running Time [*Psychology*]
mrt........... Mean Radiant Temperature (AD)
MRT .... Mean Radiant Temperature
MRT .... Mean Radiative-Transfer [*Meteorology*]
MRT .... Mean Ready Time (MCD)
MRT .... Mean Recovery Time [*Communications term*] (DCT)
MRT .... Mean Repair Time
MRT .... Mean Residence Time [*Kinetics*]
MRT .... Mean Resolvable Temperature (ACAE)
MRT .... Mean Retention Time [*Physiology*]
MRT .... Measured Rate of Time (PDAA)
MRT .... Median Reaction Time (MELL)
MRT .... Median Recognition Threshold (MAE)
MRT .... Median Relapse Time (MELL)
MRT .... Medical Records Technician (DAVI)
MRT .... Medical Relief Train [*Indian Railway*] (TIR)
MRT .... Medium Range Truck [*Military*]
MRT .... Medium-Range Typhon [*Missile*] (NG)
MRT .... Meetings, Reviews, and Training (ALAC)
MRT .... Meridional Ray Trace
Mrt........... Merit [*Record label*]
MRT .... Metropolitan Readiness Test
mrt........... Mid-Range Trajectory (AD)
mrt........... Mildew-Resistant Thread (AD)
MRT .... Mildew-Resistant Thread
MRT .... Milestones Reporting Techniques
MRT .... Military Rated Thrust (NG)
mrt........... Military-Rated Thrust (AD)
MRT .... Military Reserve Technician (GFGA)
MRT .... Military Review Team (AD)
MRT .... Milk Ring Test (PDAA)
MRT .... Miniature Receiver Terminal
MRT .... Minimal Resolvable Temperature
MRT .... Minimum Resolvable Temperature (MCD)
MRT .... Missile Round Trainer (MCD)
MRT .... Missile Round Transporter (MCD)
mrt........... Mission Readiness Tester (AD)
MRT .... Mobile RADAR Target
MRT .... Mobile Radio Terminal (SAUO)
MRT .... Mobile Repair Team (SAUO)
MRT .... Modified Rhyme Test
MRT .... Modulus of Rupture Test (AD)
MRT .... Mortgage & Realty Trust (EFIS)
MRT .... Movimento Revolucionario Tiradentes [*Revolutionary Tiradentes Movement*] [*Brazil*] [*Political party*] (PD)
MRT .... Multiple Rectangle Technique (GART)
MRT .... Multiple Requests Terminal [*Computer science*] (HGAA)
MRT .... Multi-Radar Tracking (SAUS)
MRT .... Murotomisaki [*Japan*] [*Seismograph station code, US Geological Survey*] (SEIS)
MRT .... Muscle Response Test
MRT .... Reformed Theological Seminary, Jackson, MS [*OCLC symbol*] (OCLC)
MRT 6....... Metropolitan Readiness Tests-Sixth Edition [*J. R. Nurss*] (DIPS)
MRTA........ Maintenance Requirements Task Analysis (AD)
MRTA........ Marietta Corp. [*NASDAQ symbol*] (NQ)
MRTA........ Marketing Research Trade Association [*Later, MRA*] (EA)
MRTA........ Mechanical Response Tissue Analyzer [*For measuring bone strength*]

MRTA........ Movimiento Revolucionario Tupac Amaru [*Peru*] [*Political party*] (EY)
MRTA........ Tamarindo de Bagaces [*Costa Rica*] [*ICAO location identifier*] (ICLI)
MRTA........ Tupac Amaru Revolutionary Movement [*Government term*] (GA)
MRTAF ...... Marshal of the Royal Air Force (SAUO)
MRTB........ Metallic Return Transfer Breaker (ACAE)
MRTB........ Missile Research Test Building (ACAE)
MRTB........ Ticaban [*Costa Rica*] [*ICAO location identifier*] (ICLI)
MRTC........ Marine Corps Reserve Training Center
MRTC........ Medical Replacement Training Center (SAUO)
MRTC........ Military Real-Time Computer (AAG)
MRTC........ Multiple Real-Time Commands (NASA)
MRTCB ...... Machine Ruling Trade Conciliation Board (SAUO)
MRTCS ...... Miniaturized Real Time Computational System (ACAE)
MRTD........ Minimum Resolvable Temperature Difference (PDAA)
MRTE........ Master of Radio and Television Engineering
MRTE........ Missile Round Test Equipment
MRTE........ Motorette [*NCIC motorcycle make code*]
MRT Eng.... Master of Radio and Television Engineering
MRTF........ Mean Rounds To Failure (SAUS)
MRTF/A ..... Manual Radar Terrain Following/Avoidance (ACAE)
MRTFB ...... Major Range and Test Facility Base [*Military*] (CAAL)
MRTFL ...... Medium Rough Terrain Forklift (SAUS)
MRTFM...... Mean Rounds to First Maintenance [*Army*]
MRTG........ Mortgage
MRTG........ Multi Router Traffic Grapher (SAUS)
MRTG........ Taboga [*Costa Rica*] [*ICAO location identifier*] (ICLI)
MRTHN...... Marathon
MRTI......... Martin Lowboy Semi-Trailer [*NCIC trailer make code*]
MRTI......... Moscow Radio Technical Institute (SAUO)
MRTI......... Multirole Thermal Imager [*Defense electronics*]
MRTK........ Movimiento Revolucionario Tupaj Katari [*Tupaj Katari Revolutionary Movement*] [*Bolivia*] [*Political party*] (PPW)
MRTKL ...... Tupak Katari Revolutionary Liberation Movement (Bolivia) [*Political party*] (PSAP)
mrtm .... Maritime (AD)
MRTM........ Maritime
MRTM........ Tamarindo de Santa Cruz [*Costa Rica*] [*ICAO location identifier*] (ICLI)
MRTN........ Marten Transport [*NASDAQ symbol*] (TTSB)
MRTN........ Marten Transport Ltd. [*NASDAQ symbol*] (NQ)
Mrtnz........ Martinez (AD)
mrto .... Miscellaneous Reference Tool (AD)
MRTP........ Master of Regional and Town Planning
MRTP........ Master of Rural and Town Planning (GAGS)
MRTP........ Military Reliable Tube Program
MRTPI....... Member of the Royal Town Planning Institute [*British*]
MRTR........ Mortar [*Technical drawings*] (DAC)
MRTR........ Tambor [*Costa Rica*] [*ICAO location identifier*] (ICLI)
MRTRY...... Mortuary
mrts .... Marginal Rate of Technical Substitution (AD)
MRTS........ Marginal Rate of Technical Substitution [*Ecology*]
MRTS........ Mass Rapid Transit System (AD)
MRTS........ Master RADAR Tracking Station
Mrts .... Mauritius (AD)
MRTS........ Member of the Royal Television Society (SAUO)
MRTS........ Meteorological Real-Time System [*Computer science*] (KSC)
MRTS........ Microwave Repeater Test Set (DA)
MRTS........ Missile Round Test Set
MRTS........ Monthly Retail Trade Survey (SAUO)
MRTS........ Multi-Media Remote Teaching System [*AT & T Co., Illinois Institute of Technology*]
MRT-S....... Multi-Role Turret System (SAUS)
MRTT........ Modified Rushton Towed Target (SAUS)
MRTT........ Modular Record Traffic Terminal [*Formerly, COED*] [*Army*] (MCD)
MRTT........ Multi-Role Tanker Transport (SAUS)
MRTU........ Multiple Remote Terminal Unit (SAUS)
MRTU........ Multiplex Remote Terminal Unit (MCD)
MRTZ........ Martinez Trailer [*NCIC trailer make code*]
MRU......... Machine Records Unit [*Computer science*]
MRU......... Main Resource Unit
MRU......... Maintenance Recorder Unit (SAUS)
MRU......... Maintenance Replaceable Unit (MCD)
MRU......... Mano River Union [*See also UFM*] (EAIO)
MRU......... Maritime Reconnaissance Unit [*British military*] (DMA)
mru .... Mass Radiography Unit (AD)
MRU......... Mass Radiography Unit
MRU......... Material Recovery Unit
MRU......... Mauritius [*Airport symbol*] (OAG)
MRU......... Medical Rehabilitation Unit (AD)
MRU......... Medical Resistance Union [*Medicine*] (EDAA)
MRU......... Message Retransmission Unit
MRU......... Meteorological Research Unit
MRU......... Microfilm Recording Unit
MRU......... Microwave Relay Unit
MRU......... Migration Research Unit [*University College London*] [*United Kingdom*] (RCD)
MRU......... Military RADAR Unit [*Aviation*] (FAAC)
mru .... Minimal Reproductive Unit (AD)
MRU......... Minimal Reproductive Units [*Bacteriology*]
MRU......... Minimum Replacement Unit
mru .... Mobile Radio Unit (AD)
MRU......... Mobile Radio Unit [*Air Force*]
MRU......... Mobile Receiving Unit (SAUS)
MRU......... Mobile Refrigeration Unit (KSC)
MRU......... Mobile Remote Unit [*From computer game "Hacker II"*]
MRU......... Most Recently Used Data [*Computer science*] (PCM)
MRU......... Motion Reference Unit (MCD)
MRU......... Mountain Rescue Unit (COE)
MRU......... Movement Release Unit [*MTMC*] (TAG)
MRU......... Much Regret, I Am Unable
MRU......... Multifunction Reference Unit (MCD)
MRUA .... Mobile Radio Users' Association (IAA)
MRUASTAS... Medium-Range Unmanned Aerial Surveillance and Target Acquisition System (NATG)
MR-UAV..... Medium Range UAV (SAUS)
MRUB .... Maruba [*Common carrier symbol*]
M Ru E...... Master of Rural Engineering
M Ru Eng... Master of Rural Engineering
MRUP .... Upala [*Costa Rica*] [*ICAO location identifier*] (ICLI)
MRurSc ..... Master of Rural Science [*British*] (ADA)
MRUS .... Maximal Rate of Urea Synthesis [*Medicine*] (EDAA)
MRUSI ...... Member of the Royal United Service Institution [*British*]
MRV .... Maintenance-Recovery Vehicle (SAUS)
MRV .... Maneuvering Reentry Vehicle
MRV .... Mark V Petroleums & Mines [*Vancouver Stock Exchange symbol*]
MRV .... Mars Roving Vehicle [*NASA*] (PDAA)
MRV .... Marvel [*Telegraphy*] (PCTE)
MRV .... Marvel Entertainment Group [*NYSE symbol*] (SPSG)
MRV .... Marysville, CA [*Amtrak Busline code*]
mrv .... Material Receipt Voucher (AD)
MRV .... Middlesex Rifle Volunteers [*Military*] [*British*] (ROG)
MRV .... Mineral Nyye Vody [*Former USSR*] [*Airport symbol*] (OAG)
MRV .... Mini-Rotary Viscometer [*Mechanical engineering*]
MRV .... Mini-Rotator Viscometer [*Fuels and lubricants*]
MRV .... Minirotavirus [*Medicine*] (EDAA)
MRV .... Minute Respiratory Volume
MRV .... Miravia Ltd. [*Romania*] [*FAA designator*] (FAAC)
MRV .... Missile Recovery Vessel (AD)
mrv .... Missile Re-Entry Vehicle (AD)
MRV .... Missouri River Division (SAUO)
mrv .... Mixed Respiratory Vaccine [*Medicine*] (AD)
MRV .... Mixed Respiratory Vaccine
MRV .... Mouvement de Regroupement Voltaique [*Upper Volta Regroupment Movement*] [*Political party*]
MRV .... Mulberry Ringspot Virus [*Plant pathology*]
MRV .... Multiple Re-entry Vehicle (SAUO)
MRVA........ Member of the Rating and Valuation Association [*British*] (DI)
MRVA........ Minerva Transfer Company [*Common carrier symbol*]
MRVA........ Minimum Radar Vectoring Altitude (SAUS)
MRVC .... Member of the Royal Veterinary College [*British*]
MRVC .... MRV Communications, Inc. [*NASDAQ symbol*] (SAG)
MRVC .... Multiple Rate Voice Card (SAUS)
MRVC .... Mumbai Rail Vikas Corporation [*Indian Railway*] (TIR)
MRV Cm.... MRV Communications, Inc. [*Associated Press*] (SAG)
MRVD .... Thousand Recreation Visitor Days [*USDA Forest Service*] (ALAC)
MRVI .... Mixed Respiratory Virus Infection [*Medicine*] (EDAA)
MRVI .... Monte Reale Valcellina [*Italy*] [*Seismograph station code, US Geological Survey*] (SEIS)
MRVL........ Marvell Technology Group [*NASDAQ symbol*]
MRVLP...... Maneuvering Reentry Vehicle for Low-Level Penetration (MCD)
MRVP .... Mean Right Ventricular Pressure [*Cardiology*]
mrV-P .... Methyl Red Voges-Proskauer [*Bacteriology*] (AD)
MRVP .... Methyl-Red, Voges-Proskauer [*Medium*] [*Bacteriology*]
MRVR .... Mechanised Repair & Recovery Vehicle (SAUS)
MRVT........ Miravant [*NASDAQ symbol*]
MRVT........ Miravant Medical Technologies
MRVT........ Multiple Rate Voice Terminal [*Telecommunications*] (LAIN)
MRVTB...... Maximally Restrictive Verifiable Test Ban [*For nuclear bombs*]
MRVX .... Marvelous [*Telegraphy*] (PCTE)
MRW .... Maranao [*Language symbol*] (ETLW)
MRW .... Maximum Ramp Weight (SAUO)
mrw.......... Morale, Recreation, and Welfare (AD)
MRW .... Morale, Recreation, and Welfare [*Military*] (AFM)
MRW .... Morioka [*Japan*] [*Airport symbol*] (OAG)
mr/w......... Multiple Read/Write (AD)
MRWA....... Midland Railway of Western Australia (AD)
mrwc .... Multiple Reading, Writing, Compiling (AD)
MRWC....... Multiple Read-Write Compute
MRWG ...... Mission Requirements Working Group (ACAE)
MRWS....... Mobile RADAR Weather System (DNAB)
MRWS....... Monoscopic Revision Workstation (SAUO)
MRWY....... Mid State Raceway [*OTCBB symbol*]
MRX .... Hermens/Markair Express [*ICAO designator*] (FAAC)
MRX .... Magnetoresistive Extended [*Computer science*]
MRX .... Marks, MS [*Amtrak rail station code*]
MRX .... Medicis Pharmaceutical "A" [*NYSE symbol*]
MRX .... Memorex Corp. (IAA)
MRX .... Midlands Railroad [*Federal Railroad Administration identification code*]
MRX .... Mineiros [*Brazil*] [*Airport symbol*] (AD)
MRX .... Mobil Oil Corp., Toxicology Division, Information Center, Princeton, NJ [*OCLC symbol*] (OCLC)
MRX .... Movement Research Exchange
MRX .... Riverside, CA [*Location identifier*] [*FAA*] (FAAL)
MRXS .... Mental Retardation, X-Linked, Syndrome [*Medicine*] (DMAA)
MRY .... Marilyn Resources [*Vancouver Stock Exchange symbol*]
MRY .... Marry [*Telegraphy*] (PCTE)

MRY .... Mary [*Former USSR*] [*Seismograph station code, US Geological Survey*] [*Closed*] (SEIS)
MRY .... Merry Land & Invest [*NYSE symbol*] (TTSB)
MRY .... Merry Land & Investment [*NYSE symbol*] (SAG)
MRY .... Monterey [*California*] [*Airport symbol*] (OAG)
MRY .... Monterey Transit Plaza, CA [*Amtrak Busline code*]
MRYPr .... Merry Land & Inv Sr'A'Cv Pfd [*NYSE symbol*] (TTSB)
MRYPrC ..... Merry Land & Inv Sr'C'Cv Pfd [*NYSE symbol*] (TTSB)
mrytm .... Must Have Reply Here by Tomorrow Morning (AD)
mrz .... Marzo [*March*] [*Spanish*] (AD)
MRZ .... Moree [*Australia*] [*Airport symbol*] (OAG)
MRZ .... Syracuse, NY [*Location identifier*] [*FAA*] (FAAL)
MRZP .... Zapotal De Guanacaste [*Costa Rica*] [*ICAO location identifier*] (ICLI)
MRZU .... Marenzana Trasporti [*Intermodal shipping container symbol*] (TVRC)
MS .... Brody Medical Science Building (SAUS)
MS .... Egyptair [*ICAO designator*] (AD)
MS .... IEEE Magnetics Society (EA)
MS .... Ma'aser Sheni (BJA)
MS .... Machinery Survey [*Shipping*]
ms .... Machine Screw (AD)
MS .... Machine Screw
MS .... Machine Selection (IEEE)
ms .... Machine Steel (AD)
MS .... Machine Steel
MS .... Machining System (IAA)
MS .... Macromodular System [*Computer science*] (IEEE)
MS .... Macro Society (EA)
MS .... Magnetic South
MS .... Magnetic Stirrer [*Biotechnology*]
MS .... Magnetic Storage [*Computer science*]
MS .... Magnetic Strip (IAA)
MS .... Magnetic Susceptibility (SAUS)
MS .... Magnetic Synchron (IAA)
MS .... Magnetostatic [*Telecommunications*] (IAA)
MS .... Magnetostriction
MS .... Mail Station (ACAE)
MS .... Mail Steamer
M/S .... Mail Stop
MS .... Main Sequence [*Astronomy*]
M/S .... Mainstage [*NASA*] (KSC)
MS .... Main Station (SAUS)
MS .... Main Steam (NRCH)
MS .... Main Storage
ms .... Main Switch (AD)
MS .... Main Switch
MS .... Main Synchronizer [*Navigation systems*]
ms .... Maintenance and Service (AD)
MS .... Maintenance and Service
MS .... Maintenance Schedule (DA)
MS .... Maintenance Squadron
MS .... Maintenance Standard
MS .... Maintenance Superintendent [*Military*] (AFIT)
MS + ... Maintenance Support Positive
MS .... Maintenance System (ACII)
MS .... Majority Stockholder
ms .... Major Subject (AD)
MS .... Major Subject [*Military*]
MS .... Maladjustment Score [*Psychology*]
MS .... Male Servant
MS .... Malone Society (EA)
MS .... Mammal Society (EAIO)
MS .... Management Science [*Computer science*] (BUR)
MS .... Management Services (KSC)
MS .... Management Staff [*Environmental Protection Agency*] (GFGA)
MS .... Management System (OICC)
MS .... Manic State [*Medicine*] (DB)
MS .... Manned Station (IAA)
M/S .... Mannlicher-Schoenauer (AD)
MS .... Mannose Sensitive [*Biochemistry*]
MS .... Mano Sinistra [*With the Left Hand*] [*Music*]
M/S .... Manslaughter
MS .... Man Station [*Military*]
MS .... Man System (SAUS)
MS .... Manual Sequential (NRCH)
MS .... Manual Supplement
MS .... Manual System (DCTA)
MS .... Manufacturing in Space
MS .... Manufacturing Specification (AAG)
MS .... Manufacturing Standard
MS .... Manufacturing Status (AAG)
MS .... Manufacturing Support
Ms .... Manuscript (AL)
MS .... Manuscript (WDAA)
ms .... Manuscript (VRA)
MS .... Manuscript Reports [*A publication*] (DLA)
MS .... Manuscript Society (EA)
MS .... Manuscriptum [*Manuscript*] [*Latin*]
MS .... Mare Serenitatis [*Sea of Serenity*] [*Lunar area*]
MS .... Marfan's Syndrome [*Syndromes*] [*Medicine*] (QSUL)
ms .... Margin of Safety (AD)
MS .... Margin of Safety [*Engineering*]
MS .... Marian Sisters of the Diocese of Lincoln (TOCD)
MS .... Marie-See [*Syndrome*] [*Medicine*] (DB)
MS .... Marie-Struempell [*Disease*] [*Medicine*] (DB)
MS .... Marijuana Smoke
Ms .... Mariners [*Seattle Baseball Team*] (AD)
MS .... Marine Stratus (ARMP)
MS .... Marital Status
MS .... Maritime Surveillance (SAUS)
MS .... Marker Switch (IAA)
MS .... Marketing Society (COBU)
m/s .... Marking and Stenciling (AD)
MS .... Mark Sense (NITA)
MS .... Mark Sensing (MSA)
MS .... Marquandia Society (EA)
MS .... Marshall Steel Ltd. [*Toronto Stock Exchange symbol*]
MS .... Mass Spectrography
MS .... Mass Spectrometer (AAEL)
Ms .... Mass Spectrometer (NAKS)
ms .... Mass Spectrometric (AD)
MS .... Mass Spectrometry
MS .... Mass Spectroscopy
MS .... Mass Storage [*Computer science*]
MS .... Master of Science (GAGS)
MS .... Master of Sociology
MS .... Master of Surgery (ODA)
MS .... Master Scene [*Major script sequence*] (NTCM)
MS .... Master Scheduler (CMD)
MS .... Master Sequencer (AAG)
MS .... Master Sergeant
M-S .... Master-Servant [*Legal shorthand*] (LWAP)
MS .... Master Shot [*Film production*] (NTCM)
MS .... Master-Slave [*Computer science*] (MHDI)
ms .... Master Switch (AD)
MS .... Master Switch
MS .... Master Synchronizer (CET)
MS .... Mast Section (IAA)
ms .... Matched Set (AD)
MS .... Matched Set [*Philately*]
MS .... Match Station (VLIE)
Ms .... Material Specification (NAKS)
MS .... Materials Science
MS .... Material Standard (AD)
MS .... Material Support
MS .... Mathis Society [*Defunct*] (EA)
Ms .... Mating Sequence and Control [*NASA*] (NAKS)
MS .... Mating Sequence and Control (NASA)
MS .... Matrix Spike
Ms .... Mature Motion Pictures (AD)
Ms .... Mauritius (MILB)
MS .... Mauritius
MS .... Maxillary Sinus [*Medicine*] (MELL)
ms .... Maximum Stress (AD)
MS .... Maximum Stress
MS .... Maybee Society [*Association*] (EA)
MS .... Mean Score [*Medicine*] (EDAA)
ms .... Mean Square (AD)
MS .... Mean Square
MS .... Measured Service Pricing [*Telecommunications*] (TEL)
M/S .... Measurement Stimuli (NASA)
MS .... Measurement Systems Inc. (SAUS)
MS .... Measuring Set
MS .... Measuring System
MS .... Mechanical Seal
MS .... Mechanical Stimulation (DB)
MS .... Mechanized Scheduling [*Telecommunications*] (TEL)
MS .... Meckel Syndrome [*Medicine*] (DMAA)
MS .... Medial Septum [*Anatomy*]
MS .... Media-Service GmbH [*Database producer*] (IID)
MS .... Media Society [*British*] (DBA)
MS .... Mediastinal Shift [*Medicine*] (EDAA)
MS .... Medical Science (DAVI)
MS .... Medical Service Corps [*Military*] (POLM)
MS .... Medical Services [*Navy*] [*British*]
MS .... Medical Staff [*British military*] (DMA)
MS .... Medical Student (DAVI)
MS .... Medical Supplies [*Military*]
MS .... Medical Survey [*Navy*]
MS .... Medicine and Surgery [*Navy*] (IEEE)
MS .... Medium Sand [*Soil biology*] [*Soil texture*] (QSUL)
MS .... Medium-Scale (IAA)
MS .... Medium Set [*Adhesives*]
MS .... Medium Setting [*Asphalt grade*]
ms .... Medium Shot (AD)
MS .... Medium Shot
MS .... Medium Soft (IAA)
MS .... Medium-Speed (IAA)
ms .... Medium Steel (AD)
MS .... Medium Steel
MS .... Meeting of Signatories [*INTELSAT*]
MS .... Meeting Series [*Online database field identifier*]
MS .... Megalosperm [*Medicine*] (MELL)
MS .... Megasecond (IAA)
MS .... Mega Society (EA)
MS .... Megasporocyte [*Botany*]
MS .... Melville Society (EA)
M/S .... Member State (DCTA)
M/S .... Memorandum Slip [*for informal interoffice communications*]

MS .... Memoriae Sacrum [*Sacred to the Memory Of*] [*Latin*]
MS .... Memory Store [*Computer science*] (PCM)
MS .... Memory System
MS .... Mencken Society (EA)
Ms .... Mendes (AD)
MS .... Menkes' Syndrome [*Medicine*] (MELL)
MS .... Men of the Stones (EA)
MS .... Mental Status [*Psychology*]
MS .... Merchant Shipping
MS .... Mercury-Scout [*Spacecraft*] [*NASA*]
MS .... Merit System (OICC)
MS .... Mesa [*Type of transistor*] (MDG)
Ms .... Mesothorium (AD)
MS .... Message Store [*Telecommunications*] (OSI)
MS .... Message Switch (SAUS)
MS .... Message Switching [*Telecommunications*] (IAA)
MS .... Messaging Services (VLIE)
MS .... Mess Management Specialist [*Military*] (MUSM)
MS .... Mestome Sheath [*Botany*]
Ms .... Mesyl [*Organic chemistry*]
MS .... Metallurgical Society (NADA)
m/s .... Metal Shank (AD)
MS .... Metals Society [*Later, IOM*] (EAIO)
MS .... Metal Stamping
MS .... Meteoritical Society (EA)
MS .... Meteoroid Shield (KSC)
MS .... Meteor Scatter (PDAA)
ms .... Meters per Second (AD)
M/S .... Meters per Second
MS .... Methionine Synthase [*An enzyme*]
MS .... Method of Sale
MS .... Methyl Salicylate [*Organic chemistry*]
MS .... Methyl Silicone [*Medicine*] (EDAA)
MS .... Metric Size (IAA)
ms .... Metric System (AD)
MS .... Metric System
MS .... Mezzo Soprano [*Music*] (ROG)
MS .... Michigan State University of Agriculture and Applied Sciences (AD)
MS .... Microbial Susceptibility [*Medicine*] (DB)
MS .... Microcirculatory Society (EA)
MS .... Microprogram Storage [*Computer science*] (MDG)
MS .... Microscope Slide (DMAA)
MS .... Microscopic System
ms .... Microsecond (VLIE)
ms .... Microseismic (AD)
MS .... Microsoft Corporation (WDMC)
MS .... Microsphere
MS .... Microwave Scanner [*Marine science*] (OSRA)
MS .... Microwave Spectrum
MS .... Mid-Shot
ms .... Mild Steel (AD)
MS .... Mild Steel
m/s .... Milestone (AD)
Ms .... Milestone (NAKS)
M/S .... Milestone (POLM)
MS .... Milestone (KSC)
MS .... Milestone Scientific [*AMEX symbol*] (SG)
MS .... Military Science (AABC)
MS .... Military Secretary [*British*]
MS .... Military Service
MS .... Military Service Act [*British*]
MS .... Military Show
MS .... Military Specification (AAG)
MS .... Military Staff [*British military*] (DMA)
Ms .... Military Standard (NAKS)
MS .... Military Standard [*Parts designation*]
MS .... Military Surgeon [*Medicine*] (EDAA)
MS .... Military Survivors (EA)
MS .... Milk Sugar (MELL)
MS .... Millbrook Society [*Mid-Atlantic states*] (EARSL)
MS .... Millennium Society (EA)
Ms .... Millisecond (NAKS)
ms .... Millisecond
MS .... Milliseconds (ACAE)
mS .... Millisiemens
MS .... Minesweeper [*or Minesweeping*]
MS .... Miniature Screw [*Lamp base*] (NTCM)
m/s .... Miniature Sheet of Stamps (AD)
MS .... Minimal Support (DAVI)
ms .... Minimum Stress (AD)
MS .... Minister of State [*British*]
MS .... Ministry of Shipping [*British*]
MS .... Ministry of Supply [*Also, MOS*] [*British*]
MS .... Minority Stockholder
M/S .... Minor Support (KSC)
MS .... Minor Surgery (SAUS)
ms .... Mint State (AD)
MS .... Mint State
MS .... Minus
MS .... Minutes (AAG)
MS .... Miscellaneous
MS .... Miscellaneous Services [*Department of Employment*] [*British*]
MS .... Missile Station (AAG)
MS .... Missile Support (SAUS)
MS .... Missile System
ms .... [*The*] Missionaries of Our Lady La Salette (TOCD)
MS .... Missionaries of Our Lady of LaSalette [*Roman Catholic religious order*]
MS .... Missionary Sisters of Our Lady of Africa [*White Sisters*] [*Roman Catholic religious order*]
MS .... Missionary Society [*British*]
MS .... Mission Sequencer (SAA)
MS .... Mission Simulator
MS .... Mission Specialist (MCD)
Ms .... Mission Specialist [*NASA*] (NAKS)
MS .... Mission Station (MCD)
Ms .... Mission Station [*NASA*] (NAKS)
MS .... Missions to Seamen (EA)
MS .... Mission Support
MS .... Mississippi [*Postal code*]
Ms .... Mississippi State Library, Jackson, MS [*Library symbol*] [*Library of Congress*] (LCLS)
Ms .... Mistress (DAVI)
ms .... Mitral Stenosis (AD)
MS .... Mitral Stenosis [*Cardiology*]
MS .... Mittelsatz [*Middle Movement*] [*Music*]
M-S .... Mitte-Seite [*Stereo*] (IEEE)
MS .... Mobile Searchlight [*British*]
MS .... Mobile Service [*Telecommunications*] (TEL)
MS .... Mobile Station (VLIE)
MS .... Mobile Surgery [*British*]
MS .... Mobilization Station [*DoD*]
MS .... Modal Sensation [*Psychology*]
MS .... Modal Sensitivity [*Medicine*]
MS .... Model Station
MS .... Modem Sharing (ACAE)
MS .... Moderately Susceptible [*Plant pathology*]
MS .... Modern Science [*A publication*]
MS .... Modulation Sensitivity
MS .... Moessbauer Spectroscopy
MS .... Molar Degree of Substitution [*Organic chemistry*]
MS .... Molar Solution [*Dentistry*]
MS .... Molar Substitution (DB)
MS .... Molecular Sieve (MCD)
MS .... Molecular Staffing [*Optics*] (EECA)
MS .... Molecular Stuffing (VLIE)
MS .... Molecular Substitution
M-S .... Monday through Saturday (AD)
MS .... Money Supply
MS .... Mongolian Spot [*Medicine*]
MS .... Monitor Station
MS .... Monorail Society (EA)
Ms .... Monosomy (QSUL)
m/s .... Month after Sight (AD)
ms .... Months after Sight (AD)
MS .... Months after Sight [*or Month's Sight*] [*Business term*]
MS .... Montserrat [*ANSI two-letter standard code*] (CNC)
MS .... Morel Syndrome [*Medicine*] (MELL)
MS .... More of the Same (SAUS)
M/S .... More Segments [*Open Systems Interconnection*] (ODAA)
MS .... More Segments (VLIE)
MS .... More Significant [*Statistics*]
MS .... Morgan Stanley Group, Inc. [*NYSE symbol*] (SPSG)
ms .... Morphine Sulfate [*Medicine*] (BCRP)
MS .... Morphine Sulfate [*Narcotic*]
MS .... Morquio-Silverkioeld [*Syndrome*] [*Medicine*] (DB)
MS .... Morse Society [*Association*] (EA)
MS .... Morse Tape (IAA)
MS .... Most [*Telegraphy*] (PCTE)
MS .... Most Severe [*Automotive engineering*]
MS .... Most Significant
MS .... Motile Sperm
MS .... Motion Sensitivity (KSC)
MS .... Motor Ship
m/s .... Motorskib [*Motorship*] [*Norwegian*] (AD)
MS .... Motor Starting (IAA)
MS .... Motor Supports
MS .... Mucosubstance (MAE)
MS .... Muenster [*Westfalen*] [*German license plate city code*]
MS .... Multilateral Staff [*Environmental Protection Agency*] (GFGA)
ms .... Multiple Sclerosis (AD)
MS .... Multiple Sclerosis [*Medicine*]
MS .... Multiple Section (MSA)
ms .... Multiple Starters (AD)
MS .... Multiplexer Section (SAUS)
MS .... Multiplexer Storage (IAA)
MS .... Multistart [*Optimization method*]
Ms .... Multistring (NAKS)
MS .... Multistring (NASA)
MS .... Munchausen's Syndrome [*Medicine*] (MELL)
MS .... Murashige-Skoog [*Medium*] [*Botany*]
Ms .... Murmurs [*Medicine*] (DMAA)
MS .... Murphy-Sturm [*Lymphosarcoma*] [*Medicine*] (DB)
MS .... Muscle Shortening [*Medicine*]
ms .... Muscle Strength (AD)
MS .... Muscle Strength
MS .... Musculactive Substance [*Medicine*]
MS .... Musculoskeletal [*Medicine*]

MS .... Music Sales Corporation [*Publisher*]
Ms .... Mussels [*Quality of the bottom*] [*Nautical charts*]
MS .... Mustard Seed (EA)
MS .... Mycoplasma Synoviae [*A pathogen*]
MS .... Myelosclerosis [*Medicine*] (MELL)
MS .... Mythopoeic Society (EA)
ms .... Nail Steamer (ODA)
MS .... Ship Station [*ITU designation*] (CET)
MS .... Somerset Library [*Bibliotheque Somerset*], Manitoba [*Library symbol*] [*National Library of Canada*] (BIB)
MS .... Springfield City Library, Springfield, MA [*Library symbol*] [*Library of Congress*] (LCLS)
MS1 .... Mess Management Specialist, First Class [*Navy rating*] (DNAB)
MS-2 .... Mare Serenitatis [*Sea of Serenity*] [*Lunar area*]
MS2 .... Mess Management Specialist, Second Class [*Navy rating*] (DNAB)
M/S² .... Meters per Second Squared
MS2 .... Micro-Set System 2 (NITA)
MS3 .... Mess Management Specialist, Third Class [*Navy rating*] (DNAB)
MS-3 .... Military Staffing Standards System
MS3 .... Munitions Support Structure Study [*Army*]
MS3 .... Munitions System Support Structure
MS3-X .... Munitions System Support Structure - Extended [*Army*]
MS04 .... Morphine Sulfate (SAUS)
mS-222 ..... Tricaine Methane Sulphonate [*Chemistry*] (DAVI)
MSA .... Magazine Shippers Association
MSA .... Mahri, Suqutri, and Shahri (BJA)
MSA .... Maine Snowmobile Association (EARSL)
MSA .... Main Store Allocator
MSA .... Maintenance Support Activity
MSA .... Major Serologic Antigen [*Medicine*] (MELL)
MSA .... Major System Acquisition (COE)
MSA .... Malaysia-Singapore Airlines
MSA .... Male Specific Antigen (PDAA)
MSA .... Malta Standardisation Authority (SAUS)
MSA .... Management Science America, Inc. (HODG)
MSA .... Management Science Associates, Inc. [*Information service or system*] (IID)
MSA .... Management Science of America (HGAA)
MSA .... Management Service Architecture (SAUS)
MSA .... Management System Analysis
MSA .... Management System Audits (EEVL)
MSA .... Mandusa Resources Ltd. [*Vancouver Stock Exchange symbol*]
MSA .... Manitoba Society of Artists [*1925*] [*Canada*] (NGC)
MSA .... Mannitol Salt Agar (MAE)
MSA .... Marigold Society of America (EA)
MSA .... Marine Safety Agency (WDAA)
MSA .... Marine Science Activities [*Program*] [*Coast Guard*]
MSA .... Marine Stewards' Association [*Australia*]
MSA .... Mariological Society of America (EA)
MSA .... Maritime Safety Agency (NADA)
MSA .... Maritime Safety Authority (SAUS)
MSA .... Marker Signal Attenuation
MSA .... Market Science Associates, Inc. [*Information service or system*] (IID)
MSA .... Marlowe Society of America (EA)
MSA .... Marquetry Society of America (EA)
MSA .... Marshal Sprayable Ablative [*NASA*]
MSA .... Masonic Service Association of the United States (EA)
MSA .... Massachusetts School of Art
MSA .... Mass-Separating Agent [*Chemical engineering*]
MSA .... Mass Storage Adapter
MSA .... Master of School Administration (PGP)
MSA .... Master of Science Administration (PGP)
MSA .... Master of Science and Arts
MSA .... Master of Science in Accountancy
MSA .... Master of Science in Accounting (GAGS)
MSA .... Master of Science in Administration (GAGS)
MSA .... Master of Science in Agriculture
MSA .... Master of Science in Anesthesia (PGP)
MSA .... Master of Science in Anthropology (PGP)
MSA .... Master of Scientific Agriculture
MSA .... Master of Sport Administration (GAGS)
MSA .... Material Service Area
MSA .... Material Stores Area (KSC)
MSA .... Material Surveillance Assembly [*Nuclear energy*] (NRCH)
MSA .... Matrix Scheme for Algorithms (PDAA)
MSA .... Mature Students' Association [*British*] (BI)
MSA .... Mean Spherical Approximation [*Physical chemistry*]
MSA .... Measure of Sampling Adequacy Index (EDAC)
MSA .... Mechanical Signature Analysis
MSA .... Media Studies Association [*British*]
MSA .... Medical Savings Account
MSA .... Medical Scientists' Association [*Australia*]
MSA .... Medical Service Agency (WYGK)
MSA .... Medical Services Account
MSA .... Medical Services Administration [*HEW*]
MSA .... Medusa Corp. [*NYSE symbol*] (CTT)
MSA .... Member of the Society of Apothecaries [*British*]
MSA .... Member of the Society of Architects [*British*] (DAS)
MSA .... Member of the Society of Arts [*British*]
MSA .... Membrane-Stabilizing Activity [*Cardiology*]
MSA .... Membrane Surface Area [*Cytology*]
MSA .... Merchant Shipping Act
MSA .... Mercury Singapore Airlines
MSA .... Mermaid Series [*A publication*]
MSA .... Mesa Public Library, Mesa, AZ [*OCLC symbol*] (OCLC)
MSA .... Metaphysical Society of America (EA)
MSA .... Meteorological Satellite Activity (IAA)
MSA .... Meteorological Support Activity [*Army Electronics Command*]
MSA .... Methacrylate Structural Adhesive
MSA .... Methanesulfonic Acid [*Organic chemistry*]
MSA .... Method of Standard Additions
MSA .... Methyltrimethylsilylacetamide [*Organic chemistry*]
MSA .... Metropolitan Service Area [*Telecommunications*] (TSSD)
MSA .... Metropolitan Statistical Area [*Census Bureau*]
MSA .... Metropolitan Statistical Area Standard
MSA .... Michigan Statutes Annotated [*A publication*] (AAGC)
MSA .... Microcomputer Software Association (EA)
MSA .... Microgravity Science and Applications
MSA .... Microscopy Society of America (NTPA)
MSA .... Microsomal Antibody
MSA .... Microwave System Analyzer (ACAE)
MSA .... Middle Sacral Artery [*Medicine*] (MELL)
MSA .... Middle States Association (NADA)
MSA .... Middle States Association of Colleges and Schools (EA)
MSA .... Middle Stone Age [*Anthropology*]
MSA .... Midsystolic Click [*Medicine*] (DB)
MSA .... Military Service Act [*British*] (DMA)
MSA .... Military Subsistence Agency [*Merged with Defense Supply Agency*]
MSA .... Millennium Star Atlas [*A publication*]
MSA .... Milton Society of America (EA)
MSA .... Mineralogical Society of America (EA)
MSA .... Mine Safety Appliance
MSA .... Minesweeper, Auxiliary [*Navy symbol*] [*Obsolete*]
MSA .... Minimum Safe Altitude [*Aviation*]
MSA .... Minimum Sector Altitude [*Aviation*] (PIPO)
MSA .... Minimum Surface Area (KSC)
MSA .... Minimun Sector Altitude [*Aviation*] (PIAV)
MSA .... Minnesota Statutes, Annotated [*A publication*] (DLA)
MSA .... Misce Secundum Artem [*Mix Pharmaceutically*] [*Latin*]
MSA .... Missile Support Activity (MCD)
MSA .... Missile System Analyst (SAA)
MSA .... Missile System Availability (MCD)
MSA .... Missionary Sisters of the Assumption [*Roman Catholic religious order*]
MSA .... Mission Services Association (EA)
MSA .... Mission Support Area [*NASA*]
MSA .... Mistral Air SRL [*Italy*] [*ICAO designator*] (FAAC)
MSA .... Mobile Subscriber Access (MCD)
MSA .... Modern Standard Arabic [*Linguistics*] (IEL)
MSA .... Modern Studies Association [*British*] (DBA)
MSA .... Monitor and Switching Assembly
MSA .... Morale Support Activities [*Military*] (AABC)
MSA .... Most Seriously Affected [*Food-deficient nations*]
MSA .... Motor Schools' Association of Great Britain (BI)
MSA .... Motor Sports Association
MSA .... Mount Pleasant, TX [*Location identifier*] [*FAA*] (FAAL)
MSA .... Mount San Antonio [*New Mexico*] [*Seismograph station code, US Geological Survey*] (SEIS)
MSA .... Mouse Serum Albumin [*Clinical chemistry*]
MSA .... Mouvement Socialiste Africain [*African Socialist Movement*] [*Political party*]
MSA .... Mouvement Souverainete Association [*Canada*] (PPW)
MSA .... Multichannel Signal Averager [*Computer science*]
MSA .... Multiple System Atrophy [*Medicine*]
MSA .... Multiplication Stimulating Activity [*Cytochemistry*]
MSA .... Multisubsystem Adapter [*Sperry UNIVAC*]
MSA .... Multivariate Survival Analysis [*Statistics*]
MSA .... Municipal Saleyards Association [*Victoria, Australia*]
MSA .... Muscle Sympathetic Activity [*Medicine*] (DMAA)
MSA .... Museum Store Association (EA)
MSA .... Muslim Students' Association of the US and Canada (EA)
MSA .... Mutual Security Act [*1954*]
MSA .... Mutual Security Agency [*Functions transferred to Foreign Operations Administration, 1953*]
MSA .... Mutual Society of Arts (NADA)
MSA .... Mycological Society of America (EA)
MSA .... Royal Automobile Club Motor Sports Association [*United Kingdom*] (EAIO)
MSa .... Salem Public Library, Salem, MA [*Library symbol*] [*Library of Congress*] (LCLS)
MSA-1 .... Marshall Sprayable Ablator (SAUS)
MSA-2 .... Improved Marshall Sprayable Ablator (SAUS)
MSAA .... Master of Science in Astronautics and Aeronautics (PGP)
MSAA .... Membrane Structures Association of Australasia
MSAA .... Microsoft Active Accessibility [*Computer science*]
MSAA .... Moderately Severe Aplastic Anemia [*Hematology*]
MSAA .... Multiple-Sclerosis-Associated Agent [*A virus*]
MSAA .... Multiple Sclerosis Association of America
MSAAB ..... Military Services Ammunition Allocation Board (AABC)
MSAAC ..... Mower Specialists' Association of Australia Cooperative
MSAAE ..... Master of Science in Aeronautical and Astronautical Engineering (GAGS)
MSAAP ..... Mississippi Army Ammunition Plant (AABC)
MSAAT ..... Member of the Society of Architectural and Allied Technicians [*British*] (DI)
MsAb .... Evans Memorial Library, Aberdeen, MS [*Library symbol*] [*Library of Congress*] (LCLS)
MS/AB ...... Massenet Society/American Branch (EA)
MSAc .... Master of Science in Accounting

MSAC........ Mid-State Athletic Conference (PSS)
MSAC........ Missile System Analyst Console (AAG)
MSAC........ Moore School of Automatic Computers [*University of Pennsylvania*]
MSAC........ Mount Saint Agnes College [*Maryland*] [*Merged with Loyola College*]
MSAC........ Murray State Agricultural College [*Oklahoma*]
MSAC........ Sonsonate/Acajutla [*El Salvador*] [*ICAO location identifier*] (ICLI)
MSACC...... Master of Science in Accounting (PGP)
MS Acct..... Master of Science in Accounting (PGP)
MS/Accy.... Master of Science in Accountancy
MSACHA.... Mid-South Automated Clearing House Association
MSACM..... Master of Science in Acquisition and Contract Management (PGP)
MSACS...... Middle States Association of Colleges and Schools (DHP)
MSAD....... Materials Summary Acceptance Document (MCD)
MSAD....... Microgravity Science and Applications Division (SAUS)
MSAD....... Motor Safe and Arm Device
MSAD....... Multisatellite Attitude Determination [*NASA*]
MS Admin... Master of Science in Administration (PGP)
MSADY...... Mid-States plc ADS [*NASDAQ symbol*] (TTSB)
MSaE........ Essex Institute, Salem, MA [*Library symbol*] [*Library of Congress*] (LCLS)
MSAE........ Master of Science in Aeronautical Engineering
MSAE........ Master of Science in Aerospace Engineering (GAGS)
MSAE........ Master of Science in Agricultural Engineering (PGP)
MSAE........ Master of Science in Architectural Engineering (PGP)
MSAE........ Master of Science in Art Education (PGP)
MSAE........ Member of the Society of Automotive Engineers
MSAER...... Master of Science in Aerospace Engineering (PGP)
MSAES...... Michigan Sheriffs' Association Educational Services (EARSL)
MSAF........ Meconium Stained Amniotic Fluid [*Neonatology*] (DAVI)
MSafetySc... Master of Safety Science
MSAFP....... Maternal Serum Alpha Fetoprotein [*Clinical chemistry*]
MSAfrica.... Morgan Stanley Africa Investment Fund [*Associated Press*] (SAG)
MSafSc...... Master of Safety Science
MS (Ag)..... Master of Science in Agriculture
MSAG........ MEECN Senior Advisory Group (SAUS)
MSAG........ Multifunction Self-Aligned Gate (SAUS)
MS (Ag E)... Master of Science in Agricultural Engineering
MS Agr...... Master of Science in Agriculture
MSAgrEng... Master of Science in Agricultural Engineering (NADA)
MSAH........ Michigan Sportsmen Against Hunger
MSAI........ American International College, Springfield, MA [*Library symbol*] [*Library of Congress*] (LCLS)
MSAI........ Management Science America, Inc. [*NASDAQ symbol*] (COMM)
MSAI........ Master of Science in Artificial Intelligence (GAGS)
MSAICE..... Member of the South African Institution of Civil Engineers
MSAInstMM... Member of the South African Institute of Mining and Metallugy
MSAL........ Mammal Serum Albumin (DB)
MSALAS.... Medical Sickness Annuity & Life Assurance Society (WDAA)
MSALT...... Mean Sea Level Altitude (ACAE)
MsAM........ Alcorn Agricultural and Mechanical College, Lorman, MS [*Library symbol*] [*Library of Congress*] (LCLS)
MSAM....... Master of Science in Applied Mechanics
MSAM....... Medium-range Surface-to-Air Missile (SAUS)
M-SAM...... Medium Surface-to-Air Missile [*Army*]
MSAM....... Microsoft Screen Access Model (SAUS)
MSAM....... Mobile Surface-to-Air Missile
MSAM....... Morgan Stanley Asset Management [*Commercial firm*]
MSAM....... Morpholinomethyl Salicyclamide [*Analgesic compound*]
MSAM....... Multi-Indexed Sequential Access Method [*Computer science*]
MSAM....... Multiple Sequential Access Method (NITA)
MSAMP..... Master Ship Acquisition Milestone Plan
MSAMS..... Mobile Surface-to-Air Missile System (MCD)
M San....... Master of Sanitation
MSAN....... Medical Student's Admission Note [*Medicine*] (EDAA)
MSAN....... Microwave Steerable Null Antenna Array (ACAE)
MS & C..... Marley, Scrooge, and Cratchit [*Accounting agency*]
MS & E..... Materials Science and Engineering
MS & FR.... Missile Stability and Frequency Response
MS & LR.... Manchester, Sheffield & Lincolnshire Railway [*Later, Great Central*] [*British*] (ROG)
MS & NI.... Michigan Southern & Northern Indiana Railroad
MS & P..... Materials Synthesis and Processing [*National Science Foundation*]
MS&R....... Merchant Shipbuilding and Repairs (ODA)
MS & R..... Merchant Shipbuilding and Repairs
MS & W.... Maintenance Shop and Warehouse (NRCH)
MSanHi..... Sandwich Historical Society, Sandwich, MA [*Library symbol*] [*Library of Congress*] (LCLS)
MSANS...... Multiple Small-Angle Neutron Scattering [*Surface analysis*]
M San Sc... Master of Sanitary Science
MSanSc&PH... Master of Sanitary Science and Public Health (GAGS)
MSAO....... Medical Services Accountable Officer
MSAO....... Morale Support Activities Office
MSAP........ MAC Sublayer Service Access Point [*Open Systems Interconnection*] (ODAA)
MSAP........ Master of Science in Applied Physics (PGP)
MSAP........ Master of Science in Applied Psychology (PGP)
MSAP........ Master Space Allocation Plan (MCD)
MSAP........ Mean Systemic Arterial Pressure [*Cardiology*]
MSAP........ Military Security Assistance Projection [*Military*]
MSAP........ Multisatellite Attitude Prediction [*NASA*]
MSaP........ Peabody Museum of Salem, Salem, MA [*Library symbol*] [*Library of Congress*] (LCLS)
MSA PAC... Mine Safety Appliances Company PAC [*Pittsburgh, PA*] (PACS)
MSApSc..... Master of Science in Applied Science (GAGS)
MSAR....... Microwave Spectrometer and Radiometer (ACAE)
MSAR....... Mines Safety Appliance Research (IEEE)
MSAR....... Miniature Synthetic Aperture Radar (SAUS)
Ms-Ar........ Mississippi Department of Archives and History, Jackson, MS [*Library symbol*] [*Library of Congress*] (LCLS)
MSARC...... Marine Systems Acquisition Review Council (MCD)
MS Arch.... Master of Science in Architecture
MS Arch St... Master of Architectural Studies (PGP)
MSAS........ Malaysia Singapore Australia Society
MSAS........ Mandel Social Adjustment Scale [*Psychology*]
MSAS........ Marine Sciences Affairs Staff [*A publication*]
MSAS........ Master of Science in Architectural Studies (GAGS)
MSAS........ Maternal Separation Anxiety Scale
MSa/s....... MegaSamples per Second (CDE)
MSAS........ Microwave Signature Acquisition System (MCD)
MSAS........ Military Sponsored Air Service
MSAS........ Minnesota School Attitude Survey [*Educational test*]
MSAS........ Modal Suppression Augmentation System [*Aerospace*]
M Sa Sc.... Master of Sacred Sciences
MSAsia...... Morgan Stanley Asia Pacific Fund [*Associated Press*] (SAG)
MSAT........ Master of Science in Advanced Technology (PGP)
MSAT........ Medical School Aptitude Test [*Medicine*] (EDAA)
MSAT........ Minnesota Scholastic Aptitude Test
MSAT........ Missile System Analyst Technician (SAA)
MSAT........ Mobile Service Satellite [*Open Systems Interconnection*] (ODAA)
MSaT........ Salem State College, Salem, MA [*Library symbol*] [*Library of Congress*] (LCLS)
MSATA...... Motorcycle, Scooter, and Allied Trades Association [*Later, MIC*]
MSAT-A..... Multisensor Aided Targeting-Air [*Army*] (DOMA)
MSAT-Air.... Multi-Sensor Aided Targeting-Airborne (SAUS)
MSATF...... Missile Site Activation Task Force (SAA)
MSATS...... Marksman Small Arms Training System (SAUS)
MSATT...... Martian Surface and Atmosphere through Time [*NASA*]
MSAT-X..... Mobile Satellite Experiment (MCD)
MSAU....... Marcella Shipping [*Intermodal shipping container symbol*] (TVRC)
MSAU....... Multistation Access Unit [*Telecommunications*] (TSSD)
MSAUSC.... Muslim Students' Association of the United States and Canada (EA)
MSAutE..... Member of the Society of Automobile Engineers [*British*]
MSAV........ Medical Scientists' Association of Victoria [*Australia*]
MSAV........ Microsoft Anti-Virus [*Microsoft Corp.*] [*Computer science*] (PCM)
MSAW....... Minimum Safe Altitude Warning [*Aviation*]
MSAWA..... Migrant and Seasonal Agricultural Worker Act of 1983 (WYGK)
MSAWS..... Mobile Surface-to-Air Weapon System (MCD)
MSAZ........ National Motor Freight Traffic Association [*Intermodal trailer symbol*]
MsB.......... Biloxi Public Library, Biloxi, MS [*Library symbol*] [*Library of Congress*] (LCLS)
MSB.......... Iola, KS [*Location identifier*] [*FAA*] (FAAL)
MSB.......... Magnetic Susceptibility Bridge
MSB.......... Main Steamline Break [*Nuclear energy*] (NRCH)
MSB.......... Main Support Base [*Air Force*] (AFM)
MSB.......... Main Support Battalion [*Army*] (DOMA)
MSB.......... Main Switchboard
MSB.......... Maintenance Standard Book
MSB.......... Maintenance Support Base [*Military*]
MSB.......... Male Sexual Biomass [*Botany*]
MSB.......... Manpower Services Branch [*Military*] (MCD)
MSB.......... Maritime Safety Board (ODA)
MSB.......... Maritime Subsidy Board [*Maritime Administration*] [*Department of Commerce*]
MS/B........ Marshall and Swift/Boeckh (IID)
MSB.......... Martin's Scarlet Blue [*Histologic stain*]
MSB.......... Mass Spectrometry Bulletin [*Mass Spectrometry Data Centre*] [*Bibliographic database*] [*British*]
Ms B......... Master of Bacteriology
MSB.......... Master of Science in Business
MSB.......... Material Support Branch [*NASA*] (KSC)
MSB.......... Mediterranean Shipping Board [*World War II*]
MSB.......... Member of the School Board [*British*] (ROG)
MSB.......... Memory Storage Buffer [*Computer science*] (CAAL)
MSB.......... Mesabi Tr Ctfs SBI [*NYSE symbol*] (TTSB)
MSB.......... Mesabi Trust [*NYSE symbol*] (SAG)
MSB.......... Methylstyrylbenzene [*Fluorescent compound*]
MSB.......... Metropolitan Separate School Board [*UTLAS symbol*]
MSB.......... Metropolitan Society for the Blind (ODA)
MSB.......... Michael Stanley Band [*Musical group*]
MSB.......... Mid-Small Bowel [*Gastroenterology*] (DAVI)
MSB.......... Military Security Board
MSB.......... Military Service Branch [*World War I*] [*Canada*]
MSB.......... Mine Subsidence Board [*New South Wales, Australia*]
MSB.......... Minesweeping Boat [*Navy symbol*]
MSB.......... Minority Small Business (BARN)
MSB.......... Missile Storage Building (NATG)
MSB.......... Missile Support Base (SAA)
MSB.......... Mission Simulator Building (MCD)
MSB.......... Mobile Support Base (DNAB)
MSB.......... Montadale Sheep Breeders Association (EA)
MSB.......... Most Significant BIT [*Binary Digit*] [*Computer science*]
MSb.......... Most Significant Bit (RALS)
MSB.......... Motor Surfboat
MSB.......... Mouvement de Saintete Biblique [*Association*] [*Canada*] (EAIO)
MSB.......... Multi-Step Industries [*Vancouver Stock Exchange symbol*]
MSB.......... Multnomah School of the Bible [*Oregon*]
MSB.......... Municipal Securities Board [*Approved by Congress May 22, 1975*] [*Securities and Exchange Commission*]

MSB .... Museum of Southwestern Biology [*University of New Mexico*] [*Research center*] (RCD)
MSB .... Music Sound Books [*Record label*]
MSB .... Mutual Savings Bank
MSBA .... Malaysia, Singapore, and Brunei Association [*British*] (DBA)
MSBA .... Master of Science in Business Administration
MSBA .... Michigan State Bowling Association (EARSL)
MSBA .... Military School Band Association (EA)
MSBA .... Missouri School Boards' Association (EARSL)
MSBAE ...... Master of Science in Biological and Agricultural Engineering (PGP)
MSBAE ...... Master of Science in Biosystems and Agricultural Engineering (PGP)
MsBB .... Beauvoir, the Jefferson Davis Shrine, Biloxi, MS [*Library symbol*] [*Library of Congress*] (LCLS)
MSBB .... MSB Bancorp [*NASDAQ symbol*] (TTSB)
MSBB .... MSB Bancorp, Inc. [*NASDAQ symbol*] (SAG)
MSB Bcp .... MSB Bancorp, Inc. [*Associated Press*] (SAG)
MSBC .... MainStreet BankGroup [*NASDAQ symbol*] (TTSB)
MSBC .... MainStreet BankGroup, Inc. [*NASDAQ symbol*] (SAG)
MSBC .... Master of Science in Building Construction
MSBC .... Maximum Specific Binding Capacity [*Medicine*] (EDAA)
MSBC .... Steinbach Bible College, Manitoba [*Library symbol*] [*National Library of Canada*] (BIB)
MSBCA ...... Maryland State Board of Contract Appeals (AAGC)
MSB-COD ... Minority Small Business-Capital Ownership Development Program [*Small Business Administration*]
MSBDC ...... Mississippi Small Business Development Centers State Office (EARSL)
MSBE .... Master of Science in Biomedical Engineering (GAGS)
MSBE .... Master of Science in Business Education (PGP)
MSBE .... Molten-Salt Breeder Experiment [*Nuclear energy*]
MsBel .... Humphreys County Library, Belzoni, MS [*Library symbol*] [*Library of Congress*] (LCLS)
MSBENG .... Master of Science in Bioengineering (PGP)
MSBF .... Mean Sorties between Flights (MCD)
MSBF .... MSB Financial [*NASDAQ symbol*] (TTSB)
MSBF .... MSB Financial, Inc. [*NASDAQ symbol*] (SAG)
MSB Fn ..... MSB Financial, Inc. [*Associated Press*] (SAG)
MSBHS ...... Mountain State Behavioral Health Services, LLC (MHID)
MSBI .... Montclair Savings Bank (New Jersey) [*NASDAQ symbol*] (COMM)
MSBIC .... Minority Small Business Investment Company (AAGC)
MSBJC ...... Missabe Junction, MN [*American Association of Railroads railroad junction routing code*]
MSBK .... Mutual Savings Bank [*NASDAQ symbol*] (TTSB)
MSBK .... Mutual Savings Bank FSB [*NASDAQ symbol*] (SAG)
MSBL .... Member of the School Board, London [*Defunct*] [*British*] (ROG)
MSBLA ...... Mouse Specific B Lymphocyte Antigen [*Immunology*]
MSBLK ...... Mild Steel, Black Finish (IAA)
MSBLMS .... Multi Station Boundary Layer Model System (PDAA)
MSBLS ...... Microwave Scanning Beam Landing Station [*or System*] [*NASA*] (NASA)
MSBLS ...... Microwave Scanning Beam Land Station [*NASA*]
MSBLS-GS ... Microwave Scanning Beam Landing System Ground Station [*NASA*]
MsBm .... Blue Mountain College, Blue Mountain, MS [*Library symbol*] [*Library of Congress*] (LCLS)
MSBM .... Master of Science in Business Management (PGP)
MSBME ..... Master of Science in Biomedical Engineering (PGP)
MSBMS ..... Master of Science in Basic Medical Science (PGP)
MSBNSW ... Maritime Services Board of New South Wales [*Australia*]
MSBO .... Michigan School Business Officials (EARSL)
MSBO .... Mooring and Salvage Officer [*Navy*] [*British*]
MSBOA ...... Michigan School Band and Orchestra Association (EARSL)
MSBP .... Munchausen Syndrome by Proxy [*Medicine*]
Ms-BPH ..... Mississippi Library Commission, Services for the Handicapped, Jackson, MS [*Library symbol*] [*Library of Congress*] (LCLS)
MsBr .... Lincoln-Lawrence-Franklin Regional Library, Brookhaven, MS [*Library symbol*] [*Library of Congress*] (LCLS)
MSBR .... Maximum Storage Bus Rate
MSBR .... Military Strength Balance Report (AFM)
MSBR .... Molten-Salt Breeder Reactor
MSbrA .... American Optical Corp., Southbridge, MA [*Library symbol*] [*Library of Congress*] (LCLS)
MSBRT ...... Mild Steel, Bright Finish (IAA)
MsBs .... City-County Memorial Library, Bay St. Louis, MS [*Library symbol*] [*Library of Congress*] (LCLS)
MSBS .... Minimum Social Behavior Scale [*Psychology*]
MsBsNA ..... National Aeronautics and Space Administration, NASA/NSTL Research Library, NSTL Station, Bay St. Louis, MS [*Library symbol*] [*Library of Congress*] (LCLS)
MsBsNO ..... United States Naval Oceanographic Office NSTL Station, Bay St. Louis, MS [*Library symbol*] [*Library of Congress*] (LCLS)
MsBsS .... Divine Word Seminary, Bay St. Louis, MS [*Library symbol*] [*Library of Congress*] (LCLS)
MSBT .... Missionary Servants of the Most Blessed Trinity [*Roman Catholic women's religious order*]
MSBTh ...... Member of the Society of Health and Beauty Therapists [*British*] (DBQ)
MSBU .... Market Buoyant but Unsettled [*Telegraphy*] (PCTE)
MSBu .... Thousand Standard Bushels (EG)
MS Bus ..... Master of Science in Business
MSBV .... Mooring Salvage and Boom Vessel (PDAA)
MSBVW ..... Magnetostatic Backward Volume Wave [*Telecommunications*] (TEL)
MSBY .... Most Significant Byte [*Computer science*]
MSC .... Chief Mess Management Specialist [*Formerly, CSC, CST, SDC*] [*Navy rating*]
MSC .... College de St.-Boniface, Manitoba [*Library symbol*] [*National Library of Canada*] (NLC)
MSC .... Congregation of the Marianites of the Holy Cross (TOCD)
MSC .... Congregation of the Sisters Marianites of Holy Cross [*Roman Catholic religious order*]
MSC .... [*The*] MacNeal-Schwendler Corp.
MSC .... Macro Selection Compiler [*Computer science*] (BUR)
MSC .... Madras Staff Corps [*British*]
MSC .... Magnetically Settable Counter
MSC .... Magnetic Surface Current
MSC .... Magnitude Square of the Complex Coherence (PDAA)
MSC .... Maharashtra Socialist Congress [*India*] [*Political party*] (PPW)
MSC .... Mailstop Code
MSC .... Maine Sardine Council (EA)
MSC .... Main Storage Control [*Computer science*] (BUR)
MSC .... Main Switching Centre [*Telecommunications*] (NITA)
MSC .... Maintenance Support Center (MCD)
MSC .... Maisach [*Federal Republic of Germany*] [*Geomagnetic observatory code*]
MSC .... Major Subcontract (MCD)
MSC .... Major Subordinate Command [*Military*]
MSC .... Major Subordinate Commander (SAUS)
MSC .... Malaysian Multimedia Super Corridor
MSC .... Management Sectional Center
MSC .... Management Service Center [*Marine science*] (OSRA)
MSC .... Management Services Contractor [*INTELSAT*]
MSC .... Manchester Ship Canal
MSC .... Mandatory Settlement Conference [*Insurance*]
MSC .... Mandatum sine Clausula [*Authority without Restriction*] [*Latin*]
MSC .... Mankato State College [*Later, Mankato State University*] [*Minnesota*]
MSC .... Manned Spacecraft (ACAE)
msc .... Manned Spacecraft Center [*NASA*] (NAKS)
MSC .... Manned Spacecraft Center [*Later, Johnson Space Center*] [*NASA*]
MSC .... Manpower Services Commission [*British*]
MSC .... Maple Syrup Council (EA)
MSC .... Marine Safety Committee (SAUS)
MSC .... Marine Safety Council [*Coast Guard*]
MSC .... Marine Science Center [*Oregon State University*] [*Research center*] (RCD)
MSC .... Marine Science Council [*Marine science*] (MSC)
MSC .... Marine Stewardship Council
MSC .... Marital Status Code [*IRS*]
MSC .... Maritime Safety Committee [*Advisory Committee on Pollution of the Sea*]
MSC .... Maritime Service Committee [*New York, NY*] (EA)
MSC .... Maritime Surveillance Capability (CCCA)
MSC .... Marketing Services Conference [*LIMRA*]
MSC .... Marquise [*Marchioness*] [*French*] (ROG)
MSC .... Marrow Stromal Cell [*Biochemistry*]
MSC .... Maryland State College [*Merged with University of Maryland*]
MSC .... Mass Storage Control [*Computer science*] (BUR)
MSC .... Mass Storage Controller (NITA)
MSc .... Master of Science [*Academic degree*] (AIE)
MSC .... Master of Science in Commerce (DD)
MSC .... Master of Science in Communication (PGP)
MSC .... Master of Science in Counseling (GAGS)
MSc .... Master of Science in Epidemiology & Biostatistics (CMD)
MSC .... Master of Speech Communication (GAGS)
msc .... Master Sequence Controller (NAKS)
MSC .... Master Sequence Controller (NASA)
MSC .... Master Status Chart
MSC .... Material Sciences [*NYSE symbol*] (TTSB)
MSC .... Material Sciences Corp. [*NYSE symbol*] (SPSG)
MSC .... Material Source Code
MSC .... Materials Science Center [*Cornell University*]
msc .... Materials Service Center (NAKS)
MSC .... Materials Service Center [*NASA*] (NASA)
MSC .... Materiel Screening Code [*DoD*] (AFIT)
MSC .... Materiel Status Committee [*Military*] (AABC)
MSC .... Materiel Support Center (MCD)
MSC .... Materiel Support Command (MCD)
MSC .... Mathematics, Science, and Computer [*Education*]
MSC .... Mathematics/Science/Computer
MSC .... Mean Spherical Candlepower [*Computer science*] (IAA)
MSC .... Mechanical Super-Calendered Paper (DGA)
MSC .... Medical Service Commission [*Canada*]
MSC .... Medical Service Corps [*Military*]
MSC .... Medical Social Coordinator
MSC .... Medical Specialist Corps [*Military*]
MSC .... Medical Staff Corps [*British*]
MSC .... Mediterranean Society of Chemotherapy (EAIO)
MSC .... Mediterranean Sub-Commission [*Silva Mediterranea*] [*FAO*]
MSC .... Medium-Scale Computer (IAA)
MSC .... Memory Storage Control [*Computer science*]
MSC .... Memphis Service Center [*IRS*]
MSC .... Meritorious Service Cross [*Canada*] (FOTI)
MSC .... Mesa [*Arizona*] [*Airport symbol*] [*Obsolete*] (OAG)
MSC .... Mesenchymal Stem Cell
MSC .... Mesitylenesulfonyl Chloride [*Biochemistry*]
MSC .... Message Sequence Chart [*Telecommunications*] (TEL)
MSC .... Message Switching Center [*Telecommunications*]
MSC .... Message Switching Computer [*Telecommunications*] (TEL)
MSC .... Message Switching Concentration
MSC .... Metal Shielded Cabinet

MSC .... Meteorological Satellite Center [*Aerospace*] (IAA)
MSC .... Methane Sulfonyl Chloride [*Organic chemistry*]
MSC .... Metric System - Conversion (NATG)
MSC .... Metropolitan Special Constabulary (ODA)
MSC .... Metropolitan State College [*Denver, CO*]
MSC .... Microgravity Smoldering Combustion Experiment (SAUS)
MSC .... Micronesia Support Committee [*Later, MC*] (EA)
MSC .... Microscale Cloud [*Module*] [*Air Force*]
MSC .... Microsystems Centre (NITA)
MSC .... Microwave Semiconductors Corporation (ACAE)
MSC .... Microwave Stripline-Circuit (PDAA)
MSC .... Mid-South Conference (PSS)
MSC .... Midwestern Simulation Council
MSC .... Migent Software [*Vancouver Stock Exchange symbol*]
MSC .... Mile of Standard Cable
MSC .... Milestone Schedule Charts (MCD)
MSC .... Military Scout Car [*British*]
msc .... Military Sealift Command (NAKS)
MSC .... Military Sealift Command [*Formerly, MSTS, NTS*] [*Navy*] (NOAA)
MSC .... Military Staff Committee [*United Nations*] (DLA)
MSC .... Military Studies Center (EA)
msc .... Millisecond (WGA)
MSC .... Milliwatts per Square Centimeter
MSC .... Minesweeper, Coastal [*Nonmagnetic*] [*Navy symbol*]
MSC .... Minor Suma Corp. [*Kansas City, MO*] (TSSD)
MSC .... Mirror Sign Convention
MSC .... Mirror Streak Camera
MSC .... Miscellaneous (ADA)
MSC .... Missile and Space Council [*Defunct*] (AAG)
MSC .... Missile Sequence Charts (AAG)
MSC .... Missile Support Co. [*Army*]
MSC .... Missile System Checkout (AAG)
MSC .... Missionaries of the Sacred Heart (TOCD)
msc .... Missionaries of the Sacred Heart (TOCD)
MSC .... Missionarii Sacratissimi Cordis [*Missionaries of the Most Sacred Heart*] [*Roman Catholic men's religious order*]
MSC .... Missionarii Sancti Caroli [*Missionaries of St. Charles*] [*Roman Catholic men's religious order*]
msc .... Missionary Servants of Christ (TOCD)
MSC .... Missionary Sisters of the Most Sacred Heart of Jesus [*Roman Catholic religious order*]
MSC .... Missionary Sisters of the Most Sacred Heart of Jesus of Hiltrup (TOCD)
MSC .... Missionary Sisters of the Sacred Heart [*Cabrini Sisters*] [*Roman Catholic religious order*]
MSC .... Mississippi Central R. R. [*AAR code*]
Ms-C .... Mississippi Library Commission, Jackson, MS [*Library symbol*] [*Library of Congress*] (LCLS)
MSC .... Mississippi Southern College
MSC .... Mixing Smoke Chamber (MCD)
MSC .... Mobile Servicing Center [*Canada*]
MSC .... Mobile Switching Center (ACRL)
MSC .... Mode Selector Controller (MCD)
MSC .... Modified Stirling Cycle (ACAE)
MSC .... Moding Sequencing and Control (MCD)
msc .... Moding Sequencing and Control (NAKS)
MSC .... Modular Spacecraft Computer (ACAE)
MSC .... Monitor Sugar [*Federal Railroad Administration identification code*]
MSC .... Mono-Stereo Compatible (PDAA)
MSC .... Montana State College (MCD)
MSC .... Moorhead State College [*Minnesota*]
MSC .... Morgan State College [*Later, Morgan State University*] [*Baltimore, MD*]
MSC .... Morpheme Structure Constraint [*Linguistics*] (IEL)
MSC .... Moscow Airways [*Russian Federation*] [*ICAO designator*] (FAAC)
MSC .... Most Significant Character [*Computer science*] (MDG)
MSC .... Motor Speed Changer (IAA)
MSC .... Motor Speed Control
MSC .... Motor Starting Contractor
MSC .... Motor Submersible Canoe [*British Marines' Special Forces*] [*World War II*]
MSC .... Mountain Safety Council (SAUS)
MSC .... Moved, Seconded, and Carried
MSC .... Multimedia Super Corridor [*Proposed, Malaysia*]
MSC .... Multiple Scan Correlator
MSC .... Multiple Spindle Chucker
MSC .... Multiple Systems Coupling [*Computer science*]
MSC .... Multipotential Stem Cells [*Hematology*]
MSC .... Multisensor Correlator (CAAL)
MSC .... Multiservice Center
MSC .... Multistrip Coupler [*Telecommunications*] (TEL)
MSC .... Multisystem Coupling [*Computer science*]
MSC .... Murray State College [*Later, MSU*] [*Kentucky*]
MSC .... Museum Support Center [*Smithsonian Institution*]
MSC .... Muskingum College, New Concord, OH [*OCLC symbol*] (OCLC)
Msc .... New York Miscellaneous Reports [*A publication*] (DLA)
MSC .... Social Christian Movement (Ecuador) [*Political party*] (PSAP)
MSC .... Springfield College, Springfield, MA [*Library symbol*] [*Library of Congress*] (LCLS)
Msc 2d ...... New York Miscellaneous Reports. Second Series [*A publication*] (DLA)
MsCa .... Canton Public Library, Canton, MS [*Library symbol*] [*Library of Congress*] (LCLS)
MScA .... Maitre es Sciences Appliquees [*Master of Applied Science*] [*French*]
MSCA .... Make or Subcontract Authorization (AAG)
MScA .... Master of Applied Science (DD)
M Sc A ...... Master of Science (Applied) (PGP)
MScA .... Master of Science in Agriculture (CPGU)
MScA .... Master of Social Administration (GAGS)
MSCA .... McCarthy Scales of Children's Abilities [*Education*]
MSCA .... Mechanical Service Contractors of America (NTPA)
MSCA .... Microwave Switch Control Assembly
MSCA .... Military Support to Civil Authorities (AABC)
MSCA .... Missile Site Construction Agency [*Army*]
msca .... Missing Cargo (DS)
MSCA .... Mixed Spectrum Critical Assembly [*Nuclear energy*]
MSCA .... M.S Carriers [*NASDAQ symbol*] (TTSB)
MSCA .... MS Carriers, Inc. [*NASDAQ symbol*] (NQ)
MSCA .... Multi-Site Cooperative Agreement (COE)
MSCAC ...... Massachusetts State Collegiate Athletic Conference (PSS)
MSc(Acoustics)... Master of Science (Acoustics) (ADA)
MSc(AeroMed)... Master of Science (Aeromedicine)
MSc(Ag) .... Master of Science (Agriculture)
MScAgri ..... Master of Science in Agriculture
MSc(Agric)... Master of Science in Agriculture
MSc(AgricE)... Master of Science (Agricultural Economics) (ADA)
MSc(AgricEc)... Master of Science (Agricultural Economics) (ADA)
MSCAJC ..... Martin Steinberg Center of the American Jewish Congress (EA)
MsCaM ...... Madison County Library, Canton, MS [*Library symbol*] [*Library of Congress*] (LCLS)
MSc(Appl)... Master of Science (Applied) (ADA)
MsCar .... Leake County Library, Carthage, MS [*Library symbol*] [*Library of Congress*] (LCLS)
MSc(Arch)... Master of Science (Architecture)
MSc(Arch)(Cons)... Master of Science (Architectural) (Conservation)
M Sc (Architecture)... Master of Science in Architecture
MS Carr ..... MS Carriers, Inc. [*Associated Press*] (SAG)
MSCAT ...... Minesweeper Catamaran [*Military*]
MSCB .... Missile Site Control Building (AABC)
MsCba .... Shelby Memorial Library, Columbia, MS [*Library symbol*] [*Library of Congress*] (LCLS)
MSc(Biochem)... Master of Science (Biochemistry)
MSc(Biotech)... Master of Science (Biotechnology) (ADA)
M Sc BMC.. Master of Science in Biomedical Communications (PGP)
MSc(BuildServ)... Master of Science (Building Services) (ADA)
MSCC .... Major Subcontract Change Coordination (MCD)
MSCC .... Manned Space Flight Control Center [*Air Force*]
MSCC .... Master of Science in Christian Counseling (PGP)
MScC .... Master of Science in Commerce (DD)
MSCC .... Master Simulator Control Console (MCD)
MSCC .... Microsemi Corp. [*NASDAQ symbol*] (NQ)
MSCC .... Midstream Clean Catch [*Urine Sample*] (DAVI)
MSCC .... Military Space Surveillance Control Center (IAA)
MSCC .... Missile Site Control Center (MCD)
MSCC .... Morgan Sports Car Club (EA)
MSCC .... MS Carriers [*Common carrier symbol*]
MSCCC ...... Minimum Shuffle Control Cell Core [*Nuclear energy*] (NUCP)
M Sc CE .... Master of Science in Chromo-Electronic Science
MScCE ...... Master of Science in Civil Engineering [*British*] (ADA)
MSc(Cer) ... Master of Science in Ceramics (ADA)
MScChemTech... Master of Science in Chemical Technology [*British*] (ADA)
MScCom .... Master in Commercial Sciences
MScComm.. Master in Commercial Science (DD)
MSc(CommMed)... Master of Science (Community Medicine)
M Sc CS .... Master of Science in Computer Science (PGP)
MScD .... Doctor of Medical Science (DAVI)
MScD .... Doctor of Science in Medicine (DAVI)
M Sc D ...... Doctor of the Science of Medicine
MScD .... Magister Scientia Dentalis [*Master of Dental Science*] [*British*]
MScD .... Master of Dental Science
MSCD .... Master of Science in Communication Disorders (PGP)
MScD .... Master of Science in Dentistry (GAGS)
MSCD .... Military Support of Civil Defense (AABC)
MSCD .... Mobile Source Control Division
MSCDC ...... Missouri State Census Data Center [*Information service or system*] (IID)
MSc(Dent)... Master of Science in Dentistry
MSCDEX .... Microsoft Compact Disc Extension [*Computer science*] (DOM)
MSCDEX .... MicroSoft Compact Disc Read Only Memory Extensions [*Computer science*] (IGQR)
MSCDEX .... MS-DOS, CD-ROM Extension [*Computer science*]
MSCDIS ..... Master of Science in Communication Disorders (PGP)
MSCDR ...... Minimum Standardized Crash Data Reporting
MSCDR ...... Mohawk Synchronous Communication Data Recorder [*Military*] (PDAA)
MSCE .... Main Storage Control Element [*Computer science*] (IEEE)
MSCE .... Master of Science in Civil Engineering
MSCE .... Master of Science in Clinical Engineering (PGP)
MSCE .... Master of Science in Clinical Epidemiology (PGP)
MSCE .... Master of Science in Computer Engineering (GAGS)
MScE .... Master of Science in Engineering (DD)
MSCE .... Microsoft Site Commerce Edition (VLIE)
MSCE .... Modular, Standard Control Electronics (SAUS)
M Sc (Econ)... Master of Science in Economics
MSCEd ...... Master of Science in Continuing Education (GAGS)
M Sc Ed ..... Master of Science in Education
MSc(EdPsych)... Master of Science in Educational Psychology (CMD)
MSCEE ...... Master of Science in Civil and Environmental Engineering (PGP)
M Sc EE ..... Master of Science in Electrical Engineering

MSc(Elec)... Master of Science in Electronics [*British*] (ADA)
M Sc (Elec Eng)... Master of Science in Electrical Engineering
MSCELM.... Military Sealift Command, Eastern Atlantic and Mediterranean (DNAB)
MSCEM..... Master of Science in Civil Engineering Management (PGP)
M Sc (Eng)... Master of Science (Engineering)
MSc(Engg)... Master of Science (Engineering)
M Sc Engr... Master of Science in Engineering (PGP)
MSc(Epid)... Master of Science (Epidemiology)
MS (Cer E)... Master of Science in Ceramic Engineering
MSCF........ Master of Science in Computational Finance (PGP)
MScF........ Master of the Science of Forestry [*or Master of Science in Forestry*]
MSCF........ Millions of Standard Cubic Feet (AAG)
MSCF........ Multisource Correlation Facility (MCD)
MSCFAM.... Royal Canadian Army Museum, Canadian Forces Base, Shilo, Manitoba [*Library symbol*] [*National Library of Canada*] (NLC)
MSCFD...... Thousand Standard Cubic Feet per Day (SAUS)
M Sc FE...... Master of Science in Forest Engineering (PGP)
MSCFE...... Military Sealift Command, Far East (DNAB)
MSCFH...... Thousand Standard Cubic Feet per Hour (SAUS)
MSCFM..... Thousand Standard Cubic Feet per Minute (SAUS)
M Sc (For)... Master of Science in Forestry
MSCGpe.... Missionaries of the Sacred Heart of Jesus and of Our Lady of Guadalupe (TOCD)
msch........ Microscheduler (MHDI)
MSCH....... Mode Switch Chassis
MsCh........ Tallahatchie County Library, Charleston, MS [*Library symbol*] [*Library of Congress*] (LCLS)
MSCHAP.... Microsoft Challenge Handshake Authentication Protocol (SAUS)
MSChE...... Master of Science in Chemical Engineering
M Sch Mus... Master of School Music
MSc(HomeScience)... Master of Science (Home Science)
MSc(Hort)... Master of Science in Horticulture [*British*] (ADA)
MSCI........ Madrid Stock-Exchange Index [*Spain*] (ECON)
MSCI........ Master Ships Configuration Index (MCD)
MSCI........ Mediterranean Secret Convoy Instructions [*World War II*]
MSCI........ Military Science
MSCI........ Missile Status Control Indicator [*Military*] (CAAL)
M/SCI........ Mission/Safety Critical Item [*NASA*] (NASA)
MSCI........ Mission Scientist (SAUS)
MSCI........ Mississippi Central Railroad [*Federal Railroad Administration identification code*]
MSCI........ Molten Steel Coolant Interaction (NRCH)
MSCI........ Morgan Stanley Capital Index (NUMA)
MSCI........ Morgan Stanley Capital International
MSCI-EAFE... Morgan-Stanley Capital International - Europe, Australia, Far East [*Free*] [*Index - Financial*]
M Sci Mil... Master of Military Science
M Sc in Agr Eng... Master of Science in Agricultural Engineering
M Sc in Agr Ex... Master of Science in Agricultural Extension
MSC(IndDes)... Master of Science (Industrial Design) (ADA)
M Sc in ME... Master of Science in Mechanical Engineering
MSC/I/O/R... Minesweeper, Coastal/Inshore/Offshore/Riverine (MILB)
MSCIS....... Master of Science in Computer Information Science (PGP)
MSCIS....... Master of Science in Computer Information Systems
MSCIS....... Model Spinal Cord Injury Systems (SAUS)
MScitHi..... Scituate Historical Society, Scituate, MA [*Library symbol*] [*Library of Congress*] (LCLS)
MSCJ........ Master of Science in Criminal Justice (WGA)
MSCJA...... Master of Science in Criminal Justice Administration (PGP)
MSCJA-AJC... Martin Steinberg Center for Jewish Artists - American Jewish Congress [*Defunct*] (EA)
MSCK........ Missionary Sisters of Christ the King (TOCD)
MSCK........ MST Trucking [*Common carrier symbol*]
MSCKC...... Measurement of Self Concept in Kindergarten Children [*Psychology*]
M Sc L...... Master of the Science of Law
MSCL........ Master Ships Configuration List (MCD)
MSCL........ Mathematical and Statistical Computing Laboratory [*Center for Information Technology*] (RCD)
MSCL........ Mississippi State Chemical Laboratory [*Mississippi State University*] [*Research center*] (RCD)
MSCL........ Springlfied City Library, Springfield, MA [*Library symbol*] [*Library of Congress*] (LCLS)
MSCLANT... Military Sealift Command, Atlantic (DNAB)
MSCLANTDET... Military Sealift Command, Atlantic Detachment (DNAB)
MsCld....... Carnegie Public Library, Clarksdale, MS [*Library symbol*] [*Library of Congress*] (LCLS)
MsCle....... Bolivar County Library, Cleveland, MS [*Library symbol*] [*Library of Congress*] (LCLS)
MSCLE...... Maximum Space Charge Limited Emission (IAA)
MsCleD..... Delta State College, Cleveland, MS [*Library symbol*] [*Library of Congress*] (LCLS)
MsCleP...... Presbyterian Church Library, Cleveland, MS [*Library symbol*] [*Library of Congress*] (LCLS)
MsCliBHi.... Mississippi Baptist Historical Society, Clinton, MS [*Library symbol*] [*Library of Congress*] (LCLS)
MsCliM...... Mississippi College, Clinton, MS [*Library symbol*] [*Library of Congress*] (LCLS)
MSC LNO... Major Subordinate Command Liaison Officer
M Sc (Lond)... Master of Science, London
MSCLS...... Master of Science in Clinical Laboratory Science (PGP)
MSCLS...... Master of Science in Clinical Laboratory Studies (PGP)
MSCLS...... Michigan Society for Clinical Laboratory Science (EARSL)
MSCM....... Master Chief Mess Management Specialist [*Formerly, SDCM*] [*Navy rating*]
M Sc M..... Master of the Science of Medicine
MSCM....... Mobile Station Class Mark (CGWS)
MSCM....... Mobile Surface Contamination Monitor
MSCM....... MOSCOM Corp. [*NASDAQ symbol*] (NQ)
MSCM....... Multi-System Configuration Manager [*Computer science*] (HODG)
M Sc (Mech Eng)... Master of Science in Mechanical Engineering
M Sc Med... Master of Medical Science
MScMed.... Master of Science in Medicine [*British*] (ADA)
MSc(Med)... Master of Science (Medical)
M Sc Met... Master of Science in Metallurgy
MSc(Min)... Master of Science in Mining [*British*] (ADA)
MSCN....... Manned Satellite Communication Network (ACAE)
MScN........ Master of Science in Nursing
MSCN....... Misconnection [*Travel industry*] (TRID)
MSc(NatResMgt)... Master of Science in Natural Resources Management
MSc(NeuChem)... Master of Science (Neurochemistry)
MSCNS...... Methicillin-Susceptible Coagulase-Negative Staphylococcus [*Medicine*] (PALA)
MSCNU...... Master of Science in Clinical Nutrition (PGP)
MSc(Nut)... Master of Science (Nutrition)
MSc(Nutr)... Master of Science in Nutrition [*British*] (ADA)
MSCNY...... Marine Society of the City of New York (EA)
MSCO....... Manned Spacecraft Operations [*NASA*] (KSC)
MSCO....... Manual Sustainer Cutoff [*NASA*] (KSC)
MSCO....... Masstor Systems (EFIS)
M Sc O...... Master of the Science of Oratory
MSC(O)..... Minesweeper, Coastal (Old) [*Navy symbol*]
MSc(OccMed)... Master of Science (Occupational Medicine)
MsCol....... Lowndes County Library System, Columbus, MS [*Library symbol*] [*Library of Congress*] (LCLS)
MsColS...... Mississippi State College for Women, Columbus, MS [*Library symbol*] [*Library of Congress*] (LCLS)
MS Cons.... Master of Science in Conservation
MSCOP...... Missile Systems Checkout Program [*Aerospace*] (IAA)
MSc(Ophth)... Master of Science (Ophthalmology)
MScOptom.. Master of Science in Optometry (ADA)
MsCor....... Northeast Regional Library, Corinth, MS [*Library symbol*] [*Library of Congress*] (LCLS)
M Sc (Ost)... Master of Science in Osteopathy
MSCOTSG... Medical Service Corps, Office of the Surgeon General
MS Coun.... Master of Science in Counseling (PGP)
MSCOW..... Moscow, TX [*American Association of Railroads railroad junction routing code*]
MSCP........ Mass Storage Control Protocol (NITA)
MSCP........ Master of Science in Community Planning
MSCP........ Master of Science in Counseling Psychology (PGP)
M Sc P....... Master of Science in Planning (PGP)
mscp........ Mean Spherical Candle Power [*Medicine*] (EDAA)
MSCP........ Mean Spherical Candlepower
MSCP........ Member of the Society of Certified Professionals [*British*] (DBQ)
MSCP........ Missile Systems Checkout Programmer [*Aerospace*] (IAA)
MSCP........ Motor Short-Circuit Protector (IAA)
MSCPA...... Mississippi Society of Certified Public Accountants (EARSL)
MSCPA...... Montana Society of Certified Public Accountants (EARSL)
MSCPAC.... Military Sealift Command, Pacific (DNAB)
MSCPAC.... MS Consultants Inc. PAC [*Youngstown, OH*] (PACS)
MS Cp E.... Master of Science in Computer Engineering (PGP)
MScPhm.... Master of Science in Pharmacy (ADA)
M Sc Pl...... Master of Science in Planning (PGP)
M/S CPO.... Master/Senior Chief Petty Officer (SAUS)
M/S/CPO.... Master/Senior/Chief Petty Officer of the Command (DNAB)
MSCPR...... Mixed-Suspension, Classified-Product Removal [*Crystallizer*] [*Chemical engineering*]
M Sc PT.... Master of Science in Physical Therapy (PGP)
MSCR....... Machine Screw
MSCR....... Measurement/Stimuli Change Request (MCD)
MSCR....... Multilayer Side-Cladded Ridge Waveguide (PDAA)
MSCR/A..... Major Subcontract Change Request/Approval (MCD)
MSc(Rehab)... Master of Science (Rehabilitation Medicine)
MSCREP.... Military Sealift Command Representative (DNAB)
MSCRP...... Master of Science in City and Regional Planning (PGP)
MSCRP...... Master of Science in Community and Regional Planning (PGP)
MsCs........ Crystal Springs Library, Crystal Springs, MS [*Library symbol*] [*Library of Congress*] (LCLS)
MSCS........ Management Scheduling and Control System [*Telecommunications*] (TEL)
MSCS........ Manual SHORAD [*Short Range Air Defense*] Control System (RDA)
MSCS........ Mass Storage Control System [*Computer science*] (IAA)
MSCS........ Master of Science in Computer Science
MSCS........ Merchant Ship Control Service [*Navy*]
MSCS........ Microsoft Clustering Server [*Computer science*]
MSCS........ Microsoft Cluster Server
MSCS........ Microsoft Commerce Server (AGLO)
MSCS........ Miner Sentence Completion Scale [*Psychology*]
MSCS........ Mobile Service Communications Satellite (ACAE)
MSCS........ Multiple Satellite Communications System (ACAE)
MSCS........ Multiservice Communications Systems (RDA)
MSCS........ Senior Chief Mess Management Specialist [*Formerly, CSCS, SDCS*] [*Navy rating*]
MS CSCO... Morgan Stanley Group, Inc. [*Associated Press*] (SAG)
MSCSD...... Master of Science in Communication Sciences and Disorders (PGP)
MSCSE...... Master of Science in Computer and Systems Engineering (PGP)
MSCSE...... Master of Science in Computer Science and Engineering (PGP)
MScSoc..... Master of Social Science (CPGU)

M Sc (Social Sciences)... Master of Science in the Social Sciences
M Sc (Soc Sci)... Master of Science (Social Science)
MSCSO-M & R... Military Sealift Command Service Office - Maintenance and Repair (DNAB)
MSCSO-OCPO... Military Sealift Command Service Office - Operations Cargo Passenger Office (DNAB)
MSCSO-SA... Military Sealift Command Service Office - Supply Assistant (DNAB)
MScSt....... Master of Scientific Studies (ADA)
MSCT........ Malignant Small Cell Tumor [*Oncology*]
MScT........ Master of Science in Teaching (GAGS)
MScT........ Master of Science Teaching (GAGS)
MSCT........ Member of the Society of Cardiological Technicians [*British*]
MSCT........ Miniature Synaptic Calcium Transient [*Neurophysiology*]
MSCTC....... Mass Storage Control Table Create [*Computer science*] (MHDI)
M Sc Tech... Master of Science in Technology
M Sc Tech... Master of Technical Science
MSCTRANSU... Military Sealift Command Transportation Unit (DNAB)
MSCU....... Medical Special Care Unit (DMAA)
MSCU....... Mediterranean Shipping [*Intermodal shipping container symbol*] (TVRC)
MSCU....... Mediterranean Shipping Corporation [*Common carrier symbol*]
MSCU....... Military Sealift Command Unit (DNAB)
MSCU....... Modular Store Control Unit
MSCU....... Multistation Control Unit [*Telecommunications*] (IAA)
MSC(UN).... Military Staff Committee of the United Nations
MSCV........ Connecticut Valley Historical Museum, Springfield, MA [*Library symbol*] [*Library of Congress*] (LCLS)
MSCVAN.... [*An*] MSC [*Military Sealift Command*] Leased/Controlled Seavan or Milvan
MSCW...... Marked Stack Control Word
MSCW...... Mississippi State College for Women [*Columbus*]
MSCWP..... Musculoskeletal Chest Wall Pain [*Medicine*] (EDAA)
MSCX........ Michigan Star Clipper [*Federal Railroad Administration identification code*]
MSCZ........ Mediterranean Shipping [*Intermodal trailer symbol*]
MSCZ........ Montana Sulfur & Chemical [*Federal Railroad Administration identification code*]
MSD......... Doctor of Medical Science
Ms D........ Doctor of Metaphysics
MsD......... Holmes County Library, Durant, MS [*Library symbol*] [*Library of Congress*] (LCLS)
MSD......... Magnetic Storage Drum [*Computer science*]
MSD......... Major Seismic Disturbance
MSD......... Management Services Department [*British*] (DCTA)
MSD......... Management Systems Division [*Environmental Protection Agency*] (EPA)
MSD......... Mansfield, LA [*Location identifier*] [*FAA*] (FAAL)
MSD......... Manual SHORAD [*Short Range Air Defense*] Control System [*Army*]
MsD......... Manuscript Decisions [*Comptroller General*] [*United States*] [*A publication*] (DLA)
MSD......... Maple-Syrup Disease [*Medicine*] (MELL)
MSD......... Marginal Support Date (COE)
MSD......... Marine Sanitation Device
MSD......... Marine Sciences Directorate [*Canada*] (MSC)
MSD......... Marine Signal Detachment (SAA)
MSD......... Maritime-Self-Defense
MSD......... MARS [*Modular Airborne Recorder System*] Supplemental Data (GFGA)
MSD......... Maryland School for the Deaf (MHID)
MSD......... Mass Selector Detector [*Gas chromatography*]
MSD......... Mass Sensor Demonstration
MSD......... Mass Spectral Detector (ABAC)
MSD......... Mass Storage Device [*Computer science*]
MSD......... Master of Dietetics (GAGS)
MSD......... Master of Science in Dentistry
MSD......... Master of Science in Design (PGP)
MSD......... Master of Science in Dietetics (PGP)
MSD......... Master of Scientific Didactics
MSD......... Master Resources & Developments Ltd. [*Vancouver Stock Exchange symbol*]
MSD......... Master Standard Data
MSD......... Master Surgeon Dentist
MSD......... Material Safety Data
MSD......... Materials and Structures Division [*NASA*]
MSD......... Materials Science Department [*Brookhaven National Laboratory*] (RCD)
MSD......... Material Support Data (MCD)
MSD......... Material Support Date (DOMA)
MSD......... Matrix Spike Duplicate
MSD......... Maxillary Sinus Disease [*Medicine*] (EDAA)
MSD......... McNaney Spectroelectric Device
MSD......... Mean Solar Day
MSD......... Mean Squared Distance [*Data analysis*]
MSD......... Mean Square Deviation [*or Difference*]
MSD......... Mean-Square Displacement [*Statistical graphing*]
MSD......... Measurex Management Systems Division (EFIS)
MSD......... Mechanical Setting Device
MSD......... Medical Stores Department [*Tanzania*]
MSD......... Medium Screen Display (SAUS)
MSD......... Merck, Sharpe and Dohme [*Medicine*] [*Pharmaceutical firm*] (EDAA)
MSD......... Metal Sensor Detection
MSD......... Meteorological Systems Development Group [*National Oceanic and Atmospheric Administration*] (RCD)
MSD......... Metering Suction Differential (NG)
MSD......... Method of Steepest Descent
MSD......... Metropolitan Sewer District (GNE)
MSD......... Microdata Software Development (MCD)
MSD......... Microelectronics Systems Division (ACAE)
MSD......... Microsoft Diagnostics [*Microsoft Corp.*] [*Computer science*] (PCM)
MSD......... Microsoft System Diagnostics (VLIE)
MSD......... Microsurgical Discectomy [*Medicine*] (MELL)
MSD......... Mid-Sleep Disturbance [*Medicine*] (EDAA)
MSD......... Mid-Summer Drought (SAUS)
MSD......... Mild Sickle Cell Disease (AAMN)
MSD......... Military Sales Department
MSD......... Military Store Department [*British military*] (DMA)
MSD......... Military Support Detachment [*Emergency Management*] (EMA)
MSD......... Military Support Division [*of Materiel Testing Directorate*] (RDA)
MSD......... Minesweeper, Drone [*Navy symbol*]
MSD......... Minimal Steric Difference [*Organic chemistry*]
MSD......... Minimum Safe Distance (AABC)
MSD......... Misce, Signa, Da [*Mix, Write (the Directions), and Give (to the Patient)*] [*Pharmacy*] (ROG)
MSD......... Missed [*Telegraphy*] (PCTE)
MSD......... Missiles and Space Division [*NASA*] (KSC)
MSD......... Missile Support Days (AAG)
MSD......... Missile Systems Development (AAG)
MSD......... Mission Sensor Data (ACAE)
MSD......... Mission Systems Data (SAA)
MSD......... Mixed Service Drive [*Tire design*]
MSD......... Mobilization Stores Depot (SAUS)
MSD......... Molecular Size Distribution [*Chemistry*]
MSD......... Molecular Structures and Dimensions [*A publication*]
MSD......... Molten Salt Destruction [*Incineration process*]
MSD......... Monorail and Suspension Device [*British*]
MSD......... Morale Support Detachment [*Army*]
MSD......... Morgan Stanley Emerging Markets Debt Fund, Inc. [*NYSE symbol*] (SAG)
MSD......... Morgan Stanley Emer'g Mkt Debt [*NYSE symbol*] (TTSB)
MSD......... Mossoro [*Brazil*] [*Airport symbol*] (AD)
MSD......... Most Significant Decade (IAA)
MSD......... Most Significant Digit [*Computer science*]
MSD......... Motor Storage Dolly
MSD......... Motor System Disease [*Medicine*] (EDAA)
MSD......... Mount Pleasant [*Utah*] [*Airport symbol*] (OAG)
MSD......... Movimento Social Democrata [*Social Democrat Movement*] [*Portugal*] [*Political party*] (PPE)
MSD......... Moving Scene Display
MSD......... Multifrequency Signal Detector [*Telecommunications*]
MSD......... Multimode Silent Digital (SAUS)
MSD......... Multiple Sensor Discrimination (ACAE)
MSD......... Multiple Spark Discharge [*Autotronic Controls Corp.*] [*Automotive engineering*]
MSD......... Multiple Sulfatase Deficiency [*Medicine*] (AAMN)
MSD......... Multisatellite Dispenser (MCD)
MSD......... Multisensor Display
MSD......... Multisensory Disorder
MSD......... Multi-Site Damage (SAUS)
MSD......... Munitions Systems Division (SAUS)
MSD......... Musculoskeletal Disorder (LDOE)
MSDA....... Maryland State Dental Association (SAUS)
MSDA....... Masada Security Holdings, Inc. [*NASDAQ symbol*] (SAG)
MSDA....... Michigan Soft Drink Association (EARSL)
MSDAC..... Minnesota State Drafting Advisory Committee (EDAC)
MSDB....... Main Storage Database
MSDBP..... Mean Squared Distance Between Pairs [*Statistics*] (PDAA)
MSDC....... Maintenance Signal Data Cassette (MCD)
MSDC....... Maintenance Signal Data Converter (MCD)
MSDC....... Manual Slave Direction Center [*RADAR site*]
MSDC....... Mass Spectrometry Data Centre [*Royal Society of Chemistry*] (IID)
MSDC....... Microwave Spectra Data Center [*National Institute of Standards and Technology*]
MSDC....... Molten Salts Data Center [*Rensselaer Polytechnic Institute*] [*National Institute of Standards and Technology*] [*Research center*] (IID)
MSDD....... Master of Science in Design and Development (PGP)
MSDD....... Milli-Second Delay Detonator [*Military*] (PDAA)
MSDD....... Multi-Sensory Developmental Delays
MSDE....... Microsoft Data Engine (VLIE)
MSde....... Tilton Library, South Deerfield, MA [*Library symbol*] [*Library of Congress*] (LCLS)
MSDE-BSNT... Department of Education-Business Services (SAUS)
MSDE-CA... Department of Education-C & A (SAUS)
MSDE-DORS... Department of Education-Rehabilitation (SAUS)
MSDEF...... Missile System Development and Evaluation Facility (MCD)
MSDE-LBRY... Department of Education-Libraries (SAUS)
MS Dent.... Master of Science in Dentistry
MSDE-PRIM... Department of Education-Planning, Results (SAUS)
MSDEQ...... Mothers' Sensory Developmental Expectation Questionnaire [*Occupational therapy*]
MSDerm.... Master of Science in Dermatology (NADA)
MS Des..... Master of Science in Design
MSDES...... Multi-Spectral Document Examination System [*Police and security equipment*]
MSDE-SCO... Department of Education-Community Outreach (SAUS)
MSDE-SIS... Department of Education-Improvement (SAUS)
MSDF....... Maritime Self-Defense Force [*Japan*]
MSDF....... Maritime Staff Defense Force (CINC)
MSDF....... Multi-Sensor Data Fusion (ACAE)

MSDFF ...... Master Slave D Flip Flop (NITA)
MSDG .... Multiple Sensor Display Group (MCD)
MSDHS...... Mission System Data Handling Subsystem (SAUS)
MSDI .... Mainstream Data, Inc. [*NASDAQ symbol*] (SAG)
MSDI .... Martin Suicide Depression Inventory (MELL)
MS Di .... Master of Scientific Didactics
MSDI .... Mayonnaise and Salad Dressings Institute [*Later, Association for Dressings and Sauces*] (EA)
MSDIF....... Modeling and Simulation Data Interchange Format (SAUS)
MSDIG ...... McGuire Safe Driver Interview Guide (AEBS)
MSDL........ Magnetostrictive Delay Line
MSDL........ Microsoft Download [*Computer science*] (AGLO)
MSDL........ Microsoft Download Library (MWOL)
MSD licence... Music, Singing & Dancing Licence (WDAA)
MSDM....... Medium-Speed DynaBIT [*Binary Digit*] Memory [*Computer science*]
MSDM....... Morgan Stanley Group, Inc. [*Associated Press*] (SAG)
MSDN .... Microbial Strain Data Network [*Information service or system*] (IID)
MSDN .... Microsoft Developer's Network [*Computer science*] (PCM)
MSDNA...... Multicopy Single-Stranded Deoxyribonucleic Acid [*Biochemistry, genetics*]
MSDO .... Management Systems Development Office
MS-DOS.... Microsoft Disk Operating System [*IBM Corp.*] [*Computer science*]
MSDP .... Missile Site Data Processor (AABC)
MSDPS...... Missile Site Data Processing System (AABC)
MSDPSS .... Missile Site Data Processing Subsystem (AABC)
MSDR .... Main Storage Data Register [*Computer science*] (IAA)
MSDR .... Maintenance Signal Data Recorder (MCD)
MSDR .... Master Sensor Data Record [*For spacecraft*]
MSDR .... Materials Science Double Rack
MSDR .... Mississippi Delta Railroad [*Federal Railroad Administration identification code*]
MSDR .... Multiplexer Storage Data Register [*Computer science*] (IAA)
MSDR .... Multi-Spectral Scanner Data Redundancy (ACAE)
MSDRS...... Maintenance Signal Data Recording Set [*or System*] (MCD)
MSDS .... Magnetic Storage Drum System [*Computer science*]
MSDS .... Maintenance Safety Data Sheets (MCD)
MSDS .... Manufacturer's Safety Data Sheet (WDAA)
MSDS .... Marconi Space and Defence Systems (MUSM)
MSDS .... Master Simulation Data System (Model) [*Army*]
MSDS .... Material Safety Data Sheet
MSDS .... Material Safety Data Sheets [*Occupational Health Services, Inc.*] [*Information service or system*]
MSDS .... McGuire Safe Driver Scale (AEBS)
MSDS .... Message Switching Data Service
MSDS .... Microsoft Developer Support (VLIE)
MSDS .... Missile Static Development Site (AAG)
MSDS .... Missile System Development Stand (AAG)
MSDS .... Mission Specific Data Set [*Army*]
MSDS .... Multisolvent Delivery System
MSDS .... Multispectral Scanner and Data System
MSDSS...... Microsoft Directory Synchronization Services (GART)
MSDT........ Maintenance Strategy Diagraming Technique (IEEE)
MSDT........ Mean Supply Downtime (CAAL)
MSDT........ Meshless Storage Display Tube
MSDU .... Chemique Merck [*Intermodal shipping container symbol*] (TVRC)
MSDX .... Mason-Dixon Bancshares [*NASDAQ symbol*] (TTSB)
MSDX .... Mason-Dixon Bancshares, Inc. [*NASDAQ symbol*] (SAG)
MSE .... Magnetic Strain Energy
MSE .... Maintenance Support Equipment [*Deep Space Instrumentation Facility, NASA*]
MSE .... Major Source of Employment
MSE .... Major Support Element (DOMA)
MSE .... Malaysia Shipyard & Engineering (SAUS)
MSE .... Manned Spacecraft Engineer (MCD)
MSE .... Manston [*England*] [*Airport symbol*] (AD)
MSE .... Manufacturing Support Equipment (ACAE)
MSE .... Manufacturing Systems Engineering
MSE .... Marshall Energy Ltd. [*Vancouver Stock Exchange symbol*]
MSE .... Mask Superposition Error [*Computer science*] (IAA)
MSE .... Massachusetts Studies in English [*A publication*] (ANEX)
MSE .... Mass Storage Editor [*Computer science*] (MCD)
MSE .... Master of Sanitary Engineering
MSE .... Master of Science in Chemical Engineering
MSE .... Master of Science in Education
MSE .... Master of Science in Engineering
MSE .... Master of Software Engineering (GAGS)
MSE .... Master of Systems Engineering
MSE .... Materials Science and Engineering (ACAE)
MSE .... Materiel Status Evaluation [*Army*] (AABC)
MSE .... Mean Square Error [*Statistics*]
MSE .... Measurement Systems Engineering, Inc. (EFIS)
MSE .... Measuring and Stimuli Equipment (NASA)
MSE .... Mechanical Support Equipment (KSC)
MSE .... Medical Support Equipment (NASA)
MSE .... Member of the Society of Engineers [*British*]
MSE .... Mental Status Examination [*Neurology*] (DAVI)
MSE .... Merck, Sharp & Dohme [*Later, Merck & Co., Inc.*] Research Laboratory, Rahway , NJ [*OCLC symbol*] (OCLC)
MSE .... Merit Students Encyclopedia [*A publication*]
MSE .... Metaphloem Sieve Element [*Botany*]
MSE .... Mexican Stock Exchange (MHDW)
MSE .... Microsoft Exchange server (SAUS)
MSE .... Mid-Song Element [*Ornithology*]
MSE .... Midwest Stock Exchange [*Chicago, IL*] (EA)
MSE .... Military Specification Exception (RDA)
MSE .... Military Standard Engines
MSE .... Milk-Sensitive Enteropathy [*Medicine*]
MSE .... Milwaukee School of Engineering [*Wisconsin*]
MSE .... Minus Sense (SAA)
MSE .... Missile Support Element (AABC)
MSE .... Missile Support Equipment
MSE .... Mission Staff Engineer (MCD)
MSE .... Mission Support Element (MCD)
MSE .... Mississippi Export Railroad Co. [*AAR code*]
MSE .... Mobile Subscriber Equipment [*Military*]
MSE .... Modern Ship Equivalent
MSE .... Montana Society of Engineers (EARSL)
MSE .... Montreal Stock Exchange (CDAI)
MSE .... Moose
MSE .... Morgan Stan Fin 8.40% Cp Uts [*NYSE symbol*] (TTSB)
MSE .... Morgan Stanley Finance PLC Capital Unit [*NYSE symbol*] (SAG)
MSE .... M-scan Echocardiogram [*Medicine*] (EDAA)
MSE .... Multiple Sample Exchanger (SAUS)
MSE .... Multiple Simultaneous Engagement (MCD)
MSE .... Multi-Position Small Engine [*Automotive engineering*]
MSE .... Muscle-Specific Enhancer [*Genetics*]
MSE .... Muscle-Specific Enolase [*Medicine*] (DMAA)
MSE .... Muscle Strengthening Exercise (MELL)
MSEA........ Maine State Employees Association (EARSL)
MSEA........ M & S [*Modeling and Simulation*] Executive Agent [*Army*]
M Se A...... Master of Secretarial Arts
MSEA........ Medical Society Executives Association [*Later, AAMSE*] (EA)
MSEA........ Metropolitan Bancorp [*NASDAQ symbol*] (TTSB)
MSEA........ Metropolitan Bancorp Seattle [*NASDAQ symbol*] (SAG)
MSEA........ Michigan State Employees Association (EARSL)
MSEC........ Maintenance Support Equipment Center
MSEC........ Master of Science in the Economic Aspects of Chemistry
MSEC........ Master Separation Events Controller (MCD)
MSEC........ Materials Science and Engineering Commission [*British*]
MSEC........ Message Security (ACAE)
MSEC........ Michelin Stress Equilibrium Casing [*Tire design*]
MSEC........ Millisecond (GOBB)
msec .... Millisecond
MSEC........ Motorsports Engineering Conference
MSEC........ Mountain States Employers Council (EARSL)
MSECE ...... Master of Science in Electrical and Computer Engineering (PGP)
MS Eco...... Master of Science in Economics (PGP)
MS Econ .... Master of Science in Economics (PGP)
MSecSchSci... Master of Secondary School Science (GAGS)
MsecSP ..... Managed Security Service Provider
MS Ed .... Master of Sanitary Education
MSEd........ Master of Science Education (GAGS)
MS Ed .... Master of Science in Education
MSED........ Minimum Signal Element Duration [*Telecommunications*] (TEL)
MSED........ Ministry of State for Economic Development [*Canada*]
MSED........ Mobile Source Enforcement Division [*Environmental Protection Agency*]
MS EdU ..... Master of Science in Education (PGP)
MSEE........ Major Source Enforcement Effort [*Environmental Protection Agency*] (GFGA)
MSEE........ Master of Science in Electrical Engineering
MSEE........ Master of Science in Environmental Engineering (GAGS)
MSEE........ Mean Square Error Efficiency [*Statistics*]
MSE (Elec)... Master of Science in Engineering - Electrical
MSEF........ Missile System Evaluation Flight (MUGU)
MSEG........ Medical Service Group [*Military*]
MSEG........ Memory-Segment [*Computer science*]
MSEG........ Missile Systems Evaluation Group (CINC)
MSEH........ Master of Science in Environmental Health (PGP)
MSEI......... Mean Square Error Inefficiency [*Statistics*]
MSEIS....... Microgravity Systems Engineering Information System (SAUS)
MSEL........ Lord Selkirk Regional School, Selkirk, Manitoba [*Library symbol*] [*National Library of Canada*] (NLC)
MSEL........ Master of Science and English Literature
MSEL........ Master of Science in Environmental Law (PGP)
MSEL........ Master Scenario Events List (MCD)
MSEL........ Master Sequence of Events List [*Emergency Management*] (EMA)
MSEL........ Merisel, Inc. [*NASDAQ symbol*] (SPSG)
MSEL........ Mullen Scales of Early Learning [*Child development test*] [*Psychology*]
MSEL........ Selkirk Community Library, Manitoba [*Library symbol*] [*National Library of Canada*] (NLC)
MS Elect E... Master of Science in Electrical Engineering
MSEM .... Mainstreamed Special Educator Model (EDAC)
MSEM .... Master of Science in Engineering and Mining (GAGS)
MSEM .... Master of Science in Engineering Management (PGP)
MSEM .... Master of Science in Engineering Mechanics
MSEM .... Master of Science in Engineering of Mines (PGP)
MSEM .... Master of Science in Environmental Management (PGP)
MSEM .... Metrology Specific Equipment Model (AAEL)
MSEM .... Mission Status and Evaluation Module
MS EMD .... Morgan Stanley Emerging Markets Debt Fund, Inc. [*Associated Press*] (SAG)
MSEMech... Master of Science in Engineering Mechanics (GAGS)
MSEMgt.... Master of Science in Engineering Management (GAGS)
MSEMH ..... Selkirk Mental Health Centre, Manitoba [*Library symbol*] [*National Library of Canada*] (NLC)
MS/EMI ..... Mission Sequence/Electromagnetic Interference

MSEMPR.... Missile Support Equipment Manufacturers Planning Reports (MCD)
MSEN........ Media Status Event Notification (MWOL)
MS En E.... Master of Science in Environmental Engineering (PGP)
MS Eng..... Master of Sanitary Engineering
MS Eng..... Master of Science in Engineering
MS Engr.... Master of Science in Engineering (PGP)
MS Engr Sci... Master of Science in Engineering Science (PGP)
MS Ent...... Master of Science in Entomology
MS Env E... Master of Science in Environmental Engineering (PGP)
MSEnvrE.... Master of Science in Environmental Engineering (GAGS)
MSEO........ Marine Services Engineer Officer [*Navy*] [*British*]
MSEP........ Maintenance Standardization Evaluation Program [*Air Force*] (AFM)
MSEP........ Mean Square Error of Prediction [*Statistics*] (PDAA)
MSEP........ Mercury Scientific Experiment Panel
MSEP........ Military Standard Evaluation Program
MSEPN...... School of Psychiatric Nursing, Selkirk, Manitoba [*Library symbol*] [*National Library of Canada*] (NLC)
MSEPS...... Modular Space Electrical Power Station
M/SEQ....... Master Sequencer
MSER........ Management System Evaluation Review (NG)
MSER........ Master of Science in Energy Resources (GAGS)
MSER........ Mean Systolic Ejection Rate [*Cardiology*]
MSER........ Mental Status Examination Report (DIPS)
MSER........ Multiple Stores Ejection Rack [*For munitions*] (MCD)
MSERD...... Ministry of State for Economic and Regional Development [*Canada*]
MSERT...... Member of the Society of Electronic and Radio Technicians [*British*] (DBQ)
MSES........ Marine Scientific Equipment Service [*British*]
MSES........ Master of Science in Engineering Science (PGP)
MSES........ Master of Science in Environmental Studies (PGP)
MSES........ Medical School Environmental Stress
MSES........ Medical Service Squadron [*Military*]
MSES........ Mobile Status Entry System
M Se Sc.... Master of Secretarial Science
MSESM..... Master of Science in Engineering Science and Mechanics (PGP)
MSESS...... Master of Science in Exercise and Sport Studies (GAGS)
M Se St..... Master of Secretarial Studies
MSET........ Maintenance Standardization and Evaluation Team (MCD)
MSET........ Multistage Exercise Test [*Medicine*] (CPH)
MSETM...... Master of Science in Environmental Technology Management (PGP)
MSE TPN... Mobile Subscriber Equipment Tactical Packet Network [*Computer science*] [*Military*] (RDA)
MSEUE...... Mouvement Socialiste pour les Etats Unis d'Europe
MSEuro..... Morgan Stanley European Emerging Markets Ltd. [*Associated Press*] (SAG)
MSEVM..... Master of Science in Environmental Management (PGP)
MSEW....... Medical Service Wing [*Military*]
MSEX........ Middlesex Water [*NASDAQ symbol*] (TTSB)
MSEX........ Middlesex Water Co. [*NASDAQ symbol*] (NQ)
MS Exp Surg... Master of Science in Experimental Surgery (PGP)
MSF......... Congregatio Missionariorum a Sancta Familia [*Congregation of the Missionaries of the Holy Family*] [*Roman Catholic men's religious order*]
MSF......... Construction Education Foundation [*Formerly, Merit Shop Foundation*] (EA)
MSF......... Macrophage Spreading Factor [*Hematology*]
MSF......... Magnetic Silencing Facility [*Kingsburg, GA*] (DWSG)
MSF......... Maintenance Source File (MCD)
MSF......... Manned Space Flight [*NASA*] (KSC)
MSF......... Manufacturing, Science, and Finance Union [*British*] (WA)
MSF......... Mark Sense Form (MCD)
MSF......... Mass Storage Facility [*Computer science*] (IBMDP)
MSF......... Master of Science in Finance
MSF......... Master of the Science of Forestry
MSF......... Master Source File [*Computer science*] (BUR)
MSF......... Matched Spatial Filter [*Optics*]
MSF......... Maximum Shear Force
MSF......... Max Sea Food SA de CV [*El Salvador*] [*ICAO designator*] (FAAC)
MSF......... Measurement Summarization Function [*Open Systems Interconnection*] (ODAA)
MSF......... Medecins sans Frontieres [*Doctors without Borders - DWB*] [*France*] (EAIO)
MSF......... Medium Standard Frequency (DEN)
MSF......... Member of the Society of Floristry [*British*] (DI)
MSF......... Merit Shop Foundation [*Washington, DC*] (EA)
MSF......... Metal Space-Frame (MCD)
MSF......... MetaScience Foundation (EA)
MSF......... Metastasis-Stimulating Factor [*Immunosuppressant*]
MSF......... Methanesulfonyl Fluoride [*Organic chemistry*]
MSF......... Migration Stimulating Factor [*Cytology*]
MSF......... Militarily Significant Fallout (SAUS)
MSF......... Military Support Fund (MCD)
MSF......... Mind Science Foundation (EA)
MSF......... Minesweeper, Fleet [*Steel hull*] [*Navy symbol*]
MSF......... Minimum Sustaining Field [*Atomic reactor*]
MSF......... Missionary Sisters of the Holy Family (TOCD)
MSF......... Mission Simulator Facility
MSF......... Mobile Striking Force [*Military*]
MSF......... Mobility Support Forces [*Military*]
MSF......... Moisture Seekers Foundation [*Later, Sjogren's Syndrome Foundation - SSF*] (EA)
MSF......... Month-Second-Foot [*Measurement*]
MSF......... Morale Support Funds (MCD)
MSF......... Morgan Stanley Emerging Market [*NYSE symbol*] (SPSG)
MSF......... Moroccan Sea Frontier [*Navy*] [*World War II*]
MSF......... Motorcycle Safety Foundation (EA)
MSF......... Mott Scattering Formula [*Physics*]
MSF......... Multiaxial Stress Field
MSF......... Multi-Sensor Fusion (ACAE)
MSF......... Multiservice Switching Forum [*Association*] (EA)
MSF......... Multi-Stage Filter [*Automotive engineering*]
MSF......... Multistage Flash [*Desalination method*]
MSF......... Muscle Shock Factor
MsFa........ Jefferson County Library, Fayette, MS [*Library symbol*] [*Library of Congress*] (LCLS)
MSFA........ Massachusetts State Firemen's Association (EARSL)
MSFA........ Michigan State Firemen's Association (EARSL)
MSFA........ Mid-States Football Association (PSS)
MSFAM...... Master of Science in Family Studies (PGP)
MSFB........ Multi-Solids Fluidized Bed [*Chemical engineering*]
MSFC........ George C. Marshall Space Flight Center (SAUS)
MSFC........ Mark Slade Fan Club (EA)
MSFC........ Marshall Space Flight Center [*Also known as GCMSC*] [*NASA*]
MSFC........ McCarver Sisters Fan Club (EA)
MSFC........ Medical Students for Choice
MSFC........ Mid-South Football Conference (PSS)
MSFC........ Mobile Strike Force Command [*Military*] (VNW)
MSFC........ Morale Support Fund Council [*Military*] (AABC)
MSFC........ Mutual Society of the French Community (EA)
MSFCV...... Main Stream Flow Control Valve [*Nuclear energy*] (NUCP)
MSFD........ Millimeter Wave Seeker Feasibility Demonstration
MSFDC...... Microsoft and First Data Corp.
MSFDPS.... Manned Space Flight Data Processing System [*NASA*]
MSFE........ Mechanisms of Soil Formation and Evolution (SAUS)
MSFEB...... Manned Space Flight Experiments Board [*NASA*] (KSC)
MSFET...... Metal-on-Silicon Field-Effect Transistor [*Electronics*] (IAA)
MSFET...... Metal Schottky Gate Field Effect Transistor [*Electronics*] (IAA)
MSFF........ Master Slave Flipflop [*Nuclear energy*] (IAA)
MSFF........ Miles Since First Fail (HAWK)
MSFF........ Miles Since First Failure [*Automotive engineering*]
MSFH........ Manned Space Flight Headquarters [*NASA*]
MSFHA...... Morgan Single-Footing Horse Foundation [*Association*] (EA)
MSFI......... MS Financial [*NASDAQ symbol*] (TTSB)
MSFI......... MS Financial Corp. [*NASDAQ symbol*] (SAG)
MS Fin...... Morgan Stanley Finance PLC Capital Unit [*Associated Press*] (SAG)
MSFIS....... Microsoft Fax Information Service (SAUS)
MSFL........ Main Station Field Laboratories [*University of Nevada, Reno*] (RCD)
MSFL........ Manned Space Flight Laboratory [*NASA*] (IAA)
MSFLS...... Microwave Scanning Beam Landing System (SAUS)
MSFLS...... Microwave Scanning Beam Land Station (SAUS)
MSFLV....... Manned Space Flight and Launch Vehicles [*Panel*]
MSFM....... Master of Financial Management (PGP)
MSFM....... Master of Science in Forest Management
MSFN........ Manned Space Flight Network [*NASA*]
MSFn........ Morgan Stanley Finance PLC Capital Unit [*Associated Press*] (SAG)
MS Fncl..... MS Financial, Inc. [*Associated Press*] (SAG)
MSFNOC.... Manned Space Flight Network Operations Center [*NASA*] (KSC)
MSFO........ Manned Space Flight Operations [*NASA*] (KSC)
MSFOR...... Master of Science in Forestry (PGP)
MS For...... Master of Science in Forestry
MSFP........ Manned Space Flight Program [*NASA*] (KSC)
MSFP........ Migrant and Seasonal Farmworkers Program [*Title III*] (OICC)
MSFP........ Mosaic-Staring Focal Plane (SAUS)
MSFRSP.... Male Sterile-Facilitated Recurrent Selection Population [*Plant breeding*]
MSFS........ Main Steam and Feed Water System (IEEE)
MSFS........ Manned Space Flight Subcommittee [*NASA*] (AAG)
MSFS........ Manned Space Flight System [*NASA*] (IAA)
MSFS........ Master of Science in Family Studies (PGP)
MSFS........ Master of Science in Financial Services (PGP)
MSFS........ Master of Science in Foreign Service (GAGS)
MSFS........ Master of Science in Forensic Science (GAGS)
MSFS........ Missionaries of St. Francis of Sales [*Roman Catholic religious order*]
MSFSA...... American School Food Service Association - Mideast Regional Chapter (EARSL)
MSFSG...... Manned Space Flight Support Group (MCD)
MSFSRD.... Manned Space Flight Support Requirements Documentation [*NASA*]
MSFT........ Microsoft [*Company symbol*]
MSFT........ Microsoft Corp. [*NASDAQ symbol*] (NQ)
MSFT P..... Microsoft Corp. [*NASDAQ symbol*]
MSFU........ Merchant Service Fighter Unit [*Air Force*] [*British*]
MSFVW..... Magnetostatic Forward Volume Wave [*Telecommunications*] (TEL)
MSFW....... Migrant and Seasonal Farmworkers
MSFX........ Master Fixture
MSG......... [*The*] Imperial Merchant Service Guild [*British*]
MSG......... Madison Square Garden [*New York, NY*] (NADA)
MSG......... Madison Square Garden Network [*Cable-television system*]
MSG......... Maintenance Steering Group (MCD)
MSG......... Management Steering Group (AAEL)
MSG......... Manufacturers Standard Gauge
MSG......... Mapper Sweep Generator
MSG......... Mapping Supervisor Gap Filler (SAA)
MSG......... Marine Security Guard
MSG......... Maritime Studies Group [*Military*] (VNW)
MSG......... Mascot Gold Mines Ltd. [*Toronto Stock Exchange symbol*] [*Vancouver Stock Exchange symbol*]
MSG......... Massage (DAVI)
MSG......... Master of Science in Gerontology (GAGS)
MSG......... Master Sergeant [*Army*] (AABC)

MSG .... Maximum Stable Gain (IAA)
MSG .... Mechanical Subsystem Group [*NASA*] (NASA)
MSG .... Message (AFM)
msg .... Message (IDOE)
MSG .... Message Switch [*Communications term*] (DCT)
MSG .... Methysergide [*A serotonin antagonist*] [*Pharmacology*] (DAVI)
MSG .... Microcephaly Support Group [*British*] (NRGU)
MSG .... Microcomputer Support Group
MSG .... Microwave Signal Generator
MSG .... Miners' Support Group (WDAA)
MSG .... Miniature Sub-machine Gun [*Police and security equipment*]
MSG .... Ministry of Solicitor General [*Canada*]
MSG .... Ministry of the Solicitor General Library [*UTLAS symbol*]
MSG .... Miscellaneous Simulation Generator
MSG .... Missile Systems Group [*of General Motors Corp.*]
MSG .... Missing [*Telegraphy*] (PCTE)
MSG .... Missing [*Military*]
MSG .... Mission Support Groups (MCD)
MSG .... Missouri State Guard [*Civil War term*]
MSG .... Mobile Support Group [*Military*] (NVT)
MSG .... Modular Steam Generator (NRCH)
MSG .... Modulation Signal Generator (NITA)
MSG .... Moessingen [*Federal Republic of Germany*] [*Seismograph station code, US Geological Survey*] (SEIS)
MSG .... Monosodium Glutamate [*Food additive*] [*Pharmacology*]
MSG .... Mycoses Study Group [*Medicine*] (HVTR)
MsG .... William Alexander Percy Memorial Library, Greenville, MS [*Library symbol*] [*Library of Congress*] (LCLS)
MSGA .... Master Gauge
MSGA .... Merchant Service Guild of Australia
MSGA .... Montana Stockgrowers Association (EARSL)
MSGB .... Manorial Society of Great Britain (EAIO)
MSGB .... Muslim Society in Great Britain
MSGBI ...... Mineralogical Society of Great Britain and Ireland (EAIO)
MSGC .... Maine Space Grant Consortium (RCD)
MSGC .... Maryland Space Grant Consortium (RCD)
MSGC .... Massachusetts Space Grant Consortium (RCD)
MSGC .... Master of Science in Genetic Counseling (PGP)
MSGC .... Michigan Space Grant Consortium (RCD)
MSGC .... Missouri Space Grant Consortium (RCD)
MSGC .... Multinucleated Stromal Giant Cell
MSGCEN .... Message Center
MSGCTR .... Message Center [*Aviation*] (FAAC)
MSGDPU .... Message-Drop and Pick-Up [*Military*] (IAA)
MSGE .... Master of Science in Geological Engineering (NADA)
MS Geo E ... Master of Science in Geological Engineering (PGP)
MSGeolE .... Master of Science in Geological Engineering [*Education*] (FOTI)
MSGFLG .... Message Flag [*Computer science*] (MHDI)
MSGFM ..... Message Form (MUGU)
MS-GFW .... Memory for Sequence Subtest of the Goldman-Fristoe-Woodcock Auditory Skills TestBattery (EDAC)
MSGG .... Message Generator (MSA)
MSGI .... Marketing Services Group
MSGID ...... Message Identifier
MSGL .... Multi-Salvo Grenade Launcher (SAUS)
MSGL .... Multishot Grenade Launcher (RDA)
MSGL .... Thousand Square Feet of Single Glueline (WPI)
MSGlobl .... Morgan Stanley Global Opportunities Bond Fund, Inc. [*Associated Press*] (SAG)
MSGM .... Master of Science in Government Management
MSG Mgt ... Master of Science in Game Management
MSGO .... Mediterranean Secret General Orders
MSGO .... Miskimins Self-Goal-Other Discrepancy Scale [*Psychology*] (DHP)
MsGoH ...... Holmes Junior College, Goodman, MS [*Library symbol*] [*Library of Congress*] (LCLS)
MSGP .... Mobile Support Group [*Military*]
MSGQ .... Marin Storage and Trucking [*Common carrier symbol*]
MSGR .... Messenger (AFM)
MSGR .... Mobile Support Group [*Military*]
MSGR .... Monseigneur
Msgr .... Monsignor (SHCU)
MSGR .... Monsignor
MsGren ..... Grenada County Library, Grenada, MS [*Library symbol*] [*Library of Congress*] (LCLS)
M Sgt .... Master Sergeant (NTIO)
MSGT .... Master Sergeant
MsGu .... Gulfport-Carnegie-Harrison County Library, Gulfport, MS [*Library symbol*] [*Library of Congress*] (LCLS)
MSGV .... Mouse Salivary Gland Virus [*Medicine*] (DMAA)
MsGW .... Washington County Library System, Greenville, MS [*Library symbol*] [*Library of Congress*] (LCLS)
MSGWA ..... Military and Sporting Gun Workers' Association [*A union*] [*British*]
MsGwL ...... Greenwood-Leflore Public Library, Greenwood, MS [*Library symbol*] [*Library of Congress*] (LCLS)
MSG/WTG ... Message Waiting (MDG)
MSh .... Ma'aser Sheni (BJA)
MSH .... Magnetoelastic Static Hysteresis (MCD)
MSH .... Management Sciences for Health
MSH .... Mashhad [*Iran*] [*Seismograph station code, US Geological Survey*] [*Closed*] (SEIS)
MSH .... Masikoro Maalgasy [*Language symbol*] (ETLW)
MSH .... Master of Science in Horticulture (NADA)
MSH .... Master of Science in Hospice (PGP)
MSH .... Master of Science in Hygiene (NADA)
MSH .... Master of Staghounds
MSH .... Mauler Seeker Head
MSH .... Medical Self-Help [*Defunct*]
MSH .... Melanocyte-Stimulating Hormone [*Also, MH*] [*Endocrinology*]
MSH .... Melanophore-Stimulating Hormone [*Endocrinology*] (AAMN)
MSH .... Men of the Sacred Hearts (EA)
MSH .... Metastable Helium (MCD)
MSH .... Metropolitan Cooperative Library System, Pasadena, CA [*OCLC symbol*] (OCLC)
MSH .... Minesweeper Hunter Vessel
MSH .... Mishibishu Resources [*Vancouver Stock Exchange symbol*]
MSH .... Missionaries of the Sacred Heart [*Roman Catholic men's religious order*]
Ms-H .... Mississippi State Board of Health, Jackson, MS [*Library symbol*] [*Library of Congress*] (LCLS)
MSH .... Mont Saint-Hilaire
MSH .... Mount St. Helens [*Washington*] [*Geology*]
MSH .... US Marshal Service [*Department of Justice*] [*ICAO designator*] (FAAC)
MsHa .... Hattiesburg Public Library, Hattiesburg, MS [*Library symbol*] [*Library of Congress*] (LCLS)
MSHA ...... Mannose-Sensitive Hemagglutination [*Medicine*] (DMAA)
MSHA ...... Master of Science in Health Administration (PGP)
MSHA ...... Master of Science in Hospital Administration
MSHA ...... Michigan Speech-Language-Hearing Association (EARSL)
MSHA ...... Mine Safety and Health Administration [*Department of Labor*]
MSHA ...... Minnesota Speech-Language-Hearing Association (EARSL)
MSha .... Sharon Public Library, Sharon, MA [*Library symbol*] [*Library of Congress*] (LCLS)
MSHAA ..... Member of the Society of Hearing Aid Audiologists [*British*] (DBQ)
MSHAA ..... Morocco Spotted Horse Association of America [*Defunct*] (EA)
MShaK ..... Kendall Whaling Museum, Sharon, MA [*Library symbol*] [*Library of Congress*] (LCLS)
MSH & Ph Ed ... Master of Science in Health and Physical Education
MsHaP ..... [*The*] Library-Hattisburg, Petal Forrest County, Hattiesburg, MS [*Library symbol*] [*Library of Congress*] (LCLS)
MsHaU ..... University of Southern Mississippi, Hattiesburg, MS [*Library symbol*] [*Library of Congress*] (LCLS)
MsHaW ..... William Carey College, Hattiesburg, MS [*Library symbol*] [*Library of Congress*] (LCLS)
MSHB ...... Minimum Safe Height of Burst [*Military*]
MSHCS ..... Master of Science in Human and Consumer Science (PGP)
MsHe .... First Regional Library, Hernando, MS [*Library symbol*] [*Library of Congress*] (LCLS)
MSHE .... Master of Science in Home Economics
MSHE .... Master of Science in Hydraulic Engineering
MSH Ec .... Master of Science in Home Economics
MSH Ed .... Master of Science in Health Education (PGP)
MSHES ..... Master of Science in Human Environmental Sciences (PGP)
MSHF2 ..... Matrix Switch Host Facility 2 [*Communications term*] (DCT)
MSHG ...... Meshing
MSHI .... Medium Scale Hybrid Integration [*Computer science*] (IAA)
MSH-IF ..... Melanocyte-Stimulating Hormone-Inhibiting Factor [*Endocrinology*] (MAE)
MSH-IF ..... Melanophore-Stimulating Hormone [*Intermedin*] Inhibiting Factor [*Laboratory science*] (DAVI)
MSHJ .... Medical Staff Hospital Joint Venture
MSHK ...... Megadata Corp. (MHDW)
MSHK ...... Morgan Stanley Group, Inc. [*Associated Press*] (SAG)
Mshl .... Marshal (BARN)
MShM ...... Mount Holyoke College, South Hadley, MA [*Library symbol*] [*Library of Congress*] (LCLS)
MS Hort .... Master of Science in Horticulture
MsHos ...... Marshall County Library, Holly Springs, MS [*Library symbol*] [*Library of Congress*] (LCLS)
MsHosR .... Rust College, Holly Springs, MS [*Library symbol*] [*Library of Congress*] (LCLS)
MsHou ..... Houston Carnegie Public Library, Houston, MS [*Library symbol*] [*Library of Congress*] (LCLS)
Mshp .... Machine Shop (MHDB)
MSHP ...... Maintain System History Program [*IBM Corp.*]
MSHP ...... Master of Science in Health Professions (PGP)
MSHP ...... Missionary Sisters of the Holy Family (Poland) (TOCD)
MSHR ...... Master of Science in Human Resources (PGP)
MSHR ...... Melanocyte Stimulating Hormone Receptor [*Medicine*] (DMAA)
MSHR ...... Miniature Secure Hand-held Radio [*Police and security equipment*]
MSHR ...... Missionary Sisters of Our Lady of the Holy Rosary [*Blackrock, County Dublin, Republic of Ireland*] (EAIO)
MSHRF ..... Melanocyte-Stimulating Hormone Releasing Factor (DB)
MSHRH ..... Melanocyte-Stimulating-Hormone Regulating Hormone (QSUL)
MSHRM .... Master of Science in Human Resources Management (PGP)
MSHS ...... Master of Science in Health and Safety (GAGS)
MSHS ...... Master of Science in Health Science (PGP)
MSHS ...... Master of Science in Health Systems (GAGS)
MSHS ...... Medical Sciences History Society [*British*] (DBA)
MSHS ...... Michigan State Horticultural Society (EARSL)
MSHSA ..... Master of Science in Human Service Administration (PGP)
MSHSE ..... Master of Science in Health Science Education (PGP)
mshsks ..... Mesh Sacks
MSHU ...... Malaysian Shipping Sentirian [*Intermodal shipping container symbol*] (TVRC)
MS-HUG .... Microsoft Healthcare Users Group [*Association*] (EA)
MSHy ...... Master of Science in Hygiene (DAVI)
MS Hyg .... Master of Science in Hygiene
MsHz .... Copiah-Jefferson Regional Library, Hazelhurst, MS [*Library symbol*] [*Library of Congress*] (LCLS)
MSI .... Magnetic Source Imaging [*Neuroscience*]

msi .... Maintenance Significant Item (NAKS)
MSI .... Maintenance Significant Items (NASA)
MSI .... Maintenance Supply Item
MSI .... Maintenance Support Index
MSI .... ManagedStorage International Inc
MSI .... Management Style Inventory [*Test*] (TMMY)
MSI .... Management Systems Italia (EFIS)
MSI .... Manned Satellite Inspector
MSI .... Man System Integration (IAA)
MSI .... Manufacturing Standing Instructions (ACAE)
MSI .... Manufacturing Support Item
MSI .... Marine Science Institute [*University of California, Santa Barbara*] [*Research center*] (RCD)
MSI .... Marine Science Institute [*Philippines*]
MSI .... Marine Specialty Inc. (SAUS)
MSI .... Marital Satisfaction Inventory [*Psychology*]
MSI .... Marketing Science Institute [*Cambridge, MA*] (EA)
MSI .... Master of Science in Instruction (PGP)
MSI .... Master of Science in Insurance
MSI .... Mathematical Sciences Institute [*Cornell University*] [*Research center*] (RCD)
MSI .... Mattoon Services [*Federal Railroad Administration identification code*]
MSI .... Maximum Speed Indicator
MSI .... Maxwell Scientific International [*Inc.*]
MSI .... Mean Spleen Index
MSI .... Medical Seminars International (EA)
MSI .... Medium Scale Integrated [*Communications term*] (DCT)
msi .... Medium Scale Integration (NAKS)
MSI .... Medium-Scale Integration [*Circuit packaging*]
MSI .... Megapounds per Square Inch
MSI .... Member of the Chartered Surveyors Institution (ODA)
MSI .... Member of the Sanitary Institute [*British*] (ROG)
MSI .... Member of the Surveyors' Institution [*British*] (ROG)
MSI .... Mentoring Style Indicator [*Test*] (TMMY)
MSI .... Meritorious Service Increase (SAUS)
MSI .... Messina ING [*Istituto Nazionale Geodetico*] [*Sicily*] [*Seismograph station code, US Geological Survey*] (SEIS)
MSI .... Metal Support Interaction [*Catalysis*]
MSI .... Micorsoft Installer [*Computer science*]
MSI .... Microbiological Safety Index (DB)
MSI .... Micro-Star International (SAUS)
MSI .... Microwave Services International, Inc. [*Denville, NJ*] [*Telecommunications*] (TSSD)
MSI .... Middle-Scale Integration [*Computer science*] (IAA)
MSI .... Military Service Indicator (MCD)
MSI .... Military Standard Item (MCD)
MSI .... Military Static Inverter
MSI .... Mill Service, Inc. (EFIS)
MSI .... Minesweeper, Inshore [*Navy symbol*]
MSI .... Missile Status Indicator
MSI .... Missile Subsystem Integration (SAA)
MSI .... Mission Success Indicator (MCD)
MSI .... Moderate Scale Integration [*Electronics*]
MSI .... Molecular Sciences Institute
MSI .... Molecular Simulations (IID)
MSI .... Molecular Surface Ionization
MSI .... Money Store (EFIS)
MSI .... Moon Sphere of Influence (KSC)
MSI .... Moshi [*Tanzania*] [*Airport symbol*] (AD)
MSI .... Mother Symptom Inventory [*Psychology*]
MSI .... Motor Sich [*Ukraine*] [*FAA designator*] (FAAC)
MSI .... Motor Skills Inventory [*Sensorimotor skills test*]
MSI .... Movie Star, Inc. (SPSG)
MSI .... Movimento Sociale Italiano [*Italian Social Movement*] [*Political party*] (PPE)
MSI .... MSI Data Corp. [*AMEX symbol*] (COMM)
MSI .... M-System [*NCIC trailer make code*]
MSI .... Multicomm Sciences International, Inc. [*Denville, NJ*] (TSSD)
MSI .... Multiple Spark Igniter
MSI .... Multiple Subcutaneous Injections [*Medicine*] (MELL)
MSI .... Multiple Subcutaneous Insulin [*Medicine*]
MSI .... Multisensor Imagery
MSI .... Multi Sensor Integration (ACAE)
MSI .... Multispectral Imagery (DOMA)
MSI .... Multispectral Scan Imaging (ACAE)
MSI .... Multisystem Involvement [*Medicine*]
MSI .... Museum of Science and Industry [*Chicago, IL*]
MSI .... Museum Services Institute [*Department of Education*] (OICC)
MSI .... Mustang Software International [*California*] [*Bulletin board system*]
MSI .... Second Independence Movement [*Ecuador*] [*Political party*] (PPW)
MSIA .... Church of the Movement for Spiritual Inner Awareness (ECON)
MSIA .... Mass Spectrometric Immunoassay
MSIA .... Master of Institutional Administration (GAGS)
MSIA .... Master of Science in Industrial Administration
MSIA .... Master of Science in International Adminstration (PGP)
MSIA .... Master of Science in International Affairs (GAGS)
MSIA .... Member of the Society of Industrial Artists [*British*]
MSIA .... Michigan School Investment Association (EARSL)
MSIA .... Mississippi Crop Improvement Association (EARSL)
MSIA .... Multispectral Image Analyzer (ACAE)
MSIAD....... Member of the Society of Industrial Artists and Designers [*British*] (DBQ)
MSIB .... Master of Science in International Business (PGP)
MSIB .... Modular Systems Interface Bus (NITA)
MSIBK....... Master of Science in International Banking (PGP)
MsIbM....... Mississippi Valley State College, Itta Bena, MS [*Library symbol*] [*Library of Congress*] (LCLS)
MSIC .... Mid-South Independent Conference (PSS)
MSIC .... Missile and Space Intelligence Center [*DoD*]
MSIC .... Mixed-Signal Integrated Circuit [*Electronics*]
MSIC .... Mobile Subscriber Indentification Number (CGWS)
M-SID ...... Magnetic Sensing Intrusion Device [*Remote sensor*] [*Also, MAGNA-SID*] [*Military*] (VNW)
MSID .... Manufacturing Systems Integration Division [*National Institute of Standards and Technology*] (RCD)
MSID .... Mass Spectrometric Isotope Dilution
MSID .... Measurement Stimulation Identification (MCD)
MSID .... Medium-Scale Integration Device [*Circuit packaging*]
MSI-DN ..... Movimento Sociale Italiano-Destra Nazionale [*Italian Social Movement-National Right*] [*Political party*] (EY)
MSIE......... Master of Science in Industrial Engineering
MSIE......... Master of Science in International Economics (PGP)
MSIEOR..... Master of Science in Industrial Engineering and Operations Research (GAGS)
MSIF......... MSI Freight Forwarding [*Common carrier symbol*]
MSIF......... Multi-Systems Integration Facility (SSD)
MSIG .... Most Significant (IAA)
MSIG .... Multiple Spark-Ignition Gasket [*Automotive engineering*]
MSIGM...... Macintosh Special Interest Group of Mensa (EA)
MS IGT...... Morgan Stanley Group, Inc. [*Associated Press*] (SAG)
MSIGX....... Oppenheimer Main Street Inc. & Growth [*Mutual fund ticker symbol*] (SG)
MSII .... Medicine Shoppe International (EFIS)
MSIIP........ Missile System Installation Interrupted for Parts (NVT)
MS IIS....... Microsoft Internet Information Server (SAUS)
MSIL......... Master of Science in International Logistics (PGP)
MSIM........ Master of Science in Industrial Management
MSIM........ Master of Science in Information Management (GAGS)
MSIMC ...... Master of Science in Information Management and Communication (PGP)
MSIMD ...... Multiple Single Instruction, Multiple Data (MCD)
MsIn......... Henry M. Seymour Library, Indianola, MS [*Library symbol*] [*Library of Congress*] (LCLS)
MSIN .... Mail Stop Identification Number (ABAC)
MS in Aero E... Master of Science in Aeronautical Engineering
MS in Ag ... Master of Science in Agriculture
MS in Ag E... Master of Science in Agricultural Education
MS in Ag Ec... Master of Science in Agricultural Economics
MS in Agr... Master of Science in Agriculture
MS in Agr Ed... Master of Science in Agricultural Education
MS in AN ... Master of Science in Agricultural Engineering
MS in Aud & Sp... Master of Science in Audiology and Speech
MS in BA ... Master of Science in Business Administration
MS in Bl Sc... Master of Science in Biological Sciences
MS in C..... Master of Science in Commerce
MS in C & BA... Master of Science in Commercial and Business Administration
MS in CE ... Master of Science in Civil Engineering
MS in Cer... Master of Science in Ceramics
MS in Cer E... Master of Science in Ceramic Engineering
MS in Cer Tech... Master of Science in Ceramic Technology
MS in Ch ... Master of Science in Chemistry
MS in Ch E... Master of Science in Chemical Engineering
MS in Ch Eng... Master of Science in Chemical Engineering
MS in Con... Master of Science in Conservation
MS in CRP... Master of Science in City and Regional Planning
MS Ind E.... Master of Science in Industrial Engineering
MSIndEng... Master of Science in Industrial Engineering (NADA)
MS in Derm... Master of Science in Dermatology
MS India.... Morgan Stanley India Investment Fund [*Associated Press*] (SAG)
MS in Dt.... Master of Science in Dietetics
MS in E..... Master of Science in Education
MS in E..... Master of Science in Engineering
MS in Ed.... Master of Science in Education
MS in EE.... Master of Science in Electrical Engineering
MS in EM... Master of Science in Engineering Mechanics
MS in EM... Master of Science in Engineering of Mines
MS in E Mgt... Master of Science in Engineering Management
MS in EP ... Master of Science in Engineering Physics
MS in ES ... Master of Science in Engineering Science [*or Sciences*]
MS in For... Master of Science in Forestry
MS in GE ... Master of Science in General Engineering
MS in Gp Engr... Master of Science in Geophysical Engineering
MS in GSM... Master of Science in General Science and Mathematics
MS in HE ... Master of Science in Home Economics
MS in H Ec... Master of Science in Home Economics
MS in HR... Master of Science in Human Relations
MS in ID.... Master of Science in Industrial Design
MS in IE.... Master of Science in Industrial Engineering
MS in IM ... Master of Science in Industrial Management
MS in Ind Ed... Master of Science in Industrial Education
MS in LS ... Master of Science in Library Science
MS in ME... Master of Science in Mechanical Engineering
MS in Mech... Master of Science in Engineering Mechanics
MS in Med... Master of Science in Medicine
MS in Met... Master of Science in Metallurgy
MS in Met E... Master of Science in Metallurgical Engineering
MS in Mus... Master of Science in Music
MS in Mus Ed... Master of Science in Music Education

MS in N ..... Master of Science in Nursing
MS in NE ... Master of Science in Nursing Education
MS in N Ed... Master of Science in Nursing Education
MS in Nr Ed... Master of Science in Nursing Education
MS in NT ... Master of Science in Nuclear Technology
MS in Nucl E... Master of Science in Nuclear Engineering
MS in PA ... Master of Science in Public Administration
MS in PE ... Master of Science in Petroleum Engineering
MS in PE ... Master of Science in Physical Education
MS in P Ed... Master of Science in Physical Education
MS in Pet E... Master of Science in Petroleum Engineering
MS in PH ... Master of Science in Public Health
MS in Phar... Master of Science in Pharmacy
MS in Phy... Master of Science in Physics
MS in PRE... Master of Science in Petroleum Refining Engineering
MS in PSM... Master of Science in Public School Music
MS in Py Sc... Master of Science in Poultry Science
MS in Rad... Master of Science in Radiology
MS in Rec... Master of Science in Recreation
MS in Ret... Master of Science in Retailing
MS in Sp ... Master of Science in Speech
MS in SS ... Master of Science in Sanitary Science
MS in SS ... Master of Science in Social Service
MS in SW... Master of Science in Social Work
MS in T & I... Master of Science in Trade and Industrial Education
MS in Trans E... Master of Science in Transportation Engineering
MSINZ....... Member of the Surveyors' Institute of New Zealand
MSIO .... Mass Storage Input-Output [*Computer science*] (IEEE)
MSIO .... Medical Systems Integration Office [*Army*] (RDA)
MSIP .... Mechanical Stress Improvement Process [*Nuclear energy*] (NUCP)
MSIP .... Minority Science Improvement Program [*Department of Education*] (GFGA)
MSIP .... Modeling and Simulation Investment Plan [*Army*]
MSIP .... Monitoring and State Improvement Planning Division [*Office of Special Education and Rehabilitative Services*] (RCD)
MSIP .... Multinational Staged Improvement Program (MCD)
MSIP .... Multistage Improvement Program (DOMA)
MSIPC....... Master of Science in Information Processing and Communications (PGP)
MSIR .... Machine Survey and Installation Report
MSIR .... Master of Science in Industrial Relations (GAGS)
MSIR .... Master of Social and Industrial Relations
MSIR .... Master Stock Item Record
MSIS .... MacSiss Delivery [*Common carrier symbol*]
MSIS .... Main Steam Isolation Signal [*Nuclear energy*] (NRCH)
MSIS .... Manned Satellite Inspection System
MSIS .... Man-Systems Integration Standard (SSD)
MSIS .... Marine Safety Information System [*Coast Guard*] (MSC)
MSIS .... Mask Shop Information System [*Bell Laboratories*]
MSIS .... Mass Spectral Information System
MSIS .... Mass Spectrometer and Incoherent Scatter (SAUS)
MSIS .... Mass Spectrometer Incoherent Scatter (ACAE)
MSIS .... Master of Science in Computer-Based Information Systems
MSIS .... Master of Science in Information Science (GAGS)
MSIS .... Master of Science in Information Systems (PGP)
MSIS .... Master of Science in Interdisciplinary Studies (PGP)
MSIS .... Model State Information System [*Environmental Protection Agency*] (GFGA)
MSIS .... Multi-Sensor Integrated Surveillance (SAUS)
MSIS .... Multi-sensor Stabilised Integrated Sensor (SAUS)
MSIS .... Multisensor Stabilized Integrated System
MSIS .... Multistate Information System [*Patient records*]
MSISDN...... Mobile Station Integrated Service Digital Network Number (CGWS)
MSISL....... Moore School Information Systems Laboratory
Ms IT........ Manuscript, Inner Temple [*A publication*] (DLA)
MSIT......... Master of Science in Industrial Technology (PGP)
MSIT......... Member of the Society of Instrument Technology [*British*]
MSIT......... Missile Subsystem Integration Technology (ACAE)
MSITTL...... Medium Scale Integration Transistor-Transistor Logic (CIST)
MSIU .... Modular Storage [*Intermodal shipping container symbol*] (TVRC)
MSIV .... Main Steam Isolation Valve [*Nuclear energy*] (NRCH)
MSIVLCS... Main Steam Isolation Valve Leakage Control System [*Nuclear energy*] (NRCH)
MS/IWS ..... Master of Science/Industry Work Study
MSIX .... Mining Services International Corp. [*NASDAQ symbol*] (NQ)
MSIX .... Mining Svcs Intl [*NASDAQ symbol*] (TTSB)
MSIX .... Morton International [*Private rail car owner code*]
MSIZ......... Matador Services [*Federal Railroad Administration identification code*]
MsJ .... Jackson Municipal Library, Jackson, MS [*Library symbol*] [*Library of Congress*] (LCLS)
MSJ.......... Machine Screw Jack
MSJ.......... Master of Science in Journalism
MSJ.......... Medical Sisters of St. Joseph (TOCD)
MSJ.......... Message [*Telegraphy*] (PCTE)
MSJ.......... Misawa [*Japan*] [*Airport symbol*] (OAG)
MSJ.......... Mission San Jose [*California*] [*Seismograph station code, US Geological Survey*] (SEIS)
MSJ.......... Multiple Subsonic Jet
MSJ96....... Morgan Stanley Group, Inc. [*Associated Press*] (SAG)
MSJA........ Master of Science in Judicial Administration (GAGS)
MsJB .... Belhaven College, Jackson, MS [*Library symbol*] [*Library of Congress*] (LCLS)
MSJBS ...... Master of Science in Japanese Business Studies (PGP)
MsJG .... Mississippi Bureau of Geology, Jackson, MS [*Library symbol*] [*Library of Congress*] (LCLS)
MsJMC...... Millsaps College, Jackson, MS [*Library symbol*] [*Library of Congress*] (LCLS)
MsJPED ..... Episcopal Diocese of Mississippi, Jackson, MS [*Library symbol*] [*Library of Congress*] (LCLS)
MSJPS ...... Master of Science in Justice and Public Safety (PGP)
MSJPS ...... Master of Science in Justice and Public Service (GAGS)
MSJR........ Messenger [*Telegraphy*] (PCTE)
MsJRD ...... Research and Development Center Library, Jackson, MS [*Library symbol*] [*Library of Congress*] (LCLS)
MsJRT....... Reformed Theological Seminary, Jackson, MS [*Library symbol*] [*Library of Congress*] (LCLS)
MsJS .... Jackson State College [*Later, Jackson State University*], Jackson, MS [*Library symbol*] [*Library of Congress*] (LCLS)
MSJS .... Master of Science in Jewish Studies (PGP)
MsJV .... United States Veterans Administration Hospital, Jackson, MS [*Library symbol*] [*Library of Congress*] (LCLS)
MsJW .... Wesley Biblical Seminary, Jackson, MS [*Library symbol*] [*Library of Congress*] (LCLS)
MSK .... Grupo Indl Maseca ADS [*NYSE symbol*] (TTSB)
MSK .... Grupo Industrial Maseca SA de CV [*NYSE symbol*] (SAG)
MSK .... Magyar Statisztikai Kozlemenyek [*Hungary*]
MSK .... Major Subcontractor
MSK .... Manual Select Keyboard [*Computer science*] (KSC)
MSK .... Mask [*Computer science*] (IAA)
MSK .... Master of Science in Kinesiology (GAGS)
MSK .... Mastic Point [*Andros Islands, Bahamas*] [*Airport symbol*] (AD)
MSK .... Medullary Sponge Kidney [*Anatomy*] (MAE)
MSK .... Medvedev, Sponheuer, Karnick [*Earthquake intensity scale*]
MSK .... Memorial Sloan-Kettering Cancer Center [*New York*] (AGLO)
MSK .... Mesick, MI [*Amtrak Busline code*]
MsK.......... Mid-Mississippi Regional Library, Kosciusko, MS [*Library symbol*] [*Library of Congress*] (LCLS)
MSK .... Minimal Shift Keying (NITA)
MSK .... Minimum Shift Keying
MSK .... Minimum Spares Kit (ACAE)
MSK .... Misaki [*Japan*] [*Seismograph station code, US Geological Survey*] [*Closed*] (SEIS)
MSK .... Mission Support Kit
MSK .... Mistake [*Telegraphy*] (PCTE)
MSK .... Mobility Support Kit
MSK .... Modern Standard Khmer [*Linguistics*] (IEL)
MSK .... Mostek Corporation (NITA)
MSK .... Musculoskeletal [*Orthopedics*] (DAVI)
MSKB........ Microsoft Knowledge Base [*Computer science*] (PCM)
MSKC........ Memorial Sloan-Kettering Cancer Center [*Research center*] (RCD)
MSKCC ...... Memorial Sloan-Kettering Cancer Center [*New York*]
MSKCH...... Memorial Sloan-Kettering Cancer Hospital [*Medicine*] (EDAA)
MSKCP...... Missionary Sisters of Christ the King of Polonia (TOCD)
MSKM....... Minimum Shift Keyed Modulation (NITA)
MSKN .... Mistaken [*Telegraphy*] (PCTE)
MSKP........ Management Skills - Knowledge Profile [*Business term*]
MSKP........ Medical Sciences Knowledge Profile (DAVI)
MSKX........ Milwaukee Solvay Coke [*Private rail car owner code*]
MsL.......... Laurel Library Association, Laurel, MS [*Library symbol*] [*Library of Congress*] (LCLS)
MSL .... Machine Specification Language
MSL .... Macromolecular Structure Laboratory [*National Cancer Institute*] (RCD)
MSL .... Magnetic Surfaces Laboratory
MSL .... Main Sea Level (AAG)
MSL .... Main Steam Line [*Nuclear energy*] (NRCH)
MSL .... Maintenance Supply Liaison [*Air Force*] (AFM)
MSL .... Major Soccer League (BARN)
MSL .... Management Selection Ltd.
MSL .... Management Systems Laboratories [*Virginia Polytechnic Institute and State University*] [*Research center*] (RCD)
MSL .... Manned Space Laboratory [*NASA*] (IAA)
MSL .... Manpower Source Listing (MCD)
MSL .... Marine Systems Laboratory [*Smithsonian Institution*]
MSL .... Master of Sacred Literature
MSL .... Master of Science in Language
MSL .... Master of Science in Librarianship (PGP)
MSL .... Master of Science in Limnology (PGP)
MSL .... Master of Science in Linguistics
MSL .... Master of Studies in Law (PGP)
MSL .... Master Save List [*Military*] (AFIT)
MSL .... Master Scheduling Letter
MSL .... Masterseal [*Record label*]
MSL .... Master Support List (MCD)
MSL .... Master Symbol List (SAUS)
MSL .... Materialien zum Sumerischen Lexikon. B. Landsberger. Patrologiae Cursus Completus. Series Latina [*A publication*] (BJA)
MSL .... Materials and Structures Laboratory [*Texas A & M University*] [*Research center*] (RCD)
MSL .... Materials Science Laboratory (TIMI)
MSL .... Maximum Service Life [*or Limit*] (AAG)
MSL .... Maximum Stillwater Level [*Nuclear energy*] (NRCH)
MSL .... Maximum Street Load (CTAS)
msl .... Mean Sea Level (PIAV)
MSL .... Mean Sea Level
MSL .... Measurement Standards Laboratory
MSL .... Measurement System Laboratory (MCD)
MSL .... Mechanical Systems Laboratory [*NASA*] (NASA)

MSL .... Medical Skills Library [*Medicine*] (EDAA)
MSL .... Medicine, Science and the Law [*Medicine*] [*BAFS*] [*Journal*] (EDAA)
MSL .... Message Switched Line (MCD)
MSL .... Meteorological Satellite Laboratory
MSL .... Methuen's Standard Library [*A publication*]
MSL .... Microcomputer Sales and Leasing, Inc.
MSL .... Microgravity Science Laboratory [*NASA*]
MSL .... Microstar Software Ltd. [*Nepean, ON*] [*Telecommunications*] (TSSD)
MSL .... Microwave Systems Laboratory (ACAE)
MSL .... Midsouth Bancorp, Inc. [*AMEX symbol*] (SAG)
MSL .... Midsternal Line
MSL .... Military Shipping Label
MSL .... Military Side Loader [*Air transport*] [*British*]
MSL .... Military Support List (MCD)
MSL .... Minesweeping Launch [*Navy ship symbol*]
MSL .... Minimum Size Limit [*Pisciculture*]
MSL .... Minneapolis & St. Louis [*Railroad*] (MHDB)
MSL .... Minnesota State Law Library, St. Paul, MN [*OCLC symbol*] (OCLC)
MSL .... Missile (AFM)
msl .... Missile (MILB)
MSL .... Missile Sea Level
MSL .... Missile Site Load (MCD)
MSL .... Modify System Logging (AAEL)
MSL .... Moisture Sensitivity Level (AGLO)
MSL .... Molecular Spectroscopy Laboratory [*Fisk University*] [*Research center*] (RCD)
MSL .... Mouvement des Sociaux-Liberaux [*Movement of Social Liberals*] [*France*] [*Political party*] (PPW)
MSL .... Multimedia Software Laboratory [*University of Wisconsin--Milwaukee*] (RCD)
MSL .... Multiple Stinger Launcher
MSL .... Multiple Symmetric Lipomatosis [*Medicine*] (DMAA)
MSL .... Municipal Savings & Loan Corp. [*Toronto Stock Exchange symbol*]
MSL .... Murphy-Sturm Lymphosarcoma [*Medicine*] (QSUL)
MSL .... Muscle Shoals [*Alabama*] [*Airport symbol*] (OAG)
MSL .... Myelomonocytic Subacute Leukemia [*Medicine*] (EDAA)
MSL .... Snow Lake Community Library, Manitoba [*Library symbol*] [*National Library of Canada*] (NLC)
MSlA .... Atlantic Union College, South Lancaster, MA [*Library symbol*] [*Library of Congress*] (LCLS)
MSLA .... Main Steam Line Accident [*Nuclear energy*] (NRCH)
MSLA .... Manitoba School Library Association
MSLA .... Master of Science in Legal Administration (PGP)
MSLA .... Missionary Sisters of Our Lady of the Angels [*Lennoxville, PQ*] (EAIO)
MSLA .... Mouse Specific Lymphocyte Antigen [*Immunology*]
MSLA .... Multisample Luer Adapter [*Medicine*] (MEDA)
MSLAET ..... Member of the Society of Licensed Aircraft Engineers and Technologists [*British*] (DBQ)
MsLb .... Long Beach Public Library, Long Beach, MS [*Library symbol*] [*Library of Congress*] (LCLS)
MSLB .... Main Steam Line Break [*Nuclear energy*] (NRCH)
MsLbU ...... University of Southern Mississippi, Gulf Park, Richard G. Cox Library, Long Beach, MS [*Library symbol*] [*Library of Congress*] (LCLS)
MSLC .... Master Synchronizer and Load Control [*Electrical generation*]
MSLC .... Minnesota Short Lines Co. [*AAR code*]
MSLC .... Missile Sites Labor Commission [*A federal government body*] [*Abolished 1967; functions transferred to Federal Mediation and Conciliation Service*]
MSLC .... Multi-Loop Sidelobe Cancellation (SAUS)
MSLCOMD ... Missile Command [*Army*]
MSLD .... Masland Corp. [*NASDAQ symbol*] (SAG)
MSLD .... Mass Spectrometer Leak Detector (NRCH)
MsLE .... Lauren Rogers Library and Museum of Art, Laurel, MS [*Library symbol*] [*Library of Congress*] (LCLS)
MSLEX ...... Missile Exercise (DOMA)
MSLF .... Miles Since Last Fail (HAWK)
MSLF .... Miles Since Last Failure [*Automotive engineering*]
MSLF .... Mountain States Legal Foundation (EA)
MSLFM ...... Massenet Society and Lovers of French Music [*Later, MSAB*] (EA)
MSLG .... Maintenance Support Logistics Group [*Military*] (CAAL)
Ms Ll .... Manuscript, Lincoln's Inn [*A publication*] (DLA)
MsLi .... Microfilm Services Ltd., Auckland, New Zealand [*Library symbol*] [*Library of Congress*] (LCLS)
MSLIR .... Master of Science in Labor and Industrial Relations
MS Litt ...... Master of Sacred Letters
MSLIVSS ... Main Steam Line Isolation Valve Sealings System [*Nuclear energy*] (NRCH)
MSLM .... Microchannel Spatial Light Modulator [*Electronics*]
MSLMAINTSq ... Missile Maintenance Squadron [*Air Force*]
MSLN .... Mari Sandoz Library Network [*Library network*]
MSLN .... Meridian Shipping Line [*Common carrier symbol*]
MSLO .... Master Layout
MSLO .... Medical Service Liaison Officer [*Air Force*]
MSLOUG .... Medium-Sized Libraries/OCLC [*Online Computer Library Center*] Users Group
MSLP .... Malawi Socialist Labour Party [*Political party*] (EY)
MSLP .... Master of Speech-Language Pathology (PGP)
MSLP .... Mean Sea Level Pressure (WEAT)
MSLP .... San Salvador/El Salvador Internacional [*El Salvador*] [*ICAO location identifier*] (ICLI)
MSLPr .... MidSouth Bancorp Sr'A'Cv Pfd [*AMEX symbol*] (TTSB)
MSLPU ...... Medium-Speed Line Processing Unit [*Communications term*] (DCT)
MSLQ .... Motivated Strategies for Learning Questionnaire [*Test*] (TMMY)
MSLR .... Mixed Skin Cell-Leukocyte Reaction [*Medicine*] (DMAA)
MSLS .... Maneuverable Satellite Landing System (MUGU)
MSLS .... Master of Science in Law and Society (DLA)
MSLS .... Master of Science in Library Science
MSLS .... Master of Science in Logistics Systems (PGP)
MSLS .... Missile Site Location System (MCD)
MSLS .... Modular Site Location System (ACAE)
MSLS .... Multi-Slice Least Squares [*Software for crystallography*]
MSLSc ...... Master of Science in Library Science
MSLT .... Military Solid Logic Technology (IAA)
MSLT .... Multiple Sleep Latency Test
MSLWARNINGSq ... Missile Warning Squadron [*Air Force*]
MSLY .... Mostly (MSA)
MSLZ .... Mississippi Lime [*Federal Railroad Administration identification code*]
MSM .... Maastricht School of Management [*Netherlands*]
MSM .... Major System Mode (CAAL)
MSM .... Managed Security Monitoring
MSM .... Manhattan School of Music
msm .... Manned Support Module [*NASA*] (NAKS)
MSM .... Manned Support Module [*NASA*] (NASA)
MSM .... Manufacturing Shop Manual (SAA)
MSM .... Manufacturing Standards Manual
MSM .... Marine Safety Manual [*Coast Guard*] [*A publication*] (DLA)
MSM .... Mars Surface Module (MCD)
MSM .... Mass Scatterable Mine (RDA)
MSM .... Master of Medical Science
MSM .... Master of Sacred Ministry (PGP)
MSM .... Master of Sacred Music
MSM .... Master of Science in Management
MSM .... Master of Science in Music
MSM .... Master of Service Management (PGP)
MSM .... Master Scheduling Manager
MSM .... Master Slave Manipulator [*Nuclear energy*]
MSM .... Mauritian Socialist Movement [*Political party*]
MSM .... Meal Semiconductor Metal (IAA)
MSM .... Mechanically Separated Meat [*Food technology*]
MSM .... Medium Minesweeper (NATG)
MSM .... Medium-Size Molecule [*Medicine*] (EDAA)
MSM .... Memory Seat Module
MSM .... Memory Storage Module
MSM .... Men Who Have Sex with Men [*Australia*] [*An association*]
MSM .... Mercury Specialist Management [*Commercial firm*] [*British*]
MsM .... Meridian Public Library, Meridian, MS [*Library symbol*] [*Library of Congress*] (LCLS)
MSM .... Meritorious Service Medal [*Military decoration*]
MSM .... Message Switching Multiplexing (RALS)
MSM .... Messman
MSM .... Metal-Semiconductor-Metal (IEEE)
MSM .... Methyl Sulfonylmethane [*Biochemistry*]
MSM .... Microsoft Systems Management (GART)
MSM .... Micro Surface Mapping [*Software package*] (NCC)
MSM .... Microwave Switch Matrix (LAIN)
MSM .... Mid-Systolic Murmur [*Medicine*] (MELL)
MSM .... Millimeter and Submillimeter Conference (MCD)
MSM .... Mineral Salts Medium [*Medicine*] (DMAA)
MSM .... Minesweeper, River [*Navy symbol*] [*Obsolete*]
MSM .... Missile Standards Manual [*Military*] (IAA)
MSM .... Mission Simulation Model
MSM .... Mission Support Manager (ACAE)
MSM .... Missouri School of Mines
MSM .... Modified Source Multiplication (NRCH)
MSM .... Montana School of Mines
MSM .... Morehouse School of Medicine [*Atlanta, GA*]
MSM .... Motorized Switching Matrix
MSM .... Motorsteuermonolith
MSM .... Mott's Super Markets, Inc. [*AMEX symbol*] (COMM)
MSM .... Mount St. Mary's College, Emmitsburg, MD [*OCLC symbol*] (OCLC)
MSM .... Mouvement Social Mohutu [*Mohutu Social Movement*]
MSM .... Mouvement Solidaire Muluba [*Muluba Solidarity Movement*] [*Political party*]
MSM .... MSC Industrial Direct'A' [*NYSE symbol*] (TTSB)
MSM .... MSC Industrial Direct Co. [*NYSE symbol*]
MSM .... Multi-Speed Module [*Automotive ignition systems*]
MSM .... Muscat Securities Market
MSM .... Mystic Seaport Museum (EA)
MSM .... Thousand Feet Surface Measure [*Lumber*]
MSMA .... Mail Systems Management Association [*New York, NY*] (EA)
MSMA .... Maine School Management Association (EARSL)
MSMA .... Major Symphony Managers Association (EA)
MSMA .... Margarine and Shortening Manufacturers Association (EAIO)
MSMA .... Master Sign Makers' Association (NADA)
MSMA .... Medical-Surgical Manufacturers Association [*Later, HIMA*]
MSMA .... Metal Sink Manufacturers Association [*British*] (DBA)
MSMA .... Meteorological Services to Marine Activities [*WMO*] (MSC)
MSMA .... Metropolitan Symphony Managers Association (EA)
MSMA .... Minnesota/Missouri State Medical Association [*Medicine*] (EDAA)
MSMA .... Monosodium Methyl Arsonate [*Herbicide*]
MSMA .... Monosodium Salt of Methylarsonic Acid [*Agriculture*]
MsMac ...... Noxubee County Library, Macon, MS [*Library symbol*] [*Library of Congress*] (LCLS)
MSMAE ..... Master of Science in Materials Engineering (PGP)
MSMAN ..... Master Sign Makers' Association [*British*] (BI)
MsMar ...... Quitman County Library, Marks, MS [*Library symbol*] [*Library of Congress*] (LCLS)

MSMAS ..... Master of Science in Media Arts and Sciences (PGP)
MS Mat ..... Master of Science in Materials Engineering (PGP)
MS Mat E... Master of Science in Materials Engineering (PGP)
MS Mat SE... Master of Science in Material Science and Engineering (PGP)
MSMatSE... Master of Science in Materials Science Engineering (GAGS)
MSMAV ..... Master Stone Masons' Association of Victoria [*Australia*]
MSMB .... Mortgage Secondary Market Board [*Australia*]
MSMC .... Master of Science in Marketing Communication (GAGS)
MSMC .... Master of Science in Mass Communication (GAGS)
MSMC .... Master Schedule and Milestone Chart (MCD)
MSMC .... Member of the Spectacle Makers Co. [*British*] (ROG)
MSMC .... Migrant Studies and Media Center [*Australia*]
MSMC .... Military Subsistence Market Center (MUGU)
MSMC .... Mount Sinai Medical Center [*Medicine*] [*New York, NY*] (EDAA)
MsMc........ Pike-Amite Library System, McComb, MS [*Library symbol*] [*Library of Congress*] (LCLS)
MSMCS ..... Master of Science in Management and Computer Science (PGP)
MSMD....... Madras Subordinate Medical Department [*British military*] (DMA)
MSMDA ..... Mutual Sewing Machine Dealers Association (EA)
MSME .... Master of Science in Mathematics Education (PGP)
MSME .... Master of Science in Mechanical Engineering
MSMEA ..... Multiwall Sack Manufacturers Employers Association [*British*] (DBA)
MS Mech E... Master of Science in Mechanical Engineering
MSMed...... Master of Medical Science (NADA)
MS Met E... Master of Science in Metallurgical Engineering
MS Metr .... Master of Science in Meteorology (PGP)
MSMF .... Maintenance Support Management File (MCD)
MSMFE...... Master of Science in Manufacturing Engineering (PGP)
MS Mfg E... Master of Science in Manufacturing Engineering (PGP)
MsMFM ..... Masonic Library, Meridian, MS [*Library symbol*] [*Library of Congress*] (LCLS)
MS Mf SE... Master of Science in Manufacturing Systems Engineering (PGP)
MSMG....... Missionary Sisters of the Mother of God [*Roman Catholic religious order*]
MSMgt ...... Master of Science in Management (GAGS)
MS Mgt E... Master of Science in Management Engineering
MSMI........ Master of Science in Medical Illustration (GAGS)
MSMIA ...... Medical and Sports Music Institute of America (EA)
MS Min ..... Master of Science in Mining (PGP)
MS Min E... Master of Science in Mining Engineering (PGP)
MSMIS ...... Master of Science in Management Information Systems (PGP)
MS/MIS ..... Master of Science/Management Information Systems
MSML .... Minesweeping Motorlaunch [*Navy*]
MSMLCS.... Mass Service Mainline Cable Systems
MSMM ...... Master of Science in Manufacturing Management (PGP)
MsMM....... Meridian Junior College, Meridian, MS [*Library symbol*] [*Library of Congress*] (LCLS)
MsMo .... Lawrence County Public Library, Monticello, MS [*Library symbol*] [*Library of Congress*] (LCLS)
MS Mot ..... Master of Science in Management of Technology (PGP)
MSMP....... Master Sensitized Material Print (MSA)
MSMP....... Modeling and Simulation Master Plan [*Army*]
MSMP....... Multispectral Measurements Program (MCD)
MSMPR ..... Mixed-Suspension, Mixed-Product Removal [*Crystallizer*] [*Chemical engineering*]
MSMQ....... Microsoft Message Queue Server [*Computer science*]
MSMR....... Madras and Southern Mahratta Railway [*Indian Railway*] (TIR)
MSMR....... Massachusetts Society for Medical Research (GVA)
MSMR....... Missouri School of Mines Reactor
MSMS....... Machine Strap Makers' Society [*A union*] [*British*]
MSMS....... Magnetic Signature Measurement System (SAUS)
MSMS....... Marine Safety Management System [*BTS*] (TAG)
MSMS....... Maritime Shipping Services [*Common carrier symbol*]
MSMS....... Master of Science in Management Science (PGP)
MSMS....... Master of Science in Medical Sciences (PGP)
MS/MS ...... Materials Science and Manufacturing in Space [*Program*] [*NASA*]
MSMS....... Max Steiner Memorial Society (EA)
MSMS....... Membership Section for Multihospital Systems [*Later, HCS*] (EA)
MSMS....... Meteorological Systems Management Section
MSMS....... Michigan State Medical Society (SAUS)
MSMS....... Microwave Self-Mixing Sensor (ACAE)
MSMS....... Mutual Security Military Sales
MS-MS...... Tandem Mass Spectroscopy
MSMSA ..... Master of Science in Management Systems Analysis (PGP)
MSMSE ..... Master of Science in Manufacturing Systems Engineering (PGP)
MSMSE ..... Master of Science in Material Science Engineering (PGP)
MSMSEd.... Master of Science in Mathematics and Science Education (GAGS)
MSMSP ..... Project Manager, Surface Missile Systems [*Navy*]
MsMStA..... Saint Aloysius Academy, Meridian, MS [*Library symbol*] [*Library of Congress*] (LCLS)
MS MT ...... Manuscript, Middle Temple [*A publication*] (DLA)
MSMT .... Master of Science in Medical Technology (GAGS)
MSMT .... Measurement (KSC)
MS Mt E .... Master of Science in Materials Engineering (PGP)
MSMTH ..... Metalsmith [*Navy*]
MsMU .... Mississippi State University, Meridian Branch, Meridian, MS [*Library symbol*] [*Library of Congress*] (LCLS)
MSMU....... Mobile Spectrum Monitoring Unit
MSMU....... Norpol Marine [*Intermodal shipping container symbol*] (TVRC)
MSMus...... Master of Science in Music (NADA)
MSMusEd... Master of Science in Music Education (NADA)
MSMV....... Monk Seal Morbillivirus
MSMV....... Monostable Multivibrator
MSMW ...... Magnetically Suspended Momentum Wheel
MSN .... Dane County Regional-Truax Field [*FAA*] (TAG)
MSN .... Emerson Radio Corp. [*AMEX symbol*] (SAG)
MSN .... Madison [*Wisconsin*] [*Airport symbol*] (OAG)
MSN .... Madison, WI [*Amtrak Busline code*]
MSN .... Main Sensory Nucleus [*Medicine*] (EDAA)
MSN .... Main-Stem Node [*Botany*]
MSN .... Maintenance and Support Network
MSN .... Manned Space Network [*NASA*] (MCD)
MSN .... Manufacturing Sequence Number (TIMI)
MSN .... Mason
MSN .... Master of Science in Nursing
MSN .... Master Serial Number (AAG)
MSN .... Material Supply Notice (AAG)
MSN .... Mechanical Serial Number [*Computer science*] (FOTI)
MSN .... Medial Septal Nucleus [*Medicine*] [*Brain*] (EDAA)
MSN .... Median Sample Number (PDAA)
MSN .... Medicare Summary Notice
MSN .... Merchant Shipping Notice (SAUS)
MSN .... Message Sequence Number (CAAL)
MSN .... Microsoft Network [*Microsoft Corp.*]
MSN .... Mildly Subnormal [*Medicine*] (MAE)
MSN .... Military Serial Number
MSN .... Military Service Number
MSN .... Mission (AFM)
MSN .... Mobil Showcase Network [*Television*]
MSN .... Modern Satellite Network [*Cable-television system*]
MSN .... Morrison Minerals Ltd. [*Toronto Stock Exchange symbol*]
MSN .... Movimiento de Salvacion Nacional [*National Salvation Movement*] [*Colombia*] [*Political party*] (EY)
MSN .... Mozambique Support Network (EA)
MSN .... Multiple Subscriber Number [*Telecommunications*] (DOM)
MSN .... Multiservice Network (GART)
MSN .... Music, Sport, News [*Radio broadcasting format*]
MsN .... Public Library of Natchez and Adams County, Natchez, MS [*Library symbol*] [*Library of Congress*] (LCLS)
MsNa........ Jennie Belle Stephens Smith Library, New Albany, MS [*Library symbol*] [*Library of Congress*] (LCLS)
MSNA .... Maine State Nurses' Association (EARSL)
MSNA .... Master of Science in Nurse Anesthesia (GAGS)
MSNA .... Master of Science in Nursing Administration (GAGS)
MSNA .... Mission Accomplished [*Military*] (AABC)
MSNAP...... Merchant Ship Naval Augmentation Program [*Navy*]
MSNAP...... Microwave Steerable Null Antenna Processor (MCD)
MSNBC...... Microsoft Corp. National Broadcasting Co. [*Cable news channel*]
MSNC .... Masonic
MSNCDRFAIRECONRON... Mission Commander, Fleet Air Reconnaissance Squadron (DNAB)
MSND .... Mercury Substitution and Nucleonic Detection (PDAA)
MSND .... Mouvement Social pour la Nouvelle Democratie [*Cameroon*] [*Political party*] (EY)
MSNE........ Master of Science in Nuclear Engineering (GAGS)
MsNe........ Newton Public Library, Newton, MS [*Library symbol*] [*Library of Congress*] (LCLS)
MsNeC ...... Clarke Memorial College, Newton, MS [*Library symbol*] [*Library of Congress*] (LCLS)
MSNEd ...... Master of Science in Nursing Education (NADA)
MS-Net...... Microsoft Network [*Computer science*] [*Also, MSN*] (CDE)
MSNF........ Milk Solids - Not Fat [*Food industry*]
MSNF........ Multisystem Networking Facility [*Computer science*]
MSNGR ..... Messenger (ADA)
MSNHP...... Mississippi Natural Heritage Program [*Mississippi State Department of Wildlife Conservation*] [*Jackson, MS*] [*Information service or system*] (IID)
MSNI .... (Mesitylenesulfonyl)nitroimidazole [*Organic chemistry*]
MSNik 97... Morgan Stanley Group, Inc. [*Associated Press*] (SAG)
MSN(R)..... Master of Science in Nursing (Research) (PGP)
MSNRY...... Masonry (MSA)
MSNS .... Master of Science in Natural Science (PGP)
MSNS .... MediSense, Inc. [*NASDAQ symbol*] (SAG)
MSN/SSN... Military Service Number / Social Security Number (DNAB)
MS Nsurg... Master of Science in Neurosurgery (PGP)
MSNT........ (Mesitylenesulfonyl)nitrotriazolide [*Biochemistry*]
MSNuclEng... Master of Science in Nuclear Engineering (NADA)
MSNY .... Massena [*New York*] [*Seismograph station code, US Geological Survey*] (SEIS)
MSNY .... Mattachine Society of New York [*Defunct*] (EA)
MSNY .... Missionary [*Telegraphy*] (PCTE)
MSO .... Main Signal Office [*British*]
MSO .... Maintenance Standard Order
MSO .... Maintenance Support Office [*Navy*]
MSO .... Malaysian Students' Organization [*Australia*]
MSO .... Managed Service Organization [*Health Insurance*]
MSO .... Management Science Office
MSO .... Management Service Organization
MSO .... Management Systems Office [*NASA*]
MSO .... Management Systems Operations (ACAE)
MSO .... Mandatory Second Surgical Opinion [*Health insurance*] (GHCT)
MSO .... Manned Solar Observatory (MCD)
MSO .... Manned Spacecraft Operations [*NASA*] (KSC)
MSO .... Manufacturer's Statement of Origin
MSO .... Manufacturing Sequence Outline (MCD)
MSO .... Marginally Stable Orbit [*Physics*]
MSO .... Marine Safety Office (MCD)
MSO .... Marine Staff Officers (EA)

MSO .... Maritime Staff Office (ACAE)
MSO .... Marketing Service Office (SAUS)
MSO .... Marketing Services Officer [*Insurance*]
MSO .... Mars Surface Operation
MSO .... Martha Stewart Living Omnimedia
MSO .... Massachusetts Society of Optometrists (EARSL)
MSO .... Mass Spectrometer Outgasing (KSC)
MSO .... Master of Science in Orthodontics (GAGS)
M So .... Master of Sociology
MSO .... Master of the Science of Oratory
MSO .... Master Specification Officer (SAUS)
MSO .... Material Sales Order
MSO .... Materiel Status Office (MCD)
MSO .... Mazur Surname Organization [*Association*] (EA)
MSO .... Medial Superior Olive [*Brain anatomy*]
MSO .... Medical Services Organization (MHCS)
MSO .... Medical Staff Organization (HCT)
MSO .... Member of the Society of Osteopaths [*British*]
MSO .... Mentally Stable and Oriented (MELL)
MSO .... Mesityl Oxide [*Also, MO*] [*Organic chemistry*]
MSO .... Methionine Sulfoxime [*Biochemistry*]
MSO .... Michigan Southern Railroad [*Federal Railroad Administration identification code*]
MSO .... Military Satellite Organization
MSO .... Military Service Obligation (AFM)
MSO .... Military Supply Officer (AFM)
MSO .... Minesweeper, Ocean [*Nonmagnetic*] [*Navy symbol*]
MSO .... Missabe Southern Railroad
MSO .... Missile Safety Officer (AFM)
MSO .... Missoula [*Montana*] [*Seismograph station code, US Geological Survey*] (SEIS)
MSO .... Mixed Services Organisation [*British Armed Services*]
MSO .... Mixed Signal Oscilloscope [*Automotive engineering*]
MSO .... Mobile Switching Office [*Bell System*]
MSO .... Model for Spare Optimization (MCD)
MSO .... Morale Support Officer [*Military*] (AABC)
MSO .... Moss Resources Ltd. [*Vancouver Stock Exchange symbol*]
MSO .... Mouvement Socialiste Occitan [*Occitanian Socialist Movement*] [*France*] [*Political party*] (PPE)
MSO .... Mozambique Solidarity Office (EA)
MSO .... Multiple System Operator [*Cable television*]
MSO .... Multiple Systems Operator (ACRL)
MSO .... Multistage Operation (MHDI)
MSo .... Public Library of the City of Somerville, Somerville, MA [*Library symbol*] [*Library of Congress*] (LCLS)
MSOA .... Military Studies and Operational Analysis (ADA)
MSOA .... Missouri State Orthopaedic Association (SAUS)
MSOB .... Manned Spacecraft Operations Building [*NASA*] (KSC)
MSOB .... Master of Science in Organizational Behavior
MSobPR .... New England Regional Primate Research Center, Harvard University, Southborough, MA [*Library symbol*] [*Library of Congress*] (LCLS)
MSOC .... MANPRINT [*Manpower and Personnel Integration*] Staff Officer Course [*Military*] (RDA)
MSOC .... Marine Systems Operational Compiler
MSOC .... Maritime Sector Operations Center [*NATO*] (NATG)
MSoc .... Master of Sociology (ADA)
MSOC .... Mechanized Smoke Obscurants Carrier (SAUS)
MSocAdmin... Master of Social Administration
msocc .... Multisatellite Operations Control Center [*NASA*] (NAKS)
MSOCC ...... Multisatellite Operations Control Center [*NASA*]
M Soc E ...... Member of the Society of Engineers [*British*]
MSocPol .... Master of Social Policy
M Soc Sc ... Master of Social Science (PGP)
MSocSc ..... Master of Social Sciences
MSocSci .... Master of Social Sciences
MSocSt ..... Master of Social Studies
MSocStud... Master of Social Studies (ADA)
MSocWk .... Master of Social Work
MSOD .... Master of Science in Organizational Development (GAGS)
MSOD .... Military Service Obligation Date (AFM)
MSOD .... Mobile Source Operations Division
MSOE .... Master of Science in Ocean Engineering (PGP)
MSOE .... Milwaukee School of Engineering [*Wisconsin*]
MSOE .... Multiband Spectral Observation Equipment
MSOF .... Multi Soft, Inc. [*NASDAQ symbol*] (QUAN)
MSOF .... Multisystem Organ Failure [*Medicine*] (CPH)
MSOFPA .... Massachusetts Society of the Order of Founders and Patriots of America (EARSL)
MSOG .... Glenwood and Souris Regional Library, Souris, Manitoba [*Library symbol*] [*National Library of Canada*] (NLC)
MSOG .... Molecular Sieve Oxygen Generating (PDAA)
MSohG ...... Gordon-Conwell Theological Seminary Library, South Hamilton, MA [*Library symbol*] [*Library of Congress*] (LCLS)
MSOINST... Maintenance Support Office Instructions [*Navy*]
MSOK .... Masson Trucking [*Common carrier symbol*]
MSOL .... Manned Scientific Orbital Laboratory [*NASA*] (IAA)
MSOLA ...... Missionary Sisters of Our Lady of Africa (TOCD)
MSOM .... Master of Science in Organization and Management (PGP)
MSOM .... Modernized Systems Operations Manual [*Computer science*]
MSom .... Somerset Public Library, Somerset, MA [*Library symbol*] [*Library of Congress*] (LCLS)
MSON .... Misonix, Inc. [*NASDAQ symbol*] (SAG)
MSonHi ..... South Natick Historical, Natural History, and Library Society, South Natick, MA [*Library symbol*] [*Library of Congress*] (LCLS)
MSONW ..... Misonix Inc. Wrrt [*NASDAQ symbol*] (TTSB)
MSOP .... Measurement System Operating Procedure (NG)
MSOP .... Medical School Objectives Project (DMAA)
MSOP .... Mezzo Soprano [*Music*]
MSOP .... Mutual Security Objectives Plan (CINC)
MSOPF ...... Multicast Open Shortest Path First (SAUS)
MSOphthal... Master of Ophthalmological Surgery (NADA)
M Sopr ...... Mezzo Soprano [*Music*]
MSOR .... Master of Science in Operations Research (GAGS)
MSOR .... Maximum System Operational Range
MSOR .... Missile Systems Operational Report [*Military*] (IAA)
MS Orn Hort... Master of Science in Ornamental Horticulture
MSORS ...... Mechanized Sales Office Record System [*Telecommunications*] (TEL)
MS(Orth) .... Master of Surgery (Orthopedic)
MSOS .... Mass Storage Operating System [*Control Data Corp.*] [*Computer science*] (NVT)
M So Sc .... Master of Social Science
M So Se .... Master of Social Service
MSOT .... Master of Science in Occupational Technology (PGP)
MSOT .... Master of Science in Occupational Therapy (GAGS)
MS Otol ..... Master of Science in Otolaryngology (PGP)
M So W ..... Master of Social Work
MSOW .... Modular Standoff Weapon [*Ballistic missile*]
MsP .... Jackson County - Pascagoula City Library, Pascagoula, MS [*Library symbol*] [*Library of Congress*] (LCLS)
MSP .... Macrophage Stimulating Protein [*Biochemistry*]
MSP .... Magnetic Scalar Potential
MSP .... Main-Spessart [*German license plate city code*]
MSP .... Maintenance Service Plan
MSP .... Maintenance Support Plan [*or Program*] [*Army*]
MSP .... Maintenance Surveillance Procedure (IEEE)
MSP .... Managed-Service Provider [*Computer science*] (GART)
MSP .... Management Service Provider
MSP .... Management System Programmers Ltd. (NITA)
MSP .... Manager Software Products Ltd. (NITA)
MSP .... Manager Support Programs (MCD)
MSP .... Manual Switching Position (IAA)
MSP .... Manufacturing Systems Products (ACAE)
MSP .... Marine Security Program [*FHWA*] (TAG)
MSP .... Marine Shale Processors, Inc. (EFIS)
MSP .... Maritime Shore Patrol
MSP .... Market Stabilization Price [*Department of Agriculture*]
MSP .... Mark-Sensed Punching (SAUS)
MSP .... Maryland State Police [*Motor vehicle violation code used in state of Maryland*] (MVRD)
MSP .... Mass Storage Processor [*Honeywell, Inc.*]
MSP .... Master of School Psychology (PGP)
MSP .... Master of Science in Pharmacy
MSP .... Master of Science in Planning (PGP)
MSP .... Master of Social Psychology (PGP)
M Sp .... Master of Speech
MSP .... Master of Speech Pathology (PGP)
MSP .... Master Shuttle Verification Plan (MCD)
MSP .... Master Simulator Program (NVT)
MSP .... Matched Sale-Purchase Agreement [*Business term*]
MSP .... Material Support Plan [*or Program*]
MSP .... Maximum Silo Price [*Farming terminology*]
MSP .... Maximum Sound Pressure
MSP .... Measurement Sensitive Products (DICI)
MSP .... Mededelingen Spinozahuis [*A publication*] (BJA)
MSP .... Media Signal Processor (SAUS)
MSP .... Media Suite Pro [*Computer software*] (CDE)
MSP .... Medical Specialist
MSP .... Medium Side Prong [*Lamp base type*] (NTCM)
MSP .... Medium-Speed Printer (AABC)
MSP .... Medium Stressed Platform
MSP .... Merozoite Surface Protein [*Of protozoa*]
MSP .... Message Security Protocol (SAUS)
MSP .... Metal Splash Pan (AAG)
MSP .... Microsoft Paint [*Computer science*] (CDE)
MSP .... Microsoft Solution Provider [*Computer science*] (CDE)
MSP .... Microspectrophotometry
MSP .... Microsuspension Seeded Polymerization (DICI)
MSP .... Military Space Program (AAG)
MSP .... Millisecond Pulsar [*Astronomy*]
MSP .... Minesweeper, Patrol [*Navy*] (DNAB)
MSP .... Miniature Series of Painters [*A publication*]
MSP .... Minimum Service Period (TIMI)
MSP .... Minimum Sustaining Power
MSP .... Minneapolis-St. Paul [*Minnesota*] [*Airport symbol*]
MSP .... Miscellaneous Small Parts
MSP .... Missile Setting Panel [*Military*] (CAAL)
MSP .... Missile Simulator Plug
MSP .... Missile Status Panel (ACAE)
MSP .... Missile Support Plan
MSP .... Missionaries of St. Paul (TOCD)
msp .... Missionaries of St. Paul (TOCD)
MSP .... Mission Specific Processing Program [*Defense Advanced Research Projects Agency*] (RCD)
MSP .... Mission Support Plan (MCD)
MSP .... Mississippi [*Telegraphy*] (PCTE)
MSP .... Mobile Support Package (MCD)

MSP .... Moderata Samlingspartiet [*Moderate Unity Party*] [*Sweden*] [*Political party*] (PPE)
MSP .... Mode Select Panel (IAA)
MSP .... Modular Switching Peripheral (ACAE)
MSP .... Modular System Programs [*IBM Corp.*]
MSP .... Monosodium Orthophosphate [*Inorganic chemistry*]
MSP .... Monosodium Phosphate (EDCT)
MSP .... Morgan Stan Fin 8.20% Cp Uts [*NYSE symbol*] (TTSB)
MSP .... Morgan Stanley Finance PLC Capital Unit [*NYSE symbol*] (SAG)
msp .... Mortuus sine Prole [*Dead without Issue*] [*Latin*] (WGA)
MSP .... Mosaic Sensor Program (MCD)
MSP .... Most Significant Position (CMD)
MSP .... Motorized Set Point (IAA)
MSP .... Motor, Sensory, Pulse
MSP .... Mount St. Thomas [*Philippines*] [*Seismograph station code, US Geological Survey*] (SEIS)
MSP .... Mouse Serum Protein [*Biochemistry*] (DAVI)
MSP .... Movement for a Peaceful Society (Algeria) [*Political party*] (PSAP)
MSP .... Movement Support Plans (ACAE)
MSP .... Movimento Socialista Popular [*Popular Socialist Movement*] [*Portugal*] [*Political party*] (PPE)
MSP .... Multicamera Synthesizing Projector (ACAE)
MSP .... Multiprocessing Server Pack [*Computer science*] (CDE)
MSP .... Multipurpose Semi-Submersible Platform (DNAB)
MSP .... Multisensor Processor (CAAL)
MSP .... Multi-Tech Supervisory Protocol [*Telecommunications*] (PCM)
MSP .... Munchausen Syndrome by Proxy [*Child abuse*] (DIPS)
MSP .... Mutual Security Program
MSP .... Mutual Support Program
MSP .... Servicio de Vigilancia Aerea del Ministerio de Seguridad Publica [*Costa Rica*] [*ICAO designator*] (FAAC)
MSPA .... Maine Sardine Packers Association (EA)
MSPA .... Marin Self-Publishers Association (EA)
MSPA .... Master of Science in Professional Accountancy (PGP)
MSPA .... Master of Science in Public Administration (GAGS)
MSPA .... Master of Speech Pathology and Audiology (PGP)
MSPA .... Member, Society of Pension Actuaries [*American Society of Pension Actuari es*] [*Designation awarded by*]
MSPA .... Mid-States Port Authority [*Federal Railroad Administration identification code*]
MSPA .... Migrant and Seasonal Worker Protection Act (WPI)
MSPA .... Modified Sodium Polyacrylate [*Organic chemistry*]
MSPA .... Mystery Shopping Providers Association (EA)
MSP & SSM ... Minneapolis, St. Paul & Sault Ste. Marie Railway Co. (IIA)
MSPAP ...... Maryland School Performance Assessment Program
MSPAW ..... Miedzynarodowe Stowarzyszenie Przyjaciele Angkor Wat [*International Association of Friends of Angkor Wat*] [*Multinational association based in Poland*] (EAIO)
MSPB .... Medical Specialist Preference Blank
MSPB .... Merit Systems Protection Board [*Formerly, Civil Service Commission*]
MSPC .... Manufacturer Standard Paint Color [*Motor vehicle specification*]
MSPC .... Medical Specialist Corps [*Military*]
MSPC .... MOPAR Scat Pack Club (EA)
MSPC .... Multivariate Statistical Process Control
MSPCL ...... Lower Fort Garry National Historic Park, Parks Canada [*Parc Historique National Lower Fort Garry, Parcs Canada*] Selkirk, Manitoba [*Library symbol*] [*National Library of Canada*] (NLC)
MSPCP ...... Mobile Source Pollution Control Program [*Environmental Protection Agency*]
MSPD .... Master of Social Planning and Development (ADA)
MSPD .... Matrix Solid-Phase Dispersion [*Analytical chemistry*]
MSPD .... Maximum Speed
MSPD .... Mulheres Portuguesas Social-Democratas [*An association*] (EAIO)
MSPE .... Maintenance Safety and Protection Equipment (AFIT)
MSPE .... Maryland Society of Professional Engineers (EARSL)
MSPE .... Massachusetts Society of Professional Engineers (EARSL)
MSPE .... Master of Science in Petroleum Engineering (PGP)
MSPE .... Master of Science in Physical Education
MSPE .... Master Plate [*Tool*] (AAG)
MSPE .... Michigan Society of Professional Engineers (EARSL)
MSpecEd .... Master of Special Education
MSpEd ...... Master of Special Education
MsPeM ...... Mississippi Gulf Coast Junior College, Perkinston, MS [*Library symbol*] [*Library of Congress*] (LCLS)
MSPEQ ...... Morgan Stanley Group [*Associated Press*] (SAG)
MSpeSJ ..... Saint Joseph's Abbey, Spencer, MA [*Library symbol*] [*Library of Congress*] (LCLS)
MSPetE ..... Master of Science in Petroleum Engineering (GAGS)
MSPetEng ... Master of Science in Petroleum Engineering (NADA)
MSP Ex ..... Master of Science in Exercise Physiology (PGP)
MSPEx ...... Master of Science in Physiology of Exercise (GAGS)
MSPF .... Maritime Special Purpose Force (COE)
MSPF .... Multispectral Photographic Facility
MSPFW ..... Multishot Portable Flame Weapon (DNAB)
MSPG .... Magnetic Shock Pulse Generator (IAA)
MSPG .... Master of Science in Psychology (PGP)
MSPG .... Materiel Support Planning Guidance [*Military*] (AABC)
MSPG .... Measure Specific Performance Guarantee [*Calculation*] (AAGC)
MSPG .... MindSpring Enterprises [*NASDAQ symbol*] (TTSB)
MSPG .... MindSpring Enterprises, Inc. [*NASDAQ symbol*] (SAG)
MSPGN ...... Mesangial Proliferative Glomerulonephritis [*Nephrology*]
MSPH .... Master of Science in Poultry Husbandry
MSPH .... Master of Science in Public Health
MsPh .... Neshoba County Library, Philadelphia, MS [*Library symbol*] [*Library of Congress*] (LCLS)
MSPhar ..... Master of Science in Pharmacy [*Education*] (FOTI)
MSPharm ... Master of Science in Pharmacy (NADA)
MSPHE ...... Master of Science in Public Health Engineering
MSPH Ed ... Master of Science in Public Health Education
MS Phr ...... Master of Science in Pharmacy (PGP)
MS Phys Op ... Master of Science in Physiological Optics (PGP)
MsPi .... Crosby Memorial Library, Picayune, MS [*Library symbol*] [*Library of Congress*] (LCLS)
MSPI .... M&T Software Partner International (SAUS)
MSPI .... Modified Ship Plan Index
MSPIR .... Master of Science in Personnel and Industrial Relations
MSPLT .... Master Source Program Library Tape [*Computer science*] (BUR)
MsPMF ...... United States Department of Commerce, National Marine Fisheries Service, Pascagoula, MS [*Library symbol*] [*Library of Congress*] (LCLS)
MSPM Rehab ... Master of Science in Physical Medicine and Rehabilitation (PGP)
MSPN .... Medical Student's Progress Note (DMAA)
MSPNGE .... Master of Science in Petroleum and Natural Gas Engineering (PGP)
MSPO .... Mercury Support Planning Office (MUGU)
MSPO .... Meridian Sports [*NASDAQ symbol*] (TTSB)
MSPO .... Meridian Sports, Inc. [*NASDAQ symbol*] (SAG)
MSPO .... Military Support Planning Officer [*Civil Defense*]
MSPO .... Mission System Project Office [*Military*] (CAAL)
MsPog .... Harriette Person Memorial Library, Port Gibson, MS [*Library symbol*] [*Library of Congress*] (LCLS)
MSPoly ...... Master of Science in Polymers (GAGS)
MsPon .... Dixie Regional Library, Pontotoc, MS [*Library symbol*] [*Library of Congress*] (LCLS)
MsPop .... Poplarville Public Library, Poplarville, MS [*Library symbol*] [*Library of Congress*] (LCLS)
MSPP .... Merit System Protection Plan
MSPP .... Michigan Screening Profile of Parenting [*Psychology*]
MsPr .... Jefferson Davis County Library, Prentiss, MS [*Library symbol*] [*Library of Congress*] (LCLS)
MSPR .... Master Spares Positioning Resolver [*Data processing*]
MSPR .... Medical System Program Review [*Army*] (RDA)
MSPR .... Model State Packaging Regulation [*National Institute of Standards and Technology*]
MSPr .... Morgan Stanley 9.36% Pfd [*NYSE symbol*] (TTSB)
MSPRB ...... Meteorological Satellite Program Review Board [*NOAA and NASA*]
MSPrB ...... Morgan Stanley 8.88% Dep Pfd [*NYSE symbol*] (TTSB)
MSPrC ...... Morgan Stanley 8.75% Dep Pfd [*NYSE symbol*] (TTSB)
MSPrD ...... Morgan Stanly 7.375% Dep Pfd [*NYSE symbol*] (TTSB)
MSPRS ...... Multispectral Photographic Reconnaissance (MCD)
MSPS .... Maneuvering Satellite Propulsion System (MCD)
MSPS .... Master of Science in Planning Studies (PGP)
MSPS .... Master of Science in Psychological Services (GAGS)
MSPS .... Megasample per Second (IAA)
MSPS .... Mega Symbols per Second (MCD)
MSpS .... Misioneros del Espiritu Santo [*Missionaries of the Holy Spirit*] [*Mexico*] (EAIO)
MSpS .... Missionaries of the Holy Spirit (TOCD)
msps .... Missionaries of the Holy Spirit (TOCD)
MSPS .... Mobilization Station Planning System [*MTMC*] (TAG)
MSPS .... Modular Self-Protection System (SAUS)
MSPS .... Modular Space Power Station
MSPS .... Multisource Processing System (MCD)
MSPS .... Multi-Spectral Point Scanner (ACAE)
MSPS .... Myocardial Stress Perfusion Scintigram [*Medicine*]
MSPT .... Marine Silent Power Transmission (SAUS)
MSPT .... Master of Science in Physical Therapy (GAGS)
MSPTA ...... Michigan State Police Troopers Association (EARSL)
MSpThy ..... Master of Speech Therapy (ADA)
MS Pw ...... Mississippi Power Co. [*Associated Press*] (SAG)
MSPWS ..... Microsoft Personal Web Server [*Computer science*] (AGLO)
MSPX .... Solutia [*Private rail car owner code*]
MSQ .... Managing Service Quality (ODA)
Msq .... Masque [*Record label*]
MSQ .... Minnesota Satisfaction Questionnaire
MSQ .... Minsk [*Former USSR*] [*Airport symbol*] (OAG)
MSQ .... Mosquito Construction Gold [*Vancouver Stock Exchange symbol*]
MSQL .... Multilevel Structured Query Language (SAUS)
MSQT .... Missile Ship Qualification Test [*Navy*] (NVT)
MSQT .... Modified Ship Qualification Test
MSQU .... Military Sealift Command [*Intermodal shipping container symbol*] (TVRC)
MsR .... Capital Area Regional Library, Raymond, MS [*Library symbol*] [*Library of Congress*] (LCLS)
MSR .... Egypt Air [*ICAO designator*] (FAAC)
MSR .... Machine Specific Register (SAUS)
MSR .... Machine Status Register [*Computer science*] (OA)
MSR .... Machine Stress Rated
MSR .... Macrophage Scavenger Receptor [*Immunology*]
MSR .... Magnetic Shift Register
MSR .... Magnetic Silencing Range [*Navy*] (DOMA)
MSR .... Magnetic Silencing Ranger (DWSG)
MSR .... Magnetic Storage Ring [*Computer science*]
MSR .... Magnetic Stripe Reader (IAA)
MSR .... Magnetic Superresolution
MSR .... Main Status Register [*Computer science*] (VLIE)
MSR .... Main Supply Road [*or Route*]
MSR .... Makassar [*Sulawesi, Indonesia*] [*Airport symbol*] (AD)

MSR .... Male Seniors [*International Bowhunting Organization*] [*Class equipment*]
MSR .... Mammalian Selectivity Ratio (FFDE)
MSR .... Management Summary Report (ABAC)
MSR .... Management Systems Representative (MCD)
MSR .... Manual Sliding Roof [*Automotive accessory*]
MSR .... Manufacturing Service Request (MCD)
MSR .... Manufacturing Specification Request (AAG)
MSR .... Marketing Service Representative
MSR .... Marketing Support Representative
MSR .... Market Share Reporter [*A publication*]
MSR .... Mark Sense Reading
MSR .... Mark Sheet Reader [*Computer science*] (BUR)
MSR .... Mark-to-Space Ratio (VLIE)
MSR .... Mass Storage Resident [*Computer science*] (IEEE)
MS (R) ...... Master of Science in Research
MSR .... Master Stock Record (DNAB)
MSR .... Material Status Report [*AEC*]
MSR .... Maximum Steam Rate [*Nuclear energy*] (NRCH)
MSR .... McDonnell Simulator Recorder [*McDonnell Douglas Corp.*] (MCD)
MSR .... Mean Spring Rise [*Tides and currents*]
MSR .... Mean Square Residual
MSR .... Mean Square Root (IAA)
MSR .... Measure [*Telegraphy*] (PCTE)
MSR .... Mechanically Steered Radar (ACAE)
MSR .... Mechanized Storage and Retrieval [*Computer science*]
MSR .... Medium Stocking Rate [*Agriculture*] (OA)
MSR .... Member of the Society of Radiographers [*British*]
MSR .... Membrane-Spanning Region [*Cytology*]
MSR .... Memory Select Register (NITA)
MSR .... Merchant Ship Reactor [*Navy*]
MSR .... Message Has Been Misrouted [*Communications*]
MSR .... Metal Seal Ring
MSR .... Metalsmith, Ship Repair [*Navy*]
MSR .... Meteorological Sounding Rocket
MSR .... Michigan Shore Railroad [*Federal Railroad Administration identification code*]
MSR .... Microsoft Research Center
MSR .... Micro Support Resource Corp. [*Atlanta, GA*]
MSR .... Microwave Scanning Radiometer (ACAE)
MSR .... Midwest Sunbeam Registry (EA)
MSR .... Milestone Status Report [*Military*] (AFIT)
MSR .... Mineral-Surface Roof [*Technical drawings*]
MSR .... Mine Smelter and Refinery Databank [*Commodities Research Unit Ltd.*] [*Information service or system*] (CRD)
MSR .... Minesweeper, Patrol [*Navy symbol*] [*Obsolete*]
MSR .... Minesweeper River [*Navy symbol*] (VNW)
MSR .... Minimum Sales Responsibility [*Automotive sales quotas*]
MSR .... Minimum Security Requirement
MSR .... Minimum Sustaining Rate (MCD)
MSR .... Missile Scoring Reliability (MCD)
MSR .... Missile Simulation Round (ACAE)
MSR .... Missile Site RADAR [*Army*] (MCD)
MSR .... Missile Site Range
MSR .... Missile Surface RADAR (MCD)
MSR .... Mission Success Ratio [*Military*] (CAAL)
MSR .... Mission Support Recording [*Deep Space Instrumentation Facility, NASA*]
MSR .... Mission Support Room [*NASA*] (KSC)
MSR .... Mobile Sea Range (NVT)
MSR .... Mobile Support Router (SAUS)
MSR .... Mode Status Register (IAA)
MSR .... Modification Status Report (KSC)
MSR .... Modular Survivable Radar (SAUS)
MSR .... Module Support Rack (NASA)
MSR .... Moisture Separator Reheater (NRCH)
MSR .... Molten-Salt Reactor
MSR .... Monthly Status Report [*Navy*]
MSR .... Montserrat [*ANSI three-letter standard code*] (CNC)
MSR .... Movimiento Socialista Revolucionario [*Revolutionary Socialist Movement*] [*Panama*] [*Political party*] (PPW)
MSR .... MSR Exploration [*AMEX symbol*] (TTSB)
MSR .... MSR Exploration Ltd. [*Associated Press*] (SAG)
MSR .... Multi-Carrier Station Radio [*or Remote*] Control Equipment (PDAA)
MSR .... Multicomet Sample Return [*Space science*]
MSR .... Multijunction Semiconductor Rectifier
MSR .... Multisensor Reconnaissance (SAUS)
MSR .... Multispeed Repeater
MSR .... Multi-Surface Reflector [*Automotive lighting*]
MSR .... Multitrack Serpentine Recording (VLIE)
MSR .... Munster [*Germany*] [*Airport symbol*] (OAG)
MSR .... Muscle Stretch Reflexes [*Medicine*] (DAVI)
MSR .... Musicians for Social Responsibility (EA)
MSR .... Mysore State Railway [*Indian Railway*] (TIR)
MSR .... St. Louis Art Museum, St. Louis, MO [*OCLC symbol*] (OCLC)
MSRA .... Master of Science in Recreation Administration (PGP)
MSRA .... Middle States Regatta Association (EA)
MSRA .... Midwest Ski Representatives Association (EA)
MSRA .... Multiple Shoe Retailers' Association [*British*] (BI)
MSRad ...... Master of Science in Radiology [*Education*] (FOTI)
MSRadSc ... Master of Science in Radiation Science (GAGS)
MSR/ASR ... Main Supply Route/Alternative Supply Route (MCD)
MSRB .... Margaret Sanger Research Bureau [*Defunct*] (EA)
MSRB .... Metalsmith, Ship Repair, Blacksmith [*Navy*]
MSRB .... Metrology Standards Requirements Board (ACII)
MSRB .... Municipal Securities Rulemaking Board [*Securities and Exchange Commission*]
MSRC .... Management Science Research Centre [*McGill University*] [*Canada*] (RCD)
MSRC .... Marine Sciences Research Center [*State University of New York at Stony Brook*] [*Research center*] (RCD)
MSRC .... Marine Spill Response Corp. [*An association*]
MSRC .... Master of Science in Resource Conservation (PGP)
MSRC .... Materiel Studies Review Committee [*Army*]
MSRC .... Medical and Surgical Relief Committee [*Defunct*] (EA)
MSRC .... Membre, Societe Royale du Canada [*French*] (CPGU)
MSRC .... Metalsmith, Ship Repair, Coppersmith [*Navy*]
MSRC .... Microelectronic Systems Research Center [*West Virginia University*] (RCD)
MSRC .... Mid-South Railroad [*Federal Railroad Administration identification code*]
MSRD .... Marine Services Research Division [*Now Coastal and Arctic Research Division*] (USDC)
MSRD .... Mean Square Relative Displacement [*Spectra*]
MSRD .... Measured [*Telegraphy*] (PCTE)
MSRD .... Mobile Service & Repair Depot (SAUS)
MSRD .... Mobile Servicing and Repair Detachment [*Military*] [*British*]
MSRE........ Master of Science in Real Estate and Urban Affairs
MSRE........ Master of Science in Religious Education (PGP)
MSRE........ Mir Sample Return Experiment [*NASA*] (SPST)
MSRE........ Molten Salt Reactor Experiment
MSRE........ Moon Signal Rejection Equipment (AFM)
MSRec ...... Master of Science in Recreation (NADA)
MSRet....... Master of Science in Retailing (NADA)
MSRF........ Metalsmith, Ship Repair, Forger-Anglesmith [*Navy*]
MSRF........ Microwave Space Research Facility
MSRFT ...... Minesweeper Refresher Training [*Navy*] (NVT)
MSRG .... Measuring [*Telegraphy*] (PCTE)
MSRG .... Medieval Settlement Research Group [*British*] (DBA)
MSRG .... Member of the Society of Remedial Gymnasts [*British*]
MSRG .... Moated Sites Research Group (EA)
MSRG .... Modular Shift Register Generator
MSRGSN.... Mountain States Regional Genetic Services Network (SAUS)
MsRH........ Hinds Junior College, Raymond, MS [*Library symbol*] [*Library of Congress*] (LCLS)
MSRI .... Mathematical Sciences Research Institute [*University of California, Berkeley*] (PDAA)
MSRI .... Mathematical Sciences Research Institute [*University of Minnesota*] (PDAA)
MSRI .... Mid-States Rail Car [*Federal Railroad Administration identification code*]
MsRi......... Pine Forest Regional Library, Richton, MS [*Library symbol*] [*Library of Congress*] (LCLS)
MSRIS....... Molten-Salt Reactor Information System
MSRJE ...... Multiple Session Remote Job Entry [*Computer science*] (VLIE)
MSRK .... Mathias-Soave-Redlich-Kwong [*Equation of state*]
MSRL........ Marine Sciences Research Laboratory [*Canada*] (MSC)
MSRL........ Materials Science Research Laboratory (TIMI)
MSRL........ Mobile Secondary Reference Laboratory
MSRM....... Main Steam Radiation Monitor (IEEE)
MSRM....... Mars Sample Return Mission [*NASA*]
MSRM....... Measurement [*Telegraphy*] (PCTE)
MSRM....... Mixture and Systemic Toxicant Risk Model [*Environmental term*] (EAGT)
MSRMNT ... Measurement
MSRMP ..... Master of Science in Radiological Medical Physics (PGP)
MSRN .... Mobile Station Roaming Number (CGWS)
MSRNW..... North-West Regional Library, Swan River, Manitoba [*Library symbol*] [*National Library of Canada*] (NLC)
MSRO .... Missile System Requirements Outline (MCD)
MSRP .... Management Sciences Research Project [*University of California*] (MCD)
MSRP .... Manufacturer's Suggested Retail Price
MSRP .... Massive Selective Retaliatory Power (NATG)
MSRP .... Meteorological Sounding Rocket Program [*NASA*]
MSRP .... Missile, Space and Range Pioneers (EA)
MSRP .... Mission Support Real Property [*NASA*] (KSC)
MSRP .... Multi Stage Retrofit Program (ACAE)
MSRPC...... Microsoft Remote Procedure Call (SAUS)
MSRPP...... Multidimensional Scale for Rating Psychiatric Patients
MSRPS...... State Retirement & Pension System (SAUS)
MS(R)PT.... Master of Science (Research) in Physical Therapy (PGP)
MSR (R) .... Member of the Society of Radiographers (Radiography) [*British*]
MSRR .... Mission and System Requirements Review [*NASA*]
MSRR .... Modeling and Simulation Resource Repository (SAUS)
MSRS .... Main Steam Radiation System (IEEE)
MSRS .... Master of Science in Recreational Studies (PGP)
MSRS .... Materiel System Requirements Specification [*Military*]
MSRS .... Metalsmith, Ship Repair, Sheet Metal Worker [*Navy*]
MSRS .... Meteoroid Shield Release System (MCD)
MSRS .... Military Spending Research Services, Inc. [*Information service or system*] (IID)
MSRS .... Military System Requirement Specification (ACAE)
MSRS .... Miniature Sonobuoy Receiver System (SAUS)
MSRS .... Missile Strike Reporting System
MSRS .... Multiple Stylus Recording System (OA)
MSRSIM .... Missile Site RADAR Simulation [*Missile system evaluation*] (RDA)
MSRT........ Master Standard Reference Tape [*Computer science*] (VLIE)
MSRT........ Mean Supply Response Time
MSR (T)..... Member of the Society of Radiographers (Radiotherapy) [*British*]

MSRT........ Mini System Real-Time (VLIE)
MSRT........ Minnesota Spatial Relations Test (DIPS)
MSRT........ Missile System Readiness Test (IEEE)
MSRT........ Mobile Subscriber Radio Terminal [*Army*]
MSRT........ Mobile Subscriber Receiver/Transmitter (SAUS)
MSRTE...... Misroute
MS-RTP..... Micelle-Stabilized Room-Temperature Phosphorescence
MSRTS...... Migrant Student Records Transfer System (GFGA)
MSRU....... Marine Sales [*Intermodal shipping container symbol*] (TVRC)
MS Russ.... Morgan Stanley Russia & New Europe Fund, Inc. [*Associated Press*] (SAG)
MSRV....... Main Steam Relief Valve [*Nuclear energy*] (NRCH)
MSRW....... Mississippian Railway Co-Operative [*Federal Railroad Administration identification code*]
MSRX....... Missouri Southeastern Railroad [*Federal Railroad Administration identification code*]
MSRY....... Masonry
MSS......... Magnetic Spark Spectrometer (PDAA)
MSS......... Magnetic Stereotaxis System [*Surgery*]
MSS......... Magnetic Storm Satellite [*Air Force/NASA*]
MSS......... Magnetic Strip Storage [*Computer science*] (VLIE)
MSS......... Main Steam System [*Nuclear energy*] (NRCH)
MSS......... Main Support Structure (NRCH)
MSS......... Maintenance Standards Study (MCD)
MSS......... Maintenance Status System (MCD)
mss......... Maintenance Status System (NAKS)
MSS......... Maintenance Support Schedule [*Air Force*] (AFM)
MSS......... Major Stationary Source [*Environmental Protection Agency*]
MSS......... Make Suitable Substitution
MSS......... Managed Security Services
MSS......... Management Science Systems (IEEE)
MSS......... Management Statistics Subsystem (TEL)
MSS......... Management Summary Sheets (MCD)
MSS......... Management Supplier Selection (AAG)
MSS......... Management Support Services (ACAE)
MSS......... Management Support Staff [*Social Security Administration*]
MSS......... Management Support System (USDC)
MSS......... Management Systems Staff (EAGT)
MSS......... Management Systems Study (MCD)
MSS......... Manassas, VA [*Amtrak rail station code*]
MSS......... Manned Space Station [*NASA*]
MSS......... Manual Safety Switch
MSS......... Manufacturers Standardization Society (AAGC)
mss......... Manufacturers Standardization Society (NAKS)
MSS......... Manufacturers Standardization Society of the Valve and Fittings Industry (EA)
MSS......... Manuscripta [*Manuscripts*] [*Latin*]
mss......... Manuscripts [*Linguistics*] (IEL)
MSS......... Manuscript, Signed
MSS......... MAP [*Manufacturing Automation Protocol*]/One System Software [*Industrial Networking, Inc.*]
MSS......... Marine Safety Services [*British*] (DCTA)
MSS......... Marital Satisfaction Scale [*Psychology*] (DAVI)
MSS......... Maritime Support Service
MSS......... Maryland Spectral Services, Inc. (EFIS)
MSS......... Mary Stuart Society of America (EA)
MSS......... Massage
MSS......... Massena [*New York*] [*Airport symbol*] (OAG)
MSS......... Mass Storage Service [*Computer science*]
MSS......... Mass Storage System [*Computer science*]
MSS......... Mastergroup Surveillance System [*AT & T*]
MSS......... Master of Sanitary Science
MSS......... Master of Science in Safety (GAGS)
MSS......... Master of Selected Studies (PGP)
MSS......... Master of Social Science
MSS......... Master of Social Service
MSS......... Master of Social Studies
MSS......... Master of Sport Science (GAGS)
MSS......... Master Station Subsystem
MSS......... Master Surveillance Station [*Air Force*]
MSS......... Master Switching Station (MCD)
MSS......... Master System Schedule (MCD)
MSS......... Matrix Switch System [*Electronics*]
MSS......... Maximum Segment Size [*Computer science*] (VLIE)
MSS......... Mayo Smith Society (EA)
MSS......... Mean Solar Second (IAA)
MSS......... Measurement Specialities, Inc. [*AMEX symbol*] (SAG)
MSS......... Measurement Specialties [*AMEX symbol*] (TTSB)
MSS......... Measurement Standard Sensitivity (DICI)
MSS......... Mechanical and Structural Subsystems (MCD)
MSS......... Mechanically Separated Spleen [*Food technology*]
MSS......... Mechanical Speed Switch
MSS......... Mechanical Support System (MCD)
mss......... Mechanical Support Systems (NAKS)
MSS......... Medical Service School [*Air Force*] (AFM)
MSS......... Medical Social Services
MSS......... Medical Superintendents' Society (DAVI)
MSS......... Medical Supply Section (SAUS)
MSS......... Medium Survey Ship [*Marine science*] (MSC)
MSS......... Megasample per Second (IAA)
MSS......... Member of the Statistical Society [*British*] (ROG)
MSS......... Memory System Security [*Computer science*] (ECII)
MSS......... Men's Social Services [*Salvation Army*]
MSS......... Mental Status Schedule [*Psychology*]
MSS......... Message Support Subsystem (MCD)
MSS......... Message Switching Station [*Telecommunications*] (CET)
MSS......... Message Switching System
MSS......... Messtetten [*Federal Republic of Germany*] [*Seismograph station code, US Geological Survey*] (SEIS)
MSS......... Metal Silicone Silicon (VLIE)
MSS......... Metal Spring Seal
MSS......... Metastable State (IAA)
MSS......... Meteorological Satellite Section
MSS......... Meter Stamp Society (EA)
MSS......... Methylprednisolone Sodium Succinate [*Antirheumatoid compound*]
MSS......... Metropolitan Speleological Society [*Australia*]
MSS......... Metropolitan Switching System (VLIE)
MSS......... Mexican-Spanish Speaking (OICC)
MSS......... Microwave Switching Station
MSS......... Midcourse Surveillance System (MCD)
MSS......... Midwest Sociological Society (AEBS)
MSS......... Military Security Service [*RVNAF*]
MSS......... Military Supply Standards [*DoD*] (MCD)
MSS......... MIMOLA Software System (SAUS)
MSS......... Mine Search System [*Navy*] (DOMA)
MSS......... Minesweeper, Special [*Device*] [*Navy symbol*]
MSS......... Miniature Signaling System [*Railway term*] (DCTA)
MSS......... Miniature Stepping Switch
MSS......... Miniature Surveillance System (SAUS)
MSS......... Ministry of Social Security [*British*]
MSS......... Minnesota Satisfactoriness Scale [*Job performance test*]
MSS......... Minor Surgery Suite [*Medicine*] (DAVI)
MSS......... Missile Safety Set (IAA)
MSS......... Missile Security Squadron
MSS......... Missile Select Switch
MSS......... Missile Sensor Study (ACAE)
MSS......... Missile Sight System [*Army*]
MSS......... Missile Stabilization System
MSS......... Missile Station Select
MSS......... Missile Subsystem
MSS......... Missile Support Stand (MCD)
MSS......... Missile Support Subsystem (SAUS)
MSS......... Mission Simulator System
mss......... Mission Specialist Station [*NASA*] (NAKS)
MSS......... Mission Specialist Station [*NASA*] (NASA)
MSS......... Mission Status Summary (MCD)
mss......... Mission Status Summary [*NASA*] (NAKS)
MSS......... Mission Support Site [*Army*]
MSS......... Mission Support System (ACAE)
MSS......... Mission System Simulator (MCD)
MSS......... Mississauga Public Library [*UTLAS symbol*]
MSS......... Mixed Spectrum Superheater [*Nuclear energy*]
MSS......... Mobile Satellite Service
MSS......... Mobile Satellite System (DA)
MSS......... Mobile Service Structure (KSC)
mss......... Mobile Service Structure (NAKS)
MSS......... Mobile Servicing System [*For space station*]
MSS......... Mobile Subscriber Equipment System (SAUS)
MSS......... Mobile Subscriber Subsystem (ACAE)
MSS......... Mobility Subsystem (KSC)
MSS......... Modelling and Simulation Studies [*Marine science*] (MSC)
MSS......... Model Skin Surface [*Artificial skin*]
MSS......... Modern Satellite Systems, Inc. [*Whitehouse Station, NJ*] [*Telecommunications*] (TSSD)
MSS......... Mode Selection Switch (KSC)
MSS......... Mode Sickness Susceptibility (KSC)
MSS......... Modified Scram System [*Nuclear energy*] (NRCH)
MSS......... Modify System State (AAEL)
MSS......... Modularized Simulation System (ACAE)
MSS......... Modular Space Station
MSS......... Modulation Semiconductor Structure
MSS......... Moored Sonobuoy System (MCD)
MSS......... Moored Surveillance System [*To detect and destroy enemy submarines*] [*Navy*]
MSS......... Morris Air Service [*ICAO designator*] (FAAC)
MSS......... Motion Sickness Susceptibility (MCD)
MSS......... Motor Start-Stop [*Automotive engineering*]
MSS......... Motor Surveillance Service [*MTMC*] (TAG)
MSS......... Movement Shorthand Society [*Later, Center for Sutton Movement Writing*] (EA)
MSS......... Mucus-Stimulating Substance
MSS......... Multibeam Steering System
MSS......... Multimedia Systems Services (RALS)
MSS......... Multiple Sclerosis Society [*British*]
MSS......... Multiple Selling Service (OA)
MSS......... Multiple Steady States [*Chemical engineering*]
MSS......... Multi-Satellite System (ACAE)
MSS......... Multispectral Scanner [*or Sensor*]
MSS......... Multispectral Scanner System
MSS......... Multispectral/Spin Scanner (SAUS)
MSS......... Multistatic Sonar System (SAUS)
MSS......... Multitask Single Stream System (NITA)
MSS......... Muscular Subaortic Stenosis [*Cardiology*]
MSS......... Music Story Series [*A publication*]
MSS......... Special Minesweeper [*Navy symbol*]
MSs......... Swansea Free Public Library, Swansea, MA [*Library symbol*] [*Library of Congress*] (LCLS)
MSS......... West Masela [*Language symbol*] (ETLW)

MSSA........ Maintenance Supply Services Agency (NATG)
MSSA........ Manchester Scales of Social Adaptation [*Psychology*]
MSSA........ Master of Science in Social Administration (GAGS)
MSSA........ Master Safeguards and Security Agreements (DOMA)
MSSA........ Methicillin-Susceptible Staphylococcus Aureus [*Medicine*] (PALA)
MSSA........ Midland Steel Stockholders Association [*British*] (DBA)
MSSA........ Military Selective Service Act (OICC)
MSSA........ Military Subsistence Supply Agency [*Later, Defense Subsistence Supply Center*]
mssa .... Missionaries of the Holy Apostles (TOCD)
MSsA........ Missionaries of the Holy Apostles [*Roman Catholic men's religious order*]
MSSA........ Missionary Servants of St. Anthony [*Roman Catholic women's religious order*]
MSSA........ Modification of Special Service Authorization [*FCC*] (NTCM)
MSSA........ Multi-Sensor Surveillance Aircraft (SAUS)
MSS & H ... Master of Science in Speech and Hearing
MSSanE..... Master of Science in Sanitary Engineering
MSS AS ..... Multistatic Sonar System Acoustic Source (DOMA)
MSSB........ Mid-State Federal Savings Bank (EFIS)
MSSB........ Missile Servicing and Storage Building [*Military*] (IAA)
MSSBR...... Multi-Purpose Supersonic Beamrider (ACAE)
MSSC........ Main Storage Stock Control [*Computer science*] (IAA)
MSSC........ Management System for Support Contracts [*Social Security Administration*]
MSSC........ Maritime Surface Surveillance Capability (SAUS)
MSSC........ Mass Storage System Communications (NITA)
MSSC........ Mass Storage System Communicator [*Computer science*] (IBMDP)
MSSC........ Mass Storage System Control [*Computer science*] (BUR)
MS Sc....... Master of Sanitary Science
MS Sc....... Master of Social Science
MSSc........ Master of Surgical Science, University of Dundee [*British*] (DBQ)
MSSC........ Medium SEAL [*Sea, Air, and Land*] Support Craft [*Navy symbol*]
MSSC........ Metropolitan School Study Council [*Columbia University*] (AEE)
MSSC........ Military Standard and Specification Committee
MSSC........ Military Store Staff Corps [*British military*] (DMA)
MSSC........ Missile System Software Center
MSSC........ Missionary Society of St. Columban (EAIO)
MSSC........ Mobile Service Switching Center
MSSC........ Multiple Sclerosis Society of Canada
MSSC........ Multi-Spectral Scanning Camera (ACAE)
MSSCB...... Missionary Sisters of St. Charles Borromeo (TOCD)
MSSCC...... Military Space Surveillance Control Center (MUGU)
MSSCC...... Missionaries of the Sacred Hearts of Jesus and Mary (TOCD)
msscc .... Missionaries of the Sacred Hearts of Jesus and Mary (TOCD)
MSSCC...... Missionarii a Sacris Cordibus Jesus et Mariae [*Missionaries of the Sacred Hearts of Jesus and Mary*] [*Roman Catholic men's religious order*]
MSSCC...... Multicolor Spin-Scan Cloudcover Camera
MSSCE...... Mixed Spectrum Superheater Critical Experiment [*Nuclear energy*]
MSSCIC..... National Multiple Sclerosis Society, Channel Islands Chapter (EARSL)
MSS-CPA... National Multiple Sclerosis Society, Central Pennsylvania Chapter (EARSL)
MSSCS...... Manned Space Station Communications System [*NASA*]
MSSD....... Model Secondary School for the Deaf (EA)
MSSE........ Mass Storage System Extensions [*Computer science*] (HODG)
MSSE........ Master of Science in Sanitary Engineering
MSSE........ Master of Science in Secondary Education of Students (who are Deaf or Hard of Hearing)
MSSE........ Message Submission Service Element [*Open Systems Interconnection*] (ODAA)
MSSE........ Missile System Support Equipment
MSSE........ Multi-Sensor Situation Elaboration (SAUS)
MSS/EC..... Missile System Supervisor/Engagement Controller [*Military*] (CAAL)
MSSEng..... Master of Science in Sanitary Engineering (NADA)
MSSFA...... Michigan Steelhead and Salmon Fisherman's Association
MSSG....... Marine Expeditionary Unit Service Support Group (DOMA)
MSSG....... Message
MSSG....... Messina Shipping Company [*Common carrier symbol*]
MSSG....... Multiple Sclerosis Susceptibility Gene [*Medicine*] (DB)
MSSG....... Stanford Medical Student Survival Guide (SAUS)
MSSH....... Master of Science in Speech and Hearing (PGP)
MSSH....... Springfield Hospital, Medical Center Library, Springfield, MA [*Library symbol*] [*Library of Congress*] (LCLS)
MSSI........ Master of Science in Strategic Intelligence (PGP)
MSSI........ MSSI TeleScience International [*OTCBB symbol*]
MSSJ........ Missionary Servants of St. Joseph [*Roman Catholic women's religious order*]
MSSJ........ Multiple Subsonic Jet
MSSL........ Management Systems Summary List
MSSL........ Master of Science in Speech and Language (PGP)
MSSL........ Mid-State Federal S&L Assn. [*NASDAQ symbol*] (COMM)
MSSL........ Missile System Stockage List (AFIT)
MSSL........ Mullard Space Science Laboratory [*University of London*] (PDAA)
MSSM....... Mars Spinning Support Module [*NASA*] (KSC)
MSSM....... Master of Science in Science Management (PGP)
MSSM....... Master of Science in Systems Management (PGP)
MSSM....... Missionary Sisters of the Society of Mary [*Italy*] (EAIO)
MsSM....... Mississippi State University, State College, MS [*Library symbol*] [*Library of Congress*] (LCLS)
MSSM....... Mount Sinai School of Medicine [*New York*] (PDAA)
MSSM....... Multiple-Sine-Slit Microdensitometer (PDAA)
MSSMS...... Munitions Section of Strategic Missile Squadron (AAG)
MSSN....... Mean Square Signal-to-Noise (IAA)
MSSN....... Mission
MSSN....... Mission Resources Corp. [*NASDAQ symbol*]
MSSNRY.... Missionary
MSSNSW... Multiple Sclerosis Society of New South Wales [*Australia*]
MSSNY...... Medical Society of the State of New York [*Medicine*] (EDAA)
MSSP........ Managed Security Service Provider
MSSP........ Miscellaneous Small Special Projects (AAG)
MSSP........ Missionary Society of Saint Paul [*Australia*]
MSSp........ Mission Sisters of the Holy Spirit [*Roman Catholic religious order*]
MSSP........ Model Seafood Surveillance Project [*National Marine Fisheries Service*]
MSSPA...... Master of Speech Pathology and Audiology (GAGS)
MSSPA...... Missionary Society of St. Paul the Apostle (EA)
MSSPC...... Missionary Sisters of St. Peter Claver (EA)
MS Sp Ed... Master of Science in Special Education (PGP)
MS-SPRING... Multiplex-Section, Shared-Protection Rings
MSSQ....... Mission Support Squadron
MSSQ....... Multiple Sclerosis Society of Queensland [*Australia*]
MSSR....... Mars Soil [*or Surface*] Sample Return
MSSR....... Medical Society for the Study of Radiesthesia (EA)
MSSR....... Mixed Spectrum Superheat Reactor
MSSR....... Mobility, Survivability, Sizing Recommendations (MCD)
MSSR....... Monopulse Secondary Surveillance RADAR (DA)
MSSS........ Main Steam Supply System [*Nuclear energy*] (NRCH)
MSSS........ Maintenance and Service Subsystem (IAA)
MSSS........ Maintenance Supply Services System (NATG)
MSSS........ Manned Space Station Simulator [*NASA*] (MUGU)
MSSS........ Manned Static Space Simulator
MSSS........ Manuscripts, Signed
MSSS........ Mass Spectral Search System [*National Bureau of Standards, Environmental Protection Agency, and National Institutes of Health*] [*Database*]
MSSS........ Master of Science in Social Science
MSSS........ Maui Space Surveillance System [*Air Force Research Laboratory*] (RCD)
MSSS........ Midcourse Surveillance Satellite Study (ACAE)
MSSS........ Missionary Sisters of the Most Blessed Sacrament [*Roman Catholic religious order*]
MSSS........ Mobile Spectrum Search System
MSSS........ Mobile Submarine Simulator System (DWSG)
MSSS........ Multiple-Start Systematic Sampling [*Statistics*]
MSSS........ San Salvador/Ilopango Internacional [*El Salvador*] [*ICAO location identifier*] (ICLI)
MSSSE...... Message Submission and Storage Service Element [*Open Systems Interconnection*] (ODAA)
MSSSM-MMS... Missionary Sisters of the Society of Saint Mary - Marist Missionary Sisters (EA)
MSSST...... Meeting Street School Screening Test [*Used to detect learning disabilities*]
MSSSW..... Mass Spectral Search System-Wiley [*Cornell University*] [*Database*]
MSST........ JAMCO Ltd. [*NASDAQ symbol*] (COMM)
MSST........ Manufacturing Standards and Specifications for Textbooks
MSST........ Master of Science in Science Teaching
MSST........ Mean Sea Surface Temperature
MSST........ Meldesammelstelle [*Message Center*] [*German military - World War II*]
MSST........ Member of the Society of Surveying Technicians [*British*] (DBQ)
MSST........ Ministry of State for Science and Technology [*Canada*]
MSST........ Missionary Servants of the Most Holy Trinity [*Roman Catholic men's religious order*]
MSST........ Multiple Sclerosis Society of Tasmania [*Australia*]
MsSt......... Oktibbeha County Library System, Starkville, MS [*Library symbol*] [*Library of Congress*] (LCLS)
MSST........ Springfield Technical Community College, Springfield, MA [*Library symbol*] [*Library of Congress*] (LCLS)
MSSTA...... Multispectra Solar Telescope Array (SAUS)
MSStat...... Master of Science in Statistics (GAGS)
MSSTC...... Master of Science in Science and Technology Commercialization [*Military*] [*Army*]
MSSTC...... Mobile Service Structure Test Conductor (KSC)
MSStEng.... Master of Science in Structural Engineering (NADA)
MsStL....... Oktibbeha County Library System, Starkville, MS [*Library symbol*] [*Library of Congress*] (LCLS)
MSSTM..... Military Space Systems Technology Model (MCD)
MSSTS...... McMurdo Sound Sediment and Tectonic Studies (SAUS)
MSSU....... Meteorology on Stamps Study Unit [*American Topical Association*] (EA)
MSSU....... Midstream Specimen of Urine [*Medicine*]
MSSU....... Mississippi State University (PDAA)
MsSu........ Sunflower County Library, Sunflower, MS [*Library symbol*] [*Library of Congress*] (LCLS)
MS Surg.... Master of Science in Surgery (PGP)
MSSV........ Maize Sterile Stunt Virus [*Plant pathology*]
MSSV........ Maximum Safe Sampling Volume [*Analytical chemistry*]
MSSV........ Multiple Sclerosis Society of Victoria [*Australia*]
MSSVD...... Medical Society for the Study of Venereal Diseases [*Leeds, England*] (EAIO)
MSSVFI..... Manufacturers Standardization Society of the Valve and Fittings Industry (EA)
MSSW....... Magnetostatic Surface Wave [*Telecommunications*] (TEL)
MSSW....... Master of Science in Social Work
MSSWA..... Multiple Sclerosis Society of Western Australia
MS Sy Sc... Master of Science in Systems Science (PGP)
MST......... Aeroamistad SA de CV [*Mexico*] [*ICAO designator*] (FAAC)
MST......... Association of Maximum Service Telecasters (EA)

MsT......... Lee-Itawamba Regional Library, Tupelo, MS [*Library symbol*] [*Library of Congress*] (LCLS)
MST......... Maastricht [*Netherlands*] [*Airport symbol*] (OAG)
MST......... Machinery Safety Tag
MST......... Machine Shock Test
MST......... Machine Steel
MST......... Magnetostrictive Transducer
MST......... Maintenance Standard Tests [*Military*]
MST......... Maintenance Support Team (MCD)
MST......... Management Survey Team (AAG)
MST......... Manifold Surface Temperature [*Automotive engineering*]
MST......... Marconi Self-Tuning (IAA)
MST......... Marine Science Technician [*Coast Guard*] (MUSM)
MST......... Mass Spectrometer Tube
MST......... Mass Storage Task [*Computer science*] (NOAA)
MST......... Master (MCD)
MST......... Master of Sacred Theology
MST......... Master of Science in Taxation (GAGS)
MST......... Master of Science in Teaching
MST......... Master of Science in Tourism (GAGS)
MST......... Master of Science Teaching (GAGS)
MST......... Master of Science Technology (PGP)
MST......... Master of Secondary Teaching (GAGS)
MST......... Master of Speech Therapy (GAGS)
M St......... Master of Statistics
MSt......... Master of Studies, University of Oxford [*British*] (DBQ)
MST......... Master of Systems Technology (PGP)
MST......... Master of Teaching
MST......... Maximal Stimulation Test (DMAA)
MST......... Maximum Service Telecasters
MST......... Maximum Summer Temperature [*Climatology*]
MST......... McCarthy Screening Test [*Intended to diagnose academic potentials and disabilities*] (DIPS)
MST......... Mean Selected Temperature
MST......... Mean Service Time (CIST)
MST......... Mean Solar Time
MST......... Mean Spring Tide (ODA)
MST......... Mean Survival Time
MST......... Mean Swell Time [*Botulism test*] [*Food analysis*]
MST......... Measurement
MST......... Measurement Status Table (NASA)
MST......... Mechanics Support Team [*Military*] (GFGA)
MST......... Mecklenburg-Strelitz [*German license plate city code*]
MST......... Medial Superior Temporal [*Brain Anatomy*]
MST......... Median Survival Time
MST......... Media Systems Technology (HGAA)
MST......... Medium-Scale Technology
MST......... Medium STOL [*Short Takeoff and Landing*] Transport [*Aircraft*]
MST......... Memotron Storage Tube
MST......... Mercantile Stores Co., Inc. [*NYSE symbol*] (SPSG)
MST......... Mercury System Test [*NASA*]
MST......... Mesosphere-Stratosphere-Troposphere [*Marine science*] (OSRA)
MST......... Message Status Table (MCD)
MST......... Microprocessor Simulation Technology (SAUS)
MST......... Microsecond Trip
MST......... Micro System Technology (AAEL)
MST......... Microwave Satellite Technologies, Inc. [*Wellington, NJ*] (TSSD)
MST......... Midsummer Time
MST......... Military Science Training
MST......... Military Shipping Tag
MST......... Military Support Team (SAUS)
MST......... Miniature Situations Test (EDAC)
MST......... Minimal Spanning Tree [*Computer science*]
MST......... Minimum Spawning Time [*Pisciculture*]
MST......... Ministry, Society, and Theology [*A publication*] (APTA)
MST......... Missile Surveillance Technology (MCD)
MST......... Missile System Test
MST......... Mission Sequence Test (SAUS)
MST......... Mission Simulator Test (MCD)
MST......... Mission Support Team (MCD)
MST......... Mistral Resources Ltd. [*Vancouver Stock Exchange symbol*]
MST......... Mobile Service Tower [*Aerospace*]
MST......... Mobile Strike Team
MST......... Mobile Support Team (NVT)
MST......... Mobile Systems Technology (SAUS)
MST......... Modal Survey Test (MCD)
MST......... Modern Standard Telugu [*Linguistics*] (IEL)
MST......... Module Service Tool (NASA)
MST......... Module Systems Trainer (SAUS)
MST......... Moisture-Proof Heat-Sealing Transparent [*Flexography*] (DGA)
MST......... Monolithic Systems Technology
M St......... More's Notes on Stair's Institutes of Scotland [*A publication*] (ILCA)
MST......... Morphine Sulphate [*Medicine*] (WDAA)
MST......... Mostar [*Yugoslavia*] [*Seismograph station code, US Geological Survey*] [*Closed*] (SEIS)
MST......... Mountain Standard Time
MST......... Movement of Landless Rural Workers [*Brazil*]
MST......... Movimento Sem Terra [*Political party*] [*Brazil*]
MST......... Multimode Storage Tube
MST......... Multi Sensor Track (ACAE)
MST......... Multi-Sensor Tracking (SAUS)
MST......... Multisystem Test [*Military*]
MST......... Must [*Telegraphy*] (PCTE)
MST......... Mutual Security Treaty (MCD)
MST......... St. Cloud State University, St. Cloud, MN [*OCLC symbol*] (OCLC)
MST......... Therapeutic Massage Therapist (NUJO)
MST3K...... Mystery Science Theater 3000 [*Cable television program*]
MSTA........ Manufacturers Surgical Trade Association [*Later, HIMA*] (EA)
MSTA........ Master of Science in Statistics (PGP)
MSTA........ Master Tape (AAG)
MSTA........ Member of the Swimming Teachers' Association [*British*] (DBQ)
MSTA........ Mumps Skin Test Antigen [*Clinical chemistry*]
MSTAB...... Manufacturing Systems Technical Advisory Board (AAEL)
MSTACCMB... Master Aircraft Crewman Badge [*Military decoration*] (GFGA)
MSTAN...... Modal Stamen Number per Flower [*Botany*]
MST & E.... Multiservice Test and Evaluation [*Military*]
MSTAR...... Manportable Surveillance & Target Acquisition Radar (SAUS)
MSTAR...... MLRS [*Multiple Launch Rocket System*] Smart Tactical Rocket [*USA*]
MSTARAVB... Master Army Aviator Badge [*Military decoration*] (GFGA)
MSTART..... Missile System to Attack Relocatable Targets (ACAE)
MSTAT....... Marine Safety Training and Assistance Team [*RSPA*] (TAG)
M Stat....... Master of Statistics (PGP)
mstb......... Mastaba (VRA)
MSTB........ Mission Simulator and Training Building
MS TBR..... Morgan Stanley Group [*Associated Press*] (SAG)
MSTC........ Management Systems Training Council [*British*]
MSTC........ Manned Spacecraft Test Center [*NASA*] (KSC)
MSTC........ Manufacturing Systems and Technology Center [*Baltimore, MD*] [*Westinghouse Electric Corp.*]
MSTC........ Maryland State Teachers College
MSTC........ Massachusetts State Teachers College
MSTC........ Master of Science in Telecommunications (PGP)
MSTC........ Mastic
MSTC........ Microwave Sensitivity Time Control [*Circuit*]
MSTC........ Midwest Securities Trust Co.
MSTC........ Mistletoe Tex-Pack Express [*Common carrier symbol*]
MSTC........ Multi-Spectral Target Cueing (ACAE)
MSTCS(GB)... Member of the Society of Thoracic and Cardiovascular Surgeons (Great Britain)
MSTD........ Marine Safety Technology Division [*Medicine*] [*Coast Guard*] (EDAA)
MSTD........ Master Steward [*Marine Corps*]
MSTD........ Member of the Society of Typographic Designers (DGA)
MSTDIVB... Master Diver Badge [*Military decoration*] (GFGA)
MSTE........ Master of Science in Technical Education (GAGS)
MSTE........ Master of Science in Transportation Engineering (GAGS)
M St E....... Master of Structural Engineering
MSTE........ Steinbach Public Library, Manitoba [*Library symbol*] [*National Library of Canada*] (NLC)
MS (T Ed)... Master of Science in Teacher Education
MSTEd...... Master of Science in Technical Education (GAGS)
MSTEL...... Member of the Society of Telegraph Engineers, London [*British*] (ROG)
M St Eng.... Master of Structural Engineering
MSTEODBAD... Master Explosive Ordnance Disposal Badge [*Military decoration*] (GFGA)
M-STEP..... Multi-State Teacher Education Project
MSText..... Master of Science in Textiles (GAGS)
MS Text Chem... Master of Science in Textile Chemistry (PGP)
MSTFA...... (Methyl)trimethylsilyltrifluoroacetamide [*Organic chemistry*]
MSTFLSB... Master Flight Surgeon Badge [*Military decoration*] (GFGA)
MSTG........ Mass Storage Task Group [*CODASYL*]
MstG........ Master Glaziers Karate International [*Associated Press*] (SAG)
MSTG........ Material Safety Task Group [*Air Force*] (AFM)
MSTG........ Melbourne Screen and Theatre Guild [*Australia*]
MSTG........ Mustang Software [*NASDAQ symbol*] (TTSB)
MSTG........ Mustang Software, Inc. [*NASDAQ symbol*] (SAG)
MSTGA...... Library Allard, St. Georges, Manitoba [*Library symbol*] [*National Library of Canada*] (BIB)
MstGlaz..... Master Glaziers Karate International [*Associated Press*] (SAG)
MSTGP...... Material Safety Task Group [*Air Force*]
MSTh........ Mesothorium [*Radioelement*]
MsTI......... Itawamba Junior College, Tupelo Campus, Tupelo, MS [*Library symbol*] [*Library of Congress*] (LCLS)
MSTI......... Main Street Trust [*OTCBB symbol*]
MSTI......... Miniature Sensor Technology Integration [*Orbital satellites*]
MSTI......... Multiple Soft Tissue Injuries [*Medicine*] (DMAA)
M ST J...... Ordinary Member of the Order of St. John of Jerusalem
MSTJ......... Public Library, St. James-Assiniboia, Manitoba [*Library symbol*] [*National Library of Canada*] (NLC)
MSTK........ MOS Specific Tool Kit (SAUS)
MSTL........ Military Subvention Type Lorry [*British*]
MSTL........ Minneapolis & St. Louis Railway Co. [*Later, MSL Industries, Inc.*] [*AAR code*]
MSTLAB..... Materials and Science Toxicology Laboratory [*University of Tennessee*] [*Research center*] (RCD)
MSTLY....... Mostly [*NWS*] (FAAC)
mstly........ Mostly
MSTM....... Master of Science in Teaching Mathematics (PGP)
MSTM....... Master of Science in Technology Management (GAGS)
MSTM....... Master of Science in Tropical Medicine (GAGS)
MSTM....... Mennonite Village Museum, Steinbach, Manitoba [*Library symbol*] [*National Library of Canada*] (NLC)
MSTM....... Missile Service Test Model [*Military*] (IAA)
MS TMX.... Morgan Stanley Group, Inc. [*Associated Press*] (SAG)
MSTO........ Main-Sequence Turnoff [*Stellar physics*]
MSTO........ Military System Training Organization (SAA)
MStoc....... Stockbridge Library Association, Stockbridge, MA [*Library symbol*] [*Library of Congress*] (LCLS)

MStocA...... Austen Riggs Center, Inc., Stockbridge, MA [*Library symbol*] [*Library of Congress*] (LCLS)
MSTOL...... Medium-Slow Takeoff and Landing
MSTOS...... South Interlake Regional Library, Stonewall, Manitoba [*Library symbol*] [*National Library of Canada*] (NLC)
MsToT...... Tougaloo College, Tougaloo, MS [*Library symbol*] [*Library of Congress*] (LCLS)
MSTP........ Maintenance Support Test Package [*Military*]
MStp........ Maize Stripe [*Plant pathology*]
MSTP........ Manual System Training Program (SAA)
MSTP........ Master Template
MSTP........ Medical Scientist Training Program [*National Institutes of Health*]
MSTP........ Michigan State Trust for Railway Preservation [*Federal Railroad Administration identification code*]
MSTP........ Multimission Software Transmission Project (SAUS)
MStP & A... Minneapolis, St. Paul & Ashland Railway
MSTP & SSM... Minneapolis, St. Paul & Sault Ste. Marie Railway Co.
MSTPHC.... Multistop Time-to-Pulse Height Converter [*NASA*]
MSTPJ...... Jolys Regional Library, St. Pierre, Manitoba [*Library symbol*] [*National Library of Canada*] (NLC)
MSTPRCHT... Master Parachutist Badge [*Military decoration*] (GFGA)
MStpV...... Maize Stripe Virus [*Plant pathology*]
MSTR........ [*The*] Massena Terminal Railroad Co. [*AAR code*]
mstr........ Master (VRA)
MSTR........ Master
MSTR........ MicroStrategy [*NASDAQ symbol*]
MSTR........ MicroStrategy Inc'A' [*NASDAQ symbol*] (SG)
MSTR........ Moisture [*NWS*] (FAAC)
MSTR........ Morningstar Group [*NASDAQ symbol*] (SAG)
MSTR........ Multivariable Self-Tuning Regulator [*Control technology*]
MSTR........ Ste-Rose Regional Library, Manitoba [*Library symbol*] [*National Library of Canada*] (NLC)
MSTrans.... Master of Science in Transportation (NADA)
MSTransE... Master of Science in Transportation Engineering (NADA)
MSTRE...... Moisture (MSA)
MSTRP...... Motor Sports Technology Research Program [*Automotive engineering*]
MSTS........ Manifold Surface Temperature Sensor [*Automotive engineering*]
MSTS........ McDonnell Scrap Tool System [*McDonnell Douglas Corp.*] (MCD)
MSTS........ Mean Standard Toxicity Score (MCD)
MSTS........ Microprocessor Spark Timing System
MSTS........ Microsoft Terminal Server (SAUS)
MSTS........ Midcourse Surveillance Tracking System (SAUS)
MSTS........ Military Sea Transportation Service [*Later, MSC*] [*Navy*]
MSTS........ Minuteman System Test Station (ACAE)
MSTS........ Missile Simulator Test Set (MCD)
MSTS........ Missile Static Test Site [*Air Force*]
MSTS........ Missile Station Test Set (MCD)
MSTS........ Missile Subsystem Test Set [*Military*] (CAAL)
MSTS........ Multi-Source Tactical Systems (SAUS)
MSTS........ Multisubscriber Time-Sharing Systems [*Computer system*]
MSTS........ Multisystem Training System
MSTS........ Musculoskeletal Tumor Society [*Association*] (EA)
MSTSFE..... Military Sea Transport Service, Far East
MSTSL...... Master of Science in Teaching a Second Language (GAGS)
MSTSO...... Military Sea Transportation Service Office [*Obsolete*]
MSTT........ Multi-Spectral Tracking Telescope (ACAE)
MSTU........ Metanolsko Sircetni Kompleks Kikinda [*Intermodal shipping container symbol*] (TVRC)
MSTU........ Military Sea Transport Union
MStuO...... Old Sturbridge Village Library, Sturbridge, MA [*Library symbol*] [*Library of Congress*] (LCLS)
MSTV........ Maize Stripe Virus [*Plant pathology*]
MSTV........ Manned Supersonic Test Vehicle (MCD)
MSTV........ Master-Scale Television
MSTV........ Multi-Spectral Television (ACAE)
MsTy........ Walthall County Library, Tylertown, MS [*Library symbol*] [*Library of Congress*] (LCLS)
MSTZ........ Metropolitan Stevedore [*Federal Railroad Administration identification code*]
MSu......... Goodnow Library, Sudbury, MA [*Library symbol*] [*Library of Congress*] (LCLS)
MSU......... Main Storage Unit [*Computer science*]
MSU......... Main Switching Unit [*Telecommunications*] (NITA)
MSU......... Maintenance and Status Unit [*Telecommunications*] (TEL)
MSU......... Maintenance Service Unit (IAA)
MSU......... Maintenance Signal Unit [*Telecommunications*] (TEL)
MSU......... Maintenance Station Unit (ACAE)
MSU......... Malaria Survey Unit [*Army*] [*World War II*]
MSU......... Management Signal Unit [*Telecommunications*] (TEL)
MSU......... Management Support Unit
MSU......... Management Systems Unit
MSU......... Maple Sugar [*or Syrup*] Urine [*Medicine*] (DMAA)
MSU......... Marysvale [*Utah*] [*Seismograph station code, US Geological Survey*] (SEIS)
MSU......... Maseru [*Lesotho*] [*Airport symbol*] (OAG)
MSU......... Masonic Study Unit [*American Topical Association*] (EA)
msu......... Mass Storage Unit (NAKS)
MSU......... Mass Storage Unit [*Computer science*] (NASA)
MSU......... Material Salvage Unit
MSU......... Mathematical Study Unit [*American Topical Association*] (EA)
MSU......... Measurable System Unit (TIMI)
msu......... Measuring Stimuli Unit (NAKS)
MSU......... Measuring Stimuli Units (NASA)
MSU......... Medical Service Unit [*Air Force*] (AFM)
MSU......... Medical Studies Unit (DAVI)
MSU......... Medical Subjects Unit [*American Topical Association*] (EA)
MSU......... Medical Support Unit [*Department of Emergency Management*] (DEMM)
MSU......... Memory Service Unit [*Computer science*]
MSU......... Memphis State University [*Tennessee*]
MSU......... Message Signal Unit [*Communications term*] (DCT)
MSU......... Message Switching Unit
MSU......... Meteorology on Stamps Study Unit [*American Topical Association*] (EA)
MSU......... Michigan State University [*East Lansing*]
MSU......... Microelectronics Support Unit [*Department of Education and Science*] (NITA)
MSU......... Microwave Sounding Unit [*Telecommunications*] (TEL)
MSU......... Middle South Utilities, Inc. [*NYSE symbol*] (COMM)
MSU......... Midstream Specimen of Urine [*Medicine*]
MSU......... Mid-Stream Urine [*Medicine*] (DMAA)
MSU......... Million Service Units [*Computer science*] (GART)
MSU......... Mill Sawyers' Union [*British*]
MSU......... Ministerial Services Unit (SAUS)
MSU......... Mission Systems Update (SAUS)
msu......... Mississippi [*MARC country of publication code*] [*Library of Congress*] (LCCP)
MSU......... Mobile Signals Unit [*British military*] (DMA)
MSU......... Modern Sharing Unit [*Computer science*] (OA)
MSU......... Mode Selector Unit
MSU......... Monitored Stroke Unit (SAUS)
MSU......... Monosodium Urate [*Organic chemistry*]
MSU......... Montana State University [*Bozeman*]
MSU......... Morgan Stan Fin 7.82% Cp Uts [*NYSE symbol*] (TTSB)
MSU......... Morgan Stanley Financial [*NYSE symbol*] (SPSG)
MSU......... Morgan State University, Baltimore, MD [*OCLC symbol*] (OCLC)
MSU......... Motor-Switching Unit (MCD)
MSU......... Multiblock Synchronization Signal Unit [*Telecommunications*] (TEL)
MSU......... Multiple Signal Unit [*Telecommunications*] (TEL)
MSU......... Multipoint Signaling Unit [*Communications term*] (DCT)
MSU......... Murray State University [*Kentucky*]
MSU......... Myocardial Substrate Uptake [*Medicine*] (DMAA)
MsU......... University of Mississippi, University, MS [*Library symbol*] [*Library of Congress*] (LCLS)
MSUA....... Mobile Satellite Users Association (EA)
MSUAG...... Michigan State University Advisory Group [*Contracted with the Government of South Vietnam to provide-civilian training*] (VNW)
MSU Business Topics... Michigan State University Business Topics [*A publication*] (DLA)
MSUCLE.... Missouri State University Continuing Legal Education (DLA)
MSU/COM... College of Osteopathic Medicine [*Michigan State University*] (MHID)
MSUD....... Maple Syrup Urine Disease Family Support Group [*Founded in 1982*] (NRGU)
MSUD....... Master of Science in Urban Design (GAGS)
MSUDC...... Michigan State University Discrete Computer
MSUDFSG... MSUD [*Maple Syrup Urine Disease*] Family Support Group (EA)
MSUESM.... Master of Science in Urban Environmental Systems Management (PGP)
MSuL........ Goodnow Library, Sudbury, MA [*Library symbol*] [*Library of Congress*] (LCLS)
MSUL........ Medical Schools of the University of London (DAS)
MsU-L....... University of Mississippi, Law School, University, MS [*Library symbol*] [*Library of Congress*] (LCLS)
MSUM....... Mission Society for United Methodists (EA)
MSUM....... Monosodium Urate Monohydrate [*Organic chemistry*]
MsU-M...... University of Mississippi, Medical Center, Jackson, MS [*Library symbol*] [*Library of Congress*] (LCLS)
MSUP....... Mouvement pour la Solidarite, l'Union et le Progres [*Benin*] [*Political party*] (EY)
MsU-P....... University of Mississippi, School of Pharmacy, University, MS [*Library symbol*] [*Library of Congress*] (LCLS)
MSU-PVMA... Michigan State University Pre-Veterinary Medical Association (GVA)
M Sur....... Master of Surgery
MSUR....... Masur Trucking [*Common carrier symbol*]
MSURC...... Mulberry Street Urban Renewal Corp. (EFIS)
MSurg...... Master of Surgery (BABM)
MSurgery... Master of Surgery (NADA)
MSurv...... Master of Surveying
MSurvMap... Master of Surveying and Mapping
MSurvSc.... Master of Surveying Science
MSUS....... Mouvement Socialiste d'Union Senegalaise [*Senegalese Socialist Movement*] [*Political party*]
MSUSM..... Medical Society of the United States and Mexico (EA)
MSUS/PALS... Minnesota State Universities System Project for Automated Library Systems [*Mankato State University Library*] [*Mankato, MN*] [*Information service or system*]
MSuSR...... Sperry Rand Research Center, Sudbury, MA [*Library symbol*] [*Library of Congress*] (LCLS)
MSUU....... Municipal Services [*Intermodal shipping container symbol*] (TVRC)
MSV......... Catskills/Sullivan County [*New York*] [*Airport symbol*] [*Obsolete*] (OAG)
MSV......... Magnetically Supported Vehicle
MSV......... Maintenance Support Vessel
MSV......... Maize Streak Virus [*Plant pathology*]
MSV......... Manned Space Vehicle [*NASA*] (AAG)
MSV......... Manufacturers Services [*NYSE symbol*]
MSV......... Martian Surface Vehicle
MSV......... Mass Stimulated Vehicles (MCD)
MSV......... Mass Storage Volume

MSV .... Materials Screening Vehicle (SAUS)
MSV .... Maximal Sustained Level of Ventilation [*Medicine*]
MSV .... Mean Scale Value [*Medicine*] (EDAA)
MSV .... Mean Square Velocity
MSV .... Mean Square Voltage (NRCH)
MSV .... Medical Society of Virginia (SAUS)
MSV .... Meteor Simulation Vehicle (SAA)
MSV .... Micro Surveillance system (SAUS)
mSv........ Millisievert [*Radiation dose*]
MSV .... Miniature Solenoid Valve
MSV .... Missionary Sisters of Verona [*Roman Catholic religious order*]
MSV .... Mississippi & Skuna Valley Railroad Co. [*AAR code*]
MSV .... Mobile Surface Vehicle (AAG)
MSV .... Mobile Surveillance Vehicle [*Police and security equipment*]
MSV .... Modular Support Vehicle (SAUS)
MSV .... Molecular Solution Volume
MSV .... Molinia Streak Virus
MSV .... Moloney Sarcoma Virus (AAMN)
MSV .... Monitored Sine Vibration [*Test*] (MCD)
msv........ Monitored Sine Vibration [*Test*] (NAKS)
MSV .... Monticello, NY [*Location identifier*] [*FAA*] (FAAL)
MSV .... Morgan Stan Fin 9% Cp Uts [*NYSE symbol*] (TTSB)
MSV .... Morgan Stanley Finance Markets Ltd. Capital Units [*NYSE symbol*] (SAG)
MSV .... Mouse Sarcoma Virus
MSV .... Multifunctional Service Vessel [*Off-shore drilling technology*]
MSV .... Multipurpose Support Vessel [*Offshore drilling*]
MSV .... Multi-Service Vendor (VLIE)
MSV .... Murine Sarcoma Virus
MsV........ Vicksburg Public Library, Vicksburg, MS [*Library symbol*] [*Library of Congress*] (LCLS)
MSVA........ Magnetic Speed Variable Assist [*General Motors*] [*Power steering*]
MSVA........ Magnetic Steering Variable Assist [*Automotive engineering*]
MSVC........ Mass Storage Volume Control [*Computer science*] (BUR)
MSVC........ Master of Vocational Counseling (GAGS)
MSVC........ Maximal Sustained Ventilatory Capacity [*Medicine*] (DMAA)
MSVC........ Meta-Signalling Virtual Channel (VLIE)
MSVC........ Mount St. Vincent College [*New York*]
MSVCS ...... Missile Sight Video Camera Systems (MCD)
MSVD ...... Missile and Space Vehicle Department [*NASA*] (KSC)
MsVE........ United States Army, Corps of Engineers, Waterways Experiment Station, Vicksburg,MS [*Library symbol*] [*Library of Congress*] (LCLS)
MSVI .... Mass Storage Volume Inventory [*Computer science*] (IAA)
MSV(M)..... Murine Sarcoma Virus (Moloney)
MSVO .... Missile and Space Vehicle Office [*NASA*] (IAA)
MsVO........ Old Court House Museum Library, Vicksburg, MS [*Library symbol*] [*Library of Congress*] (LCLS)
MSVP........ Master Shuttle Verification Plan (MCD)
MSVR .... Mandatory Securities Valuation Reserve [*National Association of Insurance Commissioners*]
MSW .... Machine Status Word [*Computer science*]
MSW .... Magnetostatic Waves [*Telecommunications*] (TEL)
MSW .... Mammal Species of the World (SAUS)
MSW .... Massawa [*Ethiopia*] [*Airport symbol*] (OAG)
MSW .... Master of Social Welfare
MSW .... Master of Social Work
MSW .... Master's in Social Work
MSW .... Master Switch
MSW .... Maximum Shipping Weight [*MTMC*] (TAG)
MSW .... Mean Sea Water
MSW .... Mean Shallow Water
MSW .... Medical Social Worker [*British*]
MSW .... Medical Solid Waste (EEVL)
MSW .... Meters of Seawater [*Deep-sea diving*]
MSW .... Microswitch
MSW .... Microwave Spectrometer (TEL)
MSW .... Mikheyev-Smirnov-Wolfenstein Theory [*Oscillation effect*] [*Particle physics*]
MSW .... MI Software Co. [*Vancouver Stock Exchange symbol*]
MSW .... Mission West Properties [*AMEX symbol*] (SPSG)
MSW .... Modified Sinewave (SAUS)
MSW .... Most Significant Word (GART)
MSW .... Multiple Shrapnel Wounds
MSW .... Multiple Stab Wounds [*Emergency medicine*] (DAVI)
MSW .... Municipal Solid Waste
MSW .... Western Massachusetts Regional Public Library System, Springfield, MA [*Library symbol*] [*Library of Congress*] (LCLS)
MSWAMD... Market Steady With Moderate Demand [*Telegraphy*] (PCTE)
MSWAP ..... Master of Social Welfare and Administration Planning
MSWD....... Mean Square Weighted Deviation [*Statistics*]
MSWD....... Multisystem Weapon Delivery [*Air Force*]
M Sw En.... Master of Software Engineering (PGP)
MSWG....... Manpower Systems Work Group
MSWG....... Materials Science Working Group (SAUS)
MSWG....... Military Spending Working Group
MSWG....... Military Strategy Working Group (SAUS)
MSWG....... Modeling and Simulation Working Group
MS/WG...... Module Select/Write Gate [*Computer science*] (VLIE)
MS Windows... Microsoft Windows [*Computer science*] (DCOM)
MsWJ .... Jefferson College, Washington, MS [*Library symbol*] [*Library of Congress*] [*Obsolete*] (LCLS)
MSWJ .... Midland and South Western Junction Railway [*British*]
MSWL....... Municipal Solid Waste Landfill
MSWLF ..... Municipal Solid Waste Landfill
MSWLFS.... Municipal Solid Wast Landfills (BCP)
MSWM ...... Men Who Have Sex With Men [*AIDS transmission group*]
MsWov...... Wilkinson County Library System, Woodville, MS [*Library symbol*] [*Library of Congress*] (LCLS)
MsWp .... Tombigbee Regional Library, West Point, MS [*Library symbol*] [*Library of Congress*] (LCLS)
MsWpCt..... Court House Library, West Point, MS [*Library symbol*] [*Library of Congress*] (LCLS)
MsWpMH ... Mary Holmes College, West Point, MS [*Library symbol*] [*Library of Congress*] (LCLS)
MSWREE.... Master of Science in Water Resources and Environmental Engineering (PGP)
MSWT....... Minimum-Speed Wind Tunnel (MCD)
MsWv .... Water Valley Public Library, Water Valley, MS [*Library symbol*] [*Library of Congress*] (LCLS)
MSWYE ..... Modified Seawater Yeast Extract [*Agar*] [*Microbiology*] (DAVI)
MSX .... Mascota [*Mexico*] [*Airport symbol*] (AD)
MSX .... MascoTech, Inc. [*NYSE symbol*] (SPSG)
MSX .... MicroSoft Extended [*Computer science*] (VLIE)
MSX .... Microsoft Extended Basic (NITA)
MSX .... Midcourse Space Experiment (MCD)
MSX .... Minesweeper, Experimental [*Navy symbol*]
MSX .... Mossendjo [*Congo*] [*Airport symbol*] (OAG)
MSX .... Multinucleate Nature, Spherical Shape, Unknown History
MSXN .... Mid-States Express [*Common carrier symbol*]
MSXPr....... Masco Tech Inc. Cv Pfd [*NYSE symbol*] (TTSB)
MSXU .... Marine Spill Response [*Intermodal shipping container symbol*] (TVRC)
MSY .... Massey University School of Aviation [*New Zealand*] [*ICAO designator*] (FAAC)
MSY .... Maximum Sustainable Yield
MSY .... Minimum Sustainable Yield [*Pisciculture*]
MSY .... Morgan Stanley High Yield Fund [*NYSE symbol*] (SPSG)
MSY .... Morgan Stanley Hi Yld Fd [*NYSE symbol*] (TTSB)
MSY .... Mostly [*Telegraphy*] (PCTE)
MSY .... New Orleans [*Louisiana*] [*Airport symbol*]
MsY......... Yazoo-Sharkey Library System, Yazoo City, MS [*Library symbol*] [*Library of Congress*] (LCLS)
MSYN .... Master Synchronization (VLIE)
MSYNC...... Master Synchronization [*Telecommunications*] (TEL)
MSYNC...... Master Synchronizer (MSA)
MSYS........ Marketing Systems USA [*OTCBB symbol*]
MSYS........ Medical Technology Systems, Inc. [*NASDAQ symbol*] (NQ)
M-SysFD.... M-Systems Flash Disk Pioneers Ltd. [*Associated Press*] (SAG)
M Sy Th.... Master of Systematic Theology
MSZ .... Massive Surf Zone
MSZ .... McLouth Steel [*Federal Railroad Administration identification code*]
MSZ .... Milford Sound [*New Zealand*] [*Seismograph station code, US Geological Survey*] (SEIS)
MSZ .... Moga Stan Fin 7.80% Cp Uts [*NYSE symbol*] (TTSB)
MSZ .... Morgan Stanley Finance Markets Ltd. Capital Unit [*NYSE symbol*] (SAG)
MSZ .... Mossamedes [*Angola*] [*Airport symbol*] (OAG)
MSZDP...... Magyar Szocial Demokrata Part [*Hungarian Social Democratic Party*] [*Political party*] (PPE)
MSZMP ..... Magyar Szocialista Munkaspart [*Hungarian Socialist Workers' Party*] [*Political party*] (PPE)
MSzP .... Magyar Szocialista Part [*Hungarian Socialist Party*] [*Political party*] (EY)
MT........... Core Melt Through [*Nuclear energy*] (IEEE)
MT........... Empty [*Slang*]
MT........... Flame Tight
MT........... Internacia Asocio Monda Turismo [*International Association for World Tourism*] (EAIO)
MT........... Internal Revenue Bureau Miscellaneous Tax Ruling [*United States*] [*A publication*] (DLA)
MT........... Machine Tool
MT........... Machine Tool Technology Program [*Association of Independent Colleges and Schools specialization code*]
MT........... Machine Translation [*Computer science*]
MT........... Mac Knight Airlines [*ICAO designator*] (AD)
M-T.......... Macroglobulin-Trypsin [*Complex*] (DAVI)
M-T.......... Macroglobulin-Trypsin Complex [*Medicine*] (BABM)
MT........... Magic Tee (IAA)
MT........... Magnetic
MT........... Magnetic Particle Testing [*Nuclear energy*] (IEEE)
MT........... Magnetic Tape
MT........... Magnetic Tube
mt........... Magnetite [*CIPW classification*] [*Geology*]
MT........... Magnetotelluric [*Geological surveying*]
MT........... Mail Transfer
MT........... Mail Tray (AAG)
MT........... Main Telescope
MT........... Maintenance Technician (MUGU)
MT........... Maintenance Time
MT........... Maintenance Trailer
MT........... Maintenance Trainer (MCD)
MT........... Malaria Therapy [*British*]
MT........... Malignant Teratoma [*Oncology*]
MT........... Malta [*IYRU nationality code*] [*ANSI two-letter standard code*] (CNC)
MT........... Mammary Tumor [*Medicine*]
MT........... Mammilothalamic Tract [*Anatomy*]
MT........... Management Team
MT........... Mandated Territory
MT........... Mannesman Tally (NITA)
MT........... Mantle Tentacle

MT .... Manual Test
MT .... Manual Traction (SAUS)
M/T .... Manual Transmission [*Automotive engineering*]
MT .... Manufacturing Technology (RDA)
MT .... Marathoner's Toe (MELL)
MT .... Mare Tranquillitatis [*Sea of Tranquility*] [*Lunar area*]
MT .... Maritime Tropical Air Mass
MT .... Market Town [*Geographical division*] [*British*]
MT .... Mark Trunk (IAA)
MT .... Masking Template (MCD)
MT .... Masoretic Text [*of the Bible*] [*Hebrew tradition*]
M/T .... Masses or Tumors [*Medicine*] (CPH)
MT .... Mast (IAA)
MT .... Master of Taxation (GAGS)
MT .... Master of Teaching (GAGS)
MT .... Master of Technology (GAGS)
MT .... Master of Textiles (PGP)
MT .... Master Teacher (ADA)
MT .... Master Timer
MT .... Master Tool (NASA)
MT .... Mat
MT .... Materials Test (IEEE)
MT .... Material Test (IAA)
MT .... Material Transfer (NRCH)
MT .... Mathematics Teacher [*A publication*]
Mt .... Matthew [*New Testament book*]
MT .... Maximal Therapy [*Medicine*]
MT .... Maximum Torque
MT .... Maximum Total (VLIE)
MT .... Maximum Traction [*Tire design*]
MT .... Mean Tide [*Tides and currents*]
MT .... Mean Time
MT .... Measured Time
MT .... Measurement (IAA)
MT .... Measurement Ton (MUGU)
M/T .... Measurement Tons (COE)
MT .... Measuring Transformer (IAA)
MT .... Mechanical Technician (KSC)
MT .... Mechanical Test (MCD)
MT .... Mechanical Time [*Fuse*] (AABC)
MT .... Mechanical Traction [*British military*] (DMA)
MT .... Mechanical Translation [*Computer science*]
MT .... Mechanical Transport
MT .... Mediaeval Towns [*A publication*]
MT .... Medial Triceps Brachii [*Medicine*]
MT .... MediaTel [*Database*] [*British*]
MT .... Medical Technician [*British military*] (DMA)
MT .... Medical Technologist
MT .... Medical Transcriptionist (DAVI)
MT .... Medical Transfer (WDAA)
MT .... Meditrust Corp. [*NYSE symbol*] [*Formerly, Meditrust SBI*] (SG)
MT .... Meditrust SBI [*NYSE symbol*] (SPSG)
MT .... Meditsinskaya Tekhnika [*Medicine*] [*Former USSR*] [*Journal*] (EDAA)
MT .... Medium Truck [*British*]
MT .... Meet [*Telegraphy*] (PCTE)
MT .... Megaton [*Nuclear equivalent of one million tons of high explosive*] (AFM)
Mt .... Megaton [*Emergency Management*] (EMA)
Mt .... Megatonnes [*Atmosphere*]
MT .... Megatron (CET)
Mt .... Meitnerium [*Proposed name and symbol for recently-discovered element*]
MT .... Melatonin (MELL)
MT .... Melt Through [*Nuclear energy*] (NRCH)
MT .... Membrana Tympani [*Anatomy*]
MT .... Mesenteric Traction [*Medicine*]
MT .... Mesotocin [*Endocrinology*]
MT .... Message Table [*Computer science*] (OA)
MT .... Message Terminal [*Police and security equipment*]
MT .... Message Transfer [*Computer science*] (VLIE)
MT .... Message Type (CGWS)
MT .... Metallothionein [*Biochemistry*]
MT .... Metal Threshold (AAG)
MT .... Metatarsal [*Anatomy*]
MT .... Meteor Construzioni Aeronautiche & Elettroniche SpA [*Italy*] [*ICAO aircraft manufacturer identifier*] (ICAO)
MT .... Meter (MCD)
MT .... Metering Truss (SAUS)
MT .... Methoxytryptamine [*Biochemistry*]
MT .... Methoxytyramine [*Biochemistry*]
MT .... Methyltryptophan [*Biochemistry*]
MT .... Methyltyrosine [*Biochemistry*]
Mt .... Metical (ODBW)
mt .... Metric Ton (SHCU)
MT .... Metric Ton [*1,000 kilograms*]
MT .... Michaelmas Term [*British*] [*Legal term*] (ROG)
MT .... Microptic Theodolite
MT .... Microsyn Torquer (SAA)
MT .... Microthrombus [*Hematology*]
MT .... Microtome [*Instrumentation*]
MT .... Microtubule [*Cytology*]
MT .... Microwave Thermograph [*Medical instrumentation*]
MT .... Middle Temple [*London*] [*One of the Inns of Court*]
MT .... Middle Temporal [*Anatomy*]
MT .... Middle Temporal Lobe [*of the brain*]
MT .... Middle Turbinate [*Otorhinolaryngology*] (DAVI)
MT .... Midland Terminal Railroad (IIA)
MT .... Midrash Tanna'im (BJA)
MT .... Midship Deep Tank
MT .... Might
MT .... Migraine Trust [*Medicine*] [*United Kingdom*] (EDAA)
MT .... Migratory Trout
MT .... Military Tanker [*British*]
MT .... Military Technician
MT .... Military Tractor [*British*]
MT .... Military Train [*British military*] (DMA)
MT .... Military Training
MT .... Military Transport
MT .... Million Tonne (CARB)
mT .... Millitesla
MT .... Miniature Tube (NTCM)
MT .... Minimum Tax Credit Adjustment [*Electric utility company*]
MT .... Minimum Temperature (DS)
MT .... Minimum Threshold [*Medicine*] (DB)
MT .... Minimum Transfer (DCTA)
MT .... Ministry of Transport [*Later, DOE*] [*British*]
MT .... Mishneh Torah [*Maimonides*] (BJA)
MT .... Missile Target (SAUS)
MT .... Missile Technician [*Navy rating*]
MT .... Missile Test
MT .... Missile Tilt
MT .... Mission Time (MCD)
MT .... Mission Trainer (ACAE)
MT .... Mission Trajectory (MCD)
MT .... Mississippi & Tennessee Railnet Railroad [*Federal Railroad Administration identification code*]
mt .... Mitochrondrial [*Medicine*]
MT .... Mitomycin [*Also, M, MC*] [*Antineoplastic drug*]
MT .... Mitotic Time (DB)
MT .... Mitral [*Valve*] [*Cardiology*]
MT .... Mitsubishi [*Society of Automotive Engineers auto manufacturer code for service information interchange*]
MT .... Mobile Target (SAUS)
MT .... Mobile Team
MT .... Mobile Terminal (DA)
MT .... Mobile Termination (SAUS)
MT .... Mobile/Transportable (CCCA)
MT .... Mobile Traveler [*Recreational vehicle*]
MT .... Mode Transducer
MT .... Modified Tape Armor [*Telecommunications*] (TEL)
MT .... Modus Tolens [*Rule of inference*] [*Logic*] [*Latin*]
MT .... Moluccas Time (SAUS)
MT .... Mongolia [*Civil aircraft markings - international*] (PIPO)
MT .... Monroe Tidal Drainage [*Medicine*] (DMAA)
MT .... Montana [*Postal code*]
MT .... Montana Reports [*A publication*] (DLA)
Mt .... Montana State Library, Helena, MT [*Library symbol*] [*Library of Congress*] (LCLS)
MT .... More Than
MT .... Morse Taper (IAA)
MT .... Morton Toe (MELL)
MT .... Moscow Time (SAUS)
MT .... Most (WGA)
MT .... Motilin [*Biochemistry*]
MT .... Mo Time [*An association*] (EA)
MT .... Motor Driver [*British military*] (DMA)
MT .... Motor Tanker
MT .... Motor Terminal (IAA)
MT .... Motor Threshold [*Medicine*]
MT .... Motor Transport [*Military*]
MT .... Motor Trend Magazine [*A publication*]
MT .... Mount [*Maps and charts*] (KSC)
Mt .... Mount (ODBW)
Mt .... Mountain (SHCU)
MT .... Mountain [*Board on Geographic Names*]
mt .... Mountain (VRA)
MT .... Mountain Time
MT .... Mounted [*Technical drawings*]
MT .... Mountings [*JETDS nomenclature*] [*Military*] (CET)
MT .... Mounting Tray
MT .... Movement Time [*Physical education*]
MT .... Moxalactam/Ticarcillin (DB)
MT .... MTC Electronic [*Vancouver Stock Exchange symbol*]
MT .... Mud Traction [*Tires*]
MT .... Muertos Trough [*Geology*]
MT .... Multi-frequency Transducer (SAUS)
MT .... Multiple Tics (MELL)
MT .... Multiple Transfer
MT .... Multiple Twin (IAA)
MT .... Multitasking
MT .... Muscle and Tendon [*Medicine*] (MAE)
MT .... Muscles and Tendons (SAUS)
MT .... Muscle Testing (MELL)
MT .... Muscle Trauma (MELL)
mt .... Music-Theatre Piece (GROV)
MT .... Music Therapist [*or Therapy*]
MT .... MUX [*Multiplex*] Terminal (MCD)
Mt .... Mycobacterium Tuberculosis [*Bacteriology*]

MT .... Myelotomography [*Medicine*]
MT .... Transcona Public Library, Manitoba [*Library symbol*] [*National Library of Canada*] (NLC)
MT .... Traverse City Public Library (SAUS)
MT1 .... Missile Technician, First Class [*Navy rating*]
MT2 .... Missile Technician, Second Class [*Navy rating*]
MT3 .... Missile Technician, Third Class [*Navy rating*]
MT6 .... Mercaptomerin [*Pharmacology*] (DAVI)
MTA .... Mackenzie Tribbeck Associates Ltd. (SAUS)
MTA .... MAC [*Military Airlift Command*] Transportation Authorization (AFM)
MTA .... Magnetic Tape Accessory [*General Electric Co.*]
MTA .... Magnetic Torquer Assembly (SAUS)
MTA .... Magyar TavKozlesi ADS [*NYSE symbol*] (SG)
MTA .... Mail Transfer Agent [*Computer science*]
MTA .... Maintenance Task Analysis
MTA .... Maintenance Training Aid (SAUS)
MTA .... Major Test Article (NASA)
MTA .... Major Trading Area (CGWS)
MTA .... Major Training Area [*Army*]
MTA .... Malignant Teratoma, Anaplastic [*Medicine*] (DMAA)
MTA .... Mammary Tumor Agent (DOG)
MTA .... Managed Thermactor Air [*Automotive engineering*]
MTA .... Management by Talking Around [*Business term*]
MTA .... Management Transactions Audit [*Test*]
MTA .... Manpower Training Association (AEBS)
MTA .... Man-Tended Approach (SSD)
MTA .... Manual Target Acquisition (MCD)
MTA .... Manufacturing Technical Assistance
MTA .... Marine Trades Association [*British*] (DBA)
MTA .... Maritime Training Association (EA)
MTA .... Market Technicians Association (NADA)
MTA .... Mark Twain Association (EA)
MTA .... Marshall Trowelable Ablator (SAUS)
MTA .... Mass Thermal Analysis (MCD)
MTA .... Master of Tax Accounting (GAGS)
MTA .... Master of Teaching Arts (GAGS)
MTA .... Master of Theater Arts (GAGS)
MTA .... Master Timer Assembly
MTA .... Materials Testing Activity (MCD)
MTA .... Materiel Transfer Agreement [*DoD*]
MTA .... Mean Tryptic Activity (PDAA)
MTA .... Measurement Tolerance Allowed (ACAE)
MTA .... Media Technology Associates Ltd. [*Bethesda, MD*] [*Telecommunications service*] (TSSD)
MTA .... Medical Technical Assistant (DMAA)
MTA .... Medical Technology Assessment (DMAA)
MTA .... Melamine Tableware Association (EA)
MTA .... Message Terminal Area (MCD)
MTA .... Message Transfer Agent [*Telecommunications*] (PCM)
MTA .... Message Transfer Architecture [*Computer science*]
MTA .... Message Transport Agent [*Telecommunications*] (PCM)
MTA .... Meta Communications Group, Inc. [*Toronto Stock Exchange symbol*]
MTA .... Metatarsus Adductus [*Anatomy*] (DAVI)
MTA .... MetaTechnologies Associates [*Oakland, CA*] [*Telecommunications service*] (TSSD)
MTA .... Methods-Time Analysis [*Industrial engineering*]
MTA .... Methylthionadenosine [*Biochemistry*]
MTA .... Metric Tons per Annum
MTA .... Metropolitan Transit Authority [*Later, MBTA*] [*Initialism also title of folk song about Boston's transit system*]
MTA .... Metropolitan Transportation Authority [*Greater New York City*]
MTA .... Metropolitan Travel Agents [*Inactive*] (EA)
MTA .... Michigan Tooling Association (EARSL)
MTA .... Michigan Towing Association (EARSL)
MTA .... Michigan Townships Association (EARSL)
MTA .... Michigan Trucking Association (EARSL)
MTA .... Midterm Availability
MTA .... Mid-West Truckers Association (EA)
MTA .... Military Technical Advisor (DNAB)
MTA .... Military Testing Association (MCD)
MTA .... Military Training Airspace (NATG)
MTA .... Military Training Area (DA)
MTA .... Military Transportation Authorization [*Air Force*]
MTA .... Miniature Truck Association [*Defunct*] (EA)
MTA .... Minimum Terms Agreement
MTA .... Minimum Terrain-Clearance Altitude [*Aviation*]
MTA .... Minimum Time Ashore (SAUS)
MTA .... Minor Task Authorization [*Navy*]
MTA .... Missile Transfer Area (IAA)
MTA .... Missile Tube Air
MTA .... Mississippi Test Area [*Aerospace*] (AAG)
MTA .... Mitchell Aero, Inc. [*ICAO designator*] (FAAC)
MTA .... Mobile Training Assistance (CINC)
MTA .... Mobility Test Article [*Lunar-surface rover*] [*NASA*]
MTA .... Modified Tape Armor [*Telecommunications*] (IAA)
MTA .... Monopulse Tracking Antenna
MTA .... Montana (automobile) [*NCIC car model code*]
MTA .... Motion-Time Analysis
MTA .... Motorhome Travelers Association [*Defunct*] (EA)
MTA .... Motor Trade Association (NADA)
MTA .... Mount Allison University Library [*UTLAS symbol*]
MTA .... Mount Auburn Hospital, Cambridge, MA [*OCLC symbol*] (OCLC)
MTA .... Movimiento Teresiano de Apostolado [*Teresian Apostolic Movement - TAM*] [*Italy*] (EAIO)
MTA .... M Technology Association
MTA .... Multilateral Trade Agreement (AAGC)
MTA .... MultiMedia Telecommunications Association [*Computer science*] (FOTI)
MTA .... Multiple Tailors Association [*British*] (BI)
MTA .... Multiple-Terminal Access [*Computer science*] (IBMDP)
MTA .... Multiterminal Adapter (IEEE)
MTA .... Multitumor Antibody [*Clinical chemistry*]
MTA .... Municipal Treasurers Association of the United States and Canada
MTA .... Museum Trustee Association (EA)
MTA .... Musical Theatres Association
MTA .... Music Teachers' Association [*British*] (BI)
MTA .... Music Trades' Association [*British*] (BI)
MTA .... Muslim Teachers' Association (AIE)
MTA .... Myoclonic Twitch Activity [*Neurology*] (DAVI)
MTA .... Reference My Talk Address [*Military*] (IAA)
MTa .... Taunton Public Library, Taunton, MA [*Library symbol*] [*Library of Congress*] (LCLS)
MTA 4 .... Medical Technician, Acting, 4th Class [*British military*] (DMA)
MTAA .... Mopar Trans-Am Association [*Commercial firm*] (EA)
MTaB .... Bristol County Law Library, Taunton, MA [*Library symbol*] [*Library of Congress*] (LCLS)
MTAB .... Marginal Terrain Assault Bridge [*Military*] (RDA)
MTAB .... Military Technical Acceptance Board (MCD)
MTAC .... Mailers Technical Advisory Committee (EA)
MTAC .... Mathematical Tables and Other Aids to Computation
MTAC .... Michigan Test of Aural Comprehension [*J. Upshur*] (TES)
MTAC .... Mid-Atlantic Technology Applications Center [*University of Pittsburgh*] [*Research center*] (RCD)
MTAC .... Minatitlan Al Carmen Railroad [*Federal Railroad Administration identification code*]
MTAC .... Motor Transport Association of Connecticut (EARSL)
MTAC .... Multiple Test Acceptance Code [*Lubricants testing*] [*Automotive engineering*]
MTAC .... Multiple Test Acceptance Criteria
MTAC .... Multiple Time Around Clutter
MTAC .... Office of Technology Management [*University of Pittsburgh*] (IID)
MTACC ...... Modular Tactical Air Control Centre (SAUS)
MTACCS ..... Marine Tactical Command and Control System (MCD)
MTACLS ..... Marine Tactical Air Control and Landing System
MTACP ...... Magnetic Tape Ancillary Control Process [*Computer science*] (CIST)
MTACS ...... Marine Tactical Air Control System (SAUS)
MTAD .... Multi-Trace Analysis Display (SAUS)
MTAD .... N-methyl-triazolinedione
MTADS ...... Marine Corps Tactical Data System (AFIT)
MTADS ...... Mass Tactical Aerial Delivery System (SAUS)
MTAE .... Message Transfer Agent Entity [*Telecommunications*] (OSI)
MTAE .... Multiple-Time-Around Echoes (SAUS)
MTAE .... Multiple Time Around Elimination (ACAE)
MTAF .... Mediterranean Tactical Air Force Headquarters
MTAG .... Manufacturing Technology Advisory Group [*DoD*] (RDA)
MTAG .... Mission Theological Advisory Group (WDAA)
MTaHi .... Old Colony Historical Society, Taunton, MA [*Library symbol*] [*Library of Congress*] (LCLS)
MtAHS .... Alberton High School, Alberton, MT [*Library symbol*] [*Library of Congress*] (LCLS)
MTAI .... Meal Tickets Authorized and Issued [*Army*] (AABC)
MTAI .... Member of the Institute of Travel Agents [*British*]
MTAI .... Minnesota Teacher Attitude Inventory
MTAIF .... Member of the Australasian Institute for Fundraising (NFD)
MTAK .... Magyar Tudomanyos Akademia Konyvtara [*Hungarian Academy of Sciences Library*] (IID)
mTAL .... Medullary Thick Ascending Limb [*Anatomy*]
MTAM .... Maritime Tropical Air Mass (MSA)
MTAM .... Multileaving Telecommunications Access Method (VLIE)
MTAMP ...... Matamoros, TM [*American Association of Railroads railroad junction routing code*]
MTAMRI ..... Machine Tool Agile Manufacturing Research Institute (RCD)
MT(AMT) .... Medical Technologist (American Medical Technologists) (DAVI)
MT & AETF ... Missile Tilt and Azimuth Error Test Fixture
MT & CE .... Missile Test and Checkout Equipment
MT&RC ..... Marine Training and Replacement Command (SAA)
MT & SE .... Maintenance Test and Support Equipment
MTANSW .... Motor Trades Association of New South Wales [*Australia*]
MTANSW .... Music Teachers' Association of South Australia
MTAP .... Machine Timing Analysis Program (VLIE)
MTAP .... Management Technical Applications Plan (MCD)
MTAP .... Methylthioadenosine Phosphorylase [*An enzyme*]
MTAP .... Multifunction Target Acquisition Processor (ACAE)
MTAR .... Manual Terrain Avoidance RADAR
MTAR .... Moving Target Acquisition RADAR (MCD)
MTARRI ..... MTA Remedial Resources, Inc. (EFIS)
MTAS .... Membrana Tympana Auris Sinistrae [*Medicine*] (DMAA)
MTAS .... Microwave Transistor Amplifiers (ACAE)
MTAS .... Modular Target Acquisition System (TIMI)
MTAS .... Multisensor Target Acquisition System [*Military*] (RDA)
MTASA ...... Motor Trade Association of South Australia
MTASC ...... Mercer Trenton Addiction Science Center (MHID)
MT(ASCP) ... Registered Medical Technologist (American Society of Clinical Pathologists)
MT(ASCP)SBB ... Medical Technologist (American Society of Clinical Pathologists) Specialist in Blood Bank [*Technology*] (DAVI)
MTase .... Methyltransferase [*An enzyme*]
MTA/SME ... Machining Technology Association of the Society of Manufacturing Engineers (EA)

MTAT .... Mean Turn-Around Time [*Quality control*]
MTAT .... Mixing Tee Acceptance Test [*Automotive emissions*]
MTAU .... Metallic Test Access Unit [*Communications term*] (DCT)
MTA US & C... Municipal Treasurers Association of the US and Canada (EA)
MTAWA ...... Motor Trade Association of Western Australia
MTAX .... Massachusetts Transit Administration [*Federal Railroad Administration identification code*]
M Tax .... Master of Taxation (PGP)
MtB .... Bozeman Pubic Library, Bozeman, MT [*Library symbol*] [*Library of Congress*] (LCLS)
MTB .... Maintenance of True Bearing
MTB .... Maintenance Time Budget
MTB .... Main Terminal Board
MTB .... Main Time Base [*Electronics*]
MTB .... Malaysian Tin Bureau [*Defunct*] (EA)
MTB .... M&T Bank [*NYSE symbol*] [*Formerly, First Empire State*]
MTB .... M&T Bank Corp. [*NYSE symbol*]
MTB .... Maori Trust Board (SAUS)
MTB .... Marcaptan Terminated Polybutadiene (PDAA)
MTB .... Marine Test Boat
MTB .... Mark Twain Bancshares, Inc. [*NYSE symbol*] (SAG)
MTB .... Materials Testing Branch [*NASA*]
MTB .... Materials Transportation Bureau [*Department of Transportation*]
MTB .... Maximum Theoretical Bandwidth (MHDI)
MTB .... Mechanical Time Base
MTB .... Medium Tank Battalion
MTB .... Message to Base
MTB .... Methantheline [*or Methanthine*] Bromide [*Pharmacology*]
MTB .... Methoxy(trifluoromethyl)butyrophenone [*Biochemistry*]
MTB .... Methylthymol Blue [*An indicator*] [*Chemistry*]
MTB .... Missile Torpedo Boat (SAUS)
MTB .... Mobility Test-Bed (SAUS)
MTB .... Modified Tyrode's Buffer [*Clinical chemistry*]
MTB .... Module Test Bed [*Military*] (CAAL)
MTB .... Monte Libano [*Colombia*] [*Airport symbol*] (OAG)
MTB .... Monterey, CA [*Location identifier*] [*FAA*] (FAAL)
MTB .... (Morpholinylthio)benzothiazole [*Organic chemistry*]
MTB .... Motor Tariff Bureau, Charleston WV [*STAC*]
MTB .... Motor Torpedo Boat
MTB .... Mountain Bike (ODA)
MTB .... Multichannel Triple Bridge
MTB .... Seaplane Bomber [*Russian symbol*]
MTBA .... Machine Tool Builders' Association
MTBA .... Master Test Bed Aircraft (ACAE)
MTBA .... Mean Time Between Assists (AAEL)
MTBA .... Melbourne Tenpin Bowling Association [*Australia*]
MTBA .... Methyl-tert-butylaniline [*Organic chemistry*]
MTBA .... Multi-Threat Body Armor [*Army*]
MtBaF .... Fallon County Library, Baker MT [*Library symbol*] [*Library of Congress*] (LCLS)
MtBaHS ..... Baker High School, Baker, MT [*Library symbol*] [*Library of Congress*] (LCLS)
MTBAMA .... Mean Time between Any Maintenance Actions [*Quality control*] (MCD)
MTBAP ...... Mean Productive Time Between Assists
MTBASIC .... Multitasking BASIC [*Computer science*]
MTBC .... Mean Time Between Calls [*Computer science*] (ELAL)
MTBC .... Mitsubishi Trust and Banking Corporation (EFIS)
MtBC .... Montana State University at Bozeman, Bozeman, MT [*Library symbol*] [*Library of Congress*] (LCLS)
MTBCA ...... Mean Time between Corrective Action (MCD)
MTBCA ...... M.T. Bottle Collectors Association (EA)
MTBCD ...... Mean Time Between Confirmed Defects [*Quality control*] (MHDI)
MTBCF ...... Mean Time between Confirmed Failures [*Quality control*]
MTBCF ...... Mission Time between Critical Failures
MTBCMA .... Mean Time Between Corrective Maintenance (ACAE)
MTBCME .... Mean Time between Corrective Maintenance Events [*Quality control*] (CAAL)
MTBCMI .... Mean Time between Corrective Maintenance Interrupts [*Quality control*] (CAAL)
MTBD .... Mean Time between Defects [*Quality control*] (PDAA)
MTBD .... Mean Time between Degradations [*Quality control*] [*Telecommunications*] (TEL)
MTBD .... Mean Time between Demands [*Quality control*] (MCD)
MTBD .... Mean Time between Discrepancies [*Quality control*]
MTBD .... Methyl(triazabicyclo)decene [*Organic chemistry*]
MTBDE ...... Mean Time between Downing Events [*Quality control*]
MTBDR ...... Mean Time between Depot Repair [*Quality control*] (PDAA)
MTBDU ...... Mean Time between Data Unavailability [*Computer science*] (GART)
MTBE .... Mean Time between Errors [*Quality control*]
MTBE .... Mean Time between Events [*Quality control*]
MTBE .... Meningeal Tick-Borne Encephalitis [*Medicine*] (DMAA)
MTBE .... Methyl Tertiary Butyl Ether [*Fuel additive*]
MTBE .... Motobecane [*NCIC motorcycle make code*]
MTBEF ...... Mean Time Between Equipment Failures (ACAE)
MtBeHS ..... Rocky Boy Tribal High School, Box Elder, MT [*Library symbol*] [*Library of Congress*] (LCLS)
MTBEMA .... Mean Time between Essential Maintenance Actions [*Quality control*]
MTBER ...... Mean Time between Engine Removal [*Quality control*] (DNAB)
MTBERA .... Mean Time between Essential Replacement Actions [*Quality control*]
MtBeS .... Stone Child Community College, Box Elder, MT [*Library symbol*] [*Library of Congress*] (LCLS)
MTBETF ..... Methyl Tertiary Butyl Ether Task Force (EA)
MTBF .... Mean Time between Failure [*Computer science*] (DCOM)
MTBF .... Mean Time Between Failures [*Communications term*] (DCT)
MTBFA ...... Mean Time between False Alarms [*Quality control*] (AABC)
MTBFC ...... Mean Time between Failures, Critical [*Military*]
MTBFC ...... Mean Time between Flight Cancellations [*Quality control*]
MTBFEC ..... Motor Truck, Bus, and Fire Engine Club [*Defunct*] (EA)
MTBFL ...... Mean Time between Function Loss [*Quality control*]
MTBFMI ..... Mean Time Between False Maintenance Indicators (ACAE)
MTBFP ...... Mean Productive Time Between Failures
MTBFRO .... Mean Time between Failures Requiring Overhaul [*Quality control*]
MTBHA ...... Mark Twain Boyhood Home Associates (EA)
MTBHMF .... Maintenance between Hardware Mission Failures [*Quality control*]
MTBHQ ...... Mono-Tertiarybutylhydroquinone [*Also, TBHQ*] [*Organic chemistry*]
MTBI .... Mean Time Between Incident
MTBI .... Mean Time between Interrupts [*Quality control*]
MTBI .... Mild Traumatic Brain Injury
MtBil .... Billings Public Library, Billings, MT [*Library symbol*] [*Library of Congress*] (LCLS)
MtBilB .... Bureau of Land Management, Billings, MT [*Library symbol*] [*Library of Congress*] (LCLS)
MtBilBH ..... Big Sky Hospice, Billings, MT [*Library symbol*] [*Library of Congress*] (LCLS)
MtBilC .... Billings Clinic, Billings, MT [*Library symbol*] [*Library of Congress*] (LCLS)
MtBilD .... Deaconess Medical Center, Billings, MT [*Library symbol*] [*Library of Congress*] (LCLS)
MtBilE .... Eastern Montana College, Billings, MT [*Library symbol*] [*Library of Congress*] (LCLS)
MtBilFW .... United States Fish and Wildlife, Billings, MT [*Library symbol*] [*Library of Congress*] (LCLS)
MtBilGS ..... Church of Jesus Christ of Latter-Day Saints, Genealogical Society Library, Billings Branch, Billings, MT [*Library symbol*] [*Library of Congress*] (LCLS)
MtBilMH .... Billings Mental Health Center, Billings, MT [*Library symbol*] [*Library of Congress*] (LCLS)
MtBilNC ..... Northern Rockies Cancer Center, Billings, MT [*Library symbol*] [*Library of Congress*] (LCLS)
MtBilPP ..... Planned Parenthood of Billings, Billings, MT [*Library symbol*] [*Library of Congress*] (LCLS)
MtBilR .... Rocky Mountain College, Billings, MT [*Library symbol*] [*Library of Congress*] (LCLS)
MtBilRF ..... Rimrock Foundation Library, Billings, MT [*Library symbol*] [*Library of Congress*] (LCLS)
MtBils .... Billings Public Schools, Billings, MT [*Library symbol*] [*Library of Congress*] (LCLS)
MtBilSV ..... Saint Vincents Hospital, Billings, MT [*Library symbol*] [*Library of Congress*] (LCLS)
MtBilY .... Yellowstone Treatment Center, Billings, MT [*Library symbol*] [*Library of Congress*] (LCLS)
MtBilYH ..... Yellowstone City-County Helth Department, Billings, MT [*Library symbol*] [*Library of Congress*] (LCLS)
MTblack ..... Medium Thermal Black (EDCT)
MTBM .... Mean Time between Maintenance [*Quality control*] (AFM)
MTBM .... Mean Time between Malfunctions [*Quality control*]
MTBM .... Microtunneling Boring Machine (RDA)
MTBMA ..... Mean Time between Maintenance Actions [*Quality control*]
MTBMAF .... Mean Time between Mission Affecting Failures [*Quality control*]
MTBMCF .... Mean Time between Mission Critical Failure [*Quality control*]
MTBME ...... Mean Time between Malfunction Events [*Quality control*] (CAAL)
MTBN .... Motor Transportation Battalion [*Military*]
MTBN .... Mountbatten, Inc. [*NASDAQ symbol*] (SAG)
MTBO .... Mean Time Before Obsolescence [*Navy*] (DOMA)
MTBO .... Mean Time between Outages [*Quality control*] [*Telecommunications*] (TEL)
MTBO .... Mean Time between Overhauls [*Quality control*] (MCD)
MTBO .... Minimum Time before Overhaul [*Quality control*]
MTBOF ...... Mean Time between Operational Failures [*Quality control*]
MTBOMF .... Mean Time between Operational Mission Failures [*Quality control*] (MCD)
MTBPER .... Mean Time between Permanent Engine Removal [*Quality control*] (DNAB)
MTBPM ..... Mean Time Between Planned Maintenance [*Engineering*]
MtBr .... Broadus Public Library, Broadus, MT [*Library symbol*] [*Library of Congress*] (LCLS)
MTBR .... Mean Time between Removal [*or Repair or Replacement*] [*Quality control*]
MTBR .... Mean Time Between Replacement
MTBRDR .... Mean Time between Removal for Depot Repair [*Quality control*] (MCD)
MTBRON .... Motor Torpedo Boat Squadron [*Navy*]
MTBS .... Mean Time between Service [*Quality control*] (MCD)
MTBS .... Mean Time Between Stops [*Quality control*] (IAA)
MTBS .... Methuen's Text-Books of Science [*A publication*]
MTBSD ...... Mean Time between Supply Demands [*Quality control*] (MCD)
MTBSE ...... Mean Time Between Software Errors [*Quality control*] (MHDI)
MTBSF ...... Mean Time between Software Failures [*Quality control*] (CAAL)
MTBSF ...... Mean Time between System Failures [*Quality control*]
MTBSHF .... Mean Time between System Hardware Failures [*Quality control*] (MCD)
MTBSOF .... Mean Time between System Operational Failures [*Quality control*] (MCD)
MTBSP ...... Mobilization Troop Basic Stationing Plan (MCD)
MTBSTC .... Motor Torpedo Boat Squadrons Training Center [*Melville, RI*] [*Navy*]
MTBT .... Miniature Thermal Bar Torch [*Army*] (RDA)
MTBTF ...... Mean Time between Testable Failures [*Quality control*]
MtBu .... Butte Free Public Library, Butte, MT [*Library symbol*] [*Library of Congress*] (LCLS)
MtBuE .... Montana Energy Research and Development Institute, Butte, MT [*Library symbol*] [*Library of Congress*] (LCLS)

MTBUF ...... Mean Time Between Undetected Failures [*Quality control*] (IAA)
MtBULM .... Union List of Montana Serials, Bozeman, MT [*Library symbol*] [*Library of Congress*] (LCLS)
MTBUM ..... Mean Time Between Unscheduled Maintenance [*Quality control*] (MHDI)
MtBuM ...... Montana College of Mineral Science and Technology, Butte, MT [*Library symbol*] [*Library of Congress*] (LCLS)
MTBUMA.... Mean Time between Unscheduled Maintenance Actions [*Quality control*]
MTBUR...... Mean Time between Unscheduled Removals [*or Replacements*] [*Quality control*]
MtBwB ...... Blackfeet Community College Library, Browning, MT [*Library symbol*] [*Library of Congress*] (LCLS)
MTC .... Carroll College, Library, Helena, MT [*OCLC symbol*] (OCLC)
MTC .... Machine Tool Control
MTC .... Machine Trim Compensator (AAG)
MTC .... Mackinac Transportation [*Federal Railroad Administration identification code*]
MTC .... Magnetic Tape Cassette [*Computer science*]
MTC .... Magnetic Tape Channel [*Computer science*]
MTC .... Magnetic Tape Command [*Computer science*] (IAA)
MTC .... Magnetic Tape Control [*Computer science*]
MTC .... Magnetic Tape Controller (NITA)
MTC .... Magnetization Transfer Contrast [*Imaging technique*]
MTC .... Maintenance Task Cycle
MTC .... Maintenance Time Constraint (IEEE)
MTC .... Main Trunk Circuit [*World Meteorological Organization*] [*Telecommunications*] (TEL)
MTC .... Majestic Resources [*Vancouver Stock Exchange symbol*]
MTC .... Make Today Count (EA)
MTC .... Maneuver Training Command [*Army*] (AABC)
MTC .... Manhattan Theater Club
MTC .... Manitowoc, WI [*Amtrak Busline code*]
MTC .... Man-Tended Capability (SSD)
MTC .... Man-Tended Committee (SSD)
MTC .... Manual Traffic Control (MCD)
MTC .... Manufacturing Technology Center
MTC .... Manufacturing Technology Centre of New Brunswick [*Research center*] (RCD)
MTC .... Marcus Tullius Cicero [*Roman orator and author, 106-43 BC*]
MTC .... Maritime Transport Committee [*OECD*] (DS)
MTC .... Mass Transfer Coefficient
MTC .... Master of Textile Chemistry
MTC .... Master Table of Contents (IAA)
MTC .... Master Tape Control
MTC .... Master Test Component (SAUS)
MTC .... Master Thrust Control [*or Controller*] [*NASA*] (NASA)
MTC .... Master Training Concept [*Problem solving*]
MTC .... Material Testing Center
MTC .... Materiel Testing Command [*Merged with Weapons and Mobility Command*] [*Army*]
MTC .... Maximum Tolerable Concentration [*Toxicology*]
MTC .... Maximum Toxic Concentration [*Medicine*]
MTC .... Maximum Track Capacity
MTC .... Mazda Technical Center [*Automotive industry*]
MTC .... Mechanical Torpedo Countermeasure [*Military*] (CAAL)
MTC .... Mechanical Training Centre (SAUS)
MTC .... Mechanical Transport Corps
MTC .... Medical Test Cabinet
MTC .... Medical Training Center [*Later, Academy of Health Sciences*] [*Army*]
MTC .... Mediterranean Third Countries (EURO)
MTC .... Medium Terminal Complexes (MCD)
MTC .... Medullary Thyroid Carcinoma [*Medicine*]
MTC .... Meet the Composer (EA)
MTC .... Member of Technical College [*British*] (DI)
MTC .... Memory Test Computer [*SAGE*]
MTC .... Message Table of Contents (MCD)
MTC .... Message Transmission Controller
MTC .... Meteorological Training Center
Mtc .... Methylthiocarbamoyl [*Biochemistry*]
MTC .... Metocurine [*A muscle relaxant*]
MTC .... MIDI [*Musical Instrument Digital Interface*] Time Code
MTC .... Military Tactical Computer (MCD)
MTC .... Military Training Cadets [*A boys' World War II organization*]
MTC .... Military Transportation Command
MTC .... Military Transportation Committee [*NATO*] (NATG)
mtC .... Million Tonnes Carbon (EES)
MTC .... Mini Tele-Copter (SAUS)
MTC .... Minor Transaction Code (VLIE)
MTC .... Missile Technician, Chief [*Navy rating*]
MTC .... Missile Test Center
MTC .... Missile Transfer Car
MTC .... Missile Tube Control
MTC .... Mission and Test Computer
MTC .... Mission and Traffic Control
MTC .... Mitomycin C [*Mutamycin*] [*Also, Mi, MMC*] [*Antineoplastic drug*]
MTC .... Mitsui Toatsu Chemicals, Inc. [*Japan*]
MTC .... Mobile Tactical Computer (PDAA)
MTC .... Mobile Target Carrier
MTC .... Mobile Terminated Call (CGWS)
MTC .... Moderator Temperature Coefficient (NRCH)
MTC .... Modulation Transfer Curve (OA)
MTC .... Monostable Trigger Circuit (VLIE)
MTC .... Monsanto Co. [*NYSE symbol*] (SPSG)
MTC .... Morgan Territory [*California*] [*Seismograph station code, US Geological Survey*] (SEIS)
MTC .... Morse Telegraph Club (EA)
MTC .... Motor Transport Corps [*Military*]
MTC .... Mount Clemens, MI [*Location identifier*] [*FAA*] (FAAL)
MTC .... MOUT [*Military Operations on Urbanized Terrain*] Training Complex [*Army*] (INF)
MTC .... Mouvement Traditionaliste Congolais [*Congolese Traditionalist Movement*]
MTC .... Moving Target Carrier (MCD)
MTC .... Multicomm Telecommunications Corp. [*Formerly, Mutual Satellite Services*]
MTC .... Multiple Tube Counts
MTC .... Multistate Tax Commission (EA)
MTC .... Music Teacher's Certificate [*British*] (DI)
MTC .... Mutating Transformation Converter (IAA)
MTC .... Mystic Terminal Co. [*AAR code*]
MTC .... Ontario Ministry of Transportation and Communications [*Canada*] (TSSD)
MTCA........ Cayes [*Haiti*] [*ICAO location identifier*] (ICLI)
MTCA........ Methyltetrahydrocarbolinecarboxylic Acid [*Organic chemistry*]
MTCA........ Methylthiazolidinecarboxylic Acid [*Organic chemistry*]
MTCA........ Military Terminal Control Area
MTCA........ Minimum Terrain-Clearance Altitude [*Aviation*]
MTCA........ Ministry of Transport and Civil Aviation [*Later, MT*] [*British*] (MCD)
MTCA........ Monitor and Test Control Area [*NASA*] (NASA)
MTCA........ Multiple-Terminal Communication Adapter [*Computer science*]
MtCaC....... Little Big Horn College, Crow Agency, MT [*Library symbol*] [*Library of Congress*] (LCLS)
MTCACS .... Marine Corps Tactical Command and Control System (MCD)
MTCAR...... Mount Carmel, IL [*American Association of Railroads railroad junction routing code*]
MTCAS ...... Marine Corps Tactical Command and control System (SAUS)
MTCB........ Master Timer Control Block [*Computer science*] (VLIE)
MTCB........ Metropolitan Taxicab Board (NADA)
MTCC........ Magnetics Technology [*NASDAQ symbol*] (SAG)
MTCC........ Magnetic Technologies [*NASDAQ symbol*] (TTSB)
MTCC........ Master Timing and Control Circuit
MTCC........ Military Air Transport Service [*later, Military Airlift Command*] TransportControl Center
MTCC........ Modular Tactical Communications Center
MTCD........ Microvolume Thermal Conductivity Detector [*Instrumentation*]
MTCE........ Maintenance [*Telecommunications*] (TEL)
MTCE........ Michigan Transit Center for Excellence [*Michigan State University*] (RCD)
MTCE........ Million Tonnes of Carbon Equivalent (CARB)
MTCE........ Million Tons of Coal Equivalent [*A comparative unit of energy content widely used in the oil industry*]
MTCEF ...... MTC Electronic Technology (EFIS)
MTCF........ Mean Time to Catastrophic Failure [*Quality control*]
MTCF........ Missile Tube Comparator Fixture
MtCG .... Glacier County Library, Cut Bank, MT [*Library symbol*] [*Library of Congress*] (LCLS)
MtCh......... Blaine County library, Chinook, MT [*Library symbol*] [*Library of Congress*] (LCLS)
MTCH........ Cap Haitien Internacional [*Haiti*] [*ICAO location identifier*] (ICLI)
MTCH........ Magnetic Tape Channel (NITA)
MT Ch........ Master of Textile Chemistry
MTCH........ Matchless [*NCIC motorcycle make code*]
MTCH........ Mining Technology Clearing House [*British*] [*Information service or system*] (IID)
MtchBnc .... Mitchell Bancorp, Inc. [*Associated Press*] (SAG)
MtChe .... Liberty County Library, Chester, MT [*Library symbol*] [*Library of Congress*] (LCLS)
MtchlE....... Mitchell Energy & Development Corp. [*Associated Press*] (SAG)
MtCi .... George McCone Memorial County Library, Circle, MT [*Library symbol*] [*Library of Congress*] (LCLS)
MTCI......... Magnetic Tape Control Interface (MCD)
MTCI......... Management Technologies [*NASDAQ symbol*] (TTSB)
MTCI......... Management Technologies, Inc. [*NASDAQ symbol*] (NQ)
MTCI......... Member of the Trust Companies Institute (DD)
MTCI......... Mississippi Tank Company [*NCIC trailer make code*]
MTCK........ Matlack [*Common carrier symbol*]
MTCL........ Motorcycle
MTCLO ...... Monticello, IL [*American Association of Railroads railroad junction routing code*]
MTCM .... Master of Traditional Chinese Medicine (PGP)
MTCM .... Missile Technician, Master Chief [*Navy rating*]
MTCN........ Minimum Throughput Class Negotiation (VLIE)
MTCNOLD... Minimum Tax Credit Net Operating Loss Deduction [*Business term*]
MTCO........ Macon Terminal Co. [*AAR code*]
MTCOECD... Maritime Transport Committee of the Organization for Economic Cooperation and Development [*France*] (EAIO)
MtCoHS ..... Columbus High School, Columbus, MT [*Library symbol*] [*Library of Congress*] (LCLS)
MtCol........ Colstrip Bicentennial Library, Colstrip, MT [*Library symbol*] [*Library of Congress*] (LCLS)
MtCon .... Conrad Public Library, Conrad, MT [*Library symbol*] [*Library of Congress*] (LCLS)
MTCON...... Microwave Aeropace Terminal Control [*Air Force*] (IAA)
MTCP........ Master of Town and Country Planning (ADA)
MTCP........ Ministry of Town and Country Planning [*British*]
MTCR........ Million Tonnes of Coal Replacement (CARB)
MTCR........ Missile Technology Control Regime [*US, Canada, Britain, France, West Germany, Japan*]
MTCS........ Madelian Thomas Completion Stories [*Psychology*] (DAVI)

MTCS........ Mean Time to Cycle Slip (ACAE)
MTCS........ Melbourne Theatre Cooperative Society [*Australia*]
MTCS........ Meteor Trail Communications System
MTCS........ Minimal Terminal Communications System (NVT)
MTCS........ Minimum Teleprocessing Commmunications System
MTCS........ Missile Technician, Senior Chief [*Navy rating*]
MTCT........ Manipulator/Teleoperator Control Technology (SSD)
MTCU........ Magnetic Tape Control Unit [*Computer science*]
MTCU........ Mobile Temperature Conditioning Units (ACAE)
MTCV........ Main Turbine Control Valve (IEEE)
MTCV........ Modified Total Containment Vessel (SAUS)
MTCW........ Major 20th-Century Writers [*A publication*]
MTCX........ Mallard Transportation [*Private rail car owner code*]
MTCZ........ Matlack Transportation [*Federal Railroad Administration identification code*]
MTCZ........ Mayflower Transit and Storage [*Intermodal trailer symbol*]
MTD......... Macknight Airlines [*Australia*] [*ICAO designator*] (FAAC)
MTD......... Magnetic Tape Disk (MCD)
MTD......... Main Technical Directorate (RDA)
MTD......... Maintenance Task Demand File (MCD)
MTD......... Maintenance Tasks Distribution
MTD......... Maintenance Technical Directive (SAA)
MTD......... Maintenance Technology Development
MTD......... Maintenance Training Department
MTD......... Manager, Traffic Department
MTD......... Manager, Transportation Department
MTD......... Maneuvering Technology Demonstrator (ACAE)
MTD......... Manufacturing and Test Documentation (ACAE)
MTD......... Manufacturing Technology Development (RDA)
MTD......... Manufacturing Technology Directorate [*Army*] (RDA)
MTD......... Manufacturing Technology Division [*Air Force*]
MTD......... Marine Technology Directorate [*British*]
MTD......... Maritime Trades Department, AFL-CIO [*American Federation of Labor and Congress of Industrial Organizations*] (EA)
MTD......... Mass Tape Duplicator/Verifier [*Computer science*] (MCD)
MTD......... Master of Textile Dyeing
MTD......... Master of Transport Design
MTD......... Master Tape Data
MTD......... Master Time Display
MTD......... Master Tracking Data [*NASA*]
MTD......... Materiel Testing Directorate [*Army*] (RDA)
MTD......... Maximum Tolerated Dose [*Medicine*]
MTD......... Mean Temperature Difference
MTD......... Mean Therapeutic Dose [*Medicine*]
MTD......... Mean Time Down [*Computer science*] (VLIE)
MTD......... Mean Tolerated Dose [*Medicine*]
MTD......... Mean Total Dose [*Medicine*] (DMAA)
MTD......... Mean Tubular Diameter
MTD......... Mechanical Road Transport Driver [*British military*] (DMA)
MTD......... Memory Technology Driver [*Computer science*] (MWOL)
MTD......... Metacarpal Total Density [*Anatomy*]
MTD......... Metal Trades Department, AFL-CIO [*American Federation of Labor and Congress of Industrial Organizations*] (EA)
MTD......... Metastatic Trophoblastic Disease [*Medicine*] (AAMN)
MTD......... Meta-Toluenediamine [*Organic chemistry*]
MTD......... Methyltriazolinedione [*Organic chemistry*]
MTD......... Mettler-Toledo Intl. [*NYSE symbol*] (SG)
MTD......... Microwave Target Designator
MTD......... Midwife Teacher's Diploma [*British*]
MTD......... Military Test Directorate [*Program*] [*Army*] (RDA)
MTD......... Minimal Toxic Dose (IEEE)
MTD......... Mintel International Development Corp. [*Vancouver Stock Exchange symbol*]
MTD......... Mitte Tales Doses [*Send Such Doses*] [*Pharmacy*]
MTD......... Mobile Target Division [*Mine Force*] [*Navy*]
MTD......... Mobile Training Detachment
MTD......... Mobilization Table of Distribution [*Military*]
MTD......... Modern Tool & Die [*NCIC motorcycle make code*]
MTD......... Monroe Tidal Drainage [*Urology*] (DAVI)
MTD......... Month to Date (VLIE)
MTD......... Mount Darwin [*Zimbabwe*] [*Seismograph station code, US Geological Survey*] (SEIS)
mtd......... Mounted (VRA)
MTD......... Mounted
MTD......... Moving Target Detector [*RADAR*]
MTD......... Mualang [*Language symbol*] (ETLW)
MTD......... Multimodal Transport Document [*Computer science*] (VLIE)
MTD......... Multiple Target Deception (MCD)
MTD......... Multiple Target Discrimination (MCD)
MTD......... Multiple Tile Duct [*Telecommunications*] (TEL)
MTD......... Right Ear Drum [*Medicine*] (BCRP)
MTD......... Togolese Movement for Democracy [*Political party*] (PSAP)
MTDA........ Marine Tactical Data (IAA)
MTDA........ Methyl Trimethylsilyl Dimethylketene Acetal [*Organic chemistry*]
MTDA........ Modification Table of Distribution and Allowances [*Army*] (AABC)
MTDAS...... Multi-Tier Distributed Application Services Suite [*Computer science*] (HODG)
MTDB........ Machine Type Data Base [*Computer science*] (VLIE)
MTDB........ Metropolitan Transit Development Board (NADA)
MTDC........ Modified Total Direct Costs [*Economics*]
MTDDA...... Minnesota Test for Differential Diagnosis of Aphasia [*Psychology*]
MTDDIS..... Mesoscale Transport Diffusion and Deposition Model for Industrial Sources [*Environmental Protection Agency*] (GFGA)
MTDDP...... Molecular Targets Drug Discovery Program [*National Cancer Institute*] (RCD)
MTDE........ Maritime Tactical Data Exchange (NATG)
MTDE........ Modern Technology Demonstration Engine
MT Des..... Master of Textile Design
MtDeSP..... Montana State Prison, Conley Lake, Deer Lodge, MT [*Library symbol*] [*Library of Congress*] (LCLS)
MTDF........ Master Tracking Data File [*NASA*]
MTDF........ Mobile Tank Depermer Facility (DWSG)
MtDi......... Dillon City Library, Dillon, MT [*Library symbol*] [*Library of Congress*] (LCLS)
MTDI......... Maximum Tolerable Daily Intake [*Medicine*] (EDAA)
MtDiGS...... Church of Jesus Christ of Latter-Day Saints, Genealogical Society Library, ButteStake Branch, Dillon Chapel, Dillon, MT [*Library symbol*] [*Library of Congress*] (LCLS)
MtDiW....... Western Montana College, Dillon, MT [*Library symbol*] [*Library of Congress*] (LCLS)
MTDL........ Maintenance Task Description List (ACAE)
MTDL........ Multiple Tap Delay Line
MT-DN....... Multitest, Dermatophtes and Nocardia [*Medicine*] (EDAA)
mtDNA...... Deoxyribonucleic Acid, Mitochondrial [*Biochemistry, genetics*]
mtDNA...... Mitochondrial DNA [*Deoxyribonucleic acid*] (USDC)
MTDP........ Medium Term Defense Plan (NATG)
MTDP........ Medium Term Development Plan [*Economics*] (FEA)
MTDP........ Mid-Term Defence build-up Project (SAUS)
MTDP........ National Revival Democratic Party (Uzbekistan) [*Political party*] (PSAP)
MTDS........ Manufacturing Test Data System (IEEE)
MTDS........ Marine Tactical Data System
MTDS........ Marine Toebreak Data System (NG)
MTDS........ Metallurgical and Thermochemical Data Service [*Department of Trade and Industry*] [*Information service or system*] (IID)
MTDS........ Missile Trajectory Data System (MUGU)
MTDSK...... Magnetic Tape Disk [*Computer science*] (NASA)
MTDT........ Modified Tone Decay Test (MAE)
MTE.......... AirTran Airways, Inc. [*FAA designator*] (FAAC)
MtE.......... Ekalaka Public Library, Ekalaka, MT [*Library symbol*] [*Library of Congress*] (LCLS)
MTE.......... Machine Transaction Entry [*Computer science*] (VLIE)
MTE.......... Magnetic Tape Encoder [*Computer science*] (IAA)
MTE.......... Magnetosphere-Thermosphere Explorer [*NASA*]
MTE.......... Maintenance Test Equipment (MCD)
MTE.......... Maintenance Training Equipment (MCD)
MTE.......... Manteigas [*Portugal*] [*Seismograph station code, US Geological Survey*] (SEIS)
MTE.......... Manual Test Equipment (ACAE)
MTE.......... Mass Transport Experiment (SAUS)
MTE.......... Master of Teacher Education (PGP)
MTE.......... Master of Textile Engineering
MTE.......... Maximum Temperature Engine
MTE.......... Maximum Tracking Error
MTE.......... Maximum Tractive Effort [*Equipment design*]
MTE.......... Measurement and Test Equipment [*Environmental science*] (COE)
MTE.......... Megaton-Equivalent (SAUS)
MTE.......... Member of the Telegraph Engineers [*British*] (ROG)
MTE.......... Merit Technologies Ltd. [*Vancouver Stock Exchange symbol*]
MTE.......... Mesophere-Thermosphere Explorer (ACAE)
mte.......... Metal-Engraver [*MARC relator code*] [*Library of Congress*] (LCCP)
MtE.......... Metropolitan Edison Co. [*Associated Press*] (SAG)
MTE.......... Microwave Test Equipment
MTE.......... Missile Test Engineer (MUGU)
MTE.......... Missing Time Experience
MTE.......... Mitre Corp., Bedford Operations Library, Bedford, MA [*OCLC symbol*] (OCLC)
MTE.......... Mobile Telephone Exchange [*Nordic Mobile Telephone*]
MTE.......... Modern Technology Engine
MTE.......... Modular Threat Emitter (DWSG)
MTE.......... Module Table Entry [*Computer science*] (BYTE)
MTE.......... Monte Alegre [*Brazil*] [*Airport symbol*] (AD)
MTE.......... Multiple Terminal Emulator
MTE.......... Multiple Terminator Emulator (NITA)
MTE.......... Multiple Trace Elements [*Medicine*] (MELL)
MTE.......... Multipurpose Test Equipment
MTE.......... Multisystem Test Equipment [*Military*]
MTE.......... Multithreshold Element (IAA)
MTE-5....... Multielectrolyte Concentrate [*Pharmacology*] (DAVI)
MTEA........ Maintenance Training Effectiveness Analysis [*Army*]
MTEA........ Metal Trades Employers Association (NADA)
MTEA........ Minimum Target Elevation Angle (MCD)
MTEAA...... (Methylthio)ethyl Acetoacetate [*Organic chemistry*]
MTEC........ Machine Technology, Inc. [*NASDAQ symbol*] (COMM)
MTEC........ Maintenance Test Equipment Catalog (MCD)
MTEC........ Meridian Medical Tech. [*NASDAQ symbol*] (SG)
MTec......... Metric Tons Energy Consumption
MTEC........ Microtec Research, Inc. [*NASDAQ symbol*] (SAG)
MTEC........ Monash Timber Engineering Center [*Australia*]
MTEC........ Motorola Training and Education Center (SAUS)
M Tech...... Master of Technology
MTECP...... Maintenance Test Equipment Certification Procedure (SAA)
MTECR...... Maintenance Test Equipment Certification Requirement (SAA)
MTEE........ Maintenance Test Equipment, Electrical (NASA)
MTEE........ Mean Transverse Emmission Energy (PDAA)
MTEE........ Mission Time Extreme Environment [*NASA*] (KSC)
MTEEC...... Maintenance Test Equipment, Electronic (NASA)
MTEF........ Maintenance Test Equipment, Fluid (NASA)
MTEG........ Mickey Thompson Entertainment Group [*Auto racing*]
MTEG........ Port-Au-Prince [*Haiti*] [*ICAO location identifier*] (ICLI)

MTEK........ Monitek Technologies, Inc. [*NASDAQ symbol*] (COMM)
MTEL........ Manning Table and Equipment List
MTEL........ Maximum Tolerable Exposure Level [*Toxicology*]
MTEL........ Methyltriethyllead [*Organic chemistry*]
MTEL........ Mobile Telecommunications & Technology Corp. [*NASDAQ symbol*] (SAG)
MTEL........ Mobile Telecommun Tech [*NASDAQ symbol*] (TTSB)
MTelEng.... Master of Telecommunications Engineering (NADA)
MtELH....... Lincoln County Senior High School, Eureka, MT [*Library symbol*] [*Library of Congress*] (LCLS)
MTELP...... Michigan Test of English Language Proficiency [*J. Upshur*] (TES)
MTEM....... Magnetosphere-Thermosphere Explorer Mission (SAUS)
MTEM....... Maintenance Test Equipment Module (MCD)
MTEM....... Mechanical Maintenance Test Equipment (NASA)
MTEM....... Mesosphere-Thermosphere Explorer Mission (SAUS)
MT Eng...... Master of Textile Engineering
MTEO........ Maintenance Test Equipment, Optical (NASA)
M'TER....... Manchester [*City in England*] (ROG)
MTER........ Multitest Evaluation Report [*Nuclear energy*] (NRCH)
MTES........ Metastable Transfer Emission Spectroscopy
MTES........ Methyltriethoxysilane [*Organic chemistry*]
MTESL...... Master in Teaching English as a Second Language (PGP)
MTET........ Maximal Treadmill Exercise Test
MTET........ Modified Treadmill Exercise Test [*Medicine*] (EDAA)
MTEU........ Monsanto Europe [*Intermodal shipping container symbol*] (TVRC)
Mtewan..... Matewan BancShares [*Associated Press*] (SAG)
MTEWS/AD... Mobile Tactical Early Warning System for Air Defense [*NATO*]
MTEX........ Mannatech, Inc. [*NASDAQ symbol*] (NASQ)
MTEX........ Mission Template Expert (SSD)
MText........ Master of Textiles (NADA)
MTF.......... Fairbanks, AK [*Location identifier*] [*FAA*] (FAAL)
MTF.......... Machine Tool Forum
MTF.......... Maintenance Test Facility [*Telecommunications*] (OTD)
MTF.......... Maintenance Test Flight (MCD)
MTF.......... Maintenance Training Flight [*Military*]
MTF.......... Manufacturing Technology Facility [*US Army Communications-Electronics Command*] [*Fort Monmouth, NJ*] (RDA)
MTF.......... Matrix Test Facility (MCD)
MTF.......... Maximum Terminal Flow (MAE)
MTF.......... Mean Time to Failure [*Quality control*]
MTF.......... Mechanical Time Fuze
MTF.......... Medical Treatment Facility (AABC)
MTF.......... Medical Treatment Faculty (DAVI)
MTF.......... Megawatt Transmitter Filter
MTF.......... Men's Tie Foundation [*Later, NAA*] (EA)
MTF.......... Merger Task Force
MTF.......... Message Text Format [*Computer science*] (POLM)
MTF.......... Message Text Formatting
MTF.......... Message Transfer Facility [*Telecommunications*] (OSI)
MTF.......... Metal Trades Federation (NADA)
MTF.......... Metastable Time of Flight
MTF.......... Meteorological Task Force (MCD)
MTF.......... Microsoft Tape Format [*Microsoft Corp.*] [*Computer science*] (PCM)
MTF.......... Microwave Test Facility
MTF.......... Mild Thyroid Failure [*Medicine*] (MELL)
MTF.......... Military Treatment Facility [*DoD*]
MTF.......... Minimum Toggle Frequency [*Computer science*] (ELAL)
MTF.......... Missile Track File (ACAE)
MTF.......... Mississippi Test Facility [*Later, NSTL*] [*NASA*]
MTF.......... Mizan Teferi [*Ethiopia*] [*Airport symbol*] [*Obsolete*] (OAG)
MTF.......... Mock-Up Test Facility (MCD)
MTF.......... Modulation Transfer Function [*Resolution measure*]
MtF.......... Monitoring the Future [*University of Michigan project*]
mtf........... More to Follow [*Copyediting*] (WDMC)
MTF.......... Motif
MTF.......... Moulded Fiber Technology
MTF.......... Multiple Tube Fermentation
MTF.......... Multitarget Frequency
MTF.......... Murine Typhus Fever [*Medicine*] (MELL)
MTFA........ Medium-Term Financial Assistance
MTFA........ Modulation Transfer Function Analyzer
MTFA........ Modulation Transfer Function Area (ACAE)
MtFb......... Chouteau County Free Library, Fort Benton, MT [*Library symbol*] [*Library of Congress*] (LCLS)
MTFC........ Masters Track and Field Committee (EA)
MTFC........ Missouri Tree Farm Committee (EARSL)
MTFCA...... Model "T" Ford Club of America (EA)
MTFCI....... Model T Ford Club International (EA)
MTFD........ Minimum Tracking Flux Density
MTFE........ Mercury Thin Film Electrode [*Electrochemistry*]
MTFEX...... Mountain Field Exercise [*Military*] (NVT)
MTFF........ Man-Tended Free Flyer (MCD)
MTFF........ Mean Time to First Failure [*Quality control*] (AAG)
MTFG........ Mitsubishi Tokyo Financial Group
MtFhV....... United States Veterans Administration Center, Fort Harrison, MT [*Library symbol*] [*Library of Congress*] (LCLS)
MTFL........ Mean Time to Fault Locate [*Quality control*] (CAAL)
MTFM....... Morris Transfer [*Common carrier symbol*]
MTFMPP.... Meta-Trifluoromethylphenylpiperazine [*Biochemistry*]
MTFO........ Modular Training Field Option (NASA)
MTFP........ Marema Tlou Freedom Party [*Lesotho*]
MTFR........ Mean Time for Repair [*Quality control*] (IAA)
MTFR........ Message Text Formatting Reporting
MTFR........ Metal Furring [*Technical drawings*]
MTFR........ [*The*] Minnesota Transfer Railway Co. [*AAR code*]
MtFR......... Rosebud County Library, Forsyth, MT [*Library symbol*] [*Library of Congress*] (LCLS)
MtFrHS...... Frenchtown High School, Frenchtown, MT [*Library symbol*] [*Library of Congress*] (LCLS)
MTFS........ Marine Terminal Fuel Separator (MCD)
MTFS........ Medium-Term Financial Strategy
MTFSC...... Ministerial Task Force on Soil Conservation [*Australia*]
MTFT........ Mean Time to Functional Test (ACAE)
MTFTS...... Marine Terminal Fuel Tankage System (MCD)
MTG......... Aviation Co. Mostransgas [*Former USSR*] [*FAA designator*] (FAAC)
MtG.......... Glendive Public Library, Glendive, MT [*Library symbol*] [*Library of Congress*] (LCLS)
MTG......... Main Tank Gun [*Army*]
MTG......... Main Traffic Group [*Telecommunications*] (TEL)
MTG......... Main Turbogenerator
MTG......... Media Task Group [*Environmental Protection Agency*] (GFGA)
MTG......... Meeting (AFM)
mtg.......... Meeting (BEE)
MTG......... Melt-Textured Growth [*Chemistry*]
MTG......... Methanol-to-Gasoline [*Process*] [*Mobil Oil Corp.*]
MTG......... Methoxytriglycol [*Organic chemistry*]
MTG......... Methyl Tetradecylglycidate [*Biochemistry*]
MTG......... (Methyl)thiogalactoside [*Biochemistry*]
MTG......... MGIC Investment [*NYSE symbol*] (TTSB)
MTG......... MGIC Investment Co. [*NYSE symbol*] (SPSG)
MTG......... Microsyn Torque Generator (SAA)
MTG......... Mid-thigh Girth [*Medicine*] (EDAA)
MTG......... Montague Island [*Alaska*] [*Seismograph station code, US Geological Survey*] (SEIS)
Mtg.......... Mortgage (EBF)
mtg.......... Mortgage (GEAB)
MTG......... Mortgage [*Finance*] (SPSG)
MTG......... Motorsports Technology Group [*General Motors Corp.*]
MTG......... Motor-Torque Generator
MTG......... Mounting
MTG......... Multiple-Trigger Generator
MTG......... Multipurpose Target Generator
MTGAS...... Mechanical Transport Gasoline [*Military*] [*British*]
MTGBKT.... Mounting Bracket (IAA)
MTGC....... Mounting Center (MSA)
MTGCF...... Mobile Transportation Ground Command Facility (MCD)
MtGD........ Dawson College, Glendive, MT [*Library symbol*] [*Library of Congress*] (LCLS)
MTGD....... Mortgaged (ROG)
MtGDH...... Dawson County High School, Glendive, MT [*Library symbol*] [*Library of Congress*] (LCLS)
mtge......... Mortgage (DD)
Mtge......... Mortgage (TBD)
MTGE........ Mortgage
MTGEE...... Mortgagee
MTGF........ Mouse Transforming Growth Factor [*Biochemistry*]
MTGHS..... Magnetic, True, and Grid Heading Select (MCD)
MtGl......... TIGR [*The Institute of Genomic Research*] Medicago truncatula Gene Index [*Database*] (GDD)
MtGl......... Glasgow City-County Library, Glasgow, MT [*Library symbol*] [*Library of Congress*] (LCLS)
MTGN....... Modern Times Group MTG AB [*NASDAQ symbol*] (NASQ)
MTGOR...... Mortgagor
MTGP........ Monitor Table Generator Program (MCD)
MtGr......... Great Falls Public Library, Great Falls, MT [*Library symbol*] [*Library of Congress*] (LCLS)
MtGrCE...... College of Great Falls, Great Falls, MT [*Library symbol*] [*Library of Congress*] (LCLS)
MtGrCH..... Columbus Hospital, Health Sciences Library, Great Falls, MT [*Library symbol*] [*Library of Congress*] (LCLS)
MtGrGS..... Church of Jesus Christ of Latter-Day Saints, Genealogical Society Library, GreatFalls Branch, Great Falls, MT [*Library symbol*] [*Library of Congress*] (LCLS)
MtGrPS...... Great Falls Public Schools, Great Falls, MT [*Library symbol*] [*Library of Congress*] (LCLS)
MTGS........ Metal-to-Glass Seal
MTGS........ Midcourse and Terminal Guidance System [*NASA*]
MTGU....... Australian Master Tax Guide Updater [*A publication*]
MTGU....... Main Turbine / Gearing Unit (PDAA)
MTGW....... Maximum Total Gross Weight (MCD)
MTG/WESS... Main Tank Gunfire/Weapon Effects Signature Simulator (MCD)
MtH.......... Helena Public Library, Helena, MT [*Library symbol*] [*Library of Congress*] (LCLS)
MTH......... Magnetic Tape Handler [*Computer science*]
MTH......... Marathon [*Florida*] [*Airport symbol*] (OAG)
MTH......... Marathon (automobile) [*NCIC car model code*]
MTH......... Marathon, FL [*Amtrak Busline code*]
MTH......... Massachusetts Institute of Technology [*ICAO designator*] (FAAC)
M Th......... Master of Theology
MTH......... Master of Tropical Health
MTH......... Meath [*County in Ireland*] (ROG)
MTH......... Meritage Corp. [*Formerly, Monterey Homes Corp.*] [*NYSE symbol*]
MTH......... Metharbital [*An anticonvulsant*] [*Pharmacology*] (DAVI)
MTH......... Methylthiohydantoin [*Organic chemistry*]
MTH......... Microptic Theodolite
MTH......... Mithramycin [*Medicine*] (DMAA)
MTH......... Mithramycin (Aureolic acid, mithracin) [*Antineoplastic drug*]
MTH......... Monterey Homes Corp. [*NYSE symbol*] (SAG)
MTH......... Month

MTH .... Mount Holyoke College, South Hadley, MA [*OCLC symbol*] (OCLC)
MTH .... Mount Hood Railway Co. [*Later, MH*] [*AAR code*]
Mth .... Mouth [*Maps and charts*]
MTH .... Thompson Public Library, Manitoba [*Library symbol*] [*National Library of Canada*] (NLC)
MtHa .... Havre Hill County Library, Havre, MT [*Library symbol*] [*Library of Congress*] (LCLS)
MThA .... Master of Theatre Arts
MtHam ...... Bitter Root Public Library, Hamilton, MT [*Library symbol*] [*Library of Congress*] (LCLS)
MtHamRL... United States National Institute of Health, Rocky Mountain Laboratory Library, Hamilton, MT [*Library symbol*] [*Library of Congress*] (LCLS)
MtHaN....... Northern Montana College, Havre, MT [*Library symbol*] [*Library of Congress*] (LCLS)
MtHar .... Big Horn County Public Library, Hardin, MT [*Library symbol*] [*Library of Congress*] (LCLS)
MtHarC...... Fort Belknap College, Harlem, MT [*Library symbol*] [*Library of Congress*] (LCLS)
MtHarIF ..... Fort Belknap Community College, Harlem, MT [*Library symbol*] [*Library of Congress*] (LCLS)
MTHB........ Mark Twain Home Board (EA)
MTHBD...... Motherboard (MSA)
MtHC .... Carroll College, Helena, MT [*Library symbol*] [*Library of Congress*] (LCLS)
MtHCE....... Montana Census and Economic Information Center, Helena, MT [*Library symbol*] [*Library of Congress*] (LCLS)
MTHD .... Method (MSA)
MtHe .... Laurie Hill Library, Heron, MT [*Library symbol*] [*Library of Congress*] (LCLS)
M Theol..... Master of Theology
MTHF........ Methyltetrahydrofolate [*or Methyltetrahydrofolic*] [*Biochemistry*]
MTHF........ Methyltetrahydrofuran [*Organic chemistry*]
MTHFR ...... Methylene Tetrahydrofolate Reductase [*An enzyme*]
MtHG .... United States Geological Survey, Water Resources Division, Helena, MT [*Library symbol*] [*Library of Congress*] (LCLS)
MThGH ...... Metallothionein-Human Growth Hormone [*Endocrinology*]
MtHGS ...... Church of Jesus Christ of Latter-Day Saints, Genealogical Society Library, Helena Branch, Helena, MT [*Library symbol*] [*Library of Congress*] (LCLS)
MTHHF...... Methyltetrahydrohomofolate [*Biochemistry*]
MtHHS ...... Helena High School, Helena, MT [*Library symbol*] [*Library of Congress*] (LCLS)
MtHi .... Montana Historical Society, Helena, MT [*Library symbol*] [*Library of Congress*] (LCLS)
MTHK........ Merchants Transport of Hickory [*Common carrier symbol*]
MTHL........ Medial Thyrohyoid Ligament [*Medicine*] (MELL)
Mthly........ Monthly (DLA)
MTHM........ Metric Ton of Heavy Metal (NUCP)
MTHM........ Million Tons Heavy Metal
MtHMv ...... Mountain View School, Helena, MT [*Library symbol*] [*Library of Congress*] (LCLS)
Mt Holyoke C... Mount Holyoke College (GAGS)
MTHOS...... Mount Holly Springs, PA [*American Association of Railroads railroad junction routing code*]
MTHPA...... Methyltetrahydrophthalic Anhydride [*Organic chemistry*]
MThPast .... Maitre en Theologie Pastorale [*Master in Pastoral Theology*] [*French*]
M Th Past... Master of Pastoral Theology (PGP)
MtHPI .... Montana Office of Public Instruction, Resource Center, Helena, MT [*Library symbol*] [*Library of Congress*] (LCLS)
MTHR .... Merthyr [*Cardiff*] [*Welsh depot code*]
MTHR .... Mother
MTHRD...... Male Threaded
MtHs......... Hot Springs Public Library, Hot Springs, MT [*Library symbol*] [*Library of Congress*] (LCLS)
MTHS........ Middle Turbinate Headache Syndrome [*Medicine*] (MELL)
MtHS .... Shodair Children's Hospital, Helena, MT [*Library symbol*] [*Library of Congress*] (LCLS)
MtHSH ...... Shodair Hospital, Helena, MT [*Library symbol*] [*Library of Congress*] (LCLS)
MtHsHS ..... Hot Springs High School, Hot Springs, MT [*Library symbol*] [*Library of Congress*] (LCLS)
MtHSP....... Saint Peter's Community Hospital, Helena, MT [*Library symbol*] [*Library of Congress*] (LCLS)
MTHWL ..... Motherwell [*Scotland*]
mthy......... Monthly [*Publishing*] (WDMC)
MTI .... Arturo Rodriguez Martinez [*Mexico*] [*FAA designator*] (FAAC)
MTI .... Islamic Tendency Movement (Tunisia) [*Political party*] (PSAP)
MTI .... Machine Tools Industry (MCD)
MTI .... Maeventec Travel Information [*Maeventec*] [*Information service or system*] (CRD)
MTI .... Magyar Tavviati Iroda [*Hungarian News Agency*] (BARN)
MTI .... Main Tank Injection
MTI .... Maintenance Team Inspection [*Environmental science*] (COE)
MTI .... Malignant Teratoma Intermediate [*Oncology*] (MAE)
MTI .... Manitoba Technical Institute [*Canada*]
MTI .... Manpower Training Institute
MTI .... Manufacturing Technologies Inc. (SAUS)
MTI .... Manufacturing Technology Initiative (ACAE)
MTI .... Marked Temperature Inversion [*Aviation*] (DA)
MTI .... Marketing and Training Institute (EA)
MTI .... Materials Technology Institute of the Chemical Process Industries (EA)
MTI .... Material Thickness Indicator
MTI .... Maximum Therapeutic Index (EDCT)
MTI .... Mechanical Technology, Inc.
MTI .... Mechanical Tolerance Index [*Food technology*]
MTI .... Media Technology International [*British*]
MTI .... Medium Tip-In [*Automotive testing*]
MTI .... Member of the Trust Institute (DD)
MTI .... Metal Treating Institute (EA)
MTI .... Methylthioinosine [*Biochemistry*]
MTI .... Methyltransferase I [*An enzyme*]
MTI .... Military Training Instructor (AFM)
MTI .... Mineta Transportation Institute [*San Jose State University*] (RCD)
MTI .... Minimum Time Interval [*Medicine*]
MTI .... Ministry of Trade and Industry [*Canada*]
MTI .... MIPS Technologies Inc. (SAUS)
MTI .... Missile Training Installation (NATG)
MTI .... Mission Training International (EA)
MTI .... Mobile Training Institute [*Klamath Falls, OR*] [*Telecommunications service*] (TSSD)
MTI .... Modern Telecommunications, Inc. [*New York, NY*] (TSSD)
MTI .... Morton Thiokol, Inc. (SAUS)
MTI .... Mosteiros [*Cape Verde Islands*] [*Airport symbol*] (OAG)
MTI .... Mouvement de la Tendance Islamique [*Islamic Trend Movement*] [*Tunisia*] (PD)
MTI .... Moving Target Indicator
MTI .... Multichannel Time Intervalometer (VLIE)
MTI .... Multigraphics, Inc. [*AMEX symbol*] (SG)
MTI .... Multiple Target Interception (SAUS)
MTI .... Multispectral Thermal Imager
MTI .... Multi-Spectral Thermal Imager Spacecraft [*Department of Energy*]
MTI .... Multi-Terminal Interface [*Computer science*] (VLIE)
MTI .... MuniYield Insured Fund II [*NYSE symbol*] (SPSG)
MTIA......... Medical Transcription Industry Alliance [*Association*] (EA)
MTIA......... Metal Trades Industry Association (NADA)
MTIAA....... Metal Trades Industry Association of Australia
MTIAC .... Manufacturing Technology Information Analysis Center [*DoD*] [*Information service or system*] (IID)
MTIC......... Malaysia Tourist Information Center (EA)
MTIC......... Moving Target Indicator Coherent (IEEE)
MTIC......... MTI Technology
MTICFAR.... Moving Target Indicator Constant False Alarm Rate (CET)
MTID .... Machine Type Identification Data [*Computer science*] (VLIE)
MTID .... Master of Technology for International Development (PGP)
MTIE......... Microthrust Ion Engine
Mties .... Empties (SAUS)
MTIF......... Maritime Technical Information Facility [*Maritime Administration*] [*Database producer*] (IID)
MTIF......... Master Tailored Interest File [*Navy*] (NG)
MTIF......... Mission Time Improvement Factor (VLIE)
MTIG .... MTI Technology [*NASDAQ symbol*] (TTSB)
MTIHM ...... Metric Tons Initial Heavy Metal (GAAI)
MTIK......... Miller Building Sys [*NASDAQ symbol*] (TTSB)
MTIK......... Miller Building Systems, Inc. [*NASDAQ symbol*] (NQ)
MTIK......... Missile Test Installation Kit
MTIK......... Modular Technology, Inc. [*NASDAQ symbol*] (COMM)
MTIK......... Moving Target Indicator Kit
MTIL......... Maximum Tolerable Insecurity Level (OA)
MTIM........ Manual Trim in Motion [*Aviation*]
MTIM........ Massage Therapy Institute of Missouri (MHID)
MTIN .... Martin Industries [*NASDAQ symbol*] (TTSB)
MTIN .... Martin Industries, Inc. [*NASDAQ symbol*] (SAG)
MTIN .... Mountain [*Commonly used*] (OPSA)
MTIP......... Moving Target Indication Processor (ACAE)
MTIP......... MTI [*Common carrier symbol*]
MTI PAC .... Minerals Technologies Inc. PAC [*New York, NY*] (PACS)
MTIQ .... Manito Transit Company [*Common carrier symbol*]
MTIRA....... Machine Tool Industry Research Association [*Research center*] [*British*]
MTIRI........ Multispectral Thermal Infrared Imager (SSD)
MTIS......... Maintenance Task Information System (NG)
MTIS......... Manufacturing and Trade Inventories and Sales (SAUS)
MTIS......... Material Turned into Stores
MTIS......... Mean Time in Shop [*Quality control*] (MCD)
MTIS......... Multimodal Traveler Information Systems [*FTA*] (TAG)
MTIS......... Multiplex Transmitter Input Signals (PDAA)
MTI Tch ..... MTI Technology Corp. [*Associated Press*] (SAG)
MTIU .... Miller Transporters [*Intermodal shipping container symbol*] (TVRC)
MTIX......... Mechanical Technology (EFIS)
MTIX......... Micro Therapeutics
MTIZ......... American Marine Industries [*Intermodal trailer symbol*]
MTIZ......... Mississippi Transportation [*Federal Railroad Administration identification code*]
MTJ.......... Magnetic Tunnel Junction
MTJ.......... Mark Twain Journal [*A publication*] (ANEX)
MTJ.......... Mesifta Tifereth Jerusalem (BJA)
MTJ.......... Midtarsal Joint [*Anatomy*] (DAVI)
MTJ.......... Missile Track Jamming [*Military*] (CAAL)
MTJ.......... Montrose [*Colorado*] [*Airport symbol*] (OAG)
MTJ.......... Mount Tsukuba [*Japan*] [*Seismograph station code, US Geological Survey*] (SEIS)
MTJA........ Jacmel [*Haiti*] [*ICAO location identifier*] (ICLI)
MTJE........ Jeremie [*Haiti*] [*ICAO location identifier*] (ICLI)
MtJG......... Garfield County Library, Jordan, MT [*Library symbol*] [*Library of Congress*] (LCLS)
MTK .... Camp Ripley/Little Falls, MN [*Location identifier*] [*FAA*] (FAAL)
MtK.......... Flathead County Free Library, Kalispell, MT [*Library symbol*] [*Library of Congress*] (LCLS)
MTK .... Main-Taunus-Kreis [*German license plate city code*]

MTK......... Makin [*Kiribati*] [*Airport symbol*] (OAG)
MTK......... Mechanical Time Keeping (NASA)
MTK......... Medium Tank
MTK......... Mintek Resources [*Vancouver Stock Exchange symbol*]
MTK......... Mitaka [*Japan*] [*Seismograph station code, US Geological Survey*] [*Closed*] (SEIS)
mtk......... Tropical Maritime Cold Air Mass [*Meteorology*] (BARN)
MtKF......... Flathead Valley Community College, Kalispell, MT [*Library symbol*] [*Library of Congress*] (LCLS)
MtKFH....... Flathead Senior High School, Kalispell, MT [*Library symbol*] [*Library of Congress*] (LCLS)
MtKGS....... Church of Jesus Christ of Latter-Day Saints, Genealogical Society Library, Kalispell Branch, Kalispell, MT [*Library symbol*] [*Library of Congress*] (LCLS)
MtKH........ Kalispell Regional Hospital, Kalispell, MT [*Library symbol*] [*Library of Congress*] (LCLS)
MTKN........ Tom Mason Trucking [*Common carrier symbol*]
MTKX........ Metrolink [*Federal Railroad Administration identification code*]
MTL.......... Magnetic Tape Loader
MTL.......... Main Transfer Line (MCD)
MTL.......... Maitland [*Australia*] [*Airport symbol*] (OAG)
MTL.......... Mantle Zone Lymphoma [*Medicine*] (DMAA)
MTL.......... Manufacturing and Technology Laboratory
MTL.......... Mass-Transport-Limited [*Chemical engineering*]
MTL.......... Master Tape Loading
MTL.......... Master Test Line [*Communications term*] (DCT)
MTL.......... Matched Transmission Line
MTL.......... Material (KSC)
MTL.......... Materials Research Corp. [*AMEX symbol*] (COMM)
MTL.......... Materials Technology Laboratory [*Watertown, MA*] [*Army*] (RDA)
MTL.......... Materials Test Loop [*Nuclear energy*] (NRCH)
MTL.......... Mating Type-Like Locus
MTL.......... Mean Tide Level [*Tides and currents*]
MTL.......... Mean Time Level
MTL.......... Medial Temporal Lobe [*Brain anatomy*]
MTL.......... Median Threshold Limit (EEVL)
MTL.......... Median Tolerance Limit [*Toxicity*]
MTL.......... Medium Term Loan (DCTA)
MTL.......... Mercantile Bancorp, Inc. [*NYSE symbol*] (SPSG)
MTL.......... Merged-Transistor Logic
MTL.......... Message Transfer Layer [*Telecommunications*] (OSI)
MTL.......... Metal (AAG)
MTL.......... Microelectronic Test Laboratory (IAA)
MTL.......... Minimum Time Limit
MTL.......... Minimum Triggering Level [*Aviation*] (DA)
MTL.......... Mobilization Training Loss [*Military*]
MTL.......... Mobiltherm Light (NRCH)
Mt-L......... Montana State Law Library, Helena, MT [*Library symbol*] [*Library of Congress*] (LCLS)
MTL.......... Motel
MTL.......... Motivation and Training Laboratory [*Army*] (RDA)
MTL.......... Mount Taylor [*New Mexico*] [*Seismograph station code, US Geological Survey*] (SEIS)
MTL.......... Muldentalkreis [*German license plate city code*]
MTL.......... Multiple Conductor Transmission Line (PDAA)
MTL.......... Raf-Avia [*Latvia*] [*ICAO designator*] (FAAC)
MTLA........ Maine Trial Lawyers Association (EARSL)
MTLA........ Melton Truck Lines [*Common carrier symbol*]
MTLA........ Micropublishers' Trade List Annual [*A publication*]
MTLC........ Mass Transfer Limiting Current (PDAA)
MTLC........ Metalclad Corp. [*NASDAQ symbol*] (SAG)
MTLC........ Metallic (MSA)
MTLD........ Mouvement pour le Triomphe des Libertes Democratiques [*Movement for the Triumph of Democratic Liberties*] [*Algeria*]
MtLdD....... Dull Knife Memorial College Library, Lame Deer, MT [*Library symbol*] [*Library of Congress*] (LCLS)
MtLe......... Lewistown City Library, Lewistown, MT [*Library symbol*] [*Library of Congress*] (LCLS)
MTLG........ Metrologic Instruments [*NASDAQ symbol*] (TTSB)
MTLG........ Metrologic Instruments, Inc. [*NASDAQ symbol*] (SAG)
Mtlg......... Mitteilung [*Report*] [*German*] (BJA)
MTLGY...... Metallurgy
MTLI......... Marine Transport Lines, Inc. [*NASDAQ symbol*] (COMM)
MTLI......... MTL, Inc. [*NASDAQ symbol*] (SAG)
MtLib........ Lincoln County Free Library, Libby, MT [*Library symbol*] [*Library of Congress*] (LCLS)
MtLibH...... Libby High School, Libby, MT [*Library symbol*] [*Library of Congress*] (LCLS)
MtLibJ....... Libby Junior High School, Libby, MT [*Library symbol*] [*Library of Congress*] (LCLS)
MTL Inc..... MTL, Inc. [*Associated Press*] (SAG)
MTLM........ Metal Management [*NASDAQ symbol*] (TTSB)
MTLN........ Merchants Truckload Company [*Common carrier symbol*]
MTLNG...... Metallizing
MTLP........ Malignant Toxemia of Late Pregnancy [*Medicine*] (EDAA)
MTLP........ Master Tape Loading Program
MTLP........ Metabolic Toxemia of Late Pregnancy [*Medicine*]
MTLP........ Monitor Table Listing Program (NASA)
MTLQ........ Mount Lassen Motor Transit [*Common carrier symbol*]
MTLR........ Moving Target Locating RADAR (AABC)
MTLS........ Magazine Torpedo Launch System (SAUS)
MTLS........ Mesial Temporal Lobe Seizure [*Medicine*]
MTLS........ MetaTools Inc. [*NASDAQ symbol*] (TTSB)
MTLS........ Munitions Transfer [*or Transporter*] and Loading System (MCD)
MTLU........ Montgomery Tank Lines [*Intermodal shipping container symbol*] (TVRC)
MtLv......... Livingston Public Library, Livingston, MT [*Library symbol*] [*Library of Congress*] (LCLS)
MTLV........ Missile Transport & Loading Vehicle (SAUS)
MtLvHS..... Park High School, Livingston, MT [*Library symbol*] [*Library of Congress*] (LCLS)
MtLvMS..... Livingston Middle School, Livingston, MT [*Library symbol*] [*Library of Congress*] (LCLS)
MtLvSD..... Livingston Elementary Schools, Livingston, MT [*Library symbol*] [*Library of Congress*] (LCLS)
MTLX........ Marine Transport Corp. [*NASDAQ symbol*] (NASQ)
M-TLX....... Mitsubishi Transfer-Line Heat Exchanger
MTLZ........ Metallize (MSA)
MTM......... Machine Type Model (VLIE)
MTM......... Magnetic Tape Message
MTM......... Magnetic Tape System [*Communications term*] (DCT)
MTM......... Maintenance Task Monitor (MCD)
MTM......... Maintenance Test Module
MTM......... Management Team Meeting (ALAC)
MTM......... Manpower Tradeoff Methodology [*Military*]
MTM......... Manual of Tropical Medicine [*Medicine*] [*A publication*] (EDAA)
MTM......... Mark-to-Market [*Securities*]
MTM......... Mark Twain Memorial (EA)
MTM......... Marlborough Technical Management [*British*]
MTM......... Mary Tyler Moore [*Actress after whom film studio MTM Enterprises is named*]
MTM......... Masked Terrain Map [*Military*]
MTM......... Master in the Teaching of Mathematics (PGP)
MTM......... Master of Theology and Ministry (PGP)
MTM......... Master of Transport Management
MTM......... Master of Tropical Medicine
MTM......... Matsumoto [*Japan*] [*Seismograph station code, US Geological Survey*] (SEIS)
MTM......... Mean Time Measurement
MTM......... Mechanical Road Transport Mechanic [*British military*] (DMA)
MTM......... Mechanical Test Model
MTM......... Memphis Transportation Museum [*Federal Railroad Administration identification code*]
MTM......... Methods-Time Measurement [*Industrial engineering*]
MTM......... Methylthiomethyl [*Organic chemistry*]
MTM......... Metlakatla [*Alaska*] [*Airport symbol*] (OAG)
MTM......... Metlakatla, AK [*Location identifier*] [*FAA*] (FAAL)
MTM......... Metric Ton of Metal (ABAC)
MTM......... Michelin Tire Monitor [*System*] [*Automotive engineering*]
MTM......... Million Ton Miles
MTM......... Million Train Miles
MTM......... Mission Test Module (IAA)
MTM......... Mobile Transfer Method (AAG)
MTM......... Model Test-Model (VLIE)
MTM......... Modified Thayer-Martin [*Medium*] [*Microbiology*]
MTM......... Modular Torque Motor
MTM......... Moving Target Mechanism (SAUS)
MTM......... Moving Terrain Model
MTM......... Mt. Grant Mines Ltd. [*Vancouver Stock Exchange symbol*]
MTM......... MTM [*Methods-Time Measurement*] Association for Standards and Research (EA)
MTM......... MTM Aviation GMBH Munchen [*Federal Republic of Germany*] [*FAA designator*] (FAAC)
MTM......... MTM Productions, Inc. [*Named for actress Mary Tyler Moore*]
MTM......... Multiple Terminal Manager (NITA)
MTM......... Multiple Threat Modulation [*Military*] (CAAL)
MTM......... Multiple Time Measurement (VLIE)
MTM......... Multi-Taper Method [*Spectroscopy*]
MTM......... Multi-Tasking Monitor (NITA)
MTM......... Multi-Terminal Monitor (NITA)
MTM......... Myotubular Myopathy [*Medicine*] (DMAA)
MTM......... Thayer-Martin, Modified [*Agar*] (DMAA)
MTMA....... Methods Time-Measurement Association (IAA)
MTMA....... Military Terminal Major Aerodromes (NATG)
MTMA....... Military Terminal Manoeuvring Area (SAUS)
MTMA....... Military Traffic Management Agency [*Later, DTMS*]
MtMa........ Phillips County Library, Malta, MT [*Library symbol*] [*Library of Congress*] (LCLS)
MTMAINTCO... Motor Maintenance Company (DNAB)
MTMASR.... MTM [*Methods-Time Measurement*] Association for Standards and Research [*Later, MTM*] (EA)
MTMB........ Military Traffic Management Bulletin (SAA)
MTMC........ (Methylthio)-meta-Cresol [*Organic chemistry*]
MTMC........ Micros-To Mainframe, Inc. [*NASDAQ symbol*] (SAG)
MTMC........ Micros To Mainframes [*NASDAQ symbol*] (TTSB)
MtMc......... Miles City Public Library, Miles City, MT [*Library symbol*] [*Library of Congress*] (LCLS)
MTMC........ Military Traffic Management Command [*DoD*]
MtMcC....... Miles Community College, Miles City, MT [*Library symbol*] [*Library of Congress*] (LCLS)
MTMCEA.... Military Traffic Management Command, Eastern Area [*Bayonne, NJ*]
MTMC-OA... Military Traffic Management Command Operations Analysis Division [*Newport News, VA*]
MtMcPh..... Pine Hill School, Miles City, MT [*Library symbol*] [*Library of Congress*] (LCLS)
MTMCTEA... Military Traffic Management Command Transportation Engineering Agency (AABC)
MTMCTTC... Military Traffic Management Command Transportation Terminal Command, Europe [*MTMC*] (TAG)

MTMCTTU... Military Traffic Management Command Transportation Terminal Unit (AABC)
MTMCWA... Military Traffic Management Command, Western Area [*Oakland, CA*]
MTM/D...... Million Ton Miles/Day (MCD)
MTM/D...... Million Ton Miles per Day (ACAE)
MT/MF...... Magnetic Tape to Microfilm
MTMF....... Multiple Task Management Feature (NITA)
MTM-GPD... Methods Time Measurement and General Purpose Data (PDAA)
MTMH....... Master of Tropical Medicine and Hygiene (GAGS)
MTMI........ Microtek Medical [*NASDAQ symbol*] (TTSB)
MTMI........ Microtek Medical, Inc. [*NASDAQ symbol*] (SAG)
MtMis....... Missoula Public and Missoula County Free Library, Missoula, MT [*Library symbol*] [*Library of Congress*] (LCLS)
MtMisGS.... Church of Jesus Christ of Latter-Day Saints, Genealogical Society Library, Missoula Branch, Missoula, MT [*Library symbol*] [*Library of Congress*] (LCLS)
MtMisSP.... Saint Patrick Hospital, Missoula, MT [*Library symbol*] [*Library of Congress*] (LCLS)
MtMisW..... Western Montana Clinic, Missoula, MT [*Library symbol*] [*Library of Congress*] (LCLS)
MTMM...... Multitrait-Multimethod Model
MTMOD.... Magnetic Tape Module (IAA)
MTMP....... MACOM [*Major Command*] Telephone Modernizations Program
MTMR....... Military Traffic Management Regulation
mt mRNA... Mitochondrial Messenger RNA[*Ribonucleic Acid*] [*Genetics*] (DOG)
MTMS....... Machine Tool Management System (VLIE)
MTMS....... Made2Manage Systems, Inc. [*NASDAQ symbol*] (NASQ)
MTM's....... Magnetic Tape Transmissions (CET)
MTMS....... Memorex Tape Management System [*Computer science*] (IAA)
MTMS....... Metal-to-Metal Seal
MTMS....... Methyltrimethoxysilane [*Organic chemistry*]
MTMS....... Military Traffic Management Service (MCD)
MTMS....... Mobilization Training Management System [*DoD*]
MTMS....... Multi-Terminal Modular System (DGA)
MTMT....... Mail and Telephone Mode Test (SAUS)
MTMT....... Multiple Target & Missile Tracker (SAUS)
MTMT....... Multiple Terminal Monitor Task [*Computer science*] (VLIE)
MTMTS...... Military Traffic Management and Terminal Service [*Later, MTMC*] [*Army*]
MTMTS-TSP... Military Traffic Management and Terminal Service Transportation Strike Plan (DNAB)
MTMU....... March [*Intermodal shipping container symbol*] (TVRC)
MTN......... Baltimore, MD [*Location identifier*] [*FAA*] (FAAL)
MTN......... Main Telecommunication Network [*United Nations*] (EY)
MTN......... Manton [*Australia*] [*Seismograph station code, US Geological Survey*] (SEIS)
MTN......... Medical Television Network (BARN)
MTN......... Medium-Term Note [*Finance*]
MTN......... Message Transport Network [*Computer science*] (VLIE)
MTN......... Metatolylnitrile [*Organic chemistry*]
MTN......... Midwest Treaty Network [*Association*] (EA)
MTN......... Mirtone International, Inc. [*Toronto Stock Exchange symbol*]
MTN......... Mizlou Television Network
MTN......... Mobil Producing TX & NM, Inc., Houston, TX [*OCLC symbol*] (OCLC)
MTN......... Motion (MSA)
mtn......... Mountain (MILB)
Mtn......... Mountain (TBD)
MTN......... Mountain
MTN......... Mountain Air Cargo, Inc. [*FAA designator*] (FAAC)
MTN......... Mountaineer [*NCIC car model code*]
MTN......... Mountain Medical Equipment, Inc. [*AMEX symbol*] (COMM)
MTN......... Move Trace Number (TIMI)
MTN......... Multilateral Trade Negotiations
MTN......... Multinational Trade Negotiations (IAA)
MTN......... Vail Resorts [*Company symbol*]
MTNA....... Music Teachers National Association (EA)
MTND....... Mercury Tube Nutation Damper
MTNFC...... Mel Tillis National Fan Club (EA)
MTNHP...... Montana Natural Heritage Program [*Helena, MT*] [*Information service or system*] (IID)
MTNHP...... Montana State Library (IID)
MTNK....... Main Tank [*Automotive emissions*]
MT-NMR.... Magnetic Transfer Nuclear Magnetic Resonance (DB)
MtnPkFn.... Mountain Parks Financial Corp. [*Associated Press*] (SAG)
MTNR....... Mountaineer Bankshares of West Virginia, Inc. [*NASDAQ symbol*] (COMM)
MTNS....... Manportable Thermal Night Sight (ACAE)
MTNS....... Metal-Thick Nitride Semiconductor (IAA)
MTNS....... Metal-Thick Nitride-Silicon (IAA)
MTNS....... Metal-Thick Oxide-Nitride-Silicon
MTNS....... Mountains [*Postal Service standard*] (OPSA)
MTNT....... Metro Networks, Inc. [*NASDAQ symbol*] (SAG)
MTNW....... Maritime Theater Nuclear Warfare (CARL)
MTNX....... MeltroniX [*OTCBB symbol*]
MTNX....... Rocky Mountain Transportation Service [*Private rail car owner code*]
MtNxPS..... Noxon Public School, Noxon, MT [*Library symbol*] [*Library of Congress*] (LCLS)
MTO......... Made to Order (ODBW)
MTO......... Magnetic Tape Operator (MCD)
MTO......... Maintenance Technology Office [*Air Force Logistics Command*]
MTO......... Manitoulin Air Services Ltd. [*Canada*] [*ICAO designator*] (FAAC)
MTO......... Man-Tended Operation (SSD)
MTO......... Manufacturing Technical Order (SAA)
MTO......... Manufacturing Technology Objective
MTO......... Master Terminal Operator (IAA)
MTO......... Master Timing Oscillator (MCD)
MTO......... Mattoon [*Illinois*] [*Airport symbol*] (OAG)
MTO......... Maximum Time Out (MCD)
MTO......... Medical Transport Officer [*Navy*]
MTO......... Mediterranean Theater of Operations (ADWA)
MTO......... Mediterranean Theater of Operations, United States Army [*Shortened form of MTOUSA*] [*World War II*]
MTO......... Message Template Object [*Computer science*] (AGLO)
MTO......... Message Terminal Operation [*Military*] (CAAL)
MTO......... Message to Observer (SAUS)
MTO......... Methanol-to-Olefin [*Process*]
MTO......... Microsystems Technology Office [*Defense Advanced Research Projects Agency*] (RCD)
MTO......... Mid Term Objective (ACAE)
MTO......... Missile Test Operator (SAA)
MTO......... Mission, Task, Objective
MTO......... Mission Type Order (DOMA)
MTO......... Mississippi Test Operations [*NASA*]
MTO......... Modification Task Outline (KSC)
MTO......... Motor Transport Officer [*Military*]
MTO......... Mouvement Togolais pour la Democratie [*Togolese Movement for Democracy*] [*Political party*] (PD)
MTO......... Movement Transfer Order (MCD)
MTO......... Muffin-Tin Orbital [*Physics*]
MTO......... Multilateral Trading Organization (ECON)
MTO......... Multimodal Transport Operator
MTO......... Totontepec Mixe [*Language symbol*] (ETLW)
MTOAL...... Mobilization Table of Allowance Listing [*Military*] (DNAB)
MTOB....... Manned Test Operations Board [*NASA*]
MTOC....... Microtubular Organizing Complex [*Physiology*]
MTOC....... Microtubule Organizing Center [*Cytology*]
MTOC....... Mitotic Organizing Center [*Cytology*]
MTOC....... Monitoring Transport of Ocean Currents [*Project*] [*Marine science*] (OSRA)
MTOCs...... Microtubule Organizing Centers (DOG)
MTOE....... Mid-Term Operations Estimate (SAUS)
MTOE....... Million Tons of Oil Equivalent
MTOE....... Modification Table of Organization and Equipment [*Army*] (AABC)
MTOGW..... Maximum Takeoff Gross Weight [*Aviation*] (MCD)
MTOL....... Mean Time off Line (AAEL)
MTOL....... Mean Time on Line (AAEL)
MTOM....... Master of Traditional Oriental Medicine (PGP)
MTOM....... Maximum Take-Off Mass (SAUS)
MTOM....... Melton Transportation [*Common carrier symbol*]
MTON....... Measurement Ton
MTON....... Metro One Telecommunications, Inc. [*NASDAQ symbol*] (SAG)
MTONS...... Metal-Thick Oxide-Nitride-Silicon (MSA)
MTONS...... Metric Tonnes (RIMS)
MTOP....... Maximal Time to Open [*Medicine*] (EDAA)
MTOP....... Molecular Total Overlap Population (IEEE)
MTOPS...... Million Theoretical Operations per Second [*Computer science*]
MTOR....... Meritor Savings Bank [*NASDAQ symbol*] (COMM)
MTORQ..... Maximum Torque
MTOS....... Magnetic Tape Operating System (NITA)
MTOS....... Magnetic Tape Operations System [*Computer science*] (NRCH)
MTOS....... Major Trauma Outcome Study [*American College of Surgeons Committee on Trauma*]
MTOS....... Metal-Thick Oxide Semiconductor (IAA)
MTOS....... Metal-Thick Oxide-Silicon
MTOS....... Multi-Tasking Operating System (NITA)
MTOSFET... Metal-Thick Oxide Semiconductor Field Effect Transistor (IAA)
MTOUSA.... Mediterranean Theater of Operations, United States Army [*Sometimes shortened to MTO*] [*World War II*]
MTOW....... Maximum Takeoff Weight [*Aviation*] (MCD)
MTox........ Master of Toxicology (GAGS)
MTP......... Island Helicopters, Inc. [*ICAO designator*] (FAAC)
MTP......... Magnetic Tape Processor (NITA)
MTP......... Maintenance Test Package (MCD)
MTP......... Manual Troubleshooting Procedures [*Army*]
MTP......... Manufacturing Technical Procedure [*NASA*] (NASA)
MTP......... Manufacturing Technology Program [*Aviation Systems Command*] (RDA)
MTP......... Manufacturing Technology Projects [*Manufacturing Technology Information Analysis Center*] [*Information service or system*] (CRD)
MTP......... Manufacturing Test Procedure
MTP......... Master of Town and Country Planning
MTP......... Master of Town Planning
MTP......... Master of Transpersonal Psychology (PGP)
MTP......... Master Test Plan (KSC)
MTP......... Master Training Plan [*Navy*] (ANA)
MTP......... Master Transportation Plan (AAG)
MTP......... Master Typography Program (DNAB)
MTP......... Materiel Test Procedure [*Army*]
MTP......... Materiel Transfer Plan [*Army*]
MTP......... Maximum Tire Pressure (ADA)
MTP......... Maximum Tolerated Pressure (MELL)
MTP......... Maximum Total Trihalomethane Potential (EG)
MTP......... Mechanical Thermal Pulse (IEEE)
MTP......... Medical Termination of Pregnancy (MELL)
MTP......... Message Transfer Part [*Computer science*] (GART)
MTP......... Message Transfer Point [*Communications term*] (DCT)
MTP......... Message Transfer Protocol [*Telecommunications*] (OSI)
MTP......... Message Transmission Part [*Telecommunications*] (TEL)

MTP .... Metatarsophalangeal [*Anatomy*]
MTP .... Methods Test Panel [*Bureau of the Census*] (GFGA)
MTP .... (Methylthio)phenol [*Organic chemistry*]
MTP .... Metropolitan Transport Project [*Bombay*] [*Indian Railway*] (TIR)
MTP .... Microsomal Triglyceride Transfer Protein [*Biochemistry*]
MTP .... Microtubule Protein [*Cytology*]
MTP .... Microwave Temperature Profiler (ARMP)
MTP .... Military Toxics Project [*Association*] (EA)
MTP .... Military Type Property
MTP .... Miniature Trimmer Potentiometer
MTP .... Minimum Time Path (OA)
MTP .... Missile Transfer Panel (AAG)
MTP .... Missile Tube Pressurization
MTP .... Mission Tailored Product
MTP .... Mission Tasking Package (COE)
MTP .... Mission Test Plan (KSC)
MTP .... Mission Training Plan [*Military*] (INF)
MTP .... Mobilization Training Program [*Military*]
MTP .... Mobilization Troop Program [*Army*]
MTP .... Modular Terminal Processor (NITA)
MTP .... Montana Power Co. [*NYSE symbol*] (SPSG)
MTP .... Montauk Point [*New York*] [*Airport symbol*] [*Obsolete*] (OAG)
MTP .... Monte Pirata [*Puerto Rico*] [*Seismograph station code, US Geological Survey*] (SEIS)
MTP .... MOS [*Military Occupation Specialty*] Training Plan
MTP .... Mother Tongue Project (AIE)
MTP .... Mount Pleasant, IA [*Amtrak rail station code*]
MTP .... Movimiento Todos par la Patria [*Argentina*] [*Political party*] (EY)
MTP .... Multiple-Task Performance
MTP .... Multiply Twinned Particles (DICI)
MTP .... Multipoint (DNAB)
MTP .... Muramyl Tripeptide (DB)
MtP .... Plains Public Library, Plains, MT [*Library symbol*] [*Library of Congress*] (LCLS)
MTP .... [*The*] Pas Public Library, Manitoba [*Library symbol*] [*National Library of Canada*] (NLC)
MTPA .... Master Textile Printers Association (EA)
MTPA .... Maxwell Trailers & Pickup Accessories [*NCIC trailer make code*]
MTPA .... (Methoxy)trifluoromethylphenylacetic Acid [*Organic chemistry*]
MTPA .... Mobile Transponder Performance Analyzer [*Aviation*] (DA)
MtPaS .... Salish Kootenai College Library, Pablo, MT [*Library symbol*] [*Library of Congress*] (LCLS)
MtPaTS ..... Two Eagle School, Pablo, MT [*Library symbol*] [*Library of Congress*] (LCLS)
MTPB .... Malaysia Tourism Promotion Board (EA)
MTPC .... Metal Tube Packaging Council of North America [*Later, TCNA*] (EA)
MTPC .... Minimal Total Processing Time (NITA)
MTPCNA .... Metal Tube Packaging Council of North America [*Later, TCNA*]
MTPE .... Mission to Planet Earth [*Proposed NASA satellite*]
MTPF .... Maximum Total Peaking Factor [*Nuclear energy*] (NRCH)
MTP FET .... Metal/Tunnelling-Nitride Polysilicon Gate FET (NITA)
MTPH .... Maximum Temperature of Previous Heating [*Archaeology*]
MTPI .... Member of the Town Planning Institute [*British*]
MTPJ .... Metatarsophalangeal Joint [*Medicine*] (DMAA)
MTPK .... Keewatin Community College, The Pas, Manitoba [*Library symbol*] [*National Library of Canada*] (NLC)
MTPLE ...... Mount Pleasant, MI [*American Association of Railroads railroad junction routing code*]
MTPM .... Mean Time to Provide Manpower (DNAB)
MT/PMP .... Mobile Transporter/Permanent Manned Presence (SAUS)
MtPoF .... Fort Peck Community College, Poplar, MT [*Library symbol*] [*Library of Congress*] (LCLS)
MtPol .... Polson City Library, Polson, MT [*Library symbol*] [*Library of Congress*] (LCLS)
MTPP .... Marine Transport [*Common carrier symbol*]
MTPP .... Material Test Procedure Pamphlet
MTPP .... Missile-to-Target Patch Panel
MTPP .... Port-Au-Prince/Internacional [*Haiti*] [*ICAO location identifier*] (ICLI)
MTP-PE ..... Muramyl Tripeptide Phosphatidylethanolamine [*Antineoplastic drug*] (CDI)
MTPPI .... Medical Technology and Practice Patterns Institute (SAUS)
MtPPS .... Plains Public School Library, Plains, MT [*Library symbol*] [*Library of Congress*] (LCLS)
MTPR .... Miniature Temperature Pressure Recorder [*Marine science*] (OSRA)
MTPS .... Magnetic Tape Programming System [*Computer science*] (IEEE)
MTPS .... Maintenance Test Packages (ACAE)
MTPS .... Modern Talking Picture Service, Inc. [*Funded by U.S. Department of Education*] (PAZ)
MTPSI .... Master Test Program Set Index (ACAE)
MTPT .... Mickey Thompson Performance Tires
MTPT .... Minimal Total Processing Time (IEEE)
MTPTA ...... Montana Congress of Parents and Teachers (EARSL)
MTPU .... Missile Tank Pressurization Unit (AAG)
MTPUG ...... Pascal/MT Users Group [*Defunct*] (EA)
MTPW .... Master of Technical and Professional Writing (GAGS)
MtPw .... Sheridan County Free Library, Plentywood, MT [*Library symbol*] [*Library of Congress*] (LCLS)
MTPX .... Port-De-Paix [*Haiti*] [*ICAO location identifier*] (ICLI)
MTPY .... Millions of Tons per Year [*of solids, e.g., coal*]
MTQ .... CAAA Air Martinique [*France*] [*ICAO designator*] (FAAC)
MTQ .... Greenville, MS [*Location identifier*] [*FAA*] (FAAL)
MTQ .... Martinique [*ANSI three-letter standard code*] (CNC)
MTQ .... Methaqualone [*or Methyltolylquinazolone, or Metolquizolone*] [*Sedative*]
MTQ .... Mitchell [*Australia*] [*Airport symbol*] (OAG)
MTQ .... Mount Allard Resources [*Vancouver Stock Exchange symbol*]
MTQAS ...... Methadone Treatment Quality Assurance System [*National Institute on Drug Abuse*]
MTQM .... Master of Total Quality Management (PGP)
MTQT .... Mount Tabor Trucking [*Common carrier symbol*]
MTR .... Magic-Tone Records [*Record label*]
MTR .... Magnetic Core Transistor Relay (IAA)
MTR .... Magnetic Tape Reader (NITA)
MTR .... Magnetic Tape Recorder
MTR .... Magnetisation Transfer Ratio (SAUS)
MTR .... Main Timing Register
MTR .... Major Trouble Report (MCD)
MTR .... Marine Transportation-Related (EAGT)
MTR .... Marked Target Receiver (SAUS)
MTR .... Mass, Tenderness, Rebound [*On abdominal examination*] [*Gastroenterology*] (DAVI)
MTR .... Mass-Transfer Rate [*Chemical engineering*]
MTR .... Mass Transit Railway (DS)
MTR .... Master Tool Record (SAA)
MTR .... Materials Testing Reactor
MTR .... Materials Testing Report
MTR .... Material Transfer Recorder [*LASER*] [*Army*]
MTR .... Matter [*Telegraphy*] (PCTE)
MTR .... Maximum Tracking Range
MT/R .... Maximum Traction/Reinforced [*Automotive tires*]
MTR .... Mean Time to Removal [*Quality control*]
MTR .... Mean Time to Restore [*Quality control*] (IAA)
MTR .... Measa Royalty Trust [*NYSE symbol*] (SAG)
MTR .... Meinicke Turbidity Reaction [*Obsolete test for syphilis*]
MTR .... Mental Treatment Rules [*British*]
MTR .... Mesa Royaty Tr UBI [*NYSE symbol*] (TTSB)
MTR .... Meter [*or Metering*] (AAG)
mtr .... Meter (IDOE)
MTR .... Methylthioribose [*Biochemistry*]
MTR .... Metroflight, Inc. [*ICAO designator*] (FAAC)
Mtr .... Metronome [*Record label*] [*Scandinavia, Germany, etc.*]
MTR .... Michael T. Robinson & Associates, Inc. (EFIS)
MTR .... Mid-Term Review
MTR .... Migration Traffic Rate (OA)
MTR .... Military Technical Revolution (DOMA)
MTR .... Military Temperature Range
MTR .... Military Training Route [*Aviation*] (FAAC)
MTR .... Milliammeter (IAA)
MTR .... Miniature Temperature Recorder (USDC)
MTR .... Minimum Technological Requirement
MTR .... Minimum Time Rate
MTR .... Miscellaneous Tax Ruling [*IRS*] (AAGC)
MTR .... Missile Track [*or Tracking*] RADAR [*Air Force*]
MTR .... MITRE Corp., Library Department, McLean, VA [*OCLC symbol*] (OCLC)
MTR .... Mobile Test Rig (SAUS)
MTR .... Mobile Tracking Range [*Military*] (CAAL)
MTR .... Modification Traceability Record (MCD)
MTR .... Modular Tree Representation (MHDI)
MTR .... Monitor [*Computer science*] (BUR)
mtr .... Monitor (ELAL)
MTR .... Monopulse Tracking Receiver
MTR .... Monteria [*Colombia*] [*Airport symbol*] (OAG)
MTR .... Monterrey [*California*] [*Seismograph station code, US Geological Survey*] (SEIS)
MTR .... Montour Railroad Co. [*AAR code*]
MTR .... Montreal, Quebec, Canada [*Amtrak rail station code*]
MTR .... Motor (AABC)
MTR .... Moving Target Reactor
MTR .... Moving Target Resolver (MCD)
MT-R .... Mud Traction-Reinforced [*Truck tires*]
MTR .... Multiple Thermocouple Reference
MTR .... Multiple Token Ring [*Telecommunications*] (OSI)
MTR .... Multiple Tracking Range
MTR .... Multiple Track RADAR
MTR .... Museum of Television and Radio [*New York*]
MTR .... Mutual Resources [*Vancouver Stock Exchange symbol*]
MTR .... Universite de Montreal, Bibliotheque [*UTLAS symbol*]
MTRA .... Machine Tools Research Association (WDAA)
MTRA .... Master Track [*NCIC trailer make code*]
MTRA .... Meta Biosystems [*NASDAQ symbol*] (SAG)
MTRA .... Metra Biosystems [*NASDAQ symbol*] (SAG)
MTRA .... Metra Biosystems, Inc. [*NASDAQ symbol*] (NASQ)
MTRA .... Michigan Trail Riders Association (EARSL)
MTRACS .... Multiple input Tracking Control System (SAUS)
M/TRANS ... Manual Transmission [*Automotive engineering*]
MTransEc ... Master of Transport Economics
MTRAT ...... Maverick Target Recognition and Acquisition Trainer (ACAE)
MTRB .... Man-Tended Review Board (SSD)
MTRB .... Maritime Transportation Research Board [*National Research Council*]
MTRB .... Motor Truck Rate Bureau
MTRC .... Man-Tended Reference Configuration (SSD)
MTRC .... Metric
MTRC .... Myeloma and Transplantation Research Center [*University of Arkansas for Medical Sciences*] (RCD)
MTRCL ...... Motorcycle (AABC)
Mtrclt .... Motorcyclist [*Army*]
MTRCYL .... Motorcycle

MtRd .... Community Library, Roundup, MT [*Library symbol*] [*Library of Congress*] (LCLS)
MtRd-E ...... Roundup Central Elementary School Library, Roundup, MT [*Library symbol*] [*Library of Congress*] (LCLS)
MTRDN ...... Motor-Driven
MTRE .... Magnetic Tape Recorder End
MTRE .... Missile Test and Readiness Equipment
MTRE .... Missile Test and Readiness Evaluation [*Military*] (IAA)
MTREC ...... Multi-Throttle Responsive Engine Control [*Automotive engineering*]
Mt Res Dev ... Mountain Research and Development (SAUS)
MT REVD ... Most Reverend (ROG)
MTRF .... Mark Twain Research Foundation (EA)
MTRF .... Master Training File [*Computer science*]
MTRG .... Masses, Tenderness, Rebound, Guarding (SAUS)
MTRG .... Metering (MSA)
MTRG .... Motor Cargo [*Common carrier symbol*]
MTRI .... Missile Test Range Instrumentation
MTRJC ...... Montour Junction, PA [*American Association of Railroads railroad junction routing code*]
MTRK .... Minitrack (KSC)
MTRL .... Material
MTRM .... Modulated Throat-Rocket Motor (MCD)
MTRM .... Moniterm Corp. [*NASDAQ symbol*] (COMM)
MTRN .... Metrotrans Corp. [*NASDAQ symbol*] (SAG)
mtRNA ...... Ribonucleic Acid, Mitochondrial [*Biochemistry, genetics*]
MTRNTY .... Maternity
MTRO .... Metro-Tel Corp. [*NASDAQ symbol*] (COMM)
MtRo .... Ronan City Library, Ronan, MT [*Library symbol*] [*Library of Congress*] (LCLS)
MtroOne .... Metro One Telecommunications, Inc. [*Associated Press*] (SAG)
MTR OP ..... Motor Operated [*Freight*]
MTRP .... Machine Tool Retrofit Program
MTRP .... Master of Town and Regional Planning [*British*] (ADA)
MTRP .... Maximum Transfer Rate Performance (SAUS)
MTRR .... Miller Transfer and Rigging Company [*Common carrier symbol*]
mtrRNA ..... Mitochondrial Ribosomal RNA[*Ribonucleic Acid*] [*Genetics*] (DOG)
MTRS .... Magnetic Tape Recorder Set
MTRS .... Magnetic Tape Recorder Start
MTRS .... Magnetic Tape Reformatting System [*Hewlett-Packard Co.*]
MTRS .... Mattress (MSA)
MTRS .... Metris Companies, Inc. [*NASDAQ symbol*] (SAG)
MTRS .... Multimode Tactical Radar Simulator (ACAE)
MTRU .... Martec International Trading [*Intermodal shipping container symbol*] (TVRC)
MT Rulings ... Miscellaneous Tax Rulings [*Australia*] [*A publication*]
MTRUW ..... Mixed Transuranic Waste (GAAI)
MtrVac ...... MotorVac Technologies, Inc. [*Associated Press*] (SAG)
MTRX .... Matrix Service [*NASDAQ symbol*] (TTSB)
MTRX .... Matrix Service Corp. [*NASDAQ symbol*] (NQ)
MTRY .... Momentary (FAAC)
MTS .... Left Ear Drum [*Medicine*] (BCRP)
MTS .... Machine-Tractor Stations
MTS .... Magnetic Tape Station [*Computer science*] (CET)
MTS .... Magnetic Tape Storage [*Computer science*] (IAA)
MTS .... Magnetic Tape System [*Computer science*]
MTS .... Magnetic Type System [*Computer science*] (IAA)
MTS .... Mainsborne Telecontrol System (NITA)
MTS .... Maintenance Training Set (MCD)
MTS .... Maintenance Transmittal Sheet
MTS .... Main Trunk System [*Telecommunications*] (TEL)
MTS .... Management Tracing System (COE)
MTS .... Management Tracking System [*Environmental Protection Agency*] (EPA)
MTS .... Manager, Technical Support (SAUS)
MTS .... Manitoba Telephone System [*Telecommunications service*] (TSSD)
MTS .... Manned Teller System
MTS .... Manpower Training Services
MTS .... Mantrust Asahi Airways PT [*Indonesia*] [*ICAO designator*] (FAAC)
MTS .... Manual Testing System [*Sports medicine*]
MTS .... Manufacturing Technology Section [*Navy*]
MTS .... Manzini [*Swaziland*] [*Airport symbol*] (OAG)
MTS .... Mardan Test Set
MTS .... Marine Tactical System (SAUS)
MTS .... Marine Technology Society (EA)
MTS .... Maritime Tactical Schools (MCD)
MTS .... Marked Target Seeker (SAUS)
MTS .... Marketing and Transportation Situation [*Series*] [*A publication*]
MTS .... Marketing Technical Services
MTS .... Mark Ten Saloon [*NCIC car model code*]
MTS .... Mark Twain Society [*Defunct*] (EA)
MTS .... MARS [*Military Affiliate Radio System*] Technical Service (CET)
MTS .... Mass Target Sensor
MTS .... Mass Termination System [*Computer science*] (IEEE)
MTS .... Master of Teaching of Science (GAGS)
MTS .... Master of Theological Studies (WGA)
MTS .... Master Test Station
MTS .... Master Timing Schedule
MTS .... Master Timing System
MTS .... Matching to Sample [*Psychology*] (QSUL)
MTS .... Material Test Specification (MSA)
MTS .... Material Tracking Standard (AAEL)
MTS .... Matsue [*Japan*] [*Seismograph station code, US Geological Survey*] (SEIS)
MTS .... Mechanical Test Systems [*Automotive industry*]
MTS .... Medical Testing Systems [*Commercial firm*]
MTS .... Medicare Transaction System (DMAA)
MTS .... Meets [*Telegraphy*] (PCTE)
MTS .... Member of the Technical Staff [*A generic term*]
MTS .... Memory Test System
MTS .... Meridian Telecommunication Services [*Indianapolis, IN*] (TSSD)
MTS .... Merlin Training System (SAUS)
MTS .... Message Telecommunications Service
MTS .... Message Telephone Service (NITA)
MTS .... Message Toll Service [*Communications*]
MTS .... Message Traffic Study
MTS .... Message Transfer Service
MTS .... Message Transfer System [*Telecommunications*] (OSI)
MTS .... Message Transmission Subsystem [*Telecommunications*] (TEL)
MTS .... Message Transport System [*Communications term*] (DCT)
MTS .... Meteoroid Technology Satellite [*NASA*]
MTS .... Methods-Time Study [*Industrial engineering*]
MTS .... Methyltrichlorosilane [*Organic chemistry*]
MTS .... Metric Time System (NASA)
MTS .... Metropolitan Transportation System (PA)
MTS .... Michigan Terminal System [*Computer science*]
MTS .... Microprocessor Training System [*Integrated Computer Systems*] (NITA)
MTS .... Microsoft Transaction Server [*Computer science*]
MTS .... Microtubule-Stabilizing Solution [*Cytology*]
MTS .... Microwave Temperature Sounder (EOSA)
MTS .... Microwave Test Set (MCD)
MTS .... Military Tactical Systems (SAUS)
MTS .... Military Test Satellite
MTS .... Military Training Standard (AFM)
MTS .... Million (10^6) Transitions Per Second [*Of magnetic storage*] (NITA)
MTS .... Minimum Spanning Tree [*Communications term*] (DCT)
MTS .... Missile Test Set
MTS .... Missile Test Stand
MTS .... Missile Test Station
MTS .... Missile Tracking Station [*DoD*]
MTS .... Missile Tracking System (IEEE)
MTS .... Missile Training Squadron
MTS .... Missile Tube Supply
MTS .... Missions to Seamen [*British*]
MTS .... Mississippi Test Site [*Aerospace*] (AAG)
MTS .... Mobile Telephone Service
MTS .... Mobile Terminal System [*IBM Corp.*]
MTS .... Mobile Tracking Station [*NASA*]
MTS .... Mobile Training Set (AFM)
MTS .... Mobil-Trac System [*MTMC*] (TAG)
MTS .... Modem Test Set (NITA)
MTS .... Moderate Tactile Stimulus [*Neurology*] (DAVI)
MTS .... Modernization through Spares [*Army program*]
MTS .... Modular Tactical Switch (SAUS)
MTS .... Modular Television System [*Telecommunications*] (CDE)
MTS .... Modular Terminal System (NITA)
MTS .... Module Test Set (MCD)
MTS .... Module Test System (IAA)
MTS .... Module Tracking System (NRCH)
MTS .... Money Transfer System (IAA)
MTS .... Monosyllable, Trochee, Spondee Test [*Of speech discrimination*] (DAVI)
MTS .... Montgomery Street Income Securities, Inc. [*NYSE symbol*] (SPSG)
MTS .... Monthly Treasury Statement [*Government*] (AFM)
MTS .... Morale Tendency Score (AEE)
MTS .... Motion-Time Standards [*Industrial engineering*]
MTS .... Motor-Operated Transfer Switch
MTS .... Motor Tariff Service
MTS .... Motor Turbine Ship (IIA)
MTS .... Mountains [*Board on Geographic Names*]
MTS .... Movement Tracking System
MTS .... Moving Target Screen (MCD)
MTS .... Moving Target Simulator (RDA)
MTS .... Moving Time Series
MTS .... MTS Systems Corp. [*Associated Press*] (SAG)
MTS .... Multicellular Tumor Spheroid [*Medicine*] (DB)
MTS .... Multichannel Television Sound [*or Stereo*]
MTS .... Multichannel TV Sound (WDMC)
MTS .... Multichannel TV Stereo (WDMC)
MTS .... Multimedia Teleschool (SAUS)
MTS .... Multiple Target Screen
MTS .... Multiple Terminal System (NITA)
MTS .... Multiple Time Scale
MTS .... Multiple Tumor Suppressor [*Oncology*]
MTS .... Multipoint Terminal Software [*Computer science*] (VLIE)
MTS .... Muscle Testing System [*Myology*]
MTS .... Musculotendinous Structure (DMAA)
MTS .... State Law Library of Montana, Helena, MT [*OCLC symbol*] (OCLC)
MTS1 .... Multiple Tumour Suppressor 1 [*Genetics*] (ECON)
MTSA .... Mantissa (VLIE)
MTSA .... Seaman Apprentice, Missile Technician, Striker [*Navy rating*]
MTSAA ...... Multidiscipline Technical Safety Assurance Appraisal [*Environmental science*] (COE)
MTSAT ...... Multi-functional Transport Satellite
MTSAT ...... Multi-function Transport Satellite
MTSB .... Meridial Trans-Sonic Boundary-Layer [*Aerodynamics*]
MtSc .... Daniels County Free Library, Scobey, MT [*Library symbol*] [*Library of Congress*] (LCLS)

MTSC........ Magnetic Tape Selectric Composer [*IBM Corp.*]
MTSC........ Master of Teaching Speech Communication (GAGS)
MTSC........ Master of Technical and Scientific Communication (GAGS)
MTSC........ Master of Theological Studies Counseling (PGP)
MTSC........ MTS Systems [*NASDAQ symbol*] (TTSB)
MTSC........ MTS Systems Corp. [*NASDAQ symbol*] (NQ)
MTSD........ Military Transmission Systems Department [*NORAD*]
MTSE........ Magnetic Trap Stability Experiment (IEEE)
MTSE........ Message Transfer Service Element [*Computer science*] (VLIE)
MTSF........ Mean Time to System Failure [*Quality control*] (PDAA)
MTS/GMS... Module Test Set / Guided Missile System (DWSG)
MTSGT...... Master Technical Sergeant [*Marine Corps*]
MTSGT(C)... Master Technical Sergeant (Commissary) [*Marine Corps*]
MtSh......... Toole County Free Library, Shelby, MT [*Library symbol*] [*Library of Congress*] (LCLS)
MTSI......... Mean Time to System Interrogation (VLIE)
MTSI......... Micro Touch Systems [*NASDAQ symbol*] (TTSB)
MTSI......... Microtouch Systems, Inc. [*NASDAQ symbol*] (SAG)
MtSid........ Sidney Public Library, Sidney, MT [*Library symbol*] [*Library of Congress*] (LCLS)
Mt Sinai Sch Med... Mount Sinai School of Medicine of The City University of New York (GAGS)
MTSL........ Message Transfer Sublayer [*Telecommunications*] (OSI)
MTSL........ Monitoring and Technical Support Laboratory [*Environmental Protection Agency*] (GFGA)
MTSN........ Machine Type and Serial Number (VLIE)
MTSN........ Mattson Technology [*NASDAQ symbol*] (TTSB)
MTSN........ Mattson Technology, Inc. [*NASDAQ symbol*] (SAG)
MTSN........ Seaman, Missile Technician, Striker [*Navy rating*]
MTSO........ Mean Time to Switch-Over (VLIE)
MTSO........ Mobile Telephone Switching Office [*Telecommunications*]
MTSO........ Multiprogramming Time-Sharing Operating System [*Computer science*] (VLIE)
MTSP........ Maintenance Test Support Package [*Army*]
MTSP........ Microelectronics Technology Support Program (SAUS)
MTSP........ Microelectronic Technology Support Program (ACAE)
MTSPS...... Multiple Transducer Seismic Profiling System
MTSQ........ Mechanical Time, Superquick [*Fuse*] [*Weaponry*]
MTSQF...... Mechanical Time, Superquick Fuze [*Weaponry*] (MCD)
MTSR........ Maximal Temperature of the Synthesis Reaction [*Chemical engineering*]
MTSR........ Mean Time to Service Restoral [*Quality control*] [*Telecommunications*] (TEL)
MTSR........ Mean Time to System Restoration [*Computer science*] (VLIE)
MTSR........ Mid-Term Status Reports
MTSS........ Magnetic Tape Storage System
MTSS........ Manned Test Space System [*See also MOD, MODS, MOSS*] [*Air Force/NASA*]
MTSS........ Medial Tibial Stress Syndrome [*Medicine*] (MELL)
MTSS........ Military Test Space Station [*See also MOD, MODS, MOSS*] [*Air Force/NASA*]
MTSS........ Mine Warfare Tactical Support System (SAUS)
MTSS........ Modular Torpedo Support System (SAUS)
MTSSL...... Methanethiosulphonate Spin Label [*Analytical chemistry*]
MTST........ Magnetic Tape Selectric Typewriter [*IBM Corp.*]
MTST........ Maximal Treadmill Stress Test [*Medicine*] (DMAA)
MTST........ Microtest, Inc. [*NASDAQ symbol*] (SAG)
MTSTA...... Mount Shasta, CA [*American Association of Railroads railroad junction routing code*]
Mt St Mary's C... Mount St. Mary's College (GAGS)
MtStrS....... St. Regis School, St. Regis, MT [*Library symbol*] [*Library of Congress*] (LCLS)
MTSU........ Magnetic Tape Search Unit [*Computer science*]
MTSU........ Marine Transport Service [*Intermodal shipping container symbol*] (TVRC)
MTSU........ Middle Tennessee State University
MtSu......... Mineral County Public Library, Superior, MT [*Library symbol*] [*Library of Congress*] (LCLS)
MTSV........ Merlin Transportation Services [*Common carrier symbol*]
MTS/VO..... Motor Transportation Supervisor/Vehicle Operator (AAG)
MTSX........ MAX Transportation Service [*Private rail car owner code*]
MTT.......... Magnetic Tape Terminal [*Computer science*]
MTT.......... Magnetic Tape Transport [*Computer science*] (IEEE)
MTT.......... Maintenance Training Team (MCD)
MTT.......... Malignant Trophoblastic Teratoma [*Oncology*] (MAE)
MTT.......... Mammillothalamic Tract [*Neuroanatomy*]
MTT.......... Manned Target Tank (SAUS)
MTT.......... Maritime Telegraph & Telephone Co. Ltd. [*Toronto Stock Exchange symbol*]
MTT.......... Masked Terrain Trainer [*Military*]
MTT.......... Master of Textile Technology
MTT.......... Material Testing Technology (MCD)
MTT.......... Maximal Treadmill Test (CPH)
MTT.......... Maximum Touch Temperature (MCD)
MTT.......... Mean Transit Time
MTT.......... Mediterranean Tours and Travel [*Egypt*]
MTT.......... Medium Tactical Transport [*Army*]
MTT.......... Medium Tactical Truck [*Army*] (RDA)
MTT.......... Message Transfer Time (NITA)
MTT.......... Methyl(thio)tetrazole [*Biochemistry*]
MTT.......... Metropolitan Edison Co. [*NYSE symbol*] (SPSG)
MTT.......... Microprogram Trace Tape [*Computer science*] (VLIE)
MTT.......... Microsoft Travel Technologies [*Computer science*] (VLIE)
MTT.......... Microwave Theory and Technique (MCD)
MTT.......... Military Training Team (MCD)
MTT.......... Minatitlan [*Mexico*] [*Airport symbol*] (OAG)
MTT.......... Missionary Tech Team (EA)
MTT.......... Mi-Tsiyon Tetse Torah [*Tel Aviv*] (BJA)
MTT.......... Mobile Training Team
MTT.......... Mobile Travel Team (MCD)
MTT.......... Monetta Fire Tower [*South Carolina*] [*Seismograph station code, US Geological Survey*] (SEIS)
MTT.......... Monotetrazolium [*Medicine*] (MAE)
MTT.......... Moving Target Tracking (ACAE)
MTT.......... Moving Turning Target (SAUS)
MTT.......... Multiple Target Tracker
MTT.......... Munitions Transfer Truck (MCD)
MTT.......... Orion SpA [*Italy*] [*ICAO designator*] (FAAC)
MtT.......... Prairie County Library, Terry, MT [*Library symbol*] [*Library of Congress*] (LCLS)
MTTA........ Machine Tool Technologies Association [*British*] (EAIO)
MTTA........ Machine Tool Trades Association (ACII)
MTTA........ Mean Time to Accomplish [*Quality control*] (NASA)
MTTA........ Mean Time to Arrive [*Computer science*] (ELAL)
MTTA........ Mean Time to Assist (AAEL)
MTTA........ Multi-Tenant Telecommunications Association (EA)
MTTB........ Mean Time to Bench [*Repair*] [*Quality control*]
MTTC........ Manufacturing Technology Technical Council
MTTC........ Mean Time to Change Parts [*Quality control*] (MCD)
MTTC........ Mean Time to Correct (AAEL)
MTTC........ Mechanised Transport Training Corps [*British military*] (DMA)
MtTcES...... Trout Creek Elementary School, Trout Creek, MT [*Library symbol*] [*Library of Congress*] (LCLS)
MTTD........ Mean Time to Detect [*Quality control*] (MCD)
MTTD........ Mean Time to Diagnosis [*Quality control*] (BUR)
MTTE........ Magnetic Tape Terminal Equipment [*Computer science*] (CET)
MTTE........ Mean Time to Exchange [*Quality control*] (MCD)
MTTEA...... Marine Towing and Transportation Employers Association [*Defunct*] (EA)
MTTF........ Mean Time to Failure [*Quality control*]
MTTF........ Microbuoy Transportable Test Facility (SAUS)
MtTf......... Thompson Falls Public Library, Thompson Falls, MT [*Library symbol*] [*Library of Congress*] (LCLS)
MTTFF...... Mean Time to First Failure [*Quality control*]
MtTfS........ Thompson Falls Schools, Thompson Falls, MT [*Library symbol*] [*Library of Congress*] (LCLS)
MTTFSF..... Mean Time to First System Failure [*Quality control*] (PDAA)
MTTFSR..... Mean Time to First System Repair [*Quality control*] (PDAA)
MTTHS...... Modern Transport Technical and Historical Society [*Later, SFCH*] (EA)
MTTI......... Magnetic Tape Transport Interface [*Computer science*] (MCD)
MTTI......... Mean Time to Inspect [*Quality control*] (CAAL)
MTTI......... Mean Time to Install [*Computer science*] (GART)
MTTI......... Mean Time to Isolate [*Computer science*] (GART)
MTTI......... Modified Tension Time Index [*Cardiology*]
MTTL........ Motorola Transistor-Transistor Logic (IAA)
MTTM........ Magnetic Tape and Telemetry (MCD)
MTTM........ Mean Time to Maintain [*Quality control*] (CMD)
MTTN........ Multi-Tranche Tap Note [*Finance*] [*British*]
MTTO........ Minuetto [*Slow Air*] [*Music*] (ROG)
MTTOP...... Machine Tool Trigger Order Program (MHDB)
MTTP........ Materials Testing and Technology Program
MTTP........ Maximum Total Trihalomethane Potential (FFDE)
MTTPO...... Mean Time to Planned Outage (IEEE)
MTTPrC..... Metropol Ed 3.90% cm Pfd [*NYSE symbol*] (TTSB)
MTTPrZ..... Met-Ed Capital L.P.'MIPS' [*NYSE symbol*] (TTSB)
MTTR........ Magnetic Tape Transport Replacement (DWSG)
MTTR........ Maximum Time to Repair (MCD)
MTTR........ Maximum Time to Replace [*Navy*] (IAA)
MTTR........ Mean Time to Removal [*Quality control*]
MTTR........ Mean Time to Repair [*Quality control*] (CAAL)
MTTR........ Mean Time to Replacement [*Quality control*]
MTTR........ Mean Time to Restore [*Quality control*] (IEEE)
MTTR........ Missile Target Tracking RADAR (MCD)
MTTR........ Multi-Target Tracking Radar (SAUS)
MTTRF...... Mission Time to Restore Function
mttRNA..... Mitochondrial Transfer RNA[*Ribonucleic Acid*] [*Genetics*] (DOG)
MTTRS...... Mean Time to Restore Software [*Quality control*] (CAAL)
MTTRS...... Mean Time to Restore System [*Quality control*]
MTTS........ Magnetic Tape Terminal System [*Communications term*] (DCT)
MTTS........ Marine Terminal Tankage System (MCD)
MTTS........ Mean Time to Service [*Quality control*]
MTTS........ Mean Time to Trouble Shoot (ACAE)
MTT-S....... Microwave Theory and Techniques Society (ACAE)
MTTS........ Mobile Target Tracking System
MTTS........ Multi-media Target Training System [*Police and security equipment*]
MTTS........ Multiple Target Tracking System
MTTS........ Multiplexed Tactical Telephone System (SAUS)
MTTS........ Multitask Terminal System
MTTS........ Multi-Task Training System (SAUS)
MTTSF...... Mean Time to System Failure [*Quality control*] (PDAA)
MTTT........ Mean Time to Test (MCD)
MTTU........ Modular Timing Terminal Unit
MTTUO...... Mean Time to Unplanned Outage (IEEE)
MTTV........ Maneuvering Target Test Vechicle
MTTW........ Mean Time to Wait for Parts [*Quality control*] (MCD)
MtTyrSH..... Troy Senior High School, Troy, MT [*Library symbol*] [*Library of Congress*] (LCLS)
MTTZ........ Mount Tom [*Federal Railroad Administration identification code*]
MTU......... Magnetic Tape Unit [*Computer science*]

MTU .... Magnetometer Test Unit (ACAE)
MTU .... Maintenance Training Unit
MTU .... malignant Teratoma Undifferentiated [*Oncology*] (DAVI)
MTU .... Managed Municipal Portfolio II [*NYSE symbol*] (SPSG)
MTU .... Managed Muni Portfolio II [*NYSE symbol*] (TTSB)
MTU .... Manchester Terminal Unit (NITA)
MTU .... Master Terminal Unit [*Instrumentation*]
MTU .... Master Time Unit
MTU .... Master Timing Unit [*Aerospace*] (NAKS)
MTU .... Master Trigger Unit (IAA)
MTU .... Maximum Transmission Unit [*Computer science*] (IGQR)
MTU .... Medical Therapy Unit (DMAA)
MTU .... Memory Transfer Unit (NITA)
MTU .... Methylthiouracil [*Pharmacology*]
MTU .... Metric Tons of Uranium
MTU .... Metric Ton Unit
MTU .... Metric Units (DFIT)
MTU .... Michigan Technological University [*Houghton*]
MTU .... Microwave Transmission Unit (ACAE)
MTU .... MIRA [*Multifunctional Inertial Reference Assembly*] Transport Unit [*Air Force*] (MCD)
MTU .... Missile Tracking Unit (MCD)
MTU .... Missile Training Unit [*Air Force*]
MTU .... Mist Therapy Unit [*Medicine*]
MTU .... Mobile Technical Unit (MCD)
MTU .... Mobile Test Unit [*Army*] (RDA)
MTU .... Mobile Training Unit
MTU .... Mobile Treatment Unit [*Environmental Protection Agency*] (GFGA)
MTU .... Module Test Unit [*Nuclear energy*] (NRCH)
mtu .... Montana [*MARC country of publication code*] [*Library of Congress*] (LCCP)
MTU .... Montreal Trustco, Inc. [*Toronto Stock Exchange symbol*]
MTU .... Mosquito Training Unit [*British military*] (DMA)
MTU .... Motorinen Turbo-Union [*Germany*]
MTU .... Multiplexer and Terminal Unit
MTU .... Multiterminal Unit (TEL)
MTU .... Myton, UT [*Location identifier*] [*FAA*] (FAAL)
MtU .... University of Montana at Missoula, Missoula, MT [*Library symbol*] [*Library of Congress*] (LCLS)
M TUBERC... Mycobacterium Tuberculosis [*Bacteriology*] (CPH)
MtU-L .... University of Montana at Missoula, Law School, Missoula, MT [*Library symbol*] [*Library of Congress*] (LCLS)
MTUMR ..... MIRA [*Multifunctional Inertial Reference Assembly*] Transport Unit MountingRack [*Air Force*] (MCD)
MTUOP...... Mobile Training Units Out for Parts
MTUR .... Mean Time between Unscheduled Removals [*or Replacements*] [*Quality control*] (IIA)
MTUR .... Mean Time to Unscheduled Replacement [*Quality control*] (PDAA)
MTV .... Conference des Ministres Europeens du Travail [*Conference of European Ministers of Labour*] (EAIO)
MTV .... Mammary Tumor Virus
MTV .... Management Television [*Air Force*] (AFM)
MTV .... Maneuvering Technology Vehicle
MTV .... Manifold Tuning Valve [*Automotive term*] (HAWK)
MTV .... Marginal Terrain Vehicle
MTV .... Martinsville, VA [*Location identifier*] [*FAA*] (FAAL)
M TV .... Master of Television
MTV .... Mean Transformed Value
MTV .... Media Transforming Virus [*Alleged virus causing immunodeficiency disease*]
MTV .... Medium Tactical Vehicle [*Army*] (RDA)
MTV .... Metatarsus Varus [*Anatomy*] (DAVI)
MTV .... Miniature Test Vehicle (ACAE)
MTV .... Missile Test Vehicle
MTV .... Missile Training Vehicle
MTV .... Mobile Test Vehicle (SAUS)
MTV .... Modular Tactical Vest [*Police and security equipment*]
MTV .... Modulated Throttle Valve [*Automotive engineering*]
MTV .... Molecular Tagging Velocimetry
MTV .... Mota Lava [*Vanuatu*] [*Airport symbol*] (OAG)
MTV .... Motor Test Vehicle (IAA)
MTV .... Motor Torpedo Vessel [*British*]
MTV .... Motor Transport Volunteers [*Military unit*] [*British*]
MTV .... Mountain Valley Air Service, Inc. [*ICAO designator*] (FAAC)
MTV .... Mount Tassie [*Australia*] [*Seismograph station code, US Geological Survey*] [*Closed*] (SEIS)
MTV .... Mouse Mammary Tumor Virus (DMAA)
MTV .... Multicultural Television (ADA)
MTV .... Munitions Tow Vehicle (MCD)
MTV .... Munition Test Vehicle
MTV .... Music Television [*Warner Amex Satellite Entertainment Co.*] [*Cable-television system*]
MTV .... Mutatur Terminatio Versiculi [*The Termination of the Little Verse Is Changed*]
MTVAL ...... Master Tape Validation
MTVC .... Main Thrust Vector Control (SAUS)
MTVC .... Manned [*or Manual*] Thrust Vector Control (MCD)
MTVER ...... Mount Vernon, IL [*American Association of Railroads railroad junction routing code*]
MTVIS .... Monte Vista, CO [*American Association of Railroads railroad junction routing code*]
MTVL .... Mountain Valley Express Company [*Common carrier symbol*]
MTVP .... Moving Target Video Processor
MTVS .... Mission Test and Video System
MTVT .... Medium Tactical Vehicle Trailer (SAUS)
MTVT .... Mount Vernon Terminal Railway [*Federal Railroad Administration identification code*]
MTVU .... Module Thruster Valve Unit
MTW .... Machine Tool Wire
MTW .... Main Trawl Winch
MTW .... Manitowoc [*Wisconsin*] [*Airport symbol*] (OAG)
MTW .... Manitowoc Co. [*NYSE symbol*] (SPSG)
MTW .... Marinette, Tomahawk & Western Railroad Co. [*AAR code*]
MTW .... Maximum Taxi Weight [*Aviation*]
MTW .... Mean Tumor Weight [*Medicine*] (DB)
MTW .... Military Transport Wagon [*British*]
MTW .... Mission to the World (EA)
MTW .... Mobile Training Wing [*Air Force*]
MTW .... Mountain Waves (WEAT)
MTW .... Music Treasures of the World [*Record label*]
mtw .... Tropical Maritime Warm Air Mass [*Meteorology*] (BARN)
MtW .... Wibaux Public Library, Wibaux, MT [*Library symbol*] [*Library of Congress*] (LCLS)
MTWA .... Maximum Total Weight Authorized [*Aviation*] (AIA)
MTWC .... Morgan Three-Wheeler Club (EA)
MTWF .... Metal Thru-Wall Flashing [*Technical drawings*]
MtWfSH ..... Whitefish Senior High School, Whitefish, MT [*Library symbol*] [*Library of Congress*] (LCLS)
MTWLW ..... Manufacturer's Treadwear Limited Warranty [*Tire marketing*]
MTWN .... Mark Twain Bancshares, Inc. [*NASDAQ symbol*] (NQ)
MTWN .... Mark Twain Bancshrs [*NASDAQ symbol*] (TTSB)
MTWO .... Material Test Work Order (SAA)
MTWO .... Melamine Chemicals [*NASDAQ symbol*] (TTSB)
MTWO .... Melamine Chemicals, Inc. [*NASDAQ symbol*] (NQ)
M-T WP ..... Medium-Term Work Programme (SAUS)
MTWP .... Multiplier Traveling Wave Phototube (IAA)
MtWp .... Roosevelt County Library, Wolf Point, MT [*Library symbol*] [*Library of Congress*] (LCLS)
MTWR .... Micro-Thrust Water Rocket (ACAE)
MTWS .... MAGTF [*Marine Air-Ground Task Force*] Tactical Warfare Simulation [*DoD*]
MTWS .... Manual Track While Scan
MtWs .... Montana State Hospital, Patient Library, Warm Springs, MT [*Library symbol*] [*Library of Congress*] (LCLS)
MTWV .... Metawave Communications [*NASDAQ symbol*] (SG)
MTWX .... Mechanized Teletypewriter Exchange (TEL)
MTWY .... Motorway [*Postal Service standard*] (OPSA)
MTX .... Fairbanks [*Alaska*] Metro Field [*Airport symbol*] [*Obsolete*] (OAG)
MTX .... Manual Transaxle
MTX .... Manual Transmission
MTX .... Master of Taxation
MTX .... Matrix (IAA)
MTX .... Message Text Format (COE)
MTX .... Methotrexate [*Antineoplastic drug*]
MTX .... Microwave TOKAMAK [*Toroidal Kamera Magnetic*] Experiment [*Plasma physics*]
MTX .... Mighty Max [*NCIC car model code*]
MTX .... Military Traffic Expediting Service (AABC)
MTX .... Minerals Technologies [*NYSE symbol*] (SPSG)
MTX .... Mobile Telephone Exchange (CGWS)
MTX .... Morrell Tank Line [*AAR code*]
MTX .... Multi-Tasking Executive [*Computer science*] (VLIE)
MTX .... Multi-Terminal Executive [*Computer science*] (VLIE)
MTX4 .... Manual Transaxle-Four Speed [*Automotive engineering*]
MTX5 .... Manual Transaxle-Five Speed [*Automotive engineering*]
MTXC .... Matrix Capital Corp. [*NASDAQ symbol*] (SAG)
MTX-CF ..... Methotrexate with Citrovorum Factor Rescue [*Antineoplastic drug regimen*]
MTX + MP... Methotrexate and Mercaptopurine [*Antineoplastic drug regimen*] (DAVI)
MTX + MP + CTX... Methotrexate, Mercaptopurine, and Cytoxan [*Cyclophosphamide*] [*Antineoplastic drug regimen*] (DAVI)
MTY .... Empty
MTY .... Marlton Technologies [*AMEX symbol*] (TTSB)
MTY .... Marlton Technologies, Inc. [*AMEX symbol*] (SPSG)
MTY .... Materially [*Telegraphy*] (PCTE)
MTY .... Matsuyama [*Japan*] [*Seismograph station code, US Geological Survey*] (SEIS)
Mty .... Maturity (EBF)
MTY .... Maturity [*Business term*]
MTY .... Mekhon ha-Tekanim ha-Yisre'eli (BJA)
MTY .... Million Tons per Year
MTY .... Monterrey [*Mexico*] [*Airport symbol*] (OAG)
mtydm .... Martyrdom (VRA)
MTYU .... Interpool Container [*Intermodal shipping container symbol*] (TVRC)
MTZ .... Martinez, CA [*Amtrak rail station code*]
MTZ .... Mass Transfer Zone [*Chemical engineering*]
MTZ .... MasTec, Inc. [*NYSE symbol*] (SG)
MTZ .... Materialize [*Telegraphy*] (PCTE)
MTZ .... Mitsui Osaka Shosen Kaisha Lines [*Intermodal trailer symbol*]
MTZ .... Montezuma [*Chile*] [*Seismograph station code, US Geological Survey*] [*Closed*] (SEIS)
MTZ .... Montgomery Tank [*Federal Railroad Administration identification code*]
MTZ .... Motorized (AAG)
MTZ .... Motortechnische Zeitschrift [*Engine Technical Journal*] [*Automotive industry*]
MTZ .... Tacaneco [*Language symbol*] (ETLW)
MTZ .... Tuskegee, AL [*Location identifier*] [*FAA*] (FAAL)
MTZN .... Materialization [*Telegraphy*] (PCTE)

MTZZ........ Marine Terminal [*Federal Railroad Administration identification code*]
MU........... Akaflieg Muenchen Mitsubishi Heavy Industries [*Germany*] [*Japan*] [*ICAO aircraft manufacturer identifier*] (ICAO)
MU........... China Eastern Airlines [*ICAO designator*] (AD)
Mu........... Mache Unit [*Measure of radium emanation from solutions*] (AAMN)
MU........... Machine Unit
MU........... Mail Unit (KSC)
MU........... Maintenance Unit [*Military*]
MU........... Makeup (NRCH)
MU........... Management Unit [*Aviation*]
MU........... Maneuvering Unit (KSC)
mu........... Map Unit (DOG)
MU........... Marginal Utility [*Economics*]
MU........... Markup
MU........... Marvel Universe
MU........... Mass Units
mu........... Master Unit (NAKS)
MU........... Master Unit (NASA)
mu........... Mauritania [*MARC country of publication code*] [*Library of Congress*] (LCCP)
MU........... Mauritius [*ANSI two-letter standard code*] (CNC)
MU........... Measurement Unit
MU........... Memory Unit [*Computer science*] (MCD)
MU........... Mental Units of Growth [*Psychology*]
MU........... Mescaline Unit (DB)
MU........... Message Unit [*Telecommunications*]
MU........... Methylene Unit
MU........... Methylumbelliferone [*Biochemistry*]
MU........... Methylurea [*Organic chemistry*]
MU........... Micro [*One millionth*] (WDAA)
mu........... Micron [*Micrometer*] (AAMN)
MU........... Micron Technology, Inc. [*NYSE symbol*] (SPSG)
MU........... Microwave Unit (CARB)
MU........... Midcourse Update (ACAE)
mu........... Millimicro- [*Now nano*] (IDOE)
Mu........... Millimicron (AAG)
mu........... Millimicron [*Nanometer*] (IDOE)
MU........... Million Units
mU........... Milliunit (AAMN)
MU........... Misrair [*ICAO designator*] (AD)
MU........... Missing Upper (VLIE)
mu........... Mobile Unit (NAKS)
MU........... Mobile Unit
MU........... Mock-Up (AAG)
mu........... Mockup (NAKS)
MU........... Modular Unit (IAA)
MU........... Monetary Unit (ADA)
M/U.......... Monitor Unit [*Telecommunications*] (TEL)
MU........... Montevideo Units [*Of uterine activity*]
MU........... Mothers' Union [*Episcopalian*]
MU........... Motor Union
MU........... Motor Unit
MU........... Mouse Unit [*Medicine*] (DMAA)
mu........... Mouse Unit (LDT)
MU........... Mueller Cell [*Eye anatomy*]
MU........... Mulching [*Environmental science*] (COE)
MU........... Multidestination [*Carrier*]
mu........... Multiple Unit (NAKS)
MU........... Multiple Unit
MU........... Multiple Use (IAA)
MU........... Multiplexing Unit
MU........... Multi-Unit (SAUS)
mu........... Multiuser [*Computer science*] (ELAL)
MU........... Munitions Command [*Later, Armaments Command*] [*Army*] (MCD)
MU........... Murder [*Telegraphy*] (PCTE)
Mu........... Muscle [*Anatomy*] (DAVI)
MU........... Musical Union [*Oberlin College*] [*Ohio*]
MU........... Musician [*Navy rating*]
MU........... Musicians' Union [*British*] (DCTA)
MU........... Music Program [*Association of Independent Colleges and Schools specialization code*]
MU........... Muster [*Business term*] (DCTA)
Mu........... Mutator [*A bacteriophage*]
MU........... University of Massachusetts, Amherst, MA [*Library symbol*] [*Library of Congress*] (LCLS)
MU1.......... Musician, First Class [*Navy rating*]
MU2.......... Musician, Second Class [*Navy rating*]
MU3.......... Musician, Third Class [*Navy rating*]
MUA.......... Machinery Users' Association [*British*] (BI)
MUA.......... Mail User Agent [*Computer science*] (DCDG)
MUA.......... Mail Users' Association [*British*]
MUA.......... Manipulation Under Anesthesia [*Medicine*] (DMAA)
MUA.......... Manned Undersea [*or Underwater*] Activity [*Marine science*]
MUA.......... Maritime Union of Australia
MUA.......... Master of Urban Affairs (GAGS)
MUA.......... Master of Urban Architecture (GAGS)
MUA.......... Materials Usage Agreement (NASA)
MUA.......... Material Utilization Agreement (SAUS)
MUA.......... Maximum Usable Altitude [*Aviation*]
MUA.......... Memorandum of Understanding and Agreement
MUA.......... Metallurgistes Unis d'Amerique [*United Steelworkers of America - USWA*]
MU A......... Microampere (WDAA)
MUA.......... Middle Uterine Artery [*Medicine*] (DMAA)
MUA.......... Military Utility Assessment
MUA.......... Ministry of State for Urban Affairs [*Canada*]
MUA.......... Mixed Underachievers [*Education*]
MUA.......... Monotype Users' Association (NADA)
MUA.......... Mothers' Union in Australia
MUA.......... Motor Unit Activity (DMAA)
MUA.......... Multiple Unit Activity [*Neurophysiology*]
MUA.......... Munda [*Solomon Islands*] [*Airport symbol*] (OAG)
MUA.......... Muniassets Fund [*NYSE symbol*] (SPSG)
MUA.......... Murray Aviation, Inc. [*ICAO designator*] (FAAC)
MUAA......... Major Unit Assembly Area (MCD)
MUAA......... Marquette University Alumni Association (EA)
MUAC......... Mid Upper Arm Circumference [*Anatomy*]
MUACS........ Manpower Utilization and Control System
MUADEE....... [*The*] Mars Upper Atmosphere Dynamics, Energetics and Evolution Spacecraft [*NASA*] (ECON)
MUAG......... Central Agramonte [*Cuba*] [*ICAO location identifier*] (ICLI)
MU/AG........ Mid-Upper [*Turret*] Air Gunner [*British military*] (DMA)
MU & P....... Makeup and Purification [*Nuclear energy*] (NRCH)
MUAP......... Motor Unit Action Potential [*Physiology*]
MUARC........ Monash University Accident Research Center [*Australia*]
MUART........ Microprocessor Universal Asynchronous Receiver Transmitter (IAA)
MUAT......... Antilla [*Cuba*] [*ICAO location identifier*] (ICLI)
MUAT......... Mobile Underwater Acoustic Unit (NATG)
MUB.......... Maun [*Botswana*] [*Airport symbol*] (OAG)
MUB.......... University of Maryland, Baltimore County Campus, Catonsville, MD [*OCLC symbol*] (OCLC)
MUBA......... Baracoa/Oriente [*Cuba*] [*ICAO location identifier*] (ICLI)
MU BAR....... Microbar (WDAA)
MUBE......... El Caribe [*Cuba*] [*ICAO location identifier*] (ICLI)
MUBEN........ Mutual Benefit Life Insurance Company (EFIS)
MUBI......... Cayo Mambi [*Cuba*] [*ICAO location identifier*] (ICLI)
MUBIS........ Multiple Beam Interval Scanner
MUBO......... Batabano [*Cuba*] [*ICAO location identifier*] (ICLI)
MUBR......... Mean Units between Replacement [*Quality control*]
MUBUS........ Microprocessor Bus [*Computer science*] (VLIE)
MUBY......... Bayamo [*Cuba*] [*ICAO location identifier*] (ICLI)
MUC.......... Map Unit Characteristics [*USDA Forest Service*] (ALAC)
MUC.......... Maximum Urinary Concentration [*Medicine*]
MUC.......... Maximum Use Concentration (LDOE)
MUC.......... Meritorious Unit Citation [*Military decoration*]
MUC.......... Meritorious Unit Commendation [*Military decoration*] (AFM)
MUC.......... Missionary Union of the Clergy [*British*] (BI)
MUC.......... Mount Union College [*Alliance, OH*]
MUC.......... Mucilage [*Medicine*] (EDAA)
muc.......... Mucilage [*Medicine*] (EDAA)
MUC.......... Mucilaginous (ROG)
MUC.......... Mucosal Ulcerative Colitis [*Medicine*]
MUC.......... Multicoupler
MUC.......... Multiple Use Counter (IAA)
MUC.......... Munich [*Germany*] [*Airport symbol*] (OAG)
MUC.......... Musician, Chief [*Navy rating*]
MUCA......... Ciego De Avila [*Cuba*] [*ICAO location identifier*] (ICLI)
MuCA2........ Muniyield California Insured Fund II [*Associated Press*] (SAG)
MuCAIns...... MuniYield California Insured Fund [*Associated Press*] (SAG)
MUCAR........ Mustang Car [*Automotive parts*]
MUCB......... Caibarien [*Cuba*] [*ICAO location identifier*] (ICLI)
MUCC......... Cunagua [*Cuba*] [*ICAO location identifier*] (ICLI)
MUCC......... Michigan United Conservation Clubs
MUCF......... Cienfuegos [*Cuba*] [*ICAO location identifier*] (ICLI)
MUCG......... Macquarie University Caving Group [*Australia*]
MUCG......... Management/Union Consultative Group [*Australia*]
Much D & S... Muchall's Doctor and Student [*A publication*] (DLA)
MUCHFET...... Multichannel Field Effect Transistor (IAA)
MUCIA........ Midwest Universities Consortium for International Activities [*University of Indiana*]
MUCILAG...... Mucilaginous (ROG)
MUCK......... Multi-User Chat Kingdom (SAUS)
MUCL......... Cayo Largo Del Sur [*Cuba*] [*ICAO location identifier*] (ICLI)
MUCL......... Mycological Collection of the UCL (SAUS)
MUCM......... Camaguey/Ignacio Agramonte [*Cuba*] [*ICAO location identifier*] (ICLI)
MUCM......... Musician, Master Chief [*Navy rating*]
MUCN......... Ciego De Avila Norte [*Cuba*] [*ICAO location identifier*] (ICLI)
MUCO......... Colon [*Cuba*] [*ICAO location identifier*] (ICLI)
MUCO......... Materiel Utilization Control Office (AFIT)
MUCOM........ Munitions Command [*Later, Armaments Command*] [*Army*]
Mu Corp Ca... Municipal Corporation Cases [*United States*] [*A publication*] (DLA)
Mu Corp Cir... Municipal Corporation Circular [*England*] [*A publication*] (DLA)
MUCP......... MSU Corp. [*NASDAQ symbol*] (QUAN)
MUCROMAF..... Multiple Critical Root Maximally Flat (PDAA)
MUCS......... Central Noel Fernandez [*Cuba*] [*ICAO location identifier*] (ICLI)
MUCS......... Manufacturers Consolidation Services [*Common carrier symbol*]
MUCS......... Musician, Senior Chief [*Navy rating*]
MUCU......... Santiago De Cuba/Antonio Maceo [*Cuba*] [*ICAO location identifier*] (ICLI)
MUCUSA....... Missionary Union of the Clergy in the United States of America [*Later, PMUPR*] (EA)
MUCV......... Las Clavellinas [*Cuba*] [*ICAO location identifier*] (ICLI)
MUCX......... Murro Chemical [*Private rail car owner code*]
MUCY......... Cayajabo [*Cuba*] [*ICAO location identifier*] (ICLI)
MUCZ......... Murphy [*Federal Railroad Administration identification code*]
MUD.......... Macromind Utility Disk
MUD.......... Map Unit Description [*USDA Forest Service*] (ALAC)
MUD.......... Master of Urban Design (GAGS)

MUD .... Master User Directory (MHDI)
MUD .... Matched Unrelated Donor [*Medicine*] (MELL)
MUD .... Memory Unit Drum [*Computer science*]
MUD .... Mercaptoundecanol [*Organic chemistry*]
MUD .... Middle, Up, Down [*in game of bridge*]
MUD .... Minimum Urticarial Dose [*Medicine*] (DMAA)
MUD .... Mouvement pour l'Unite et la Democratie [*Djibouti*] [*Political party*] (EY)
MUD .... Mouvement Union Democratique [*Democratic Union Movement*] [*Monaco*] [*Political party*] (PPE)
MUD .... Multiple User Dimension [*Computer science*]
MUD .... Multiple-User Domain (SAUS)
MUD .... Multiple User Dungeon [*Computer science*]
MUD .... Multi-User Device (ABAC)
MUD .... Multiuser Dialogue [*Computer science*] (IGQR)
MUD .... Multi-User Dimension [*Computer simulation environment for multi-users*] (NETL)
MUD .... Multi-User Domain [*Computer science*]
MUD .... Multi-User Dungeon [*Computer game*]
MUD .... Municipal Utility District [*Investment term*] (DFIT)
MUD .... Murchison Falls [*Uganda*] [*Airport symbol*] (AD)
MUD .... Murdered [*Telegraphy*] (PCTE)
MUDAID ..... Multivariate, Univariate, and Discriminant Analysis of Irregular Data [*Statistics*] (IAA)
MUDAR ..... Mulheres por um Desenvolvimento Alternativo [*Development Alternatives with women for a New Era - DAWN*] [*Brazil*] (EAIO)
MUDAS ...... Modular Universal Data Acquisition System (SAUS)
MUDD .... Multisource Unified Data Distribution (PDAA)
MUDDC ..... Multiunit Direct Digital Control (IAA)
MUDET ...... Militarized Universal Digital Element Tester (MCD)
MUDL .... Microwave Ultrasonic Delay Line
MUDPAC .... Modular Unit Deployable Package (SAUS)
MUDPIE ..... Museum and University Data Processing Information Exchange (IAA)
MUDR .... Multidetail Drawing (MSA)
MUDS .... Multiple Usage Data Sheet (MCD)
MUDSS ...... Mobile Underwater Debris Survey System
Mudst .... Mudstone Soil [*Agronomy*]
MUDWNT ... Makeup Demineralizer Waste Neutralizer Tank (IEEE)
MUE .... Kamuela [*Hawaii*] [*Airport symbol*] (OAG)
MUE .... Medication Use Evaluated (MELL)
MUE .... Meritorious Unit Emblem [*Military decoration*]
MUE .... Microcomputer Users in Education (AIE)
MUE .... Motor Unit Estimate (DB)
MUE .... Motor Unit Estimated (DMAA)
MUe .... Muehldorf am Inn [*German license plate city code*]
MUEI .... Micron Electronics, Inc. [*NASDAQ symbol*] (SAG)
MUEI .... Micron Electronics [*NASDAQ symbol*] (TTSB)
MUEL .... Mueller [*Paul*] Co. [*NASDAQ symbol*] (NQ)
Mueller ..... Mueller Industries [*Associated Press*] (SAG)
MuellerInd ... Muller Industries [*Associated Press*] (SAG)
MuellerP ..... Mueller [*Paul*] Co. [*Associated Press*] (SAG)
MUeR .... Mueritz [*German license plate city code*]
MUERI .... Murdoch University Energy Research Institute [*Australia*]
MUEU .... H Mueller [*Intermodal shipping container symbol*] (TVRC)
MUEW .... eW MonopolUEbertragungsWeg (SAUS)
MUEXEC .... Multi-User Executive [*Computer science*] (VLIE)
MUF .... Makeup Feed [*Boiler*]
MUF .... Marksmanship Under Fire (SAUS)
MUF .... Material Unaccounted For [*Nuclear energy*]
MUF .... Maximum Usable Frequency [*Signal transmission*]
MU F .... Microfarad (WDAA)
MUF .... Muffler
MUF .... Munivest Fund, Inc. [*AMEX symbol*] (COMM)
MUF .... Muting [*Indonesia*] [*Airport symbol*] (OAG)
MuFAR ...... Multi-target Field Artillery Radar (SAUS)
MUFC .... Central Amancio Rodriguez [*Cuba*] [*ICAO location identifier*] (ICLI)
MUFD .... Makeup Feed [*Boiler*]
MUFFIN ..... Multi-Use Interagency News [*FSS database*] (AAGC)
MUFFLIR ... Multi-Function Forward Looking Infrared (ACAE)
MUFFS ...... Multiple Frequency Firing System (ACAE)
MUFL .... Florida [*Cuba*] [*ICAO location identifier*] (ICLI)
MuFLIn ...... MuniYield Florida Insured Fund [*Associated Press*] (SAG)
MUFLNG .... Mouvement pour l'Unification des Forces de Liberation de la Guadeloupe [*Movement for the Unification of National Liberation Forces of Guadeloupe*] [*Political party*] (PD)
MUFLR ...... Muffler
MUFM .... Mouvement Universal pour une Federation Mondiale [*World Association of World Federalists - WAWF*] [*Netherlands*]
MUFON ...... Mutual UFO [*Unidentified Flying Object*] Network (EA)
MUFON ...... Mutual UFO Network, Inc.
MUFT .... Multigroup Fourier Transform [*Code*] [*Nuclear energy*] (NRCH)
MUFTI .... Minimum Use of Force Tactical Intervention [*British police*]
MUG .... Macintosh User Group [*Computer science*] (WDMC)
MUG .... Make-Up Gas [*Chemical engineering*]
mug .... Mammogram [*Medicine*] (BCRP)
MUG .... Manning Unit Group [*Air Force*] (AFM)
MUG .... Marcive Users Group [*Library network*]
MUG .... MARC Users Group (NITA)
MUG .... Maximum Unilateral Gain (IAA)
MUG .... Maximum Usable Gain [*Bell System*]
MUG .... Methylumbelliferylglucuronide [*Biochemistry*]
MUG .... Microcomputer User's Group (ACAE)
MU G .... Microgram (WDAA)
MUG .... Ministry of Useless Gestures [*Organization to increase number of voters*] [*British*]
MUG .... Mitosis with Unreplicated Genome [*Cytology*]
MUG .... Mulege [*Mexico*] [*Airport symbol*] [*Obsolete*] (OAG)
MUG .... Multiset Users Group (EA)
MUG .... MUMPS [*Massachusetts General Hospital Utility Multiprogramming System*] Users' Group (EA)
MUG .... Murdering [*Telegraphy*] (PCTE)
MUG .... Murgor Resources, Inc. [*Vancouver Stock Exchange symbol*]
MUGA .... Multigated Angiogram [*Cardiology*] (DAVI)
MUGA .... Multiple Gate Acquisition Analysis [*Scan*] (DAVI)
MUGA .... Multiple-Gated Acquisition [*Nuclear medicine*]
MU-GAL ..... Methylumbelliferyl-B-Galactosidase [*Biochemistry*] (MAE)
MUGA scan ... Multiple-Gated Arteriography Scan [*Medicine*] (WDAA)
MUGB .... Methylumbelliferyl Guanidinobenzoate [*Biochemistry*]
MUGD .... MUMPS User Group Deutschland (SAUS)
MUGEx ...... Multigated Blood Pool Image during Exercise [*Hematology*] (DMAA)
MUGM .... Guantanamo, US Naval Air Base [*Cuba*] [*ICAO location identifier*] (ICLI)
MUGN .... Giron [*Cuba*] [*ICAO location identifier*] (ICLI)
MUGR .... Multigated Blood Pool Image at Rest [*Medicine*] (DMAA)
MUGSE ...... Multimission-Unique Ground Support Equipment (MCD)
MUGT .... Guantanamo [*Cuba*] [*ICAO location identifier*] (ICLI)
MUGX .... Multiple Gated Acquisition Exercise [*Scan*] [*Cardiology*] (DAVI)
MUH .... Memorial University of Newfoundland, Health Sciences Library [*UTLAS symbol*]
MUH .... Mersa Matruh [*Egypt*] [*Airport symbol*] (AD)
MU H .... Microhenry (WDAA)
MUHA .... Habana/Jose Marti [*Cuba*] [*ICAO location identifier*] (ICLI)
MUHG .... Holguin [*Cuba*] [*ICAO location identifier*] (ICLI)
MUHL .... Muhlberg [*NCIC motorcycle make code*]
MUI .... Fort Indiantown Gap (Annville), PA [*Location identifier*] [*FAA*] (FAAL)
MUI .... Machine Utilization Index [*Computer science*]
MUI .... Mashhad University [*Iran*] [*Seismograph station code, US Geological Survey*] (SEIS)
MUI .... Mass Unbalance Input [*Computer science*]
MUI .... Metals USA [*NYSE symbol*] (SG)
MUI .... Mode-Independent Unnumbered Information
MUI .... Monsoonal Upwelling Index [*Paleoceanography*]
MUI .... Movement for the Unity of the Left [*Ecuador*] [*Political party*] (PPW)
MUI .... Multimedia User Interface (GART)
MUI .... Trans Air [*FAA designator*] (FAAC)
MUIFX .... Nationwide Fund [*Mutual fund ticker symbol*] (SG)
MUIG .... Minicomputer Users Interest Group [*Later, Mini/Micro Special Interest Group*] (EA)
MU IN .... Microinch (WDAA)
MuInI .... Muniyield Insured Fund [*Associated Press*] (SAG)
MUIR .... Microinstruction Register (MHDI)
Muir Gai .... Muirhea's Institutes of Gaius [*A publication*] (DLA)
MUIS .... Isabella [*Cuba*] [*ICAO location identifier*] (ICLI)
MuIT .... Municipal Income Trust [*Associated Press*] (SAG)
MuIT2 .... Municipal Income Trust II [*Associated Press*] (SAG)
MuIT3 .... Municipal Income Trust III [*Associated Press*] (SAG)
MUJ .... Mui [*Ethiopia*] [*Airport symbol*] (OAG)
MUJA .... Majana [*Cuba*] [*ICAO location identifier*] (ICLI)
MUK .... Alamogordo, NM [*Location identifier*] [*FAA*] (FAAL)
MUK .... Mauke [*Cook Islands*] [*Airport symbol*] (OAG)
MUK .... MEPC International Capital LP [*NYSE symbol*] (SAG)
MUK .... Muk Air Taxi [*Denmark*] [*ICAO designator*] (FAAC)
MUK .... Mukerian [*India*] [*Seismograph station code, US Geological Survey*] [*Closed*] (SEIS)
MUKPrA ..... MEPC Intl Cap 9.125%'QUIPS' [*NYSE symbol*] (TTSB)
MUL .... Manned Underwater Laboratories [*Marine science*] (MSC)
MUL .... Manufacturing under Licence [*British*] (DS)
MUL .... Master Urgency List [*Navy*]
MUL .... Mobile-Moored Undersea Laboratory
MUL .... Mobile User Link (SAUS)
MUL .... Modify User Login (AAEL)
MUL .... Moultrie, GA [*Location identifier*] [*FAA*] (FAAL)
MUL .... Mullan [*Idaho*] [*Seismograph station code, US Geological Survey*] (SEIS)
MUL .... Mulsanne [*NCIC car model code*]
MUL .... MULS [*Minnesota Union List of Serials*], Minneapolis, MN [*OCLC symbol*] (OCLC)
MUL .... Multicare Cos. [*NYSE symbol*] (TTSB)
mul .... Multilingual [*MARC language code*] [*Library of Congress*] (LCCP)
MUL .... Multiplexer
MUL .... Multiply (MDG)
MUL .... Mumuye [*Language symbol*] (ETLW)
MULASSS ... Multiple LASER Source Signature Simulator (MCD)
MULB .... Habana [*Cuba*] [*ICAO location identifier*] (ICLI)
MULC .... Measured Usage License Charge [*For software*] (GART)
MULDEM .... Multiplexer/Demultiplexer [*Bell Laboratories*]
MULDEX .... Multiplexer/Demultiplexer
MULDEX .... Multipoint Cross-Reference Index
MULE .... Manned-Unmanned Lunar Explorer
MULE .... Modular Universal LASER Equipment (MCD)
MULE .... Multech Corporation [*NCIC trailer make code*]
MULE .... Multilingual Enhancement of GNU EMACS (SAUS)
MULE .... Multiple-Use Linear Engergizer [*Automotive engineering*]
MULE .... Multi-Use Lightsat Environment (SAUS)
MULH .... Habana [*Cuba*] [*ICAO location identifier*] (ICLI)
Mu LJ .... Municipal Law Journal [*A publication*] (DLA)
MULL .... Modern Uses of Logic in Law
MULL .... Mullion [*Technical drawings*]

MULM .... La Coloma [*Cuba*] [*ICAO location identifier*] (ICLI)
MulMR ...... Multi-Market Radio, Inc. [*Associated Press*] (SAG)
MulMRad ... Multi-Market Radio, Inc. [*Associated Press*] (SAG)
MULO .... Multipurpose Lightweight Overboot [*Army*]
MULQUAL... Multiple Goal Water Quality Model (PDAA)
MULR .... Malayan Union Law Reports [*1946-47*] [*A publication*] (ILCA)
MULR .... Muller
MULS........ Mobile Unit Launch Site (IAA)
MULS........ Signed Multiplication [*Computer science*]
MULSF ...... Macquarie University Law School Foundation [*Australia*]
MULSP ...... Missouri Union List of Serial Publications [*St. Louis Public Library*] [*Missouri*] [*Information service or system*] (IID)
mult .... Multiple (MIST)
MULT .... Multiple
MULT .... Multiple Schedule of Reinforcement (DIPS)
MULT .... Multiply (NASA)
MULT .... Multi Solutions, Inc. [*NASDAQ symbol*] (QUAN)
MULT .... Multi Trailer [*NCIC trailer make code*]
MULTA....... Multiple-Use Land Alliance (EA)
MULTACK... Multiple Target Attack (ACAE)
MULTACK... Multiple Target Attack System Integration and Simulation (ACAE)
MULTACKS... Multi-Attack System (ACAE)
MULTAM .... Multiple Target Assessment Model (ACAE)
MultClr...... Multi-Color Corp. [*Associated Press*] (SAG)
MULTEWS... Multiple Electronics Warfare Surveillance [*DoD*]
MULTEWS... Multitarget Electronic Warfare System
MULTH ...... Multilith
multi......... Multicolored [*Philately*]
MULTI .... Multiple (DAVI)
multi......... Multiple (ELAL)
MULTI .... Multiplexer
Multicne .... Multicare Companies [*Associated Press*] (SAG)
MULTICOR... Multinational Finance Corp. [*Indonesia*] (EY)
MultiCp ..... Multi-Corp, Inc. [*Associated Press*] (SAG)
Multicre..... Multicare Companies [*Associated Press*] (SAG)
MULTICS... Multiplexed Information and Computing Service [*Honeywell, Inc.*]
MultiCul R... MultiCultural Review [*A publication*] (BRI)
Multilink PPP... Multichannel Connection Protocol Based on the Point-to-Point Protocol [*Computer science*]
Multilink PPP... Multilink Point-to-Point Protocol [*Computer science*]
MultiMC...... MultiMedia Concepts International, Inc. [*Associated Press*] (SAG)
MultiMed ... MultiMedia Concepts International, Inc. [*Associated Press*] (SAG)
MULTIMED... Multimedia Exposure Assessment Model [*Environmental Protection Agency*] (AEPA)
Multinat Finance J... Multinational Finance Journal [*A publication*] (JLIT)
multip .... Multiparous [*Obstetrics*]
MULTIPAC... Multiple Pool Processor and Computer (PDAA)
MULTIPLE... Multipurpose Program that Learns [*Computer science*] (PDAA)
MULTI-SDF... Multiple Signal Direction Finder (ACAE)
MULTIV...... Multivibrator (IAA)
multivits... Multivitamins [*Pharmacy*]
MultM .... Multi-Market Radio, Inc. [*Associated Press*] (SAG)
MultMC ..... MultiMedia Concepts International, Inc. [*Associated Press*] (SAG)
Multmd...... Multimedia Concepts International, Inc. [*Associated Press*] (SAG)
MultMT...... Multi-Media Tutorial Services, Inc. [*Associated Press*] (SAG)
MULTOS..... Multimedia Office Server (SAUS)
MULTOTS... Multiple Units Link 11 Test and Operational Training System [*Navy*] (NVT)
MULTP ...... Multiplier (NITA)
MultPb ...... Multicom Publishing [*Associated Press*] (SAG)
MULTR ...... Multimeter (AAG)
MULTR ...... Multiplier
MULTS ...... Mobile Universal Link 11 Translator System (SAUS)
MultZns .... Multiple Zones International, Inc. [*Associated Press*] (SAG)
MULU .... Unsigned Multiplication [*Computer science*]
MuLv .... Murine Leukemia Virus [*Medicine*] (DB)
Mum......... Chrysanthemum [*Horticulture*]
MUM .... Mass Memory Unit Manager (SAUS)
MUM .... Maximum Useful Magnification (MCD)
MUM .... Method of Unweighted Means [*Statistics*]
MUM .... Methodology for Unmanned Manufacture [*Robotics project*] [*Japan*]
MUM .... Multiple Unit Message [*Telecommunications*] (IEEE)
MUM .... Multiuse Manuscript
MUM .... Multiuse Mnemonics (IAA)
MUM .... Multi-User Message (NITA)
MUM .... Multiuser Monitor
MUM .... Mumias [*Kenya*] [*Airport symbol*] [*Obsolete*] (OAG)
MUM .... University of Mississippi, University, MS [*OCLC symbol*] (OCLC)
MU M^2 ...... Square Micrometer (WDAA)
MU M^3 ...... Cubic Micrometer (WDAA)
MUMA....... Punta De Maisi [*Cuba*] [*ICAO location identifier*] (ICLI)
MUMAD..... Museum Angkatan Darat [*Indonesia*]
MUME....... Murphy Motor Express [*Common carrier symbol*]
Mumf........ Mumford's Jamaica Reports [*A publication*] (DLA)
MUMG....... Managua [*Cuba*] [*ICAO location identifier*] (ICLI)
MUMH....... Matahambre [*Cuba*] [*ICAO location identifier*] (ICLI)
MUMH....... Minute Man Transport [*Common carrier symbol*]
MUMI........ Manzanillo [*Cuba*] [*ICAO location identifier*] (ICLI)
MUMJ .... Mayajigua [*Cuba*] [*ICAO location identifier*] (ICLI)
Mum Jam... Mumford's Jamaica Reports [*A publication*] (DLA)
MUMLIB .... Multimedia Technology in Libraries (TELE)
MUMM ...... Management Unit of the Mathematical Model of the North Sea and Scheldt Estuary (SAUS)
MUMMERS... Manned-Unmanned Environmental Research Station (MSC)
MUMMS .... Marine Corps Unified Materiel Management System
Mummy ..... Mature Upwardly Mobile Mommy [*Lifestyle classification*]
MUMO....... Moa [*Cuba*] [*ICAO location identifier*] (ICLI)
MUMP....... Marshall - University of Michigan Probe [*Rocket flight*]
MUMPS ..... Massachusetts General Hospital Utility Multiprogramming System [*Programming language*]
MUMPS ..... Multiple-Unit, Moving-Projectile System (MCD)
MUMS....... Mobile Utility Module System (IEEE)
MUMS....... Modular Underwater Measurement System (SAUS)
MUMS....... Mothers United for Moral Support
MUMS....... Multiple Unguided Mine System (MCD)
MUMS....... Multiple-Use MARC [*Machine-Readable Cataloging*] System [*Online retrieval system*] [*Information service or system*] [*Library of Congress*]
MUMSU ..... Monash University Malaysian Students' Union [*Australia*]
MUMT....... Matanzas [*Cuba*] [*ICAO location identifier*] (ICLI)
MuMTV...... Murine Mammary Tumor Virus
MUMU....... Multi-Modal Transport Equipment [*Intermodal shipping container symbol*] (TVRC)
MUMZ....... Manzanillo [*Cuba*] [*ICAO location identifier*] (ICLI)
MUN......... Aeromundo Ejecutivo, SA de CV [*Mexico*] [*FAA designator*] (FAAC)
MUN......... Maturin [*Venezuela*] [*Airport symbol*] (OAG)
MUN......... Memorial University of Newfoundland [*Marine science*] (MSC)
MUN......... Memorial University of Newfoundland Library [*UTLAS symbol*]
MUN......... Mission of National Unity (Panama) [*Political party*] (PSAP)
MUN......... Mundaring [*Australia*] [*Seismograph station code, US Geological Survey*] (SEIS)
Mun.......... Munford's Reports [*15-20 Virginia*] [*A publication*] (DLA)
mun.......... Municipal (SHCU)
Mun.......... Municipal (TBD)
MUN......... Municipal
MUN......... Municipal Court [*Court type found in state of Virginia*] (MVRD)
Mun.......... Municipal Law Reporter [*A publication*] (DLA)
MUN......... Munitions (AFM)
Mun.......... Munitions Appeals Reports [*England*] [*A publication*] (DLA)
MUN......... Munsingwear, Inc. [*NYSE symbol*] (SPSG)
MUNA .... La Cubana [*Cuba*] [*ICAO location identifier*] (ICLI)
MUNA .... United Nations Association of Mauritius (EAIO)
MunAdv .... Municipal Advantage Fund [*Associated Press*] (SAG)
MUNAF...... Movimento de Unidade Nacional Antifacista [*National United Antifascist Movement*] [*Portugal*] [*Political party*] (PPE)
Mun & El Cas... Municipal and Election Cases [*India*] [*A publication*] (DLA)
MUNAP...... Multi-National Approved Program
Mun App .... Munitions Appeals Reports [*England*] [*A publication*] (DLA)
Mun App Rep... Munitions Appeals Reports [*England*] [*A publication*] (DLA)
Mun App Sc... Munitions of War Acts, Appeal Reports [*1916-20*] [*Scotland*] [*A publication*] (DLA)
MUNB .... San Nicolas De Bari [*Cuba*] [*ICAO location identifier*] (ICLI)
MUNBG ..... Munitions Building [*Washington, DC*] [*Obsolete*]
MUNBLDG... Munitions Building [*Obsolete*] [*Washington, DC*] (DNAB)
MUNC .... Muncy Homes [*NCIC trailer make code*]
MUNC .... Munitions Command [*Later, Armaments Command*] [*Army*]
MUNC .... Nicaro [*Cuba*] [*ICAO location identifier*] (ICLI)
MunCA ...... MuniYield California Fund [*Associated Press*] (SAG)
MUNCI ...... Muncie, IN [*American Association of Railroads railroad junction routing code*]
Mun Corp Cas... Municipal Corporation Cases [*A publication*] (DLA)
Mun Ct ...... Municipal Court (DLA)
Mun Ct App Dist Col... Municipal Court of Appeals for the District of Columbia (DLA)
Mund .... De Mundo [*of Aristotle*] [*Classical studies*] (OCD)
MUND .... Model Urban Neighborhood Demonstration
Mundy....... Abstracts of Star Chamber Proceedings [*1550-58*] [*A publication*] (DLA)
MUNE .... Multiple Negative [*Circuit*] (AAG)
MUNEX...... Munitions Allocation and Expenditure Tracking System (ACAE)
Munf......... Munford's Reports [*15-20 Virginia*] [*A publication*] (DLA)
MunFL....... MuniYield Florida Fund [*Associated Press*] (SAG)
MUNFLA .... Memorial University of Newfoundland Folklore and Language Archive [*Research center*] [*Canada*] (RCD)
Munf (VA)... Munford's Reports [*15-20 Virginia*] [*A publication*] (DLA)
MUNG .... Mush until No Good [*Describes destruction of computer software*]
MUNG .... Nueva Gerona [*Cuba*] [*ICAO location identifier*] (ICLI)
MUNGE...... Movimiento para la Unificacion Nacional de Guinea Ecuatorial [*Movement for National Unification of Equatorial Guinea*] [*Political party*] (EY)
MUNGE...... Munger, IL [*American Association of Railroads railroad junction routing code*]
Mung Pay... Munger on Application of Payments [*A publication*] (DLA)
MUNHA ..... Munhall, PA [*American Association of Railroads railroad junction routing code*]
MunHi....... Municipal High Income Fund, Inc. [*Associated Press*] (SAG)
MUNI .... Municipal (AFM)
Muni......... Municipal (EBF)
muni......... Municipal (ELAL)
MUNI .... Municipal Development Corp. [*NASDAQ symbol*] (COMM)
muni......... Municiple (SHCU)
Muniast ..... Muniassets Fund, Inc. [*Associated Press*] (SAG)
munic .... Municipal (MIST)
MUNIC ...... Municipal
Munic & PL... Municipal and Parish Law Cases [*England*] [*A publication*] (DLA)
Munic LR (PA)... Municipal Law Reporter [*Pennsylvania*] [*A publication*] (DLA)
MUNIDB..... Municipal Bonds Databank (NITA)
MuniFd...... MuniEnhanced Fund [*Associated Press*] (SAG)

MuniIn ...... Muni Insured Fund, Inc. [*Associated Press*] (SAG)
MUNIMT .... Muniment (ROG)
MuniMtg .... Municipal Mortgage & Equity LLC [*Associated Press*] (SAG)
MunIns ...... MuniYield Insured Fund [*Associated Press*] (SAG)
MUNIREP... Munitions Report [*Worldwide report of location and status of air munitions*] [*Military*]
MUniv .... Master of the University
Muniv2 ...... Munivest Fund II [*Associated Press*] (SAG)
Muniyld ..... MuniYield Fund, Inc. [*Associated Press*] (SAG)
MUNJC ...... Munising Junction, MI [*American Association of Railroads railroad junction routing code*]
MuNJIn ...... MuniYield New Jersey Insured Fund [*Associated Press*] (SAG)
Munk Emp Liab... Munkman's Employer's Liability at Common Law [*8th ed.*] [*1975*] [*A publication*] (DLA)
Mun LJ ...... Municipal Law Journal [*A publication*] (DLA)
Mun LR ..... Municipal Law Reporter [*Pennsylvania*] [*A publication*] (DLA)
Mun LR ..... Municipal Law Reports [*1903-13*] [*Scotland*] [*A publication*] (DLA)
Mun L Rep... Chrostwaite's Pennsylvania Municipal Law Reporter [*A publication*] (DLA)
MunMI ...... MuniYield Michigan Fund [*Associated Press*] (SAG)
MunMIIn .... MuniYield Michigan Insured Fund [*Associated Press*] (SAG)
MunNJ ...... MuniYield New Jersey Fund [*Associated Press*] (SAG)
MunNY ...... MuniYield New York Insured Fund [*Associated Press*] (SAG)
MunPA ...... MuniYield Pennsylvania Fund [*Associated Press*] (SAG)
MunPrt ...... Municipal Partners Fund [*Associated Press*] (SAG)
MunPrt2..... Municipal Partners Fund 2 [*Associated Press*] (SAG)
MunQ12..... Muniyield Quality Fund II, Inc. [*Associated Press*] (SAG)
MunQlty..... MuniYield Quality Fund, Inc. [*Associated Press*] (SAG)
Mun Rep.... Municipal Reports [*Canada*] [*A publication*] (DLA)
Munsng ..... Munsingwear, Inc. [*Associated Press*] (SAG)
MUNSS...... Munition Support Squadron
MUNT .... Muntz [*NCIC truck make code*]
MUNT .... Muntz [*NCIC car make code*]
Mun Tort Lib... Municipal, School, and State Tort Liability [*A publication*] (DLA)
MUNU .... Central Brasil [*Cuba*] [*ICAO location identifier*] (ICLI)
Munvst ...... MuniVest Fund, Inc. [*Associated Press*] (SAG)
MuNY2 ...... Muniyield New York Insured Fund II [*Associated Press*] (SAG)
MuNY3 ...... Muniyield New York Insured Fund III [*Associated Press*] (SAG)
MunyAZ ..... Muniyield Arizona Fund II [*Associated Press*] (SAG)
MunyIAZ .... Muniyield Arizona Fund [*Associated Press*] (SAG)
MUO .... Maximal Urinary Osmolality [*Medicine*] (EDAA)
MUO .... Maximum Undistorted Output
MUO .... Mountain Home, ID [*Location identifier*] [*FAA*] (FAAL)
MUO .... Municipal University of Omaha [*Later, University of Nebraska at Omaha*]
MUO .... Myocardiopathy of Unknown Origin [*Medicine*] (EDAA)
MUO .... Pioneer Interest Shares [*Formerly, Mutual of Omaha Interest Shares, Inc.*] [*NYSE symbol*] (SPSG)
MUO .... Pioneer Interest Shs [*NYSE symbol*] (TTSB)
MUOD .... Mean Unplanned Outage Duration (IEEE)
MUOD .... Mine and Unexploded Ordnance Detector [*Police and security equipment*]
MUON .... Mu-Meson [*An elementary particle*]
MUP .... Major Urinary Protein (DB)
MUP .... Make-Up Pay (MHDB)
MUP .... Manchester University Press [*Manchester, England*]
MUP .... Manufacturing-Use Product (EEVL)
MUP .... Master of Urban Planning
MUP .... Maximal Urethral Pressure [*Medicine*] (MELL)
MUP .... Metalworking under Pressure (PDAA)
MUP .... Methyl-Umbelliferyl Phosphate [*Medicine*] (EDAA)
MUP .... Modify User Password (AAEL)
MUP .... Molded Urea Plastics
MUP .... Motor Unit Potential
MUP .... Mouse Urine Protein [*Biochemistry*] (DAVI)
MUP .... Mouvement de l'Unite Populaire [*Popular Unity Movement*] [*Tunisia*] [*Political party*] (PD)
MUP .... Movimiento da Unidade Progressiva [*Brazil*] [*Political party*] (EY)
MUP .... Multiple Utility Peripheral (NITA)
MUPA........ Punta Alegre [*Cuba*] [*ICAO location identifier*] (ICLI)
MUPAD...... Multi Processing Algebra Data (SAUS)
MuPAIns .... MuniVest Pennsylvania Insured Fund [*Associated Press*] (SAG)
MUPB .... Baracoa Playa/Habana [*Cuba*] [*ICAO location identifier*] (ICLI)
MUPDD ..... Master of Urban Planning, Design, and Development (PGP)
MUPEJARS... Multiple Peanut-Butter Jars [*Unconventional musical instrument used in performance by the "Music for Homemade Instruments" ensemble*]
MUPF........ Modified Ultrapherical Polynominal Filter (IAA)
MUPID ...... Multiple Universally Programmable Intelligent Decoder [*Telecommunications*] (TSSD)
MUPID ...... Multi-Purpose Universal Programmable Intelligent Decoder (NITA)
MuPIT .... Municipal Premier Income Trust [*Associated Press*] (SAG)
MUPL........ Military Urgency Planning List (NG)
MUPL........ Mock-Up Planning
MUPL........ Pilon [*Cuba*] [*ICAO location identifier*] (ICLI)
MUPO .... Maximum Undistorted Power Output
MUPO .... Multiple Positive [*Circuit*] (AAG)
MUPP .... Master of Urban Planning and Policy (GAGS)
MUPPATS... Multiparticle Position- and Time- Sensitive Detector
MUPPET .... Marionette and Puppet
MUPPET .... Most Useless Police Probationer Ever Trained (BB)
Muppie...... Mennonite Urban Professional [*Lifestyle classification*]
Muppie...... Middle-Aged Urban Pinhead [*Lifestyle classification*]
Muppie...... Middle-Aged Urban Professional [*Lifestyle classification*]
Muppy....... Male Urban Professional [*Lifestyle classification*]
MUPR .... Pinar Del Rio [*Cuba*] [*ICAO location identifier*] (ICLI)
MUPROF.... Multiple Projected Fibonacci [*Microwave circuit*]
MUPS .... Central Guatemala [*Cuba*] [*ICAO location identifier*] (ICLI)
MUPS .... Manpower Utilisation and Payment Structure [*Imperial Chemical Industries*] [*British*]
MUPS .... Mechanized Unit Property System [*Telecommunications*] (TEL)
MUPS .... Metastases with Unknown Primary Site [*Medicine*] (MELL)
MUPS .... Minimum Universal Pension System [*Proposed to reform pension coverage*]
MUPS .... Multiple Utility Peripheral System [*Computer science*]
MUPT........ Patria [*Cuba*] [*ICAO location identifier*] (ICLI)
MuPV........ Murine Polyomavirus [*Medicine*]
MUR......... Aerolinea Muri [*Mexico*] [*ICAO designator*] (FAAC)
MUR......... Management Update and Retrieval System (NRCH)
MUR......... Manpower Utilization Report (MCD)
MUR......... Marudi [*Malaysia*] [*Airport symbol*] (OAG)
MUR......... Mock-Up Reactor [*NASA*]
MUR......... Montana Utilities Reports [*A publication*] (DLA)
MUR......... Movimiento de Unidad Revolucionaria [*Guerrilla forces*] [*Honduras*] (EY)
mur .... Mural (VRA)
Mur .... Muramic Acid [*Also, MurA*] [*Biochemistry*]
MUR......... Murder [*FBI standardized term*]
MUR......... Murderer [*Telegraphy*] (PCTE)
MUR......... Murgab [*Former USSR*] [*Seismograph station code, US Geological Survey*] [*Closed*] (SEIS)
Mur .... Murlyn [*Record label*]
Mur .... Murphey's Reports [*5-7 North Carolina*] [*A publication*] (DLA)
MUR......... Murphy Oil [*NYSE symbol*] (TTSB)
MUR......... Murphy Oil Corp. [*NYSE symbol*] (SPSG)
Mur .... Murray's Ceylon Reports [*A publication*] (DLA)
Mur .... Murray's Jury Court Cases [*1815-30*] [*Scotland*] [*A publication*] (DLA)
MUR......... Mustang Resources, Inc. [*Vancouver Stock Exchange symbol*]
Mur .... Pro Murena [*of Cicero*] [*Classical studies*] (OCD)
MUR......... Radio Relay Message Unit [*Telecommunications*] (TEL)
MURA .... Midwestern Universities Research Association
MurA .... Muramic Acid [*Also, Mur*] [*Biochemistry*]
Mur & H .... Murphy and Hurlstone's English Exchequer Reports [*1836-37*] [*A publication*] (DLA)
Mur & Hurl... Murphy and Hurlstone's English Exchequer Reports [*1836-37*] [*A publication*] (DLA)
MURAT...... Munitions a Risques Atenues (SAUS)
Murat Antiq Med Aevi... Muratori's Antiquitates Medii Aevi [*A publication*] (DLA)
MURATREC... Multi-RADAR Track Reconstitution [*Aviation*] (DA)
MURB .... Multiple Unit Residential Building [*Canada*]
MUrbDes(Arch)... Master of Urban Design
MUrbRegPlg... Master of Urban and Regional Planning
MURC .... Measurable Undesirable Respiratory Contaminants [*Pollution index*] [*Superseded by PSI*]
MURC .... Murdock Communications Corp. [*NASDAQ symbol*] (SAG)
MURCO .... Murphy Oil Corp. (EFIS)
MURD .... Multi-Use Ranger/Designator (ACAE)
MURD .... Murder (ROG)
Murdck ...... Murdock Communications Corp. [*Associated Press*] (SAG)
Murd Epit... Murdoch's Epitome Canada [*A publication*] (DLA)
MURDER.... Murray basin Disposal by Evaporation Resource (SAUS)
Murdock .... Murdock Communications Corp. [*Associated Press*] (SAG)
MURE .... Murena [*NCIC car make code*]
MURF .... Material Utilization Reference File [*Military*]
MURFAAM... Mutual Reduction of Forces and Armaments and Associated Measures
MURFAAMCE... Mutual Reduction of Forces and Armaments and Associated Measures in Central Europe
Murfree Off Bonds... Murfree on Official Bonds [*A publication*] (DLA)
MURG .... Machine Utilization Report Generator
MURI .... Mild Upper Respiratory Illness [*Virus*] [*Obsolete usage*]
MURIEL..... Multimedia Remote Interactive Electronic Documents (TELE)
MURL .... Major Urban Resource Library [*Department of Education*] (GFGA)
MURL .... Mock-Up Release
MurNAc ..... N-Acetylmuramate [*Laboratory science*] (DAVI)
MURP .... Manned Upperstage Reusable Payload
MURP .... Master of Urban and Regional Planning
MURP .... Master of Urban and Rural Planning (GAGS)
MURPAC .... Murphy Oil Corporation PAC [*Formerly known as Murphy Oil USA PAC*] [*El Dorado, AR*] (PACS)
Murp & H... Murphy and Hurlstone's English Exchequer Reports [*1836-37*] [*A publication*] (ILCA)
Murph .... Murphey's Reports [*5-7 North Carolina*] [*A publication*] (DLA)
MURPH ..... Murphy, NC [*American Association of Railroads railroad junction routing code*]
Murph & H... Murphy and Hurlstone's English Exchequer Reports [*1836-37*] [*A publication*] (DLA)
Murph (NC)... Murphey's Reports [*5-7 North Carolina*] [*A publication*] (DLA)
MURPL....... Master of Urban and Regional Planning (PGP)
MurpO....... Murphy Oil Corp. [*Associated Press*] (SAG)
MURR .... Murray [*NCIC motorcycle make code*]
Murr .... Murray's Ceylon Reports [*A publication*] (DLA)
Murr .... Murray's Jury Court Cases [*1815-30*] [*Scotland*] [*A publication*] (DLA)
Murr .... Murray's Laws and Acts of Parliament [*Scotland*] [*A publication*] (DLA)
MURR .... University of Missouri Research Reactor
MURRA ..... Murray, KY [*American Association of Railroads railroad junction routing code*]
Murray ...... Murray's Scotch Jury Court Reports [*A publication*] (DLA)

Murray (Ceylon)... Murray's Ceylon Reports [*A publication*] (DLA)
Murray (Scot)... Murray's Scotch Jury Trials [*A publication*] (DLA)
Murray's Eng Dict... Murray's English Dictionary [*A publication*] (DLA)
Murray St U... Murray State University (GAGS)
Murr Over Cas... Murray's Overruled Cases [*A publication*] (DLA)
MURS .... Machine Utilization Reporting System (PDAA)
MURS .... Machine Utilization Report System [*Computer science*] (IAA)
MURS .... Minority Undergraduate Research Support
MURS .... Mouvement Universel de la Responsabilite Scientifique [*Universal Movement for Scientific Responsibility - UMSR*] (EAIO)
MURS .... Mursley [*England*]
MURT........ Murray Trailers [*NCIC trailer make code*]
Mur Tab Cas... Murray's Table of United States Cases [*A publication*] (DLA)
MURTF...... Nur Advanced Technologies [*NASDAQ symbol*] (TTSB)
MURTS...... Multiple User Remote Terminal Supervisor (MHDI)
Mur Us...... Murray's History of Usury [*A publication*] (DLA)
Mur US Ct... Murray's Proceedings in the United States Courts [*A publication*] (DLA)
MURXF...... International Murex Technologies [*NASDAQ symbol*] (SAG)
MURXF...... Intl Murex Technologies [*NASDAQ symbol*] (TTSB)
MUS .... A. G. Ruthven Museums Building (SAUS)
MUS .... Magnetic Unloading System
MUS .... Maintenance Utilization Sheet
MUS .... Major Use Stations (ACAE)
MUS .... Manned Underwater Station
MUS .... Manual Update Service (NITA)
MUS .... Martech USA (EFIS)
MUS .... Mass Unbalance Spin
MUS .... Master of Urban Studies (ADA)
MUS .... Mauritius [*ANSI three-letter standard code*] (CNC)
MUS .... Methylumbelliferone Sulfate [*Biochemistry*]
MU S .... Microsecond (WDAA)
MUS .... Midstream Urine Specimen [*Medicine*] (MELL)
MUS .... Mission Upgrade System (SAUS)
MUS .... Monetary Unit Sampling (ADA)
Mus.......... Mouse [*Medicine*] (EDAA)
MUS .... Mouse Urologic Syndrome (DMAA)
MUS .... Multiprogramming Utility System [*Regnecentralen*] [*Denmark*]
MUS .... Multiutility System (MCD)
MUS .... Murders [*Telegraphy*] (PCTE)
Mus.......... Musca [*Constellation*]
MUS .... Muschocho Explorations Ltd. [*Toronto Stock Exchange symbol*]
MUS .... Muscimol [*Biochemistry*]
MUS .... Muscle (SAUS)
mus.......... Musee (VRA)
mus.......... Museen (VRA)
mus.......... Museo (VRA)
Mus.......... Museum (AL)
mus.......... Museum (VRA)
MUS .... Museum
mus.......... Music (SHCU)
MUS .... Music
MUS .... Musician (GOBB)
MUS .... Music Show
MUS .... Muskinabad [*Former USSR*] [*Seismograph station code, US Geological Survey*] [*Closed*] (SEIS)
mus.......... Muskogee [*MARC language code*] [*Library of Congress*] (LCCP)
Mus.......... Muslim
MUS .... Mustang [*NCIC car model code*]
MUS .... University of Southern Mississippi, Hattiesburg, MS [*OCLC symbol*] (OCLC)
MUSA .... Manufacturing USA [*A publication*]
MUSA .... Mentoring USA
MUSA .... Multiple Unit Steerable Antenna [*Electronics*]
MUSA .... Multiple Unit Steerable Array (NITA)
MUSA .... San Antonio De Los Banos [*Cuba*] [*ICAO location identifier*] (ICLI)
MUSA .... Seaman Apprentice, Musician, Striker [*Navy rating*]
Mus AD ..... Doctor of Musical Arts
MUS & T.... Manned Undersea Science and Technology [*Marine science*] (MSC)
MUSAP...... Multisatellite Augmentation Program [*NASA*]
MUSARC.... Major United States Army Reserve Command (AABC)
MUSAT...... Multiple Station Analytical Triangulation (PDAA)
MUSAT...... Multipurpose UHF [*Ultra High Frequency*] Satellite (IAA)
MUSB .... Mobile Unit Support Base (AAG)
Mus B .... Musicae Baccalaureus [*Bachelor of Music*] [*Latin*]
Mus Bac.... Musicae Baccalaureus [*Bachelor of Music*] [*Latin*]
Mus Bach... Musicae Baccalaureus [*Bachelor of Music*] [*Latin*]
Mus Belge... Musee Belge [*A publication*] (OCD)
MUSC .... Medical University of South Carolina
MUSC .... Memphis Union Station Co. [*AAR code*]
MUSC .... Multiunit Supervisory Control (IAA)
Musc .... Musca [*Constellation*]
MUSC .... Muscarine [*Alkaloid*]
MUSC .... Muscles [*or Muscular*]
MUSC .... Music
MUSC .... Santa Clara [*Cuba*] [*ICAO location identifier*] (ICLI)
MUSCL...... Musical
MUSCLE .... Millions of Unusual Small Creatures Lurking Everywhere [*Toy by Mattel, Inc.*]
MUSCM ..... Missile Unit Simulated Combat Mission (SAA)
muscm ...... Musical Comedy (GROV)
MUSCO...... Muhoroni Sugar Co. Ltd.
Mus D....... Doctor of Music (SAUS)
Mus D....... Musicae Doctor [*Doctor of Music*] [*Latin*]
Mus Doc .... Doctor of Music (SAUS)
Mus Doc .... Musicae Doctor [*Doctor of Music*] [*Latin*]
MUSE........ Mace Utilities Sector Editor [*Computer science*]
MUSE........ Machine User Symbiotic Environment (PDAA)
MUSE........ Machine User Symbolic Environment (IAA)
MUSE........ Medical Urethral System for Erection
MUSE........ Medical Use of Simulation Electronics
MUSE........ Microcomputer Users in Education
MUSE........ Micromuse, Inc. [*NASDAQ symbol*] (SG)
MUSE........ MIDI [*Musical Instrument Digital Interface*] Users Sequencer/Editor [*Roland International Corp.*]
MUSE........ Minimum Uniform Standards for Education [*Medicine*] (EDAA)
MUSE........ Mobile Utilities Support Equipment [*Navy*] (NG)
MUSE........ Model to Understand Simple English (PDAA)
MUSE........ Modular Utilities for Systems Education (IAA)
MUSE........ Monitor of Ultraviolet Solar Energy
MUSE........ Multimedia User Environment [*Computer science*]
MUSE........ Multiple Sub-Nyquist Subsampling Encoding [*Digital recording system introduced 1984*]
MUSE........ Multiuser Shared Environment [*Computer science*] (IGQR)
MUSE........ Multi-User-Simulated Environment (PS)
MUSE........ Musicians United for Safe Energy (EA)
MUSE........ Musicians United to Stop Exclusion [*Defunct*] (EA)
MUSE........ Mustang Resources Corp. [*NASDAQ symbol*] (COMM)
Mus Ed B ... Bachelor of Music Education
Mus Ed D ... Doctor of Music Education
MUSEDET... Mobile Utilities Support Equipment Detachment [*Navy*] (DNAB)
Mus Ed M... Master of Music Education
MUSF........ Habana/Santa Fe [*Cuba*] [*ICAO location identifier*] (ICLI)
MUSG .... Mustang Trailer Manufacturing [*NCIC trailer make code*]
MUSG .... Sagua La Grande [*Cuba*] [*ICAO location identifier*] (ICLI)
Mus G Paed... Musicae Graduatus Paedagogus [*Graduate Teacher in Music*]
MUSH .... Mail Users Shell [*Computer science*] (VLIE)
MUSH .... Multiuser Shared Hallucination [*Computer science*] (IGQR)
MusH........ Music Hall [*Record label*] [*Argentina*]
MUSHes .... Multiuser Shared Hallucinations [*Computer game players*]
MUSI .... Mexico-United States Institute (EA)
MUSI .... Multi User Shared Illusion [*Computer science*] (VLIE)
musi......... Musical (GROV)
MUSIC...... Machine Utilization Statistical Information Collection (IAA)
MUSIC...... Mass Unity Sounding in Concert [*Duke Ellington definition of music*]
MUSIC...... McGill University System for Interactive Computing
MUSIC...... Multiple Signal Classification (VLIE)
MUSIC...... Multiple Signal Identification and Classification
MUSIC...... Multiple System Intelligent Controller [*Computer science*]
MUSIC...... Multisensor Intelligence Correlator (IAA)
MUSIC...... Multi-Spectral Infrared Camera (ACAE)
MUSIC...... Multi-User System for Integrated Control [*Computer science*] (VLIE)
Music........ Musicology (DIAR)
MUSICAM... Masking Pattern Universal Sub-Band Integrated Coding and Multiplexing [*Broadcasting*]
MusicLd..... Musicland Stores [*Associated Press*] (SAG)
MUSICOL... Musical Instruction Composition Oriented Language (NITA)
MUSICOMP... Music Composition
MUSIL....... Multiprogramming Utility System Interpretive Language [*Regnecentralen*] [*Denmark*]
MUSJ........ San Julian (Escuela de Aviacion) [*Cuba*] [*ICAO location identifier*] (ICLI)
MUSKE...... Muskegon, MI [*American Association of Railroads railroad junction routing code*]
MUSKO...... Muskogee, OK [*American Association of Railroads railroad junction routing code*]
MUSL........ Marconi Underwater Systems Ltd. [*British*]
MUSL........ Multiple Stinger Launcher
MUSL........ Musician's Library [*A publication*]
MUSL........ Muslin (ROG)
musl......... Muslin (VRA)
MUSL........ Santa Lucia [*Cuba*] [*ICAO location identifier*] (ICLI)
MUSLE ...... Modified Universal Soil Loss Equation [*Agricultural Research Service*]
MUSLO...... Morocco-United States Liaison Office (AFM)
musm .... Museum (BEE)
Mus M ...... Musicae Magister [*Master of Music*] [*Latin*]
MusM-Comp........ Master of Music Composition, University of Manchester [*British*] (DBQ)
MUSMF ..... Muscocho Explorations Ltd. [*NASDAQ symbol*] (COMM)
MusMPerf... Master of Music Performance, University of Manchester [*British*] (DBQ)
Musn .... Musician [*British military*] (DMA)
MUSN .... Seaman, Musician, Striker [*Navy rating*]
MUSN .... Siguanea, Isla De La Juventud [*Cuba*] [*ICAO location identifier*] (ICLI)
MUSR .... Simon Reyes [*Cuba*] [*ICAO location identifier*] (ICLI)
MUSRP...... McGill University Savanna Research Project (MCD)
MUSS .... Manchester University Software System (NITA)
MUSS .... Missile Unit Support System
MUSS .... Mobile Unit Support System (IAA)
muss .... Module Utility Support Structure (NAKS)
MUSS .... Module Utility Support Structure (NASA)
MUSS .... Musical Series [*A publication*]
MUSS .... Sancti Spiritus [*Cuba*] [*ICAO location identifier*] (ICLI)
MUST........ Machine Utilization Report Generator (DNAB)
MUST........ Malaysian University of Science and Technology
MUST........ Manned Undersea Science and Technology [*Marine science*] (OSRA)

MUST........ Manned Undersea Station
MUST........ Manpower Utilization System and Techniques [*Department of State*]
MUST........ Maust Transfer [*Common carrier symbol*]
MUST........ Maximum Utilization of Skills and Training [*Civil Service Commission*]
MUST........ Medical Unit Self-Contained Transportable [*Field hospital*] [*Army*]
MUST........ Meeting Updates in Skill Training [*International Labor Organization*] [*Information service or system*] [*United Nations*] (DUND)
MUST........ Message User Service Transcriber (IAA)
MUST........ Mobile Undersea Systems Test (ACAE)
MUST........ Mobile Underwater Surveillance Team (MCD)
MUST........ Mobile Unit Sanitation Trailer
MUST........ Multi-Mission UHF [*Ultra High Frequency*] SATCOM [*Satellite Command*] Terminal
MUST........ Multiple Source Technique
MUST........ Multipurpose User-Oriented Software Technology (MHDI)
MUST........ Mustang (motorcycle) [*NCIC motorcycle make code*]
MUSTA....... Mock-Up Spallation Target Assembly (PDAA)
MUSTARD... Multi-Racial Union of Squatters to Alleviate Racial Discrimination [*British*] (DI)
MUSTARD... Multiunit Space Transport and Recovery Device (MCD)
MUSTARD... Museum and University Storage and Retrieval of Data (NITA)
MUSTPAC-1... Medical Ultrasound, Three-Dimensional and Portabel with Advanced Communications [*An imaging device*] (INF)
MUSTRAC... Multiple-Simultaneous-Target Steerable Telemetry Tracking System [*Navy*]
MUSTRAN... Music Translation (NITA)
MUSTRS.... Multi-Sensor Target Recognition System (SAUS)
MustSft...... Mustang Software, Inc. [*Associated Press*] (SAG)
MUSU....... Multitrade Container Services [*Intermodal shipping container symbol*] (TVRC)
MUSWTCH... Mussel Watch (EAGT)
MUSY....... Multiple Use-Sustained Yield (ALAC)
MUSYA...... Multiple-Use Sustained-Yield Act of 1960
MU Sys E... Master of Urban Systems Engineering (PGP)
Mut......... De Mutatione Nominum [*Philo*] (BJA)
MUT......... Makeup Tank [*Nuclear energy*] (NRCH)
MUT......... Master Upper Tester (SAUS)
MUT......... Mean Up Time [*NASA*] (KSC)
MUT......... Mercury Unit Test
MUT......... Mock-Up Template
MUT......... Modular Universal Terminal (IAA)
MUT......... Module under Test
MUT......... Monitor Under Test (VLIE)
MUT......... Multinational Resources [*Vancouver Stock Exchange symbol*]
MUT......... Multiservicios Aeronauticos SA de CV [*Mexico*] [*ICAO designator*] (FAAC)
MUT......... Muntinlupa [*Philippines*] [*Geomagnetic observatory code*]
MUT......... Muscatine, IA [*Location identifier*] [*FAA*] (FAAL)
MUT......... Mutagen (DMAA)
MUT......... Mutilated
MUT......... Mutual (ADA)
Mut......... Mutual (TBD)
Mut......... Mutukisna's Ceylon Reports [*A publication*] (DLA)
MUTA........ Made-Up Textiles Association [*British*] (DBA)
Muta........ Marijuana [*Medicine*] (EDAA)
MUTA........ Military Upper Traffic Control Area (DA)
MUTA........ Multiple Unit Training Assembly [*Army*] (AABC)
MUTA........ Multi-Unit Training Assembly [*Army*]
MUTACI..... Mutuelle des Autochtones de la Cote d'Ivoire [*Mutual Association of the Natives of the Ivory Coast*]
MUTCD...... Manual on Uniform Traffic Control Devices [*Highway engineering*] [*A publication*]
MUTCD...... Manual on Uniform Traffic Control Traffic Control Devices [*Federal Housing Adminstration*]
MUTD....... Trinidad [*Cuba*] [*ICAO location identifier*] (ICLI)
MUTE........ Mobile Universal Test Equipment (PDAA)
MUTE........ Multiple Unit for Transmission Elimination [*Military*] (CAAL)
MUTES...... Multiple Threat Emitter System [*Air Force*]
MUTEX...... Multiuser Terminal Executive (MHDI)
MUTEX...... Multi-User Transaction Executive (NITA)
MUTEX...... Mutually Exclusive (VLIE)
MUTHX...... Mutual Shares Fund [*Mutual fund ticker symbol*] (SG)
MUTI........ Manati [*Cuba*] [*ICAO location identifier*] (ICLI)
MUTL........ Mutual (ROG)
MUTN....... Munitions [*Telegraphy*] (PCTE)
MUTP........ Mumbai Urban Transport Project [*Indian Railway*] (TIR)
MUTR....... Makai Undersea Test Range (DNAB)
MutRisk..... Mutual Risk Management Ltd. [*Associated Press*] (SAG)
MUTS........ Manual Unit Test Set
MUTS........ Multiple Target Simulation (MCD)
MutSvg...... Mutual Savings Bank FSB [*Associated Press*] (SAG)
MUTT........ Military Utility Tactical Transport
MUTT........ Military Utility Tactical Truck
MUTT........ Mobile Utility Transfer Tank [*To collect used oils*]
MUTT........ Multiuse Terminal Translator (MHDI)
mutt......... Mutton [*An em space*] [*Typesetting*] (WDMC)
MUTT/JEFF... Multi-Use Tactical Terminal/Judiciary Efficient Fixed Frame (ACAE)
MUTTS...... Multiple Unit Terminal Test Set (MCD)
MUTU....... Mutualista Acoreana [*Intermodal shipping container symbol*] (TVRC)
MutualB..... Mutual Bancompany, Inc. [*Associated Press*] (SAG)
Mutukisna... Mutukisna's Ceylon Reports [*A publication*] (DLA)
MUTY........ Mutually [*Telegraphy*] (PCTE)
MUU......... Main User Unit (SAUS)
MUU......... Mount Union, PA [*Location identifier*] [*FAA*] (FAAL)
MUU......... Mouse Uterine Unit [*Gynecology*] (MAE)
MUU......... University of Missouri, Columbia, Columbia, MO [*OCLC symbol*] (OCLC)
MUV......... Marine Unit Vietnam (VNW)
MUV......... Mechanized Utility Vehicle (MCD)
MU V........ Microvolt (WDAA)
MUV......... Middle Ultraviolet
MUV......... Mobile Underwater Vehicle
MUV......... Philadelphia, PA [*Location identifier*] [*FAA*] (FAAL)
MUVA........ Central Primero De Enero [*Cuba*] [*ICAO location identifier*] (ICLI)
MUVA........ Muv-All Trailer [*NCIC trailer make code*]
MuvCAIn.... Munivest California Insured Fund [*Associated Press*] (SAG)
MuvMIIn.... MuniVest Michigan Insured Fund [*Associated Press*] (SAG)
MuvNJFd.... MuniVest New Jersey Fund [*Associated Press*] (SAG)
MuvNYIn.... MuniVest New York Insured Fund [*Associated Press*] (SAG)
MUVR....... Varadero [*Cuba*] [*ICAO location identifier*] (ICLI)
MUVT........ Las Tunas [*Cuba*] [*ICAO location identifier*] (ICLI)
MUW........ Mascara [*Algeria*] [*Airport symbol*] (OAG)
MU W....... Microwatt (WDAA)
MUW........ Mouse Uterine Weight [*Medicine*] (EDAA)
MUW........ Mundari [*Language symbol*] (ETLW)
MUW........ Music Wire
MUW........ Mutarara [*Mozambique*] [*Airport symbol*] (AD)
MUW........ University of Mississippi, School of Law Library, University, MS [*OCLC symbol*] (OCLC)
MUWO...... Muir Woods National Monument
MUWQ...... Murphy Warehouse Company [*Common carrier symbol*]
MUWS....... Manned Underwater Station
MUWU...... Mouse Uterine Weight Unit [*Gynecology*]
MUX......... Multan [*Pakistan*] [*Airport symbol*] (OAG)
mux.......... Multiplex (NAKS)
MUX......... Multiplex [*or Multiplexer*] [*Telecommunications*]
Mux.......... Multiplexer (AAEL)
MUX......... Multiplexer (PIPO)
MUX......... Murderous [*Telegraphy*] (PCTE)
MUX......... Musto Explorations Ltd. [*Toronto Stock Exchange symbol*]
MUXARC.... Multiplexing Automatic Error Correction (IAA)
MUXART.... Multiplexed Asynchronous Receiver/Transmitter (MCD)
MUX/DEMUX... Multiplexer and Demultiplexer
MUXER...... Multiplexer
MUXES...... Multiplexes [*or Multiplexers*] [*Telecommunications*]
MUXIC....... Multiplex/Multiple Voice Interior Communications (DNAB)
MUXMOD... Multiplex Modulation
MUXP....... Music Express [*Common carrier symbol*]
MUX/PRI/SEC... Multiplexer/Priority/Second
MUY......... Lehman Br Micron'YEELD"97 [*AMEX symbol*] (TTSB)
MUY......... Lehman Brothers, Inc. [*AMEX symbol*] (SAG)
MUY......... Municipality [*Telegraphy*] (PCTE)
MUY......... Toolik, AK [*Location identifier*] [*FAA*] (FAAL)
MUYD....... Mercury Distribution Carriers [*Common carrier symbol*]
MUYP....... Macoupin County Asphalt [*Common carrier symbol*]
MUYS....... Municipalities [*Telegraphy*] (PCTE)
MUZ......... Mine Workers Union of Zambia [*Political party*] (PSAP)
MuZ......... Motorrad und Zweiradwerk [*Motorcycle and Two-wheel Works*]
MUZ......... Musoma [*Tanzania*] [*Airport symbol*] (OAG)
Muza........ Muza and Other Labels [*Record label*] [*Poland*]
MUZAK...... Music and Kodak [*Terms combined to coin brand name for canned music*]
MUZEE...... MUSE Technologies, Inc. [*NASDAQ symbol*] (QUAN)
MUZG....... Zaragoza [*Cuba*] [*ICAO location identifier*] (ICLI)
MUZH....... Muzzle Hatch
MUZM....... Makerere-University Zoology Museum [*Uganda*]
MV........... Airlines of Western Australia [*Australia*] [*ICAO designator*] (ICDA)
MV........... Great American Airways (ODA)
MV........... MacRobertson-Miller Airline Service [*ICAO designator*] (AD)
M/V.......... Magnetic Variation (MCD)
MV........... Mahzor Vitry [*A publication*] (BJA)
MV........... Maintenance Version (IAA)
MV........... Main Verb [*Linguistics*]
MV........... Majority-Vote Technique [*Parapsychology*]
MV........... Maldives [*ANSI two-letter standard code*] (CNC)
MV........... Manifold Vacuum [*Automotive engineering*]
MV........... Manned Vehicle
MV........... Manpower Voucher [*Army*] (AABC)
MV........... Mantle Vessel
MV........... Manual Valve (MCD)
mv........... Manual Valve (NAKS)
mv........... Manufacturing Verification (NAKS)
MV........... Manufacturing Verification (NASA)
MV........... Mare Vaporum [*Sea of Vapor*] [*Lunar area*]
MV........... Mariner Venus Project [*NASA*]
MV........... Market Value
MV........... Mauve [*Philately*] (ROG)
MV........... Mean Value
MV........... Mean Variation
MV........... Mean Voltage (IAA)
MV........... Measles Virus
MV........... Measured Value
MV........... Meccanica Verghera [*Motorcycles*]
MV........... Mechanical Ventilation [*Medicine*]
MV........... Medial Vestibular Nucleus [*Neuroanatomy*]
MV........... Medicus Veterinarius [*Veterinary Physician*]
MV........... Medium Voltage

MV .... Medium Volume
MV .... Megavolt
Mv .... Mendelevium [*Symbol is Md*] [*Chemical element*]
MV .... Mentor Exploration & Development Co. Ltd. [*Toronto Stock Exchange symbol*]
MV .... Merchant Vessel
MV .... Mercury Vapor
MV .... Methyl Violet [*A dye*]
MV .... Methyl Viologen [*Organic chemistry*]
MV .... Metropolitan Vickers [*Indian Railway*] (TIR)
MV .... Mezza Voce [*Half the Power of the Voice*] [*Music*]
MV .... Microvascular [*Medicine*] (EDAA)
MV .... Microvilli [*Cytology*]
mV .... Microvolt
MV .... Microwave [*Physics*] (DAVI)
MV .... Midland Valley R. R. [*AAR code*]
MV .... Military Vehicle
MV .... Military Vigilance (NATG)
MV .... Million Volts
mv .... Millivolt (NAKS)
mV .... Millivolt
MV .... Miniature Vehicle (MCD)
MV .... Minimal Variant (IAA)
MV .... Minimum Viscosity
MV .... Minute Ventilation [*Medicine*]
MV .... Minute Volume [*Medicine*]
MV .... Mitoxantrone, VePesid [*Antineoplastic drug*] (CDI)
MV .... Mitral Valve [*Cardiology*]
MV .... Mixed Venous [*Blood*]
MV .... Modern Varieties [*Agriculture*]
MV .... Modus Vivendi [*Way of Living*] [*Latin*]
MV .... Molar Volume [*Chemistry*]
MV .... Money Velocity [*Economics*]
MV .... Monochromatic Vision (WDAA)
MV .... Montevideo [*City in Uruguay*] (ROG)
MV .... Mostly Verbatim [*FAR clauses*] (AAGC)
MV .... Motorized Valve (KSC)
MV .... Motor Vehicle (CDAI)
MV .... Motor Vehicle Mishap (DNAB)
M/V .... Motor Vessel (ALAC)
mv .... Motor Vessel (ODBW)
MV .... Motor Vessel
MV .... Motor Volunteers [*British military*] (DMA)
MV .... Move [*Telecommunications*] (TEL)
MV .... Moving Violation [*Motor vehicle violation code used in state of Maryland*] (MVRD)
MV .... Multiconverter Vector [*Computer science*] (IAA)
MV .... Multivesicular [*Medicine*] [*Body*] (EDAA)
MV .... Multivessel [*Medicine*] (DB)
MV .... Multivibrator
MV .... Multivitamins [*Nutrition*]
mv .... Multivolt (ELAL)
MV .... Musica Viva (ADA)
MV .... Muzzle Velocity [*Ballistics*]
MV .... Mycoplasmatales Virus
MV-678 .... Agricultural Research Service (SAUS)
MVA .... Machine Vision Association [*Later, MVA/SME*] (EA)
MVA .... Machining Variation Analysis
MVA .... Machinists Vise Association [*Later, HTI*] (EA)
MVA .... Main Valve Actuator (NASA)
MVA .... Malignant Ventricular Arrhythmias [*Cardiology*] (DAVI)
MVA .... Manifold Vacuum Assist [*Automotive engineering*]
MVA .... Manufacturing Value Added
MVA .... Marginal Value Analysis (MCD)
MVA .... Market-Value Accounting [*Banking*] (ECON)
MVA .... Market Value Added
MVA .... Market Value Appraiser (DD)
MVA .... Master of Visual Arts (GAGS)
MVA .... Mean Vertical Acceleration
MVA .... Mechanical Ventricular Assistance [*Medicine*] (DMAA)
MVA .... Megavolt-Ampere
MVA .... Mercury Volatilizing Activity
MVA .... Merrimack Valley College Library, Manchester, NH [*OCLC symbol*] (OCLC)
MVA .... Mevalonic Acid [*Organic chemistry*]
MVA .... Million Volt Amperes
MVA .... Millivolt Ampere [*Nuclear energy*] (IAA)
MVA .... Mina, NV [*Location identifier*] [*FAA*] (FAAL)
MVA .... Minimum Vectoring Altitude [*FAA*] (TAG)
MVA .... Minnova, Inc. [*Toronto Stock Exchange symbol*] (SPSG)
MVa .... Minute Ventilatory Volume for Experimental Animal Species
MVA .... Mississippi Valley Airlines, Inc. [*ICAO designator*] (FAAC)
MVA .... Missouri Valley Authority
MVA .... Mitral Valve Area [*Cardiology*]
MVA .... Modern Volunteer Army
MVA .... Modified Vaccinia Ankara [*Medical term*]
MVA .... Modified Vaccinia (virus strain) Ankara [*Medicine*] (EDAA)
MVA .... Monovinylacetylene [*Organic chemistry*]
MVA .... Motor Vehicle Accident [*Medicine*] (AFM)
MVA .... Motor Vehicle Administration [*Motor vehicle violation code used in state of Maryland*] (MVRD)
MVA .... Motor Vehicle Allowance
MVA .... Motor Vehicle Assembly [*Military*] [*World War II*]
MVA .... Multivariate Analysis (GFGA)
MVA .... Music Video Association (EA)
MVA .... Myvatn [*Iceland*] [*Airport symbol*] [*Obsolete*] (OAG)
M-VAC .... Methotrexate, Vinblastine, Adriamiacin [*Doxorubicin*] Cisplatin [*Antineoplastic drug regimen*] (DAVI)
MVAC .... Methotrexate, Vinblastine, Adriamycin, Cisplatin [*Antineoplastic drug*] (CDI)
MVAC .... MotorVac Technologies [*NASDAQ symbol*] (TTSB)
MVAC .... MotorVac Technologies, Inc. [*NASDAQ symbol*] (SAG)
MVAC .... Motor Vehicle Air Conditioner (EEVL)
MVACS .... Mars Volatiles and Climate Survey [*NASA*]
MVAK .... Module Vertical Access Kit [*NASA*] (SPST)
MVal .... Market Value [*Insurance*]
MV & P .... Morton's Vendors and Purchasers [*1837*] [*A publication*] (DLA)
MVAP .... Modern Volunteer Army Program (AABC)
MVAPCA .... Motor Vehicle Air Pollution Control Act (GFGA)
MVAR .... Megavar
MVAR .... Megavolt-Ampere Reactive [*Nuclear energy*] (IAA)
MVARH .... Megavar-Hour
MVAS .... Multipurpose Ventricular Actuating System (NASA)
MVAS .... Murray Valley Air Service [*Australia*]
MVA/SME .... Machine Vision Association [*Society of Manufacturing Engineers*] (EA)
MVAT .... MediVators, Inc. [*NASDAQ symbol*] (SAG)
MVAT .... Metacyclic Variant Antigen Type [*Immunology*]
MVAT .... Multiple Vandal Assembly Terminal (ACAE)
MVAU .... Maximum Volt-Ampere Utilization [*Electronics*]
MVAU .... MV Agusta [*NCIC motorcycle make code*]
MVB .... Martin Van Buren [*US president, 1782-1862*]
MVB .... Mechanical Vacuum Booster
MVB .... Mississippi Valley Motor Freight Bureau, Saint Louis MO [*STAC*]
MVB .... Mixed Venous Blood [*Medicine*] (DAVI)
MVB .... Motor V-Belt
MVB .... Motor Vessel Boat
MVB .... Multimedia Viewer Book (VLIE)
MVB .... Multivesicular Body
MVB .... Multivibrator
MVB .... Mvengue [*Gabon*] [*Airport symbol*] (OAG)
MVBD .... Multiple V-Belt Drive
MVBF .... Motor Vehicle Brake Fluid [*Automotive engineering*]
MVBFC .... Martin Van Buren Fan Club (EA)
MVBI .... Mississippi Valley Bancshares [*NASDAQ symbol*] (TTSB)
MVBI .... Mississippi Valley Bancshares, Inc. [*NASDAQ symbol*] (SAG)
MVBL .... Movable (MSA)
MVBR .... Motor Vehicle Body Repair (HEAS)
MVBR .... Multivibrator
MVC .... Management Verification Consortium (AIE)
mvc .... Manual Volume Control (NAKS)
MVC .... Maryville College, St. Louis, MO [*OCLC symbol*] (OCLC)
MVC .... Master Vellum Center [*Jet Propulsion Laboratory, NASA*]
MVC .... Master Volume Control (NASA)
MVC .... Maui Volcanic Complex [*Geology*]
MVC .... Maximal Voluntary Contraction
MVC .... Maximum Vital Capacity [*Medicine*] (DAVI)
MVC .... Mechanical Vapor Compressor [*Engineering*]
MVC .... Michigan Veal Committee (EARSL)
MVC .... Micro Ventures Ltd. [*Vancouver Stock Exchange symbol*]
MVC .... Mid-size Vehicle Center [*Automotive industry*]
MVC .... Miniature Video Camera [*Police and security equipment*]
MVC .... Mississippi Vocational College
MVC .... Missouri Valley College
MVC .... Missouri Valley Conference [*Sports*]
MVC .... Mitral Valve Cusps [*Medicine*] (MELL)
MVC .... Model-View-Controller [*Computer science*]
MVC .... Monroeville, AL [*Location identifier*] [*FAA*] (FAAL)
MVC .... Motor vehicle Collision (or Crash) (SAUS)
MVC .... Motor Volunteer Corps [*British military*] (DMA)
MVC .... Move Character [*Computer science*] (VLIE)
MVC .... Multiple Variate Counter (IEEE)
MVC .... Multiport Video Controller (GART)
MVC .... MuniVest California Insured Fund [*NYSE symbol*] (SPSG)
MVC .... Myocardial Vascular Capacity [*Cardiology*] (MAE)
MVCC .... Military Vehicle Collectors Club [*Later, MVPA*] (EA)
MVCC .... Mountain Valley Collegiate Conference (PSS)
MVCM .... Millivolt per Centimeter [*Nuclear energy*] (IAA)
MVCMB .... Murray Valley Citrus Marketing Board [*Australia*]
MVCN .... Multi-Vendor Computer Networks (AGLO)
MVCO .... Meadow Valley [*NASDAQ symbol*] (TTSB)
MVCO .... Meadow Valley Corp. [*NASDAQ symbol*] (SAG)
MVCOW .... Meadow Valley Wrrt [*NASDAQ symbol*] (TTSB)
MVCS .... Marine Vapor Control System
MVCS .... Motor Vehicle Certification System
MVCU .... Multivariable Control Unit [*Computer science*]
MVD .... Doctor of Veterinary Medicine
MVD .... Map and Visual Display
MVD .... Metal Vapor Deposition (EDCT)
MVD .... Microvascular Decompression [*Medicine*] (MELL)
MVD .... Mineralny Vody Department of Cibil Aviation [*Former USSR*] [*FAA designator*] (FAAC)
MVD .... Minimum-Variance Deconvolution (MCD)
MVD .... Mission Variation Drawing (MCD)
MVD .... Mitral Valve Disease [*Cardiology*]
MVD .... Montevideo [*Uruguay*] [*Airport symbol*] (OAG)
MVD .... Motor Vehicle Department (DLA)
MVD .... Motor Vehicle Distributing [*Military*]

MVD .... Motor Vehicle Driver Selection Battery [*Army*]
MVD .... Motor Voltage Drop (IAA)
mvd .... Moved (GEAB)
MVD .... Moved [*Telegraphy*] (PCTE)
MVDA .... Motor Vehicle Dealers Act
MVDA .... Motor Vehicles Dismantlers Association [*British*] (BI)
MVDA .... Multivariate Variance and Discriminant Analysis [*Mathematics*]
MVDC .... Megavolt Direct Current [*Nuclear energy*] (IAA)
MVDC .... Millivolt Direct Current [*Nuclear energy*] (IAA)
MVDF .... Medium- and Very-High-Frequency Direction-Finding Station
MVDFC ...... Mamie Van Doren Fan Club (EA)
MVDI .... Microfield Virtual Device Interface [*Computer science*] (HGAA)
MVDLB ...... Motor Vehicle Dealers' Licensing Board [*Western Australia*]
MVDM .... Multiple Virtual DOS [*Disk Operating System*] Machine [*Computer science*] (PCM)
MVD-MGB ... Ministerstvo Vnutrennikh Del-Ministerstvo Gosudarstvennoe Bezopasnosti [*Later, KGB*]
MVDr .... Medicus Veterinarius Doctor [*Doctor of Veterinary Medicine*]
MVDS .... Modular Vault Dry Store [*Nuclear energy*] (NUCP)
MVDS .... Modular Video Data System [*Sperry UNIVAC*]
MVDS .... Multipoint Video Distribution Service (AAEL)
MVE .... Maple Valley Explorations Ltd. [*Vancouver Stock Exchange symbol*]
MVE .... Master of Vocational Education (NADA)
MVE .... Mauve [*Philately*] (ROG)
MVE .... Methyl Vinyl Ether [*Organic chemistry*]
MVE .... Mitral Valve Echogram [*Cardiology*]
MVE .... Mobile Vocational Evaluation [*Vocational guidance test*]
MVE .... Modified Vehicle Engineering
MVE .... Montevideo, MN [*Location identifier*] [*FAA*] (FAAL)
MVE .... Multivariate Exponential Distribution [*Statistics*]
MVE .... Murray Valley Encephalitis [*Virus*]
MVE .... Virden-Elkhorn Regional Library, Virden, Manitoba [*Library symbol*] [*National Library of Canada*] (NLC)
MVEA .... Missouri Valley Electric Association
MV Ed .... Master of Vocational Education
MVEE .... Military Vehicles and Engineering Establishment [*Research center*] [*British*]
MVEFS ...... Motor Vehicle Emission and Fuel Standards (COE)
MVEG .... Motor Vehicle Emission Group [*Fuels and lubricants*]
MVEL .... Motor Vehicle Emission Laboratory [*Environmental Protection Agency*]
MVEMJSUNP ... My Very Excellent Mother Just Served Us Nine Pies [*Mnemonic guide to the nine planets: Mercury, Venus, Earth, Mars, Jupiter, Saturn, Uranus, Neptune, Pluto*]
MVEN .... Marine Venture [*NCIC trailer make code*]
MVetClinStud ... Master of Veterinary Clinical Studies
MVetMed ... Master of Veterinary Medicine (NADA)
M Vet Sc ... Master of Veterinary Science (PGP)
MVetSci ..... Master of Veterinary Science (NADA)
MVetSt ...... Master of Veterinary Studies
MVF .... Manned Vertical Flight (MCD)
MVF .... Missile Verification Firing
MVF .... Mitral Valve Flow [*Medicine*] (DMAA)
MVF .... Moisture Volume Fraction (PDAA)
MVF .... MuniVest Fund [*AMEX symbol*] (TTSB)
MVF .... MuniVest Fund, Inc. [*AMEX symbol*] (SPSG)
MVFC .... Mack Vickery Fan Club (EA)
MVFC .... Mr. V Fan Club [*Defunct*] (EA)
MVFC .... Municipal Valuation Fees Committee [*Victoria, Australia*]
MVFV .... Manned Venus Flyby Vehicle
MVG .... Mengenverbrauchsguttern [*Mass Consumption Goods*] [*German*]
MVG .... Minven Gold Corp. [*Toronto Stock Exchange symbol*]
MVG .... Most Valuable Girl
MVG .... Moving
MVG .... Mycoplasmatales Virus [*from*] Goat
MVGA .... Monochrome Video Graphics Array [*Computer science*] (CDE)
MVGF .... Myxoma Virus Growth Factor [*Biochemistry*]
MV Grad .... Mitral Valve Gradient [*Cardiology*] (MAE)
MVGVT ...... Mated Vertical Ground Vibration Test [*NASA*] (NASA)
MVH .... Massive Vitreous Hemorrhage [*Medicine*] (DMAA)
MVH .... Methotrexate, VP-16 Hyxamethylmelamine [*Antineoplastic drug regimen*] (DAVI)
MVh .... Minute Ventilatory Volume for Human
MVH .... Mire [*Language symbol*] (ETLW)
MVH .... Mohave Gold, Inc. [*Vancouver Stock Exchange symbol*]
MVH .... Mountain View [*Hawaii*] [*Seismograph station code, US Geological Survey*] (SEIS)
MVh .... Vineyard Haven Public Library, Vineyard Haven, MA [*Library symbol*] [*Library of Congress*] (LCLS)
MVHD .... Hospital District Number 10, Virden, Manitoba [*Library symbol*] [*National Library of Canada*] (NLC)
MVho .... Minute Ventilatory Volume for Human in an Occupational Environment
MVI .... Macrotrends Ventures, Inc. [*Vancouver Stock Exchange symbol*]
MVI .... Maranatha Volunteers International [*Association*] (EA)
MvI .... Marcive, Inc., San Antonio, TX [*Library symbol*] [*Library of Congress*] (LCLS)
MVI .... Massachusetts Volunteer Infantry [*Civil War term*]
MVI .... Maximum Visual Impact (DNAB)
MVI .... Medium Value Item (NATG)
MVI .... Medium Viscosity Index (PDAA)
MVI .... Melt Volume Index [*Materials science*]
MVI .... Merchant Vessel Inspection Division [*Coast Guard*]
MVI .... Mercury Vapor Isolator
MVI .... Metal Ventilator Institute (EA)
MV/I .... Millivolt to Current [*Converter*] [*Nuclear energy*] (NRCH)
MVI .... Minami Daito Jima [*Volcano Islands*] [*Seismograph station code, US Geological Survey*] (SEIS)
MVI .... Miniature Variable Inductor
MVI .... Motion Video Instructions (SAUS)
MVI .... Motor Vehicle Inspection
MVI .... Multiple Vitamin Infusion [*Pharmacology*] (DAVI)
MVI .... Multivalvular Involvement [*Medicine*] (DMAA)
MVI .... Multivitamin (AMHC)
MVI .... Multivitamins Intravenously [*Pharmacology*] (DAVI)
MVIACSA ... Motor Vehicle Information and Cost Saving Act (EEVL)
MVIC .... Mitsubishi Variable Intake System [*Automotive engine design*]
MVICSA ..... Motor Vehicle Information and Cost Saving Act
MVICSA ..... Motor Vehicle Information and Cost Savings Act (EG)
MVII .... Mark VII [*NASDAQ symbol*] (TTSB)
MVII .... Mark VII, Inc. [*NASDAQ symbol*] (SAG)
MVII .... Minnesota Vocational Interest Inventory
MVIJC .... Motor Vehicle Industry Joint Council [*British*] (DCTA)
MVI/M .... Motor Vehicle Inspection/Maintenance (GFGA)
MVIN .... Medium Viscosity Index-Naphthenic (PDAA)
MVIP .... Medium Viscosity Index-Paraffinic (PDAA)
MVIP .... Multi-Vendor Integration Protocol [*Computer science*]
MVIS .... Maximum Voluntary Isometric Strength
MVIS .... Microvision, Inc. [*NASDAQ symbol*] (SAG)
MVIS .... Murrumbidgee Irrigation Area Vine Improvement Society [*Australia*]
MVJ .... Mandeville [*Jamaica*] [*Airport symbol*] [*Obsolete*] (OAG)
MVJ .... MuniVest New Jersey Fund [*NYSE symbol*] (SPSG)
MVJ .... MuniVest NJ Fund [*NYSE symbol*] (TTSB)
MVJC .... Mount Vernon Junior College [*Washington, DC*]
MVK .... Maverick Tube [*NYSE symbol*]
MVK .... Methyl Vinyl Ketone [*Organic chemistry*]
MVK .... Mulka [*Australia*] [*Airport symbol*] [*Obsolete*] (OAG)
MVL .... Magadan Airlines [*Russian Federation*] [*ICAO designator*] (FAAC)
MVL .... Man-Vehicle Laboratory [*Massachusetts Institute of Technology*] [*Research center*] (RCD)
MVL .... Manville Corp. [*NYSE symbol*] (CTT)
MVL .... Marley Vehicle Leasing [*Commercial firm*] [*British*]
MVL .... Marvel Enterprises [*NYSE symbol*] (SG)
MVL .... Mecklenburg-Vorpommern [*German license plate city code*]
MVL .... Mercury Vapor Lamp
MVL .... Metal Vapor LASER
MVL .... Mitral Valve Leaflet (DMAA)
MVL .... Moderate Visual Loss (SAUS)
MVL .... Morrisville, VT [*Location identifier*] [*FAA*] (FAAL)
MVL .... Mountain Valley Library System, Sacramento, CA [*OCLC symbol*] (OCLC)
MVL .... Moveable [*Telegraphy*] (PCTE)
MVL .... Multiple-Valued Logic [*Computer science*]
MVL .... Multiple Virtual Line [*Developed by Paradyne Corporation*] (DCDG)
MVL .... Murray Valley League [*Australia*]
MVL .... Mycoplasmatales Virus [*from*] Acholeplasma laidlawii
MVL .... Mylan Ventures Ltd. [*Vancouver Stock Exchange symbol*]
MVL .... Naval
MVLA .... Mount Vernon Ladies' Association of the Union (EA)
MVLD .... Man Worn Laser Detector (SAUS)
MVLDC ...... Murray Valley League for Development and Conservation [*Australia*]
MVLP .... Microsoft Variable License Pak (GART)
MVLPS ...... Manual Valve Lever Position Sensor [*Automotive term*] (HAWK)
MVLS .... Magic Valley Regional Library System [*Library network*]
MVLS .... Mandibular Vestibulolingual Sulcoplasty [*Surgery*]
MVLS .... Meecham Verbal Language Scale (DAVI)
MVLT .... Morse/Voice Language Trainer (SAUS)
MVLU .... Minimum Variance Linear Unbiased [*Statistics*]
MVLUE ...... Minimum Variance Linear Unbiased Estimator [*Statistics*] (OA)
MVM .... Air Cargo America, Inc. [*ICAO designator*] (FAAC)
MVM .... Manager Virtual Machine [*Computer science*] (CIST)
mvm .... Mariner Venus/Mercury (NAKS)
MVM .... Mariner Venus-Mercury Project [*NASA*]
MVM .... Massachusetts Volunteer Militia (HGAA)
MVM .... Master of Veterinary Medicine
MVM .... Medium-Voltage Mode
MVM .... Microvillous Membrane [*Cytology*] (MAE)
MVM .... Million Vehicle Miles
mV/m .... Millivolts per Meter (DEN)
MVM .... Minimum Virtual Memory
MVM .... Minute Virus of Mice
MVM .... Multiple Virtual Modem [*Computer science*] (CIST)
MVM .... Multivolume Monographs
MVM .... MuniVest Michigan Insured Fund [*NYSE symbol*] (SPSG)
MVMA .... Mississippi Veterinary Medical Association (EARSL)
MVMA .... Motor Vehicle Manufacturers Association (NADA)
MVMA .... Motor Vehicle Manufacturers Association of the United States (EA)
MVMC .... Motor Vehicle Maintenance Course
MVMF .... Ministerstvo Voenno-Morskogo Flota [*Ministry of the Navy*] [*1950-53; merged into the MO*] [*Former USSR*]
MVMFB ..... Mississippi Valley Motor Freight Bureau
MVMNT ..... Movement
MVMT .... Movement (AFM)
MVN .... Magna Ventures Ltd. [*Vancouver Stock Exchange symbol*]
MVN .... Malvern, AR [*Amtrak rail station code*]
MVN .... Marvin Ltd. [*British*] [*ICAO designator*] (FAAC)
MVN .... Medial Ventromedial Nucleus [*Medicine*] (DMAA)
MVN .... Median Ventricular Nerve [*Medicine*]
MVN .... Mount Vernon [*Illinois*] [*Airport symbol*] (OAG)

MVNT........ Movement (SAUS)
MVO......... Maximum Venous Outflow [*Medicine*]
MVO......... Member of the Royal Victorian Order [*British*]
MVO......... Military Vehicles Operation [*of General Motors Corp.*]
MVO......... Mitral Valve Opening [*Medicine*] (DMAA)
MVO......... MMC Video One Canada Ltd. [*Toronto Stock Exchange symbol*] [*Vancouver Stock Exchange symbol*]
MVO......... Money Value Only (AFIT)
MVO......... Mongo [*Chad*] [*Airport symbol*] (AD)
MVO_2........ Myocardial Oxygen Consumption [*Cardiology*] (DAVI)
MVo_2........ Myocardial Oxygen Ventilation Rate [*Cardiology*] (MAE)
MVOA........ Mitral Valve Orifice Area [*Cardiology*] (DMAA)
MVOC........ Microbial Volatile Organic Compounds (SAUS)
MVP......... Machine Vision Processor
MVP......... Magnetic Vector Potential
MVP......... Magnum Venus Products [*Plastics*]
MVP......... Maintenance Verification Plan
MVP......... Manpower Validation Program
MVP......... Marginal Value of Product [*Agriculture*]
MVP......... Master Verification Plan (MCD)
MVP......... Mechanical Vacuum Pump
MVP......... Methylvinylpyridine [*Organic chemistry*]
MVP......... Methyl-Violet Paper (MSA)
MVP......... Microvascular Pressure [*Medicine*] (DMAA)
MVP......... Micro Vector Processor (TIMI)
MVP......... Millivolt Potentiometer (IDOE)
MVP......... Minimum Viable Population [*Demographics*]
MVP......... Minority Vendors Program
MVP......... Mitral Valve Prolapse [*Cardiology*]
MVP......... Mitu [*Colombia*] [*Airport symbol*] (OAG)
MVP......... Modular Voice Processor (SAUS)
MVP......... Most Valuable Player [*Athletics*] [*Facetious translation: "Most Volatile Player"*]
MVP......... Most Valuable Princess [*Princess Diana*] [*British*] [*Slang*]
MVP......... Most Valuable Product (PCM)
MVP......... Motor Vehicle Plant (SAUS)
MVP......... Mountain View Public Library, Mountain View, CA [*OCLC symbol*] (OCLC)
MVP......... Multimedia Video Processor [*Texas Instruments*] (PS)
MVP......... Multiple Virtual Processing (NITA)
MVP......... Multivalue Program [*Computer science*]
MVP......... Multivariable Program [*Computer science*] (IAA)
MVP......... MuniVest Pennsylvania Insured Fund [*NYSE symbol*] (SPSG)
MVP......... MVP Capital Corp. [*Toronto Stock Exchange symbol*]
MVPA........ Military Vehicle Preservation Association (EA)
MVPA........ Motor Vehicle Plan Administration
MVPC........ Motor Vehicle Personal Computer [*Mobile communications*]
MVPCB....... Motor Vehicle Pollution Control Board (NADA)
MVPCCS...... Motor Vehicle Post Crash Communications System (PDAA)
MVPD-26..... metrotrexate, Citrovorum Factor, VM-26, Procarbazine, Dexamethasone [*Antineoplastic drug regimen*] (DAVI)
MVPE........ Market Value of Portfolio Equity
MVPP........ Mechlorethamine/Vinblastine/Procarbazine/Prednisone (DB)
MVPP........ Mustargen [*Nitrogen mustard*], Vinblastine, Procarbazine, Prednisone [*Antineoplastic drug regimen*]
MVPp........ Mustine, Vinblastine, Procarbazine, prednisone [*Antineoplastic drug regimen*] (DAVI)
MVPR........ Master Verification Process Requirement (SSD)
MVPS........ Manually Variable Phase Shifter
MVPS........ Mechanical Vacuum Pump System
MVPS........ Medicare Volume Performance Standard
MVPS........ Medium-Voltage Power Supply (IAA)
MVPS........ Mitral Valve Prolapse Syndrome [*Cardiology*]
MVPS........ Multiple Vertical Protective Shelter [*for missiles*] (MCD)
MVPT........ Motor-Free Visual Perception Test
MVPTG....... Medial Vascularized Patellar Tendon Graft [*Sports medicine*]
MVQ......... Malvern, AR [*Location identifier*] [*FAA*] (FAAL)
MVR......... Fifth Republic Movement (Venezuela) [*Political party*] (PSAP)
MVR......... Malabar Volunteer Rifles [*British military*] (DMA)
MVR......... Maneuver (AABC)
MVR......... Maroua [*Cameroon*] [*Airport symbol*] (OAG)
MVR......... Massive Vitreous Retraction (MAE)
MVR......... Massive Vitreous Retractor [*Blade*] [*Ophthalmology*] (DAVI)
MVR......... Master Verification Requirement (SSD)
MVR......... Maverick Airways Corp. [*FAA designator*] (FAAC)
MVR......... Maximum Ventilation Rate [*Medicine*] (DAVI)
MVR......... Mean Value Reference [*Mathematics*]
MVR......... Mechanical Vapor Recompression [*For evaporators*]
MVR......... Microvitreoretinal (DMAA)
MVR......... Minimal Vascular Resistance [*Medicine*] (DMAA)
MVR......... Minisatellite Variant Repeat [*Genetics*]
MVR......... Missing Volume Report
MVR......... Mitral Valve Regurgitation [*Cardiology*] (DAVI)
MVR......... Mitral Valve Replacement [*Cardiology*]
mvr......... Moldavian Soviet Socialist Republic [*MARC country of publication code*] [*Library of Congress*] (LCCP)
MVR......... Mondavi Resources Ltd. [*Vancouver Stock Exchange symbol*]
MVR......... Monthly Variance Report (ABAC)
MVR......... Motor Vehicle Repair (HEAS)
MVR......... Motor Vehicle Report
MVR......... Mover
MVR......... Mussoorie Volunteer Rifles [*British military*] (DMA)
MVRA........ Metropolitan Visiting and Relief Association [*British*]
MVRA........ Motor Vehicle Repairers' Association (ODA)
MVRCA....... Magnalink Variable Resource Compression Algorithm (SAUS)
MVRD........ My Virtual Reference Desk [*Internet resource*]
MVRDC....... Motor Vehicle Repair Disputes Committee [*New South Wales, Australia*]
MVRF........ Maverig Freight [*Common carrier symbol*]
MVRG........ Medieval Village Research Group (EA)
MVRI........ Mixed Vaccine, Respiratory Infection [*Medicine*]
MVRIAG...... Murray Valley Rural Industry Assistance Group [*Australia*]
MVRIC....... Motor Vehicle Repair Industry Council [*New South Wales, Australia*]
MVRO........ Minimum-Variance Reduced-Order [*Statistics*] (PDAA)
MVRS........ Marine Vapor Recovery System (GNE)
MVRS........ Mechanical Vapor Recovery System [*Engineering*]
MVRS........ Mystic Valley Railway Society (EA)
MVRT........ Multivoltage Radiation Therapy (MELL)
MVRY........ Mahoning Valley Railroad [*Federal Railroad Administration identification code*]
MVS......... Magnetic Valve System [*Diesel engines*]
MVS......... Magnetic Voltage Stabilizer
MVS......... Manifold Vacuum Sensor [*Automotive engineering*]
MVS......... Massep [*Language symbol*] (ETLW)
MVS......... Master of Valuation Sciences (GAGS)
MVS......... Master of Veterinary Studies
MVS......... Master of Veterinary Surgery
MVS......... Mature Vesicular Follicle [*Medicine*] (MELL)
MVS......... Mechanical Vibration System
MVS......... Megastar Ventures [*Vancouver Stock Exchange symbol*]
MVS......... Mennonite Voluntary Service
MVS......... Mesenteric Venous System [*Medicine*] (MELL)
MVS......... Metal Vapour Synthesis [*Chemistry*]
MVS......... Metering Valve Sensor [*Automotive engineering*]
mvs......... Middle Value Select (NAKS)
MVS......... Middle Valve Select (MCD)
MVS......... Midvoid Stream [*Medicine*] (MELL)
MVS......... Military Vehicle Systems (ACAE)
MVS......... Millersville State College, Millersville, PA [*OCLC symbol*] (OCLC)
MVS......... Mine Ventilation System [*Engineering*]
MVS......... Miniature Vehicle Sensor (ACAE)
MVS......... Minimum Visual Signal
MVS......... Ministerstvo Vooruzhennykh Sil [*Ministry of the Armed Forces*] [*1946-50; superseded by VM, MVMF*] [*Former USSR*]
MVS......... Missile Velocity Servo
MVS......... Mission Verification System (SAUS)
MVS......... Mission Video System [*NASA*]
MVS......... Mitral Valve Stenosis [*Cardiology*] (DAVI)
MVS......... Mobile Video Services Ltd. [*Washington, DC*] [*Telecommunications*] (TSSD)
MVS......... Modular 8mm Video System [*Eastman Kodak Co.*]
MVS......... Modularized Vehicle Stimulation [*Program*]
MVS......... Most Valued Supplier [*Mazda Motor Corp.*]
MVS......... Moves [*Telegraphy*] (PCTE)
MVS......... Multiple Vibration System
mvs......... Multiple Virtual Storage (NAKS)
MVS......... Multiple Virtual Storage [*IBM Corp.*] [*Computer science*]
MVS......... Multiple Virtual System [*Computer science*]
MVS......... Multiprogramming with Virtual Storage [*Computer science*] (ECII)
MVS......... Multivariable Storage [*Computer science*]
MVS......... Multivendor Service (DMAA)
MVS......... MuniVest Florida Fund [*NYSE symbol*] (SPSG)
MVS......... Muzzle Velocity System (SAUS)
MVSA........ Motor Vehicle Safety Act [*Automotive engineering*]
MVSB........ Motor Vehicle Storage Building
MVSc........ Master of Veterinary Science [*Canada*] (ASC)
MVS/ESA..... Multiple Virtual Storage/Enterprise System Architecture [*Computer science*] (VLIE)
MVS/ESA..... Multiple Virtual Storage/Enterprise Systems Architecture [*Introduced by IBM in 1988*] (GART)
MVSESASP... Multiple Virtual Storage/ Extended System Architecture System Product (SAUS)
MVSI........ MVSI, Inc. [*NASDAQ symbol*] (SAG)
MVSL........ Mouse Visible Specific Locus [*Test for mutagenesis*]
MVSMA....... Mechanical Vibrating Screen Manufacturers Association [*Later, Vibrating Screen Manufacturers Association*] (EA)
MVSN........ Macrovision Corp. [*NASDAQ symbol*] (NASQ)
MVSN........ Milizia Volontaria per la Sicurezza Nazionale [*Italian Voluntary Militia for National Security*] (WDAA)
MVSP........ Maintain Visual Separation [*Aviation*]
MVSPC....... Multi-Variate Statistical Process Control [*Computer science*] (VLIE)
MVSR........ Monthly Vital Statistics Report [*A publication*] (DHSM)
MVSRF....... Man-Vehicle Systems Research Facility (SAUS)
MVSS........ Mazda Vehicle Security System
MVSS........ Motor Vehicle Safety Standard
MVSS........ Motor Vehicle Storage Shed [*Army*] (AABC)
MVSSE....... Multiple Virtual Storage System Extension
MVS/SE...... MVS/System Extension (NITA)
MVS/SP...... MVS/System Product (NITA)
MVSt........ Master of Veterinary Studies (ADA)
MVS/TSO..... Multiple Virtual Storage/Time Sharing Option (SAUS)
MVS/TSO..... Multiple Virtual Storage/Time-Sharing Option [*Computer science*] (VLIE)
MVS/XA...... MVS/Extended Architecture (NITA)
MVSZGA...... Mein Vertrauen Steht zu Gott Allein [*My Trust Is in God Alone*] [*Motto of Johann Adolf II, Duke of Saxony-Weissenfels (1649-97)*] [*German*]
MVT......... Malfunction Verification Test (MCD)

MVT .... Marginal Value Theorem [*Mathematical model developed by Dr. Eric Charnov*]
MVT .... Market-Value Transmission [*Pricing concept*]
MVT .... Mataiva [*French Polynesia*] [*Airport symbol*] (OAG)
MVT .... Maximal Ventilation Time [*Medicine*] (DAVI)
MVT .... Miscellaneous Vector Table
MVT .... Mission Verification Test [*NASA*] (NASA)
MVT .... Mississippi Valley Type [*Ore deposits*] [*Geology*]
MVT .... Moisture Vapor Transmission (EDCT)
MVT .... Moisture Vapor Transmission Rate
MVT .... Monte Vettore [*Italy*] [*Seismograph station code, US Geological Survey*] (SEIS)
MVT .... Motor Vehicle Theft (GOBB)
MVT .... Motor Vehicle Title
MVT .... Mount Vernon Terminal [*AAR code*]
mvt .... Movement (IDYL)
MVT .... Movement (MSA)
MVT .... Multinational Volunteer Teams
MVT .... Multiprogramming with a Variable Number of Tasks [*IBM Corp.*] [*Control program*] [*Computer science*]
MVT .... Multivariable Task (MCD)
MVT .... Munivest Fund II [*NYSE symbol*] (SAG)
MVT .... MuniVest Fund, Inc. [*NYSE symbol*] (SPSG)
MVTE .... Master of Vocational Technical Education (GAGS)
MVT Ed ..... Master of Vocational and Technical Education (PGP)
MVTL .... Minnesota Valley Testing Labs, Inc. (EFIS)
MVTL .... Modified Variable-Threshold Logic [*Computer science*]
MVTLEA ..... Motor Vehicle Theft Law Enforcement Act [*1984*]
MVTR .... Moisture Vapor Transmission Rate
MVTS .... Motor Vehicle Tampering Survey (EEVL)
MVTS .... Motor Vehicle Test Station (COE)
MVT/TSO .... MVT/Time Sharing Option (NITA)
MVTV .... MetroVision of North America, Inc. [*NASDAQ symbol*] (SAG)
MVU .... Michigan Virtual University
MVU .... Minimum Variance Unbiased [*Statistics*]
MVU .... Mulege [*Mexico*] [*Airport symbol*] (AD)
MVU .... Musgrave [*Australia*] [*Airport symbol*] [*Obsolete*] (OAG)
MVUE .... Man/Vehicular User Equipment
MVUE .... Minimum Variance Unbiased Estimate [*Statistics*]
MVULE ...... Minimum Variance Unbiased Linear Estimator [*Statistics*]
MVV .... Maximum Volume Ventilation (SAUS)
MVV .... Maximum Voluntary Ventilation
MVV .... Maximum Voluntary Volume [*Medicine*] (DAVI)
MVV .... Mean Vertical Velocity
MVV .... Mitsubishi Vertical Vortex [*Automotive engineering*]
MVV .... Mixed Vespid Venom [*Pharmacology*] (DAVI)
MVV_1 .... Maximal Ventilatory Volume (MAE)
MVVF .... Maximum Voluntary Ventilation Free [*Medicine*] [*Formerly MBC*] (EDAA)
MVVPP ...... Mustargen [*Nitrogen mustard*], Vincristine, Vinblastine, Procarbazine, Prednisone [*Antineoplastic drug regimen*]
MVW .... Minot-Von Willebrand [*Syndrome*] [*Medicine*] (DB)
MVW .... Missile Viewing Window
MVW .... Mount Vernon [*Washington*] [*Airport symbol*] (OAG)
MVW .... Mud Volcano [*Wyoming*] [*Seismograph station code, US Geological Survey*] (SEIS)
MVWDU ..... Missile Viewing Window Deicing Unit
MVWGS ..... Multi-Vintage Wine Growers Society [*British*] (DBA)
MVX .... Media Videotex [*Vancouver Stock Exchange symbol*]
MVX .... Minvoul [*Gabon*] [*Airport symbol*] (OAG)
MVX .... Multiplex
MVY .... Martha's Vineyard [*Massachusetts*] [*Airport symbol*] (OAG)
MVY .... MuniVest New York Insured Fund [*NYSE symbol*] (SPSG)
MVY .... MuniVest NY Insured Fund [*NYSE symbol*] (TTSB)
MVYR .... Roger L. Mulvaney [*Common carrier symbol*]
MVYS .... Merit Moving Systems [*Common carrier symbol*]
MVZ .... Manifold Vacuum Zone [*Automotive engineering*]
MVZ .... Move Zones (VLIE)
MVZ .... Museum of Vertebrate Zoology [*University of California, Berkeley*]
MVZG .... Mein Verlangen zu Gott [*My Desires (I Give) to God*] [*Motto of Anna Marie, Margravine of Brandenburg (1609-80)*] [*German*]
MVZS .... Manifold Vacuum Zone Switch [*Automotive engineering*]
MW .... Machine Word (IAA)
MW .... Magnesiowustite [*Mineralogy*]
MW .... Malawi [*ANSI two-letter standard code*] (CNC)
mw .... Malawi [*MARC country of publication code*] [*Library of Congress*] (LCCP)
M-W .... Mallory-Weiss Syndrome [*Medicine*] (MEDA)
MW .... Management World [*Administrative Management Society*] [*A publication*]
MW .... Manual Word
MW .... Manufacturing Week (MCD)
MW .... Man Watchers (EA)
mw .... Man Week (NAKS)
MW .... Man-Week (NASA)
MW .... Marginal Wage [*Economics*]
MW .... Marginal Wings [*Botany*]
MW .... Master of Wine [*Bestowed by the Worshipful Company of Vintners, one of the ancient guilds in the City of London*]
M/W .... Mate With (MCD)
MW .... Maya Airways [*ICAO designator*] (AD)
MW .... Meanwhile [*Telegraphy*] (PCTE)
MW .... Media Watch [*An association*] (EA)
MW .... Medium Wall
MW .... Medium Wave (WA)
MW .... Medium Wave Band
MW .... Meetings Word (NITA)
MW .... Megawatt [*Also, MEGW*]
MW .... Memory Write [*Computer science*]
MW .... Men's Wearhouse [*NYSE symbol*]
M-W .... Merriam-Webster [*Publisher*]
MW .... Message Waiting
MW .... Metachrondral Wave [*Physiology*]
MW .... Metalworker [*British military*] (DMA)
M/W .... Methanol/Water
mW .... Microwatt
M/W .... Microwave [*Communications term*] (DCT)
mw .... Microwave (NAKS)
MW .... Microwave
MW .... Middle Ware (VLIE)
MW .... Middle Welsh [*Language, etc.*]
MW .... Midwife (MELL)
MW .... Midwing [*Aviation*] (AIA)
MW .... Migratory Worker (OICC)
MW .... Milliwatt (ACAE)
mw .... Milliwatt (NAKS)
mW .... Milliwatt
MW .... Mine Warfare
MW .... Mine Warning (NATG)
MW .... Ministry of Works [*British*]
MW .... Minnesota Western Railroad (IIA)
MW .... Mittweida [*German license plate city code*]
MW .... Mixed Wastes [*Environmental science*] (COE)
mw .... Mixed Widths [*Forest industry*] (WPI)
MW .... Mixed Widths
MW .... Mobile Workshop [*British*]
MW .... Modulated Wave (IAA)
MW .... Moewe Flugzeugbau, Heini Dittmar [*Germany*] [*ICAO aircraft manufacturer identifier*] (ICAO)
mw .... Molecular Weight (LDOE)
MW .... Molecular Weight [*Also, M, MOL WT*]
MW .... Money Wages [*Economics*]
MW .... Monier-Williams Method (RDA)
MW .... Montana Western Railway (IIA)
MW .... Mosaic Wart [*Medicine*] (MELL)
MW .... Most Worshipful [*Freemasonry*]
MW .... Most Worthy
MW .... Motor Wagon [*British*]
MW .... Mud Weight [*Well drilling technology*]
MW .... Multiple Warts [*Medicine*] (MELL)
MW .... Multiple Wounds
MW .... Multipurpose Weapon (MCD)
MW .... Multi-Wink (VLIE)
MW .... Multiwire (IAA)
MW .... Music of the World [*American Forces Radio and Television Service*] (DNAB)
MW .... Music Wire
Mw .... Weighted Mean [*Psychology*]
MW .... Winnipeg Centennial Library, Manitoba [*Library symbol*] [*National Library of Canada*] (NLC)
MW .... Worcester Public Library and Central Massachusetts Regional Library System Headquarters, Worcester, MA [*Library symbol*] [*Library of Congress*] (LCLS)
MWA .... American Antiquarian Society, Worcester, MA [*Library symbol*] [*Library of Congress*] (LCLS)
MWA .... Major World Authors [*A publication*]
MWA .... Management by Walking Around
MWA .... Manitoba Department of Agriculture, Winnipeg, Manitoba [*Library symbol*] [*National Library of Canada*] (NLC)
MWA .... Manufacturing Work Authority
MWA .... Marion [*Illinois*] [*Airport symbol*] (OAG)
MWA .... Married Women's Association [*British*] (DBA)
MWA .... Mayflower Warehousemen's Association (EA)
MWA .... Media Women's Association
MWA .... Meteorological Watch Advisory
MWA .... Mid-West Abrasive Co. (EFIS)
MWA .... Midwest Area (SARE)
MWA .... Mineral Workings Act [*Town planning*] [*British*]
MWA .... Modern Woodmen of America (EA)
MWA .... Momentum-Wheel Assembly
MWA .... Movers' & Warehousemen's Association of America Inc., Washington DC [*STAC*]
MWA .... Multiple Weapons Adapter (SAUS)
MWA .... Munitions of War Act [*British*]
MWA .... Mystery Writers of America (NADA)
MW/AA ...... Missile Warning/Attack Assessment (MCD)
MWAA ...... Movers' and Warehousemen's Association of America [*Defunct*] (EA)
MWAC ...... Air Command Headquarters, Canadian Forces Base, Westwin, Manitoba [*Library symbol*] [*National Library of Canada*] (NLC)
MWAC ...... Assumption College, Worcester, MA [*Library symbol*] [*Library of Congress*] (LCLS)
MWAC ...... Midwest Archeological Center [*National Park Service*] (GRD)
MWAD ...... Alcohol and Drug Education Service, Winnipeg, Manitoba [*Library symbol*] [*National Library of Canada*] (NLC)
MWAE ...... Minimum-Weighted-Absolute Error [*Statistics*] (PDAA)
MWAF ...... Alcoholism Foundation of Manitoba, Winnipeg, Manitoba [*Library symbol*] [*National Library of Canada*] (NLC)
MWAG ...... Research Station, Agriculture Canada [*Station de Recherches, Agriculture Canada*] Winnipeg, Manitoba [*Library symbol*] [*National Library of Canada*] (NLC)

MWAI........ Mystery Writers of America Inc. (NADA)
MWal........ Waltham Public Library, Waltham MA [*Library symbol*] [*Library of Congress*] (LCLS)
MWalA........ American Jewish Historical Society, Waltham, MA [*Library symbol*] [*Library of Congress*] (LCLS)
MWalAF..... African Studies Association, Brandeis University, Waltham, MA [*Library symbol*] [*Library of Congress*] (LCLS)
MWalB...... Brandeis University, Waltham, MA [*Library symbol*] [*Library of Congress*] (LCLS)
MWalBe..... Bentley College, Waltham, MA [*Library symbol*] [*Library of Congress*] (LCLS)
MWalFAR... Federal Archives and Records Center, General Services Administration, Waltham, MA [*Library symbol*] [*Library of Congress*] (LCLS)
MWalG...... General Telephone & Electronics Laboratories, Inc., Waltham Research Center Library, Waltham, MA [*Library symbol*] [*Library of Congress*] (LCLS)
MWalK...... John F. Kennedy Library, Waltham, MA [*Library symbol*] [*Library of Congress*] (LCLS)
MWalMT.... Mobil Tyco Solar Energy Corp., Waltham, MA [*Library symbol*] [*Library of Congress*] (LCLS)
MWAMA..... Administration Branch, Manitoba Department of Municipal Affairs, Winnipeg, Manitoba [*Library symbol*] [*National Library of Canada*] (NLC)
MWAMT..... Aikins, MacAulay, and Thorvaldson Law Firm, Winnipeg, Manitoba [*Library symbol*] [*National Library of Canada*] (NLC)
MW&E PAC... McDermott, Will and Emery PAC [*Washington, DC*] (PACS)
MWAR....... Microware Systems Corp. [*NASDAQ symbol*] (SAG)
MWAR....... Microwave Systems [*NASDAQ symbol*] (TTSB)
MWar........ Wareham Free Library, Wareham, MA [*Library symbol*] [*Library of Congress*] (LCLS)
MWARA..... Major World Air Route Area
MWARN..... Manitoba Association of Registered Nurses, Winnipeg, Manitoba [*Library symbol*] [*National Library of Canada*] (NLC)
MWARS..... Major Command Worldwide Ammunition Reporting System [*Army*]
MWARS..... Synod Office, Diocese of Rupert's Land, Anglican Church of Canada, Winnipeg, Manitoba [*Library symbol*] [*National Library of Canada*] (NLC)
MWAS....... Arthritis Society, Winnipeg, Manitoba [*Library symbol*] [*National Library of Canada*] (NLC)
MWASD..... Assiniboine South School Division No. 3, Winnipeg, Manitoba [*Library symbol*] [*National Library of Canada*] (NLC)
MWat........ Watertown Free Public Library, Watertown, MA [*Library symbol*] [*Library of Congress*] (LCLS)
MWatM...... Massachusetts Bay Community College, Watertown, MA [*Library symbol*] [*Library of Congress*] (LCLS)
MWatP...... Perkins School for the Blind, Watertown, MA [*Library symbol*] [*Library of Congress*] (LCLS)
MWatP-BP... Massachusetts Regional Library for the Blind and Physically Handicapped, PerkinsSchool for the Blind, Watertown, MA [*Library symbol*] [*Library of Congress*] (LCLS)
MWatP-BPH... Regional Library for the Blind and Physically Handicapped, Perkins School for the Blind, Watertown, MA [*Library symbol*] [*Library of Congress*] (LCLS)
MWAV....... M-Wave, Inc. [*NASDAQ symbol*] (SAG)
MWAVE..... Microwave
M-Wave..... M-Wave, Inc. [*Associated Press*] (SAG)
MWAX....... Martin Marietta Materials [*Private rail car owner code*]
MWAX....... Mountain West Airline [*Air carrier designation symbol*]
M-Way...... Motorway [*British*]
MWayR...... Raytheon Co., Wayland, MA [*Library symbol*] [*Library of Congress*] (LCLS)
MWB........ Maintenance Workbench [*Computer science*] (HODG)
MWB........ Master Work Book (NASA)
MWB........ Maxwell-Wien Bridge [*Electronics*]
MWB........ Metropolitan Water Board [*British*]
MWB........ Middlewest Motor Freight Bureau, Kansas City MO [*STAC*]
MWB........ Military War Book (SAUS)
MWB........ Ministry of Works and Buildings [*British*]
MWB........ Motor Whale Boat
MWB........ Multilayer Wiring Board
MWBA....... Bristol Aerospace Ltd., Winnipeg, Manitoba [*Library symbol*] [*National Library of Canada*] (NLC)
MWBA....... Michigan Women's Bowling Association (EARSL)
MWBAS..... Mail Will Be Addressed to Show
MWBC....... Mean Wafers Between Cleans (AAEL)
MWBC....... Technical Library, Boeing of Canada Ltd., Winnipeg, Manitoba [*Library symbol*] [*National Library of Canada*] (NLC)
MWBe....... Becker Junior College, Worcester, MA [*Library symbol*] [*Library of Congress*] (LCLS)
MWBH....... Bethel Hospital, Winkler, Manitoba [*Library symbol*] [*National Library of Canada*] (NLC)
MWBH....... Midwest Bookhunters (EARSL)
MWBI........ Midwest Bacshares Del [*NASDAQ symbol*] (TTSB)
MWBI........ Midwest Bancshares [*NASDAQ symbol*] (SAG)
MWBL....... Mounted Warfighting Battlespace Laboratory [*Army*] (RDA)
MWBM....... Bethania Mennonite Personal Care Home, Winnipeg, Manitoba [*Library symbol*] [*National Library of Canada*] (NLC)
MWBMT..... Mint with Both Mint Tags [*Collectibles*]
MWBP....... Missile Warning Bypass (DWSG)
MWbriM.... Massasoit Community College, West Bridgewater, MA [*Library symbol*] [*Library of Congress*] (LCLS)
MWC........ Clark University, Worcester, MA [*Library symbol*] [*Library of Congress*] (LCLS)
MWC........ Mad World Campaign [*An association*] [*Defunct*] (EA)
MWC........ Magnetoionic Wave Component
MWC........ Major Wingfield Club (EA)
MWC........ Mary Washington College [*University of Virginia*]
MWC........ Maximum Weight Capacity [*Nautical term*] (NTA)
MWC........ Maxwell Communication Corp. [*Toronto Stock Exchange symbol*]
MWC........ Medium Weight Coated Paper (DGA)
MWC........ Melbourne Walking Club [*Australia*]
MWC........ Midwest Conference (PSS)
MWC........ Miltonvale Wesleyan College [*Kansas*]
MWC........ Milwaukee, WI [*Location identifier*] [*FAA*] (FAAL)
MWC........ Minister for [*or Ministry of*] War Communications [*British*] [*World War II*]
MWC........ Missile Warning Center (ACAE)
MWC........ Missile Weapons Control (MCD)
MWC........ Monod-Wyman-Changeux [*Model*] [*Enzymology*]
MWC........ Mount Wilson [*California*] [*Seismograph station code, US Geological Survey*] (SEIS)
MWC........ Moving-Withdrawal Chromatography
MWC........ Multiple Water Connector (KSC)
MWC........ Multiway Calling [*Communications term*] (DCT)
MWC........ Multi-Wire Cable (VLIE)
MWC........ Municipal Waste Combustor (GFGA)
MWC........ Music and Record Library, Canadian Broadcasting Corp. [*Musicotheque et Discotheque, Societe Radio-Canada*] Winnipeg, Manitoba [*Library symbol*] [*National Library of Canada*] (NLC)
MWCA....... Monetary Working Capital Adjustment [*British*]
MWCA....... Monterey Wine Country Association (EA)
MWCAC..... Midwest Collegiate Athletic Conference (PSS)
MWCB....... Cayman Brac/Gerrard Smith [*Cayman Islands*] [*ICAO location identifier*] (ICLI)
MWCB....... Manufacturer's Working Cell Bank [*Cell line*]
MWCC....... Mauchline Ware Collectors' Club [*Association*] (EA)
MWCC....... Metropolitan Wrestling Coach's Conference (PSS)
MWCC....... Mineral Water Co. of Canada (ECON)
MWCCA..... Manitoba Department of Consumer and Corporate Affairs, Winnipeg, Manitoba [*Library symbol*] [*Obsolete*] [*National Library of Canada*] (NLC)
MWCCAC... Midwest Community College Athletic Conference (PSS)
MWCCI...... Manitoba Consumer's Bureau, Winnipeg, Manitoba [*Library symbol*] [*National Library of Canada*] (NLC)
MWCCIR.... Central Region Information Resources Center, Canada Department of Communications[*Centre de Documentation Region du Centre, Ministere des Communications*] Winnipeg, Manitoba [*Library symbol*] [*National Library of Canada*] (NLC)
MWC/CS.... Mechanized Wire Centering/Cross Section [*AT & T*] [*Telecommunications*] (TEL)
MWCE....... Controlled Environments Ltd., Winnipeg, Manitoba [*Library symbol*] [*National Library of Canada*] (NLC)
MWCE....... Millimeter Wave Communications Experiment
MWCF....... Canadian Forces Aerospace and Navigation School, Canadian Forces Base Winnipeg, Westwin, Manitoba [*Library symbol*] [*National Library of Canada*] (NLC)
MWCG....... Grand Cayman [*Cayman Islands*] [*ICAO location identifier*] (ICLI)
MWCH....... Concordia Hospital, Winnipeg, Manitoba [*Library symbol*] [*National Library of Canada*] (NLC)
MWCHA..... Charles Howard & Associates, Winnipeg, Manitoba [*Library symbol*] [*National Library of Canada*] (NLC)
MWCHD..... Charleswood Public Library, Winnipeg, Manitoba [*Library symbol*] [*National Library of Canada*] (NLC)
MWCI........ Canertech, Inc., Winnipeg, Manitoba [*Library symbol*] [*National Library of Canada*] (NLC)
MWCL....... Little Cayman/Boddenfield [*Cayman Islands*] [*ICAO location identifier*] (ICLI)
MWCL....... Midwest Coal Handling [*Federal Railroad Administration identification code*]
MWCL....... Worcester County Law Library Association, Worcester, MA [*Library symbol*] [*Library of Congress*] (LCLS)
MWCLC..... Midwest Classic Conference (PSS)
MWCM...... Canadian Mennonite Bible College, Winnipeg, Manitoba [*Library symbol*] [*National Library of Canada*] (NLC)
MWCM...... Milliwatt per Square Centimeter (IAA)
MWCMS.... Centre for Mennonite Brethren Studies in Canada, Winnipeg, Manitoba [*Library symbol*] [*National Library of Canada*] (NLC)
MWCNT..... Multiwalled Carbon Nanotube
MWCO....... Medium Weight Coated Offset Paper (DGA)
MWCO....... Molecular Weight Cutoff [*Chemistry*]
MWCR....... Georgetown/Owen Roberts International [*Cayman Islands*] [*ICAO location identifier*] (ICLI)
MWCR....... Mercury-Wetted Contact Relay
MWCS....... Marine Wing Communication Squadron
MWCS....... Mental Welfare Commission for Scotland
MWCS....... Midwest Cable & Satellite, Inc. [*Minneapolis, MN*] [*Telecommunications*] (TSSD)
MWCS....... Millimeter Wave Contrast Seeker (MCD)
MWCS....... Missile Weapons Control System (MCD)
MWCS....... Mobile Weapons Control System
MWCSC..... Midwest Collegiate Ski Conference (PSS)
MWCSCC... Midwest Council of Sports Car Clubs
MWCSJ..... Minimum Wage Coalition to Save Jobs [*Defunct*] (EA)
MWCSS..... Mine Warfare Command Support System (SAUS)
MWCT....... Manitoba Cancer Treatment and Research Foundation, Winnipeg, Manitoba [*Library symbol*] [*National Library of Canada*] (NLC)
MWCU....... AP Moller [*Intermodal shipping container symbol*] (TVRC)
MWCU....... Credit Union Central of Manitoba, Winnipeg, Manitoba [*Library symbol*] [*National Library of Canada*] (NLC)
MWCU....... Molecular Weight Cut-Off [*Metallurgy*]
MWCWB.... Canadian Wheat Board [*Commission Canadienne du Ble*] Winnipeg, Manitoba [*Library symbol*] [*National Library of Canada*] (NLC)

MWCX .... Midwest Central Railroad [*Federal Railroad Administration identification code*]
MWD .... Magnetostatic Wave Device (ACAE)
MWD .... Measurement-While Drilling [*Drilling technology*]
MWd .... Megawatt-Day (ABAC)
MWD .... Megawatt-Day
MWD .... Megaword
MWD .... Metering Water Dispenser [*Apollo*] [*NASA*]
MWD .... Meters Water Depth
MWD .... Metropolitan Water District
MWD .... Microwave Diathermy [*Medicine*] (EDAA)
MWD .... Military Working Dog (DOMA)
MWD .... Millimeter Wave Device
MWD .... Molecular Weight Distribution
MWD .... Morgan Stanley [*NYSE symbol*]
MWD .... Morgan Stanley Dean Witter [*NYSE symbol*] [*Formerly, Dean Witter Discover & Co.*] (SG)
MWD .... Moving Window Display (MCD)
MWD .... Rochester, NY [*Location identifier*] [*FAA*] (FAAL)
MWDA .... Montana Wholesale Distributors Association (EARSL)
MWDAC ..... Mountain West Desegregation Assistance Centers (EDAC)
MWDC ...... Market Without Decided Change [*Telegraphy*] (PCTE)
MWDCA ..... Midwest Decoy Collectors Association (EA)
MWDDEA ... Mutual Weapons Development Data Exchange Agreement [*NATO*]
MWDDEP ... Mutual Weapons Development Data Exchange Procedures [*NATO*]
MWDEA ..... Mutual Weapons Data Exchange Agreement (TIMI)
MWDGP ..... Manly Warringah Division of General Practice (SAUS)
MWDGP ..... Mid West Division of General Practice (SAUS)
MWDI .... Master Water Data Index [*US Geological Survey*] [*Information service or system*] (CRD)
MWDL .... Deer Lodge Hospital, Winnipeg, Manitoba [*Library symbol*] [*National Library of Canada*] (NLC)
MWD/MTU .. Megawatt-Days per Metric Ton of Uranium
MWDO ...... Minewarfare Tactical Development Group (SAUS)
MWDP .... Master Warning Display Panel (SAUS)
MWDP .... Mutual Weapons Development Program [*NATO*]
MWDRR ..... Manitoba Department of Renewable Resources, Winnipeg, Manitoba [*Library symbol*] [*National Library of Canada*] (NLC)
MWDS .... Man-Worn Detector System (SAUS)
MWDS .... Med/Waste Inc. [*NASDAQ symbol*] (TTSB)
MWDS .... Missile Warning and Display System [*or Subsystem*] (MCD)
MWDSQ ..... Med/Waste [*OTCBB symbol*]
MWDSW .... Med/Waste Inc. Wrrt'A' [*NASDAQ symbol*] (TTSB)
MWD/T ...... Megawatt-Days per Ton
MWDT .... Mutual Weapons Development Team [*Military*]
MWDU ...... Ducks Unlimited, Winnipeg, Manitoba [*Library symbol*] [*National Library of Canada*] (NLC)
MWE .... Manitoba Department of Education, Winnipeg, Manitoba [*Library symbol*] [*National Library of Canada*] (NLC)
MWE .... Manufacturer's Weight Empty (DA)
MWE .... Megawatt Electric (LDOE)
MWe .... Megawatts of Electric Power
MWE .... Merowe [*Sudan*] [*Airport symbol*] (OAG)
MWE .... Meters of Water Equivalent
MWE .... Millimeter Wave Experiment
MWE .... Mwera [*Language symbol*] (ETLW)
MWEA .... Montana Water Environment Association (EARSL)
MWeA .... Westfield Athenaeum, Westfield, MA [*Library symbol*] [*Library of Congress*] (LCLS)
MWEAC ..... Mount Weather Emergency Assistance Center [*Emergency Management*] (EMA)
MWEAE ..... Central Region Headquarters, Atmospheric Environment Service, Environment Canada[*Quartier-General de la Region Centrale, Service de l'Environnement Atmosphe rique, Environnement Canada*] Winnipeg, Manitoba [*Library symbol*] [*National Library of Canada*] (NLC)
MWeba ...... Whelden Memorial Library, West Barnstable, MA [*Library symbol*] [*Library of Congress*] (LCLS)
MWebaC .... Cape Cod Community College, West Barnstable, MA [*Library symbol*] [*Library of Congress*] (LCLS)
MWECW .... Canadian Wildlife Service, Environment Canada [*Service Canadien de la Faune, Environnement Canada*] Winnipeg, Manitoba [*Library symbol*] [*National Library of Canada*] (NLC)
MWEE .... Mechanised Warfare Experimental Establishment [*British military*] (DMA)
MWEEP ..... Environmental Protection Service, Environment Canada [*Service de la Protection de l'Environnement, Environnement Canada*] Winnipeg, Manitoba [*Library symbol*] [*National Library of Canada*] (NLC)
MWEIA ...... Montessori World Educational Institute Australia
MWelC ...... Wellesley College, Wellesley, MA [*Library symbol*] [*Library of Congress*] (LCLS)
MWelD ...... Dana Hall School Library, Wellesley, MA [*Library symbol*] [*Library of Congress*] (LCLS)
MWeldI ...... Member of the Welding Institute [*British*] (DBQ)
MWEM ...... Major Work Element Manager (ACAE)
MWEM ...... Manitoba Environmental Management Division, Winnipeg, Manitoba [*Library symbol*] [*National Library of Canada*] (NLC)
MWEM ...... Mine Warfare Evaluation Model
MWEMM .... Manitoba Energy and Mines, Winnipeg, Manitoba [*Library symbol*] [*National Library of Canada*] (NLC)
MWenhG .... Gordon College, Wenham, MA [*Library symbol*] [*Library of Congress*] (LCLS)
MWenhHi ... Wenham Historical Society and Museum, Wenham, MA [*Library symbol*] [*Library of Congress*] (LCLS)
MWES .... Member of the Women's Engineering Society [*British*] (DBQ)
MWESM ..... Special Materials Services, Manitoba Department of Education, Winnipeg, Manitoba [*Library symbol*] [*National Library of Canada*] (NLC)
MWesR ...... Regis College, Weston, MA [*Library symbol*] [*Library of Congress*] (LCLS)
MWestonGS ... Church of Jesus Christ of Latter-Day Saints, Genealogical Society Library, Boston Branch, Weston, MA [*Library symbol*] [*Library of Congress*] (LCLS)
MWestonR ... Regis College, Weston, MA [*Library symbol*] [*Library of Congress*] (LCLS)
MWeT .... Westfield State College, Westfield, MA [*Library symbol*] [*Library of Congress*] (LCLS)
MWEU .... Moving Wall Electrophoresis Unit (SAUS)
MWEWSH ... Manitoba Department of Environment, Workplace Safety and Health, Winnipeg, Manitoba [*Library symbol*] [*National Library of Canada*] (NLC)
MWEX .... Mineral Wells & Eastern [*Federal Railroad Administration identification code*]
MWeyAA .... Abigail Adams Historical Society, Weymouth, MA [*Library symbol*] [*Library of Congress*] (LCLS)
MWEZ .... Midwest Energy Loop [*Federal Railroad Administration identification code*]
MWF .... Make-a-Wish Foundation [*Later, MWFA*] (EA)
MWF .... Marine General Workers' Federation
MWF .... Medical Women's Federation [*British*] (DAS)
MWF .... Medical Working File (DOMA)
MWF .... Metalworking Fluid [*Fuels and lubricants*]
MWF .... Military Works Force (SAUS)
MWF .... Monday, Wednesday, Friday (BARN)
MWFA .... Make-a-Wish Foundation of America (EA)
MWFC .... Malcolm Wain Fan Club [*Association*] (EA)
MWFC .... Mary Wilson Fan Club (EA)
MWFC .... Midwest Football Conference (PSS)
MWFCA ..... Motor Wheel and Flyer Club of America [*Defunct*] (EA)
MWFCS ..... Multiweapons Fire Control System (DNAB)
MWFD .... Fred Douglas Lodge Nursing Home, Winnipeg, Manitoba [*Library symbol*] [*National Library of Canada*] (NLC)
MWFD .... Midwest Federal Financial [*NASDAQ symbol*] (SAG)
MWFD .... Midwest Fed Finl [*NASDAQ symbol*] (TTSB)
MWFG .... Fort Garry Public Library, Winnipeg, Manitoba [*Library symbol*] [*National Library of Canada*] (NLC)
MWFI .... Manitoba Department of Finance, Winnipeg, Manitoba [*Library symbol*] [*National Library of Canada*] (NLC)
MWFM ...... Microwave Window Failure Mechanism
MWfo .... J. V. Fletcher Library, Westford, MA [*Library symbol*] [*Library of Congress*] (LCLS)
MWFOPS ... Mine Warfare Operations (NVT)
MWFP .... Winnipeg Free Press Co. Ltd., Manitoba [*Library symbol*] [*National Library of Canada*] (NLC)
MWFRS ..... Manitoba Department of Fitness, Recreation and Sport, Winnipeg, Manitoba [*Library symbol*] [*National Library of Canada*] (NLC)
MWFS .... Marine Wing Facilities Squadron
MWFS .... Maritime Warfare School [*Canadian Navy*]
MWFSD ..... Frontier School Division, Winnipeg, Manitoba [*Library symbol*] [*National Library of Canada*] (NLC)
MWFW ...... Freshwater Institute, Fisheries and Oceans Canada [*Institut des Eaux Douces, Peches et Oceans Canada*] Winnipeg, Manitoba [*Library symbol*] [*National Library of Canada*] (NLC)
MWG .... Maintenance Analyzer Working Group (MCD)
MWG .... Maintenance Working Group (VLIE)
MWG .... Management Working Group [*Army*] (RDA)
MWG .... Maternal Weight Gain (MELL)
MWG .... Meteorological Working Group
MWG .... Missile-Warning Group [*Military*]
MWG .... Model Work Group [*Environmental Protection Agency*] (GFGA)
MWG .... Muenster-Westfalen [*Federal Republic of Germany*] [*Seismograph station code, US Geological Survey*] (SEIS)
MWG .... Music Wire Gauge
MWGBP ..... Guertin Brothers Paint Library, Winnipeg, Manitoba [*Library symbol*] [*National Library of Canada*] (NLC)
MWGC .... Midwestern Governors Conference
MWGCP ..... Most Worthy Grand Chief Patriarch
MWGH ...... Grace Hospital, Winnipeg, Manitoba [*Library symbol*] [*National Library of Canada*] (NLC)
MWGHA ..... Gunn Hoffer & Associates Law Firm, Winnipeg, Manitoba [*Library symbol*] [*National Library of Canada*] (NLC)
MWGM ...... Most Worshipful [*or Worthy*] Grand Master [*Freemasonry*]
MWGP .... Midwest Grain Products [*NASDAQ symbol*] (TTSB)
MWGP .... Midwest Grain Products, Inc. [*NASDAQ symbol*] (CTT)
MWGR ...... Canadian Grain Commission, Agriculture Canada [*Commission Canadienne des Grains, Agriculture Canada*] Winnipeg, Manitoba [*Library symbol*] [*National Library of Canada*] (NLC)
MWGW ...... Great West Life Assurance Co., Winnipeg, Manitoba [*Library symbol*] [*National Library of Canada*] (NLC)
MWH .... Baycorp Holdings [*AMEX symbol*] (SG)
MWH .... College of the Holy Cross, Worcester, MA [*Library symbol*] [*Library of Congress*] (LCLS)
MWH .... Main Wiring Harness [*Automotive engineering*]
MWH .... Manitoba Hydro, Winnipeg, Manitoba [*Library symbol*] [*National Library of Canada*] (NLC)
MWH .... Megawatt Hour [*Electric utility company*]
Mwh .... Megawatt Hour
MWh .... Megawatt-Hour (MCD)
MW(H) ...... Megawatts (Heat) (IEEE)
MWH .... Milliwatt Hour
MWH .... Model Wave Height

MWH........ Mokuaweoweo [*Hawaii*] [*Seismograph station code, US Geological Survey*] (SEIS)
MWH........ Moses Lake [*Washington*] [*Airport symbol*] (OAG)
MWHB....... Hudson's Bay House, Winnipeg, Manitoba [*Library symbol*] [*National Library of Canada*] (NLC)
MWhB....... Marine Biological Laboratory, Woods Hole, MA [*Library symbol*] [*Library of Congress*] (LCLS)
MWHD...... Maw's Warehouse and Delivery Service [*Common carrier symbol*]
MWHF....... Michigan Wildlife Habitat Foundation
MWHG...... Marine Wing Headquarters Group
MWHGL...... Multiple Wheel Heavy Gear Loading [*Aviation*]
MWHi....... Worcester Historical Society, Worcester, MA [*Library symbol*] [*Library of Congress*] (LCLS)
MWHL....... Madrigal-Wan Hai Line [*Common carrier symbol*]
MWhN....... United States National Marine Fisheries Service, Northeast Fisheries Center, Woods Hole, MA [*Library symbol*] [*Library of Congress*] (LCLS)
MWHO...... Manitoba Health Organizations, Winnipeg, Manitoba [*Library symbol*] [*National Library of Canada*] (NLC)
MWHP....... Information Resources Center, Manitoba Health, Winnipeg, Manitoba [*Library symbol*] [*National Library of Canada*] (NLC)
MWHQ...... Mobile War Headquarters (SAUS)
MWHR...... Henderson Regional Library, Winnipeg, Manitoba [*Library symbol*] [*National Library of Canada*] (NLC)
MWHS....... Library Services, Health Sciences Centre, Winnipeg, Manitoba [*Library symbol*] [*National Library of Canada*] (NLC)
MWHS....... Marine Wing Headquarters Squadron (NVT)
MWHS....... Micro Warehouse [*NASDAQ symbol*] (TTSB)
MWHS....... Micro Warehouse, Inc. [*NASDAQ symbol*] (SAG)
MWHS....... Modified Warhead Section (MCD)
MWHSC..... Manitoba Health Services Commission, Winnipeg, Manitoba [*Library symbol*] [*National Library of Canada*] (NLC)
MWHSDET... Marine Wing Headquarters Squadron Detachment (DNAB)
MWHT....... Miscellaneous Waste Holdup Tank [*Nuclear energy*] (NRCH)
MWHU...... Mitsui Warehouse [*Intermodal shipping container symbol*] (TVRC)
MWHX....... MarkWest Hydrocarbon, Inc. [*NASDAQ symbol*] (SAG)
MWHZ....... Merchandise Warehouse [*Federal Railroad Administration identification code*]
MWI......... Insurance Institute of Winnipeg, Manitoba [*Library symbol*] [*National Library of Canada*] (NLC)
MWI......... Malawi [*ANSI three-letter standard code*] (CNC)
MWI......... Mantle Width Index
MWI......... Many Worlds Interpretation [*Term coined by authors John Barrow and Frank Tipler in their book, "The Anthropic Cosmological Principle"*]
MWI......... Marinette, WI [*Amtrak Busline code*]
MWI......... Master Weavers Institute (EA)
MWI......... Measured Workload Index [*Aviation*]
MWI......... Medical Walk-in [*Medicine*] [*Clinic*] (EDAA)
MWI......... Medical Waste Incinerator (EEVL)
MWI......... Message-Waiting Indicator
MWI......... Missionary Women International (EA)
MWI......... Mobil Wax Isomerization [*Petroleum engineering*]
MWI......... Montserrat [*West Indies*] [*Seismograph station code, US Geological Survey*] (SEIS)
MWI......... Motor-Ways Inc., Des Moines IA [*STAC*]
MWI......... Municipal-Waste Incineration (ODA)
MWIA....... Medical Women's International Association [*See also AIFM*] [*Cologne, Federal Republic of Germany*] (EAIO)
MWIAP...... Prairie Regional Office, Parks Canada [*Bureau Regional des Pres, Parcs Canada*] Winnipeg, Manitoba [*Library symbol*] [*National Library of Canada*] (NLC)
MWIC....... Manitoba Department of Economic Development, Winnipeg, Manitoba [*Library symbol*] [*National Library of Canada*] (NLC)
MWiCA...... Sterling and Francine Clark Art Institute, Williamstown, MA [*Library symbol*] [*Library of Congress*] (LCLS)
MWIDE...... IDE Engineering Co., Winnipeg, Manitoba [*Library symbol*] [*National Library of Canada*] (NLC)
MWIE....... Indus Electronic, Winnipeg, Manitoba [*Library symbol*] [*National Library of Canada*] (NLC)
MWIF....... Ivan Franko Museum & Library, Winnipeg, Manitoba [*Library symbol*] [*National Library of Canada*] (NLC)
MWIFC...... Midwest Intercollegiate Football Conference (PSS)
MWIN....... Indian and Northern Affairs Canada [*Affaires Indiennes et du Nord Canada*],Winnipeg, Manitoba [*Library symbol*] [*National Library of Canada*] (BIB)
MWIP........ Mixed Waste Integrated Program [*Department of Energy*]
MWIR....... Medium-Wavelength Infrared
MWIR....... Midwave Infrared Sensor (MCD)
MWIR....... Mixed Waste Inventory Report [*Department of Energy*]
MWIS........ National Network of Minority Women in Science (EA)
MWIV........ Mean Wildlife Index Value [*Statistics*] (PDAA)
MWIVA...... Midwest Intercollegiate Volleyball Association (PSS)
MWiW....... Williams College, Williamstown, MA [*Library symbol*] [*Library of Congress*] (LCLS)
MWiW-C.... Williams College, Chapin Library, Williamstown, MA [*Library symbol*] [*Library of Congress*] (LCLS)
MWIZ........ Meijer Wines [*Federal Railroad Administration identification code*]
MWJ......... Canada Department of Justice [*Ministere de la Justice*] Winnipeg, Manitoba [*Library symbol*] [*National Library of Canada*] (NLC)
MWJ......... Matthews Ridge [*Guyana*] [*Airport symbol*] (OAG)
MWJC....... Marjorie Webster Junior College [*Washington, DC*]
MWJCAC.... Midwestern Junior College Athletic Conference (PSS)
MWJHS..... Jewish Historical Society of Western Canada, Winnipeg, Manitoba [*Library symbol*] [*National Library of Canada*] (NLC)
MWJP....... Jewish Public Library, Winnipeg, Manitoba [*Library symbol*] [*National Library of Canada*] (NLC)
MWK........ Kelvin High School, Winnipeg, Manitoba [*Library symbol*] [*National Library of Canada*] (NLC)
MWK........ Mill Work [*Technical drawings*]
MWK........ Milwaukee Land [*AMEX symbol*] (TTSB)
MWK........ Milwaukee Land Co. [*AMEX symbol*] (SPSG)
MWK........ Mount Airy, NC [*Location identifier*] [*FAA*] (FAAL)
MWL......... Law Society of Manitoba, Winnipeg, Manitoba [*Library symbol*] [*National Library of Canada*] (NLC)
MWL......... Mail-Well, Inc. [*NYSE symbol*] (SG)
MWL......... Malawi Women's League
MWL......... Mean Water Level
MWL......... Meteoric Water Line [*Geology*]
MWL......... Milled-Wood Lignin
mWL......... Milliwatt Logic
MWL......... Mineral Wells [*Texas*] [*Airport symbol*] (AD)
MWL......... Mineral Wells, TX [*Location identifier*] [*FAA*] (FAAL)
MWL......... Miniature Warning Light (HEAS)
MWL......... Minimum Wage Laws (OICC)
MWL......... Motor Water Lighter (ADA)
MWL......... Municipal Waste Leachate (GNE)
MWL......... Muslim World League (BJA)
MWL......... Mutual Welfare League (NADA)
MWLAE..... Millimeter Wave Large Antenna Experiment [*NASA*] (PDAA)
MWLCC..... Lutheran Council in Canada, Winnipeg, Manitoba [*Library symbol*] [*National Library of Canada*] (NLC)
MWLD....... Man Worn LASER Detector [*Assembly*] (MCD)
MWLD....... Man-Worn LASER Device [*Army*]
MWLDA..... Maine Wholesale Lobster Dealers Association [*Defunct*] (EA)
MWLG....... Midwest Women's Legal Group (EA)
MWLMV..... Maize White Line Mosaic Virus [*Plant pathology*]
MWLR....... Labour Research Library, Manitoba Department of Labour and Manpower, Winnipeg, Manitoba [*Library symbol*] [*National Library of Canada*] (NLC)
MWLS....... Faculty of Law, University of Manitoba, Winnipeg, Manitoba [*Library symbol*] [*National Library of Canada*] (NLC)
MWLT....... Modified Word Learning Test [*Medicine*] (EDAA)
MWLX....... Midwest Locomotive Leasing and Sales [*Private rail car owner code*]
MWLZ....... Madrigal-Wan Hai Lines [*Intermodal trailer symbol*]
MWM........ Maxwell-Wagner Mechanism [*Physics*]
MWM........ Medical Library, University of Manitoba, Winnipeg, Manitoba [*Library symbol*] [*National Library of Canada*] (NLC)
MWM........ Millimeter Wave Mixer
MWM........ Minskoff, Wiseman, Minskoff [*Program for the development of language abilities*]
MWM........ Mode-Woche-Muenchen [*Munich Fashion Week - International Fashion Fair*] [*Germany*] (TSPED)
MWM........ Moments with Meredith - Meredith Baxter-Birney Fan Club [*Defunct*] (EA)
MWM........ Morfee Wheel Manufacturing [*Vancouver Stock Exchange symbol*]
MWM........ Motif Window Manager [*Computer science*] (VLIE)
MWM........ Motoren Werke Mannheim [*Motors Works of Mannheim*] [*Automotive supplier*]
MWM........ Windom, MN [*Location identifier*] [*FAA*] (FAAL)
MWM........ Worcester Art Museum, Worcester, MA [*Library symbol*] [*Library of Congress*] (LCLS)
MWMA...... Manitoba Department of Municipal Affairs, Winnipeg, Manitoba [*Library symbol*] [*National Library of Canada*] (NLC)
MWMA...... Michigan Weights and Measures Association (EARSL)
MWMA...... Multiple Wine Merchants Association [*British*] (BI)
MWMA...... Municipal Waste Management Association (NTPA)
MWM & R... Metal-Working Machine and Robot
MWMBC.... Mennonite Brethren Bible College, Winnipeg, Manitoba [*Library symbol*] [*National Library of Canada*] (NLC)
MWMC...... M & W Manufacturing Company [*NCIC trailer make code*]
MWMC...... Metropolitan Waste Management Council [*Melbourne, Australia*]
MwMC....... Midwest Microfilm Service, Co., Springfield, IL [*Library symbol*] [*Library of Congress*] (LCLS)
MWMCA.... Michigan Women for Medical Control of Abortion (EA)
MWME...... Maclaren Engineering, Winnipeg, Manitoba [*Library symbol*] [*National Library of Canada*] (NLC)
MWMF...... Mixed Waste Management Facility [*Environmental science*] (COE)
MWMFB..... Middlewest Motor Freight Bureau
MWMFOC... Multiwavelength Multifield of View (SAUS)
MWMG...... Misericordia General Hospital, Winnipeg, Manitoba [*Library symbol*] [*National Library of Canada*] (NLC)
MWMH...... Winnipeg Municipal Hospital, Manitoba [*Library symbol*] [*National Library of Canada*] (NLC)
MWMHC.... Mennonite Heritage Centre, Winnipeg, Manitoba [*Library symbol*] [*National Library of Canada*] (NLC)
MWMM..... Manitoba Museum of Man & Nature, Winnipeg, Manitoba [*Library symbol*] [*National Library of Canada*] (NLC)
MWMMP.... Meadowood Manor Personal Care Home, Winnipeg, Manitoba [*Library symbol*] [*National Library of Canada*] (NLC)
MWMP...... City of Winnipeg Metro Planning Division, Manitoba [*Library symbol*] [*National Library of Canada*] (NLC)
MWMPE..... Manitoba Pool Elevators Library, Winnipeg, Manitoba [*Library symbol*] [*National Library of Canada*] (NLC)
MWMR...... Multiple Write, Multiple Read (SAUS)
MWMRC.... Manitoba Research Council, Winnipeg, Manitoba [*Library symbol*] [*National Library of Canada*] (NLC)
MWMRTL... Milliwatt Motorola Resistor Transistor Logic (IAA)
MWMS...... Mid-West Motor Service Company of Illinois [*Common carrier symbol*]
MWMSE..... Minimum-Weighted Mean Square Error (IAA)

MWMT ...... Metal-Working Machine Tool
MWMT ...... Mint with Mint Tag [*Collectibles*]
MWMT ...... Monotonic Word Memory Test [*Medicine*] (EDAA)
MWMTC..... Manitoba Theater Center, Winnipeg, Manitoba [*Library symbol*] [*National Library of Canada*] (NLC)
MWMTS..... Manitoba Teachers Socity, Winnipeg, Manitoba [*Library symbol*] [*National Library of Canada*] (NLC)
MWMU ...... University of Massachusetts, Medical Center, Worcester, MA [*Library symbol*] [*Library of Congress*] (LCLS)
MWn......... GAR Memorial Library, West Newbury, MA [*Library symbol*] [*Library of Congress*] (LCLS)
MWN .... Gordon College, Wenham, MA [*Inactive*] [*OCLC symbol*] (OCLC)
MWN .... Madras Weekly Notes [*India*] [*A publication*] (DLA)
MWN .... Medical World News [*Medicine*] [*Journal*] (EDAA)
MWN .... Message Waiting Notification (SAUS)
MWN .... Mount Washington, NH [*Location identifier*] [*FAA*] (FAAL)
MWNCC..... Madras Weekly Notes, Criminal Cases [*India*] [*A publication*] (DLA)
MWNR ...... Missouri Women's Network (EARSL)
MWNT....... Multi-Walled Carbon Nanotube
MWNT....... Multiwalled Nanotube [*Materials science*]
MWNT....... Multiwall Nanotube [*Materials science*]
MWO .... Maintenance Work Order
MWO .... Manufacturing Work Order
MWO .... Master Warrant Officer [*Canadian Forces, since 1964*]
MWO .... Master Work Order (AAG)
MWO .... Mental Welfare Officer [*British*]
MWO .... Meteorological Watch Office (ODA)
MWO .... Middletown, OH [*Location identifier*] [*FAA*] (FAAL)
MWO .... Millimeter Wavelength Oscillator
MWO .... Millimeter Wave Observatory [*University of Texas at Austin*] [*Research center*] (RCD)
MWO .... Modification Work Order
MWO .... Mount Wilson Observatory (NADA)
MWO .... Rev. Peres Oblats, Winnipeg, Manitoba [*Library symbol*] [*National Library of Canada*] (NLC)
MWo......... Woburn Public Library, Woburn, MA [*Library symbol*] [*Library of Congress*] (LCLS)
MWOA....... Mizrachi Women's Organization of America [*Later, AMW*] (EA)
MWOC....... Mothers without Custody (EA)
MWOFP..... Modification Work Order Fielding Plan
MWolIE..... Eastern Nazarene College, Wollaston, MA [*Library symbol*] [*Library of Congress*] (LCLS)
MWOP....... Mixed Waste Office Paper [*Pulp and paper technology*]
MWOT....... Master Warrant Officer Training [*DoD*]
MWOU ...... Midwest Ocean Lines [*Intermodal shipping container symbol*] (TVRC)
MWP .... Kala Lagaw Ya [*Language symbol*] (ETLW)
MWP .... Legislative Library of Manitoba, Winnipeg, Manitoba [*Library symbol*] [*National Library of Canada*] (NLC)
MWP .... Malta Workers Party [*Political party*] (PPE)
MWP .... Maneuvering Work Platform [*NASA*]
MWP .... Mangla [*Pakistan*] [*Airport symbol*] (AD)
MWP .... Master of Welfare Policy
MWP .... Maximum Working Pressure
MWP .... Mean Wedge Pressure (DMAA)
MWP .... Mechanical Wood Pulp [*Paper*]
MWP .... Medieval Warm Period [*Geoscience*]
MWP .... Membrane Waterproofing
MWP .... Metabolic Waste Production
MWP .... Meteorological Weather Processor (GAVI)
MWP .... Meteorologist Weather Processor [*FAA*] (TAG)
MWP .... Mexican Water Plan [*Land use*]
MWP .... Midwest Processing [*Federal Railroad Administration identification code*]
MWP .... Millimeter Wave Propagation
MWP .... Ministry of Works and Planning [*British*]
MWP .... Missile Warning Position (MCD)
MWP .... Mixed Waste Project (ABAC)
MWP .... Momentum Wheel Platform (ACAE)
MWP .... Most Worthy Patriarch
MWP .... Worcester Polytechnic Institute, Worcester, MA [*Library symbol*] [*Library of Congress*] (LCLS)
MWPA....... Married Women's Property Act [*1882*] [*British*] (AIA)
MWPA....... Provincial Archives of Manitoba, Winnipeg, Manitoba [*Library symbol*] [*National Library of Canada*] (NLC)
MWPC....... Moorepark Whey Protein Concentrate (OA)
MWPC....... Multiple Wire Proportional Counter
MWPC....... Multiwire Proportional Chamber (IAA)
MWPCPA.... Archaeology Subsection Office, Prairie Region Library, Parks Canada [*Recherches Archeologiques, Bibliotheque de la Region des Pres, Parcs Canada*] Winnipeg, Manitoba [*Library symbol*] [*National Library of Canada*] (NLC)
MWPCPH ... Historic Resources Conservation Subsection Office, Prairie Region Library, ParksCanada [*Ressources et Conservation Historiques, Bibliotheque de la Region de s Pres, Parcs Canada*] Winnipeg, Manitoba [*Library symbol*] [*National Library of Canada*] (NLC)
MWPCR..... Riding Mountain National Park, Parks Canada [*Parc National Riding Mountain, Parcs Canada*] Wasagaming, Manitoba [*Library symbol*] [*National Library of Canada*] (NLC)
MWPE....... Mental Workload and Performance (SAUS)
MWPF....... Marine Wildlife Preservation Fund
MWPI....... Munson-Williams-Proctor Institute [*Utica, NY*]
MWPL....... Public Library Services, Manitoba Department of Culture, Heritage and Recreation, Winnipeg, Manitoba [*Library symbol*] [*National Library of Canada*] (NLC)
MWPNR..... Park Management Library, Manitoba Department of Natural Resources, Winnipeg, Manitoba [*Library symbol*] [*National Library of Canada*] (NLC)
MWPO....... Mine Warfare Project Office [*Naval Material Command*]
MWpP....... Westport Free Public Library, Westport, MA [*Library symbol*] [*Library of Congress*] (LCLS)
MWPPH..... Provincial Public Health Nursing Services, Winnipeg, Manitoba [*Library symbol*] [*National Library of Canada*] (NLC)
MWPR....... Monthly Work Package Report [*NASA*] (NASA)
MWPS....... Manitoba Probation Services, Winnipeg, Manitoba [*Library symbol*] [*National Library of Canada*] (NLC)
MWPS....... Master of Wood and Paper Science (GAGS)
MWPS....... Multimeter Wave Power Source
MWQ .... Magwe [*Myanmar*] [*Airport symbol*] (OAG)
MWQ .... Quinsigamond Community College, Worcester, MA [*Library symbol*] [*Library of Congress*] (LCLS)
MWQCG..... Media and Information Services, Quadraplegic Communications Group, Inc., Winnipeg, Manitoba [*Library symbol*] [*National Library of Canada*] (NLC)
MWR .... Magnetic Tape Write [*Computer science*] (VLIE)
MWR .... Maintenance Work Request [*or Requirement*]
MWR .... Man-Worn Receiver (MCD)
mwr......... Marwari [*MARC language code*] [*Library of Congress*] (LCCP)
MWR .... Mean Width Ratio
MWR .... Metal Whisker Reinforcement
MWR .... Method of Weighted Residual
MWR .... Microwave Radiation (MELL)
MWR .... Microwave Radiometer (CARB)
MWR .... Midwest Resources Inc. (EFIS)
MWR .... Millimeter-Wave Radar (DOMA)
MWR .... Mine Warfare Range (SAUS)
MWR .... Mine Watching RADAR (NATG)
MWR .... Mini Web Reel (DGA)
MWR .... Missile-Warning Receiver (MCD)
MWR .... Morale, Welfare, and Recreation [*DoD*]
MWR .... Mountain-West Resources [*Vancouver Stock Exchange symbol*]
MWR .... Mower
MWR .... Muncie & Western Railroad Co. [*AAR code*]
MWR .... Royal Winnipeg Ballet, Manitoba [*Library symbol*] [*National Library of Canada*] (NLC)
MWRA....... Master of Water Resources Administration (PGP)
MWRA....... Morale, Welfare, and Recreation Activity [*DoD*] (AFIT)
MWRAILS... Microwave Remote Area Instrument Landing System (IAA)
MWRC....... Maintain Well to Right of Course [*Aviation*] (FAAC)
MWRC....... Melbourne Western Region Commission [*Australia*]
MWRC....... Mount Washington Railway Co. [*AAR code*]
MWRC....... RCMP [*Royal Canadian Mounted Police*] Crime Laboratory, Winnipeg, Manitoba [*Library symbol*] [*National Library of Canada*] (NLC)
MWRCC..... Roman Catholic Chancery Office, Winnipeg, Manitoba [*Library symbol*] [*National Library of Canada*] (NLC)
MWRK....... Mothers Work [*NASDAQ symbol*] (TTSB)
MWRK....... Mothers Work, Inc. [*NASDAQ symbol*] (SAG)
MWRL....... Molalla Western Railway [*Federal Railroad Administration identification code*]
MWRN ...... Midwest Transport [*Common carrier symbol*]
MWroxV..... United States Veterans Administration Hospital, West Roxbury, MA [*Library symbol*] [*Library of Congress*] (LCLS)
MWRR ...... Learning Resources Centre, Red River Community College, Winnipeg, Manitoba [*Library symbol*] [*National Library of Canada*] (NLC)
MWRR ...... Montana Western Railway [*Federal Railroad Administration identification code*]
MWRRC..... Montana Water Resources Research Center [*Montana State University, University ofMontana, and Montana College of Mineral Science and Technology*] [*Research center*] (RCD)
MWRRL..... Library Technician Program, Red River Community College, Winnipeg, Manitoba, LS [*National Library of Canada*] (NLC)
MWRS....... Millimeter Wave Radio System (MCD)
MWRS....... Richardson Securities of Canada, Winnipeg, Manitoba [*Library symbol*] [*National Library of Canada*] (NLC)
MWRT....... Mobile Wing Reconnaissance Technical [*Squadron*]
mWRTL ..... Milliwatt Resistor-Transistor Logic (IDOE)
MWRX....... Midwest Rail Holding [*Private rail car owner code*]
MWRY....... Mineral Wells & Eastern Railway [*Federal Railroad Administration identification code*]
MWRZ....... Metropolitan Water Reclamation District [*Federal Railroad Administration identification code*]
MWS .... Major Weapon System [*Manager*] (MCD)
MWS .... Mallory-Weiss Syndrome [*Medicine*] (MELL)
MWS .... Management Work Station (BUR)
MWS .... Manned Weapons Station (ACAE)
MWS .... Marden-Walker Syndrome [*Medicine*] (DMAA)
MWS .... Marine Weather Service (NOAA)
MWS .... Master of Women's Studies (PGP)
MWS .... Master Warning System (SAUS)
MWS .... Mawashi [*Ryukyu Islands*] [*Seismograph station code, US Geological Survey*] [*Closed*] (SEIS)
MWS .... Maximum Wind Speed
MWS .... Medium Wide Shot [*Photography*]
MWS .... Megawatt Waveguide Switch
MWS .... Member of the Wernerian Society [*British*] (ROG)
MWS .... Meridional Wind Stress (SAUS)
MWS .... Microwave Scatterometer [*Telecommunications*] (TEL)
MWS .... Microwave Station
MWS .... Microwave Wind Spectrometer

MWS .... Mikity-Wilson Syndrome [*Neonatology*] (DAVI)
MWS .... Mini Weapon Sight (SAUS)
MWS .... Mini-Weapon Sight [*Police and security equipment*]
MWS .... Mini Workstation (SSD)
MWS .... Missile Warning Set (SAUS)
MWS .... Missile Warning Squadron
MWS .... Missile Warning System (SAUS)
MWS .... Missile Weapon System [*Military*] (CAAL)
MWS .... Missouri Western State College, St. Joseph, MO [*OCLC symbol*] (OCLC)
MWS .... Mobile Weapon System
MWS .... Modular Weapons System (MCD)
MWS .... Modular Workstation (SAUS)
MWS .... Moersch-Woltman Syndrome [*Medicine*] (DMAA)
MWS .... Molecular Wake Shield (SAUS)
MWS .... Most Wise Sovereign [*Freemasonry*]
MWS .... Most Worshipful Scribe [*Freemasonry*] (ROG)
MWS .... Mount Wilson, CA [*Location identifier*] [*FAA*] (FAAL)
MWS .... Muckle-Wells Syndrome [*Medicine*] (MELL)
MWS .... Multiwork Station
MWSA .... Michigan Women's Studies Association (EARSL)
MWSA .... St. Andrew's College, Winnipeg, Manitoba [*Library symbol*] [*National Library of Canada*] (NLC)
MWSAC ..... St. Amant Center, Winnipeg, Manitoba [*Library symbol*] [*National Library of Canada*] (NLC)
MWSACB ... Salvation Army Catherine Booth Bible College, Winnipeg, Manitoba [*Library symbol*] [*National Library of Canada*] (BIB)
MWSB .... Saint Boniface Public Library, Winnipeg, Manitoba [*Library symbol*] [*National Library of Canada*] (NLC)
MWSBM .... Saint Boniface General Hospital Medical Library, Winnipeg, Manitoba [*Library symbol*] [*National Library of Canada*] (NLC)
MWSBN ..... Saint Boniface General Hospital School of Nursing Library, Winnipeg, Manitoba [*Library symbol*] [*National Library of Canada*] (NLC)
MWSC .... American Men and Women of Science [*Database*] [*R. R. Bowker Co.*] [*Information service or system*] (CRD)
MWSC .... Midwest Cargo Systems [*Common carrier symbol*]
MWSC .... Midwestern Simulation Council
MWSC .... Mine Warfare Support Centre (SAUS)
MWSC .... Mine Warfare Systems Centre (SAUS)
MWSC .... Society for Manitobans with Disabilities, Inc., Winnipeg, Manitoba [*Library symbol*] [*National Library of Canada*] (NLC)
MWSCS ..... Midwestern Signal Corps School
MWSD .... Missile and Weapons Systems Division [*Military*] (IAA)
MWSD .... Teachers' Library and Resource Centre, Winnipeg School Division No. 1, Manitoba [*Library symbol*] [*National Library of Canada*] (NLC)
MWSE .... Midwest Stock Exchange, Inc. (HGAA)
MWSF .... Molecular Wake Shield Facility (SAUS)
MWSG .... Marine Wing Support Group (NVT)
MWSGDET ... Marine Wing Support Group Detachment (DNAB)
MWSGR ..... Marine Wing Staff Ground (MCD)
MWSH .... Worcester State Hospital, Worcester, MA [*Library symbol*] [*Library of Congress*] (LCLS)
MWSJ .... St. John's College, Winnipeg, Manitoba [*Library symbol*] [*National Library of Canada*] (NLC)
MWSM .... Stony Mountain Institution Library, Winnipeg, Manitoba [*Library symbol*] [*National Library of Canada*] (NLC)
MWSOGH ... Educational Services, Seven Oaks General Hospital, Winnipeg, Manitoba [*Library symbol*] [*National Library of Canada*] (NLC)
MWSP .... St. Paul's College, Winnipeg, Manitoba [*Library symbol*] [*National Library of Canada*] (NLC)
MWSPA ..... Spiece Associates, Winnipeg, Manitoba [*Library symbol*] [*National Library of Canada*] (NLC)
MWSPC ..... Social Planning Council of Winnipeg, Manitoba [*Library symbol*] [*National Library of Canada*] (NLC)
MW Sprg ... Mid-West Spring Manufacturing Co. [*Associated Press*] (SAG)
MWSR .... Magnetic Wire Shift Register
MWSR .... Microwave Water Substance Radiometer [*Marine science*] (OSRA)
MWSRA ..... Midwest Winter Sports Representatives Association (EARSL)
MWSS .... Manitoba Regional Library, Secretary of State Canada [*Bibliotheque Regionale du Manitoba, Secretariat d'Etat*], Winnipeg, Manitoba [*Library symbol*] [*National Library of Canada*] (NLC)
MWSS .... Marine Wing Support Squadron [*Navy*] (ANA)
MWSS .... Metropolitan Waterworks and Sewerage System [*Philippines*]
MWSS .... Metwork Six [*NASDAQ symbol*] (TTSB)
MWSS .... Mid-West Spring Manufacturing Co. [*NASDAQ symbol*] (SAG)
MWSS .... Millimeter Wave Signal Source (ACAE)
MWSSE ..... Mid-West Spring Mfg [*NASDAQ symbol*] (TTSB)
MWSSP ..... Maned Wolf Species Survival Plan [*Smithsonian Institution*] (RCD)
MWST .... Martco Waste System Equipment [*NCIC trailer make code*]
MWST .... Mean Weighted Skin Temperature
MWST .... Miscellaneous Waste Storage Tank [*Nuclear energy*] (NRCH)
MWST .... Missile Warning System Test (MCD)
MWSV .... St. Vital Public Library, Winnipeg, Manitoba [*Library symbol*] [*National Library of Canada*] (NLC)
MWT .... Maintenance of Wakefulness Test (MELL)
MWT .... Makeup Water Treatment (IEEE)
MWT .... Malpositioned Wisdom Teeth [*Medicine*] (EDAA)
MWT .... Marconi Wireless Telegraph [*Telecommunications*] (IAA)
MWT .... Master of Wood Technology
MWT .... Maximum Walking Time (on treadmill) [*Medicine*] (EDAA)
MWT .... McWhorter Technologies, Inc. [*NYSE symbol*] (SAG)
MWT .... Mean Water Temperature
MWT .... Medium Wheeled Tractor (SAUS)
MWT .... Megawatt Thermal [*Nuclear energy*] (NRCH)
MWT .... Michigan Walleye Tour
MWT .... Midwest Aviation [*Southwest Aviation, Inc.*] [*ICAO designator*] (FAAC)
MWT .... Millimeter Wave Technology (ACAE)
MWT .... Millimeter Wave Tube
MWT .... Ministry of War Transport [*Terminated, 1956*] [*British*]
MWt .... Molecular Weight [*Also, M, MOL WT, MW*] (AAMN)
MWT .... Monitor Wafer Turner (AAEL)
MWT .... Moolawatana [*Australia*] [*Airport symbol*] [*Obsolete*] (OAG)
MWT .... Mountain War Time
MWT .... Myocardial Wall Thickness [*Cardiology*] (DMAA)
Mwt .... Thermal Megawatt [*Also, TMW*]
MWT .... Winnipeg Tribune, Manitoba [*Library symbol*] [*National Library of Canada*] (NLC)
MWTA .... Airworthiness Library, Central Region, Transport Canada [*Bibliotheque de la Navigabilite Aerienne, Region Centrale, Transports Canada*], Winnipeg, Manitoba [*Library symbol*] [*National Library of Canada*] (NLC)
MWTA .... Medical Waste Tracking Act [*1988*] (FFDE)
MWTA .... Medical Waste Treatment Act
MWTC .... Ministry of War Time Communications [*British*] [*World War II*]
MWTC .... Teshmount Consultants, Winnipeg, Manitoba [*Library symbol*] [*National Library of Canada*] (NLC)
M-WTCA .... Mid-West Tool Collectors Association (EA)
MWTCR ..... Central Regional Library, Transport Canada [*Bibliotheque Regionale du Centre,Transports Canada*], Winnipeg, Manitoba [*Library symbol*] [*National Library of Canada*] (NLC)
MWTCS ..... Modernized Weather Teletypewriter Communications System (FAAC)
MWTE .... Interdisciplinary Engineering, Winnipeg, Manitoba [*Library symbol*] [*National Library of Canada*] (NLC)
MWTE .... Modern Weapons Training Exercises (MCD)
MWTGM .... Milimeter Wage Terminal Guided Missile (ACAE)
MW(th) ...... Megawatts (Thermal)
MWTHA ..... Michigan Wild Turkey Hunters Association
MWTP .... Mixed Waste Treatment Project
MWTR .... Mean Waiting Time for Supply Replacement (DNAB)
MWTR .... Monthly Wholesale Trade Report [*A publication*]
MWTS .... Manitoba Telephone System, Winnipeg, Manitoba [*Library symbol*] [*National Library of Canada*] (NLC)
MWTS .... Midwest Transit Service [*Common carrier symbol*]
MWTS .... Millimeter Wave Transmitting Subsystem (ACAE)
MWTS .... Monthly Wholesale Trade Survey (SAUS)
MWTU .... Marble Workers' Trade Union [*British*]
MWU .... Maccabi World Union [*Ramat Gan, Israel*] (EAIO)
MWU .... Mercer University, Southern School of Pharmacy, Atlanta, GA [*OCLC symbol*] (OCLC)
MWU .... Merriam-Webster Unabridged [*A publication*]
MWU .... Mine Workers Union [*South Africa*] (IMH)
MWU .... Modified Wohlgemuth Unit [*Of hydrolytic enzyme activity*]
MWU .... Mussau [*Papua New Guinea*] [*Airport symbol*] (OAG)
MWU .... University of Manitoba, Winnipeg, Manitoba [*Library symbol*] [*National Library of Canada*] (NLC)
MWUA .... Ukrainian Academy of Arts and Science, Winnipeg, Manitoba [*Library symbol*] [*National Library of Canada*] (NLC)
MWUAF ..... Architecture and Fine Arts Library, University of Manitoba, Winnipeg, Manitoba [*Library symbol*] [*National Library of Canada*] (NLC)
MWUC .... University of Winnipeg, Manitoba [*Library symbol*] [*National Library of Canada*] (NLC)
MWUCE ..... Ukrainian Cultural and Educational Centre, Winnipeg, Manitoba [*Library symbol*] [*National Library of Canada*] (NLC)
MWUD .... Dental Library, University of Manitoba, Winnipeg, Manitoba [*Library symbol*] [*National Library of Canada*] (NLC)
MWUG .... Department of Geography, University of Manitoba, Winnipeg, Manitoba [*Library symbol*] [*National Library of Canada*] (NLC)
MWUGG ..... United Grain Growers, Winnipeg, Manitoba [*Library symbol*] [*National Library of Canada*] (NLC)
MWUM .... Map and Atlas Collection, University of Manitoba, Winnipeg, Manitoba [*Library symbol*] [*National Library of Canada*] (NLC)
MWUML ..... Underwood McLellan Ltd., Winnipeg, Manitoba [*Library symbol*] [*National Library of Canada*] (NLC)
MWUSA ..... Minute Women of the United States of America (EA)
MWV .... Maximum Working Voltage [*Electronics*]
MWV .... Meadwestvaco [*Company symbol*]
MWV .... Mexican War Veteran
MWV .... Milkweed Virus
MWV .... Minor War Vessels (SAUS)
MWV .... Modulated Wavy Vortex [*Fluid mechanics*]
MWV .... Motor Tariff Bureau of West Virginia, Charleston WV [*STAC*]
MWV .... Multifit Weapons Vehicle (SAUS)
MWVCO ..... Microwave Voltage Controlled Oscillator
MWVGH ..... Victoria General Hospital, Winnipeg, Manitoba [*Library symbol*] [*National Library of Canada*] (NLC)
MWVP .... Minor War Vessels Programme (SAUS)
MWVS .... Branch Library, Manitoba Veterinarian Services, Winnipeg, Manitoba [*Library symbol*] [*National Library of Canada*] (NLC)
MWVS .... Mission Weapon Visionics System (SAUS)
MWW .... Majestic Wine Warehouses [*Commercial firm*] [*British*]
MWW .... Manual Wire Wrap
MWW .... Mark's Work Wearhouse Ltd. [*Toronto Stock Exchange symbol*]
MWW .... Marquis Who's Who [*Marquis Who's Who, Inc.*] [*Information service or system*] [*A publication*]
MWW .... Mastering the Wired World (EURO)
MWW .... [*The*] Merry Wives of Windsor [*Shakespearean work*] (BARN)
MWW .... Municipal Wastewater
MWW .... William Ave. Branch, Winnipeg Public Library, Manitoba [*Library symbol*] [*National Library of Canada*] (NLC)

MWW .... Worcester State College, Worcester, MA [*Library symbol*] [*Library of Congress*] (LCLS)
MWWA ...... Winnipeg Art Gallery, Manitoba [*Library symbol*] [*National Library of Canada*] (NLC)
MWWC ...... Military Weather Warning Center (NOAA)
MWWC ...... Winnipeg Clinic, Manitoba [*Library symbol*] [*National Library of Canada*] (NLC)
MWWF ...... Manual Wire Wrap Fixture
MWWII ...... Mothers of World War II
MWWK ...... West Kildonan Public Library, Winnipeg, Manitoba [*Library symbol*] [*National Library of Canada*] (NLC)
MWWLW .... W. L. Wardrop & Associates, Winnipeg, Manitoba [*Library symbol*] [*National Library of Canada*] (NLC)
MWWR ...... Water Resources Division, Manitoba Department of Natural Resources, Winnipeg, Manitoba [*Library symbol*] [*National Library of Canada*] (NLC)
MWWSH .... Manitoba Workplace Safety and Health Division, Winnipeg, Manitoba [*Library symbol*] [*National Library of Canada*] (NLC)
MWWU ...... Marine Wing Weapon Unit
MWWV ...... Movement of Working Women and Volunteers [*Tel Aviv, Israel*] (EAIO)
MWX .... Montpelier, VT [*Location identifier*] [*FAA*] (FAAL)
MWY .... Midway Games, Inc. [*NYSE symbol*] (SAG)
MWY .... Miranda Downs [*Australia*] [*Airport symbol*] [*Obsolete*] (OAG)
MWYE .... Megawatt Year of Electricity (IAA)
MWyr .... Megawatt-Year (ABAC)
MWZ .... Mwanza [*Tanzania*] [*Airport symbol*] (OAG)
MX .... Compania Mexicana de Aviacion [*ICAO designator*] (OAG)
MX .... Magnavox (SAUS)
MX .... Mail Exchange [*Computer science*]
mx .... Management (DAVI)
MX .... Master Agility Excellent
MX .... Matrix (BUR)
Mx .... Maxwell [*Unit of magnetic flux*] [*Also, abWb*]
MX .... Measurex Corp. [*NYSE symbol*] (SPSG)
MX .... Metaxylene
MX .... Methanex Corp. [*Toronto Stock Exchange symbol*] [*Canada*]
MX .... Mexicana [*Airline*] (DS)
MX .... Mexicana de Aviacion [*ICAO designator*] (AD)
MX .... Mexican L & P Co. Ltd. [*Toronto Stock Exchange symbol*]
MX .... Mexico [*ANSI two-letter standard code*] (CNC)
mx .... Mexico [*IYRU nationality code*] [*MARC country of publication code*] [*Library of Congress*] (LCCP)
MX .... Middlesex [*Region of London*]
MX .... Missile, Experimental
MX .... Mix
MX .... Motocross (WGA)
MX .... Multiple Address
mx .... Multiplex (NAKS)
MX .... Multiplex [*or Multiplexer*]
MX .... Murexide [*An indicator*] [*Chemistry*]
MX .... Mutually Exclusive (ACAE)
MX .... Peacekeeper Missile (SAUS)
MXA .... Compania Mexicana de Aviacion SA [*Mexico*] [*ICAO designator*] (FAAC)
MXA .... Manila, AR [*Location identifier*] [*FAA*] (FAAL)
MXA .... Minnesota Municipal Income Portfolio [*AMEX symbol*] (SPSG)
MXA .... Minnesota Muni Inc. Portfolio [*AMEX symbol*] (TTSB)
MXA .... Mobile Exercise Area [*Military*] (NVT)
MXA .... Oaxaca Noroeste Mixteco [*Language symbol*] (ETLW)
MXAL .... Mercury Xenon Arc Lamp
MXB .... Masamba [*Indonesia*] [*Airport symbol*] (OAG)
MXB .... Medix Resources [*AMEX symbol*] (SG)
MXB .... Multimedia Extension Board (SAUS)
MXBIF ...... MFC Bancorp Ltd. [*NASDAQ symbol*]
MXC .... Maintenance [*Telegraphy*] (PCTE)
MXC .... MATEC Corp. [*AMEX symbol*] (SPSG)
MXC .... Maxon Computer Systems, Inc. [*Toronto Stock Exchange symbol*]
MXC .... Mexair SA [*Switzerland*] [*ICAO designator*] (FAAC)
MXC .... Monticello [*Utah*] [*Airport symbol*] (OAG)
MXC .... Multimedia Extension Connector (SAUS)
MXC .... Multiplexer Channel [*Computer science*]
MXC .... University of Cincinnati, Medical Center, Cincinnati, OH [*OCLC symbol*] (OCLC)
MxChGS ..... Church of Jesus Christ of Latter-Day Saints, Genealogical Society Library, Colonia Juarez Branch, Chihuahua, Mexico [*Library symbol*] [*Library of Congress*] (LCLS)
MXCPEC .... Mexico National Committee for Pacific Economic Cooperation
MXD .... Marion Downs [*Queensland*] [*Airport symbol*] (AD)
MXD .... Maximum-Latewood-Density
MXD .... Mixed
mxd .... Mixed
MXD .... Mixed Artillery [*Military*] (VNW)
MXD .... Mixed Use Development (PA)
MXD .... Multiple Transmitter Duplicator
MXDA .... Meta-Xylenediamine [*Organic chemistry*]
MXD CL ..... Mixed Carload [*Freight*]
MXDCR ...... Mode Transducer (MSA)
MXDL .... Micro Xenon Driving Lamp [*Automotive engineering*]
MXDTH ...... Maximum Depth (NOAA)
MXDY .... Maximum Dynamics [*OTCBB symbol*]
MXE .... Excision of Myoma [*Medicine*] (EDAA)
MXE .... Manx Airlines (Europe) Ltd. [*British*] [*ICAO designator*] (FAAC)
MXE .... Mexico Eqty & Income Fd [*NYSE symbol*] (TTSB)
MXE .... Mexico Equity & Income Fund [*NYSE symbol*] (SPSG)
MXE .... Modena, PA [*Location identifier*] [*FAA*] (FAAL)
MXF .... Mexico Fund [*NYSE symbol*] (TTSB)
MXF .... [*The*] Mexico Fund, Inc. [*NYSE symbol*] (SPSG)
MXF .... Montgomery, AL [*Location identifier*] [*FAA*] (FAAL)
MXFL .... Mixed Flow
MXG .... Mixing (MSA)
MxGuBF ..... Biblioteca Benjamin Franklin, Guadalajara, Mexico [*Library symbol*] [*Library of Congress*] (LCLS)
MXIC .... Macronix International Co., Ltd. [*NASDAQ symbol*] (NASQ)
MXIC .... MX Information Center [*Defunct*] (EA)
MXICY ...... Macronix Intl ADR [*NASDAQ symbol*] (TTSB)
MXIM .... Maxim Integrated Prod [*NASDAQ symbol*] (TTSB)
MXIM .... Maxim Integrated Products, Inc. [*NASDAQ symbol*] (NQ)
MXIS .... Maxis, Inc. [*NASDAQ symbol*] (SAG)
MXK .... Camp Springs, MD [*Location identifier*] [*FAA*] (FAAL)
MXK .... Metekel [*Ethiopia*] [*Airport symbol*] (AD)
MXK .... Multiple-Frequency X- and K-Band
MXL .... Maxi Gbe [*Language symbol*] (ETLW)
MXL .... Mexicali [*Mexico*] [*Airport symbol*] (OAG)
MXL .... Mixed Workload [*Computer science*] (PCM)
MXLU .... Malcolm X Liberation University
MXLU .... Mexican Line [*Common carrier symbol*]
MXM .... Matrix Memory (MHDI)
MXM .... Maximum (ADA)
MXM .... MAXXAM, Inc. [*AMEX symbol*] (SPSG)
MXM .... Morombe [*Madagascar*] [*Airport symbol*] (OAG)
MxMBF ...... Biblioteca Benjamin Franklin, Mexico City, Mexico [*Library symbol*] [*Library of Congress*] (LCLS)
MxMBN ..... Biblioteca Nacional de Mexico, Mexico City, Mexico [*Library symbol*] [*Library of Congress*] (LCLS)
MxMC .... Centro de Investigacion y de Estudios Avanzados, Instituto Politecnico Nacional,Mexico City, Mexico [*Library symbol*] [*Library of Congress*] (LCLS)
MxMCM ..... Colegio de Mexico, Mexico, Mexico City, Mexico [*Library symbol*] [*Library of Congress*] (LCLS)
MXMF .... Maximum Freight Systems [*Common carrier symbol*]
MxMGS ..... Church of Jesus Christ of Latter-Day Saints, Genealogical Society Library, Mexico City Branch, Mexico City, Mexico [*Library symbol*] [*Library of Congress*] (LCLS)
MxMI .... Universidad Iberoamericana, Mexico [*Library symbol*] [*Library of Congress*] (LCLS)
MX/MM ..... Missile X/Minuteman Missile
MxMoT ...... Instituto Tecnologico y de Estudios Superiores de Monterrey, Monterrey, Mexico [*Library symbol*] [*Library of Congress*] (LCLS)
MX/MPS .... Missile X [*Deploy In*] Multiple Protective Shelters
MXN .... Maintain [*Telegraphy*] (PCTE)
MxN .... Maxillary Nerve [*Neuroanatomy*]
MXN .... Morlaix [*France*] [*Airport symbol*] (OAG)
MXND .... Maintained [*Telegraphy*] (PCTE)
MXNG .... Maintaining [*Telegraphy*] (PCTE)
MX-NM ...... Matrix - National Module
MXO .... Maxtor [*Company symbol*]
MXO .... Monticello, IA [*Location identifier*] [*FAA*] (FAAL)
MXP .... MaxPharma, Inc. [*AMEX symbol*] (COMM)
MXP .... May Air Xpress, Inc. [*ICAO designator*] (FAAC)
MXP .... Mesa, Inc. [*NYSE symbol*] (SAG)
MXP .... Milan [*Italy*] Malpensa Airport [*Airport symbol*] (OAG)
MXPC .... Maritime Express [*Common carrier symbol*]
MXPE .... Metro Area Express [*Common carrier symbol*]
MXPS .... Magnum Xpress [*Common carrier symbol*]
MXPST ...... Maximum Possible Storm (NOAA)
MXQ .... Modular X-Ray Quantometer
MXQ .... Wilmington, OH [*Location identifier*] [*FAA*] (FAAL)
MXR .... Mask Index Register
MXR .... Mass X-Ray
MXR .... Merrix Air Ltd. [*British*] [*ICAO designator*] (FAAC)
MXR .... Mixer (MSA)
MXR .... Moussoro [*Chad*] [*Airport symbol*] (AD)
MXR .... Raton, NM [*Location identifier*] [*FAA*] (FAAL)
MXRAN ...... Maximum Rainfall (NOAA)
M-X/RES .... M-X [*Missile*] Renewable Energy System
MXRV .... Middlesex Rifle Volunteers [*Military*] [*British*] (DMA)
MXS .... Max Minerals, Inc. [*Vancouver Stock Exchange symbol*]
MXS .... Maxus Energy Corp. [*NYSE symbol*] (SPSG)
MXS .... Mixes [*Telegraphy*] (PCTE)
MXSBP ...... Maxus Energy [*NASDAQ symbol*] (SAG)
MXSBP ...... Maxus Energy $4 Cv Pfd [*NASDAQ symbol*] (TTSB)
MXSPrA ..... Maxus Energy $2.50 Pfd [*NYSE symbol*] (TTSB)
MXSV .... Maxserv, Inc. [*NASDAQ symbol*] (SAG)
MXT .... Chicago, IL [*Location identifier*] [*FAA*] (FAAL)
MXT .... Maintirano [*Madagascar*] [*Airport symbol*] (OAG)
MXT .... Message Exchange Terminal
MXT .... Metris Cos. [*NYSE symbol*] (SG)
MXT .... Mixture
MXT .... Morgan StanGp 6.00% Tele'PERQS' [*AMEX symbol*] (TTSB)
MXT .... Morgan Stanley Group, Inc. [*AMEX symbol*] (SAG)
MXTF .... Max-24 LTL [*Common carrier symbol*]
MXTMP ..... Maximum Temperature (NOAA)
MXTR .... Maxtor Corp. [*NASDAQ symbol*] (NQ)
MXU .... Mobile Exhibition Unit (NITA)
MXU .... Mullewa [*Australia*] [*Airport symbol*] [*Obsolete*] (OAG)
MXU .... Multiplexer Unit [*Telecommunications*]
MxU .... Universidad Nacional Autonoma de Mexico, Mexico City, Mexico [*Library symbol*] [*Library of Congress*] (LCLS)
MXVRC ..... Middlesex Volunteer Rifle Corps [*British military*] (DMA)

MXW Mari [*Language symbol*] (ETLW)

MXW Maxwell, CA [*Location identifier*] [*FAA*] (FAAL)

MXWL Maxwell Laboratories, Inc. [*NASDAQ symbol*] (NQ)

MXWL Maxwell Labs [*NASDAQ symbol*] (TTSB)

MXWL Maxwell Technologies, Inc. [*NASDAQ symbol*] (SAG)

MXWND Maximum Wind (NOAA)

MXX International Murex Technologies (SAUS)

MXX Merchant Express Aviation [*Nigeria*] [*ICAO designator*] (FAAC)

MXX Mora [*Sweden*] [*Airport symbol*] (OAG)

MXXX Mars Stores, Inc. [*NASDAQ symbol*] (COMM)

MXY McCarthy [*Alaska*] [*Airport symbol*] (OAG)

MXY McCarthy, AK [*Location identifier*] [*FAA*] (FAAL)

MXY [*The*] Yarumal Foreign Mission Institute (Colombia) (TOCD)

MY Air Mali [*ICAO designator*] (AD)

My All India Reporter, Mysore Series [*A publication*] (ILCA)

MY Machine Yield [*Agriculture*] (OA)

MY Mahzor Yanai (BJA)

MY Malaysia [*IYRU nationality code*] [*ANSI two-letter standard code*] (CNC)

my Malaysia [*MARC country of publication code*] [*Library of Congress*] (LCCP)

MY Man-Year (AFM)

M/Y Marshaling Yards [*Military*]

My May (RION)

MY May

my Mayer [*A unit of heat capacity*]

MY Mean Year (IAA)

MY Mean Yield [*Agriculture*]

MY Miller-Yoder Language Comprehension Test

MY Million Years

MY Miss You [*Internet lingo*] (NETL)

MY Model Year [*Automotive industry*]

MY Montgomeryshire Yeomanry [*British military*] (DMA)

MY Motorized Yacht (TRID)

MY Motor Yacht

MY Muddy [*Track condition*] [*Thoroughbred racing*]

My Myanmar (Burma) (MILB)

My Myopia (DIPS)

MY Myopia

MY Myria [*A prefix meaning multiplied by 10^4*]

MY Myxedematous [*Endocrinology*] (DAVI)

MYA Million Years Ago

MYA Model Yachting Association [*British*] (DBA)

MYA Monterey Aquarium, CA [*Amtrak Busline code*]

MYA Moruya [*Australia*] [*Airport symbol*] (OAG)

MYA Myasishchev [*Aircraft*] [*Commonwealth of Independent States*]

MYA Myflug HF [*Iceland*] [*ICAO designator*] (FAAC)

mya Myiare (BARN)

MYAB Clarence Bain, Andros Island [*Bahamas*] [*ICAO location identifier*] (ICLI)

MYAF Andros Town, Andros Island [*Bahamas*] [*ICAO location identifier*] (ICLI)

MYAG Gorda Cay, Abaco Island [*Bahamas*] [*ICAO location identifier*] (ICLI)

MYAK Congo Town, Andros Island [*Bahamas*] [*ICAO location identifier*] (ICLI)

MYAM Marsh Harbour, Abaco Island [*Bahamas*] [*ICAO location identifier*] (ICLI)

MYAN San Andros, Andros Island [*Bahamas*] [*ICAO location identifier*] (ICLI)

My & C Mylne and Craig's English Chancery Reports [*A publication*] (DLA)

My & Cr Mylne and Craig's English Chancery Reports [*A publication*] (DLA)

My & K Mylne and Keen's English Chancery Reports [*A publication*] (DLA)

MYAO Moores Island, Abaco Island [*Bahamas*] [*ICAO location identifier*] (ICLI)

MYAP Spring Point [*Bahamas*] [*ICAO location identifier*] (ICLI)

MYAPP Main Yankee Atomic Power Plant (NRCH)

MYAS Sandy Point, Abaco Island [*Bahamas*] [*ICAO location identifier*] (ICLI)

MYAT Treasure Cay, Abaco Island [*Bahamas*] [*ICAO location identifier*] (ICLI)

MYAW Walker Cay, Abaco Island [*Bahamas*] [*ICAO location identifier*] (ICLI)

MYB Aerolineas Del Mayab, SA de CV [*Mexico*] [*FAA designator*] (FAAC)

MYB Mayoumba [*Gabon*] [*Airport symbol*] (OAG)

MYBC Chub Cay, Berry Island [*Bahamas*] [*ICAO location identifier*] (ICLI)

MYBC Myosin-Binding Protein C (DMAA)

MYBG Bullocks Harbour/Great Harbour Cay, Berry Island [*Bahamas*] [*ICAO location identifier*] (ICLI)

MYBK Maybank Shipping Corporation [*Common carrier symbol*]

MYBO Ocean Cay, Bimini Island [*Bahamas*] [*ICAO location identifier*] (ICLI)

MYBP Million Years before Present [*Geology*]

MYBS Alice Town/South Bimini, Bimini Island [*Bahamas*] [*ICAO location identifier*] (ICLI)

MYBT Cistern Cay, Berry Island [*Bahamas*] [*ICAO location identifier*] (ICLI)

MYBW Big Whale Cay, Berry Island [*Bahamas*] [*ICAO location identifier*] (ICLI)

MYBX Little Whale Cay, Berry Island [*Bahamas*] [*ICAO location identifier*] (ICLI)

MYC Malartic Hygrade Gold Mines Ltd. [*Vancouver Stock Exchange symbol*]

MYC Maracay [*Venezuela*] [*Airport symbol*] (OAG)

MYC Massenya [*Chad*] [*Airport symbol*] (AD)

MYC Middlesex Yeomanry Cavalry [*British military*] (DMA)

MYC Montgomeryshire Yeomanry Cavalry [*British military*] (DMA)

MYC Multiyear Contract

MYC MuniYield California Fund [*NYSE symbol*] (SPSG)

MYC Mycology (WGA)

MYCA Arthur's Town, Eleuthera Island [*Bahamas*] [*ICAO location identifier*] (ICLI)

MYCB New Bight, Cat Island [*Bahamas*] [*ICAO location identifier*] (ICLI)

MYCCI Mid Yorkshire Chamber of Commerce and Industry [*United Kingdom*] (EAIO)

MYCH Hawks Nest Creek/Hawks Nest, Cat Island [*Bahamas*] [*ICAO location identifier*] (ICLI)

MYCI Colonel Hill, Crooked Island [*Bahamas*] [*ICAO location identifier*] (ICLI)

MYCI Mirrer Yeshiva Central Institute (EA)

MYCO Mycobacterium

MYCO Mycogen Corp. [*NASDAQ symbol*] (NQ)

MYCO Myco Industries [*NCIC trailer make code*]

Myco Mycoplasma [*A bacterium*] (DAVI)

Mycogn Mycogen Corp. [*Associated Press*] (SAG)

MYCOL Mycology

Mycol Res Mycological Research (SAUS)

MYCOS My Compact Operating System [*Toshiba*]

MYCOS/SS MYCOS Support System (NITA)

MYCP Pittsdown, Crooked Island [*Bahamas*] [*ICAO location identifier*] (ICLI)

MYCS Cay Sal [*Bahamas*] [*ICAO location identifier*] (ICLI)

MYCX Cutlass Bay, Cat Island [*Bahamas*] [*ICAO location identifier*] (ICLI)

MYD Malindi [*Kenya*] [*Airport symbol*] (OAG)

MYD Maryland [*Telegraphy*] (PCTE)

MYD Miyadu [*Japan*] [*Seismograph station code, US Geological Survey*] [*Closed*] (SEIS)

MYD MuniYield Fund [*NYSE symbol*] (SPSG)

MYD Myotonic Muscular Dystrophy [*Medicine*] (DB)

MYDP Multi-Year Development Plan [*Environmental Protection Agency*] (ERG)

MYDW Multiple Yield Defense Weapon

MYE Man Year Equivalent (SPST)

MYE Mary Ellen Resources Ltd. [*Vancouver Stock Exchange symbol*]

MYE Miyake Jima [*Japan*] [*Airport symbol*] (OAG)

MYE Myers Indus [*AMEX symbol*] (TTSB)

MYE Myers Industries, Inc. [*AMEX symbol*] (SPSG)

MYEC Cape Eleuthera, Eleuthera Island [*Bahamas*] [*ICAO location identifier*] (ICLI)

MYEG George Town, Exuma Island [*Bahamas*] [*ICAO location identifier*] (ICLI)

MYEH North Eleuthera, Eleuthera Island [*Bahamas*] [*ICAO location identifier*] (ICLI)

MYEL Mulitple Myeloma [*Hematology*] (DAVI)

MYEL Myelin [*or Myelinated*] [*Medicine*]

MYEL Myelocyte [*Hematology*]

MYEL Myelogram [*Medicine*] (AAMN)

MYEL Staniel Cay, Exuma Island [*Bahamas*] [*ICAO location identifier*] (ICLI)

myelo Myelocyte [*Hematology*]

Myelo Myelogram (AMHC)

MYEM Governor's Harbour, Eleuthera Island [*Bahamas*] [*ICAO location identifier*] (ICLI)

MYEN Norman's Cay, Exuma Island [*Bahamas*] [*ICAO location identifier*] (ICLI)

MYER Rock Sound/International, Eleuthera Island [*Bahamas*] [*ICAO location identifier*] (ICLI)

Myer Dig Myer's Texas Digest [*A publication*] (DLA)

Myer Fed Dec Myer's Federal Decisions [*A publication*] (DLA)

MyerL [*The*] Myers [*L. E.*] Co. Group [*Associated Press*] (SAG)

Myer's Fed Dec Myer's Federal Decisions [*United States*] [*A publication*] (DLA)

MyersInd Myers Industries, Inc. [*Associated Press*] (SAG)

MYES Lee Stocking Island, Exuma Island [*Bahamas*] [*ICAO location identifier*] (ICLI)

MYEY Hog Cay, Exuma Island [*Bahamas*] [*ICAO location identifier*] (ICLI)

MYF Methodist Youth Fellowship

MYF MuniYield Florida Fund [*NYSE symbol*] (SPSG)

MYF Myogenic Factor (DMAA)

MYF San Diego [*California*] Montgomery Field [*Airport symbol*] [*Obsolete*] (OAG)

MYFA Mayfairer [*NCIC truck make code*]

MYFC Mike Yager Fan Club (EA)

MYFR Mary's Freight Lines [*Common carrier symbol*]

MYFRA Mayfair Super Markets, Inc. (Class A) [*NASDAQ symbol*] (COMM)

MYFV Melandrium Yellow Fleck Virus [*Plant pathology*]

MYG Massachusetts Institute of Technology, Cambridge, MA [*OCLC symbol*] (OCLC)

MYG Matka [*Yugoslavia*] [*Seismograph station code, US Geological Survey*] (SEIS)

MYG Mayaguana [*Bahamas*] [*Airport symbol*] (OAG)

MYG Maytag [*NYSE symbol*] (SAG)

MYG Maytag Corp. [*NYSE symbol*] (TTSB)

MyG Myasthenia Gravis [*Medicine*] (MELL)

MYG Myriagram [*Ten Thousand Grams*]

MYGD Deep Water Cay, Grand Bahama Island [*Bahamas*] [*ICAO location identifier*] (ICLI)

MYGF Freeport/International, Grand Bahama Island [*Bahamas*] [*ICAO location identifier*] (ICLI)

MYGM Grand Bahama Auxiliary Air Force Base, Grand Bahama Island [*Bahamas*] [*ICAO location identifier*] (ICLI)

MYGN Myriad Genetics [*NASDAQ symbol*] (TTSB)

MYGN Myriad Genetics, Inc. [*NASDAQ symbol*] (SAG)

MYGW West End, Grand Bahama Island [*Bahamas*] [*ICAO location identifier*] (ICLI)

MYH Monterey Hyatt Regency, CA [*Amtrak Busline code*]

MYH Rosh-Pina [*Israel*] [*Airport symbol*] (AD)

MYHD Macy's Light Delivery [*Common carrier symbol*]

MYHEC Michigan Youth Hunter Education Challenge

MY I .... First Multiyear Contract [*Military*] (RDA)
MYI .... Magical Youths International (EA)
MYI .... Metallic Yarns Institute [*Defunct*]
MYI .... Mina [*Language symbol*] (ETLW)
MYI .... MuniYield Insured Fund [*NYSE symbol*] (SPSG)
MYID .... Safe ID Corp. [*OTCBB symbol*]
MYIG .... Matthew Town, Great Inagua Island [*Bahamas*] [*ICAO location identifier*] (ICLI)
MY II .... Second Multiyear Contract [*Military*] (RDA)
MYIM .... Mylar Insulation Material
MYJ .... Matsuyama [*Japan*] [*Airport symbol*] (OAG)
MYJ .... MuniYield New Jersey Fund [*NYSE symbol*] (SPSG)
MYK .... May Creek [*Alaska*] [*Airport symbol*] (OAG)
MYK .... May Creek, AK [*Location identifier*] [*FAA*] (FAAL)
MYK .... Mayen-Koblenz [*German license plate city code*]
MYK .... Miyakojima [*Ryukyu Islands*] [*Seismograph station code, US Geological Survey*] (SEIS)
MYL .... Aeromyl SA de CV [*Mexico*] [*ICAO designator*] (FAAC)
MYL .... McCall, ID [*Location identifier*] [*FAA*] (FAAL)
Myl .... Myeloid [*Medicine*] (QSUL)
MYL .... Mylan Laboratories, Inc. [*NYSE symbol*] (SPSG)
MYL .... Mylan Labs [*NYSE symbol*] (TTSB)
MYL .... Myrialiter [*Unit of measurement*]
Mylan .... Mylan Laboratories, Inc. [*Associated Press*] (SAG)
Myl & C..... Mylne and Craig's English Chancery Reports [*A publication*] (DLA)
Myl & C (Eng)... Mylne and Craig's English Chancery Reports [*A publication*] (DLA)
Myl & Cr.... Mylne and Craig's English Chancery Reports [*A publication*] (DLA)
Myl & K..... Mylne and Keen's English Chancery Reports [*A publication*] (DLA)
Myl & K (Eng)... Mylne and Keen's English Chancery Reports [*A publication*] (DLA)
MYLAN LABS PAC... Mylan Laboratories Inc. PAC [*Canonburg, PA*] (PACS)
MYLD........ Deadman's Cay, Long Island [*Bahamas*] [*ICAO location identifier*] (ICLI)
Mylex........ Mylex Corp. [*Associated Press*] (SAG)
My LJ .... Mysore Law Journal [*India*] [*A publication*] (DLA)
Mylne & K... Mylne and Keen's English Chancery Reports [*A publication*] (DLA)
MYLR........ Diamond Roads, Long Island [*Bahamas*] [*ICAO location identifier*] (ICLI)
MYLS......... Mid-York Library System [*Library network*]
MYLS......... Stella Maris, Long Island [*Bahamas*] [*ICAO location identifier*] (ICLI)
MYLU......... Mayan Line [*Intermodal shipping container symbol*] (TVRC)
MYLX......... Mylex Corp. [*NASDAQ symbol*] (NQ)
MYM.......... Managing Your Money [*MECA Software, Inc.*] (PCM)
MYM.......... Marley Mines Ltd. [*Vancouver Stock Exchange symbol*]
MYM.......... Monkey Mountain [*Guyana*] [*Airport symbol*] (OAG)
MYM.......... Monterey Marriott, CA [*Amtrak Busline code*]
MYM.......... MONY Real Estate Investors [*NYSE symbol*] (COMM)
MYM.......... Muniyield Michigan Fund [*NYSE symbol*] (SAG)
MYM.......... Myriameter
MyMD........ Myotonic Muscular Dystrophy [*See also MD*] [*Medicine*]
MYMD........ New York Military District (SAUS)
MYMI......... Meyers Motor Trans [*Common carrier symbol*]
MYMM .... Mayaguana Auxiliary Air Force Base, Mayaguana Island [*Bahamas*] [*ICAO location identifier*] (ICLI)
MYMS........ Mothers of Young Mongoloids [*Later, PODSC*] (EA)
MYMV........ Mungbean Yellow Mosaic Virus [*Plant pathology*]
MYN .... Mareb [*Yemen*] [*Airport symbol*] [*Obsolete*] (OAG)
myn........... Mayan [*MARC language code*] [*Library of Congress*] (LCCP)
MYN .... Mayan Energy, Inc. [*Vancouver Stock Exchange symbol*]
MYN .... Million [*Telegraphy*] (PCTE)
MYN .... MuniYield New York Insured Fund [*NYSE symbol*] (SPSG)
MYN .... MuniYield NY Insured Fund [*NYSE symbol*] (TTSB)
MYNA .... Nassau [*Bahamas*] [*ICAO location identifier*] (ICLI)
MYNN .... Nassau/International, New Providence Island [*Bahamas*] [*ICAO location identifier*] (ICLI)
MYO .... Myocardial [*or Myocardium*] [*Cardiology*] (AAMN)
MYO .... Myoglobin (DB)
MYOB .... Mind Your Own Business [*Slang*]
MYOBB....... Mind Your Own Business, Buster [*Slang*]
MYOC-A...... Myocarditis, Pericarditis [*Cardiology*] (DAVI)
MYOGLB .... Myoglobin [*hematology*] (DAVI)
MYOP .... Multiyear Operational Plan [*Long-range forecast produced by the Canadian government*]
myop .... Myopia [*Ophthalmology*] (DAVI)
MYOQ .... MYO Trucking Company [*Common carrier symbol*]
MYOT........ Myo-Tech Corp. (EFIS)
MYP .... Malawi Young Pioneers [*Political party*] (PSAP)
MYP .... Mannito-Egg Yolk Polymyxin (OA)
MY/P .... Mean Yield/Plants [*Agriculture*]
MYP .... Montgomery [*Pakistan*] [*Airport symbol*] (AD)
MYP .... Multiyear Procurement [*DoD*]
MYPO .... Multiyear Procurement Objective [*DoD*]
MYQ.......... Windsor Locks, CT [*Location identifier*] [*FAA*] (FAAL)
MYR.......... Maximum Yield Research [*Agricultural technology*]
MYR.......... Mayor's Jewelers [*AMEX symbol*]
m/yr .... Milli-Inches per Year [*Corrosion technology*]
MYR.......... Millionaire [*Telegraphy*] (PCTE)
Myr........... Million Years
MYR.......... Million Years [*Also, MY*]
MYR.......... Miriadair [*France*] [*ICAO designator*] (FAAC)
MYR.......... [*The*] Myers [*L. E.*] Co. Group [*NYSE symbol*] (SPSG)
MYR.......... MYR Group [*NYSE symbol*] (TTSB)
Myr .... Myrick's California Probate Court Reports [*1872-79*] [*A publication*] (DLA)
myr .... Myrtle [*Philately*]
MYR.......... Myrtle Beach [*South Carolina*] Myrtle Air Force Base [*Airport symbol*] (OAG)
MYRA .... Multiyear Rescheduling Agreement [*Banking*]
MYRAA...... Model Yacht Racing Association of America (EA)
Myr Cal Prob... Myrick's California Probate Court Reports [*1872-79*] [*A publication*] (DLA)
MYRD .... Duncan Town, Exuma Island [*Bahamas*] [*ICAO location identifier*] (ICLI)
Myriad ...... Myriad Genetics, Inc. [*Associated Press*] (SAG)
Myrick (Cal)... Myrick's California Probate Court Reports [*1872-79*] [*A publication*] (DLA)
Myrick Prob (Cal)... Myrick's California Probate Court Reports [*1872-79*] [*A publication*] (DLA)
Myrick's Prob Rep... Myrick's California Probate Court Reports [*1872-79*] [*A publication*] (DLA)
MYRP .... Port Nelson, Exuma Island [*Bahamas*] [*ICAO location identifier*] (ICLI)
Myr Prob.... Myrick's California Probate Court Reports [*1872-79*] [*A publication*] (DLA)
Myr Prob Rep... Myrick's California Probate Court Reports [*1872-79*] [*A publication*] (DLA)
MYRTL ...... Myrtlewood, AL [*American Association of Railroads railroad junction routing code*]
Mys .... All India Reporter, Mysore [*A publication*] (DLA)
MYS .... Maderas y Sinteticos [*NYSE symbol*] (SPSG)
MYS .... Maderas y Sinteticos ADS [*NYSE symbol*] (TTSB)
MYS .... Malaysia [*ANSI three-letter standard code*] (CNC)
MYS .... Man-Year-Space [*Army*] (AABC)
MYS .... Masisa S.A. ADS [*Formerly, Maderas y Sinteticos ADS*] [*NYSE symbol*]
MYS .... Myasthenic Syndrome [*Neurology*]
MYS .... Mystery [*Telegraphy*] (PCTE)
MYS .... Mystery Mountain Minerals [*Vancouver Stock Exchange symbol*]
MYS .... Mystic, CT [*Amtrak rail station code*]
MYS .... Mystic, KY [*Location identifier*] [*FAA*] (FAAL)
MYS .... Mystic Marinelife Aquarium, New London, CT [*OCLC symbol*] (OCLC)
MYS .... Mystique (automobile) [*NCIC car model code*]
Mys Ch Ct... Mysore Chief Court Reports [*India*] [*A publication*] (DLA)
Mys HCR.... Mysore High Court Reports [*India*] [*A publication*] (DLA)
Mys LJ ...... Mysore Law Journal [*India*] [*A publication*] (DLA)
Mys LR...... Mysore Law Reports [*India*] [*A publication*] (DLA)
MYSM .... Cockburn Town, San Salvador Island [*Bahamas*] [*ICAO location identifier*] (ICLI)
MySoft ...... MySoftware Co. [*Associated Press*] (SAG)
MYSOLN.... Mysoline [*An anticonvulsant*] [*Wyeth-Ayerst Laboratorie*] (DAVI)
Mysore...... Mysore Law Reports [*India*] [*A publication*] (DLA)
Mysore LJ... Mysore Law Journal [*India*] [*A publication*] (DLA)
Mys R (R).... Mysore Reports (Reprint) [*1878-1923*] [*India*] [*A publication*] (DLA)
MYST......... Mystery
MYST......... Mystic Financial, Inc. [*NASDAQ symbol*] (NASQ)
MYSTIC ..... Mystic
MYSTIC STAR... Presidential Support AirGround Communications System (SAUS)
MYSW....... MySoftware Co. [*NASDAQ symbol*] (SAG)
Mys WN...... Mysore Weekly Notes [*1891-92*] [*India*] [*A publication*] (DLA)
MYT .... Monterey Travelodge, CA [*Amtrak Busline code*]
MYT .... MuniYield New York Insured Fund II [*NYSE symbol*] (SPSG)
MYT .... MuniYield NY Insured Fund II [*NYSE symbol*] (TTSB)
MYT .... Myitkyina [*Myanmar*] [*Airport symbol*] (OAG)
MYT .... Mytec Technologies [*Toronto Stock Exchange symbol*] [*Canada*]
MYT .... Mytec Technology, Inc. [*Vancouver Stock Exchange symbol*]
MYT .... Mythology
MYT .... Sangab Mandaya [*Language symbol*] (ETLW)
MYTA........ Maintainability Task Analyses (NASA)
MYTAB ...... Myristyltrimethylammonium Bromide [*Organic chemistry*]
MYTD........ Model Year to Date
MYTGC...... Miller-Yoder Test of Grammatical Comprehension [*Speech and lanaguage therapy*] (DAVI)
MYTH........ Mythical (GOBB)
Myth......... Mythology (BEE)
myth......... Mythology (ELAL)
MYTH........ Mythology
MYTHOL .... Mythology (WGA)
Myth Vat.... Mythographi Vaticani [*A publication*] (OCD)
MYTK........ Mitek Surgical Products (EFIS)
MYU .... Mekoryuk [*Alaska*] [*Airport symbol*] (OAG)
MYV .... Malva Yellows Virus [*Plant pathology*]
MYV .... Marysville [*California*] [*Airport symbol*] (AD)
MYV .... Marysville, CA [*Location identifier*] [*FAA*] (FAAL)
MYVAL ...... Maintainability Evaluation (NASA)
MYVC........ Metro Recycling Service [*Common carrier symbol*]
MYW .... Mtwara [*Tanzania*] [*Airport symbol*] (OAG)
MYW .... Multiple Yield Weapon
MYWA........ My-Way Corporation [*NCIC trailer make code*]
MYWF........ Masonic Youth Welfare Fund [*Australia*]
MYX .... Marion, VA [*Location identifier*] [*FAA*] (FAAL)
MYX .... Menyamya [*Papua New Guinea*] [*Airport symbol*] (OAG)
MYX .... Methotrexate [*Antineoplastic drug*] (CDI)
MYX .... Mysterious [*Telegraphy*] (PCTE)
MYXO .... Myxomatosis (DSUE)
MYY .... Miri [*Malaysia*] [*Airport symbol*] (OAG)
MYY .... MuniYield MY Insured Fund III [*NYSE symbol*] (TTSB)
MYY .... MuniYield New York Insured Fund III [*NYSE symbol*] (SPSG)
MYY .... Philadelphia, PA [*Location identifier*] [*FAA*] (FAAL)
MYZ .... Marysville, KS [*Location identifier*] [*FAA*] (FAAL)

MYZ .... Mayoko [*Gabon*] [*Airport symbol*] (AD)
MYZ .... Miyazaki [*Japan*] [*Seismograph station code, US Geological Survey*] (SEIS)
Mz .... Geology Mesozoic (ODA)
MZ .... Mainz [*German license plate city code*]
MZ .... Mantle Zone
MZ .... Marginal Zone [*Neurology*]
m-z .... Mass to Charge Ratio
MZ .... Merpati Nusatnara Airlines [*ICAO designator*] (AD)
Mz .... Methoxyphenylazobenzyloxycarbonyl [*Biochemistry*]
MZ .... Meziocillin [*Medicine*] (EDAA)
MZ .... Mezzo [*Moderate*] [*Music*] (ROG)
Mz .... Mezzo Soprano
MZ .... Middle Zone (HEAS)
MZ .... Midzone Phenomenon [*Immunology*]
MZ .... Miesiecznik Zydowski (BJA)
MZ .... Milacron, Inc. [*NYSE symbol*] (SG)
MZ .... Minus Zero (IAA)
MZ .... Monozygotic [*Genetics*]
MZ .... Monozygotic Twins (DIPS)
MZ .... Motorrad Zschopau [*Motorcycles*]
MZ .... Mozambique [*ANSI two-letter standard code*] (CNC)
mz .... Mozambique [*MARC country of publication code*] [*Library of Congress*] (LCCP)
MZ .... Museum of Zoology (NADA)
MZA .... Air Zory [*Bulgaria*] [*FAA designator*] (FAAC)
MZA .... Mariazell [*Austria*] [*Seismograph station code, US Geological Survey*] (SEIS)
MZA .... Monozygotic Twins Reared Apart [*Genetics*]
MZa .... Monozygotic Twins Reared or Raised Apart (DIPS)
MZA .... MuniYield Arizona Fund [*AMEX symbol*] (TTSB)
MZA .... MuniYield Arizona Fund, Inc. [*AMEX symbol*] (SPSG)
MZAD .... Mains Army Depot [*Germany*]
MZB .... Mocimboa da Praia [*Mozambique*] [*Airport symbol*] (AD)
MZB .... San Diego, CA [*Location identifier*] [*FAA*] (FAAL)
MZBO .... Menezes Brothers [*Common carrier symbol*]
MZBZ .... Belize/International [*Belize*] [*ICAO location identifier*] (ICLI)
MZC .... Mitzic [*Gabon*] [*Airport symbol*] (OAG)
MZCP .... Mean Zonal Candlepower (IAA)
MZE .... Multifunctional Zone Evaluation (ACAE)
MZF .... Aiku [*Language symbol*] (ETLW)
MZF .... Manganese Zinc Ferrite
MZF .... Mazirat [*France*] [*Seismograph station code, US Geological Survey*] (SEIS)
MZFR .... Mehrzweck Forschungs [*Reactor*] [*Germany*] (NRCH)
MZFW .... Maximum Zero Fuel Weight [*Aviation*] (MCD)
MZG .... Makung [*Taiwan*] [*Airport symbol*] (OAG)
MZG .... Merzig [*Saar*] [*German license plate city code*]
MZI .... Mopti [*Mali*] [*Airport symbol*] (OAG)
MZIZ .... Marko B. Zanovich [*Intermodal trailer symbol*]
MZJ .... Marana, AZ [*Location identifier*] [*FAA*] (FAAL)
MZK .... Marakei [*Kiribati*] [*Airport symbol*] (OAG)
MZL .... Aerovias Montes Azules, SA de CV [*Mexico*] [*FAA designator*] (FAAC)
MZL .... Manizales [*Colombia*] [*Airport symbol*] (OAG)
MZL .... Minnesota Zephyr [*Federal Railroad Administration identification code*]
MZL .... Muzzle (MSA)
MZM .... Metz [*France*] [*Airport symbol*] (OAG)
MZM .... Movado Zenith Mondia
MZM INC PAC ... MZM, Inc. [*Washington, DC*] (PACS)
MZN .... Maruzen Co. Ltd. [*UTLAS symbol*]
MZN .... Minj [*New Guinea*] [*Airport symbol*] (AD)
MZN .... Mount Vernon Nazarene College, Mount Vernon, OH [*OCLC symbol*] (OCLC)
MZO .... Manzanillo [*Cuba*] [*Airport symbol*] (OAG)
MZO .... Mazie Landing [*Oklahoma*] [*Seismograph station code, US Geological Survey*] (SEIS)
MZOA .... Masada of the Zionist Organization of America (EA)
MZON .... Multiple Zones International, Inc. [*NASDAQ symbol*] (SAG)
M-ZONE ..... Manufacturing Zone (MHDB)
MZP .... Meta-Azidopyrimethamine [*Biochemistry*]
MZP .... Modulated Zone Plate (PDAA)
MZPI .... Microwave Zone Position Indicator (IAA)
MZQ .... Mori Atas [*Language symbol*] (ETLW)
MZQ .... Mozambique [*Mozambique*] [*Airport symbol*] (AD)
MZR .... Mazar-I-Sharif [*Afghanistan*] [*Airport symbol*] (OAG)
MZR .... Monroe, LA [*Location identifier*] [*FAA*] (FAAL)
MZR .... Multi-Zone Recording (CIST)
MZS .... Mahfooz Aviation [*Gambia*] [*FAA designator*] (FAAC)
MZS .... Master of Zoology Science (GAGS)
MZS .... Spokane, WA [*Location identifier*] [*FAA*] (FAAL)
MZ Sc .... Master of Zoological Science
MZSCS ...... Martinek-Zaichkowsky Self-Concept Scale for Children [*Child development test*]
MZSH .... Missionary Zelatrices of the Sacred Heart [*Roman Catholic women's religious order*]
MZsL .... Magyar Zsido Lexikon [*A publication*] (BJA)
MZSU .... Zelesnicko Transportono Pretprijatie [*Intermodal shipping container symbol*] (TVRC)
MZT .... Mazatlan [*Mexico*] [*Airport symbol*] (OAG)
MZt .... Monozygotic Twins Reared or Raised Together (DIPS)
MZT .... Monozygotic Twins Reared Together [*Genetics*]
MZU .... Muzaffarpur [*India*] [*Airport symbol*] (AD)
MZV .... Magyar Zsidok Vilagszovetsege [*World Federation of Hungarian Jews*] (EAIO)
MZV .... Moline, IL [*Location identifier*] [*FAA*] (FAAL)
MZWTWD ... Multi-Zone Walk-Through Weapon Detector [*Police and security equipment*]
MZX .... Augusta, GA [*Location identifier*] [*FAA*] (FAAL)
MZX .... Massio [*Ethiopia*] [*Airport symbol*] (AD)
MZY .... Mzimba [*Malawi*] [*Airport symbol*] (AD)
MZZ .... Marion [*Indiana*] [*Airport symbol*] (AD)
MZZ .... Marion, IN [*Location identifier*] [*FAA*] (FAAL)
M~of~M ..... Ministry of Munitions (SAUO)

N
By Acronym

N .... All India Reporter, Nagpur Series [*A publication*] (ILCA)

n .... Amino [*As substituent on nucleoside*] [*Biochemistry*]

n .... Amount of Substance [*Molecular quantity*] [*Symbol*] [*IUPAC*]

N .... Anthraquic [*Soil biology*] [*Soil phases*] (QSUL)

N .... Asparagine [*Biochemistry*] (DAVI)

N .... Asparaginyl (SAUS)

N .... Avogadro Number [*Number of molecules in one gram-molecular weight of a substance*]

N .... Blood Factor in the MNS Blood Group System [*Medicine*] (EDAA)

N .... Carbon Star [*Astronomy*] (BARN)

N .... Cementex [*Research code symbol*]

N .... Clearance Hot Delivered (SAUS)

N .... Cranial Nerve (DIPS)

N .... Digestum Novum [*A publication*] [*Authority cited in pre-1607 legal work*] (DSA)

N .... Dr. Karl Thomae GmbH [*Germany*] [*Research code symbol*]

N .... Dumb [*Auxiliary craft suffix*] [*British*] [*Navy*]

N .... Educational Premises [*Public-performance tariff class*] [*British*]

N .... Efficiency [*Physics*] (BARN)

N .... Electron N-Type Semiconductor Material

N .... Employment [*Economics*]

N .... En [*Typography*] (WDAA)

n .... En [*Printing measurement*] (WDMC)

n .... Fallout Decay Exponent [*Emergency Management*] (EMA)

N .... Flying Boat [*Russian aircraft symbol*]

n .... Footnote (DLA)

N .... Haploid Chromosome Number (DOG)

N .... Haploid Number [*Genetics*]

N .... H. Lundbeck [*Denmark*] [*Research code symbol*]

N .... INCO Ltd. [*Formerly, International Nickel Co. of Canada Ltd.*] [*NYSE symbol*] [*Toronto Stock Exchange symbol*] (SPSG)

n .... [*An*] Indefinite Quantity [*Mathematics*] (ROG)

n .... index of refraction (SAUS)

N .... Knight [*Chess*]

N .... Loudness [*Medicine*] (EDAA)

N .... Magnetic Flux [*Symbol*] (ROG)

N .... Nail

N .... Name

N .... Nan [*Phonetic alphabet*] [*World War II*] (DSUE)

n .... Nano [*A prefix meaning divided by one billion*] [*SI symbol*]

N .... Narcolepsy

N .... Naringenin [*Organic chemistry*]

N .... Naris [*Nostril*] [*Pharmacy*]

N .... Narrow

N .... Nasal

N .... Nasion (MELL)

N .... National [*Screw threads*]

N .... Nationalist (ROG)

N .... Nationalist Party [*British*] [*Political party*]

N .... National League [*Baseball*]

N .... Native [*Ecology*]

N .... Natural Division [*Geography*]

N .... Naturalization (DNAB)

N .... Natural Number (IDOE)

N .... Natus [*Birth*] [*Latin*]

N .... Nautical

N .... Naval [*British military*] (DMA)

N .... Navigation

N .... Navigational Aids [*JETDS nomenclature*]

N .... Navy

N .... Nay [*Vote*]

N .... Near [*Optics*] (WDAA)

N .... Near the Nut (or Heel) of the Bow [*Music*] (ROG)

N .... Necrotic

n .... Need (DIPS)

N .... Need [*Psychology*]

N .... Negative (PIPO)

n .... Negative [*Crystal*]

N .... Negro

N .... Neisseria [*Medicine*]

N .... Nematic Phase [*Physical chemistry*]

N .... Nematocyst [*Zoology*]

N .... Neomycin [*Medicine*] (EDAA)

N .... Nepal (MILB)

N .... Neper [*A unit on a natural logarithmic scale*] (DEN)

n .... Nephew (GEAB)

N .... Nephew

N .... Nepos [*Grandson*] [*Latin*]

N .... Nervus [*Nerve*] [*Anatomy*]

N .... Nested [*Freight*]

N .... Nesting [*Ornithology*]

N .... Net

N .... Network [*FCC program source designation*] (NTCM)

n .... Network (WDMC)

N .... Neuraminidase [*An enzyme*]

N .... Neurogenic Element

N .... Neurology

N .... Neuropathy [*Medicine*] (DAVI)

N .... Neuroticism

N .... Neuroticism Index (SAUS)

n .... Neuter (ODA)

N .... Neuter

n .... Neutral (MEC)

N .... Neutral

n .... Neutrino (SAUS)

N .... Neutron (NAKS)

n .... Neutron [*A nuclear particle*]

N .... Neutron Number [*Physics*] (DAVI)

N .... Neutrophil [*Hematology*]

N .... Nevus (MELL)

N .... New [*Stock exchange term*] (SPSG)

N .... New Issue [*Investment term*] (DFIT)

N .... New Persian

n .... News (WDMC)

N .... News

N .... Newspaper

N .... News Program (NTCM)

N .... Newton [*Symbol*] [*SI unit of force*]

N .... New York State Library, Albany, NY [*Library symbol*] [*Library of Congress*] (LCLS)

N .... New York Stock Exchange [*New York, NY*]

n .... Next [*Computer science*] [*Telecommunications*]

N .... Ngultrum [*Monetary unit*] [*Bhutan*] (BARN)

N .... Nichrome (IAA)

N .... Nickel (NTIO)

n .... Nickel (SHCU)

N .... Nicolaus Furiosus [*Flourished, 12th century*] [*Authority cited in pre-1607 legal work*] (DSA)

N .... Nicotinamide [*Also, NAA*] [*Vitamin*]

N .... Niece (ADA)

N .... Nifedipine [*Pharmacology*]

n .... Night (WDMC)

N .... Night [*Approach and landing charts*] [*Aviation*]

N .... Night [*Broadcasting term*]

N .... Night Fighter [*When suffix to plane designation*] [*Navy*]

N .... Night Game [*Baseball*]

N .... Nighttime (NTCM)

N .... Nitrogen [*Chemical element*]

N .... Nitrogen Peroxide (SAUS)

N .... Nitrogen Tetroxide (SAUS)

n .... No [*Therapy term*] (CTAA)

N .... No

N .... Nocardia [*Genus of bacteria*] (MAE)

N .... Nocte [*At Night*] [*Pharmacy*]

N .... Nodal [*Oncology*]

N .... Node [*Lymphatic*] [*Anatomy*]

N .... Noise [*Broadcasting*]

N .... Nomen [*Name*] [*Latin*]

N .... Nominal [*Stock exchange term*] (SPSG)

N .... Nominally Labeled [*Compound, with radioisotope*]

n .... Nominative (ODA)

N .... Nominative

N .... None

N .... Nonmalignant [*Of tumors*] [*Medicine*]

N .... Nonne [*Globulin test*]

N .... Nontactical [*Military*]

n .... Noon (WDMC)

N .... Noon

N .... Norein [*Geology*]

N .... Norland Potato

N .... Norm (WDAA)

N .... Normal [*Solute concentration*] [*Chemistry*]

n .... Normal [*Molecular structure*] [*Chemistry*]

N .... Normal Depth [*Earthquakes*]

N .... Normal Horsepower

N .... Normality (SAUS)

N .... Normal Solution (DOG)
N .... Norse [*Language, etc.*]
N .... Norske Veritas [*Norwegian ship classification society*] (ROG)
N .... North [*or Northern*]
n---- .... North America [*MARC geographic area code*] [*Library of Congress*] (LCCP)
N .... Northeastern Reporter [*Commonly cited NE*] [*A publication*] (DLA)
N .... Northern Ireland Law Reports [*A publication*] (DLA)
N .... Northern latitude (SAUS)
N .... Northgate Exploration Ltd. [*Gold producer*] [*Canada*]
N .... Northing (SAUS)
N .... North London [*Postcode*] (ODBW)
N .... Northwestern Reporter [*Commonly cited NW*] [*A publication*] (DLA)
N .... Norway [*IYRU nationality code*]
N .... Noster [*Our*] [*Latin*]
N .... Nostril (AAMN)
N .... Not (DAVI)
N .... Notative Speed (WDAA)
n .... Note (WDMC)
N .... Note
n .... Noun (WDMC)
N .... Noun
N .... No Uniform [*For schoolgirls*] [*British*]
N .... No Vegetation [*Soil biology*] [*Vegetation*] (QSUL)
N .... Novellae [*Novels*] [*New Constitutions of Justinian*] [*A publication*] (DLA)
N .... Novelty [*Insulation*]
N .... November [*Phonetic alphabet*] [*International*] (DSUE)
N .... Novice Slope [*Skiing*]
N .... Nu [*Thirteenth letter of the Greek alphabet*] (DAVI)
N .... Nuclear
N .... Nuclear Propelled [*When following vessel classification, as CAG(N)*] [*Navy*]
N .... [*A*] Nucleoside [*One-letter symbol; see Nuc*]
N .... Nucleus [*of a cell*] [*Biology*]
n .... Nucleus [*Psychology*]
N .... Nucleus (of Syllable) [*Linguistics*]
N .... Nuernberg [*German license plate city code*]
N .... Nullity [*Divorce cases*] [*British*] (ROG)
n .... Number [*Usually integer*] (IDOE)
N .... Number
N .... Number Factor (DIPS)
N .... Number (of Bits) [*Computer science*] (ECII)
N .... Number of Molecules [*Symbol*] [*IUPAC*]
n .... Number of Observations [*Statistics*] (DAVI)
N .... Number (of Turns) [*Electronics*] (ECII)
N .... Numeric
N .... Numerical Ability (DIPS)
N .... Nun [*Buoy*]
N .... Nunnery
N .... Nupta [*Married*] [*Latin*]
N .... Nurse (ADA)
N .... Nuts [*Phonetic alphabet*] [*Royal Navy*] [*World War I*] [*Pre-World War II*] (DSUE)
N .... Nylon (AAG)
N .... Nymph [*Entomology*]
N .... Nystatin [*Antifungal antibiotic*]
N .... Population Size [*Symbol*] (MAE)
n .... Principal Quantum Number [*Atomic physics*] (DEN)
N .... Probe [*Missile vehicle type symbol*]
n .... Refractive Index [*Symbol*] [*Physics*]
N .... Rockwell International Corp. [*ICAO aircraft manufacturer identifier*] (ICAO)
N .... Size of Sample [*Statistics*] (DAVI)
N .... Sound in Air [*JETDS nomenclature*]
N .... South African Law Reports, Natal Province Division [*1910-46*] [*A publication*] (DLA)
N .... Special Test, Permanent [*Aircraft classification letter*]
N .... Stauffer Chemical Co. [*Research code symbol*]
N .... Tilt Correction
N .... United States of America [*Civil aircraft markings - international*] (PIPO)
n.c.u.p. ..... No Commission Until Paid (ODA)
N1 .... Low Pressure Compressor [*Aviation*] [*Fan speed*] (PIPO)
N1 .... Staff Officer for Administration [*Navy*] (POLM)
N1E .... Nosed One Edge [*Lumber*] (DAC)
N2 .... High Pressure Compressor Speed [*Aviation*] [*Core speed*] (PIPO)
N_2 .... Molecular Nitrogen [*Chemistry*] (DAVI)
N2 .... Nitrogen
N2 .... Staff Officer for Intelligence [*Navy*] (POLM)
N2E .... Nosed Two Edges [*Lumber*] (DAC)
N2H04 .... Nitrogen Peroxide (NAKS)
N2H4 .... Hydrazine (NAKS)
N2N .... Neighbor to Neighbor [*An association*] (EA)
N2N .... Project Neighbor to Neighbor (EA)
N20 .... Distickstoffoxid (SAUS)
N_2O .... Nitrous Oxide [*An Anesthetic*] (DAVI)
$N_2O:O_2$ ...... Nitrous Oxide to Oxygen Ratio [*Anesthesiology*] (DAVI)
N3 .... Cyclophosphamide, Vincristine, Triflurothymidine, Papaverine [*Antineoplastic drug regimen*] (DAVI)
N3 .... Staff Officer for Operations [*Navy*] (POLM)
N3F .... National Fantasy Fan Federation (EA)
N4 .... Staff Officer for Supply/Logistics [*Navy*] (POLM)
N4A .... National Academic Athletic Advisors' Association (NTPA)
N4A .... National Association of Academic Advisors for Athletics (EA)
N4A .... National Association of Area Agencies on Aging [*Also, NAAAA*] (EA)
N4-HC .... National 4-H Council (EA)
N4WDA ...... National 4 Wheel Drive Association (EA)
N5 .... Staff Officer for Plans [*Navy*] (POLM)
N6 .... Staff Officer for Communications [*Navy*] (POLM)
n/30 .... Net in 30 Days (FOTI)
N/30 .... Net in Thirty Days
N204 .... Nitrogen Tetroxide (NAKS)
NA .... Academician of the National Academy of Design, New York [*1825*] (NGC)
NA .... Anatomic Nomenclature [*Medicine*] (BCRP)
Na .... Avogadro's Number [*Chemistry*] (DAVI)
NA .... De Natura Animalium [*of Aelianus*] [*Classical studies*] (OCD)
Na .... Exchangeable Body Sodium (AD)
NA .... Nabisco Holdings'A' [*NYSE symbol*] (TTSB)
NA .... Nabisco Holdings Corp. [*NYSE symbol*] (SAG)
Na .... Nachrichten (SAUS)
NA .... Nachrichtenabteilung [*Signal battalion*] [*German military - World War II*]
NA .... Nachrichten-Aufklaerung [*Signal intelligence*] [*German military - World War II*]
NA .... Nadir (WGA)
Na .... Nahum [*Old Testament book*]
NA .... Nailable [*Technical drawings*]
Na .... Naira [*Monetary unit*] [*Nigeria*]
NA .... Nalidixic Acid [*Medicine*] (EDAA)
NA .... Name [*Telegraphy*] (PCTE)
N/A .... Name and Address
NA .... Namibia [*ANSI two-letter standard code*] (CNC)
nA .... Nanoampere [*One billionth of an ampere*]
NA .... Naphthalene Dicarboxylic Acid
NA .... Naphthylacetamide [*Organic chemistry*]
NA .... Naphthylamine [*Organic chemistry*]
NA .... Napoleonic Association [*Enfield, Middlesex, England*] (EAIO)
NA .... Narcolepsy Association [*British*] (DBA)
NA .... Narcotics Anonymous (EA)
NA .... Narrow Angle
NA .... Nasal Allergy (MELL)
NA .... Nash Papyrus (BJA)
NA .... National Academician
NA .... National Academy (ROG)
NA .... National Acme [*Thread*]
NA .... National Action [*Australia*]
NA .... National Aerospace Standards Committee (AAGC)
NA .... National Airlines, Inc. [*ICAO designator*]
NA .... National Airport [*Under control of BAA*] [*British*]
NA .... National Alliance (EA)
NA .... National Ambucs (EA)
NA .... [*The*] National Archives [*of the United States*]
NA .... National Army
NA .... National Assistance [*British*]
NA .... National Association [*National Bank*]
NA .... National Bank of Canada [*Toronto Stock Exchange symbol*] [*Vancouver Stock Exchange symbol*]
NA .... Nationale Aktion fuer Volk und Heimat [*National Action for People and Homeland*] [*Switzerland*] [*Political party*] (PPE)
NA .... Native American (GOBB)
Na .... Natrium [*Sodium*] [*Chemical element*]
NA .... Natural Axis
na .... Naturalized (GEAB)
NA .... Naturally Aspirated [*Diesel engines*]
NA .... Nautical Almanac
NA .... Nautical Archaeology [*Oceanography*]
NA .... Naval Academy
NA .... Naval Accounts [*British*]
NA .... Naval Adviser (SAUS)
NA .... Naval Aircraft
NA .... Naval Airman [*Navy rating*] [*British*]
NA .... Naval Air Systems Command Manual
NA .... Naval Architect
NA .... Naval Assistant [*Navy rating*] [*British*]
NA .... Naval Attache [*Diplomacy*]
NA .... Naval Auxiliary
NA .... Naval Aviator
NA .... Navigation Aid (IAA)
NA .... Navion Aircraft Co. [*ICAO aircraft manufacturer identifier*] (ICAO)
NA .... Navy Aircraft (IAA)
NA .... Needle Aspiration [*Surgery*]
NA .... Needs Assessment (OICC)
NA .... Nelson Associates [*Also, an information service or system*] (IID)
NA .... Neo-Assyrian [*or New Assyrian*] [*Language, etc.*] (BJA)
NA .... Net Absolutely (MARI)
NA .... Net Assessment Organization [*Navy*]
NA .... Net Assets [*Banking*]
na .... Netherlands Antilles [*MARC country of publication code*] [*Library of Congress*] (LCCP)
NA .... Network Adapter (MCD)
NA .... Network Administrator (DMAA)
NA .... Neuraminidase (DMAA)
NA .... Neuraminidase Activity [*An enzyme*]
NA .... Neurologic Age (DMAA)
NA .... Neuropathology [*Medicine*] (DHSM)
NA .... Neurotics Anonymous (NADA)
NA .... Neutral Axis

NA .... Neutrality Act (SAUS)
NA .... Neutralizing Antibody [*Immunochemistry*]
NA .... Neutron Absorption (SAUS)
NA .... Neutrophil Antibody [*Immunology*] (DAVI)
NA .... New Account
NA .... New African [*A publication*]
NA .... New Age [*Later, LR*] [*An association*] (EA)
NA .... New Alliance (Slovakia) [*Political party*] (PSAP)
NA .... New Alternative Party [*Venezuela*] [*Political party*]
NA .... New Associations [*Later, NAP*] [*A publication*]
NA .... Newsletter Association (EA)
NA .... Newton Abbot [*British depot code*]
NA .... Next Action (NASA)
NA .... Next Address (VLIE)
NA .... Next Assembly
NA .... Ney-Allen [*Astronomy*]
NA .... Nickel Alloy (SAUS)
NA .... Nicotinic Acid [*Biochemistry*]
NA .... Night Alarm [*Telecommunications*] (TEL)
NA .... Night Answer (WDMC)
NA .... Niro Atomizer Ltd., Copenhagen (SAUS)
NA .... Nitric Acid (SAUS)
NA .... Nitrobenzene Association [*Defunct*] (EA)
NA .... Nizamut Adalat Reports [*India*] [*A publication*] (DLA)
NA .... No Abnormalities (SAUS)
NA .... No Abnormality [*Medicine*] (MAE)
NA .... No Access [*Telecommunications*] (TEL)
NA .... No Account [*Banking*]
N/A........... No Action
NA .... No Activity (ELAL)
N/A........... No Advice [*Business term*]
N/A........... No Alternative (DAVI)
NA .... No Answer (WDMC)
NA .... No Approval Required (MHDW)
NA .... No Assets (AFIT)
NA .... Noctes Atticae [*of Gellius*] [*Classical studies*] (OCD)
NA .... Nomina Anatomica [*System of anatomical terminology*]
N/A........... Nominative/Accusative [*Linguistics*] (IEL)
NA .... Nonabrasive (SAUS)
N/A........... Nonacceptance [*Business term*]
NA .... Nonacosadiynoic Acid (SAUS)
NA .... Nonacquiescence [*Legal term*] (DLA)
NA .... Nonactivated
NA .... Nonadherent [*Medicine*] (EDAA)
NA .... Nonagglomerating (SAUS)
NA .... Nonalcoholic
NA .... Non Allocatur [*Legal*] [*Latin*] (ROG)
NA .... Non-AM [*Automated Meter*] Read - After Hours [*Electric utility company*]
NA .... Nonaqueous (SAUS)
NA .... Non-Attached [*European political movement*] (ECON)
NA .... Nonattainment (COE)
NA .... Nonattendance
NA .... Non-Australian (SAUS)
NA .... Nora Alice [*DoD satellite*]
NA .... Noradrenaline [*Also known as NE: Norepinephrine*] [*Biochemistry*]
NA .... Normal Adult
NA .... Normal Alarm (SAA)
NA .... Normalized Air (SAUS)
NA .... Normally Aspirated [*Automotive engineering*]
NA .... North Africa
NA .... North African (SAUS)
NA .... North America
NA .... North American Watch Corp. (EFIS)
NA .... Northanger Abbey [*Novel by Jane Austen*]
NA .... North Atlantic Industries
NA .... North Australia (SAUS)
NA .... North Australian (SAUS)
NA .... Northern Alberta Railways Co. (IIA)
NA .... Northern Athabaskan [*Linguistics*] (IEL)
NA .... Norwegian metrology and Accreditation service (SAUS)
NA .... Nostra Aetate [*Declaration on the Relationship of the Church to the Non-Christian Religions*] [*Vatican II document*]
NA .... Nostro Account [*Our Account*] [*An account maintained by a bank with a bank in a foreign country*]
N/A........... Not Above
NA .... Not Absolutely (SAUS)
NA .... Not Accepted (FOTI)
NA .... Not Accurate (CIST)
NA .... Not Active (ELAL)
NA .... Not Actual (ELAL)
NA .... Not Adjustable (SAUS)
NA .... Not Adjusted (SAUS)
NA .... Not Admitted [*Medicine*] (MAE)
N/A........... Not Affected (AAG)
N/A........... Not Affiliated (NETL)
NA .... Not Allowed
NA .... Not And [*Logical operator*] [*Computer science*]
N/A........... Not Applicable [*Motor vehicle violation status code used in state of Arkansas*] (MVRD)
n/a .... Not Applicable (WA)
NA .... Not Applicable
NA .... Not Apply (ACAE)
NA .... Not Appropriated
NA .... Not Assigned
NA .... Not Authorized
n/a .... Not Available (WA)
NA .... Not Available
NA .... Noticias Argentinas SA [*News agency*] [*Argentina*] (EY)
NA .... Novice Agility
NA .... Nozzle Assembly
NA .... Nuclear Antibody (DMAA)
NA .... Nuclear Antigen (MELL)
NA .... Nuclear Assessment (SAUS)
NA .... Nucleic Acid [*Biochemistry*]
NA .... Nucleus Accumbens [*Neuroanatomy*]
NA .... Nucleus Ambiguus [*Neuroanatomy*]
NA .... Nueva Alternativa [*Venezuela*] [*Political party*] (EY)
NA .... Number of Aimpoints [*Military*]
NA .... Numerical Analysis [*Computer science*] (BUR)
NA .... Numerical Aperture [*Microscopy*]
NA .... Nurse Anesthetist (AAMN)
NA .... Nurse's Aide
NA .... Nurses Almanac
NA .... Nursing Assistant
NA .... Nursing Auxiliary [*British*]
NA .... Nurturant-Authoritative [*Psychotherapy*]
NA .... Nutrient Agar [*Microbiology*]
NA .... Organon, Inc. [*Research code symbol*]
Na .... Sodium [*Chemical element*] (AAMN)
nA........... Transitional Antarctic Coastal Air Mass [*Meteorology*] (BARN)
NA1 .... Neutrophil-specific Antigen [*Medicine*] (EDAA)
NA 1SL...... Naval Assistant to the First Sea Lord [*British military*] (DMA)
Na5 DTPA... Pentasodium Diethylenetriaminepentaacetic Acid (SAUS)
NAA.......... 1-Naphthaleneacetic Acid (LDT)
NAA.......... Naalehu [*Hawaii*] [*Seismograph station code, US Geological Survey*] [*Closed*] (SEIS)
NAA.......... N-Acetyl Aspartate (MELL)
NAA.......... Name and Address (VLIE)
NAA.......... Nanny Academy of America [*Defunct*] (EA)
NAA.......... Naphthaleneacetic Acid [*Biochemistry*] (DAVI)
NAA.......... Naphthylacetic [*or Napthaleneacetic*] Acid [*Organic chemistry*]
NAA.......... Narrabri [*Australia*] [*Airport symbol*] (OAG)
NAA.......... Narrow-Angle Acquisition
NAA.......... National Academy of Arbitrators (EA)
NAA.......... National Academy of Astrology [*Defunct*] (EA)
NAA.......... National Aeronautic Association (NADA)
NAA.......... National Aeronautic Association of the USA (EA)
NAA.......... National Aeronautics and Space Administration, Washington, DC [*OCLC symbol*] (OCLC)
NAA.......... National Aeronca Association (EA)
NAA.......... National Aerosol Association (EA)
NAA.......... National Aftermarket Audit Co.
NAA.......... National Aggregates Association (NTPA)
NAA.......... National Airspace Analysis [*FAA*] (TAG)
NAA.......... National Aldrich Association (EA)
NAA.......... National Alumni Association (EA)
NAA.......... National Apartment Association (EA)
NAA.......... National Aphasia Association (NRGU)
NAA.......... National Arborist Association (AGLO)
NAA.......... National Archery Association of the United States (EA)
NAA.......... National Arthritis Act (1974) [*Medicine*] (EDAA)
NAA.......... National Ash Association (EA)
NAA.......... National Association of Accountants [*Montvale, NJ*] (EA)
NAA.......... National Auctioneers Association (EA)
NAA.......... National Automobile Association (NADA)
NAA.......... National Oceanic and Atmospheric Administration [*Department of Commerce*] [*ICAO designator*] (FAAC)
NAA.......... Natural Areas Association (EA)
NAA.......... Naval Air Arm [*British*]
NAA.......... Naval Airship Association (EA)
NAA.......... Naval Attache for Air
NAA.......... Nebraska Arborists Association (EARSL)
NAA.......... Neckwear Association of America (EA)
NAA.......... Network Analysis Area [*Space Flight Operations Facility, NASA*]
NAA.......... Neuron Activation Analysis [*Neurology*] (DAVI)
NAA.......... Neutral Amino Acid [*Biochemistry*]
NAA.......... Neutron Activation Analysis
NAA.......... Neutrophil Aggregation Activity (MELL)
NAA.......... New Art Association (EA)
NAA.......... Newburyport Art Association [*Amateur and professional artists*] [*Connecticut, Maryland, Maine, Massachusetts, and New Hampshire*] (EARSL)
NAA.......... Newsletter Association of America (EA)
NAA.......... Newspaper Association of America [*Reston, VA*] (WDMC)
NAA.......... Next Available Agent (DINT)
NAA.......... Nicotinic Acid Amide [*Also, N*]
NAA.......... Nigerian-American Alliance (EA)
NAA.......... Nitroanthranilic Acid [*Organic chemistry*]
NAA.......... No Apparent Abnormalities [*Medicine*]
NAA.......... Nocturnal Acid Accumulation [*Botany*]
NAA.......... Nocturnal Apnoeic Attack [*Medicine*] (EDAA)
NAA.......... Noise Analysis Approach (ELAL)
NAA.......... Nonattainment Area [*Environmental Protection Agency*] (EPA)
NAA.......... Nord Africa Aviazione
NAA.......... North American Aviation, Inc. [*Later, Rockwell International Corp.*]
NAA.......... North Atlantic Alliance
NAA.......... North Atlantic Area (SARE)

NAA .... North Atlantic Assembly
NAA .... Northeast Atlantic Airlines, Inc. (SAUS)
NAA .... Northern Attack Area
NAA .... Norway-America Association (EA)
NAA .... Notable Asian Americans [*A publication*]
naa .... Not Always Afloat [*Shipping*] (ODBW)
NAA .... Not Always Afloat [*Shipping*]
NAA .... Not at All (SAUS)
NAA .... Nuclear Accidents Agreement (SAUS)
NAA .... Nuclear Activation Analysis (PDAA)
NAA .... Nurses Auxiliaries Association (SAUS)
NAAA .... National Agricultural Aviation Association (EA)
NAAA .... National Alarm Association of America (EA)
NAAA .... National Alliance of Athletic Associations [*Defunct*] (EA)
NAAA .... National Association of American Academicians (NADA)
NAAA .... National Association of Arab Americans (EA)
NAAA .... National Auto Auction Association [*Lincoln, NE*] (EA)
NAAAA ...... National Association for the Advancement of Aardvarks in America [*Defunct*] (EA)
NAAAA ...... National Association of Area Agencies on Aging [*Also, N4A*] (EA)
NAAACC ..... National Association of Antique Automobile Clubs of Canada
NAAACPA ... National Association of Asian American Certified Public Accountants (EA)
NAAAD ...... National Association of Athletes Against Drugs (EA)
NAAAHR .... National Association of African Americans in Human Resources (EA)
NAAAID ..... National Association of Americans of Asian Indian Descent (EA)
NAAAP ...... National Association of Asian-American Professionals (EA)
NAAAP ...... North American Association of Alcoholism Programs [*Later, ADPA*] (EA)
NAAAPI ...... National Association of African Americans for Positive Imagery (EA)
NAAAS ...... National Association for Applied Arts and Sciences (EA)
NAAAS ...... National Association of African American Studies (NTPA)
NAAAS ...... National Association of Air Ambulance Services (SAUS)
NAAASL ..... National Association of African American Students of Law (EA)
NAAB .... National Alliance Against Blacklisting [*Association*] (EA)
NAAB .... National Architectural Accrediting Board (EA)
NAAB .... National Archival Appraisal Board [*Canada*]
NAAB .... National Association of Animal Breeders (EA)
NAABA ...... National Association for the Advancement of the Black Aged (EA)
NAABAVE ... National Association for the Advancement of Black Americans in Vocational Education (EA)
NAABC ...... National Association American Business Clubs [*High Point, NC*]
NAABCV ..... National Association American Balloon Corps Veterans (EA)
NAABI .... National Association of Alcoholic Beverage Importers [*Later, NABI*] (EA)
NAABSA ..... Not Always Afloat but Safe Aground [*Shipping*]
NAAC .... National Accessible Apartment Clearinghouse [*Association*] (EA)
NAAC .... National Adoption Assistance Center (EA)
NAAC .... National Affiliated Corp. [*NASDAQ symbol*]
NAAC .... National Agricultural Advisory Commission (NADA)
NAAC .... National Air Access Council (NTPA)
NAAC .... National Albanian American Council [*Association*] (EA)
NAAC .... National Association for Ambulatory Care (EA)
NAAC .... National Association of Agricultural Contractors [*British*] (BI)
NAAC .... National Association of Avon Collectors (EA)
NAAC .... Navy Aeroballistics Advisory Committee (MCD)
NAAC .... No Apparent Anesthesia Complication [*Medicine*] (MELL)
NAAC .... North American Adoption Congress (EA)
NAACC ...... National Association for American Composers and Conductors (EA)
NAACC ...... National Association of Angling and Casting Clubs [*Later, ACA*]
NAACC ...... Northwest Athletic Association of Community Colleges (PSS)
NAACCR ..... North American Association of Central Cancer Registries
NAACE ...... National Association of Advisers in Computer Education (AIE)
NAACLS ..... National Accrediting Agency for Clinical Laboratory Sciences (EA)
NAACO ...... National Association of American Community Organizations (EA)
NAACO ...... North American Arms Corporation of Canada (SAUS)
NAACOG .... NAACOG: the Organization for Obstetric, Gynecologic, and Neonatal Nurses [*Formerly, Nurses Association of the American College of Obstetricians and Gynecologists*] (EA)
NAACOG .... Nurses Association of the American College of Obstetrics and Gynecology (SAUS)
NAACOGBN ... Nurses Association of the American College of Obstetricians and Gynecologists Bulletin News [*Medicine*] (EDAA)
NAACP ...... National Association for the Advancement of Colored People (EA)
NAACP ...... Neoplasia, Allergy, Addison's Disease, Collagen Disease, and Parasites [*Medicine*]
NAACPA ..... National Association of Asian American Certified Public Accountants (MHDB)
NAACS ...... National Association of Accredited Cosmetology Schools (EA)
NAACS ...... National Association of Adult College Students (EA)
NAACS ...... National Association of Aircraft and Communications Suppliers [*Defunct*] (EA)
NAACSS ..... National Association for the Accreditation of Colleges and Secondary Schools (EA)
NAACSW .... North American Association of Christians in Social Work [*Later, NACSW*] (EA)
NAACT .... National Association of Assessors and Collectors of Taxes [*A union*] [*British*]
NAAD .... National Association of Aluminum Distributors (EA)
NAAD .... Navajo Army Depot [*Arizona*] (AABC)
NAAD .... Nicotine Acid Adenine Dinucleotide (SAUS)
NAAD .... Nicotinic Acid Adenine Dinucleotide [*Biochemistry*]
NAAD .... North American Association for the Diaconate (EA)
NAADAA ..... National Antique and Art Dealers Association of America (EA)
NAADAC ..... National Association of Alcoholism and Drug Abuse Counselors (EA)
NAADAC ..... National Association of Alcoholism and Drug Addiction Counselors (SEAT)
NAADC ...... National Association of Art and Design Companies (EA)
NAADC ...... North American Aerospace Defense Command (SAUS)
NAADC ...... North American Air Defense Command (AAG)
NAADC ...... North American Area Defense Command (SAUS)
NAADD ...... National Association of Athletic Development Directors
NAADD ...... National Association on Alcohol, Drugs & Disability (SAUS)
NAADI .... National Association of Approved Driving Instructors [*British*] (DBA)
NAADM ...... North American Air Defense Modernization (SAUS)
NAADM ...... North American Defense Modernization (SAUS)
NAADMP .... North American Air Defense Master Plan (CCCA)
NAADS ...... New Army Authorization Documents System (AABC)
NAADS ...... New Army Automatic Data System
NAAE .... Agricultural Education National Headquarters [*Association*] (EA)
NAAE .... National Association of Aeronautical Examiners (EA)
NAAE .... National Association of Afro-American Educators
NAAE .... National Association of Agriculture Employees (EA)
NAAE .... Nordic Association for Adult Education (EAIO)
NAAE .... North American Academy of Ecumenists (EA)
NAAEC .... North American Agreement on Environmental Cooperation (EPAT)
NAAEE .... North American Association of Environmental Educators
NAAF .... National Aboriginal Achievement Foundation [*Canada*] (EAIO)
NAAF .... National Alopecia Areata Foundation (EA)
NAAF .... Naval Auxiliary Air Facility
NAAF .... New Amino Acid Formula [*Nutrition*]
NAAF .... North African Air Force [*World War II*]
NAAFA .... National Association of Agricultural Fair Agencies (NTPA)
NAAFA .... National Association to Advance Fat Acceptance (EA)
NAAFA .... National Association to Aid Fat Americans [*Medicine*] (EDAA)
NAAFE .... North American Association of Fisheries Economists (EA)
NAAFETEE ... North American Association For Exports To Eastern Europe (SAUS)
Naafi .... Navy, Army & Air Force Institute (WDAA)
NAAFI .... Navy, Army, and Air Force Institutes [*Responsible for clubs, canteens, and provision of some items for messing of British armed forces*]
NAAFW ...... National Association of Air Forces Women
NAAG .... N-Acetylaspartylglutamic Acid [*Biochemistry*]
NAAG .... National Association of Attorneys General (EA)
NAAG .... NATO Army Advisory Group (NATG)
NAAG .... NATO Army Armaments Group (AABC)
NAAG .... Nordic Association of Applied Geophysics (EA)
NAAG .... North African Adjutant General [*World War II*]
NAAGA ...... North African Adjutant General, Analysis and Control Division [*World War II*]
NAAGC ...... North African Adjutant General, Casualty Branch [*World War II*]
NAAG-DPG ... North Atlantic-Arctic Gateways Detailed Planning Group (SAUS)
NAAGE ...... North African Adjutant General, Personnel Division [*World War II*]
NAAGE ...... North American Alliance for Green Education
NAAGG ...... North African Adjutant General, Executive Division [*World War II*]
NAAGO ...... North African Adjutant General, Operations Division [*World War II*]
NAAGP ...... North African Adjutant General, Postal Division [*World War II*]
NAAGS ...... North African Adjutant General, Statistical Division [*World War II*]
NAAHE ...... National Association for the Advancement of Humane Education [*LA NAHEE*] (EA)
NAAHL ...... National Association of Affordable Housing Lenders (NTPA)
NAAHP ...... National Association for the Advancement of Hispanic People (EA)
NAAHP ...... National Association of Advisors for the Health Professions (EA)
NAAHSC ..... North American Association of Hunter Safety Coordinators
NAAI .... National Alliance of Arts and Industry
NAAI .... National Association of Accountants in Insolvencies (EA)
NAA-ICIF ... North American Association of the ICIF [*International Cooperative Insurance Federation*] [*Detroit, MI*] (EA)
NAAIS .... National Aircraft Accident Investigation School [*FAA*]
NAAIS .... North American Association of Inventory Services [*Greensboro, NC*] (EA)
NAAJ .... National Association of Agricultural Journalists (NTPA)
NAAJHHA ... North American Association of Jewish Homes and Housing for the Aging (EA)
NAAJS .... National Academy for Adult Jewish Studies (EA)
NAAK .... Nerve Agent Antidote Kit [*Military*] (RDA)
NAAL .... National Alliance for Animal Legislation [*Defunct*] (EA)
NAAL .... North American Academy of Liturgy (EA)
NAAL .... North American Aerodynamic Laboratory [*Wind tunnel*] (NASA)
NAALA .... North American Aviation Los Angeles (SAUS)
NAALBWV ... National Association for the Advancement of Leboyer's Birth Without Violence (EA)
NAALC .... National Afro-American Labor Council [*Later, NALC*]
NAALS .... Navigational Aids and Landing Systems (MCD)
NAAM .... National Association of Alternative Medicines (EA)
NAAM .... National Association of Anvil Makers [*A union*] [*British*]
NAAM .... National Association of Architectural Metal Manufacturers (IAA)
NAAM .... North American Aliyah Movement (EA)
NAAMA ...... National Agricultural Advertising and Marketing Association [*Later, NAMA*]
NAAMACC ... National Association for the Accreditation of Martial Arts Colleges and Curriculum (EA)
NAAMCS .... National Association of Air Medical Communication Specialists (EA)
NAAMIC ..... National Association of Automotive Mutual Insurance Companies [*Later, American Insurers Highway Safety Alliance*] (EA)
NAAMM ..... National Association of Architectural Metal Manufacturers (EA)
NAAMM ..... North American Academy of Musculoskeletal Medicine (EA)
NAAMO ..... National Association Agricultural Marketing Officials (NTPA)
NAAN .... National Advertising Agency Network [*New York, NY*] (EA)

NAAN .... North American Advertising Agency Network (NTPA)
NAAN .... Nuclear Arms Alert Network [*Defunct*] (EA)
NAANACM... National Association for the Advancement of Native American Composers and Musicians
NAANAD .... National Association of Anorexia Nervosa and Associated Disorders (DHP)
NAANBW.... National Amalgamated Association of Nut and Bolt Workers [*A union*] [*British*]
NAAND ...... North American Association for the Diaconate (EA)
NA & D C & O... Selection of Cases Decided in the Native Appeal and Divorce Court, Cape and Orange Free State [*A publication*] (DLA)
NA & DT & N... Transvaal and Natal Native Appeal and Divorce Court Decisions [*A publication*] (DLA)
NA&G........ Norgulf Lines (SAUS)
NA & G....... Norgulf Lines (North Atlantic & Gulf) (AD)
NA & G....... North Atlantic & Gulf Steamship Co. (MHDW)
Na & K...... Sodium and Potassium [*Urine test*] [*Biochemistry*] (DAVI)
Na & KSP... Sodium and Potassium Spot [*Urine Test*] (DAVI)
NAANGHT... National Association of Air National Guard Health Technicians (EA)
NAANP ...... National Alliance for the Advancement of Nodnarbian Philosophy (EA)
NAAO........ National Association of Amateur Oarsmen [*Later, USRA*] (EA)
NAAO........ National Association of Artists' Organizations (EA)
NAAO........ National Association of Assessing Officers [*Later, IAAO*]
NAAO........ Navy Area Audit Office [*London*]
NAAO........ North America Aircraft Operations (SAUS)
NAAO........ North American Aircraft Operations (SAUS)
NAAO........ North American Automotive Operations [*Ford Motor Co.*]
NAAOJ....... National Association for the Advancement of Orthodox Judaism (EA)
NAAOP ...... National Association for the Advancement of Older People (EA)
NAAOSE..... National Association of Advisory Officers Special Education [*British*] (DBA)
NAAP .... N-Acetylaminophenazone [*Organic chemistry*]
NAAP .... National Association for Accreditation in Psychoanalysis (EA)
NAAP .... National Association fot the Advancement of Psychoanalysis (NTPA)
NAAP .... National Association of Activity Professionals (EA)
NAAP .... National Association of Advertising Publishers [*Later, AFCP*] (EA)
NAAP .... National Association of Apnea Professionals (EA)
NAAP .... Netherlands Antarctic Programme (SAUS)
NAAP .... Newport Army Ammunition Plant (AABC)
NAAPABAC... National Association for the Advancement of Psychoanalysis and the American Boards for Accreditation and Certification (EA)
NAAPABAP... National Association for the Advancement of Psychoanalysis and the American Board for Accreditation in Psychoanalysis (EA)
NAA PAC.... National Apartment Association PAC [*Alexandria, VA*] (PACS)
NAAPAE..... National Association for Asian and Pacific American Education (EA)
NAAPHE..... National Association for the Advancement of Private Higher Education [*Later, United Student Association*] (EA)
NAAPI .... National Association of Accountants for the Public Interest [*Later, API*] (EA)
NAAPM...... National Association for the Advancement of Perry Mason (EA)
NAAPPA..... North American Association for the Protection of Predatory Animals (SAUS)
NAAPPB..... National Association of Amusement Parks, Pools, and Beaches [*Later, IAAPA*]
NAAPS ...... Nozzle Actuator Auxiliary Power Supply (SAA)
NAAQS ...... National Ambient Air Quality Standards [*Environmental Protection Agency*]
NAAQS ...... National Ambient Air Quality Standards Program (EAGT)
NAAR........ National Alliance for Autism Research (NRGU)
NAAR........ National Association of Advertising Representatives (DGA)
NAAR........ Night Air-to-Air Refueling (SAUS)
NAARD ...... North American Aviation Rocketdyne Division (SAA)
Naar Elec... Naar on Suffrage and Elections [*A publication*] (DLA)
NAARFC..... National Association of Auto Racing Fan Clubs
NAARMC.... National Association of Auto Racing Memorabilia Collectors (EA)
NAARPR .... National Alliance Against Racist and Political Repression (EA)
NAARS ...... National Association of Radio Reading Services (SAUS)
NAARS ...... National Automated Accounting Research System [*American Institute of Certified Public Accountants*] [*Database*] [*Information service or system*] (IID)
NAAS .... National Academy of American Scholars (EA)
NAAS .... National Agricultural Advisory Service [*Later, ADAS*] [*British*]
NAAS .... National Air Audit System [*Environmental Protection Agency*] (GFGA)
NAAS .... National Anorexic Aid Society (EA)
NAAS .... National Association of Academies of Science (EA)
NAAS .... National Association of Art Services [*Later, NAADC*] (EA)
NAAS .... National Aviation Assistance
NAAS .... Naval Area Audit Service
NAAS .... Naval Auxiliary Air Station
NAAS .... Navy Aircraft Accounting System
NAAS .... Navy Area Audit Service (DNAB)
NAAS .... New Academic Appointments Scheme (SAUS)
NAAS .... Newsletter of the Association for Asian Studies (SAUS)
NAAS .... Nordic Association for American Studies (EAIO)
NAAS .... North American Apiotherapy Society (EA)
NAAS .... North American Automated Systems co. (SAUS)
NAASA ...... National African American Speakers Association (EA)
NAASA ...... Native American Art Studies Association (EA)
NAA S&ID... North American Aviation Space and Information Division (SAUS)
NAASC ...... North American Aviation Science Center (SAA)
NAASC ...... Northwest African Air Service Command [*World War II*]
NaAsc .... Sodium Ascorbate (SAUS)
NAASD ...... North American Aviation Space Division (SAA)
NAASER..... National Association of American School Employees and Retirees (EA)
NAASERLDC... National Association of American School Employees and Retirees Legal Defense Counsel (EA)
NAASFEP... National Association of Administrators of State and Federal Education Programs (EA)
NAASL....... North American Academy of the Spanish Language (EA)
NAASLANT... Navy Auxiliary Air Stations, Atlantic
NAASLN..... National Association for Adults with Special Learning Needs (EA)
NAASMWB... National Amalgamated Association of Sheet Metal Workers and Blaziers [*A union*] [*British*]
NAASPAC... Navy Auxiliary Air Stations, Pacific
NAASPL..... North American Association of State and Provincial Lotteries (EA)
NAASR ...... National Association for Armenian Studies and Research (EA)
NAASR ...... North American Association for the Study of Jean-Jacques Rousseau (EA)
NAASS ...... North American Association of Summer Sessions (EA)
NAASTOR... Non-Addressable Auxiliary Storage [*Computer science*] (VLIE)
NAASW...... Nonacoustic Antisubmarine Warfare [*Military*]
NAASW...... Non-Acoustic ASW (SAUS)
NAAT .... National Association of Agricultural Teachers [*Australia*]
NAAT .... Naval Air Advance Training (SAA)
NAATA....... National Asian American Telecommunications Association (EA)
NAATC....... Naval Air Advanced Training Command
NAATD....... North-American Association of Telecommunications Dealers (NTPA)
NAATP....... National Association of Addiction Treatment Providers (EA)
NAATP....... National Association of Alcoholism Treatment Programs (EA)
NAATP....... New African Air Transport Policy (SAUS)
NAATPWB... National Amalgamated Association of Tin Plate Workers and Blaziers [*A union*] [*British*]
NAATS....... National Association of Air Traffic Specialists (EA)
NAATS....... National Association of Auto Trim Shops (EA)
NAATTFO... National Association of Alcohol and Tobacco Tax Field Officers
NAAUG ...... North American Autocad User's Group [*Computer science*] (VLIE)
NAAUS ...... National Archery Association of the United States (NADA)
NAAUSA..... National Association of Assistant United States Attorneys (NTPA)
NAAUTC..... National Amateur Athletic Union Taekwondo Committee [*Later, NAAUTUUSA*] (EA)
NAAUTUUSA... National AAU [*Amateur Athletic Union*] Taekwondo Union of the United Statesof America [*Formerly, NAAUTC*] (EA)
NAAV .... National Alliance Against Violence (EA)
NAAV .... National Association of Atomic Veterans (EA)
NAAV .... North American Association of Ventriloquists (EA)
NAAW .... National Association of Accordion Wholesalers [*Defunct*] (EA)
NAAWER.... National Association of Arc Welding Equipment Repairers [*British*] (DBA)
NAAWFS .... Naval Air All Weather Flight Squadron
NAAWP...... National Association for the Advancement of White People [*Defunct*] (EA)
NAAWS...... NATO Anti-Air Warfare System (DOMA)
NAAWS...... North American Association of Wardens and Superintendents (EAIO)
NAAWU...... National Automobile and Allied Workers' Union [*South Africa*] (SAFN)
NAAWUL .... National Agricultural and Allied Workers' Union of Liberia (IMH)
NAB.......... Mina Airline Company [*Egypt*] [*FAA designator*] (FAAC)
Nab .... Nabatean (BJA)
NAB.......... National Accreditation Board (SAUS)
NAB.......... National Acoustics Board (MUGU)
NAB.......... National Advisory Board (ACII)
NAB.......... National Advisory Body [*British*]
NAB.......... National Aircraft Beacon
NAB.......... National Alliance of Business [*Washington, DC*] (EA)
NAB.......... National Alliance of Businessmen (NADA)
NAB.......... National Apex Body [*India*] (BUAC)
NAB.......... National Associated Businessmen [*Defunct*] (EA)
NAB.......... National Association of Bioengineers [*Defunct*] (EA)
NAB.......... National Association of Boards of Examiners for Nursing Home Administrators (EA)
NAB.......... National Association of Bookmakers Ltd. [*British*] (BI)
NAB.......... National Association of Broadcasters (EA)
NAB.......... National Audience Board [*An association*] (NTCM)
NAB.......... National Australia Bank (EFIS)
NAB.......... National Australia Bank ADS [*NYSE symbol*] (SPSG)
NAB.......... Naval Advanced Base
NAB.......... Naval Air Base
NAB.......... Naval Amphibious Base
NAB.......... Navigational Aid to Bombing [*Air Force*]
NAB.......... Needle Aspiration Biopsy [*Surgery*]
NAB.......... Net Asset Backing
NAB.......... Netware Asynchronous Board (SAUS)
Nab .... Neutralizing Antibodies [*Medicine*] (MELL)
NAB.......... New American Bible
NAB.......... News Agency of Burma
NAB.......... Newspaper Advertising Bureau [*New York, NY*] (EA)
NAB.......... Nickel Alkaline Battery
NAB.......... Nigeria-Arab Bank Ltd.
NAB.......... Nitric Acid Burns [*Medicine*] (MELL)
NAB.......... Nitrosoanabasine [*Organic chemistry*]
NAB.......... Non-A, Non-B [*Hepatitis*] [*Infectious diseases*] (DAVI)
NAB.......... None of the Above
NAB.......... North American Biologicals, Inc.
NAB.......... North American Blastomycosis [*Medicine*] (MELL)
NAB.......... North American Bowhunter [*Association*] (EA)
NAB.......... North Atlantic Base (SAUS)
NAB.......... Not Above [*Aviation*]

NAB .... Not at Bedside [*Medicine*] (MELL)
NAB .... Novarsenobenzene (DMAA)
NAB .... Nuclear Air Burst
NAB .... Nuclear Assembly Building
NAB .... Nut and Bolt
NAB .... Southern Nambikuara [*Language symbol*] (ETLW)
NAB$2CC ... National Association of Bicentennial $2 Cancellation Collectors (EA)
NAB A .... NAB Asset Corp. [*Associated Press*] (SAG)
NABA .... National Alliance of Black Americans
NABA .... National Amateur Basketball Association (EA)
NABA .... National Association of Black Accountants [*Washington, DC*] (EA)
NABA .... National Association of Breweriana Advertising (EA)
NABA .... Native American Business Alliance [*Association*] (EA)
NABA .... Naval Amphibious Base Annex
NABA .... Nitro-(amino)butyric Acid
NABA .... North American Ballet Association [*Defunct*] (EA)
NABA .... North American Benefit Association [*Port Huron, MI*] (EA)
NABA .... North American Broadcasters Association (SAUS)
NABA .... North American Bungee Association (EA)
NABA .... North American Butterfly Association
NABA .... Woman's Life Insurance Society
NABAC ...... National Association for Bank Auditors and Comptrollers [*Later, BAI*] (EA)
NABADA ..... Association of Container Reconditioners
NABARD .... National Bank for Agricultural and Rural Development [*India*] (BUAC)
NABAS ...... National Association of Ballon Suppliers (BUAC)
NABAS ...... National Association of Balloon Artists and Suppliers [*Great Britain*]
NABATRA ... Naval Air Basic Training Center
NABB .... National Association for Better Broadcasting (EA)
NABB .... National Association of Barber Boards (EA)
NABB .... National Association of Business Brokers (EA)
NABBA ...... National Amateur Body Building Association [*British*] (BI)
NABBA ...... North American Brass Band Association (EA)
NABBEA ..... National Association of Boards of Barbers Examiners of America [*Later, NABB*] (EA)
NABBP ...... National Association of Base Ball Players (NDBD)
NABBS ...... National Association of Bench and Bar Spouses (EA)
NABC .... NAB Asset Corp. [*NASDAQ symbol*] (SAG)
NABC .... National Association of Basketball Coaches of the United States (EA)
NABC .... National Association of Bingo Clubs [*British*] (BI)
NABC .... National Association of Boys' Clubs [*British*]
NABC .... Normative Adaptive Behavior Checklist (TES)
NABC .... North American Blueberry Council (EA)
NABC .... North American Bridge Championships (SAUS)
NABC .... North American Broadcasting Corp. (SAUS)
NABCA ...... National Alcoholic Beverage Control Association (EA)
NABCA ...... National Association for Bank Cost Analysis (EA)
NABCA ...... National Association for Bank Cost and Management Accounting (EA)
NABCA ...... National Association of Black Catholic Administrators (EA)
NABCE .... National Association of Black Consulting Engineers (EA)
NABCEO .... National Association of Black Customs Enforcement Officers (EA)
NABCJ .... National Association of Blacks in Criminal Justice (EA)
NABCM ..... National Association of Baby Carriage Manufacturers (EA)
NABCM ..... National Association of Brattice Cloth Manufacturers (EA)
NABCO ...... National Alliance of Breast Cancer Organizations (EA)
NABCO ...... National Association of Black County Officials (EA)
NABCO ...... National Association of Building Cooperatives [*Ireland*] (BUAC)
NABCO ...... Nippon Air Brake Co. Ltd. [*Tokyo, Japan*]
NABCP ...... North American Bat Conservation Partnership
NAB curve ... National Association of Broadcasters Curve (MED)
NABD .... National Association of Bank Directors [*Later, ASBD*] (EA)
NABD .... National Association of Blood Donors (BUAC)
NABD .... National Association of Brick Distributors (EA)
NABD .... Naval Advanced Base Depot
NABD .... North American Band Directors (SAUS)
NABDC ...... National Association of Blueprint and Diazotype Coaters [*Later, ARMM*]
NABDCC ..... North American Band Directors Coordinating Committee (EA)
NABE .... National Association for Bilingual Education (EA)
NABE .... National Association for Business Economics
NABE .... National Association of Bar Executives (EA)
NABE .... National Association of Biological Engineering
NABE .... National Association of Boards of Education (EA)
NABE .... National Association of Book Editors [*Defunct*] (EA)
NABE .... National Association of Business Economists (EA)
NABE .... National Association of Business Education (IAA)
nabe .... Neighborhood (ADWA)
NABE .... North Atlantic Bloom Experiment (SAUS)
NABE .... Nuclear Air Burst Effect
NABEA ...... North American Bicycle Exhibitor Association [*Defunct*] (EA)
NABER ...... National Association of Business and Educational Radio (EA)
NABESS ..... National Association of Business Education State Supervisors [*Stillwater, OK*] (EA)
NABET .... National Association Broadcast Employees and Technicians (EA)
NABEWD .... North American Board for East-West Dialogue (SAUS)
NABEX .... National Bellas Hess Inc. (EFIS)
NABF .... National Alliance of Black Feminists (EA)
NABF .... National Amateur Baseball Federation (EA)
NABF .... North American Baptist Fellowship (EA)
NABF .... North American Boxing Federation (EA)
NABG .... National Association of Blacks within Government (EA)
NABGG ...... National Association of Black Geologists and Geophysicists (EA)
NABHP ...... National Association of Black Hospitality Professionals (EA)
NABI .... Nabi Biopharmaceuticals [*NASDAQ symbol*]
NABI .... NABI, Inc. [*NASDAQ symbol*] (SAG)
NABI .... National Association of Beverage Importers (EA)
NABI .... National Association of Biblical Instructors [*Later, American Academy of Religion*] (EA)
NABI .... National Association of Bunco Investigators
NABI .... North American Biologicals, Inc. (EFIS)
NABIC .... National Association of Bail Insurance Companies (EA)
NABIE .... National Academy of Building Inspection Engineers [*Association*] (EA)
NABIL .... Nepal Arab Bank Ltd. (BUAC)
NABIM .... National Association of Band Instrument Manufacturers (EA)
NABIM .... National Association of British and Irish Millers [*Incorporated*] (DBA)
NABIN .... North Alabama Biomedical Information Network (SAUS)
NABio .... North American Biologicals, Inc. [*Associated Press*] (SAG)
NABIPB ..... National Association of Blacks in Public Broadcasting (SAUS)
NABIR .... Natural and Accelerated Bioremediation Research [*Department of Energy*]
NABIS .... National Association of Business and Industrial Saleswomen [*Denver, CO*] (EA)
NABIS .... National Biological Survey
NABIS .... Northern Alberta Brain Injury Society (SAUS)
NABISCO ... National Biscuit Co. [*Acronym now used as company name*]
NabisH ...... Nabisco Holdings Corp. [*Associated Press*] (SAG)
NABJ .... National Association of Black Journalists (EA)
NAB-JOBS ... National Alliance of Business - Job Opportunities in the Business Sector (OICC)
NABL .... National Accreditation Board for Testing and Calibration Laboratories (SAUS)
NABL .... National Association of Bond Lawyers (EA)
NABL .... National Association of Builders' Labourers [*A union*] [*British*]
NABL .... National Association of Business Leaders (EA)
NABLOC ..... Brussels Tariff Nomenclature for the Latin American Free Trade Association (BARN)
NABLT .... National Association of Business Law Teachers [*Later, NBLC*] (EA)
NABM .... National Association of Bedding Manufacturers [*Later, ISPA*] (EA)
NABM .... National Association of Biscuit Manufacturers (BUAC)
NABM .... National Association of Black Manufacturers (EA)
NABM .... National Association of Blouse Manufacturers (EA)
NABM .... National Association of Boating Magazines [*Defunct*] (EA)
NABM .... National Association of Boat Manufacturers (EA)
NABM .... National Association of Book Manufacturers [*Defunct*] (EA)
NABM .... National Association of British Manufacturers
NABM .... National Association of Building Manufacturers [*Later, HMC*] (EA)
NABMA ...... National Association of British Market Authorities
NABMCC .... National Association of Black and Minority Chambers of Commerce [*Later, NBCC*] (EA)
NABMO ...... NATO Bullpup Management Office [*Missiles*] (NATG)
NABMP ...... National Association of Black Media Producers
NABN .... EMSL-RTP National Atmospheric Background Network (SAUS)
NABO .... Nabors Trailer [*NCIC trailer make code*]
NABO .... National Alliance of Black Organizations (EA)
NABO .... National Association of Bankshot Operators (EA)
NABO .... National Association of Boat Owners (BUAC)
NABO .... North Atlantic Biocultural Organization [*A research cooperative*]
NABOB ...... National Association of Black Owned Broadcasters (EA)
NABOM ...... National Association of Building Owners and Managers [*Later, BOMA*] (EA)
NABOR ...... National Association of Bank Club Organization
Nabors ...... Nabors Industries, Inc. [*Associated Press*] (SAG)
NABP .... National Association of Black Professors (EA)
NABP .... National Association of Boards of Pharmacy (EA)
NABP .... National Association of Book Publishers (NADA)
NABPAC ..... National Association of Business Political Action Committees (EA)
NABPARS ... Navy Automatic Broadcasting, Processing, and Routing System (NG)
NABPLEX ... National Association of Boards of Pharmacy Licensure Examination
NABPO ...... NATO Bullpup Production Organization [*Missiles*] (NATG)
NABPP ...... National Association of Black Procurement Professionals (NTPA)
NABPR ...... National Association of Baptist Professors of Religion (EA)
NABPS ...... National Association of Business and Industrial Saleswomen (NTPA)
NABPULP ... National Book Pulping Centre (BUAC)
NABR .... National Alliance for Belizean Rights [*Political party*] (PSAP)
NABR .... National Association for BioMedical Research (EA)
NABR .... National Association of Baby Sitter Registries [*Later, NASR*] (EA)
NABR .... National Association of Basketball Referees (EA)
NABR .... National Association of Beverage Retailers (NTPA)
NABR .... Natural Bridges National Monument
NaBr .... Sodium Bromide [*Pharmacology*] (DAVI)
NABREP ..... National Association of Black Real Estate Professionals (EA)
NaBRO ...... National Bridge Research Organization [*University of Nebraska--Lincoln*] (RCD)
NABRPAC ... National Association of Beverage Retailers PAC [*Bethesda, MD*] (PACS)
NABRT .... National Association for Better Radio and Television (NADA)
NABRTI ...... National Association of Bar-Related Title Insurers [*San Diego, CA*] (EA)
NABS .... National Advertising Benevolent Society [*British*]
NABS .... National AIDS Behavioral Survey
NABS .... National Alliance of Blind Students (EA)
NABS .... National Association of Bank Servicers (EA)
NABS .... National Association of Barber Schools [*Later, NABSS*] (EA)
NABS .... National Association of Bereavement Services (BUAC)
NABS .... National Association of Black Students (EA)
NABS .... National Association of Breeders Services (DBA)

NABS .... National Association of Business Services [*Baldwin, NY*] (EA)
NABS .... National Association of Buying Services (EA)
NABS .... NATO Airborne SATCOM (MCD)
NABS .... Nordic Association for British Studies (BUAC)
NABS .... Normal Abdominal Bowel Sound [*Medicine*] (CPH)
NABS .... Normoactive Bowel Sounds [*Gastroenterology*] (DAVI)
NABS .... North American Benthological Society (EA)
NABS .... North American Blue-Bird Society (EA)
NABS .... Nuclear-Armed Bombardment Satellite [*Study*] [*Air Force*] (AAG)
NABSC .... National Association of Building Service Contractors [*Later, BSCA*]
NABSCAN... National Advertised Brands Scanning Reports [*Research project*]
NABSE....... National Alliance of Black School Educators (EA)
NABSE....... National Association of Black School Educators (SEAT)
NABSE....... Norwegian Artillery Battery Survey Equipment (SAUS)
NABS/GMF... NATO Airbase Satellite/Ground Mobile Force (MCD)
NABSMSW... National Alliance of Black Salesmen and Saleswomen (NTPA)
NABSP ...... National Association of Blue Shield Plans [*Later, BCBSA*] (EA)
NABSS ...... National Alliance of Black School Superintendents (AEE)
NABSS ...... National Association of Barber Styling Schools (EA)
NABST....... National Advisory Board on Science and Technology [*Canada*]
NABSTP ..... Navy Adult Basic Skills Training Program (NVT)
NABSW...... National Association of Black Social Workers (EA)
NABT .... National Association of Bankruptcy Trustees (EA)
NABT .... National Association of Biology Teachers (EA)
NABT .... National Association of Black Professors (BUAC)
NABT .... National Association of Blind Teachers (EA)
NABTA....... National Association of Business Travel Agents (EA)
NABTC....... National Associated Building Trades Council [*A union*] [*British*]
NABTC....... Naval Air Base Training Command
NABTC....... North American Brain Tumor Coalition (SAUS)
NABTE....... National Association for Business Teacher Education [*Reston, VA*] (EA)
NABTFP ..... National Association of Black Television and Film Producers (NTCM)
NABTMS .... North American Branch of the Maple Society [*Horticulture*]
NABTO ...... National Association of Bar and Tavern Owners (NTPA)
NABT PAC... National Association of Bankruptcy Trustees PAC [*Columbia, SC*] (PACS)
NABTRACOM... Naval Air Basic Training Command (DNAB)
NABTS....... National Alliance Building Trades Society [*A union*] [*British*]
NABTS....... National Association of Broadcast Transmission Standards (PCM)
NABTS....... North American Basic Teletext Specification (WDMC)
NABTS....... North American Broadcasting Teletext Standard (SAUS)
NABTS....... North American Broadcast Teletext Specification (SAUS)
NABTS....... North American Broadcast Teletext Standard (NTCM)
NABTTI ...... National Association of Business Teacher-Training Institutions
NABU .... Express Container Services and Trading [*Intermodal shipping container symbol*] (TVRC)
NABU .... Naval Advanced Base Unit
NABU .... Nonadjusting Ball-Up [*A hopeless state of confusion*] [*Military slang*]
NABUG ...... National Association of Broadcast Unions and Guilds (EA)
NABV .... National Association for Black Veterans (EA)
NABVICU... National Association of Blind and Visually Impaired Computer Users [*Defunct*] (EA)
NABW .... National Association of Bank Women [*Chicago, IL*] (EA)
NABWA...... National Association of Black Women Attorneys (EA)
NABWE...... National Association of Black Women Entrepreneurs [*Detroit, MI*] (EA)
NABWMT ... National Association of Black and White Men Together: A Gay Multiracial Organiz ation for All People (EA)
NABWS...... National Amalgamated Brass Workers' Society [*A union*] [*British*]
NABWU ..... North American Baptist Women's Union (BUAC)
NABX .... Narragansett Bay [*Federal Railroad Administration identification code*]
NABX .... Needle Aspiration Biopsy [*Medicine*] (MELL)
NABZ .... Nabisco [*Federal Railroad Administration identification code*]
NAC.......... Association of Chiropodists (NADA)
NAC.......... CDC National AIDS Clearinghouse (EA)
NAC.......... Nacelle [*Aviation*]
NAC.......... N-Acetyl-L-Cysteine [*Biochemistry*]
NAC.......... Naples Alcofuel Club [*Defunct*] (EA)
NAC.......... NASA Advisory Council (SAUS)
NAC.......... Nashville & Ashland City Railroad [*Federal Railroad Administration identification code*]
NAC.......... National Ability Center (EA)
NAC.......... National Abortion Campaign [*British*] (DBA)
NAC.......... National Academy of Conciliators (EA)
NAC.......... National Accelerator Center [*South Africa*] [*Research center*]
NAC.......... National Access Center [*Defunct*] (EA)
NAC.......... National Accreditation Council (SAUS)
NAC.......... National Accreditation Council for Agencies Serving the Blind and Visually Handicapped (EA)
NAC.......... National Achievement Clubs (EA)
NAC.......... National Action Committee on the Status of Women [*Canada*] (CROSS)
NAC.......... National Addiction Centre [*United Kingdom*] (RCD)
NAC.......... National Adoption Center [*Information service or system*] (IID)
NAC.......... National Advertising Campaign [*Army*]
NAC.......... National Advisory Committee
NAC.......... National Advisory Council
NAC.......... National Aero Club (EA)
NAC.......... National Aeronautical Corp.
NAC.......... National Agency Check [*Security clearance*]
NAC.......... National Agricultural Centre [*British*] (CB)
NAC.......... National Agricultural Council (BUAC)
NAC.......... National Air Carrier Association (MCD)
NAC.......... National Air Charters [*Zambia*] (BUAC)
NAC.......... National Air Communications [*British*]
NAC.......... National Alliance for Caregiving [*An association*]
NAC.......... National Alumni Council of the United Negro College Fund (EA)
NAC.......... National Amusements Council (BUAC)
NAC.......... National Anglers' Council [*British*]
NAC.......... National Anxiety Center (EA)
NAC.......... National Aquaculture Council (EA)
NAC.......... National Archives Council (BUAC)
NAC.......... National Arts Centre [*Canada*]
NAC.......... National Arts Club (EA)
NAC.......... National Asbestos Council (EA)
NAC.......... National Association for the Childless [*British*] (DBA)
NAC.......... National Association of Cemeteries [*Later, ACA*] (EA)
NAC.......... National Association of Choirs [*British*] (BI)
NAC.......... National Association of Composers, USA (EA)
NAC.......... National Association of Concessionaires (EA)
NAC.......... National Association of Conveyancers [*British*] (DBA)
NAC.......... National Association of Coopers [*A union*] [*British*]
NAC.......... National Association of Coroners (EA)
NAC.......... National Association of Counselors (EA)
NAC.......... National Association of Counties
NAC.......... National Asthma Campaign (BUAC)
NAC.......... National Asthma Center [*Later, NJCIRM*]
NAC.......... National Audience Composition [*Nielsen Television Index*] (NTCM)
NAC.......... National Audiovisual Center [*General Services Administration*]
NAC.......... National Automotive Center [*Army*] (RDA)
NAC.......... National Aviation Club (EA)
NAC.......... National Aviation Corp.
NAC.......... Native American Church (ECON)
NAC.......... Native Appeal Courts [*South Africa*] [*A publication*] (DLA)
NAC.......... NATO Alert Committee (SAUS)
NAC.......... Natural Area Council (EA)
NAC.......... Naval Academy
NAC.......... Naval Air Center
NAC.......... Naval Air Command [*British*]
NAC.......... Naval Aircraftman [*British*]
NAC.......... Naval Amyloid Component [*Medicine*]
NAC.......... Naval Avionics Center (MCD)
NAC.......... Navy Acquisition Circular (AAGC)
NAC.......... Navy Activity Control (DNAB)
NAC.......... Navy Advanced Concept (CAAL)
NAC.......... NCAR Administrators Committee (SAUS)
NAC.......... Nebraska Administrative (Code) Rules and Regulations [*A publication*] (AAGC)
NAC.......... Negative Acknowledge Character [*Computer science*] (VLIE)
NAC.......... Negative Air Cushion [*Aviation*] [*Air Force*]
NAC.......... Neighbourhood Advice Council
NAC.......... Neo-American Church (EA)
NAC.......... Net Advertising Circulation (DOAD)
NAC.......... Network Access Center [*Telecommunications*]
NAC.......... Network Access Controller
NAC.......... Network Adapter Card [*Computer science*] (VLIE)
NAC.......... Network Administration Center [*Computer science*] (VLIE)
NAC.......... Network Advisory Committee [*to Library of Congress and Council on Library Resources*]
NAC.......... Network Analysis Center [*Contel, Inc.*] [*Telecommunications service*] (TSSD)
NAC.......... Network Analysis Corporation (CCCA)
NAC.......... Network Appliance Corp. [*Commercial firm*]
NAC.......... Networks and Communications (SAUS)
NAC.......... Nevada Administrative Code (SAUS)
NAC.......... New American Community (MHDB)
NAC.......... New Apostolic Church
NAC.......... New Assembly of Churches (BUAC)
NAC.......... Nielson Audience Composition
NAC.......... Nipple Areolar Complex [*Oncology*]
NAC.......... Nitric Acid Concentrator (MCD)
NAC.......... Nitrogen Mustard [*Mustargen*], Adriamycin, CCNU [*Lomustine*] [*Antineoplastic drug regimen*]
NAC.......... NMCS [*Nuclear Material Control System*] Automatic Control
NAC.......... No Action (SAUS)
NAC.......... No Action Taken on Communication [*Travel industry*] (TRID)
NAC.......... No Additional Charge
NAC.......... No Apparent Change (MCD)
NAC.......... Noise Advisory Council [*British*]
NAC.......... Nonairline Carrier [*Aerospace*]
NAC.......... Nordic Academic Council [*Defunct*] (EA)
NAC.......... Nordic Actors' Council (EAIO)
NAC.......... Nordic Association for Campanology (EA)
NAC.......... Normal Approach Course [*Navy*] (NVT)
NAC.......... North American Collectors (EA)
NAC.......... North American Committee [*An association*] (EA)
NAC.......... North American Craton (ODA)
NAC.......... North American Mortgage Co. [*NYSE symbol*] (SPSG)
NAC.......... North Atlantic Coast
NAC.......... North Atlantic Conference (PSS)
NAC.......... North Atlantic Council
NAC.......... North Atlantic Current [*Oceanography*]
NAC.......... North Atlantic Nickel Corp. [*Toronto Stock Exchange symbol*] [*Canada*]
NAC.......... North Atlantic Shipping Conference (DS)
NAC.......... Northeast Air Command

NAC......... Northern Air Cargo, Inc. [*ICAO designator*] (FAAC)
NAC......... Norwegian-American Council (SAUS)
NAC......... Norwegian American Cruises (SAUS)
NAC......... Nous Autres Canada [*Association*] [*Canada*] (EAIO)
NAC......... Nozzle Area Control
NAC......... Nuclear Assurance Corp.
NAC......... Null Attached Concentrator (SAUS)
NAC......... Null Attachment Concentrator (SAUS)
NAC......... Nursing Audit Committee (MEDA)
NAC......... US Catholic Bishops' National Advisory Council (EA)
NACA........ National Academy of Chiropractic Assistants [*An association*]
NACA........ National Academy of Code Administration (EA)
NACA........ National Acoustical Contractors Association [*Later, CISCA*] (EA)
NACA........ National Advisory Committee for Aeronautics [*Functions transferred to NASA, 1958*]
NACA........ National Advisory Committee on Aeronautics [*OST*] (TAG)
NACA........ National Advisory Council on Aging (SAUS)
NACA........ National Agricultural Chemicals Association (EA)
NACA........ National Air Carrier Association (EA)
NACA........ National Animal Control Association (EA)
NACA........ National Armored Car Association (EA)
NACA........ National Association for Campus Activities (EA)
NACA........ National Association for Children of Alcoholics (DHP)
NACA........ National Association for Clean Air [*South Africa*] (BUAC)
NACA........ National Association for Court Administration (EA)
NACA........ National Association of Catastrophe Adjusters [*Comfort, TX*] (EA)
NACA........ National Association of Cellular Agents (EA)
NACA........ National Association of Child Advocates (EA)
NACA........ National Association of Childbirth Assistants (EA)
NACA........ National Association of Chinese Americans
NACA........ National Association of Chiropractic Attorneys
NACA........ National Association of Christian Athletes
NACA........ National Association of Christians in the Arts (EA)
NACA........ National Association of Consumer Advocates (EA)
NACA........ National Association of Cost Accountants [*Later, NAA*]
NACA........ National Association of County Administrators (EA)
NACA........ National Association of Cuban Architects (in Exile) [*Defunct*] (EA)
NACA........ National Athletic and Cultural Association [*Ireland*] (EAIO)
NACA........ National Athletic and Cycling Association (BUAC)
NACA........ National Autosound Challenge Association [*Later, IASCA*] (EA)
NACA........ Native American Casino Association
NACA........ Naval Aviation Cadet Act of 1942
NACA........ Neighborhood Assistance Corporation of America
NACA........ Netherlands-America Community Association (EA)
NACA........ Network of Aquaculture Centres in Asia (BUAC)
NACA........ North American Center on Adoption [*Defunct*] (EA)
NACA........ North American Coastal Alliance
NACA........ North American College of Acupuncture
NACA........ North American Comente Association (SAUS)
NACA........ North American Corriente Association (EA)
NACA........ North American Currach Association (EA)
NACA........ North Australian Canine Association
NACA........ Nunavut Arts and Crafts Association [*Canada*]
NACAA...... National Assembly of Community Arts Agencies (EA)
NACAA...... National Association of Community Action Agencies (EA)
NACAA...... National Association of Computer-Assisted Analysis (IAA)
NACAA...... National Association of Consumer Agency Administrators (EA)
NACAA...... National Association of County Agricultural Agents (EA)
NACAB...... National Accreditation Council for Agencies Serving the Blind and Visually Handicapped [*New York, NY*]
NACAB...... National Agricultural Centre Advisory Board (BUAC)
NACAB...... National Association of Citizens Advice Bureaus [*British*] (DBA)
NACAB...... National Association of Citizens Advice Bureaux (ODA)
NACA BCA... Nationalo Advisory Commission for Aeronautics Board of Contract Appeals (AAGC)
NACAC...... National Association of Catholic Alumni Clubs [*Later, CACI*] (EA)
NACAC...... National Association of College Admission Counselors (EA)
NACAC...... North African Antiaircraft Section [*World War II*]
NACAC...... North American Council on Adoptable Children (EA)
NACACP..... National Cash Register Applied COBOL [*Common Business-Oriented Language*] Package (IAA)
NACADA..... National Academic Advising Association (EA)
NACAE....... National Advisory Council on Adult Education [*Washington, DC*]
NACAE....... National Advisory Council on Art Education (BUAC)
NACAF....... Northwest African Coastal Air Force [*World War II*]
NACAL....... Navy Air Cooperation and Liaison Committee
NACAM...... National Association of Corn and Agricultural Merchants (BUAC)
NAC & O.... Cape and Orange Free State Native Appeal Court, Selected Decisions [*A publication*] (DLA)
NACAO...... National Association of County Arts Officers (BUAC)
NACAP...... National Association of Claims Assistance Professionals (EA)
NACAP...... National Association of Co-Op Advertising Professionals [*Defunct*] (EA)
NACAR...... National Advisory Committee on Aeronautical Research [*South Africa*] (BUAC)
NACARM.... Northwest America Civil Air Routes Manual
NACAS...... National Advisory Committee on Agricultural Services [*Canada*] (BUAC)
NACAS...... National Association of College Auxiliary Services (EA)
NACAT....... National Association of College Automotive Teachers (EA)
NACAT....... North American Council of Automotive Teachers (NTPA)
NACATS..... North American Clear Air Turbulence Tracking System [*Aviation*]
NACAWM-USA... National Association of Cuban Women and Men of the United States (EA)
NACAW-USA... National Association of Cuban-American Women of the USA (EA)
NACB........ National Academy of Clinical Biochemistry (NTPA)
NACB........ National Association of Catering Butchers [*British*] (DBA)
NACB........ National Association of College Broadcasters (EA)
NACB........ National Association of Convention Bureaus (NADA)
NACB........ Native American Community Board (EA)
NACB........ Navy and Army Canteen Board [*British military*] (DMA)
NACBA...... National Association of Church Business Administration (EA)
NACBC...... Natinal Advisory Centre on the Battered Child (BUAC)
NACBFAA... National Association of Customs Brokers and Forwarders Association of America
NACBHD.... National Association of County Behavioral Health Directors (EA)
NACBO...... National Association of Cosmetic Boutique Owners (EA)
NACBP...... No-Adjust Car Building Process [*Ford Motor Co.*] [*Automotive engineering*]
NACBS...... National Affiliation of Concerned Business Students [*Defunct*] (EA)
NACBS...... National Association and Council of Business Schools
NACBS...... North American Conference on British Studies (EA)
NACBT....... National Association of Cognitive-Behavioral Therapists (SAUS)
NACC........ National Aboriginal Consultative Committee [*Australia*] (BUAC)
NACC........ National Advisory Cancer Council
NACC........ National Agency Check Center (AFM)
NACC........ National Air Conservation Commission (EA)
NACC........ National Alliance of Czech Catholics (EA)
NACC........ National Association for Colitis and Crohn's Disease (BUAC)
NACC........ National Association for Core Curriculum (EA)
NACC........ National Association of Career Colleges [*Canada*] (EAIO)
NACC........ National Association of Catholic Chaplains (EA)
NACC........ National Association of Childbearing Centers (EA)
NACC........ National Association of Colitis and Crohn's Disease [*United Kingdom*] (EAIO)
NACC........ National Association of Collegiate Commissioners [*Later, CCA*] (EA)
NACC........ National Association of Counsel for Children (EA)
NACC........ National Automatic Controls Conference
NACC........ Naval Academy Computer Center
NACC........ Nigerian-American Chamber of Commerce (NTPA)
NACC........ North America Control Committee (SAUS)
NACC........ North American Calibration Cooperation (SAUS)
NACC........ North American Car [*Federal Railroad Administration identification code*]
NACC........ North American-Chilean Chamber of Commerce (EA)
NACC........ North Atlantic Christian Conference (PSS)
NACC........ North Atlantic Co-operation Council (SAUS)
NACC........ North Atlantic Council for Cooperation (SAUS)
NACC........ Norwegian American Chamber of Commerce
NACC........ Novel Architectures Computing Committee [*British*]
NAC (C)..... Selected Decisions of the Native Appeal Court (Central Division) [*1948-51*] [*South Africa*] [*A publication*] (DLA)
NACCA...... National Association for Creative Children and Adults (EA)
NACCA...... National Association of Claimants' Counsel of America [*Also known as NACCA Bar Association*] [*Later, ATLA*]
NACCA...... National Association of Consumer Credit Administrators (EA)
NACCA...... National Association of County 4-H Club Agents [*Later, NAE4-HA*] (EA)
NACCA...... National Association of County Civil Attorneys (EA)
NACCA...... North American Council of Chemical Associations (SAUS)
NACCAC..... National Community College Athletic Conference (PSS)
NACCALJ... National Association of Claimants' Compensation Attorneys. Law Journal [*A publication*] (DLA)
NACCAM.... National Coordinating Committee for Aviation Meteorology
NACCAN..... National Association of Christian Councils and Networks (BUAC)
NAC (C & O)... Reports of the Decisions of the Native Appeal Courts, Cape Province and the Orange Free State [*South Africa*] [*A publication*] (ILCA)
NACCAS..... National Accrediting Commission of Cosmetology Arts and Sciences (EA)
NACCB...... National Accreditation Council for Certification Bodies (AIE)
NACCB...... National Association of Computer Consultant Businesses (EA)
NACCB HIGH TECH PAC... National Association of Computer Consultant Businesses High-Tech PAC [*Alexandria, VA*] (PACS)
NACCC...... National Association of Citizens Crime Commissions (EA)
NACCC...... National Association of Congregational Christian Churches [*Later, CCCNA*] (EA)
NACCC...... Network of Access and Child Contact Centres (BUAC)
NACCC...... North American-Chilean Chamber of Commerce (NTPA)
NACCCA..... National Association of Civilian Conservation Corps Alumni (EA)
NACCCA..... North American Chinese Clinical Chemists Association (EA)
NACCCAN... National Centre for Christian Communities and Networks [*Westhill College*] [*British*] (CB)
NACCD...... National Advisory Commission on Civil Disorders (NADA)
NACCDD.... National Association of County Community Development Directors (EA)
NACCE....... National Advisory Council on Continuing Education (OICC)
NACCE....... North American Conference on Christianity and Ecology (EA)
NACCED..... National Association for County Community and Economic Development (NTPA)
NACCES..... Naval Air Crew Combat Ejection Seat (DWSG)
NACCG...... National Association of Crankshaft and Cylinder Grinders [*British*] (BI)
NACCHO.... National Aboriginal Community-Controlled Health Organization [*Australia*]
NACCHO.... National Association of County and City Health Officials (NTPA)
NACCIC...... National Association of County Intergovernmental Relations Officials (NTPA)

NACCIMA... Nigerian Association of Chambers of Commerce, Industry, Mines and Agriculture (SAUS)
NACCM...... National Association for Child Care Management [*Defunct*] (EA)
NACCMHC... National Academy of Certified Clinical Mental Health Counselors (DHP)
NACCO...... NACCO Industries, Inc. [*Associated Press*] (SAG)
NACCO...... North American Coal Corp. (EFIS)
NACCP...... North American Cambridge Classics Project (SAUS)
NACCRRA... National Association of Child Care Resource and Referral Agencies (EA)
NACCRT..... North America Coordinating Center for Responsible Tourism (EA)
NACCS...... National Association for Chicana and Chicano Studies (NTPA)
NACCSMA... NATO Command and Control Systems Management Agency (PDAA)
NACCSS..... National Association of Commodity Cargo Superintendents and Surveyors [*British*] (DBA)
NACCT...... North American Congress of Clinical Toxicology (SAUS)
NACCU...... National Association of Campus Card Users (EA)
NACCU...... National Association of Canadian Credit Unions (BUAC)
NACCW...... National Advisory Centre on Careers for Women [*British*] (CB)
NACCWO.... National Association of Civil Court Welfare Officers (BUAC)
NACD........ National Academy for Child Development (SAUS)
NACD........ National Alliance of Cleaning Distributors [*Commercial firm*] (EA)
NACD........ National Association for Cave Diving [*Inactive*]
NACD........ National Association for Community Development [*Defunct*] (EA)
NACD........ National Association of Chemical Distributors (EA)
NACD........ National Association of Computer Dealers (ROAS)
NACD........ National Association of Conservation Districts
NACD........ National Association of Container Distributors (EA)
NACD........ National Association of Corporate Directors [*Washington, DC*] (EA)
NACD........ Not Acidified [*Biochemistry*] (DAVI)
NACDA...... National Archive for Computerized Data on Aging [*Department of Health and Human Services*] (GFGA)
NACDA...... National Archive of Computerized Data on Aging (MHID)
NACDA...... National Arts and Cultural Development Act of 1964
NACDA...... National Association of Collegiate Directors of Athletics (EA)
NACDAC..... National Association for City Drug and Alcohol Coordination [*Defunct*] (EA)
NACDAP..... National Advisory Council for Drug Abuse Prevention [*Terminated, 1975*] (EGAO)
NACDC...... National Association of Career Development Consultants (EA)
NACDD...... National Advisory Council on Services and Facilities for the Developmentally Disabled [*Terminated, 1978*] [*HEW*] (EGAO)
NACDE...... National Action Committee for Drug Education [*Medicine*] [*USOE*] (EDAA)
NACDE...... National Association for Child Development and Education [*Later, NACCM*] (EA)
NACDET..... National Association of Colleges in Distributive Education and Training (BUAC)
NACDFB..... National Association of Canada Dry Franchise Bottlers (EA)
NACDFLM... National Association of Catholic Diocesan Family Life Ministers [*Later, NACFLM*] (EA)
NACDL...... National Association of Criminal Defense Lawyers (EA)
NACDLF..... National Association of Community Development Loan Funds (EA)
NACDPA..... National Association of County Data Processing Administrators (EA)
NACD PAC... National Association of Chemical Distributors [*Arlington, VA*] (PACS)
NAC/DPC.... North Atlantic Council/Defense Planning Committee (SAUS)
NACDR...... National Association of College Deans and Registrars [*Later, NACDRAO*] (EA)
NACDRAO... National Association of College Deans, Registrars, and Admissions Officers (EA)
NACDS...... National Association of Chain Drug Stores (EA)
NACDS...... North American Clinical Dermatologic Society (EA)
NACE........ Nace International
NACE........ National Advisory Committee for Electronics
NACE........ National Advisory Committee on Electronics [*India*] (BUAC)
NACE........ National Association for Career Education (EA)
NACE........ National Association for Curriculum Enrichment and Extension [*British*] (EAIO)
NACE........ National Association of Catering Executives (EA)
NACE........ National Association of Childbirth Education [*Defunct*] (EA)
NACE........ National Association of Colleges and Employers
NACE........ National Association of Corrosion Engineers (EA)
NACE........ National Association of Counsellors in Education (AIE)
NACE........ National Association of County Engineers (EA)
NACE........ National Autobody Congress and Exposition [*Precision Planning and Sales, Inc.*] (TSPED)
NACE........ Native Americans for a Clean Environment (EA)
NACE........ Neutral Atmospheric Composition Experiment [*Geophysics*]
NACE........ North American Commission on the Environment
NACE........ North American Cycle Exhibitor Association (EA)
NACEBE..... National Association of Classroom Educators in Business Education [*Cambridge City, IN*] (EA)
NACEC...... National Association of Charitable Estate Counselors (EA)
NACEC...... North American Center for Emergency Communications (EA)
NACEC...... North American Commission for Environmental Cooperation (SAUS)
NACEC...... North American Committee of Enamel Creators (EA)
NACECE..... National Advisory Council on Extension and Continuing Education
NACED...... National Advisory Committee on the Education of the Deaf [*Terminated, 1973*] [*HEW*] (EGAO)
NACED...... National Advisory Council on the Employment of Disabled People (BUAC)
NACED...... National Advisory Council on the Employment of the Disabled [*British*]
NACEDC..... National Advisory Council on Education of Disadvantaged Children (OICC)
NAC/EDP.... National Advisory Council on Education Professions Development [*HEW*] (EGAO)
NAC-EDTA... N-Acetyl-L-Cysteine Ethylenediaminetetra-Acetic Acid [*Biochemistry*] (MAE)
NACEEO..... National Advisory Council on Equality of Educational Opportunity [*Termina ted, 1979*] [*HEW*] (EGAO)
NACEHC..... National Accreditation Council for Environmental Health Curricula (EA)
NACEIC...... National Advisory Council on Education for Industry and Commerce (MCD)
NACEL....... Navy Air Crew Equipment Laboratory [*Philadelphia, PA*]
NACEO...... National Advisory Council on Economic Opportunity (EA)
NACEPD..... National Advisory Council on Education Professions Development [*Terminate d, 1976*] [*HEW*] (OICC)
NACEPE..... National Association of Creamery Proprietors and Wholesale Dairymen (BUAC)
NACEPT..... National Advisory Committee for Environmental Policy and Technology [*Environmental Protection Agency*]
NACERI...... National Advisory Council for Educational Research and Improvement [*Washington, DC*] [*Department of Education*] (GRD)
NACES....... National Association of Credential Evaluation Services (EA)
NACES....... Navy Aircrew Common Ejection Seat [*British*]
NACES....... Navy Aircrew Escape System (POLM)
NACESA..... Navarra de Componentes Electronicos (EFIS)
NACESW.... National Association of Chief Education Social Workers (AIE)
NACETA..... National Association of County Employment and Training Administrators [*Later, NACTEP*] (EA)
NACEW...... National Advisory Council on the Employment of Women [*New Zealand*] (BUAC)
NACF........ National Agricultural Cooperative Federation [*Republic of Korea*] (BUAC)
NACF........ National Art-Collectors' Fund [*British*]
NACF........ National Association of Church Furnishers [*British*] (BI)
NACF........ Navy Air Combat Fighter (MCD)
NACFA....... North American Clun Forest Association (EA)
NACFAM.... National Coalition for Advanced Manufacturing [*Association*] (EA)
NACFE....... National Association of Certified Fraud Examiners (EA)
NACFFA..... National Advisory Committee for the Flammable Fabrics Act
NACFI....... North American Council on Fishery Investigations (SAUS)
NACFL....... National Advisory Committee on Farm Labor [*Defunct*] (EA)
NACFLM.... National Association of Catholic Family Life Ministers (EA)
NACFR...... National Association of Casual Furniture Retailers (EA)
NACFRC..... North Atlantic Coastal Fisheries Research Center (SAUS)
NACFRC..... North Atlantic Coastal Fisheries Research Centre (BUAC)
NACFT....... National Academy for Certified Family Therapists (SEAT)
NACFT....... National Academy of Counselors and Family Therapists (EA)
NACFT....... National Association of Cattle Foot Trimmers (GVA)
NACG........ National Association of Conservative Graduates (AIE)
NACG........ National Association of County Governments (OICC)
NACG........ North African Commanding General [*World War II*]
NACGC...... National Association of Collegiate Gymnastics Coaches (Men) (EA)
NACGC...... National Association of Colored Girls Clubs [*Later, NAGC*] (EA)
NACGG...... North American Commercial Gladiolus Growers [*Later, CGD-NAGC*] (EA)
NACGM...... National Association of Chewing Gum Manufacturers (EA)
NACGS...... North American Cottage Garden Society
NACGS/NADS... Combined North American Cottage Garden Society and North American Dianthus Society [*Association*] (EA)
NACGT...... National Association of Careers and Guidance Teachers [*British*] (DBA)
NACH........ National Academy of Clinicians and Holistic Health (EA)
NACH........ National Advisory Committee on the Handicapped
NACH........ National Advisory Council for the Handicapped (NADA)
NACH........ National Association for the Craniofacially Handicapped (EA)
NACH........ National Association of Clergy Hypnotherapists (EA)
NACH........ National Association of Coal Haulers [*Defunct*] (EA)
nAch......... Need for Achievement
NACHA...... National Automated Clearing House Association [*Washington, DC*] (EA)
NACHA...... National Collegiate Hockey Association (PSS)
NACHC...... National Advisory Committee on Handicapped Children [*Terminated, 1973*] [*HEW*] (EGAO)
NACHC...... National Association of Christian Colleges (PSS)
NACHC...... National Association of Community Health Centers (EA)
Nach Chem Tech... Nachrichten aus Chemie, Technik und Laboratorium (MEC)
NACHES..... Association of Jewish Family, Children's Agency Professionals (EA)
NACHFA..... National Association of County Health Facility Administrators (EA)
NACHGR.... National Advisory Council for Human Genome Research (HGEN)
NACHM...... Nachmittags [*Afternoon*] [*German*]
NACHO...... National Association of Chemical Hygiene Officers (SARE)
NACHO...... National Association of County Health Officials (EA)
NACHP...... National Association of Counsellors, Hypnotherapists and Psychotherapists (BUAC)
NACHP...... North African Chaplain's Section [*World War II*]
NAChR...... Nicotinic Acetylcholine Receptor [*Immunology*]
NACHRI..... National Association of Children's Hospitals and Related Institutions (EA)
NACHRK.... North American Coalition for Human Rights in Korea (EA)
NACHSA..... National Association of County Human Services Administrators (EA)
NACHVRO... National Air Conditioning, Heating, Ventilating, and Refrigeration Officials (EA)
NACI......... NACAL [*Common carrier symbol*]
NACI......... Naphthenic Acid Corrosion Index
NACI......... National Agency Check and Inquiry (EAGT)
NACI......... National Agency Check and Written Inquiries
NACI......... National Association for the Cottage Industry (EA)

NACIA .... National Association of Crop Insurance Agents [*Anoka, MN*] (EA)
NACIA PAC... National Association of Crop Insurance PAC [*Memphis, TN*] (PACS)
NACIE .... National Advisory Council on Indian Education (OICC)
NACIFO...... National Association of Church and Institutional Financing Organizations [*Atlanta, GA*] (EA)
NACIME..... North American Committee for IME [*Institut Medical Evangelique*] [*Defunct*] (EA)
NACIO .... National Association of County Information Officers (EA)
NACIO .... Naval Air Combat Information Office [*or Officer*]
NACIP .... Navy Assessment and Control of Installation Pollutants
NACIS .... National Credit Information Service [*TRW, Inc.*] [*Long Beach, CA*] [*Credit-information databank*] (IID)
NACIS .... Naval Air Combat Information School
NACIS .... Navy Air Control and Identification System
NACIS .... Networking Analytical and Computing Information Systems [*National Aeronautics and Space Administration*]
NACIS .... North American Cartographic Information Society (EA)
NACISA...... North Atlantic Communications and Information Systems Agency [*NATO*]
NACISO ..... NATO Communications and Information Systems Organization (EAIO)
NACITA...... National Association of County Information Technology Administrators (NTPA)
NACJ .... National Association of Costume Jewelers [*Defunct*] (EA)
NACJD....... National Archive of Criminal Justice Data [*Database*] (GDD)
NACJP....... National Association of Criminal Justice Planners [*Defunct*] (EA)
NACK .... National Advisory Committee on Kangaroos (BUAC)
NACK .... Negative Acknowledgment [*Telecommunications*]
NACK .... Nonacknowledgment Character [*Computer science*]
NACL .... National Advisory Commission on Libraries
NACL .... National Association for Community Leadership (EA)
NACL .... Navy/ARPA [*Advanced Research Projects Agency*] Chemical LASER (MCD)
NACL .... Nippon Aviatronics Corp. Ltd. [*Japan*]
NaCl .... Sodium Chloride [*Salt*] [*Chemistry*] (DAVI)
NACLA....... National Cooperation for Laboratory Accreditation (SAUS)
NACLA....... North American Congress on Latin America (EA)
NACLC....... National Association of Community Legal Centers [*Australia*]
NACLE....... National Association of Chimney Lining Engineers [*British*] (DBA)
NACLEO..... National Association of Coin Laundry Equipment Operators (EA)
NACLIS...... National Commission on Libraries and Information Science [*Washington, DC*]
NACLM...... North African Claims Section [*World War II*]
NACLO ...... National Association of Canoe Liveries and Outfitters (EA)
NACLO ...... National Association of Community Leadership Organizations [*Later, National Association for Community Leadership*] (EA)
NACLP....... North American Conference on Logic Programming (SAUS)
NACLS....... National Association of Commission Lumber Salesmen
NACLS....... North Alabama Cooperative Library System [*Library network*]
NACLS....... North American Canon Law Society (NTPA)
NACLSO..... National Assembly of Chief Livestock Sanitary Officials [*Later, United States Animal Health Association*] (EA)
NACM .... National Association for Court Management (EA)
NACM .... National Association of Chain Manufacturers (EA)
NACM .... National Association of Charcoal Manufacturers [*British*] (DBA)
NACM .... National Association of Cider Makers [*British*] (BI)
NACM .... National Association of Colliery Managers [*British*] (DBA)
NACM .... National Association of Cotton Manufacturers (BUAC)
NACM .... National Association of Credit Management ,
NACM .... Networks and Communications Marketing (SAUS)
NACMA...... National Armored Cable Manufacturers Association (EA)
NACMA...... National Association of Collegiate Marketing Administrators
NACMA...... NATO ACCS Management Agency (SAUS)
NACMB...... National Association of Certified Mortgage Bankers [*Later, NSREF*] (EA)
NACMC...... National Association for Church Management Consultants (EA)
NACMC...... National Association of Christian Marriage Counselors [*Defunct*] (EA)
NACMCF .... National Advisory Committee on Microbiological Criteria for Foods
NACME...... National Action Council for Minorities in Engineering (EA)
NACMEMS... National Association of Continuing Medical Education Meetings and Seminars [*Defunct*] (EA)
NACMHD.... National Association of County Mental Health Directors (NTPA)
NACMIS..... Navy Automated Civilian Management Information System
NACM-NCR... National Association of Credit Management - East Coast [*Maryland, the District of Columbia, and Virginia*] (EARSL)
NACMO...... National Association of Cigarette Machine Operators [*British*] (DBA)
NACMO...... National Association of Competitive Mounted Orienteering (EA)
NACMO...... NATO ACCS Management Organisation (SAUS)
NACMW..... North American Council for Muslim Women (EA)
NACM-WM... National Association of Credit Management - Western Michigan (EARSL)
NACN........ Newspaper Advertising Co-Op Network (EA)
NACN........ North American Cellular Network (CGWS)
NAC (N & T)... Decisions of the Native Appeal and Divorce Court (Transvaal and Natal) [*South Africa*] [*A publication*] (ILCA)
NAC (NE) ... Decisions of the Native Appeal Court (North Eastern Division) [*South Africa*] [*A publication*] (ILCA)
NACNE ...... National Advisory Council on Nutrition Education [*British*]
NACNEMS... North American Cooperative Network of Enhanced Measurement Sites (SAUS)
NACNS ...... National Association of Clinical Nurse Specialists (NTPA)
NACO........ Name Authority Co-Operative (NITA)
NACO........ National Advisory Committee on Oceanography [*Marine science*] (MSC)
NACO........ National Agricultural Co. [*St. Christopher and Nevis*] (BUAC)
NACO........ National Agricultural Credit Office [*Vietnam*] (BUAC)
NACO........ National Association of Charterboat Operators (EA)
NACO........ National Association of Condominium Owners
NACO........ National Association of Consumer Organizations
NACO........ National Association of Cooperative Officials [*A union*] [*British*] (DCTA)
NACO........ National Association of Counties [*Emergency Management*] (EMA)
NACO........ National Coordinated Cataloging Operations [*Library science*]
NACO........ Navy Acquisition-Contracting Officer (MCD)
NACO........ Navy Coolant [*Gunpowder*]
NACO........ Night Alarm Cut-Off (SAUS)
NACO........ Noise Abatement and Control Office (SAUS)
NACOA ...... If Not Available Your Command, Obtain Accounting Data from Administrative Command [*Army*] (AABC)
NACOA ...... National Advisory Committee on Oceans and Atmosphere [*Marine science*] (MSC)
NACOA ...... National Association for Children of Alcholics (BUAC)
NACoA....... National Association for Children of Alcoholics (EA)
NACOA ...... National Association for Children of Alcoholism and Other Addictions (EA)
NACOA ...... National Association of Cruise Oriented Agents (TVEL)
NACODS .... National Association of Colliery Overmen, Deputies, and Shotfirers [*A union*] [*British*] (DCTA)
NACOEJ ..... North American Conference on Ethiopian Jewry (EAIO)
NACOI .... National Association of Canadians of Origins in India
NACOL ...... National Advisory Commission on Libraries
NACOLADS... National Council on Libraries, Archives and Documentation Services [*Jamaica*] (BUAC)
NACOM...... National Communications [*System*]
NACOM...... Northern Area Command
NACOMEX... National Computer Exchange
NACON ...... Newspaper Advertising Co-Op Network (EA)
NACOP ...... National Association of Chiefs of Police (NTPA)
NACOPRW... National Conference of Puerto Rican Women (EA)
NACOR ...... National Advisory Committee on Radiation
NaCOR ...... National Center on Occupational Readjustment [*Defunct*] (EA)
NACORE..... National Association of Corporate Real Estate Executives (EA)
NACORF..... National Association of Counties Research Foundation
NACOS ...... National Communications Schedule
NACOS ...... NATO Courier Service (NATG)
NACOS ...... North African Chief of Staff [*World War II*]
NACOSH .... National Advisory Committee on Occupational Safety and Health
NACOSH .... National Advisory Committee on Scouting for the Handicapped (EA)
NACOSS..... National Approval Council for Security Systems (BUAC)
NACP .... National Academy of Cable Programming (NTCM)
NACP .... National Accounts Capability Programme [*United Nations*] (EY)
NACP .... National Association of Chiefs of Police (AD)
NACP .... National Association of County Planners (EA)
NACP .... National Attack Civil Preparedness [*Emergency Management*] (EMA)
NACP .... Navy Acoustical Communication Program (MCD)
NACP .... Network Against Coercive Psychiatry (EA)
NACP .... Nordic Association of Clinical Physics [*Medicine*] (EDAA)
NACP .... North Atlantic Consultive Process (OSI)
NACPA....... National Association of Church Personnel Administrators (EA)
NACPA....... National Association of County and Prosecuting Attorneys [*Later, NDAA*]
NACPA....... North American Concert Promoters Association (NTPA)
NACPAC..... National Action Committee [*Hollywood, FL*] (PACS)
NACPAC..... North American Chronic Pain Association of Canada (SAUS)
NACPAC..... North American Coal Corporation PAC [*Dallas, TX*] (PACS)
NACPAF..... National Associated CPA Firms [*Association*] (EA)
NACPC ...... North American Christian Peace Conference (EA)
NACPCC..... National Advisory Committee for Pig Carcase Competitions (BUAC)
NACPD ...... National Association of County Planning Directors [*Later, NACP*] (EA)
NACPDCG... National Association of Catholic Publishers and Dealers in Church Goods (EA)
NACPDE..... National Advice Centre for Postgraduate Dental Education (BUAC)
NACPR ...... National Association of Corporate and Professional Recruiters (EA)
NACPRO .... National Association of County Park and Recreation Officials (EA)
NACPU ...... National Amalgamated Coal Porters' Union [*British*]
NACPUISCW... National Amalgamated Coal Porters' Union of Inland and Seaborne Coal Workers [*British*]
NACR........ Nashville & Ashland City Railroad [*Federal Railroad Administration identification code*]
NACR........ National Advisory Committee on Radiation
NACR........ Native American Cancer Research [*Association*] (EA)
NACRA ...... North American Case Research Association (EA)
NACRC ...... National Association of Community Relations Council (BUAC)
NACRC ...... National Association of County Recorders and Clerks (EA)
NACRCD .... National Advisory Council on Rural Civil Defense
NAC Re ..... NAC RE Corp. [*Associated Press*] (SAG)
NACRE ...... North American Coalition on Religion and Ecology (EA)
NACRF ...... National Association of Counties Research Foundation (OICC)
NACRMR.... National Advisory Committee on Rhesus Monkey Requirements
NACRO ...... National Association for the Care and Resettlement of Offenders [*British*]
nacro .... Night-Alarm Cutoff (AD)
NACRS ...... National Asbestos-Contractor Registration System (COE)
NACRS ...... North African Censorship Section, US [*World War II*]
NACR (SR)... Native Appeal Court Reports (Southern Rhodesia) [*A publication*] (ILCA)
NACRT....... National Association of Canadian Race Tracks
NACRU ...... North American Committee for Reconciliation in Ulster (EA)
NACS .... National Advisory Committee on Semiconductors

NACS .... National Ambulatory Care Survey [*Medicine*] (EDAA)
NACS .... National Association for Check Safekeeping [*Washington, DC*] (EA)
NACS .... National Association for Chicano Studies (EA)
NACS .... National Association of Carpet Specialists [*Defunct*]
NACS .... National Association of Chimney Sweeps [*British*] (DBA)
NACS .... National Association of Christian Schools [*Defunct*] (EA)
NACS .... National Association of Christian Singles (EA)
NACS .... National Association of Civic Secretaries (EA)
NACS .... National Association of Collection Sites (EA)
NACS .... National Association of College Stores (EA)
NACS .... National Association of Computer Stores [*Later, IVCI*] [*Defunct*] (EA)
NACS .... National Association of Concession Services (EA)
NACS .... National Association of Consumer Shows (NTPA)
NACS .... National Association of Convenience Stores (EA)
NACS .... National Association of Cosmetology Schools (EA)
NACS .... National Association of County Surveyors (NTPA)
NACS .... Natural Areas of Canadian Significance [*NPPAC*]
NACS .... NetWare Asynchronous Communication Service [*Novell, Inc.*]
NACS .... Network Assisted Coordinated Science (ACAE)
NACS .... Neurologic and Adaptive Capacity Scoring [*System*]
NACS .... Nonlinear Automatic Control System (SAUS)
NACS .... Nordic Association for Clinical Sexology (BUAC)
NACS .... North American Catalysis Society (NTPA)
NACS .... North American Communications Corp. (SAUS)
NACS .... North Atlantic Current System [*Oceanography*]
NACS .... Northern Area Communications System (MCD)
NACS .... Nucleic Acid Chromatography System
NAC (S) ..... Selected Decisions of the Native Appeal Court (Southern Division) [*South Africa*] [*A publication*] (ILCA)
NACSA ...... National Advisory Committee on Safety in Agriculture
NACSA ...... National Association for Corporate Speaker Activities (EA)
NACSA ...... National Association of Casualty and Surety Agents [*Bethesda, MD*] (EA)
NACSA ...... North American Computer Service Association (EA)
NACSAA..... National Advisory Council for South Asian Affairs (EA)
NACSAP..... National Alliance Concerned with School-Age Parents [*Defunct*] (EA)
NACSARS... National Association of Companion Sitter Agencies and Referral Services [*Later, PCA*] (EA)
NACSB ...... Naval Aviation Cadet Selection Board
NACSC ...... National Association of Cold Storage Contractors (EA)
NACSCAOM... National Accreditation Commission for Schools and Colleges of Acupuncture and Oriental Medicine (EA)
NACSCC..... National Association of Community Schools, Colleges, and Centres [*British*] (DBA)
NACSCS..... National Advisory Council on Supplementary Centers and Services
NACSDA..... National Association of Commissioners, Secretaries, and Directors of Agriculture[*Later, NASDA*] (EA)
NACSDC..... North American Conference of Separated and Divorced Catholics (EA)
NACSE....... National Association of Casualty and Surety Executives [*New York, NY*] (EA)
NACSE....... National Association of Civil Service Employees (EA)
NACSE....... Non-Avionics Common Support Equipment (MCD)
NACSI .... National Communications Security Instruction (COE)
NACSI .... National COMSEC Information (SAUS)
NACSIC...... National Association of Cold Storage Insulation Contractors (EA)
NACSIM..... NATO Communications Security Information (NATG)
NACSIS...... National Academic Center for Science Information Systems (SAUS)
NACSIS...... National Center for Science Information Systems [*Japan*]
NACSM...... National Association of Catalog Showroom Merchandisers (EA)
NACSN ...... North American Commission on Stratigraphic Nomenclature (SAUS)
NACSPMR... National Association of Coordinators of State Programs for the Mentally Retarded[*Later, National Association of State Mental Retardation Program Directors*] (EA)
NACSS ...... National Approved Council for Security Systems (WDAA)
NACSS ...... National Association of Clerical and Supervisory Staffs (BUAC)
NACST....... National Association of Catholic School Teachers (EA)
NACSW...... National Action Committee on the Status of Women [*Canada*] (AD)
NACSW...... North American Association of Christians in Social Work (EA)
NACT .... NASA Activities [*A publication*]
NACT .... National Alliance of Cardiovascular Technologists (EA)
NACT .... National Association of Careers Teachers (AD)
NACT .... National Association of Chapter 13 Trustees (MHDB)
NACT .... National Association of Clinical Tutors [*British*] (DBA)
NACT .... National Association of Consumers and Travelers (EA)
NACT .... National Association of Corporate Treasurers [*Washington, DC*] (EA)
NACT .... National Association of Craftsman Tailors [*British*] (BI)
NACT .... National Association of Cycle Traders [*British*] (BI)
NACT .... National Association of Cycle Trades (AD)
NACT .... National Automatic Controller for Testing (MUGU)
NACT .... Normalized from Actual Read [*Electric utility company*]
NACTA....... National Association of Colleges and Teachers of Agriculture (EA)
NACTA....... National Association of Commissioned Travel Agents (TVEL)
NACTAC..... Navy Antenna Computer Tracking and Command
NAC (T & N)... Reports of the Decisions of the Native Appeal Courts (Transvaal and Natal) [*South Africa*] [*A publication*] (ILCA)
NACTEFL... National Advisory Council on the Teaching of English as a Foreign Language (EA)
NACTEP..... National Association of County Training and Employment Professionals [*Washington, DC*] (EA)
NACTFO..... National Association of County Treasurers and Finance Officers (EA)
NACTP....... National Association of Computerized Tax Processors (EA)
NACTST..... National Advisory Council on the Training and Supply of Teachers (AD)
NACTU ...... National Affiliation of Carpet Trade Unions (BUAC)
NACTU ...... National Council of Trade Unions [*South Africa*] (BUAC)
NACTU ...... Night Attack Combat Training Unit [*Navy*]
NACU .... National Association of Colleges and Universities
NACU .... Navigazione Alga [*Intermodal shipping container symbol*] (TVRC)
NACUA ...... National Association of College and University Administrators [*Superseded by NEA Higher Education Council*] (EA)
NACUA ...... National Association of College and University Attorneys (EA)
NACUBO .... National Association of College and University Business Office Associations (AD)
NACUBO .... National Association of College and University Business Officers [*Washington, DC*] (EA)
NACUC ...... National Association of College and University Chaplains and Directors of Religious Life (EA)
NACUC ...... National Association of Credit Union Chairmen (NTPA)
NACUFS..... National Association of College and University Food Services (EA)
NACUP ...... National Association of Credit Union Presidents (EA)
NACUSA..... National Association of Composers, USA (EA)
NACUSAC... National Association of Credit Union Supervisory and Auditing Committees (EA)
NACUSIP.... National Congress of Union in the Sugar Industry of the Philippines (BUAC)
NACUSO .... National Association of Credit Union Service Organizations (NTPA)
NACUSS..... National Association of College and University Summer Sessions [*Later, NAASS*]
NACUTCD... National Advisory Committee on Uniform Traffic Control Devices [*Terminated, 1979*] [*Department of Transportation*] (EGAO)
NACUTSO... National Association of College and University Traffic and Security Officers (EA)
NACV .... National Association of Concerned Veterans (EA)
NACVA....... National Association of Certified Valuation Analysts (NTPA)
NACVCB..... National Association of Crime Victim Compensation Boards (EA)
NACVE....... National Advisory Council on Vocational Education
NA-CVR ..... National Association for Crime Victims Rights (EA)
NACVS ...... National Association of Councils for Voluntary Service (BUAC)
NACW .... National Advisory Committee on Women (AD)
NACW .... National Association of College Women [*Later, NAUW*] (EA)
NACW .... National Association of Commissions for Women (EA)
NACWAA..... National Association of Collegiate Women Athletic Administrators (NTPA)
NACWC...... National Association of Colored Women's Clubs (EA)
NACWD ..... National Association of County Welfare Directors [*Later, NACHSA*] (EA)
NACWEP .... National Advisory Council on Women's Educational Programs (OICC)
NACWIS..... Navy Controlled Waste Information System
NACWPI..... National Association of College Wind and Percussion Instructors (EA)
NACWPI..... National Association of College Wind and Percussion Instruments (AD)
NACWRR.... National Advisory Committee on Water Resources Research [*Canada*]
NACWS...... Naval Aircraft Collision Warning System (SAUS)
NACWS...... North African Chemical Warfare Section [*World War II*]
NACX .... Northern Air Cargo, Inc. [*Air carrier designation symbol*]
NACYS ...... National Advisory Council for Youth Services (AIE)
NACZ .... Northwest Alloy [*Federal Railroad Administration identification code*]
NAd.......... Addison Public Library, Addison, NY [*Library symbol*] [*Library of Congress*] (LCLS)
nad .... Nadir (AD)
NAD.......... Nadir (WDAA)
NAD.......... Named [*Telegraphy*] (PCTE)
NAD.......... Nansen Arctic Drilling program (SAUS)
NAD.......... Nansen Arctic Drilling Project (SAUS)
NAD.......... Naphthaleneacetamide [*Herbicide*]
NAD.......... National Academy of Design (EA)
NAD.......... National Advertising Division [*of the Council of Better Business Bureaus*]
NAD.......... National Alliance for Democracy [*Political party*] (AD)
NAD.......... National Armaments Director (NATG)
NAD.......... National Association of Druggists [*Medicine*] (EDAA)
NAD.......... National Association of the Deaf (EA)
NAD.......... National Audience Demographics Report [*Nielsen Television Index*] (NTCM)
NAD.......... NATO Air Doctrine (NATG)
NAd.......... Naval Adviser [*British*]
NAD.......... Naval Air Defense (NATG)
NAD.......... Naval Air Depot
NAD.......... Naval Air Detachment (MCD)
NAD.......... Naval Air Detail
NAD.......... Naval Air Development Center, Warminster, PA [*OCLC symbol*] (OCLC)
NAD.......... Naval Air Division [*British*]
NAD.......... Naval Ammunition Depot [*Charleston, SC*]
NAD.......... Naval Armament Depot [*British*]
NAD.......... Naval Aviation Depot (AAGC)
Nad .... Nedezhda (AD)
NAD.......... Network Access Device
nad .... Networking Addressing Device [*Computer science*] (AD)
NAD.......... New Antigenic Determinant [*Immunochemistry*]
NAD.......... New Audio Dimension
NAD.......... Nicotene-Adenine Dinucleotide (SAUS)
NAD.......... Nicotinamide-Adenine Dinucleotide [*Preferred form, but also see ARPPRN, DPN, NADH*] [*Biochemistry*]
NAD.......... Nicotinamide Adenine Dinucleotide Oxidized (EDCT)
NAD.......... Nicotinic Acid Dehydrogenase [*An enzyme*] (AAMN)
NAD.......... Nielson Audience Demographic Report [*A publication*] (DOAD)
NAD.......... Night Air Defence [*British*] [*World War II*]

NAD .... Nitric Acid Dihydrate [*Inorganic chemistry*]
Nad .... Nitrosamide [*Biochemistry*]
NAD .... No Abnormal Discovery [*Medicine*] (DB)
NAD .... No Abnormality Demonstrable (SAUS)
NAD .... No Abnormality Detected [*Medicine*]
NAD .... No-Acid Descaling (IEEE)
NAD .... No Active Disease (DAVI)
NAD .... No Acute Distress [*Medicine*]
nad .... No Apparent Defect (AD)
NAD .... No Apparent Defect [*Shipping*]
NAD .... No Apparent Distress [*Medicine*]
nad .... No Appreciable Difference (AD)
nad .... No Appreciable Disease (AD)
NAD .... No Appreciable Disease [*Medicine*]
NAD .... Nobelair [*Turkey*] [*ICAO designator*] (FAAC)
NAD .... Node Administration (NITA)
NAD .... Noise Amplitude Distribution
NAD .... Nordiska Namden for Alkohol- och Drogforskning [*Nordic Council for Alcohol and Drug Research - NCADR*] (EAIO)
NAD .... Normal Axis Deviation [*Medicine*]
NAD .... North American Aero Dynasty [*Vancouver Stock Exchange symbol*]
NAD .... North American Datum
NAD .... North Atlantic Division [*Army Engineers*]
nad .... Nothing Abnormal Detected (AD)
NAD .... Nothing Abnormal Detected [*or Discovered*] [*Medicine*]
NAD .... Nothing Abnormal Discovered (SAUS)
nad .... Not on Active Duty [*Military*] (AD)
NAD .... Not on Active Duty
NAD .... Nuclear Accident Dosimeter (SAUS)
NAD .... Nuclear Accident Dosimetry
NaD .... Sodium Dialysate [*Medicine*] (EDAA)
NAD 27 ...... North American Datum of 1927 (CARB)
NAD83 .... North American Datum of 1983 (USDC)
NADA .... Dealers Election Action Committee of the National Auto Dealers Association [*McLean, VA*] (PACS)
NADA .... N-Acetyldopamine [*Biochemistry*]
NADA .... National Art Dealers Association [*Later, ADA*] (EA)
NADA .... National Association for Disabled Athletes (EA)
NADA .... National Association of Dealers in Antiques (EA)
NADA .... National Association of Dental Assistants (EA)
NADA .... National Association of Drama Advisers [*British*]
NADA .... National Association of Drug Addiction (AD)
NADA .... National Automobile Dealers Association [*McLean, VA*] (EA)
NADA .... National Democratic Alliance [*Zambia*] [*Political party*] (EY)
NADA .... Navajo Army Depot Activity [*Arizona*] [*Army*]
NADA .... New Animal Drug Application [*Food and Drug Administration*]
NADA .... North American Datacom [*NASDAQ symbol*] (QUAN)
NADA .... Numerical Analysis and Computing Science (SAUS)
NADABA ..... N-Adenosyldiaminobutyric Acid [*Biochemistry*] (DB)
NADABB ..... National Alzheimer's Disease Autopsy and Brain Bank (AD)
NADAC ...... National Air Duct Cleaners Association
NADAC ...... National Anti-Drug Abuse Campaign (AD)
NADAC ...... National Automotive Dealer Advisory Council
NADAC ...... National Damage Assessment Center
NADAC ...... Naval ASW [*Antisubmarine Warfare*] Data Center (NVT)
NADAC ...... Navigation Data Assimilation Computer (IAA)
NADAC ...... Pacific Command, North Vietnam Air Defense Analysis and Coordinating Group (CINC)
NADACS ..... National Air Defense and Airspace Control System (ACAE)
NADAF ...... National Association of Decorative Architectural Finishes (EA)
NADAG ...... National Association of Diocesan Altar Guilds of the Protestant Episcopal Church (EA)
NADAP ...... National Association on Drug Abuse Problems (EA)
NADAPI ..... National Alcoholism and Drug Abuse Program Inventory [*Department of Health and Human Services*] (GFGA)
NADAR ...... No After Duty Action Required [*Military*]
NADAR ...... North American Data Airborne Recorder
NADase ..... Nicotinamide Adenine Dinucleosidase (SAUS)
NADase ..... Nicotinamide-Adenine Dinucleotide Glycohydrolase [*Also, DPNase*] [*An enzyme*]
NADASO .... National Association Drug and Allied Sales Organizations [*Wyncote, PA*] (EA)
NADASO .... National Association of Design and Art Service Organizations (EA)
NADB .... National Aerometric Data Bank [*Office of Air and Radiation*] (COE)
NADB .... National Air Data Branch [*Environmental Protection Agency*] [*Information service or system*] (IID)
NADB .... National Archeological Database (GDD)
NADB .... National Atmospheric Data Bank (GNE)
NADB .... National Audience Data Bank [*Newspaper Marketing Bureau*] [*Information service or system*] (CRD)
NADB .... North American Development Bank
NADB .... US EPA National Air Data Branch (SAUS)
NADBR ...... National Association for the Deaf, Blind, and Rubella [*British*]
NADBRH .... National Association for Deaf-Blind and Rubella Handicapped (BUAC)
NADC .... National Advisory Drug Committee [*HEW*]
NADC .... National Animal Data Centre (BUAC)
NADC .... National Animal Disease Center [*Ames, IA*] [*Department of Agriculture*] [*Research center*] (GRD)
NADC .... National Anti-Drug Coalition [*Defunct*] (EA)
NADC .... National Anti-Dumping Committee (EA)
NADC .... National Arctic and Antarctic Data Centres (SAUS)
NADC .... National Arts and Disability Center (SAUS)
NADC .... National Association of Demolition Contractors (EA)
NADC .... National Association of Demonstration Companies (NTPA)
NADC .... National Association of Dredging Contractors (EA)
NADC .... NATO Air Defense Committee
NADC .... NATO Defense College [*Also, NADEFCOL, NDC*]
NADC .... Naval Aide-de-Camp [*British military*] (DMA)
NADC .... Naval Air Development Center [*Also, NADEVCEN, NAVAIRDEVCEN*] [*Warminster, PA*]
NADC .... Naval Ammunition Depot, Concord [*California*]
NADC .... Non-Associated Developing Countries (EURO)
NADC .... North American Digital Cellular (CGWS)
NADC .... North American Digital Cellular system (SAUS)
NADC .... Northern Agricultural Development Corp. (AD)
NADC .... Northern Region Agricultural Development Centre [*Thailand*] (BUAC)
NADC .... Nothern Alberta Development Council (SAUS)
NADC .... Nuclear Affairs Defence Council (SAUS)
NADCA ...... National Air Duct Cleaners Association
NADCA ...... National Animal Damage Control Association (EA)
NADCA ...... North American Die Casting Association (SAUS)
NADCA ...... North American Draft Cross Association (EA)
NADC-AC ... Naval Air Development Center - Aerospace Crew Equipment Department
NADC-ACL ... Naval Air Development Center - Aeronautical Computer Laboratory (DNAB)
NADC-AE ... Naval Air Development Center - Aero-Electronic Technology Department
NADC-AI ... Naval Air Development Center - Aeronautical Instruments Laboratory
NADC-AM ... Naval Air Development Center - Aero-Mechanics Department
NADC-AML ... Naval Air Development Center - Aeronautical Materials Laboratory (DNAB)
NADCAP ..... National Aerospace and Defense Contractors Accreditation Procedures (SAUS)
NADCAP ..... National Aerospace and Defense Contractors Accreditation Program [*DoD*]
NADC-AP ... Naval Air Development Center - Aeronautical Photographic Experimental Laboratory
NADC-AR ... Naval Air Development Center - Aviation Armament Laboratory
NADC-ASL ... Naval Air Development Center - Aeronautical Structures Laboratory (DNAB)
NADC-ASW ... Naval Air Development Center - Antisubmarine Warfare Laboratory
NADC-AW ... Naval Air Development Center - Air Warfare Research Department
NADC-AWG ... Naval Air Development Center - Acoustical Working Group
NADC-CS .... Naval Air Development Center - Crew Systems Department
NADC-ED .... Naval Air Development Center - Engineering Development Laboratory
NADC-EL .... Naval Air Development Center - Aeronautical Electronic and Electrical Laboratory
NADCI .... North American Die Casting Institute (SAUS)
NADC-LS .... Naval Air Development Center - Life Sciences and Bio-Equipment Group
NADC-ML ... Naval Air Development Center - Aviation Medical Acceleration Laboratory
NADC-MR ... Naval Air Development Center - Aerospace Medical Research Department
NADCO ...... National Agricultural Development Co. [*Saudi Arabia*] (BUAC)
NADCO ...... National Association of Development Companies (EA)
NAD-CO ..... Naval Ammunition Depot, Concord [*California*]
NADCORP ... National Development Corp. [*Ireland*] (BUAC)
NADCP ...... National Association of Drug Court Programs (SEAT)
NAD-CR ..... Naval Ammunition Depot, Crane [*Indiana*]
NADCRC .... National Advisory Dental & Craniofacial Research Council (SAUS)
NADCs .... National Antarctic Data Centres (SAUS)
NADC-SD ... Naval Air Development Center - Systems Analysis and Engineering Department
NADC-ST .... Naval Air Development Center - Aero Structures Department
NADC-SY .... Naval Air Development Center - Systems Project Department
NADC-WR ... Naval Air Development Center - Air Warfare Research Department
NADD .... National Association for the Dually Diagnosed (PAZ)
NADD .... National Association of Deputising Doctors [*British*] (DBA)
NADD .... National Association of Diemakers and Diecutters [*Formerly, DDA*] (EA)
NADD .... National Association of Disco Disc Jockeys [*Defunct*] (EA)
NADD .... National Association of Distributors and Dealers of Structural Clay Products [*Later, NABD*] (EA)
NADD .... NNational Association of Diaconante Directors (NTPA)
NADDC ...... National Association of Developmental Disabilities Councils (EA)
NADDIS ..... Narcotics and Dangerous Drugs Intelligence File (AD)
NADDM ..... National Association of Daytime Dress Manufacturers [*Defunct*]
NADDMI/MR ... National Association for the Dually Diagnosed Mental Illness/Mental Retardation (NTPA)
NADDRG .... North American Deep Drawing Research Group [*Automotive metal stampings*]
NADE .... National Association for Design Education [*British*]
NADE .... National Association for Developmental Education (EA)
NADE .... National Association for Drama in Education [*Australia*]
NADE .... National Association of Disability Examiners (EA)
NADE .... National Association of Document Examiners (EA)
NADEC ...... National Agricultural Development Co. [*Saudi Arabia*] (BUAC)
NADEC ...... National Association of Development Education Centres [*British*] (DBA)
NADEC ...... Navy Decision Center
NADEC ...... Navy Development Center (CAAL)
NaDEC ...... Sodium Diethyl Dithiocarbamate (SAUS)
NADECO .... National Development Co. [*Ghana*] (BUAC)

NADECT..... National Association for Drama in Education and Children's Theatre (BUAC)
NADEE....... National Association of Divisional Executives for Education [*British*]
NADEEC..... NATO Air Defense Electronic Environment Committee
NADeFA..... North American Deer Farmers Association (NTPA)
NaDefCo.... NATO [*North Atlantic Treaty Organization*] Defense College (AD)
NADEFCOL... NATO Defense College [*Also, NADC, NDC*] [*Rome, Italy*]
NADEL....... National Association of Democratic Lawyers [*South Africa*] (SAFN)
NADEM...... National Association of Dairy Equipment Manufacturers [*Later, DFISA*] (EA)
NADEO...... National Association of Diocesan Ecumenical Officers (EA)
NADEP...... National Association of Disability Evaluating Professionals (NTPA)
NADEP...... Naval Aviation Depot (MCD)
NADEPA..... National Democratic Party [*Solomon Islands*] [*Political party*] (PPW)
NADET....... National Association of Distributive Education Teachers
NADE(V).... National Association for Drama in Education (Victoria) [*Australia*]
NaDevCen... Naval Air Development Center (AD)
NADEVCEN... Naval Air Development Center [*Also, NADC, NAVAIRDEVCEN*]
NADEX...... NATO Data Exchange (NATG)
NADF........ National Addison's Disease Foundation (EA)
NADF........ National Adrenal Diseases Foundation (EA)
NADF........ National Alzheimer's Disease Foundation (AD)
NADF........ National Arbor Day Foundation (EA)
NADF........ North American Directory Forum
NADFA....... North American Deer Farmers Association (EA)
NADFAS..... [*The*] National Association of Decorative and Fine Arts Societies [*British*]
NADFAS..... National Association of Design and Fine Art Societies (AD)
NADFD...... National Association of Decorative Fabric Distributors (EA)
NADFPM.... National Association of Domestic and Farm Pump Manufacturers [*Later, WSC*]
NADFS...... National Association of Drop Forgers and Stampers (AD)
NADG........ Nicotinamide Adenine Dinucleotide Glycohydrolase [*An enzyme*] (DMAA)
NADGE...... NATO Air Defense Ground Environment
NADGE...... NATO Air Defense Ground Equipment
NADGECO... NATO Air Defense Ground Environment Consortium
NADGEMO... NADGE [*NATO Air Defense Ground Environment*] Management Office [*Belgium*]
NADGEMO... NATO Air Defense Ground Environment Management Organization (NATG)
NADH........ Dihydronicotinamide Adenine Dinucleotide (AD)
NADH........ Naval Ammunition Depot, Hawaii
NADH........ Nicotinamide-Adenine Dinucleotide (Reduced) [*See also NAD*] [*Biochemistry*]
NADHCI..... North American District Heating and Cooling Institute [*Defunct*] (EA)
NADHPRS... Naval Ammunition Depot Hawthorne Police Records System (DNAB)
NADI......... National Association of Display Industries [*New York, NY*] (EA)
NADI......... Naval Ammunition Depot, Indiana
NADIB....... North American Defense Industrial Base
NADIBO..... North American Defense Industrial Base Organization
NADIDE..... Nicotinamide Adenine Dinucleotide (SAUS)
NADIN....... National Airspace Data Interchange Network [*FAA*] (TAG)
NADIN II... National Airspace Data Interchange Network II [*National digital message switching network for aeronautical data*] (GAVI)
NADIP....... Navy Display Improvement Program
NADIS....... National Aerometric Data Information System [*Environmental Protection Agency*]
NADJ........ National Association of Disk Jockeys (BUAC)
NADL........ National Animal Disease Laboratory [*Iowa*]
NADL........ National Association of Dental Laboratories (EA)
NADL........ Navy Authorized Data List (NG)
NADL........ Navy Avionics Development Laboratory (SAUS)
NADLCC..... National Association of Defense Lawyers in Criminal Cases [*Later, NACDL*] (EA)
NADLJ....... National Association of Dental Laboratories Journal [*Medicine*] (EDAA)
NAD-LLL.... Naval Ammunition Depot - Lwalualei [*Hawaii*] (DNAB)
NADM....... National Association of Discount Merchants [*Defunct*] (EA)
NADM....... National Association of Doll Manufacturers [*Later, NADSTM*] (EA)
NADM....... Naval Administration
NADMAP.... Naval Architecture Design & Material Assistance Programme (SAUS)
NADMC...... Naval Air Development and Material Center
NaDMC...... Sodium Dimethyl Dithiocarbamate (SAUS)
NADME...... Noise Amplitude Distribution Measuring Equipment (PDAA)
NADMR..... National Association of Diversified Manufacturers Representatives [*Later, NAGMR*] (EA)
NADMW..... National Association of Direct Mail Writers
NAD/NADH... Nicotinamide Adenine Dinucleotide (AD)
NADO........ National Association of Development Organizations (EA)
NADO........ Navy Accounts Disbursing Office
NADO........ New Airport Development Office (SAUS)
NADO........ New Airport Development Organization (SAUS)
NADOA...... National Association of Division Order Analysts (EA)
NADOC...... Naval Aviation Depot Operations Center (DOMA)
NADOI....... National Association of Dog Obedience Instructors (EA)
NADONA/LTC... National Association of Directors of Nursing Administration in Long Term Care (EA)
NADOP...... Natural Disaster Operations Plan [*Emergency Management*] (EMA)
NADOP...... North American Defense Operational Plan (SAUS)
NADOP...... North American Defense Operation Plan [*NORAD*]
NADOR...... Notification of Accidents and Dangerous Occurrences Regulations 1980 (HEAS)
NADORF.... National Association of Development Organization Research Fund
NADORF.... National Association of Development Organizations Research Foundation (EA)
NADOT...... North Atlantic Deepwater Oil Terminal (PDAA)
NADOW..... National Association for Training the Disabled in Office Work (AD)
NADP........ National Acid Deposition Program [*Air pollution*]
NADP........ National Association of Deafened People (BUAC)
NADP........ National Association of Dental Plans (NTPA)
NADP........ National Association of Desktop Publishers (EA)
NADP........ National Association of Doctors in Practice [*British*] (DI)
NADP........ National Atmospheric Deposition Program [*Department of Agriculture*]
NADP........ NAVAIR Advanced Development Plan (MCD)
nadp......... Nicotinamide Adenine Dinucleotide Phosphate (AD)
NADP........ Nicotinamide-Adenine Dinucleotide Phosphate [*Preferred form, but see also TPN*] [*Biochemistry*]
NADP........ Northern Alberta Dairy Pool (SAUS)
NADPAC..... National Association of Dental Plans [*Dallas, TX*] (PACS)
NADPAS..... National Association of Discharged Prisoners' Aid Societies [*British*] (DI)
NADPB...... North Atlantic Defense Production Board (NATG)
NADPH...... Dihydronicotinamide Adenine Dinucleotide Phosphate (AD)
nadph....... Dihydronicotinamide Adenine Dinucleotide Phosphate (AD)
NADPH...... Nicotinamide-Adenine Dinucleotide Phosphate (Reduced) [*Preferred form, but see also TPNH*] [*Biochemistry*]
NADR........ Normalized Aggregate Data Rate (SAUS)
NADREG.... National Alliance for Democratic Restoration in Equatorial Guinea [*Switzerland*] (EAIO)
NADREPS... National Armaments Directors Representatives
NADS........ National Advanced Driver Simulator [*NHTSA*] (TAG)
NADS........ National Armament Directors [*NATO*]
NADS........ National Association Diaper Services (EA)
NADS........ National Association for Down Syndrome (EA)
NADS........ National Automobile Driving Simulator
NADS........ Naval Air Development Station
NADS........ Nevada Automated Diagnostics System (SAUS)
NADS........ North American Data Systems (SAUS)
NADS........ North American Dostoevsky Society (EA)
NADS........ North Atlantic Defense System
NADSA...... National Agricultural Diversification and Settlement Authority [*Sri Lanka*] (BUAC)
NADSA...... National Association of Dramatic and Speech Arts (EA)
NADSA...... North American Dairy Sheep Association (NTPA)
NADSC...... National Association of Direct Selling Companies [*Later, DSA*] (EA)
NADSIC..... No Apparent Disease Seen in Chest [*Medicine*] (EDAA)
NADSP...... National Association of Dental Service Plans [*Insurance*] (DHSM)
NADSTM.... National Association of Doll and Stuffed Toy Manufacturers (EA)
NADT........ National Association for Drama Therapy (EA)
NADTC...... North Atlantic Air Defense Technical Center (SAUS)
NADTCA..... North American Diecast Toy Collectors Association (EA)
NADTP...... National Association of Desktop Publishers (NTPA)
NADU........ Naval Aircraft Delivery Unit
NADU........ Naval Air Development Unit (MUGU)
NADU........ Redon [*Intermodal shipping container symbol*] (TVRC)
NADUC...... Nimbus/Ats Data Utilization Center (SAUS)
NADUG...... North American Datamanager Users Group (EA)
NADUS...... National Association of Doctors in the United States (EA)
NADUSM.... National Association of Deputy United States Marshals (EA)
NADVH...... National Association of Drama with the Visually Handicapped (BUAC)
NADW....... National Association of Disabled Writers (BUAC)
NADW....... North Atlantic Deep Water [*Oceanography*]
NADWAGNS... National Association of Deans of Women and Advisors to Girls in Negro Schools [*Defunct*] (EA)
NADWARN... National Disaster Warning System (AD)
NADWARN... Natural Disaster Warning
NADWARN... Natural Disaster Warning System (IAA)
NADWAS.... Natural Disaster Warning Survey (NOAA)
NADWAS.... North American Dr. Who Appreciation Society (EA)
NADX........ National Dentex Corp. [*NASDAQ symbol*] (SAG)
NADX........ Natl Dentex [*NASDAQ symbol*] (TTSB)
NADX........ North American Car [*Private rail car owner code*]
NADZ........ REDON [*Intermodal trailer symbol*]
Nae.......... Exchangeable Body Sodium (MAE)
NAE.......... N-Acylethanolamine [*Organic chemistry*]
NAE.......... Nake [*Tuamotu Archipelago*] [*Seismograph station code, US Geological Survey*] (SEIS)
NAE.......... National Academy of Education
NAE.......... National Academy of Engineering [*Washington, DC*] (GRD)
nae.......... National Administrative Expenses (AD)
NAE.......... National Administrative Expenses (NATG)
NAE.......... National Adoption Exchange (EA)
NAE.......... National Aeronautical Establishment [*Research center*] [*Canada*] (IRC)
NAE.......... National Association of Entrepreneurs
NAE.......... National Association of Evangelicals (EA)
NAE.......... Nations Air Express, Inc. [*FAA designator*] (FAAC)
NAE.......... Naval Aeronautical Establishment [*Canada*] (AD)
NAE.......... Naval Aircraft Establishment (AD)
NAE.......... Navy Acquisition Executive (MCD)
NAE.......... Net Acid Excretion (DMAA)
NAE.......... Netware Application Engine [*Networth, Inc.*]
NAE.......... New Age Encyclopedia [*A publication*]
NAE.......... No American Equivalent [*Language*]
NAE.......... Noise Acoustic Emitter [*Military*] (CAAL)
NAE.......... Noram Energy Corp. [*Formerly, Arkla, Inc.*] [*NYSE symbol*] (SAG)
NAE.......... Noram Financing I [*NYSE symbol*] (SAG)

NAE .... North American Environmental, Inc. (SAUS)
NAE .... Not Above or Equal (SAUS)
nae .... Not Always Excused (AD)
NAE .... Nursery Association Executives [*Later, NAENA*] (EA)
NAE4-HA .... National Association of Extension 4-H Agents (EA)
NAEA .... National Aerospace Education Association [*Formerly, NAEC*] [*Defunct*]
NAEA .... National Art Education Archive (AIE)
NAEA .... National Art Education Association (EA)
NAEA .... National Artists Equity Association (EA)
NAEA .... National Association of Enrolled Agents (EA)
NAEA .... National Association of Estate Agents [*British*] (EAIO)
NAEA .... National Association of Extension 4-H Agents (EA)
NAEA .... Newspaper Advertising Executives Association [*Later, INAME*] (EA)
NAEA .... Newspaper Advertising Executives Association of Canada (BUAC)
NAEA News ... Newspaper Advertising Executives Association News (SAUS)
NAE-ASEB ... National Academy of Engineering Aeronautics and Space Engineering Board
NAEB .... National Association of Educational Broadcasters [*Formerly, Association of Collegeand University Broadcasting Stations (1934)*] (EA)
NAEB .... National Association of Educational Buyers [*Woodbury, NY*] (EA)
NAEB .... Naval Aviation Evaluation Board
NAEB .... North African Economic Board [*World War II*]
NAEB .... North American EDIFACT (Electronic Data Interchange for Administration, Commerce, and Transport) Board [*Open Systems Interconnection*] (ODAA)
NAEBA .... National Association of Exclusive Buyer Agents (EA)
NAEBA .... North American Elk Breeders Association (EA)
NAEBM ...... National Association of Engine and Boat Manufacturers [*Later, NMMA*] (EA)
NAEC .... Hungarys National Atomic Energy Commission (SAUS)
NAEC .... National Aboriginal Education Committee (BUAC)
NAEC .... National Advisory Eye Council
NAEC .... National Aeronautical Establishment, Canada (BUAC)
NAEC .... National Aerospace Education Council [*Later, NAEA*] (EA)
NAEC .... National Agricultural Engineering Corp. [*China*] (BUAC)
NAEC .... National Association Executives Club (EA)
NAEC .... National Association for Educational Computing (EA)
NAEC .... National Association of Electric Companies [*Later, EEI*] (EA)
NAEC .... National Association of Elevator Contractors (EA)
NAEC .... National Association of Engineering Companies (EA)
NAEC .... National Association of Exhibition Contractors [*British*] (BI)
NAEC .... National Atomic Energy Commission (SAUS)
NAEC .... National Aviation Education Council [*Later, National Aerospace Education Council*] (AEBS)
NAEC .... Naval Air Engineering Center [*Closed*]
NAEC .... Northern Agricultural Energy Center
NAEC .... Novell Authorized Education Center (SAUS)
NAECA .... National Appliance Energy Conservation Act [*1987*]
NAEC-ACEL ... Naval Air Engineering Center Aerospace Crew Equipment Laboratory [*Lakehurst, NJ*]
NAEC-AEL ... Naval Air Engineering Center Aeronautical Engine Laboratory [*Lakehurst, NJ*]
NAEC-AML ... Naval Air Engineering Center Aeronautical Materials Laboratory [*Lakehurst, NJ*]
NAEC-ASL ... Naval Air Engineering Center Aeronautical Structures Laboratory [*Lakehurst, NJ*]
NAEC-ENG ... Naval Air Engineering Center Engineering Department [*Lakehurst, NJ*]
NAECFO ..... Naval Air Engineering Center Field Office (DNAB)
NAEC-GSED ... Naval Air Engineering Center Ground Support Equipment Department [*Lakehurst, NJ*]
NAECOE ..... National Academy of Engineering Committee on Ocean Engineering
NAECON ..... National Aerospace Electronics Conference [*IEEE*] (MCD)
NAEd .... National Academy of Education (EA)
NAED .... National Association of Electrical Distributors (EA)
NAED .... National Association of Engravers and Diestampers (BUAC)
NAEDA ...... National American Eskimo Dog Association (EA)
NAEDA ...... North American Equipment Dealers Association (EA)
NAEDS ...... National Association of Educational Data Systems (IAA)
NAEDS ...... National Association of Engravers and Die-Stampers [*British*] (BI)
NAEDS ...... Nonaqueous Equipment Decontamination System (ACAE)
NAEE .... National Association of Environmental Education [*British*] (DBA)
NAEE .... North American Association for Environmental Education (EA)
NAEE .... North American Association of Environmental Education (SAUS)
NAEEO .... National Association for Equal Educational Opportunities (EA)
NAEF .... Naval Air Engineering Facility (MCD)
NAEF .... North American Environmental Fund (SAUS)
NAEFA .... North American Economics and Finance Association (EA)
NAEF-ENG ... Naval Air Engineering Facility Ship Installations Engineering Department [*Philadelphia, PA*]
NAEFR .... North American English Ford Registry (EA)
NAEFTA ..... National Association of Enrolled Federal Tax Accountants (EA)
NAEG .... Nevada Applied Ecology Group (SAUS)
NAEGA ...... North American Export Grain Association (EA)
NAEGS ...... National Association of Educational Guidance Services for Adults [*British*] (DBA)
NAEH .... National Alliance to End Homelessness (EA)
NAEHCA ..... National Association of Employers on Health Care Action
NAEHCA ..... National Association of Employers on Health Care Alternatives (EA)
NAEHE .... National Association of Extension Home Economists (EA)
NAEHMO .... National Association of Employers on Health Maintenance Organizations [*Later, NAEHCA*] (EA)
NAEIAC ...... National Association of Educational Inspectors, Advisers, and Consultants (AIE)
NAEIC .... Nevada Applied Ecology Information Center [*Department of Energy*] (IID)
NAEIR .... National Association for the Exchange of Industrial Resources (EA)
NAEKM ...... National Association of Electronic Keyboard Manufacturers (EA)
NAEL .... Naval Air Engineering Laboratory (MCD)
NAEL .... No-Adverse-Effect Level [*Toxicology*] (LDT)
NAELA .... National Academy of Elder Law Attorneys (EA)
NAELB .... National Association of Equipment Leasing Brokers (NTPA)
NAELC .... National Architect-Engineer Liaison Commission [*Defunct*] (EA)
NAEL-ENG ... Naval Air Engineering Laboratory Ship Installations Engineering Department [*Philadelphia, PA*]
NAELSI ...... Naval Air Electronics Shipboard Installation
NAEM .... National Association for Environmental Management
NAEM .... National Association of Exposition Managers (EA)
NAEM .... Naval Air Effect Model (PDAA)
NAEMB ...... National Academy of Engineering Marine Board
NAEMD ...... National Academy of Emergency Medical Dispatch [*Association*] (EA)
NAEMSE .... National Association of EMS Educators (EA)
NAEMSP .... National Association of Emergency Medical Service Physicians (EA)
NAEMSPA ... National EMS Pilots Association (SAUS)
NAEMT ...... National Association of Emergency Medical Technicians (EA)
NAEN .... National Association of Educational Negotiators (EA)
NAENA ...... Nursery Association Executives of North America (EA)
NAE-NEPP ... National Academy of Engineering Navy Environmental Protection Program Study Group
NAENG ...... North African Engineer Section [*World War II*]
NAEO .... National Activity Education Organization (EA)
NAEO .... National Association of Extradition Officials (EA)
NAEOM ...... National Association of Electronic Organ Manufacturers
NAEOP ...... National Association of Educational Office Personnel (EA)
NAEP .... National Assessment of Educational Progress (AD)
NAEP .... National Assessment of Educational Progress, The Nation's Report Card (EA)
NAEP .... National Association of Educational Programs [*Carnegie Foundation*] (AD)
NAEP .... National Association of Entrepreneurial Parents (EA)
NAEP .... National Association of Environmental Professionals (EA)
NAEP .... National Asthma Education Program (DMAA)
NAEPC .... National Association of Estate Planning Councils (EA)
NAEPDC ..... National Adult Education Professional Development Consortium (NTPA)
NAEPIRS ... National Assessment of Educational Progress Information Retrieval System [*National Institute of Education*] [*Database*]
NAEPIS ...... North America Engineering Parts Inquiry System
NAEPrA ...... Noram Energy $3 Cv Ex A Pfd [*NYSE symbol*] (TTSB)
NAEPS .... National Academy of Economics and Political Science (EA)
NAER .... National Association for Employee Recognition (EA)
NAER .... National Association of Executive Recruiters (EA)
NAERC ...... North American Electric Reliability Council (EA)
NAERG ...... North American Emergency Response Guidebook (SAUS)
NAERIC ...... North American Equine Ranching Information Council (GVA)
NaEry .... Sodium Erythorbate (SAUS)
NAES .... National Association for Ethnic Studies (EA)
NAES .... National Association of Ecumenical Staff (EA)
NAES .... National Association of Educational Secretaries [*Later, NAEOP*] (EA)
NAES .... National Association of Episcopal Schools (EA)
NAES .... National Association of Executive Secretaries (EA)
NAES .... Native American Educational Service [*Later, NAESC*] (EA)
NAES .... Naval Air Experimental Station
NAES .... Nevada Agricultural Experiment Station [*University of Nevada - Reno*] [*Research center*] (RCD)
NAES .... North African Army Exchange Service [*World War II*]
NAES .... North American Electronic Systems (SAUS)
NAESA .... National Association of Elevator Safety Authorities (EA)
NAESA .... North American Economic Studies Association (EA)
NAESB .... National Association of Equity Source Banks (EA)
NAESC .... National Association of Energy Service Companies (EA)
NAESC .... Native American Educational Services College (EA)
NAESCO ..... National Association of Energy Service Companies (EA)
NAESP .... National Association of Elementary School Principals (EA)
NAEST .... National Archives for Electrical Science and Technology (PDAA)
NAESU ...... Naval Aviation Electronic Service Unit (MCD)
NAESU ...... Naval Aviation Engineering Service Unit [*Philadelphia, PA*]
NAESUDET ... Naval Aviation Engineering Service Unit Detachment (DNAB)
NAET .... National Association for Educational Television (NTCM)
NAET .... National Association of Educational Technicians [*British*]
NAETS .... Naval Air Emission-Tracking System
NAETV .... National Association for Educational Television [*Defunct*]
NAEUSA ..... National Academy of Engineering of the United States of America (NTPA)
NAEW .... NATO Airborne Early Warning
NAEWS ...... NATO Airborne Early Warning System
NAEWTF .... NATO Aircrew Electronic Warfare Tactics Facility (NATG)
NAEYC ...... National Association for the Education of Young Children (EA)
NAF .... Guilder [*Florin*] [*Monetary unit*] [*Netherlands Antilles*]
NAF .... Nafimidone [*Biochemistry*]
NAF .... Name and Address File [*IRS*]
NAF .... Name Authority File
NAF .... National Abortion Federation (EA)
NAF .... National Abortion Foundation (AD)

NAF.......... National Aging Foundation (EA)
NAF.......... National Amputation Foundation (EA)
NAF.......... National Analytical Facility [*National Oceanic and Atmospheric Administration*]
NAF.......... National Angling Federation [*British*]
NAF.......... National Anxiety Foundation (NRGU)
NAF.......... National Arts Foundation (EA)
NAF.......... National Ataxia Foundation (EA)
NAF.......... National Automotive Finance Association (EA)
NAF.......... National Aviation Forum
NAF.......... Naval Aircraft Factory
NAF.......... Naval Air Facility
NAF.......... Naval Airfield (PIPO)
NAF.......... Naval Air Force
NAF.......... Naval Avionics Facility [*Later, NAC*] [*Indianapolis, IN*]
NAF.......... Nernst Approximation Formula [*Physics*]
NAF.......... Net Acid Flux [*Medicine*] (DMAA)
NAF.......... Netherland-America Foundation [*Later, Netherlands-America Community Association*] (EA)
NAF.......... Network Access Facility
NAF.......... Neutrophil-Activating Factor [*Animal physiology*] (QSUL)
NAF.......... New Age Federation (EA)
NAF.......... New Age Media Fund [*NYSE symbol*] (SPSG)
NAF.......... No Abnormal Findings [*Medicine*]
NAF.......... Nonadjacent Form (SAUS)
NAF.......... Nonappropriated Fund [*or Funds*]
naf.......... Nonappropriated Funds (AD)
NAF.......... Non-urea Adducting Fatty Acid [*Food science*]
NAF.......... Nordisk Anaestesiologisk Forening [*Scandinavian Society of Anaesthesiologists - SSA*] (EA)
NAF.......... Norges Automobil Fornund [*Norway Automobile Association*] (AD)
NAF.......... North American Federation of Third Order Franciscans (EA)
NAF.......... North American Fire [*Vancouver Stock Exchange symbol*]
NAF.......... North Anatolian Fault (SAUS)
NAF.......... Northern Africa (CARB)
NAF.......... Northern Africa Region (SAUS)
NAF.......... Northern Attack Force [*Navy*]
NAF.......... North West Atlantic Fisheries, Memorial University [*UTLAS symbol*]
NAF.......... Norwegian Employers' Association [*Political party*] (PSAP)
NAF.......... Notice of Adverse Finding [*Food and Drug Administration*]
NAF.......... Nouvelle Action Francaise [*New French Action*] [*Political party*] (PPE)
NAF.......... Numbered Air Force (AFM)
NAF.......... Royal Netherlands Air Force [*ICAO designator*] (FAAC)
NaF.......... Sodium Fluoride [*Chemistry*] (DAVI)
NAFA........ National Academy of Foreign Affairs (AD)
NAFA........ National Aerobic Fitness Award (AD)
NAFA........ National Aircraft Finance Association (EA)
NAFA........ National Air Filtration Association (EA)
NAFA........ National American Farmers Association [*Defunct*] (EA)
NAFA........ National Association of Fine Arts [*Defunct*] (EA)
NAFA........ National Association of Fleet Administrators [*Iselin, NJ*] (EA)
NAFA........ National Association of Forensic Accountants (EA)
NAFA........ National Association of Furniture Agents [*Australia*]
NAFA........ National Association to Aid Fat Americans [*Bellrose, NY*]
NAFA........ Net Acquisition of Financial Assets (ADA)
NAFA........ Nonappropriated Fund Activity (CINC)
NAFA........ North American Falconers Association (EA)
NAFA........ North American Farm Alliance (EA)
NAFA........ Northwest Atlantic Fisheries Act of 1950
NAFAC....... National Association for Ambulatory Care [*Formerly, NAFEC*] (EA)
NAFAD....... National Association of Fashion and Accessory Designers (EA)
NAFAG....... NATO Air Force Advisory Group (NATG)
NAFAG....... NATO Air Force Armaments Group
NAFAPAC.... National Association for Association Political Action Committees (EA)
NAFARE..... National Association for Families and Addiction Research and Education (PAZ)
NAFAS....... National Association of Flower Arrangement Societies (AD)
NAFAS....... National Association of Flower Arrangement Societies of Great Britain (BI)
NAFAS....... Nonappropriated Fund Accounting System [*Military*] (DNAB)
NAFAWU.... National Food and Allied Workers' Union [*South Africa*] (SAFN)
NAFAX....... National Facsimile Network [*National Weather Service*]
NAFB........ National Association of Farm Broadcasters (EA)
NAFB........ National Association of Franchised Businessmen [*Defunct*] (EA)
NAFB........ Norton Air Force Base [*California*]
NAFB & AE... National Association of Farriers, Blacksmiths, and Agricultural Engineers [*British*] (DBA)
NAFBO...... National Association for Business Organizations [*Baltimore, MD*] (EA)
NAFBRAT... National Association for Better Radio and Television [*Later, NABB*] (EA)
NAFC........ Nash Finch Co. [*NASDAQ symbol*] (TTSB)
NAFC........ National Accounting and Finance Council [*Alexandria, VA*] (EA)
NAFC........ National Anthropological Film Center [*Smithsonian Institution*] (GRD)
NAFC........ National Anti-Fluoridation Campaign [*British*] (DBA)
NAFC........ National Association of Fan Clubs (EA)
NAFC........ National Association of Financial Consultants (EA)
NAFC........ National Association of Food Chains (NADA)
NAFC........ National Association of Forensic Counselors (SEAT)
NAFC........ National Association of Formwork Contractors [*British*] (DBA)
NAFC........ National Association of Friendship Centres [*Canada*]
NAFC........ National Average Fuel Consumption
NAFC........ Naval Air Ferry Command [*World War II*]
NAFC........ Navy Accounting and Finance Center
NAFC........ North American Fishing Club (EA)
NAFC........ North American Forestry Commission [*UN Food and Agriculture Organization*]
NAFC........ North American Forum on the Catechumenate (EA)
NAFC........ Northern Attack Force Commander [*Navy*]
NAFC........ Northwest Atlantic Fisheries Center (SAUS)
NAFCA....... North American Family Campers Association (EA)
NAFCA....... North American Poultry Cooperative Association (SAUS)
NAFCC....... National Association for Family Child Care (NTPA)
NAFCD...... National Association of Floor Covering Distributors (EA)
NAFCE...... National Association of Federal Career Employees [*Defunct*] (EA)
NAFCI....... National Association of Floor Covering Installers [*Later, AIDS International*] (EA)
NAFCM...... National Association for Community Mediation (NTPA)
NAFCO...... National Association of Franchise Companies (EA)
NAFCO...... National Floor Products Co., Inc.
NAFCO...... North Atlantic Fisheries Consultative Committee (SAUS)
NAFCO...... Northwest Atlantic Fishery Consultative Organization (SAUS)
NAFCOM.... Northern Africa Committee (SAUS)
NAFCOM.... Northern Africa Regional Committee for START (SAUS)
NAFCR...... National Association of Foster Care Reviewers (EA)
NAFCU...... National Association of Federal Credit Unions (EA)
NAFCUPAC... National Association of Federal Credit Unions PAC [*Arlington, VA*] (PACS)
NAFD........ National Air Forwarding Division [*Institute of Freight Forwarders*] (AD)
NAFD........ National Association of Farm Directors (NTCM)
NAFD........ National Association of Flour Distributors (EA)
NAFD........ National Association of Funeral Directors [*British*] (BI)
NAFD........ New America Fund (SAUS)
NAFDA...... National Association of Future Doctors of Audiology (EA)
NAFDC...... National Association for Family Day Care (EA)
NAFDI....... National Foundation for Depressive Illness (EA)
NAFDMA.... North American Farmers' Direct Marketing Association (EA)
NAFE........ National Association for Female Executives [*New York, NY*] (EA)
NAFE........ National Association for Film in Education [*British*]
NAFE........ National Association for Free Enterprise [*Defunct*] (EA)
NAFE........ National Association of Forensic Economists (EA)
NAFE........ Non-Advanced Further Education [*British*]
NAFEA....... National Association for the Education and Advancement of Cambodian, Laotian, and Vietnamese Americans
NAFEC....... National Association of Farmer Elected Committeemen (EA)
NAFEC....... National Association of Freestanding Emergency Centers [*Later, NAAC*] (EA)
NAFEC....... National Aviation Facilities Experimental Center [*of FAA*] [*Atlantic City, NJ*]
NAFEC....... North American Fund for Environmental Cooperation (SAUS)
NAFED....... National Association of Fire Equipment Distributors (EA)
NAFEM....... National Association of Food Equipment Manufacturers (EA)
NAFEMS.... National Agency for Finite Element Methods and Standards [*British*] (IRUK)
NAFEO....... National Association for Equal Opportunity in Higher Education (EA)
NAFEPA..... National Association of Federal Education Program Administrators (NTPA)
NAFEX....... North American Fruit Explorers (EA)
NAFF........ National Association for Freedom [*British*]
nAff......... Need for Affection
naff......... Need for Affiliation (AD)
N Aff........ Need for Affiliation (DIPS)
NAFF........ Need for Affiliation (MHDB)
nAffil........ Need for Affiliation [*Psychology*] (QSUL)
NAFFP....... National Association of Frozen Food Packers [*Later, AFFI*] (EA)
NAFFP....... National Association of Frozen Food Producers (AD)
NAFFS....... National Association of Fruits, Flavors, and Syrups (EA)
NAFFW...... National Association of Full Figured Women (EA)
NAFGDA..... National Auto and Flat Glass Dealers Association [*Later, NGA*]
NAFGPD..... National Association of Foster Grandparent Program Directors (EA)
NAFI......... National Association of Fire Investigators (EA)
NAFI......... National Association of Flight Instructors (EA)
NAFI......... Naval Air Fighting Instructions
NAFI......... Naval Avionics Facility, Indianapolis [*Later, NAC*]
NAFI......... Nonappropriated Fund Instrumentalities [*DoD*] (MCD)
NAFI......... Northern Air Freight, Inc. (SAUS)
NAFIC....... National Association of Fraternal Insurance Counsellors [*Sheboygan, WI*] (EA)
NAFIN....... Nacional Financiera (EFIS)
NAFIN....... North African Finance Section [*World War II*]
NAFINSA.... Nacional Financiera [*National Finance Coro.*] [*Spanish*] (AD)
NAFIP....... National Foreign Intelligence Program [*DoD*] (MCD)
NAFIPS...... North American Fuzzy Information Processing Society (EA)
NAFIS....... National Association of Federally Impacted Schools (EA)
NAFIS....... National Automated Fingerprint Identification System
NAFIS....... Naval Forces Intelligence Study (MCD)
NAFIS....... Navigational Aid Flight Inspection System (AFM)
NAFISS...... Nonappropriated Funds Information Standard System [*Army*]
NAFL........ National Alliance for Family Life [*Later, NACFT*] (EA)
NAFLAC..... Navy Department Fuel and Lubricants Advisory Committee [*Ministry of Defense*] [*British*] (PDAA)
NAFLANT... Naval Air Facilities, Atlantic
NAFLFD..... National Association of Federally Licensed Firearms Dealers (EA)
NAFLI........ Natural Flight Indication (MCD)
NAFLI........ Natural Flight Instrument System
NAFLIR...... Navigation Forward Looking Infrared (ACAE)
NAFM........ National Armed Forces Museum (AD)
NAFM........ National Association of Fan Manufacturers [*Later, AMCA*]

NAFM .... National Association of Farmers' Markets (GVA)
NAFM .... National Association of Flag Manufacturers
NAFM .... National Association of Furniture Manufacturers [*Later, AFMA*] (EA)
NAFMA ...... NATO European Fighter Management Agency
NAFMAB .... National Armed Forces Museum Advisory Board [*Smithsonian Institution*]
NAFMB ...... National Association of FM [*Frequency Modulation*] Broadcasters [*Later, NRBA*] (EA)
NAFMC ...... Nonappropriated Funds, Marine Corps (DNAB)
NAFMDA .... North American Folk Music and Dance Alliance (NTPA)
NAFMG ...... National Association of Foreign Medical Graduates [*Later, ACIP*]
NAFMIS ..... Nonappropriated Funds Management Information System
NAFMOW ... National Action Forum for Midlife and Older Women (EA)
NAFMW ..... National Action for Former Military Wives (EA)
NAFN .... Norton Administrator for Networks [*Symantec Corp.*] [*Telecommunications*] (PCM)
NAFO .... National Association of Farmworker Organizations [*Defunct*] (EA)
NAFO .... National Association of Fire Officers [*British*] (DI)
NAFO .... Northwest Atlantic Fisheries Organization (EA)
NAFO .... Organizaci"n de Pesca del Atl ntico Noroeste (SAUS)
NAFOW ...... National Action Forum for Midlife and Older Women (EA)
NAFOW ...... National Action Forum for Older Women [*Later, NAFMOW*] (EA)
NAFP .... National Association of Factoring Professionals (NTPA)
NAFP .... National Association of Food Processors (ECON)
NAFP .... Naval Air Force, Pacific Fleet (DNAB)
NAFP .... Nebraska Academy of Family Physicians (EARSL)
NAFP .... New Armed Forces of the Philippines (AD)
NAFPA .... National Alcohol Fuels Producers Association [*Defunct*] (EA)
NAFPA .... National Association of Federal Education Program Administrators (EA)
NAFPAC ..... Naval Air Facilities, Pacific
NAFPB .... National Association of Freight Payment Banks [*Pittsburgh, PA*] (EA)
NAFPC .... National Academy for Fire Prevention and Control [*of FEMA*]
NAFPD .... National Association of Family Planning Doctors [*British*] (DBA)
NAFPP .... National Accelerated Food Production Project [*Agency for International Development*]
NAFPP .... National Association of Fresh Produce Processors (EA)
NAFPU .... North American Friends of Palestinian Universities [*Defunct*] (EA)
NAFR .... National Association of First Responders (NTPA)
N Afr .... North Africa
NAFRC ...... National Association of Fiscally Responsible Cities [*Defunct*] (EA)
NAFRC ...... North Atlantic Fisheries Research Center (PDAA)
NAFRD ...... National Association of Fleet Resale Dealers [*Los Angeles, CA*] (EA)
NAFRF .... Navy Alternate Fuel Reference File [*Battelle Memorial Institute*] [*Information service or system*] [*Defunct*] (IID)
NAFRLG ..... National Alliance of Financially-Responsible Local Governments (AD)
NAFRTM .... National Association of Farm and Ranch Trailer Manufacturers [*Defunct*] (EA)
NAFS .... National Association of Fastener Stockholders [*British*] (DBA)
NAFS .... National Association of Foot Specialists (AD)
NAFS .... National Association of Forensic Sciences (AD)
NAFS .... Naval Air Fighter School
NA/FS .... Naval Aviator/Flight Surgeon (MCD)
NAFS .... Newark Air Force Station [*Ohio*]
NAFS .... North American Fichte Society [*Association*] (EA)
NAFSA .... National Association for Foreign Student Affairs (EA)
NAFSA .... National Association of Fire Science and Administration [*Defunct*] (EA)
NAFSA .... National Association of Foreign Student Advisors (AD)
NAFSA .... No American Flag Shipping Available
NAFSC .... North American Farm Show Council (NTPA)
NAFSLAC ... National Association of Federations of Syrian and Lebanese American Clubs (EA)
NAFSMA .... National Association of Flood and Stormwater Management Agencies (NTPA)
NAFSO .... National Association of Field Studies Officers [*British*] (DBA)
NAFSONW ... Nonappropriated Fund Statement of Operations and Net Worth
NAFSWMA ... National Association of Flood and Storm Water Management Agencies (EA)
NAFT .... National Alternative Fuel Test (AD)
NAFT .... Natural Adjuvant Factor Toxoid [*Medicine*]
NAFT .... Network for Analysis of Fireball Trajectories (EA)
NAFT .... No Accounting for Taste (GOBB)
NAFTA .... National Amalgamated Furnishing Trades Association [*A union*] [*British*]
NAFTA .... National Association of Futures Trading Advisors [*Defunct*] (EA)
NAFTA .... National Association of Future Teachers of America [*Later, Student National Education Association*] (AEBS)
NAFTA .... New Zealand-Australia Free Trade Agreement (AD)
NAFTA .... North America Free Trade Agreement (SAUS)
NAFTA .... North American Free Trade Agreement [*Passed in 1993*]
NAFTA .... North American Free-Trade Area (ECON)
NAFTA .... North Atlantic Free Trade Area
NAFTAT ...... National Association for the Advancement of Time (EA)
NAFTC .... National Association of Freight Transportation Consultants (EA)
NAFTC .... North American Forging Technology Conference (SAUS)
NAFTCO ..... National Ford Tool Collectors [*Automotive hobby group*]
NAFTF .... National Association of Finishers of Textile Fabrics [*Later, ATMI*] (EA)
NAFTM ...... National Association of Fund Raising Ticket Manufacturers (NTPA)
NAFTOC ..... NORAD Automated Forward Tell Output to Canada (MCD)
NAFTRAC ... National Foreign Trade Council (EA)
NAFTS .... National Association of Fleet Tug Sailors (EA)
NAFTZ .... National Association of Foreign-Trade Zones [*Washington, DC*] (EA)
NAFU .... Safe Container [*Intermodal shipping container symbol*] (TVRC)
NAFV .... National Association of Federal Veterinarians (EA)
NAFW .... National Association of Future Women [*Later, NAFWIC*] (EA)
NAFWA ...... North American Flowerbulb Wholesalers Association (EA)
NAFWIC ..... National Association for Women in Careers (EA)
NAFWR ...... National Association of Furniture Warehousemen and Removers (AD)
NAFWS ...... Native American Fish and Wildlife Society [*An association*] (ALAC)
Nag .... All India Reporter, Nagpur [*A publication*] (DLA)
NAG .... Goddard Space Flight Center, Greenbelt, MD [*OCLC symbol*] (OCLC)
Nag .... Indian Law Reports, Nagpur Series [*A publication*] (DLA)
Nag .... Indian Rulings, Nagpur Series [*A publication*] (DLA)
NAG .... N-Acetylglucosamine [*Biochemistry*]
NAG .... N-Acetylglucosaminidase [*An enzyme*]
NAG .... Nachrichten der Akademie der Wissenschaften in Goettingen. Philologisch-Historische Klasse [*A publication*] (BJA)
Nag .... Nagasaki [*Japan*] (AD)
Nag .... Nagoya [*Japan*] (AD)
NAG .... Nagoya [*Japan*] [*Seismograph station code, US Geological Survey*] (SEIS)
NAG .... Nagpur [*India*] [*Airport symbol*] (OAG)
NAG .... Naming [*Telegraphy*] (PCTE)
NAG .... Narrow Angle Glaucoma [*Medicine*]
NAG .... National Academy of Geosciences (EA)
NAG .... National Acquisitions Group [*Libraries*] [*British*]
NAG .... National Action Group [*Antibusing organization*]
NAG .... National Advisory Group, Convenience Stores/Petroleum Companies (EA)
NAG .... National Air-Racing Group (EA)
NAG .... National Assessment Group (SAUS)
NAG .... National Association of Gagwriters (EA)
NAG .... National Association of Gardeners [*Later, PGMS*] (EA)
NAG .... National Association of Goldsmiths [*British*]
NAG .... National Association of Grooms [*British*] (DI)
NAG .... National Association of Groundsmen [*British*] (DI)
NAG .... Natural Assessments Group (SAUS)
NAG .... Naval Advisory Group
NAG .... Naval Analysis Group (MCD)
NAG .... Naval Applications Group
NAG .... Navy Astronautics Group (MUGU)
NAG .... Negro Actors Guild (NADA)
NAG .... Negro Actors Guild of America (EA)
NAG .... Neighborhood Action Group (AD)
NAG .... NERVA [*Nuclear Engine for Rocket Vehicle Application*] Advisory Group [*NASA*] (KSC)
nag .... Net Annual Gain (AD)
NAG .... Net Annual Gain [*Business term*] (PDAA)
NAG .... Netherlands Aerospace Group (SAUS)
NAG .... Networking Advisory Group [*Library of Congress*]
N-Ag .... Neutralization Antigenic Site [*Immunogenetics*]
Nag .... No-Acronym Sort of Guy [*Term coined by William F. Doescher, publisher of "D & B Reports"*] [*Lifestyle classification*]
NAG .... Nonagglutinable [*or Nonagglutinating*] [*Immunochemistry*]
NAG .... Nonagglutinable (or Nonagglutinating) (SAUS)
NAG .... Nor-Acme Gold Mines Ltd. [*Toronto Stock Exchange symbol*]
NAG .... Northern Army Group (NATG)
NAG .... Nova Scotia Agricultural College Library [*UTLAS symbol*]
NAG .... Numerical Algorithms Group (CIST)
NAG .... Nystagmus Action Group [*British*] (DBA)
NAGA .... National Advertising Golf Association (EA)
NAGA .... National Amputee Golf Association (EA)
NAGA .... North American Gamebird Association (EA)
NAGA .... North American Ginseng Association [*Defunct*] (EA)
NAGAP ...... National Association of Gay Alcoholism Professionals [*Later, NALGAP*] (EA)
NAGAP ...... National Association of Graduate Admissions Professionals (NTPA)
NAGARA .... National Association of Government Archives and Records Administrators (EA)
NAGARD .... NATO Advisory Group for Aeronautical Research and Development
Nagas .... Nagasaki [*Japan*] (AD)
NAGASA ..... North American Graphic Arts Suppliers Association (NTPA)
NAGB .... National Assessment Governing Board
NAGB & SPA ... North American Game Breeders and Shooting Preserve Association [*Later, NAGA*] (EA)
NAGBM ...... National Association of Golf Ball Manufacturers (EA)
NAGC .... National Association for Gifted Children (EA)
NAGC .... National Association of Gas Chlorinators (EA)
NAGC .... National Association of Girls Clubs (EA)
NAGC .... National Association of Government Communicators (EA)
NAGC .... National Gaming Corp. [*NASDAQ symbol*] (SAG)
NAGC .... Naval Armed Guard Center
NAGC .... Navy Astronautics Group Conference [*Navy*]
NAGC .... North American Gladiolus Council (EA)
NAGCD ...... National Association of Glass Container Distributors [*Later, NACD*] (EA)
NAGCM ...... National Association of Golf Club Manufacturers (EA)
NAGCO ...... Naval Air Ground Center
NAGCP ...... National Association of Greeting Card Publishers [*Later, GCA*] (EA)
NAGCR ...... North American Guild of Change Ringers (EA)
NAGDCA .... National Association of Government Deferred Compensation Administrators (EA)
NAGDM ..... National Association of Garage Door Manufacturers (EA)
NAGE .... National Association of Government Employees (EA)
NAGE .... NATO Air Defense Group Environment (AABC)
N-age .... Nuclear Age (AD)
NAGGL ...... National Association of Government Guaranteed Lenders (NTPA)

NagHammSt... Nag Hammadi Studies [*A publication*] (BJA)
NAGHSR.... National Association of Governors' Highway Safety Representatives (EA)
NAGI......... National Association of Government Inspectors [*Later, National Association of Government Inspectors and Quality Assurance Personnel*] (EA)
NAGI......... Not A Good Idea (SAUS)
NAGIM...... North American Gunnery Instruction Monitor
NAGI/QAP... National Association of Government Inspectors and Quality Assurance Personnel (EA)
NAGIS....... National Airport Grant Information System [*FAA*] (TAG)
Nag LJ...... Nagpur Law Journal [*India*] [*A publication*] (DLA)
Nag LN...... Nagpur Law Notes [*India*] [*A publication*] (DLA)
NAGLO...... National Association of Governmental Labor Officials (EA)
Nag LR...... Nagpur Law Reports [*India*] [*A publication*] (DLA)
NAGM....... National Association of Glove Manufacturers (EA)
NAGM....... National Association of Glue Manufacturers [*Defunct*] (EA)
NAGM....... National Association of Governors and Managers [*British*] (DBA)
NAGMC...... North Atlantic Council and Military Committee (SAUS)
NAGMR..... National Association of General Merchandise Representatives [*Chicago, IL*] (EA)
NAGO........ National Association of Greyhound Owners (GVA)
Nagp......... Nagpur, India (AD)
NAGPFS..... National Association of Governors' Councils on Physical Fitness and Sports (NTPA)
NAGPIPM... National Association of Graphic and Product Identification Manufacturers (NTPA)
NAGPM...... National Association of Grained Plate Makers (AD)
NAGP/NCP... North American Great Plains/North China Plain Project [*Agriculture*]
NAGPRA.... Native American Graves Protection and Repatriation Act [*Enacted 1990*]
NAGPTDU... National Action Group for the Prevention and Treatment of Decubitus Ulcers (EA)
NAGRA...... National Association of Gambling Regulatory Agencies (EA)
NAGRA...... Nationalen Genossenschaft fuer die Lagerung Radioaktiver Abfaelle [*National Cooperative Society for the Storage of Radioactive Wastes*] [*Germany*] (AD)
NAGRA...... Nation Association of Govenment Archives and Records Administration (TELE)
NAGRP...... National Animal Genome Research Program (SAUS)
NAGS........ National Allotments and Gardens Society Ltd. [*British*] (BI)
NAGS........ National Association of Government Secretaries [*Defunct*]
NAGS........ Naval Air Gunners School
NAGSC...... National Association of Government Service Contractors [*Defunct*] (EA)
NAGSCT..... National Association of Guidance Supervisors and Counselor Trainers
NAGT........ National Association of Geology Teachers (EA)
NAGT........ National Association of Geoscience Teachers (NTPA)
NAGTAD..... National Association for Government Training and Development (EA)
NAGTADD... National Association of Government Training and Development Directors (NTPA)
NAGTC...... North American Gasoline Tax Conference (EA)
NAGUA...... Numerical Algorithms Group Users Association (SAUS)
Nag UCL Mag... Nagpur University. College of Law. Magazine [*1933-34*] [*India*] [*A publication*] (DLA)
NAGVG...... National Association Greenhouse Vegetable Growers (EA)
NAGWS..... National Association for Girls and Women in Sport (EA)
NAH.......... Autism Services Center [*Formerly, National Autism Hotline*] (EA)
NAH.......... Naha [*Ryukyu Islands*] [*Airport symbol*] (OAG)
NAH.......... Nahanni Air Services Ltd. [*Canada*] [*ICAO designator*] (FAAC)
nah........... Nahuatlan [*MARC language code*] [*Library of Congress*] (LCCP)
Nah........... Nahum [*Old Testament book*]
NAH.......... National Association of Homebuilders (AD)
NAH.......... National Autism Hotline (EA)
NAH.......... Night Adoration in the Home (EA)
NAH.......... No-Antihalation Film
NAH.......... Nordic Association for Hydrology (EA)
NAH.......... Nordic Association for the Handicapped (EA)
NAH.......... Nordic Association of Hairdressers [*Sweden*] (EAIO)
NAH.......... Not at Home
NAH.......... Nutrition Action Health Letter (SAUS)
NAHA........ National Association for Holistic Aromatherapy (NTPA)
NAHA........ National Association of Handwriting Analysts
NAHA........ National Association of Health Authorities [*British*] (EAIO)
NAHA........ National Association of Health Authorities in England and Wales (AIE)
NAHA........ National Association of Hotel Accountants [*Later, International Association of Hospitality Accountants*] (EA)
NAHA........ North American Highway Association
NAHA........ Norwegian-American Historical Association (EA)
NAHAD...... National Association of Hose and Accessories Distributors (EA)
Nahal........ Na'or Halutsi Lohem [*Fighting Pioneer Youth*] [*Israel*] (AD)
NAHAL...... Noar Halutzi Lohem [*Pioneering Fighting Youth*] [*Israel*]
NAHAM...... National Association of Healthcare Access Management (EA)
NAHAM...... National Association of Hospital Admitting Managers (EA)
NAHAT....... National Association of Health Authorities and Trusts [*British*] (EAIO)
NAHAWA.... North American Heating and Airconditioning Wholesalers Association
NAHB........ National Alliance of Homebased Businesswomen [*Defunct*] (EA)
NAHB........ National Association of Home Builders (NADA)
NAHB........ National Association of Home Builders of the United States (EA)
NAHB........ National Association of Homes for Boys [*Later, NFCCE*]
NAHBB...... National Association of Home Based Businesses [*Baltimore, MD*] (EA)
NAHBE...... Naval Academy Heat Balanced Engine [*Pronounced "knobby"*]
NAHBO...... National Association of Hospital Broadcasting Organizations [*British*] (DBA)
NAHB/RC.... NAHB Remodelers Council (EA)
NAHC........ National Advisory Health Council
NAHC........ National Anti-Hunger Coalition (EA)
NAHC........ National Association for Home Care (EA)
NAHC........ National Association of Holiday Centres [*British*] (DBA)
NAHC........ National Association of Homes for Children (EA)
NAHC........ National Association of Housing Cooperatives (EA)
NAHC........ North American Hunting Club (EA)
NAHCAC..... National Ad Hoc Committee Against Censorship (AD)
NAHCO...... National Association of Hispanic County Officials (NTPA)
NAHCR...... National Association of Healthcare Recruitment (EA)
NAHCS...... National Association of Health Career Schools (EA)
NAHCS...... National Association of Health Center Schools (DMAA)
NAHCSP..... National Association of Hospital Central Service Personnel [*Later, IAHCSM*] (EA)
NAHD........ National Association for Hospital Development (EA)
NAHD........ National Association for Human Development (EA)
NAHD........ National Association of Hillel Directors [*Later, IAHD*] (EA)
NAHDDM.... National Association of House and Daytime Dress Manufacturers (EA)
NAHDO...... National Association of Health Data Organizations (EA)
NAHDSA.... National Association of Hebrew Day School Administrators (EA)
NAHE........ Nash-Healey [*NCIC car make code*]
NAHE........ National Alliance for Hydroelectric Energy (EA)
NAHE........ National Association for Holocaust Education (EA)
NAHE........ National Association for Humanities Education (EA)
NAHEE....... National Association for Humane and Environmental Education (EA)
NAHEM...... National Association of Health Estates Managers [*British*] (DBA)
NAHEMA.... NATO Helicopter Management Agency (SAUS)
NAHES...... National Association of Home Economics Supervisors [*Later, NASSVHE*] (EA)
NAHFAGIF... National Archives and Historical Foundation of the American GI Fo rum (EA)
NAHFE....... National Association of Hispanic Federal Executives (EA)
NAHFO...... National Association of Hospital Fire Officers [*British*] (DBA)
NAHG........ National Association of Homoeopathic Groups [*British*] (DBA)
NAHG........ National Association of Humanistic Gerontology (EA)
NAHGT...... National Aboriginal Health Goals and Targets [*Australia*]
NAHHA...... National Association of Home Health Agencies [*Later, NAHC*] (EA)
NAHHH...... National Association of Hospital Hospitality Houses (EA)
NAHHIC..... National Association of House to House Installment Companies [*Later, NAIC*] (EA)
NAHI......... National Association of Home Inspectors (NTPA)
NAHI......... National Athletic Health Institute (EA)
NAHICUS... Nuclear Attack Hazards in the Continental United States
NAHIM...... National Association of Housing Information Managers (NTPA)
NAHIS....... National Arts and Handicapped Information Service (EA)
NAHJ........ National Association of Hispanic Journalists (EA)
NAHL........ North American Hockey League
NAHL........ North American Holding Corp. (SAUS)
NAHLA...... North American Holding Corp. (Class A) [*NASDAQ symbol*] (COMM)
NAHLS...... National Association of Hispanic and Latino Studies (NTPA)
NAHM....... National Association of Home Manufacturers [*Later, HMC*] (EA)
NAHM....... National Association of Hosiery Manufacturers (EA)
NAHM....... Norwegian-American Historical Museum (SAUS)
NAHMA...... National Affordable Housing Management Association (NTPA)
NAHMA...... National Assisted Housing Management Association (NTPA)
NAHMA...... National Association of Hotel and Motel Accountants [*Later, International Association of Hospitality Accountants*]
NAHMOR.... National Association of HMO [*Health Maintenance Organization*] Regulators
NAHMS...... National Animal Health Monitoring System (SAUS)
NAHN........ National Association of Hispanic Nurses (EA)
NAHNS...... National Association of the Holy Name Society (EA)
NAHO........ National Association of Hearing Officials (NTPA)
NAHO........ National Association of Homeowners [*British*] (DBA)
NAHOD...... N-Acetylhexosamine Oxidase (DB)
NAHP........ National Association of Hispanic Publications (EA)
NAHP........ National Association of Horseradish Packers [*Defunct*] (EA)
NAHP........ National Association of Hypnotists and Psychotherapists [*British*] (DBA)
NAHPA...... National Association of Hospital Purchasing Agents [*Later, NAHPMM*] (EA)
NAHPM...... National Association of Hospital Purchasing Management [*Later, NAHP MM*] (EA)
NAHPMM... National Association of Hospital Purchasing Materials Management (EA)
NAHPS...... North American Habitat Preservation Society (EA)
NAHQ........ National Association for Healthcare Quality (EA)
NAHREP.... National Association of Hispanic Real Estate Professionals (EA)
NAHRMP.... National Association of Hotel and Restaurant Meat Purveyors [*Later, NAMP*] (EA)
NAHRO...... National Association of Housing and Redevelopment Officials (EA)
NAHRW..... National Association of Human Rights Workers (EA)
NAHS........ National Aboriginal Health Strategy [*Australia*]
NAHS........ National Association of Health Stores [*British*] (DBA)
NAHS........ National Association of Horological Schools (EA)
NAHS........ New American High Schools [*Initiative*]
NAHS........ North American Heather Society (EA)
NAHS........ North American Hernia Society (NTPA)
NAHS........ North American Hyperthermia Society (SAUS)
NAHSA...... National Association for Hearing and Speech Action (EA)
NAHSA...... National Association of Hearing and Speech Agencies (AEBS)

NAHSA ...... North American Horticultural Supply Association (EA)
NAHSC ...... National Association of Homes and Services for Children (EA)
NAHSC ...... National Automated Highway System Consortium
NAHSE ...... National Association of Health Services Executives (EA)
NAHSL ...... North Atlantic Health Sciences Libraries
NAHSO ...... National Association of Hospital Supplies Officers [*British*] (BI)
NAHSPO .... National Association of Health Service Personnel Officers [*British*] (DBA)
NAHSQCD... National Association of Human Service Quality Control Directors (NTPA)
NAHSSO .... National Association of Health Service Security Officers [*British*] (DBA)
NAHST ...... National Association of Human Services Technologies [*Defunct*] (EA)
NAHSTA...... National Hiking and Ski Touring Association (AD)
NAHSWP.... National Aboriginal Health Strategy Working Party [*Australia*]
NAHT .... National Association of Head Teachers [*British*]
NAHU........ NAHU, an Association of Bull Users [*Formerly, North American Honeywell Users Association*] (EA)
NAHU........ National Association of Health Underwriters [*Washington, DC*] (EA)
NAHU........ North American Honeywell Users Association (SAUS)
NAHUC ...... National Association of Health Unit Clerks-Coordinators (EA)
NAHUC ...... National Association of Health Unit Coordinators [*Formerly, National Association of Health Unit Clerks-Coordinators*] (EA)
NAHW .... National Association of Hardwood Wholesalers [*Defunct*]
NAHWMUMC... National Association of Health and Welfare Ministries of the United Methodist Church [*Later, United Methodist Association of Health and Welfare Ministries - UMA*] (EA)
NAHWW..... National Association of Home and Workshop Writers (EA)
NAI........... Annai [*Guyana*] [*Airport symbol*] (OAG)
NAI........... N-Acetylimidazole [*Organic chemistry*]
NAI........... Nairobi [*Kenya*] [*Seismograph station code, US Geological Survey*] (SEIS)
NAI........... Named Areas of Interest [*Army intelligence matrix*] (INF)
NAI........... Nanjing Aeronautical Institute [*China*] (BUAC)
NAI........... National Agricultural Institute [*Later, ACA*] (EA)
NAI........... National Apple Institute [*Later, IAI*] (EA)
NAI........... National Association of Independent Insurance Auditors and Engineers (NTPA)
NAI........... National Association of Instructors (BUAC)
NAI........... National Association of Interpretation (EA)
NAI........... Natural Alternatives International [*AMEX symbol*] (SPSG)
NAI........... Negro Airmen International (EA)
NAI........... Net Acid Input [*Medicine*] (DB)
NAI........... Net Annual Inflow [*Pensions*]
NAI........... Netherlands Arbitration Institute (ILCA)
NAI........... Network Associates, Inc. [*Computer science*]
NAI........... New Acronyms and Initialisms [*Later, NAIA*] [*A publication*]
NAI........... New Alchemy Institute [*Defunct*] (EA)
NAI........... No Accidental Injury (DMAA)
nai .... No Action Indicated (AD)
NAI........... No Action Indicated
NAI........... No Acute Infection (SAUS)
NAI........... No Acute Inflammation [*Medicine*] (DMAA)
nai .... No Address Instruction (AD)
NAI........... No-Address Instruction (AAG)
NAI........... No Airborne Intercept [*Fighter aircraft lacking airborne intercept RADAR*]
NAI........... Nonaccidental Injury
NAI........... Nonadherence Index (DMAA)
NAI........... Nonproliferation, Arms Control, and International Security [*Lawrence Livermore National Laboratory*] (RCD)
nai .... North American Indian [*MARC language code*] [*Library of Congress*] (LCCP)
NAI........... North American Internet Co.
NAI........... Northern Alberta Institute of Technology [*UTLAS symbol*]
NAI........... Northrop Aeronautical Institute [*Later, Northrop University*]
NAI........... Northrop Aircraft, Inc. (MCD)
NAI........... N'shei Agudath Israel (BJA)
NAI........... Nurse Attitudes Inventory (TES)
NAI........... Sodium Iodide (SAUS)
NAIA......... National Agricultural and Industrial Association [*Australia*]
NAIA......... National Animal Interest Alliance [*Association*] (EA)
NAIA......... National Association of Industrial Artists [*Later, IG*]
NAIA......... National Association of Insurance Agents [*Later, IIAA*] (EA)
NAIA......... National Association of Intercollegiate Athletics (EA)
NAIA......... New Acronyms, Initialisms, and Abbreviations [*Formerly, NAI*] [*A publication*]
NAIA......... North American Indian Association (EA)
NAIAD .... Nerve Agent Immobilised Enzyme Alarm and Detector (PDAA)
NAIB .... National Association of Independent Business [*Defunct*]
NAIB .... National Association of Insurance Brokers [*Washington, DC*] (EA)
NAIBD .... National Association of Industries for the Blind and Disabled [*British*] (DBA)
NAIC .... National Adoption Information Clearinghouse (EA)
NAIC .... National Advice and Information Centre for Outdoor Education [*Doncaster Metropolitan Institute of Higher Education*] [*British*] (CB)
NAIC .... National Aging Information Center
NAIC .... National AIDS [*Acquired Immune Deficiency Syndrome*] Information Clearinghouse [*Information service or system*] (IID)
NAIC .... National Air Intelligence Center
NAIC .... National Art Industry Council [*Australia*]
NAIC .... National Association of Installment Companies [*New York, NY*] (EA)
NAIC .... National Association of Insurance Commissioners [*Kansas City, MO*] (EA)
NAIC .... National Association of Intercollegiate Commissioners (EA)
NAIC .... National Association of Investment Clubs [*British*] (DBA)
NAIC .... National Association of Investment Companies
NAIC .... National Association of Investors Corp. (EA)
NAIC .... National Astronomy and Ionosphere Center [*Ithaca, NY*] [*National Science Foundation*]
NAIC .... NATO Intelligence Centre (SAUS)
NAIC .... Naval Aircraft Investigation Center (AD)
NAIC .... Network Applications and Information Center
NAIC .... Newly Agro-Industrialized Country (SAUS)
NAIC .... Nigerian Army Intelligence Corps (SAUS)
NAIC .... Nuclear Accident and Incident Control [*Army*] (AABC)
NAICA .... National American Indian Cattlemen's Association (EA)
NAICC .... National Alliance of Independent Crop Consultants (EA)
NAICC .... National Association of Independent Computer Companies
NAICC .... Navigation-Aided Intelligent Cruise Control [*Automotive engineering*]
NAICC .... Nuclear Accident and Incident Control Center [*Army*] (AABC)
NAICCA..... National American Indian Court Clerks Association (EA)
NAIC/DXLS... National Air Intelligence Center/DXLS [*US Air Force*] (IID)
NAICJA ...... National American Indian Court Judges Association (EA)
NAICO .... Nuclear Accident and Incident Control Officer [*Army*] (AABC)
NAICOM/MIS... Navy Integrated Command Management Information System
NAICP .... Nuclear Accident and Incident Control Plan [*Army*]
NAICPS...... National Association of Independent Colleges and Private Schools (EA)
NAICS .... North American Industry Classification System (AAGC)
NAICU .... National Association of Independent Colleges and Universities (EA)
NAICV .... National Association of Ice Cream Vendors [*Defunct*] (EA)
NAID .... National Associates for Informed Depressives [*Defunct*] (EA)
NAID .... National Association for Information Destruction (EA)
NAID .... National Association of Industrial Distributors [*British*] (DBA)
NAID .... National Association of Installation Developers (EA)
NAID .... National Association of Interior Designers [*Defunct*] (EA)
NAID .... North American Integration and Development Center [*University of California, Los Angeles*] (RCD)
NAIDA .... National Agricultural and Industrial Development Association [*Republic of Ireland*] (BI)
NAIDM ...... National Association of Insecticide and Disinfectant Manufacturers (BUAC)
NAIDS .... North Atlantic Institute for Defense Studies (or Study) (SAUS)
NAIDST...... National AIDS Trust [*British*]
NAIEA .... National Association of Inspectors and Educational Advisers [*British*]
NAIEC .... National Association for Industry-Education Cooperation [*Buffalo, NY*] (EA)
NAIEHS...... National Association of Importers and Exporters of Hides and Skins [*Later, USHSLA*] (EA)
NAIEM....... National Association of Insect Electrocutor Manufacturers (EA)
NAIEO .... National Association of Inspectors of Schools and Educational Organisers [*British*] (BI)
NAIES .... National Adoption Information Exchange System [*Formerly, ARENA*] (EA)
NAIES .... National Association of Interdisciplinary Ethnic Studies (EA)
NAIF .... National Association for Irish Freedom (EA)
NAIF .... Navigation Ancillary Information Facility (ACAE)
NAIF .... Navigation and Ancillary Information Facility (RALS)
NAIF .... Nordiska Akademiska Idrottsforbund [*Scandinavian Federation for University Sport*] (EA)
NAIFA........ National Association of Independent Fee Appraisers (EA)
NAIFR .... National Association of Independent Food Retailers [*Defunct*] (EA)
NAIG......... National Information Group [*NASDAQ symbol*]
NAIG......... National Insurance Group [*NASDAQ symbol*] (NQ)
NAIG......... Natl Insurance Group [*NASDAQ symbol*] (TTSB)
NAIG......... Nippon Atomic Industry Group [*Japan*]
NAIHC .... National American Indian Housing Council (EA)
NAII.......... National Association of Ice Industries [*Later, PIA*]
NAII.......... National Association of Independent Insurance Adjusters
NAII.......... National Association of Independent Insurers [*Des Plaines, IL*] (EA)
NAII.......... Natural Alternatives International [*NASDAQ symbol*] (SAG)
NAIIA .... National Association of Independent Insurance Adjusters [*Chicago, IL*] (EA)
NAIIAE....... National Association of Independent Insurance Auditors and Engineers (EA)
NAII PAC.... National Association of Independent Insurers PAC [*Des Plaines, IL*] (PACS)
NAIIU .... Not Authorized If Issued Under [*Army*]
NAIJ .... National Association for Irish Justice [*Superseded by National Association for Irish Freedom*] (EA)
NAIL .... National Argo Industries Ltd. [*Seychelles*] (BUAC)
NAIL .... National Association for Independent Living (EA)
NAIL .... National Association of Independent Lubes (EA)
NAIL .... National Association of Independent Lumbermen [*Defunct*] (EA)
NAIL .... Naval Aircraft Inventory Log (AD)
NAIL .... Neurotics Anonymous International Liaison (EA)
NAIL .... New African Investments, Ltd (SAUS)
NAIL .... North American Indian Landmarks [*A publication*]
NAILBA...... National Association of Independent Life Brokerage Agencies [*Washington, DC*] (EA)
NAILD .... National Association of Independent Lighting Distributors (EA)
NAILDD ..... North American Interlibrary Loan and Document Delivery [*Project*] (TELE)
NAILG .... National Awards for Innovation in Local Government [*Australia*]
NAILM....... National Association of Institutional Laundry Managers [*Later, National Association of Institutional Linen Management*] (EA)
NAILM....... National Association of Institutional Linen Management (EA)
NAILS .... Albany Law School (SAUS)
NAILS .... National Airspace Integrated Logistics Support [*FAA*] (TAG)
NAILS .... National Automated Immigration Lookout System [*Immigration and Naturalization Service*]

NAILS .... Naval Aviation Integrated Logistic Support Task Force (NG)
NAILSC ...... Naval Aviation Integrated Logistic Support Center (MCD)
NAILTE ...... National Association of Instructional Leaders in Technical Education (EA)
NAIM .... NAIM [*North American Indian Mission*] Ministries (EA)
NAIM .... National Association Insurance Managers, Inc. (EFIS)
NAIM .... Number Allocation and Inspection Module (PDAA)
NAIMA .... North American Indian Museums Association (EA)
NAIMA .... North American Insulation Manufacturers Association (NTPA)
NAIMD ...... National Association of Independent Music Dealers [*Defunct*] (EA)
NAIME .... National Association of Independent Maritime Educators (EA)
NAIMIS ...... NAVAIRSYSCOM [*Naval Air Systems Command*] Integrated Management InformationSystem (DNAB)
NAIMS .... National Airspace Information System [*BTS*] (TAG)
NAIMSAL ... National Anti-Imperialist Movement in Solidarity with African Liberation (EA)
NAION .... Nonarteritic Anterior Ischemic Optic Neuropathy
NAIOP .... National Association of Industrial and Office Parks (EA)
NAIOP .... Navigational Aid Inoperative for Parts
naiop .... Navigational Aids Inoperative for Parts (AD)
NAIP .... National Assault on Illiteracy Program (EA)
NAIP .... National Association of Independent Publishers (EA)
NAIP .... National Association of Industrial Parks [*Later, NAIOP*]
NAIP .... National Association of Inpatient Physicians (EA)
NAIP .... National Association of Insured Persons [*Defunct*] (EA)
NAIP .... National Association of Investment Professionals (EA)
NAIP .... Neuronal Apoptosis Inhibitory Protein [*Genetics*]
NAIP .... Neuronal Apoptpsos Inhibitory Protein [*Cytology*]
NAIPFA ...... National Association of Independent Public Finance Advisors
NAIPR .... National Association of Independent Publishers Representatives (NTPA)
NAIPRC ..... Netherlands Automated Information Processing Research Centre (NITA)
NAIPTS ...... National Amalgamated Iron Plate Trade Society [*A union*] [*British*]
NAIR .... Nairobi Trailer [*NCIC trailer make code*]
NAIR .... Narrow Absorption Infrared
NAIR .... National Arrangements for Incidents Involving Radioactivity [*Nuclear energy*] (NUCP)
NAIR .... National Association of Independent Resurfacers (EA)
NAIR .... National Association of Independent Retailers [*Ireland*] (BUAC)
NAIR .... Naval Air Systems Command Headquarters (ACAE)
NAIR .... Network Action Item Report (MCD)
NAIR .... Nonadrenergic Inhibitory Response (DB)
NAIRA .... Northamerican Industrial Representatives Association (NTPA)
NAIRD .... National Association of Independent Record Distributors and Manufacturers (EA)
NAIRDM ..... National Association of Independent Record Distributors and Manufacturers (EA)
NAIRE .... National Association of Internal Revenue Employees [*Later, NTEU*] (EA)
NAIREC ..... Nimbus Arctic Ice Reconnaissance [*Canadian project*]
Nairns .... Nairnshire, Scotland (AD)
NAIRO .... National Association of Intergroup Relations Officials [*Later, NAHRW*] (EA)
NAIRS .... National Athletic Injury/Illness Reporting System [*Pennsylvania State University*] [*Defunct*]
NAIRS .... Navy Aircraft and Readiness System
NAIRU .... Naval Air Intelligence Reserve Units
NAIRU .... Non-Accelerating-Inflation Rate of Unemployment
NAIS .... National Administrative Information System [*Computer science*] (IID)
NAIS .... National Aquaculture Information System (NOAA)
NAIS .... National Association for Information Services (EA)
NAIS .... National Association of Independent Schools (EA)
NAIS .... National Association of Investigative Specialists (EA)
NAIS .... Navy Attitudinal Information System (NVT)
NAIS .... Neutral Administrative Inspection Scheme (COE)
NAIS .... Neutral Administrative Inspection System (SAUS)
NAIS .... Night Attack Interdiction System
NAISC .... National American Indian Safety Council (EA)
NAISEO ..... National Association of Inspectors of Schools and Educational Organisers [*British*]
NAISS .... National Association of Iron and Steel Stockholders (AD)
NAIT .... National Alliance for Infusion Therapy [*An association*]
NAIT .... National Association of Industrial Technologists
NAIT .... National Association of Industrial Technology (EA)
NAIT .... Naval Air Intermediate Training
NAIT .... North American Islamic Trust (EA)
NAIT .... Northern Alberta Institute of Technology [*Edmonton, AB*]
NAITA .... National Association of Independent Travel Agents (BUAC)
NAI Tc ...... NAI Technologies [*Associated Press*] (SAG)
NAIT(C) ..... Naval Air Intermediate Training (Command)
NAITE .... National Association of Industrial Teacher Educators [*Later, NAITTE*] (EA)
NAI Tech .... NAI Technologies [*Associated Press*] (SAG)
NAITF .... Naval Air Intercept Training Facility (MUGU)
NAITP .... National Association of Income Tax Preparers [*Defunct*] (EA)
NAITPD ..... National Association of Independent Television Producers and Distributors [*Defunct*] (EA)
NAITTE ...... National Association of Industrial and Technical Teacher Educators (EA)
NAIU .... Nigeria America Line [*Intermodal shipping container symbol*] (TVRC)
NAIVPP ..... National Association of Independent Veterinary Practices and Practitioners (GVA)
NAIW .... National Association of Insurance Women (International) [*Tulsa, OK*] (EA)
NAIWA ...... North American Indian Women's Association (EA)
NAIWC ...... National Association of Inland Water Carriers [*British*] (BI)
NAIWC ...... National Association of Inland Waterway Carriers [*British*] (DBA)
NaIX .... Sodium Isopropyl Xanthogenate (SAUS)
NAIY .... National Association of Indian Youth (BUAC)
NAJ .... Napierville Junction Railway Co. [*Later, NJ*] [*AAR code*]
NAJ .... National Academy of Jazz (EA)
NAJ .... National Aeronautics and Space Administration, Johnson Space Center, Houston, TX [*OCLC symbol*] (OCLC)
NAJ .... National Association for Justice
NAJA .... National Association of Jewelry Appraisers (EA)
NAJA .... National Association of Junior Auxiliaries (EA)
NAJA .... Native American Journalists Association (EA)
NAJA .... North American Judges Association [*Later, AJA*]
NAJAE .... National Association of Jai Alai Frontons (NTPA)
NAJAFRA ... National Jazz Fraternity
NAJAG .... North African Judge Advocate General's Section [*World War II*]
NAJAKS ..... Nordic Association for Japanese and Korean Studies (BUAC)
NAJAS .... National Association of Japan-America Societies
NAJC .... National Assessment of Juvenile Correction [*University of Michigan*] (AD)
NAJC .... Northern Australia Jockey Club (AD)
NAJC .... Northwest Alabama Junior College (AD)
NAJCA .... National Association of Juvenile Correctional Agencies (EA)
NAJCW ...... National Association of Jewish Center Workers [*Later, AJCW*] (EA)
NAJD .... National Association of Journalism Directors [*Later, JEA*] (EA)
NAJD/MBAP ... National Association of JD/MBA [*Juris Doctor/Master of Business Administration*] Professionals [*Defunct*] (EA)
NAJE .... National Association of Jazz Education (AD)
NAJE .... National Association of Jazz Educators [*Later, IAJE*] (EA)
NAJEM ...... North African Joint Economic Mission [*World War II*]
NAJF .... National Association of Jai Alai Frontons (EA)
NAJFCHP ... National Association of Jewish Family, Children's, and Health Professionals (EA)
NAJHA .... National Association of Jewish Homes for the Aged [*Later, NAA-JHHA*] (EA)
NAJHHA ..... North American Association of Jewish Homes and Housing for the Aging (EA)
NAJIT .... National Association of Judiciary Interpreters and Translators (NTPA)
NAJLA .... North American Junior Limousin Association (EA)
NAJRC .... North African Joint Rearmament Committee [*World War II*]
NAJSA .... North American Jewish Students Appeal (EA)
NAJSN .... North American Jewish Students' Network (EA)
NAJU .... Nordic Association of Journalists' Unions (EA)
NAJVS .... National Association of Jewish Vocational Services (EA)
NAJYC .... North American Jewish Youth Council [*Defunct*] (EA)
NAK .... Nakhichevan [*Former USSR*] [*Seismograph station code, US Geological Survey*] [*Closed*] (SEIS)
NAK .... National Auto Credit, Inc. [*NYSE symbol*] (SAG)
NAK .... Negative Acknowledge [*or Acknowledgment*] [*Data communication*]
nak .... Negative Acknowledge Character [*Computer science*] (AD)
NAK .... Negative Acknowledge Character (ECII)
nak .... Negative Knowledge (AD)
NAK .... Network Acknowledgment
NAK .... No Acknowledgement (SAUS)
NAK .... Non-Acknowledge (SAUS)
NAK .... Non-Acknowledgment (SAUS)
NAK .... Not Acknowledged (SAUS)
nak .... Nothing Adverse Known (AD)
NAK .... Nothing Adverse Known (ADA)
NaK .... Sodium-Potassium (SAUS)
NaK .... Sodium-Potassium Alloy (SAUS)
NaK .... Sodium-Potassium Eutectic [*Medicine*] (EDAA)
NAKA .... National Association of Korean Americans (EA)
Na K-ATPase ... Adenosine Triphosphatase (Na, K-Activated) [*An enzyme*]
NAKBA ...... National Association to Keep and Bear Arms (EA)
nakl .... Naklad [*Edition*] [*Polish*] (AD)
nakl .... Nakladatel [*Edition*] [*Czech*] (AD)
NAKMAS .... National Association of Karate & Martial Arts Schools (BUAC)
NAKN .... National Anti-Klan Network (EA)
NAKOSTA ... Natural Convection in the Stationary Condition [*Computer program*]
NAKS .... North American Kant Society (EA)
NAl .... Albany Public Library, Albany, NY [*Library symbol*] [*Library of Congress*] (LCLS)
NAL .... N-Acetyllactopamine [*Biochemistry*]
NAL .... Naloxone [*A drug*]
NAL .... Name, Address, and Legal File [*Real estate*]
NAL .... National [*Telegraphy*] (PCTE)
NAL .... National Accelerator Laboratory [*AEC*]
NAL .... National Acoustics Laboratory [*Australia*] (ECON)
NAL .... National Aeronautical Laboratory (MCD)
NAL .... National Aerospace Laboratory (AD)
NAL .... National Agricultural Library [*Department of Agriculture*] [*Beltsville, MD*]
NAL .... National Airlines (AD)
NAL .... National Assistance League (EA)
NAL .... National Association of Laity (EA)
NAL .... National Association of Landowners (EA)
NAL .... National Astronomical League
NAL .... Naval Aeronautical Laboratory
NAL .... Negro American League [*Baseball*] (NDBD)
NAL .... NetWare Application Launcher [*Computer science*] (VLIE)
NAL .... New Aalesund [*Norway*] [*Geomagnetic observatory code*]
NAL .... Newalta Corp. [*Toronto Stock Exchange symbol*]
NAL .... New American Library [*Publisher*]

NAL .... New Assembly Language
NAL .... Nigeria America Line (AD)
NAL .... Niue Airways Ltd. (EY)
NAL .... No Activity Log (MCD)
NAL .... Noise Abatement League (SAUS)
NAL .... Nonadherent Leukocyte (DB)
NAL .... Non-Associated Labor (WDAA)
NAL .... North American Library (SAUS)
NAL .... North American Lighting [*Automotive industry supplier*]
NAL .... Northway Aviation Ltd. [*Canada*] [*ICAO designator*] (FAAC)
NAL .... Northwest Air Lines (SAUS)
NAL .... Norwegian America Line
NAL .... Novell Application Launcher [*Computer science*]
NAL .... Numerical Analysis Laboratory (MCD)
nal .... Sodium Iodide [*Pharmacology*] (DAVI)
NAL .... US Department of Agriculture (MHID)
NAlA .... Albany Medical College, Albany, NY [*Library symbol*] [*Library of Congress*] (LCLS)
NALA .... National Academy of Literary Arts (EA)
NALA .... National Adult Literacy Agency [*Ireland*] (BUAC)
NALA .... National Affiliation for Literacy Advance (EA)
NALA .... National Agricultural Limestone Association [*Later, National Limestone Institute*]
NALA .... National Association of Language Advisers [*British*]
NALA .... National Association of Legal Assistants (EA)
NALAA .... National Assembly of Local Arts Agencies (EA)
NALAC .... National Association of Local Arts Councils (BUAC)
NALAM ...... National Association of Livestock Auction Markets
NAlb .... Shelter Rock Public Library, Albertson, NY [*Library symbol*] [*Library of Congress*] (LCLS)
NALBA .... North American Log Builders Association (EA)
NAlBC .... Albany Business College, Albany, NY [*Library symbol*] [*Library of Congress*] (LCLS)
NAlbH .... Human Resources Center, Albertson, NY [*Library symbol*] [*Library of Congress*] (LCLS)
NAlbHM ..... Herricks Middle School, Albertson, NY [*Library symbol*] [*Library of Congress*] (LCLS)
NAlbi .... Swan Library, Albion, NY [*Library symbol*] [*Library of Congress*] (LCLS)
NAlbiH ...... Arnold Gregory Memorial Hospital, Albion, NY [*Library symbol*] [*Library of Congress*] (LCLS)
NAlbME ..... Meadow Drive Elementary School, Albertson, NY [*Library symbol*] [*Library of Congress*] (LCLS)
NALBOH ..... National Association of Local Boards of Health
NAlbSE ...... Searington Elementary School, Albertson, NY [*Library symbol*] [*Library of Congress*] (LCLS)
NALBY .... New Albany, MS [*American Association of Railroads railroad junction routing code*]
NALC .... National Afro-American Labor Council (EA)
NALC .... National Association of Ladies Circles of Great Britain and Ireland (BUAC)
NALC .... National Association of Laryngectomee Clubs [*British*] (DBA)
NALC .... National Association of Lawyers for Children (BUAC)
NALC .... National Association of Letter Carriers of the USA (EA)
NALC .... National Association of Life Companies [*Washington, DC*] (EA)
NALC .... National Association of Litho Clubs (EA)
NALC .... National Association of Local Councils [*British*]
NALC .... National Association of Louisiana Catahoulas (EA)
NALC .... National Carriers [*Common carrier symbol*]
NALC .... Natl Lodging [*NASDAQ symbol*] (TTSB)
NALC .... Naval Aviation Logistics Center (NVT)
NALC .... Navy Ammunition Logistics Code
NALC .... New Age Learning Center [*Defunct*] (EA)
NALC .... North American Landscape Characterization (SAUS)
NALCC .... National Automatic Laundry and Cleaning Council (EA)
NALCD ...... National Agricultural Library and Centre for Documentation [*Hungary*] (BUAC)
NALCDVE ... National Association of Large City Directors of Vocational Education (EA)
NAlCI .... Center for International Studies, Albany, NY [*Library symbol*] [*Library of Congress*] (LCLS)
NAlCJ .... New York State Division of Criminal Justice Services, Albany, NY [*Library symbol*] [*Library of Congress*] (LCLS)
NALCM ...... National Association of Lace Curtain Manufacturers [*Defunct*]
Nalco .... Nalco Chemical Co. [*Associated Press*] (SAG)
NALCO ...... Naval Air Logistics Control Office
NALCO ...... Newfoundland & Labrador Corp.
NALCOEASTPAC... Naval Air Logistics Control Office Eastern Pacific (DNAB)
NALCOEURREP... Naval Air Logistics Control Office European Representative
NALCOLANT... Naval Air Logistics Control Office Atlantic
NALCOM .... Naval Logistics Command (SAUS)
NALCOMIS... Naval Aviation Logistics Command Management Information System (MCD)
NALCOMIS-OS... Naval Air Logistics Command Management Information System for Operating and Support (DNAB)
NALCON ..... Navy Laboratory Computer Network
NALCOPAC... Naval Air Logistics Control Office Pacific
NALCOPACREP... Naval Air Logistics Control Office Pacific Representative
NALCOREP... Naval Air Logistics Control Office Representative
NALCOWESTPAC... Naval Air Logistics Control Office Western Pacific (DNAB)
NALCOWESTPACREP... Naval Air Logistics Control Office Western Pacific Representative (DNAB)
NAlCSR ..... College of Saint Rose, Albany, NY [*Library symbol*] [*Library of Congress*] (LCLS)
NAlD .... Dudley Observatory, Albany, NY [*Library symbol*] [*Library of Congress*] (LCLS)
NALD .... National Association of Limbless and Disabled [*British*] (DBA)
NALD .... National Association of Limbless Disabled (BUAC)
NALD .... Neonatal Adrenoleukodystrophy [*Medicine*] (EDAA)
NALD .... Nonattainment Areas Lacking Demonstrations [*Environmental science*] (COE)
NALDA ...... Naval Aviation Logistics Data Analysis (NVT)
NaLDAP ..... National Learning Disabilities Assistance Project
NALDEF ..... Native American Legal Defense and Education Foundation (EA)
NAlDH .... New York State Department of Health, Division of Laboratories and Research, Albany, NY [*Library symbol*] [*Library of Congress*] (LCLS)
NAlDS .... New York State Department of State, Community Affairs Library, Albany, NY [*Library symbol*] [*Library of Congress*] (LCLS)
NALE .... National Lead [*Federal Railroad Administration identification code*]
NALEAO ..... National Association of Latino Elected and Appointed Officials (AD)
NALECOM... National Law Enforcement Telecommunications System
NALED .... National Association of Limited Edition Dealers (EA)
NAleNH ..... E. J. Noble Hospital, Medical Library, Alexandria Bay, NY [*Library symbol*] [*Library of Congress*] (LCLS)
NALEO .... National Association of Latino Elected and Appointed Officials (EA)
NAlf .... Alfred University, Alfred, NY [*Library symbol*] [*Library of Congress*] (LCLS)
NALF .... NAL Financial Group, Inc. [*NASDAQ symbol*] (SAG)
NALF .... National Agricultural Legal Fund [*Defunct*] (EA)
NALF .... National Association of Lively Families (EA)
NALF .... Naval Auxiliary Landing Field (NG)
NALF .... Negro American Literature Forum [*A publication*] (ANEX)
NALF .... North American Limousin Foundation (EA)
NALF .... North American Loon Fund (EA)
NAlfC .... State University of New York, College of Ceramics at Alfred University, Alfred, NY [*Library symbol*] [*Library of Congress*] (LCLS)
NALFMA .... National Association of Law Firm Marketing Administrators (EA)
NAL Fn ...... NAL Financial Group, Inc. [*Associated Press*] (SAG)
NAlf-ST ...... Alfred University, School of Theology, Alfred, NY [*Library symbol*] [*Library of Congress*] [*Obsolete*] (LCLS)
NAlfUA ...... State University of New York, Agricultural and Technical College at Alfred, Alfred, NY [*Library symbol*] [*Library of Congress*] (LCLS)
NALG .... National Association for Loss and Grief [*Australia*]
NALG .... National Association of Left-Handed Golfers (EA)
NALGA ...... National Association of Local Government Auditors (NTPA)
NALGAP ..... National Association of Lesbian/Gay Alcoholism Professionals (EA)
NALGBTCC... National Association of Lesbian, Gay, Bisexual and Transgender Community Centers (EA)
NALGEP ..... National Association of Local Government Environmental Professionals (EA)
NALGG ...... National Association for Lesbian and Gay Gerontology (AD)
NALGHW .... National Association of Local Governments on Hazardous Wastes (EA)
NALGM ...... National Association of Lawn and Garden Manufacturers [*Defunct*] (EA)
NALGM ...... National Association of Leather Glove Manufacturers [*Later, NAGM*]
NALGO ...... National and Local Government Officers' Association [*British*]
NALGO ...... National Association of Local Government Officers (AIE)
NAlGS .... United States Geological Survey, Water Resources Services, New York District, Albany, NY [*Library symbol*] [*Library of Congress*] (LCLS)
NALGWC .... National Association of Local Government Women's Committees (BUAC)
NAlH .... Hospital Educational and Research Fund, Inc., Albany, NY [*Library symbol*] [*Library of Congress*] (LCLS)
NALHC ...... National Acoustic Laboratories Hearing Center [*Australia*]
NALHC ...... North American Log Homes Council (EA)
NALHF .... National Association of Leagues of Hospital Friends [*British*] (DI)
NALHI .... National Authority for the Ladies Handbag Industry (EA)
NALHM ...... National Association of Licensed House Managers [*Pronounced "nalem"*] [*A union*] [*British*] (DCTA)
NAlI .... Albany Institute of History of Art, Albany, NY [*Library symbol*] [*Library of Congress*] (LCLS)
NALI .... National Agricultural Limestone Institute [*Later, National Limestone Institute*]
NALI .... National Association of Legal Investigators (EA)
NALI .... National Association of the Launderette Industry [*British*] (DBA)
NALI .... North Atlantic Lobster Institute (EA)
NALIC .... National Association of Loft Insulation Contractors [*British*] (DI)
NALIN .... National Library Information Network (TELE)
NALIS .... Nevada Academic Libraries Information System (SAUS)
NAlJ .... Junior College of Albany, Albany, NY [*Library symbol*] [*Library of Congress*] (LCLS)
NALJS .... Nordic Atomic Libraries Joint Secretariat [*Information service or system*] (IID)
NALLA .... National Long-Lines Agency (NATG)
NALLADS... Norway Army Low Level Air Defense System (ACAE)
NALLADS... Norwegian Army Low Level Air Defence System (SAUS)
NALLD .... National Association of Learning Laboratory Directors [*Later, IALL*]
NAlLL .... New York State Department of Law Library, Albany, NY [*Library symbol*] [*Library of Congress*] (LCLS)
NALLO .... National Association of License Law Officials [*Later, NARELLO*] (EA)
NAlLS .... Albany Law School, Albany, NY [*Library symbol*] [*Library of Congress*] (LCLS)
NALLS .... National Aboriginal Literacy and Language Strategy [*Australia*]
NAlM .... Maria College, Albany, NY [*Library symbol*] [*Library of Congress*] (LCLS)
NALM .... National Association for Lay Ministry (EA)
NALM .... National Association of Lift Makers [*British*] (BI)
NALMA ...... North American Land Mammal Age [*Geological epoch*]

NALMC ...... National Association of Labor-Management Committees (EA)
NALMCO .... International Association of Lighting Management Companies (EA)
NALMCO .... National Association of Lighting Maintenance Contractors (EA)
NAlMem .... Memorial Hospital, Medical Library, Albany, NY [*Library symbol*] [*Library of Congress*] (LCLS)
NAIMH ...... New York State Department of Mental Hygiene, Mental Hygiene Research Library, Albany, NY [*Library symbol*] [*Library of Congress*] (LCLS)
NALMS ...... North American Lake Management Society (EA)
NAIMV .... New York State Department of Motor Vehicles, Research Library, Albany, NY [*Library symbol*] [*Library of Congress*] (LCLS)
NALN .... National Agricultural Libraries Network [*National Agricultural Library*]
NALN .... Native Authority Legal Notice [*Northern Nigeria*] [*A publication*] (DLA)
NALN .... North African Liaison Section [*World War II*]
NALNET ..... NASA Library Network [*NASA*] [*Washington, DC*] [*Library network*] (MCD)
NALO .... National Association of Launderette Owners (BUAC)
NALO .... National Association of Launderette Owners Ltd. [*British*] (BI)
NALO .... Naval Air Liaison Officer
NALO .... Naval Air Logistics Office (DOMA)
NALO .... Nitride Assisted Lift-Off (TIMI)
NALOG ...... Natural Logarithm (IAA)
NALOH ...... National Association Legions of Honor (EA)
NALOP ...... NATO Letter of Promulgation
NALOPKT ... Not a lot of people know that (SAUS)
NALOXONE... N-Allylnoroxymorphone [*Narcotic antagonist*]
NAIP .... Albany College of Pharmacy, Albany, NY [*Library symbol*] [*Library of Congress*] (LCLS)
NALP .... National Association for Law Placement (EA)
NALPA .... National American Legion Press Association (EA)
NALPM ...... National Association of Lithographic Plate Manufacturers [*Defunct*] (EA)
NALPN ...... National Association of Licensed Practical Nurses (EA)
NALR .... National Acid Lakes Registry [*Environmental Protection Agency*]
NALR .... National Association of Lighting Representatives (EA)
NALR .... North American Liturgy Resources (BUAC)
NALRET ..... National Association for Learning Resources Educational Technology (BUAC)
NALS .... National Advisory Logistics Staff (NATG)
NALS .... National Association of Laboratory Suppliers [*Defunct*] (EA)
NALS .... National Association of Labor Students [*British*] (DI)
NALS .... National Association of Legal Secretaries (International) [*Tulsa, OK*] (EA)
NALS .... National Association of Lumber Salesmen (EA)
NALS .... Neonatal Advanced Life Support (NUJO)
NALS .... North American Lily Society (EA)
NAIS .... Saint Peter's Hospital, Albany, NY [*Library symbol*] [*Library of Congress*] (LCLS)
NALSA .... Native American Law Students Association (EA)
NALSA .... North American Land Sailing Association (AD)
NALSAP ..... National Association of Leadership for Student Assistance Programs (NTPA)
NALSAS ..... National Association for Legal Support of Alternative Schools (EA)
NALSAT ..... National Association of Land Settlement Association Tenants (AD)
NALSC .... National Association of Legal Search Consultants (NTPA)
NALSF .... National ALS [*Amyotrophic Lateral Sclerosis*] Foundation (EA)
NALSI .... National Association of Life Science Industries [*Defunct*] (EA)
NALSO ...... National Association of Labour Student Organisations [*British*] (BI)
NAISS .... New York State Department of Social Sciences, Social Services and Statistics Library, Albany, NY [*Library symbol*] [*Library of Congress*] (LCLS)
Nal St P ..... Nalton's Collection of State Papers [*A publication*] (DLA)
NAISU .... State University of New York, Union List of Serials, Albany, NY [*Library symbol*] [*Library of Congress*] (LCLS)
NALSVHE ... National Association of Local Supervisors of Vocational Home Economics (EA)
NALT .... Naltrexone [*A drug*]
NALT .... National Association of the Legitimate Theatre [*Defunct*] (EA)
Nal (Tl) ..... Thallium-Activated Sodium Iodide [*Scintillation detector*] [*Medicine*] (MEDA)
NAltL .... La Salette Seminary, Altamont, NY [*Library symbol*] [*Library of Congress*] (LCLS)
NALTOACS... Navy Laboratory Technical Office for ADP and Communication Systems (GFGA)
NALTS .... National Advertising Lead Tracking System [*Navy*] (NVT)
NALU .... National Association of Life Underwriters [*Washington, DC*] (EA)
NALU .... National Association of Life Underwriting
NALU .... Norske Amerikalinje [*Intermodal shipping container symbol*] (TVRC)
NAIU .... State University of New York at Albany, Albany, NY [*Library symbol*] [*Library of Congress*] (LCLS)
NALUAS ..... North American Life Union Assurance Society (EA)
NAIU-F ...... State University of New York at Albany, Filmdex, Albany, NY [*Library symbol*] [*Library of Congress*] (LCLS)
NAIUHL ..... Upper Hudson Library Federation, Albany, NY [*Library symbol*] [*Library of Congress*] (LCLS)
NAIU-L ...... State University of New York at Albany Library School, Albany, NY [*Library symbol*] [*Library of Congress*] (LCLS)
NAIULS ...... New York State Union List of Serials, Albany, NY [*Library symbol*] [*Library of Congress*] (LCLS)
NAIU-PA ..... State University of New York at Albany, Graduate School of Public Affairs, Albany, NY [*Library symbol*] [*Library of Congress*] (LCLS)
NALUS ...... National Association of Leagues, Umpires, and Scorers (EA)
NALV .... National Association of Legal Vendors (NTPA)
NAIVA .... United States Veterans Administration Hospital, Albany, NY [*Library symbol*] [*Library of Congress*] (LCLS)
NALW .... Not an A-List Writer [*Screenwriter's lexicon*]
NALX .... Nalco Chemical [*Private rail car owner code*]
NALZ .... Naval Lead [*Federal Railroad Administration identification code*]
NALZ .... Neptune Orient Lines [*Intermodal trailer symbol*]
NAM .... N-Acetylmethionine [*Organic chemistry*]
NAM .... N-(Acridinyl)maleimide [*Organic chemistry*]
NAM .... Namangan [*Former USSR*] [*Seismograph station code, US Geological Survey*] [*Closed*] (SEIS)
NAM .... NAM Corp. [*Associated Press*] (SAG)
NAM .... Name and Address Module [*Computer science*] (VLIE)
NAM .... Named
NAM .... Namibia [*ANSI three-letter standard code*] (CNC)
NAM .... Namlea [*Indonesia*] [*Airport symbol*] (OAG)
NAM .... Nampa, ID [*Amtrak Busline code*]
NAM .... Nangikurrunggurr [*Language symbol*] (ETLW)
NAM .... NASA Access Mechanism (ITCA)
NAM .... National Account Management [*Bell System*]
NAM .... National Aero Manufacturing (AD)
NAM .... National Air Museum [*of the Smithsonian Institution*] [*Later, NASM*]
NAM .... National Apple Month (EA)
NAM .... National Arbitration & Mediation
NAM .... National Army Museum [*British military*] (DMA)
NAM .... National Association of Manufacturers (NTCM)
NAM .... National Average Maintenance (VLIE)
NAM .... Natural Actomyosins [*Biochemistry*]
NAM .... Nautical Air Miles
NAM .... Naval Aircraft Modification
NAM .... Naval Air Material (SAA)
NAM .... Naval Air Mechanic [*British military*] (DMA)
NAM .... Naval Aviation Museum [*Pensacola, FL*]
NAM .... Navy Achievement Medal [*Military decoration*]
NAM .... Nederlandsche Aluminium Maatschappij [*Netherlands Aluminum Co.*] (AD)
NAM .... Negro Adult Male [*Medicine*] (EDAA)
nam .... Network Access Machine [*Computer science*] (AD)
NAM .... Network Access Machine [*National Institute of Standards and Technology*] [*Computer science*]
NAM .... Network Access Method [*Control Data Corp.*] [*Telecommunications*] (TEL)
NAM .... Network Analysis Model
NAM .... New Account Memorandum
NAM .... New America Movement (EA)
NAM .... New American Man [*Lifestyle classification coined by Robert Bly*] (ECON)
NAM .... New Architectural Movement [*British*] (DI)
NAM .... Newspaper Association Managers (EA)
NAM .... Nicotinamide (SAUS)
NAM .... NOAA [*National Oceanic and Atmospheric Administration*] Accounting Manual (NOAA)
NAM .... Node Address Memory (SAUS)
NAM .... Nonadditive Mixing (DICI)
NAM .... Non-Addressable Memory (SAUS)
nam .... Non-Aligned Movement (AD)
NAM .... Nonaligned Movement
NAM .... Non-Alignment Movement (SAUS)
NAM .... Normal Adult Male (MELL)
N Am .... North America (AD)
NAM .... North America
NAM .... North American Metals Corp. [*Vancouver Stock Exchange symbol*]
NAM .... North American Movement (AD)
NAM .... North American Museum Corp. (SAUS)
NAM .... North American Region [*USTTA*] (TAG)
NAM .... Nortland Air Manitoba [*Canada*] [*ICAO designator*] (FAAC)
NAM .... Norwegian American Museum Corp. (EA)
NAM .... Number Assignment Module (VLIE)
NAM .... Numerical Assignment Number [*Computer science*]
NAM .... Nurses Against Misrepresentation (EA)
NAM .... State University of New York at Albany, Albany, NY [*OCLC symbol*] (OCLC)
Nam .... Vietnam
NAma .... Amagansett Free Library, Amagansett, NY [*Library symbol*] [*Library of Congress*] (LCLS)
NAMA .... National Account Marketing Association (EA)
NAMA .... National Agenda for a Multicultural Australia
NAMA .... National Agri-Marketing Association (EA)
NAMA .... National Air-Monitoring Audit [*Environmental Protection Agency*] (GFGA)
NAMA .... National Assistance Management Association [*Washington, DC*] (EA)
NAMA .... National Association of Master Appraisers (EA)
NAMA .... National Association of Mathematics Advisers [*British*] (DBA)
NAMA .... National Automatic Merchandising Association [*Chicago, IL*] (EA)
NAMA .... National Automotive Muffler Association [*Defunct*] (EA)
NAMA .... Naval Aeronautical Material Area (NG)
NAMA .... New Amsterdam Musical Association (AD)
NAMA .... North American Manx Association (EA)
NAMA .... North American Maritime Agencies (AD)
NAMA .... North American Mycological Association (EA)
NAMA .... Northern Air Material Area (SAUS)
NAMA .... Northwest Atlantic Marine Alliance (EARSL)
NAMAB ...... National Air Museum Advisory Board (MUGU)
NAMAC ...... National Alliance for Media Arts and Culture (NTPA)
NAMAC ...... National Alliance of Media Arts Centers (EA)
NAMAC ...... National Amateur Missile Analysis Center
NAMAC ...... National Association of Men's Apparel Clubs [*Later, NAMBAC, Bureau of WholesaleSales Representatives*]
NAMAC ...... National Association of Merger and Acquisition Consultants (EA)

NAMAD...... National Association of Minority Automobile Dealers [*Detroit, MI*] (EA)
NAMAD PAC... National Association of Minority Automobile Dealers PAC [*Detroit, MI*] (PACS)
NAMAE...... Northern Air Material (or Materiel) Area, Europe (SAUS)
NAMAE...... Northern Air Materiel Area, Europe [*Army*]
NAmaHi..... Amagansett Historical Association, Amagansett, NY [*Library symbol*] [*Library of Congress*] (LCLS)
NAMAINTRADET... Naval Air Maintenance Training Detachment (DNAB)
NAMAINTRAGRU... Naval Air Maintenance Training Group (DNAB)
NAMAP...... Northern Air Material (or Materiel) Area, Pacific (SAUS)
NAMAP...... Northern Air Materiel Area, Pacific [*Army*]
NAMAPAC... National Automatic Merchandising Association PAC [*Chicago, IL*] (PACS)
NAMAPUS... Naval Assistant to the Military Aide to the President of the United States
NAMAR...... North American Mustang Association and Registry (EA)
NAMARA.... Navy and Marine Corps Appellate Review Activity (DNAB)
NAMARCO... National Marketing Corp [*Philippines*] (BUAC)
NAMAS...... National Accreditation of Measurement and Sampling (SAUS)
NAMAS...... National Measurement Accreditation Service [*Research center*] [*British*] (IRC)
NAMAST.... System of National Accounts and System of Material Product Balances [*United Nations Statistical Office*] [*Information service or system*] (CRD)
NAMAT...... Normal Material (SAUS)
NAMATCEN... Naval Air Material Center [*Also, NAMC, NAVAIRMATCEN*]
NAMATE..... Naval Air Material Command
NAMB....... National Agricultural Marketing Board [*Canada*] (BUAC)
NAMB....... National Association of Master Bakers [*British*] (DI)
NAMB....... National Association of Master Bakers, Confectioners, and Caterers [*British*] (DBA)
NAMB....... National Association of Media Brokers (EA)
NAMB....... National Association of Minority Businesses (AAGC)
NAMB....... National Association of Mortgage Brokers [*Washington, DC*] (EA)
NAMB....... Naval Academy Midshipmen Branch
NAMB....... Naval Amphibious Base
NAMB....... North American Bank & Trust Co. [*NASDAQ symbol*] (QUAN)
NAMBAC.... National Association of Men's and Boys' Apparel Clubs [*Later, Bureau of Wholesale Sales Representatives*] (EA)
NAMBC...... National Association of Milk Bottle Collectors (EA)
NAMBLA.... North American Man-Boy Love Association
NAMBLA.... North American Men-Boy Love Association (BUAC)
NAMBO...... National Association of Motor Bus Operators (AD)
NAMBO...... National Association of Motor Bus Owners [*Later, ABA*] (EA)
NAMB PAC... National Association of Mortgage Brokers PAC [*Bloomington, MN*] (PACS)
NaMBT...... Sodium-2-Mercaptobenzothiazole (SAUS)
NAMC....... NAM Corp. [*NASDAQ symbol*] (SAG)
NAMC....... Nanchang Aircraft Manufacturing Co. (SAUS)
NAMC....... N & Ha Manufacturing Company [*NCIC trailer make code*]
NAMC....... National Air Material Center (KSC)
NAMC....... National Association of Management Consultants (EA)
NAMC....... National Association of Minority Contractors (EA)
NAMC....... National Association of Mothers' Centers (EA)
NAMC....... Naval Aerospace Medical Center
NAMC....... Naval Air Material Center [*Also, NAMATCEN, NAVAIRMATCEN*]
NAMC....... Naval Air Materiel Command
NAMC....... Nihon Aeroplane Manufacturing Co. (AD)
NAMC....... North American National Corp. (SAUS)
NAMC....... North Atlantic Military Committee
NAMC....... Northern Association of Management Consultants (COBU)
NAMCA...... National Association for Middle Class Americans (EA)
NAMCA...... Norfolk Area Medical Center Authority [*Medicine*] (EDAA)
NAMCA...... North America Missing Children Association [*Canada*] (EAIO)
NAMC-AEL... Naval Air Material Center - Aeronautical Engine Laboratory
NAMC-AIL... Naval Air Material Center - Aeronautical Instruments Laboratory [*Philadelphia, PA*]
NAMC-AML... Naval Air Material Center - Aeronautical Materials Laboratory
NAMC-APEL... Naval Air Material Center - Aeronautical Photographic Experimental Laboratory
NAMCAR.... North America/Caribbean
NAMC-ARRL... Naval Air Material Center - Aeronautical Radio and RADAR Laboratory
NAMC-ASL... Naval Air Material Center - Aeronautical Structures Laboratory
NAMCC...... National Association of Mutual Casualty Companies (EA)
NAM-CDH... Non Absorbing Mirror Constricted Double Heterostructure (NITA)
NAMCF...... National Association of Minority CPA [*Certified Public Accounting*] Firms
NAMCO...... Air-Cushion Vehicle built by Nakamura Seisakusho [*Usually used in com bination with numerals*] [*Japan*]
NAMCO...... Namibian Minerals Corporation (EFIS)
NAMCO...... Naval and Mechanical Co. (AD)
NAMCO...... North American Management Council (BUAC)
NAMCO...... North Atlantic Marine Cooperative Commission (BUAC)
NAM Cp..... NAM Corp. [*Associated Press*] (SAG)
NAMCP...... National Association of Managed Care Physicians (EA)
NAMCPAF... National Association of Minority Certified Public Accounting Firms (EA)
NAMCS...... National Ambulatory Medical Care Survey [*National Center for Health Statistics*]
NAMCU...... National Association of Minority Consultants and Urbanologists [*Defunct*] (EA)
NAMC-UM... National Association of Minority Contractors of Upper Midwest (EARSL)
NAMCW..... National Association of Maternal and Child Welfare [*British*]
NAMD....... National Association for Membership Development (NTPA)
NAMD....... National Association of Marble Dealers [*Later, MIA*] (EA)
NAMD....... National Association of Marine Dealers
NAMD....... National Association of Market Developers [*New York, NY*] (EA)
NAMD....... National Association of Membership Directors of Chambers of Commerce [*Defunct*] (EA)
NAMD....... Naval Ammunition Depot [*Charleston, SC*]
NAMD....... Newsletter of the Army Medical Department
NAMDA...... North American Medical/Dental Association (EA)
NAMDAR.... North American Data Airborne Recorder (IAA)
NAMDB...... National Association of Medical-Dental Bureaus [*Later, MDHBA*]
NAMDDU.... Naval Air Mine Defense Development Unit (MUGU)
NAMDEX.... Name Index
NAMDI...... National Marine Data Inventory
NAMDRA.... National American Motors Drivers and Racers Association (EA)
NAMDRC.... National Association for Medical Direction of Respiratory Care (NTPA)
NAMDRC.... National Association of Medical Directors for Respiratory Care (EA)
NAMDRP.... Naval Aviation Maintenance Discrepancy Reporting Program (DNAB)
NAMDT...... National Association of Milliners, Dressmakers, and Tailors (EA)
NAME........ National Anti-Racist Movement in Education [*British*] (DBA)
NAME........ National Association for Mediation in Education (EA)
NAME........ National Association for Minority Education
NAME........ National Association for Multiracial Education [*British*]
NAME........ National Association of Management/Marketing Educators [*Defunct*] (EA)
NAME........ National Association of Marine Enginebuilders [*British*] (BI)
NAME........ National Association of Marine Engineers (AD)
NAME........ National Association of Marine Engineers of Canada (BUAC)
NAME........ National Association of Maritime Educators (NTPA)
NAME........ National Association of Media Educators (EA)
NAME........ National Association of Medical Examiners (EA)
NAME........ National Association of Metal Name Plate Manufacturers (AD)
NAME........ National Association of Miniature Enthusiasts (EA)
NAME........ National Association of Minority Entrepreneurs (EA)
NAME........ National Association of Mobile Entertainers (EA)
NAME........ National Association of Modeling and Entertainment (EA)
NAME........ National Association of Name Plate Manufacturers, Inc.
NAME........ Nevi, Atrial Myxoma, Myxoid Neurofibroma, and Ephilides [*Syndrome*] [*Medicine*] (MELL)
NAME........ New American Music in Europe [*An association*] (BUAC)
NAME........ Nitroarginine Methyl Ester [*Organic chemistry*]
NAME........ North American Monogrammers and Embroiderers [*Defunct*] (EA)
NAME........ Nuclear Accident Modelling Exercise (SAUS)
NAMEB...... National Association of Marine Engine Builders (AD)
NAMEC...... National Association of Marine Engineers of Canada
NAMED...... North African Medical Section [*World War II*]
NAMEDCEN... Naval Aviation Medical Center (DNAB)
NAMEPA.... National Association of Minority Engineering Program Administrators (EA)
N Amer J Econ Finance... North American Journal of Economics and Finance [*A publication*] (JLIT)
NAMES...... National Association of Medical Equipment Suppliers (EA)
NAMES...... NAVDAC [*Naval Data Automation Command*] Assembly, Monitor, Executive System (PDAA)
NAMESAKES... Naval Aviators Must Energetically Sell Aviation to Keep Effective Strength
NAMESU.... National Association of Music Executives in State Universities (EA)
NAMET...... Naval Mathematics and English Test [*British military*] (DMA)
NAMF........ National Association of Metal Finishers (EA)
NAMF........ Naval Aviation Museum Foundation (DNAB)
NAMF........ North American Multi-Frequency (SAUS)
NAMFAX.... National and Aviation Meteorological Facsimile Network [*National Weather Service*]
NAMFC...... North Atlantic Mediterranean Freight Conference (EA)
NAMFI....... NATO Missile Firing Installation
NAMFREL... National Citizens' Movement for Free Elections [*Philippines*] [*Political party*]
NAMFSM.... National Association of Meat and Food Seasoning Manufacturers [*Later, NSMA*] (EA)
NAMG....... Narrow-Angle Mars Gate [*NASA*]
NAMG....... National Association of Mining Groups (EA)
NAMG....... National Association of Multiple Grocers [*British*] (BI)
NAMG....... North American Group Ltd. (SAUS)
NAMGAR.... North American MGA [*Morris Garage Automobile*] Register (EA)
NAMH....... National Association for Mental Health (EA)
NAMHA...... North American Morab Horse Association (EA)
NAMHH..... National Association of Methodist Hospitals and Homes
NAMHI...... National Association for the Mentally Handicapped of Ireland (EAIO)
NAMHO..... National Association of Mining History Organizations [*British*] (DBA)
NAmi........ Amityville Public Library, Amityville, NY [*Library symbol*] [*Library of Congress*] (LCLS)
NAMI........ National Alliance for the Mentally Ill (EA)
NAMI........ National Association of Malleable Ironfounders [*British*] (BI)
NAMI........ National Association of Marine Investigators [*Association*] [*Nautical term*] (NTA)
NAMI........ Naval Aerospace Medical Institute
NAMIA....... National Association of Mutual Insurance Agents [*Later, PIA*] (EA)
NAMI - Arkansas... National Alliance for the Mentally Ill, Arkansas (EARSL)
Namib....... Namibia (AD)
NAMIC....... National Association of Minorities in Communications (EA)

NAMIC....... National Association of Mutual Insurance Companies [*Indianapolis, IN*] (EA)
NAMIC CAP... National Association of Mutual Insurance Companies Congressional Action Program [*Washington, DC*] (PACS)
NAMID ...... National Moving Image Database [*American Film Institute*] [*Information service or system*] (IID)
NAMIEP ..... National AIDS Minority Information and Education Program (SAUS)
NAmiGH..... Brunswick General Hospital, Amityville, NY [*Library symbol*] [*Library of Congress*] (LCLS)
NAmiHS..... Amityville Memorial High School, Amityville, NY [*Library symbol*] [*Library of Congress*] (LCLS)
NAmiJH ..... Amityville Junior High School, Amityville, NY [*Library symbol*] [*Library of Congress*] (LCLS)
NAMilCom... North Atlantic Military Committee (AD)
NAMILCOM... North Atlantic Military Committee
NAMILPO... NATO Military Posture (AABC)
NAMIM ...... National Association of Musical Instrument Mechanics (EA)
NAMIMASS... National Alliance for the Mentally Ill, AMI of Massachusetts (EARSL)
NAMI-NYS... NAMI New York State (EARSL)
NAMIRL..... Naval Aerospace Medical Institute and Research Laboratory [*Medicine*] (EDAA)
NAMIS....... Nitride-Barrier Avalanche Injection Missile (MCD)
NAmiSH..... South Oaks Hospital, Amityville, NY [*Library symbol*] [*Library of Congress*] (LCLS)
NAMISTESTCEN... Naval Air Missile Test Center
naml......... Namligen [*Namely*] [*Swedish*] (AD)
NAML........ National Applied Mathematics Laboratory [*National Institute of Standards and Technology*] (MCD)
NAML........ National Association of Marine Laboratories (BUAC)
NAML........ Naval Aircraft Materials Laboratory (MCD)
NAML Dig... National Association of Manufacturers Law Digest [*A publication*] (DLA)
NAMLM ..... National Association for Multi-Level Marketing (EA)
NAMLNC.... National Association of Medical Legal Nurse Consultants (EA)
NAMM....... National Association of Margarine Manufacturers (EA)
NAMM....... National Association of Mass Merchandisers (EA)
NAMM....... National Association of Master Masons [*British*] (DBA)
NAMM....... National Association of Mirror Manufacturers (EA)
NAMM....... National Association of Music Merchandisers (AD)
NAMM....... National Association of Music Merchants (EA)
NAMM....... North African Military Mission [*World War II*]
NAMM....... North American Music Merchants (SAUS)
NAMMA..... NATO Multi-Role Combat Aircraft Development and Production Management Agency
NAMMA..... North American Maritime Ministry Association (EA)
NAMMC..... Natural Asphalt Mineowners' and Manufacturers' Council (AD)
NAMMC..... North Atlantic Marine Mammal Commission (BUAC)
NAMMD..... National Association of Marinas and Marine Dealers (EA)
NAMME..... National Association of Medical Minority Educators (EA)
NAMME..... National Association of Minority Media Executives (NTPA)
NAMMIS .... Navy Aviation Maintenance and Material Support System (NG)
NAMMM .... National Association of Musical Merchandise Manufacturers [*Later, GAMA*] (EA)
NAMMMR... North American Midget Magna Magnette Register [*Automotive hobby group*]
NAMMO..... NATO Multi-Role Combat Aircraft Management Organization (PDAA)
NAMMO..... North Atlantic Treaty Organization [*NATO*] Multi-Role Combat Aircraft Development and Production Management Organization (AAGC)
NAMMO Development a... NATO [*North Atlantic Treaty Organization*] Multi-Role Combat Aircraft Development a (AD)
NAMMOS ... Navy Manpower Mobilization System
NAMMR..... National Association for Milk Marketing Reform [*Later, NIDA*] (EA)
NAMMR..... North American Mini Moke Registry (EA)
NAMMS..... Navy Aviation Maintenance and Material Support System
NAMMU..... National Association of Major Mail Users [*Canada*] (EAIO)
NAMMW .... National Association of Musical Merchandise Wholesalers [*Later, MDA*] (EA)
NAMN....... Nicotinic Acid Mononucleotide (DMAA)
NAMNPM ... National Association of Metal Name Plate Manufacturers
NAMO .... Namco Industries [*NCIC trailer make code*]
NAMO .... National Agricultural Marketing Officials [*Richmond, VA*] (EA)
NAMO .... National Association of Manufacturing Opticians (EA)
NAMO .... National Association of Multifamily Owners
NAMO .... Naval Aircraft Maintenance Orders
NAMOA...... National Association of Miscellaneous Ornamental and Architectural Products Contractors (EA)
NAMOC...... Northwest Atlantic Mid-Ocean Canyon (SAUS)
NAMORB.... North Atlantic Mid-Ocean-Ridge Basalt [*Geology*]
NAMOS...... National Art Museum of Sport (EA)
NAMP .... National Alliance of Mental Patients [*Later, NAPS*] (EA)
NAMP .... National Antibiotic Minimization Program [*Australia*]
NAMP .... National Association of Magazine Publishers [*Later, Magazine Publishers Association*]
NAMP .... National Association of Marble Producers (EA)
NAMP .... National Association of Married Priests (AD)
NAMP .... National Association of Mature People (EA)
NAMP .... National Association of Meal Programs (EA)
NAMP .... National Association of Meat Purveyors (EA)
NAMP .... National Association of Midwifery Practitioners [*Defunct*] (EA)
NAMP .... NATO Annual Manpower Plan (NATG)
NAMP .... Naval Aviation Maintenance Program (MCD)
NAMP .... Nonaccounting Majors Program
NAMP .... North American Meat Processors Association (NTPA)
NAMP .... North Atlantic Missiology Project
NAMPA...... NATO Maritime Patrol Aircraft Agency (NATG)
NAMPBG.... National Association of Manufacturers of Pressed and Blown Glassware [*Defunct*] (EA)
NAMP-CV... NAPM - Carolinas - Virginia (EARSL)
nampg....... Nautical Air Miles per Gallon (AD)
NAMPI....... National Association of Missing Persons Investigators [*Defunct*] (EA)
NAMPMW... Vietnam Prisoners of War [*An association*] (AD)
NAMPPF .... Nautical Air Miles per Pound of Fuel (AAG)
namppf...... Nautical Air Miles per Pound of Fuel (AD)
NAMPS...... Narrow Advanced Mobile Phone Service
NAMPS...... Narrowband Advanced Mobile Phone Service (CGWS)
NAMPS...... Narrow-Band Analog Mobile Phone Service [*Computer science*] (VLIE)
NAMPS...... National Association of Marine Products and Services (EA)
NAMPS...... Navy Manpower Planning System (NVT)
NAMPUS.... National Association of Master-Plumbers of the United States (BUAC)
NAMPW..... National Association of Meat Processors and Wholesalers (EA)
NAMPW..... National Association of Minority Political Women (EA)
NAMRA...... North American Mini-Champ Racing Association (EA)
NAMRAD.... Non-Atomic Military Research and Development [*Subcommittee*]
NAMRC...... National Association of Multicultural Rehabilitation Concerns (EA)
NAMRC...... North American Marten Rabbit Club (EA)
NAMRI ...... Naval Aerospace Medical Research Institute (DNAB)
NAMRI ...... North American Manufacturing Research Institute (SAUS)
NAMRI/SME... North American Manufacturing Research Institution of SME [*Society of Manufacturing Engineers*] (EA)
NAMRL...... Naval Aerospace Medical Research Laboratory
NAMRP...... National Apostolate with Mentally Retarded Persons (EA)
NAMRU...... Navy Aerospace Medical Research Unit [*Medicine*] (EDAA)
NAMRU ..... Navy Medical Research Unit [*World War II*]
NAMRU ..... Navy Medical Reserve Unit (DAVI)
NAMRU-2... Naval Medical Research Unit No. 2, Jakarta, Indonesia
NAMRU-3... Naval Medical Research Unit No. 3, Cairo, Egypt
NAms........ Amsterdam Free Library, Amsterdam, NY [*Library symbol*] [*Library of Congress*] (LCLS)
NAMS .... National Account Management Society (NTPA)
NAMS .... National Air Monitoring Station [*Environmental Protection Agency*] (ERG)
NAMS .... National Air Monitoring System (EEVL)
NAMS .... National Ambient Air Monitoring Station [*or System*] [*Environmental Protection Agency*]
NAMS .... National Association of Marine Services (EA)
NAMS .... National Association of Marine Surveyors (EA)
NAMS .... National Association of Military Spouses (EA)
NAMS .... National Association of Municipal Securities Dealers
NAMS .... Network Analysis and Management System [*Computer science*] (VLIE)
NAMS .... North American Membrane Society (EA)
NAMS .... North American Menopause Society (EA)
NAMS .... North American Micropaleontology Section (SAUS)
NAMS .... Nurses and Army Medical Specialists
NAMSA...... National Ambulance Medical Suppliers Association [*Medicine*] (EDAA)
NAMSA...... NATO Maintenance and Supply Agency
NAMSA...... North American Multihull Sailing Association (EA)
NAMSB...... National Association of Men's Sportswear Buyers (EA)
NAMSB...... National Association of Mutual Savings Banks (EA)
NAMSC...... North American Maple Syrup Council (EA)
NAMSCO.... National Association of MDS [*Multipoint Distribution System*] Service Companies [*Later, MDSIA*] (EA)
NAMSDIC... National Arthritis and Musculoskeletal and Skin Diseases Information Clearinghouse [*Later, NAMSIC*] (EA)
NAMSE...... National Association of Minority Students and Educators in Higher Education (EA)
NAMSIC..... National Arthritis and Musculoskeletal and Skin Diseases Information Clearinghouse (EA)
NAmsM ..... Mohasco Corp., Corporate Planning Library, Amsterdam, NY [*Library symbol*] [*Library of Congress*] (LCLS)
NAMS/MIS... National Air Monitoring Stations Management Information System (EAGT)
NAMSO...... NATO Maintenance and Supply Organization [*Formerly, NATO Maintenance Supply Service Agency*] [*Luxembourg*]
NAMSO...... Navy Maintenance Support Office
NAMSOINST... Navy Maintenance Support Office Instruction (MCD)
NAMSP...... National Association of Mail Service Pharmacies [*Later, AMCPA*] (EA)
NAMSR...... National Association of Multiple Shoe Repairers [*British*] (DBA)
NAMSRC.... National AM Stereophonic Radio Committee
NAMSS...... National Association Medical Staff Services (EA)
NAmSv...... North American Savings Bank [*Associated Press*] (SAG)
NAMT........ National Association for Music Therapy (EA)
NAMT........ National Association for Music Therapy, Inc. [*Medicine*] (EDAA)
NAMT........ Naval Aircraft Mobile Trainer
NAMT........ Naval Air Maintenance Trainer (MUGU)
NAMT........ Norwegian Association of Microbiological Technologists (BUAC)
NAMTA...... National Art Materials Trade Association (EA)
NAMTAC .... National Association of Management and Technical Assistance Centers [*Washington, DC*] (EA)
NamTai...... Nam Tai Electronics, Inc. [*Associated Press*] (SAG)
NAMTC...... National Association of Media and Technology Centers (EA)
NAMTC...... Naval Air Missile Test Center
NAmTch..... North American Technologies Corp. [*Associated Press*] (SAG)
NAMTD...... Naval Air Maintenance Training Detachment
NAMTD...... Naval Air Maintenance Training Devices

NAMTG ...... Naval Air Maintenance Training Group (MCD)
NAMTGD .... Naval Air Maintenance Training Group Detachment (DNAB)
NAMtge ..... North American Mortgage Co. [*Associated Press*] (SAG)
NAMTM ..... Naval Air Mobile Training Maintenance
NAMTRA .... Naval Air Maintenance Training
NAMTRADET... Naval Air Maintenance Training Detachment (MCD)
NAMTRAGRU... Naval Air Maintenance Training Group (MCD)
NAMTRAGRUDET... Naval Air Maintenance Training Group Detachment (DNAB)
NAMTRAGRUP... Naval Air Maintenance Training Group (SAA)
NAMTRATCLOFLT... Naval Air Maintenance Training Type Commander Liaison Office, Fleet (DNAB)
NAMTRATCLOLANT... Naval Air Maintenance Training Type Commander Liaison Officer, Atlantic (DNAB)
NAMTRATCLOPAC... Naval Air Maintenance Training Type Commander Liaison Office, Pacific (DNAB)
NAMTS ...... Nippon Automatic Mobile Telephone System (SAUS)
NAMU .... Naval Aircraft Material Utility
NAMU .... Naval Aircraft Modification Unit
NAMU .... Nederlandse Aardolie Maatschappij [*Intermodal shipping container symbol*] (TVRC)
NAMV .... Narcissus Mosaic Virus [*Plant pathology*]
NAMVF ...... North American Metals Corp. [*NASDAQ symbol*] (COMM)
NAMW .... National Association of Media Women (EA)
NAMW .... National Association of Military Widows (EA)
NAMW .... National Association of Ministers' Wives [*Later, NAMWMW*] (EA)
NAMWB ..... National Association of Minority Women in Business [*Kansas City, MO*] (EA)
NAMWMW... National Association of Ministers' Wives and Ministers' Widows (EA)
NAMZ .... Neue Allgemeine Missions-Zeitschrift [*A publication*] (BJA)
NAN .... N-Acetylneuraminic Acid [*Also, AcNeu, NANA*] [*Biochemistry*]
NAN .... Nadi [*Fiji*] [*Airport symbol*] (OAG)
Nan .... Nancy (AD)
Nan .... Nanette (AD)
Nan .... Nanking [*China*] (AD)
NAN .... Nanking [*Republic of China*] [*Seismograph station code, US Geological Survey*] (SEIS)
NAN .... Nantucket Industries, Inc. [*AMEX symbol*] (SPSG)
NAN .... National Academy of Needlearts (EA)
NAN .... National Academy of Neuropsychology (EA)
NAN .... National AIDS [*Acquired Immune Deficiency Syndrome*] Network [*Defunct*] (EA)
NAN .... National Airlines, Inc. [*ICAO designator*] (FAAC)
NAN .... National Area Network [*Computer science*] (VLIE)
NAN .... National Association of Neighborhoods (EA)
NAN .... Network Application Node
NAN .... Neuraminidase (SAUS)
NAN .... News Agency of Nigeria (EY)
NAN .... Nisi Aliter Notetur [*Unless Otherwise Noted*] [*Latin*]
nan .... Nisi Aliter Notetur [*Unless It is Otherwise Noted*] [*Latin*] (AD)
Nan .... Nitrosamine [*Biochemistry*]
NAN .... No Action Necessary [*Military*] (CINC)
NAN .... Non-Ammonia-Nitrogen (PDAA)
NAN .... North American Nippon Technologies Corp. [*Vancouver Stock Exchange symbol*]
NAN .... North Atlantic Network (EA)
NAN .... Norton Administrator for Networks [*Computer software*] [*Symantec Corp.*] (PCM)
NaN .... Not a Number [*Computer programming*] (BYTE)
NAN .... Not a Number
nana .... N-Acetylneuraminic Acid (AD)
NANA .... N-Acetylneuraminic Acid [*Also, AcNeu, NAN*] [*Biochemistry*]
NANA .... National Advertising News Association (AD)
NANA .... National Advertising Newspaper Association [*Later, SNA*] (EA)
NANA .... National Association of Nail Artists [*Later, NANAA*] (EA)
NANA .... Newsagents' Association of New South Wales and the Australian Capital Territory,Inc.
NANA .... North American Newspaper Alliance
NANA .... North American Normande Association (EA)
NANA .... Northwest Alaska Native Association [*Later, MA*]
NANAA ...... National Aesthetician and Nail Artist Association [*Formerly, NANA*] [*WINBA*] [*Absorbed by*] (EA)
NANAC ...... National Aircraft Noise Abatement Council [*Defunct*] (EA)
NANAC ...... National Aviation Noise Abatement Council (AD)
NANACA ..... National Association for Native American Children of Alcoholics (EA)
NANACOA... National Association for Native American Children of Alcoholics (EA)
NANAI .... Dutch Actiongroup for Indians of North America
NANAP ...... Non-Aligned News Agency Pool (BUAC)
NANAPAC... NANA Regional Corp PAC [*Anchorage, AK*] (PACS)
NANASP ..... National Association of Nutrition and Aging Services Programs (EA)
NANAWO .... Namibia National Women's Organzation (BUAC)
NAnB .... Bard College, Annandale-On-Hudson, NY [*Library symbol*] [*Library of Congress*] (LCLS)
NANB .... Non-A, Non-B [*Virology*]
NANB .... Nurses Association of New Brunswick (SAUS)
NANBA ...... North American Native Bankers Association (EA)
NANBH ...... Non-A, Non-B Hepatitis [*Medicine*]
NANBPWC... National Association of Negro Business and Professional Women's Clubs [*Washington, DC*] (EA)
NANBV ...... Non-A, Non-B Hepatic Virus
NANC .... National Association of New Careerists (EA)
NANC .... Non-Adrenergic, Non-Cholinergic [*Neurology*]
NANC .... North American Numbering Council (CGWS)
NANCA ...... North American Natural Casing Association (EA)
NANCB ...... National Association of Negotiated Commissioned Brokers [*Defunct*] (EA)
NANCF ...... North Atlantic Naval Coastal Frontier
NANCI .... New Aeronautical and Nautical Chart Investigations (NOAA)
NANCO ...... National Association of Noise Control Officials (EA)
NANCRFUG... North American NCR [*National Cash Register Co.*] Financial Users Group (EA)
NAND .... Inverted And Gate, Not And (SAUS)
NAND .... Naval Ammunition and Net Depot
NAND .... NOT-AND (SAUS)
NAND .... Not And [*Logical operator*] [*Computer science*]
N & A .... Nautical & Aviation Publishing Co.
N&A .... Nipple and Areola [*Medicine*] (MELL)
N&A .... Normal and Active [*Medicine*] (EDAA)
NANDA ...... North American Nursing Diagnosis Association (EA)
N&A .... Notes and Application (SAUS)
N&CR .... [*The*] Nash and Cibinic Report [*A publication*] (AAGC)
N&D .... Nelly Don Inc. (EFIS)
N&D .... Nodular and Diffuse [*Medicine*] (MELL)
N & D .... Nodular and Diffuse Lymphoma [*Oncology*]
N&D .... Noise and Distortion (SAUS)
N&G .... Navigation and Guidance
NAND Gate... NOT-AND Gate (SAUS)
N & GS ...... Navigation and Guidance Subsystem [*NASA*] (KSC)
N & H .... Nott and Hopkins' Reports [*United States Court of Claims*] [*A publication*] (DLA)
N & H .... Nott and Huntington's Reports [*1-7 United States Court of Claims*] [*A publication*] (DLA)
N & Hop .... Nott and Hopkins' Reports [*United States Court of Claims*] [*A publication*] (DLA)
N & Hunt ... Nott and Huntington's Reports [*1-7 United States Court of Claims*] [*A publication*] (DLA)
N&M .... Nerves and Muscles (DMAA)
N & M .... Nevile and Manning's English King's Bench Reports [*A publication*] (DLA)
N&M .... Night and Morning (DMAA)
N & M .... November and May [*Denotes semiannual payments of interest or dividends in these months*] [*Business term*]
N & Macn .. Neville and Macnamara's Railway and Canal Cases [*1855-1950*] [*A publication*] (DLA)
N & MC ..... Navy and Marine Corps [*Medal*]
N & Mc ..... Nott and McCord's South Carolina Reports [*A publication*] (DLA)
N & McC .... Nott and McCord's South Carolina Reports [*A publication*] (DLA)
N & MCM... Navy and Marine Corps Medal [*Military decoration*]
N & McN.... Neville and Macnamara's Railway and Canal Cases [*1855-1950*] [*A publication*] (DLA)
N & M Mag... Nevile and Manning's English Magistrates' Cases [*A publication*] (DLA)
N & MMC... Nevile and Manning's English Magistrates' Cases [*A publication*] (DLA)
N & P .... Nevile and Perry's English King's Bench Reports [*1836-38*] [*A publication*] (DLA)
N & P Mag... Nevile and Perry's English Magistrates' Cases [*1836-37*] [*A publication*] (DLA)
N & PMC ... Nevile and Perry's English Magistrates' Cases [*1836-37*] [*A publication*] (DLA)
N&PNWR ... Ninepipe and Pablo National Wildlife Refuge (SAUS)
N&Q .... Nostrums and Quackery [*Medicine*] [*Book*] (EDAA)
N&Q .... Notes and Queries [*A publication*] (ANEX)
N&R Indication... Normal and Reverse Indication (SAUS)
N&RS .... Nuclear and Radiological Sciences Program [*Idaho National Engineering and Environmental Laboratory*] (RCD)
N & S .... Nicholls and Stops' Reports [*1897-1904*] [*Tasmania*] [*A publication*] (DLA)
N&S .... North & South [*Publcation*] [*Civil War term*]
N & SDCP... Neurological and Sensory Disease Control Program
N & SE ...... Nacogdoches & Southeastern Railroad (IIA)
N & T .... Navigation and Timing
N&T .... Nicotine and Tobacco (MELL)
N & T .... Nose and Throat [*Medicine*]
n&v .... Nausea and Vomiting [*Therapy term*] (CTAA)
N & V .... Nausea and Vomiting
N & W .... Norfolk & Western Railway Co.
NANE .... National Association for Nursery Education [*Later, NAEYC*] (EA)
NANEAP ..... North Africa, Near East, Asia, and Pacific Region [*Program of ACTION, an independent government agency*]
NANEP ...... Navy Air Navigation Electronic Project
NANEWS .... Naval Aviation News
NANFA .... North American Native Fishes Association (EA)
NANFAC ..... Naval Air Navigation Facility Advisory Committee
NANFM ...... National Association of Non-Ferrous Scrap Metal Merchants (BUAC)
NANFORMS... Naval Aviator/Naval Flight Officer Reporting Management System (DNAB)
NANFPT ..... National Association of Natural Family Planning Teachers (BUAC)
NAng .... Angelica Free Library, Angelica, NY [*Library symbol*] [*Library of Congress*] (LCLS)
NANGL ...... Nanty Glo, PA [*American Association of Railroads railroad junction routing code*]
NANHC ...... National Association of Neighborhood Health Centers [*Later, NACHC*] (EA)
NANHPH .... National Association of Nursing Homes and Private Hospitals [*Australia*]
NANI .... National Academy of Nannies, Inc. (EA)
NANIME ..... Norfolk and Norwich Institute for Medical Education (SAUS)
NA/NLP ..... National Association of Neuro-Linguistic Programming (EA)
NANM .... N-Allylnormetazocine [*Biochemistry*]
NANM .... N-Allylnormorphine [*Narcotic antagonist*]

NANM .... National Association of Negro Musicians (EA)
NANMT...... National Association of Nurse Massage Therapists
NANMV...... Nandina Mosaic Virus [*Plant pathology*]
NANN........ National Association of Neonatal Nurses (EA)
NANN........ National Association of Nursery Nurses (BUAC)
NANNP ...... Nordic Association of Non-Commercial Phonogram Producers (EA)
nano-........ Billionth (IDOE)
NANO........ Nanometrics, Inc. [*NASDAQ symbol*] (NQ)
NANO........ Non-linear AND, Non-linear OR (SAUS)
nano......... One billionth [*From the Latin nanus*] (WDMC)
NANOG...... North American Network Operators Group (SAUS)
NanomtR.... Nanometrics, Inc. [*Associated Press*] (SAG)
NANOS...... North American Neuro-Ophthalmology Society [*Association*] (EA)
NANOSAT... Nanosatellite
nanova...... Non-Orthogonal Analysis of Variance (AD)
NANP........ National Alliance of Nurse Practitioners (EA)
NANP........ National Association of Naturopathic Physicians [*Defunct*] (EA)
NANP........ North American Numbering Plan [*A set of rules for the assignment of telephone area codes and the method by which calls are routed*] (DCDG)
NANPA...... North American Nature Photography Association
NANPCA.... Nonindigenous Aquatic Nuisance Prevention (LDOE)
NANPE...... National Association of Newspaper Purchasing Executives [*Later, NPMA*] (EA)
NANPMA.... North American Nutrition and Preventive Medicine Association (EA)
NANPRH.... National Association of Nurse Practitioners in Reproductive Health (EA)
NANPS...... North American Native Plant Society [*Canada*] (EAIO)
NANR........ National Association of Nurse Recruiters [*Later, NAHCR*] (EA)
NANS........ National Association for Neighborhood Schools (EA)
NANS........ National Association of Nigerian Students (BUAC)
NANS........ National Association of Non-Smokers (EA)
NANS........ National Catholic News Service (EA)
NANS........ Naval Air Navigation School
NANs........ Negative Axillary Node [*Medicine*] (MELL)
NANS........ Nevada Academy of Natural Sciences (SAUS)
NANS........ Night Attack Navigation System (ACAE)
NANS........ North American Nietzsche Society (EA)
NANS........ North Atlantic and Neighboring Seas
NANSI....... Nordic Automated Network of Shell Installation (SAUS)
NANSIM..... Nonlinear Active Network Simulation (SAUS)
NANT........ National Association of Nephrology Technologists (EA)
NANT........ National Associaton of Nephrology Technicians/Technologists (EA)
Nantck...... Nantucket Industries, Inc. [*Associated Press*] (SAG)
NANTDDDC... National Association of Negro Tailors, Designers, Dressmakers, and Dry Cleaners (EA)
NANTIS...... Nottignham and Nottinghamshire Technical Information Service [*British*] (AD)
NANTS...... National Association of Naval Technical Supervisors (EA)
NANU........ National Association of NIDS [*National Investor Data Service*] Users (EA)
NANU........ National Association of Non-Unionists (BUAC)
NANU........ Naviera Lavinel [*Intermodal shipping container symbol*] (TVRC)
NANU........ Notice Advisory to NAVSTAR (Navigation Satellite Tracking and Ranging) Users
NANU........ Notice Advisory to NAVSTAR User (SAUS)
NANVH&SWO... National Assembly of National Voluntary Health and Social Welfare Organizations (AD)
NANWEP.... Navy Numerical Weather Prediction [*Computer system*] [*Control Data Corp.*]
NANWEP.... Navy Numerical Weather Problems [*Group*]
NANWR..... North American Network of Women Runners (EA)
NANX........ Nanophase Technologies Corp. [*NASDAQ symbol*]
NAO.......... Charleston, SC [*Location identifier*] [*FAA*] (FAAL)
NAO.......... Her Majesty's Nautical Almanac Office [*British*] (PDAA)
NAO.......... National Academy of Opticianry (EA)
NAO.......... National Accordion Organisation of the United Kingdom (BUAC)
NAO.......... National Accordion Organization [*British*] (DBA)
NAO.......... National Adhering Organization
NAO.......... National Association of Outfitters (AD)
NAO.......... National Astronomical Observatory [*Japan*]
NAO.......... National Audit Office [*British*] (ECON)
NAO.......... Nautical Almanac Office (BUAC)
NAO.......... Naval Audit Office (DNAB)
NAO.......... Naval Aviation Observer [*Obsolete*]
NAO.......... NOAA [*National Oceanic and Atmospheric Administration*] Administrative Order (USDC)
NAO.......... Noise Abatement Office (AD)
NAO.......... Non-Asbestos Organic [*Friction materials*]
NAO.......... Normal Alpha Olefin [*Fuels and lubricants*]
NAO.......... Norsar Array Site 01A00 [*Norway*] [*Seismograph station code, US Geological Survey*] (SEIS)
NAO.......... North American Airlines, Inc. [*ICAO designator*] (FAAC)
NAO.......... North American Operations [*Automotive industry*]
NAO.......... North Atlantic Oscillation [*Climatology*]
NAO.......... Nurse Aide/Orderly (OICC)
NAOA........ National Apartment Owners Association [*Later, NAA*] (EA)
NAOA........ National Association of Older Americans [*Later, Heartline/National Association of Older Americans*] (EA)
NAOA........ Naval Aviation Observer Aerology (SAA)
NAOA........ Navy Officers Accounts Office (AD)
NAOAG...... North American Official Airline Guide (TRID)
NAOB........ Naval Aviation Observer Bombardier (MUGU)
NAOBMISB... National Association of Operative Boiler Makers and Iron Ship Builders [*A union*] [*British*]
NAOC........ National Antique Oldsmobile Club (EA)
NAOC........ National Association of Ordnance and Explosive Waste Contractors (EA)
NAOC........ Naval Aviation Observer Controller (MUGU)
NAOC........ Naval Aviation Officer Candidate
NAOC........ Nigerian Agip Oil Co. (AD)
NAOC........ North Absheron Operating Co.
NAOCJ....... National Association of Operative Carpenters and Joiners [*A union*] [*British*]
NAOCP...... Novice Amateur Operator's Certificate of Proficiency [*Radio*]
NAOE........ National Association for Outdoor Education [*British*]
NAOEJ....... National Association of Oil Equipment Jobbers [*Later, PEI*] (EA)
NAOFD...... National Association of Office Furniture Dealers (NTPA)
NAOGE...... National Association of Government Engineers [*Defunct*] (EA)
NAOGTC..... North American Opel GT [*Gran Turismo*] Club (EA)
NAOH........ National Alliance for Oral Health (NTPA)
NaOH........ Sodium Hydroxide
NAOHSM.... National Association of Oil Heating Service Managers (EA)
NAOI......... Naval Aviation Observer Intercept (MUGU)
NAOIG....... North African Inspector General's Section [*World War II*]
NAOJ........ National Astronomical Observatory of Japan
NAOL........ National Association of Orchestra Leaders (EA)
NAOMI...... National Association of Ovulation Method Instructors [*British*] (DBA)
NAON........ National Association of Orthopaedic Nurses (EA)
NAON........ Naval Aviation Observer Navigator (MUGU)
NAOO........ National Association of Optometrists and Opticians (EA)
NAOO........ National Oceanic and Atmospheric Administration (SAUS)
NAOODA.... North American Offshore One-Design Association (EA)
NAOP........ National Alliance for Optional Parenthood (DAVI)
NAOP........ National Association for Olmsted Parks (EA)
NAOP........ National Association of Operative Plasterers
NAOP........ National Association of Operative Plumbers [*A union*] [*British*]
NAOP........ Nonadditive Operational Project [*Military*]
NAOPL...... National Association of Operative Plasterers' Labourers [*A union*] [*British*]
NAOPS...... North Atlantic Ocean Prediction Systems (SAUS)
NAOR........ Naval Aviation Observer RADAR (MUGU)
NAORD...... North African Ordnance Section [*World War II*]
NAORPB.... North Atlantic Ocean Regional Planning Board [*NATO*]
NAORPG.... North Atlantic Ocean Regional Planning Group [*NATO*] (NATG)
NAORTS..... Naval Aviation Ordnance Test Station
NAOS........ NASA Aircrew Oxygen System
NAOS........ North American Atmospheric Observing System (SAUS)
NAOS........ North Atlantic Ocean Station [*WMO*]
NAOSH...... Naitonal Authority for Occupational Safety and Health [*Ireland*] (BUAC)
NAOSMM... National Association of Scientific Material Managers (EA)
NAOSOF.... National Association of Soap Opera Fans
NAOSW..... National Association of Oncology Social Workers (EA)
NAOT........ National Association of Organ Teachers [*Later, IAOT*]
NAOT........ National Association of Orthopaedic Technologists (EA)
NAOT........ Naval Air Operational Training
NAOT........ Naval Aviation Observer Tactical (SAA)
NAOTB...... National Association of Off-Track Betting (EA)
NAOTC...... National Association of OTC [*Over-the-Counter*] Companies [*Later, APTC*] (EA)
NAOTC...... National Association of Timetable Collectors (EA)
NAOTC...... Naval Air Operational Training Command
NAOTD...... National Alliance of the Disabled (SAUS)
NAOTS...... Naval Aviation Ordnance Test Station
NAOWES.... National Association of Older Worker Employment Services [*Washington, DC*] (EA)
NAP.......... Armed Proletarian Nuclei [*Italy*]
NAP.......... Bangladesh National Awami Party [*Political party*] (PPW)
nap.......... Knapsack (AD)
NAP.......... Napa, CA [*Amtrak Busline code*]
nap.......... Napalm (AD)
NAP.......... Napa Resources, Inc. [*Vancouver Stock Exchange symbol*]
NAP.......... Napay [*Former USSR*] [*Seismograph station code, US Geological Survey*] [*Closed*] (SEIS)
nap.......... Naphtha (AD)
NAP.......... Napier Air Service, Inc. [*ICAO designator*] (FAAC)
Nap.......... Naples (AD)
NAP.......... Naples [*Italy*] [*Airport symbol*] (OAG)
Nap.......... Napoleon (AD)
NAP.......... Napoleon [*or Napoleonic*]
NAP.......... Napoleonic Age Philatelists (EA)
NAP.......... [*The*] Narragansett Pier Railroad Co., Inc. [*AAR code*]
NAP.......... Narrative, Assessment, and Plan [*Medicine*] (EDAA)
NAP.......... Nasion Pogonion [*Anatomy*] (MAE)
NAP.......... National Academies of Practice (NTPA)
NAP.......... National Action Party [*Sierra Leone*] [*Political party*] (EY)
NAP.......... National Action Party [*Turkey*] [*Political party*] (PD)
NAP.......... National Action Plan [*Salinity and water quality*]
NAP.......... National Advertising Program
NAP.......... National Aerospace Plane (AD)
NAP.......... National Afforestation Program (BUAC)
NAP.......... National Agency for Privatisation [*Romania*] (BUAC)
NAP.......... National Alliance Party [*Sierra Leone*] [*Political party*] (BUAC)
NAP.......... National Apprenticeship Program [*Bureau of Apprenticeship and Training*] [*Department of Labor*]
NAP.......... National Archives Publication
NAP.......... National Association for the Paralysed (AD)
NAP.......... National Association of Parents (EA)
NAP.......... National Association of Parliamentarians (EA)

NAP National Association of Planners [*Defunct*] (EA)
NAP National Association of Postmasters (NADA)
NAP National Association of Postmasters of the United States
NAP National Association of Publishers [*Defunct*] (EA)
NAP National Association of the Professions (EA)
NAP National Audit Plan
NAP National Awami Party [*Pakistan*] [*Political party*] (PD)
NAP National Awami Party-Bashani [*Bangladesh*] [*Political party*] (FEA)
NAP National Awareness Partner (TELE)
NAP National Processing, Inc. [*NYSE symbol*] (SAG)
NAP Native American Program (OICC)
NAP Native Americans in Philanthropy
NAP Naval Academy Preparatory Student (DNAB)
NAP Naval Air Plan (CAAL)
NAP Naval Airplane Pusher [*Slang*] (DNAB)
NAP Naval Air Priorities
NAP Naval Auxiliary Patrol [*British military*] (DMA)
nap Naval Aviation Pilot (AD)
NAP Naval Aviation Pilot
NAP Naval Aviation Plan (NVT)
NAP Navigation Analysis Program [*NASA*] (NASA)
NAP Neighborhood Action Program [*New York City*] (EA)
NAP Neighborhood Awareness Program (AD)
NAP Nerve Action Potential [*Medicine*] (MELL)
NAP Network Access Point [*Telecommunications*]
NAP Network Access Pricing [*Telecommunications*] (TEL)
NAP Network Access Program [*Computer science*] (CIST)
NAP Network Access Protocol
NAP Network Applications Platform [*Computer science*] (CIST)
NAP Neutrophil Activating Protein
NAP Neutrophil Alkaline Phosphatase [*An enzyme*]
NAP New Age Patriot [*An association*] (EA)
NAP New Aspiration Party [*Thailand*]
NAP New Associations and Projects [*Formerly, NA*] [*A publication*]
NAP Niger Agricultural Project [*Nigeria*] (BUAC)
NAP Night Attack Program [*Military*]
NAP Nitroaminophenol [*Organic chemistry*]
NAP Noise Abatement Procedure (AAG)
NAP Nomina Anatomica Parisiensia [*Medicine*]
NA-P Nonabrasive-Polishing (SAUS)
NAP Nonacquisition Project [*Military*] (CAAL)
NAP Nonadvertising Promotion [*Public relations*] (WDMC)
nap Non-Agency Purchase (AD)
NAP Nonagency Purchase
NAP Nonaggression Pact
NAP Non-Arboreal Pollen [*Palynology*] (QUAC)
NAP Nonarborescent Pollen (SAUS)
NAP Nonnuclear Armament Plan (MCD)
NAP Normal Administrative Practice
NAP Normalized Abundance Pattern [*Geochemistry*]
NAP North American Philips Corp. (IAA)
NAP North Atlantic Pact (SAUS)
NAP North Australia Program
NAP Northern Agricultural Producers (BUAC)
NAP Not Applicable (SAUS)
NAP Not a Priori
nap Not at Present (AD)
NAP Not at Present
NAP Not Authorized POMCUS (SAUS)
NAP Nuclear Action Project (EA)
NAP Nuclear-Active Particles [*Astrophysics*]
NAP Nuclear Auxiliary Power
NAP Nuclei Armati Proletari [*Armed Proletarian Nuclei*] [*Italian*] (PD)
NAP Nucleic Acid Phosphate (or Phosphorus) (SAUS)
NAP Nucleic Acid Phosphorus [*Biochemistry*]
NAP Nucleoacidic Protein [*Cytochemistry*]
NAP Null Amsterdam Pegel (SAUS)
NAPA N-Acetyl-p-aminophenol [*Organic chemistry*]
NAPA N-Acetylprocainamide [*Cardiac depressant*]
NAPA National Academy of Public Administration (EA)
NAPA National Agricultural Plastics Association [*Later, ASP*] (EA)
NAPA National Agricultural Press Association (EA)
NAPA National Alcohol Producers' (BUAC)
NAPA National Alliance of Postal & Federal Employees National Alliance for Political Action [*Washington, DC*] (PACS)
NAPA National Amateur Press Association (EA)
NAPA National Asphalt Pavement Association (EA)
NAPA National Association for Photographic Art [*Canada*] (EAIO)
NAPA National Association for the Practice of Anthropology (EA)
NAPA National Association of Park Administrators [*British*] (BI)
NAPA National Association of Performing Artists
NAPA National Association of Polish Americans
NAPA National Association of Press Agencies (BUAC)
NAPA National Association of Pro America (EA)
NAPA National Association of Purchasing Agents [*Later, NAPM*] (EA)
NAPA National Association of the Partners of the Alliance [*Later, Partners of the Americas*] (EA)
NAPA National Automotive Parts Association (EA)
NAPA National Police Officers Association of America
NAPA Native American Press Association (EA)
NAPA Naval Association of Physician Assistants (EARSL)
NAPA Network Against Psychiatric Assault (EA)
NAPA Network Automated Problem Application [*Computer science*] (HODG)
NAPA North American Photonics Association [*Defunct*] (EA)
NAPA North American Pizza Association [*Defunct*]
NAPA North Atlantic Ports Association (EA)
NAPAA National Association for Promotional and Advertising Allowances, Inc. (NTPA)
NAPA/AIM Network Automated Problem Applications/Automatic Inventory Manager [*Computer science*] (HODG)
NAPAAW National Association of Professional Asian-American Women (EA)
NAPABA National Asian Pacific American Bar Association (EA)
NAPAC National Arson Prevention and Action Coalition (EA)
NAPAC National Association for Professional Associations and Corporations (EA)
NAPAC National Association of Paper and Advertising Collectors (EA)
NAPAC National Program for Acquisitions and Cataloging [*Library of Congress*]
NAPAEO National Association of Principal Agricultural Education Officers [*British*]
NAPAF National Association of Private Art Foundations [*Defunct*] (EA)
NAPAFASA National Asian Pacific American Families Against Substance Abuse [*Association*] (EA)
NAPAG National Academies Policy Advisory Group
NAPALC National Asian Pacific American Legal Consortium [*Association*] (EA)
NAPall North American Palladium [*Associated Press*] (SAG)
napalm Naphthene Palmitate (AD)
NAPALM Naphthenic and Palmitic Acids [*Major constituents of flame thrower*]
NAPALM National ADP [*Automatic Data Processing*] Program for AMC Logistics Management [*Army Materiel Command*]
NAPALM National Automatic Data Processing Program for Army Material Command Logistics Management (IAA)
NAPALSA National Asian Pacific American Law Student Association (EA)
NAPAMA National Association of Performing Arts Managers and Agents (EA)
NAPAMS Navy Automated Pilot Aptitude Measurement System
NAPAN National Association for the Prevention of Addiction to Narcotics [*Later, NADAP*]
NAPAP National Acidic Precipitation Assessment Program (BUAC)
NAPAP National Acid Precipitation Assessment Program [*Council on Environmental Quality*] [*Washington, DC*]
NAPAP National Atmospheric and Precipitation Assessment Program
NAPAP Noyaux Armes pour l'Autonomie Populaire [*Armed Cells for Popular Autonomy*] [*France*] (PD)
NAPARE National Association for Perinatal Addiction Research and Education (EA)
NAPAS National Association of Protection and Advocacy Systems (EA)
NAPATMO NATO Patriot Management Office
NAPAVHEE National Association of Postsecondary and Adult Vocational Home Economics Educators (EA)
NAPAW North American Process Algebra Workshop (SAUS)
NAPB National Agricultural Products Boards [*Tanzania*] (BUAC)
NAPB National Association for the Preservation of Baseball (EA)
NAPB National Association of Professional Bureaucrats [*Later, INATAP-ROBU*]
NAPBC National Action Plan on Breast Cancer
NAPBC Native American Public Broadcasting Consortium (EA)
NAPBFC National Association of Pat Boone Fan Clubs (EA)
NAPBIRT National Association of Professional Band Instrument Repair Technicians (EA)
NAPBL National Association of Professional Baseball Leagues (EA)
NAPBN National Air Pollution Background Network [*Environmental Protection Agency*] (GFGA)
NAPBTA National American Pit Bull Terrier Association (EA)
NAPBX ING International Small-Cap Growth
NAPC National Air Pollution Control (KSC)
NAPC National Alliance of Preservation Commissions (EA)
NAPC National Assault Prevention Center (EA)
NAPC National Association of Parish Councils [*British*] (BI)
NAPC National Association of Pastoral Counselors [*Defunct*] (EA)
NAPC National Association of Personnel Consultants [*Defunct*] (EA)
NAPC National Association of Pet Cemeteries [*Later, IAPC*]
NAPC National Association of Plumbing Contractors [*Later, NAPHCC*]
NAPC National Association of Precancel Collectors (EA)
NAPC Naval Air Photographic Center (DNAB)
NAPC Naval Air Priorities Center (DNAB)
NAPC Naval Air Project Coordinator (ACAE)
NAPC Naval Air Projects Co-ordination office (SAUS)
NAPC Naval Air Propulsion Center [*Trenton, NJ*]
NAPC Non-Adherent Peritoneal Cell (PDAA)
napc Non-Adherent Peritoneal Cells (AD)
NAPC North American Paleontological Convention
NAPC North American Paleontology Convention (SAUS)
NAPC North American Philips Corp. (SAUS)
NAPCA National Air Pollution Control Administration (AAGC)
NAPCA National Asian Pacific Center on Aging (EA)
NAPCA National Association of Pension Consultants and Administrators [*Atlanta, GA*] (EA)
NAPCA National Association of Pipe Coating Applicators (EA)
NAPCA National Association of Professional Contracts Administrators (AAGC)
NAPCA National Automatic Pistol Collectors Association (EA)
NAPCA North American Poultry Cooperative Association [*Defunct*] (EA)
NAPCAE National Association for Public Continuing and Adult Education (EA)
NAPCC National Association for Poison Control Centers [*Medicine*] (EDAA)
NAPCE National Association of Pastoral Care in Education [*British*] (DBA)
NAPCE National Association of Professors of Christian Education (EA)
NAPCIS National Association of Private Catholic and Independent Schools (EA)
NAPCMM-ELCA Native American Program Commission for Multicultural Ministries of ELCA [*Evangelical Lutheran Church in America*] (EA)

NAPC/MS ... Naval Air Propulsion Center Measurement and Information Systems Department [*Trenton, NJ*]
Napco .... Napco Security Systems, Inc. [*Associated Press*] (SAG)
NAPCO .... North American Publishing Co. (IID)
NAPCOR .... National Association for Plastic Container Recovery (EA)
NAPC-PE ... Naval Air Propulsion Center Propulsion Engineering Department [*Trenton, NJ*]
NAPCR ...... National Association for Puerto Rican Civil Rights
NAPCRG .... North American Primary Care Research Group (EA)
NAPCRO .... National Association of Police Community Relations Officers (EA)
NAPCS ...... National Association of Postpartum Care Services (PAZ)
NAPCTAC ... National Air Pollution Control Techniques Advisory Committee [*Environmental Protection Agency*] (GFGA)
NAPCU ...... Northwest Association of Private Colleges and Universities [*Library network*] (EA)
NAPCWA .... National Association of Public Child Welfare Administrators (EA)
NAPD .... National Association of Pharmaceutical Distributors [*British*] (BI)
NAPD .... National Association of Plastics Distributors (EA)
NAPD .... National Association of Police Driving (AD)
NAPD .... National Association of Precollege Directors (EA)
NAPD .... North American Pollen Database (QUAC)
NAPDA ...... North American Professional Driver's Association [*Defunct*] (EA)
NAPDD ...... Non-Acquisition Program Definition Document [*Navy*] (DOMA)
NAPDEA ..... North American Professional Driver Education Association (EA)
NAPDP ...... National Association of Prepaid Dental Plans (DMAA)
NAPE .... Naphthenic-Palmitic Acid [*Mixture used in flame-throwing weapons and bombs*] [*Also, NAPALM*] (VNW)
NAPE .... National Alliance of Postal Employees [*Later, NAPFE*]
NAPE .... National Association for Pseudoxanthoma Elasticum (NRGU)
NAPE .... National Association of Partners in Education
NAPE .... National Association of Physicians for the Environment (EA)
NAPE .... National Association of Port Employers [*British*]
NAPE .... National Association of Power Engineers (EA)
NAPE .... National Association of Primary Education [*British*] (DBA)
NAPE .... National Association of Private Enterprise [*Fort Worth, TX*] (EA)
NAPE .... National Association of Probation Executives (EA)
NAPE .... National Association of Professional Educators (EA)
NAPE .... National Association of Professional Engravers (EA)
NAPE .... National Properties Corp. [*NASDAQ symbol*] (COMM)
NAPE .... Nuclear Attack Preparedness Evaluation
NAPEC .... National Association of Professional Environmental Communicators (NTPA)
NAPEC .... Naval Ammunition Production Engineering Center
NAPECW .... National Association for Physical Education of College Women [*Later, NAPEHE*] (EA)
NAPEDNC ... National Association of Political Ex-Deportees of the Nazi Camps [*Italy*] [*Political party*] (EAIO)
NAPEGG ..... Association of Professional Engineers, Geologists & Geophysicists of the Northwest Territories (AC)
NAPEHE ..... National Association for Physical Education in Higher Education (EA)
NAPEM ...... National Association of Public Exposition Managers [*Later, HGSEI*] (EA)
NAPENA ..... National Association of Public Employer Negotiators and Administrators [*Later, NAPPENA*] (EA)
Na Pent ..... Sodium Pentothal [*Thiopental Sodium*] [*A brand name*] [*Pharmacology*] (DAVI)
NAPEO ...... National Association of Professional Employer Organizations (NTPA)
NAPEP .... National Association of Planners, Estimators, and Progressmen (EA)
NAPET .... National Association of Photo Equipment Technicians (EA)
NAPEX .... National Philatelic Exhibition
NAPF .... National Association of Pension Funds [*British*] (DI)
NAPF .... National Association of Petroleum Funds [*British*]
NAPF .... National Association of Pipe Fabricators (EA)
NAPF .... National Association of Plastic Fabricators (EA)
NAPF .... Naval Aviation Publication Facility
NAPF .... Nonappropriated Funds (DNAB)
NAPF .... North Atlantic Polar Front (SAUS)
NAPF .... Nuclear Age Peace Foundation (EA)
NAPFA .... National Association of Personal Financial Advisors (EA)
NAPFE .... National Alliance of Postal and Federal Employees (EA)
NAPFM ...... National Association of Packaged Fuel Manufacturers [*Defunct*] (EA)
NAPFR ...... National Association of Professional Fund Raisers (EA)
NAPFSC ..... National Association of Professional Forestry Schools and Colleges (WPI)
NAPG .... National Association of Professional Gardeners [*Later, PGMS*]
NAP(G) ...... Naval Aviation Pilot (Glider)
NAPG .... News America Publishing Group
NaPG .... Sodium Pregnanediol Glucuronide [*Medicine*] (DMAA)
NAPGC ...... National Association of Public Golf Courses [*British*] (BI)
NAPGCM .... National Association of Private Geriatric Care Managers (EA)
NAPGCW .... National Association of Plasters, Granolithic, and Cement Workers [*A union*] [*British*]
naph .... Naphtha (AD)
NAPH .... Naphtha (ADA)
naph .... Naphthyl (AD)
NAPH .... Naphthyl [*Organic chemistry*] (MAE)
NAPH .... National Association of Professors of Hebrew (EA)
NAPH .... National Association of Public Hospitals (EA)
NAPH .... National Association of the Physically Handicapped (EA)
NAPH .... Nicotinamide Adenine Dinucleotide Phosphate [*An enzyme*] (DMAA)
NAPHA .... National Amusement Park Historical Association (EA)
NAPhA .... North American Photonics Association (EA)
NAPH & MSC ... National Association of Plumbing, Heating, and Mechanical Service Contractors [*British*] (DBA)
NAPHC ...... National Association of Plumbing/Heating/Cooling Contractors (AD)
NAPHCC ..... National Association of Plumbing-Heating-Cooling Contractors [*Formerly, NAPC*] (EA)
NAPHS ...... National Association of Psychiatric Health Systems (NTPA)
NAPHSIS ... National Association for Public Health Statistics and Information Systems (SAUS)
NAPHS/PAC ... National Association of Psychiatric Health Systems PAC [*Washington, DC*] (PACS)
NAPHT ...... National Association of Patients on Hemodialysis and Transplantation [*Later, AAKP*] (EA)
NAPI .... National Appaloosa Pony (EA)
NAPI .... National Association of Property Inspectors (NTPA)
NAPI .... National Association of the Pet Industry [*Defunct*] (EA)
NAPI .... Naval Aeronautical Publications Index (DNAB)
NAPI .... Neurobehavioral Assessment of the Preterm Infant [*Test*] (TMMY)
NAPI .... Numbering and Addressing Plan Identifier (SAUS)
NAPIA .... National Affiliate of Printing Industries of America (AD)
NAPIA .... National Association of Public Insurance Adjusters [*Baltimore, MD*] (EA)
NAPIAP ...... National Agricultural Pesticide Impact Assessment Program [*Department of Agriculture*]
NAPIC .... National Association of Private Industry Councils [*Washington, DC*] (EA)
NAPIL .... National Association for Public Interest Law (EA)
NAPIM .... National Association of Printing Ink Manufacturers (EA)
NAPIS .... National Agricultural Pest Information System (AUEG)
NAPJPO .... National Aerospace Plane Joint Programs Office
NAPL .... National Air Photo Library [*Canada*] (PDAA)
NAPL .... National Association of Photolithographers (IAA)
NAPL .... National Association of Police Laboratories (EA)
NAPL .... National Association of Printers and Lithographers (EA)
NAPL .... Nonaqueous Phase Liquid [*Chemistry*]
NAPLIB ...... National Association Aerial of Photographic Libraries [*British*] (DBA)
NAPLO ...... National Association of Power Loom Overlookers [*British*] (DBA)
NAPLP .... National Association of Para-Legal Personnel (AD)
NAP-LP ..... National Association of Para-Legals Personnel (EA)
NAPLPS ..... North American Presentation Layer Protocol Suite (SAUS)
NAPLPS ..... North American Presentation Level Protocol Standard (DOM)
NAPLPS ..... North American Presentation Level Protocol Syntax [*Computer display system*] [*Pronounced "naplips"*]
NAPLS .... North American Presentation Level Protocol Syntax (ELAL)
NAPM .... National Association of Paper Merchants [*British*]
NAPM .... National Association of Pastoral Musicians (BUAC)
NAPM .... National Association of Pattern Manufacturers [*LA PPTBA*] (EA)
NAPM .... National Association of Perry Makers [*British*] (DBA)
NAPM .... National Association of Pharmaceutical Manufacturers (EA)
NAPM .... National Association of Photographic Manufacturers (EA)
NAPM .... National Association of Punch Manufacturers (EA)
NAPM .... National Association of Purchasing Management (EA)
NAP-M ...... National Awami Party-Muzaffar [*Bangladesh*] [*Political party*] (FEA)
NAPMA ...... NATO AEWC [*Airborne Early Warning and Control*] Program Management Agency
NAPMA ...... North American Punch Manufacturers Association (NTPA)
NAPMDAC ... National Air Pollution Manpower Development Advisory Committee [*Terminate d, 1976*] [*HEW*] (EGAO)
NAPMECA ... National Association of Postgraduate Medical Education Centre Administrators (BUAC)
NAPMG ...... North African Provost Marshal General [*World War II*]
NAPM-JN ... National Association of Purchasing Management, New Jersey Chapter (EARSL)
NAPMM ..... National Association of Produce Market Managers [*Hartford, CT*] (EA)
NAPM-O ..... Institute for Supply Management-Oregon (EARSL)
NAPMO ...... NATO Airborne Early Warning and Control Programme Management Organization [*Brunssum, Netherlands*]
NAPMR ...... National Apostolate with People with Mental Retardation (EA)
NAPMT ...... National Association of Pregnancy Massage Therapy (EA)
NAPMW ..... National Association of Professional Mortgage Women
NAPN .... National Association of Physician Nurses (EA)
NAPN .... Native American Policy Network (EA)
NAPN .... Native Authority Public Notice [*Nigeria*] [*A publication*] (ILCA)
NAPN .... North American Poetry Network (EA)
NAPNAP ..... National Association of Pediatric Nurse Associates and Practitioners (EA)
NAPNE ...... National Association for Practical Nurse Education (DAVI)
NAPNES ..... National Association for Practical Nurse Education and Service (EA)
NAPNM ...... National Association of Pipe Nipple Manufacturers [*Defunct*] (EA)
NAPNOC .... Neighborhood Arts Program National Organizing Committee (EA)
NAPNSC ..... National Association of Private, Nontraditional Schools and Colleges (EA)
NAPNW ..... Nurses Alliance for the Prevention of Nuclear War [*Defunct*] (EA)
NAPO .... NASA Pasadena Office
NAPO .... National Association of Performing Artists (AD)
NAPO .... National Association of Pizza Operators [*Commercial firm*] (EA)
NAPO .... National Association of Police Organizations (EA)
NAPO .... National Association of Pool Owners
NAPO .... National Association of Prison Officers [*British*] (DI)
NAPO .... National Association of Probation Officers [*British*] (DI)
NAPO .... National Association of Professional Organizers (EA)
NAPO .... National Association of Property Owners (EA)
NAPO .... National Association of Purchasing Agents (AD)
NAPO .... NATO Airborne Early Warning Program Office (NATG)
NAPO .... Naval Air Priorities Office
NAPO .... New Afrikan People's Organization (EA)
NAPO .... United National Association of Post Office Craftsmen [*Later, APWU*]

NAPOCU .... National Association of Parliamentarians, Oil Capital Unit [*Oklahoma*] (EARSL)
NAPOG ...... Naval Airborne Project Press Operations Group [*Hickam AFB, HI*]
NAPOL ...... Napoleon, OH [*American Association of Railroads railroad junction routing code*]
NAPOL ...... North Atlantic Policy Working Group (SAUS)
NAPOLI...... National Politics [*Behavioral science game*]
NAPOMHWMGL... National Association of Post Office Mail Handlers, Watchmen, Messengers, and Group Leaders [*Later, NPOMHWMGL*] (EA)
NAPOTS..... National Aboriginal Project Officer Training Scheme [*Australia*]
NAPP .... National Association for the Protection of Punters (BUAC)
NAPP .... National Association of Paralegal Personnel (NTPA)
NAPP .... National Association of Patient Participation [*British*] (DBA)
NAPP .... National Association of Play Publishers
NAPP .... National Association of Poultry Packers Ltd. [*British*] (BI)
NAPP .... National Association of Priest Pilots (EA)
NAPP .... National Association of Printing Purchasers [*Defunct*] (EA)
NAPP .... National Association of Private Process Servers (EA)
NAPP .... Native American Publishing Program [*of Harper & Row, Publishers, Inc.*]
NAPP .... Naval Aviation Preparatory Program
NAPP .... Neighborhood Adult Participation Project
NAPP .... Net Aerial Primary Productivity [*Forestry*]
NAPP .... Non-Agricultural Pesticides Panel (HEAS)
NAPP .... Nonattainment Plan Provision [*Environmental Protection Agency*]
NAPPA....... National Association of Physical Plant Administrators of Universities and Colleges [*Later, Association of Physical Plant Administrators of Universities and Colleges*] (EA)
NAPPA....... National Association of Prevention Professionals and Advocates (NTPA)
NAPPA....... National Association of Pupil Personnel Administrators [*Later, NAPSA*] (EA)
NAPPA....... North American Potbellied Pig Association (EA)
NAPPB ...... National Association of Professional Print Buyers (EA)
NAPPC ...... National Association of Party Plan Companies [*Defunct*] (EA)
NAPPC ...... North American Plant Preservation Council (NTPA)
NAPPENA... National Association of Public and Private Employer Negotiators and Administrators (EA)
NAPPF....... North American Power Petroleums, Inc. (SAUS)
NAPPH ...... National Association of Private Psychiatric Hospitals (EA)
NAPPHJ..... National Association of Private Psychiatric Hospitals Journal [*Medicine*] (EDAA)
NAPPHN .... National Association of Private Psychiatric Hospitals Newsletter [*Medicine*] (EDAA)
Nappie ...... Neuilly, Auteil, and Passy [*Elegant Paris neighborhoods; the term, Nappie, is used as a nickname for French Yuppies*]
Nappies..... New Age Professional People in Esoteric Studies [*Lifestyle classification*]
NAPPO ...... National Association of Plant Patent Owners (EA)
NAPPO ...... North American Plant Protection Organization [*Canada*] (BUAC)
Nap Pres.... Napier. Prescription [*A publication*] (ILCA)
NAPPS ...... National Association for the Preservation and Perpetuation of Storytelling (EA)
NAPPS ...... National Association of Private Placement Syndicators [*Later, California Investment Real Estate Forum*] (EA)
NAPPS ...... National Association of Private Process Servers (NTPA)
NAPPS ...... National Association of Professional Pet Sitters (NTPA)
NAPPS ...... National Association of Professional Process Servers (EA)
NAPPS ...... North American Pediatric Pseudo-Obstruction Society (EA)
na pr .... Na Priklad [*For Example*] [*Czech*] (AD)
NAPR........ NASA Procurement Regulation
NAPR........ National Association for Pastoral Renewal [*Defunct*] (EA)
NAPR........ National Association of Park Rangers (EA)
NAPR........ National Association of Physician Recruiters (EA)
NAPR........ National Association of Pram Retailers (BUAC)
NAPR........ National Association of Publishers' Representatives (EA)
NAPR........ NATO Armaments Planning Review (NATG)
NAPRA ...... National Association of Progressive Radio Announcers (EA)
NAPRA ...... New Age Publishing and Retailing Alliance (EA)
NAPRA Int'l... New Age Publishing and Retailing Alliance International (NTPA)
NAPRALERT... Natural Products Alert [*University of Illinois at Chicago*] [*Information service or system*] (IID)
NAPRC ...... National Association for the Prevention of Rape by Castration (AD)
NAPRCR .... National Association for Puerto Rican Civil Rights (EA)
NAPRE ...... National Association Practical Refrigerating Engineers [*Later, RETA*] (EA)
NAPRECA... Natural Products Research Network for Eastern and Central Africa [*UNESCO*] [*Ethiopia*] (BUAC)
NAPRFMR... National Association of Private Residential Facilities for the Mentally Retarded (EA)
NAPRI .... National Animal Production Research Institute [*Nigeria*] (BUAC)
NAPRI .... North American Pollutant Release Inventory (SAUS)
NaPro .... NaPro BioTherapeutics, Inc. [*Associated Press*] (SAG)
NaProBio ... NaPro BioTherapeutics, Inc. [*Associated Press*] (SAG)
NAPRS ...... National Airspace Performance Reporting System [*Aviation*] (FAAC)
NAPRW ..... Northwest African Photographic Reconnaissance Wing [*World War II*]
NAPS .... National Air Pollution Surveillance (EPAT)
NAPS .... National Alliance of Postal Supervisors (AD)
NAPS .... National Association for Premenstrual Syndrome (BUAC)
NAPS .... National Association for Professional Saleswomen (EA)
NAPS .... National Association of Personal Secretaries (BUAC)
NAPS .... National Association of Personnel Services (NTPA)
NAPS .... National Association of Pet Sitters (EA)
NAPS .... National Association of Postal Supervisors (EA)
NAPS .... National Association of Premenstrual Syndrome [*British*] (DBA)
NAPS .... National Association of Presbyterian Scouters (EA)
NAPS .... National Association of Private Secretaries [*British*] (BI)
NAPS .... National Association of Psychiatric Survivors (EA)
NAPS .... National Auricula and Primula Society (BUAC)
NAPS .... National Auxiliary Publications Service [*American Society for Information Science*]
NAPS .... Nationwide Association of Preserving Specialists [*British*] (DBA)
NAPS .... Naval Academy Preparatory School
NAPS .... Navy Acquisition Procedures Supplement [*A publication*] (AAGC)
NAPS .... Navy Automated Publications System (ACAE)
NAPS .... Nerve Agent Pre-Treatment Set [*A cholinergic drug*] [*Used for protective immunization by the military*]
NAPS .... Nerve Agent Pre-treatment Tablets (SAUS)
NAPS .... New Abstracts and Papers in Sleep (SAUS)
NAPS .... Night Aerial Photographic System
NAPS .... Nimbus Automatic Programming System (IEEE)
NAPS .... Nissan Air Pollution System (AD)
NAPS .... Nonspecific Air Pollution Syndrome
NAPS .... North American Patristic Society (EA)
NAPS .... North American Precis Syndicate
NAPS .... North American Pro Series [*Auto racing*]
NAPS .... North Anna Power Station [*Virginia*] [*Nuclear energy*] (NRCH)
NAPSA ...... National Appliance Parts Suppliers Association (EA)
NAPSA ...... National Association of Pretrial Service Agencies (AD)
NAPSA ...... National Association of Public Service Advertisers [*British*] (DBA)
NAPSA ...... National Association of Pupil Services Administrators (EA)
NAPSA ...... North American Pediatric Subspecialty Association (SAUS)
NAPSAA..... National Association of Public School Adult Administrators [*Later, NAPSAE*]
NAPSAC..... International Association of Parents and Professionals for Safe Alternatives in Childbirth [*Association retains acronym of its former name*] (EA)
NAPSAC..... National Association for the Protection from Sexual Abuse of Adults and Children with Learning Disabilities (BUAC)
NAPSAC..... Naval Atomic Planning, Support, and Capabilities Report (NG)
NAPSAE..... National Association for Public School Adult Educators [*Later, NAPCAE*] (EA)
NAPSAP..... Naval Airship Program for Sizing and Performance (MCD)
Nap's bones... Napier's Bones [*First slide rule*] (AD)
NAPSEC..... National Association of Private Schools for Exceptional Children (EA)
NAPSEO..... National Association of Public Sector Equal Opportunity Officers
NAPSG ...... National Association of Principals of Schools for Girls (EA)
NAPSIC...... North American Power Systems Interconnection Committee [*US and Canada*] [*Electric power*]
NAPSIS...... Navy Air Pollution Source Information System
NAPSLO..... National Association of Professional Surplus Lines Offices (EA)
NAPSOE..... National Association of Public Service Organization Executives (EA)
NAPSS ...... National Association of Professional Secretarial Services [*Later, PASS*] (EA)
NAPSS ...... Numerical Analysis Problem Solving System
NAPSV ...... National Association of Private Security Vaults (EA)
Napt .... Napton's Reports [*4 Missouri*] [*A publication*] (DLA)
NAPT .... National Association for Poetry Therapy (EA)
NAPT .... National Association for Proton Therapy (NTPA)
NAPT .... National Association for Pupil Transportation (EA)
NAPT .... National Association for the Prevention of Tuberculosis [*British*] (DI)
NAPT .... National Association of Percussion Teachers (BUAC)
NAPT .... National Association of Physical Therapists (EA)
NAPT .... Native American Public Telecommunications, Inc. (SAUS)
NAPT .... Naval Air Primary Training
NAPT .... Nordic Association of Plumbers and Tinsmiths (EAIO)
NAPTC....... Naval Air Primary Training Command
NAPTC....... Naval Air Propulsion Test Center [*Later, NAPC*]
NAPTCA..... National Alliance for the Prevention and Treatment of Child Abuse (EA)
NAPTC-AED... Naval Air Propulsion Test Center - Aeronautical Engine Department
NAPTC-ATD... Naval Air Propulsion Test Center - Aeronautical Turbine Department
NAPTCC ..... National Association of Psychiatric Treatment Centers for Children (EA)
NAPTC-OP... Naval Air Propulsion Test Center - Operations and Plant Engineering Department
NAPTC-PE... Naval Air Propulsion Test Center - Propulsion Technology and Project EngineeringDepartment
NAPTCRO... Naval Air Primary Training Command Regional Office
NAPTDC..... National Association of Professional Truck Driving Champions (EA)
NAPTE....... National Association of Part-Time and Temporary Employees
NaPTEC ..... National Primary Teacher Education Conference (AIE)
NAPTIC...... National Air Pollution Technical Information Center [*of National Air Pollution Control Administration*] [*Also, APTIC*] (DIT)
Napton ...... Napton's Reports [*4 Missouri*] [*A publication*] (DLA)
NAPTR ...... National Association of Property Tax Representatives [*Defunct*] (EA)
NAPTS....... National Association of Public Television Stations [*Later, APB*] (EA)
NAPTW...... National Association of Pet Trade Wholesalers (BUAC)
NAPU........ National Association of Professional Upholsterers [*Defunct*] (EA)
NAPU........ Naviera Pacifico [*Intermodal shipping container symbol*] (TVRC)
NAPU........ Nuclear Auxiliary Power Unit
NAPUBFAC... Naval Air Publication Facility (MCD)
NAPUS ...... National Association of Postmasters of the United States (EA)
NAPUS ...... Nuclear Auxiliary Power Unit System
NAPV........ National Association of Prison Visitors [*British*] (BI)
NAPVD ...... National Association for the Prevention of Venereal Disease (AD)

NAPVI .... National Association for Parents of the Visually Impaired (EA)
NAPVO ...... National Association of Passenger Vessel Owners (EA)
NAPW .... National Association of Personnel Workers (EA)
NAPWA ...... National Association of People with AIDS (EA)
NAPWDA .... North American Police Work Dog Association (EA)
NAPWPT .... National Association of Professional Word Processing Technicians [*Philadelphia, PA*] (EA)
NAPX .... North American Plastics [*Private rail car owner code*]
NAQ .... Narssarssuaq [*Denmark*] [*Geomagnetic observatory code*]
NAQ .... Never Answered Questions (SAUS)
NAQ .... North American Quotations (IID)
NAQ .... Nursing Administration Quarterly (SAUS)
NAQAP ...... National Association of Quality Assurance Professionals (EA)
NAQDC ...... National Air Quality Data Center [*Australia*]
NAQI .... National Air Quality Index (AD)
NAQMC ...... North African Quartermaster Section [*World War II*]
NAQP .... National Association of Quick Printers (EA)
NAQUADAT ... National Water Quality Data Bank [*Environment Canada*] [*Information service or system*] (IID)
NAR .... Air Continental, Inc. [*ICAO designator*] (FAAC)
NAR .... Nagase Analbuminemia Rat
NAR .... Nara [*Japan*] [*Seismograph station code, US Geological Survey*] (SEIS)
NAR .... Narcotic (ROG)
NAR .... Nare [*Colombia*] [*Airport symbol*] (OAG)
Nar .... Narragansett (AD)
NAR .... Narration [*Films, television, etc.*]
nar .... Narrator (GROV)
NAR .... Narrow (AAG)
nar .... Narrow (AD)
NAR .... Nasal Airway Resistance [*Medicine*]
NAR .... National Alliance for Reconstruction (Trinidad and Tobago) [*Political party*] (PSAP)
NAR .... National Amniocentesis Registry [*Medicine*] (EDAA)
NAR .... National Archives and Records Service, Washington, DC [*OCLC symbol*] (OCLC)
NAR .... National Asbestos Registry [*Environmental Protection Agency*] (GFGA)
NAR .... National Association for the Retarded (DMAA)
NAR .... National Association of Realtors (EA)
NAR .... National Association of Rocketry (EA)
NAR .... Naval Air Reserve
NAR .... Naval Auxiliary Reserve
NAR .... Naval Research and Development
NAR .... Navy Ammunition Reclassification
NAR .... Nelson Aldrich Rockefeller (AD)
NAR .... Neo Aristero Revma [*Greece*] [*Political party*] (ECED)
NAR .... Net Advertising Revenue [*Television*] [*British*]
nar .... Net Assimilation Rate (AD)
NAR .... Net Assimilation Rate [*Botany*]
NAR .... New American Review (SAUS)
NAR .... New Arrival Information [*Travel industry*] (TRID)
NAR .... No Action [*or Answer*] Required (NVT)
nar .... No Adverse Reaction [*Therapy term*] (CTAA)
NAR .... No Adverse Reaction [*Medicine*] (MELL)
NAR .... No Answer Required (SAUS)
nar .... No Apparent Rate (AD)
NAR .... No Apparent Reason (SAUS)
NAR .... Noise-Adding Radiometer
NAR .... Nominal Acceleration Radar (SAUS)
NAR .... Non-Addressable Register (SAUS)
NAR .... Non-Advocacy Review (ACAE)
NAR .... Non-Advocate Review (SAUS)
NAR .... Nordic Association for Rehabilitation [*Denmark*] (EAIO)
NAR .... Nordiska Akademiker Radet [*Nordic Academic Council - NAC*] [*Defunct*] (EA)
NAR .... North American Review [*A publication*] (BRI)
NAR .... North American Rockwell Corp. [*Later, Rockwell International Corp.*] (MCD)
NAR .... North American Route [*Aviation*]
NAR .... North American Royalties (AD)
NAR .... North Australia Railway
NAR .... Northern Alberta Railways Co. [*AAR code*]
NAR .... Nose Alone Reference [*Aviation*] (MCD)
NAR .... Not According to Routine
NAR .... Not at Risk (MELL)
NAR .... Notice of Ammunition Reclassification [*Navy*] (NG)
NAR .... Notification of Ammunition Reclassification [*Military*]
NAR .... Nuclear Acoustic Resonance
NAR .... Nuclear Androgen Receptor [*Endocrinology*]
NAR .... Nuclear Assessment Routine (MCD)
NAR .... Nuclei Armati Rivoluzionari [*Armed Revolutionary Nuclei*] [*Italian*] (PD)
NAR .... Nucleic Acids Research [*A publication*]
NAR .... Numerical Analysis Research (MCD)
NARA .... N3N Restorers Association (EA)
NARA .... Narcotics Addict Rehabilitation Act [*1966*]
NARA .... National Agrichemical Retailers Association (EPAT)
NARA .... National Aircraft Resale Association (EA)
NARA .... National Air Resources Act (GFGA)
NARA .... National Alliance for Rural Action (EA)
NARA .... National Aquatic Resources Agency [*Sri Lanka*] [*Marine science*] (OSRA)
NARA .... National Archives and Records Administration [*Independent government agency*] [*Formerly, NARS*]
NARA .... National Association for the Rescue of Animals [*British*] (DI)
NARA .... National Association of Recovered Alcoholics [*Defunct*] (EA)
NARA .... National Association of Rehabilitation Agencies (EA)
NARA .... National Association of Republican Attorneys (EA)
NARA .... National Association of Review Appraisers (EA)
NARA .... Naval Aircraft Restorers Association (EA)
NARA .... Navy Appellate Review Activity (ACAE)
NARA .... Nippon Australian Relations Agreement (AD)
NARA .... North American Radio Archives (EA)
NARA .... North American Radon Association [*Defunct*] (EA)
NARA .... North American Regional Alliance of IATA [*International Amateur Theatre Association*] (EA)
NARA .... North American Rhea Association (NTPA)
NARA .... Northern Auto Racing Association [*Sanctioning organization*]
NARAA ...... National Association of Recruitment Advertising Agencies [*Defunct*] (EA)
NARAC ...... National Atmospheric Release Advisory Center [*Lawrence Livermore National Laboratory*] (RCD)
NARACC ..... National Association for Research and Action in Community Care [*British*] (DI)
NARACS ..... National Radio Communications System [*FAA*] (TAG)
NARAD ...... Naval Air Research and Development (MUGU)
NARAD ...... Navy Research and Development (AD)
NARADCOM ... Natick Research and Development Command [*Army*]
NARAG ...... National Association of Ratepayers' Action Groups [*British*] (DI)
NARAL ...... National Abortion and Reproductive Rights Acion League
NARAL ...... National Abortion Rights Action League (EA)
NARAL ...... National Association for the Repeal of Abortion Laws
NARAL ...... Net Advertising Revenue after Levy [*Television*] [*British*]
NARAL PAC ... National Abortion and Reproductive Rights Action League-Political Action Committee
NARAMU .... National Association of Review Appraisers and Mortgage Underwriters (NTPA)
NARANEXOS ... Name, Rate, Service Number, and Expiration of Obligated Service [*Navy*]
NARANO .... Name, Rate, and Service Number [*Navy*]
NarAnon .... Narcotics Anonymous (MELL)
NARAS ...... National Academy of Recording Arts and Sciences (EA)
NARASO .... Nevada Association Race and Sports Book Operators (EA)
NARASPO ... Navy Regional Airspace Officer (MUGU)
NARAT .... NATO Request for Air Transport Support [*Military*]
NARATE ..... Navy Advanced Radar Automatic Test Equipment (SAUS)
NARATE ..... Navy Automatic RADAR Test Equipment (KSC)
NARATE ..... Northrop Automatic RADAR Test System (SAA)
NARAVA ..... National Archives and Records Administration Volunteer Association (EA)
NARB .... Narcotic Addict Rehabilitation Branch [*National Institute of Mental Health*]
NARB .... National Advertising Review Board [*New York, NY*] (EA)
NARB .... National Assembly of Religious Brothers (EA)
NARB .... National Assocation of Radio Broadcasters (NTCM)
NARB .... National Association for Regional Ballet [*Later, RDA*]
NARB .... National Association of Referees in Bankruptcy [*Later, National Conference of Bankruptcy Judges*] (EA)
NARB .... National Association of Retired Bankers [*Later, RBA*] (EA)
NARB .... Navy Art Review Board (DNAB)
NARB .... Nonazeotropic Refrigerant Blend
NARBA ...... North American Rare Bird Alert (SAUS)
NARBA ...... North American Regional Broadcasting Agreement [*To minimize interference between AM stations*]
NARBC ...... National Angora Rabbit Breeders Club (EA)
NARBEC ..... North American Regional Broadcasting Engineering Committee (SAUS)
NARBHA .... Northern Arizona Regional Behavioral Health Authority (MHID)
NARBL ...... Net Advertising Revenue before Levy [*Television*] [*British*]
NARBS ...... Night/Day Angle Rate Bombing System (ACAE)
NARBW ..... National Association of Railway Business Women (EA)
narc .... Narcotic (AD)
NARC .... Narcotics [*FBI standardized term*]
NARC .... Narcotics Addiction Rehabilitation Center [*Medicine*] (EDAA)
narc .... Narcotics Agent (AD)
NARC .... Narcotism [*Chemical dependency*] (DAVI)
NARC .... Nasal Airway Resistance Computer [*Medicine*] (EDAA)
NARC .... National Agricultural Research Center
NARC .... National Amateur Retriever Club (EA)
NARC .... National Archives and Records Service (AD)
NARC .... National Army Revolutionary Committee [*or Council*] [*Laos*]
NARC .... National Association for Retarded Citizens [*Later, ARC*] (EA)
NARC .... National Association of Regional Councils (EA)
NARC .... National Association of Retired Catholics (AD)
NARC .... Naval Air Research Center (DNAB)
NARC .... Naval Air Reserve Center (DNAB)
NARC .... Naval Alcohol Rehabilitation Center (DNAB)
NARC .... Ninth Area Radio Club (SAUS)
NARC .... Nonautomatic Relay Center (AABC)
NARC .... North American Riders Club (EA)
NARC .... North American Rockwell Corp. [*Later, Rockwell International Corp.*] (MCD)
NARC .... North Atlantic Route Chart (PIPO)
NARC .... Northern Automobile Racing Club [*Sanctioning organization*]
NARC .... Nuclear Age Resource Center (EA)
NARC .... Nucleus Arcuatus [*Medicine*] (EDAA)
NARCA ...... National Antidrug Reorganization and Coordination Act
NARCA ...... National Association of Retail Collection Attorneys (NTPA)
NARCE ...... National Association of Retired Civil Employees [*Later, NARFE*] (EA)

NARCF ...... National Association of Residential Care Facilities (NTPA)
NARCF ...... National Association of Retail Clothiers and Furnishers [*Later, MRA*] (EA)
NARCINT... Narcotics Intelligence [*Military*] (ADDR)
NARCL ...... Nuclear Accident Response Capability Listing (MCD)
narco .... Narcolepsy [*Neurology*] (DAVI)
narco .... Narcotic (AD)
NARCO ...... Narcotics Commission [*United Nations*] (AD)
narco .... Narcotics Hospital (DAVI)
narco .... Narcotics Officer (AD)
narco .... Narcotics Treatment Center (DAVI)
NARCO .... National Aeronautical Corp. (MCD)
narcocard... Narcotic-Addict Registration Card (AD)
narcodollars... Narcotic Traffic Dollars (AD)
NARCOG .... Narcotics Coordination Group [*CIA*]
NARCOM.... Narration, Commentary [*Motion pictures*]
NARCOM.... North Atlantic Relay Communication (SAUS)
NARCOM.... North Atlantic Relay Communication Satellite
NARCOM Satellite... North Atlantic Relay Communication Satellite (SAUS)
NARCOM System... North Atlantic Relay Communication System (SAUS)
Narconon ... Narcotics Anonymous [*An association*] (AD)
Nar Conv.... Nares' Penal Convictions [*1815*] [*A publication*] (DLA)
NAR CORP... North American Rockwell Corp. [*Later, Rockwell International Corp.*]
narcos....... Narcotics (AD)
narcos....... Narcotics Police Officers (AD)
narcot .... Narcotic (AD)
narcotest... Narcotics Test (AD)
Narcotics L Bull... Narcotics Law Bulletin [*A publication*] (DLA)
narco-traf... Narcotics Traffick (AD)
narcs .... Narcotics (AD)
Narcs........ Narcotics (MILB)
narcs .... Narcotics Agents (AD)
narcs .... Narcotics Hospital (AD)
narcs .... Narcotics Officers (AD)
narcs .... Narcotics Treatment Centers (AD)
NARCU ...... National Association of Railroad and Utility Commissioners (NTCM)
NARCUP .... National Association for Retired Credit Union People (EA)
NArd......... Ardmore Industrial Air Park (SAUS)
NArd......... Ardsley Public Library, Ardsley, NY [*Library symbol*] [*Library of Congress*] (LCLS)
NARD........ Nardi-Danese [*NCIC car make code*]
NARD........ National Association of Regimental Drummers (AD)
NARD........ National Association of Retail Druggists (EA)
NARD........ National Association of Rudimental Drummers [*Defunct*]
NARD........ Navy Alcohol Rehabilitation Drydock (DNAB)
NARD........ Nonarticular Rheumatic Disorder [*Medicine*] (MELL)
nard .... Spikenard (AD)
NARDA...... National Appliance and Radio TV Dealers Association (IAA)
NARDA...... National Association of Retail Dealers of America (EA)
NARDA...... Naval Air Research and Development Activities (SAA)
NARDAC .... Navy Regional Data Automation Center
NARDACWASHDC... Navy Regional Data Automation Center, Washington, DC (DNAB)
NArdCG ..... CIBA-GEIGY Corp., Corporate Library, Ardsley, NY [*Library symbol*] [*Library of Congress*] (LCLS)
NARDELOG... Navy Rapid Delivery Logistics (AFIT)
NARDET..... Naval Air Reserve Detachment (DNAB)
NARDIC ..... Navy Acquisition, Research, and Development Information Center (POLM)
NARDIC ..... Navy Research and Development Information Center
NARDIS ..... Navy Automated Research and Development Information System [*Later, NAVWUIS*]
Nar Div...... Narodni Divadlo [*National Theater*] [*Czechoslavakia*] (AD)
NARDIV ..... Naval Air Reserve Divisions
NARDIV(FA)... Naval Air Reserve Division (Fleet Air) (DNAB)
NARDV ...... National Association Rainbow Division Veterans (EA)
NARE .... National Association for Recreational Equality (EA)
NARE .... National Association for Remedial Education [*British*]
NARE .... North Atlantic Regional Experiment [*Ozone measurement*]
NAREA ...... National Association of Real Estate Appraisers (EA)
Na_{reab}........ Sodium Reabsorption Rate [*Biochemistry*] (DAVI)
NAREB ...... National Association of Real Estate Boards [*Later, National Association of Realtors*] (EA)
NAREB ...... National Association of Real Estate Brokers
NAREBB..... National Association of Real Estate Buyer Brokers (EA)
NAREC ...... National Association of Real Estate Companies (EA)
narec .... Naval Research Electronic Computer (AD)
NAREC ...... Naval Research Electronic Computer
NAREE....... National Association of Real Estate Editors (EA)
NAREF....... National Anti-Repression Forum [*South Africa*] (SAFN)
NAREFA ..... North Atlantic Reference Fares (SAUS)
NaREIA...... National Real Estate Investors Association (NTPA)
NAREIF...... National Association of Real Estate Investment Funds [*Later, NAREIT*] (EA)
NAREIM ..... National Association of Real Estate Investment Managers (NTPA)
NAREIT...... National Association of Real Estate Investment Trusts (EA)
NAREIT PAC... National Association of Real Estate Investment Trusts Inc. PAC [*Washington, DC*] (PACS)
NAREL....... National Air and Radiation Environmental Laboratory (IID)
NARELLO... National Association of Real Estate License Law Officials (EA)
NAREMCO... National Records Management Council (EA)
NAREP ...... National Association of Real Estate Professionals (NTPA)
NARES ...... Nonallergic Rhinitis-Eosinophilia Syndrome [*Medicine*] (EDAA)
NARESU..... Naval Air Reserve Unit (DNAB)
NARETPA... National Agricultural Research, Extension, and Teaching Policy Act of 1977
NARETU..... Naval Air Reserve Electronics Training Unit (DNAB)
NARF .... American Rehabilitation Association [*Formerly, National Association of Rehabilitation Facilities*] (EA)
NARF .... National Association of Rehabilitation Facilities (EA)
NARF .... National Association of Retail Furnishers (AD)
NARF .... Native American Rights Fund (EA)
NARF .... Natural Axial Resonant Frequency (PDAA)
narf .... Natural Axial-Resonant Frequency (AD)
NARF .... Naval Aerospace Recovery Facility (SAUS)
NARF .... Naval Aerospace Research Facility
NARF .... Naval Air Reserve Force
NARF .... Naval Air Rework Facility
NARF .... Navy Arctic Research Facility
NARF .... Nuclear Aerospace Research Facility (IEEE)
NARF .... Nuclear Aircraft Research Facility (AD)
NARFE....... National Association of Retired Federal Employees (EA)
NARFE PAC... National Association of Retired Federal Employees PAC [*Alexandria, VA*] (PACS)
NARFFO..... Naval Air Rework Facility Field Office (DNAB)
NARFS ...... Naval Air Reserve Force Squadron (DNAB)
NARGA ...... National Association of Retail Grocers of Australia (AD)
NARGOM.... North American Research Group on Management (PDAA)
NARGS ...... North American Rock Garden Society (EA)
NARGUS .... National Association of Retail Grocers of the United States [*Later, NGA*] (EA)
NARHA ...... North American Riding for the Handicapped Association (EA)
NARHC ...... National Association of River and Harbor Contractors [*Later, NADC*] (EA)
NARHS ...... National Auto Racing Historical Society (EA)
NARI......... National Ageing Research Institute (SAUS)
NARI......... National Agriculture Research Institute (WDAA)
NARI......... National AIDS Research Institute [*India*]
NARI......... National Alliance for Reduction of Imprisonment [*Defunct*] (EA)
NARI......... National Association of Recycling Industries [*Later, ISRI*] (EA)
NARI......... National Association of Rehabilitation Instructors (EA)
NARI......... National Association of Residents and Interns (EA)
NARI......... National Association of the Remodeling Industry (EA)
NARI......... National Atmospheric Research Institute (AD)
NARI......... Native American Research Institute (EA)
NARI......... Nuclear Aerospace Research Institute [*Air Force*]
NARIC .... National Academic Recognition Information Centre (AIE)
NARIC .... National Rehabilitation Information Center (EA)
NARICM..... National Association of Retail Ice Cream Manufacturers [*Later, NICYRA*] (EA)
Nar Inv...... Narcotics Investigation (AD)
NARISCO... North American Rockwell Information Systems Co.
NARIST...... Naristillae [*Nasal Drops*] [*Pharmacy*]
narist........ Naristillae [*Nasal Drops*] [*Latin*] (AD)
NARK........ Nikolai Andreyvich Rimsky-Korsakov (AD)
Narkomvneshtorg... Narodny Komissariat Vneshney Torgovli [*People's Commissariate of Foreign Trade*] [*Russian*] (AD)
NARKOMVNUDEL... Narodnyi Komissariat Vnutrennikh Del [*People's Commissariat of Internal Affairs (1917-1946)*] [*Also known as NKVD*] [*Soviet secret police organization*]
NARL........ National Aero Research Laboratory [*Canada*] (PDAA)
NARL........ National Air and Radiation Laboratory (AUEG)
NARL........ National Association for Rehabilitation Leadership (EA)
NARL........ Naval Arctic Research Laboratory
NARL........ No Adverse Response Level [*Medicine*] (HCT)
NARM .... National Association of Recording Merchandisers (EA)
NARM .... National Association of Relay Manufacturers (EA)
NARM .... National Association of Restaurant Managers [*Scottsdale, AZ*] (EA)
NARM .... National Association of Retail Merchants (AD)
NARM .... National Association of Reunion Managers (EA)
NARM .... Naturally Occurring or Accelerator-Produced Radioactive Material
NARM .... Naval Resource Model (MCD)
NARM .... North American Registry of Midwives [*Association*] (EA)
NARM .... Nuclear Accelerator-generated Radioactive Material (SAUS)
N-arm .... Nuclear Armament (AD)
NARMA...... North American Russian Motorcycle Association
NARMC...... National Association of Regional Media Centers (EA)
NARMC...... National Association of Resident Management Corporations (NTPA)
NARMC...... Naval Aerospace and Regional Medical Center [*Bureau of Medicine*]
NARMC...... North Atlantic Regional Medical Center (SAUS)
NARMCO.... National Research and Manufacturing Co. (AD)
NARM-DPG... North Atlantic Rifted Margins Detailed Planning Group (SAUS)
N-armed .... Nuclear-Armed (AD)
NARMFD .... National Association of Retail Meat and Food Dealers
NARMH ..... National Association for Rural Mental Health (EA)
NARMIC..... National Action/Research on the Military Industrial Complex (EA)
NArmN ...... North Castle Library, Armonk, NY [*Library symbol*] [*Library of Congress*] (LCLS)
NARMP...... National Antibacterial Residue Minimization Program [*Australia*]
NARM-PAC... PAC of National Association of Recording Merchandisers [*Marlton, NJ*] (PACS)
NARMPU.... Naval Air Reserve Mobile Photographic Unit (DNAB)
NARMS...... National Association for Retail Marketing Services (EA)
N-Arms Control... Nuclear Arms Control (SAUS)
N-Arms Race... Nuclear Arms Race (SAUS)
NARMU ..... Naval Air Reserve Maintenance Units
NARN........ National Association of Registered Nurses (EA)
NARND...... National Association of Radio News Directors (IAA)

NARO........ National Agricultural Research Organization [*Netherlands*] (ECON)
NARO........ National Association of Reimbursement Officers [*Washington, DC*] (EA)
NARO........ National Association of Royalty Owners (EA)
NARO........ Naval Aircraft Repair Organisation (SAUS)
NARO........ North American Regional Office (AD)
NARO........ North American Representative Office (EFIS)
NAROCTESTSTA... Naval Air Rocket Test Station
NARP........ National Administrative Rehabilitation Programme [*United Nations program*]
NARP........ National Association for Registered Plans (EA)
NARP........ National Association of Railroad Passengers (EA)
NARP........ National Association of Reunion Managers (NTPA)
NARP........ Neurogenic Muscle Weakness, Ataxia, and Retinitis Pigmentosa [*Medicine*]
NARP........ Neuropathy, Ataxia, Retinitis Pigmentosa (SAUS)
NARP........ New Australian Republican Party [*Political party*]
NARP........ Nonaqueous Reversed Phase [*Chromatography*]
NARP........ Non-Broadcast Multiple Access Address Resolution Protocol (SAUS)
NARP........ Nuclear Weapons Accident Report Procedures (AD)
NARPA...... National Air Rifle and Pistol Association [*British*]
NARPA...... National Association for Rights Protection and Advocacy (EA)
NARPD...... National Association for the Relief of Paget's Disease [*British*]
NARPM...... National Association of Residential Property Managers (NTPA)
NARPO...... National Association of Retired Police Officers [*British*] (DBA)
NARPO...... National Association of Reversionary Property Owners (EA)
NARPPS..... National Association of Rehabilitation Professionals in the Private Sector (EA)
NARPS...... Northampton Air Raid Precautions Standard (SAUS)
NARPTR..... National Association of Railroad Property Tax Representatives (NTPA)
NARPV...... National Association for Remotely Piloted Vehicles (MCD)
NARR........ Narrator [*or Narration*]
NARRD...... National Association of Record Retailer Dealers [*Defunct*] (EA)
Nar Rep Bul... Narodna Republika Bulgaria [*Bulgarian People's Republic*] [*Political party*] (AD)
Narr Mod... Narrationes Modernae [*Style's English King's Bench Reports*] [*1646-55*] [*A publication*] (DLA)
NARRP...... National Association of Recreation Resource Planners (NTPA)
NARRS...... National Association of Radio Reading Services (EA)
NARS........ Narrative Accomplishment Reporting System [*Department of Agriculture*] [*Information service or system*] (IID)
NARS........ National Acupuncture Research Society (EA)
NARS........ National Agricultural Research Systems (ECON)
NARS........ National Annual Report Service [*NYSE*]
NARS........ National Archives and Records Service [*of GSA*] [*Washington, DC*] [*Later, NARA*]
NARS........ National Asbestos-Contractor Registry System (EAGT)
NARS........ National Association of Radiation Survivors (EA)
NARS........ National Association of Radiator Specialists [*British*] (DBA)
NARS........ National Association of Radiotelephone Systems [*Later, Telocator Network of America*] (EA)
NARS........ National Association of Rail Shippers (EA)
NARS........ National Association of Refunders and Shoppers [*Defunct*] (EA)
NARS........ National Association of Rehabilitation Secretaries (EA)
NARS........ Naval Air Rescue Service (MUGU)
NARS........ New Atlantean Research Society [*Defunct*] (EA)
NARS........ Non-Affiliated Reserve Section (SAUS)
NARS........ Northampton Activity Rating Scale [*Psychology*]
NARS........ North Atlantic Radio System
NARSA...... National Automotive Radiator Service Association (EA)
NARS-A1.... National Archive and Record Service-Automation 1 (NITA)
NARSAB..... National Association of Rail Shippers Advisory Boards (EA)
NARSAD.... National Alliance for Research on Schizophrenia and the Depressions (EA)
NARSAP..... National Advanced Remote Sensing Application Program
NARSC...... National Association of Reinforcing Steel Contractors (EA)
NARSI....... Native American Recreation and Sport Institute [*Association*] (EA)
NARSID..... Non-Avalanche-Related Snow-Immersion Death
NARSIS..... National Association for Road Safety Instruction in Schools (AD)
NARSLL..... National Association to Reform State Liquor Laws [*Later, National Association to Reform State Drinking Ages*] [*Defunct*] (EA)
NARSNDF... North Atlantic Regional Study Narrative Data File (SAUS)
NARSS...... National Association of Rehabilitation Support Staff (EA)
NARST...... National Association for Research in Science Teaching (EA)
NARSTC..... Naval Air Rescue Training Command
NARSTO..... North American Research Strategy for Tropospheric Ozone
NARSUP.... Navy Acquisition Regulations Supplement
NARSVA..... National Archives and Record Service Volunteer Association [*Later, NARAVA*] (EA)
NARSVPD... National Association of Retired Senior Volunteer Program Directors (EA)
NART........ National Association for Remedial Teaching (AEBS)
NART........ National Association of Recreation Therapists [*Later, NTRS*] (EA)
NART........ National Retail Transportation [*Common carrier symbol*]
NART........ New Adult Reading Test
NART........ North American Racing Team [*Auto racing*]
NARTA...... North American Restaurant and Tavern Alliance (EA)
NARTB...... National Association of Radio and Television Broadcasters [*Later, NAB*]
NARTC...... National Association of Railroad Trial Counsel (EA)
NARTC...... Naval Air Research Training Command
NARTC...... Naval Air Rocket Test Center (MUGU)
NARTC...... North American Regional Test Center (SAUS)
NARTC...... North America Regional Test Center (NATG)
NARTCE..... National Association for Released Time Christian Education (EA)
NARTE....... National Association of Radio and Telecommunications Engineers (EA)
NARTH...... National Association of Research and Therapy of Homosexuality (EA)
NARTM...... National Association of Rope and Twine Merchants (AD)
NARTRANS... North American Rockwell Training and Services [*Obsolete*]
NARTS....... National Association of Radio Telephone Systems [*Later, Telocator Network of America*] (IAA)
NARTS....... National Association of Reporter Training Schools [*Defunct*] (EA)
NARTS....... National Association of Resale and Thrift Shops (EA)
NARTS....... Naval Aeronautics Test Station
NARTS....... Naval Air Rocket Test Station
NARTU...... Naval Air Reserve Training Unit
NARU........ Natural Rate of Unemployment [*Economics*]
NARU........ Naval Air Reserve Unit (NVT)
NARU........ North Australian Research Unit (AD)
NARUC...... National Association of Regulatory Utility Commissioners (EA)
NARUCE..... National Association of Regulatory Utility Commission Engineers (IAA)
NARUS...... Navy Aircraft Resources Utilization Study
NARVRE..... National Association of Retired and Veteran Railroad Employees (EA)
NARW....... National Assembly of Religious Women (EA)
NARW....... National Association of Refrigerated Warehouses [*Later, IARW*] (EA)
NARWA...... Nordic Agricultural Research Workers Association (EA)
NARWA...... Northern Arizona Romance Writers of America (EARSL)
NARWACL... North American Regional World Anti-Communist League (AD)
NARZ........ North Alabama Railroad Museum [*Federal Railroad Administration identification code*]
NAS.......... Advanced Supercomputing Division [*Ames Research Center*] (RCD)
NAS.......... N-Acetylserotonin [*Biochemistry*]
NAS.......... Names [*Telegraphy*] (PCTE)
NAS.......... Narcotics Affairs Section [*Foreign service*]
NAS.......... Narrow-Angle Sensor
nas.......... Nasal (AD)
NAS.......... Nasal
NAS.......... Nasangga [*Fiji*] [*Seismograph station code, US Geological Survey*] (SEIS)
NAS.......... Nassau [*Bahamas*] [*Airport symbol*] (OAG)
NAS.......... Nasta International, Inc. [*AMEX symbol*] (COMM)
NAS.......... National Abatement Services, Inc. (EFIS)
NAS.......... National Academy of Sciences [*Washington, DC*]
NAS.......... National Academy of Songwriters (EA)
NAS.......... National Academy of Sports (EA)
NAS.......... National Accreditation Service (SAUS)
NAS.......... National Adoption Society (WDAA)
NAS.......... National Advanced Systems (HGAA)
NAS.......... National Advocates Society (EA)
NAS.......... National Aerospace Standards Industrial Association (AAGC)
NAS.......... National Agricultural Society (NADA)
NAS.......... National Aircraft Standard (SAUS)
NAS.......... National Aircraft Standards
NAS.......... National Airspace System [*NASA*]
NAS.......... National Alliance for Salvation [*Sudan*] [*Political party*] (MENA)
NAS.......... National Aquarium Society (EA)
NAS.......... National Aquatic School [*Red Cross*]
NAS.......... National Association of Sanitarians [*Later, NEHA*] (EA)
NAS.......... National Association of Scholars (EA)
NAS.......... National Association of Schoolmasters [*British*]
NAS.......... National Association of Shopfitters [*British*] (BI)
NAS.......... National Association of Shopkeepers [*British*] (DBA)
NAS.......... National Association of Specialized Carriers, Marietta GA [*STAC*]
NAS.......... National Association of Stevedores (EA)
NAS.......... National Association of Supervisors [*Later, Federal Managers Association*] (EA)
NAS.......... National Astrological Society [*Defunct*] (EA)
NAS.......... National Audubon Society (EA)
NAS.......... National Autistic Society [*British*]
NAS.......... National Aviation System [*FAA*]
NAS.......... National Avionics Society (EA)
NAS.......... National Seastar [*Vancouver Stock Exchange symbol*]
NAS.......... Native American Studies (AD)
NAS.......... Nautical Archaeology Society [*United Kingdom*] (EAIO)
NAS.......... Naval Air Service
NAS.......... Naval Air Squadron (SAUS)
NAS.......... Naval Air Station
NAS.......... Naval Air Systems Command, Washington, DC [*OCLC symbol*] (OCLC)
NAS.......... Naval Audit Service (DOMA)
NAS.......... Navigation Avoidance System (KSC)
NAS.......... Navy Advisory Section [*Vietnam*] (VNW)
NAS.......... Navy Anesthesia Society [*Association*] (EA)
NAS.......... Neonatal Abstinence Syndrome (DAVI)
NAS.......... Neonatal Airleak Syndrome [*Medicine*] (DMAA)
NAS.......... NetWare Access Server [*Computer science*]
NAS.......... Network Access Switch [*Telecommunications*] (MCD)
NAS.......... Network Administration Station (ELAL)
NAS.......... Network Analyzer Software
NAS.......... Network Application Support [*Computer science*] (BTTJ)
NAS.......... Network-Attached Storage [*Computer science*]
NAS.......... Neuroallergic Syndrome [*Medicine*] (DMAA)
NAS.......... New American Schools
NAS.......... New Attack Submarine [*Navy*] (MUSM)
NAS.......... Newport Aeronautical Sales (SAUS)

NAS.......... Newsreel Access Systems, Inc. [*Also, an information service or system*] (IID)
NAS.......... No Abnormality Seen [*Medicine*] (MELL)
n-a-s.......... No Added Salt (AD)
NAS.......... No Added Salt [*Medicine*]
NAS.......... Nocturnal Adoration Society (EA)
NAS.......... Noise Abatement Society [*British*]
NAS.......... Nominal Aggregate Signal (SAUS)
NAS.......... Non-Assessable Stock [*Investment term*] (MHDW)
NAS.......... Nonavailability Statement [*Military*]
NAS.......... Non-Indigenous Aquatic Species [*Marine science*] (OSRA)
NAS.......... Nonlinear Aerial System (SAUS)
NAS.......... Nonlinear Antenna System
NAS.......... Nord Amerikanischer Sangerbund (EA)
NAS.......... Normalized Alignment Score
NAS.......... North American Shale [*Geology*]
NAS.......... North American Supply [*World War II*]
NAS.......... North Arabian Sea (SAUS)
NAS.......... Northeast Aviation Services Ltd. [*British*] [*ICAO designator*] (FAAC)
NAS.......... Nozzle Actuating System [*Aerospace*] (MCD)
NAS.......... Numencal Analysis Subroutines (SAUS)
NAS.......... Numerical Aerodynamic Simulation [*NASA supercomputer system*]
NAS.......... Numerical Aerodynamics Simulator (SAUS)
NAS.......... Numerical Analysis Subroutines [*Computer science*] (BUR)
NAS.......... Numerical and Atmospheric Sciences Network [*NASA*]
NAS.......... Nursery Association Secretaries [*Later, Nursery Association Executives*] (EA)
NAS.......... Nursing Auxiliary Service [*British*]
NASA........ Nasan Trailer [*NCIC trailer make code*]
NASA........ National Acoustical Suppliers Association [*Defunct*] (EA)
NASA........ National Advertising Sales Association (EA)
NASA........ National Aeronautics and Space Act of 1958
NASA........ National Aeronautics and Space Administration [*Washington, DC*]
NASA........ National Aerospace Services Association [*Defunct*] (MCD)
NASA........ National Appliance Service Association (EA)
NASA........ National Association of School Affiliates (EA)
NASA........ National Association of Schools of Art (EA)
NASA........ National Association of Securities Administrators
NASA........ National Association of Shippers' Agents [*Washington, DC*] (EA)
NASA........ National Association of State Archeologists (EA)
NASA........ National Association of Student Anthropologists (SAUS)
NASA........ National Association of Synagogue Administrators (EA)
NASA........ National Automobile Salesmen's Association
NASA........ National Auto Sport Association
NASA........ Naval Aircraft Safety Activity (SAA)
NASA........ Newspaper Advertising Sales Association (EA)
NASA........ Nitrogen Atmosphere Sampling Analysis (SAUS)
NASA........ North American Sailing Association (AD)
NASA........ North American Savings Association (SAUS)
NASA........ North American Saxophone Alliance (EA)
NASA........ North American Securities Administrators Association [*Also, NASAA*] (EA)
NASA........ North American Shippers Association (EA)
NASA........ North American Singers Association (EA)
NASA........ North American Swiss Alliance (EA)
NASA........ North Atlantic Seafood Association [*Defunct*] (EA)
NASA........ North Atlantic Shippers Association (DS)
NASAA...... National Aeronautics and Space Administration Act (AD)
NASAA...... National Assembly of State Arts Agencies (EA)
NASAA...... National Association of State Approval Agencies (EA)
NASAA...... National Association of Student Activity Advisers (EA)
NASAA...... North American Securities Administrators Association [*Topeka, KS*] (EA)
NASA-AEC... National Aeronautics and Space Administration and Atomic Energy Commission (SAA)
NASAB...... National Association of Shippers Advisory Boards (EA)
NASABCA... National Aeronautics and Space Administration Board of Contract Appeals
NASABF..... North America Statistical Areas Boundary File (SAUS)
NASA-CF Florida... National Aeronautics and Space Administration - Cocoa Beach, Florida (AD)
NASA-CO... National Aeronautics and Space Administration - Cleveland, Ohio (AD)
NASACOM... NASA Communications System (SAUS)
NASACRE... National Association for Standing Advisory Councils for Religious Education (AIE)
NASACT..... National Association of State Auditors, Comptrollers, and Treasurers (EA)
NASACU..... National Association of State Approved Colleges and Universities (EA)
NASAD...... National Association of Schools of Art and Design (EA)
NASAD...... National Association of Sport Aircraft Designers (EA)
NASADAD... National Association of State Alcohol and Drug Abuse Directors (EA)
NASAE....... National Association of Supervisors of Agricultural Education (EA)
NASA-EC California... National Aeronautics and Space Administration - Edwards, California (AD)
NASAEN..... National Association for State-Enrolled Assistant Nurses (AD)
NASAERC... NASA Electronic Research Center (IAA)
NASAF....... Northwest African Strategic Air Force [*British military*] (DMA)
NASA FAR Supp... National Aeronautics and Space Administration FAR Supplement [*A publication*] (AAGC)
NASA FTCSC... NASA Food Technology Commercial Space Center [*Iowa State University of Science and Technology*] (RCD)
NASAGA..... North American Simulation and Gaming Association (EA)
NASA-GM Maryland... National Aeronautics and Space Administration - Greenbelt, Maryland (AD)
NASA-HA Alabama... National Aeronautics and Space Administration - Huntsville, Alabama (AD)
NASAHOE... National Association of Supervisors and Administrators of Health Occupations Education (EA)
NASA-HT... National Aeronautics and Space Administration - Houston, Texas (AD)
NASAKOM... Nasional, Agama, Kommunist [*Indonesian President Sukarno's policy of unity among National, Religious, and Communist forces*]
Nasakom.... Nationalist-Communist (AD)
NASA-KSC... National Aeronautics and Space Administration - Kennedy Space Center
NASAL....... National Association of Single Adult Leaders (EA)
NASAL....... Network of Single Adult Leaders (EA)
NASA LST Telescope... National Aeronautics and Space Administration Large Space Telescope (AD)
NASA-LV Virginia... National Aeronautics and Space Administration - Langley Field, Virginia (AD)
NASA-MC California... National Aeronautics and Space Administration - Moffett Field, California (AD)
NASAMECU... Natura Sanat, Medicus Curat [*Nature Heals, the Doctor Cures*] [*Title of collected talks by Dr. Georg Groddeck, published in 1913*]
NASAMS.... Norwegian Advanced Surface to Air Missile System (ACAE)
NASAMS.... Norwegian Advanced Surface-to-Air Missile System (SAUS)
NASA-MSC... National Aeronautics and Space Administration - Manned Spacecraft Center
NAS & FCA... National Automatic Sprinkler and Fire Control Association (AD)
NASANX..... Naval Air Station Annex (DNAB)
NASAO...... National Association of State Aeronautics and Organizations (SAUS)
NASAO...... National Association of State Aviation Officials (EA)
NASAOCARE... National Association of State Aviation Officials Center for Aviation Research and Education (EA)
NASAP...... National Association of Student Affairs Professionals (NTPA)
NASAP...... National Association of Student Assistance Professionals (EA)
NASAP...... Navy Alcohol Safety Action Program (DNAB)
NASAP...... Network Analysis for Systems Applications Program [*Computer program*] [*NASA*]
NASAP...... Nonproliferation Alternative Systems Assessment Program [*Nuclear energy*] (NRCH)
NASAP...... North American Society of Adlerian Psychology (EA)
NASAP...... Nuclear Alternative System Assessment Program
NASAP...... Nuclear Alternative Systems Assessment Program (SAUS)
NASAPOFF... Navy Alcohol Safety Action Program Office (DNAB)
NASAPR..... National Aeronautics and Space Administration Procurement Regulations
NASAPRD... National Aeronautics and Space Administration Procurement Regulations Directive
NASAR...... National Association for Search and Rescue (EA)
NASA/RECON... National Aeronautics and Space Administration Remote Console
NASARR.... North American Search and Range RADAR [*Military*]
NASA-SC California... National Aeronautics and Space Administration - Santa Monica, California (AD)
NASASP..... National Association State Agencies for Surplus Property (EA)
NASASPS... National Association of State Administrators and Supervisors of Private Schools (EA)
NASA-STAR... NASA Scientific and Technical Reports (NITA)
NASA/STIF... National Aeronautics and Space Administration/Scientific and Technical Information Facility
NASATE..... National Association of Substance Abuse Trainers and Educators (EA)
NASA-TR... NASA Tank Reactor
NASB........ Nancy Ann Story Book [*Doll collecting*]
NASB........ National Association of School Boards (OICC)
NASB........ National Association of Spanish Broadcasters (EA)
NASB........ National Association of State Boards of Accountancy (AAGC)
NASB........ Navigational Aid Support Base
NASB........ Nebraska Association of School Boards (EARSL)
NASB........ New American Standard Bible [*A publication*] (BJA)
NASB........ North American Savings Bank FSB [*NASDAQ symbol*] (SAG)
NASB........ North Amer Svgs Bk [*NASDAQ symbol*] (TTSB)
NASBA...... NASBA - The Association of System Builders and Integrators (EA)
NASBA...... National Association of State Boards of Accountancy [*New York, NY*] (EA)
NASBA...... National Automobile Safety Belt Association [*British*]
NASBA...... Nucleic Acid Sequence-Based Amplification [*Biochemistry*]
NASBCO..... National Association of School Bus Contract Operators [*Later, NSTA*] (EA)
NASBE....... National Association of State Boards of Education (EA)
NASBE....... National Association of Supervisors of Business Education [*Fort Lauderdale, FL*] (EA)
NASBERM... Naval Air Station, Bermuda
NASBHC..... National Assembly on School-Based Health Care (SAUS)
NASBIC...... National Association of Small Business Investment Companies [*Washington, DC*] (EA)
NASBITE... National Association of Small Business International Trade Educators (NTPA)
NASBLA..... National Association of State Boating Law Administrators (EA)
NASBO...... National Association of State Budget Officers (EA)
NASBO...... North African Shipping Board [*World War II*]
NASBOE..... National Association of Supervisors of Business and Office Education [*Later, NASBE*]
NASBOSA... National Academy of Sciences Board on Ocean Science Affairs (PDAA)

NASBP ...... National Association of Surety Bond Producers [*Bethesda, MD*] (EA)
NASBS ...... North American Skull Base Society (EA)
NASC .... National Aeronautics and Space Council [*Terminated, 1973*]
NASC .... National Aircraft Standards Committee
NASC .... National Alliance for Safer Cities (EA)
NASC .... National Alliance of Senior Citizens (EA)
NASC .... National Aloe Science Council [*Later, IASC*] (EA)
NASC .... National Amalgamated Society of Coopers [*A union*] [*British*]
NASC .... National Aquatic Sports Camps (EA)
NASC .... National Association of Scaffolding Contractors [*British*] (DBA)
NASC .... National Association of School Counselors [*Defunct*] (EA)
NASC .... National Association of Service Contractors [*Defunct*] (EA)
NASC .... National Association of Solar Contractors (EA)
NASC .... National Association of Specialized Carriers [*Defunct*] (EA)
NASC .... National Association of Student Councils (EA)
NASC .... National Athletic Steering Committee (EA)
NASC .... Native American Sports Council [*Association*] (EA)
NASC .... NATO Supply Center
NASC .... Naval Aircraft Standards Committee (AFIT)
NASC .... Naval Air Systems Command
NASC .... Navy Aviation Safety Center (MUGU)
NASC .... Network Access Solutions [*NASDAQ symbol*] (SG)
NASC .... North American Shale Composite [*Geology*]
NASC .... North American Sporting Clays [*An association*]
NASC .... North American Sports Camps
NASC .... North American Stratigraphic Code (SAUS)
NASC .... North American Supply Council (SAUS)
NASC .... North America Supply Council
NASC .... North Atlantic Salmon Convention [*Marine science*] (OSRA)
NASC .... Northwest Association of Schools and Colleges (EA)
NASCA ...... National Association for Corporate Speaker Activities [*Reston, VA*] (WDMC)
NASCA ...... National Association of State Cable Agencies (EA)
NASCA ...... National Association of State Conservation Agencies [*Washington, DC*]
NASCA ...... North American Swing Club Association (EA)
NASCAD..... NASA Computer Aided Design (SAUS)
NASCAP..... NASA Charging Analyzer Program (MCD)
NASCAR..... National Association for Stock Car Advancement and Research (AD)
NASCAR..... National Association for Stock Car Auto Racing (EA)
NASCAR..... National Association of Sports Car Racing (AD)
NASCAS..... NAS Committee on Atmospheric Sciences (SAUS)
NASCAS..... National Academy of Sciences Committee on Atmospheric Science
NASCAT ..... National Association of Securities and Commercial Law Attorneys (EA)
NASCAT PAC... National Association of Securities and Commercial Law Attorneys PAC [*New York, NY*] (PACS)
NASCC ...... National Association of Service and Conservation Corps (EA)
NASCCD..... National Association of State Catholic Conference Directors (EA)
NASCCEN... Naval Air Systems Command Representative, Central
NAS-CD ..... National Academy of Sciences - Chemistry Division
NASCD ...... National Association for Sickle Cell Disease (EA)
NASCD ...... National Association of Soil Conservation Districts [*Later, National Association of Conservation Districts*]
NASCDC..... National Association for Sick Child Daycare Centers (PAZ)
NASCDD .... National Association of State Civil Defense Directors [*Later, NEMA*] (EA)
NASCE....... Network Access Solutions Corp. [*NASDAQ symbol*] (QUAN)
NASCH ...... National Association of Swimming Clubs for the Handicapped [*British*] (DBA)
NASCI .... North American Society for Cardiac Imaging (SAUS)
NASCIS...... National Acute Spinal Cord Injury Study
NASCL....... North American Student Cooperative League
NASCLANT... Naval Air Systems Command Representative, Atlantic
NASCMVE... National Academy of Sciences Committee on Motor Vehicle Emissions (PDAA)
NASCO ...... National Academy of Sciences Committee on Oceanography
NASCO ...... National Association of Security Companies (NTPA)
NASCO ...... National Association of Smaller Communities (EA)
NASCO ...... National Association of State Charity Officials (EA)
NASCO ...... National Automotive Service Co. (AD)
NASCO ...... National Scientific Committee on Oceanography [*Marine science*] (MSC)
NASCO ...... North American Students of Cooperation (EA)
NASCO ...... North Atlantic Salmon Commission (SAUS)
NASCO ...... North Atlantic Salmon Conservation Organization [*Edinburgh, Scotland*] (EAIO)
NASCOE..... National Association of ASCS [*Agricultural Stabilization and Conservation Service*] County Office Employees (EA)
Nascom ..... NASA Communications
NASCOM.... NASA Communications Network
NASCOM.... NASA Worldwide Communications Network (MCD)
NASCOM.... National Aeronautics and Space Administration Tracking Network (AD)
NASCOM.... National Airspace Communications System
NASCom .... Naval Air Systems Command (AD)
NASCOM.... Naval Air Systems Command (MCD)
NASCOMIS... Naval Air Station/Command Management Information System (MCD)
NASCOP..... NASA Communications Operating Procedures (MCD)
NAS/COW... National Academy of Sciences/Committee on Water [*Marine science*] (MSC)
NASCP ...... National Association of Sports for Cerebral Palsy [*Later, USCPAA*] (EA)
NASCP ...... North American Society for Corporate Planning [*Later, PF*] (EA)
NASCPA..... North American Study Center for Polish Affairs (EA)
NASCPAC... Naval Air Systems Command Representative, Pacific
NASCPD..... National Association of Senior Companion Project Directors (EA)
NASCPNCLA... Naval Air Systems Command Representative, Naval Air Training Command, Pensacola [*Florida*]
NASCRIST... Naval Air Station Corpus Christi
NASCRL..... Naval Air Systems Command Representative, Atlantic
NASCRP..... Naval Air Systems Command Representative-Pacific (MCD)
NASCS ...... National Association of Shoe Chain Stores [*Later, FDRA*] (EA)
NASCSA..... National Association of State Controlled Substance Authorities (EA)
NASCSP..... National Association for State Community Service Programs (EA)
NASCUMC... National Association of Schools and Colleges of the United Methodist Church (EA)
NASCUS..... National Association of State Credit Union Supervisors (EA)
NASD .... National AG Safety Database (GDD)
NASD .... National Amalgamated Stevedores and Dockers (AD)
NASD .... National Association for Staff Development [*British*] (DET)
NASD .... National Association of Schools of Dance (EA)
NASD .... National Association of Schools of Design [*Later, NASA*]
NASD .... National Association of Securities Dealers [*Washington, DC*] (EA)
NASD .... National Association of Selective Distributors [*Defunct*] (EA)
NASD .... National Association of Service Dealers (EA)
NASD .... Naval Air [*or Aviation*] Supply Depot
NASD .... Naval Aviation Supply Depot (AD)
NASD .... Network-Attached Storage Device [*Computer science*] (GART)
NASDA ...... National Association of Sign and Display Advertisers [*Defunct*]
NASDA ...... National Association of State Departments of Agriculture (EA)
NASDA ...... National Association of State Development Agencies (EA)
NASDA ...... National Space Development Agency [*Japan*]
NASDA ...... North American South Devon Association (EA)
NASDAC..... National Aviation Safety Data Analysis Center [*FAA*] (TAG)
NASDAD .... National Association of Seventh-Day Adventist Dentists (EA)
NASDAGS... National Association of State Directors of Administration and General Service (EA)
NASDAPC... National Association of State Drug Abuse Program Coordinators [*Later, NASADAD*] (EA)
nasdaq ...... Medical Registry Services [*NASDAQ symbol*]
Nasdaq...... National Association of Securities Dealers Automated Quotations [*The full name is the Nasdaq Stock Market*] [*Washington, DC*] (WDMC)
NASDAQ .... National Association of Securities Dealers Automated Quotations [*Over-the-counter stock quotations*] [*Bunker Ramo Corp.*] [*Trumbell, CT*] [*Information service or system*]
NASDAQS... National Association of Security Dealers Automated Quotation System (AD)
NASDCD .... National Association of State Directors of Child Development
NASDDDS... National Association of State Directors of Developmental Disability Services (NTPA)
NASDDP .... National Association of State Directors for Disaster Preparedness [*Later, NEMA*] (EA)
NASDI .... National Association of Selective Distributors (EA)
NASDIEGO... Naval Air Station San Diego
NASDIM..... National Association of Securities Dealers and Investment Managers [*Securities and Investment Board*] [*British*]
NASDLET ... National Association of State Directors of Law Enforcement Training
NASDM...... National Association of Special Delivery Messengers [*Later, APWU*] [*AFL-CIO*] (EA)
NASDME.... National Association of State Directors of Migrant Education (EA)
NASDQ ...... National Association of Securities Dealers Automated Quotations (SAUS)
NASDS ...... National Amalgamated Stevedores' and Dockers' Society [*A union*] [*British*]
NASDS ...... National Association of Scuba Diving Schools [*Later, CA*] [*Commercial firm*] (EA)
NASDS ...... Naval Aviation Supply Distribution System (AFIT)
NASDS ...... North American Sheep Dog Society (EA)
NASDSE..... National Association of State Directors of Special Education [*Database producer*] (EA)
NASDSSE... National Association of State Directors and Supervisors of Secondary Education [*Later, NASSDSE*] (EA)
NASDT ...... Naval Aviators' Speech Discrimination Test
NASDT ...... North American Society for Dialysis and Transplantation (EA)
NASDTEC ... National Association of State Directors of Teacher Education and Certification (EA)
NASDU ...... National Amalgamated Stevedores and Dockers Union [*British*] (BI)
NASDVA..... National Association of State Directors of Veterans Affairs (EA)
NASDVE..... National Association of State Directors of Vocational Education (EA)
NASDVTEC... National Association of State Directors of Vocational-Technical Education (NTPA)
NASE .... National Academy of School Executives [*of American Association of School Administrators*]
NASE .... National Academy of Stationary Engineers [*British*] (DAS)
NASE .... National Association for the Self-Employed [*Fort Worth, TX*] (EA)
NASE .... National Association for the Study of Epilepsy (DAVI)
NASE .... National Association of Stationary Engineers (AD)
NASE .... National Association of Steel Exporters [*Defunct*] (EA)
nase .... Neutral Atom Space Engine (AD)
NASE .... Nonacoustic Submarine Effects (NVT)
NASEA....... National Association of Student Employment Administrators (EA)
NASEA....... Native American Science Education Association [*Defunct*] (EA)
NASEAB..... Naval Air Systems Effectiveness Advisory Board
NASEAN..... National Association for State Enrolled Assistant Nurses
NASECODE... Numerical Analysis of Semiconductor Devices and Integrated Circuits [*Computer science*]
NASED ...... National Association of State Election Directors (EA)

NASEDIO.... National Association of State Education Department Information Officers (EA)
NASEES..... National Association for Soviet and East European Studies [*British*]
NASEM...... National Association of Satellite Equipment Manufacturers [*Defunct*] (EA)
NASEMP.... National Association of State Educational Media Professionals (EA)
NASEMSD... National Association of State EMS Directors (EA)
NASEN...... National Association for Special Educational Needs (AIE)
NASEN...... National Association of State Enrolled Nurses [*British*] (BI)
NASEO...... National Association of State Energy Officials (NTPA)
NASEPA..... National Association of State Environmental Programs Agencies [*Marine science*] (MSC)
n-ASER...... Neutron-Accelerated Soft-Error Rate (SAUS)
NAS/ESB.... National Academy of Sciences/Environmental Studies Board [*Marine science*] (MSC)
NASF........ National Aboriginal Sports Foundation (AD)
NASF........ National American Studies Faculty [*Defunct*] (EA)
NASF........ National Arts Stabilization Fund [*Defunct*] (EA)
NASF........ National Association of State Foresters (EA)
NASF........ Native American Scholarship Fund [*An association*] (EA)
NASF........ Navigation & Attack Systems Flight (SAUS)
NASF........ NIC [*Naval Intelligence Center*] Analyst Support Facility
NASF........ North American Soccer Foundation [*Defunct*] (EA)
NASF........ Numerical Aerodynamic Simulation Facility
NASFA....... National Association of State Facilities Administrators (EA)
NASFA....... National Association of State Farm Agents Inc. [*Baltimore, MD*] (PACS)
NASFAA..... National Association of Student Financial Aid Administrators (EA)
NASFCA..... National Automatic Sprinkler and Fire Control Association (EA)
NASFCB..... National Association of Specialty Food and Confection Brokers (EA)
NASFHA..... North American Selle Fran(ais Horse Association, Inc [*Equine term*] (TED)
NASFM...... National Association of State Fire Marshals (EA)
NASFM...... National Association of Store Fixture Manufacturers (EA)
NASFO...... National Asset Seizure and Forfeiture Office (AD)
NASFT....... National Association for the Specialty Food Trade (EA)
NASFW...... National Association of Solid Fuel Wholesalers [*British*] (DBA)
NASG........ National Alliance for Spiritual Growth (EA)
NASG........ New-Age Sensitive Guy (SAUS)
NASGA...... North American Strawberry Growers Association (EA)
NAS-GB..... Noise Abatement Society of Great Britain (AD)
NASGC...... National Association of Small Government Contractors (EA)
NaSGIM..... National Study of Graduate Education in Internal Medicine (SAUS)
NAS/GRB.... National Academy of Sciences/Geophysical Research Board [*Marine science*] (MSC)
NASGS...... North African Secretary General Staff [*World War II*]
NASGTMO... Naval Air Station Guantanamo
NASGW..... National Association of Sporting Goods Wholesalers (EA)
NASH........ Nahariya to Ashkelon [*Proposed name for possible "super-city" formed by the urban sprawl between these two*] [*Israel*]
NASH........ Nash [*NCIC car make code*]
NASH........ Nashua Motor Express [*Common carrier symbol*]
Nash......... Nashville [*Tennessee*] (AD)
NASH........ National Association of Safety at Home [*British*] (DBA)
NASH........ National Association of Specimen Hunters (AD)
NASH........ North American Society of Homeopaths [*Association*] (EA)
NASHA...... National Association for Speech and Hearing Action (EA)
NASHA...... North American Survival and Homesteading Association (AD)
NASHAC..... National Association for Safety and Health in the Arts and Crafts (EA)
NASHAW.... National Association for Statewide Health and Welfare (EA)
NASHC...... National All States Hobby Club [*Defunct*] (EA)
NashCtr..... Nashville Country Club [*Associated Press*] (SAG)
NashF....... Nash Finch Co. [*Associated Press*] (SAG)
NASHL...... Nashville, TN [*American Association of Railroads railroad junction routing code*]
NASHOC.... North American Student Humanist Organizing Committee [*Defunct*] (EA)
NASHP...... National Academy for State Health Policy (RCD)
Nash Pl..... Nash's Ohio Pleading and Practice [*A publication*] (DLA)
NASHRD.... National Association of State Human Resource Directors (EA)
Nashua..... Nashua Corp. [*Associated Press*] (SAG)
Nashvl....... Nashville (BEE)
NASI......... National A (CDE)
NASI......... NetWare Asynchronous Services Interface [*Computer science*] (PCM)
NASI......... Nigerian Army School of Infantry
NASI......... North American Scientific [*NASDAQ symbol*]
NASI......... Novell Asynchronous Services Interface
NASIB....... Naval Air Station, Imperial Beach (DNAB)
NASIC....... Northeast Academic Science Information Center
NASID....... National Association of the Sixth Infantry Division (EA)
NASIG....... North African Signal Section [*World War II*]
NASIG....... North American Serials Group (EA)
NASIG....... North American Serials Interest Group
NASILP...... National Association of Self-Instructional Language Programs (EA)
NASIMD..... National Association of the Sixth Infantry/Motorized Division [*Later, NASID*] (EA)
Nas Inst..... Nasmith's Institutes of English Private Law [*1873*] [*A publication*] (DLA)
Nas Inst Priv... Nasmith's Institutes of English Private Law [*1873*] [*A publication*] (DLA)
Nas Inst Pub... Nasmith's Institutes of English Public Law [*1873*] [*A publication*] (DLA)
NASIP....... National Aviation Safety Inspection Program [*RSPA*] (TAG)
NASIP....... NATO AEW System Improvement Programme (SAUS)
NASIR....... Nuclear Amplification by Stimulated Isomer Radiation (SAA)
NASIRC..... NASA Automated Systems Incident Response Capability
NASIRE...... National Association of State Information Resource Executives (AAGC)
NASIS....... NASA Aerospace Safety Information System
NASIS....... National Association for State Information Systems (EA)
NASIS....... NATO Subject Indicator System (NATG)
NASIS....... Nevada Statewide Information Service (SAUS)
NASIS....... Northeast Australian Satellite Imagery System (SAUS)
NASISS...... National Association of Sailing Instructors and Sailing Schools (EA)
NASJA....... North American Ski Journalists Association (EA)
NASJAX..... Naval Air Station Jacksonville
NASJE....... National Association of State Judicial Educators
NASL........ Nasal (DAVI)
NASL........ National Association for the Support of Long Term Care (EA)
NASL........ National Association of State Lotteries (EA)
NASL........ Naval Applied Science Laboratory
NASL........ North American Soccer League [*Defunct*] (EA)
NASLAKE... Naval Air Station Lakehurst
NASLAT..... National Association of Securities and Commercial Law Attorneys (NTPA)
NASLI....... National Association for Senior Living Industries (EA)
NASLPA..... North American Soccer League Players Association [*Defunct*] (EA)
NASLR...... National Association of State Land Reclamationists (EA)
NASLS....... National Association of Small Loan Supervisors (EA)
NASM....... Nash Manufacturing [*NCIC trailer make code*]
NASM....... National Air and Space [*Warfare*] Model [*Air Force*]
NASM....... National Air and Space Museum [*Smithsonian Institution*] [*Formerly, NAM*]
NASM....... National Association for School Magazines [*British*] (BI)
NASM....... National Association of Sandwich Manufacturers [*Defunct*] (EA)
NASM....... National Association of Schools of Music (EA)
NASM....... National Association of Service Managers (EA)
NASM....... National Association of Service Merchandising (EA)
NASM....... National Association of State Militia (EA)
NASM....... National Association of Surrogate Mothers (EA)
NASM....... Naval Aviation School of Medicine
NASMA...... Parti Nasionalis Malaysia [*Political party*] (FEA)
NASMAC.... Naval Air Software Management Advisory Committee (MCD)
NASMAP.... NAS Management Automation Program [*FAA*] (TAG)
NASMAR.... National Association of Sack Merchants and Reclaimers [*British*] (BI)
NASMBCM... National Association of Sanitary Milk Bottle Closure Manufacturers [*Defunct*] (EA)
NASMD...... National Association of Medicaid Directors (EA)
NASMD...... National Association of School Music Dealers (EA)
NASMD...... National Association of Sewing Machine Dealers [*Defunct*] (EA)
NASMD...... National Association of Sewing Machine Distributors [*Defunct*] (EA)
NASMD...... National Association of Sheet Music Dealers [*Later, NAMM*] (EA)
NASMD...... National Association of State Medicaid Directors (EA)
NASMD...... Northamerican Association of Sheet Metal Distributors [*Later, division of NHAW*] (EA)
NASMHPD... National Association of State Mental Health Program Directors (EA)
NASMI....... National Association of Secondary Material Industries [*Later, NARI*] (EA)
NAS(MISC)... North American Supply Committee, Miscellaneous [*World War II*]
NASML...... National Air and Space Museum Library [*Smithsonian Institute*] (AD)
NASMO...... National Association of School Meals Organisers [*British*] (DBA)
NASMO...... NATO Starfighter Management Office
NASMP...... National Association of Sales and Marketing Professionals [*Defunct*] (EA)
NASMV...... National Association on Standard Medical Vocabulary (EA)
NASN........ Nason's Delivery [*Common carrier symbol*]
NASN........ National Air Sampling Network [*Public Health Service*]
NASN........ National Air Surveillance Network [*Environmental Protection Agency*]
NASN........ National Association of School Nurses (EA)
NAS/NAE.... National Academy of Sciences/National Academy of Engineering [*Marine science*] (MSC)
NAS/NAE-SECAN... NAS/NAE [*National Academy of Sciences/National Academy of Engineering*] Science and Engineering Committee Advisory to NOAA [*National Oceanic and Atmospheric Administration*] [*Defunct*] (USDC)
NAS/NAE-SECAN... National Academy of Sciences/National Academy of Sciences Engineering Science and Engineering Committee Advisory to NOAA[*National Oceanic and Atmospheric Administration*] [*Marine science*] (OSRA)
NASNI....... Naval Air Station North Island
NAS-NRC... National Academy of Sciences - National Research Council (EA)
NASNSA..... National Association of Special Needs State Administrators (EA)
NASO........ Natchez & Southern Railway Co. [*AAR code*] [*Terminated*]
NASO........ National Adult School Organisation [*British*]
NASO........ National Association of Sports Officials (EA)
NASO........ National Astrological Society [*Defunct*] (EA)
NASO........ National Astronomical Space Observatory
NASO........ Naval Aviation Supply Office
NASO........ Nonacoustic Sensor Operator [*Military*] (CAAL)
NASO........ North American Space Operations (SAUS)
NAS/OAB.... National Academy of Sciences/Ocean Affairs Board [*Marine science*] (MSC)
NASOC...... North American Singer Owners Club (EA)
NASOH...... North American Society for Oceanic History (EA)
NASOH...... North America Society for Oceanic History (SAUS)
NASOPT..... Network Analysis System with Optimization Facility [*NASA*] (IAA)
NA So Rhod... Southern Rhodesia Native Appeal Court Reports [*A publication*] (DLA)

NASORLO.... National Association of State Outdoor Recreation Liaison Officers (EA)
NAS/OSB.... National Academy of Sciences/Ocean Sciences Board [*Marine science*] (MSC)
NASP........ NASI [*Common carrier symbol*]
NASP........ National Achievement Scholarship Program [*National Merit Scholarship Corp.*] (AEBS)
NASP........ National Aerospace Plane (AAGC)
NASP........ National Aerospace Plane Program [*NASA, DoD*]
NASP........ National Airport System Plans [*Department of Transportation*]
NASP........ National Airspace System Plan [*FAA*] (TAG)
NASP........ National Alternative Schools Program
NASP........ National Association for the Southern Poor (EA)
NASP........ National Association of School Psychologists (EA)
NASP........ National Association of Schools and Publishers (EA)
NASP........ National Association of Securities Professionals (EA)
NASP........ National Association of Settlement Purchasers (EA)
NASP........ National Association of Single Persons (EA)
NASP........ National Association of Subrogation Professionals (EA)
NASP........ National Atmospheric Sciences Program
NASP........ National Aviation System Plan [*A publication*]
NASP........ Naval Air Survivability Program (MCD)
NASP........ Navy Advanced SATCOM [*Satellite Communications*] Program (ANA)
NASP........ Navy Airship Program (SAUS)
NASP........ Negro, Anglo-Saxon Protestant
NA-SP....... Nonabrasive-Slightly Polishing (SAUS)
NASP........ North Atlantic Seaboard Program (QUAC)
NASP........ North Atlantic Seaboard Programme (SAUS)
NASPA....... National Association for Public Accountants (HGAA)
NASPA....... National Association of Student Personnel Administrators (EA)
NASPA....... National Society of Public Accountants (MCD)
NaSPA....... National Systems Programmers Association (EA)
NASPA....... North American Soccer Players Association [*Later, NASLPA*] (EA)
NASPAA..... National Association of Schools of Public Affairs and Administration (EA)
NASPAC..... National Airspace System Performance Analysis Capability [*FAA*] (TAG)
NASPALS... Nas Precision Approach and Landing System [*FAA*] (TAG)
Nas Par..... Nasionale Party [*National Party*] [*Political party*] (AD)
NASPCS..... National Advisory Service for Parents of Children with a Stoma (NRGU)
NASPD...... National Association of Plumbing Specialty Distributors (NTPA)
NASPD...... National Association of State Park Directors (EA)
NASPD...... National Association of Steel Pipe Distributors (EA)
NASPE....... National Association for Sport and Physical Education (EA)
NASPE....... National Association of State Personnel Executives (EA)
NASPE....... North American Society of Pacing and Electrophysiology (EA)
NASPENSA... Naval Air Station Pensacola
Nas Pers.... Nasionale Pers [*National Press*] [*South Africa*] (AD)
NASPG...... North American Society for Pediatric Gastroenterology [*Later, NASPGN*] (EA)
NASPGN.... North American Society for Pediatric Gastroenterology and Nutrition (EA)
NASPHV..... National Association of State Public Health Veterinarians (EA)
NASP JPO... NASP Joint Program Office (SAUS)
NASPL....... North American Association of State and Provincial Lotteries (NTPA)
NASPM...... National Association of Seed Potato Merchants [*British*] (BI)
NASPM...... National Association of Slipper and Playshoe Manufacturers (EA)
NASPO...... National Airspace System Program Office [*FAA*] (MCD)
NASPO...... National Alliance of Statewide Preservation Organizations (EA)
NASPO...... National Association of State Purchasing Officials (EA)
NASPO...... NATO Starfighter Production Organization
NASPO...... Naval Air System Program Office (SAUS)
NASPOG.... North American Society for Psychosocial Obstetrics and Gynecology (SEAT)
NASPP...... National Association of Stock Plan Professionals (EA)
NASPPR..... National Association of Service Providers in Private Rehabilitation (NTPA)
NASPR...... NASA Procurement Regulation (KSC)
NASPRFMR... National Association of Superintendents of Public Residential Facilities for theMentally Retarded
NASPSM.... National Association of Shirt, Pajama, and Sportswear Manufacturers [*Later, AAMA*]
NASPSO..... National Association of Special Police and Security Officers (EA)
NASPSPA... North American Society for the Psychology of Sport and Physical Activity (EA)
Na-Spt....... Sodium Spot [*Urine Test*] [*Biochemistry*] (DAVI)
NASQAN.... National Stream Quality Accounting Network [*Department of the Interior*]
NASQUON... Naval Air Station Quonset Point
NASR........ National Annual Symposium on Reliability [*IEEE*] (MCD)
NASR........ National Association of Sitter Registries [*Defunct*] (EA)
NASR........ National Association of Solvent Recyclers (EA)
NASR........ National Association of Swine Records (EA)
NASR........ Naval & Air Staff Requirement (SAUS)
NASRA...... National Association of State Retirement Administrators (EA)
NASRC...... National Association of State Racing Commissioners [*Later, ARCI*] (EA)
NASRC...... North American Salmon Research Center [*Later, Atlantic Salmon Research Institute*] [*Canada*] [*Research center*] (RCD)
NASRC...... North Atlantic Salmon Research Center [*Marine science*] (MSC)
NASRN...... National Association of State Radio Networks (EA)
NASRO...... National Association of Shooting Range Owners (EA)
NASRP...... National Association of Special and Reserve Police [*Defunct*]
NASRP...... National Association of State Recreation Planners (EA)
NASRPM.... National Association of State River Program Managers (EA)
NASRR...... North American Search and Range RADAR [*Military*]
NASRS...... Non-Available Status Reporting System (SAUS)
NASRS...... Not Available Status Report System [*DoD*]
NASRU...... Naval Air Systems Command Reserve Unit (MCD)
NASRWCBL... National Amalgamated Society of Railway Wagon and Carriage Builders and Lifters [*A union*] [*British*]
NASS........ Narrow Angle Sun Sensor (SAA)
NASS........ Nassau (ROG)
Nass......... Nassau, Bahamas (AD)
NASS........ National Accident Sampling System [*National Highway Traffic Safety Admini stration*] [*Washington, DC*]
NASS........ National Agricultural Statistics Service [*Department of Agriculture*] [*Information service or system*] (IID)
NASS........ National Aids Support System [*Military*] (SAA)
NASS........ National Alliance for Safe Schools (EA)
NASS........ National Alliance of Supermarket Shoppers (EA)
NASS........ National Ankylosing Spondylitis Society [*British*] (DBA)
NASS........ National Association for Small Schools [*British*] (DI)
NASS........ National Association of Saw Shops (EA)
NASS........ National Association of School Superintendents (AD)
NASS........ National Association of Secretarial Services [*St. Petersburg, FL*] (EA)
NASS........ National Association of Secretaries of State (EA)
NASS........ National Association of Specialized Schools [*Defunct*] (EA)
NASS........ National Association of Steel Stockholders (MHDB)
NASS........ National Association of Suggestion Systems (EA)
NASS........ National Association of Summer Sessions [*Later, NAASS*]
NASS........ National Automotive Sampling System
NASS........ Naval Air Signal School
NASS........ Naval Anti-Submarine School (SAUS)
NASS........ Naval Armaments Stores System (PDAA)
NASS........ Navigation Satellite System (PDAA)
NASS........ Navy Advent Ship Station (SAA)
NASS........ Network Access Switching Subsystem [*Telecommunications*] (MCD)
NASS........ North African Special Service Section [*World War II*]
NASS........ North American Shagya-Arabian Society (EA)
NASS........ North American Spine Society (EA)
NASS........ North American Super Sports [*Defunct*] (EA)
NAS(S)...... North American Supply Committee, Scientific Subcommittee [*World War II*]
NASSA...... National Aerospace Services Association [*Defunct*] (EA)
NASSA...... National Art School Students' Association [*Australia*]
NASSA...... North American State Securities Administrators
NASSAM.... National Association for the Self-Supporting Active Ministry (EA)
NASS & LS... National Association of State Savings and Loan Supervisors [*Later, ACSSS*] (EA)
NASSB...... National Association of Supervisors of State Banks [*Later, CSBS*] (EA)
NASSC...... National Alliance on Shaping Safer Cities [*Later, NASC*] (EA)
NASSCO..... National Association of Sewer Service Companies (EA)
NASSCO..... National Steel & Shipbuilding Co.
NASSCOM... National Association of Software and Service Companies
NASSD...... National Association of School Security Directors (EA)
NASSD...... National Association of Sign Supply Distributors (NTPA)
NASSD...... North American Society of Scaffold Professionals (NTPA)
NASSDC..... National Social Science Documentation Centre [*Information service or system*] (IID)
NASSDE..... National Association of State Supervisors of Distributive Education (EA)
NASSDOC... National Social Science Documentation Centre [*Information service or system*] (IID)
NASSDSE... National Association of State Supervisors and Directors of Secondary Education (EA)
NAS/SEC.... National Academy of Sciences' Site Evaluation Committee
NASSH...... North American Society for Sport History (EA)
NASSHE..... National Association of State Supervisors of Home Economics [*Later, NASSVHE*]
NASSL....... National Association of Spanish Speaking Librarians (EA)
NASSLEO... National Association of School Safety and Law Enforcement Officers (NTPA)
NASSM...... National Association of Scissors and Shears Manufacturers (EA)
NASSM...... National Association of State Supervisors of Music (EA)
NASSM...... North American Society for Sport Management (EA)
NASSNC..... National Association of State School Nurse Consultants (EA)
NASSO...... National Association of Socialist Students' Organizations [*Political party*] (AD)
NASSP...... National Association of Secondary School Principals (EA)
NASSP...... North American Society for Social Philosophy (EA)
NASSP-B.... National Association of Secondary School Principals. Bulletin [*A publication*] (BRI)
NASSPE..... National Alliance of Spanish-Speaking People for Equality (EA)
NASSR...... Nahichevan Autonomous Soviet Socialist Republic (AD)
NASSS...... National Association of Support for Small Schools [*British*] (DBA)
NASSS...... North American Society for the Sociology of Sport (EA)
NASSSA..... National Association of State Social Security Administrators [*Later, NCSSSA*] (EA)
NASSTA..... National Association of Secretaries of State Teachers Associations [*Later, NCSEA*] (EA)
NASSTIE.... National Association of State Supervisors of Trade and Industrial Education (EA)
NASSTRAC... National Small Shipments Traffic Conference [*Acronym now used as official name of association*] (EA)
NASSTRAC... National Small Shipments Traffic Council
NASSVHE... National Association of State Supervisors of Vocational Home Economics (EA)

NAST........ National Association of Schools of Theatre (EA)
NAST........ National Association of State Treasurers (EA)
NAST........ Naval & Air Staff Target (SAUS)
NAST........ Navigation/Attack Systems Trainer (PDAA)
NAST........ Navy Advent Ship Terminal (SAA)
NAST........ Nuclear Accident Support Team [*Canada*]
NASTA....... National Association of State Text Book Administrators (EA)
NASTAD..... National Alliance of State and Territorial AIDS [*Acquired Immune-Deficiency Syndrome*] Directors (NTPA)
NASTAD..... Naval Acoustic Sensor Training Aids Department (DNAB)
NASTAR..... National Standard Race [*Skiing*]
NASTART... Normal After Start (SAUS)
NASTAT..... North American Society of Teachers of the Alexander Technique (EA)
NASTBD..... National Association of State Text Book Directors [*Later, NASTA*] (EA)
Nastc........ Nastech Pharmaceutical Co., Inc. [*Associated Press*] (SAG)
NASTC....... Naval Air Station Twin Cities (DNAB)
NASTD...... National Association of State and Territorial Apprenticeship Directors [*Bureau of Apprenticeship and Training*] [*Department of Labor*]
NASTD...... National Association of State Telecommunications Directors (EA)
Nastech..... Nastech Pharmaceutical Co., Inc. [*Associated Press*] (SAG)
NASTEMP... National Association of State Educational Media Professionals (EA)
NASTI....... Naval Air Station, Terminal Island (AD)
NASTI....... Next Assembly Support Table Index [*Aerospace*] (MCD)
NASTI....... North American Society for Trenchless Technology (SAUS)
NASTL....... National Anti-Steel-Trap League (AD)
NASTOCK... North American Stock Market [*I. P. Sharp Associates*] [*Canada*] [*Information service or system*]
NASTPHV... National Association of State and Territorial Public Health Veterinarians [*Later, NASPHV*] (EA)
NASTRAN... NASA Structural Analysis [*Computer program*]
NAS/TRB.... National Academy of Sciences/Transportation Board [*Marine science*] (MSC)
NASTS....... National Association for Science, Technology, and Society (EA)
NASTT....... North American Society for Trenchless Technology (EA)
NASTX....... Phoenix Equity Opportunities Cl.A [*Mutual fund ticker symbol*] (SG)
NASU........ Nashua Manufacturing Company [*NCIC trailer make code*]
NASU........ Nassau Leasing [*Intermodal shipping container symbol*] (TVRC)
NASU........ National Adult School Union [*British*] (DAS)
NASU........ National Association of State Universities [*Later, NASULGC*]
NASU........ National Association of System 3 Users (IAA)
NASU........ Navy Air Support Unit
NASU........ Navy Underwater Sound Laboratory (MUGU)
NASU........ North American Singers Union (EA)
NASUA....... National Association of State Units on Aging (EA)
NASUCA..... National Association of State Utility Consumer Advocates (EA)
NASULGC... National Association of State Universities and Land-Grant Colleges (EA)
NASUP...... National Association on Service to Unmarried Parents (EA)
NAS-UWT... National Association of Schoolmasters - Union of Women Teachers [*British*]
NASV........ International Academy of Sports Vision [*Formerly, National Academy of Sports Vision*] (EAIO)
NASV........ National Academy of Sports Vision (EA)
NASVG...... Nordic Association for Study and Vocational Guidance [*See also NRSY*] (EAIO)
NASVH...... National Association of State Veterans Homes (EA)
NASVL....... Nashville, IL [*American Association of Railroads railroad junction routing code*]
NASVO...... National Association of State Vocal Organizations (EA)
NASW....... National Association of Science Writers (EA)
NASW....... National Association of Social Workers (EA)
NASW....... National Association of Social Workers National Committee on Lesbian and Gay Issues (EA)
NASW....... North American Slope Water [*Oceanography*] (MSC)
NASWA...... North American Shortwave Association (EA)
NASW-AZ... National Association of Social Workers, Arizona Chapter (EARSL)
NASW-CT... National Association of Social Workers - Connecticut Chapter (EARSL)
NASWDU.... Naval Air/Sea Warfare Development Unit (SAUS)
NASWF...... Naval Air Special Weapons Facility
NASWHP.... National Association of Sheltered Workshops and Homebound Programs [*Later, NARF*] (EA)
NASWM..... National Association of Scottish Woollen Manufacturers [*British*] (BI)
NASW-M.... National Association of Social Workers - Massachusetts Chapter (EARSL)
NASW-NYS... National Association of Social Workers - New York State Chapter (EARSL)
NASW-OC... National Association of Social Workers - Ohio Chapter (EARSL)
NASWS...... National Aeronautics and Space Administration White Sands [*Proving ground*]
NASWS...... Naval Anti Submarine Warfare Systems (ACAE)
NASWSC.... North American Society for Water and Soil Conservation
NASWSO.... National Association of Soft Water Service Operators [*Later, WQA*]
NASW-VA... National Association of Social Workers - Virginia Chapter (EARSL)
NASW-VT... National Association of Social Workers, Vermont Chapter (EARSL)
NASW-WI... National Association of Social Workers - Wisconsin Chapter (EARSL)
NASX........ NASA Railroad [*Federal Railroad Administration identification code*]
NAT.......... Information Content Natural Unit [*Information theory*]
NAT.......... N-Acetyltransferase [*An enzyme*]
NAT.......... N-Acetyltryptophan [*Biochemistry*]
NAT.......... NASA Apollo Trajectory (KSC)
NAT.......... NASA STI [*Scientific and Technical Information*] Facility, BWI Airport, MD [*Baltimore-Washington International*] [*OCLC symbol*] (OCLC)
NAT.......... Natal [*Brazil*] [*Airport symbol*] (OAG)
Nat.......... Natalia (AD)
Nat.......... Natalie (AD)
Nat.......... Natasha (AD)
Nat.......... Nathalie (AD)
Nat.......... Nathan (AD)
Nat.......... Nathaniel (AD)
nat.......... Nation (AD)
Nat.......... Nation [*A publication*] (BRI)
NAT.......... Nation
Nat.......... National (AD)
nat.......... National (AD)
NAT.......... National
NAT.......... National Academy of Teaching (EA)
NAT.......... National Agency for Tourism
NAT.......... National AIDS Trust (SAUS)
NAT.......... National Air Transport (SAA)
NAT.......... National Arbitration Tribunal [*British*]
NAT.......... National Association of Toolmakers [*A union*] [*British*]
NAT.......... National Drug Co. [*Research code symbol*]
Nat.......... Nationalist (ODBW)
NAT.......... Nationalist (WDAA)
NAT.......... Nationality (AAG)
Nat.......... National Party [*Australia*] [*Political party*]
NAT.......... National Transport, Inc.
NAT.......... Native (AAG)
nat.......... Native (AD)
NAT.......... Nativity [*Church calendars*] (ROG)
NAT.......... Natrolite [*A zeolite*]
NAT.......... Natural (AAG)
nat.......... Natural (AD)
Nat.......... Natural (ODBW)
nat.......... Naturalist (AD)
nat.......... Naturalization (AD)
Nat.......... Naturalized [*Botany*]
NAT.......... Natural Unit (IAA)
nat.......... Nature (AD)
Nat.......... Nature [*or Naturalist*]
NAT.......... Naturist (WDAA)
NAT.......... Natus [*Birth*] [*Latin*]
nat.......... Natuurkunde [*Natural Science*] [*Dutch*] (AD)
NAT.......... Naval Air Technical Services Facility (MUGU)
NAT.......... Naval Air Terminal
NAT.......... Naval Air Training
NAT.......... Naval Anthropomorphic Teleoperater (DNAB)
NAT.......... Navigational Aids Technician (DNAB)
NAT.......... Nearly Airborne Truck (PDAA)
NAT.......... Neonatal Alloimmune Thrombocytopenia [*Medicine*] (EDAA)
NAT.......... Network Address Transaction [*Computer science*] (AGLO)
NAT.......... Network Address Translation [*Computer science*]
NAT.......... Network Analysis Team
NAT.......... Network Analysis Technique (IAA)
NAT.......... Neuralgic Amyotrophy [*Medicine*] (EDAA)
NAT.......... New Age Thinking
NAT.......... New Attainment Target (AIE)
NAT.......... Nitric Acid Trihydrate [*Inorganic chemistry*]
NAT.......... Nitrosoanatabine [*Also, NAtB*] [*Organic chemistry*]
NAT.......... No Action Taken
NAT.......... Node Attached Table (SAUS)
NAT.......... Non-accidental Trauma [*Medicine*] (EDAA)
NAT.......... Non-Verbal Ability Tests [*Intelligence test*]
NAT.......... Nordic American Tanker Shipping Ltd. [*AMEX symbol*] (SAG)
nat.......... Normal Allowed Time (AD)
NAT.......... Normal Allowed Time (IEEE)
NAT.......... North African Theater [*World War II*]
NAT.......... North Atlantic Air, Inc. [*ICAO designator*] (FAAC)
NAT.......... North Atlantic Region [*USTTA*] (TAG)
NAT.......... North Atlantic Regional Area [*Aviation*]
NAT.......... North Atlantic Tracks (HLLA)
NAT.......... North Atlantic Traffic (PIPO)
NAT.......... North Atlantic Treaty
NAT.......... Northern Airborne Technology Ltd. (SAUS)
NAT.......... Not Air Transportable (ACAE)
NAT.......... Not Attending Training
NAT3......... Naturally Aspirated Tier 3 [*Auto industry consortium*]
NATA......... N-Acetyl-Tryptophan-Amide [*Organic chemistry*]
NATA......... N-Acetyltyramine [*Biochemistry*]
NATA......... Narcotic Addict Treatment Act of 1974
NATA......... National Airfreight Trucking Alliance (EA)
NATA......... National Air Transportation Association (EA)
NATA......... National Association of Tax Accountants [*Defunct*] (EA)
NATA......... National Association of Tax Administrators (EA)
NATA......... National Association of Teachers' Agencies (EA)
NATA......... National Association of Teachers of Agriculture [*Australia*]
NATA......... National Association of Temple Administrators (EA)
NATA......... National Association of Testing Authorities (IAA)
NATA......... National Association of Transportation Advertising [*Later, Transit Advertising Association*]
NATA......... National Athletic Trainers Association (EA)
NATA......... National Automated Transportation Association (AD)
NATA......... National Automobile Transporters Association [*Detroit, MI*] (EA)
NATA......... National Automotive Trade Association
NATA......... National Aviation Trades Association
NATA......... Natural Alternatives, Inc. [*NASDAQ symbol*] (COMM)

NATA......... North American Tasar Association (EA)
NATA......... North American Telecommunications Association (EA)
NATA......... North American Telephone Association (EA)
NATA......... North American Trakehner Association (EA)
NATA......... North American Travel Association [*Defunct*] (EA)
NATA......... North Atlantic Treaty Alliance
NATA......... Northern Air Transport Association (SAUS)
NATA......... Numerical Analysis Thermal Application (VLIE)
Nat Absten... National Abstentionalist (AD)
NATAC....... North Atlantic Chemistry Experiment (QUAC)
NATACMS... Navy Tactical Missile System (SAUS)
NATAD....... National Association of Textile and Apparel Distributors [*Defunct*] (EA)
NATAF....... Northwest African Tactical Air Force [*World War II*]
Natal LJ..... Natal Law Journal [*South Africa*] [*A publication*] (DLA)
Natal LM.... Natal Law Magazine [*South Africa*] [*A publication*] (DLA)
Natal LQ.... Natal Law Quarterly [*South Africa*] [*A publication*] (DLA)
Natal LR.... Natal Law Reports [*South Africa*] [*A publication*] (DLA)
NatAlt....... Natural Alternatives International [*Associated Press*] (SAG)
NA T & N... Selected Decisions of the Native Appeal Court, Transvaal and Natal [*A publication*] (DLA)
NATAP....... North American Trade Automation Prototype
NATAPROBU... National Association of Professional Bureaucrats [*Later, INATAPROBU*]
Nat Arc...... National Archives (AD)
NATARI...... National Association of Traffic Accident Reconstructionists and Investigators (EA)
NATAS....... National Academy of Television Arts and Sciences (EA)
NATAS....... National Appropriate Technology Assistance Service [*Butte, MT*] [*Department of Energy*] (GRD)
NATAS....... NOAA AVHRR Transcription and Archive System (SAUS)
NATAS....... North American Thermal Analysis Society (EA)
Nat Assn.... National Association (AD)
natat......... Natation (AD)
NATaT....... National Association of Towns and Townships (EA)
NatAutoC.... National Auto Credit, Inc. Holding [*Associated Press*] (SAG)
NATAW...... National Association of Textile and Apparel Wholesalers [*Later, NATAD*] (EA)
NATB........ National Association of Ticket Brokers (EA)
NATB........ National Automobile Theft Bureau (EA)
NATB........ Naval Air Training Base
NATB........ Naval Training Bulletin
NAtB......... Nitrosoanatabine [*Organic chemistry*]
NATB........ Nonreading Aptitude Test Battery [*US Employment Service*] [*Department of Labor*]
Nat Bank Reg... National Bankruptcy Register Reports [*United States*] [*A publication*] (DLA)
Nat Bankr Law... National Bankruptcy Law [*A publication*] (DLA)
Nat Bankr N & R... National Bankruptcy News and Reports [*A publication*] (DLA)
Nat Bankr R... National Bankruptcy Register [*United States*] [*A publication*] (DLA)
Nat Bankr Reg... National Bankruptcy Register [*United States*] [*A publication*] (DLA)
Nat Bankr Rep... National Bankruptcy Register Reports [*United States*] [*A publication*] (DLA)
Nat Bar J... National Bar Journal [*A publication*] (DLA)
NATBASES... Naval Air Training Bases
Nat BC...... National Bank Cases [*United States*] [*A publication*] (DLA)
NatBev...... National Beverage Corp. [*Associated Press*] (SAG)
NATBF....... Northwest African Tactical Bomber Force [*World War II*]
Nat BJ....... National Bar Journal [*A publication*] (DLA)
NATBM....... Navy Anti-Tactical Ballistic Missile (SAUS)
Nat BR...... National Bankruptcy Register [*United States*] [*A publication*] (DLA)
Nat Brev.... Fitzherbert's Natura Brevium [*A publication*] (DLA)
Nat Bur Econ Res... National Bureau of Economic Research (AD)
NAT BUR ECON RES... National Bureau of Economic Research (WDAA)
Nat Bur Stand Circ... National Bureau of Standards Circular [*A publication*] (AD)
NAtC......... Columbia-Greene Community College, Athens, NY [*Library symbol*] [*Library of Congress*] (LCLS)
NATC........ National Air Taxi Conference (SAA)
NATC........ National Air Traffic Controllers (AD)
NATC........ National Air Transportation Conferences [*Later, NATA*]
NATC........ National Alcohol Tax Coalition (EA)
NATC........ National Association of Taurine Clubs
NATC........ National Association of Tax Consultors (EA)
NATC........ National Association of Telemarketing Consultants [*Defunct*] (EA)
NATC........ Naval Air Technical Training Center (ACAE)
NATC........ Naval Air Test Center
NATC........ Naval Air Training Center
NATC........ Naval Air Training Command (CAAL)
NATC........ Nevada Automotive Test Center (SAUS)
NATC........ Nordic Amateur Theatre Council (EAIO)
NATC........ Nordic Automobile Technical Committee [*Defunct*] [*Denmark*] (EAIO)
NATC........ North Atlantic Treaty Council (NATG)
NATC........ Northwest African Training Command [*World War II*]
NATC........ Noval Air Test Center (IAA)
NATCA....... National Air Traffic Control Administration (SAUS)
NATCA....... National Air Traffic Controllers Association (EA)
NATCA....... National Association of Trial Court Administrators (EA)
NATCA....... North American Trap Collector Association (EA)
NATCA PAC... National Air Traffic Controllers Association PAC [*Washington, DC*] (PACS)
NAT-CAT..... Consortium for Natural and Technological Catastrophes [*Emergency Management*] (EMA)
NATCC....... North American Touring Car Championship [*Automobile racing*]
NATCC....... Northwest African Troop Camer Command (SAUS)
NATCC....... Northwest African Troop Carrier Command [*World War II*]
NATCD....... National Association of Tobacco & Confectionery Distributors (AC)
NATCECT... National Centre for English Cultural Tradition [*University of Sheffield*] [*United Kingdom*] (RCD)
NATCEM..... National Cemetery
NATCENTATHLIT... National Centre for Athletic Literature (NITA)
NATCG....... National Association of Training Corps for Girls [*British*] (BI)
Natch........ Natchez (AD)
NATCH....... Natchez, MS [*American Association of Railroads railroad junction routing code*]
natch........ Naturally (AD)
NATCO....... National Association of Transit Consumer Organizations (EA)
NATCO....... National Automatic Tool Co.
NATCO....... National Coordinator [*Marine science*] (MSC)
NATCO....... National Tank Co. (AD)
NATCO....... Navy Air Traffic Coordinating Officer
NATCO....... North American Transplant Coordinators Organization (EA)
NATCO....... Northern Advanced Technologies Corp. [*Research center*] (RCD)
NATCO....... Nuclear Auditing and Testing Co.
natcol....... Natural Color (AD)
NATCOL..... Natural Food Colours Association [*Basel, Switzerland*] (EAIO)
natcom...... National Communications (AD)
NATCOM.... National Communications Symposium [*IEEE*]
NATCOM.... National Conference on Communications (MCD)
NATCOM.... NATO Communication (NATG)
Nat Con..... Nature Conservancy (BARN)
NatConv..... National Convenience Stores [*Associated Press*] (SAG)
NATCS....... National Air Traffic Control Service (IEEE)
NATCS....... National Air Traffic Control System (NATG)
Nat D........ De Natura Deorum [*of Cicero*] [*Classical studies*] (OCD)
NATD........ National Association of Teachers of Dancing [*British*] (DBA)
NATD........ National Association of Telecommunications Dealers (EA)
NATD........ National Association of Test Directors (EA)
NATD........ National Association of Tobacco Distributors (EA)
NATD........ National Association of Tool Dealers [*British*] (BI)
NATD........ National Diagnostics, Inc. [*NASDAQ symbol*] (SAG)
NATD........ North American Association of Telecommunications Dealers (EA)
NATD........ Nuclear and Advanced Technology Division (SAUS)
NATDEC..... Naval Air Training Division Engineering Command (DNAB)
NATDEFSM... National Defense Service Medal [*Military decoration*]
Nat Dem.... National Democrats [*Political party*] (AD)
NatDiag..... National Diagnostics, Inc. [*Associated Press*] (SAG)
NATDP....... National Agricultural Text-Digitizing Project [*National Agricultural Library*]
NATDS....... National Association of Truck Driving Schools (EA)
NATDS....... Naval Air Tactical Data System (MCD)
NATDS....... Navy Automated Transportation Data System (DNAB)
NATDW...... National Diagnostics Wrrt [*NASDAQ symbol*] (TTSB)
NATE......... National Association for Teachers of Electronics [*Defunct*] (EA)
NATE......... National Association for the Teaching of English (AD)
NATE......... National Association of Teachers of English
NATE......... National Association of Temple Educators (EA)
NATE......... National Association of Trade Exchanges
NATE......... Native American Teacher Education (AD)
NATE......... Neutral Atmosphere Temperature Experiment
NATE......... North American Technician Excellence [*Association*] (EA)
NATEBE..... National Association of Teacher Educators for Business Education [*DeKalb, IL*] (EA)
NATEBOE... National Association of Teacher Educators for Business and Office Education [*Later, NATEBE*] (EA)
NATEC....... Naval Air Technical Evaluation Center (IAA)
NATEC....... Naval Air Training and Experimental Command
NATECHTRA... Naval Air Technical Training (DNAB)
NATECHTRACEN... Naval Air Technical Training Center
NATECHTRAU... Naval Air Technical Training Unit
NATECOM... Naval Airship Training and Experimentation Command
NatEdu....... National Education Corp. [*Associated Press*] (SAG)
NATEF....... National Automotive Technicians Education Foundation (EA)
NATEFACS... National Association of Teacher Educators for Family and Consumer Sciences (NTPA)
NATEL....... Nortronics Automatic Test Equipment Language [*Computer science*]
NATELCA... National Association for Teaching English and other Community Languages to Adults [*Formerly, NATELSA*] (AIE)
NATELO..... NATO maritime air Telecommunications Organization (SAUS)
NatEng...... National Energy Group [*Associated Press*] (SAG)
NATES....... National Analysis of Trends in Emergency Systems [*Canada*] (MSC)
NATESA..... National Alliance of Television and Electronics Services Associations (IAA)
NATESA..... National Association of Television and Electronic Servicers of America [*N ESSDA*] [*Absorbed by*] (EA)
NATESLA... National Association for Teaching English as a Secondary Language to Adults [*British*] (DI)
NATESOL... National Association of Teachers of English for Speakers of Other Languages [*England*]
NATESTCEN... Naval Air Test Center
NATEVHE... National Association of Teacher Educators for Vocational Home Economics (EA)
NATEX....... National Stock Exchange [*Dissolved, 1975*]
NATF......... National Automobile Theft Bureau
NATF......... Naval Advanced Tactical Fighter (SAUS)
NATF......... Naval Air Test Facility
NATF......... Navy Advanced Tactical Fighter (MCD)
NATF......... New Arrivals Task Force (MCD)

NATFACS... National Association of Teachers of Family and Consumer Sciences (NTPA)
NATFARMPAC... National Farmers Union PAC [*Aurora, CO*] (PACS)
NATFB .... National Archives Trust Fund Board
NATFC .... North American Toyah Fan Club (EA)
Nat Fed ..... National Federation (AD)
NatFGs ...... National Fuel Gas Co. [*Associated Press*] (SAG)
NATFHE ..... National Association of Teachers in Further and Higher Education [*British*]
Nat For ...... National Forum [*A publication*] (BRI)
NATFREQU... Natural Frequency (IAA)
NATF-SI... Naval Air Test Facility - Ship Installations
NATG .... National Association of Training Groups [*British*] (DBA)
NATGA .... National Amateur Tobacco Growers' Association [*British*] (BI)
Nat Gal ...... National Gallery (AD)
NAT GAL .... National Gallery [*London*] (WDAA)
NatGam ..... National Gaming Corp. [*Associated Press*] (SAG)
Nat Geog Mag... National Geographic Magazine [*A publication*] (AD)
NatGeogRes... National Geographic Research [*A publication*] (ABAR)
Nat Geogr Mag... National Geographic Magazine (SAUS)
NatGolf ...... National Golf Properties [*Associated Press*] (SAG)
NatGsO ...... National Gas & Oil Co. [*Associated Press*] (SAG)
NATH .... Nathan's Famous [*NASDAQ symbol*] (TTSB)
NATH .... Nathan's Famous, Inc. [*NASDAQ symbol*] (NQ)
Nathan ...... Nathan's Common Law of South Africa [*A publication*] (DLA)
Nathans ..... Nathan's Famous, Inc. [*Associated Press*] (SAG)
Nath B .... Nathaniel Bowditch (AD)
NATHE .... National Associations of Teachers of Home Economics [*British*]
NATHHAN... National Challenged Homeschoolers Associated Network (PAZ)
nat hist ...... Natural History (AD)
Nathl .... Nathaniel (AD)
NatHlth ...... Natural Health Trends Corp. [*Associated Press*] (SAG)
NatHme ..... National Home Centers [*Commercial firm*] [*Associated Press*] (SAG)
NatHP .... Nationwide Health Properties, Inc. [*Associated Press*] (SAG)
NATI .... National Instrument Corp. [*NASDAQ symbol*] (SAG)
NATIBO ...... North American Technology and Industrial Base Organization
NATICH ...... National Air Toxics Information Clearinghouse [*Environmental Protection Agency*] (GFGA)
NATIDC ...... Netherlands-Australia Trade and Industrial Development Council (AD)
NATIE .... National Association for Trade and Industrial Education (EA)
NATII .... National Association of Trade and Industrial Instructors (EA)
NATINADS... NATO Integrated Air Defense System (NATG)
Nat Inc Tax Mag... National Income Tax Magazine [*A publication*] (DLA)
Nat Inf .... Nature Information (SAUS)
NatInst ...... National Instrument Corp. [*Associated Press*] (SAG)
Nat Inst Econ Rev... National Institute Economic Review [*A publication*] (JLIT)
nation .... Nationality (AD)
National ADDA... National Attention-Deficit Disorder Association (EA)
National PTA... National Congress of Parents and Teachers (PAZ)
NATIP .... NATO Information & Press office (SAUS)
NATIP .... Navy Technical Information Program
NATIS .... National Information Systems [*Later, GIP*] [*UNESCO*]
NATIS .... Naval Air Training Information System
NATIS .... North Atlantic Treaty Information Service (NATG)
Nativ .... Nativity (AD)
NATIV .... Nativity
NATIV .... North American Test Instrument Vehicle [*Air Force test rocket*]
NATIVE ...... North American Test Instrument Vehicle [*Air force test rocket*] (IAA)
Nat J Leg Ed... National Journal of Legal Education [*A publication*] (DLA)
NATK .... North American Technologies Corp. [*NASDAQ symbol*] (SAG)
NATK .... North Amer Technologies Group [*NASDAQ symbol*] (TTSB)
NATKE .... National Association of Theatrical and Kine Employees (AD)
NATKE .... National Association of Theatrical and Kinema Employees [*British*] (DI)
NATL .... NAI Technologies [*NASDAQ symbol*] (SAG)
NATL .... National (AAG)
natl .... National (AD)
Natl .... National (AL)
NATL .... National Agricultural Transportation League [*Defunct*] (EA)
NATL .... National Mobile Homes [*NCIC trailer make code*]
NATI .... Natl Instruments [*NASDAQ symbol*] (TTSB)
NATL .... Naval Aeronautical Turbine Laboratory
N Atl .... North Atlantic (AD)
NATL .... North Atlantic Industries, Inc. [*NASDAQ symbol*] (COMM)
N Atlantic Reg Bus L Rev... North Atlantic Regional Business Law Review [*A publication*] (DLA)
NATLAS ..... National Testing Laboratory Accreditation Scheme [*Military*] [*British*]
Nat Law Guild Q... National Lawyers Guild Quarterly [*A publication*] (DLA)
NatlBev ..... National Beverage Corp. [*Associated Press*] (SAG)
NatlCity ..... National City Corp. [*Associated Press*] (SAG)
Natl Civ Rev... National Civic Review [*A publication*] (ILCA)
N Atl Cur... North Atlantic Current (AD)
NATL FOP PAC... National Fraternal Order of Police PAC [*Washington, DC*] (PACS)
Nat L Guild Q... National Lawyers Guild Quarterly [*A publication*] (DLA)
Nat Lib ...... National Liberal (AD)
NatLib .... National Liberal Party [*Australia*] [*Political party*]
Nat Lib ...... National Library of Canada (AD)
NATLIBCAN... National Library of Canada (AD)
NATLIBNZ... National Library of New Zealand (AD)
Nat'l Income Tax Mag... National Income Tax Magazine [*A publication*] (DLA)
Nat LJ .... Natal Law Journal [*South Africa*] [*A publication*] (DLA)
Nat'l Legal Mag... National Legal Magazine [*A publication*] (DLA)
Nat LM ...... Natal Law Magazine [*South Africa*] [*A publication*] (DLA)
Natlm .... Naturalism (VRA)
Natl Meas Lab Tech Pap CSIRO Anst... Australia. Commonwealth Scientific and Industrial Research Organisation. National Measurement Laboratory. Technical Pape (SAUS)
Nat Louis U... National-Louis University (GAGS)
Nat'l Pub Empl Rep... National Public Employment Reporter [*A publication*] (DLA)
Nat LQ ...... Natal Law Quarterly [*South Africa*] [*A publication*] (DLA)
Nat LR ...... Natal Law Reports [*South Africa*] [*A publication*] (ILCA)
Nat L Rec... National Law Record [*A publication*] (DLA)
NatlReg ..... National Registry [*Associated Press*] (SAG)
Nat L Rep... National Law Reporter [*A publication*] (DLA)
Natl Rep Sys... National Reporter System (DLA)
Nat L Rev... National Law Review [*A publication*] (DLA)
NatlRV ...... National R.V. Holdings, Inc. [*Associated Press*] (SAG)
Nat'l School L Rptr... National School Law Reporter [*A publication*] (DLA)
NATLSCO... National Loss Control Service Corporation (EFIS)
NATLSEMICON... National Semiconductor Corp. (IAA)
Natl Stand Lab Tech Pap CSIRO Aust... Australia Commonwealth Scientific and Industrial Research Organisation. National Standards Laboratory. Technical Paper (SAUS)
NatlStl .... National Steel Corp. [*Associated Press*] (SAG)
Natl Wildlife... National Wildlife [*A publication*] (PABS)
NATM .... National Association of Trailer Manufacturers (NTPA)
NATM .... New Austrian Tunneling Method (SAUS)
NATM .... New Austrian Tunnel Method [*Civil engineering*]
NATMA .... National Award and Trophy Manufacturers Association (EA)
NATMAC .... National Air Traffic Management Advisory Committee [*British*]
NATMAP .... Division of National Mapping (SAUS)
NATMAP .... National Mapping (AD)
NATMATMUS... National Automotive and Truck Model and Toy Museum of the United States
NATMC ...... National Advanced Technology Management Conference
NatMFS ..... National Medical Financial Services Corp. [*Associated Press*] (SAG)
NATMH ...... National Association of Teachers of the Mentally Handicapped [*British*]
NatMicr ..... Natural Microsystems Corp. [*Associated Press*] (SAG)
NATMILCOMSYS... National Military Command System
Nat Mon .... National Monument (AD)
NAT MON .... National Monument (WDAA)
NATMSACT... Naval Air Training Support Facility (AAGC)
Nat Mus .... Natal Museum (AD)
NATMUS .... National Automobile and Truck Museum of the United States
NATMUS .... National Automotive and Truck Museum of United States (EA)
Nat Mus .... National Museum (AD)
NATN .... National Association of Theatre Nurses [*British*] (BI)
NATN .... National Association of Traveling Nurses
NATNAV ..... North Atlantic Navigation
NATNAVDENCEN... National Naval Dental Center (DNAB)
NATNAVMEDCEN... National Naval Medical Center [*Bethesda, MD*]
NATNAVRESMASTCONRADSTA... National Naval Reserve Master Control Radio Station (DNAB)
Natn Bank Mon Sum... National Bank. Monthly Summary [*A publication*]
Natn Bank Mon Sum Aust Cond... National Bank of Australasia. Monthly Summary of Australian Conditions [*A publication*]
Nat Neotrop... Natura Neotropicalis [*A publication*] (PABS)
Natnet .... National Network [*Telecommunications*] [*British*]
Natn Farmer... National Farmer [*A publication*]
NatnGv03 .... Nations Government Income Term 2003 [*Associated Press*] (SAG)
NatnGv04 .... Nations Government Income Term 2004 [*Associated Press*] (SAG)
Natn Hosp... National Hospital [*A publication*]
NATNN ...... National Association of Theatre Nurses News [*Medicine*] [*United Kingdom*] (EDAA)
Natn Parks J... National Parks Journal [*A publication*]
Natn Rehab Digest... National Rehabilitation Digest [*A publication*]
NatnsBal .... Nations Balanced Target Maturity Fund [*Associated Press*] (SAG)
NatnsBk ..... NationsBank Corp. [*Associated Press*] (SAG)
Natn Times Mag... National Times Magazine [*A publication*]
NATO .... Narrow-Angle Target of Opportunity [*Photography*] [*NASA*]
NATO .... National Association of Taxicab Owners [*Later, ITA*] (EA)
NATO .... National Association of Telephone Operators [*A union*] [*British*]
NATO .... National Association of Theatre Owners (EA)
NATO .... National Association of Trailer Owners (EA)
NATO .... National Association of Travel Organizations [*Later, TIA*] (EA)
NATO .... No Action, Talk Only (DICI)
NATO .... North African Theater of Operations [*World War II*]
NATO .... North Atlantic Treaty Organization [*Facetious translation: "No Action, Talk Only"*] [*Brussels, Belgium*]
NATO .... Not a Team Operator (BB)
NATOA .... National Association of Telecommunications Officers and Advisors (EA)
NATO AEW... North Atlantic Treaty Organization Airborne Early Warning Program
NATO-AGARD... North Atlantic Treaty Organization - Advisory Group for Aeronautical Research and Development
NATO-ARW... NATO Advanced Research Workshop (SAUS)
Nat Obs ..... National Observer [*A publication*] (AD)
NATODC ..... North Atlantic Treaty Organization Defense College (DNAB)
NATODEFCOL... North Atlantic Treaty Organization Defense College (DNAB)
NATOELLA... North Atlantic Treaty Organization - European Long Lines Agency
NatOilwll ... National Oilwell, Inc. [*Associated Press*] (SAG)
NAT-OJT ..... National On-the-Job Training Program [*Department of Labor*]
NATO Letter... North Atlantic Treaty Organization Letter (SAUS)
NATO-LRSS... North Atlantic Treaty Organization - Long-Range Scientific Studies

NATO MC ... North Atlantic Treaty Organization Military Committee
NATOMILOCGRP... North Atlantic Treaty Organization - Military Oceanography Group (NATG)
NATOPA ..... National Association of Theatre Owners of Pennsylvania (EARSL)
NATOPS ..... Naval Air Training and Operating Procedures Standardization (MCD)
NATOPS ..... Naval Air Training Operating Practices (SAUS)
Nat Ord ..... Natural Order [*Botany*] (BARN)
NATO-RDPP... North Atlantic Treaty Organization - Multilateral Research and Development Production Program
NATO-RDPP... North Atlantic Treaty Organization-Research and Development Production Program (SAUS)
NATOSAT... North Atlantic Treaty Organization Satellite
NATO-SC ... North Atlantic Treaty Organization - Science Committee
NATOUSA... North African Theater of Operations, United States Army [*World War II*]
NATP .... National Association of Tax Practitioners (EA)
NATP .... Natl Power plc [*LO, exchange symbol*] (TTSB)
NATPA....... North America Taiwanese Professors' Association (EA)
NAT PAC .... National PAC [*Political Action Committee*] (EA)
NATPE....... National Association of Television Program Executives (NTCM)
NATPE....... NATPE [*National Association of Television Program Executives*] International (EA)
Nat Peop.... Native Peoples [*A publication*] (BRI)
nat phil ..... Natural Philosophy (AD)
Nat Phil..... Natural Philosophy (BARN)
Nat Pk....... National Park (BARN)
NATPN....... North African Transportation Section [*World War II*]
NatProc ..... National Processing, Inc. [*Associated Press*] (SAG)
NatProp ..... National Propane Partners LP [*Associated Press*] (SAG)
NATPS....... National Association of Trade Protection Societies [*British*] (DBA)
NATR .... Natchez Trace Parkway [*National Park Service designation*]
NATR .... National Association of Tenants and Residents [*British*] (BI)
NATR .... National Association of Toy Retailers [*British*] (BI)
NATR .... National Representative [*Red Cross*]
Nat R .... National Review [*A publication*] (BRI)
NATR .... Natrium [*Sodium*] [*Pharmacy*]
natr .... Natrium [*Sodium*] [*Latin*] (AD)
NATR .... Natural Resources
NATR .... Nature's Sunshine Prod [*NASDAQ symbol*] (TTSB)
NATR .... Nature's Sunshine Products, Inc. [*NASDAQ symbol*] (NQ)
NATR .... No Additional Traffic Reported [*Aviation*]
NATR .... Nordischer Amator Theater Rat [*Nordic Amateur Theatre Council - NATC*] (EAIO)
NATRA....... National Association of Television and Radio Announcers (NTCM)
NATRA....... National Association of Television and Radio Artists [*Inactive*]
NATRA....... Naval Air Training Command (AFIT)
NATRACOM... Naval Air Training Command (DNAB)
NATRADIVENGCOM... Naval Air Training Division Engineering Command (DNAB)
NATRAP..... Narrow-Band Transmission of RADAR Pictures (MCD)
NATRC....... North American Trail Ride Conference (EA)
NatRe .... National Re Corp. [*Associated Press*] (SAG)
NATRE .... North Atlantic Tracer Release Experiment (SAUS)
NatRecd..... National Record Mart, Inc. [*Associated Press*] (SAG)
Nat Reg..... National Register, Edited by Mead [*1816*] [*A publication*] (DLA)
Nat Rept Syst... National Reporter System (DLA)
Nat Resources... Nature and Resources (SAUS)
Nat Resour Environ... Natural Resources & Environment [*A publication*] (PABS)
Nat Resour J... Natural Resources Journal [*A publication*] (PABS)
Nat Resour Model... Natural Resource Modeling [*A publication*] (PABS)
NATRFD ..... National Association of Television-Radio Farm Directors [*Later, NAFB*] (EA)
NATRI .... National Association of Treasurers of Religious Institutes (EA)
NATRI .... Navy Training Requirements Information
NATRIP...... National Association of Tax Reducing Income Plans (NTPA)
NatrlHlth... Natural Health Trends Corp. [*Associated Press*] (SAG)
NATRON..... National Cash Register Electronic Data Processing System (MCD)
NAT-RPG.... North Atlantic Treaty Regional Planning Group (NATG)
NatrSun ..... Natures Sunshine Products [*Associated Press*] (SAG)
NATS .... National Activity to Test Software
NATS .... National Air Toxics Strategy [*Environmental Protection Agency*] (GFGA)
NATS .... National Air Traffic Services [*British*]
NATS .... National Association of Teachers of Singing (EA)
NATS .... National Association of Temporary Services [*Alexandria, VA*] (EA)
NATS .... National Association of Textile Supervisors (EA)
Nats .... Nationalists (AD)
NATS .... National Securities Corp. [*NASDAQ symbol*] (NQ)
Nats .... Natsionalnyii [*National*] [*Russian*] (AD)
NATS .... Naval Air Test Station (AD)
NATS .... Naval Air Transport Service
NATS .... NCAR Airborne Telemetry System (SAUS)
NATS .... NCAR Aircraft Telemetry System (SAUS)
NATS .... Needlework and Accessories Trade Show (ITD)
NATS .... Negative Authorization Terminal System [*Computer science*] (MHDB)
NATS .... New Aircraft Tool System [*Army*]
NATS .... Noise Abatement Test System (FAAC)
NATS .... Nordisk Avisteknisk Samarbetsnamnd [*Nordic Joint Technical Press Board*] [*Sweden*] (EAIO)
NATS .... North American Truffling Society (EA)
NATS .... North Atlantic Track System (SAUS)
NATSA....... National Associated Truck Stops and Associates (EA)
NATSAA ..... NATO Air Traffic Service Advisory Agency (NATG)
NATSC....... National Association of Training School Chaplains (EA)
NATSC....... National Association of Trap and Skeet Clubs (EA)
NAT SC...... Natural Sciences (WDAA)
Nat ScD..... Doctor of Natural Science (AD)
Nat Sci Fdn... National Science Foundation (AD)
NATSECM... National Security Medal
Nat Sec Soc... National Secular Society (AD)
Nat Semi ... National Semiconductor Corp.
NATSEMI ... National Semiconductor Inc. (AD)
NATSF....... Naval Air Technical Services Facility (MCD)
NATSFERRY... Naval Air Transport Service, Ferry Command [*World War II*]
NATSFQADIVLANT... Naval Air Technical Services Facility, Quality Assurance Division, Atlantic (DNAB)
NATSFQADIVPAC... Naval Air Technical Services Facility, Quality Assurance Division, Pacific (DNAB)
NATSIEP... National Aboriginal and Torres Strait Islander Education Policy [*Australia*]
NATSILCO... National Silver Industries, Inc. (EFIS)
NATSJA ..... National Association of Training School and Juvenile Agencies [*Later, NAJCA*] (EA)
NATSLANT... Naval Air Transport Service, Atlantic Wing [*World War II*]
NATSO....... National Association of Truck Stop Operators (EA)
NATSOPA ... National Society of Operative Printers and Assistants [*British*]
NAT sound... Natural Sound [*Broadcasting*] (WDMC)
NATSPAC ... Naval Air Transport Service, Pacific Wing [*World War II*]
NATSPG..... North Atlantic Systems Planning Group [*Military*] (WDAA)
NATSRA..... North American Thermal Soil Recycling Association (NTPA)
NATSS....... National Association of Temporary and Staffing Services (NTPA)
NAT-STD .... NATO STANAG International Standards
NATSU....... Naval Air Technical Services Unit (NVT)
NATSU....... Nominated Air Traffic Service Unit (DA)
Nat Sup ..... National Superannuation (AD)
NatSurg ..... National Surgery Centers, Inc. [*Associated Press*] (SAG)
NATSY....... National Stock Yards, IL [*American Association of Railroads railroad junction routing code*]
NATSYN ..... Natural and Synthetic [*Type of long-wearing rubber, which is actually wholly synthetic*]
NATT......... National Association of Teachers of Travellers [*British*] (DBA)
NATT......... National Association of Tinsmiths and Tilers [*Canada*] (EAIO)
NATT......... National Association of Towns and Township Officials (EA)
NATT......... Naval Air Technical Training
N Att......... Naval Attache (AD)
N ATT......... Naval Attache (WDAA)
NATT......... North Atlantic Technology, Inc. (SAUS)
NATT......... Northern Australian Tropical Transect (QUAC)
NATT......... Northern Australia Tropical Transect (SAUS)
NAtt.......... Stevens Memorial Library, Attica, NY [*Library symbol*] [*Library of Congress*] (LCLS)
NATTA .... Network of Alternative Technology and Technology Assessment (EAIO)
NATTA .... North American Trackless Trolley Association (EA)
N-attack..... Nuclear Attack (AD)
Nat Tax J... National Tax Journal [*A publication*] (JLIT)
Nat Tax Mag... National Tax Magazine [*A publication*] (DLA)
NATTC....... National Tank Truck Carriers (AD)
NATTC....... Naval Air Technical Training Center
NATTCDET... Naval Air Technical Training Center Detachment (DNAB)
NATTCL ..... Naval Air Technical Training Center, Lakehurst (DNAB)
NAT/TFG .... North Atlantic Traffic Forecasting Group (SAUS)
NATTFU ..... National Transsexual-Transvestite Feminization Union (EA)
NATTKE ..... National Association of Theatrical, Television, and Kine Employees [*A union*] [*British*] (DCTA)
NATTS....... National Association of Trade and Technical Schools (EA)
NATTS....... Naval Air Turbine Test Station
NATTS....... North American Transvestite/Transsexual Society [*Defunct*] (EA)
NATTS-ATL... Naval Air Turbine Test Station - Aeronautical Turbine Laboratory
NATTU....... Naval Air Technical Training Unit
NATU .... Nasso [*Common carrier symbol*]
NATU .... Natal African Teachers' Union [*South Africa*] (SAFN)
Nat U .... Nations Unies [*United Nations*] [*French*] (AD)
NATU .... Naval Aircraft Torpedo Unit
Nat UL Rev... National University. Law Review [*1921-31*] [*A publication*] (DLA)
Nat Uni...... National University (AD)
natur......... Naturalist (AD)
NATUR .... Naturalist (WDAA)
Natural Res J... Natural Resources Journal [*A publication*] (JLIT)
Natural Res Modeling... Natural Resource Modeling [*A publication*] (JLIT)
NATURBTESTSTA... Naval Air Turbine Test Station
Nature Struct Biol... Nature Structural Biology (MEC)
NaturlAlt... Natural Alternatives International [*Associated Press*] (SAG)
NATUS....... Naturalized United States Citizen
NATUS....... US message dealing with NATO subject matter (SAUS)
NATUSA..... North African Theater of Operations (AD)
NATUSA..... North African Theater, United States Army [*World War II*]
NATVA....... National All Terrain Vehicle Association (EA)
NATVAS ..... National Academy of Television Arts and Sciences (EA)
NatVisn ..... National Vision Associates [*Associated Press*] (SAG)
NATW........ National Association of Texaco Wholesalers (EA)
NATW........ National Association of Town Watch (EA)
NATW........ Nationwide [*NCIC trailer make code*]
NATW........ Natural Wonders [*NASDAQ symbol*] (TTSB)
NATW........ Natural Wonders, Inc. [*NASDAQ symbol*] (SAG)
NATWA....... National Auto and Truck Wreckers Association [*Later, ADRA*] (EA)
NATwA....... North American Tiddlywinks Association (EA)
NATWARCOL... National War College [*Later, UND*] [*DoD*] (DNAB)
NATWC...... National War College [*Later, UND*] [*DoD*]

NatWest..... National Westminster [*Bank*]
NATWF...... North American Tug of War Federation (EA)
NATWJ...... National Alliance of Third World Journalists (EA)
NatWndr.... Natural Wonders, Inc. [*Associated Press*] (SAG)
NATWP...... Naval Air Transport Wing, Pacific
NAT WS..... Nordic Amer Tanker Ship Wrrt [*AMEX symbol*] (TTSB)
NATX........ General Electric Capital Railcar Services [*Private rail car owner code*]
naty......... Naturally (AD)
NaTY........ Sodium Hydrogen Phosphate-Tryptone-Yeast Extract [*Growth medium*] [*Microbiology*]
NATZ......... North American Transportation [*Intermodal trailer symbol*]
Natzd....... Naturalized [*Biology*] (BARN)
NAU.......... Confederation Nordique des Cadres, Techniciens, et Autres Responsables [*Nordic Confederation of Supervisors, Technicians, and Other Managers*] (EAIO)
NAU.......... Nalcus Resources [*Vancouver Stock Exchange symbol*]
NAU.......... Napuka [*Marquesas Islands*] [*Airport symbol*] (OAG)
NAU.......... Narcotics Assistance Unit [*Department of State*]
Nau.......... Nauruan (AD)
Nau.......... Nauru Island (AD)
nau.......... Nautica [*Nautical*] [*Spanish*] (AD)
NAU.......... Naval Administrative Unit
NAU.......... Network Access Unit [*Telecommunications*]
NAU.......... Network Address [*or Addressable*] Unit [*Computer science*] (BUR)
NAU.......... Network Administration Utilities [*Honeywell*] (NITA)
NAU.......... Noise Augmentation Unit [*Military*] (CAAL)
NAU.......... Nordic Confederation of Supervisors, Technicians, and Other Managers [*Formerly, Nordic Union of Foremen*] (EA)
NAU.......... North Arizona University (AD)
NAU.......... Northern Arizona University (SAUS)
NAu.......... Seymour Library, Auburn, NY [*Library symbol*] [*Library of Congress*] (LCLS)
NAUA........ National Aircraft Underwriters' Association (AD)
NAUA........ National Automobile Underwriters Association [*Later, ISO*] (EA)
NAUB........ National Association of Urban Bankers (EA)
NAuC........ Cayuga County Community College, Auburn, NY [*Library symbol*] [*Library of Congress*] (LCLS)
NAUE........ New and Unused Equipment (MCD)
NAUF........ Name and Address Update File [*IRS*]
NAUFMA.... National Association of Urban Flood Management Agencies [*Later, NAFSWMA*] (EA)
NAUFOF..... North American UFO Federation [*Defunct*] (EA)
NAUFRED... National Association of Used Fitness and Rehabilitation Equipment Dealers (NTPA)
NAUFWP.... National Association of University Fisheries and Wildlife Programs (NTPA)
NAUG........ National AppleWorks Users Group (EA)
NAUG........ Naugatuck Railroad [*Federal Railroad Administration identification code*]
nauga....... Naugahide (AD)
NAUHF...... Northern Area Ultrahigh Frequency Radio System [*Green Pine*] (MCD)
NAuHi....... Cayuga County Historical Society, Auburn, NY [*Library symbol*] [*Library of Congress*] (LCLS)
NAUI......... National Association of Underwater Instructors (EA)
NAUL........ Netherland-America University League [*Defunct*] (EA)
NAULAS..... North American Union Life Assurance Society [*Chicago, IL*] (EA)
NAUM........ National Association of Uniform Manufacturers [*Later, NAUMD*] (EA)
NAUMD..... National Association of Uniform Manufacturers and Distributors (EA)
NAuMH...... Auburn Memorial Hospital, Learning Resources Center, Auburn, NY [*Library symbol*] [*Library of Congress*] (LCLS)
NAUN........ Nearest Active Upstream Neighbor [*Computer science*]
NAUN........ Nearest Available Upstream Neighbor (MLOA)
NAU-OLC.... North American Union of Sisters of Our Lady of Charity (TOCD)
NAUP........ National Association of Unemployed Persons [*Defunct*] (EA)
NAUPA...... National Amalgamated Union of Shop Assistants [*A union*] [*British*]
NAUPA...... National Association of Unclaimed Property Administrators (EA)
NAURI....... Nonaccelerating-Unemployment Rate of Inflation [*Economics*]
NAurW...... Wells College, Aurora, NY [*Library symbol*] [*Library of Congress*] (LCLS)
NAUS........ National Aerospace Utilization System (NOAA)
NAUS........ National Association for Uniformed Services (EA)
NAuS........ Seward House, Auburn, NY [*Library symbol*] [*Library of Congress*] (LCLS)
NAUSAWC... National Amalgamated Union of Shop Assistants, Warehousemen, and Clerks [*A union*] [*British*]
NAUS/SMW... National Association for Uniformed Services and Society of Military Widows (NTPA)
NAuT........ Auburn Theological Seminary, Auburn, NY [*Library symbol*] [*Library of Congress*] [*Obsolete*] (LCLS)
NAUT........ Nautica Enterprises [*NASDAQ symbol*] (TTSB)
NAUT........ Nautica Enterprises, Inc. [*NASDAQ symbol*] (SAG)
NAUT........ Nautical (AAG)
naut......... Nautical (AD)
Naut......... Nautical (DIAR)
NAUTEL..... Nautical Electronic Laboratories Ltd. (SAUS)
NAUTIC...... Naval Autonomous Intelligent Console (PDAA)
Nautica...... Nautica Enterprises, Inc. [*Associated Press*] (SAG)
NAUTIS...... Naval Autonomous Information System (SAUS)
NAUTIS-F.... Naval Autonomous Information System-Frigate (DOMA)
NAUTO...... Nautophone
NAUTS...... Nautical Miles (ROG)
NAUTT....... National Association of Unions in the Textile Trade [*British*] (DCTA)
NAUW....... National Association of University Women (EA)
NAUWS..... Naval Advanced Undersea Weapons School
n aux b...... New Auxiliary Boiler (AD)
NAV.......... Association of Private Practitioners of Germany [*Medicine*] (EDAA)
NAV.......... Narrows [*Virginia*] [*Seismograph station code, US Geological Survey*] (SEIS)
NAV.......... National American Veterans
NAV.......... National Association of Videographers [*Defunct*] (EA)
NAV.......... Natividade [*Brazil*] [*Airport symbol*] (AD)
Nav.......... Navaho (AD)
nav.......... Navajo [*MARC language code*] [*Library of Congress*] (LCCP)
NAV.......... Navajo (automobile) [*NCIC car model code*]
Nav.......... Naval (AD)
NAV.......... Naval (MSA)
nav.......... Naval (AD)
NAV.......... Naval Artillery Volunteers [*British*] (ROG)
Nav.......... Navarra (AD)
Nav.......... Navarre (AD)
Nav.......... Navassa Island (AD)
NAV.......... Nav Flight Planning [*Czech Republic*] [*FAA designator*] (FAAC)
nav.......... Navigable (AD)
NAV.......... Navigate (AAG)
nav.......... Navigation (AD)
NAV.......... Navigation (GAVI)
NAV.......... Navigator (DSUE)
NAV.......... Navigator (automobile) [*NCIC car model code*]
NAV.......... Navistar International Corp. [*NYSE symbol*] (SPSG)
NAV.......... Navy (AAG)
NAV.......... Net Annual Value [*Business term*] (ADA)
NAV.......... Net Asset Value
NAV.......... Next Generation Advanced Vehicle [*Nippon Steel Corp.*]
NAV.......... Nonalcoholic Volunteers
NAV.......... Non-Aqueous Volatiles (SAUS)
NAV.......... North American Ventures, Inc. [*Vancouver Stock Exchange symbol*]
NAV.......... North American Veterinarian [*Medicine*] [*Journal*] (EDAA)
NAV.......... Norton Anti-Virus [*Computer science*] (VLIE)
NAV.......... Nurserymens Association of Victoria (SAUS)
NAV.......... Visual Navigation (MCD)
NAVA........ National Association for Variable Annuities
NAVA........ National Association for Veterinary Acupuncture (EA)
NAVA........ National Association of Veterinary Assistants [*Defunct*] (EA)
NAVA........ National Audio-Visual Association [*Later, ICIA*] (EA)
NAVA........ Navajo National Monument
NAVA........ Navieras NPR [*Common carrier symbol*]
NAVA........ Net Asset Value (AD)
NAVA........ Non-Added Value Activity (VLIE)
NAVA........ North American Vexillological Association (EA)
NAVABSCOLLU... Navy Absentee Collection Unit (DNAB)
NAVAC....... National Audiovisual Aids Centre [*British*]
NAVAC....... North American Vaccine, Inc. (SAUS)
NAVACAD... Naval Academy
NA Vacc..... North American Vaccine, Inc. [*Associated Press*] (SAG)
NAVACCTGFINCEN... Navy Accounting and Finance Center (DNAB)
NAVACD..... Naval Academy (DNAB)
navaco...... Navigation Action Cutout (AD)
NAVACO..... Navigation Action Cutout Switchboard
NAVACT..... All Navy Activities [*A dispatch to all activities in an area*]
NAVACTDET... Naval Activities Detachment (DNAB)
NAVAD....... Naval Administrator At [*Place*]
NAVADCOM... Naval Administrative Command
NAVADGP... Naval Advisory Group
NAVADGRU... Naval Advisory Group (CINC)
NAVADGRU... Navy Administrative Group
NAV-ADMIN... Navigation-Administration [*Inquiry program*] (AFIT)
NAVADMINCOM... Naval Administrative Command (DNAB)
NAVADMINO... Navy Administrative Office [*or Officer*]
NAVADMINU... Naval Administration Unit (MUGU)
NAVADMINUANX... Naval Administrative Unit Annex (DNAB)
NAVADS..... Navy Automated Transport Documentation System (DNAB)
NAVADUNIT... Naval Administrative Unit
NAVADUNSEAWPNSCOL... Naval Advanced Undersea Weapons School (DNAB)
NAVADVUSEAWPNSCOL... Naval Advanced Undersea Weapons School (MUGU)
NAVAE....... National Association for Vietnamese American Education (EA)
NAVAER..... Navy Aeronautics
NAVAERAUDOFC... Navy Area Audit Office [*London*] (DNAB)
NAVAEROMEDCEN... Naval Aeronautical Medical Center
NAVAERORECOV... Naval Aerospace Recovery Facility
NAVAERORECOVF... Naval Aerospace Recovery Facility (AD)
NAVAERORECOVFAC... Naval Aerospace Recovery Facility
NAVAEROSPMEDINST... Naval Aerospace Medical Institute
NAVAEROSPMEDRSCHINST... Naval Aerospace Medical Research Institute (DNAB)
NAVAERO(SP)OMEDRSCHLAB... Naval Aerospace Medical Research Laboratory (DNAB)
NAVAERO(SP)RECFAC... Naval Aerospace Recovery Facility (DNAB)
NAVAERO(SP)REGMEDCEN... Naval Aerospace Medical Center (DNAB)
NAVAGLOBE... Long-Distance Navigation System, Global [*Air Force*]
NAVAID...... Air Navigation Facilities (or Facility) (SAUS)
NAVAID...... Navigation Aid
NAVAID...... Navigational Aid (DNAB)
NAVAIDE... Naval Aide
NavAide..... Naval Aide
NAVAIDS... Navigation Aids (VLIE)
NAVAIDSUPPUNIT... Navigational Aids Support Unit (DNAB)

NAVAIR....... Naval Air Systems Command
NAVAIR....... Naval Air Systems Command Headquarters (USDC)
NAVAIRANDACT... Naval Air Research and Development Activities (MUGU)
NAVAIRDEVCEN... Naval Air Development Center [*Also, NADC, NADEVCEN*] (MUGU)
NAVAIRDEVU... Naval Air Development Unit (MUGU)
NAVAIRECONTECHSUPCEN... Naval Air Reconnaissance Technical Support Center
NAVAIRENGCEN... Naval Air Engineering Center [*Closed*]
NAVAIRENGCENFO... Naval Air Engineering Center Field Office (DNAB)
NAVAIRENGLAB... Naval Air Engineering Laboratory (DNAB)
NAVAIRENGRCEN... Naval Air Engineering Center [*Closed*]
NAVAIRENGRFAC... Naval Air Engineering Facility (MUGU)
NAVAIRESCEN... Naval Air Reserve Center (DNAB)
NAVAIRESFORRON... Naval Air Reserve Force Squadron (DNAB)
NAVAIRESMOPIXU... Naval Air Reserve Mobile Photographic Unit (DNAB)
NAVAIRESU... Naval Air Reserve Unit (DNAB)
NAVAIREWORKF... Naval Air Rework Facility
NAVAIREWORKFAC... Naval Air Rework Facility
NAVAIRFAC... Naval Air Facility
NAVAIRINST... Naval Air Systems Command Instruction
NavAirInstr... Naval Air Command Instruction (AAGC)
NAVAIRINTO... Naval Air Intelligence Office (MUGU)
NAVAIRLANT... Naval Air Force, Atlantic Fleet
NAVAIRLOGOFF... Naval Air Logistics Office (DNAB)
NAVAIRLOGTASKFORREP... Naval Air Logistics Task Force Representative (DNAB)
NAVAIRMAINTRAGRU... Naval Air Maintenance Training Group (DNAB)
NAVAIRMATCEN... Naval Air Material Center [*Also, NAMATCEN, NAMC*] (MUGU)
NAVAIRMINDEFDEVU... Naval Air Mine Defense Development Unit (MUGU)
NAVAIRNEWS... Naval Aviation News [*A publication*] (DNAB)
NAVAIRPAC... Naval Air Force, Pacific Fleet
NAVAIRPROPCEN... Naval Air Propulsion Center (GRD)
NAVAIRPROPTESTCEN... Naval Air Propeller Test Center
NAVAIRRES... Naval Air Reserve
NAVAIRREWORKF... Naval Air Rework Facility (AD)
NAVAIRSTA... Naval Air Station (DNAB)
NAVAIRSUPPU... Naval Air Support Unit
NAVAIRSYSCO... Naval Air Systems Command (MCD)
NAVAIR SYSCOM... Naval Air System Command (DOMA)
NAVAIRSYSCOM... Naval Air Systems Command
NAVAIRSYSCOMFLEREADREP... Naval Air Systems Command Fleet Readiness Representative (DNAB)
NAVAIRSYSCOMFLESUPREPCEN... Naval Air Systems Command Fleet Supply Representative Center (DNAB)
NAVAIRSYSCOMHQ... Naval Air Systems Command Headquarters
NAVAIRSYSCOMMETSYSDIV... Naval Air Systems Command, Meteorological Systems Division (DNAB)
NAVAIRSYSCOMREP... Naval Air Systems Command Representative
NAVAIRSYSCOMREPAC... Naval Air Systems Command Representative, Pacific
NAVAIRSYSCOMREPCENT... Naval Air Systems Command Representative, Central
NAVAIRSYSCOMREPLANT... Naval Air Systems Command Representative, Atlantic
NAVAIRSYSCOMREP PNCLA... Naval Air Systems Command Representative, Naval Air Training Command, Pensacola [*Florida*]
NAVAIRSYSCOMTARANDSYSDIV... Naval Air Systems Command Target and Range Systems Command (DNAB)
NAVAIRTECHREP... Naval Air Systems Command Technical Representative (DNAB)
NAVAIRTECHSERVFAC... Naval Air Technical Services Facility (MUGU)
NAVAIRTERM... Naval Air Terminal (DNAB)
NAVAIRTESTCEN... Naval Air Test Center (MUGU)
NAVAIRTESTCENT... Naval Air Test Center (GRD)
NAVAIRTESTFAC... Naval Air Test Facility (MUGU)
NAVAIRTESTFACSHIPINSTAL... Naval Air Test Facility - Ship Installations (DNAB)
NAVAIRTORPU... Naval Aircraft Torpedo Unit (MUGU)
NAVAIRTRACEN... Naval Air Training Center
NAVAIRTU... Naval Air Training Unit (DNAB)
NAVAIRTURBTESTSTA... Naval Air Turbine Test Station (MUGU)
NAVAL....... National Audio Visual Aids Library (AIE)
Naval E..... Naval Engineer (PGP)
NAVALOT... Allotment Division [*Navy*]
NAVALREHCEN... Naval Alcohol Rehabilitation Center (DNAB)
NAVALREHDRYDOCK... Navy Alcohol Rehabilitation Drydock (DNAB)
NAVALT... Navy Alterations
NAVAMDEP... Naval Ammunition Depot [*Charleston, SC*]
NAVAMPROENGCEN... Naval Ammunition Production Engineering Center (DNAB)
NAVAN....... National Association of Vascular Access Networks (EA)
NAVANTRA... Naval Air Advanced Training Center
NAVANTRACOM... Naval Air Advanced Training Command
NAVAP....... National Association of VA [*Veterans Administration*] Physicians (EA)
NAVAPD....... National Association of VA [*Veterans' Administration*] Physicians and Dentists (NTPA)
NAVAPI...... North American Voltage and Phase Indicator (IEEE)
NAVAPSCIENCLAB... Naval Applied Science Laboratory (DNAB)
NAVAR....... Combined Navigation and Radar system (SAUS)
NAVAR....... Navigation Air RADAR (IAA)
NAVAR....... Navigation and Ranging (IAA)
NAVAR....... Navigation RADAR
NAVAR....... Radar Air Navigation and Control System (SAUS)
NAVARA..... Navy Appellate Review Activity
Nav Arch.... Naval Architect [*Academic degree*]
NAVAREAAUDSVC... Naval Area Audit Service
NAVAREP... Natural Variability, Resilience and Buffer Capacity of the Bodden Ecosystem (SAUS)
NAVARHO... Navigation and Radio Homing [*Aviation*]
NAVARMDEP... Naval Armament Depot
Navarre..... Navarre Corp. [*Associated Press*] (SAG)
NAVAS....... Navasota, TX [*American Association of Railroads railroad junction routing code*]
NAVASCOPE... Airborne RADARscope Used in NAVAR (SAUS)
NAVASCOPE... Navigation Airborne RADAR Scope [*Air Force*]
NAVASCREEN... Navigation RADAR Screen [*Air Force*]
NAVASTROGRU... Navy Astronautics Group (MUGU)
NAVASTROGRUHQTRINJFAC... Navy Astronautics Group Headquarters, Tracking and Injection Facility (DNAB)
NAVASTROGRUP... Navy Astronautics Group (SAA)
NAVASWDATACEN... Navy Antisubmarine Warfare Data Center
NAVASWDATCEN... Navy Antisubmarine Warfare Data Center (DNAB)
NAVATAC... Naval Antiterrorism Tactical Alert Center [*U.S. Navy*] (CARL)
NAVATAC... Navy Antiterrorism Analysis Center (COE)
NAVATR..... Naval Air Systems [*Command Headquarters*] [*Marine science*] (OSRA)
NAVAUD..... Navy Auditor
NAVAUDO... Navy Audit Office (DNAB)
NAVAUDSVC... Director, Naval Audit Service
NAVAUDSVCAP... Naval Audit Service, Capital Area (DNAB)
NAVAUDSVCHQ... Naval Audit Service Headquarters (DNAB)
NAVAUDSVCNE... Naval Audit Service, Northeast Area (DNAB)
NAVAUDSVCSE... Naval Audit Service, Southeast Area (DNAB)
NAVAUDSVCWEST... Naval Audit Service, Western Area (DNAB)
NavAus...... Navigation in Australian Waters (AD)
NAVAUTH... Naval Authority
NAVAUTODINSCEN... Navy Automatic Digital Network Switching Center (DNAB)
NAVAVCEN... Naval Audio-Visual Center (DNAB)
NAVAVENGSERVU... Naval Aviation Engineering Services Unit [*Philadelphia, PA*] (DNAB)
NAVAVENGSERVUDET... Naval Aviation Engineering Service Unit Detachment (DNAB)
NAVAVIONICFAC... Naval Avionics Facility [*Later, NAC*] (MUGU)
NAVAVIONICSCEN... Naval Avionics Center (DNAB)
NAVAVMEDCEN... Naval Aviation Medical Center (DNAB)
NAVAVMUSEUM... Naval Aviation Museum [*Pensacola, FL*] (DNAB)
NAVAVNENGRSERVU... Naval Aviation Engineering Service Unit [*Philadelphia, PA*] (DNAB)
NAVAVNLOGCEN... Naval Aviation Logistics Center (NVT)
NAVAVNLOGCENDET... Naval Aviation Logistics Center Detachment (DNAB)
NAVAVNLOGCENFSO... Naval Aviation Logistics Center Field Service Office (DNAB)
NAVAVNLOGCENMETALABOPS... Naval Aviation Logistics Center Meteorology Calibration Laboratory Operations (DNAB)
NAVAVNMEDCEN... Naval Aviation Medical Center (DNAB)
NAVAVNSAFECEN... Naval Aviation Safety Center
NAVAVNSCOLCOM... Naval Aviation School Command
NAVAVNWEPSFAC... Naval Aviation Weapons Facilities
NAVAVNWPNSFAC... Naval Aviation Weapons Facilities (DNAB)
NAVAVNWPNSFACDET... Naval Aviation Weapons Facility Detachment (DNAB)
NAVB....... National Association of Volunteer Bureaux [*British*] (EAIO)
NAVBALTAP... Allied Naval Forces, Baltic Approaches [*NATO*] (NATG)
NAVBALTAP... Naval Forces Baltic Approaches [*NATO*] (AD)
nav bar...... Navigation Bar [*Internet tool*] (NETL)
NAVBASE... Naval Base
NAVBASELANT... Naval Bases Atlantic
NAVBASEPAC... Naval Bases Pacific
NAVBCHGRU... Naval Beach Group (DNAB)
NAVBCHPHIBREFTRAGRU... Navy Beach Amphibious Refresher Training Group (DNAB)
NAVBCSTSVCDET... Navy Broadcasting Service Detachment (DNAB)
NAVBCSTSVCDETTASA... Navy Broadcasting Service Detachment Television Audio Support Activity (DNAB)
NAVBCSTSVCWASHDC... Navy Broadcasting Service, Washington, DC (DNAB)
NAVBE....... National Association for Vocational Business Education (AEBS)
NAVBEACHGRU... Naval Beach Group (CINC)
NAVBIODYNLAB... Naval Biodynamics Laboratory (DNAB)
NAVBIOLAB... Naval Biological Laboratory (MUGU)
NAVBIOSCILAB... Naval Biosciences Research Laboratory (DNAB)
NAVBIT....... Naval Basic Instrument Trainer (PDAA)
navbm....... Naval Ballistic Missile (AD)
NAVBM....... Navy Ballistic Missile
NAVBMC.... Navy Ballistic Missile Committee
NAVBOILAB... Navy Boiler Laboratory
nav brz...... Naval Bronze (AD)
Nav Bs...... Naval Base (AD)
NAVC........ National Audiovisual Center [*Medicine*] [*GSA*] (EDAA)
NAVC........ Naval Audio Visual Center (ACAE)
NAVC........ Naval Aviation Cadet
NAVC........ North American Voyageur Council (EA)
NAVCA....... North American Veterinary College Administrators (GVA)
NAVCAD..... Naval Aviation Cadet
NavCad...... Naval Cadet (AD)
NAVCALAB... Navy Calibration Laboratory (DNAB)
NAVCALABANX... Navy Calibration Laboratory Annex (DNAB)
NAVCALABMSG... Navy Calibration Laboratory Meteorology Support Group (DNAB)
NAVCALABOPS... Navy Calibration Laboratory Operations (DNAB)
NAVCALS... Naval Communication Area Local Station (NVT)
NAVCAMS... Naval Communication Area Master Station (NVT)

NAVCAMSEASTPAC... Naval Communication Area Master Station, Eastern Pacific (DNAB)
NAVCAMSLANT... Naval Communication Area Master Station, Atlantic (DNAB)
NAVCAMSMED... Naval Communication Area Master Station, Mediterranean (DNAB)
NAVCAMSOAM... Naval Communication Area Master Station, South America (DNAB)
NAVCAMSSPECCOMDIVLANT... Naval Communication Area Master Station, Special Communications Division, Atlantic (DNAB)
NAVCARGOHANBN... Naval Cargo Handling Battalion
NAVCAT..... Naval Career Appraisal Team (MUGU)
NAVCAT..... Naval Construction Action Team [*Vietnam*] (VNW)
NAVCBCEN... Naval Construction Battalion Center
NAVCC....... Naval Communications Center (MCD)
NAVCENFRACO... Navy Central Freight Control Office
NAVCENT... Allied Naval Forces, Central Europe [*NATO*]
NAVCENT... Naval Forces [*US*] Central [*Command*] (DOMA)
NAVCENT... Navy, Central Command (SAUS)
NAVCG...... Coast Guard Publication [*Formerly, NCG*]
NAVCHAPGRU... Navy Cargo Handling and Port Group (NVT)
NAVCHAPGRUDET... Navy Cargo Handling and Port Group Detachment (DNAB)
NAVCINSUPPACT... Navy Counterintelligence Support Activity (DNAB)
NAVCINTSUPPCEN... Navy Counterintelligence Support Center (DNAB)
NAVCINTSUPPGRU... Navy Counterintelligence Support Unit (DNAB)
NAVCIVENGLAB... Navy Civil Engineering Laboratory (DNAB)
NAVCIVENGRLAB... Naval Civil Engineering Laboratory
NAVCJ....... National Association on Volunteers in Criminal Justice [*Later, IAJV*] (EA)
NAVCLODEP... Naval Clothing Depot
NAVCLOTEXTOFC... Navy Clothing and Textile Office (DNAB)
NAVCLOTEXTRSCHFAC... Navy Clothing and Textile Research Facility [*Natick, MA*] (DNAB)
NAVCLOTEXTRSCHU... Navy Clothing and Textile Research Unit
NAVCLOTHTEXOFC... Navy Clothing and Textile Office (DNAB)
NAVCM...... Navigation Countermeasure (IAA)
NavCm...... Navigation Countermeasures and Deception (AD)
NAVCM...... Navigation Countermeasures and Deception
NAVCMD.... Navigation Command (MCD)
NAVCO...... National Valve & Mfg. Co. (EFIS)
NAVCOASTSYSCEN... Naval Coastal Systems Center [*Panama City, FL*] (DNAB)
NAVCOM.... Naval Communications [*System*]
navcom..... Navigation Communication (AD)
NAV/COM... Navigation Communications Radio
NAVCOM.... Navigator/Communications operator (SAUS)
NAVCOMCOM... Naval Communications Command
NAVCOMM... Naval Communications [*System*]
NAVCOMMAREA... Naval Communications Area (NVT)
NAVCOMMCOM... Naval Communications Command
NAVCOMMDET... Naval Communication Station Detachment (DNAB)
NAVCOMMDETSPECCOMMDIV... Naval Communication Station Detachment, Special Communications Division (DNAB)
NAVCOMMFAC... Naval Communications Facility (NVT)
NAVCOMMHQ... Naval Communications Headquarters (DNAB)
NAVCOMMIS... Naval Communications Command Management Information System (MCD)
NAVCOMMOPNET... Naval Communications Operation Network (DNAB)
NAVCOMMSTA... Naval Communication Station
NAVCOMMSTASPECCOMMDIV... Naval Communication Station, Special Communications Division (DNAB)
NAVCOMMSYS... Naval Communication System (MUGU)
NAVCOMMSYSSUPPACT... Naval Communications System Support Activity (DNAB)
NAVCOMMTRACEN... Naval Communications Training Center (MUGU)
NAVCOMMU... Naval Communication Unit
NAVCOMMUNR... Naval Communications Unit, Naval Reserve (IAA)
NAVCOMPARS... Naval Communications Processing and Routing System (MCD)
NAVCOMPT... Office of the Comptroller of the Navy
NAVCOMPTINST... Office of the Comptroller of the Navy Instruction
NAVCOMPTMAN... Naval Comptroller Manual
NAVCOMSAT... Naval Communications Satellite (VLIE)
NAVCOMSTA... Naval Communications Station (CCCA)
NAVCOMSYSSUPPACT... Naval Command Systems Support Activity (DNAB)
NAVCOMSYSSUPPCEN... Naval Command Systems Support Center (DNAB)
NAVCOMSYSTO... Navy Commissary Store (DNAB)
NAVCOMSYSTORE... Navy Commissary Store
NAVCOMU... Naval Communications Unit
NAVCON..... Naval Countermeasures (CINC)
NAVCON..... Navigation Control Systems (RDA)
Nav Const... Naval Constructor [*Academic degree*]
NAVCONSTRACEN... Naval Construction Training Center (DNAB)
NAVCONSTRAU... Naval Construction Training Unit (DNAB)
NAVCONSTREGT... Naval Construction Regiment (DNAB)
NAVCONTDEP... Navy Contracting Department (DNAB)
NAVCONTRACEN... Naval Construction Training Center
NAVCONVHOSP... Naval Convalescent Hospital
NAVCORCOURSECEN... Naval Correspondence Course Center (DNAB)
NAVCORRCUSUNIT... Navy Correctional Custody Unit (DNAB)
NAVCOSSACT... Naval Command Systems Support Activity
NAVCOSSCEN... Naval Command Systems Support Center (DNAB)
NAVCRUITAREA... Navy Recruiting Area
NAVCRUITBRSTA... Navy Recruiting Branch Station (DNAB)
NAVCRUITCOM... Navy Recruiting Command (DNAB)
NAVCRUITCOMORIENTUNIT... Navy Recruiting Command Orientation Unit (DNAB)
NAVCRUITCOMSAT... Navy Recruiting Command Standardization and Audit Team (DNAB)
NAVCRUITCOMYPFLDREP... Navy Recruiting Command Youth Programs Field Representative (DNAB)
NAVCRUITDIST... Navy Recruiting District (DNAB)
NAVCRUITEXHIBCEN... Navy Recruiting Exhibit Center (DNAB)
NAVCRUITEXHIBCENCAT... Navy Recruiting Exhibit Center Catalog (DNAB)
NAVCRUITRACOM... Navy Recruit Training Command (DNAB)
NAVCRUITSTA... Navy Recruiting Station
NAVCSG..... National Archives Volunteers Constitution Study Group [*Defunct*] (EA)
NAVCURRSUPPGRULANTFLT... Naval Current Support Group, Atlantic Fleet (DNAB)
NAVCURRSUPPGRUNAVEUR... Naval Current Support Group, Naval Forces, Europe (DNAB)
NAVCURRSUPPGRUPACFLT... Naval Current Support Group, Pacific Fleet (DNAB)
NAVCURSERV... Naval Courier Service
NAVCURSERVDET... Naval Courier Service Detachment (DNAB)
NAVCURSERVHQ... Naval Courier Service Headquarters
NAVD........ National Association of Video Distributors (EA)
NAVD........ North American Vertical Datum [*National Oceanic and Atmospheric Administration*]
NAVD88..... North American Vertical Datum of 1988 (USDC)
NAVDAB..... Navy Ocean Experimental Acoustic Data Bank (MSC)
NAVDAC..... Naval Data Automation Command (MCD)
NAVDAC..... Navigation Data Assimilation Center (AD)
navdac...... Navigation Data Assimilation Computer (AD)
NAVDAC..... Navigation Data Assimilation Computer
NAVDAD..... Navigationally-Derived Air Data (MCD)
NAVDAF..... Navy Data Automation Center (DNAB)
NAVDAMCONTRACEN... Navy Damage Control Training Center
NAVDAR..... Naval Defense Acquisition Regulations (MCD)
NAVDATACEN... Naval Data Center (DNAB)
NAVDEFEASTPAC... Naval Defense Forces, Eastern Pacific (DNAB)
NAVDEGSTA... Navy Degaussing Station (DNAB)
NAVDEGSTALANT/PAC... Naval Degaussing Station, Atlantic/Pacific
NAVDENCEN... Naval Dental Center
NAVDENCLINIC... Naval Dental Clinic
NAVDENSCOL... Naval Dental School
NAVDENTECHSCOL... Naval Dental Technicians School
Nav Dep.... Naval Deputy [*NATO*] (AD)
NAVDEP..... Naval Deputy [*NATO*] (NATG)
NAVDEPCENT... Naval Deputy to Commander-in-Chief, Allied Forces, Central Europe [*NATO*] (NATG)
NAVDEPNOAA... Naval Deputy National Oceanic and Atmospheric Administration (DNAB)
NAVDEPT... Navy Department
NAVDES..... Navy Design Selection List
NAVDESCOL... Naval Destroyer School (NVT)
NAVDESSCOL... Naval Destroyer School
NAVDET..... Naval Detachment
NAVDEVTRACEN... Navy Development Training Center
NAVDI....... National Association for Ventilator Dependent Individuals (EA)
NAVDIS...... Naval District
NAVDISBAR... Navy Disciplinary Barracks (DNAB)
NAVDISCBAR... Naval Disciplinary Barracks
NAVDISCOM... Navy Disciplinary Command
NAVDISEAVECTORCONCEN... Navy Disease Vector Control Center
NAVDISP... Naval Dispensary
NAVDIST... Naval District
NAVDISVECTTECOLCONCEN... Navy Disease Vector Ecology and Control Center (DNAB)
NAVDIVSALVTRACEN... Naval Diving and Salvage Training Center (DNAB)
NAVDOC.... Navy Department Orientation Course (NG)
NAVDOCKS... Bureau of Yards and Docks Publications [*Obsolete*] [*Navy*]
NAVDOCSP... Bureau of Yards and Docks Publications [*Obsolete*] [*Navy*]
NAVDRUGREHCEN... Naval Drug Rehabilitation Center (DNAB)
NAVE........ National Assessment of Vocational Education [*Department of Education*] (GFGA)
Nav E........ Naval Engineer [*Academic degree*]
NAVEA....... National Adult Vocational Education Association (EA)
NAVEAMS... Navigational Warning East Atlantic and Mediterranean [*Navy*] (PDAA)
NavEams... Navigation in the Eastern Atlantic and the Mediterranean (AD)
NAVEARB... Navy Employee Appeals Review Board (DNAB)
NavEast..... Navigation along the East Coast of Asia (AD)
NAVEASTOCEANCEN... Naval Eastern Oceanography Center (DNAB)
NAVED....... National Association of Visual Education Dealers [*Later, National Audio-Visual Association*] (AEBS)
NAVEDTRA... Naval Education and Training Command (MCD)
NAVEDTRA... Naval Education and Training Program Development Center [*Pensacola, FL*]
NAVEDTRACOM... Naval Education and Training Center [*or Command*] (DNAB)
NAVEDTRAPRODEVCEN... Naval Education and Training Program Development Center [*Pensacola, FL*] (DNAB)
NAVEDTRAPRODEVCENCODIV... Naval Education and Training Program Development Center Coordination Division (DNAB)
NAVEDTRAPRODEVCENDET... Naval Education and Training Program Development Center Detachment (DNAB)
NAVEDTRASUPPCEN... Naval Education and Training Support Center (DNAB)
NAVEDTRASUPPCENLANT... Naval Education and Training Support Center, Atlantic (DNAB)
NAVEDTRASUPPCENPAC... Naval Education and Training Support Center, Pacific (DNAB)
NAVEDTRASUPPCENPACNCFA... Naval Education and Training Support Center, Pacific, Navy Campus for Achievement (DNAB)

NAVEL .... Naloxone, Atropine, Valium, Epinephrine, Lidocaine [*Medicine*] (DMAA)
NAVELEC... Naval Electronics System Command (IAA)
NAVELECS... Naval Electronic Systems Command (SAA)
NAVELECSYSCOM... Naval Electronics Systems Command
NAVELECSYSCOMCENLANTDIV... Naval Electronics Systems Command, Central Atlantic Division
NAVELECSYSCOMHQ... Naval Electronics Systems Command Headquarters
NAVELECSYSCOMNEDIV... Naval Electronics Systems Command, Northeast Division
NAVELECSYSCOMSEDIV... Naval Electronics Systems Command, Southeast Division
NAVELECSYSCOMWESTDIV... Naval Electronics Systems Command, Western Division
NAVELEM... Navy Element (DNAB)
NAVELEX... Naval Electronics Systems Command
NAVELEX... Naval Electronic Systems Command Headquarters (USDC)
NAVELEXACTS... Naval Electronic Systems Command Activities (DNAB)
NAVELEXDET... Naval Electronic Systems Command Detachment (DNAB)
NAVELEXENGOFF... Naval Electronics Engineering Office (DNAB)
NAVELEXINST... Naval Electronics Systems Command Instruction
NAVELEXSITEREP... Naval Electronic Systems Command, Site Representative (DNAB)
NAVELEXSYSCOMCENDET... Naval Electronic Systems Command Center Detachment (DNAB)
NAVELEXSYSCOMDIV... Naval Electronic Systems Command Division (DNAB)
NAVELEXSYSCOMMIDWESTDIV... Naval Electronic Systems Command, Midwest Division (DNAB)
NAVELEXSYSCOMSEDIV... Naval Electronic Systems Command, Southeast Division (DNAB)
NAVELEXSYSTRAPUBMO... Naval Electronic Systems Command Training and Publications Management Office (DNAB)
NAVELEXTECHREP... Naval Electronic Systems Command Technical Representative (DNAB)
NAVELXSYSCOMTECHLREP... Naval Electronic Systems Command Technician Liaison Representative (DNAB)
NAVEMSCEN... Navy Electromagnetic Spectrum Center (DNAB)
NAVENENVSA... Navy Energy and Environmental Support Activity (DNAB)
NAVENGRXSTA... Naval Engineering Experiment Station
NAVENPVNTMEDU... Navy Environmental and Preventive Medicine Unit (DNAB)
NAVENVPREDRSCHFAC... Naval Environmental Prediction Research Facility (MCD)
NAVENVRHLTHCEN... Navy Environmental Health Center (DNAB)
NAVENVSUPPCEN... Navy Environmental Support Center (DNAB)
NAVENVSUPPO... Navy Environmental Support Office [*Obsolete*] (DNAB)
NAVEODFAC... Naval Explosive Ordnance Disposal Facility
NAVEODTECHCE... Naval Explosive Ordnance Disposal Technology Center [*Indian Head, MD*]
NAVEODTECHCEN... Naval Explosive Ordnance Disposal Technology Center [*Indian Head, MD*] (DNAB)
NAVEONIC... Nautical Auto Vessel Environmental Ocean Naval Information Communications System (ACAE)
NAVESNP... National Association of Vocational Education Special Needs Personnel (EA)
NAVETC ..... Navy Educational Tape Catalog (DNAB)
NAVEUR..... Naval Forces, Europe (CCCA)
NAVEURWWMCCS DP... Naval Forces, Europe, Worldwide Military Command Control System, Data Processing (DNAB)
NAVEURWWMCCS EMSKD... Naval Forces, Europe, Worldwide Military Command Control System, Employment Schedule (DNAB)
NAVEURWWMCCS MOVREP... Naval Forces, Europe, Worldwide Military Command Control System, Movement Reports (DNAB)
NAVEURWWMCCS NAVFORSTA... Naval Forces, Europe, Worldwide Military Command Control System, Naval Forces Status (DNAB)
navex........ Navigation Exercise (AD)
NAVEX........ Navigation Exercise [*Navy*] (NVT)
NAVEX........ Norton AntiVirus Extension
NAVEXAM... Naval Examining Board
NAVEXAMBD... Naval Examining Board (DNAB)
NAVEXAMCEN... Navy Examination Center
NAVEXAMCENADVAUTHLIST... Naval Examining Center Advancement Authorization List (DNAB)
NAVEXENGLANDCOM... Navy Exchange, England Complex (DNAB)
NAVEXHIBCEN... Naval Exhibit Center
NAVEXOS... Executive Office of the Secretary [*Navy*]
NAVF .... Naval Avionics Facility [*Later, NAC*] (AFIT)
NAVF .... Norges Allmennvitenskapelige Forskningsrad [*Norwegian Research Council for Science and the Humanities*] [*Information service or system*] (IID)
NAVF .... Norwegian Natural Science Research Council (SAUS)
NAVFAC ..... Naval Facilities Engineering Command [*Formerly, Bureau of Yards and Docks*]
NAVFAC ..... Naval Facilities Engineering Command Headquarters (USDC)
NAVFAC ..... Naval Facility
NAVFAC ..... Navy Faces (NITA)
NAVFACCHESDIV... Naval Facilities Engineering Command, Chesapeake Division (DNAB)
NAVFACDM... Naval Facilities Engineering Command Design Manuals
NAVFACENG... Naval Facilities Engineering Command (CAAL)
NAVFACENGCOM... Naval Facilities Engineering Command [*Formerly, Bureau of Yards and Docks*]
NAVFACENGCOMCHESDIV... Naval Facilities Engineering Command, Chesapeake Division (DNAB)
NAVFACENGCOMCONTR... Naval Facilities Engineering Command Contractor (DNAB)
NAVFACENGCOMHQ... Naval Facilities Engineering Command Headquarters
NAVFACENGCOMLANTDIV... Naval Facilities Engineering Command, Atlantic Division (DNAB)
NAVFACENGCOMNORDIV... Naval Facilities Engineering Command, Northern Division (DNAB)
NAVFACENGCOMPACDIV... Naval Facilities Engineering Command, Pacific Division (DNAB)
NAVFACENGCOMSODIV... Naval Facilities Engineering Command, Southern Division (DNAB)
NAVFACENGCOMWESDIV... Naval Facilities Engineering Command, Western Division (DNAB)
NAVFACENSYSCOM... Naval Facilities Engineering Systems Command
NAVFACINST... Naval Facilities Engineering Command Instructions
NAVFACLANTDIV... Naval Facilities Engineering Command, Atlantic Division (DNAB)
NAVFACLANT/PAC... Naval Facilities Atlantic/Pacific
NAVFACNORDIV... Naval Facilities Engineering Command, Northern Division (DNAB)
NAVFACOC... Naval Facility Operational Center (DNAB)
NAVFACP... Naval Facilities Engineering Command Publications
NAVFAC P-68... Naval Facilities Engineering Command Contracting Manual [*A publication*] (AAGC)
NAVFACSODIV... Naval Facilities Engineering Comamnd, Southern Division (DNAB)
NAVFAC SYSCOM... Naval Facilities Engineering Command (POLM)
NAVFAC-TP-AD... Naval Facilities Engineering Command Technical Publications - Administration
NAVFAC-TP-MO... Naval Facilities Engineering Command Technical Publications - Maintenance Operation
NAVFAC-TP-PL... Naval Facilities Engineering Command Technical Publications - Planning
NAVFAC-TP-PU... Naval Facilities Engineering Command Technical Publications - Public Utilities
NAVFACWESDIV... Naval Facilities Engineering Command, Western Division (DNAB)
NAVFAMALWACT... Navy Family Allowance Activity
NAVFE....... Naval Forces Far East (AD)
NAVFEC ..... Naval Facilites (AD)
NAVFEC ..... Naval Facilities Engineering Command [*Formerly, Bureau of Yards and Docks*]
NAVFECENGCOM... Naval Facilities Engineering Command (AD)
NAVFECO... Naval Facilities Engineering Command (PDAA)
NAVFINCEN... Navy Finance Center
NAVFINCEN-CLEVE... Navy Finance Center - Cleveland [*Ohio*] (DNAB)
NAVFINCEN-WASH... Navy Finance Center - Washington, DC (DNAB)
NAVFINOFF... Navy Finance Office
NAVFITWEPSCOL... Navy Fighter Weapons School (DNAB)
NAVFLDINTO... Navy Field Intelligence Office (DNAB)
NAVFLDOPINTO... Naval Field Operational Intelligence Office
NAVFLDOPSUPPGRU... Naval Field Operations Support Group
NAVFLIGHTPREPSCOL... Naval Flight Preparatory School
NAVFLIR... Navigational Forward Looking Infrared (ACAE)
NAVFLITHTDEMORON... Navy Flight Demonstration Squadron (DNAB)
NAVFOODMGTM... Navy Food Management Team (DNAB)
NAVFOR..... Naval Forces (AD)
NAVFORJAP... Naval Air Forces, Japan (AD)
NAVFORKOR... Naval Air Forces, Korea (AD)
NAVFORSTAT... Naval Force Status Report (NVT)
NAVFRCOORD... Navy Frequency Coordinator (DNAB)
NAVFROF... Navy Freight Office
NAVFSSO... Navy Food Services Office (DNAB)
NAVFSSO... Navy Food Service Systems Office
NAVFUELDEP... Naval Fuel Depot
NAVFUELSUPO... Naval Fuel Supply Office
NAVFW...... Norton AntiVirus for Firewalls [*Symantec*] [*Computer science*]
NAVG .... Navigators Group [*NASDAQ symbol*] (TTSB)
NAVG .... [*The*] Navigators Group, Inc. [*NASDAQ symbol*] (NQ)
NAVGDENSCOL... Naval Graduate Dental School (DNAB)
NAVGEN..... Navy General Publications
NavgGp ..... [*The*] Navigators Group, Inc. [*Associated Press*] (SAG)
NAVGMSCHOL... Navy Guided Missile School
NAVGMU .... Navy Guided Missile Unit
NAVGP ...... Naval Advisory Group
NAVGRU .... Naval Group
NAVGSUP... Navigational Guidance Support (NVT)
NAVGUN .... Naval Gun Factory [*Later, NWF*]
NAVH .... National Aid to Visually Handicapped (AD)
NAVH .... National Association for Visually Handicapped (EA)
NAVH .... National Association of Voluntary Hostels [*British*] (DBA)
NAVHARS... Navigation Heading and Altitude Reference System [*Aviation*] (PDAA)
NAVHET ..... National Association of Vocational Home Economics Teachers (EA)
NAVHISTCEN... Naval History Center (DNAB)
NAVHISTDISPLAYCEN... Navy Historical Display Center
NAVHLTHRSCHC... Naval Health Research Center
NAVHLTHRSCHCEN... Naval Health Research Center (DNAB)
NAVHO ...... National Association of Voluntary Help Organisers [*British*] (DBA)
NAVHOME... Naval Home [*Philadelphia, PA*]
NAVHOME... Naval Home Command (SAUS)
NAVHOMERESINFOSYS... Naval Home Resident Information System (DNAB)
NAVHOSINGACT... Naval Housing Activity (DNAB)
NAVHOSP... Naval Hospital
NAVHOSPCORPSCOL... Naval Hospital Corps School
NAVHOUSINGACT... Naval Housing Activity
NAVHT....... National Association of Vocational Homemakers Teachers [*Later, National Association of Vocational Home Economics Teachers*] (EA)

Nav I .... Navassa Island (AD)
NAVI .... Navistar [*NCIC truck make code*]
NAVI .... North American Ventures, Inc. (SAUS)
NAVI .... Norton AntiVirus
NAVIC .... Navy Information Center (MCD)
navicert ..... Naval Inspection Certificate (AD)
NAVICERT... Navigation Certificate [*Paper issued by British government to merchant vessel, certifying that cargo was non-contraband, that is, not consigned to Germany*] [*World War II*]
NAVID .... Navigation Aid (NASA)
NAVIG .... Navigation
NAVIGA...... Welt Organisation fur Schiffsmodellbau und Schiffsmodellsport [*World Organization for Modelship Building and Modelship Sport*] [*Austria*] (EAIO)
NAVILCO... Navy International Logistics Control Office (MCD)
NAVIMAC... Naval Immediate Area Coordinator (DNAB)
NAVIMOS... Nissan Advanced Vehicle Management Object-oriented System [*Automotive engineering*]
NavInd ...... Navigation in the Indian Ocean (AD)
NAVINFO... Navy Information Office (DNAB)
NAVINFONET... Navigation Information Network [*Nautical term*] (NTA)
NAVINRELACT... Navy Internal Relations Activity (DNAB)
NAVINSGEN... Naval Inspector General
NAVINTCOM... Naval Intelligence Command
NAVINTCOMINST... Naval Intelligence Command Instructions
NAVINTCOMM... Naval Intelligence Command
NAVINTEC... Naval de Investigacion Y Tecnologia (EFIS)
NAVINTEL... Naval Intelligence
NAVINTSUPPCEN... Naval Intelligence Support Center (DNAB)
NAVINVSERV... Naval Investigative Service (DNAB)
NAVINVSERVHQ... Naval Investigative Service Headquarters (NVT)
NAVINVSERVO... Naval Investigative Service Office
NAVINVSERVOREP... Naval Investigative Service Office Representative (DNAB)
NAVINVSERVRA... Naval Investigative Service Resident Agent (DNAB)
NAVION ..... North American Aviation, Inc. [*Later, Rockwell International Corp.*] [*Acronym also used to refer to light aircraft of World War II*]
NAVISLO... Naval Interservice Liaison Office (DNAB)
NAVISTAR... formerly International Harvester (SAUS)
Navistar..... Navistar International Corp. [*Associated Press*] (SAG)
NAVIXS...... Navy Information Transfer System (POLM)
NAVJ......... Navajo Horse Trailer [*NCIC trailer make code*]
NAVJAC ..... North American Vane Jump Angle Computer
NAVJAG ..... Judge Advocate General's Office Publications [*Navy*]
NAVJIT ...... Naval Jet Instrument Trainer
NAVJNTSERVACT... Naval Joint Services Activity (DNAB)
NAVJUSTSCOL... Naval Justice School
NAVL .... National Anti-Vaccination League [*British*] (BI)
NAVL .... National Van Lines [*Common carrier symbol*]
NAVL .... Navigation Light (IAA)
NAVLEGSERVOFF... Naval Legal Service Office (DNAB)
NAVLEGSERVOFFDET... Naval Legal Service Office Detachment (DNAB)
NAVLIAGRU... Naval Liaison Group (DNAB)
NAVLINKSTA... Naval Link Station (DNAB)
NAVLIS....... Navy Logistics Information System
NAVLO....... Naval Liaison Officer
NAVLOGENGRU... Naval Logistics Engineering Group (DNAB)
NAVLOGSIP... Navy Logistic Support Improvement Plan (NG)
NAVLOS..... Navy Liaison Officer for Scouting (DNAB)
NAVMAA .... Naval Mutual Aid Association (DNAB)
NAVMAC .... Navy Manpower and Material Analysis Center (DNAB)
NAVMACPAC... Navy Manpower and Material Analysis Center, Pacific (DNAB)
NAVMACS... Naval Modular Automated Communications System (NVT)
NAVMAIRCOMCON... Naval and Maritime Air Communications-Electronics Conference [*NATO*]
NAVMAP .... Navy Missile Analysis Program (MCD)
NAVMAR .... Naval Forces, Marianas (AD)
NAVMARCORESTRACEN... Navy and Marine Corps Reserve Training Center
NAVMAREXHIBCEN... Navy-Marine Corps Exhibit Center (DNAB)
NAVMARJUDACT... Navy-Marine Corps Judiciary Activity
NAVMARTRIJUDCIR... Navy-Marine Corps Trial Judiciary Court (DNAB)
NAVMARTRIJUDCIRBROFF... Navy-Marine Corps Trial Judiciary Court Branch Office (DNAB)
NAVMARTRIJUDIC... Navy-Marine Corps Trial Judiciary (DNAB)
NAVMASSO... Navy Maintenance and Supply Systems Office (DNAB)
NAVMASSO... Navy Management Systems Support Office (AAGC)
NAVMASSODET... Navy Maintenance and Supply Systems Office Detachment (DNAB)
NAVMASSODETPAC... Navy Maintenance and Supply Systems Office Detachment, Pacific (DNAB)
NAVMAT..... Naval Material Command [*Formerly, NMSE*] (MCD)
NAVMAT..... Office of Naval Materiel (SAUS)
NAVMATCOM... Naval Material Command [*Formerly, NMSE*]
NAVMATCOMSUPPACT... Naval Material Command Support Activity
NAVMAT COOPLAN... Naval Material Command Contingency/Emergency Planning (DNAB)
NAVMATDATASYSGRU... Naval Material Data Systems Group (DNAB)
NAVMATDET... Naval Material Command Detachment (DNAB)
NAVMATEVALU... Naval Material Evaluation Unit (DNAB)
NAVMATINST... Naval Material Command Instruction
NAVMATMOCON... Navy Material Movement Control Plan
NAVMATRANSOFC... Naval Material Transportation Office (DNAB)
NAVMC...... Navy-Marine Corps
NAVMEC .... Naval Manpower Engineering Center (MCD)
NAVMED .... Naval Aerospace Medical Institute (MCD)
NAVMED .... Naval Medicine
NAVMEDADMINU... Navy Medical Administrative Unit (DNAB)
NAVMEDATASERVCEN... Naval Medical Data Service Center
NAVMEDCEN... Navy Medical Center (DNAB)
NAVMEDCOM... Naval Medical Command (ANA)
NAVMEDFLDRSCHLAB... Navy Medical Field Research Laboratory (DNAB)
NAVMEDIS... Navy Medical Information System
NAVMEDLAB... Naval Medical Laboratory (DNAB)
NAVMEDLABDET... Naval Medical Laboratory Detachment (DNAB)
NAVMEDMATSUPPCOM... Naval Medical Materiel Support Command (DNAB)
NAVMEDNPRSCHU... Navy Medical Neuropsychiatric Research Unit (DNAB)
NAVMEDRSCHDEVCOM... Naval Medical Research and Development Command (DNAB)
NAVMEDRSCHINST... Naval Medical Research Institute
NAVMEDRSCHINSTDET... Navy Medical Research Institute Detachment (DNAB)
NAVMEDRSCHU... Naval Medical Research Unit
NAVMEDRSCHUDET... Naval Medical Research Unit Detachment (DNAB)
NAVMEDRSHCHLAB... Navy Medical Research Laboratory (DNAB)
NAVMEDSCOL... Naval Medical School
NAVMEDSUPPU... Navy Medical Support Unit (DNAB)
NAVMGTSYSCEN... Naval Management Systems Center (MCD)
NAVMIC ..... Naval Maritime Intelligence Center [*Formerly, NISC and then NTIC*] (DOMA)
NAVMILPERSCOM... Naval Military Personnel Command (MCD)
NAVMINCOMEASTA... Navy Mine Countermeasures Station
NAVMINDEFLAB... Navy Mine Defense Laboratory [*Later, NCSC*]
NAVMINDEP... Naval Mine Depot
NAVMINENGRFAC... Naval Mine Engineering Facility
NAVMINWARTRACEN... Naval Mine Warfare Training Center
NAVMIRO... Naval Material Industrial Resources Office
NAVMIS ..... Naval Mission
NAVMIS ..... Navy Management Information System (MCD)
NavMisCen... Naval Missile Center (AD)
NAVMISCEN... Naval Missile Center [*Point Mugu, CA*] (MCD)
NAVMISFAC... Naval Missile Facility [*Also, NMF*] (MUGU)
NAVMMAC... Navy Manpower and Material Analysis Center (NVT)
NAVMMACLANT... Navy Manpower and Material Analysis Center, Atlantic
NAVMMACPAC... Navy Manpower and Material Analysis Center, Pacific
NAVMOBCONSTBN... Navy Mobile Construction Battalion
NAVMORTOFF... Naval Mortuary Office (DNAB)
NAVMOVE... Navigational Movements (SAUS)
NAVMTO .... Navy Material Transportation Office
NAVMTO .... Navy Movement and Transportation Office
NAVMTONORVA... Naval Military Transportation Office, Norfolk, Virginia (DNAB)
NAVMTOREP... Naval Military Transportation Office Representative (DNAB)
NAVMUTAID... Navy Mutual Aid
NAVN .... Naval Aviation News
NAVN .... Navigation [*Telegraphy*] (PCTE)
NAVNET ..... Naval Network (VLIE)
NAVNET ..... Navigation Network (NVT)
NAVNET ..... Navy Network (DOMA)
NAVNETDEP... Naval Net Depot
NAVNON .... Allied Naval Forces, North Norway [*NATO*] (NATG)
NAVNON .... Naval Forces, Northern Norway [*NATO*] (AD)
NavNoPac .. Navigation in the North Pacific (AD)
NavNorlant... Navigation in the North Atlantic (AD)
NAVNORTH... Allied Naval Forces, Northern Europe [*NATO*]
NAVNUPWRSCOL... Navy Nuclear Power School (DNAB)
NAVNUPWRTRAU... Naval Nuclear Power Training Unit (MCD)
NAVNUPWRU... Naval Nuclear Power Unit
NAVO .... National Association of Volvo Owners [*Defunct*] (EA)
NAVO .... Naval Oceanographic Office (USDC)
NAVOBS..... Naval Observatory (MUGU)
NAVOBSY... Naval Observatory [*Navy*]
NAVOBSYFLAGSTAFFSTA... Naval Observatory Flagstaff [*Arizona*] Station
NAVOBSYSTA... Naval Observatory Station (DNAB)
NAVOCEANCOM... Naval Oceanography Command Support System (GFGA)
NAVOCEANCOMCEN... Naval Oceanography Command Center (DNAB)
NAVOCEANCOMDET... Naval Oceanography Command Detachment (MCD)
NAVOCEANCOMFAC... Naval Oceanography Command Facility (DNAB)
NAVOCEANCOMMDET... Naval Oceanography Communications Detachment (DNAB)
NAVOCEANDISTO... Naval Oceanographic District Office
NAVOCEANO... Naval Oceanographic Office [*Also known as NOO; formerly, HO, NHO, USNHO*] [*Bay St. Louis, MS*]
NavOceanO... Naval Oceanographic Officer (AD)
NAVOCEANOAIRSUPPGRU... Naval Oceanographic Office Aircraft Support Squadron (DNAB)
NAVOCEANODET... Naval Oceanographic Office Detachment (DNAB)
NAVOCEANOFC... Naval Oceanographic Office (DNAB)
NAVOCEANPROFAC... Naval Ocean Processing Facility (DNAB)
NAVOCEANSURVINFOCEN... Naval Ocean Surveillance Information Center (DNAB)
NAVOCEANSYSCEN... Naval Ocean Systems Center [*Formerly, NELC*] (DNAB)
NAVOCEANSYSCENLAB... Naval Ocean Systems Center Laboratory (DNAB)
NAVOCEANSYSCENLABDET... Naval Ocean Systems Center Laboratory Detachment (DNAB)
NAVOCFORMED... Naval On-Call Force, Mediterranean [*NATO*] (NATG)
NAVOCS..... Naval Officer Candidate School
NAVOLF ..... Navy Outlying Landing Field (DNAB)
NAVOPFAC... Naval Operating Facility
NAVOPHTHALSUPPTRACT... Naval Ophthalmic Support and Training Activity (DNAB)
NAVOPNET... Naval Operations Network (CINC)

NAVOPSUPPGRU... Naval Operations Support Group (DNAB)
NAVOPSUPPGRULANT... Naval Operations Support Group, Atlantic
NAVOPSUPPGRUPAC... Naval Operations Support Group, Pacific
NAVOPTINCEN... Naval Operations Intelligence Center (ACAE)
NAVORD .... Naval Ordnance (MUGU)
NAVORD .... Naval Ordnance Systems Command [*Later, Naval Sea Systems Command*]
NAVORD .... Naval Ordnance Systems Command Headquarters (USDC)
NAVORDCH... Naval Ordnance Chart (MCD)
NAVORDENGFAC... Naval Ordnance Engineering Facility (DNAB)
NAVORDFAC... Naval Ordnance Facility
NAVORD ILS/MIS... Naval Ordnance Systems Command, Integrated Logistics Support / Management Information System (DNAB)
NAVORDINST... Naval Ordnance Systems Command Instruction
NAVORDLABFIELDIV... Naval Ordnance Laboratory Field Division (DNAB)
NAVORDLIST... Navy Ordnance List (DNAB)
NAVORDMISTESTFAC... Naval Ordnance Missile Test Facility
NAVORDSTA... Naval Ordnance Station
NAVORDSTADET... Naval Ordnance Station Detachment (DNAB)
NAVORD-SWOP... Naval Ordnance Systems Command, Special Weapons Ordnance Publication
NAVORDSYSCO... Naval Ordnance Systems Command [*Later, Naval Sea Systems Command*] (MCD)
NAVORDSYSCOM... Naval Ordnance Systems Command [*Later, Naval Sea Systems Command*]
NAVORDSYSCOMHQ... Naval Ordnance Systems Command Headquarters
NAVORDSYSSUPPO... Naval Ordnance Systems Support Office
NAVORDSYSUPPO... Naval Ordnance Systems Support Office (DNAB)
NAVORDSYSUPPOLANT... Naval Ordnance Systems Support Office, Atlantic (DNAB)
NAVORDSYSUPPOPAC... Naval Ordnance Systems Support Office, Pacific (DNAB)
NAVORDTECHREP... Naval Ordnance Technical Representative (MCD)
NAVORDTESTU... Naval Ordnance Test Unit
NAVORDU... Naval Ordnance Unit
NAVORECSUPPACT... Naval Officer Record Support Activity (DNAB)
NAVOROUS... Naval Order of the United States [*Later, NOUS*] [*An association*] (EA)
NAVOSH..... Navy Occupational Safety and Health (MCD)
NAVOSH DAP/MIS... Navy Occupational Safety and Deficiency Abatement/ Management Information System
NAVOSTAT... Navigation by Visual Observation of Satellites (DNAB)
NAVP .... National Association of Vision Professionals (EA)
NAVPA........ National Association of Veterans Program Administrators (EA)
NAVPAC ..... Navigation Package (DNAB)
NAVPACEN... Navy Public Affairs Center (DNAB)
NAVPAOEASCO... Naval Public Affairs Office, East Coast
NAVPAOMWEST... Naval Public Affairs Office, Midwest
NAVPAOWESCO... Naval Public Affairs Office, West Coast
NAVPBRO... Naval Plant Branch Representative Officer (DNAB)
NAVPC....... National Association of Vision Program Consultants [*Later, NAVP*] (EA)
NAVPECO... Naval Production Equipment Control Office
NAVPECOS... Navy Pentagon Computer Services Division (DNAB)
NAVPEP ..... Navy Program Evaluation Procedures
NAVPERS... Bureau of Naval Personnel [*Also, BNP, BUPERS*]
NAVPERS... Naval Personnel (AD)
NAVPERSCEN... Naval Personnel Center
NAVPERSINST... Bureau of Naval Personnel Instruction
NAVPERS-PRD... Bureau of Naval Personnel - Personnel Research Division
NAVPERSPROGSUPPACT... Naval Personnel Program Support Activity
NAVPERSRANDCEN... Naval Personnel Research and Development Center
NAVPERSRANDCENWB... Naval Personnel Research and Development Center, Washington [*DC*] Branch (DNAB)
NAVPERSRANDLAB... Navy Personnel Research and Development Laboratory
NAVPERSREACT... Naval Personnel Research Activity
NAVPERSRSCHACT... Naval Personnel Research Activity
NAVPETOFF... Navy Petroleum Office
NAVPETRAU... Naval Petroleum Training Unit (DNAB)
NAVPETRES... Naval Petroleum Reserves
NAVPETRESO... Naval Petroleum Reserves Office
NAVPGCOL... Navy Postgraduate College
NAVPGSCOL... Naval Postgraduate School
NAVPHIBASE... Naval Amphibious Base (MUGU)
NAVPHIBASELANT... Naval Amphibious Base Atlantic
NAVPHIBSCOL... Naval Amphibious School (NVT)
NAVPHIL... Naval Forces - Philippines (AD)
NAVPHOTOCEN... Naval Photographic Center
NAVPLANTDEVU... Naval Plant Development Unit (DNAB)
NAVPLANTREP... Naval Plant Representative Office [*or Officer*] (MCD)
NAVPLANTREPO... Naval Plant Representative Office [*or Officer*]
NAVPLANTTECHREP... Naval Plant Technical Representative (DNAB)
NAVPO ...... National Association of Van Pool Operators [*Later, Association of Commuter Transportation*] (EA)
NAVPOLAROCEANCEN... Naval Polar Oceanography Center (DNAB)
NAVPOOL... Navigation Parameter Common Pool (NASA)
NAVPOOL... Navigation [*Parameter Common*] Pool
NAVPORCO... Naval Port Control Office [*or Officer*]
NAVPORCOF... Naval Port Control Office [*or Officer*]
NAVPORTCO... Naval Port Control Office [*Or officer*] (DNAB)
NAVPOSTGRADSCOL... Naval Postgraduate School
NAVPOWFAC... Naval Powder Factory
NAVPrD ..... Navistar Intl Cv Jr D Pref [*NYSE symbol*] (TTSB)
NAVPREFLIGHTSCOL... Naval Preflight School
NAVPrG ..... Navistar Intl $6 cm Cv Pfd [*NYSE symbol*] (TTSB)
NAVPRIMSTDEPT... Navy Primary Standards Department (DNAB)
NAVPRIS... Naval Prison
NAVPRO..... Naval Plant Representative Office [*or Officer*]
NAVPRO..... Naval Procurement Office (SAUS)
NAVPROPLT... Naval Propellant Plant (DNAB)
NAVPROV... Naval Proving Ground [*Dahlgren, VA*]
NAVPTO..... Navy Passenger Transportation Office (DNAB)
NAVPUB..... Naval Publications (AD)
NAVPUB..... Navy Publications and Printing Service
NAVPUBFORMCEN... Naval Publications and Forms Center (MCD)
NAVPUBINST... Navy Publications and Printing Service Instruction
NAVPUBPRINTO... Navy Publications and Printing Office
NAVPUBPRINTSERV... Naval Publications and Printing Service (DNAB)
NAVPUBPRINTSERVO... Navy Publications and Printing Service Office
NAVPUBSCONBD... Navy Department Publications Control Board
NAVPUBWKSCEN... Navy Public Works Center
NAVPUBWKSDEPT... Navy Public Works Department (DNAB)
NAVPUR..... Navy Purchasing Office
NAVPURDEP... Navy Purchasing Department (DNAB)
NAVPURO... Navy Purchasing Office
NAVPVNTMEDU... Navy Preventive Medicine Unit
NAVR........ Navarre Corp. [*NASDAQ symbol*] (SAG)
NAVR........ Navigator (WGA)
NAVRA ...... National Association of Volunteer Referral Agencies [*Australia*]
NAVRADCO... Naval Regional Active Duty Cryptologic Officer (DNAB)
NAVRADCON... Naval Radiological Control
NAVRADLDEFLAB... Navy Radiological Defense Laboratory
NAVRADRECFAC... Naval Radio Receiving Facility (DNAB)
NAVRADSTA... Naval Radio Station
NAVRADTRANSFAC... Naval Radio Transmitting Facility (DNAB)
NAVRDSATCOMMGRU... Naval Research and Development Satellite Communications Group (MUGU)
NAVRECCEN... Naval Recreation Center (DNAB)
NAVRECONTACSUPPCENLANT... Naval Reconnaissance and Tactical Support Center, Atlantic (DNAB)
NAVRECONTECHSUPPCEN... Naval Reconnaissance and Technical Support Center
NAVRECONTECHSUPPCENLANT... Naval Reconnaissance and Technical Support Center, Atlantic (DNAB)
NAVRECONTECHSUPPCENPAC... Naval Reconnaissance and Technical Support Center, Pacific (DNAB)
NAVRECSTA... Naval Receiving Station (NVT)
NAVREF..... National Association of Veterans' Research and Education Foundations (NTPA)
NAVREGAIRCARCONO... Navy Regional Air Cargo Central [*or Control*] Office (DNAB)
NAVREGCONTO... Navy Regional Contracting Office (DNAB)
NAVREGCONTODET... Navy Regional Contracting Office Detachment (DNAB)
NAVREGDENCEN... Navy Regional Dental Center (DNAB)
NAVREGDENCENBRFAC... Navy Regional Dental Center Branch Facility (DNAB)
NAVREGDENCLIN... Navy Regional Dental Clinic (DNAB)
NAVREGFINCEN... Navy Regional Finance Center
NAVREGFINCENBRKLN... Navy Regional Finance Center, Brooklyn [*New York*] (DNAB)
NAVREGFINCENGLAKES... Navy Regional Finance Center, Great Lakes (DNAB)
NAVREGFINCENNORVA... Navy Regional Finance Center, Norfolk, Virginia (DNAB)
NAVREGFINCENPEARL... Navy Regional Finance Center, Pearl Harbor [*Hawaii*] (DNAB)
NAVREGFINCENSDIEGO... Navy Regional Finance Center, San Diego [*California*] (DNAB)
NAVREGFINCENSFRAN... Navy Regional Finance Center, San Francisco [*California*] (DNAB)
NAVREGFINOFC... Navy Regional Finance Office (DNAB)
NAVREGMEDCEN... Naval Regional Medical Center (DNAB)
NAVREGMEDCENBRCLINIC... Naval Regional Medical Center Branch Clinic (DNAB)
NAVREGMEDCENBRHOSP... Naval Regional Medical Center Branch Hospital (DNAB)
NAVREGMEDCENCLINIC... Naval Regional Medical Center Clinic (DNAB)
NAVREGMEDCENDET... Naval Regional Medical Center Detachment (DNAB)
NAVREGPEO... Naval Regional Plant Equipment Office [*or Officer*] (DNAB)
NAVREGPROCO... Navy Regional Procurement Office (DNAB)
NAVREGS... Navy Regulations
NAVREL..... Navy Relief Society
NAVREPFAC... Naval Repair Facility (MCD)
NAVRES..... Naval Reserve
NAVRESCEN... Naval Research Center (DNAB)
NAVRESCEN... Naval Reserve Center (DNAB)
NAVRESCOMICEDEFOR... Naval Reserve Commander, Iceland Defense Force (DNAB)
NAVRESFOR... Naval Reserve Force (DNAB)
NAVRESLAB... Naval Research Laboratory [*ONR*]
NAVRESMANPOWERCEN... Naval Reserve Manpower Center
NAVRESMANPWRCEN... Naval Reserve Manpower Center (DNAB)
NAVRESMIDSCOL... Naval Reserve Midshipmen's School
NAVRESO... Navy Resale System Office (PDAA)
NAVRESO... Navy Resale Systems Office (DNAB)
NAVRESOFSO... Navy Resale Systems Field Support Office (DNAB)
NAVRESOREACT... Naval Reserve Officer Recording Activity (DNAB)
NAVRESOREP... Navy Resale Systems Office Representative (DNAB)
NAVRESREDCOM... Naval Reserve Readiness Command (DNAB)
NAVRESREDCOMREG... Naval Reserve Readiness Command Region (DNAB)
NAVRESSECGRP... Naval Reserve Security Group (DNAB)
NAVRESSO... Navy Resale and Services Support Office
NAVRESSOFO... Navy Resale and Services Support Office, Field Office (DNAB)

NAVRESSOFO... Navy Resale and Service Support Office, Field Support Office (POLM)
NAVRESTRA... Naval Reserve Training (DNAB)
NAVRESTRACEN... Naval Reserve Training Center
NAVRESTRACOM... Naval Reserve Training Command
NAVRESTRAFAC... Naval Reserve Training Facility
NAVRESUBDET... Naval Reserve Submarine Detachment (DNAB)
NAVRESUPPOFC... Naval Reserve Support Office (DNAB)
NAVRESUPPOFCDET... Naval Reserve Support Office Detachment (DNAB)
NAVRETRAINCOM... Naval Retraining Command
NAVROM.... Romanian Merchant Marine (AD)
NAVROUTE... Navy Routing Office
NAVRSCHLAB... Naval Research Laboratory [*ONR*]
NAVS........ National Anti-Vivisection Society (EA)
NAVS........ National Association of Variety Stores [*Defunct*] (EA)
NAVS........ Navigation System
NAVS........ North American Vegetarian Society (EA)
NAVSAFECEN... Naval Safety Center
NAVSANDA... Bureau of Supplies and Accounts [*Later, NSUPSC*] [*Navy*]
navsat....... Navigational Satellite (AD)
NAVSAT..... Navigational Satellite [*NASA*]
NavSat...... Navigation in the South Atlantic (AD)
NAVSATCOMMDET... Navy Satellite Communications Detachment (DNAB)
NAVSATCOMMFAC... Navy Satellite Communications Facility (DNAB)
NAVSATCOMMNET... Navy Satellite Communications Network (DNAB)
NAVSCAP... Allied Naval Forces, Scandinavian Approaches [*NATO*] (NATG)
NAVSCAP... Naval Forces, Scandinavian Approaches [*NATO*] (AD)
NAVSCIADV... Naval Science Advisor (DNAB)
NAVSCIENTECHINTCEN... Naval Scientific and Technical Intelligence Center
NAVSCITECHGRUFE... Naval Scientific and Technical Group, Far East (DNAB)
NAVSCOLCEOFF... Naval Civil Engineer Corps Officers School (DNAB)
NAVSCOLCOM... Naval Schools Command
NAVSCOLCOM NORVA... Naval Schools Command, Norfolk, Virginia
NAVSCOLCONST... Naval Schools Construction
NAVSCOLCRYPTOREP... Naval School of Cryptographic Repair (DNAB)
NAVSCOLCYROGENICS... Naval School of Cryogenics (DNAB)
NAVSCOLDEEPSEADIVER... Navy School for Deep Sea Divers (DNAB)
NAVSCOLEOD... Naval School of Explosive Ordnance Disposal (DNAB)
NAVSCOLHOSPADMIN... Naval School of Hospital Administration (DNAB)
NAVSCOLMINWAR... Naval School of Mine War (DNAB)
NAVSCOLMINWARFARE... Naval Mine Warfare School
NAVSCOLPHYDISTMGT... Naval School of Physical Distribution Management (DNAB)
NAVSCOLTRANSMGT... Naval School of Transportation Management (DNAB)
NAVSCSCOL... Naval Supply Corps School
NAVSCSCOLDET... Naval Supply Corps School Detachment (DNAB)
NAVSEA..... Naval Avionics Support Equipment Appraisal (NG)
NAVSEA..... Naval Sea [*formerly, Ship*] Systems Command (MCD)
NAVSEAADSO... Naval Sea Systems Command Automated Data Systems Office (DNAB)
NAVSEAADSODET... Naval Sea Systems Command Automated Data Systems Office Detachment (DNAB)
NAVSEACARCOORD... Naval Sea Cargo Coordinator (DNAB)
NAVSEACARCOR... Navy Sea Cargo Coordinator (NVT)
NAVSEACEN... Naval Sea Support Center (DNAB)
NAVSEACENFSO... Naval Sea Support Center, Fleet Support Office (DNAB)
NAVSEACENHAWLAB... Naval Sea Support Center, Hawaii Laboratory (DNAB)
NAVSEACENLANT... Naval Sea Support Center, Atlantic (MCD)
NAVSEACENLANTDET... Naval Sea Support Center, Atlantic Detachment (DNAB)
NAVSEACENPACDET... Naval Sea Support Center, Pacific Detachment (DNAB)
NAVSEACENREP... Naval Sea Support Center Representative (DNAB)
NAVSEACENTLANT... Naval Sea Support Center - Atlantic (AD)
NAVSEACENTPAC... Naval Sea Support Center - Pacific (AD)
NAVSEACOHREP... Naval Sea Systems Command Complex Overhaul Representative (DNAB)
NAVSEADET... Naval Sea Systems Command Detachment (DNAB)
NAVSEAMATREP... Naval Sea Systems Command Material Representative (DNAB)
NAVSEAMQAO... Naval Sea Systems Command Material Quality Assessment Office (DNAB)
NAVSEASYSCOM... Naval Sea [*Formerly, Ship*] Systems Command (DNAB)
NAVSEASYSCOMGTOWESTPAC... Naval Sea Systems Command Management Office, Western Pacific (DNAB)
NAVSEASYSCOMHQ... Naval Sea Systems Command Headquarters (DNAB)
NAVSEATECHREP... Naval Sea Systems Command Technical Representative (DNAB)
NAVSEC..... Naval Ship Engineering Center
NAVSECENGRFAC... Naval Security Engineering Facility
NAVSECGRU... Naval Security Group
NAVSECGRUACT... Navy Security Group Activity
NAVSECGRUACTFO... Naval Security Group Activity Field Office (DNAB)
NAVSECGRUACTSPECOMMDIV... Naval Security Group Activity, Special Communications Division (DNAB)
NAVSECGRUCOM... Naval Security Group Command (MCD)
NAVSECGRUDET... Naval Security Group Detachment
NAVSECGRUHQ... Navy Security Group Headquarters
NAVSECGRUMGDAT... Naval Security Group Command Management Data (DNAB)
NAVSECGRU MIS... Naval Security Group Management Information System (DNAB)
NAVSECINST... Naval Ship Engineering Center Instruction
NAVSECMECHSDIV... Naval Ship Engineering Center, Mechanicsburg [*Pennsylvania*] Division (DNAB)
NAVSECNORDIV... Naval Ship Engineering Center, Norfolk Division
NAVSECPHILA... Naval Ship Engineering Center, Philadelphia Division
NAVSECPHILAD... Naval Ship Engineering Center Philadelphia Division
NAVSECPHILADIV... Naval Ship Engineering Center, Philadelphia Division
NAVSECSDIEGODIV... Naval Ship Engineering Center, San Diego [*California*] Division (DNAB)
NAVSECSTA... Naval Security Station
NAVSEEACT... Naval Shore Electronics Engineering Activity
NAVSEEC... Naval Electronics Systems Command Headquarters
NAVSEG..... Navigation Satellite Executive Steering Group
NAVSERVSCOLCOM... Naval Service School Command
NAVSEX..... Naval Standing Exercises (NATG)
NAVSHIP... Naval Ship Systems Command [*Later, NAVSEA, NSSC*]
NAVSHIPCOM... Naval Ship Systems Command (AD)
NAVSHIPENGCEN... Naval Ship Engineering Center
NAVSHIPENGSUPPACT... Naval Ship Engineering Support Activity
NAVSHIPLO... Navy Shipbuilding Office
NAVSHIPMISENGSYS... Naval Ships Missile Systems Engineering System (DNAB)
NAVSHIPMISYSENGSTA... Naval Ship Missile System Engineering Station
NAVSHIPREPFAC... Naval Ship Repair Facility
NAVSHIPREPO... Naval Ship Repair Officer (DNAB)
NAVSHIPRSCHDEVCEN... Naval Ship Research and Development Center [*Also, DTNSRDC*] (DNAB)
NAVSHIPRSCHDEVCENANNA... Naval Ship Research and Development Center, Annapolis [*Maryland*] Division (DNAB)
NAVSHIPS... Naval Ship Systems Command [*Later, NAVSEA, NSSC*]
NAVSHIPS... Naval Ship Systems Command Headquarters [*Formerly, BuShips*] (USDC)
NAVSHIPSA... Navy Shipbuilding Scheduling Activity
NAVSHIPSINST... Naval Ship Systems Command Instruction
NAVSHIPSO... Navy Shipbuilding Scheduling Office
NAVSHIPSTO... Navy Ships' Store Office (DNAB)
NAVSHIPSYSCOM... Naval Ship Systems Command [*Later, NAVSEA, NSSC*]
NAVSHIPSYSCOMHQ... Naval Ship Systems Command Headquarters
NAVSHIPTECHSMAN... Navy Ship Technical Manual (DNAB)
NAVSHIPWPNSYSENGSTA... Naval Ship Weapon Systems Engineering Station [*Port Hueneme, CA*] (DNAB)
NAVSHIPWPNSYSENGSTADET... Naval Ship Weapon Systems Engineering Station Detachment (DNAB)
NAVSHIPWPNSYSENGSTAREP... Naval Ship Weapon Sytems Engineering Station Representative (DNAB)
NAVSHIPY... Naval Shipyard (SAA)
NavShipyd... Naval Shipyard (AD)
NAVSHIPYD... Naval Shipyard
NAVSIT... Navy Scholarship Information Team (DNAB)
NAVSITSUM... Naval Situation Summary (SAUS)
NAVSMO.... Navigation Satellite Management Office
NAVSO...... Naval Supply Office
NAVSO...... Navy, Secretary's Office
NAVSO...... Navy Staff Offices
NAVSONOR... Allied Naval Forces, South Norway (SAUS)
NavSoPac... Navigation of the South Pacific (AD)
NAVSOUTH... Allied Naval Forces, Southern Europe [*NATO*] (NATG)
NAVSOUTH... Naval Forces, Southern Europe (AD)
NAVSPACCOM... Naval Space Command (DOMA)
NAVSPASUR... Naval Space Surveillance [*Center or System*]
NAVSPASYSAC... Naval Space Systems Activity (DNAB)
NAVSPEC... Navy Specification (AAGC)
NAVSPECWAR... Naval Special Warfare (MUSM)
NAVSPECWARCOM... Navy Special Warfare Command (SAUS)
NAVSPECWARGP... Naval Special Warfare Group (AABC)
NAVSPECWARGRAUDET... Naval Special Warfare Group Detachment (DNAB)
NAVSPECWARGRU... Naval Special Warfare Group (NVT)
NAVSPECWARU... Naval Special Warfare Unit (DNAB)
NAVSPECWARUDET... Naval Special Warfare Unit Detachment (DNAB)
NAVSPOC... Naval Space Operations Center (ACAE)
NAVSSES... Naval Ship Systems Engineering Station
NAVSSESDET... Naval Ship Systems Engineering Station Detachment (DNAB)
NAVSSI...... Navigation Sensor System Interface
NAVSTA..... Naval Station
NAVSTAG... Naval Standardization Agreement [*NATO*]
NAVSTALANT... Naval Stations Atlantic
NAVSTAPAC... Naval Stations Pacific
NAVSTAR... Navigational Star (SAUS)
NAVSTAR... Navigation Satellite Timing and Ranging (POLM)
NAVSTAR... Navigation Satellite Tracking and Ranging [*Later, GPS*] [*Air Force*]
NAVSTAR... Navigation System Using Time and Ranging (AD)
NAVSTAR... Navy Study of Transport Aircraft Requirements
NAVSTARCODE... Naval Staff Target and Requirement Code (SAUS)
NAVSTAR GPS... Navigation Satellite Timing and Ranging Global Positioning System (POLM)
NAVSTAR-GPS... Navigation Satellite Tracking and Ranging Global Positioning System [*Air Force*] (MCD)
NAVSTD..... Navy Standard (AAGC)
NAVSTIC... Naval Scientific and Technical Intelligence Center
NAVSTKWARCEN... Naval Strike Warfare Center (DOMA)
NAVSTRIP... Navy Standard Requisitioning and Issuing Procedure
NAVSUBBASE... Naval Submarine Base
NAVSUBINSURV... Naval Sub-Board of Inspection and Survey (DNAB)
NAVSUBMEDCEN... Naval Submarine Medical Center
NAVSUBMEDRSCHLAB... Naval Submarine Medical Research Laboratory (DNAB)
NAVSUBSCOL... Naval Submarine School
NAVSUBSUPPBASE... Naval Submarine Support Base (DNAB)
NAVSUBSUPPBASEDET... Naval Submarine Support Base Detachment (DNAB)
NAVSUBSUPPFAC... Navy Submarine Support Facility (DNAB)
NAVSUBTRACENPAC... Naval Submarine Training Center, Pacific (DNAB)

NAVSUP..... Naval Supplies
NAVSUP..... Naval Supply Systems Command [*Formerly, Bureau of Supplies and Accounts*] (MCD)
NAVSUPACT... Naval Support Activity (NVT)
NAVSUPCEN... Naval Supply Center
NAVSUPDEP... Naval Supply Depot (DNAB)
NAVSUPDEPT... Naval Supply Department (DNAB)
NAVSUPFORANT... Naval Support Forces, Antarctica
NAVSUPGRU... Naval Support Group (NVT)
NAVSUPINST... Naval Supply Systems Command Instruction
NAVSUPMIS... Navy Supply Management Information System
NAVSUPO... Navy Supply Office (DNAB)
NAVSUPOANX... Navy Supply Office Annex (DNAB)
NAVSUPORANT... Naval Support Forces, Antarctica (AD)
NAVSUPPACT... Naval Supply [*or Support*] Activity
NAVSUPPACTDET... Naval Support Activity Detachment (DNAB)
NAVSUPPFOR... Naval Support Force
NAVSUPPFORANTARCTIC... Naval Support Forces, Antarctic
NAVSUPRANDDFAC... Navy Supply Research and Development Facility (DNAB)
NAVSUPRANDFA... Naval Supply Research and Development Facility
NAVSUPSYSCOM... Naval Supply Systems Command [*Formerly, Bureau of Supplies and Accounts*]
NAVSUPSYSCOMHQ... Naval Supply System Command Headquarters
NAVSURFAC... Naval Surface Force, Pacific
NAVSURFLANT... Naval Surface Force, Atlantic (DNAB)
NAVSURFLANTREADSUPPGRU... Naval Surface Force, Atlantic Readiness Support Group (DNAB)
NAVSURFPACDAT... Naval Surface Force, Pacific Dependents' Assistance Team (DNAB)
NAVSURFWPNCEN... Naval Surface Weapons Center (PDAA)
NAVSURMISYS... Naval Surface Missile Systems (MCD)
NAVSWC.... Naval Surface Warfare Center [*Silver Spring, MD*]
NAVSWC.... Naval Surface Weapons Center [*Later, NSWC*] (CAAL)
NAVSWCFAC... Naval Surface Weapons Center Facility (DNAB)
NAVSWCREP... Naval Surface Weapons Center Representative (DNAB)
NAVSWOP... Naval Special Weapons Ordnance Publication
NAVSYD..... Naval Shipyard
NAVTA....... National Association of Veterinary Technicians in America (EA)
NAVTA....... National Automatic Vendors' Trade Association (EA)
NAVTA....... North American Veterinary Technician Association (GVA)
NAVTAC..... Navigation Tactical (AD)
navtac....... Navigation Tactical (AD)
NAVTAC..... Tactical Navigation System
NAVTACDATASYSDEVSITE... Naval Tactical Data Systems Development and Evaluation Site (DNAB)
NAVTACDOCACT... Navy Tactical Doctrine Activity
NAVTACDOCDEVPRODACT... Navy Tactical Doctrine Development and Production Activity (DNAB)
NAVTACINTEROPSUPPACT... Navy Tactical Interoperability Support Activity (DNAB)
NAVTACINTEROPSUPPACTDET... Navy Tactical Interoperability Support Activity Detachment (DNAB)
NAVTACSAT... Naval Tactical Satellite (DNAB)
NAVTACSTANS... Naval Tactical Standards (MCD)
NAVTACSUPPACT... Navy Tactical Support Activity (NVT)
NAVTAG..... Naval Tactical Game
NAVTAG..... Navy Tactical Action Game
NAVTAS..... Navigation and Target Acquisition System (ACAE)
NAVTASC... Naval Telecommunications Automation Support Center (DNAB)
NAVTASCDETLANT... Naval Telecommunications Automation Support Center, Atlantic (DNAB)
NAVTASCDETPAC... Naval Telecommunications Automation Support Center, Pacific (DNAB)
NAVTEC..... National Association of Vocational-Technical Education Communicators (EA)
NAVTECHJAP... Naval Technical Mission to Japan
NAVTECHMISJAP... Naval Technical Mission to Japan (DNAB)
NAVTECHREP... Naval Technical Representative
NAVTECHTRACEN... Naval Air Technical Training Center
NAVTECHTRACENDET... Naval Technical Training Center Detachment (DNAB)
NAVTECMISEU... Naval Technical Mission in Europe
NAVTELCOM... Naval Telecommunications Command
NAVTELSYSIC... Naval Telcommunications System Integration Center (DNAB)
NAVTEX..... Navigational and meteorological warning broadcast service (SAUS)
NAVTIS...... National Vessel Traffic Information System (AD)
NAVTIS...... Naval Training Information System (MCD)
NAVTIS ADS... Naval Training Information System with Automated Data Systems (DNAB)
NAVTNG..... Navigator Training [*Air Force*]
NAVTNGSq.. Navigator Training Squadron [*Air Force*]
NAVTORPSTA... Naval Torpedo Station
NAVTP....... National Association of Vertical Transportation Professionals
NAVTRA..... Naval Training Command
NAVTRACEN... Naval Training Center (DNAB)
NAVTRACOM... Naval Training Command
NAVTRADEV... Naval Training Device Center
NAVTRADEVCEN... Naval Training Device Center
NAVTRADEVSUPCEN... Naval Training Devices Supply Center (DNAB)
NAVTRADISTCEN... Naval Training and Distribution Center
NAVTRAEQUIPC... Naval Training Equipment Center
NAVTRAEQUIPCEN... Naval Training Equipment Center
NAVTRAEQUIPCENFEO... Naval Training Equipment Center Field Office (DNAB)
NAVTRAEQUIPCENREPCEN... Naval Training Equipment Center, Representative for the Center (DNAB)
NAVTRAEQUIPCENREPLANT... Naval Training Equipment Center Representative, Atlantic (DNAB)
NAVTRAEQUIPCENREPPAC... Naval Training Equipment Center Representative, Pacific (DNAB)
NAVTRAFSAT... Navigational/Traffic-Control Satellite (MCD)
NAVTRAIDSCEN... Naval Training Aids Center
NAVTRAINST... Naval Training Support Command Instruction (MCD)
NAVTRANSCO... Naval Transportation Coordinating Office
NAVTRAPUBCEN... Naval Training Publications Center (MCD)
NAVTRASAT... Navigation/Traffic Control Satellite (MCD)
NAVTRASCOL... Naval Training School
NAVTRASTA... Naval Training Station
NAVTRASYSCEN... Naval Training Systems Center [*Orlando, FL*]
NAVU........ Naviera Interamericana Navicana [*Intermodal shipping container symbol*] (TVRC)
NAVU........ Naviera Interamericana Navigana [*Common carrier symbol*]
NAVUSEARANDCEN... Naval Undersea Research and Development Center (MCD)
NAVUSEARESDEVCEN... Naval Undersea Research and Development Center
NAVUSEAWARCEN... Naval Undersea Warfare Center
NAVUWSEC... Naval Underwater Weapons Systems Engineering Center (AD)
NAVUWSES... Naval Underwater Systems Engineering Center
NAVUWSOUNDLAB... Naval Underwater Sound Laboratory [*Later, NUSC*]
NAVVF....... National Association of the Van Valkenburg Family (EA)
NAVWAG.... Naval Warfare Analysis Group
NAVWARCOL... Naval War College
Nav War C Rev... Naval War College. Review [*A publication*] (DLA)
NAVWASS... Navigation and Weapon-Aiming Subsystem (MCD)
NAVWEARSCHFA... Navy Weather Research Facility
NAVWEASERV... Naval Weather Service Command
NAVWEPEVALFAC... Naval Weapons Evaluation Facility [*Kirtland Air Force Base, NM*] (DNAB)
NAVWEPS... Bureau of Naval Weapons [*Obsolete*]
NAVWESA... Naval Weapons Engineering Support Activity
NAVWESS... National Aviation Weather System Study (NOAA)
NAVWESTOCEANCEN... Naval Western Oceanographic Center (DNAB)
NAVWPNCEN... Naval Weapons Center (MCD)
NAVWPNENGSUPPACT... Naval Weapons Engineering Support Activity (DNAB)
NAVWPNEVALFAC... Naval Weapons Evaluation Facility [*Kirtland Air Force Base, NM*]
NAVWPNLAB... Naval Weapons Laboratory [*Later, NSWC*]
NAVWPNQAO... Naval Weapons Quality Assurance Office [*Washington, DC*]
NAVWPNQUALASSURO... Naval Weapons Quality Assurance Office [*Washington, DC*]
NAVWPNSCEN... Naval Weapons Center
NAVWPNSERVO... Naval Weapons Services Office [*Also, NWSO, WEPSO*]
NAVWPNSTA... Naval Weapons Station (MCD)
NAVWPNSTRACEN... Naval Weapons Training Center (DNAB)
NAVWPNSUPPACT... Naval Weapons Support Activity (DNAB)
NAVWPNSUPPCEN... Naval Weapons Support Center (DNAB)
NAVWPNSYSANALO... Naval Weapons Systems Analysis Office
NAVWUIS... Navy Work Unit Information Service (IID)
NAVXDIVINGU... Navy Experimental Diving Unit
NAVY........ Never Again Volunteer Yourself (SAUS)
NAVYCAB... Navy Contract Adjustment Board (AAGC)
NAVYEO..... Navigator's Yeoman [*British military*] (DMA)
NAW......... Narathiwat [*Thailand*] [*Airport symbol*] (OAG)
NAW......... National Agricultural Workers Union
NAW......... National Association for Women (NADA)
NAW......... National Association of Wholesaler-Distributors [*Washington, DC*] (EA)
NAW......... National Association of Wholesalers (NADA)
NAW......... National Association of Widows [*British*] (DI)
NAW......... Negative Afterwave [*Microelectrode recording*]
NAW......... Newair [*Denmark*] [*ICAO designator*] (FAAC)
N/AW........ Night/Adverse Weather (SAUS)
N/AW........ Night/Adverse Weather Evaluator (IEEE)
N/AW........ Night/All-Weather (SAUS)
NAW......... Non Acid Washed (SAUS)
NAW......... Non-All-Weather (CINC)
NAW......... North African Waters
NAW......... Northwest African Waters
NAW......... Nutzfahrzeuggesellschaft Arbon & Wetzikon (EFIS)
NAWA....... National Academy of Western Art (EA)
NAWA....... National Apple Week Association [*Later, NAM*] (EA)
NAWA....... National Association of Women Artists (EA)
NAWA....... North American Warmblood Association (EA)
NAWAC...... National Aviation Weather Advisory Committee [*Marine science*] (OSRA)
NAWAC...... National Weather Analysis Center [*Air Force, Navy*]
NAWAF...... Navy with Air Force
NAWAPA.... North American Water and Power Alliance
NAWAR..... Navy with Army
NAWARCOL... Naval War College (MUGU)
NAWAS...... National Attack Warning System [*Military*] (IAA)
NAWAS...... National Warning System [*Civil Defense*]
NAWatch.... North American Watch Corp. [*Associated Press*] (SAG)
NAWAU...... National Aviation Weather Advisory Unit [*Federal Aviation Administration*] (USDC)
NAWB....... National Association of Wine and Beer Makers [*British*] (DBA)
NAWB....... National Association of Wine Bottlers [*Later, NWA*] (EA)
NAWBM..... National Association of Window Blind Manufacturers [*British*] (BI)
NAWBO...... National Association of Women Business Owners [*Chicago, IL*] (EA)
NAWBO PAC... National Association of Women Business Owners PAC [*St. Louis, MO*] (PACS)

NAWC .... National Art Workers Community [*Later, FCA*] (EA)
NAWC .... National Association for Women in Careers [*Later, NAFWIC*] (EA)
NAWC .... National Association of Water Companies (EA)
NAWC .... National Association of Waterproofing Contractors (NTPA)
NAWC .... National Association of Women's Centers [*Defunct*] (EA)
NAWC .... National Association of Women's Clubs [*British*] (DBA)
NAWC .... Naval Air Warfare Center (DOMA)
NAWC .... Naval War College
NAWC .... North American Watch Corp. [*NASDAQ symbol*] (SAG)
NAWC .... North American Weather Consultants (SAUS)
NAWC .... North Atlantic Women's Conference (PSS)
NAWC .... Number of Additional Words Coming (CGWS)
NAWCAS .... National Association of Women's and Children's Apparel Salesmen [*Later, Bureau of Wholesale Sales Representatives*] (EA)
NAWCC ...... National Association of Watch and Clock Collectors (EA)
NAWCC ...... National Association of Women in Chambers of Commerce (EA)
NAWCC ...... North American Wetlands Conservation Council (COE)
NAWCH ...... National Association for the Welfare of Children in Hospital [*British*]
NAWCJ ...... National Association of Women in Criminal Justice (EA)
NAWCM ..... National Association of Wiping Cloth Manufacturers [*Later, IAWCM*] (EA)
NAWC-PAC ... National Association of Water Companies PAC [*Washington, DC*] (PACS)
NAWCWD ... Naval Air Warfare Center Weapons Divison
NAWCWPNS ... Naval Air Warfare Center Weapons Division
NAWD .... National Association of WIC Directors (EA)
NAWD .... Notice of Award
NAWDA ...... North American Working Dog Association (EA)
NAWDAC .... National Association for Women Deans, Administrators, and Counselors (EA)
NAWDC ...... National Association of Waste Disposal Contractors [*British*] (DCTA)
NAWDC ...... National Association of Women Deans and Counselors [*Later, NAWDAC*] (EA)
NAWDEX .... National Water Data Exchange [*United States Geological Survey*] [*Reston, VA*] [*Information service or system*]
NAWDEX .... National Weather Data Exchange (ACAE)
NAWDP ...... National Association of Workforce Development Professionals (NTPA)
NAWE .... National Association for Women in Education (NTPA)
NAWE .... National Association of Waterfront Employers (NTPA)
NAWESA .... Naval Weapons Engineering Support Activity (PDAA)
NAWF .... National Aborigine Welfare Fund [*Australia*] (NADA)
NAWF .... Nodes Above White Flower [*Botany*]
NAWF .... North American Waterfowl Federation
NAWF .... North American Wildlife Foundation (EA)
NAWF .... North American Wolf Society (EA)
NAWFA ...... North Atlantic Westbound Freight Association (DS)
NAWFC ...... National Association of Wholesale Fur Cleaners
NAWFC ...... National Association of Women Federal Contractors [*Later, NAWGC*] (EA)
NAWFMP .... North American Waterfowl Management Plan of 1986 (COE)
NAWG .... National Association of Wheat Growers (EA)
NAWGA ...... National-American Wholesale Grocers' Association (EA)
NAWGC ...... National Association of Women Government Contractors [*Defunct*] (EA)
NAWGF ...... National Association of Wheat Growers Foundation (EA)
NAWGP ...... National Agenda for Women's Grants Program [*Australia*]
NAWH .... National Association for Women's Health (EA)
NAWH .... National Association of Women in Horticulture [*Defunct*] (EA)
NAWH .... Norwegian-American Historical Museum (AD)
NAWHO ..... National Asian Women's Health Organization [*Association*] (EA)
NAWHP ..... National Association of Women's Health Professionals (NTPA)
NAWHSL .... National Association of Women Highway Safety Leaders (EA)
NAWiC .... National Association for Women in Careers [*Later, NAFWIC*] (EA)
NAWIC .... National Association of Women in Construction (EA)
NAWID ...... National Association of Water Institute Directors (EA)
NAWID ...... National Association of Writing Instrument Distributors (EA)
NAWJ .... National Association of Women Judges (EA)
NAWK .... National Association of Warehouse Keepers [*British*] (DBA)
NAWL .... National Association of Women Lawyers (EA)
NAWL .... North American Iterative Weighted Least Squares (SAA)
NAWLA ...... North American Wholesale Lumber Association (EA)
NAWLD ...... North American Women's Letters and Diaries
NAWLT ...... Nitric Acid Weight Loss Test (SAUS)
NAWM .... National Association of Wool Manufacturers [*Later, American Textile Manufacturers Institute*] (EA)
NAWM .... Naval Air Weapons Meet (MUGU)
NAWMD ..... National Association of Waste Material Dealers [*Later, NARI*]
NAWME ..... National Average Weekly Male Earning
NAWMP ..... National Association of Waste Material Producers [*Defunct*] (EA)
NAWMP ..... Naval Aviation Weapons Maintenance Program (MCD)
NAWMP ..... North American Waterfowl Management Plan (SAUS)
NAWND ..... National Association of Wholesale Newspaper Distributors (DGA)
NAWP .... National Anti-Waste Programme [*British*] (DCTA)
NAWP .... National Association for Widowed People [*Later, IAWP*] (EA)
NAWP .... National Association of Women Pharmacists [*British*] (DBA)
NAWP .... North American Woodperson (SAUS)
NAWPA ...... North American Water and Power Alliance
NAWPB ...... National Association of Wholesale Pie Bakers (EA)
NAWPB ...... National Association of Wine Producers and Bottlers [*Later, NWA*] (EA)
NAWPC ...... National Aircraft War Production Council [*World War II*]
NAWPF ...... National Aviation Weather Processing Facility [*FAA*] (TAG)
NAWPF ...... North American Wildlife Park Foundation (EA)
NAWPM ..... National Association of Wholesale Paint Merchants [*British*] (BI)
NAWPS ...... National Association of Word Processing Specialists [*Later, WPS*] (EA)
NAWPU ...... National Association of Water Power Users [*British*] (DBA)
NAWQC ...... National Ambient Water Quality Criteria (WPI)
NAWR .... National Assembly of Women Religious (EA)
NAWRSRF ... New Age World Religious and Scientific Research Foundation (EA)
NAWS .... National Agricultural Workers Survey
NAWS .... National Aviation Weather System
NAWS .... Naval Air Weapons Station
NAWS .... North African War Shipping [*World War II*]
NAWS .... North American Wolf Society (EA)
NAWSS ...... North American Wilderness Survival School
NAWST ...... Night Attack Weapon Systems Trainer (SAUS)
NAWT .... National Animal Welfare Trust (WDAA)
NAWT .... National Association of Waste Transporters (NTPA)
NAWTPD .... Naval All Weather Testing Program Detachment
NAWTS ..... National Association of World Trade Secretaries [*Later, AWTCE*] (EA)
NAWU .... National Agricultural Workers Union (EA)
NAWU .... National Asphalt Workers' Union [*A union*] [*British*]
NAWU .... North American West African Line [*Intermodal shipping container symbol*] (TVRC)
NAWU .... Ovambo Namibia Workers Union (SAUS)
NAWW .... National Association of Wheat Weavers (EA)
NAWW, Inc. ... National Association of Wheat Weavers (EA)
NAWWO ..... National Association of Woolen and Worsted Overseers [*Later, NATS*] (EA)
NAX .... Ewa, HI [*Location identifier*] [*FAA*] (FAAL)
NAX .... Nakwi [*Language symbol*] (ETLW)
NAX .... New Arcadia Explorations [*Vancouver Stock Exchange symbol*]
NAX .... Norwegian Air Shuttle, AS [*FAA designator*] (FAAC)
NAXSTA ..... Naval Air Experimental Station
NAXU .... Naphtachimie [*Intermodal shipping container symbol*] (TVRC)
NAY .... Navegacion y Servicios Aereos Canarios SA [*Spain*] [*ICAO designator*] (FAAC)
NAY .... New Alster Energy [*Vancouver Stock Exchange symbol*]
NAY .... Not Available Yet [*Numismatic term*]
NAYA .... North American Yngling Association (EA)
NAYC .... National Association of Youth Clubs [*British*] (DI)
NAYCEO .... National Association of Youth and Community Education Officers [*British*] (DI)
NAYGTA ..... North American Youth Glider Training Association
NAYO .... National Association of Youth Orchestras (EAIO)
NAYPCAS ... National Association of Young People's Counselling and Advisory Services [*British*] (DI)
NAYPIC ...... National Association of Young People in Care [*British*]
NAYRE .... National Association for Year-Round Education (EA)
NAYRU ...... North American Yacht Racing Union (EA)
NAYSI .... North American Youth Sport Institute (EA)
NAYT .... National Association of Youth Theatres [*British*] (DBA)
NAYTA ...... National Association of Youth Training Agencies (AIE)
NAYW .... National Association for Young Writers [*Defunct*] (EA)
NAZ .... Nazarene
Naz .... Nazir (BJA)
NAZ .... Normal Analytical Zone [*Chemistry*]
NAZ .... North American [*Federal Railroad Administration identification code*]
NAZ .... Nuveen Arizona Premium Income [*NYSE symbol*] (SAG)
NAZ .... Nuveen AZ Prem Inc. Muni Fd [*NYSE symbol*] (TTSB)
NAZ .... Servicios Aereos del Nazas SA de CV [*Mexico*] [*ICAO designator*] (FAAC)
NAZI .... Nationalsozialistische Deutsche Arbeiterpartei [*National Socialist German Workers' Party, 1919-45*] [*Political party*]
NB .... Brooklyn Public Library, Brooklyn, NY [*Library symbol*] [*Library of Congress*] (LCLS)
NB .... Nabonidus and Belshazzar (BJA)
NB .... Nail Bed (DMAA)
NB .... Nanobarn [*Unit of Measure*]
nb .... Narrowband (IDOE)
NB .... Narrowband
NB .... Narrow Beam (NATG)
NB .... Narrow-Bore (ODA)
NB .... National Battlefield (BARN)
NB .... National Board
NB .... National Body (AG)
NB .... NationsBank Corp. [*NYSE symbol*] (SPSG)
NB .... Naval Base
NB .... Navigation Base (NASA)
NB .... Navy Band
NB .... Neath and Brecon Railway [*Wales*]
NB .... Nebraska (IAA)
Nb .... Nebraska State Library, Lincoln, NE [*Library symbol*] [*Library of Congress*] (LCLS)
NB .... Needle Biopsy [*Surgical procedure*] (DAVI)
NB .... Negative Binomial Distribution [*Statistics*]
NB .... Negri Body (AAMN)
NB .... Nemzeti Bank [*National Bank*] [*Hungarian*]
NB .... Neo-Babylonian [*or New Babylonian*] (BJA)
NB .... Nephroblastoma [*Medicine*] (MELL)
NB .... Nerve Block [*Medicine*] (MELL)
NB .... Network Booter [*Computer science*] (BYTE)
NB .... Neubrandenburg [*German license plate city code*]
NB .... Neuro-Behcet [*Syndrome*] [*Medicine*] (DMAA)
NB .... Neuroblast [*Cytology*]
NB .... Neuroblastoma [*Medicine*] (DMAA)
NB .... Neurometric Battery (DMAA)
NB .... Neurometric Test Battery [*Neurometrics*]

NB .... Neutral Beam (ACAE)
NB .... Neutral Buoyancy [*Navy*] (SSD)
NB .... Neutron Beam (SAUS)
NB .... New Benloe's Reports, English King's Bench [*1531-1628*] [*A publication*] (DLA)
NB .... New Boiler
NB .... Newborn
NB .... New Bottom [*On ships*]
NB .... New Brunswick [*Canadian province*] [*Postal code*]
NB .... New Brunswick Power Corporation (EFIS)
NB .... New Brunswick Reports [*A publication*] (DLA)
NB .... New Business
NB .... New Haven Airways [*ICAO designator*] (AD)
NB .... Next Brochure
NB .... Nigerian Bonny [*Crude oil*]
NB .... Night Blindness (MELL)
NB .... Night Bomber (or Bombing) (SAUS)
NB .... Nimbus [*Cloud*] [*Meteorology*]
Nb........... Niobium [*See Cb*] [*Chemical element*]
NB .... Nitrobenzene [*Organic chemistry*]
NB .... Nitrogen Base (NASA)
NB .... Nitrous Oxide-Barbiturate [*Organic chemistry*] (MAE)
NB .... No Ball [*Cricket*]
NB .... No Bias [*Relay*] [*Electronics*]
NB .... No Bid [*or Bidders*]
NB .... No Bowel Movement [*Gastroenterology*] (DAVI)
NB .... No Box
N/B........... No Brands (SAUS)
NB .... Noise Blanker
NB .... Noise Block (ELAL)
N/B........... Noise Power/Bandwidth
NB .... Nomenclature Board [*Tasmania, Australia*]
NB .... Nominal Bone (SAUS)
NB .... Nominal Bore [*Tubing*]
NB .... Nonbargaining (SAUS)
NB .... Nonbattle [*Army*] (AABC)
NB .... Nonbusiness [*IRS*]
NB .... Nopol Benzyl (SAUS)
NB .... Nordiska Batradet [*Nordic Boat Council*] [*Sweden*] (EAIO)
NB .... Nordlands Bank [*Norway*]
NB .... Normal Bowel Movement [*Gastroenterology*] (DAVI)
NB .... Normal Bus (SAUS)
NB .... Normoblast [*Hematology*] (AAMN)
NB .... Northampton & Bath Railroad Co. [*AAR code*]
NB .... Northbound
NB .... North Britain [*i.e., Scotland*]
NB .... Nosebleed (MELL)
NB .... Not a Bean [*Penniless*] [*Facetious translation of NB, Nota Bene (Note Well)*] (DSUE)
nb........... Nota Bene [*Note Well*] [*Latin*] (WDMC)
NB .... Nota Bene [*Note Well*] [*Latin*]
NB .... Not Be [*Telegraphy*] (PCTE)
NB .... Not Bent [*Freight*]
NB .... Not Blind [*Experimental conditions*]
NB .... Notch Bend (SAUS)
NB .... Notch-Bend (PDAA)
NB .... Nuclear Blank (NRCH)
NB .... Nuclear Boiler (NRCH)
NB .... Nucleus Basalis [*Brain anatomy*]
NB .... Nulla Bona [*No Goods*] [*Latin*] [*Legal term*] (DLA)
Nb........... Number (SAUS)
Nb........... Numbered (SAUS)
NB .... Number of Bits (SAUS)
NB .... Number of Bytes (SAUS)
Nb........... Numbers [*Old Testament book*] (BJA)
NB .... Nursing Building (SAUS)
NB .... Nutrient Broth (MELL)
NB2.......... Norsar Array Site 02B00 [*Norway*] [*Seismograph station code, US Geological Survey*] (SEIS)
NB 2d .... New Brunswick Reports, Second Series [*A publication*] (DLA)
NB3.......... Norsar Array Site 03B00 [*Norway*] [*Seismograph station code, US Geological Survey*] (SEIS)
NB4.......... Norsar Array Site 04B00 [*Norway*] [*Seismograph station code, US Geological Survey*] (SEIS)
NB5.......... Norsar Array Site 05B00 [*Norway*] [*Seismograph station code, US Geological Survey*] (SEIS)
NBA.......... Amateur Astronomers Association, Brooklyn, NY [*Library symbol*] [*Library of Congress*] (LCLS)
NBa.......... Davenport Library, Bath, NY [*Library symbol*] [*Library of Congress*] (LCLS)
Nba.......... Nambia (MILB)
NBA.......... Narrowband Allocation
NBA.......... Narrowband Analyzer
NBA.......... Narrow-Beam Adapter
NBA.......... National Ballet of America
NBA.......... National Band Association (EA)
NBA.......... National Bank Act of 1863
NBA.......... National Bankers Association [*Washington, DC*] (EA)
NBA.......... National Bankruptcy Act [*1898*]
NBA.......... National Bar Association (EA)
NBA.......... National Basketball Association (EA)
NBA.......... National Beef Association (GVA)
NBA.......... National Beefmaster Association (EA)
NBA.......... National Benevolent Association of the Christian Church [*Disciples of Christ*] (EA)
NBA.......... National Benzole and Allied Products Association [*British*] (BI)
NBA.......... National Biographical Association (EA)
NBA.......... National Bison Association (NTPA)
NBA.......... National Boat Association (EA)
NBA.......... National Book Awards [*Discontinued*]
NBA.......... National Bowling Association (EA)
NBA.......... National Boxing Association of America [*Later, WBA*]
NBA.......... National Braille Association (EA)
NBA.......... National Brassfoundry Association [*British*] (BI)
NBA.......... National Broadcasting Authority [*Bangladesh*] (EY)
NBA.......... National Broiler Association [*Later, NBC*]
NBA.......... National Buffalo Association (EA)
NBA.......... National Building Agency [*British*]
NBA.......... National Business Association (EA)
NBA.......... National Butterfly Association (EA)
NBA.......... National Button Association
NBA.......... N-Bromoacetamide [*Organic chemistry*]
NBA.......... N-Butylamine [*Organic chemistry*]
NBA.......... Nebraska Bankers Association (EARSL)
NBA.......... Net Book Agreement [*British*]
NBA.......... Net Building Area (ADA)
NBA.......... Neuromuscular Blocking Agent (SAUS)
NBA.......... New Brunswick Area (SAA)
NBA.......... Nickel-Base Alloy
NBA.......... Non-Weight-Bearing Ambulation [*Orthopedics*] (DAVI)
NBA.......... Normal Butyl Alcohol (SAUS)
NBA.......... North British Academy
NBA.......... North East Bolivian Airways [*ICAO designator*] (FAAC)
NBAA........ Amateur Astronomers Association, Brooklyn, NY [*Library symbol*] [*Library of Congress*] (LCLS)
NBAA........ National Business Aircraft Association (EA)
NBAA-PAC... National Business Aviation Association Inc. PAC [*Washington, DC*] (PACS)
NBab........ Babylon Public Library, Babylon, NY [*Library symbol*] [*Library of Congress*] (LCLS)
NBAB........ Biological Station, Fisheries and Oceans Canada [*Station de Biologie, Peches et Oceans Canada*] St. Andrews, New Brunswick [*Library symbol*] [*National Library of Canada*] (NLC)
NBab........ Neo-Babylonian [*or New Babylonian*] (BJA)
NBAC........ National Bioethics Advisory Commission
NBAC........ National Bioethics Advisory Committee
NBAC........ National Biotechnology Advisory Committee [*Canada*]
NBAC........ National Black Alcoholism Council (EA)
NBACA...... National Broadcast Association for Community Affairs (NTPA)
NBACCH..... Charlotte County Historical Society, Inc., St. Andrews, New Brunswick [*Library symbol*] [*National Library of Canada*] (NLC)
NBACSTT... New Brunswick Association of Certified Survey Technicians and Technologists (SAUS)
NBACY...... North Bay City, MI [*American Association of Railroads railroad junction routing code*]
NBAD........ National Bank of Abu Dhabi
NBAD........ Naval Bases Air Defense
NBAD........ N-beta-Alanyldopamine [*Biochemistry*]
NBADA...... National Barrel and Drum Association [*Later, NABADA - The Association of Container Reconditioners*] (EA)
NBAE........ National Basketball Association Entertainment
NBAE........ New Business Acquisition Expenditures (ACAE)
NBAF........ National Blonde d'Aquitaine Foundation (EA)
NBAGLE..... National Black Alliance for Graduate Level Education [*Defunct*] (EA)
NBAJ........ National Buffalo Association Juniors [*Defunct*] (EA)
NBAK........ National Bancorp of Alaska, Inc. [*NASDAQ symbol*] (NQ)
NBAK........ National Bancorporation of Alaska [*NASDAQ symbol*]
NBAK........ Natl Bancorp(AK) [*NASDAQ symbol*] (TTSB)
N balance... Nitrogen Balance [*Medicine*] (WDAA)
NBald........ Baldwin Public Library, Baldwin (SAUS)
NBald........ Baldwin Public Library, Baldwin, NY [*Library symbol*] [*Library of Congress*] (LCLS)
NBaldBE.... Brookside Elementary School, Baldwin, NY [*Library symbol*] [*Library of Congress*] (LCLS)
NBaldCE.... Collidge Elementary School, Baldwin, NY [*Library symbol*] [*Library of Congress*] (LCLS)
NBaldGE.... Grand Avenue Elementary School, Baldwin, NY [*Library symbol*] [*Library of Congress*] (LCLS)
NBaldHE.... Harbor Elementary School, Baldwin, NY [*Library symbol*] [*Library of Congress*] (LCLS)
NBaldHJ.... Harbor Junior High School, Baldwin, NY [*Library symbol*] [*Library of Congress*] (LCLS)
NBaldLE.... Lenox Elementary School, Baldwin, NY [*Library symbol*] [*Library of Congress*] (LCLS)
NBaldME.... Meadow Elementary School, Baldwin, NY [*Library symbol*] [*Library of Congress*] (LCLS)
NBaldMiE... Milburn Elementary School, Baldwin, NY [*Library symbol*] [*Library of Congress*] (LCLS)
NbaldPE.... Plaza Elementary School, Baldwin, NY [*Library symbol*] [*Library of Congress*] (LCLS)
NBaldPrE... Prospect Elementary School, Baldwin, NY [*Library symbol*] [*Library of Congress*] (LCLS)
NBaldSE.... Shubert Elementary School, Baldwin, NY [*Library symbol*] [*Library of Congress*] (LCLS)
NBaldSH.... Baldwin Senior High School, Baldwin, NY [*Library symbol*] [*Library of Congress*] (LCLS)
NBaldStE.... Steele Elementary School, Baldwin, NY [*Library symbol*] [*Library of Congress*] (LCLS)
NB Alsk..... National Bancorp of Alaska, Inc. [*Associated Press*] (SAG)
NB & BA.... National Bed-and-Breakfast Association (EA)
NB & C...... Norfolk, Baltimore & Carolina Line [*Steamship*] (MHDB)

NBAO........ New Brunswick Area Office [*Later, NBL*] [*AEC*]
NBAPA....... National Black American Paralegal Association (NTPA)
NBar......... Barker Free Library, Barker, NY [*Library symbol*] [*Library of Congress*] (LCLS)
nbar......... Nanobar [*One billionth of a bar*]
NBAR........ Non-Binding Allocation of Responsibility (COE)
NBAR........ Nonbinding Preliminary Allocation of Responsibility [*Environmental Protection Agency*] (FFDE)
NBARN...... New Brunswick Association of Registered Nurses (SAUS)
NBaryU...... Unified Theological Seminary, Barrytown, NY [*Library symbol*] [*Library of Congress*] (LCLS)
NBAs........ National Bioindustries Associations (SAUS)
NBAS........ Neonatal Behavioural Assessment Scale [*Developed by Brazelton*]
NBAS-K..... Neonatal Behavioral Assessment Scale-Kansas Revision (EDAC)
NBASLH..... National Black Association for Speech, Language and Hearing (EA)
NBat......... Richmond Memorial Library, Batavia, NY [*Library symbol*] [*Library of Congress*] (LCLS)
NBatC....... Genesee Community College, Batavia, NY [*Library symbol*] [*Library of Congress*] (LCLS)
NBatGB...... Genesse-Wyoming Board of Cooperative Education Services, Batavia, NY [*Library symbol*] [*Library of Congress*] (LCLS)
NBatGH..... Genesee Memorial Hospital, Batavia, NY [*Library symbol*] [*Library of Congress*] (LCLS)
NBatHHi..... Holland Purchase Historical Society, Batavia, NY [*Library symbol*] [*Library of Congress*] (LCLS)
NBatStJ..... Saint Jerome Hospital, Medical Library, Batavia, NY [*Library symbol*] [*Library of Congress*] (LCLS)
NBatV....... United States Veterans Administration Hospital, Library Service, Batavia, NY [*Library symbol*] [*Library of Congress*] (LCLS)
NBAU........ No Business as Usual (EA)
NBaVA....... United States Veterans Administration Hospital, Bath, NY [*Library symbol*] [*Library of Congress*] (LCLS)
NBAW....... Notable Black American Women [*A publication*]
NBAWADU... National Black Anti-War Anti-Draft Union (EA)
NBAY........ North Bay, ON [*American Association of Railroads railroad junction routing code*]
NBayr........ Bayville Free Library (SAUS)
NBayv....... Bayville Free Library, Bayville, NY [*Library symbol*] [*Library of Congress*] (LCLS)
NBayvE...... Bayville Elementary School, Bayville, NY [*Library symbol*] [*Library of Congress*] (LCLS)
NBayvI...... Bayville Intermediate School, Bayville, NY [*Library symbol*] [*Library of Congress*] (LCLS)
NBayvP...... Bayville Primary School, Bayville, NY [*Library symbol*] [*Library of Congress*] (LCLS)
NbB.......... Beatrice Public Library, Beatrice, NE [*Library symbol*] [*Library of Congress*] (LCLS)
NBB.......... Brooklyn Museum, Brooklyn, NY [*Library symbol*] [*Library of Congress*] (LCLS)
NBB.......... Narrowband Beam [*Physics*]
NBB.......... National Bank of Bahrain (EY)
NBB.......... National Bank of Brunei
NBB.......... National Biodiesel Board [*Alternative fuels*]
NBB.......... New Bedford Institution for Savings (SAUS)
NBB.......... New Business Beat (ACAE)
NBB.......... Nike/Black Brant (SAUS)
NBB.......... Number of Bytes of Binary (SAUS)
NBBA........ National Bed and Breakfast Association (NTPA)
NBBA........ National Beep Baseball Association (EA)
NBBA........ National Black Business Alliance (EA)
NBB & L.... National Bath, Bed, and Linen Show (ITD)
NBBB........ National Better Business Bureau (NADA)
NBBC........ Bibliotheque Medicale, Hopital Regional Chaleur [*Medical Library, Chaleur Regional Hospital*] Bathurst, New Brunswick [*Library symbol*] [*National Library of Canada*] (NLC)
NBBC........ National Black Business Council
NBBCC...... College Communautaire du New Brunswick, Bathurst, New Brunswick [*Library symbol*] [*National Library of Canada*] (NLC)
NBBCN...... New Brunswick Breast Cancer Network (SAUS)
NBBDA...... National Burlap Bag Dealers Association [*Later, Textile Bag and Packaging Association*] (EA)
NbBe........ Bellevue Public Library, Bellevue, NE [*Library symbol*] [*Library of Congress*] (LCLS)
NBB-E....... Brooklyn Museum, Wilbour Library of Egyptology, Brooklyn, NY [*Library symbol*] [*Library of Congress*] (LCLS)
NBBE........ National Board for Bakery Education [*British*] (BI)
NbBea....... Beatrice Public Library, Beatrice, NE [*Library symbol*] [*Library of Congress*] (LCLS)
NbBeL....... Bellevue Public Library, Bellevue, NE [*Library symbol*] [*Library of Congress*] (LCLS)
NBBI......... National Blue Books, Inc. [*Canoga Park, CA*] [*Publisher*]
NBBI......... National Board of Boiler and Pressure Vessel Inspectors (NTPA)
NBBI......... Nederlands Bureau voor Bibliotheekwezen en Informatieverzorging [*Netherlands Organization for Libraries and Information Services*] [*Information service or system*] (IID)
NBBL........ National Bath, Bed, and Linen Association (EA)
NbBla........ Blair Public Library, Blair, NE [*Library symbol*] [*Library of Congress*] (LCLS)
NBBLA....... National Bath, Bed, and Linen Association [*Later, NBBL*] (EA)
NbBlaD...... Dana College, Blair, NE [*Library symbol*] [*Library of Congress*] (LCLS)
NBBLC....... National Black on Black Love Campaign (EA)
NBBMA...... National Beauty and Barber Manufacturers Association [*Later, ABA*] (EA)
NBBMK...... Mussee de Kent, Bouctouche, New Brunswick [*Library symbol*] [*National Library of Canada*] (NLC)
NBBN........ Nepisiguit Centennial Public Library, Bathurst, New Brunswick [*Library symbol*] [*National Library of Canada*] (NLC)
NBBP........ National Board of Boiler & Pressure Vessel Inspectors
Nb-BPH..... Nebraska Library Commission, Library for Blind and Physically Handicapped, Lincoln, NE [*Library symbol*] [*Library of Congress*] (LCLS)
NBBPVI...... National Board of Boiler and Pressure Vessel Inspectors (EA)
NBBQA...... National Barbecue Association
NbBro....... Broken Bow Carnegie Library, Broken Bow, NE [*Library symbol*] [*Library of Congress*] (LCLS)
NBBS........ New British Broadcasting Station (NADA)
NBBU........ New Brunswick Board of Underwriters (SAUS)
NBBWM..... Central New Brunswick Woodmen's Museum, Boiestown, New Brunswick [*Library symbol*] [*National Library of Canada*] (NLC)
NBC.......... Beaufort, SC [*Location identifier*] [*FAA*] (FAAL)
NBC.......... Brooklyn College, Brooklyn, NY [*Library symbol*] [*Library of Congress*] (LCLS)
NBC.......... Concordia College, Seward, NE [*OCLC symbol*] (OCLC)
NBC.......... Cook [*N. B.*] Corp. Ltd. [*Toronto Stock Exchange symbol*] [*Vancouver Stock Exchange symbol*]
NBC.......... Narrowband Conducted (IEEE)
NBC.......... Nasobiliary Catheter [*Medicine*] (MELL)
NBC.......... National Bank of Canada [*Canada*] (EFIS)
NBC.......... National Baseball Congress (EA)
NBC.......... National Basketball Congress (NADA)
NBC.......... National Battlefields Commission [*See also CCBN*]
NBC.......... National Beagle Club (EA)
NBC.......... National Beef Congress
NBC.......... National Bibliographic Control
NBC.......... National Biscuit Co. (EFIS)
NBC.......... National Board for Certification in Dental Laboratory Technology (EA)
NBC.......... National Book Committee [*Defunct*]
NBC.......... National Book Council [*Later, NBL*] [*United Kingdom*]
NBC.......... National Bowling Council (EA)
NBC.......... National Boxing Council [*British*]
NBC.......... National Boys' Club (WDAA)
NBC.......... National Braille Club [*Later, NBA*] (EA)
NBC.......... National Broadcasters' Club (NTCM)
NBC.......... National Broadcasting Co., Inc. [*New York, NY*]
NBC.......... National Broadcasting Commission (NADA)
NBC.......... National Broiler Council (EA)
NBC.......... National Broom Council [*Later, NBMC*] (EA)
NBC.......... National Building Code
NBC.......... National Building Code of Canada (HGAA)
NBC.......... National Bus Co. [*British*]
NBC.......... Natural Background Clutter
NBC.......... Natural Birth Control
NBC.......... Navy Beach Commando
NBC.......... Navy Branch Clinic (ACAE)
NBC.......... Neumann Boundary Conditions
NBC.......... Newfoundland Base Command [*Army*] [*World War II*]
NBC.......... Nies Babylonian Collection [*Yale University*] (BJA)
NBC.......... Nigeria Broadcasting Corp. (SAUS)
NBC.......... Nigerian Broadcasting Corp.
NBC.......... No Back Cover
NBC.......... Noise Balancing Circuit (DEN)
NBC.......... Noise Balancing Control (IAA)
NBC.......... Nonbattle Casualty (NVT)
NBC.......... Nonbleeding Cable (SAUS)
NBC.......... Nordic Boat Council (EA)
NBC.......... Norwegian Bulk Carrier (SAUS)
NBC.......... Nostalgia Book Club
NBC.......... Not Backward-Compatible (SAUS)
NBC.......... Nothing but Chaos (SAUS)
NBC.......... Nuclear, Biological, and Chemical [*Warfare*]
NBC.......... Number Base Conversion
NBC.......... Nursing Bottle Caries [*Medicine*] (MELL)
NBCA........ Campbellton Centennial Public Library, New Brunswick [*Library symbol*] [*National Library of Canada*] (NLC)
NBCA........ National Band Council of Australia
NBCA........ National Bareboat Charter Association (NTPA)
NBCA........ National Baseball Congress of America (NADA)
NBCA........ National Beagle Club of America (EA)
NBCA........ National Bituminous Concrete Association [*Later, NAPA*] (EA)
NBCA........ National Business Circulation Association (EA)
NBCA........ Navy Department Board of Contract Appeals [*1944-50*] (AAGC)
NBCAA...... National Bible College Athletic Association (PSS)
NBCAC...... Chaleur Library Region, Campbellton, New Brunswick [*Library symbol*] [*National Library of Canada*] (NLC)
NBCAM...... Campobello Public Library, New Brunswick [*Library symbol*] [*National Library of Canada*] (BIB)
NBCAP...... National Becaon Code Allocation Plan (FAAC)
NBCBP...... Bibliotheque Publique Mgr. Paquet, Caraquet, New Brunswick [*Library symbol*] [*National Library of Canada*] (NLC)
NBCC........ National Baby Care Council [*Defunct*] (EA)
NBCC........ National Bank of Commerce Co. (West Virginia) [*NASDAQ symbol*] (COMM)
NBCC........ National Beauty Career Center (EA)
NBCC........ National Bidders Control Center
NBCC........ National Bituminous Coal Commission [*Functions transferred to Department of the Interior, 1939*]
NBCC........ National Black Chamber of Commerce (EA)
NBCC........ National Board for Certified Counselors (EA)
NBCC........ National Book Critics Circle (EA)
NBCC........ National Breast Cancer Centre (SAUS)

NBCC .... National Breast Cancer Coalition
NBCC .... National Budget and Consultation Committee [*Defunct*] (EA)
NBCC .... National Building Code of Canada
NBCC .... National Bureau for Co-Operation in Child Care [*British*]
NBCC .... National Business Career Center (EA)
NBCC .... Netherlands British Chamber of Commerce (DS)
NBCC .... Nevoid Basal-Cell Carcinoma [*Oncology*]
NBCC .... New Brunswick Community College (SAUS)
NBCC .... Nigerian British Chamber of Commerce [*London*] (DCTA)
NBCC .... Nuclear, Biological, and Chemical Center
NBCC .... Nuclear, Biological, and Chemical Contamination (DOMA)
NBCC .... Nuclear, Biological, Chemical, Conventional [*Warfare*]
NBCCA ...... National Business Council for Consumer Affairs [*Terminated, 1974*] [*Department of Commerce*] (EGAO)
NBCCA ...... Northern British Columbia Construction Association (SAUS)
NBCCC ...... Miramichi Campus, New Brunswick Community College [*Campus Miramichi, College Communautaire du Nouveau-Brunswick*], Chatham, New Brunswick [*Library symbol*] [*National Library of Canada*] (NLC)
NBCCC ...... National Black Catholic Clergy Caucus (EA)
NBCCC ...... National Bureau for Co-Operation in Child Care [*British*] (BI)
NBCCC ...... Nuclear, Biological, and Chemical Control Center [*Military*] [*Chemical warfare*]
NBC-CDTP... National Board for Certification - Certified Dental Technician Program (EA)
NBCCEDP... National Breast and Cervical Cancer Early Detection Program (SAUS)
NBCCH ...... National Board for Certified Clinical Hypnotherapists (NTPA)
NBCCS ...... Nevoid Basal Cell Carcinoma Syndrome [*Oncology*] (DMAA)
NBCCW...... Nuclear, Biological, Chemical, Conventional Warfare (SAUS)
NBCD .... Natural Binary-Coded Decimal
NBCD .... Negate BCD [*Binary-Coded Decimal*] Number [*Computer science*]
NBCD .... Normal Binary Coded Decimal (SAUS)
NBCD .... Nuclear, Biological, and Chemical Defense (NATG)
NBCDC3..... NBCD Command, Control & Communications (SAUS)
NBCDC3T ... NBC defence & Damage C3 Trainer (SAUS)
NBCDCE..... Nuclear, Biological, and Chemical Defense Control Element [*Military*]
NBCDCODING... Normal Binary Coded Decimal Coding (SAUS)
NBC defense... Nuclear defense, Biological defense and Chemical defense (SAUS)
NBCDI .... National Black Child Development Institute (EA)
NBCDL ...... National Board for Certification of Dental Laboratories [*Later, CDL*] (EA)
NBCDX ...... Nuclear, Biological, and Chemical Defense Exercise [*NATO*] (NATG)
NBCE .... National Board of Chiropractic Examiners [*Association*] (EA)
NBCE .... Nuclear, Biological, and Chemical Element
NbCen....... Hards Memorial Library, Central City, NE [*Library symbol*] [*Library of Congress*] (LCLS)
NbCenC ..... Nebraska Central College, Central City, NE [*Library symbol*] [*Library of Congress*] [*Obsolete*] (LCLS)
NBCF .... Nuclear, Biological, Chemical & Fire (SAUS)
NBCFAE ..... National Black Coalition of Federal Aviation Employees (EA)
NBCFD ...... Naval Base Consolidated Fire Department (DNAB)
NBCFWRU... New Brunswick Cooperative Fish and Wildlife Research Unit [*University of New Brunswick*] [*Canada*] (RCD)
NBCG .... National Bulk Commodities Group [*Australia*]
NBCGT ...... National Business Consortium for the Gifted and Talented [*Defunct*] (EA)
NbCh .... Chadron Public Library, Chadron, NE [*Library symbol*] [*Library of Congress*] (LCLS)
NBCH .... Historical Society Nicolas Denys, Societe Historique Nicolas Denys, Caraquet, New Brunswick [*Library symbol*] [*National Library of Canada*] (NLC)
NBCHD ...... Chatham, Hotel-Dieu Hospital, New Brunswick (SAUS)
NBCHD ...... Health Sciences Library, Hotel-Dieu Hospital, Chatham, New Brunswick [*Library symbol*] [*National Library of Canada*] (BIB)
NBCHR ...... Bibliotheque de la Sante, Centre Hospitalier Restigouche, Campbellton, New Brunswick [*Library symbol*] [*National Library of Canada*] (BIB)
NbChS....... Chadron State College, Chadron, NE [*Library symbol*] [*Library of Congress*] (LCLS)
NBCI......... NBC Internet
NBCi......... NBC Internet Inc.
NBCI......... Nigerian Bank for Commerce and Industry
NBCIA .... National Blue Crab Industry Association (EA)
NBCL .... National Beauty Culturists' League (EA)
NBCL .... National Birth Control League
NBCLEO..... National Black Caucus of Local Elected Officials (NTPA)
NBCM .... Miramichi Natural History Society, Chatham, New Brunswick [*Library symbol*] [*National Library of Canada*] (NLC)
NBCMA...... Mussee Acadien, Caraquet, New Brunswick [*Library symbol*] [*National Library of Canada*] (NLC)
NBC/MMT... Nuclear Biological Contamination/Manufacturing Methods Technology (ACAE)
NBCMu...... Brooklyn Children's Museum, Brooklyn, NY [*Library symbol*] [*Library of Congress*] (LCLS)
NbCo .... Columbus Public Library, Columbus, NE [*Library symbol*] [*Library of Congress*] (LCLS)
NbCoC....... Platte Technical Community College, Columbus, NE [*Library symbol*] [*Library of Congress*] (LCLS)
NBCOT ...... National Board for Certification of Orthopaedic Technologists (EA)
NBCP .... Brooklyn College of Pharmacy, Brooklyn, NY [*Library symbol*] [*Library of Congress*] (LCLS)
NBCP .... National Bladder Cancer Project [*National Cancer Institute*]
NBCP .... Niagara Bancorp, Inc. [*NASDAQ symbol*] (NASQ)
NBCPC ...... National Board for Cardiovascular and Pulmonary Credentialing [*Later, Cardiovascular Credentialing International - CCI*] (EA)
NBCPC ...... Nuclear, Biological & Chemical Protective Cover (SAUS)
NbCr......... Crete Public Library, Crete, NE [*Library symbol*] [*Library of Congress*] (LCLS)
NBCR........ Nominal Balance Credit Write-Off [*Electric utility company*]
NbCrD .... Doane College, Crete, NE [*Library symbol*] [*Library of Congress*] (LCLS)
NBCRS ...... Nuclear-Biological-Chemical Reconnaissance System [*Military*]
NBCS .... National Black Communicators Society (EA)
NBCS .... St. Thomas University, Fredericton, New Brunswick [*Library symbol*] [*National Library of Canada*] (NLC)
NBCSA ...... National Black Catholic Seminarians Association (EA)
NBCSDA..... National Broom Corn and Supply Dealers Association (EA)
NBCSH ...... La Societe Historique de Clair, Inc., New Brunswick [*Library symbol*] [*National Library of Canada*] (NLC)
NBCSI .... National Board of the Coat and Suit Industry [*Defunct*] (EA)
NBCSL....... National Black Caucus of State Legislators (EA)
NBCSS ...... Nuclear, Biological & Chemical Shelter System (SAUS)
NBcs TX..... National Bancshares Corp. of Texas [*Associated Press*] (SAG)
NBCU .... National Bureau of Casualty Underwriters [*Later, ISO*] (EA)
NBC USA.... National Baptist Convention, USA (EA)
NBCV .... Narrowband Coherent Video (IEEE)
NBCVHA..... Le Village Historique Acadien, Caraquet, New Brunswick [*Library symbol*] [*National Library of Canada*] (NLC)
NBCW .... National Bird Cage Week
NBCW .... National Board of Catholic Women [*British*]
NBCWARN... Nuclear, Biological, and Chemical Warning
NBCWRS.... Nuclear, Biological, and Chemical Warning and Reporting System
NBD.......... Doane College, Crete, NE [*OCLC symbol*] (OCLC)
NBD.......... Narrowband Detector
NBD.......... National Bank of Detroit (EFIS)
NBD.......... National Bank of Dubai
NBD.......... National Detroit Corp. (EFIS)
NBD.......... NBD Bancorp, Inc. [*NYSE symbol*] (SPSG)
NBD.......... Negative Binomial Distribution [*Statistics*]
NBD.......... Neurogenic Bladder Dysfunction [*Medicine*]
NBD.......... Neurologic Bladder Dysfunction [*Medicine*] (DB)
NBD.......... Neutral Beam Divider
NBD.......... Nitrobenzoxadiazole [*Organic chemistry*]
nbd .... No Big Deal [*Internet language*] [*Computer science*]
NBD.......... No Brain Damage (MELL)
NBD.......... Nondirectional Beacon
NBD.......... Norbornadiene [*Organic chemistry*]
NBD.......... Normal Business Day [*Communications term*] (DCT)
NBD.......... Nucleotide Binding Domain [*Biochemistry*]
NBDA........ National Barrel and Drum Association
NBDA........ National Bicycle Dealers Association (EA)
NBDA........ National Black Deaf Advocates (EA)
NBDC........ National Blood Data Center [*American Blood Commission*] [*Information service or system*] (IID)
NBDC .... National Bomb Data Center
NBDC........ Nebraska Business Development Center [*University of Nebraska at Omaha*] (RCD)
NBDC........ Nebraska Business Development Center [*University of Nebraska at Kearney*] (RCD)
NBDC........ Nebraska Business Development Center [*Wayne State College*] (RCD)
NBDC........ Nebraska Business Development Center [*Chadron State College*] (RCD)
NBDC........ New Brunswick Development Corp. (SAUS)
NBDCA ...... National Baptist Deacons Convention of America (EA)
NBDE .... National Bureau of Document Examiners (EA)
NBDEA ...... National Beverage Dispensing Equipment Association (EA)
NB Dep Nat Resour Repr... New Brunswick Department of Natural Resources. Reprint (SAUS)
NBDF........ Narrow Band Device - Fix
NBDF........ Narrowband Dicke-Fix [*Electronics*] (CET)
NBDFB ...... Nitrobenzenediazonium Tetrafluoroborate [*Organic chemistry*]
NBDFX ...... Narrowband Dicke-Fix [*Electronics*] (MSA)
NBDKH ...... Keillor House Museum, Dorchester, New Brunswick [*Library symbol*] [*National Library of Canada*] (NLC)
NBDL........ Narrowband Data Line
NBDL........ Narrowband Data Link (IAA)
NBDL........ Naval Biodynamics Laboratory (GRD)
NBDM .... Miramichi Salmon Museum, Inc., Doaktown, New Brunswick [*Library symbol*] [*National Library of Canada*] (NLC)
NBDMO ..... N-Bromo(dimethyl)oxazolidinone [*Organic chemistry*]
NBDN........ Nuclear Blast Detector Network (SAUS)
NB-DNJ ..... N-Butyldeoxynojirimycin [*Biochemistry*]
NBDP........ Narrow-Band Direct Printing (OTD)
NBD-PS ..... Nitrobenzoxadiazole Phosphatidylserine [*Biochemistry*]
NBDR........ Nominal Balance Debit Write-Off [*Electric utility company*]
NBDRRM.... Restigouche Regional Museum, Dalhousie, New Brunswick [*Library symbol*] [*National Library of Canada*] (NLC)
NBDS .... Nuclear Burst Detection Systems (MCD)
NBDVS ...... Narrow Band Digital Voice System [*Telecommunications*] (LAIN)
NBE.......... Dallas, TX [*Location identifier*] [*FAA*] (FAAL)
NbE .... Exeter Public Library, Exeter, NE [*Library symbol*] [*Library of Congress*] (LCLS)
NBE.......... Near Band Edge (AAEL)
NBE.......... Neutron Binding Energy
NBE.......... Newburyport Birders' Exchange (EA)
NBE.......... Nominal Band Edge
NBE.......... Normal Binocular Experience [*Ophthalmology*]

NbE .... North by East
NBE .... Not Below or Equal (SAUS)
NBE .... Nova Beaucage Mines Ltd. [*Toronto Stock Exchange symbol*]
NBE .... Nuclear Binding Energy
NBEA .... National Ballroom and Entertainment Association (EA)
NBEA .... National Black Evangelical Association (EA)
NBEA .... National Broadcast Editorial Association (EA)
NBEA .... National Business Education Association [*Reston, VA*] (EA)
NBEBR .... Bibliotheque Regionale du Haut Saint-Jean, Edmundston, New Brunswick [*Library symbol*] [*National Library of Canada*] (NLC)
NBEC .... National Business and Education Council (OICC)
NBEC .... New Brunswick East Coast Railway [*Federal Railroad Administration identification code*]
NBECC .... New Brunswick Community College, Edmundston, New Brunswick [*Library symbol*] [*National Library of Canada*] (NLC)
NBECN .... New Brunswick Education Computer Network (SAUS)
NBECS .... Nonresidential Building Energy Comsumption Survey [*Department of Energy*] (GFGA)
NBed .... Bedford Free Library, Bedford, NY [*Library symbol*] [*Library of Congress*] (LCLS)
NBEDC .... National Black Economic Development Conference
NBedh .... Bedford Hills Free Library, Bedford Hills, NY [*Library symbol*] [*Library of Congress*] (LCLS)
NBEF .... National Bowhunter Education Foundation (EA)
NBEI-Syndr ... Non Butanol Extractable Iodine-Syndrome (SAUS)
NBel .... Bellport Memorial Library, Bellport, NY [*Library symbol*] [*Library of Congress*] (LCLS)
NBelf .... Belfast Public Library, Belfast, NY [*Library symbol*] [*Library of Congress*] (LCLS)
NBelL .... Long Island Library Resources Council, Inc., Bellport, NY [*Library symbol*] [*Library of Congress*] (LCLS)
NBellm .... Bellmore Memorial Library, Bellmore, NY [*Library symbol*] [*Library of Congress*] (LCLS)
NBellmCM .. Wellington C. Mepham High School, Bellmore, NY [*Library symbol*] [*Library of Congress*] (LCLS)
NBellmGJ ... Grand Avenue Junior High School, Bellmore, NY [*Library symbol*] [*Library of Congress*] (LCLS)
NBellmKH .. John F. Kennedy High School, Bellmore, NY [*Library symbol*] [*Library of Congress*] (LCLS)
NBellmR .... C.H. Reinhard School, Bellmore, NY [*Library symbol*] [*Library of Congress*] (LCLS)
NBellmSE ... Shore Road Elementary School, Bellmore, NY [*Library symbol*] [*Library of Congress*] (LCLS)
NBellmWE .. Winthrop Avenue Elementary School, Bellmore, NY [*Library symbol*] [*Library of Congress*] (LCLS)
NBelS .... Suffolk Cooperative Library System, Bellport, NY [*Library symbol*] [*Library of Congress*] (LCLS)
NBEMM .... Musee de Madawaska, Edmundston, New Brunswick [*Library symbol*] [*National Library of Canada*] (NLC)
N Ben .... New Benloe's Reports, English King's Bench [*1531-1628*] [*A publication*] (DLA)
N Benl .... New Benloe's Reports, English King's Bench [*1531-1628*] [*A publication*] (DLA)
NBEO .... National Board of Examiners in Optometry (EA)
NBEOPS .... National Board of Examiners for Osteopathic Physicians and Surgeons [*Later, NBOME*] (EA)
NBEPC .... New Brunswick Electric Power Commission (SAUS)
NB Eq .... New Brunswick Equity Reports [*A publication*] (DLA)
NB Eq Ca ... New Brunswick Equity Cases [*A publication*] (DLA)
NB Eq R ..... New Brunswick Equity Reports [*A publication*] (DLA)
NB Eq Rep ... New Brunswick Equity Reports [*A publication*] (DLA)
NBER .... National Bureau of Economic Research (EA)
NBER .... National Bureau of Engineering Registration
NBER .... Nittany & Bald Eagle [*Federal Railroad Administration identification code*]
NBERA .... National Bicentennial Ethnic-Racial Alliance
NBerG .... Gillam-Grant Community Center Library, Bergen, NY [*Library symbol*] [*Library of Congress*] (LCLS)
NBernN .... Bernardsville News, Bernardsville, NJ [*Library symbol*] [*Library of Congress*] (LCLS)
NBerR .... Bergen Reading Center, Bergen, NY [*Library symbol*] [*Library of Congress*] (LCLS)
NBES .... N and B Express [*Common carrier symbol*]
NBES .... National Business Equipment Survey [*British*]
NBES .... Near-Bottom Echo Sounder (SAUS)
NBESLM .... Centre Universitaire Saint-Louis Maillet, Edmundston, New Brunswick [*Library symbol*] [*National Library of Canada*] (NLC)
NBESS .... North Bessemer, PA [*American Association of Railroads railroad junction routing code*]
NBet .... Bethpage Public Library, Bethpage, NY [*Library symbol*] [*Library of Congress*] (LCLS)
NBET .... National Business Entrance Test [*Education*] (AEBS)
NBetCaE .... Campagne Elementary School, Bethpage, NY [*Library symbol*] [*Library of Congress*] (LCLS)
NBetCE .... Central Elementary School, Bethpage, NY [*Library symbol*] [*Library of Congress*] (LCLS)
NBETF .... Neutral-Beam Engineering Test Facility [*Lawrence Berkeley Laboratory*] [*Terminated*] [*Department of Energy*] (GRD)
NBetG .... Grumman Aerospace Corp., Bethpage, NY [*Library symbol*] [*Library of Congress*] (LCLS)
NBetH .... Mid-Island Hospital, Bethpage, NY [*Library symbol*] [*Library of Congress*] (LCLS)
NBethKJ ..... John F. Kennedy Junior High School, Bethpage, NY [*Library symbol*] [*Library of Congress*] (LCLS)
NBethSH .... Bethpage Senior High School, Bethpage, NY [*Library symbol*] [*Library of Congress*] (LCLS)
NBetKE .... Kramer Elementary School, Bethpage, NY [*Library symbol*] [*Library of Congress*] (LCLS)
NBetKJ .... John F. Kennedy Junior High School, Bethpage, NY [*Library symbol*] [*Library of Congress*] (LCLS)
NBetSH .... Bethpage Senior High School, Bethpage, NY [*Library symbol*] [*Library of Congress*] (LCLS)
NBetWE .... John H. West Elementary School, Bethpage, NY [*Library symbol*] [*Library of Congress*] (LCLS)
NBF .... Brooklyn Friends School, New York, NY [*Library symbol*] [*Library of Congress*] (LCLS)
NBF .... Narrowband Filter
NBF .... Nathan Bedford Forrest [*Civil War term*]
NBF .... National Bed Federation [*British*] (DBA)
NBF .... National Birman Fanciers (EA)
NBF .... National Blood Foundation [*Association*] (EA)
NBF .... National Boating Federation (EA)
NBF .... National Burn Federation (EA)
NBF .... Netbios Frame (SAUS)
NBF .... Neutral Buoyancy Facility [*Navy*] (MCD)
NBF .... New Biotechnology Firm
NBF .... New Business Funds (MCD)
NBF .... Nordisk Barnkirurgisk Forening [*Scandinavian Association of Paediatric Surgeons - SAPS*] [*Denmark*] (EAIO)
NBF .... Northbay Financial Corp. [*AMEX symbol*] (SPSG)
NBF .... North Bergen Federation of Public Libraries [*Library network*]
NBF .... Northwest AHEC [*Area Health Education Center*] - Bowman Gray School of Medicine, Taylorsville, NC [*OCLC symbol*] (OCLC)
NBF .... Not Breast Fed (MELL)
NBF .... Now Batting For [*Telegraphy*] (PCTE)
NBF .... Nucleotide Binding Fold [*Genetics*]
NBFA .... National Baseball Fan Association (EA)
NBFA .... National Business Forms Association [*Alexandria, VA*] (EA)
NBFA .... New Business Fund Authorization (MCD)
NBFA .... Provincial Archives of New-Brunswick Fredericton (SAUS)
NBFA .... Provincial Archives of New-Brunswick [*Archives Provinciales du Nouveau-Brunswick*] Fredericton, New Brunswick [*Library symbol*] [*National Library of Canada*] (NLC)
NBFAA .... National Burglar and Fire Alarm Association (EA)
NBFAFA .... Archives, Diocese of Fredericton, Anglican Church of Canada, New Brunswick [*Library symbol*] [*National Library of Canada*] (NLC)
NBFAG .... Research Station, Agriculture Canada [*Station de Recherches, Agriculture Canada*] Fredericton, New Brunswick [*Library symbol*] [*National Library of Canada*] (NLC)
NBFB .... Beaverbrook Collection, New Brunswick Archives, Fredericton, New Brunswick [*Library symbol*] [*National Library of Canada*] (NLC)
NbFb .... Fairbury Public Library, Fairbury, NE [*Library symbol*] [*Library of Congress*] (LCLS)
NbFbC .... Southeast Community College, Fairbury, NE [*Library symbol*] [*Library of Congress*] (LCLS)
NBFBS .... New Brunswick Barristers Society, Fredericton, New Brunswick [*Library symbol*] [*National Library of Canada*] (NLC)
NbFC .... Central Lutheran Theological Seminary, Fremont, NE [*Library symbol*] [*Library of Congress*] (LCLS)
NBFC .... New Brunswick Library Service, Fredericton, New Brunswick (SAUS)
NbFc .... Woods Memorial Library, Falls City, NE [*Library symbol*] [*Library of Congress*] (LCLS)
NBFCE .... NETBIOS Frames Control Program (SAUS)
NbFcP .... Woods Memorial Library, Falls City, NE [*Library symbol*] [*Library of Congress*] (LCLS)
NBFDEC .... Dr. Everett Chalmers Hospital, Fredericton, New Brunswick [*Library symbol*] [*National Library of Canada*] (NLC)
NBFE .... Maritimes Forest Research Centre, Environment Canada [*Centre de Recherches Forestieres des Maritimes, Environnement Canada*] Fredericton, New Brunswick [*Library symbol*] [*National Library of Canada*] (NLC)
NBFED .... New Brunswick Department of Education, Fredericton, New Brunswick [*Library symbol*] [*National Library of Canada*] (NLC)
NBFFO .... National Board of Fur Farm Organizations (EA)
NBFHR .... New Brunswick Department of Historical Resources, Fredericton, New Brunswick [*Library symbol*] [*National Library of Canada*] (NLC)
NBFI .... Non-Bank Financial Institution (SAUS)
NBFI .... Non-Bank Financial Institutions [*Ghana*]
NBFI .... Non-Bank Financial Intermediary (ADA)
NBFJS .... Sunbury West Historical Society, Fredericton Junction, New Brunswick [*Library symbol*] [*National Library of Canada*] (NLC)
NBFJWO ..... National Bureau of Federated Jewish Women's Organizations (EA)
NBFKL .... Kings Landing Historical Settlement, Fredericton, New Brunswick [*Library symbol*] [*National Library of Canada*] (NLC)
NBFL .... Legislative Library [*Bibliotheque Legislative*] Fredericton, New Brunswick [*Library symbol*] [*National Library of Canada*] (NLC)
NBFL .... New Brunswick Federation of Labour (SAUS)
NBFLM .... Photogrammetry Branch, New Brunswick Department of Lands and Mines, Fredericton,New Brunswick [*Library symbol*] [*National Library of Canada*] (NLC)
NBFM .... Narrowband Frequency Modulation [*Radio*]
NBFMM .... Medley Memorial Library, Christ Church Cathedral, Fredericton, New Brunswick [*Library symbol*] [*National Library of Canada*] (NLC)
NBFNR .... New Brunswick Department of Natural Resources and Energy, Fredericton, New Brunswick [*Library symbol*] [*National Library of Canada*] (NLC)
NBFO .... National Black Feminist Organization
NBFO .... Norbert Barrie Family Organization [*Association*] (EA)
NBFP .... New Brunswick Power, Fredericton, New Brunswick [*Library symbol*] [*National Library of Canada*] (NLC)
NBFPO .... Premier's Office, Province of New Brunswick, Fredericton, New Brunswick [*Library symbol*] [*National Library of Canada*] (NLC)

NbFr......... Fremont Public Library, Fremont, NE [*Library symbol*] [*Library of Congress*] (LCLS)
NBFR........ Neutral Balance Force Reductions (SAUS)
NBFR........ Not Before [*ICAO designator*] (FAAC)
NbFrM....... Midland Lutheran College, Fremont, NE [*Library symbol*] [*Library of Congress*] (LCLS)
NBFRP...... New Brunswick Research and Productivity Council, Fredericton, New Brunswick [*Library symbol*] [*National Library of Canada*] (NLC)
NBFS........ National Bird-Feeding Society (EA)
NBFS........ New Balanced File Organization Scheme (MHDB)
NBFS........ Societe d'Histoire de la Riviere Saint Jean, Fredericton, New Brunswick [*Library symbol*] [*National Library of Canada*] (BIB)
NBFSS....... New Brunswick Department of Social Services, Fredericton, New Brunswick [*Library symbol*] [*National Library of Canada*] (NLC)
NBFT........ Bureau de Traduction, Gouvernement du Nouveau-Brunswick [*Translation Bureau, Governement of New Brunswick*] Fredericton, New Brunswick [*Library symbol*] [*National Library of Canada*] (NLC)
NBFTR....... New Brunswick Department of Transportation, Fredericton, New Brunswick [*Library symbol*] [*National Library of Canada*] (NLC)
NBFU........ National Board of Fire Underwriters [*Later, AIA*] (EA)
NBFU........ Newfoundland Board of Fire Underwriters (SAUS)
NBFU........ University of New Brunswick, Fredericton, New Brunswick [*Library symbol*] [*National Library of Canada*] (NLC)
NBFUA...... Archives and Special Collections Department, University of New Brunswick, Fredericton, New Brunswick [*Library symbol*] [*National Library of Canada*] (NLC)
NBFUE....... Engineering Library, University of New Brunswick, Fredericton [*Library symbol*] [*National Library of Canada*] (BIB)
NBFUL....... Law Library, University of New Brunswick, Fredericton, New Brunswick [*Library symbol*] [*National Library of Canada*] (NLC)
NBFUM...... Map Room, Government Documents Department, University of New Brunswick, Fredericton, New Brunswick [*Library symbol*] [*National Library of Canada*] (NLC)
NBFY........ York-Sunbury Historical Society, Fredericton, New Brunswick [*Library symbol*] [*National Library of Canada*] (NLC)
NBFYR...... York Regional Library, Fredericton, New Brunswick [*Library symbol*] [*National Library of Canada*] (NLC)
NBFYRC..... New Brunswick Department of Youth, Recreation and Cultural Resources, Fredericton, New Brunswick [*Library symbol*] [*National Library of Canada*] (NLC)
NBG.......... Bowman Gray School of Medicine, Winston-Salem, NC [*OCLC symbol*] (OCLC)
NBG.......... Brooklyn Botanic Garden, Brooklyn, NY [*Library symbol*] [*Library of Congress*] (LCLS)
NbG.......... Grand Island Public Library, Grand Island, NE [*Library symbol*] [*Library of Congress*] (LCLS)
NBG.......... National Bank of Greece
NBG.......... Naval Beach Group (NVT)
NBG.......... Networking Business Group (SAUS)
NBG.......... New Burlington Gallery (SAUS)
NBG.......... New Orleans, LA [*Location identifier*] [*FAA*] (FAAL)
NBG.......... Niederohmig Begrabenes Gebiet (SAUS)
NBG.......... Nieuwe Vertaling Nederlands Bijbelgenootschap [*A publication*] (BJA)
NBG.......... No Blasted Good [*Slang*]
NBG.......... No Bloody Good [*British slang*]
NBG.......... Not Being [*Telegraphy*] (PCTE)
nbg.......... Treatment Not Working (SPVS)
NBGA........ National Bingo Game Association [*British*] (DBA)
NBGACF..... Canadian Forces Base, Gagetown, New Brunswick [*Library symbol*] [*National Library of Canada*] (NLC)
NBGFCC..... New Brunswick Community College, Grand Falls, New Brunswick [*Library symbol*] [*National Library of Canada*] (NLC)
NBGFH...... Grand Falls Historical Society, New Brunswick [*Library symbol*] [*National Library of Canada*] (NLC)
NBGG........ Grand Manan Historical Society, Grand Harbour, Grand Manan Island, New Brunswick [*Library symbol*] [*National Library of Canada*] (NLC)
NbGi......... Grand Island Public Library, Grand Island, NE [*Library symbol*] [*Library of Congress*] (LCLS)
NBGMM..... Grand Manan Museum, Grand Harbour, Grand Manan Island, New Brunswick, [*Library symbol*] [*National Library of Canada*] (NLC)
NBGQA...... National Building Granite Quarries Association (EA)
NBGRN...... Narrow Band Gaussian Random Noise (PDAA)
NBGS........ New Bedford Glass Society [*Defunct*] (EA)
NBGSA...... National Black Graduate Student Association (EA)
NBH.......... Board on Neuroscience and Behavioral Health [*National Academy of Sciences*] (RCD)
NBH.......... Hastings College, Hastings, NE [*OCLC symbol*] (OCLC)
NbH.......... Hastings Public Library (SAUS)
NbH.......... Hastings Public Library, Hastings, NE [*Library symbol*] [*Library of Congress*] (LCLS)
NBH.......... National Bank of Hungary
NBH.......... National Bellas Hess [*Inc.*] [*Commercial firm*]
NBH.......... Neighborhood [*Telegraphy*] (PCTE)
NBH.......... Network Busy Hour [*Telecommunications*] (TEL)
NBH.......... North Bay [*Hawaii*] [*Seismograph station code, US Geological Survey*] [*Closed*] (SEIS)
NBHA........ National Barrel House Association
NBHA........ National Bicentennial Hospitality Alliance [*American Revolution Bicentennial Administration*]
NBHA........ National Builders' Hardware Association [*Later, DHI*] (EA)
NbHC........ Hastings College, Hastings, NE [*Library symbol*] [*Library of Congress*] (LCLS)
NBHCA...... Albert County Historical Society, Inc., Hopewell Cape, New Brunswick [*Library symbol*] [*National Library of Canada*] (NLC)
NBHCA...... National Belgian Hare Club of America [*Defunct*] (EA)
NbHCC...... Central Technical Community College, Hastings, NE [*Library symbol*] [*Library of Congress*] (LCLS)
NbHCro..... Crosier Fathers' Library, Hastings, NE [*Library symbol*] [*Library of Congress*] (LCLS)
NBHF........ Narrowband High Frequency Communications System (ACAE)
NbHi......... Nebraska State Historical Society, Lincoln, NE [*Library symbol*] [*Library of Congress*] (LCLS)
NbHo........ Holdrege-Phelps County Library, Holdrege, NE [*Library symbol*] [*Library of Congress*] (LCLS)
NBHPA...... National Black Health Planners Association (EA)
NBHS........ National Bureau for Handicapped Students [*British*] (CB)
NBHU........ Nitrogen Blower Heater Unit (SAUS)
NBi........... Binghamton Public Library, Binghamton, NY [*Library symbol*] [*Library of Congress*] (LCLS)
NBI........... Mao Naga [*Language symbol*] (ETLW)
NBI........... Nabisco Brands, Inc. [*Toronto Stock Exchange symbol*]
NBI........... Nathaniel Branden Institute
NBI........... National BankAmericard, Inc. [*Later, Visa USA, Inc.*]
NBI........... National Benevolent Institution (ODA)
NBI........... National Bridge Inventory [*FHWA*] (TAG)
NBI........... NBI, Inc. [*NYSE symbol*] (COMM)
NBI........... Neutral Beam Injection (MCD)
NBI........... Nielsen Broadcast Index [*A. C. Nielsen Co.*] (NTCM)
NBI........... No Bone Injury [*Medicine*]
NBI........... Nonbattle Injuries
NBI........... Non-Battle-Injury (SAUS)
NBI........... Northern Business Information, Inc. [*New York, NY*] [*Information service or system*] (TSSD)
NBI........... Nothing but Initials [*Initialism is name of commercial word processor firm*]
NBI........... Nuclear Burst Indicator (NATG)
NBIA......... National Business Incubation Association
NBIAP....... National Biological Impact Assessment Program [*Computer science*] (IID)
NBiBT....... Broome Technical Community College, Binghamton, NY [*Library symbol*] [*Library of Congress*] (LCLS)
NBIC......... National Business Information Center [*Dun & Bradstreet*]
NBIC......... Northeast Bancorp, Inc. (SAUS)
NBICU....... Newborn Intensive Care Unit (MELL)
NBIE......... National Burn Information Exchange [*Information service or system*] (CRD)
NBIEU....... Natal Baking Industry Employees Union [*South Africa*] (SAFN)
NBiF......... Four County Library System, Binghamton, NY [*Library symbol*] [*Library of Congress*] (LCLS)
NBIF......... National Biotechnology Information Facility (SAUS)
NBII......... National Biological Information Infrastructure
NBiL......... Our Lady of Lourdes Hospital, Binghamton, NY [*Library symbol*] [*Library of Congress*] (LCLS)
NBIO......... North American Biologicals, Inc. [*NASDAQ symbol*] (NQ)
NBIP......... National Biomonitoring Inventory Program [*Department of Energy*] (MSC)
NBIRF....... National Brain Injury Research Foundation (EA)
NBiRM....... Roberson Museum and Science Center, Binghamton, NY [*Library symbol*] [*Library of Congress*] (LCLS)
NBIS......... National Bridge Inspection Standards [*FHWA*] (TAG)
NBIS......... Neutral Beam Injection System (SAUS)
NBIS......... New Brunswick Information Service (SAUS)
NBIS......... New Brunswick Land Surveyors (SAUS)
NBIS......... Northern Biosphere Information System (EOSA)
NBiSC....... New York State Supreme Court Law Library, Binghamton, NY [*Library symbol*] [*Library of Congress*] (LCLS)
NBiSEG..... New York State Electric & Gas Corp., Binghamton, NY [*Library symbol*] [*Library of Congress*] (LCLS)
NBiSL....... Singer Co., Link Division, Binghamton, NY [*Library symbol*] [*Library of Congress*] (LCLS)
NBiSU....... State University of New York at Binghamton, Binghamton, NY [*Library symbol*] [*Library of Congress*] (LCLS)
NBIT......... New Bedford Institute of Technology [*Massachusetts*]
NBIT......... New Brunswick Institute of Technology (SAUS)
NBIX......... Neurocrine Biosciences [*NASDAQ symbol*] (TTSB)
NBIX......... Neurocrine Biosciences, Inc. [*NASDAQ symbol*] (SAG)
NBJ.......... Kingsbrook Jewish Medical Center, Brooklyn, NY [*Library symbol*] [*Library of Congress*] (LCLS)
NBJ.......... National Bar Journal [*A publication*] (DLA)
NBJ.......... New Brunswick Judgments [*Database*] [*Canada*] (GDD)
NbK.......... Kearney Public Library, Kearney, NE [*Library symbol*] [*Library of Congress*] (LCLS)
NBK.......... Kingsborough Community College of the City University of New York, Brooklyn, NY [*Library symbol*] [*Library of Congress*] (LCLS)
NBK.......... Nabu Network Corp. [*Toronto Stock Exchange symbol*]
NBK.......... National Bank of Kuwait
NBK.......... Natural Born Killers [*Movie title*]
NBK.......... Nebelkerze [*Smoke-Candle*] [*German military - World War II*]
NBK.......... New Brunswick, NJ [*Amtrak rail station code*]
NBK.......... Nordisk Bilteknisk Kommitte [*Nordic Automobile Technical Committee - NATC*] [*Defunct*] [*Denmark*] (EAIO)
NBKC........ Kingsborough Community College of the City University of New York, Brooklyn, NY [*Library symbol*] [*Library of Congress*] (LCLS)
NBKC........ New England Bancorp, Inc. (SAUS)
NBkCmce... Northern Bank of Commerce [*Associated Press*] (SAG)
NBkCmce... Northwest Bank of Commerce [*Oregon*] [*Associated Press*] (SAG)
NbKi......... Kimball Public Library, Kimball, NE [*Library symbol*] [*Library of Congress*] (LCLS)
NBKI......... Neutral Buffered Potassium Iodide (SAUS)

N Bkpt R.... National Bankruptcy Register Reports [*United States*] [*A publication*] (DLA)
N Bkpt Reg... National Bankruptcy Register Reports [*United States*] [*A publication*] (DLA)
N Bk R...... National Bankruptcy Register Reports [*United States*] [*A publication*] (DLA)
NbKS........ Kearney State College, Kearney, NE [*Library symbol*] [*Library of Congress*] (LCLS)
NBL......... Brooklyn Law School, Brooklyn, NY [*Library symbol*] [*Library of Congress*] (LCLS)
NbL......... Lincoln City Libraries, Lincoln, NE [*Library symbol*] [*Library of Congress*] (LCLS)
NBL......... National Basketball League (NADA)
NBL......... National Bicycle League (EA)
NBL......... National Book League [*Formerly, NBC*]
NBL......... National Business League [*Washington, DC*] (EA)
NBL......... Naval Biological Laboratory (TIMI)
NBL......... Naval Biosciences Laboratory [*Research center*]
NBL......... Navy Basic Logistic [*Plan*]
NBL......... Nebraska Library Commission, Lincoln, NE [*OCLC symbol*] (OCLC)
NBL......... Neutral Beam Line (SAUS)
NBL......... Neutral Buoyancy Laboratory [*NASA*] (SPST)
NBL......... New Brunswick Laboratory [*Formerly, NBAO*] [*Argonne, IL*] [*Department of Energy*]
NBL......... Night Bombardment - Long Distance [*Air Force*]
NBL......... No Berth List [*Shipping*] (DS)
NBL......... Noble Affiliates, Inc. [*NYSE symbol*] (SPSG)
NBL......... Noble Energy [*Company symbol*]
NBL......... Nocturnal Boundary Layer (SAUS)
NBL......... Norbaska Mines Ltd. [*Toronto Stock Exchange symbol*]
nbl......... Normoblast [*Hematology*]
NBL......... North British Locomotive Co. [*Indian Railway*] [*Glasgow*] (TIR)
NBL......... Not Bloody Likely [*British slang*]
NBL......... Nuclear Bomb Line (CINC)
NBla........ Blauvelt Free Library, Blauvelt, NY [*Library symbol*] [*Library of Congress*] (LCLS)
NBLA........ National Businesswomen's Leadership Association [*Defunct*] (EA)
NBlaD....... Dominican College, Blauvelt, NY [*Library symbol*] [*Library of Congress*] (LCLS)
NBLB........ Nebraska Law Bulletin [*A publication*] (DLA)
NBLC........ National Business Law Council [*Formerly, NABLT*] (EA)
Nb-LC....... Nebraska Public Library Commission, Lincoln, NE [*Library symbol*] [*Library of Congress*] (LCLS)
NBLCC....... National Black Lay Catholic Caucus (EA)
NBLD........ Narrowband Linear Detector (MCD)
NblD........ Noble Drilling Corp. [*Associated Press*] (SAG)
NBLE........ Nearly Best Linear Estimator [*Statistics*]
NbleDr...... Noble Drilling Corp. [*Associated Press*] (SAG)
NBLIC....... National Black Leadership Initiative on Cancer [*Association*] (EA)
NBLIC....... National Black Leadership Initiative on Cancer II (RCD)
NBLiCH...... Long Island College Hospital, Brooklyn, NY [*Library symbol*] [*Library of Congress*] (LCLS)
NBLiHi...... Long Island Historical Society, Brooklyn, NY [*Library symbol*] [*Library of Congress*] (LCLS)
NBLiU....... Long Island University, Brooklyn, NY [*Library symbol*] [*Library of Congress*] (LCLS)
NbLL........ Lincoln City Libraries, Lincoln, NE [*Library symbol*] [*Library of Congress*] (LCLS)
NbLNP....... United States Department of the Interior, National Park Service, Midwest Archaeological Center, Lincoln, NE [*Library symbol*] [*Library of Congress*] (LCLS)
NbLo........ Loup City Township Library, Loup City, NE [*Library symbol*] [*Library of Congress*] (LCLS)
NBLP........ National Bureau for Lathing and Plastering [*Later, International Institute for Lath and Plaster*] (EA)
NBLR........ National Black Leadership Roundtable (EA)
Nb-LR....... Nebraska Legislative Council, Reference Library, Lincoln, NE [*Library symbol*] [*Library of Congress*] (LCLS)
NBLR........ North Borneo Law Reports [*A publication*] (DLA)
NBLSA....... National/Black Law Student Association (EA)
NbLSc....... Southeast Community College, Lincoln, NE [*Library symbol*] [*Library of Congress*] (LCLS)
NbLU........ Union College, Lincoln, NE [*Library symbol*] [*Library of Congress*] (LCLS)
NbLVA....... United States Veterans Administration Hospital, Lincoln, NE [*Library symbol*] [*Library of Congress*] (LCLS)
NbLW........ Nebraska Wesleyan University, Lincoln, NE [*Library symbol*] [*Library of Congress*] (LCLS)
NBm......... Briarcliff Manor Public Library, Briarcliff Manor, NY [*Library symbol*] [*Library of Congress*] (LCLS)
NbM......... McCook Public Library, McCook, NE [*Library symbol*] [*Library of Congress*] (LCLS)
NBM......... Medical Research Library of Brooklyn, Brooklyn, NY [*Library symbol*] [*Library of Congress*] (LCLS)
NBM......... National Book Month
NBM......... National Building Museum (EA)
NBM......... National Bureau of Metrology
NBM......... Nation's Balanced Target Maturity Fund [*NYSE symbol*] (SAG)
NBM......... Navy Basic Modernization [*Plan*]
nbm......... Net Board Measure [*Construction term*] (MIST)
NBM......... New Beginnings Movement (Jamaica) [*Political party*] (PSAP)
NBM......... New Brunswick Museum (SAUS)
NBM......... New Buffalo, MI [*Amtrak rail station code*]
NBM......... Nitro-Form Bind Medium [*Analytical biochemistry*]
NBM......... No Bowel Movement [*Medicine*] (DMAA)
NBM......... Normal Bone Marrow [*Medicine*] (DMAA)
NBM......... Normal Bowel Movement [*Medicine*] (DMAA)
NBM......... Nothing by Mouth
NBM......... Nuclear Ballistic Missile
NBM......... Nucleus Basalis Magnocellularis [*Cytology*]
nbM......... Nucleus Basalis of Meynert [*Brain anatomy*]
NBMA........ Non-Broadcast Multiple Access (VLIE)
NBMAIA...... National Broom Manufacturers and Allied Industries Association [*Later, NBMC*] (EA)
NBmB........ Briarcliff College, Briarcliff Manor, NY [*Library symbol*] [*Library of Congress*] (LCLS)
NBMB........ National Bus Military Bureau (EA)
NBMB........ N Binary Digits-M Binary Digits (NITA)
NBMBAA...... National Black MBA [*Master of Business Administration*] Association [*Chicago, IL*] (EA)
NbMC........ McCook Community College, McCook, NE [*Library symbol*] [*Library of Congress*] (LCLS)
NBMC........ National Bar Mitzvah Club [*Later, AZYF*] (EA)
NBMC........ National Black Media Coalition (EA)
NBMC........ National Black Music Caucus - of the Music Educators National Conference (EA)
NBMC........ National Broom and Mop Council [*Defunct*]
NBMC........ National Businessmen's Council [*Defunct*] (EA)
NBMCM....... Minto Coal Museum, New Brunswick [*Library symbol*] [*National Library of Canada*] (NLC)
NBMCR....... Non-Book Materials Cataloguing Rules (NITA)
NBMDA....... National Building Material Distributors Association (EA)
NBMDR....... National Bone Marrow Donor Registry (EA)
NBME........ Medgar Evers College of the City University of New York, Brooklyn, NY [*Library symbol*] [*Library of Congress*] (LCLS)
NBME........ National Board of Medical Examiners (EA)
NBMG........ Navigational Bombing and Missile Guidance (MCD)
NBMGS....... Navigational Bombing and Missile Guidance System (AAG)
NBMHD....... Hopital Docteur Georges - L. Dumont [*Docteur Georges - L. Dumont Hopital*]Moncton, New Brunswick [*Library symbol*] [*National Library of Canada*] (NLC)
NbMi........ Milford Public Library, Milford, NE [*Library symbol*] [*Library of Congress*] (LCLS)
NB Miner Resour Branch Inf Circ... New Brunswick. Mineral Resources Branch Information Circular (SAUS)
NbMiS....... Southeast Community College, Milford, NE [*Library symbol*] [*Library of Congress*] (LCLS)
NBmK........ King's College, Briarcliff Manor, NY [*Library symbol*] [*Library of Congress*] (LCLS)
NbML........ McCook Public Library, McCook, NE [*Library symbol*] [*Library of Congress*] (LCLS)
NBmlA....... Adirondack Historical Association Museum Library, Blue Mountain Lake, NY [*Library symbol*] [*Library of Congress*] (LCLS)
NBMMH....... Health Sciences Library, The Moncton Hospital, New Brunswick [*Library symbol*] [*National Library of Canada*] (NLC)
NBMO........ Nonbonding Molecular Orbital [*Physical chemistry*]
NBMOA....... National Black McDonald's Operators Association (EA)
NBMOAL...... Atlantic Lottery Corp. [*Societe des Loteries de l'Atlantique*], Moncton, New Brunswick [*Library symbol*] [*National Library of Canada*] (NLC)
NBMOCC...... New Brunswick Community College, Moncton, New Brunswick [*Library symbol*] [*National Library of Canada*] (NLC)
NBMOF....... Fisheries and Oceans Canada [*Peches et Oceans Canada*] Moncton, New Brunswick [*Library symbol*] [*National Library of Canada*] (NLC)
NBMOLM...... Lutz Mountain Heritage Foundation, Inc., Moncton, New Brunswick [*Library symbol*] [*National Library of Canada*] (NLC)
NBMOM....... Moncton Museum, New Brunswick [*Library symbol*] [*National Library of Canada*] (NLC)
NBMORE...... Canada Department of Regional Industrial Expansion [*Ministere de l'Expansion Industrielle Regionale*] Moncton, New Brunswick [*Library symbol*] [*National Library of Canada*] (NLC)
NBMOTA...... Airworthiness Library, Atlantic Region, Transport Canada [*Bibliotheque de la Navigabilite Aerienne, Region de l'Atlantique, Transports Canada*], Moncton, New Brunswick [*Library symbol*] [*National Library of Canada*] (NLC)
NBMOTAR..... Atlantic Regional Library, Transport Canada [*Bibliotheque Regionale de l'Atlantique, Transports Canada*], Moncton, New Brunswick [*Library symbol*] [*National Library of Canada*] (NLC)
NBMOU....... Universite de Moncton, New Brunswick [*Library symbol*] [*National Library of Canada*] (NLC)
NBMOUA...... Archives Acadiennes, Universite de Moncton, New Brunswick [*Library symbol*] [*National Library of Canada*] (NLC)
NBMOUD...... Bibliotheque de Droit, Universite de Moncton, New Brunswick [*Library symbol*] [*National Library of Canada*] (NLC)
NBMOW....... Albert-Westmorland-Kent Regional Library, Moncton, New Brunswick [*Library symbol*] [*National Library of Canada*] (NLC)
NBMR........ NATO Basic Military Requirements (AABC)
NBMR........ Northern Bengal Mounted Rifles [*British military*] (DMA)
NBMS........ National Bulk Mail System [*Postal Service*]
NBMT........ NATO Basic Military Techniques (NATG)
NBmtT....... Bear Mountain Trailside Museum, Bear Mountain, NY [*Library symbol*] [*Library of Congress*] (LCLS)
NBMUX....... Neub. & Berman Munic. Secs. Trust [*Mutual fund ticker symbol*] (SG)
NBMV&NSL.... New Bedford, Marthas Vineyard and Nantucket Steamship Line (SAUS)
Nbn......... Nabonidus (BJA)
NBN......... Narrow Band Nerve [*Neurology*] (DAVI)
NBN......... Narrowband Network
NBN......... Narrowband Noise
NBN......... National Bank of Nigeria Ltd.
NBN......... National Bibliography Number

NBN National Black Network [*A radio network*]
NBN National Book Number [*British*]
NBN Nationality Broadcasting Network [*Cable-television system*]
NBN Network for Better Nutrition (EA)
NBN Neubabylonisches Namenbuch zu den Geschaeftsurkunden [*A publication*] (BJA)
NBN New Bad News (SAUS)
NBN Newbern, TN [*Amtrak rail station code*]
NBN New Biological Nomenclature (SAUS)
NBN Newborn Nursery [*Medicine*]
NBN Newcastle Broadcasting Network [*Australian company broadcasting in Papua New Guinea*] (FEA)
NBN Nicolet Badger Northern Railroad [*Federal Railroad Administration identification code*]
NBN Nixdorf Broadband Network [*Communications*] [*British*]
NBN North British Airlines Ltd. [*ICAO designator*] (FAAC)
NBN Northeast Bancorp [*AMEX symbol*] (NASQ)
NBN Old Manse Library, Newcastle, New Brunswick [*Library symbol*] [*National Library of Canada*] (NLC)
NBNA National Bank of North America [*New York*]
NBNA National Black Nurses Association (EA)
NBNAM Archives of the Miramichi Historical Society, Newcastle, New Brunswick [*Library symbol*] [*National Library of Canada*] (NLC)
NbNb Neubabylonisches Namenbuch zu den Geschaeftsurkunden [*A publication*] (BJA)
NbNc Nebraska City Public Library, Nebraska City, NE [*Library symbol*] [*Library of Congress*] (LCLS)
NBNC New York City Community College of the City University of New York, Brooklyn, NY [*Library symbol*] [*Library of Congress*] (LCLS)
NBNC Noted but Not Corrected (MCD)
NbNcM Morton-James Public Library, Nebraska City, NE [*Library symbol*] [*Library of Congress*] (LCLS)
NBND Northbound (SAUS)
NBNDH New Denmark Historical Museum, New Brunswick [*Library symbol*] [*National Library of Canada*] (NLC)
NbNf Norfolk Public Library, Norfolk, NE [*Library symbol*] [*Library of Congress*] (LCLS)
NbNfN Northeast Technical Community College, Norfork, NE [*Library symbol*] [*Library of Congress*] (LCLS)
NBNM Health Sciences Library, Miramichi Hospital, Newcastle, New Brunswick [*Library symbol*] [*National Library of Canada*] (NLC)
NbNp North Platte Public Library, North Platte, NE [*Library symbol*] [*Library of Congress*] (LCLS)
NbNpM Mid-Plains Community College, North Platte, NE [*Library symbol*] [*Library of Congress*] (LCLS)
NBNR National Bankruptcy News and Reports [*A publication*] (DLA)
NBN Rep National Bankruptcy News and Reports [*A publication*] (DLA)
NBNS NetBIOS Name Service (SAUS)
NBo Bolivar Free Library, Bolivar, NY [*Library symbol*] [*Library of Congress*] (LCLS)
NBO Nairobi [*Kenya*] [*Airport symbol*] (OAG)
NBO National Bank of Oman Ltd. SAO (EY)
NBO Navy Bureau of Ordnance [*Obsolete*]
NBO Nebo Air Co. Ltd. [*Former USSR*] [*FAA designator*] (FAAC)
NBO Network Buildout (IEEE)
NBO Network Business Opportunity (VLIE)
NBO Network Byte Order (SAUS)
NBO New Business Opportunity (TIMI)
NBO Nonbed Occupancy (AAMN)
NBO Nonbonding Orbital (SAUS)
NBO Nonbridging Oxygen [*Materials science*]
NBO Nordiska Kooperativa och Allmannyttiga Bostadsforetags Organisation [*Organization of Cooperative and Non-Profit Making Housing Enterprises in the Nordic Countries*] (EAIO)
NBO Normal-Branch Oscillation [*Astronomy*]
NBO Norsar Array Site 01B00 [*Norway*] [*Seismograph station code, US Geological Survey*] (SEIS)
NbO Omaha Public Library, Omaha, NE [*Library symbol*] [*Library of Congress*] (LCLS)
NBO Omaha Public Library, Omaha, NE [*OCLC symbol*] (OCLC)
NBO Oromocto Public Library, New Brunswick [*Library symbol*] [*National Library of Canada*] (NLC)
NBOA National Ballroom Operators Association [*Later, National Ballroom and Entertainment Association*]
NBOA National Business Officers Association (EA)
NBOA National Business Owners Association (EA)
NbOB Boys Town Center for the Study of Youth Development, Omaha, NE [*Library symbol*] [*Library of Congress*] (LCLS)
NbOC Creighton University, Omaha, NE [*Library symbol*] [*Library of Congress*] (LCLS)
NBOC Network Building Out Capacitor [*Telecommunications*] (TEL)
NBOC Newman Communications Corp. (SAUS)
NBOC Northern Bank of Commerce [*NASDAQ symbol*] (SAG)
NBOC Northern Bk Comm Ore [*NASDAQ symbol*] (TTSB)
NBOC Northwest Bank of Commerce [*Oregon*] [*NASDAQ symbol*] (SAG)
NbOC-A Creighton University, Alumni Library, Omaha, NE [*Library symbol*] [*Library of Congress*] (LCLS)
NbOC-D Creighton University, School of Dentistry, Omaha, NE [*Library symbol*] [*Library of Congress*] (LCLS)
NbOC-H Creighton University, Health Sciences Library, Omaha, NE [*Library symbol*] [*Library of Congress*] (LCLS)
NbOC-L Creighton University, School of Law, Omaha, NE [*Library symbol*] [*Library of Congress*] (LCLS)
NbOC-M Creighton University, School of Medicine and School of Pharmacy, Omaha, NE [*Library symbol*] [*Library of Congress*] (LCLS)
NbOD Duchesne College, Omaha, NE [*Library symbol*] [*Library of Congress*] (LCLS)
NBOFC National Board of Forensic Chiropractors [*Association*] (EA)
NbOg Goodall City Library, Ogallala, NE [*Library symbol*] [*Library of Congress*] (LCLS)
NbOGS Church of Jesus Christ of Latter-Day Saints, Genealogical Society Library, OmahaBranch, Omaha, NE [*Library symbol*] [*Library of Congress*] (LCLS)
NBoh Connetquot Public Library, Bohemia, NY [*Library symbol*] [*Library of Congress*] (LCLS)
NBohCH Connetquot High School, Bohemia, NY [*Library symbol*] [*Library of Congress*] (LCLS)
NbOJ Joslyn Art Museum, Omaha, NE [*Library symbol*] [*Library of Congress*] (LCLS)
NBoL Bolivar Free Library, Bolivar, NY [*Library symbol*] [*Library of Congress*] (LCLS)
NBolS Marcella Sembrich Memorial Studio, Bolton Landing, NY [*Library symbol*] [*Library of Congress*] (LCLS)
N-BOMB Neutron Bomb (GOBB)
N (Bomb) Neutron Bomb
N-Bomb Nuclear Bomb (SAUS)
NbOMC Metropolitan Technical Community College, Omaha, NE [*Library symbol*] [*Library of Congress*] (LCLS)
NBOME National Board of Osteopathic Medical Examiners (EA)
NbONPS United States National Park Service, Midwest Regional Office, Omaha, NE [*Library symbol*] [*Library of Congress*] (LCLS)
NbOP Presbyterian Theological Seminary, Omaha, NE [*Library symbol*] [*Library of Congress*] (LCLS)
NBOR Network Building Out Resistor [*Telecommunications*] (TEL)
NBOR Nucleus of Basal Optic Root [*Neuroanatomy*]
NbOsc Osceola Public Library, Osceola, NE [*Library symbol*] [*Library of Congress*] (LCLS)
NBOT National Board of Orthopaedic Technologists [*British*] (DAVI)
NbOU University of Nebraska at Omaha, Omaha, NE [*Library symbol*] [*Library of Congress*] (LCLS)
NBoU-E State University of New York at Buffalo, Educational Opportunity Center (SAUS)
NBoU-RP State University of New York at Buffalo, Roswell Park Memorial Institute (SAUS)
NbOV United States Veterans Administration Hospital, Omaha, NE [*Library symbol*] [*Library of Congress*] (LCLS)
NbOW Westside Community Schools, Omaha, NE [*Library symbol*] [*Library of Congress*] (LCLS)
NBp Bayport-Blue Point Public Library, Blue Point, NY [*Library symbol*] [*Library of Congress*] (LCLS)
NBP Name Binding Protocol [*Computer science*]
NBP National Battlefield Park (BARN)
NBP National Booster Program (AAG)
NBP National Braille Press (EA)
NBP National Business Publications [*Later, ABP*] (EA)
NBP Needle Biopsy of Prostate [*Medicine*] (MELL)
NBP Needs-Based Payment [*Job Training and Partnership Act*] (OICC)
NBP Net Biome Production (SAUS)
NBP Neutral Bitter Principle [*Pharmacy*]
NBP New Birth Party [*Cyprus*] [*Political party*]
NBP New Brooklyn Philharmonic (SAUS)
NBP (Nitrobenzyl)pyridine [*Organic chemistry*]
NBP No Baseband Processing (ACAE)
NBP NonBacterial Prostatis [*Medicine*]
NBP Non-invasive Blood Pressure (SAUS)
NBP Normal Boiling Point
NBP Northern Border Partners Ltd. [*NYSE symbol*] (SPSG)
NBP Nucleic Acid Binding Protein [*Biochemistry*]
NBP Nude Beach Pest (SAUS)
NBP Peru State College Library, Peru, NE [*OCLC symbol*] (OCLC)
NBP Pratt Institute, Brooklyn, NY [*Library symbol*] [*Library of Congress*] (LCLS)
NBPA National Back Pain Association (EAIO)
NBPA National Bark Producers Association (EA)
NBPA National Basketball Players Association (EA)
NBPA National Beverage Packaging Association (EA)
NBPA National Black People's Assembly (EA)
NBPA National Black Police Association (EA)
NBPA National Building Products Association [*Defunct*] (EA)
NBPA Navy Board for Production Awards
NBPA New Brunswick Potato Agency (SAUS)
NBPA Northeastern Bancorp (SAUS)
NBPASV Southern Victoria Historical Society, Perth-Andover, New Brunswick [*Library symbol*] [*National Library of Canada*] (NLC)
NBPB National Biotechnology Policy Board
NBPC National Black Political Convention [*1972*]
NBPC National Black Programming Consortium (EA)
NBPC National Border Patrol Council (EA)
NBPC Neutral Beam Power Conversion (SAUS)
NBPDW National Brotherhood of Packinghouse and Dairy Workers [*Formerly, NBPW*] (EA)
NBPE National Board of Podiatry Examiners
NBPE National Board of Polygraph Examiners [*Later, APA*] (EA)
NbPerS Peru State College, Peru, NE [*Library symbol*] [*Library of Congress*] (LCLS)
NBPHA N-Benzoyl(phenyl)hydroxylamine [*Organic chemistry*]
NBPI National Board for Prices and Incomes [*British*]
NBPI Newspaper Benevolent and Provident Institution [*British*] (DGA)
NBPIW National Brotherhood of Packinghouse and Industrial Workers (EA)
NbPl Plattsmouth Public Library, Plattsmouth, NE [*Library symbol*] [*Library of Congress*] (LCLS)
NBPM Narrowband Phase Modulation (MCD)
NBPM Network-Based Project Management (PDAA)

NBPMC ...... National Bureau of Professional Management Consultants (NTPA)
NBPME ...... National Board of Podiatric Medical Examiners (EA)
NBPNPA ..... National Board of Pediatric Nurse Practitioners and Associates [*Later, NCBPNP/N*] (EA)
NBPO .... NATO Bullpup Production Organization [*Missiles*] (NATG)
NBPol .... Polytechnic Institute of New York, Brooklyn, NY [*Library symbol*] [*Library of Congress*] (LCLS)
NBPol-G ..... Polytechnic Institute of New York, Long Island Graduate Center, Farmingdale, NY [*Library symbol*] [*Library of Congress*] (LCLS)
NBpP .... Bayport-Blue Point Public Library, Blue Point, NY [*Library symbol*] [*Library of Congress*] (LCLS)
NBPP .... National Black Political Party
NBPRP ...... National Board for the Promotion of Rifle Practice (EA)
NBPRS ...... National Black Public Relations Society (NTPA)
NBPS .... National Backgammon Players Society [*British*] (DBA)
NBPS .... Neutral Beam Power Systems (SAUS)
NBPTE ...... National Board of Physical Therapy Examiners (EA)
NBPTS ...... National Board for Professional Teaching Standards (EA)
NBPu .... Brooklyn Public Library, Brooklyn, NY [*Library symbol*] [*Library of Congress*] (LCLS)
NBPW .... National Brotherhood of Packinghouse Workers [*Later, NBPDW*]
NBPZ .... Neches Butane Products [*Federal Railroad Administration identification code*]
NBQ .... Nitro(benzothiazolo)quinolinium Perchlorate [*Antineoplastic drug*]
NBQ .... No Broken Quantities (SAUS)
NBR .... Nabors Industries, Inc. [*AMEX symbol*] (SPSG)
NBR .... Narrowband Radiated (IEEE)
NBR .... National Bankruptcy Register Reports [*United States*] [*A publication*] (DLA)
NBR .... National Board of Review of Motion Pictures
NBR .... National Buildings Record [*British*]
NBR .... National Bureau of Asian Research (RCD)
NBR .... Neighbor [*Telegraphy*] (PCTE)
NBR .... Neighborhood Business Revitalization [*Program*]
NBR .... Net Borrowing Requirement [*Banking*] (MHDW)
NBR .... New Beginnings Resources [*Vancouver Stock Exchange symbol*]
NBR .... New Brunswick Reports [*Maritime Law Book Co. Ltd.*] [*Canada*] [*Information service or system*] [*A publication*] (CRD)
NBR .... [*The*] Nightly Business Reports [*Television program*]
NBR .... Nitrile Based Rubber (SAUS)
NBR .... Nitrile Butadiene-Acrylonitrile Rubber (AAEL)
NBR .... Nitrile Butadiene Rubber (SAUS)
NBR .... Nonborrowed Reserve [*Banking*]
NBR .... Nonbreathing
NBR .... North British Railway
NBR .... Nuclear Boiler Rated (NRCH)
NBR .... Null Balance Recorder
nbr .... Number (ELAL)
NBR .... Number (KSC)
NBR .... Number of Bids Received [*DoD*]
NBR .... Nursing Boards Review [*Course*] [*American Journal of Nursing*]
NBR 2d ...... New Brunswick Reports, Second Series [*A publication*] (DLA)
NBRA .... National Barrel Racing Association
NBRA .... National Basketball Referees Association (NTPA)
NBRA .... National Brain Research Association (EA)
NbRal .... Ralston Public Library, Ralston, NE [*Library symbol*] [*Library of Congress*] (LCLS)
NBR All ..... Allen's New Brunswick Reports [*Canada*] [*A publication*] (DLA)
NBR Ber .... Berton's New Brunswick Reports [*A publication*] (DLA)
NBRC .... National Black Republican Council (EA)
NBRC .... National Board for Respiratory Care (EA)
NBRCA ...... Atlantic Institution, Correctional Service Canada [*Etablissement Atlantique, Service Correctionnel Canada*], Renous, New Brunswick [*Library symbol*] [*National Library of Canada*] (BIB)
NBR Carl .... Carleton's New Brunswick Reports [*A publication*] (DLA)
NBR Chip ... Chipman's New Brunswick Reports [*1825-35*] [*A publication*] (DLA)
NbRcW ...... Willa Cather Pioneer Memorial, Red Cloud, NE [*Library symbol*] [*Library of Congress*] (LCLS)
NBre .... Brewster Public Library, Brewster, NY [*Library symbol*] [*Library of Congress*] (LCLS)
NBREH ...... L'Eglise Historique St-Henri-De-Barachois, Robichaud, New Brunswick [*Library symbol*] [*National Library of Canada*] (NLC)
NBren .... Brentwood Public Library, Brentwood, NY [*Library symbol*] [*Library of Congress*] (LCLS)
NBrenEJ ..... East Junior High School, Brentwood, NY [*Library symbol*] [*Library of Congress*] (LCLS)
NBrenIMC ... District Instructional Media Center, Brentwood, NY [*Library symbol*] [*Library of Congress*] (LCLS)
NBrenSJ .... Saint Joseph's College, Brentwood, NY [*Library symbol*] [*Library of Congress*] (LCLS)
NBrenST .... Saint Josephs College, Brentwood (SAUS)
NB Rep ...... New Brunswick Reports [*A publication*] (DLA)
NB Rev Stat ... New Brunswick Revised Statutes [*Canada*] [*A publication*] (DLA)
NBRF .... National Biomedical Research Foundation [*Georgetown University*] [*Research center*]
NBRG .... National Basic Reference Graphic (MCD)
NBRG .... Neighboring [*Telegraphy*] (PCTE)
NBR Han .... Hannay's New Brunswick Reports [*12, 13 New Brunswick*] [*A publication*] (DLA)
NBri .... Bay Shore-Brightwaters Public Library, Brightwaters, NY [*Library symbol*] [*Library of Congress*] (LCLS)
NBRI .... National Building Research Institute (ODA)
NBrih .... Hampton Library, Bridgehampton, NY [*Library symbol*] [*Library of Congress*] (LCLS)
NBR Kerr ... Kerr's New Brunswick Reports [*A publication*] (DLA)
NBRL .... Naval Biomedical Research Laboratory
NBRL .... Naval Blood Research Laboratory [*Bureau of Medicine*]
NBRMP ...... National Board of Review of Motion Pictures (EA)
NBRN .... Nestart Library, Richibucto, New Brunswick [*Library symbol*] [*National Library of Canada*] (NLC)
NBrockU .... State University of New York, College at Brockport, Brockport, NY [*Library symbol*] [*Library of Congress*] (LCLS)
NBron .... Bronxville Public Library, Bronxville, NY [*Library symbol*] [*Library of Congress*] (LCLS)
NBronC ...... Concordia College, Bronxville, NY [*Library symbol*] [*Library of Congress*] (LCLS)
NBronSL .... Sarah Lawrence College, Bronxville, NY [*Library symbol*] [*Library of Congress*] (LCLS)
NBroo .... Brookhaven Free Library, Brookhaven, NY [*Library symbol*] [*Library of Congress*] (LCLS)
NBrooHS .... Bellport Senior High School, Brookhaven, NY [*Library symbol*] [*Library of Congress*] (LCLS)
NBRP .... National Blood Research Program [*Medicine*] (EDAA)
NBRP & B ... Pugsley and Burbridge's New Brunswick Reports [*A publication*] (DLA)
NBRP & T ... Pugsley and Trueman's New Brunswick Reports [*A publication*] (DLA)
NBRPC ...... New Brunswick Research and Productivity Council
NBR Pug .... Pugsley's New Brunswick Reports [*A publication*] (DLA)
NBR Pugs ... Pugsley's New Brunswick Reports [*1876-93*] [*Canada*] [*A publication*] (DLA)
NBRS .... Next Basic Records System [*Computer science*] (VLIE)
NBRSA ...... National Bench Rest Shooters Association (EA)
NBRT .... National Board for Respiratory Therapy [*Formerly, ARIT*] [*Later, NBRC*] (EA)
NBR Tru ..... Trueman's New Brunswick Reports [*A publication*] (DLA)
N Bruns ..... New Brunswick Reports [*A publication*] (DLA)
NBrunS ...... New Brunswick Scientific Co., Inc. [*Associated Press*] (SAG)
NbRVt .... Neubabylonische Rechts- und Verwaltungstexte [*A publication*] (BJA)
NbRVu .... Neubabylonische Rechts- und Verwaltungsurkunden Uebersetzt und Erlaeutert [*A publication*] (BJA)
NBS .... Bureau of Ships Publications [*Obsolete*] [*Navy*]
NBS .... Kekaha, Kauai, HI [*Location identifier*] [*FAA*] (FAAL)
NBS .... Narrowband Search (MCD)
NBS .... Narrowband Socket (SAUS)
NBS .... Narrowband Sockets Specification (GART)
NBS .... Narrow Beam Sounder (SAUS)
NBS .... National Australia Bank. Monthly Summary [*A publication*] (ADA)
NBS .... National Bakery School [*British*] (BI)
NBS .... National Battlefield Site (BARN)
NBS .... National Bibliographic Service [*British Library*] (IID)
NBS .... National Biological Service
NBS .... National Biological Survey [*Department of the Interior*]
NBS .... National Bird-Feeding Society (EA)
NBS .... National Blood Service (WDAA)
NBS .... National Board for Nursing, midwifery and health visiting (SAUS)
NBS .... National Bookkeepers' Society (EA)
NBS .... National Book Sale [*British*]
NBS .... National Bridal Service (EA)
NBS .... National Broadcasting Service [*Trinidad and Tobago*] (EY)
NBS .... National Broadcasting Service [*New Zealand*]
NBS .... National Broadcasting System
NBS .... National Brotherhood of Skiers (EA)
NBS .... National Bureau of Standards [*Department of Commerce*] [*Later, NIST*]
NBS .... National Bureau of Standards, Gaithersburg, MD [*OCLC symbol*] (OCLC)
NBS .... National Business Systems, Inc. [*Toronto Stock Exchange symbol*]
NBS .... National Button Society (EA)
NBS .... Natural Black Slate (MSA)
NBS .... Navigational Bombing System [*British military*] (DMA)
NBS .... Navy Broadcasting Service (ACAE)
NBS .... N-Bromosuccinimide [*Organic chemistry*]
NBS .... Needs-Based Staffing (ADA)
NBS .... Neighborhood Bible Studies (EA)
NBS .... Netherland Benevolent Society of New York [*Later, Netherlands-America CommunityAssociation*] (EA)
NBS .... Neurobehavioral Scale
NBS .... Neutral Buoyancy Simulator [*Navy*] (MCD)
NBS .... Nevoid Basal Cell Carcinoma Syndrome [*Oncology*] (DMAA)
NBS .... New British Standard [*Imperial wire gauge*]
NBS .... New Brunswick Scientific Co., Inc.
NBS .... Newcastle Business School [*British*] (ODBW)
NBS .... New South Capital Trust I [*AMEX symbol*] (NASQ)
NBS .... Nickel-Bonded Steel (SAUS)
NBS .... Night Bombardment - Short Distance [*Air Force*]
NBS .... Nijmegen Breakage Syndrome [*Medicine*] (DMAA)
NBS .... Nile Blue Sulfate (SAUS)
NBS .... Nimbus Aviation [*British*] [*ICAO designator*] (FAAC)
NBS .... No Bacteria Seen [*Clinical microbiology*]
NBS .... Nonbaseline Software Library (MCD)
NBS .... Nordiska Byggforskningsorgans Samarbetsgrupp [*Nordic Building Research Cooperation Group*] [*Iceland*] (EAIO)
NBS .... Normal Blood Serum (MAE)
NBS .... Normal Bowel Sounds [*Gastroenterology*] (DAVI)
NBS .... Normal Brain Stem [*Medicine*] (EDAA)
NBS .... Normal Breath Sounds (SAUS)
NBS .... Normal Burm Serum (SAUS)
NBS .... Normal Burro Serum [*Biochemistry*] (DAVI)
NBS .... Normandy Base Section [*World War II*]
NBS .... Nothing Before Something [*Library cataloguing*] (DGA)

NBS .... Nuclear Backscattering Spectroscopy (EDCT)
NBS .... Nucleotide Binding Site [*Genetics*]
NBS .... Numeric Backspace (SAUS)
NBS .... Numeric Backspace Character [*Computer science*]
NBS .... Numismatic Bibliomania Society (EA)
NBS .... Nystagmus Blockage Syndrome [*Medicine*] (EDAA)
NBS .... Saint John Regional Library, New Brunswick [*Library symbol*] [*National Library of Canada*] (NLC)
NbS .... Scottsbluff Public Library, Scottsbluff, NE [*Library symbol*] [*Library of Congress*] (LCLS)
NBSA .... National Bakery Suppliers Association (EA)
NBS-A .... National Bureau of Standards - Atomic (SAA)
NBSA .... Normalized Body Surface Area (SAUS)
NBSA .... Nurses' Board of South Australia
NBSAB ...... Fort Beausejour Museum, Sackville, New Brunswick [*Library symbol*] [*National Library of Canada*] (NLC)
NBSAC ...... National Boating Safety Advisory Council [*Department of Transportation*] [*Washington, DC*] (EGAO)
NBSACW .... Canadian Wildlife Service, Environment Canada [*Service Canadien de la Faune, Environnement Canada*] Sackville, New Brunswick [*Library symbol*] [*National Library of Canada*] (NLC)
NBSAE .... Norwegian-British-Swedish Antarctic Expedition [*1949-52*]
NBSAM ...... Mount Allison University, Sackville, New Brunswick [*Library symbol*] [*National Library of Canada*] (NLC)
NBSAP ...... National Biodiversity Strategy and Action Plan (SAUS)
NBSARM .... Ross Memorial Library, St. Andrews, New Brunswick [*Library symbol*] [*National Library of Canada*] (BIB)
NBSBL .... National Bureau of Standards Boulder Laboratories
NBSC .... Health Sciences Library, Centracare Saint John, Inc., New Brunswick [*Library symbol*] [*National Library of Canada*] (NLC)
NBSC .... National Bank of South Carolina (EFIS)
NBSC .... National Black Sisters' Conference (EA)
NBSC .... New Brunswick Safety Council (SAUS)
NBSC .... New Brunswick Scientific Co. [*NASDAQ symbol*]
NBSC .... New Brunswick Scientific Co., Inc. [*NASDAQ symbol*] (NQ)
NBSC .... Nitrobenzenesulfenyl Chloride [*Organic chemistry*]
NBSCA ...... National Beauty Salon Chain Association [*Later, ICSA*] (EA)
NBSCCST ... National Bureau of Standards Center for Computer Sciences and Technology (DIT)
NBSCETT ... New Brunswick Society of Certified Engineering Technicians and Technologists (SAUS)
NBSCM ...... Centre Marin, Shippagan, New Brunswick [*Library symbol*] [*National Library of Canada*] (NLC)
NBSC PAC ... National Bank of South Carolina PAC [*Columbia, SC*] (PACS)
NBSCU ...... Centre Universitaire de Shippagan, New Brunswick [*Library symbol*] [*National Library of Canada*] (NLC)
NBSD .... Night Bombardment - Short Distance [*Air Force*] (IEEE)
NBSDI .... National Brands Soft Drinks Institute (EA)
NBsdQ .... Queensborough Community College of the City University of New York, Bayside, NY [*Library symbol*] [*Library of Congress*] (LCLS)
NbSe .... Seward Public Library, Seward, NE [*Library symbol*] [*Library of Congress*] (LCLS)
NbSeT .... Concordia Teachers College, Seward, NE [*Library symbol*] [*Library of Congress*] (LCLS)
NBSF .... Nitrobenzenesulfonyl Fluoride [*Organic chemistry*]
NBSFS .... National Bureau of Standards Frequency Standard (IEEE)
NBSG .... National Biotherapy Study Group (EA)
NbSHS ...... Hiram Scott College, Scottsbluff, NE [*Library symbol*] [*Library of Congress*] [*Obsolete*] (LCLS)
NBSI .... North Bancshares, Inc. [*NASDAQ symbol*] (SAG)
NbSi .... Sidney Public Library, Sidney, NE [*Library symbol*] [*Library of Congress*] (LCLS)
NBSIR .... National Bureau of Standards Interagency Reports
NBSL .... New York City School Library System, Brooklyn, NY [*Library symbol*] [*Library of Congress*] (LCLS)
NBSLD ...... National Bureau of Standards Load Determination [*Computer program*]
NBSM .... New Brunswick Museum, Saint John, New Brunswick [*Library symbol*] [*National Library of Canada*] (NLC)
NBSMA ...... National Boot and Shoe Manufacturers' Association [*Later, FIA*]
NbSN .... Nebraska Western College, Scottsbluff, NE [*Library symbol*] [*Library of Congress*] (LCLS)
NBSP .... Non-Breaking Space (VLIE)
NBSPA ...... National Bark and Soil Producers Association (NTPA)
NBSQH ...... Quaco Historical and Library Society, St. Martins, New Brunswick [*Library symbol*] [*National Library of Canada*] (NLC)
NBSR .... National Bureau of Standards Reactor
NBSR .... New Brunswick Southern Railroad [*Federal Railroad Administration identification code*]
NBSRH ...... Health Sciences Library, Saint John Regional Hospital [*Bibliotheque des Sciences de la Sante, Hopital Regional de Saint-Jean*], New Brunswick [*Library symbol*] [*National Library of Canada*] (NLC)
NBSS .... Narrowband Switching System (SAUS)
NBSS .... National Bank Surveillance System
NBSS .... National British Softbill Society (BI)
NBSS .... Naval Beach Signal Section
NBsSH .... Southside Hospital, Bay Shore, NY [*Library symbol*] [*Library of Congress*] (LCLS)
NBS-SIS .... NBS-Standard Information Services (NITA)
NBSSSC .... St. Croix Public Library, St. Stephen, New Brunswick [*Library symbol*] [*National Library of Canada*] (NLC)
NBSSX ...... Neub. & Berman Focus Fund [*Mutual fund ticker symbol*] (SG)
NBST .... Narrow Band Secure Terminal (ACAE)
NBST .... Narrowband Subscriber Terminal (CET)
NBST .... National Board for Science and Technology [*Ireland*] (PDAA)
NBST .... [*The*] New Braunfels & Servtex Railroad, Inc. [*AAR code*]
NbSt .... Nimbostratus [*Cloud*] [*Meteorology*] (AIA)
NBSTAC ..... St. Andrews Campus, New Brunswick Community College [*Library symbol*] [*National Library of Canada*] (BIB)
NBS/TAD .... National Bureau of Standards/Technical Analysis Division (NOAA)
NB Stat ...... New Brunswick Statutes [*Canada*] [*A publication*] (DLA)
NBSTC .... National Black State Troopers Coalition [*Association*] (EA)
NBStF .... Saint Francis College, Brooklyn, NY [*Library symbol*] [*Library of Congress*] (LCLS)
NBSTIM ..... Le Musee de St-Isidore, Inc., New Brunswick [*Library symbol*] [*National Library of Canada*] (NLC)
NBStJC ...... Saint Joseph's College, Brooklyn, NY [*Library symbol*] [*Library of Congress*] (LCLS)
NBS TN ..... United States Department of Commerce. National Bureau of Standards. Technial Notes (SAUS)
NbSu .... Superior Carnegie Library, Superior, NE [*Library symbol*] [*Library of Congress*] (LCLS)
NBSU .... University of New Brunswick, Saint John, New Brunswick [*Library symbol*] [*National Library of Canada*] (NLC)
NBSUH ...... Kings County Historical Society, Sussex, New Brunswick [*Library symbol*] [*National Library of Canada*] (NLC)
NBSU-M ..... State University of New York at Brooklyn, Medical Research Library, Brooklyn, NY [*Library symbol*] [*Library of Congress*] (LCLS)
NBSUS ...... Sussex Public Library, New Brunswick [*Library symbol*] [*National Library of Canada*] (NLC)
NBSV .... Narrowband Secure Voice System [*Army*] (CAAL)
NBSVS ...... Narrowband Secure Voice System [*Army*] (MCD)
NBSVS ...... Saint John Vocational School, New Brunswick [*Library symbol*] [*National Library of Canada*] (NLC)
NBSX .... New Braunfels-Servtex Railroad [*Federal Railroad Administration identification code*]
NBT .... Brunswick, ME [*Location identifier*] [*FAA*] (FAAL)
NBT .... Na [*Language symbol*] (ETLW)
NBT .... Nagoya Bumpy Torus [*Military*]
NBT .... Narrow-Beam Transducer [*National Ocean Survey*]
NBT .... National Bancshares Corp. of Texas [*AMEX symbol*] (SAG)
NBT .... Navigator Bombardier Training [*Air Force*] (AFM)
NBT .... Neale's Ball Token [*Indian Railway*] (TIR)
NBT .... Negative Balance Test (IAA)
NBT .... Netherlands Board of Tourism (EA)
NBT .... Networks for Biotechnology
NBT .... Neurobiotin [*Biochemical labelling compound*]
NBT .... Neutral Buoyancy Trainer [*Navy*] (MCD)
NBT .... New Brunswick Telephone Co. Ltd. [*Toronto Stock Exchange symbol*]
NBT .... Nimbus Beacon Transmitter
NBT .... Nitro Blue Tetrazolium (SAUS)
NBT .... Nitroblue Tetrazolium [*A stain*] [*Hematology*]
NBT .... Non-Selective Bottom-to-Top (SAUS)
NBT .... Non-tumor-bearing [*Medicine*] (EDAA)
NBT .... Normal Breast Tissue [*Medicine*] (DB)
NBT .... Northern Ballet Theatre [*England*]
NBT .... Null-Balance Transmissometer (IEEE)
NBTA .... National Basketball Trainers Association (EA)
NBTA .... National Baton Twirling Association (EA)
NBTA .... National Board of Trial Advocacy (EA)
NBTA .... National Business Teachers Association (NADA)
NBTA .... National Business Travel Association (EA)
NBTA .... National Bus Traffic Association (EA)
NBTB .... NBT Bancorp. [*NASDAQ symbol*] (SAG)
NBTB .... NBT Bancorporation [*NASDAQ symbol*]
NBT Bcp .... NBT Bancorp [*Associated Press*] (SAG)
NBTC .... Nanobiotechnology Center (RCD)
NBTC .... New Brands and Their Companies [*Formerly, NTN*] [*A publication*]
NBTC .... New Brunswick Teachers College
NBTD .... Nothing Better To Do (SAUS)
NBT-DF ..... Nitroblue Tetrazolium Diformazan [*A stain*] [*Hematology*]
NBTDR ...... Narrowband Time Domain Reflectometry (MCD)
NBTE .... Nonbacterial Thrombotic Endocarditis [*Cardiology*]
NbTe .... Tekamah Carnegie Public Library, Tekamah, NE [*Library symbol*] [*Library of Congress*] (LCLS)
NBTEL ...... New Brunswick Telephone Company (EFIS)
NBTF .... National Brain Tumor Foundation (EA)
NBTF .... National Building Trades Federation [*A union*] [*British*]
NBTF .... NB&T Financial Group, Inc. [*NASDAQ symbol*] (QUAN)
NBTF .... Neutral Beam Test Facility (SAUS)
NBTH .... Bibliotheque Medicale, Hotel-Dieu Saint-Joseph-De-Tracadie, New Brunswick [*Library symbol*] [*National Library of Canada*] (BIB)
NbTi .... Niobium Titanium (SAUS)
NBTI .... Nitrobenzylthioinosine [*Organic chemistry*]
NBTL .... National Battery Test Laboratory [*Department of Energy*]
NBTL .... Naval Boiler and Turbine Laboratory
NBTM .... Le Musee Historique de Tracadie, New Brunswick [*Library symbol*] [*National Library of Canada*] (NLC)
NBT Meter ... Null-Balance Transmission Meter (SAUS)
NBTNF ...... Newborn, Term, Normal, Female [*Obstetrics*]
NBTNM ..... Newborn, Term, Normal, Male [*Obstetrics*]
NBTPI .... National Book Trade Provident Institution [*British*] (DGA)
NBTPS ...... National Book Trade Provident Society [*British*] (DI)
NBTR .... Narrowband Tape Recorder
NBTS .... National Blood Transfusion Service
NBTS .... Neutral Beam Test Stand (SAUS)
NBTS .... New Boston Tracking Station (SAA)
NBTS .... New Brunswick Theological Seminary [*New Jersey*]
NBTS .... Northern Baptist Theological Seminary [*Lombard, IL*]
NBTT .... Net Barter Terms of Trade

NBTY .... Nature's Bounty, Inc. [*NASDAQ symbol*] (COMM)
NBTY .... NBTY, Inc. [*NASDAQ symbol*] (SAG)
NBu .... Buffalo and Erie County Public Library, Buffalo, NY [*Library symbol*] [*Library of Congress*] (LCLS)
NBU .... Glenview, IL [*Location identifier*] [*FAA*] (FAAL)
NBU .... Natural Business Unit (VLIE)
NBU .... NBU Mines Ltd. [*Toronto Stock Exchange symbol*]
nbu .... Nebraska [*MARC country of publication code*] [*Library of Congress*] (LCCP)
NBU .... Net Built Units (TIMI)
NBU .... New Better than Used [*Statistics*]
NBU .... Nordiska Bankmannaunionen [*Confederation of Nordic Bank Employees' Unions*] (EA)
NBU .... University of Nebraska at Omaha, Omaha, NE [*OCLC symbol*] (OCLC)
NbU .... University of Nebraska, Lincoln, NE [*Library symbol*] [*Library of Congress*] (LCLS)
NBuA .... Allied Corp., Specialty Chemicals Division, Buffalo, NY [*Library symbol*] [*Library of Congress*] (LCLS)
NbU-A .... University of Nebraska, Agriculture Library, Lincoln, NE [*Library symbol*] [*Library of Congress*] (LCLS)
NBuAA .... Acres American, Inc., Buffalo, NY [*Library symbol*] [*Library of Congress*] (LCLS)
NBuACE ..... United States Army, Corps of Engineers, Buffalo, NY [*Library symbol*] [*Library of Congress*] (LCLS)
NBuAK .... Albright-Knox Art Gallery Library, Buffalo Fine Arts Academy, Buffalo, NY [*Library symbol*] [*Library of Congress*] (LCLS)
NBuAn .... Andco, Inc., Buffalo, NY [*Library symbol*] [*Library of Congress*] (LCLS)
NBuB .... Buffalo Society of Natural Sciences, Buffalo Museum of Science, Buffalo, NY [*Library symbol*] [*Library of Congress*] (LCLS)
NBuBA .... Bell Aerosystems Co., Buffalo, NY [*Library symbol*] [*Library of Congress*] (LCLS)
NBuBE .... Buffalo and Erie County Public Library, Buffalo, NY [*Library symbol*] [*Library of Congress*] (LCLS)
NBuBLH ..... Bry-Lin Hospital, Buffalo, NY [*Library symbol*] [*Library of Congress*] (LCLS)
NBuBM ...... Brystol-Myers Pharmaceuticals R & D, Buffalo, NY [*Library symbol*] [*Library of Congress*] (LCLS)
NBuBO ...... Buffalo Organization for Social and Technological Innovation, Inc. (BOSTI), Buffalo, NY [*Library symbol*] [*Library of Congress*] (LCLS)
NBuBR ...... Biblial Research Institute, Inc., Buffalo, NY [*Library symbol*] [*Library of Congress*] (LCLS)
NBuC .... State University of New York, College at Buffalo, Buffalo, NY [*Library symbol*] [*Library of Congress*] (LCLS)
NBuCA .... Cornell Aeronautical Laboratory, Buffalo, NY [*Library symbol*] [*Library of Congress*] (LCLS)
NBuCBL ..... Christel, Bean & Linihan, Buffalo, NY [*Library symbol*] [*Library of Congress*] (LCLS)
NBuCC .... Canisius College, Buffalo, NY [*Library symbol*] [*Library of Congress*] (LCLS)
NBuCEC ..... CECOS International, Buffalo, NY [*Library symbol*] [*Library of Congress*] (LCLS)
NBuCH ...... Children's Hospital, Buffalo, NY [*Library symbol*] [*Library of Congress*] (LCLS)
NBuCo .... Buffalo Color Corp., Buffalo, NY [*Library symbol*] [*Library of Congress*] (LCLS)
NBuCoH ..... Buffalo Columbus Hospital, Buffalo, NY [*Library symbol*] [*Library of Congress*] (LCLS)
NBuD .... D'Youville College, Buffalo, NY [*Library symbol*] [*Library of Congress*] (LCLS)
NBuDa .... Daemen College, Buffalo, NY [*Library symbol*] [*Library of Congress*] (LCLS)
NBuDD ...... DeLancey Divinity School, Buffalo, NY [*Library symbol*] [*Library of Congress*] [*Obsolete*] (LCLS)
NBuDY ...... E. I. Du Pont de Nemours & Co., Yerkes Research Laboratory, Buffalo, NY [*Library symbol*] [*Library of Congress*] (LCLS)
NBUE .... New Better than Used in Expectation [*Statistics*]
NBuEC .... Erie Community College-North, Buffalo, NY [*Library symbol*] [*Library of Congress*] (LCLS)
NBuEC-C .... Erie Community College-North, City Campus, Buffalo, NY [*Library symbol*] [*Library of Congress*] (LCLS)
NBuEC-U .... Erie Community College-North, Urban Center, Buffalo, NY [*Library symbol*] [*Library of Congress*] (LCLS)
NBuEE .... Ecology and Environment, Inc., Buffalo, NY [*Library symbol*] [*Library of Congress*] (LCLS)
NBuEMH .... Edward J. Meyer Memorial Hospital Medical Library, Buffalo, NY [*Library symbol*] [*Library of Congress*] (LCLS)
NBuF .... Falcon Research & Development, Inc., Buffalo, NY [*Library symbol*] [*Library of Congress*] (LCLS)
NBUF .... National Black United Front (EA)
NBUF .... National Black United Fund (EA)
NBUFC ...... National Black United Federation of Charities [*Association*] (EA)
NBuG .... Grosvenor Reference Division, Buffalo and Erie County Public Library, Buffalo, NY [*Library symbol*] [*Library of Congress*] (LCLS)
NBuGC ...... Graphic Controls Corp., Buffalo, NY [*Library symbol*] [*Library of Congress*] (LCLS)
NBuGD ...... Goldome FSB, Bufflo, NY [*Library symbol*] [*Library of Congress*] (LCLS)
NBuGH ...... Buffalo General Hospital, Buffalo, NY [*Library symbol*] [*Library of Congress*] (LCLS)
NBuGH-N ... Buffalo General Hospital, School of Nursing, Buffalo, NY [*Library symbol*] [*Library of Congress*] (LCLS)
NBuHi .... Buffalo and Erie County Historical Society, Buffalo, NY [*Library symbol*] [*Library of Congress*] (LCLS)
NBuHSA ..... Health Systems Agency of Western New York, Inc., Buffalo, NY [*Library symbol*] [*Library of Congress*] (LCLS)
NBuKMH .... Kenmore Mercy Hospital, Medical Library, Buffalo, NY [*Library symbol*] [*Library of Congress*] (LCLS)
NbU-L .... University of Nebraska, College of Law, Lincoln, NE [*Library symbol*] [*Library of Congress*] (LCLS)
NBuLH .... Lafayette General Hospital, Buffalo, NY [*Library symbol*] [*Library of Congress*] (LCLS)
NBuLTV ...... LTV Aerospace & Defense Co., Buffalo, NY [*Library symbol*] [*Library of Congress*] (LCLS)
NBuM .... Medaille College, Buffalo, NY [*Library symbol*] [*Library of Congress*] (LCLS)
NbU-M ...... University of Nebraska, College of Medicine, Omaha, NE [*Library symbol*] [*Library of Congress*] (LCLS)
NBuMM ..... Marine Midland Services Corp., Technical Information Center, Buffalo, NY [*Library symbol*] [*Library of Congress*] (LCLS)
NBuNCE ..... National Center for Earthquake Engineering, Research Information Services, State, Buffalo, NY [*Library symbol*] [*Library of Congress*] (LCLS)
NBuPC .... Buffalo Psychiatric Center, Buffalo, NY [*Library symbol*] [*Library of Congress*] (LCLS)
NBuPL .... Pennwalt Corp., Lucidol Division, Buffalo, NY [*Library symbol*] [*Library of Congress*] (LCLS)
NBuRH ...... Rosary Hill College, Buffalo, NY [*Library symbol*] [*Library of Congress*] [*Obsolete*] (LCLS)
NBuRSI ...... Reichert Scientific Instruments, Buffalo, NY [*Library symbol*] [*Library of Congress*] (LCLS)
NBUSA ...... United States Army, Fort Hamilton Post Library, Fort Hamilton, Brooklyn, NY [*Library symbol*] [*Library of Congress*] (LCLS)
NBuSCA ..... SCA Chemical Services, Inc., Buffalo, NY [*Library symbol*] [*Library of Congress*] (LCLS)
NBuSCH ..... Sisters of Charity Hospital, Buffalo, NY [*Library symbol*] [*Library of Congress*] (LCLS)
NBuSD ...... Buffalo City School District, Buffalo, NY [*Library symbol*] [*Library of Congress*] (LCLS)
NBuSFH ..... St. Francis Hospital of Buffalo, Buffalo, NY [*Library symbol*] [*Library of Congress*] (LCLS)
NBuSK .... Spencer Kellogg Division, Textron, Inc., Buffalo, NY [*Library symbol*] [*Library of Congress*] (LCLS)
NBuSMH .... Sheehan Memorial Emergency Hospital, Buffalo, NY [*Library symbol*] [*Library of Congress*] (LCLS)
NBuSR ...... Sierra Research Corp., Buffalo, NY [*Library symbol*] [*Library of Congress*] (LCLS)
NBuStM ..... Saint Mary's School for the Deaf, Buffalo, NY [*Library symbol*] [*Library of Congress*] (LCLS)
NBuTC .... Trocaire College, Buffalo, NY [*Library symbol*] [*Library of Congress*] (LCLS)
NBuU .... State University of New York at Buffalo, Buffalo, NY [*Library symbol*] [*Library of Congress*] (LCLS)
NBuU-A ..... State University of New York at Buffalo, Art Library, Buffalo, NY [*Library symbol*] [*Library of Congress*] (LCLS)
NBuU-AR .... State University of New York at Buffalo, Archives, Buffalo, NY [*Library symbol*] [*Library of Congress*] (LCLS)
NBuU-BA .... State University of New York at Buffalo, Bell Annex, Buffalo, NY [*Library symbol*] [*Library of Congress*] (LCLS)
NBuU-BS .... State University of New York at Buffalo, Bell Science Library, Buffalo, NY [*Library symbol*] [*Library of Congress*] (LCLS)
NBuU-C ..... State University of New York at Buffalo, Chemistry Library, Buffalo, NY [*Library symbol*] [*Library of Congress*] (LCLS)
NBuU-CT .... University of Buffalo Foundation, Inc., Center for Tomorrow, State University of New York at Buffalo, Amherst, NY [*Library symbol*] [*Library of Congress*] (LCLS)
NBuU-D ..... State University of New York at Buffalo, Documents Library, Buffalo, NY [*Library symbol*] [*Library of Congress*] (LCLS)
NBuU-E ...... State University of New York at Buffalo, Educational Opportunity Center, Buffalo, NY [*Library symbol*] [*Library of Congress*] (LCLS)
NBuU-H ..... State University of New York at Buffalo, Health Sciences Library, Buffalo, NY [*Library symbol*] [*Library of Congress*] (LCLS)
NBuU-HA .... State University of New York at Buffalo, Harriman Library, Buffalo, NY [*Library symbol*] [*Library of Congress*] (LCLS)
NBuU-L ...... State University of New York at Buffalo, Law Library, Buffalo, NY [*Library symbol*] [*Library of Congress*] (LCLS)
NBuU-LL .... State University of New York at Buffalo, Library Literature Library, Buffalo, NY [*Library symbol*] [*Library of Congress*] (LCLS)
NBuU-LS .... State University of New York at Buffalo, Library Science Library, Buffalo, NY [*Library symbol*] [*Library of Congress*] (LCLS)
NBuU-Mu ... State University of New York at Buffalo, Music Library, Buffalo, NY [*Library symbol*] [*Library of Congress*] (LCLS)
NBuU-P ..... State University of New York at Buffalo, Physics Library, Buffalo, NY [*Library symbol*] [*Library of Congress*] (LCLS)
NBuU-PO .... State University of New York at Buffalo, Poetry Library, Buffalo, NY [*Library symbol*] [*Library of Congress*] (LCLS)
NBuU-R ..... State University of New York at Buffalo, Reference, Buffalo, NY [*Library symbol*] [*Library of Congress*] (LCLS)
NBuU-RL .... State University of New York at Buffalo, Ridge Lea, Buffalo, NY [*Library symbol*] [*Library of Congress*] (LCLS)
NBuU-RP .... State University of New York at Buffalo, Roswell Park Memorial Institute, Buffalo, NY [*Library symbol*] [*Library of Congress*] (LCLS)
NBuU-SE .... State University of New York at Buffalo, Science and Engineering Library, Buffalo, NY [*Library symbol*] [*Library of Congress*] (LCLS)
NBuVA .... United States Veterans Administration Hospital, Buffalo, NY [*Library symbol*] [*Library of Congress*] (LCLS)
NBuVM ...... Villa Maria College of Buffalo, Buffalo, NY [*Library symbol*] [*Library of Congress*] (LCLS)
NBuVNA ..... Visiting Nursing Association of Buffalo, Buffalo, NY [*Library symbol*] [*Library of Congress*] (LCLS)
NBuW .... Worthington Compressor & Engine International, Buffalo, NY [*Library symbol*] [*Library of Congress*] (LCLS)
NBuWeP .... Westwood Pharmaceuticals, Inc., Buffalo, NY [*Library symbol*] [*Library of Congress*] (LCLS)

NBUWH ..... Carleton County Historical Society, Upper Woodstock, New Brunswick [*Library symbol*] [*National Library of Canada*] (NLC)
NBuWNED .. WNED-TV, Buffalo, NY [*Library symbol*] [*Library of Congress*] (LCLS)
NBuX .... XACO, Inc., Buffalo, NY [*Library symbol*] [*Library of Congress*] (LCLS)
NBV .... Net Book Value (TEL)
NbV .... Valentine Public Library, Valentine, NE [*Library symbol*] [*Library of Congress*] (LCLS)
NBVA .... National Bulk Vendors Association (EA)
NBVA .... United States Veterans Administration Hospital, Brooklyn, NY [*Library symbol*] [*Library of Congress*] (LCLS)
NBV Ad ...... New Brunswick Vice Admiralty Reports [*A publication*] (DLA)
NBVA-O ..... United States Veterans Administration Hospital, Outpatient Clinic, Brooklyn, NY [*Library symbol*] [*Library of Congress*] (LCLS)
NBVCXO ..... Narrowband Voltage-Controlled Crystal Oscillator
NBVF .... National Burn Victim Foundation (EA)
NBVM .... Narrow-Band Voice Modulation (VLIE)
NBVO .... National Black Veterans Organization [*Defunct*] (EA)
NBVOAD .... Nebraska Voluntary Organizations Active in Disaster [*Emergency Management*] (EMA)
NBVS .... Neutral Beam Vacuum System (SAUS)
NBW .... L. P. Fisher Public Library, Woodstock, New Brunswick [*Library symbol*] [*National Library of Canada*] (NLC)
NBW .... National Barristers' Wives [*Later, NABBS*] (EA)
NBW .... National Book Week (NTCM)
NBW .... Natural Bandwidths [*Spectroscopy*]
NBW .... Nebraska Wesleyan University, Lincoln, NE [*OCLC symbol*] (OCLC)
nbw .... Noise Bandwidth (IDOE)
NBW .... Noise Bandwidth
NBW .... Normal Birth Weight
NbW .... North by West
NBWA .... National Beer Wholesalers' Association (EA)
NBWA .... National Blacksmiths and Welders Association (EA)
NBWA .... National Buddhist Women's Associations (EA)
NBWA PAC ... National Beer Wholesalers' Association PAC [*Alexandria, VA*] (PACS)
NbWayS ..... Wayne State College, Wayne, NE [*Library symbol*] [*Library of Congress*] (LCLS)
NBWH .... Carleton Memorial Hospital, Woodstock, New Brunswick [*Library symbol*] [*National Library of Canada*] (BIB)
NBWHP ..... National Black Women's Health Project (EA)
NbWi .... Dvoracek Memorial Library, Wilber, NE [*Library symbol*] [*Library of Congress*] (LCLS)
NBWPLC .... National Black Women's Political Leadership Caucus (EA)
NBWROP .... Naval Bureau of Weapons Reserve Ordnance Plant
NBWTAU .... National British Women's Total Abstinence Union (EAIO)
NBWV .... Victoria-Carleton Courthouse, Woodstock, New Brunswick [*Library symbol*] [*National Library of Canada*] (NLC)
NBWY .... York Regional Library, Headquarters No. 2, Woodstock, New Brunswick [*Library symbol*] [*National Library of Canada*] (NLC)
NBX .... Jeffersn-Pilot 7.25% 'ACES' [*NYSE symbol*] (TTSB)
NBX .... Jefferson Pilot [*NYSE symbol*] (SAG)
NBX .... Nabire [*Indonesia*] [*Airport symbol*] (OAG)
NBY .... NBC Capital [*AMEX symbol*] (SG)
NBY .... Nearest Besselian Year
NBY .... Nutrient Broth Yeast [*Microbiology*]
NbY .... York Public Library, York, NE [*Library symbol*] [*Library of Congress*] (LCLS)
NbYC .... York College, York, NE [*Library symbol*] [*Library of Congress*] (LCLS)
NBYLC .... National Black Youth Leadership Council (EA)
NBysSH ..... Bay Shore Senior High School, Bay Shore, NY [*Library symbol*] [*Library of Congress*] (LCLS)
NBZ .... National By-Products [*Federal Railroad Administration identification code*]
nc--- .... Central America [*MARC geographic area code*] [*Library of Congress*] (LCCP)
NC .... Chloropicrin Stannic Chloride [*Inorganic chemistry*]
NC .... La Nouvelle Clio [*Brussels*] [*A publication*] (BJA)
NC .... NACCO Indus Inc. Cl'A' [*NYSE symbol*] (TTSB)
NC .... Name Control [*IRS*]
NC .... Naming Context (MWOL)
NC .... Nanocomposite [*Plastics*]
NC .... Nano Crystal (AAEL)
NC .... Nanocrystal (SAUS)
nc .... Nanocurie [*Pne billionth of a curie*]
NC .... Narrowband Communicative Services [*Telecommunications*]
NC .... Narrow Coverage
NC .... Nasal Cannula [*Medicine*] (MEDA)
NC .... Nasal Catheter [*Medicine*] (MELL)
NC .... Nashville, Chattanooga & St. Louis [*Louisville & Nashville Railroad Co.*] [*AAR code*]
NC .... Natal Carabiniers [*British military*] (DMA)
NC .... National Catholic News Service
NC .... National Cemetery (IIA)
NC .... National Center (IAA)
NC .... National Certificate (WDAA)
NC .... National Churches [*A publication*]
NC .... National City Corporation (EFIS)
NC .... National Coarse [*Thread*]
NC .... National Colonialist Party [*Australia*] [*Political party*]
NC .... National Cooperatives [*Later, UNICO*] [*An association*]
NC .... National Course (SAUS)
NC .... National Curriculum [*Education*] (AIE)
NC .... Native Cavalry [*British military*] (DMA)
NC .... NATO Center (NATG)
NC .... NATO Confidential (NATG)
NC .... Natural Cytotoxic [*Cells*] [*Immunochemistry*]
NC .... Nature Conservancy [*NERC*] [*British*]
NC .... Naval Cadet [*British*] (ROG)
NC .... Naval Correspondence
NC .... Navigation Computer
NC .... Navigation Console
NC .... Navy Component
NC .... Navy Counselor [*Military*] (POLM)
NC .... Navy Cross
NC .... Neanderthal Conservative [*Slang*]
NC .... Nearly Commensurate Model [*Physics*]
NC .... Nebraska Cattlemen (EARSL)
NC .... Neck Complaint [*Medicine*] (EDAA)
NC .... Necrosis
Nc .... Negative Wave in Children [*Neurophysiology*]
NC .... Neighborhood Coalition (EA)
NC .... Neonatal Cholestasis [*Medicine*] (EDAA)
NC .... Nerve Center [*An association*] (EA)
NC .... Nerve Conduction
NC .... Net Capital [*Business term*]
NC .... Net Charter [*Business term*] (DS)
NC .... Net Control (MCD)
NC .... Net Cost
NC .... Netilmicin-Clindamycin [*Antibiotic combination*]
NC .... Network Card [*British Rail*]
NC .... Network Channel [*Broadcasting*] (NTCM)
NC .... Network Computer (PCM)
NC .... Network Computing
NC .... Network Concept [*Communications term*] (DCT)
NC .... Network Congestion [*Telecommunications*] (TEL)
NC .... Network Connect
NC .... Network Connection [*Computer science*] (VLIE)
NC .... Network Control (IAA)
NC .... Network Controller
NC .... Network Countdown
NC .... Neural Crest [*Anatomy*]
NC .... Neurocirculatory [*Medicine*] (DAVI)
NC .... Neurologic Check [*Medicine*]
NC .... Neutral Current [*Physics*]
NC .... Neutralization Capacitor (IAA)
NC .... Neutralizing Capacitance [*or Coil*] (DEN)
NC .... Neutralizing Capacitance (or Capacitor) (SAUS)
NC .... Neutron Content (SAUS)
NC .... Neutron Contrast (SAUS)
NC .... Neutron Controller [*Nuclear energy*] (NRCH)
NC .... Nevus Comedonicus [*Medicine*] (EDAA)
N/C .... New Account (ROG)
NC .... Newair [*ICAO designator*] (AD)
NC .... Newark College (SAUS)
NC .... New Caledonia [*ANSI two-letter standard code*] (CNC)
NC .... New Canada Press
NC .... New Cases (Bingham's New Cases) in Common Pleas [*1834-40*] [*A publication*] (DLA)
NC .... Newcastle Connection (SAUS)
NC .... New Cavendish Books [*Publisher*] [*British*]
N/C .... New Charter [*Navigation*]
NC .... New Church (ROG)
NC .... New College (SAUS)
NC .... Newcomb College (SAUS)
NC .... New Construction [*Navy*]
NC .... New Consultants [*A publication*]
NC .... New Crop
NC .... Newnham College (SAUS)
NC .... Neylan Conference (EA)
NC .... Nichols College (SAUS)
NC .... Nickel Cadmium (IAA)
NC .... Nickel Clad
NC .... Nickel-clad Copper (SAUS)
NC .... Nickel Copper (SAUS)
NC .... Niger-Congo [*Linguistics*] (IEL)
NC .... Night Coach [*Airline designation*]
N-C .... Nightingale-Conant [*Audio publisher*]
NC .... Nippon Club (EA)
NC .... Nitrocellulose [*Organic chemistry*]
NC .... Nitrocompound (SAUS)
NC .... Nixdorf Computer (IAA)
NC .... NOAA [*National Oceanic and Atmospheric Administration*] Corps (USDC)
NC .... No Card (SAUS)
NC .... No Carry (SAUS)
NC .... No Casualty (MAE)
NC .... No Change
NC .... No Charge
NC .... No Coil (MSA)
NC .... No Collaterals [*Medicine*]
NC .... No Comment (NASA)
NC .... No Complaint (SAUS)
N/C .... No Complaints [*Medicine*]
NC .... No Computers
nc .... No Connection (IDOE)
NC .... No Connection [*Valve pins*] [*Radio*] [*Technical drawings*]
NC .... No Contact
NC .... No Contest [*Sports*]

NC .... No Correction (SAUS)
NC .... No Cost (AAG)
NC .... No Credit (WGA)
NC .... Node Centre (SAUS)
NC .... Node Consistency (SAUS)
NC .... Noise Correlation (MSA)
NC .... Noise Criteria (or Criterion) (SAUS)
NC .... Noiseless Camera (NTCM)
NC .... Nolo Contendere [*Motor vehicle violation code used in state of Maryland*] (MVRD)
NC .... Nominal Correction
NC .... Nominating Committee [*American Occupational Therapy Association*]
NC .... Noncallable (EBF)
NC .... Noncallable Bond [*Investment term*]
NC .... Noncarcinogen (SAUS)
NC .... Noncoin (IAA)
NC .... Noncollectable
NC .... Non-Collectible (SAUS)
NC .... Non-Color Sensitized Emulsion [*Also called color-blind emulsion*] (WDMC)
NC .... Noncommercial [*Rate*] [*Value of the English pound*]
NC .... Noncommissioned
NC .... Noncomplex (MCD)
NC .... Noncompliance [*Noncompliant*] (DAVI)
N/C .... Non-Concur (SAUS)
NC .... Non-Condensing (SAUS)
NC .... Nonconforming
NC .... Nonconformist [*Indicating religious preference*] [*Military*] [*British*]
NC .... Non-Contact (SAUS)
NC .... Non-Continuous Liner [*Shipping*] (DS)
NC .... Noncontributory (DAVI)
NC .... Non Conversational (SAUS)
NC .... Nonconversational (IAA)
NC .... Noncorrodible (SAUS)
NC .... Non-Crystalline (OA)
NC .... Non-Curling [*Photographic film*] (ROG)
NC .... Nonlinear Capacitance
NC .... Nonrecurring Costs (AAGC)
NC .... Nordic Council
NC .... NORDLEK Council (EAIO)
NC .... Norfolk College (SAUS)
NC .... Normal Children
NC .... Normal Control
NC .... Normal Cooling (SAUS)
NC .... Normal Copy [*Oncology*]
NC .... Normal Corrective Maneuver (SAUS)
NC .... Normally Closed [*Switch*]
NC .... Norman College (SAUS)
NC .... Norman Conquest [*of England, 1066*]
NC .... Normocephalic [*On physical examination*] [*Medicine*] (DAVI)
NC .... North Carolina [*Postal code*]
NC .... North Carolina Railroad
NC .... North Carolina Reports [*A publication*] (DLA)
Nc .... North Carolina State Library, Raleigh, NC [*Library symbol*] [*Library of Congress*] (LCLS)
NC .... North Carolina Supreme Court Reports [*A publication*] (DLA)
NC .... North Central Airlines, Inc. [*ICAO designator*] (OAG)
NC .... North Coast (ADA)
NC .... Northcor Resources Ltd. [*Vancouver Stock Exchange symbol*]
NC .... North Country (ROG)
NC .... Northern Cascades (SAUS)
NC .... Northern Command
NC .... Northern Consolidated Airlines, Inc.
NC .... Northern Counties (SAUS)
NC .... Northern County (SAUS)
NC .... Northland College (SAUS)
NC .... Northrop Corp. (KSC)
NC .... Northwestern College (SAUS)
NC .... Norton Commander (SAUS)
NC .... Norwegian Club (EA)
NC .... Nose Clip (MELL)
NC .... Nose Cone [*Aviation*] (AFM)
N/C .... Nose Cone [*Aerospace*] (NAKS)
NC .... Not Calculated (SAUS)
NC .... Not Carried
NC .... Not Classified [*Auto racing*]
NC .... Not Coded (MCD)
NC .... Not Competitive [*Rejected research proposals*] [*National Institutes of Health*]
NC .... Not Complete (SAUS)
NC .... Not Completed [*Medicine*] (DMAA)
NC .... Not Connected [*Electronics*] (DEN)
NC .... Not Controlled [*Experimental conditions*]
N/C .... Not Critical (NASA)
NC .... Not Cultured (MAE)
NC .... Notes of Cases at Madras (Strange) [*A publication*] (DLA)
NC .... Notes of Cases, English Ecclesiastical and Maritime Courts [*1841-50*] [*A publication*] (DLA)
NC .... Novo Cruzado [*Brazilian currency*]
NC .... Nuclear Capability
NC .... Nuclear Congress
NC .... Nuclear-Cytoplasmic [*Ratio*] [*Cytology*] (MAE)
NC .... Nucleocapsid (DB)
NC .... Nucleus of Ciliated Cell
NC .... Nuestra Cuenta [*Our Account*] [*Business term*] [*Spanish*]
NC .... "Nuff Ced" [*Enough Said*] [*Slang*]
NC .... Nuffield College (SAUS)
NC .... Number Cruncher (SAUS)
NC .... Number Crusher (SAUS)
NC .... Numbering Counter [*Computer science*] (OA)
NC .... Number of unallocated channels at node (SAUS)
NC .... Numerical Code (SAUS)
NC .... Numerical Coding (SAUS)
NC .... Numerical Control [*Computer science*]
NC .... Numeric Coding (SAUS)
NC .... Numeric Control (SAUS)
NC .... Numismatic Chronicle [*A publication*] (ABAR)
NC .... Nurse Corps [*Military*]
NC .... Sagrada Biblia [*1944*] [*Eloino Nacar Fuster and Alberto Colunga*] (BJA)
NC .... Sandoz Pharmaceuticals [*Research code symbol*]
nc .... Sodium Carbonate [*CIPW classification*] [*Geology*]
NC .... Warner-Lambert Pharmaceutical Co. [*Research code symbol*]
NC1 .... Navy Counselor First Class (DNAB)
NC1 .... Nominal Correction 1 [*Phasing Maneuver*] [*NASA*] (NAKS)
NC3 .... Norsar Array Site 03C00 [*Norway*] [*Seismograph station code, US Geological Survey*] (SEIS)
NC^{3}A .... Nuclear Command, Control, and Communications Assessment (COE)
NC^{3}D .... National Coordinating Center for Curriculum Development
NC5 .... Norsar Array Site 05C00 [*Norway*] [*Seismograph station code, US Geological Survey*] (SEIS)
NC-17 .... No Children under 17 Admitted [*Movie rating*]
NC$_{50}$ .... Median Narcotic Concentration [*Pharmacology*] (QSUL)
NCa .... Canton Free Library, Canton, NY [*Library symbol*] [*Library of Congress*] (LCLS)
NCA .... College of New Caledonia Library [*UTLAS symbol*]
NCA .... Jacksonville, NC [*Location identifier*] [*FAA*] (FAAL)
NCA .... National Campaign for the Arts [*British*] (DBA)
NCA .... National Camp Association (EA)
NCA .... National Camping Association (EA)
NCA .... National Candle Association (EA)
NCA .... National Canners Association [*Later, NFPA*] (EA)
NCA .... National Capital Award
NCA .... National Carousel Association (EA)
NCA .... National Cashmere Association [*Defunct*] (EA)
NCA .... National Caterers Association [*Later, ICA*] (EA)
NCA .... National Catfishing Association (EA)
NCA .... National Cathedral Association (EA)
NCA .... National Cattlemens Association (EA)
NCA .... National Caves Association (EA)
NCA .... National Caving Association [*British*] (DBA)
NCA .... National Cemetery Administration
NCA .... National Center on Accessibility [*Indiana University Bloomington*] (RCD)
NCA .... National Ceramic Association [*Later, ICA*] (EA)
NCA .... National Certificate of Agriculture [*British*]
NCA .... National Certification Agency (DMAA)
NCA .... National Certification Agency for Medical Laboratory Personnel (EA)
NCA .... National Chaplain's Association (EA)
NCA .... National Charcoal Association
NCA .... National Chastity Association (EA)
NCA .... National Cheerleaders Association (EA)
NCA .... National Childminding Association [*British*] (EAIO)
NCA .... National Chiropractic Association [*Universal Chiropratic Association and American Chiropratic Association*] [*Later, American Chiropractic Association*] [*Formed by a merger of*]
NCA .... National Christian Association (EA)
NCA .... National Civic Association
NCA .... National Climate Archive (QUAC)
NCA .... National Club Association (EA)
NCA .... National Coal Association (EA)
NCA .... National Coal Authority [*Australia*]
NCA .... National Coffee Association of the United States of America (EA)
NCA .... National Color-Bred Association (EA)
NCA .... National Command Authorities
NCA .... National Command Authorization [*Communications term*] (DCT)
NCA .... National Commission on Accrediting [*Later, COPA*] (EA)
NCA .... National Communication Agencies (NATG)
NCA .... National Communication Association (IID)
NCA .... National Communications Association (EA)
NCA .... National Composition Association [*Later, NCPA*] (EA)
NCA .... National Computer Association (EA)
NCA .... National Concierge Association (EA)
NCA .... National Concilio of America (EA)
NCA .... National Confectioners Association of the United States (EA)
NCA .... National Conference of Artists (EA)
NCA .... National Congressional Analysis Corp. (IID)
NCA .... National Constables Association (EA)
NCA .... National Constructors Association (EA)
NCA .... National Contesters Association (EA)
NCA .... National Contingency Account (OICC)
NCA .... National Control Authority (SAUS)
NCA .... National Cosmetology Association (EA)
NCA .... National Costumers Association (EA)
NCA .... National Council for Aviculture [*British*] (DBA)
NCA .... National Council on Alcoholism [*Later, NCADD*] (EA)
NCA .... National Council on the Aging [*Washington, DC*]

NCA......... National Council on the Arts [*of NFAH*]
NCA......... National Courier Association [*United Kingdom*] (EAIO)
NCA......... National Coursing Association [*Later, NGA*] (EA)
NCA......... National Cranberry Association
NCA......... National Creameries Association [*Later, NMPF*] (EA)
NCA......... National Credit Association (NADA)
NCA......... National Cricket Association [*British*]
NCA......... National Crop Acreage Program [*Department of Agriculture*]
NCA......... Naval Center for Cost Analysis
NCA......... Naval Command Assistant
NCA......... Naval Communications Annex
NCA......... Navy Contract Administrator
NCA......... NCA Minerals [*Vancouver Stock Exchange symbol*]
NCA......... N-Carboxy Anhydride [*Organic chemistry*]
NCA......... N-Chloroacetamide [*Organic chemistry*]
NCA......... N-Chloroethylnorapomorphine [*Organic chemistry, biochemistry*]
NCA......... Netherlands Centre Alternatives to Animal Use (GVA)
NCA......... Network Career Advancement Institute [*Telecommunications service*] (TSSD)
NCA......... Network Communications Adapter [*Computer science*] (VLIE)
NCA......... Network Computer Architecture [*Computer science*] (VLIE)
NCA......... Network Computing Architecture [*Computer science*] (TNIG)
NCA......... Network for Community Activities
NCA......... Neurocirculatory Asthenia [*Medicine*]
NCA......... Neutralized Current Acid (ABAC)
NCA......... Neutrophil Chemotactic Activity [*Clinical chemistry*]
NCA......... Nevada Correctional Association (SAUS)
NCA......... New Communities Administration [*HUD*]
NCA......... Newfoundland Club of America (EA)
NCA......... News & Current Affairs (WDAA)
NCA......... Ngorongoro Conservation Area (SAUS)
NCA......... Nickel-Copper Alloy (MSA)
NCA......... Nippon Cargo Airlines Co. Ltd. [*Japan*] [*ICAO designator*] (FAAC)
NCA......... No Congenital Abnormalities [*Medicine*] (MELL)
NCA......... No Copies Available (ADA)
NCA......... No Coupons Attached (DLA)
NCA......... Nodulocystic Acne [*Medicine*] (DMAA)
NCA......... Noise Control Act (EG)
NCA......... Noise Control Association (EA)
NCA......... Noncombat Aircraft [*Military*] (MCD)
NCA......... Noncommutative Algebra (SAUS)
NCA......... Non-Continuous Action (CCCA)
NCA......... Noncontractile Area (DB)
NCA......... Noncontractual Authorization
NCA......... Noncorrodible Aluminum (SAUS)
NCA......... Nonorganic Ceramic Adhesive
NCA......... Nonspecific Cross-Reacting Antigen [*Immunology*]
NCA......... Nor-Cal Aviation, Inc. (SAUS)
NCA......... Normal Coordinate Analysis
NCA......... North Caicos [*British West Indies*] [*Airport symbol*] (OAG)
NCA......... North Carolina Court of Appeals Reports [*A publication*] (DLA)
NCA......... North Central Airlines (SAUS)
NCA......... North Central Association (SAUS)
NCA......... North Central Association of Colleges and Secondary Schools [*Later, NCACS*]
NCA......... North Central Bible College, Minneapolis, MN [*OCLC symbol*] (OCLC)
NCA......... North Coast Airlines [*Australia*]
NCA......... Northern Communications Area [*Military*]
NCA......... Northern Consolidated Airlines, Inc.
NCA......... Northern Consultancy Association (COBU)
NCA......... Northwest Computing Association
NCA......... Norwegian Council for Africa
NCA......... Novell Certification Alliance (SAUS)
NCA......... Nuclear and Chemical Agency [*Army*]
NCA......... Nuclear Cerebral Angiogram [*Medicine*] (DMAA)
NCA......... Nurse Consultants Association (EA)
NCA......... Nuveen California Municipal Fund [*NYSE symbol*] (SPSG)
NcA......... Pack Memorial Public Library, Asheville, NC [*Library symbol*] [*Library of Congress*] (LCLS)
NCAA........ National Center for Audio Tapes Archive (EA)
NCAA........ National Center on Arts and the Aging (EA)
NCAA........ National Change of Address Association [*Commercial firm*] [*New York, NY*] (EA)
NCAA........ National Collegiate Athletic Association (EA)
NCAA........ National Command Authority Aircraft-747 [*MTMC*] (TAG)
NCAA........ National Credit Adjustment Association [*New York, NY*] (EA)
NCAA........ NATO Civil Air Augmentation (DOMA)
NCAA........ Naval Civilian Administrators Association [*Later, NCMA*] (EA)
NCAA........ Non-Nuclear Consumable Annual Analysis System (SAUS)
NCAA........ North Carolina Aggregates Association (EARSL)
NCAA........ Northern Counties Athletic Association (ODA)
NCAAA...... National Center of Afro-American Artists
NCAAA...... National Council of Affiliated Advertising Agencies [*Later, First Network of Affiliated Advertising Agencies*] (EA)
NcAAB....... Asheville-Buncombe Technical Institute, Asheville, NC [*Library symbol*] [*Library of Congress*] (LCLS)
NCaaC....... Community College of the Finger Lakes, Canandaigua (SAUS)
NCAAC...... Northern California Athletic Conference (PSS)
NCAADA..... National Community Action Agency Directors Association [*Formerly, NCAAEDA*] [*Later, NACAA*] (EA)
NCAADACCB... National Commission on Accreditation of Alcoholism and Drug Abuse Counselor Credentialing Bodies (EA)
NCAAE....... National Council of Administrators of Adult Education (EA)
NCAAEDA... National Community Action Agency Executive Directors Association (EA)
NcAAH....... Appalachian Hall Medical Library, Asheville, NC [*Library symbol*] [*Library of Congress*] (LCLS)
NCAAL....... National Conference of African American Librarians
NcAAP....... Amcel Propulsion Co., Asheville, NC [*Library symbol*] [*Library of Congress*] (LCLS)
NCAAP...... National Coalition for Adequate Alcoholism Programs [*Defunct*] (EA)
NC-AAPSO... Nigerian Committee of the Afro-Asian Peoples Solidarity Organization (SAUS)
NCAARL..... National Council for African American Republican Leadership [*Canton, MI*] (PACS)
NCAB........ National Association of Citizen Advice Bureaux [*British*]
NCAB........ National Cancer Advisory Board
NCAB........ National Collegiate Athletic Bureau [*Later, NCSS*] (EA)
NCAB........ National Committee for Amateur Baseball [*Later, USBF*]
NCAB........ Navy Contract Adjustment Board
NCABC...... National Catholic Association for Broadcasters/Communicators (EA)
NCABC...... National Citizens' Advice Bureaux Committee [*British*] (BI)
NcAbd....... Page Memorial Library, Aberdeen, NC [*Library symbol*] [*Library of Congress*] (LCLS)
NCABHP..... National Center for the Advancement of Blacks in the Health Professions (EA)
NcAbMR.... North Carolina Marine Resources Center, Bogue Banks Library, Atlantic Beach, NC [*Library symbol*] [*Library of Congress*] (LCLS)
NcAC........ Cecils Junior College, Asheville, NC [*Library symbol*] [*Library of Congress*] (LCLS)
NCAC........ National Cancer Advisory Committee [*Australia*]
NCAC........ National Catholic Action Coalition [*Defunct*] (EA)
NCAC........ National Center on Accessing the General Curriculum
NCAC........ National Certified Addiction Counselor (SEAT)
NCAC........ National Christian Action Coalition [*Defunct*] (EA)
NCAC........ National Civil Aviation Council [*British*] (BI)
NCAC........ National Clean Air Coalition [*Defunct*] (EA)
NCAC........ National Coalition Against Censorship (EA)
NCAC........ National Consumer Advisory Council
NCAC........ National Copyright Advisory Committee (NADA)
NCAC........ National Council Against Conscription [*World War I*] [*British*]
NCAC........ National Council of Acoustical Consultants (EA)
NCAC........ Navy Combat Art Collection (DNAB)
NCAC........ Nordic Customs Administrative Council (EA)
NCAC........ North Carolina Administrative Code [*A publication*] (AAGC)
NCAC........ North Coast Athletic Conference (PSS)
NCAC........ Northern Combat Area Command [*Myanmar*]
NCA-CASI... North Central Association Commission on Accreditation and School Improvement (EA)
NCACC...... National Collection of Animal Cell Cultures (DB)
NCACC...... National Conference of Appellate Court Clerks (EA)
NCACCT..... North Carolina Association of Community College Trustees (EARSL)
NCACE....... National Capital Association for Cooperative Education (MCD)
NC/AC-EC... Narrow Coverage/Area Coverage to Earth Coverage (SAUS)
NCACME.... National Center for Adult, Continuing, and Manpower Education [*Office of Education*]
NC/AC-NC/AC... Narrow Coverage/Area Coverage to Narrow Coverage/Area Coverage (SAUS)
NCACP...... National Campaign for the Abolition of Capital Punishment [*Founded in 1955*] [*British*]
NCACPS..... National Coalition to Abolish Corporal Punishment in Schools (EA)
NCACS...... National Coalition of Alternative Community Schools (EA)
NCACS...... North Central Association of Colleges and Schools (EA)
NCAD........ New Cumberland Army Depot [*Pennsylvania*] (AABC)
NCAD........ Northrop Computer Aided Design (ACAE)
NCAD........ Notice of Cancellation at Anniversary Date [*Insurance*] (DCTA)
NCADC...... National Coalition of Anti-Deportation Campaigns [*United Kingdom*] (EAIO)
NCADD...... National Commission Against Drunk Driving (EA)
NCADD...... National Council on Alcoholism and Drug Dependence (EA)
NCADH...... National Committee Against Discrimination in Housing [*Defunct*] (EA)
NCADI....... National Clearinghouse for Alcohol and Drug Abuse Information (PAZ)
NCADI....... National Clearinghouse for Alcohol and Drug Information [*US Public Health Service*] [*Information service or system*] (IID)
NC Admin Code... North Carolina Administrative Code [*A publication*] (DLA)
NCADP...... National Coalition Against the Death Penalty (EA)
NCADP...... National Coalition to Abolish the Death Penalty (EA)
NCADS...... Numerical Control Advisory and Demonstration Service (SAUS)
NCADV...... National Coalition Against Domestic Violence (EA)
NC Adv Legis Serv... North Carolina Advance Legislative Service (SAUS)
NC Adv Legis Serv... North Carolina Advance Legislative Service (Michie) [*A publication*] (DLA)
NCAE........ National Center for Alcohol Education [*National Institutes of Health*]
NCAE........ National Center for Audio Experimentation [*Defunct*] (EA)
NCAE........ National College of Agricultural Engineering [*British*] (ARC)
NCAE........ National Conference on Airborne Electronics (MCD)
NCAE........ National Council for Alcohol Education (DMAA)
NCAE........ National Council of Agricultural Employers (EA)
NCAE........ North Carolina Association of Educators (SAUS)
NCAEE...... National Committee on Art Education for the Elderly [*Defunct*] (EA)
NCAEF...... National Ceramic Association Educational Foundation (EA)
NCAEG...... National Confederation of American Ethnic Groups (EA)
NCAEI....... National Conference on the Application of Electrical Insulation
NCAES....... National Center for Analysis of Energy Systems (HGAA)
NCAF........ National Clean Air Fund (GFGA)
NCAF........ National Committee Against Fluoridation [*National Health Federation - NHF*] [*Absorbed by*] (EA)

NCAF .... National Community Action Foundation (EA)
NCAF .... Nationalist Chinese Air Force (SAUS)
NCAFB .... Normal Crop Acreage Farm Base
NCAFP .... National Committee on American Foreign Policy (EA)
NCAG .... National Council on the Arts and Government (EA)
NcAh .... Ahoskie Public Library, Ahoskie, NC [*Library symbol*] [*Library of Congress*] (LCLS)
NCAH .... National Child Abuse Hotline (MELL)
NCAH .... National Committee, Arts for the Handicapped [*Later, VSA*] (EA)
NCAHCP ...... National Council on Alternative Health Care Policy (EA)
NcAHE .... Mountain Area Health Education Center, Health Sciences Library, Asheville, NC [*Library symbol*] [*Library of Congress*] (LCLS)
NCAHE .... National Commission on Allied Health Education [*American Occupational Therapy Association*]
NCAHF .... National Council Against Health Fraud (EA)
NcAHH .... Highland Hospital, Medical Library, Asheville, NC [*Library symbol*] [*Library of Congress*] (LCLS)
NcAhRC ...... Roanoke-Chowan Technical Institute, Ahoskie, NC [*Library symbol*] [*Library of Congress*] (LCLS)
NCAHRN ...... National Central American Health Rights Network (EA)
NCAHUAC ..... National Committee to Abolish the House Un-American Activities Committee [*Later, NCARL*] (EA)
NCAI .... Aitutaki [*Cook Islands*] [*ICAO location identifier*] (ICLI)
NCAI .... Appraisal Institute, North Carolina Chapter (EARSL)
NCAI .... National Clearinghouse for Alcohol Information [*Rockville, MD*] [*National Institutes of Health*]
NCAI .... National Coalition for Adult Immunization
NCAI .... National Congress of American Indians (EA)
NCAI .... National Council of American Importers [*Later, AAEI*] (EA)
NCAI .... National Council on Alcoholism, Inc. (NADA)
NCA-I .... Neighborhood Cleaners Association-International (NTPA)
NCAIAE ...... National Center for American Indian Alternative Education (EA)
NCAIANMHR ... National Center for American Indian and Alaska Native Mental Health Research (EA)
NCAIC .... Nuclear Chemical Accident Incident Control (MCD)
NCAICU ...... North Carolina Association of Independent Colleges and Universities (SAUS)
NCAIE .... National Center for American Indian Education [*Later, NCAIAE*] (EA)
NCAIE .... National Council of the Arts in Education [*Later, ACAE*] (EA)
NCAIED ...... National Center for American Indian Enterprise Development (EA)
NCAIL .... National Council Against Illegal Liquor [*Defunct*] (EA)
NCAIP .... National Consumer Affairs Internship Program [*Defunct*] (EA)
NCAIR .... National Center for Automated Information Retrieval (IID)
NCAIR .... North Carolina Association for Institutional Research (EDAC)
NCAJ .... National Center for Administrative Justice [*Formerly, CAJ*] (EA)
NCA/JCS ..... National Command Authorities and Joint Chiefs of Staff
NCAJL .... National Council on Art in Jewish Life (EA)
NCaL .... Canton Free Library, Canton, NY [*Library symbol*] [*Library of Congress*] (LCLS)
NCAL .... National Centre for Athletics Literature (AIE)
NCAL .... National Committee for Adult Literacy [*British*] (DI)
N Cal .... New Caledonia
NcAlb .... Albemarle-Stanly County Public Library, Albemarle, NC [*Library symbol*] [*Library of Congress*] (LCLS)
NcAlbS ...... Stanly Technical Institute, Albemarle, NC [*Library symbol*] [*Library of Congress*] (LCLS)
NCALC .... North Carolina Association of Launderers and Cleaners (EARSL)
NCALHBCU .... National Consortium of Arts and Letters for Historically Black Colleges and Universities (EA)
NCALI .... National Clearinghouse for Alcohol Information [*National Institutes of Health*] (IID)
NCALL .... National Council on Agricultural Life and Labor Research Fund (EA)
NcAlP .... Pamlico Technical Institute, Alliance, NC [*Library symbol*] [*Library of Congress*] (LCLS)
NCalv .... Baiting Hollow Free Library, Calverton, NY [*Library symbol*] [*Library of Congress*] (LCLS)
NCAM .... National Center for Accessible Media (SAUS)
NCAM .... National Center for Advanced Materials [*Later, Berkeley Center for A dvanced Materials*]
NCAM .... Network Communication Access Method
N-CAM .... Neural Cell Adhesion Molecule [*Biochemistry*]
NCAM .... Neurall Cell Adhesion Molecule (SAUS)
NCAMI .... National Committee Against Mental Illness [*Defunct*] (EA)
NCAMLP ...... National Certification Agency for Medical Laboratory Personnel (MAE)
NCAMP .... National Coalition Against the Misuses of Pesticides (EA)
NCAMR .... Nordic Council for Arctic Medical Research (EA)
NCAN .... Incan Superior Ltd. [*AAR code*]
NCAN .... National Catholic AIDS Network (EA)
NCAN .... National Citizens Action Network (EA)
NCAN .... National Coalition of American Nuns (EA)
NCAN .... National Committee for Amnesty Now (EA)
NCaN .... North Country Reference and Research Resources Council, Canton, NY [*Library symbol*] [*Library of Congress*] (LCLS)
NCAN .... Number of Canisters [*Automotive emissions*]
NcAnA .... Anson Technical Institute, Ansonville, NC [*Library symbol*] [*Library of Congress*] (LCLS)
NCanC .... Community College of the Finger Lakes, Canandaigua, NY [*Library symbol*] [*Library of Congress*] (LCLS)
NcANCC ...... United States National Oceanic and Atmospheric Administration, National ClimaticCenter, Ashville, NC [*Library symbol*] [*Library of Congress*] (LCLS)
NcAnd .... Andrews Carnegie Library, Andrews, NC [*Library symbol*] [*Library of Congress*] (LCLS)
NC & B ...... Naval Courts and Boards
NC&C .... Normal Coitus and Climax (MELL)
NC & CS ..... Navigation Command and Control System
NC & SL ..... Nashville, Chattanooga & St. Louis Railway (IIA)
NC & ST L ... Nashville, Chattanooga & St. Louis Railway
NCANH .... National Council for the Accreditation of Nursing Homes (NADA)
NCanHi ...... Ontario County Historical Society, Canandaigua, NY [*Library symbol*] [*Library of Congress*] (LCLS)
NCaNNH ...... Northern New York Health Information Cooperative, Canton, NY [*Library symbol*] [*Library of Congress*] (LCLS)
NCanV .... United States Veterans Administration Hospital, Canandaigua, NY [*Library symbol*] [*Library of Congress*] (LCLS)
NCAO .... National Commission on Air Quality [*Environmental Protection Agency*] (ERG)
NCAO .... Naval Civil Affairs Officer [*World War II*]
NCAP .... Nansen Centennial Arctic Program (SAUS)
NCAP .... Nasal Continuous Airway Pressure [*Medicine*] (MELL)
N-CAP .... National Coalition Against Pornography (EA)
NCAP .... National Coalition of Abortion Providers (NTPA)
NCAP .... Naval Combat Air Patrol (DNAB)
NCAP .... Neighborhood Community Action Program
NCAP .... Nematic Curvilinear Aligned Phase [*Emulsion film used in windows*] [*Taliq Corp.*]
NCAP .... New Car Assessment Program [*Automobile testing*]
NCAP .... Night Combat Air Patrol [*Military*]
NCAP .... Nordic Council for Animal Protection (EA)
NCAP .... Northwest Coalition for Alternatives to Pesticides (GNE)
NCAP .... Nucleotide Column Affinity for Purification [*Biochemical analysis*]
N-CAP .... Nurses Coalition for Action in Politics
NCAPC .... National Center for Air Pollution Control [*Public Health Service*] [*Obsolete*]
NCAPC .... NATO Conventional Armaments Planning Committee (SAUS)
NCAPHCC ..... North Carolina Association of Plumbing-Heating-Cooling Contractors (EARSL)
NCAPI .... Nuveen California Premium Income Municipal Fund [*Associated Press*] (SAG)
NCAPO .... National Council of Adoptive Parents Organizations [*NACAC*] [*Absorbed by*]
NC App ...... North Carolina Appellate Reports [*A publication*] (AAGC)
NC App ...... North Carolina Court of Appeals Reports [*A publication*] (DLA)
NCAPS .... Naval Control and Protection of Shipping (NVT)
NCAPS .... Non-Contact Angular Position Sensor [*Automotive engineering*]
NCapV .... United States Veterans Administration Hospital, Medical Library, Castle Point, NY [*Library symbol*] [*Library of Congress*] (LCLS)
NCAQ .... National Commission on Air Quality (GNE)
NCAR .... National Center for Association Resources (EA)
NCAR .... National Center for Atmospheric Research [*Boulder, CO*] [*National Science Foundation*] (GRD)
NCAR .... National Conference on the Advancement of Research (EA)
NCAR .... Navy Center for Acquisition Research [*Monterey, CA*]
NCAR .... Nonconformance and Corrective Action Reporting System [*NASA*] (KSC)
N Car .... North Carolina (DLA)
N Car .... North Carolina Reports [*A publication*] (DLA)
Nc-Ar .... North Carolina State Department of Archives and History, Raleigh (SAUS)
Nc-Ar .... North Carolina State Department of Archives and History, Raleigh, NC [*Library symbol*] [*Library of Congress*] (LCLS)
NcAr .... Sallie H. Jenkins Memorial Public Library, Aulander, NC [*Library symbol*] [*Library of Congress*] (LCLS)
NCARAI ...... Navy Center for Applied Research in Artificial Intelligence [*Washington, DC*] (GRD)
NCARB .... National Council of Architectural Registration Boards (EA)
NCARC .... NATO Conventional Armament Review Committee (SAUS)
NCaRC .... North Country Reference and Research Resources Council, Canton, NY [*Library symbol*] [*Library of Congress*] [*Obsolete*] (LCLS)
NCARF .... National Committee for Amish Religious Freedom (EA)
NCARL .... National Committee Against Repressive Legislation (EA)
N Car Law Rep ... Carolina Law Repository (Reprint) [*North Carolina*] [*A publication*] (DLA)
NCARMD ...... National Commission on Arthritis and Related Musculoskeletal Disease
NCarNG ...... North Carolina Natural Gas Corp. [*Associated Press*] (SAG)
NCarol Dent Gaz ... North Carolina Dental Gazette (SAUS)
N Carolina Cases ... North Carolina Reports [*A publication*] (DLA)
NCARP .... Collegiate Association for Research of Principle (EA)
N Car Rep ... North Carolina Reports [*A publication*] (DLA)
NCARRV ...... North Carolinians Against Racist and Religious Violence (SAUS)
NCAR System ... Non-conformance and Corrective Action Reporting System (SAUS)
NCAS .... National Coalition Against Surrogacy (EA)
NCAS .... National Coalition of Advocates for Students (EA)
NCAS .... National Collegiate Association for Secretaries [*Defunct*] (EA)
NCAS .... Neocarzinostatin [*Zinostatin*] [*Antineoplastic drug*]
NCas .... North Cascades (SAUS)
NcA-S .... Pack Memorial Public Library, Sondley Reference Library, Asheville, NC [*Library symbol*] [*Library of Congress*] (LCLS)
NCaS .... Saint Lawrence University, Canton, NY [*Library symbol*] [*Library of Congress*] (LCLS)
NCASA .... National Campaign Against Solvent Abuse [*British*] (DBA)
NCASA .... National Coalition Against Sexual Assault (EA)
NCASA .... Naval Civil Affairs Staging Area
NCASAA ...... National Court Appointed Special Advocates Association (EA)
NcAsbC ...... Randolph Public Library, Asheboro, NC [*Library symbol*] [*Library of Congress*] (LCLS)
NcAsbH ...... Randolph Hospital, Inc., Asheboro, NC [*Library symbol*] [*Library of Congress*] (LCLS)

NcAsbR ..... Randolph Technical Institute, Asheboro, NC [*Library symbol*] [*Library of Congress*] (LCLS)
NCASC ...... National Capital Administrative Support Center [*Marine science*] (OSRA)
NCASC ...... National Council of Acupuncture Schools and Colleges (EA)
NCASC ...... Nordic Council for Adult Studies in Church [*See also NKS*] (EAIO)
NCASEPS ... North Central Alaskan Seasonal Earned Premium Scale [*Aviation*] (AIA)
NCASF....... National Council of American-Soviet Friendship (EA)
NCASI .... National Council of the Paper Industry for Air and Stream Improvement (EA)
NCAT .... Atiu [*Cook Islands*] [*ICAO location identifier*] (ICLI)
NCAT .... National Catalog (AEPA)
NCAT .... National Catalog [*Database*] [*Environment term*] (EGA)
NCAT .... National Center for Advanced Technology [*Vienna, VA*]
NCAT .... National Center for Appropriate Technology (EA)
NCAT .... National Center for Audiotape [*Later, NCATA*] (EA)
NCAT .... National Centre for Alternative Technology [*British*]
NCAT .... National Council of Athletic Training (NTPA)
NCAT .... National Program for Clear Air Turbulence [*Air Force*]
NCAT .... Naval College Aptitude Test (NVT)
NC/AT........ Normal Cephalic Atraumatic [*Medicine*] (DMAA)
NCAT .... Northampton College of Advanced Technology (SAUS)
NCATA....... National Cable Antenna Television Association of Canada (NTCM)
NCATA....... National Center for Audiotape Archive [*Defunct*] (EA)
NCATA....... National Coalition of Arts Therapy Associations (EA)
NCATB....... National Congress of Animal Trainers and Breeders (EA)
NCATE....... National Council for Accreditation of Teacher Education (EA)
NCATH....... National Campaign Against Toxic Hazards (EA)
NcATH....... Thoms Rehabilitation Hospital, Medical Library, Asheville, NC [*Library symbol*] [*Library of Congress*] (LCLS)
NCATL....... North Carolina Academy of Trial Lawyers (EARSL)
NCAU........ Colonial Atlantic [*Intermodal shipping container symbol*] (TVRC)
NcAu......... Sallie H. Jenkins Memorial Public Library, Aulander, NC [*Library symbol*] [*Library of Congress*] (LCLS)
NcAU .... University of North Carolina at Asheville, Asheville, NC [*Library symbol*] [*Library of Congress*] (LCLS)
NCaUA ...... State University of New York, Agricultural and Technical College, Canton, NY [*Library symbol*] [*Library of Congress*] (LCLS)
NCAV .... National Coursing Association of Victoria [*Australia*]
NcAV......... United States Veterans Administration, Hospital Library Service, Asheville, NC [*Library symbol*] [*Library of Congress*] (LCLS)
NCAVAE ..... National Committee for Audio-Visual Aids in Education [*British*]
NCAVC....... National Center for the Analysis of Violent Crime [*Quantico, VA*] [*Department of Justice*] (GRD)
NCAW .... National Council for Animal Welfare (NADA)
NCAW .... Neutralized Current Acid Waste (ABAC)
NCAWA...... National Coinamatic Auto Wash Association [*Later, ICA/NCC*]
NCAWE...... National Council of Administrative Women in Education (EA)
NCAWP...... National Council for Alternative Work Patterns (EA)
NCAWRR.... National Committee Against War, Racism, and Repression
NCAYR ...... National Chaplains Association for Youth Rehabilitation [*Defunct*]
NCAZ .... NCA Leasing Company [*Intermodal trailer symbol*]
NCazC .... Cazenovia College, Cazenovia, NY [*Library symbol*] [*Library of Congress*] (LCLS)
NCB.......... Barber-Scotia College, Concord, NC [*OCLC symbol*] (OCLC)
NCB.......... Name Continuation Block (TIMI)
NCB.......... Nanyang Commercial Bank [*China*]
NCB.......... National Cargo Bureau (EA)
NCB.......... National Center for Biodefense [*George Mason University*] (RCD)
NCB.......... National Central Bureau [*INTERPOL term*]
NCB.......... National Certification Bodies (AG)
NCB.......... National Children's Bureau [*British*]
NCB.......... National Classification Board [*American Trucking Association*]
NCB.......... National Coal Board [*British*]
NCB.......... National Codification Bureau [*NATO*] (NATG)
NCB.......... National Collection of Industrial Bacteria [*British*]
NCB.......... National College of Business (IAA)
NCB.......... National Commercial Bank [*Saudi Arabia*]
NCB.......... National Commercial Bank [*Jamaica*]
NCB.......... National Compliance Board [*New Deal*]
NCB.......... National Conservation Bureau [*Defunct*]
NCB.......... National Cooperative Bank (USGC)
NCB.......... NATO Codification Bureau (SAUS)
NCB.......... Naval Communications Board
NCB.......... Naval Construction Battalion
NCB.......... Navy Comptroller Budget (NG)
NCB.......... NCNB Corp. [*NYSE symbol*] (COMM)
NCB.......... NCNB Corp. [*AMEX symbol*] (NASQ)
NCB.......... Nederlandse Credietbank NV [*Financial institution*] [*Netherlands*] (EY)
NCB.......... NetBIOS [*Network Basic Input/Output System*] Control Block [*Computer science*]
NCB.......... Net Change of Biomass (CARB)
NCB.......... Net Clearing Balance [*Finance*]
NCB.......... Net Conservation Benefit (SAUS)
NCB.......... Netherlands Convention Bureau (EA)
NCB.......... Network Connect Block [*Computer science*] (CIST)
NCB.......... Network Control Block
NCB.......... Nevrite Cervico-Brachial (SAUS)
NCB.......... New Century Bible [*A publication*] (BJA)
NCB.......... New Crime Buffer
NCB.......... Nickel-Cadmium Battery
NCB.......... Nippon Credit Bank [*Japan*]
NCB.......... Nippon Cultural Broadcasting (SAUS)
NCB.......... No Claim Bonus [*Insurance*] (ADA)
NCB.......... No Code Blue [*For terminal cases*] [*Medicine*] (DAVI)
NCB.......... Noncallable Bond [*Investment term*]
NCB.......... North Caribou Flying Service Ltd. [*Canada*] [*ICAO designator*] (FAAC)
NCB.......... Northwest Cherry Briners (SAUS)
NCB.......... Northwest Cherry Briners Association (EA)
NCB.......... Nuclear Contingency Branch (SAUS)
NcBa......... Mitchell County Library, Bakersville, NC [*Library symbol*] [*Library of Congress*] (LCLS)
NCBA........ National Candy Brokers Association (EA)
NCBA........ National Catholic Band Association (NTPA)
NCBA........ National Catholic Bandmasters' Association (EA)
NCBA........ National Cattle Breeders Association [*British*] (DBA)
NCBA........ National Cattlemen's Beef Association (GVA)
NCBA........ National Caucus and Center on Black Aged (EA)
NCBA........ National Chinchilla Breeders of America [*Later, ECBC*] (EA)
NCBA........ National Color-Bred Association (EA)
NCBA........ National Commodity and Barter Association (EA)
NCBA........ National Cooperative Business Association (EA)
NCBA........ National Council on Black Aging (EA)
NCBA........ Northern California Booksellers Association (SAUS)
NCBAE....... No-Claim Bonus as Earned [*Insurance*] (ODBW)
NcBaneL.... Lees-McRae College, Banner Elk, NC [*Library symbol*] [*Library of Congress*] (LCLS)
NCBA-PAC... National Cattlemen's Beef Association PAC [*Centennial, CO*] (PACS)
NCBBC ...... National Council of Bible Believing Churches [*Later, CBBC*] (EA)
NcBc......... Marianna Black Library, Bryson City, NC [*Library symbol*] [*Library of Congress*] (LCLS)
NCBC .... National Commerce Bancorp [*NASDAQ symbol*] (NQ)
NCBC .... National Committee for the Berne Convention [*Defunct*] (EA)
NCBC .... Natl Commerce Bancorp [*NASDAQ symbol*] (TTSB)
NCBC .... Naval Construction Battalion Center
NCBC .... New Century Bible Commentary [*A publication*]
NCBC .... North Carolina Biotechnology Center [*Research center*] (RCD)
NcBcF .... Fontana Regional Library, Bryson City, NC [*Library symbol*] [*Library of Congress*] (LCLS)
NCBCS ...... National Conference of States on Building Codes and Standards (OICC)
NCBDE ...... National Certification Board for Diabetes Educators (SAUS)
NcBe......... Belmont Abbey College, Belmont, NC [*Library symbol*] [*Library of Congress*] (LCLS)
NCBE .... National City Bancshares [*NASDAQ symbol*] (SAG)
NCBE .... National Clearinghouse for Bilingual Education [*Wheaton, MD*]
NCBE .... National Conference of Bar Executives [*Later, NABE*] (EA)
NCBE .... National Council for Better Education (EA)
NCBE .... North County Business Exchange
NcBea .... Cateret County Public Library, Beaufort, NC [*Library symbol*] [*Library of Congress*] (LCLS)
NCBEA....... National Catholic Business Education Association [*Emporia, KS*] (EA)
NCBEA....... North Central Business Education Association (AEBS)
NcBeaAE.... United States Marine Fisheries Service, Southeast Fisheries Center, Beaufort Laboratory, Beaufort, NC [*Library symbol*] [*Library of Congress*] (LCLS)
NCBEC....... National Center for Business and Economic Communication [*American University*] [*Research center*] (RCD)
NCBEE....... National Council of State Boards of Engineering Examiners [*Later, NCEE*] (IAA)
NCBEL....... [*The*] New Cambridge Bibliography of English Literature [*A publication*]
NCBES....... National Council of Black Engineers and Scientists (NTPA)
NcBeSH .... Sacred Heart College, McCarthy Library, Belmont, NC [*Library symbol*] [*Library of Congress*] (LCLS)
NcBesL...... Lithium Corp. of America, Ellestad Research Library, Bessemer City, NC [*Library symbol*] [*Library of Congress*] (LCLS)
NCBF .... National Conference of Bar Foundations (EA)
NCBF .... Non-Conventional Brake Fluid [*Automotive engineering*]
NCBFAA..... National Customs Brokers and Forwarders Association of America [*New York, NY*] (EA)
NCBFE....... National Center for a Barrier Free Environment (EA)
NCBG .... National Coalition of Black Gays (EA)
ncbh-........ British Honduras [*MARC geographic area code*] [*Library of Congress*] (LCCP)
NCBH........ National Coalition to Ban Handguns [*Later, CSGV*] (EA)
NCBHC ...... National Committee on Black and Hispanic Concerns (EA)
NCBI......... National Center for Biotechnology Information (IID)
NCBI......... National Cotton Batting Institute (EA)
NCBIAE..... National Council of BIA [*Bureau of Indian Affairs*] Educators (EA)
NCBJ .... National Conference of Bankruptcy Judges (EA)
NCBJS....... National Council of Beth Jacob Schools [*Later, FCBJS*] (EA)
NcBl .... Bridger Memorial Public Library, Bladenboro, NC [*Library symbol*] [*Library of Congress*] (LCLS)
NCBL .... National Conference of Black Lawyers (EA)
NCBL .... Natural Convection Boiling Loops
NCBLG ...... National Coalition of Black Lesbians and Gays (EA)
NcBlm....... Black Mountain Public Library, Black Mountain, NC [*Library symbol*] [*Library of Congress*] (LCLS)
NCBLRDC... National Coalition of Black Lung and Respiratory Disease Clinics (EA)
NcBlv........ Phillip Leff Memorial Library, Beulaville, NC [*Library symbol*] [*Library of Congress*] (LCLS)
NCBM .... National City Bancorp [*NASDAQ symbol*] (NQ)
NCBM .... National Conference of Black Mayors (EA)
NCBM .... National Council on Business Mail (EA)
NCBM .... Natl City Bancorp'n [*NASDAQ symbol*] (TTSB)

NCBMP ...... National Coalition of Black Meeting Planners (EA)
NCBMP ...... National Council of Building Material Producers [*A union*] [*British*]
NcBo .... Watauga County Library, Boone, NC [*Library symbol*] [*Library of Congress*] (LCLS)
NcBoA .... Appalachian State University, Boone, NC [*Library symbol*] [*Library of Congress*] (LCLS)
NcBoHE ..... Northwest Area Health Education Center, Boone, NC [*Library symbol*] [*Library of Congress*] (LCLS)
NcBoNM .... New River Area Mental Health, Boone, NC [*Library symbol*] [*Library of Congress*] (LCLS)
NCBOR ...... No Claim Bonus on Renewal [*Insurance*] (AIA)
NCBP .... National Conference of Bar Presidents (EA)
NCBPD ...... National Consortium for Black Professional Development (EA)
Nc-BPH ...... North Carolina Library for the Blind and Physically Handicapped, Raleigh, NC [*Library symbol*] [*Library of Congress*] (LCLS)
NCBPNP/N... National Certification Board of Pediatric Nurse Practitioners and Nurses (EA)
NCBR .... National Center for Bilingual Research [*National Institute of Education*] [*Research center*] (RCD)
NCBR .... National Community Banks (EFIS)
NCBR .... Near Commercial Breeder Reactor [*Also, PLBR*]
NCBR .... Nitride Cooled Breeder Reactor (SAUS)
NCBR .... Nordic Committee on Building Regulations (SAUS)
NcBre .... Transylvania County Library, Brevard, NC [*Library symbol*] [*Library of Congress*] (LCLS)
NcBreC ...... Brevard College, Brevard, NC [*Library symbol*] [*Library of Congress*] (LCLS)
NCBS .... National Cage Bird Show (EA)
NCBS .... National Consumer Board for Stuttering (EA)
NCBS .... National Council for Black Studies (EA)
NCBS .... New Commerce Bancorp [*NASDAQ symbol*] (QUAN)
NCBSA ...... National Candy Brokers and Salesmen's Association [*Later, NCBA*] (EA)
NcBsG .... Gardner-Webb College, Boiling Springs, NC [*Library symbol*] [*Library of Congress*] (LCLS)
NCBTA .... Nordic Cooperative of Brick and Tilemakers Associations (SAUS)
NCBTMB .... National Certification Board for Therapeutic Massage and Bodywork [*Association*] (EA)
NCBU .... Northbrook Container Leasing [*Intermodal shipping container symbol*] (TVRC)
NcBuC .... Campbell College, Buies Creek, NC [*Library symbol*] [*Library of Congress*] (LCLS)
NcBuC-L .... Campbell University, Law Library, Buies Creek, NC [*Library symbol*] [*Library of Congress*] (LCLS)
NcBur .... Central North Carolina Regional Library, Burlington, NC [*Library symbol*] [*Library of Congress*] (LCLS)
NcBurAT ..... AT&T Technologies Inc., Technical Library, Burlington, NC [*Library symbol*] [*Library of Congress*] (LCLS)
NcBurgP .... Pender County Library, Burgaw, NC [*Library symbol*] [*Library of Congress*] (LCLS)
NcBurgP-H... Pender County Library, Hampstead Branch Library, Hampstead, NC [*Library symbol*] [*Library of Congress*] (LCLS)
NcBurT ...... Technical Institute of Alamance, Burlington, NC [*Library symbol*] [*Library of Congress*] (LCLS)
NcBurWE.... Western Electric Co., Technical Library, Burlington, NC [*Library symbol*] [*Library of Congress*] (LCLS)
NcButM ..... Murdoch Center, School Library, Butner, NC [*Library symbol*] [*Library of Congress*] (LCLS)
NcBv .... Yancey County Public Library, Burnsville, NC [*Library symbol*] [*Library of Congress*] (LCLS)
NCBVA .... National Concrete Burial Vault Association (EA)
NCBVP ...... National Coalition on Black Voter Participation (EA)
NCBW .... National Cage Bird Week Association [*Defunct*] (EA)
NCBW .... National Coalition of 100 Black Women (EA)
NCBWA ...... National Collegiate Baseball Writers Association (EA)
NcBy .... Palmico County Library, Bayboro, NC [*Library symbol*] [*Library of Congress*] (LCLS)
NCC .... Chadron State College, Chadron, NE [*OCLC symbol*] (OCLC)
NCC .... Dutch national computer catalogue (SAUS)
NCC .... NAACOG [*Nurses Association of the American College of Obstetricians and Gynecologists*] Certification Corp. (EA)
NCC .... Nanoose Conversion Campaign [*Canada*] (EAIO)
NCC .... NASA Class Code (NASA)
NCC .... NASA Communications Control (SAUS)
NCC .... National Cadet Corps (NADA)
NCC .... National Cambridge Collectors (EA)
NCC .... National Cancer Center (EA)
NCC .... National Can Corp. (EFIS)
NCC .... National Capital Commission [*Canada*]
NCC .... National Capon Council [*Defunct*] (EA)
NCC .... National Caravan Council Ltd. [*British*] (BI)
NCC .... National Carbon Co. (MCD)
NCC .... National Career Center (EA)
NCC .... National Carwash Council [*Later, ICA*] (EA)
NCC .... National Castings Council [*Defunct*] (EA)
NCC .... National Certification Commission (NTPA)
NCC .... National Certification Corporation for the Obstetric, Gynecologic and Neonatal Nursing Specialties (EA)
NCC .... National Certified Counselor (DHP)
NCC .... National Chile Center [*Formerly, NCCSC*] (EA)
NCC .... National Citizens Coalition [*Canada*]
NCC .... National Citizens Committee. Bulletin [*A publication*]
NCC .... National City Corp. [*NYSE symbol*] (CTT)
NCC .... National Clearing Corp. [*National Association of Securities Dealers*]
NCC .... National Clients Council (EA)
NCC .... National Climatic Center [*National Oceanic and Atmospheric Administration*]
NCC .... National Coaches Council [*Later, ANCC*] (EA)
NCC .... National Coal Council [*Department of Energy*] [*Arlington, VA*] (EGAO)
NCC .... National Command Center (ACAE)
NCC .... National Communications Club (EA)
NCC .... National Communications Command [*Army*] (RDA)
NCC .... National Communications Commission [*Uganda*] (ECON)
NCC .... National Company of Crossbowmen [*Defunct*] (EA)
NCC .... National Computer Center [*IRS*]
NCC .... National Computer Conference
NCC .... National Computer Council (NADA)
NCC .... National Computing Centre [*Manchester, England*]
NCC .... National Conference on Citizenship (EA)
NCC .... National Congressional Club (EA)
NCC .... National Consumer Council [*British*] (ILCA)
NCC .... National Consumers Congress [*Later, NCL*]
NCC .... National Container Committee [*Later, Uniform Classification Committee*] (EA)
NCC .... National Control Center (ELAL)
NCC .... National Coordinating Center [*Emergency Management*] (EMA)
NCC .... National Coordinating Committee (USGC)
NCC .... National Coordinating Committee for the Promotion of History (EA)
NCC .... National Coordinating Committee to End the War [*Organization formed in 1965*] (VNW)
NCC .... National Coordinating Council on Drug Abuse Education and Information [*Later, NCCDE*] (EA)
NCC .... National Coordination Committee [*Responsible for administering the Work Incentive Program*]
NCC .... National Cotton Council of America (EA)
NCC .... National Council Against Conscription [*World War I*] [*British*]
NCC .... National Council of Churches (SHCU)
NCC .... National Council of Churches of Christ in the USA (EA)
NCC .... National Counselor Certification [*Psychology*]
NCC .... National Crime Commission
NCC .... National Cryptologic Command [*National Security Agency*]
NCC .... National Cultural Center [*Later, John F. Kennedy Center for the Performing Art s*]
NCC .... National Curriculum Council [*British*] (ECON)
NCC .... Native Council of Canada
NCC .... Natural Circulation Cooldown [*Nuclear energy*] (NUCP)
NCC .... Naturally Commutated Cycloconverter [*Electronics*] (EECA)
NCC .... Nature Conservancy Council [*British*]
NCC .... Navajo Community College [*Chinle, AZ*]
NCC .... Naval Command College (POLM)
NCC .... Naval Component Command (CINC)
NCC .... Navigation Computer Control
NCC .... Navigation Control Console
NCC .... Navy Command Center (MCD)
NCC .... Navy Cost Center
NCC .... NetWare Console Commander [*Frye Computer Systems*] [*Telecommunications*] (PCM)
NCC .... NetWare Control Center [*Novell, Inc.*] [*Computer science*] (PCM)
NCC .... Network Communications Corp.
NCC .... Network Computer Center (OA)
NCC .... Network Control Center [*Telecommunications*]
NCC .... Network Control Computer (HGAA)
NCC .... Network Coordination Center [*NASA*]
NCC .... Network Cybernetics Corp. (IID)
NCC .... Network of Concerned Correspondents (EA)
NCC .... Neural Crest Cell [*Cytology*]
NCC .... Neuronal Correlate of Consciousness
NCC .... New Chancery Cases (Younge and Collyer) [*1841-43*] [*England*] [*A publication*] (DLA)
NCC .... New Chemical Compound [*Food science*]
NCC .... New Common Carriers
NCC .... New Computer Center [*Social Security Administration*]
NCC .... New Construction and Conversion [*Navy*] (AFIT)
NCC .... New Consultants and Consulting Organizations Directory [*A publication*]
NCC .... Newfoundland Capital Corp. Ltd. [*Toronto Stock Exchange symbol*]
NCC .... Newhouse Communications Center (SAUS)
NCC .... Newspaper Comics Council [*Later, NFC*] (EA)
NCC .... Niagara County Community College [*UTLAS symbol*]
NCC .... Nitrogen Carbon Cycle (SAUS)
NCC .... Nitrogen Charging Console
NCC .... Noise Control Committee
NCC .... Noise Criterion Curve (LDOE)
NCC .... Nominal Corrective Combination (MCD)
NCC .... Noncarbohydrate Craver [*Nutrition*]
NCC .... Noncombatant Corps [*British*]
NCC .... NORAD Control Center [*Military*]
NCC .... Nordic Choral Committee (EAIO)
NCC .... Nordic Construction Co. (EFIS)
NCC .... Normal-Control Children [*Psychology*]
NCC .... Normal Corrective Combination (SAUS)
NCC .... Normally Closed Contact [*Switch*] (IAA)
NCC .... North Calotte Committee [*See also NKK*] [*Nordic Council of Ministers*] [*Finland*] (EAIO)
NCC .... North Central Caucasian [*Linguistics*] (IEL)
NCC .... North Central College [*Naperville, IL*]
NCC .... North Central Conference (PSS)
NCC .... North Coast Air Services Ltd. [*Canada*] [*ICAO designator*] (FAAC)
NCC .... Northwest Christian College [*Oregon*]
NCC .... Northwest Community College (SAUS)

NCC.......... Northwood Control Centre (SAUS)
NCC.......... Notre Cause Commune [*Benin*] [*Political party*] (EY)
NCC.......... Numerical Control Code
NCC.......... Nursing Clerical Coordinator
NCC.......... Our Common Cause (Benin) [*Political party*] (PSAP)
NcC.......... Public Library of Charlotte and Mecklenburg County, Charlotte, NC [*Library symbol*] [*Library of Congress*] (LCLS)
NcCA........ Arthur Andersen & Co., Carolinas Central Library, Charlotte, NC [*Library symbol*] [*Library of Congress*] (LCLS)
NCCA........ Nash Car Club of America (EA)
NCCA........ National Carpet Cleaners Association [*British*] (EAIO)
NCCA........ National Catholic Camping Association [*Defunct*] (EA)
NCCA........ National Catholic Council on Alcoholism and Related Drug Problems (EA)
NCCA........ National Cedar Chest Association [*Defunct*] (EA)
NCCA........ National Center for Child Advocacy
NCCA........ National Center for Community Action (EA)
NCCA........ National Centre for Clinical Audit (SAUS)
NCCA........ National Centre for Computer Animation [*Bournemouth University*] [*United Kingdom*] (RCD)
NCCA........ National Chemical Credit Association (EA)
NCCA........ National Child Care Association (NTPA)
NCCA........ National Clergy Council on Alcoholism and Related Drug Problems (EA)
NCCA........ National Club Cricket Association [*British*] (BI)
NCCA........ National Coil Coaters Association (EA)
NCCA........ National Collegiate Conference Association (EA)
NCCA........ National Columbia Challenger Association (EA)
NCCA........ National Commission for Certifying Agencies (SAUS)
NCCA........ National Commission for the Certification of Acupuncture (EA)
NCCA........ National Commission for the Certification of Acupuncturists (EA)
NCCA........ National Committee on Central America (EA)
NCCA........ National Concrete Contractors Association [*Later, ASCC*] (EA)
NCCA........ National Cotton Council of America [*Memphis, TN*]
NCCA........ National Council for Critical Analysis [*Defunct*] (EA)
NCCA........ National Council for Culture and Art (EA)
NCCA........ National Court Clubs Association [*Later, IRSA*] (EA)
NCCA........ Naval Center for Cost Analysis
NCCA........ Nebraska Community College Association (EARSL)
NCCA........ Negligence and Compensation Cases, Annotated [*A publication*] (DLA)
NCCA........ Nordic Committee for Central Africa [*Defunct*] (EA)
NCCA........ North Carolina Classical Association (SAUS)
NCCA........ North Carolina Coaches Association (EARSL)
NCCA........ North Carolina Correctional Association (SAUS)
NCCA 3d.... Negligence and Compensation Cases, Annotated, Third Series [*A publication*] (DLA)
NCCAA...... National Christian College Athletic Association (EA)
NCCAC...... National Catholic Conference of Airport Chaplains (EA)
NCCACS..... National Council of Columbia Associations in Civil Service (EA)
NCCAE...... National Conference of Catholic Art Educators (AEBS)
NCCAE...... National Council of County Association Executives (EA)
NCCAFV..... National Council on Child Abuse and Family Violence (EA)
NcCaLM..... United States Naval Medical Field Research Laboratory, Camp Lejeune, NC [*Library symbol*] [*Library of Congress*] (LCLS)
NcCaLMC... United States Marine Corps, Marine Corps Base General Library, Camp Lejeune, NC [*Library symbol*] [*Library of Congress*] (LCLS)
NcCaLNM... United States Navy, Naval Regional Medical Center, Library, Camp Lejeune, NC [*Library symbol*] [*Library of Congress*] (LCLS)
NCCAM...... National Center for Complementary and Alternative Medicine
NCCAN...... National Center on Child Abuse and Neglect [*Department of Health and Human Services*] [*Washington, DC*]
NCCAN...... National Clearinghouse on Child Abuse and Neglect Information (PAZ)
NCCA NS.... Negligence and Compensation Cases, Annotated, New Series [*A publication*] (DLA)
NCCAOM.... National Certification Commission for Acupuncture and Oriental Medicine
NCCAP...... National Certification Council for Activity Professionals (NTPA)
NcCar........ Moore County Library, Carthage, NC [*Library symbol*] [*Library of Congress*] (LCLS)
NCCAS...... National Center of Communication Arts and Sciences (EA)
NCCAS...... National Council for Clean Air and Streams
NCCAT...... National Committee for Clear Air Turbulence (KSC)
NCCB........ National Carpenters Craft Board [*Defunct*] (EA)
NCCB........ National Citizens Committee for Broadcasting (EA)
NCCB........ National Conference of Catholic Bishops (EA)
NCCB........ National Consumer Cooperative Bank
NCCB........ National Council to Combat Blindness [*Also known as Fight for Sight - FS*] (EA)
NCCB........ Netherlands Culture Collection of Bacteria (SAUS)
NCCBA...... National Caucus and Center on Black Aged (EA)
NCCBH...... National Council for Community Behavioral Healthcare (SAUS)
NCCBI....... National Coordinating Committee of the Beverage Industry
NCCBI....... North Carolina Citizens for Business and Industry (EARSL)
NCCBMI..... National Consortium for Computer Based Music Instruction [*University of Delaware*] [*Research clearinghouse*] (EA)
NCCBN...... National Council of Churches Broadcasting Network (NTCM)
NCCC........ National Cambodia Crisis Committee [*Defunct*] (EA)
NCCC........ National Cancer Cytology Center [*Later, NCC*] (EA)
NCCC........ National Catholic Cemetery Conference (EA)
NCCC........ National Certified Career Counselor (DHP)
NCCC........ National Cervical Cancer Coalition (NRGU)
NCCC........ National Civilian Community Corps
NCCC........ National Conference of Catholic Charities (EA)
NCCC........ National Conservative Congressional Committee (EA)
NCCC........ National Consumer Credit Consultants (EA)
NCCC........ National Council of Churches of Christ in the USA [*Later, NCC*] (EA)
NCCC........ National Council of Community Churches [*Later, ICCC*] (EA)
NCCC........ National Council of Corvette Clubs (EA)
NCCC........ Niagara County Community College (SAUS)
NCCC........ Norris Cotton Cancer Center [*Dartmouth-Hitchcock Medical Center*] [*Research center*] (RCD)
NCCCC...... National Coalition for Campus Child Care (EA)
NCCCC...... National Council for Credentialing Career Counselors (DHP)
NCCCC...... Naval Command, Control Communications Center (IAA)
NCCCC...... North Central Community College Conference (PSS)
NCCCCA..... National Collegiate Cross Country Coaches Association [*Later, USC-CCA*] (EA)
NCCCD...... National Center Confraternity of Christian Doctrine (EA)
NCCCD...... National Center for Computer Crime Data (EA)
NcCCed..... Cedalion Systems, Inc., Information Resources, Charlotte, NC [*Library symbol*] [*Library of Congress*] (LCLS)
NcCCel...... Celanese Fibers Co., Technical Information Center, Charlotte (SAUS)
NcCCel...... Celanese Fibers Co., Technical Information Center, Charlotte, NC [*Library symbol*] [*Library of Congress*] (LCLS)
NCCCHE..... National Certification Commission in Chemistry and Chemical Engineering (IAA)
NCCCLC..... Naval Command Control Communications Laboratory Center
NcCCP....... Central Piedmont Community College, Charlotte, NC [*Library symbol*] [*Library of Congress*] (LCLS)
NCCCP...... National Center for Community Crime Prevention (EA)
NCCCR...... National Citizens Committee for Community Relations [*Defunct*]
NCCCSA..... National Council for the Care of Cripples in South Africa [*Medicine*] (EDAA)
NCCCTC..... Non-Corrosive Cyclic Corrosion Test Chamber
NCCCWA.... National Cotton Compress and Cotton Warehouse Association [*Later, CWAA*] (EA)
NcCD........ Duke Power Co., Information Systems Library, Charlotte, NC [*Library symbol*] [*Library of Congress*] (LCLS)
NCCD........ National Center for Chronic Disease Control [*Public Health Service*]
NCCD........ National College for Criminal Defense (EA)
NCCD........ National Council for Community Development (EA)
NCCD........ National Council for Criminal Defense (EA)
NCCD........ National Council on Crime and Delinquency (EA)
NCCDC...... National Center for Chronic Disease Control (DAVI)
NcCDD...... Duke Power Co., David Nabow Library, Charlotte, NC [*Library symbol*] [*Library of Congress*] (LCLS)
NCCDE...... National Coordinating Council on Drug Education [*Formerly, NCC*]
NCCDL...... National College of Criminal Defense Lawyers and Public Defenders (DLA)
NCCDN...... National Consortium of Chemical Dependency Nurses (EA)
NCCDPC..... NATO Command, Control, and Information Systems and Automatic Data Processing Committee (NATG)
NCCDPHP... National Center for Chronic Disease Prevention and Health Promotion
NCCD-R & I... National Council on Crime and Delinquency, Research and Information Division [*Research center*] (RCD)
NCCDS...... National Cooperative Crohn's Disease Study
NCCDS...... Network Control Center Data System (SSD)
NCCE........ National Center for Community Education (EA)
NCCE........ National Center for Computational Electronics [*University of Illinois at Urbana-Champaign*] (RCD)
NCCE........ National Coalition for Consumer Education (EA)
NCCE........ National Commission for Cooperative Education (EA)
NCCE........ National Committee for Citizens in Education (EA)
NCCE........ Nordic Committee for Commercial Education [*See also NKH*] [*Odense, Denmark*] (EAIO)
NCCEA....... Neurosensory Center Comprehensive Examination for Aphasia (DAVI)
NCCED...... National Congress for Community Economic Development (EA)
NCCEM...... National Coordinating Council on Emergency Management (EA)
NCCEM...... National Council of Catholic Employers and Managers (EA)
NCCEWV.... National Coordinating Committee to End the War in Vietnam [*Defunct*]
NCCF........ National Cancer Care Foundation (EA)
NCCF........ National Childhood Cancer Foundation (NRGU)
NCCF........ National Commission on Consumer Finance [*Terminated*]
NCCF........ National Council on Community Foundations [*Later, CF*] (EA)
NCCF........ Network Communications Control Facility [*IBM program product*]
NCC-FC..... National Computer Center - Fort Collins [*Colorado*] (ALAC)
NCCFL....... National Catholic Conference on Family Life (EA)
NCCG........ National Council on Compulsive Gambling [*Later, NAPG*] (EA)
NCCG........ Navy Central Clearance Group (DNAB)
NCCGDP.... National Council of Chairmen of Graduate Departments of Psychology
NcCGS....... Church of Jesus Christ of Latter-Day Saints, Genealogical Society Library, Charlotte North Carolina Branch, Charlotte, NC [*Library symbol*] [*Library of Congress*] (LCLS)
NcCh......... Chapel Hill Public Library, Chapel Hill, NC [*Library symbol*] [*Library of Congress*] (LCLS)
NCCH........ National Council of Community Hospitals (EA)
NCCH........ National Council to Control Handguns [*Later, HCI*] (EA)
NCCH........ Nurses' Central Clearing House (AIE)
NCCHB...... National Committee on Concerns of Hispanics and Blacks [*Defunct*] (EA)
NCCHC...... National Commission on Correctional Health Care (EA)
NCCHE...... National Chicano Council for Higher Education [*Defunct*] (EA)
NCCHI....... National Cap and Cloth Hat Institute (EA)
NcCHM...... Helms, Mullis & Johnston Law Library, Charlotte, NC [*Library symbol*] [*Library of Congress*] (LCLS)

NCCHR ...... National Commission on Confidentiality of Health Records [*Defunct*] (EA)
NCCHS ...... National Commission on Community Public Health Services
NCCHS ...... Nonirradiated Core Component Handling System (SAUS)
NCCHTA ..... National Coordinating Centre for Health Technology Assessment (SAUS)
NcCI .... IBM Corp., Library/15C, Charlotte, NC [*Library symbol*] [*Library of Congress*] (LCLS)
NCCI .... Nashville Country Club [*NASDAQ symbol*] (SAG)
NCCI .... National Center for Creativity [*Association*] (EA)
NCCI .... National Commission on Coping with Interdependence (EA)
NCCI .... National Council on Compensation Insurance [*New York, NY*] (EA)
NCCI .... North Central Computer Institute [*Research center*] (RCD)
NCCI .... Nutri-Cheese Co. [*NASDAQ symbol*] (COMM)
NCCIA .... North Carolina Crop Improvement Association (SAUS)
NCC/IBL ..... Nederlandse Centrale Catalogus/Interbibliothecair Leenverkeer System [*Netherlands Central Catalogue/Interlibrary Loan System*] [*Consortium of the Royal Library and University Libraries*] [*Information service or system*] (IID)
NCCIC .... National Child Care Information Center (SAUS)
NCCIDSA ... North Central Chapter Infectious Diseases Society of America (SAUS)
NCCIHE ...... North Carolina Center for Independent Higher Education (SAUS)
NCCIJ .... National Catholic Conference for Interracial Justice (EA)
NCCIP .... National Center for Clinical Infant Programs (EA)
NCCIP .... Nordic Cooperation Committee for International Politics, Including Conflict and Peace Research (EA)
NCCIR .... National Catholic Commission for Industrial Relations [*Australia*]
NCCIS .... NATO Command, Control, and Information System (NATG)
NCCIW .... Nashville Country Club Wrrt [*NASDAQ symbol*] (TTSB)
NcCJ .... Johnson C. Smith University, Charlotte, NC [*Library symbol*] [*Library of Congress*] (LCLS)
NCCJ .... National Conference of Christians and Jews (EA)
NCCJ .... Native Code Compiler for Java (GART)
NCCJP & A... National Clearinghouse for Criminal Justice Planning and Architecture [*Defunct*] (EA)
NCCK .... Noncoherent Carrier Keying (IAA)
NCC-KC ..... National Computer Center - Kansas City (ALAC)
NCCL .... National Citizen Communication Lobby (EA)
NCCL .... National Conference of Catechetical Leadership (NTPA)
NCCL .... National Council for Civil Liberties [*British*]
NCCL .... National Council of Canadian Labour
NCCL .... National Council of Catholic Laity [*Defunct*] (EA)
NCCL .... National Council of Coal Lessors (EA)
NcCla .... Hocutt-Ellington Memorial Library, Clayton, NC [*Library symbol*] [*Library of Congress*] (LCLS)
NCC-LAW ... North Carolina Center for Laws Affecting Women, Inc. [*Research center*] (RCD)
NcClH .... Haywood Technical Institute, Clyde, NC [*Library symbol*] [*Library of Congress*] (LCLS)
NcCli .... Sampson-Clinton Public Library, Clinton, NC [*Library symbol*] [*Library of Congress*] (LCLS)
NcCliS .... Sampson Technical Institute, Clinton, NC [*Library symbol*] [*Library of Congress*] (LCLS)
NCCLS .... National Committee for Clinical Laboratory Science
NCCLS .... National Committee for Clinical Laboratory Standards (EA)
NCCLS .... National Consumer Center for Legal Services [*Later, NRCCLS*] (EA)
NCCLS .... Nevada Center for Cooperative Library Services (SAUS)
NCCLVP ..... National Coordinating Committee on Large Volume Parenterals (BABM)
NCCM .... Master Chief Navy Counselor [*Navy rating*] (DNAB)
NcCM .... Mecklenburg County Medical Society, Charlotte, NC [*Library symbol*] [*Library of Congress*] (LCLS)
NCCM .... National Council of Catholic Men (EA)
NCCMA ...... National Corporate Cash Management Association (EA)
NCCMAG .... National Computer Center Management Advisory Group (EAGT)
NCCMC ...... Navy Civilian Career Management Center (ACAE)
NCCMCU .... National Committee to Commemorate the Millenium of Christianity in the Ukraine (EA)
NCCMGI ..... National Clearinghouse for Corporate Matching Gift Information (EA)
NCCMHC .... National Council of Community Mental Health Centers (EA)
NCCMHS .... National Consortium for Child Mental Health Services (EA)
NCCMIRS... Navy Civilian Career Management Inventory and Referral System (DNAB)
NcCML ...... Medical Library of Mecklenburg County, Inc., Charlotte, NC [*Library symbol*] [*Library of Congress*] (LCLS)
NCCML ...... National Committee for Careers in the Medical Laboratory [*Defunct*] (EA)
NCCMP ...... National Coordinating Committee for Multiemployer Plans (EA)
NCCMP ...... Navy Civilian Career Management Program (DNAB)
NCCMT ...... National Committee for Careers in Medical Technology [*Later, NCCML*] (EA)
NCCN .... National Comprehensive Cancer Network [*Medical*]
NCCN .... National Council of Catholic Nurses [*Defunct*] (EA)
NCCN .... New Century Cyclopedia of Names [*A publication*]
NCCNA ...... National Clearinghouse on Child Neglect and Abuse [*HEW*]
NC/CNC ..... Numerical Control/Computer Numerical Control (SAUS)
NCCNHR .... National Citizens Coalition for Nursing Home Reform (EA)
NcCo .... Concord Public Library, Concord, NC [*Library symbol*] [*Library of Congress*] (LCLS)
NCCO .... Enseco, Inc. (SAUS)
NCCO .... Navy Command and Control System (POLM)
NCCO .... Neodymium, Cerium, Copper, Oxide [*Inorganic chemistry*]
NcCoB .... Barber-Scotia College, Concord, NC [*Library symbol*] [*Library of Congress*] (LCLS)
NcCoC .... Cabarrus County Library, Concord, NC [*Library symbol*] [*Library of Congress*] (LCLS)
NcCoCH ..... Cabarrus County Health Department, Concord, NC [*Library symbol*] [*Library of Congress*] (LCLS)
NcCoi .... Currituck County Public Library, Coinjock, NC [*Library symbol*] [*Library of Congress*] (LCLS)
NcCol .... Polk County Public Library, Columbus (SAUS)
NcCol .... Polk County Public Library, Columbus, NC [*Library symbol*] [*Library of Congress*] (LCLS)
NcCola ...... Tyrrell County Public Library, Columbia, NC [*Library symbol*] [*Library of Congress*] (LCLS)
NC Computer... Numerical Control Computer (SAUS)
NcConC ..... Concordia College, Conover, NC [*Library symbol*] [*Library of Congress*] [*Obsolete*] (LCLS)
NC Conf ..... North Carolina Conference Reports [*A publication*] (DLA)
NC Conf Rep... North Carolina Conference Reports [*A publication*] (DLA)
NCCOP ...... National Corporation for the Care of Old People [*British*] (BI)
NCCOP ...... North Carolina Computer Orientation Project (SAUS)
NcCorD ...... Duke Power Co., Information Resource Center, Cornelius, NC [*Library symbol*] [*Library of Congress*] (LCLS)
NCCOS ...... National Committee for Certificates in Office Studies [*British*]
NCCOSC .... Naval Command, Control, and Ocean Surveillance Center [*Formerly, NOSC and other activities*] (DOMA)
NCCP .... National Center for Children in Poverty (EA)
NCCP .... National Chinese Curriculum Project [*Australia*]
NCCP .... National Clearinghouse for Commuter Programs (EA)
NCCP .... National Coordinated Cataloging Program [*Library science*]
NCCP .... National Council on City Planning
NCCP .... NATO Commanders Communications Publication (NATG)
NCCP .... Navigation Control Console Panel
NCCP .... Northern California Cancer Program [*Research center*] (RCD)
NCCPA .... National Cinder Concrete Products Association (EA)
NCCPA .... National Commission on Certification of Physician's Assistants (EA)
NCCPA .... National Council of College Publications Advisers (EA)
NCCPAP ..... National Conference of CPA [*Certified Public Accountant*] Practitioners [*New York, NY*] (EA)
NCCPB ...... National Council of Commercial Plant Breeders (EA)
NCCPC ...... NATO Civil Communications Planning Committee (NATG)
NCCPG ...... National Council for the Conservation of Plants and Gardens (PDAA)
NCCPL .... National Community Crime Prevention League (EA)
NcCpM ...... United States Marine Corps, Air Station, Cherry Point, NC [*Library symbol*] [*Library of Congress*] (LCLS)
NCCPS ...... National Citizens Commission for the Public Schools (AEBS)
NCCPT .... National Congress of Colored Parents and Teachers (AEBS)
NCCPV ...... National Commission on the Causes and Prevention of Violence (EA)
NcCQ .... Queens College, Charlotte, NC [*Library symbol*] [*Library of Congress*] (LCLS)
nccr- .... Costa Rica [*MARC geographic area code*] [*Library of Congress*] (LCCP)
NCCR .... National Coalition for Cancer Research (EA)
NCCR .... National Committee for Cultural Resources
NCCR .... National Convention for Constitutional Reform (Tanzania) [*Political party*] (PSAP)
NCCR .... National Council for Children's Rights (EA)
NCCR .... National Council for Community Relations [*Later, NCMPR*] (EA)
NCCR .... National Council of Chain Restaurants (NTPA)
NCCR .... Network Control Center Representative (SSD)
NCCR .... New Construction/Conversion Requirements System [*Navy*]
NCCRE ...... National Consumers Committee for Research and Education [*Later, NCL*] (EA)
NCCRI .... National Catholic Coalition for Responsible Investment (EA)
NCCR System... New Construction/Conversion Requirements System (SAUS)
NcCS .... Charlotte-Mecklenburg Schools, Staff Development Center, Charlotte, NC [*Library symbol*] [*Library of Congress*] (LCLS)
NCCS .... NASA Center for Computational Sciences (SAUS)
NCCS .... National Carriers Contract Services [*National Freight Consortium*] [*British*]
NCCS .... National Catholic Committee on Scouting (EA)
NCCS .... National Catholic Community Service [*Defunct*] (EA)
NCCS .... National Catholic Conference for Seafarers (EA)
NCCS .... National Center for Charitable Statistics (EA)
NCCS .... National Center for Constitutional Studies (EA)
NCCS .... National Christ Child Society (EA)
NCCS .... National Climbing Classification System
NCCS .... National Coalition for Cancer Survivorship (EA)
NCCS .... National Command and Control System
NCCS .... National Council for Community Services to International Visitors [*Later, NCIV*]
NCCS .... Navigation/Command & Control System (SAUS)
NCCS .... Navy Camera Control System
NCCS .... Navy Command and Control System (NVT)
NCCS .... Network Computing Client/Server [*Computer science*] (GART)
NCCS .... Network Control Center System [*Communications term*] (DCT)
NCCS .... Nordic Church Council for Seamen [*Denmark*] (EAIO)
NCCS .... Nordic Council for Church Studies (EA)
NCCS .... Nuclear Command and Control System (SAUS)
NCCS .... Numerical Control Computer Sciences (SAUS)
NCCSA ...... National Council for the Church and Social Action (EA)
NCCSA ...... Nature Conservation Council of South Australia
NCCS-A ..... Navy Command and Control System-Ashore (SAUS)
NCCSC ...... National Coordinating Center in Solidarity with Chile [*Later, NCC*] (EA)
NCCSC ...... Northern California Collegiate Ski Conference (PSS)
NcCSC .... Sandoz Chemical, Charlotte, NC [*Library symbol*] [*Library of Congress*] (LCLS)

NCCSCE..... National Council on Community Services and Continuing Education (EA)
NcCSH....... Sun-Health, Inc., Charlotte, NC [*Library symbol*] [*Library of Congress*] (LCLS)
NcCSI........ SIM International Resource Center, Charlotte, NC [*Library symbol*] [*Library of Congress*] (LCLS)
NCCSL....... National Center for Cross-Cultural Studies in Law [*Monash University*] [*Australia*]
NCCSS ...... North Central Conference on Summer Schools (EA)
NCCT .... National Council for Civic Theatres Ltd. [*British*] (BI)
NCCTA........ National Council of Chemical Technician Affiliates
NCCTS....... National Catholic Conference for Total Stewardship (EA)
NCCU .... National Conference of Canadian Universities
NCCU .... Neurosurgical Critical Care Unit (NUJO)
NCCU .... Newborn Convalescent Care Unit [*Medicine*]
NCCU .... North Carolina Central University [*Durham*]
NcCU .... University of North Carolina at Charlotte, Charlotte, NC [*Library symbol*] [*Library of Congress*] (LCLS)
NC Curves... Noise Criterion Curves (SAUS)
NCC/USA.... National Council of Churches of Christ in the USA (NTCM)
NCCUSL..... National Commission for Creation of Uniform State Laws
NCCUSL..... National Conference of Commissioners on Uniform State Laws (EA)
NcCuW...... Western Carolina University, Cullowhee, NC [*Library symbol*] [*Library of Congress*] (LCLS)
NCCV .... National Center for Church Vocations [*Later, NCVC*] (EA)
NCCV .... New Construction and Conversion [*Navy*]
NCCVL....... Northern California Collegiate Volleyball League (PSS)
NCCW .... National Chamber of Commerce for Women [*New York, NY*] (EA)
NCCW .... National Council of Career Women (EA)
NCCW .... National Council of Catholic Women (EA)
NCCWAO.... National Council of Community World Affairs Organizations (EA)
NCCWHO.... National Citizens Committee for the World Health Organization [*Later, AAWH*] (EA)
NCCWS...... Nuclear Component Cooling Water System (SAUS)
NCCX .... North American Car [*Private rail car owner code*]
NCCY .... National Committee for Children and Youth [*Later, NCOCY*] (EA)
NCCY .... National Council of Catholic Youth [*Defunct*] (EA)
NcCyL .... Lord Corp. Research and Development Library, Cary, NC [*Library symbol*] [*Library of Congress*] (LCLS)
NcCyS .... SAS Institute, Inc., Cary, NC [*Library symbol*] [*Library of Congress*] (LCLS)
NCCYSA..... National Conference of Catholics in Youth Serving Agencies [*Defunct*] (EA)
nccz-......... Canal Zone [*MARC geographic area code*] [*Library of Congress*] (LCCP)
NCCZ .... Northwestern Chemical [*Federal Railroad Administration identification code*]
NCD.......... AT&T Capital 8.25% 'PINES' [*NYSE symbol*] (SG)
NcD .... Duke University, Durham, NC [*Library symbol*] [*Library of Congress*] (LCLS)
NCD.......... National Center for the Diaconate [*Later, NAAND*] (EA)
NCD.......... National Commission for Democracy [*Ghana*] [*Political party*]
NCD.......... National Commission on Diabetes
NCD.......... National Compliance Database [*Environmental Protection Agency*] (AEPA)
NCD.......... National Control Data
NCD.......... National Council on Disability (SAUS)
NCD.......... National Council on Drugs [*Defunct*] (EA)
NCD.......... Natural Circular Dichroism [*Optics*]
NCD.......... Navy Cargo Document (DNAB)
NCD.......... Navy Contracting Directives (MCD)
NCD.......... Negotiable Certificate of Deposit (ADA)
NCD.......... Negotiated Critical Dates [*Telecommunications*] (TEL)
NCD.......... Nemine Contradicente [*No One Contradicting*] [*Latin*] [*Legal term*] (DLA)
NCD.......... Network Computing Device (DCDG)
NCD.......... Network Computing Devices (DCOM)
NCD.......... Network Computing Devices, Inc. (EFIS)
NCD.......... Network Cryptographic Device
NCD.......... Networked Computing Device [*Computer science*] (GART)
NCD.......... Neurocirculatory Dystonia [*Medicine*] (DMAA)
NCD.......... New Chemicals Database (SAUS)
NCD.......... New Collegiate Dictionary (SAUS)
NCD.......... New Component Design (IAA)
NCD.......... Nicotinamide Cytosine Dinucleotide [*Biochemistry*]
NCD.......... Nitrogen Clearance Delay (DMAA)
NCD.......... No Can Do [*From pidgin English*]
NCD.......... No Claim Discount [*Insurance*] (AIA)
NCD.......... No Computed Data (HLLA)
NCD.......... Noncallable Deposit [*Investment term*]
NCD.......... Non Coasting Drive
NCD.......... Non-Communicable Disease
NCD.......... Non-Cumulative Dividend [*Business term*] (MHDW)
NCD.......... Nonlinear Circular Dichroism (SAUS)
NCD.......... Nonlinear Control Design [*Computer science*]
NCD.......... Nordic Committee on Disability (EAIO)
NCD.......... Nordic Council for the Deaf [*See also DNR*] (EAIO)
NCD.......... Normal Childhood Diseases (DAVI)
NCD.......... Normal Childhood Disorders [*Medicine*]
NCD.......... Normalized Cumulative Deviation
NCD.......... North Canadian Oils Ltd. [*AMEX symbol*] (COMM)
NCD.......... North Central Dairy Forwarders Tariff Bureau, Minneapolis MN [*STAC*]
NCD.......... North Central Division [*Army Engineers*]
NCD.......... Norton Change Directory [*Computer science*]
NCD.......... Not Considered Disabling [*Medicine*] (MAE)
NCD.......... Not Considered Disqualifying
NCD.......... Notice of Credit Due
NCD.......... Nova Scotia College of Art and Design Library [*UTLAS symbol*]
NCD.......... Nuclear Commission Date (DNAB)
NCD.......... Numerically Controlled Drafting (MCD)
NCDA........ National Career Development Association (EA)
NCDA........ National Center for Drug Analysis [*St. Louis*] [*FDA*]
NCDA........ National Ceramic Dealers Association (EA)
NCDA........ National College of District Attorneys (EA)
NCDA........ National Community Development Association (EA)
NCDA........ National Council on Drug Abuse [*Defunct*] (EA)
NCDA........ North Carolina Department of Agriculture (ROAS)
NCDAC ...... National Civil Defense Advisory Council (EA)
NcDaD....... Davidson College, Davidson, NC [*Library symbol*] [*Library of Congress*] (LCLS)
NCDAD ...... National Council for Diplomats in Art and Design [*British*] (BI)
NCDAI .... National Clearinghouse for Drug Abuse Information [*Public Health Service*] [*Rockville, MD*]
NcDalG...... Gaston College, Dallas, NC [*Library symbol*] [*Library of Congress*] (LCLS)
NcDan....... Stokes County Public Library, Danbury, NC [*Library symbol*] [*Library of Congress*] (LCLS)
NCDAPA..... National Curtain, Drapery, and Allied Products Association [*Later, HFPA*]
NcD-B .... Duke University, Fuqua School of Business, Durham, NC [*Library symbol*] [*Library of Congress*] (LCLS)
NCDB........ Find a Pediatric Cancer Center [*American Cancer Society database*] (MHID)
NCDB........ National Center for Drugs and Biologics [*FDA*]
NCDB........ National Commercial and Development Bank [*Dominica*]
NCDB........ National Compliance Database [*Environmental Protection Agency*] (AEPA)
NCDBC ...... National Center for the Development of Bilingual Curriculum (EA)
NCDC........ National Catholic Development Conference (EA)
NCDC........ National Center for Disease Control [*Public Health Service*]
NCDC........ National Climatic Data Center [*National Oceanic and Atmospheric Administration*] [*Information service or system*] (IID)
NCDC........ National Coalition for a Democratic Constitution [*Political group*] [*South Korea*]
NCDC........ National Committee for the Day Care of Children [*Later, DCCA*]
NCDC........ National Communicable Disease Center (MCD)
NCDC........ National Criminal Defense College (EA)
NCDC........ Naval Contract Distribution Center
NCDC........ New Community Development Corp. [*HUD*]
NCDC........ Nitro(carboxyphenyl)diphenylcarbamate [*Biochemistry*]
NCDC........ Norchenodeoxycholic Acid [*Biochemistry*]
NCDCA...... National Child Day Care Association (EA)
NCDCF...... National Civil Defense Computer Facility
NCDCR...... North Carolina Department of Cultural Resources
NCDCV...... Neonatal Calf Diarrhea Coronavirus
NcD-D....... Duke University, Divinity School, Durham, NC [*Library symbol*] [*Library of Congress*] (LCLS)
NCDD........ No Change in the Due Date (AFM)
NCDD-CCD... National Conference of Diocesan Directors of Religious Education (EA)
NCDDR...... National Center for the Dissemination of Disability Research (SAUS)
NCDDRE-CCD... National Conference of Diocesan Directors of Religious Education - CCD [*Continuing Christian Development*] (EA)
NcDe........ Denton Public Library, Denton, NC [*Library symbol*] [*Library of Congress*] (LCLS)
NCDE........ National Coalition for Democracy in Education [*Defunct*] (EA)
NCDF........ National Computer Dealer Forum (EA)
NCDF........ New Crop Development Fund (SAUS)
NCDF........ Non-Coded Digital Facsmile (SAUS)
NCDH........ National Committee Against Discrimination in Housing (EA)
NCDHM ..... National Children's Dental Health Month [*American Dental Association*]
NCDHW..... National Children's Dental Health Week [*Medicine*] (EDAA)
NCDI........ Network Computing Devices, Inc. [*NASDAQ symbol*] (SAG)
NCDIE....... Network Computing Devices [*NASDAQ symbol*] (TTSB)
NC Dir Ground Water Ground Water Circ... North Carolina. Division of Ground Water. Ground Water Circular (SAUS)
NC Dir Miner Resour Inf Circ... North Carolina. Division of Mineral Resources. Information Circular (SAUS)
NC Div Resour Plann Eval Miner Resour Sect Bull... North Carolina. Division of Resource Planning and Evaluation. Mineral Resources Section. Bulletin (SAUS)
NC Div Resour Plann Eval Miner Resour Sect Educ Ser... North Carolina. Division of Resource Planning and Evaluation. Mineral Resources Section. Educational Series (SAUS)
NC Div Resour Plann Eval Miner Resour Sect Reg Geol Ser... North Carolina. Division of Resource Planning and Evaluation. Mineral Resources Section. Regional Geology Series (SAUS)
NcD-L .... Duke University, School of Law, Durham, NC [*Library symbol*] [*Library of Congress*] (LCLS)
NCDL........ National Canine Defence League [*British*] (DI)
NCDM .... National Center for Data Mining [*University of Illinois at Chicago*] (RCD)
NCDM .... Numerical Control Drafting Machine (SAUS)
NCDM .... Numerically Controlled Drafting Machine (MCD)
NcD-MC..... Duke University, Medical Center, Durham, NC [*Library symbol*] [*Library of Congress*] (LCLS)
NcDnrUC.... Union Carbide Agricultural Products Co., Inc., Research Triangle Park, Durham (SAUS)
NCDO........ Navy Central Disbursing Office

NcDo .... Surry County-Dobson Library, Dobson, NC [*Library symbol*] [*Library of Congress*] (LCLS)
NcDoS .... Surry Community College, Dobson, NC [*Library symbol*] [*Library of Congress*] (LCLS)
NCDP .... Namibie Christelike Demokratiese Party [*Namibian Christian Democratic Party*] [*Political party*] (PPW)
NCDP .... Navigation Control/Display Panel (MCD)
NCDPEH ..... National Coalition for Disease Prevention and Environmental Health
NCDRC ...... National Catholic Disaster Relief Committee (EA)
NCDRE ...... National Conference of Directors of Religious Education (NTPA)
NCDS .... National Center for Disability Services (EA)
NCDS .... National Center for Dispute Settlement [*American Arbitration Association*] [*Later, CDS*]
NCDS .... National Child Development Study [*British*]
NCDS .... National Council for the Divorced and Separated [*British*] (DBA)
NCDS .... Naval Combat Data System
NCDS .... Navy Combat Direction System (MCD)
NCDS .... North Carolina Dental Society (SAUS)
NCDS .... Numerical Control Distribution System [*Computer science*] (MHDI)
NCDT .... National Council for Drama Training [*British*]
NCDT .... Noble-Collip Drum Trauma [*Physiology*]
NCDT .... Non-Chargeable Downtime
NCDT .... North Carolina Dance Theater
NCDT & E... Naval Combat Demolition Training and Experimental Base [*Maui, HI*] (KSC)
NCDT & EBASE... Naval Combat Demolition Training and Experimental Base [*Maui, HI*]
NCDTO ...... National Council of Dance Teacher Organizations [*Later, NDCA*] (EA)
NcDu .... Dunn Public Library, Dunn, NC [*Library symbol*] [*Library of Congress*] (LCLS)
NCDU .... Naval Combat Demolition Unit
NCDU .... Navigational Control & Display Unit (SAUS)
NcDubB ..... Bladen Technical College, Dublin, NC [*Library symbol*] [*Library of Congress*] (LCLS)
NcDur .... Durham City-County Public Library, Durham, NC [*Library symbol*] [*Library of Congress*] (LCLS)
NcDurBC .... Blue Cross & Blue Shield of North Carolina, Durham, NC [*Library symbol*] [*Library of Congress*] (LCLS)
NcDurBD .... Becton, Dickinson & Co., Research Center Library, Research Triangle Park, Durham, NC [*Library symbol*] [*Library of Congress*] (LCLS)
NcDurC ...... North Carolina Central University, Durham, NC [*Library symbol*] [*Library of Congress*] (LCLS)
NcDurCG .... Ciba-Geigy Corp., Biotechnology Library, Durham, NC [*Library symbol*] [*Library of Congress*] (LCLS)
NcDurCL .... North Carolina Central University, School of Library Science, Durham, NC [*Library symbol*] [*Library of Congress*] (LCLS)
NcDurCR .... Chemstrand Research Center, Inc., Durham, NC [*Library symbol*] [*Library of Congress*] (LCLS)
NcDurEP .... United States Environmental Protection Agency, Office of Administration, LibraryServices Branch, Park, Durham, NC [*Library symbol*] [*Library of Congress*] (LCLS)
NcDurF ...... Forest History Society, Inc., Durham, NC [*Library symbol*] [*Library of Congress*] (LCLS)
NcDurG ...... Glaxo, Inc., Durham, NC [*Library symbol*] [*Library of Congress*] (LCLS)
NcDurGH .... Durham County General Hospital, Medical Library, Durham, NC [*Library symbol*] [*Library of Congress*] (LCLS)
NcDurHS .... United States National Environmental Health Sciences Center, Durham, NC [*Library symbol*] [*Library of Congress*] (LCLS)
NcDurIBM... International Business Machines Corp., IBM CPD Library, Durham, NC [*Library symbol*] [*Library of Congress*] (LCLS)
NcDurIF ..... International Fertility Research Program, Durham, NC [*Library symbol*] [*Library of Congress*] (LCLS)
NcDurIT ..... Chemical Industry institute of Toxicology, Durham, NC [*Library symbol*] [*Library of Congress*] (LCLS)
NcDurL ...... Liggett & Myers, Inc. [*Later, Liggett Group, Inc.*], Durham, NC [*Library symbol*] [*Library of Congress*] (LCLS)
NcDurM ..... Monsanto Triangle Park Development Center, Durham, NC [*Library symbol*] [*Library of Congress*] (LCLS)
NcDurMi .... Microelectronics Center Library, Durham, NC [*Library symbol*] [*Library of Congress*] (LCLS)
NcDurNH .... National Humanities Center, Durham, NC [*Library symbol*] [*Library of Congress*] (LCLS)
NcDurRa .... Radian Corp. Library, Durham, NC [*Library symbol*] [*Library of Congress*] (LCLS)
NcDurRT .... Research Triangle Institute, Technical Library, Durham, NC [*Library symbol*] [*Library of Congress*] (LCLS)
NcDurSci.... North Carolina School of Science and Mathematics, Durham, NC [*Library symbol*] [*Library of Congress*] (LCLS)
NcDurST .... North Carolina Science and Technology Research Center, Durham, NC [*Library symbol*] [*Library of Congress*] (LCLS)
NcDurT ...... Durham Technical Institute, Durham, NC [*Library symbol*] [*Library of Congress*] (LCLS)
NcDurUC .... Union Carbide Agricultural Products Co., Inc., Research Triangle Park, Durham, NC [*Library symbol*] [*Library of Congress*] (LCLS)
NcDurV ...... United States Veterans Administration Hospital, Durham, NC [*Library symbol*] [*Library of Congress*] (LCLS)
NcDurW ..... Wellcome Research Laboratories, Durham, NC [*Library symbol*] [*Library of Congress*] (LCLS)
NcDurW-Gv... Burroughs Wellcome & Co., Greenville, NC [*Library symbol*] [*Library of Congress*] (LCLS)
NCDV .... Nebraska Calf Diarrhea Virus
NCDVD ...... National Conference of Diocesan Vocation Directors (EA)
NcD-W ...... Duke University, Woman's College, Durham, NC [*Library symbol*] [*Library of Congress*] (LCLS)
NCDX .... North County Transit District [*Federal Railroad Administration identification code*]
NCDZ .... NC Distribution [*Federal Railroad Administration identification code*]
NcE .... Bladen County Public Library, Elizabethtown, NC [*Library symbol*] [*Library of Congress*] (LCLS)
NCe .... Middle Country Public Library, Centereach, NY [*Library symbol*] [*Library of Congress*] (LCLS)
NCE .... Nasa Cotopaxi [*Ecuador*] [*Seismograph station code, US Geological Survey*] (SEIS)
NCE .... National College of Education [*Illinois*]
NCE .... National Commission for Education (AIE)
NCE .... National Committee on the Emeriti (EA)
NCE .... National Conference of Executives of the Arc [*Association*] (EA)
NCE .... National Council of Exchangors (EA)
NCE .... National Counselor Examination for Licensure & Certification (SAUS)
NCE .... Naughton Cardiac Exercise (MELL)
NCE .... Navigation & Command Equipment (SAUS)
NCE .... Navy Calibration Equipment List
NCE .... Navy Civil Engineer [*A publication*]
NCE .... Negative Contrast Echocardiography [*Medicine*] (DB)
NCE .... Network Communications Engineer (ACAE)
NCE .... Network Connection Element
NCE .... Network Control Elements (MCD)
NCE .... Network Control Engine [*Synoptics Communications, Inc.*]
NCE .... Neuritis of the Cauda Equina [*Medicine*]
NCE .... Neurologic Clinical Examination [*Medicine*] (MELL)
NCE .... Newark College of Engineering [*New Jersey*]
NCE .... New Catholic Edition [*Bible*]
NCE .... New Catholic Encyclopedia [*A publication*]
NCE .... New Century Energies [*NYSE symbol*] (SG)
NCE .... New Chemical Entity
NCE .... Nice [*France*] [*Airport symbol*] (OAG)
NCE .... No Change in Estimates
NCE .... Nomadic Computing Environment
NCE .... Noncommercial Education [*FCC*] (NTCM)
NCE .... Nonconvulsive Epilepsy [*Medicine*]
NCE .... Normal Calomel Electrode [*Electrochemistry*]
NCE .... Normal Chick Embryo
NCE .... Normal Curve Equivalent [*Testing*] (EDAC)
NCE .... Northcoast Executive Airlines [*ICAO designator*] (FAAC)
NCE .... NTID [*National Technical Institute for the Deaf*] Center on Employment (PAZ)
NCE .... Nuclear Capability Evaluation
NCE .... Nuclear Capability Exercise [*Army*] (AABC)
NCE .... Nuclear/Chemical Environment [*Battlefield condition*] (RDA)
NCEA .... National Catholic Educational Association (EA)
NCEA .... National Center for Economic Alternatives (EA)
NCEA .... National Center for Environmental Assessment (AEPA)
NCEA .... National Center on Elder Abuse [*Association*] (EA)
NCEA .... National Christian Education Association (EA)
NCEA .... National College Education and Admissions Foundation (EA)
NCEA .... National Community Education Association (EA)
NCEA .... National Consortium for Education Access (EA)
NCEA .... National Council for Educational Awards [*Ireland*]
NCEA .... N-(Carboxyethyl)alanine [*Biochemistry*]
NCEA .... North Carolina Education Association (SAUS)
NCEA .... North Central Electric Association (SAUS)
NCEarc ...... National Conference of Executives of the Arc (NTPA)
NCEAS .... National Center for Ecological Analysis and Synthesis
NcEB .... Bladen Technical Institute, Elizabethtown, NC [*Library symbol*] [*Library of Congress*] (LCLS)
NcEb .... East Bend Public Library, East Bend, NC [*Library symbol*] [*Library of Congress*] (LCLS)
NCEB .... National Center for Educational Brokering [*Defunct*] (EA)
NCEB .... National Council for Environmental Balance (EA)
NCEB .... NATO Communications Electronics Board
NCEB .... North Coast Energy [*NASDAQ symbol*] (TTSB)
NCEBP .... North Coast Energy Cv'B'Pfd [*NASDAQ symbol*] (TTSB)
NCEBVS ..... National Chronic Epstein-Barr Virus Syndrome Association (EA)
NCEBW ...... North Coast Energy Wrrt [*NASDAQ symbol*] (TTSB)
NC EB Welder... Numerically Controlled Electron Beam Welder (SAUS)
NCEC .... National Center for Educational Communication [*Office of Education*]
NCEC .... National Chemical Emergency Centre [*Atomic Energy Authority*] [*Didcot, Oxon., England*]
NCEC .... National Christian Education Council [*Church of England*]
NCEC .... National Clearinghouse on Environmental Carcinogenesis [*Medicine*] [*NCI*] (EDAA)
NCEC .... National Commission for Electrologist Certification (EA)
NCEC .... National Committee for an Effective Congress (EA)
NCEC .... National Construction Employers Council [*Defunct*] (EA)
NCEC .... North Coast Environment Centre (SAUS)
NCEC .... North Coast Export Co. [*An association*] [*Defunct*] (EA)
NCECA ...... National Council on Education for the Ceramic Arts (EA)
NCECC ...... National Committee for Emergency Coronary Care [*Medicine*] (EDAA)
NC Ecc ...... Notes of Cases, English Ecclesiastical and Maritime Courts [*1841-50*] [*A publication*] (DLA)
NCECD ...... National Commission for Economic Conversion and Disarmament (EA)
NCECE .... National Council of Elected County Executives (EA)
NCECF .... National Children's Eye Care Foundation (EA)
NCECG ...... National Coalition to Expand Charitable Giving [*Defunct*] (EA)
NCECS .... North Carolina Educational Computing Services (NITA)
NCECS .... North Carolina Educational Computing System (SAUS)
NCECW ...... National Center for the Early Childhood Work Force (EA)
NcEd .... Eden Public Library, Eden, NC [*Library symbol*] [*Library of Congress*] (LCLS)

NCED .... National Center on Employment of the Deaf (EA)
NCEDC ...... Northern California Earthquake Data Center
NCedHS ..... Lawrence High School, Cedarhurst, NY [*Library symbol*] [*Library of Congress*] (LCLS)
NCEDL .... National Committee for Effective Design Legislation (EA)
NcEdR .... Rockingham County Public Library, Eden, NC [*Library symbol*] [*Library of Congress*] (LCLS)
NcEdR-M .... Mayodan Public Library, Mayodan, NC [*Library symbol*] [*Library of Congress*] (LCLS)
NcEdR-R .... Rockingham County Public Library, Reidsville Branch Library, Reidsville, NC [*Library symbol*] [*Library of Congress*] (LCLS)
NcEdR-S .... Stoneville Public Library, Stoneville, NC [*Library symbol*] [*Library of Congress*] (LCLS)
NcEdt .... Shepard-Pruden Memorial Library, Edenton, NC [*Library symbol*] [*Library of Congress*] (LCLS)
NCEE .... National Catholic Educational Exhibitors (EA)
NCEE .... National Center on Education and Employment [*New York, NY*] [*Department of Education*] (GRD)
NCEE .... National Center on Education and the Economy
NCEE .... National Congress for Educational Excellence (EA)
NCEE .... National Council of Engineering Examiners (EA)
NCEE .... Northeast Consortium for Engineering Education (SAUS)
NCEEA .... Northwest Career Educators and Employers Association (SEAT)
NCEEC .... Nested Cone Extendable Exit Cone (MCD)
NCEEER ..... National Council for Eurasian and East European Research
NCEEF .... National Committee for Electrical Engineering Films
NCEER .... National Center for Earthquake Engineering Research [*Buffalo, NY*] (GRD)
NCEES .... National Council of Examiners for Engineering and Surveying (NTPA)
NCEET .... National Consortium for Environmental Education Training
NCEF .... National Calling and Emergency Frequencies (CET)
NCEF .... National Commission on Electronic Funds Transfers (MHDW)
NCEF .... Nomads' Charitable and Educational Foundation [*Australia*]
NCEF .... Non-Circumcision Educational Foundation (EA)
NCEFF .... National Committee for Education in Family Finance (EA)
NCE-FM ..... Noncommercial Educational FM [*Frequency Modulation*] [*Telecommunications*] (OTD)
NCEFR .... National Council of Erectors, Fabricators, and Riggers (EA)
NCEFT .... National Commission on Electronic Fund Transfers
NCEG .... Numerical C Extensions Group (SAUS)
NCEHAI ..... National Committee on Ethics of the Hearing Aid Industry [*Defunct*] (EA)
NCEHELP ... National Conference of Executives of Higher Education Loan Plans [*Later, NCHELP*] (EA)
NCEHP ...... National Center for the Exploration of Human Potential (EA)
NCEHPHP ... National Council on the Education of Health Professionals in Health Promotion (DAVI)
NCEHR ...... National Council on Ethics in Human Research (MHID)
NCEHS ...... National Center for Environmental Health Strategies (EA)
NCEI .... National Center for Education Information (RCD)
NcEl .... Kemp Memorial Library, Ellerbe, NC [*Library symbol*] [*Library of Congress*] (LCLS)
NCEL .... Naval Civil Engineering Laboratory
NCEL .... Navy Contractor Experience List
NCEL .... Nuclear Certified Equipment List (DNAB)
NCELALIEP ... National Clearinghouse for English Language Acquisition and Language Instruction Educational Programs [*Association*] (EA)
NcElc .... East Albemarle Regional Library, Elizabeth City, NC [*Library symbol*] [*Library of Congress*] (LCLS)
NcElcA ...... College of the Albemarle, Elizabeth City, NC [*Library symbol*] [*Library of Congress*] (LCLS)
NcElcE ...... Elizabeth City State University, Elizabeth City, NC [*Library symbol*] [*Library of Congress*] (LCLS)
NcElcP ...... Pasquotank-Camden Library, Elizabeth City, NC [*Library symbol*] [*Library of Congress*] (LCLS)
NcElcR ...... Roanoke Bible College, Mary E. Griffith Memorial Library, Elizabeth City, NC [*Library symbol*] [*Library of Congress*] (LCLS)
NcElk .... Elkin Public Library, Elkin, NC [*Library symbol*] [*Library of Congress*] (LCLS)
NcElon ...... Elon College, Elon College, NC [*Library symbol*] [*Library of Congress*] (LCLS)
NcElonCH ... Historical Society of the Southern Convention, Congregation of Christian Churches, Elon College (SAUS)
NcElonCH ... Historical Society of the Southern Convention, Congregation of Christian Churches, Elon College, NC [*Library symbol*] [*Library of Congress*] (LCLS)
NcElonP ..... Primitive Baptist Library, Elon College, NC [*Library symbol*] [*Library of Congress*] (LCLS)
NCEM .... National Center for Electron Microscopy [*Berkeley, CA*] [*Lawrence Berkeley Laboratory*] [*Department of Energy*]
NCEMC ...... National Committee on the Education of Migrant Children [*of the National Child Labor Committee*] (EA)
NCEMCH .... National Center for Education in Maternal and Child Health (EA)
NCEMMH ... National Center, Educational Media and Materials for the Handicapped [*Defunct*] (EA)
NCEMP ...... National Center for Energy Management and Power
NCEMSF .... National Collegiate Emergency Medical Services Foundation (SAUS)
NCEMT ...... National Center for Excellence in Metalworking Technology [*Navy*]
NcEn .... Lilly Pike Sullivan Municipal Library, Enfield, NC [*Library symbol*] [*Library of Congress*] (LCLS)
NCEN .... National Commission on Egg Nutrition
NCEN .... Network Compatibility Engineer (ACAE)
NCEN .... New Century Financial
NCEN .... North Central
NC ENA ..... North Carolina Emergency Nurses Association (SAUS)
NCen Assn Q ... North Central Association. Quarterly (SAUS)
NcEnk .... American Enka Corp., Enka, NC [*Library symbol*] [*Library of Congress*] (LCLS)
NCent .... Nineteenth Century (SAUS)
NCentBsh ... North Central Bancshares, Inc. [*Associated Press*] (SAG)
N Cent School L Rev ... North Central School Law Review [*A publication*] (DLA)
NCEO .... National Center for Employee Ownership (EA)
NCEO .... National Center for Exploitation of the Oceans
NCEO .... Non-Conforming End Office (CCCA)
NCEOA ...... National Council of Educational Opportunity Associations (EA)
NCEP .... National Center for Education in Politics [*Defunct*] (EA)
NCEP .... National Centers for Environmental Prediction [*Marine science*] (OSRA)
NCEP .... National Cholesterol Education Program
NCEP .... National Cholesterol Education Program Coordinating Committee [*National Institutes of Health*] (EGAO)
NCEP .... National Council for the Encouragement of Patriotism (EA)
NCEP .... National Council on Employment Policy (EA)
NCEPI .... National Center for Environmental Publications and Information (AEPA)
NcEr .... Erwin Public Library, Erwin, NC [*Library symbol*] [*Library of Congress*] (LCLS)
NCER .... National Center for Earthquake Research [*US Geological Survey*]
NCER .... National Center for Environmental Research [*Environmental Protection Agency*] (RCD)
NCER .... National Conference on Electromagnetic Relays
NCER .... National Council on Educational Research [*Later, NCERI*] [*Department of Education*] [*Washington, DC*]
NCERACCS ... National Coalition to End Racism in America's Child Care System (EA)
NCERC ...... North Carolina Occupational Safety and Health Education and Research Center [*University of North Carolina at Chapel Hill*] (RCD)
NCERD ...... National Center for Educational Research and Development [*HEW*]
NCERI .... National Center on Educational Restructuring and Inclusion [*City University of New York*] (RCD)
NCERT .... National Council for Educational Research and Training (WDAA)
nces- .... El Salvador [*MARC geographic area code*] [*Library of Congress*] (LCCP)
NCES .... National Center for Education Standards
NCES .... National Center for Education Statistics [*Office of Education*] [*Later, CES*]
NCES .... National Council for Educational Standards (AIE)
NCES .... New Careers in Employment Security (OICC)
NCES .... Normal Curve Equivalent Scores [*Testing*] (EDAC)
NCES .... North Central Experiment Station [*University of Minnesota*] [*Research center*] (RCD)
NCES .... North Country Educational Services [*Library network*]
NCES .... NovaCare Employee Services [*NASDAQ symbol*]
NCESA .... National Class E Scow Association (EA)
NCESGR ..... National Committee for Employer Support of the Guard and Reserve (EA)
NCET .... National Center for Educational Technology [*Office of Education*]
NCET .... National Coastal Ecosystems Team [*Office of Biological Services, United States Fish and Wildlife Service*] (MSC)
NCET .... National Conference of English Teachers (BARN)
NCET .... National Council for Educational Technology [*British*]
NCETA .... National Center for Education and Training in Addictions [*Australia*]
NCEU .... North American Container System-XTRA [*Intermodal shipping container symbol*] (TVRC)
NCEUS ...... National Commission on Employment and Unemployment Statistics [*Bureau of Labor Statistics*] (GFGA)
NCEW .... National Conference of Editorial Writers (EA)
NCEY .... National Committee on Employment of Youth [*National Child Labor Committee*] (EA)
NCEZ .... National Coalition for Enterprise Zones [*San Diego, CA*] (EA)
NCEZ .... New Co-Operative Elevator [*Federal Railroad Administration identification code*]
NCF .... AT&T Capital 8.125% 'PINES' [*NYSE symbol*] (SG)
NCF .... Narramore Christian Foundation (EA)
NCF .... National Cancer Foundation
NCF .... National Capital FreeNet [*Canada*] (EAIO)
NCF .... National Chamber Foundation (EA)
NCF .... National Civics Federation
NCF .... National Clayware Federation [*British*] (DBA)
NCF .... National Commerce Financial [*Company symbol*]
NCF .... National Commerce Financial Corp. [*NASDAQ symbol*]
NCF .... National Commission on a Free and Responsible Media (EA)
NCF .... National Communications Forum [*National Engineering Consortium, Inc.*] [*Chicago, IL*] [*Telecommunications*] (TSSD)
NCF .... National Conservative Foundation (EA)
NCF .... National Consumer Federation (NADA)
NCF .... National Control Facility [*FAA*] (TAG)
NCF .... National Craniofacial Foundation [*Later, ICF*] (EA)
NCF .... National Cristina Foundation (EA)
NCF .... NATO Composite Force
NCF .... Naval Communications Facility (MUGU)
NCF .... Naval Construction Force (NVT)
NCF .... Naval Contingency Force (SAUS)
NCF .... Nerve Cell Food
NCF .... Net Cash Flow
NCF .... NetWare Command File [*Computer science*] (VLIE)
NCF .... NetWare Configuration File [*Computer science*]
NCF .... Network-Computing Framework [*Computer science*] (GART)
NCF .... Network Control Facility (COE)
NCF .... Neutrophil Chemotactic Factor [*Hematology*]
NCF .... Neutrophil Cytosol Factor [*Cytology*]

NCF .... Newton-Cotes Formula [*Mathematics*]
NCF .... Nineteenth-Century Fiction [*A publication*] (ANEX)
NCF .... No Clean Flux (SAUS)
NCF .... No Clean Flux Process [*Computer manufacturing*] (PCM)
NCF .... No Conscription Fellowship [*England, World War I*]
NCF .... No Containment Failure [*Environmental science*] (COE)
NCF .... Nominal Characteristics File (IEEE)
NCF .... Noncold Front [*Meteorology*]
NCF .... Non-Crimp Fabric [*Plastics*]
NCF .... Nonflammable Cellulosic Foam
NCF .... Nordic Youth Center Association [*Political party*] (PSAP)
NCF .... Notsi [*Language symbol*] (ETLW)
NCF .... Now Catching For [*Telegraphy*] (PCTE)
NCF .... Nuclear Capable Forces (MCD)
NCF .... Nucleonia Calibration Facility (SAUS)
NCF .... Nucleonics Calibration Facility (RDA)
NCF .... Nugget Coombs Foundation for Indigenous Studies [*Australia*]
NCF .... Nurses Christian Fellowship (EA)
NCFA .... Narcolepsy and Cataplexy Foundation of America (EA)
NCFA .... National Cat Fanciers' Association [*Defunct*] (EA)
NCFA .... National Collection of Fine Arts [*Later, National Mus eum of American Art*]
NCFA .... National Collegiate Football Association (EA)
NCFA .... National Commercial Finance Association (EA)
NCFA .... National Commission of Fine Arts (NADA)
NCFA .... National Committee for Adoption (EA)
NCFA .... National Consumer Finance Association (EA)
NCFA .... National Council for Adoption [*Formerly National Committee for Adoption*] (PAZ)
NCFA .... Naval Campus for Achievement (NVT)
NCFA .... North Carolina Forestry Association (WPI)
NCFA .... North Central Field Area
NCFA .... Nurses' Christian Fellowship of Australia
NCFAE .... National Council of Forestry Association Executives (EA)
NCFAP .... Naval Campus for Achievement Program (MCD)
NcFayC ...... Cumberland County Public Library, Fayetteville, NC [*Library symbol*] [*Library of Congress*] (LCLS)
NcFayC-F ... Cumberland County Public Library, North Carolina Foreign Language Center, Fayetteville, NC [*Library symbol*] [*Library of Congress*] (LCLS)
NcFayCFH .. Cape Fear Valley Hospital, Medical Library, Fayetteville, NC [*Library symbol*] [*Library of Congress*] (LCLS)
NcFayH ...... Fayetteville Area Health Education Foundation, Inc., Fayetteville, NC [*Library symbol*] [*Library of Congress*] (LCLS)
NcFayM ..... Methodist College, Fayetteville, NC [*Library symbol*] [*Library of Congress*] (LCLS)
NcFayR ...... Rutledge College, Fayetteville, NC [*Library symbol*] [*Library of Congress*] (LCLS)
NcFayS ...... Fayetteville State University, Fayetteville, NC [*Library symbol*] [*Library of Congress*] (LCLS)
NcFayT ...... Fayetteville Technical Institute, Fayetteville, NC [*Library symbol*] [*Library of Congress*] (LCLS)
NcFayV ...... United States Veterans Administration Medical Center, Fayetteville, NC [*Library symbol*] [*Library of Congress*] (LCLS)
NCFB .... National Collection of Food Bacteria (MELL)
NcFb .... United States Army, Special Services Library System, Fort Bragg, NC [*Library symbol*] [*Library of Congress*] (LCLS)
NcFbH .... United States Army, Womack Army Hospital, Fort Bragg, NC [*Library symbol*] [*Library of Congress*] (LCLS)
NcFbIM ...... United States Army, Institute for Military Assistance, Marquat Memorial Library,Fort Bragg, NC [*Library symbol*] [*Library of Congress*] (LCLS)
NcFc .... Mooneyham Public Library, Forest City, NC [*Library symbol*] [*Library of Congress*] (LCLS)
NCFC .... National Coalition for a Free Cuba (EA)
NCFC .... National Commercial Finance Conference [*Later, NCFA*] (EA)
NCFC .... National Congress for Fathers and Children [*Association*] (EA)
NCFC .... National Congress for Men and Children [*An association*] (PAZ)
NCFC .... National Council of Farmer Cooperatives (EA)
NCFCA .... National Congress of Floor Covering Associations [*Defunct*] (EA)
NCFD .... National Corporate Fund for Dance (EA)
NCFD .... New Computer Family D (SAA)
NCFDA ...... National Council on Federal Disaster Assistance
NCFDAL ..... National Committee for Fair Divorce and Alimony Laws (EA)
NCFDITFS ... National Committee for the Full Development of Instructional Television Fixed Services [*ITFS regulation*] (NTCM)
NCFE .... National Campaign for Freedom of Expression
NCFE .... National Center for Financial Education (EA)
NCFE .... National Committee for Full Employment [*Defunct*] (EA)
NCFE .... National Commodity Futures Examination
NCFEA .... North Carolina Federation of Electronic Associations (SAUS)
NCFEAD ..... National Council for Foundation Education in Art and Design (AIE)
NCFEPS ..... National Commission for Full Employment Policy Studies (OICC)
NCFES .... North Central Forest Experiment Station [*St. Paul, MN*] [*Department of Agriculture*] (GRD)
NCFFR .... National Commission on Fraudulent Financial Reporting [*Defunct*] (EA)
NCFI .... National Cold Fusion Institute [*Closed June 30, 1991*]
NCFI .... North Carolina Alliance of Community (TBD)
NCFI .... North Carolina Foam Insulation (SAUS)
NCFIRB ...... North Carolina Fire Insurance Rating Bureau (SAUS)
NCFIS .... National Center for Freedom of Information Studies (EA)
NCFJE .... National Committee for the Furtherance of Jewish Education (EA)
NCFL .... National Catholic Forensic League (EA)
NCFL .... National Center for Family Literacy
NCFLIS ...... National Council on Foreign Language and International Studies (EA)
NCFM .... National Coalition of Free Men (EA)
NCFM .... National Commission on Food Marketing
NCFMF ...... National Committee for Fluid Mechanics Films
NCFMS ...... Naval Comptroller Financial Management Service
NCFNP ...... National Committee for a Freedom Now Party [*Defunct*] (EA)
NCFO .... National Conference of Firemen and Oilers (NTPA)
NCFP .... National Conference on Fluid Power (EA)
NCFPC .... National Center for Fish Protein Concentrate [*Fish and Wildlife Service*]
NCFPC .... National Commission on Fire Prevention and Control
NCFPI .... National Clearinghouse for Family Planning Information [*Database*]
NCFPO ...... Northern California Field Procurement Office (ACAE)
NCFPS .... National Center for Family Planning Services [*Health Services and Mental Health Administration, HEW*]
NCFPV .... Non-Continuous Flow Primer Valve (SAUS)
NcFr .... Macon County Public Library, Franklin, NC [*Library symbol*] [*Library of Congress*] (LCLS)
NCFR .... National Campaign for Firework Reform [*British*] (DBA)
NCFR .... National Council for Family Reconciliation (EA)
NCFR .... National Council on Family Relations (EA)
NCF Receiver ... Non-Frequency-Conversion Receiver (SAUS)
NCFRF .... National Cystic Fibrosis Research Foundation [*Later, Cystic Fibrosis Foundation*] (EA)
NcFrt .... Franklinton Public Library, Franklinton, NC [*Library symbol*] [*Library of Congress*] (LCLS)
NCFS .... National Center for Forensic Science [*University of Central Florida*] (RCD)
NCFS .... National College of Foot Surgeons (EA)
NCFS .... National Committee on Films for Safety [*Defunct*] (EA)
NCFS .... National Conference of Friendly Societies [*British*] (DBA)
NCFS .... Near Constant Force Suspension
NCFS .... Noncontingent Footshock
NCFS .... North Country Educational Services (SAUS)
NCFSA .... National Chronic Fatigue Syndrome Association (EA)
NCFSD .... NORAD Cost Factors and System Data [*Military*] (MCD)
NCFSFA ..... National Chronic Fatigue Syndrome and Fibromyalgia Association [*Formerly, National Chronic Fatigue Syndrome Association*] (EA)
NCFSK .... Noncoherent Frequency Shift Keying
NCFSU ...... Naval Construction Force Support Unit (NVT)
NCFT .... National Council for Families and Television (EA)
NCFTF .... National Consumer Fraud Task Force (EA)
NCFTJ .... National Conference on Federal Trial Judges (EA)
NcFv .... Farmville Public Library, Farmville, NC [*Library symbol*] [*Library of Congress*] (LCLS)
NCFVP .... National Center for Film and Video Preservation (EA)
NCFVSI ...... National Council for Fishing Vessel Safety and Insurance (EA)
NCFZ .... North Central Farm Service [*Federal Railroad Administration identification code*]
NCG .... Coast Guard Publication [*Later, NAVCG*]
NcG .... Greensboro Public Library, Greensboro, NC [*Library symbol*] [*Library of Congress*] (LCLS)
NCG .... Nacogdoches, TX [*Amtrak Busline code*]
NCG .... Nanochannel Glass
NCG .... National Contractors Group [*British*] (DBA)
NCG .... National Council for the Gifted (EA)
NCG .... Network Control Group [*Manned Space Flight Network*]
NCG .... New College Graduate (BARN)
NCG .... Nickel-Coated Graphite [*Materials technology*]
NCG .... Nicotine Chewing Gum (PDAA)
NCG .... Non-Condensable Gas (SAUS)
NCG .... Noncondensible Gases
NCG .... North Carolina Nat Gas [*NYSE symbol*] (TTSB)
NCG .... Nova-Cogesco Resources, Inc. [*Toronto Stock Exchange symbol*]
NCG .... Nuclear Cratering Group [*Later, EERA*] [*Army*]
NCG .... Nueva Casas Grandes [*Mexico*] [*Airport symbol*] (AD)
NCG .... Null Command Generator
NCG .... Numerical Control Graphics (MCD)
NcGa .... Gaston-Lincoln Regional Library, Gastonia, NC [*Library symbol*] [*Library of Congress*] (LCLS)
NCGA .... National Church Goods Association (EA)
NCGA .... National Collegiate Gymnastics Association (PSS)
NCGA .... National Computer Graphics Association (EA)
NCGA .... National Corn Growers Association (EA)
NCGA .... National Cotton Ginners' Association (EA)
NCGA .... National Council on Governmental Accounting (EA)
NcGA .... North Carolina Agricultural and Technical State University, Greensboro, NC [*Library symbol*] [*Library of Congress*] (LCLS)
NcGaH .... Gaston Memorial Hospital, Inc., Medical Library, Gastonia (SAUS)
NcGaH .... Gaston Memorial Hospital, Inc., Medical Library, Gastonia, NC [*Library symbol*] [*Library of Congress*] (LCLS)
NcGaL .... Gaston-Lincoln Regional Library, Gastonia, NC [*Library symbol*] [*Library of Congress*] (LCLS)
NcGAT .... AT&T Technologies Inc., Legal Library, Greensboro, NC [*Library symbol*] [*Library of Congress*] (LCLS)
NcGatr .... Gates County Library, Gatesville (SAUS)
NcGav .... Gates County Library, Gatesville, NC [*Library symbol*] [*Library of Congress*] (LCLS)
NcGB .... Bennett College, Greensboro, NC [*Library symbol*] [*Library of Congress*] (LCLS)
NcGBI .... Burlington Industries, Inc., Information Services Library, Greensboro, NC [*Library symbol*] [*Library of Congress*] (LCLS)
NcGBur ...... Burlington Industries, Inc., Information Services Library, Greensboro (SAUS)

NcGBur...... Burlington Industries, Inc., Information Services Library, Greensboro, NC [*Library symbol*] [*Library of Congress*] (LCLS)
NcGC........ Greensboro College, Greensboro, NC [*Library symbol*] [*Library of Congress*] (LCLS)
NCGC........ National Catholic Guidance Conference [*Later, ARVIC*] (EA)
NCGC........ National Certified Gerontological Counselor (SEAT)
NCGCC...... National Convention of Gospel Choirs and Choruses (EA)
NcGCG...... Ciba-Geigy Corp., Technical Information Service, Greensboro, NC [*Library symbol*] [*Library of Congress*] (LCLS)
NcGCH...... Wesley Long Community Hospital, Inc., Greensboro, NC [*Library symbol*] [*Library of Congress*] (LCLS)
NcGCL....... Center for Creative Leadership, Greensboro, NC [*Library symbol*] [*Library of Congress*] (LCLS)
NcGCM...... Cone Mills Corp., Greensboro, NC [*Library symbol*] [*Library of Congress*] (LCLS)
NCGE........ National Council for Geographic Education (EA)
NCGE/J...... Journal of Geography. National Council of Geographic Education (journ.) (SAUS)
NC Gen Stat... General Statutes of North Carolina [*A publication*] (DLA)
NCGEP...... National Council on Graduate Education in Psychology
NcGf......... Granite Falls Public Library, Granite Falls, NC [*Library symbol*] [*Library of Congress*] (LCLS)
NCGF........ Nickel-Coated Graphite Fiber (SAUS)
NcGG........ Guilford College, Greensboro, NC [*Library symbol*] [*Library of Congress*] (LCLS)
NCGG........ National Committee for Geodesy and Geophysics (MCD)
NcGGil...... Gilbarco Corp. Library, Greensboro, NC [*Library symbol*] [*Library of Congress*] (LCLS)
NcGGT....... Guilford Technical Community College, Learning Resource Center, Greensboro, NC [*Library symbol*] [*Library of Congress*] (LCLS)
NcGH........ Moses H. Cone Memorial Hospital, Medical Library, Greensboro, NC [*Library symbol*] [*Library of Congress*] (LCLS)
NcGI......... TIGR [*The Institute of Genomic Research*] Neospora caninum Gene Index [*Database*] (GDD)
NCGIC....... National Cartographic and Geographic Information Center [*Geological Survey*] [*Reston, VA*] [*Database*]
NCGIF....... National Cherry Growers and Industries Foundation (EA)
NCGIS....... National Council of Guilds for Infant Survival (EA)
NcGL........ Lorillard Research Center, Greensboro, NC [*Library symbol*] [*Library of Congress*] (LCLS)
NCGLC...... National Caucus of Gay and Lesbian Counselors (EA)
NCGMCTC... National Chevy/GMC Truckin' Club [*Defunct*] (EA)
NCGNP...... National Conference of Gerontological Nurse Practitioners (SAUS)
NcGo........ Wayne County Public Library, Goldsboro, NC [*Library symbol*] [*Library of Congress*] (LCLS)
NcGoCH..... Cherry Hospital, Learning Resource Center, Goldsboro, NC [*Library symbol*] [*Library of Congress*] (LCLS)
NcGoO....... O'Berry Center, Professional Library, Goldsboro, NC [*Library symbol*] [*Library of Congress*] (LCLS)
NcGoW...... Wayne Community College, Goldsboro, NC [*Library symbol*] [*Library of Congress*] (LCLS)
NcGPS....... Greensboro Public Schools, Greensboro, NC [*Library symbol*] [*Library of Congress*] (LCLS)
NCGR........ National Center for Genome Resources
NCGR........ National Clonal Germplasm Repository [*Corvallis, OR*] [*Agricultural Research Service*] [*Department of Agriculture*] (GRD)
NCGR........ National Council for GeoCosmic Research (EA)
NCGR........ National Council on Gene Resources (EA)
NcGrE....... East Carolina University, Greenville, NC [*Library symbol*] [*Library of Congress*] (LCLS)
NcGrE-H..... East Carolina University, Health Sciences Library, Greenville, NC [*Library symbol*] [*Library of Congress*] (LCLS)
NcGrP....... Pitt Technical Institute, Greenville, NC [*Library symbol*] [*Library of Congress*] (LCLS)
NcGrS....... Sheppard Memorial Library, Greenville, NC [*Library symbol*] [*Library of Congress*] (LCLS)
NCGS........ National Coalition of Girls Schools (NTPA)
NCGS........ National Cooperative Gallstone Study
NCGS........ New Century Gilders Society [*A union*] [*British*]
NCGS........ North Carolina Genealogical Society (EARSL)
NCGS........ Nuclear Criteria Group Secretariat [*Air Force Weapons Laboratory*] [*Kirtland Air Force Base, NM*]
NCGS........ Nuclear Criteria Group Secretary (NAKS)
NCGSTDS... National Coalition of Gay Sexually Transmitted Disease Services [*Defunct*] (EA)
ncgt-......... Guatemala [*MARC geographic area code*] [*Library of Congress*] (LCCP)
NCGT........ Nitrogen-cooled Closed-cycle Gas Turbine (SAUS)
NCGU........ North American Container System-Genstar [*Intermodal shipping container symbol*] (TVRC)
NcGU........ University of North Carolina at Greensboro, Greensboro, NC [*Library symbol*] [*Library of Congress*] (LCLS)
NCGUR...... National Coalition Government Union of Burma (Myanmar) [*Political party*] (PSAP)
NcGWE...... Western Electric Co., Legal Library, Greensboro, NC [*Library symbol*] [*Library of Congress*] (LCLS)
NCGWR..... National Center for Ground Water Research [*Stillwater, OK*] [*Environmental Protection Agency*] (GRD)
NCH.......... Hamilton & Kirkland Colleges, Clinton, NY [*Library symbol*] [*Library of Congress*] (LCLS)
NCH.......... Nachingwea [*Tanzania*] [*Airport symbol*] (OAG)
NCH.......... National Center for Homeopathy (EA)
NCH.......... National Center on Educational Media and Materials for the Handicapped, Columbus, OH [*Inactive*] [*OCLC symbol*] (OCLC)
NCH.......... National Chemsearch (EFIS)
NCH.......... National Children's Home [*British*]
NCH.......... National Clearinghouse [*Public Health Service*]
NCH.......... National Coalition for the Homeless (EA)
NCH.......... National Cocaine Hotline
NCH.......... National Committee on Housing
NCH.......... National Council on the Humanities [*Washington, DC*]
NCH.......... NCH Corp. [*Formerly, National Chemsearch Corp.*] [*NYSE symbol*] (SPSG)
NCH.......... Negative Channel [*Computer science*] (IAA)
NCH.......... Network Connection Handler
NCH.......... Nielson Clearing House [*A.C. Nielson Co.*] (DOAD)
NCH.......... Notched
NCH.......... Number [*or Name*] Changed [*Telephone Listing*] (BARN)
NCH.......... Nylon Clay Hydride [*Plastics*]
NCha........ Chatham Public Library, Chatham, NY [*Library symbol*] [*Library of Congress*] (LCLS)
NcHa........ Hamlet Public Library, Hamlet, NC [*Library symbol*] [*Library of Congress*] (LCLS)
NCHA........ National Campers and Hikers Association (EA)
NCHA........ National Capital Housing Authority
NCHA........ National Crossbow Hunters Association (EA)
NCHA........ National Cutting Horse Association (EA)
NCHA........ Northern Collegiate Hockey Association (PSS)
NCHAA...... National Cutting Horse Association of Australia
NChaL....... Chatham Public Library, Chatman, NY [*Library symbol*] [*Library of Congress*] (LCLS)
NcHal........ Halifax County Library, Halifax, NC [*Library symbol*] [*Library of Congress*] (LCLS)
NChap....... Chappaqua Library, Chappaqua, NY [*Library symbol*] [*Library of Congress*] (LCLS)
NcHaR....... Richmond Technical Institute, Hamlet, NC [*Library symbol*] [*Library of Congress*] (LCLS)
NcHav....... Havelock-Craven County Public Library, Havelock, NC [*Library symbol*] [*Library of Congress*] (LCLS)
NcHavCr.... Craven Community College, Havelock Learning Center, Havelock, NC [*Library symbol*] [*Library of Congress*] (LCLS)
NcHay....... Moss Memorial Library, Hayesville, NC [*Library symbol*] [*Library of Congress*] (LCLS)
NCHC........ National Clogging and Hoedown Council (EA)
NCHC........ National Collegiate Honors Council (EA)
NCHC........ National Council of Health Centers [*Formerly, NCHCS*] [*Later, AHCA*] (EA)
NCHC........ North Carolina Humanities Council (EARSL)
NCHCA....... National Commission for Health Certifying Agencies (EA)
NCHCS....... National Council of Health Care Services (EA)
NCHCT....... National Center for Health Care Technology [*US Congress agency*]
NCHDI........ National Center for Hearing Dog Information [*Later, HDRC*] (EA)
NcHe........ H. Leslie Perry Memorial Library, Henderson, NC [*Library symbol*] [*Library of Congress*] (LCLS)
NCHE........ National Center for Health Education (EA)
NCHE........ National Committee on Household Employment
NCHE........ National Council for History Education (EA)
NCHEC....... National Commission for Health Education Credentialing, Inc. (SEAT)
NCheH....... Saint Joseph Intercommunity Hospital, Cheektowaga, NY [*Library symbol*] [*Library of Congress*] (LCLS)
NCHELP..... National Council of Higher Education Loan Programs (EA)
NCHEML..... National Chemical Laboratory (MCD)
NCHEMS.... National Center for Higher Education Management Systems (EA)
NCHER...... National Center for Homecare Education and Research [*Defunct*] (EA)
NCHES...... National Child Health and Education Study [*University of Bristol*] [*British*]
NcHeV....... Vance County Technical Institute, Henderson, NC [*Library symbol*] [*Library of Congress*] (LCLS)
NCHF........ Navy Cargo Handling Force (COE)
NCHF........ Northern California Hemophilia Foundation (SAUS)
NcHf......... Perquimans County Library, Hertford, NC [*Library symbol*] [*Library of Congress*] (LCLS)
NCHFCI...... National Committee to Honor the Fourteenth Centennial of Islam (EA)
NCHFFA..... National Council of Health Facilities Finance Authorities (NTPA)
N CHG....... Normal Charge (MHDB)
NCHGD...... National Clearinghouse for Human Genetic Diseases [*Later, NCEMCH*] [*Public Health Service*] [*Information service or system*] (IID)
NCHGR...... National Center for Human Genome Research
NCHHA...... National Council of Homemakers and Home Health Aides
NCHHAS... National Council for Homemaker-Home Health Aid Services, Inc. [*Medicine*] (EDAA)
NCHHHSO... National Coalition of Hispanic Health and Human Services Organizations (EA)
NCHI......... National Council of the Housing Industry (EA)
NcHil........ Confederate Memorial Library, Hillsboro, NC [*Library symbol*] [*Library of Congress*] (LCLS)
NCHLA...... National Committee for a Human Life Amendment (EA)
NCHLRR.... National Commission on Human Life, Reproduction, and Rhythm (EA)
NCHLS...... National Council on Health Laboratory Services (EA)
NCHM........ National Center for Housing Management (EA)
NCHMHHSO... National Coalition of Hispanic Mental Health and Human Services Organizations [*Later, NCHHHSO*]
NCHMI...... National Centers for Health and Medical Information, Inc. [*Research center*] (RCD)
NCHMOS.... Negative Channel Metal-Oxide Semiconductor (IAA)
NCHMT...... National Capital Historical Museum of Transportation (EA)
ncho-........ Honduras [*MARC geographic area code*] [*Library of Congress*] (LCCP)
NCHO........ National Chicano Health Organization (EA)

NcHp .... High Point Public Library, High Point, NC [*Library symbol*] [*Library of Congress*] (LCLS)
NCHP .... National Corp. for Housing Partnerships
NCHP .... National Council of Hospice Professionals (SAUS)
NCHP .... Nickel-Chromium Honeycomb Panel
NCHPA ...... National Center for Health Promotion and Aging (EA)
NcHpC .... High Point College, High Point, NC [*Library symbol*] [*Library of Congress*] (LCLS)
NCHPC ...... National Consortium for High Performance Computing (DDC)
NCHPD ...... National Council on Health Planning and Development
NcHpH .... High Point Regional Hospital Medical Library, High Point, NC [*Library symbol*] [*Library of Congress*] (LCLS)
NCHR .... National Coalition for Haitian Refugees (EA)
NCHR .... National Coalition for Haitian Rights (EA)
N Ch R ...... Nelson's English Chancery Reports [*A publication*] (DLA)
Nchr .... Numismatic Chronicle (SAUS)
NCHRP ...... National Cooperative Highway Research Program
NCHRTM .... National Clearing House of Rehabilitation Training Materials [*Oklahoma State University*] [*Information service or system*] (IID)
NcHs .... Hudson Library, Highlands, NC [*Library symbol*] [*Library of Congress*] (LCLS)
NCHS .... National Center for Health Statistics [*Public Health Service*] [*Hyattsville, MD*] [*Originator and database*]
NCHS .... National Committee on Homemaker Service [*Superseded by NHC*] (EA)
NCHS .... New Canaan Historical Society [*Association*] (EA)
NCHSR ...... Australian National Centre in HIV Social Research (SAUS)
NCHSR ...... National Center for Health Services Research
NCHSR ...... National Center for Health Services Research and Health Care Technology Assessment [*Rockville, MD*] [*Public Health Service*] (GRD)
NCHSR & D... National Center for Health Services Research and Development [*Later, NCHSR*] [*HEW*]
NCHSRD .... National Center for Health Services Research and Development [*Later, NCHSR*] [*HEW*]
NcHu .... Hudson Public Library, Hudson, NC [*Library symbol*] [*Library of Congress*] (LCLS)
NcHv .... Henderson County Public Library, Hendersonville, NC [*Library symbol*] [*Library of Congress*] (LCLS)
NcHvH .... Blue Ridge Technical Institute, Hendersonville, NC [*Library symbol*] [*Library of Congress*] (LCLS)
NcHvME ..... Mother Earth News, Hendersonville, NC [*Library symbol*] [*Library of Congress*] (LCLS)
NCHVR ...... National Center for HIV [*Human Immunodeficiency Virus*] Virology Research [*Australia*]
NCHVRFE... National College for Heating, Ventilating, Refrigeration, and Fan Engineering (MCD)
NCHW .... National Council of Hispanic Women (EA)
NCHWPPTA... National Conference of Health, Welfare, and Pension Plans, Trustees and Administrators [*Later, International Foundation of Employee Benefit Plans*] (EA)
NcHy .... Elbert Ivey Memorial Library, Hickory, NC [*Library symbol*] [*Library of Congress*] (LCLS)
NcHyC .... Catawba Valley Technical Institute, Hickory, NC [*Library symbol*] [*Library of Congress*] (LCLS)
NcHyCH ..... Catawba Memorial Hospital, Northwest AHEC Library at Hickory, Hickory, NC [*Library symbol*] [*Library of Congress*] (LCLS)
NcHyCM ..... Catawba Area Mental Health Center, Hickory, NC [*Library symbol*] [*Library of Congress*] (LCLS)
NcHyFH ..... Glenn R. Frye Memorial Hospital, Hickory, NC [*Library symbol*] [*Library of Congress*] (LCLS)
NcHyL .... Lenoir Rhyne College, Hickory, NC [*Library symbol*] [*Library of Congress*] (LCLS)
NcHyMH .... Hickory Memorial Hospital Library, Hickory, NC [*Library symbol*] [*Library of Congress*] (LCLS)
NcHyS .... Siecor Corp., Technical Information Center, Hickory, NC [*Library symbol*] [*Library of Congress*] (LCLS)
NCl .... Camden County Library, Voorhees (SAUS)
NCi .... Central Islip Public Library, Central Islip, NY [*Library symbol*] [*Library of Congress*] (LCLS)
nCi .... Nanocurie [*One billionth of a curie*]
NCI .... Naphthalene Creosote, Iodoform [*Powder for lice*]
NCI .... National Cancer Institute [*Database producer*] [*Bethesda, MD*] [*National Institutes of Health*] [*Department of Health and Human Services*]
NCI .... National Captioning Institute (EA)
NCI .... National Cheese Institute (EA)
NCI .... National Components, Inc. (EFIS)
NCI .... National Computer Index [*National Computing Centre Ltd.*] [*British*] [*Information service or system*] (CRD)
NCI .... National Computer Institute (MCD)
NCI .... National Computing Industries (NITA)
NCI .... National Council for Inordinacy (EA)
NCI .... National Critics Institute (EA)
NCI .... Natural Casing Institute [*Later, International Natural Sausage Casing Institute*] (EA)
NCI .... Naval Cost Inspector
NCI .... Navigant Consulting [*NYSE symbol*] (SG)
NCI .... Navigation Control Indicator (MCD)
NCI .... Necocli [*Colombia*] [*Airport symbol*] (OAG)
NCI .... Negative Chemical Ionization [*Spectrometry*]
NCI .... Network Channel Interface (SAUS)
NCI .... Network Communications International [*Telecommunications service*] (TSSD)
NCI .... Network Computer, Inc. (IGQR)
NCI .... Neutral Countries Intelligence [*of Ministry of Economic Warfare*] [*British*] [*World War II*]
NCI .... New Community Instrument [*European Community*] (MHDB)
NCI .... New Concepts Initiative (ACAE)
NCI .... New Creation Institute (EA)
NCI .... No Common Interest
NCI .... No-Cost Item (AAG)
NCI .... Nodular Cast Iron (SAUS)
NCI .... Nomenclature Control Index (MCD)
NCI .... Nominal Correction I [*Phasing maneuver*] (MCD)
NCI .... Noncoded Information [*Computer science*] (IBMDP)
NCI .... Noncoherent Integration
NCI .... Noncriterion Ischemic (DMAA)
NCI .... North Conway Institute (EA)
NCI .... Northeast Computer Institute (HGAA)
NCI .... Northern Crops Institute (EARSL)
NCI .... Norton Corrosion Limited, Inc. (EFIS)
NCI .... Notice of Change Inception (MCD)
NCI .... Notice of Change Incorporation (MCD)
NCI .... Nuclear Capability Inspection (CINC)
NCI .... Nuclear Contour Index [*Cytology*]
NCI .... Nuclear Control Institute (EA)
NCI .... Numerical Coded Instruction (SAUS)
NCI .... Nurse Competency Inventory
NCI .... Nursing Care Integration [*Medicine*] (DMAA)
NCI .... Nursing Citation Index
NCI .... Office of New Concepts and Initiatives [*Air Force*] (TEL)
NCI .... Southwest New Jersey Consortium for Health Information Service, Voorhees, NJ [*OCLC symbol*] (OCLC)
NCIA .... National Cavity Installation Association [*British*]
NCIA .... National Center on Institutions and Alternatives (EA)
NCIA .... National Crop Insurance Association [*Shawnee Mission, KS*] (EA)
NCIAC .... National Construction Industry Arbitration Committee (EA)
NCIAC .... North Central Intercollegiate Athletic Conference (PSS)
NCIAED...... National Center for Information and Advice on Educational Disadvantage
NCIB .... National Charities Information Bureau (EA)
NCIB .... National Collection of Industrial Bacteria [*British*]
NCI Bldg .... NCI Building Systems [*Associated Press*] (SAG)
NCIBRD ..... National Center for Integrated Bioremediation Research & Development [*Initiated in Michigan with government funding, 1994*]
NCIC .... National Cancer Institute of Canada
NCIC .... National Career Information Center [*Defunct*] (EA)
NCIC .... National Cartographic Information Center [*United States Geological Survey*] [*Reston, VA*]
NCIC .... National Commission on the Indian Canadian
NCIC .... National Congress of Italian Canadians
NCIC .... National Construction Industry Council (EA)
NCIC .... National Crime Information Center [*FBI*] [*Washington, DC*]
NCIC .... National Crime Information Computer (SAUS)
NCIC .... National Crop Insurance Council [*Inactive*] (EA)
NCIC .... Network Communications Interface, Common (MCD)
NCIC .... Network Control Interface Channel [*Computer science*] (VLIE)
NCIC .... Non-Circumcision Information Center (EA)
NCIC .... Nonconfidential Information Center (AEPA)
NCIC .... Northwest Coastal Information Center [*Marine science*] (MSC)
NCIC .... Northwest Conference of Independent Colleges (PSS)
NCICA .... National Counter Intelligence Corps Association (EA)
NCIC Ops ... North Carolina Industrial Commission Advance Sheets [*A publication*] (DLA)
NCICU .... National Council of Independent Colleges and Universities [*Later, NAICU*]
NCID .... National Council for Industrial Defense (EA)
NCID .... Non-Cooperative Identification (ACAE)
NCIDQ .... National Council for Interior Design Qualification (EA)
NCIE .... National Coalition for Indian Education (EA)
NCIES .... National Center for the Improvement of Educational Systems [*Office of Education*]
NCIES .... National Committee for International Education through Satellites (EA)
NCIESD...... National Conference on International Economic and Social Development [*Later, IDC*]
NCIH .... National Conference on Industrial Hydraulics
NCIH .... National Council for International Health (EA)
NCIHC .... National Council for Interior Horticultural Certification (EA)
NCII .... National Council for Industrial Innovation (EA)
NCII .... National Council of Individual Investors
NCIJ .... National Cancer Institute Journal [*Medicine*] (EDAA)
NCIJC........ National Council of Independent Junior Colleges [*Defunct*]
nCi/L......... Nanocuries per Liter (EEVL)
NCIL .... National Council on Independent Living (EA)
NCILT .... National Centre for Industrial Language Training [*British*] (DI)
NCIM .... National Commission on Infant Mortality (MELL)
NCIMA....... National Cellulose Insulation Manufacturers Association
NCIMC....... National Council of Industrial Management Clubs [*Later, IMC*] (EA)
NCIMS....... National Conference on Interstate Milk Shipments
NCIMS....... Negative Chemical Ionization Mass Spectra
NCIMS....... Numerical Control Information Management System (MCD)
NCIN .... National Credit Information Network
NCIN .... North Carolina Information Network [*Library network*]
NCINAS ..... National Council of Industrial Naval Air Stations (EA)
NCINASEO... National Council of Industrial Naval Air Stations Employee Organizations [*Formerly, NCNASEO*] (EA)
NCIO .... National Congress of Inventors Organizations (EA)
NCIO .... National Council on Indian Opportunity (EA)
NCIP .... National Center to Improve Practice (SAUS)
NCIP .... National Council for Industrial Peace [*Defunct*] (EA)

NCIP......... No Change in Price (MCD)
NCIP......... Non-Contributory Invalid Pension [*British*] (DI)
NCIP......... North American Collections Inventory Project [*Established 1982*] [*Library science*]
NCIP......... Northeast Corridor Improvement Program (SAUS)
NCIP......... Novell Certified Internet Professional (SAUS)
NCIPA........ National Committee for Independent Political Action (EA)
NCIPLA...... National Council of Intellectual Property Law Associations (EA)
NCIR......... National Center for Immigrants' Rights [*Later, NILC*] (EA)
NCIR......... National Center for Initiative Review (EA)
NCIR......... National Conference on Industrial Research
NCirc........ Numismatic Circular [*A publication*] (ABAR)
NCIRE........ Northern California Institute for Research and Education (RCD)
NCIRF........ National Center for Initiative Review Foundation [*Defunct*] (EA)
NCIRLS...... North Central Regional Library System [*Library network*]
NCIS......... Nadir Climate Interferometer Spectrometer (MCD)
NCIS......... National Chemical Information System (DIT)
NCIS......... National Coalition of Independent Scholars
NCIS......... National Council of Independent Schools [*Later, National Association of Independent Schools*] (AEBS)
NCIS......... National Credit Information Service [*TRW, Inc.*] [*Long Beach, CA*] [*Credit-information databank*]
NCIS......... National Criminal Intelligence Service (WA)
NCIS......... National Criminal Investigation Service (WDAA)
NCIS......... National Crop Insurance Services (EA)
NCIS......... Naval Criminal Investigative Service
NCIS......... Navy Cost Information System
NCIS......... Nuclear Criticality Information System [*Lawrence Livermore National Laboratory*] [*Information service or system*] (IID)
NCISC........ Naval Counterintelligence Support Center
NCISD........ National Coalition on Immune System Disorders (EA)
NCISE........ National Center for Improving Science Education (EA)
NCiSH........ Central Islip State Hospital, Central Islip, NY [*Library symbol*] [*Library of Congress*] (LCLS)
NCISS........ National Council of Investigation and Security Services (EA)
NCIT......... National Committee for Insurance Taxation (EA)
NCIT......... National Council of Independent Truckers [*Defunct*] (EA)
NCIT......... National Council of Inland Transport [*British*] (DBA)
NCIT......... Numerical Control Inspection Tape (MCD)
NCITC........ National Clothing Industry Training Committee [*Australia*]
NCITD........ National Committee on International Trade Documentation [*MARAD*] (TAG)
NCITD........ National Council on International Trade Development [*Association*] (EA)
NCITD........ National Council on International Trade Documentation [*In association name: NCITD - The International Trade Facilitation Council*] (EA)
NCITR........ National Center for Intermedia Transport Research [*Los Angeles, CA*] (GRD)
NCITRP...... National Center for Interpretation Testing, Research, and Policy [*University of Arizona*] (RCD)
NCITS........ National Committee for Information Technology Standards [*Washington, DC*] (DDC)
NCITT........ National Committee for the In-Service Training of Teachers [*Scotland*] (AIE)
NCIU......... Network Common Interface Unit
NCIU......... Network Common Interference Unit (MCD)
NCIU......... Network Communications Interface, Unique
NCIU......... North American Container System-Trac Lease [*Intermodal shipping container symbol*] (TVRC)
NCIV......... National Council for International Visitors (EA)
NCIX......... Nova Chemicals [*Private rail car owner code*]
NCIZ......... Nucor Industries [*Federal Railroad Administration identification code*]
NcJ.......... Jamestown Public Library, Jamestown, NC [*Library symbol*] [*Library of Congress*] (LCLS)
NCJ.......... Johnson C. Smith University, James B. Duke Memorial Library, Charlotte, NC [*OCLC symbol*] (OCLC)
NCJ.......... Needle Catheter Jejunostomy [*Medicine*] (DMAA)
NCJA......... National Criminal Justice Association (EA)
NcJa......... Onslow County Public Library, Jacksonville, NC [*Library symbol*] [*Library of Congress*] (LCLS)
NcJaC........ Coastal Carolina Community College, Jacksonville, NC [*Library symbol*] [*Library of Congress*] (LCLS)
NcJac........ Northampton County Memorial Library, Jackson, NC [*Library symbol*] [*Library of Congress*] (LCLS)
NcJacL...... Northampton County Memorial Library, Jackson, NC [*Library symbol*] [*Library of Congress*] (LCLS)
NcJaMC...... United States Marine Corps, Marine Corps Air Station, Special Services for Station Library, New River Base, Jacksonville, NC [*Library symbol*] [*Library of Congress*] (LCLS)
NCJAR........ National Council for Japanese American Redress [*Defunct*] (EA)
NCJAVM..... National Council on Jewish Audio-Visual Materials (EA)
NCJC......... National Conference of Judicial Councils [*Defunct*] (EA)
NCJCC........ National Council of Jewish Correctional Chaplains [*Later, AJCCA*] (EA)
NCJCJ........ National Council of Juvenile Court Judges [*Later, NCJFCJ*] (EA)
NCJCS........ National Conference of Jewish Communal Service [*Later, CJCS*] (EA)
NCJD......... National Coalition for a Just Draft (EA)
NCJD......... National Congress of Jewish Deaf (EA)
NCJE......... National Council for Jewish Education [*Later, CJE*] (EA)
NCJF......... National Center for Jewish Film (EA)
NCJFCJ...... National Council of Juvenile and Family Court Judges (EA)
NcJG......... Guilford Technical Institute, Jamestown, NC [*Library symbol*] [*Library of Congress*] (LCLS)
NCJISN...... National Council of Jewish Invalids Survivors of Nazism [*Later, CHSD*] (EA)
NCJISS...... National Criminal Justice Information and Statistics Service
NCJJ......... National Center for Jobs and Justice (EA)
NCJJ......... National Center for Juvenile Justice (EA)
NCJMS........ National Center for Job Market Studies [*Commercial firm*] [*Washington, DC*] (EA)
NcJo......... Jonesville-Arlington Public Library, Jonesville, NC [*Library symbol*] [*Library of Congress*] (LCLS)
NCJO......... National Council of Junior Outdoorsmen (EA)
NCJ of L.... North Carolina Journal of Law [*A publication*] (DLA)
NCJPS........ National Center for Jewish Policy Studies
NCJR......... National Coalition for Jail Reform [*Defunct*] (EA)
NCJRS........ National Criminal Justice Reference Service [*Department of Justice*] [*Information service or system*]
NcJRS........ Ragsdale Senior High School, Jamestown, NC [*Library symbol*] [*Library of Congress*] (LCLS)
NCJSB........ National Commission on Jobs and Small Business [*Defunct*] (EA)
NCJSC........ National Criminal Justice Statistics Center
NCJT......... Nordic Committee of Journalism Teachers (EA)
NCJW......... National Council of Jewish Women (EA)
NCJWA........ National Council of Jewish Women of Australia
NCK.......... Camden County College, Voorhees, NJ [*OCLC symbol*] (OCLC)
NcK.......... Kinston-Lenoir County Public Library, Kinston, NC [*Library symbol*] [*Library of Congress*] (LCLS)
NCK.......... Nagycenk [*Hungary*] [*Geomagnetic observatory code*]
NCK.......... Neck
NCK.......... Nickelodeon Industries Corp. [*Vancouver Stock Exchange symbol*]
NCK.......... Norman, Craig & Kummel [*Advertising agency*]
NcKa......... Cannon Memorial YMCA Public Library, Kannapolis, NC [*Library symbol*] [*Library of Congress*] (LCLS)
NCKA......... National Catholic Kindergarten Association (AEBS)
NcKbMR.... North Carolina Marine Resources Center, Fort Fisher, Kure Beach, NC [*Library symbol*] [*Library of Congress*] (LCLS)
NcKC......... Kinston-Lenoir County Public Library, Caswell Center Library, Kinston, NC [*Library symbol*] [*Library of Congress*] (LCLS)
NCKE......... North Central Kentucky Express [*Common carrier symbol*]
NcKeD........ Duplin County, Dorothy Wightman Library, Kenansville, NC [*Library symbol*] [*Library of Congress*] (LCLS)
NcKeS........ James Sprunt Technical Institute, Kenansville, NC [*Library symbol*] [*Library of Congress*] (LCLS)
NcKg......... King Public Library, King, NC [*Library symbol*] [*Library of Congress*] (LCLS)
NcKiK........ Kittrell College, Kittrell, NC [*Library symbol*] [*Library of Congress*] (LCLS)
NcKL......... Lenoir Community College, Kinston, NC [*Library symbol*] [*Library of Congress*] (LCLS)
NCKL......... North Central Kansas Libraries System [*Library network*]
NcKm......... Jacob S. Mauney Memorial Library, Kings Mountain, NC [*Library symbol*] [*Library of Congress*] (LCLS)
NcKn......... Kenly Public Library, Kenly, NC [*Library symbol*] [*Library of Congress*] (LCLS)
NCKWM...... National Committee for the Korean War Memorial [*Later, KWVM*] (EA)
NCL.......... Camden County Library, Voorhees, NJ [*OCLC symbol*] (OCLC)
NCL.......... Financial
NCL.......... National Carriers Ltd. [*British*] (DCTA)
NCL.......... National Center for the Laity (EA)
NCL.......... National Central Library [*United Kingdom*]
NCL.......... National Character Laboratory (EA)
NCL.......... National Chemical Laboratory
NCL.......... National Church League (ODA)
NCL.......... National Civic League (EA)
NCL.......... National Coalition for Literacy (EA)
NCL.......... National Commuter Airways [*British*] [*ICAO designator*] (FAAC)
NCL.......... National Consumers League (EA)
NCL.......... National Council of Labour [*British*] (DCTA)
NCL.......... National Cycle League (EA)
NCL.......... Navy Calibration Laboratory
NCL.......... Navy Code Logistic [*Plan*]
NCL.......... Network Control Language [*Computer science*] (GART)
NCL.......... Neuronal Ceroid Lipofuscinoses Mutations (MHID)
NCL.......... Neuronal Ceroid Lipofuscinosis [*Medicine*]
NCL.......... New Caledonia [*ANSI three-letter standard code*] (CNC)
NCL.......... Newcastle [*England*] [*Airport symbol*] (OAG)
NCL.......... Node Compatibility List [*Telecommunications*] (TEL)
NCL.......... Node Control Logic [*Computer science*] (VLIE)
NCL.......... Noise Control Laboratory [*Pennsylvania State University*] [*Research center*] (RCD)
NCL.......... Norfolk, VA [*Location identifier*] [*FAA*] (FAAL)
NCL.......... Normal Card Listing (SAUS)
NCL.......... Norwegian Caribbean Lines
NCL.......... Norwegian Cruise Line (TVEL)
NCL.......... Norwegian Cruise Lines (TRID)
NCL.......... Nuclear Cardiology Laboratory [*Medicine*] (EDAA)
NCL.......... Nucleolin (DMAA)
NCL.......... Null Convention Logic (SAUS)
NCL.......... Numerical Control Language [*Computer science*] (VLIE)
NCL.......... Numerically Controlled Lathe
NCL.......... NuVeen Ins CA Prem Inc Muni 2 [*NYSE symbol*] (TTSB)
NCL.......... Nuveen Insured California Premium Income Municipal II [*NYSE symbol*] (SPSG)
NcL.......... Scotland County Memorial Library, Laurinburg, NC [*Library symbol*] [*Library of Congress*] (LCLS)
NCL.......... S.E. Nichols, Inc. [*AMEX symbol*] (COMM)
NCLA......... National C-Lark Association (EA)
NCLA......... National Council of Local Administrators of Vocational Education and Practical Arts (EA)

NCLA .... North Carolina Library Association (SAUS)
NCLAB .... National Center for Laboratory Animal Sciences (SAUS)
NCLAC .... North Central Louisiana Arts Council (EARSL)
NCLAN ...... National Crop Loss Assessment Network
NCL & SW .. National Conference of Lawyers and Social Workers
NC Law Repos ... North Carolina Law Repository [*A publication*] (DLA)
NC Law Repository ... North Carolina Law Repository (Reprint) [*A publication*] (DLA)
NCLB .... No Child Left Behind
NCLB .... North Central Laboratories, Inc. (SAUS)
NCLC .... National Catholic Liturgical Conference (EA)
NCLC .... National Caucus of Labor Committees
NCLC .... National Chamber Litigation Center (EA)
NCLC .... National Child Labor Committee (EA)
NCLC .... National Christian Life Community of the United States of America (EA)
NCLC .... National Consumer Law Center (EA)
NCLC .... National Council of Labour Colleges
NCLC .... National Council on Legal Clinics [*Later, CLEPR*]
NCLC .... Nineteenth Century Literary Criticism [*A publication*]
NCLC .... Noncombatant Labour Corps [*British*]
NCLC .... NorCal Community Bancorp [*NASDAQ symbol*] (QUAN)
NCLCH .... National Civil Liberties Clearing House [*Defunct*] (EA)
NCLCI .... National Christian Leadership Conference for Israel (EA)
NCLD .... National Center for Law and Deafness [*Formerly, National Center for Law and the Deaf*] (EA)
NCLD .... National Center for Law and the Deaf (EA)
NCLD .... National Center for Learning Disabilities (EA)
NCLD .... Williamsport District Library Center [*Library network*]
NCLE .... National Contact Lens Examiners (EA)
NcLeC .... Caldwell County Public Library, Lenoir, NC [*Library symbol*] [*Library of Congress*] (LCLS)
NcLeCT ...... Caldwell Community College and Technical Institute, Lenoir, NC [*Library symbol*] [*Library of Congress*] (LCLS)
NCLEHA ..... National Conference of Local Environmental Health Administrators (EA)
NCLER .... National Clearinghouse on Licensure, Enforcement, and Regulation (EA)
NCLEX .... National Council Licensure Examination
NCLEX-RN ... National Council Licensure Examination for Registered Nurses
NCLF .... National Coalition to Legalize Freedom (EA)
NCLG .... National Committee for Latin and Greek (EA)
NCLG .... National Conference of Lieutenant Governors (EA)
NCLH .... National Center for Law and the Handicapped [*Defunct*] (EA)
NCLHA .... National Conference of Law Historians of America (EA)
NCLHA ...... North Carolina Literary and Historical Association (EARSL)
NCLI .... National Committee for Labor Israel [*Later, NCLIIHC*] (EA)
NCLIIHC ..... National Committee for Labor Israel-Israel Histadrut Campaign (EA)
NcLil .... Harnett County Public Library, Lillington, NC [*Library symbol*] [*Library of Congress*] (LCLS)
NcLiL .... Lincoln County Memorial Library, Lincolnton, NC [*Library symbol*] [*Library of Congress*] (LCLS)
NClinc .... Clinton Corners Reading Center, Clinton Corners, NY [*Library symbol*] [*Library of Congress*] (LCLS)
NCLIP .... North Coast Life Ins Cv'A'Pfd [*NASDAQ symbol*] (TTSB)
NCLIP .... North Coast Life Insurance Co. [*NASDAQ symbol*] (SAG)
NCLIS .... National Commission on Libraries and Information Science [*Washington, DC*]
NCLIS .... National Council for Languages and International Studies (EA)
NcLit .... Littleton Public Library, Littleton, NC [*Library symbol*] [*Library of Congress*] (LCLS)
NCLJ .... North Carolina Law Journal [*A publication*] (DLA)
NcLjUM ..... United Methodist Church, Commission on Archives and History, Lake Junaluska, NC [*Library symbol*] [*Library of Congress*] (LCLS)
NcLk .... Rockingham County Library, Leakesville, NC [*Library symbol*] [*Library of Congress*] (LCLS)
NCLLF .... National Civil Liberties Legal Foundation [*Inactive*] (EA)
NCLM .... North Carolina League of Municipalities (EARSL)
NcLo .... Franklin County Library, Louisburg, NC [*Library symbol*] [*Library of Congress*] (LCLS)
NCLO .... Naval Communication Liaison Officer (IAA)
NcLo-B ...... Franklin County Library, Bunn Branch Library, Bunn, NC [*Library symbol*] [*Library of Congress*] (LCLS)
NcLoC .... Louisburg College, Louisburg, NC [*Library symbol*] [*Library of Congress*] (LCLS)
NCLP .... National Conference on Law and Poverty
NCLP .... National Contract Laboratory Program (COE)
NCLP .... Numerically Controlled Line Plotter
NCLPWA .... National Council of Local Public Welfare Administrators (EA)
NCLR .... National Center for Legislative Research [*Defunct*] (EA)
NCLR .... National Center for Lesbian Rights (EA)
NCLR .... National Coalition for Land Reform (EA)
NCLR .... National Council for Labor Reform (EA)
NCLR .... National Council of La Raza (EA)
NCL Rep .... North Carolina Law Repository [*A publication*] (DLA)
NCL Reps ... North Carolina Law Repository (Reprint) [*A publication*] (DLA)
NCLS .... National Clearinghouse for Legal Services [*Legal Services Corp.*] [*Information service or system*] (IID)
NCLS .... National Committee for Liberation of Slovakia (EA)
NCLS .... National Conference of Lawyers and Scientists [*Joint project of the American Association for the Advancement of Science and the American Bar Association*]
NCLS .... National Conference of State Legislatures [*Australia*]
NCLS .... North Country Library System [*Library network*]
NcLS .... Saint Andrews Presbyterian College, Laurinburg, NC [*Library symbol*] [*Library of Congress*] (LCLS)
NCLT .... Night Carrier Landing Trainer [*Navy*]
NCLTA .... National Cigar Leaf Tobacco Association [*Defunct*] (EA)
NCLU .... Namucar Line [*Intermodal shipping container symbol*] (TVRC)
NcLu .... Robeson County Public Library, Lumberton, NC [*Library symbol*] [*Library of Congress*] (LCLS)
NcLuH .... Southeastern General Hospital, Medical Library, Lumberton, NC [*Library symbol*] [*Library of Congress*] (LCLS)
NcLuR .... Robeson Technical Institute, Lumbarton, NC [*Library symbol*] [*Library of Congress*] (LCLS)
NCLX .... Nova Chemicals [*Private rail car owner code*]
NcLxD .... Davidson County Public Library, Lexington, NC [*Library symbol*] [*Library of Congress*] (LCLS)
NcLxDC ..... Davidson County Community College, Lexington, NC [*Library symbol*] [*Library of Congress*] (LCLS)
NCm .... Center Moriches Free Public Library, Center Moriches, NY [*Library symbol*] [*Library of Congress*] (LCLS)
NCM .... Court Martial Reports, Navy Cases [*A publication*] (DLA)
NCM .... Mars Hill College, Mars Hill, NC [*OCLC symbol*] (OCLC)
NCM .... Nailfold Capillary Microscope (DAVI)
NCM .... National Center for Men (EA)
NCM .... National City Lines Inc. (EFIS)
NCM .... National Coal Model [*Department of Energy*] (GFGA)
NCM .... National Coastal Monitoring (USDC)
NCM .... National College of Music [*British*] (DI)
NCM .... National Congress for Men (EA)
NCM .... National Corvette Museum
NCM .... National Cursillo Movement (EA)
NCM .... Natural Clay Mosaic (DICI)
NCM .... Navy Commendation Medal
NCM .... Navy Correspondence Manual
NCM .... Nazarene Compassionate Ministries International [*Association*] (EA)
NCM .... Necanicum, OR [*Amtrak Busline code*]
NCM .... Net Control Master (MCD)
NCM .... Network Connection Management [*Computer science*] (VLIE)
NCM .... Network Control Module
NCM .... Newcastle Conservatorium of Music [*Australia*]
NCM .... New Moon [*Queensland*] [*Airport symbol*] (AD)
NCM .... Nicaraguan Campaign Medal
NCM .... Nippon Calculating Machine Co. [*Japan*] (PDAA)
NCM .... Nitrocellulose Membrane
NCM .... No Compromise Majority [*An association*] (EA)
NCM .... Node Controller Module (SAUS)
NCM .... Noise Canceling Microphone
NCM .... Noise Cancelling Microphone (SAUS)
NCM .... Non Compos Mentis [*Not of Sound Mind*] [*Latin*] (LWAP)
NCM .... Noncorrosive Metal
NCM .... Noncrew Member
NCM .... Nordic Council of Ministers (EAIO)
NCM .... Nordic Council on Medicines [*See also NLN*] (EAIO)
NCM .... Normal Human Colon Mucosal [*Cells*]
NCM .... North Carolina Motor Carriers Association [*STAC*]
NCM .... Northern Conservatory of Music [*Maine*]
NCM .... Northern Cruise Master (SAA)
NCM .... Notice of Commencement of Manufacture [*Toxic Substances Control Act*] [*Environmental Protection Agency*] (EPA)
NCM .... Numerical Controlled Machine
NCM .... Nurse Case Manager (DMAA)
NCM .... Nuveen California Municipal Income [*NYSE symbol*] (SPSG)
NCMA .... National Campus Ministry Association (EA)
NCMA .... National Catalog Managers Association (EA)
NCMA .... National Ceramic Manufacturers Association
NCMA .... National Childminding Association [*British*] (DBA)
NCMA .... National Concrete Masonry Association (EA)
NCMA .... National Contract Management Association (EA)
NCMA .... National Corporate Medical Associates [*An association*]
NCMA .... National Council of Millinery Associations (EA)
NCMA .... National Council of Moving Associations (EA)
NCMA .... Naval Civilian Manager's Association (EA)
NCMA .... Newspaper Credit Managers' Association (EA)
NCMA .... North Carolina Museum of Art (SAUS)
NcMad ...... Madison Public Library, Madison, NC [*Library symbol*] [*Library of Congress*] (LCLS)
NCMAF ...... National Conference on Ministry to the Armed Forces (EA)
NCMAG ...... National Computer Center Management Advisory Group (COE)
NcMaM ...... McDowell Technical Institute, Marion, NC [*Library symbol*] [*Library of Congress*] (LCLS)
NcMaMC .... McDowell County Public Library, Marion, NC [*Library symbol*] [*Library of Congress*] (LCLS)
NcMan ...... Dare County Library, Manteo, NC [*Library symbol*] [*Library of Congress*] (LCLS)
NcManA ..... College of the Albemarle, Dare County Center Library, Manteo, NC [*Library symbol*] [*Library of Congress*] (LCLS)
NcManMR .. North Carolina Marine Resources Center, Roanoke Island Resource Library, Manteo,NC [*Library symbol*] [*Library of Congress*] (LCLS)
NcMarM ..... Madison County Public Library, Marshall, NC [*Library symbol*] [*Library of Congress*] (LCLS)
NcMauDC ... North Carolina Department of Corrections, Eastern Correctional Center Library, Maury, NC [*Library symbol*] [*Library of Congress*] (LCLS)
NcMax .... Gilbert Patterson Memorial Public Library, Maxton, NC [*Library symbol*] [*Library of Congress*] (LCLS)
NCMC .... Nassau County Medical Center [*Medicine*] [*New York, NY*] (EDAA)
NCMC .... National Capital Management Corp. [*NASDAQ symbol*] (NQ)
NCMC .... National Capital Market (EFIS)

NCMC .... National Center on Missing Children (NADA)
NCMC .... National Coalition for Marine Conservation (EA)
NCMC .... National Conference of Metropolitan Courts
NCMC .... Natl Capital Mgmt [*NASDAQ symbol*] (TTSB)
NCMC .... Natural Cell-Mediated Cytotoxicity [*Immunochemistry*]
NCMC .... N-Carboxymethylchitosan [*Biochemistry*]
NCMC .... Non-Classical Mesoscale Circulations (SAUS)
NCMC .... NORAD Cheyenne Mountain Complex [*Military*] (AABC)
NCMC .... Nordic Council for Music Conservatories (EA)
NCMC .... Numerically-Controlled Machine Center (IAA)
NCMC .... Numeric Control Machining Center (SAUS)
NCMCA ...... North Carolina Mason Contractors Association (EARSL)
NcMcC ...... Carteret Technical Institute, Morehead City (SAUS)
NcMcC ...... Carteret Technical Institute, Morehead City, NC [*Library symbol*] [*Library of Congress*] (LCLS)
NcMccH ..... McCain Hospital, Medical Library, McCain, NC [*Library symbol*] [*Library of Congress*] (LCLS)
NcMccS ..... Sandhills Youth Center, McCain, NC [*Library symbol*] [*Library of Congress*] (LCLS)
NCMCE ...... National Council of Minority Consulting Engineers (IAA)
NCMCG ...... National Construction Machinery Credit Group [*Park Ridge, IL*] (EA)
NCM Company ... Nippon Calculating Machine Co. (SAUS)
NCMD .... National Center for Municipal Development (EA)
NCMDA ...... National Coin Machine Distributors Association (EA)
NCMDA ...... National Commission on Marijuana and Drug Abuse [*Presidential advisory committee, terminated 1973*]
NCMDLRJO ... National Council of Marriage and Divorce Law Reform and Justice Organizations (EA)
NCME .... National Center for Mediation Education (EA)
NCME .... National Council on Measurement in Education (EA)
NCME .... Network for Continuing Medical Education (EA)
NCME .... Northern Counties Motor & Engineering Co. Ltd. [*British*] (DCTA)
NCME .... Numerically Controlled Machine Equipment
NCMEA ...... National Catholic Music Educators Association [*Later, NPM*] (EA)
NCMEC ...... National Center for Missing and Exploited Children (EA)
NCMES ...... Numerically Controlled Measuring and Evaluating System (SAUS)
NCMESD .... National Coalition for More Effective School Discipline (EA)
NCMET ...... Nonclosed Shell Many Electron Theory [*Physics*]
NcMf .... Murfreesboro Public Library, Murfreesboro, NC [*Library symbol*] [*Library of Congress*] (LCLS)
NCMF .... National Carvers Museum Foundation [*Defunct*] (EA)
NCMF .... National Church Music Fellowship [*Defunct*]
NcMfC .... Chowan College, Murfreesboro, NC [*Library symbol*] [*Library of Congress*] (LCLS)
NCMFST .... National Committee for Motor Fleet Supervisor Training (EA)
NcMG .... Graham Evangelistic Association, Montreat, NC [*Library symbol*] [*Library of Congress*] (LCLS)
NCMG .... Mangaia [*Cook Islands*] [*ICAO location identifier*] (ICLI)
NCMH .... National Clearinghouse for Mental Health Information (NITA)
NCMH .... National Committee for Mental Health (DAVI)
NCMH .... National Committee for Mental Hygiene (DAVI)
NCMH .... National Committee on Maternal Health (EA)
NCMH .... National Council for Monday Holidays
NCMHA ...... North Carolina Mobile Home Association
NcMhC ...... Mars Hill College, Mars Hill, NC [*Library symbol*] [*Library of Congress*] (LCLS)
NCMHC ...... National Community Mental Healthcare Council (NTPA)
NCMHC ...... National Community Mental Heathcare Council (EA)
NCMHCE .... National Clinical Mental Health Counseling Examination (SAUS)
NCMHD ..... National Center on Minority Health and Health Disparities (RCD)
NcMHi .... Historical Foundation of the Presbyterian and Reformed Churches, Montreat, NC [*Library symbol*] [*Library of Congress*] (LCLS)
NCMHI ...... National Clearinghouse for Mental Health Information [*Public Health Service*] [*Rockville, MD*] [*Database*] [*HEW*]
NCMHS ...... National Conference on Mental Health Statistics [*Department of Health and Human Services*] (GFGA)
NCMI .... National Coin Machine Institute (EA)
NCMI .... National Committee Against Mental Illness (EA)
NCMI .... National Council of Music Importers [*Later, NCMIE*]
NCMI .... National Country Maintenance Index (IAA)
NCMIE .... National Council of Music Importers and Exporters (EA)
NcMiP .... Pfeiffer College, Misenheimer, NC [*Library symbol*] [*Library of Congress*] (LCLS)
NCMIR ...... National Center for Microscopy and Imaging Research [*University of California, San Diego*] (RCD)
NCMJ .... National Contract Management Journal [*A publication*] (AAGC)
NCMK .... Mauke [*Cook Islands*] [*ICAO location identifier*] (ICLI)
NCMLB ...... National Council of Mailing List Brokers [*Later, MLBPA*] (EA)
NcMM .... Montreat-Anderson College, Montreat, NC [*Library symbol*] [*Library of Congress*] (LCLS)
NCmM .... Museum Manor of Saint George, Center Moriches, NY [*Library symbol*] [*Library of Congress*] (LCLS)
NCMM .... National Council on Medical Malpractice [*Medicine*] (EDAA)
NCMM .... Nuveen California Municipal Market Opportunity Fund [*Associated Press*] (SAG)
NCmMM .... Museum Manor of Saint George, Center Moriches, NY [*Library symbol*] [*Library of Congress*] (LCLS)
NCMN .... Manuae [*Cook Islands*] [*ICAO location identifier*] (ICLI)
NCMO .... National Case Mix Office (SAUS)
NCMO .... Navigational Aids/Communications Management Office [*Air Force*] (CET)
NcMoBH .... Broughton Hospital, Staff Library, Morganton, NC [*Library symbol*] [*Library of Congress*] (LCLS)
NcMoc .... Davie County Public Library, Mocksville, NC [*Library symbol*] [*Library of Congress*] (LCLS)
NcMoFM .... Foothills Area Mental Health, North Carolina School for the Deaf, Morganton, NC [*Library symbol*] [*Library of Congress*] (LCLS)
NcMoGH .... Grace Hospital, Medical Library, Morganton, NC [*Library symbol*] [*Library of Congress*] (LCLS)
NcMoM ...... Morganton-Burke Library, Inc., Morganton, NC [*Library symbol*] [*Library of Congress*] (LCLS)
NcMon ...... Union County Public Library, Monroe, NC [*Library symbol*] [*Library of Congress*] (LCLS)
NcMorB ..... Bell Northern Research, Inc., Learning Resources Center, Morrisville, NC [*Library symbol*] [*Library of Congress*] (LCLS)
NcMoW ..... Western Piedmont Community College, Morganton, NC [*Library symbol*] [*Library of Congress*] (LCLS)
NcMoWC .... Western Carolina Center, Staff Library, Morganton, NC [*Library symbol*] [*Library of Congress*] (LCLS)
NcMoWCC ... Western Correctional Center, Morganton, NC [*Library symbol*] [*Library of Congress*] (LCLS)
NCMP .... National Commission for Manpower Policy [*Department of Labor*]
NCMP .... National Commission on Materials Policy
NCMP .... Navy Capabilities and Mobilization Plan (DOMA)
NCMPA ...... National Corrugated Metal Pipe Association [*Later, NCSPA*] (EA)
NCMPR ...... National Council for Marketing and Public Relations (EA)
NCMPs ...... Non-Constituency Members of Parliament (Singapore) [*Political party*] (PSAP)
NCMR .... Matiaro [*Cook Islands*] [*ICAO location identifier*] (ICLI)
NCMR .... National Center for Microgravity Research (RCD)
NCMR .... National Centre for Marine Research (SAUS)
NCMR .... National Committee for Monetary Reform (EA)
NCMR .... Nonconforming Material Report
NCMR .... North Canterbury Mounted Rifles [*British military*] (DMA)
NCMRED .... National Council on Marine Resources and Engineering Development [*Later, ICMSE*]
NCMRR ..... National Center for Medical Rehabilitation Research [*National Institute of Child Health and Human Development*] (RCD)
NCMRWF ... National Centre for Medium Range Weather Forecasting [*New Delhi, India*]
NCMS .... National Center for Manufacturing Sciences [*Research center*]
NCMS .... National Classification Management Society (EA)
NCMS .... National Council of Marine Sciences
NCMS .... Network Control and Management Systems [*Open Systems Interconnection*] (ODAA)
NCMS .... North Carolina Medical Society (EARSL)
NCMS .... Numerically-Controlled Machine System (IAA)
NCMS .... Numerically Controlled Machining System (SAUS)
NCMS .... Numerically-Controlled Manufacture System (IAA)
NCMS .... Numerically Controlled Manufacturing System (SAUS)
NCMT .... Numerical Controlled Machine Tool (SAUS)
NCMT .... Numerical Control of Machine Tools (SAUS)
NCMT .... Numerically Controlled Machine Tool
NcMta .... Mount Airy Public Library, Mount Airy, NC [*Library symbol*] [*Library of Congress*] (LCLS)
NCMTA ...... National Council of Marine Trade Associations
NcMtaC ..... Crossroads Center, Mount Airy, NC [*Library symbol*] [*Library of Congress*] (LCLS)
NcMtC .... Mount Olive College, Mount Olive, NC [*Library symbol*] [*Library of Congress*] (LCLS)
NCMTE ...... National Council on Medical Technology Education [*Defunct*]
NCMTI ...... Noncoherent Moving Target Indicator (MCD)
NCMTT ...... National Council for Mother Tongue Teaching (AIE)
NcMu .... Murphy Public Library, Murphy, NC [*Library symbol*] [*Library of Congress*] (LCLS)
NCMU .... North American Container System-CN RAIL [*Intermodal shipping container symbol*] (TVRC)
NCMUE ...... National Council on Measurements Used in Education [*Later, National Council on Measurement in Education*] (AEBS)
NcMuN ...... Nantahala Regional Library, Murphy, NC [*Library symbol*] [*Library of Congress*] (LCLS)
NcMuT ...... Tri-County Technical Institute, Murphy, NC [*Library symbol*] [*Library of Congress*] (LCLS)
NcMv .... Mooresville Public Library, Mooresville, NC [*Library symbol*] [*Library of Congress*] (LCLS)
NCMV .... Northern Cereal Mosaic Virus [*Plant pathology*]
NCMX .... North Carolina Transportation Museum [*Federal Railroad Administration identification code*]
N/cmy .... Newton per Square Centimeter (SAUS)
n-cn- .... Canada [*MARC geographic area code*] [*Library of Congress*] (LCCP)
NCN .... Nasociliary Nerve [*Medicine*] (MELL)
NCN .... National Airlines (Chile), SA [*FAA designator*] (FAAC)
NCN .... National Cardiovascular Network
NCN .... National Christian Network [*Cable-television system*]
NCN .... National Computer Network Corp. [*Information service or system*] (IID)
NCN .... National Council of Nurses [*British*] (DI)
NCN .... Navy Control Number (MCD)
NCN .... Network Control Node
NCN .... New Caledonian Nickel (SAUS)
NCN .... New Century Network (SAUS)
NCN .... Nitrocarbonitrate (EEVL)
NCN .... Nixdorf Communications Network [*Nixdorf*] [*Germany*]
NCN .... Non-Casein Nitrogen (OA)
NCNA .... National Council of Nonprofit Associations
NCNA .... National Council on Noise Abatement (EA)
NCNA .... New China News Agency
NCNA .... North Carolina Nurses Association (SAUS)
NCNA .... Nursing Clinics of North America [*Medicine*] [*Journal*] (EDAA)
n-cn-ab ...... Alberta [*MARC geographic area code*] [*Library of Congress*] (LCCP)

NCNASEO.... National Council of Naval Air Stations Employee Organizations [*Later, NCINASEO*] (EA)
NCNB........ National Center for Nonprofit Boards (EA)
NCNB........ North Carolina National Bank (EFIS)
n-cn-bc...... British Columbia [*MARC geographic area code*] [*Library of Congress*] (LCCP)
NcNbC....... Craven Technical Institute, New Bern, NC [*Library symbol*] [*Library of Congress*] (LCLS)
NcNbCP..... Craven-Pamlico-Carteret Regional Library, New Bern, NC [*Library symbol*] [*Library of Congress*] (LCLS)
NCNC........ National Captive Nations Committee (EA)
NCNC........ National Council of Nigeria and the Cameroons [*Political party*]
NCNC........ Normochromic Normocytic [*Medicine*] (MEDA)
NCNC........ Normochromic, Normocytic Anemia [*Hematology*] (DAVI)
NCNCA...... Normochromic, Normocytic Anemia [*Hematology*] (DAVI)
NCNCD...... National Center for Neurogenic Communication Disorders [*University of Arizona*] (RCD)
NC/NCI...... Network Channel/Network Channel Interface [*Communications term*] (DCT)
NCND........ Neither Confirm nor Deny
NCNE........ National Campaign for Nursery Education [*British*]
NCNE........ National Center for Neighborhood Enterprise (EA)
NcNep....... Newport Public Library, Newport, NC [*Library symbol*] [*Library of Congress*] (LCLS)
NCNEVAW... National Communications Network for the Elimination of Violence Against Women [*NCADV*] [*Absorbed by*] (EA)
NcNew...... Avery-Morrison Public Library, Newland, NC [*Library symbol*] [*Library of Congress*] (LCLS)
NCNG........ North Carolina Natural Gas Corp. (SAUS)
NCNGD...... Not Crushed or Not Ground
n-cnh-....... Hudson Bay [*MARC geographic area code*] [*Library of Congress*] (LCCP)
NCNIA....... Northern California Nursing Informatics Association (SAUS)
n-cnm-...... Maritime Provinces [*MARC geographic area code*] [*Library of Congress*] (LCCP)
n-cn-mb..... Manitoba [*MARC geographic area code*] [*Library of Congress*] (LCCP)
NCNMLG.... Northern California and Nevada Medical Group (SAUS)
n-cn-nf...... Newfoundland [*MARC geographic area code*] [*Library of Congress*] (LCCP)
n-cn-nk...... New Brunswick [*MARC geographic area code*] [*Library of Congress*] (LCCP)
n-cn-ns...... Nova Scotia [*MARC geographic area code*] [*Library of Congress*] (LCCP)
n-cn-nt...... Northwest Territories [*MARC geographic area code*] [*Library of Congress*] (LCCP)
N/CNO....... Navy/Chief of Naval Operations (AAG)
n-cn-on..... Ontario [*MARC geographic area code*] [*Library of Congress*] (LCCP)
NCNP........ National Child Nutrition Project (EA)
NCNP........ National Conference for New Politics [*Organization formed in 1966 to support peace candidates*] (VNW)
NCNP........ North Cascades National Park (SAUS)
n-cnp-....... Prairie Provinces [*MARC geographic area code*] [*Library of Congress*] (LCCP)
n-cn-pi...... Prince Edward Island [*Canada*] [*MARC geographic area code*] [*Library of Congress*] (LCCP)
NCNPR...... National Center for Natural Products Research [*University of Mississippi*] (RCD)
NCNPSA.... National Conference of Non-Profit Shipping Associations (EA)
ncnq-........ Nicaragua [*MARC geographic area code*] [*Library of Congress*] (LCCP)
n-cn-qu..... Quebec [*MARC geographic area code*] [*Library of Congress*] (LCCP)
NCNR........ National Center for Nursing Research [*Bethesda, MD*] [*Department of Health and Human Services*] (GRD)
NCNS........ Nassau [*Cook Islands*] [*ICAO location identifier*] (ICLI)
NCNS........ National Catholic News Service (EA)
NCNS........ No Complications, No Sequelae (SAUS)
NCNS........ North Central Name Society (EA)
n-cn-sn..... Saskatchewan [*MARC geographic area code*] [*Library of Congress*] (LCCP)
NcNt......... Catawba County Library, Newton, NC [*Library symbol*] [*Library of Congress*] (LCLS)
NCNT........ Netcentives
NCNTUCW... National Commission on New Technological Uses of Copyrighted Works [*Terminated, 1978*] [*Library of Congress*]
NCNU........ Grupo Libra USA [*Common carrier symbol*]
NcNv......... Harold D. Cooley Library, Nashville, NC [*Library symbol*] [*Library of Congress*] (LCLS)
NCNW....... National Congress of Neighborhood Women (EA)
NCNW....... National Council of Negro Women (EA)
NCNW....... Nearly Certain New Work (MCD)
NcNw........ Wilkes County Public Library, North Wilkesboro, NC [*Library symbol*] [*Library of Congress*] (LCLS)
NcNwA...... Appalachian Regional Library, North Wilkesboro, NC [*Library symbol*] [*Library of Congress*] (LCLS)
NCNY........ Netherland Club of New York (EA)
NCNY........ Newswomen's Club of New York (EA)
n-cn-yk...... Yukon Territory [*MARC geographic area code*] [*Library of Congress*] (LCCP)
NCo.......... Commack Public Library, Commack, NY [*Library symbol*] [*Library of Congress*] (LCLS)
NCO.......... National Commission for Information and Conscientization on Development Cooperation [*Netherlands*]
NCO.......... National Council of Obesity (EA)
NCO.......... Nationalist Chams Organization (EA)
NCO.......... Negotiated Consent Order [*Environmental Protection Agency*] (ERG)
NCO.......... Net Control (CAAL)
NCO.......... Net Control Operator (CCCA)
NCO.......... Net Control Outstation [*Military*] (DOMA)
NCO.......... Network Control Office [*Telecommunications*] (TEL)
NCO.......... New Consultants [*A publication*]
NCO.......... No Complaints Offered (SAUS)
NCO.......... No-Cost Option (SAUS)
NCO.......... No Crossing Over (SAUS)
NCO.......... Noncombatant Evacuation Order [*Navy*] (CINC)
NCO.......... Noncombat Operations [*Military*] (CAAL)
NCO.......... Noncommissioned Officer [*Military*]
NCO.......... Noncommissioned Officers
NCO.......... Non Compliance Order [*Environmental Protection Agency*]
NCO.......... Norsar Array Site 01C00 [*Norway*] [*Seismograph station code, US Geological Survey*] (SEIS)
NCO.......... North Canadian Oils Ltd. [*Toronto Stock Exchange symbol*]
NCO.......... North Carolina Department of Transportation, Raleigh, NC [*OCLC symbol*] (OCLC)
NCO.......... Nuclear Control Order [*Military*] (MUSM)
NCO.......... Number-Controlled Oscillator
NCO.......... Numerically Controlled Oscillator (SAUS)
NCO.......... Nuveen California Municipal Market Opportunities [*NYSE symbol*] (SPSG)
NCO.......... Nuveen CA Muni Mkt Oppt [*NYSE symbol*] (TTSB)
NCOA........ National Campground Owners Association (EA)
NCOA........ National Change of Address
NCOA........ National Change of Address Service [*US Postal Service*]
NCOA........ National Chevelle Owners Association (EA)
NCOA........ National Condominium Owners Association [*Defunct*]
NCOA........ National Corvette Owners' Association (EA)
NCOA........ National Council on the Aging (EA)
NCOA........ Noncommissioned Officer Academy [*Military*] (AABC)
NCOA........ Non-Commissioned Officers Association of the United States of America (EA)
NCOAUSA... Non-Commissioned Officers Association of the United States of America (SAUS)
NCOB........ No Cargo On Board (SAUS)
NCoBJ....... Burr Junior High School, Commack, NY [*Library symbol*] [*Library of Congress*] (LCLS)
NCOBPS..... National Conference of Black Political Scientists (EA)
NCOBQ...... Noncommissioned Officer Bachelor Quarters [*Military*] (AFM)
N'COBRA.... National Coalition of Blacks for Reparations in America (ECON)
NCobUA..... State University of New York, Agricultural and Technical College at Cobleskill, Cobleskill, NY [*Library symbol*] [*Library of Congress*] (LCLS)
NCOC........ National Commission on Organized Crime (NADA)
NCOC........ National Council on Organized Crime (EA)
NCOC........ Noncommissioned Officer Course (VNW)
NCoCE....... Cedar Road Elementary School, Commack, NY [*Library symbol*] [*Library of Congress*] (LCLS)
NCOCY...... National Council of Organizations for Children and Youth (EA)
NCOD........ National Catholic Office for the Deaf (EA)
NCOD........ National Coming Out Day [*An association*] (EA)
NCOD........ National Coming Out Day Campaign (EA)
NCOD........ National Commission on Orphan Diseases [*Department of Health and Human Services*] (GFGA)
NCODE...... National Clearinghouse on Development Education [*Information service or system*] (IID)
NCODP...... Noncommissioned Officer Development Program [*Army*] (INF)
NCOE........ National Council for Occupational Education [*Association*] (EA)
NCOER...... Noncommissioned Officer Evaluation Report [*Army*]
NCO-ER..... Noncommissioned Officer Evaluation Reporting [*Army*] (INF)
NCOES...... Noncommissioned Officer Education System [*Military*] (AABC)
NC of A..... Newfoundland Club of America (EA)
NCOFF....... National Center on Fathers and Families [*University of Pennsylvania*] (RCD)
NCOG........ NCO Group, Inc. [*NASDAQ symbol*] (NASQ)
NcOG........ Richard H. Thornton Memorial Library, Oxford, NC [*Library symbol*] [*Library of Congress*] (LCLS)
NCOGD...... National Council for the Observance of Grandparent's Day (EA)
NCO Grp.... NCO Group, Inc. [*Associated Press*] (SAG)
NCOHC...... Northern California Occupational Health Center [*University of California*] [*Research center*] (RCD)
NCO/HPCC... National Coordination Office for High Performance Computing and Communications
NCoHS-N.... North High School, Commack, NY [*Library symbol*] [*Library of Congress*] (LCLS)
NCoHS-S.... South High School, Commack, NY [*Library symbol*] [*Library of Congress*] (LCLS)
NCOI......... National Council for the Omnibus Industry [*British*]
NCOIC....... Noncommissioned Officer-in-Charge [*Military*]
NCoIE....... Indian Hollow Elementary School, Commack, NY [*Library symbol*] [*Library of Congress*] (LCLS)
NCOIL....... National Conference of Insurance Legislators (EA)
NCOK........ North Central Oklahoma Railway [*Federal Railroad Administration identification code*]
NCOL........ National Council on Occupational Licensing [*Formerly, COL*] [*Defunct*] (EA)
NCol......... New Colophon (SAUS)
NCO Lamp.. Non-Cut-Off Lamp (SAUS)
NCOLANT... Net Control Officer, Atlantic [*Navy*] (DNAB)
NCOLCTL... National Council of Organizations of Less Commonly Taught Languages [*Association*] (EA)
NCOLG...... National Coordinating Office for Latin and Greek [*Later, NCLG*] (EA)
NColnA...... Albany Area Board of Cooperative Education Services, Colonie, NY [*Library symbol*] [*Library of Congress*] (LCLS)

NCOLP ...... Noncommissioned Officer Logistics Program [*Army*] (AABC)
NCOLS ...... Noncommissioned Officers' Leadership School [*Air Force*] (AFM)
NCOLUG .... North Carolina Online User Group (NITA)
NCOM .... NEC Computerised Operation and Maintenance System (NITA)
NCOM .... News Communications [*NASDAQ symbol*] (TTSB)
NCOM .... News Communications, Inc. [*NASDAQ symbol*] (SAG)
NCOMBL .... Noncombustible (MSA)
NCOMD ..... National Committee on the Observance of Mothers' Day [*Later, MDC*] (EA)
NCOMDR.... National Clearinghouse on Marital and Date Rape (EA)
NCOMED .... Net Control Officer, Mediterranean [*Navy*] (DNAB)
NCOMM ..... Naval Communications Command
NCOMP...... National Catholic Office for Motion Pictures [*Later, Office for Film and Broadcasting*]
NCOMR ..... National Clearinghouse on Marital Rape [*Later, NCOMDR*] (EA)
NCON........ Encon Systems [*NASDAQ symbol*] (SAG)
NCONE ...... ENCON Systems [*OTCBB symbol*]
NCoNE....... North Ridge Elementary School, Commack, NY [*Library symbol*] [*Library of Congress*] (LCLS)
NConL .... Notes on Contemporary Literature [*A publication*] (ANEX)
NCoOE....... Old Farms Elementary School, Commack, NY [*Library symbol*] [*Library of Congress*] (LCLS)
NCooHi...... New York State Historical Association, Cooperstown, NY [*Library symbol*] [*Library of Congress*] (LCLS)
NCOOM ..... Noncommissioned Officers' Open Mess [*Military*] (AFM)
NCop .... Copiague Memorial Public Library, Copiague, NY [*Library symbol*] [*Library of Congress*] (LCLS)
NCOP........ National Council on Philanthropy [*Later, IS*] (EA)
NCOP........ Network Code of Practice [*Computer science*] (GART)
NCOP........ New Choreographers On Point
NCOPA ...... National Conference of Police Associations (EA)
NCOPAC..... Net Control Officer, Pacific [*Navy*] (DNAB)
NCOPD ...... National Catholic Office for Persons with Disabilities (EA)
NCOPDP .... Noncommissioned Officer Professional Development Program [*Army*] (INF)
NCOPDR .... NCO [*Noncommissioned Officer*] Professional Development Ribbon [*Military decoration*] (GFGA)
NCOPE ...... National Council of Preservation Executives (EA)
NCOPF ...... National Council for One Parent Families [*British*]
NCOPGC .... North Central Ohio Planned Giving Council (EARSL)
NCopH....... Lakeside Hospital, Copiague, NY [*Library symbol*] [*Library of Congress*] (LCLS)
NCopHS..... Copiague High School, Copiague, NY [*Library symbol*] [*Library of Congress*] (LCLS)
NCOPP ...... National Committee on Pot Bellied Pigs [*Association*] (EA)
NCOQ........ Non-Cost of Quality (SAUS)
NCORE ...... National Center for Caribbean Coral Reef Research [*University of Miami*] (RCD)
NCoRE....... Rolling Hills Elementary School, Commack, NY [*Library symbol*] [*Library of Congress*] (LCLS)
NCorf........ Corfu Free Library, Corfu, NY [*Library symbol*] [*Library of Congress*] (LCLS)
NCorn .... Cornwall Public Library, Cornwall, NY [*Library symbol*] [*Library of Congress*] (LCLS)
NCornB...... Harvard Black Rock Forest, Cornwall, NY [*Library symbol*] [*Library of Congress*] (LCLS)
NCorni....... Corning Public Library, Corning, NY [*Library symbol*] [*Library of Congress*] (LCLS)
NCorniC..... Corning Glass Works, Corning, NY [*Library symbol*] [*Library of Congress*] (LCLS)
NCorniCC ... Corning Community College, Corning, NY [*Library symbol*] [*Library of Congress*] (LCLS)
NCorniFL.... College Center of the Finger Lakes, Corning, NY [*Library symbol*] [*Library of Congress*] (LCLS)
NCorniM .... Corning Museum of Glass, Corning, NY [*Library symbol*] [*Library of Congress*] (LCLS)
NCorniS..... Southern Tier Library System, Corning, NY [*Library symbol*] [*Library of Congress*] (LCLS)
NCort........ Cortland Free Library (SAUS)
NCort........ Cortland Free Library, Cortland, NY [*Library symbol*] [*Library of Congress*] (LCLS)
NCORT ...... National Catholic Office for Radio and Television [*Later, Office for Film and Broadcasting*]
NCortHi ..... Cortland County Historical Society, Cortland, NY [*Library symbol*] [*Library of Congress*] (LCLS)
NCortSC..... Smith-Corona Laboratory, Cortland, NY [*Library symbol*] [*Library of Congress*] (LCLS)
NCortU ...... State University of New York, College at Cortland, Cortland, NY [*Library symbol*] [*Library of Congress*] (LCLS)
NCOS........ Comite de Liaison des Organisations Non-Gouvernmentales de Developpement aupres des Communautes Europeennes [*Liaison Committee of Development Non-Governmental Organizations to the European Communities*] (EAIO)
NCOS........ National Centre for Orchestral Studies [*Goldsmiths' College*] [*British*] (CB)
NCOS........ National Commission on Space [*Terminated, 1986*] (EGAO)
NCOS........ National Commission on Superconductivity [*Presidential advisory commission*] (EGAO)
NCOS........ National Council on Stuttering (EA)
NCOS........ Non-Concurrent Operating System [*Sperry UNIVAC*]
NCOSCC.... National Central Office for the Suppression of Counterfeit Currency [*British*]
NCoSJ....... Saw Mill Junior High School, Commack, NY [*Library symbol*] [*Library of Congress*] (LCLS)
NCOSTA..... National Council of Officers of State Teachers Associations (EA)
NcOtV .... United States Veterans Administration Hospital, Oteen, NC [*Library symbol*] [*Library of Congress*] (LCLS)
NCOU........ Somincor [*Intermodal shipping container symbol*] (TVRC)
NCOVR ...... National Consortium on Violence Research
NCOWC ..... Noncommissioned Officers' Wives Club [*An association*]
NCoWE...... Wood Park Elementary School, Commack, NY [*Library symbol*] [*Library of Congress*] (LCLS)
NCOWFL.... National Center on Women and Family Law (EA)
NCOX........ North Central Oklahoma & Midlands Railway [*Federal Railroad Administration identification code*]
NCOX........ Tenneco Chemicals [*Private rail car owner code*]
NCoxHi...... Greene County Historical Society, Inc., Coxsakie, NY [*Library symbol*] [*Library of Congress*] (LCLS)
NcP.......... Given Memorial Library, Pinehurst, NC [*Library symbol*] [*Library of Congress*] (LCLS)
NCP.......... National Cancer Program [*National Institutes of Health*]
NCP.......... National Caries Program [*Public Health Service*] (GRD)
NCP.......... National Car Parks [*British*]
NCP.......... National Choreography Project
NCP.......... National Circus Project (EA)
NCP.......... National Climate Program [*Rockville, MD*] [*National Oceanic and Atmospheric Administration*]
NCP.......... National Collegiate Players (EA)
NCP.......... National Command Post (ACAE)
NCP.......... National Commission on Population (SAUS)
NCP.......... National Commission on Productivity [*Later, National Productivity Council*]
NCP.......... National Commodity-Processing Program [*Department of Agriculture*] (GFGA)
NCP.......... National Conservative Party (Finland) [*Political party*] (PSAP)
NCP.......... National Constitutional Party (Jordan) [*Political party*] (PSAP)
NCP.......... National Contingency Plan [*Hazardous wastes*] [*Environmental Protection Agency*]
NCP.......... National Convention Party [*Gambia*] [*Political party*] (PPW)
NCP.......... National Council of Psychotherapists and Hypnotherapy Register [*British*] (DBA)
NCP.......... National Council on Philanthropy [*Later, IS*]
NCP.......... National Curriculum Project
NCP.......... National Cycling Proficiency (BARN)
NCP.......... National Inventory Control Point [*Military*]
NCP.......... National Oil and Hazardous Substances Contingency Plan
NCP.......... Natural Clay Pavers (DICI)
NCP.......... Naval Capabilities Plan
NCP.......... N-Chlorothiophosphoramide [*Organic chemistry*]
NCP.......... N-Cholorpiperidine [*Organic chemistry*]
NCP.......... Neomycin, Chlorhexidine, and Polymyxin B [*Medicine*] [*Cream*] (EDAA)
NCP.......... Nepali Congress Party [*Political party*] (EY)
NCP.......... Net Combat Power
NCP.......... Net Community Productivity (FFDE)
NCP.......... Net Control Procedure
NCP.......... Netherlands and Colonial Philately
NCP.......... NetWare Core Protocol [*Computer science*]
NCP.......... Network Communications Program (TIMI)
NCP.......... Network Control Point [*Telecommunications*]
NCP.......... Network Control Processor [*Telecommunications*] (TSSD)
NCP.......... Network Control Program [*IBM Corp.*] [*Telecommunications*] (BUR)
NCP.......... Network Control Protocol [*Telecommunications*]
NCP.......... New Call to Peacemaking (EA)
NCP.......... New Communities Program [*Defunct*] (EA)
NCP.......... New Community Projects [*A publication*]
NCP.......... Nickel-Chromium Panel
NCP.......... Nitrogen Charge Panel [*Later, MRAC*] (AAG)
NCP.......... No Caffeine [*or*] Pepper (DAVI)
NCP.......... No-Copy Paper
NCP.......... Noctilucent Cloud Particles
NCP.......... Noise Control Plan (SAUS)
NCP.......... Non Carbon Paper (SAUS)
NCP.......... Noncarbon Paper (IAA)
NCP.......... Noncollagen Protein
NCP.......... Noncompliance Penalties (EEVL)
NCP.......... Noncompliance Penalty [*Environmental Protection Agency*] (EPA)
NCP.......... Non-Conformance Penalties [*Automotive emissions standards*]
NCP.......... Nonconformance Penalty (EEVL)
NCP.......... Nonconformance Pickup (SAUS)
NCP.......... Non-Consultative Party (SAUS)
NCP.......... Non-Custodial Parent
NCP.......... Non-United States Coalition Partner (DOMA)
NCP.......... Normal Circular Pitch (MSA)
NCP.......... North Celestial Pole [*Astronomy*]
NCP.......... North Central Pacific (TVEL)
NCP.......... Not Copy Protected [*Computer science*] (IGQR)
NCP.......... Nuclear Civil Protection [*Emergency Management*] (EMA)
NCP.......... Nuclear Contingency Plan (MCD)
NCP.......... Number of Channel Programs (SAUS)
NCP.......... Numerically-Controlled Peripheral (IAA)
NCP.......... Nursing Care Plan
NCP.......... Nutation Control Processor (ACAE)
NCP.......... Nutrition Center of the Philippines (SAUS)
NCP.......... Nutrition in Clinical Practice (SAUS)
NCP.......... Nuveen California Performance Plus Municipal [*NYSE symbol*] (SPSG)
NCP.......... Nuveen CA Perf Plus Muni [*NYSE symbol*] (TTSB)
NCPA .... National Center for Policy Alternatives [*Later, CPA*] (EA)
NCPA .... National Center of Policy Analysis [*Association*] (EA)
NCPA .... National Chincoteague Pony Association (EA)
NCPA .... National Coalition of Patriotic Americans (EA)

NCPA........ National Committee for the Prevention of Alcoholism and Drug Dependency [*Later,NCPADD*] (EA)
NCPA........ National Composition and Prepress Association (EA)
NCPA........ National Conservation Policy Act [*1979*]
NCPA........ National Cottonseed Products Association (EA)
NCPA........ National Crime Prevention Association [*Defunct*] (EA)
NCPA........ North Carolina Psychological Association (EARSL)
NC PAC...... National City Corporation PAC [*Cleveland, OH*] (PACS)
NCPAC....... National Conservative Political Action Committee (EA)
NCPACE..... Navy College Program for Afloat College Education
NCPAD ...... National Council on Psychological Aspects of Disability (EA)
NCPADD..... National Committee for the Prevention of Alcoholism and Drug Dependency (EA)
NCPAG ...... National CPA [*Certified Public Accountant*] Group [*Later, BKR International*] (EA)
NCPAMA .... Noise Control Product and Materials Association [*Later, NCA*] (IAA)
NCPAMT .... National Coalition of Psychiatrists Against Motorcoach Therapy (EA)
N-CPAP...... Nasal Continuous Positive Airway Pressure [*Medicine*] (DMAA)
NCPAPAC ... National Community Pharmacists Association PAC [*Alexandria, VA*] (PACS)
NCPAS....... National Computer Program Abstract Service, Inc. (IID)
NC/PAT ...... National Council for the Public Assessment of Technology [*Defunct*]
NCPB........ National Cancer Policy Board
NCPB........ Navy Council of Personnel Boards (ACAE)
NcPb......... Pinebluff Public Library, Pinebluff, NC [*Library symbol*] [*Library of Congress*] (LCLS)
NCPC........ National Cancer Pain Coalition
NCPC........ National Capital Planning Commission [*Formerly, NCPPC*]
NCPC........ National Chrysler Products Club (EA)
NCPC........ National Citizens Participation Council (EA)
NCPC........ National Coal Policy Conference [*Defunct*] (EA)
NCPC........ National Collegiate Poultry Club
NCPC........ National Crime Prevention Council (EA)
NCPC........ Naval Civilian Personnel Command (ACAE)
NCPC........ Northern Canada Power Commission (SAUS)
NCPC........ Nose Cone Protective Covering [*Aviation*]
NCPCA ...... National Center for the Prosecution of Child Abuse (EA)
NCPCA ...... National Committee for Peace in Central America [*Defunct*] (EA)
NCPCA ...... National Committee for Prevention of Child Abuse (EA)
NCPCA ...... National Committee to Prevent Child Abuse (EA)
NCPCC ...... National Clearinghouse for Poison Control Centers (EA)
NCpCE....... Cherry Lane Elementary School, Carle Place, NY [*Library symbol*] [*Library of Congress*] (LCLS)
NCPCF....... National Coalition for the Protection of Children and Families (EA)
NCPCINST... Naval Civilian Personnel Command Instructions (MCD)
NCPCO ...... National Climate Program Coordinating Office
NCPCR ...... National Center for Prevention and Control of Rape [*National Institutes of Health*]
NCPCU ...... National Council of Postal Credit Unions (NTPA)
NCPD........ National Catholic Office for Persons with Disabilities (EA)
NCPD........ Navy Current Procurement Directive
NCPDI .... National Coastal Pollutant Discharge Inventory (CARB)
NCPDM...... National Council of Physical Distribution Management
NCPDP ...... National Council for Prescription Drug Programs (EA)
NCPDS ...... Navy Civilian Personnel Data System
NCPE........ National Center on Public Education and Social Policy [*University of Rhode Island*] (RCD)
NCPE........ National Committee on Pay Equity (EA)
NCPE........ National Council for Preservation Education
NCPE........ Netware Core Protocol Extension (SAUS)
NCPE........ Noncardiac Pulmonary Edema [*Medicine*]
NCPEA....... National College Physical Education Association [*Later, NCPEAM*] (EA)
NCPEA....... National Conference of Professors of Educational Administration [*Later, NAPEHE*] (EA)
NCPEAM .... National College Physical Education Association for Men [*Later, NAPEHE*]
NCPEARL ... National Coalition for Public Education and Religious Liberty (EA)
NCPEG ...... Navy Contractor Performance Evaluation Group
NCPEP...... New Century Policies Educational Programs (EA)
NCPERL..... National Coalition for Public Education and Religious Liberty (EA)
NCPERS..... National Conference on Public Employee Retirement Systems (EA)
NcPeS....... Pembroke State University, Pembroke, NC [*Library symbol*] [*Library of Congress*] (LCLS)
NCPF........ National Council on Private Forests (EA)
NcPfO .... Olin Corp., Ecusta-Film Technical Library, Pisgah Forest, NC [*Library symbol*] [*Library of Congress*] (LCLS)
NCPG........ National Catholic Pharmacists Guild of the United States (EA)
NCPG........ National Committee on Planned Giving (NFD)
NCPG........ National Council on Problem Gambling (EA)
NCPG........ Nozzleless Center-Perforated Grain (MCD)
NCPGA ...... North Carolina Personnel and Guidance Association (SAUS)
NCPGG ...... National Center for Petroleum Geology and Geophysics [*Australia*]
NCPH........ National Council on Public History [*Database producer*] (EA)
NCPhA....... North Carolina Pharmacists Association (EARSL)
NCpHS ...... Carle Place High School, Carle Place, NY [*Library symbol*] [*Library of Congress*] (LCLS)
NCPHU ...... North Coast Public Health Unit (SAUS)
NCPI......... National Center for Postsecondary Improvement (RCD)
NCPI......... National Clay Pipe Institute (EA)
NCPI......... National Committee on Property Insurance [*Boston, MA*] (EA)
NCPI......... National Computer Program Index (IAA)
NCPI......... National Conference on Parent Involvement (EA)
NCPI......... National Crime Prevention Institute (EA)
NCPI......... Navy Civilian Personnel Instructions
NCPIE .... National Coalition for Parent Involvement in Education
NCPIE .... National Conference on Prescription Medicine Information and Education
NCPIE .... National Council of Patient Information and Education (EA)
NCPIM....... National Commission to Prevent Infant Mortality
NCPIRG ..... North Carolina Public Interest Research Group (EARSL)
NCPISA...... National Collaborative Project for Indicators of Sustainable Development (SAUS)
NCPL .... Kirkland Town Library, Clinton, NY [*Library symbol*] [*Library of Congress*] (LCLS)
NCPL .... National Center for Preservation Law (EA)
NCPL .... National Collegiate Parachuting League (EA)
NCPLA....... National Council of Patent Law Associations [*Later, NCIPLA*] (EA)
NCPLD ...... Noncoupled
NCPLF....... National Congenital Pulmonary Lymphangiectasis Foundation (NRGU)
NcPly........ Washington County Library, Plymouth, NC [*Library symbol*] [*Library of Congress*] (LCLS)
NcPlyP ...... Pettigrew Regional Library, Plymouth, NC [*Library symbol*] [*Library of Congress*] (LCLS)
NcPm........ Charles H. Stone Memorial Library, Pilot Mountain, NC [*Library symbol*] [*Library of Congress*] (LCLS)
NCPM .... National Centre for Popular Music [*England*] (WDAA)
NCPM .... National Clay Pot Manufacturers (EA)
NCPM .... National Conference of Personal Managers (EA)
NCPM .... Noncritical Phase Matching (IAA)
NCPMA...... National Clay Pot Manufacturers Association (NTPA)
NCPMA...... Noise Control Products and Materials Association [*Later, NCA*] (EA)
NCPMA...... North Carolina Petroleum Marketers Association (EARSL)
ncpn-........ Panama [*MARC geographic area code*] [*Library of Congress*] (LCCP)
NCPNFUNW... National Coalition for a Policy of No-First-Use of Nuclear Weapons (EA)
NCPO........ National Chronic Pain Outreach Association (EA)
NCPO........ National Client Protection Organization [*Association*] (EA)
NCPO........ National Climate Program Office [*National Oceanic and Atmospheric Administration*]
NCPO........ National Climate Project Office (SAUS)
NCPO........ Nordic Council for Physical Oceanography (EA)
NcPo......... United States Air Force, Pope Air Force Base, Base Library, Pope AFB, NC [*Library symbol*] [*Library of Congress*] (LCLS)
NCPOA ...... National Chief Petty Officers' Association (EA)
NCPOA ...... National Chronic Pain Outreach Association, Inc. (PAZ)
NcPolA ...... Anson Technical College, Learning Resources Center, Polk Campus, Polkton (SAUS)
NcPolA ...... Anson Technical College, Learning Resources Center, Polk Campus, Polkton, NC [*Library symbol*] [*Library of Congress*] (LCLS)
NCPP........ National Coal Policy Project
NCPP........ National Council on Public Policy (EA)
NCPP........ National Council on Public Polls (EA)
NCPP........ New Cinema Partners, Inc. [*NASDAQ symbol*] (QUAN)
NCPPA....... National Coalition for Promoting Physical Activity (MELL)
NCP PAC.... North Carolina Pork Council PAC [*Formerly known as North Carolina Pork Producers Association Inc. PAC*] [*Raleigh, NC*] (PACS)
NCPPB ...... National Collection of Plant Pathogenic Bacteria (DMAA)
NCPPC ...... National Capital Park and Planning Commission [*Later, NCPC*]
NCPPL....... Numerical Control Parts Programming Language (SAUS)
NCPPP ...... National Council for Public-Private Partnerships (EA)
NCPPR ...... National Center for Public Policy Research (EA)
NCP PU ADDR... Network Control Program Physical Unit Address [*Communications term*] (DCT)
NCP PU IDNUM... Network Control Program Physical Unit ID Number [*Communications term*] (DCT)
NCPQWL.... National Center for Productivity and Quality of Working Life [*Later, National Productivity Council*]
NCPR........ National Center for Patient's Rights (MELL)
NCPR........ National Championship Poker Run [*American Motorcyclists Association*]
NCPR........ National Congress of Petroleum Retailers [*Later, SSDA*] (EA)
NCPR........ No Cardiopulmonary Resuscitation [*For terminal patients*] (DAVI)
NCPR........ North Carolina Ports Railway [*Federal Railroad Administration identification code*]
NCpRE....... Rushmore Elementary School, Carle Place, NY [*Library symbol*] [*Library of Congress*] (LCLS)
NCPRP ...... National Coastal Pollution Research Program [*Environmental Protection Agency*] (MSC)
NCPRR ...... National Congress for Puerto Rican Rights (EA)
NCPRV ...... National Congress of Puerto Rican Veterans (EA)
NCPRV ...... National Council of Puerto Rican Volunteers [*Defunct*] (EA)
NCPS........ National Cat Protection Society (EA)
NCPS........ National Circus Preservation Society (EA)
NCPS........ National Coalition to Prevent Shoplifting (EA)
NCPS........ National Commission on Product Safety
NCPS........ National Commission on the Public Service [*Defunct*] (EA)
NCPS........ Netware Cross-Platform Services (SAUS)
NCPS........ Nigerian College of Petroleum Studies [*Kaduna, Northern Nigeria*]
NCPS........ Non-Contributory Pension Scheme (DLA)
NCPS........ North Carolina Pediatric Society (EARSL)
NCPS........ Nuclear Contingency Planning System (MCD)
NCPSA ...... National Child Passenger Safety Association [*Later, NPSA*] (EA)
NCPSA ...... National Council for Private School Accreditation [*Association*] (EA)
NCPSC ...... National Committee on Paper Stock Conservation
NCPSD ...... Normalized Cross-Power Spectral Density (SAUS)
NCPSF....... National Council of Professional Services Firms [*Later, PSC*] (EA)
NCPSIDS ... National Center for the Prevention of Sudden Infant Death Syndrome (EA)

NCPSSM.... National Committee to Preserve Social Security and Medicare (EA)
NCPT........ National Conference on Power Transmission (EA)
NCPT........ National Congress of Parents and Teachers [*Later, National PTA*] (EA)
NCPT........ Nationally-Certified Psychiatric Technician
NCPT........ Navy Central Planning Team [*NATO*] (NATG)
NCPTA....... National Confederation of Parent Teacher Associations [*British*]
NCPTCAN... National Center for the Prevention and Treatment of Child Abuse and Neglect (EA)
NCPTF....... National Campaign for a Peace Tax Fund (EA)
NCPTO...... National China Painting Teachers Organization [*Later, IPAT*] (EA)
NCPTSD..... National Center for Post Traumatic Stress Disorder (IID)
NCPTT....... National Center for Preservation Technology and Training (SAUS)
NCPTWA.... National Clearinghouse for Periodical Title Word Abbreviations [*ANSI*]
NCPU........ Navicon [*Intermodal shipping container symbol*] (TVRC)
NCPUA...... National Committee on Pesticide Use in Agriculture [*Canada*]
NCP/VS...... NCP Virtual Storage (NITA)
NCPVS...... Network Control Program Virtual Storage [*Telecommunications*] (IAA)
NCPW....... National Country Party of Western Australia [*Political party*]
NCPWB...... National Certified Pipe Welding Bureau (EA)
NCPWSF.... National Congenital Port Wine Stain Foundation (EA)
NCPY........ Penrhyn [*Cook Islands*] [*ICAO location identifier*] (ICLI)
NCPYA....... National Conference of Public Youth Agencies [*Defunct*] (EA)
NCQ.......... Marietta, GA [*Location identifier*] [*FAA*] (FAAL)
NCQA........ National Committee for Quality Assurance (EA)
NCQHC...... National Committee for Quality Health Care (EA)
NCQIE....... National Coalition for Quality Integrated Education (EA)
NCQR........ National Council for Quality and Reliabiltiy [*British*] (BI)
NCQU........ Northbrook Container Leasing [*Intermodal shipping container symbol*] (TVRC)
NCR.......... Air Sur [*Spain*] [*ICAO designator*] (FAAC)
NCR.......... National Capital Region
NCR.......... National Cash Register [*Computer science*] (NADA)
NCR.......... National Cash Register Co. [*Later, NCR Corp.*] [*Computer manufacturer*]
NCR.......... National Civic Review [*A publication*] (BRI)
NCR.......... National Coalition for Research in Neurological and Communicative Disorders (EA)
NCR.......... National Coalition for Research in Neurological Disorders (EA)
NCR.......... National Council of Resistance for Liberty and Independence [*Iran*] (PD)
NCR.......... Naval Construction Regiment (NVT)
NCR.......... Navy Code Room
NCR.......... Ncane [*Language symbol*] (ETLW)
NCR.......... NCR Corp. [*NYSE symbol*] (SG)
NCR.......... Network Change Request [*NASA*] (KSC)
NCR.......... Network Control Room [*Television*]
NCR.......... Neutrophil Complement Rosettes [*Hematology*]
NCR.......... New Carrollton, MD [*Amtrak rail station code*]
NCR.......... New Christian Right (SAUS)
NCR.......... New Cinema Review [*A publication*]
N Cr......... New York Criminal Reports [*A publication*] (DLA)
NCR.......... Nickerson, C. R., San Francisco CA [*STAC*]
NCR.......... Nicorandil [*Biochemistry*]
NCR.......... Nippon Cataloguing Rules (SAUS)
NCR.......... Nitrile-Chloroprene Rubber
NCR.......... No Calibration Required (MCD)
NCR.......... No Canadian Rights
NCR.......... No Carbon Required (NG)
NCR.......... No Circuit Request (SAUS)
NCR.......... Noncoding Region [*Genetics*]
NCR.......... Non-Combat Ready [*Military*] (SAA)
NCR.......... Non-Combustible Residue [*Automotive engineering*]
NCR.......... Non-Communist Resistance (SAUS)
NCR.......... Noncompliance Report [*Environmental Protection Agency*] (EPA)
NCR.......... Non-Compliance request (SAUS)
NCR.......... Nonconformance Record [*NASA*] (KSC)
NCR.......... Nonconformance Report [*Nuclear energy*] (NRCH)
NCR.......... Non-Conforming Reports (SAUS)
NCR.......... Nonconserved Region [*Genetics*]
NCR.......... Non-Selective Catalyst Reduction [*Diesel engine emissions*]
NCR.......... Normotensive Control (DB)
NCR.......... North Carolina Register [*A publication*] (AAGC)
NCR.......... Northern Capital Region (SAUS)
NCR.......... Northern Central Railway [*British*] (ROG)
NCR.......... Not Combat Ready (SAUS)
NCR.......... Notification of Change Report (NRCH)
NCR.......... Nucal Resources Ltd. [*Vancouver Stock Exchange symbol*]
NCR.......... Nuclear (AAG)
NCR.......... Nuclear Cytoplasmic Ratio [*Cytology*]
NCR.......... Number of Collisions Register (SAUS)
NCR.......... Ontario Library Service - Voyageur [*UTLAS symbol*]
NcR.......... Wake County Public Libraries, Raleigh, NC [*Library symbol*] [*Library of Congress*] (LCLS)
NCR3........ National Center for Remanufacturing and Resource Recovery [*Rochester Institute of Technology*] (RCD)
NcRa........ Hoke County Public Library, Raeford, NC [*Library symbol*] [*Library of Congress*] (LCLS)
NCRA........ National Cancer Registrar's Association (NTPA)
NCRA........ National Cellular Resellers' Association (EA)
NCRA........ National Center on Rural Aging (EA)
NCRA........ National Championship Racing Association [*Auto racing*]
NCRA........ National Coalition of Redevelopment Agencies (EA)
NCRA........ National Coal Resource Assessment
NCRA........ National Cooperative Refinery Association [*Commercial firm*] (EA)
NCRA........ National Cooperative Research Act [*1984*]
NCRA........ National Correctional Recreational Association (EA)
NCRA........ National Council of Research Administrators
NCRA........ National Court Reporters Association
NCRA........ National Crew and Rowing Association (PSS)
NCRA........ North Carolina Restaurant Association (EARSL)
NCRAC...... National Community Relations Advisory Council [*Later, NJCRAC*] (EA)
NCRB........ North Campus Recreation Building (SAUS)
NCRC........ National Calibration Reference Centre for In Vivo Monitoring [*Health Canada*] (RCD)
NCRC........ National Catholic Resettlement Council (EA)
NCRC........ National Cave Rescue Commission
NCRC........ National Climate Research Committee (QUAC)
NCRC........ National Committee for a Representative Congress (EA)
NCRC........ National Community Reinvestment Coalition
NCRC........ Nebraska Central Railroad [*Federal Railroad Administration identification code*]
NCRC........ Nephrology Clinical Research Center [*University of Virginia*] (RCD)
NCRC........ Nickel-Cadmium Rechargeable Cell
NCRC........ Non-Child-Resistant Container (MELL)
NcR-C....... Wake County Public Libraries, Cameron Village Regional Library, Raleigh, NC [*Library symbol*] [*Library of Congress*] (LCLS)
NCRC/AODA... National Certification Reciprocity Consortium/Alcoholism and Other Drug Abuse (EA)
NCRCH...... Nordic Committee of the Research Councils for the Humanities (EA)
NcRCPL..... Carolina Power & Light Co., Technical Library, Raleigh, NC [*Library symbol*] [*Library of Congress*] (LCLS)
NCRCRD.... North Central Regional Center for Rural Development [*Iowa State University*] [*Research center*] (RCD)
NCRD........ National Council on Resource Development (EA)
NCRD........ National Council to Repeal the Draft [*Defunct*] (EA)
NCRDA...... National Center for Research into Drug Abuse [*Australia*]
NCRDC...... National Capital Region, District of Columbia (MCD)
NcRDC...... North Carolina Department of Corrections, Central Prison School, Raleigh, NC [*Library symbol*] [*Library of Congress*] (LCLS)
NCRDC...... Northern Colorado Research-Demonstration Center [*Colorado State University*] [*Research center*] (RCD)
NcRDD...... North Carolina Department of Human Resources, Dorothea Dix Hospital, F. T. Fuller Staff Library, Raleigh, NC [*Library symbol*] [*Library of Congress*] (LCLS)
NCRDL...... Nautical Charting Research and Development Laboratory [*National Oceanic and Atmospheric Administration*]
NCR-DNA... Corp-Distributed Network Architecture [*Communications term*] (DCT)
NCRDP...... Nimba County Rural Development Plan (SAUS)
NCRDS...... National Coal Resources Data System [*Geological Survey*] [*Databank*] [*Information service or system*] (IID)
NCRDTA..... National Council of Refuse Disposal Trade Associations
NCRE........ National Conference on Research in English (EA)
NCRE........ National Council on Rehabilitation Education (EA)
NCRE........ Naval Construction Research Establishment [*British*] (AAG)
NCRE........ Noncephalic Reference Electrode [*Medicine*] (EDAA)
NCREE....... National Center for Research in Earthquake Engineering [*Emergency Management*] (EMA)
NC Reg...... North Carolina Register [*A publication*] (AAGC)
NcReH....... Annie Penn Hospital, Medical Library, Reidsville, NC [*Library symbol*] [*Library of Congress*] (LCLS)
NCREIF...... National Council of Real Estate Investment Fiduciaries (EA)
NCREL....... North Central Regional Educational Laboratory [*Elmhurst, IL*] [*Department of Education*] (GRD)
NC Rep...... North Carolina Reports [*A publication*] (DLA)
NC Rep Appendix... North Carolina Reports, Appendix [*A publication*] (DLA)
NC Reports... North Carolina Reports [*A publication*] (DLA)
NcRf......... Eden Public Library, Eden, NC [*Library symbol*] [*Library of Congress*] (LCLS)
NCRF........ National Court Reporters Foundation
NcR-F....... Wake County Public Libraries, Fuquay-Varina Public Library, Fuquay-Varina, NC [*Library symbol*] [*Library of Congress*] (LCLS)
NCRFCL..... National Commission on Reform of Federal Criminal Laws
NCRFP...... National Council for a Responsible Firearms Policy [*Defunct*] (EA)
NCRFRA..... National Committee to Repeal the Federal Reserve Act (EA)
NCRFSCU... National Commission on the Role and Future of State Colleges and Universities [*Defunct*] (EA)
NCRG........ Avarua/Rarotonga International [*Cook Islands*] [*ICAO location identifier*] (ICLI)
NcrGI........ TIGR [*The Institute of Genomic Research*] Neurospora crassa Gene Index [*Database*] (GDD)
NcRGM...... North Carolina Department of Human Resources, The Governor Morehead School, Raleigh, NC [*Library symbol*] [*Library of Congress*] (LCLS)
NcRGP...... State of North Carolina, Governor's Press Office State Capital Building, Raleigh, NC [*Library symbol*] [*Library of Congress*] (LCLS)
NcRGS...... Church of Jesus Christ of Latter-Day Saints, Genealogical Society Library, Raleigh Branch, Raleigh, NC [*Library symbol*] [*Library of Congress*] (LCLS)
NCRH........ National Center for Radiological Health [*Public Health Service*]
NCRH........ National Conference on Rural Health [*Medicine*] (EDAA)
NCRH........ North Coast Railroad Historical Society (EA)
NcRH........ W. W. Holding Technical Institute, Raleigh, NC [*Library symbol*] [*Library of Congress*] (LCLS)
NCRHI....... National Council for Reliable Health Information (SAUS)
NcRHR...... North Carolina Department of Human Resources, Public Health Library, Raleigh, NC [*Library symbol*] [*Library of Congress*] (LCLS)
NCRI......... National Center for Resource Innovations

NCRI National Coastal Resources Research and Development Institute [*Newport, OR*] [*Department of Commerce*] (GRD)
NCRI National Consumer Research Institute (EA)
NCRI National Coral Reef Institute [*Nova Southeastern University*] (RCD)
NCRIB Naval Communications Improvement Review Board (DNAB)
NCRIC National Chemical Response and Information Center [*Established by the Chemical Manufacturers Association to provide information and advice during emergencies*]
NCRICT Northern China Research Institute of Computer Technology (SAUS)
NCRIPTAL National Center for Research to Improve Postsecondary Teaching and Learning [*Ann Arbor, MI*] [*Department of Education*] (GRD)
NCRIS National Committee to Restore Internal Security (EA)
NcRJP Jaakko Poyry, Inc., Raleigh, NC [*Library symbol*] [*Library of Congress*] (LCLS)
NCRK Rakahanga [*Cook Islands*] [*ICAO location identifier*] (ICLI)
NCRL National Canners Association Research Laboratory
NCRL National Citizens Radio League (IAA)
NCRLC National Catholic Rural Life Conference (EA)
NCRLC National Committee on Regional Library Cooperation
NCRLL National Conference on Research in Language and Literacy (NTPA)
NCRLS National Committee for Russian Language Study [*American Association for the Advancement of Slavic Studies*] (EDAC)
NCRLS National Committee of Religious Leaders of Safety (EA)
NcRM Meredith College, Raleigh, NC [*Library symbol*] [*Library of Congress*] (LCLS)
NCRM National Conference on Radiation Measurements
NCRM Nordic Council for Railway Music (EA)
NcRm Thomas Hackney Braswell Memorial Library, Rocky Mount, NC [*Library symbol*] [*Library of Congress*] (LCLS)
NcRMA North Carolina Museum of Art in Raleigh, Raleigh, NC [*Library symbol*] [*Library of Congress*] (LCLS)
NcRMC Meredith College, Raleigh, NC [*Library symbol*] [*Library of Congress*] (LCLS)
NCRMD National Capital Region, Maryland (MCD)
NcRmE Edgecombe Technical College, Learning Resources Center, Rocky Mount, NC [*Library symbol*] [*Library of Congress*] (LCLS)
NcRMG Measurements Group, Inc., Raleigh, NC [*Library symbol*] [*Library of Congress*] (LCLS)
NcRmHE Area L AHEC Library, Rocky Mount, NC [*Library symbol*] [*Library of Congress*] (LCLS)
NcRmN Nash Technical Institute, Rocky Mount, NC [*Library symbol*] [*Library of Congress*] (LCLS)
NcRMNH North Carolina State Museum of Natural History, Raleigh, NC [*Library symbol*] [*Library of Congress*] (LCLS)
NcRMNH-B North Carolina State Museum of Natural History, H. H. Brimley Memorial Library, Raleigh, NC [*Library symbol*] [*Library of Congress*] (LCLS)
NcRmW North Carolina Wesleyan College, Rocky Mount, NC [*Library symbol*] [*Library of Congress*] (LCLS)
NCRND National Committee for Research in Neurological Disorders [*Later, NCR*] (EA)
NCRNE National Campaign for Real Nursery Education [*United Kingdom*] (EAIO)
NcRNO News and Observer Publishing Co., Raleigh, NC [*Library symbol*] [*Library of Congress*] (LCLS)
NcRNR North Carolina Department of Natural Resources and Community Development, Raleigh, NC [*Library symbol*] [*Library of Congress*] (LCLS)
NCRNT National Committee for Rescue from NAZI Terror [*British*]
NcRo Rockingham-Richmond County Library, Rockingham, NC [*Library symbol*] [*Library of Congress*] (LCLS)
NcRob Bemis Memorial Library, Robbinsville, NC [*Library symbol*] [*Library of Congress*] (LCLS)
NCROBOT Numerically Controlled Robot (SAUS)
NcRobS Snowbird Community Library, Robbinsville, NC [*Library symbol*] [*Library of Congress*] (LCLS)
NCroh Croton Free Library, Croton-On-Hudson, NY [*Library symbol*] [*Library of Congress*] (LCLS)
NCrohH Hudson Institute, Croton-On-Hudson, NY [*Library symbol*] [*Library of Congress*] (LCLS)
NcRop Roper Community Library and Resource Center, Inc., Roper, NC [*Library symbol*] [*Library of Congress*] (LCLS)
NCROPA National Campaign for the Reform of the Obscene Publications Acts [*British*] (DBA)
NcRoS Sandhills Regional Library, Rockingham, NC [*Library symbol*] [*Library of Congress*] (LCLS)
NcRov Robersonville Public Library, Robersonville, NC [*Library symbol*] [*Library of Congress*] (LCLS)
NcRox Person County Public Library, Roxboro, NC [*Library symbol*] [*Library of Congress*] (LCLS)
NcRoxP Person Technical Institute, Roxboro, NC [*Library symbol*] [*Library of Congress*] (LCLS)
NCRP National Climatic Research Program
NCRP National Commission on Radiological Protection
NCRP National Committee for Responsible Patriotism (EA)
NCRP National Committee for Responsive Philanthropy (EA)
NCRP National Corrections Reporting Program Series [*Database*] (GDD)
NCRP National Council for Research and Planning (EA)
NCRP National Council on Radiation Protection (LDOE)
NCRP National Council on Radiation Protection and Measurements [*Later, NCRPM*]
NCRP Non-Compulsory Reporting Point (PIPO)
NCRP Non-Residential Conditional Purchase (SAUS)
NcRP Peace College, Raleigh, NC [*Library symbol*] [*Library of Congress*] (LCLS)
NCR paper No Carbon Required Paper
NCRPC National Capital Regional Planning Council [*Terminated, 1966*]
NCRPCV National Council of Returned Peace Corps Volunteers (EA)
NCRPDA National Centre for Research into the Prevention of Drug Abuse (SAUS)
NCRPE National Council on Religion and Public Education (EA)
NcRPI North Carolina Department of Public Instruction, Education Information Services, Raleigh, NC [*Library symbol*] [*Library of Congress*] (LCLS)
NCRPM National Council on Radiation Protection and Measurements (EA)
NCRPS Non-Contact Rotary Position Sensor [*Automotive engineering*]
NCRPS North Carolina Recreation and Park Society (EARSL)
NcRPS Pointer & Spruill Library, Raleigh, NC [*Library symbol*] [*Library of Congress*] (LCLS)
NCRR National Center for Research Resources [*National Institutes of Health*]
NCRR National Center for Resource Recovery [*Defunct*]
NCRR National Credit Union Administration Rules and Regulations
NCRR Nordic Council of Reindeer Research (EAIO)
NCRR North Coast Railroad [*Federal Railroad Administration identification code*]
NcRr Roanoke Rapids Public Library, Roanoke Rapids, NC [*Library symbol*] [*Library of Congress*] (LCLS)
NCRRC National Committee to Reopen the Rosenberg Case (EA)
NCRRF Norris Communications Corp. [*NASDAQ symbol*] (SAG)
NcRRH Rex Hospital Library, Raleigh, NC [*Library symbol*] [*Library of Congress*] (LCLS)
NCRRHA National Confederation of Registered Rest Home Associations [*British*] (DBA)
NCRRRC North Country Reference and Research Resources Council [*Information service or system*] (IID)
NCRS National Clearinghouse on Revenue Sharing [*Defunct*]
NCRS National Committee for Radiation Safety [*Medicine*] (EDAA)
NCRS National Committee for Rural Schools [*Defunct*] (EA)
NCRS National Corvette Restorers Society (EA)
NcRS North Carolina State University at Raleigh, Raleigh, NC [*Library symbol*] [*Library of Congress*] (LCLS)
NCRSA National Commercial Refrigeration Sales Association (EA)
NcRSA Saint Augustine's College, Raleigh, NC [*Library symbol*] [*Library of Congress*] (LCLS)
NcRSh Shaw University, Raleigh, NC [*Library symbol*] [*Library of Congress*] (LCLS)
NcRSM Saint Mary's Junior College, Raleigh, NC [*Library symbol*] [*Library of Congress*] (LCLS)
NcRS-P North Carolina State University at Raleigh, Photocopy Services, Raleigh, NC [*Library symbol*] [*Library of Congress*] (LCLS)
NCR SPTG National Capital Regional Support Group [*Air Force*] (POLM)
NCRSR National Congenital Rubella Syndrome Registry [*Centers for Disease Control*]
NcRS-V North Carolina State University, School of Veterinary Medicine, Raleigh, NC [*Library symbol*] [*Library of Congress*] (LCLS)
NCRT National College of Rubber Technology (PDAA)
NCRTE National Center for Research on Teacher Education [*East Lansing, MI*] [*Department of Education*] (GRD)
NCRTM National Clearinghouse of Rehabilitation Training Materials [*Oklahoma State University*] (IID)
NCR/TSI NCR Telecommunication Services, Inc. (TSSD)
NcRu Norris Public Library, Rutherfordton, NC [*Library symbol*] [*Library of Congress*] (LCLS)
NCRU North American Container System-Transamerica [*Intermodal shipping container symbol*] (TVRC)
NCRUCE National Conference of Regulatory Utility Commission Engineers (EA)
NcRuR Rutherford County Library, Inc., Rutherfordton, NC [*Library symbol*] [*Library of Congress*] (LCLS)
NCRV National Committee for Radiation Victims (EA)
NCRVA National Capital Region, Virginia (MCD)
NCRVD National Conference of Religious Vocation Directors [*Later, NRVC*] (EA)
NCRVDM National Conference of Religious Vocation Directors of Men [*Later, NCRVD*] (EA)
NCRVE National Center for Research in Vocational Education (EA)
NCRW National Council for Research on Women (EA)
NCRW Neutralized Cladding Removal Waste (ABAC)
NCRW Nuclear Cladding Removal Waste (SAUS)
NcRWCM Wake County Hospital System, Wake County Medical Center, Raleigh, NC [*Library symbol*] [*Library of Congress*] (LCLS)
NcRWHD Wake County Health Department, Raleigh, NC [*Library symbol*] [*Library of Congress*] (LCLS)
NCRWS National Campaign for Radioactive Waste Safety (EA)
NCRY National Commission on Resources for Youth
NCS INMARSAT Network Coordination Station (SAUS)
NCS National Cancer Survey [*Medicine*] (EDAA)
NCS National Cartoonists Society (EA)
NCS National Cemetery System
NCS National Center for Stuttering (EA)
NCS National Chrysanthemum Society (EA)
NCS National Cockatiel Society (EA)
NCS National Collaborative Study [*Medicine*] (EDAA)
NCS National Commemorative Society [*Defunct*]
NCS National Committee on Safety
NCS National Communications System [*DoD*]
NCS National Compliance Strategy (GNE)
NCS National Computer Services
NCS National Computer Systems, Inc.
NCS National Conference of States on Building Codes and Standards, Inc.
NCS National Conference on Solicitations (EA)
NCS National Consensus Standards (MCD)

NCS.......... National Conservation Strategy (GNE)
NCS.......... National Convenience Stores, Inc. [*NYSE symbol*] (SPSG)
NCS.......... National Corrosion Service [*British*] (IRUK)
NCS.......... National Council of Stutterers [*Later, NCOS*] (EA)
NCS.......... National Crime Squad (WDAA)
NCS.......... National Crime Stoppers [*Later, ACF*] (EA)
NCS.......... National Crime Survey [*University of Michigan*] [*Database*]
NCS.......... National Cryptologic School [*National Security Agency*]
NCS.......... Nationwide Cellular Service, Inc. (EFIS)
NCS.......... NATO Codification System (SAUS)
NCS.......... Naval Canteen Service [*British military*] (DMA)
NCS.......... Naval Combat System (SAUS)
NCS.......... Naval Communications Station [*or System*]
NCS.......... Naval Compass Stabilizer (PDAA)
NCS.......... Naval Control of Shipping [*NATO*] (NATG)
NCS.......... Navigational Computer Set (MCD)
NCS.......... Navigation Control Simulator
NCS.......... N-Chlorosuccinimide [*Organic chemistry*]
NCS.......... NCI Building Systems [*NYSE symbol*] (SG)
NCS.......... NCR [*NCR Corp.*] Century Software
NCS.......... Nearest Cross Street (ADA)
NCS.......... Needlework and Craft Showcase (ITD)
NCS.......... Neocarzinostatin [*Zinostatin*] [*Antineoplastic drug*]
NCS.......... NERC Computing Service (SAUS)
NCS.......... Nerve Conduction Studies [*Neurology*] (DAVI)
NCS.......... Net Control Station [*Communications*] [*Amateur radio*]
NCS.......... Network and Communications Services [*McGill University*] (IID)
NCS.......... Network Clock Signal (CCCA)
NCS.......... Network Communications Server [*J & L Information Systems*]
NCS.......... Network Communication Standard (AAEL)
NCS.......... Network Communication System (IAA)
NCS.......... Network Computer System (ACAE)
NCS.......... Network Computing System [*Computer science*] (AGLO)
NCS.......... Network Control Station (IAA)
NCS.......... Network Control System
NCS.......... Network Coordination Station
NCS.......... Network Co-ordination System (NITA)
NCS.......... Newborn Calf Serum [*Immunology*]
NCS.......... Newcastle [*South Africa*] [*Airport symbol*] (OAG)
NCS.......... New Concept Sedan [*Automotive engineering*]
NCS.......... Nielsen Coverage Service [*A.C. Nielson Co.*] (DOAD)
NCS.......... Nineteenth Century Series [*A publication*]
NCS.......... NMIC [*National Military Intelligence Center*] Control Subsystem
NCS.......... No Checking Signal [*Telecommunications*] (TEL)
NCS.......... No Concentrated Sweets [*Medicine*] (DMAA)
NCS.......... Node Centre Switch (SAUS)
NCS.......... Noncallable Security [*Investment term*]
NCS.......... Noncircumferential Stenosis [*Medicine*] (DMAA)
NCS.......... Non-Collimated Source (PDAA)
NCS.......... Non-Conventional System [*Post coordinate indexing*] (NITA)
NCS.......... Noncoronary Sinus [*Cardiology*] (AAMN)
NCS.......... Noncritical Sensitive [*DoD*]
NCS.......... Noncrystalline Solid [*Physics*]
NCS.......... Noncrystallographic Symmetry [*Chemistry*]
NCS.......... Nonwater Cooling System
NCS.......... North Carolina State (SAUS)
NCS.......... North Carolina State Library, Raleigh, NC [*OCLC symbol*] (OCLC)
NCS.......... Northern Cross Society (EA)
NCS.......... Northwest Communication System (SAUS)
NCS.......... Norwegian Certification System (SAUS)
NCS.......... Norwegian Continental Shelf (RIMS)
NCS.......... Nuclear-Chicago Solubilizer
NCS.......... Nuclear Components Spare (IAA)
NCS.......... Nuclear Components Spares (SAUS)
NCS.......... Nuclear Criticality Safety (NRCH)
NCS.......... Nuclear-Powered Container Ship (PDAA)
NCS.......... Nucleolar Channel System
NCS.......... Nucleus Support Crew [*Navy*] (DNAB)
NCS.......... Nueva Concepcion [*El Salvador*] [*Seismograph station code, US Geological Survey*] [*Closed*] (SEIS)
NCS.......... Numerical Category Scaling
NCS.......... Numerical Control Society [*Later, NCS/AIMTECH*] (EA)
NCS.......... Numerical Control System (IAA)
NCS.......... Nutation Control System (MCD)
NCS.......... Simmons Adult Study [*Database*] (GDD)
NCS.......... Simpson Air Ltd. [*Canada*] [*ICAO designator*] (FAAC)
NCSA........ National Capital Speakers Association (EA)
NCSA........ National Carl Schurz Association [*Defunct*] (EA)
NCSA........ National Center for Statistics and Analysis [*National Highway Traffic Safety Administration*] [*Washington, DC*] (GRD)
NCSA........ National Center for Supercomputer Applications (NITA)
NCSA........ National Center for Supercomputing Applications [*University of Illinois*] [*National Science Foundation*] [*Research center*] (RCD)
NCSA........ National Church Secretaries Association [*Defunct*] (EA)
NCSA........ National Club Sports Association (EA)
NCSA........ National Coffee Service Association [*Vienna, VA*] (EA)
NCSA........ National Collegiate Ski Association (EA)
NCSA........ National Committee for Senior Americans (EA)
NCSA........ National Committee of State Associations
NCSA........ National Computational Science Alliance [*Supercomputing center*]
NCSA........ National Computer Security Association [*Computer science*] (PCM)
NCSA........ National Confectionery Salesmen's Association of America (EA)
NCSA........ National Construction Software Association (EA)
NCSA........ National Contract Sweepers Association [*Later, NCSI*] (EA)
NCSA........ National Council of Seamen's Agencies [*Later, ICOSA*] (EA)
NCSA........ National Crushed Stone Association [*Later, NSA*] (EA)
NCSA........ National Cued Speech Association (EA)
NCSA........ National Customer Service Association (SAUS)
NCSA........ National Customs Service Association [*Later, NTEU*] (EA)
NCSA........ National Strength and Conditioning Association
NCSA........ Navajo-Churro Sheep Association (EA)
NCSA........ Newsagency Council of South Australia
NCSA........ Newspaper Collectors Society of America (EA)
NCSA........ No Charge Storage Agreement (AAGC)
NCSA........ Non-Chemical Shift Anisotropy [*Physical chemistry*]
NCSA........ Noncommercial Spot Announcement [*Public service announcement*] (NTCM)
NCSA........ North Carolina School of the Arts (SAUS)
NCSA........ North Carolina Sheriffs' Association (EARSL)
NCSA........ North Coast of South America (SAUS)
NCSAB...... National Council of State Agencies for the Blind (EA)
NCSABMT... National Campaign to Save the ABM [*Antiballistic missile*] Treaty [*Defunct*] (EA)
NcSaC....... Central Carolina Technical Institute, Sanford, NC [*Library symbol*] [*Library of Congress*] (LCLS)
NCSAC...... National Catholic Social Action Conference [*Defunct*] (EA)
NCSAC...... National Child Support Advocacy Coalition (EA)
NCSAC...... Nuclear Cross Sections Advisory Committee
NcSaCi..... Cilco, Sanford, NC [*Library symbol*] [*Library of Congress*] (LCLS)
NCSAG...... Nuclear Cross Section Advisory Group (NRCH)
NCS/AIMTECH... Numerical Control Society/AIMTECH [*Association for Integrated Manufacturing Technology*] (EA)
NcSaL....... Lee County Library, Sanford, NC [*Library symbol*] [*Library of Congress*] (LCLS)
NcSal........ Rowan Public Library, Salisbury, NC [*Library symbol*] [*Library of Congress*] (LCLS)
NcSalC...... Catawba College, Salisbury, NC [*Library symbol*] [*Library of Congress*] (LCLS)
NcSaLCL.... Lee County Library, Sanford, NC [*Library symbol*] [*Library of Congress*] (LCLS)
NcSal-E..... Rowan Public Library East Branch, Rockwell, NC [*Library symbol*] [*Library of Congress*] (LCLS)
NcSalL...... Livingstone College, Salisbury, NC [*Library symbol*] [*Library of Congress*] (LCLS)
NcSalR...... Rowan Technical Institute, Salisbury, NC [*Library symbol*] [*Library of Congress*] (LCLS)
NcSalRH.... Rowan Memorial Hospital Area, Health Education Center, Salisbury, NC [*Library symbol*] [*Library of Congress*] (LCLS)
NcSal-S..... Rowan Public Library, South Rowan Branch, Landis, NC [*Library symbol*] [*Library of Congress*] (LCLS)
NcSalTM.... Tri-County Mental Health Center, Salisbury, NC [*Library symbol*] [*Library of Congress*] (LCLS)
NcSalVA..... United States Veterans Administration Center, Medical Library, Salisbury, NC [*Library symbol*] [*Library of Congress*] (LCLS)
NCSAnet..... [*The*] National Center for Supercomputing Applications Network [*Computer science*] (TNIG)
NCSAP...... National Council for Single Adoptive Parents (EA)
NCSASR..... National Center for Small-Angle Scattering Research [*Oak Ridge, TN*] [*Department of Energy*] (GRD)
NCSAW...... National Catholic Society for Animal Welfare [*Later, ISAR*] (EA)
NCSB........ National Centre for School Biotechnology (AIE)
NCSBA...... North Carolina School Boards Association (SAUS)
NCSBCS..... National Conference of States on Building Codes and Standards (EA)
NCSBEE..... National Council of State Boards of Engineering Examiners [*Later, NCEE*] (EA)
NCSBI....... National Council for Small Business Innovation
NcSbJ....... North Carolina Justice Academy, Salemburg, NC [*Library symbol*] [*Library of Congress*] (LCLS)
NCSBMD.... National Council for Small Business Management Development [*Later, ICSB*] (EA)
NCSBN...... National Council of State Boards of Nursing (EA)
NCSBN...... National Council of State Boards of Nursing, Inc.
NcSbP....... Southwood College, Salemburg, NC [*Library symbol*] [*Library of Congress*] (LCLS)
NCSC........ National Cargo Security Council [*Association*] (EA)
NCSC........ National Catholic Stewardship Council (EA)
NCSC........ National Center for Schools and Communities [*Fordham University*] (RCD)
NCSC........ National Center for State Courts (EA)
NCSC........ National Certified School Counselor (SEAT)
NCSC........ National Child Safety Council (EA)
NCSC........ National Communications Security Committee (ACAE)
NCSC........ National Communication System Circulars
NCSC........ National Computer Security Center (IGQR)
NCSC........ National Computer Security Council
NCSC........ National Council of Senior Citizens (EA)
NCSC........ National Council on Schoolhouse Construction [*Later, CEFP*] (EA)
NCSC........ Naval Coastal Systems Center [*Panama City, FL*]
NCSC........ Navy Command Support Center (MCD)
NCSC........ Neighborhood Community Service Centers
NCSC........ Neural Crest Stem Cell
NCSC........ North Carolina State College
Nc-SC....... North Carolina State Supreme Court, Raleigh, NC [*Library symbol*] [*Library of Congress*] (LCLS)
NCSC........ North Carolina Supercomputing Center (SAUS)
NCSC........ North Central Superpave Center [*Purdue University*] (RCD)
NCSC........ Nuclear Criticality Safety Committee (SAUS)
NCSCBHEP... National Center for the Study of Collective Bargaining in Higher Education and the Professions (EA)

NCSCC ...... National Championship Stock Car Racing [*Later, NASCAR*]
NCSCCY ..... National Council of State Committees for Children and Youth (EA)
NCSCEE ..... National Council of State Consultants in Elementary Education [*Defunct*] (EA)
NCSCI .... National Center for Standards and Certification Information [*Gaithersburg, MD*] [*Database*] [*National Institute of Standards and Technology*]
NCSCJ .... National Conference of Special Court Judges (EA)
NCSCJPA ... National Conference of State Criminal Justice Planning Administrators [*Later, NCJA*] (EA)
NCSCL .... National Committee for Sexual Civil Liberties (EA)
NcScn .... Scotland Neck Memorial Library, Scotland Neck, NC [*Library symbol*] [*Library of Congress*] (LCLS)
NCSCPAS ... National Center for the Study of Corporal Punishment and Alternatives in the Schools (EA)
NCSCR ...... North Carolina State College Reactor
NCSCS ...... Non-compressive Spinal Cord Syndrome [*Medicine*] (EDAA)
NCSCT .... National Center for School and College Television
NCSD .... National Child Safety Development [*British*]
NCSD .... National Council on Student Development (EA)
NCSDCJC ... National Council of State Directors of Community Junior Colleges (NTPA)
NCS/DISA-GOSC... NCS/Defense Information Systems Agency-Global Operations Security Center [*Emergency Management*] (EMA)
NCSDR ...... National Commission on Sleep Disorders Research
NCSE .... National Center for Science Education (EA)
NCSE .... National Commission on Safety Education [*Defunct*] (EA)
NCSE .... National Committee on Secondary Education [*of NASSP*]
NCSE .... National Council for Special Education [*British*]
NCSE .... Nonconvulsive Status Epilepticus [*Medicine*] (MELL)
NCSE .... North Carolina Society of Engineers (SAUS)
NcSe .... Selma Public Library, Selma, NC [*Library symbol*] [*Library of Congress*] (LCLS)
NCSEA .... National Child Support Enforcement Association (EA)
NCSEA .... National Community School Education Association [*Later, NCEA*] (EA)
NCSEA .... National Council of State Education Associations (EA)
NCSEA .... National Council of Structural Engineers Associations (EA)
NcSEA .... North Carolina Society of Enrolled Agents (SAUS)
NCSEE .... National Coalition for Sex Equity in Education (EA)
NCSEER ..... National Council for Soviet and East European Research (EA)
NCSEES ..... Nordic Committee for Soviet and East European Studies (EA)
NCSEMSTC... National Council of State Emergency Medical Services Training Coordinators (EA)
NC Sess Laws... Session Laws of North Carolina [*A publication*] (DLA)
NCSEX .... Naval Control of Shipping Exercises
NCSF .... National Catholic Society of Foresters (EA)
NCSF .... National Cold Storage Federation [*British*] (DBA)
NCSF .... National College Student Foundation [*Defunct*] (EA)
NCSFA .... National Conference of State Fleet Administrators (EA)
NCSFI .... National Coalition to Stop Food Irradiation (EA)
NCSFP .... National Council on Synthetic Fuels Production [*Later, CSF*] (EA)
NCSFWI ..... National Coalition to Stop Food and Water Irradiation (EA)
NCSG .... National Carcinoid Support Group, Inc. (NRGU)
NCSG .... National Chimney Sweep Guild (EA)
NCSGC ...... National Council of State Garden Clubs (EA)
NCSGC ...... North Carolina Space Grant Consortium (RCD)
NCSGSO .... National Conference of State General Service Officers [*Later, NASDAGS*] (EA)
NcSh .... Cleveland County Memorial Library, Shelby, NC [*Library symbol*] [*Library of Congress*] (LCLS)
NCsh .... Cold Spring Harbor Public Library, Cold Spring Harbor, NY [*Library symbol*] [*Library of Congress*] (LCLS)
NCSH .... National Clearinghouse for Smoking and Health [*Public Health Service*]
NCSH .... Newton College of the Sacred Heart [*Later, Newton College*] [*Massachusetts*]
NCSHA ...... National Council of State Housing Agencies (NTPA)
NCSHA ...... Naval Communications System Headquarters Activity (SAA)
NCshB .... Cold Spring Harbor Biological Laboratory, Cold Spring Harbor, NY [*Library symbol*] [*Library of Congress*] (LCLS)
NcShC .... Cleveland County Technical Institute, Shelby, NC [*Library symbol*] [*Library of Congress*] (LCLS)
NCshL .... Cold Spring Harbor Public Library, Cold Spring Harbor, NY [*Library symbol*] [*Library of Congress*] (LCLS)
NCS Hlt ..... NCS Healthcare, Inc. [*Associated Press*] (SAG)
NCSHPO .... National Conference of State Historic Preservation Officers (EA)
NCSHSA .... National Council of State Human Service Administrators (EA)
NCshWM .... Whaling Museum Society, Inc., Cold Spring Harbor, NY [*Library symbol*] [*Library of Congress*] (LCLS)
NCSI .... National Communication System Instructions
NCSI .... National Contract Sweepers Institute (EA)
NCSI .... National Convenience Stores, Inc. [*NASDAQ symbol*] (SAG)
NCSI .... National Council for Stream Improvement (EA)
NCSI .... National Council of Savings Institutions (EMRF)
NCSI .... National Council of Self-Insurers [*Chicago, IL*] (EA)
NCSI .... National Curriculum Study Institute [*Associaton for Supervision and Curriculum Development*] (EDAC)
NCSI .... Network Communications Services Interface [*Computer science*] (PCM)
NCSIT .... National Coalition to Support Indian Treaties (EA)
NCSITSG ... National Community Services Industry Training Steering Group [*Australia*]
NCSJ .... National College of the State Judiciary (DLA)
NCSJ .... National Conference on Soviet Jewry (EA)
NCSJ .... Naval Communication Station, Japan
NcSj .... United States Air Force, Seymour Johnson Air Force Base, Base Library, Seymour Johnson AFB, NC [*Library symbol*] [*Library of Congress*] (LCLS)
NCSL .... National Center for Service-Learning [*Defunct*] (EA)
NCSL .... National Civil Service League [*Defunct*] (EA)
NCSL .... National Computer Systems Laboratory (VLIE)
NCSL .... National Conference of Standards Laboratories (EA)
NCSL .... National Conference of State Legislatures (EA)
NCSL .... National Council of State Legislatures (WPI)
NCSL .... Naval Coastal Systems Laboratory [*Later, NCSC*]
NCSL .... Naval Code and Signal Laboratory
NCSL .... Near-Coincident Site Lattice [*Crystallography*]
NCSLA .... National Conference of State Liquor Administrators (EA)
NCSLL .... National Conference of State Legislative Leaders [*Later, NCSL*] (EA)
NCSLO ...... Naval Control of Shipping Liaison Officer
NCSM .... National Communication System Memoranda
NCSM .... National Council of Supervisors of Mathematics (EA)
NCSMA ...... Nonadaptive Carrier Sensing Multiple Access (SAUS)
NCSMA ...... Nonpersistent Carrier Sensing Multiple Access (SAUS)
NCSMHC .... National Council for the Single Mother and Her Child [*Australia*]
NcSmJ ...... Johnston County Technical Institute, Smithfield (SAUS)
NCSMX ...... National Campaign to Stop the MX [*Defunct*] (EA)
NcSn .... Greene County Public Library, Snow Hill (SAUS)
NCSN .... National Computer Service Network (EA)
NCSN .... National Council for School Nurses [*of AAHPER*]
NCSNE ...... Naval Control of Shipping in Northern European Command Area [*NATO*] (NATG)
NCSO .... National Council of Salesmen's Organizations [*New York, NY*] (EA)
NCSO .... Naval Control of Shipping Officer
NCSO .... Naval Control of Shipping Operations
NCSO .... Naval Control Service Office [*World War II British Routing Service*]
NCSO .... North Carolina Symphony Orchestra (SAUS)
NCSOICC... North Carolina State Occupational Information Coordinating Committee (EDAC)
NcSopS-L ... Southport-Brunswick County Library, Leland Branch Library, Leland, NC [*Library symbol*] [*Library of Congress*] (LCLS)
NcSopS-W... Southport-Brunswick County Library, West Brunswick Branch Library, Shallotte, NC [*Library symbol*] [*Library of Congress*] (LCLS)
NCSORG .... Naval Control of Shipping Organization
NCSP .... National Center for Surrogate Parenting [*Later, IAI*] [*Commercial firm*] (EA)
NCSP .... National Conference on State Parks [*Later, NRPA*] (EA)
NCSP .... National Crime Stop Program (EA)
NCSP .... Naval Communication Station, Philippines (DNAB)
NCSP .... NOMESKO Classification of Surgical Procedure (SAUS)
NCSP .... Nordic Committee on Salaries and Personnel [*Nordic Council of Ministers*] [*Copenhagen, Denmark*] (EAIO)
NCSP .... Northern Cod Science Program (SAUS)
NcSp .... Southern Pines Public Library, Southern Pines, NC [*Library symbol*] [*Library of Congress*] (LCLS)
NcSpa .... Alleghany County Public Library, Sparta, NC [*Library symbol*] [*Library of Congress*] (LCLS)
NCSPA .... National Corrugated Steel Pipe Association (EA)
NCSPA .... North Carolina State Ports Authority
NCSPAA ..... National Council of School Press and Advisers Association
NCSPAE ..... National Council of State Pharmaceutical Association Executives (EA)
NCSPAE ..... National Council of State Pharmacy Association Executives (NTPA)
NCSPAS ..... National Conference of State Pharmaceutical Association Secretaries [*Later, NCSPAE*]
NCSPE .... National Center for the Study of Privatization in Education [*Columbia University*] (RCD)
NcSph .... Spring Hope Public Library, Spring Hope, NC [*Library symbol*] [*Library of Congress*] (LCLS)
NcSpi .... Spindale Public Library, Spindale, NC [*Library symbol*] [*Library of Congress*] (LCLS)
NcSpiI .... Isothermal Community College, Spindale, NC [*Library symbol*] [*Library of Congress*] (LCLS)
NcSpiR ...... Rutherford County Library, Inc., Spindale, NC [*Library symbol*] [*Library of Congress*] (LCLS)
NCSPP ...... National Center for Social Policy and Practice (EA)
NcSppA ..... Avery-Mitchell-Yancey Regional Library, Spruce Pine, NC [*Library symbol*] [*Library of Congress*] (LCLS)
NcSppM ..... Mayland Technical Institute, Spruce Pine, NC [*Library symbol*] [*Library of Congress*] (LCLS)
NcSpr .... Spray Public Library, Spray, NC [*Library symbol*] [*Library of Congress*] (LCLS)
NCSPS ...... National Committee for Support of the Public Schools [*Later, NCCE*] (EA)
NcSpS .... Sandhills Community College, Southern Pines, NC [*Library symbol*] [*Library of Congress*] (LCLS)
NCSPWA .... National Council of State Public Welfare Administrators [*Later, NCSHSA*] (EA)
NCSR .... National Centre for Systems Reliability [*Research center*] [*British*] (CB)
NCSRA ...... National Conference of State Retail Associations (EA)
NCSRLL ..... North Carolina Studies in Romance Languages and Literatur (SAUS)
NCSRM ...... National Communications System Regional Manager [*Emergency Management*] (EMA)
NCSRP ...... North Central Soybean Research Program (SAUS)
NCSS .... National Cactus and Succulent Society [*British*] (BI)
NCSS .... National Center for Social Statistics [*HEW*]
NCSS .... National Collegiate Sports Services (EA)
NCSS .... National Commission on Supplies and Shortages [*Terminated, 1977*]
NCSS .... National Computer Security System (ACAE)

NCSS .... National Conference of Shomrim Societies (EA)
NCSS .... National Conference of State Societies (EA)
NCSS .... National Conference on Student Services (EA)
NCSs .... National Conservation Strategies (SAUS)
NCSS .... National Conversational Software Systems, Inc.
NCSS .... National Cooperative Soil Survey
NCSS .... National Council for the Social Studies (EA)
NCSS .... National Council of Social Service [*British*]
NCSS .... National Council of Social Studies
NCSS .... National Crash Severity Study [*National Highway Traffic Safety Administration*]
NCSS .... National CSS, Inc. (EFIS)
NCSS .... Navy Command Support System (MCD)
NCSS .... NCS Healthcare, Inc. [*NASDAQ symbol*] (SAG)
NCSS .... NCS HealthCare 'A' [*NASDAQ symbol*] (TTSB)
NCSS .... NGT Command and Status System (SAUS)
NCSS .... Non Commentary Sources Statements (SAUS)
NCSS .... Non-Contact Smart Sensor
NCSS .... Nordic Council of Ski Schools (EAIO)
NCSS .... Number Cruncher Statistical System [*Computer software*] (PCM)
NCSS .... Number Crunching Statistical System (SAUS)
NCSSA ...... Naval Command Systems Support Activity
NCSSAD..... National Council of Secondary School Athletic Directors (EA)
NCSSB ...... National Coalition for Seat Belts on School Buses (EA)
NCSSC ...... Naval Command Systems Support Center
NCSSE....... National Coalition to Support Sexuality Education [*Fact sheet published by the Sexuality Information and Education Coalition of the United States (SIECUS)*] (PAZ)
NCSSFL ..... National Council of State Supervisors of Foreign Languages (EA)
NCSSIA...... National Council of State Self-Insurers Associations [*Later, NCSI*] (EA)
NCSSM...... National Council of State Supervisors of Music (EA)
NCSSM...... North Carolina School of Science and Mathematics [*Free, residential public high school for gifted students*]
NCSSMA .... National Council of Social Security Management Associations (EA)
NCSSSA..... National Conference of State Social Security Administrators (EA)
NCSSW...... Nordic Committee of Schools of Social Work (EAIO)
NcSt .... Iredell Public Library, Statesville, NC [*Library symbol*] [*Library of Congress*] (LCLS)
NCST .... National Center for Software Technology [*India*] (DDC)
NCST .... National Certification Skills Test [*Psychiatry*]
NCST .... National Coalition for Science and Technology [*Defunct*] (EA)
NCSTAR ..... National Committee of Shatnez Testers and Researchers (EA)
NCSTAS ..... National Council of Scientific and Technical Art Societies [*Later, IG*] (EA)
NC State Univ Sch Agric Life Sci Annu Rep... North Carolina State University. School of Agriculture and Life Sciences. Annual. Report (SAUS)
NCSTD ...... National Council of State Travel Directors (EA)
NcStH .... Iredell Memorial Hospital, Statesville, NC [*Library symbol*] [*Library of Congress*] (LCLS)
NCSTL....... New Castle, IN [*American Association of Railroads railroad junction routing code*]
NCstLf....... North Coast Life Insurance Co. [*Associated Press*] (SAG)
NcStMC ..... Mitchell College, Statesville, NC [*Library symbol*] [*Library of Congress*] (LCLS)
NcStpR...... Robeson Technical Institute, St. Pauls, NC [*Library symbol*] [*Library of Congress*] [*Obsolete*] (LCLS)
NCSTR ...... NATO Communication System Technical Recommendation (NATG)
NC Str....... Strange's Notes of Cases, Madras [*1798-1816*] [*A publication*] (DLA)
NC/STRC.... North Carolina Science and Technology Research Center [*North Carolina Department of Commerce*] [*Research center*] (RCD)
NCSTRL..... Networked Computer Science Technical Reference Library
NCSTS....... National Conference of State Transportation Specialists (EA)
NCSTSR..... National Conference of Superintendents of Training Schools and Reformatories [*Later, International Conference of Administrators Residential Centers for Youth -ICA*] (EA)
NCSU .... Network Channel Service Unit [*Computer science*] (TNIG)
NCSU .... North Carolina State University [*Raleigh*]
NCSU .... Sato [*Intermodal shipping container symbol*] (TVRC)
NC SU CAPPS... North Carolina State University Center for Aseptic Processing and Packaging Studies (SAUS)
NcSupB ..... Brunswick Technical College, Supply, NC [*Library symbol*] [*Library of Congress*] (LCLS)
NCSW .... National Conference of Social Workers
NCSW .... National Conference on Social Welfare [*Defunct*] (EA)
NCSW .... National Council for the Single Woman and Her Dependants Ltd. [*British*] (BI)
NcSw .... Swannanoa Public Library, Swannanoa, NC [*Library symbol*] [*Library of Congress*] (LCLS)
NcSwC ...... Chemtronics, Inc., Swannanoa, NC [*Library symbol*] [*Library of Congress*] (LCLS)
NCSWCL .... National [*Presidential*] Commission on State Workmen's Compensation Laws
NCSWD ..... National Center for Solid Waste Disposal [*Later, National Center for Resource Recovery*] (EA)
NCSWD ..... National Center for the Study of Wilson's Disease (EA)
NCSWD ..... National Council for the Single Woman and Her Dependants (EA)
NCSWDI..... National Combination Storm Window and Door Institute [*Defunct*] (EA)
NCSW-ECO... Naval Warfare Center, East Coast Operations (SAUS)
NC Switch... Normally Closed Switch (SAUS)
NcSwW...... Warren Wilson College, Swannanoa, NC [*Library symbol*] [*Library of Congress*] (LCLS)
NCSX .... Shipping Control Exercise [*NATO exercises*] (NATG)
NcSy......... Jackson County Public Library, Sylva, NC [*Library symbol*] [*Library of Congress*] (LCLS)
NCSY .... National Conference of Synagogue Youth (EA)
NcSyS .... Southwestern Technical Institute, Sylva, NC [*Library symbol*] [*Library of Congress*] (LCLS)
NCT.......... Name Changed To
NCT.......... National Centre of Tribology [*Risley Nuclear Laboratories*] [*British*] (CB)
NCT.......... National Chamber of Trade [*British*] (BI)
NCT.......... National Childbirth Trust [*British*]
NCT.......... National College Television [*Cable-television system*] (WDMC)
N Ct.......... Native Court [*Ghana*] [*A publication*] (DLA)
NCT.......... NATO Comparative Testing (RDA)
NCT.......... NATO Comparative Test programme (SAUS)
NCT.......... Necessitate [*Telegraphy*] (PCTE)
NCT.......... Neoclassical Radiation Theory
NCT.......... Nerve Conduction Tests [*Neurology*] (DAVI)
NCT.......... Nerve Conduction Time [*neurology*] (DAVI)
NCT.......... Net Cost of Transport
NCT.......... Network Computing Tools (TIMI)
NCT.......... Network, Control and Timing [*Communications term*] (DCT)
NCT.......... Network Control Terminal (MCD)
NCT.......... Neural Crest Tumor [*Oncology*]
NCT.......... Neutral Contour Technology [*Automotive engineering*]
NCT.......... Neutron-Capture Therapy (ODA)
NCT.......... Newcourt Credit Group [*NYSE symbol*] (SG)
NCT.......... New Curing Technology
NCT.......... Nicoya [*Costa Rica*] [*Airport symbol*] (AD)
NCT.......... Night Closing Trunks [*Telecommunications*] (TEL)
NCT.......... Nitrocellulose Tubular (SAUS)
nct........... No Charge for Terms (SAUS)
nct........... No Civil Twilight (SAUS)
NCT.......... Noise Cancellation Technology (PS)
NCT.......... Non-Chargeable Time (DGA)
NCT.......... Non-Competitive Tenders [*Business term*] (MHDW)
NCT.......... Non-Contact Time (AIE)
NCT.......... Noncontact Tonometer (SAUS)
NCT.......... Noncontact Tonometry (MELL)
NCT.......... Non-Co-operative Target (SAUS)
NCT.......... Nordic Cooperation on Telecommunications (EAIO)
NCT.......... North Charleston Terminal [*Federal Railroad Administration identification code*]
NCT.......... North Coast Industries Ltd. [*Vancouver Stock Exchange symbol*]
NCT.......... Northern Cultural Trust [*South Australia*]
NCT.......... Number Connection Test
NCT.......... Nursing Care Technician (MELL)
NcTA......... Edgecombe County Memorial Library, Tarboro (SAUS)
NcTA......... Edgecombe County Memorial Library, Tarboro, NC [*Library symbol*] [*Library of Congress*] (LCLS)
NCTA .... National Cable Television Association
NCTA .... National Cable Television Association, Inc.
NCTA .... National Capital Transportation Agency [*Functions transferred to Washington Metropolitan Area Transit Authority*]
NCTA .... National Cattle Theft Act
NCTA .... National Ceramic Teachers Association (EA)
NCTA .... National Child Transport Association (NTPA)
NCTA .... National Christmas Tree Association (EA)
NCTA .... National Council for Technological Awards [*British*]
NCTA .... National Council for the Traditional Arts (EA)
NCTA .... Navajo Code Talkers Association (EA)
NCTA .... North Carolina Trucking Association (EARSL)
NCTA .... North Country Trail Association (EA)
NCTA .... Northern California Translators Association (EARSL)
NcTaE........ Edgecombe County Technical Institute, Tarboro, NC [*Library symbol*] [*Library of Congress*] (LCLS)
NCTAF .... Nuclear Communications Task Force (SAUS)
NcTaH .... Edgecomb General Hospital Library, Tarboro, NC [*Library symbol*] [*Library of Congress*] (LCLS)
NCTAM ...... National Committee for Theoretical and Applied Mechanics [*British*]
NCTAMS .... Naval Computer and Telecommunications Area Master Station (DOMA)
NcTa-P ...... Edgecombe County Memorial Library, Pinetops Branch, Pinetops, NC [*Library symbol*] [*Library of Congress*] (LCLS)
NCTA PAC... National Cable and Telecommunications Association PAC [*Washington, DC*] (PACS)
NcTayA...... Alexander County Public Library, Taylorsville, NC [*Library symbol*] [*Library of Congress*] (LCLS)
NCTC .... National Cancer Institute Tissue Culture [*Medium*]
NCTC .... National Catholic Theatre Conference (EA)
NCTC .... National Collection of Type Cultures [*British*]
NCTC .... Naval Communications Training Center
NCTC .... Naval Computer and Telecommunications Command (DOMA)
NCTC .... Naval Construction Training Center
NCTCA....... National Collegiate Track Coaches Association (EA)
NCTCA....... National Council of Teachers for Critical Analysis (AEBS)
NCTCP....... National Coalition of Title I/Chapter I Parents (EA)
NCTD .... National College of Teachers of the Deaf [*British*]
NCTE .... National Council for Textile Education (EA)
NCTE .... National Council for Torah Education (EA)
NCTE .... National Council of Teachers of English
NCTE .... Network Channel Terminating Equipment [*Telecommunications*]
NCTE .... No-Cost Time Extension (MCD)
NCTE .... North Central Turfgrass Exposition [*Illinois Turfgrass Foundation*] (TSPED)
NCTEC....... Northern Counties Technical Examinations Council (SAUS)
NC Telephone... Non-Coin Telephone (SAUS)

NCTEPS ..... National Commission on Teacher Education and Professional Standards [*Defunct*] (EA)
NC Term R ... North Carolina Term Reports [*A publication*] (DLA)
NC Term Rep ... North Carolina Term Reports [*A publication*] (DLA)
NCTET .... National Coalition for Technology Education and Training
NCTF .... National Check Traders Federation [*British*] (BI)
NCTF .... National Corporate Theatre Fund (EA)
NCTFC .... North Central Texas Film Cooperative [*Library network*]
NCTGA ...... National Christmas Tree Growers Association [*Later, National Christmas Tree Association*] (EA)
NcTh .... Thomasville Public Library, Thomasville, NC [*Library symbol*] [*Library of Congress*] (LCLS)
NcThCH ..... Community General Hospital Library, Thomasville, NC [*Library symbol*] [*Library of Congress*] (LCLS)
NcThDM ..... Davidson Area Mental Health Center, Thomasville, NC [*Library symbol*] [*Library of Congress*] (LCLS)
NCTI .... National Cable Television Institute (EA)
NCTI .... National Consumer Testing Institute (BARN)
NCTI .... Noise Cancellation Tech [*NASDAQ symbol*] (TTSB)
NCTI .... Noise Cancellation Technologies, Inc. [*NASDAQ symbol*] (SAG)
NCTI .... Non-Co-operative Target Identification (SAUS)
NCTIA .... North Carolina Telecommunications Industry Association (EARSL)
NCTIP .... National Center for Transportation and Industrial Productivity [*New Jersey Institute of Technology*] (RCD)
NCTIP .... National Coalition of ESEA [*Elementary and Secondary Education Act*] Title I Parents (EA)
NCTIP .... National Committee on the Treatment of Intractable Pain (EA)
NCTI/R ...... Non-Cooperative Target Identification/ Recognition (SAUS)
NCTJ .... National Council for the Training of Journalists [*British*]
NCTL .... National Commercial Temperance League [*British*] (BI)
NCTL .... National Computer and Telecommunications Laboratory (VLIE)
NCTM .... National Council of Teachers of Mathematics (EA)
NCTM .... Non-Contact Temperature Measurements (SAUS)
NCTO .... Naval Central Torpedo Office
NCTO .... Navy Clothing and Textile Supply Office
NCTOG ...... North Central Texas Council of Governments
NCTP .... National Center for Technology Planning (RCD)
NCTP .... National Cryptologic Training Plan (MCD)
NCTPD ...... National Council for Teacher-Centred Professional Development [*British*] (DBA)
NCTPI .... Nuveen Connecticut Premium Income Municipal Fund [*Associated Press*] (SAG)
NcTr .... Montgomery County Public Library, Troy, NC [*Library symbol*] [*Library of Congress*] (LCLS)
NCTR .... National Center for Telephone Research [*Louis Harris and Associates*] [*Commercial firm*] (EA)
NCTR .... National Center for Therapeutic Riding (EA)
NCTR .... National Center for Toxicological Research [*Department of Health and Human Services*] [*Jefferson, AR*]
NCTR .... National Council on Teacher Retirement (EA)
NCTR .... Naval Commercial Traffic Regulations
NCTR .... Noncooperative Target Recognition (MCD)
NCTR .... Non-Cooperative Target Resolution (POLM)
NCTR .... Nordic Council for Tax Research (EA)
NCTR .... Taylor's North Carolina Term Reports [*A publication*] (DLA)
NCTRC ...... National Council for Therapeutic Recreation Certification (EA)
NcTrDC ...... North Carolina Department of Corrections, Troy, NC [*Library symbol*] [*Library of Congress*] (LCLS)
NCT Rep .... North Carolina Term Reports [*A publication*] (DLA)
NCTRF .... Navy Clothing and Textile Research Facility [*Natick, MA*]
NCTRH ...... National Council for Therapy and Rehabilitation through Horticulture (EA)
NcTrM .... Montgomery Technical Institute, Troy, NC [*Library symbol*] [*Library of Congress*] (LCLS)
NCTRP ...... National Cooperative Transit Research and Development Program [*TRB*] (TAG)
NCTRU ...... Navy Clothing and Textile Research Unit (MCD)
NCTS .... National Center for Tourism Studies [*Australia*]
NCTS .... National Council of Technical Schools (EA)
NCTS .... Naval Computer & Telecommunications Station (SAUS)
NCTS .... Navy Civilian Technical Specialist (MCD)
NCTS .... Non-Contacting Test System (VLIE)
NCTS .... Northeast Corridor Transportation System [*Boston to Washington high-speed transportation*]
NCTSI .... National Council of Technical Service Industries [*Later, Contract Services Association of America - CSA*]
NCTT .... National Committee on Tunneling Technology
NCTT .... Norwegian Council for Technical Terminology (SAUS)
NCTT .... Nuclear Certification Test Team (MCD)
NCTTA .... National Competitiveness Technology Transfer Act [*1989*] [*Department of Energy*]
NCTTF .... Northern Counties Textile Trades' Federation [*British*] (DCTA)
NCTU .... Northbrook Container Leasing [*Intermodal shipping container symbol*] (TVRC)
NCTU .... Northern Carpet Trades Union [*British*] (DCTA)
NCTV .... National Coalition on Television Violence (EA)
NCTV .... National College Television [*Cable-television system*]
NCTW .... National Conference of Tuberculosis Workers [*Later, CLAS*] (EA)
NCTWU ...... National Cigar and Tobacco Workers' Union [*British*]
NCTWX ...... Nicholas II Fund [*Mutual fund ticker symbol*] (SG)
NCTX .... North Central Texas [*Federal Railroad Administration identification code*]
NcTy .... Lanier Library Association, Inc., Tryon, NC [*Library symbol*] [*Library of Congress*] (LCLS)
NCtyB .... National City Bancorp [*Associated Press*] (SAG)
NCtyBn ...... National City Bancshares [*Associated Press*] (SAG)
NcTyI .... Isothermal Community College, Polk Campus, Tryon, NC [*Library symbol*] [*Library of Congress*] (LCLS)
NcTyI .... Isothermal Community College, Polk Campus, Tryon (SAUS)
NCTYL .... National College for the Training of Youth Leaders [*British*] (BI)
NCu .... Cuba Library, Cuba, NY [*Library symbol*] [*Library of Congress*] (LCLS)
NCU .... John Nuveen & Co., Inc. [*AMEX symbol*] (NASQ)
NCU .... National Communications Union [*British*]
NCU .... National Conference for Unification [*South Korea*] [*Political party*] (PPW)
NCU .... National Cutlery Union [*British*]
NCU .... National Cyclists' Union [*British*]
NCU .... Naval Communications Unit (IAA)
NCU .... Navigation Computer Unit
NCU .... Navigation Control and Display Unit (MCD)
NCU .... Network Configuration Utility [*Telecommunications*]
NCU .... Network Control Unit [*Computer science*]
NCU .... New Cinch Uranium [*Vancouver Stock Exchange symbol*]
NCU .... Nitrogen Control Unit (AAG)
NCU .... Nonconforming Use (ADA)
ncu .... North Carolina [*MARC country of publication code*] [*Library of Congress*] (LCCP)
NCU .... North Carolina University (SAUS)
NCU .... Nozzle Control Unit [*NASA*]
NCU .... Number Crunching Unit (MHDB)
NCU .... Numerical Control Unit (SAUS)
NCU .... Nuveen California Premium Income Municipal Fund [*AMEX symbol*] (SAG)
NCU .... Nuveen CA Prem Inc. Muni [*AMEX symbol*] (TTSB)
NCU .... Union College, Lincoln, NE [*OCLC symbol*] (OCLC)
NcU .... University of North Carolina, Chapel Hill, NC [*Library symbol*] [*Library of Congress*] (LCLS)
NCU .... University of North Carolina, Mathematics-Physics Library (SAUS)
NCUA .... National Credit Union Administration
NCUA .... National Credit Union Association (NADA)
NCUAAE ..... National Council of Urban Administrators of Adult Education (OICC)
NCUAS ...... Northwest College and University Association for Science (SAUS)
NcU-BPR .... University of North Carolina, Bureau of Public Records, Collection and Research,Chapel Hill, NC [*Library symbol*] [*Library of Congress*] (LCLS)
NCUC .... National Center for the Urban Community (RCD)
NCUC .... National Commission on Unemployment Compensation (NADA)
NCUC .... North Carolina Utilities Commission Reports [*A publication*] (DLA)
NCUC .... Nuclear Chemistry Users Committee
NCUCIF ..... National Credit Union Share Insurance Fund (EBF)
NCU(E) ..... National Communications Union, Engineering Group [*British*]
NCUEA ...... National Center for Urban Ethnic Affairs (EA)
NCUEA ...... National Council of Urban Education Associations (EA)
NCUES ...... National Center for Urban Environmental Studies [*Defunct*] (EA)
NCUF .... National Computer Users Forum [*National Computing Center*] (PDAA)
NCUG .... National Centrex Users Group (CIST)
NCUG .... Nevada COBOL [*Common Business-Oriented Language*] Users Group [*Defunct*] (EA)
NCUGAE ..... National Computer User Group in Agricultural Education (NITA)
NcU-H .... University of North Carolina, Division of Health Affairs, Chapel Hill, NC [*Library symbol*] [*Library of Congress*] (LCLS)
NCUI .... National Center for Urban and Industrial Health [*Public Health Service*]
NCUIC .... National Council for Uniform Interest Compensation [*Association*] (EA)
NcU-IG ...... University of North Carolina, Institute of Government Library, Chapel Hill, NC [*Library symbol*] [*Library of Congress*] (LCLS)
NCuL .... Cuba Library, Cuba, NY [*Library symbol*] [*Library of Congress*] (LCLS)
NcU-L .... University of North Carolina, Law Library, Chapel Hill, NC [*Library symbol*] [*Library of Congress*] (LCLS)
NCULA ...... Nebraska Credit Union League and Affiliates (EARSL)
NCULPAC ... Nebraska Credit Union League Inc. PAC [*Omaha, NE*] (PACS)
NcU-LS ...... University of North Carolina at Chapel Hill, Library School, Chapel Hill, NC [*Library symbol*] [*Library of Congress*] (LCLS)
NCUMA ...... National Credit Union Management Association (EA)
NCUMC ...... National Council for the Unmarried Mother and Her Child [*British*] (ILCA)
NcU-MS ..... University of North Carolina, Institute of Marine Sciences, Morehead City, NC [*Library symbol*] [*Library of Congress*] (LCLS)
NCUP .... National Conference of University Professors (AIE)
NCUP .... No Commission until Paid
NCUPI .... National Coalition for Universities in the Public Interest [*Defunct*] (EA)
NCUPM ...... National Council of United Presbyterian Men (EA)
NcU-Pop .... University of North Carolina, Carolina Population Center, Technical Information Service, Chapel Hill, NC [*Library symbol*] [*Library of Congress*] (LCLS)
NCUPRSE ... National Consortium of Universities Preparing Rural Special Educators [*Defunct*] (EA)
NCUR .... National Committee for Utilities Radio (MCD)
NCUR .... National Conferences on Undergraduate Research [*An association*]
NCURA ...... National Council of University Research Administrators (EA)
NCURSRV ... Naval Courier Service (ACAE)
NCUS .... Normalized from Customer Read [*Electric utility company*]
NCUSA ...... Navy Club of the United States of America (EA)
NCUSAA .... Navy Club of the United States of America Auxiliary (EA)
NCUSAR .... National Council on US-Arab Relations (EA)
NCUSCR .... National Committee on United States-China Relations (EA)
NCUSCT .... National Council for US-China Trade [*Later, USCBC*] (EA)

NCUSIF...... National Credit Union Share Insurance Fund
NCUSIOGT... National Council of the United States, International Organization of Good Templars (EA)
NCUTLO..... National Committee on Uniform Traffic Laws and Ordinances (EA)
NCUU........ North American Container System-Greenbriar Capital [*Intermodal shipping container symbol*] (TVRC)
NCUUA...... National Council for Universal and Unconditional Amnesty [*For Vietnam-War resisters*] [*Defunct*] (EA)
NCUX........ Trinity Rail Management [*Private rail car owner code*]
NCV.......... Navigation Computer Unit
NCV.......... Nebraska Center for Virology [*University of Nebraska--Lincoln*] (RCD)
NCV.......... Nerve Conduction Velocity [*Electrophysiology*]
NCV.......... Net Calorific Value (PDAA)
NCV.......... New Century Value [*Automotive design*]
NCV.......... New Concept Van
NCV.......... No Commercial Value [*Business term*]
NCV.......... No Cone Value (SAUS)
NCV.......... No Core Value [*Business term*]
NCV.......... No Customs Value (DS)
NCV.......... Non-Cholera Vibrios [*Microbiology*]
NCV.......... Normalized Critical View
NCV.......... Noze Control Vehicle (SAUS)
NCVA........ National Center for Voluntary Action [*Later, NVC*]
NCVA........ National Crime Victim Bar Association (IID)
NCVA........ North Carolina & Virginia Railroad [*Federal Railroad Administration identification code*]
NCVA........ North Carolina Vending Association (EARSL)
NcVal........ Valdese Public Library, Valdese, NC [*Library symbol*] [*Library of Congress*] (LCLS)
NcValH...... Valdese General Hospital, Valdese, NC [*Library symbol*] [*Library of Congress*] (LCLS)
NCVC........ National Catholic Vocation Council [*Defunct*] (EA)
NCVC........ National Congress on Volunteerism and Citizenship [*Bicentennial event, 1976*]
NCVCCO..... National Council of Voluntary Child Care Organizations (ODA)
NCVE........ National Council on Vocational Education [*Department of Education*] [*Washington, DC*] (EGAO)
NCVECS..... National Center for Vehicle Emissions Control and Safety [*Colorado State University*]
NCVG........ National Council for Vocational Qualifications (COBU)
NCVHS...... National Committee on Vital and Health Statistics [*Department of Health and Human Services*] (GFGA)
NCVL........ Northeast College Volleyball League (PSS)
NCVMA...... North Carolina Veterinary Medical Association (GVA)
NCVME...... Nova Communications Ltd. [*OTCBB symbol*]
NCVO........ National Council for Voluntary Organisations [*British*] (ILCA)
NCVOTE..... National Center for Vocational, Occupational, and Technical Education [*Office of Education*]
NCVP........ Natural Circulation Verification Program [*Nuclear energy*] (NRCH)
NCVP........ Noncapsid Viral Protein [*Biochemistry*]
NCVQ........ National Council for Vocational Qualifications [*British*]
NCVR........ National Conference of Vicars for Religious (EA)
NCVS........ National Center for Voice and Speech [*Association*] (EA)
NCVS........ National Credential Verification Service (MCD)
NCVS........ National Crime Victimization Survey [*Department of Justice*] (ECON)
NCVS........ Nerve Conduction Velocity Studies [*Medicine*] (MEDA)
NCW......... National Council of Women of Great Britain (BI)
NCW......... National Council of Women of the United States (EA)
NCW......... Newberry College, Newberry, SC [*OCLC symbol*] (OCLC)
NCW......... No Change in Weather (SAUS)
NCW......... Non-Code Word (SAUS)
NCW......... North Central Washington (SAUS)
NCW......... North City West (SAUS)
NCW......... Nose Cone Warhead [*Aviation*] (NATG)
NCW......... Not Complied With [*Military*]
NcW......... Wilmington Public Library, Wilmington, NC [*Library symbol*] [*Library of Congress*] (LCLS)
NcWa........ George H. and Laura E. Brown Library, Washington, NC [*Library symbol*] [*Library of Congress*] (LCLS)
NCWA....... National Candy Wholesalers Association (EA)
NCWA....... National Children's Wear Association [*British*] (EAIO)
NCWA....... NATO Civil Wartime Agency (NATG)
NCWA....... Newsagency Council of Western Australia
NCWA....... Northeast College Wrestling Association (PSS)
NcWaB...... Beaufort County Technical Institute, Washington, NC [*Library symbol*] [*Library of Congress*] (LCLS)
NcWaBHM.. Beaufort, Hyde, Martin Regional Library, Washington, NC [*Library symbol*] [*Library of Congress*] (LCLS)
NcWad...... Anson County Library, Wadesboro, NC [*Library symbol*] [*Library of Congress*] (LCLS)
NcWadAS... Anson County Senior High School, Medial Center, Wadesboro, NC [*Library symbol*] [*Library of Congress*] (LCLS)
NcWal....... Thelma Dingus Bryant Library, Wallace, NC [*Library symbol*] [*Library of Congress*] (LCLS)
NCWAO...... National Council of World Affairs Organizations (EA)
NcWarW.... Warren County Memorial Library, Warrenton, NC [*Library symbol*] [*Library of Congress*] (LCLS)
NCWAS...... National Coal Workers Autopsy Study
NcWaw...... Warsaw Public Library, Warsaw, NC [*Library symbol*] [*Library of Congress*] (LCLS)
NcWayH..... Haywood County Public Library, Waynesville, NC [*Library symbol*] [*Library of Congress*] (LCLS)
NcWayH-C.. Haywood County Public Library, Canton Branch, Canton, NC [*Library symbol*] [*Library of Congress*] (LCLS)
NCWBA...... National Conference of Women's Bar Associations (EA)
NCWC....... National Carwash Council
NCWC....... National Catholic Welfare Conference [*Later, USCC*] (EA)
NCWC....... National Catholic Welfare Conference News Service (NTCM)
NCWC....... National Council of Women Chiropractors (EA)
NCWC....... National Council of Women of Canada
NcWc........ Walnut Cove Public Library, Walnut Cove, NC [*Library symbol*] [*Library of Congress*] (LCLS)
NcW-C....... Wilmington Public Library, College Square Branch, Wilmington (SAUS)
NcWC........ Wilmington Public Library, College Square Branch, Wilmington, NC [*Library symbol*] [*Library of Congress*] (LCLS)
NCWCC...... North Central Weed Control Committee (SAUS)
NcWCF...... Cape Fear Technical Institute, Wilmington, NC [*Library symbol*] [*Library of Congress*] (LCLS)
NcWcL....... Walnut Cove Public Library, Walnut Cove, NC [*Library symbol*] [*Library of Congress*] (LCLS)
NCWD....... National Coalition for Women in Defense (EA)
NcWea...... Bess Tilson Sprinkle Memorial Library, Weaverville, NC [*Library symbol*] [*Library of Congress*] (LCLS)
NcWek....... North Davidson Public Library, Welcome (SAUS)
NcWel....... Weldon Memorial Library, Weldon, NC [*Library symbol*] [*Library of Congress*] (LCLS)
NcWelc...... North Davidson Public Library, Welcome, NC [*Library symbol*] [*Library of Congress*] (LCLS)
NcWelH..... Halifax County Technical Institute, Weldon, NC [*Library symbol*] [*Library of Congress*] (LCLS)
NcWeR...... Rockingham Community College, Wentworth, NC [*Library symbol*] [*Library of Congress*] (LCLS)
NCWF....... Northern California Womens Facility (SAUS)
NCWFC...... National Council of Women of Free Czechoslovakia (EA)
NCWFD...... National Committee for World Food Day [*Later, USNCWFD*] (EA)
NcWfSB..... Southeastern Baptist Theological Seminary, Wake Forest, NC [*Library symbol*] [*Library of Congress*] (LCLS)
NCWGA..... Natural Colored Wool Growers Association (EA)
NCWGB..... National Council of Women of Great Britain (DI)
NcWGE..... General Electric Co., WMD Technical Library, Wilmington (SAUS)
NCWGE..... National Coalition for Women and Girls in Education (EA)
NcWhC...... Columbus County Public Library, Whiteville, NC [*Library symbol*] [*Library of Congress*] (LCLS)
NcWHE...... Wilmington Area Health Education Center Medical Library, Wilmington, NC [*Library symbol*] [*Library of Congress*] (LCLS)
NcWhS...... Southeastern Community College, Whiteville, NC [*Library symbol*] [*Library of Congress*] (LCLS)
NcWil........ Wilson County Public Library, Wilson, NC [*Library symbol*] [*Library of Congress*] (LCLS)
NcWilA...... Atlantic Christian College, Wilson, NC [*Library symbol*] [*Library of Congress*] (LCLS)
NcWilB...... Beddingfield High School Library, Wilson, NC [*Library symbol*] [*Library of Congress*] (LCLS)
NcWilC...... Carolina Discipliana Library, Wilson, NC [*Library symbol*] [*Library of Congress*] (LCLS)
NcWilE...... North Carolina Department of Human Resources, Eastern North Carolina School for the Deaf, Wilson (SAUS)
NcWilE...... North Carolina Department of Human Resources, Eastern North Carolina School for the Deaf, Wilson, NC [*Library symbol*] [*Library of Congress*] (LCLS)
NcWilF...... Fike High School Library, Wilson, NC [*Library symbol*] [*Library of Congress*] (LCLS)
NcWilH...... Wilson Memorial Hospital, Wilson, NC [*Library symbol*] [*Library of Congress*] (LCLS)
NcWilHS.... Hunt High School Library, Wilson, NC [*Library symbol*] [*Library of Congress*] (LCLS)
NcWill....... Martin Memorial Library, Williamston, NC [*Library symbol*] [*Library of Congress*] (LCLS)
NcWillM.... Martin Technical Institute, Williamston, NC [*Library symbol*] [*Library of Congress*] (LCLS)
NcWilW..... Wilson County Technical Institute, Wilson, NC [*Library symbol*] [*Library of Congress*] (LCLS)
NcWin....... Wingate College, Wingate, NC [*Library symbol*] [*Library of Congress*] (LCLS)
NcWind..... Lawrence Memorial Library, Windsor, NC [*Library symbol*] [*Library of Congress*] (LCLS)
NcWintA.... Albermarle Regional Library, Winton, NC [*Library symbol*] [*Library of Congress*] (LCLS)
NCWIS...... New Computerized World Information Service [*Information service or system*] (IID)
NcWiW...... Wilkes Community College, Wilkesboro, NC [*Library symbol*] [*Library of Congress*] (LCLS)
NcWj........ Ashe County Public Library, West Jefferson, NC [*Library symbol*] [*Library of Congress*] (LCLS)
NCWM....... National Conference on Weights and Measures (EA)
NCWM....... National Congress of Women in Music (EA)
NcWMM..... Miller-Motte Business College, Wilmington, NC [*Library symbol*] [*Library of Congress*] (LCLS)
NcWN....... New Hanover County Public Library, Wilmington, NC [*Library symbol*] [*Library of Congress*] (LCLS)
NcWN-C.... New Hanover County Public Library, Carolina Beach Branch Library (SAUS)
NcWNC..... New Hanover County Public Library, Carolina Beach Branch Library, Carolina Beach, NC [*Library symbol*] [*Library of Congress*] (LCLS)
NCWNSW... National Council of Women of New South Wales [*Australia*]
NCWO....... National Council of Women's Organizations
NCWP....... National Center for Women and Policing [*Association*] (EA)
NCWP....... National Communications Working Party [*Australia*] [*Political party*]
NCWP....... Near Coastal Waters Program (WPI)
NCWPA..... National Committee for Women in Public Administration (EA)
NCWPA..... National Council for the Welfare of Prisoners Abroad [*British*] (DI)
NCWPTF.... National Council for a World Peace Tax Fund (EA)

NCWQ .... National Commission on Water Quality [*National Academy of Sciences*]
NCWQ .... National Council of Women of Queensland [*Australia*]
NCWR .... Nordic Council for Wildlife Research (EAIO)
NCWRU ..... North Central Watershed Research Unit [*Department of Agriculture*] (GRD)
NcWs .... Forsyth County Public Library System, Winston-Salem, NC [*Library symbol*] [*Library of Congress*] (LCLS)
NCWS .... Non-Community Water System [*Environmental Protection Agency*]
NCWSA ...... National Collegiate Water Ski Association (EA)
NcWsA ...... North-West AHEC Library at Winston-Salem, Bowman-Gray School of Medicine, Winston-Salem, NC [*Library symbol*] [*Library of Congress*] (LCLS)
NcWsAT ..... AT & Technologies, Inc., Winston-Salem, NC [*Library symbol*] [*Library of Congress*] (LCLS)
NcWsAT-R ... AT & T Technologies, Inc., Winston-Salem, NC [*Library symbol*] [*Library of Congress*] (LCLS)
NCWSBA .... National Council of Wool Selling Brokers of Australia
NcWs-C ..... Forsyth County Public Library, Clemmons Branch Library, Clemmons, NC [*Library symbol*] [*Library of Congress*] (LCLS)
NcWs-E ..... Forsyth County Public Library, East Winston Branch, Winston-Salem, NC [*Library symbol*] [*Library of Congress*] (LCLS)
NcWsF ...... Forsyth Technical Institute, Winston-Salem, NC [*Library symbol*] [*Library of Congress*] (LCLS)
NcWsFM .... Forsyth-Stokes Area Mental Health Center, Winston-Salem, NC [*Library symbol*] [*Library of Congress*] (LCLS)
NcWs-K ..... Forsyth County Public Library, Kernersville Branch Library, Kernersville, NC [*Library symbol*] [*Library of Congress*] (LCLS)
NcWsM ...... Moravian Archives, Winston-Salem, NC [*Library symbol*] [*Library of Congress*] (LCLS)
NcWsMES .. Museum of Early Southern Decorative Arts, MESDA Library, Winston-Salem, NC [*Library symbol*] [*Library of Congress*] (LCLS)
NcWsMM ... Moravian Music Foundation, Winston-Salem, NC [*Library symbol*] [*Library of Congress*] (LCLS)
NcWsN ...... North Carolina School of the Arts, Winston-Salem, NC [*Library symbol*] [*Library of Congress*] (LCLS)
NcWs-R ..... Forsyth County Public Library, Reynolda Manor Branch, Winston-Salem, NC [*Library symbol*] [*Library of Congress*] (LCLS)
NcWsR ...... Reynolds Tobacco Co., Winston-Salem, NC [*Library symbol*] [*Library of Congress*] (LCLS)
NcWsRI ..... Reynolds Industries, Corporate Library, Winston-Salem, NC [*Library symbol*] [*Library of Congress*] (LCLS)
NcWsR-M ... Reynolds Tobacco Co., Marketing Development Intelligence Center, Winston-Salem, NC [*Library symbol*] [*Library of Congress*] (LCLS)
NcWsR-R ... Reynolds Tobacco Co., Research and Development Technical Information Services, Winston-Salem, NC [*Library symbol*] [*Library of Congress*] (LCLS)
NcWs-RS ... Forsyth County Public Library, Rural Hall/Stanleyville Branch Library, Rural Hall, NC [*Library symbol*] [*Library of Congress*] (LCLS)
NcWs-S ..... Forsyth County Public Library, Southside Branch, Winston-Salem, NC [*Library symbol*] [*Library of Congress*] (LCLS)
NCWSS ...... North Central Weed Science Society (SAUS)
NcWsS ...... Salem College, Winston-Salem, NC [*Library symbol*] [*Library of Congress*] (LCLS)
NcWs-T ..... Forsyth County Public Library, Thruway Branch, Winston-Salem, NC [*Library symbol*] [*Library of Congress*] (LCLS)
NcWsU ...... Winston-Salem State University, Winston-Salem, NC [*Library symbol*] [*Library of Congress*] (LCLS)
NcWsW ..... Wake Forest University, Winston-Salem, NC [*Library symbol*] [*Library of Congress*] (LCLS)
NcWsW-B ... Wake Forest University, Babcock Graduate School of Management, Winston-Salem, NC [*Library symbol*] [*Library of Congress*] (LCLS)
NcWsWE .... Western Electric Co., Lexington Road Technical Library, Winston-Salem, NC [*Library symbol*] [*Library of Congress*] (LCLS)
NcWsWE-R . Western Electric Co., Reynolda Road Technical Library, Winston-Salem, NC [*Library symbol*] [*Library of Congress*] (LCLS)
NcWsW-L ... Wake Forest University, Law Library, Winston-Salem, NC [*Library symbol*] [*Library of Congress*] (LCLS)
NcWsW-M .. Wake Forest University, Bowman Gray School of Medicine, Wake Forest, NC [*Library symbol*] [*Library of Congress*] (LCLS)
NCWT .... National Council of Women of Tasmania [*Australia*]
NCWTF ...... Naval Commander Western Task Force
NCWTM ..... National Council on Wholistic Therapeutics and Medicine [*Defunct*] (EA)
NCW Trf Cy ... New Control Word Transfer Cycle (SAUS)
NCWU .... National Catholic Women's Union (EA)
NcWU .... University of North Carolina at Wilmington, Wilmington, NC [*Library symbol*] [*Library of Congress*] (LCLS)
NCWUS ..... National Council of Women of the United States (WDAA)
NCWUSA .... National Council of Women of the United States of America (DI)
NCWV .... National Council of Women of Victoria [*Australia*]
NCWW ...... National Commission on Working Women (EA)
NCWWA ..... National Council of Women of Western Australia
NCWX .... No Change in Weather [*Weather codes - aviation*] (PIPO)
NCX .... Corpus Christi, TX [*Location identifier*] [*FAA*] (FAAL)
NCX .... NCN Exploration & Development [*Vancouver Stock Exchange symbol*]
NCX .... North Carolina Central University, Durham, NC [*OCLC symbol*] (OCLC)
NCX .... NOVA Chemicals [*NYSE symbol*] (SG)
NCX .... Nova Chemicals Corp. [*NYSE symbol*]
NCXL .... Northcoast Express Line [*Common carrier symbol*]
NCXU .... Nor-Cargo [*Intermodal shipping container symbol*] (TVRC)
NCY .... Annecy [*France*] [*Airport symbol*] (OAG)
NcY .... Hyconeechee Regional Library, Yanceyville, NC [*Library symbol*] [*Library of Congress*] (LCLS)
NCY .... Nancy Aviation [*France*] [*ICAO designator*] (FAAC)
NCY .... National Collaboration for Youth (EA)
N-CY .... Natural-Colored Yellow [*Diamonds*]
NCY .... Necessity [*Telegraphy*] (PCTE)
NCY .... New Century Resources [*Vancouver Stock Exchange symbol*]
NCY .... North Central Yiddish (BJA)
NCY .... Yorktown, VA [*Location identifier*] [*FAA*] (FAAL)
NCYA .... National Catholic Youth Association [*British*] (BI)
NcYad .... Yadkin County Public Library, Yadkinville, NC [*Library symbol*] [*Library of Congress*] (LCLS)
NCYC .... National Catholic Youth Council
NCYC .... National Collection of Yeast Cultures [*AFRC Institute of Food Research*] [*British*] [*Information service or system*] (IID)
NCYC .... National Council of Yacht Clubs (EA)
N CYC BN ... Northern Cyclist Battalion [*British military*] (DMA)
NCYC CAT ... National Collection of Yeast Cultures Catalogue [*Norwich Laboratory*] [*Norfolk, England*] [*Information service or system*] [*A publication*] (IID)
NCYD .... National Center for Youth with Disabilities (EA)
NCYF .... National Crusaders Youth Federation (EA)
NCYFS .... National Children and Youth Fitness Study [*HHS*]
NcYG .... Gunn Memorial Public Library, Yanceyville, NC [*Library symbol*] [*Library of Congress*] (LCLS)
NCYI .... National Council of Young Israel (EA)
NCYL .... National Center for Youth Law (EA)
NCYL .... Number of Cylinders [*Automotive emissions*]
NcYo .... Youngsville Public Library, Youngsville, NC [*Library symbol*] [*Library of Congress*] (LCLS)
NCYOF ...... National CYO [*Catholic Youth Organizations*] Federation (EA)
NCYP .... National Conference of Yeshiva Principals (EA)
NCYR .... Nash County Railroad [*Federal Railroad Administration identification code*]
NCYRE ...... National Council for Year-Round Education [*Later, NAYRE*] (EA)
NCYSI .... National Clearinghouse for Youth Sports Information [*Operated by the National Alliance for Youth Sports*] (PAZ)
NCYSP ...... National Committee on Youth Suicide Prevention (EA)
NCYWA ..... Nordic Child and Youth Welfare Alliance (EA)
NCYX .... National Cylinder Gas [*Private rail car owner code*]
NCz .... New Cruzado [*Monetary unit*] [*Brazil*] (BARN)
NcZG .... Glaxo, Inc., Zebulon, NC [*Library symbol*] [*Library of Congress*] (LCLS)
ND .... Aerospatiale [*Societe Nationale Industrielle Aerospatiale*] [*France*] [*ICAO aircraft manufacturer identifier*] (ICAO)
ND .... Diploma in Naturopathy [*British*]
ND .... Doctor of Naturopathic Medicine (PGP)
ND .... Doctor of Naturopathy
ND .... Doctor of Nursing (PGP)
ND .... Environment Near Death (SAUS)
ND .... Named (ROG)
ND .... Narrowband Distributive Services [*Telecommunications*]
ND .... NASA [*National Aeronautics and Space Administration*] Document
ND .... Nasal Deformity (DAVI)
ND .... National Debt
ND .... National Diploma [*Academic degree*] (AIE)
ND .... Native Defect (AAEL)
ND .... Natural Death [*Medicine*]
ND .... Natural Draught
ND .... Naturopathic Diploma (ODA)
ND .... Naval Dispensary
ND .... Naval Distillate Fuel (NVT)
ND .... Naval District
ND .... Naval Draftsman (ROG)
ND .... Navigation Display (MCD)
ND .... Navy Department
N-D .... N-Dimensional (MCD)
ND .... Nea Demokratia [*New Democracy*] [*Greece*] [*Political party*] (PPE)
ND .... Need [*Telegraphy*] (PCTE)
N/D .... Need Date (MCD)
ND .... Negative Declaration (NRCH)
ND .... Negatives and Deposition (DGA)
Nd .... Neodymium [*Chemical element*]
ND .... Neonatal Death [*Medicine*] (MAE)
ND .... Neoplastic Disease [*Medicine*]
ND .... Nervous Debility [*Medicine*]
ND .... Net Debt
ND .... Network Development [*Computer science*] (VLIE)
ND .... Network Digit [*Open Systems Interconnection*] (ODAA)
ND .... Network Directorate (SSD)
ND .... Neuburg [*Donau*] [*German license plate city code*]
ND .... Neurologic Deficit [*Medicine*]
ND .... Neuropathic Doctor (BARN)
ND .... Neurotic Depression [*Psychiatry*]
nd .... Neutral Density (ODA)
ND .... Neutral Density [*Photography*]
ND .... Neutral Density Filter (WDMC)
ND .... Neutral-Drive [*Automotive engineering*]
ND .... Neutron Density
ND .... Neutron Detector (SAUS)
ND .... Neutron Diffraction (MCD)
ND .... Newcastle Disease [*Virus*] [*Also, NDV*]
ND .... New Dawn [*An association*] (EA)
ND .... New Deal (DAS)
ND .... New Deck [*On ships*]

ND .... New Democracy [*European political movement*] (ECON)
ND .... New Developments Research Branch [*Bureau of Naval Personnel*] [*Washington, DC*]
ND .... New Directions [*Later, Democratic Alternatives - DA*] (EA)
ND .... New Donor (AAEL)
ND .... New Dramatists (EA)
ND .... New Drug
ND .... New Drugs [*A publication*]
Nd.......... Newfoundland Reports [*A publication*] (DLA)
ND .... News Director (NTCM)
ND .... Newsletters Directory [*Later, NIP*] [*A publication*]
ND .... Next Day [*Stock exchange term*] (SPSG)
ND .... Next Day's Delivery
ND .... Nhan Dan Newspaper [*A publication*]
ND .... Nickajack Dam [*TVA*]
ND .... Night Differential [*Payroll term*] (ALAC)
ND .... Nippondenso Co. [*Toyota Motor Corp.*]
ND .... No Data
nd.......... No Date (VRA)
ND .... No Date [*of publication*]
ND .... No Decision [*Sports*]
ND .... Node Dissection [*Medicine*]
nd.......... No Deed [*Or not Deeded*] (ODA)
ND .... No Deed (SAUS)
N/D .... No Defects
ND .... No Degree Objective (SAUS)
ND .... No Delay (SAUS)
ND .... No Delivery (SAUS)
ND .... No Detect
ND .... No Discharge (SAUS)
ND .... No Discount [*Business term*] (DS)
ND .... No Disease [*Medicine*]
ND .... No Drawing [*Engineering*]
ND .... No Drinking (SAUS)
ND .... No Drugs (SAUS)
ND .... Nondelay [*Military*]
ND .... Nondelivery [*Shipping*]
nd.......... non-delivery (SAUS)
ND .... Non-Denominational
ND .... Non-Descript (WDMC)
N/D .... Non-Destructive (SAUS)
ND .... Nondestructive Count (ACAE)
ND .... Nondetect (SAUS)
ND .... Nondetectable [*Medicine*] (DB)
ND .... Nondeterministic (IAA)
ND .... Nondiabetic [*Medicine*]
ND .... Nondirectional (IAA)
ND .... Nondirectional Antenna
ND .... Nondirectional Microphone (WDMC)
ND .... Nondirector (IAA)
ND .... Nondisabling [*Medicine*]
ND .... Non Disponible [*Not Available*] [*French*]
ND .... Non-Distended (SAUS)
N/D .... Non-Drinker [*Medicine*]
ND .... Nonduty [*Military*]
ND .... Nordair [*ICAO designator*] (AD)
ND .... Nordair Ltd. [*Canada*] [*ICAO designator*] (OAG)
ND .... Normal Delivery [*Obstetrics*]
ND .... Normal Deployability Posture (SAUS)
ND .... Normal Detail (ELAL)
ND .... Normal Development [*Pediatrics*] (DAVI)
ND .... Normal Direction (SAUS)
ND .... Normal Distribution (SAUS)
ND .... Normal Duty (SAUS)
ND .... Normalized Difference (SAUS)
ND .... North Dakota [*Postal code*]
Nd.......... North Dakota State Library, Bismarck, ND [*Library symbol*] [*Library of Congress*] (LCLS)
ND .... North Dakota Supreme Court Reports [*1890-1953*] [*A publication*] (DLA)
ND .... Northern District (DLA)
ND .... Nose Down [*Aviation*]
ND .... Nose Drops [*Pharmacy*] (DAVI)
ND .... Nostra Domina [*Our Lady*] [*Latin*]
nd.......... Not Dated (EBF)
ND .... Not Dated [*Banking, bibliography*]
ND .... Not Deeded (SAUS)
ND .... Not Desirable (ELAL)
ND .... Not Detected [*or Detectable*] [*Medicine*]
ND .... Not Determinable (SAUS)
ND .... Not Determined [*Medicine*]
ND .... Not Diagnosed [*Medicine*]
ND .... Not Directly (DGA)
ND .... Not Done
ND .... Not Drawn (SAUS)
nd.......... Nothing Doing (ODA)
ND .... Nothing Doing [*Amateur radio slang*]
ND .... Notre Dame (NTIO)
ND .... Notre Dame Sisters (TOCD)
ND .... Nouvelle Droite [*New Right*] [*France*] [*Political party*] (WDAA)
ND .... Nuclear Data Corp. (SAUS)
ND .... Nuclear Detonation (SAUS)
ND .... Nuclear Device (AAG)
ND .... Nucleotidase (SAUS)
ND .... Number Detector (SAUS)
Nd.......... Number of Dissimilar Matches
ND .... Number of Document [*Online database field identifier*]
ND .... Numerical Data (SAUS)
ND .... Numerical Display (SAUS)
ND .... Nursing Doctorale (SAUS)
ND .... Nursing Doctorate
ND .... Nutritionally Deprived (MELL)
ND .... Nutrition Disorder (MELL)
ND .... Ny Demokrati [*New Democracy*] [*Sweden*] [*Political party*] (EY)
ND .... Romania [*License plate code assigned to foreign diplomats in the US*]
ND .... University of Notre Dame [*Indiana*]
nd.......... Updated (VRA)
Nd2.......... Nord-Aviation 262 [*Airplane code*]
NDA.......... Bandanaira [*Indonesia*] [*Airport symbol*] (OAG)
NDA.......... Naphthalenedicarboxaldehyde [*Organic chemistry*]
NDA.......... National Dairy Association (NADA)
NDA.......... National Dairymen's Association, Inc. [*British*] (BI)
NDA.......... National Dance Association (EA)
NDA.......... National Defense Act
NDA.......... National Defense Area (AABC)
NDA.......... National Democratic Alliance [*Sierra Leone*] [*Political party*] (EY)
NDA.......... National Democratic Alliance [*Sudan*] [*Political party*]
NDA.......... National Dental Association (EA)
NDA.......... National Denturist Association (EA)
NDA.......... National Diploma in Agriculture [*British*]
NDA.......... National Dome Association [*Later, NDC*] (EA)
NDA.......... National Door Association [*Defunct*]
NDA.......... National Drilling Association (NTPA)
NDA.......... NAUI [*National Association of Underwater Instructors*] Diving Association (EA)
NDA.......... Naval Discipline Act [*British military*] (DMA)
NDA.......... Nebraska Dressage Association (EARSL)
NDA.......... Network Delivery Access (SAUS)
NDA.......... Neutral Detector Assembly
NDA.......... Nevada (ROG)
NDA.......... New Desk Accessories [*Utility program*] [*Apple Computers, Inc.*] [*Computer science*]
NDA.......... New Drug Application [*FDA*]
NDA.......... New Drug Approval (MELL)
NDA.......... Newspaper Design Award (DGA)
NDA.......... Nigerian Defense Academy (SAUS)
NDA.......... Night Driving Aid (ACAE)
NDA.......... Ninos de las Americas [*Children of the Americas*] (EAIO)
NDA.......... No Data Available [*Computer science*]
NDA.......... No Demonstrable Antibody [*Medicine*] (MAE)
NDA.......... No Detectable Activity
NDA.......... No Diagnosis of Anything
NDA.......... Nonadecanoic Acid [*Organic chemistry*]
NDA.......... Non-Destructive Addition (SAUS)
NDA.......... Nondestructive Analysis (SAUS)
NDA.......... Nondestructive Assay
NDA.......... Nondimensional Analysis
NDA.......... Non Disclosure Agreement (SAUS)
NDA.......... Non-Disclosure Agreement (WDMC)
NDA.......... Nonresonant Deflection Amplifier
NDA.......... Nordair Ltd. [*Toronto Stock Exchange symbol*]
NDA.......... Northern Airways, Inc. [*ICAO designator*] (FAAC)
NDA.......... Not Diagnosed with Anything
NDA.......... Nuclear Development Associates, Inc. (SAUS)
NDA.......... Nuclear Device Association (AAG)
NDA.......... [*The*] Nuzi Dialect of Akkadian [*A publication*] (BJA)
NDAA.......... National Dental Assistants Association (EA)
NDAA.......... National District Attorneys Association (EA)
NDAA.......... Non-Developmental Airlift Aircraft [*Military*]
NDAA.......... Not Dated At All (SAUS)
NDAAC.......... Navy Drug and Alcohol Advisory Council (DNAB)
NDA & LB... Naval District Affairs and Logistics Branch
NDAB.......... North Dakota Association of Builders (EARSL)
NDAB.......... Numerical Data Advisory Board [*National Academy of Sciences*] [*Information service or system*] (IID)
NDAC.......... National Defense Advisory Commission [*World War II*]
NDAC.......... National Defense Advisory Committee (NADA)
NDAC.......... National Defense Advisory Council (SAUS)
NDAC.......... NATO Data-Buoy System [*National Oceanic and Atmospheric Administration*]
NDAC.......... Naval Data Automation Command (ACAE)
NDAC.......... No Data Accepted [*Computer science*] (IAA)
NDAC.......... Normalized Differential Absorption Cross-section (SAUS)
NDAC.......... North Dakota Administrative Code [*A publication*] (AAGC)
NDAC.......... North Dakota Agricultural College
NDAC.......... Not Data Accepted (SAUS)
NDAC.......... Nuclear Defense Affairs Committee [*NATO*]
NDACAN .... National Data Archive on Child Abuse and Neglect [*Database*] (GDD)
NDACO.......... North Dakota Association of Counties (EARSL)
NDACP.......... Navy Drug Abuse Control Program (DNAB)
NDACS.......... Navy Drug Abuse Counselor School (DNAB)
NDACS.......... Network Diagnostic and Control Systems (ADA)
NDACSS..... Navy Department Advisory Committee on Structural Steel
NdAD.......... Nicotinamide Deoxyadenosine Dinucleotide (SAUS)
ND Admin Code... North Dakota Administrative Code [*A publication*] (DLA)
NDADS.......... NSSDC Data Archive and Distribution System (SAUS)

NDAFA....... National Directory of Accounting Firms and Accountants [*A publication*]
ND Agr E.... National Diploma in Agricultural Engineering [*British*]
NDAIS....... Nondestructive assay isotopic system (SAUS)
N DAK....... North Dakota (AAG)
N Dak....... North Dakota (NTIO)
N Dak....... North Dakota Reports [*A publication*] (DLA)
ND Ala...... United States District Court for the Northern District of Alabama (DLA)
ND ALV...... Nondefective Avian Leucosis Virus (SAUS)
NDAM....... New Disk Access Method [*Computer science*] (MHDI)
NDANG...... North Dakota Air National Guard (MUSM)
NDANO...... North Dakota Association of Nonprofit Organizations (EARSL)
NDAP....... Nationalsozialistische Deutsche Arbeiterpartei [*National Socialist German Workers' Party, 1919-45*] [*Political party*] (PPW)
NDAPTA..... National Drivers Association for the Prevention of Traffic Accidents [*Defunct*] (EA)
NDAR....... North Dakota Association of Realtors (EARSL)
NDARC...... National Drug and Alcohol Research Center [*University of New South Wales*] [*Australia*]
NDAREC..... North Dakota Association of Rural Electric Cooperatives (EARSL)
NDASSP..... North Dakota Association of Secondary School Principals (SAUS)
ND ASV..... Nondefective Avian Sarcoma Virus (SAUS)
NDAT....... Neighborhood Disaster Action Team [*Emergency Management*] (EMA)
NDAT....... Nondestructible Aiming Target
NDAT....... Non-Destructive Assay Technique [*Military*] (PDAA)
NData....... National Data Corp. [*Associated Press*] (SAG)
NDATC....... North Dakota Association of Telephone Cooperatives (EARSL)
NDATUS..... National Drug and Alcohol Treatment Utilization Survey [*Department of Health and Human Services*] (GFGA)
NDB......... Name Definition Block (TIMI)
NDB......... National Discount Brokers Group [*NYSE symbol*] [*Formerly, Sherwood Group*] (SG)
NDB......... Nautical Directional Beacon (IAA)
NDB......... Naval Disciplinary Barracks
NDB......... Navy Department Bulletin [*A publication*]
NDB......... Net Debit Balance
NDB......... Net Decision Benefit (NUCP)
NDB......... New Domestic Boiler (SAUS)
NDB......... New Donkey Boiler (SAUS)
NDB......... Niger Delta Congress (SAUS)
NDB......... Niue Development Board (SAUS)
NDB......... Non Directional Beacon (SAUS)
NDB......... Nondirectional Beacon (AFM)
NDB......... Non-Directional Radio Beacon (PIPO)
NDB......... Nouadhibou [*Mauritania*] [*Airport symbol*] (OAG)
NDB......... Nuclear Depth Bomb (NVT)
NDB......... Numeric Data Base [*INPADOC*] [*Computer science*]
NDBA........ National Data Base on Aging (EDAC)
NDBA........ National Deaf Bowling Association (EA)
NDBA........ New Directions in Biblical Archaeology [*A publication*] (BJA)
NDBA........ Nitrosodibutylamine [*Organic chemistry*]
NDBA........ North Dakota Bankers Association (EARSL)
NDB-ADF.... Non-Directional Beacon-Automatic Direction Finder (SAUS)
NDBB........ North Dakota Bar Brief [*A publication*] (DLA)
NdBC........ Bismarck Junior College, Bismarck, ND [*Library symbol*] [*Library of Congress*] (LCLS)
NDBC........ National Data Buoy Center [*National Oceanic and Atmospheric Administration*] [*Also, an information service or system*] (IID)
NDBC........ National Day of Bread Committee [*Defunct*] (EA)
NDBC........ National Dry Bean Council (EA)
NDBC........ National Duckpin Bowling Congress (EA)
NDBC........ NOAA Data Buoy Center (SAUS)
NDBCA...... Navy Department Board of Contract Appeals
NDBDM..... Navy Department Board of Decorations and Medals (DNAB)
NDBDP...... National Data Buoy Development Project [*Later, NDBO*] [*Coast Guard*] (MSC)
NdBH........ Bismarck Hospital, School of Nursing Library, Bismarck, ND [*Library symbol*] [*Library of Congress*] (LCLS)
NdBHD...... North Dakota State Health Department, Bismarck, ND [*Library symbol*] [*Library of Congress*] (LCLS)
NdBHwy..... North Dakota State Highway Department, Bismarck, ND [*Library symbol*] [*Library of Congress*] (LCLS)
NDBI......... National Dairymen's Benevolent Institution, Inc. [*British*] (BI)
NDBL........ National Deaf-Blind League [*British*] (EAIO)
NDB/L....... Nondireetional Beacon/Locator (SAUS)
NDBLO...... Not to Descend Below [*Aviation*] (FAAC)
NdBM........ Mary College, Bismarck, ND [*Library symbol*] [*Library of Congress*] (LCLS)
NDBMS...... Network Database Management System
NDBMS...... Nonstandard Database Management System (SAUS)
NDBO........ National Data Buoy Office [*Marine science*] (OSRA)
NdBoU....... North Dakota State University, Bottineau Branch, Bottineau, ND [*Library symbol*] [*Library of Congress*] (LCLS)
NDBP........ National Data Buoy Program [*National Oceanic and Atmospheric Administration*] (GFGA)
NdBPI........ North Dakota State Department of Public Instruction, Bismarck, ND [*Library symbol*] [*Library of Congress*] (LCLS)
NDBPSA..... Non-Denominational Bible Prophecy Study Association (EA)
NdBPW...... North Dakota State Public Welfare Board, Bismarck, ND [*Library symbol*] [*Library of Congress*] (LCLS)
NdBQ........ Quain and Ramstad Clinic, Bismarck, ND [*Library symbol*] [*Library of Congress*] (LCLS)
Nd-BR....... Butadiene Rubber Based on Neodymium Catalyst (SAUS)
NDBS........ National Data Buoy System
NDBS........ Naval Despatch Boat Service
NDBS........ Non-standard Database System (SAUS)
NDBULCUMED... Navy Department Bulletins, Cumulative Editions [*A publication*]
NdBV........ Bismarck [*Veterans Memorial*] Public Library, Bismarck, ND [*Library symbol*] [*Library of Congress*] (LCLS)
NDC.......... Air Nordic SWE Aviation, AB [*Sweden*] [*FAA designator*] (FAAC)
NDC.......... Naphthalene Dicarboxylate [*Organic chemistry*]
NDC.......... Natick Development Center [*Massachusetts*] [*Army*]
NDC.......... National Dairy Council (EA)
NDC.......... National Data Communication
NDC.......... National Data Corp. [*NYSE symbol*] (SPSG)
NDC.......... National Debt Commission [*Australia*]
NDC.......... National Defence College [*British*]
NDC.......... National Defence Committee [*Ghana*] [*Political party*] (PPW)
NDC.......... National Defence Company [*British military*] (DMA)
NDC.......... National Defence Contribution [*British*]
NDC.......... National Defence Corps [*British*]
NDC.......... National Defense College [*Australia*]
NDC.......... National Defense Council (KSC)
NDC.......... National Democratic Club (EA)
NDC.......... National Democratic Congress [*Ghana*] [*Political party*] (ECON)
NDC.......... National Democratic Congress [*Grenada*] [*Political party*] (EY)
NDC.......... National Design Council [*Canada*]
NDC.......... National DeSoto Club (EA)
NDC.......... National Development Corp. [*Dominica*] (EY)
NDC.......... National Development Council (EA)
NDC.......... National Directory of Churches, Synagogues, and Other Houses of Worship [*A publication*]
NDC.......... National Disaster Coalition
NDC.......... National Distributing Co., Inc. (EFIS)
NDC.......... National Distribution Circuit (ACAE)
NDC.......... National Diving Council
NDC.......... National Dome Council (EA)
NDC.......... National Drug Code [*FDA*]
NDC.......... National Duckling Council [*Defunct*] (EA)
NDC.......... Natl Data [*NYSE symbol*] (TTSB)
NDC.......... NATO Defense College [*Also, NADC, NADEFCOL*] (NATG)
NDC.......... Natural Distribution Certificate (WDAA)
NDC.......... Naval Data Center
NDC.......... Naval Dental Clinic
NDC.......... Naval Doctrine Command (COE)
NDC.......... Navigation Display and Computer (MCD)
NDC.......... Negative Differential Conductivity (OA)
NDC.......... Network Data Collection (SAUS)
NDC.......... Network Data Control (MCD)
NDC.......... Network Diagnostic Control
NDC.......... Networked Data Center [*Computer science*] (GART)
NDC.......... Neurologic Disease Control
NDC.......... New Democratic Coalition
NDC.......... New Die Cast [*Honda Motor Co. Ltd.*]
NDC.......... New Directions in Creativity Program (EDAC)
NDC.......... New Dramatists Committee [*Later, ND*] (EA)
NDC.......... Newport Design Center (ACAE)
NDC.......... Nippon Decimal Classification [*Library science*]
NDC.......... No Date Club [*Brooklyn girls - no dates for the duration*] [*World War II*]
NDC.......... Node Data Controller (SAUS)
NDC.......... No Direct Charge
NDC.......... Noise Dose Count (IAA)
NDC.......... Nondairy Cattle (CARB)
NDC.......... Nondestructive Characterization (SAUS)
NDC.......... Non-Destructive Cleaning (SAUS)
NDC.......... Non-Destructive Cursor (SAUS)
NDC.......... Nondifferentiated Cell [*Medicine*] (DMAA)
NDC.......... Non-Double-Couple [*Seismology*]
NDC.......... NORAD Direction Center [*Military*]
NDC.......... Normalized Device Coordinates [*Computer science*]
NDC.......... Northern Development Co. [*British*] (ECON)
NDC.......... Northwest Drama Conference (EA)
NDC.......... Notice of Drawing Change [*Navy*] (DNAB)
NDC.......... Notre Dame College [*Missouri, New Hampshire, Ohio*]
NDC.......... Notre Dame College, Manchester, NH [*Inactive*] [*OCLC symbol*] (OCLC)
NDC.......... Noyes Data Corp.
NDC.......... Nuclear Data Committee (NRCH)
NDC.......... Nuclear Design and Construction [*British*]
NDC.......... Nuclear Design Calculations [*Program*]
NDC.......... Nuclear Detector Circuit (SAUS)
NDC.......... Nuclear Development Corp. (SAUS)
NDCA........ Naphthalenedicarboxylic Acid [*Organic chemistry*]
NDCA........ National Dance Council of America (EA)
NDCA........ National Deaf Children's Association [*British*]
NDCA........ National Drilling Contractors Association (EA)
NDCA........ Nuclear Development Corp. of America
NDCAC...... North Dakota College Athletic Conference (PSS)
ND Cal...... United States District Court for the Northern District of California (DLA)
NdCan....... Cando Public Library, Cando, ND [*Library symbol*] [*Library of Congress*] (LCLS)
NDCC........ National Defense Cadet Corps
NDCC........ National Defined Contribution Council [*Association*] (EA)
NDCC........ National Disaster Coordinating Council [*Emergency Management*] (EMA)
NDCC........ Navy Department Corrosion Committee
NDCC........ Nondirectional Cross-Country (MCD)

NDCC North Dakota Century Code [*A publication*]
NDCCC National Defense Communications Control Center (MCD)
NDCD National Drug Code Directory [*FDA*] [*A publication*]
NDCDAR National Defense Committee of the Daughters of the American Revolution (EA)
NDCEAA North Dakota County Extension Agents Association (EARSL)
NDCEE National Defense Center for Environmental Excellence [*DoD*] (RDA)
ND Cent Code North Dakota Century Code [*A publication*] (DLA)
NDCF National Defense Council Foundation (EA)
NDCG Nursing Development Conference Group (DMAA)
NDCMP North Dakota Cloud Modification Project (SAUS)
NdCo Cooperstown Public Library, Cooperstown, ND [*Library symbol*] [*Library of Congress*] (LCLS)
NDCO Noble Drilling Corp. (SAUS)
NDColl National Defence College [*British*]
NDCP Navy Decision Coordinating Paper
NDCP Navy Development Concept Paper (CAAL)
NDCPD North Dakota Center for Persons with Disabilities [*Minot State University*] (RCD)
NDC Program Nuclear Design Calculations Program (SAUS)
NDC-PS No Drawing Change Project Slip
NdCr Divide County Library, Crosby, ND [*Library symbol*] [*Library of Congress*] (LCLS)
NDCR NDC Railroad [*Federal Railroad Administration identification code*]
NDCR Noise Distortion Clearance Range (SAUS)
NDCS National Deaf Children's Society [*British*] (BI)
NDCT Natural Draft Cooling Tower [*Nuclear energy*] (NRCH)
NDCT Non-Secure Data Communication Terminal (DWSG)
NDCUL North Dakota Credit Union League (EARSL)
NDCX Nickel & Dime Railway [*Federal Railroad Administration identification code*]
NDD Duke University Library, Durham, NC [*OCLC symbol*] (OCLC)
NDd Dundee Library, Dundee, NY [*Library symbol*] [*Library of Congress*] (LCLS)
NDD National Diploma in Dairying [*British*]
NDD National Diploma in Design [*British*]
NDD NATO Deducible Directory (SAUS)
NDD Navigation and Direction Division [*British military*] (DMA)
NDD Negotiation Decision Document [*Environmental Protection Agency*] (EPA)
NDD Net Defence Department [*Navy*] [*British*]
NDD Neutron Density Distribution (SAUS)
NDD New Democratic Dimensions (EA)
NDD Nitro(dimethyl)dihydrobenzofuran [*Organic chemistry*]
NDD No Dialysis Days [*Nephrology*] (DAVI)
NDD Nondeferred Development (MCD)
NDD Norton Disk Doctor [*Computer science*]
NDD Novo Redondo [*Angola*] [*Airport symbol*] (AD)
NDD Nuclear Detection Device (MCD)
NDD Sumbe [*Angola*] [*Airport symbol*] (OAG)
NDd Woman's Study Club & Library, Dundee, NY [*Library symbol*] [*Library of Congress*] (LCLS)
NDDA National Demolition Derby Association (EA)
NDD & RF Naval Dry Dock and Repair Facility
NDDC National Defeat Dukakis Campaign (EA)
NDDC Navy Department Duty Chaplain (DNAB)
NDDC NORAD Division Direction Center [*Military*] (AABC)
NdDe Devils Lake Carnegie Library, Devils Lake, ND [*Library symbol*] [*Library of Congress*] (LCLS)
NdDeH Mercy Hospital, Devils Lake, ND [*Library symbol*] [*Library of Congress*] (LCLS)
NDDEIC National Digestive Diseases Education and Information Clearinghouse [*Public Health Service*] [*Later, NDDIC*] (IID)
NdDeL Lake Region Junior College, Devils Lake, ND [*Library symbol*] [*Library of Congress*] (LCLS)
NDDF National Drug Data File Knowledge Base [*Database*] (GDD)
NDDF The National Drug Data File Knowledge Base (MHID)
NDDG National Diabetes Data Group [*British*]
NdDi Dickinson Public Library, Dickinson, ND [*Library symbol*] [*Library of Congress*] (LCLS)
NDDIC National Digestive Diseases Information Clearinghouse (EA)
NdDiS Dickinson State College, Dickinson, ND [*Library symbol*] [*Library of Congress*] (LCLS)
NdDiStJ Saint Joseph Hospital, Dickinson, ND [*Library symbol*] [*Library of Congress*] (LCLS)
NDDL Neutral Data Definition Language [*Computer science*] (VLIE)
NDDN National Dry Deposition Network (GNE)
NDDN Norwegian Defence Digital Network (SAUS)
NDDO Neglect of Diatomic Differential Overlap [*Quantum mechanics*]
NDDP NATO Defense Data Program (AABC)
NDDS National Disability Data System [*Social Security Administration*] (GFGA)
NDDS National Driving Distractions Survey [*Automotive safety*]
NDDS Nuclear Detonation Detection System (DOMA)
NDE IndyMac Bancorporation [*NYSE symbol*]
NDE IndyMac Mortgage Holdings [*NYSE symbol*] [*Formerly, INMC Mortgage Holdings*]
NDE Mandera [*Kenya*] [*Airport symbol*] (OAG)
NDE National Defense Education
NDE National Defense Emergency [*Headquarters*] (MCD)
NDE National Dinghy Exhibition [*British*]
NDE Navy Department Establishments [*British*]
NDE N-Demethylencainide [*Organic chemistry*]
NDE Near-Death Experience
NDE Nevada Desert Experience (EA)
NDE News Development Environment (SAUS)
NDE Nissan Design Europe [*Automotive industry*]
NDE No Date Established
NDE No Delay Expected
NDE Nondestructive Evaluation
NDE Nondestructive Examination [*Nuclear energy*] (NRCH)
NDE Nondiabetic Extremity [*Medicine*] (DMAA)
NDE Notodden [*Norway*] [*Airport symbol*] (AD)
NDEA National Defense Education Act [*1958*]
NDEA National Defense Emergency Authorization
NDEA National Display Equipment Association [*British*] (BI)
NDEA Nitrosodiethylamine [*Organic chemistry*]
nDEA No Deviation of Electrical Axis [*On electrocardiogram*] [*Cardiology*] (DAVI)
NDEA-PACE North Dakota Education Association PAC for Education [*Bismarck, ND*] (PACS)
N de Aqi Nicholas de Aquila [*Flourished, 1197-1217*] [*Authority cited in pre-1607 legal work*] (DSA)
NDEC National Disaster Education Coalition [*Emergency Management*] (EMA)
NDEC NDE Environmental Corp. [*NASDAQ symbol*] (NQ)
NDEC Nursing Diagnosis and Extension Classification (SAUS)
NDEDIC National Dental EDI Council [*Association*] (EA)
n def Nerve Deficit (SPVS)
NDEF Not Defined (SAUS)
NDEF Not to be Defined (VLIE)
N-Defense Nuclear Defense (SAUS)
NDEI National Defense Education Institute
NDEITA National Dance-Exercise Instructor's Training Association (EA)
NDEL Non-Destructive Evaluation Laboratory [*NASA*]
NDELA Nitrosodiethanolamine [*Also, NDEOL*] [*Organic chemistry*]
NdEIN State Normal and Industrial School, Ellendale, ND [*Library symbol*] [*Library of Congress*] [*Obsolete*] (LCLS)
NdEIT Trinity Bible Institute, Ellendale, ND [*Library symbol*] [*Library of Congress*] (LCLS)
NDemP National Democratic Party [*British*]
NDEO Naval Disability Evaluation Office (ACAE)
NDEOA National Drug Enforcement Officers Association (EA)
NDEOL Nitrosodiethanolamine [*Also, NDELA*] [*Organic chemistry*]
NDEP Nevada Division of Environmental Protection
NDER National Defense Executive Reserve
NDERR National Defense Executive Reserve Roster [*of the CSC*]
NDERWF Navy Department Employees Recreation and Welfare Fund (MCD)
NDES Normal Digital Echo Suppressor [*Telecommunications*] (TEL)
NDETP National Drug Education Training Program [*HEW*]
NDeUA State University of New York, Agricultural and Technical College at Delhi, Delhi, NY [*Library symbol*] [*Library of Congress*] (LCLS)
NDEW Nuclear-Driven Directed-Energy Weapon
NDEWT Nuclear Directed Energy Weapon Technology programme (SAUS)
NDex Dexter Free Library, Dexter, NY [*Library symbol*] [*Library of Congress*] (LCLS)
NDEX Newspaper Index [*Bell & Howell Co.*] [*Database*]
NDf Dobbs Ferry Public Library, Dobbs Ferry, NY [*Library symbol*] [*Library of Congress*] (LCLS)
NdF Fargo Public Library, Fargo, ND [*Library symbol*] [*Library of Congress*] (LCLS)
NDF Nacelle Drag Efficiency [*Factor*] [*Aerospace*]
NDF Namibian Defense Force [*Political party*] (PSAP)
NDF Nandi [*Fiji*] [*Seismograph station code, US Geological Survey*] (SEIS)
NDF Narrative Data File (CARB)
NDF National Democratic Front [*Guyana*] [*Political party*] (EY)
NDF National Democratic Front [*Iran*] [*Political party*] (PD)
NDF National Democratic Front [*Yemen*] [*Political party*] (PD)
NDF National Democratic Front [*Myanmar*] [*Political party*] (FEA)
NDF National Democratic Front [*Pakistan*] [*Political party*] (FEA)
NDF National Democratic Front [*Philippines*] [*Political party*] (FEA)
NDF National Diploma in Forestry [*British*]
NDF National Dividend Foundation (EA)
NDF National Drilling Federation [*Later, IDF*] (EA)
NDF Naval Dairy Farm
NDF Naval Defence Force [*British military*] (DMA)
NDF Navy Distillate Fuel (DNAB)
NDF NCP/EP Definition Facility [*Communications term*] (DCT)
NDF Ndebele [*Language symbol*] (ETLW)
NDF Needful [*Telegraphy*] (PCTE)
NDF Network Distributed Function [*Computer science*] (GART)
NDF Network Dynamic Functionality [*Computer science*] (GART)
NDF Neutral Density Factor (SAUS)
NDF Neutral Density Filter
NDF Neutral Detergent Fiber [*Food analysis*]
NDF New Democratic Forum (EA)
NDF New Dimensions Foundation (EA)
NDF New Dosage Form [*Medicine*] (MAE)
NDF Nicolas-Durand-Favre [*Disease*] [*Medicine*] (DB)
NDF Night Defense Fire (DNAB)
NDF No Diagnostic Findings [*Medicine*] (DMAA)
NDF No Disease Found (DAVI)
NDF Non-Deterministic Fortran [*Computer science*] (VLIE)
NDF Nondipole Field [*Electromagnetism*]
NDF Non-linear Discriminant Function (SAUS)
NDF Nonlinear Distortion Factor [*Telecommunications*] (OA)
NDF Nonrecursive Digital Filter [*Navy*] (IAA)
NDF Number of Discontinuity Functions (SAUS)
NDFA National Dietary Foods Association [*Later, NNFA*] (EA)

NDFA .... National Drama Festivals Association [*British*] (BI)
NDFA .... North Dakota Family Alliance (RCD)
NdFA .... North Dakota State University, Fargo, ND [*Library symbol*] [*Library of Congress*] (LCLS)
NdFC .... Cass County Court House, Fargo (SAUS)
NDFC .... National Days Fan Club (EA)
NDF/CAD .... Nondestructive Evaluation/Computer-Aided Design (SAUS)
NdFD .... Dakota Clinic, Fargo, ND [*Library symbol*] [*Library of Congress*] (LCLS)
NDFEA .... Northwest Dried Fruit Export Association [*Defunct*] (EA)
NDFFRA ..... North Dakota Flying Farmers and Ranchers Association (EARSL)
nd filter ..... Neutral-Density Filter [*Photography*] (WDMC)
NDfL .... Dobbs Ferry Public Library, Dobbs Ferry, NY [*Library symbol*] [*Library of Congress*] (LCLS)
NDFL .... National Defense Foreign Language [*Fellowship*]
ND Fla ...... United States District Court for the Northern District of Florida (DLA)
NdFM .... Masonic Grand Lodge Library, Fargo, ND [*Library symbol*] [*Library of Congress*] (LCLS)
NDfM .... Mercy College, Dobbs Ferry, NY [*Library symbol*] [*Library of Congress*] (LCLS)
NdFMG ...... Masonic Grand Lodge, Fargo, ND [*Library symbol*] [*Library of Congress*] (LCLS)
NdFN .... Neuropsychiatric Hospital, Fargo, ND [*Library symbol*] [*Library of Congress*] (LCLS)
NDFS .... Non-Dwelling Floor Space (SAA)
NDfS .... Stauffer Chemical Co., Eastern Research Center, Dobbs Ferry, NY [*Library symbol*] [*Library of Congress*] (LCLS)
NdFStJ ...... Saint John's Hospital, Fargo, ND [*Library symbol*] [*Library of Congress*] (LCLS)
NdFStL ...... Saint Luke's Hospital, Fargo, ND [*Library symbol*] [*Library of Congress*] (LCLS)
NdFStLN .... Saint Luke's School of Nursing, Fargo, ND [*Library symbol*] [*Library of Congress*] (LCLS)
NDFTA .... National Dried Fruit Trade Association [*British*] (DBA)
NdFVA .... United States Veterans Administration Hospital, Fargo, ND [*Library symbol*] [*Library of Congress*] (LCLS)
NDFYP ...... Navy Department Five Year Plan
NdG .... Grand Forks Public Library, Grand Forks, ND [*Library symbol*] [*Library of Congress*] (LCLS)
NDG .... National Dance Guild [*Later, ADG*]
NDG .... National Distribution Guide [*Mailing technique*]
NDG .... Needing [*Telegraphy*] (PCTE)
NDG .... No Date Given (AFM)
NDGA .... National Depression Glass Association (EA)
NDGA .... National Dog Groomers Association (EA)
NDGA .... Nordihydroguaiaretic Acid [*Antioxidant, food additive*]
ND GA .... United States District Court for the Northern District of Georgia (DLA)
NDGAA ...... National Dog Groomers Association of America (EA)
NDGC .... National Design Graphics Competition (VLIE)
NDGE .... NATO Air Defense Ground Environment
NdGIT .... United States Air Force Institute of Technology, Grand Forks AFB, ND [*Library symbol*] [*Library of Congress*] (LCLS)
NDGL .... Neodymium-Doped Glass LASER
NDGO .... Navy Department General Order
NDGP .... Nepean Division of General Practice (SAUS)
NDGPS ...... Nationwide Differential Global Positioning System [*Navigation systems*]
NdGrC .... Carnegie Bookmobile Library, Grafton, ND [*Library symbol*] [*Library of Congress*] (LCLS)
NDGS .... National Defense General Staff (NATG)
NDGS .... National Duncan Glass Society (EA)
NdGUH ...... Grand Forks United Hospital, Grand Forks, ND [*Library symbol*] [*Library of Congress*] (LCLS)
NDGW .... Native Daughters of the Golden West (EA)
NDH .... Delhi [*India*] [*Airport symbol*] (AD)
NDH .... National Defense Headquarters [*Canada*]
NDH .... National Diploma in Horticulture [*British*]
NDH .... Natural Disaster Hospitals [*Public Health Service*]
NDH .... New Departure Hyatt Division [*General Motors Corp.*]
NDH .... No Damage History [*Aviation*] (PIPO)
NDH .... Nordhausen [*German license plate city code*]
NDH .... Royal North Devonshire Yeomanry Hussars [*British military*] (DMA)
NdHa .... Harvey Public Library, Harvey, ND [*Library symbol*] [*Library of Congress*] (LCLS)
NDHA .... National Dental Hygienists' Association (EA)
NDHA .... National District Heating Association [*Later, IDHCA*] (EA)
NDHA .... North Dakota Hospitality Association (EARSL)
NDHECN .... North Dakota Higher Education Computer Network (VLIE)
NDHFP ...... New Developments Human Factors Program [*Navy*]
NdHi .... State Historical Society of North Dakota, Bismarck, ND [*Library symbol*] [*Library of Congress*] (LCLS)
NDHIA .... National Dairy Herd Improvement Association (GVA)
NDHQ .... National Defence Headquarters [*Canada*]
NDHS .... New Drop High School (SAUS)
NDHS .... Nimbus Data Handling System
NDHX .... Natural Draft Heat Exchanger [*Nuclear energy*] (NRCH)
NDI .... Dickinson State College, Dickinson, ND [*OCLC symbol*] (OCLC)
NDI .... KS Nordic Air, Denmark [*ICAO designator*] (FAAC)
NDI .... Namudi [*Papua New Guinea*] [*Airport symbol*] (OAG)
NDI .... National Dance Institute (EA)
NDI .... National Death Index [*Department of Health and Human Services*] (GFGA)
NDI .... National Democratic Institute for International Affairs
NDI .... National Design, Inc. (PCM)
NDI .... Nephrogenic Diabetes Insipidus [*Endocrinology*]
NDI .... Network Development and Implementation Group [*National Research Council of Canada*]
NDI .... Network Distributed ISDN (SAUS)
NDI .... New Delhi [*India*] [*Seismograph station code, US Geological Survey*] (SEIS)
NDI .... Nielsen Drug Index [*Marketing*] (DOAD)
NDI .... Nissan Design International
NDI .... No-Dig International [*A publication*]
NDI .... Noise Depreciation Index
NDI .... Non-Combat Development Item
NDI .... Nondestructive Inspection (AFM)
NDI .... Non-Developmental Item [*Military*] (INF)
NDI .... Non-Developmental Items (SAUS)
NDI .... Non-Development [*or Developmental*] Issue [*or Item*]
NDI .... Nuclear Data, Inc. (SAUS)
NDI .... Numerical Designation Index (IEEE)
NDI .... Numerical Design Index (SAUS)
NDIA .... National Defender Investigator Association (EA)
NDIA .... National Defense Industrial Association
NDIA .... New Denver International Airport (COE)
NDiag .... National Diagnostics, Inc. [*Associated Press*] (SAG)
NDIAG .... Norton Diagnostics (SAUS)
NDIC .... National Defence Industries Council (SAUS)
NDIC .... National Diabetes Information Clearinghouse [*Public Health Service*] (IID)
NDIC .... National Drug Intelligence Center [*Department of Defense*] (SEAT)
NDIC .... NATO Defense Information Complex (NATG)
NDIC .... Nuclear Data Information Center [*ORNL*]
NDIC .... Nuclear Desalination Information Center
NDICE .... Non-Developmental Items Candidate Evaluation
NDICF .... North Dakota Independent College Fund (SAUS)
n Dicke ...... des n-ten Farbfilters (SAUS)
NDIIA .... National Democratic Institute for International Affairs (EA)
NDIL .... Non-Destructive Inspection Laboratory (SAUS)
ND Ill .... United States District Court for the Northern District of Illinois (DLA)
NDIMC ...... NATO Defense Information Management Committee (NATG)
NDIN .... National Disaster Information Center [*Emergency Management*] (EMA)
ND Ind ...... United States District Court for the Northern District of Indiana (DLA)
ND Iowa .... United States District Court for the Northern District of Iowa (DLA)
NDIR .... Nondispersive Infrared [*Analyzer*]
NDIR .... Nondispersive Infrared Analysis (EEVL)
NDIR .... Non-Dispersive Infrared Radiation (SAUS)
NDIR .... Non-Dispersive Infrared Spectroscopy (AAEL)
NDIRA .... Nondispersive Infrared Analysis (COE)
NDIR Analyzer ... Nondispersive Infrared Analyzer (SAUS)
NDIRS .... North Dakota Institute for Regional Studies (SAUS)
NDIS .... National Document and Information Service [*Australia*]
NDIS .... Network Driver Interface Specification [*Computer science*] (PCM)
NDIS .... Nissan Direct Ignition System [*Automotive engineering*]
NDIS .... North Dakota State Industrial School
NDIU .... National Drugs Intelligence Unit [*Metropolitan Police*] [*British*]
NDIY .... North Devon Imperial Yeomanry [*British military*] (DMA)
NdJ .... Alfred Dickey Free Library, Jamestown, ND [*Library symbol*] [*Library of Congress*] (LCLS)
NDJ .... Jamestown College, Jamestown, ND [*OCLC symbol*] (OCLC)
NDJ .... N'Djamena [*Chad*] [*Airport symbol*] (OAG)
NdJC .... Jamestown College, Jamestown, ND [*Library symbol*] [*Library of Congress*] (LCLS)
NDJCC .... North Dakota Junior College Conference (PSS)
NdJF .... North Dakota Farmers Union Resource Library, Jamestown, ND [*Library symbol*] [*Library of Congress*] (LCLS)
NdJN .... Northern Prairie Wildlife Research Center, Jamestown, ND [*Library symbol*] [*Library of Congress*] (LCLS)
NdJSH .... State Hospital, Jamestown, ND [*Library symbol*] [*Library of Congress*] (LCLS)
NDK .... Nachrichtendienstkonzept (SAUS)
NDK .... Namorik [*Marshall Islands*] [*Airport symbol*] (OAG)
NDK .... Network Developer's Kit [*Computer science*] (AGLO)
NDK .... Network Development Kit [*Computer science*] (VLIE)
NDK .... Nucleoside Diphosphate Kinase [*An enzyme*]
NDK .... South Weymouth, MA [*Location identifier*] [*FAA*] (FAAL)
NDKSBX ..... Journal. Agricultural Laboratory (journ.) (SAUS)
NDL .... Duke University, Law Library, Durham, NC [*OCLC symbol*] (OCLC)
NDL .... National Defence Headquarters Library [*UTLAS symbol*]
NDL .... National Democratic League [*Early British political party*]
NDL .... National Demographics & Lifestyles, Inc.
NDL .... National Diet Library [*Japan*]
NDL .... National Digital Library (TELE)
NDL .... Natural Daylight
NDL .... Needle (MSA)
NDL .... Needles, CA [*Amtrak rail station code*]
NDL .... Neon Discharge Lighting [*Automotive lighting*]
NDL .... Network Database Language [*Telecommunications*] (OSI)
NDL .... Network Definition Language [*Burroughs Corp.*]
NDL .... Ni-Cal Developments Ltd. [*Vancouver Stock Exchange symbol*]
NDL .... No Decompression Limit
NDL .... Nonconductive Data Link (SAUS)
NDL .... Norddeutscher Lloyd [*German steamship company*]
Nd-L .... North Dakota State Law Library, Bismarck (SAUS)
Nd-L .... North Dakota State Law Library, Bismarck, ND [*Library symbol*] [*Library of Congress*] (LCLS)
NDL .... Nuclear Data Link System [*Nuclear Regulatory Commission*]
NDL .... Nuclear Defense Laboratory [*Army*]
NDL .... Nuclear Diagnostic Laboratories, Inc. (EFIS)

NDL.......... Numerical Drawing List
NDLA........ North Dakota Library Association
NDLB........ National Dock Labour Board [*British*]
NDLC........ Network Data Link Control
NDLC........ North Dakota League of Cities (EARSL)
ND Lens.... Night & Day Lens (SAUS)
NdLibC...... North Dakota State Library Commission, Bismarck, ND [*Library symbol*] [*Library of Congress*] (LCLS)
NDLM....... Nondestructive Laser Mapping (SAUS)
NDLOA...... National Disabled Law Officers Association (EA)
NDLP........ NDL Products, Inc. [*NASDAQ symbol*] (COMM)
NDLT......... N-Channel Depletion-Load Triode Inverter
NDLTA....... North Dakota Land Title Association (EARSL)
NDLTD....... Networked Digital Library of Theses and Dissertations
NDLUP...... Nonduplicate (SAUS)
ndlwk........ Needlework (VRA)
NDM......... Ferrocarriles Nacionales de Mexico [*AAR code*]
NDM......... Mary College, Library, Bismarck, ND [*OCLC symbol*] (OCLC)
NDM......... Nadym Airlines [*Russian Federation*] [*ICAO designator*] (FAAC)
NDM......... National Data Manager (SAUS)
NDM......... National Democratic Movement (Jamaica) [*Political party*] (PSAP)
NDM......... National Dried (Milk) [*Brand name for the British government's dried milk for babies - manufacturer undisclosed*]
NDM......... N-Desmethyl-Methsuximide [*Biochemistry*] (AAMN)
NDM......... Negative Differential Mobility (IEEE)
NDM......... Network Database Management [*Computer science*] (VLIE)
NDM......... Network Data Mover [*Computer science*] (HODG)
NDM......... Neutron Dose Monitor
NDM......... New Democratic Movement (EA)
NDM......... New Dimensions in Medicine
NDM......... Newspaper Designated Market (WDMC)
NDM......... Nigerian Democratic Movement (SAUS)
NDM......... Nomad Energy & Resources [*Vancouver Stock Exchange symbol*]
NDM......... Normal Data Mode (SAUS)
NDM......... Normal Disconnected Mode (SAUS)
NDM......... Normal Disconnect Mode (SAUS)
NDM......... North Durham Militia [*British military*] (DMA)
NDMA....... National Dimension Manufacturers Association (EA)
NDMA....... National Door Manufacturers Association [*Later, NWWDA*]
NDMA....... National Dress Manufacturers Association [*Later, AMA*] (EA)
NDMA....... Nitrosodimethylaniline [*Chemistry*] (DAVI)
NDMA....... N-Nitrosodimethylamine [*Also, DMN, DMNA*] [*Organic chemistry*]
NDMA....... Nonprescription Drug Manufacturers Association (EA)
NDMAC...... Nonprescription Drug Manufacturers Association of Canada (SAUS)
NdMan...... Mandan Public Library, Mandan, ND [*Library symbol*] [*Library of Congress*] (LCLS)
NdManMH.. North Dakota Memorial Mental Health and Retardation Center, Mandan, ND [*Library symbol*] [*Library of Congress*] (LCLS)
NdManN.... North Dakota Industrial School, Mandan, ND [*Library symbol*] [*Library of Congress*] (LCLS)
NdManNG... United States Northern Great Plains Research Center, Mandan, ND [*Library symbol*] [*Library of Congress*] (LCLS)
NdMayS..... Mayville State College, Mayville, ND [*Library symbol*] [*Library of Congress*] (LCLS)
NDMB....... National Defense Mediation Board [*World War II*]
NDMC....... National Drought Mitigation Center
NDMC....... NATO Defense Manpower Committee (NATG)
NDMC....... N-Desmethylclobazam [*Biochemistry*]
NDMC....... Nissan Diesel Motor Company [*NCIC truck make code*]
NDMDA..... National Depressive and Manic Depressive Association (EA)
NDMHA..... Nondirectional Microphone Hearing Aid [*Medicine*] (EDAA)
N/DMI BOS... Network/Digital Multiplex Interface Bit Ordered Signaling [*Communications term*] (DCT)
NdMin....... Minot Public Library, Minot, ND [*Library symbol*] [*Library of Congress*] (LCLS)
NdMinAF.... United States Air Force, Base Library, Minot AFB, ND [*Library symbol*] [*Library of Congress*] (LCLS)
NdMinIT..... United States Air Force Institute of Technology, Minot AFB, ND [*Library symbol*] [*Library of Congress*] (LCLS)
NdMinN..... Northwest Bible College, Minot, ND [*Library symbol*] [*Library of Congress*] (LCLS)
NdMinS..... Minot State College, Minot, ND [*Library symbol*] [*Library of Congress*] (LCLS)
NdMinT-M.. Trinity Medical Center, August Cameron Medical Library, Minot, ND [*Library symbol*] [*Library of Congress*] (LCLS)
NdMinT-N... Trinity Medical Center, School of Nursing, Minot, ND [*Library symbol*] [*Library of Congress*] (LCLS)
ND Miss.... United States District Court for the Northern District of Mississippi (DLA)
NDML....... Neutral Data Manipulation Language [*Computer science*]
NDML....... Never During My Lifetime (SAUS)
NdMo........ Mott Public Library, Mott, ND [*Library symbol*] [*Library of Congress*] (LCLS)
NDMP....... Network Data Management Protocol (SAUS)
NDMPI...... Nitrosodimethylpiperazinium Iodide [*Organic chemistry*]
NDMREA.... National Diabetes Mellitus Research and Education Act (1974) [*Medicine*] (EDAA)
NDMS....... National Debt Management System [*Social Security Administration*] (GFGA)
NDMS....... National Disaster Medical System
NDMS....... National Drug Monitoring System [*Medicine*] [*FDA*] (EDAA)
NDMS....... Navigation Data Management System (SAUS)
NDMS....... Netware Distributed Management Services [*Novell, Inc.*] (PCM)
NDMS....... Network Design and Management System
NDMS....... Noise Deficiency Management System
NDMS....... Non-Directional Mud-and-Snow (PDAA)
NDMSOSC... National Disaster Medical System Operations Support Center [*Emergency Management*] (EMA)
NDMSP...... Navy Department Mobilization Security Plan (NG)
NDMTB...... Nondeployment Mobilization Troop Basis (AABC)
NDMTP...... National Defense Manufacturing Technology Plan
NDMWC..... National Domestic Meatworks Wholesalers Council [*Australia*]
NDMZ....... Ferrocarriles Nacionales [*Intermodal trailer symbol*]
NDMZ....... National Dominion of Mexico [*Federal Railroad Administration identification code*]
NDN......... 99 Cents Only Stores [*NYSE symbol*]
NDN......... National Diffusion Network [*Department of Education*] [*Information service or system*] (IID)
NDN......... National Directory of Newsletters and Reporting Services [*A publication*]
NDN......... Naval Digital Network (SAUS)
NDN......... New Data Network (IAA)
NDN......... Ninety-Nine Cent Only Stores [*NYSE symbol*] (SAG)
NDN......... Nodal Data Network (SAUS)
NDN......... Non-Delivery Notice (SAUS)
NDN......... Non-Delivery Notification (SAUS)
NDN......... Noninvasive Diagnostics Newsletter [*Medicine*] (EDAA)
NDN......... Nonsynaptic Diffusion Neurotransmission [*Neurology*]
NDN......... Nordic Data Network (SAUS)
NDN......... Nu-Dawn Resources, Inc. [*Vancouver Stock Exchange symbol*]
nDNA........ Deoxyribonucleic Acid, Nuclear [*Biochemistry, genetics*]
NDNA........ Native (double-strand) Deoxyribonucleic Acid [*Medicine*] (EDAA)
nDNA........ Native (double-strand) Deoxyribonucleic Acid [*Medicine*] (EDAA)
NDNHI....... North Dakota Natural Heritage Inventory [*North Dakota State Department of Natural Resources*] [*Bismarck*] [*Information service or system*] (IID)
NDNO........ National Directory of Nonprofit Organizations [*A publication*]
NDN PAC.... The New Democrat Network PAC [*Washington, DC*] (PACS)
NDNR........ Normalized Differences of Nadir Reflectivity (SAUS)
NDNT........ Not Dressed nor Tanned
NDNY........ United States District Court for the Northern District of New York (DLA)
NDO......... Abu Nidal Organization [*International terrorist group*] (EMA)
NDO......... National Debt Office [*British*]
NDO......... National Diving Officer (SAUS)
NDO......... Navy Disbursing Office
NDO......... Negotiate Downward Only (MCD)
NDO......... Netherlands Development Organization (SAUS)
NDO......... Network Development Office [*Library of Congress*]
NDO......... Neuro-Developmental Observation [*Medicine*] (EDAA)
NDOA........ National Dog Owners' Association [*British*] (BI)
NDOC........ National Defense Operations Center (ACAE)
NDOC........ Neurological Dysfunctions of Children [*Test*]
NDOC........ Non Departmental Output Class (SAUS)
NDOCP...... Non-Dispersant Olefin Copolymer [*Fuels and lubricants*]
ND Ohio..... United States District Court for the Northern District of Ohio (DLA)
ND Okla..... United States District Court for the Northern District of Oklahoma (DLA)
NDOP........ Navy Designated Overhaul Point (CAAL)
NDOS........ National Defense Operations Section [*FCC*]
NDOS........ New Disc Operating System (NITA)
NDOW....... Nevada Division of Wildlife (SAUS)
NDp.......... Deer Park Public Library (SAUS)
NDp.......... Deer Park Public Library, Deer Park, NY [*Library symbol*] [*Library of Congress*] (LCLS)
NDP.......... National Democracy Party [*Thailand*] [*Political party*] (PPW)
NDP.......... National Democratic Party [*Iraq*] [*Political party*] (BJA)
NDP.......... National Democratic Party [*Sierra Leone*] [*Political party*] (EY)
NDP.......... National Democratic Party [*Pakistan*] [*Political party*] (PD)
NDP.......... National Democratic Party [*Solomon Islands*] [*Political party*] (PPW)
NDP.......... National Democratic Party [*Namibia*] [*Political party*] (PPW)
NDP.......... National Democratic Party [*Egypt*] [*Political party*] (PPW)
NDP.......... National Democratic Party [*India*] [*Political party*] (PPW)
NDP.......... National Democratic Party [*Morocco*] [*Political party*] (PPW)
NDP.......... National Democratic Party [*Grenada*] [*Political party*] (PPW)
NDP.......... National Democratic Party [*Rhodesia and Nyasaland*] [*Political party*]
NDP.......... Nationaldemokratische Partei [*National Democratic Party*] [*Austria*] [*Political party*] (PPW)
NDP.......... National Determination Party (EA)
NDP.......... National Development Party [*Montserrat*] [*Political party*] (EY)
NDP.......... National Diocesan Press [*Later, Episcopal Communicators*] (EA)
NDP.......... National Diploma in Poultry Husbandry [*British*]
NDP.......... National Disclosure Policy [*Military*] (MCD)
NDP.......... Nationalist Democracy Party [*Turkey*] [*Political party*] (PPW)
NDP.......... Nationwide Demonstration Program
NDP.......... Naval Doctrine Publication (DOMA)
NDP.......... Navy Department Personnel
NDP.......... Neighborhood Development Program [*Urban renewal*]
NDP.......... Net Dietary Protein (MAE)
NDP.......... Net Domestic Product [*Business term*] (PDAA)
NDP.......... Neurological Disorders Program [*National Institute of Neurological and Communicative Disorders and Stroke*]
NDP.......... Neutron Depth Profiling [*Analytical chemistry*]
NDP.......... New Democratic Party [*Seychelles*] [*Political party*] (EY)
NDP.......... New Democratic Party [*South Korea*] [*Political party*] (PPW)
NDP.......... New Democratic Party [*St. Vincent*] [*Political party*] (PPW)
NDP.......... New Democratic Party [*Facetious translations: "Never Dies Politically," "No Dreams of Prosperity"*] [*Canada*] [*Political party*] (PPW)
NDP.......... New Development Policy (Malaysia) [*Political party*] (PSAP)
NDP.......... Night Defensive Position [*Military*]

NDP......... Normal Diametral Pitch (MSA)
ndp......... Normal Diametric Pitch (ODA)
NDP......... Normal Diametric Pitch (SAUS)
NDP......... Nuclear Desalination Plant
NDP......... Nuclear Disarmament Party [*Australia*] [*Political party*]
NDP......... Nucleoside Diphosphatase (SAUS)
NDP......... Nucleoside Diphosphate [*Biochemistry*]
NDP......... Numerical Data Processing (SAUS)
NDP......... Numerical Data Processor (SAUS)
NDP......... Numeric Data Package (SAUS)
NDP......... Numeric Data Processor
NDP......... Pensacola, FL [*Location identifier*] [*FAA*] (FAAL)
NDPA........ National Decorated Packaging Association
NDPA........ National Decorating Products Association (EA)
NDPA........ National Directory Publishing Association (NTPA)
NDPA........ Network Problem Determination Application (SAUS)
NDPA........ Nitrosodipropylamine [*Also, DPN, DPNA*] [*Organic chemistry*]
NDPB........ National Drug Policy Board [*Department of Justice*] (GFGA)
NDPB........ Non-Departmental Public Body [*British*]
NDPBC...... National Duck Pin Bowling Congress [*Later, NDBC*] (EA)
NDPC........ National Democratic Policy Committee (EA)
NDPC........ National [*Military Information*] Disclosure Policy Committee
NDPC........ National Dropout Prevention Center (EA)
NDPC........ National Drought Policy Commission [*Emergency Management*] (EMA)
NDPC........ National Drowning Prevention Coalition (EA)
NDPC........ Network Data Processing Center (TIMI)
NDpCal...... Net Dietary Protein Energy Ratio (WDAA)
NDPD........ National Data Processing Division [*Environmental Protection Agency*] (GFGA)
NDPD........ Nationaldemokratische Partei Deutschlands [*German National Democratic Party*] [*Political party*]
NDPEA...... North Dakota Public Employees Association (EARSL)
NDPF........ NASA Data Processing Facility (MCD)
NDPGA...... North Dakota Personnel and Guidance Association (SAUS)
NDPhA...... N-Nitrosodiphenylamine [*Organic chemistry*]
NDPhA...... North Dakota Pharmaceutical Association (EARSL)
NDpHS...... Deer Park High School, Deer Park, NY [*Library symbol*] [*Library of Congress*] (LCLS)
NDPIC....... Navy Department Program Information Center
NDPK........ Nucleoside Diphosphate Kinase (SAUS)
NDPK........ Nucleoside Diphosphokinase [*An enzyme*]
NDPK........ Nucleotide Diphosphate Kinase [*An enzyme*]
NDPL........ National Democratic Party of Liberia [*Political party*] (EY)
NDPMA...... Non-Dispersant Polymethacrylate [*Fuels and lubricants*]
NDPN........ National Dropout Prevention Network (EA)
NDPO........ National Defence Programme Outline (SAUS)
NDPO........ National Domestic Preparedness Office [*Emergency Management*] (EMA)
NDPP........ (Nitrobenzyl)(Diethylaminophenylazo)-pyridinium Bromide [*Reagent*]
NDPR........ NATO Defense Planning Review (NATG)
NDPR........ Nuclear Duty Position Roster (MCD)
NDPRP...... National Defense Project Rating Plan
NDPS........ National Data Processing Service [*British*] (DCTA)
NDPS........ NetWare Distributed Print Services [*Communications term*] (DCT)
NDPS........ Non-Disruptive Path Switching (SAUS)
NDPS........ Novell Distributed Print Services [*Computer science*]
NDPU........ Frigo Leasing [*Intermodal shipping container symbol*] (TVRC)
NDP Zheltoksan... December National Democratic Party (Kazakhstan) [*Political party*] (PSAP)
NDQ......... NASA Delta Quotation (MCD)
NDQ......... Ndombe [*Language symbol*] (ETLW)
ND(Q)....... Nominal Defendant (Queensland) [*Australia*]
NDQ......... North Dakota Quarterly [*A publication*] (ANEX)
NDR......... Andrea Airlines SA [*Peru*] [*ICAO designator*] (FAAC)
NDR......... Nador [*Morocco*] [*Airport symbol*] (AD)
NDR......... National Derby Rallies (EA)
NDR......... National Dialysis Registry [*Medicine*] (EDAA)
NDR......... National Dog Registry (EA)
NDR......... National Driver Register
NDR......... National Drug Co. [*Research code symbol*]
NDR......... Nazarene Disaster Response [*Emergency Management*] (EMA)
NDR......... Negative Differential Resistance [*Electronics*]
NDR......... Neonatal Death Rate [*Medicine*] (DMAA)
NDR......... Net Difference Report (IAA)
NDR......... Network Data Reduction
NDR......... Network Data Representation [*Computer science*]
NDR......... Neurotic Depressive Reaction [*Medicine*] (EDAA)
NDR......... Neutral Detergent Residue [*Food analysis*]
NDR......... New Dimensions Radio (EA)
NDR......... New Document Reference (SAUS)
NDR......... Non-Delivery Report (SAUS)
NDR......... Nondestructive Read [*Computer science*]
NDR......... Non-Destructive Readout (SAUS)
NDR......... Norddeutscher Rundfunk [*Radio network*] [*Germany*]
NDR......... Normal Daily Requirement [*Military*]
NDR......... Normal Detrusor Reflex (DMAA)
NDR......... Normotensive Donor Rat
NDR......... Nuclear Double Resonance [*Analytical chemistry*]
NDRA........ National Deafblind & Rubella Association (WDAA)
NDRA........ North Dakota Retail Association (EARSL)
NDRA........ Nostalgia Drag Race Association (EA)
NDRB........ New Developments Research Branch [*Navy*] (MCD)
NDRC........ National Defense Research Committee [*of Office of Scientific Research and Development*] [*World War II*]
NDRC........ Non Destructive Read Character [*Computer science*] (ELAL)
NDRC........ Nutrient Data Research Center (SAUS)
NDRE........ Norwegian Defense Research Establishment
ND Res Found Bull... North Dakota Research Foundation Bulletin [*A publication*]
NDRF........ National Debt Repayment Foundation (EA)
NDRF........ National Defense Reserve Fleet [*Maritime Administration, Department of Commerce*]
NDRG........ NATO Defense Research Group (NATG)
NDRI......... National Defense Research Institute (POLM)
NDRI......... National Diabetes Research Interchange [*Research center*] (RCD)
NDRI......... National Disease Research Interchange (MHID)
NDRI......... Naval Dental Research Institute
NDRL........ North Dakota Right-to-Life Association (EARSL)
NDRL........ Notre Dame Radiation Laboratory [*University of Notre Dame*] [*Research center*] (RCD)
NDRM........ Neesby Delayed Release Mechanism [*Medicine*]
NDRM........ Non-Destructive Readout Memory (SAUS)
NDRO........ Nondestructive Read Only [*Computer science*] (IAA)
NDRO........ Nondestructive Readout [*Computer science*]
NDROS...... Non-Destructive Read-Only Storage (SAUS)
NDRP........ New Democratic Republican Party [*South Korea*] [*Political party*] (EY)
NDRS........ National Driver Register Service [*Department of Transportation*]
NDRS........ Nuclear Definition and Reporting System (AAG)
NDRSWG... NATO Data Requirements and Standards Working Group (NATG)
NDRT........ Nelson-Denny Reading Test (EDAC)
NDRW........ Non-Destructive Read and Write (SAUS)
NDRW........ Nondestructive Read/Write [*Computer science*]
NDRX........ National Defense Railroad [*Federal Railroad Administration identification code*]
NDryT....... Tompkins-Cortland Community College, Division of Instructional and Learning Resources, Dryden, NY [*Library symbol*] [*Library of Congress*] (LCLS)
NDS.......... Congregation of Notre Dame de Sion [*Roman Catholic women's religious order*]
NDS.......... Name Definition Segment (TIMI)
NDS.......... National Dahlia Society [*British*] (DBA)
NDS.......... National Decision Systems [*Information service or system*] (IID)
NDS.......... National Defense Stockpile [*Collection of materials essential to the defense industry*]
NDS.......... National Democratic Party (Slovakia) [*Political party*] (PSAP)
NDS.......... National Design Specification [*For wood construction*] (WPI)
NDS.......... National Dioxin Study [*Environmental Protection Agency*] (GFGA)
NDS.......... National Disposal Site [*Environmental Protection Agency*] (GFGA)
NDS.......... Naval Dental School
NDS.......... Navigation Data Systems Inc. (SAUS)
NDS.......... Navigation Development Satellite (MCD)
NDS.......... Navigation Display System
NDS.......... Navy Data System
NDS.......... Navy Directive System (NVT)
NDS.......... Navy Display System
NDS.......... Needs [*Automotive advertising*]
NDS.......... NetWare Directory Services [*Novell, Inc.*] [*Computer science*] (PCM)
NDS.......... Network Data Series (MHDI)
NDS.......... Network Data System (SAUS)
NDS.......... Network Development System (IAA)
NDS.......... Neurologic Disability Score
NDS.......... Neutral Drive Switch [*Automotive engineering*]
NDS.......... Neutral-Drive Switch [*Automotive engineering*]
NDS.......... Neutron Doped Silicon (IAA)
NDS.......... New Drug Submission [*Medicine*] (DB)
NDS.......... Newport Design System (ACAE)
NDS.......... News Distribution Service [*Reuters*] (STAH)
NDS.......... Nicholas Data [*Vancouver Stock Exchange symbol*]
NDS.......... Nominal Detectable Signal (IAA)
NDS.......... Noncommunications Detection System (MCD)
NDS.......... Non-Developmental Software
N-DS......... Non-Dust Storm (SAUS)
NDS.......... Nonparametric Detection Scheme [*Communication signal*]
NDS.......... Non-selective Direct Substitution (SAUS)
NDS.......... Nordic Demographic Society (EA)
NDS.......... Nordstress (Australia) Pt Ltd. [*FAA designator*] (FAAC)
NDS.......... Normal Dog Serum [*Medicine*] (DMAA)
NDS.......... North Dakota State (SAUS)
NDS.......... North Dakota State Library Commission, Bismarck, ND [*OCLC symbol*] (OCLC)
NDS.......... Novell Directory Service [*Computer Networking*] (PCM)
NDS.......... Nuclear Data Sheets [*National Academy of Sciences*]
NDS.......... Nuclear Detection Satellite
NDS.......... Nuclear Detection System (MCD)
NDS.......... Nuclear Detonation Detection System
NDS.......... Nuclear Detonation System (SAUS)
NDSA........ National Disposal Services Association (EA)
NDSB........ Narcotic Drugs Supervisory Body [*UN*]
NDSB........ Navy Dependents School Branch
ND/SB....... Nuclear Depth/Strike Bomb (DOMA)
NDSBA...... North Dakota School Boards Association (SAUS)
NDSC........ National Down Syndrome Congress (EA)
NDSC........ Network for the Detection of Stratospheric Change [*New Zealand*] (USDC)
NDSCS...... National Duck Stamp Collectors Society
NDSDF...... National Disaster Search Dog Foundation [*Association*] (EA)
NDSE........ Nondeliverable Support Equipment

NdSEA....... North Dakota Society of Enrolled Agents (SAUS)
NDSEG...... National Defense Science and Engineering
NDSEG...... National Defense Science and Engineering Graduate
ND Sess Laws... Laws of North Dakota [*A publication*] (DLA)
NDSF........ National Defense Sealift Fund (DOMA)
NDSF........ North Dakota School of Forestry
NDSHS...... North Dakota State Horticultural Society (SAUS)
NDSL........ National Direct [*formerly, Defense*] Student Loan [*later, Perkins Loan*] [*Department of Education*]
NDSL........ Networking and Distributed Systems Laboratory [*University of Kansas*] (RCD)
NDSL........ New Domestic Substance List [*Fuels and lubricants*]
NDSL........ Non Domestic Substances List [*Canada*]
NDSM........ National Defense Service Medal [*Military decoration*]
NDSM........ Nondeterministic State Machine (SAUS)
NDSN........ National Drug Strategy Network (EA)
NDSN........ Nobody Don't Say Nothing
NDSN........ Nordson Corp. [*NASDAQ symbol*] (NQ)
NDSO........ Special Olympics, North Dakota (EARSL)
NDSOS...... Navy Deep Sea Oceanographic System
NDSPE...... North Dakota Society of Professional Engineers (SAUS)
NDSS........ National Down Syndrome Society (EA)
NDSS........ National DS Society
NDSs........ Nuclear Delivery Systems (SAUS)
NDSSS...... North Dakota State School of Science (SAUS)
NDST........ Nondimensional Special Tooling (SAUS)
NDSTC...... National Defence Science & Technology Commission (SAUS)
NDSTC...... Naval Dive and Salvage Training Center (SAUS)
NDSTC...... Naval Diving and Salvage Training Center (DNAB)
NDSTIC...... National Defence Science Technology & Industry Commission (SAUS)
NDSU........ North Dakota State University
NDSUAA.... North Dakota State University Alumni Association (EA)
NDT.......... Ferrocarril Nacional de Tehuantepec [*AAR code*]
NDT.......... National Diploma in the Science and Practice of Turfculture and Sports Ground Management [*British*]
NDT.......... National Nondestructive Testing Centre [*AEA Technology PLC Engineering Solutions*] (IID)
NDT.......... Nephrology Dialysis Transplantation (SAUS)
NDT.......... Net Data Throughout
NDT.......... Network Description Table (MHDI)
NDT.......... Network Design Tool (ACAE)
NDT.......... Neuro-Developmental Treatment [*Physical therapy*]
NDT.......... Nevada Dance Theatre
NDT.......... New Dictionary of Thoughts [*A publication*]
NDT.......... New Dimensions [*Vancouver Stock Exchange symbol*]
NDT.......... Newfoundland Daylight Time (SAUS)
NDT.......... Nil-Ductility Temperature [*Metallurgy*]
NDT.......... Nil-Ductility Transition [*Metallurgy*] (IEEE)
NDT.......... No Dial Tone [*Of a telephone*] (WDMC)
NDT.......... Noise Detection Threshold (DMAA)
NDT.......... Nondestructive Test (DMAA)
NDT.......... Nondestructive Testing
NDT.......... Non-Distributive Trade (SAUS)
NDT.......... Non-Lethal Disabling Technology
NDT.......... Normal Device Termination (SAUS)
NDT.......... Nuclear Detection Test (IAA)
NDTA........ National Defense Transportation Association (EA)
NDTA........ National Dental Technicians Association [*Defunct*] (EA)
NDTA........ Neurodevelopmental Treatment Association (EA)
NDTA........ Night Driving Training Aid [*Army*]
NDTA........ Non Destructive Testing Association (SAUS)
NDTA........ Nondestructive Testing Association (SAUS)
NDTA........ Non-Destructive Testing Association of Australia
NDT & E.... Nondestructive Testing and Evaluation Programs [*Pennsylvania State University*] [*Research center*] (RCD)
NDTC........ National Drug Trade Conference (EA)
NDTC........ Naval Device Training Center
NDTC........ Nondestructive Testing Center (IEEE)
NDTC........ Nottingham and District Technical College (SAUS)
NDTE........ Nondestructive Testing Equipment (SAUS)
NDTE........ North Dakota Tracer Experiment (USDC)
ND Tex...... United States District Court for the Northern District of Texas (DLA)
NDTF........ Nondestructive Test Facility (MCD)
Ndthl........ Neanderthal (VRA)
NDTI......... New Denaeyer Thermal Industries (EFIS)
NDTI......... Nondestructive Testing and Inspection
NDTIAC...... Non-Destructive Testing Information Center [*Army Materials and Mechanics Research Center*] (PDAA)
NDTIB....... Nondestructive Testing and Inspection Building
NDTL........ Nondestructive Test Laboratory (MCD)
NDTMA...... National Drain Tile Manufacturers Association [*Defunct*] (EA)
NDTMA...... Non Destructive Testing Management Association (NTPA)
NDTP........ Network Development Test Plan (ACAE)
NDTP........ North Dakota Thunderstorm Project (SAUS)
NDTP........ Nuclear Data Tape Program
NDTRAN.... Notre Dame Translator [*Programming language*] [*1977*] [*Computer science*] (CSR)
NDTS........ Nonlinear Dynamics Time Series (SAUS)
NDTT........ Nil-Ductility Transition Temperature [*Metallurgy*]
NDU......... National Defense University, Washington, DC [*OCLC symbol*] (OCLC)
NDU......... National Democratic Union [*Zimbabwe*] [*Political party*] (PPW)
NDU......... Navigation Display Unit [*Military*]
NDU......... NDU Resources [*Vancouver Stock Exchange symbol*]
NDU......... Nederlandse Dagbladunie
NDU......... Network Device Utility (SAUS)
N/D/U....... None Done Up [*Bookselling*]
ndu.......... North Dakota [*MARC country of publication code*] [*Library of Congress*] (LCCP)
NDU......... Notre Dame University (SAUS)
NDU......... Nuclear Data Unit [*International Atomic Energy Agency*] (DIT)
NDU......... Rundu [*Namibia*] [*Airport symbol*] (OAG)
NdU.......... University of North Dakota, Grand Forks, ND [*Library symbol*] [*Library of Congress*] (LCLS)
NDUC........ Nimbus Data Utilization Center
NdU-El...... University of North Dakota, Ellendale Branch, Ellendale, ND [*Library symbol*] [*Library of Congress*] [*Obsolete*] (LCLS)
NDUF........ National Democratic United Front [*Later, FNDF*] [*Myanmar*] [*Political party*] (PD)
NdU-L....... University of North Dakota, Law Library, Grand Forks, ND [*Library symbol*] [*Library of Congress*] (LCLS)
NdU-M...... University of North Dakota, Medical Library, Grand Forks, ND [*Library symbol*] [*Library of Congress*] (LCLS)
NDunBH..... Brooks Memorial Hospital Medical Center, Dunkirk, NY [*Library symbol*] [*Library of Congress*] (LCLS)
NDUP........ Nonduplicate
NDUP........ Nonduplication (SAUS)
NDUSTA..... New Duty Station [*Navy*]
NDUV........ Nondispersion Ultraviolet (EEVL)
NDUV........ Nondispersive Ultraviolet
NDUV........ Non-Dispersive Ultraviolet Spectroscopy (AAEL)
NDV.......... NASP [*National AeroSpace Plane*] Derived Vehicle [*Astronomy term*]
NDV.......... Newcastle Disease Virus [*Also, ND*]
NDV.......... Not to Delay Delivery
NDV.......... Not to Delay Vessel
NDV.......... Nuclear Delivery Vehicle
NDV.......... Valley City State College, Valley City, ND [*OCLC symbol*] (OCLC)
NDV.......... Washington, DC [*Location identifier*] [*FAA*] (FAAL)
NDVC........ Northland Services [*Common carrier symbol*]
NdVc......... Valley City Public Library, Valley City, ND [*Library symbol*] [*Library of Congress*] (LCLS)
NdVcT....... Valley City State College, Valley City, ND [*Library symbol*] [*Library of Congress*] (LCLS)
NDVH........ National Domestic Violence Hotline [*Association*] (EA)
NDVI......... Normalized Difference Vegetation Index [*Plant biota*]
NDVOAD.... North Dakota Voluntary Organizations Active in Disaster [*Emergency Management*] (EMA)
NDW......... Naval District Washington
NDW......... North Dakota State School of Science, Mildred Johnson Library, Wahpeton, ND [*OCLC symbol*] (OCLC)
NDW......... Norton Desktop for Windows [*Symantec Corp.*] [*Computer science*] (PCM)
NDWAC...... National Drinking Water Advisory Council [*Environmental Protection Agency*]
NdWah...... Leach Public Library, Wahpeton, ND [*Library symbol*] [*Library of Congress*] (LCLS)
NdWahS..... North Dakota State School of Science, Wahpeton, ND [*Library symbol*] [*Library of Congress*] (LCLS)
NDWB....... North Devon Water Board (SAUS)
NDWBA..... National Deaf Women's Bowling Association (EA)
NDWF....... North Dakota Wildlife Federation (EARSL)
NdWi........ James Memorial Library, Williston, ND [*Library symbol*] [*Library of Congress*] (LCLS)
NdWiU...... University of North Dakota, Williston Branch, Williston, ND [*Library symbol*] [*Library of Congress*] (LCLS)
NdWiW..... West Plains Rural Library, Williston, ND [*Library symbol*] [*Library of Congress*] (LCLS)
NDWP....... National Demonstration Water Project (EA)
NDWRRI.... North Dakota Water Resources Research Institute [*Fargo, ND*] [*Department of the Interior*] (GRD)
NDWU....... National Domestic Workers Union (EA)
NDWUA..... North Dakota Water Users Association (EARSL)
NDX.......... Northern Dynasty Explorations Ltd. [*Toronto Stock Exchange symbol*] [*Vancouver Stock Exchange symbol*]
NDxhBJ..... Burr's Lane Junior High School, Dix Hills, NY [*Library symbol*] [*Library of Congress*] (LCLS)
NDxhFE..... Forest Park Elementary School, Dix Hills, NY [*Library symbol*] [*Library of Congress*] (LCLS)
NDxhH....... Half Hollow Hills Community Public Library, Dix Hills, NY [*Library symbol*] [*Library of Congress*] (LCLS)
NDxhHH-E... Half Hollow Hills High School East, Dix Hills, NY [*Library symbol*] [*Library of Congress*] (LCLS)
NDxhHH-W... Half Hollow Hills High School West, Dix Hills, NY [*Library symbol*] [*Library of Congress*] (LCLS)
NDxhHT..... Half Hollow Hills District Teacher's Center, Dix Hills, NY [*Library symbol*] [*Library of Congress*] (LCLS)
NDY.......... Dahlgren, VA [*Location identifier*] [*FAA*] (FAAL)
NDY.......... Needy [*Telegraphy*] (PCTE)
NDY.......... Neodymium-Doped Yttralox [*Ceramic*]
NDY.......... Nonresonant Deflection Yoke
NDY.......... Not Diagnosed Yet (SAUS)
NDY.......... Sanday [*Scotland*] [*Airport symbol*] (OAG)
Nd:YAG..... Neodymium-Doped: Yttrium Aluminum Garnet [*LASER technology*]
NDYL........ Neodymium-Doped YAG [*Yttrium Aluminum Garnet*] LASER
NDYX........ First Union Rail [*Private rail car owner code*]
NDZ.......... Milton, FL [*Location identifier*] [*FAA*] (FAAL)
NE............ Air New England [*ICAO designator*] (AD)
Ne............ Algemeen Rijksarchief te s'Gravenhage (Central State Archives), The Hague, Netherlands [*Library symbol*] [*Library of Congress*] (LCLS)

NE........... Left Nationalists [*Spain*] [*Political party*] (PPW)
NE........... Narcotics Education [*An association*] (EA)
NE........... National Emergency
NE........... National Estate
NE........... National Exchequer [*British*]
NE........... National Executive (ADA)
NE........... National Exhibition [*British*]
NE........... Naval Engineer [*Academic degree*]
NE........... Navy Evaluation
NE........... Near East (BJA)
NE........... Near Effect (DIPS)
NE........... Nebraska [*Postal code*]
NE........... Necrotic Enteritis [*Medicine*] (MELL)
NE........... Negative Expectancy [*Psychometrics*]
NE........... Negatives and Etching (DGA)
NE........... Negotiated Exit [*Telecommunications*] (OSI)
Ne........... Nehemiah [*Old Testament book*] (BJA)
NE........... Neiva [*Sociedade Construtora Aeronautica Neiva Ltda.*] [*Brazil*] [*ICAO aircraft manufacturer identifier*] (ICAO)
NE........... Neomycin [*Antibacterial compound*]
Ne........... Neon [*Chemical element*] (ODBW)
ne........... Neon (VRA)
NE........... Neon [*Chemical element*]
ne........... Nephelite [*CIPW classification*] [*Geology*]
NE........... Nephropathia Epidemica [*Medicine*]
NE........... Nerve Ending (MAE)
NE........... Nerve Excitability [*Test*]
NE........... Nervous Exhaustion (MELL)
NE........... Net Earnings
ne........... Netherlands [*MARC country of publication code*] [*Library of Congress*] (LCCP)
NE........... Netherlands
NE........... Network Element (MLOA)
NE........... Neumann-Electroporation [*Gene technology*]
NE........... Neural Excitation [*neurology*] (DAVI)
NE........... Neurologic Examination [*Medicine*]
NE........... Neuss [*German license plate city code*]
NE........... Neutral Endopeptidase [*An enzyme*]
NE........... Neutral Excitation
NE........... Neutrophil Elastase
NE........... New Edition
NE........... New Editions [*Record label*]
NE........... New Engine [*On ships*]
NE........... New England
NE........... New England Patriots [*National Football League*] [*1971-present*] (NFLA)
NE........... New English [*Linguistics*] (IEL)
NE........... [*The*] New English Bible [*1961*] [*A publication*] (BJA)
NE........... New Executable [*Computer science*] (PCM)
NE........... News Editor (ADA)
NE........... Niacin Equivalent
NE........... Nickel Equivalent [*Coinage*]
NE........... Niger [*ANSI two-letter standard code*] (CNC)
NE........... Night Experimental [*British military*] (DMA)
NE........... Noble Drilling Corp. [*NYSE symbol*] (SG)
NE........... Nodal Exchange (MCD)
NE........... No Earthly Chance (DSUE)
NE........... No Ectopy [*Medicine*] (MEDA)
NE........... No Effects
NE........... No Equal (ELAL)
NE........... Noise-Equivalent (IAA)
NE........... Non-Effective (SAUS)
NE........... Nonelastic [*Medicine*] (MAE)
NE........... Nonelastic Elongation (SAUS)
NE........... Non-English Speaker [*Airline notation*]
NE........... Nonessential
NE........... Non Exempt (SAUS)
NE........... Nonexempt (TIMI)
NE........... Norepinephrine [*Also known as NA: Noradrenaline*] [*Biochemistry*]
NE........... Normal Excitability [*Medicine*]
NE........... Normally Energized (NRCH)
NE........... North East (SAUS)
NE........... Northeast
NE........... Northeast Airlines, Inc. [*Obsolete*]
NE........... North Eastern (SAUS)
NE........... North Eastern Reporter [*A publication*] (DLA)
NE........... Northern Electric (SAUS)
NE........... Not Editable (SAUS)
NE........... Not Elevated [*Laboratory science*] (DAVI)
NE........... Not Employed
NE........... Not Engaged
NE........... Not Enlarged [*Medicine*]
NE........... Not Entered (MARI)
NE........... Not Entitled [*British military*] (DMA)
NE........... Not Equal [*Relational operator*]
NE........... Not Equal To (NITA)
NE........... Not Essential (SAUS)
NE........... Not Evaluated (INF)
NE........... Not Examined [*Medicine*]
ne........... Not Exceeding (MARI)
N/E........... Not Exceeding
NE........... Not Explosive
NE........... Notice of Exception (MCD)
N/E........... Not to Exceed (SAUS)
NE........... Nuclear Electric (WDAA)
NE........... Nuclear Energy (COE)
NE........... Nuclear Engineer
NE........... Nuclear Envelope [*Cytology*]
NE........... Nuclear Equipment (SAUS)
NE........... Nuclear Explosive
NE........... Nuclear Extract [*Cytology*]
NE........... Numeric Editing (SAUS)
NE........... Nursing Educator (AAMN)
NE........... Office of Nuclear Energy (SAUS)
NE 2d........ North Eastern Reporter, Second Series [*West*] [*A publication*] (AAGC)
ne/4 mos ... new edition expected in four months (SAUS)
ne/6m .... new edition in preparation, expected in 6 months (SAUS)
ne/6 mos ... new edition expected in six months (SAUS)
NE-10........ Northeast-10 Conference (PSS)
NE311 .... Non-Emergency 311 [*Telephone service*]
NEa .... Eastchester Public Library, Eastchester, NY [*Library symbol*] [*Library of Congress*] (LCLS)
NEA.......... Nashville Entertainment Association (EA)
NEA.......... National Economic Association (EA)
NEA.......... National Editorial Association [*Later, NNA*] (EA)
NEA.......... National Education Association (EA)
NEA.......... National Electronic Associations [*Later, NESSDA*]
NEA.......... National Employment Association [*Later, NAPC*] (EA)
NEA.......... National Endowment for the Arts
NEA.......... National Energy Accounts [*Department of Commerce*] [*Information service or system*] (IID)
NEA.......... National Energy Act (GFGA)
NEA.......... National Erectors Association (EA)
NEA.......... Natural Energy Association [*British*]
NEA.......... Nearctic Resources, Inc. [*Toronto Stock Exchange symbol*]
NEA.......... Near-Earth Asteroid [*Astronomy*]
NEA.......... Near Eastern Affairs [*Department of State*]
NEA.......... Near Eastern Archaeology [*A publication*] (ABAR)
NEA.......... Neath [*Welsh depot code*]
NEA.......... Negative Electron Affinity [*Photocathode*]
NEA.......... Nelson & Albemarle Railway [*AAR code*]
NEA.......... Nenana [*Alaska*] [*Seismograph station code, US Geological Survey*] (SEIS)
NEA.......... Neoplasm Embryonic Antigen (DB)
NEA.......... Network Equivalent Analysis
NE-a......... Neuroepithelioma (SAUS)
NEA.......... Neustadt an der Aisch [*German license plate city code*]
NEA.......... New England Airlines, Inc. [*ICAO designator*] (FAAC)
NEA.......... New England Aquarium (SAUS)
NEA.......... New Entitlement Authority
NEA.......... Newsletter Editors' Association [*Australia*]
NEA.......... Newspaper Enterprise Association [*A syndicate*]
NEA.......... Nitrogen Enriched Air (ACAE)
NEA.......... No Evidence of Abnormality [*Medicine*] (DMAA)
NEA.......... Noise-Equivalent Angle (MCD)
NEA.......... Northeast Airlines, Inc. [*Obsolete*]
NEA.......... Northeast Asia (CINC)
NEA.......... Northern Electric Authority (SAUS)
NEA.......... Northern Examining Association [*British*]
NEA.......... Nuclear Energy Agency [*See also AEN*] [*Organization for Economic Cooperation and Development*] (EAIO)
NEA.......... Nuclear Engineering Associates (SAUS)
NEA.......... Null Error Amplifier
NEA.......... Nurse Education Act
NEA.......... Nutrition Education Association (EA)
NeAA .... Gemeente Archief van Amsterdam, Amsterdam, Netherlands [*Library symbol*] [*Library of Congress*] (LCLS)
NEAA .... National Employment Assistance Act (OICC)
NEAA .... Non-Essential Amino Acid (SAUS)
NEAA .... Northeastern Anthropological Association (SAUS)
NEAA .... Norwegian Elkhound Association of America (EA)
NEAAN ...... Non-Essential Amino Acid N [*Biochemistry*] (PDAA)
NEAATS ..... Northeast Asia Association of Theological Schools
NEAB .... Northern Examinations and Assessment Board (AIE)
NEABFGP... New England Advisory Board for Fish and Game Problems [*Defunct*] (EA)
NEabG....... Genesee County Landmark Society, East Bethany (SAUS)
NEabG....... Genesee County Landmark Society, East Bethany, NY [*Library symbol*] [*Library of Congress*] (LCLS)
NEAC .... National Episcopal AIDS Coalition [*Association*] (EA)
NEAC .... New English Art Club [*British*]
NEAC .... Nippon Electric Automatic Computer (IEEE)
NEAC .... Northeast Air Command
NEACDS..... Naval Emergency Air Cargo Delivery System (CAAL)
NEACH ...... New England Automated Clearing House Association
NEACP....... National Emergency Airborne Command Post [*Pronounced "kneecap"*] [*Modified Boeing 747 jet to be used as a military control center by the President or Vice President during a nuclear war or other crisis*]
NEACRP..... Nuclear Energy Agency Committee on Reactor Physics [*OECD*] (EY)
NEACSS..... New England Association of Colleges and Secondary Schools [*Later, NEASC*] (EA)
NEADA ...... National Energy Assistance Directors' Association (EA)
NEA-DB ..... NEA [*Nuclear Energy Agency*] Data Bank [*OECD*] [*Information service or system*] (IID)
NEADS ...... National Educational Association of Disabled Students (SAUS)
NEADS ...... National Education for Assistance Dog Services [*Formerly, New England Assistance Dog Service*] (PAZ)
NEADS ...... Near East and African Development Service

NEADS ...... Network Engineering Administrative Data System [*AT & T*]
NEADS ...... Northeast Air Defense Sector (SAUS)
NEADS ...... North East Atlantic Dynamics Studies (SAUS)
NEADS ...... Northeast Atlantic Dynamics Studies [*Marine science*] (MSC)
NEADW...... Northeast Atlantic Deep Water [*Oceanography*]
NEAF .... Near East Air Force [*British*]
NEAF .... New Era Aboriginal Fellowship (SAUS)
NEAFC....... North-East Atlantic Fisheries Commission [*British*] (EAIO)
NEAFC....... North East Atlantic Fisheries Convention (SAUS)
NEAFCS ..... National Extension Association of Family & Consumer Sciences (NTPA)
NEAG .... Nevada Environmental Advisory (SAUS)
NEAG .... Nevada Environmental Advisory Group (SAUS)
NEAG .... New English Art Gallery (SAUS)
NEAGC ...... National Early American Glass Club (EA)
NEAHI .... Near East Animal Health Institute
NEA HIN .... NEA Health Information Network [*Association*] (EA)
NEAIS .... National Elder Abuse Incidence Study (SAUS)
NEAL .... Neal Manufacturing Company [*NCIC trailer make code*]
NEAM........ Nonvolatile Electrically Alterable Memory
NEAN .... National Execution Alert Network (EA)
NEAN .... North European ADS-B Network (SAUS)
NE&B .... New Engines and Boilers (SAUS)
NEANDC..... Nuclear Energy Agency Nuclear Data Committee [*OECD*] (EY)
NEANMCC... Navy Element Alternate National Military Command Center (MCD)
NEanpHE.... Harley Avenue Elementary School, East Northport, NY [*Library symbol*] [*Library of Congress*] (LCLS)
NeAO .... Rijksinstituut voor Orlogsdocumentatie, Amsterdam, Netherlands [*Library symbol*] [*Library of Congress*] (LCLS)
NEAP .... National Energy Audit Program [*Canada*]
NEAP .... National Environmental Action Plan [*Environmental planning*]
NEAP .... Near Earth Asteroid Prospector (SAUS)
NEAP .... Novell Education Academic Partner (VLIE)
NEAPACC... North East Atlantic Palaeooceanography and Climate Change (SAUS)
NEAPD ...... Northeastern Air Procurement District
NEAPs .... National Environmental Action Plans (SAUS)
NEAQ .... Northern Electricity Authority of Queensland [*Australia*]
NEAR .... National Electronic Accounting and Reporting System (VLIE)
NEAR .... National Emergency Alarm Repeater [*Civil defense warning system for homes*]
NEAR .... Nationwide/Worldwide Emergency Ambulance Return
NEAR .... Near-Earth Asteroid Rendezvous (MCD)
NEAR .... New England Action Research Project
NEAR .... Nielsen Engineering & Research, Inc.
NEARA ...... New England Antiquities Research Association (EA)
NEARA ...... New England Archeological Research Association (SAUS)
NEARELF ... Near East Land Forces [*British military*] (DMA)
NEARGOOS... North East Asian Regional GOOS (SAUS)
NEARNAVDIST... Nearest Naval District
NEARnet .... [*The*] New England Academic and Research Network [*Computer science*] (TNIG)
NEARO ...... New England Albanian Relief Organization
NEARP ...... New England Appalachian Research Project [*University of Maine at Orono*] [*Research center*] (RCD)
NEARS ...... Navy Evaluation of Advanced Reconnaissance Systems
NEARS ...... Near Earth Asteroid Returned Samples [*NASA, proposed*]
NEARSS..... Northeast Area Remote Sensing System Association (SAUS)
NEARTIP ... Near-Term Improvement Program [*For torpedos*] (MCD)
NEARYP..... National Employers Association of Rayon Yarn Producers [*British*] (BI)
NEAS .... National Engineering Aptitude Search
NEAS .... National European American Society (EA)
NEAS .... Near East Archaeological Society (EA)
NEAS .... Newsletter of Engineering Analysis Software [*A publication*] (MCD)
NEASA....... Near Eastern, African, and South Asian Affairs [*Department of State*]
NEASC ...... New England Association of Schools and Colleges (EA)
NEA/SCEC... NEA/Salleri-Chialsa Electricity Co. (SAUS)
NEASCUS ... New England Association of School, College and University Staffing (SAUS)
NE Asiat J Th... Northeast Asia Journal of Theology (SAUS)
NEASIM ..... Network Analytical Simulator (PDAA)
NEASP....... Navy Enlisted Advanced School Program
NEaspHS.... Eastport High School, Eastport, NY [*Library symbol*] [*Library of Congress*] (LCLS)
NeAT........ Koninklijk Instituut voor de Tropen, Amsterdam, Netherlands [*Library symbol*] [*Library of Congress*] (LCLS)
NEAT......... National Cash Register Electronic Autocoding Technique [*Computer science*] (IAA)
NEAT......... National Electronic Autocoding Technique (MHDB)
NEAT......... Navy Electronics Application Trainer
NEAT......... Navy Embarked Advisory Team
NEAT......... NCR [*NCR Corp.*] Electronic Autocoding Technique [*Computer science*]
NEAT......... Near-Earth Asteroid Tracking
NEAT......... Network Expert Advisory Tool [*Communications term*] (DCT)
NEAT......... New Eindhoven Architectural Toolbox (VLIE)
NEAT......... New Enhanced Advanced Technology (CIST)
NEAT......... New Enhanced Technology
NEAT......... New Equipment Advisory Team (ACAE)
NEAT......... Next Advanced Technology (SAUS)
NEAT......... Nonexercise activity thermogenesis
NEAT......... Novell Easy Administration Tool (SAUS)
NEATE .... New England Association of Teachers of English (AEBS)
NEATICC .... Northeast Asia Tactical Information Communications Center (DNAB)
NEATO....... North East Asian Treaty Organization (NATG)
NeAU........ University of Amsterdam, Amsterdam, Netherlands [*Library symbol*] [*Library of Congress*] (LCLS)
NEAuC....... Christ the King Seminary, East Aurora, NY [*Library symbol*] [*Library of Congress*] (LCLS)
NEAuF....... Fisher-Price Toys, East Aurora, NY [*Library symbol*] [*Library of Congress*] (LCLS)
NEAuH....... Elbert Hubbard Library Museum, East Aurora, NY [*Library symbol*] [*Library of Congress*] (LCLS)
NEAuS....... Saint John Vianney Seminary, East Aurora, NY [*Library symbol*] [*Library of Congress*] (LCLS)
NEawNE..... North Side Elementary School, East Williston, NY [*Library symbol*] [*Library of Congress*] (LCLS)
NEB .... Bank of New England Corp. [*NYSE symbol*] (COMM)
NEB .... Department of Aeronautics State of Nebraska [*FAA designator*] (FAAC)
NEB .... National Electricity Board (ODA)
NEB .... National Energy Board [*Canada*]
NEB .... National Enterprise Board [*Later, BTG*] [*British*]
NEB .... Nebelwerfer [*German six-barrelled mortar*] (DSUE)
Neb .... Nebraska (ODBW)
NEB .... Nebraska
Neb .... Nebraska Supreme Court Reports [*A publication*] (DLA)
NEB .... Nebula [*Spray*] [*Pharmacy*]
NEB .... Neuroepithelial Bodies [*Anatomy*]
NEB .... New England Biolabs (IID)
NEB .... New England Business Service [*NYSE symbol*]
NEB .... New England Business Services [*NYSE symbol*] (SAG)
NEB .... New England Bus Svc [*NYSE symbol*] (TTSB)
NEB .... New England Motor Rate Bureau Inc., Burlington MA [*STAC*]
NEB .... New England Review and Bread Loaf Quarterly (SAUS)
NEB .... [*The*] New English Bible [*1961*] [*A publication*]
NEB .... Nissim Ezra Benjamin [*Shanghai*] (BJA)
NEB .... Noise-Equivalent Bandwidth
NEB .... Nonenzymatic Maillard Browning [*Food technology*]
NEB .... Nonisothermal Energy Balance (SAUS)
NEB .... North-Eastbound [*Aviation*] (FAAC)
NEB .... North Equatorial Belt [*Planet Jupiter*]
NEB .... Nuclear, Electronic, Biological (SAUS)
NEB .... Nuclear Energy Board [*Republic of Ireland*] (NUCP)
NEB .... Nuclear Envelope Breakdown [*Also, NEBD*] [*Cytology*]
NEB .... Nuclear Exoatmospheric Burst (SAUS)
NEB .... Toura [*Language symbol*] (ETLW)
Neb .... United States District Court for the District of Nebraska (DLA)
NEBA .... NASA Employee Benefit Association (SAUS)
NEBA .... New England Booksellers Association (EARSL)
NEBA .... North East Bolivian Airways [*ICAO designator*] (FAAC)
Neb Admin R... Nebraska Administrative Rules and Regulations [*A publication*] (DLA)
NEBB .... National Environmental Balancing Bureau (EA)
NEBBA....... Northeastern Bird-Banding Association [*Later, AFO*] (EA)
NEBBS....... Naval Environmental Bulletin Board System
Nebby .... Negative-Equity Baby Boomer [*Lifestyle classification*]
nEbC......... no-European-before-Columbus (SAUS)
NEBCY....... Nebraska City, NE [*American Association of Railroads railroad junction routing code*]
NEBD .... Nuclear Envelope Breakdown [*Also, NEB*] [*Cytology*]
NEbE......... Northeast by East
NEBFARMPAC... Nebraska Farmers Union PAC [*Lincoln, NE*] (PACS)
NEBHE....... New England Board of Higher Education [*Information service or system*]
NEBI .... National Employee Benefits Institute [*Washington, DC*] (EA)
NEBIC .... New England Bibliographic Instruction Collection
NEBIS .... North of England Biotechnology Information Service [*University of Newcastle-Upon-Tyne Medical School*] [*England*] [*Information service or system*] (IID)
NEBIT........ New and Expanding Business and Industry Training (OICC)
NEBK......... National Enterprise Bank [*Washington, DC*] (NQ)
Neb LB....... Nebraska Law Bulletin [*A publication*] (DLA)
Neb Leg N... Nebraska Legal News [*A publication*] (DLA)
NEBM........ New Bame Trailer [*NCIC trailer make code*]
NEBM........ No Eating between Meals
NEBMA...... Neben-Munitionsanstalt [*Branch ammunition depot*] [*German military - World War II*]
NEbN .... Northeast by North
NEBOSH..... National Examination Board in Occupational Safety and Health (PDAA)
NEBP .... Nicaraguan Exile Relocation Program (SAUS)
NEBR .... Nebraska (AAG)
Nebr .... Nebraska (ODBW)
Nebr .... Nebraska Reports [*A publication*] (DLA)
Neb RC...... Nebraska Railway Commission Reports [*A publication*] (DLA)
Neb Rev Stat... Revised Statutes of Nebraska [*A publication*] (DLA)
Nebr J Econ Bus... Nebraska Journal of Economics and Business [*A publication*] (JLIT)
Nebr LB..... Nebraska Law Bulletin [*A publication*] (DLA)
NEBS .... Network Equipment Building Specifications (TIMI)
NEBS .... Network Equipment-Building System
NEBS .... New England Business Service, Inc. [*NASDAQ symbol*] (NQ)
NEBS .... New Equipment Building System (SAUS)
NEBS .... New Exporters to Border States (SAUS)
NEBSS....... National Examinations Board in Supervisory Studies [*British*]
Neb Sup Ct J... Nebraska Supreme Court Journal [*A publication*] (DLA)
NEBT .... Nebraska Transport Company [*Common carrier symbol*]
NEBUL....... Nebula [*Spray*] [*Pharmacy*]

NEBULA..... Natural Electronic Business User's Language [*International Computers Ltd.*]
Neb (Unof)... Nebraska Unofficial Reports [*A publication*] (DLA)
Neb Unoff... Nebraska Unofficial Reports [*A publication*] (DLA)
NE Bus...... New England Business Services [*Associated Press*] (SAG)
NEBW....... Nonvacuum Electron Beam Welding
Neb WCC... Nebraska Workmen's Compensation Court. Bulletin [*A publication*] (DLA)
NEC.......... National Economic Council [*Defunct*] (EA)
NEC.......... National Economists Club (EA)
NEC.......... National Ecumenical Coalition (EA)
NEC.......... National Education Center for Paraprofessionals in Mental Health (EA)
NEC.......... National Education Corp. [*NYSE symbol*] (SPSG)
NEC.......... National Egg Council [*Later, PEIA*] (EA)
NEC.......... National Election Commission (Nigeria) [*Political party*] (PSAP)
NEC.......... National Electoral Commission [*Nigeria*] (ECON)
NEC.......... National Electrical Code
NEC.......... National Electronics Conference (AEBS)
NEC.......... National Electronics Council (NITA)
NEC.......... National Emblem Club (EA)
NEC.......... National Emergency Council [*Abolished, 1939*]
NEC.......... National Emissions Ceiling [*Air quality*]
NEC.......... National Employers' Committee
NEC.......... National Empowerment Consortium [*Investment group*] [*South Africa*]
NEC.......... National Engineering Consortium (EA)
NEC.......... National Entertainment Conference [*Later, NECAA*] (EA)
NEC.......... National Exchange Club (EA)
NEC.......... National Executive Committee [*British*] (DCTA)
NEC.......... National Executive Council (WDAA)
NEC.......... National Exhibition Centre [*British*]
NEC.......... National Extension College [*England*]
NEC.......... Natl Education [*NYSE symbol*] (TTSB)
NEC.......... Naval Examining Center
NEC.......... Naval Exercise Coordinator (CINC)
NEC.......... Naval Exhibit Center
NEC.......... Navy Enlisted Classification (NG)
NEC.......... Navy Enlisted Code
NEC.......... Nebraska State Railway Commission [*STAC*]
NEC.......... NEC Corp. [*Associated Press*] (SAG)
NEC.......... Necessary (AABC)
NEC.......... Necessity
NEC.......... Necochea [*Argentina*] [*Airport symbol*] (OAG)
NEC.......... Necrotizing Enterocolitis [*Medicine*]
NEC.......... Negro Ensemble Company [*A theatre group*]
NEC.......... Netherlands Electrotechnical Committee
NEC.......... Nett Explosives Content (HEAS)
NEC.......... Network Emergency Co-Ordinator (HEAS)
NEC.......... Neuroendocrine Cell [*Cytology*]
NEC.......... Neuroendocrine Convertase (DMAA)
NEC.......... Never Ending Conflict (VLIE)
NEC.......... New England College, Henniker, NH [*OCLC symbol*] (OCLC)
NEC.......... New England Commuter, Inc. (SAUS)
NEC.......... New England Conservatory of Music (BARN)
NEC.......... New England Council (EA)
NEC.......... Newspaper Editor's Course [*Defense Information School*] (DNAB)
NEC.......... Nippon Electric Co. [*Japan*]
NEC.......... Nippon Electronic Corp. (SAUS)
NEC.......... No-Error Check (IAA)
NEC.......... No Essential Changes (DMAA)
NEC.......... No Eye Contact [*Psychology*]
NEC.......... Noise-Equivalent Charge (PDAA)
NEC.......... Nonengineering Change (DNAB)
NEC.......... Non-Error Check (VLIE)
NEC.......... Nonesterified Cholesterol (DMAA)
NEC.......... Northcoast Environmental Center [*Conservation*] [*California and Oregon*] (EARSL)
NEC.......... Northeast Coast (SAUS)
NEC.......... Northeast Conference (PSS)
NEC.......... Northeast Conference on the Teaching of Foreign Languages (EA)
NEC.......... North East Corner [*Freemasonry*]
NEC.......... Northeast Corridor [*Railroad line*] (EGAO)
NEC.......... Northeast Corridor-Amtrak [*Federal Railroad Administration identification code*]
NEC.......... North Equatorial Current [*Oceanography*] (MSC)
NEC.......... Northern European Command [*NATO*] (NATG)
NEC.......... Northern European Countries
NEC.......... Northern Europe Committee [*NATO*] (NATG)
NEC.......... Not Else Classified (DMAA)
nec.......... Not Elsewhere Classified (ODBW)
NEC.......... Not Elsewhere Classified
NEC.......... Notes of English Ecclesiastical Cases [*A publication*] (DLA)
NEC.......... Nuclear Energy Center (NRCH)
NEC.......... Nuclear Energy Commission (USDC)
NEC.......... Nuclear Equipment Corp. (SAUS)
NEC.......... Nucleus of Epidermal Cell
NEC.......... Nursing Ethics Committee (DMAA)
NECA........ National Electrical Contractors Association (EA)
NECA........ National Employment Counseling Association (EA)
NECA........ National Employment Counselors Association (EA)
NECA........ National Episcopal Coalition on Alcohol [*Later, NECAD*] (EA)
NECA........ National Exchange Carrier Association (EA)
NECA........ National Explorers and Collectors Association (EA)
NECA........ Near East College Association (EA)
NECA........ N-Ethylcarboxamide Adenosine [*Biochemistry*]
NECA........ Numismatic Error Collectors of America (EA)
NECAA....... National Entertainment and Campus Activities Association [*Formerly, NEC*] (EA)
NECAC....... New England College Athletic Conference (PSS)
NECAD...... National Episcopal Coalition on Alcohol and Drugs (EA)
NECAF....... National Electromagnetic Compatibility Analysis Facility [*Department of Commerce*] (PDAA)
NECAH...... Northern Educational Centre for Aging and Health [*Lakehead University*] [*Canada*] (RCD)
NECA Newsletter... Numismatic Error Collectors of America Newsletter (SAUS)
NECAP....... NASA Energy-Cost Analysis Program
NECAP....... Navigation Equipment Capability Analysis (KSC)
NECAP....... Nutmeg Electric Companies Atomic Project
NECAR...... National Engineers Commission on Air Resources (PDAA)
NECAR...... New Electric Car [*Automotive engineering*]
NECB........ New England Coastal Basins (SAUS)
NECB........ New England Comm Bancorp'A' [*NASDAQ symbol*] (TTSB)
NECB........ New England Community Bancorp, Inc. [*NASDAQ symbol*] (SAG)
NE CBcp.... New England Community Bancorp, Inc. [*Associated Press*] (SAG)
NECBS....... Northeast Conference on British Studies (EARSL)
NECC........ National Education Computer Center
NECC........ National Education Computing Conference
NECC........ National Emergency Coordination Center (BARN)
NECC........ New England Collegiate Conference (PSS)
NECC........ New England Congressional Caucus [*Defunct*] (EA)
NECC........ New England Critical Care, Inc. [*NASDAQ symbol*] (COMM)
NECC........ North East Chamber of Commerce [*United Kingdom*] (EAIO)
NECC........ Northeast Computer Center [*Military*] (AABC)
NECC........ North Equatorial Countercurrent [*Oceanography*]
NECC........ Northern Essex Community College [*Haverhill, MA*]
NECCAC..... Northeast Community College Athletic Conference (PSS)
NECCB....... National Education Council of the Christian Brothers [*Later, RECCB*] (EA)
NECCC....... New England Correetional Coordinating Council (SAUS)
NECCC....... New Jersey State Department of Education (IID)
NEC CCIS... Northern European Command, Command & Control System (SAUS)
NECCO...... New England Confectionery Co.
NECCO...... Northern Essex Community College [*Haverhill, MA*]
NECCR...... North of England Children's Cancer Research Unit
NECCTA..... National Educational Closed-Circuit Television Association [*British*]
NECCWA.... New England College Conference Wrestling Associaton (PSS)
NECDC...... New England Consumer Development Council
NECEA....... National Engineering Construction Employers Association [*British*] (DBA)
NECEC....... New England Catholic Education Center (AEBS)
NECEL....... New England Coalition of Educational Leaders (SAUS)
NECEPT..... Northeast Center of Excellence for Pavement Technology [*Pennsylvania State University*] (RCD)
NECF........ National Exchange Club Foundation for the Prevention of Child Abuse (EA)
NECF........ New England College of Finance
NECG........ National Engineering Council for Guidance (EA)
NECH........ National Employment Clearing House [*American Chemical Society*]
NECH........ National Event Clearinghouse Database [*National Event Clearinghouse, Inc.*] [*Information service or system*] (CRD)
NECHE....... Northeastern Colorado Hail Experiment
NECHI........ Northeastern Consortium for Health Information [*Library network*]
NECI......... Noise Exposure Computer Integrator (PDAA)
NECIEB...... Northeast Coast Institution of Engineers and Shipbuilders (SAUS)
NECIES...... North East Coast Institution of Engineers and Shipbuilders (EAIO)
NECIP....... Northeast Corridor Improvement Project [*Department of Transportation*]
NECIS....... Naval Environmental Compliance Information System
NECIS....... NEC Information Systems, Inc. [*Boxborough, MA*]
NECIS....... Nippon Electric Company Information Systems, Inc. (SAUS)
NECJ......... New England Classical Journal (SAUS)
NECJC....... New Castle Junction, PA [*American Association of Railroads railroad junction routing code*]
NECK........ Neck [*Commonly used*] (OPSA)
NECK........ Neckar [*NCIC car make code*]
NECL........ Nonepitheliotropic Cutaneous Lymphosarcomas (SAUS)
NECLC....... National Emergency Civil Liberties Committee (EA)
NECM........ New England Conference Management [*Australia*]
NECM........ New England Conservatory of Music [*Boston, MA*]
NECMA...... New England County Metropolitan Areas
NECMD...... Newark Contract Management District (SAA)
NECMG...... Northeast Computer Measurement Group (SAUS)
NECN........ National Emergency Coordination Net [*Emergency Management*] (EMA)
NECNVA..... New England Committee for Nonviolent Action [*Later, CNVA*] (EA)
NECO........ National Ethnic Coalition of Organizations [*Association*] (EA)
NECO........ Nippon Electric Co. (IAA)
NECO........ Nuclear Engineering Co., Inc.
NECO........ Nuclear Engineering Company, Inc. (SAUS)
NECOE....... New England Center for Organizational Effectiveness (EA)
NECON...... Northeastern Conference (SAUS)
NECOP...... Nutrient-Enhanced Coastal Ocean Productivity [*Marine science*] (OSRA)
NECOR...... North East Consortium (SAUS)
NECOS...... Communication Net Control Station [*Navy*] (NVT)
NECOS...... Nepal Community Support Group (SAUS)
NECOS...... Northern European Chiefs of Staff [*NATO*] (NATG)
NECOS...... Northern Europe Chiefs of Staff (SAUS)

NECP .... National Eye Care Project [*Foundation of the American Academy of Ophthalmology*] (EA)
NECP .... New England College of Pharmacy
NECP .... Nonengineering Change Proposal
NECPA .... National Emergency Command Post Afloat
NECPA .... National Energy Conservation Policy Act [*1978*]
NEC PAC .... National Elevator Constructions PAC/International Union of Elevator Constructers [*Columbia, MD*] (PACS)
NECPL .... NATO Exploratory Conference on Production Logistics (NATG)
NECPR .... New External Cardiopulmonary Resuscitation
NECPUC ..... New England Conference of Public Utility Commissioners (SAUS)
NECPWA .... Northeast Club for Pre-War Austins [*British*] (EAIO)
NECQ .... National Electronics Component Qualification System (AAEL)
NECR .... New England Central Railroad [*Federal Railroad Administration identification code*]
NEC Research... Nippon Electric Company Research (SAUS)
NECRMP .... Northeast Corridor Regional Modeling Project [*Environmental Protection Agency*] (GFGA)
Necro .... Necrofile [*A publication*]
NECROL ..... Necrology (WDAA)
necrp .... Necropolis (VRA)
NECS .... National Electrical Code Standards
NECS .... National Elephant Collectors Society (EA)
NECS .... Nationwide Educational Computer Service (IEEE)
NECS .... Navy Embedded Computer System (ACAE)
NECS .... NetCom AB [*NASDAQ symbol*] (NASQ)
NECS .... New England Collectors Society (SAUS)
NECS .... Normal Environmental Control System (SAUS)
NECSA .... Navigational Electronic Chart System Association (SAUS)
NECSS .... Nuclear Energy Center Site Survey (NRCH)
NECT .... Neckover Trailer Manufacturing Company [*NCIC trailer make code*]
NECT .... North East China Transect (SAUS)
NECTA .... National Electric Comfort Trade Association [*Defunct*] (EA)
NECTA .... Naval Environmental Command Tactical Aid (SAUS)
NECTAR ..... Network of European CNS [*Central Nervous System*] Transplantation and Restoration
NECTAR ..... Network of European Communications and Transport Activities Research (SAUS)
NECTEC ..... National Electronics and Computer Technology Center [*Thailand*] (DDC)
NECTFL ..... Northeast Conference on the Teaching of Foreign Languages (EARSL)
NECTP .... North East Corridor Transportation Project (SAUS)
NECTP .... Northeast Corridor Transportation Project
NECU .... Deutsche Nah-Oest Linien [*Intermodal shipping container symbol*] (TVRC)
NECWA ...... New England College Wrestling Association (PSS)
NECY .... Necessary
NECY .... Necessity (WDAA)
NED .... Naphthylethylenediamine Dihydrochloride [*Organic chemistry*]
NED .... NASA/IPAC Extragalactic Database (GDD)
NED .... National Endowment for Democracy (EA)
NED .... Naval Equipment Department [*British military*] (DMA)
NED .... Navigation Error Data (MUGU)
Ned .... Nedarim (BJA)
NED .... Network Engineering Division (ACAE)
NED .... NeverEnding Disk [*Computer software*] [*Sytron Corp.*] (PCM)
NED .... Newark [*Delaware*] [*Seismograph station code, US Geological Survey*] (SEIS)
N Ed .... New Edition (SAUS)
NED .... New Editor [*Computer program*] [*Air Force*] (MCD)
NED .... New England Division [*Army Engineers*]
NED .... New English Dictionary [*i.e., the Oxford English Dictionary*]
NED .... No-Effect Dose [*Medicine*] (LDT)
NED .... No Evidence of Disease
NED .... No Expiration Date
NED .... No Export Demand [*Telegraphy*] (PCTE)
NED .... Noise Emitting Diode (SAUS)
NED .... Nonenzymatic Glycosylation [*Biochemistry*] (DAVI)
NED .... Normal Equivalent Deviate (or Deviation) (SAUS)
NED .... North, East, and Down
NED .... Northeastern University, Boston, MA [*OCLC symbol*] (OCLC)
NED .... Northrop Electronics Division (ACAE)
NED .... Nuclear Energy Division [*General Electric Co.*]
NED .... Nuclear Engineering Directorate [*Army*]
NEDA .... National Economic Development Association
NEDA .... National Electronic Distributors Association (EA)
NEDA .... National Emergency Defense Airlift
NEDA .... National Environmental Development Association (EA)
NEDA .... National Equipment Distributors Association [*Defunct*] (EA)
NEDA .... National Exhaust Distributors Association [*Later, NEDA/USA*] (EA)
Neda .... Nedarim (BJA)
NEDA/CAAP... National Environmental Development Association/Clean Air Act Project [*Defunct*] (EA)
NEDA/GRND... National Environmental Development Association/Ground Water Project (EA)
NEDAM ...... Nuclear Effects Damage Assessment Methodologies (SAUS)
NEDA/USA... National Exhaust Distributors Association/Undercar Specialists Association [*Defunct*] (EA)
NEDAX ...... Nippon Electric Data Exchange (SAUS)
NEDB .... National Exposure Data Base (HEAS)
NEDC .... National Economic Development Council [*Nickname: Neddie*] [*British*]
NEDC .... National Engineering Design Challenge (VLIE)
NeDC .... New England Document Conservation Center, Andover, MA [*Library symbol*] [*Library of Congress*] (LCLS)
NEDC .... New European Driving Cycle [*Automotive emissions*]
NEDCC ...... New England Document Conservation Center [*Information service or system*] (IID)
NEDCC ...... Northeast Document Conservation Center
NEDCO ...... Newport European Distribution Co. (EFIS)
NEDCO ...... Non-Electronic Part Data Collection (PDAA)
NEDCO ...... Northeast Dairy Cooperative Federation [*Defunct*] (EA)
NEDD .... NATO & European Defence Directorate (SAUS)
NEDECO .... Netherlands Engineering Consultants
NEDED ...... Naval Explosive Development Engineering Department (DNAB)
NEDEL .... No Epidemiologically Detectable Exposure Level [*Medicine*] (HCT)
NEDELA ..... Network Definition Language [*Computer science*] (PDAA)
NEDEP .... Navy Enlisted Dietetic Education Program
NEDEPA ..... Nea Demokratiki Parataxi [*Cyprus*] [*Political party*] (PPE)
NeDF .... New England Data Film, Inc., Milford, CT [*Library symbol*] [*Library of Congress*] (LCLS)
NEDGP ...... New England Division of General Practice (SAUS)
NEDH .... New England Deaconess Hospital [*Medicine*] (EDAA)
NEDI .... Nobel Education Dynamics, Inc. [*NASDAQ symbol*] (SAG)
NEDIPA ...... Nea Demokratiki Parataxi [*Cyprus*] [*Political party*] (PPW)
NEDIPS ...... NEC Dataflow Image Processing System (NITA)
NEDIS .... National Environmental Data and Information Service [*Marine science*] (MSC)
NEDL .... New England Deposit Library
NEDI .... Nobel Ed Dynamics [*NASDAQ symbol*] (TTSB)
NEDLC .... National Economic Development and Law Center [*Berkeley, CA*] [*Research center*] (EA)
NEDLIB ...... Networked European Deposit Library (TELE)
NEDN .... Naval Environmental Data Network
NEDN .... Naval Worldwide Environmental Data Network (MCD)
NEDNA ...... National Emergency Department Nurses Association [*Medicine*] (EDAA)
NEDO .... National Eating Disorders Organization (EA)
NEDO .... National Economic Development Office [*British*]
NEDO .... New Energy and Industrial Technology Development Organization
NEDPS ...... Nacken Electronic Data Processing System (SAUS)
NEDR .... Noise Equivalent Delta Reflectivity (SAUS)
NEDRES .... National Environmental Data Referral Service [*Online database*] [*National Oceanic and Atmospheric Administration*] [*Washington, DC*]
NEDRES .... National Environmental Data Referral Service/NODC (IID)
NEDRIX ..... Northern New England Disaster Recovery Information Exchange [*Emergency Management*] (EMA)
NEDS .... National Emissions Data System [*Environmental Protection Agency*] [*Information service or system*]
NEDS .... Naval Environmental Data System (CAAL)
NEDS .... Naval Environmental Display Station (CAAL)
NEDS .... New Enlisted Distribution System (NVT)
NEDS .... Nonviolent Explosive Destructive System (MCD)
NEDSA ...... Non-Erasing Determination (or Deterministic) Stack Automation (SAUS)
NEDSA ...... Nonerasing Deterministic Stack Automation [*Computer science*] (IAA)
NEDT .... National Educational Development Test
NEDT .... Noise-Equivalent Differential Temperature
NeDTH ...... Technische Hogeschool Delft, Delft, Netherlands [*Library symbol*] [*Library of Congress*] (LCLS)
NEDTRA ..... Naval Education and Training Command (MCD)
NEDU .... Naval Experimental Diving Unit (SAUS)
NEDU .... Navy Experimental Diving Unit [*Panama City, FL*]
NEDU .... Nedrac Container Lines [*Intermodal shipping container symbol*] (TVRC)
NEDWSA .... Non-Erasing Deterministic Writing Stack Acceptor (SAUS)
NEE .... National Electrical Effect
NEE .... National Electrology Educators (EA)
NEE .... Needle Electrode Examination [*Medicine*] (DMAA)
NEE .... Net Ecosystem Exchange [*Biology*]
NEE .... New England Express [*Steamship*] (MHDW)
NEE .... Noise-Equivalent Energy (MCD)
NEE .... Noise Equivalent Exposure [*Photonics*]
NEE .... Norethindrone Enanthate [*Medicine*] (EDAA)
NEE .... Norethindrone/Ethinyl Estradiol [*Oral contraceptive*]
NEE .... Normalized Error Energy (SAUS)
NEE .... Northeast Airlines [*FAA designator*] (FAAC)
NEE .... Northeast Express Regional Airlines, Inc. [*ICAO designator*] (FAAC)
NEE .... North Enter Earth (ACAE)
NEEA .... North-East Electricity Authority (SAUS)
NEEB .... National Expressway Engineering Bureau [*Highway operations*]
NEEB .... North East Engineering Bureau (SAUS)
NEEB .... North Eastern Electricity Board [*British*]
NEEB .... Northeastern Electricity Board (SAUS)
NEEC .... National Environmental Enforcement Council [*National Association of Attorneys General*] (EPA)
NEEC .... National Export Expansion Council [*Terminated, 1973*] [*Department of Commerce*]
NEEC .... NEECO, Inc. [*NASDAQ symbol*] (COMM)
NEEC .... Not Entailing Excessive Cost [*Environmental technology*]
NEEC .... Nuclear Explosion Effects Center
NEED .... National Energy Education Development Project (EA)
NEED .... National Environmental Education Development [*Program of National Park Service*] [*Defunct*]
NEED .... Native Employment and Educational Development [*Canada*]
NEED .... Near East Emergency Donations
Need .... Needham's Annual Summary of Tax Cases [*England*] [*A publication*] (DLA)

NEED .... Need, Inc. [*An association*] (EA)
NEED .... Negro Education Emergency Drive
NEED .... New Employment Expansion and Development [*Canada*]
NEEDA....... National Emergency Equipment Dealers Association (EA)
NEEDHA..... National Electrical Engineering Department Heads Association (EA)
NEEDIS...... National Enterprise Education Development and Information Service (AIE)
NEEDS....... NASA End-to-End Data Systems
NEEDS....... National Emergency Equipment Data System (NITA)
NEEDS....... Navy Education and Employment Development System (MCD)
NEEDS....... Neighborhood Environmental Evaluation and Decision System [*Health Services and Mental Health Administration*]
NEEDS....... New England Electronic Data System (SAUS)
NEEDS....... Nikkei Economic Electronic Databank System (SAUS)
NEEDS-IR... NIKKEI Economic Electronic Databank Service - Information Retrieval [*Information service or system*] [*Japan*] (IID)
NEEDS-TS... NIKKEI Economic Electronic Databank Service - Time Sharing [*Information service or system*] [*Japan*] (IID)
NEEE......... Near East Equine Encephalomyelitis [*Medicine*] (DMAA)
NEEEV....... Near East Equine Encephalomyelitis Virus [*Virology*] (QSUL)
NeEinP...... Philips Research Laboratories, Eindhoven, Netherlands [*Library symbol*] [*Library of Congress*] (LCLS)
NeEinT ...... Technische Hogeschool te Eindhoven, Eindhoven, Netherlands, [*Library symbol*] [*Library of Congress*] (LCLS)
NEEITC ...... National Electrical and Electronic Industry Training Committee [*Australia*]
NEEJ......... National Environmental Enforcement Journal [*National Association of Attorneys General*] [*A publication*] (EPA)
NEEL......... National Environmental Education Landmarks [*Department of the Interior*]
NEELS .... National Emergency Equipment Locator System [*Environment Canada*] [*Information service or system*] (CRD)
NEEMA ...... New England Educational Media Association
NEEMIS ..... New England Energy Management Information System
NEENA....... Neenah, WI [*American Association of Railroads railroad junction routing code*]
NEEP .... Negative End Expiratory Pressure [*Medicine*]
NEEP .... New England Economic Project (NITA)
NEEP .... Nuclear Dectronics Effects Program (SAUS)
NEER .... National Environmental Evaluation and Remediation Consortium (RCD)
NE'ER .... Never (ROG)
NEERI .... National Environmental Engineering Research Institute
NEERS....... National Earthquake Early Reporting System (NOAA)
NEERS....... New England Estuarine Research Society (SAUS)
NEES .... Naval Engineering Experiment Station
NEES .... Nett Emissions Eliminator System [*Off-Highway equipment*]
NEES .... Network for Earthquake Engineering Simulation [*Emergency Management*] (EMA)
NEES .... New England Electric Service (SAUS)
NEES .... New England Electric System
NEESA....... Naval Energy and Environmental Support Activity
NEESAB ..... National Energy Extension Service Advisory Board [*Department of Energy*] [*Washington, DC*] (EGAO)
NEET......... Navy Extended Electrode Technique (PDAA)
NEET......... Nonlinear Estimation for Exoatmospheric Trajectories (ACAE)
NEETF .... National Environmental Education and Training Foundation [*An association*] (PS)
NEETRAC... National Electric Energy Testing, Research, and Applications Center [*Georgia Institute of Technology*] (RCD)
NEETS....... Naval Electronics Environmental Training System (MCD)
NEETU....... National Engineering and Electrical Trade Union [*Republic of Ireland*] (BI)
NEEWSSOP... NATO Europe Early Warning System Standard Operating Procedures (NATG)
NEF .... National Economic Forum (SAFN)
NEF .... National Educators Fellowship [*Later, CEAI*]
NEF .... National Energy Foundation (EA)
NEF .... National Extra Fine [*Thread*]
NEF .... Naval Emergency Fund [*A budget category*]
NEF .... Near East Foundation (EA)
NEF .... Negative Expiratory Force [*Medicine*] (EDAA)
NEF .... Negative-Regulatory Factor [*Genetics*]
NeF .... Nephritic Factor [*Clinical medicine*]
NEF .... Network Element Function [*Computer science*] (VLIE)
NEF .... New Economics Foundation [*United Kingdom*] (RCD)
NEF .... New Education Fellowship [*Later, WEF*]
NEF .... No Further Clearance Required [*Aviation*] (FAAC)
NEF .... Noise Equivalent Flux (SAUS)
NEF .... Noise-Equivalent Flux
NEF .... Noise Exposure Forecast [*Aircraft*]
NEF .... Nordiska Ekonomiska Forskningsradet [*Nordic Economic Research Council - NERC*] (EAIO)
NEF .... Northern Elders Forum (SAUS)
NEF .... Nurses Educational Funds (EA)
NEF .... Scudder New Europe Fund [*NYSE symbol*] (SPSG)
NEFA......... Narcotic Educational Foundation of America (EA)
NEFA......... New European Fighter Aircraft (PS)
NEFA......... Nonesterified Fatty Acid [*Biochemistry*]
NEFA......... North East Forest Alliance (SAUS)
NEFA......... Northeast Frontier Agency (SAUS)
NEFARS ..... Nuclear Effects from Analysis of Residual Signatures
NEFBRACS... Nearfield Bearing and Range Accuracy Calibration System (PDAA)
NEFC .... NATO Electronic Warfare Fusion Cell (SAUS)
NEFC .... Near East Forestry Commission
NEFC .... New England Football Conference (PSS)
NEFC .... Northeast Fisheries Center [*Department of Commerce*] [*Woods Hole, MA*]
NEFCCO..... New England Fish Co. (SAUS)
NEFCO....... New England Fish Co.
NEFCO....... Nordic Environment Finance Corp. (SAUS)
NEFD .... Noise-Equivalent Flux Density
NEFDA....... New England Fisheries Development Association (EA)
NEFDF....... New England Fisheries Development Foundation [*Later, NEFDA*] (EA)
NEFE......... New England Fish Exchange (EA)
NEFEC....... Northeast Fisheries Center [*National Marine Fisheries Service*] (USDC)
NEFES....... Northeastern Forest Experiment Station [*Department of Agriculture*] [*Broomall, PA*] (GRD)
NEFFS....... Northeastern Forest Experiment Station (SAUS)
NEFGX....... New England Growth [*Mutual fund ticker symbol*] (SG)
NEFI .... New England Fuel Institute
NEFIRA...... New England Fire Insurance Rating Association (SAUS)
NEFLIN...... North East Florida Library Network
NEFMA ...... NATO EFA Management Agency (SAUS)
NEFMC ...... New England Fisheries Management Council
NEFMO ...... NATO European Fighter Management Organization (MCD)
NEFO .... National Electronics Facilities Organization
NEFOS....... New Emerging Forces
NEFP .... New England Free Press [*Publisher*]
NEFPO....... New England Field Procurement Office (ACAE)
NEFPS....... National Enginemen and Firemen's Protection Society [*A union*] [*British*]
NEFR .... North-East Frontier Railway [*Indian Railway*] (TIR)
NEFS .... Network Extensible File System [*Computer science*] (VLIE)
NEFSA....... National Education Field Service Association [*Defunct*] (EA)
NEFSG....... Northeastern Forest Soils Group (SAUS)
NEFTIC ...... Northeastern Forest Tree Improvement Conference (SAUS)
NEFX .... Northeast Corridor Foundation [*Private rail car owner code*]
NEFZ......... New Fand Plant [*Federal Railroad Administration identification code*]
NEG.......... Energy East [*NYSE symbol*] [*Formerly, New York State E&G*]
NEG.......... National Environmental Group (EFIS)
Neg .... Nega'im (BJA)
NEG.......... Negate a Binary Number [*Computer science*]
NEG.......... Negation (WDAA)
NEG.......... Negative (AAG)
neg .... Negative (VRA)
NEG.......... Neglect [*FBI standardized term*]
NEG.......... Negligible (AAG)
NEG.......... Negotiable (ADA)
NEG.......... Negril [*Jamaica*] [*Airport symbol*] (OAG)
NEG.......... Negro
NEG.......... Nitrogen Efficiency for Growth (SAUS)
NEG.......... Nonevaporable Getter (SAUS)
NEG.......... Numerical Experimentation Group [*Marine science*] (OSRA)
NEGA .... National Ex-Offender Grant Alliance [*Defunct*] (EA)
NEGA .... New England Gerontological Association (EA)
NEGAU ...... Negaunee, MI [*American Association of Railroads railroad junction routing code*]
Negb.......... Negotiable
NEGB .... Northeastern Gas Board (SAUS)
Neg C .... Negligence Cases [*Commerce Clearing House*] [*A publication*] (DLA)
Neg Cas..... Bloomfield's Manumission (or Negro) Cases [*New Jersey*] [*A publication*] (DLA)
NEGD........ Negotiated (ROG)
NEGDEF..... Navy Enlisted Ground Defense Emergency Force
NEGEA....... New England Gas & Electric Association (EFIS)
NEGF .... Neurite Growth-Promoting Factor (DMAA)
NEGFC....... New England Grain and Feed Council [*Connecticut, Maine, Massachusetts, New Hampshire, Rhode Island, and Vermont*] (EARSL)
NEGFIRE... Negligible Fire [*Emergency Management*] (EMA)
NEGI .... National Federation of Engineering and General Ironfounders [*British*] (BI)
Neg Inst..... Negotiable Instrument [*Legal term*] (DLA)
NEGISTOR... Negative Resistor (PDAA)
NEGIT .... Negative Impedance Transistor [*Electronics*] (IAA)
Negl .... Negligence
NEGL .... Negligent [*Motor vehicle violation code used in state of Maryland*] (MVRD)
Negl & Comp Cas Ann... Negligence and Compensation Cases, Annotated [*A publication*] (DLA)
Negl & Comp Cas Ann 3d... Negligence and Compensation Cases, Annotated, Third Series [*A publication*] (DLA)
Negl & Comp Cas Ann (NS)... Negligence and Compensation Cases, Annotated, New Series [*A publication*] (DLA)
Negl Cas.... Negligence Cases [*Commerce Clearing House*] [*A publication*] (DLA)
Negl Cas 2d... Negligence Cases, Second Series [*Commerce Clearing House*] [*A publication*] (DLA)
NEGN........ Negotiation (ROG)
NEGOA ...... Northeast Gulf of Alaska [*Marine science*] (MSC)
NEGOT ...... Negotiable [*Legal shorthand*] (LWAP)
NEGPED..... Negotiator's Planned Execution Date (MCD)
NEGPR ...... Negative Print
NEGPT....... Negative Print (VRA)
NEGR .... Negrini [*NCIC motorcycle make code*]
NEGRAD .... Negligible Radiation [*Emergency Management*] (EMA)
NEGRO ...... National Economic Growth and Reconstruction Organization [*Black entrepreneurial organization*]

NEGRO ...... New England Grass Roots Organization
Negro Cas... Bloomfield's Manumission (or Negro) Cases [*New Jersey*] [*A publication*] (DLA)
NEGRS ...... Negative Report Submitted [*Army*] (AABC)
NEGRSBM... Negative Report Submitted [*Army*] (AABC)
negs .... Negatives [*Film*] (WDMC)
NEGS .... New England Southern Railroad [*Federal Railroad Administration identification code*]
NEGTAX ..... Negative Tax (MHDW)
NEGU .... North Europe-United States Gulf Freight Association [*Intermodal shipping container symbol*] (TVRC)
NEGX .... National Energy Group [*NASDAQ symbol*] (SAG)
NEGX .... Natl Energy Group'A' [*NASDAQ symbol*] (TTSB)
NEGX .... Negate a Binary Number with Extend [*Computer science*]
NEGY .... Neutral-Equivalent Gasoline Yield [*Petroleum chemistry*]
NEH .... East Carolina University, Health Sciences Library, Greenville, NC [*OCLC symbol*] (OCLC)
NEh .... East Hampton Free Library, East Hampton, NY [*Library symbol*] [*Library of Congress*] (LCLS)
NEH .... National Endowment for the Humanities
Neh .... Nehemiah [*Old Testament book*]
NEH .... Nuclear Effects Handbook
NEHA .... National Environmental Health Association (EA)
NEHA .... National Executive Housekeepers Association (EA)
NeHaCa ..... New Hampshire Campground Owners Association (EARSL)
NeHB .... Bureau voor de Industriele Eigendom, Bibliotheek Octrooiraad, The Hague, Netherlands [*Library symbol*] [*Library of Congress*] (LCLS)
NEHC .... National Extension Homemakers Council (EA)
NEHCA ...... Northeast Highland Cattle Association (EARSL)
NEHE .... Nurses for Environmental Health Education (DAVI)
NEHEP....... National Eye Health Education Program [*Information service or system*] (IID)
NEHF .... National Eye and Health Foundation (EA)
NEHGS ...... New England Historic Genealogical Society (EA)
NEHI .... Northwest Educators of the Hearing Impaired (EDAC)
NeHKB ...... Koninklijke Bibliotheek [*Royal Library*], The Hague, Netherlands [*Library symbol*] [*Library of Congress*] (LCLS)
NEHM .... Northeast Health Management (MHID)
NEHRC ...... New England History Resources Center [*University of New England*] [*Australia*]
NEHRP ...... National Earthquake Hazards Reduction Program [*Federal Emergency Management Agency*] [*Washington, DC*] (EGAO)
NeHSU ...... Staatsuitgeverij Christoffel Plantijnstaat (State Printing Office), The Hague, Netherlands [*Library symbol*] [*Library of Congress*] (LCLS)
NEi .... East Islip Public Library, East Islip, NY [*Library symbol*] [*Library of Congress*] (LCLS)
NEI .... Narcotics Education, Inc. (EA)
NEI .... National Elevator Industry (NTPA)
NEI .... National Enterprises (EFIS)
NEI .... National Estuarine Inventory
NEI .... National Eye Institute [*Formerly, NINDB*] [*Department of Health and Human Services*] [*Bethesda, MD*] [*National Institutes of Health*]
NEI .... Nature Expeditions International (GNE)
NEI .... Neipperg [*Federal Republic of Germany*] [*Seismograph station code, US Geological Survey*] (SEIS)
NEI .... Netherlands East Indies
NEI .... New England Institute (SAUS)
NEI .... New England Instrument (SAUS)
NEI .... New Enterprise Institute [*University of Southern Maine*] [*Research center*] (RCD)
NEI .... New Equipment Introduction [*Army*] (AABC)
NEI .... Noise Equivalent Input (SAUS)
NEI .... Noise-Equivalent Input
NEI .... Noise Equivalent Intensity (SAUS)
NEI .... Noise-Equivalent Intensity
NEI .... Noise Equivalent Irradiance (CIST)
NEI .... Noise Exposure Index (SAUS)
NEI .... Non Est Inventus [*It Has Not Been Found or Discovered*] [*Latin*]
NEI .... Non Explosive Initiator (ACAE)
NEI .... Non-Explosive Initiator (LDOE)
NEI .... Nordic Energy Index [*Database*] [*Nordic Atomic Libraries Joint Secretariat*] [*Denmark*] [*Information service or system*] (IID)
NEI .... Northern Electric Industries [*British*]
NEI .... Northern Engineering Industries [*Commercial firm*] [*British*]
NEI .... Not Elsewhere Included (SAUS)
nei .... Not Elsewhere Included or Indicated (EBF)
NEI .... Not Elsewhere Indicated
NEI .... Nouvelles Equipes Internationales [*Later, European Christian Democratic Union*]
NEI .... Nuclear Energy Institute (NTPA)
NEI .... US National Eye Institute (SAUS)
NEIAL........ North East Iowa Academic Libraries [*Library network*]
NEIB .... Northeast Indiana Banc [*NASDAQ symbol*] (TTSB)
NEIB .... Northeast Indiana Bancorp, Inc. [*NASDAQ symbol*] (SAG)
NEIC .... National Earthquake Information Center [*US Geological Survey*]
NEIC .... National Electronic Information Corp. [*Information service or system*] (IID)
NEIC .... National Energy Information Center [*Department of Energy*] [*Washington, DC*]
NEIC .... National Enforcement Investigations Center [*Environmental Protection Agency*] (EG)
NEIC .... National Equivalence Information Centre (AIE)
NEIC .... NATO Equipment Interpretation Course (MCD)
NEIC .... New England Information Center [*Information service or system*]
NEIC .... New England Investment Companies, Inc. (EFIS)
NEIC .... Northeast Independent Conference (PSS)
NEIC .... North East Insurance [*NASDAQ symbol*] (TTSB)
NEIC .... North East Insurance Co. [*NASDAQ symbol*] (NQ)
NEICA .... National Energy Information Center Affiliate [*University of New Mexico*] (IID)
NEICE........ North of England Institute for Christian Education
NEIDA .... Network of Educational Innovation for Development in Africa (EAIO)
NEIDS .... North East Interim Data System (WDAA)
NEIED .... National Educational Institute for Economic Development (EA)
NEIETC ...... New England Interstate Environmental Training Center
NEIF .... Near-Earth Instrumentation Facility [*NASA*] (KSC)
NEII .... National Elevator Industry, Inc. (EA)
NEII .... National Engineering Information Initiative (SAUS)
NEIL .... Neon Indicating Light
NEIL .... Nordic Energy Index, Literature [*Database*] [*Nordic Atomic Libraries Joint Secretariat*] [*Information service or system*] (CRD)
NEILC........ New England Interstate Library Compact (SAUS)
NeimM ...... Neiman-Marcus Group [*Associated Press*] (SAG)
NEIMME...... North of England Institute of Mining and Mechanical Engineers (SAUS)
NeINBc ...... Northeast Indiana Bancorp, Inc. [*Associated Press*] (SAG)
NE Ins .... North East Insurance Co. [*Associated Press*] (SAG)
NEIP .... National Environmental Indicators Programme (SAUS)
NEIPG .... National Electronic Industries Procurement Group
NEIR .... Narrative End Item Report [*NASA*] (KSC)
NEIR .... Neither (ROG)
NEIRIS ...... Northeast Regional Library System (SAUS)
NEIRLS...... Northeast Regional Library System [*Library network*]
NEIS .... National Earthquake Information Service [*United States Geological Survey*] (IID)
NEIS .... National Emissions Inventory System [*Database*] [*Environment Canada*] [*Information service or system*] (CRD)
NEIS .... National Engineering Information System (BUR)
NEIS .... National Environmental Information Symposium
NEIS .... Nuclear Energy Information Service [*An association*] (EA)
NEISA .... New England Intercollegiate Sailing Association
NEISS .... National Electronic Injury Surveillance System [*Consumer Product Safety Commission*] [*Washington, DC*] [*Databank*]
NEIT .... New Equipment Introductory Team [*Army*] (AABC)
NEITA........ National Excellence in Teaching Award [*Australia*]
NEIULS...... Northeast Iowa Union List of Serials
NEIWPCC... New England Interstate Water Pollution Control Commission
NEIX .... Nordic Energy Index [*Database*] [*Nordic Atomic Libraries Joint Secretariat*] [*Information service or system*] (CRD)
NEJ .... Neuroeffector Junction [*Medicine*] (EDAA)
NEJ .... Seattle, WA [*Location identifier*] [*FAA*] (FAAL)
NEJA......... James Nelms [*Common carrier symbol*]
NEJA......... National Entertainment Journalists Association [*Defunct*] (EA)
NEJM......... New England Journal of Medicine [*A publication*]
NEJO .... New England Journal of Optometry [*Medicine*] [*NECO*] (EDAA)
NEJS......... Near Eastern and Judaistic Studies (BJA)
NEK.......... Naval Equerry to the King
NEKASA..... New England Knitwear and Sportswear Association (EA)
NEKDA ...... Neurotech Development Corp. [*OTCBB symbol*]
NEKDA ...... New England Kiln Drying Association (EA)
NEKL .... Northeast Kansas Library System [*Library network*]
NEKM........ Northeast Kansas & Missouri [*Federal Railroad Administration identification code*]
NEKOA ...... New England Knitted Outerwear Association [*Later, NEKASA*] (EA)
NEKOO ...... Nekoosa, WI [*American Association of Railroads railroad junction routing code*]
NEL .... East Carolina University, Department of Library Science, Greenville, NC [*OCLC symbol*] (OCLC)
NEl........... Greenburgh Public Library, Elmsford, NY [*Library symbol*] [*Library of Congress*] (LCLS)
NEL .... Lakehurst, NJ [*Location identifier*] [*FAA*] (FAAL)
NEL .... National Electronics Laboratory (IDOE)
NEL .... National Emancipation League [*Nigeria*]
NEL .... National Engineering Laboratory [*Scotland*]
NEL .... National Engineering Laboratory [*Superseded IAT*] [*Gaithersburg, MD*] [*National Institute of Standards and Technology*]
NEL .... National Epilepsy League [*Later, EFA*] (EA)
NEL .... National Epilepsy Library [*Epilepsy Foundation*] (IID)
NEL .... Naval Command Control Communications Laboratory Center
NEL .... Naval Electronics Laboratory
NEL .... Naval Explosive Laboratory
NEL .... Navy Electronics Laboratory [*San Diego, CA*]
NEL .... Nelson [*Nevada*] [*Seismograph station code, US Geological Survey*] (SEIS)
Nel .... Nelson's English Chancery Reports [*A publication*] (DLA)
NEL .... Neon Light (IAA)
NEL .... New England Mutual Life Insurance Co. (EFIS)
NEL .... New English Library [*Publishers*] [*British*]
NEL .... NewTel Enterprises Ltd. [*Toronto Stock Exchange symbol*]
NEL .... No Effect Level (ADA)
NEL .... Noise Exposure Level (SAUS)
NEL .... Non-English Language
NEL .... Nonspecific Excitability Level [*Animal behavior*]
NEL .... Northern Extratropical Land [*Geography*]
NEL .... Nuclear Electronics Laboratory (SAUS)
NEL .... Nuclear Energy Laboratory [*Research center*] (RCD)
NEL .... Nuclear Engineering Laboratory [*University of Utah*] [*Research center*] (RCD)
NELA .... National Electric Light Association

NELA .... National Employment Lawyers Association (EA)
NELA .... New England Library Association
NELA .... Northeastern Loggers Association (EA)
NELAC .... National Environment Laboratory Accreditation Conference [*Environmental Protection Agency*]
NELAT .... Navy Electronics Laboratory Assembly Tester
NELATS ..... Naval Electronics Laboratory Automatic Tester System (DNAB)
NELB .... New England Library Board [*Library network*]
NELC .... Naval Electronics Center (TIMI)
NELC .... Naval Electronics Laboratory Center [*Later, NOSC*]
NELC .... New England Life Companies, Inc. (EFIS)
NELCON ..... New-Zealand Electronics Convention (SAUS)
NELCON NZ ... National Electronics Conference, New Zealand [*IEEE*]
Nel CR ...... Nelson's English Chancery Reports [*A publication*] (DLA)
NEld .... Sunshine Hall Free Library, Eldred, NY [*Library symbol*] [*Library of Congress*] (LCLS)
NELDIC ...... Nippon Electric Layout Design for Integrated Circuits (SAUS)
NELEC .... Nonelectric
NELEX .... Naval Electronics Systems Command Headquarters
NeLH .... National Electronic Library for Health (SAUS)
NELIA .... Nuclear Energy Liability Insurance Association [*Later, ANI*] (EA)
NELIAC ...... Naval Electronics Laboratory International ALGOL Compilers
NELINET ... New England Library Information Network
NELIS .... Noncommunications Emitter Location and Identification System (MCD)
NELIS-A ..... Noncommunications Emitter Location and Identification System - Airborne
NELL .... Nallej of Florida [*NCIC trailer make code*]
NELL .... Nellcor, Inc. [*NASDAQ symbol*] (NQ)
NELL .... Nellcor Puritan Bennett [*NASDAQ symbol*] (TTSB)
Nell .... Nell's Reports [*1845-55*] [*Ceylon*] [*A publication*] (DLA)
NELL .... North East Lancashire Libraries (SAUS)
NELLCO ..... New England Law Library Consortium (IID)
NELLCO ..... New England Law Library Consortium, Inc. [*Harvard Law School*] [*Information service or system*] (IID)
Nellcor ...... Nellcor, Inc. [*Associated Press*] (SAG)
NElle .... Ellenville Public Library, Ellenville, NY [*Library symbol*] [*Library of Congress*] (LCLS)
NELM .... Northeastern Lumber Manufacturers Association
NElm ...... Steele Memorial Library of Elmira and Chemung County, Elmira, NY [*Library symbol*] [*Library of Congress*] (LCLS)
NELMA ...... Northeastern Lumber Manufacturers Association (EA)
NElmC .... Elmira College, Elmira, NY [*Library symbol*] [*Library of Congress*] (LCLS)
NElmhC ..... City Hospital at Elmhurst, Elmhurst, NY [*Library symbol*] [*Library of Congress*] (LCLS)
NElmHi ...... Chemung County Historical Society, Elmira, NY [*Library symbol*] [*Library of Congress*] (LCLS)
NElmM ...... Mount Saviour Monastery, Elmira, NY [*Library symbol*] [*Library of Congress*] (LCLS)
NElmo .... Elmont Public Library, Elmont, NY [*Library symbol*] [*Library of Congress*] (LCLS)
NElmoAE .... Alden Terrace Elementary School, Elmont, NY [*Library symbol*] [*Library of Congress*] (LCLS)
NElmoCCE .. Clara H. Carlson Elementary School, Elmont, NY [*Library symbol*] [*Library of Congress*] (LCLS)
NElmoCE .... Covert Elementary School, Elmont, NY [*Library symbol*] [*Library of Congress*] (LCLS)
NElmoDE .... Dutch Broadway Elementary School, Elmont, NY [*Library symbol*] [*Library of Congress*] (LCLS)
NElmoGE .... Gotham Avenue Elementary School, Elmont, NY [*Library symbol*] [*Library of Congress*] (LCLS)
NElmoMH ... Elmont Memeorial High School, Elmont, NY [*Library symbol*] [*Library of Congress*] (LCLS)
NElmoSE .... Stewart Elementary School, Elmont, NY [*Library symbol*] [*Library of Congress*] (LCLS)
NElmP .... Elmira Psychiatric Center, Elmira, NY [*Library symbol*] [*Library of Congress*] (LCLS)
NElmsAr .... Weschester County Archives, Elmsford, NY [*Library symbol*] [*Library of Congress*] (LCLS)
NElmSC ..... Supreme Court Law Library-Elmira, Elmira, NY [*Library symbol*] [*Library of Congress*] (LCLS)
NElmsSW ... Southern Westchester BOCES School, Elmsford, NY [*Library symbol*] [*Library of Congress*] (LCLS)
NELN .... Nelson-Dykes Company [*NCIC trailer make code*]
NELNET PAC ... Nelnet Inc. PAC [*Washington, DC*] (PACS)
NELOS .... Navy Electronics Laboratory Operating System
NELP .... National Employment Law Project [*New York, NY*] (EA)
NELP .... Navy Environmental Leadership Program
NELP .... North East London Polytechnic [*School*] [*England*]
NELPA .... Northwest Electric Light and Power Association (SAUS)
NELPAC ..... National Engineering Laboratory's Thermophysical Properties Package [*British*] [*Information service or system*] (IID)
NELPAC ..... Nebraska Leadership PAC [*Omaha, NE*] (PACS)
NELPAC ..... New England League of Savings Institutions PAC [*Boston, MA*] (PACS)
NELPAC ..... New England Life Insurance Company PAC [*Boston, MA*] (PACS)
NELPIA ...... Nuclear Energy Liability Property Insurance Association [*Later, ANI*]
NeLR .... Rijksuniversiteit Leiden, Leiden, Netherlands [*Library symbol*] [*Library of Congress*] (LCLS)
NELRC .... National Epilepsy Library and Resource Center [*Epilepsy Foundation of America*] [*Information service or system*] (IID)
NELS .... National Educational Longitudinal Survey
NELS .... National Environmental Laboratories [*Proposed*]
NELS .... Nelson Manufacturing Company [*NCIC trailer make code*]
Nels .... Nelson's English Chancery Reports [*A publication*] (DLA)
NELS .... Northwest Europe Loran Steering Committee (SAUS)
NELS .... Nuclear Effects Link Simulator (SAUS)
Nels 8vo .... Nelson's English Chancery Reports [*A publication*] (DLA)
NELS:88 ..... National Education Longitudinal Study of 1988 [*Department of Education*] (GFGA)
NELSA .... Northeast Library Service Area [*Library network*]
Nels Abr .... Nelson's Abridgment of the Common Law [*A publication*] (DLA)
Nels Cler ... Nelson's Rights of the Clergy [*A publication*] (DLA)
Nels F .... Finch's English Chancery Reports, by Nelson [*1673-81*] [*A publication*] (DLA)
Nels Fol ..... Finch's English Chancery Reports, by Nelson [*1673-81*] [*A publication*] (DLA)
Nels Lex Man ... Nelson's Lex Maneriorum [*A publication*] (DLA)
NelsnB ...... Nelson [*Thomas*], Inc. [*Associated Press*] (SAG)
NelsnT ...... Nelson [*Thomas*], Inc. [*Associated Press*] (SAG)
NELSON ..... News Editing and Layout System of Newspapers (DGA)
Nelson (Eng) ... Nelson's English Chancery Reports [*A publication*] (DLA)
Nelson's Rep ... Nelson Tempore Finch [*1673-81*] [*A publication*] (DLA)
NELTAS ...... North East Lancashire Technical Advisory Services (SAUS)
NELTS .... Number of Elements Loaded [*Army*]
NELU .... New England Express Lines [*Intermodal shipping container symbol*] (TVRC)
NeLV .... Koninklijk Instituut voor Taal-, Land-, en Volkenkunde, Leiden, Netherlands [*Library symbol*] [*Library of Congress*] (LCLS)
NELV .... Nerine Latent Virus [*Plant pathology*]
NELWA ...... New England Lumber Women's Association [*Defunct*] (EA)
NEm .... East Meadow Public Library, East Meadow, NY [*Library symbol*] [*Library of Congress*] (LCLS)
NEM .... Metropolitan Technical Community College, Omaha, NE [*OCLC symbol*] (OCLC)
nem .... Nahrungs Einheit Milch [*Nahrungsteinheit Milch*] [*Nutritional milk unit*] [*Dietetics*] (DAVI)
NEM .... Nederlandsche Elektrolasch Maatschappig (EFIS)
Nem .... Nemean [*of Pindar*] [*Classical studies*] (OCD)
NEM .... Nemuro [*Japan*] [*Seismograph station code, US Geological Survey*] (SEIS)
NEM .... N-Ethylmaleimide [*Also, NEMI*] [*Organic chemistry*]
NEM .... N-Ethylmorpholine [*Organic chemistry*]
nEM .... NetworkMCI Enterprise Management
NEM .... New Electronic Media (NTCM)
NeM .... New England Micrographics, Inc., Waltham, MA [*Library symbol*] [*Library of Congress*] (LCLS)
NEM .... Newmont Mining [*NYSE symbol*] (TTSB)
NEM .... Newmont Mining Corp. [*NYSE symbol*] (SPSG)
NEM .... Nickel Electroformed Mold
NEM .... Nitrogen Ethylmorpholine (SAUS)
NEM .... No Evidence of Malignancy [*Medicine*] (MELL)
NEM .... Noise Equivalent to Man (SAUS)
NEM .... Nonelectronic Maintenance
NEM .... Non-Erasable Memory (SAUS)
NEM .... Noram Environment [*Vancouver Stock Exchange symbol*]
nem .... Not Elsewhere Mentioned (EBF)
NEM .... Not Elsewhere Mentioned
NEM .... Nothing Else Matters (SAUS)
NEM .... Numbered Error Message (SAUS)
NEM .... Numerical Exerciser for Memory (TIMI)
NEMA .... National Early Music Association [*British*] (DBA)
NEMA .... National Eclectic Medical Association [*Defunct*] (EA)
NEMA .... National Educational Management Association (EA)
NEMA .... National Electrical Manufacturers Association (EA)
NEMA .... National Electricity Manufacturers' Association (NITA)
NEMA .... National Emergency Management Association (EA)
NEMA .... National Emergency Medicine Association (EA)
NEMA .... Nebraska Emergency Management Agency [*Emergency Management*] (EMA)
NEMA .... Nematode [*Threadworm*]
NEMA .... Nematron Corp. [*NASDAQ symbol*] (SAG)
NEMAC ...... National Energy Management Advisory Committee [*British*]
NEMAC ...... Normal Error Model Analysis Chart
NEMAG ...... Negative Effective Mass Amplifiers and Generators
NEMA PAC ... National Electrical Manufacturers Association PAC [*Rosslyn, VA*] (PACS)
NEM Area ... Northeastern Mediterranean Area (SAUS)
NEMAS ...... New England Marine Advisory Service
NEMAS ...... Nursing Education Module Authoring System
NEMATOL ... Nematology
NEmBGE .... Bowling Green Elementary School, East Meadow, NY [*Library symbol*] [*Library of Congress*] (LCLS)
NEmBWE .... Barnum Woods Elementary School, East Meadow, NY [*Library symbol*] [*Library of Congress*] (LCLS)
NEMC .... National Export Meatworks Council [*Australia*]
NEMC .... New England Medical Center [*Boston, MA*]
NEMCA ...... NATO Electromagnetic Compatibility Agency (NATG)
NEMCA ...... Non-Faradaic Electrochemical Modification of Catalytic Activity [*Chemistry*]
NEMCC ...... Nonessential Motor Control Center (AAG)
NEMCH ...... New England Medical Center Hospitals
NEmCJS ..... W. T. Clarke Junior-Senior High School, East Meadow, NY [*Library symbol*] [*Library of Congress*] (LCLS)
nem con .... Nemine Contradicente [*No One Contradicting*] [*Latin*] (WA)
NEM CON ... Nemine Contradicente [*No One Contradicting*] [*Latin*] [*Legal term*]
NEMD .... Nonequilibrium Molecular Dynamics [*Chemical property simulation technique*]
NEMD .... Nonspecific Esophageal Motility Disorder [*Gastroenterology*] (DAVI)
NEMD .... Nonspecific Esophageal Motor Dysfunction [*Medicine*]

NEMDA...... Northeastern Minnesota Development Association
NEMDGP.... Northeast Melbourne Division of General Practice (SAUS)
NEM DISS... Nemine Dissentiente [*No One Dissenting*] [*Latin*]
NEMEA...... New England Media Evaluators Association
NEMEDRI... North European and Mediterranean Routing Information [*Naval Oceanographic Office*]
NEMEX...... National Energy Management Exhibition and Conference (ITD)
NEMF........ New England Motor Freight [*Common carrier symbol*]
NEMFB...... New England Motor Freight Bureau (SAUS)
NEMG....... New England Medical Gazette (SAUS)
NEMG T RL... New England MG "T" Register Ltd. (EA)
NEmH....... Meadowbrook Hospital, East Meadow, NY [*Library symbol*] [*Library of Congress*] (LCLS)
NEMI........ National Elevator Manufacturing Industry [*Later, NEII*] (EA)
NEMI........ N-Ethylmaleimide [*Also, NEM*] [*Organic chemistry*]
NEMI........ North European Management Institute (SAUS)
NEMI........ Nuclear Electromagnetic Interference (SAUS)
NEMIC....... New England Materials-Instruction Center
NEMIS....... National Emergency Management Information System [*Emergency Management*] (EMA)
NEMISYS... New Mexico Information System [*Library network*]
NEmL........ East Meadow Public Library, East Meadow, NY [*Library symbol*] [*Library of Congress*] (LCLS)
NEMLA...... New England Modern Language Association (AEBS)
NEmMC..... Nassau County Medical Center, East Meadow, NY [*Library symbol*] [*Library of Congress*] (LCLS)
NEmMcE.... McVey Elementary School, East Meadow, NY [*Library symbol*] [*Library of Congress*] (LCLS)
NEMMCO... National Electricity Market Management Company, Ltd. [*Australia*] [*Commercial firm*]
NEmME..... Meadowbrook Elementary School, East Meadow, NY [*Library symbol*] [*Library of Congress*] (LCLS)
NEmMH..... East Meadow High School, East Meadow, NY [*Library symbol*] [*Library of Congress*] (LCLS)
NEmNHi..... Nassau County Historical Museum, East Meadow, NY [*Library symbol*] [*Library of Congress*] (LCLS)
NEMO....... Naval Earth Map Observer [*Geographic systems*]
NEMO....... Naval Experimental Manned Observatory
NEMO....... Navy EarthMap Explorer
NEMO....... Never Ever Mention Outside [*Secret computer toy project of Axlon, Inc.*]
NeMO....... New Millennium Observatory
NEMO....... Nonempirical Molecular Orbitals [*Atomic physics*]
NEMO....... Not Emanating from Main Office (SAUS)
NEMO....... Not Emanating Main Office [*Remote broadcast*] (NTCM)
NEMO....... Nuclear Exchange Model
NEMOS...... Network Management Operations Support [*Computer science*] (AGLO)
NEMP........ Nuclear Electromagnetic Propagation
NEMP........ Nuclear Electromagnetic Pulse (AABC)
NEMPA...... North-Eastern Master Printers Alliance (SAUS)
NEMPAC.... National Emergency Medicine Political Action Committee (SAUS)
NEMPAC.... Nevada Medical PAC [*Reno, NV*] (PACS)
NEMPAC.... New Mexico Medical Society PAC [*Albuquerque, NM*] (PACS)
NEmPE...... Parkway Elementary School, East Meadow, NY [*Library symbol*] [*Library of Congress*] (LCLS)
NEMPET..... Northeast Microbial Physiologists, Ecologists and Taxonomists (SAUS)
NEMPS...... National Environmental Monitoring and Prediction System (MCD)
NEMPs...... National Environment Management Plans (SAUS)
NEMQO...... Non Est Mortale Quod Opto [*It Is No Mortal Thing I Desire*] [*Motto of Friedrich III, Duke of Schleswig-Holstein-Gottorp (1597-1659)*] [*Latin*]
NEMR....... National E [*Electronic*]-Mail Registry [*Information service or system*] (TSSD)
NEMRA...... National Electrical Manufacturers Representatives Association (EA)
NEMRB...... New England Motor Rate Bureau
NEMRIP..... New England Marine Resources Information Program [*University of Rhode Island*] [*Later, NEMAS*]
NEMRL...... New England Marine Research Laboratory (ABAC)
NEMS........ National Aeronautics and Space Administration [*NASA*] Equipment Management System (AAGC)
NEMS........ National Emergency Management System (ACAE)
NEMS........ National Exchange Market System
NEMS........ Navigation and Environmental Monitoring System (ACAE)
NEMS........ Near-Earth Magnetospheric Satellite
NEMS........ Nimbus E Microwave Spectrometer [*Meteorology*]
NEMS........ Non-External-Moving Surface (SAUS)
NEMS........ North East Medical Services (MHID)
NEMSPA.... National EMS [*Emergency Medical Service*] Pilots Association (EA)
NEMT........ Naval Emergency Monitoring Teams (PDAA)
NEMTA...... New England Marine Trade Association (EARSL)
NEMTA...... New England Men's Track Association (PSS)
NEMVAC.... Noncombatant Emergency and Evacuation Plan (NVT)
NE-MWCC... Northeast-Midwest Congressional Coalition (EA)
NEmWJ..... Woodland Junior High School, East Meadow, NY [*Library symbol*] [*Library of Congress*] (LCLS)
NEMX........ Ogden Martin Systems [*Private rail car owner code*]
NEN.......... Nengone [*Language symbol*] (ETLW)
NEN.......... New England Nuclear Corp. (SAUS)
NEN.......... New Eyes for the Needy (EA)
nen.......... Noise and Exposure Number (SAUS)
NEN.......... North-East Airlines Ltd. [*Nigeria*] [*FAA designator*] (FAAC)
NEN.......... Northstar Energy Corp. [*Toronto Stock Exchange symbol*]
NEN.......... Nursing Ethics Network (SAUS)
NEN.......... Whitehouse, FL [*Location identifier*] [*FAA*] (FAAL)
NENA........ National Emergency Number Association (CGWS)
NENA........ National Emergency Nurses Affiliation (SAUS)
NENA........ Northeast Neighborhood Association [*Medicine*] (EDAA)
NENB........ Nevada National Bancorporation (SAUS)
NENCL....... Nonenclosed (SAUS)
NENCL....... Nonenclosure
ne/nd........ new edition in preparation-no date can be given (SAUS)
NE/ND....... New Edition / No Date [*of Publication*] (DGA)
NENE........ Nebraska Northeastern Railway [*Federal Railroad Administration identification code*]
NENEP....... Navy Enlisted Nursing Education Program
N-Energy.... Nuclear Energy (SAUS)
NENG........ New England
NEngEl...... New England Electric System [*Associated Press*] (SAG)
NEngInv..... New England Investment Companies Ltd. [*Associated Press*] (SAG)
N Eng J Med... New England Journal of Medicine (MEC)
N Eng J Prison L... New England Journal on Prison Law [*A publication*] (DLA)
N Engl Fruit Meet Proc Annu Meet Mass Fruit Grow Assoc... New England Fruit Meetings. Proceedings. Annual Meeting. Massachusetts Fruit Growers Association (SAUS)
N Eng M Gaz... New England Medical Gazette (SAUS)
N Eng Rep... New England Reporter [*A publication*] (DLA)
N EnI........ International Business Machines Corp., Systems Development Library, Endicott (SAUS)
NEnI......... International Business Machines Corp., Systems Development Library, Endicott, NY [*Library symbol*] [*Library of Congress*] (LCLS)
N ENMLD... Not Enameled [*Freight*]
NENOA8..... Japanese Journal of Tropical Agriculture (journ.) (SAUS)
NEnoVM..... James Vernon Middle School, East Norwich, NY [*Library symbol*] [*Library of Congress*] (LCLS)
NENP........ New England National Park (SAUS)
NEO.......... National Electrolysis Organization [*Later, SCME*] (EA)
NEO.......... National Energy Office [*Executive Office of the President*]
NEO.......... Near-Earth Object [*Astronomy*]
NEO.......... Near-Earth Orbit
NEO.......... Neoarsphenamine [*or Neosalvarsan*] [*Medicine*]
NEO.......... Neocomian [*Paleontology*]
NEO.......... Neomycin [*Antibiotic compound*]
NEO.......... Neonatal [*Medicine*]
NEO.......... Neonatology [*Medicine*] (MELL)
NEO.......... Neon (automobile) [*NCIC car model code*]
NEO.......... Neopharm, Inc. [*AMEX symbol*] (SAG)
neo........... neovascularization (SAUS)
NEO.......... New Employee Orientation (TIMI)
NEO.......... Noncombatant Evacuation Operation [*Army*] (INF)
NEO.......... Noncombatant Evacuation Order [*Army*] (AABC)
NEO.......... Northeastern Operations Office [*NASA*]
NEO.......... Northeast Oklahoma R. R. [*AAR code*]
NEO.......... Pensacola, FL [*Location identifier*] [*FAA*] (FAAL)
NEOB........ New Executive Office Building [*Washington, DC*]
NEOC........ National Earth Observations Center [*National Oceanic and Atmospheric Administration*]
NEOC........ Network Emergency Operations Center [*Emergency Management*] (EMA)
NEOCOMP... New Computational Formulas
NEOCON.... National Exposition of Contract Interior Furnishings
NEOCON.... Neoconservative
NEOCON.... Neomycin, Colistin, Nystatin [*Antineoplastic drug regimen*]
NEOCS...... Navy Enlisted Occupational Classification System (NVT)
NEODA...... National Edible Oil Distributors Association [*British*] (DBA)
NEODA...... Naval Explosive Ordnance Disposal Association
NEODE...... Neodesha, KS [*American Association of Railroads railroad junction routing code*]
NEODF...... Naval Explosive Ordnance Disposal Facility
NEO-DHC... Neohesperidin Dihydrochalcone [*Also, NHDC*] [*Sweetening agent*]
NEODTC..... Naval Explosive Ordnance Disposal Technology Center [*Indian Head, MD*] (DNAB)
NEOEA....... North Eastern Ohio Education Association (EARSL)
NEOF........ Neoforma.com, Inc. [*NASDAQ symbol*] (SG)
NEOF........ No Evidence of Failure (MCD)
NEOF........ Nordic Engineer Officers' Federation (EA)
NEOG........ Neogen Corp. [*NASDAQ symbol*] (NQ)
NEOGA...... Neoga, IL [*American Association of Railroads railroad junction routing code*]
Neogen...... Neogen Corp. [*Associated Press*] (SAG)
Neo ICU..... Neonatal Intensive Care Unit [*Health care*] (MHCS)
NEOL........ Neolens, Inc. [*NASDAQ symbol*] (NQ)
Neol......... Neolithic (VRA)
NEOL........ Neologism
NEOM....... NeoMedia Technologies, Inc. [*NASDAQ symbol*] (SAG)
NEOM....... No Evidence of Malignancy [*Medicine*] (MELL)
NEOMAL.... Northeastern Ohio Major Academic Libraries [*The College of Wooster*] [*Wooster, OH*] [*Later, NEOMARL*] [*Library network*]
NEOMARL... Northeast Ohio Major Academic and Research Libraries [*Library network*] [*Information service or system*] (IID)
NeoMd...... NeoMedia Technologies, Inc. [*Associated Press*] (SAG)
NeoMdia.... NeoMedia Technologies, Inc. [*Associated Press*] (SAG)
NEOME....... New Electroactive Organic Materials for Electronics [*Esprit*]
NEON........ Neon Systems [*NASDAQ symbol*]
NEON........ New Era of Networks [*NASDAQ symbol*] (SG)
NEON........ Northeast Ohio Neighborhood Health Services (MHID)
Neonat...... Neonatology [*Medicine*] (IDYL)
NEOP........ Neoplan [*NCIC truck make code*]

NEOP........ Neoprobe Corp. [*NASDAQ symbol*] (SAG)
NEOP........ New Earth Observation Projects
NEOP........ New Employees Orientation Program (SAUS)
NEOP........ New England Order of Protection [*Later, Woodmen of the World Life Insurance Society*] (EA)
NEOP........ Nuclear Emergency Operations Plan [*Emergency Management*] (EMA)
NEOPAPE PAC... National Federation of Public and Private Employees [*Plantation, FL*] (PACS)
NeoPath..... NeoPath, Inc. [*Associated Press*] (SAG)
Neophrm.... Neopharm, Inc. [*Associated Press*] (SAG)
NEO-PI...... NEO [*Neuroticism, Extraversion, Openness to Experience*] Personality Inven tory [*Personality development test*] [*Psychology*]
Neopr........ Neoprobe Corp. [*Associated Press*] (SAG)
Neoprobe... Neoprobe Corp. [*Associated Press*] (SAG)
NEOPW...... Neoprobe Corp. Wrrt'E' [*NASDAQ symbol*] (TTSB)
NEORMP.... Northeastern Ohio Regional Medical Program (SAUS)
NeoRx....... NeoRx Corp. [*Associated Press*] (SAG)
NEOS........ National Earth Orientation Service (ACAE)
NEOS........ NeoStar Retail Group [*NASDAQ symbol*] (SAG)
NEOS........ New Employee Orientation Seminars (TIMI)
NEOSH...... Neosho, MO [*American Association of Railroads railroad junction routing code*]
NeoStar..... NeoStar Retail Group [*Associated Press*] (SAG)
NEO SULF... Neomycin Sulfate (SAUS)
NEOT........ NeoTherapeutics, Inc. [*NASDAQ symbol*] (SAG)
NEOT........ Otto Nelson and Sons [*Common carrier symbol*]
NeoTher..... NeoTherapeutics, Inc. [*Associated Press*] (SAG)
NeoThr...... NeoTherapeutics, Inc. [*Associated Press*] (SAG)
NEOU........ Navigators' and Engineering Officers' Union [*British*]
Neoz......... Neozyme Corp. [*Associated Press*] (SAG)
N/EP......... Name on End-Paper [*Antiquarian book trade*]
NEP.......... National Education Program (EA)
NEP.......... National Emphasis Program [*Occupational Safety and Health Administration*]
NEP.......... National Energy Plan (COE)
NEP.......... National Energy Program [*or Plan*] [*Canada*]
NEP.......... National Estuary Program [*Federal government*]
NEP.......... Natural Effects Processor
NEP.......... Near-Earth Phase [*NASA*]
NEP.......... Nearest Equivalent Product
NEP.......... Needle Exchange Program
NEP.......... Negative Equally Probable
NEP.......... Negative Expiratory Pressure [*Medicine*]
NEP.......... Nekoosa-Edwards Paper [*Federal Railroad Administration identification code*]
NEP.......... Nemzeti Egyseg Partja [*Party of National Unity*] [*Hungary*] [*Political party*] (PPE)
Nep.......... Nepal (VRA)
nep.......... Nepali [*MARC language code*] [*Library of Congress*] (LCCP)
NEP.......... NEPC Airlines [*India*] [*FAA designator*] (FAAC)
NEP.......... Nepean Public Library [*UTLAS symbol*]
NEP.......... Nephrology [*Medical specialty*] (DHSM)
Nep.......... Nepos [*First century BC*] [*Classical studies*] (OCD)
NEP.......... Neptune (ROG)
NEP.......... Nerve-Ending Particle (OA)
NEP.......... Net Earned Premiums [*Insurance*] (MARI)
NEP.......... Net Ecosystem Production [*Biology*]
NEP.......... N-Ethylpyrrolidinone [*Organic chemistry*]
NEP.......... Network Entry Point (AAGC)
NEP.......... Neutral Endopeptidase [*An enzyme*]
N-Ep......... Neutralizing Epitope [*Immunogenetics*]
NEP.......... Neverending Program (IAA)
NEP.......... New Ecological Paradigm (SAUS)
NEP.......... New Economic Plan (SAUS)
NEP.......... New Economic Policy [*Program of former USSR, 1921-28; also US wage/price freeze and controls of Nixon Administration, 1971*]
NEP.......... New Edition Pending [*Publishing*]
NEP.......... New England Pathology (SAUS)
NEP.......... New England Plant (NRCH)
NEP.......... New Equipment Practice
NEP.......... Newton Extrapolation Polynominal (SAUS)
NEP.......... Nixon Economic Policy (SAUS)
NEP.......... No Evidence of Pathology [*Medicine*] (DMAA)
NEP.......... Noise-Equivalent Power
NEP.......... Nominal Entry Point [*Aerospace*] (NAKS)
NEP.......... Nonelectronic Part
NEP.......... Nonelutable Polar Compounds [*Analytical chemistry*]
NEP.......... Non-Employee Pass (ACAE)
NEP.......... Non-English-Proficient
NEP.......... Normal Entry Point (MCD)
NEP.......... Northeast Pennsylvania Finl. [*AMEX symbol*] (SG)
NEP.......... Not Elsewhere Provided (SAUS)
NEP.......... Nuclear Earth Penetration programme (SAUS)
NEP.......... Nuclear Electric Propulsion [*System*]
NEP.......... Nuclear Environment Protection (SAUS)
NEP.......... Nude-Encounter Parlor (SAUS)
NEP.......... Numerical Experimentation Panel (SAUS)
NEP.......... Nu Pacific Resources Ltd. [*Vancouver Stock Exchange symbol*]
NEP.......... Nurse Education in Practice [*Database*] (GDD)
NEPA........ National Enginemen's Protection Association [*A union*] [*British*]
NEPA........ National Environmental Policy Act (EG)
NEPA........ National Environmental Policy Act of 1969
NEPA........ National Environmental Protection Agency [*China*]
NEPA........ National Euchre Players Association (EA)
NEPA........ New England Poultry Association [*Connecticut, Maine, Massachusetts, New Hampshire, Rhode Island, and Vermont*] (EARSL)
NEPA........ New England Press Association (EARSL)
NEPA........ Northeast Pacific Area
NEPA........ Nuclear Energy for Propulsion of Aircraft
NEPA........ Nuclear Energy Powered Aircraft (SAUS)
NEPA........ Nuclear Energy Propulsion of Aircraft (SAUS)
NEPA........ Nuclear Environmental Protection Agency (SAUS)
NEPAC....... Northeast-Purdue Agricultural Center [*Purdue University*] (RCD)
NEPACCO... Northeastern Pharmaceutical Chemical Co. (EFIS)
Nepad....... New Partnership for Africa's Development [*Political group*]
NEPAL....... National Egg Packers' Association Ltd. [*British*] (BI)
NEP & P.... New England Printer and Publisher [*A publication*] (DGA)
NEPASU..... Northeastern Pennsylvania Society of Ultrasound (EARSL)
NEPB........ National Energy Protection Board
NEPBC....... Northeastern Pennsylvania Bibliographic Center [*King's College*] [*Wilkes-Barre, PA*] [*Library network*]
NEPC........ National Environment Protection Council [*Atmosphere*]
NEPC........ New England Power Co.
NEPCA....... New England Pest Management Association (EARSL)
NEPCC....... North East Pacific Culture Collection [*of marine organisms*] [*University of British Columbia*]
NEPCO...... New England Provision Co.
NEPCO...... New England Provision Company (EFIS)
NEPCON.... National Electronic Packaging and Production Conference
NEPD........ No Evidence of Pulmonary Disease (DAVI)
NEPD........ Noise-Equivalent Power Density
NEPDB...... Navy Environmental Protection Data Base [*Obsolete*]
NEPE........ National Emergency Planning Establishment [*Canada*]
NEPE........ Nez Perce National Historical Park
NEPE........ Nitrate Ester Plasticized Polyethylene (PDAA)
NEPEA....... New England Project on Education of the Aging [*Defunct*] (EA)
NEPEC....... Curran Memorial Library, Port Au Port East, Newfoundland (SAUS)
NEPEC....... National Earthquake Prediction Evaluation Council [*US Geological Survey*]
NEPEX....... New England Power Exchange
NEPH........ Nephelometer (SAUS)
neph......... Nephew (GEAB)
neph......... Nephrite (VRA)
NEPH........ Nephrology
NEPHAT..... Northeastern Pacific Hurricane Analog Tracker
NEPHGE..... Nonequilibrium pH Gradient Gel Electrophoresis
NEPHIS..... Nested Phrase Indexing System [*Automated indexing system*] [*University of Western Ontario*]
NEPI......... National Environmental Policy Institute [*Washington, D.C.*]
NEPIA....... Nuclear Energy Property Insurance Association [*Later, ANI*] (EA)
NEPIRC..... Northeastern Pennsylvania Industrial Resource Center
NEPIS....... N-Ethyl(phenylisoxazolium)sulfonate [*Organic chemistry*]
NEPL........ National Endowment for the Preservation of Liberty [*Foundation created by Carl Channell to collect funds for Nicaraguan CONTRAs*]
NEPLG....... Nuclear Emergency Planning Liaison Group [*Emergency Management*] (EMA)
NEPM........ National Environmental Protection Measure
NEPM........ National Environment Protection Measure [*Atmosphere*]
NEPMA...... National Engine Parts Manufacturers Association (EA)
NEPMU...... Navy Environmental and Preventive Medicine Unit (NVT)
NEPN........ Near-Earth Phase Network [*NASA*] (KSC)
NEPO........ NATO Equipment Policy Objective (NATG)
NEPO........ New Entrant Prison Officer (WDAA)
NEPOOL..... New England Power Pool
NEPP........ National Energy Policy Plan
NEPP........ Nuclear Effects Post Processor (ACAE)
NEPPCO..... Northeastern Poultry Producers Council [*Later, PEIA*] (EA)
NEPPS....... National Environmental Performance Partnership System
NEPR........ NATO Electronic Parts Recommendations (AABC)
NEPr......... Noble Drilling $1.50 Cv Pfd [*NYSE symbol*] (TTSB)
NEPR........ Nuclear Explosion Pulse Reaction (AAG)
NEPRA...... National Electric Power Regulatory Authority [*Pakistan*]
NEPRAC..... National Electron Probe Resource for Analysis of Cells [*Harvard University*] [*Research center*] (RCD)
NEPRF....... Naval Environmental Prediction Research Facility
NEPRS....... New Equipment Personnel Requirements Summary [*Army*]
NEPS........ National Economic Projections Series [*NPA Data Services, Inc.*] [*Information service or system*] (CRD)
NEPS........ National Estuarine Pollution Study [*Federal Water Quality Administration*] (MSC)
NEPSS....... Navy Environmental Protection Support Service
NEPSWL.... New England Plant, Soil, and Water Laboratory [*Department of Agriculture*] [*Research center*] (RCD)
NEP System... Nuclear Electric Propulsion System (SAUS)
NEPT........ Neosho Custom Coach NEOS Materials Neptune Corporation [*NCIC trailer make code*]
NEPT........ Neptune (WDAA)
NEPT........ No Evidence of Pulmonary Tuberculosis [*Medicine*]
NEPTUNE... North-Eastern Electronic Peak Tracing Unit and Numerical Evaluator (IEEE)
NEPU........ Neptune Orient Lines [*Intermodal shipping container symbol*] (TVRC)
NEPU........ Northern Elements Progression Union [*Nigeria*] [*Political party*]
NEPX........ National Fruit Product [*Private rail car owner code*]
NEPZ........ New England Produce Center [*Federal Railroad Administration identification code*]
NEQ.......... New England Quarterly [*A publication*] (BRI)

NEQ.......... Non-Equivalence (SAUS)
NEQ.......... Northeast Quadrant (SAUS)
NEQ.......... Not Equal (EECA)
NER.......... Air Newark, Inc. [*ICAO designator*] (FAAC)
NEr.......... East Rockaway Public Library, East Rockaway, NY [*Library symbol*] [*Library of Congress*] (LCLS)
NER.......... National Educational Radio
NER.......... National Emissions Report [*Environmental Protection Agency*] (GFGA)
NER.......... National Engineers Register (IAA)
NER.......... Near East Report [*A publication*] (BJA)
NER.......... NERCO, Inc. [*NYSE symbol*] (COMM)
Ner.......... Neriglissar (BJA)
Ner.......... Nero [*of Suetonius*] [*Classical studies*] (OCD)
NER.......... Nervine [*Medicine*] (ROG)
NER.......... Network for Economic Rights [*Defunct*] (EA)
NER.......... Neutral External Rotation [*Sports medicine*]
NER.......... Never-Exceed Redline [*Aerospace*] (AAG)
NER.......... Newcor, Inc. [*AMEX symbol*] (NASQ)
NER.......... New Employee Registry (SAUS)
NER.......... New England Reporter [*A publication*] (DLA)
NER.......... New English Review (SAUS)
NER.......... Niger [*ANSI three-letter standard code*] (CNC)
NER.......... No Evidence of Recurrence [*Medicine*] (MAE)
NER.......... Noise-Equivalent Radiance
NER.......... Nonconformance Event Record [*NASA*] (KSC)
NER.......... Nondestructive Examination Report (SAUS)
NER.......... Nonionizing Electromagnetic Radiation
NER.......... North Eastern Railway [*British*]
NER.......... Northeastern Regional Library, Cimarron, NM [*OCLC symbol*] (OCLC)
NER.......... North Eastern Reporter [*Commonly cited NE*] [*A publication*] (DLA)
NER.......... Not Economically Repairable
NER.......... Nuclear Electric Resonance (PDAA)
NER.......... Nucleotide-Excision Repair
NERA........ National Economic Research Associates
NERA........ National Emergency Relief Administration
NERA........ National Employers' Resource Alliance [*Association*] (EA)
NERA........ Naval Enlisted Reserve Association (EA)
Nera......... Nera & Musica [*Record label*] [*Norway*]
NERA........ Nera AS [*NASDAQ symbol*] (NASQ)
NERA........ Nevada Education Reform Act
NERA........ New England Reading Association (AEBS)
NeraAS...... Nera AS [*Associated Press*] (SAG)
NERAC...... New England Research Application Center [*University of Connecticut*]
NERAIC...... Northern European Region Air Information Center (SAUS)
NERAIC...... North European Region Air Information Center (NATG)
NERAM...... Network Reliability Assessment Model (PDAA)
NERAy....... Nera-AS [*NASDAQ symbol*] (SAG)
NERAY....... Nera AS ADS [*NASDAQ symbol*] (TTSB)
NERB........ North East Regional Board of Dental Examiners (SAUS)
NERB........ North East Regional Boards [*Medicine*] (EDAA)
NERBA...... New England Road Builders Association (SAUS)
NERBC...... New England River Basin Commission
NERBS...... National Electric Rate Book by States [*A publication*]
NERC........ National Electronic Reliability Council (NTCM)
NERC........ National Electronics Research Council
NERC........ National English Rabbit Club [*British*] (BI)
NERC........ National Environmental Research Center [*Later, CERL*] [*Environmental Protection Agency*]
NERC........ National Environmental Research Council (NITA)
NERC........ National Environmental Respiratory Center [*Environmental Protection Agency*] (RCD)
NERC........ National Environment Resource Council [*British*] (NRCH)
NERC........ National Equal Rights Council (EA)
NERC........ National Eye Research Centre [*United Kingdom*] (RCD)
NERC........ Natural Environment Research Council [*Research center*] [*British*] (IRC)
NERC........ Nerco Trailer [*NCIC trailer make code*]
NERC........ New England Regional Commission [*Terminated, 1981*] [*Department of Commerce*]
NERC........ New England Research Center (SAUS)
NERC........ New En-Route Center (SAUS)
NERC........ Newton-Evans Research Co., Inc. [*Ellicott City, MD*] [*Information service or system*] (TSSD)
NERC........ Nordic Economic Research Council (EA)
NERC........ North American Electric Reliability Council (EA)
NERC........ Nuclear Energy Research Center [*Also, CEEN, SCK*] [*Belgium*]
NERC........ Regional Conference for the Near East [*UN Food and Agriculture Organization*]
NErCE....... Centre Elementary School, East Rockaway, NY [*Library symbol*] [*Library of Congress*] (LCLS)
NERCIC...... Northeast Regional Coastal Information Center [*Marine science*] (MSC)
NERCOE..... New England Resource Center for Occupational Education
NERCOM.... New England Regional Commission [*Department of Commerce*] [*Terminated, 1981*] (EGAO)
NERCOMM... New England Regional Commission [*Terminated, 1981*] [*Department of Commerce*] (NOAA)
NERComP... New England Regional Computing Program, Inc. [*Boston, MA*]
NERCP...... Naval European Research Contract Program (NG)
NERD........ National Establishment for Real Dorks (SAUS)
NERD........ Neuro-Evolutionary Rostral Developer (ACAE)
NERD........ Newman's Electronic Rhyming Dictionary [*Computer software*] (PCM)
NERD........ No Evidence of Recurrent Disease [*Medicine*] (MAE)
NERDA...... New England Rural Development Association
NERDAS..... NASA Earth Resources Data Annotation System (MCD)
NERDC...... Northeast Regional Data Center [*University of Florida*] [*Research center*] (RCD)
NERDLab... Neuro Engineering Research and Development Laboratory [*University of Texas at Austin*] (RCD)
NEREIS...... European deep-sea drilling program ship (SAUS)
NEREIS...... Novel European Research Ship (SAUS)
NEREM...... Northeast Electronics Research and Engineering Meeting
NEREN...... Nebraska Research and Education Network (SAUS)
NE Rep...... New England Reporter [*A publication*] (DLA)
NE Rep...... North Eastern Reporter [*Commonly cited NE*] [*A publication*] (DLA)
NEREP....... Nuclear Execution and Reporting (SAUS)
NEREP....... Nuclear Execution and Reporting Plan (COE)
NE Reporter... North Eastern Reporter [*Commonly cited NE*] [*A publication*] (DLA)
NE Repr..... North Eastern Reporter [*Commonly cited NE*] [*A publication*] (DLA)
NERF........ National Eye Research Foundation [*Later, NEHF*] (EA)
NERFC....... North East River Forecast Center (SAUS)
NERGG...... New England Regional Genetics Group (NRGU)
NERHL...... Northeastern Radiological Health Laboratory [*Massachusetts*]
NErHS....... East Rockaway High School, East Rockaway, NY [*Library symbol*] [*Library of Congress*] (LCLS)
NERI......... National Electronics Research Initiative [*British*]
NERICOMP... Northeast Rhode Island Computer Project (SAUS)
NERIF....... Newstar Resources [*NASDAQ symbol*]
NERIS....... National Educational Resources Information Service [*British*]
NERIS....... National Energy Referal Information System (NITA)
NERIT....... Northeast Regional Implementation Team [*Army Corps of Engineers*]
NERL........ National Ecological Research Laboratory [*Environmental Protection Agency*]
NERL........ Northeast Research Libraries
NERL........ Nuclear Engineering Research Laboratory (SAUS)
NE Rlty...... New England Realty Associates Ltd. [*Associated Press*] (SAG)
NERMLS.... New England Regional Medical Library Service (EA)
NERN........ National Educational Radio Network [*Defunct*] (NTCM)
NERO........ National Energy Resources Organization (EA)
NERO........ Near-Earth Rescue and Operations [*NASA*]
NERO........ Noninvasive Evaluation of Radiation Output [*Medicine*] (DMAA)
NERO........ Nuclear Effects Rocket Operations
NERO........ Nutrition Education Research Organization (SAUS)
NERO........ Sodium [*Na*] Experimental Reactor of Zero Power [*British*] (DEN)
NEROC...... Northeast Radio Observatory Corp.
NEROS...... ASRL-RTP Northeast Regional Oxidant Study (SAUS)
NEROS...... Northeast Regional Oxidant Study [*Environmental Protection Agency*] (GFGA)
NERP........ National Environmental Research Park [*Marine science*] (MSC)
NERP........ New Economic Recovery Program (Zambia) [*Political party*] (PSAP)
NERP........ Nicaraguan Exile Relocation Program [*CIA*]
NERPG...... Northern European Regional Planning Group [*NATO*] (NATG)
NERPRC..... New England Regional Primate Research Center [*Harvard University*] [*Research center*] (RCD)
NERR........ Nashville & Eastern Railroad [*Federal Railroad Administration identification code*]
NERRA...... New England Roentgen Ray Association (SAUS)
NERRA...... New Equipment Resources Requirements Analysis [*Army*] (AABC)
NErRE....... Rhame Elementary School, East Rockaway, NY [*Library symbol*] [*Library of Congress*] (LCLS)
NERRS...... National Estuarine Research Reserve System (USDC)
NERRS...... New England Roentgen Ray Society (SAUS)
NERRT....... Nuclear Energy Reactor Review Team (SAUS)
NERS........ Neurotic/Endogenous Rating Scale (DB)
NERSA...... Centrale Nucleaire Europeenne a Neutrons Rapides SA [*France*] (PDAA)
NERSA...... European Fast Reactor Power Station (SAUS)
NERSA...... Northeast Rail Service Act [*1981*] [*Also, NRSA*]
NERSC...... Nansen Environmental and Remote Sensing Center (SAUS)
NERSC...... National Energy Research Scientific Computing Center
NERSE....... Nutrition, Exercise, Relaxation, Sleep, and Enjoyment
NERSICA... National Established Repair, Service, and Improvement Contractors Association [*Later, National Remodelers Association*]
NERSP...... Navy Environmental Remote Sensing Program
NERT........ National Emergency Response Team [*Emergency Management*] (EMA)
NERU........ Nursing Education Research Unit
NERV........ Nervous [*Medicine*]
NERV........ Nuclear Emergency Recovery Vehicle (NUCP)
NERV........ Nuclear Emulsion Recovery Vehicle (MUGU)
NERV........ Nuclear Energy Research Vehicle
NERV........ Nuclear Engine Recovery Vehicle (SAUS)
NERVA....... Nuclear Engine for Rocket Vehicle Application [*NASA*]
NErWE....... Waverly Park Elementary School, East Rockaway, NY [*Library symbol*] [*Library of Congress*] (LCLS)
NERX........ NeoRx Corp. [*NASDAQ symbol*] (NQ)
NE-Rx....... Northeast Regional Exchange (SAUS)
NERX........ Transportation Management Services [*Private rail car owner code*]
NERXP...... NeoRx $2.4375 Cv Exch Pfd [*NASDAQ symbol*] (TTSB)
NERXW...... Neorx Corp. Wrrt [*NASDAQ symbol*] (TTSB)
NERZ........ General Electric Capital Corporation [*Intermodal trailer symbol*]
NES.......... National Eczema Society [*British*]
NES.......... National Election Studies [*University of Michigan*] (RCD)
NES.......... National Energy Software [*Department of Energy*] [*Information service or system*] (CRD)
NES.......... National Energy Strategy [*Department of Energy*] (ECON)
NES.......... National Enuresis Society (EA)
NES.......... National Estimating Society [*Later, SCEA*] (EA)

NES National European American Society
NES National Eutrophication Survey [*Environmental Protection Agency*]
NES Naval Engineering Standard (SAUS)
NES Naval Examination Service [*British military*] (DMA)
NES Naval Experimenting Station
NES Near Eastern Society (EA)
NES Near Eastern Studies [*A publication*] (BJA)
NES Near-End Suppressor (IAA)
NES Nesmont Industry [*Vancouver Stock Exchange symbol*]
NES Net Encryption System (SAUS)
NES Netherlands' Ecological Society [*Multinational association*] (EAIO)
NES N-Ethylsuccinimide [*Organic chemistry*]
NES Netscape Enterprise Server [*Computer science*] (GART)
NES Network Environmental Systems, Inc. (EFIS)
NES Neurobehavioral Evaluation System
NES Neustadt [*Saale*] [*German license plate city code*]
NES New Earnings Survey [*British*]
NES New Editorial System
NES New England Electric System [*NYSE symbol*] (SPSG)
NES New England El Sys [*NYSE symbol*] (TTSB)
NES New Enlisted System [*Navy*] (DNAB)
NES News Election Service [*Vote-counting consortium of the major TV networks and two wire services*]
NES News Electronic Service (SAUS)
NES Night Effects Simulator (SAUS)
NES Nintendo Entertainment System [*Video game*]
NES Noise-Equivalent Signal (IEEE)
NES Non-English-Speaking (ADA)
NES Nonerasable Storage [*Computer science*]
NES Nordeste, Linhas Aereas Regionais SA [*Brazil*] [*ICAO designator*] (FAAC)
NES Nordiska Ergonomisallskapet [*Nordic Ergonomic Society*] (EAIO)
NES Northeast Environmental Services, Inc. (EFIS)
NES Northern Eurasia Study (SAUS)
NES North of 60. Environmental Studies (SAUS)
NES Not Elsewhere Specified
NES Not Elsewhere Stated (SAUS)
NES Nowhere Else Specified (SAUS)
NES Nowhere Else Stated (SAUS)
NES Nuclear Elastic Scattering (ODA)
NES Nuclear Energy System (SAUS)
NES Nuclear Estate with Small holdings (SAUS)
NES Nuclear Export Signal [*Biochemistry*]
NES Nucleus Estate and Smallholders (SAUS)
NES Numerical Engineering Society [*British*] (DBA)
NESA John H. Nelson Environmental Study Area [*University of Kansas*] [*Research center*] (RCD)
NESA National Eagle Scout Association (EA)
NESA National Electric Sign Association (EA)
NESA National Emission Standards Act [*1967*]
NESA National Employment Service Act [*1933*]
NESA National Energy Services Association (NTPA)
NESA National Energy Specialist Association (EA)
NESA National Environmental Specialist Association (EA)
NESA National Environmental Study Areas Program [*National Park Service*] [*Defunct*]
NESA Near East and South Asia [*Department of State*]
NE/SA Near East/South Asia Council of Overseas Schools (EA)
NESA New England School of Art
NESAC National Environmental Services Administration Committee [*Marine science*] (MSC)
NESAF Office of Near Eastern, South Asian, and African Analysis [*Central Intelligence Agency*] (RCD)
NES&L Nuclear Engineering, Safety & Licensing (SAUS)
NESB National Environmental Specimen Bank [*Energy Research and Development Administration*]
NESB NESB Corp. [*NASDAQ symbol*] (COMM)
NESB Non-English-Speaking Background (ADA)
NESB Number of Equally Strong Beams [*Military*] (CAAL)
NESB1 First Generation Non-English-Speaking Background
NESB2 Second Generation Non-English-Speaking Background
NESBA National Earth Shelter Builders Association [*Defunct*] (EA)
NESBA National Executive of Small Business Agencies [*Australia*]
NESBAC Northeast Shetland Basin Area Communications (SAUS)
NESBU Nuclear Energy Systems Business Unit Westinghouse (SAUS)
NESC National Electrical Safety Code [*Also, NEC*] (NTCM)
NESC National Electric Safety Code (SAA)
NESC National Energy Software Center [*Department of Energy*] [*Information service or system*] (IID)
NESC National Enquiry into Scholarly Communication
NESC National Environmental Satellite Center [*Formerly, National Weather Satellite Center*] [*Later, National Environmental Satellite Service*]
NESC National Environmental Supercomputing Center (AEPA)
NESC National Environmental Svc. [*NASDAQ symbol*] (TTSB)
NESC National Executive Service Corps [*New York, NY*] (EA)
NESC Naval Electronics Systems Command
NESC Navy Electromagnetic Spectrum Center (DNAB)
NESC Neuroepithelial Stem Cells [*Medicine*]
NESC Newcastle Electric Supply Co. (SAUS)
NESC New England Science Center (SAUS)
NESC Non-English-Speaking Country
NESC Nuclear and Environmental Safety Council (SAUS)
NESC Nuclear Engineering and Science Conference (SAUS)
NESC Nuclear Engineering and Scientific Congress (MCD)
NESCA National Environmental Systems Contractors Association [*Later, ACCA*] (EA)
NESCA Northeastern Subcontractors Association (EARSL)
NESCA North Escanaba, MI [*American Association of Railroads railroad junction routing code*]
NESCAC New England Small College Athletic Conference
NESCAUM North East States for Coordinated Air Use Management
NESCH New England Society of Clinical Hypnosis (SAUS)
NESCNSC Net Evaluation Subcommittee, National Security Council (AABC)
NESCO National Energy Supply Corp. [*Proposed*]
NESCO National Engineering Science Co.
NESCO National Environmental Service Company (EFIS)
NESCO Naval Environmental Support Office [*Marine science*] (MSC)
NESCO Nigerian Electricity Supply Corp. African Workers' Union
NesCom IEEE-SA Standards Board New Standards Committee (SAUS)
NESCOM New Standards Projects Committee (SAUS)
NESCTM National Environmental Satellite Center Technical Memoranda (NOAA)
NESCWS Nonessential Services Chilled Water System [*Nuclear energy*] (NRCH)
NESDA National Electronic Service Dealers Association [*Later, NESSDA*] (EA)
NESDA National Equipment Servicing Dealers Association (EA)
NESDA Network for Environment and Sustainable Development for Africa (SAUS)
NESDA Northeast Scotland Development Authority (SAUS)
NESDEC New England School Development Council (EA)
NESDIS National Earth Satellite Data and Information System (SAUS)
NESDIS National Environmental Satellite, Data, and Information Service [*Washington, DC*] [*National Oceanic and Atmospheric Administration*] (GRD)
NESDRES National Environmental Data Referral Service [*Marine science*] (OSRA)
NESE Neue Ephemeris fuer Semitische Epigraphik [*Wiesbaden*] [*A publication*] (BJA)
NESEA Naval Electronic Systems Engineering Activity
NESEA Northeast Sustainable Energy Association (SAUS)
NESEC Naval Electronics Systems Engineering Center (MCD)
NESEC Northeast States Emergency Consortium [*Emergency Management*] (EMA)
NESEP Navy Enlisted Scientific Education Program
NESF Normal Engineered Safety Features [*Nuclear energy*] (NRCH)
NESFD Noise Equivalent Spectral Flux Density (SAUS)
NESHAP National Emission Standards for Hazardous Air Pollutants [*Environmental Protection Agency*]
NESHAPS National Emission Standard for Hazard Air Pollutants [*Environmental science*] (COE)
NESHAPS National Emission Standards for Hazardous Air Pollutants (WPI)
NESHCo New England Society for Healthcare Communications (EARSL)
NESHS New England Society for Healthcare Strategy (EARSL)
NESIP Naval Explosive Safety Improvement Program
NESIP/POA & M Naval Explosive Safety Improvement Program / Plan of Action and Milestones (DNAB)
NESL Networked and Embedded Systems Laboratory [*University of California, Los Angeles*] (RCD)
NESL Northeast Shipbuilders Ltd. [*Commercial firm*] [*British*]
NESLA New England Shoe and Leather Association (EA)
NESLI National Electronic Site License Initiative
NESLS North East of Scotland Library Service (SAUS)
NEsM Mount Saint Alphonsus Seminary, Esopus, NY [*Library symbol*] [*Library of Congress*] (LCLS)
NESMRA New England Super-Modified Racing Association
NESN NATO English-Speaking Nations
NESN New England Sports Network [*Cable-television system*]
NESNE New England Society of Newspaper Editors (SAUS)
NESO Naval Air Engineering Support Office [*Norfolk, VA*]
NESO Naval Electronic Sensor Operator [*Canadian Navy*]
NESO Naval Engineering Service Office (MCD)
NESO Navy Environmental Support Office [*Obsolete*]
NESO New Employee Safety Orientation (SAUS)
NESO Northeastern Society of Orthodontists (DMAA)
NESOSC New England Society of Open Salts Collectors (EA)
NESP National Environmental Studies Project [*Defunct*] (EA)
NESP Navy EHF [*Extremely High Frequency*] Satellite Program (DOMA)
NESP Northeastern Society of Periodontists (SAUS)
NESP Nurse Education Support Program
NESPA National Elementary Schools Press Association (EA)
NE-SPIDR New England Chapter of the Association for Conflict Resolution (EARSL)
NESR Natural Environment Support Room (MCD)
NESR Noise-Equivalent Spectral Radiance [*Physics*]
NESRA National Employee Services and Recreation Association (EA)
NESRF Northern Environmental Studies Revolving Fund (SAUS)
NESS NASA Expert Simulation System (NITA)
NESS National Easter Seal Society (EA)
NESS National Emergency Steel Specification [*World War II*]
NESS National Environmental Satellite Service [*National Oceanic and Atmospheric Administration*] [*Telecommunications*] (TEL)
NESS Naval Engineering Support System (SAUS)
NESS Network and Evaluation Simulation System (NITA)
NESS Northeast Satellite Systems [*Avoca, PA*] [*Telecommunications*] (TSSD)
NESS Nuclear Effects Simulation Study
NESSCCA National Easter Seal Society for Crippled Children and Adults [*Medicine*] (EDAA)

NESSDA..... National Electronic Sales and Service Dealers Association (EA)
NEssDS..... Dunlap Society, Essex, NY [*Library symbol*] [*Library of Congress*] (LCLS)
NESSEC..... Naval Electronics Systems Security Engineering Center (MCD)
NESSUS..... Nonlinear Evaluation of Stochastic Structures Under Stress (ACAE)
NEST........ National Emergency Survivable Troop System (AABC)
NEST........ Naval Experimental Satellite Terminal (IEEE)
NEST........ Nestor, Inc. [*NASDAQ symbol*] (COMM)
NEST........ Network for Environmental Science Training [*California State University at San Bernardino - College of Education*] (EARSL)
NEST........ New and Emerging Sciences and Technologies
NEST........ New El Salvador Today (EA)
NEST........ New Expanding Shelter Technology [*Residential construction*]
NEST........ Node Execution Selection Table (SAUS)
NEST........ Nonelectric Stimulus Transfer
NEST........ Non-surgical Embryonic Selective Thinning (SAUS)
NEST........ Novell Embedded Systems Technology [*Novell, Inc.*] [*Computer science*]
NEST........ Nuclear Effects Support Team
NEST........ Nuclear Emergency Search Team [*Department of Energy*]
NEST........ Nuclear Energy Search Team (SAUS)
NEST........ Nuclear Explosive Simulation Technique
NESTA....... National Earth Science Teachers Association (EA)
NESTED..... Naval Electronic Systems Test and Evaluation Detachment
NESTEF..... Naval Electronic Systems Test and Evaluation Facility
NESTEV..... Naval Electronics Systems Test and Evaluation (IAA)
NESTOR..... Netherlands Educational and Scientific Titles for Online Retrieval (TELE)
NESTOR..... Neutron Source Thermal Reactor [*British*] (DEN)
NESTOR..... Newsagent Project under eLib (SAUS)
NESTOR..... Nuclear Reactor Winfrith (SAUS)
NESTS....... Nonelectric Stimulus Transfer System
NestU........ Northeast Utilities [*Associated Press*] (SAG)
NESU........ Neste Polyeten [*Intermodal shipping container symbol*] (TVRC)
NESW....... Non-Essential Service Water (SAUS)
NESW....... Nonessential Service Water Relay Pump [*Nuclear energy*] (IAA)
NESX........ Nestle Brands [*Private rail car owner code*]
NESY........ NEON Systems, Inc. [*NASDAQ symbol*] (NASQ)
NET.......... Centre for Agricultural Publications and Documents, Wageningen, Netherlands [*OCLC symbol*] (OCLC)
Net.......... Internet (DCDG)
NET.......... NASA Employee Team (SAUS)
NET.......... Nasoendotracheal Tube [*Medicine*]
NET.......... National Educational Television [*Later, EBC*]
NET.......... National Empowerment Television
NET.......... National Environmental Testing, Inc. (EFIS)
NET.......... National Estate Tasmania [*Australia*]
NET.......... National Evangelization Teams (EA)
NET.......... Negative Entropy Trap
NET.......... Nerve Excitability Test [*Medicine*] (DMAA)
NET.......... Net Energy Thrust
NET.......... Net Equivalent Temperature
NET.......... Net Explosive Weight (MSA)
NET.......... NETI Technologies, Inc. [*Vancouver Stock Exchange symbol*]
NET.......... Netto [*Lowest*]
NET.......... Network [*Telecommunications*] (AAG)
net.......... Network (WDMC)
NET.......... Network Associates [*Company symbol*]
NET.......... Network Aviation Services (NIG) Ltd. [*FAA designator*] (FAAC)
NET.......... Network-Entity Title [*Computer science*] (VLIE)
NET.......... Network Equipment Technologies [*Computer science*] (VLIE)
NET.......... Neuroectodermal Tumor [*Medicine*] (DMAA)
NET.......... Neuroelectric Therapy [*Substance detoxification*]
NET.......... Neuroendocrine Transducer [*Medicine*] (MELL)
NET.......... Neuroendocrine Tumor [*Medicine*] (DMAA)
NET.......... New England Telephone (SAUS)
NET.......... New Equipment Training [*Army*] (AABC)
NET.......... New Era Technologies, Inc. [*Washington, DC*] [*Telecommunications*] (TSSD)
NET.......... Newton Emission Theory [*Physics*]
NET.......... Next European Torus [*Formerly, Joint European Torus (JET)*]
NET.......... Nimbus Experiment Team [*NASA*]
NET.......... Nippon Educational Television Co. Ltd. (SAUS)
NET.......... Nitrigin Eireann Teoranta [*Nationalized industry*] [*Ireland*] (EY)
NET.......... No Earlier Than (SAUS)
NET.......... No Electronic Theft [*Act*]
NET.......... No Evidence of Tumor [*Medicine*]
NET.......... Noise Enforcement Team (SAUS)
NET.......... Noise Equivalent Target (CCCA)
NET.......... Noise Equivalent Temperature (SAUS)
NET.......... Noise-Equivalent Temperature
NET.......... Noise Evaluation Test (IAA)
NET.......... Nonlethal Entanglement Technology
NET.......... Nonradiative Energy Transfer [*Physics*]
NET.......... Norepinephrine Transporter [*Medicine*] (DMAA)
NET.......... Norethisterone [*Oral contraceptive ingredient*]
NET.......... Normal Environmental Temperature (SAUS)
NET.......... Norme Europeene de Telecommunications [*Telecommunications*] (OSI)
NET.......... North European Oil Royalty Trust [*NYSE symbol*] (SPSG)
NET.......... North Europn Oil Rty Tr [*NYSE symbol*] (TTSB)
net.......... Not Earlier Than (ODA)
NET.......... Not Earlier Than
NET.......... Nuclear Effects Test
NET.......... Nuclear Electronic Transistor (SAUS)
NET.......... Nuclear Emergency Teams [*DASA*]
NET.......... Nuclear Energy Team
NET.......... Nuclear Engineer Trainee
NET.......... Number of Element Types
NET.......... Nutrition Education Training (SAUS)
NETA......... International Electrical Testing Association (EA)
NETA......... National Educational Telecommunications Association (AGLO)
NETA......... National Employment and Training Association [*Upland, CA*] (EA)
NETA......... National Environmental Training Association (EA)
NETA......... Network Associates [*NASDAQ symbol*] [*Formerly, McAfee Associates*] (SG)
NETA......... New England Telecommunications Association (CIST)
NETA......... Northeast Test Area [*Military*] (MCD)
NETA......... Northwest Electronic Technical Association (SAUS)
NETAC....... Nuclear Energy Trade Associations' Conference
NETANAL... Network Analysis (PDAA)
NETAPPS... Net Ad-Produced Purchases [*Advertising*]
NETAS....... Northern Electric Telekomunikasyon (EFIS)
NetBEUI..... NetBIOS [*Network Basic Input/Output System*] Extended User Interface [*Microsoft Corp.*] (PCM)
NetBIOS..... Network Basic Input/Output System [*Computer science*] (DOM)
NETBIOS... Network Basic Input/Output System [*Computer software*]
NETBLT...... Network Block Transfer [*Computer science*] (VLIE)
NETC........ National Emergency Training Center
NETC........ National Emergency Transportation Center
NETC........ Naval Education and Training Center [*or Command*] (NVT)
NETC........ NETCM On-Line Comm Svcs [*NASDAQ symbol*] (TTSB)
NETC........ Netcom On-Line Communications Services, Inc. [*NASDAQ symbol*] (SAG)
NETC........ New England Theatre Conference (EA)
NETC........ New England Trail Conference (EA)
NETC........ No Explosion of the Total Contents [*Business term*] (DCTA)
NETC........ Northeast Transportation Coalition
NETCAP..... National Exploitation of Technical Capabilities (CARL)
NET CDF.... Network Common Data Format [*Computer science*]
NETCHE..... Nebraska Educational Television Council for Higher Education, Inc. [*Library network*]
NETCO....... North Western Employes Transportation Corp. [*Successor to Chicago & North Western Railway*]
Netcom...... Netcom On-Line Communictions Services, Inc. [*Associated Press*] (SAG)
NETCOM.... Network Communications
NETCOM.... Network Control Communications [*Deep Space Instrumentation Facility, NASA*]
NETCON..... Network Control [*Computer science*] (MHDB)
NETCONSTA... Net Control Station [*Computer science*] (VLIE)
NETD........ Noise Equivalent Temperature Difference (SAUS)
NETD........ Noise-Equivalent Temperature Difference [*Thermography*]
NETD........ Noneffective Transit Depot (SAUS)
NETDA....... Network Design and Analysis [*Computer science*] (VLIE)
NETDC....... New England Trophoblastic Disease Center
NetDDE...... Network Dynamic Data Exchange [*Computer science*] (VLIE)
NETDP....... National Environmental Technology Demonstration Program (BCP)
NETDS....... Near-Earth Tracking and Data System
NETE......... Naval Engineering Test Establishment [*Canadian Armed Forces*] (PDAA)
NETE......... Network of European Teacher Education (AIE)
NETEP....... Northern European Terrestrial Ecosystem Profile (SAUS)
NETF......... Netframe Systems [*NASDAQ symbol*] (SAG)
NETF......... Nuclear Energy Test Facility (AFM)
NETF......... Nuclear Engineering Test Facility (AAG)
NETFIPCBR... Naval Education and Training Financial Information Processing Branch (DNAB)
NETFMS..... Naval Education and Training Financial Management System (DNAB)
Netframe.... Netframe Systems [*Associated Press*] (SAG)
NETFS....... National Educational Television/Film Service (WGA)
NETG........ National Education Training Group (EFIS)
NETG........ NetGravity, Inc. [*NASDAQ symbol*] (SG)
NETG........ Network General [*NASDAQ symbol*] (TTSB)
NETG........ Network General Corp. [*NASDAQ symbol*] (CTT)
NetGALA.... Network of Gay and Lesbian Alumni Associations (EA)
NETGEN..... Network Generation [*Computer science*] (MHDB)
NETH........ National Employ the Handicapped Week
Neth......... Netherlands (ODBW)
NETH........ Netherlands
Neth Ant.... Netherlands Antilles
Netherl Intl L Rev... Netherlands Yearbook of International Law [*The Hague, Netherlands*] [*A publication*] (DLA)
Neth Int'l L Rev... Netherlands International Law Review [*A publication*] (DLA)
Nethl........ Netherlands (VRA)
Neth P....... Netherlands Pharmacopoeia [*A publication*]
NETHW...... National Employ the Handicapped Week (OICC)
Neth YB Int'l Law... Netherlands Yearbook of International Law [*A publication*] (DLA)
NETI......... Network Technologies International, Inc. [*Ann Arbor, MI*] [*Telecommunications*] (TSSD)
NETI......... Newton Enterprises [*Common carrier symbol*]
NETIC........ Nonretentive Nonshocksensitive (SAUS)
NETIF........ NETI Technologies, Inc. [*NASDAQ symbol*] (COMM)
NetIP........ Network of Indian Professionals [*Association*] (EA)
Netiquette... Internet Etiquette [*Computer science*]
NETISA...... Naval Education and Training Information Systems Activity (DNAB)
NET IVHU... Next European Torus/In-Vessel Handling Unit (SAUS)
NETK........ Network Express [*NASDAQ symbol*] (TTSB)

NETK .... Network Express, Inc. [*NASDAQ symbol*] (SAG)
NETL .... National Energy Technology Laboratory
NETL .... National Export Traffic League [*New York, NY*] (EA)
NETL .... NetLive Communications, Inc. [*NASDAQ symbol*] (SAG)
NETL .... Nuclear Engineering Teaching Laboratory [*University of Texas at Austin*] [*Research center*] (RCD)
NETLAB ..... Networking and Telecommunications Research Laboratory [*Ohio State University*] (RCD)
NetLive ...... NetLive Communications, Inc. [*Associated Press*] (SAG)
NETLS .... Northeast Texas Library System [*Library network*]
NETLS/DPL ... Northeast Texas Library System/Dallas Public Library Film Service [*Library network*]
NETLSS ..... Northeast Texas Library System (SAUS)
NET Ltd ..... Nigerian External Telecommunications Ltd. [*Lagos*]
NETM .... NetManage, Inc. [*NASDAQ symbol*] (SAG)
n et m .... Nocte et Mane [*Night and Morning*] [*Latin*] [*Pharmacy*] (DAVI)
N et M .... Nocte et Mane [*Night and Morning*] [*Pharmacy*]
NETMA ...... Nobody Ever Tells Me Anything [*Executive complaint*]
Netmed ..... Netmed, Inc. [*Associated Press*] (SAG)
NETMIS ..... Naval Education and Training Management Information System (MCD)
Netmng ..... NetManage, Inc. [*Associated Press*] (SAG)
NETMUX .... Network Multiplexer (NITA)
NETN .... Networks North [*NASDAQ symbol*] (SG)
NETN .... Newton Transportation Company [*Common carrier symbol*]
NET/NLT ..... No Earlier Than/No Later Than (MCD)
NETO .... NetObjects, Inc. [*NASDAQ symbol*] (SG)
NETOP .... Network Operator Process [*Computer science*] (MHDB)
NETOPS ..... Nuclear Emergency Team Operations (AFM)
NETOR ...... New Toronto, ON [*American Association of Railroads railroad junction routing code*]
NETP .... Net Perceptions [*NASDAQ symbol*] (SG)
NETP .... New Equipment Training Plan (SAUS)
NETP .... New Equipment Training Program [*Army*] (AABC)
NETPARS ... Network Performing Analysis Reporting System (SAUS)
NetPC .... Network Personal Computer (IGQR)
NETPDC ..... Naval Education and Training Program Development Center [*Pensacola, FL*] (DNAB)
NETR .... NATO Electronic Technical Recommendation (PDAA)
NETR .... No Essential Traffic Reported [*Aviation*]
NETR .... Nuclear Engineering Test Reactor [*Air Force*]
NETRA .... Network of Electrification -- Testing and Recording Apparatus [*Indian Railway*] (TIR)
NETRA .... New England Trail Rider Association (EA)
NETRAS ..... Nuclear Electric Transfer Stage (SAUS)
NETRB .... New England Territory Railroad Bureau
NETRC .... National Educational Television and Radio Center [*Later, EBC*] (EA)
NETREM .... Net Requirementes Estimation Model (PDAA)
NETR-FTC ... New England Territory Railroads Freight Traffic Committee
Netrix .... Netrix Corp. [*Associated Press*] (SAG)
NETRJE ..... Network Remote Job Entry [*Telecommunications*] (OSI)
NE TR S NUM ... Ne Tradas sine Nummo [*Cash on Delivery*] [*Latin*]
NETRZ .... NetRadio Corp. [*OTCBB symbol*]
nets .... Communication Networks (SAUS)
NETS .... National Educational Technology Standards for Administrators
NETS .... National Education Technology Standards
NETS .... National Electronics Teachers' Service [*Defunct*]
NETS .... National Emergency Telecommunications System (CCCA)
NETS .... Nationwide Emergency Telecommunications System [*DoD*]
NETS .... Navy Engineering Technical Services (NG)
NETS .... Nebraska Electronic Transfer System
NETS .... Network Electrical Technique System (IAA)
NETS .... Network Event Theatre, Inc. [*NASDAQ symbol*] (SAG)
NETS .... Network for Electronic Transfers System
NETS .... Network of Employees for Traffic Safety [*NHTSA*] (TAG)
NETS .... Network Techniques
NETS .... Network Testing Section [*Social Security Administration*]
NETS .... Neurodysfunction Eye Test System [*Medical*]
NETS .... New Examiner Training School [*Federal Home Loan Bank Board*]
NETS .... New Threats Simulator (ACAE)
NETSC .... Naval Education and Training Support Center (DNAB)
NETSCL ..... Naval Education and Training Support Center, Atlantic (DNAB)
NETSCP ..... Naval Education and Training Support Center, Pacific (DNAB)
Netscpe ..... Netscape Communications Corp. [*Associated Press*] (SAG)
NETSET ..... Network Synthesis and Evaluation Technique [*Computer science*]
NETSET ..... Network Systems and Evaluation Technique (NITA)
NETSIM ..... [*Traffic*] Network Simulation [*TXDOT*] (TAG)
NETSL .... New England Technical Services Librarians
Netsmrt ..... Netsmart Technologies, Inc. [*Associated Press*] (SAG)
NETSO .... Northern European Transhipment Organization [*NATO*] (NATG)
NETSO .... Northern European Transshipment Organization (SAUS)
NETSP .... New Equipment Training Support Package
NetSrce ..... NetSource Communications, Inc. [*Associated Press*] (SAG)
NETSS .... National Electronic Telecommunications System for Surveillance [*Center for Disease Control*]
NETSS .... National Electronic Telecommunication Surveillance System (SAUS)
NetStar ...... NetStar, Inc. [*Associated Press*] (SAG)
NETSW ...... Network Event Theater Wrrt [*NASDAQ symbol*] (TTSB)
NETSYO ..... Network Security Officer (SAUS)
NETT .... Nasal Endotracheal Tube [*Medicine*] (EDAA)
NETT .... National Emphysema Treatment Trial (SAUS)
NETT .... Netter Digital Entertainment, Inc. [*NASDAQ symbol*] (SAG)
NETT .... Net Tons [*Shipping*]
NETT .... Network Environmental Technology Transfer [*Europe*] [*An association*]
NETT .... New Employment, Transition, and Training [*Department of Labor*] (OICC)
NETT .... New Equipment Training Team [*Army*]
NETT .... Notes on Elementary Tactical Training (SAUS)
NETTEL ...... Network Telecommunications, Inc. [*Denver, CO*] [*Telecommunications*] (TSSD)
Netter .... Netter Digital Entertainment, Inc. [*Associated Press*] (SAG)
NetterD ...... Netter Digital Entertainment, Inc. [*Associated Press*] (SAG)
NETTING ... Emission trading used to avoid PSD/NSR permit review requirements (SAUS)
NETTL .... Nettleton, AR [*American Association of Railroads railroad junction routing code*]
NETTO .... Network Training Officer (SAUS)
NETTSP ..... New Equipment Training Test Support Package (MCD)
NETTW ...... Netter Digital Entm't Wrrt [*NASDAQ symbol*] (TTSB)
NETU .... Netumar Lines [*Common carrier symbol*]
NETV .... Nebraska ETV [*Educational Television*] Network [*Lincoln, NE*] [*Telecommunications*] (TSSD)
NetV .... NetVantage, Inc. [*Associated Press*] (SAG)
NETVA .... NetVantage, Inc. [*NASDAQ symbol*] (SAG)
NETVA .... NetVantage Inc.'A' [*NASDAQ symbol*] (TTSB)
NetVant ..... NetVantage, Inc. [*Associated Press*] (SAG)
NETVU .... NetVantage Inc. Unit [*NASDAQ symbol*] (TTSB)
NETVW ...... NetVantage Inc. Wrrt'A' [*NASDAQ symbol*] (TTSB)
NETVZ .... NetVantage Inc. Wrrt'B' [*NASDAQ symbol*] (TTSB)
NetwkAp .... Network Appliance Corp. [*Associated Press*] (SAG)
NetwkE ...... Network Event Theatre, Inc. [*Associated Press*] (SAG)
Networth .... Networth, Inc. [*Associated Press*] (SAG)
netwrkg ..... Networking (BARN)
NETX .... Network Equipment Technologies, Inc. (MHDW)
NETZ .... Netzee, Inc. [*NASDAQ symbol*] (QUAN)
NETZ .... Northeast Terminal [*Federal Railroad Administration identification code*]
NEU .... (Naphthyl)ethyl Urea [*Organic chemistry*]
NEU .... Neuchatel [*Switzerland*] [*Seismograph station code, US Geological Survey*] [*Closed*] (SEIS)
Neu .... Neural [*Medicine*] (QSUL)
Neu .... Neuraminic Acid [*Biochemistry*]
neu .... Neurilemma [*Neurology*] (DAVI)
NEU .... Neuroscience (SAUS)
Neu .... Neutrality (SAUS)
NEU .... Transportes Aereos Neuquinos Sociedad de Estado [*Argentina*] [*ICAO designator*] (FAAC)
NeuAc .... N-Acetylneuraminic Acid
NEUC .... National Engine Use Council [*Defunct*] (EA)
NEUCC ...... Northern European Universities Computer Centre [*Denmark*] (PDAA)
NEUCC ...... Northern Europe University Computing Centre (SAUS)
NEUCC ...... Northern Europe University Computing Complex (SAUS)
Neucrine .... Neurocrine Biosciences, Inc. [*Associated Press*] (SAG)
NEUDATA ... Neutron Data Under Direct Access (NITA)
Neu-Epi-a ... Neuroepithelioma (SAUS)
NEUF .... Neufeld [*NCIC trailer make code*]
NEUFCH .... Neufchatel [*Imprint*] (ROG)
NEUG .... National Epson Users Group (EA)
NEUIC .... National Employee Union Information Center (EA)
NEUM .... Non-European Unity Movement [*South Africa*] (PD)
NEUMAG .... Neumunstersche Maschinen-Und Anlagenbau (EFIS)
Neumed ..... Neuromedical Systems, Inc. [*Associated Press*] (SAG)
Neur .... Neuralgia (SAUS)
Neur .... Neurasthenia (SAUS)
Neur .... Neuritis (SAUS)
neur .... Neurology [*Medicine*] (MAE)
NeUR .... Rijksuniversiteit te Utrecht, Utrecht, Netherlands [*Library symbol*] [*Library of Congress*] (LCLS)
NEUR-A ..... Neurogenic Battery Acute (DAVI)
Neural Netw ... Neural Networks (SAUS)
Neurex ...... Neurex Corp. [*Associated Press*] (SAG)
Neurgn ...... Neurogen Corp. [*Associated Press*] (SAG)
Neuro .... Neurologic [*Medicine*] (AMHC)
neuro .... Neurological [*Therapy term*] (CTAA)
NEURO ...... Neurology [*or Neurological*]
Neuro .... Neurosurgery [*Medicine*] (IDYL)
neuro .... neurotic (SAUS)
NEurO .... North European Oil Royalty Trust [*Associated Press*] (SAG)
neurobio ..... neurobiological (SAUS)
Neurobio .... neurobiologist (SAUS)
Neurobio .... Neurobiology (SAUS)
NEUROBIOL ... Neurobiology
Neurobiol Biochem Morphol ... Neurobiology, Biochemistry and Morphology (SAUS)
Neurol .... Neurologist (SAUS)
NEUROL ..... Neurology
NEUROLGST ... Neurobiologist
Neurol India ... Neurology India (SAUS)
Neuropath ... Neuropathology [*or Neuropathologist*] (DAVI)
neurophys ... neurophysiological (SAUS)
Neuropsychiat ... Neuropsychiatry (SAUS)
neuropsycho ... neuropsychological (SAUS)
NEURO SC ... Neuroscience Building (SAUS)
neurosci .... neuroscientist (SAUS)
Neurosci Res ... Neuroscience Research (SAUS)
Neurospora Newsrl ... Neurospora Newsletter (SAUS)

Neuro-Surg... Neurosurgeon (BABM)
Neuro-Surg... Neurosurgery [*or Neurosurgeon*] (DAVI)
NeuroTc..... Neurobiological Technologies, Inc. [*Associated Press*] (SAG)
NEURS...... Navy Energy Usage Reporting System (DNAB)
neurs........ neurosis (SAUS)
NEUS........ New Extensions for Utilizing Scientists, Inc.
NEUS........ Northeastern United States
NEUS........ Nuclear Electric Unmanned Spacecraft (SAUS)
NEUS........ Nuclear-Electric Unmanned Spacecraft
NEUSSN..... Northeastern United States Seismic Network (NRCH)
neut.......... Neuter (BEE)
NEUT........ Neuter
NEUT........ Neutral (AAG)
neut.......... Neutral (SHCU)
neut.......... neutralize (SAUS)
NEUT........ Neutralizer (SAUS)
NEUT........ Neutralizing (SAUS)
neut.......... Neutrophil [*Hematology*]
neut equiv... Neutralization Equivalent [*Chemistry*]
NEUTN...... Neutralization [*Electronics*] (ECII)
Neutr........ Neutralization (SAUS)
Neutron..... Neutral Ion (SAUS)
NEV.......... Nederlandse Ecologen Vereniging [*Netherlands Ecological Society*] [*Multinational association*] (EAIO)
NEV.......... Negative Expected Value
NEV.......... Neighborhood Electric Vehicle
NEV.......... Net Economic Value
NEV.......... Neutral-to-Earth Voltage [*Electrical power transmission*]
NEV.......... Nevada (AAG)
Nev.......... Nevada (ODBW)
NEV.......... Nevada Airlines, Inc. (SAUS)
NEV.......... Nevada (automobile) [*NCIC car model code*]
NEV.......... Nevada City, CA [*Amtrak Busline code*]
Nev.......... Nevada Supreme Court Reports [*A publication*] (DLA)
NEV.......... Nevis [*Leeward Islands*] [*Airport symbol*] (OAG)
NEV.......... Nieghborhood Electric Vehicle
NEV.......... Non-Equivalent (SAUS)
NEV.......... Nuevo Energy Co. [*NYSE symbol*] (SPSG)
NEV.......... Nuevo Financing I [*NYSE symbol*] (SAG)
NEVA........ Nevada Air Products Company [*NCIC trailer make code*]
NEVA........ Nevada Resources (SAUS)
NEVA........ North Eastern Vecturists Association
NEVA........ North of England Veterinary Association (GVA)
NEVAD....... Nevada, MO [*American Association of Railroads railroad junction routing code*]
NEVADA..... Net Energy Verification and Determination Analyzer (ACAE)
Nevada Rep... Nevada Reports [*A publication*] (DLA)
Nevada Repts... Nevada Reports [*A publication*] (DLA)
Nev Admin Code... Nevada Administrative Code [*A publication*] (DLA)
Nev & M.... Nevile and Manning's English King's Bench Reports [*A publication*] (ILCA)
Nev & Mac... Neville and Macnamara's Railway Cases [*1855-1950*] [*A publication*] (DLA)
Nev & MacN... Neville and Macnamara's Railway and Canal Cases [*1855-1950*] [*A publication*] (DLA)
Nev & Man... Nevile and Manning's English King's Bench Reports [*A publication*] (DLA)
Nev & Man Mag Cas... Nevile and Manning's English Magistrates' Cases [*A publication*] (DLA)
Nev & Mcn... Neville and Macnamara's Railway Cases [*England*] [*A publication*] (DLA)
Nev & M (Eng)... Nevile and Manning's English King's Bench Reports [*A publication*] (DLA)
Nev & MKB... Nevile and Manning's English King's Bench Reports [*A publication*] (DLA)
Nev & MMC... Nevile and Manning's English Magistrates' Cases [*A publication*] (DLA)
Nev & P..... Nevile and Perry's English King's Bench Reports [*1836-38*] [*A publication*] (DLA)
Nev & P..... Nevile and Perry's English Magistrates' Cases [*1836-37*] [*A publication*] (DLA)
Nev & PKB... Nevile and Perry's English King's Bench Reports [*1836-38*] [*A publication*] (DLA)
Nev & P Mag Cas... Nevile and Perry's English Magistrates' Cases [*1836-37*] [*A publication*] (DLA)
Nev & PMC... Nevile and Perry's English Magistrates' Cases [*1836-37*] [*A publication*] (DLA)
NEVATV..... Nebraska VA Television Network [*Telecommunications service*] (TSSD)
NEVD........ Nevadan Manufacturing Company [*NCIC trailer make code*]
NEVDGP..... North East Valley Division of General Practice (SAUS)
NEVE........ Nonempirical Valence-Electron [*Physics*]
NevEngy.... Nevada Energy Co., Inc. [*Associated Press*] (SAG)
NEVIL........ Neville Island, PA [*American Association of Railroads railroad junction routing code*]
NEVL........ Nevlen Company [*NCIC trailer make code*]
NEVLESS... Nevertheless (ROG)
NEVM........ Neval Motorcycles [*NCIC motorcycle make code*]
Nev Nurses Assoc Q Newslett... Nevada Nurses Association. Quarterly Newsletter (SAUS)
NEVOT....... Network Voice Terminal [*Telecommunications*]
Nev PSC Op... Nevada Public Service Commission Opinions [*A publication*] (DLA)
NevPw....... Nevada Power Co. [*Associated Press*] (SAG)
Nev Rev Stat... Nevada Revised Statutes [*A publication*] (DLA)
NEVRLS..... Nevertheless (SAUS)
Nev SBJ..... Nevada State Bar Journal [*A publication*] (DLA)
Nev Stats... Statutes of Nevada [*A publication*] (DLA)
Nev St Bar J... Nevada State Bar Journal [*A publication*] (DLA)
NEVU........ Consent Equipment [*Intermodal shipping container symbol*] (TVRC)
Nev Univ Dp G M B... Nevada University. Department of Geology and Mining Bulletin (SAUS)
NEVX........ Nerine Virus X [*Plant pathology*]
NEW......... Hawarden BAE [*British*] [*ICAO designator*] (FAAC)
NEW......... National Electronics Week
NEW......... National Energy Watch [*Edison Electric Institute*]
NEW......... Native Egg White
NEW......... Natural Engineering Workbench [*Computer science*] (HODG)
NEW......... Navy Early Warning
NEW......... Net Economic Welfare [*Economic indicator*]
NEW......... Net Explosive Weight (AFM)
NEW......... Neustadt an der Waldnaab [*German license plate city code*]
new.......... Newari [*MARC language code*] [*Library of Congress*] (LCCP)
NEW......... Newark [*Diocesan abbreviation*] [*New Jersey*] (TOCD)
NEW......... Newberg [*Federal Railroad Administration identification code*]
NEW......... New College of California, San Francisco, CA [*OCLC symbol*] (OCLC)
New.......... New College, Oxford (SAUS)
New.......... Newell's Illinois Appeal Reports [*A publication*] (DLA)
NEW......... New England Air Express, Inc. [*ICAO designator*] (FAAC)
NEW......... New England Inv Cos. L.P. [*NYSE symbol*] (TTSB)
NEW......... New England Investment Companies [*Formerly, Reich & Tang Ltd.*] [*NYSE symbol*] (SPSG)
NEW......... New Experimental Wagon [*Automotive engineering*]
NEW......... New Information (SAUS)
NEW......... New Orleans, LA [*Location identifier*] [*FAA*] (FAAL)
NEW......... Newport [*Washington*] [*Seismograph station code, US Geological Survey*] (SEIS)
NEW......... Newport [*Quebec*] [*Geomagnetic observatory code*]
NEW......... Newport [*NCIC car model code*]
NEW......... Newtec Industries Ltd. [*Vancouver Stock Exchange symbol*]
NEW......... Newton
NEW......... Newton, KS [*Amtrak rail station code*]
NEW......... Non-Traditional Employment for Women
NEW......... Northeast Water (SAUS)
NEW......... Nuclear Energy Women [*Defunct*] (EA)
NEW......... Nursery Education Week (AEBS)
NEW......... Nvest Cos. LP [*NYSE symbol*]
NEW......... Nvest L.P. [*NYSE symbol*] [*Formerly, New England Investment Companies*]
NEw.......... Thomas E. Ryan Public Library, East Williston, NY [*Library symbol*] [*Library of Congress*] (LCLS)
NEW8C...... New England Women's 8 Conference (PSS)
NEWA....... National Electrical Wholesalers Association
NEWA....... Nuclear Energy Writers Association [*Defunct*]
NEWAC...... NATO Electronic Warfare Advisory Committee (NATG)
NEWAC...... New England Women's Athletic Conference (PSS)
New ACP.... New American and Canadian Poetry (SAUS)
NEW-ACTE... Northeast Wisconsin Association for Career and Technical Education (EARSL)
New Ad..... New Advocate [*A publication*] (BRI)
NewAD...... Newspaper Archive Developments Ltd., New Haven, CT [*Library symbol*] [*Library of Congress*] (LCLS)
NEWAG...... New Augusta, MS [*American Association of Railroads railroad junction routing code*]
New Age.... New Age Journal [*A publication*] (BRI)
NewAge..... New Age Media Fund [*Associated Press*] (SAG)
NEWAL...... New Albany, IN [*American Association of Railroads railroad junction routing code*]
NEW AM.... Berlin, VT [*AM radio station call letters*] (BROA)
NEW AM.... Madisonville, TX [*AM radio station call letters*] (BROA)
NewAm...... New America High Income Fund [*Associated Press*] (SAG)
New Am Cyc... New American Cyclopaedia [*A publication*] (ROG)
New Am Lib... New American Library (SAUS)
New Ann Reg... New Annual Register [*London*] [*A publication*] (DLA)
NEWAR...... Newark, OH [*American Association of Railroads railroad junction routing code*]
Newark L Rev... University of Newark. Law Review [*A publication*] (DLA)
New Asian Post... New Australasian Post (SAUS)
NEWAU...... New Augusta, AR [*American Association of Railroads railroad junction routing code*]
NEWB....... Newberry Bancorp [*NASDAQ symbol*] (TTSB)
NEWB....... Newberry Bancorp, Inc. [*NASDAQ symbol*] (SAG)
Newb......... Newberry's United States District Court, Admiralty Reports [*A publication*] (DLA)
NEWB....... Newbury [*Municipal borough in England*]
Newb Adm.. Newberry's United States District Court, Admiralty Reports [*A publication*] (DLA)
NEWBE...... Newberry, SC [*American Association of Railroads railroad junction routing code*]
New Benl... New Benloe's Reports, English King's Bench [*1531-1628*] [*A publication*] (DLA)
New B Eq Ca... New Brunswick Equity Cases [*A publication*] (DLA)
New B Eq Rep... New Brunswick Equity Reports [*A publication*] (DLA)
Newberry... Newberry's United States District Court, Admiralty Reports [*A publication*] (DLA)
Newberry Adm (F)... Newberry's United States District Court, Admiralty Reports [*A publication*] (DLA)
Newberry's Ad Rep... Newberry's United States District Court, Admiralty Reports [*A publication*] (DLA)
New Biol.... New Biologist (SAUS)

NEWBN...... New Bern, NC [*American Association of Railroads railroad junction routing code*]
NewbNk..... Newbridge Networks, Inc. [*Associated Press*] (SAG)
NEWBO...... New England Women Business Owners (EARSL)
Newbon..... Newbon's Private Bills Reports [*1895-99*] [*England*] [*A publication*] (DLA)
NEWBR...... New Braunfels, TX [*American Association of Railroads railroad junction routing code*]
New Br...... New Brunswick Reports [*A publication*] (DLA)
New Br Eq (Can)... New Brunswick Equity Reports [*Canada*] [*A publication*] (DLA)
New Br Eq Cas (Can)... New Brunswick Equity Cases [*Canada*] [*A publication*] (DLA)
New Br R... New Brunswick Reports [*A publication*] (DLA)
Newbyth.... Newbyth's Manuscript Decisions, Scotch Session Cases [*A publication*] (DLA)
NEWC....... Newcastle [*Name of two cities in England*]
NEWC....... New Comer Industries [*NCIC trailer make code*]
NEWC....... Newcor, Inc. [*NASDAQ symbol*] (SAG)
NEWCA...... New Castle, PA [*American Association of Railroads railroad junction routing code*]
NewCare.... New Care Health Corp. [*Associated Press*] (SAG)
New Cas.... New Cases (SAUS)
New Cas.... New Cases (Bingham's New Cases) [*A publication*] (DLA)
New Cas Eq... New Cases in Equity [*8, 9 Modern Reports*] [*1721-55*] [*A publication*] (DLA)
Newcastle Inst Ed J... Institutes of Education of the Universities of Newcastle Upon Tyne and Durham. Journal (journ.) (SAUS)
New Cath World... New Catholic World (SAUS)
NEWCC...... Northeastern Weed Control Conference [*Later, NEWSS*] (EA)
NEWC L..... Newcastle-Under-Lyme [*City in England*] (ROG)
NEWCN...... New Construction [*Navy*]
New Col..... New Columbia (SAUS)
Newcor...... Newcor, Inc. [*Associated Press*] (SAG)
NEW-CUE... Nature and Environmental Writers - College and University Educators [*Association*] (EA)
NEWD....... New Dimension [*NCIC trailer make code*]
NewDay..... New Day Beverage, Inc. [*Associated Press*] (SAG)
NEWE........ New England [*NCIC trailer make code*]
NEWE........ Newport Electronics, Inc. (SAUS)
New Ed Rev and Enl... New Edition, Revised and Enlarged (SAUS)
Newell...... Newell Co. [*Associated Press*] (SAG)
Newell...... Newell's Appeals Reports [*48-90 Illinois*] [*A publication*] (DLA)
Newell Defam... Newell on Defamation, Slander, and Libel [*A publication*] (DLA)
Newell Eject... Newell's Treatise on the Action of Ejectment [*A publication*] (DLA)
Newell Mal Pros... Newell's Treatise on Malicious Prosecution [*A publication*] (DLA)
Newell Sland & L... Newell on Slander and Libel [*A publication*] (DLA)
New Eng.... New England Reporter [*A publication*] (DLA)
New Eng Cons Music... New England Conservatory of Music (GAGS)
NEWENGGRU... New England Group (DNAB)
New Eng J Crim&Civil Confinement... New England Journal on Criminal and Civil Confinement (SAUS)
New England Econ Rev... New England Economic Review [*A publication*] (JLIT)
New Engl Univ Bull... New England University. Bulletin [*A publication*]
New Eng R... New England Reporter [*A publication*] (DLA)
New Eng Rep... New England Reporter [*A publication*] (DLA)
New Eng Sch Law... New England School of Law (GAGS)
New ER..... New England Review [*A publication*] (BRI)
Newf.......... Newfoundland (SHCU)
NEWF........ Newfoundland [*with Labrador, a Canadian province*]
NEWF........ North-East-West-South Transport [*Common carrier symbol*]
NewfEx...... Newfield Exploration [*Associated Press*] (SAG)
NEWFLD.... Newfoundland [*with Labrador, a Canadian province*]
Newfld LR... Newfoundland Law Reports [*A publication*] (DLA)
Newf LR.... Newfoundland Law Reports [*A publication*] (DLA)
NEW FM.... Alberta, VA [*FM radio station call letters*] (BROA)
NEW FM.... Pukatawagan, Manitoba [*FM radio station call letters*] (BROA)
NEWFO...... Newfoundland [*with Labrador, a Canadian province*]
New For..... New Forests (SAUS)
Newfoundland and Labrador Mineral Resources Div Bull... Newfoundland and Labrador. Department of Mines, Agriculture and Resources. Mineral Resources Division. Bulletin (SAUS)
Newfoundland Geol Survey Inf Circ Rept... Newfoundland Geological Survey. Information Circular. Report (SAUS)
Newfoundl LR... Newfoundland Law Reports [*A publication*] (DLA)
Newfoundl R... Newfoundland Reports [*A publication*] (DLA)
Newfoundl Sel Cas... Newfoundland Select Cases [*A publication*] (DLA)
NEWFPS.... New England Wild Flower Preservation Society (SAUS)
NEWFS...... New England Wild Flower Society (EA)
Newf S Ct... Newfoundland Supreme Court Decisions [*A publication*] (DLA)
Newf Sel Cas... Newfoundland Select Cases [*A publication*] (DLA)
NEWG....... New Georgia Railroad [*Federal Railroad Administration identification code*]
New Gener Comput... New Generation Computing (SAUS)
New Grove... New Grove Dictionary of Music and Musicians [*A publication*]
NEWGU...... Newgulf, TX [*American Association of Railroads railroad junction routing code*]
New Guinea Austral Pacific SE Asia... New Guinea and Australia, the Pacific and South East Asia (SAUS)
NEWH....... New Holland [*NCIC trailer make code*]
NEWH....... New Horizons Worldwide, Inc. [*NASDAQ symbol*] (SAG)
Newhal...... Newhall Land & Farming Co. [*Associated Press*] (SAG)
New Hamp. New Hampshire Reports [*A publication*] (DLA)
New Hamp Profiles... New Hampshire Profiles (SAUS)
New Hamp R... New Hampshire Reports [*A publication*] (DLA)
New Hamp Rep... New Hampshire Reports [*A publication*] (DLA)
New Hampshire Rep... New Hampshire Reports [*A publication*] (DLA)
New Heb Con... New Hebrides Condominium (SAUS)
New Hebr... New Hebrides (NTIO)
NewHrz...... New Horizons Savings & Loan Association [*Associated Press*] (SAG)
NEWI........ New West Eyeworks [*NASDAQ symbol*] (TTSB)
NEWI........ New West Eyeworks, Inc. [*NASDAQ symbol*] (SAG)
NEWIB....... New Iberia, LA [*American Association of Railroads railroad junction routing code*]
NEWIL....... Northeast Wisconsin Intertype Libraries [*Library network*]
New Ind..... New International Review (SAUS)
New Ir Jur... New Irish Jurist and Local Government Review [*1900-05*] [*A publication*] (DLA)
NEWISA..... New England Women's Intercollegiate Sailing Association
New J Chem... New Journal of Chemistry (MEC)
New Jersey... New Jersey Law Reports [*A publication*] (DLA)
New Jersey Eq... New Jersey Equity Reports [*A publication*] (DLA)
New Jersey Equity... New Jersey Equity Reports [*A publication*] (DLA)
New Jersey Leg Rec... New Jersey Legal Record [*A publication*] (DLA)
New Jersey L Rev... New Jersey Law Review [*A publication*] (DLA)
New Jersey SBA Qu... New Jersey State Bar Association. Quarterly [*A publication*] (DLA)
New Journ... New Journalist [*A publication*]
New J Stat&Oper Res... New Journal of Statistics and Operational Research (SAUS)
NEWK....... New Yorker Homes Corporation [*NCIC trailer make code*]
NEWL........ Newell [*NCIC truck make code*]
NEWLAND... Northeast Water Polynya Project, land based (SAUS)
NEWLC...... NATO Electronic Warfare Liaison Committee
Newl Ch PR... Newland's Chancery Practice [*A publication*] (DLA)
Newl Ch Prac... Newland's Chancery Practice [*A publication*] (DLA)
Newl Cont... Newland on Contracts [*1806*] [*A publication*] (DLA)
NEWLNE.... New Line Cinema Corp. (SAUS)
NEWLON.... New London, Connecticut [*Navy*]
NEWM....... New England and World Missions (EA)
NEWM....... Newham Enterprises [*NCIC trailer make code*]
NEW M...... New Mexico (ROG)
New Mag Cas... New Magistrates' Cases (Bittleston, Wise, and Parnell) [*1844-51*] [*A publication*] (DLA)
NEWMAST... National Education Workshop for Math and Science Teachers (SAUS)
New Mat World... New Materials World (SAUS)
Newm Conv... Newman on Conveyancing [*A publication*] (DLA)
New Mex BA... New Mexico State Bar Association, Minutes [*A publication*] (DLA)
New Mexico Bur Mines and Mineral Resources Bull... New Mexico. Bureau of Mines and Mineral Resources. Bulletin (SAUS)
New Mexico Bur Mines and Mineral Resources Circ... New Mexico. Bureau of Mines and Mineral Resources. Circular (SAUS)
New Mexico Bur Mines and Mineral Resources Geol Map... New Mexico. Bureau of Mines and Mineral Resources. Geologic Map (SAUS)
New Mexico Bur Mines and Mineral Resources Mem... New Mexico. Bureau of Mines and Mineral Resources. Memoir (SAUS)
New Mexico Bus... New Mexico Business [*A publication*] (JLIT)
New Mex Magazine... New Mexico Magazine (SAUS)
New Mex SBA... New Mexico State Bar Association, Report of Proceedings [*A publication*] (DLA)
NEWMOA... Northeast Waste Management Officials Association
NEW MOONS... NASA Evaluation with Models of Optimized Nuclear Spacecraft
NewmtM.... Newmont Mining [*Associated Press*] (SAG)
NEWN....... Newman Trailers [*NCIC trailer make code*]
Newn........ Newnham College, Oxford (SAUS)
NEWNA...... Newnan, GA [*American Association of Railroads railroad junction routing code*]
New Nat Brev... New Natura Brevium [*A publication*] (DLA)
New NB..... New Natura Brevium [*A publication*] (DSA)
NEwNE...... North Side Elementary School, East Williston, NY [*Library symbol*] [*Library of Congress*] (LCLS)
NEWOR..... New Orleans, LA [*American Association of Railroads railroad junction routing code*]
NEWOT...... Naval Electronic Warfare Operator Trainer (MCD)
NewOv...... Newscorp Overseas Ltd. [*Associated Press*] (SAG)
NEWP....... Newport [*England*]
NEWP....... Newport [*NCIC truck make code*]
NEWP....... Newport Corp. [*NASDAQ symbol*] (NQ)
NEWP....... Newport Homes [*NCIC trailer make code*]
NEWPA...... New Paris, IN [*American Association of Railroads railroad junction routing code*]
NEWPAC.... Newhall Land and Farming Company PAC [*Valencia, CA*] (PACS)
New Par.... New Paragraph (SAUS)
NEWPEX.... Northeast Wood Products Expo [*In company name, NEWPEX, Inc.*] (TSPED)
New Phil Orch... New Philharmonia Orchestra (SAUS)
NEWPIL..... NADGE [*NATO Air Defense Ground Environment*] Early Warning Program Information Leaflet (NATG)
NEWPIN..... New Parent-Infant Network (AIE)
NEWPO...... Newport, KY [*American Association of Railroads railroad junction routing code*]
New Polit Economy... New Political Economy [*A publication*] (JLIT)
NEWPOSITREP... New [*Corrected*] Position Report (NVT)
New Pract Case... New Practice Cases [*1844-48*] [*A publication*] (DLA)
New Pr Cases... New Practice Cases [*1844-48*] [*A publication*] (DLA)
Newpt....... Newport Corp. [*Associated Press*] (SAG)
NEWPT...... Newport, VT [*American Association of Railroads railroad junction routing code*]
NEWQ....... Newquay [*Urban district in England*]

NEWR .... New England Realty Associates Ltd. [*NASDAQ symbol*] (NQ)
New R .... New Republic [*A publication*] (BRI)
NEWRAD .... New Radiometry
NEWRADS ... Nuclear Explosion Warning and Radiological Data System
New Rep .... Bosanquet and Puller's New Reports, English Common Pleas [*1804-07*] [*A publication*] (DLA)
New Rep .... New Reports [*1862-65*] [*England*] [*A publication*] (DLA)
NEWRIT ..... Northeast Water Resources Information Terminal (IID)
NEWRZ ..... New Englad Rlty Assoc L.P. [*NASDAQ symbol*] (TTSB)
NEWRZ ...... New England Realty Associates LP [*NASDAQ symbol*]
NEWS .... National Extreme Weather Systems (SAUS)
NEWS .... Naval Electronic Warfare Simulator
NEWS .... Navy Electronic Warfare Simulator (SAUS)
NEWS .... Neighborhood Environmental Workshops (EA)
NEWS .... NetWare Early-Warning System [*Frye Computer Systems, Inc.*] [*Computer science*] (PCM)
NEWS .... Network Extensible Window System [*Computer science*]
NEWS .... New England Wild Flower Society (EA)
NEWS .... New European Wide Warranty System [*General Motors Corp.*]
NEWS .... New Product Early Warning System
NEWS .... Newspaper/Microcopy Library (SAUS)
NEWS .... New Style Homes [*NCIC trailer make code*]
NEWS .... Novell Electronic Webcasting Service (SAUS)
NewSAfr .... New South Africa Fund [*Associated Press*] (SAG)
NEWS AMERICA-FOX PAC... News America Holdings Inc. - Fox PAC [*Washington, DC*] (PACS)
NEWSAR .... Nuclear Energy Waste Space Transportation and Removal (GFGA)
New Sci ..... New Scientist [*A publication*] (BRI)
NewsCm .... News Communictions, Inc. [*Associated Press*] (SAG)
NewsCorp... News Corp Ltd. [*Associated Press*] (SAG)
NewsCp ..... [*The*] News Corp. Ltd. [*Associated Press*] (SAG)
New Series... Martin's Louisiana Reports, New Series [*A publication*] (DLA)
New Sess Cas... New Session Cases (Carrow, Hamerton, and Allen) [*1844-51*] [*A publication*] (DLA)
News For Hist... News of Forest History (SAUS)
NEWSL ...... Newsletter
Newsl Aust Coll Ed Qd... Australian College of Education. Queensland Chapter. Newsletter [*A publication*]
Newsl Aust Natn Ass Ment Hlth... Australian National Association for Mental Health. Newsletter [*A publication*]
Newsl Commonw Sci Counc Earth Sci Programme... Newsletter. Commonwealth Science Council. Earth Sciences Programme (SAUS)
News Lepid Soc... News. Lepidopterists Society (SAUS)
Newslett .... Newsletter (DIAR)
Newslett Environ Mutagen Soc... Newsletter of the Environmental Mutagen Society (SAUS)
Newsl Inst Foresters Aust... Institute of Foresters of Australia. Newsletter (journ.) (SAUS)
Newsl Leg Act... Newsletter on Legislative Activities [*Council of Europe*] [*A publication*] (DLA)
Newsl R&D Uranium Explor Tech... Newsletter. R and D in Uranium Exploration Techniques (SAUS)
Newsl Statist Soc Aust... Statistical Society of Australia. Newsletter [*A publication*]
NEWSLTR... Newsletter
NewsML .... News Markup Language
News Nisshin Steel... News from Nisshin Steel (SAUS)
New South Wales Univ Sch Civ Eng UNICIV Rep... University of New South Wales. School of Civil Engineering UNICIV Report (SAUS)
Newsp .... Newspaper (SAUS)
News Physiol Sci... News in Physiological Sciences (SAUS)
News Rohde Schwarz... News from Rohde and Schwarz (SAUS)
NEWSS ...... Northeastern Weed Science Society [*Formerly, NEWCC*] (EA)
NEWSTAR... Nuclear Energy Waste Space Transportation and Removal (GOBB)
NewSvg ..... Newnan Savings Bank [*Associated Press*] (SAG)
NEW T .... Newcastle-Upon-Tyne [*City in England*] (ROG)
NEWT .... New EBI Web Taxonomy [*Database*] [*United Kingdom*] (GDD)
NEWT .... New Paris Traveler Corporation [*NCIC trailer make code*]
NEWT .... News Terminal (SAUS)
NEWT .... Newton [*England*]
NEWT .... Not Environmentally Worse Than (WDAA)
New TB ..... New Technical Books [*A publication*] (BRI)
New Technol Jpn... New Technology Japan (SAUS)
New Term Rep... Dowling and Ryland's English King's Bench Reports [*A publication*] (DLA)
New Term Rep... New Term Reports [*A publication*] (DLA)
New Test .... New Testament (NTIO)
NEWTO ...... Newton, KS [*American Association of Railroads railroad junction routing code*]
NEWTS ...... Naval Electronic Warfare Training System
NEWU .... Sin Chiao Shipping [*Intermodal shipping container symbol*] (TVRC)
NEWV F ..... The News Corporation Ltd. [*OTCBB symbol*]
NEWW .... Network of East West Women [*Association*] (EA)
NEWW .... New World Computer (SAUS)
NEWWA ..... New England Water Works Association (SAUS)
NewWrld .... New World Communictions Corp. [*Associated Press*] (SAG)
New York ... New York Magazine [*A publication*] (BRI)
New York Acad of Sci Annals... New York Academy of Sciences, Annals (SAUS)
New York Att'y Gen Annual Rep... New York Attorney General Reports [*A publication*] (DLA)
New York City BA Bul... Bulletin. Association of the Bar of the City of New York [*A publication*] (DLA)
New York R... New York Court of Appeals Reports [*A publication*] (DLA)
New York Rep... New York Court of Appeals Reports [*A publication*] (DLA)
New York Supp... New York Supplement [*A publication*] (DLA)
New Yugo L... New Yugoslav Law [*A publication*] (DLA)
NEWZ .... NewsEDGE Corp. [*NASDAQ symbol*] (NASQ)
NEWZAD .... New Zealand Army Detachment (CINC)
New Zealand... Dominion of New Zealand (SAUS)
New Zealand Archit... New Zealand Architect (SAUS)
New Zeal Jur R... New Zealand Jurist Reports [*A publication*] (DLA)
New Zeal L... New Zealand Law Reports [*A publication*] (DLA)
New Zeal LR... New Zealand Law Reports [*A publication*] (DLA)
NEX .... National Exchange, Inc. [*McLean, VA*] [*Telecommunications*] (TSSD)
NEX .... Non-Cyclic Executive Lover Level Computer Software Component (SAUS)
NEX .... Nonepoxide Xanthophyll [*Organic chemistry*]
NEX .... Nonexempt (TIMI)
NEX .... Nonfueled experiment (SAUS)
NEX .... Northern Executive Aviation Ltd. [*British*] [*ICAO designator*] (FAAC)
NEX .... Nose to Ear to Xiphoid [*Medicine*]
N EX .... Not Exceeding [*Freight*]
NEXAFS ..... Near-Edge X-Ray Absorption Fine Structure [*For study of surfaces*]
NEXAIR ...... Next Generation Upper Air System [*National Weather Service*]
NEXAIR System... Next-generation upper Air System (SAUS)
NEXCO ...... National Association of Export Companies [*New York, NY*] (EA)
NEXCOM .... Navy Exchange Service Command
NEXD .... Next Day Motor Freight [*Common carrier symbol*]
NexGen ..... NexGen, Inc. [*Associated Press*] (SAG)
NexGen ..... Next Generation (SAUS)
N-Exports... Nuclear Exports (SAUS)
NEXQ .... NEXIQ Technologies [*OTCBB symbol*]
NEXR .... Nexar Technologies [*OTCBB symbol*]
NEXRAD ..... Next Generation Weather RADAR [*National Weather Service*]
NEXS .... Nexus Distribution Corporation [*Common carrier symbol*]
Nexstar ...... NeXstar Pharmaceuticals [*Associated Press*] (SAG)
NEXT .... Hooker Enterprises, Inc. (SAUS)
NEXT .... Nationwide Evaluation of X-Ray Trends
NEXT .... NATO Experimental Tactics (NATG)
NEXT .... Near-End Crosstalk [*Bell System*]
NExt .... New Experiences in Teaching [*Mathematics*]
NEXT .... New/Experimental Techniques (MCD)
NEXT .... New Extended Technology (SAUS)
NEXT .... NextHealth, Inc. [*NASDAQ symbol*] (SAG)
NexT .... Nexus Telecommunication Systems Ltd. [*Associated Press*] (SAG)
NextelCm ... Nextel Communications [*Commercial firm*] [*Associated Press*] (SAG)
NextHlth .... NextHealth, Inc. [*Associated Press*] (SAG)
NEXTUP ..... Next Higher Emergency Operating Center [*Emergency Management*] (EMA)
NEXU .... Neptunia [*Intermodal shipping container symbol*] (TVRC)
NEXUS ...... NASA Engineering Extendible United Software system (SAUS)
NEXUS ...... Nature and Earth United with Science [*Brand of hair products*]
NEXUS ...... Nucleus Expert User System (NITA)
NEXUS ...... Numerical Examination of Urban Smog (IAA)
NexusTel .... Nexus Telecommunication Systems Ltd. [*Associated Press*] (SAG)
NEY .... Neomycin Egg Yolk [*Agar*] [*Microbiology*]
NEY .... Neyland [*British depot code*]
NEY .... Northeastern Yiddish [*Language, etc.*] (BJA)
NEYA .... Neomycin Egg Yolk Agar [*Medicine*] (EDAA)
NEYAL .... North East and Yorkshire Academic Libraries Consortium (SAUS)
NEYO .... New York City National Park Service Group
NEZ .... Northern Economic Zone (SAUS)
NEZC .... New England Zoological Club (SAUS)
NEZP .... Net Euphotic Zone Production [*Oceanography*]
NEZP .... Nez Perce Railroad [*Federal Railroad Administration identification code*]
NEZP .... Nezperce Railroad Co. [*AAR code*]
NEZs .... New Economic Zones (SAUS)
NEZS .... North of England Zoological Society [*United Kingdom*] (EAIO)
NF .... Air Vanuatu [*Airline code*] [*Australia*]
NF .... Eaton Laboratories, Inc. [*Research code symbol*]
NF .... EJA/Newport [*ICAO designator*] (AD)
NF .... Fujisawa Pharmaceutical Co. [*Japan*] [*Research code symbol*]
NF .... Nafcillin [*An antibiotic*]
nF .... Nanofarad [*One billionth of a farad*]
NF .... Nanofiltration
NF .... Narodni Fronta [*National Front*] [*Former Czechoslovakia*] [*Political party*] (PPE)
NF .... National Federation of Nonpublic School State Accrediting Associations (NTPA)
NF .... National Fine [*Thread*]
NF .... National Forest (IIA)
NF .... National Formulary [*A publication listing standard drugs*]
NF .... National Foundation
NF .... National Front [*British*] [*Political party*] (CDAI)
NF .... Natural Flat
NF .... Natural Flood (MCD)
NF .... Natural Food (MCD)
NF .... Near Face [*Technical drawings*]
NF .... Nebramycin Factor [*An antibacterial compound*]
NF .... Necrotising Fasciitis [*Medicine*] (WDAA)
NF .... Negro Female
NF .... Neighborhood Final Fade
NF .... Nephritic Factor [*Clinical medicine*]
NF .... Nested or Flat [*Freight*]
NF .... Neue Folge [*New Series*] [*Bibliography*] [*German*]
NF .... Neurofibromatosis [*Medicine*]
NF .... Neurofibromatosis, Inc. [*An association*] (EA)

NF........... Neurofilament [*Neurophysiology*]
NF........... Neutral Filter (SAUS)
NF........... Neutral Fraction
NF........... Neutron Filter (SAUS)
NF........... Neutron Flux [*Nuclear energy*] (NRCH)
N/F........... Neutrons per Fission
NF........... Nevrofibromatosis (SAUS)
NF........... New Face [*Collectibles*]
NF........... Newfoundland [*with Labrador, a Canadian province*] [*Postal code*]
NF........... Newfoundland Reports [*A publication*] (DLA)
NF........... New French [*Language, etc.*] (ROG)
NF........... Newspaper Fund (EA)
NF........... Nichibei Fujinkai [*An association*] (EA)
NF........... Nickel Faced (DGA)
NF........... Niederfrequenz [*Audio Frequency*] [*German military - World War II*]
NF........... Nieman Foundation (EA)
NF........... Nieuw Front [*New Front*] [*Suriname*] [*Political party*] (EY)
NF........... Night Fighter (SAUS)
NF........... Night Fighter Aircraft
NF........... Night Frequency [*Aviation*] (IAA)
NF........... Nitrofluoranthene [*Organic chemistry*]
NF........... Nobel Foundation (EA)
NF........... No Flash [*Phototypesetting*] (DGA)
NF........... No Fly [*Shrewd tradesman*] [*Slang*] [*British*] (DSUE)
NF........... No Fool
NF........... No Form (AAG)
NF........... No Fracture (SAUS)
n/f........... No Funds (WDMC)
NF........... No Funds [*Banking*]
NF........... Noise Factor [*Medicine*] (EDAA)
NF........... Noise Factor
NF........... Noise Figure
NF........... Noise Frequency (MSA)
NF........... Noise Fuse (MCD)
NF........... None Found [*Medicine*]
NF........... Nonferrous
NF........... Nonfiction (NTCM)
NF........... Nonfiler [*IRS*]
NF........... Nonfiltered
N-F........... Nonfordable (SAUS)
NF........... Non-Forested [*USDA Forest Service*] (ALAC)
NF........... Non-Fragments (NITA)
NF........... Nonfunction (AAMN)
NF........... Nonfundable
NF........... Nonne-Froin [*Syndrome*] [*Medicine*] (DB)
NF........... Nonwhite Female
NF........... Noranda Forest, Inc. [*Toronto Stock Exchange symbol*] [*Vancouver Stock Exchange symbol*]
NF........... Nordfriesland [*German license plate city code*]
NF........... Nordiska Fabriksarbetarefederationen [*Nordic Federation of Factory Workers Unions - NFFWU*] (EAIO)
NF........... Nordmanns-Forbunder [*Norsemen's Federation*] (EA)
NF........... Norfolk [*Virginia*] [*Navy Yard*]
NF........... Norfolk Island [*ANSI two-letter standard code*] (CNC)
NF........... Normal Flow [*Medicine*]
NF........... Normal Form [*Database design rule*] [*Computer science*] (PCM)
NF........... Normal Format (SAUS)
NF........... Normal Formula
NF........... Normal Frequency [*Telecommunications*] (NTCM)
NF........... Norman French [*Language, etc.*]
NF........... Norsk Front [*Norwegian Front*] (PD)
NF........... Northern Foundation [*Canada*] (EAIO)
NF........... Northern French [*Language, etc.*] (ROG)
NF........... North Following [*Astronomy*]
NF........... Northumberland Fusiliers [*British military*] (DMA)
NF........... Nose Fairing [*Missiles*]
NF........... Nose Fuse [*Aviation*]
NF........... Nose Fuse (or Fuze) (SAUS)
NF........... Not Fertilized
NF........... Not Filtered [*Medicine*] (EDAA)
NF........... Not Finished [*Open Systems Interconnection*] (ODAA)
nf........... Not Followed (SAFN)
NF........... Not Fordable [*Maps and charts*]
NF........... Not Forgeable (SAUS)
NF........... Not Found [*Telephone listing*] [*Telecommunications*] (TEL)
NF........... Notify [*Telegraphy*] (PCTE)
NF........... Not Releasable to Foreign Nationals (SAUS)
NF........... Nouveau Franc [*New Franc*] [*Monetary unit*] [*Introduced in 1960*] [*France*]
NF........... Nozzle Flow (SAUS)
NF........... Nuclear Factor [*Cytology*]
NF........... Nuclear Fission (SAUS)
NF........... Nuclear Red Fast [*A dye*]
NF........... Number Format (SAUS)
NF........... Nursed Fair [*Medicine*] (EDAA)
NF........... Nursing Forum [*Medicine*] (EDAA)
NF........... Nutrition Foundation [*Later, ILSI-NF*]
NF........... Royal Northumberland Fusiliers [*Military unit*] [*British*]
NF1.......... Neurofibromatosis Type 1 [*Medicine*]
NFA.......... Cast Metals Association (EA)
NFA.......... Naga Federal Army [*India*]
NFA.......... Name Field Address (SAUS)
NFA.......... Natal Field Artillery [*British military*] (DMA)
NFA.......... National Faculty Association (NADA)
NFA.......... National Faculty Association of Community and Junior Colleges [*Later, NEA Higher Education Council*]
NFA.......... National Families in Action (EA)
NFA.......... National Farmers' Association [*Republic of Ireland*] (BI)
NFA.......... National Federation of Anglers [*British*] (BI)
NFA.......... National Film Archive [*British Film Institute*]
NFA.......... National Film, Television, and Sound Archives [*Ottawa*] [*UTLAS symbol*]
NFA.......... National Finance Adjusters (NTPA)
NFA.......... National Fire Academy (COE)
NFA.......... National Firearms Act
NFA.......... National Firearms Association [*Canada*]
NFA.......... National Fishermen's Association [*Australia*]
NFA.......... National Fitness Association [*Later, NHCA*] (EA)
NFA.......... National Florist Association (EA)
NFA.......... National Flute Association (EA)
NFA.......... National Food Administration
NFA.......... National Foremen's Association [*A union*] [*British*]
NFA.......... National Forensic Association (EA)
NFA.......... National Foundation for Asthma (EA)
NFA.......... National Foundry Association (EA)
NFA.......... National Franchisee Association (EA)
NFA.......... National Freedom Academy (EA)
NFA.......... National Front of Ahvaz [*Iran*]
NFA.......... National Frumps of America (EA)
NFA.......... National Futures Association (EA)
NFA.......... Natural Food Associates (EA)
NFA.......... Naval Fuel Annex
NFA.......... Net Financial Assets (BARN)
NFA.......... Net Fixed Assets (TIMI)
NFA.......... New Farmers of America [*Later, FFA*] (EA)
NFA.......... New Fighter Aircraft (MCD)
NFA.......... News and Feature Assistant (WDMC)
nfa.......... News and Feature Assistant [*An employee of a TV network*] (WDMC)
NFA.......... New South Wales Farmers Association (SAUS)
NFA.......... Night Fighter Association
NFA.......... Nitrogen Filling Assembly
NFA.......... Nixon Family Association (EA)
NFA.......... No Fire Area [*Military*] (INF)
NFA.......... No Fixed Abode
NFA.......... No Flow Assemblies (COE)
NFA.......... No Further Action
NFA.......... Nondeterministic Finite Automaton
NFA.......... Non-Financial Agreement (OICC)
NFA.......... Non-Food Agricultural [*Commodity Price Index*] (ECON)
NFA.......... Nonhydroxylated Fatty Acid [*Organic chemistry*]
NFA.......... Northern Forum Academy (SAUS)
NFA.......... North Flying AS [*Denmark*] [*ICAO designator*] (FAAC)
NFA.......... Northwest Festivals Association (EA)
NFA.......... Northwest Fisheries Association (EA)
NFA.......... Northwest Florists Association [*Alaska, Idaho, Montana, Oregon, Utah, Washington, Wyoming, and British Columbia and Alberta, Canada*] (EARSL)
NFA.......... Northwest Forestry Association (EA)
NFA.......... Not for Attribution [*Military*]
NFA.......... Not Forgotten Association [*British*] (DBA)
NFA.......... Nuclear Free America (EA)
NFA.......... Nutritional Foods Association [*Australia*]
NFAA......... National Fashion Accessories Association (NTPA)
NFAA......... National Federation of Advertising Agencies [*Later, IFAA*] (EA)
NFAA......... National Field Archery Association (EA)
NFAA......... National Forum for the Advancement of Aquatics (EA)
NFAA......... National Foundation for Advancement in the Arts (EA)
NFAA......... Neuro-Fibromatosis Association of Australia
NFAA......... Nordic Forwarding Agents Association [*Defunct*] (EA)
NFAA......... Northern Federation of Advertisers Associations [*Stockholm, Sweden*] (EAIO)
NFAA......... Nuclear Fuel Assurance Act
NFAARr........ Nuclear Flash Absorber Arrester Resister reflector (SAUS)
NFAAUM....... National Federation of Asian American United Methodists (EA)
NFAC......... Arnolds Cove Public Library, Newfoundland [*Library symbol*] [*National Library of Canada*] (NLC)
NFAC......... National Federation of Access Centres [*United Kingdom*] (EAIO)
NFAC......... National Food and Agricultural Council (NADA)
NFAC......... National Foreign Assessment Center [*CIA*]
NFAC......... National Foundation for Asthmatic Children at Tucson [*Later, NFA*] (EA)
NFAC......... National Franchise Association Coalition (EA)
NFAC......... National Full-Scale Aerodynamics Complex [*Ames Research Center, CA*] [*NASA*]
NFAC......... Naval Facilities Engineering Command Headquarters
NFAC......... NFA Corp. (SAUS)
NFACJC....... National Faculty Association of Community and Junior Colleges [*Later, NEA Higher Education Council*]
NFADB........ National Family Association for Deaf-Blind [*Sponsored by the Helen Keller National Center for Deaf-Blind Youths and Adults (HKNC)*] (PAZ)
NFAF......... Naval Fleet Auxiliary Force
NFAH......... National Federation of American Hungarians (EA)
NFAH......... National Federation of Hungarian-Americans
NFAH......... National Foundation on the Arts and Humanities
NFAHA........ National Foundation on the Arts and Humanities Act [*1965*]
NFAHS........ National Foundation for Affordable Housing Solutions (EA)
NFaiB........ Board of Cooperative Educational Services - Monroe I, Fairport, NY [*Library symbol*] [*Library of Congress*] (LCLS)

NFAIO .... National Federation of Asian Indian Organizations in America [*Later, NFIAA*] (EA)
NFAIS .... National Federation of Abstracting and Indexing Services (NITA)
NFAIS .... National Federation of Abstracting and Information Services (EA)
NFAIS .... National Federation of American Information Services [*International Council of Scientific Unions*]
NFAL .... National Foundation of Arts and Letters (WDAA)
N-Fallout ... Nuclear Fallout (SAUS)
NFAM .... National Foundation for the Australian Musical
NFAM .... Network File Access Method
NFAN .... National Filter Analysis Network [*Environmental Protection Agency*] (GFGA)
NFANA .... Norwegian Fjord Association of North America (EA)
NF & F .... Natural Food and Farming [*A publication*]
NF&M .... Nuclear Fuels & Materials Department (SAUS)
NFAP .... Nationwide Forestry Applications Program [*USDA Forest Service*] (ALAC)
NFAP .... Nerve Fiber Action Potentials [*Neurophysiology*]
NFAP .... Network File Access Protocol
NFAP .... Nuclear Free Australia Party [*Political party*]
NFAPC .... National Fisheries Adjustment Program Committee [*Australia*]
NFAPP .... National Food and Agricultural Policy Project [*Arizona State University*] (RCD)
NFar .... Farmingdale Public Library, Farmingdale, NY [*Library symbol*] [*Library of Congress*] (LCLS)
NFAR .... No Further Action Required (DAVI)
NFarB .... BioResearch, Inc., Farmingdale, NY [*Library symbol*] [*Library of Congress*] (LCLS)
NFarEE .... East Memorial Elementary School, Farmingdale, NY [*Library symbol*] [*Library of Congress*] (LCLS)
NFarF .... Fairchild-Hiller Corp. [*Later, Fairchild Industries, Inc.*], Republic Aviati on Division, Farmingdale, NY [*Library symbol*] [*Library of Congress*] (LCLS)
NFarHS .... Howitt School, Farmingdale, NY [*Library symbol*] [*Library of Congress*] (LCLS)
NFarNE .... Northside Elementary School, Farmingdale, NY [*Library symbol*] [*Library of Congress*] (LCLS)
NFarSH .... Farmingdale Senior High School, Farmingdale, NY [*Library symbol*] [*Library of Congress*] (LCLS)
NFarUA .... State University of New York, Agricultural and Technical College at Farmingdale,Farmingdale, NY [*Library symbol*] [*Library of Congress*] (LCLS)
NFarWP .... Woodward Parkway School, Farmingdale, NY [*Library symbol*] [*Library of Congress*] (LCLS)
NFAS .... National Field Archery Society [*British*] (DBA)
NFAS .... Non Facilities-Associated Signaling (SAUS)
NFASG .... National Fashion Accessories Salesmen's Guild (EA)
NFAT .... Nuclear Factor of Activated T-Cells [*Genetics*]
NFAWSR .... North Fork American Wild and Scenic River (COE)
NFay .... Fayetteville Free Library, Fayetteville (SAUS)
NFay .... Fayetteville Free Library, Fayetteville, NY [*Library symbol*] [*Library of Congress*] (LCLS)
NFB .... Booth Memorial Hospital, Flushing, NY [*Library symbol*] [*Library of Congress*] (LCLS)
NFB .... Mount Clemens, MI [*Location identifier*] [*FAA*] (FAAL)
NFB .... National Federation of the Blind (EA)
NFB .... National Film Board [*Canada*] (WDMC)
NFB .... National Film Board of Canada [*UTLAS symbol*]
NFB .... National Foundation for the Blind (DMAA)
NFB .... Naval Frontier Base
NFB .... Negative Feedback (DEN)
NFB .... New Fibers International [*Vancouver Stock Exchange symbol*]
NFB .... Niagara Frontier Tariff Bureau, Inc., Buffalo NY [*STAC*]
NFB .... Node of First-Fruiting Branch [*Botany*] (OA)
NFB .... No Feed Back (AEBS)
NFB .... Nonfermenting Bacteria
NFB .... North Fork Bancorp [*NYSE symbol*] (SPSG)
NFBA .... National Family Business Association [*Tarzana, CA*] (EA)
NFBA .... National Farm Borrowers Association (EA)
NFBA .... National Food Brokers Association (EA)
NFBA .... National Frame Builders Association (EA)
NFBC .... National Family Business Council [*Northbrook, IL*] (EA)
NFBC .... National Film Board of Canada
NFBC .... Newfoundland Base Command [*Army*] [*World War II*]
NFBC .... North Fork Bancorp (MHDW)
NFBCA .... National Federation of Blind Citizens of Australia
NFBF .... Bishops Falls Public Library, Newfoundland [*Library symbol*] [*National Library of Canada*] (NLC)
NFBF .... National Farm Bureau Federation
NFBF .... Noninverting Feedback Bridging Fault (SAUS)
NFBG .... National Federation of Badger Groups [*British*] (DBA)
NFBI .... Bell Island Public Library, Newfoundland [*Library symbol*] [*National Library of Canada*] (NLC)
NFBI .... Netherlands Flower-Bulb Institute [*Defunct*] (EA)
NFBI .... Nonresidential Fixed Business Investment (MCD)
NFBN .... National Food Bank Network (EA)
NFBO .... Bonavista Public Library, Newfoundland [*Library symbol*] [*National Library of Canada*] (NLC)
NfBoo .... Holmes Library, Boonton (SAUS)
NFBOT .... Botwood Public Library, Newfoundland [*Library symbol*] [*National Library of Canada*] (NLC)
NFBPA .... National Forum for Black Public Administrators (EA)
NFBPM .... National Federation of Builders' and Plumbers' Merchants [*British*] (BI)
NFBPT .... National Federation for Biblio/Poetry Therapy (EA)
NFBPW ...... National Federation of Business and Professional Women's Clubs (WGA)
NFBPWC .... National Federation of Business and Professional Women's Clubs (EA)
NFBQ .... Rural District Memorial Library, Badgers Quay, Newfoundland [*Library symbol*] [*National Library of Canada*] (NLC)
NFBR .... Bay Roberts Public Library, Newfoundland [*Library symbol*] [*National Library of Canada*] (NLC)
NFBR .... National Foundation for Biomedical Research [*An association*]
NFBR .... National Foundation for Brain Research (EA)
NFBRI .... Brigus Public Library, Newfoundland [*Library symbol*] [*National Library of Canada*] (NLC)
NFBS .... National Freehold Building Society [*British*]
NFBSS .... National Federation of Bakery Students' Societies [*British*] (BI)
NFBTE .... National Federation of Building Trades Employers [*British*] (DCTA)
NFBTO .... National Federation of Building Trades Operatives [*British*]
NFBU .... Buchans Public Library, Newfoundland [*Library symbol*] [*National Library of Canada*] (NLC)
NFBU .... National Federation of Bus Users [*British*]
NFBU .... National Fire Brigades Union (ROG)
NFBUK .... National Federation for the Blind [*British*] (DBA)
NFBUR .... Burgeo Public Library, Newfoundland [*Library symbol*] [*National Library of Canada*] (NLC)
NFBURI ..... Burin Public Library, Newfoundland [*Library symbol*] [*National Library of Canada*] (NLC)
NFBV .... Baie Verte Public Library, Newfoundland [*Library symbol*] [*National Library of Canada*] (NLC)
NFBWA .... National Federation of Buddhist Women's Associations [*Later, BCAFBWA*] (EA)
NFBWW ..... Nordic Federation of Building and Wood Workers (EA)
NFC .... Carbonear Public Library, Newfoundland [*Library symbol*] [*National Library of Canada*] (NLC)
NFC .... Name Formula Card
NFC .... National Farm Coalition [*Defunct*] (EA)
NFC .... National Federated Craft (EA)
NFC .... National Fenestration Council [*Later, PGMC*] (EA)
NFC .... National Fertility Center (DAVI)
NFC .... National Field Communication (TIMI)
NFC .... National Film Carriers (EA)
NFC .... National Finance Center [*USDA center in New Orleans*] (ALAC)
NFC .... National Firebird Club (EA)
NFC .... National Fire Code
NFC .... National Food Conference Association (EA)
NFC .... National Football Conference [*of NFL*]
NFC .... National Forensic Center (EA)
NFC .... National Fraternal Congress [*Later, NFCA*]
NFC .... National Freight Consortium (WDAA)
NFC .... National Freight Corp. [*British*]
NFC .... National Fructose Center (EA)
NFC .... National Fund Chairman [*or Co-chairman*] [*Red Cross*]
NFC .... Native Forest Council (EA)
NFC .... Navy Federal Credit Union
NFC .... Navy Finance Center
NFC .... NCF Financial Corp. [*AMEX symbol*] (COMM)
NFC .... Near-Frictionless Carbon
NFC .... Negative Factor Counting
NFC .... Negative Feedback Circuit
nfc .... Newfoundland [*MARC country of publication code*] [*Library of Congress*] (LCCP)
NFC .... News for Farmer Cooperatives [*A publication*]
NFC .... Newsline Fan Club (EA)
NFC .... Newsline II Fan Club (EA)
NFC .... Newspaper Features Council (EA)
NFC .... NFC Ltd. [*Associated Press*] (SAG)
NFC .... NFC PLC [*AMEX symbol*] (SPSG)
NFC .... NFC plc ADS [*AMEX symbol*] (TTSB)
NFC .... Nighttime Fatal Crash
NFC .... No Frequency Conversion (SAUS)
NFC .... No Front Cover
NFC .... No Further Clearance Required (KSC)
NFC .... No Further Consequences (NRCH)
NFC .... Nonfavorably Considered (DAVI)
NFC .... Nordisk Forening for Cellforskning [*Nordic Society for Cell Biology - NSCB*] (EAIO)
NFC .... Nose Fairing Container [*Missiles*]
nfc .... Not Favourably Considered (ODA)
NFC .... Nuclear Fuel Cycle (NUCP)
NFC .... Numbered Fleet Commander (DOMA)
NFCA .... Carmanville Public Library, Newfoundland [*Library symbol*] [*National Library of Canada*] (NLC)
NFCA .... National Family Caregivers Association (NTPA)
NFCA .... National Federation of Community Associations [*British*] (DI)
NFCA .... National Floor Covering Association [*Canada*] (EAIO)
NFCA .... National Foster Care Association [*British*] (EAIO)
NFCA .... National Fraternal Congress of America [*Naperville, IL*] (EA)
NFCA .... National Fuel Credit Association [*Defunct*]
NFCA .... Near-Field Calibration Array (PDAA)
NFCA .... Nonfuel Core Array [*Nuclear energy*] (NRCH)
NFCA .... Northern Fishing Companies Association (SAUS)
NFCAA .... National Fencing Coaches Association of America (EA)
NFCADA ..... National Family Council Against Drug Abuse [*Formerly, NFCDA*] (EA)
NFC(ALLOT) ... Navy Finance Center (Allotments Division) (DNAB)
NFCARW .... National Federation of Cuban-American Republican Women (EA)
NFCAT .... Joseph E. Clouter Memorial Library, Catalina, Newfoundland [*Library symbol*] [*National Library of Canada*] (NLC)

NFCB .... Corner Brook City Public Library, Newfoundland [*Library symbol*] [*National Library of Canada*] (NLC)
NFCB .... National Federation of Community Broadcasters (EA)
NFCBF .... Newfoundland Department of Forest Resources and Lands, Corner Brook, New Foundland [*Library symbol*] [*National Library of Canada*] (NLC)
NFCBFT ..... Fisher Institute of Applied Arts and Technology, Corner Brook, Newfoundland [*Library symbol*] [*National Library of Canada*] (NLC)
NFCBM ...... Sir Wilfred Grenfell College, Memorial University, Corner Brook, Newfoundland [*Library symbol*] [*National Library of Canada*] (NLC)
NFCBR ...... Regional Library, Corner Brook, Newfoundland [*Library symbol*] [*National Library of Canada*] (NLC)
NFCBRO ..... National Federation of Citizen Band Radio Operators (EA)
NFCBW ...... Western Memorial Hospital, Corner Brook, Newfoundland [*Library symbol*] [*National Library of Canada*] (NLC)
NFCC .... National Family Conciliation Council [*British*] (DI)
NFCC .... National Farm-City Council (EA)
NFCC .... National Foundation for Consumer Credit [*Silver Spring, MD*] (EA)
NFCC .... National Foundation for Credit Counseling
NFCC .... National Free Clinic Council [*Superseded by NCAHCP*]
NFCC .... Navy Finance Center, Cleveland (ACAE)
NFCC .... Neighborhood Family-Care Center (MEDA)
NFC(CAD) ... Navy Finance Center (Central Accounts Division) (DNAB)
NFCCE .... National Fellowship of Child Care Executives (EA)
NFC-CLEVE ... Navy Finance Center - Cleveland [*Ohio*] (DNAB)
NFCCS .... National Federation of Catholic College Students [*Defunct*] (EA)
NFCDA ...... National Family Council on Drug Addiction [*Later, NFCADA*] (EA)
NFCDCU ..... National Federation of Community Development Credit Unions [*New York, NY*] (EA)
NFCDS ...... National Federation of Clubs for Divorced and Separated [*British*] (BI)
NFCE .... Centreville Public Library, Newfoundland [*Library symbol*] [*National Library of Canada*] (NLC)
NFCEO .... National Foundation for Conservation and Environmental Officers [*Defunct*] (EA)
NFCF .... Churchill Falls Public Library, Newfoundland [*Library symbol*] [*National Library of Canada*] (NLC)
NFCF .... National Federation of City Farms [*British*] (EAIO)
NFCG .... National Federation of Consumer Groups [*British*] (ILCA)
NFCGA ...... National Federation of Constructional Glass Associations [*British*] (BI)
NFCGC ...... National Federation of Coffee Growers of Colombia [*See also FNCC*] (EA)
NFCGH ...... Carbonear General Hospital, Newfoundland [*Library symbol*] [*National Library of Canada*] (NLC)
NFCH .... Corner Brook City Public Library, Newfoundland (SAUS)
NFCH .... Cow Head Public Library, Newfoundland [*Library symbol*] [*National Library of Canada*] (NLC)
NFCH .... National Foundation for the Chemically Hypersensitive (EA)
NFCI .... Change Islands Public Library, Newfoundland [*Library symbol*] [*National Library of Canada*] (NLC)
NFCI .... National Federation of Clay Industries [*British*] (BI)
NFCIS .... Nuclear Fuel Cycle Information System [*Database*] [*International Atomic Energy Agency*] [*United Nations*] (DUND)
NFCJ .... National Forum on Criminal Justice [*Formerly, NICD*] [*Inactive*] (EA)
NFCL .... Clarenville Public Library, Newfoundland [*Library symbol*] [*National Library of Canada*] (NLC)
NFC-L .... National Fisheries Center - Leetown [*Department of the Interior*] (GRD)
NFCM .... National Front Constitutional Movement [*British*]
NFCO .... Cormack Public Library, Newfoundland [*Library symbol*] [*National Library of Canada*] (NLC)
NFCO .... National Federation of Community Organizations [*British*] (EAIO)
NFCP .... Channel/Port Aux Basques Public Library, Newfoundland [*Library symbol*] [*National Library of Canada*] (NLC)
NFCP .... Nuclear Fuel Cycle and Production Division (SAUS)
NFCPG ...... National Federation of Catholic Physicians' Guilds (EA)
NFCPO ...... National Forum of Catholic Parent Organizations [*Defunct*] (EA)
NFCR .... Narrow Cold-Frontal Rainbands (SAUS)
NFCR .... National Foundation for Cancer Research (EA)
NFCRC ...... National Fisheries Contaminant Research Center (EA)
NFCRC ...... National Fuel Cell Research Center [*University of California, Irvine*] (RCD)
NFC Receiver ... No-Frequency-Conversion Receiver (SAUS)
NFCS .... National Federation of Catholic Seminarians [*Defunct*] (EA)
NFCS .... National Federation of Construction Supervisors [*British*] (BI)
NFCs .... National Focal Centres (SAUS)
NFCS .... Naval Field Contracting System (AAGC)
NFCS .... Night-Fire [*Rifle*] Control Sight [*Army*]
NFCS .... Nuclear Forces Communications Satellite
NFCSG ...... Cape St. George Public Library, Newfoundland [*Library symbol*] [*National Library of Canada*] (NLC)
NFCSIT ...... National Federation of Cold Storage and Ice Trades [*British*] (BI)
NFCSP .... National Family Caregiver Support Program
NFCT .... National Federation of Class Teachers (AIE)
NFCT .... Nonfederal Control Tower [*For chart use only*]
NFCTA .... National Federation of Continuative Teachers' Associations [*British*]
NFCTA .... National Federation of Corn Trade Associations [*British*] (BI)
NFCTA .... National Fibre Can and Tube Association [*Later, CCTI*] (EA)
NFCU .... Navy Federal Credit Union
NFCUS ...... National Federation of Canadian University Students
NFCW .... Cartwright Public Library, Newfoundland [*Library symbol*] [*National Library of Canada*] (BIB)
NFC-WASH ... Navy Finance Center - Washington, DC (DNAB)
NFCYM ...... National Federation for Catholic Youth Ministry (EA)
NFD .... Dover Public Library, Newfoundland [*Library symbol*] [*National Library of Canada*] (BIB)
NFD .... Eurowings (NFD & RFG Luftverhehrs AG) [*Germany*] [*ICAO designator*] (FAAC)
NFD .... National Faculty Directory [*A publication*]
NFD .... National Fax Directory [*A publication*]
NFD .... National Federation for Decency (EA)
NFD .... National Federation of Drapers and Allied Traders Ltd. [*Republic of Ireland*] (BI)
NFD .... Naval Fuel Depot
NFD .... Network Flow Diagrams (CTAS)
NFD .... Neurofibrillary Degeneration [*Medicine*]
NFD .... Neutron Flux Density [*Nuclear energy*]
NFD .... New Democratic Force (Colombia) [*Political party*] (PSAP)
NFD .... Newfoundland [*with Labrador, a Canadian province*]
NFD .... Newfoundland Tracking Station
NFD .... No Family Doctor (MELL)
NFD .... No Fixed Date
NFD .... No Foreign Dissemination [*Intelligence classification*] (MCD)
NFD .... No Further Description (SAUS)
NFD .... No Further Details (GOBB)
NFD .... Noise-Free Device (SAUS)
NFD .... Non-Familial Disease (MELL)
NFD .... Non-Fatal Defect (VLIE)
NFD .... Nonfat Dry (SAUS)
NFD .... Norfolk, Franklin & Danville Railway Co. [*AAR code*]
NFD .... Northern Frontier District [*Kenya*]
NFD .... Notified [*Telegraphy*] (PCTE)
NFD .... Nuclear Energy and Surplus Facilities DOE-RL Management Division (SAUS)
NFD .... Nuclear Fuels Division (SAUS)
NFD .... Nueva Fuerza Democratica [*New Democratic Force*] [*Colombia*] [*Political party*] (EY)
NFDA .... National Fastener Distributors Association (EA)
NFDA .... National Food Distributors Association (EA)
NFDA .... National Funeral Directors Association (EA)
NFDA-PAC ... National Funeral Directors Association of the US Inc. PAC [*Brookfield, WI*] (PACS)
NFDC .... Dark Cove Public Library, Newfoundland [*Library symbol*] [*National Library of Canada*] (NLC)
NFDC .... National Father's Day Committee (EA)
NFDC .... National Federation of Demolition Contractors [*British*] (EAIO)
NFDC .... National Fertilizer Development Center [*Tennessee Valley Authority*] [*Muscle Shoals, AL*]
NFDC .... National Flight Data Center [*FAA*]
NFDCAMD ... National Food, Drug, and Cosmetic Association of Manufacturers and Distributors [*Defunct*] (EA)
NFDD .... National Flight Data Digest [*FAA*] (TAG)
NFDF .... National Flag Day Foundation (EA)
NFDH .... Daniels Harbour Public Library, Newfoundland [*Library symbol*] [*National Library of Canada*] (NLC)
NFDH .... National Foundation of Dentistry for the Handicapped (EA)
NFDL .... Deer Lake Public Library, Newfoundland [*Library symbol*] [*National Library of Canada*] (NLC)
NFDLF .... Northern Frontier District Liberation Front (SAUS)
NFDM .... Nonfat Dry Milk
NFDMA ...... National Funeral Directors and Morticians Association (EA)
NFDPM ...... National Federation of Data Processing Manufacturing (NITA)
NFDPS ...... National Flight Data Processing System [*ICAO*] (DA)
NFDR .... Neurofacial-Digitorenal Syndrome [*Medicine*] (DMAA)
NFDRS ...... National Fire Danger Rating System [*US Forest Service*]
NFDW .... National Federation of Democratic Women (EA)
NFE .... Fentress, VA [*Location identifier*] [*FAA*] (FAAL)
NFE .... National Faculty Exchange (EA)
NFE .... Naval Facilities Engineering Command, Alexandria, VA [*OCLC symbol*] (OCLC)
NFE .... Near Free Electron (AAEL)
NFE .... Nearly Free Electron [*Physics*] (OA)
NFE .... Network Front End
NFE .... Neutron Flux Experiment (SAUS)
NFE .... News from Ethiopia [*A publication*]
NFE .... Nitride Forming Element [*Metal treating*]
NFE .... Nitrogen-Free Extract [*Analytical chemistry*]
NFE .... No First Error (VLIE)
NFE .... Nonferrous Extract (DMAA)
NFE .... Nonformal Education
NFE .... Northwest Fruit Exporters (NTPA)
NFE .... Nose Fairing Exit [*Missiles*]
NFE .... Not Fully Equipped [*of aircraft*] [*Air Force*]
NFE .... Nuclear Faraday Effect (SAUS)
NFEA .... National Federated Electrical Association (MHDB)
NFEA .... National Federation of Export Associations [*New York, NY*] (EA)
NFEA .... Newspaper Farm Editors of America (EA)
NFEA .... Non-Fleet Experienced Aviator (NVT)
NFEAC .... National Foundation for Education in American Citizenship (EA)
NF-EBM ..... Noise Forced Energy Balance Model (SAUS)
NFEC .... National Food and Energy Council (EA)
NFEC .... National Foundation for Environmental Control (EA)
NFEC .... Naval Facilities Engineering Command [*Formerly, Bureau of Yards and Docks*] (IEEE)
NFEC .... Newspaper Food Editors Conference (EA)
NFECC .... National Fusion Energy Computer Center [*Lawrence Livermore National Laboratory*] (MCD)
NFED .... National Foundation for Ectodermal Dysplasias (EA)
NFEF .... National Free Enterprise Foundation [*Australia*]

NFEJ........ Nepal Forum of Environmental Journalists (SAUS)
NFER........ National Foundation for Educational Research [*British*] (DET)
NFER........ National Foundation for Educational Research in England and Wales (IID)
NFER........ National Foundation for Eye Research (EA)
NFER........ Nonferrous
NFERC....... National Fertilizer and Environmental Research Center (CARB)
NFERF....... National Fisheries Education and Research Foundation (EA)
NFERO....... Non Ferrous (VLIE)
NFES........ No Fire, Empty Seat [*Automotive safety, air bags*]
NFESC....... Naval Facilities Engineering Service Center (BCP)
NFET........ N-Channel Junction Field-Effect Transistor (IDOE)
NFETA....... National Foundry and Engineering Training Association [*British*]
NFETM....... National Federation of Engineers' Tools Manufacturers (MHDB)
NFEW........ National Forum for Executive Women [*Washington, DC*] (EA)
NFEWA....... Newspaper Food Editors and Writers Association (EA)
NFF......... Fogo Public Library, Newfoundland [*Library symbol*] [*National Library of Canada*] (NLC)
NFF......... Jacksonville, FL [*Location identifier*] [*FAA*] (FAAL)
NFF......... Natal Field Force [*British military*] (DMA)
NFF......... National Farmers Federation
NFF......... National Fatherland Front [*Afghanistan*] [*Political party*] (FEA)
NFF......... National Federation of Fishermen [*Inactive*] (EA)
NFF......... National Federation of Fishmongers [*British*] (DBA)
NFF......... National Fitness Foundation (EA)
NFF......... National Flag Foundation (EA)
NFF......... National Flood Frequency Program [*Computer science*]
NFF......... National Football Foundation and Hall of Fame (EA)
NFF......... National Forum Foundation (EA)
NFF......... National Froebel Foundation [*British*] (BI)
NFF......... Naval Fuel Facility
NFF......... Neff Corp'A' [*NYSE symbol*] (SG)
NFF......... Negation as Finite Failure (RALS)
NFF......... Nemzeti Fueggetlensegi Front [*National Independence Front*] [*Hungary*] [*Political party*] (PPE)
NFF......... Neutral File Format [*Computer science*] (VLIE)
NFF......... New Forests Fund (EA)
NFF......... No Failures Found (SAUS)
NFF......... No Fault Found (MCD)
NFF......... No Form Feed (VLIE)
NFF......... No Frills Fund
Nff......... Nordisk Forening for Folkendansforskning [*Nordic Association for Folk Dance Research*] [*Sweden*] (EAIO)
NFF......... Normal Freezing Furnace (SAUS)
NFF......... Nuclear Freeze Foundation [*Defunct*] (EA)
NFF......... Numbered Fleet Flagship [*Navy*]
NFFA........ Ba [*Fiji*] [*ICAO location identifier*] (ICLI)
NFFA........ National Flying Farmers Association [*Later, International Flying Farmers*]
NFFA........ National Folk Festival Association [*Later, National Council for the TraditionalArts*]
NFFA........ National Frozen Food Association (EA)
NFFAO....... National FFA [*Future Farmers of America*] Organization (EA)
NFFA PAC... National Frozen Food Association PAC [*Harrisburg, PA*] (PACS)
NFFAW....... Newfoundland Fishermen, Food and Allied Workers Union (SAUS)
NFFC........ Nancy Fisher Fan Club (EA)
NFFC........ National Family Farm Coalition (EA)
NFFC........ National Fantasy Fan Club for Disneyana Enthusiasts
NFFC........ National Film Finance Corp. [*British*] (BI)
NFFDA....... National Frozen Food Distributors Association [*Later, NFFA*]
NFFDF....... National Fraternal Flag Day Foundation [*Defunct*] (EA)
NFFE........ National Federation of Federal Employees (EA)
NFFF........ Nandi [*Fiji*] [*ICAO location identifier*] (ICLI)
NFFF........ National Fantasy Fan Federation
NFFF........ National Federation of Fish Friers [*British*] (BI)
NFFGB....... National Federation of Flemish Giant Breeders [*Later, NFFGRB*]
NFFGRB...... National Federation of Flemish Giant Rabbit Breeders (EA)
NFFH........ Fox Harbour Public Library, Newfoundland [*Library symbol*] [*National Library of Canada*] (NLC)
NFFI........ Not Fit for Issue [*Navy*]
NFFL........ Northern Forest Fire Laboratory [*Later, Intermountain Fire Sciences Laboratory*] [*Research center*] (RCD)
NFFN........ Nandi/International [*Fiji*] [*ICAO location identifier*] (ICLI)
NFFO........ Fortune Public Library, Newfoundland [*Library symbol*] [*National Library of Canada*] (NLC)
NFFO........ Malolo Lailai [*Fiji*] [*ICAO location identifier*] (ICLI)
NFFO........ National Federation of Fishermen's Organisations (EAIO)
NFFO........ Non-Fossil Fuel Obligation [*Pronounced "Noffo"*] [*Nuclear power*]
NFFPT....... National Federation of Fruit and Potato Trades [*British*] (BI)
NFFQO....... National Federation of Freestone Quarry Owners [*British*] (BI)
NFFR........ Freshwater Public Library, Newfoundland [*Library symbol*] [*National Library of Canada*] (NLC)
NFFR........ National Foundation for Facial Reconstruction (EA)
NFFR........ Rabi [*Fiji*] [*ICAO location identifier*] (ICLI)
NFFS........ National Foundation of Funeral Service (EA)
NFFS........ Nonfederal Financial Support (SAUS)
NFFS........ Non-Ferrous Founders Society (EA)
NFFTU....... National Federation of Furniture Trade Unions [*British*] (BI)
NFFWU....... Nordic Federation of Factory Workers Unions (EA)
NFFZ........ Nalley's Fine Foods [*Federal Railroad Administration identification code*]
NFG......... Gander Public Library, Newfoundland [*Library symbol*] [*National Library of Canada*] (NLC)
NFG......... Nagaland Federal Government [*India*]
NFG......... National Freight Group
NFG......... National Fuel Gas Co. [*NYSE symbol*] (SPSG)
NFG......... Natl Fuel Gas [*NYSE symbol*] (TTSB)
NFG......... Network Flow Graph [*Computer science*] (VLIE)
NFG......... Nichols, Fayette & Greenbriar [*Federal Railroad Administration identification code*]
NFG......... No Flux Gate (SAUS)
NFG......... Northwest Fruit Growers (EA)
NFG......... Not Functioning Good (SAUS)
NFG......... Notifying [*Telegraphy*] (PCTE)
NFG......... Oceanside, CA [*Location identifier*] [*FAA*] (FAAL)
NFGA........ Garnish Public Library, Newfoundland [*Library symbol*] [*National Library of Canada*] (NLC)
NFGAU....... Gaultois Public Library, Newfoundland [*Library symbol*] [*National Library of Canada*] (BIB)
NFGB........ Grand Bank Public Library, Newfoundland [*Library symbol*] [*National Library of Canada*] (NLC)
NFGBM....... Medical Library, Melville Hospital, Goose-Bay, Newfoundland [*Library symbol*] [*National Library of Canada*] (BIB)
NFGBM....... National Fellowship of Grace Brethren Ministers (EA)
NFGC........ National Federation of Grain Cooperatives [*Later, NCFC*] (EA)
NFGCA....... National Federation of Grandmother Clubs of America (EA)
NFGF........ Regional Library, Grand Falls, Newfoundland [*Library symbol*] [*National Library of Canada*] (NLC)
NFGFC....... Central Region Libraries, Grand Falls, Newfoundland [*Library symbol*] [*National Library of Canada*] (NLC)
NFG FEDPAC... National Fuel Gas Company Federal PAC [*Buffalo, NY*] (PACS)
NFGFH....... Central Newfoundland Hospital, Grand Falls, Newfoundland [*Library symbol*] [*National Library of Canada*] (NLC)
NFGFHA...... Harmsworth Public Library, Grand Falls, Newfoundland [*Library symbol*] [*National Library of Canada*] (NLC)
NFGJPH...... James Paton Memorial Hospital, Gander, Newfoundland [*Library symbol*] [*National Library of Canada*] (NLC)
NFGL........ Glenwood Public Library, Newfoundland [*Library symbol*] [*National Library of Canada*] (NLC)
NFGLO....... Glovertown Public Library, Newfoundland [*Library symbol*] [*National Library of Canada*] (NLC)
NFGMIC...... National Federation of Grange Mutual Insurance Companies [*Glastonbury, CT*] (EA)
NFGND....... National Foundation for Genetics and Neuromuscular Disease [*Later, NGF*]
NFGNE....... National Fund for Graduate Nursing Education [*Defunct*]
NFGO........ Goulds Public Library, Newfoundland [*Library symbol*] [*National Library of Canada*] (BIB)
NFGOCM...... National Forum of Greek Orthodox Church Musicians (EA)
NFGOPC...... National Federation of the Grand Order of Pachyderm Clubs (EA)
NFGR........ Greenspond Public Library, Newfoundland [*Library symbol*] [*National Library of Canada*] (NLC)
NFGS........ National Federation of Gramophone Societies (EAIO)
NFGS........ National Fenton Glass Society (EA)
NFH......... Holyrood Public Library, Newfoundland [*Library symbol*] [*National Library of Canada*] (BIB)
NFH......... National Federation of Hairdressers (WDAA)
NFH......... National Fish Hatchery
NFH......... Native Field Hospital [*British military*] (DMA)
NFH......... Nonfamilial Hematuria [*Medicine*] (DMAA)
NFHA........ National Federation of Housing Associations [*British*] (DBA)
NFHA........ National Fox Hunters Association (EA)
NFHANA...... Norwegian Fjord Horse Association of North America [*Later, NFANA*] (EA)
NFHAS....... National Faculty of Humanities, Arts, and Sciences (EA)
NFHB........ Harbour Breton Public Library, Newfoundland [*Library symbol*] [*National Library of Canada*] (NLC)
NFHBA....... Hare Bay Public Library, Newfoundland [*Library symbol*] [*National Library of Canada*] (NLC)
NFHC........ National Federation of Hispanics in Communication (EA)
NFHC........ National Federation of Housing Coops [*British*] (DBA)
NFHC........ National Federation of Housing Counselors (EA)
NFHC........ National Foot Health Council [*Defunct*] (EA)
NFHC........ National Foundation for History of Chemistry (EA)
NFHCF....... National Flotation Health Care Foundation (EA)
NFHD........ National Foundation for the Handicapped and Disabled [*Defunct*] (EA)
NFHE........ Hermitage Public Library, Newfoundland [*Library symbol*] [*National Library of Canada*] (NLC)
NFHE........ Non-Irradiated Fuel Handling Equipment [*Nuclear energy*] (NRCH)
NFHEA....... National Farm Home Editors Association [*Defunct*] (EA)
NFHG........ Harbour Grace Public Library, Newfoundland [*Library symbol*] [*National Library of Canada*] (NLC)
NFHH........ Harrys Harbour Public Library, Newfoundland [*Library symbol*] [*National Library of Canada*] (NLC)
NFhM........ Medical Society of the County of Queens, Forest Hills, NY [*Library symbol*] [*Library of Congress*] (LCLS)
NFHO........ Caaf Ho Nandi [*Fiji*] [*ICAO location identifier*] (ICLI)
NFHO........ National Federation of Housestaff Organizations (EA)
NFHON....... National Federation of Hispanic Owned Newspapers (NTPA)
NFHPER...... National Foundation for Health, Physical Education, and Recreation [*Defunct*]
NFHRL....... National Fish Health Research Laboratory [*Department of the Interior*] [*Kearneysville, WV*] (GRD)
NFHTP....... National Federation of Hebrew Teachers and Principals [*Defunct*] (EA)
NFHV........ Happy Valley Public Library, Newfoundland [*Library symbol*] [*National Library of Canada*] (NLC)
NFI......... Narrow Fabrics Institute (EA)
NFI......... National Fatherhood Initiative [*Association*] (EA)
NFI......... National Fisheries Center [*Marine science*] (OSRA)
NFI......... National Fisheries Institute (EA)

NFI .... Natural Food Institute [*Defunct*] (EA)
NFI .... Naturfreunde-Internationale [*International Friends of Nature - IFN*] (EAIO)
NFI .... Net Fundable Issues (DNAB)
NFI .... News Features of India [*Press agency*]
NFI .... New Signet Resources [*Vancouver Stock Exchange symbol*]
NFI .... Nielsen Food Index [*Marketing*] (DOAD)
NFI .... Noise Figure Indicator
NFI .... Not Further Identified (MCD)
NFI .... NovaStar Financial [*NYSE symbol*] (SG)
NFI .... Nutrition Foundation of India (SAUS)
NFIA .... National Families in Action [*An association*] (EA)
NFIA .... National Feed Ingredients Association (EA)
NFIA .... National Flood Insurance Act of 1968 (COE)
NFIA .... National Flood Insurers Association [*Defunct*] (EA)
NFIA .... National Forest Industries Association [*Australia*]
NFIA .... Nonappropriated Fund Instrumentalities Act
NFIAA .... National Federation of Indian American Associations (EA)
NFIB .... National Federation of Independent Business [*San Mateo, CA*] (EA)
NFIB .... National Foreign Intelligence Board [*Formerly, USIB*] [*Military*]
NFIB/NJ .... National Federation of Independent Business, New Jersey (EARSL)
NFIC .... National Foundation for Ileitis and Colitis (EA)
NFIC .... National Fraud Information Center
NFICA .... National Federation Interscholastic Coaches Association (EA)
NFICA .... National Forest Industries Campaign Association [*Australia*]
NFICSC .... National Foundation for Ileitis and Colitis Sports Council (EA)
NFID .... National Foundation for Infectious Diseases (EA)
NFIE .... National Foundation for the Improvement of Education (EA)
NFIEC .... Niagara Frontier Industry Education Council (SAUS)
NFIL .... Nuclear Factor Interleukin [*Genetics*]
NFIMA .... National Federation Interscholastic Music Association (EA)
NFIMA .... Nonferrous Ingot Metal Institute (SAUS)
NFIOA .... National Federation Interscholastic Officials Association (EA)
NFIP .... National Flood Insurance Program [*Federal Emergency Management Agency*]
NFIP .... National Foreign Intelligence Program [*DoD*]
NFIP .... National Foreign Intelligence Programme (SAUS)
NFIP .... National Foundation for Infantile Paralysis [*Later, MDBDF*]
NFIPA .... National Fire Protection Association (WPI)
NFIPS .... National Flood Insurance Program System [*Federal Emergency Management Agency*] (GFGA)
NFIR .... National Federation of Indian Railwaymen
NFIRF .... Nature Farming International Research Foundation (EAIO)
NFIRS .... National Fire Incident Reporting System [*Federal Emergency Management Agency*] (GFGA)
NFIS .... Naval Fighting Instruction School
NFIS .... Nicolet Federated Library System (SAUS)
NFIS .... Non-Formatted Information System [*Computer science*] (VLIE)
NFISDA .... National Federation Interscholastic Speech and Debate Association (EA)
NFisi .... Fishers Island Library Association, Fishers Island, NY [*Library symbol*] [*Library of Congress*] (LCLS)
NFisk .... Blodgett Memorial Library, Fishkill, NY [*Library symbol*] [*Library of Congress*] (LCLS)
NFISM .... National Federation of Iron and Steel Merchants [*British*] (BI)
NFISYD .... National Federation of Independent Scrap Yard Dealers (EA)
NFITC .... National Forest Industries Training Council [*Australia*]
NFIU .... National Federation of Independent Unions (EA)
NFJ .... Milton, FL [*Location identifier*] [*FAA*] (FAAL)
NFJC .... National Foundation for Jewish Culture (EA)
NFJGD .... National Foundation for Jewish Genetic Diseases (EA)
NFJM .... National Foundation for Junior Museums [*Later, NSYF*]
NFJMC .... National Federation of Jewish Men's Clubs (EA)
NFJU .... Nordic Federation of Journalists Unions (SAUS)
NFK .... Neuer Fundamentalkatalog (SAUS)
NFK .... Niederfrequenz-Koppelfeld (SAUS)
NFK .... Norfolk [*Telegraphy*] (PCTE)
NFK .... Norfolk Island [*ANSI three-letter standard code*] (CNC)
NFK .... Norfolk, VA [*Amtrak Busline code*]
NFK .... Nuclear Factor Kappa (DMAA)
NFKK .... Nordisk Forening for Klinisk Kemi [*Scandinavian Society for Clinical Chemistry - SSCC*] [*Finland*] (EAIO)
NFKP .... Kings Point Public Library, Newfoundland [*Library symbol*] [*National Library of Canada*] (NLC)
NFKPA .... National Federation of Kidney Patients Association [*British*] (DI)
NFL .... Ayiwo [*Language symbol*] (ETLW)
NFL .... Fallon, NV [*Location identifier*] [*FAA*] (FAAL)
NFL .... Labrador City Public Library, Newfoundland [*Library symbol*] [*National Library of Canada*] (NLC)
NFL .... National Federation of Laymen (EA)
NFL .... National Film Library (NADA)
NFL .... National Football League (EA)
NFL .... National Forensic League (EA)
NFL .... National Foresters League (NADA)
NFL .... National Fund Leadership [*Group*] [*Red Cross*]
NFL .... Naval Standard Flange (MSA)
NFL .... Nerve Fiber Layer [*Neurology*] (DAVI)
NFL .... Neurofilament Protein, Light Polypeptide (DMAA)
NFL .... New Foreign Launch (ACAE)
NFL .... Newfoundland and Prince Edward Island Reports [*Maritime Law Book Co. Ltd.*] [*Canada*] [*Information service or system*] (CRD)
NFL .... Newfoundland Federation of Labour (SAUS)
NFL .... Newfoundland Light & Power Co. Ltd. [*Toronto Stock Exchange symbol*]
NFL .... Newlands Field Laboratory [*University of Nevada - Reno*] [*Research center*] (RCD)
NFL .... Niagara Falls, NY [*Amtrak rail station code*]
NFL .... No Field Lubrication (PDAA)
NFL .... No Fire Line [*Military*]
NFL .... No Phone Listed [*Cablegram marking*] [*British*]
NFL .... Normal Female Liver [*Hepatology*]
NFL .... Normal for Londoners (BB)
NFL .... Northaire Freight Lines Ltd. [*ICAO designator*] (FAAC)
NFL .... Nurses for Laughter
NFL .... Nuveen Ins FL Prem Inc. Muni [*NYSE symbol*] (TTSB)
NFL .... Nuveen Insured Florida Premium Income Municipal [*NYSE symbol*] (SPSG)
NFLA .... L'Anse Au Loup Public Library, Newfoundland [*Library symbol*] [*National Library of Canada*] (NLC)
NFLA .... National Football League Alumni (EA)
NFLA .... National Front for the Liberation of Angola (EA)
NFLA .... Nuclear-Free Local Authorities (WDAA)
NFL Alumni ... National Football League Alumni [*An association*] (EA)
NFLC .... National Federation of Land Councils [*Australia*]
NFLC .... Northern Forest Lands Council (WPI)
NFLCC .... National Fishing Lure Collectors Club (EA)
NFLCP .... National Federation of Local Cable Programmers (EA)
NFLD .... Enfield [*NCIC motorcycle make code*]
NFLD .... Nerve Fiber Layer Defect [*Medicine*] (DMAA)
Nfld .... Newfoundland [*Canada*] (DD)
NFLD .... Newfoundland [*with Labrador, a Canadian province*]
Nfld .... Newfoundland Supreme Court Decisions [*Canada*] [*A publication*] (DLA)
NFLD .... Northfield Laboratories [*NASDAQ symbol*] (TTSB)
NFLD .... Northfield Laboratories, Inc. [*NASDAQ symbol*] (SAG)
Nfld LR .... Newfoundland Law Reports [*A publication*] (DLA)
Nfld R .... Newfoundland Reports [*A publication*] (DLA)
Nfld Rev Stat ... Newfoundland Revised Statutes [*Canada*] [*A publication*] (DLA)
NFLDS .... National Fire Loss Data System [*Military*] (PDAA)
Nfld Sel Cas ... Newfoundland Select Cases [*A publication*] (DLA)
Nfld Stat ... Newfoundland Statutes [*Canada*] [*A publication*] (DLA)
NFLE .... Lewisporte Public Library, Newfoundland [*Library symbol*] [*National Library of Canada*] (NLC)
NFLF .... National Family Life Foundation (EA)
NFLF .... Nylon Full-Line Filter
NFLHB .... Blow Me Down School/Public Library, Lark Harbour, Newfoundland [*Library symbol*] [*National Library of Canada*] (NLC)
NFLI .... Northern Fraternal Life Insurance (EA)
NFLI .... Nutrition For Life International, Inc. [*NASDAQ symbol*] (SAG)
NFLI .... Nutrition For Life Intl. [*NASDAQ symbol*] (TTSB)
NFLIO .... Training Department, Iron Ore Co. of Canada, Labrador City, Newfoundland [*Library symbol*] [*National Library of Canada*] (NLC)
NFLIW .... Nutrition For Life Intl. Wrrt [*NASDAQ symbol*] (TTSB)
NflkSo .... Norfolk Southern Corp. [*Associated Press*] (SAG)
NFLO .... Lourdes Public Library, Newfoundland [*Library symbol*] [*National Library of Canada*] (NLC)
NFlp .... Floral Park Public Library, Floral Park (SAUS)
NFlp .... Floral Park Public Library, Floral Park, NY [*Library symbol*] [*Library of Congress*] (LCLS)
NFLPA .... National Football League Players Association (EA)
NFLPA .... National Free Lance Photographers Association (EA)
NFlpBE .... Floral Park-Bellerose Elementary School, Floral Park, NY [*Library symbol*] [*Library of Congress*] (LCLS)
NFlpCE .... John Lewis Childs Elementary School, Floral Park, NY [*Library symbol*] [*Library of Congress*] (LCLS)
NFlpMH .... Floral Park Memeorial High School, Floral Park, NY [*Library symbol*] [*Library of Congress*] (LCLS)
NFLPN .... National Federation of Licensed Practical Nurses (EA)
NFlpSH .... Sewanhaka High School, Floral Park, NY [*Library symbol*] [*Library of Congress*] (LCLS)
NFLQI .... Nuveen Florida Quality Income Municipal Fund [*Associated Press*] (SAG)
NFLS .... La Scie Public Library, Newfoundland [*Library symbol*] [*National Library of Canada*] (NLC)
NFLS .... Nicolet Federated Library System [*Library network*]
NFLSV .... National Front for the Liberation of South Vietnam
NFLTHC .... National Foundation for Long Term Health Care [*Defunct*] (EA)
NFLU .... Lumsden Public Library, Newfoundland [*Library symbol*] [*National Library of Canada*] (NLC)
NFM .... Conception Bay South Public Library, Manuels, Newfoundland [*Library symbol*] [*National Library of Canada*] (NLC)
NFM .... Midland Lutheran College, Fremont, NE [*OCLC symbol*] (OCLC)
NFM .... Narrowband Frequency Modulation [*Radio*]
NFM .... Network File Manager [*Computer science*] (VLIE)
NFM .... Neurofilament Protein, Medium Polypeptide (DMAA)
NFM .... New Frontiers of Medicine [*An association*] (EA)
NFM .... Next Full Moon [*Freemasonry*] (ROG)
NFM .... Neyrpic Framatome Mecanique (EFIS)
NFM .... Noise Figure Meter
NFM .... Nonfat Milk (OA)
NFM .... Nonferromagnetic (SAUS)
NFM .... Nonferrous Metal
NFM .... Normal Fundamental Mode (SAUS)
NFM .... Northern Fowl Mite [*Immunology*]
NFM .... North-Finding Module (RDA)
NFM .... Nuclear Ferromagnetism (SAUS)
NFMA .... Marystown Public Library, Newfoundland [*Library symbol*] [*National Library of Canada*] (NLC)
NFMA .... National Federation of Municipal Analysts (NTPA)
NFMA .... National Fireplace Makers Association [*British*] (BI)

NFMA........ National Footwear Manufacturers Association [*Later, FIA*]
NFMA........ National Forest Management Act (GFGA)
NFMA........ Needleroom Felt Manufacturers Association [*British*] (DBA)
NFMA........ Northwest Farm Managers Association (EA)
NFMA........ Norwegian Furniture Manufacturers Association (SAUS)
NFMA........ November, February, May, and August [*Denotes quarterly payments of interest or dividends in these months*] [*Business term*]
NFMAA...... National Federation Music Adjudicator Association (EA)
NFMAS...... National Fire Management Analysis System [*Fire-planning*] [*USDA Forest Service*] (ALAC)
NFMC........ National Federation of Music Clubs (EA)
NFMC........ National Film Music Council [*Defunct*]
NFMC........ National Foundation for Mortuary Care [*Emergency Management*] (EMA)
NFMC........ Not Fully Mission Capable (ACAE)
NFMC........ Nutritious Food Management Committee (SAUS)
NFMCS...... Not Fully Mission Capable Supply (SAUS)
NFMD....... National Foundation for Muscular Dystrophy
NFMD....... National Foundation for the March of Dimes (NADA)
NFME........ National Fund for Medical Education (EA)
NFME........ Nordic Federation for Medical Education [*Denmark*] (EAIO)
NFMHA...... National Federation of Milk Hauler Associations (EA)
NFMHJ...... John B. Wheeler Memorial Library, Musgrave Harbour, Newfoundland [*Library symbol*] [*National Library of Canada*] (NLC)
NFMHO...... National Foundation Manufactured Home Owners (EA)
NFMLTA..... National Federation of Modern Language Teachers Associations (EA)
NFMM....... National Fellowship of Methodist Musicians (EA)
NFMN....... National Fallout Monitoring Network
NFMOA...... National Fish Meal and Oil Association (EA)
NFMP........ Mount Pearl Public Library, Newfoundland [*Library symbol*] [*National Library of Canada*] (NLC)
NFMP........ National Federation of Master Painters and Decorators of England and Wales (BI)
NFMP........ Nonferrous Metal Powder
NFMPC...... Non-Ferrous Metals Producers Committee (EA)
NFMPS...... National Federation of Marriage Preparation Services [*Canada*] (EAIO)
NFMR....... National Foundation for Metabolic Research [*Defunct*] (EA)
NFMR....... Non-Linear Ferromagnetic Resonance (PDAA)
NFMR....... Nordisk Forening for Medisinsk Radiologi [*Scandinavian Radiological Society - SRS*] (EAIO)
NFMRAD.... Null Filter Mobile RADAR (PDAA)
NFMS........ National Federation of Music Societies [*British*]
NFMS........ National Fetal Mortality Survey [*Department of Health and Human Services*] (GFGA)
NFMS........ Navy Fleet Material Support (MCD)
NFMS........ Nitrogen Flow Measuring System
NFMS........ Noise Figure Meter System
NFMS........ Nonfat Milk Solids (OA)
NFMSAEG... Naval Fleet Missile System Analysis and Evaluation Group
NFMSAEGA... Naval Fleet Missile System Analysis and Evaluation Group Annex (MCD)
NFMSO...... Navy Fleet Material Support Office (DNAB)
NFMT........ National Federation of Meat Traders [*British*] (BI)
NFMT........ Navy Food Management Team (DNAB)
NFMWC..... National Federation of Master Window Cleaners [*British*] (DBA)
NFMY........ National Festival of Music for Youth (AIE)
NFN.......... National Fathers' Network [*An association*] (PAZ)
NFN.......... National Federation of Non-Profits (NTPA)
NFN.......... Newly Founded Nest [*Ornithology*]
NFN.......... No Form Necessary
NFN.......... No Further Need (MUGU)
NFn.......... Not for Resuscitation [*Medicine*] (WDAA)
NFN.......... Notification [*Telegraphy*] (PCTE)
NFN.......... Nouvelle Front NAZI [*New NAZI Front*] [*French*] (PD)
NFNA........ National Facilities Needs Assessment (ALAC)
NFNA........ National Flight Nurses Association (EA)
NFNA........ Nausori/International [*Fiji*] [*ICAO location identifier*] (ICLI)
NFNA........ Norris Arm Public Library, Newfoundland [*Library symbol*] [*National Library of Canada*] (NLC)
NFNB........ Bureta [*Fiji*] [*ICAO location identifier*] (ICLI)
NFND........ Deumba [*Fiji*] [*ICAO location identifier*] (ICLI)
NFND........ National Foundation for Neuromuscular Diseases [*Later, NGF*] (EA)
NFNG........ Ngau [*Fiji*] [*ICAO location identifier*] (ICLI)
NFNH........ Lauthala Islands [*Fiji*] [*ICAO location identifier*] (ICLI)
NFNID....... National Foundation for Non-Invasive Diagnostics (EA)
NFNK........ Lakemba [*Fiji*] [*ICAO location identifier*] (ICLI)
NFNL........ Lambasa [*Fiji*] [*ICAO location identifier*] (ICLI)
NFNLI....... Labrador Inuit Association, Nain, Newfoundland [*Library symbol*] [*National Library of Canada*] (NLC)
NFNLI....... Labrador Unit Association, Nain, Newfoundland [*Library symbol*] [*National Library of Canada*] (NLC)
NFNM....... Matei [*Fiji*] [*ICAO location identifier*] (ICLI)
NFNMD...... National Foundation for Neuromuscular Diseases, Inc. [*Medicine*] (EDAA)
NFNN........ Vanuabalavu [*Fiji*] [*ICAO location identifier*] (ICLI)
NFNO........ Koro [*Fiji*] [*ICAO location identifier*] (ICLI)
NFNP........ National Food and Nutrition Policy [*Australia*]
NFNP........ Norris Point Public Library, Newfoundland [*Library symbol*] [*National Library of Canada*] (NLC)
NFNR........ Rotuma [*Fiji*] [*ICAO location identifier*] (ICLI)
NFNS........ Neurofibromatosis-Noonan Syndrome [*Medicine*] (DMAA)
NFNS........ Savusavu [*Fiji*] [*ICAO location identifier*] (ICLI)
N FNSHD... Not Finished [*Freight*]
NFNT........ New Font Numbering Table (SAUS)
NFNTU...... National Federation of Furniture Trade Union [*British*]
NFNU........ Bua [*Fiji*] [*ICAO location identifier*] (ICLI)
NFNU........ National Federation of Nurses' Unions [*See also FNSII*]
NFNV........ Vatukoula [*Fiji*] [*ICAO location identifier*] (ICLI)
NFNW........ Wakaya [*Fiji*] [*ICAO location identifier*] (ICLI)
NFNWF...... Navy Fleet Numerical Weather Facility [*Marine science*] (MSC)
NFO.......... National Family Opinion
NFO.......... National Farmers Organization (EA)
NFO.......... Naval Flight Officer
NFO.......... Navy Finance Office
NFO.......... News from the Ukraine [*A publication*]
NFO.......... NFO Worldwide [*NYSE symbol*] (SG)
NFO.......... Non-Fluid Oil (SAUS)
NFO.......... Non Free Out (SAUS)
NFO.......... Normal Fuel Oil (DNAB)
NFO.......... Norvell Family Organization (EA)
NFO.......... Not Fully Open (MCD)
NFOAPA..... National Federation of Old Age Pensioners' Associations [*British*] (BI)
NFO(B)...... Naval Flight Officer (Bombardier) (DNAB)
NFOBA...... National Fats and Oils Brokers Association [*Defunct*] (EA)
NFOC........ Naval Facility Operational Center (DNAB)
NFOC........ Naval Flight Officer Candidate (DNAB)
NFO(C)...... Naval Flight Officer (Controller) (DNAB)
NFOF........ Fiji [*Fiji*] [*ICAO location identifier*] (ICLI)
NFOF........ New Face of Fitness [*Medicine*] [*Exercise program*] (EDAA)
NFOFL....... National Federation of Officers for Life (EA)
NFOHA...... National Federation of Off-Licence Holders Associations of England and Wales (BI)
NFO(I)....... Naval Flight Officer (RADAR Intercept) (DNAB)
NFOIO....... Naval Field Operational Intelligence Office (NVT)
NFOIODET... Naval Field Operational Intelligence Office Detachment (DNAB)
NFOM........ Near Field Optical Microscopy (AAEL)
NFO(N)...... Naval Flight Officer (Navigator) (DNAB)
NFOO........ Naval Forward Observing Officer [*British military*] (DMA)
NFOP........ National Fraternal Order of Police (NTPA)
NFOP........ Old Perlican Public Library, Newfoundland [*Library symbol*] [*National Library of Canada*] (NLC)
NFoPA....... National Forest Products Association [*Washington, DC*]
NFOR........ National Forest Products Association
NFOR........ NFO Research [*NASDAQ symbol*] (TTSB)
NFOR........ NFO Research, Inc. [*NASDAQ symbol*] (SAG)
NFOR........ NFO Worldwide [*NYSE symbol*]
NFO Rs...... NFO Research, Inc. [*Associated Press*] (SAG)
NFOS........ National Federation of Opticianry Schools [*Association*] (EA)
NFOSG...... Naval Field Operations Support Group
NFOU........ Number of Fourier Coefficients (SAUS)
NFOV........ Narrow Field of View
NFP.......... Marietta, GA [*Location identifier*] [*FAA*] (FAAL)
NFP.......... Nandrolone Furylpropionate [*Pharmacology*]
NFP.......... National Family Partnership [*An association*] (EA)
NFP.......... National Federation of Parents for Drug-Free Youth (EA)
NFP.......... National Federation Party [*Fiji*] [*Political party*] (PPW)
NFP.......... National Financial Partners Corp. [*NYSE symbol*]
NFP.......... National Fire Academy Library, Emmitsburg, MD [*OCLC symbol*] (OCLC)
NFP.......... National Fire Plan (RCD)
NFP.......... National Focal Points (DCTA)
NFP.......... Nationalist Front for Progress [*Solomon Islands*] [*Political party*] (FEA)
NFP.......... Natural Family Planning
NFP.......... Neighborhood Facilities Program (OICC)
NFP.......... Network Facilities Package [*Computer science*] (ELAL)
NFP.......... Network for Fitness Professionals [*Australia*]
NFP.......... Neurofilament Protein [*Neurophysiology*]
NFP.......... New Federalist Party (EA)
NFP.......... New Forests Project (EA)
NFP.......... New Frontier Party [*Japan*] [*Political party*]
NFP.......... New Frontier Petroleum Corp. (SAUS)
NFP.......... N-Formylmethionylphenylalanine [*Biochemistry*]
NFP.......... No Family Physician [*Medicine*] (EDAA)
NFP.......... No File Protect [*Computer science*] (VLIE)
NFP.......... Nonflare Proton
NFP.......... Norfolk Petroleum Ltd. [*Vancouver Stock Exchange symbol*]
NFP.......... Normal Failure Period
NFP.......... Nortestosteronefuryl-propionate [*Medicine*] (EDAA)
NFP.......... Northern Frontier Province [*Kenya*]
NFP.......... Not for Profit (ADA)
NFP.......... Not for Publication (ADA)
NFP.......... Nuclear Fire Plan (SAUS)
NFP.......... Nuclear Fuel Processing (SAUS)
NFP.......... Placentia Public Library, Newfoundland [*Library symbol*] [*National Library of Canada*] (NLC)
NFPA........ National Federation of Paralegal Associations (EA)
NFPA........ National Fire Protection Association (EA)
NFPA........ National Flaxseed Processors Association (EA)
NFPA........ National Flexible Packaging Association [*Later, FPA*] (EA)
NFPA........ National Flight Paramedics Association (EA)
NFPA........ National Fluid Power Association (EA)
NFPA........ National Food Processors Association (EA)
NFPA........ National Forest Products Association (EA)
NFPA........ National Foster Parent Association (EA)
NFPA........ Natural Family Planning Association of Connecticut (EA)
NFPA........ New Forest Pony Association and Registry (EA)
NFPA........ Niagara Frontier Port Authority (SAUS)

NFPA .... Pasadena Public Library, Newfoundland [*Library symbol*] [*National Library of Canada*] (NLC)
NFPAC .... National Food Processors Association PAC [*Washington, DC*] (PACS)
NFPB .... National Friends of Public Broadcasting (EA)
NFPC .... National Federation of Plastering Contractors [*British*] (BI)
NFPC .... National Federation of Priests' Councils (EA)
NFPC .... National Forest Planning Committee (WPI)
NFPC .... Niagara Falls Power Co. (SAUS)
NFPC .... Pouch Cove Public Library, Newfoundland [*Library symbol*] [*National Library of Canada*] (NLC)
NFPCA .... National Fire Prevention and Control Administration [*Later, United States Fire Administration*] [*Department of Commerce*]
NFPDC ...... National Federation of Painting and Decorating Contractors [*British*] (DBA)
NFPDHE ..... National Federation of Plumbers and Domestic Heating Engineers [*British*] (BI)
NFPE .... NATO Force Planning Exercise (NATG)
NFPE .... Non-Financial Public Enterprise [*British*]
NFPEC .... Curran Memorial Library, Port Au Port East, Newfoundland [*Library symbol*] [*National Library of Canada*] (NLC)
NFPEDA ..... National Farm and Power Equipment Dealers Association [*Later, NAEDA*] (EA)
NF/PFOG .... National Federation of Parents and Friends of Gays (EA)
NFPHC ...... National Federation of Permanent Holiday Camps Ltd. [*British*] (BI)
NFPI .... National Frozen Pizza Institute (EA)
NFPL .... Point Leamington Public Library, Newfoundland [*Library symbol*] [*National Library of Canada*] (NLC)
NFPLA .... National Foundation for Professional Legal Assistants (EA)
NFPM .... Nuclear Flight Propulsion Module (KSC)
NFPMA ...... National Feeder Pig Marketing Association (EA)
NFPMA ...... National Foundation for Peroneal Muscular Atrophy (EA)
NFPMC ...... National Farm Products Marketing Council [*Canada*]
NFPNS ...... Natural Family Planning National Secretariat [*Australia*]
NFPO .... National Federation of Professional Organizations (EA)
NFPO .... National Federation of Property Owners [*British*] (BI)
NFPOC ...... National Federation of Post Office Clerks [*Later, APWU*]
NFPOD ...... National Foundation for the Prevention of Oral Disease [*Defunct*] (EA)
NFPPE .... Nuclear Force Policy, Planning and Execution (SAUS)
NFPR .... National Fund for Research into Poliomyelitis and Other Crippling Diseases [*British*] (BI)
NFPRHA ..... National Family Planning and Reproductive Health Association (EA)
NFPs .... National Focal Points (SAUS)
NFPS .... Naval Flight Preparatory School
NFPS .... Naval Future Policy Staff [*British*]
NFPS .... Navy Field Purchase Systems (NG)
NFPS .... Nuclear Flight Propulsion System (AAG)
NFPS .... Port Saunders Public Library, Newfoundland [*Library symbol*] [*National Library of Canada*] (NLC)
NFPTC .... National Federation of Postal and Telegraph Clerks [*A union*] [*British*]
NFPW .... National Federation of Press Women (EA)
NFPW .... National Federation of Professional Workers [*British*] (DI)
NFPW .... Port Au Port West School/Public Library, Newfoundland [*Library symbol*] [*National Library of Canada*] (NLC)
NFPZ .... Newton Falls Paper [*Federal Railroad Administration identification code*]
NFQ .... Night Frequency (FAAC)
NFQC .... Queens College, Flushing, NY [*Library symbol*] [*Library of Congress*] (LCLS)
NFR .... National Field Research [*British*]
NFR .... National Film Board Reference Library [*UTLAS symbol*]
NFR .... National Finals Rodeo
NFR .... National Fire Rating (SARE)
NFR .... NATO Frigate Replacement (SAUS)
NFR .... Naturvetenskapliga forskingsradet [*Swedish Natural Science Research Council*]
NFR .... Near-Field Recording [*Computer science*] (PCM)
NFR .... Negative Flux Rate (IEEE)
NFR .... Nephron Filtration Rate [*Physiology*]
NFR .... Net Financing Requirement
NFR .... Net Flux Radiometer [*Instrumentation*]
NFR .... New Frontier Petroleum Corp. [*Vancouver Stock Exchange symbol*]
nfr .... no further record found (SAUS)
NFR .... Nordisk Forening for Rehabilitering [*Nordic Association for Rehabilitation*] (EAIO)
NFR .... Northeast Frontier Railway (SAUS)
N FR .... Northern French [*Language, etc.*] (ROG)
NFR .... Norwegian Research Council (SAUS)
NFR .... Not a Functional Requirement (SAUS)
NFR .... Not for Report (SAUS)
NFR .... Not for Resuscitation [*Hospital patient classification*]
NFR .... Nothing Further to Report (SAUS)
NFR .... Nuclear Fission Reactor
NFR .... Nuclear Fuel Reprocessing (SAUS)
NFR .... Nursing Field Representative [*Red Cross*]
NFR-90 ...... NATO Frigate for the 1990s
NFRA .... National Forest Recreation Association (EA)
NFRA .... Robert's Arm Public Library, Newfoundland [*Library symbol*] [*National Library of Canada*] (BIB)
NFR&T ...... National Forest Roads & Trails [*Act of 1964*] (ALAC)
NFRAP ...... No Further Remedial Action Planned (EEVL)
NFRAP ...... No Further Response Action Planned (BCP)
NFRBMEA ... National Farm and Ranch Business Management Education Association (EA)
NFRC .... National Federation of Roofing Contractors [*British*] (EAIO)
NFRC .... National Fenestration Rating Council (EA)
NFRC .... National Finals Rodeo Committee (EA)
NFRC .... National Forest Research Council (WPI)
NFRC .... National Forest Reservation Commission [*Terminated, 1976; functions transferred to Department of Agriculture*]
NFRC .... Northeast Financial Resources Corp. (SAUS)
NFRC .... Northwest First Regional Consultants (SAUS)
NFRCD ...... National Fund for Research into Crippling Diseases [*British*] (DI)
NFred .... Darwin R. Barker Library Association, Fredonia, NY [*Library symbol*] [*Library of Congress*] (LCLS)
NFredCB .... Chautauqua County Board of Cooperative Educational Services, Fredonia, NY [*Library symbol*] [*Library of Congress*] (LCLS)
NFredU ...... State University of New York, College at Fredonia, Fredonia, NY [*Library symbol*] [*Library of Congress*] (LCLS)
NFree .... Freeport Memorial Library, Freeport, NY [*Library symbol*] [*Library of Congress*] (LCLS)
NFreeAE .... Archer Elementary School, Freeport, NY [*Library symbol*] [*Library of Congress*] (LCLS)
NFreeAtE .... Caroline G. Atkinson Elementary School, Freeport, NY [*Library symbol*] [*Library of Congress*] (LCLS)
NFreeBE .... Bayview Avenue Elementary School, Freeport, NY [*Library symbol*] [*Library of Congress*] (LCLS)
NFreeCE .... Columbus Elementary School, Freeport, NY [*Library symbol*] [*Library of Congress*] (LCLS)
NFreeDH .... Doctors Hospital, Freeport, NY [*Library symbol*] [*Library of Congress*] (LCLS)
NFreeDJ .... Dodd Junior High School, Freeport, NY [*Library symbol*] [*Library of Congress*] (LCLS)
NFreeEC .... Early Childhood Center, Freeport, NY [*Library symbol*] [*Library of Congress*] (LCLS)
NFreeGE .... Leo F. Giblyn Elementary School, Freeport, NY [*Library symbol*] [*Library of Congress*] (LCLS)
NFreeH ...... Freeport Hospital, Freeport, NY [*Library symbol*] [*Library of Congress*] (LCLS)
NFreeHS .... Freeport High School, Freeport, NY [*Library symbol*] [*Library of Congress*] (LCLS)
NFRH .... Rocky Harbour Public School, Newfoundland [*Library symbol*] [*National Library of Canada*] (NLC)
NFRM .... National Foundation for Research in Medicine (EA)
NFRMC ...... National Foundation for Rural Medical Care [*Defunct*] (EA)
NFRN .... National Federation of Retail Newsagents [*British*]
NFRP .... Marie S. Penney Memorial Library, Ramea, Newfoundland [*Library symbol*] [*National Library of Canada*] (NLC)
NFRRC ...... Nuclear Fuel Recovery and Receiving Center (NRCH)
NFRS .... National Fancy Rat Society [*British*] (DBA)
NFRW .... National Federation of Republican Women (EA)
NFS .... Fayetteville State University, Fayetteville, NC [*OCLC symbol*] (OCLC)
NFs .... Franklin Square Public Library, Franklin Square, NY [*Library symbol*] [*Library of Congress*] (LCLS)
NFS .... National Aeronautics and Space Administration FAR Supplement [*A publication*] (AAGC)
NFS .... National Facility Survey [*Emergency Management*] (EMA)
NFS .... National Federation of Settlements [*Later, UNCA*]
NFS .... National Fertility Study
NFS .... National Field Service Corp. [*Suffern, NY*] [*Telecommunications*] (TSSD)
NFS .... National Film Society [*Defunct*] (EA)
NFS .... National Fire Service [*British*]
NFS .... National Flying Service [*British*]
NFS .... National Food Situation [*Series*] [*A publication*]
NFS .... National Food Survey [*British*]
NFS .... National Forest Service (COE)
NFS .... National Forest System (GNE)
NFS .... National Fuchsia Society (EA)
NFS .... Nationwide Finl Svcs'A' [*NYSE symbol*] (SG)
NFS .... Naval Flying Station [*British*]
NFS .... Navy Facilities System
NFS .... Navy Field Service
NFS .... Network Facilities Services (SAUS)
NFS .... Network File System
NFS .... Neutron Flux Spectra [*Nuclear energy*]
NFS .... Neutron Flux Spectrum (SAUS)
NFS .... New Fighter Squadron (SAUS)
NFS .... New Financial Status (SAUS)
NFS .... Niagara Falls, Ontario, Canada [*Amtrak rail station code*]
NFS .... Niagara Frontier Services, Inc. (EFIS)
NFS .... Nitrofuraldehyde Semicarbazone [*Germicide*]
NFS .... Nitrogen Flow System
NFS .... No Fracture Seen [*Medicine*] (DMAA)
NFS .... Noise Frequency Spectrum
NFS .... Nonfriendly Submarines (MCD)
NFS .... Non Functional Status (SAUS)
NFS .... Nordiska Forbundet for Statskunskap [*Nordic Political Science Association - NPSA*] [*Norway*] (EAIO)
NFS .... Not for Sale
NFS .... Not Fully Successful (SAUS)
NFS .... Not on Flying Status
NFS .... Nozzle Flow Sensor (MCD)
NFS .... Nuclear Facility Safety (SAUS)
NFS .... Nuclear Fuel Services, Erwin, Tennessee (SAUS)
NFS .... Nuclear Fuel Services Fuel Fabrication Plant
NFS .... Nuclear Fuel Services Plant (NRCH)
NFS .... Number Field Sieve (SAUS)
NFS .... NWFS Capital Financing Trust [*NYSE symbol*] (SAG)
NFSA .... National Federation of Sea Anglers [*British*]
NFSA .... National Fertilizer Solutions Association (EA)

NFSA .... National Field Selling Association (NTPA)
NFSA .... National Fire Sprinkler Association (EA)
NFSA .... National Food Service Association (EA)
NFSA .... National Food Standards Agreement [*Australia*]
NFSA .... Navy Field Safety Association (EA)
NFSA .... New Fuel Storage Area (NRCH)
NFSA .... News from Saudi Arabia [*A publication*] (BJA)
NFSA .... Provincial Archives of Newfoundland and Labrador, St. John's, Newfoundland [*Library symbol*] [*National Library of Canada*] (NLC)
NFSAG ...... Research Station, Agriculture Canada [*Station de Recherches, Agriculture Canada*] St. John's, Newfoundland [*Library symbol*] [*National Library of Canada*] (NLC)
NFSAIC...... Charles Curtis Memorial Hospital, International Grenfell Association, St. Anthony, Newfoundland [*Library symbol*] [*National Library of Canada*] (NLC)
NFSAIS...... National Federation of Science Abstracting and Indexing Services [*Later, NFAIS*] (EA)
NFSAL....... St. Alban's Public Library, Newfoundland [*Library symbol*] [*National Library of Canada*] (NLC)
NFSAN ...... St. Anthony Public Library, Newfoundland [*Library symbol*] [*National Library of Canada*] (NLC)
NFS & NC... National Federation of Settlements and Neighborhood Centers [*Later, UNCA*] (EA)
NFSANS..... Naskapi School/Public Library, Sops Arm, Newfoundland [*Library symbol*] [*National Library of Canada*] (NLC)
NFSB .... Spaniards Bay Public Library, Newfoundland [*Library symbol*] [*National Library of Canada*] (NLC)
NFSBC....... Boys' Club, St. John's, Newfoundland [*Library symbol*] [*National Library of Canada*] (NLC)
NFSBCS..... Cape Shore Public Library, St. Brides, Newfoundland [*Library symbol*] [*National Library of Canada*] (NLC)
NFSBS....... Bay St. George Community College, Stephenville, Newfoundland [*Library symbol*] [*National Library of Canada*] (NLC)
NFSC .... National Federation of Stamp Clubs (EA)
NFSC .... Nuclear Fuel Services Corporation (ABAC)
NFSC .... Seal Cove Public Library, Newfoundland [*Library symbol*] [*National Library of Canada*] (NLC)
NFSCA....... Children's and Adults' Library, St. John's, Newfoundland [*Library symbol*] [*National Library of Canada*] (NLC)
NFSCAEE ... Environment Division, Newfoundland Department of Consumer Affairs and Environment, St. John's, Newfoundland [*Library symbol*] [*National Library of Canada*] (NLC)
NFSCCU..... National Federation of Savings and Cooperative Credit Unions [*British*] (DBA)
NFSCF....... Newfoundland and Labrador Institute of Fisheries and Marine Technology (Marine Institute), St. John's, New Foundland [*Library symbol*] [*National Library of Canada*] (NLC)
NFsCH....... H. Frank Carey High School, Franklin Square, NY [*Library symbol*] [*Library of Congress*] (LCLS)
NFSCJ....... Dr. Charles A. Janeway Child Health Centre, St. John's, Newfoundland [*Library symbol*] [*National Library of Canada*] (NLC)
NFSCR ...... Children's Rehabilitation Centre, St. John's, Newfoundland [*Library symbol*] [*National Library of Canada*] (NLC)
NFSCSW .... National Federation of Societies for Clinical Social Work (EA)
NFSCT....... Cabot Institute of Applied Arts and Technology, St. John's, Newfoundland [*Library symbol*] [*National Library of Canada*] (NLC)
NFSCTM .... Topsail Campus Resource Centre, Cabot Institute of Applied Arts and Technology, St. John's, Newfoundland [*Library symbol*] [*National Library of Canada*] (NLC)
NFSD .... National Aeronautics and Space Administration FAR Supplement Directive (AAGC)
NFSD .... National Federation of Spiritual Directors (EA)
NFSD .... National Food Safety Database (SAUS)
NFSD .... National Fraternal Society of the Deaf [*Mount Prospect, IL*] (EA)
NFSD .... Nonfused (MSA)
NFSE .... National Federation for the Self-Employed and Small Businesses [*British*] (DBA)
NFSE .... National Federation of Sales Executives [*Later, Sales and Marketing Executives International*]
NFSE .... National Federation of Self Employed [*British*]
NFSEC....... Newfoundland Forest Research Centre, Environment Canada [*Centre de RecherchesForestieres de Terre-Neuve, Environnement Canada*] St. John's, Newfoundland [*Library symbol*] [*National Library of Canada*] (NLC)
NFSEEP ..... National Foundation for the Study of Equal Employment [*Washington, DC*] (EA)
NFSF .... National Freedom Shrine Foundation (EA)
NFSF .... NFS Financial Corp. [*NASDAQ symbol*] (NQ)
NFSF .... North-West Atlantic Fisheries Centre, Fisheries and Oceans Canada [*Centre de Pecheries de l'Atlantique du Nord-Ouest, Peches et Oceans Canada*] St. John's,Newfoundland [*Library symbol*] [*National Library of Canada*] (NLC)
NFSFJG ..... St. Judes Central High School Public Library/Bay St. George South Public LibraryLibrary, St. Fintans, Newfoundland [*Library symbol*] [*National Library of Canada*] (NLC)
NFSFS....... Newfoundland Forest Service, St. John's, Newfoundland [*Library symbol*] [*National Library of Canada*] (NLC)
NFSG .... National Federation of Students of German (EA)
NFSG .... Newfoundland Public Library Services, St. Johns, Newfoundland (SAUS)
NFSG .... Provinical Reference and Resource Library, Newfoundland Public Library Services,St. John's, New Foundland [*Library symbol*] [*National Library of Canada*] (NLC)
NFSGE....... St. Georges Public Library, Newfoundland [*Library symbol*] [*National Library of Canada*] (NLC)
NFSGGH .... C. A Pippy Jr. Medical Library, Grace General Hospital, St. John's, Newfoundland [*Library symbol*] [*National Library of Canada*] (NLC)
NFSGGHN... School of Nursing, Grace General Hospital, St. John's, Newfoundland [*Library symbol*] [*National Library of Canada*] (NLC)
NFSGH ...... General Hospital Corp., St. John's, Newfoundland [*Library symbol*] [*National Library of Canada*] (NLC)
NFSGHN .... Nursing Education, General Hospital Corp., St. John's, Newfoundland [*Library symbol*] [*National Library of Canada*] (NLC)
NFSGO ...... Gosling Library, St. John's, Newfoundland [*Library symbol*] [*National Library of Canada*] (NLC)
NFSH .... National Federation of Spiritual Healers (EA)
NFSH .... National Federation of State High School Associations
NFSH .... Southern Harbour Public Library, Newfoundland [*Library symbol*] [*National Library of Canada*] (NLC)
NFSHC ...... National Federation of State Humanities Councils (EA)
NFSHE....... Health Education Division, Newfoundland Department of Health, St. John's, Newfoundland [*Library symbol*] [*National Library of Canada*] (NLC)
NFSHPH..... Public Health Nursing Division, Newfoundland Department of Health, St. John's, Newfoundland [*Library symbol*] [*National Library of Canada*] (NLC)
NFSHSA..... National Federation of State High School Associations (EA)
NFSHSAA... National Federation of State High School Athletic Associations [*Later, NFSHSA*] (EA)
NFSI .... National Floor Safety Institute [*Association*] (EA)
NFSICA...... Institute of Chartered Accountants of Newfoundland, St. John's, Newfoundland [*Library symbol*] [*National Library of Canada*] (NLC)
NFSID .... National Foundation for Sudden Infant Death [*Medicine*] (EDAA)
NFsJE .... John Street Elementary School, Franklin Square, NY [*Library symbol*] [*Library of Congress*] (LCLS)
NFSJL .... Law Library, Newfoundland Department of Justice, St. John's, Newfoundland [*Library symbol*] [*National Library of Canada*] (NLC)
NFSK .... Kindale Public Library, Stephenville, Newfoundland [*Library symbol*] [*National Library of Canada*] (NLC)
NFSK .... Narrowband Frequency Shift Keying (MCD)
NFSL .... Legislative Library, St. John's, Newfoundland [*Library symbol*] [*National Library of Canada*] (NLC)
NFSL .... National Front for the Salvation of Libya [*Political party*] (PSAP)
NFSL .... Newnan Savings Bank [*NASDAQ symbol*] (NQ)
NFSL .... Newnan Svgs Bank FSB [*NASDAQ symbol*] (TTSB)
NFSL .... No Fighter Suitably Located (SAA)
NFSL .... Nucleus Fleet Sealift
NFSLA....... St. Lawrence Public Library, Newfoundland [*Library symbol*] [*National Library of Canada*] (NLC)
NFSLG....... St. Lunaire-Griquet Public Library, St. Lunaire, Newfoundland [*Library symbol*] [*National Library of Canada*] (NLC)
NFSLP....... Central Records Library, Newfoundland Light and Power Co. Ltd., St. John's, Newfoundland [*Library symbol*] [*National Library of Canada*] (NLC)
NFSLS....... Law Society of Newfoundland, St. John's, Newfoundland [*Library symbol*] [*National Library of Canada*] (NLC)
NFSM........ Memorial University, St. John's, Newfoundland [*Library symbol*] [*National Library of Canada*] (NLC)
NFSM........ National Fraternity of Student Musicians (EA)
NFSM........ Queen Elizabeth II Library, Memorial University of Newfoundland, St. John's, Newfoundland [*Library symbol*] [*National Library of Canada*] (NLC)
NFSMA...... National Fruit and Syrup Manufacturers Association (EA)
NFSMA...... Provincial Planning Office, Newfoundland Department of Municipal Affairs, St. John's, Newfoundland [*Library symbol*] [*National Library of Canada*] (NLC)
NFSME ...... Newfoundland Department of Mines and Energy, St. John's, Newfoundland [*Library symbol*] [*National Library of Canada*] (NLC)
NFSMEC .... Curriculum Materials Centre, Education Library, Memorial University, St. John's,Newfoundland [*Library symbol*] [*National Library of Canada*] (NLC)
NFSMED .... Education Library, Memorial University, St. John's, Newfoundland [*Library symbol*] [*National Library of Canada*] (NLC)
NFSMEM.... Publications and Information Section, Mineral Development Division Library, Newfoundland Department of Mines and Energy, St. John's, Newfoundland [*Library symbol*] [*National Library of Canada*] (NLC)
NFSMG...... Department of Geography, Memorial University, St. John's, Newfoundland [*Library symbol*] [*National Library of Canada*] (NLC)
NFSMLS .... Library Studies Program, Memorial University of Newfoundland, St. John's, Newfoundland [*Library symbol*] [*National Library of Canada*] (BIB)
NFSMM ..... Health Sciences Library, Memorial University, St. John's, Newfoundland [*Library symbol*] [*National Library of Canada*] (NLC)
NFSMMH ... Maritime History Archive, Memorial University, St. John's, Newfoundland [*Library symbol*] [*National Library of Canada*] (BIB)
NFSMO...... Ocean Engineering Centre, Memorial University, St. John's, Newfoundland [*Library symbol*] [*National Library of Canada*] (NLC)
NFSN........ NATO French-Speaking Nations
NFsNH....... North Junior-Senior High School, Franklin Square, NY [*Library symbol*] [*Library of Congress*] (LCLS)
NFSNI .... National Research Council IRAP [*Industrial Research Assistance Program*], St. John's, Newfoundland [*Library symbol*] [*National Library of Canada*] (NLC)
NFSNL....... Newfoundland and Labrador Hydro, St. John's, Newfoundland [*Library symbol*] [*National Library of Canada*] (NLC)
NFSNLD..... Newfoundland and Labrador Development Corp., St. John's, Newfoundland [*Library symbol*] [*National Library of Canada*] (NLC)
NFSNO ..... National Federation for Specialty Nursing Organizations (EA)
NFSO .... Navy Fuel Supply Office

NFSP .... National Federation of Sub-Postmasters [*British*] (DBA)
NFSP .... Netware File Service Protocol (SAUS)
NFSP .... Non-Flight Switch Panel
NFSP .... Nuclear Fuel Services Plant (SAUS)
NFSP .... Springdale Public Library, Newfoundland [*Library symbol*] [*National Library of Canada*] (NLC)
NFsPE .... Polk Street Elementary School, Franklin Square, NY [*Library symbol*] [*Library of Congress*] (LCLS)
NFSPR ...... Provincial Reference Library, St. John's, Newfoundland [*Library symbol*] [*National Library of Canada*] (NLC)
NFSPS....... National Federation of State Poetry Societies (EA)
NFSQ .... Queen's College, St. John's, Newfoundland [*Library symbol*] [*National Library of Canada*] (NLC)
NFSR .... National Finals Steer Roping
NFSRA ...... National Fitness Southern Recreation Association [*Australia*]
NFSRD ...... Newfoundland Department of Rural Development, St. John's, Newfoundland [*Library symbol*] [*National Library of Canada*] (NLC)
NFSREX..... Canada Department of Regional Industrial Expansion [*Ministere de l'Expansion Industrielle Regionale*] St. John's, Newfoundland [*Library symbol*] [*National Library of Canada*] (NLC)
NFSS .... National Fallout Shelter Survey [*Civil Defense*]
NFSS .... National Federation of Sailing Schools [*British*]
NFSS .... National Finch and Softbill Society (EA)
NFSS .... New Font Selection Scheme (SAUS)
NFSS .... Nucleus Fleet Scientific Support
NFSSC....... St. Clare's Mercy Hospital, St. John's, Newfoundland [*Library symbol*] [*National Library of Canada*] (NLC)
NFSSCN..... School of Nursing, St. Clare's Mercy Hospital, St. John's, Newfoundland [*Library symbol*] [*National Library of Canada*] (NLC)
NFSSO ...... Navy Food Service System Office (ACAE)
NFSSW...... Newfoundland Status of Women Council, St. John's, Newfoundland [*Library symbol*] [*National Library of Canada*] (NLC)
NFST .... Newfoundland Department of Tourism, St. John's, Newfoundland [*Library symbol*] [*National Library of Canada*] (NLC)
NFST .... Nuclear Effects Support Team (SAUS)
NFSTA....... Newfoundland Teachers' Association, St. John's, Newfoundland [*Library symbol*] [*National Library of Canada*] (NLC)
NFSTC....... National Food Safety and Toxicology Center [*Michigan State University*] (RCD)
NFSTC....... Stephenville Crossing Public Library, Newfoundland [*Library symbol*] [*National Library of Canada*] (NLC)
NFSTCG ..... Canadian Coast Guard [*Garde Cotiere Canadienne*] St. John's, Newfoundland [*Library symbol*] [*Obsolete*] [*National Library of Canada*] (NLC)
NFSTPG ..... National Foundation for the Study and Treatment of Pathological Gambling [*Defunct*] (EA)
NFSTR....... Medical Library, Sir Thomas Roddick Hospital, Stephenville, Newfoundland [*Library symbol*] [*National Library of Canada*] (NLC)
NFSU .... Nonflying Support Unit
NFSU .... Summerford Public Library, Newfoundland [*Library symbol*] [*National Library of Canada*] (NLC)
NFSU .... Suva/Nausori [*Fiji*] [*ICAO location identifier*] (ICLI)
NFSVP....... National Forest Service Volunteers Program (EA)
NFsWE ...... Washington Street Elementary School, Franklin Square, NY [*Library symbol*] [*Library of Congress*] (LCLS)
NFSWH...... Health Services, Waterford Hospital, St. John's, Newfoundland [*Library symbol*] [*National Library of Canada*] (NLC)
NFSWMM... National Federation of Scale and Weighing Machine Manufacturers [*British*] (DBA)
NFsWS ...... Willow Road School, Franklin Square, NY [*Library symbol*] [*Library of Congress*] (LCLS)
NFSX .... Nuclear Fuel Services [*Private rail car owner code*]
NFT .... National Film and Television Sound Archives [*National Film Board of Canada*] [*UTLAS symbol*]
NFT .... National Film Theatre [*British*]
NFT .... National Foundation for Transplants [*Established in 1983 as the Liver Organ Transplant Fund*] (NRGU)
NFT .... Navigation Flight Test [*Aviation*] (DA)
NFT .... Navy Flight Test (MCD)
NFT .... Nefteyugansk Aviation Division [*Russian Federation*] [*ICAO designator*] (FAAC)
NFT .... Networks File Transfer
NFT .... Neurofibrillary Tangle [*Brain anatomy*]
NFT .... Newfoundland Telephone Co. Ltd. [*Toronto Stock Exchange symbol*]
NFT .... Newfoundland Time (SAUS)
NFT .... New Frontiers in Theology [*A publication*] (BJA)
NFT .... N-Formimidoylthienamycin [*Biochemistry*]
NFT .... No Filing Time [*Aviation*]
NFT .... No Fixed Time (SAUS)
NFT .... No Forwarding Time (SAUS)
NFT .... No Further Treatment [*Medicine*] (MELL)
NFT .... Non-Firing Test [*Military*]
NFT .... Non-Functional Test (SAA)
NFT .... Normal Fuel-Oil Tank (MSA)
NFT .... Northern Foods plc (EFIS)
NFT .... Nutrient Film Technique
nft3 .... normal cubic feet (SAUS)
NFTA......... National Federation of Taxicab Associations [*British*] (DBA)
NFTA......... National Feminist Therapist Association (EA)
NFTA......... National Fillings Trades Association [*British*] (DBA)
NFTA......... National Freight Transportation Association [*Rocky River, OH*] (EA)
NFTA......... New Feminist Talent Associates (EA)
NFTA......... Niagara Falls Transit Authority [*Federal Railroad Administration identification code*]
NFTA......... Niagara Frontier Transportation Authority (SAUS)
NFTA......... Night-Fire [*Rifle*] Training Aid [*Army*] (INF)
NFTA......... Nitrogen Fixing Tree Association [*University of Hawaii*] [*Research center*] (RCD)
NFTB .... National Federation of Temple Brotherhoods (EA)
NFTB .... Naval Fleet Training Base
NFTB .... Niagara Frontier Tariff Bureau
NFTB .... Nuclear Flight Test Base
NFTC .... National Foreign Trade Council [*New York, NY*] (EA)
NFTC .... National Furniture Traffic Conference (EA)
NFTD .... Normal, Full Term Delivery [*Obstetrics*]
NFTE......... Eua [*Tonga*] [*ICAO location identifier*] (ICLI)
NFTE......... National Foundation for Teaching Entrepreneurship [*Association*] (EA)
NFTF......... Night Fighting Training Facility [*Army*] (INF)
NFTF......... Tongatapu/Fua'Amotu International [*Tonga*] [*ICAO location identifier*] (ICLI)
NFTI .... Naval Firefighters Thermal Imager (ACAE)
NFTI .... NoFire Technologies [*OTCBB symbol*]
NFTL......... Ha'Apai Lifuka [*Tonga*] [*ICAO location identifier*] (ICLI)
NFTMS ...... National Federation of Terrazzo-Mosaic Specialists [*British*] (BI)
NFTN .... Nuku'Alofa [*Tonga*] [*ICAO location identifier*] (ICLI)
NFTO .... Niuafo'Ou [*Tonga*] [*ICAO location identifier*] (ICLI)
NFTO .... Torbay Public Library, Newfoundland [*Library symbol*] [*National Library of Canada*] (NLC)
NFTP .... Niuatoputapu [*Tonga*] [*ICAO location identifier*] (ICLI)
NFTR .... Trepassey Public Library, Newfoundland [*Library symbol*] [*National Library of Canada*] (NLC)
NFTS .... National Federation of Temple Sisterhoods (EA)
NFTS .... National Film and Television School [*British*]
NFTS .... Naval Fixed Telecommunications System (SAUS)
NFTS .... Naval Flight Training School
NFTS .... Women of Reform Judaism, the Federation of Temple Sisterhoods (EA)
NFTSA....... National Film, Television, and Sound Archives [*Canada*]
NFTSD....... Normal Full-Term Spontaneous Delivery [*Obstetrics*] (DAVI)
NFtT .... Fort Ticonderoga Association Museum and Library, Fort Ticonderoga, NY [*Library symbol*] [*Library of Congress*] (LCLS)
NFTT......... Nonorganic Failure to Thrive [*Neonatology*] [*Pediatrics*] (DAVI)
NFT UK...... Norsk Forsvarsteknologi A/S (SAUS)
NFTV .... Vava'u [*Tonga*] [*ICAO location identifier*] (ICLI)
NFTW........ National Federation of Telephone Workers [*Later, CWA*]
NFTW........ National Federation of Tobacco Workers [*A union*] [*British*]
NFTW........ Twillingate Public Library, Newfoundland [*Library symbol*] [*National Library of Canada*] (NLC)
NFTWO...... North Fort Worth, TX [*American Association of Railroads railroad junction routing code*]
NFTY .... North American Federation of Temple Youth (EA)
NFTZ......... Non Free Trade Zone (DS)
NFU.......... National Farmers' Union [*British*]
NFU.......... National Film Unit (BARN)
NFU.......... National Formulary Unit(s) [*Medicine*] (EDAA)
NFU.......... Niho Fukushi University [*UTLAS symbol*]
NFU.......... Non First Use (SAUS)
NFU.......... Not for Us [*Communications*]
NFUCWC.... National Foundation for Unemployment Compensation and Workers Compensation (EA)
N-Fuel....... Nuclear Fuel (SAUS)
NFUF .... Codroy Valley Public Library, Upper Ferry, Newfoundland [*Library symbol*] [*National Library of Canada*] (NLC)
NFUI .... Upper Island Cove Public Library, Newfoundland [*Library symbol*] [*National Library of Canada*] (NLC)
NFV .... National Field Volunteer [*Red Cross*]
NFV .... Naval Forces Vietnam (VNW)
NFV .... No Further Visits [*Medicine*]
NFV .... Nordischer Friseurverband [*Nordic Association of Hairdressers*] [*Sweden*] (EAIO)
NFV .... Point Barrow, AK [*Location identifier*] [*FAA*] (FAAL)
NFV .... Victoria Public Library, Newfoundland [*Library symbol*] [*National Library of Canada*] (NLC)
NFVA .... Net Free Vent Area [*Roofing*]
NFVC .... National Frozen Vegetable Council [*Later, FVC*] (EA)
NFVLS....... National Federation of Voluntary Literacy Schemes [*British*]
NFVOA ...... Northern Fishing Vessel Owners Association [*Defunct*] (EA)
NFVP .... National Film and Video Productions [*Australia*]
NFVT .... National Federation of Vehicle Trades [*British*] (BI)
NFW .... Lakehurst, NJ [*Location identifier*] [*FAA*] (FAAL)
NFW .... National Fishing Week (ALAC)
NFW .... New Field Wildcat (SAUS)
NFW .... No Feasible Way [*Internet lingo*] (NETL)
NFW .... Non-Fuel-Wasting (MCD)
NFW .... Nursed Fairly Well [*Medicine*] (DMAA)
NFWA........ National Farm Workers of America
NFWA........ National Furniture Warehousemen's Association [*Later, NMSA*] (EA)
NFWA........ Neuromuscular Foundation of Western Australia
NFWA........ Wabush Public Library, Newfoundland [*Library symbol*] [*National Library of Canada*] (NLC)
NFWBO...... National Foundation for Women Business Owners
NFWC .... National Fire Waste Council
NFWD .... New Field Wildcat Drilling [*Petroleum technology*]
NFWE........ Edgar L. M. Roberts Memorial Library, Woodypoint, Newfoundland [*Library symbol*] [*National Library of Canada*] (NLC)
NFWE........ National Federation of Woman's Exchanges (EA)
NFWF........ National Fish and Wildlife Foundation (EPA)
NFWG .... National Federation of Wholesale Grocers and Provision Merchants [*British*] (BI)
NFWH .... National Foundation for Wholistic Medicine [*Defunct*] (EA)

NFWH .... Whitbourne Public Library, Newfoundland [*Library symbol*] [*National Library of Canada*] (NLC)
NFWHF ...... National Fresh Water Fishing Hall of Fame
NFWI .... National Federation of Women's Institutes [*British*]
NFWI .... Windsor Memorial Public Library, Newfoundland [*Library symbol*] [*National Library of Canada*] (NLC)
NFWIN .... Winterton Public Library, Newfoundland [*Library symbol*] [*National Library of Canada*] (NLC)
NFWL......... National Foundation for Women Legislators [*Association*] (EA)
NFWM........ National Farm Worker Ministry (EA)
NFWPM ..... National Federation of Wholesalers and Poultry Merchants [*British*] (DBA)
NFWS .... Navy Fighter Weapons School (DNAB)
NFWT......... National Foundation of Wheelchair Tennis (EA)
NFWV .... Wesleyville Public Library, Newfoundland [*Library symbol*] [*National Library of Canada*] (NLC)
NFWW........ National Federation of Women Workers [*British*]
NFWY .... Wesleyville Public Library, Newfoundland (SAUS)
NFX........... Newfield Exploration [*NYSE symbol*] (TTSB)
NFX........... Newfield Exploration Co. [*NYSE symbol*] (SPSG)
NFX........... Nuclear Factor X (DMAA)
NFXD .... National Fax Directory [*A publication*]
NFXF .... National Fragile X Foundation (EA)
NFY .... Notify [*Telecommunications*] (TEL)
NFYD .... Notified [*Telecommunications*] (TEL)
NFYFC........ National Federation of Young Farmers' Clubs (EAIO)
NFYG .... Notifying (SAUS)
NFZ .... National Front of Zimbabwe (PPW)
NFZ .... (Nitro)furfuralsemicarbazone [*Organic chemistry*]
NFZ .... No Fire Zone [*Military*]
NFZ .... Nuclear Free Zone (AFM)
NFZ .... Nuclear Weapons Free Zone (SAUS)
NFZR .... Nuclear Free Zone Registry [*Defunct*] (EA)
NG .... Gill Aviation Ltd. (SAUS)
NG .... Green Hills Aviation [*ICAO designator*] (AD)
ng .... Nanogram [*One billionth of a gram*]
NG .... Narrow Gage (NAKS)
NG .... Narrow Gauge
N/G .... Nasogastric [*Medicine*] (IDYL)
NG .... Nasogastric [*Medicine*]
NG .... National Gallery [*London*]
NG .... National Gathering [*Jordan*] [*A publication*] (BJA)
NG .... National Grange (EA)
NG .... National Grid [*British Ordnance Survey maps*]
NG .... National Guard [*or Guardsman*]
NG .... Natural Gas
NG .... Natural Gas Shutoff [*NFPA pre-fire planning symbol*] (NFPA)
NG .... Natural, Grazed [*Agriculture*]
NG .... Naval Gunfire (SAA)
NG .... Navy General [*MCD files*]
NG .... NAZI Government (BJA)
NG .... Negative Glow (IDOE)
NG .... Negotiate [*Telegraphy*] (PCTE)
NG .... Neopentyl Glycol [*Organic chemistry*]
NG .... Nephridial Gland
NG .... New Genus
NG .... New Gnostics Special Interest Group (EA)
NG .... New Granada
NG .... New Group
NG .... New Growth [*Medicine*] (EDAA)
NG .... New Guinea
NG .... Newly Generated
NG .... Newsgroup (SAUS)
NG .... Next Generation (SAUS)
Ng............. Ngoko [*Linguistics*] (IEL)
ng .... Niger [*MARC country of publication code*] [*Library of Congress*] (LCCP)
NG .... Nigeria [*ANSI two-letter standard code*] (CNC)
NG .... Nitrogen Gauge (MCD)
NG .... Nitroglycerin [*Also, GTN, NTG*] [*Explosive, vasodilator*]
N-G .... Nitro-Glycerine (SAUS)
NG .... Nitroguanidine [*Organic chemistry*]
NG .... Noble Gases [*Nuclear energy*] (NRCH)
NG .... Noble Grand
NG .... Noble Guard [*Freemasonry*] (ROG)
NG .... Nodose Ganglion [*Medicine*] (DB)
NG .... Nodular Goiter [*Medicine*] (MELL)
NG .... No Go [*i.e., an unacceptable arrangement*]
NG .... No Good [*Similar to IC - Inspected and Condemned*]
NG .... No Growth [*Medicine*] (EDAA)
NG .... No Gum [*Philately*]
NG .... Non-Government (OTD)
NG .... Nongraduate
NG .... Non-Groupable [*Medicine*] (EDAA)
NG .... Normal Graduate
NG .... Normoglycemia [*Medicine*] (MELL)
NG .... Normotensive Group [*Cardiology*]
NG .... Norwegian
NG .... Norwegium [*Chemistry*] (ROG)
NG .... Nose Gear [*Aviation*] (MCD)
NG .... Nose Guard (SAUS)
NG .... Not Given (ADA)
NG .... Not Good
NG .... Not Greater (SAUS)
NG .... Not Ground (SAUS)
NG .... Not Guilty
NG .... Nottingham [*Postcode*] (ODBW)
NG .... No Window Glazing
NG .... Nuclear Galaxy (BARN)
NG .... Nut Grounds (SAUS)
NG .... Royal North Gloucestershire Militia [*British military*] (DMA)
NGA........... Associated Natural Gas Corp. (SAUS)
NGA........... National Gallery of Art [*Washington, DC*]
NGA........... National Gallery of Art, Washington, DC [*OCLC symbol*] (OCLC)
NGA........... National Gallery of Australia
NGA........... National Gallery of Canada Library [*UTLAS symbol*]
NGA........... National Gardening Association (EA)
NGA........... National Glass Association (EA)
NGA........... National Gliding Association [*Later, SSA*]
NGA........... National Governors' Association (EA)
NGA........... National Grant Agency
NGA........... National Graphical Association [*British printers' union*]
NGA........... National Greyhound Association (EA)
NGA........... National Grocers Association (EA)
NGA........... National Guardianship Association (NTPA)
NGA........... NATO Guidelines Area (NATG)
NGA........... Natural Gas Association (EPA)
NGA........... Naval Gunfire Assistant
NGA........... Needlework Guild of America [*Later, NGAI*] (EA)
NGA........... Never Go Away (SAUS)
NGA........... New Generation Alliance (SAUS)
NGA........... Next Generation Accounting (TIMI)
NGA........... Nigeria [*ANSI three-letter standard code*] (CNC)
Nga .... Nigeria (MILB)
NGA........... Nutrient Gelatin Agar [*Microbiology*]
NGA........... WAAC (Nigeria) Ltd. Nigeria Airways [*ICAO designator*] (FAAC)
NGA........... Young [*Australia*] [*Airport symbol*] (OAG)
NGAA .... National Girls Athletic Association [*Defunct*]
NGAA .... Natural Gasoline Association of America [*Later, GPA*]
NGAB .... Abaiang [*Kiribati*] [*ICAO location identifier*] (ICLI)
NGaC .... Capuchin Theological Seminary, Garrison, NY [*Library symbol*] [*Library of Congress*] (LCLS)
NGAC .... National Greenhouse Advisory Committee [*Australia*]
NGAC .... National Guard Air Corps (WDAA)
NGAD .... Nobody Gives a Damn
NGAD .... Notice Given Arrival Date (MARI)
NGADA .... National Graphic Arts Dealers Association (EA)
NGAI .... NGA [*Needlework Guild of America*], Inc. (EA)
NGAL .... Chestatee Regional Library [*Library network*]
NGAM .... Noble Gas Activity Monitor (IEEE)
NG & A....... National Gift and Art Association (EA)
NGAO......... New Governmental Advisory Organizations [*A publication*]
NGAPI .... Nuveen Georgia Premium Income Municipal Fund [*Associated Press*] (SAG)
NGARP .... National Guard and Army Reserve Policy
NGAS .... Naval Gunfire Air Spotting
NGAS .... Needs-Based Goal Attainment Scale (EDAC)
NGAS .... North General Area Services (SAUS)
NGASR .... Navy, Army & Air Staff Requirement (SAUS)
NGAST .... Navy, Army & Air Staff Target (SAUS)
NGAT .... National Guard Association of Texas (EARSL)
NGATE........ Northgate, ND [*American Association of Railroads railroad junction routing code*]
NGATM .... New Generation Air Traffic Manager (GAVI)
NGAUS .... National Guard Association of the United States (EA)
NGAYA........ National Gay Alliance for Young Adults (EA)
NGAZ .... NATO Gazetteer (MCD)
NGB........... Army National Guard Bureau (BCP)
NGB........... National Garden Bureau (EA)
NGB........... National Governing Body [*United States Olympic Committee*]
NGB........... National Guard Base
NGB........... National Guard Bureau [*Army*]
ngb .... Natural Gum Blend [*Philately*]
NGB........... Neues Goettinger Bibelwerk [*A publication*] (BJA)
NGB........... Neurogenic Bladder [*Medicine*] (MELL)
NGB........... Nordic Gene Bank (CARB)
NGB........... Northern Gas Board (SAUS)
NGB2B .... Newport and Gwent Chamber of Commerce and Industry [*United Kingdom*] (EAIO)
NGBR......... Beru [*Kiribati*] [*ICAO location identifier*] (ICLI)
NGBRI........ Not Guilty by Reason of Insanity
NGc .... Garden City Public Library, Garden City, NY [*Library symbol*] [*Library of Congress*] (LCLS)
NGC........... Gloucester County College, Voorhees, NJ [*OCLC symbol*] (OCLC)
NGC........... National Gallery of Canada
NGC........... National Gambling Commission (NADA)
NGC........... National Gasohol Commission [*Defunct*] (EA)
NGC........... National General Corp. (EFIS)
NGC........... National Giro Centre [*British*] (DCTA)
NGC........... National Glass Clubs (EA)
NGC........... National Gloster Club (EA)
NGC........... National Goose Council (NTPA)
NGC........... National Governors Conference [*Later, NGA*]
NGC........... National Grid Company (ODA)
NGC........... National Guideline Clearinghouse (SAUS)
NGC........... National Guild of Churchmen (EA)
NGC........... National Guinea Club
NGC........... National Gypsy Council [*British*] (DBA)

NGC .... Natural Gas Clearinghouse
ngc .... Natural Gum Crease [*Philately*]
NGC .... Naval Gunfire Control (SAUS)
NGC .... Near Galactic Catalog
NGC .... New General Catalogue [*Astronomy*]
NGC .... New Generation Computer (SAUS)
NGC .... Newmont Gold Co. [*NYSE symbol*] (SPSG)
NGC .... Next Generation Controller (TIMI)
NGC .... Next Group Clause (SAUS)
NGC .... Noise Generator Card
NGC .... Nordic Geodetic Commission (EA)
NGC .... North Georgia College [*Dahlonaga*]
NGC .... Nozzle Gap Control [*Aerospace*] (AAG)
NGC .... Nucleus Gigantocellularis (SAUS)
NGC .... Nucleus Reticularis Gigantocellularis [*Brain anatomy*]
NGC .... Numismatic Guarantee Corp. (SAUS)
NGcA .... Adelphi University, Garden City, NY [*Library symbol*] [*Library of Congress*] (LCLS)
NGCAA ...... National Golf Clubs Advisory Association [*British*] (DBA)
NGCADMM ... Next Generation Computer-Aided Design (SAUS)
Ng-CAM ..... Neuralglial Cell Adhesion Model [*Biochemistry*]
NgCAM ...... Neural-Glial Cell Adhesion Molecule (SAUS)
NGCC .... National Guard Computer Center
NGCC .... Network Group for Composites in Construction [*Plastics industry*]
NGCC .... North German Coal Control [*Post-World War II*]
NGcCC .... Nassau Community College, Garden City, NY [*Library symbol*] [*Library of Congress*] (LCLS)
NGC Cp ..... NGC Corp. [*Associated Press*] (SAG)
NGCDC ...... North Georgia CDC (EARSL)
NGCDO ...... North German Coal Distribution Organization [*Post-World War II*]
NGcE .... Endo Laboratories, Inc., Garden City, NY [*Library symbol*] [*Library of Congress*] (LCLS)
NGcG .... George Mercer, Jr., School of Theology, Garden City, NY [*Library symbol*] [*Library of Congress*] (LCLS)
NGcHE .... Homestead Elementary School, Garden City, NY [*Library symbol*] [*Library of Congress*] (LCLS)
NGCIC .... Natural Gas Consumers Information Center (EA)
NGcJ .... Garden City Junior High School, Garden City, NY [*Library symbol*] [*Library of Congress*] (LCLS)
NGcLE .... Locust Elementary School, Garden City, NY [*Library symbol*] [*Library of Congress*] (LCLS)
NGCM .... Navy Good Conduct Medal
NGCMA ...... National Golf Car Manufacturers Association (NTPA)
NGcMH ...... Mineola High School, Garden City Park, NY [*Library symbol*] [*Library of Congress*] (LCLS)
NGCMS ...... National Guild of Community Music Schools [*Later, NGCSA*] (EA)
NGcN .... Nassau Academy of Medicine, Garden City, NY [*Library symbol*] [*Library of Congress*] (LCLS)
NGcNe .... Newsday, Garden City, NY [*Library symbol*] [*Library of Congress*] (LCLS)
NGcNLS ..... Nassau Library System, Garden City, NY [*Library symbol*] [*Library of Congress*] (LCLS)
NGCOW ..... National Gypsum Wrrt [*NASDAQ symbol*] (TTSB)
NGCP .... National Guild of Catholic Psychiatrists (EA)
NGcpMH .... Mineola High School, Garden City Park, NY [*Library symbol*] [*Library of Congress*] (LCLS)
NGcR .... Nassau County Research Library, Garden City, NY [*Library symbol*] [*Library of Congress*] (LCLS)
NGCR .... Next Generation Computer Resources (DWSG)
NGCSA ...... National Guild of Community Schools of the Arts (EA)
NGcSAE ..... Stratford Avenue Elementary School, Garden City, NY [*Library symbol*] [*Library of Congress*] (LCLS)
NGcSE .... Stewart Avenue Elementary School, Garden City, NY [*Library symbol*] [*Library of Congress*] (LCLS)
NGcSH .... Garden City Senior High School, Garden City, NY [*Library symbol*] [*Library of Congress*] (LCLS)
NGcSS .... Scully, Scott, Murphy, and Presser, Garden City, NY [*Library symbol*] [*Library of Congress*] (LCLS)
NGcStP ...... Saint Paul's School, Garden City, NY [*Library symbol*] [*Library of Congress*] (LCLS)
NGCT .... Navy General Classification Test (DNAB)
NGCZ .... Northwest Grain Co-Operative [*Federal Railroad Administration identification code*]
NGD .... National Grassland Demonstration [*British*]
NGD .... National Guild of Decoupeurs (EA)
NGD .... Negotiated [*Telegraphy*] (PCTE)
NGD .... New Geographical Dictionary (SAUS)
NGD .... New Golden Sceptre Minerals Ltd. [*Toronto Stock Exchange symbol*] [*Vancouver Stock Exchange symbol*]
NGD .... Nicotinamide Guanine Dinucleotide (SAUS)
Ngd .... Nitrosoguanidine [*Biochemistry*]
NGDA .... National Glass Dealers Association [*Later, NGA*] (EA)
NGDA .... New Generation Design Automation (SAUS)
NGDA .... Non-Grounded Disc and Annulus (SAUS)
NGDA .... Nordihydroguaiaretic Acid (ACAE)
NGDA Arrangement ... Non-Grounded Disc and Annulus Arrangement (SAUS)
NGDB .... National Geochemical Data Bank [*Natural Environment Research Council*] [*Information service or system*] (IID)
NGDBFC ..... Nitty Gritty Dirt Band Fan Club (EA)
NGDC .... National Geophysical Data Center [*Later, NGSDC*] [*Boulder, CO*] [*National Oceanic and Atmospheric Administration*] (MCD)
NGDD .... New Generation Desktop Design (SAUS)
NGDF .... National Geospatial Data Framework [*Emergency Management*] (EMA)
NGDF .... National Grave's Disease Foundation (EA)
NGDI .... National Geo Data Information (SAUS)
NGDM&M ... New Grove Dictionary of Music and Musicians (SAUS)
NGDO .... Non-Governmental Development Organisation (EURO)
NGDS .... Naval Graduate Dental School
NGE .... National Grain Exchange [*Australia*]
NGE .... Navigation Guidance Equipment (MCD)
NGE .... New York State Electric & Gas Corp. [*NYSE symbol*] (SPSG)
NGE .... N'Gaoundere [*Cameroon*] [*Airport symbol*] (OAG)
NGE .... Noise Generation Equipment (ACAE)
NGE .... Not Greater or Equal (SAUS)
NGEA .... Next Generation Electric Architecture [*Automotive engineering*]
NGEC .... National Gypsy Education Council [*British*]
NGEDA ...... National Guard Executive Directors Association (NTPA)
NG-EGDN ... Nitroglycerine Ethylene Glycol Dinitrate (SAUS)
NGEN .... Nanogen, Inc. [*NASDAQ symbol*] (NASQ)
NGEN .... New Generation Foods, Inc. (SAUS)
n gen .... New Genus [*Biology*] (BARN)
NGEN .... Noise Generator (MSA)
NGeno .... Wadsworth Library, Geneseo, NY [*Library symbol*] [*Library of Congress*] (LCLS)
NGenoA ..... Livingston County Archives, Geneseo, NY [*Library symbol*] [*Library of Congress*] (LCLS)
NGenoLS .... Livingston-Steuben-Wyoming Educational Communication Center (BOCES), Geneseo, NY [*Library symbol*] [*Library of Congress*] (LCLS)
NGenoU ..... State University of New York, College at Geneseo, Geneseo, NY [*Library symbol*] [*Library of Congress*] (LCLS)
NGEO .... Natural Gas Engine Oil [*Fuels and lubricants*]
NGEPr .... N.Y. State E&G, 3.75% Pfd [*NYSE symbol*] (TTSB)
NGEPrD ..... N.Y. State E&G Adj Rt B Pfd [*NYSE symbol*] (TTSB)
NGEPrE ...... N.Y. State E&G 7.40% Pfd [*NYSE symbol*] (TTSB)
NGEPSSC ... Navy Graduate Education Program Select Study Committee [*Terminated, 1975*] (EGAO)
NGF .... Kaneohe, HI [*Location identifier*] [*FAA*] (FAAL)
NGF .... National Gaucher Foundation (EA)
NGF .... National Genetics Foundation [*Defunct*] (EA)
NGF .... National Golf Foundation (EA)
NGF .... Nations Government Income Term Trust 2004 [*NYSE symbol*] (SAG)
NGF .... Nations Gvt Inc. Term Tr 2004 [*NYSE symbol*] (TTSB)
NGF .... Natural Guard Fund [*Defunct*] (EA)
NGF .... Naval Gun Factory [*Later, NWF*]
NGF .... Naval Gunfire
NGF .... Nerve Growth Factor [*A protein*] [*Biochemistry*]
NGF .... Nevada Goldfields Corp. [*Toronto Stock Exchange symbol*]
NGF .... New Games Foundation [*Defunct*] (EA)
NGF .... New Guinea Force [*Army*] [*World War II*]
NGF .... Nordic Gunners Federation (SAUS)
NGF .... Normalized Gain Function (SAUS)
NGF .... Northern Group of Forces [*Commonwealth of Independent States*] (NATG)
NGFA .... National Grain and Feed Association (EA)
NGFCF ...... Nevada Goldfields Corp. (MHDW)
NGFEX ...... Naval Gunfire Exercise (NVT)
NGFF .... Funafuti [*Tuvalu*] [*ICAO location identifier*] (ICLI)
NGFLO ...... Naval Gunfire Liaison Officer
NGFLT ...... Naval Gunfire Liaison Team
NGFO .... Nanumea [*Tuvalu*] [*ICAO location identifier*] (ICLI)
NGFO .... Naval Gunfire Officer
NGFP .... National Graduate Fellowship Program [*Department of Education*] (GFGA)
NGFR .... Nerve Growth Factor Receptor [*Neurobiology*]
NGFS .... National Grigsby Family Society (EA)
NGFS .... Naval Gunfire Support (NVT)
NGFT .... National Guard on Field Training Exercises
NGFT .... Naval Gunfire Liaison Team (MUGU)
NGFU .... Funafuti/International [*Tuvalu*] [*ICAO location identifier*] (ICLI)
NGG .... Air Trans NG Group Moldova [*FAA designator*] (FAAC)
NGG .... National Grid Group [*NYSE symbol*]
NGG .... Negative Grid Generator
NGG .... Negotiating [*Telegraphy*] (PCTE)
NGG .... Network Group Germany (SAUS)
NGGA .... National Greentown Glass Association (EA)
NGGC .... National Grape Growers Cooperative (NTPA)
NGGI .... National Greenhouse Gas Inventory
NGGR .... Nonglucogenic/Glucogenic Ratio (DB)
NGH .... Hobart and William Smith Colleges, Geneva, NY [*Library symbol*] [*Library of Congress*] (LCLS)
NGH .... Nabisco Group Holdings [*NYSE symbol*] (SG)
NGH .... Nabisco Group Holdings Corp. [*NYSE symbol*]
NGH .... NASA Grant Handbook
NGH .... National Guard [*Hawaii*] [*Seismograph station code, US Geological Survey*] (SEIS)
NGH .... National Guild of Hypnotists (EA)
NGHA .... 91st General Hospital Association (EA)
NGHBRHD ... Neighborhood
NGHEF ...... National Gay Health Education Foundation (EA)
NGHGS ...... Northwest Georgia Historical and Genealogical Society (EARSL)
NGHK .... Night Hawk [*Common carrier symbol*]
NGI .... Nasogastric Intubation [*Medicine*] (MELL)
NGI .... National Garden Institute
NGI .... National Genomics Institute (SAUS)
NGI .... Nations Government Income Term Trust [*NYSE symbol*] (SPSG)
NGI .... Nations Gvt Inc. Term Tr 2003 [*NYSE symbol*] (TTSB)
NGI .... Natural Gas Industry [*Australia*]
NGI .... Next General Internet Program [*Defense Advanced Research Projects Agency*] (RCD)

NGI Next Generation Internet [*Computer science*]
NGI Next-Generation Internet [*Clinton Administration project*] (NETL)
NGI Ngau [*Fiji*] [*Airport symbol*] (OAG)
NGI Ngizim [*Language symbol*] (ETLW)
NGI Non-Government Institution (SAUS)
NGI Not Guilty by Reason of Insanity
NGI Not Guilty, Insanity (SAUS)
NGI Nuclear Globulin Inclusions (DMAA)
NGI Nurses' Global Impressions (DB)
NGI N-W Group, Inc. [*Toronto Stock Exchange symbol*]
NGIB National Geodetic Information Branch [*National Oceanic and Atmospheric Administration*]
NGIC National Geodetic Information Center [*National Oceanic and Atmospheric Administration*] (IID)
NGIC National Guard Intelligence Center [*USA*]
NGIFF Next Generation IFF (SAUS)
NGiG Gibco/Invenex, Grand Island (SAUS)
NGiG Gibco/Invenex, Grand Island, NY [*Library symbol*] [*Library of Congress*] (LCLS)
NGiHC Hooker Chemicals & Plastics Corp., Corporate Technical and Services Center Research Library, Grand Island, NY [*Library symbol*] [*Library of Congress*] (LCLS)
NGIO Next Generation Input Output (SAUS)
NGIPSCA National GI Pipe Smokers Club of America (EA)
NGIS Next Generation Information System (SAUS)
NGISC National Gambling Impact Study Commission
NgIU University of Ibadan, Ibadan, Nigeria [*Library symbol*] [*Library of Congress*] (LCLS)
n giv Not Given (DAVI)
NGJ Beaufort, SC [*Location identifier*] [*FAA*] (FAAL)
NGJ Nigerian Geographical Journal [*A publication*]
NGJA National Gymnastics Judges Association (EA)
NGJC North Greenville Junior College [*South Carolina*]
NGK New Greek [*Language, etc.*]
NGK Niemegk [*German Democratic Republic*] [*Geomagnetic observatory code*]
NGK Nippon Gaishi Kabushiki [*Japanese Insulator Company*] [*Automotive supplier*]
n-gl- Greenland [*MARC geographic area code*] [*Library of Congress*] (LCCP)
NGl Harborfields Public Library, Greenlawn, NY [*Library symbol*] [*Library of Congress*] (LCLS)
NGL Natural Gas Liquids
NGL Natural Ground Level
NGL Neodymium Glass LASER
NGL Neon Glow Lamp
NGL NGC Corp. [*NYSE symbol*] (TTSB)
NGL No Gimbal Lock
NGL No Greater Love (EA)
NGL Normalair-Garrett Ltd. [*British*] (IRUK)
NGL North Gasline [*Alaska*] [*Seismograph station code, US Geological Survey*] (SEIS)
NGL North German Lloyd Line (SAUS)
NGL Nose Gear Launch (MCD)
NGL Trident NGL Holdings, Inc. [*NYSE symbol*] (SPSG)
NGlc Glen Cove Public Library, Glen Cove, NY [*Library symbol*] [*Library of Congress*] (LCLS)
NGLC Next Generation Level Control (SAUS)
NGlcC Community Hospital at Glen Cove, Glen Cove, NY [*Library symbol*] [*Library of Congress*] (LCLS)
NGlcCE Coles Elementary School, Glen Cove, NY [*Library symbol*] [*Library of Congress*] (LCLS)
NGlcCoE Connolly Elementary School, Glen Cove, NY [*Library symbol*] [*Library of Congress*] (LCLS)
NGlcDE Deasy Elementary School, Glen Cove, NY [*Library symbol*] [*Library of Congress*] (LCLS)
NGlcF-L Friends Academy, Lower School, Glen Cove, NY [*Library symbol*] [*Library of Congress*] (LCLS)
NGlcF-U Friends Academy, Upper School, Glen Cove, NY [*Library symbol*] [*Library of Congress*] (LCLS)
NGlcGE Gribbin Elementary School, Glen Cove, NY [*Library symbol*] [*Library of Congress*] (LCLS)
NGlcHS Glen Cove High School, Glen Cove, NY [*Library symbol*] [*Library of Congress*] (LCLS)
NGlcLE Landing Elementary School, Glen Cove, NY [*Library symbol*] [*Library of Congress*] (LCLS)
NGlcM Garvie's Point Museum, Glen Cove, NY [*Library symbol*] [*Library of Congress*] (LCLS)
NGlcMS Glen Cove Middle School, Glen Cove, NY [*Library symbol*] [*Library of Congress*] (LCLS)
NGlcP Pall Corp., Glen Cove, NY [*Library symbol*] [*Library of Congress*] (LCLS)
NGlcW Webb Institute of Naval Architecture, Glen Cove, NY [*Library symbol*] [*Library of Congress*] (LCLS)
NGlf Crandall Library, Glens Falls, NY [*Library symbol*] [*Library of Congress*] (LCLS)
NGlfAC Adirondack Community College, Glens Falls, NY [*Library symbol*] [*Library of Congress*] (LCLS)
NGlH Hazeltine Corp., Greenlawn, NY [*Library symbol*] [*Library of Congress*] (LCLS)
NGlhC New York Chiropractic College, Glen Head, NY [*Library symbol*] [*Library of Congress*] (LCLS)
NGlhES Glen Head Elementary School, Glen Head, NY [*Library symbol*] [*Library of Congress*] (LCLS)
NGlhGE Glenwood Landing Elementary School, Glen Head, NY [*Library symbol*] [*Library of Congress*] (LCLS)
NGlhNH North Shore High School, Glen Head, NY [*Library symbol*] [*Library of Congress*] (LCLS)
NGlhNJ North Shore Junior High School, Glen Head, NY [*Library symbol*] [*Library of Congress*] (LCLS)
NGlHS Harborfields High School, Greenlawn, NY [*Library symbol*] [*Library of Congress*] (LCLS)
NGLIOGT National Grand Lodge, International Order of Good Templars [*Later, NCUSIOGT*] (EA)
NGlo Gloversville Free Library, Gloversville, NY [*Library symbol*] [*Library of Congress*] (LCLS)
NGLO Naval Gunfire Liaison Officer
NGLR Neodymium Glass LASER Rod
NGLS Non-Governmental Liaison Service [*World Resources Institute*]
NGLTF National Gay and Lesbian Task Force (EA)
NGlwES Glenwood Landing Elementary School, Glenwood Landing, NY [*Library symbol*] [*Library of Congress*] (LCLS)
N GLZD Not Glazed [*Freight*]
NGM Agana Naval Air Station [*FAA*] (TAG)
ngm Nanogram [*Measurement*] (DAVI)
NGM Naval General Message (SAUS)
NGM Nested Grid Model [*Marine science*] (OSRA)
NGM NetWare Global Messaging [*Computer science*] (CDE)
NGM Neutron-Gamma Monte Carlo [*Computer science*]
NGM New Ridge Resources [*Vancouver Stock Exchange symbol*]
NGM Nitrogen Generation Module (NASA)
NGM Noise Generation Mechanism
NGMA Maiana [*Kiribati*] [*ICAO location identifier*] (ICLI)
NGMA National Gadget Manufacturers Association
NGMA National Gas Measurement Association (EA)
NGMA National Geoscience Mapping Accord [*Australia*]
NGMA National Gospel Music Association (EA)
NGMA National Grants Management Association (AAGC)
NGMA National Greenhouse Manufacturers Association (EA)
NGMC Next Generation Media Corp. [*OTCBB symbol*]
N Gmc North Germanic (SAUS)
NGMEX Northern Gulf of Mexico (SAUS)
NGMH New Generation Military Hospital (SAUS)
NGMK Marakei [*Kiribati*] [*ICAO location identifier*] (ICLI)
ng/ml Nanograms [*One billionth of a gram*] per Milliliter
NGMN Makin [*Kiribati*] [*ICAO location identifier*] (ICLI)
NGMP New Guinea Marine Products (SAUS)
NGMRD New Generation Mark Reader (or Reading) (SAUS)
NGN Nagano [*Japan*] [*Seismograph station code, US Geological Survey*] (SEIS)
NGN Nargana [*Panama*] [*Airport symbol*] (OAG)
NGN National Geographic Names Data Base [*Geological Survey*] [*Database*]
NGN Negotiation [*Telegraphy*] (PCTE)
NGN News Group Newspapers [*British*]
NGN NRG Resources Ltd. [*Vancouver Stock Exchange symbol*]
NGNA National Gerontological Nursing Association (NTPA)
NGNA Neutrogena Corp. (SAUS)
NGNC Non-Government Non-Catholic [*School*]
NGNF National Guard Not in Federal Service
NGNF Next Generation Navy Fighter (ACAE)
NG/NS Next Generation/Notional System [*Army*]
NGNU Nikunau [*Kiribati*] [*ICAO location identifier*] (ICLI)
NGO Nago [*Ryukyu Islands*] [*Seismograph station code, US Geological Survey*] (SEIS)
NGO Nagoya [*Japan*] [*Airport symbol*] (OAG)
NGO National Gas & Oil Company (EFIS)
NGO National Gas Outlet [*Thread*]
NGO Naval Gunfire Officer
NGO Navy Guidance Official [*British*]
NGO Neuro-Genetic Optimizer (PCM)
NGO Nitroglycerin Ointment [*Pharmacy*] (CPH)
NGO Non-Gazetted Officer [*India*] (WDAA)
NGO Nongovernmental Observer
NGO Nongovernmental Organization [*Generic term*]
NGOC Naval Gunfire Operations Center
NGOC North German Oil Control [*Post-World War II*]
NGOCD Non-Governmental Organization Committee on Disarmament (EA)
NGO Committee Non-Governmental Organizations Committee on UNICEF (EA)
NGOCS National Guard Officer Candidate School
NGO/GO Non Governmental Organisation/ Governmental Organisation (SAUS)
NGoH Hillside Hospital, Glen Oaks, NY [*Library symbol*] [*Library of Congress*] (LCLS)
NGON Onotoa [*Kiribati*] [*ICAO location identifier*] (ICLI)
NGos Goshen Library and Historical Society, Goshen, NY [*Library symbol*] [*Library of Congress*] (LCLS)
NGOS Non-Governmental Organisations
NGosA Arden Hill Hospital Medical Library, Goshen, NY [*Library symbol*] [*Library of Congress*] (LCLS)
NGOU Natural Gas Odorizing [*Intermodal shipping container symbol*] (TVRC)
NGou Reading Room Association Library, Gouveneur, NY [*Library symbol*] [*Library of Congress*] (LCLS)
NGowH Tri-County Memorial Hospital, Gowanda, NY [*Library symbol*] [*Library of Congress*] (LCLS)
NGP Corpus Christi, TX [*Location identifier*] [*FAA*] (FAAL)
NGP Greensboro Public Library, Greensboro, NC [*OCLC symbol*] (OCLC)
NGP Nano Glass Pellet
NGP Natural Gas Pressure
NGP Natural Generative Phonology [*Linguistics*] (IEL)
NGP Navigation Processor (ISAK)

NGP.......... Nearest Grid Point (PDAA)
NGP.......... Network Graphics Protocol
NGP.......... Neue Grosse Partei [*New Great Party*] [*Germany*] [*Political party*] (PPW)
NGP.......... New Gatineau Pulp [*Pulp and paper technology*]
NGP.......... Next Generation Processor (ACAE)
NGP.......... N-Glycidylpyrrolidone [*Organic chemistry*]
Ngp.......... Nominal Group [*Linguistics*]
NGP.......... Northern Galactic Pole
NGP.......... North Galactic Pole
NGPA........ National Gas Policy Act (GFGA)
NGPA........ National Guard Personnel, Army
NGPA........ Natural Gas Policy Act [*1978*]
NGPA........ Natural Gas Processors Association [*Later, GPA*] (EA)
NGPE........ Neurogenic Pulmonary Edema [*Medicine*] (MELL)
NGPEC...... National Guard Professional Education Center [*North Little Rock, AR*]
NGPF........ North General Purpose Facilities (SAUS)
NGPL........ Natural Gas Plant Liquids [*DOE*] (TAG)
NGPP........ National Guild of Professional Paperhangers (EA)
NGPRP...... Northern Great Plains Resource Program [*Dept. of the Interior, Dept. of Agriculture and Environmental Protection Agency*] (PDAA)
NGPRS...... Northern Great Plains Research Center [*Department of Agriculture*] [*Research center*] (RCD)
NGPS........ Navstar Global Positioning System (SAUS)
NGPSA...... Natural Gas Pipeline Safety Act [*1968*]
NGPSA...... Natural Gas Processors Suppliers Association [*Later, GPSA*] (EA)
NGPT........ National Guild of Piano Teachers (EA)
NGQ......... Nongovernment Quarters (AFM)
NGR......... Narrow Gauge Railways Ltd. [*Wales*]
NGR......... Narrow Gauze Roll [*Medicine*]
NGR......... Nasogastric Replacement [*Medicine*] (DMAA)
NGR......... National Guard Register
NGR......... National Guard Regulations
NGR......... Neutral Grounding Resistor (SAUS)
NGR......... Newbold General Refractories (SAUS)
NGr.......... New Greek (ODA)
N GR........ New Greek [*Language, etc.*] (ROG)
N-GR........ New York State Library, General Reference Library, Albany, NY [*Library symbol*] [*Library of Congress*] (LCLS)
Ngr........... Niger (MILB)
NGR......... Nigerum [*Papua New Guinea*] [*Airport symbol*] (OAG)
NGR......... Night-Goggle Readable (SAUS)
ngr........... Non-Geared (SAUS)
NGR......... Non-Grain-Raising [*Coating technology*]
NGR......... Nongrain-Raising Stain (SAUS)
NGR......... Nongrain Rating (SAUS)
NGR......... Norgold Resources [*Vancouver Stock Exchange symbol*]
NGR......... Nuclear Gamma-ray Resonance (SAUS)
NGR......... Nuclear Gamma Ray Spectroscopy (EDCT)
NGR......... Nuclear Gamma Resonance (SAUS)
NGRA........ National Gay Rights Advocates [*Defunct*] (EA)
NGRAF...... North Grafton, MA [*American Association of Railroads railroad junction routing code*]
NGRC........ National Government of the Republic of China
NGRC........ National Greyhound Racing Club [*British*] (DI)
NGRE........ Negative Glucocorticoid Response Element [*Biochemistry*]
NGRF........ National Ghost Ranch Foundation (EA)
NGRI......... Not Guilty by Reason of Insanity
NGrl......... Greenwood Lake Public Library, Greenwood, NY [*Library symbol*] [*Library of Congress*] (LCLS)
NGrlHS...... Harborfields High School, Greenlawn, NY [*Library symbol*] [*Library of Congress*] (LCLS)
NGrn......... Great Neck Library, Great Neck, NY [*Library symbol*] [*Library of Congress*] (LCLS)
NGrnBE...... Baker Elementary School, Great Neck, NY [*Library symbol*] [*Library of Congress*] (LCLS)
NGrnKE...... Kennedy Elementary School, Great Neck, NY [*Library symbol*] [*Library of Congress*] (LCLS)
NGrnKJE.... Kensington-Johnson Elementary School, Great Neck, NY [*Library symbol*] [*Library of Congress*] (LCLS)
NGrnLE...... Lakeville Elementary School, Great Neck, NY [*Library symbol*] [*Library of Congress*] (LCLS)
NGrnMiS.... John L. Miller-Great Neck North High School, Great Neck, NY [*Library symbol*] [*Library of Congress*] (LCLS)
NGrnMS..... Great Neck South Middle School, Great Neck, NY [*Library symbol*] [*Library of Congress*] (LCLS)
NGrnNA..... Network Analysis Corp., Great Neck, NY [*Library symbol*] [*Library of Congress*] (LCLS)
NGrnNM..... Great Neck North Middle School, Great Neck, NY [*Library symbol*] [*Library of Congress*] (LCLS)
NGrnPE...... Parkville Elementary School, Great Neck, NY [*Library symbol*] [*Library of Congress*] (LCLS)
NGrnS....... Sperry Rand Corp., Sperry Gyroscope Division, Great Neck, NY [*Library symbol*] [*Library of Congress*] (LCLS)
NGrnSH..... Great Neck South Senior High School, Great Neck, NY [*Library symbol*] [*Library of Congress*] (LCLS)
NGrnSRE.... Saddle Rock Elementary School, Great Neck, NY [*Library symbol*] [*Library of Congress*] (LCLS)
NGroT....... Tompkins-Cortland Community College, Groton, NY [*Library symbol*] [*Library of Congress*] [*Obsolete*] (LCLS)
NGrpAg...... United States Department of Agriculture, Plum Island Animal Disease Laboratory Library, Greenport, NY [*Library symbol*] [*Library of Congress*] (LCLS)
NGrpEH..... Eastern Long Island Hospital, Greenport, NY [*Library symbol*] [*Library of Congress*] (LCLS)
NGRS........ Narrow Gauge Railway Society [*British*]
NGRS........ National Geodetic Reference System [*National Oceanic and Atmospheric Administration*]
NGRS........ National Goals Research Staff
NGS.......... General Air Services Ltd. [*Nigeria*] [*ICAO designator*] (FAAC)
NGS.......... Nagasaki [*Japan*] [*Airport symbol*] (OAG)
NGS.......... National Gardens Scheme Charitable Trust (EAIO)
NGS.......... National Gas Straight [*Thread*]
NGS.......... National Genealogical Society (EA)
NGS.......... National Geodetic Survey [*National Oceanic and Atmospheric Administration*]
NGS.......... National Geodetic System (OTD)
NGS.......... National Geographic Service
NGS.......... National Geographic Society (EA)
NGS.......... National Geriatrics Society (EA)
NGS.......... National Gladiolus Society (EA)
NGS.......... National Goldfish Society
NGS.......... National Graniteware Society (EA)
NGS.......... Natural Ground Surface
NGS.......... Naval Gunfire Support
NGS.......... Naval Gun Support (SAUS)
NGS.......... Negotiates [*Telegraphy*] (PCTE)
NGS.......... Neutral Gear Switch [*Automotive engineering*]
NGS.......... Neutral Grain Spirits
NGS.......... New-Generation STAR (Self-Test Automatic Readout) [*Automotive engineering*]
NGS.......... New Generation System (SAUS)
NGS.......... New Guidance System (SAUS)
NGS.......... Niagara Share Corp. [*NYSE symbol*] (COMM)
NGS.......... No Gallstones [*Medicine*]
NGS.......... Nominal Guidance Scheme (OA)
NGS.......... Non-Immune [*or Normal*] Goat Serum
NGS.......... Normal Goat Serum (DMAA)
NGS.......... Nuclear Generating Site (SAUS)
NGS.......... Nuclear Generating Station (BARN)
NGS.......... Nucleonic Gauging System
NGS.......... Numerical Geometry System (SAUS)
NGSA........ National Golf Salesmen Association [*Defunct*] (EA)
NGSA........ Natural Gas Supply Association (EA)
NGSA........ Nerve Growth Stimulating Activity [*Biochemistry*]
NGSB........ Non-Government Standards Bodies (SAUS)
NGSC........ National Gay Student Center [*Defunct*] (EA)
NGSC........ National Gender Selection Center (EA)
NGSC........ Next-Generation Speed Control [*Automotive engineering*]
NGSCO...... National Geodetic Survey Operations Center [*National Oceanic and Atmospheric Administration*]
NGSDC...... National Geophysical and Solar-Terrestrial Data Center [*National Oceanic and Atmospheric Administration*] (IID)
NGSEF....... National Geographic Society Education Foundation (EA)
NGSF........ Noble Gas Storage Facility (NRCH)
NGSFO...... Naval Gunfire Support Forward Observer [*British*]
NGSIC....... National Geodetic Survey Information Center [*National Oceanic and Atmospheric Administration*] (IID)
NGSLO...... Naval Gunfire Support Forward Observer (SAUS)
NGSLO...... Naval Gunfire Support Liaison Officer
NGSM........ National Gold Star Mothers [*Defunct*] (EA)
NGSMA...... Natural Gasoline Supply Men's Association [*Later, GPSA*]
NGSNY...... National Guard State of New York (HGAA)
NGSP........ National Geodetic Satellite Program [*NASA*]
NGSP........ National Glycohemoglobin Standardization Program (SAUS)
NGSP........ National Grain Sorghum Producers (NTPA)
NGSP........ National Guilds of St. Paul (EA)
NGSP........ Next Generation Signal Processor (SAUS)
NGSP........ Nonglycosylated Serum Protein
NGSQ........ National Genealogical Society Quarterly [*A publication*] (BRI)
NGSR........ Nizams Guaranteed State Railway (SAUS)
NGSS........ Next Generation Sky Survey (SAUS)
NGSS........ Non-Government Schools' Secretariat [*South Australia*]
NGSSLO..... Naval Gunfire Support Senior Liaison Officer (SAUS)
NGSSO...... Naval Gunfire Support Staff Officer
NGST........ Next Generation Space Telescope [*NASA*]
NGSTDC..... National Geophysical and Solar-Terrestrial Data Center [*National Oceanic and Atmospheric Administration*]
NGSU........ Nigerian Star Line [*Intermodal shipping container symbol*] (TVRC)
NGT.......... Berclair, TX [*Location identifier*] [*FAA*] (FAAL)
NGT.......... Eastern American Natural Gas Trust [*NYSE symbol*] (SAG)
NGT.......... Eastern AmerNatlGasTr'SPERs' [*NYSE symbol*] (TTSB)
NGT.......... Nagatsuro [*Irozaki*] [*Japan*] [*Seismograph station code, US Geological Survey*] (SEIS)
NGT.......... NASA Ground Terminal (MCD)
NGT.......... Nasogastric Tube [*Medicine*] (CPH)
NGT.......... National Gas Taper [*Thread*]
NGT.......... National Guard Technician (MCD)
NGT.......... National Guild of Telephonists [*British*] (BI)
NGT.......... Natural Gas Temperature
NGT.......... Neon Globe Tube
NGT.......... Neue Gebaudetechnik (EFIS)
NGT.......... New Generation Technology (SAUS)
NGT.......... New Generation Trainer (SAUS)
NGT.......... New Generation Truck [*Concept vehicle*]
NGT.......... Next Generation Technology (SAUS)
NGT.......... Next Generation Trainer [*Air Force*]
NGT.......... Ngeq [*Language symbol*] (ETLW)

NGT.......... Night
NGT.......... Noise Generator Tube
NGT.......... Nominal Grouping Technique
NGT.......... Nonsymmetrical Growth Theory (SAUS)
NGT.......... Nonsymmetric Gravitational Theory
NGT.......... Northern General Transport Co. [*British*] (DCTA)
NGT.......... North German Traders (SAUS)
NGT.......... Not Greater Than
NGTA........ National Gas Transportation Association (NTPA)
NGTA........ Next Generation Trainer Aircraft (MCD)
NGTA........ Nonguaranteed Trade Arrears (IMH)
NGTA........ Tarawa/Bonriki International [*Kiribati*] [*ICAO location identifier*] (ICLI)
NGTB........ Abemama [*Kiribati*] [*ICAO location identifier*] (ICLI)
NGTC........ National Grain Trade Council (EA)
NGTE........ National Gas Turbine Establishment [*British*]
NGTE........ Northgate Innovations [*OTCBB symbol*]
NGTE........ Tabiteuea (North) [*Kiribati*] [*ICAO location identifier*] (ICLI)
NGTF........ National Gay Task Force [*Later, NGLTF*] (EA)
NGTG........ NCAR [*National Center for Atmospheric Research*] GARP Task Group [*Global Atmospheric Research Program*]
NGTM....... Tamana [*Kiribati*] [*ICAO location identifier*] (ICLI)
NGTO........ Nonouti [*Kiribati*] [*ICAO location identifier*] (ICLI)
NGTOW..... Normal Gross Take-Off Weight (SAUS)
NGTP........ Natural Gas Tank Pressure
NGTR........ Arorae [*Kiribati*] [*ICAO location identifier*] (ICLI)
NGTS........ Tabiteuea (South) [*Kiribati*] [*ICAO location identifier*] (ICLI)
NGTT........ Natural Gas Tank Temperature
NGTT........ Tarawa/Betio [*Kiribati*] [*ICAO location identifier*] (ICLI)
NGTU........ Butaritari [*Kiribati*] [*ICAO location identifier*] (ICLI)
NGTX........ Suburban Propane [*Private rail car owner code*]
NGU......... Geological Survey of Norway (SAUS)
NGU......... Nachalnik Glavnoyo Upravlenia [*Chief of Main Directorate*] [*Soviet military rank*]
nGU.......... Nano-Goldblatt Units [*Clinical chemistry*]
NGU......... Nongonococcal Urethritis [*Medicine*]
NGU......... Norfolk, VA [*Location identifier*] [*FAA*] (FAAL)
NGU......... University of North Carolina, Greensboro, Greensboro, NC [*OCLC symbol*] (OCLC)
NGUAX...... Neub. & Berman Guardian Fund [*Mutual fund ticker symbol*] (SG)
NGUI......... New-Generation Electronic Unit Injector [*Automotive fuel systems*]
N GUI........ New Guinea Territory (WDAA)
N Guin...... New Guinea
NGUK........ Aranuka [*Kiribati*] [*ICAO location identifier*] (ICLI)
NGuNA...... New York State Nurses Association, Guilderland, NY [*Library symbol*] [*Library of Congress*] (LCLS)
NGUS........ National Guard of the United States
NGUT........ National Group of Unit Trusts [*British*] (DI)
NGV.......... Angoavia Angola [*FAA designator*] (FAAC)
NGV.......... Natural Gas for Vehicles
NGV.......... Natural Gas Vehicle
NGV.......... New-Generation Vehicle [*Automotive engineering*]
NGV.......... New Goldcore Ventures [*Vancouver Stock Exchange symbol*]
NGV.......... Nongonococcal Vulvovaginitis (SAUS)
NGV.......... Nozzle Guide Vanes [*Aviation*] (AIA)
NGVC........ National Guard Volunteer Corps [*British military*] (DMA)
NGVC........ Natural Gas Vehicle Coalition (NTPA)
NGVD........ National Geodetic Vertical Datum [*National Oceanic and Atmospheric Administration*]
NGvHI....... Harbor Hill Intermediate School, Greenvale, NY [*Library symbol*] [*Library of Congress*] (LCLS)
NGVIA....... Natural Gas Vehicle Industry Alliance
NGVL........ National Gene Vector Laboratories [*National Center for Research Resources*] (RCD)
NGVM....... Natural Gas Vehicle Module [*Automotive engineering*]
NGvP........ Long Island University, C. W. Post Center, Greenvale, NY [*Library symbol*] [*Library of Congress*] (LCLS)
NGVP........ Natural Gas Vehicle Partnership
NGVR........ New Guinea Volunteer Reserve
NGVTP...... Natural Gas Vehicle Technology Partnership [*Automotive industry cooperative research*]
NGW......... Corpus Christi, TX [*Location identifier*] [*FAA*] (FAAL)
NGW......... Gardner-Webb College, Boiling Springs, NC [*OCLC symbol*] (OCLC)
NGW......... National Gallery of Art, Washington, DC
NGW......... Newly Generated Waste (SAUS)
NGW......... No Gift Wrap [*Mail-order catalogs*]
NGW......... Nuclear Gravity Weapon (SAUS)
NGWA....... National Ground Water Association (NTPA)
NGWASOREP... Ngwane Socialist Revolutionary Party (SAUS)
NGWIC...... National Ground Water Information Center [*National Water Well Association*] [*Information service or system*] (IID)
NGWLM..... Next Generation Water Level Measurement system (SAUS)
NGWS....... Next Generation Windows Services [*Computer science*] (VLIE)
NGX......... Northgate Explor [*NYSE symbol*] (TTSB)
NGX......... Northgate Exploration Ltd. [*NYSE symbol*] [*Toronto Stock Exchange symbol*] (SPSG)
NGYN........ National Gay Youth Network (EA)
NGZ......... Alameda, CA [*Location identifier*] [*FAA*] (FAAL)
NH........... All Nippon [*ICAO designator*] (AD)
NH........... All Nippon Airways Co. Ltd. (SAUS)
NH........... Editions Nouveaux Horizons [*US government imprint*]
NH........... Hamilton Public Library, Hamilton, NY [*Library symbol*] [*Library of Congress*] (LCLS)
NH........... Hydrazine (SAUS)
NH........... Nahum [*Bible*]
nH............ Nanohenry [*One billionth of a henry*] (IEEE)
NH........... Nash-Healey [*Model of automobile, now out of production*]
NH........... National Health Labs (EFIS)
NH........... National Heritage [*British*] [*An association*] (DBA)
NH........... National Highway
NH........... National Hunt [*British*]
NH........... NATO Helicopter [*NH-90*] (DOMA)
NH........... Natriuretic Hormone (DB)
NH........... Natural Hazard [*Emergency Management*] (EMA)
NH........... Natural Health (SAUS)
NH........... Natural History [*A publication*] (BRI)
NH........... Naval Home [*Philadelphia, PA*]
NH........... Naval Hospital
NH........... Neo-Hebrew (BJA)
NH........... Neonatal Hepatitis [*Medicine*] (DB)
NH........... Neonatal Hypothyroidism [*Cretinism*] [*Medicine*]
NH........... Neurohormone [*Medicine*] (MELL)
NH........... Neurologic History (SAUS)
NH........... Never Hinged [*Philately*]
NH........... New Hampshire [*Postal code*]
Nh............ New Hampshire State Library, Concord, NH [*Library symbol*] [*Library of Congress*] (LCLS)
NH........... New Hampshire Supreme Court Reports [*A publication*] (DLA)
NH........... New Haven [*Connecticut*]
NH........... New Haven Elm City (SAUS)
NH........... New Head [*Also, NL*] [*News stories*] (NTCM)
NH........... New High [*Investment term*]
NH........... New Holland N.V. [*NYSE symbol*] (SG)
NH........... New York, New Haven & Hartford R. R. [*AAR code*]
N/H.......... Next Higher Assembly [*Engineering*]
NH........... Nike Hercules [*Surface-to-air missile system*] (MCD)
NH........... Nippon Airways (SAUS)
NH........... Nodal-His [*Medicine*] (MEDA)
NH........... Nodular Histiocytic [*Lymphoma*] [*Oncology*] (DAVI)
NH........... No Hurry (SAUS)
NH........... Nominal Height (MCD)
NH........... Non-Busy Hour (VLIE)
NH........... Nonhandicapped
NH........... Nonhuman (MAE)
NH........... Nonhygroscopic
NH........... Norfolk Howard [*Refers to a bed-bug*] [*Slang*] (DSUE)
NH........... Northern Canada Mines Ltd. [*Toronto Stock Exchange symbol*]
NH........... Northern Hemisphere
Nh............ Northern Hogsucker [*Ichthyology*]
N H.......... North Hall (SAUS)
NH........... Northumberland Hussars [*British military*] (DMA)
NH........... Not at Home [*Telegraphy*] (PCTE)
NH........... Not Held
NH........... Novikoff Hepatoma [*Medicine*] (DB)
NH........... Nursing Home
NH_3.......... Ammonia (GNE)
NH4 ClO4... Ammonium Perchlorate (SAUS)
NHA.......... American Foundation for Management Research, Hamilton, NY [*Library symbol*] [*Library of Congress*] (LCLS)
NHA.......... Nahanni Mines Ltd. [*Toronto Stock Exchange symbol*]
NHA.......... National Fashion Accessories Association (EA)
NHA.......... National Hairdressers' Association [*British*] (BI)
NHA.......... National Handbag Association (EA)
NHA.......... National Hay Association (EA)
NHA.......... National Health Agencies (EA)
NHA.......... National Health Association
NHA.......... National Hearing Association (EA)
NHA.......... National Hemophilia Association (DAVI)
NHA.......... National Heritage Act [*Protects national treasures from sale out of the country*] [*British*]
NHA.......... National Hide Association [*Later, USHSLA*] (EA)
NHA.......... National Hobo Association (EA)
NHA.......... National Hockey Association [*to 1917*]
NHA.......... National Holiness Association [*Later, CHA*] (EA)
NHA.......... National Homeowners Association (EA)
NHA.......... National Homeschool Association (EA)
NHA.......... National Horse Association of Great Britain (ODA)
NHA.......... National Housewives Association [*British*] (DBA)
NHA.......... National Housing Act [*1934, 1954*]
NHA.......... National Housing Administration
NHA.......... National Housing Agency [*Superseded by HHFA, 1947; then by HUD, 1965*]
NHA.......... National Humanities Alliance (EA)
NHA.......... National Hunters Association (EA)
NHA.......... National Hydrogen Association (NTPA)
NHA.......... National Hydropower Association (EA)
NHA.......... National Hypertension Association (EA)
NHA.......... National Hypoglycemia Association (EA)
NHA.......... Nationwide Hotel Association
NHA.......... Never Has Anything (SAUS)
NHA.......... New Homemakers of America [*Later, FHA*] (EA)
NHA.......... New Humanity Alliance (EA)
NHA.......... Next Higher Assembly [*Engineering*]
NHA.......... Next Higher Authority (MUGU)
NHA.......... Nhatrang [*Vietnam*] [*Seismograph station code, US Geological Survey*] [*Closed*] (SEIS)
NHA.......... Nigerian Housing Administration (SAUS)
NHA.......... Nitrohippuric Acid [*Organic chemistry*]
NHA.......... Nonhydrogen Atom [*Chemistry*]
NHA.......... Nonspecific Hepatocellular Abnormality [*Medicine*] (MAE)

NHA......... Northwest Hardwood Association [*Later, WHA*] (EA)
NHA......... Nursing Home Administration (SAUS)
NHA......... Nutritional Health Alliance
NHAAP...... National Heart Attack Alert Program
NHAC........ National Health Awareness Center [*Later, NHSAC*] (EA)
NHACC...... New Hampshire Association of Conservation Commissions (EARSL)
NHACE...... National Hispanic Association of Construction Enterprises (EA)
NHACES..... New Hampshire Association for Computer Education Statewide (EDAC)
NHACFC..... National Health Agencies for the Combined Federal Campaign [*Formerly, FSCNHA*] [*Later, NVHA*] (EA)
NH Act...... National Housing Act [*1934, 1954*] (DLA)
NH Admin Code... New Hampshire Code of Administrative Rules [*A publication*] (DLA)
NH Admin Rules Ann... New Hampshire Code of Administrative Rules Annotated [*A publication*] (AAGC)
NHAES...... New Hampshire Agricultural Experiment Station [*University of New Hampshire*] [*Research center*] (RCD)
NHaHS...... Harborfields High School, Harborfields, NY [*Library symbol*] [*Library of Congress*] (LCLS)
NHAIAC..... National Highway Accident and Injury Analysis Center
NHAM....... National Hose Assemblies Manufacturers Association [*Defunct*]
NHamB...... Hampton Bays Public Library, Hampton Bays, NY [*Library symbol*] [*Library of Congress*] [*Obsolete*] (LCLS)
NHamH...... Hilbert College, Hamburg, NY [*Library symbol*] [*Library of Congress*] (LCLS)
NHAMM..... North Hammond, IN [*American Association of Railroads railroad junction routing code*]
N Hamp..... New Hampshire Reports [*A publication*] (DLA)
NHampB.... Hampton Bays Public Library, Hampton Bays, NY [*Library symbol*] [*Library of Congress*] (LCLS)
N Hamp Rep... New Hampshire Reports [*A publication*] (DLA)
N Hampshire Rep... New Hampshire Reports [*A publication*] (DLA)
NH & C...... Railway and Canal Cases [*1835-55*] [*England*] [*A publication*] (DLA)
NH&RA...... National Housing & Rehabilitation Association (NTPA)
NH & S...... Needham, Harper & Steers [*Advertising agency*]
NH & S...... Nuclear Hardening and Survivability
NH&S........ Nuclear Hardness and Survivability (SAUS)
NHANES..... National Health and Nutritional Examination Survey
NHANG...... New Hampshire Air National Guard (MUSM)
NHaOM...... Oldfield Middle School, Harborfield, NY [*Library symbol*] [*Library of Congress*] (LCLS)
NHAP........ National High-Altitude Photography Program (CARB)
NHAP........ National High Altitude Program (ALAC)
NHapS....... Suffolk County Department of Health Service, Hauppauge, NY [*Library symbol*] [*Library of Congress*] (LCLS)
NHapSA..... Suffolk Academy of Medicine, Hauppauge, NY [*Library symbol*] [*Library of Congress*] (LCLS)
NHAPTA..... American Physical Therapy Association, New Hampshire Chapter (EARSL)
NHAR........ New Hampshire Association of Realtors (EARSL)
Nh-Ar........ New Hampshire Department of Administration and Control, Division of Archives andRecords Management, Concord, NH [*Library symbol*] [*Library of Congress*] (LCLS)
NHAR........ Next Higher Assembly Removal Frequency [*Engineering*] (MCD)
NHarC....... Harriman College, Harriman, NY [*Library symbol*] [*Library of Congress*] (LCLS)
NHARC...... Nursing Home Advisory and Research Council (EA)
NHarn....... Harrison Public Library, Harrison, NY [*Library symbol*] [*Library of Congress*] (LCLS)
NHarnC...... Westchester County Courthouse, Harrison, NY [*Library symbol*] [*Library of Congress*] (LCLS)
NHas........ Hastings-On-Hudson Public Library, Hastings-On-Hudson, NY [*Library symbol*] [*Library of Congress*] (LCLS)
NHAS........ National Healthcare Antifraud Association [*Address unknown*] (EA)
NHAS........ National Hearing Aid Society (EA)
NHASA...... National Handbag and Accessories Salesmen's Association (EA)
NHasI........ Institute of Society, Ethics, and Life Sciences, The Hastings Center, Hastings- On-Hudson, NY [*Library symbol*] [*Library of Congress*] (LCLS)
NHAT........ Neutron Hardness Assurance Test
NHauS....... Suffolk County Department of Health Service, Hauppauge, NY [*Library symbol*] [*Library of Congress*] (LCLS)
NHAW....... Northamerican Heating and Airconditioning Wholesalers Association (EA)
NHAW....... Notable Hispanic American Women [*A publication*]
NHB.......... Kodiak [*Alaska*] [*Airport symbol*] (AD)
NHB.......... NASA Handbook (KSC)
NHB.......... National Harbours Board [*Canada*]
NHB.......... National Health Board
NHB.......... National Naval Medical Center [*Maryland*] [*Seismograph station code, US Geological Survey*] [*Closed*] (SEIS)
NH-B......... Naval Hospital-Bethesda (ACAE)
NHB.......... New Hibernian [*Vancouver Stock Exchange symbol*]
NHB.......... Nitro(hydroxy)benzoic Acid [*Organic chemistry*]
NHB.......... Northland Harbour Board (SAUS)
NHBC........ National House Building Council [*British*]
NHBE........ Normal Human Bronchial Epithelial [*Cells*]
NHBIA....... New Hampshire Brain Injury Association (SAUS)
NHBPCC.... National High Blood Pressure Coordinating Committee
NHBPEP..... National High Blood Pressure Education Program
NHBPM...... National Housebuilders' and Plumbers' Merchants [*British*] (DI)
NHBRA...... National Housebuilders' Registration Association [*British*] (DI)
NHBRC...... National House-Builders' Registration Certificate (ODA)
NHBRC...... National House-Builders Registration Council [*British*] (ILCA)
NHBS........ Natural History Book Service Ltd.
NHBS........ Navy Headquarters Budgeting System (GFGA)
NHBS/NHPS... Navy Headquarters Budgeting System/Navy Headquarters Programming System (GFGA)
NHBU........ New Hampshire Board of Underwriters (SAUS)
NHBW....... National Hook-Up of Black Women (EA)
NHC.......... Colgate University, Hamilton, NY [*Library symbol*] [*Library of Congress*] (LCLS)
NHC.......... National Havurah Committee (EA)
NHC.......... National Healthcare Ltd. [*AMEX symbol*] (SPSG)
NHC.......... National Healthcorp (EFIS)
NHC.......... National Health Council (EA)
NHC.......... National Heart Council (EA)
NHC.......... National Homecaring Council [*Later, FHH*] (EA)
NHC.......... National Homes Corporation (EFIS)
NHC.......... National Horse Carriers Association, Inc., Frankfort KY [*STAC*]
NHC.......... National Housing Center (EA)
NHC.......... National Housing Conference (EA)
NHC.......... National Housing Council [*of the HHFA*] [*Abolished, 1965*]
NHC.......... National Humanities Center (EA)
NHC.......... National Hunt Committee [*British*] (DI)
NHC.......... National Hunt Cup [*British*] (ROG)
NHC.......... National Hurricane Center [*National Weather Service*]
NHC.......... Native High Court Reports [*South Africa*] [*A publication*] (DLA)
NHC.......... Natl Healthcare L.P. [*AMEX symbol*] (TTSB)
NHC.......... Natural Hydrocarbon [*Organic chemistry*]
NHC.......... Navy Department Library, Naval Historical Center, Washington, DC [*OCLC symbol*] (OCLC)
NHC.......... Neighborhood Health Center [*Generic term*] (DHSM)
NHC.......... Neohemocyte [*An artificial red blood cell*]
NHC.......... Neonatal Hypocalcemia [*Medicine*] (DB)
NHC.......... New Hall College (SAUS)
NHC.......... New Haven [*Connecticut*] [*Seismograph station code, US Geological Survey*] [*Closed*] (SEIS)
NHC.......... New Hope Corporation Ltd. [*Australian Stock Exchange symbol*]
NHC.......... New Zealand National Health Committee (SAUS)
NHC.......... Next Hop Client (SAUS)
NHC.......... N-Hexylcarborane [*Rocket fuel*] (RDA)
NHC.......... Nicaraguan Humanitarian Coalition (EA)
NHC.......... Nonhistone Chromosomal Protein [*Genetics*] (MAE)
NHC.......... Normal-Hexylcarbane (MCD)
NHC.......... Northwest Horticultural Council (EA)
NHC.......... Northwest Hydraulic Consultants (SAUS)
NHC.......... Numatec Hanford Corp. (SAUS)
NHC.......... Nursing Home Care (MELL)
NHC.......... United States National Hurricane Center (SAUS)
NHCA........ National Hairdressers and Cosmetologists Association (EA)
NHCA........ National Health Club Association (EA)
NHCA........ National Hearing Conservation Association (EA)
NHCA........ National Hispanic Congress on Alcoholism [*Defunct*] (EA)
NHCA........ National Hispanic Council on Aging (EA)
NHCA........ Nebraska Health Care Association (EARSL)
NHCAA...... National Health Care Anti-Fraud Association (EA)
NHCAA...... New Hampshire Community Action Association (EARSL)
NHCAP...... Native Hawaiian Culture and Arts Program [*An association*] (EA)
NHCBS...... New Hampshire Council for Better Schools (SAUS)
NHCC........ NASA Headquarters Computer Center
N-HCC....... Nash-Healey Car Club (EA)
NHCC........ National Havurah Coordinating Committee (EA)
NHCC........ National Health Care Campaign [*Defunct*] (EA)
NHCC........ National Hebrew Culture Council (EA)
NHCC........ National Hepatitis C Coalition [*Association*] (EA)
NHCC........ National Hispanic Corporate Council (EA)
NHCCOEP... National Hispanic Colorectal Cancer Outreach and Education Project (SAUS)
NHCE........ Native Hawaiian Center of Excellence [*University of Hawaii*] (RCD)
NHCE........ Non-Highly Compensated Employee
NHCES...... National Health Care Expenditures Study (DHSM)
NHCFD...... National Health Care Foundation for the Deaf [*Later, Deaf-REACH*] (EA)
NHCH........ Newmark Homes Corp. [*NASDAQ symbol*] (NASQ)
NHCHC...... National Health Care for the Homeless Council [*Association*] (EA)
NHCI......... National Home Centers [*NASDAQ symbol*] (SAG)
NhCla........ Fiske Free Library, Claremont, NH [*Library symbol*] [*Library of Congress*] (LCLS)
NHCoA...... National Hispanic Council on Aging (EA)
NHCP........ National HUMINT Collection Plan (MCD)
NHCP........ Nonhistone Chromosomal Protein [*Genetics*]
NHCPPS.... New Hampshire Center for Public Policy Studies (RCD)
NHCQA...... National Healthcare Cost & Quality Association (EA)
NHCR........ New Hampshire Central Railroad [*Federal Railroad Administration identification code*]
NHCS........ National Health Care Survey [*Department of Health and Human Services*] (GFGA)
NHCS........ National Home Center Show (ITD)
NHCSA...... National Historic Communal Societies Association [*Later, CSA*] (EA)
NhCSp....... Saint Paul's School, Concord, NH [*Library symbol*] [*Library of Congress*] (LCLS)
NhCT........ New Hampshire Technical Institute, Concord, NH [*Library symbol*] [*Library of Congress*] (LCLS)
NHCU........ Nursing Home Care Unit [*Veterans Administration*]
NHCUC...... New Hampshire College and University Council, Library Policy Committee [*Library network*]
NhD.......... Dartmouth College, Hanover (SAUS)
NhD.......... Dartmouth College, Hanover, NH [*Library symbol*] [*Library of Congress*] (LCLS)

NHD .... Doctor of Natural History (WDAA)
NHD .... National History Day (EA)
NHD .... Nevada Highway Department (SAUS)
NHD .... New Harding Group, Inc. [*Toronto Stock Exchange symbol*]
NHD .... Normal Hair Distribution [*Medicine*] (DAVI)
NHD .... Not Heard [*Communications*]
NHDA .... National Huntington's Disease Association [*Later, HDSA*] (EA)
NHDAA ...... National Home Demonstration Agents' Association [*Later, NAEHE*] (EA)
NhD-BE ...... Dartmouth College, Business Administration and Engineering Library, Hanover, NH [*Library symbol*] [*Library of Congress*] (LCLS)
NHDC .... Connecticut History Day (EARSL)
NHDC .... National Hansen's Disease Center (DMAA)
NHDC .... National Home Demonstration Council [*Later, NEHC*] (EA)
NHDC .... NATO HAWK Documentation Center [*Missiles*] (NATG)
NHDC .... Naval Historical Display Center
NHDC .... Neohesperidin Dihydrochalcone [*Also, NEO-DHC*] [*Sweetening agent*]
NhD-D .... Dartmouth College, Dana Biomedical Library, Hanover, NH [*Library symbol*] [*Library of Congress*] (LCLS)
NHDF .... Normal Human Diploid Fibroblast [*Medicine*] (DMAA)
NhD-H .... Dartmouth College, Hood Museum, Hanover, NH [*Library symbol*] [*Library of Congress*] (LCLS)
NHDI .... NHD Stores, Inc. [*NASDAQ symbol*] (COMM)
NHDI .... Notch Die [*Tool*] (AAG)
NhD-K .... Dartmouth College, Kresge Physical Sciences Library, Hanover, NH [*Library symbol*] [*Library of Congress*] (LCLS)
NHDL .... Nonhigh Density Lipoprotein [*Medicine*] (DMAA)
NHDNA ...... Nucleohistone Deoxyribonucleic Acid
NhDo .... Dover Public Library, Dover, NH [*Library symbol*] [*Library of Congress*] (LCLS)
NhD-P .... Dartmouth College, Paddock Music Library, Hanover, NH [*Library symbol*] [*Library of Congress*] (LCLS)
NHDS .... National Health Data System (DMAA)
NHDS .... National Hospital Discharge Survey
NHDS .... New Hampshire Dental Society (EARSL)
NHDS .... Nonhazardous Dry Solid [*Shipping classification*]
NHDSC ...... National Hot Dog and Sausage Council (EA)
NHDX .... New Hampshire Department of Transportation [*Federal Railroad Administration identification code*]
NHE .... National Health Expenditures (IDYL)
NHE .... National Housing Endowment (EA)
NHE .... Nitrogen Heat Exchange
NHE .... Normal Hydrogen Electrode
NHE .... North Hennepin Community College Library, Brooklyn Park, MN [*OCLC symbol*] (OCLC)
NHE .... Nuclease-Hypersensitive Element [*Biochemistry*]
NHEA .... National Higher Education Association (EA)
NHEA .... New Hampshire Education Association (SAUS)
NHEB .... National Home Enlargement Bureau [*British*] (DI)
N HEB .... New Hebrew [*Language, etc.*] (ROG)
N HEB .... New Hebrides (ROG)
N Heb .... New Hebrides (SHCU)
NHEC .... Northern Hemisphere Exchange Center (SAUS)
NHEC Station... North Hemispheric Central Station (SAUS)
NHEDLP ..... National Housing and Economic Development Law Project
NHEF .... National Health Education Foundation
NHEIAP ..... New Hampshire Educational Improvement and Assessment Program
NHEIAY ...... Japanese Journal of Smooth Muscle Research (journ.) (SAUS)
NHEJ .... Non-Homologous End Joining
NHEK .... Normal Human Epidermal Keratinocyte
NHeLP .... National Health Law Program (EA)
NHELP .... New Hitachi Effective Library for Programming (NITA)
NHELTR ..... National High Energy Laser Test Range (ACAE)
NHem .... Hempstead Public Library, Hempstead, NY [*Library symbol*] [*Library of Congress*] (LCLS)
NHEM .... Normal Human Epidermal Melanocyte [*Cytology*]
NHEMA PAC... National Home Equity Mortgage Association Federal PAC [*Washington, DC*] (PACS)
NHemB ...... Burns & Roe, Inc., Branch Library, Hempstead, NY [*Library symbol*] [*Library of Congress*] (LCLS)
NHemCE .... William S. Covert School, Hempstead, NY [*Library symbol*] [*Library of Congress*] (LCLS)
NHemFE .... Franklin School, Hempstead, NY [*Library symbol*] [*Library of Congress*] (LCLS)
NHemFuE ... Fulton School, Hempstead, NY [*Library symbol*] [*Library of Congress*] (LCLS)
NHemGH .... Hempstead General Hospital, Medical Center, Hempstead, NY [*Library symbol*] [*Library of Congress*] (LCLS)
NHemH ...... Hofstra University, Hempstead, NY [*Library symbol*] [*Library of Congress*] (LCLS)
NHemJE ..... Jackson Elementary School, Hempstead, NY [*Library symbol*] [*Library of Congress*] (LCLS)
NHEML ...... National Hurricane and Experimental Meteorology Laboratory [*Marine science*] (MSC)
NHEML ...... United States National Hurricane Experimental Meteorological Laboratory (SAUS)
NHemLE .... Ludlum School, Hempstead, NY [*Library symbol*] [*Library of Congress*] (LCLS)
NHemLJ ..... Lawrence Road Junior High School, Hempstead, NY [*Library symbol*] [*Library of Congress*] (LCLS)
NHemME .... Marshall School, Hempstead, NY [*Library symbol*] [*Library of Congress*] (LCLS)
NHemMS ... Hempstead Middle School, Hempstead, NY [*Library symbol*] [*Library of Congress*] (LCLS)
NHemNH .... Nassau County Department of Health, Hempstead, NY [*Library symbol*] [*Library of Congress*] (LCLS)
NHemNHR .. Nassau County Department of Health, Division of Laboratories and Research, Hempstead, NY [*Library symbol*] [*Library of Congress*] (LCLS)
NHemPE .... Prospect School, Hempstead, NY [*Library symbol*] [*Library of Congress*] (LCLS)
NHemSH .... Hempstead Senior High School, Hempstead, NY [*Library symbol*] [*Library of Congress*] (LCLS)
NHemWE ... Washington School, Hempstead, NY [*Library symbol*] [*Library of Congress*] (LCLS)
NHen .... Henderson Free Library, Henderson, NY [*Library symbol*] [*Library of Congress*] (LCLS)
NHEN .... National Holistic Education Network (EA)
NHENMA .... National Hand Embroidery and Novelty Manufacturers Association [*Defunct*] (EA)
NHEP .... Nicaragua-Honduras Education Project (EA)
NHEP .... Nuclear Hardness Evaluation Procedures Program (ACAE)
NHEPLC ..... Nepal Hydro and Electric Production Limited Company (SAUS)
NHERI .... National Home Education Research Institute (EA)
NHerkCHi ... Herkimer County Historical Society, Herkimer, NY [*Library symbol*] [*Library of Congress*] (LCLS)
NHerrSH .... Herricks Senior High School, Herricks, NY [*Library symbol*] [*Library of Congress*] (LCLS)
NHES .... National Health Enhancement Systems, Inc. [*NASDAQ symbol*] (NQ)
NHES .... National Health Examination Survey [*Department of Health and Human Services*] (GFGA)
NHES .... National Humane Education Society (EA)
NHES .... Natl Health Enhacement Sys [*NASDAQ symbol*] (TTSB)
NHESA ...... National Higher Education Staff Association [*Defunct*] (EA)
NHESP ...... Natural Heritage and Endangered Species Program [*Massachusetts State Division of Fisheries and Wildlife*] [*Also, an information service or system*] (IID)
NHew .... Hewlett-Woodmere Public Library, Hewlett, NY [*Library symbol*] [*Library of Congress*] (LCLS)
NHewE ...... Hewlett Elementary School, Hewlett, NY [*Library symbol*] [*Library of Congress*] (LCLS)
NHewFC ..... Franlin Early Childhood Center, Hewlett, NY [*Library symbol*] [*Library of Congress*] (LCLS)
NHewFE ..... Franklin Elementary School, Hewlett, NY [*Library symbol*] [*Library of Congress*] (LCLS)
NHewLD .... Lawrence Country Day School, Hewlett, NY [*Library symbol*] [*Library of Congress*] (LCLS)
NHewOE .... Ogden Elementary School, Hewlett, NY [*Library symbol*] [*Library of Congress*] (LCLS)
NHewSH .... G. W. Hewlett Senior High School, Hewlett, NY [*Library symbol*] [*Library of Congress*] (LCLS)
NHewWM ... Woodmere Middle School, Hewlett, NY [*Library symbol*] [*Library of Congress*] (LCLS)
NhExP .... Phillips Exeter Academy, Exeter, NH [*Library symbol*] [*Library of Congress*] (LCLS)
NHF .... National Hairdressers' Federation [*British*] (BI)
NHF .... National Handicapped Foundation (EA)
NHF .... National Headache Foundation (EA)
NHF .... National Health Federation (EA)
NHF .... National Health Foundation (NADA)
NHF .... National Heart Foundation (NADA)
NHF .... National Hemophilia Foundation (EA)
NHF .... National Humanities Faculty [*Later, NFHAS*] (EA)
NHF .... National Hunting and Fishing [*In "NHF" Day*] [*National Rifle Association*]
NHF .... National Hydrocephalus Foundation (EA)
NHF .... Natural Heritage Fund (SAUS)
NHF .... Nausori Highlands [*Fiji*] [*Seismograph station code, US Geological Survey*] (SEIS)
NHF .... Naval Historical Foundation (EA)
NHF .... New Halfa [*Sudan*] [*Airport symbol*] (OAG)
NHF .... Nonimmune Hydrops Fetalis [*Medicine*] (DMAA)
NHF .... Nordic Hydrological Association (SAUS)
NHF .... Nordiska Handikappforbundet [*Nordic Association for the Handicapped - NAH*] (EAIO)
NHF .... Nordisk Herpetologisk Forening [*Scandinavian Herpetological Society - SHS*] (EAIO)
NHF .... Nordisk Hydrologisk Forening [*Nordic Association for Hydrology - NAH*] [*Denmark*] (EAIO)
NHFA .... National Home Furnishings Association (EA)
NHFF .... National Historical Fire Foundation (EA)
NHFL .... National Home Fashions League (EA)
NHFP .... New Hebrides Federal Party [*Political party*] (PPW)
NHFPL .... New Haven Free Public Library (SAUS)
NhFr .... Franklin Public Library, Franklin, NH [*Library symbol*] [*Library of Congress*] (LCLS)
NHFRA ...... National Hay Fever Relief Association [*Defunct*] (EA)
NHG .... Newhawk Gold Mines Ltd. [*Toronto Stock Exchange symbol*] [*Vancouver Stock Exchange symbol*]
NHG .... New High German [*Language, etc.*]
NHG .... Normal Human Globulin [*or anticancer substance derived from NHG*] [*Biochemistry*]
NHG .... Northern Hemisphere Glaciation
NHG .... Tetelcingo Nahuatl [*Language symbol*] (ETLW)
NHGJ .... Normal Human Gastric Juice [*Medicine*] (DMAA)
NHGRI .... National Human Genome Research Institute (HGEN)
NHGS .... Non-Hydrogenous Gas Delivery System (SAUS)
NHH .... Neither Help nor Hinder
NHH .... Neurohypophyseal Hormone (DB)

NhHaCR..... United States Army, Cold Regions Research and Engineering Laboratory, Hanover, NH [*Library symbol*] [*Library of Congress*] (LCLS)
NHHC........ National Home Health Care Corp. [*NASDAQ symbol*] (SPSG)
NHHC........ Natl Home Health Care [*NASDAQ symbol*] (TTSB)
NHHCA...... New Hampshire Health Care Association (EARSL)
NhHen....... Tucker Free Library, Henniker, NH [*Library symbol*] [*Library of Congress*] (LCLS)
NhHenN...... New England College, Henniker, NH [*Library symbol*] [*Library of Congress*] (LCLS)
NhHi......... New Hampshire Historical Society, Concord, NH [*Library symbol*] [*Library of Congress*] (LCLS)
NH His S.... New Hampshire Historical Society. Prroceedings (SAUS)
NhHopA..... New Hampshire Antiquarian Society, Hopkinton, NH [*Library symbol*] [*Library of Congress*] (LCLS)
NHHRA...... National Hereford Hog Record Association (EA)
NHHS........ New Hampshire Historical Society (SAUS)
NHHS........ Non-Household Sources (SAUS)
NH-HY....... Harvard University, Harvard-Yenching Institute [*Chinese-Japanese Library*],Cambridge, MA [*Library symbol*] [*Library of Congress*] (LCLS)
NHI.......... Jacksonville, FL [*Location identifier*] [*FAA*] (FAAL)
NHI.......... Naphtali Herz Imber (BJA)
NHI.......... Nathan Hale Institute (EA)
NHI.......... National Health Insurance [*British*]
NHI.......... National Health Investors [*NYSE symbol*] (SPSG)
NHI.......... National Heart Institute [*Later, NHLI, NHLBI*] [*National Institutes of Health*]
NHI.......... National Highway Institute
NHI.......... National Hobby Institute [*Defunct*]
NHI.......... National Housing Institute (EA)
NHI.......... National Humanities Institute (EA)
NHI.......... NATO Helicopter Industries (SAUS)
NHI.......... Nelson Holdings International Ltd. [*Toronto Stock Exchange symbol*] [*Vancouver Stock Exchange symbol*]
NHi.......... New York Historical Society, New York, NY [*Library symbol*] [*Library of Congress*] (LCLS)
NHI.......... Nielsen Home Video Index [*A. C. Nielsen Co.*] (NTCM)
NHI.......... No Humans Involved (SAUS)
NHIA......... National Holography and Imaging Association (EA)
NHIBAC..... National Health Insurance Benefits Advisory Council [*Medicine*] (EDAA)
NHIC......... NASA Hazards Identification Committee (KSC)
NHIC......... National Health Information Center [*US Department of Health and Human Services*] [*Office of Disease Prevention and Health Promotion*] (IID)
NHIC......... National Health Information Clearinghouse [*Public Health Service*] [*Later, ODPHP Health Information Center*] (IID)
NHIC......... National Heritage Insurance Co.
NHIC......... National Home Improvement Council [*Later, NARI*] (EA)
NHIC......... Nichols-Homeshield, Inc. (SAUS)
NHick........ Hicksville Free Public Library, Hicksville, NY [*Library symbol*] [*Library of Congress*] (LCLS)
NHickAd..... Hicksville Administration, Hicksville, NY [*Library symbol*] [*Library of Congress*] (LCLS)
NHickBE..... Burns Elementary School, Hicksville, NY [*Library symbol*] [*Library of Congress*] (LCLS)
NHickCE..... Old Country Elementary School, Hicksville, NY [*Library symbol*] [*Library of Congress*] (LCLS)
NHickDLE... Dutch Lane Elementary School, Hicksville, NY [*Library symbol*] [*Library of Congress*] (LCLS)
NHickEE..... East Elementary School, Hicksville, NY [*Library symbol*] [*Library of Congress*] (LCLS)
NHickFE..... Fork Elementary School, Hicksville, NY [*Library symbol*] [*Library of Congress*] (LCLS)
NHickHT.... Holy Trinity Diocesan High School, Hicksville, NY [*Library symbol*] [*Library of Congress*] (LCLS)
NHIckL...... Long Island Lighting Co., Hicksville, NY [*Library symbol*] [*Library of Congress*] (LCLS)
NHickLE..... Lee Elementary School, Hicksville, NY [*Library symbol*] [*Library of Congress*] (LCLS)
NHickOL.... Our Lady of Mercy School, Hicksville, NY [*Library symbol*] [*Library of Congress*] (LCLS)
NHickSH.... Hicksville Senior High School, Hicksville, NY [*Library symbol*] [*Library of Congress*] (LCLS)
NHickWE.... Willet Elementary School, Hicksville, NY [*Library symbol*] [*Library of Congress*] (LCLS)
NHickWoE.. Woodland Avenue Elementary School, Hicksville, NY [*Library symbol*] [*Library of Congress*] (LCLS)
NHID......... National Healthcare Identifier (GART)
NHIDA....... No-Hands-in-the-Die-Area (SAUS)
NHIF......... Brain Injury Association [*Formerly, National Head Injury Foundation*] (EA)
NHIF......... National Head Injury Foundation (EA)
NHig......... Highland Free Library, Highland, NY [*Library symbol*] [*Library of Congress*] (LCLS)
NHigfL....... Ladycliff College, Highland Falls, NY [*Library symbol*] [*Library of Congress*] (LCLS)
NHigm....... Rushmore Memorial Library, Highland Mills, NY [*Library symbol*] [*Library of Congress*] (LCLS)
NHIP......... National Health Insurance Plan [*Medicine*] (EDAA)
NHIP......... Natl Hlth Inv 8.50%Cv Pfd [*NYSE symbol*] (TTSB)
NHIP......... Nursing Home Improvement Program [*National Institute of Mental Health*]
NHIR......... Natural History Information Retrieval System [*Smithsonian Institution*]
NHIR......... New Hope & Ivyland Railroad Co. [*AAR code*]
NHIS......... National Health Interview Survey [*Department of Health and Human Services*] (GFGA)
NHIS......... Navy Hazardous Materials Information System (DNAB)
NHIS......... New Hampshire International Speedway [*Loudon*]
NHIS......... Nuclear Hardening Interceptor Structure
NHIS......... Nursing Home Information Service (EA)
NHISCH..... National Health Interview Survey of Child Health [*Department of Health and Human Services*]
NHIU......... Norse Hydrogas [*Intermodal shipping container symbol*] (TVRC)
NHIY......... Northumberland Hussars Imperial Yeomanry [*British military*] (DMA)
NHJ.......... Nathaniel Hawthorne Journal [*A publication*] (ANEX)
NHJA......... National Hunter and Jumper Association (EA)
NHJC......... National Hunter/Jumper Council [*Association*] (EA)
NHjI.......... International Business Machines Corp., Components Division Library, Hopewell Junction, NY [*Library symbol*] [*Library of Congress*] (LCLS)
NHK.......... Frank Aviation, Inc. (SAUS)
NHK.......... Nippon Hoso Kyokai [*Japanese national broadcasting system*] (NTCM)
NHK.......... Normal Human Kidney [*Medicine*] (DMAA)
NHK.......... Patuxent River, MD [*Location identifier*] [*FAA*] (FAAL)
NhKe......... Keene Public Library, Keene, NH [*Library symbol*] [*Library of Congress*] (LCLS)
NhKeHi...... Historical Society of Cheshire County, Keene (SAUS)
NhKeHi...... Historical Society of Cheshire County, Keene, NH [*Library symbol*] [*Library of Congress*] (LCLS)
NhKeK....... Keene State College, Keene, NH [*Library symbol*] [*Library of Congress*] (LCLS)
NHKidQ..... New Horizon Kids Quest, Inc. [*Associated Press*] (SAG)
NHK Lab Note... NHK Laboratories Note (SAUS)
NHK Tech J... NHK Technical Journal (SAUS)
NHKYA...... National Hand Knitting Yarn Association [*Later, NHKYC*] (EA)
NHKYC...... National Hand Knitting Yarn Committee [*Defunct*] (EA)
NHL.......... Hamilton Public Library, Hamilton, NY [*Library symbol*] [*Library of Congress*] (LCLS)
NHL.......... National Historic Landmark
NHL.......... National Hockey League (EA)
NHL.......... Negro Heritage Library
NHL.......... Newhall, CA [*Amtrak Busline code*]
NHL.......... Newhall Land & Farming Co. [*NYSE symbol*] (SPSG)
NHL.......... Nodular Histiocytic Lymphoma [*Oncology*]
NHL.......... Noise Interference Level (MELL)
NHL.......... Non-Hodgkin's Lymphoma [*Oncology*]
NHL.......... Nordic Federation of Heart and Lung Associations (EA)
NHL.......... Normal Hearing Level (MELL)
NHL.......... Normal Hormone Level (MELL)
NHL.......... Normal Human Lymphocyte
NHL.......... Northcal Resources [*Vancouver Stock Exchange symbol*]
NHL.......... Notes from Hume's Lectures [*A publication*] (DLA)
NHLA......... National Hardwood Lumber Association (EA)
NHLA......... National Health Lawyers Association (EA)
NHLA......... National Hispanic Leadership Agenda (EA)
NHLA......... National Housewives' League of America (EA)
NHLA......... National Housewives League of America for Economic Security (EA)
NHLA......... Norwegian Heart and Lung Association (SAUS)
NHLBAC..... National Heart, Lung, and Blood Advisory Council [*National Institutes of Health*]
NHLBCA..... National Hockey League Booster Clubs Association (EA)
NHLBI....... National Heart, Lung, and Blood Institute [*Bethesda, MD*] [*National Institutes of Health*]
NHLBIC...... National Heart, Lung, and Blood Information Center (PAZ)
NHLBI OEI... NHLBI Obesity Education Initiative (SAUS)
NHLC......... National Hispanic Leadership Conference (EA)
NHLC......... National Home Loans Corp. [*British*]
NhLe......... Lebanon Public Library, Lebanon, NH [*Library symbol*] [*Library of Congress*] (LCLS)
NhLeHi...... Lebanon Historical Society, Lebanon, NH [*Library symbol*] [*Library of Congress*] (LCLS)
NHLF......... National Heritage Lottery Fund [*British*] (WDAA)
NHLI......... National Heart and Lung Institute [*Later, NHLBI*] [*National Institutes of Health*]
NHLN......... Not at Home - Left Notice [*Telegraphy*] (PCTE)
NHLP......... National Housing Law Project (EA)
NHLPA....... National Hockey League Player's Association (EA)
NHL Rep.... New Hampshire Law Reporter [*A publication*] (DLA)
NHltCre..... National Healthcare Ltd. [*Associated Press*] (SAG)
NhM.......... Manchester City Library, Manchester, NH [*Library symbol*] [*Library of Congress*] (LCLS)
NHM.......... Natural History Museum [*British*]
NHM.......... Niihama [*Japan*] [*Seismograph station code, US Geological Survey*] [*Closed*] (SEIS)
NHM.......... Nitrosohexamethyleneimine [*Organic chemistry*]
NHM.......... No Hot Metal [*Photocomposition*]
NHM.......... Nonhostile Missing [*Military*] (CINC)
NHM.......... Normal Human Milk
NHM.......... Nozzle Hinge Moment
NHM.......... Nuclear Hyperfine Magnetic [*Rare-earth alloy*]
NHM.......... University of New Hampshire, Durham, NH [*OCLC symbol*] (OCLC)
NHMA........ National Handle Manufacturers Association [*Defunct*] (EA)
NHMA........ National Hispanic Medical Association (SAUS)
NHMA........ National Housewares Manufacturers Association (EA)
NHMA........ New Hampshire Medical Association (SAUS)
NHMC........ National Hispanic Media Coalition (EA)
NHMC........ National Hispanic Media Conference (EA)
NHMC........ National Hotline for Missing Children (MELL)

NHMC .... Normal Human Mammary Cell
NHMEL ...... National High Magnetic Field Laboratory
NHMF .... National Heritage Memoiral Fund (WDAA)
NHMF .... National Heritage Memorial Fund (AIE)
NHMFL ...... National High Magnetic Field Laboratory [*Florida State University*]
NHMIE .... National Hazardous Materials Information Exchange (EEVL)
NHMILCOM ... NATO HAWK Military Committee [*Missiles*] (AABC)
NHML .... Non-Hodgkin's Malignant Lymphoma [*Oncology*] (DMAA)
NhMND ..... Notre Dame College, Manchester, NH [*Library symbol*] [*Library of Congress*] (LCLS)
NHMO .... National HMO Corp. [*NASDAQ symbol*] (COMM)
NHMO .... NATO HAWK Management Office [*Missiles*] (NATG)
NHMP .... National Human Milk Monitoring Program (EAGT)
NHmpTh .... New Hampshire Thrift Bancshares, Inc. [*Associated Press*] (SAG)
NHMRC ..... National Health and Medical Research Council (DAVI)
NHMRC ..... National Hotel & Motel Reservations Corp.
NHMRCA .... National Health and Medical Research Council of Australia (ODA)
NHMS .... New Hampshire Medical Society (SAUS)
NhMSA ...... Saint Anselm's College, Manchester, NH [*Library symbol*] [*Library of Congress*] (LCLS)
NHMT .... Nuclear-Hardened Mosaic Technology (SAUS)
NhMV .... United States Veterans Administration Hospital, Manchester, NH [*Library symbol*] [*Library of Congress*] (LCLS)
NHN .... National Homes Network [*British*] (DI)
NHN .... Natural Heritage Network (SAUS)
NHN .... Nebraska HealthNetwork [*Information service or system*] (IID)
NHN .... New Hampshire North Coast Railroad [*Federal Railroad Administration identification code*]
NHN .... Northern Horizon [*Vancouver Stock Exchange symbol*]
NhNa .... Nashua Public Library, Nashua, NH [*Library symbol*] [*Library of Congress*] (LCLS)
NHNA .... New Hampshire Nurses Association (SAUS)
NhNaR ...... Rivier College, Nashua, NH [*Library symbol*] [*Library of Congress*] (LCLS)
NhNaS .... Sanders Associates, Inc., Technical Library, Nashua, NH [*Library symbol*] [*Library of Congress*] (LCLS)
NhNelC ...... Colby Junior College for Women [*Later, CSC*], New London, NH [*Library symbol*] [*Library of Congress*] (LCLS)
NHNP .... New Hebrides National Party [*Political party*] (FEA)
NHNR .... National Highway Needs Report [*Department of Transportation*]
NHO .... M/I Schottenstein Homes [*NYSE symbol*] (TTSB)
NHO .... National Hospice and Palliative Care Organization (NRGU)
NHO .... National Hospice Organization (EA)
NHO .... Native Habitat Organization [*Association*] (EA)
NHO .... Navy Hydrographic Office [*Later, NOO*]
NHO .... Northern Hemisphere Observatory [*Canary Islands*] (PDAA)
NHOA .... National Hemi Owners Association (EA)
NHOB .... Nonspecific Hierarchical Operational Binding [*Open Systems Interconnection*] (ODAA)
NHOH .... Never Heard of Him (or Her) (SAUS)
NHolbHS .... Sachem High School North, Holbrook (SAUS)
NHolb .... Sachem Public Library, Holbrook, NY [*Library symbol*] [*Library of Congress*] (LCLS)
NHolbHS .... Sachem High School North, Holbrook, NY [*Library symbol*] [*Library of Congress*] (LCLS)
NHolbSJ .... Seneca Junior High School, Holbrook, NY [*Library symbol*] [*Library of Congress*] (LCLS)
NHoll .... Community Free Library, Holley, NY [*Library symbol*] [*Library of Congress*] (LCLS)
NHOP .... National Hurricane Operations Plan (DNAB)
NHOP .... New Hope Steam Railway [*Federal Railroad Administration identification code*]
NHorizn ..... New Horizon Kids Quest, Inc. [*Associated Press*] (SAG)
NHorW ...... Westinghouse Electric Corp., Engineering Library, Horseheads, NY [*Library symbol*] [*Library of Congress*] (LCLS)
NHOS .... Naval Hospital
NHOS .... Nuclear Hardened Optical Sensor (ACAE)
NHOYOA .... National Home of Your Own Alliance (NRGU)
NHP .... National Hamiltonian Party (EA)
NHP .... National Historic Park (BARN)
NHP .... National Housing Partnership [*HUD*]
NHP .... National Humanitarian Party [*Political party*] [*Australia*]
NHP .... Nationwide Health Prop [*NYSE symbol*] (TTSB)
NHP .... Nationwide Health Properties, Inc. [*NYSE symbol*] (SPSG)
NHP .... Natural Hazards Project [*Emergency Management*] (EMA)
NHP .... Natural History Press (DGA)
NHP .... Neighborhood Health Program [*Generic term*]
NHP .... Net Horsepower [*Engineering*]
NHP .... Network Host Protocol
NHP .... New Haven Free Public Library, New Haven, CT [*OCLC symbol*] (OCLC)
NHP .... New Health Practitioners [*Nurse practitioners and physician assistants*]
NHP .... New Hebrides Protectorate (SAUS)
NHP .... NHP, Inc. [*Associated Press*] (SAG)
NHP .... Nitrogen High Pressure
NHP .... Nodular Hyperplasia of Prostate [*Medicine*] (MELL)
NHP .... Nominal Horsepower
NHP .... Non-health Practitioner [*Medicine*] (EDAA)
NHP .... Nonhemoglobin Protein [*Medicine*] (MELL)
NHP .... Nonhistone Protein (DB)
NHP .... Nonhuman Primate
NHP .... Noninverted Hand Position [*Neuropsychology*]
NHP .... Normal Hearing Peer [*of the hearing-impaired*]
NHP .... Normal Human-Pooled Plasma
NHP .... Nuclear Heart Pacer
NHP .... Numeric Hand-Printing (SAUS)
NHP .... Nursing Home Placement (DAVI)
NHPA .... National Hispanic Psychological Association [*Defunct*] (EA)
NHPA .... National Historic Preservation Act (GNE)
NHPA .... National Historic Preservation Act of 1966
NHPA .... National Horseshoe Pitchers Association of America (EA)
NH-PA .... Nurse Healers - Professional Associates (NTPA)
NHPA .... Nurse Healers - Professional Association (EA)
NHPAA ...... National Historic Preservation Act Amendments of 1980 (COE)
NHPAA ...... National Horseshoe Pitchers Association of America (EA)
NHPC .... National Health Planning Council (DMAA)
NHPC .... National Historical Publications Commission [*Later, NHPRC*]
NHPDA ...... National Honey Packers and Dealers Association (EA)
NHPDPA ..... National Health Promotion and Disease Prevention Act of 1976 (COE)
NHPE .... Nuclear Hardening Evaluation Procedures (SAUS)
NHPF .... National Health Policy Forum (EA)
NHPGA ...... New Hampshire Personnel and Guidance Association (SAUS)
NhPHi .... Peterborough Historical Society, Peterborough, NH [*Library symbol*] [*Library of Congress*] (LCLS)
NHPI .... NHP, Inc. [*NASDAQ symbol*] (SAG)
NHPIC .... National Health Planning Information Center [*Public Health Service*] [*Database*] (IID)
NHpJR .... James Roosevelt Library, Hyde Park, NY [*Library symbol*] [*Library of Congress*] [*Obsolete*] (LCLS)
NHPL .... New Hampshire Public Library (SAUS)
NHPL .... New Haven Public Library (SAUS)
NHPL Bul ... New Hampshire Public Library Bulletin (SAUS)
NHPLO ...... NATO HAWK Production and Logistics Organization [*France*] (NATG)
NhPlS .... Plymouth State College of the University of New Hampshire, Plymouth, NH [*Library symbol*] [*Library of Congress*] (LCLS)
NHPMA ..... New Hampshire Podiatric Medical Association (EARSL)
NHPMA ..... Northern Hardwood and Pine Manufacturers Association [*Defunct*] (EA)
NHPN .... National Highway Planning Network [*FHWA*] (TAG)
NHPO .... National Health Program for Orthopaedics [*Medicine*] [*AAOS*] (EDAA)
NHPO .... NATO HAWK Production Organization [*Missiles*]
NhPoA .... Portsmouth Athenaeum, Portsmouth, NH [*Library symbol*] [*Library of Congress*] (LCLS)
NhPoS .... Strawbery Banke, Portsmouth, NH [*Library symbol*] [*Library of Congress*] (LCLS)
NHPP .... National Health Professions Placement Network
NHPP .... National Hormone and Pituitary Program (EA)
NHPP .... Non-Homogeneous Poisson Process (SAUS)
NHpR .... Franklin D. Roosevelt Library, Hyde Park, NY [*Library symbol*] [*Library of Congress*] [*Obsolete*] (LCLS)
NHPRC ...... National Historical Publications and Records Commission [*Formerly, NHPC*] [*Washington, DC*]
NHPRO ...... National Historical Publications and Records Commission
NHPRO ...... Nitrosohydroxyproline [*Organic chemistry*]
NHPS .... New Hampshire Pharmaceutica Association (SAUS)
NHPSCR .... New Hampshire Public Service Commission Reports [*A publication*] (DLA)
NHPYR ...... Nitrosohydroxypyrrolidine [*Organic chemistry*]
NHQ .... NASA Headquarters
NHQ .... National Headquarters
NHQ .... Naval Headquarters (SAUS)
NHQ .... Nuclear Hyperfine Quadrupolar [*Rare-earth alloy*]
NHQC .... National Hispanic Quincentennial Commission (EA)
NHQRA ...... Nursing Home Quality Reform Act
NHR .... Naro [*Language symbol*] (ETLW)
NHR .... National Handwriting Recognition (VLIE)
NHR .... National Heritage (EFIS)
NHR .... National Housewives Register [*British*]
NHR .... National Hunt Rules [*British*]
NHR .... Natl Health Realty [*AMEX symbol*] (SG)
NHR .... Naval High Refresh display system (SAUS)
NHR .... Net Histocompatibility Ratio
NHR .... New Hampshire Reports [*A publication*] (DLA)
NHR .... Non Hierarchial Routing (SAUS)
NHR .... Non-Hierarchical Routing (VLIE)
NHR .... North Hart Resources [*Vancouver Stock Exchange symbol*]
NHR .... Nova/Husky Research Corp. (SAUS)
NHR .... Nova/Husky Research Corp. Ltd. [*UTLAS symbol*]
NHRA .... National Hot Rod Association (EA)
NHRA .... National Housing and Rehabilitation Association (EA)
NHRA .... National Human Resources Association (NTPA)
NHRA .... Next Higher Recoverable Assembly (SAUS)
NHRA .... Next Higher Repairable Assembly (MCD)
NHRAC ...... National Health Resources Advisory Committee [*Terminated, 1978*] [*General Services Administration*] (EGAO)
NHRAIC ..... Natural Hazards Research and Applications Information Center [*University of Colorado - Boulder*] [*Research center*] (RCD)
NHRAW ..... Northamerican Heating, Refrigeration, and Airconditioning Wholesalers Association (NTPA)
NHRB .... National Health Review Board [*Proposed medical-care price regulator*] (ECON)
NHRC .... National Health Research Center (DAVI)
NHRC .... National Human Rights Committee (EA)
NHRC .... National Human Rights Congress [*Australia*]
NHRC .... National Hydrology Research Centre (CARB)
NHRC .... Naval Health Research Center (GRD)
NHRC .... Nigerian Human Rights Community (SAUS)
NHRCPPUS ... National Human Rights Campaign for Political Prisoners in the US (EA)

NHRD........ National Health Planning and Resource Development Act [*1974*] (DHSM)
NHRDP...... National Health Research and Development Program [*Canada*]
NHRE........ National Hail Research Experiment
NHRE........ United States National Hail Research Experiment (SAUS)
NH Rep..... New Hampshire Reports [*A publication*] (DLA)
NH Rev Stat... New Hampshire Revised Statutes [*A publication*] (AAGC)
NH Rev Stat Ann... New Hampshire Revised Statutes, Annotated [*A publication*] (DLA)
NHRI........ National Health Research Institutes [*Taiwan*]
NHRI........ National Hydrology Research Institute [*Canada*]
NHRIC....... National Health Related Items Code [*Medicine*] [*Other than drugs*] (EDAA)
NHRL........ National Hurricane Research Laboratory [*Later, AOML*]
NHRL........ Northern Hemisphere Reference Line [*Geology*]
NHRP........ National Heart Research Project (EA)
NHRP........ National Hurricane Research Project
NHRP........ Next Hop Resolution Protocol [*Computer science*]
NHRP........ Next Hop Routing Protocol (SAUS)
NHRR........ New Haven Railroad
NHRR........ New Hope & Ivyland Rail Road [*Federal Railroad Administration identification code*]
NHRRC...... National Hybrid Rice Research Center [*China*]
NHRS........ National Hospital Reserve Service [*Emergency Management*] (EMA)
NHRS........ New Hampshire Revised Statutes [*A publication*] (DLA)
NHrzWrld... New Horizons Worldwide, Inc. [*Associated Press*] (SAG)
NHS.......... Das Nordhebraeische Sagenbuch [*A publication*] (BJA)
NHS.......... International Society for the Prevention and Mitigation of Natural Hazards (SAUS)
NhS.......... Kelley Memorial Library, Salem, NH [*Library symbol*] [*Library of Congress*] (LCLS)
NHS.......... Nag Hammadi Studies [*A publication*] (BJA)
NHS.......... Nathaniel Hawthorne Society (EA)
NHS.......... National Handcraft Society [*Commercial firm*] (EA)
NHS.......... National Handicapped Sports (EA)
NHS.......... National Health Service [*British*]
NHS.......... National Health Survey
NHS.......... National Helicopter Services (SAUS)
NHS.......... National Highway System
NHS.......... National Historical Society [*Commercial firm*] (EA)
NHS.......... National Historic Site (BARN)
NHS.......... National Honor Society (EA)
NHS.......... National Huguenot Society (EA)
NHS.......... Native Human Serum Pooled [*Hematology*] (DAVI)
NHS.......... Natural Human Serum
NHS.......... Naval Honor Schools (AFIT)
NHS.......... Neighborhood Housing Services [*Generic term*]
NHS.......... New Hampshire Tracking Station (SAUS)
NHS.......... New Hampshire State Library, Concord, NH [*OCLC symbol*] (OCLC)
NHS.......... New Hampshire Tracking Station
NHS.......... Newport Historical Society (SAUS)
NHS.......... Next Hop Server (SAUS)
NHS.......... N-Hydroxysuccinimide [*Organic chemistry*]
NHS.......... Nikon Historical Society (EA)
NHS.......... Normal Horse Serum
NHS.......... Normal Human Sera (or Serum) (SAUS)
NHS.......... Normal Human Serum
NHS.......... North Hampton [*South Carolina*] [*Seismograph station code, US Geological Survey*] [*Closed*] (SEIS)
NHSA........ National Handicapped Skiers Association [*British*] (DBA)
NHSA........ National Head Start Association (EA)
NHSA........ National Heart Savers Association (EA)
NHSA........ National Highway Safety Administration [*Formerly, NHSB; later, NHTSA*] [*Department of Transportation*]
NHSA........ National Home Service Association [*Defunct*] (EA)
NHSA........ National Horse Show Association of America (EA)
NHSA........ Natural Health Society of Australia
NHSA........ Naval Historical Society of Australia
NHSA........ Negro Historical Society of America
NHSA........ Neighborhood Housing Services of America (EA)
NHSAA...... National Horse Show Association of America (EA)
NHSAA...... New Hampshire School Administrators Association (SAUS)
NHSAC...... National Health and Safety Awareness Center [*Defunct*] (EA)
NHSAC...... National Highway Safety Advisory Committee
NHSACA..... National High School Athletic Coaches Association (EA)
NHSAS...... National Health Service Audit Staff [*Department of Health and Social Security*] [*British*]
NHSB........ National High School Band Institute (EA)
NHSB........ National Highway Safety Bureau [*Later, NHSA, NHTSA*] [*Department of Transportation*]
NHSB........ New Hampshire Savings Bank Corp. (SAUS)
NHSBA...... New Hampshire School Boards Association (SAUS)
NHsBE....... Birchwood Elementary School, Huntington Station, NY [*Library symbol*] [*Library of Congress*] (LCLS)
NHSBVA..... National High School Boys Volleyball Association (EA)
NHSC........ National Health Service Corps [*Department of Health and Human Services*]
NHSC........ National Highway Safety Council (NADA)
NHSC........ National Historic Site of Canada
NHSC........ National Home Study Council (EA)
NHSC........ National Horse Show Commission (EA)
NHsCE....... Countrywood Elementary School, Huntington Station, NY [*Library symbol*] [*Library of Congress*] (LCLS)
NHSCP...... National Household Survey Capability Program [*United Nations*]
NHSCVO.... National Health Screening Council for Volunteer Organizations (EA)
NHSD........ National Health Survey Division [*of OSG*]
NHSD........ NATO HAWK Support Department [*Missiles*] (NATG)
NhSEA....... New Hampshire Society of Enrolled Agents (SAUS)
NHSF........ National Hispanic Scholarship Fund (EA)
NHSF........ National Horse Show Foundation (EA)
NHSGC...... New Hampshire Space Grant Consortium (RCD)
NHsH........ Half Hollow Hills Community Public Library, Huntington Station, NY [*Library symbol*] [*Library of Congress*] (LCLS)
NHsK........ KLD Associates, Inc., Huntington Station, NY [*Library symbol*] [*Library of Congress*] (LCLS)
NHSL........ New Hampshire State Library (SAUS)
NHSL........ New Horizons Savings & Loan Association [*NASDAQ symbol*] (SPSG)
NHSL........ NHS Financial [*NASDAQ symbol*] (TTSB)
NHSM....... No Hepatosplenomegaly [*On physical examination*] [*Gastroenterology*] (DAVI)
NHsME...... Maplewood Elementary School, Huntington Station, NY [*Library symbol*] [*Library of Congress*] (LCLS)
NHsMJ...... Memorial Junior High School, Huntington Station, NY [*Library symbol*] [*Library of Congress*] (LCLS)
NHsOE....... Oakwood Elementary School, Huntington Station, NY [*Library symbol*] [*Library of Congress*] (LCLS)
NHSP........ N-Hydroxysuccinimidyl Palmitate [*Organic chemistry*]
NHSR........ National Hospital Service Reserve [*British*]
NHSRA...... National Handicapped Sports and Recreation Association [*Later, NHS*] (EA)
NHSRA...... National High School Rodeo Association (EA)
NHSRP...... National Hail Suppression Research Program (SAUS)
NHSS........ National Herb Study Society (EA)
NHsS........ South Huntington Public Library, Huntington Station, NY [*Library symbol*] [*Library of Congress*] (LCLS)
NHsSAHS... Saint Anthony's High School, Huntington Station, NY [*Library symbol*] [*Library of Congress*] (LCLS)
NHsSE....... Silaswood Elementary School, Huntington Station, NY [*Library symbol*] [*Library of Congress*] (LCLS)
NHsSJH..... Henry L. Stinson Junior High School, Huntington Station, NY [*Library symbol*] [*Library of Congress*] (LCLS)
NHST........ Null Hypothesis Significance Testing (DIPS)
NHSV........ Normal Hourly Space Velocity [*Emission control*]
NHsW........ Walt Whitman Birthplace Association, Huntington Station, NY [*Library symbol*] [*Library of Congress*] (LCLS)
NHsWH...... Walt Whitman High School, Huntington Station, NY [*Library symbol*] [*Library of Congress*] (LCLS)
NHT.......... Corpus Christi, TX [*Location identifier*] [*FAA*] (FAAL)
NHT.......... Nationwide Housing Trust [*British*]
NHT.......... Natural Heritage Trust (SAUS)
NHT.......... Nernst Heat Theorem [*Physics*]
NHT.......... Nonpenetrating Head Trauma [*Medicine*] (DMAA)
NHT.......... Now Hear This (EFIS)
NHT.......... Nursing Home Type (ADA)
NHTAC...... Natural Heritage Trust Advisory Committee (SAUS)
NHTB........ New Hampshire Thrift [*NASDAQ symbol*] (TTSB)
NHTB........ New Hampshire Thrift Bancshares, Inc. [*NASDAQ symbol*] (NQ)
NHTC........ Natural Health Trends Corp. [*NASDAQ symbol*] (SAG)
NHTCW..... Natural Health Trends Wrrt'A' [*NASDAQ symbol*] (TTSB)
NHTCZ...... Natural Health Trends Wrrt'B' [*NASDAQ symbol*] (TTSB)
NHTD........ NASA Headquarters Telephone Directory
NHTI......... New Hampshire Technical Institute (SAUS)
NHTP........ Nursing Home-Type Patient
NHTPC...... National Housing and Town Planning Council [*British*]
NHTS........ New Hampshire Tracking Station (SAA)
NHTSA...... National Highway Traffic Safety Act (EEVL)
NHTSA...... National Highway Traffic Safety Administration [*Formerly, NHSB, NHSA*] [*Department of Transportation*]
NHTSA...... National Highway Transportation Safety Administration (EBF)
NHTU........ Naval Hovercraft Trials Unit
NH Turn..... New Hampshire Turnpike (SAUS)
NHu.......... Huntington Public Library, Huntington, NY [*Library symbol*] [*Library of Congress*] (LCLS)
nhu.......... New Hampshire [*MARC country of publication code*] [*Library of Congress*] (LCCP)
NhU.......... University of New Hampshire, Durham, NH [*Library symbol*] [*Library of Congress*] (LCLS)
NHUBW..... National Hook-Up of Black Women (EA)
NHUC........ National Highway Users Conference [*Later, HUF*]
NHuCE....... Cuba Hill Elementary School, Huntington, NY [*Library symbol*] [*Library of Congress*] (LCLS)
NHudC....... Columbia-Greene Community College, Hudson, NY [*Library symbol*] [*Library of Congress*] (LCLS)
NHudDAR... Daughters of the American Revolution, Hendrick Hudson Chapter, Hudson, NY [*Library symbol*] [*Library of Congress*] (LCLS)
NHudHi...... Columbia County, New York Official Historian, Hudson, NY [*Library symbol*] [*Library of Congress*] (LCLS)
NHudO....... Olana State Historic Site, Hudson, NY [*Library symbol*] [*Library of Congress*] (LCLS)
NHuEJ....... Elwood Junior High School, Huntington, NY [*Library symbol*] [*Library of Congress*] (LCLS)
NHuFE....... Flower Hill Elementary School, Huntington, NY [*Library symbol*] [*Library of Congress*] (LCLS)
NHuFJ....... Finley Junior High School, Huntington, NY [*Library symbol*] [*Library of Congress*] (LCLS)
NHuGH...... John H. Glenn High School, Huntington, NY [*Library symbol*] [*Library of Congress*] (LCLS)
NHuH........ Huntington Hospital, Huntington, NY [*Library symbol*] [*Library of Congress*] (LCLS)
NHuHAE..... Harley Avenue Elementary School, Huntington, NY [*Library symbol*] [*Library of Congress*] (LCLS)

NHuHE ...... Huntington Elementary School, Huntington, NY [*Library symbol*] [*Library of Congress*] (LCLS)
NHuHi .... Huntington Historical Society, Huntington, NY [*Library symbol*] [*Library of Congress*] (LCLS)
NHuHS ...... Huntington High School, Huntington, NY [*Library symbol*] [*Library of Congress*] (LCLS)
NHuI .... Immaculate Conception Seminary, Huntington, NY [*Library symbol*] [*Library of Congress*] (LCLS)
NHuJE .... Jefferson Elementary School, Huntington, NY [*Library symbol*] [*Library of Congress*] (LCLS)
NHuL .... Huntington Public Library, Huntington, NY [*Library symbol*] [*Library of Congress*] (LCLS)
NHuMHS .... Madonna Heights High School, Huntington, NY [*Library symbol*] [*Library of Congress*] (LCLS)
NhuSE .... Southdown Elementary School, Huntington, NY [*Library symbol*] [*Library of Congress*] (LCLS)
NHusk .... KLD Associates, Inc., Huntington Station, NY [*Library symbol*] [*Library of Congress*] (LCLS)
NHusMJ ..... Memorial Junior High School, Huntington Station, NY [*Library symbol*] [*Library of Congress*] (LCLS)
NHusWH .... Walt Whitman High School, Huntington Station, NY [*Library symbol*] [*Library of Congress*] (LCLS)
NHuTJ .... R. K. Toaz Junior High School, Huntington, NY [*Library symbol*] [*Library of Congress*] (LCLS)
NHV .... Natural Hazard Vulnerability Survey [*Emergency Management*] (EMA)
NHV .... New Haven Clock and Watch (SAUS)
NHV .... New Haven, CT [*Amtrak rail station code*]
NHV .... Nuku Hiva [*French Polynesia*] [*Airport symbol*] (OAG)
NHvL .... Long Island Lighting Co., Hicksville, NY [*Library symbol*] [*Library of Congress*] (LCLS)
NHVT .... New Hampshire & Vermont Railroad [*Federal Railroad Administration identification code*]
NHVX .... New Hope Valley Railway [*Federal Railroad Administration identification code*]
NHW .... National Health and Welfare Mutual Life Insurance Association [*Formerly, NHWRA*] (EA)
NHW .... Neuhebraeisches Woerterbuch [*A publication*] (BJA)
NHW .... New Hospital for Women [*1904*] [*British*] (ROG)
NHW .... Night Hawk Resources Ltd. [*Vancouver Stock Exchange symbol*]
NhWalHi .... Walpole Historical Society, Walpole, NH [*Library symbol*] [*Library of Congress*] (LCLS)
NHWC .... New Highway Carrier [*Common carrier symbol*]
NHWK .... Harris Computer Systems [*NASDAQ symbol*] (TTSB)
NHWK .... Harris Computer Systems Corp. [*NASDAQ symbol*] (SAG)
NHWM ...... Normal Human White Matter (DB)
NHWP .... Northeast Hazardous Waste Project [*Environmental Protection Agency*] (GFGA)
NHWRA ..... National Health and Welfare Retirement Association [*Later, NHW*] (EA)
NHWRDDC... NW Hazardous Waste Research, Development & Demonstration Center (SAUS)
NHWS .... National Hurricane Warning Service [*National Weather Service*]
NHWU .... Non-Heatset Web Unit (EA)
NHWZSP .... National Highway Work Zone Safety Program
NHX .... Albany, GA [*Location identifier*] [*FAA*] (FAAL)
nhx .... Narthex (VRA)
NHY .... NIPSCO Industries [*NYSE symbol*] (TTSB)
NHY .... Norsk Hydro AS [*NYSE symbol*] (SPSG)
NHY .... Northumberland Hussars Yeomanry [*British military*] (DMA)
NHYD .... Northern Hydrolics [*NCIC trailer make code*]
NHyF .... General Services Administration, National Archives and Record Service, Franklin D. Roosevelt Library, Hyde Park, NY [*Library symbol*] [*Library of Congress*] (LCLS)
NHZ .... Brunswick, ME [*Location identifier*] [*FAA*] (FAAL)
nhz .... Nanohertz (ELAL)
NHZ .... Nominal Hazard Zone [*Environmental science*] (COE)
NI .... [*First*] Cranial Nerve [*Second cranial nerve is NII, etc., through NVIII*] [*Medicine*] (DAVI)
NI .... Das Neue Israel [*A publication*] (BJA)
NI .... Inversion of the Note series (SAUS)
NI .... NAMBA [*North American Model Boating Association*] International (EA)
NI .... National Income
NI .... National Insurance [*British*]
NI .... National Interest
NI .... National Intervenors [*Defunct*] (EA)
NI .... Nation Institute (EA)
NI .... Nation of Ishmael [*An association*] (EA)
NI .... Native Infantry [*Indian Armed Forces regiment*]
NI .... Natural Intelligence (VLIE)
NI .... Nautical Institute [*British*] (EAIO)
NI .... Naval Infantry (SAUS)
NI .... Naval Instructor [*British*]
NI .... Naval Intelligence
NI .... Near Instantaneous (VLIE)
NI .... Need International [*An association*] (EA)
NI .... Negotiable Instrument
NI .... Neighbourhood Interchangeability (SAUS)
NI .... Netherlands Indies [*Later, Republic of Indonesia*]
NI .... Net Income
NI .... Net Interest
NI .... Network Identification [*Broadcasting*] (NTCM)
NI .... Network Interface [*Computer science*] (VLIE)
NI .... Network International (EA)
NI .... Neuraminidase Inhibition [*Medicine*] (DMAA)
NI .... Neurointermediate Lobe [*Of the pituitary*]
NI .... Neurological Impairment
NI .... Neurological Institute
NI .... Neurologically Intact [*Medicine*]
NI .... Neutralization Index [*Medicine*] (DMAA)
NI .... Neutraminidase Inhibition (PDAA)
NI .... New Impression [*Publishing*]
NI .... New Initiatives
NI .... New Internationalist [*Australia*] [*A publication*]
NI .... New Ireland
NI .... New Issue [*Publishing*]
NI .... News International [*An association*] (EA)
NI .... Niagara Institute (EA)
NI .... Nicaragua [*ANSI two-letter standard code*] (CNC)
NI .... Nicaraguan Airways (SAUS)
ni .... Nickel (VRA)
Ni .... Nickel [*Chemical element*]
Ni .... Nicolaus de Tudeschis [*Deceased, 1445*] [*Authority cited in pre-1607 legal work*] (DSA)
Ni .... Nicolaus Furiosus [*Flourished, 12th century*] [*Authority cited in pre-1607 legal work*] (DSA)
NI .... Nienburg [*Weser*] [*German license plate city code*]
NI .... Night (AABC)
Ni .... Nike (SAUS)
NI .... NIPSCO Industries [*NYSE symbol*] (SPSG)
NI .... NiSource, Inc. [*NYSE symbol*] (SG)
NI .... Nissho Iwai Corporation (EFIS)
NI .... Nitrogen [*Chemical element*]
NI .... No Imprint (ADA)
NI .... No Information
NI .... No Interaction [*Medicine*]
NI .... Noise Index
N/I .... Noise to Interference (SAUS)
N/I .... Noise to Interference Ratio [*Telecommunications*] (TEL)
NI .... No Issue
NI .... Non-Aligned [*Political group*] [*EC*] (ECED)
NI .... Non Indicate (VLIE)
NI .... Non-Indicate (SAUS)
NI .... Noninductive (DEN)
NI .... Noninhibit (SAUS)
NI .... Non-Inhibitable Interrupt (MHDB)
NI .... Non-Interlaced (CDE)
NI .... Non-Interlocked [*Indian Railway*] (TIR)
NI .... Nonintervention
NI .... Noninvasive Index [*Medicine*]
NI .... Non-inverting Input (SAUS)
NI .... Nonviolence International (EA)
NI .... Normal Impurity [*Metals*]
NI .... Normal Inferior
NI .... Normal Limits (IDYL)
NI .... Northern Illinois Gas Company (EFIS)
NI .... Northern Indiana Public Service Co. [*NYSE symbol*] (SAG)
NI .... Northern Indiana Railway
NI .... Northern Ireland Law Reports [*A publication*] (DLA)
NI .... Northern Island (SAUS)
NI .... North Indiana Public Service Co. [*AMEX symbol*] (SAG)
NI .... North Island [*New Zealand*] (BARN)
NI .... Notice of Information [*Computer science*]
NI .... Not Identified
NI .... Notifiable Installation (HEAS)
NI .... Not Illustrated [*Publishing*]
NI .... Not In
NI .... Not Indicated [*Laboratory science*] (DAVI)
N/I .... Not Indicated (IDYL)
NI .... Not Informed
NI .... Not Inoculated
NI .... Not Interested
NI .... Not Isolated
NI .... Not Issued (AAG)
NI .... Nuclear Instrumentation (NRCH)
NI .... Nuclear Island (NRCH)
NI .... Numerical Index (BUR)
NI .... Numeric Information (SAUS)
NI .... Numeric Item (SAUS)
NI .... Numismatics International (EA)
NI .... Tompkins County Public Library, Ithaca, NY [*Library symbol*] [*Library of Congress*] (LCLS)
NIA .... National Ice Association [*Later, PIA*] (EA)
NIA .... National Iceboat Authority
NIA .... National Impala Association (EA)
NIA .... National Income Accounts
NIA .... National Industrial Automation (GART)
NIA .... National Inholders Association [*Database producer*] (EA)
NIA .... National Institute on Aging [*Bethesda, MD*] [*National Institutes of Health*]
NIA .... National Insulation Association (NTPA)
NIA .... National Insulator Association (EA)
NIA .... National Insurance Association [*Chicago, IL*] (EA)
NIA .... National Intelligence Authority [*1946-1947*]
NIA .... National International Academy
NIA .... National Involvement Association (EA)
NIA .... National Irrigation Administration (NADA)
NIA .... Naval Intelligence Activity (DOMA)
NIA .... Navy Industrial Association [*Later, NSIA*]

NIA.......... Neighborhood Improvement Association (BARN)
NIA.......... Neighborhoods-in-Action [*An association*] (EA)
NIA.......... Nephelometric Immunoassay [*Analytical chemistry*]
NIA.......... Nephelometric Inhibition Assay [*Analytical chemistry*] (MAE)
NIA.......... Net Internal Area
NIA.......... Network Information Access (SAUS)
NIA.......... Network Interface Adapter [*Computer science*] (AGLO)
NIA.......... Neuromuscular Integrative Action
NIA.......... New Indo-Aryan [*Linguistics*] (IEL)
NIA.......... Newspaper Institute of America (EA)
NIA.......... Next Instruction Address (SAUS)
nia.......... Niacin (MELL)
NIA.......... Niagara [*NCIC car model code*]
NIA.......... Nickel-Iron Alloy
NIA.......... Nitroisatoic Anhydride [*Organic chemistry*]
NIA.......... No Information Available
NIA.......... No Input Acknowledge [*Computer science*]
NIA.......... Noise Impact Area (SAUS)
NIA.......... Norfolk Island [*Australia*] [*Seismograph station code, US Geological Survey*] [*Closed*] (SEIS)
NIA.......... Norfolk Island Airlines [*Australia*] [*ICAO designator*] (FAAC)
NIA.......... Not in Action (SAUS)
NIA.......... NOVA Interface Adapter (SAUS)
NIA.......... Nutrition Institute of America [*Inactive*] (EA)
NIAA........ National Independent Agents' Association [*Australia*]
NIAA........ National Indian Athletic Association (EA)
NIAA........ National Industrial Advertisers Association [*Later, B/PAA*]
NIAA........ National Institute of Animal Agriculture [*Defunct*] (EA)
NIAA........ National Institute on Alcohol Abuse and Alcoholism (SAUS)
NIAA........ No Idea At All (SAUS)
NIAA........ Northern Iowa Athletic Association (PSS)
NIAA........ Nuclear Industries Association of America (SAUS)
NIAAA...... National Institute on Alcohol Abuse and Alcoholism [*Rockville, MD*] [*Public Health Service*] [*Department of Health and Human Services*]
NIAAA...... National Interscholastic Athletic Administrators Association (EA)
NIAAA...... Northern Ireland Amateur Athletic Association (ODA)
NIAA-DTF... National Industry Associations Anti-Dumping Task Force [*Australia*]
NIAAP...... Indian Army Ammunition Plant (SAUS)
NIAB........ National Institute of Agricultural Botany (WDAA)
NIAB........ Naval Intelligence Advisory Board (DNAB)
NIABA...... National Italian American Bar Association (EA)
NIABS...... National Institute for Applied Behavioral Science
NIABY...... Not in Anyone's Back Yard (PA)
NIAC........ NASA Industrial Application Center [*University of Southern California*] [*Los Angeles*] [*Information service or system*] (IID)
NIAC........ NASA Industrial Applications Center [*University of Pittsburgh*] [*Pittsburgh, PA*]
NIAC........ National Industry Advisory Committee [*Terminated, 1986*] [*FCC*]
NIAC........ National Information and Analysis Center
NIAC........ National Infrastructure Assurance Council [*Emergency Management*] (EMA)
NIAC........ National Insulation and Abatement Contractors Association (EA)
NIAC........ National Insurance Advisory Committee [*British*] (DCTA)
NIAC........ Nebraska-Iowa Athletic Conference (PSS)
NIAC........ Nissho-Iwai American Corp. (SAUS)
NIAC........ Northern Ireland Automation Centre [*Queen's University of Belfast*] (CB)
NIAC........ Nuclear Insurance Association of Canada
NIAC........ Nutritional Information and Analysis Center [*Illinois Institute of Technology and Institute of Food Technologists*] (IID)
NIACA...... National Indirect Air Carrier Association [*Defunct*] (EA)
NIACE...... National Institute for the Advancement of Career Education [*Defunct*] (EA)
NIACE...... National Institute of Adult Continuing Education [*British*]
NIACRO.... Northern Ireland Association for the Care and Resettlement of Offenders (DI)
NIACT...... Night Action [*American diplomat's jargon*]
NIAD........ National Institute on Adult Daycare (EA)
NIADA...... National Independent Automobile Dealers Association (EA)
NIADA...... National Institute of American Doll Artists (EA)
NIADDK.... National Institute of Arthritis, Diabetes, and Digestive and Kidney Diseases [*National Institutes of Health*] (EA)
NIAE........ National Institute for Architectural Education (EA)
NIAE........ National Institute of Agricultural Engineering [*Research center*] [*British*] (IRC)
NIAF........ National Italian American Foundation (EA)
NIAFS...... Niagara Falls, NY [*American Association of Railroads railroad junction routing code*]
NIAG........ NATO Industrial Advisory Group (MCD)
NIAG........ Niagara (ROG)
NIAG........ Niagara Corp. [*NASDAQ symbol*] (SAG)
Niag........ Niagara Corp. [*Associated Press*] (SAG)
NIAG........ Niagara Trailer Company [*NCIC trailer make code*]
NI AG....... Nickel Silver (SAUS)
Niagara..... Fort Niagara, Niagara Falls, Niagara-on-the-Lake, Niagara River, Niagara University (SAUS)
Niagara U... Niagara University (GAGS)
NiagCp..... Niagara Corp. [*Associated Press*] (SAG)
NIAGRC..... National Institute on Aging's Gerontology Research Center (MELL)
NIAGW..... Niagar Corp. Wrrt [*NASDAQ symbol*] (TTSB)
NIAH........ National Indian AIDS Hotline (EA)
NIAID....... National Institute of Allergy and Infectious Diseases [*of National Institutes of Health*] [*Department of Health and Human Services*] [*Bethesda, MD*]
NIAISA..... Northwest Indiana Area Library Services Authority (SAUS)
NIAJ........ Niagara Junction Railway Co. [*Absorbed into Consolidated Rail Corp.*] [*AAR code*]
NIAL........ National Institute of Arts and Letters [*Later, AAIAL*] (EA)
NIAL........ Network for Informal Adult Learning (AIE)
NIAL........ Not In Active Labor [*Obstetrics*] (DAVI)
NIALSA..... Northwest Indiana Area Library Services Authority [*Library network*]
NIAM........ National Imaging, Inc. [*NASDAQ symbol*] (COMM)
NIAM........ National Institute of Advertising Management
NiaM........ Niagara Mohawk Power Corp. [*Associated Press*] (SAG)
NIAMDD.... National Institute of Arthritis, Metabolism, and Digestive Diseases [*Formerly, NIAMD*] [*Later, NIADDK*] [*National Institutes of Health*]
NiaMP...... Niagara Mohawk Power Corp. [*Associated Press*] (SAG)
NIAMS...... National Institute of Arthritis and Musculoskeletal and Skin Diseases [*Bethesda, MD*] [*Department of Health and Human Services*] (GRD)
NIAMSD.... National Institute of Arthritis and Musculoskeletal and Skin Diseases [*Department of Health and Human Services*] (GFGA)
NIAMSK.... National Institute of Arthritis and Musculoskeletal and Skin Diseases
NI&C........ Hippon Information and Communication (SAUS)
NI & C...... Nippon Information and Communication [*Joint venture of IBM Corp. Japan and Nippon Telegraph and Telephone*]
NI&C........ Nippon Information & Communication Corp. (SAUS)
NI & RT.... Numerical Index and Requirement Table (MCD)
NIANSW.... Nursery Industry Association of New South Wales [*Australia*]
NIAP........ National Income and Products [*Economics*]
NIAP........ National Information Assurance Partnership
NIAP........ Noninverting Amplifier Pair
NIAR........ National Institute of Agrobiological Resources [*Japan*]
NIAR........ National Institute of Atmospheric Research
NIAR........ Neutron-Induced Autoradiography
NIAS........ National Institute for Advanced Studies (EA)
NIAS........ National Institute of Aeronautical Sciences
NIAS........ National Institute of Airworthiness Surveyors [*Australia*]
NIAS........ Netware Internet Access Server (SAUS)
NIASA...... National Insurance Actuarial and Statistical Association [*Later, ISO*]
NIASE...... National Institute for Automotive Service Excellence
NIAT........ Non-Indexable Address Tag (SAA)
NIAT........ Nursery Industry Association of Tasmania [*Australia*]
NIATT...... National Institute for Advanced Transportation Technology [*University of Idaho*] (RCD)
NIAWA..... Nursery Industry Association of Western Australia [*Australia*]
NIAWR..... National Institute on Aging, Work, and Retirement [*Washington, DC*] (EA)
NIB.......... National Identification Bureau [*British*]
NIB.......... National Industries for the Blind (EA)
NIB.......... National Information Bureau [*Information service or system*] (EA)
NIB.......... National Institute for the Blind (EA)
NIB.......... National Investment Bank [*Ghana*] (EY)
NIB.......... Navigation Information Bulletin
NIB.......... Negative Impedance Booster [*Electronics*]
NIB.......... Negative Ion Beam
NIB.......... Negative Ion Blemish
NIB.......... Network Interface Board
NIB.......... New Iberia Bancorp [*AMEX symbol*] (TTSB)
NIB.......... New Iberia Bancorp, Inc. [*AMEX symbol*] (SAG)
NIB.......... New Iberia, LA [*Amtrak rail station code*]
NIB.......... New in Box [*Watch collecting*]
NIB.......... Nigeria International Bank Ltd.
NIB.......... Node Initialization Block [*Computer science*] (IBMDP)
NIB.......... Noise Investigation Bureau (SAUS)
NIB.......... Noninterference Basis
NIB.......... Norddeutsche Innovations-Und Beteiligungsgesellschaft (EFIS)
NIB.......... Nordic Investment Bank (GNE)
NIB.......... North Ingalls Building (SAUS)
NIB.......... Not to Interface Base
NIBA........ National Industrial Belting Association (EA)
NIBA........ National Insurance Buyers Association
NIBA........ Nebraska Independent Bankers Association (TBD)
NIBAA...... National Insurance Brokers' Association of Australia
NIBC........ Northern Ireland Base Command [*World War II*]
NIBCA...... National Intercollegiate Boxing Coaches Association (EA)
NIberia..... New Iberia Bancorp, Inc. [*Associated Press*] (SAG)
NIberiaB.... New Iberia Bancorp [*Associated Press*] (SAG)
NIBESA..... National Independent Bank Equipment and Systems Association [*Park Ridge, IL*] (EA)
NIBGE...... National Institute of Biotechnology and Genetic Engineering [*Pakistan*]
NIBID....... National Investment Bank for Industrial Development [*Greece*]
NIBJL....... National Information Bureau for Jewish Life (EA)
NIBL........ National Industrial Basic Language (MHDB)
NIBL........ National Industrial Basketball League (EA)
NIBM........ National Institute for Burn Medicine (EA)
NIBMAR.... No Independence before Majority African Rule [*British policy in regard to Rhodesia*]
NIBOR...... New York Interbank Official Rate
NIBP........ Noninvasive Blood Pressure [*Medicine*] (DMAA)
Ni-BR........ Butadiene Rubber Based on Nickel Catalyst (SAUS)
NIBRA...... National Independent Bicycle Rep Association [*Defunct*] (EA)
NIBS........ National Institute of Building Sciences (EA)
NIBS........ National Institute of Business Sciences [*Industrial hygiene term*] (OHS)
NIBS........ National Interim Bankruptcy System (AAGC)
NIBS........ Neural, Informational, and Behavioral Science
NIBS........ Neutral Industry Booking System (AAGC)

NIBS .... Nippon Institute of Biological Sciences (DAVI)
NIBS .... Nuffield Interactive Book System [*British*] (TELE)
NIBS Bulletin... Nippon Institute for Biological Science Bulletin (SAUS)
NIBSC .... National Institute for Biological Standards and Control [*British*]
NIBTN .... Nitroisobutametriol Trinitrate [*An explosive*]
NIC.......... Cornell University, Ithaca, NY [*Library symbol*] [*Library of Congress*] (LCLS)
NIC.......... Naphthylisocyanate [*Organic chemistry*]
NIC.......... National Impeachment Coalition [*Defunct*] (EA)
NIC.......... National Incomes Commission [*Nickname: Nicky*] [*British*]
NIC.......... National Indications Center [*Disbanded*] [*DoD*]
NIC.......... National Industrial Council (EA)
NIC.......... National Informatics Center [*India*] [*Information service or system*]
NIC.......... National Information Center [*Emergency Management*] (EMA)
NIC.......... National Information Clearinghouse [*for Infants with Disabilities and Life-Threatening Conditions*] (PAZ)
NIC.......... National Information Clearinghouse for Infants with Disabilities and Life-Threatening Conditions
NIC.......... National Institute of Corrections [*Department of Justice*]
NIC.......... National Institute of Creativity [*Defunct*] (EA)
NIC.......... National Institute of Credit [*New York, NY*] (EA)
NIC.......... National Insurance Certificate [*British*]
NIC.......... National Insurance Contribution [*British*] (ECON)
NIC.......... National Insurance Contributions [*British*]
NIC.......... National Integrated Services Digital Network Council
NIC.......... National Intelligence Committee
NIC.......... National Intelligence Council (POLM)
NIC.......... National Interagency Council on Smoking and Health [*New York, NY*]
NIC.......... National Interfraternity Conference (EA)
NIC.......... National Interrogation Center [*Military*]
NIC.......... National Interstate Council of State Boards of Cosmetology (EA)
NIC.......... National Inventors Council [*Terminated, 1974*] [*National Institute of Standards and Technology*]
NIC.......... Natural Image Computer (PDAA)
NIC.......... Nauru Island Council [*Australia*]
NIC.......... Naval Intelligence Code [*World War II*] [*British*]
NIC.......... Naval Intelligence Command
NIC.......... Navigation Information Center
NIC.......... Navy Information Center
NIC.......... Nearly Instantaneous Compounding (MCD)
NIC.......... Neck Injury Criteria [*Automotive safety testing*]
NIC.......... Negative Immittance Converter [*Electronics*]
NIC.......... Negative Impedance Converter [*Electronics*]
NIC.......... Negative Ion Chamber
NIC.......... Neighborhood Info Centers Project (EA)
NIC.......... Neonatal Inclusion Conjunctivitis [*Medicine*] (MELL)
NIC.......... Neonatal Intensive Care
NIC.......... Netherlands Information Combine [*Delft*] [*Information service or system*] (IID)
NIC.......... Net Interest Cost [*Investment term*]
NIC.......... Networked Information Center (NETL)
NIC.......... Network Information Center [*Advanced Research Projects Agency*] [*DoD*]
NIC.......... Network Interface Card [*Computer science*]
NIC.......... Network Interface Control
NIC.......... Neurogenic Intermittent Claudication [*Medicine*] (DMAA)
NIC.......... Nevada Institute for Children (RCD)
NIC.......... New Community Instrument for Borrowing & Lending (WDAA)
NIC.......... New Initial Commissions [*Business term*]
NIC.......... New International Clinics [*Medicine*] [*Journal*] (EDAA)
NIC.......... New International Commentary on the New Testament [*A publication*] (BJA)
NIC.......... New Internet Computer
NIC.......... New Internet Computers
NIC.......... Newly Industrialised (or Industralized, or Industrializing) Coutries (or Country) (SAUS)
NIC.......... Newly Industrializing Country (ECON)
NIC.......... Newspaper Indexing Center [*Flint, MI*]
NIC.......... Newsprint Information Committee [*Defunct*] (EA)
NIC.......... Niagara International Center (or Centre) (SAUS)
Nic.......... Nicander [*Second century BC*] [*Classical studies*] (OCD)
NIC.......... Nicaragua [*ANSI three-letter standard code*] (CNC)
Nic.......... Nicaragua (VRA)
NIC.......... Nicaraguan Information Center (EA)
NIC.......... Nickling Resources, Inc. [*Vancouver Stock Exchange symbol*]
Nic.......... Nicolaus de Tudeschis [*Deceased, 1445*] [*Authority cited in pre-1607 legal work*] (DSA)
NIC.......... Nicolet Instrument Corp. (SAUS)
NIC.......... Nicosia [*Cyprus*] [*Airport symbol*] (AD)
Nic.......... Nicotinyl (SAUS)
Nic.......... Nicotinyl Alcohol [*Biochemistry*] (MAE)
nic.......... Niger-Congo [*MARC language code*] [*Library of Congress*] (LCCP)
NIC.......... Nineteen-Hundred Indexing and Cataloging (DIT)
NIC.......... Nippon International Containers (SAUS)
NIC.......... NIPSCO Capital Markets [*NYSE symbol*] (SAG)
NIC.......... NIPSCO Cap Mkt 7.75% Debt Sec [*NYSE symbol*] (TTSB)
NIC.......... Nisa [*Language symbol*] (ETLW)
NIC.......... Nissho Iwai Corporation (EFIS)
NIC.......... Noise Isolation Class (PDAA)
NIC.......... Nomarski Interference Contrast (SAUS)
NIC.......... Nominal Index Card (WDAA)
NIC.......... Non-Intel [*Corp.*]-Compatible Chips [*Computer science*]
NIC.......... Non-Intervention in Chile [*An association*] (EA)
NIC.......... Noninvasive Carotid [*Study*] [*Cardiology*] (DAVI)
NIC.......... Nonisothermal Calorimeter (SAUS)
NIC.......... Northern Illinois Commuter [*ICAO designator*] (FAAC)
NIC.......... Northern Intercollegiate Conference (PSS)
NIC.......... Not in Contact [*Electronics*] (DEN)
NIC.......... Not in Contract [*Technical drawings*]
NIC.......... Nudist Information Center [*Defunct*] (EA)
NIC.......... Numerical Interactive Controller [*Medicine*] (EDAA)
NIC.......... Numeric Intensive Computing (SAUS)
N i C......... Nurse in Charge (SAUS)
NIC.......... Nursing Interim Care (MELL)
NIC.......... Nursing Interventions Classification (SAUS)
NIC.......... US National Ice Centre (SAUS)
NICA......... National Ice Carving Association (EA)
NICA......... National Indian Counselors Association (EA)
NICA......... National Institute of Conveyancing Agents [*British*] (DBA)
NICA......... National Insulation Contractors Association [*Later, NIAC*] (EA)
NICA......... National Interfaith Coalition on Aging (EA)
NICA......... Netherlands Indies Civil Affairs Organization [*World War II*]
NICA......... Nicaragua Interfaith Committee for Action (EA)
NICA......... Nicaraguense de Aviacion SA [*Nicaragua*] [*ICAO designator*] (FAAC)
NICA......... Non-Interactive Computer Applications (SAUS)
NICAC .... Nebraska Intercollegiate Athletic Conference (PSS)
NICAD .... Nickel Cadmium (NG)
NiCad........ Nickel-Cadmium
NiCad Battery... Nickel Cadmium Battery (SAUS)
Ni-cad Cell... Nickel Cadmium Cell (SAUS)
Nic Adult Bast... Nicolas' Adulterine Bastardy [*1836*] [*A publication*] (DLA)
NICAM....... Near-Instantaneous Companded Audio Multiplex (WDAA)
NICAM....... Near-Instantaneous Companding Audio Multiplex (WDAA)
NICAM....... Near Instantaneously Companded Audio Multiplex
Nic & Fl Reg... Nicoll and Flaxman on Registration [*A publication*] (DLA)
NICAP .... National Investigations Committee on Aerial Phenomena
NICAP .... Nuveen Insured California Premium Income Municipal [*Associated Press*] (SAG)
NICAP2...... Nuveen Insured California Premium Income Municipal Fund 2 [*Associated Press*] (SAG)
NICAR .... Nicaragua
NICARD ..... Navy/Industry Cooperative Research and Development Program (MCD)
NICAS .... Nuveen Insured California Select Tax Free [*Associated Press*] (SAG)
NICATELSAT... Nicaraguan Telecommunication by Satellite [*Commercial firm*]
NICB......... National Industrial Conference Board [*Later, TCB*] (EA)
NICB......... National Insurance Crime Bureau (NTPA)
Nic Bel...... Nicolaus Bellonus [*Flourished, 1542-47*] [*Authority cited in pre-1607 legal work*] (DSA)
Nic Boe ..... Nicolaus Boerius [*Authority cited in pre-1607 legal work*] (DSA)
NICC......... National Incident Coordination Center [*USDA Forest Service*] [*Boise, ID*] (ALAC)
NICC......... National Industrial Conservation Conference
NICC......... National Interagency Coordination Center [*Emergency Management*] (EMA)
NICC......... National Inventory Control Center (MCD)
NICC......... Nationalized Industries Computer Committee (NITA)
NICC......... Neonatal Intensive Care Center (DAVI)
NICC......... Nevis Island Cultural Center of the US (EA)
NICCF........ National Ice Core Curatorial Facility (SAUS)
NICCW ...... Nuclear Island Closed Cooling Water (SAUS)
NICCWS..... Nuclear Island Closed Cooling Water System (SAUS)
NICCYH ..... National Information Center for Children and Youth with Handicaps (EA)
NICD......... National Information Center on Deafness (EA)
NICD......... National Institute on Crime and Delinquency [*Later, NFCJ*] (EA)
NICD......... Nickel Cadmium (MCD)
Ni-Cd........ Nickel-Cadmium
NICD......... Northern Indiana Commuter Transportation District [*Federal Railroad Administration identification code*]
NICDA .... National Imported Car Dealers Association (EA)
Nice .... Eunice (SAUS)
NICE .... National Information Conference and Exposition [*Associated Information Managers*]
NICE......... National Institute for Clinical Excellence
NICE......... National Institute for Computers in Engineering [*Defunct*] (EA)
NICE......... National Institute for Consumer Education
NICE......... National Institute of Careers, Inc. [*NASDAQ symbol*] (COMM)
NICE......... National Institute of Ceramic Engineers (EA)
NICE......... National Institute of Clinical Excellence
NICE......... Nationally-Integrated Caring Employees [*Union*] [*British*] (DI)
NICE......... National Society of Fund Raisers Institute of Continuing Education [*Former name of the National Society of Fund Raising Executives Foundation*] (NFD)
NICE......... Network Information and Control Exchange [*Computer science*] (CIST)
NICE......... Niceson Boat Trailer [*NCIC trailer make code*]
NICE......... NICE-Systems ADR [*NASDAQ symbol*] (SG)
NICE......... Noninvasive Carotid Examination [*Cardiology*] (DAVI)
NICE......... Noninvasive Cerebrovascular Examination [*Cardiology*] (DAVI)
NICE......... Nonlinear, Iterative Constrained Estimator (MCD)
NICE......... Nonprofit International Consortium for Eiffel (EA)
NICE......... Normal Input-Output Control Executive [*Computer science*]
NICE......... Northern Indiana Consortium for Education [*Library network*]
NICE......... Nosocomial Infection Control in Europe (SAUS)
NICE^3........ National Industrial Competitiveness through Efficiency: Energy, Environment, andEconomics [*Environmental Protection Agency*]
NICEC .... National Institute for Careers Education and Counselling [*Research center*] [*British*] (IRC)

NICEDD ..... National Institute for Continuing Education in Developmental Disabilities (EA)
NICEIC .... National Inspection Council for Electrical Installation Contracting [*British*]
NICEL .... National Institute for Citizen Education in the Law (EA)
Nic Elec ..... Nicolsons Dections in Scotland (SAUS)
Nic Elec ..... Nicolson's Elections in Scotland [*A publication*] (DLA)
NICEM .... National Information Center for Educational Materials (NITA)
NICEM .... National Information Center for Educational Media [*Access Innovations*] (IID)
NICEM .... National Information Center for Educational Media [*Later, AV Online*] (EA)
NICER .... Northern Ireland Council for Educational Research (AIE)
NICET .... National Institute for Certification in Engineering Technologies (EA)
NICEY .... NICE-Systems ADR [*NASDAQ symbol*] (TTSB)
NICF .... National Institute of Carpet Fitters [*British*] (DBA)
NICF .... Northern Ireland Cycling Federation (SAUS)
NICG .... National Interagency Coordination Group [*National Atmospheric Electricity Hazards Program*] (MCD)
NICH .... National Information Center for the Handicapped (EA)
NICH .... Nitches, Inc. [*NASDAQ symbol*] (SAG)
NICH .... Non-Intervention in Chile [*An association*] (EA)
NICHA .... Northern Ireland Chest and Heat Association (SAUS)
Nic Ha C ...... Nicholl, Hare, and Carrow's Railway and Canal Cases [*1835-55*] [*A publication*] (DLA)
Nich Adult Bast... Nicholas on Adulterine Bastardy [*A publication*] (DLA)
Nic H & C... Nicholl, Hare, and Carrow's Railway and Canal Cases [*1835-55*] [*A publication*] (ILCA)
NICHCY ..... National Information Center for Children and Youth with Disabilities (PAZ)
NICHD .... National Institute of Child Health and Human Development [*Bethesda, MD*] [*National Institutes of Health*] (GRD)
Nich H & C... Nicholl, Hare, and Carrow's Railway and Canal Cases [*1835-55*] [*A publication*] (DLA)
NICHHD ..... National Institute of Child Health and Human Development [*National Institutes of Health*]
NICHINS ... Nichols Institute (SAUS)
NICHO .... Nicholson, MS [*American Association of Railroads railroad junction routing code*]
Nicholl H & C... Nicholl, Hare, and Carrow [*1835-55*] [*A publication*] (DLA)
Nichols-Cahill... Nichols-Cahill's Annotated New York Civil Practice Acts [*A publication*] (DLA)
Nicholson... Nicholson's Manuscript Decisions, Scotch Session Cases [*A publication*] (DLA)
NICHROME... Nickel Chromium [*Alloy*] [*Trade name*]
NichRs .... Nichols Research Corp. [*Associated Press*] (SAG)
NICI .... National Insulation Certification Institute (EA)
NICI .... National Interagency Counterdrug Institute [*Camp San Luis Obispo, CA*] (DOMA)
NICI .... Negative Ion Chemical Ionization [*Spectrometry*]
NICIA .... Northern Ireland Coal Importers Association (SAUS)
NICIMS .... Negative Ion Chemical Ionization Mass Spectroscopy
NICIS .... Nikon Intracellular Calcium Ion System
NICJ .... National Institute for Consumer Justice
NICK .... Name Information Correlation Key
NICK .... Nature's Initial Cosmic Kickstart
NICK .... Nicholas Financial [*NASDAQ symbol*]
NICK .... Nickel & Holman [*NCIC trailer make code*]
NICK .... Nickelodeon [*Cable television channel*]
nick .... Nickname
NICKA .... Codeword, Nickname and Exercise Term System (SAUS)
NICKA3 ...... Japanese Journal of Zootechnical Science (journ.) (SAUS)
NICKE .... Nickerson, KS [*American Association of Railroads railroad junction routing code*]
NICL .... National Ice Core Laboratory (SAUS)
NICL .... Nickel Resoures Development Corp. (SAUS)
NICLC .... National Institute on Community-Based Long-Term Care (EA)
NICLF .... Ni-Cal Developments Ltd. (MHDW)
NICLOG ..... National Information Center for Local Government Records [*Canada*]
NICM .... National Institute for Campus Ministries (EA)
NICM .... National Institute of Comparative Medicine (DAVI)
NICM .... Nuffield Institute of Comparative Medicine (SAUS)
NICMA .... National Ice Cream Mix Association (EA)
NICMA .... National Industrial Cafeteria Managers Association [*Later, SFM*] (EA)
NICMC .... National Institute of Certified Moving Consultants (NTPA)
NICMOS ..... Near-Infrared Camera and Multiobject Spectrograph [*Astronomy*]
NICMOS ..... Near-Infrared Camera and Multiobject Spectrometer
NICN .... Navy Item Control Number (MCD)
NICNT .... New International Commentary on the New Testament [*A publication*] (BJA)
NICO .... National Insurance Consumer Organization (EA)
NICO .... Navy Indochina Clearing Office (DNAB)
NICO .... Navy Inventory Control Office
Nico .... Nicolaus de Tudeschis [*Deceased, 1445*] [*Authority cited in pre-1607 legal work*] (DSA)
NICO .... Nissan Infiniti Car Owners Club [*Association*] (EA)
NICOA .... National Independent Coal Operators Association [*Defunct*] (EA)
NICOA .... National Indian Council on Aging (EA)
Nico Alex... Nicolaus de Alexandria [*Authority cited in pre-1607 legal work*] (DSA)
NICOL .... National Insurance Corp. of Liberia (EY)
NICOL .... Network Information Center On-Line (SAUS)
NICOL .... New Integrated Computer Language
NICOL .... New International Commercial Language (SAUS)
NICOL .... Nineteen-Hundred Commercial Language
Nicolas ...... Proceedings and Ordinances of the Privy Council, Edited by Sir Harry Nicolas [*A publication*] (DLA)
Nicollet ..... Nicollet Process Engineering, Inc. [*Associated Press*] (SAG)
NICOP .... Navy Industry Cooperation Plan
NICOP .... Nickel Copper
NICOR .... NICOR, Inc. [*Formerly, Northern Illinois Gas Co.*] [*Associated Press*] (SAG)
NICORD ..... Navy/Industry Cooperative Research and Development Program
NICOS .... Newfoundland Institute for Cold Ocean Science [*Memorial University of Newfoundland*] [*Canada*] [*Research center*] (RCD)
NICOV .... National Information Center on Volunteerism [*Later, NVC*] (EA)
NICP .... National Inventory Control Point [*Military*]
NICP .... Nuclear Incident Contingency Plan [*Emergency Management*] (EMA)
NICP .... Nuclear Incident Control Plan
NIC-PAC ..... Northville Industries Corporation PAC [*Melville, NY*] (PACS)
Nic R .... Nicolaus Rufulus [*Flourished, 13th century*] [*Authority cited in pre-1607 legal work*] (DSA)
NICRA .... National Ice Cream Retailers Association [*Later, NICYRA*] (EA)
NICRA .... Northern Ireland Civil Rights Association
NICRAD ..... Navy/Industry Cooperative Research and Development
Nicralloy... Nickel-Chrome Alloy (SAUS)
NICRISP ... Navy Integrated Comprehensible Repairable Item Scheduling Program
NICRO .... National Institute for Crime Prevention and Rehabilitation of Offenders
Ni-Cr S ...... Nickel-Chromium Steel (SAUS)
NICS .... NAS Interfacility Communications System [*FAA*] (TAG)
NICS .... National Airspace System Interfacility Communications System (FAAC)
NICS .... National Instant Check System
NICS .... National Institute for Chemical Studies (EA)
NICS .... National Insurance Contributions System [*Department of Health and Social Security*] [*British*]
NICS .... NATO Integrated Communications System (NATG)
NICS .... Network Integrity Control System
NICS .... Newly Industrialized Countries (DFIT)
NICS .... Nissan's Induction Control System [*Automotive engineering*]
NICSA .... National Investment Company Service Association (NTPA)
NICSA .... Northern Ireland Countryside Staff Association [*United Kingdom*] (EAIO)
NICSBC ...... National Interstate Council of State Boards of Cosmetology (NTPA)
NICS COA... NICS Control Operating Authority (SAUS)
NICSE .... National Institute for Child Support Enforcement [*Commercial firm*] (EA)
NICSEM ..... National Information Center for Special Education Materials [*University of Southern California*] [*Los Angeles, CA*]
NICSEM/NIMIS... National Information Center for Special Education Material/ National Instructional Material Information System (EDAC)
NICSH .... National Interagency Council on Smoking and Health [*Defunct*] (EA)
Nic Sic Do... Nicolaus (Siculus Doctor) de Tudeschis [*Deceased, 1445*] [*Authority cited in pre-1607 legal work*] (DSA)
NICSMA ..... NATO Integrated Communications System Management Agency (NATG)
NICSO .... NATO Integrated Communications System Organization [*Brussels, Belgium*] (NATG)
NICSOI ...... NICS Operating Instruction (SAUS)
NICSS .... Nellis Integrated Communications Switching System (ACAE)
NICSS .... Northern Ireland Council of Social Science (SAUS)
NICSX .... Nicholas Fund [*Mutual fund ticker symbol*] (SG)
NICT .... National Incident Coordination Team [*Environmental science*] (EPAT)
NIC-TRANS... Naval Intelligence Command - Translation Division
NICU .... Neonatal [*or Newborn*] Intensive Care Unit
NICU .... Neurological Intensive Care Unit [*Medicine*]
NICU .... Neurosurgical Intensive Care Unit [*Medicine*] (DMAA)
NICU .... Newborn Intensive Care Unit [*Medicine*] (DB)
NICU .... NIC Leasing [*Intermodal shipping container symbol*] (TVRC)
NICU .... Nippon International Container Unit (SAUS)
NICU .... Nonimmunologic Contact Urticaria [*Medicine*] (DMAA)
NI-CU Alloy... Nickel-Copper Alloy (SAUS)
NICUFO ..... National Investigations Committee on Unidentified Flying Objects (EA)
NIC US ...... National Ice Centre (SAUS)
NICWA .... National Indian Child Welfare Association (EA)
NICWJ .... National Interfaith Committee for Worker Justice [*Association*] (EA)
NICWM ...... National Information Center on Women and the Military [*Later, WMP*] (EA)
NICX .... Niles Canyon Railway [*Federal Railroad Administration identification code*]
NICYRA ..... National Ice Cream and Yogurt Retailers Association (EA)
NICZ .... Northwest Iowa Co-Operative [*Federal Railroad Administration identification code*]
NID .... Inyokern, CA [*Location identifier*] [*FAA*] (FAAL)
NID .... Namespace Identifier (SAUS)
NID .... National Institute for the Deaf (WDAA)
NID .... National Institute of Drycleaning [*Later, IFI*] (EA)
NID .... National Institute of Dyslexia [*Defunct*] (EA)
NID .... National Intelligence Daily [*CIA*] [*A publication*] (MUSM)
NID .... National Intelligence Digest [*Central Intelligence Agency classified daily newspaper*] (CARL)
NID .... Naval Intelligence Database (DOMA)
NID .... Naval Intelligence Division [*British*]
NID .... Negligible Individual Dose [*Environmental Protection Agency*]
NID .... Network In-Dial [*Automatic Voice Network*] (CET)
NID .... Network Interface Device [*Telecommunications*]
NID .... New Interactive Display [*NEC*] [*Computer science*] (PCM)

NID .... New International Dictionary [*Webster's*] [*A publication*]
NID .... Next ID (SAUS)
Nid .... Niddah (BJA)
NID .... Nonequilibrium Ionospheric Disturbance [*Geophysics*]
NID .... Non Illusion Direction (SAUS)
NID .... Nonillusion Direction [*Ophthalmology*]
NID .... Non-Immunologic Disease [*Medicine*] (MELL)
NID .... Noninsulin-Dependent [*Diabetes*] [*Endocrinology*] (DAVI)
NID .... Non-Interactive Display (CCCA)
NID .... Non-Internal Development [*DoD*]
NID .... Noninvasive Diagnostics [*Medicine*] (EDAA)
NID .... Northern Ireland District
NID .... Not in Distress [*Medicine*] (MELL)
NID .... Nuclear Instruments and Detectors [*IEEE*] (MCD)
NIDA .... 99th Infantry Division Association (EA)
NIDA .... National Independent Dairy-Food Association (EA)
NIDA .... National Industrial Distributors Association [*Philadelphia, PA*] (EA)
NIDA .... National Institute on Drug Abuse [*Department of Health and Human Services*] [*Rockville, MD*]
NIDA .... National Insurance Development Act of 1975
NIDA .... Northeastern Industrial Developers (or Development) Association (SAUS)
NIDA .... Northern Ireland Development Agency (SAUS)
NIDA .... Numerically Integrated Differential Analyzer [*Computer science*]
NIDA .... Numerically Integrating Differential Analyzer (SAUS)
NIDA Res Mono ... National Institute on Drug Abuse Research Monographs (MEC)
NIDA Res Monogr ... NIDA Research Monograph (SAUS)
NIDAS .... Nixdorf Integrated Data Accounting System (SAUS)
NIDC .... National Insurance Development Corp. [*Government-sponsored organization*]
NIDC .... Newly Industrialized Developing Country
NIDC .... Northern Ireland Development Council (SAUS)
NIDCC .... National Internal Defense Coordination Center [*Army*] (AABC)
NIDCD .... National Institute on Deafness and Other Communication Disorders [*National Institutes of Health*] (EGAO)
NIDCR .... National Institute of Dental and Craniofacial Research
NIDCR .... National Institute of Dental Craniofacial Research
NIDD .... Non-Insulin-Dependent Diabetes [*Medicine*]
NIDDK .... National Institute of Diabetes and Digestive and Kidney Diseases [*Public Health Service*] [*Also, an information service or system*] (IID)
NIDDKD .... National Institute of Diabetes and Digestive and Kidney Diseases [*Department of Health and Human Services*] (GFGA)
NIDDM .... Non-Insulin-Dependent Diabetes Mellitus [*Medicine*]
NIDDY .... Non-Insulin-Dependent Diabetes in the Young [*Medicine*] (DMAA)
NIDE .... Numerical Integration of Differential Equation (VLIE)
NIDE .... Numerical Integration of Differential Equations (SAUS)
NIDEC .... Nippon Densan (EFIS)
NiDI .... Nickel Development Institute (EAIO)
NIDIR .... Nike Digital Instrumentation Radar (SAUS)
NIDL .... Network Interface Definition Language [*Computer science*]
NIDLR .... Office of the Director of Law Reform, Northern Ireland (DLA)
NIDM .... National Institute for Disaster Mobilization (EA)
NIDM .... Noninsulin-Dependent Diabetes Mellitus [*Endocrinology*] (DAVI)
NIDN .... Navy Intelligence Data Network (MCD)
NIDOC .... National Information and Documentation Center
NIDOCD .... National Institute on Deafness and Other Communication Disorders [*NIH*]
NIDR .... National Institute for Dispute Resolution (EA)
NIDR .... National Institute of Dental and Craniofacial Research (IID)
NIDR .... National Institute of Dental Research [*Public Health Service*] [*Bethesda, MD*]
NIDR .... Networked Information Discovery and Retrieval (TELE)
NIDRR .... National Institute on Disability and Rehabilitation Research [*Washington, DC*] [*Department of Education*] (GRD)
NIDS .... National Institute for Defense Studies (SAUS)
NIDS .... National Institute of Diaper Services [*Defunct*] (EA)
NIDS .... National Institutional Delivery System
NIDS .... National Intelligence Display System (ACAE)
NIDS .... National Inventory of Documentary Sources [*British*]
NIDS .... National Investor Data Service (EA)
NIDS .... Navigation Instrument Development Unit
NIDS .... Network Interface Data System [*NASA*]
NIDS .... NEXRAD Information Dissemination Service (SAUS)
NIDS .... Nonionic Detergent Soluble (DMAA)
NIDS .... Nuclear Integrated Data System
NIDX .... Network Intrusion Detection Expert system (SAUS)
NIE .... NASA Interface Equipment (MCD)
NIE .... National Index of Ecosystems [*Australia*]
NIE .... National Institute for the Environment [*Proposed government agency*]
NIE .... National Institute of Education [*Department of Education*] [*Washington, DC*]
NIE .... National Institute of Education, Washington, DC [*OCLC symbol*] (OCLC)
NIE .... National Intelligence Estimate
NIE .... Natural and Induced Environment (SPST)
NIE .... Negative Ion Erosion
NIE .... Netherlands Institute of Ecology
NIE .... Neutron Ionization Effect
NIE .... Newly-Industrialized Economy
NiE .... Newspaper in Education (SAUS)
NIE .... Newspaper in Education Program
NIE .... Newton Internet Enabler (SAUS)
NIE .... Niedzica [*Poland*] [*Seismograph station code, US Geological Survey*] (SEIS)
NIE .... Non-Interference Experiment (SAUS)
NIE .... Not Included Elsewhere
NIEA .... National Indian Education Association (EA)
NIEAC .... National Indian Education Advisory Committee [*Terminated, 1974*] [*Department of the Interior*] (EGAO)
NIECC .... National Industrial Energy Conservation Council (MCD)
NIEF .... National Ironfounding Employers Association [*British*] (BI)
NIEHS .... National Institute of Environmental Health Sciences [*Research Triangle Pa rk, NC*] [*National Institutes of Health*]
NIEHS .... National Institute of Environmental Health Service [*Marine science*] (OSRA)
NIEI .... National Indoor Environmental Institute (EPA)
NIEI .... National Institute of Electromedical Information (EA)
niel .... Niello (VRA)
NIEL .... Non-Ionizing Energy Loss (SAUS)
NIEM .... National Industrial Engineering Mission (AABC)
NIEM .... Northern Institute for Environmental and Minority Law (SAUS)
NIEMR .... Non-Ionizing Electro-Magnetic Radiation (VLIE)
Nient Cul ... Nient Culpable [*Not Guilty*] [*Latin*] [*Legal term*] (DLA)
NIEO .... New International Economic Order
NIEO .... Nieto and Sons Trucking [*Common carrier symbol*]
NIEO .... Non-Incorporated Engineering Order (SAUS)
NIEP .... National Independent Energy Producers (NTPA)
NIEP .... Natural and Induced Environments Panel (SPST)
NIER .... National Industrial Equipment Reserve [*of DMS*]
NIER .... National Institute for Educational Research (NITA)
NIERC .... Northern Ireland Economic Research Centre
NIES .... National Institute for Environmental Studies (CARB)
NIES .... National Intelligence Estimates [*Summaries of foreign policy information and advice prepared for the president*] [*Known informally as "knees"*]
NIESO .... Non-materiel Individual Enhancement for the SOF Operator (SAUS)
NIESR .... National Institute of Economic and Social Research [*British*]
NIETB .... National Imagery Exploitation Target Base (MCD)
NIETS .... National Imagery Exploitation Tasking Study
NIETU .... National Independent Enginemen's Trade Union [*British*]
NIEU .... Negro Industrial and Economic Union
NIEWS .... NTCS-A Imagery Exploitation Workstation (SAUS)
NIEX .... Niagara Exchange Corp. (SAUS)
NIF .... National Ichthyosis Foundation (EA)
NIF .... National Ignition Facility [*Lawrence Livermore National Laboratory*] [*Department of Energy*] (PS)
NIF .... National Income Forecasting (ADA)
NIF .... National Innovation Fund [*South Africa*]
NIF .... National Institute for the Family (EA)
NIF .... National Interfraternity Foundation (EA)
NIF .... National Inventors Foundation (EA)
NIF .... National Investment Fund [*Poland*] [*Finance*]
NIF .... National Iranian Front [*Political party*]
NIF .... National Islamic Front [*Sudan*] [*Political party*]
NIF .... National Issues Forums (EA)
NIF .... Navy Industrial Fund
NIF .... Negative Inspiratory Force [*Medicine*]
NIF .... Network Information Files [*Burroughs Corp.*]
NIF .... Network Information Frame (SAUS)
NIF .... Network Interface Function (SPST)
NIF .... Neutrophil Immobilizing Factor (DMAA)
NIF .... Neutrophil Migration Inhibition Factor
NIF .... New Israel Fund (EA)
NIF .... Nickel-Iron Film
NIF .... Nifedipine [*Pharmacology*]
nif .... Nitrogen-Fixing [*Biology*] (BARN)
NIF .... Noise Improvement Factor (IEEE)
NIF .... Nonindustrial Facility [*Emergency Management*] (EMA)
NIF .... Nonintestinal Fibroblast [*Medicine*] (DMAA)
NIF .... Note-Issuance Facility [*Banking*]
NIF .... Notice of Intent to Fine (SAUS)
NIF .... Not Industrially Funded [*Military*]
NIF .... Not in File
NIF .... Nuclear Information File (AFM)
NIF .... Nuveen Prem Insured Muni Inc. [*NYSE symbol*] (TTSB)
NIF .... Nuveen Premium Insured Municipal Income [*NYSE symbol*] (SPSG)
NIFA .... National Intercollegiate Flying Association (EA)
NIFAC .... Night Forward Air Controller [*Aircraft*]
NIFADCS ... National Institute of Furnace and Air Duct Cleaning Specialists (EA)
NIFAST .... National Industrial Fire and Safety Centre (ACII)
NIFB .... National Institute of Farm Brokers [*Later, NIFLB*] (EA)
NIFC .... National Interagency Firefighting Center
NIFDA .... National Independent Flag Dealers Association (NTPA)
NIFDA .... National Institutional Food Distributor Associates (EA)
NIFDA .... Northern Ireland Food and Drink Association [*United Kingdom*] (EAIO)
NIFE .... Nomenclature-in-Federal Employment
NIFEGS .... Northern Ireland Further Education Guidance Service (AIE)
NIFER .... National Institute for Full Employment Research [*Department of Labor*] (OICC)
NIFES .... National Industrial Fuel Efficiency Service [*British*]
NIFF .... Nordiska Ickekommersielles Fonogramproducenters Forening [*Nordic Association of Non-Commercial Phonogram Producers - NANPP*] (EAIO)
NIFF .... Notation Interchange File Format [*Computer science*] (VLIE)
NIFFTE .... Noncooperative Identification Friend or Foe Technology Evaluation (RDA)

NIFHA .... Northern Ireland Federation of Housing Associations [*United Kingdom*] (EAIO)
NIFI .... National Institute for the Foodservice Industry (EA)
NIFL .... Finger Lakes Library System, Ithaca, NY [*Library symbol*] [*Library of Congress*] (LCLS)
NIFLB .... National Institute of Farm and Land Brokers [*Later, FLI*] (EA)
NIFLP .... Nuveen Insured Florida Premium Income Municipal Fund [*Associated Press*] (SAG)
NIFM .... Northwest Independent Forest Manufacturers (WPI)
NIFMA .... Nigerian Furniture Manufacturers Association (SAUS)
NIFMS .... NAVAIR [*Naval Air Systems Command*] Industrial Finance Management System (MCD)
NIFO .... Next In, First Out [*Queuing technique*]
NIFOB .... Non-Injurious Free-on-Board
NIFP .... National Institute for Federal Procurement (AAGC)
NIFP .... National Institute of Fresh Produce [*British*] (DBA)
NIFRS .... Navy Industrial Fund-Reporting System (MCD)
NIFS .... National Institute for Farm Safety (EA)
NIFS .... NT [*New Technology*] File System [*Microsoft Corp.*]
NIFTE .... Neon Indicator Functional Test Equipment
NIFTI .... Near-Isotropic Flux Turbulence Instrument [*Oceanography*]
NIFTP .... File transfer network in the United Kingdom (SAUS)
NIFTP .... Network Independent File Transfer Program (HGAA)
NIFTP .... Network Independent File Transfer Protocol (PDAA)
NIFTS .... Naval Integrated Flight Training System (MCD)
NI/FWM ..... New, Incorporated/Fourth World Movement (EA)
NIG .... Aero Contractors Company of Nigeria Ltd. [*ICAO designator*] (FAAC)
NIG .... National Institute of Genetics [*Japan*]
NIG .... National Interest Group (HEAS)
NIG .... Nationwide Investigations Group [*British*]
NIG .... Naval Inspector General
NIG .... Negative Ion Generator (ADA)
Nig .... Niger [*African nation*] (NTIO)
NIG .... Niger [*Black*] [*Pharmacy*]
NIG .... Nigeria
Nig .... Nigerian (SAUS)
NIG .... Nikunau [*Kiribati*] [*Airport symbol*] (OAG)
NIG .... Nonimmunoglobulin [*Medicine*] (DB)
NIG .... Non Isolated Gate (SAUS)
NIG .... Nordic Industrial Group (SAUS)
NIG .... Nude Ionization Gauge
NIGA .... National Indian Gaming Association (NTPA)
NIGA .... Neutron-Induced Gamma Activity (AABC)
NIGA .... Nuclear Indirect Gamma Activity (SAUS)
NIGA .... Nuclear-Induced Ground Radioactivity (NATG)
NIGAB .... Annual Report. National Institute of Genetics (journ.) (SAUS)
NIG&P .... Nanjing Institute of Geology and Paleontology [*China*]
Nig Ann Int'l L ... Nigerian Annual of International Law [*A publication*] (DLA)
Nig Bar J ... Nigerian Bar Journal [*A publication*] (DLA)
Nig BJ .... Nigerian Bar Journal [*A publication*] (DLA)
NIGC .... National Indian Gaming Commission (AGLO)
NIGCS .... National Imperial Glass Collectors Society (EA)
NIGDA .... National Industrial Glove Distributors Association (EA)
NIGEC .... National Institute for Global Environmental Change [*University of Southern California and Department of Energy*]
Niger .... Nigerian (DIAR)
Nigeria ...... Federal Republic of Nigeria (SAUS)
Nigeria Bar J ... Nigerian Bar Journal. Annual Journal of the Nigeria Bar Association [*Lagos, Nigeria*] [*A publication*] (DLA)
Nigeria Fed Dep For Res Annu Rep ... Nigeria Federal Department of Forest Research Annual Report (SAUS)
Nigeria LR ... Nigeria Law Reports [*A publication*] (DLA)
Nigerian Ann Int'l L ... Nigerian Annual of International Law [*A publication*] (DLA)
Nigerian LJ ... Nigerian Law Journal [*A publication*] (DLA)
NIGFET ...... Non-Insulated-Gate Field-Effect Transistor (SAUS)
NIGHTCAP ... Night Combat Air Patrol [*Military*] (NVT)
NIGL .... NERC Isotope Geosciences Laboratory (SAUS)
Nig Lawy Q ... Nigeria Lawyer's Quarterly [*A publication*] (DLA)
Nig LJ .... Nigerian Law Journal [*A publication*] (DLA)
Nig LQ .... Nigeria Lawyer's Quarterly [*A publication*] (ILCA)
Nig LQR ..... Nigerian Law Quarterly Review [*A publication*] (DLA)
Nig LR .... Nigeria Law Reports [*A publication*] (DLA)
NIGMS .... National Institute of General Medical Sciences [*National Institutes of Health*] [*Bethesda, MD*]
NIGP .... Nanjing Institute of Geology and Paleontology [*China*]
NIGP .... National Institute of Governmental Purchasing (EA)
Nigr .... Nigeria (VRA)
Nigr .... Nigrinus [*of Lucian*] [*Classical studies*] (OCD)
NIGRA .... Northern Ireland Gay Rights Association [*United Kingdom*] (EAIO)
NIGRO .... Northern Ireland General Register Office (SAUS)
NIGS .... Non-Inertial Guidance Set (SAA)
NIH .... Hoffmann-La Roche, Inc. [*Research code symbol*]
NIH .... National Institute for the Humanities [*Yale University*] [*National Endowment for the Humanities*]
NIH .... National Institute of Biomedical Imaging and Bioengineering (RCD)
NIH .... National Institute of Hardware [*British*] (BI)
NIH .... National Institute of Housecraft [*British*] (BI)
NIH .... National Institute on the Holocaust [*Later, AFIP*] (EA)
NIH .... National Institutes of Health [*Public Health Service*] [*Bethesda, MD*]
NIH .... New Inn Hall [*British*] (ROG)
NIH .... Nonimmune Hydrops [*Medicine*]
NIH .... Nonirradiated Handling (SAUS)
NIH .... North Irish Horse [*Military unit*] [*British*]
NIH .... Not Invented Here (NITA)
NIH .... Not Invented Here Syndrome [*Business Management*]
NIHB .... National Indian Health Board (EA)
NIHBC .... Northern Ireland House Building Council (SAUS)
NIH BSA .... NIH Black Scientists Association (EA)
NIHC .... Northern Ireland House of Commons
NIHCA .... Northern Ireland Hotels and Caterers Association (ODBW)
NIHD .... Noise-Induced Hearing Damage [*Medicine*] (MEDA)
NIHE .... National Institute for Higher Education [*Defunct*] (ACII)
NIHE .... Northern Ireland Housing Executive (SAUS)
NIHEC .... Northern Ireland Higher Education Council (SAUS)
NIHERST ... National Institute of Higher Education (Research, Science, and Technology) [*Spain*]
NIHF .... Nonimmune Hydrops Fetalis [*Medicine*]
NIHGR .... National Institute for Human Genome Research [*National Institutes of Health*] (BARN)
NIHHD .... National Institute of Health and Human Development
NIHHS .... Notification of Installations Handling Hazardous Substances Regulations 1982 (HEAS)
NIHi .... DeWitt Historical Society of Tompkins County, Ithaca, NY [*Library symbol*] [*Library of Congress*] (LCLS)
NIHL .... Noise-Induced Hearing Loss
NIHN .... National Interfaith Hospitality Network [*Association*] (EA)
NIHOE .... Nitrogen, Helium, and Oxygen Experiment (DNAB)
NIHPC .... National Institute of Health Plateletpheresis Center [*Medicine*] (EDAA)
NIHQ .... Nautical Institute Headquarters (SAUS)
NIHR .... National Institute of Handicapped Research [*Department of Health and Human Services*] [*Later, NIDRR*] [*Washington, DC*]
NIHS .... National Institute of Health Sciences (SAUS)
NIHS .... National Institute of Hypertension Studies - Institute of Hypertension School ofResearch (EA)
NIHS .... NAVEUR Intelligence Highlights Summary (MCD)
NIHSA .... Newfoundland Industrial Health and Safety Association (SAUS)
NIHT .... Northern Ireland Housing Trust (SAUS)
NIHTA .... Northern Ireland Head Teachers' Association
NIHYSOB ... Now I Have You, Son of a Bitch [*Term coined by Kenneth Blanchard, author of "The One-Minute Manager"*]
NII .... National Industries, Inc. (EFIS)
NII .... National Information Infrastructure [*Proposed 1992*] [*Telecommunications*]
NII .... National Intergroup (EFIS)
NII .... NATO Item Identification (NATG)
NII .... Negative Immittance Inverter (PDAA)
NII .... Neruonal Intranuclear Inclusion [*Neurophysiology*]
NII .... Net Interest Income (TDOB)
NII .... Niigata [*Japan*] [*Seismograph station code, US Geological Survey*] (SEIS)
NII .... Nuclear Installations Inspectorate [*British*]
NIIA .... Nonisotropic Immunoassay
NIIC .... Ithaca College, Ithaca, NY [*Library symbol*] [*Library of Congress*] (LCLS)
NIIC .... National Injury Information Clearinghouse [*Consumer Product Safety Commission*]
NIIC .... NORAD Intelligence Indications Center (MCD)
NIIC .... Northern Illinois Intercollegiate Conference (PSS)
NIICP .... No Increase in Contract Price
NIICU .... National Institute of Independent Colleges and Universities (EA)
NIID .... Netherlands Defense Manufacturers Association (SAUS)
NIIG .... NATO Item Identification Guide (NATG)
NIIIP .... National Industrial Information Infrastructure Protocol [*Computer science*] (VLIE)
NIIMS .... National Interagency Incident Management System [*Emergency Management*] (EMA)
NIIN .... National Item Identification Number (MCD)
NII Nor ...... NII Norsat International, Inc. [*Associated Press*] (SAG)
NIIO .... New International Information Order (NITA)
NIIP .... National Institute of Industrial Psychology (PDAA)
NIIP .... Net International Investment Position
NIIPA .... Native Indian/Inuit Photographers' Association [*Canada*] (EAIO)
NIIR .... Non-Imaging Infrared Sensor (SAUS)
NIIRS .... National Image Interpretability Rating Scale
NIIRS .... National Imagery Interpretation Rating Scale (MCD)
NIIS .... National Institute of Infant Services [*Later, NADS*]
NIIS .... New Image Industries [*NASDAQ symbol*] (TTSB)
NIIS .... New Image Industries, Inc. [*NASDAQ symbol*] (NQ)
NIIS .... New Item Introductory Schedule (AAGC)
NIIS .... Niagara Institute for International Studies [*Canada*]
NIIS .... Nigeria Institute for International Studies (SAUS)
NIIS .... Nuclear Issues Information Service (IID)
NIIT .... National Information Infrastructure Testbed [*Telecommunications*] (PCM)
NIIU .... Neozyme Corp. [*NASDAQ symbol*] (SAG)
NIJ .... National Institute of Justice (USGC)
NIJ .... New Irish Jurist [*A publication*] (DLA)
NIJC .... North Idaho Junior College (SAUS)
NIJD .... National Institute of Judicial Dynamics [*Defunct*] (EA)
NIJH .... National Institute for Jewish Hospice (EA)
NIJJDP ...... National Institute for Juvenile Justice and Delinquency Prevention
NIJR .... New Irish Jurist [*A publication*] (DLA)
NIK .... Boston, MA [*Location identifier*] [*FAA*] (FAAL)
NIK .... Nicaragua [*Telegraphy*] (PCTE)
NIK .... Nickel [*Watchmaking*] (ROG)
NIK .... Nickel Rim Mines Ltd. [*Toronto Stock Exchange symbol*]
NIK .... Nikolski [*Alaska*] [*Seismograph station code, US Geological Survey*] [*Closed*] (SEIS)

NIK........... No Information Keeping [*Medicine*] (BCRP)
nik........... Northern Ireland [*MARC country of publication code*] [*Library of Congress*] (LCCP)
NIK........... Novye Inostrannyye Knigi [*New Foreign Books*] [*A publication*]
NIKA........ Northern Ireland Korfball Association (EAIO)
NikeB........ Nike, Inc. [*Associated Press*] (SAG)
NIKKEI....... Nihon Keizai Shimbun, Inc. [*Tokyo, Japan*] (IID)
Nikkei Electron... Nikkei Electronics (SAUS)
NIKO......... Nigerian Korean Co. (SAUS)
NIKOS........ New Internet Knowledge Systems [*Computer science*] (DDC)
NIKT......... Neue Informations- und Kommunikationstechnologien (SAUS)
NIKU......... Niku Corp. [*NASDAQ symbol*] (SG)
NIL........... Negotiable Instruments Law (DLA)
NIL........... Network Interface Layer [*Computer science*] (VLIE)
NIL........... Neurointermediate Lobe [*Neuroanatomy*]
NIL........... Nilore [*Pakistan*] [*Seismograph station code, US Geological Survey*] (SEIS)
NIL........... Nitrogen Inerting Line (IEEE)
NIL........... Noble International, Ltd. [*AMEX symbol*] (NASQ)
NIL........... Noise Immission Level (SAUS)
NIL........... Noise Immunity Level (SAUS)
NIL........... No Limit (NASA)
NIL........... Nothing in Light Disease [*Nephrotic Syndrome*] (DAVI)
NIL........... Nothing in Light Microscopy (MELL)
NIL........... Nothing to Send [*Amateur radio shorthand*] (WDAA)
NIL........... Not in Labor [*Medicine*]
NIL........... Nuclear-Induced Lightning
NILA......... National Industrial Leather Association [*Later, NIBA*] (EA)
NILab........ Northern Ireland Labour Party [*Political party*] [*Defunct*]
NILB......... National Indian Lutheran Board (EA)
NILC......... National Immigration Law Center (EA)
NILE......... National Institute of Labor Education [*Defunct*] (EA)
NILE......... NATO Improved Link 11 (SAUS)
NILE......... Naval Inflatable Liferaft Equipment (SAUS)
NILE......... Naval Inflatable Life-Saving Equipment [*British military*] (DMA)
NILE......... Number of Inverters Along Any Loop is Even (MHDI)
NILE & CJ... National Institute of Law Enforcement and Criminal Justice [*Law Enforcement Assistance Administration*]
NILECJ...... National Institute of Law Enforcement and Criminal Justice [*Law Enforcement Assistance Administration*]
NILES........ Niles, OH [*American Association of Railroads railroad junction routing code*]
Niles Reg... Niles' Weekly Register [*A publication*] (DLA)
NILF......... Not in Labor Force (GFGA)
NILFP........ National Institute of Locker and Freezer Provisioners [*Later, AAMP*] (EA)
NILGOSC... Northern Ireland Local Government Officers Superannuation Committee
NIIH.......... Herkimer County Community College, Ilion, NY [*Library symbol*] [*Library of Congress*] (LCLS)
NILI.......... Netsah Israel Lo Yeshakker (BJA)
NILI.......... Newark Island Layered Intrusion [*Geology*] [*Canada*]
NILI.......... Northern Interior Lumber Industries (SAUS)
NILIC........ Northern Illinois Iowa Conference (PSS)
NILKY....... No Income, Lots of Kids [*Lifestyle classification*]
N Ill U Pr... Northern Illinois University Press (SAUS)
NILN......... Nylon Insert Lock Nut
NILO......... Naval Intelligence Liaison Officer (NVT)
NILP......... Northern Ireland Labour Party [*Political party*] [*Defunct*] (PPW)
NILPT........ National Institute for Low Power Television [*Defunct*] (EA)
NILR......... Netherland International Law Review [*A publication*] (SAFN)
NILR......... Northern Ireland Law Reports [*A publication*] (DLA)
NILRC....... Northern Illinois Learning Resources Cooperative [*Library network*]
Nil Reg...... Niles' Weekly Register [*A publication*] (DLA)
NILRR....... National Institute for Labor Relations Research (RCD)
NILS......... Naval Intelligence Locating Summary (MCD)
NILS......... Newsletter of International Labour Studies [*Netherlands*]
NILS......... Northern Illinois Library System [*Library network*]
NILS......... Nuclear Instrument Landing System
NILT......... National Institute for Lay Training [*Defunct*] (EA)
NILT......... Nursing Intervention Lexicon and Taxonomy (SAUS)
NILTC........ National Industrial Language Training Centre (AIE)
NILU......... National Intelligence Liaison Unit (SAUS)
NILU......... Norwegian Institute for Air Research (SAUS)
NILU......... Norwegian Institute for/of Air Research (SAUS)
NILUG....... National Independent Lynx User Group (NITA)
NIM.......... National Impact Model [*Environmental Protection Agency*] (ERG)
NIM.......... National Islamic Movement (SAUS)
NIM.......... Naval Inspector of Machinery
NIM.......... Net Interest Margin [*Banking*]
NIM.......... Networked Interactive Multimedia
NIM.......... Network Injection Molding
NIM.......... Network Installation Manager [*Computer science*] (VLIE)
NIM.......... Network Interface Machine [*Datapac*]
NIM.......... Network Interface Module [*Telecommunications*] (TSSD)
NIM.......... Network Interface Monitor
NIM.......... Neurological Impress Method (EDAC)
NIM.......... Newspapers in Microform (NITA)
NIM.......... Niamey [*Niger*] [*Airport symbol*] (OAG)
NIM.......... Night Intruder Mission [*Air Force*]
NIM.......... No Immediate Miracles [*Acronym and facetious translation derived from turning President Gerald Ford's anti-inflation WIN buttons upside down*] [*See WIN entry*]
NIM.......... No Internal Message [*E-mail lingo denoting that no Internet message is included*] (NETL)
NIM.......... Noninterrupt Mode
NIM.......... NORAD Intelligence Memorandum (MCD)
NIM.......... Normal-Incidence Monochromator
NIM.......... Normal Integration Mode
NIM.......... North Irish Militia [*Military unit*] [*British*]
NIM.......... Nothing in Mind [*Acronym and facetious translation derived from turning President Gerald Ford's anti-inflation WIN buttons upside down*] [*See WIN entry*]
NIM.......... Nuclear Instrumentation Module
NIM.......... Nuclear Instrument Module (SAUS)
NIM.......... Nuveen Select Maturities Municipal [*NYSE symbol*] (SPSG)
NIM.......... Nylon Insulation Material
NIM.......... University of North Carolina at Asheville, Asheville, NC [*OCLC symbol*] (OCLC)
NIM.......... US Neutron Interactive Materials Program (SAUS)
NIMA......... National Imagery and Mapping Agency [*Military*]
NIMA......... National Institute on Mental Health
NIMA......... National Insulation Manufacturers Association [*Later, Thermal Insulation Manufacturers Association*] (EA)
NIMA......... Noninherited Maternal Antigen [*Genetics*] [*Immunology*]
NIMA......... Northern Ireland Ministry of Agriculture (SAUS)
NIMAB....... National Indian Manpower Advisory Board
NIMAC....... National Interscholastic Music Activities Commission [*Defunct*] (EA)
NIMAJ....... National Integrated Medical Association Journal [*Medicine*] (EDAA)
NIMAT....... Newfoundland Institute for Management Advancement and Training (SAUS)
NIMBAS..... [*The*] Netherlands Insitute for MBA Studies
NIMBIN...... Nuclear Instrumentation Modular Bin
NIMBUS..... Network Information Management Client-Based User Service [*Marine science*] (OSRA)
Nimbus...... Nimbus CD International, Inc. [*Associated Press*] (SAG)
NIMBUS..... United States Meteorological Satellite (SAUS)
NIMBUS-7.. NOAA [*National Oceanic and Atmospheric Administration*] Satellite (USDC)
Nimby....... Nembutal Capsule [*Medicine*] (EDAA)
NIMBY....... Not in My Back Yard [*i.e., garbage incinerators, prisons, roads, etc.*]
NIMC......... Naparano Iron & Metal [*Federal Railroad Administration identification code*]
NIMC......... National Institute of Management Counsellors (EA)
NIMC......... National Institute of Materials and Chemical Research [*Japan*]
NIMC......... National Institute of Municipal Clerks [*Later, IIMC*]
NIMC......... Nodding Image Motion Compensation [*Instrumentation*]
NIMC......... Noninventoriable Manufacturing Cost (TIMI)
NIMCGA..... Northern Indiana Muck Crop Growers Association [*Defunct*] (EA)
NIMCO....... Northeastern Industrial Maintenance Co. (EFIS)
NIMCP....... NATO Information Management Control Point (NATG)
NIMCSSC... National Military Command Systems Support Center (SAUS)
NIMD......... Not in My District (SAUS)
NIME......... National Institute for Multicultural Education [*Defunct*] (EA)
NIMEA....... Northern Ireland Meat Exporters Association [*United Kingdom*] (EAIO)
NIMEX....... Nomenclature for Imports and Exports [*European Community*] (PDAA)
NIMEY....... Not in My Election Year [*Slang*]
NIMFR....... National Institutes of Marriage and Family Relations (EA)
NIMFR....... Normal Incidence Multifilter Radiometer (SAUS)
NIMFY....... Not in My Front Yard [*i.e., Garbage incinerators, landfills, etc.*]
NIMH......... National Institute of Medical Herbalists [*British*]
NIMH......... National Institute of Mental Health [*Rockville, MD*] [*Department of Health and Human Services*]
NiMH......... Nickel-Metal Hydride [*Organic chemistry*] (PS)
NIMHDIS... National Institute for Mental Health Diagnostic Interview Schedule [*Medicine*] (EDAA)
NIMIC........ NATO [*North Atlantic Treaty Organization*] Insensitive Munitions Information Center
NIMIC........ NATO Insensitive Munitions Information Centre (SAUS)
NIMIC........ Not in My Insurance Company [*Insurance slang*]
NIMIS........ National Instructional Materials Information System
NIMIT........ Nimbus Integration and Test [*NASA*] (KSC)
NIMJ......... Near Infrared Miniaturized Jammer
NIML......... National Independence Movement of Latvia [*Political party*]
NIMLO....... National Institute of Municipal Law Officers (EA)
NIMLO Mun L Rev... National Institute of Municipal Law Officers. Municipal Law Review [*A publication*] (DLA)
NIMM........ Nuclear-Induced Missile Malfunction (SAUS)
NIMMA...... Northern Ireland Mixed Marriage Association
NIMMP...... National Institute of Marine Medicine and Pharmacology [*Proposed*] [*National Institutes of Health*]
NIMMS...... New Integrated Modular Management System (SAUS)
NIMMS...... Nineteen-Hundred Integrated Modular Management System
NIMN......... Not in My Neighborhood (SAUS)
NIMO......... Numerical Indicator Multiple Oscilloscope (SAUS)
NiMoV....... Nickel-Molybdenum-Vanadium (SAUS)
NIMP......... National Intern Matching Program [*Later, NRMP*] (EA)
NIMP......... NATO Interoperability Management Plan (SAUS)
NIMP......... New and Improved Materials and Processes (PDAA)
N IMP........ New Impression [*Publishing*] (DGA)
NIMPA....... National Independent Meat Packers Association [*Later, NMA*] (EA)
NIMPA....... Newly Installed Machine Performance Analysis (SAUS)
NIMPH....... Network Interface Message Processing Host [*NERComP*]
NIMPHE..... Nuclear Isotope Monopropellant Hydrazine Engine
NIMQ......... Not in My Queue (WDAA)
NIMR......... National Institute for Medical Research [*British*]

NIMR .... Navy Industrial Management Reviews (NG)
NIMR .... Nimrod Tent Trailer [*NCIC trailer make code*]
NIMROD .... National Institute for Medical Research Online Database (PDAA)
NIMROD .... Nineteen-Hundred [*Computer*] Management and Recovery of Documentation (PDAA)
NIMROD .... Northern Illinois Meteorological Research on Downbursts [*National Center for Atmospheric Research*]
NIMRS ...... Navy Integrated Message Reporting System (MCD)
NIMS .... Fairhaven International Ltd. (SAUS)
NIMS .... National Infant Mortality Survey [*Department of Health and Human Services*] (GFGA)
NIMS .... National Information Management System
NIMS .... National Ingredient Marketing Specialists (EA)
NIMS .... Nationwide Improved Mail Service [*Postal Service*]
NIMS .... Near Infrared Mapping Spectrometer [*Instrument on Galileo spacecraft*] [*NASA*]
NIMS .... Nevada Information Management System (SAUS)
NIMS .... Noiseless Integral Magnetic Scanners (ACAE)
NIMS .... Non-Invasive Monitoring Systems [*Medicine*]
NIMS .... Nuclear Instrumentation Modular System (MCD)
NIMSC....... Nonconsumable Item Materiel Support Code [*Military*] (AFIT)
NIMSCO..... NODC [*National Oceanographic Data Center*] Index to Instrument Measures Subsurface Current Observations [*Marine science*] (MSC)
NIMSDP..... Non-Innovator Multiple Source Drug Product
NIMSR ...... Nonconsumable Item Materiel Support Request [*Military*] (AFIT)
NIMT .... National Institute for Management Technology (SAUS)
NIMT .... National Institute for Music Theater [*Defunct*] (EA)
NIMTECH ... New and Improved Technology [*British*]
NIMTOF..... Not in My Term of Office [*Government slang*]
NIMTOO..... Not in My Term of Office (PA)
NIMU .... Non-Invasive Monitoring Systems, Inc. (SAUS)
NIMU .... North Island Mutual Insurance (SAUS)
NIN .... National Information Network [*ASTIA*]
NIN .... National Inservice Network
NIN .... Neighbors in Need [*An association*]
NIN .... Nine Inch Nails [*Rock music group*]
NIN .... Nine West Group [*NYSE symbol*] (TTSB)
NIN .... Nine West Group, Inc. [*NYSE symbol*] (SPSG)
NIN .... Ninhydrine [*Chemical agent used in espionage*]
NIN .... Ninilchik [*Alaska*] [*Seismograph station code, US Geological Survey*] [*Closed*] (SEIS)
NIN .... Ninilchik, AK [*Location identifier*] [*FAA*] (FAAL)
NIN .... Ninzam [*Language symbol*] (ETLW)
NIN .... Norsat International, Inc. [*Vancouver Stock Exchange symbol*]
NINA......... National Institute Northern Accelerator (PDAA)
NINA......... Neutron Instruments for Nuclear Analysis (PDAA)
NINA......... No Irish Need Apply [*Classified advertising*]
NINA......... Norwegian Institute for Nature Research (SAUS)
NINB......... National Institute of Neurology and Blindness (WDAA)
NINCDS ..... National Institute of Neurological and Communicative Disorders and Stroke [*Formerly, NINDS*] [*Public Health Service*] [*Bethesda, MD*]
NINDB....... National Institute of Neurological Diseases and Blindness [*Later, NEI, NINDS*] [*National Institutes of Health*]
NINDC....... Northern Independence Conference (PSS)
NInDE .... Elementary School No. 2, Inwood, NY [*Library symbol*] [*Library of Congress*] (LCLS)
NINDS....... National Institute of Neurological Diseases and Stroke [*Formerly, NINDB*] [*Later, NINCDS*] [*National Institutes of Health*]
NINDS....... National Institute of Neurological Disorders and Stroke
NIndTP ..... National Independent Teenage Party [*British*]
NINE......... National Infertility Network Exchange [*An association*] (EA)
NINE......... Ninth-Plate (VRA)
NINE......... Number Nine Visual Tech [*NASDAQ symbol*] (TTSB)
NINE......... Number Nine Visual Technology, Inc. [*NASDAQ symbol*] (SAG)
Nine-C Lit... Nineteenth-Century Literature [*A publication*] (BRI)
NINES .... Norfolk Information Exchange Scheme (NITA)
NineWest ... Nine West Group, Inc. [*Associated Press*] (SAG)
NINFRA ..... National Independent Nursery Furniture Retailers Association (EA)
NINIA........ Nephelometric Inhibition Immunoassay [*Analytical chemistry*]
Nink .... No Income, No Kids [*Lifestyle classification*]
NINO......... No Input, No Output (SAUS)
NINO......... No Inspector, No Operator (ODBW)
NINO......... Nothing In Nothing Out (SAUS)
NINOW ...... Non-Interest-Bearing Negotiable Order of Withdrawal [*Banking*]
NINR......... National Institute for Nursing Research
NINS......... Northern Ireland News Service [*Information service or system*] (IID)
NINST .... Non-Instrument Runway [*Aviation*] (DA)
NINST .... Nose Instantaneous [*Aerospace*]
N Instr Meth... Nuclear Instruments and Methods (SAUS)
NINU......... Neuro-intermediate Nursing Unit [*Medicine*] (EDAA)
NINVS .... Noninvasive Neurovascular Study [*Medicine*] (DAVI)
NInWE....... Elementary School No. 4, Inwood, NY [*Library symbol*] [*Library of Congress*] (LCLS)
NINYP .... Nuveen Insured New York Premium Income Municipal [*Associated Press*] (SAG)
NINYS .... Nuveen Insured New York Select Tax Free Income [*Associated Press*] (SAG)
NIO .... National Institute of Oceanography [*British*] (IID)
NIO .... National Intelligence Officer (MCD)
NIO .... Naval Inspector of Ordnance
NIO .... Navigational Information Office
NIO .... Navy Institute of Oceanography
NIO .... Network Input-Output (TIMI)
NIO .... Nieuwe Internationale Orde [*Netherlands*]
NIO .... Niobium [*See Cb*] [*Chemical element*] (ROG)
NIO .... Nioki [*Zaire*] [*Airport symbol*] (OAG)
NIO .... Non-Ionic Oil [*Fuels and lubricants*]
NIO .... Northern Ireland Office
NIO .... Nuveen Ins Muni Oppt Fd [*NYSE symbol*] (TTSB)
NIO .... Nuveen Insurance Municipal Opportunity Fund (SAUS)
NIO .... Nuveen Insured Municipal Opportunity Fund [*NYSE symbol*] (SPSG)
NIOA......... Northern Ireland Orienteering Association [*United Kingdom*] (EAIO)
NIOBE .... Numerical Integration of the Boltzmann Transport Equation
NIOC......... National Iranian Oil Company
NIOD......... Network In-Out Dial [*Automatic Voice Network*] (CET)
NIOF......... National Institute of Oceanography and Fisheries [*Egypt*] [*Marine science*] (OSRA)
NIOG......... Nationalized Industries Overseas Group [*British*] (DCTA)
NIOK......... National Institute for Overseas Koreans (EA)
NIOK......... Nederlands Instituut voor Onderzoek in de Katalyse [*Netherlands Institute for Catalysis Research*]
NIOP......... National Institute of Oilseed Products (EA)
NIOPSWL... New Input/Output Program Status Word Location [*Computer science*] (MHDI)
NIOS......... Nixdorf Integrated Office System (HGAA)
NIO-S........ Non-Ionic Oil-Soluble [*Fuels and lubricants*]
NIOS......... Northern Ireland Orchid Society (EAIO)
NIOSH....... National Institute for Occupational Safety and Health [*Public Health Service*] [*Cincinnati, OH*] [*Database producer*]
NIOSH....... National Institute of Occupational Safety and Health [*Emergency Management*] (EMA)
NIOSHTIC... National Institute for Occupational Safety and Health Technical Information Center [*Database*] [*NIOSH*] [*Information service or system*] (CRD)
NIOST .... National Institute on Out-of-School Time [*Association*] (EA)
NIOTC .... Naval Inshore Operations Training Center (NVT)
NIOZ......... Institute of Marine Scientific Research (SAUS)
NIOZ......... Netherlands Institute for Sea Research [*Marine science*] (OSRA)
NIp........... Island Park Public Library, Island Park, NY [*Library symbol*] [*Library of Congress*] (LCLS)
NIP........... Jacksonville, FL [*Location identifier*] [*FAA*] (FAAL)
NIP........... Mononitroiodophenyl [*Organic chemistry*] (DAVI)
NIP........... NADGE [*NATO Air Defense Ground Environment*] Improvement Plan (NATG)
NIP........... Namibia Independence Party [*Political party*] (PPW)
NIP........... National and International Program (SAUS)
NIP........... National Identification Program for the Advancement of Women in Higher EducationAdministration (EA)
NIP........... National Impatient Profile (MEDA)
NIP........... National Implementation Plan (SAUS)
NIP........... National Independence Party [*Namibia*] [*Political party*] (PPW)
NIP........... National Industrial Partner
NIP........... National Inspection Plan [*RSPA*] (TAG)
NIP........... National Institute for the Psychotherapies (SEAT)
NIP........... National Institute of Polarology [*Research center*] [*British*] (IRUK)
NIP........... National Integration Party [*Liberia*] [*Political party*] (EY)
NIP........... National Intelligence Priorities (MCD)
NIP........... National Inventory Programme [*National Museums of Canada*] [*Later, CHIN*]
NIP........... Naval Institute Press [*Publisher*]
NIP........... Naval Intelligence Professionals (EA)
NIP........... Navy Interceptor Program
NIP........... Negative Inspiratory Pressure [*Medicine*] (DAVI)
NIP........... Neighbourhood Improvement Program [*Canada*]
NIP........... Network Input Processor [*Computer science*] (MCD)
NIP........... Network Interface Processor (MCD)
NIP........... Neuroleptic-Induced Parkinsonism (SAUS)
NIP........... Newhall Investment Properties (SAUS)
NIP........... New Impact Resources, Inc. [*Vancouver Stock Exchange symbol*]
NIP........... New Incentive Package (ADA)
NIP........... Newsletters in Print [*Formerly, ND*] [*A publication*]
NIP........... Nipple (AAG)
Nip........... Nippon (SAUS)
NIP........... Nipponese
NIP........... No Infection Present [*Medicine*] (DMAA)
NIP........... No Inflammation Present (SAUS)
NIP........... Nonimpact Printer
NIP........... Non-Indexing Part (SAUS)
NIP........... Non-invasive Procedure [*Medicine*] (EDAA)
NIP........... Normal Impact Point
NIP........... Normal Incidence Pyrheliometer (PDAA)
NIP........... Normal Investment Practice
NIP........... Northern Ireland Parliament (SAUS)
NIP........... Notice of Intelligence Potential [*Military*] (AFM)
NIP........... Notice of Intent to Purchase [*DoD*]
NIP........... Not in Plan
NIP........... Not in Possession (SAUS)
NIP........... Not in Practice (CMD)
NIP........... Nucleus Initialization Procedure (SAUS)
NIP........... Nucleus Initialization Program [*Computer science*]
NIP........... Numeric Indicator Performance
NIP........... Numero d'Identification Personnel [*Personal Identification Number - PIN*]
NIP........... Numismatic Indexes Project (SAUS)
NIPA......... National Income and Product Accounts [*The WEFA Group*] [*Information service*] [*Information service or system*] (CRD)
NIPA......... National Institute of Pension Administrators [*Santa Ana, CA*] (EA)
NIPA......... National Institute of Public Affairs

NIPA .... N-Isopropylacrylamide [*Organic chemistry*]
NIPA .... Noninherited Paternal Antigen [*Genetics*] [*Immunology*]
NIPA .... Noninterference Performance Assessment
NIPA .... Non-local Independent Pixel Approximation (SAUS)
NIPA .... Nordens Institut pa Aland [*Nordic Institute in Aland - NIA*] [*Finland*] (EAIO)
NIPA .... Northern Ireland Ploughing Association (EAIO)
NIPA .... Northern Ireland Police Authority
NIPA .... Notice of Initiation of Procurement Action (NRCH)
NIPAC .... Northern Indiana Public Service Company PAC [*Columbus, OH*] [*Columbia Gas of Ohio Inc. PAC*] (PACS)
NIPAGRAM... National Income and Product Account Data by Mailgram [*NTIS*]
NIPALS ...... Noniterative Partial Least Squares [*Algorithm*]
NIPALS ...... Nonlinear Iterative Partial Least Squares (SAUS)
NIP & TB ... Northern Ireland Postal and Telecommunications Board
NIPAW .... National Inhalants & Poisons Awareness Week (SAUS)
NIPC .... National Infrastructure Protection Center
NIPC .... National Inhalant Prevention Coalition [*Association*] (EA)
NIPC .... N-Isopropylcarbazole [*Organic chemistry*]
NIPCC .... National Industrial Pollution Control Council [*Terminated, 1973*] [*Department of Commerce*]
NIPCI .... National Infrastructure Protection and Computer Intrusion Program [*Emergency Management*] (EMA)
NIPD .... Nightly Intermittent Peritoneal Dialysis (SAUS)
NIPD .... Not in the Public Domain
NIPDE .... National Initiative for Product Data Exchange
NIPDWR .... National Interim Primary Drinking Water Regulations [*Environmental Protection Agency*]
NIPDWS..... National Interim Primary Drinking Water Standards [*Environmental Protection Agency*]
NIPE .... National Intelligence Programs Evaluation (CARL)
NIPE .... Noninvasive Peripheral Vascular Examination [*or Evaluation*] (DAVI)
NIPER .... National Institute for Petroleum and Energy Research [*Formerly, BETC*] [*Department of Energy*] [*Bartlesville, OK*]
NIPERA...... Nickel Producers Environmental Research Association
NIPF .... Nonindustrial Private Forest Owners (WPI)
NIPF .... Non-Industrial Private Forests (ALAC)
NIPF .... Northern Ireland Peace Forum
NIPFDA...... National Independent Poultry and Food Distributors Association (EA)
NIPGM ...... National Institute on Park and Grounds Management (EA)
NIPH .... National Institute of Poultry Husbandry [*British*] (BI)
NIPH .... National Institute of Public Health
NIpHE .... Francis X. Hegarty Elementary School, Island Park, NY [*Library symbol*] [*Library of Congress*] (LCLS)
NIPHL .... Noise-Induced Permanent Hearing Loss (PDAA)
NIPHLE...... National Institute of Packaging, Handling, and Logistic Engineers (EA)
NIPHYS ..... Nitrogen Physiology of Forest Plants and Soils (SAUS)
NIPILS....... New Irish Professionals in London [*Lifestyle classification*]
NIPIM2...... Nuveen Insured Premium Income Municipal Fund 2 [*Associated Press*] (SAG)
NIPIMn...... Nuveen Insured Premium Income Municipal Fund [*Associated Press*] (SAG)
NIPIMS...... NAVMAT Instructional Procurement Inventory Monitoring System (MCD)
NIPIR........ Nuclear Immediate Photo Interpretation Report (MCD)
NIpL .... Lincoln Orens School, Island Park, NY [*Library symbol*] [*Library of Congress*] (LCLS)
NIPM .... National Institute of Public Management (EA)
NIPN......... NEC Corp. [*NASDAQ symbol*] (SAG)
NIP/NLG.... National Immigration Project of the National Lawyers Guild (EA)
NIPNY .... NEC Corp. ADR [*NASDAQ symbol*] (TTSB)
NIPO......... Navy International Program Office (SAUS)
NIPO......... Negative Input, Positive Output
NIPOLOS... Nonimpact Off-Line Operating System [*Computer science*]
NIPP......... National Institute for Public Policy (EA)
NIPP......... National Intelligence Projection for Planning (AFM)
NIPP......... Net Income per Partner [*Business term*]
NIPP......... Nonimpact Printing Process (MCD)
NIPPE .... National Income per Person Employed
NIPPI .... Japan Aircraft Manufacturing Co. Ltd. (SAUS)
NIPPING .... Nonimpact Printing (DGA)
NippnTT..... Nippon Telegraph & Telephone Co. [*Associated Press*] (SAG)
Nippon Kokan Tech Rep... Nippon Kokan Technical Report (SAUS)
Nippon Stainless Tech Rep... Nippon Stainless Technical Report (SAUS)
Nippon Steel Tech Rep... Nippon Steel Technical Report (SAUS)
Nippon Tungsten Rev... Nippon Tungsten Review (SAUS)
NIPR......... National Industrial Plant Reserve
NIPR......... Naval Intelligence Publication Register (NVT)
ni pr .... Nisi Prius [*Unless Before*] [*Legal term*] [*Latin*] (WGA)
NIPr.......... North'n Ind Pub Sv.4 1/4%cmPfd [*AMEX symbol*] (TTSB)
NIPR......... Revolutionary Proletarian Initiative Nuclei [*Government term*] (GA)
NIPrA........ North'n Ind Pub Sv Adj RtA Pfd [*NYSE symbol*] (TTSB)
NI PRI .... Nisi Prius [*Unless Before*] [*Legal term*] [*Latin*]
NIPRNET... Non-classified Internet Protocol Router Network [*Computer science*]
NIPS .... National Information Processing System [*Military*]
NIPS .... National Institute for Public Services
NIPS .... National Inventory of Pollution Sources [*Database*] [*Environment Canada*] [*Information service or system*] (CRD)
NIPS .... Nationwide Integrated Postal Service [*Postal Service*]
NIPS .... Naval Intelligence Processing System
NIPS .... Navy Information Policy Summaries (NG)
NIPS .... Neuroleptic-induced Parkinson Syndrome [*Medicine*] (EDAA)
NIPS .... New Inventory Pricing Systems (MCD)
NIPS .... News in Physiological Sciences [*Database*] (GDD)
NIPS .... Nippon Information Processing System [*Nippon Shuppan Hanbai, Inc.*] [*Database*]
NIPS .... NIPSCO Capital Markets [*Associated Press*] (SAG)
NIPS .... Nixdorf Inventory and Production-control System (SAUS)
NIPS .... Northern Indiana Public Service Co. [*Associated Press*] (SAG)
NIPS .... Not in Profile Students (SAUS)
NIPS .... Nottingham Image Processing System (SAUS)
NIPS .... NTCS-A Intelligence Processing System (SAUS)
NIPSA .... Northern Ireland Public Service Alliance (EAIO)
NIPSCO ..... NIPSCO Industries [*Associated Press*] (SAG)
NIPSCO ..... Northern Indiana Public Service Co. (EFIS)
NIPSSA...... Naval Intelligence Processing System Support Activity
NIPT .... New Information Processing Technologies (SAUS)
NIPT .... New Information Processing Technology Project [*Japan*] (ECON)
NIPTS .... Noise-Induced Permanent Threshold Shift [*Hearing*]
NIQU......... Nuuk Imeq [*Intermodal shipping container symbol*] (TVRC)
NIR .... Acrylonitrile-Isoprene Rubber (SAUS)
NIR .... Beeville, TX [*Location identifier*] [*FAA*] (FAAL)
NIr .... Irvington Public Library, Irvington, NY [*Library symbol*] [*Library of Congress*] (LCLS)
NIR .... Napier Environmental Technologies [*Toronto Stock Exchange symbol*] [*Canada*]
NIR .... National Inventory Record [*DoD*]
NIR .... Near Infrared (ECII)
NIR .... Near-Infrared Reflectance (DB)
NIR .... Near Infrared Region
NIR .... Nerve Impulse Recorder
NIR .... Networked Information Resource (TELE)
NIR .... Network Information Registry [*Computer science*] (VLIE)
NIR .... Network Information Retrieval
NIR .... New Ireland Review [*A publication*] (ROG)
NIR .... Next Inferior Rank
NIR .... Next Instruction Register (NITA)
NIR .... Nickel-Iron Refinery (SAUS)
NIR .... Nighttime Infrared (SAUS)
NIR .... Nitrile Isoprene Rubber (SAUS)
NIR .... Nitrite Reductase [*An enzyme*]
NIR .... No Individual Requirement (MSA)
NIR .... Noninductive Resistor
NIR .... Non-Insulin-Requiring [*Medicine*]
NIR .... Non-Ionizing Radiant (SAUS)
NIR .... Non-Ionizing Radiation (SAUS)
NIR .... Norskair [*Norway*] [*ICAO designator*] (FAAC)
NIR .... Northeast Illinois Railroad [*Federal Railroad Administration identification code*]
N Ir .... Northern Ireland Law Reports [*A publication*] (DLA)
NIR .... Northern Ireland Railways Co. Ltd.
NIR .... Nose Impact Rocket (NATG)
NIRA......... Designer of SUPERPHENIX with Novatome (SAUS)
NIRA......... Italian Fast Nuclear Reactor Co Genova (SAUS)
NIRA......... National Industrial Recovery Act [*1933*]
NIRA......... National Industrial Recovery Administration (WDAA)
NIRA......... National Industrial Recreation Association [*Later, NESRA*] (EA)
NIRA......... National Industrial Reserve Act of 1948
NIRA......... National Institute for Research Advancement
NIRA......... National Intercollegiate Rodeo Association (EA)
NIRA......... National Iridology Research Association (NTPA)
NIRA......... Navy Industrial Relations Activity (DNAB)
NIRA......... Navy Internal Relations Activity (DNAB)
NIRA......... Near Infrared Reflectance Analysis
NIRA......... Newspaper Industries Research Association (SAUS)
NIRA......... Niravoice, Inc. (SAUS)
NIRA......... Nitrite Reductase (DB)
NIRA......... North American Industrial Representatives Association (EA)
NIRAA....... Niravoice, Inc. (Class A) [*NASDAQ symbol*] (COMM)
NIRAP .... Naval Industrial Reserve Aircraft Plant (MUGU)
NIRAS .... National Institute of Research and Advanced Studies [*Proposed*]
NIRB......... National Industrial Recovery Board [*Terminated, 1935*]
NIRB......... National Intelligence Resources Board (CARL)
NIRB......... Nuclear Insurance Rating Bureau
NIRC......... National Industrial Relations Court [*British*]
NIRC......... National Information Retrieval Colloquium [*Later, Benjamin Franklin Colloquium on Information Science*]
NIRC......... National Institute of Rug Cleaning [*Superseded by AIDS International*] (EA)
NIRC......... Negative Ion Recombination Chamber
NIRC......... Northeast Illinois Regional Commuter Rail [*Federal Railroad Administration identification code*]
NIRCF .... National Immigration, Refugee and Citizenship Forum (EA)
NIRD......... National Institute for Research in Dairying [*British*]
NIRD......... Nonimmune Renal Disease [*Medicine*] (DMAA)
NIRDR....... Nonintegrated Radar (SAUS)
NIRE .... National Institute for Rehabilitation Engineering (EA)
N Ire......... Northern Ireland (NTIO)
N IRE........ Northern Ireland
N Ire......... North Ireland (SHCU)
NIREB .... National Institute of Real Estate Brokers [*Later, Realtors National Marketing Institute*] (EA)
NIREX .... Nuclear Industry Radioactive Waste Executive [*British*] (ECON)
NIRFOODPS... Nonscanning Infrared Focal Plan Options Study (ACAE)
NIRI......... National Information Research Institute
NIRI......... National Investor Relations Institute [*Washington, DC*] (EA)
NIRL......... Negligible Individual Risk Level (GNE)
NIRL......... Netherlands International Law Review [*A publication*] (SAFN)

N Ir LR...... Northern Ireland Law Reports [*A publication*] (DLA)
NIRM........ Network for Information Retrieval in Mammology
NIRMA...... Nuclear Information and Records Management Association (EA)
NIRMP...... National Intern and Resident Matching Program (DAVI)
NIRMS...... Noble Gas-Ion Reflection Mass Spectroscopy (SAUS)
NIRNS....... National Institute for Research in Nuclear Science [*British*]
NIRO......... Nike-Iroquois [*Rockets*]
NIROC....... National Institute of Red Orange Canaries and All Other Cage Birds (EA)
NIROP....... Naval Industrial Reserve Ordnance Plant (MCD)
NIRO Rocket... Nike-Iroquois Rocket (SAUS)
NIROS....... Near Infrared Oxygen Sufficiency Scope [*Monitors oxygen delivery to brain during surgery*] (DAVI)
NIROS....... Nixdorf Real-Time Operating System (NITA)
NIRPL....... Navy Industrial Readiness Planning List (NG)
N Ir Pub Gen Acts... Northern Ireland Public General Acts [*A publication*] (DLA)
NIRRL....... Northern Ireland Regional Research Laboratory (SAUS)
NIRS......... National Information Research Institute (ELAL)
NIRS......... National Inorganic and Radionuclides Survey [*Environmental Protection Agency*]
NIRS......... National Institute for Radiological Science [*Japan*]
NIRS......... Near Infrared Reflectance Spectroscopy [*Britton Chance*]
NIRS......... Normal Inactivated Rabbit Serum [*Medicine*] (EDAA)
NIRS......... Nuclear Information and Resource Service (EA)
NIRSA....... National Intramural-Recreational Sports Association (EA)
N Ir Stat.... Northern Ireland Statutes [*A publication*] (DLA)
NIRTS....... National Income Realty Trust [*NASDAQ symbol*] (NQ)
NIRTS....... Natl Inc. Rlty Tr SBI [*NASDAQ symbol*] (TTSB)
NIRTS....... New Integrated Range Timing System
NIrvH........ Lake Shore Hospital, Irving, NY [*Library symbol*] [*Library of Congress*] (LCLS)
NIs........... Islip Public Library, Islip, NY [*Library symbol*] [*Library of Congress*] (LCLS)
NIS........... Names Information Socket (VLIE)
NIS........... NASA Interface System (MCD)
NIS........... National Immunisation Strategy (SAUS)
NIS........... National Income Statistics [*British*]
NIS........... National Information Systems [*Later, GIP*] [*UNESCO*] (BUR)
NIS........... National Information Systems, Inc. [*Information service or system*] (IID)
NIS........... National Institute of Science (EA)
NIS........... National Insurance Surcharge [*A separately accounted tax on employment*] [*British*]
NIS........... National Intelligence Scale (DIPS)
NIS........... National Intelligence Service (NADA)
NIS........... National Intelligence Summary (MCD)
NIS........... National Intelligence Survey
NIS........... National Interdepartmental Seminar [*Military*]
NIS........... National Inventory System [*Department of Agriculture*] (GFGA)
NIS........... NATO Identification System
NIS........... NATO International Staff (SAUS)
NIS........... Naval Intelligence School
NIS........... Naval Investigative Service
NIS........... Navy Inspection Service
NIS........... Negative Ion Source
NIS........... Negotiation Information System
NIS........... Neighborhood Information Service
NIS........... Net Identification Sign (SAUS)
NIS........... Network Information Service
NIS........... Network Information System [*AT & T*]
NIS........... Network Interface System
NIS........... Neutron Inelastic Scattering
NIS........... Neutron Instrumentation System (IEEE)
NIS........... New Independent States of the former Soviet Union (SAUS)
NIS........... Newly-Independent States [*Of former Soviet Union*]
NIS........... News and Information Service [*National Broadcasting Co.*]
NIS........... Nicaraguense de Aviacion SA [*Nicaragua*] [*ICAO designator*] (FAAC)
NIS........... Nickel-Iron System
NIS........... Night Illumination System
NIS........... N-Iodosuccinimide [*Organic chemistry*]
NIS........... Nippon Information System (SAUS)
NIS........... Nissin Co ADS [*Stock exchange symbol*]
NIS........... No Inflammatory signs [*Medicine*] (MELL)
NIS........... No Intermediate Storage [*Industrial engineering*]
NIS........... Noise Information System [*Environmental Protection Agency*] (IID)
NIS........... Nonconsumable Item Subgroup [*Military*] (AFIT)
NIS........... Nonimmune Sheep Serum (DB)
NIS........... Normal Incidence Spectrometer (PDAA)
NIS........... Norton Internet Security [*Symantec Corp.*]
NIS........... Norwegian International Shipsregister (RIMS)
NIS........... Not in Scope (SAUS)
NIS........... Not in Specification [*Training term*] (LPT)
NIS........... Not in Stock
NIS........... Not in System (SAUS)
NIS........... NOVA Corp. [*NYSE symbol*] (TTSB)
NIS........... Nova Corp. (Georgia) [*NYSE symbol*] (SAG)
NIS........... Nuclear Instrumentation System (NRCH)
NIS........... Number Indicating System (SAUS)
NIS........... Numerical Information Storage (SAUS)
NIS........... Shekel (ODBW)
NISA......... National Inconvenienced Sportsmen's Association [*Later, NHSRA*] (EA)
NISA......... National Industrial Sand Association (EA)
NISA......... National Industrial Service Association [*Later, EASA*]
NISA......... National Industrial Stores Association (EA)
NISA......... National Institute of Supply Associations
NISA......... New Information Services Architecture (SAUS)
NISA......... Northeast Intercollegiate Sailing Association (PSS)
NISA......... Numerically Integrated Elements for System Analysis (MCD)
NISAC....... National Industrial Security Advisory Committee (EAGT)
NISAC....... National Infrastructure Simulation and Analysis Center
NISARC..... National Information Storage and Retrieval Center
NISBCO..... National Interreligious Service Board for Conscientious Objectors (EA)
Nisbet....... Nisbet of Dirleton's Scotch Session Cases [*1665-77*] [*A publication*] (DLA)
NISBS....... National Institute of Social and Behavioral Science (EA)
NISC......... National Independent Study Center [*Civil Service Commission*]
NISC......... National Industrial Space Committee
NISC......... National Industry Safety Committee (NADA)
NISC......... National Information Services Corp. (IID)
NISC......... National Institute of Senior Centers (EA)
NISC......... National Intelligence Study Center (EA)
NISC......... National Inter Seminary Council
NISC......... National Intramural Sports Council
NISC......... Naval Intelligence Support Center (TIMI)
NISC......... Network Information and Support Center [*Computer science*] (VLIE)
NISC......... Network Information Systems Center (AGLO)
NISCA....... National Interscholastic Swimming Coaches Association of America (EA)
NISCA....... Northeastern Illinois Sheet Metal Contractors Association (EARSL)
N I S C N E... Nursing Information Systems Council of New England (SAUS)
NISCO....... Nissho Iwai Corporation (EFIS)
NISCO....... Nuclear Installation Services Co. (NRCH)
NISCON..... National Industrial Safety Conference (PDAA)
NISCR....... South Central Research Library Council, Ithaca, NY [*Library symbol*] [*Library of Congress*] (LCLS)
NISC-TRANS... Naval Intelligence Support Center Translation Division
NISCUE...... National Institute for State Credit Union Examination [*McLean, VA*] (EA)
NISD......... National Institute of Steel Detailing (EA)
NISDA....... Northeast Intercollegiate Swimming and Diving Association (PSS)
N-ISDN...... National ISDN [*Integrated Services Digital Network*] [*Telecommunications*]
NISE......... Naval In-Service Engineering (IGSL)
NISE......... Navel In-Service Engineering (ISAK)
NISE......... NCCOSC In-Service Engineering (SAUS)
NISE......... Neighborhood Information Sharing Exchange [*Defunct*] (EA)
NISE......... Normalized Integral Squared Error
NISEC....... National Institute for the Study of Educational Change
NISEC....... Northern Ireland Schools Examination Council (AIE)
NISEE........ National Information Service for Earthquake Engineering (EA)
NISG......... National Institute of Student Governments [*Defunct*] (EA)
NISG......... Navy Installation Survey Group
NISGAZ...... National Intelligence Survey Gazetteer
NISGUA..... Network in Solidarity with the People of Guatemala (EA)
NISH......... National Industries for the Severely Handicapped (EA)
NISH......... National Information Sources on the Handicapped [*Clearinghouse on the Handicapped*] [*Database*]
NISH......... National Institute of Senior Housing (EA)
NISH......... Naval Intelligence Support Headquarters (CCCA)
NISH......... Nonisotopic In Situ Hybridization [*Analytical biochemistry*]
NISHQ....... Naval Investigative Service Headquarters
NISI.......... Network Information Services Infrastructure (SAUS)
NISI.......... Northwest Instrument Systems, Inc. (SAUS)
NI-SIL....... Nickel-Silver
NIS-IPP..... Newly Independent States-Initiatives for Proliferation Prevention [*Brookhaven National Laboratory*] (RCD)
Nisi Prius & Gen T Rep... Nisi Prius and General Term Reports [*Ohio*] [*A publication*] (DLA)
Nisi Prius Rep... Ohio Nisi Prius Reports [*A publication*] (DLA)
NISL......... National Indoor Soccer League [*Australia*]
NISL......... National Intercollegiate Swimming League (PSS)
NISLAPP... National Institute for Science, Law, and Public Policy (EA)
NISM........ Non-Deterministic Incomplete Sequential Machine (PDAA)
NISMART... National Incidence Studies of Missing, Abducted, Runnaway, and Thrownaway Children
NISMF....... Naval Inactive Ship Maintenance Facility
NISMO...... Nissan Motorsports
NISO......... National Individual Standing Offer (ACAE)
NISO......... National Information Standards Organization
NISO......... National Information Standards Organization - Z39 (EA)
NISO......... Naval Investigative Service Office (NVT)
NISOA....... National Intercollegiate Soccer Officials Association (EA)
NISOD....... National Institute for Staff and Organizational Development (OICC)
NISOR....... Naval Investigative Service Office Representative (DNAB)
NISORS..... Nigerian Society of Remote Sensing (SAUS)
NISP......... National Industrial Security Program [*A publication*] (AAGC)
NISP......... National Information System for Psychology
NISP......... National Intelligence Situation Report (CARL)
NISP......... Navy Integrated Space Program (NG)
NISP......... Networked Information Services Project [*Computer science*] (VLIE)
NISP......... Nuclear Weapons Intelligence Support Plan (COE)
NISP......... Number of Identified Specimens (SAUS)
NISP......... NUWEP [*Nuclear Weapon*] Intelligence Support Plan [*Military*]
NISPA....... National Information System for Physics and Astronomy (NITA)
NISPOM..... National Industrial Security Program Manual [*A publication*] (AAGC)
NISR......... National Intelligence Situation Report (MCD)
NISR......... Navy Initial Support Requirement (AFIT)
NISRA....... National Industrial Salvage and Recovery Association [*British*] (BI)

NISRA .... National Intercollegiate Squash Racquets Association (EA)
NISRA .... Naval Investigative Service Resident Agent (NVT)
NISREGFORENSICLAB ... Naval Investigative Service Regional Forensic Laboratory (DNAB)
NISS .... National Information of Software and Services (AIE)
NISS .... National Institute of Social Sciences (EA)
NISS .... National ITV Satellite Schedule (SAUS)
NISS .... Navigation Interface Subsystem (SAUS)
NISS .... New Information Systems and Services [*A publication*]
NISS .... Nissan [*NCIC truck make code*]
NISS .... Nissan [*NCIC car make code*]
NISS .... Nosocomial Infection Surveillance System [*Medicine*] (MELL)
Nissan .... Nissan Motor Co. Ltd. [*Associated Press*] (SAG)
NISSM .... Navy Interim Surface Ship Model (CAAL)
NISSOL ...... NAVAIR [*Naval Air Systems Command*] Initial Supply Support Outfitting List (MCD)
NISSPAC ... NISS Public Access Collections (SAUS)
NISSPO ..... NATO Identification System Special Project Office
NISSU .... Naval Investigative Service Satellite Unit (DNAB)
NIST .... National Information System for Science and Technology (NITA)
NIST .... National Institute for Standardisation Technology (SAUS)
NIST .... National Institute for Standards and Technology
NIST .... National Institute for Standards and Testing (EEVL)
NIST .... National Institute of Science and Technology (NADA)
NIST .... National Institute of Standards and Technology [*Formerly, NBS*] [*Gaithersburg, MD*] [*Department of Commerce*]
NIST .... National Intelligence Support Team (COE)
NIST .... Naval Institute of Standards & Technology (SAUS)
NIST .... Non-Interchangeable Screw Thread (SAUS)
NIST .... North-American Institute for Standards and Telecommunications (SAUS)
NIST-7 .... National Institute of Standards and Technology, Seventh Generation (MED)
N/ISTA .... National/International Safe Transit Association (NTPA)
NISTA .... Northern Independent Steel Training Association (AIE)
NISTARS ... Naval Integrated Storage Tracking and Retrieval System
NISTAV ...... Niederschlags-Verzeichnis der Niederschlagsstationen (SAUS)
NIST Connection ... Non-Interchangeable Screw Threaded Connection (SAUS)
NIST-EEEL ... National Institute of Standards & Technology - Electronics and EE Lab
NISTF .... National Information Systems Task Force [*Society of American Archivists*] [*Information service or system*] (IID)
NISTIR ...... National Institute of Standards and Technology Interagency Report
NISU .... National Injury Surveillance Unit [*Australia*]
NISU .... Norsul Internacional [*Intermodal shipping container symbol*] (TVRC)
NISUCO ..... Nigerian Sugar Co. (SAUS)
NISUS .... Neutron Intermediate Standard Uranium Source (PDAA)
NISW .... National Institute for Social Work (SAUS)
NISW .... National Institute of Social Work [*British*]
NISW .... Naval In-Shore Warfare (PDAA)
NISWA .... National Indian Social Workers Association (EA)
NISZ .... National Industrial Services [*Federal Railroad Administration identification code*]
NIT .... Midwest Aviation Corp. [*ICAO designator*] (FAAC)
NIT .... National Institute of Technology
NIT .... National Institute of Transplantation [*Association*] (EA)
NIT .... National Instructional Television [*Superseded by AIT*] (EA)
NIT .... National Intelligence Test [*Psychology*]
NIT .... National Intelligence Topic (MCD)
NIT .... National Invitation Tournament [*Basketball*]
NIT .... Native Interface Tester [*Computer science*] (VLIE)
NIT .... Nearly Intelligent Terminal [*Computer science*] (ELAL)
NIT .... Negative Income Tax
NIT .... Network Information Technology
NIT .... Network Interface Task [*Computer science*] (CIST)
NIT .... Nevada Institute of Technology (SAUS)
NIT .... New Industrial Technology (SAUS)
NIT .... New Information Technologies (or Technology) (SAUS)
NIT .... New Information Technology
NIT .... New Investment Technology
NIT .... New Technology, Incorporated (ACAE)
NIT .... Nippon Institute of Technology (SAUS)
NIT .... Nitrate (SAUS)
NIT .... Nitrum [*Chemistry*] (ROG)
NIT .... None in Town [*Bookselling*]
NIT .... Non-Intelligent Terminal (NITA)
NIT .... Nonlinear Inertialess Three-Pole [*Telecommunications*] (OA)
NIT .... Norfolk International Terminal
NIT .... Normal Incidence Technique [*Structural testing*]
NIT .... Nortel Institute for Telecommunications [*University of Toronto*] [*Canada*] (RCD)
NIT .... Northrop Institute of Technology (SAUS)
NIT .... Northrop International Terminals (SAUS)
NIT .... Norwegian Institute of Technology (SAUS)
NIT .... Not In Therapy (SAUS)
NIT .... Nuclear Irradiation Test
NIT .... Numerical Indicator Tube (SAUS)
NIT .... Nurses in Transition (EA)
NITA .... National Indoor Tennis Association [*Formerly, ITA*] [*Later, NTA*] (EA)
NITA .... National Industrial Television Association [*Later, ITVA*] (EA)
NITA .... National Institute for Trial Advocacy (EA)
NITA .... National Instructional Television Association (NTCM)
NITA .... National Intravenous Therapy Association [*Later, INS*] (EA)
NITAT .... Northern Ireland Training & Advisory Team (SAUS)
NITB .... Northern Ireland Tourist Board
NITB .... Tompkins-Seneca-Tioga Board of Cooperative Educational Services, Ithaca, NY [*Library symbol*] [*Library of Congress*] (LCLS)
NITC .... National Information Technology Committee [*Thailand*] (DDC)
NITC .... National Information Transfer Centre (NITA)
NITC .... National Instructional Television Center (NTCM)
NITC .... National Intelligence Tasking Center [*CIA*]
NITCA .... Northern Ireland Training Council Association [*United Kingdom*] (EAIO)
NITCCU ...... Northern Information Technology Centre Consultancy Unit (NITA)
Nitches ...... Nitches, Inc. [*Associated Press*] (SAG)
NITD .... Noninsulin-Treated Disease [*Medicine*] (MELL)
NITE .... Knight Trading Group [*NASDAQ symbol*]
NITE .... Knight/Trimark Group, Inc. [*NASDAQ symbol*] (NASQ)
NITE .... National Institute of Technology & Evaluation (SAUS)
NITE .... Navy Integrated Terminal Evaluation
NITE .... Night Imaging Thermal Equipment [*Army*] (INF)
NITEC .... National Information Technology in Education Centre (ACII)
NITEDEVRON ... Night Development Squadron
NITEOP ...... Night Imaging Through Electro-Optic Package [*Military*] [*British*]
NITE-OP .... Night Imaging Trough Electro-Optics (SAUS)
NITEP .... National Incinerator Testing and Evaluation Program [*Environmental Protection Agency*] (GFGA)
NITES .... NTCS-A/Navy Integrated Tactical Environmental (SAUS)
NITEWOG ... Naval Integrated Test and Evaluation Working Group (MCD)
NITF .... National Imagery Transmission Format (DOMA)
NITF .... National Interreligious Task Force (EA)
NITF .... News Industry Text Format
NITF .... Nuclear Instrument Test Facilities (SAUS)
NITFSJ ...... National Interreligious Task Force on Soviet Jewry (EA)
NITHC .... Northern Ireland Transport Holding Co. (SAUS)
NITINOL ... Nickel Titanium Naval Ordnance Laboratory [*An alloy named by William Buehler of the NOL*] (KSC)
Nitinol .... Nitinol Medical Technologies, Inc. [*Associated Press*] (SAG)
NITL .... National Industrial Traffic League (EA)
NITL .... National Industrial Transportation League (EA)
NITM .... National Income Tax Magazine [*A publication*] (DLA)
NIT-MCS .... Nippon Telephone and Telegraph-Mobile Cellular System (CGWS)
NITMDA ..... National Indoor Track Meet Directors Association (EA)
NITOL .... Norway-net with IT for Open Learning (SAUS)
NITO/W ...... National Intelligence Tasking Office, Warning and Crisis Management (ACAE)
NIT OX ...... Nitmus Oxide (SAUS)
NIT OX ...... Nitrous Oxide [*Laughing gas*] (AAMN)
NITP .... National Industrial Training Program [*Canada*]
NITP .... National Institutional Training Program [*Canada*]
NITP .... Nibbling Template
NITPA .... National Institutional Teacher Placement Association [*Later, ASCUS*]
NITPICKERS ... National Institute of Technical Processors, Information Consultants, Keyword Experts, and Retrieval Specialists [*Fictitious organization*]
NITR .... Nitrite (SAUS)
NITR .... Nonimmune Transfusion Reaction [*Medicine*] (MELL)
NITRAS ...... Navy Integrated Training Resources and Administration System (NVT)
NITRC .... National Indian Training and Research Center (EA)
NITREX ...... Nitrogen Saturation Experiments (SAUS)
NITRO .... National Independent Textiles Retailers Organizations (NTPA)
NITRO .... Nitrocellulose (WDAA)
NITRO .... Nitrogen [*Chemical element*]
nitro .... Nitroglycerin [*Pharmacy*]
Nitro .... Nitroglycerine (SAUS)
NITRO .... Sodium Nitroprusside [*Pharmacology*] (DAVI)
NITROS ..... Nitrostarch (AAG)
NITS .... National Interstate Truck Summary
NITS .... Niederbrach Truck Service [*Common carrier symbol*]
NITSTL ...... Nitride Steel
NITTS .... Noise Induced Temporary Threshold Shift (SAUS)
NITU .... Notice of Interim Trail Use [*Interstate Commerce Commission*]
NITUC .... National Independent Truckers Unity Council [*Defunct*] (EA)
NITV .... National Iranian Television (NADA)
NITV .... Network for Instructional Television (SAUS)
NITZ .... Norfolk International Terminal [*Federal Railroad Administration identification code*]
NIU .... NATO Interface Unit (MCD)
NIU .... Naval Intelligence Unit
NIU .... Navigation Interface Unit [*Navy*] (CAAL)
NIU .... Network Interface Unit [*Computer science*]
NIU .... Niue [*ANSI three-letter standard code*] (CNC)
NIU .... Niumate [*Tonga*] [*Seismograph station code, US Geological Survey*] [*Closed*] (SEIS)
NIU .... North american ISDN Users (SAUS)
NIU .... Northern Illinois University [*Dekalb, IL*]
NIU .... Northern Interparliamentary Union (SAUS)
NIU .... University of Northern Iowa, Cedar Falls, IA [*OCLC symbol*] (OCLC)
NIUC .... National Independent Union Council [*Later, NFIU*]
NIUE .... Alofi/Niue International [*Niue Island*] [*ICAO location identifier*] (ICLI)
NIUF .... National Inshore Union of Fishermen [*British*]
NIUF .... North American ISDN Users Forum (SAUS)
NIULPE ...... National Institute for Uniform Licensing of Power Engineers'
NIUS&R ..... National Institute for Urban Search and Rescue [*Emergency Management*] (EMA)
NIUSR .... National Institute for Urban Search and Rescue (SAUS)
NIUW .... National Institute for Urban Wildlife (EA)
NIV .... National Institute for Virology [*South Africa*]

NIV National Institute of Victimology (EA)
NIV Negative Ion Vacancy
NIV Neutron-Induced Voltagwe (NUCP)
NIV Newbury International Ventures, Inc. [*Vancouver Stock Exchange symbol*]
NIV New International Version [*of the Bible*] [*A publication*]
NIV Niva [*NCIC car model code*]
NIV Nivalenol [*A mycotoxin*]
NIV Nodule-Inducing Virus
NIV Non-Immigrant Visa (SAUS)
NIV Non-Invasive Ventilation (SAUS)
NIVA National Independent Vendors Association [*Defunct*] (EA)
NIVA North of Ireland Veterinary Association (GVA)
NIVA Norwegian Institute for Water Research (SAUS)
NIVC National Interactive Video Centre [*British*]
NIVEA Night Vision Equipment for Armor
NIVR Netherlands Agency for Aerospace Programs
NIW National Industrial Workers Union
NIW Naval Inshore Warfare Project
NIW Night in Weather (ACAE)
NIW Non-Ionic Water [*Fuels and lubricants*]
NIW Nonlethal Incapacitating Weapon
NIWA New Zealand National Institue for Water and Atmospheric Research (SAUS)
NIWAA Northern Ireland Women's Amatuer Athletic Association (ODA)
NIWAR National Institute of Water and Atmospheric Research (SAUS)
NIWC National Institute for Women of Color (EA)
NIWC Naval Inshore Warfare Command (NVT)
NIWC Northern Ireland Womens Coalition (SAUS)
NIWF Network Interworking Function (MLOA)
NIWFA National Intercollegiate Women's Fencing Association (EA)
NIWG National Institute for the Word of God (EA)
NIWKC National Institute of Wood Kitchen Cabinets [*Later, KCMA*]
NIWL National Institute for Work and Learning (EA)
NIWR National Institutes for Water Resources (NTPA)
NIWS National Institute on Workshop Standards [*Defunct*] (EA)
NIWS National Integrated Wage Structure (ADA)
NIWS News Information Weekly Service
NIW-S Non-Ionic Water-Soluble [*Fuels and lubricants*]
NIWTU Naval Inshore Warfare Task Unit (MCD)
NIWU National Industrial Workers Union (EA)
NIX Nioro [*Mali*] [*Airport symbol*] (OAG)
Nix Nixa [*Record label*] [*Great Britain, etc.; including Vanguard label re-issues*]
NIX Nix-O-Tine Pharmaceuticals Ltd. [*Vancouver Stock Exchange symbol*]
NIX Nix-o-Tine Pharmacy (SAUS)
NIX Pacific Beach, WA [*Location identifier*] [*FAA*] (FAAL)
Nix Dig Nixon's Digest of Laws [*New Jersey*] [*A publication*] (DLA)
Nix F Nixon's Forms [*A publication*] (DLA)
NIXSW Normal Incidence X-ray Standing Wave (SAUS)
NIXT Normal Incidence X-Ray Telescope
NIXX Nix-O-Tine Pharmaceuticals Ltd. (SAUS)
NIY Ngiti [*Language symbol*] (ETLW)
NIY Norfolk, VA [*Location identifier*] [*FAA*] (FAAL)
NIY Northamptonshire Imperial Yeomanry [*British military*] (DMA)
NIY Northumberland Imperial Yeomanry [*British military*] (DMA)
NIYC National Indian Youth Council (EA)
NIZ Nalley's [*Federal Railroad Administration identification code*]
NIZ Nizhne-Angarsk [*Former USSR*] [*Seismograph station code, US Geological Survey*] (SEIS)
NIZC National Industrial Zoning Committee (EA)
NJ Namakwaland Lugdiens [*ICAO designator*] (AD)
NJ Namakwaland Lugdiens Bpk [*South Africa*] [*ICAO designator*] (ICDA)
nJ Nanojoule [*One billionth of a joule*]
NJ Napierville Junction Railway Co. [*AAR code*]
NJ Nasojejunal [*Medicine*]
NJ Network Junction [*Telecommunications*] (OA)
NJ Neue Justiz. Zeitschrift fuer Recht und Rechtswissenschaft [*Berlin, German Democratic Republic*] [*A publication*] (DLA)
NJ Newfoundland and Labrador Judgments [*Canada*] [*Database*] (GDD)
NJ New Jaguar [*Jaguar PLC*]
NJ New Japan Aircraft Maintenance Co. Ltd. [*Japan*] [*ICAO aircraft manufacturer identifier*] (ICAO)
NJ New Jason [*Charter-party clause*] [*Business term*] (DS)
NJ New Jersey [*Postal code*]
Nj New Jersey State Library, Trenton, NJ [*Library symbol*] [*Library of Congress*] (LCLS)
NJ New Jersey Supreme Court Reports [*A publication*] (DLA)
NJ New Journalism [*Refers to specific style, as that of writer Tom Wolfe*]
NJ Non Justifying [*Typography*] (DGA)
NJ Non-Juxtaposed (SAUS)
NJ Notice of Judgment (Official) [*Legal term*] (DLA)
NJ Nylon Jacket
NJA National Jail Association [*Later, AJA*] (EA)
NJA National Jewellers' Association [*British*] (BI)
NJA National Jogging Association [*Later, ARFA*] (EA)
NJA National Jousting Association (EA)
NJA National Judges Association (EA)
NJA Network Interoperability Alliance [*Communications term*] (DCT)
NJA New Jewish Agenda (EA)
NJA Nozzle Jetevator Assembly
NJA Sky Air Cargo Services (UK) Ltd. [*British*] [*ICAO designator*] (FAAC)
NJAA National Junior Angus Association (EA)
NJABR New Jersey Association for Biomedical Research (EARSL)
NjAc Atlantic City Free Public Library, Atlantic City, NJ [*Library symbol*] [*Library of Congress*] (LCLS)
NJAC National Joint Action Committee (Trinidad and Tobago) [*Political party*] (PSAP)
NJAC National Joint Advisory Council [*on labor-management relations*] [*British*]
NJAC New Jersey Administrative Code [*A publication*]
NJAC New Jersey Athletic Conference (PSS)
NjAcCoC Atlantic County Clerk, Atlantic City, NJ [*Library symbol*] [*Library of Congress*] (LCLS)
NJACE New Jersey Association of Corvair Enthusiasts (EARSL)
NjAcFA United States Federal Aviation Administration, National Aviation Facilities Experimental Center, Atlantic City, NJ [*Library symbol*] [*Library of Congress*] (LCLS)
NjAcJ Jewish Record, Atlantic City, NJ [*Library symbol*] [*Library of Congress*] (LCLS)
NjAcP Press Publishing Co., Atlantic City, NJ [*Library symbol*] [*Library of Congress*] (LCLS)
NjAcPI Popolo Italiano, Atlantic City, NJ [*Library symbol*] [*Library of Congress*] (LCLS)
NjAcR Atlantic City Reporter, Atlantic City, NJ [*Library symbol*] [*Library of Congress*] (LCLS)
NJACU New Jersey Association of Colleges and Universities (SAUS)
NJAD Nozzle Joint Assembly Demonstration (SAUS)
NJ Admin Code New Jersey Administrative Code [*A publication*] (DLA)
NJAG National Jewish Artisans Guild [*Defunct*] (EA)
NJAHCF Health Care Association of New Jersey (EARSL)
NJAHS National Japanese American Historical Society [*Association*] (EA)
NJAIC New Jersey Asparagus Industry Council (EA)
NJAIS New Jersey Association of Independent Schools (SAUS)
NjAl Allentown Public Library, Allentown, NJ [*Library symbol*] [*Library of Congress*] (LCLS)
NjAlA Allentown Printing Service, Allentown, NJ [*Library symbol*] [*Library of Congress*] (LCLS)
NjAlB Allentown Borough Hall, Allentown, NJ [*Library symbol*] [*Library of Congress*] (LCLS)
NjAlHi Allentown Historical Society, Allentown, NJ [*Library symbol*] [*Library of Congress*] (LCLS)
NJam James Prendergast Free Library, Jamestown, NY [*Library symbol*] [*Library of Congress*] (LCLS)
NJamC Chautauqua-Cattaraugus Library System, Jamestown, NY [*Library symbol*] [*Library of Congress*] (LCLS)
NJamCC Jamestown Community College, Jamestown, NY [*Library symbol*] [*Library of Congress*] (LCLS)
NJamH Jamestown General Hospital, Jamestown, NY [*Library symbol*] [*Library of Congress*] (LCLS)
NJamW Woman's Christian Association Hospital, Jamestown, NY [*Library symbol*] [*Library of Congress*] (LCLS)
NJANG New Jersey Air National Guard (MUSM)
NJAOPS New Jersey Association of Osteopathic Physicians and Surgeons (MHID)
NJAR New Jersey Administrative Reports [*A publication*]
NJARA New Jersey Animal Rights Alliance (EARSL)
NjAs Asbury Park Free Public Library, Asbury Park, NJ [*Library symbol*] [*Library of Congress*] (LCLS)
NJASBO New Jersey Association of School Business Officials (SAUS)
NjAsP Asbury Park Press, Asbury Park, NJ [*Library symbol*] [*Library of Congress*] (LCLS)
NjAsS Spotlight Magazine, Asbury Park, NJ [*Library symbol*] [*Library of Congress*] (LCLS)
NJASSPS New Jersey Association of Secondary School Principals and Supervisors (SAUS)
NjAt Atlantic Highlands Public Library Association, Atlantic Highlands, NJ [*Library symbol*] [*Library of Congress*] (LCLS)
NjAuV Weekly Visitor, Audubon, NJ [*Library symbol*] [*Library of Congress*] (LCLS)
NjAveT Tabloid Lithographers, Inc., Avenel, NJ [*Library symbol*] [*Library of Congress*] (LCLS)
NjAvH Herald, Avalon, NJ [*Library symbol*] [*Library of Congress*] (LCLS)
NJB Appalachian State University, Boone, NC [*OCLC symbol*] (OCLC)
NjB Bridgeton Free Public Library, Bridgeton, NJ [*Library symbol*] [*Library of Congress*] (LCLS)
NJB New Jerusalem Bible [*1985*] [*A publication*] (ODCC)
NjBa Bayonne Free Public Library, Bayonne, NJ [*Library symbol*] [*Library of Congress*] (LCLS)
NjBaF Facts of Bayonne Publishing Co., Bayonne, NJ [*Library symbol*] [*Library of Congress*] (LCLS)
NjBaFAR Federal Archives and Records Center, General Services Administration, Bayonne, NJ [*Library symbol*] [*Library of Congress*] (LCLS)
NjBaNSRF United States Naval Supply Research and Development Facility, Bayonne, NJ [*Library symbol*] [*Library of Congress*] (LCLS)
NjBAP Cumberland County Advertiser-Press, Inc., Bridgeton, NJ [*Library symbol*] [*Library of Congress*] (LCLS)
NjBarHi Barrington Historical Society (SAUS)
NjBarHi Barrington Historical Society, Barrington, NJ [*Library symbol*] [*Library of Congress*] (LCLS)
NjBas Bernards Township Library, Inc., Basking Ridge, NJ [*Library symbol*] [*Library of Congress*] (LCLS)
NjBb Bound Brook Memorial Library, Bound Brook, NJ [*Library symbol*] [*Library of Congress*] (LCLS)
NjBbA American Cyanamid Co., Organic Chemicals Division, Bound Brook, NJ [*Library symbol*] [*Library of Congress*] (LCLS)
NjBbC Bound Brook Chronicle, Bound Brook, NJ [*Library symbol*] [*Library of Congress*] (LCLS)
NJBBF National Judo Black Belt Federation of the USA (EA)
NjBbU Union Carbide Plastics Co., Bound Brook, NJ [*Library symbol*] [*Library of Congress*] (LCLS)

NjBCoC ...... Cumberland County Clerk, Bridgeton, NJ [*Library symbol*] [*Library of Congress*] (LCLS)
NjBe .... Belleville Free Public Library, Belleville, NJ [*Library symbol*] [*Library of Congress*] (LCLS)
NjBeA .... Ad-Print, Belleville, NJ [*Library symbol*] [*Library of Congress*] (LCLS)
NjBeacO .... Daily Observer, Beachwood, NJ [*Library symbol*] [*Library of Congress*] (LCLS)
NjBel .... Belmar Public Library, Belmar, NJ [*Library symbol*] [*Library of Congress*] (LCLS)
NjBelvCoC... Warren County Clerk, Belvidere, NJ [*Library symbol*] [*Library of Congress*] (LCLS)
NjBelvW .... Warren County Library, Belvidere, NJ [*Library symbol*] [*Library of Congress*] (LCLS)
NjBer .... Bergenfield Free Public Library, Bergenfield, NJ [*Library symbol*] [*Library of Congress*] (LCLS)
NjBerl .... Marie Fleche Memorial Library, Berlin, NJ [*Library symbol*] [*Library of Congress*] (LCLS)
NjBern....... Bernardsville Library Association, Bernardsville, NJ [*Library symbol*] [*Library of Congress*] (LCLS)
NjBernN..... Bernardsville News, Bernardsville, NJ [*Library symbol*] [*Library of Congress*] (LCLS)
NjBeT........ Belleville Telegram, Belleville, NJ [*Library symbol*] [*Library of Congress*] (LCLS)
NjBh .... Berkley Heights Public Library, Berkley Heights, NJ [*Library symbol*] [*Library of Congress*] (LCLS)
NJBIA........ New Jersey Business and Industry Association (EARSL)
NjBl.......... Bloomfield Public Library, Bloomfield, NJ [*Library symbol*] [*Library of Congress*] (LCLS)
NjBla .... Gloucester Township [*Blackwood*] Library, Blackwood, NJ [*Library symbol*] [*Library of Congress*] (LCLS)
NjBlaC....... Camden County College, Blackwood, NJ [*Library symbol*] [*Library of Congress*] (LCLS)
NjBlaCG..... Camden-Gloucester Newspapers, Blackwood, NJ [*Library symbol*] [*Library of Congress*] (LCLS)
NjBlaiP...... Blairstown Press, Blairstown, NJ [*Library symbol*] [*Library of Congress*] (LCLS)
NjBlC .... Bloomfield College, Bloomfield, NJ [*Library symbol*] [*Library of Congress*] (LCLS)
NjBlHi .... Historical Society of Bloomfield, Bloomfield, NJ [*Library symbol*] [*Library of Congress*] (LCLS)
NjBlI .... Independent Press, Bloomfield, NJ [*Library symbol*] [*Library of Congress*] (LCLS)
NjBlM .... Academy of Medicine of New Jersey, Bloomfield, NJ [*Library symbol*] [*Library of Congress*] (LCLS)
NjBlS .... Shering Corp., Bloomfield, NJ [*Library symbol*] [*Library of Congress*] (LCLS)
NjBlW .... Westinghouse Electric Corp., Lamp Division, Bloomfield, NJ [*Library symbol*] [*Library of Congress*] (LCLS)
NjBN......... Bridgeton Evening News, Bridgeton, NJ [*Library symbol*] [*Library of Congress*] (LCLS)
NjBo .... Bogota Public Library, Bogota, NJ [*Library symbol*] [*Library of Congress*] (LCLS)
NjBoo........ Holmes Library, Boonton, NJ [*Library symbol*] [*Library of Congress*] (LCLS)
NjBooT...... Times-Bulletin, Boonton, NJ [*Library symbol*] [*Library of Congress*] (LCLS)
NjBorHi ..... Bordentown Historical Society, Bordentown, NJ [*Library symbol*] [*Library of Congress*] (LCLS)
NjBorL....... Lorraine Publishing, Inc., Bordentown, NJ [*Library symbol*] [*Library of Congress*] (LCLS)
NjBriCN ..... Plainfield Courier-News, Bridgewater, NJ [*Library symbol*] [*Library of Congress*] (LCLS)
NjBrigT...... Brigantine Times, Brigantine, NJ [*Library symbol*] [*Library of Congress*] (LCLS)
NjBro .... Mendham Township Library, Brookside, NJ [*Library symbol*] [*Library of Congress*] (LCLS)
NjBrS........ Seacoast Newspapers, Brick Town, NJ [*Library symbol*] [*Library of Congress*] (LCLS)
NjBu .... Library Co. of Burlington, Burlington, NJ [*Library symbol*] [*Library of Congress*] (LCLS)
NjBuHi ...... Burlington County Historical Society, Burlington, NJ [*Library symbol*] [*Library of Congress*] (LCLS)
NjButA....... Argus Printing & Publishing Co., Butler, NJ [*Library symbol*] [*Library of Congress*] (LCLS)
NjC........... Chatham Public Library, Chatham, NJ [*Library symbol*] [*Library of Congress*] (LCLS)
NJC .... Natchez Junior College [*Mississippi*]
NJC .... National Jewish Center [*Australia*]
NJC .... National Jewish Coalition (EA)
NJC .... National Joint Council (AIE)
NJC .... National Judicial College (EA)
NJC .... National Security Caucus Institute (EA)
NJC .... Navarro Junior College [*Texas*]
NJC .... Navy Job Classification Manual
NJC .... New Jersey Central Railroad
NJC .... Newton Junior College [*Massachusetts*]
NJC .... Nordic Journal of Computing (SAUS)
NJC .... Norfolk Junior College [*Nebraska*]
NJC .... Not Just Cows (SAUS)
NjCa .... Camden Free Public Library, Camden, NJ [*Library symbol*] [*Library of Congress*] (LCLS)
NJCAA....... National Job Corps Alumni Association [*Washington, DC*] (EA)
NJCAA....... National Junior College Athletic Association (EA)
NjCaC .... Cooper Medical Center, Camden, NJ [*Library symbol*] [*Library of Congress*] (LCLS)
NjCaHi ..... Camden County Historical Society, Camden, NJ [*Library symbol*] [*Library of Congress*] (LCLS)
NjCal .... Caldwell Free Public Library, Caldwell, NJ [*Library symbol*] [*Library of Congress*] (LCLS)
NjCalC....... Caldwell College, Caldwell, NJ [*Library symbol*] [*Library of Congress*] (LCLS)
NjCalP....... Caldwell Progress, Caldwell, NJ [*Library symbol*] [*Library of Congress*] (LCLS)
NjCaN .... Camden News, Camden, NJ [*Library symbol*] [*Library of Congress*] (LCLS)
NjCapS...... Star and Wave, Cape May, NJ [*Library symbol*] [*Library of Congress*] (LCLS)
NJCAPT & C... National Joint Council for Administrative, Professional, Technical, and ClericalStaff [*British*]
NjCaRD ..... Radio Corp. of America, Communications Systems Division, Camden, NJ [*Library symbol*] [*Library of Congress*] (LCLS)
NjCarpD..... E. I. Du Pont de Nemours & Co., Carney's Point Development Laboratory, Carney's Point, NJ [*Library symbol*] [*Library of Congress*] (LCLS)
NjCaSH...... Catholic Star Herald, Camden, NJ [*Library symbol*] [*Library of Congress*] (LCLS)
NjCaUR ..... Union Reporter, Camden, NJ [*Library symbol*] [*Library of Congress*] (LCLS)
NJCBI........ National Joint Council for the Building Industry [*British*] (DCTA)
NJCBSPT... New Jersey College Basic Skills Placement Test (EDAC)
NjCC......... Chatham Courier, Chatham, NJ [*Library symbol*] [*Library of Congress*] (LCLS)
NJCC .... National Joint Computer Committee [*of ACM, AIEE, IRE*] [*Superseded by AFIPS*]
NJCC .... National Joint Consultative Committee (ODA)
NJCC .... Northeastern Junior College of Colorado [*Sterling*]
NJCCA....... National Japanese Canadian Citizens' Association
NJCCOE ..... Nordic Joint Committee of Commercial and Office Executives (EA)
NJCDE....... Nordic Joint Committee for Domestic Education (EA)
NjCE .... Chatham Township Echoes, Chatham, NJ [*Library symbol*] [*Library of Congress*] (LCLS)
NJCEC ...... NATO Joint Communications-Electronics Committee (NATG)
NJCF......... National Juvenile Court Foundation (EA)
NJCF......... New Jersey Conservation Foundation (SAUS)
NjCg .... Cedar Grove Public Library, Cedar Grove, NJ [*Library symbol*] [*Library of Congress*] (LCLS)
NjCh .... Cherry Hill Free Public Library, Cherry Hill, NJ [*Library symbol*] [*Library of Congress*] (LCLS)
NJ Ch........ New Jersey Equity Reports [*A publication*] (DLA)
NJCHC....... National Joint Council for Handicapped Children [*British*]
NjChCP...... Courier Post, Cherry Hill, NJ [*Library symbol*] [*Library of Congress*] (LCLS)
NjChe........ Chester Free Public Library, Chester, NJ [*Library symbol*] [*Library of Congress*] (LCLS)
NjChJ........ Jewish Federation of Camden County, Cherry Hill, NJ [*Library symbol*] [*Library of Congress*] (LCLS)
NjChM....... Cherry Hill Medical Center, Cherry Hill, NJ [*Library symbol*] [*Library of Congress*] (LCLS)
NjChSG...... Shoppers Guide, Cherry Hill, NJ [*Library symbol*] [*Library of Congress*] (LCLS)
NjChSN...... Suburban Newspaper Group, Cherry Hill, NJ [*Library symbol*] [*Library of Congress*] (LCLS)
NjCiL .... Cinnaminson Little Paper, Cinnaminson, NJ [*Library symbol*] [*Library of Congress*] (LCLS)
NjCl.......... Clark Free Public Library, Clark, NJ [*Library symbol*] [*Library of Congress*] (LCLS)
NJCL......... Network Job Control Language [*Computer science*]
NJCLAFB ... National Joint Council for Local Authority Fire Brigades [*British*]
NJCLD....... National Joint Committee for Learning Disabilities
NJCLE........ Institute for Continuing Legal Education, New Jersey (DLA)
NjClif .... Clifton Public Library, Clifton, NJ [*Library symbol*] [*Library of Congress*] (LCLS)
NjClifB ...... New Jersey Business Review, Clifton, NJ [*Library symbol*] [*Library of Congress*] (LCLS)
NjClifI .... Clifton Independent Prospector, Clifton, NJ [*Library symbol*] [*Library of Congress*] (LCLS)
NjClifL....... Clifton Leader, Clifton, NJ [*Library symbol*] [*Library of Congress*] (LCLS)
NjClifP ...... Clifton Publishing Co., Clifton, NJ [*Library symbol*] [*Library of Congress*] (LCLS)
NjClifPE..... Post Eagle Publishing Co., Clifton, NJ [*Library symbol*] [*Library of Congress*] (LCLS)
NjClifW...... Woodward-Clyde Consultants, Clifton, NJ [*Library symbol*] [*Library of Congress*] (LCLS)
NjClinH...... Hunterdon Review, Clinton, NJ [*Library symbol*] [*Library of Congress*] (LCLS)
NjClp .... Cliffside Park Public Library, Cliffside Park, NJ [*Library symbol*] [*Library of Congress*] (LCLS)
NjClpP...... Palisades Printing Corp., Cliffside Park, NJ [*Library symbol*] [*Library of Congress*] (LCLS)
NjCmCo ..... Cape May County Library, Cape May Court House, NJ [*Library symbol*] [*Library of Congress*] (LCLS)
NjCmCoC ... Cape May County Clerk, Cape May Court House, NJ [*Library symbol*] [*Library of Congress*] (LCLS)
NjCmG ...... Cape May County Gazette, Cape May Court House, NJ [*Library symbol*] [*Library of Congress*] (LCLS)
NJCMS ..... New Jersey Chamber Music Society (SAUS)
NjCo......... Collingswood Free Public Library, Collingswood, NJ [*Library symbol*] [*Library of Congress*] (LCLS)
NjCoB .... Christian Beacon, Collingswood, NJ [*Library symbol*] [*Library of Congress*] (LCLS)
NjCoC .... Collingswood Publishing Co., Collingswood, NJ [*Library symbol*] [*Library of Congress*] (LCLS)
NjColS...... South Jersey Ad-Visor, Cologne, NJ [*Library symbol*] [*Library of Congress*] (LCLS)

NjConC ...... College of Saint Elizabeth, Convent Station, NJ [*Library symbol*] [*Library of Congress*] (LCLS)
NJCOS ...... National Jewish Committee on Scouting (EA)
NjCoT .... Camden County Times, Collingswood, NJ [*Library symbol*] [*Library of Congress*] (LCLS)
NjCr .... Cranford Public Library, Cranford, NJ [*Library symbol*] [*Library of Congress*] (LCLS)
NJCRAC ..... National Jewish Community Relations Advisory Council (EA)
NjCrbP ...... Cranbury Press, Cranbury, NJ [*Library symbol*] [*Library of Congress*] (LCLS)
NjCrC .... Cranford Citizen & Chronicle, Cranford, NJ [*Library symbol*] [*Library of Congress*] (LCLS)
NjCrHi .... Cranford Historical Society, Cranford, NJ [*Library symbol*] [*Library of Congress*] (LCLS)
NJCRI .... North Jersey Community Research Initiative (MHID)
NjCrU .... Union College, Cranford, NJ [*Library symbol*] [*Library of Congress*] (LCLS)
NJCS .... National Jewish Committee on Scouting (EA)
NJCSA .... National Juvenile Court Services Association (EA)
NJCSE .... National Jewish Civil Service Employees (EA)
NjD .... Dover Public Library, Dover, NJ [*Library symbol*] [*Library of Congress*] (LCLS)
NjDA .... Daily Advance, Dover, NJ [*Library symbol*] [*Library of Congress*] (LCLS)
NJDA .... National Juvenile Detention Association (EA)
NJDA .... New Jersey Dental Association (SAUS)
NjDC .... County College of Morris, Dover, NJ [*Library symbol*] [*Library of Congress*] (LCLS)
NJDDC ...... New Jersey Development Disabilities Council (EDAC)
NjDe .... Denville Free Public Library, Denville, NJ [*Library symbol*] [*Library of Congress*] (LCLS)
NjDeC .... Citizen of Morris County, Denville, NJ [*Library symbol*] [*Library of Congress*] (LCLS)
NJDEP .... New Jersey Department of Environmental Protection
NJDEPE ..... New Jersey Department of Environmental Protection and Energy (SAUS)
NJDFC .... New Jersey Devils Fan Club (EA)
NJDOT .... New Jersey Department of Transport (SAUS)
NjDPA .... United States Army, Armament Research and Development Command, Science and Technical Library, Dover Site Dover (SAUS)
NjDPA .... United States Army, Armament Research and Development Command, Science and Technical Library, Dover Site, Dover, NJ [*Library symbol*] [*Library of Congress*] (LCLS)
NJE .... Network Job Entry
NJE .... New Jersey Equity Reports [*A publication*] (DLA)
NJE .... New Jersey Experiment (SAUS)
Nj-E .... New Jersey State Library, Department of Education, Trenton, NJ [*Library symbol*] [*Library of Congress*] (LCLS)
NJE .... Office of Cancer and Toxic Substances Research, Trenton, NJ [*OCLC symbol*] (OCLC)
NjEa .... Eatontown Public Library, Eatontown, NJ [*Library symbol*] [*Library of Congress*] (LCLS)
NjEb .... East Brunswick Public Library, East Brunswick, NJ [*Library symbol*] [*Library of Congress*] (LCLS)
NjEbGS ...... Church of Jesus Christ of Latter-Day Saints, Genealogical Society Library, East Brunswick Stake Branch, East Brunswick, NJ [*Library symbol*] [*Library of Congress*] (LCLS)
NjEbS .... Sentinel Publishing Co., East Brunswick, NJ [*Library symbol*] [*Library of Congress*] (LCLS)
NjEdE .... Engelhard Minerals & Chemicals Corp. [*Later, Engelhard Corp.*], Research Library, Edison, NJ [*Library symbol*] [*Library of Congress*] (LCLS)
NjEdM .... Middlesex County College, Edison, NJ [*Library symbol*] [*Library of Congress*] (LCLS)
NjEgN .... Egg Harbor News, Egg Harbor City, NJ [*Library symbol*] [*Library of Congress*] (LCLS)
NjEh .... East Hanover Public Library, East Hanover, NJ [*Library symbol*] [*Library of Congress*] (LCLS)
NjEli .... Elizabeth Free Public Library, Elizabeth, NJ [*Library symbol*] [*Library of Congress*] (LCLS)
NjEliCoC .... Union County Clerk, Elizabeth, NJ [*Library symbol*] [*Library of Congress*] (LCLS)
NjEliJ .... Daily Journal, Elizabeth, NJ [*Library symbol*] [*Library of Congress*] (LCLS)
NjElT .... Elmer Times, Elmer, NJ [*Library symbol*] [*Library of Congress*] (LCLS)
NjEn .... Englewood Library, Englewood, NJ [*Library symbol*] [*Library of Congress*] (LCLS)
NjEncL ...... Thomas J. Lipton, Inc., Englewood Cliffs, NJ [*Library symbol*] [*Library of Congress*] (LCLS)
NjEncStP .... Saint Peter's College, Englewood Cliffs, NJ [*Library symbol*] [*Library of Congress*] (LCLS)
NJE/NJI ..... Network Job Entry, Including Network Job Interface
NjEnP .... Englewood Press, Englewood, NJ [*Library symbol*] [*Library of Congress*] (LCLS)
NjEnPa ...... Palisades Newspapers, Englewood, NJ [*Library symbol*] [*Library of Congress*] (LCLS)
NjEnS .... North Jersey Suburbanite, Englewood, NJ [*Library symbol*] [*Library of Congress*] (LCLS)
NjEo .... East Orange Free Public Library, East Orange, NJ [*Library symbol*] [*Library of Congress*] (LCLS)
NjEoA .... Advocate, East Orange, NJ [*Library symbol*] [*Library of Congress*] (LCLS)
NjEoS .... Sokol USA, East Orange, NJ [*Library symbol*] [*Library of Congress*] (LCLS)
NjEoU .... Upsala College, East Orange, NJ [*Library symbol*] [*Library of Congress*] (LCLS)
NjEoV .... United States Veterans Administration Hospital, East Orange, NJ [*Library symbol*] [*Library of Congress*] (LCLS)
NJ Eq .... New Jersey Equity Reports [*A publication*] (DLA)
NJ Eq R ..... New Jersey Equity Reports [*A publication*] (DLA)
NJ Equity ... New Jersey Equity Reports [*A publication*] (DLA)
NJer .... Jericho Public Library, Jericho, NY [*Library symbol*] [*Library of Congress*] (LCLS)
NJerC .... Long Island Association of Commerce and Industry, Jericho, NY [*Library symbol*] [*Library of Congress*] (LCLS)
NJerCE ...... Cantiague Elementary School, Jericho, NY [*Library symbol*] [*Library of Congress*] (LCLS)
NJerHS ...... Jericho Senior High School, Jericho, NY [*Library symbol*] [*Library of Congress*] (LCLS)
NJERHS ..... North Jersey Electric Railway Historical Society (EARSL)
NJerJE ...... George Jackson Elementary School, Jericho, NY [*Library symbol*] [*Library of Congress*] (LCLS)
NJerS .... Staff Supermarket Associates, Inc., Jericho, NY [*Library symbol*] [*Library of Congress*] (LCLS)
N Jersey R ... New Jersey Law Reports [*A publication*] (DLA)
NJES .... Nozzle Joint Environmental Simulators (SAUS)
NJESS .... Nigerian Journal of Economic and Social Studies [*A publication*]
NjEwB .... Bergen Citizen, Edgewater, NJ [*Library symbol*] [*Library of Congress*] (LCLS)
NjEwJJ ...... Johnson & Johnson Dental Product Co., East Windsor, NJ [*Library symbol*] [*Library of Congress*] (LCLS)
NJF .... Cherry Point, NC [*Location identifier*] [*FAA*] (FAAL)
NjF .... Fair Lawn Free Public Library, Fair Lawn, NJ [*Library symbol*] [*Library of Congress*] (LCLS)
NJF .... Nordiska Journalistforbundet [*Nordic Association of Journalists Unions - NAJU*] (EAIO)
NJF .... Nordiske Jordbrugsforskeres Forening [*Nordic Agricultural Research Workers Association - NARWA*] (EAIO)
NJF .... Scandinavian Agricultural Research Workers' Association
NJFA .... National Justice Foundation of America (EA)
NJFAA .... Federal Aviation Administration, Eastern Region Library, Jamaica, NY [*Library symbol*] [*Library of Congress*] (LCLS)
NJFC .... New Jetson's Fan Club [*Association*] (EA)
NJFC .... Norma Jean Fan Club (EA)
NJFD .... Notices of Judgment, United States Food and Drug Administration [*A publication*] (DLA)
NjFdA .... United States Army, Special Services Post Library, Fort Dix, NJ [*Library symbol*] [*Library of Congress*] (LCLS)
NjFf .... Fairfield Free Public Library, Fairfield, NJ [*Library symbol*] [*Library of Congress*] (LCLS)
NjFhUGA .... United States Golf Association, Far Hills, NJ [*Library symbol*] [*Library of Congress*] (LCLS)
NjFlCoC ..... Hunterdon County Clerk, Flemington, NJ [*Library symbol*] [*Library of Congress*] (LCLS)
NjFlD .... Hunterdon County Democrat, Flemington, NJ [*Library symbol*] [*Library of Congress*] (LCLS)
NjFlH .... Hunterdon County Library, Flemington, NJ [*Library symbol*] [*Library of Congress*] (LCLS)
NjFlHi .... Hunterdon County Historical Society, Flemington, NJ [*Library symbol*] [*Library of Congress*] (LCLS)
NjFlM .... Hunterdon Medical Center, Flemington, NJ [*Library symbol*] [*Library of Congress*] (LCLS)
NjFmE-TD ... United States Army, Electronics Command, Technical Documents Branch, Fort Monmouth, NJ [*Library symbol*] [*Library of Congress*] (LCLS)
NjFmS .... United States Army, Signal School, Fort Monmouth (SAUS)
NjFmS .... United States Army, Signal School, Fort Monmouth, NJ [*Library symbol*] [*Library of Congress*] (LCLS)
NjFNB .... Shopper-News Beacon, Fair Lawn, NJ [*Library symbol*] [*Library of Congress*] (LCLS)
NjFp .... Florham Park Public Library, Florham Park, NJ [*Library symbol*] [*Library of Congress*] (LCLS)
NjFpEx ...... Exxon Research & Engineering Co., Engineering Information Center, Florham Park, NJ [*Library symbol*] [*Library of Congress*] (LCLS)
NjFpN .... Florham Park Community News, Florham Park, NJ [*Library symbol*] [*Library of Congress*] (LCLS)
NjFr .... Freehold Public Library, Freehold, NJ [*Library symbol*] [*Library of Congress*] (LCLS)
NJFR .... National Joint Fiction Reserve
NjFraS .... Suburban News, Franklin Lakes, NJ [*Library symbol*] [*Library of Congress*] (LCLS)
NjFrCoC ..... Clerk of Monmouth County, Freehold, NJ [*Library symbol*] [*Library of Congress*] (LCLS)
NjFrHi .... Monmouth County Historical Association, Freehold, NJ [*Library symbol*] [*Library of Congress*] (LCLS)
NjFrM .... Monmouth County Library, Freehold, NJ [*Library symbol*] [*Library of Congress*] (LCLS)
NjFrS .... Schreiber Publishing Co., Freehold, NJ [*Library symbol*] [*Library of Congress*] (LCLS)
NjFrtD .... Delaware Valley News, Frenchtown, NJ [*Library symbol*] [*Library of Congress*] (LCLS)
NjFrvA .... Advertiser, Franklinville, NJ [*Library symbol*] [*Library of Congress*] (LCLS)
NjFvW .... West New Yorker, Inc., Fairview, NJ [*Library symbol*] [*Library of Congress*] (LCLS)
NJG .... Glassboro State College, Glassboro, NJ [*OCLC symbol*] (OCLC)
NJG .... Nachtjagugeschwader [*Night Fighter*] [*German*]
NJG .... Nice Jewish Girl [*Slang*]
NjGaB .... Bergen Gazette, Inc., Garfield, NJ [*Library symbol*] [*Library of Congress*] (LCLS)
NjGaG .... Garfield Guardian, Garfield, NJ [*Library symbol*] [*Library of Congress*] (LCLS)
NjGaS .... Glassboro State College, Glassboro (SAUS)

NjGb .... Glassboro Public Library, Glassboro, NJ [*Library symbol*] [*Library of Congress*] (LCLS)
NjGbS .... Glassboro State College, Glassboro, NJ [*Library symbol*] [*Library of Congress*] (LCLS)
NJGFE .... Nordic Joint Group for Forest Entomology (EA)
NjGiD .... E. I. Du Pont de Nemours & Co., Eastern Laboratory Library, Gibbstown, NJ [*Library symbol*] [*Library of Congress*] (LCLS)
NjGl .... Gloucester City Library, Gloucester City, NJ [*Library symbol*] [*Library of Congress*] (LCLS)
NjGlN .... Gloucester City News, Gloucester City, NJ [*Library symbol*] [*Library of Congress*] (LCLS)
NjGlri .... Glen Ridge Free Public Library, Glen Ridge, NJ [*Library symbol*] [*Library of Congress*] (LCLS)
NjGlriA ...... Associated Technical Services, Inc., Glen Ridge, NJ [*Library symbol*] [*Library of Congress*] (LCLS)
NJGRA ...... Special Account New Jersey Gasoline Retailers Association [*Springfield, NJ*] (PACS)
NjGrbR ...... Raritan Valley Hospital, Greenbrook, NJ [*Library symbol*] [*Library of Congress*] (LCLS)
NjGrHi .... Cumberland County Historical Society, Greenwich, NJ [*Library symbol*] [*Library of Congress*] (LCLS)
NJGSC .... National Jewish Girl Scout Committee (EA)
NjH .... Haddonfield Public Library, Haddonfield, NJ [*Library symbol*] [*Library of Congress*] (LCLS)
NJHA .... National Junior Horticultural Association (EA)
NJHA .... New Jersey Hospital Association (SAUS)
NjHaC .... Centenary College for Women, Hackettstown, NJ [*Library symbol*] [*Library of Congress*] (LCLS)
NjHack ...... Johnson Free Public Library, Hackensack, NJ [*Library symbol*] [*Library of Congress*] (LCLS)
NjHackR .... Bergen Record, Hackensack, NJ [*Library symbol*] [*Library of Congress*] (LCLS)
NjHam .... Hammonton Public Library, Hammonton, NJ [*Library symbol*] [*Library of Congress*] (LCLS)
NjHamN ..... News Publishing Co., Hammonton, NJ [*Library symbol*] [*Library of Congress*] (LCLS)
NjHanS ...... Sandoz, Inc., Hanover, NJ [*Library symbol*] [*Library of Congress*] (LCLS)
NjHarN ...... Diamond Shamrock Corp., Harrison, NJ [*Library symbol*] [*Library of Congress*] (LCLS)
NjHarR ...... Radio Corp. of America, Electronics Division, Harrison, NJ [*Library symbol*] [*Library of Congress*] (LCLS)
NjHas .... Hasbrouck Heights Free Public Library, Hasbrouck Heights, NJ [*Library symbol*] [*Library of Congress*] (LCLS)
NjHaS .... Star Gazette, Hackettstown, NJ [*Library symbol*] [*Library of Congress*] (LCLS)
NjHaSG ..... Star Gazette, Hackettstown, NJ [*Library symbol*] [*Library of Congress*] (LCLS)
NjHasO ...... Observer, Hasbrouck Heights, NJ [*Library symbol*] [*Library of Congress*] (LCLS)
NjHawD ..... Dodds Publishing Co., Hawthorne, NJ [*Library symbol*] [*Library of Congress*] (LCLS)
NjHawP ..... Hawthorne Press, Inc., Hawthorne, NJ [*Library symbol*] [*Library of Congress*] (LCLS)
NjHb .... Hillsborough Public Library, Hillsborough, NJ [*Library symbol*] [*Library of Congress*] (LCLS)
NJHC .... National Jewish Hospitality Committee (EA)
NjHh .... Haddon Heights Public Library, Haddon Heights, NJ [*Library symbol*] [*Library of Congress*] (LCLS)
NJHHCC ..... National Joint Heavy and Highway Construction Committee (EA)
NjHHi .... Historical Society of Haddonfield, Haddonfield, NJ [*Library symbol*] [*Library of Congress*] (LCLS)
NjHi .... New Jersey Historical Society, Newark, NJ [*Library symbol*] [*Library of Congress*] (LCLS)
NjHibP .... High Bridge Painting Co., High Bridge, NJ [*Library symbol*] [*Library of Congress*] (LCLS)
NjHig .... Hightstown Memorial Library, Hightstown, NJ [*Library symbol*] [*Library of Congress*] (LCLS)
NjHigG ...... Hightstown Gazette, Hightstown, NJ [*Library symbol*] [*Library of Congress*] (LCLS)
NjHigN ...... NL Industries, Inc., Hightstown, NJ [*Library symbol*] [*Library of Congress*] (LCLS)
NjHigP ...... Peddie School, Hightstown, NJ [*Library symbol*] [*Library of Congress*] (LCLS)
NjHil .... Hillside Free Public Library, Hillside, NJ [*Library symbol*] [*Library of Congress*] (LCLS)
NjHilT .... Hillside Times, Hillside, NJ [*Library symbol*] [*Library of Congress*] (LCLS)
NJ Hist Soc... New Jersey Historical Society (SAUS)
NJHMFA..... New Jersey Housing & Mortgage Finance Agency
NJH/NAC .... National Jewish Hospital/National Asthma Center [*Later, National Jewish Center for Immunology and Respiratory Medicine*] (EA)
NjHo .... Hoboken Free Public Library, Hoboken, NJ [*Library symbol*] [*Library of Congress*] (LCLS)
NjHoGF ...... General Foods Corp., Hoboken, NJ [*Library symbol*] [*Library of Congress*] (LCLS)
NjHolB ...... Bell Telephone Laboratories, Inc., Technical Information Library, Holmdel, NJ [*Library symbol*] [*Library of Congress*] (LCLS)
NjHop .... Hopewell Public Library, Hopewell, NJ [*Library symbol*] [*Library of Congress*] (LCLS)
NjHopM ..... Hopewell Museum, Hopewell, NJ [*Library symbol*] [*Library of Congress*] (LCLS)
NjHopN ...... Hopewell Valley News, Hopewell, NJ [*Library symbol*] [*Library of Congress*] (LCLS)
NjHoS .... Stevens Institute of Technology, Hoboken, NJ [*Library symbol*] [*Library of Congress*] (LCLS)
NjHowB ..... Booster Press, Howell, NJ [*Library symbol*] [*Library of Congress*] (LCLS)
NJHS .... New Jersey Historical Society (SAUS)
NjI .... Free Public Library of Irvington, Irvington, NJ [*Library symbol*] [*Library of Congress*] (LCLS)
NJI .... Network Job Interface
NJI .... New Jersey Institute of Technology, Newark, NJ [*OCLC symbol*] (OCLC)
NJIC .... National Joint Industrial Council [*Pharmacology*] [*British*]
NJIFR .... Notices of Judgment, Federal Insecticide, Fungicide, and Rodenticide Act [*A publication*] (DLA)
NJII .... New Jersey, Indiana & Illinois Railroad Co. [*AAR code*]
NJIS .... National Jewish Information Service (for the Propagation of Judaism) [*Defunct*] (EA)
NJIT .... New Jersey Institute of Technology (GAGS)
NjJ .... Jersey City Free Public Library, Jersey City, NJ [*Library symbol*] [*Library of Congress*] (LCLS)
NJJ .... Jersey City State College, Jersey City, NJ [*OCLC symbol*] (OCLC)
NJJ .... Niijima [*Japan*] [*Seismograph station code, US Geological Survey*] [*Closed*] (SEIS)
NjJa .... Library at Jamesburg, Jamesburg, NJ [*Library symbol*] [*Library of Congress*] (LCLS)
NjJacN ...... Jackson News, Jackson, NJ [*Library symbol*] [*Library of Congress*] (LCLS)
NjJacP ...... Jackson Township Publishing Co., Jackson, NJ [*Library symbol*] [*Library of Congress*] (LCLS)
NjJJ .... Jewish Standard, Jersey City, NJ [*Library symbol*] [*Library of Congress*] (LCLS)
NjJJJ .... Jersey Journal, Jersey City, NJ [*Library symbol*] [*Library of Congress*] (LCLS)
NjJS .... Jersey City State College, Jersey City, NJ [*Library symbol*] [*Library of Congress*] (LCLS)
NjJStP .... Saint Peter's College, Jersey City, NJ [*Library symbol*] [*Library of Congress*] (LCLS)
NjJUB .... Urner-Barry Publications, Jersey City, NJ [*Library symbol*] [*Library of Congress*] (LCLS)
NJK .... El Centro, CA [*Location identifier*] [*FAA*] (FAAL)
NJK .... Kean College of New Jersey, Union, NJ [*OCLC symbol*] (OCLC)
NjK .... Kearny Public Library, Kearny, NJ [*Library symbol*] [*Library of Congress*] (LCLS)
NJK .... Not Just Kidding (SAUS)
NjKeHS ...... Keansburg High School, Keansburg, NJ [*Library symbol*] [*Library of Congress*] (LCLS)
NjKey .... Keyport Free Public Library, Keyport, NJ [*Library symbol*] [*Library of Congress*] (LCLS)
NjKO .... Kearny Observer, Kearny, NJ [*Library symbol*] [*Library of Congress*] (LCLS)
NjKWT .... Western Electric Co., Kearny, NJ [*Library symbol*] [*Library of Congress*] (LCLS)
NjL .... Lodi Memorial Library, Lodi, NJ [*Library symbol*] [*Library of Congress*] (LCLS)
NJL .... New Jersey Law Reports [*A publication*] (DLA)
NJL .... New Jersey State Library, Trenton, NJ [*OCLC symbol*] (OCLC)
NJLA .... New Jersey Library Association
NjLaHi .... Lake Hopatcong Historical Society, Lake Hopatcong, NJ [*Library symbol*] [*Library of Congress*] (LCLS)
NjLak .... Lakewood Public Library, Lakewood, NJ [*Library symbol*] [*Library of Congress*] (LCLS)
NjLakC ...... Ocean County Citizen, Lakewood, NJ [*Library symbol*] [*Library of Congress*] (LCLS)
NjLakG ...... Georgian Court College, Lakewood, NJ [*Library symbol*] [*Library of Congress*] (LCLS)
NjLakhM .... Manchester Publishing Co., Lakehurst, NJ [*Library symbol*] [*Library of Congress*] (LCLS)
NjLakT ...... Ocean County Daily Times, Lakewood, NJ [*Library symbol*] [*Library of Congress*] (LCLS)
NjLamB ..... Lambertville Beacon, Lambertville, NJ [*Library symbol*] [*Library of Congress*] (LCLS)
NJ Law ...... New Jersey Law Reports [*A publication*] (DLA)
NJ Law N ... New Jersey Law News [*A publication*] (DLA)
NjLawR ..... Rider College, Lawrenceville, NJ [*Library symbol*] [*Library of Congress*] (LCLS)
NJ Law Rep... New Jersey Law Reports [*A publication*] (DLA)
NJLC .... National Juvenile Law Center [*Later, NCYL*] (EA)
NjLe .... Leonia Public Library, Leonia, NJ [*Library symbol*] [*Library of Congress*] (LCLS)
NjLedW ..... West Morris Star Journal, Ledgewood, NJ [*Library symbol*] [*Library of Congress*] (LCLS)
NJ Leg Rec... New Jersey Legal Record [*A publication*] (DLA)
NjLF .... Felician College, Lodi, NJ [*Library symbol*] [*Library of Congress*] (LCLS)
NjLf .... Little Falls Free Public Library, Little Falls, NJ [*Library symbol*] [*Library of Congress*] (LCLS)
NJLFC .... New Jersey Film Circuit [*Library network*]
NjLh .... Lake Hiawatha Public Library, Lake Hiawatha, NJ [*Library symbol*] [*Library of Congress*] (LCLS)
NjLhP .... Pennysaver Publishing Co., Lake Hiawatha, NJ [*Library symbol*] [*Library of Congress*] (LCLS)
NjLi .... Free Public Library of Livingston, Livingston, NJ [*Library symbol*] [*Library of Congress*] (LCLS)
NjLin .... Linden Free Public Library, Linden, NJ [*Library symbol*] [*Library of Congress*] (LCLS)
NjLincB ..... Brookdale Community College, Lincroft, NJ [*Library symbol*] [*Library of Congress*] (LCLS)
NjLinEx ...... Exxon Research & Engineering Co., Company and Literature Information Center Library, Linden, NJ [*Library symbol*] [*Library of Congress*] (LCLS)
NjLinEx-M... Exxon Research & Engineering Co., Medical Research Library, Linden, NJ [*Library symbol*] [*Library of Congress*] (LCLS)

NjLivStB .... Saint Barnabas Medical Center, Staff Library, Livingston, NJ [*Library symbol*] [*Library of Congress*] (LCLS)
NjLiW .... West Essex Tribune, Livingston, NJ [*Library symbol*] [*Library of Congress*] (LCLS)
NjLob .... Long Branch Public Library, Long Branch, NJ [*Library symbol*] [*Library of Congress*] (LCLS)
NjLp .... Lincoln Park Public Library, Lincoln Park, NJ [*Library symbol*] [*Library of Congress*] (LCLS)
NjLP .... Paci Press, Lodi, NJ [*Library symbol*] [*Library of Congress*] (LCLS)
NjLpBHi ...... Beavertown Historical Society, Lincoln Park, NJ [*Library symbol*] [*Library of Congress*] (LCLS)
NjLpH .... Lincoln Herald, Lincoln Park, NJ [*Library symbol*] [*Library of Congress*] (LCLS)
NjLPP .... Paci Press, Lodi, NJ [*Library symbol*] [*Library of Congress*] (LCLS)
NJL Rep .... New Jersey Law Reports [*A publication*] (DLA)
NJL Rev..... New Jersey Law Review [*A publication*] (DLA)
NjLwR .... Record Breeze, Lindenwold, NJ [*Library symbol*] [*Library of Congress*] (LCLS)
NjLy.......... Lyndhurst Public Library, Lyndhurst, NJ [*Library symbol*] [*Library of Congress*] (LCLS)
NjLyL .... Leader Publications, Lyndhurst, NJ [*Library symbol*] [*Library of Congress*] (LCLS)
NjLyoV ...... United States Veterans Administration Hospital, Lyons, NJ [*Library symbol*] [*Library of Congress*] (LCLS)
NjM .... Free Public Library of the Borough of Madison, Madison, NJ [*Library symbol*] [*Library of Congress*] (LCLS)
NJM .... Montclair State College, Upper Montclair, NJ [*OCLC symbol*] (OCLC)
NJM .... New Jersey Miscellaneous Reports [*A publication*] (DLA)
NJM .... New JEWEL Movement (SAUS)
NJM .... Swansboro, NC [*Location identifier*] [*FAA*] (FAAL)
NJMA......... National Jail Managers Association [*Later, AJA*] (EA)
NjMah .... Free Public Library of the Township of Mahwah, Mahwah, NJ [*Library symbol*] [*Library of Congress*] (LCLS)
NjMahR ..... Ramapo College of New Jersey, Mahwah, NJ [*Library symbol*] [*Library of Congress*] (LCLS)
NjMal......... Franklin Township Public Library, Malaga, NJ [*Library symbol*] [*Library of Congress*] (LCLS)
NjMan .... Manasquan Public Library, Manasquan, NJ [*Library symbol*] [*Library of Congress*] (LCLS)
NjManhT.... Times Beacon Co., Manahawkin, NJ [*Library symbol*] [*Library of Congress*] (LCLS)
NjManS ..... Coast Star, Manasquan, NJ [*Library symbol*] [*Library of Congress*] (LCLS)
NjMap....... Maplewood Memorial Library, Maplewood, NJ [*Library symbol*] [*Library of Congress*] (LCLS)
NjMapW .... Worrall Publishing Co., Maplewood, NJ [*Library symbol*] [*Library of Congress*] (LCLS)
NjMat........ Matawan Joint Free Public Library, Matawan, NJ [*Library symbol*] [*Library of Congress*] (LCLS)
NjMatB ...... Bayshore Independent, Matawan, NJ [*Library symbol*] [*Library of Congress*] (LCLS)
NjMatHi ..... Madison Township Historical Society, Matawan, NJ [*Library symbol*] [*Library of Congress*] (LCLS)
NjMayO ..... Our Town, Maywood, NJ [*Library symbol*] [*Library of Congress*] (LCLS)
NJMC........ National Jewish Music Council [*Later, Jewish Welfare Board Jewish Music Council*] (EA)
NjMcUSAF... United States Air Force, Base Library, McGuire Air Force Base, NJ [*Library symbol*] [*Library of Congress*] (LCLS)
NjMD .... Drew University, Madison, NJ [*Library symbol*] [*Library of Congress*] (LCLS)
NJMDC...... NORAD Joint Manual Direction Center [*Military*]
NjMD-T...... Drew University, Theological School, Madison, NJ [*Library symbol*] [*Library of Congress*] (LCLS)
NjMe .... Free Public Library, Metuchen, NJ [*Library symbol*] [*Library of Congress*] (LCLS)
NjME .... Madison Eagle, Madison, NJ [*Library symbol*] [*Library of Congress*] (LCLS)
NjMedR ..... Central Record, Medford, NJ [*Library symbol*] [*Library of Congress*] (LCLS)
NjMen....... Mendham Public Library, Mendham, NJ [*Library symbol*] [*Library of Congress*] (LCLS)
NjMenO ..... Observer-Tribune, Mendham, NJ [*Library symbol*] [*Library of Congress*] (LCLS)
NjMF .... Fairleigh Dickinson University, Madison, NJ [*Library symbol*] [*Library of Congress*] (LCLS)
NjMhB....... Burlington County Area Reference Library, Mount Holly, NJ [*Library symbol*] [*Library of Congress*] (LCLS)
NjMhCoC.... Burlington County Clerk, Mount Holly, NJ [*Library symbol*] [*Library of Congress*] (LCLS)
NjMhH....... Burlington County Herald, Mount Holly, NJ [*Library symbol*] [*Library of Congress*] (LCLS)
NjMHi .... Madison Historical Society, Madison, NJ [*Library symbol*] [*Library of Congress*] (LCLS)
NjMhL........ Burlington County Lyceum [*Mount Holly Public Library*], Mount Holly, NJ [*Library symbol*] [*Library of Congress*] (LCLS)
NjMhPM .... Burlington County Prison Museum, Mount Holly, NJ [*Library symbol*] [*Library of Congress*] (LCLS)
NJMI......... Catholic Medical Center of Brooklyn & Queens, Inc., Jamaica, NY [*Library symbol*] [*Library of Congress*] (LCLS)
NJMI......... Mary Immaculate Hospital, School of Nursing, Jamaica, NY [*Library symbol*] [*Library of Congress*] (LCLS)
NjMi .... Middletown Township Free Public Library, Middletown, NJ [*Library symbol*] [*Library of Congress*] (LCLS)
NJMI......... New Junior Maudsley Inventory [*Psychology*]
NjMiA .... Advisor, Middletown, NJ [*Library symbol*] [*Library of Congress*] (LCLS)
NjMiC .... Courier, Middletown, NJ [*Library symbol*] [*Library of Congress*] (LCLS)
NjMid........ Middlesex Public Library, Middlesex, NJ [*Library symbol*] [*Library of Congress*] (LCLS)
NjMil .... Millburn Free Public Library, Millburn, NJ [*Library symbol*] [*Library of Congress*] (LCLS)
NjMilt .... Milltown Public Library, Milltown, NJ [*Library symbol*] [*Library of Congress*] (LCLS)
NjMilv .... Millville Public Library, Millville, NJ [*Library symbol*] [*Library of Congress*] (LCLS)
NjMilvHi .... Wheaton Historical Association, Millville, NJ [*Library symbol*] [*Library of Congress*] (LCLS)
NjMilvM..... Millville Daily, Millville, NJ [*Library symbol*] [*Library of Congress*] (LCLS)
NjMiP .... Middletown Township Public Library, Middletown, NJ [*Library symbol*] [*Library of Congress*] (LCLS)
NJ Mis ...... New Jersey Miscellaneous Reports [*A publication*] (DLA)
NJ Misc ..... New Jersey Miscellaneous Reports [*A publication*] (DLA)
NJ Mis R ... New Jersey Miscellaneous Reports [*A publication*] (DLA)
NjMj .... South Brunswick Free Public Library, Monmouth Junction, NJ [*Library symbol*] [*Library of Congress*] (LCLS)
NjMlA .... Atlantic County Library, Mays Landing, NJ [*Library symbol*] [*Library of Congress*] (LCLS)
NjMlAC...... Atlantic Community College, Mays Landing, NJ [*Library symbol*] [*Library of Congress*] (LCLS)
NjMlCoC .... Atlantic County Clerk, Mays Landing, NJ [*Library symbol*] [*Library of Congress*] (LCLS)
NjMlR .... Atlantic County Record, Mays Landing, NJ [*Library symbol*] [*Library of Congress*] (LCLS)
NjMo .... Joint Free Public Library of Morristown and Morris Township, Morristown, NJ [*Library symbol*] [*Library of Congress*] (LCLS)
NjMoAT ..... American Telephone & Telegraph Co., Morristown Corporate Marketing Library, Morristown, NJ [*Library symbol*] [*Library of Congress*] (LCLS)
NjMoCoC.... Morris County Clerk, Morristown, NJ [*Library symbol*] [*Library of Congress*] (LCLS)
NjMoH....... Morristown Memorial Hospital, Morristown, NJ [*Library symbol*] [*Library of Congress*] (LCLS)
NjMoHP ..... Morristown National Historical Park, Morristown, NJ [*Library symbol*] [*Library of Congress*] (LCLS)
NjMon .... Montclair Free Public Library, Montclair, NJ [*Library symbol*] [*Library of Congress*] (LCLS)
NjMonM..... Montclair Times, Montclair, NJ [*Library symbol*] [*Library of Congress*] (LCLS)
NJ Monthly... New Jersey Monthly (SAUS)
NjMor .... Moorestown Free Library, Moorestown, NJ [*Library symbol*] [*Library of Congress*] (LCLS)
NjMorR...... Radio Corp. of America, Missile and Surface Radar Division, Moorestown, NJ [*Library symbol*] [*Library of Congress*] (LCLS)
NjMou .... Mountain Lakes Public Library, Mountain Lakes, NJ [*Library symbol*] [*Library of Congress*] (LCLS)
NjMouHi .... Mountain Lakes Historical Society, Mountain Lakes, NJ [*Library symbol*] [*Library of Congress*] (LCLS)
NjMov .... Montvale Free Public Library, Montvale, NJ [*Library symbol*] [*Library of Congress*] (LCLS)
NjMovL...... Lehn & Fink Products Co., Montvale, NJ [*Library symbol*] [*Library of Congress*] (LCLS)
NjMp .... Morris Plains Public Library, Morris Plains, NJ [*Library symbol*] [*Library of Congress*] (LCLS)
NJMP........ New Jersey Marine Police (SAUS)
NJMP........ New Jewish Media Project [*JMS*] [*Absorbed by*] (EA)
NjMpN....... Morris News-Bee, Morris Plains, NJ [*Library symbol*] [*Library of Congress*] (LCLS)
NjMpW ...... Warner-Lambert Research Institute, Morris Plains, NJ [*Library symbol*] [*Library of Congress*] (LCLS)
NJMR........ Nordisk Verbane Musik Rad [*Nordic Council for Railway Music - NCRM*] (EAIO)
NjMs......... Maple Shade Public Library, Maple Shade, NJ [*Library symbol*] [*Library of Congress*] (LCLS)
NJMS........ New Jersey Medical School [*Newark*]
NJMSC ...... New Jersey Sea Grant College Program [*National Oceanic and Atmospheric Administration*] (RCD)
NjMsP .... Maple Shade Progress Press, Maple Shade, NJ [*Library symbol*] [*Library of Congress*] (LCLS)
NjMuA....... Air Reduction Co., Inc., Central Research Department Library, Murray Hill, NJ [*Library symbol*] [*Library of Congress*] (LCLS)
NjMuB....... Bell Telephone Laboratories, Inc., Murray Hill, NJ [*Library symbol*] [*Library of Congress*] (LCLS)
NjMuhHi .... Harrison Township Historical Society, Mullica Hill, NJ [*Library symbol*] [*Library of Congress*] (LCLS)
NJMX........ New Jersey Marine Terminals [*Federal Railroad Administration identification code*]
NJN .... College of Medicine and Dentistry of New Jersey, Newark, NJ [*OCLC symbol*] (OCLC)
NjN .... Newark Public Library, Newark, NJ [*Library symbol*] [*Library of Congress*] (LCLS)
NJN.......... New Jersey Network [*Trenton*] [*Telecommunications service*] (TSSD)
NjNA......... United States Attorney's Office, Law Library, Newark, NJ [*Library symbol*] [*Library of Congress*] (LCLS)
NjNAA .... New Jersey Afro-American, Newark, NJ [*Library symbol*] [*Library of Congress*] (LCLS)
NjNb .... New Brunswick Free Public Library, New Brunswick, NJ [*Library symbol*] [*Library of Congress*] (LCLS)
NjNbH .... Home News, New Brunswick, NJ [*Library symbol*] [*Library of Congress*] (LCLS)
NjNbJJ ...... Johnson & Johnson, Research Center, New Brunswick, NJ [*Library symbol*] [*Library of Congress*] (LCLS)
NjNbM....... Middlesex General Hospital, New Brunswick, NJ [*Library symbol*] [*Library of Congress*] (LCLS)

NjNbS .... New Brunswick Theological Seminary, New Brunswick, NJ [*Library symbol*] [*Library of Congress*] (LCLS)
NjNbSI ...... Squibb-Beechnut, Inc., New Brunswick, NJ [*Library symbol*] [*Library of Congress*] (LCLS)
NjNbSp ...... New Brunswick Spokesman, New Brunswick, NJ [*Library symbol*] [*Library of Congress*] (LCLS)
NjNbStP ..... Saint Peter's Medical Center, New Brunswick, NJ [*Library symbol*] [*Library of Congress*] (LCLS)
NJNC .... National Joint Negotiating Committee (ODA)
NjNC .... New Jersey Institute of Technology, Newark, NJ [*Library symbol*] [*Library of Congress*] (LCLS)
NjNCM ...... New Jersey College of Medicine and Dentistry, Newark, NJ [*Library symbol*] [*Library of Congress*] (LCLS)
NjNE .... Essex County College, Newark, NJ [*Library symbol*] [*Library of Congress*] (LCLS)
NjNeP .... New Egypt Press, New Egypt, NJ [*Library symbol*] [*Library of Congress*] (LCLS)
NjNet .... Dennis Memorial Library, Newton, NJ [*Library symbol*] [*Library of Congress*] (LCLS)
NjNetcN ..... News Leader, Netcong, NJ [*Library symbol*] [*Library of Congress*] (LCLS)
NjNetCoC ... Sussex County Clerk, Newton, NJ [*Library symbol*] [*Library of Congress*] (LCLS)
NjNetDB ..... Don Bosco College, Newton, NJ [*Library symbol*] [*Library of Congress*] (LCLS)
NjNetH ...... New Jersey Herald, Newton, NJ [*Library symbol*] [*Library of Congress*] (LCLS)
NjNetS ...... Sussex County Library, Newton, NJ [*Library symbol*] [*Library of Congress*] (LCLS)
NjNetSHi .... Sussex County Historical Society, Newton, NJ [*Library symbol*] [*Library of Congress*] (LCLS)
NjNhBHi ..... Bergen County Historical Society, North Hackensack, NJ [*Library symbol*] [*Library of Congress*] (LCLS)
NjNI .... Ironbound Crier, Newark, NJ [*Library symbol*] [*Library of Congress*] (LCLS)
NjNIJS .... Institute of Jazz Studies, Rutgers, the State University, Newark, NJ [*Library symbol*] [*Library of Congress*] (LCLS)
NjNIM .... International Musician, Newark, NJ [*Library symbol*] [*Library of Congress*] (LCLS)
NjNIT .... Italian Tribune, Newark, NJ [*Library symbol*] [*Library of Congress*] (LCLS)
NjNJL .... Jewish Ledger, Newark, NJ [*Library symbol*] [*Library of Congress*] (LCLS)
NjNJN .... Jewish News, Newark, NJ [*Library symbol*] [*Library of Congress*] (LCLS)
NjNL .... Luso-Americano, Newark, NJ [*Library symbol*] [*Library of Congress*] (LCLS)
NjNLH .... New Jersey Labor Herald, Newark, NJ [*Library symbol*] [*Library of Congress*] (LCLS)
NjNN .... Nite-Lite, Newark, NJ [*Library symbol*] [*Library of Congress*] (LCLS)
NjNoA .... Atlantic County Advertiser, Northfield, NJ [*Library symbol*] [*Library of Congress*] (LCLS)
NjNoa .... North Arlington Free Public Library, North Arlington, NJ [*Library symbol*] [*Library of Congress*] (LCLS)
NjNoaP ..... North Arlington Free Public Library, North Arlington, NJ [*Library symbol*] [*Library of Congress*] (LCLS)
NjNor .... Norwood Public Library, Norwood, NJ [*Library symbol*] [*Library of Congress*] (LCLS)
NjNp .... New Providence Memorial Library, New Providence, NJ [*Library symbol*] [*Library of Congress*] (LCLS)
NjNpD .... Dispatch, New Providence, NJ [*Library symbol*] [*Library of Congress*] (LCLS)
NjNpHi ...... New Providence Historical Society, New Providence, NJ [*Library symbol*] [*Library of Congress*] (LCLS)
NjNpI .... Independent Press, New Providence, NJ [*Library symbol*] [*Library of Congress*] (LCLS)
NjNPSE ...... Public Service Electric & Gas Co., Newark, NJ [*Library symbol*] [*Library of Congress*] (LCLS)
NjNT .... Tribuna di North Jersey, Newark, NJ [*Library symbol*] [*Library of Congress*] (LCLS)
NjNu .... Nutley Free Public Library, Nutley, NJ [*Library symbol*] [*Library of Congress*] (LCLS)
NjNuH .... Hoffmann-La Roche, Inc., Scientific Library, Nutley, NJ [*Library symbol*] [*Library of Congress*] (LCLS)
NjNuHi ...... Nutley Historical Society, Nutley, NJ [*Library symbol*] [*Library of Congress*] (LCLS)
NjNuS .... Sun-Bank Newspapers, Nutley, NJ [*Library symbol*] [*Library of Congress*] (LCLS)
NJNY .... New Jersey & New York R. R. [*AAR code*]
NjO .... Free Public Library of the City of Orange, Orange, NJ [*Library symbol*] [*Library of Congress*] (LCLS)
NjOak .... Oakland Public Library, Oakland, NJ [*Library symbol*] [*Library of Congress*] (LCLS)
NjOaS .... Shore Publishers, Inc., Oakhurst, NJ [*Library symbol*] [*Library of Congress*] (LCLS)
NjOcM .... Ocean City Historical Museum, Ocean City, NJ [*Library symbol*] [*Library of Congress*] (LCLS)
NjOcS .... Sentinel Ledger, Ocean City, NJ [*Library symbol*] [*Library of Congress*] (LCLS)
NjOgT .... Ocean Grove Times, Ocean Grove, NJ [*Library symbol*] [*Library of Congress*] (LCLS)
NjOrd .... Oradell Public Library, Oradell, NJ [*Library symbol*] [*Library of Congress*] (LCLS)
NjOrdB ...... Burns & Roe, Inc., Oradell, NJ [*Library symbol*] [*Library of Congress*] (LCLS)
NJosnU ..... United Health Services, Wilson Hospital, Johnson City, NY [*Library symbol*] [*Library of Congress*] (LCLS)
NJostF .... Fulton-Montgomery Community College, Johnstown, NY [*Library symbol*] [*Library of Congress*] (LCLS)
NjOtR .... Fleming H. Revell Co., Old Tappan, NJ [*Library symbol*] [*Library of Congress*] (LCLS)
NjOW .... Worrall Publications, Inc., Orange, NJ [*Library symbol*] [*Library of Congress*] (LCLS)
NJP .... National Jury Project (EA)
NJP .... Network Job Processing
NJP .... Nonjudicial Punishment [*Military*]
NjP .... Princeton University, Princeton, NJ [*Library symbol*] [*Library of Congress*] (LCLS)
NJP .... Warminster, PA [*Location identifier*] [*FAA*] (FAAL)
NJP .... William Patterson College of New Jersey, Wayne, NJ [*OCLC symbol*] (OCLC)
NjPA .... American Cyanamid Co., Agricultural Division, Princeton, NJ [*Library symbol*] [*Library of Congress*] (LCLS)
NjP-A .... Art Museum of Princeton University, Princeton, NJ [*Library symbol*] [*Library of Congress*] (LCLS)
NJPA .... National Juice Products Association (EA)
NjPalN ...... Bergen News, Palisades Park, NJ [*Library symbol*] [*Library of Congress*] (LCLS)
NjPar .... Paramus Public Library, Paramus, NJ [*Library symbol*] [*Library of Congress*] (LCLS)
NjParB ...... Bergen Community College, Paramus, NJ [*Library symbol*] [*Library of Congress*] (LCLS)
NjParkHi .... Pascack Historical Society and Museum, Park Ridge, NJ [*Library symbol*] [*Library of Congress*] (LCLS)
NjParkP ..... Pascack Publications Corp., Park Ridge, NJ [*Library symbol*] [*Library of Congress*] (LCLS)
NjParR ...... Ridgewood Newspapers, Paramus, NJ [*Library symbol*] [*Library of Congress*] (LCLS)
NjParT .... Town News, Paramus, NJ [*Library symbol*] [*Library of Congress*] (LCLS)
NjPas .... Passaic Public Library, Passaic, NJ [*Library symbol*] [*Library of Congress*] (LCLS)
NjPasC ...... Passaic Citizen, Passaic, NJ [*Library symbol*] [*Library of Congress*] (LCLS)
NjPasCS .... Catholic Sokol Printing Co., Passaic, NJ [*Library symbol*] [*Library of Congress*] (LCLS)
NjPasE ...... Eastern Catholic Life, Passaic, NJ [*Library symbol*] [*Library of Congress*] (LCLS)
NjPasH ...... Herald News, Passaic, NJ [*Library symbol*] [*Library of Congress*] (LCLS)
NjPat .... Paterson Free Public Library, Paterson, NJ [*Library symbol*] [*Library of Congress*] (LCLS)
NjPatCoC ... Passaic County Clerk, Paterson, NJ [*Library symbol*] [*Library of Congress*] (LCLS)
NjPatNe ..... News, Paterson, NJ [*Library symbol*] [*Library of Congress*] (LCLS)
NjPatPHi .... Passaic County Historical Society, Paterson, NJ [*Library symbol*] [*Library of Congress*] (LCLS)
NjPatSA ..... Saint Anthony's Guild, Franciscan Monastery, Paterson, NJ [*Library symbol*] [*Library of Congress*] (LCLS)
NjPatV .... Voce Italiana, Paterson, NJ [*Library symbol*] [*Library of Congress*] (LCLS)
NjPauR ...... Record, Paulsboro, NJ [*Library symbol*] [*Library of Congress*] (LCLS)
NjPauS ...... Mobil Research & Development Corp., Paulsboro, NJ [*Library symbol*] [*Library of Congress*] (LCLS)
NJPBA .... New Jersey Public Broadcasting Authority (SAUS)
NJPC .... National Joint Practice Commission (DMAA)
NjPD .... Daily Princetonian, Princeton, NJ [*Library symbol*] [*Library of Congress*] (LCLS)
NJPDDATC ... National Joint Painting, Decorating, and Drywall Apprenticeship and Training Committee (EA)
NjPE .... Educational Testing Service, Princeton, NJ [*Library symbol*] [*Library of Congress*] (LCLS)
NjPeB .... Burlington County College, Pemberton, NJ [*Library symbol*] [*Library of Congress*] (LCLS)
NjPegR ...... Penns Grove Record, Penns Grove, NJ [*Library symbol*] [*Library of Congress*] (LCLS)
NjPenP ...... Pennsauken Resume, Pennsauken, NJ [*Library symbol*] [*Library of Congress*] (LCLS)
NjPeqB ...... Beacon, Pequannock, NJ [*Library symbol*] [*Library of Congress*] (LCLS)
NjPera .... Perth Amboy Free Public Library, Perth Amboy, NJ [*Library symbol*] [*Library of Congress*] (LCLS)
NjPeraSo ... Universum Sokol Publishers, Perth Amboy, NJ [*Library symbol*] [*Library of Congress*] (LCLS)
NjPERS ...... E. R. Squibb & Sons, Princeton, NJ [*Library symbol*] [*Library of Congress*] (LCLS)
NjPeT .... Times Advertising Printing Co., Pemberton, NJ [*Library symbol*] [*Library of Congress*] (LCLS)
NjPF .... FMC Corp., Princeton (SAUS)
NjP-G .... Princeton University, Gest Library, Princeton, NJ [*Library symbol*] [*Library of Congress*] (LCLS)
NJPGA .... New Jersey Personnel and Guidance Association (SAUS)
NjPh .... Phillipsburg Free Public Library, Phillipsburg, NJ [*Library symbol*] [*Library of Congress*] (LCLS)
NJPHA .... National Junior Polled Hereford Association (EA)
NJPHC .... National Junior Polled Hereford Council [*Later, NJPHA*] (EA)
NjPHi .... Historical Society of Princeton, Princeton, NJ [*Library symbol*] [*Library of Congress*] (LCLS)
NjPhP .... Free Press, Phillipsburg, NJ [*Library symbol*] [*Library of Congress*] (LCLS)
NjPI .... Institute for Advanced Study, Princeton, NJ [*Library symbol*] [*Library of Congress*] (LCLS)
NjPi .... McCowan Memorial Library, Pitman, NJ [*Library symbol*] [*Library of Congress*] (LCLS)
NjPiM .... McCowan Memorial Library, Pitman, NJ [*Library symbol*] [*Library of Congress*] (LCLS)

NjPJ .... Robert Wood Johnson Foundation Library, Princeton, NJ [*Library symbol*] [*Library of Congress*] (LCLS)
NjPl .... Emanuel Einstein Free Public Library, Pompton Lakes (SAUS)
NjPl .... Emanuel Einstein Free Public Library, Pompton Lakes, NJ [*Library symbol*] [*Library of Congress*] (LCLS)
NjPla .... Plainfield Public Library, Plainfield, NJ [*Library symbol*] [*Library of Congress*] (LCLS)
NjPlaM ...... Muhlenberg Hospital, Plainfield, NJ [*Library symbol*] [*Library of Congress*] (LCLS)
NjPlaSDB ... Seventh Day Baptist Historical Society, Plainfield, NJ [*Library symbol*] [*Library of Congress*] (LCLS)
NjPlaT .... Plainfield Times, Plainfield, NJ [*Library symbol*] [*Library of Congress*] (LCLS)
NjPlaV .... Voice, Plainfield, NJ [*Library symbol*] [*Library of Congress*] (LCLS)
NjPleM ...... Mainland Journal, Pleasantville, NJ [*Library symbol*] [*Library of Congress*] (LCLS)
NjPM .... Mobil Research & Development Corp., Central Research Division Library, Princeton, NJ [*Library symbol*] [*Library of Congress*] (LCLS)
NJPMB ...... Navy Jet-Propelled-Missile Board
NjPMC .... Medical Center at Princeton, Princeton, NJ [*Library symbol*] [*Library of Congress*] (LCLS)
NjPoiO ...... Ocean County Leader, Point Pleasant Beach, NJ [*Library symbol*] [*Library of Congress*] (LCLS)
NjPoR .... Richard Stockton State College, Pomona, NJ [*Library symbol*] [*Library of Congress*] (LCLS)
NjPP .... Princeton Packet, Inc., Princeton, NJ [*Library symbol*] [*Library of Congress*] (LCLS)
NjPpE .... Eastern Historical Commission, Prospect Park, NJ [*Library symbol*] [*Library of Congress*] (LCLS)
NjP-Pop ..... Princeton University, Office of Population Research, Princeton, NJ [*Library symbol*] [*Library of Congress*] (LCLS)
NjPPP .... Princeton Public Library, Princeton, NJ [*Library symbol*] [*Library of Congress*] (LCLS)
NjPRCA ..... Radio Corp. of America, Laboratories Division, Princeton, NJ [*Library symbol*] [*Library of Congress*] (LCLS)
NjPS .... Princeton Shopping News, Princeton, NJ [*Library symbol*] [*Library of Congress*] (LCLS)
NjP-SC ...... Princeton University, Princeton Special Collection, Princeton, NJ [*Library symbol*] [*Library of Congress*] (LCLS)
NjPStJ .... Saint Joseph's College, Princeton, NJ [*Library symbol*] [*Library of Congress*] (LCLS)
NjPT .... Princeton Theological Seminary, Princeton, NJ [*Library symbol*] [*Library of Congress*] (LCLS)
NjPTe .... Textile Research Institute, Princeton, NJ [*Library symbol*] [*Library of Congress*] (LCLS)
NjPTT .... Town Topics, Inc., Princeton, NJ [*Library symbol*] [*Library of Congress*] (LCLS)
NjPW .... Western Electric Co., Inc., Engineering Research Center, Princeton, NJ [*Library symbol*] [*Library of Congress*] (LCLS)
NjPwAT ...... American Telephone & Telegraph Co. Resource Center, Piscataway, NJ [*Library symbol*] [*Library of Congress*] (LCLS)
NjPwC .... Colgate-Palmolive Co., Technical Information Center, Piscataway, NJ [*Library symbol*] [*Library of Congress*] (LCLS)
NjPwIE ...... Institute of Electrical and Electronics Engineers, Piscataway, NJ [*Library symbol*] [*Library of Congress*] (LCLS)
NJQ .... Queens Borough Public Library, Jamaica, NY [*Library symbol*] [*Library of Congress*] (LCLS)
NJQH .... Queens Hospital Center, Jamaica, NY [*Library symbol*] [*Library of Congress*] (LCLS)
NJR .... New Jersey Register [*A publication*] (DLA)
NJR .... New Jersey Resources [*NYSE symbol*] (TTSB)
NJR .... New Jersey Resources Corp. [*NYSE symbol*] (SPSG)
NJR .... New JEWEL Regime [*Grenada*]
NJR .... Njerep [*Language symbol*] (ETLW)
NJR .... Noise-to-Jammer Ratio (SAUS)
NJR .... Nonjob Routed [*Military*] (AFIT)
NjR .... Rutgers-[*The*] State University, New Brunswick, NJ [*Library symbol*] [*Library of Congress*] (LCLS)
NJRA .... National Juvenile Restitution Association [*Later, ARA*] (EA)
NjRah .... Rahway Public Library, Rahway, NJ [*Library symbol*] [*Library of Congress*] (LCLS)
NjRahB ...... Bauer Publishing & Printing Ltd., Rahway, NJ [*Library symbol*] [*Library of Congress*] (LCLS)
NjRahM ..... Merck, Sharp & Dohme [*Later, Merck & Co., Inc.*] Research Laboratory, Research Library, Rahway, NJ [*Library symbol*] [*Library of Congress*] (LCLS)
NjRam .... Ramsey Free Public Library, Ramsey, NJ [*Library symbol*] [*Library of Congress*] (LCLS)
NjRamH ..... Home and Store News, Ramsey, NJ [*Library symbol*] [*Library of Congress*] (LCLS)
NjRamI ...... Immaculate Conception Theological Seminary, Ramsey, NJ [*Library symbol*] [*Library of Congress*] (LCLS)
NjRarO ...... Ortho Pharmaceutical Corp., Raritan, NJ [*Library symbol*] [*Library of Congress*] (LCLS)
NjRarOD .... Ortho Diagnostics, Raritan, NJ [*Library symbol*] [*Library of Congress*] (LCLS)
NjRb .... Red Bank Public Library, Red Bank, NJ [*Library symbol*] [*Library of Congress*] (LCLS)
NjRbR .... Daily Register, Red Bank, NJ [*Library symbol*] [*Library of Congress*] (LCLS)
NJRC .... National Jewish Resource Center (EA)
NJRC .... New Jersey Board of Railroad Commissioners Annual Reports [*A publication*] (DLA)
NjRdR .... Riverdale Publishing Co., Riverdale, NJ [*Library symbol*] [*Library of Congress*] (LCLS)
NJ Rep ...... New Jersey Law Reports [*A publication*] (DLA)
NJ Re Tit N... New Jersey Realty Title News [*A publication*] (DLA)
NJ Rev Stat... New Jersey Revised Statutes [*A publication*] (DLA)
NjRf .... Ridgefield Public Library, Ridgefield, NJ [*Library symbol*] [*Library of Congress*] (LCLS)
NjRh .... Rocky Hill Public Library, Rocky Hill, NJ [*Library symbol*] [*Library of Congress*] (LCLS)
NjRiv .... Riverside Public Library, Riverside, NJ [*Library symbol*] [*Library of Congress*] (LCLS)
NjRive .... River Edge Free Public Library, River Edge, NJ [*Library symbol*] [*Library of Congress*] (LCLS)
NjR-L .... Rutgers-[*The*] State University, Rutgers-Camden School of Law, Camden, NJ [*Library symbol*] [*Library of Congress*] (LCLS)
NJRMA ...... New Jersey Retail Merchants Association (EARSL)
NjR-NL ...... Rutgers, The State University, Law School Library-Newark, Newark, NJ [*Library symbol*] [*Library of Congress*] (LCLS)
NjRo .... Roseland Public Library, Roseland, NJ [*Library symbol*] [*Library of Congress*] (LCLS)
NjRocM ..... Morris County News, Rockaway, NJ [*Library symbol*] [*Library of Congress*] (LCLS)
NjRos .... Roselle Free Public Library, Roselle, NJ [*Library symbol*] [*Library of Congress*] (LCLS)
NJROTC ..... Naval Junior Reserve Officer Training Corps
NjRp .... Ridgefield Park Free Public Library, Ridgefield Park, NJ [*Library symbol*] [*Library of Congress*] (LCLS)
NjRpS .... Sun Bulletin, Ridgefield Park, NJ [*Library symbol*] [*Library of Congress*] (LCLS)
NjR-S .... Rutgers-[*The*] State University, College of South Jersey, Camden, NJ [*Library symbol*] [*Library of Congress*] (LCLS)
NJRsc .... New Jersey Resources [*Associated Press*] (SAG)
NjRu .... Rutherford Free Public Library, Rutherford, NJ [*Library symbol*] [*Library of Congress*] (LCLS)
NjRuB .... Becton, Dickinson & Co., Rutherford, NJ [*Library symbol*] [*Library of Congress*] (LCLS)
NjRuF .... Fairleigh Dickinson University, Rutherford, NJ [*Library symbol*] [*Library of Congress*] (LCLS)
NJRW .... New Jersey Romance Writers (EARSL)
NjRw .... Ridgewood Library, Ridgewood, NJ [*Library symbol*] [*Library of Congress*] (LCLS)
NjRwN .... Ridgewood News, Ridgewood, NJ [*Library symbol*] [*Library of Congress*] (LCLS)
NjRwPHi .... Paramus Historical and Preservation Society, Ridgewood, NJ [*Library symbol*] [*Library of Congress*] (LCLS)
NJS .... New Jersey Superior Court Reports [*A publication*] (DLA)
NJS .... Noise Jammer Simulator [*Telecommunications*] (TEL)
NJS .... Stockton State College, Pomona, NJ [*OCLC symbol*] (OCLC)
NjS .... Summit Free Public Library, Summit, NJ [*Library symbol*] [*Library of Congress*] (LCLS)
NJSA .... New Jersey Statutes, Annotated [*A publication*]
NjSabN ...... News Dispatch, Saddle Brook, NJ [*Library symbol*] [*Library of Congress*] (LCLS)
NjSalCoC ... Salem County Clerk, Salem, NJ [*Library symbol*] [*Library of Congress*] (LCLS)
NjSalHi ...... Salem County Historical Society, Salem, NJ [*Library symbol*] [*Library of Congress*] (LCLS)
NjSalS .... Sunbeam Publishing Co., Salem, NJ [*Library symbol*] [*Library of Congress*] (LCLS)
NJSB .... New Jersey Savings Bank [*NASDAQ symbol*] (COMM)
NJSBA .... New Jersey School Boards Association (SAUS)
NJSBAQ ..... New Jersey State Bar Association. Quarterly [*A publication*] (DLA)
NjSbB .... Beachcomber, Ship Bottom, NJ [*Library symbol*] [*Library of Congress*] (LCLS)
NjSbbU ...... Saint Sophia Ukrainian Orthodox Seminary, South Bound Brook, NJ [*Library symbol*] [*Library of Congress*] (LCLS)
NJSBJ .... New Jersey State Bar Journal [*A publication*] (DLA)
NJSBTA Ops... New Jersey State Board of Tax Appeals, Opinions [*A publication*] (DLA)
NjSC .... Ciba Pharmaceutical Co., Research Library, Summit, NJ [*Library symbol*] [*Library of Congress*] (LCLS)
NjSCC .... Summit City Clerk, Summit, NJ [*Library symbol*] [*Library of Congress*] (LCLS)
NjScp .... Scotch Plains Public Library, Scotch Plains, NJ [*Library symbol*] [*Library of Congress*] (LCLS)
NjScpT ...... Times, Scotch Plains, NJ [*Library symbol*] [*Library of Congress*] (LCLS)
NJSD .... National Joint Service Delegations (NATG)
NJSDC .... New Jersey State Data Center [*New Jersey State Department of Labor*] [*Trenton*] [*Information service or system*] (IID)
NjSe .... Secaucus Free Public Library, Secaucus, NJ [*Library symbol*] [*Library of Congress*] (LCLS)
NJSEA .... New Jersey Society of Enrolled Agents (SAUS)
NjSeH .... Secaucus Home News, Secaucus, NJ [*Library symbol*] [*Library of Congress*] (LCLS)
NJ Sess Law Serv... New Jersey Session Law Service [*A publication*] (DLA)
NjSewG ..... Gloucester County College, Sewell, NJ [*Library symbol*] [*Library of Congress*] (LCLS)
NjSewHi .... Washington Township Historical Society, Sewell, NJ [*Library symbol*] [*Library of Congress*] (LCLS)
NJSGA .... National Junior Santa Gertrudis Association (EA)
NJSGC .... New Jersey Space Grant Consortium (RCD)
NjSGS .... Church of Jesus Christ of Latter-Day Saints, Genealogical Society Library, Caldwell Branch, Summit, NJ [*Library symbol*] [*Library of Congress*] (LCLS)
NjSH .... Summit Herald, Summit, NJ [*Library symbol*] [*Library of Congress*] (LCLS)
NjShO .... Ocean County Review, Seaside Heights, NJ [*Library symbol*] [*Library of Congress*] (LCLS)
NJSHP .... New Jersey Society of Health-System Pharmacists (EARSL)
NJSHS .... National Junior Science and Humanities Symposium
NJSHS .... New Jersey State Horticultural Society (SAUS)

NjSicTR ..... Cape May County Times and Seven Mile Beach Reporter, Sea Isle City, NJ [*Library symbol*] [*Library of Congress*] (LCLS)
NJSLPAC... New Jersey State Laborers' PAC/Laborers' Political League [*Monroe Township, NJ*] (PACS)
NJSN .... National Job Sharing Network (EA)
NJSNA....... New Jersey State Nurses Associaton (SAUS)
NJSO .... National Jazz Service Organization (EA)
NjSo .... Somerville Free Public Library, Somerville, NJ [*Library symbol*] [*Library of Congress*] (LCLS)
NjSoa........ South Amboy Public Library, South Amboy, NJ [*Library symbol*] [*Library of Congress*] (LCLS)
NjSoaP...... South Amboy Publishing Co., South Amboy, NJ [*Library symbol*] [*Library of Congress*] (LCLS)
NjSobC...... Central Post, South Brunswick, NJ [*Library symbol*] [*Library of Congress*] (LCLS)
NjSoCo...... Somerset County Library, Somerville, NJ [*Library symbol*] [*Library of Congress*] (LCLS)
NjSoCoC .... Somerset County Clerk, Somerville, NJ [*Library symbol*] [*Library of Congress*] (LCLS)
NjSoE........ Ethicon, Inc., Somerville (SAUS)
NjSoH .... Somerset Hospital, Somerville, NJ [*Library symbol*] [*Library of Congress*] (LCLS)
NjSoHR ..... Hoechst-Roussel Pharmaceuticals, Inc., Somerville, NJ [*Library symbol*] [*Library of Congress*] (LCLS)
NjSoM....... Somerset Messenger-Gazette, Somerville, NJ [*Library symbol*] [*Library of Congress*] (LCLS)
NjSoo......... South Orange Public Library, South Orange, NJ [*Library symbol*] [*Library of Congress*] (LCLS)
NjSooS...... Seton Hall University, South Orange, NJ [*Library symbol*] [*Library of Congress*] (LCLS)
NjSooS-L ... Seton Hall University, Law Library, Newark, NJ [*Library symbol*] [*Library of Congress*] (LCLS)
NjSop........ South Plainfield Free Public Library, South Plainfield, NJ [*Library symbol*] [*Library of Congress*] (LCLS)
NjSopA...... American Smelting & Refining Co., Research Department Library, South Plainfield,NJ [*Library symbol*] [*Library of Congress*] (LCLS)
NjSopP...... PAMCAM, Inc., South Plainfield, NJ [*Library symbol*] [*Library of Congress*] (LCLS)
NjSoS .... Somerset County College, Somerville, NJ [*Library symbol*] [*Library of Congress*] (LCLS)
NjSosS ...... Somerset Spectator, Somerset, NJ [*Library symbol*] [*Library of Congress*] (LCLS)
NjSoVA...... United States Veterans Administration Supply Depot, Somerville, NJ [*Library symbol*] [*Library of Congress*] (LCLS)
NJSP .... New Jersey State Police (SAUS)
NjSp .... Springfield Free Public Library, Springfield, NJ [*Library symbol*] [*Library of Congress*] (LCLS)
NJSPE....... New Jersey Society of Professional Engineers (SAUS)
NjSpl .... Spring Lake Public Library, Spring Lake, NJ [*Library symbol*] [*Library of Congress*] (LCLS)
NjSpW....... Western Electric Co., Springfield, NJ [*Library symbol*] [*Library of Congress*] (LCLS)
NJSSPA ..... New Jersey State Society of Physician Assistants (EARSL)
NJST......... New Jersey Steel [*NASDAQ symbol*] (TTSB)
NJST......... New Jersey Steel Corp. [*NASDAQ symbol*] (NQ)
NjSt.......... Passaic Township Public Library, Stirling, NJ [*Library symbol*] [*Library of Congress*] (LCLS)
NJ Stat Ann (West)... New Jersey Statutes, Annotated (West) [*A publication*] (DLA)
NJ St BJ .... New Jersey State Bar Journal [*A publication*] (DLA)
NJ Stl .... New Jersey Steel Corp. [*Associated Press*] (SAG)
NjStR........ Recorder Publishing Co., Stirling, NJ [*Library symbol*] [*Library of Congress*] (LCLS)
NjStrK....... John F. Kennedy Memorial Hospital, Stratford, NJ [*Library symbol*] [*Library of Congress*] (LCLS)
NjSu .... Roxbury Public Library, Succasunna, NJ [*Library symbol*] [*Library of Congress*] (LCLS)
NJ Sup ...... New Jersey Superior Court Reports [*A publication*] (DLA)
NJ Super.... New Jersey Superior Court Reports [*A publication*] (DLA)
NjSw......... Swedesboro Free Public Library, Swedesboro, NJ [*Library symbol*] [*Library of Congress*] (LCLS)
NjSwN....... Swedesboro News, Swedesboro, NJ [*Library symbol*] [*Library of Congress*] (LCLS)
NJT .... National Jewish Television [*Cable-television system*]
NJT .... New Jersey Department of Transportation [*Federal Railroad Administration identification code*]
NJT .... Societe Novajet [*France*] [*ICAO designator*] (FAAC)
NjT........... Trenton Free Public Library, Trenton, NJ [*Library symbol*] [*Library of Congress*] (LCLS)
NJT .... Trenton State College, Trenton, NJ [*OCLC symbol*] (OCLC)
NjTCP .... Commercial Printing Co., Trenton, NJ [*Library symbol*] [*Library of Congress*] (LCLS)
NjTea .... Teaneck Public Library, Teaneck, NJ [*Library symbol*] [*Library of Congress*] (LCLS)
NjTeaF....... Fairleigh Dickinson University, Teaneck, NJ [*Library symbol*] [*Library of Congress*] (LCLS)
NjTeaL....... Luther College, Teaneck, NJ [*Library symbol*] [*Library of Congress*] (LCLS)
NjTen .... Tenafly Public Library, Tenafly, NJ [*Library symbol*] [*Library of Congress*] (LCLS)
NJTL......... National Junior Tennis League (EA)
NJTL Bulletin... New Jersey Tuberculosis League Bulletin (SAUS)
NjTM .... Monitor, Trenton, NJ [*Library symbol*] [*Library of Congress*] (LCLS)
NjTMC....... Mercer County Community College, Trenton, NJ [*Library symbol*] [*Library of Congress*] (LCLS)
NjTPP .... Planned Parenthood of Mercer Area, Trenton, NJ [*Library symbol*] [*Library of Congress*] (LCLS)
NJTR .... New Jersey Transit Rail [*Federal Railroad Administration identification code*]
NjTR......... Rider College, Trenton, NJ [*Library symbol*] [*Library of Congress*] (LCLS)
NjTrCo...... Ocean County Public Library, Toms River, NJ [*Library symbol*] [*Library of Congress*] (LCLS)
NjTrCoC .... Ocean County Clerk, Toms River, NJ [*Library symbol*] [*Library of Congress*] (LCLS)
NjTrO .... Ocean County College, Toms River, NJ [*Library symbol*] [*Library of Congress*] (LCLS)
NjTrR .... Reporter, Toms River, NJ [*Library symbol*] [*Library of Congress*] (LCLS)
NjTS .... Trenton State College, Trenton, NJ [*Library symbol*] [*Library of Congress*] (LCLS)
NjTSch ...... Schweats, Inc., Trenton, NJ [*Library symbol*] [*Library of Congress*] (LCLS)
NjTStF....... Saint Francis Medical Center, Health Science Library, Trenton, NJ [*Library symbol*] [*Library of Congress*] (LCLS)
NjTTr......... Trentonian, Trenton, NJ [*Library symbol*] [*Library of Congress*] (LCLS)
NjTTT........ Trenton Times Newspapers, Trenton, NJ [*Library symbol*] [*Library of Congress*] (LCLS)
NJTU .... J Theriot Nolty [*Intermodal shipping container symbol*] (TVRC)
NJ Turn...... New Jersey Turnpike (SAUS)
nju .... New Jersey [*MARC country of publication code*] [*Library of Congress*] (LCCP)
NJU .... Nordic Judo Union (EAIO)
NJU .... Northern Jiaotong University [*China*]
NjU .... Union Township Public Library, Union, NJ [*Library symbol*] [*Library of Congress*] (LCLS)
NjUbI .... International Flavors & Fragrances, Inc., Union Beach, NJ [*Library symbol*] [*Library of Congress*] (LCLS)
NjUc .... Union City Free Public Library, Union City, NJ [*Library symbol*] [*Library of Congress*] (LCLS)
NjUcD .... Dispatch, Union City, NJ [*Library symbol*] [*Library of Congress*] (LCLS)
NjUcS .... Shield, Union City, NJ [*Library symbol*] [*Library of Congress*] (LCLS)
NjUcSM ..... Saint Michael's Passionist Monastery, Union City, NJ [*Library symbol*] [*Library of Congress*] (LCLS)
NJUDS ...... North Judson, IN [*American Association of Railroads railroad junction routing code*]
NjUJ .... Jewish Community News, Union, NJ [*Library symbol*] [*Library of Congress*] (LCLS)
NjUN......... Kean College of New Jersey, Union, NJ [*Library symbol*] [*Library of Congress*] (LCLS)
NjUpM....... Montclair State College, Upper Montclair, NJ [*Library symbol*] [*Library of Congress*] (LCLS)
NjUpM-C.... China Institute of New Jersey, Montclair State College, Upper Montclair, NJ [*Library symbol*] [*Library of Congress*] (LCLS)
NJUS .... Netherlands Jurisprudence (NITA)
NjUS......... Suburban Publishing Co., Union, NJ [*Library symbol*] [*Library of Congress*] (LCLS)
NjUsrHi ..... Upper Saddle River Historical Committee, Upper Saddle River, NJ [*Library symbol*] [*Library of Congress*] (LCLS)
NJUZA9..... Japanese Journal of Veterinary Science (journ.) (SAUS)
NJV .... Nederlandse Juristenvereniging [*Netherlands Lawyers Association*] (ILCA)
NjV........... Vineland Free Public Library, Vineland, NJ [*Library symbol*] [*Library of Congress*] (LCLS)
NjVC .... Cumberland County College, Vineland, NJ [*Library symbol*] [*Library of Congress*] (LCLS)
NjVcP........ Ventnor City Public Library, Ventnor City, NJ [*Library symbol*] [*Library of Congress*] (LCLS)
NJVGA....... National Junior Vegetable Growers Association [*Later, NJHA*] (EA)
NjVHi .... Vineland Historical and Antiquarian Society, Vineland, NJ [*Library symbol*] [*Library of Congress*] (LCLS)
NJVOAD..... New Jersey Voluntary Organizations Active in Disaster [*Emergency Management*] (EMA)
NjVT .... Times Journal, Vineland, NJ [*Library symbol*] [*Library of Congress*] (LCLS)
NJW .... Norris Junction [*Wyoming*] [*Seismograph station code, US Geological Survey*] (SEIS)
NjW.......... Wayne Public Library, Wayne, NJ [*Library symbol*] [*Library of Congress*] (LCLS)
NjWa .... Warren Township Public Library, Warren, NJ [*Library symbol*] [*Library of Congress*] (LCLS)
NjWas .... Washington Free Public Library, Washington, NJ [*Library symbol*] [*Library of Congress*] (LCLS)
NjWasW..... Washington Star, Washington, NJ [*Library symbol*] [*Library of Congress*] (LCLS)
NJWB........ National Jewish Welfare Board [*Later, JWB*]
NjWdHi...... Gloucester County Historical Society, Woodbury, NJ [*Library symbol*] [*Library of Congress*] (LCLS)
NjWdT....... Woodbury Daily Times, Woodbury, NJ [*Library symbol*] [*Library of Congress*] (LCLS)
NjWef........ Westfield Memorial Library, Westfield, NJ [*Library symbol*] [*Library of Congress*] (LCLS)
NjWefW ..... Wyckoff Printing Co., Westfield, NJ [*Library symbol*] [*Library of Congress*] (LCLS)
NjWem ...... Haddon Township Free Library, Westmont, NJ [*Library symbol*] [*Library of Congress*] (LCLS)
NjWemT..... Camden County Times, Westmont, NJ [*Library symbol*] [*Library of Congress*] (LCLS)
NjWesny .... West New York Public Library, West New York, NJ [*Library symbol*] [*Library of Congress*] (LCLS)
NjWew ...... Westwood Free Public Library, Westwood, NJ [*Library symbol*] [*Library of Congress*] (LCLS)
NjWewP..... Pascack Valley Community Life, Westwood, NJ [*Library symbol*] [*Library of Congress*] (LCLS)

NjWewW.... Westwood Publications, Westwood, NJ [*Library symbol*] [*Library of Congress*] (LCLS)
NjWF........ Fairleigh Dickinson University, Wayne, NJ [*Library symbol*] [*Library of Congress*] (LCLS)
NjWhi....... Whippanong Public Library, Whippany, NJ [*Library symbol*] [*Library of Congress*] (LCLS)
NjWhiB...... Bell Telephone Laboratories, Inc., Technical Information Library, Whippany, NJ [*Library symbol*] [*Library of Congress*] (LCLS)
NjWhiM..... Morris County Free Library, Whippany, NJ [*Library symbol*] [*Library of Congress*] (LCLS)
NjWhiR...... Regional Weekly News, Whippany, NJ [*Library symbol*] [*Library of Congress*] (LCLS)
NjWhsH..... Hunterdon Review, Whitehouse Station, NJ [*Library symbol*] [*Library of Congress*] (LCLS)
NjWi......... Willingboro Public Library, Willingboro, NJ [*Library symbol*] [*Library of Congress*] (LCLS)
NjWilH...... Williamstown High School, Williamstown, NJ [*Library symbol*] [*Library of Congress*] (LCLS)
NjWiT....... Burlington County Times, Willingboro, NJ [*Library symbol*] [*Library of Congress*] (LCLS)
NjWlM....... Monmouth College, West Long Beach, NJ [*Library symbol*] [*Library of Congress*] (LCLS)
NjWMN...... Matzner Suburban Newspapers, Wayne, NJ [*Library symbol*] [*Library of Congress*] (LCLS)
NjWo........ West Orange Free Public Library, West Orange, NJ [*Library symbol*] [*Library of Congress*] (LCLS)
NjWoE....... Edison National Historic Site, West Orange, NJ [*Library symbol*] [*Library of Congress*] (LCLS)
NjWolA...... Alphonsus College, Woodcliff Lake, NJ [*Library symbol*] [*Library of Congress*] (LCLS)
NjWoo....... Free Public Library of Woodbridge, Woodbridge, NJ [*Library symbol*] [*Library of Congress*] (LCLS)
NjWooN..... News-Tribune, Woodbridge, NJ [*Library symbol*] [*Library of Congress*] (LCLS)
NjWor....... Wood Ridge Memorial Library, Wood Ridge, NJ [*Library symbol*] [*Library of Congress*] (LCLS)
NjWP........ William Paterson College of New Jersey, Wayne, NJ [*Library symbol*] [*Library of Congress*] (LCLS)
NJWPC....... National Jobs with Peace Campaign (EA)
NjWw........ Wildwood Crest Public Library, Wildwood, NJ [*Library symbol*] [*Library of Congress*] (LCLS)
NjWwHi...... Wildwood Historical Commission, Wildwood, NJ [*Library symbol*] [*Library of Congress*] (LCLS)
NjWwL...... Wildwood Leader, Wildwood, NJ [*Library symbol*] [*Library of Congress*] (LCLS)
NjWwP...... National Association of Precancel Collectors, Wildwood, NJ [*Library symbol*] [*Library of Congress*] (LCLS)
NjWy........ Wyckoff Free Public Library, Wyckoff, NJ [*Library symbol*] [*Library of Congress*] (LCLS)
NjWyN....... Wyckoff News, Wyckoff, NJ [*Library symbol*] [*Library of Congress*] (LCLS)
NJY.......... Newjay Resources Ltd. [*Vancouver Stock Exchange symbol*]
NJY.......... York College of the City University of New York, Jamaica, NY [*Library symbol*] [*Library of Congress*] (LCLS)
NJZ.......... New Jersey Zinc (SAUS)
NjZaA........ Alma White College, Zarephath, NJ [*Library symbol*] [*Library of Congress*] (LCLS)
NJZX......... New Jersey Zinc [*Private rail car owner code*]
Nk............ Naik [*British military*] (DMA)
NK........... Natural Killer [*Cell*] [*Immunochemistry*]
NK........... Neck (AAG)
NK........... Neon Komma [*New Party*] [*Greek*] [*Political party*] (PPE)
NK........... Neunkirchen [*Saar*] [*German license plate city code*]
NK........... Neurokinin [*Biochemistry*]
NK........... New Kingdom [*Egyptology*] (ROG)
NK........... Next of Kin
NK........... Nielsen-Kellerman
NK........... Nippon Kaiji Kyokai [*Japanese ship classification society*] (DS)
NK........... No Ketones [*Organic chemistry*] (DAVI)
NK........... No Kidding [*An association*] [*Canada*] (EAIO)
NK........... Nomemklatur Kommission [*Commission on Nomenclature*] [*Germany*] (DAVI)
NK........... Nordiska Kemistradet [*Chemical Societies of the Nordic Countries*] (EAIO)
NK........... Normalized Kinetic (SAUS)
NK........... Normal Keratinocyte (DB)
n/k.......... Not Known (DMAA)
NK........... Not Known
NK........... Nuclear Kill
NKa.......... Katonah Village Library, Katonah, NY [*Library symbol*] [*Library of Congress*] (LCLS)
NKA.......... National Kindergarten Association [*Defunct*] (EA)
NKA.......... Neurokinin A [*Biochemistry*]
NKA.......... Nikiskha [*Alaska*] [*Seismograph station code, US Geological Survey*] (SEIS)
NKA.......... No Known Allergies [*Medicine*]
NKA.......... Norcanair [*Canada*] [*ICAO designator*] (FAAC)
NKA.......... Nordic Liaison Committee for Atomic Energy (SAUS)
NKA.......... Nordisk Kontaktorgan for Atomenergisporgsmal [*Nordic Liaison Committee for Atomic Energy*] (EAIO)
NKA.......... North Korean Army
NKA.......... Now Known As (DLA)
nka.......... Now Known As (SAFN)
NKABEA..... National Korean American Bilingual Educators Association [*Defunct*] (EA)
NKAF........ Natural Killer-Cell Activating Factor [*Immunology*]
NKAF........ North Korean Air Force
NKAO........ Nagorno-Karabakh Autonomous Oblast
NKB.......... Bear Stearns Companies, Inc. [*AMEX symbol*] (SAG)
NKB.......... Neurokinin B [*Biochemistry*]
NKB.......... No Known Basis (MELL)
NKB.......... Nordiska Kommitten for Byggbestammelser [*Nordic Committee on Building Regulations - NCBR*] [*Finland*] (EAIO)
NKB.......... Norges Kommunalbank [*Bank*] [*Norway*]
NKBA........ National Kitchen and Bath Association (EA)
NKC.......... Merrill Lynch & Co. [*AMEX symbol*] (SAG)
NKC.......... National Kidney Centre [*British*] (CB)
NKC.......... Natural Killer Cells [*Microbiology*] (DAVI)
nkc.......... New Brunswick [*MARC country of publication code*] [*Library of Congress*] (LCCP)
NKC.......... Newtek Capital [*AMEX symbol*]
NKC.......... Nonketotic Coma [*Medicine*] (DMAA)
NKC.......... Nouakchott [*Mauritania*] [*Airport symbol*] (OAG)
NKCA........ National Kidney Cancer Association
NKCA........ National Kitchen Cabinet Association [*Later, KCMA*] (EA)
NKCA........ National Knife Collectors Association (EA)
NKCA........ Natural Killer Cell Activity [*Medicine*] (DMAA)
NKCF........ National Keratoconus Foundation (NRGU)
NKCF........ Natural Killer (Cell) Cytotoxic Factor [*Immunochemistry*]
NKCP........ North Kalimantan Communist Party [*Malaysia*] [*Political party*] (PD)
NKCR........ Nebraska, Kansas, Colorado Railnet [*Federal Railroad Administration identification code*]
NKD.......... No Known Disease (SAUS)
NKDA........ No Known Drug Allergies [*Medicine*]
NKDC........ Nonketotic Diabetic Coma [*Medicine*] (CPH)
NKDF........ National Kidney Disease Foundation [*Later, NKF*] (EA)
NKDS........ Navy Key Distribution System (CAAL)
NKE.......... Nake [*Ryukyu Islands*] [*Seismograph station code, US Geological Survey*] [*Closed*] (SEIS)
NKE.......... Nike [*NYSE symbol*]
NKE.......... Nike, Inc. Class B [*NYSE symbol*] (SPSG)
NKE.......... NIKE, Inc. Cl'B' [*NYSE symbol*] (TTSB)
NKE.......... Nortek Capital Corp. [*Formerly, Nortek Energy Corp.*] [*Vancouver Stock Exchange symbol*]
NKendOHi.. Orleans County Historical Society, Kendall, NY [*Library symbol*] [*Library of Congress*] (LCLS)
NKEW........ Nuclear Kinetic Energy Weapon (SAUS)
NKEWA...... New Kuban Education and Welfare Association (EA)
NKEZA4..... Japanese Journal of Public Health (journ.) (SAUS)
NKF.......... National Kidney Foundation (EA)
NKF.......... Nordiske Kvinners Fredsnettverk [*Nordic Women's Peace Network*] [*Denmark, Finland, Norway, and Sweden*] (EAIO)
NKF.......... Nordisk Konstforbund [*Nordic Art Association*] [*Norway*] (EAIO)
NKFA........ National Kidney Foundation of Arkansas (EARSL)
NKFA........ No Known Food Allergies [*Medicine*] (DMAA)
NKF-DOQI... National Kidney Foundation-Dialysis Outcomes Quality Initiative (SAUS)
NKFN........ National Kidney Foundation of Nebraska (EARSL)
NKFO........ Nordisk Kollegium for Fysisk Oceanografi [*Nordic Council for Physical Oceanography - NCPO*] (EAIO)
NKFTA....... National Kosher Food Trade Association [*Defunct*] (EA)
NKG.......... Nanjing [*China*] [*Airport symbol*] (OAG)
NkG.......... Newton K. Gregg, Novato, CA [*Library symbol*] [*Library of Congress*] (LCLS)
NKGB........ Peoples Commissariat for State Security (SAUS)
NKGB-NKVD... Narodnyi Komissariat Gosudarstvennoe Bezopasnosti-Narodnyi Komissariat Vnutrennikh Del [*Later, KGB*]
NKH.......... Kaneohe Bay, HI [*Location identifier*] [*FAA*] (FAAL)
NKH.......... Nonketotic Hyperglycemia [*Endocrinology*] (DAVI)
NKH.......... Nonketotic Hyperosmotic [*Medicine*] (MAE)
NKH.......... Nordisk Komite for Handelsundervisning [*Nordic Committee for Commercial Education - NCCE*] [*Odense, Denmark*] (EAIO)
NKHA........ National Kerosene Heater Association (EA)
NKHA........ Nonketotic Hyperosmolar Acidosis [*Medicine*]
NKHHC...... Nonketotic Hyperosmolar Hyperglycemis Coma [*Also, HHNK*] [*Medicine*]
NKHS........ Nonketotic Hyperosmolar Syndrome [*Biochemistry*] (DAVI)
NKHS........ Normal Krebs-Henseleit Solution (DB)
NKI.......... Nash-Kelvinator International [*Automobile manufacturer, now out of production*]
NKI.......... Nikolski [*Alaska*] [*Seismograph station code, US Geological Survey*] (SEIS)
NKI.......... Thangal Naga [*Language symbol*] (ETLW)
NKiB......... Benedictine Hospital, Medical Library, Kingston, NY [*Library symbol*] [*Library of Congress*] (LCLS)
NKiC......... Children's Home of Kingston, Kingston, NY [*Library symbol*] [*Library of Congress*] (LCLS)
NKID......... Narodnyy Komissariat Inostrannykh Del [*People's Commissariat of Foreign Affairs*] [*Former USSR*] (LAIN)
NKID......... Noodle Kidoodle [*NASDAQ symbol*] (TTSB)
NKID......... Noodle Kidoodle, Inc. [*NASDAQ symbol*] (SAG)
NKiHL....... Kingston Hospital Libraries, Kingston, NY [*Library symbol*] [*Library of Congress*] (LCLS)
NKiI......... International Business Machines Corp., Kingston, NY [*Library symbol*] [*Library of Congress*] (LCLS)
NKIM......... Nederlandsche Kali-Import Maatschappij (EFIS)
NKipM....... United States Merchant Marine Academy, Kings Point, NY [*Library symbol*] [*Library of Congress*] (LCLS)
NKJV......... New King James Version of the Bible [*A publication*]
NKK.......... Nippon Kokan (EFIS)
NKK.......... Nordkalottkommitten [*North Calotte Committee - NCC*] [*Finland*] (EAIO)
NKK.......... North Calotte Committee (SAUS)

NKK.......... Novo-Kazalinsk [*Former USSR*] [*Geomagnetic observatory code*]
NKK.......... People's Congress of Kazakhstan [*Political party*] (PSAP)
NKKGAB..... Japanese Poultry Science (journ.) (SAUS)
NKK Tech Rep... NKK Technical Report (SAUS)
NKK Tech Rev... NKK Technical Review (SAUS)
NKL.......... Nemeth-Kellner Leukemia
NKL.......... New Keel [*On ships*]
NKL.......... New Kelore Mines Ltd. [*Toronto Stock Exchange symbol*]
NKL.......... Nickel
NKL.......... Nkolo [*Zaire*] [*Airport symbol*] (AD)
NKL C....... Nickel Copper [*Freight*]
NKL FCD.... Nickel Faced (DGA)
NKLU........ Northern Lights Shipping [*Intermodal shipping container symbol*] (TVRC)
NKM......... Nakhla [*Morocco*] [*Seismograph station code, US Geological Survey*] (SEIS)
NKM......... New Park Mining (SAUS)
NKM......... University of North Carolina at Charlotte, Charlotte, NC [*OCLC symbol*] (OCLC)
NKMA....... National Knitwear Manufacturers Association (EA)
NKMA....... No Known Medication Allergies (DAVI)
NKMB....... Nordisk Kollegium for Marinbiologi [*Nordic Council for Marine Biology - NCMB*] (EAIO)
NKMU....... National Kangaroo Monitoring Unit [*Australia*]
NKN.......... Neurokinin (DMAA)
NKN.......... North Korean Navy
NKNO........ Nakano Express Service [*Common carrier symbol*]
NKNU........ Niznekamsk Neftechimexport [*Intermodal shipping container symbol*] (TVRC)
NKO.......... Narodnyi Komissariat Oborony [*People's Commissariat of Defense*] [*Existed until 1946*] [*Former USSR*]
NKO.......... Need to Know Only [*Espionage*]
NKOA........ National Knitted Outerwear Association [*Later, NKSA*] (EA)
NKOT........ Nu-kote Holding'A' [*NASDAQ symbol*] (TTSB)
NKOT........ Nu-Kote Holding, Inc. [*NASDAQ symbol*] (SAG)
NKOTB...... New Kids on the Block [*Music group*]
NKOU........ Nikou Shipping [*Common carrier symbol*]
NKP.......... Nakorn Phanom [*Air base northeast of Bangkok*]
NKP.......... Nasionale Konserwatiewe Party [*National Conservative Party*] [*South Africa*] [*Political party*] (PPW)
NKP.......... New Kensington [*Pennsylvania*] [*Seismograph station code, US Geological Survey*] [*Closed*] (SEIS)
NKP.......... New Korea Party [*South Korea*]
NKP.......... Nickel Plate Railroad (SAUS)
NKP.......... Norges Kommunistiske Parti [*Norwegian Communist Party*] [*Political party*] (PPE)
NKPA........ National Kraut Packers Association (EA)
NKPA........ North Korean Peoples Army (SAUS)
NKpaH....... Kings Park State Hospital, Kings Park, NY [*Library symbol*] [*Library of Congress*] (LCLS)
NKpK........ Keuka College, Keuka Park, NY [*Library symbol*] [*Library of Congress*] (LCLS)
NKPR........ Innkeepers USA Trust [*NASDAQ symbol*] (SAG)
NKP RTAB... Nakhon Phanom Royal Thai Air Base [*Leased by USAF during the Vietnam War*] (VNW)
NKR.......... Nakanohara [*Japan*] [*Seismograph station code, US Geological Survey*] (SEIS)
NKR.......... New Kenrell Resources [*Vancouver Stock Exchange symbol*]
NKR.......... Nordisk Konservatorierad [*Nordic Council for Music Conservatories - NCMC*] (EAIO)
NKR.......... Normal Rat Kidney (DB)
N KR......... Norwegian Krone [*Monetary unit*]
NKRC........ No Known Relatives or Concerned
NKRD........ Robert Nikrandt and Daughters Trucking Company [*Common carrier symbol*]
NKS.......... Needle-Knife Sphincterotomy [*Medicine*] (MELL)
NKS.......... Network of Kindred Spirits (EA)
NKS.......... Nordic Nuclear Safety Project (SAUS)
NKS.......... Nordisk Kirkelig Studierad [*Nordic Council for Adult Studies in Chruch - NCASC*] (EAIO)
NKSA........ National Knitwear and Sportswear Association (EA)
NKSC........ National Korean Studies Center [*Australia*]
NKSF........ Natural Killer-Cell Stimulatory Factor [*Immunology*]
NKSR........ Non-Kernel Security Related (SAUS)
NKSRS...... Non-Kernel Security Related Software (ACAE)
NKT.......... Cherry Point, NC [*Location identifier*] [*FAA*] (FAAL)
NKT.......... Nankipoo [*Tennessee*] [*Seismograph station code, US Geological Survey*] (SEIS)
NKT.......... National Kakapo Team (SAUS)
NKT.......... Nihon Kai Telecasting (SAUS)
NKT.......... None Kept in Town
NKTAD....... Journal. Gyeongsang National University. Natural Sciences (journ.) (SAUS)
NKU.......... Nakusp Resources Ltd. [*Vancouver Stock Exchange symbol*]
NKU.......... Nkaus [*Lesotho*] [*Airport symbol*] (OAG)
NKUDIC..... National Kidney and Urologic Diseases Information Clearinghouse (EA)
NKUSA...... Neturei Karta of USA (EA)
NKVD........ Narodnyi Kommissariat Vnutrennikh Del [*People's Commissariat for Internal Affairs*] [*Former USSR*] (NADA)
NKVMF...... Narodnyy Komissariat Voyenno-Morskogo Flota [*People's Commissariat of the Navy*] [*Former USSR*] (LAIN)
NKX.......... Nkoroo [*Language symbol*] (ETLW)
NKX.......... San Diego, CA [*Location identifier*] [*FAA*] (FAAL)
N Ky St LF... Northern Kentucky State Law Forum [*A publication*] (DLA)
NKYu........ Narodnyy Komissariat Yustitsii [*People's Commissariat of Justice*] [*Former USSR*] (LAIN)
NKYZA2..... Jaganese Journal of Thoracic Diseases (SAUS)
NKz.......... Kwanza (ODBW)
NKZ.......... Nuclear Killing Zone [*Military*] [*British*]
NL............ Air Liberia [*ICAO designator*] (AD)
nl---.......... Great Lakes [*MARC geographic area code*] [*Library of Congress*] (LCCP)
NL............ Lamborghini [*Society of Automotive Engineers auto manufacturer code for service information interchange*]
NL............ Lima Public Library, Lima, NY [*Library symbol*] [*Library of Congress*] (LCLS)
NL............ Nailable [*Technical drawings*]
nl............. Nanoliter [*One billionth of a liter*] (MAE)
NL............ Nasolacrimal [*Medicine*] (DAVI)
NL............ Natick Laboratories [*Army*] (MCD)
NL............ National Lakeshore (BARN)
NL............ National Lead (EFIS)
NL............ National League (NTIO)
NL............ National League of Professional Baseball Clubs (EA)
NL............ National Liberal [*British politics*]
NL............ National Library [*Canada*]
NL............ Native Language (BARN)
NL............ Natural [*Telegraphy*] (PCTE)
NL............ Naturalist's Library [*A publication*]
NL............ Natural Language [*Computer software*]
NL............ Natural Log [*or Logarithm*] (WDAA)
NL............ Naval Lighter
NL............ Navigating Lieutenant [*Navy*] [*British*] (ROG)
N/L........... Navigation/Localizer (IEEE)
NL............ Navy League of the United States
NL............ Navy Library (WDAA)
NL............ Navy List [*British military*] (DMA)
NL............ Nebenlager [*Branch Camp*] [*German military - World War II*]
NL............ Nelson's Lutwyche, English Common Pleas Reports [*A publication*] (DLA)
NL............ Neon Lamp (KSC)
NL............ Netherlands [*ANSI two-letter standard code*] (CNC)
Nl............. Netherlands (MILB)
NL............ Net Loss
NL............ Neural Lobe [*Medicine*] (EDAA)
NL............ Neurilemmona [*Oncology*]
NL............ Neuroleptic (SAUS)
NL............ Neutral Lipid (DB)
NL............ Neutron Log (SAUS)
nl............. New Caledonia [*MARC country of publication code*] [*Library of Congress*] (LCCP)
NL............ New Latin [*Language, etc.*]
NL............ New Lead [*Also, NH*] [*News stories*] (NTCM)
NL............ New Leader [*A publication*] (BRI)
nl............. New Line (WDMC)
NL............ New Line [*Computer science*]
NL............ New London, Connecticut [*Navy*]
NL............ Newsletter (WDMC)
N-L........... New York State Library, Law Library, Albany, NY [*Library symbol*] [*Library of Congress*] (LCLS)
NL............ Niedersachsen [*German license plate city code*]
NL............ Night Letter
NL............ NL Industries, Inc. [*Formerly, National Lead Co.*] [*NYSE symbol*] (SPSG)
NL............ Nodular Lymphoma [*Oncology*] (DAVI)
NL............ Noiseless (SAUS)
NL............ Noise Level (SAUS)
NL............ No Label (SAUS)
NL............ No Layers (SAUS)
N/L........... No Ledger (SAA)
NL............ No Liability (ADA)
NL............ No License [*Traffic offense charge*]
NL............ No Limit (NASA)
NL............ No Liner (DS)
NL............ No Load
NL............ Non-Labeled [*Tape*] [*Computer science*]
NL............ Non Licet [*It Is Not Permitted*] [*Latin*]
NL............ Nonlinear
NL............ Non Liquet [*It Is Not Clear*] [*Latin*]
NL............ Non-Loaded (NITA)
NL............ Nonlocking
NL............ Non Longe [*Not Far*] [*Latin*]
NL............ Non-Lubricant (SAUS)
NL............ Nonprogrammer Language [*Computer science*] (PDAA)
NL............ Normal Libido [*Medicine*] (EDAA)
n/l............ Normal Limits
NL............ Normal Lungs
NL............ North Latitude
NL............ North Library (SAUS)
NL............ Nose Left [*Aviation*] (MCD)
NL............ Notless (SAUS)
NL............ Not Licensed (SAUS)
NL............ Not Listed (AFM)
NL............ Not Located
NL............ Nulead [*Journalism*] [*Slang*] (WDMC)
NL............ Number Language (SAUS)
NL............ Number Lines (SAUS)
NL............ Number of unallocated channels on link (SAUS)
NL............ Nurses for Laughter [*Defunct*] (EA)

NL.......... Nyhan-Lesch [*Syndrome*] [*Medicine*] (DB)
NL/1.......... Non-programmer Language 1 (SAUS)
NLA.......... Children's Leukemia Research Association [*Formerly, National Leukemia Association*] (EA)
NLA.......... National Laboratory Accreditation Service (SAUS)
NLA.......... National Landscape Association (EA)
NLA.......... National Leather Association (EA)
NLA.......... National Leukemia Association (EA)
NLA.......... National Liberation Army [*Bolivia*]
NLA.......... National Librarians Association (EA)
NLA.......... National Libraries Authority
NLA.......... National Library Act
NLA.......... National Library of Australia (NITA)
NLA.......... National Library of Canada, Cataloguing Branch [*UTLAS symbol*]
NLA.......... National Lime Association (EA)
NLA.......... National Limousine Association (EA)
NLA.......... National Locksmiths Association (EA)
NLA.......... NATO Lot Acceptance (MCD)
NLA.......... Navy League of Australia
NLA.......... Ndola [*Zambia*] [*Airport symbol*] (OAG)
NLA.......... Neiltown Air Ltd. [*Canada*] [*ICAO designator*] (FAAC)
NLA.......... Net Lettable Area
NLA.......... Neuroleptanalgesia [*Altered state of awareness*] [*Medicine*] (AAMN)
NLA.......... Neuroleptic Anesthesia
NLA.......... Neuroleptoanesthesia [*Medicine*] (DMAA)
NLA.......... Nevada Library Association (SAUS)
NLA.......... Newfoundland Library Association (SAUS)
NLA.......... New Large Airplane
NLA.......... New Larger Aeroplanes (SAUS)
NLA.......... New Libertarian Alliance (EA)
NLA.......... New Libertian Alliance (SAUS)
NLA.......... Next Lower Assembly (MCD)
NLA.......... Nine Lives Associates (EA)
NLA.......... Nonlinear Amplifier
NLA.......... Nonlinear Analysis (SAUS)
NLA.......... Nonuniform Linear Array
NLA.......... Normalized Load Access (NITA)
NLA.......... Normalized Local Address [*Computer science*] (CIST)
NLA.......... Normal Lactase Activity [*Medicine*] (DMAA)
NLA.......... Norris-LaGuardia Act (MHDB)
NLA.......... Not Long Ago (SAUS)
NLAA.......... National Legal Aid Association
NLAAM.......... N-Desmethyl-levo-alpha-Acetylmethadol [*Opiate*]
NLAB.......... National Laboratory Accreditation Bureau (SAUS)
NLAB.......... NuOncology Labs, Inc. [*NASDAQ symbol*] (QUAN)
NLABS.......... Natick Laboratories [*Army*] (AABC)
NLAC.......... National Listen America Club (EA)
NLAC.......... Northeast Louisiana Arts Council (EARSL)
NLacOH.......... Our Lady of Victory Hospital, Lackawanna, NY [*Library symbol*] [*Library of Congress*] (LCLS)
NLADA.......... National Legal Aid and Defender Association (EA)
NLADA Brief... National Legal Aid and Defender Association Briefcase [*A publication*] (DLA)
NLAES.......... National Longitudinal Alcohol Epidemiologic Survey (SAUS)
NLakrHS.......... Sachem High School South, Lake Ronkonkoma, NY [*Library symbol*] [*Library of Congress*] (LCLS)
NLAL.......... Nodule-Like Alveolar Lesion [*Medicine*] (DB)
NLanEB.......... Erie No. 1 Board of Coopertive Educational Services, Lancaster, NY [*Library symbol*] [*Library of Congress*] (LCLS)
NLANR.......... National Laboratory for Applied Network Research (DDC)
NLanS.......... Scott Aviation, Lancaster, NY [*Library symbol*] [*Library of Congress*] (LCLS)
NLAP.......... National Lab Audit Program (COE)
NLAPW.......... National League of American Pen Women (EA)
NLar.......... Larchmont Public Library, Larchmont, NY [*Library symbol*] [*Library of Congress*] (LCLS)
NLAS.......... National Laboratory Accreditation Service (SAUS)
NLAS.......... National Lum and Abner Society (EA)
N Lat.......... North Latitude (ODA)
NLaw.......... Peninsula Public Library, Lawrence, NY [*Library symbol*] [*Library of Congress*] (LCLS)
NLawBS.......... Brandeis School, Lawrence, NY [*Library symbol*] [*Library of Congress*] (LCLS)
NLawCE.......... Central Elementary School, Lawrence, NY [*Library symbol*] [*Library of Congress*] (LCLS)
NLawChE.......... Cedarhurst Elementary School, Lawrence, NY [*Library symbol*] [*Library of Congress*] (LCLS)
NLawDE.......... Donahue Elementary School, Lawrence, NY [*Library symbol*] [*Library of Congress*] (LCLS)
NLawJH.......... Lawrence Junior High School, Lawrence, NY [*Library symbol*] [*Library of Congress*] (LCLS)
NLawPE.......... Peninsula Elementary School, Lawrence, NY [*Library symbol*] [*Library of Congress*] (LCLS)
NLawrPE.......... Peninsula Elementary School, Lawrence (SAUS)
NLawSH.......... Lawrence Senior High School, Lawrence, NY [*Library symbol*] [*Library of Congress*] (LCLS)
NLawWE.......... Wansee Elementary School, Lawrence, NY [*Library symbol*] [*Library of Congress*] (LCLS)
NLB.......... National Labor Board (WDAA)
NLB.......... National Library for the Blind
NLB.......... National Library of Canada, Locations Division [*UTLAS symbol*]
NLB.......... National Lighting Bureau (EA)
NLB.......... Needle Liver Biopsy [*Medicine*] (DMAA)
NLB.......... Network Load Balancing
NLB.......... No Lunch Break
NLB.......... Nonlinear Buckling (SAUS)
NLB.......... Northern Lighthouse Board (SAUS)
NLB.......... Nuclear Light Bulb
NLB.......... Number of Lines of Binary (SAUS)
NLBA.......... National Lead Burning Association (EA)
NLBA.......... National Licensed Beverage Association (EA)
NLBA.......... Nonlinear Buckling Analysis (SAUS)
NLBA BAR-PAC... National Licensed Beverage Association Beverage Alcohol Retailer PAC [*Bathesda, MD*] (PACS)
NLB & D.......... National League for the Blind and Disabled [*British*] (DBA)
NLBC.......... National Livestock Brand Conference [*Later, International Livestock Brand Conference*]
NLBD.......... National League of the Blind and Disabled [*A union*] [*British*] (DCTA)
NLBI.......... National League of the Blind of Ireland (EAIO)
NLBK.......... National Loan Bank (Texas) [*NASDAQ symbol*] (COMM)
NLBMDA.......... National Lumber and Building Material Dealers Association (EA)
NLBRA.......... National Little Britches Rodeo Association (EA)
NLBU.......... Ned-Lloyd Lines [*Common carrier symbol*]
NLC.......... Lemoore, CA [*Location identifier*] [*FAA*] (FAAL)
NLC.......... NADGE [*NATO Air Defense Ground Environment*] Logistics Committee (NATG)
NLC.......... Nalco Chemical [*NYSE symbol*] (TTSB)
NLC.......... Nalco Chemical Co. [*NYSE symbol*] (SPSG)
NLC.......... National Laboratory Census [*Medicine*] [*ASMT*] (EDAA)
NLC.......... National Laboratory Center [*Bureau of Alcohol, Tobacco, and Firearms*] [*Rockville, MD*] (GRD)
NLC.......... National Labour Congress [*Nigeria*] (ECON)
NLC.......... National Law Center for Children and Families [*Association*] (EA)
NLC.......... National Lawyers Club (EA)
NLC.......... National Leadership Committee [*Military*]
NLC.......... National Leadership Council [*Defunct*] (EA)
NLC.......... National League of Cities (EA)
NLC.......... National Legislative Conference [*Later, NCSL*] (EA)
NLC.......... National Legislative Council [*Later, NCSL*]
NLC.......... National Liberal Club [*British*]
NLC.......... National Liberation Committee [*South Africa*]
NLC.......... National Liberty Committee (EA)
NLC.......... National Library of Canada
NLC.......... National Library of Canada, Ottawa, ON, Canada [*OCLC symbol*] (OCLC)
NLC.......... National Library of China
NLC.......... National Lifeguard Championships (EA)
NLC.......... National Liturgical Commission [*Catholic Church*] [*Australia*]
NLC.......... National Location Code [*Civil Defense*]
NLC.......... National Logistical Command (MCD)
NLC.......... National Lutheran Council [*Later, LC/USA*] (EA)
NLC.......... Natural Language Command [*Computer science*]
NLC.......... Navy Law Center (DNAB)
NLC.......... Negro Labor Committee [*Defunct*] (EA)
NLC.......... Nematic Liquid Crystal [*Physical chemistry*]
NLC.......... Network Language Center (MHDB)
NLC.......... New Liberal Club [*Shin Jiyu Club*] [*Japan*] (PPW)
NLC.......... New Line Character [*Keyboard*] [*Computer science*] (MDG)
NLC.......... New Location Code [*Military*]
NLC.......... New London, CT [*Amtrak rail station code*]
NLC.......... New Orleans & Lower Coast Railroad Co. [*AAR code*]
NLC.......... News and Letters Committee (EA)
NLC.......... Next Linear Collider [*Proposed*]
NLC.......... Nocturnal Leg Cramps [*Medicine*] (MELL)
NLC.......... Node Location Code (PDAA)
NLC.......... Noise-Level Cable
NLC.......... Non-Linear Capacitor (SAUS)
NLC.......... Non-Linear Condenser (SAUS)
NLC.......... Nonlinear Control (SAUS)
NLC.......... Nordic Literature Committee [*Copenhagen, Denmark*] (EAIO)
NLC.......... Northern Libraries Colloquy (EA)
NLC.......... Northland Library System [*Library network*]
NLCA.......... Norlaudanosolinecarboxylic Acid [*Biochemistry*]
NLCA.......... Norlithocholic Acid [*Biochemistry*]
NLCA.......... Norwegian Lutheran Church of America (IIA)
NLCAA.......... National Little College Athletic Association [*Later, NSCAA*] (EA)
NLCAB.......... National Library of Canada Advisory Board
NLCACBC... National League of Cuban American Community-Based Centers (EA)
NLC&C.......... Normal Libido, Coitus and Climax [*Medicine*] (MELL)
NLCC.......... National Latino Communications Center (SAUS)
NLCC.......... Navy League Cadet Corps (EA)
NLCC.......... NORTHAG Logistics Command Center (SAUS)
NLCD.......... National Liberation Council Decree [*1966-69*] [*Ghana*] [*A publication*] (DLA)
NLCEA.......... Naval Laboratory Centers' Employee Association (DNAB)
NLCH.......... National Legislative Council for the Handicapped (EA)
NLCHP.......... National Law Center on Homelessness and Poverty [*Association*] (EA)
NLCI.......... Nobel Learning Communities [*NASDAQ symbol*]
NLCIF.......... National Light Castings Ironfounders' Federation [*British*] (BI)
NLCM.......... National Lutheran Campus Ministry (EA)
NLCM.......... Non-Lethal Countermeasures (SAUS)
NLCMDD.......... National Legal Center for the Medically Dependent and Disabled (EA)
NLCOA.......... National Leadership Coalition on AIDS [*Acquired Immune Deficiency Syndrome*] (EA)
NLCP.......... Navy Logistics Capabilities Plan
NLCP-FY... Navy Logistics Capabilities Plan - Fiscal Year (DNAB)
NLCPI.......... National Legal Center for the Public Interest (EA)
NLCQ.......... L Neill Cartage Company [*Common carrier symbol*]

NLCR .... New Line, Carriage Return (SAUS)
NLCS .... National Computer Systems, Inc. [*NASDAQ symbol*] (NQ)
NLCS .... National League Championship Series [*Baseball*]
NLCS .... National Lutheran Commission on Scouting [*Defunct*] (EA)
NLCS .... Natl Computer Sys [*NASDAQ symbol*] (TTSB)
NLCS .... Nordic Leather Chemists Society [*Formerly, IVLIC Scandinavian Section*] (EA)
NLCS .... North London Collegiate School (SAUS)
NLCSDHRES... National Labor Committee in Support of Democracy and Human Rights in El Salvador (EA)
NLCSE....... Non-Linear Charge Storage Element (PDAA)
NLCSJ....... National Lawyers Committee for Soviet Jewry (EA)
NLCU .... Natural le Coultre [*Intermodal shipping container symbol*] (TVRC)
NLCWC..... National Lincoln-Civil War Council (EA)
NLD.......... Namakwaland Lugdiens (EDMS) BPK [*South Africa*] [*ICAO designator*] (FAAC)
NLD.......... NASA Launch Director
NLD.......... Nasolabial Distance [*Medicine*] (MELL)
NLD.......... Nasolacrimal Duct [*Medicine*] (DAVI)
NLD.......... National League for Democracy [*Myanmar*] [*Political party*] (EY)
NLD.......... National Legal Databases (IID)
NLD.......... National Legion of Decency [*Later, National Catholic Office for Motion Pictures*] (EA)
NLD.......... Naval Electrical Department [*British military*] (DMA)
NLD.......... Naval Lighter [*Pontoon*] Dock
NLD.......... Necrobiosis Lipoidica Diabeticorum [*Medicine*]
NLD.......... Netherlands [*ANSI three-letter standard code*] (CNC)
NLD.......... No Load (MSA)
NLD.......... Nonlinear Distortion (SAUS)
NLD.......... Nonverbal Learning Disability
NLD.......... Northland Bank [*Toronto Stock Exchange symbol*] [*Vancouver Stock Exchange symbol*]
NLD.......... Not in Line of Duty [*as of an injury*] [*Military*]
NLD.......... Nuevo Laredo [*Mexico*] [*Airport symbol*] (OAG)
NLD.......... Nunn-Lugar-Domenici [*Emergency Management*] (EMA)
NLDA........ National Livestock Dealers Association [*Later, Livestock Marketing Association*] (EA)
NLDA........ National Luggage Dealers Association (EA)
NLDB........ Natural Language Data Base
NLDC........ National Legal Data Center [*Defunct*] (EA)
NLDC........ Newfoundland and Labrador Development Corp. (SAUS)
NLDDE...... Non-Linear Differential-Difference Equation (SAUS)
NLDF........ National Leigh's Disease Foundation (EA)
NLDF........ Naval Local Defense Forces
NLDGP...... Non-Linear Discrete Goal Programming (SAUS)
NLDI......... Nasolacrimal Duct Impatency [*Medicine*] (MELL)
NLDL........ Normal Low-density Lipoprotein [*Medicine*] (EDAA)
NLDM....... Network Logical Data Manager (NITA)
NLDN....... National Lightning Detection Network
NLDO........ Nasolacrimal Duct Obstruction [*Medicine*] (MELL)
NLDP........ National Launch Development Program [*Astronomy term*]
NLDS........ National Lightning Detection System (SAUS)
NLDTS....... Nonlinear Discrete-Time System (SAUS)
NLDU........ Nexus Logistics [*Intermodal shipping container symbol*] (TVRC)
NLDV........ National League of Disabled Voters (EA)
NLE.......... National Library of Education
NLE.......... National Livestock Exchange [*Defunct*] (EA)
NLE.......... Neonatal Lupus Erythematosus [*Medicine*] (MELL)
NLE.......... Nonlinear Editing (SAUS)
NLE.......... Nonlinear Element
NLE.......... Nonlinear Equation (SAUS)
NLE.......... Nonlinear Estimation (SAUS)
Nle.......... Norleucine [*A nonessential amino acid*] [*Biochemistry*]
Nle.......... Norleucyl (SAUS)
NLE.......... Northern Commuter Airlines [*New Zealand*] [*ICAO designator*] (FAAC)
NLE.......... North Leave Earth (ACAE)
NLE.......... Not Less or Equal (SAUS)
NLE.......... Nursing Late Entry [*Medicine*] (EDAA)
NLEA........ National Lumber Exporters Association [*Later, AHEC*] (EA)
NLEA........ National Lupus Erythematosus Association (MELL)
NLEA........ Nutrition Labeling Act (SAUS)
NLEA........ Nutrition Labeling and Education Act [*1990*] [*Food and Drug Administration*]
NLEACH..... Northleach [*England*]
NLEC........ National Law Enforcement Council (EA)
NLEC........ National Lutheran Educational Conference [*Later, LECNA*] (EA)
NLEEF....... National Law Enforcement Emergency Frequency (LAIN)
NLEF........ National Legislative Education Foundation (EA)
NLEF........ National Lupus Erythematosus Foundation [*Defunct*] (EA)
NLEF........ Nonlinear Electric Field (SAUS)
NLEFM...... Nonlinear Elastic Fracture Mechanics (SAUS)
NLEMA...... National Lutheran Editors and Managers Association [*Defunct*] (EA)
NLEOMF.... National Law Enforcement Officers Memorial Fund (EA)
NLer.......... Woodward Memorial Library, LeRoy, NY [*Library symbol*] [*Library of Congress*] (LCLS)
NLerHi...... LeRoy Historical Society, LeRoy, NY [*Library symbol*] [*Library of Congress*] (LCLS)
NLETS....... National Law Enforcement Telecommunications System
NLETS....... National Law Enforcement Teletype System (COE)
Nleu......... Norleucine (DB)
NLev......... Levittown Public Library, Levittown, NY [*Library symbol*] [*Library of Congress*] (LCLS)
NLEV........ National Low-Emission Vehicles
NLevAE...... Abbey Lane Elementary School, Levittown, NY [*Library symbol*] [*Library of Congress*] (LCLS)
NLevDH..... Division Avenue High School, Levittown, NY [*Library symbol*] [*Library of Congress*] (LCLS)
NLevEC...... Levittown Memorial Education Center, Levittown, NY [*Library symbol*] [*Library of Congress*] (LCLS)
NLevGE..... Gardiners Avenue Elementary School, Levittown, NY [*Library symbol*] [*Library of Congress*] (LCLS)
NLevGGE.... Geneva N. Gallow Elementary School, Levittown, NY [*Library symbol*] [*Library of Congress*] (LCLS)
NLevI........ Island Trees Public Library, Levittown, NY [*Library symbol*] [*Library of Congress*] (LCLS)
NLevIH...... Island Trees High School, Levittown, NY [*Library symbol*] [*Library of Congress*] (LCLS)
NLevIJ....... Island Trees Memorial Junior High School, Levittown, NY [*Library symbol*] [*Library of Congress*] (LCLS)
NLevJSE.... J. Fred Sparke Elementary School, Levittown, NY [*Library symbol*] [*Library of Congress*] (LCLS)
NLevLE...... Lee Road Elementary School, Levittown, NY [*Library symbol*] [*Library of Congress*] (LCLS)
NLevMH..... General Douglas McArthur High School, Levittown, NY [*Library symbol*] [*Library of Congress*] (LCLS)
NLevMSE... Michael F. Stokes Elementary School, Levittown, NY [*Library symbol*] [*Library of Congress*] (LCLS)
NLevNE..... Northside Elementary School, Levittown, NY [*Library symbol*] [*Library of Congress*] (LCLS)
NLevSJ...... Jonas E. Salk Junior High School, Levittown, NY [*Library symbol*] [*Library of Congress*] (LCLS)
NLevSLE.... Summit Lane Elementary School, Levittown, NY [*Library symbol*] [*Library of Congress*] (LCLS)
NLevSNE.... Seaman Neck Elementary School, Levittown, NY [*Library symbol*] [*Library of Congress*] (LCLS)
NLevWM.... Wisdom Middle School, Levittown, NY [*Library symbol*] [*Library of Congress*] (LCLS)
NLew........ Lewiston Public Library, Lewiston, NY [*Library symbol*] [*Library of Congress*] (LCLS)
NLewStM... Mount Saint Mary's Hospital, Lewiston, NY [*Library symbol*] [*Library of Congress*] (LCLS)
NLf........... Little Falls Public Library, Little Falls, NY [*Library symbol*] [*Library of Congress*] (LCLS)
NLF.......... Nasolabial Fold [*Medicine*] (DAVI)
NLF.......... National Fuelcorp Ltd. [*Vancouver Stock Exchange symbol*]
NLF.......... National Laser Facility
NLF.......... National League of Families of Prisoners and Missing in Southeast Asia
NLF.......... National Legal Foundation (EA)
NLF.......... National Liberal Federation [*British*]
NLF.......... National Liberation Front [*South Africa*] [*Political party*] (PD)
NLF.......... National Liberation Front [*Myanmar*] [*Political party*] (PD)
NLF.......... National Liberation Front [*Aden*] [*Political party*]
NLF.......... National Liberation Front [*Vietnam*] [*Political party*]
NLF.......... Navigation Light Flasher
nlf........... Nearest Landing Field (ODA)
NLF.......... Nearest Landing Field
NLF.......... Neonatal Lung Fibroblast [*Medicine*] (DMAA)
NLF.......... Neutral Lipid Fraction [*Biochemistry*]
NLF.......... New Leadership Fund (EA)
NLF.......... No-Load Field (SAUS)
NLF.......... No-Load Funds
NLF.......... Nonlactose Fermenting [*Organism*] [*Medicine*] (DB)
NLF.......... Non-Linear Filter (SAUS)
NLF.......... North Luzon Force [*Army*] [*World War II*]
NLF.......... Westair Aviation, Inc. [*Canada*] [*ICAO designator*] (FAAC)
NLFA........ National Lamb Feeders Association (EA)
NLFA........ National Livestock Feeders Association [*Later, NCA*] (EA)
NLFED...... Naval Landing Force Equipment Depot
NLFM....... Noise-Level Frequency Monitor
NLFMA..... National Law Firm Marketing Association (EA)
NLFPA...... National Liberation Front Party Apparatus [*Algeria*]
NLFS........ Nucleus Landing Force Staff (DNAB)
NLFSV...... National Liberation Front of South Vietnam [*Political party*]
NLFT........ No-Load Frame Time
NLFX........ National Lead [*Private rail car owner code*]
NLG.......... National Gas & Oil Corp. [*AMEX symbol*] (SPSG)
NLG.......... National Lawyers Guild (EA)
NLG.......... Natl Gas & Oil [*AMEX symbol*] (TTSB)
NLG.......... Nelson Lagoon [*Alaska*] [*Airport symbol*] (OAG)
NLG.......... No-Load Governed [*Equipment design*]
NLG.......... North Louisiana & Gulf Railroad Co. [*AAR code*]
NLG.......... Nose Landing Gear [*Aviation*]
NLG.......... Null Line Gap
NLG.......... Numismatic Literary Guild (EA)
NLGA........ National Lumber Grading Agency [*Canada*]
NLGAWVA... National Legion of Greek-American War Veterans in America (EA)
NLGC........ Nauru Local Government Council [*Australia*]
NLGC........ Noise-Level Gain Control (MCD)
NLGDA...... National Lawn and Garden Distributors Association (EA)
NLGHA...... National Lesbian and Gay Health Association (EA)
NLGHF...... National Lesbian and Gay Health Foundation (EA)
NLGI......... National Lubricating Grease Institute (EA)
NLGLA...... National Lesbian and Gay Lawyers Association (NTPA)
NLGLP...... National Laboratory Gene Library Project (HGEN)
NLGPDC..... National Lawyer's Guild Peace and Disarmament Committee [*Later, NLGPDS*] (EA)
NLGPDS..... National Lawyer's Guild Peace and Disarmament Society (EA)

NLGPDS ..... National Lawyer's Guild Peace and Disarmament Subcommittee (EA)
NLGQ .... National Lawyers Guild Quarterly [*A publication*] (DLA)
NLGU .... Transoceanique Suisse [*Intermodal shipping container symbol*] (TVRC)
NLH .... Natural Language Habits [*Medicine*] (EDAA)
NLH .... New Lao Hak [*Lao Patriotic Front*] [*Vietnam*] [*Political party*]
NLH .... New Life Hamlet [*See also NLHS, NLHZ*] [*Vietnam*] [*Military*]
NLH .... New Literary History: A Journal of Theory and Interpretation [*A publication*] (ANEX)
NLH .... Non-Locating Head [*Engineering*] (OA)
NLHA .... National Leased Housing Association [*Washington, DC*] (EA)
NLHO .... National Latina Health Organization (EAIO)
NLHP .... National Literacy and Health Program (SAUS)
NLHRSA ..... National Left-Handers Racquet Sports Association (EA)
NLHS .... New Lao Hak Sat [*New Life Hamlet*] [*See also NLH*] [*Vietnam*] [*Military*]
NLHZ .... New Lao Hak Zat [*New Life Hamlet*] [*See also NLH, NLHS*] [*Vietnam*] [*Military*]
NLI .... National Landscape Institute
NLI .... National Language Interface (NITA)
NLI .... National Leadership Institute [*Defunct*] (EA)
NLI .... National Library of Ireland (AIE)
NLI .... National Limestone Institute [*Later, NSA*] (EA)
NLI .... Natural Language Interface [*Linguistics*] (IEL)
NLI .... Neodymium LASER Illuminator
NLI .... New Learning Initiative (AIE)
NLI .... Newmark & Lewis Co. [*AMEX symbol*] (COMM)
NLI .... Nippon Life Insurance Company (EFIS)
NLI .... NL Industries [*Federal Railroad Administration identification code*]
NLI .... Noise Limit Indicator
NLI .... Nonlinear Interpolating (IEEE)
NLI .... Non-Linear Interpolator (SAUS)
NLI .... Northern Lights College Library [*UTLAS symbol*]
NLI .... Not Logged In (SAUS)
NLI .... NovaNET Learning
NLI .... NTL, Inc. [*NYSE symbol*]
NLI .... Nursing Literature Index (SAUS)
NLIA .... National Languages Institute of Australia
NLib .... Liberty Public Library, Liberty, NY [*Library symbol*] [*Library of Congress*] (LCLS)
NLIBE .... North Liberty, IN [*American Association of Railroads railroad junction routing code*]
NLIC .... National Landslide Information Center [*US Geological Survey*]
NLIC .... National Lead Information Center (AEPA)
NLicL .... LaGuardia Community College of the City University of New York, Long Island Cit y, NY [*Library symbol*] [*Library of Congress*] (LCLS)
NLicP .... PepsiCo, Inc., Research Library, Long Island, NY [*Library symbol*] [*Library of Congress*] (LCLS)
NLIEC .... Not Like I Even Care [*Internet lingo*] (NETL)
NLIF .... Nonlinear Interference Filter [*Electronics*]
NLIHC .... National Low Income Housing Coalition (EA)
NLIMT .... Newfoundland and Labrador Institute of Marine Technology (SAUS)
NLin .... Lindenhurst Memorial Library, Lindenhurst, NY [*Library symbol*] [*Library of Congress*] (LCLS)
NLIN .... NOAA [*National Oceanic and Atmospheric Administration*] Library and Information Network [*Marine science*] (OSRA)
NLin .... Nonlinear
NL Ind .... NL Industries, Inc. [*Formerly, National Lead Co.*] [*Associated Press*] (SAG)
N-lines ...... Regions in Striated Muscle Sarcomere [*Cell biology*] (QSUL)
NLinHS ...... Lindenhurst High School, Lindenhurst, NY [*Library symbol*] [*Library of Congress*] (LCLS)
NLinJS ...... Lindenhurst Junior High School, Lindenhurst, NY [*Library symbol*] [*Library of Congress*] (LCLS)
NLIRO .... North Little Rock, AR [*American Association of Railroads railroad junction routing code*]
NLIS .... National Lesbian Information Service
NLIS .... Navy Logistics Information System
NLISA .... National League of Insured Savings Associations [*Later, NSLL*] (EA)
NLIZ .... National Limestone [*Federal Railroad Administration identification code*]
NLJ .... Nagpur Law Journal [*India*] [*A publication*] (DLA)
NLJ .... New Law Journal [*A publication*] (ILCA)
NLK .... Neuroleukin [*Biochemistry*]
NLK .... Norfolk Island [*Airport symbol*] (OAG)
NLK .... Norlink Air Ltd. [*British*] [*ICAO designator*] (FAAC)
NLKF .... Nonlinear Kalman Filter
NLL .... National Aeronautical Research Institute [*Netherlands*] (SAA)
NLL .... National Lacrosse League [*Disbanded*]
NLL .... National Lending Library for Science and Technology [*Later, BLLD*] [*British Library*]
NLL .... National Liberal League [*Later, NLSCS*] (EA)
NLL .... Negative Logic Level
NLL .... New England School of Law Library, Boston, MA [*OCLC symbol*] (OCLC)
NLL .... New Library of Law [*Harrisburg, PA*] [*A publication*] (DLA)
NLL .... New Library of Law and Equity [*England*] [*A publication*] (DLA)
NLL .... New Life League (EA)
NLL .... New London [*Connecticut*] Laboratory [*Navy*] (DNAB)
NLL .... Night Low Level (SAUS)
NLL .... Normal Liquid Level [*Engineering*]
NLL .... Northern Limit Line [*Korea*]
NLL .... Nullagine [*Australia*] [*Airport symbol*] (OAG)
NLLAP .... National Lead Laboratory Accreditation Program
NLLC .... National Labor Law Center (EA)
NLLC .... National Languages and Literacy Council [*Australia*]
NLLS .... Nonlinear Least Square [*Mathematics*]
NLLSQ .... Nonlinear Least Squares [*Computer program*]
NLLST .... National Lending Library for Science and Technology [*Later, BLL*] [*British*]
NL LT .... Net Laying Light (SAA)
NLLTF .... Night Low-Level Terrain-Following (SAUS)
NLLU .... Nippon Liner Systems [*Common carrier symbol*]
NLLX .... Northern Line Layers [*Private rail car owner code*]
NLM .... National Labor Movement (Saint Lucia) [*Political party*] (PSAP)
NLM .... National Language Mediator
NLM .... National Library of Medicine [*Public Health Service*] [*Bethesda, MD*] [*Database producer*]
NLM .... National Library of Medicine, Bethesda, MD [*OCLC symbol*] (OCLC)
NLM .... Natural Language Mode [*Computer science*]
NLM .... Naval Ordnance Lab [*Maryland*] [*Seismograph station code, US Geological Survey*] [*Closed*] (SEIS)
NLM .... Nederlands Luchtvaart Maatschappij [*Airline*] [*Netherlands*]
NLM .... NetWare Loadable Module [*Computer science*] (DDC)
NLM .... Network Loadable Module (GAVI)
NLM .... New Library of Music [*A publication*]
NLM .... Noise Level Monitor (DMAA)
NLM .... Nonlinear Mapping (MCD)
NLM .... Nuclear Level Mixing [*Physics*]
NLM .... U.S. National Library of Medicine [*National Network of Libraries of Medicine*] (IID)
NLMA .... National Lumber Manufacturers Association [*Later, NFPA*] (EA)
NLMA .... Northeastern Lumber Manufacturers Association
NLMBX ...... Neub. & Berman Ltd. Maturity Bond Fund [*Mutual fund ticker symbol*] (SG)
NLMC .... National Latino Media Coalition [*Citizen's group*] (NTCM)
NLMC .... National League of Masonic Clubs (EA)
NLMC .... Nocturnal Leg Muscle Cramp [*Medicine*] (MELL)
NLMC .... Nordic Labor Market Committee (SAUS)
NLMC .... Nordic Labour Market Committee (EAIO)
NLMC .... North Lilly Mining Co. [*NASDAQ symbol*] (NQ)
NLMC .... North Lily Mining [*NASDAQ symbol*] (TTSB)
NLME .... Non-Linear Material Effect (PDAA)
NLMF .... National Labor-Management Foundation (EA)
NLMF .... Nonlinear Magnetic Field (SAUS)
NLMF .... Nucleus of Longitudinal Muscle Fiber
NLMFA ...... No-Load Mutual Fund Association (EA)
NLMI .... Newfoundland and Labrador Marine Institute (SAUS)
NLMIAF ..... National League of Missing in Action Families [*Medicine*] (EDAA)
NLMS .... Navigational Lane Marking System [*Navy*] (DOMA)
NLMS .... Navy Logistics Management School
NLMS .... Numerical Largeness of More Significant [*Statistics*]
NLM Server ... NetWare Loadable Module Server [*Computer science*] (HODG)
NLMWT ..... National Liberation Movement of Western Togoland
NLN .... National League for Nursing (EA)
NLN .... National Library Network
NLN .... National Lymphedema Network (SAUS)
NLN .... Navy Learning Network
NLN .... New Line Cinema (EFIS)
NLN .... New Lintex Minerals [*Vancouver Stock Exchange symbol*]
NLN .... No Longer Needed (AABC)
NLN .... Nordiska Lakemedelsnamnden [*Nordic Council on Medicines - NCM*] (EAIO)
NLN .... Northwest Missouri Library Network [*Library network*]
NLNA .... National Landscape Nurserymen's Association [*Later, NLA*] (EA)
NLNE .... National League for Nursing Education (DAVI)
NLnet .... [*The*] Newfoundland and Labrador Network [*Canada*] [*Computer science*] (TNIG)
NLNGNE ..... National League of Nursing Graduate Nursing Examination (GAGS)
NLNP .... National Library Network Program (AEPA)
NLNR .... Nonlinear (MSA)
NLNS .... New Lightweight Night Sight (INF)
NLO .... Nasolacrimal Occlusion [*Medicine*]
NLO .... Naval Liaison Officer
NLO .... No-Limit Order
NLO .... Non-Linear Operator (CCCA)
NLO .... Nonlinear Optics (IEEE)
NLO .... Non-Linear Optimizer (SAUS)
NLO .... Nonlocalized Orbital (SAUS)
NLob .... Long Beach Public Library, Long Beach, NY [*Library symbol*] [*Library of Congress*] (LCLS)
NLobBK ..... Blackhealth Kindergarten School, Long Beach, NY [*Library symbol*] [*Library of Congress*] (LCLS)
NLobES ..... East School, Long Beach, NY [*Library symbol*] [*Library of Congress*] (LCLS)
NLobH ...... Long Beach Memorial Hospital, Long Beach, NY [*Library symbol*] [*Library of Congress*] (LCLS)
NLobJH ..... Long Beach Junior High School, Long Beach, NY [*Library symbol*] [*Library of Congress*] (LCLS)
NLobLE ...... Lido Elementary School, Long Beach, NY [*Library symbol*] [*Library of Congress*] (LCLS)
NLobLS ..... Lindell Boulevard School, Long Beach, NY [*Library symbol*] [*Library of Congress*] (LCLS)
NLobM ...... Long Beach Middle School, Long Beach, NY [*Library symbol*] [*Library of Congress*] (LCLS)
NLobMS ..... Magnolia School, Long Beach, NY [*Library symbol*] [*Library of Congress*] (LCLS)
NLobSH ..... Long Beach Senior High School, Long Beach, NY [*Library symbol*] [*Library of Congress*] (LCLS)

NLobWE..... West Elementary School, Long Beach, NY [*Library symbol*] [*Library of Congress*] (LCLS)
NLock........ Lockport Public Library, Lockport, NY [*Library symbol*] [*Library of Congress*] (LCLS)
NLockH...... Lockport Memorial Hospital, Doctor's Library, Lockport, NY [*Library symbol*] [*Library of Congress*] (LCLS)
NLockMt.... Mount View Health Facility, Lockport, NY [*Library symbol*] [*Library of Congress*] (LCLS)
NLockNHi... Niagara County Historical Society, Lockport, NY [*Library symbol*] [*Library of Congress*] (LCLS)
NLOGM...... Navy Liaison Office for Guided Missiles (MCD)
NLOMA...... National Lutheran Outdoors Ministry Association (EA)
NLOMTF.... Non-Linear Optical Monomer Thin Films (SAUS)
NLON........ New London, Inc. (SAUS)
NLOND...... New London, CT [*American Association of Railroads railroad junction routing code*]
NLONTEVDET... New London Test and Evaluation Detachment [*Navy*]
NLOOC...... Non-Linear Optical Organic Crystals (SAUS)
NLOP........ Nonlinear Optical Polymer
NLOrLanyard... Netherlands Orange Lanyard [*Military decoration*]
NLOS........ Natural Language Operating System
NLOS........ Nonline of Sight
NLOS-AT/AD... Nonline-of-Sight Antitank/Air Defense Vehicle [*Army*]
NLOS-CA... Non-Line-of-Sight-Combined Arms System (INF)
NLOS/IOE... Nonline-of-Sight / Internal Operator Equipment (DWSG)
NLOS-R..... Non-Line-of-Sight-Rear [*Army*] (DOMA)
NLouvGS.... Church of Jesus Christ of Latter-Day Saints, Genealogical Society Library, Albany New York Stake Branch, Loudonville, NY [*Library symbol*] [*Library of Congress*] (LCLS)
NLouvS...... Siena College, Loudonville, NY [*Library symbol*] [*Library of Congress*] (LCLS)
NLowLH..... Lewis County General Hospital, Medical Library, Lowville, NY [*Library symbol*] [*Library of Congress*] (LCLS)
NLp.......... Lake Placid Public Library, Lake Placid, NY [*Library symbol*] [*Library of Congress*] (LCLS)
NLP.......... Narodnoliberalna Partiia [*National Liberal Party*] [*Bulgaria*] [*Political party*] (PPE)
NLP.......... National Labour Party [*Sierra Leone*] [*Political party*] (EY)
NLP.......... National Land for People [*An association*] (EA)
NLP.......... National League of Postmasters of the United States
NLP.......... National Liberal Party [*Bermuda*] [*Political party*] (EY)
NLP.......... National Liberation Party [*Gambia*] [*Political party*] (PPW)
NLP.......... National Realty Ltd. [*AMEX symbol*] (SPSG)
NLP.......... Natl Realty L.P. [*AMEX symbol*] (TTSB)
NLP.......... Natural Language Parsing (IDAI)
NLP.......... Natural Language Processing [*Computer science*]
NLP.......... Natural Law Party [*Australia*] [*Political party*]
NLP.......... Neglected Language Program
NLP.......... Neighborhood Loan Program
NLP.......... Nelspruit [*South Africa*] [*Airport symbol*] (OAG)
NLP.......... Net Level Premium [*Insurance*]
nlp.......... Neuro-Linguistic Programmers (SAUS)
NLP.......... Neurolinguistic Programming
NLP.......... New Left Party [*Political party*] [*Australia*]
NLP.......... Nodular Liquifying Panniculitis [*Dermatology*] (DAVI)
NLP.......... No Light Perception [*Ophthalmology*]
NLP.......... Non-Linear Programming [*Computer science*] (VLIE)
NLP.......... Normal Light Perception [*Physiology*] (MAH)
NLP.......... Normal Link Pulse (SAUS)
NLPC........ National Legal and Policy Center (RCD)
NLPC........ n-Laurylpyridinium Chloride [*Detergent*]
NLPCA....... Nonlinear Principal Components Analysis (IDAI)
NLPGA...... National LP-Gas Association (EA)
NLPI......... National Lampoon, Inc. [*NASDAQ symbol*] (COMM)
NLPID....... Network Layer Protocol Identifier [*Computer science*] (VLIE)
NLPM........ National League of Postmasters of the United States (EA)
NLPM........ Newspaper Lines per Minute (DGA)
NLPNEF..... National Licensed Practical Nurses Educational Foundation [*Defunct*] (EA)
NLPOA...... National Latino Peace Officers Association (EA)
NLPQ........ Natural Language Processing System for Queuing Problems [*Computer science*] (PDAA)
NLPR........ National Laboratory of Psychical Research [*British*]
NLPS........ Natural Language Processing Segment [*Computer science*]
NLpSA....... Lake Placid School of Art, Fine Arts Library, Lake Placid, NY [*Library symbol*] [*Library of Congress*] (LCLS)
NLpT......... Tissue Culture Association, Lake Placid, NY [*Library symbol*] [*Library of Congress*] (LCLS)
NLPTL....... National Lutheran Parent-Teacher League (EA)
NLQ.......... Natural Language Query [*Software*] [*Battelle Software Products Center*]
NLQ.......... Near Letter Quality [*Computer printer*]
NLQ.......... Nigeria Lawyer's Quarterly [*A publication*] (DLA)
NLQ.......... Nonlinear Quantization [*Telecommunications*] (NTCM)
NLQ.......... Not Letter Quality (NITA)
NLQP........ Natural Language Query Processor (ACAE)
NLQR........ Nigeria Law Quarterly Review [*A publication*] (DLA)
NLR.......... Nagpur Law Reports [*India*] [*A publication*] (DLA)
NLR.......... Natal Law Reports [*India*] [*A publication*] (DLA)
NLR.......... National Liquid Reserves Money Market Fund
NLR.......... National Research Laboratory [*Netherlands*] (GAVI)
NLR.......... NATO Liaison Representative (MCD)
NLR.......... Nearest Living Relative (SAUS)
NLR.......... Neodymium LASER Range-Finder
NLR.......... Net Liquidity Ratio (PDAA)
NLR.......... Newfoundland Law Reports [*A publication*] (DLA)
NLR.......... New Law Reports [*Ceylon*] [*A publication*] (DLA)
N-LR......... New York State Library, Legislative Reference Library, Albany, NY [*Library symbol*] [*Library of Congress*] (LCLS)
NLR.......... Ngarla [*Language symbol*] (ETLW)
NLR.......... Nigeria Law Reports [*A publication*] (DLA)
NLR.......... Noise Load Ratio
NLR.......... Nolan Resources Ltd. [*Vancouver Stock Exchange symbol*]
NLR.......... No Load Ratio (VLIE)
NLR.......... No-Load Ratio (SAUS)
NLR.......... Non-Linear Refraction
NLR.......... Nonlinear Regression [*Mathematics*]
NLR.......... Nonlinear Resistance (IDOE)
NLR.......... Nonlinear Resistive
NLR.......... Nonlinear Resistor [*Electronics*] (ECII)
NLR.......... Northern Central Railway [*Federal Railroad Administration identification code*]
NLR.......... North London Railway [*British*]
NLR.......... Nyasaland Law Reports [*A publication*] (DLA)
NLR.......... South African Law Reports, Natal Province Division [*1910-46*] [*A publication*] (DLA)
NLRA........ National Labor Relations Act [*1935*]
NLRA........ National Lakes and Rivers Association [*Defunct*] (EA)
NLRA........ Northern Late Model Racing Association (EA)
NLRB........ National Labor Relations Board [*Department of Labor*] [*Washington, DC*]
NLRB........ National Labor Relations Board Decisions and Orders [*A publication*] (DLA)
NLRB Ann Rep... National Labor Relations Board Annual Report [*A publication*] (DLA)
NLRB Dec.. National Labor Relations Board Decisions [*A publication*] (DLA)
NLRBP...... National Labor Relations Board Professional Association
NLRBPA..... National Labor Relations Board Professional Association (EA)
NLRBU...... National Labor Relations Board Union (EA)
NLRCA...... National Lilac Rabbit Club of America (EA)
NLRCCAP... National Legal Resource Center for Child Advocacy and Protection [*Later, ABACCL*] (EA)
NLREG...... Non-Linear Regression (SAUS)
Nl Res Men Health&Behav Sc... Newsletter for Research in Mental Health and Behavioral Sciences (SAUS)
NL Rev...... Northeastern Law Review [*A publication*] (DLA)
NLRG........ Narrow-Line Radio Galaxy
NLRG........ Navy Long-Range Guidance
NLRI......... Network Layer Reachability Information [*Computer science*] (VLIE)
NLRO........ North Liberty Radio Observatory (SAUS)
NLROG...... Navy Long-Range Objectives Group (DNAB)
NLR (OS)... Natal Law Reports, Old Series [*1867-72*] [*South Africa*] [*A publication*] (DLA)
NLRSS...... Navy Long-Range Strategic Study
NLRU........ Nordens Liberale og Radikale Ungdom [*Nordic Liberal and Radical Youth*] (EAIO)
NLRX........ New London Railroad & Village [*Federal Railroad Administration identification code*]
NLS.......... Holland Schreiner International Air Training (SAUS)
NLS.......... Nassau Library System [*Library network*]
NLS.......... National Language Support [*Computer science*] (PCM)
NLS.......... National Launch System (ECON)
NLS.......... National Library of Scotland (NITA)
NLS.......... National Library Service for the Blind and Physically Handicapped [*Also, NLS /BPH*] [*Library of Congress*]
NLS.......... National Longitudinal Survey [*Statistics*]
NLS.......... National Longitudinal Surveys of Labor Market Experience [*Ohio State University*] [*Columbus*] [*Information service or system*] (IID)
NLS.......... Native Language System (VLIE)
NLS.......... Natural-Language Search [*Computer science*] (GART)
NLS.......... Natural-Language System (GART)
NLS.......... Natural Law Society (EA)
NLS.......... Navigating Light System
NLS.......... Navigation Light Satellite
NLS.......... Negative Lens Systems
NLS.......... Neodymium LASER System
NLS.......... NetWare Link State Protocol (DCOM)
NLS.......... Network Library System
NLS.......... Network License System [*Computer science*] (CIST)
NLS.......... New Launch System (SAUS)
NLS.......... New Least Square (PDAA)
NLS.......... New Least Squares (SAUS)
NLs.......... New Leftists (SAUS)
NLS.......... Niles, MI [*Amtrak rail station code*]
NLS.......... Node Logic Shelf (VLIE)
NLS.......... Noise Line State (SAUS)
NLS.......... No-Load Speed
NLS.......... No-Load Start
NLS.......... Non-Linear Least Squares [*Statistics*]
NLS.......... Nonlinear Smoothing
NLS.......... Non-Linear Systems (SAUS)
NLS.......... Nordic Language Secretariat [*See also SLN*] [*Norway*] (EAIO)
NLS.......... Nordiske Laererorganisationers Samrad [*Council of Nordic Teachers' Association*] [*Sweden*] (EAIO)
NLS.......... Normal Lymphocyte Supernatant (DB)
NLS.......... North Carolina Central University, School of Library Science, Durham, NC [*OCLC symbol*] (OCLC)
NLS.......... Nuclear Localization Signal [*Biochemistry*]
NLS.......... Nuclear Location Sequence [*Cytology*]
NLS.......... On-Line System [*Stanford Research Institute*] [*Computer science*]

NLSA .... National Liquor Stores Association (EA)
NLSA .... National Lithuanian Society of America (EA)
NLSA .... National Locksmith Suppliers Association (EA)
NLSBA....... National Lincoln Sheep Breeders' Association (EA)
NLS/BPH.... National Library Service for the Blind and Physically Handicapped [*Also, NLS*] [*Library of Congress*] [*Computer science*] (IID)
NLSC .... National Language Services Center (VLIE)
NLSC .... National Logistics Supply Center [*Marine science*] (OSRA)
NLSC .... Navy Lockheed Service Center
NLSC .... Non-Locking Shift Character [*Computer science*] (VLIE)
NLSC .... Northeastern Louisiana State College
NLSCS....... National League for Separation of Church and State (EA)
NLSDAP..... Non-Linear System Data Presentation [*Computer science*] (VLIE)
NLSF .... National Life Share Foundation (EA)
NLSF .... Navy Logistics Support Force (DOMA)
NLsH .... Frederic R. Harris, Inc., Lake Success, NY [*Library symbol*] [*Library of Congress*] (LCLS)
NLSI .... National Library of Science and Invention [*British*] (DIT)
NLSI .... Nationwide Legal Services, Inc. [*NASDAQ symbol*] (COMM)
NLS Inc ..... Non-Linear Systems, Inc. (SAUS)
NLSL .... North Land Savings & Loan Association (SAUS)
NLSLS....... National Library of Scotland Lending Services (NITA)
NLsM........ Medical Society of the State of New York, Lake Success, NY [*Library symbol*] [*Library of Congress*] (LCLS)
NLSMA...... National Lamp and Shade Manufacturers' Association (IAA)
NLSMA...... National Longitudinal Study of Mathematical Abilities
NLSMB...... National Live Stock and Meat Board (EA)
NLSO .... Naval Legal Service Office (ACAE)
NLSP .... Neighborhood Legal Services Program
NLSP .... NetWare Link Services Protocol [*Novell, Inc.*] (PCM)
NLSP .... Network Layer Security Protocol [*Computer science*] (GART)
NLSPA....... National Live Stock Producers Association (EA)
NLSPN ...... National List of Scientific Plant Names [*Department of Agriculture*] (IID)
NLSS .... Navy Logistics Systems School
NLSS .... New London Submarine School [*Navy*] (MCD)
NLSSA....... National Litigation Support Services Association (NTPA)
NLSST....... Nonlinear Sea Surface Temperature (USDC)
NLSSTUF ... Non-Linear System Statistical Utility Feature (SAUS)
NLST .... National Lung Screening Trial
NLST .... Nonlisted Name [*Telecommunications*] (TEL)
NLSU .... National League for Social Understanding (EA)
NLSU .... Nautilus Leasing Services [*Intermodal shipping container symbol*] (TVRC)
NLSX .... National Starch and Chemical [*Private rail car owner code*]
NLSY .... National Longitudinal Study of Youth
NLSY .... National Longitudinal Survey of Youth
NLSZ .... Trans Ocean Chassis [*Intermodal trailer symbol*]
NLT .... National Life & Accident Insurance Co. (EFIS)
NLT .... Negative Line Transmission [*Noise limiter*] (IAA)
NLT .... Net Long Ton
NLT .... Newfoundland Labrador Air Transport Ltd. [*Canada*] [*ICAO designator*] (FAAC)
NLT .... New Logic Technology (SAUS)
NLT .... New London Training Unit [*Navy*]
NLT .... Night Letter [*Telegraphic communications*]
NLT .... Noise Limiter (IAA)
NLT .... No Later Than (SAUS)
NLT .... No Left Turn (SAUS)
NLT .... Non Light-Tight (SAUS)
NLT .... Non-Linear Time Sequence (ABAC)
NLT .... Normal Lube-Oil Tank (MSA)
NLT .... Normal Lymphocyte Transfer [*Immunochemistry*]
NLT .... Not Later Than
NLT .... Not Less Than
NLT .... Not Losing Time [*Indian Railway*] (TIR)
NLT .... Not Lower Than (SAUS)
NLT .... Nucleus Lateralis Tuberis (DMAA)
NLT .... Nucleus Load Table (SAUS)
NLTA......... National Lawn Tennis Association (WDAA)
NLTA......... National League of Teachers' Associations [*Defunct*] (EA)
NLTC......... National Livestock Tax Committee [*Later, NCA*] (EA)
NLTCDP ..... National Long-Term Care Channeling Demonstration Program [*Department of Health and Human Services*] (GFGA)
NLTE......... Nonlocal Thermodynamic Equilibrium
NLTF......... National Leather Trades Federation [*A union*] [*British*]
NLT-HP ...... New Logic Technology-High Performance (SAUS)
NLTI.......... Non-Linear Time-Invariant (SAUS)
NLTNIF ...... National Low-Temperature Neutron Irradiation Facility [*Oak Ridge, TN*] [*Department of Energy*] (GRD)
NLTRA....... National Land Title Reclamation Association (EA)
NLT Reaction... Normal Lymphocyte Transfer Reaction (SAUS)
NLTS......... Near Launch Tracking System
NLT-S........ New Logic Technology-Slow (SAUS)
NLTU......... New London Training Unit (SAUS)
NLTV......... Non-Linear Time-Varying (SAUS)
NLU.......... Natural-Language Understanding (GART)
NLU.......... Naval Field Liaison Unit (DNAB)
NLU.......... Normal Latch Up (COE)
NLUC .... National Land Use Classification (PDAA)
NLUF .... National LASER Users Facility [*Rochester, NY*] [*Department of Energy*] (GRD)
NLUPP ...... Northern Land Use Planning Program (SAUS)
NLUS .... Navy League of the United States (EA)
NLUTS....... National Labourers' Union Trade Society [*British*]
NLv .... Locust Valley Public Library, Locust Valley, NY [*Library symbol*] [*Library of Congress*] (LCLS)
NLV .... Narcissus Latent Virus
NLVA......... National Licensed Victualers Association [*British*] (DBA)
NLvBI........ Bayville Intermediate School, Locust Valley, NY [*Library symbol*] [*Library of Congress*] (LCLS)
NLVF......... North Las Vegas Facility (SAUS)
NLVF......... Norway Agricultural Research Council (SAUS)
NLvHS........ Locust Valley High School, Locust Valley, NY [*Library symbol*] [*Library of Congress*] (LCLS)
NLvI .... Locust Valley Intermediate School, Locust Valley, NY [*Library symbol*] [*Library of Congress*] (LCLS)
NLvMP ...... A.M. MacArthur Primary School, Locust Valley, NY [*Library symbol*] [*Library of Congress*] (LCLS)
NLVP......... NASA Launch Vehicle Planning Project (MCD)
NLVR .... Nonlinear Vacuum Regulator Valve [*Automotive engineering*]
NLW .... National Lawyers Wives (EA)
NLW .... National Library of Wales (WDAA)
NLW .... National Library Week
NLW .... New London, WI [*Amtrak Busline code*]
NLW .... Nominal Line Width
NLW .... Nonlinear Wave (SAUS)
NLWF........ Futuna/Pointe Vele [*Wallis and Futuna Islands*] [*ICAO location identifier*] (ICLI)
NLWM....... Non-Linear Wave Mixing (SAUS)
NLWRA...... National Land and Water Resources Audit (SAUS)
NLWRAAC... National Land and Water Resources Audit Advisory Committee (SAUS)
NLWW....... Wallis/Hififo [*Wallis and Futuna Islands*] [*ICAO location identifier*] (ICLI)
NLX.......... NLX Resources, Inc. [*Toronto Stock Exchange symbol*]
NLXI .... Nelx [*OTCBB symbol*]
NLXI .... Northland Express [*Common carrier symbol*]
NLXU .... Norton Line [*Common carrier symbol*]
NLY .... Annaly Mortgage Management [*NYSE symbol*]
NLY .... Annaly Mortgage Mgmt [*NYSE symbol*] (SG)
NLY .... Naturally [*Telegraphy*] (PCTE)
NLY .... Northerly
NLynAE...... Atlantic Avenue School, Lynbrook, NY [*Library symbol*] [*Library of Congress*] (LCLS)
NLynd .... Yates Community Library, Lyndonville, NY [*Library symbol*] [*Library of Congress*] (LCLS)
NLynDE...... Davidson Avenue Elementary School, Lynbrook, NY [*Library symbol*] [*Library of Congress*] (LCLS)
NLyndHi..... Lyndonville Historical Society, Lyndonville, NY [*Library symbol*] [*Library of Congress*] (LCLS)
NLynHS ..... Lynbrook High School, Lynbrook NY [*Library symbol*] [*Library of Congress*] (LCLS)
NLynME..... Marion Street Elementary School, Lynbrook, NY [*Library symbol*] [*Library of Congress*] (LCLS)
NLynNM..... North Middle School, Lynbrook, NY [*Library symbol*] [*Library of Congress*] (LCLS)
NLynSM..... Lynbrook South Middle School, Lynbrook, NY [*Library symbol*] [*Library of Congress*] (LCLS)
NLynWPE ... Waverly Park Elementary School, Lynbrook, NY [*Library symbol*] [*Library of Congress*] (LCLS)
NLZ.......... Naturalize [*Telegraphy*] (PCTE)
NLZN........ Naturalization [*Telegraphy*] (PCTE)
nm--- .... Gulf of Mexico [*MARC geographic area code*] [*Library of Congress*] (LCCP)
NM........... Mt. Cook Airlines [*ICAO designator*] (AD)
NM........... Nachmittag [*Afternoon*] [*German*]
NM........... Nanomemory (IAA)
NM........... Nano Meter (ACAE)
NM........... Nanometer (DIPS)
nm .... Nanometer [*One billionth of a meter*]
nM .... Nanomole [*One billionth of a mole*]
NM........... Narrow Market [*Investment term*]
NM........... Nationalist Movement (EA)
NM........... National Magazine Co. Ltd. [*Publisher*] [*British*]
NM........... National Match
NM........... National Media Corp. [*NYSE symbol*] (SPSG)
NM........... National Monument (GNE)
NM........... National Motor Volunteers [*British military*] (DMA)
NM........... National Mutual Holdings Limited (EFIS)
NM........... Nations Ministries (EA)
NM........... Natl Media Corp. [*NYSE symbol*] (TTSB)
NM........... Natriuretic Material [*Physiology*]
NM........... Naturally Occurring Mutants
NM........... Natural Morphology [*Linguistics*] (IEL)
nm .... Nautical Mile (MILB)
NM........... Nautical Mile [*6,080 feet*]
NM........... Naval Mission (AFIT)
NM........... Navigation Multiplexer [*Navy*] (CAAL)
NM........... Navy Mines (MCD)
NM........... Near Match (MCD)
nm .... Near-Metacentric [*Botany*]
NM........... Near Mint [*Condition*] [*Numismatics, deltiology, etc.*]
NM........... Negro Male
NM........... Neiman-Marcus
NM........... Neomycin [*Medicine*] (MELL)
NM........... Neonatal Meningitis [*Medicine*] (MELL)
NM........... Netherlands Museum [*Later, HHT*] (EA)
NM........... Net Imports [*Economics*]
NM........... Network Management (MLOA)
NM........... Network Manager (MCD)

NM.......... Neumarkt [*Oberpfalz*] [*German license plate city code*]
NM.......... Neuromotor [*Neurology*] (DAVI)
NM.......... Neuromuscular
NM.......... Nevermind (SAUS)
NM.......... Newly Molded
NM.......... New Majority (Peru) [*Political party*] (PSAP)
NM.......... New Material [*FAR clauses*] (AAGC)
NM.......... New Measurement
NM.......... New Mexico [*Postal code*]
Nm.......... New Mexico State Library, Santa Fe, NM [*Library symbol*] [*Library of Congress*] (LCLS)
NM.......... New Mexico Supreme Court Reports [*A publication*] (DLA)
NM.......... New Mexico Territorial Court (DLA)
NM.......... New Moon [*Moon phase*]
Nm.......... Newton-Meter (SAUS)
N/m.......... Newton per Meter (or Metre) (SAUS)
N-M.......... New York State Library, Medical Library, Albany, NY [*Library symbol*] [*Library of Congress*] (LCLS)
NM.......... Nickeloid Metals (SAUS)
Nm.......... Nicotiana mesophilia [*Tobacco*]
NM.......... Nictitating Membrane [*Animal anatomy*]
NM.......... Nigeria Museum (SAUS)
NM.......... Night and morning (DAVI)
NM.......... Night Message
NM.......... Nilsson Model (SAUS)
NM.......... Nitrogen Mustard [*Also, HN, M, MBA*] [*Antineoplastic drug, war-gas base*]
NM.......... Nitromethane [*Organic chemistry*]
NM.......... Noble Metal (SAUS)
NM.......... Nocte et Mane [*Night and Morning*] [*Pharmacy*]
NM.......... Nocturnal Myoclonus [*Medicine*] (MELL)
NM.......... Nodular Melanoma [*Oncology*]
NM.......... Nodular Mixed Lymphoma [*Onocology*] (DAVI)
NM.......... Noise Margin (SAUS)
NM.......... Noise Meter (MSA)
N/m.......... No Mark (EBF)
NM.......... No Mark
NM.......... No Match (SAUS)
NM.......... No Measurement (SAUS)
NM.......... Nomenclature (SAUS)
NM.......... Nomen Masculinam [*Masculine Name*] [*Latin*] (ROG)
NM.......... No Message
NM.......... Nominate [*Telegraphy*] (PCTE)
NM.......... None Minted [*Numismatic term*]
NM.......... Nonmagnetic (IAA)
NM.......... Nonmalignant [*Medicine*] (MELL)
NM.......... Nonmember (SAUS)
NM.......... Nonmetal (SAUS)
NM.......... Nonmetallic
NM.......... Nonmetallic Sheathed [*Construction term*] (MIST)
NM.......... Nonmotile [*Microbiology*]
NM.......... Nonwhite Male
NM.......... Nordiska Metallarbetaresekretariatet [*Nordic Metalworkers Secretariat - NMS*] (EAIO)
NM.......... Normal Mode (SAUS)
NM.......... Normetadrenaline [*Biochemistry*] (DAVI)
NM.......... Northeastern Mortgage Co., Inc. (SAUS)
NM.......... Notice to Mariner
N/M.......... Not Marked [*Business term*]
NM.......... Not Married
NM.......... Not Meaningful
NM.......... Not Measurable [*or Measured*]
NM.......... Not Measured (SAUS)
NM.......... Not Mentioned (SAUS)
n/m.......... Not Mentioned [*Medicine*]
NM.......... Noun Modifier [*Linguistics*]
NM.......... Nuclear Magnetic
NM.......... Nuclear Magnetism (SAUS)
nm.......... Nuclear Magneton (ABAC)
NM.......... Nuclear Magnetron (MSA)
NM.......... Nuclear Materials (SAUS)
NM.......... Nuclear Measurement (IAA)
NM.......... Nuclear Medicine
NM.......... Nuclear Membrane (DB)
NM.......... Nuclear Model (SAUS)
NM.......... Null Matrix (SAUS)
NM.......... Numbering Machine (SAUS)
NM.......... Number Module (SAUS)
NM.......... Number of Matrices (SAUS)
Nm.......... Numbers [*Old Testament book*]
NM.......... Numerical Machining (SAUS)
NM.......... Numeric Move (SAUS)
NM.......... Nutmeg (ADA)
NM.......... Nutrient Medium (SAUS)
NM.......... Nux Moschata [*Nutmeg*] [*Pharmacology*] (ROG)
N/m^2.......... Newtons per Square Meter [*Pascals*] (IDOE)
NmA.......... Albuquerque Public Library, Albuquerque, NM [*Library symbol*] [*Library of Congress*] (LCLS)
NMA.......... Miami, FL [*Location identifier*] [*FAA*] (FAAL)
NMA.......... Minute Men of America (NADA)
NMA.......... Naphthalenemethylamine [*Reagent*] [*Organic chemistry*]
NMA.......... Nashville Music Association [*Later, NEA*] (EA)
NMA.......... National Malaria Association (DAVI)
NMA.......... National Management Association [*Dayton, OH*] (EA)
NMA.......... National Management Award [*GAMC*]
NMA.......... National Marina Association [*Defunct*] (EA)
NMA.......... National Maritime Alliance (NTPA)
NMA.......... National Maritime Authority [*Australia*]
NMA.......... National Meat Association [*Formerly, NIMPA*] (EA)
NMA.......... National Medical Association (EA)
NMA.......... National Microfilm Association [*Later, National Micrographics Association, now AIIM*] [*Trade association*]
NMA.......... National Microform Association (NITA)
NMA.......... National Micrographics Association [*Later, AIIM*] [*Trade association*] (EA)
NMA.......... National Midwives Association (EA)
NMA.......... National Military Authority (NATG)
NMA.......... National Mime Association [*Later, NMTA*] (EA)
NMA.......... National Mining Association (NTPA)
NMA.......... National Motorists Association (EA)
NMA.......... National Museum of Antiquities in Scotland
NMA.......... National Music Academy [*Australia*]
NMA.......... National Mustang Association (EA)
NMA.......... NATO Military Authorities (NATG)
NMA.......... Natural Marketing Association [*Woodland Hills, CA*] (EA)
NMA.......... Navy Mutual Aid Association (EA)
NMA.......... Needle Makers Association [*British*] (BI)
NMA.......... Negligee Manufacturers Association [*Later, IAMA*]
NMA.......... Netherlands Military Administration [*World War II*]
NMA.......... Network Management and Administration [*Communications term*] (DCT)
NMA.......... Network Management Architecture [*Communications term*] (DCT)
NMA.......... Neue Mozart-Ausgabe [*A publication*]
NMA.......... Neurogenic Muscular Atrophy [*Medicine*]
NMA.......... New Music Articles [*A publication*]
NMA.......... Nicaragua Medical Aid (EA)
NMA.......... N-Methylaspartate [*Organic chemistry*]
NMA.......... N-Methylaspartic Acid [*An amino acid*]
NMA.......... N-Methylolacrylamide [*Organic chemistry*]
NMA.......... Nobeyama Millimeter Array (SAUS)
NMA.......... Noma Industries Ltd. [*Toronto Stock Exchange symbol*]
NMA.......... Non-Marine Association [*Lloyd's Underwriters*] (AIA)
NMA.......... Nonmass Analysed (SAUS)
NMA.......... Nonmass Analyzed [*Photovoltaic energy systems*]
NMA.......... Nonmedical Attendant (AABC)
NMA.......... Nonprofit Management Association (EA)
NMA.......... Nonresonant Magnetic Amplifier
NMA.......... Normal Method of Acquisition (MCD)
NMA.......... Northwest Mining Association (EA)
NMA.......... Nuclear Materials Accountability (SAUS)
NMA.......... Nuveen Muni Advantage Fd [*NYSE symbol*] (TTSB)
NMA.......... Nuveen Municipal Advantage Fund [*NYSE symbol*] (SPSG)
NMA.......... University of Albuquerque, Albuquerque, NM [*OCLC symbol*] (OCLC)
NMa.......... Wead Library, Malone, NY [*Library symbol*] [*Library of Congress*] (LCLS)
NMAA.......... National Machine Accountants Association [*Later, DPMA*]
NMAA.......... National Metal Awning Association [*Defunct*] (EA)
NMAA.......... National Mobilization Against AIDS [*Acquired Immune Deficiency Syndrome*] (EA)
NMAA.......... National Multimedia Association of America (DDC)
NMAA.......... National Museum of African Art [*Smithsonian Institution*]
NMAA.......... National Museum of American Art [*Internet resource*] [*Web site*]
NMAA.......... Navy Mutual Aid Association
NMAA.......... Nursing Mothers' Association of Australia
NmAAc.......... Albuquerque Academy, Albuquerque, NM [*Library symbol*] [*Library of Congress*] (LCLS)
NmAACF.......... ACF Industries, Inc., Albuquerque, NM [*Library symbol*] [*Library of Congress*] (LCLS)
NmAAF.......... United States Air Force, Weapons Laboratory, Kirtland Air Force Base, Albuquerque, NM [*Library symbol*] [*Library of Congress*] (LCLS)
NmAAM.......... United States Army, Medical Library, Sandia Base, Albuquerque, NM [*Library symbol*] [*Library of Congress*] (LCLS)
NMAA Newsletter... Nursing Mothers Association of Australia. Newsletter (SAUS)
NMAB.......... National Market Advisory Board [*SEC*]
NMAB.......... National Materials Advisory Board (EA)
N-MAb.......... Neutralizing Monoclonal Antibody [*Immunology*]
NMAB.......... N-Monochloro(amino)butyric Acid [*Organic chemistry*]
NmABD.......... BDM Corp., Albuquerque, NM [*Library symbol*] [*Library of Congress*] (LCLS)
NMAC.......... National Medical Audiovisual Center [*of the National Library of Medicine*] [*LHNCBC*] [*Absorbed by*] (EA)
NMAC.......... National Minority AIDS [*Acquired Immune Deficiency Syndrome*] Council (EA)
NMAC.......... Naval Missile and Astronautics Center
NMAC.......... Near Midair Collision
NMAC.......... Nissan Motor Acceptance Corp.
NMAC.......... Nissan Motor Acceptance Corporation [*Automotive financing*]
NMAC.......... Nuclear Materials Accounting and Control
NMACS.......... Nuclear Materials Accounting Cost System (SAUS)
NMACT.......... Nuclear Materials Accounting Control Team [*British*] (NUCP)
NmADAS.......... United States Defense Atomic Support Agency, Sandia Base, Albuquerque, NM [*Library symbol*] [*Library of Congress*] (LCLS)
NmA-EP.......... Albuquerque Public Library, Ernie Pyle Memorial Branch, Albuquerque, NM [*Library symbol*] [*Library of Congress*] (LCLS)
NMAF.......... National Medical Association Foundation [*Defunct*] (EA)
NMAFA.......... National Museum of African Art [*Smithsonian Institution*] (GFGA)
NMAG.......... Nonmagnetic (MSA)
N Mag Ca... New Magistrates' Cases [*England*] [*A publication*] (DLA)

NmAGen .... New Mexico Genealogical Society, Inc., Albuquerque, NM [*Library symbol*] [*Library of Congress*] (LCLS)
NM Ag Exp... New Mexico. Agricultural Experiment Station. Publiations (SAUS)
NmAGS...... Church of Jesus Christ of Latter-Day Saints, Genealogical Society Library, Albuquerque Branch, Albuquerque, NM [*Library symbol*] [*Library of Congress*] (LCLS)
NMah........ Mahopac Library Association, Mahopac, NY [*Library symbol*] [*Library of Congress*] (LCLS)
NmAHS...... Honeywell Sperry Inc., Defense System Division, Albuquerque, NM [*Library symbol*] [*Library of Congress*] (LCLS)
NMAHSTC... National Museum of American History, Science, Technology, and Culture [*Smithsonian Institution*]
NMAI .... National Museum of the American Indian
NmAl .... Alamogordo Public Library, Alamogordo, NM [*Library symbol*] [*Library of Congress*] (LCLS)
NmAL........ Lovelace Foundation for Medical Education and Research, Albuquerque, NM [*Library symbol*] [*Library of Congress*] (LCLS)
NMAL........ Northeast Marine Animal Lifeline
NMALC...... National Mexican-American Leadership Council [*El Centro, CA*] (PACS)
NmA-LG..... Albuquerque Public Library, Los Griegos Branch, Albuquerque, NM [*Library symbol*] [*Library of Congress*] (LCLS)
NMalv .... Malverne Public Library, Malverne, NY [*Library symbol*] [*Library of Congress*] (LCLS)
NMalvDE.... Davison Elementary School, Malverne, NY [*Library symbol*] [*Library of Congress*] (LCLS)
NMalvHM... Howard T. Herber Middle School, Malverne, NY [*Library symbol*] [*Library of Congress*] (LCLS)
NMalvLE.... Lindner Elementary School, Malverne, NY [*Library symbol*] [*Library of Congress*] (LCLS)
NMalvSH.... Malverne Senior High School, Malverne, NY [*Library symbol*] [*Library of Congress*] (LCLS)
NMam....... Mamaroneck Free Library, Mamaroneck, NY [*Library symbol*] [*Library of Congress*] (LCLS)
NmAM....... Montessori School, Albuquerque, NM [*Library symbol*] [*Library of Congress*] (LCLS)
NMAM....... NIOSH Manual of Analytical Methods [*Database*] (GDD)
NMamL ..... Mamaroneck Free Library, Mamaroneck, NY [*Library symbol*] [*Library of Congress*] (LCLS)
NM & S..... Bureau of Medicine and Surgery Publications [*Navy*]
NM&SA ..... National Moving & Storage Association [*MTMC*] (TAG)
NManh ...... Manhasset Public Library, Manhasset, NY [*Library symbol*] [*Library of Congress*] (LCLS)
NManhH .... North Shore Hospital, Manhasset, NY [*Library symbol*] [*Library of Congress*] (LCLS)
NManhJH... Manhasset Junior High School, Manhasset, NY [*Library symbol*] [*Library of Congress*] (LCLS)
NManhJSH... Manhasset Junior-Senior High School, Manhasset, NY [*Library symbol*] [*Library of Congress*] (LCLS)
NManhM.... Manhasset Medical Center Hospital, Manhasset, NY [*Library symbol*] [*Library of Congress*] (LCLS)
NManhME... Munsey Park Elementary School, Manhasset, NY [*Library symbol*] [*Library of Congress*] (LCLS)
NManhSE... Shelter Rock Elementary School, Manhasset, NY [*Library symbol*] [*Library of Congress*] (LCLS)
NManhSH... Manhasset Senior High School, Manhasset, NY [*Library symbol*] [*Library of Congress*] (LCLS)
NManhSM... Saint Mary's Boys High School, Manhasset, NY [*Library symbol*] [*Library of Congress*] (LCLS)
NMANX...... Neub. & Berman Manhattan Fund [*Mutual fund ticker symbol*] (SG)
NMAP .... Navy Military Assistance Programs
NMAP .... Network Menuing Administration Pack [*Computer science*] (HODG)
NmA-PP..... Albuquerque Public Library, Prospect Park Branch, Albuquerque, NM [*Library symbol*] [*Library of Congress*] (LCLS)
NM App..... New Mexico Court of Appeals (DLA)
NMAQCR.... New Mexico Air Quality Control Region (SAUS)
NMAQD ..... New Mexico Air Quality District (SAUS)
NmAr........ Artesia Public Library, Artesia, NM [*Library symbol*] [*Library of Congress*] (LCLS)
NMar .... Marcellus Free Library, Marcellus, NY [*Library symbol*] [*Library of Congress*] (LCLS)
Nm-Ar....... New Mexico State Records Center and Archives, Santa Fe, NM [*Library symbol*] [*Library of Congress*] (LCLS)
NMARC...... Navy and Marine Corps Acquisition Review Committee [*Terminated, 1975*] (MCD)
NMarcP ..... Marcy Psychiatric Center, Marcy, NY [*Library symbol*] [*Library of Congress*] (LCLS)
NmArP ...... Artesia Public Library, Artesia, NM [*Library symbol*] [*Library of Congress*] (LCLS)
NMas........ Henry H. Warren Memorial Library, Massena (SAUS)
NMAS .... National Map Accuracy Standards (PDAA)
NMAS .... National Marine Advisory Service [*National Oceanic and Atmospheric Administration*] (MSC)
NMAS .... Norwegian Metrology and Accreditation Service (SAUS)
NmAS .... Sandia Corp., Albuquerque, NM [*Library symbol*] [*Library of Congress*] (LCLS)
NMasL ...... Massena Public Library, Massena, NY [*Library symbol*] [*Library of Congress*] (LCLS)
NMasMH.... Massena Memorial Hospital, Massena, NY [*Library symbol*] [*Library of Congress*] (LCLS)
NMass....... Massapequa Public Library, Massapequa, NY [*Library symbol*] [*Library of Congress*] (LCLS)
NMassAJ.... J. Lewis Ames Junior High School, Massapequa, NY [*Library symbol*] [*Library of Congress*] (LCLS)
NMassBE ... Birch Elementary School, Massapequa, NY [*Library symbol*] [*Library of Congress*] (LCLS)
NMassBH ... Berner High School, Massapequa, NY [*Library symbol*] [*Library of Congress*] (LCLS)
NMassELE.. East Lake Elementary School, Massapequa, NY [*Library symbol*] [*Library of Congress*] (LCLS)
NMassFE.... Fairfield Elementary School, Massapequa, NY [*Library symbol*] [*Library of Congress*] (LCLS)
NMassHE ... Hawthorn Elementary School, Massapequa, NY [*Library symbol*] [*Library of Congress*] (LCLS)
NMassHS ... Masspequa High School, Massapequa, NY [*Library symbol*] [*Library of Congress*] (LCLS)
NMassLE.... Lockhart Elementary School, Massapequa, NY [*Library symbol*] [*Library of Congress*] (LCLS)
NmassMJ ... J.P. McKenna Junior High School, Massapequa, NY [*Library symbol*] [*Library of Congress*] (LCLS)
NMassSE ... Charles E. Schwarting Elementary School, Massapequa, NY [*Library symbol*] [*Library of Congress*] (LCLS)
NMassUE ... Unqua Elementary School, Massapequa, NY [*Library symbol*] [*Library of Congress*] (LCLS)
NMat .... Mattituck Free Library, Mattituck, NY [*Library symbol*] [*Library of Congress*] (LCLS)
NMAT........ Night-Time Marine Air Temperature
N-Materials... Nuclear Materials (SAUS)
NMATP ...... Navy Military Assistance Training Program (NG)
Nmatrn ...... Nematron Corp. [*Associated Press*] (SAG)
NMAU .... Naval Medical Administration Unit (DNAB)
NmAU .... University of Albuquerque, Albuquerque, NM [*Library symbol*] [*Library of Congress*] (LCLS)
NmAVA ...... United States Veterans Administration Hospital, Albuquerque, NM [*Library symbol*] [*Library of Congress*] (LCLS)
NMAVC...... National Medical Audiovisual Center [*Medicine*] [*NLM*] (EDAA)
NMAX .... Nonwireline Multiple-Access Communications Exchange System (PDAA)
NMb .... Mastics-Moriches-Shirley Community Library, Mastic Beach, NY [*Library symbol*] [*Library of Congress*] (LCLS)
NMB .... Namib Air (Pty) Ltd. [*Namibia*] [*ICAO designator*] (FAAC)
NMB .... National Marine Board [*British*] [*World War II*]
NMB .... National Maritime Board
NMB .... National Meat Brokers [*Australia*]
NMB .... National Mediation Board [*Department of Labor*]
NMB .... National Metric Board
NMB .... National Motel Brokers (EA)
NMB .... National Mutual Benefit [*Madison, WI*] (EA)
NMB .... Naval Meteorological Branch [*British*]
NMB .... Naval Minecraft Base
NMB .... Naval Model Basin
NMB .... Neuromuscular Blockade [*Medicine*]
NMB .... New Methylene Blue [*Organic chemistry*]
NMB .... Nippon Miniature Bearing (SAUS)
NMB .... Nippon Miniature Bearing Corp. (EFIS)
NMB .... Noise, Measurement Buoy
NMB .... No Military Branch
NMB .... Non-Maturing Balance
NMB .... Not Member of a Branch
nmb.......... Number Book
NMBA .... National Marine Bankers Association [*Chicago, IL*] (EA)
NMBA .... Neuromuscular Blocking Agent
NMBA .... (Nitrosomethylamino) Butyric Acid [*Organic chemistry*]
NMBC .... National Minority Business Campaign [*Later, NMBD*] (EA)
NMBC .... National Minority Business Council [*New York, NY*] (EA)
NMbCH...... Bayview Community Hospital, Mastic Beach, NY [*Library symbol*] [*Library of Congress*] (LCLS)
NMBD .... National Minority Business Directories [*Minneapolis, MN*] (EA)
NmBeN...... Northwestern Regional Library, Belen, NM [*Library symbol*] [*Library of Congress*] (LCLS)
NMBF........ National Manufacturers of Beverage Flavors [*Defunct*] (EA)
NMBHF...... Naismith Memorial Basketball Hall of Fame (EA)
NMB Journal... Nigerian Marketing Board Journal (SAUS)
NMBMMR... New Mexico Bureau of Mines and Mineral Resources [*New Mexico Institute of Mining and Technology*] [*Research center*] (RCD)
NMbr .... Millbrook Library, Millbrook, NY [*Library symbol*] [*Library of Congress*] (LCLS)
NMBR .... NATO Military Basic Requirement (MCD)
NMbrB....... Bennett College, Millbrook, NY [*Library symbol*] [*Library of Congress*] (LCLS)
NMBS .... Nationale Maatschappij der Belgische Spoorwegen [*Railway*] [*Belgium*] (EY)
NMBS .... Nimbus CD International, Inc. [*NASDAQ symbol*] (SAG)
NMBS .... Nimbus CD Intl. [*NASDAQ symbol*] (TTSB)
NMBT........ New Main Battle Tank [*Military*] (RDA)
NMBT........ New Milford Bank & Trust Co. [*NASDAQ symbol*] (CTT)
NMBT........ New Milford BK & Tr Conn [*NASDAQ symbol*] (TTSB)
NMBU .... Navigation Maritime Burgare [*Intermodal shipping container symbol*] (TVRC)
NM Bur Mines Miner Resour Hydrol Rep... New Mexico. Bureau of Mines and Mineral Resources Hydrologic Report (SAUS)
NM Bur Mines Miner Resour Prog Rep... New Mexico. Bureau of Mines and Mineral Resources Report (SAUS)
NMBWCA ... New Mexico Barbed Wire Collectors Association (EA)
NmC .... Carlsbad Public Library, Carlsbad, NM [*Library symbol*] [*Library of Congress*] (LCLS)
NMC .... Marine Corps Publications [*Later, NAVMC*]
NMC .... Meredith College, Raleigh, NC [*OCLC symbol*] (OCLC)
NMC .... Nail Manufacturers Council (EA)
NMC .... Natal Medical Corps [*British military*] (DMA)
NMC .... National Magazine Co.
NMC .... National Mail Centers, Inc. [*Telecommunications service*] (TSSD)

NMC .... National Manpower Council
NMC .... National Marine Center (USDC)
NMC .... National Maritime Council [*Defunct*] (EA)
NMC .... National Mastitis Council (EA)
NMC .... National Medical Care
NMC .... National Medical Center [*Medicine*] (EDAA)
NMC .... National Memorials Committee [*Australia*]
NMC .... National Message Center [*Overland Park, KS*] (TSSD)
NMC .... National Meteorological Center [*National Oceanic and Atmospheric Administration*] [*Information service or system*] (IID)
NMC .... National Migrant Clearinghouse (OICC)
NMC .... National Military Council [*Surinam*] (PD)
NMC .... National Missionary Council [*Australia*]
NMC .... National Motorsports Committee (EA)
NMC .... National Mouse Club [*British*] (BI)
NMC .... National Museum of Canada
NMC .... National Music Camp [*Interlochen, MI*]
NMC .... National Music Council (EA)
NMC .... NATO Manual on Codification (NATG)
NMC .... Naval Material Command [*Formerly, NMSE*]
NMC .... Naval Medical Center [*Bethesda, MD*]
NMC .... Naval Memorandum Correction (NVT)
NMC .... Naval Missile Center [*Point Mugu, CA*]
NMC .... Naval Mission Center (KSC)
NMC .... NAVA [*National Audio-Visual Association*] Materials Council (EA)
NMC .... Navigation Map Computer
NMC .... Navy Mail Clerk
NMC .... Navy Memorandum Correction
NMC .... Nebraska Motor Carriers Association, Petroleum Carriers' Conference, Inc., OmahaNE [*STAC*]
NMC .... Net Matchable Cost
NMC .... Network Management Center [*Computer science*]
NMC .... Network Management Computer (SAUS)
NMC .... Network Management Console [*Industrial Networking, Inc.*]
NMC .... Network Measurement Center
NMC .... Neuromuscular Control [*Medicine*] (DMAA)
NMC .... New Muon Collaboration (SAUS)
NMC .... Nine Mile Canyon [*California*] [*Seismograph station code, US Geological Survey*] (SEIS)
NMC .... Noble Metal Catalyst [*Automotive engineering*]
NMC .... No More Credit [*Business term*] (ADA)
NMC .... Non-Marginal Check (SAUS)
NMC .... Nonmetallic Cable (SAUS)
NMC .... Non-Metropolitan Counties [*British*]
NMC .... Non-Mission Capable [*Military*] (INF)
NMC .... Nonmotor Condition [*Medicine*] (DMAA)
NMC .... Northern Mining Corp. (SAUS)
NMC .... Northern Montana College [*Havre*]
NMC .... Northwestern Michigan College [*Traverse City*]
NMC .... Northwestern Motor Company [*Off-Highway equipment*]
NMC .... Not Mission Capable (MCD)
NMC .... NSSDC Master Catalog (SAUS)
NMC .... Nuclear Material Control (SAUS)
NMC .... Nuclear Material Convention (SAUS)
NMC .... Nuclear Medical Committee [*Medicine*] (EDAA)
NMC .... Nuclear Metal Conference
NMC .... Nucleus Reticularis Magnocellularis [*Medicine*] (DMAA)
NMC .... Numac Energy [*AMEX symbol*] (SPSG)
NMC .... Numac Oil & Gas Ltd. (SAUS)
NMC .... Numeric (SAUS)
NMC .... Numerical Modelling Center (SAUS)
NMC .... Nurse Managed Center (MEDA)
NMC .... Nursery Marketing Council (EA)
NMC .... Nursing Mothers Counsel [*An association*] (EA)
NMC .... Public Archives of Canada, National Map Collection [*UTLAS symbol*]
NMC .... San Francisco, CA [*Location identifier*] [*FAA*] (FAAL)
NMCA .... National Marble Club of America (EA)
NMCA .... National Meat Canners Association (EA)
NMCA .... National Military Command Authority (NVT)
NMCA .... National Mossberg Collectors Association (EA)
NMCA .... National Motorcycle Commuter Association [*Defunct*] (EA)
NMCA .... National Musclecar Association (EA)
NMCA .... Navy Mothers' Clubs of America (EA)
N-McAb ..... Neutralizing Monoclonal Antibody [*Immunology*]
NMCAC ...... National Motor Carrier Advisory Committee [*MTMC*] (TAG)
NM CAMP .. University Division, National Music Camp, Interlochen (SAUS)
NMC&A ..... Nuclear Material Control and Accountability (SAUS)
NMCB .... National Metric Conversion Board (NADA)
NMCB .... National Munitions Control Board [*World War II*]
NMCB .... National Museum of Canada Bulletin [*A publication*]
NMCB .... Navy Mobile Construction Battalion (CINC)
NMCC .... National Management Career Curriculum [*Office of Personnel Management*] (GFGA)
NMCC .... National Manpower Coordinating Committee [*Department of Labor*]
NMCC .... National Military Command Center [*DoD*]
NMCC .... National Military Communications Center [*Communications term*] (DCT)
NMCC .... Navy-Marine Corps Council [*Defunct*] (EA)
NMCC .... Network Management Command and Control [*Communications term*] (DCT)
NMCC .... Network Management Control Center [*Telecommunications*]
NMCC .... Nonmyeloid Cell Content (DB)
NMCC .... Northeast-Midwest Congressional Coalition (EA)
NMCCDDA... National Model Cities Community Development Directors Association [*Later, NCDA*] (EA)
NMCCIS ..... NATO Military Command and Control and Information System (NATG)
NMCC/MC... NMCC/Message Center (SAUS)
NMCCS ...... Nuclear Materials Control Computer System (SAUS)
NMCDA ...... National Model Cities Directors Association [*Later, NCDA*] (EA)
NMCEC ...... Navy-Marine Corps Exhibit Center
NMCEM ..... New Mexico Certified Emergency Manager [*Emergency Management*] (EMA)
NMCES ...... National Medical Care Expenditures Survey [*Department of Health and Human Services*] (GFGA)
NMCGB ...... National Music Council of Great Britain (EAIO)
NMCGRF .... Navy-Marine Corps-Coast Guard Residence Foundation
NMCHC ...... National Maternal and Child Health Clearinghouse (EA)
NMCI .... National Multicultural Institute (EA)
NmCiN ...... Northeastern Regional Library, Cimarron, NM [*Library symbol*] [*Library of Congress*] (LCLS)
NMCIRD ..... Naval Material Command Industrial Resources Detachment (DNAB)
NMCJS ...... Naval Member, Canadian Joint Staff
NmCl .... Clovis-Carver Public Library, Clovis, NM [*Library symbol*] [*Library of Congress*] (LCLS)
NMCL .... Navy Missile Center Laboratory (KSC)
NmCla .... Albert W. Thompson Memorial Library, Clayton, NM [*Library symbol*] [*Library of Congress*] (LCLS)
NMCLA ...... Bethesda Military Librarians Group [*Library network*]
NmClA .... United States Air Force, Cannon Air Force Base, Clovis, NM [*Library symbol*] [*Library of Congress*] (LCLS)
NmClaP ..... Albert W. Thompson Memorial Library, Clayton, NM [*Library symbol*] [*Library of Congress*] (LCLS)
NMCLK ...... Navy Mail Clerk
NMCM .... Navy and Marine Corps Medal [*Military decoration*]
NMCM .... Noble Metals Compatibility Melters (SAUS)
NMCM .... Not Mission Capable, Maintenance (NVT)
NMCMS ...... Not Mission Capable Maintenance Scheduled (SAUS)
NMCMU ...... Not Mission Capable Maintenance Unscheduled (SAUS)
NMCNCR .... Naval Medical Command National Capital Region (ACAE)
NMCO .... Namibian Minerals Corp. [*NASDAQ symbol*] (NASQ)
NMCO .... Navy Material Cataloging Office
NMCOC ...... National Media Corp. [*NASDAQ symbol*] (COMM)
NMCOM ..... Naval Material Command [*Formerly, NMSE*] (MCD)
NmCP .... United States Potash Co., Carlsbad, NM [*Library symbol*] [*Library of Congress*] (LCLS)
NMCPAC .... Nuclear Management Company PAC [*Hudson, WI*] (PACS)
NMCPP ...... New Mexico Center for Particle Physics (SAUS)
NMCRB ...... Navy Military Construction Review Board
NMCRC ...... Navy-Marine Corps Reserve Center (NVT)
NMCRC ...... North McKees Rocks, PA [*American Association of Railroads railroad junction routing code*]
NMCRS ...... Navy-Marine Corps Relief Society
NMCRTC .... Navy and Marine Corps Reserve Training Center
NMCS .... National Medic-Card [*Commercial firm*] (EA)
NMCS .... National Medicinal Chemistry Symposium
NMCS .... National Military Command System
NMCS .... Navy Mine Countermeasures Station (MUGU)
NMCS .... Nickel Manganese Chromium Steel (SAUS)
NMCS .... Not Mission Capable, Supply (MCD)
NMCS .... Nuclear Materials Control System (IEEE)
NMCSA ...... Navy Material Command Support Activity
NMC SEB ... New Media Center, School of Education Building (SAUS)
NMCSHA .... National Morgan Cutting and Stock Horse Association (EA)
NMCSS ...... National Military Command System Standards (AFM)
NMCSSC .... National Military Command System Support Center (AABC)
NMCTE ...... New Mexico Council of Teachers of English (EARSL)
NMCU .... NAMA [*Intermodal shipping container symbol*] (TVRC)
NMCUES .... National Medical Care Utilization and Expenditure Survey [*Department of Health and Human Services*] [*A publication*] (DHSM)
NMCZ .... Northshore Mining [*Federal Railroad Administration identification code*]
NmD .... Deming Public Library, Deming, NM [*Library symbol*] [*Library of Congress*] (LCLS)
NMD .... NASA Management Delegations (MCD)
NMD .... National Mapping Division (SAUS)
NMD .... National Missile Defense [*DoD*]
NMD .... National Museum of Dentistry (SAUS)
NMD .... Naval Mine Depot
NMD .... Navy Marine Diesel Fuel
NMD .... Neosynephrine/Mydriacil Dilation [*Medicine*] (MELL)
NMD .... Netmed, Inc. [*AMEX symbol*] (SAG)
NMD .... NeuroMotor Disease (SAUS)
NMD .... Neuromuscular Disease [*Medicine*] (MELL)
NMD .... Neuromyodysplasia [*Medicine*] (MELL)
NMD .... Nominated [*Telegraphy*] (PCTE)
NMD .... Nonmonetary Determination [*Unemployment insurance*] (OICC)
NMD .... Normal Muscle Development (DAVI)
NMD .... Norwegian Maritime Directorate (RIMS)
NMD .... Nuclear Medicine Department (SAUS)
NMD .... Nu-Media Industry International [*Vancouver Stock Exchange symbol*]
NMD .... Nutritional Muscular Dystrophy (SAUS)
NMD .... Nutrition Monitoring Division [*Department of Agriculture*] (GFGA)
NMDA .... National Marine Distributors Association (EA)
NMDA .... National Medical and Dental Association (EA)
NMDA .... National Metal Decorators Association (EA)
NMDA .... National Midas Dealers Association (EA)
NMDA .... National Motorcycle Dealers Association [*Later, NMRA*] (EA)

NMDA .... National Motorcycle Dismantelers Association (EA)
NMDA .... National Motor Drivers' Association [*A union*] [*British*]
NMDA .... N-Methyl-D-Aspartate [*Medicine*] (MELL)
NMDA .... N-Methyl-D-Aspartic Acid [*An amino acid*]
NMDA .... Nonresonant Magnetic Deflection Amplifier
NMDAB....... National Medical and Dental Association Bulletin [*Medicine*] (EDAA)
NMDAR ..... N-Methyl-D-Aspartic Acid Receptor [*Neurochemistry*]
nMDC........ Native Macrophage-Derived Chemokine [*Immunology*]
NMDC .... Nonmagnetic Drill Collar [*Well drilling technology*]
NMDCEF .... National Medico-Dental Conference for the Evaluation of Fluoridation [*Later, Medical-Dental Committee on Evaluation of Fluoridation*] (EA)
NM Dep Game Fish Bull... New Mexico. Department of Game and Fish Bulletin (SAUS)
NMDF .... Navy Management Data File (DNAB)
NMDG .... N-Methyl-D-Glucamine [*Biochemistry*]
NMD/GBR... National Missile Defense-Ground Based RADAR [*Army*] (RDA)
NMDIS ...... National Marine Data and Information Service [*China*] [*Marine science*] (OSRA)
NMDIS ...... National Music and Disability Information Service [*British*]
NMDL .... Naval Mine Defense Laboratory [*Naval Facilities Engineering Command*] [*Panama City, FL*]
NMDL .... Navy Management Data List (NG)
NMDL .... Navy Material Data List
NMDOY ..... National Midget Driver of the Year
NMDP .... National Marrow Donor Program [*Department of Health and Human Services*]
NMDP .... Neomenthyldiphenylphosphine [*Organic chemistry*]
NMDPI ...... Nuveen Maryland Premium Income Municipal Fund [*Associated Press*] (SAG)
NMDR .... Nuclear Magnetic Double Resonance
NMDRP ..... National Military Discharge Review Project (EA)
NMDS .... Naval Mine Disposal School
NMDS .... Network Management Directory Services (NITA)
NMDS .... New Music Distribution Service (EA)
NMDS .... Nonmetric Multidimensional Scaling [*Statistics*]
NMDS .... Nursing Minimum Data Set (SAUS)
NMDSC....... Naval Medical Data Service Center (DNAB)
NMDSG ..... Naval Material Data Systems Group (DNAB)
NMDU .... Newspaper and Mail Deliverers Union of New York and Vicinity (EA)
NMDY .... Nonresonant Magnetic Deflection Yoke
NMDY .... Normandy Oil & Gas Co. (SAUS)
NMDZ .... NATO Maritime Defense Zone (NATG)
NmE .... Espanola Public Library, Espanola, NM [*Library symbol*] [*Library of Congress*] (LCLS)
NME .... National Marriage Encounter (EA)
NME .... National Medical Enterprises, Inc. [*NYSE symbol*] (COMM)
NME .... National Military Establishment [*Designated Department of Defense, 1949*]
NME .... Naval Material Establishment (DOMA)
NME .... Necrolytic Migratory Erythema [*Dermatology*]
NME .... Neiman Marcus
NME .... Network Management Entity (MLOA)
NME .... Newly Maturing Economy [*Business term*]
NME .... New Molecular Entity [*Chemistry*]
NME .... New Musical Express [*A publication*] (WDAA)
NME .... Nightmute [*Alaska*] [*Airport symbol*] (OAG)
NME .... Nissan Motorsports Europe
NME .... Noise-Measuring Equipment
NME .... Nominee [*Telegraphy*] (PCTE)
NME .... Nonlinear Mesoscopic Elastic
NME .... Non-Market Economy (JAGO)
NME .... Nonsupervisory Manufacturing Engineer
NME .... Norton Mobile Essentials [*Symantec*]
NMEA........ National Marine Educators Association (EA)
NMEA........ National Marine Electronics Association (EA)
NMEBA....... National Marine Engineers' Beneficial Association (EA)
NMEC........ National Metric Education Center [*Western Michigan University*]
NMEC........ Nuclear Material Control Center (NUCP)
NMED .... Inmed Corp. (SAUS)
NMed........ Lee-Whedon Memorial Library, Medina, NY [*Library symbol*] [*Library of Congress*] (LCLS)
NMED .... New Mexico Environmental Department
NMEDA...... National Mobility Equipment Dealers Association (NTPA)
NMedH....... Medina Memorial Hospital, Medina, NY [*Library symbol*] [*Library of Congress*] (LCLS)
NMedia ..... National Media Corp. [*Associated Press*] (SAG)
N-Medicine... Nuclear Medicine (SAUS)
N-Med Tech... Nuclear-Medicine Technician (SAUS)
NMEF........ Naval Mine Engineering Facility
NMEFC ...... National Marine Environmental Forecasting Center [*China*] [*Marine science*] (OSRA)
NMEG .... Nisei Mass Evacuation Group
NMEIA....... National Machine Embellishment Instructors and Artists (NTPA)
NMEIA....... National Machine Embroidery Instructors Association (EA)
NMEIAA ..... National Machine Embroidery Instructors Association of America (EA)
NMEIB....... New Mexico Environmental Improvement Board (SAUS)
NMEL........ Navy Marine Engineering Laboratory [*Later, David W. Taylor Naval Ship Research and Development Center*] (KSC)
NMEL........ Nuclear Mechano-Electronic Laboratory (SAUS)
NMelA....... Airborne Institute Laboratories, Melville, NY [*Library symbol*] [*Library of Congress*] (LCLS)
NMelH....... Holzmacher, McLendon & Murrell, Inc., Melville, NY [*Library symbol*] [*Library of Congress*] (LCLS)
NMelL....... Litcom Library, Melville, NY [*Library symbol*] [*Library of Congress*] (LCLS)
NMelS....... Suffolk State School, Melville, NY [*Library symbol*] [*Library of Congress*] (LCLS)
NMelSC ..... Sagamore Children's Center, Melville, NY [*Library symbol*] [*Library of Congress*] (LCLS)
NMEMA ..... New Mexico Emergency Management Association [*Emergency Management*] (EMA)
NmEN .... Northern Regional Library, Espanola, NM [*Library symbol*] [*Library of Congress*] (LCLS)
NMERI....... New Mexico Engineering Research Institute [*University of New Mexico*] [*Research center*] (RCD)
NMerk....... Merrick Public Library, Merrick, NY [*Library symbol*] [*Library of Congress*] (LCLS)
NMerkBE.... Birch Elementary School, Merrick, NY [*Library symbol*] [*Library of Congress*] (LCLS)
NMerk CE... Chatterton Elementary School, Merrick, NY [*Library symbol*] [*Library of Congress*] (LCLS)
NMerkCH ... Sanford H. Calhoun High School, Merrick, NY [*Library symbol*] [*Library of Congress*] (LCLS)
NMerkF ..... Five Towns College, Merrick, NY [*Library symbol*] [*Library of Congress*] (LCLS)
NMerkLE.... Lakeside Elementary School, Merrick, NY [*Library symbol*] [*Library of Congress*] (LCLS)
NMerkMJ ... Merrick Avenue Junior High School, Merrick, NY [*Library symbol*] [*Library of Congress*] (LCLS)
NMES........ National Medical Expenditure Survey [*Department of Health and Human Services*] (GFGA)
NMES........ Naval Marine Engineering Station
NMET........ Naval Mobile Environmental Team (COE)
NMEU .... Naval Material Evaluation Unit (DNAB)
N Mex....... New Mexico (SHCU)
NMEX........ New Mexico
N Mex Highlands U... New Mexico Highlands University (GAGS)
N Mex Inst M&T... New Mexico Institute of Mining and Technology (GAGS)
NMexMilDist... New Mexico Military District (SAUS)
N Mex State Engineer Office Tech Rept... New Mexico State Engineer Office. Technical Report (SAUS)
N Mex St U... New Mexico State University (GAGS)
NMF .... Boston, MA [*Location identifier*] [*FAA*] (FAAL)
NmF .... Farmington Public Library, Farmington, NM [*Library symbol*] [*Library of Congress*] (LCLS)
NMF .... National Marfan Foundation (EA)
NMF .... National Medical Fellowships (EA)
NMF .... National Migraine Foundation [*Later, National Headache Foundation - NHF*] (EA)
NMF .... National Motor Freight Traffic Association Inc., Agent, Washington DC [*STAC*]
NMF .... National Myoclonus Foundation [*Defunct*] (EA)
NMF .... Naval Missile Facility [*Also, NAVMISFAC*]
NMF .... Navy Management Fund
NMF .... Network Management Forum [*Computer science*] (VLIE)
NMF .... Networks Messaging Facility [*Computer science*] (HODG)
NMF .... Neutron Multiplier Facility (SAUS)
NMF .... New Master File
NMF .... N-Methylformamide [*Antineoplastic compound*]
NMF .... N-Methyl Fucosamine [*Organic chemistry*]
NMF .... Nonmaster File [*Computer science*]
NMF .... Nonmember Firm [*of NYSE*]
NMF .... Nonmigrating Fraction [*of spermatozoa*] [*Medicine*]
NMF .... Non-Negative Matrix Factorization
NMF .... Nonprofit Mailers Federation (EA)
NMF .... Nonuniform Magnetic Field
NMF .... Nordiska Maskinbefalsfederationen [*Nordic Engineer Officers' Federation - NEOF*] (EAIO)
NMF .... Normal Mode Functions (SAUS)
NMFA........ National Military Family Association (EA)
NMFC........ National Magazine and Film Carriers (NTPA)
NMFC........ National Magazine, Book, and Film Carriers Conference (NTPA)
NMFC........ National Motor Freight Classification
NMFCR...... National Motor Freight Classification Rules
NMFEC ...... National Medical Foundation for Eye Care [*Later, AAO*] (EA)
NMFECC .... National Magnetic Fusion Energy Computer Center [*Department of Energy*] (MCD)
NmFGS...... Church of Jesus Christ of Latter-Day Saints, Genealogical Society Library, Farmington Branch, Farmington, NM [*Library symbol*] [*Library of Congress*] (LCLS)
NMFHAWAREA... Naval Missile Facility, Hawaiian Area (MUGU)
NMFHG...... National Master Farm Homemakers Guild (EA)
NMFI .... National Master Facility Inventory [*Department of Health and Human Services*] (GFGA)
NmfL .... National Microfilms Ltd., Dublin, Ireland [*Library symbol*] [*Library of Congress*] (LCLS)
NMFMA ..... National Mutual Fund Managers Association [*Defunct*] (EA)
NMFMA ..... New Mexico Floodplain Management Association [*Emergency Management*] (EMA)
NMFP........ Nuclear Mean Free Path (SAUS)
NMFPA ...... Naval Missile Facility, Point Arguello
NMFPM ..... Naval Missile Facility, Point Mugu [*California*] (SAA)
NMFR .... NAPALM [*National ADP Program for AMC Logistics Management*] Master File Record
NMFRL...... Naval Medical Field Research Laboratory [*Camp Lejeune, NC*]
NmFs........ Fort Sumner Public Library, Fort Sumner, NM [*Library symbol*] [*Library of Congress*] (LCLS)

NMFS........ National Marine Fisheries Service [*Formerly, Bureau of Commercial Fisheries*] [*National Oceanic and Atmospheric Administration*] [*Washington, DC*]
NMFS........ National Medical Financial Services Corp. [*NASDAQ symbol*] (SAG)
NMFS........ National Mortality Followback Survey [*National Center for Health Statistics*]
NMFS........ Natl Medical Finl Svcs [*NASDAQ symbol*] (TTSB)
NMFS........ Night Missile Flash Simulator (MCD)
NMFS........ Nuclear Materials Faclities Stabilization (SAUS)
NMFT........ New Material Flight Tests
NMFTA...... National Motor Freight Traffic Association [*Alexandria, VA*] (EA)
NMFWA..... National Military Fish and Wildlife Association (EA)
NMFWA..... Neuromuscular Foundation of Western Australia
NmG......... Gallup Public Library, Gallup, NM [*Library symbol*] [*Library of Congress*] (LCLS)
NMG......... Navy Metrication Group (DNAB)
NMG......... Navy Military Government
NMG......... Neiman-Marcus Group [*NYSE symbol*] (SPSG)
NMG......... New Maruti Goods [*Indian Railway*] (TIR)
NM (G)...... New Mexico Reports (Gildersleeve) [*1852-89*] [*A publication*] (DLA)
NMG......... New Modified Goods [*Indian Railway*] (TIR)
NMG......... New Orleans, LA [*Location identifier*] [*FAA*] (FAAL)
NMG......... Nominating [*Telegraphy*] (PCTE)
NMG......... Numerical Master Geometry [*System*]
NMG......... San Miguel [*Panama*] [*Airport symbol*] (OAG)
NMGA....... National Military Guidance Association (EA)
NMGA....... Neiman Marcus Group [*Company symbol*]
NMGC....... National Marriage Guidance Council [*British*] (ILCA)
NMGC....... NeoMagic Corp. [*NASDAQ symbol*] (SG)
NMGCS...... National Milk Glass Collectors Society
NM Geol Soc Field Conf Guideb... New Mexico Geological Society. Feld Conference Guidebook (SAUS)
NMGO....... New Millenium Global Outreach [*Association*] (EA)
NmGr........ Mother Whiteside Memorial Library, Grants, NM [*Library symbol*] [*Library of Congress*] (LCLS)
NMGRA..... National Museum and Gallery Registration Association (EA)
NMG System... Numerical Master Geometry System (SAUS)
NMh......... Library of Poultney Bigelow, Malden-On-Hudson, NY [*Library symbol*] [*Library of Congress*] (LCLS)
NMH......... Monsang Naga [*Language symbol*] (ETLW)
NMH......... Nautical Miles per Hour
NMH......... Neurally Mediated Hypotension
NMH......... New Mexico Highlands [*New Mexico*] [*Seismograph station code, US Geological Survey*] (SEIS)
NMH......... New Mexico Highlands University, Las Vegas, NM [*OCLC symbol*] (OCLC)
NMH......... N-Methylhydroxylamine [*Organic chemistry*]
NMH......... No-Mar Hammer (SAUS)
NMH......... Northwestern Memorial Hospital (SAUS)
NmHa....... Hatch Public Library, Hatch, NM [*Library symbol*] [*Library of Congress*] (LCLS)
NMHA....... National Mental Health Association (EA)
NMHA....... National Minority Health Association (EA)
NMHA....... National Mobile Home Association (EA)
NMHAG..... National Mental Health Association of Georgia (EARSL)
NmHARL.... Aeromedical Library, 6571st Aeromedical Research Laboratory, Holloman AFB, NM [*Library symbol*] [*Library of Congress*] (LCLS)
NMHC....... National Materials Handling Centre [*Cranfield Institute of Technology*] [*British*] (CB)
NMHC....... National Multi Housing Council (EA)
NMHC....... Nonmethane Hydrocarbons [*Organic chemistry*]
NMHCA...... National Mental Health Consumers' Association (EA)
NMHCA...... New Mexico Health Care Association (EARSL)
NMHCC...... National Managed Health Care Congress (HGEN)
NMHCE...... Non-Methane Hydrocarbon Equivalent (EEVL)
NMHCSHC... National Mental Health Consumer Self-Help Clearinghouse (EA)
NMHF....... National Manufactured Housing Federation (EA)
NMHFA...... National Manufactured Housing Finance Association [*Defunct*] (EA)
NmHi........ Historical Society of New Mexico, Santa Fe (SAUS)
NmHi........ Historical Society of New Mexico, Santa Fe, NM [*Library symbol*] [*Library of Congress*] (LCLS)
NMHID...... National Mental Health Institute on Deafness (SAUS)
NmHo....... Hobbs Public Library, Hobbs, NM [*Library symbol*] [*Library of Congress*] (LCLS)
NmHoC...... New Mexico Junior College, Hobbs, NM [*Library symbol*] [*Library of Congress*] (LCLS)
NmHORA.... United States Air Force, Office of Research Analyses, Technical Library, Holloman AFB, Albuquerque, NM [*Library symbol*] [*Library of Congress*] (LCLS)
NmHoSW... College of the Southwest, Hobbs, NM [*Library symbol*] [*Library of Congress*] (LCLS)
NM/HR...... Nautical Mile/Hour (MCD)
NMHS....... National Maritime Historical Society (EA)
NMHS....... National Mental Health Strategy (SAUS)
NMHS....... National Meteorologicial and Hydrological Service (SAUS)
NMHS....... Not-Made-Here Syndrome (VLIE)
NMHSPE.... New Mexico High School Proficiency Examination (EDAC)
NMHT....... National Museum of History and Technology [*Later, National Museum of American History*] (GRD)
NMHU....... New Mexico Highlands University [*Las Vegas, NM*]
NMHWMS.. New Mexico Hazardous Waste Management Society (SAUS)
NMI.......... Minot State College, Minot, ND [*OCLC symbol*] (OCLC)
NMI.......... NASA Management Instruction (KSC)
NMI.......... NASA Management Issuance (MCD)
NMI.......... National Macaroni Institute (EA)
NMI.......... National Maglev Initiative [*Department of Transportation*]
NMI.......... National Maintenance Index (IAA)
NMI.......... National Manpower Institute [*Later, NIWL*] (EA)
NMI.......... National Maritime Institute [*British*]
NMI.......... Native Method Invocation (VLIE)
nmi.......... Nautical Mile (NAKS)
NMI.......... Nautical Mile
NMI.......... New Material Introductory [*Team*] [*Military*]
NMI.......... New Millennium Interferometer (SAUS)
NMI.......... New Model Introduction (VLIE)
NMI.......... Nissan Motorsports International [*Automotive competition*]
NMI.......... No Meaningful Improvement (MELL)
nmi.......... No Middle Initial (SHCU)
NMI.......... No Middle Initial
NMI.......... Nonmajor Item (MCD)
NMI.......... Non Maskable Interrupt (SAUS)
NMI.......... Nonmasking [*or Nonmaskable*] Interrupt
NMI.......... Northeast-Midwest Institute (EA)
NMI.......... Northwest Microfilm, Inc. [*Information service or system*] (IID)
NMI.......... Nuclear Magnetic Imaging
NMI.......... Nuclear Materials Information (SAUS)
NMI.......... Nuclear Metals, Inc.
NMI.......... Nutritional Metabolic Index [*Therapy term*] (CTAA)
NMI.......... Nuveen Municipal Income Fund [*NYSE symbol*] (SPSG)
NMi.......... Thrall Library, Middletown, NY [*Library symbol*] [*Library of Congress*] (LCLS)
NMIA........ National Military Intelligence Association (EA)
NMIA........ Northeast Michigan Industrial Association (EARSL)
NMIAPO..... New Montreal International Airport Project [*Canada*]
NMIB........ New Material Introductory Briefing [*Military*] (MCD)
NMIBT...... New Material Introductory Briefing Team [*Military*] (MCD)
NMIC........ National Maritime Intelligence Center [*Created in 1992 from intelligence activities in the Washington, D.C., area*] [*Navy*] (DOMA)
NMIC........ National Meat Industry Council (EA)
NMIC........ National Micronetics, Inc. [*NASDAQ symbol*] (COMM)
NMIC........ National Military Information Center
NMIC........ National Military Intelligence Center (CCCA)
NMIC........ National Missile Industry Conference (AAG)
NMIC........ Not Made in Canada [*Business term*]
NMICA....... New Mexico Independent College Association (SAUS)
NMICC....... National Military Intelligence Collection Center (SAUS)
NMICSS..... NMIC [*National Military Information Center*] Support System (MCD)
NMIDA...... N-Methyliminodiacetic Acid [*Organic chemistry*]
NMidp....... Middleport Free Library, Middleport, NY [*Library symbol*] [*Library of Congress*] (LCLS)
NMidpF..... FMC Corp., Niagara Chemical Division, R and D Library, Middleport, NY [*Library symbol*] [*Library of Congress*] (LCLS)
NMIHS...... National Maternal and Infant Health Survey [*Department of Health and Human Services*] (GFGA)
NMil......... Millerton Free Library, Millerton, NY [*Library symbol*] [*Library of Congress*] (LCLS)
NMIL........ New Materiel Introductory Letter [*Army*] (AABC)
NMILA....... NASA Merritt Island Launch Area (SAA)
NMilBc...... New Milford Savings Bank [*Associated Press*] (SAG)
NMilt........ Sarah Hull Hallock Free Library, Milton, NY [*Library symbol*] [*Library of Congress*] (LCLS)
NMILW...... North Milwaukee, WI [*American Association of Railroads railroad junction routing code*]
NMIMT...... New Mexico Institute of Mining and Technology [*Socorro*]
NMin........ Mineola Memorial Library, Mineola, NY [*Library symbol*] [*Library of Congress*] (LCLS)
NMinH....... Nassau Hospital, Mineola, NY [*Library symbol*] [*Library of Congress*] (LCLS)
NMinHe..... Hampton Elementary School, Mineola, NY [*Library symbol*] [*Library of Congress*] (LCLS)
NMinJE...... Jackson Avenue Elementary School, Mineola, NY [*Library symbol*] [*Library of Congress*] (LCLS)
NMinME..... Meadow Elementary School, Mineola, NY [*Library symbol*] [*Library of Congress*] (LCLS)
NMinMJ..... Mineola Junior High School, Mineola, NY [*Library symbol*] [*Library of Congress*] (LCLS)
NMinMS.... Mineola Middle School, Mineola, NY [*Library symbol*] [*Library of Congress*] (LCLS)
NMinNCL... Nassau County Law Library, Mineola, NY [*Library symbol*] [*Library of Congress*] (LCLS)
NMiOC...... Orange County Community College, Middletown, NY [*Library symbol*] [*Library of Congress*] (LCLS)
NMIP........ New Major Investment Program [*Australia*]
NMIPC....... National Military Intelligence Production Center (SAUS)
NMIQI....... Nuveen Michigan Quality Income Municipal Fund [*Associated Press*] (SAG)
NMiR........ Ramapo Catskill Library System, Middletown, NY [*Library symbol*] [*Library of Congress*] (LCLS)
NMIRI....... New Mexico Independence Research Institute (RCD)
NMIRO...... Naval Material Industrial Resources Office
NMIS........ National Military Indications System (MCD)
NMIS........ Naval Manpower Information System
NMIS........ Newspapers Mutual Insurance Society Ltd. [*British*] (BI)
NMIS........ Nuclear Materials Information System
NMIS........ Nuclear Materials Inventory System (NRCH)
NMIS........ Nuclear Medicine Information System [*Medicine*] [*FDA*] (EDAA)
NMIS........ Nursing Management Information System (DMAA)
NMISC....... National Military Intelligence Support Center (SAUS)
NMISMAN... Navy Manpower Information System Manual (DNAB)
NMIST...... National Military Intelligence Support Team [*Defense Intelligence Agency*] (DOMA)

NMIT .... New Materiel Introductory Team [*Army*] (AABC)
NMIT .... Nuclear Material Item Transfer (SAUS)
NMITC .... Navy and Marine Corps Intelligence Training Center (DOMA)
NMIU .... Nordic Meat Industry Union (EA)
NMIW .... Northwest Marine Iron Works (AAGC)
NmJ .... Jal Public Library, Jal, NM [*Library symbol*] [*Library of Congress*] (LCLS)
NMJ .... National Medical Journal [*Medicine*] (EDAA)
NMJ .... Neuromuscular injection (SAUS)
NMJ .... Neuromuscular Junction [*Medicine*] (EDAA)
NM (J) ...... New Mexico Reports (Johnson) [*A publication*] (DLA)
NMJ .... Northern Masonic Jurisdiction (SAUS)
NMJC .... National Men's Judo Championships [*British*]
NMJC .... Northeastern Mississippi Junior College [*Senatobia*]
NMJC .... Northwest Mississippi Junior College
NMJCT ...... Northern Maine Junction, ME [*American Association of Railroads railroad junction routing code*]
NMJL .... National Mah Jongg League (EA)
NMK .... Cape May, NJ [*Location identifier*] [*FAA*] (FAAL)
NMK .... Niagara Mohawk Power Corp. [*NYSE symbol*] (SPSG)
NMK .... Niagara Mohawk Pwr [*NYSE symbol*] (TTSB)
NMKL .... Nordisk Metodikkommitte for Livsmedel [*Nordic Committee on Food Analysis*] (EAIO)
NMKPr ...... Niagara Moh Pwr Adj Rt A Pfd [*NYSE symbol*] (TTSB)
NMKPrA ..... Niag Moh Pwr 3.40% Pfd [*NYSE symbol*] (TTSB)
NMKPrB ..... Niag Moh Pwr 3.60% Pfd [*NYSE symbol*] (TTSB)
NMKPrC ..... Niag Moh Pwr 3.90% Pfd [*NYSE symbol*] (TTSB)
NMKPrD ..... Niag Moh Pwr 4.10% Pfd [*NYSE symbol*] (TTSB)
NMKPrE ..... Niag Moh Pwr 4.85% Pfd [*NYSE symbol*] (TTSB)
NMKPrG ..... Niag Moh Pwr 5.25% Pfd [*NYSE symbol*] (TTSB)
NMKPrI ...... Niag Moh Pwr 7.72% Pfd [*NYSE symbol*] (TTSB)
NMKPrK ..... Niagara Mohawk Pwr Adj C Pfd [*NYSE symbol*] (TTSB)
NMKPrM .... Niagara Moh Pwr 9.50% Pfd [*NYSE symbol*] (TTSB)
NML .... Narragansett Marine Laboratory [*University of Rhode Island*]
NML .... National Magnet Laboratory
NML .... National Measurement Laboratory [*Gaithersburg, MD*] [*National Institute of Standards and Technology*] (GRD)
NML .... National Media Laboratory (SAUS)
NML .... National Medical Library (DAVI)
NML .... National Metrology Laboratory (ACII)
NML .... National Municipal League (EA)
NML .... National Music League (EA)
NML .... Native Machine Language [*Computer science*]
NML .... Nautical Mile
NML .... Naval Materials Management (SAA)
NML .... Naval Multiple Launcher (SAUS)
NML .... Navy Management List (AFIT)
NML .... Network Management Layer [*Computer science*] (VLIE)
NML .... New Mathematical Library [*School Mathematics Study Group*]
Nm-L .... New Mexico Supreme Court Law Library, Santa Fe, NM [*Library symbol*] [*Library of Congress*] (LCLS)
NML .... Nodular Mixed Lymphoma [*Onocology*] (DAVI)
NML .... No Mail Label
NML .... No Man's Land [*Medical slang, cardiology*]
NML .... Nominal [*Telegraphy*] (PCTE)
NML .... Nonocclusive Mesenteric Infarction [*Medicine*] (MELL)
NML .... Normal
NML .... Normal Male Infant (MELL)
NML .... Northwestern Mutual Life (SAUS)
NML .... Nuclear Magnetic Logging (IAA)
NML .... Nuclear Magnetism Log (PDAA)
NML .... University of New Mexico, School of Law, Albuquerque, NM [*OCLC symbol*] (OCLC)
NmLa .... Mesa Public Library, Los Alamos, NM [*Library symbol*] [*Library of Congress*] (LCLS)
NMLA .... New Mexico Library Association (SAUS)
NmLaS ...... Los Alamos Scientific Laboratory, Los Alamos, NM [*Library symbol*] [*Library of Congress*] (LCLS)
NmLaS-M ... Los Alamos Scientific Laboratory, Medical Library, Los Alamos, NM [*Library symbol*] [*Library of Congress*] (LCLS)
NmLaU ...... University of New Mexico, Los Alamos, NM [*Library symbol*] [*Library of Congress*] (LCLS)
NMLC .... Normalized Mass Loss Coefficient [*Nuclear energy*] (NUCP)
NmLc .... Thomas Branigan Memorial Library, Las Cruces, NM [*Library symbol*] [*Library of Congress*] (LCLS)
NMLCF ...... Nuclear Measurements & Logging Calibration (SAUS)
NmLcU ...... New Mexico State University, Las Cruces, NM [*Library symbol*] [*Library of Congress*] (LCLS)
NML FEDPAC ... Northwestern Mutual Life Insurance Company Federal PAC [*Milwaukee, WI*] (PACS)
NMLO .... National Media Liaison Officer
NMLOC ...... Non-Motorist Location [*National Highway Traffic Safety Administration Fatal Accident Recording System code*]
NmLor .... Lordsburg-Hidalgo Public Library, Lordsburg, NM [*Library symbol*] [*Library of Congress*] (LCLS)
NmLov ...... Lovington Public Library, Lovington, NM [*Library symbol*] [*Library of Congress*] (LCLS)
NmLovS ..... Southeastern Regional Library Center, Lovington, NM [*Library symbol*] [*Library of Congress*] (LCLS)
NMLR .... Nigerian Monthly Law Reports [*1964-65*] [*A publication*] (DLA)
NMLRA ...... National Muzzle Loading Rifle Association (EA)
NMLS .... National Microwave Landing System (MCD)
NMLT .... New Material Laboratory Tests
NmLv .... Las Vegas Carnegie Library, Las Vegas, NM [*Library symbol*] [*Library of Congress*] (LCLS)
NmLvH ...... New Mexico Highlands University, Las Vegas, NM [*Library symbol*] [*Library of Congress*] (LCLS)
NmLvSH .... New Mexico State Hospital, Las Vegas, NM [*Library symbol*] [*Library of Congress*] (LCLS)
NMLX .... Richmond Steel Recycling [*Private rail car owner code*]
NMLZMMAX ... Normalize by Matrix Maximum (SAUS)
NMM .... Meridian, MS [*Location identifier*] [*FAA*] (FAAL)
NMM .... NASA Management Manual
NMM .... National Maritime Museum [*British*]
NMM .... NetWare Management Map [*Computer science*] (VLIE)
NMM .... Network Measurement Machine [*Computer Network*] (IAA)
NMM .... Neutron Magnetic Moment
NMM .... New Madrid [*Missouri*] [*Seismograph station code, US Geological Survey*] [*Closed*] (SEIS)
NMM .... New Mexico Military Institute, Roswell, NM [*OCLC symbol*] (OCLC)
N-mm .... Newton-Millimeter (SAUS)
NMM .... N-Methylmorpholine [*Organic chemistry*]
NMM .... Nodular Malignant Melanoma [*Medicine*] (DB)
NMM .... Noisemont Mining (SAUS)
NMM .... Nonmetal Material (SAUS)
NMM .... Nonne-Milroy-Meige [*Syndrome*] [*Medicine*] (DB)
NMM .... Norsemont Mining [*Vancouver Stock Exchange symbol*]
NMM .... Nuclear Magnetic Moment (SAUS)
NMM .... Nuclear Materials Management
NMMA .... National Macaroni Manufacturers Association [*Later, NPA*] (EA)
NMMA .... National Maintenance Management Association [*Defunct*] (EA)
NMMA .... National Marine Manufacturers Association (EA)
NMMC .... National Adult Education Clearinghouse (NAEC)/National Multimedia Center for Adult Education [*Information service or system*] [*Defunct*] (IID)
NMMC .... National Marina Manufacturers Consortium [*Defunct*] (EA)
NMMD .... Nuclear Materials Management Department (SAUS)
NmMeB ..... Bent-Mescalero School Library, Mescalero, NM [*Library symbol*] [*Library of Congress*] (LCLS)
NMMFO ..... Navy Maintenance Management Field Office
NMMFO(W) ... Navy Maintenance Management Field Office (West) (DNAB)
NMMHMO ... Network and Mixed Model Health Maintenance Organization [*Insurance*] (WYGK)
NMMHOF ... National Mobile/Manufactured Home Owners Foundation [*Later, NFMHO*] (EA)
NMMI .... New Mexico Military Institute [*Roswell*] (MCD)
NMML .... National Marine Mammal Laboratory [*National Marine Fisheries Service*]
NMMLC ..... New Moon Matchbox and Label Club (EA)
NMMM ...... Navy Maintenance and Material Management System [*Also known as MMM, NMMMS, 3M*]
NMMMS .... Navy Maintenance and Material Management System [*Also known as MMM, NMMM, 3M*]
NMMPS ..... National Military Message Processor System (CCCA)
NmMS .... Montezuma Seminary, Montezuma, NM [*Library symbol*] [*Library of Congress*] (LCLS)
NMMS .... Navy Mast Mounted Sight (SAUS)
NMMSA ..... NASA Microgravity Materials Science Assessment Task Force (SAUS)
NMMSB ..... Non-Nuclear Munitions Safety Board
NMMSN ..... National Marine Mammal Stranding Network (EA)
NMMSS ..... Nuclear Materials Management and Safeguards System (NRCH)
NMMW ...... Near Millimeter Wave System [*Telecommunications*] (TEL)
N/mmy ..... Newton per Square Millimeter (SAUS)
NMN .... Nicotinamide-Mononucleotide [*Biochemistry*]
NMN .... No Middle Name
NMN .... Nomination [*Telegraphy*] (PCTE)
NMN .... Normetanephrine [*Also, Methylnorepinephrine*] [*Biochemistry*]
NMN .... NRD Mining Ltd. [*Vancouver Stock Exchange symbol*]
NMNA .... National Male Nurse Association [*Later, AAMN*] (EA)
NMNA .... New Mexico Nurses Association (SAUS)
NMNase .... Nicotinamidenucleotide Phosphoribohydrolase [*An enzyme*]
NMND .... Naval Magazine and Net Depot
NMNFO ..... Navy Maintenance Field Office (NVT)
NMNH .... National Museum of National History
NMNH .... National Museum of Natural History [*Smithsonian Institution*]
NMNH .... Nicotinamide Mononucleotide, Reduced Form (SAUS)
NMNRU .... National Medical Neuropsychiatric Research Unit (DMAA)
NMNRU .... Naval Medical Neuropsychiatric Research Unit
NMNS .... National Museum of Natural Sciences [*National Museums of Canada*] [*Research center*] (RCD)
NMO .... Long Beach, CA [*Location identifier*] [*FAA*] (FAAL)
NMO .... National Medical Organisation (ACII)
NMO .... National Military Objectives (SAUS)
NMO .... National Mobility Office [*British*]
NMO .... Navy Management Office
NMO .... Nitroso-Morpholin (SAUS)
NMO .... N-Methylmorpholine N-Oxide [*Organic chemistry*]
NMO .... Noble Mines & Oils Ltd. [*Toronto Stock Exchange symbol*]
NMO .... Normal Manual Operation (KSC)
NMO .... Normal Mode Operation
NMO .... Normal Move-Out (SAUS)
NMO .... Norman [*Oklahoma*] [*Seismograph station code, US Geological Survey*] [*Closed*] (SEIS)
NMO .... Number of Critical Micro-Operations [*Computer science*] (MHDI)
NMO .... Nuveen Municipal Market Opportunities [*NYSE symbol*] (SPSG)
NMO .... Nuveen Muni Mkt Oppt [*NYSE symbol*] (TTSB)
NMOA .... National Mail Order Association [*Los Angeles, CA*] (EA)
NMOC .... New Man On Campus (SAUS)
NMOC .... Non-Methane Organic Compound [*Environmental chemistry*]

NMOCOD.... [*The*] Nonmateriel Objectives Coordinating Document [*Army*] (RDA)
NMOG....... Non-Methane Organic Gas [*Organic chemistry*]
nmol........ Nanomole [*One billionth of a mole*] (MAE)
NMOMA..... New Mexico Osteopathic Medical Association (EARSL)
NMoN....... New York Ocean Science Laboratory, Montauk, NY [*Library symbol*] [*Library of Congress*] (LCLS)
NMONA..... National Mail Order Nurserymen's Association [*Later, MAN*] (EA)
NMontr...... Hendrick Hudson Free Library, Montrose, NY [*Library symbol*] [*Library of Congress*] (LCLS)
NMontrVA... United States Veterans Administration Hospital, Montrose, NY [*Library symbol*] [*Library of Congress*] (LCLS)
NMOP....... National Mission Operating Procedures (AAG)
NMOPI...... Nuveen Missouri Premium Income Municipal Fund [*Associated Press*] (SAG)
NMOR....... Nitrosomorpholine [*Also, NNM*] [*Organic chemistry*]
NMOR....... Northern Missouri Railroad [*Federal Railroad Administration identification code*]
NMOS....... Negative Channel Metal-Oxide Semiconductor
NMOS....... Network Mission and Operations Support
NMOS....... Nonvolatile Metal-Oxide Semiconductor (MCD)
NMOSAW... Naval and Military Order of the Spanish-American War (EA)
NMOS/SOS... Nitrite Metal Oxide Silicon/Silicon on Sapphire (SAUS)
NMOST...... Nitrite Metal Oxide Silicon Transistor (SAUS)
NMP......... National Maintenance Point [*Military*] (AABC)
NMP......... National Meter Programming (NRCH)
NMP......... National Military Command System Master Plan (SAUS)
NMP......... National Military Park
NMP......... National Municipal Policy [*Environmental Protection Agency*] (EPA)
NMP......... Naval Management Program
NMP......... Naval Medical Publication
NMP......... Naval Message Processing (MCD)
NMP......... Navigational Microfilm Projector
NMP......... Navy Manning Plan (NVT)
NMP......... Nederlands Middenstands Partij [*Netherlands Middle Class Party*] [*Political party*] (PPE)
NMP......... Net Material Product [*Economics*]
NMP......... Network Management Protocol [*Computer science*] (TNIG)
NMP......... Network Modem Program (SAUS)
NM/P........ New Material/Process (MCD)
NMP......... New Mediterranean Policy (EURO)
NMP......... New Millenium Program (SAUS)
NMP......... Niagara Mohawk Power [*Federal Railroad Administration identification code*]
NMP......... N-Methylphenazium [*Organic chemistry*]
NMP......... N-Methylphthalimide [*Organic chemistry*]
NMP......... N-Methylpyrrolidone [*Organic chemistry*]
NMP......... Normal Menstrual Period [*Gynecology*] (MAE)
NMP......... Not Machine Pressed
NMP......... Not My Problem [*Internet lingo*] (NETL)
NMP......... Nucleoside Monophosphate [*Biochemistry*]
NMP......... Nuveen Michigan Premium Income Municipal [*NYSE symbol*] (SPSG)
NMP......... Nuveen MI Prem Inc. Muni [*NYSE symbol*] (TTSB)
NmP......... Portales Public Library, Portales, NM [*Library symbol*] [*Library of Congress*] (LCLS)
NMPA........ National Motorsports Press Association (EA)
NMPA........ National Music Publishers' Association (EA)
NMPA........ NATO Maritime Patrol Aircraft (NATG)
NMPA........ New Mexico Philatelic Association (EA)
NMPA........ New Mexico Psychological Association (EARSL)
NMPA........ (Nitrosomethylamino) Propionic Acid [*Organic chemistry*]
NMPA........ Nitrosomethylpropylamine [*Organic chemistry*]
NM PAC..... Nuclear Medicine PAC [*Washington, DC*] (PACS)
NMPAP...... Noise Minimization Pad Assignment Problem (VLIE)
NMPASC.... NATO Maritime Patrol Aircraft Steering Committee (NATG)
NMPATA..... National Music Printers and Allied Trades Association (EA)
NMPB........ National Millinery Planning Board [*Defunct*] (EA)
NMPC........ National Maintenance Publications Center [*Army*] (AABC)
NMPC........ National Milk Publicity Council [*British*] (BI)
NMPC........ National Minority Purchasing Council [*Later, NMSDC*] (EA)
NMPC........ National Moratorium on Prison Construction [*Defunct*] (EA)
NMPC........ Naval Military Personnel Command (ANA)
NMPC........ Niagara Mohawk Power Co. (SAUS)
NMPC........ NutraMax Products, Inc. [*NASDAQ symbol*] (SAG)
NMPCA...... Nonmetric Principal Component Analysis [*Medicine*] (EDAA)
NMPCRECSREDIVREGOFF... Naval Military Personnel Command, Recreational Services Division, Regional Office (DNAB)
NMPD........ Nitromethylpropanediol [*Organic chemistry*]
NMPDN...... National Materials Property Data Network (EA)
NmPE........ Eastern New Mexico University, Portales, NM [*Library symbol*] [*Library of Congress*] (LCLS)
NMPF........ National Milk Producers Federation (EA)
NMPF........ Network Management Productivity Facility [*Computer science*] (VLIE)
NMPF........ Normal Magnitude Probability Function
NMPF PAC... National Milk Producers Federation PAC [*Arlington, VA*] (PACS)
NMPFT...... National Museum of Photography, Film & Television (WDAA)
NMPG........ New Mexico Proving Ground [*Army*]
NMPGA...... New Mexico Personnel and Guidance Association (SAUS)
NMPIS....... National Marine Pollution Information System [*Marine science*] (OSRA)
NMPIS....... National Marine Pollution Information Systems (USDC)
NMPK........ Nucleoside Monophosphate Kinase (SAUS)
NMPL........ Netscape/Mozilla Public License (SAUS)
NMPL........ New Material Planning Letter (MCD)
NMPNC...... Naval Medical Program for Nuclear Casualties
NMPNS...... Nine Mile Point Nuclear Station (NRCH)
NMPO........ Navy Motion Picture Office
NMPO........ Nordic Master Painters' Organization (EA)
NMPP........ Nautical Miles per Pound (MCD)
NMPP........ Nouvelles Messageries de la Presse Parisienne [*Paris press distribution agency*]
NMPPO...... National Marine Pollution Program Office [*Marine science*] (OSRA)
NMPR........ National Morgan Pony Registry [*Association*] (EA)
NMPRA...... National MedPeds Residents' Association (EA)
NMPS........ Matritech, Inc. [*NASDAQ symbol*] (SAG)
NMPS........ Nautical Miles per Second
NMPS........ Naval Military Pay System (ACAE)
NMPS........ Navy Motion Picture Service
NMPs........ Nominated Members of Parliament (Singapore) [*Political party*] (PSAP)
NMPS........ Nutritional and Molecular Physiology Unit [*National Institute on Aging*] (RCD)
NMPSMOPIXDISTOFF... Navy Motion Picture Service, Motion Picture Distribution Office (DNAB)
NMPTP...... N-Methyl(phenyl)tetrahydropyridine [*Biochemistry*]
NMPX........ Navy Motion Picture Exchange
NMQAAC.... National Mammography Quality Assurance Advisory Committee [*U.S. Food and Drug Administration*]
NMQR........ New Music Quarterly Review [*Record label*]
NMQUE...... Nocte Maneque [*Night and Morning*] [*Pharmacy*]
NMR......... Centre for Nuclear Magnetic Resonance [*University of Warwick*] [*British*] (CB)
NMR......... Nappamerrie [*Queensland*] [*Airport symbol*] (AD)
NMR......... Natal Mounted Rifles [*British military*] (DMA)
NMR......... National Military Representatives with SHAPE [*NATO*]
NMR......... National Milk Record [*British*] (BI)
NMR......... National Missile Range (KSC)
NMR......... National Museum of Racing (EA)
NMR......... National Museum of Racing and Hall of Fame (EA)
NMR......... Natural Magnetic Remanence [*Geophysics*]
NMR......... Naval Medical Research Institute, Washington, DC [*OCLC symbol*] (OCLC)
NMR......... Naval Missile Range
NMR......... Navy Management Review [*A publication*]
NMR......... Neomar Resources Ltd. [*Toronto Stock Exchange symbol*]
NMR......... Neonatal Mortality Rate [*Medicine*] (DMAA)
NMR......... Neonatal Mortality Risk [*Medicine*]
NMR......... New Material Release (MCD)
NMR......... New Message Request (AG)
NMR......... New Mexico Regulations (SAUS)
NMR......... New Mobile Radar (SAUS)
NMR......... News Media Representative (COE)
NMR......... Nictitating Membrane Response [*Neurophysiology*]
NMR......... Nielsen Media Research [*NYSE symbol*] [*Formerly, Cognizant Corp.*]
NMR......... Nilgiri Mountain Railway [*Indian Railway*] (TIR)
NMR......... N. M. De Rothschild & Co. [*Merchant bank*] [*British*]
NMR......... N-Modular Redundancy (RALS)
NMR......... NMR of America, Inc. [*Associated Press*] (SAG)
NMR......... No Maintenance Required (SAUS)
NMR......... No Maintenance Requirement (NVT)
NMR......... No Master Record [*Military*] (AFIT)
NMR......... Nomura Holdings [*NYSE symbol*]
NMR......... Nonconforming Material Report (MCD)
NMR......... Nordic Council of Ministers (SAUS)
NMR......... Normal Mode Rejection
NMR......... Nuclear Magnetic Relaxation
nmr......... Nuclear Magnetic Resonance (HGEN)
NMR......... Nuclear Magnetic Resonance [*Also, NUMAR*] [*Atomic physics*]
NMR......... Nuclear Magnetic Resonance Unit [*National Institute on Aging*] (RCD)
NmR......... Roswell Carnegie Library, Roswell, NM [*Library symbol*] [*Library of Congress*] (LCLS)
NMR......... San Juan, PR [*Location identifier*] [*FAA*] (FAAL)
NmRa........ Arthur Johnson Memorial Library, Raton, NM [*Library symbol*] [*Library of Congress*] (LCLS)
NMRA........ National Marine Representatives Association (EA)
NMRA........ National Mine Rescue Association
NMRA........ National Mobile Radio Association [*Defunct*] (EA)
NMRA........ National Model Railroad Association (EA)
NMRA........ National Motorcycle Racing Association (EA)
NMRA........ National Motorcycle Retailers Association [*Defunct*] (EA)
NMRA........ National Mud Racing Association
NMRA........ National Mustang Racing Association [*Motorsports*]
NMRA........ Not Mission Ready and Available (SAUS)
NMR & DA... Navy Material Redistribution and Disposition Administration
NMR & DO... Navy Material Redistribution and Disposal Office [*or Officer*]
NMRAS...... Nuclear Material Report and Analysis System [*Energy Research and Development Administration*]
NMRAS...... Nuclear Materials Report and Analysis System (SAUS)
NMRB........ National Mutual Royal Bank [*Australia*] (ADA)
NMRC........ American Health Services Corp. [*NASDAQ symbol*] (COMM)
NMRC........ National Maritime Research Center [*Maritime Administration*] [*Also, an information service or system*] (IID)
NMRC........ National Meat Retail Council [*Australia*]
NMRC........ National Men's Resource Center (EA)
NMRC........ National Microelectronics Research Centre (NITA)
NMRC........ Navy Material Redistribution Center
NMRC........ Neuromuscular Research Center [*Boston University*]
NMRCD...... Naval Medical Research Center Detachment, Lima, Peru
NMR-CT..... Nuclear Magnetic Resonance Computer Tomography (SAUS)

NMRD .... Nuclear Magnetic Relaxation Dispension [*Physics*]
NMRDC ..... Naval Medical Research and Development Command (MCD)
NmRE .... Eastern New Mexico University, Roswell Campus, Roswell, NM [*Library symbol*] [*Library of Congress*] (LCLS)
NMREC...... National Maritime Resource Center [*MARAD*] (TAG)
NM Reg..... New Mexico Register [*A publication*] (AAGC)
NMRF .... Navy-Marine Corps Residence Foundation (DNAB)
NMRG .... Navy Mid-Range Guidance
NMRHA ..... National Morgan Reining Horse Association (EA)
NMRI .... National Mass Retailing Institute [*New York, NY*] (EA)
NMRI .... National Medical Research Institute (MAE)
NMRI .... Naval Medical Research Institute
NMRI .... Nuclear Magnetic Resonance Imaging
NMRL .... Naval Medical Research Laboratory
NMRLIT ..... Nuclear Magnetic Resonance Literature System [*Chemical Information Systems, Inc.*] [*Information service or system*]
NmRM....... New Mexico Military Institute, Roswell (SAUS)
NmRM....... New Mexico Military Institute, Roswell, NM [*Library symbol*] [*Library of Congress*] (LCLS)
NMRN .... National Meteorological Rocket Network
NMRO .... Navy Mid-Range Objectives
NMR-ON .... Nuclear Magnetic Resonance-Oriented Nuclei (SAUS)
NMRP .... National Migrant Resource Program (EA)
NMRP .... New Mexico Research Park (SAUS)
NMRP .... Nuclear Magnetic Resonance Program
NMRR .... NMR of America [*NASDAQ symbol*] (TTSB)
NMRR .... NMR of America, Inc. [*NASDAQ symbol*] (NQ)
NMRR .... Normal-Mode Rejection Ratio [*Electronics*] (BARN)
NMRS .... National Mobile Radio System [*Later, Telocator Network of America*] (EA)
NMRS .... Navy Manpower Requirements System (NVT)
NMRS .... Nuclear Magnetic Resonance Spectroscopy (DMAA)
NMRS .... Numerous (FAAC)
NMR Spectroscopy... Nuclear Magnetic Resonance Spectroscopy (SAUS)
NMR Spectrum... Nuclear Magnetic Resonance Spectrum (SAUS)
NMRT........ New Members Round Table [*American Library Association*]
NMRT........ Nimbus Meteorological Radiation Tape [*NASA*]
NMRTC...... Navy and Marine Corps Reserve Training Center
NMRTC...... New Mexico Research and Treatment Center (SAUS)
NMRU .... Naval Medical Research Unit
NmRu .... Ruidoso Public Library (SAUS)
NmRu .... Ruidoso Public Library, Ruidoso, NM [*Library symbol*] [*Library of Congress*] (LCLS)
NMRX .... Numerex Corp. [*NASDAQ symbol*] (SAG)
NMS .... Ancient Egyptian Arabic Order Nobles of the Mystic Shrine (EA)
NMS .... Letemboi [*Language symbol*] (ETLW)
NMS .... Namsang [*Myanmar*] [*Airport symbol*] (OAG)
NMS .... National Management Systems [*Information service or system*] (IID)
NMS .... National Marine Service, Inc. (EFIS)
NMS .... National Maritime System [*MARAD*] (TAG)
NMS .... National Market System
NMS .... National Master Specification [*Construction Specifications Canada*] [*Information service or system*] (IID)
NMS .... National Measurement Service (SAUS)
NMS .... National Measurement System [*National Institute of Standards and Technology*]
NMS .... National Medicine Society [*British*]
NMS .... National Military Strategy (DOMA)
NMS .... National Mobility Scheme [*British*]
NMS .... Natural Matrix Standard
NMS .... Natural Mortality Schedule [*Biology*]
NMS .... Naval Medical School (MCD)
NMS .... Naval Meteorological Service
NMS .... Navigation and Mayday System [*Automotive engineering*]
NMS .... Navigation Management System (PDAA)
NMS .... Navy Mid-Range Study
NMS .... Neonatal Maladjustment Syndrome [*Equine term*] (TED)
NMS .... NetWare Management System [*Novell, Inc.*] (PCM)
NMS .... Network Management Services [*Ohio Bell Communications, Inc.*] [*Cleveland, OH*] [*Telecommunications*] (TSSD)
NMS .... Network Management Signal [*Telecommunications*] (TEL)
NMS .... Network Management Station (MLOA)
NMS .... Network Management System (DA)
NMS .... Network Measurement System [*Computer network*]
NMS .... Network Modeling and Simulation Program [*Defense Advanced Research Projects Agency*] (RCD)
NMS .... Network Monitoring Station (SAUS)
NMS .... Neumuenster [*German license plate city code*]
NMS .... Neuroleptic Malignant Syndrome
NMS .... Neuromuscular Stimulator [*Neurology*] (DAVI)
NMS .... Neuro-Musculo-Skeletal [*Medicine*]
NMS .... Neutral Mass Spectrometer [*Instrumentation*]
NMS .... Neutral Meson Spectrometer (SAUS)
NMS .... Neutron Monitoring System [*Nuclear energy*] (NRCH)
NMS .... New Management Strategy (SAUS)
NMS .... New Management System (SAUS)
NMS .... New Manning System [*Army*] (MCD)
NMS .... New Mexico State Library, Santa Fe, NM [*OCLC symbol*] (OCLC)
NMS .... New Mexico Statutes [*A publication*] (DLA)
NMS .... New Music Seminar
NMS .... New Music Society [*Australia*]
NMS .... Nitrogen Measuring System
NMS .... NMS Services (IID)
NMS .... Nobles of the Mystic Shrine (SAUS)
NMS .... Noise Measuring Set [*Telecommunications*] (TEL)
NMS .... Noise Monitoring System (ACAE)
NMS .... Nonmajor System (MCD)
NMS .... Nonmedical Science Category (DAVI)
NMS .... Non-Member State (SAUS)
NMS .... Non-Metric Multidimensional Scaling (PDAA)
NMS .... Nonprofit Management Strategies [*A publication*]
NMS .... Nordic Metalworkers Secretariat (EA)
NMS .... Normal Market Size (ODA)
NMS .... Normal Market Size Transaction
NMS .... Normal Mouse Serum
NMS .... Nuclear Materials Safeguards
NMS .... Nuclear Medical Science (SAUS)
NMS .... Nuclear-Powered Merchant Ship (PDAA)
NmS .... Santa Fe City and County Public Library, Santa Fe, NM [*Library symbol*] [*Library of Congress*] (LCLS)
NMSA .... National Metal Spinners Association (EA)
NMSA .... National Middle School Association (EA)
NMSA .... National Moving and Storage Association (EA)
NMSA .... New Mexico Statutes Annotated [*A publication*] (AAGC)
NMSA .... Nonnuclear Munitions Storage Area [*Air Force*] (DOMA)
NMSA .... Nonstandard Metropolitan Statistical Area
NMSA .... North Atlantic Treaty Organization [*NATO*] Mutual Support Act (AAGC)
NMSB .... Navy Manpower Survey Board
NMSB .... NewMil Bancorp [*NASDAQ symbol*] (TTSB)
NMSB .... New Milford Savings Bank [*NASDAQ symbol*] (NQ)
NmSC .... College of Santa Fe, Santa Fe, NM [*Library symbol*] [*Library of Congress*] (LCLS)
NMSC .... National Main Street Center (EA)
NMSC .... National Maple Syrup Council [*Later, NAMSC*]
NMSC .... National Merit Scholarship Corp. (EA)
NMSC .... Naval Medical Supply Unit (DNAB)
NMSC .... Navy Management Systems Center (PDAA)
NMSC .... Nerve and Muscle Stimulating Current
NMSC .... Nonferrous Metals Society of China (SAUS)
NMSC .... Nonmartensitic Structural Component (SAUS)
NMSC .... Nonmelanoma Skin Cancer [*Medicine*]
NMSC .... Non-Military Supplies Committee [*Combined Production and Resources Board*] [*British*] [*World War II*]
NMSC .... Northeast-Midwest Senate Coalition (EA)
NMSC .... Northwest Missouri State College [*Later, Northwest Missouri State University*]
NMSC .... Nutrition Management [*NASDAQ symbol*] (SAG)
NmSc........ Silver City Public Library, Silver City, NM [*Library symbol*] [*Library of Congress*] (LCLS)
NMSCA...... Navy Material Command Support Activity (PDAA)
NMSCA...... Nutrition Mgmt Svcs'A' [*NASDAQ symbol*] (TTSB)
NmSCS...... College of Santa Fe, Santa Fe, NM [*Library symbol*] [*Library of Congress*] (LCLS)
NmScSW.... Southwestern Regional Library, Silver City, NM [*Library symbol*] [*Library of Congress*] (LCLS)
NMSCW..... Nutrition Mgmt Svcs Wrrt [*NASDAQ symbol*] (TTSB)
NmScW ..... Western New Mexico University, Silver City, NM [*Library symbol*] [*Library of Congress*] (LCLS)
NMSD .... National Match Support Detachment [*Ammunition supplier*]
NMSD .... National Military Strategy Document (DOMA)
NMSD .... Naval Medical Supply Depot
NMSD .... Next Most Significant Digit [*Computer science*]
NMSDC...... National Minority Supplier Development Council (EA)
NMSE........ Naval Material Support Establishment [*After 1966, NAVMAT, NMCOM, NMC*]
NMSE........ Normalized Mean Square Error (SAUS)
NMSE........ Normalized Minimum Square Error (SAUS)
NmSEA...... New Mexico Society of Enrolled Agents (SAUS)
NMSF........ Normalized Mean Square Error (DMAA)
NMSHC...... Bureau of Medicine and Surgery Hospital Corps Publication [*Later, NAVMED*] [*Navy*]
NMSI .... National Mini-Storage Institute [*Defunct*] (EA)
NMSI .... National Museum of Science & Industry (WDAA)
NMSIDS..... Near-Miss Sudden Infant Death Syndrome [*Medicine*] (DMAA)
NMSK .... Namesake (ABBR)
NMSL........ National Maximum Speed Limit [*NHTSA*] (TAG)
NmSM....... Museum of New Mexico, Santa Fe, NM [*Library symbol*] [*Library of Congress*] (LCLS)
NMSM....... New Mexico School of Mines (AAG)
NmSM-A .... Museum of New Mexico, Laboratory of Anthropology, Santa Fe, NM [*Library symbol*] [*Library of Congress*] (LCLS)
NMSMK ..... Numismatic (ABBR)
NMSMTST... Numismaticist (ABBR)
NMSO .... NATO Maintenance and Support Operation (AFM)
NMSO .... Naval Manpower Survey Office (NVT)
NMSO .... N-Methylnitroanisole [*Organic chemistry*]
NMSO .... Nuclear Missile Safety Office [*or Officer*] (AFM)
NmSo........ Socorro Public Library (SAUS)
NmSo........ Socorro Public Library, Socorro, NM [*Library symbol*] [*Library of Congress*] (LCLS)
NmSoI....... New Mexico Institute of Mining and Technology, Socorro, NM [*Library symbol*] [*Library of Congress*] (LCLS)
NMSP .... National Marine Sanctuary Program [*Nautical term*] (NTA)
NmSP .... New Mexico State Penitentiary Library, Santa Fe, NM [*Library symbol*] [*Library of Congress*] (LCLS)
NMSP .... New Mon State Party [*Myanmar*] [*Political party*]
NMSP .... N-Methylspiperone [*Biochemistry*]
NmSp........ Springer Public Library, Springer, NM [*Library symbol*] [*Library of Congress*] (LCLS)

NmSpP ...... Springer Public Library, Springer, NM [*Library symbol*] [*Library of Congress*] (LCLS)
NMSQT ...... National Merit Scholarship Qualifying Test
NmSr .... Moise Memorial Library, Santa Rosa, NM [*Library symbol*] [*Library of Congress*] (LCLS)
NMSR .... New Mexico State Road (SAUS)
NMSRA ...... National Master Shoe Rebuilders Association (EA)
NMSRC ...... National Middle School Resource Center (EA)
NMSS .... NASCOM [*Naval Air Systems Command*] Manual Scheduling System
NMSS .... National Meteorological Satellite System (IAA)
NMSS .... National Multiple Sclerosis Society (EA)
NMSS .... National Multipurpose Space Station
NMSS .... Natural Microsystems [*NASDAQ symbol*] (TTSB)
NMSS .... Natural Microsystems Corp. [*NASDAQ symbol*] (SAG)
NMSS .... Nemesis (ABBR)
NMSS .... Nuclear Materials Safety and Safeguards (SAUS)
NMSS .... Office of Nuclear Materials Safety and Safeguards [*Nuclear Regulatory Commission*]
NMSSA ...... National Multiple Sclerosis Society of Australia
NMSSA ...... NATO Maintenance Supply Service Agency [*Later, NAMSO*]
NMSSO ...... Navy Maintenance and Supply Systems Office (DNAB)
NMSSS ...... NATO Maintenance Supply Service System
NMSST ...... Naval Manpower Shore Survey Team (NVT)
NmSStJ ..... Saint Johns College in Santa Fe (SAUS)
NMST .... Materials System Test (SAUS)
NMST .... New Materials System Test [*Obsolete*] [*Nuclear energy*]
NM Stat Ann ... New Mexico Statutes, Annotated [*A publication*] (DLA)
NM State Eng Off Tech Rep ... New Mexico State Engineer Office. Technical Report (SAUS)
NM State Univ Agric Exp Stn Res Rep ... New Mexico State University. Agricultural Experiment Station. Research Report (SAUS)
NMSU .... Naval Motion Study Unit [*British*]
NMSU .... New Mexico State University
NmSuAF .... United States Air Force, Sacramento Peak Observatory, Sunspot, NM [*Library symbol*] [*Library of Congress*] (LCLS)
NMSVA ...... Navy Mail Service Veterans Association (EA)
NMSZ .... New Madrid Seismic Zone [*Geology*]
NMT .... Barrow, AK [*Location identifier*] [*FAA*] (FAAL)
NMT .... Montedison SpA [*NYSE symbol*] (COMM)
NMT .... National Museum of Transport [*Later, TMA*] (EA)
NMT .... Neuromuscular Tension [*Medicine*]
NMT .... Neuromuscular Transmission [*Physiology*]
NMT .... New Means of Transportation
NMT .... New Mexico Institute of Mining and Technology, Socorro, NM [*OCLC symbol*] (OCLC)
NMT .... N-Methyltransferase (DB)
NMT .... N-Monomethyltryptamine [*Organic chemistry*]
NMT .... N-Myristoyl Acyltransferase [*An enzyme*]
NMT .... Noble-Metal-Coated Titanium [*Anode*]
NMT .... Noise Measurement Technique (SAUS)
NMT .... No More Than [*Pharmacy*] (DAVI)
NMT .... No More Trouble [*Coates' brand of cotton thread*] (ROG)
NMT .... Nonmetalic [*Technical drawings*]
NMT .... Nordic Mobile Telephone [*Radio-telephone system for car users*] [*Denmark, Finland, Norway, Sweden*]
NMT .... Nordic Mobile Telephone Network (NITA)
NMT .... Nordic Mobile Telephone System (SAUS)
NMT .... Norepinephrine N-Methyl-Transferase (SAUS)
NMT .... Nor More Than (SAUS)
NMT .... Northwest Marine Trade Association (EA)
NMT .... Norwegian Method of Tunnelling [*Civil engineering*]
NMT .... Notification of Master Tool (NASA)
nmt .... Not More Than (ODA)
NMT .... Not More Than
NMT .... Nuclear Medicine Technologist (MELL)
NMT .... Nuclear Medicine Technology
NMT .... Number of Module Types
NMT .... Nuveen MA Prem Inc. Muni Fd [*NYSE symbol*] (TTSB)
NMT .... Nuveen Massachusetts Premium Income Municipal Fund [*NYSE symbol*] (SPSG)
NMTA .... National Manpower Training Association [*Later, NETA*] (EA)
NMTA .... National Metal Trades Association [*Later, AAIM*] (EA)
NMTA .... National Movement Theatre Association (EA)
NMTA .... Northwest Marine Trade Association [*Association*] [*Nautical term*] (NTA)
NMTBA ...... National Machine Tool Builders' Association [*Later, AMT*] (EA)
NMTBD ...... No More to Be Done [*Medicine*]
NMTC .... Naval Mine Testing Center (MCD)
NMTC .... Naval Missile Testing Center
NMTC .... North Metropolitan Tramways Co. [*British*] (ROG)
NMTC .... Nucleon-Meson Transport Code
NMTC .... Numerical Technologies [*NASDAQ symbol*] (SG)
NMTCB ...... Nuclear Medicine Technology Certification Board (EA)
NMTD .... Nonmetastatic Trophoblastic Disease [*Medicine*] (DMAA)
NMTD .... Nuclear Materials Transfer Document
NMTF .... N and M Transfer Company [*Common carrier symbol*]
NMTF .... National Market Traders Federation [*British*] (DBA)
NMTF .... National Metal Trades Federation [*British*] (DBA)
NMTF .... Naval Mine Test Facility
NMTFA ...... National Master Tile Fixers Association [*British*] (DBA)
NMTHC ...... Nonmethane Total Hydrocarbons [*Organic chemistry*]
NmTHF ...... Harwood Foundation, Taos, NM [*Library symbol*] [*Library of Congress*] (LCLS)
NMTI .... Neuromedical Technologies, Inc. (SAUS)
NMTI .... Nitinol Medical Technologies, Inc. [*NASDAQ symbol*] (SAG)
NMTI .... NMT Medical [*NASDAQ symbol*] (SG)
NMtK .... Mount Kisco Public Library, Mount Kisco, NY [*Library symbol*] [*Library of Congress*] (LCLS)
NmTKC ...... Kit Carson Memorial Foundation, Inc., Taos, NM [*Library symbol*] [*Library of Congress*] (LCLS)
NMTLK ...... Nonmetallic (ABBR)
NMTLM ...... Nuclear Materials Transportation Logistics Model (SAUS)
NMTN .... National Music Theater Network (EA)
NMTO .... Navy Material Transportation Office
NMTP .... National Means Test Proposal
NMTR .... Nuclear Materials Transfer Report
NmTr .... Truth Or Consequences Public Library, Truth Or Consequences, NM [*Library symbol*] [*Library of Congress*] (LCLS)
NMTS .... National Milk Testing Service
NMTS .... Navy Military Technical Specialist (MCD)
NMTS .... Neuromuscular Tension State [*Medicine*] (DMAA)
NMTS .... Noise Measurement Test Set
NMTS .... Non-Matching to Sample [*Psychology*] (QSUL)
NmTu .... Tucumcari Public Library, Tucumcari, NM [*Library symbol*] [*Library of Congress*] (LCLS)
NmTuE ...... Eastern Plains Regional Library, Tucumcari, NM [*Library symbol*] [*Library of Congress*] (LCLS)
NMtv .... Mount Vernon Public Library, Mount Vernon, NY [*Library symbol*] [*Library of Congress*] (LCLS)
NMTV .... Network Multimedia Co. (IID)
NMTX .... Novametrics Medical Systems [*NASDAQ symbol*] (SAG)
NMTX .... Novametrix Medical Systems, Inc. [*NASDAQ symbol*] (NQ)
NMTX .... Novametrix Med Sys [*NASDAQ symbol*] (TTSB)
NMTXW ..... Novametrix Med Sys Wrt'A' [*NASDAQ symbol*] (TTSB)
NMTXZ ...... Novametrix Med Sys Wrrt'B' [*NASDAQ symbol*] (TTSB)
NMU .... Brunswick, ME [*Location identifier*] [*FAA*] (FAAL)
NMU .... National Maritime Union (USDC)
NMU .... National Maritime Union of America (EA)
NMU .... National Museums of Canada Library [*UTLAS symbol*]
NMU .... Navigation Management Unit (HLLA)
NMU .... Network Monitor Unit [*Telecommunications*] (TSSD)
NMU .... Neuromuscular Unit [*Medicine*]
nmu .... New Mexico [*MARC country of publication code*] [*Library of Congress*] (LCCP)
NMU .... Nitrosomethylurea [*Also, MNU*] [*Organic chemistry*]
NMU .... Nitrosomethylurethane (SAUS)
NMU .... Nordic Musicians' Union (EA)
NMU .... Northern Michigan University [*Marquette*]
NmU .... University of New Mexico, Albuquerque, NM [*Library symbol*] [*Library of Congress*] (LCLS)
NMUAA ...... Northern Michigan University Alumni Association (EA)
NMUC .... National Medical Utilization Committee [*HEW*]
NmU-L ...... University of New Mexico, Law Library, Albuquerque, NM [*Library symbol*] [*Library of Congress*] (LCLS)
NmU-M ...... University of New Mexico, Library of the Medical Sciences, School of Medicine and Bernalillo County Medical Society, Albuquerque, NM [*Library symbol*] [*Library of Congress*] (LCLS)
NMuP .... Muttontown Preserve, Muttontown, NY [*Library symbol*] [*Library of Congress*] (LCLS)
NMusic R ... New Music Review (SAUS)
NMV .... National Museum of Victoria (SAUS)
NMV .... Nitrogen Manual Valve (MCD)
NMV .... Normal Mode Voltage (SAUS)
NMVCA ...... National Military Vehicle Collectors Association [*Defunct*]
NMVD .... Null Multi-Valued Dependency (SAUS)
NMVMA ..... New Mexico Veterinary Medical Association (GVA)
NMVO .... Navy Manpower Validation Office (DNAB)
NMVOC ...... Nonmethane Volatile Organic Carbon [*Environmental chemistry*]
NMVOC ...... Non-Methane Volatile Organic Chemicals (SAUS)
NMVOC ...... Non-Methane Volatile Organic Compounds (SAUS)
NMVOLANT ... Navy Manpower Validation Office, Atlantic (DNAB)
NMVOPAC ... Navy Manpower Validation Office, Pacific (DNAB)
NMVP .... Navy Manpower Validation Program (NG)
NMVSA ...... Navy Manpower Validation Support Activity
NMVSAC .... National Motor Vehicle Safety Advisory Council (EA)
NMVT .... Network Management Vector Command (SAUS)
NMVT .... Network Management Vector Tables [*Computer science*] (GART)
NMVT .... Network Management Vector Transport [*IBM's SNA*] [*Communications term*] (DCT)
NMVTA ...... National Motor Vehicle Theft Act
NMvUA ...... State University of New York, Agricultural and Technical College at Morrisville,Morrisville, NY [*Library symbol*] [*Library of Congress*] (LCLS)
NMW .... Astoria, OR [*Location identifier*] [*FAA*] (FAAL)
NMW .... Naval Mine Warfare (DOMA)
NMW .... Normal Molecular Weight
NMW .... Notes on Mississippi Writers [*A publication*] (ANEX)
NMW .... Western Carolina University, Cullowhee, NC [*OCLC symbol*] (OCLC)
NMWA .... National Military Wives Association [*Later, NMFA*] (EA)
NMWA .... National Mineral Wool Association [*Later, MIMA*]
NMWC .... National Migrant Workers Council [*Farmington Hills, MI*] (EA)
NMWC .... Nelson, Marlborough, and West Coast Regiment [*British military*] (DMA)
NMWC .... New Mexico Western College
NMWGI ...... New Mexico Wool Growers (EARSL)
NMWIA ...... National Mineral Wool Insulation Association [*Formerly, NMWA*] [*Later, MIMA*] (EA)
NMWL .... Normal Molecular Weight, Low in Extractables

NmWM ...... White Sands Missile Range Library, White Sands Missile Range, NM [*Library symbol*] [*Library of Congress*] (LCLS)
NMWP .... National Migrant Worker Program [*Department of Labor*]
NMWP .... National Mixed Waste Program (ABAC)
NMWQL ..... National Marine Water Quality Laboratory [*Environmental Protection Agency*] (MSC)
NMWS .... Naval Meroka Weapon System (SAUS)
NMWS .... Naval Mine Warfare School
NMWTC ..... Naval Mine Warfare Training Center
NMWTS ..... Naval Mine Warfare Test Station
NMWTS ..... Naval Mine Warfare Training School
n-mx- .... Mexico [*MARC geographic area code*] [*Library of Congress*] (LCCP)
NMX .... Not Multiplexed (ACAE)
NMxAr .... New Mexico & Arizona Land Co. [*Associated Press*] (SAG)
NMxB .... Board of Cooperative Educational Services, Regional Resource Center, Mexico, NY [*Library symbol*] [*Library of Congress*] (LCLS)
NMY .... Mayville State College, Mayville, ND [*OCLC symbol*] (OCLC)
N/my .... Newton per Square Meter (or Metre) (SAUS)
NMY .... Nonresonant Magnetic Yoke
NMY .... Nuveen Maryland Premium Income Municipal Fund [*NYSE symbol*] (SPSG)
NMY .... Nuveen MD Prem Inc. Muni Fd [*NYSE symbol*] (TTSB)
NMyM .... Maryknoll Fathers Seminary, Maryknoll, NY [*Library symbol*] [*Library of Congress*] (LCLS)
NMZ .... Norman Resources Ltd. [*Vancouver Stock Exchange symbol*]
NMZ .... Willow Grove, PA [*Location identifier*] [*FAA*] (FAAL)
NN .... Air Trails [*ICAO designator*] (AD)
N:N .... Azo Group [*Chemical group with two nitrogen atoms*] (MEDA)
nn .... Footnotes (DLA)
NN .... Names (ABBR)
NN .... Narcolepsy Network
NN .... NASA Notice
NN .... National Neighbors (EA)
NN .... National Networker [*An association*] (EA)
NN .... Natural, Nongrazed [*Agriculture*]
NN .... Nearest Neighbor [*Mathematics*] [*Computer search term*]
NN .... Necessary Nuisance [*i.e., a husband*] [*Slang*]
NN .... Neonatal (DAVI)
NN .... Nerves
nn .... Nervi Nerves [*Neurology*] [*Latin*] (DAVI)
NN .... Network Node [*Communications term*] (DCT)
NN .... Neuroelectric News [*Medicine*] [*Journal*] (EDAA)
NN .... Neurotics Nomine [*British*]
NN .... Neutral and Nonaligned [*Nations*]
NN .... Neutralization Number (SAUS)
N-N .... Neutron-Neutron Logging (SAUS)
NN .... Nevada Northern Railway Co. [*AAR code*]
NN .... Nevocellular Nevus (MELL)
NN .... Nevus Network (NRGU)
NN .... Newbridge Networks [*NYSE symbol*] (TTSB)
NN .... Newbridge Networks Corp. [*NYSE symbol*]
NN .... Newbridge Networks, Inc. [*NYSE symbol*] (SAG)
nn .... New Hebrides [*MARC country of publication code*] [*Library of Congress*] (LCCP)
NN .... New Nationals [*Political party*] [*Australia*]
NN .... Newspaper News [*A publication*]
NN .... New York Public Library (SAUS)
NN .... Next Node (SAUS)
NN .... Nicaragua Network (EA)
NN .... Nicaragua Network Education Fund (EA)
NN .... Nigerian Navy
NN .... Nightmare Networker (SAUS)
NN .... Night-Night (SAUS)
NN .... noch nicht besetzt (SAUS)
NN .... Noise Network (WDAA)
N/N .... Noise-to-Noise (SAUS)
nn .... Nomen Nescio [*Unknown*] [*Latin*] (GPO)
nn .... Nomen Novum [*New Name*] [*Latin*] (DAVI)
NN .... Nomina [*Names*] [*Latin*]
NN .... No Name
NN .... No News (SAUS)
N/N .... Non-Negotiable (FOTI)
NN .... Nonnuclear (ACAE)
NN .... Non-Nuclear Lance (MCD)
N/N .... No Noting (SAUS)
NN .... Non-Participating National (OTD)
N/N .... No Number (SAUS)
NN .... Noon
NN .... Normally Nourished [*Medicine*] (EDAA)
NN .... Normalnull [*Mean Sea Level*] [*German*]
NN .... Normal Nutrition (MELL)
N/N .... Normocytic/Normochromic Anemia (DAVI)
NN .... Northampton [*Postcode*] (ODBW)
NN .... Northern Nevada Railroad [*Federal Railroad Administration identification code*]
N/N .... Northrop/Nortronics (SAUS)
NN .... Northwestern National (EFIS)
NN .... Notes [*Finance*]
NN .... Not Nested [*Freight*]
NN .... Not Normal
n N .... Not North Of (RIMS)
N/N .... Not North Of
N/N .... Not to Be Noted [*Business term*]
NN .... Nouns
NN .... Nuclear Network (EA)
NN .... Nucleon-Nucleon
NN .... Nurse Notes (SAUS)
N/N .... Nurses' Notes (MAE)
NN .... Nurturing Network [*An association*] (EA)
NN .... Nynorsk [*Linguistics*] (IEL)
NN .... Office of Nonproliferation and National Security (SAUS)
NNA .... American Geographical Society, New York, NY [*Library symbol*] [*Library of Congress*] (LCLS)
NNA .... Nana [*Peru*] [*Seismograph station code, US Geological Survey*] (SEIS)
nna .... Nanoampere (ELAL)
NNA .... National Neckwear Association (EA)
NNA .... National Needlework Association (EA)
NNA .... National Newman Apostolate
NNA .... National News Agency [*Lebanon*]
NNA .... National Newspaper Association (EA)
NNA .... National Notary Association (EA)
NNA .... National Notion Association [*Later, AHSA*] (EA)
NNA .... National Numismatic Association (EA)
NNA .... Neonatal Nurses Association (SAUS)
NNA .... Neutral/Nonaligned [*Countries*]
NNA .... Neutral Non-Allied (ACAE)
NNA .... Nevada Nurses Association (SAUS)
NNA .... New Nadina Explorations [*Vancouver Stock Exchange symbol*]
NNA .... New Network Architecture
NNA .... N-Nitrosamine [*Organic chemistry*]
NNA .... Nonhistone Nucleoprotein Antibodies [*Immunochemistry*]
NNA .... Nonnarcotic Analgesics [*Medicine*] (MELL)
NNA .... Normochromic, Normocytic Anemia (DAVI)
NNAA .... Augusta Warshaw Advertising Library, New York, NY [*Library symbol*] [*Library of Congress*] (LCLS)
NNAA .... National Newman Alumni Association [*Defunct*] (EA)
NNAA .... Native North American Almanac [*A publication*]
NNAAI .... American Alpine Club, New York, NY [*Library symbol*] [*Library of Congress*] (LCLS)
NNAAr .... American Arbitration Association, New York, NY [*Library symbol*] [*Library of Congress*] (LCLS)
NNAB .... American Bible Society, New York, NY [*Library symbol*] [*Library of Congress*] (LCLS)
NNABA ...... American Bankers Association, New York, NY [*Library symbol*] [*Library of Congress*] (LCLS)
NNA-Ber .... NNA-Berichte (SAUS)
NNAC .... National Native American Cooperative (EA)
NNAC .... National Noise Abatement Council [*Defunct*]
NNACC ..... National Native American Chamber of Commerce [*Defunct*] (EA)
NNACS ...... American Cancer Society, New York, NY [*Library symbol*] [*Library of Congress*] (LCLS)
NNAD .... Anti-Defamation League of B'nai B'rith, New York, NY [*Library symbol*] [*Library of Congress*] (LCLS)
NNADAP .... National Native Alcohol and Drug Abuse Program [*Canada*]
NNAdv .... American Association of Advertising Agencies, New York, NY [*Library symbol*] [*Library of Congress*] (LCLS)
NNAEMSA ... National Native American EMS Association (EA)
NNAF .... American Foundation for the Blind, New York, NY [*Library symbol*] [*Library of Congress*] (LCLS)
NNAF .... National Network of Abortion Funds [*Association*] (EA)
NNAFS ...... National Newman Association of Faculty and Staff [*Defunct*] (EA)
NNAG .... American Gas Association, New York, NY [*Library symbol*] [*Library of Congress*] (LCLS)
NNAG .... NATO Naval Advisory Group (NATG)
NNAG .... NATO Naval Armaments Group (NATG)
NNAI .... American Irish Historical Society, New York, NY [*Library symbol*] [*Library of Congress*] (LCLS)
NNAIA .... American Institute of Certified Public Accountants, New York, NY [*Library symbol*] [*Library of Congress*] (LCLS)
NNAIAA ..... American Institute of Aeronautics and Astronautics, Technical Information Service, New York, NY [*Library symbol*] [*Library of Congress*] (LCLS)
NNAIL .... Austrain Institute Library, New York, NY [*Library symbol*] [*Library of Congress*] (LCLS)
NNAIP .... American Institute of Physics, New York, NY [*Library symbol*] [*Library of Congress*] (LCLS)
NNAJ .... American Jewish Committee, New York, NY [*Library symbol*] [*Library of Congress*] (LCLS)
NNAJN ...... American Journal of Nursing Co., New York, NY [*Library symbol*] [*Library of Congress*] (LCLS)
NNAKC ...... American Kennel Club, New York, NY [*Library symbol*] [*Library of Congress*] (LCLS)
NNAL .... American Academy of Arts and Letters, New York, NY [*Library symbol*] [*Library of Congress*] (LCLS)
NNAMA ...... American Management Associations, New York, NY [*Library symbol*] [*Library of Congress*] (LCLS)
NNAMM ..... American Merchant Marine Library Association, New York, NY [*Library symbol*] [*Library of Congress*] (LCLS)
NNAN .... American Numismatic Society, New York, NY [*Library symbol*] [*Library of Congress*] (LCLS)
NNAn .... Anthology Film Archives, New York, NY [*Library symbol*] [*Library of Congress*] (LCLS)
NNan .... Nanuet Public Library, Nanuet, NY [*Library symbol*] [*Library of Congress*] (LCLS)
NNAnF .... Anthology Film Archives, New York, NY [*Library symbol*] [*Library of Congress*] (LCLS)
NNanL .... Nanuet Public Library, Nanuet, NY [*Library symbol*] [*Library of Congress*] (LCLS)
NNAP .... NAVAIR [*Naval Air Systems Command*] Naval Aviation Plan (MCD)
NNAPS ...... Night Navigation and Pilotage System

NNAPW ..... National Network of Asian and Pacific Women (EA)
NNAS .... Neonatal Narcotic Abstinence Syndrome [*Medicine*] (DMAA)
NNASA ...... American National Standards Institute, New York, NY [*Library symbol*] [*Library of Congress*] (LCLS)
NNASF ...... American-Scandinavian Foundation, New York, NY [*Library symbol*] [*Library of Congress*] (LCLS)
NNASovM ... American-Soviet Medical Society, New York, NY [*Library symbol*] [*Library of Congress*] [*Obsolete*] (LCLS)
NNASP ...... American Society for Psychical Research, New York, NY [*Library symbol*] [*Library of Congress*] (LCLS)
NNAT .... American Telephone & Telegraph Co., Corporate Research Library, New York, NY [*Library symbol*] [*Library of Congress*] (LCLS)
NNAT .... Naglieri Nonverbal Ability Test (DIPS)
NNAUR ...... Australian Consulate-General, Australian Reference Library, New York, NY [*Library symbol*] [*Library of Congress*] (LCLS)
NNAuS ...... National Audubon Society, New York, NY [*Library symbol*] [*Library of Congress*] (LCLS)
N/NAVEXOS... Navy/Executive Offices (AAG)
NNAVS ...... Association for Voluntary Sterilization, Inc., International Project, New York, NY [*Library symbol*] [*Library of Congress*] (LCLS)
NNAW .... Native North American Writers [*A publication*]
NNAy .... American Home Products Corp., Ayerst Medical Library, New York, NY [*Library symbol*] [*Library of Congress*] (LCLS)
NNB.......... Association of the Bar of the City of New York, New York, NY [*Library symbol*] [*Library of Congress*] (LCLS)
NNB.......... National Needlecraft Bureau (EA)
NNB.......... National News Bureau [*Commercial firm*] (EA)
NNB.......... Nature New Biology [*Medicine*] (EDAA)
NNB.......... New Natura Brevium [*A publication*] (DSA)
NN-B......... New York Public Library, Albert A. and Henry W. Berg Collection, New York, NY [*Library symbol*] [*Library of Congress*] (LCLS)
NNb.......... North Babylon Public Library, North Babylon, NY [*Library symbol*] [*Library of Congress*] (LCLS)
NNB.......... Northumberland and Newcastle Board of Education [*UTLAS symbol*]
NNBa .... Barnard College, Columbia University, New York, NY [*Library symbol*] [*Library of Congress*] (LCLS)
NNBA........ National Nurses in Business Association (EA)
NN Ball ..... NN Ball & Roller, Inc. [*Associated Press*] (SAG)
NNBBC ...... Bernard M. Baruch College of the City University of New York, New York, NY [*Library symbol*] [*Library of Congress*] (LCLS)
NNbBE....... Belmont Elementary School, North Babylon, NY [*Library symbol*] [*Library of Congress*] (LCLS)
NNBC .... Bronx Community College, New York (SAUS)
NNBC .... Bronx Community College, New York, NY [*Library symbol*] [*Library of Congress*] (LCLS)
NNBC .... National Network of Bilingual Centers (EA)
NNBC .... Node-Negative Breast Cancer (MELL)
NNBCLA..... Negative Negabinary Carry-Look-Ahead Adder [*Computer science*] (MHDI)
NNbe .... North Bellmore Public Library, North Bellmore, NY [*Library symbol*] [*Library of Congress*] (LCLS)
NNbeDE..... Dinkelmeyer Elementary School, North Bellmore, NY [*Library symbol*] [*Library of Congress*] (LCLS)
NNbeGE..... Gunther Elementary School, North Bellmore, NY [*Library symbol*] [*Library of Congress*] (LCLS)
NNbeJJ...... Jerusalem Avenue Junior High School, North Bellmore, NY [*Library symbol*] [*Library of Congress*] (LCLS)
NNbeNE..... Newbridge Road Elementary School, North Bellmore, NY [*Library symbol*] [*Library of Congress*] (LCLS)
NNbePE..... Park Elementary School, North Bellmore, NY [*Library symbol*] [*Library of Congress*] (LCLS)
NNBeS ...... Bentley School, New York, NY [*Library symbol*] [*Library of Congress*] (LCLS)
NNbeSME... Saw Mill Elementary School, North Bellmore, NY [*Library symbol*] [*Library of Congress*] (LCLS)
NNBG........ New York Botanical Garden, Bronx, NY [*Library symbol*] [*Library of Congress*] (LCLS)
NNbHS ...... North Babylon High School, North Babylon, NY [*Library symbol*] [*Library of Congress*] (LCLS)
NNBI......... Beth Israel Medical Center, New York, NY [*Library symbol*] [*Library of Congress*] (LCLS)
NNBIS .... National Narcotics Border Interdiction System
NNBL .... National Negro Business League [*Later, National Business League*]
NNbL .... North Babylon Public Library, North Babylon, NY [*Library symbol*] [*Library of Congress*] (LCLS)
NNbLE....... William E. De Luca Jr. Elementary School, North Babylon, NY [*Library symbol*] [*Library of Congress*] (LCLS)
NNBLI .... British Information Services, New York, NY [*Library symbol*] [*Library of Congress*] (LCLS)
NNBMC...... Borough of Manhattan Community College, New York, NY [*Library symbol*] [*Library of Congress*] (LCLS)
NNbMJ ...... Robert Moses Junior High School, North Babylon, NY [*Library symbol*] [*Library of Congress*] (LCLS)
NNbPE....... Parliment Place Elementary School, North Babylon, NY [*Library symbol*] [*Library of Congress*] (LCLS)
NN-Br........ New York Public Library, Branch Library System, New York, NY [*Library symbol*] [*Library of Congress*] (LCLS)
NNBR........ NN [*NASDAQ symbol*]
NNBR........ NN Ball & Roller [*NASDAQ symbol*] (TTSB)
NNBR........ NN Ball & Roller, Inc. [*NASDAQ symbol*] (SAG)
NNBS........ Biblical Seminary in New York, New York, NY [*Library symbol*] [*Library of Congress*] (LCLS)
NNBSC ...... Bank Street College of Education, New York, NY [*Library symbol*] [*Library of Congress*] (LCLS)
NNbWE...... Woods Road Elementary School, North Babylon, NY [*Library symbol*] [*Library of Congress*] (LCLS)
NNC.......... Columbia University, New York (SAUS)
NNC.......... Columbia University, New York, NY [*Library symbol*] [*Library of Congress*] (LCLS)
NNC.......... Naga National Council [*India*] (PD)
NNC.......... Natal Native Contingent [*British military*] (DMA)
NNC.......... National Namibia Concerns (EA)
NNC.......... National Neighborhood Coalition (EA)
NNC.......... National Network Congestion Signal (NITA)
NNC.......... National News Council (EA)
NNC.......... National Nomad Club [*Defunct*] (EA)
NNC.......... National Nuclear Corp. [*British*]
NNC.......... National Nudist Council [*Defunct*] (EA)
NNC.......... National Nutrition Consortium [*Defunct*] (EA)
NNC.......... Navy Nurse Corps
NNC.......... Neutral Nations Committee [*CINCPAC*] (CINC)
NN/C......... Night Noise Group C [*Aircraft*]
NNC.......... Nolan, Norton & Co., Inc., Lexington, MA [*OCLC symbol*] (OCLC)
NNC.......... Non-Noise Certificated Aircraft (DA)
NNC.......... Non-Noise Certified Aircraft (SAUS)
NNC.......... Northern Navigation Co. Ltd. [*AAR code*]
NNC.......... Northwest Nazarene College [*Nampa, ID*]
NNC.......... Notice of Noncompliance (EPA)
NNC.......... Nuance (ABBR)
NNC.......... Nudist National Committee (EA)
NNC.......... Nuveen NC Prem Inc. Muni [*NYSE symbol*] (TTSB)
NNC.......... Nuveen North Carolina Premium Income Municipal Fund [*NYSE symbol*] (SPSG)
NNC-A....... Columbia University, Avery Library of Architecture, New York, NY [*Library symbol*] [*Library of Congress*] (LCLS)
NNCA........ National Newman Chaplains Association [*Later, CCMA*] (EA)
NNCA........ Navy Nurse Corps Association (SAUS)
NNCAA...... National Negro County Agents Association (EA)
NNCAM...... Cravath, Swaine & Moore, New York, NY [*Library symbol*] [*Library of Congress*] (LCLS)
NNCar .... Carnegie Corp. of New York, New York, NY [*Library symbol*] [*Library of Congress*] (LCLS)
NNCB .... [*The*] College Board, New York, NY [*Library symbol*] [*Library of Congress*] (LCLS)
NNC-B....... Columbia University, Biological Sciences Library, New York, NY [*Library symbol*] [*Library of Congress*] (LCLS)
NNC-BE ..... Columbia University, Business-Economic Library, New York, NY [*Library symbol*] [*Library of Congress*] (LCLS)
NNCBN ...... City Bank, North America, New York, NY [*Library symbol*] [*Library of Congress*] (LCLS)
NNCBS ...... Columbia Broadcasting System, Inc., New York, NY [*Library symbol*] [*Library of Congress*] (LCLS)
NNCC........ Chemists' Club, New York, NY [*Library symbol*] [*Library of Congress*] (LCLS)
NNCC........ National Network Control Centre [*Communications*] [*British*]
NNCC........ National Nursing Consultative Committee [*Australia*]
NNCC........ Navy Nurse Corps Candidate (DNAB)
NNCCA ...... Canadian Centre for Architecture, New York, NY [*Library symbol*] [*Library of Congress*] (LCLS)
NNCCG ...... Canadian Consulate General Library, New York, NY [*Library symbol*] [*Library of Congress*] (LCLS)
NNCCVTE... National Network for Curriculum Coordination in Vocational and Technical Education (OICC)
NNCD........ Nitro-naphthalene-chlorobenzene-diazonium Sulfonate [*Medicine*] (EDAA)
NNCE .... Carnegie Endowment for International Peace, New York, NY [*Library symbol*] [*Library of Congress*] (LCLS)
NNC-EA ..... Columbia University, East Asiatic Library, New York, NY [*Library symbol*] [*Library of Congress*] (LCLS)
NNCEF....... Child Education Foundation, New York, NY [*Library symbol*] [*Library of Congress*] [*Obsolete*] (LCLS)
NNCenC ..... Century Association, New York, NY [*Library symbol*] [*Library of Congress*] (LCLS)
NNCEP ...... Centro de Estudios Puertorriquenos, New York, NY [*Library symbol*] [*Library of Congress*] (LCLS)
NNCF .... Commonwealth Fund, New York, NY [*Library symbol*] [*Library of Congress*] (LCLS)
NNCF .... National Newman Club Federation [*Defunct*] (EA)
NNCFo....... Council on Foundations, New York, NY [*Library symbol*] [*Library of Congress*] (LCLS)
NNCFR ...... Council on Foreign Relations, New York, NY [*Library symbol*] [*Library of Congress*] (LCLS)
NNC-G....... Columbia University, Lamont-Doherty Geological Observatory, Palisades, NY [*Library symbol*] [*Library of Congress*] (LCLS)
NNCG........ Norwegian Consulate General, New York, NY [*Library symbol*] [*Library of Congress*] (LCLS)
NNCh .... Chadbourne & Parke, New York, NY [*Library symbol*] [*Library of Congress*] (LCLS)
NNCI......... College of Insurance, New York, NY [*Library symbol*] [*Library of Congress*] (LCLS)
NNCit........ Cities Service Co., Corporate Library, New York, NY [*Library symbol*] [*Library of Congress*] (LCLS)
NNC-L .... Columbia University, Law Library, New York, NY [*Library symbol*] [*Library of Congress*] (LCLS)
NNC-M ...... Columbia University, Medical Library, New York, NY [*Library symbol*] [*Library of Congress*] (LCLS)
NNCN........ Northern Nigeria Case Notes [*A publication*] (DLA)
NNCo .... Collectors Club, New York, NY [*Library symbol*] [*Library of Congress*] (LCLS)
NNcoM ...... Moore-Cottrell Subscription Agencies, Inc., North Cohocton, NY [*Library symbol*] [*Library of Congress*] (LCLS)
NNConE ..... Consolidated Edison Co., Inc., New York, NY [*Library symbol*] [*Library of Congress*] (LCLS)

NNCoo .... Cooper Union for the Advancement of Science and Art, New York, NY [*Library symbol*] [*Library of Congress*] (LCLS)
NNCorI ...... Cornell University, New York State School of Industrial and Labor Relations, Sanford V. Lenz Library, New York, NY [*Library symbol*] [*Library of Congress*] (LCLS)
NNCorM ..... Cornell University, Medical College, New York, NY [*Library symbol*] [*Library of Congress*] (LCLS)
NNCorM-A ... New York Hospital-Cornell Medical Center Archives, New York, NY [*Library symbol*] [*Library of Congress*] (LCLS)
NNCorM-D ... Cornell University, Medical College, Oskar Diethelm Historical Library, New York, NY [*Library symbol*] [*Library of Congress*] (LCLS)
NNC-P .... Columbia University, College of Pharmacy, New York, NY [*Library symbol*] [*Library of Congress*] (LCLS)
NNCP .... Pfizer, Inc., New York, NY [*Library symbol*] [*Library of Congress*] (LCLS)
NNCPI .... Nuveen North Carolina Premium Income Municipal Fund [*Associated Press*] (SAG)
NNCPL ...... College of Police Science, New York, NY [*Library symbol*] [*Library of Congress*] (LCLS)
NNCPM ...... New York College of Podiatric Medicine, New York, NY [*Library symbol*] [*Library of Congress*] (LCLS)
NNC-Pop .... Columbia University, International Institute for the Study of Human Reproduction, Center for Population and Family Health, New York, NY [*Library symbol*] [*Library of Congress*] (LCLS)
NNC-Ps ...... Columbia University, Psychology Library, New York, NY [*Library symbol*] [*Library of Congress*] (LCLS)
NNCR .... North Norfolk Coast Reserves (SAUS)
NNcR .... Roberts Wesleyan College, North Chili, NY [*Library symbol*] [*Library of Congress*] (LCLS)
NNCre .... Creedmore Psychiatric Center, Queens Village, New York, NY [*Library symbol*] [*Library of Congress*] (LCLS)
NNCREW .... National Network of Commercial Real Estate Women (NTPA)
NNCS .... Child Study Association of America, New York, NY [*Library symbol*] [*Library of Congress*] (LCLS)
NNCS .... NICS Network Control System (SAUS)
NNCSC ...... National Neutron Cross Section Center [*AEC*] (MCD)
NNC-T .... Columbia University, Teachers College, New York, NY [*Library symbol*] [*Library of Congress*] (LCLS)
NNC-Typ .... Columbia University, American Typefounders' Library, New York, NY [*Library symbol*] [*Library of Congress*] (LCLS)
NNCU-C ..... City University of New York, Central Office, New York, NY [*Library symbol*] [*Library of Congress*] (LCLS)
NNCU-G ..... City University of New York, Graduate Center, New York, NY [*Library symbol*] [*Library of Congress*] (LCLS)
NNCU-L ..... City University of New York, Law School, Flushing, NY [*Library symbol*] [*Library of Congress*] (LCLS)
NNCU-T ..... City University of New York, Division of Teacher Education, New York, NY [*Library symbol*] [*Library of Congress*] (LCLS)
NNCX .... Newbridge Networks Corp. (SAUS)
NND .... Dover Publications, New York, NY [*Library symbol*] [*Library of Congress*] (LCLS)
NND .... National Network Dialing [*Telecommunications*] (TEL)
NND .... National Number Dialing [*Telecommunications*] (DCTA)
NND .... Naval Net Depot
NND .... Neo-Natal Death [*Medicine*]
NND .... New and Nonofficial Drugs [*AMA*]
NND .... Nonspecific Nonerosive Duodenitis [*Medicine*] (DMAA)
NND .... West Ambae [*Language symbol*] (ETLW)
NNDC .... National Naval Dental Center
NNDC .... National New Democratic Coalition (EA)
NNDC .... National Nuclear Data Center [*Brookhaven National Laboratory*] (IID)
NNDC .... National Nuclear Data Center [*Department of Energy*] [*Database producer*] (IID)
NNDCG ...... Danish Consultate General, Reference Library, New York, NY [*Library symbol*] [*Library of Congress*] (LCLS)
NNDE .... Nearest-Neighbor Distance Error [*Algorithm*]
NNDP .... Debevoise & Plimpton, New York, NY [*Library symbol*] [*Library of Congress*] (LCLS)
NNDP .... Naga National Democratic Party [*India*] [*Political party*] (PPW)
NNDP .... Nigerian National Democratic Party [*Political party*] (PSAP)
NNDPA ...... National New Deal Preservation Association (EA)
NNDPA ...... N-Nitrosodiphenylamine [*Organic chemistry*]
NNDPW ..... Davis, Polk & Wardwell, Law Library, New York, NY [*Library symbol*] [*Library of Congress*] (LCLS)
NNDR .... National Non-Domestic Rate [*British*]
NNDS .... NDS Group PLC [*NASDAQ symbol*]
NNDSS ...... National Notification Disease Surveillance System [*Centers for Disease Control*]
NNDTC ...... National Nondestructive Testing Centre [*Atomic Energy Authority*] [*Information service or system*] (IID)
NNDU .... Naviera Neptuno del Peru [*Intermodal shipping container symbol*] (TVRC)
NNE .... Engineering Societies Library, New York, NY [*Library symbol*] [*Library of Congress*] (LCLS)
NNE .... Neonatal Necrotizing Enterocolitis [*Medicine*] (AAMN)
NNE .... Newbridge Networks Corp. [*Toronto Stock Exchange symbol*] [*Canada*]
NNE .... Noise and Number Exposure (PDAA)
NNE .... Nonneuronal Enolase [*Medicine*] (DMAA)
NNE .... Nonneuron-Specific Enolase [*An enzyme*]
NNE .... Nonstandard Negro English
NNE .... North by North East (SAUS)
NNE .... North-Northeast
NNEA .... National Negro Evangelical Association [*Later, NBEA*]
NNEB .... National Nursery Examination Board
NNebg .... Newburgh Free Library, Newburgh, NY [*Library symbol*] [*Library of Congress*] (LCLS)
NNebgE ..... Epiphany Apostolic College, Newburgh, NY [*Library symbol*] [*Library of Congress*] (LCLS)
NNebgL ..... Ninth Judicial District Law Library, Newburgh, NY [*Library symbol*] [*Library of Congress*] (LCLS)
NNebgM .... Mount Saint Mary College, Newburgh, NY [*Library symbol*] [*Library of Congress*] (LCLS)
NNebgWM ... Washington's Headquarters Museum, Newburgh, NY [*Library symbol*] [*Library of Congress*] (LCLS)
NNebpHH ... Herricks High School, New Hyde Park (SAUS)
NNEC .... Explorers Club, New York, NY [*Library symbol*] [*Library of Congress*] (LCLS)
NNec .... New City Free Library, New City, NY [*Library symbol*] [*Library of Congress*] (LCLS)
NNECA ...... National Network of Episcopal Clergy Associations (EA)
NNECH ...... National Nutrition Education Clearing House [*Society for Nutrition Education*] (IID)
NnecL .... New City Free Library, New City, NY [*Library symbol*] [*Library of Congress*] (LCLS)
NNEDV ...... National Network to End Domestic Violence [*Association*] (EA)
NNEEDD ..... NOAA N-ROSS/ERS-1 Environmental Data Development (SAUS)
NNEF .... Educational Film Library Association, New York, NY [*Library symbol*] [*Library of Congress*] (LCLS)
NNef .... Newfane Public Library, Newfane, NY [*Library symbol*] [*Library of Congress*] (LCLS)
NNefH .... Inter-Community Memorial Hospital, Newfane, NY [*Library symbol*] [*Library of Congress*] (LCLS)
NNefL .... Newfane Free Library, Newfane, NY [*Library symbol*] [*Library of Congress*] (LCLS)
NNegbM .... Mount St. Mary College, Newburgh, NY [*Library symbol*] [*Library of Congress*] (LCLS)
NNegbWM .. Washington's Headquarters Museum, Newburgh, NY [*Library symbol*] [*Library of Congress*] (LCLS)
NNehpHH ... Herricks High School, New Hyde Park, NY [*Library symbol*] [*Library of Congress*] (LCLS)
NNEL .... Equitable Life Assurance Society of the United States, Medical Library, New York, NY [*Library symbol*] [*Library of Congress*] (LCLS)
NNEL-M ..... Equitable Life Assurance Society of the United States, Medical Library, New York, NY [*Library symbol*] [*Library of Congress*] (LCLS)
NNEM .... National Network for Environmental Management Studies (EAGT)
NNepa .... Elting Memorial Library, New Paltz, NY [*Library symbol*] [*Library of Congress*] (LCLS)
NNepaSU ... State University of New York, College at New Paltz, New Paltz, NY [*Library symbol*] [*Library of Congress*] (LCLS)
NNer .... New Rochelle Public Library, New Rochelle, NY [*Library symbol*] [*Library of Congress*] (LCLS)
NNerAIS ..... United States Army, Information School, Fort Slocum, New Rochelle, NY [*Library symbol*] [*Library of Congress*] (LCLS)
NNerC .... College of New Rochelle, New Rochelle, NY [*Library symbol*] [*Library of Congress*] (LCLS)
NNerI .... Iona College, New Rochelle (SAUS)
NNerI .... Iona College, New Rochelle, NY [*Library symbol*] [*Library of Congress*] (LCLS)
NNERN ...... North-Northeastern (SAUS)
NNES .... National Nuclear Energy Series [*of AEC-sponsored books*]
NNESCC ..... Northern New England Small College Conference (PSS)
NNET .... Nostalgia Network, Inc. [*NASDAQ symbol*] (COMM)
NNEU .... Naval Nuclear Evaluation Unit
NNEW .... Ernst & Whinney, Audit Management Services, New York, NY [*Library symbol*] [*Library of Congress*] (LCLS)
NNEWD ..... North-Northeastward (FAAC)
NNEXF ...... Newscope Resources Ltd. [*NASDAQ symbol*] (SAG)
NNF .... Fordham University, New York, NY [*Library symbol*] [*Library of Congress*] (LCLS)
NNF .... Namibia National Front [*Political party*] (PPW)
NNF .... National Nephrosis Foundation [*Later, NKF*]
NNF .... National Neurofibromatosis Foundation (PAZ)
NNF .... National Newman Foundation [*Defunct*] (EA)
NNF .... National Newspaper Foundation (EA)
NNF .... National Nothing Foundation [*Defunct*] (EA)
NNF .... Negation Normal Form (IDAI)
NNF .... Nordisk Neurokirurgisk Forening [*Scandinavian Neurosurgical Society - SNS*] (EAIO)
NNF .... Nordisk Neurologisk Forening [*Scandinavian Neurological Association - SNA*] (EAIO)
NNF .... Northern Nurses Federation [*Norway*]
NNF .... Nuveen Ins. NY Prem Inc. Muni [*NYSE symbol*] (TTSB)
NNF .... Nuveen Insured New York Premium Income Municipal [*NYSE symbol*] (SPSG)
NNFA .... National Nutritional Foods Association (EA)
NNFB .... Ford, Bacon & Davis, Inc., New York, NY [*Library symbol*] [*Library of Congress*] (LCLS)
NNFBC ...... First Boston Corporation, New York, NY [*Library symbol*] [*Library of Congress*] (LCLS)
NNFC .... Finch College, New York, NY [*Library symbol*] [*Library of Congress*] (LCLS)
NNFE .... Free Europe Committee, New York, NY [*Library symbol*] [*Library of Congress*] (LCLS)
NNFF .... Ford Foundation, New York, NY [*Library symbol*] [*Library of Congress*] (LCLS)
NNFF .... National Neurofibromatosis Foundation (EA)
NNFF .... Not Nested or Folded Flat [*Freight*]
NNFF-FL .... Ford Foundation, Ford Foundation Library, New York, NY [*Library symbol*] [*Library of Congress*] (LCLS)

NNFFu....... Franklin Furnance Archives, New York, NY [*Library symbol*] [*Library of Congress*] (LCLS)
NNFI......... French Institute/Alliance Francaise, New York, NY [*Library symbol*] [*Library of Congress*] (LCLS)
NNFIT....... Fashion Institute of Technology, New York, NY [*Library symbol*] [*Library of Congress*] (LCLS)
NNF-L....... Fordham University, Law Library, New York, NY [*Library symbol*] [*Library of Congress*] (LCLS)
NNFL........ Religious Society of Friends [*Quakers*], New York, NY [*Library symbol*] [*Library of Congress*] (LCLS)
NNF-LC...... Fordham University, Library at Lincoln Center, New York (SAUS)
NNF-LC...... Fordham University, Library at Lincoln Center, New York, NY [*Library symbol*] [*Library of Congress*] (LCLS)
NNFM....... Grand Lodge of New York, F & AM Library and Museum, New York, NY [*Library symbol*] [*Library of Congress*] (LCLS)
NNFoC....... Foundation Center Library, New York, NY [*Library symbol*] [*Library of Congress*] (LCLS)
NNFoM...... Forbes Magazine, Inc., New York, NY [*Library symbol*] [*Library of Congress*] (LCLS)
NNFP........ Nuclear Nitrogen Fixation Plant
NNFr......... Frick Art Reference Library, New York, NY [*Library symbol*] [*Library of Congress*] (LCLS)
NNF-RS..... Fordham University, Institute of Contemporary Russian Studies, New York, NY [*Library symbol*] [*Library of Congress*] (LCLS)
NNFS........ Nordic Narrow/16mm Film Society (EA)
NNFT........ National Federation of Textiles, New York, NY [*Library symbol*] [*Library of Congress*] (LCLS)
NNFU........ Nuclear Nonfirst Use
NNG......... General Theological Seminary of the Protestant Episcopal Church, New York, NY [*Library symbol*] [*Library of Congress*] (LCLS)
NNG......... Nanning [*China*] [*Airport symbol*] (OAG)
NNG......... National Network of Grantmakers (EA)
NNG......... National Number Group (NITA)
NNG......... Nonspecific Nonerosive Gastritis [*Medicine*] (DMAA)
NNG......... Northern Natural Gas (SAUS)
NNG......... Northwest Natural Gas Company (EFIS)
NNGA........ Northern Nut Growers Association (EA)
NNGBSW.... National Network of Graduate Business School Women [*Knoxville, TN*] (EA)
NNGI......... National Aeronautics and Space Administration, Goddard Institute for Space Studies, New York, NY [*Library symbol*] [*Library of Congress*] (LCLS)
NNGoe...... Goethe House, German Cultural Institute, New York, NY [*Library symbol*] [*Library of Congress*] (LCLS)
NNGr........ Grolier Club, New York, NY [*Library symbol*] [*Library of Congress*] (LCLS)
NNGS........ Church of Jesus Christ of Latter-Day Saints, Genealogical Society Library, New York Branch, New York, NY [*Library symbol*] [*Library of Congress*] (LCLS)
NNGu........ Solomon R. Guggenheim Museum, New York, NY [*Library symbol*] [*Library of Congress*] (LCLS)
NNH......... Hispanic Society of America, New York, NY [*Library symbol*] [*Library of Congress*] (LCLS)
NNH......... Natal Native Horse [*British military*] (DMA)
NNH......... National Humanities Center, Research Triangle Park, NC [*OCLC symbol*] (OCLC)
NNH......... Nordiska Namnden for Handikappfragor [*Nordic Committee on Disability - NCD*] [*Sweden*] (EAIO)
NNHA........ National Novice Hockey Association [*Later, HNA*] (EA)
NNHC........ Hostos Community College, New York, NY [*Library symbol*] [*Library of Congress*] (LCLS)
NNHC........ Natal Native High Court Reports [*1899-1915*] [*South Africa*] [*A publication*] (DLA)
NNHCF-C.... Holy Cross Friary, Juniper Carol Library, New York, NY [*Library symbol*] [*Library of Congress*] (LCLS)
NNHE........ New York City Board of Higher Education, New York, NY [*Library symbol*] [*Library of Congress*] (LCLS)
NNHeb...... Hebrew Union College - Jewish Institute of Religion, New York, NY [*Library symbol*] [*Library of Congress*] (LCLS)
NNHH........ Harlem Hospital Center, Medical Library, New York, NY [*Library symbol*] [*Library of Congress*] (LCLS)
NNHHR...... Hughes, Hubbard & Reed, New York, NY [*Library symbol*] [*Library of Congress*] (LCLS)
NNHL........ National Novice Hockey League [*Later, NNHA*] (EA)
NNHol....... Holland Society of New York, New York, NY [*Library symbol*] [*Library of Congress*] (LCLS)
NNHor....... Horticultural Society of New York, Inc., New York, NY [*Library symbol*] [*Library of Congress*] (LCLS)
NNhp........ New Hyde Park Public Library, New Hyde Park, NY [*Library symbol*] [*Library of Congress*] (LCLS)
NNhpDE..... Denton Avenue Elementary School, New Hyde Park, NY [*Library symbol*] [*Library of Congress*] (LCLS)
NNhpGE..... Garden City Park School, New Hyde Park, NY [*Library symbol*] [*Library of Congress*] (LCLS)
NNhpH...... Hillside Public Library, New Hyde Park, NY [*Library symbol*] [*Library of Congress*] (LCLS)
NNhpHE..... Hillside Grade School, New Hyde Park, NY [*Library symbol*] [*Library of Congress*] (LCLS)
NNhpHH..... Herricks High School, New Hyde Park, NY [*Library symbol*] [*Library of Congress*] (LCLS)
NNhpJ....... Long Island Jewish Hospital, New Hyde Park, NY [*Library symbol*] [*Library of Congress*] (LCLS)
NNhpME.... Manor-Oaks-William R. Bowie School, New Hyde Park, NY [*Library symbol*] [*Library of Congress*] (LCLS)
NNhpMH.... New Hyde Park Memorial High School, New Hyde Park, NY [*Library symbol*] [*Library of Congress*] (LCLS)
NNhpNE..... New Hyde Park Road School, New Hyde Park, NY [*Library symbol*] [*Library of Congress*] (LCLS)
NNHR........ New York City Human Resources Administration, New York, NY [*Library symbol*] [*Library of Congress*] (LCLS)
NNHRA...... Northern Nevada Human Resource Association (EARSL)
NNHS........ Hospital for Special Surgery, New York, NY [*Library symbol*] [*Library of Congress*] (LCLS)
NNHS........ National Nursing Home Survey [*Department of Health and Human Services*] (GFGA)
NNhS........ Special Metals Corp., New Hartford, NY [*Library symbol*] [*Library of Congress*] (LCLS)
NNHT........ Nuffield Nursing Homes Trust (ODA)
NNHuC...... Hunter College of the City University of New York, New York, NY [*Library symbol*] [*Library of Congress*] (LCLS)
NNHWW.... H.W. Wilson Co., Bronx, NY [*Library symbol*] [*Library of Congress*] (LCLS)
NNI.......... Nanaimo, British Columbia, Canada [*Amtrak Busline code*]
NNI.......... National Newspaper Index [*Information Access Co.*] [*Bibliographic database*] [*Information service or system*] (IID)
NNI.......... Net National Income [*Economics*]
NNI.......... Net-Net Income [*Business term*]
NNI.......... Network-Network Interface (RALS)
NNI.......... Network Node Interface [*Computer science*]
NNI.......... New Nickerie [*Surinam*] [*Airport symbol*] (AD)
NNI.......... Next Node Index (SAUS)
NNI.......... Next Node Indicator (SAUS)
NNI.......... Noise and Nuisance Index (SAUS)
NNI.......... Noise and Number Index
NNI.......... Noise Nuisance Index (PDAA)
NNI.......... Nonnuclear Instrumentation (NRCH)
NNI.......... Non-Numeric Information (SAUS)
NNI.......... Norwegian Nobel Institute (SAUS)
NNI.......... Nucleon-Nucleon Interaction
NNI.......... Office of Naval Intelligence Publications
NNIA......... American Institute of Aeronautics and Astronautics, New York, NY [*Library symbol*] [*Library of Congress*] (LCLS)
NNia......... Niagara Falls Public Library, Niagara Falls, NY [*Library symbol*] [*Library of Congress*] (LCLS)
NNiaA....... Airco Speer Research & Development Laboratories, Niagara Falls, NY [*Library symbol*] [*Library of Congress*] (LCLS)
NNiaB....... Bell Aerospace Textron, Technical Library, Niagara Falls, NY [*Library symbol*] [*Library of Congress*] (LCLS)
NNiaC....... Niagara County Community College, Niagara Falls, NY [*Library symbol*] [*Library of Congress*] (LCLS)
NNiaCa...... Carborundum Co., Niagara Falls, NY [*Library symbol*] [*Library of Congress*] (LCLS)
NNiaD....... E. I. Du Pont de Nemours & Co., Electrochemical Department, Niagara Falls, NY [*Library symbol*] [*Library of Congress*] (LCLS)
NNiaEM..... Elkem Metals Co., Niagara Falls, NY [*Library symbol*] [*Library of Congress*] (LCLS)
NNiaH....... Hooker Chemical Corp. [*Later, Hooker Chemicals & Plastics Corp.*], Niagara Falls, NY [*Library symbol*] [*Library of Congress*] (LCLS)
NNiaHC..... Hooker Chemicals & Plastics Corp., Business Library, Niagara Falls, NY [*Library symbol*] [*Library of Congress*] (LCLS)
NNiaM....... Moore Business Forms, Niagara Falls, NY [*Library symbol*] [*Library of Congress*] (LCLS)
NNiaMed.... Niagara Falls Memorial Medical Center, Medical Library, Niagara Falls, NY [*Library symbol*] [*Library of Congress*] (LCLS)
NNiaN....... National Lead Co., Research Library, Niagara Falls, NY [*Library symbol*] [*Library of Congress*] (LCLS)
NNiaNC..... NIACET Corporation, Niagara Falls, NY [*Library symbol*] [*Library of Congress*] (LCLS)
NNiaNL...... Nioga Library System, Niagara Falls, NY [*Library symbol*] [*Library of Congress*] (LCLS)
NNiaO....... Occidental Chemical Corp., Technical Information Center, Niagra Falls, NY [*Library symbol*] [*Library of Congress*] (LCLS)
NNiaSE...... Sohio Engineered Materials Co., Research and Development Library, Niagara Falls, NY [*Library symbol*] [*Library of Congress*] (LCLS)
NNiaTC...... TAM Ceramics, Inc., Niagara Falls, NY [*Library symbol*] [*Library of Congress*] (LCLS)
NNiaTV...... Trott Vocational High School, Niagara Falls, NY [*Library symbol*] [*Library of Congress*] (LCLS)
NNiaU....... Niagara University, Niagara University, NY [*Library symbol*] [*Library of Congress*] (LCLS)
NNiaUC..... Union Carbide Corp., Niagara Falls, NY [*Library symbol*] [*Library of Congress*] (LCLS)
NNIC......... Normalized Noise Isolation Class (SAUS)
NNICC....... National Narcotics Intelligence Consumers Committee [*Drug Enforcement Administration*] [*Washington, DC*] (EGAO)
NNIG......... Netherlands Naval Industries Group (SAUS)
NNI-I......... NASA Standard Initiator-Type I (SAUS)
NNIIC........ Istituto Italiano Di Cultura Biblioteca, New York, NY [*Library symbol*] [*Library of Congress*] (LCLS)
NNIIE........ Institute of International Education, New York, NY [*Library symbol*] [*Library of Congress*] (LCLS)
NNIMD...... Institute for Muscle Disease, New York, NY [*Library symbol*] [*Library of Congress*] [*Obsolete*] (LCLS)
NNIND....... International Nickel Co., Technical Library, New York, NY [*Library symbol*] [*Library of Congress*] (LCLS)
NNInS....... Insurance Society of New York, New York, NY [*Library symbol*] [*Library of Congress*] (LCLS)
NNIP......... Institute of Public Administration, New York, NY [*Library symbol*] [*Library of Congress*] (LCLS)
NNIPF....... International Planned Parenthood Federation, Documentation and Publications Center, New York, NY [*Library symbol*] [*Library of Congress*] (LCLS)
NNIR......... Industrial Relations Counselors, New York, NY [*Library symbol*] [*Library of Congress*] (LCLS)
NNIRR....... National Network for Immigrant and Refugee Rights (EA)

NNIS .... Library for Intercultural Studies, Inc., New York, NY [*Library symbol*] [*Library of Congress*] (LCLS)
NNIS .... National Nosocomial Infections Study [*Medicine*] (DMAA)
NNIS .... National Nosocomial Infections Surveillance [*Medicine*]
NNIS .... Nonnuclear Instrumentation System (NRCH)
NNISS .... Nosocomial Infections Surveillance System [*Center for Disease Control*]
NNIU .... Nautica Line [*Intermodal shipping container symbol*] (TVRC)
NNJ .... Jewish Theological Seminary of America, New York, NY [*Library symbol*] [*Library of Congress*] (LCLS)
NNJ .... Nakano [*Japan*] [*Seismograph station code, US Geological Survey*] (SEIS)
NNJ .... Nuveen New Jersey Premium Income Municipal [*NYSE symbol*] (SPSG)
NNJ .... Nuveen NJ Prem Inc. Muni [*NYSE symbol*] (TTSB)
NNJa .... Juilliard School of Music, New York (SAUS)
NNJef .... Jefferson School of Social Science, New York, NY [*Library symbol*] [*Library of Congress*] [*Obsolete*] (LCLS)
NNJH .... Joint Health Library, New York, NY [*Library symbol*] [*Library of Congress*] [*Obsolete*] (LCLS)
NNJHK .... Jenny Hunter's Kindergarten and Primary Training School, New York, NY [*Library symbol*] [*Library of Congress*] [*Obsolete*] (LCLS)
NNJJ .... John Jay College of Criminal Justice, New York, NY [*Library symbol*] [*Library of Congress*] (LCLS)
NNJS .... Japan Society Library, New York, NY [*Library symbol*] [*Library of Congress*] (LCLS)
NNJSCIS ... Northern New Jersey Spinal Cord Injury System (RCD)
NNJu .... Juilliard School of Music, New York, NY [*Library symbol*] [*Library of Congress*] (LCLS)
NNK .... Naknek [*Alaska*] [*Airport symbol*] (OAG)
NNK .... Nic-Nik Resources [*Vancouver Stock Exchange symbol*]
NNK .... Nicotine-Derived Nitrosaminoketone
NNK .... Nonnuclear Kill
NNK .... Notify Next of Kind (SAUS)
NNKKAA ..... Journal. Agricultural Chemical Society of Japan (journ.) (SAUS)
NNKRAS .... Non-Nuclear Kill Requirements and Applications Study [*Military*]
NNL .... Beeville, TX [*Location identifier*] [*FAA*] (FAAL)
NNL .... Herbert H. Lehman College of the City University of New York, New York, NY [*Library symbol*] [*Library of Congress*] (LCLS)
NNL .... Negro National League [*Baseball*] (NDBD)
NN-L .... New York Public Library, Research Library for the Performing Arts at Lincoln Center, New York, NY [*Library symbol*] [*Library of Congress*] (LCLS)
NNL .... Nigerian National Line (SAUS)
NNL .... Ninilchik [*Alaska*] [*Seismograph station code, US Geological Survey*] (SEIS)
NNL .... Nondalton [*Alaska*] [*Airport symbol*] (OAG)
NNL .... No Net Loss
NNL .... No New Laboratory (MELL)
NNL .... Non-Newtonian Liquid (SAUS)
NNL .... Non-Nuclear Lance Missile (PDAA)
NNLA .... Nebraska Nursery and Landscape Association
NNLBI .... Leo Baeck Institute, New York, NY [*Library symbol*] [*Library of Congress*] (LCLS)
NNLC .... Lutheran Council in the USA, New York, NY [*Library symbol*] [*Library of Congress*] (LCLS)
NNLC .... Ngwane National Liberatory Congress [*Swaziland*]
NNLDA ...... National Network of Learning Disabled Adults (EA)
NNLehman . Lehman Corp., New York, NY [*Library symbol*] [*Library of Congress*] (LCLS)
NNLH .... Lenox Hill Hospital, Medical Library, New York, NY [*Library symbol*] [*Library of Congress*] (LCLS)
NNLI .... New York Law Institute, New York, NY [*Library symbol*] [*Library of Congress*] (LCLS)
NN/LM .... National Network of Libraries of Medicine (IID)
NNLM .... National Network of Libraries of Medicine
NNLN .... Northern Nigeria Legal Notes [*A publication*] (DLA)
NNLP .... National Natural Landmarks Program (WPI)
NNLR .... Law Reprints, New York, NY [*Library symbol*] [*Library of Congress*] (LCLS)
NNLR .... Northern Nigeria Law Reports [*A publication*] (DLA)
NNLS .... New York Law School Library, New York, NY [*Library symbol*] [*Library of Congress*] (LCLS)
NNLS .... Non-Negative Least Squares (ARMP)
NNM .... American Museum of Natural History, New York, NY [*Library symbol*] [*Library of Congress*] (LCLS)
NNM .... American Numismatic Society [*A publication*] (ABAR)
NNM .... Davidson College, Davidson, NC [*OCLC symbol*] (OCLC)
NNM .... Nasdaq National Market (SG)
NNM .... Neonatal Mortality [*Medicine*] (DMAA)
NNM .... Network Node Manager [*Computer science*] (GART)
NN-M .... New York Public Library, Municipal Reference Library, New York, NY [*Library symbol*] [*Library of Congress*] (LCLS)
NNM .... Next New Moon (SAUS)
NNM .... Next (or Nearest) New Moon [*Freemasonry*] (ROG)
NNM .... Nicolle-Novy-MacNeal [*Medium*] [*Microbiology*] (DAVI)
NNM .... N-Nitrosomorpholine [*Also, NMOR*] [*Organic chemistry*]
NNM .... Node-to-Node Message (SAUS)
NNM .... No Neutral Mode
NNm .... North Merrick Public Library, North Merrick, NY [*Library symbol*] [*Library of Congress*] (LCLS)
NNM .... Nuveen New York Municipal Income [*AMEX symbol*] (SPSG)
NNMa .... Marymount Manhattan College, New York, NY [*Library symbol*] [*Library of Congress*] (LCLS)
NNMAI ...... Museum of the American Indian, New York, NY [*Library symbol*] [*Library of Congress*] (LCLS)
NNMan ...... Manhattan College, New York, NY [*Library symbol*] [*Library of Congress*] (LCLS)
NNMB .... Methodist Board of Missions, New York, NY [*Library symbol*] [*Library of Congress*] (LCLS)
NNMB .... National Nutrition Monitoring Bureau (SAUS)
NNmBJ ...... Brookside Junior High School, North Merrick, NY [*Library symbol*] [*Library of Congress*] (LCLS)
NNMC .... Mannes College of Music, New York, NY [*Library symbol*] [*Library of Congress*] (LCLS)
NNMC .... National Naval Medical Center [*Bethesda, MD*]
NNmCE ...... Camp Avenue Elementary School, North Merrick, NY [*Library symbol*] [*Library of Congress*] (LCLS)
NNMcGraw ... McGraw-Hill, Inc., New York, NY [*Library symbol*] [*Library of Congress*] (LCLS)
NNME .... Mid-European Studies Center, New York, NY [*Library symbol*] [*Library of Congress*] (LCLS)
NNMec ...... General Society of Mechanics and Tradesmen, New York, NY [*Library symbol*] [*Library of Congress*] (LCLS)
NNMel .... Andrew W. Mellon Foundation, New York, NY [*Library symbol*] [*Library of Congress*] (LCLS)
NN-Mel ...... New York Public Library, Mellon Microfilm Collection, New York, NY [*Library symbol*] [*Library of Congress*] (LCLS)
NNMer ...... Mercantile Library Association, New York, NY [*Library symbol*] [*Library of Congress*] (LCLS)
NNMF .... Markle Foundation, New York, NY [*Library symbol*] [*Library of Congress*] (LCLS)
NNmFE ...... Harold D. Fayette Elementary School, North Merrick, NY [*Library symbol*] [*Library of Congress*] (LCLS)
NNMH .... Montefiore Hospital, New York, NY [*Library symbol*] [*Library of Congress*] (LCLS)
NNMi .... Millenium Film Workshop, New York, NY [*Library symbol*] [*Library of Congress*] (LCLS)
NNMI .... Nonlinear Normal Mode Initialization (SAUS)
NNML .... Metropolitan Life Insurance Co., New York, NY [*Library symbol*] [*Library of Congress*] (LCLS)
NNMLC ...... Medical Library Center of New York, New York, NY [*Library symbol*] [*Library of Congress*] (LCLS)
NNMM ...... Metropolitan Museum of Art, New York, NY [*Library symbol*] [*Library of Congress*] (LCLS)
NNMMA ..... Museum of Modern Art, New York, NY [*Library symbol*] [*Library of Congress*] (LCLS)
NNMMA-F ... Museum of Modern Art, Film Study Center, New York, NY [*Library symbol*] [*Library of Congress*] (LCLS)
NNMMA-U ... Metropolitan Museum of Art, Uris Library and Resources Center, New York, NY [*Library symbol*] [*Library of Congress*] (LCLS)
NNMM-C .... Metropolitan Museum of Art, The Cloisters Library, New York, NY [*Library symbol*] [*Library of Congress*] (LCLS)
NNMM-CI ... Metropolitan Museum of Art, Costume Institute, New York, NY [*Library symbol*] [*Library of Congress*] (LCLS)
NNmN .... North Merrick Public Library, North Merrick, NY [*Library symbol*] [*Library of Congress*] (LCLS)
NNMO .... Mobil Oil Corp., Secretariat Library, New York, NY [*Library symbol*] [*Library of Congress*] (LCLS)
NnmOE ...... Old Mill Road Elementary School, North Merrick, NY [*Library symbol*] [*Library of Congress*] (LCLS)
NNMoMA ... Museum of Modern Art, New York, NY [*Library symbol*] [*Library of Congress*] (LCLS)
NNMP .... Motion Picture Association of America, Inc., Research Department Library, New York, NY [*Library symbol*] [*Library of Congress*] (LCLS)
NNMPA ...... Museum of Primitive Art, New York, NY [*Library symbol*] [*Library of Congress*] (LCLS)
NNmPE ...... Park Avenue Elementary School, North Merrick, NY [*Library symbol*] [*Library of Congress*] (LCLS)
NN-MPH .... New York Public Library, Public Health Division, New York, NY [*Library symbol*] [*Library of Congress*] (LCLS)
NNMR .... Missionary Research Library, New York, NY [*Library symbol*] [*Library of Congress*] (LCLS)
NNMRR ..... New York Metropolitan Reference and Research Library Agency, Inc., New York, NY [*Library symbol*] [*Library of Congress*] (LCLS)
NNMS .... Manhattan State Hospital, New York, NY [*Library symbol*] [*Library of Congress*] (LCLS)
NNMS .... National Nutrition-Monitoring System [*Department of Agriculture*] (GFGA)
NNMS .... Nazareth National Motor Speedway [*Pennsylvania*]
NNMSB ...... Nonnuclear Munitions Safety Board [*Military*]
NNMSCP .... Nonnuclear Munitions Safety Control Program [*Military*]
NNMSE ...... Network Node Manager Special Edition
NNMSG ..... Nonnuclear Munitions Safety Group [*Air Force*] (AFM)
NNMSGP .... Nonnuclear Munitions Safety Group [*Air Force*]
NNMSK ...... Memorial Sloan-Kettering Cancer Center, New York, NY [*Library symbol*] [*Library of Congress*] (LCLS)
NNMSM ..... Manhattan School of Music, New York, NY [*Library symbol*] [*Library of Congress*] (LCLS)
NNMT .... Newport News Marine Terminal
NNMtS ...... Mount Sinai Hospital, New York, NY [*Library symbol*] [*Library of Congress*] (LCLS)
NNMtSM .... Mount Sinai School of Medicine of the City University of New York, New York, NY [*Library symbol*] [*Library of Congress*] (LCLS)
NNMtSV ..... College of Mount Saint Vincent, New York, NY [*Library symbol*] [*Library of Congress*] (LCLS)
NNMus ...... Museum of the City of New York, New York, NY [*Library symbol*] [*Library of Congress*] (LCLS)
NNN .... Commercial Net Lease Realty, Inc. [*NYSE symbol*] (SAG)
NNN .... Commercial Net Lease Rlty [*NYSE symbol*] (TTSB)
NNN .... Nannies Need Nannies Association [*British*] (DBA)
NNN .... National Navy Notice

NNN .... National Nostalgic Nova (EA)
NNN .... Next Nearest Neighbor [*Chemical physics*]
NNN .... Nicolle-Novy-MacNeal [*Medium*] [*Medicine*] (MEDA)
NNN .... Nihon News Network (SAUS)
NNN .... Nitrosonornicotine [*Organic chemistry*]
NNN .... N-Nitrosonornicotine [*Organic chemistry*]
NNN .... No National Name
NNN .... No Native Named (SAUS)
NNN .... Non-Normalized Number (SAUS)
NNN .... No No Nanette [*Broadway musical*]
NNN .... Noramco Mining Corp. [*Toronto Stock Exchange symbol*] [*Vancouver Stock Exchange symbol*]
NNN .... Novy, MacNeal, and Nicolle's Medium [*Medicine*] (MAE)
NNNA........ No Name, No Address
NNNA........ Non-Native Network Attachment (SAUS)
NNNAM ..... New York Academy of Medicine, New York, NY [*Library symbol*] [*Library of Congress*] (LCLS)
NNNASA .... National Aeronautical and Space Administration, Institute for Space Studies, NewYork, NY [*Library symbol*] [*Library of Congress*] (LCLS)
NNNBC ...... National Broadcasting Co., Inc., General Library, New York, NY [*Library symbol*] [*Library of Congress*] (LCLS)
NNNBC-I .... National Broadcasting Co., Inc., Information Unit, Research Department, New York, NY [*Library symbol*] [*Library of Congress*] (LCLS)
NNNC........ New York Chamber of Commerce, New York, NY [*Library symbol*] [*Library of Congress*] (LCLS)
NNNCC-Ar .. New York County Clerk Archives, Division of Old Records, New York, NY [*Library symbol*] [*Library of Congress*] (LCLS)
NNNCL ...... New York County Lawyers Association, New York, NY [*Library symbol*] [*Library of Congress*] (LCLS)
NNNCR...... National Council for Resources on Women, New York, NY [*Library symbol*] [*Library of Congress*] (LCLS)
NNNDO...... Neglect of Non-Neighbor Differential Overlap [*Physics*]
NNNDR...... Narcotic and Drug Research, Inc., New York, NY [*Library symbol*] [*Library of Congress*] (LCLS)
NNNeI .... Netherlands Information Service, New York, NY [*Library symbol*] [*Library of Congress*] (LCLS)
NNNGB...... New York Genealogical and Biographical Society, New York, NY [*Library symbol*] [*Library of Congress*] (LCLS)
NNNH........ National Health Agencies Library, New York, NY [*Library symbol*] [*Library of Congress*] [*Obsolete*] (LCLS)
NNNHi....... Naval History Society, New York, NY [*Library symbol*] [*Library of Congress*] [*Obsolete*] (LCLS)
NNNM .... New York Medical College, Flower and Fifth Avenue Hospitals, New York, NY [*Library symbol*] [*Library of Congress*] (LCLS)
NNNMCA.... New Museum of Contemporary Art, New York, NY [*Library symbol*] [*Library of Congress*] (LCLS)
NNNN........ End of Message (SAUS)
NNNPsan ... New York Psychoanalytic Institute, New York, NY [*Library symbol*] [*Library of Congress*] (LCLS)
NNNPSC .... National No-Nukes Prison Support Collective (EA)
NNNPsI...... New York State Department of Mental Hygiene, Psychiatric Institute, New York, NY [*Library symbol*] [*Library of Congress*] (LCLS)
NNNR........ Noss National Nature Reserve (SAUS)
NNNS........ New School for Social Research, New York, NY [*Library symbol*] [*Library of Congress*] (LCLS)
NNNSB ...... National Society for the Prevention of Blindness, New York, NY [*Library symbol*] [*Library of Congress*] (LCLS)
NNNT .... New York Theological Seminary, New York, NY [*Library symbol*] [*Library of Congress*] (LCLS)
NNNTSH .... Naukove Tovarystvo Imeni Shevchenka (Shevchenko Scientific Society, Inc.), New York, NY [*Library symbol*] [*Library of Congress*] (LCLS)
NNNWA ..... N. W. Ayer & Son, New York, NY [*Library symbol*] [*Library of Congress*] (LCLS)
NNO .... Naga Nationalist Organization [*India*]
N-NO .... New York-New Orleans (SAUS)
NNO .... Ngomba [*Language symbol*] (ETLW)
NNO .... Nittobo Norplex Oak Co., Ltd (EFIS)
NNO .... No New Orders [*Medical Records*] (DAVI)
NNO .... Nord-Nord-Ouest [*North-Northwest*] [*French*]
NNO .... Northern Orion Explorations [*Vancouver Stock Exchange symbol*]
NNO .... Nuveen N.Y. Muni Market Opportunity (EFIS)
NNOA........ National Naval Officers Association (EA)
NNOC........ National Network Operations Center [*Ottawa, ON*] [*Telecommunications*] (TSSD)
NNOC........ Nigerian National Oil Co. (SAUS)
NNomAE .... Albany Avenue Elementary School, North Massapequa, NY [*Library symbol*] [*Library of Congress*] (LCLS)
NNomEE .... Eastplain Elementary School, North Massapequa, NY [*Library symbol*] [*Library of Congress*] (LCLS)
NNomPH.... Plainedge High School, North Massapequa, NY [*Library symbol*] [*Library of Congress*] (LCLS)
NNomPJ .... Sylvia Packard Junior High School, North Massapequa, NY [*Library symbol*] [*Library of Congress*] (LCLS)
NNOPE ...... Naturists and Nudists Opposing Pornographic Exploitation (EA)
NNopo....... Northport Public Library (SAUS)
NNopo....... Northport Public Library, Northport, NY [*Library symbol*] [*Library of Congress*] (LCLS)
NNopo-E .... Northport Public Library, East Northport Branch, East Northport, NY [*Library symbol*] [*Library of Congress*] (LCLS)
NNopoHS ... Northport High School, Northport, NY [*Library symbol*] [*Library of Congress*] (LCLS)
NNopoJH.... Northport Junior High School, Northport, NY [*Library symbol*] [*Library of Congress*] (LCLS)
NNopoVA.... United States Veterans Administration Hospital, Northport, NY [*Library symbol*] [*Library of Congress*] (LCLS)
NNOR........ Nonnuclear Ordnance Requirement (MCD)
NNorP .... Norwich Pharmacal Co., Norwich, NY [*Library symbol*] [*Library of Congress*] (LCLS)
nNOS .... Neuronal Nitric Oxide Synthase [*An enzyme*]
NNosCE ..... Sea Cliff Elementary School, North Shore, NY [*Library symbol*] [*Library of Congress*] (LCLS)
NNOSE ...... NanoSignal Corp. [*OTCBB symbol*]
NnosJH...... North Shore Junior High School, North Shore, NY [*Library symbol*] [*Library of Congress*] (LCLS)
NNosSH ..... North Shore Senior High School, North Shore, NY [*Library symbol*] [*Library of Congress*] (LCLS)
NNOt......... New York Orthopaedic Hospital, New York, NY [*Library symbol*] [*Library of Congress*] (LCLS)
NNot .... North Tonawanda Public Library, North Tonawanda, NY [*Library symbol*] [*Library of Congress*] (LCLS)
NNOT .... Not Necessarily on Topic (SAUS)
NNotD .... DeGraff Memorial Hospital, North Tonawanda, NY [*Library symbol*] [*Library of Congress*] (LCLS)
NNotHC ..... Hooker Chemicals & Plastics Corp., Durez Division Library, North Tonawanda, NY [*Library symbol*] [*Library of Congress*] (LCLS)
NNotL .... Lawless Container Corp., North Tonawanda, NY [*Library symbol*] [*Library of Congress*] (LCLS)
NNotP .... North Tonawanda Public Library, North Tonawanda, NY [*Library symbol*] [*Library of Congress*] (LCLS)
N NOV....... Nomen Novum [*New Name*] [*Latin*] (BABM)
n nov .... Nomen Novum [*New Name*] [*Latin*] [*Pharmacy*] (DAVI)
NNP.......... Needle-Nosed Probe
NNP.......... Negative Node Point
NNP.......... Neonatal Nurse Practitioner (DAVI)
NNP.......... Nerve Net Pulse [*Neurobiology*]
NNP.......... Net National Product [*Economics*]
NNP.......... New National Party (Grenada) [*Political party*] (PSAP)
NNP.......... Ngezi National Park (SAUS)
NNP.......... Nimule National Park (SAUS)
NNP.......... Non-Negation Property (SAUS)
NNP.......... Nuveen New York Performance Plus Municipal [*NYSE symbol*] (SPSG)
NNP.......... Nuveen NY Perform Plus Muni [*NYSE symbol*] (TTSB)
NNPA .... National Negro Press Association [*Defunct*] (EA)
NNPA .... National Newspaper Promotion Association [*Later, INPA*] (EA)
NNPA .... National Newspaper Publishers Association (EA)
NNPA .... Nuclear Nonproliferation Act [*1975*]
NNPA .... Port Authority of New York and New Jersey, New York, NY [*Library symbol*] [*Library of Congress*] (LCLS)
NNParS ..... Parsons School of Design, New York, NY [*Library symbol*] [*Library of Congress*] (LCLS)
NNPaul...... Paul, Weiss, Rifkind, Wharton & Garrison, Law Library, New York, NY [*Library symbol*] [*Library of Congress*] (LCLS)
NNPaW...... Payne Whitney Clinic, New York, NY [*Library symbol*] [*Library of Congress*] (LCLS)
NNPBD ...... National Network to Prevent Birth Defects (MELL)
NNPC .... Nigerian National Petroleum Corp. (ECON)
NNPC .... Pace College, New York, NY [*Library symbol*] [*Library of Congress*] (LCLS)
NNPCC ...... National Nutrition Policy Coordination Committee (SAUS)
NNPC-L ..... Pace University, Law Library, White Plains, NY [*Library symbol*] [*Library of Congress*] (LCLS)
NNPE-NC ... National Council of the Protestant Episcopal Church, New York, NY [*Library symbol*] [*Library of Congress*] (LCLS)
NNPennie... Pennie, Edmonds, Morton, Taylor & Adams, New York, NY [*Library symbol*] [*Library of Congress*] (LCLS)
NNPf......... Carl H. Pforzheimer Library, New York, NY [*Library symbol*] [*Library of Congress*] (LCLS)
NNPH-O ..... Institute of Ophthalmology, Presbyterian Hospital, New York, NY [*Library symbol*] [*Library of Congress*] (LCLS)
NNPHR ...... New York City Public Health Research Laboratory, New York, NY [*Library symbol*] [*Library of Congress*] (LCLS)
NNPHW ..... National New Professional Health Workers [*Later, NPSAPHA*] (EA)
NNPI......... Naval Nuclear Propulsion Information (MCD)
NNPIA .... Polish Institute of Art and Sciences in America, Inc., Research Library, New York, NY [*Library symbol*] [*Library of Congress*] (LCLS)
n-n p-i-f..... never-never pay-inful (SAUS)
NNPlan...... Planning Assistance, Inc., New York, NY [*Library symbol*] [*Library of Congress*] (LCLS)
NNPM .... Pierpont Morgan Library, New York, NY [*Library symbol*] [*Library of Congress*] (LCLS)
NNPopC .... Population Council, New York, NY [*Library symbol*] [*Library of Congress*] (LCLS)
NNPPFA..... Planned Parenthood Federation of America, Inc., Katharine Dexter McCormick Library, New York, NY [*Library symbol*] [*Library of Congress*] (LCLS)
NNPPNYC... Planned Parenthood of New York City, Inc., Abraham Stone Memorial Library, Margaret Sanger Center, New York, NY [*Library symbol*] [*Library of Congress*] (LCLS)
NNPR........ New York & New Jersey Port Railroad [*Federal Railroad Administration identification code*]
NNPRM ..... United Presbyterian Mission Library of the United Presbyterian Church in the USA, New York, NY [*Library symbol*] [*Library of Congress*] (LCLS)
NNPS .... Navy Nuclear Power School (DNAB)
NNPS .... Norco Nuclear Power Station (NRCH)
NNPSPP.... National Non-Point Source Pollution Program (GNE)
NNPTU ...... Naval Nuclear Power Training Unit (DNAB)
NNPU........ Naval Nuclear Power Unit [*Obsolete*]

NNPU........ Nigerian National Petroleum [*Intermodal shipping container symbol*] (TVRC)
NNR......... City College of City University of New York, New York, NY [*Library symbol*] [*Library of Congress*] (LCLS)
NNR......... National Narcolepsy Registry [*Founded in 1996*] (NRGU)
NNR......... National Nature Reserve [*British*]
NNR......... National Number Routed [*Telecommunications*] (TEL)
NNR......... Nearest-Neighbor Rule [*Mathematics*]
NNR......... Nevada North Resources [*Vancouver Stock Exchange symbol*]
NNR......... New and Nonofficial Remedies [*A publication*]
NNR......... Nordiska Nykterhetsradet [*Nordic Temperance Council - NTC*] (EAIO)
NNR......... Normalized Noise Reduction (SAUS)
NNR......... Northern NORAD [*North American Air Defense*] Region (SAA)
NNR......... Northwest Nonprofit Resources [*Washington, Idaho, and Montana*] (EARSL)
NNR......... Not Necessary to Return (SAUS)
NNR......... Novell Network Registry (SAUS)
NNRA........ National Negro Republican Assembly [*Defunct*]
NNRB........ National Neurological Research Bank [*Veterans Administration Medical Center*] [*Research center*] (RCD)
NNRB........ Recording for the Blind, Inc., New York, NY [*Library symbol*] [*Library of Congress*] (LCLS)
NNRC........ Neural Net Research Group [*Georgia Institute of Technology*] (RCD)
NNRC........ Neutral Nations Repatriation Commission (SAUS)
NNRDC...... National Nuclear Rocket Development Center [*Also known as NRDS*]
NNRDF...... National Nuclear Rocket Development Facility (AAG)
NNRecA..... National Recreation Association [*Later, NRPA*], New York, NY [*Library symbol*] [*Library of Congress*] (LCLS)
NNreP....... Regional Plan Association, Inc., Library, New York, NY [*Library symbol*] [*Library of Congress*] (LCLS)
NNRF........ National Neurological Research Foundation (EA)
NNRG........ Nevada Energy Co., Inc. [*NASDAQ symbol*] (SAG)
NNRGA...... Nevada Energy [*NASDAQ symbol*] (TTSB)
NNRH........ Roosevelt Hospital, Medical Library, New York, NY [*Library symbol*] [*Library of Congress*] (LCLS)
NNRIS....... Nebraska Natural Resources Information System [*Nebraska State Natural Resources Commission*] [*Lincoln*] [*Information service or system*] (IID)
NNRo........ Theodore Roosevelt Association, New York, NY [*Library symbol*] [*Library of Congress*] (LCLS)
NNRocF..... Rockefeller Foundation, New York, NY [*Library symbol*] [*Library of Congress*] (LCLS)
NNRocFA.... Rockefeller Family & Associates, Inc., Office Library, New York, NY [*Library symbol*] [*Library of Congress*] (LCLS)
NNRoI....... Rochdale Institute, New York, NY [*Library symbol*] [*Library of Congress*] (LCLS)
NNRom...... Romanian Library, New York, NY [*Library symbol*] [*Library of Congress*] (LCLS)
NNRRB...... R. R. Bowker Co., New York, NY [*Library symbol*] [*Library of Congress*] (LCLS)
NNRT........ Non-Nucleoside Reverse Transcriptase [*Biochemistry*]
NNRT........ Racquet and Tennis Club, New York, NY [*Library symbol*] [*Library of Congress*] (LCLS)
NNRTC...... Northwest Natural Resource Technologies Consortium
NNRTI....... Non-Nucleoside Reverse Transcriptase Inhibitor [*Biochemistry*]
NNRU........ Rockefeller University, New York, NY [*Library symbol*] [*Library of Congress*] (LCLS)
NNRU-P..... Rockefeller University, Population Council, Bio-Medical Library, New York, NY [*Library symbol*] [*Library of Congress*] (LCLS)
NNRX........ Nevada Northern Railway [*Federal Railroad Administration identification code*]
NNRY........ Nunnery (ABBR)
NNRYS...... National Network of Runaway and Youth Services (EA)
NNS......... National Narrowcast Service [*Public Broadcasting Service*] [*Arlington, VA*] [*Telecommunications service*] (TSSD)
NNS......... National Natality Survey
NNS......... National Network Services (NITA)
NNS......... National Newspaper Syndicate
NNS......... Navy Navigation Satellite
NNS......... Navy News Service (DOMA)
NNS......... Near Net Shape (ACAE)
NNS......... Neonatal Society [*British*] (DBA)
NNS......... Neural Network Simulator
NNS......... Newhouse News Service (WDMC)
NNS......... Newport News Shipbuilding (DOMA)
NNS......... New York Society Library, New York, NY [*Library symbol*] [*Library of Congress*] (LCLS)
NNS......... Non-Native Speakers (EDAC)
NNS......... Nonnuclear Safety (NRCH)
NNS......... Nonnutritive Sweetener
NNS......... Nonproliferation and National Security [*Brookhaven National Laboratory*] (RCD)
NNS......... Norfolk Naval Shipyard [*Portsmouth, VA*] (MCD)
NNs......... North Salem Free Library, North Salem, NY [*Library symbol*] [*Library of Congress*] (LCLS)
NNS......... Nucleon-Nucleon Scattering
NNSA........ National Nuclear Security Administration (RCD)
NNSA........ National Nurses Society on Addictions (EA)
NNSA........ National Nurses Society on Alcoholism [*Medicine*] (EDAA)
NNSaB...... Salomon Brothers, New York, NY [*Library symbol*] [*Library of Congress*] (LCLS)
NNSAE...... Society of Automotive Engineers, New York, NY [*Library symbol*] [*Library of Congress*] (LCLS)
NNS&DDC.. Newport News Shipbuilding and Dry Dock Co. (SAUS)
NNSAR...... Sons of the American Revolution, Empire State Society Library, New York, NY [*Library symbol*] [*Library of Congress*] (LCLS)
NNSAS...... Skadden, Arps, Slate, Meagher & Flom, New York, NY [*Library symbol*] [*Library of Congress*] (LCLS)
NNSB........ Simmons-Boardman Publishing Corp., New York, NY [*Library symbol*] [*Library of Congress*] [*Obsolete*] (LCLS)
NNSB & DDCO... Newport News Shipbuilding & Dry Dock Co. (DNAB)
NNSC........ Neutral Nations Supervisory Commission
NN-Sc....... New York Public Library, Schomburg Collection, New York, NY [*Library symbol*] [*Library of Congress*] (LCLS)
NNSC........ Non-Nuclear Strategic Capabilities (SAUS)
NNSC........ NSF [*National Science*] Network Service Center [*Internet*] (TNIG)
NNSC........ Smithsonian Institution, Cooper-Hewitt Museum of Decorative Arts and Design, NewYork, NY [*Library symbol*] [*Library of Congress*] (LCLS)
NNSDO...... National Nursing Staff Development Organization (NTPA)
NNSeag..... Joseph E. Seagram & Sons, Inc., New York, NY [*Library symbol*] [*Library of Congress*] (LCLS)
NNSF........ National Natural Science Foundation
NNSG........ NASCOM [*NASA Communications Network*] Network Scheduling Group
NNShA...... Shubert Archive, New York, NY [*Library symbol*] [*Library of Congress*] (LCLS)
NNSIHi...... Staten Island Historical Society, New York, NY [*Library symbol*] [*Library of Congress*] (LCLS)
NNSII........ Staten Island Institute of Arts and Sciences, New York, NY [*Library symbol*] [*Library of Congress*] (LCLS)
NNSIS....... Swedish Information Service, New York, NY [*Library symbol*] [*Library of Congress*] (LCLS)
NNSJD...... Cathedral of Saint John the Divine, New York, NY [*Library symbol*] [*Library of Congress*] (LCLS)
NNSL........ Newport News Savings Bank (SAUS)
NNSL........ Nigerian National Shipping Line (SAUS)
NNSN........ No National Stock Number (AABC)
NNSNP...... National Network in Solidarity with the Nicaraguan People (EA)
NNSP........ National Network of State Polls
NNSPG...... National Network in Solidarity with the People of Guatemala (EA)
NNSPo...... Standard & Poor's Corp., New York, NY [*Library symbol*] [*Library of Congress*] (LCLS)
NNSR........ Sons of the Revolution in the State of New York, New York, NY [*Library symbol*] [*Library of Congress*] (LCLS)
NNSS........ Navy Navigational Satellite System
NNSS........ Shearman & Sterling Library, New York, NY [*Library symbol*] [*Library of Congress*] (LCLS)
NNSSS...... South Street Seaport Museum, New York, NY [*Library symbol*] [*Library of Congress*] (LCLS)
NNSTB...... Simpson, Thacher & Bartlett, Law Library, New York, NY [*Library symbol*] [*Library of Congress*] (LCLS)
NNStJ....... St. John's University, Jamaica, NY [*Library symbol*] [*Library of Congress*] (LCLS)
NNStL....... Saint Luke's Hospital, Richard Walker Bolling Memorial Medical Library, New York, NY [*Library symbol*] [*Library of Congress*] (LCLS)
NNStOD..... Standard Oil Co. (New Jersey), New York, NY [*Library symbol*] [*Library of Congress*] (LCLS)
NNSTWG.... Nonnuclear Survivability Technology Working Group (AFIT)
NNSU-MC... State University of New York, Maritime College, Fort Schuyler, Bronx, NY [*Library symbol*] [*Library of Congress*] (LCLS)
NNSU-Op... State University of New York, College of Optometry, New York, NY [*Library symbol*] [*Library of Congress*] (LCLS)
NNS/VPP.... Non-Nuclear Survivability/ Vulnerability Program Plan (SAUS)
NNSW........ Nonnuclear Strategic Warfare
NNSWM..... National Network for Social Work Managers (EA)
NNSY........ Norfolk Naval Shipyard [*Portsmouth, VA*]
NNT......... Nan [*Thailand*] [*Airport symbol*] (OAG)
NNT......... Nanotec Canada, Inc. [*Vancouver Stock Exchange symbol*]
NNT......... Nearest Neighbor Tool [*Mathematical technique*] (USDC)
NNT......... Neonatal Tetanus [*Medicine*] (EDAA)
NNT......... New York Times, New York, NY [*Library symbol*] [*Library of Congress*] (LCLS)
NNT......... Notice Number Tracking (MCD)
NNT......... Nuclear Nonproliferation Treaty (ODA)
NNT......... Nuclei Nervi Trigemini [*Medicine*] (EDAA)
NNT......... Number Needed to Treat
NNTAICH... Technical Assistance Information Clearing House, New York, NY [*Library symbol*] [*Library of Congress*] (LCLS)
NNTAPS..... National Nuclear Targeting Policy (CCCA)
NNTax....... Tax Foundation, Inc., New York, NY [*Library symbol*] [*Library of Congress*] (LCLS)
NNTC........ National Nondestructive Testing Centre [*Atomic Energy Authority*] [*Information service or system*] (IID)
NNTC........ Norwich and Norfolk Terrier Club (EA)
NNTC........ Teachers College, New York, NY [*Library symbol*] [*Library of Congress*] (LCLS)
NNTEP....... Northern Nigeria Teacher Education Project [*University of Wisconsin*] (AEBS)
NNTF........ Traphagen School of Fashion, New York, NY [*Library symbol*] [*Library of Congress*] (LCLS)
NNTIA....... Teachers Insurance and Annuity Association of America, New York, NY [*Library symbol*] [*Library of Congress*] (LCLS)
NNTM....... Tobacco Merchants Association of the United States, New York, NY [*Library symbol*] [*Library of Congress*] (LCLS)
NNTN........ Not Necessarily the News [*Cable television comedy program*]
NNTO........ Norwegian National Travel Office (SAUS)
NNTP........ National Nuclear Test Plan [*Later, NNTRP*]
NNTP........ Network News Transfer Protocol (TELE)
NNTP........ Network News Transport Protocol [*Telecommunications*]
NNTRP...... National Nuclear Test Readiness Program [*Formerly, NNTP*]
NNTSA...... No Need to See Again (SPVS)

NNTT .... National New Technology Telescope [*Proposed*] [*National Science Foundation*]
NNttR .... Rockefeller Archive Center, Rockefeller University, North Tarrytown, NY [*Library symbol*] [*Library of Congress*] (LCLS)
NNU .... Nanuque [*Brazil*] [*Airport symbol*] (AD)
NNU .... Neonatal Unit [*Medicine*] (DMAA)
NNU .... Net Nitrogen Utilization [*Medicine*] (DAVI)
NNU .... New York University, New York, NY [*Library symbol*] [*Library of Congress*] (LCLS)
NNU .... Nordic Numismatic Union (EAIO)
NNUAA ...... Northwest Nazarene University Alumni Association (EA)
NNU-B .... New York University, Graduate School of Business Administration, New York, NY [*Library symbol*] [*Library of Congress*] (LCLS)
NNU-C .... New York University, School of Commerce, New York, NY [*Library symbol*] [*Library of Congress*] (LCLS)
NNU-D .... New York University, College of Dentistry, New York, NY [*Library symbol*] [*Library of Congress*] (LCLS)
NNU-ES ..... New York University, Engineering and Science Library, New York, NY [*Library symbol*] [*Library of Congress*] (LCLS)
NNU-F .... New York University, Fales Collection, New York, NY [*Library symbol*] [*Library of Congress*] (LCLS)
NNU-FA ..... New York University, Institute of Fine Arts, New York, NY [*Library symbol*] [*Library of Congress*] (LCLS)
NNU-G .... New York University, Wall Street Library, New York, NY [*Library symbol*] [*Library of Congress*] (LCLS)
NNU-H .... New York University, University Heights Library, Bronn, NY [*Library symbol*] [*Library of Congress*] (LCLS)
NNUH .... United Hospital Fund of New York, New York, NY [*Library symbol*] [*Library of Congress*] (LCLS)
NNU-IEM .... New York University, Institute of Environmental Medicine, Tuxedo Park, NY [*Library symbol*] [*Library of Congress*] (LCLS)
NNU-L .... New York University, School of Law, New York, NY [*Library symbol*] [*Library of Congress*] (LCLS)
NNU-LA ..... New York University, Fobert F. Wagner Labor Archives, New York Labor Records Survey, New York,NY [*Library symbol*] [*Library of Congress*] (LCLS)
NNU-M ...... New York University, Medical Center, New York, NY [*Library symbol*] [*Library of Congress*] (LCLS)
NNUN .... United Nations Library, New York, NY [*Library symbol*] [*Library of Congress*] (LCLS)
NNUnC ...... University Club, New York, NY [*Library symbol*] [*Library of Congress*] (LCLS)
NNUN-CF ... United Nations Childrens Fund, New York, NY [*Library symbol*] [*Library of Congress*] (LCLS)
NNUni .... Unipub, Inc., New York, NY [*Library symbol*] [*Library of Congress*] (LCLS)
NNUnionC ... Union Club, New York, NY [*Library symbol*] [*Library of Congress*] (LCLS)
NNUnionL ... Union League Club, New York, NY [*Library symbol*] [*Library of Congress*] (LCLS)
NNUN-PA ... United Nations Fund for Population Activities, New York, NY [*Library symbol*] [*Library of Congress*] (LCLS)
NNUN-W .... United Nations, Woodrow Wilson Memorial Library, New York, NY [*Library symbol*] [*Library of Congress*] (LCLS)
NNUP .... Nocopi Technologies [*OTCBB symbol*]
NNU-T .... New York University, Tamiment Library, New York, NY [*Library symbol*] [*Library of Congress*] (LCLS)
NNUT .... Union Theological Seminary, New York, NY [*Library symbol*] [*Library of Congress*] (LCLS)
NNUT-Mc ... Union Theological Seminary, McAlpin Collection, New York, NY [*Library symbol*] [*Library of Congress*] (LCLS)
NNUVAN .... Ukrainian Academy of Arts and Sciences in the United States, New York, NY [*Library symbol*] [*Library of Congress*] (LCLS)
NNUVE ...... Nonnegative Unbiased Variance Estimator [*Statistics*]
NNU-W ...... New York University, Washington Square Library, New York, NY [*Library symbol*] [*Library of Congress*] (LCLS)
NNU-We ..... New York University, Joe Weinstein Residence Halls Library, New York, NY [*Library symbol*] [*Library of Congress*] (LCLS)
NNV .... National Naval Volunteers
NNVAB ...... United States Veterans Administration Hospital, Bronx, NY [*Library symbol*] [*Library of Congress*] (LCLS)
NNVAM ...... United States Veterans Administration Hospital (Manhattan), New York, NY [*Library symbol*] [*Library of Congress*] (LCLS)
NNW .... North by North West (SAUS)
NNW .... North-Northwest
NNWB .... Navy Nuclear Weapons Bulletin [*A publication*]
NNWB .... Net National Well Being
NNWC .... Nonnuclear Weapons Country
NNWF .... National Network of Women's Funds (EA)
NNWFG ..... Wilkie, Farr & Gallagher, New York, NY [*Library symbol*] [*Library of Congress*] (LCLS)
NNWG .... Wenner-Gren Foundation for Anthropological Research, New York, NY [*Library symbol*] [*Library of Congress*] (LCLS)
NNWH .... Nonnormal Working Hours
NNWH .... Walter Hampden Memorial Library, New York, NY [*Library symbol*] [*Library of Congress*] (LCLS)
NNWhit ...... Whitney Museum of American Art, New York, NY [*Library symbol*] [*Library of Congress*] (LCLS)
NNWI .... Neonatal Narcotic Withdrawal Index [*Medicine*] (DMAA)
NNWM ...... William Douglas McAdams, Inc., Medical Library, New York, NY [*Library symbol*] [*Library of Congress*] (LCLS)
NNWML ..... Wagner College, Staten Island, NY [*Library symbol*] [*Library of Congress*] (LCLS)
NNWO .... Navy Nuclear Weapons Officer (DNAB)
NNWP .... National Network of Women Philanthropists (NFD)
NNWR .... Noxubee National Wildlife Refuge (SAUS)
NNWRN ..... North-Northwestern (SAUS)
NNWS .... National Network of Women in Sales [*Defunct*] (EA)
NNWS .... Nonnuclear Weapons State
NNWSI ...... Nevada Nuclear Waste Storage Investigations
NNWWD .... North-Northwestward (SAUS)
NNWWD .... North-Westward (FAAC)
NNY .... Nanyang [*China*] [*Airport symbol*] (OAG)
NNY .... Nuveen New York Municipal Fund [*NYSE symbol*] (SPSG)
NNY .... Nuveen NY Muni Val Fd [*NYSE symbol*] (TTSB)
NNy .... Nyack Library, Nyack, NY [*Library symbol*] [*Library of Congress*] (LCLS)
NNYAB ...... National Network of Youth Advisory Boards (EA)
NNYACGS ... Northern New York American-Canadian Genealogical Society [*New York, the New England states, and Quebec, Canada*] (EARSL)
NNYC .... Yale Club, New York, NY [*Library symbol*] [*Library of Congress*] (LCLS)
NNYD .... Norfolk Navy Yard [*Virginia*] [*Later, Norfolk Naval Shipyard*]
NNYI .... YIVO Institute for Jewish Research, New York, NY [*Library symbol*] [*Library of Congress*] (LCLS)
NNYIQ .... Nuveen New York Investment Quality Municipal Fund [*Associated Press*] (SAG)
NNYM .... Nuveen New York Municipal Income Fund (SAUS)
NNyM .... Nyack Missionary College, Nyack, NY [*Library symbol*] [*Library of Congress*] (LCLS)
NNYMCA .... Young Men's Christian Association, National Council Historical Library, New York, NY [*Library symbol*] [*Library of Congress*] (LCLS)
NNYMCA-GC ... Young Men's Christian Association, Grand Central Branch Library, New York, NY [*Library symbol*] [*Library of Congress*] (LCLS)
NNYMCA-NC ... Young Men's Christian Association, National Council Historical Library, New York, NY [*Library symbol*] [*Library of Congress*] (LCLS)
NNYMI ...... Nuveen New York Municipal Income Fund [*Associated Press*] (SAG)
NNYMV ...... Nuveen New York Municipal Value Fund [*Associated Press*] (SAG)
NNYSQ ...... Nuveen New York Select Quality Municipal Fund [*Associated Press*] (SAG)
NNYU .... Yeshiva University, New York, NY [*Library symbol*] [*Library of Congress*] (LCLS)
NNYU-HJ ... Yeshiva University, Mendel Gottesman Library of Hebraica Judaica, New York, NY [*Library symbol*] [*Library of Congress*] (LCLS)
NNYU-M .... Yeshiva University, Albert Einstein College of Medicine, Bronx, NY [*Library symbol*] [*Library of Congress*] (LCLS)
NNYU-S ..... Yeshiva University, Stern College, New York, NY [*Library symbol*] [*Library of Congress*] (LCLS)
NNZ .... Ndanda [*Language symbol*] (ETLW)
NNZ .... New York Zoological Society, New York, NY [*Library symbol*] [*Library of Congress*] (LCLS)
NNZ .... Point Sur, CA [*Location identifier*] [*FAA*] (FAAL)
NNZCG ...... New Zealand Consulate General, Library, New York, NY [*Library symbol*] [*Library of Congress*] (LCLS)
NNZi .... Zionist Archives and Library, New York, NY [*Library symbol*] [*Library of Congress*] (LCLS)
NO .... Air North [*ICAO designator*] (AD)
N/O .... In the Name of (SAUS)
NO .... Lifts Not Operating [*Skiing*]
NO .... Nachalnik Otdelenia [*Chief of Department*] [*Soviet military rank*]
NO .... Narcotics Officer
NO .... National Office
NO .... National Office, Office of Federal Contract Compliance Programs (AAGC)
NO .... National Outlook: an Australian Christian Monthly [*A publication*] (APTA)
NO .... Native Officer [*British military*] (DMA)
NO .... Natural Orbital [*Physical chemistry*]
NO .... Natural Order [*Botany*]
NO .... Naval Observatory [*Navy*]
NO .... Naval Officer
NO .... Navigation Officer
NO .... Negative [*British naval signaling*]
NO .... Neuromyelitis Optica (SAUS)
NO .... Neutral Officer (SAUS)
NO .... Neutral Oil
NO .... New Options (EA)
NO .... New Order [*Defunct*] (EA)
NO .... New Orleans [*Louisiana*]
NO .... New Orleans, La [*Telegraphy*] (PCTE)
NO .... New Orleans Saints [*National Football League*] [*1967-present*] (NFLA)
NO .... Night Observation (SAUS)
NO .... Nitric Oxide
NO .... Nitrogen Dioxide (SAUS)
NO .... Nitrogen Monoxide
NO .... Nitrogen Oxide [*Emission control*] [*Automotive engineering*]
NO .... Noah (ABBR)
No .... Nobelium [*Chemical element*]
No .... Nocturia [*Urology*] (DAVI)
n/o .... None Obtained [*Medicine*]
NO .... Nonobese [*Medicine*] (DMAA)
NO .... Nonofficial
NO .... Nonoriginal
NO .... No Operational (SAUS)
N/O .... No Orders [*Business term*]
NO .... No Palpable Nodes [*Oncology*]
NO .... Nord-Ouest [*Northwest*] [*French*]
NO .... Normally Open [*Switch*]
NO .... Normal Operation (SAUS)
no .... North (SHCU)

NO .... North
NO .... North Central Airlines, Inc.
NO .... Northern (ABBR)
N/O .... North Of [*In outdoor advertising*] (WDMC)
NO .... Norway [*ANSI two-letter standard code*] (CNC)
no .... Norway [*MARC country of publication code*] [*Library of Congress*] (LCCP)
No .... Norway (MILB)
No .... Norwegian [*Linguistics*] (IEL)
NO .... Nose [*Horse racing*]
NO .... Notes [*Online database field identifier*]
NO .... Not for Off [*Kennedy Space Center Distribution*] (NAKS)
N/O .... Not Observed [*Emergency Management*] (EMA)
NO .... Not Operational (SAUS)
NO .... Not Or [*Logical operator*] [*Computer science*]
N/O .... Not Otherwise
NO .... Not Our Publication
NO .... Not Ours (SAUS)
N/O .... Not Out [*Bookselling*]
NO .... November (ADA)
NO .... Nuestra Orden [*Our Order*] [*Spanish*] [*Business term*]
NO .... Nuffield Observatory (SAUS)
No .... Number (EBF)
NO .... Number (EY)
no .... Number (WDMC)
NO .... Numero [*In Number*] [*Pharmacy*] (ROG)
NO .... Nurse's Office (DMAA)
NO .... Nursing Officer [*British*]
NO .... Oneida Library (SAUS)
NO .... Oneida Library, Oneida, NY [*Library symbol*] [*Library of Congress*] (LCLS)
NO .... Stickstoffmonoxid (SAUS)
No 1 .... first (SAUS)
No 1 .... first person (SAUS)
No 1 .... first quality (SAUS)
No 1 .... first rate (SAUS)
NO2 .... Nitrogen Dioxide
NO_3 .... Nitrate (GNE)
No9Vis .... Number Nine Visual Technology, Inc. [*Associated Press*] (SAG)
NOA .... National Oceanographic Association
NOA .... National Officers Association (EA)
NOA .... National Onion Association (EA)
NOA .... National Opera Association (EA)
NOA .... National Optical Association [*Later, NAOO*]
NOA .... National Optometric Association (EA)
NOA .... National Optometry Association (EA)
NOA .... National Orchestral Association (EA)
NOA .... National Outboard Association [*Defunct*] (EA)
NOA .... National Outdoorsmen's Association [*Defunct*] (EA)
NOA .... NATO Oil Authority (NATG)
NOA .... Natural Optical Activity
NOA .... Natural Orange Aroma
NOA .... Nature of Action [*Military*] (AFM)
NOA .... Nearest Onshore Area (EEVL)
NOA .... Nebraska Optometric Association (EARSL)
NOA .... Net on Air (SAUS)
NOA .... Network-Oriented Analysis and Transformation Unit [*Computer science*] (MHDB)
NOA .... New London, CT [*Location identifier*] [*FAA*] (FAAL)
NOA .... New Obligational Authority
NOA .... Non-Operational Aircraft (SAUS)
NOA .... Norontair [*Canada*] [*ICAO designator*] (FAAC)
NOA .... Northwest Orient Airlines, Inc.
NOA .... Notice of Arrival (EEVL)
NOA .... Notice of Availability (MCD)
NOA .... Not Operationally Assigned
N-O-A .... Not-Or-And [*Computer science*]
NOA .... Not Otherwise Authorized
NOA .... NSWC Office Automation (SAUS)
NOA .... Nueva Organizacion Antiterrorista [*New Anti-Terrorist Organization*] [*Guatemala*] (PD)
NOA .... University of North Carolina, Chapel Hill Library School, Chapel Hill, NC [*OCLC symbol*] (OCLC)
NOAA .... National Oceanic and Atmospheric Administration [*Rockville, MD*] [*Pronounced "Noah"*]
NOAA .... Nonoperating Aircraft Authorization
NOAA .... US National Oceanic and Atmospheric Administration (SAUS)
NOAADN .... National Organization for Advancement of Associate Degree Nursing (EA)
NOAA-FSL ... NOAA [*National Oceanic and Atmospheric Administration*]-Forecast Systems Lab
NOAA-JTRE ... National Oceanic and Atmospheric Administration Joint Tsunami Research Effort
NOAAnet .... NOAA network (SAUS)
NOAA-NOS ... National Oceanic and Atmospheric Administration - National Ocean Service (DNAB)
NOAA-NWS ... National Oceanic and Atmospheric Administration - National Weather Service (DNAB)
NOAA-PMEL ... National Oceanic and Atmospheric Administration Pacific Marine Environmental Laboratory
NOAAport ... NOAA data-delivery system (SAUS)
NOAA-TR-NMFS-Circ ... National Oceanic and Atmospheric Administration Technical Report-National MarineFisheries Service-Circular [*A publication*] (PDAA)
NOAA-TR-NMFS-SSRF ... National Oceanic and Atmospheric Administration-Technical Report-National MarineFisheries Service-Special Scientific Report Fisheries (PDAA)
NOAB .... National Outdoor Advertising Bureau [*Defunct*] (EA)
NO-AB .... New Orleans-Algiers Bridge (SAUS)
NOAB .... North American Bancorporation, Inc. (SAUS)
NOAC .... National Operations and Automation Conference (HGAA)
NOAC .... Nature of Action Code [*Environmental science*] (EPAT)
NOAC .... Naval Officers' Association of Canada (EAIO)
No a/c .... No Account (EBF)
NOAC .... Nordic Accelerator-Based-Research Committee (SAUS)
NOAC .... Nuclear Operations Analysis Center [*Oak Ridge National Laboratory*] (IID)
NOAC .... Nuclear Operations Analysis Center [*Department of Energy*] [*Information service or system*] (IID)
NOACT .... Naval Overseas Air Cargo Terminal
NOACT .... No Action (MUGU)
NOACTLANT ... Naval Ordnance Activities, Atlantic
NOACTPAC ... Naval Ordnance Activities, Pacific
NOaD .... Dowling College, Oakdale, NY [*Library symbol*] [*Library of Congress*] (LCLS)
NOAD .... National Organization for Apraxia and Dyspraxia (EA)
NOAD .... No Other Abnormality Diagnosed (SPVS)
No Adams St C ... North Adams State College (GAGS)
NOADN .... National Oceanic and Atmospheric Data Network
NOADN .... National Organization for Associate Degree Nursing (EA)
NOADS .... Newspapers Opposed to Advertising Death by Smoking (SAUS)
No Adv .... No Advice (EBF)
NOAEL .... No Observed Adverse Effect Level [*Toxicology*] (EG)
NOAF .... No Other Abnormal Findings (SPVS)
NOaf .... Oakfield Public Library (Haxton Memorial), Oakfield, NY [*Library symbol*] [*Library of Congress*] (LCLS)
NOAFIRM ... Affirmative Replies Neither Required nor Desired (MUGU)
NOAG .... Naval Objectives Analysis Group
NO A/G .... No Air to Ground Communications
NOAH .... Narrow-Band Optimiziation of the Alignment of Highways (PDAA)
NOAH .... National Ocean Agency Headquarters
NOAH .... National Organization for Albinism and Hypopigmentation (EA)
NOAH .... New Opportunities for Animal Health scientists (SAUS)
NOAH .... New York Online Access to Health (SAUS)
NOAH .... New York Online Access to Health Home Page [*Database*]
NOAH .... Nitrous Oxide and Halocarbons Division (SAUS)
NOAH .... Noarko Resources, Inc. (SAUS)
NOAH .... Norwegian Adapted HAWK [*Hughes Aircraft Co.*]
NOAHS .... New Opportunities in Animal Health Sciences
Noahs Ark Toy Libr Handicapped Child Newsletter ... Noahs Ark Toy Library for Handicapped Children. Newsletter (SAUS)
NOaJH .... Oakdale-Bohemia Junior High School (SAUS)
NOaJH .... Oakdale-Bohemia Junior High School, Oakdale, NY [*Library symbol*] [*Library of Congress*] (LCLS)
NOALA .... Noise-Operated Automatic Level Adjuster (or Adjustment) (SAUS)
NOAM .... Noan Mizrachi [*American Zionist organization*]
NOAM .... Nuclear Ordnance Air Force Materiel [*Military*] (AFIT)
NOAMTRAC ... North America Trail Complex (EA)
NO & LC .... New Orleans & Lower Coast Railroad Co. (IIA)
NOAO .... National Optical Astronomical Observatories
NOAO .... National Optical Astronomy Observatories [*Tucson, AZ*] [*National Science Foundation*]
NOAO .... Navy Officers, Accounts Office (MUGU)
NOAP .... National Ocean Access Project (EA)
NOAP .... Naval Overseas Air Cargo Terminal, Pearl (MUGU)
NOAP .... Navy Oil Analysis Program (NG)
NOAPP .... National Organization of Adolescent Pregnancy and Parenting (EA)
NOAPP .... National Organization on Adolescent Pregnancy, Parenting, and Prevention (PAZ)
NOAPS .... National Oil and Acrylic Painters Society
NOAR .... National Organization for an American Revolution (EA)
NOARB .... New Orleans Army Base (SAA)
No Ariz U ... Northern Arizona University (GAGS)
NOARL .... National Oceanographic and Atmospheric Research Laboratory (USDC)
NOARL .... Naval Ocean and Atmosphere Research Laboratory [*USA*] [*Marine science*] (OSRA)
NOART .... New Orleans Army Terminal
NOASSR .... North Ossetian Autonomous Soviet Socialist Republic (SAUS)
NOAX .... NEOAX, Inc. [*NASDAQ symbol*] (COMM)
NOB .... National Oil Board (NATG)
NOB .... Naval Operating Base
NOB .... Naval Order of Battle
NOB .... Naval Ordnance Bulletin [*A publication*]
NOB .... Nobeoka [*Japan*] [*Seismograph station code, US Geological Survey*] (SEIS)
NOB .... Nobile [*Nobly*] [*Music*] (ROG)
NOB .... Nobility (ABBR)
NOB .... Nobis [*With Us*] [*Latin*] (ROG)
NOB .... Noble (ABBR)
NOB .... Non-Biased Optical Bistable [*Device*] (AAEL)
NOB .... Nonobese [*A diabetic mouse strain*]
NOB .... No Open Burning (SAUS)
NOB .... North Bay Cooperative Library System, Santa Rosa (SAUS)
NOB .... North Bay Cooperative Library System, Santa Rosa, CA [*OCLC symbol*] (OCLC)
NOB .... North Outpatient Building (SAUS)
NOB .... Norwest Corp. [*NYSE symbol*] (SPSG)
NOB .... Notes over Bonds [*Finance*] (NUMA)

NOB.......... Not on Board (SAUS)
NOB.......... Not on Bonus
NOB.......... Nuclear Order of Battle (AFM)
NOB.......... Number of Bursts
NOB.......... San Francisco, CA [*Location identifier*] [*FAA*] (FAAL)
NOBA........ Nitrosobenzamide [*Organic chemistry*]
NOBA........ Norwegian Zero Power Reactor Assembly (SAUS)
NOBAR...... National Organization for Birthfathers and Adoption Reform (EA)
NOBC........ National Office for Black Catholics (EA)
NOBC........ National Order of Battlefield Commissions (EA)
NOBC........ National Organization of Bar Counsel (EA)
NOBC........ Naval Officer Billet Classifications [*or Code*]
NOBC........ Norris Brothers Company [*Common carrier symbol*]
NOBCA...... National Organization of Black College Alumni (EA)
NOBCCE..... National Organization of Black Chemists and Chemical Engineers [*Later, NOPABCCE*] (EA)
NOBCChE... National Organization for Professional Advancement of Black Chemists and Chemical Engineers
NOBCO...... National Organization of Black County Officials (EA)
NOBDUCHAR... Naval Operating Base, Dutch Harbor, Aleutians
NOBE........ Nordstrom, Inc. [*NASDAQ symbol*] (NQ)
NoBeFi...... Fiskeridirektoratet [*Directorate of Fisheries*], Bergen-Nordens, Norway [*Library symbol*] [*Library of Congress*] (LCLS)
Nobel........ Nobel Insurance Ltd. [*Associated Press*] (SAG)
NobelEd..... Nobel Education Dynamics, Inc. [*Associated Press*] (SAG)
NOBELS..... New Office and Business Education Learning System
NoBeU........ Universitetet i Bergen [*University of Bergen*], Bergen, Norway [*Library symbol*] [*Library of Congress*] (LCLS)
NOBFRAN... Naval Operating Base, San Francisco, California
NOBH........ Nobility Homes [*NASDAQ symbol*] (TTSB)
NOBH........ Nobility Homes, Inc. [*NASDAQ symbol*] (NQ)
NOBI......... Nobility Homes [*NCIC trailer make code*]
NobiltyH.... Nobility Homes, Inc. [*Associated Press*] (SAG)
NOBIN....... Stichting Nederlands Orgaan voor de Bevordering van de Informatieverzorging [*Netherlands Organization for Information Policy*] [*Information service or system*] [*Defunct*] (IID)
No Biz....... No Business (SAUS)
NOBL........ Nobel Insurance Ltd. [*NASDAQ symbol*] (NQ)
NOBL........ Noble Cultivators [*NCIC trailer make code*]
NOBL........ Noble International [*NASDAQ symbol*] (SG)
NoblAf....... Noble Affiliates, Inc. [*Associated Press*] (SAG)
NOBLE....... National Organization of Black Law Enforcement Executives (EA)
Noble........ Noble's Current Court Decisions [*New York*] [*A publication*] (DLA)
NOBLE....... Noblesville, IN [*American Association of Railroads railroad junction routing code*]
NOBLE....... North of Boston Library Exchange
NobleR....... Noble Roman's, Inc. [*Associated Press*] (SAG)
NOBLF....... Nobel Insurance [*NASDAQ symbol*] (TTSB)
NOB LIB..... North Outpatient Building Library (SAUS)
NobltyH..... Nobility Homes [*Associated Press*] (SAG)
NOBMN...... Nobleman (ABBR)
NoBncshs... North Bancshares, Inc. [*Associated Press*] (SAG)
NOBNEWT... Naval Operating Base, Newport, Rhode Island
NOBO........ Nonobjecting Beneficial Owner (SAUS)
NoBordr..... Northern Border Partners Ltd. [*Associated Press*] (SAG)
NOBP........ Nitrosobenzopyrone [*Organic chemistry*]
NOBR........ Nobler (ABBR)
NOBS........ Naval Observatory [*Navy*]
NOBS........ Naval Operating Base Supplies (DNAB)
N Obs....... Nihil Obstat [*Official Approval*] [*Latin*]
NOBS........ Nonanoyloxybenzene (EDCT)
NOBS........ Nonanoyloxybenzene Sulfonate [*Laundry bleach activator*]
NOBS........ Nursing Observation of Behaviour Syndromes (DB)
NOBSOLO... Naval Operating Base, Coco Solo, Canal Zone
NOBST...... Noblest (ABBR)
NOBSY...... Naval Observatory [*Navy*]
NOBT........ New Orleans Board of Trade (EA)
NOBT........ Nobility (ABBR)
NOBT........ Nonoperative Biopsy Technique [*Medicine*] (MELL)
NOBTRIN... Naval Operating Base, Trinidad
NOBTS...... Naval Order of Battle Textual Summary (MCD)
NOBU........ Nordic Bulkers [*Intermodal shipping container symbol*] (TVRC)
NOBWN..... Noblewomen (ABBR)
NOBY........ Nobly (ABBR)
NOC.......... Ascor Flyservice AS [*Norway*] [*ICAO designator*] (FAAC)
NOC.......... National Oceanographic Center [*Marine science*] (MSC)
NOC.......... National Oceanographic Council (NADA)
NOC.......... National Offshore Council (EA)
NOC.......... National Olympic Committee (NADA)
NOC.......... National Online Circuit [*Defunct*] (EA)
NOC.......... National Opportunity Camps for the Pre-Teen Child (EA)
NOC.......... Natural Organic Carbon
NOC.......... Naval Oceanographic Command (SAUS)
NOC.......... Naval Operations Center (NVT)
NOC.......... Navy Officer's Classification
NOC.......... Network Operation Center [*Bell System*]
NOC.......... Network Operations Center [*Internet*] (NETL)
NOC.......... Network Operations Control [*NASA*] (KSC)
NOC.......... New Orleans Consortium [*Library network*]
noc........... Night [*Therapy term*] (CTAA)
NOC.......... Nippon Oil Company [*Fuels and lubricants*]
noc........... Noctis [*Night*] [*Medicine*]
noc........... Nocturnal [*Therapy term*] (CTAA)
NOC.......... Nominal Operating Cell [*Photovoltaic energy systems*]
NOC.......... Nonionic Organic Compound [*Organic chemistry*]
NOC.......... Non-Ionic Organic Contaminant [*Environmental chemistry*]
NOC.......... Normally Open Contact [*Switch*] (IAA)
NOC.......... Norris Communications Corp. [*Vancouver Stock Exchange symbol*]
NOC.......... Northrop Corp. [*NYSE symbol*] (SPSG)
NOC.......... Northrop Grumman [*NYSE symbol*] (TTSB)
NOC.......... Northrop Grumman Corp. [*NYSE symbol*] (SAG)
NOC.......... Northwest Ohio Consortium [*Library network*]
NOC.......... Norwegian Government Office of Culture [*Record label*]
NOC.......... Notation of Content [*Aerospace*]
NOC.......... Not-Carry (SAUS)
NOC.......... Notice of Cancellation (AAGC)
NOC.......... Notice of Change (MCD)
NOC.......... Notice of Commencement (EPA)
NOC.......... Notice of Construction (EEVL)
NOC.......... Notice of Contents [*Indexing*]
NOC.......... Not Otherwise Classified
NOC.......... Not Otherwise Coded (GFGA)
NOC.......... Nuclear Operations Center (MCD)
NOC.......... Nuclear Ordnance Commission [*Military*] (AFIT)
NOC.......... Number of Children (SAUS)
NOC.......... Numerical Optimisation Centre [*British*]
NOC.......... Nursing Outcomes Classification (SAUS)
NOC.......... Nuttall Ornithological Club (EA)
NOc.......... Oceanside Free Library, Oceanside, NY [*Library symbol*] [*Library of Congress*] (LCLS)
NOC.......... University of North Carolina, Chapel Hill, Chapel Hill, NC [*OCLC symbol*] (OCLC)
NOCA........ National Organization for Competency Assurance (EA)
NOCA........ National Ovarian Cancer Association [*Canada*] (EAIO)
NOCA........ Nitrosooxazolidinecarboxylic Acid [*Organic chemistry*]
NOCA........ North Cascades National Park
No Ca Ecc & Mar... Notes of Cases, English Ecclesiastical and Maritime Courts [*1841-50*] [*A publication*] (DLA)
NOCAP...... National Oral Cancer Awareness Program (SAUS)
No Car Ag & Tech... North Carolina Agricultural & Technical State University (GAGS)
No Car Cent U... North Carolina Central University (GAGS)
No Car St U (Raleigh)... North Carolina State University (Raleigh) (GAGS)
NOcaS....... Shaker Museum Foundation, Inc., Old Catham, NY [*Library symbol*] [*Library of Congress*] (LCLS)
No Cas LJ... Notes of Cases, Law Journal [*A publication*] (DLA)
NOCB........ New Orleans City Ballet
NocBE....... Walter S. Boardman Elementary School, Oceanside, NY [*Library symbol*] [*Library of Congress*] (LCLS)
NOCC........ National Ovarian Cancer Coalition, Inc. (NRGU)
NOCC........ NATO Oil Crisis Contingent (NATG)
NOCC........ Navigation Operational Checkout Computer
NOCC........ Navigation Operator's Control Console
NOCC........ Network Operations Control Center [*Manned Space Flight Network, NASA*]
NOCC........ New Orleans Crime Commission (SAUS)
NOCC........ North Peralta Community College (SAUS)
NOCCC...... No Control Circuit Contacts (MSA)
NOCCE...... No Clubbing, Cyanosis or Edema (SAUS)
NOCC/JTWC... Naval Oceanography Command Center/Joint Typhoon Warning Center
NOCD........ Not Our Class, Dear [*Slang*]
NOCE........ New Orleans Commodity Exchange (EA)
NOCEM...... National Organization for Civic Education & Election Monitoring [*Lira, Uganda*]
NOCERCC... National Organization for Continuing Education of Roman Catholic Clergy (EA)
NOCF........ National Office Computer Facility [*IRS*]
NOCF........ Naval Oceanography Command Facility (DNAB)
NocFE....... Elementary School #3, Oceanside, NY [*Library symbol*] [*Library of Congress*] (LCLS)
NOcH........ South Nassau Communities Hospital, Oceanside, NY [*Library symbol*] [*Library of Congress*] (LCLS)
NOCHA...... National Off-Campus Housing Association [*Defunct*] (EA)
NOCI......... Nederlandse Organisatie voor Chemische Informatie (NITA)
NOCI......... Non Orthogonal Configuration Interaction (AAEL)
NOCIG....... Night Only Calligraphic Image Generator
NOC II....... Nuclear Operations Concept II [*Military*]
NOCIRC..... National Organization of Circumcision Information Resource Centers (PAZ)
No-Clo Z.... No-Clone Zone (SAUS)
NOCM........ National Organization for Changing Men (EA)
NOCM........ Nuclear Ordnance Commodity Manager (AFM)
NocME....... Elementary School #8, Oceanside, NY [*Library symbol*] [*Library of Congress*] (LCLS)
NOCMIS..... NOC Management Information System (SAUS)
NocMS....... Oceanside Middle School, Oceanside, NY [*Library symbol*] [*Library of Congress*] (LCLS)
NOCN........ National Ocean Communications Network (USDC)
NOCN........ National Open College Network (AIE)
NOCN........ No Connection [*Travel industry*] (TRID)
NocNE....... Elementary School #5, Oceanside, NY [*Library symbol*] [*Library of Congress*] (LCLS)
NOCO........ Noise Correlation
NOCO........ North Coast Energy (EFIS)
NOCO........ North Country [*NCIC trailer make code*]
No Co........ Northern Counties (SAUS)
No Co........ Northern Countries (SAUS)
NOCO........ Norwegian Oil Consortium (SAUS)

NOCO........ Nuclear Ordnance Cataloging Officer [*Military*]
NOCO........ Nuclear Ordnance Catalog Office [*DoD*]
No Code .... do not resuscitate (SAUS)
NOCOL...... No Collision (SAUS)
NOCONIT... No Continuing Interest (NG)
NOCONTRACT... Not Releasable to Contractors (MCD)
NOCOPOR... Nordic Cooperation in Polar Research (SAUS)
NOCOR...... Neglect of Core Orbitals [*Physical chemistry*]
NOCP........ Network Operator Control Program
No-CPR ..... No Cardiopulmonary Resuscitation [*Medicine*] (MELL)
NOCR........ Network Operations Control Room (SAUS)
NOCSA...... National Olympic Committee of South Africa (ECON)
NOCSAE..... National Operating Committee on Standards for Athletic Equipment (EA)
NOcSE....... Florence A. Smith School, Oceanside, NY [*Library symbol*] [*Library of Congress*] (LCLS)
NocSH....... Oceanside Senior High School, Oceanside, NY [*Library symbol*] [*Library of Congress*] (LCLS)
no C/S/V/D... No Coughing, Sneezing, Vomiting or Diarrhoea (SPVS)
NOCT........ Navy Overseas Cargo Terminals
NOCT........ Nocte [*At Night*] [*Pharmacy*] (ROG)
noct.......... Nocturnal (CPH)
NOCT........ Nominal [*or Normal*] Operating Cell Temperature [*Photovoltaic energy systems*]
NOCT MANEQ... Nocte Maneque [*Night and Morning*] [*Pharmacy*]
NOCU........ Northern Container [*Intermodal shipping container symbol*] (TVRC)
NOCUS...... Nord Computer Users Society (SAUS)
NOCUS...... North Continental US (SAUS)
NOCX........ North Carolina Railroad Museum [*Federal Railroad Administration identification code*]
NOD .... National Organization on Disability (EA)
NOD .... Naval Ordnance Department [*British*]
NOD .... Naval Ordnance Depot
NOD .... Navy Operational Deception (MCD)
NOD .... Network Operations Directive [*NASA*] (KSC)
NOD .... Network Operations Division (ACAE)
NOD .... Network Out-Dial [*Automatic Voice Network*] (CET)
NOD .... New Offshore Dischargement (NATG)
NOD .... New-Onset Diabetes [*Medicine*] (MELL)
NOD .... Night Observation Device
NOD .... Nitrogenous Oxidation (SAUS)
NOD .... Noise Output Device
NOD .... Nondefinitive Pattern [*Laboratory science*] (DAVI)
NOD .... Nonobese Diabetic [*Mouse strain*]
NOD .... Non-Offensive Defence (SAUS)
NOD .... Norris Dam [*TVA*]
NOD .... Notice of Decision (COE)
NOD .... Notice of Deficiency (EPA)
NOD .... Notify of Death (DAVI)
NOD .... Not Otherwise Defined (SAUS)
NOD .... Not Otherwise Diagnosed
NODA........ National Operatic and Dramatic Association (EAIO)
NODA........ National Orientation Directors Association (EA)
NODA........ National Outdoor Drama Association [*Defunct*] (EA)
NODA........ Night Operatic and Dramatic Association (SAUS)
NODA........ Nordana Line [*Common carrier symbol*]
NODA........ Normal-Octyl & -Deyl Adipate [*Organic chemistry*]
NODAC...... Naval Ordnance Data Automation Center
NODAC...... Navy Occupational Development and Analysis Center (DNAB)
No Dak St U... North Dakota State University (GAGS)
NODAL...... Network-Oriented Data Acquisition Language
NODAN...... Noise-Operated Device for Antinoise [*Telecommunications*] (TEL)
NODAP...... Nonlinear Distortion Analysis Program [*Bell System*]
NODAR...... North Dartmouth, MA [*American Association of Railroads railroad junction routing code*]
NODAS...... Network-Oriented Data Acquisition System (MHDI)
NODB........ North Dallas Bank & Trust Co. [*NASDAQ symbol*] (QUAN)
NODC........ National Oceanographic Data Center [*Databank originator*] [*Washington, DC*] [*National Oceanic and Atmospheric Administration*]
NODC........ Naval Oceanographic Distribution Center
NODC........ Naval Operating Development Center
NODC........ Non-Oil Developing Countries (SAUS)
NODC........ Non-OPEC Developing Country (NUCP)
NODCAB .... National Oceanographic Data Center Advisory Board [*National Oceanic and Atmospheric Administration*] (NOAA)
NODCC...... Noble Order, Descendants of the Conqueror and His Companions (EA)
NODD........ Nord Orphan Drug Designation Database (SAUS)
NODDS...... Naval Oceanographic Data Distribution System
NODDY...... Notions, Oddities, Doodads & Delights of Yesterday
NODE........ National Organization of Downsized Employees
NODE........ Nodine Manufacturing [*NCIC trailer make code*]
NODE........ Noise Diode [*Electronics*] (IAA)
NODEL...... Not to Delay
NODESTA... Will Not Depart This Station [*Army*] (AABC)
NODI......... Nordic [*NCIC trailer make code*]
NODI......... Notice of Delayed [*or Delinquent*] Item
NODI......... Notice of Delayed Items (SAUS)
NODI......... Notice of Delinquent Item (SAUS)
NODIS....... No Distribution [*Military security classification*] (AFM)
NODIS....... Northern Ohio Data and Information Service [*Cleveland State University*] [*Information service or system*] (IID)
NODIS....... NSSDC Online Data and Information System (SAUS)
NODL........ National Office for Decent Literature [*Defunct*]
NODL........ Not on Drawing List (MCD)
NODLR...... Night Observation Device, LASAR Ranging (TIMI)
NODLR...... Night Observation Device, Long-Range [*Army*] (RDA)
NODM....... Ferrocarril Nor-Oeste de Mexico [*Mexico North Western Railroad*] [*AAR code*]
NODM....... National Organization of Dance and Mime [*British*] (DBA)
NODMR..... Night Observation Device, Medium-Range [*Army*]
NODO........ NASA Orbital Debris Observatory (SAUS)
NODOZ...... Nuclear Offense/Defense Operational Zone (ACAE)
NODRA...... National One Design Racing Association (EA)
NODS........ NASA Ocean Data System (EOSA)
NODS........ National Oversight Database (AEPA)
NODS........ Navy Overseas Dependents School
NODS........ Near-Object Detection Sensor [*Automotive electronics*]
NODS........ Near Obstacle Detection System [*General Motors-Delco Co.*]
NODS........ Night Observation & Detection System (SAUS)
NODU........ Nordana Line [*Intermodal shipping container symbol*] (TVRC)
NOE.......... Nap of the Earth [*Night helicopter flight*] [*Army*]
NOE.......... No Ophthalmologic Examination [*Medicine*]
NOE.......... No Other Entry (ADA)
NOE.......... NORAD Operational Evaluation (MCD)
NOE.......... Norden-Norddeich [*Germany*] [*Airport symbol*]
NOE.......... Notice of Exception
NOE.......... Notice of Exception Oceanographic Foundation (SAUS)
NOE.......... Notice of Execution
NOE.......... Not Otherwise Enumerated
NOE.......... Nuclear Overhauser Effect
NOE.......... Nuclear Overhauser Enhancement (DB)
NOE.......... Number of Employees (SAUS)
NOE.......... Number of Errors (SAUS)
NOEA........ National Outdoor Events Association [*British*] (DBA)
No East Rep... Northeastern Reporter [*Commonly cited NE*] [*A publication*] (DLA)
NOEB........ NATO Oil Executive Board (NATG)
NOEB-E..... NATO Oil Executive Board - East
NOEB-W.... NATO Oil Executive Board - West
NOEC........ No Effects Concentration [*British environmental standard*]
NOEC........ No Observed Effect Concentration [*Toxicology*]
NOECC...... Northeast College Conference (PSS)
NOECOMM... Nap-of-the-Earth Communications [*Night helicopter flight*]
NOED........ New Oxford English Dictionary [*Proposed*]
NOEDS...... Nuclear Overhauser Enhancement Difference Spectrometry
NOEF........ Naval Ordnance Engineering Facility (DNAB)
NOEHI....... No One Else Has It [*Lexicography*]
No E Ill U... Northeastern Illinois University (GAGS)
NOEL........ National Organization of Episcopalians for Life (EA)
NOEL........ National Ornament and Electric Lights Christmas Association (EA)
NOEL........ Naval Ordnance Electronics Laboratory
NOEL........ Noel Group [*NASDAQ symbol*] (TTSB)
NOEL........ Noel Group, Inc. [*NASDAQ symbol*] (SAG)
NOEL........ Noel Manufacturing [*NCIC trailer make code*]
NOEL........ Nonobservable Effect Level (SAUS)
NOEL........ No Observed Effect Level [*Toxicology*]
NOEL........ Number of Errors Left (SAUS)
No E La U... Northeast Louisiana University (GAGS)
NoelGp...... Noel Group, Inc. [*Associated Press*] (SAG)
No E Mo St U... Northeast Missouri State University (GAGS)
No E Ohio U... Northeastern Ohio University (GAGS)
NOEP........ Neue Oekonomische Politik [*New Economic Policy*] [*Germany*]
NOES........ National Operational Environmental Satellite Service (MCD)
NOESS...... National Operational Environmental Satellite System
No E St U... Northeastern State University (GAGS)
NoestUt..... Northeast Utilities [*Associated Press*] (SAG)
NOESY...... Nuclear Overhauser Effect Spectroscopy
NOESY...... Nuclear Overhauser enhancement and Exchange Spectroscopy (SAUS)
No et Vet Test... Novi et Veteris Testamenti (DSA)
NOEU........ Naval Ordnance Experimental Unit
No E U...... Northeastern University (GAGS)
NOF.......... Fonnafly AS [*Norway*] [*ICAO designator*] (FAAC)
NOF.......... National Oceanographic Facility [*Marine science*] (OSRA)
NOF.......... National Optical Font [*Typography*]
NOF.......... National Osteopathic Foundation (EA)
NOF.......... National Osteoporosis Foundation (EA)
NOF.......... Naval Operating Facility
NOF.......... Naval Ordnance Facility
NOF.......... NCR [*NCR Corp.*] Optical Font (MCD)
NOF.......... Network Operations and Facilities
NOF.......... Network Operations Forum [*Exchange Carriers Standards Association*] [*Telecommunications*]
NOF.......... Neurite Outgrowth Factor [*Biochemistry*]
NOF.......... Nickel Offsets Ltd. [*Toronto Stock Exchange symbol*]
NOF.......... Nitrogen-Oxygen-Fluorine (SAUS)
NOF.......... Nitrosyl Fluoride (SAA)
NOF.......... Node Operator Facility (SAUS)
NOF.......... Notice of Findings (SAUS)
NOF.......... Not on File (SAUS)
NOF.......... St. Petersburg, FL [*Location identifier*] [*FAA*] (FAAL)
NOFA........ National Office Furniture Association [*Later, NOPA*] (EA)
NOFA........ Natural Organic Farmers Association (EA)
NOFA........ Notice of Funding Availability [*Department of Housing and Urban Development*] (GFGA)
NOFAD...... Naval Ocean Floor Analysis Division (DNAB)
NOFA-JN ... Northeast Organic Farming Association, New Jersey (EARSL)

NOFA-NY ... Northeast Organic Farming Association of New York (EARSL)
NOFAS .... National Organization on Fetal Alcohol Syndrome (MELL)
NOFA VT .... Northeast Organic Farming Association, Vermont Chapter (EARSL)
NOFBF .... Noninverting Output Bridging Fault (SAUS)
N of Cas .... Notes of Cases at Madras (Strange) [*A publication*] (DLA)
N of Cas .... Notes of Cases, English Ecclesiastical and Maritime Courts [*1841-50*] [*A publication*] (DLA)
N of Eng .... North of England (SAUS)
NOFI .... National Oil Fuel Institute [*Later, NOJC*] (EA)
NOFIN .... No Further Information
NoFkBc ...... North Fork Bancorp [*Associated Press*] (SAG)
NOFLD .... Northfield, MN [*American Association of Railroads railroad junction routing code*]
NOFMA ...... National Oak Flooring Manufacturers Association (EA)
NOFO .... Norsk Forkonservering (EFIS)
NOFOA ...... Naval Office for Occupied Areas [*World War II*]
NOFODIS ... No Foreign Dissemination [*Intelligence classification*]
NOFORN .... No Foreign Nationals (SAUS)
NOFORN .... Not Releasable to Foreign Nationals [*Military security classification*]
NOFRC ...... Northern Forest Research Centre [*Canadian Forestry Service of Agriculture Canada*] [*Research center*] (RCD)
NOFS .... National Option and Futures Society [*Defunct*] (EA)
NOFT .... Naval Overseas Freight Terminal
NOFT .... Nonorganic Failure-to-Thrive [*Medicine*] (DMAA)
NOFT .... Notification of Foreign Travel (AFM)
NOFTT .... Nonorganic Failure-to-Thrive [*Medicine*] (MEDA)
NOFU .... Nodfos [*Intermodal shipping container symbol*] (TVRC)
NOG .... Arizona-Nogales [*Mexico*] [*Airport symbol*] (AD)
nog .... noggin (SAUS)
NOG .... North Carolina Natural Gas [*NYSE symbol*] (SAG)
NOG .... NSAPAC Operations Group
NOG .... Nuclear Oncogenes [*Medicine*] (MELL)
NOG .... Nuclear Ordnance Group [*Air Force*] (MCD)
NOG .... Numbering
NOg .... Ogdensburg Public Library, Ogdensburg, NY [*Library symbol*] [*Library of Congress*] (LCLS)
NOGA .... National Osteopathic Guild Association (EA)
NOGAD ...... Noise-Operated Gain-Adjusting Device
NOGAL ...... Nogales, AZ [*American Association of Railroads railroad junction routing code*]
Nogal .... Nogales, Sonora, Mexico (SAUS)
NOGAP ...... Northern Oil and Gas Action Plan (SAUS)
NOGAP ...... Northern Oil and Gas Action Program (SAUS)
NOGAPS .... National Oceanographic Global Atmospheric Prediction System (WEAT)
NOGAPS .... Navy Operational Global Atmospheric Prediction System
NOGC .... New Orleans & Gulf Coast Railway [*Federal Railroad Administration identification code*]
NOGC .... Nicklos Oil & Gas (SAUS)
NOGGA ...... National Ornamental Goldfish Growers Association (EA)
NOgH .... A. Barton Hepburn Hospital, Ogdensburg, NY [*Library symbol*] [*Library of Congress*] (LCLS)
NOGIC .... Night-Only Computer Image Generation (SAUS)
NOGKAV .... Agricultural Research (journ.) (SAUS)
NOGL .... Naval Ordnance Gauge Laboratory
NOGL .... Nizam's Own Golgonda Lancers [*British military*] (DMA)
NOGLSTP ... National Organization of Gay and Lesbian Scientists and Technical Professionals (EA)
NOgM .... Mater Dei College, Ogdensburg, NY [*Library symbol*] [*Library of Congress*] (LCLS)
NOGM .... No Gammopathy Detected [*Biochemistry*] (DAVI)
NOgRM ...... Remington Art Memorial Museum, Ogdensburg, NY [*Library symbol*] [*Library of Congress*] (LCLS)
NOGS .... Night Observation Gunship (MCD)
NOGS .... Night Observation Gunship System (SAUS)
NOgSH ...... Saint Lawrence State Hospital, Ogdensburg, NY [*Library symbol*] [*Library of Congress*] (LCLS)
NOgW .... Wadhams Hall Seminary College, Ogdensburg, NY [*Library symbol*] [*Library of Congress*] (LCLS)
NOH .... Chicago, IL [*Location identifier*] [*FAA*] (FAAL)
NOH .... Night Observation Helicopter (MCD)
NOH .... Nitric Oxide ferro-Hemochrome (SAUS)
NOH .... Nordhorn [*German license plate city code*]
NOH .... University of North Carolina, Health Science Library, Chapel Hill, NC [*OCLC symbol*] (OCLC)
NOHA .... Nutrition for Optimal Health Association (EA)
NOHALICE ... Nitrous Oxide and Halocarbon Intercalibration Experiment (SAUS)
NOHARMM ... National Organization to Halt the Abuse and Routine Mutilation of Males (EA)
NOHb .... Nitric Oxide Hemoglobin (SAUS)
NOHD .... Nominal Ocular Hazard Distance (SAUS)
NOHIC .... National Oral Health Information Clearinghouse (PAZ)
NOHIMS ..... Navy Occupational Health Information Management System
NOHL .... North Hills Electronics, Inc. (SAUS)
NoHo .... North of Houston Street [*Artists' colony in New York City*] [*See also SoHo, SoSo, TriBeCa*]
NOHOL ...... Not Holding [*a given course or altitude*] [*Aviation*]
NOHP .... Not Otherwise Herein Provided
NOHQI .... Nuveen Ohio Quality Income Municipal Fund [*Associated Press*] (SAG)
NOHS .... National Oceanographic Hazard Survey (NITA)
NOHS .... National Organization of Human Services [*Defunct*] (EA)
NOHSCP .... National Oil and Hazardous Substances Contingency Plan [*Environmental Protection Agency*] (ERG)
NOHSE ...... National Organization of Human Service Education (EA)
NOHSM ..... National Occupational Health Survey of Mining [*Department of Health and Human Services*] (GFGA)
NOHSN ...... National Organization of Hospital Schools of Nursing [*Defunct*] (EA)
NOI .... Detroit, MI [*Location identifier*] [*FAA*] (FAAL)
NOI .... National Oilwell, Inc. [*NYSE symbol*] (SAG)
NOI .... National Opera Institute (EA)
NOI .... Nation of Islam [*Religion*]
NOI .... NAVWEPS ORDALT Instruction (MCD)
NOI .... Netherlands Offset Industry
NOI .... Net Operating Income
NOI .... Nevus Outreach, Inc. (NRGU)
NOI .... Node Operator Interface (NITA)
NOI .... Noise Com, Inc. (SPSG)
NOI .... Nonoperational Intelligence
NOI .... No-Operation Instruction (SAUS)
NOI .... Notice of Inquiry (IEEE)
NOI .... Notice of Intent (MCD)
NOI .... Notice of Intention
NOI .... Notice of Interest (DEMM)
NOI .... Not Otherwise Identified (NG)
NOI .... Not Otherwise Indexed
NOIA .... National Ocean Industries Association (EA)
NOIA .... Newfoundland Ocean Industries Association (SAUS)
NOIAN .... National Operations Intelligence Analysis Net (CCCA)
NOIAW ...... National Organization of Italian-American Women (EA)
NOIBN .... Not Otherwise Identified [*or Indicated*] by Name [*Military*] (AABC)
NOIBN .... Not Otherwise Indexed by Name [*Tariffs*]
NOIBN .... Not Otherwise Indicated by Number (SAUS)
NOIC .... National Oceanographic Instrumentation Center [*National Oceanic and Atmospheric Administration*]
NOIC .... National Osteopathic Interfraternity Council (EA)
NOIC .... Naval Ocean Intelligence Center (DOMA)
NOIC .... Naval Officer-in-Charge
NOIC .... Navy Operational Intelligence Center [*Now Naval Maritime Intelligence Center (NAVMIC)*] (DOMA)
NOIC .... Notice of Intent to Cancel [*Environmental Protection Agency*] (EPAT)
NOICC .... National Occupational Information Coordinating Committee [*Washington, DC*]
NOIE .... Naval Ordnance Inspection Establishment [*Ministry of Defence*] [*British*] (PDAA)
NOIE .... North Iowa Express [*Common carrier symbol*]
NOIFN .... No Information Available (SAUS)
NOII .... Non-Occlusive Intestinal Ischemia [*Medicine*] (DMAA)
NOIL .... Norris Oil Co. (SAUS)
No Ill U ..... Northern Illinois University (GAGS)
NOIM .... Nuclear Ordnance Inventory Manager (SAUS)
NOIO .... Naval Ordnance Inspecting Officer
NOIS .... National Occupational Information Service
NOIS .... Notice of Intent to Suspend [*Environmental Protection Agency*] (EPAT)
NOISE .... National Organisation of Initiatives for Social Education [*British*] (DBA)
NOISE .... National Organization for Improving School Environments [*Defunct*] (EA)
NOISE .... National Organization to Insure a Sound-Controlled Environment (EA)
NOISE .... National Organization to Insure Survival Economics (EA)
NOISE .... Netscape, Oracle, IBM, Sun-and Everybody Else
NOISE .... Noise Information Service
NoiseCT ..... Noise Cancellation Technologies, Inc. [*Associated Press*] (SAG)
Noise Reg Rep ... Noise Regulation Reporter [*Bureau of National Affairs*] [*A publication*] (DLA)
Noise Reg Rep BNA ... Noise Regulation Reporter. Bureau of National Affair (SAUS)
NOIT .... Northern Illinois Transit [*Common carrier symbol*]
NOITSDSL ... Not Included in Technical Service Demand Stockage Lists (SAUS)
NOITU .... National Organization of Industrial Trade Unions (EA)
NOIWON .... National Operations and Intelligence Watch Officers Network (MCD)
NOIZ .... Micronetics, Inc. [*NASDAQ symbol*] (NQ)
NOIZ .... Micronetics Wireless [*NASDAQ symbol*] (TTSB)
NOJ .... Kodiak, AK [*Location identifier*] [*FAA*] (FAAL)
NOJ .... New Orleans Jassband (WDAA)
NOJC .... National Oil Jobbers Council [*Later, PMAA*] (EA)
NOJC .... New Orleans Jazz Club (EA)
NOJC .... Northern Oklahoma Junior College
NOJSM ...... National Office of Jesuit Social Ministries (EA)
NOK .... Next of Kin
NOK .... Nokia Corp. [*NYSE symbol*] (SAG)
NOK .... Noril'sk [*Former USSR*] [*Geomagnetic observatory code*]
NOKD .... Not Our Kind, Dear [*Slang*]
No Kent U ... Northern Kentucky University (GAGS)
Nokia .... Nokia Corp. [*Associated Press*] (SAG)
NOKL .... Northwestern Oklahoma Railroad Co. [*AAR code*]
Nok Mort .... Nokes' Mortgages and Receiverships [*3rd ed.*] [*1951*] [*A publication*] (DLA)
NOKU .... Novoktan Mineralol-Additive [*Intermodal shipping container symbol*] (TVRC)
NOKW .... NAZI Oberkommando der Wehrmacht [*NAZI Armed Forces High Command*] [*World War II*] [*German*] (BJA)
NOL .... National Old Lacers [*Later, IOL*] (EA)
NOL .... National Ordnance Laboratory
NOL .... National Overseas Airline Co. [*Egypt*] [*ICAO designator*] (FAAC)
NOL .... Naval Ordnance Laboratory [*Later, NSWC*]
NOL .... Net Operating Loss

NOL......... New Orleans - Loyola [*Louisiana*] [*Seismograph station code, US Geological Survey*] (SEIS)
NOL......... Niederschlesischer Oberlausitzkreis [*German license plate city code*]
NOL......... Noel Industries, Inc. (SAUS)
Nol......... Nolan's English Magistrates' Cases [*A publication*] (DLA)
Nol......... Nolan's English Settlement Cases [*A publication*] (DLA)
NOL......... Normal Operational Loss [*Nuclear energy*]
NOL......... Norse Oriental Lines (MHDW)
NOL......... Northland Oils Ltd. [*Toronto Stock Exchange symbol*]
NOl......... Olean Public Library, Olean, NY [*Library symbol*] [*Library of Congress*] (LCLS)
NOLA......... National Association for Outlaw and Lawman History (EA)
NOLA......... Northeastern Ohio Library Association [*Library network*]
NOLAC......... National Organization of Liaison for Allocation of Circuit (NATG)
Nolan......... Nolan on the Poor Laws [*A publication*] (DLA)
Nolan......... Nolan's English Magistrates' Cases [*A publication*] (DLA)
Noland......... Noland Co. [*Associated Press*] (SAG)
NOLAP......... Non-Linear Analysis Program (PDAA)
NOLB......... Novaferon Laboratories, Inc. (SAUS)
NOLC......... National Obscenity Law Center (IID)
NOLC......... National One-Liners Club (EA)
NOLC......... Naval Ordnance Laboratory Corona
nol con......... Nolo Contendere [*I Do Not Wish to Contend*] [*Legal term*] [*Latin*] (BARN)
NOlD......... Dresser Industries, Inc., Dresser Clark Division, Olean, NY [*Library symbol*] [*Library of Congress*] (LCLS)
NOLD......... Noland Co. [*NASDAQ symbol*] (NQ)
NOLDAR......... Noludar [*A hypnotic*] [*Roche laboratories*] (DAVI)
NOLDC......... Non-Oil Less-Developed Country
NOLDS......... Naval Ordnance Laboratory Data Service (ACAE)
NOLE......... Nolena Feeder Trailer [*NCIC trailer make code*]
NOLEO......... Notice to Law Enforcement Officials
NOLF......... Nursing Organization Liaison Forum (SAUS)
NOlH......... Olean General Hospital, Olean, NY [*Library symbol*] [*Library of Congress*] (LCLS)
NOLHGA......... National Organization of Life and Health Guaranty Associations [*An association*]
NOLM......... Nonlinear Optical Loop Mirror [*Optical computing*]
Nol Mag......... Nolan's English Magistrates' Cases [*A publication*] (DLA)
NOL-MDI......... Naval Ordnance Laboratory Miss Distance Indicator
NOLO......... No Live Operator (NG)
NOLO......... No Local Operator (SAUS)
NOLOC......... No Location (AABC)
NOLOG......... No Logging (SAUS)
NOLPE......... National Organization on Legal Problems of Education (EA)
NOLPE Sch LJ... NOLPE [*National Organization on Legal Problems of Education*] School Law Journal [*A publication*] (DLA)
NOLPE School LJ... NOLPE [*National Organization on Legal Problems of Education*] School Law Journal [*A publication*] (DLA)
Nol PL......... Nolan on the Poor Laws [*A publication*] (DLA)
NOL PROS... Nolle Prosequi [*Unwilling to Prosecute*] [*Legal term*] [*Latin*]
nol-pros......... nol-prossed (SAUS)
nol-pros......... nol prossing (SAUS)
NO-LQ......... No Living Quarters (SAUS)
NOLR......... New Orleans Lower Coast Railroad [*Federal Railroad Administration identification code*]
NOLS......... National Oceanographic Laboratory System
NOLS......... National Organization for Legal Services (EA)
NOLS......... National Outdoor Leadership School
NOLS......... Nuclear Ordnance Logistics Systems (SAUS)
NOlSFH......... Saint Francis Hospital, Olean, NY [*Library symbol*] [*Library of Congress*] (LCLS)
NolSL......... Cattaraugus-Allegany School Library System, Olean, NY [*Library symbol*] [*Library of Congress*] (LCLS)
NOLSS......... Nuclear Ordnance Logistics Support System (SAUS)
NOLSW......... National Organization Legal Services Workers (NTPA)
NOLTESTFAC... Naval Ordnance Laboratory Test Facility (SAA)
NOLTF......... Naval Ordnance Laboratory Test Facility
NOLU......... Neptune Orient Lines [*Intermodal shipping container symbol*] (TVRC)
NOL/WO......... Naval Ordnance Laboratory, White Oak [*Maryland*]
NOLZ......... Neptune Orient Lines [*Intermodal trailer symbol*]
NOM......... National Online Meeting [*Conference*] (IT)
NOM......... National Organization for Men (EA)
NOM......... National Organization for Men Legal Defense and Education Fund
NOM......... Natural Organic Matter
NOM......... Network Operations Manager [*Manned Space Flight Network, NASA*]
NOM......... Network Output Multiplexer [*Telecommunications*] (MCD)
NOM......... Newspapers on Microfilm
NOM......... Ninth October Movement (SAUS)
NOM......... Nocaman [*Language symbol*] (ETLW)
NOM......... Nomad River [*Papua New Guinea*] [*Airport symbol*] (OAG)
NOM......... Noman [*Italy*] [*FAA designator*] (FAAC)
NOM......... Nome [*Alaska*] [*Seismograph station code, US Geological Survey*] [*Closed*] (SEIS)
NOM......... Nomenclature (AAG)
NOM......... Nominal (AAG)
NOM......... Nominate (AFM)
Nom......... Nominating (AL)
nom......... Nominative (SHCU)
NOM......... Nominative
NOM......... Nonsuppurative Otitis Media [*Medicine*] (EDAA)
NOM......... No Offense Meant (SAUS)
NOM......... Norbeau Mines, Inc. [*Toronto Stock Exchange symbol*]
NOM......... Normal Extraocular Movements [*Ophthalmology*] (DAVI)
NOM......... Northeim [*German license plate city code*]
NOM......... Number of Open Microphones
NOM......... Nuveen Missouri Premium Income Municipal Fund [*AMEX symbol*] (SPSG)
NOM......... Nuveen MO Prem, Inc. Muni [*AMEX symbol*] (TTSB)
NOM......... Opa Locka, FL [*Location identifier*] [*FAA*] (FAAL)
NOMA......... National Office Management Association [*Later, AMS*]
NOMA......... National Oil Marketers Association [*Defunct*] (EA)
NOMA......... National Organization of Minority Architects (EA)
NOMAC......... Noise Modulation and Correlation (SAUS)
NOMAD......... National Organisational Management Database
NOMAD......... National Organization of Miniaturists and Dollers (EA)
NOMAD......... Naval Operations & Maintenance Aviation Deck (SAUS)
NOMAD......... Navy Oceanographic Meteorological Association (USDC)
NOMAD......... Navy Oceanographic Meteorological Automatic Device
NOMAD......... Navy Operation and Maintenance Aviation Deck (MCD)
NOMAD......... Neutrino Oscillation Magnetic Detector
NOMAD......... Nominal Michigan Algorithmic Decoder (SAUS)
NOMAD......... Northeast Music, Art and Dance [*Connecticut*] (EARSL)
NOMAD......... Nozzle Materials Application and Design (MCD)
NOMAG......... Nonmagnetic (IAA)
NOMAS......... National Organization for Men Against Sexism [*Association*] (EA)
NOMb......... Nitric Oxide Myoglobin [*Food technology*]
NOMB......... No Motorized Bicycle Permit [*Motor vehicle violation driver status code in state of North Dakota*] (MVRD)
NOMBOS......... Nonmine Bottom Objects [*Navy*] (NVT)
NOMC......... National Organization for Migrant Children [*Later, NCEMC*] (EA)
Nom Cap......... Nominal Capital (SAUS)
nom cons......... Nomen Conservandum [*Retained Name*] [*Latin*]
NOMD......... Nominated (ABBR)
NOMDA......... National Office Machine Dealers Association (EA)
Nom Dam......... Nominal Damages (SAUS)
nom dub......... Nomen Dubium [*Doubtful Name*] [*Latin*]
NOME......... National Origin Minority Education [*New Hampshire Department of Education*] (EDAC)
NOMEE......... Nominee [*Legal shorthand*] (LWAP)
NOMEN......... Nomenclature (AFM)
NOMES......... New England Offshore Mining Experiment Study (NOAA)
NOMESKO... Nordic Medico-Statistical Committee (SAUS)
NOMFS......... New England Offshore Mining Experiment Study (SAUS)
NOMG......... Nominating (ABBR)
NOMHICE... Non-Methane Hydrocarbon Intercomparison Experiment (SAUS)
NOMI......... Nonocclusive Mesenteric Infarction [*Medicine*] (AAMN)
NOMI......... Nonocclusive Mesenteric Ischemia [*Medicine*]
No Mich U... Northern Michigan University (GAGS)
nom illeg... Nomen Illegitimum [*Illegitimate Name*] [*Latin*]
NOMIN......... Nominative (WDAA)
nom inval... Nomen Invalidum [*Name Not Valid*] [*Latin*]
NOMIS......... National Online Manpower Information System [*Manpower Services Commission*] [*Information service or system*] (IID)
NOMIS......... Naval Ordnance Management Information System
NOMIS......... Nuclear Operations and Maintenance Information Service (IID)
NOML......... Nominal (ROG)
NOMLM......... Nominalism (ABBR)
NOMLT......... Nominalist (ABBR)
NOMLY......... Nominally (ABBR)
NOMMA......... National Ornamental and Miscellaneous Metals Association (EA)
NOM MUD... Nomen Nudum [*A Name without Designation*] [*Latin*] (BABM)
NOMN......... Nomanco [*NCIC trailer make code*]
NOMN......... Nomination
nom nov......... Nomen Novum [*New Name*] [*Latin*]
nom nud......... Nomen Nudum [*Invalid Name*] [*Biology, taxonomy*] [*Latin*]
NOMOP......... No Record of Mustering-Out Payment (DNAB)
NOMOTC......... National Organization of Mothers of Twins Clubs (EA)
NOMP......... Navy Ocean Modeling and Prediction Program (SAUS)
nom prov......... Nomen Provisiorum [*Provisional Name*] [*Latin*]
NOMR......... Nominator (ABBR)
nom rej......... Nomen Rejiciendum [*Rejected Name*] [*Latin*]
NOMRP......... Normal Return Point (MCD)
NOMS......... Network Operations Management System [*Computer science*]
NOMS......... Nuclear Operations Monitoring System (MCD)
NOMSA......... National Office Machine Service Association [*Paramount, CA*] (EA)
NOMSS......... National Operational Meteorological Satellite System
NOMSS......... Navy Oceanographic and Meteorological Support System (MCD)
Nom Std......... Nominal Standard (SAUS)
nom superfl... Nomen Superfluum [*Superfluous Name*] [*Latin*]
NOMSV......... National Organization on Male Sexual Victimization (SEAT)
NOMTF......... Naval Ordnance Missile Test Facility
NOMTS......... Naval Ordnanace Missile Test Station [*White Sands Missile Range, NM*] (GRD)
NOMUS......... Nordisk Musikkomite [*Nordic Music Committee*] (EAIO)
NOMV......... Nominative (ABBR)
NOMW......... National Organizational of Mall Walkers
NOMW......... National Organization of Mall Walkers (EA)
NON......... National Organization for Non-Parents [*Later, NAOP*]
Non......... Nonoc (SAUS)
NON......... Nonouti [*Kiribati*] [*Airport symbol*] (OAG)
NON......... Normine Resources Ltd. [*Vancouver Stock Exchange symbol*]
NON......... North Norway (NATG)
NON......... Notice of Noncompliance (EPA)
No N......... Novae Narrationes [*New Counts*] [*1516*] [*A publication*] (DLA)
NONA......... Notice of Nonavailability
Non Acpc... Non-Acceptance (SAUS)

Nonacq...... Nonacquiescence by Commissioner in a Tax Court or Board of Tax Appeals Decision [*United States*] [*Legal term*] (DLA)
NONADD.... Nonadditivity [*Statistics*]
NON AL OCC... Non Alibi Occurrit [*It Occurs in No Other Place*] [*Latin*] (ROG)
non-Annex I... Parties Countries without a quantified CO2 commitment (SAUS)
Nonappr..... Nonappropriated (SAUS)
non arrl..... non-arrival (SAUS)
NON-BUS... Nonbusiness [*IRS*]
NONCAN.... Noncancellable [*Insurance*]
Non-Chk..... Non Check (SAUS)
NonChk...... Noncheck (SAUS)
NONCIT..... Noncitizen (AABC)
noncm....... Non-Cumulative (SG)
NON-CM.... Noncumulative (ABBR)
NONCNST... Nonconsent
NONCOHO... Noncoherent Oscillator (MCD)
Non-Coll.... Non Collegiate (SAUS)
noncoll...... Noncollinear (MHDI)
NONCOM.... Noncommissioned Officer [*Military*]
NON COM... Non Compos Mentis [*Not in Sound Mind*] [*Latin*] (ROG)
NONCOMECM... Noncommunications Electronics Countermeasures [*Military*] (AABC)
NONCOMJAM... Noncommunications Jamming [*Military*] (AABC)
NONCON.... Nonconformist
NON COND... Non-Condensing (SAUS)
NON CUL... Non Culpabilis [*Not Guilty*] [*Latin*] (ROG)
NON-CUM... Non-Cumulative [*Business term*]
Non-cum.... Noncumulative (EBF)
NOND........ Non Detected [*Laboratory science*] (DAVI)
nondely..... non-delivery (SAUS)
Nondestr Test... Nondestructive Testing (SAUS)
Nondestr Test Commun... Nondestructive Testing Communications (SAUS)
NONE........ National Organization for Non-Enumeration (EA)
NONE........ New Orleans & Northeastern R. R. [*AAR code*]
None......... Nonesuch (SAUS)
NONE........ Not One (SAUS)
NONEG...... Negative Replies Neither Required nor Desired
NONEL...... Non-Electric (SAUS)
NOneoC..... Hartwick College, Oneonta, NY [*Library symbol*] [*Library of Congress*] (LCLS)
NOneoU..... State University of New York, College at Oneonta, Oneonta, NY [*Library symbol*] [*Library of Congress*] (LCLS)
NONF........ Nonfasting [*Laboratory science*] (DAVI)
Non Ferr Met World... Non Ferrous Metal World (SAUS)
Nonferrous Met... Nonferrous Metals (SAUS)
nonfin....... Non-Finite [*Linguistics*] (IEL)
non flam.... non-flammable (SAUS)
NONFLMB... Nonflammable
NON-FRAG... Non-Fragmentation [*Bomb*]
NONGAP.... Nonlinear Grain Analysis Program (MCD)
N/ONI........ Navy/Office of Naval Intelligence (AAG)
Non-Ind..... Nonindicate (SAUS)
Non Ind..... Non-Indication (SAUS)
NONLIN..... Nonlinear (IAA)
Nonlinear Anal Theory Appl Proc Int Summer Sch... Nonlinear Analysis. Theory and Applications. Proceedings. International Summer School (SAUS)
Nonlinear Sci Today... Nonlinear Science Today (SAUS)
NONMAGCI... Nonmagnetic Cast Iron (IAA)
NON-MSA... Non-Standard Metropolitan Statistical Area (OICC)
NON-MTI.... Non-Moving Target Indicator (SAUS)
Non Negl.... Non-Negotiable (SAUS)
NON/NOV... Notices of Noncompliance/Notices of Violation [*Navy*]
NON-NSN... Not Assigned a National Stock Number
NON OBS... Non Obstante [*Notwithstanding*] [*Latin*]
NON OBST... Non Obstante [*Notwithstanding*] [*Latin*] (ROG)
Non Op...... Non-Operational (SAUS)
NONP........ Nonpackaged
NONP........ Nonpareil (ADA)
NONP........ Non-Precision Approach Runway [*Aviation*] (DA)
NONPAR.... Nonparticipating [*Insurance*]
Non-Par.... Non-Participating Provider
Non-par..... Non-Participating Provider
NONPAYT... Nonpayment (ROG)
NONPERF... Nonperforated (ABBR)
NONPF...... National Organization of Nurse Practitioner Faculties (NTPA)
nonpoly..... Nonpolychrome (VRA)
Nonpr........ Nonprofit (PROS)
NONPROF... Nonprofessional
NON PROS... Non Prosequitur [*Does Not Prosecute*] [*Latin*]
non pyt..... non-payment (SAUS)
N/ONR...... Navy/Office of Naval Research (AAG)
Non-REM... Nonrapid Eye Movement [*Type of sleep*] (MAE)
Non Rep.... Do Not Repeat [*Medicine*] (BCRP)
NON REP... Non Repetatur [*Do Not Repeat*] [*Pharmacy*]
Non Repetat... Non Repetatur [*Do Not Repeat*] [*Pharmacy*]
NON RES... Nonresident (WDAA)
NONRET..... Nonreturnable (SAUS)
Non-Rev.... Non-Reversible (SAUS)
Non-Rev PL... Non-Reversible Plug (SAUS)
Non-Rev Skt... Non-Reversible Socket (SAUS)
NONRSNT... Nonresonant (IAA)
Non Rtnl.... Non-Returnable (SAUS)
NONS........ Nonspecific [*Laboratory science*] (DAVI)
NONSAP.... Nonlinear Structural Analysis Program [*Computer science*]
non segs.... Nonsegmented Neutrophils [*Medicine*] (CPH)
NON SEQ... Non Sequitur [*It Does Not Follow*] [*Latin*]
NONSKED... Nonscheduled (ABBR)
NON-SLIP... Non-Speech Language Initiation Program
NON-SLKG... Nonslaking (SAUS)
nonstand.... Nonstandard (BEE)
NONSTAND... Nonstandard (WDAA)
NON STD... Non Standard (SAUS)
NONSTD.... Nonstandard
NONStY..... Non-Standard Yiddish (BJA)
NONSUB.... Nonsubmarine [*Navy*] (NVT)
NONSYN.... Nonsynchronous
NONTAX..... Nontaxable (SAUS)
NONTSDSL... Not Included in Technical Service Demand Stockage Lists [*Army*] (AABC)
NONTT...... Nonentity (ABBR)
Non-U....... Not Upper Class (SAUS)
NONUM..... Notional Number (NVT)
non-vis...... Nonvisualization (DAVI)
NON-VON... Non-Von Neumann [*Experimental computer, not based on the principles of Von Neumann computer design, under construction at Columbia University*]
nonvtg....... Non-Voting (SG)
NON-VTG... Non-Voting [*Business term*]
Non-vtg..... Nonvoting (EBF)
Nonwovens Ind... Nonwovens Industry (SAUS)
Nonwovens Rep Int... Nonwovens Report International (SAUS)
NOO......... Naoro [*Papua New Guinea*] [*Airport symbol*] (OAG)
NOO......... National Organization Order (USDC)
NOO......... Naval Oceanographic Office [*Also known as NAVOCEANO; formerly, HO, NHO, USNHO*]
NOO......... Naval Oceanographic Office, Washington, DC [*Inactive*] [*OCLC symbol*] (OCLC)
NOO......... Nevada Operations Office [*Department of Energy*]
NOO......... Notice of Obligation [*Military*] (AFM)
NOOA........ New Orleans Opera Association (SAUS)
NOOB........ Not Out of Bed [*Medicine*] (DAVI)
NOOD........ National Offshore One-Design [*Boating regatta*]
NOOD........ Nitrix Oxide Optical Detector (SAUS)
NoodKid...... Noodle Kidoodle, Inc. [*Associated Press*] (SAG)
No of Cas Madras... Notes of Cases at Madras (Strange) [*A publication*] (DLA)
NOOIAC..... National Offshore Operations Industry Advisory Committee [*Coast Guard*]
Nooney...... Nooney Realty Trust, Inc. [*Associated Press*] (SAG)
NOOOA....... NORAD Office of Operational Analysis (IAA)
NO-OP....... Flight Not Operating [*Travel industry*]
NOOP........ No Operation [*Computer science*]
no-op........ No Operator [*Telemarketing*] (WDMC)
NOOP........ No Opinion (SAUS)
NO OP Instruction... No-Operation Instruction (SAUS)
NOOS........ Navy Oceanographic Observations from Space (SAUS)
NOOS........ Nuclear Orbit-to-Orbit Shuttle [*NASA*]
NOO-SP..... Naval Oceanographic Office Special Publication
NOOTER PAC... Nooter Corporation PAC [*St. Louis, MO*] (PACS)
NOOU........ Not One of Us [*Slang*]
NoOU........ Universitetet i Oslo [*University of Oslo*], Oslo, Norway [*Library symbol*] [*Library of Congress*] (LCLS)
NoOU-M..... Universitetet i Oslo, Matematisk-Naturvitenskapelige Fakultet [*University of Oslo, Department of Mathematics and Natural Sciences*], Oslo, Norway [*Library symbol*] [*Library of Congress*] (LCLS)
NOP.......... Brooklyn, NY [*Location identifier*] [*FAA*] (FAAL)
NOP.......... National Onderzoek Persmedia [*Database*] [*Stichting Nationaal Onderzoek Persmedia*] [*Netherlands*] [*Information service or system*] (CRD)
NOP.......... National Opinion Poll
NOP.......... National Oracy Project (AIE)
NOP.......... National Outpatient Profile [*Medicine*] (MEDA)
NOP.......... Naval Oceanographic Publication
NOP.......... Naval Officer Procurement
NOP.......... Naval Ordnance Plant
NOP.......... Navigation Operating Procedure
NOP.......... Navy Objectives Plan
NOP.......... Near Object Probe (SAA)
NOP.......... Net Orders Processed [*Business term*] (DOAD)
NOP.......... Network Operations Procedure [*Manned Space Flight Network, NASA*]
NOP.......... Newscorp Overseas Ltd. [*NYSE symbol*] (SPSG)
NOP.......... Noncoherent Optical Processor
NOP.......... Nonoperating (KSC)
NOP.......... No Ocular Pain (SAUS)
NOP.......... No Operation [*Computer science*]
NOP.......... Normal Operating Procedure (NRCH)
NOP.......... Normed Programming (SAUS)
NOP.......... North Oscura Peak [*White Sands Missile Range*] [*Army*]
NOP.......... Notice of Procurement [*Navy*] (NG)
NOP.......... Not on Production (SAUS)
NOP.......... Not Operative (SAUS)
nop........... Not Otherwise Provided (EBF)
NOP.......... Not Otherwise Provided
NOP.......... Not Otherwise Provided For [*Construction term*] (MIST)
NOP.......... Not Our Publication

NOP......... Novair-Aviacao Geral SA [*Portugal*] [*ICAO designator*] (FAAC)
NOP......... Nuclear Operating Plan (SAUS)
NOP......... Nuclear Operations (COE)
NOP......... Nuclear Operations Plan (MCD)
NOP......... Nuclear Ordnance Platoon [*Marine Corps*] (NVT)
NOP......... Null Operation [*Computer science*]
NOP......... Number of Openings [*Technical drawings*]
NOP......... Number of Passes (MSA)
NOP......... Numerical Oceanographic Prediction (PDAA)
NOP......... Office of the Chief of Navy Operations (SAUS)
NOPA........ National Office Products Association (EA)
NOPA........ National Oilseed Processors Association (EA)
NOPA........ Network Operations Performance Analysis [*Manned Space Flight Network, NASA*]
NOPAA...... National Office Products Association of Australia
NOPABCCE... National Organization for Professional Advancement of Black Chemists and Chemical Engineers (EA)
NOPAC...... North Pacific [*Aviation*] (FAAC)
NOPAR...... Do Not Pass to Air Defense RADAR [*Air Traffic Control*] (FAAC)
No Par...... No Paragraph (SAUS)
NOPAT....... Net Operating Profit after Tax
NOPB........ New Orleans Public Belt Railroad [*AAR code*]
NOPC........ Naval Oceanographic Processing Center (DOMA)
NOPCL...... Naval Officer Personnel Circular Letter
NOPCO...... National Oil Products Co. [*Later, NOPCO Chemical Co.*]
NOPD........ New Orleans Police Department [*Initialism also used as title of TV series*]
NOPE........ National Organization of Poll-Ettes (EA)
NOPE........ Naturists and Nudists Opposing Pornographic Exploitation (EA)
NOPE........ New Orleans Port of Embarkation
NOPE........ No Promotion [*Refers to lack of publicity in the record business*]
NOPE........ Not on Planet Earth [*Waste management slang*]
NOPEC...... Non-members of OPEC (SAUS)
NOPEC...... Non-OPEC [*Oil producing countries which are not members of OPEC*]
NOPECO..... Northern Transvaal Peoples Congress (SAUS)
NOPEOL..... National Organization to Promote English as the Official Language (EA)
NOPES...... Non-Occupational Pesticide Exposure Study [*Environmental Protection Agency*] (GFGA)
NOPEX...... Northern Hemisphere Climate Processes Experiment (SAUS)
NOPEX...... Northern Hemisphere Climate Process Land-Surface Experiment (SAUS)
NOPF........ National Oceanographic Processing Facility (DOMA)
NOPF........ Naval Oceanographic Processing Facility (ANA)
NOPF........ Naval Ordnance Plant, Forest Park [*Illinois*]
nopf.......... Not Otherwise Provided For (EBF)
N O Phil.... New Orleans Philharmonic (SAUS)
NOPHN...... National Organization for Public Health Nursing (HGAA)
NOPHYSRET... Not Required to Take New Physical Provided No Material Change since Recent Retirement Physical [*Military*]
NOPI......... Naval Ordnance Plant Institute (MCD)
NOPK........ North Park Transportation Company [*Common carrier symbol*]
NOPL........ Naval Ordnance Plant, Louisville [*Kentucky*]
NOPL........ New Orleans Public Library (SAUS)
NOPLAN..... No Operational Plan Published (SAUS)
NOPMS...... Network-Oriented Project Management System (PDAA)
NOP-N....... Nordiska Publiceringsnamnden for Naturvetenskap [*Nordic Publishing Board in Science*] (EAIO)
NOPN........ Normally Open [*Switch*]
NOPO........ New Orleans Philharmonic Orchestra (SAUS)
NOPO........ Nuclear Operations Planning Office (COE)
NOPOL...... No Pollution
NOPPA...... National Ocean Pollution Planning Act of 1978
NOPPA...... Nitroso(oxopropyl)propylamine [*Organic chemistry*]
NOPPO...... National Ocean Pollution Program Office (GNE)
NOPPrA..... Newscp Pverseas Ltd Pref [*NYSE symbol*] (TTSB)
NOPPrB..... Newscp Overseas Ltd Adj Pref [*NYSE symbol*] (TTSB)
NOPR........ Notice of Proposed Rule Making [*Federal agencies*]
NOP Region... North Pacific Region (SAUS)
NOPRI....... National Orthotic and Prosthetic Research Institute (EA)
NOPROCAN... If Not Already Processed, Orders Cancelled [*Military*]
NOPRT...... Northport, NE [*American Association of Railroads railroad junction routing code*]
NOPS........ National Ocean Policy Study [*US Senate*]
NOPS........ Network Order Processing System (TIMI)
NOPS........ New Orleans Public Service (SAUS)
NOPS........ Nike Operator Proficiency Scale [*Army*]
NOPS........ Nimbus Observation Processing System (ACAE)
NOPS........ Nimbus Observations Processing System (SAUS)
NOPS........ Noncoherent Optical Processing System
NOPT........ Naval Organisation Project Team (SAUS)
NOPT........ Neon Communications [*NASDAQ symbol*]
NOPT........ No Procedure Turn (SAUS)
NOPT........ No Procedure Turn Required [*Aviation*]
NOPU........ Nopal Lines [*Intermodal shipping container symbol*] (TVRC)
NOPUS...... National Occupant Protection Use Survey [*NHTSA*] (TAG)
NoPVDM.... N'Oubliez Pas Vos Decorations Maconniques [*Do Not Forget Your Masonic Regalia*] [*Freemasonry*] [*French*]
NOPWC..... National Old People's Welfare Council (NADA)
NO-PYR..... N-Nitrosopyrrolidine [*Also, NYPR*] [*Biochemistry, organic chemistry*]
NOQUIS..... Nucleonic Oil Quantity Indication System [*Air Force*]
NOR......... AS Norving [*Norway*] [*ICAO designator*] (FAAC)
NOR......... Logic circuit usable as either AND or OR (SAUS)
NOR......... National Organization for Rehabilitation [*British*]
NOR......... Network Operations Representative (ACAE)
nor........... Nitrogen ohne Radikal [*Chemical prefix*]
NOR......... Nitrogen Oxide Reduction [*Research in automotive air pollution*]
NOR......... Nonoperational Ready (NVT)
NOR......... Non-Ordinary Resident [*British*]
NOR......... Non-Relay (SAUS)
NOR......... Noradrenaline [*or Norepinephrine*] [*Endocrinology*] (DAVI)
NOR......... Noranda, Inc. [*Toronto Stock Exchange symbol*] [*Vancouver Stock Exchange symbol*]
NOR......... Norbornadiene [*Also, NBD*] [*Organic chemistry*]
NOR......... Nord [*Greenland*] [*Seismograph station code, US Geological Survey*] [*Closed*] (SEIS)
NOR......... Nordfjordur [*Iceland*] [*Airport symbol*] (OAG)
NOR......... Nordic Organisation for Reindeer Research (SAUS)
NOR......... Nordisk Organ for Reinforskning [*Nordic Council of Reindeer Research*] [*Norway*] (EAIO)
NOR......... Norepinephrine (SAUS)
NOR......... NORfluoxetine (SAUS)
NOR......... Norhtwestern Corp. [*NYSE symbol*] [*Formerly, Northwestern Pub. Svc.*]
Nor........... Norma [*Constellation*]
NOR......... Normal (KSC)
Nor........... Norman (SHCU)
NOR......... Norman
NOR......... Normandale Community College, Bloomington, MN [*OCLC symbol*] (OCLC)
NOR......... Norman, OK [*Amtrak rail station code*]
nor........... North (SHCU)
NOR......... North
NOR......... North Central Airlines, Inc.
NOR......... Northern (SAUS)
NOR......... Northrup Flight Strip (SAUS)
NOR......... NorthWestern Corp. [*NYSE symbol*] (SG)
NOR......... Nortriptyline [*Medicine*] (EDAA)
NOR......... Norway [*ANSI three-letter standard code*] (CNC)
Nor........... Norway (VRA)
nor........... Norwegian [*MARC language code*] [*Library of Congress*] (LCCP)
NOR......... Norwich [*City in England*] (ROG)
NOR......... Norwich [*Diocesan abbreviation*] [*Connecticut*] (TOCD)
NOR......... Not and Or (SAUS)
NOR......... Notice of Readiness [*Shipping*]
NOR......... Notice of Revision
NOR......... Notices of Revision (SAUS)
NOR......... Not Operationally Ready [*Military*] (AFM)
NOR......... Not Or [*Logical operator*] [*Computer science*]
NOR......... Not Otherwiese Rated (SAUS)
NOR......... Nucleolar Organizer Region [*in chromosomes*]
NOR......... Nucleolus Organizer Region [*Genetics*] (DOG)
NOR......... Number of Rounds [*Military*] (CINC)
NOR......... San Diego, CA [*Location identifier*] [*FAA*] (FAAL)
NORA........ National Occupation Research Agenda [*Industrial hygiene term*] (OHS)
NORA........ National Oil Recyclers Association (GNE)
NORA........ National Online Regulatory Access [*Data Development, Inc.*] [*Information service or system*] (CRD)
NORA........ Norwegian Zero Power Reactor Assembly
NORA........ Notice of Recruitment Activity (SAUS)
NORAC...... No Radio Contact [*Aviation*]
NORAD...... North American Aerospace Defense (SAUS)
NORAD...... North American Aerospace Defense Command [*FAA*] (TAG)
NORAD...... North American Air Defense [*Integrated United States-Canada command*]
NORAD...... North American Air Defense Command (AAGC)
NORAD...... North American Defense Command (SAUS)
NORAD...... North Atlantic Aerospace Defense Command (SAUS)
NORAD...... Norwegian Agency for Development Cooperation (SAUS)
NORAD...... Norwegian Agency for International Development
NORADCOC... North American Air Defense Combat Operations Center [*Military*] (AFM)
NORAD CPX... North American Air Defense Command Post Exercise (SAA)
NORADCRU... North American Air Defense Orientation Cruise (NVT)
Noradr....... Noradrenaline [*Norepinephrine*] [*Endocrinology*] (DAVI)
NorAE........ Norwegian Antarctic Expedition [*1956-*]
NORAG...... Northern Army Group (SAUS)
NORAGRIC... Norwegian Centre for International Agricultural Development (SAUS)
NORAID..... Irish Northern Aid Committee (EA)
NORAID..... Northern Aid (SAUS)
NORAID..... Norwegian Agency for International Development
NORAIL..... Northrop Overhead Rail Assembly and Installation Line (SAA)
NORAIM..... Not Operationally Ready, Aircraft Intermediate Maintenance [*Military*] (DNAB)
NOR-ALFA... Northwest Assisted Living Facilities Association (EARSL)
Noram....... Noram Energy Corp. [*Associated Press*] (SAG)
Noram....... Noram Financing I [*Associated Press*] (SAG)
NoramE..... Noram Energy Corp. [*Formerly, Arkla, Inc.*] [*Associated Press*] (SAG)
Norand...... Norand Corp. [*Associated Press*] (SAG)
Nor Ant...... Norwegian Antarctic (SAUS)
Nor Ant...... Norwegian Antarctica (SAUS)
NORAO...... National Organization of Responsible Animal Owners [*Association*] (EA)
NORAP...... Northwestern Alumni Players
NORAPS.... Navy Operational Regional Atmospheric Prediction System (MCD)
Nor Arc...... Norwegian Arctic (SAUS)
NORASDEFLANT... North American Antisubmarine Defense Force, Atlantic (NATG)
NORATS..... Navy Operational Radio and Telephone Switchboard (NVT)

NOrb......... Orangeburg Public Library, Orangeburg, NY [*Library symbol*] [*Library of Congress*] (LCLS)
NORBA...... National Off-Road Bicycle Association [*Later, USCF*] (EA)
NORBAT..... Nordic Battalion (SAUS)
NORBO...... Norborne, MO [*American Association of Railroads railroad junction routing code*]
NOrbR....... Rockland State Hospital, Medical Library, Orangeburg, NY [*Library symbol*] [*Library of Congress*] (LCLS)
NORBS...... Northern Base Section [*Corsica*]
NORC........ National Oceanographic Records Center
NORC........ National Opinion Research Center [*University of Chicago*]
NORC........ Naturally Occurring Retirement Community
NORC........ Naval Ordnance Research Computer (RALS)
NORC........ Naval Ordnance Research Calculator [*or Computer*] [*Naval Ordnance Proving Ground*]
NORC........ Nippon Ocean Racing Club (SAUS)
NORC........ Norcal Boat Trailer [*NCIC trailer make code*]
Norc......... Norcross' Reports [*23-24 Nevada*] [*A publication*] (DLA)
NORC........ Normal Curve [*Laboratory science*] (DAVI)
Norc......... Normally Occurring Retirement Community
NORC........ Nuclear Ordnance Record Card (NVT)
NOrc......... Orchard Park Public Library, Orchard Park, NY [*Library symbol*] [*Library of Congress*] (LCLS)
NorCACHA.. North Carolina Automated Clearing House Association (TBD)
NORCAISEC... Northern California Section, Western Sea Frontier (SAUS)
Nor Cal SAF... Northern California Society of American Foresters (EARSL)
NORCALSEC... Northern California Section, Western Sea Frontier
NORCANUKUS... Norway, Canada, United Kingdom, United States (DOMA)
NORCAP.... National Organisation of Counselling Adoptees and Their Parents [*British*] (DBA)
NORCCIS... Norwegian Command Control Information System (ACAE)
NOrcE....... Erie Community College-South, Orchard Park, NY [*Library symbol*] [*Library of Congress*] (LCLS)
NorcEB...... Erie-Cattaraugus Board of Cooperative Educational Services, Orchard Park, NY [*Library symbol*] [*Library of Congress*] (LCLS)
NORCEN.... Norcen Energy Resources Ltd. (SAUS)
NORCO...... National Oil Recovery Corp.
Nor Co...... Northern Command (SAUS)
NORCOM.... Nonrecurring Cost Model (SAUS)
NORCOM.... Northern Command (SAUS)
NorCran.... Northland Cranberries [*Associated Press*] (SAG)
NORCSEX... Norwegian Continental Shelf Experiment (SAUS)
Nor Cur..... Norwegian Current (SAUS)
NORCUS.... Northwest College and University Association for Science [*Richland, WA*] [*Department of Energy*] (GRD)
NORCY...... Norris City, IL [*American Association of Railroads railroad junction routing code*]
NORD........ Bureau of Ordnance Publication [*Later, NAVORD*] [*Navy*]
NORD........ National Organization for Rare Disorders (EA)
NORD........ National Organization for Rare Disorders, Inc.
NORD........ Naval Ordnance
Nord......... Nordic (DIAR)
NORD........ Nordine Manufacturing [*NCIC trailer make code*]
NORD........ Norsk Data (NITA)
NORD........ Not Ordered, This Part of Package (DAVI)
NORD........ Nursing Orderly (SAUS)
NORDA...... Naval Oceanographic Research and Development Administration [*USA*] [*Marine science*] (OSRA)
NORDA...... Naval Ocean Research and Development Activity [*Bay St. Louis, MS*]
NORDDOK... Nordic Committee on Information and Documentation (SAUS)
NordDRG.... Nordic DRG (SAUS)
NORDEC.... Nordic Economic Union (SAUS)
NORDEK.... Nordic Customs Union (EBF)
NORDEK.... Nordic Economic Community (SAUS)
NORDEK.... Norway, Denmark, Finland, Sweden [*Nordic Economic Community*] [*Trade bloc*]
NORDEL..... Nordic Electricity Union (SAUS)
NORDEL..... Organization for Nordic Electrical Cooperation (EA)
NORDIATRANS... Association for Nordic Transplant and Dialysis Personnel (EAIO)
Nordic....... Nordic American Tanker Shipping Ltd. [*Associated Press*] (SAG)
Nordic J Polit Economy... Nordic Journal of Political Economy [*A publication*] (JLIT)
NORDICOM... Nordic Documentation Center for Mass Communication Research [*Database ori ginator*] [*Finland*] [*Information service or system*] (IID)
Nordic Pulp Paper Res J... Nordic Pulp and Paper Research Journal (SAUS)
NORDIHS... Nordic Integrated Hydrographic System (SAUS)
NORDINFO... Nordic Council for Scientific Information and Research Libraries (SAUS)
NORDINFO... Nordiska Samarbetsorganet for Vetenskaplig Information [*Nordic Council for Scientific Information and Research Libraries*] [*Finland*] (EAIO)
NORDITA... Nordic Institute for Theoretic Atomic Physics [*Later, NIIP*] (EY)
NORDMAP... European Nordic Pollen Data Mapping Project (SAUS)
NORDMAP... Nordic Pollen Data Mapping Project (SAUS)
NORDO...... No Radio
Nord P...... Nordic Pharmacopoeia [*A publication*]
NordPac..... Nord Pacific Ltd. [*Associated Press*] (SAG)
NordPc...... Nord Pacific Ltd. [*Associated Press*] (SAG)
NORDPOST... Nordic Postal Union Conference (SAUS)
NORDQUA... Nordic Association for Quaternary Research (SAUS)
NordRs...... Nord Resources Corp. [*Associated Press*] (SAG)
NORDSAT... Scandinavian Countries Broadcast Satellite (MCD)
Nordser..... Nordisk Samkatalog foer Seriella Medicinska Publikationer [*Karolinska Institutets Bibliotek och Informationscentral*] [*Sweden*] [*Information service or system*] (CRD)
Nordsn...... Nordson Corp. [*Associated Press*] (SAG)
Nordst....... Nordstrom, Inc. [*Associated Press*] (SAG)
NORDTEL... Nordiskt Samarbete Inom Telekommunikation [*Nordic Cooperation on Telecommunications*] [*Finland*] (EAIO)
NORDTEST... Organisation for testing in the Nordic countries (SAUS)
NORDUNet... Nordic Countries Network
NORDUnet... [*The*] Nordic University Network (TNIG)
NORE........ Northeast
NOREA...... Nordic Radio Evangelic Association (SAUS)
NOREASTNAVFACENGCOM... Northeast Division Naval Facilities Engineering Command
NOREC...... No Record
NOREC...... Northern Environmental Council [*Defunct*] (EA)
NORECHAN... Northeast Subarea Channel (NATG)
NOREF...... No Reference
Norelco Rep... Norelco Report (SAUS)
NOREP...... No Reply (SAUS)
NOREP...... No Reply Received
NOREP...... No Report Prepared (SAUS)
NOREP...... Not Reportable
NORESS..... Norwegian Regional Seismic Array
Norex........ Norex America, Inc. [*Associated Press*] (SAG)
NOREX....... Nuclear Operational Readiness Exercise (NVT)
NORF........ National Offense Reserve Fleet (ACAE)
Norf.......... Norfolk [*County in England*] (ODBW)
NORF........ Norfolk [*County in England*]
NORFED..... National Organization for the Repeal of the Federal Reserve Act and the Internal Revenue Code [*Association*] (EA)
NORFISH... North Pacific Fisheries Project (NOAA)
NORFLK..... Norfolk [*County in England*]
NORFO...... Norfolk, NE [*American Association of Railroads railroad junction routing code*]
NORFORM... Not Releasable to Foreign Nationals
Nor Fr....... Norman French [*Language, etc.*] (DLA)
Nor Fr....... Norman-French (SAUS)
Norf S....... Norfolk Southern, Norfolk & Western, Southern Railway (SAUS)
NOR Gate... NOT OR Gate (SAUS)
NORGD...... National Organization for the Rights of Guide Dogs (EA)
NORGLAC... Northern Great Lakes Area Council
NORGRAIN... North American Grain Charter (SAUS)
NORGRAPH... Northeast Graphics Conference and Printing Show [*Printing Industry Association of Connecticut and Western Massachusetts*] (TSPED)
NORGT...... Northgate, SK [*American Association of Railroads railroad junction routing code*]
NORI......... National Office for the Rights of the Indigent [*Later, LDF*]
NORI......... Norris [*NCIC truck make code*]
NORI......... Norris Homes [*NCIC trailer make code*]
NORIANE... Normes et Reglements Informations Automatisees Accessibles en Ligne [*Automated Standards and Regulations Information Online*] [*Database*] [*French Association for Standardization*] [*Information service or system*] (IID)
NORIF....... Natural (cycle) Ovulation Retrieval in In-Vitro Fertilization [*Medicine*] (EDAA)
NORIF....... Natural Oocyte Retrieval Intravaginal Fertilization [*Alternative to traditional in-vitro fertilization (IVF)*] (PAZ)
NORIF....... Non-stimulated Oocyte Retrieval In Fertilization (SAUS)
NORIMB..... Norimberge [*Nuremberg*] [*Imprint*] (ROG)
NORINCO... Norin Corporation (EFIS)
NORIP....... NORAD Intelligence Plan [*Military*] (AABC)
NORIS....... Normal Range Information System [*Medicine*] (EDAA)
NORIS....... North Island (MUGU)
NORIV....... No Arrival Report [*Aviation*] (FAAC)
NORJ......... Norjack [*NCIC trailer make code*]
NORK........ [*The*] New Orleans Rhythm Kings [*Jazz band*]
NORKZ...... Norsk-Data AS (MHDW)
NORL........ Nordic Limited, Inc. (SAUS)
Norland..... Norland Medical Systems, Inc. [*Associated Press*] (SAG)
NORLANT... North Atlantic Area (MUGU)
NORLANT... Northern Sub-Area Eastern Atlantic Command (SAUS)
NORLANTAACS... North Atlantic Airways and Air Communications Service (SAA)
NORLANTEX... North Atlantic - Training Exercise (MCD)
NorldCr...... Northland Cranberries, Inc. [*Associated Press*] (SAG)
norleu....... Norleucine [*Biochemistry*] (DAVI)
NORLEU..... Norleucine [*A nonessential amino acid*] [*Biochemistry*]
N Orl N&S J... New Orleans Medical and Surgical Journal (SAUS)
NOR-LUCS... Northern Software Consultants-Library Updating and Compiling System (SAUS)
NORLUCS... Nother Software Consultants Library Updating and Compiling System (SAUS)
NORM....... National Office Resources Management [*IRS*]
NORM....... National Organization for Raw Materials (EA)
NORM....... National Organization of Restoring Men (SAUS)
NORM....... Naturally Occurring Radioactive Material (FFDE)
Norm........ Norma [*Constellation*]
NORM....... Normal [*or Normalize*] (AAG)
Norm........ Normal (DIAR)
norm........ Normal (ELAL)
Norm........ Normalized (SAUS)
NORM....... Norman [*or Normandy*]
NORM....... Norman [*NCIC motorcycle make code*]
Norm........ Normative Analysis (SAUS)

NORM....... Normative Operating Reporting Method
NORM....... Normetal [*AAR code*]
NORM....... Northern Ohio Railway Museum [*Federal Railroad Administration identification code*]
NORM....... Not Operationally Ready Maintenance [*Military*] (NG)
NORM....... Not Operational Ready Materiel [*Military*] (AFIT)
NORM....... Nuclear Operational Readiness Maneuver (NVT)
NORM....... Nuclear Ordnance Readiness Manpower
NORMA..... No Remote Memory Access (RALS)
NORMAGS... Northern Magnetic and Gravity Survey (SAUS)
NORMAL.... Nova Realtime Macro Language (SAUS)
NORMARSEN... Norwegian Maritime Remote Sensing (SAUS)
NORMATERM... Normalisation, Automatisation de la Terminologie [*Standardization and Automation of Terminology*] [*Databank*] [*France*] [*Information service or system*] (IID)
NORMCLSD... Normally Closed [*Switch*] [*Electronics*] (IAA)
NORMEDS... Northern Meteorological Data System (ACAE)
NORMET.... Normetanephrine [*Also, Methylnorepinephrine*] [*Biochemistry*] (AAMN)
NorMet...... Northern Metropolitan Hospital Association [*New York*] (EARSL)
NORM(F).... Not Operationally Ready Maintenance - Flyable [*Military*] (MCD)
NORM(G)... Not Operationally Ready Maintenance - Grounded [*Military*] (MCD)
NORML...... National Organization for the Reform of Marijuana Laws (EA)
NORML...... National Organization for the Reinforcement of Marijuana Laws (NADA)
NORML...... National Organization for the Repeal of Marijuana Laws (NADA)
NORML...... Normal (DAVI)
NORM/MAG... Normal/Magnified (SAUS)
NORMOPN... Normally Open [*Switch*] [*Electronics*] (IAA)
NORM OPN SW... Normally Open Switch (SAUS)
NORMSHOR... Normal Tour of Shore Duty
NORM-UK... National Organization of Restoring Men-UK (SAUS)
NORN........ North American Manufacturing Company [*NCIC trailer make code*]
NORO........ North American Shipbuilding [*NCIC trailer make code*]
NORO........ Not Operationally Ready Other [*Military*] (AFM)
NOROEC.... NORAD Operational Employment Concept [*Military*] (AABC)
Noroil....... Norwegian Oil (SAUS)
NORONTAIR... Northern Ontario Airways (SAUS)
NORP........ New Oil Reference Price (or Pricing) (SAUS)
NORP........ Nord Pacific Ltd. [*NASDAQ symbol*] (SAG)
NORP........ NORPAC Explorations Services (SAUS)
NORPA...... Norpaul, IL [*American Association of Railroads railroad junction routing code*]
NORPAC..... Naval Overhaul and Repair Pacific (MUGU)
NORPAC..... NORPAC [*Formerly known as North Jersey PAC*] [*Englewood, NJ*] (PACS)
Nor Pac..... Northern Pacific (SAUS)
NORPAC..... Northern Pacific Railway Co.
NORPAC..... North Pacific [*Military*]
NORPAC..... North Pacific Paper Corporation (EFIS)
NORPAC Project... North Pacific Project (SAUS)
Nor Pat..... Norman. Letters Patent [*1853*] [*A publication*] (DLA)
NORPAT..... Northern Patrol (SAUS)
NORPAX..... North Pacific Expedition (SAUS)
NORPAX..... North Pacific Experiment [*National Science Foundation*]
NORPF...... Nord Pacific Ltd. [*OTCBB symbol*]
NORPI...... No Pilot Balloon Observation Will Be Filed Next Collection Unless Weather Changes Siginificantly [*NWS*] (FAAC)
NOrpOHi.... Oyster Pond Historical Society, Orient Point, NY [*Library symbol*] [*Library of Congress*] (LCLS)
Nor Pro Pr... North's Probate Practice [*Illinois*] [*A publication*] (DLA)
NORPY...... Nord Pacific Ltd ADR [*NASDAQ symbol*] (TTSB)
NORQR...... NORAD Qualitative Requirement [*Military*] (AABC)
NORR........ No Reply Received (FAAC)
Norr........ Norris' Reports [*82-96 Pennsylvania*] [*A publication*] (DLA)
NORR........ Northern Cruisers [*NCIC trailer make code*]
NORRA...... National Off-Road Racing Association
NORRCA.... National Organization for Racing Radio Control Autos [*Association*] (EA)
NORRD...... No Reply Received (NOAA)
Norrell...... Norrell Corp. [*Associated Press*] (SAG)
NORRF...... Norris Communications [*NASDAQ symbol*] (TTSB)
Norris....... Norris' Reports [*82-96 Pennsylvania*] [*A publication*] (DLA)
Norris & L Perpetuities... Norris and Leach on Rule Against Perpetuities [*A publication*] (DLA)
NorrisC...... Norris Communications Corp. [*Associated Press*] (SAG)
Norris Seamen... Norris' Law of Seamen [*A publication*] (DLA)
Norr Peake... Norris' Edition of Peake's Law of Evidence [*A publication*] (DLA)
NORRS...... Naval Operational Readiness Reporting Systems
NORS........ National Organization for Rivers (EA)
NORS........ National Organization for River Sports (EA)
NORS........ New Old Replacement Stock [*Automotive parts*]
NORS........ Nonoperational Ready [*Navy*] (POLM)
NORS........ Norse Trailer [*NCIC trailer make code*]
NORS........ North Atlantic Regional Research (SAUS)
NORS........ Not Operationally Ready for Service [*Military*] (VNW)
NORS........ Not Operationally Ready, Spare parts (SAUS)
NORS........ Not Operationally Ready Supply [*Military*]
NORS........ Not Operationally Ready System [*Military*]
NORSAIR... Not Operationally Ready Supply Aeronautical Items Report (SAUS)
NORSAIR... Not Operationally Ready Supply Aviation Items Report [*Military*]
NORSAR.... Norwegian Seismic Array [*Royal Norwegian Council for Scientific and Industrial Research*]
NORSAT..... Norwegian Satellite System
NORSAT..... Norwvegian Domestic Satellite (SAUS)
NORSE...... Norsul Oil & Mining (SAUS)
NORSE...... Nuclear Optical & Radar Signature Estimation (SAUS)
NORSE...... Nuclear Optical and Radar System Effects (SAUS)
NORSEACENT... North Sea Subarea (NATG)
NORSEC..... Northern Security Exhibition [*British*] (ITD)
NORSEX..... Norwegian Remote Sensing Experiment [*in marginal ice zone*]
NORSF...... Not Operationally Ready Supply Flyable [*Military*] (MCD)
NORS-G..... Not Operationally Ready for Service - Grounded (VNW)
NORSG...... Not Operationally Ready Supply Grounded [*Military*] (NG)
NORS Group... Northern Offshore Resources Study Group (SAUS)
NORSHIPCO... Norfolk Shipbuilding & Drydock Corp. (SAUS)
NORSIB..... NORAD Space Intelligence Bulletin [*DoD*]
Norsk........ Norsk Hydro [*Associated Press*] (SAG)
Norskie...... Norwegian-American (SAUS)
NORSMAP... Norwegian Remote Sensing Spectroscopy for Mapping and Monitoring of Algal Blooms and Pollution (SAUS)
NORSN...... Not Operationally Ready Supply Nongrounded [*Military*] (NG)
NORSNET... National Oceanographic Reference Station Network (NOAA)
NORSOLS... Northern Solomons Area
NORSP...... Nora Springs, IA [*American Association of Railroads railroad junction routing code*]
NORSPEC... North Sea Spectrum (SAUS)
NORST...... No Restrictions (FAAC)
Norstan..... Norstan, Inc. [*Associated Press*] (SAG)
NORSTAR... Norden Search Terrain Avoidance RADAR (SAA)
NorSys...... Nortech Systems, Inc. [*Associated Press*] (SAG)
NORT........ Norton [*NCIC motorcycle make code*]
NORT........ Norton Drilling Services [*OTCBB symbol*]
NORT........ Nuclear Ordnance Readiness Test (NVT)
NORTAM.... Northrop Terminal Attrition Model (SAA)
NORTANA... Norwegian Researchers and Teachers Association of North America [*Canada*] (EAIO)
NORTANA... Norwegian Teachers and Researchers Association of North America (EA)
NORTEB..... Norwegian Telecommunications Users Group
Nortek....... Nortek, Inc. [*Associated Press*] (SAG)
NORTEL..... Northern Telecom
Nortel....... Northern Telecom [*Canada*]
NorTel....... Northern Telecom Ltd. [*Associated Press*] (SAG)
Nortel100... Nortel Inversora SA [*Associated Press*] (SAG)
NORTEP..... Northern Teacher Education Program (SAUS)
North........ Northampton County Reporter [*Pennsylvania*] [*A publication*] (DLA)
NORTH...... Northerly (ABBR)
NORTH...... Northern (ABBR)
NORTH...... Northern Operations of Rail Transportation and Highways [*Alaska*]
North........ Reports Tempore Northington [*Eden. English Chancery Reports*] [*1757-67*] [*A publication*] (DLA)
North Africa... Africa north of the Tropic of Cancer (SAUS)
North Africa... Algeria, Egypt, Libya, Morocco, Tunisia (SAUS)
NORTHAG... North [*European*] Army Group [*NATO*]
NORTHAG... Northern Army Group, Central Europe (SAUS)
NORTHAG... North European Army Group (SAUS)
Northam.... Northampton Law Reporter [*Pennsylvania*] [*A publication*] (DLA)
Northam Law Rep... Northampton County Law Reporter [*Pennsylvania*] [*A publication*] (DLA)
Northam L Rep... Northampton Law Reporter [*Pennsylvania*] [*A publication*] (DLA)
Northamp Co Repr... Northampton County Reporter [*Pennsylvania*] [*A publication*] (DLA)
Northampton Co Rep... Northampton County Reporter [*Pennsylvania*] [*A publication*] (DLA)
North & G... North and Guthrie's Appeals Reports [*68-80 Missouri*] [*A publication*] (DLA)
Northants... Northamptonshire (DIAR)
NORTHANTS... Northamptonshire [*County in England*]
Northbay.... Northbay Financial Corp. [*Associated Press*] (SAG)
North BH.... North Broken Hill (SAUS)
North Car J Int'l L & Comm... North Carolina Journal of International Law and Commercial Regulation [*A publication*] (DLA)
North Carolina College LJ... North Carolina College Law Journal [*A publication*] (DLA)
North Carolina Div Mineral Resources Geol Map Ser... North Carolina. Department of Conservation and Development. Division of Mineral Resources. Geologic Map Series (SAUS)
North Carolina Div Mineral Resources Inf Circ... North Carolina. Department of Conservation and Development. Division of Mineral Resources. Information Circular (SAUS)
North Carolina Div Mineral Resources Spec Pub... North Carolina. Department of Conservation and Development. Division of Mineral Resources. Special Publication (SAUS)
North Co.... Northampton County Reporter [*Pennsylvania*] [*A publication*] (DLA)
North Co Rep... Northampton County Reporter [*Pennsylvania*] [*A publication*] (DLA)
North Co R (PA)... Northampton County Reporter [*Pennsylvania*] [*A publication*] (DLA)
NORTHD.... Northumberland [*County in England*] (ROG)
Northeast Golf Sci... Northeast Gulf Science (SAUS)
Northern Institute... Northern Region Correction Institute at Fairbanks, Alaska (SAUS)
Northern J Appl Forestry... Northern Journal of Applied Forestry (SAUS)
Northerns... Burlington, Great Northern and Northern Pacific railroads (SAUS)
North Irel Gov Minist Commer Mem Geol Surv... Northern Ireland. Government. Ministry of Commerce. Memoirs. Geological Survey (SAUS)
North Jersey Coast... Atlantic City to the Atlantic Highlands (SAUS)
North Ken'y SL Rev... Northern Kentucky State Law Review [*A publication*] (DLA)

North Log Timber... Northern Logger and Timber Processor (SAUS)
NORTHM.... Northumberland (ABBR)
NORTH'N.... Northampton [*City in England*] (ROG)
Northop U... Northop University (GAGS)
North Pole... discovered by American explorers Frederick A Cook and Robert E Peary in 1909 (SAUS)
North Pr..... North's Probate Practice [*Illinois*] [*A publication*] (DLA)
Northrim .... Northrim Bank [*Associated Press*] (SAG)
Northrop ULJ... Northrop University. Law Journal of Aerospace, Energy, and the Environment [*A publication*] (DLA)
Northrop ULT Aero Energy and Envt... Northrop University. Law Journal of Aerospace, Energy and the Environment (SAUS)
North Scod Coll Agric Bull... North of Scotland College of Agriculture. Bulletin (SAUS)
North St L... North. Study of the Laws [*1824*] [*A publication*] (DLA)
NORTHUM... Northumberland [*County in England*]
Northum .... Northumberland County Legal News [*Pennsylvania*] [*A publication*] (DLA)
Northumb... Northumberland [*County in England*] (ODBW)
NORTHUMB... Northumberland [*County in England*] (ROG)
Northumb Co... Northumberland County Legal News [*Pennsylvania*] [*A publication*] (DLA)
Northumberland Co Leg Jour... Northumberland Legal Journal [*Pennsylvania*] [*A publication*] (DLA)
Northumberland LJ... Northumberland Legal Journal [*Pennsylvania*] [*A publication*] (DLA)
Northumb Legal J... Northumberland Legal Journal [*Pennsylvania*] [*A publication*] (DLA)
Northumb LJ... Northumberland Legal Journal News [*Pennsylvania*] [*A publication*] (DLA)
Northumb LN... Northumberland Legal Journal [*Pennsylvania*] [*A publication*] (DLA)
Northum Co Leg N... Northumberland County Legal News [*Pennsylvania*] [*A publication*] (ILCA)
Northum Leg J... Northumberland Legal Journal [*Pennsylvania*] [*A publication*] (DLA)
Northum Leg J (PA)... Northumberland Legal Journal [*Pennsylvania*] [*A publication*] (DLA)
Northum Leg N (PA)... Northumberland County Legal News [*Pennsylvania*] [*A publication*] (DLA)
North-West Dent... North-West Dentistry (SAUS)
Northwestern U... Northwestern University (GAGS)
NorthWest Miller... Northwestern Miller (SAUS)
North WLJ... Northwestern Law Journal [*A publication*] (DLA)
Northw Rep... Northwestern Reporter [*Commonly cited NW*] [*A publication*] (DLA)
NORTIC...... NORAD [*North American Aerospace Defense Command*] Technical Intelligence Center (DOMA)
NORTLANT... North Atlantic
Nort LC...... Norton's Leading Cases on Inheritance [*India*] [*A publication*] (DLA)
NortMc...... Norton McNaughton, Inc. [*Associated Press*] (SAG)
NORTNK..... Nortankers, Inc. (SAUS)
NORTO ...... Norton, KS [*American Association of Railroads railroad junction routing code*]
Norton....... Norton's Cases on Hindu Law of Inheritance [*1870-71*] [*India*] [*A publication*] (DLA)
NORTR ...... Nortronics Corp.
Nortraship... Norwegian Trade and Shipping Mission (SAUS)
NortrpG ..... Northrop Grumman Corp. [*Formerly, Northrup Corp.*] [*Associated Press*] (SAG)
NorTrst ...... Northern Trust Corp. [*Associated Press*] (SAG)
NorTst .... Northern Trust Corp. [*Associated Press*] (SAG)
NORTV ..... Norton, VA [*American Association of Railroads railroad junction routing code*]
NORU........ Norasia Line [*Common carrier symbol*]
NORU........ Northern Star Mobile Home [*NCIC trailer make code*]
NORV........ Northland [*NCIC trailer make code*]
NORVA ...... Norfolk, Virginia [*Navy*]
NORVAGRP... Norfolk, Virginia Group [*Navy*]
NORVAL..... Norvaline [*Biochemistry*]
NORVIC ..... Norvicensis [*Norwich*] [*Imprint*] (ROG)
NORVIPS... Northrup Voice Interruption Priority System (MUGU)
NORW....... Northwest Trailers [*NCIC trailer make code*]
NORW....... Norway [*or Norwegian*]
Norw......... Norwegian (BEE)
NORW....... Norwich [*City in England*] (ROG)
Norw Canners Export J... Norwegian Canners Export Journal (SAUS)
NORWD ..... Norwood, NY [*American Association of Railroads railroad junction routing code*]
NORWEB.... Northwestern Electricity Board (NADA)
Norweb....... NORWEB PLC [*Associated Press*] (SAG)
NORWELD... Northwest Library District [*Library network*]
NORWESSEAFRON... Northwestern Sea Frontier
NORWESSEC... Northwestern Sector, Western Sea Frontier
Norwest..... Norwest Corp. [*Associated Press*] (SAG)
NORWESTLANT... Northwest Atlantic [*Military*]
NORWESTNAVFACENGCOM... Northwest Division Naval Facilities Engineering Command
NorwFn...... Norwich Financial Corp. [*Associated Press*] (SAG)
NORWICH... Knickers Off Ready When I Come Home [*Correspondence*] (DSUE)
NorwlkSv ... Norwalk Savings Society [*Associated Press*] (SAG)
NORWO ..... Norwood, NC [*American Association of Railroads railroad junction routing code*]
Norwood .... Norwood Promotional Products [*Associated Press*] (SAG)
Norw P...... Norwegian Patent (SAUS)
Norwt........ Norwest Corp. [*Associated Press*] (SAG)
NORWY ..... NORWEB PLC [*NASDAQ symbol*] (SAG)
NORX........ Northern Indiana Public Service [*Private rail car owner code*]
NORX........ Northwestern Mobile Homes [*NCIC trailer make code*]
NOS.......... National Ocean Service [*Formerly, Coast and Geodetic Survey*] [*Washington, DC*] [*National Oceanic and Atmospheric Administration*]
NOS.......... National Ocean Survey (NOAA)
NOS.......... National Office Staff [*American Occupational Therapy Association*]
NOS.......... National Operational Satellite
NOS.......... National Oratorio Society [*Defunct*] (EA)
NOS.......... National Osteoporosis Society [*British*]
NOS,......... NATO Office of Security (NATG)
NOS.......... Naval Ordnance Station
NOS.......... Nederlandse Omroep Stichtung [*Radio and television network*] [*Netherlands*]
NOS.......... Network Operating System
NOS.......... Network Queueing System [*Computer science*] (CIST)
NOS.......... New Old Stock [*Automotive parts*]
NOS.......... Night Observation Sight [*Air Force*]
NOS.......... Night Observation Surveillance (SAUS)
NOS.......... Night Observation System [*Navy*] (CAAL)
NOS.......... Night Operation Sight (SAUS)
NOS.......... Night Operation System [*Aviation*]
NOS.......... Nimbus Operational System
NOS.......... Nine O'Clock Service (WDAA)
NOS.......... Nirtous Oxide Systems (SAUS)
NOS.......... Nitric Oxide Synthase [*An enzyme*]
NOS.......... Nodal Operating System (SAUS)
NOS.......... Nonobese Subject (MELL)
NOS.......... Non-Ocular Source [*Physiology*]
NOS.......... Nonorganspecific [*Medicine*] (EDAA)
NOS.......... Nonoriented Satellite
NOS.......... No Organisms Seen (MELL)
NOS.......... No Other Symptoms (SPVS)
NOS.......... Nopaline Synthase [*An enzyme*]
NOS.......... Northern State College Library, Aberdeen, SD [*OCLC symbol*] (OCLC)
NOS.......... Northern Tropospheric Oxidants Study (SAUS)
NOS.......... Northstar Resources Ltd. [*Toronto Stock Exchange symbol*]
NOS.......... Norway Airlines [*ICAO designator*] (FAAC)
NOS.......... Nosing (ABBR)
NOS.......... Nossi-Be [*Madagascar*] [*Airport symbol*] (OAG)
NOS.......... Nostalgia [*A radio station format*] (WDMC)
NOS.......... Not Off Sanctions (WDAA)
NOS.......... Not of Specific Origin (SAUS)
NOS.......... Not on Shelf (ADA)
NOS.......... Not on Staff [*Medicine*] (EDAA)
NOS.......... Not Otherwise Specified (AFM)
nos........... Not Otherwise Stated (EBF)
NOS.......... Not Otherwise Stated
NOS.......... Nougth Output Signal (SAUS)
NOS.......... Nouvel Ordre Social [*New Social Order*] [*Switzerland*] (PD)
NOS.......... Number of Stops (IAA)
NOS.......... Numbers (AAG)
nos........... Numbers (WDMC)
NOs.......... Oswego City Library, Oswego, NY [*Library symbol*] [*Library of Congress*] (LCLS)
NOSA........ National Occupational Safety Association (NADA)
NOSA........ National Outerwear and Sportswear Association (EA)
NOSA........ NOSAC [*Common carrier symbol*]
NOSAC ...... National Offshore Safety Advisory Committee [*Coast Guard*]
NOSAC ...... Nonsteroidal Anti-inflammatory Compound [*Medicine*] (EDAA)
NOSAD ...... National Organization for Seasonal Affective Disorder (EA)
NOSALF..... Nordiska Samfundet for Latinamerika Forskning [*Nordic Association for Research on Latin America*] [*Sweden*] (EAIO)
NOSAMS.... National Ocean Sciences AMS Facility (SAUS)
NOSAP ...... National Ocean Survey Analytical Plotter [*NOAA*] (PDAA)
NOSAR ...... No Search and Rescue required (SAUS)
NOSB........ National Organic Standards Board
NOSBE ...... Network Operating System/Batch Environment
NOSC........ Naval Oceanographic Systems Command (CCCA)
NOSC........ Naval Ocean Systems Center [*Formerly, NELC*]
NOSC........ Naval Ordnance Systems Command [*Later, Naval Sea Systems Command*]
NOSC........ Nonoscillating
NOsC .... Oswego County Library System, Oswego, NY [*Library symbol*] [*Library of Congress*] (LCLS)
NOSCAF..... New Orleans Sickle Cell Anemia Foundation (SAUS)
NOSCL ...... Naval Ocean Systems Center Laboratory (DNAB)
NosCom..... IEEE-SA Standards Board New Opportunities in Standards Committee (SAUS)
NOSCP ...... National Ocean Sediment Coring Program (NOAA)
NOSD........ Nosed (ABBR)
NoSdeSv.... North Side Savings Bank [*Associated Press*] (SAG)
NOSE........ National Odd Shoe Exchange (EA)
NOSE........ Neighbors Opposing Smelly Emissions [*Student legal action organization*]
NOSE........ Neotronics Olfactory Sensing Equipment [*Neotronics Scientific*] (PS)
NOSECS..... NAMMA Order Supply EDP Computer System (SAUS)
NOSG........ Nosing (ABBR)
NOSGLANT... Naval Operations Support Group, Atlantic
NOSGPAC... Naval Operations Support Group, Pacific
NOSH........ Hain Food Group [*NASDAQ symbol*] (TTSB)
NOSH........ Hain Food Group, Inc. [*NASDAQ symbol*] (SAG)

NOS-H....... Nordiska Samarbetsnamnden for Humanistisk Forskning [*Nordic Committee of the Research Councils for the Humanities - NCRCH*] (EA)
NOSH........ North Shore and Central Illinois Freight Company [*Common carrier symbol*]
NOSH........ No Show [*Travel industry*] (TRID)
NOsH........ Oswego Hospital, Oswego, NY [*Library symbol*] [*Library of Congress*] (LCLS)
NOsHi....... Oswego County Historical Society, Oswego, NY [*Library symbol*] [*Library of Congress*] (LCLS)
NOsI......... International Business Machines Corp., Oswego, NY [*Library symbol*] [*Library of Congress*] (LCLS)
NOSI......... Nitric Oxide Synthase Inhibitor [*Medicine*] (MELL)
NOSI......... Now Simultaneous (SAUS)
NOSIC....... Naval Ocean Surveillance Information Center
NOSIC....... Naval Ocean Surveillance Information System [*Navy*] (POLM)
NOSIC....... Naval Ocean Surveillance Intelligence Command (CCCA)
NOSIC....... Naval Operations Support Information Center [*Navy*]
NOSIC....... Neurologic Outcome Scale for Infants and Children [*Medicine*] (DMAA)
NOSIE....... Nurses Observation Scale for Inpatient Evaluation [*Psychiatry*]
NO SIG....... No Signature (SAUS)
NOSIG....... No Significant (SAUS)
NOSIG....... No Significant Change [*Used to qualify weather phenomena*]
NOSIGCHNG... No Significant Change (SAUS)
NOSIH....... Naval Ordnance Station, Indian Head (MCD)
NOSINS..... Nosiness (ABBR)
NOSL........ Naval Ordnance Station, Louisville [*Kentucky*]
NOSL........ Night-Day Optical Survey of Lightning [*NASA*]
NOSL........ Night/Day Optical Survey of Thunderstorm Lightning (NAKS)
NOSL........ Night-time Optical Survey of Lightning (SAUS)
NOSLA...... National Oil Scouts and Landmen's Association [*Later, IOSA*]
NOSL-QA... Naval Ordnance Station, Louisville Quality Assurance Department [*Kentucky*]
NOS-LSCR... National Ocean Survey Lake Survey Center [*National Oceanic and Atmospheric Administration*]
NOSM....... Navy Occupation Service Medal
NOSM....... Noise Diotic, Signal Monaural (PDAA)
NOSMO..... Norden Optics Setting, Mechanized Operation [*Air Force bombsight*]
NOSMO..... No Smoking (SAUS)
No Smoke/Drugs... No Smoking or Drugs (SAUS)
NOS-N....... Samarbetsnamnden for de Nordiska Naturvetenskapliga Forskningraden [*Joint Committee of the Nordic Natural Science Research Councils - JCNNSRC*] (EA)
NOSO........ Naval Ordnance Supply Office (MUGU)
NOSO........ Not of Specific Origin
NOSOPEX... Northern Sumatra Offshore Petroleum Exploration (SAUS)
NOSORD.... Not in Sequential Order (SAUS)
NOSP........ National Ophthalmic Speakers Programme [*Canada*]
NOSP........ Naval Ordnance Special Projects
NOSP........ Network Operations Support Plan [*NASA*] (KSC)
NOSP........ Network Operation Support Program [*Computer science*]
NOSP........ Norfolk Naval Shipyard [*Federal Railroad Administration identification code*]
NOSPI....... Newsletter on Serials Pricing Issues (SAUS)
NOSPL...... No Special Observation Taken [*NWS*] (FAAC)
NOSR........ National Office for Social Responsibility (EA)
NOSS........ National Oceanic Satellite System (MCD)
NOSS........ National Oceanic Survey Satellite (NAKS)
NOSS........ National Ocean Survey System [*Cooperative program of governmental agencies*]
NOSS........ National Office Support System (NITA)
NOSS........ National Orbiting Space Station
NOSS........ Navy Ocean Surveillance System
NOSS........ Network Operating Software System [*Computer science*] (AGLO)
NOSS........ Network Operations Support Specialist (ACAE)
NOSS........ Nimbus Operational Satellite System [*GSFC/USWB*]
NOss......... Ossining Public Library, Ossining, NY [*Library symbol*] [*Library of Congress*] (LCLS)
NOSSA...... New Orleans Steamship Association (EA)
NOSSCR.... National Organization of Social Security Claimants' Representatives (EA)
NOSSO...... Naval Ordnance Systems Support Office (MCD)
NOSSOLANT... Naval Ordnance Systems Support Office, Atlantic
NOSSOPAC... Naval Ordnance Systems Support Office, Pacific
NOSSOREP... Naval Ordnance Systems Support Office Representative (DNAB)
NOST........ Knights of the Square Table (EA)
NOST........ Near-term Optical Sensor Technology (SAUS)
NOST........ Nuclear Operational Systems Test
NOSTA....... National Ocean Science and Technology Agency
NOSTA....... Naval Ophthalmic Support and Training Activity
No St C..... Northern State College (South Dakota) (GAGS)
NoStPw..... Northern States Power Co. [*Associated Press*] (SAG)
NOSTRAC... North-South Transport Corridor [*Indian Railway*] (TIR)
NOSTS...... National Ocean Survey Tide Station [*Marine science*] (MSC)
NOSU........ Neptune Orient Lines [*Common carrier symbol*]
NOsU........ State University of New York, College at Oswego, Oswego, NY [*Library symbol*] [*Library of Congress*] (LCLS)
NOSUB...... Not Subject to load (SAUS)
NOSUM..... Notice to Airmen Summary (SAUS)
NOS/VE...... Network Operating System / Virtual Environment (HGAA)
NO Switch... Normally Open Switch (SAUS)
NOSX........ Northern Sun [*Federal Railroad Administration identification code*]
NOT.......... New Organization Training
NOT.......... New Orleans Terminal [*AAR code*]
NOT.......... Nocturnal Oxygen Therapy [*Medicine*] (DMAA)
NOT.......... Nordic Optical Telescope
NOT.......... Noront Resources Ltd. [*Vancouver Stock Exchange symbol*]
NOT.......... Notary (WDAA)
NOT.......... Notation (ROG)
NOT.......... Noted
NOT.......... Notice (ROG)
NOT.......... Notion
NOT.......... Not Oiltight (SAUS)
NOT.......... Not Our Title [*Publishing*] (WDMC)
NOT.......... Nucleus of the Optic Tract [*Eye anatomy*]
NOT.......... Number of Turns (IAA)
NOTA........ National Organ Transplant Act [*1984*]
NOTA........ None of the Above [*Politics*]
NOTACGENSEA... Nontactical Generator, Southeast Asia
NOTACK..... No Attack Area [*Military*] (NVT)
NOTAD...... Notice to Airmen Address
NOTAEI...... National Old Timers' Association of the Energy Industry (EA)
NOTAL....... Not at All
NOTAL....... Not Sent to All Addresses (SAUS)
NOTAL....... Not to, nor Needed by, All
Notam....... Notices to Airmen (PIAV)
NOTAM...... Notice to Airmen
NOTAM...... Notice to Mariners (DOMA)
NOTAMS.... Notice to Airmen and Sailors (SAUS)
NOTAP....... Navy Occupational Task Analysis Program (NVT)
not appr..... Not Approved (SAFN)
NOTAR...... No-Tail Rotor [*Helicopters*]
NOTARC..... National Old Timers Auto Racing Club (EA)
NOTAS....... Notice to Airmen Summary
NOTB........ National Ophthalmic Treatment Board [*British*]
NOTBA...... National Ophthalmic Treatment Board Association [*British*]
NOTC........ Naval Ordnance Test Center (KSC)
Not Cas..... Notes of Cases at Madras (Strange) [*A publication*] (DLA)
Not Cas..... Notes of Cases, English Ecclesiastical and Maritime Courts [*1841-50*] [*A publication*] (DLA)
Not Cas Ecc & M... Notes of Cases, English Ecclesiastical and Maritime Courts [*1841-50*] [*A publication*] (DLA)
Not Cas Madras... Notes of Cases at Madras (Strange) [*A publication*] (DLA)
NOTCOMM... Not Commissioned [*Military*]
Notc on Fac... Notcutt on Factories and Workshops [*2nd ed.*] [*1879*] [*A publication*] (DLA)
Not Dec..... Notes of Decisions [*Martin's North Carolina Reports*] [*A publication*] (DLA)
Not Dig...... Boddam and Greenwood's Notanda Digest [*A publication*] (DLA)
Not Dign.... Notitia Dignitatum [*Classical studies*] (OCD)
note.......... Footnote in Cross-Reference (DLA)
NOTEF....... National Organ Transplant Education Foundation (EA)
NOTEMPS... Nontemporary Storage of Household Goods System (SAUS)
NOTEMPS... Nontemporary Storage System (MCD)
NOTES....... National Organization of Telecommunications Engineers and Scientists [*Washington, DC*] [*Telecommunications*] (TSSD)
Notes........ Notes (Music Library Association) [*A publication*] (BRI)
Notes Higher Ed... Notes on Higher Education [*A publication*]
Notes of Ca... Notes of Cases [*England*] [*A publication*] (DLA)
Notes of Cas... Notes of Cases, English Ecclesiastical and Maritime Courts [*1841-50*] [*A publication*] (DLA)
Notes of Cases... Notes of Cases, English Ecclesiastical and Maritime Courts [*1841-50*] [*A publication*] (DLA)
Notes on US... Notes on United States Reports [*A publication*] (DLA)
Notes Read... Notes and Queries for Readers and Writers, Collectors and Librarians (SAUS)
NotesRec R... Notes and Records. Royal Society of London (SAUS)
No Test...... Novum Testamentum (DSA)
NO-TFA...... National Old-Time Fiddlers' Association (EA)
not foll...... Not Followed (SAFN)
notg.......... nothing (SAUS)
NOTH........ Nothsway Tandem Trailer [*NCIC trailer make code*]
NOTIF....... Notification
NO-TILL..... No Tillage (SAUS)
NOTIN....... Notification (ROG)
NOTIP....... Night Observation Television in a Pod
NOTIP....... Northern-Tier Integration Project [*Military*] (DNAB)
NOTIS....... Network Operations Trouble Information System [*Telecommunications*] (TEL)
NOTIS....... Northwestern Online Total Integrated System [*Northwestern University Library*] [*Library automation project*] [*Information service or system*] (IID)
Not J........ Notaries Journal [*A publication*] (DLA)
N-O-T-L..... Niagara-On-The-Lake [*Ontario*]
NOTL........ Notarial (ROG)
NOTM........ National Organization of Tutoring and Mentoring Centers (EA)
NOTM........ New Orleans, Texas & Mexico [*AAR code*]
NOTMAR.... Notice to Mariner (NVT)
NoTN........ Norges Tekniske Vitenskapsakademi [*Norwegian Academy for Technical Sciences*], Trondheim, Norway [*Library symbol*] [*Library of Congress*] (LCLS)
NOTN........ Notion (ABBR)
NoTNG...... Norges Geologiske Undersoekelse Biblioteket [*Geological Survey of Norway*], Trondheim, Norway [*Library symbol*] [*Library of Congress*] (LCLS)
NOTNO...... Notional Number (NVT)
NOTO........ Non-Official Trade Organisation [*British*]
NOTO........ Numbering Tool (AAG)

NOTOAD .... No Telegraph Office, Advise Disposition [*Telegraphy*] (PCTE)
NOTOF ...... Notice to Airmen Office
Not Op ...... Wilmot's Notes of Opinions and Judgments [*A publication*] (DLA)
NOTOPM .... No-Touch Ocular Pulse Measurement (SAUS)
notox .... non toxic (SAUS)
NOTOX ...... No Toxic Incinerator Group [*Political party*]
NOTOX ...... Not to Exceed (NOAA)
Not prat ..... Notice pour le praticien (SAUS)
Not Pub ..... Notary Public (EBF)
NOTR .... National Order of Trench Rats (EA)
NOTR .... No Traffic Rights [*Travel industry*] (TRID)
Notrad .... No Traditions [*Internet*]
Notre Dame Est Plan Inst... Notre Dame Estate Planning Institute. Proceedings [*A publication*] (DLA)
Notre Dame J Leg... Notre Dame Journal of Legislation [*A publication*] (DLA)
NOTRTR..... National Organization of Test, Research, and Training Reactors [*Later, TRTR*] (EA)
NOTS .... Naval Ocean Transport Service [*Changed to MSTS in 1949 now MSC*] (DOMA)
NOTS .... Naval Ordnance Test Station
NOTS .... Naval Overseas Transport Service
NOTS .... New Era Dianetics for OTs (SAUS)
NOTS .... NOAA [*National Oceanic and Atmospheric Administration*] Operational Telecommunications System (NOAA)
NOTS .... Norrenberns Truck Service [*Common carrier symbol*]
NOTS .... Nuclear Orbit Transfer Stage (PDAA)
NOT SAFE... National Organization Taunting Safety and Fairness Everywhere (EA)
NoTT......... Nordic Theatre Technicians (SAUS)
Nott & Hop... Nott and Hopkins' Reports [*United States Court of Claims*] [*A publication*] (DLA)
Nott & Hunt... Nott and Huntington's Reports [*1-7 United States Court of Claims*] [*A publication*] (DLA)
Nott & McC... Nott and McCord's South Carolina Reports [*A publication*] (DLA)
Nott & M'C (SC)... Nott and M'Cord's South Carolina Reports [*A publication*] (DLA)
NOTTM ...... Nottingham [*County in England*]
Nott Mech L... Non on the Mechanics Lien Law (SAUS)
Nott Mech L... Nott on the Mechanics' Lien Law [*A publication*] (DLA)
Notts......... Nottinghamshire [*County in England*] (ODBW)
NOTTS....... Nottinghamshire [*County in England*]
NOTU .... Naval Operational Training Unit
NOTU .... Naval Ordnance Test Unit
NoTU .... Universitetet i Trondheim [*University of Trondheim*], Trondheim, Norway [*Library symbol*] [*Library of Congress*] (LCLS)
NOTUN ...... Notice of Unreliability
NoTU-T...... Universitetet i Trondheim, Norges Tekniske Hogskole [*University of Trondheim,Norwegian Institute of Technology*], Trondheim-NTH, Norway [*Library symbol*] [*Library of Congress*] (LCLS)
NoTU-V...... Universitetet i Trondheim, Kongelige Norske Videnskabers Selskabs [*Universityof Trondheim, Royal Norwegian Society of Sciences and Letters*], Trondheim, N orway [*Library symbol*] [*Library of Congress*] (LCLS)
NOTWG ..... Notwithstanding
NOTWSTG... Notwithstanding
NOTWT...... Do Not Transmit by Radio (NATG)
NOTY .... Notary (ROG)
NOU .... Naval Ordnance Unit
NOU .... Noumea [*New Caledonia*] [*Airport symbol*] (OAG)
NOU .... Nouvelles (NITA)
NOU .... Sitka, AK [*Location identifier*] [*FAA*] (FAAL)
NOUE......... Notification of Unusual Event (GOBB)
nough .... enough (SAUS)
NOUP........ New Orleans Union Passenger Terminal [*Federal Railroad Administration identification code*]
NOUR........ Nourish (ABBR)
NOURD...... Nourished (ABBR)
NOURG...... Nourishing (ABBR)
NOURT ...... Nourishment (ABBR)
NOUS .... Naval Order of the United States (EA)
Nouv Rev ... Nouvelle Revue de Droit Francais [*Paris*] [*A publication*] (DLA)
NOV.......... Avianova SpA [*Italy*] [*ICAO designator*] (FAAC)
NOV.......... Huambo [*Angola*] [*Airport symbol*] (OAG)
NOV.......... Night Only Visual (ACAE)
NOV.......... Nodamura Virus
NOV.......... Non Obstante Veredicto [*Judgment Notwithstanding*] [*Latin*] [*Legal term*] (DLA)
NOV.......... Nonoccluded Virus
NOV.......... Notice of Violation [*Nuclear energy*] (NRCH)
NOV.......... Nova [*NCIC car model code*]
NOV.......... NovaCare [*NYSE symbol*] (SPSG)
NOV.......... Nova Lisboa [*Angola*] [*Airport symbol*] (AD)
NOV.......... Novamin, Inc. [*Toronto Stock Exchange symbol*]
NOV.......... Novara [*Sicily*] [*Seismograph station code, US Geological Survey*] (SEIS)
NOV.......... Novation [*Legal term*] (DLA)
NOV.......... Novel (ROG)
NOV.......... Novelist (ABBR)
Nov .... Novellae [*Classical studies*] (OCD)
NOV.......... Novello & Co. [*Publisher*]
NOV.......... November (AAG)
Nov .... November (ODBW)
nov........... Novembre [*November*] [*French*] (ASC)
NOV.......... Novitiate (ROG)
nov........... Novum [*New*] [*Latin*] (MAE)
NOVA........ National Organization for Victim Assistance (EA)
NOVA........ National Outdoor Volleyball Association [*Defunct*] (EA)
NOVA........ National Overhead Evaluation Assessment [*Term for the restructuring process begun at E. F. Hutton after the October 1987 stock market collapse*]
NOVA........ Network Organization via Advanced Architecture [*Marubeni Corp.*]
NOVA........ Northern Ohio Valley Area (SAUS)
NOVA........ Northern Valley Private Industry Council [*Sunnyvale, CA*] (ECON)
Nova......... Nova Corp. [*Associated Press*] (SAG)
NOVA........ Nova Med Eyecare [*NASDAQ symbol*]
NOVA........ Nova Natural Resources Corp. (SAUS)
NOVA........ Nova Omega Ventura Apollo [*General Motors automobiles*]
NOVA........ Nurses Organization of Veterans Affairs (EA)
NOVA........ Nutritional Oncology Vascular Access
NovaCre..... NovaCare [*Associated Press*] (SAG)
Novadig..... Novadigm, Inc. [*Associated Press*] (SAG)
NOVAM...... Navy Oceanographic Vertical Aerosol Model (SAUS)
Novatk....... Novatek International, Inc. [*Associated Press*] (SAG)
NOVATOR... Novye Torit [*Newly Flattened*] [*KGB term for newly recruited agent abroad*]
Nova U ...... Nova University (GAGS)
Novavx ...... Novavax, Inc. [*Associated Press*] (SAG)
NOVC .... Novice (ABBR)
NOVCAM .... Nonvolatile Charge-Addressed Memory [*Computer science*] (PDAA)
NOV/CD .... Notice of Violation / Compliance Demand (EPA)
Nov Com Fragm... Novae Comoediae Fragmenta in Papyris Reperta Exceptis Menandreis [*A publication*] (OCD)
Novdec ...... November and December (SAUS)
NOVE .... NOMOS Verlagskatalog [*NOMOS Datapool*] [*Information service or system*] (IID)
NOVEL....... Narrative Output Vocabulary Editing Language [*Psychiatric test*]
NOVEL....... New York Online Virtual Electronic Library
Novell .... Novell, Inc. [*Associated Press*] (SAG)
Noven .... Noven Pharmaceuticals, Inc. [*Associated Press*] (SAG)
NOVI .... Novitron International, Inc. [*NASDAQ symbol*] (SAG)
NOVICE...... Night Operational Vision and the Individual Combat Engineer (MCD)
Novitrn ...... Novitron International, Inc. [*Associated Press*] (SAG)
NOVL .... Novell, Inc. [*NASDAQ symbol*] (NQ)
NOVLT....... Novelty
Novlus....... Novellus Systems, Inc. [*Associated Press*] (SAG)
NOVM .... No Obvious Value Mail [*Postal service*]
Novmtx...... Novametrics Medical Systems [*Associated Press*] (SAG)
Novmtx...... Novametrix Medical Systems, Inc. [*Associated Press*] (SAG)
NOVN........ Noven Pharmaceuticals [*NASDAQ symbol*] (TTSB)
NOVN........ Noven Pharmaceuticals, Inc. [*NASDAQ symbol*] (NQ)
NOV N....... Novum Nomen [*New Name*] [*Latin*] (BABM)
nov n .... Novum Nomen [*New Name*] [*Latin*] (DAVI)
NOVO........ Novo Corp. [*NASDAQ symbol*] (COMM)
NovoNdk .... Novo Nordisk AS [*Associated Press*] (SAG)
Novoste ..... Novoste Corp. [*Associated Press*] (SAG)
NOVP........ Novantrone, Oncovin, Vinblastine, Prednisone [*Antineoplastic drug*] (CDI)
NOVR........ Novar Electronics Corp. (SAUS)
NOVRAM.... Non-Volatile Random Access Memory [*Computer science*]
NOVRAM.... Nonvolotile Static RAM (NITA)
NOVS........ National Office of Vital Statistics [*Public Health Service*] [*Obsolete*]
Nov Sc Dec... Nova Scotia Decisions [*A publication*] (DLA)
Nov Sc LR... Nova Scotia Law Reports [*A publication*] (DLA)
NOV SP ..... Novum Species [*New Species*] [*Latin*] (BABM)
nov sp....... Novum Species [*New species*] [*Latin*] (DAVI)
NOVST .... Novelist (ABBR)
NOVT .... Novelty (ABBR)
NOVT .... Novoste Corp [*NASDAQ symbol*] (TTSB)
NOVX........ Nova Pharmaceutical Corp. (SAUS)
NOVX........ Scios [*OTCBB symbol*]
NOW......... MAI Systems [*AMEX symbol*] (TTSB)
NOW......... MAI Systems Corp. [*AMEX symbol*] (SAG)
NOW......... National Organization for Women (EA)
NOW......... National Organizations of the World [*A publication*]
NOW......... National Overhaul Warranty [*Automotive engineering*]
NOW......... Negotiable Order of Withdrawal [*Banking*]
NOW......... Neighbors of Woodcraft [*Portland, OR*] (EA)
NOW......... Network of Workstations (RALS)
NOW......... Network Order Wire [*Military*] (CAAL)
NOW......... New Opportunities for Women (SAUS)
NOW......... News of the World [*A publication*] (DGA)
NOW......... Nonhazardous Oil Field Waste [*Environmental Protection Agency*] (FFDE)
NOW......... Northern Ohio & Western Railway [*Federal Railroad Administration identification code*]
NOW......... North Water (SAUS)
NOW......... Northway Explorations Ltd. [*Toronto Stock Exchange symbol*]
NOW......... Nurture-Outreach-Witness [*Religion*]
NOW......... Nutrition on the Web [*Internet site for teens*]
NOW......... Port Angeles, WA [*Location identifier*] [*FAA*] (FAAL)
NOW......... Royal Norwegian Air Force [*ICAO designator*] (FAAC)
NOW account... Negotiable Order of Withdrawal Account (EBF)
NOWAI ...... Neshei Ubenos Agudath Israel [*Antwerp*] (BJA)
NOWAPA.... North American Water and Power Alliance (NADA)
NOWD .... Northward (ABBR)
NOWESP.... North-West European Shelf Programme (SAUS)
No West Rep... Northwestern Reporter [*Commonly cited NW*] [*A publication*] (DLA)
NOWESTSEAFRON... Northwest Sea Frontier [*Nautical term*] (NTA)

NOweWJ.... Wheatley Junior-Senior High School, Old Westbury, NY [*Library symbol*] [*Library of Congress*] (LCLS)
NOwHC-U... Old Westbury School of the Holy Child, Upper School, Old Westbury, NY [*Library symbol*] [*Library of Congress*] (LCLS)
NOWIS...... National Older Workers Information System [*American Association of Retired Persons*] [*Information service or system*] [*Defunct*] (IID)
NOWL....... National Order of Women Legislators (EA)
NOW LDEF... NOW [*National Organization for Women*] Legal Defense and Education Fund (EA)
NOWL/NFWL... National Order of Women Legislators/National Foundation for Women Legislators (NTPA)
NOWME...... National Organisation for Women's Management Education [*British*] (DI)
No W Mo St U... Nortwest Missouri State University (GAGS)
NOwNC...... New York College of Osteopathic Medicine, Old Westbury, NY [*Library symbol*] [*Library of Congress*] (LCLS)
NOwNI....... New York Institute of Technology, Old Westbury, NY [*Library symbol*] [*Library of Congress*] (LCLS)
NOwNI-C.... New York Institute of Technology, Commack Center Library, Commack, NY [*Library symbol*] [*Library of Congress*] (LCLS)
NOwNI-CI... New York Institute of Technical, Central Islip, NY [*Library symbol*] [*Library of Congress*] (LCLS)
NOwNI-N.... New York Institute of Technology, New York, NY [*Library symbol*] [*Library of Congress*] (LCLS)
No W Okla St U... Northwestern Oklahoma State University (GAGS)
NOWPA...... National Osteopathic Women Physician's Association (EA)
NOW/PAC... National Organization for Women PAC [*Washington, DC*] (PACS)
NOWPAP.... North-West Pacific Action Plan (SAUS)
NOWP-OM... National Older Workers Programs - Operation Mainstream [*Department of Labor*]
NOWR....... Nuclear Ordnance War Reserve [*Military*] (AFIT)
NOWRA..... National Onsite Waste Water Recycling Association (AEPA)
NOWS....... NVG Operations Weather Software (SAUS)
NOWSA..... National One-Write Systems Association (EA)
Nowsc....... Nowsco Well Services Ltd. [*Associated Press*] (SAG)
No W St U La... Northwestern State University of Louisiana (GAGS)
NOWT....... North-West Telecommunications, Inc. (SAUS)
NOWU....... Nowsco Well Service [*Intermodal shipping container symbol*] (TVRC)
NOwU....... State University of New York, College at Old Westbury, Oyster Bay, NY [*Library symbol*] [*Library of Congress*] (LCLS)
NOWUS..... Normal Operation with Unscram [*Nuclear energy*] (NRCH)
NOwWJ..... Wheatley Junior-Senior High School, Old Westbury, NY [*Library symbol*] [*Library of Congress*] (LCLS)
NOWWN.... National Organization of World War Nurses (EA)
NOX.......... Air Nordic in Vasteras AB [*Sweden*] [*ICAO designator*] (FAAC)
NOx.......... generic oxides of nitrogen (SAUS)
NOx.......... Nitrogen Oxide (COE)
NOX.......... Nitrogen-Oxygen (SAUS)
NOX.......... Nitrous Oxide [*Laughing gas*]
NOX.......... Novavax, Inc. [*AMEX symbol*] (SAG)
NOX.......... Noxious (ABBR)
NOx.......... Oxford Memorial Library, Oxford, NY [*Library symbol*] [*Library of Congress*] (LCLS)
NOx.......... Oxide of Nitrogen (SAUS)
NOX.......... Stickstoffoxide (SAUS)
NOXA........ Naphth-2yl-Oxyacetic Acid (LDT)
NOXA........ Naphthoxyacetic Acid [*Organic chemistry*]
NOXL........ Noxell Corp. (SAUS)
NOXLB...... Noxell Corp. (Class B) [*NASDAQ symbol*] (COMM)
NOXO........ Noxso Corp. [*NASDAQ symbol*] (NQ)
NOXSF...... Oxides of Nitrogen Scale Factor [*Automotive emissions*]
Noxso....... Noxso Corp. [*Associated Press*] (SAG)
NOXU........ National Oxygen [*Intermodal shipping container symbol*] (TVRC)
NOXY........ Noxiously (ABBR)
NOXZEMA... Knocks Eczema [*Acronym, brand name for skin cream, said to be taken from this phrase*]
NOY.......... Not Online Yet (BEE)
NOY.......... Not Out Yet
Noy.......... Noy's English King's Bench Reports [*1559-1649*] [*A publication*] (DLA)
NOy.......... Oyster Bay-East Norwich Public Library, Oyster Bay, NY [*Library symbol*] [*Library of Congress*] (LCLS)
NOy.......... total active Nitrogen (SAUS)
NOYB........ None of Your Business [*Internet lingo*] (NETL)
Noy Ch U... Noyes on Charitable Uses [*A publication*] (DLA)
Noye......... Grounds and Maxims of English Law, by William Noye (journ.) (SAUS)
Noy (Eng)... Noy's English King's Bench Reports [*1559-1649*] [*A publication*] (DLA)
NOYES...... Noyes, MN [*American Association of Railroads railroad junction routing code*]
Noye's Max... Maxims of the Laws of England, by William Noye [*A publication*] (DLA)
NOyHS...... Oyster Bay High School, Oyster Bay, NY [*Library symbol*] [*Library of Congress*] (LCLS)
Noy Max.... Noy's Maxims [*A publication*] (DLA)
NOyRE....... Theodore Roosevelt Elementary School, Oyster Bay, NY [*Library symbol*] [*Library of Congress*] (LCLS)
NOYS........ A Unit Used in the Calculation of Perceived Noise Level [*Industrial hygiene term*] (OHS)
NOYS........ National Organization for Youth Safety [*NHTSA*] (TAG)
NOyStD...... Saint Dominic High School, Oyster Bay, NY [*Library symbol*] [*Library of Congress*] (LCLS)
NOZ.......... Elizabeth City, NC [*Location identifier*] [*FAA*] (FAAL)
NOZ.......... New Process Co. (SAUS)
NOZ.......... No Operating Zone (DA)
NOZ.......... Normal Operating Zone (SAUS)
NOZ.......... Nozzle (AAG)
NOZE........ US National Ozone Expedition [*1986*] [*McMurdo Station, Antarctica*]
NOZE-1...... National Ozone Expedition (SAUS)
NP........... Adriance Memorial Library, Poughkeepsie, NY [*Library symbol*] [*Library of Congress*] (LCLS)
NP........... Desert Pacific [*ICAO designator*] (AD)
np---......... Great Plains [*MARC geographic area code*] [*Library of Congress*] (LCCP)
NP........... Heavylift Cargo Airlines (SAUS)
NP........... Nacionalista Party [*Philippines*]
NP........... Nairobi Protocol (JAGO)
NP........... Name of Publisher (NITA)
NP........... Nameplate
NP........... NAPALM [*Naphthenic and Palmitic Acids*] (NATG)
NP........... Narayan Prediction
NP........... [*The*] Narragansett Pier Railroad Co. Inc. (IIA)
NP........... Nasal Prongs [*For administration of oxygen*] (DAVI)
NP........... Nasionale Party van Suid-Afrika [*National Party of South Africa*] [*Political party*] (PPW)
NP........... Nasionale Party van Suidwesafrika [*National Party of South West Africa*] [*Namibia*] [*Political party*] (PPW)
NP........... Nasopharyngeal [*or Nasopharynx*] [*Medicine*]
NP........... Nationalist Parnellite [*British*] (ROG)
NP........... Nationalist Party [*Malta*] [*Political party*] (PPE)
NP........... Nationalist Party [*Philippines*] [*Political party*] (PPW)
NP........... National Parks [*A publication*] (BRI)
NP........... National Party [*Papua New Guinea*] [*Political party*] (PPW)
NP........... National Pipe [*Thread*]
NP........... National Police (CINC)
NP........... National Porkettes (EA)
NP........... National Power PLC [*NYSE symbol*] (SAG)
NP........... National Primary (OTD)
NP........... National Publishing Co. [*Philadelphia*]
NP........... Nation Party [*Turkey*] [*Political party*] (PPW)
NP........... Natural Passivation [*Metallurgy*]
NP........... Naval Party [*British military*] (DMA)
NP........... Naval Patrol [*British military*] (DMA)
NP........... Naval Pattern [*British military*] (DMA)
NP........... Naval Pension [*British*] (ROG)
NP........... Naval Police [*British*] (ROG)
NP........... Naval Prison
NP........... Naval Publication (IEEE)
NP........... Navy Publications & printing service (SAUS)
NP........... Neap Tide
NP........... Near Point
NP........... Needle Position [*on dial*]
N-P.......... Need-persistence [*Medicine*] (EDAA)
NP........... Negative Prescreening [*Marketing*]
NP........... Negative Pressure (NRCH)
NP........... Neo-Punic (BJA)
NP........... Nepal [*ANSI two-letter standard code*] (CNC)
np........... Nepal [*MARC country of publication code*] [*Library of Congress*] (LCCP)
Np........... Neper [*A unit on a natural logarithmic scale*]
NP........... Neptunium (NAKS)
Np........... Neptunium [*Chemical element*]
NP........... Net Position [*Business term*]
NP........... Net Price [*Business term*] (MHDW)
NP........... Net Proceeds
NP........... Net Profit
NP........... Network Planning [*Computer science*]
NP........... Network Processor [*Communications term*] (DCT)
NP........... Network Program (NASA)
NP........... Network Project [*An association*] (EA)
NP........... Network Provider [*Computer science*] (MWOL)
NP........... Neuritic Plaque [*Pathology*]
NP........... Neuropathology [*Medicine*]
NP........... Neuropeptide (SAUS)
NP........... Neurophysin [*Biochemistry*]
NP........... Neurophysiological
NP........... Neuropsychiatric
N/P.......... Neuro-Psychiatry [*Medical Officer designation*] [*British*]
NP........... Neutral oil, Port Arthur [*Fuels and lubricants*]
NP........... Neutrino Patents (SAUS)
NP........... Neutron Porosity (CARB)
NP........... Newly Presented (DMAA)
NP........... New Page (SAUS)
np........... New Paragraph (WDMC)
NP........... New Paragraph
NP........... New Party (EA)
NP........... New Patient
NP........... New Pattern [*British military*] (DMA)
np........... New Pence [*Monetary unit in Great Britain since 1971*]
NP........... New Permutations
NP........... New Persian [*Linguistics*] (IEL)
NP........... New Perspectives (SAUS)
NP........... New Point [*Used in correcting manuscripts, etc.*]
NP........... New Police (SAUS)
NP........... Newport [*Rhode Island*]
NP........... New Position
NP........... New Providence
N/P.......... Newspaper

NP .... New Work Item Proposal in ISO/IEC (AG)
NP .... Next Page (SAUS)
NP .... Next Position (SAUS)
NP .... Nickel Plated [*Guns*]
NP .... Niemann-Pick [*Disease*] [*Medicine*] (DB)
NP .... Nifurpipone (SAUS)
NP .... Nippon Investment Corp. [*Vancouver Stock Exchange symbol*]
NP .... Nippon Paint Company Ltd (EFIS)
NP .... Nisi Prius [*Unless Before*] [*Legal term*] [*Latin*]
NP .... Nitrogen-Phosphorus [*Chemistry*] (MAE)
NP .... Nitrophenide [*Pharmacology*]
NP .... Nitrophenoacetylamino Caproate
np .... nitroproof (SAUS)
NP .... Nitropropane [*Organic chemistry*]
NP .... Nitro Proved [*Rifle mark*] (DICI)
NP .... Nitroprusside [*A vasodilator*]
NP .... Nitropyrene [*Organic chemistry*]
NP .... Nitrosopiperidine [*Organic chemistry*]
NP .... Nobel Prize
NP .... Nodal Point (SAUS)
NP .... Noise Parameter (SAUS)
NP .... Noise Power (SAUS)
NP .... Nomen Proprium [*Proper Name*] [*Latin*]
NP .... Nominal Horsepower (IAA)
NP .... Nominal Phrase (SAUS)
NP .... Nominal Pressure (SAUS)
NP .... Non-deterministic-Polynomial (SAUS)
NP .... Nondeterministic Polynomial [*Mathematics*]
NP .... Nonpapillate [*Type of seed*] [*Botany*]
NP .... Nonparental (SAUS)
NP .... Nonparticipating [*Insurance or finance*]
N-P .... Non-Partisan (SAUS)
NP .... Non-Patents (NITA)
n/p .... Non-Payment (FOTI)
N/P .... Nonpayment (ROG)
NP .... Nonpermanent (SAUS)
NP .... Nonperson
NP .... Non-Plastic (SAUS)
NP .... Nonpolarized [*Computer science*]
NP .... Nonpolice (BARN)
NP .... Non-Pooled [*Indian Railway*] (TIR)
NP .... Nonpractising Member [*Chiropody*] [*British*]
NP .... Nonprint [*Computer science*] (IAA)
NP .... Nonprinting (SAUS)
NP .... Nonprocurable
NP .... Nonproducer (SAUS)
NP .... Nonprofit (BARN)
NP .... Nonpropelled (AAG)
NP .... Nonpurgeable (SAUS)
NP .... Nonviolent Peaceforce [*Association*] (EA)
NP .... Nonylphenol [*Organic chemistry*]
NP .... No Pagination (SAUS)
NP .... No Paging
NP .... No Parity
NP .... No Parking (SAUS)
NP .... No Party with the Name of the Recipient of the Message [*International telex abbreviation*] (WDMC)
NP .... No Payment (SAUS)
NP .... No Pin [*Electronics*] (OA)
np .... No Place (WDMC)
NP .... No Place [*of publication*] [*Bibliography*]
np .... No Place of Publication (WDAA)
NP .... No Predators [*Ecology*]
NP .... No Print [*Telecommunications*] (TEL)
NP .... No Printer Listed (NTCM)
NP .... No Problem (SAUS)
NP .... No Prospect [*In sports*]
NP .... No Protest [*Banking*]
NP .... No Publisher Listed (NTCM)
NP .... Normal Phase [*Chromatography*]
NP .... Normal Pitch (ADA)
NP .... Normal Plasma [*Medicine*] (MAE)
NP .... Normal Pregnancy [*Medicine*]
NP .... Normal Pressure
NP .... Normal Profit [*Business term*] (MHDW)
NP .... Northern Pacific (SAUS)
NP .... Northern Pacific Railway Co. (MHDW)
NP .... Northern Pine [*Utility pole*] [*Telecommunications*] (TEL)
NP .... North Park (SAUS)
NP .... North Pole [*Also, PN*]
NP .... Norwegian Patent (SAUS)
NP .... Norwegian Polar Institute (SAUS)
NP .... Nose Plug (SAUS)
Np .... Notary Public (WDAA)
np .... Notary Public (WDAA)
NP .... Notary Public
NP .... Note Payable (SAUS)
N/P .... Notes Payable [*Finance*] (DFIT)
NP .... Not Paginated (SAUS)
NP .... Not Palpable (SAUS)
NP .... Not Perceptible [*Medicine*]
NP .... Not Performed
NP .... Not Planned
NP .... Not Practiced [*Medicine*]
NP .... Not Preferred
NP .... Not Present (DAVI)
NP .... Not Pressed or Glazed [*Paper*] (DGA)
NP .... Not Printed (ILCA)
NP .... Not Provably (SAUS)
N/P .... Not Provided (KSC)
NP .... Not Published (SAUS)
NP .... Noun Phrase [*Linguistics*]
NP .... Nuclear Pile (SAUS)
NP .... Nuclear Polarization (SAUS)
NP .... Nuclear Power (GOBB)
NP .... Nuclear Preparation (SAUS)
NP .... Nuclear Propulsion (SAUS)
NP .... Nucleophasmic (SAUS)
NP .... Nucleoplasmic [*Index*] [*Cytology*]
NP .... Nucleoprotein [*Biochemistry*]
NP .... Nucleoside Phosphorylase [*An enzyme*]
np .... Nucleotide Pair [*Genetics*] (DOG)
NP .... Nucleotide Phosphorylase (DB)
NP .... Nucleus Pulposus [*Medicine*] (DAVI)
NP .... Null Parameter (SAUS)
NP .... Number of Pitches [*Baseball term*] (NDBD)
NP .... Number of Primary Turns (IAA)
N_p .... Number of Primary Turns (IDOE)
NP .... Number of Steps, Polynomial Time [*Mathematics*]
NP .... Nursed Poorly [*Medicine*] (DMAA)
NP .... Nurse Practitioner
NP .... Nurse Prescriber (NUJO)
NP .... Nursing Procedure
NP .... Nurturing Parent [*Psychology*] (DHP)
NP .... Ohio Nisi Prius Reports [*A publication*] (DLA)
NP.PP .... Natl Power PLC Interim ADS [*NYSE symbol*] (TTSB)
NPO .... Negative-Positive-Zero
NPA .... Committee for a National Peace Academy [*Later, N-PAC*] (EA)
NPA .... Napan [*West Irian, Indonesia*] [*Airport symbol*] (AD)
NPA .... Naphthylphthalamic Acid [*Organic chemistry*]
NPA .... Naptalam (EDCT)
NPA .... Nar Phu [*Language symbol*] (ETLW)
NPA .... Nasal Pharyngeal Airway [*Medicine*] (EDAA)
NPA .... National PACE Association (EA)
NPA .... National Paddleball Association (EA)
NPA .... National Panel of Arbitrators
NPA .... National Paperboard Association [*Later, API*]
NPA .... National Paralegal Association (EA)
NPA .... National Parenthood Association (NADA)
NPA .... National Parents Association
NPA .... National Parking Association (EA)
NPA .... National Parks Act (SAUS)
NPA .... National Parks and Access to the Countryside Act [*Town planning*] [*British*]
NPA .... National Parks Association [*Later, NPCA*] (EA)
NPA .... National Particleboard Association (EA)
NPA .... National Pasta Association (EA)
NPA .... National Patrolmen's Association
NPA .... National Pawnbrokers Association (EA)
NPA .... National Payphone Association (EA)
NPA .... National Peace Academy
NPA .... National Peace Accord (SAFN)
NPA .... National Pediculosis Association (EA)
NPA .... National People's Action (EA)
NPA .... National Perinatal Association (EA)
NPA .... National Peripheral Association (EA)
NPA .... National Personnel Associates
NPA .... National Pet Association [*Defunct*] (EA)
NPA .... National Petroleum Association [*Later, NPRA*]
NPA .... National Pharmaceutical Alliance (NTPA)
NPA .... National Pharmaceutical Association [*Washington, DC*]
NPA .... National Phlebotomy Association (EA)
NPA .... National Physician's Association (EA)
NPA .... National Pigeon Association [*Defunct*] (EA)
NPA .... National Pilots Association [*Defunct*] (EA)
NPA .... National Pistol Association [*British*] (DI)
NPA .... National Pituitary Agency [*Later, NHPP*]
NPA .... National Planning Association (EA)
NPA .... National Plastercraft Association (EA)
NPA .... National Platelet Association (NRGU)
NPA .... National Playbus Association [*British*] (DBA)
NPA .... National Podiatry Association [*Later, NPMA*] (EA)
NPA .... National Poker Association (EA)
NPA .... National Portage Association [*British*] (DBA)
NPA .... National Ports Authority [*British*]
NPA .... National Postmasters Auxiliary (EA)
NPA .... National Poultry Association [*Australia*]
NPA .... National Prescription Audit
NPA .... National Preservers Association [*Later, International Jelly and Preserve Association*] (EA)
NPA .... National Priority Area [*Military*]
NPA .... National Proctologic Association (EA)
NPA .... National Production Authority [*Functions merged into BDSA, 1953*]
NPA .... National Productivity Authority (MHDB)
NPA .... National Prohibition Act
NPA .... National Psychological Association [*Defunct*] (EA)
NPA .... Naval Procurement Account
NPA .... Navy Postal Affairs Section Publication

NPA .... Navy Purchasing Activity (AFIT)
NPA .... Near Point Accommodation [*Ophthalmology*]
NPA .... Nebraska Pharmacists Association (EARSL)
NPA .... Neighborhood Publication Area Report [*Bureau of the Census*] (GFGA)
NPA .... Network Performance Analyzer [*Computer science*] (ITCA)
NPA .... Network Professional Association (SAUS)
NPA .... Network Program Analysis by ADI [*Area of Dominant Influence*] [*Arbitron Ratings Co.*] [*Information service or system*] (CRD)
NPA .... Neutrons per Absorption (DEN)
NPA .... New People's Army [*Philippines*] (PD)
NPA .... New Populist Action [*Defunct*] (EA)
NPA .... New Product Announcements [*Predicasts, Inc.*] [*Cleveland, OH*] [*Information service or system*] (IID)
NPA .... Newsletter Publishers Association (NTPA)
NPA .... Newspaper Publishers' Association [*British*] (DCTA)
NPA .... Nigel Press Association Ltd. (SAUS)
NPA .... Nigerian Ports Authority (SAUS)
NPA .... Nine Pin Association [*Schauenburg, Federal Republic of Germany*] (EAIO)
NPA .... Nonbuffered Pyrophosphatase Activity
NPA .... Non-Parallel Application (SAUS)
NPA .... Non-Par Approved
NPA .... Non-Partisan Association [*Political party*] [*Vancouver, British Columbia, Canada*]
NPA .... Non-Principal Axis
NPA .... No Power Alarm (SAUS)
NPA .... No Previous Admission [*Medicine*] (MEDA)
NPA .... No Price Available [*Business term*] (ADA)
NPA .... Normal Pressure Angle
NPA .... Northern Pipeline Agency [*Ottawa, ON*]
NPA .... North Pacific Airlines (SAUS)
NPA .... North Plains Area (SARE)
NPA .... Northwest Perennial Alliance [*Pacific Northwest*] (EARSL)
NPA .... Notice of Proposed Amendment (DA)
NPA .... Novel Plasminogen Activator [*Anticlotting agent*]
NPA .... N-Propylamine [*Organic chemistry*]
NPA .... Nuclear Plant Analyzer (NRCH)
NPA .... Numbering Plan Area [*Bell System*] [*Telecommunications*]
NPA .... Number Plan Area (SAUS)
NPA .... Numerical Production Analysis (IEEE)
NPA .... Nurse Practice Act (SAUS)
NPA .... Pensacola, FL [*Location identifier*] [*FAA*] (FAAL)
NPA .... PTS [*Predicasts, Inc.*] New Product Announcements/Plus [*Information service or system*] (IID)
NPAA .... National Park Academy of the Arts (EA)
NPAA .... National Photographic Art Archive [*Victoria and Albert Museum*] [*British*]
NPAA .... National Postal Arts Association (EA)
NPAA .... Noise Pollution and Abatement Act (GFGA)
NPAACT ..... National Parks Association of the Australian Capital Territory
NPAB .... Navy Price Adjustment Board
NPAB .... Nuclear Power Advisory Board (PDAA)
NPABC .... National Public Affairs Center for Television (NADA)
NPAC .... National Parks Advisory Council [*Australia*]
N-PAC .... National Peace Academy Campaign [*Formerly, NPA*] (EA)
NPAC .... National Peace Action Coalition
NPAC .... National Plantation Advisory Committee
NPAC .... National Political Action Committee (EA)
NPAC .... National Program for Acquisitions and Cataloging [*Library of Congress*]
NPAC .... National Project in Agricultural Communication (PDAA)
NPAC .... Navy Procurement Assignment Committee
NPAC .... Newcastle Photovoltaics Applications Centre [*University of Northumbria at Newcastle*] [*United Kingdom*] (RCD)
NPAC .... Nonconducted Premature Atrial Contractions [*Medicine*] (MELL)
NPAC .... Northeast Parallel Architectures Center [*Syracuse University*] [*Research center*] (RCD)
NPAC .... Northern Pipeline Agency Canada [*See also APNC*]
NPACC .... Nominated Primary Alternate Command Centre (SAUS)
N Pac Cur ... North Pacific Current (SAUS)
NPACE .... Nurse Practitioner Association for Continuing Education (SAUS)
NPACI .... National Partnership for Advanced Computational Infrastructure [*Supercomputing Center*]
NPACI .... National Production Advisory Council on Industry [*British*]
NPACOE ..... National Panhellenic Association of Central Office Executives (EA)
NPACSE ..... National Political Action Committee for Scientists and Engineers
NPACT .... National Public Affairs Center for Television [*Defunct*]
NPAED .... National Progress Association for Economic Development (EA)
NPAF .... National Peace Academy Foundation (EA)
NPAF .... National Picture & Frame Co. [*NASDAQ symbol*] (SAG)
NPAF .... National Pledge of Allegiance Foundation (EA)
NPAFC .... North Pacific Anadromous Fish Commission (SAUS)
NPA(G)R .... National Parks and Access to the Countryside (Grants) Regulations [*Town planning*] [*British*]
NPAH .... Nitrated Polycyclic Aromatic Hydrocarbons [*Automotive emissions*] [*Organic chemistry*]
NPAI .... Network Protocol Addressing Information [*Telecommunications*] (OSI)
NPAI .... Nevada Public Affairs Institute [*University of Nevada - Reno*] [*Research center*] (RCD)
NPAJGA ..... National Pan-American Junior Golf Association (EA)
NPals .... Palisades Free Library, Palisades, NY [*Library symbol*] [*Library of Congress*] (LCLS)
NPAM .... Navy Priorities and Allocations Manual (DNAB)
NPAM .... Nonpermanent Active Militia
NPAN .... National Plan for Australian Newspapers
NPAN .... Newspapers Proprietors Association of Nigeria (SAUS)
NP&AA ...... Noise Pollution and Abatement Act of 1970 (EAGT)
NP & GT Rep ... Nisi Prius and General Term Reports [*Ohio*] [*A publication*] (DLA)
NP & OSR .. Naval Petroleum and Oil Shale Reserve
NP & PA .... National Paperbox and Packaging Association (EA)
NPANX ...... Naval Potomac Annex
NPAP .... National Psychological Association for Psychoanalysis (EA)
NPAP .... Navy Public Affairs Plan (DNAB)
NPAP .... Niue People's Action Party [*Political party*] (EY)
NPA-PAC .... National Pawnbrokers Association Inc. PAC [*Roanoke, TX*] (PACS)
NPAR .... Negative-Positive Acknowledgment and Retransmission [*Telecommunications*] (IAA)
NPAR .... Nonbinding Preliminary Allocation of Responsibility (LDOE)
NPAR .... Nonstandard Part Approval Request (MCD)
NPAR .... Nuclear Plant Aging Research Program (COE)
NP/ARCA .... National Pacific/Asian Resource Center on Aging (EA)
NPAS .... National Policy Assistance Standards (AAGC)
NPAS .... National Public Awareness Strategy (SAUS)
NPAS .... New Products Analysis System (SAUS)
NPAS .... Normalized Photoacoustic Signal [*Instrumentation*]
NPASO ...... National Postsecondary Agriculture Student Organization (EA)
NPAT .... National Political Awareness Test [*Sent to all candidates in presidential, congressional, gubernatorial, and most state legislative races*]
NPAT .... Nonparoxysmal Atrial Tachycardia [*Medicine*] (EDAA)
NPat .... Patchogue Library, Patchogue, NY [*Library symbol*] [*Library of Congress*] (LCLS)
NPatB .... Brookhaven Town Hall, Historical Collection, Patchogue, NY [*Library symbol*] [*Library of Congress*] (LCLS)
NPatBH ...... Brookhaven Memorial Hospital, Patchogue, NY [*Library symbol*] [*Library of Congress*] (LCLS)
NPatSJ ...... Saint Joseph's College, Patchogue, NY [*Library symbol*] [*Library of Congress*] (LCLS)
NPAV .... National Parks Association of Victoria [*Australia*]
NPAWT ...... National Plan of Action for Women in TAFE [*Technical and Further Education*] [*Australia*]
NPB .... NADGE [*NATO Air Defense Ground Environment*] Policy Board (NATG)
NPB .... National Park Board (NADA)
NPB .... National Parole Board [*Canada*]
NPB .... National Planning Board [*Terminated, 1944; superseded by National Resources Board*]
NPB .... National Plant Board (EA)
NPB .... National Plumbing Bureau (NTPA)
NPB .... National Prayer Breakfast (EA)
NPB .... National Productivity Board (NADA)
NPB .... Neutral Particle Beam (MCD)
NPB .... Neutron Particle Beam (SAUS)
NPB .... Newport Beach, CA [*Amtrak Busline code*]
NPB .... Newspaper Bag (ROG)
NPB .... Nodal Premature Beat [*Cardiology*]
NPB .... Nonplasminogen Binding [*Hematology*]
NPB .... Nonprimate Biosatellite
NPB .... Non-Protein Bound [*Medicine*] (DMAA)
NPB .... Norfolk & Portsmouth Belt Line Railroad Co. [*AAR code*]
NPB .... North Pacific Bank (SAUS)
NPB .... Nuclear Powered Bomber (SAUS)
NPBA .... National Palomino Breeders Association [*Inactive*]
NPBA .... National Paper Box Association [*Formerly, NPBMA; later NP & PA*] (EA)
NPBA .... National Perinatal Bereavement Association [*Defunct*] (EA)
NPBA .... National Pig Breeders' Association [*British*] (BI)
NPBA .... National Pocket Billiards Association (EA)
NPBA .... National Police Bloodhound Association (EA)
NPBA .... National Poro Beautician Association [*Defunct*] (EA)
NPBA .... Natural Product Broker Association [*St. Augustine, FL*] (EA)
NPBC .... National Penn Bancshares, Inc. [*NASDAQ symbol*] (NQ)
NPBC .... National Progressive Broadcast Coalition [*Defunct*] (EA)
NPBC .... Natl Penn Bancshares [*NASDAQ symbol*] (TTSB)
NPBC .... Newer Predominantly Black College (SAUS)
NPBE .... National Political Button Exchange [*An association*] [*Defunct*] (EA)
NPBE .... Nitrophenyl Butyl Ether [*Organic chemistry*]
NPBE .... Nonlinear Poisson-Boltzmann Equation [*Physical chemistry*]
NPBEA .... National Poultry, Butter, and Egg Association [*Defunct*] (EA)
NPBF .... Nonplacental Blood Flow [*Medicine*] (EDAA)
NPBFC .... National Pat Boone Fan Club (EA)
NPBI .... National Pretzel Bakers Institute [*Defunct*] (EA)
NPBI .... Nonprotein Bound Insulin [*Medicine*] (EDAA)
NPBIE .... Nuetral Particle Beam Integration Experiment (SAUS)
NPBMA ...... National Paper Box Manufacturers Association (EA)
NPBOA ...... National Party Boat Owners Alliance (EA)
NPBRO ...... Naval Plant Branch Representative Office
NPBS .... Navy Personnel Billeting System (DNAB)
NPBSA ...... National Paper Box Supplies Association [*Defunct*] (EA)
NPBSV ...... Neutral Particle Beam Space Vehicle (SAUS)
NPBW .... Neutral Particle Beam Weapon [*Military*] (MUSM)
NPC .... Nasal Point of Conversion [*Medicine*] (MELL)
NPC .... NASA Procurement Circular
NPC .... NASA Publication Control (KSC)
NPC .... Nasopancreatic Catheter [*Medicine*] (MELL)
NPC .... Nasopharyngeal Cancer [*Medicine*] (EDAA)
NPC .... Nasopharyngeal Carcinoma [*Medicine*]
NPC .... National Packaging Confederation [*British*] (DBA)
NPC .... National Panhellenic Conference (EA)

NPC.......... National Patent Council (EA)
NPC.......... National Peace Council [*British*]
NPC.......... National Peach Council (EA)
NPC.......... National Peanut Council (EA)
NPC.......... National People's Coalition (Philippines) [*Political party*] (PSAP)
NPC.......... National People's Congress [*China*] [*Political party*] (PPW)
NPC.......... National People's Congress [*Nigeria*] [*Political party*]
NPC.......... National Periodicals Center
NPC.......... National Personnel Consultants [*Later, NAPC*] [*Defunct*] (EA)
NPC.......... National Petroleum Council [*Department of Energy*] (EA)
NPC.......... National Pharmaceutical Council (EA)
NPC.......... National Philatelic Center [*Australia*]
NPC.......... National Philatelic Collections [*Smithsonian Institution*]
NPC.......... National Pizza Co. (EFIS)
NPC.......... National Plasterers Council [*Association*] (EA)
NPC.......... National Playwrights Conference (EA)
NPC.......... National Plumbing Code
NPC.......... National Poetry Circle [*Cambridge*] [*British*]
NPC.......... National Ports Council [*British*]
NPC.......... National Potato Council (EA)
NPC.......... National Poverty Center [*University of Michigan*] (RCD)
NPC.......... National Press Club (EA)
NPC.......... National Prime Contractor (NATG)
NPC.......... National Processing Centre [*Marine science*] (MSC)
NPC.......... National Productivity Council [*Inactive*]
NPC.......... National Publicity Council for Health and Welfare Services [*Later, NPRC*]
NPC.......... Native Preacher Co. [*An association*] (EA)
NPC.......... NATO Parliamentarians' Conference
NPC.......... NATO Pipeline Committee
NPC.......... NATO Programming Center (NATG)
NPC.......... Nauru Phosphate Commission [*Australia*]
NPC.......... Naval Personnel Committee [*British military*] (DMA)
NPC.......... Naval Photographic Center
NPC.......... Navy Policy Council
NPC.......... Navy Procurement Circular
NPC.......... Near Point of Convergence [*Ophthalmology*]
NPC.......... Nebraska Potato Council (EARSL)
NPC.......... Needle Punch Card
NPC.......... Neplanocin A [*Biochemistry*]
NPC.......... Network Parameter Control (SAUS)
NPC.......... Neuropsychiatry Clerical Procedure [*Navy*]
NPC.......... Neuropsychiatry Clerical Technician [*Navy*]
NPC.......... New Peoples Center (SAUS)
NPC.......... New Practice Cases [*Legal*] [*British*]
NPC.......... New Practice Cases. Bail Court [*1844-48*] [*A publication*] (DLA)
npc.......... New Process Companys trademark (SAUS)
NPC.......... News and Periodicals Corp. (SAUS)
NPC.......... Niagara Parks Commission (SAUS)
NP-C.......... Niemann-Pick Type C [*Disease*] [*Medicine*]
NPC.......... Nigerian Population Commission (SAUS)
NPC.......... Ninety Pound Charge
NPC.......... Nippon PetroChemicals (SAUS)
NPC.......... Nisi Prius Cases [*England*] [*A publication*] (DLA)
NPC.......... Nitrogen Purge Control
NPC.......... Nitro-para-cresol [*Medicine*] (EDAA)
NPC.......... Nodal Premature Contraction [*Cardiology*] (MAE)
NPC.......... Nominal Protection Coefficient [*Business term*]
NPC.......... Nonparenchymal Cell (DB)
NPC.......... Non Participating Countries (SAUS)
NPC.......... Nonpatient Contact [*Medicine*] (EDAA)
NPC.......... Nonphased Color [*Television signals*] (NTCM)
NPC.......... Non Player Character (SAUS)
NPC.......... Nonplayer Characters [*Computer science*]
NPC.......... Nonprinting Character [*Computer science*]
npc.......... Non-Productive Cough [*Medicine*] (BCRP)
NPC.......... Nonproductive Cough [*Medicine*] (DAVI)
NPC.......... Nonproliferation Center [*Central Intelligence Agency*] (RCD)
NPC.......... No Previous Carrier [*Insurance*]
NPC.......... No Previous Complaint [*Medicine*] (DAVI)
NPC.......... Normal Phase Chromatography
NPC.......... Normal Plane Change Maneuver (SAUS)
NPC.......... Northern Pacific Conference (PSS)
NPC.......... Northern Peoples Congress (SAUS)
NPC.......... North Pacific Coast Freight Bureau, Seattle WA [*STAC*]
NPC.......... North Pacific Industry [*Vancouver Stock Exchange symbol*]
NPC.......... North Polar Cap [*A filamentary mark on Mars*]
NPC.......... NPC International, Inc. [*Associated Press*] (SAG)
NPC.......... Nuclear Pore Complex [*Protein*]
NPC.......... Nuclear Power Co. (NRCH)
NPC.......... Nuclear Propulsion Committee (SAUS)
NPC.......... Nucleonic Products Co. (SAUS)
NPC.......... Numerical Positioning Control (SAUS)
NPC.......... Numerical Print Control (SAUS)
NPC.......... Nursing and Personal Care
NPC.......... Nuveen Ins CA Prem Inc. Muni [*NYSE symbol*] (TTSB)
NPC.......... Nuveen Insured California Premium Income Municipal [*NYSE symbol*] (SPSG)
NPC.......... Public Library of Charlotte and Mecklenburg County, Charlotte, NC [*OCLC symbol*] (OCLC)
NPCa.......... Nasopharyngeal Carcinoma [*Medicine*] (MAE)
NPCA.......... National Paint and Coatings Association (EA)
NPCA.......... National Parks and Conservation Association (EA)
NPCA.......... National Peace Corps Association (EA)
NPCA.......... National Peer Counseling Association (DHP)
NPCA.......... National Pest Control Association (EA)
NPCA.......... National Pig Carvers Association (EA)
NPCA.......... National Plastercraft Association (EA)
NPCA.......... National Precast Concrete Association (EA)
NPCA.......... National Progressive Consumers Alliance (EA)
NPCBW.......... National Political Congress of Black Women (EA)
NPCC.......... National Poison Control Center (DAVI)
NPCC.......... National Pop Can Collectors (EA)
NPCC.......... National Possum Co-ordinating Committee (SAUS)
NPCC.......... National Program for Cancer Chemotherapy [*Medicine*] (EDAA)
NPCC.......... National Prostate Cancer Coalition (SAUS)
NPCC.......... Northeast Power Coordinating Council [*Regional power council*]
NPCC.......... North Peralta Community College [*California*]
NPC/CBS.......... National Planning Commission/Central Bureau of Statistics (SAUS)
NPCCI.......... Notification Procedures for Confidential Commercial Information (COE)
NPC/COES.......... National Panhellenic Conference of Central Office Executives (EA)
NPCD.......... National Association of Parish Coordinators/Directors of Religious Education (EA)
NPCDN.......... National Private Circuit Digital Network (PDAA)
NP Cells.......... Nonproducer Cells (SAUS)
NPCF.......... National Pollution Control Foundation
NPCFB.......... North Pacific Coast Freight Bureau
NPCI.......... National Potato Chip Institute [*Later, SFA*]
NPCI.......... NPC International, Inc. [*NASDAQ symbol*] (SAG)
NPCI.......... NPC Intl. [*NASDAQ symbol*] (TTSB)
NPCIL.......... Nuclear Power Corp. of India Ltd.
NPC Intl.......... NPC International, Inc. [*Associated Press*] (SAG)
NPCL.......... North Pacific Coast Line (MHDB)
N-PCL.......... Not-for-Profit Corp. Law [*New York, NY*] [*A publication*]
NP-CLT.......... Neuropsychiatry Clerical Procedure Technician [*Navy*]
NPCMW.......... North Pacific Central Mode Water [*Marine science*] (OSRA)
NPCN.......... National Poison Center Network (EA)
NPC/NCC.......... National Planning Commission/National Computer Centre (SAUS)
NPCNU.......... Neopentyl(chloroethyl)nitrosourea [*Biochemistry*]
NPCO.......... Napco International, Inc. [*NASDAQ symbol*] (COMM)
NPCO.......... Negative Patient-Care Outcome [*Medicine*] (WDAA)
NPCOA.......... National Pest Control Operators Association [*Medicine*] (EDAA)
NP Code.......... Non-Print Code (SAUS)
N-P, Complete.......... Nondeterministic Polynomial Complete Problem [*Mathematics*]
NPCP.......... Nairobi Peoples' Convention Party
NPCP.......... National Prostatic Cancer Project
NPCP.......... Non-Pneumocystis Pneumonia [*Medicine*] (EDAA)
NPCPL.......... Normal Process Complementary Pass transistor Logic (SAUS)
NPCR.......... No Periodic Calibration Required (MCD)
NPCR.......... No Programmed Calibration Required (MCD)
NPCR.......... Normalized Protein Catabolic Rate (SAUS)
NPCS.......... Narrowband Personal Communications Service (ODA)
NPCS.......... National Population Control Secretariat [*Australia*]
NPCSD.......... North Pacific Co-operative Security Dialog (SAUS)
NP-CT.......... Naval Personnel Conversion Tables
NP Cult.......... Nasopharyngeal Culture [*Bacteriology*] (CPH)
NPCW.......... National Pork Council Women (EA)
NPCX.......... Equistar Chemicals [*Private rail car owner code*]
NPD.......... Napped (ABBR)
NPD.......... Narcissistic Personality Disorder [*Medicine*] (DMAA)
NPD.......... NASA Policy Directive
NPD.......... NASA Program Director (SSD)
NPD.......... Nationaldemokratische Partei Deutschlands [*National Democratic Party of Germany*] [*Germany*] [*Political party*] (PPE)
NPD.......... National Niemann Pick Disease Foundation (EA)
NPD.......... National Paint Distributors (EA)
NPD.......... National Party for Democracy [*Zambia*] [*Political party*] (EY)
NPD.......... National Patent Development Corp. [*AMEX symbol*] (SPSG)
NPD.......... National Philanthropy Day (NFD)
NPD.......... National Policy Debate [*Nuclear energy*] (NRCH)
NPD.......... National Power Demonstration (IEEE)
NPD.......... National Program Director
NPD.......... National Program for Dermatology
NPD.......... Natl Patent Devel [*AMEX symbol*] (TTSB)
NPD.......... Natriuretic Plasma Dialysate [*Medicine*] (MAE)
NPD.......... Navy Procurement Directives
NPD.......... Nees Politikes Dynameis [*New Political Forces*] [*Greek*] [*Political party*] (PPE)
NPD.......... Negative Pressure Device [*Medicine*] (DMAA)
NPD.......... Neimann-Pick Disease (CPH)
NPD.......... Network Protection Device [*Telecommunications*] (TEL)
NPD.......... Network Protective Device (NITA)
NPD.......... Neutron Powder Diffractometer (SAUS)
NPD.......... New Product Development [*Business term*]
NPD.......... New Products Digest (SAUS)
NPD.......... New Providence Development Co. Ltd. [*Toronto Stock Exchange symbol*]
NPD.......... Newspaper Press Directory [*A publication*] (DGA)
NPD.......... Niemann-Pick Disease [*Medicine*]
NPD.......... Night Perimeter Defense
NPD.......... Nitrogen-Phosphorus Detector [*Analytical instrumentation*]
NPD.......... Nitrogen, Phosphorus Gas Chromatographic Detector [*Spectroscopy*]
NPD.......... Nocturnal Paroxysmal Dystonia [*Medicine*] (MELL)
NPD.......... Nominal Percent Defective
NPD.......... Nonparental Ditype [*Genetics*]
NPD.......... Non-Planar Dipole (SAUS)

NPD .... Nonprescription Drug (MELL)
NPD .... No Pay Due [*Military*] (ADDR)
NPD .... No Payroll Division
NPD .... North Pacific Division [*Army*] [*World War II*]
NPD .... North Pacific Drift [*Oceanography*]
NPD .... North Polar Distance
NPD .... Nouveau Parti Democratique [*New Democratic Party*] [*Canada*] [*Political party*] (EAIO)
NPD .... N-Player Prisoneris Dilemma
NPD .... Nuclear Physics Division (SAUS)
NPD .... Nuclear Power Demonstration [*of a reactor*]
NPD .... Nuclear Power Development (SAUS)
NPD .... Nuclear Power Division (SAA)
NPD .... Nuclei Postero Dorsalis (SAUS)
NPD .... South African Law Reports, Natal Province Division [*A publication*] (DLA)
NPDA .... National Pharmaceutical Distributors' Association [*Australia*]
NPDA .... National Plywood Distributors Association (EA)
NPDA .... National Privy Diggers Association (EA)
NPDA .... National Pyrotechnic Distributors Association [*APA*] [*Absorbed by*] (EA)
NPDA .... Network Problem Determination Aid (NITA)
NPDA .... Network Problem Determination Application [*Computer science*]
NPDAA ...... National Pharmaceutical Direct Advertising Association [*Defunct*] (EA)
NPDB .... National Practitioner Data Bank [*Information service or system*] (IID)
NPDB .... Nuclear Plant Databank (NRCH)
NPDBA ...... National Pet Dealers and Breeders Association [*Defunct*] (EA)
NPDC .... Dutchess Community College, Poughkeepsie, NY [*Library symbol*] [*Library of Congress*] (LCLS)
NPDC .... National Patent Development Corp.
NPDC .... National Peace Day Celebration (EA)
NPDC .... National Planning Data Corp. [*Information service or system*] (IID)
NPDC .... National Poetry Day Committee (EA)
NPDC .... Neurofibromatosis-Pheochromocytoma-Duodenal Carcinoid [*Syndrome*] [*Medicine*] (DMAA)
NPDCM ...... Dutchess County Mental Health Center, Poughkeepsie, NY [*Library symbol*] [*Library of Congress*] (LCLS)
NPDDE ...... Nitrophenyl Dodecyl Ether [*Organic chemistry*]
NPDE .... Nonlinear Partial Differential Equation
NPDEA ...... National Professional Driver Education Association (AEBS)
NPDES ...... National Pollutant Discharge Elimination System [*Environmental Protection Agency*]
NPDES ...... Nuclear Pollution Discharge Elimination Specification (SAUS)
NPDES ...... Nuclear Pollution Discharge Elimination System (SAUS)
NPDF .... Normal Probability Distribution Function
NPDFC ...... National Phyllis Diller Fan Club [*Association*] (EA)
NPDI .... Nonperformance of Duty because Imprisoned [*Navy*]
NPDI .... Non-psychotic Depressive Illness [*Medicine*] (EDAA)
NPDL .... Nodular Poorly Differentiated Lymphocyte
NPDM .... Navy Program Decision Meeting (DOMA)
NPDN .... Nordic Public Data Network [*Denmark, Finland, Iceland, Norway and Sweden*] (PDAA)
NPDNA ...... Nucleoprotamine Deoxyribonucleic Acid
NPDO .... Nacelle Product Development Organization (MCD)
NPDO .... Non-Profit Distributing Organization (PDAA)
NPDR .... Napa Drayage [*Common carrier symbol*]
NPDR .... NCO Professional Development Ribbon [*Military decoration*]
NPDR .... Nonproliferative Diabetic Retinopathy [*Medicine*] (MAE)
NPD Reactor... Nuclear Power Demonstration Reactor (SAUS)
NPDS .... National Pollutant Discharge Elimination System [*Environmental Protection Agency*] (ERG)
NPDS .... NMCC Processing and Display System (SAUS)
NPDS .... Nuclear Particle Detection Subsystem (SAUS)
NPDS .... Nuclear Particle Detection System (KSC)
NPDSA ...... National Public Domain Software Archive (AIE)
NPDU .... Naval Plant Development Unit (DNAB)
NPDU .... Network Protocol Data Unit [*Telecommunications*] (OSI)
NPDW .... North Pacific Deep Water [*Oceanography*]
NPDWG ..... Networking Project for Disabled Women and Girls (EA)
NPDWR ..... National Primary Drinking Water Regulations [*Environmental Protection Agency*]
NPDZ .... NP Drain [*Federal Railroad Administration identification code*]
NPD' .... No Pathologic Diagnosis [*Medicine*] (BARN)
NPE .... Elizabeth City State University, Elizabeth City, NC [*OCLC symbol*] (OCLC)
NPE .... Napier [*New Zealand*] [*Airport symbol*] (OAG)
NPE .... Nasal Physical Examination
NPE .... National Plastic Exposition
NPE .... National Population Enquiry
NPE .... Natural Parity Exchange [*Physics*] (OA)
NPE .... Naval Pilot Evaluation (MUGU)
NPE .... Navy Preliminary Evaluation
NPE .... Negative Pressure Enclosure [*Industrial hygiene term*] (OHS)
NPE .... Network Processing Element (NITA)
NPE .... New Preliminary Evaluation (MCD)
NPE .... New Product Engineering (SAUS)
NPE .... Nonpolluting Engine [*Rocketdyne/Commonwealth Edison Co.*]
NPE .... Nonpotential Energy [*of molecules*]
NPE .... Nonylphenol Ethoxylate [*Organic chemistry*]
NPE .... Nuclear Photographic Emulsion
NPE .... Nuclear Planning and Execution (SAUS)
NPE .... Nuclear Planning and Execution System (MCD)
NPE .... Nuclear Power Engineering (IAA)
NPE .... Nutrition Program for the Elderly
NPE .... Nuveen Ins Prem Inc. Muni [*NYSE symbol*] (TTSB)
NPE .... Nuveen Insured Premium Income Municipal [*NYSE symbol*] (SPSG)
NPEA .... National Patio Enclosure Association (EA)
NPEA .... National Printing Equipment Association [*Later, NPES*] (EA)
N-Peace ..... Nuclear Peace (SAUS)
NPEB .... Nonparametric Empirical Bayes [*Statistics*]
NPEC .... National Panhellenic Editors Conference (EA)
NPEC .... Native Plants Extracts Cooperative [*Australia*]
NPEC .... Nuclear Power Engineering Committee [*Nuclear Regulatory Commission*] (NRCH)
NPECCD ..... National Public Education Campaign on Clinical Depression
NPED .... Nuclear-Powered Energy Depot
NPee .... Field Library, Inc., Peekskill, NY [*Library symbol*] [*Library of Congress*] (LCLS)
NPEE .... NP Energy Corp. (SAUS)
NPEF .... New Product Evaluation Form
NPEGE ...... Nonyl Phenyl Eicosa-Ethylene Glycol Ether (SAUS)
NPel .... Pelham Public Library, Pelham, NY [*Library symbol*] [*Library of Congress*] (LCLS)
NPELRA ..... National Public Employer Labor Relations Association (EA)
NPEO .... Nonylphenol Polyethoxylate [*Organic chemistry*]
NPE/PES .... Nuclear Power Engineering/Power Engineering Society (SAUS)
NPER .... National Public Employment Reporter Database [*Information service or system*] (IID)
NPerbA ...... J. N. Adam Developmental Center, Perrysburg, NY [*Library symbol*] [*Library of Congress*] (LCLS)
NPES .... Association for Suppliers of Printing and Publishing Technologies (SAUS)
NPES .... National Printing Equipment and Supply Association (EA)
NPES .... National Printing Equipment Show
NPE(S) ...... Nuclear Planning and Execution (Service) (DOMA)
NPES .... Nuclear Planning and Execution System (COE)
NPESA ...... National Printing Equipment & Supply Association, Inc.
NPESO ...... NAVSHIPS [*Naval Ship Systems Command*] Plant Equipment Support Office
NPET .... Newport Petroleums (SAUS)
NPET .... Nicollet Process Engineering, Inc. [*NASDAQ symbol*] (SAG)
NPET .... Nicollet Process Engr [*NASDAQ symbol*] (TTSB)
NPET .... Nonpetroleum
NPEV .... Nonpolio Enterovirus [*Infectious Diseases*] (DAVI)
NPEX .... Normal Priority Exit (IAA)
NPF .... Names Project Foundation (EA)
NPF .... National Paraplegia Foundation (EA)
NPF .... National Park Foundation (EA)
NPF .... National Parkinson Foundation (EA)
NPF .... National Pharmaceutical Foundation (EA)
NPF .... National Piano Foundation (EA)
NPF .... National Pig Fair [*British*] (ITD)
NPF .... National Poetry Foundation (EA)
NPF .... National Police Force [*South Vietnam*] (VNW)
NPF .... National Policy Forum
NPF .... National Postal Forum [*Association*] (EA)
NPF .... National Press Foundation (EA)
NPF .... National Progressive Front [*Iraq*] [*Political party*] (PPW)
NPF .... National Psoriasis Foundation (EA)
NPF .... Naval Parachute Facility (MCD)
NPF .... Naval Powder Factory
NPF .... Naval Procurement Fund [*Budget appropriation title*]
NPF .... NAVSTAR [*Navigation Satellite Tracking and Ranging*] Processing Facility (MCD)
NPF .... Net Propulsion Force (MCD)
NPF .... Network Pulse Forming
NPF .... Neutrons per Fission (DEN)
NPF .... Newspaper Press Fund (DGA)
NPF .... Newsprint Pulp Flat (SAUS)
NPF .... Newtonian Potential Function [*Mathematics*]
NPF .... Nicaragua Peace Fleet [*Defunct*] (EA)
NPF .... Nonpublic Funds [*Canadian Forces*]
NPF .... No Private Facilities (SAUS)
NPF .... No Problem Found (SAUS)
NPF .... Nordisk Plastikkirurgisk Forening [*Scandinavian Association of Plastic Surgeons - SAPS*] (EAIO)
NPF .... North Pyrenean Fault [*Geology*]
npf .... Not Provided For (ODBW)
NPF .... Not Provided For
NPF .... Now Pitching For [*Telegraphy*] (PCTE)
NPF .... Nuclear Power Facility (NRCH)
NPF .... Nuclear Problems Forum (SAUS)
NPF .... Nuclepore Filter (SAUS)
NPF .... Nuveen Premium Municipal Income [*NYSE symbol*] (SPSG)
NPF .... Nuveen Prem Muni Income [*NYSE symbol*] (TTSB)
NPFA .... National Peanut Festival Association (EA)
NPFA .... National Playing Fields Association [*British*]
NPFA .... National Prepared Food Association (NTPA)
NPF & PP... Naval Prison Farms and Prison Personnel [*Budget appropriation title*]
NPFC .... National Pro-Family Coalition (EA)
NPFC .... Naval Publications and Forms Center
NPFC .... North Pacific Fisheries Commission (NOAA)
NPFC .... North Pacific Fur Seal Commission [*Defunct*]
NPFC .... Northwest Pacific Fisheries Center (SAUS)
NPFDA ...... National Poultry and Food Distributors Association (NTPA)
NPFF .... National Police Field Force [*Military*]
NPFF .... Normal Probability Frequency Function
NPFFA ...... National Prepared Frozen Food Association (EA)

NPFFG........ National Plant, Flower, and Fruit Guild (EA)
NPFFPA..... National Prepared Frozen Food Processors Association [*Later, NPFFA*] (EA)
NPFI......... National Plant Food Institute [*Later, TFI*] (EA)
NPFID....... Nitrogen-Phosphorus-Flame Ionization Detector [*Instrumentation*]
NPFL........ National Patriotic Front of Liberia [*Political party*] (EY)
NPFM........ Neural Pulse Frequency Modulation (PDAA)
NPFMC...... Northern Prawn Fishery Management Committee [*Australia*]
NPFMC...... North Pacific Fishery Management Council [*National Oceanic and Atmospheric Administration*] (GFGA)
NPFO........ Nuclear Power Field Office (IEEE)
N-PFPS...... Navy Portable Flight Planning Software
NPFR........ Normalized Peak Filling Rate [*Cardiology*]
NPFRC...... North Pacific Fisheries Research Center [*National Oceanic and Atmospheric Administration*]
NPFS........ Naval Preflight School
NPFS........ No Prior or Current Federal Service (AABC)
NPFSC....... North Pacific Fur Seal Commission [*Defunct*]
NPFT........ Neurotic Personality Factor Test [*Psychology*]
NPFTA....... National Personal Fitness Trainers Association (EA)
NPFVAS..... Northern Prawn Fishery Voluntary Assistance Scheme (SAUS)
NPFZ........ North Pyrenean Fault Zone [*Geology*]
NPG.......... Napping (ABBR)
NPG.......... National Peace Garden (EA)
NPG.......... National Portrait Gallery [*Smithsonian Institution*]
NPG.......... NATO Planning Group (NATG)
NPG.......... Naval Proving Ground [*Dahlgren, VA*]
NPG.......... Negative Population Growth (EA)
NPG.......... Neopentylglycol [*Organic chemistry*]
NPG.......... Nevada Proving Ground (BARN)
NPG.......... New Performance Gallery [*San Francisco*]
NPG.......... New Power Generation (SAUS)
NPG.......... New Product Group (SAUS)
NPG.......... News-Press & Gazette Company (EFIS)
NPG.......... Non-Aqueous Propylene Glycol [*Automotive coolant*]
NPG.......... Nonpregnant (MELL)
NPG.......... Nonprocessor Grant (IAA)
NPG.......... Nonunit Personnel Generator (DOMA)
NPG.......... No Pregnancy [*Medicine*] (EDAA)
NPG.......... Normalized Electron-Peak to Gamma-Peak [*Electronics*] (OA)
NPG.......... Normalized Programming Generator (IAA)
NPG.......... Not Paged [*Publishing*]
NPG.......... N-Phenylglycine [*Organic chemistry*]
NPG.......... Nuclear Planning Group [*NATO*]
NPG.......... Nuclear Power Group [*British*] [*Defunct*] (NUCP)
NP-G......... Nurse Practitioner-Generalist [*Medicine*] (EDAA)
NPG.......... Nuveen GA Prem Inc. Muni [*AMEX symbol*] (TTSB)
NPG.......... Nuveen Georgia Premium Income Municipal Fund [*AMEX symbol*] (SPSG)
NPG.......... Ontario Library Service Nipigon/Thunder Bay Public Library [*UTLAS symbol*]
NPGA........ National Propane Gas Association (NTPA)
NPGA........ National Pygmy Goat Association (EA)
NPGA........ Nevada Personnel and Guidance Association (SAUS)
NPGB........ (Nitrophenyl)guanidinobenzoate [*Organic chemistry*]
NPGC........ National Pell Grant Coalition (EA)
NPG-GMA... N-Phenylglycine Glycidyl Methacrylate [*Organic chemistry*]
NPGLINAC... Naval Postgraduate School Linear Accelerator
NPGPA....... Non-Powder Gun Products Association (EA)
NPGS........ GRIN - National Plant Germplasm System [*Database*] (GDD)
NPGS........ National Plant Germplasm System [*Department of Agriculture*]
NPGS........ Naval Postgraduate School
NPGS........ Nuclear Power Generating Station (NRCH)
NPGTC....... National Prairie Grouse Technical Council (EA)
NPH.......... Association of Nordic Paper Historians [*See also FNPH*] [*Sweden*] (EAIO)
NPH.......... Nalcap Holdings, Inc. [*Vancouver Stock Exchange symbol*]
NPH.......... Natural Period in Heave
NPH.......... Natural Protamine Hagadorn [*Insulin*]
NPH.......... Natural Protein Hagedorn (DB)
NPH.......... Nephi [*Utah*] [*Airport symbol*] (OAG)
NPH.......... Neurophysin [*Biochemistry*]
NPH.......... Neutral Protamine Hagedorn [*Insulin suspension*]
NPH.......... New Party Harbinger (Japan) [*Political party*] (PSAP)
NPH.......... Non Processed Header (SAUS)
NPH.......... No Parse Headers (SAUS)
NPH.......... No Previous History [*Medicine*] (DAVI)
NPH.......... No Profit Here [*Business term*]
NPH.......... Normal Paraffin Hydrocarbon
NPH.......... Normal Pressure Hydrocephalus [*Medicine*]
NPh.......... Northern Phoenician (BJA)
NPH.......... North Pit [*Hawaii*] [*Seismograph station code, US Geological Survey*] (SEIS)
NPHA........ Nanga Parbat/Haramosh Axis [*Himalayan geology*]
NPHA........ National Park Hospitality Association (NTPA)
NPHA........ National Peer Helpers Association (EA)
NPhA........ National Pharmaceutical Association (EA)
NPHA........ National Plott Hound Association (EA)
NPHA........ National Prison Hospice Association (NTPA)
NPHAP...... National Pesticide Hazard Assessment Program (EPAT)
NPHB........ Nonphotochemical Hole Burning [*Spectrometry*]
NPhD........ Doctor of Natural Philosophy
NPHE........ Nitrophenyl Hexyl Ether [*Organic chemistry*]
NPHOE...... Nitrophenyl Hydroxyoctyl Ether [*Organic chemistry*]
NPHP........ National Public Health Partnership (SAUS)
NPHPRS.... National Public Health Program Reporting System [*Department of Health and Human Services*]
NPHR........ National Foreign Intelligence Plan for Human Resources (MCD)
NPhR........ Neue Philologische Rundschau [*A publication*] (BJA)
NPHR........ Notice Papers-House of Representatives (SAUS)
NPHRC...... National Pediatric HIV Resource Center (PAZ)
NPHS........ Northwick Park Heart Study (DAVI)
NPHWA...... National Presbyterian Health and Welfare Association [*Later, PH-EWA*]
NPhx......... Nasopharynx [*Anatomy*] (DAVI)
NPI........... International Business Machines Corp., Systems Development Division, Poughkeepsie (SAUS)
NPI........... International Business Machines Corp., Systems Development Division, Poughkeepsie, NY [*Library symbol*] [*Library of Congress*] (LCLS)
NPI........... Nappanee, IN [*Amtrak rail station code*]
NPI........... Narcissistic Personality Inventory [*Psychology*] (EDAC)
NPI........... Nasopharyngeal Intubation [*Medicine*] (MELL)
NPI........... National Paralegal Institute (EA)
NPI........... National Parkinson Institute
NPI........... National Pollutant Inventory
NPI........... National Preservation Institute [*Association*] (EA)
NPI........... National Presto Industries, Inc. (EFIS)
NPI........... National Provident Institution [*Wales*]
NPI........... National Provider Identifier (SAUS)
NPI........... National Purchasing Institute (EA)
NPI........... Neighbourhood Partial Interchangeability (SAUS)
NPI........... Net Premium Income [*Insurance*] (AIA)
NPI........... Network Provider Interface [*Computer science*] (MWOL)
NPI........... NeuroPsychiatric Institute [*UCLA*]
NPI........... New Partnership Initiative (SAUS)
NPI........... New Policy Institute [*United Kingdom*] (RCD)
NPI........... New Product Introduction (SAUS)
NPI........... NEXRAD [*Next Generation Weather Radar*] Product Interface [*Marine science*] (OSRA)
NPI........... Nippon Pulp Industry (SAUS)
NPI........... Nonprecision Instrument (SAUS)
NPI........... Nonprocedural Interface [*Computer science*]
NPI........... No Present Illness
NPI........... No Previous Information [*to tip off a US Customs Service seizure*]
NPI........... Nordic Productivity Institute (SAUS)
NPI........... Normick Perron, Inc. [*Toronto Stock Exchange symbol*]
NPI........... Northampton Polytechnic Institute (SAUS)
NPI........... North Pocatello Valley [*Idaho*] [*Seismograph station code, US Geological Survey*] (SEIS)
NPI........... Nuclear Propulsion Initiative (ABAC)
NPI........... Nucleoplasmic Index [*Medicine*] (DMAA)
NPI........... Numbering Plan Identification (SAUS)
NPI........... Numbering Plan Indicator [*Computer science*] (TNIG)
NPI........... Number Planning Area (SAUS)
NPI........... Nuveen Prem Income Muni [*NYSE symbol*] (TTSB)
NPI........... Nuveen Premium Income Municipal Fund, Inc. [*NYSE symbol*] (SPSG)
NPIA......... Nanny Pop-Ins Association [*Defunct*] (EA)
NPIA......... National Pet Insurance Association (GVA)
NPIA......... National Photography Instructors Association (EA)
NPIA......... Norfolk Port and Industrial Authority (SAUS)
NPIAS....... National Plan of Integrated Airport Systems [*BTS*] [*FAA*] (TAG)
NPIC......... National Pesticide Information Clearinghouse [*Later, NPTN*] (EA)
NPIC......... National Pharmacy Insurance Council [*Defunct*] (EA)
NPIC......... National Photographic Intelligence Center (MUSM)
NPIC......... National Photographic Interpretation Center [*CIA*]
NPIC......... Naval Photographic Interpretation Center
NPIC......... Neurogenic Peripheral Intermittent Claudication [*Medicine*] (DMAA)
NPIC......... Nitrosopipecolic Acid [*Organic chemistry*]
NPie......... Piermont Public Library, Piermont, NY [*Library symbol*] [*Library of Congress*] (LCLS)
NPIF......... National Peace Institute Foundation (EA)
NPIG......... Nuclear Power Information Group [*British*] (NUCP)
NPIL......... Nepal Paper Industries Ltd. (SAUS)
NPIN......... National Parent Education Network
NPIN......... National Parent Information Network
NPIN......... National Prevention Information Network [*Internet resource*]
NPIN......... Negative-Positive-Intrinsic-Negative [*Electron device*] (MSA)
NPIP......... National Poultry Improvement Plan (EA)
NPIP......... Nitrosopiperidine [*Also, NP*] [*Organic chemistry*]
NPIPF....... Newspaper and Printing Industries Pension Fund [*British*] (BI)
NPiPNA..... N-Paraffins, iso-Paraffins, Naphthenes and Aromatics [*Gasoline analysis*]
NPIR......... No Periodic Inspection Required [*Military*] (AFIT)
NPIRG....... National Public Interest Research Group (EA)
NPIRI........ National Printing Ink Research Institute (EA)
NPIRS....... National Pesticide Information Retrieval System [*Purdue University*] [*West Lafayette, IN*] [*Database*]
NPIS......... National Physics Information System [*American Institute of Physics*] [*New York, NY*] (DIT)
NP/IS........ National Premium Incentive Show (ITD)
NPIS......... New Product Information Service [*Department of Commerce*]
NPIS......... Nuclear Plant Island Structure (NRCH)
NPITI........ National Project for the Improvement of Televised Instruction [*National Association of Educational Broadcasters*]
NPIU......... Network Processing and Interface Unit (NITA)
NPIU......... Numerical Processing and Interface Unit [*Computer science*] (MHDB)
NPIW......... North Pacific Intermediate Water [*Marine science*] (OSRA)

NPIX .... Network Peripherals [*NASDAQ symbol*] (TTSB)
NPIX .... Network Peripherals, Inc. [*NASDAQ symbol*] (SAG)
NPJ .... Corpus Christi, TX [*Location identifier*] [*FAA*] (FAAL)
NPJ .... Night Photo Jet (SAUS)
NPJ .... Number of Projects in the RTD-projects (SAUS)
NPj .... Port Jefferson Free Library, Port Jefferson, NY [*Library symbol*] [*Library of Congress*] (LCLS)
NPjES .... Port Jefferson Elementary School, Port Jefferson, NY [*Library symbol*] [*Library of Congress*] (LCLS)
NPjMH .... John T. Mather Memorial Hospital, Port Jefferson, NY [*Library symbol*] [*Library of Congress*] (LCLS)
NPJPA .... National Prune Juice Packers Association (EA)
NPjs .... Port Jefferson Station-Terryville Public Library, Port Jefferson Station, NY [*Library symbol*] [*Library of Congress*] (LCLS)
NPjSCH .... Saint Charles Hospital, Port Jefferson, NY [*Library symbol*] [*Library of Congress*] (LCLS)
NPJT .... Nonparoxysmal Atrioventricular Junction Tachycardia [*Cardiology*]
NPjVH .... Earl L. Vandermeulen High School, Port Jefferson, NY [*Library symbol*] [*Library of Congress*] (LCLS)
NPK .... Nationale Partij Kombinatie [*National Party Alliance*] [*Surinam*] [*Political party*] (PPW)
NPK .... National Presto Industries, Inc. [*NYSE symbol*] (SPSG)
NPK .... Natl Presto Indus. [*NYSE symbol*] (SG)
NPK .... Natrium, Phosphorus, Kalium (SAUS)
N-P-K .... Nitrogen-Phosphate-Potash (SAUS)
NPK .... Nitrogen, Phosphorus, Potassium [*Fertilizer components*]
NPK .... Noble Peak Resources Ltd. [*Vancouver Stock Exchange symbol*]
NPK .... Nodal Point Keying
NPK .... Non-Printing Key (SAUS)
NPKA .... National Paving and Kerb Association [*British*] (DBA)
NPL .... Free Public Library of Newark, Newark, NJ [*OCLC symbol*] (OCLC)
NPL .... Nameplate (MSA)
NPL .... Naples [*Italy*] [*Seismograph station code, US Geological Survey*] [*Closed*] (SEIS)
NPL .... National Physical Laboratory [*Research center*] [*British*] (IRC)
NPL .... National Physics Laboratory (KSC)
NPL .... National Priorities List [*Hazardous wastes*] [*Environmental Protection Agency*]
NPL .... National Priority List (AUEG)
NPL .... National Propane Partners LP [*NYSE symbol*] (SAG)
NPL .... National Puzzlers' League (EA)
NPL .... Natural Processing Language [*Computer science*] (HGAA)
NPL .... Neon Pilot Light
NPL .... Neoproteolipid [*Hematology*]
NPL .... Nepal [*ANSI three-letter standard code*] (CNC)
NPL .... Nepheline Resources Ltd. [*Vancouver Stock Exchange symbol*]
NPL .... Netscape Public License (SAUS)
NPL .... Newark Public Library (SAUS)
NPL .... Newfoundland Public Library Services [*UTLAS symbol*]
NPL .... New Plymouth [*New Zealand*] [*Airport symbol*] (OAG)
NPL .... New Product Line
NPL .... New Program Language (SAUS)
NPL .... New Programming Language [*1974*] [*Later, PL/1*] [*Computer science*]
NPL .... Nippon Peripherals Ltd. (SAUS)
NPL .... NOAAPORT Liaison (SAUS)
NPL .... Nodular Poorly Differentiated Lymphoma [*Oncology*] (DAVI)
NPL .... Noise Pollution Level
NPL .... Nonparametric Multipoint Linkage [*Mathematics*]
NPL .... Nonpartisan League [*Political party in North Dakota opposed by the IVA*]
NPL .... Non-Patent Literature
NPL .... Nonpersonal Liability
NPL .... Non Procedural Language (SAUS)
NPL .... Nonprocedural Language (TIMI)
NPL .... Nonprogramming Language (IAA)
NPL .... Nonstandard Parts List (MCD)
NPL .... No Perception of Light [*Ophthalmology*] (CPH)
NPL .... No Phonon Line (SAUS)
NPL .... Norfolk Public Library (SAUS)
NPL .... Normal Power Level (KSC)
NPL .... Northwest Pipeline Corp. (SAUS)
npl .... Noun, Plural [*Grammar*] (CDAI)
NPL .... Numerical Parts List (MCD)
NPL .... Numerical Preference List [*Military*] (AFIT)
NPl .... Plainview-Old Bethpage Public Library, Plainview, NY [*Library symbol*] [*Library of Congress*] (LCLS)
NPL .... Zero Phonon Line
NPLA .... National Perishable Logistics Association (NTPA)
NPLA .... New Product Line Audit (SAUS)
NPla .... Plattsburgh Public Library, Plattsburgh, NY [*Library symbol*] [*Library of Congress*] (LCLS)
NPlaB .... Bellarmine College, Plattsburgh, NY [*Library symbol*] [*Library of Congress*] (LCLS)
NPlaC .... Champlain College, Plattsburgh, NY [*Library symbol*] [*Library of Congress*] [*Obsolete*] (LCLS)
NPLAC .... National People Living with AIDS [*Acquired Immune Deficiency Syndrome*] Coalition [*Australia*]
NPlaCC .... Clinton Community College, Plattsburgh, NY [*Library symbol*] [*Library of Congress*] (LCLS)
NPlaCEF .... Clinton-Essex-Franklin Library System, Plattsburgh, NY [*Library symbol*] [*Library of Congress*] (LCLS)
NPlaCN .... Champlain Valley School of Nursing, Plattsburgh, NY [*Library symbol*] [*Library of Congress*] (LCLS)
NPL-AERO .... National Physical Laboratory, Aerodynamics Division [*British*]
NPLAN .... National Plan for Australian Newspapers
NPlaP .... Champlain Valley Physicians Hospital, Plattsburgh, NY [*Library symbol*] [*Library of Congress*] (LCLS)
NPLA-PAC .... National Pro-Life Alliance PAC [*Annandale, VA*] (PACS)
NPlaU .... State University of New York, College at Plattsburgh, Plattsburgh, NY [*Library symbol*] [*Library of Congress*] (LCLS)
NPlBE .... Old Bethpage Elementary School, Plainview, NY [*Library symbol*] [*Library of Congress*] (LCLS)
NPlBM .... Plainview-Old Bethpage Middle School, Plainview, NY [*Library symbol*] [*Library of Congress*] (LCLS)
NPLC .... National Pedigree Livestock Council (EA)
NPLC .... National Product Liability Council (EA)
NPLC .... Normal Phase Liquid Chromatography
NPlCH .... Central General Hospital, Plainview, NY [*Library symbol*] [*Library of Congress*] (LCLS)
NPLD .... National Pro-Life Democrats (EA)
NPle .... Mount Pleasant Public Library, Pleasantville, NY [*Library symbol*] [*Library of Congress*] (LCLS)
NPLEI .... National Police Law Enforcement Institute (EA)
NPleP .... Pace University Westchester, Pleasantville, NY [*Library symbol*] [*Library of Congress*] (LCLS)
NPLF .... National Preservation Loan Fund [*National Trust for Historic Preservation*]
NPLG .... Navy Program Language Group
NPLG .... Night Plane Guard Station (NVT)
NPLG .... Night Plane Landing Guard (NVT)
NPlGS .... Church of Jesus Christ of Latter-Day Saints, Genealogical Society Library, Plainview Branch, Plainview, NY [*Library symbol*] [*Library of Congress*] (LCLS)
NPLGS .... Night Plane Guard Station (SAUS)
NPLI .... Netpliance, Inc. [*NASDAQ symbol*] (SG)
NPlJE .... Jamaica Elementary School, Plainview, NY [*Library symbol*] [*Library of Congress*] (LCLS)
NPlKH .... John F. Kennedy High School, Plainview, NY [*Library symbol*] [*Library of Congress*] (LCLS)
NPlMC .... Nassau County Medical Center, Plainview Division, Plainview, NY [*Library symbol*] [*Library of Congress*] (LCLS)
NPlMM .... H.B. Mattlin Middle School, Plainview, NY [*Library symbol*] [*Library of Congress*] (LCLS)
NPlnRl .... New Plan Realty Trust [*Associated Press*] (SAG)
NPLO .... NATO Production and Logistics Organization (NATG)
NP-L PAC .... National Pro-Life Political Action Committee [*Defunct*] (EA)
NPlPE .... Pasadena Elementary School, Plainview, NY [*Library symbol*] [*Library of Congress*] (LCLS)
NPlPwE .... Parkway Elementary School, Plainview, NY [*Library symbol*] [*Library of Congress*] (LCLS)
NPLR .... Nyasaland Protectorate Law Reports [*A publication*] (ILCA)
NPLRC .... National Pro-Life Religious Council [*Association*] (EA)
NPLS .... Network Plus [*NASDAQ symbol*] (SG)
NPLS .... Non-performing Loans
NPLS .... Nonplus (ABBR)
NPLSD .... Nonplused (ABBR)
NPlSH .... Plainview-Old Bethpage Senior High School, Plainview, NY [*Library symbol*] [*Library of Congress*] (LCLS)
N/PLT .... Name Plate [*Automotive engineering*]
NPLT .... North Platte Basin (SAUS)
NPLTC .... National Public Law Training Center (EA)
NPLU .... Nauru Pacific Line [*Intermodal shipping container symbol*] (TVRC)
NPLU .... Not People Like Us (SAUS)
N PLUR .... Neuter Plural [*Grammar*] (OCD)
NPM .... Counts per Minute (IDOE)
NPM .... Marist College, Poughkeepsie, NY [*Library symbol*] [*Library of Congress*] (LCLS)
NPM .... Narrowband Phase Modulation (DEN)
NPM .... National Association of Pastoral Musicians (EA)
NPM .... National Program Manager [*Environmental Protection Agency*] (GFGA)
NPM .... Natural Particulate Matter [*Oceanography*]
NPM .... Naval Provost Marshal (SAUS)
NPM .... Naval Provost Martial [*British*]
NPM .... Navy Programming Manual
NPM .... Neonatal-Perinatal Medicine [*Medical specialty*] (DHSM)
Np/m .... Neper per Meter
NPM .... Network Performance Monitor (NITA)
NPM .... New Privateer Mines [*Vancouver Stock Exchange symbol*]
NPM .... Noise Power Meter (SAUS)
NPM .... Non-Print Media [*Advertising*]
NPM .... North Pahute Mesa [*Nevada*] [*Seismograph station code, US Geological Survey*] (SEIS)
NPM .... Nothing per Mouth [*Medicine*] (DMAA)
NPM .... Nuclear Paramagnetism (SAUS)
npm .... number of points in the point-matching method (SAUS)
NPM .... Nuveen Prem Income Muni 2 [*NYSE symbol*] (TTSB)
NPM .... Nuveen Premium Income Municipal 2 [*NYSE symbol*] (SPSG)
NPMA .... National Piano Manufacturers Association of America [*Later, PMAI*] (EA)
NPMA .... National Podiatric Medical Association (EA)
NPMA .... National Property Management Association (EA)
NPMA .... Navy Personnel Management Academy (DNAB)
NPMA .... Newspaper Purchasing Management Association (EA)
NPMC .... National Pecan Marketing Council (EA)
NPMC .... Natural Products Marketing Council [*Canada*] (EAIO)
NPMCA .... National Paper Marketing Council of Australia
NPMDX .... Navellier Mid-Cap Growth
NPME .... New Penn Motor Express [*Common carrier symbol*]
NPMG .... NATO Patriot Management Group (MCD)

NPMH .... Mid-Hudson Libraries, Poughkeepsie, NY [*Library symbol*] [*Library of Congress*] (LCLS)
NPMHU ..... National Postal Mail Handlers Union (EA)
NPMI .... Nordic Pool for Marine Insurance [*Helsinki, Finland*] (EA)
NPMP .... National Pesticide Monitoring Program [*Later, National Contaminant Biomonitoring Program*] [*US Fish and Wildlife Service*]
NPMP .... No Problem, My Pleasure [*Internet lingo*] (NETL)
NPMR .... National Premium Manufacturers Representatives [*Later, IMRA*] (EA)
NPMR .... Neutron Program for Materials Research [*National Research Council Canada*] (RCD)
NPMTC ...... Navy Pacific Missile Test Center (MCD)
NPMTC ...... Nuclear Propulsion Mobile Training Team (SAUS)
NPMTT ...... Nuclear Propulsion Mobile Training Team [*Military*] (CAAL)
NPN .... NASA Part Number (MCD)
NPN .... National Particulate Network [*Environmental Protection Agency*] (GFGA)
NPN .... National Party of Nigeria [*Political party*] (PPW)
NPN .... National Performance Network (EA)
NPN .... National Prevention Network (EA)
NPN .... National Prices Network
N-P-N .... Negative-Positive-Negative [*Transistor*] (CET)
NPN .... Newport News, VA [*Amtrak rail station code*]
NPN .... New Product Network [*Television*]
NPN .... New Pseudonyms and Nicknames [*A publication*]
NPN .... Non-Par Not Approved
NPN .... Non-Physician Practitioner (SAUS)
NPN .... Nonprotein Nitrogen [*Analytical chemistry*]
NPN .... Normal Propyl Nitrate (MCD)
NPN .... Notes Public Network (SAUS)
NPNA .... No Protest Nonacceptance [*Banking*]
NPNA .... Normalized Protein equivalent of total Nitrogen Appearance (SAUS)
NPNCA ...... National Parks and Nature Conservation Authority [*Australia*]
NPNCF ...... Nicene and Post-Nicene Christian Fathers [*A publication*] (ODCC)
NPN Compound... Nonprotein Nitrogenous Compound (SAUS)
NPND .... National Parent Network on Disabilities [*Association*] (EA)
NP/ND .... Not Published/No Date (SAUS)
NPNP .... Negative-Positive-Negative-Positive [*Transistor*]
NPNR .... Network for Psychiatric Nursing Research (SAUS)
NP NS .... Ohio Nisi Prius Reports, New Series [*A publication*] (DLA)
NPNT .... NorthPoint Communications Holdings [*NASDAQ symbol*]
NPNT .... NorthPoint Communic Grp. [*NASDAQ symbol*] (SG)
NPO .... Design & manufacturing facility (SAUS)
NPO .... Naphthylphenyloxazole [*Biochemical analysis*]
NPO .... NASA Pasadena Office (MCD)
NPO .... National [*or New*] Post Office Building
NPO .... National Project Office
NPO .... Naval Port Officer
NPO .... Navy Post Office
NPO .... Navy Program Objectives (NG)
NPO .... Navy Purchasing Office
NPO .... Negative-Positive O Temperature Coefficient (AEBE)
NPO .... Negative Positive Zero (IAA)
NPO .... Neighborhood Patrol Office [*or Officer*]
NPO .... New Personnel Orientation (MCD)
NPO .... New Philharmonic Orchestra [*British*]
NPO .... Newport, OR [*Amtrak Busline code*]
NPO .... Nil per Os [*Nothing by Mouth*] [*Medicine*]
NPO .... Nonpenetrating Orbit (SAUS)
NPO .... Non Per Os [*Nothing by Mouth*] [*Latin*] (BABM)
NPO .... Non-Profit Organization (SAUS)
NPO .... No Part on Order (MCD)
NPO .... Norpet Resources Ltd. [*Toronto Stock Exchange symbol*]
NPO .... Nothing By Mouth [*Medicine*] (BCRP)
npo .... Nothing By Mouth [*Medicine*] (BCRP)
NPO .... Nothing per Os (SAUS)
NPO .... Not Pickled Ordinary [*Metal industry*]
NPO .... Nuclear Plant Operator (NRCH)
NPO .... Nuclear Power Operator (SAUS)
NPO .... Nuclear Propulsion Office
NPO .... Nucleus Preopticus (DMAA)
NPO .... Preoptic Nucleus (DB)
NPO .... Strategic Systems Project Office, Washington, DC [*OCLC symbol*] (OCLC)
NPOAA ...... National Police Officers Association of America (EA)
NPOC .... National Point of Contact (PDAA)
NPOC .... Navy Polar Oceanographic Center (DNAB)
NPOC .... Nonpurgeable Organic Carbon
NPODS ...... Navy Publishing on Demand System (AAGC)
NPOE .... Nitrophenyl Octyl Ether [*Organic chemistry*]
NPOESS ..... National Polar-Orbiting Operational Environmental Satellite System
NPOEV ...... Nuclear-Powered Ocean Engineering Vehicle [*Minisub*]
NP Ohio ..... Ohio Nisi Prius Reports [*A publication*] (DLA)
NPO/HS ..... Nulla per Os Hora Somni [*Nothing by Mouth at Bedtime*] [*Latin*] [*Pharmacy*] (MAH)
NPOI .... Navy Prototype Optical Interferometer
NPOL .... Nuclear Pollution [*Environmental science*] (COE)
NPOLA ...... Navy Purchasing Office, Los Angeles
NPOLE .... North-seeking Pole (SAUS)
N-Pollution... Nuclear Pollution (SAUS)
NPOMHWMGL... National Post Office Mail Handlers, Watchmen, Messengers, and Group Leaders [*Later, NPMHU*] (EA)
NPO-NIA .... Nonprofit Organizations National Insurance Alliance (SAUS)
NPOP .... NASA Polar Orbiting Platform (EOSA)
NPOPR ...... Not Paid on Prior Rolls
NPoq .... Beekman Community Library Reading Center, Poughquag, NY [*Library symbol*] [*Library of Congress*] (LCLS)
NP or D ..... No Place or Date
NP or DP ... No Place or Date of Publication (SAUS)
NPORT ...... North Portland, OR [*American Association of Railroads railroad junction routing code*]
NPOS .... Nitrite Positive [*Organic chemistry*] (DAVI)
NPOS .... Nurses Professional Orientation Scale (DMAA)
NPOST ...... Nonperturbative Open-Shell Theory [*Physics*]
NPot .... Potsdam Public Library, Potsdam, NY [*Library symbol*] [*Library of Congress*] (LCLS)
NPotC .... Clarkson College of Technology, Potsdam, NY [*Library symbol*] [*Library of Congress*] (LCLS)
NPotU .... State University of New York, College at Potsdam, Potsdam, NY [*Library symbol*] [*Library of Congress*] (LCLS)
NPOU .... Ceske Zavody Gumanenske a Plastikarske [*Intermodal shipping container symbol*] (TVRC)
NPour .... Hiram Halley Memorial Library, Pound Ridge, NY [*Library symbol*] [*Library of Congress*] (LCLS)
N-Power .... Nuclear Power (SAUS)
NPP .... National Patriotic Party [*Liberia*] [*Political party*] (EY)
NPP .... National Peach Partners [*Defunct*] (EA)
NPP .... National People's Party [*Pakistan*] [*Political party*] (FEA)
NPP .... National Periodicals Publications, Inc.
NPP .... National Policy Paper [*Army*] (AABC)
NPP .... National Pretreatment Program [*Metal finishing technology*]
NPP .... National Priorities Project [*Association*] (EA)
NPP .... National Priority Pool (SAUS)
NPP .... National Priority Program [*NHTSA*] (TAG)
NPP .... National Prison Project (EA)
NPP .... National Procurement Point [*Military*] (RDA)
NPP .... National Progressive Party [*Iraq*] [*Political party*] (BJA)
NPP .... National Prohibition Party (EA)
NPP .... Naval Propellant Plant
NPP .... Navy Propellant Plant (DNAB)
NPP .... Negative Picture Phase
NPP .... Nemzeti Paraszt Part [*National Peasant Party*] [*Hungary*] [*Political party*] (PPE)
NPP .... Neodymium Pentaphosphate [*Inorganic chemistry*]
NPP .... Net Primary Production
NPP .... Net Primary Productivity
NPP .... Network Power Processor [*Acme Electric Corp.*] [*Computer science*] (PCM)
NPP .... Network Protocol Processor
NPP .... Neuropathic Pain [*Medicine*] (MELL)
NPP .... Neuroperfusion Pump [*Medicine*] (MELL)
NPP .... New Patriotic Party [*Ghana*] [*Political party*] (ECON)
NPP .... New People's Party [*North Korea*] [*Political party*] (FEA)
NPP .... New Physics Project (AIE)
NPP .... New Policy Proposal (SAUS)
NPP .... New Product Planning (IAA)
NPP .... New Progressive Party [*Puerto Rico*] [*Political party*]
NPP .... Nigerian People's Party [*Political party*] (PPW)
NPP .... Nitrogen, Phosphorus, Potassium (SAUS)
NPP .... Nitrophenyl Phosphate [*Biochemical analysis*]
NPP .... Nitrophenylprolinol [*Organic chemistry*]
NPP .... Nitropropenyl Pivalate [*Organic chemistry*]
NPP .... Non-Penetrating Periscope [*DARPA*]
NPP .... No Passed Proof
NPP .... Normal Pool Plasma [*Clinical chemistry*]
NPP .... Normal Postpartum [*Medicine*] (MELL)
NPP .... North American Power [*Vancouver Stock Exchange symbol*]
NPP .... Notice of Proposed Procurement (SAUS)
NPP .... Nozzleless Performance Program Module (MCD)
NPP .... N-Pentylpalmitamide [*Organic chemistry*]
NPP .... Nuclear Power Plant (IEEE)
NPP .... Nucleus Tegmenti Pedunculopontinus [*Medicine*] (EDAA)
NPP .... Nurse Practitioner Project
NPP .... Nuveen Performance Plus Municipal [*NYSE symbol*] (SPSG)
NPP .... Nuveen Perform Plus Muni [*NYSE symbol*] (TTSB)
NPPA .... National Parks and Primitive Areas
NPPA .... National Pickle Packers Association [*Later, PPI*]
NPPA .... National Pizza and Pasta Association (EA)
NPPA .... National Press Photographers Association (EA)
NPPA .... National Probation and Parole Association [*Later, NCCD*]
NPPA .... Northwest Pulp and Paper Association (SAUS)
NPPAC ...... National and Provincial Parks Association of Canada
NPPAG ...... National Program Production and Aquisition Grant [*Corporation for Public Broadcasting*] [*Radio*] (NTCM)
NPPase ..... Nitrophenylphosphatase (DB)
NPPB .... National Poisons and Pesticides Board [*Sweden*]
NPPB .... National Potato Promotion Board (EA)
NPPB .... Nitro(Phenylpropylamino) Benzoate [*Organic chemistry*]
NPPC .... National Pork Producers Council (EA)
NPPC .... National Power Policy Committee [*World War II*]
NPPC .... Navy Programming Planning Council
NPPC .... Northwest Power Planning Council (SAUS)
NPPC .... Nuclear Power Plant Co. Ltd.
NPPC .... Nuclear Power Plant Consultant (IDAI)
NPPC .... Numeric Parts Preference Code [*Military*] (AFIT)
NPPC .... Nursing Professional Practice Council (DMAA)
NPPD .... (Nitrophenyl)pentadienal [*Tracer chemical*] [*Organic chemistry*]
NPPD .... Nitrophenylpentadiene Aldehyde (SAUS)
NPPE .... Negative Pressure Pulmonary Edema [*Medicine*] (DMAA)
NPPE .... Nitrophenyl Pentyl Ether [*Organic chemistry*]

NPPE .... Nuclear Power Propulsion Evaluation (NG)
NP-PET ...... Nestle Purina Petcare Company Political Election Team [*St. Louis, MO*] (PACS)
NPPF .... National Poultry Producers Federation [*Defunct*] (EA)
NPPH .... Nucleotide Pyrophosphohydrolase [*Medicine*] (EDAA)
NPPI .... Navy Program Progress Item (CAAL)
NPPI .... Negative Pressure Patient Isolator [*Medicine*] (WDAA)
NPPI .... Nonpublic Personal Information (GART)
NPPI .... Norwood Promotional Prd [*NASDAQ symbol*] (TTSB)
NPPI .... Norwood Promotional Products [*NASDAQ symbol*] (SAG)
NPPL .... National Parks and Public Lands [*Victoria, Australia*]
NPPL .... National Private Pilots License (SAUS)
NPPL .... Neuropsychopharmacology Laboratory [*Wayne State University*] [*Research center*]
NPPN .... Nitroxyperoxypropyl Nitrate [*Environmental chemistry*]
NPPN .... NUDO [*Namibia United Democratic Organization*] Progressive Party of Namibia [*Political party*] (PPW)
NPPNG ...... Nonpenicillinase-producing Neisseria Gonorrhoeae [*Medicine*] (EDAA)
NPPO .... Navy Program Planning Office
NPPO .... Navy Publications and Printing Office
NPP/QAS .... Naval Propellant Plant Quality Assurance Department [*Indian Head, MD*]
NPPR .... Nationalist Party of Puerto Rico (NADA)
NPPR .... Navy Program Progress Report
NPPR .... Nonproductive Procurement Directive
NPPRE ...... Nitrophenyl Propyl Ether [*Organic chemistry*]
NPPS .... National Program for Playground Safety [*Association*] (EA)
NPPS .... Navy Planning and Programming System
NPPS .... Navy Publications and Printing Service
NPPS .... North Pacific Pediatric Society (EARSL)
NPPSA ...... Naval Personnel Program Support Activity (ACAE)
NPPSBO ..... Navy Publications and Printing Service Branch Office
NPPSIS ...... National Parent to Parent Support & Information Systems, Inc.
NPPSMO .... Navy Publications and Printing Service Management Office
NPPSO ...... Navy Publications and Printing Service Office
NPPSSOEASTDIV ... Navy Publications and Printing Service, Southeastern Division (DNAB)
NPPSWESTDIV ... Navy Publications and Printing Service, Western Division (DNAB)
NPPTA .... National Public Parks Tennis Association (EA)
NPPTS .... Nuclear Power Plant Training Simulator (PDAA)
NPPU .... Net Postprandial Protein Utilization
NPPW .... National Poison Prevention Week
NPPZ .... Northwest Power Plant [*Federal Railroad Administration identification code*]
NPQ .... Not Physically Qualified (MELL)
NPQAA ...... Natural Products Quality Assurance Alliance
NPR .... Napier [*New Zealand*] [*Seismograph station code, US Geological Survey*] [*Closed*] (SEIS)
NPR .... Napper (ABBR)
NPR .... Narodowa Partia Robotnicza [*National Workers Party*] [*Poland*] [*Political party*] (PPE)
NPR .... National Aeronautics and Space Administration Procurement Regulation [*A publication*] (AAGC)
NPR .... National Parks and Access to the Countryside Regulations [*Town planning*] [*British*]
NPR .... National Partnership for Reinventing Government
NPR .... National Performance Review [*A publication*]
NPR .... National Public Radio [*Washington, DC*] [*Telecommunications*] (TSSD)
NPR .... Naval Petroleum Reserves
NPR .... Naval Plant Representative
NPR .... Navy Payroll (DNAB)
NPR .... Navy Preliminary Revision (DNAB)
NPR .... Navy Procurement Regulation
NPR .... Negro Puerto Rican
NPR .... Neoricans in Puerto Rico (EA)
NPR .... Neptune Resources Corp. [*Toronto Stock Exchange symbol*]
NPR .... Net Pool Return
NPR .... Net Protein Ratio [*Nutrition*]
NPR .... Network Process Engineering (SAUS)
NPR .... New Plan Realty Trust SBI [*NYSE symbol*] (SPSG)
NPR .... New Plan Rlty Tr SBI [*NYSE symbol*] (TTSB)
NPR .... New Port Richey, FL [*Amtrak Busline code*]
NPR .... New Production Reactor [*Department of Energy*]
NPR .... Night Press Rate [*of newspapers*]
NPR .... Nisi Prius Reports [*A publication*] (DLA)
NPR .... Noise Pollution Ratio (SAUS)
NPR .... Noise Power Ratio
NPR .... Noise Prediction and Reduction
NPR .... Noise Preferential Route [*Aviation*] (DA)
NPR .... Nonperiodic Review (TIMI)
NPR .... Non Persistant Reference (SAUS)
NPR .... Non-Procedural Reference (SAUS)
NPR .... Nonprocessor Request (IAA)
NPR .... Nonproduction Release (MCD)
NPR .... No Power Recovery (SAUS)
NPR .... Normal Pulse Rate [*Medicine*] (DMAA)
NPR .... Northern Plains Railroad [*Federal Railroad Administration identification code*]
NPR .... North Polar Region
NPR .... Nothing Per Rectum [*Medicine*] (EDAA)
NPR .... Notice of Program Reimbursement (MEDA)
NPR .... Notice of Proposed Rule Making [*Federal agencies*] (GFGA)
NPR .... Nozzle Pressure Ratio [*Aviation*]
NPR .... Nuclear Paramagnetic Resonance (MCD)
NPR .... Nuclear Posture Review [*DoD*]
NPR .... Nuclear Power Reactor
NPR .... Nuclear Pulse Rocket [*NASA*]
NPR .... Nucleoside Phosphoribosyl (DMAA)
NPR .... Numerical Position Readout (IAA)
NPR .... Numeric Position Readout (SAUS)
NPR .... Office of New Production Reactors (SAUS)
NPr .... Pearl River Public Library, Pearl River, NY [*Library symbol*] [*Library of Congress*] (LCLS)
NPrA .... American Cyanamid Co., Lederle Laboratories, Pearl River, NY [*Library symbol*] [*Library of Congress*] (LCLS)
NPRA .... International Phase of Ocean Drilling: Seismic Line 1, Demultiplexed Data - Cape Hatteras, North Carolina to Mid-Atlantic Ridge [*Database*] (GDD)
NPRA .... National Parks and Recreation Act of 1978 (COE)
NPRA .... National Parks and Recreation Association (NADA)
NPRA .... National Personal Robot Association [*Later, NSRA*] (EA)
NPRA .... National Petroleum Refiners Association (EA)
NPRA .... National Petroleum Reserve-Alaska
NPRA .... Naval Personnel Research Activity
NPRA .... Newspaper Personnel Relations Association (EA)
NPR&D ...... Navy Property Redistribution and Disposal (AAGC)
N/P Ratio ... Nitrogen/Phosphorus Ratio (SAUS)
NPRC .... National Personnel Records Center [*National Archives and Records Service*]
NPRC .... National Pipeline Reform Coalition [*Association*] (EA)
NPRC .... National Polystyrene Recycling Co.
NPRC .... National Project on Resource Coordination for Justice Statistics and Information [*Canada*]
NPRC .... National Public Relations Council of Health and Welfare Services [*Formerly, NPC*]
NPRC .... National Puerto Rican Coalition (EA)
NPRC .... Newspaper Production and Research Center
NPRC .... Nonproliferation Program Review Committee [*US, multiagency*]
NPRC .... Nuclear Power Range Channel (IEEE)
NPRC (CPR) ... National Personnel Records Center (Civilian Personnel Records) [*National Archives and Records Service*] (AFM)
NPRCG ...... Nuclear Public Relations Contact Group
NPRC (MPR) ... National Personnel Records Center (Military Personnel Records) [*National Archives and Records Service*] (AFM)
NPRD .... NASA Procurement Regulation Directive
NPRD .... Nonelectronic Parts Reliability Data (MCD)
NPRD .... Nuclear Plant Reliability Data
NPRDA ...... National Precure Retread Dealers Association [*Defunct*] (EA)
NPRDC ...... National Public Resources Defense Council (NUCP)
NPRDC ...... Navy Personnel Research and Development Center (GRD)
NPRDL ...... Naval Personnel Research and Development Laboratory
NPRDS ...... Nuclear Plant Reliability Data System (NRCH)
NPres .... National Preserve
NPRF .... National Priority Reserve Fund [*Australia*]
NPRF .... National Puerto Rican Forum (EA)
NPRF .... Noise Power Ratio Floor (SAUS)
NPRF .... Northrop Pulse Radiation Facility
NPRFT .... Nonprofit (ABBR)
NPRH .... Nurse Practitioners in Reproductive Health (SAUS)
NPRI .... Nasopharyngeal Radium Irradiation [*Medicine*] (MELL)
NPRI .... National Psychiatric Reform Institute
NPRIS .... Nuclear Planning & Resource Information System (SAUS)
NPRL .... Navy Prosthetics Research Laboratory
NPRL .... Nonprocedural Referencing Language
NPRL .... No Parallel Traffic (SAUS)
NPRM .... Neopharm Inc. [*NASDAQ symbol*] (TTSB)
NPRM .... Notice of Proposed Rule Making [*Federal agencies*]
NPRMW ..... Neopharm Inc. Wrrt [*NASDAQ symbol*] (TTSB)
NPRN .... Neoprene [*Synthetic rubber*]
NPRN .... North American Public Relations Network (NTPA)
NPRO .... NaPro BioTherapeutics, Inc. [*NASDAQ symbol*] (SAG)
NPRO .... Naval Petroleum Reserves Office
NPRO .... Naval Representative Offices (ACAE)
NPRO .... Navy Plant Representative Office
NPRO .... N-Nitrosoproline [*Organic chemistry*]
NPRO .... Non-Process Run-Out (SAUS)
NPROA ...... Nitrosoprolylalanine [*Organic chemistry*]
N Process ... Normal Process (SAUS)
NPROCL ..... Non-Procedural Language (VLIE)
NPROG ...... Nitrosoprolylglycine [*Organic chemistry*]
N-Project ... Nuclear-power Project (SAUS)
N-Proliferation ... Nuclear Proliferation (SAUS)
N-Propulsion ... Nuclear Propulsion (SAUS)
NPROW ..... Napro Biotheraputics Wrrts [*NASDAQ symbol*] (TTSB)
NPRP .... Northern Pecan Research Program (SAUS)
NPRPA ...... Naval Petroleum Reserves Production Act (AAGC)
NPRR .... National Public Relations Roundtable [*Defunct*]
NPRR .... Net Pool Return Rule
NPRS .... NASA Procurement Regulation Supplement
NPRS .... Negative Poll Response State (IAA)
NPRS .... Newpark Resources, Inc. [*NASDAQ symbol*] (SAG)
NPRS .... Nonpersistent (FAAC)
NPRTSN ..... Nonpartisan (ABBR)
NPRTSNSP ... Nonpartisanship (ABBR)
NPRTX .... Neub. & Berman Partners Fund [*Mutual fund ticker symbol*] (SG)
NPRTZ .... Nonpolarized Return-to-Zero Recording (SAUS)

NPRV........ Nitrogen Pressure Relief Valve (MCD)
NPRWC..... National Puerto Rican Women's Caucus [*Defunct*] (EA)
NPRZ........ Non-Polarized Return-to-Zero Recording (VLIE)
NPS......... Counts per Second (IDOE)
NPS......... Honolulu, HI [*Location identifier*] [*FAA*] (FAAL)
NPS......... Nail-patella Syndrome [*Medicine*] (EDAA)
NPS......... Narcotics Prevention Service (NADA)
NPS......... NASA Planning Studies (KSC)
NPS......... Nationale Partij Suriname [*Surinam National Party*] [*Political party*] (PPW)
NPS......... National Park Service [*Department of the Interior*]
NPS......... National Parole Service [*Canada*]
NPS......... National Periodicals System
NPS......... National Permit Strategy [*Environmental Protection Agency*] (GFGA)
NPS......... National Pesticide Survey [*Environmental Protection Agency*] (GFGA)
NPS......... National Philatelic Society [*Defunct*] (EA)
NPS......... National Phone Services, Inc.
NPS......... National Poetry Secretariat [*British*] [*An association*] (DBA)
NPS......... National Poetry Series
NPS......... National Pond Society [*Association*] (EA)
NPS......... National Pony Society [*British*] (DI)
NPS......... National Prisoner Statistics [*An association*]
NPS......... Naval Postgraduate School
NPS......... Navy Personnel Survey
NPS......... Navy Primary Standards (MSA)
NPS......... Neapolis [*Greece*] [*Seismograph station code, US Geological Survey*] (SEIS)
NPS......... Negative Potential Shifts [*Neurophysiology*]
NPS......... Network Photo System (SAUS)
NPS......... Network Processing Supervisor [*Honeywell, Inc.*]
NPS......... Network Processor System (NITA)
NPS......... Network Product Support [*Computer science*] (VLIE)
NPS......... Neutral Pressure Switch
NPS......... New Products Support (VLIE)
NPS......... Newspaper Pagination System [*Typography*] (DGA)
NPS......... Night Photographic System
NPS......... Night Pilotage System (ACAE)
NPS......... Ninhydrin-Positive-Substance (SAUS)
NPS......... Nitrided Pressureless Sintering (SAUS)
NPS......... Nitrophenyl Sulfenyl [*Organic chemistry*]
Nps......... Nitrophenylthio(nitrophenylsulfonyl) [*Biochemistry*]
NPS......... Noise Power Spectra [*Spectrometry*]
NPS......... Nominal Pipe Size (SAA)
NPS......... Noncumulative Preferred Stock [*Investment term*] (MHDW)
NPS......... Non-Parallel Share (SAUS)
NPS......... Nonperishable Subsistence
NPS......... Non-Pneumatic Spare [*Automotive engineering*]
NPS......... Nonpoint Source [*Environmental Protection Agency*] (AEPA)
NPS......... Nonpoint Source Pollution [*Agricultural engineering*]
NPS......... Non-Prior Service (MCD)
NPS......... Non-Professorial Staff (SAUS)
NPS......... No-Par Stock [*Investment term*] (MHDW)
NPS......... No Prior Service [*Military*]
NPS......... Normalized Plateau Slope
NPS......... Normal Pipe Size
NPS......... North Polar Sequence
NPS......... Northwestern Public Service Co. [*NYSE symbol*] (SPSG)
NPS......... Northwestern Pub Svc [*NYSE symbol*] (TTSB)
NPs......... Notaries Public (SAUS)
NPS......... Notice Papers-Senate (SAUS)
NPS......... Novell Productivity Specialist [*Computer science*] (VLIE)
NPS......... Nuclear and Plasma Sciences (MCD)
NPS......... Nuclear Planning System (COE)
NPS......... Nuclear Power Source
NPS......... Nuclear Power Station (SAUS)
NPS......... Nuclear Power System
NPS......... Numerical Plotting System (VLIE)
NPS......... NWPS Capital Financing Tr PERCS [*NYSE symbol*] (SAG)
NPS......... US National Park Service (SAUS)
NPSA........ National Passenger Safety Association [*Defunct*] (EA)
NPSA........ National Pecan Shellers Association (EA)
NPSA........ National Pegboard Systems Association (EA)
NPSA........ National Psychic Science Association (EA)
NPSA........ New Program Status Area (IEEE)
NPSA........ Novitiate of Saint Andrew-On-Hudson, Poughkeepsie, NY [*Library symbol*] [*Library of Congress*] (LCLS)
NPSAPHA... New Professionals Section of the American Public Health Association (SAUS)
NPSAS...... National Postsecondary Student Aid Study [*Department of Education*] (GFGA)
NPSB........ National Prisoner Statistics Bulletin [*Department of Justice*]
NPSB........ News Print Service Bureau
NPS BBS.... Nonpoint Source Electronic Bulletin Board System [*Environmental Protection Agency*] (AEPA)
NPSC........ National Processing Service Center [*Emergency Management*] (EMA)
NPSC........ National Standard Pipe Straight-Couplings
NPSC........ Naval Personnel Separation Center
NPSC........ New Paradigm Software [*NASDAQ symbol*] (SAG)
NPSC........ Nursing Policy Studies Centre [*University of Warwick*] [*British*] (CB)
NPS-CL...... Nitrophenyl Sulfenyl Chloride
NPS/CPSU/UW... National Park Service Cooperative Park Studies Unit, University of Washington [*Research center*] (RCD)
NPSCW...... New Paradigm Software Wrrt [*NASDAQ symbol*] (TTSB)
NPSD........ Naval Photographic Services Depot
NPSD........ Neutron Power Spectral Density (OA)
NPSD........ Noise Power Spectre Density
NPSD........ Noise Power Spectrum Density (SAUS)
NPSD........ Normalized Power Spectral Density (SAUS)
NPSDN...... Nordic Packet Switched Data Network (NITA)
NPSE........ National Premium Sales Executives (EA)
NPSE........ Navy Peridontal Screening Examination (DNAB)
NPSF........ National Pipe Straight Fine [*Mechanical engineering*]
NPSF........ National Straight Pipe Threads for Dry Seal Pressure Tight Joints
NPSFR...... Net Public Sector Financing Requirement [*Business term*]
NPSG........ NPS Technologies Group, Inc. (SAUS)
NPSH........ National Standard Pipe Straight-Hose Couplings and Nipples
NPSH........ National Straight Pipe Threads for Hose Couplings and Nipples
NPSH........ Net Positive Suction Head [*Pumps*]
NPSH........ Niagara Parks School of Horticulture (SAUS)
NPSH........ Nonprotein Sulfhydryl [*Biochemistry*]
NPSH........ Not Positive Suction Head (COE)
NPSHA...... Net Positive Suction Head Available [*Pumps*] (PDAA)
NPSHR...... Net Positive Suction Head Required [*Chemical or food processing*]
NPSI......... National Pipe Straight Intermediate [*Mechanical engineering*]
NPSI......... National Standard Pipe Straight-Internal, Dryseal
NPSI......... Network Control Program Packet Switching Interface [*Computer science*] (HGAA)
NPSI......... Networked Picture Systems, Inc. [*NASDAQ symbol*] (COMM)
NPSI......... Network Packet Switch Interface [*Computer science*] (VLIE)
NPSI......... Network Protocol Service Interface [*Computer science*] (VLIE)
NPSI......... Nursing Performance Simulation Instrument
NPSL......... National Professional Soccer League [*Later, NASL*]
NPSL......... National Standard Pipe Straight-Lock Nuts
NPSL......... National Straight Pipe Threads for Locknuts and Locknut Pipe Threads
NPSL......... North Pacific Steamship Line [*Common carrier symbol*]
NPSM........ Non-Productive Standard Minute (PDAA)
NPSMS...... Nonpoint Source Management System (WPI)
NPSNL...... South Eastern New York Library Resources Council, Poughkeepsie, NY [*Library symbol*] [*Library of Congress*] (LCLS)
NPSO........ Nonpaired Spatial Orbitals [*Atomic physics*]
NPSP........ National People's Salvation Party [*Zambia*] [*Political party*] (EY)
NPSP........ Net Positive Static Pressure (NASA)
NPSP........ Net Positive Suction Pressure [*Cryogenics*]
NPSP........ N-Phenylselenenylphthalimide [*Organic chemistry*]
NPSP........ NPS Pharmaceuticals [*NASDAQ symbol*] (TTSB)
NPsP........ Paul Smiths College, Paul Smiths, NY [*Library symbol*] [*Library of Congress*] (LCLS)
NPSPA....... National Pecan Shellers and Processors Association (EA)
NPS Phm... NPS Pharmaceutical, Inc. [*Associated Press*] (SAG)
NPSPrA...... NWPS Cap Fin 8.125% Tr Sec 1 [*NYSE symbol*] (TTSB)
NPSR........ No Primary Staff Responsibility [*Army*] (AABC)
NPSRA...... National Professional Squash Racquets Association (EA)
NPSRC...... National Professional Standards Review Council [*Terminated, 1982*] [*HEW*] (EGAO)
NPSRI....... National Public Services Research Institute
NPSS........ IEEE Nuclear and Plasma Sciences Society (EA)
NPSS........ NASA Packet Switch System (SAUS)
NPSS........ National Police and Security Service [*Republic of Vietnam*]
NPSS........ National Proficiency Survey Series [*Scannell*] (TES)
NPSS........ Noms Propres Sud-Semitiques [*A publication*] (BJA)
NPSS........ Non-Public School Section [*American Association of School Librarians*]
NPSS........ Nordic Post Security Service
NPSS........ Nuclear and Plasma Sciences Society (SAUS)
NPSS........ Nuclear and Plasma Science Symposium (MCD)
NPST........ Native Pituitary-Derived Somatotropin [*Endocrinology*]
NPST........ Native Porcine Somatotropin [*Endocrinology*]
NPSTN...... National Public Switched Telecommunications Network (MHDI)
NPSU........ Nigel Parkes [*Intermodal shipping container symbol*] (TVRC)
NPSU........ Nuclear Plant Safety Unit (SAUS)
NPSWL...... New Program Status Word Location
NPSWU...... Newpark Resources Uts (SAUS)
NPSX........ Newport Star Clipper Dinner Train [*Federal Railroad Administration identification code*]
NPT......... Executive Aviation Services (SAUS)
NPT......... Nasal Provocation Test [*Immunology*]
NPT......... National Periodic Test [*Telecommunications*] (OTD)
NPT......... National Petroleum Corp. Ltd. [*Toronto Stock Exchange symbol*]
NPT......... National Pipe Taper [*Mechanical engineering*]
NPT......... National Pipe Thread (GOBB)
NPT......... National Taper Pipe [*Thread*]
NPT......... Navy Pointer Tracker (MCD)
NPT......... NECO Enterprises, Inc. [*AMEX symbol*] (COMM)
NPT......... Neomycin Phosphotransferase [*An enzyme*]
NPT......... Neoprecipitin Test [*Oncology*]
NPT......... Neopyrithiamine Hydrochloride [*Chemistry*] (DAVI)
NPT......... Network Planning Technique [*Computer science*] (IEEE)
NPT......... Neuroectodermal Pigmented Tumor [*Medicine*] (MELL)
NPT......... Neuropsychiatry
NPT......... Neuropsychiatry Technician [*Navy*]
NPT......... New Periodical Titles [*of British Union Catalogue of Periodicals*]
NPT......... Newport [*Rhode Island*] [*Airport symbol*] (OAG)
NPT......... Newport Ebbw Junction [*British depot code*]
NPT......... New Product Tiers [*Telecommunications*] (OTD)
NPT......... Nocturnal Penile Tumescence [*Psychiatry*]
NPT......... Noise Protection Transformer (SAUS)

NPT .... Non-Packet-making Terminal (SAUS)
NPT .... Non-Packet Mode Terminal (MHDB)
NPT .... Non-Packet-mode Terminal (SAUS)
NPT .... Nonprogrammable Terminal (SAUS)
NPT .... Non-Proliferation Treaty (MUSM)
NPT .... Non-Punch Through (AAEL)
NPT .... Nonpyramidal Tract
NPT .... Normal Pressure and Temperature
NPT .... Nuclear Non-Proliferation Treaty [*United Nations*] (ECON)
NPT .... Nuclear Proliferation Treaty (SAUS)
NPT .... Nucleoside Phosphotransferase (DB)
NPT .... Nuveen Prem Income Muni 4 [*NYSE symbol*] (TTSB)
NPT .... Nuveen Premium Income Municipal Fund IV [*NYSE symbol*] (SPSG)
NPT .... Portland Terminal R. R. Co. [*Formerly, Northern Pacific Terminal R. R.*] [*AAR code*]
NPTA .... National Paper Trade Association (EA)
NPTA .... National Passenger Traffic Association [*Later, NBTA*] (EA)
NPTA .... National Perishable Transportation Association (EA)
NPTA .... National Piano Travelers Association (EA)
NPTA .... National Postal Transport Association [*Later, APWU*]
NPTA .... Nebraska Physical Therapy Association (EARSL)
NPTA .... Nevada Parent Teacher Association (SAUS)
NPTA .... New Periodical Title Abbreviations [*A publication*]
NPTA .... Nordstrom Personal Touch America [*E-mail shopping service*]
NPTC .... National Pipe Thread Coarse (HAWK)
NPTC .... National Postal and Travelers Censorship [*Army*] (AABC)
NPTC .... National Private Truck Council (NTPA)
NPTC .... National Proficiency Test Council (AIE)
NPtc .... Port Chester Public Library, Port Chester, NY [*Library symbol*] [*Library of Congress*] (LCLS)
NPTCO ...... National Postal and Travelers Censorship Organization [*Army*] (AABC)
NPtcU .... United Hospital, Port Chester, NY [*Library symbol*] [*Library of Congress*] (LCLS)
NPTD .... Nitrogen Phosphorus Thermionic Detector [*Instrumentation*]
NPT/E .... Navy Parachute Team / East Coast (DNAB)
NPte .... Port Ewen Free Library, Port Ewen, NY [*Library symbol*] [*Library of Congress*] (LCLS)
NPTF .... National Pipe Thread Fine (SARE)
NPTF .... National Standard Pipe Tapered-Fuel
NPTF .... National Taper Pipe Threads for Dry Seal Pressure Tight Joints
NPTF .... Nuclear Power Task Force
NPTF .... Nuclear Proof Test Facility [*Proposed, but never built*] (NRCH)
NPTFB .... National Park Trust Fund Board [*Later, NPF*]
NPTG .... Nuclear Power Task Group [*Navy*] (MCD)
NPTH .... NeoPath, Inc. [*NASDAQ symbol*] (SAG)
NPTI .... Nissan Performance Technology, Inc.
NPtjer .... Port Jervis Free Public Library, Port Jervis, NY [*Library symbol*] [*Library of Congress*] (LCLS)
NPTL .... National Police Testing Laboratories (EA)
NPTL .... Nuptial (ABBR)
NPTN .... National Pesticide Telecommunication Network (EA)
NPTN .... National Public Telecomputing Network (TNIG)
NPTO .... National Petroleum Technology Office
NPTR .... National Parachute Test Range (MCD)
NPTR .... National Standard Pipe Tapered-Railroad
NPTR .... National Taper Pipe Threads for Railing Fixtures
NPTRE .... Nuclear-Powered Turbo-Reciprocating Engine
NPTRL .... Naval Personnel and Training Research Laboratory [*Formerly, Personnel Research Activity*]
NPTS .... Nationwide Personal Transportation Study [*Department of Transportation*] (GFGA)
NPTS .... Nationwide Personal Transportation Survey [*BTS*] [*FHWA*] (TAG)
NPTS .... Noise Parameter Test System (SAUS)
NPTSM ...... Nepotism (ABBR)
NPTST .... Nepotist (ABBR)
NPTT .... Nocturnal Penile Tumescence Test [*Medicine*] (MELL)
NPTTY .... Neptune Orient Lines Ltd. [*OTCBB symbol*]
NPTU .... Naval Petroleum Training Unit (DNAB)
NPTU .... Neptune Leasing [*Intermodal shipping container symbol*] (TVRC)
NPT/W .... Navy Parachute Team / West Coast (DNAB)
NPtw .... Port Washington Public Library, Port Washington, NY [*Library symbol*] [*Library of Congress*] (LCLS)
NptwDE ..... Daly Elementary School, Port Washington, NY [*Library symbol*] [*Library of Congress*] (LCLS)
NPtwGE ..... Guggenheim Elementary School, Port Washington, NY [*Library symbol*] [*Library of Congress*] (LCLS)
NPtwJSE .... John Philip Sousa Elementary School, Port Washington, NY [*Library symbol*] [*Library of Congress*] (LCLS)
NptwME ..... Manorhaven Elementary School, Port Washington, NY [*Library symbol*] [*Library of Congress*] (LCLS)
NPtwMSE ... Main Street Elementary School, Port Washington, NY [*Library symbol*] [*Library of Congress*] (LCLS)
NPtwSH ..... Paul D. Schreiber High School, Port Washington, NY [*Library symbol*] [*Library of Congress*] (LCLS)
NPtwSSE .... South Salem Elementary School, Port Washington, NY [*Library symbol*] [*Library of Congress*] (LCLS)
NPtwWJ ..... Carrie Palmer Weber Junior High School, Port Washington, NY [*Library symbol*] [*Library of Congress*] (LCLS)
NPTWZI ..... North Pacific Trade Winds Zone Investigation (NOAA)
NPTX .... Newport Steel [*Private rail car owner code*]
NPTZ .... North Pacific Transition Zone [*Marine science*] (OSRA)
NPU .... National Pharmaceutical Union (PDAA)
NPU .... National Postal Union [*Later, APWU*]
NPU .... Naval Parachute Unit
NPU .... Navigation Processor Unit (MCD)
NPU .... Ne Plus Ultra [*No Further; i.e., the pinnacle of attainment*] [*French*]
NPU .... Net Protein Utilization [*Nutrition*]
NPU .... Network Processing Unit
NPU .... Newspaper Press Union (DGA)
NPU .... Nitrogen Pressure Unit (MCD)
NPU .... Nitrogen Purge Unit (MCD)
NPU .... Nordic Postal Union (EA)
NPU .... Not Passed Urine [*Medicine*]
NPUAP ...... National Pressure Ulcer Advisory Panel [*Association*] (EA)
npubl .... no publisher (SAUS)
NPUD .... National Party for Unity and Democracy [*Mauritania*] [*Political party*] (EY)
NPUG .... National Prime User Group (GNE)
NPUI .... Nursing Process Utilization Inventory (DMAA)
NPUP .... National Progressive Unionist Party [*Egypt*] [*Political party*] (PPW)
NPur .... Purchase Free Library, Purchase, NY [*Library symbol*] [*Library of Congress*] (LCLS)
NPurMC ..... Manhattanville College, Purchase, NY [*Library symbol*] [*Library of Congress*] (LCLS)
NPurU .... State University of New York, College at Purchase, Purchase, NY [*Library symbol*] [*Library of Congress*] (LCLS)
NPurW .... Westchester Academy of Medicine, Purchase, NY [*Library symbol*] [*Library of Congress*] (LCLS)
NPV .... Naperville, IL [*Amtrak rail station code*]
NPV .... National Present Volume Method [*Management*]
NPV .... Naturpolitische Volkspartei [*People's Party for Nature Policy*] [*Germany*] [*Political party*] (PPW)
NPV .... Negative Predictive Value [*Experimentation*]
NPV .... Negative Pressure Ventilation [*Medicine*] (MELL)
NPV .... Net Present Value [*Accounting*]
NPV .... New Plymouth Ventures, Inc. [*Vancouver Stock Exchange symbol*]
NPV .... Nitrogen Pressure Valve (KSC)
NPV .... Nonpropulsive Vent (KSC)
NPV .... No Par Value [*Stock exchange term*]
NPV .... Nuclear Polyhedrosis Virus
NPV .... Nuveen VA Prem Inc. Muni Fd [*NYSE symbol*] (TTSB)
NPV .... Nuveen Virginia Premium Income Municipal Fund [*NYSE symbol*] (SPSG)
NPV .... Vassar College, Poughkeepsie, NY [*Library symbol*] [*Library of Congress*] (LCLS)
NPVCE .... Net Present Value for Current Expendable Launch Vehicles [*NASA*] (KSC)
NPVH .... Net Present Value at the Horizon (PDAA)
NPVLA .... National Paint, Varnish, and Lacquer Association [*Later, NPCA*] (EA)
NPV-Mu ..... Vassar College, George Sherman Dickerson Music Library, Poughkeepsie, NY [*Library symbol*] [*Library of Congress*] (LCLS)
NPVNE ...... Net Present Value for New Expendable Launch Vehicles [*NASA*] (KSC)
NPVS .... No-Par-Value Stock [*Stock exchange term*]
NPVSH ...... Net Present Value for Space Shuttle [*NASA*] (KSC)
NPW .... International Union of Allied Novelty and Production Workers
NPW .... National Party of Western Australia [*Political party*]
NPW .... Network for Professional Women [*Hartford, CT*] (EA)
npw .... New-Pool Wildcat (SAUS)
NPW .... Nissan Production Way [*Automotive manufacturing*]
NPW .... No Peace Without Justice [*An association*]
NPW .... Nuveen WA Prem Inc. Muni Fd [*AMEX symbol*] (TTSB)
NPW .... Nuveen Washington Premium Income Municipal Fund [*AMEX symbol*] (SPSG)
NPW .... Nuveen Washington Premium Income Muni Fund [*AMEX symbol*] (NASQ)
NPWA .... National Pure Water Association [*British*]
NPWAC ...... National Parks and Wildlife Advisory Council [*Tasmania, Australia*]
NPwADS .... National Power PLC [*Associated Press*] (SAG)
NPWC .... National Parks and Wildlife Conservation Act (SAUS)
NPWC .... National Press Women's Club (NTCM)
NPWC .... Navy Public Works Center
NPWD .... Navy Public Works Department
NPWFNSW... National Parks and Wildlife Foundation of New South Wales [*Australia*]
NPWIC .... National Prisoner of War Information Center (DOMA)
NPWOA ..... National Piggly Wiggly Operators Association (EA)
NPWRC ..... Northern Prairie Wildlife Research Center [*Jamestown, ND*] [*Department of the Interior*] (GRD)
NPWS .... NATO Planning Workshop (NATG)
NPX .... New Pioneer Exploration [*Vancouver Stock Exchange symbol*]
NPX .... Norpropoxyphene (DB)
NPX .... Numeric Processor Extension (SAUS)
NPX .... Nuveen Ins Prem Inc. Muni 2 [*NYSE symbol*] (TTSB)
NPX .... Nuveen Insured Premium Income Municipal Fund [*NYSE symbol*] (SPSG)
NPY .... Neuropeptide Y [*Biochemistry*]
NPY .... Nuveen PA Prem Inc. Muni 2 [*NYSE symbol*] (TTSB)
NPY .... Nuveen Pennsylvania Premium Income Municipal [*NYSE symbol*] (SPSG)
NPy .... Penn Yan Public Library, Penn Yan, NY [*Library symbol*] [*Library of Congress*] (LCLS)
NPYLI .... Neuropeptide Y-Like Immunoreactivity [*Medicine*] (DB)
NPYR .... Nitrosopyrrolidine [*Also, NYPYR*] [*Organic chemistry*]
NPYRR ...... N-Nitrosopyrrolidine [*Organic chemistry*]
NPZ .... Nevamar Plastic [*Federal Railroad Administration identification code*]
NPZ .... New Plymouth [*New Zealand*] [*Seismograph station code, US Geological Survey*] [*Closed*] (SEIS)
NPZ .... North Pyrenean Zone [*Geology*]
NPZD .... NAPZ Drayage [*Common carrier symbol*]

NQ .... Cumberland Airlines [*ICAO designator*] (AD)
NQ .... Net Quick Assets
NQ .... Neural Quantum [*Theory*] [*Sensory discrimination*]
NQ .... Neurological Quotient (SAUS)
nq .... Nicaragua [*MARC country of publication code*] [*Library of Congress*] (LCCP)
NQ .... Non-Quota Programme (EURO)
NQ .... No Quotations (SAUS)
NQ .... No Quote (SAUS)
NQ .... Northwest Territorial Airlines (SAUS)
NQ .... Notes and Queries [*Medicine*] (EDAA)
NQ .... Quoque Library, Quoque, NY [*Library symbol*] [*Library of Congress*] (LCLS)
NQA .... Memphis, TN [*Location identifier*] [*FAA*] (FAAL)
NQA .... National Quality Award [*LIMRA, NALU*]
NQA .... National Quilting Association (EA)
NQA .... Net Quick Assets
NQA .... No Questions Asked (SAUS)
NQA .... North Carolina Agricultural and Technical State University, Greensboro (SAUS)
NQA .... North Carolina Agricultural and Technical State University, Greensboro, NC [*OCLC symbol*] (OCLC)
NQA .... Nursing Quality Assurance (DMAA)
NQAA .... Nuclear Quality Assurance Agency
NQAPO .... Nuclear Quality Assurance Program Office (SAUS)
NQB .... National Quotation Bureau [*Stock market*]
NQB .... No Qualified Bidders [*Investment term*] (DFIT)
NQC .... NASA Quality Control (KSC)
NQC .... National Quotations Committee [*of the National Association of Securities Dealers*]
NQC .... Nuclear Quality Control (DNAB)
NQC .... Nuveen CA Inv Qual Muni [*NYSE symbol*] (TTSB)
NQC .... Nuveen California Investment Quality Municipal Fund [*NYSE symbol*] (SPSG)
NQCC .... Nuclear Quadrupole Coupling Constant [*Physics*]
NQCRRP .... North Queensland Community Rainforest Reforestation Program (SAUS)
NQD .... Nonquaded [*Telecommunications*] (TEL)
NQD .... Notice of Quality Discrepancy
NQE .... Nuclear Quality Engineering (DNAB)
NQF .... Nuveen FL Inv Qua Muni [*NYSE symbol*] (TTSB)
NQF .... Nuveen Florida Investment Quality Municipal [*NYSE symbol*] (SPSG)
NQHR .... National Quarter Horse Registry (EA)
NQHR .... Netherlands Quarterly of Human Rights [*A publication*] (SAFN)
NQI .... Kingsville, TX [*Location identifier*] [*FAA*] (FAAL)
NQI .... Nuveen Ins Qual Muni [*NYSE symbol*] (TTSB)
NQI .... Nuveen Insured Quality Municipal [*NYSE symbol*] (SPSG)
NQIC .... National Quality Information Centre [*Institute of Quality Assurance*] [*Information service or system*] (IID)
NQJ .... Nuveen New Jersey Investment Quality Municipal [*NYSE symbol*] (SPSG)
NQJ .... Nuveen NJ Inv Qua Muni [*NYSE symbol*] (TTSB)
NQKA .... Northwest Quoin Key Association [*Defunct*] (EA)
NQL .... National Quick Lube Ltd. [*Vancouver Stock Exchange symbol*]
NQL .... Neutral [*Telegraphy*] (PCTE)
NQL .... North Queensland Libraries: A Directory [*Australia*] [*A publication*]
NQL .... Nouveau Quartier Latin [*Paris bookstore*]
NQL .... Nuclear Quadrupole Interaction [*Physics*]
NQLA .... North Queensland Logging Association [*Australia*]
NQLY .... Neutrality [*Telegraphy*] (PCTE)
NQM .... Midway/Henderson Naval Station, HI [*Location identifier*] [*FAA*] (FAAL)
NQM .... Navy Quality Management
NQM .... Nuveen Investment Quality Municipal [*NYSE symbol*] (SPSG)
NQM .... Nuveen Inv Quality Muni [*NYSE symbol*] (TTSB)
NQMFP .... North Queensland Multifunction Polis [*Australia*]
NQN .... Neuquen [*Argentina*] [*Airport symbol*] (OAG)
NQN .... Nuveen New York Investment Quality Municipal Fund [*NYSE symbol*] (SPSG)
NQN .... Nuveen NY Inv Qual Muni [*NYSE symbol*] (TTSB)
NQN .... Transportes Aereos Neuquen [*Argentina*] [*ICAO designator*] (FAAC)
NQNS .... Notes & Queries, New Series (SAUS)
NQO .... Nitroquinoline Oxide [*Organic chemistry*]
NQOC .... Not Quite our Class (ODA)
NQOKD .... Not Quite Our Kind, Dear (SAUS)
NQOS .... Not Quite Our Sort (IIA)
NQOT .... Not Quite Our Type (SAUS)
NQP .... Nuveen PA Inv Qua Muni [*NYSE symbol*] (TTSB)
NQP .... Nuveen Pennsylvania Investment Quality Municipal [*NYSE symbol*] (SPSG)
NQPA .... National Quarter Pony Association (EA)
NQPC .... National Quartz Producers Council (EA)
NQPP .... National Quarantine Publicity Program [*Australia*]
NQR .... New Quebec Raglan Mines Ltd. [*Toronto Stock Exchange symbol*]
NQR .... Non-Quadratic Residues (MHDB)
NQR .... Nuclear Quadruple Resonance (SAUS)
NQR .... Nuclear Quadrupole Resonance [*Frequencies*]
NQRC .... National Quadraphonic Radio Committee
NQRC .... National Quality Research Center [*University of Michigan*] (RCD)
NQR Frequency ... Nuclear Quadrupole Resonance Frequency (SAUS)
NQRL .... Nor-Quest Resources Ltd. (SAUS)
NQRLF .... Nor-Quest Resources Ltd. [*NASDAQ symbol*] (COMM)
NQRR .... Nuclear Quadrupole Resonance Response
NQRS .... Nuclear Quadrupole Resonance Spectroscopy (SAUS)
NQS .... Nuveen Select Quality Municipal [*NYSE symbol*] (SPSG)
NQS .... Nuveen Select Qual Muni [*NYSE symbol*] (TTSB)
NQSH .... Network Shipping [*Common carrier symbol*]
NQSO .... Nonqualified Stock Options (WYGK)
NQSQ .... Nonqualified Stock Option (SAUS)
NQT .... Network Quality Tester (NITA)
NQT .... Newly Qualified to Teach (GFGA)
NQT .... Nonlanguage Qualification Test
NQT .... Nor-Quest Resources Ltd. [*Vancouver Stock Exchange symbol*]
NQTGCA .... North Queensland Tobacco Growers Cooperative Association [*Australia*]
NQ Theory ... Neural Quantum Theory (SAUS)
NQTV .... North Queensland Television [*Australia*]
NQU .... Not Quite Us [*Lower in social status*] [*Slang*] [*British*]
NQU .... Nuqui [*Colombia*] [*Airport symbol*] (OAG)
NQU .... Nuveen Qual Income Muni Fd [*NYSE symbol*] (TTSB)
NQU .... Nuveen Quality Income Municipal Fund [*NYSE symbol*] (SPSG)
NQWMI .... Non-Q-Wave Myocardial Infarction [*Cardiology*] (CPH)
NQX .... Key West, FL [*Location identifier*] [*FAA*] (FAAL)
NQY .... Newquay [*England*] [*Airport symbol*] (OAG)
NR .... Bosanquet and Puller's New Reports, English Common Pleas [*1804-07*] [*A publication*] (DLA)
NR .... CSE Aviation Ltd. (SAUS)
nr .... Do Not Repeat [*Medicine*] (BCRP)
NR .... Nachrichtenregiment [*Signal Regiment*] [*German military - World War II*]
NR .... Narrow Resonance [*Nuclear energy*] (NRCH)
NR .... Natal Reports [*South Africa*] [*A publication*] (DLA)
NR .... National Range
NR .... National Recovery Act
NR .... National Recovery Administration [*Voided by Supreme Court, 1935*]
NR .... National Register (COE)
NR .... National Report (OICC)
NR .... National Reporter [*Maritime Law Book Co. Ltd.*] [*Canada*] [*Information service or system*] (CRD)
NR .... National Reserve [*British military*] (DMA)
NR .... NATO Restricted (NATG)
NR .... Natural Resources
NR .... Natural Rubber
NR .... Nauru [*ANSI two-letter standard code*] (CNC)
NR .... Naval Rating
NR .... Naval Reactors (GAAI)
NR .... Naval Reserve
NR .... Navigational RADAR
NR .... Navy Regulations
NR .... Near (EY)
nr .... Near (VRA)
NR .... Ned-Lloyd Road Cargo [*Intermodal shipping container symbol*] (TVRC)
NR .... Negative Resistance [*Electronics*]
NR .... Negligible Risk (MELL)
NR .... Nerve Root (MELL)
NR .... Net Register [*Shipping*]
NR .... Neural Retina [*Ophthalmology*]
NR .... Neutral oil, Richmond [*Fuels and lubricants*]
NR .... Neutral Red [*An indicator*]
NR .... Neutral-Reverse [*Automotive engineering*]
NR .... Neutron Radiography (SAUS)
NR .... Neuwied [*Rhein*] [*German license plate city code*]
NR .... Newhall Resources (SAUS)
NR .... Newpark Resources [*NYSE symbol*] (TTSB)
NR .... New Range (IAA)
NR .... New Reports [*1862-65*] [*England*] [*A publication*] (DLA)
NR .... New Republic (SAUS)
NR .... New River Railway [*Federal Railroad Administration identification code*]
NR .... Next Renewal
NR .... Next to Reading Matter [*Also, NRM*] [*Advertising*] (NTCM)
NR .... Nicaraguan Resistance [*An association*] (EA)
NR .... Nicolaus Rufulus [*Flourished, 13th century*] [*Authority cited in pre-1607 legal work*] (DSA)
NR .... Nicotinamide Riboside (SAUS)
nr .... Nigeria [*MARC country of publication code*] [*Library of Congress*] (LCCP)
NR .... Nigeria Regiment [*British military*] (DMA)
NR .... Nitrate Reductase [*An enzyme*]
NR .... Nitrile Resin (SAUS)
NR .... Nitrile Rubber [*Organic chemistry*]
NR .... Nodal Rhythm [*Cardiology*] (DAVI)
NR .... No-Good Recording (SAUS)
NR .... Noise Rating (NASA)
NR .... Noise Ratio
NR .... Noise Ration
NR .... Noise Reduction (IAA)
NR .... Noise-Reduction (SAUS)
nr .... Noise Reduction [*Construction term*] (MIST)
NR .... Non-AM [*Automated Meter*] Read - Regular Hours [*Electric utility company*]
NR .... Nonconformance Report [*Nuclear energy*] (NRCH)
NR .... Nonlinear Resistance (IAA)
NR .... Nonradiative (SAUS)
NR .... Nonradioactive (SAUS)
NR .... Nonrated
NR .... Nonreactive [*Relay*]
NR .... Nonrebreathing [*Medicine*] (AAMN)
nr .... Non Recorded [*Genealogy*] (GEAB)

NR .... Nonrecoverable (IEEE)
NR .... Non-Recurring (ACAE)
NR .... Nonreduced (SAUS)
NR .... Nonredundancy (SAUS)
NR .... Nonrefundable [*Airline fare code*]
NR .... Nonregistered (AABC)
NR .... Nonreimbursement (SAUS)
NR .... Non Repetatur [*Do Not Repeat*] [*Pharmacy*]
NR .... Nonresident [*British*]
NR .... Nonresponder [*Strain of mice*]
NR .... Non-Response (WDMC)
NR .... Nonreturnable [*Beverage bottles*]
NR .... Nonreversing (IAA)
NR .... Nonspecific Gene Resistance [*Genetics*]
NR .... No Radiation (MAE)
NR .... NORAD Region (IAA)
NR .... No Rate [*Travel industry*] (TVEL)
N/R .... No Record (AAG)
NR .... No Record (CARL)
NR .... No Recurrence (SAUS)
NR .... No Refill [*Pharmacy*]
NR .... No Release (AAG)
NR .... No Remittance
NR .... No Report [*Medicine*]
NR .... No Requirement
NR .... No Residency Requirement [*Voter registration*]
NR .... No Respiration (MELL)
NR .... No Response [*Medicine*]
NR .... No Return (SAUS)
NR .... Norfolk Rangers [*British military*] (DMA)
NR .... Norgold Russet Potato
NR .... No Risk [*Business term*]
NR .... Normal (MAE)
NR .... Normal Range
N-R .... Normal-Rebroadcast (SAUS)
NR .... Normal Record [*Medicine*] (DAVI)
NR .... Normal Responder
NR .... Normotensive Rat [*Medicine*] (DMAA)
nr .... norm-referenced (SAUS)
NR .... Northern Railway [*Indian Railway*] (TIR)
NR .... Northern Range [*Navigation*]
NR .... Northern Rhodesia [*Later, Zambia*]
NR .... North Riding [*England*] (ROG)
NR .... North River [*New York, New Jersey*]
NR .... Northward Aviation Ltd. (MHDW)
NR .... Nose Right [*Aviation*] (MCD)
N/R .... Notes Receivable
NR .... Notice of Rating Required [*Civil Service*]
N/R .... Notice of Readiness [*Shipping*]
NR .... Not Ranked (SAUS)
NR .... Not Rated
NR .... Not Readable
NR .... Not Recommended (SAUS)
NR .... Not Recorded
N/R .... Not Remarkable [*Medicine*]
NR .... Not Repeat (SAUS)
NR .... Not Reported
NR .... Not Required
NR .... Not Resolved (MAE)
N/R .... Not Responsible For
NR .... Nuchal Rigidity [*Medicine*]
NR .... Nuclear Radiation
NR .... Nuclear Radiology [*Medical specialty*] (DHSM)
NR .... Nuclear Reaction (SAUS)
NR .... Nuclear Reactor
NR .... Nuclear Reporting (SAUS)
NR .... Nuclear Research Submarine (MCD)
NR .... Nuestra Remesa [*Our Remittance*] [*Spanish*] [*Business term*]
NR .... Nufort Resources, Inc. [*Toronto Stock Exchange symbol*]
NR .... Number (AAG)
NR .... Number of Report (SAUS)
NR .... Number of Runs
NR .... Nurse
NR .... Nursing Representative [*Red Cross*]
NR .... Nursing Services (HCT)
NR .... Nutritive Ratio
NR .... Nystagmus Recorder
NR .... Reynold's Number [*Viscosity*] (MAE)
NR .... Rochester Public Library, Rochester, NY [*Library symbol*] [*Library of Congress*] (LCLS)
nr--- .... Rocky Mountain Region [*MARC geographic area code*] [*Library of Congress*] (LCCP)
NR .... Submersible Research Vehicle (Nuclear Propulsion) [*Navy ship symbol*]
NRA .... Coupeville, WA [*Location identifier*] [*FAA*] (FAAL)
NRA .... Narrandera [*Australia*] [*Airport symbol*] (OAG)
NRA .... NASA Research Announcement
NRA .... National Racing Authority (NADA)
NRA .... National Reclamation Association [*Later, National Water Resources Association*] (EA)
NRA .... National Record of Achievement [*British*] (DET)
NRA .... National Recovery Act
NRA .... National Recovery Administration [*Voided by Supreme Court, 1935*]
NRA .... National Recreation Area [*National Park Service*] (GFGA)
NRA .... National Recreation Association [*Later, NRPA*] (EA)
NRA .... National Reform Association (EA)
NRA .... National Register of Archives [*Historical Manuscripts Commission*] [*British*]
NRA .... National Rehabilitation Association (EA)
NRA .... National Remodelers Association [*Later, NARI*]
NRA .... National Renderers Association (EA)
NRA .... National Republican Alliance [*Australia*]
NRA .... National Resistance Army [*Uganda*] (PD)
NRA .... National Restaurant Association (EA)
NRA .... National Retirement Association [*Australia*]
NRA .... National Rifle Association (NADA)
NRA .... National Rifle Association of America (EA)
NRA .... National Rivers Authority [*British*]
NRA .... National Roads Authority [*1997*] [*Malawi*]
NRA .... National Roommate Association [*Later, ASRS*] (EA)
NRA .... National Rounders Association [*British*] (BI)
NRA .... NATO Refugees Agency (NATG)
NRA .... Naval Radio Activity
NRA .... Naval Reserve Association (EA)
NRA .... Navy Recruiting Area (DNAB)
NRA .... Negative Resistance Amplifier (PDAA)
NRA .... Net Rentable Area (ADA)
NRA .... Network Resolution Area
NRA .... Never Refuse Anything (SAUS)
NRA .... New Era Development Ltd. [*Vancouver Stock Exchange symbol*]
NRA .... New Regional Airliner
NRA .... Nitra Air [*Slovakia*] [*FAA designator*] (FAAC)
NRA .... Nitrate Reductase (DB)
NRA .... Non-Recurrrence Action (SAA)
NRA .... Nonredundant Array
NRA .... Nonregistered Accountable [*Military*]
NRA .... Nonresident Alien
NRA .... No Repair Action [*Military*]
NRA .... Normal Retirement Age
NRA .... North River [*Alaska*] [*Seismograph station code, US Geological Survey*] (SEIS)
NRA .... Northrop Radio Service, Inc. (SAUS)
NRA .... Nothing Recorded Against [*Security investigation result*] [*British*]
NRA .... Nuclear Radiation Absorber
NRA .... Nuclear Radiation Absorber (or Adsorber) (SAUS)
NRA .... Nuclear Reaction Analysis
NRA .... Nuclear Regulatory Agency
NRA .... Nuclear Reserved Area (SAUS)
NRA .... Nucleus Raphe Alatus [*Neurology*]
NRA .... Nucleus Retroambigualis [*Neurology*] (DAVI)
NRA .... St. Augustines College, Raleigh (SAUS)
NRA .... St. Augustine's College, Raleigh, NC [*OCLC symbol*] (OCLC)
NRAA .... National Railway Appliances Association [*Later, REMSA*] (EA)
NRAA .... National Rehabilitation Administration Association (NTPA)
NRAA .... National Renal Administrators Association (EA)
NRAA .... National Rifle Association of America
NRAA-PAC .... National Renal Administrators Association PAC [*Washington, DC*] (PACS)
NRAB .... American Baptist Historical Society, Rochester, NY [*Library symbol*] [*Library of Congress*] (LCLS)
NRAB .... National Railroad Adjustment Board
NRAB .... National Railroad Adjustment Board Awards [*A publication*] (DLA)
NRAB .... Naval Reserve Aviation Base
NRAB (1st D) .... United States National Railroad Adjustment Board Awards, First Division [*A publication*] (DLA)
NRAB (2d D) .... United States National Railroad Adjustment Board Awards, Second Division [*A publication*] (DLA)
NRAB (3d D) .... United States National Railroad Adjustment Board Awards, Third Division [*A publication*] (DLA)
NRAB (4th D) .... United States National Railroad Adjustment Board Awards, Fourth Division [*A publication*] (DLA)
NRAC .... National Resources Analysis Center
NRAC .... National Rural Advisory Council (NADA)
NRAC .... Natural Resources Audit Council
NRAC .... Naval Research Advisory Committee
NRACCO .... Navy Regional Air Cargo Central [*or Control*] Office
NRAD .... National Racquetball Association of the Deaf (EA)
NRaD .... Naval Research and Development (SAUS)
NRAD .... No Risk After Discharge [*Shipping*]
NRADUSA .... National Racquetball Association of the Deaf of the USA [*Later, NRAD*] (EA)
NRAF .... Naval Reserve Auxiliary Field
NRAF .... Navy Recruiting Aids Facility (DNAB)
NRAF .... Nonrheumatic Atrial Fibrillation [*Medicine*] (MELL)
NRAF .... Not Running at Finish [*Automobile racing*]
NRAG .... Naval Research Advisory Group (KSC)
NRAHTA .... Northern Rockies Alaska Highway Tourism Association [*Canada*] (EAIO)
NRAI .... National Residential Appraisers Institute (EA)
NRAL .... New York State Appellate Division, Law Library, Rochester, NY [*Library symbol*] [*Library of Congress*] (LCLS)
NRAL .... No Risk after Landing (MARI)
NRALCC .... Northern Region Airlift Control Center (SAUS)
NRALD .... Northern Region Airlift Division (SAUS)
NRAM .... Non-Volatile Random Access Memory [*Computer science*]
NRAMEG .... National Restaurant Association Marketing Executives Group [*Defunct*] (EA)
NRAMRG .... National Restaurant Association Market Research Group [*Defunct*] (EA)

NR & HC.... National Rivers and Harbors Congress [*Later, WRC*]
NRans....... Ransomville Free Library, Ransomville, NY [*Library symbol*] [*Library of Congress*] (LCLS)
NRAO........ National Radio Astronomy Observatory [*Charlottesville, VA*] [*National Science Foundation*] (GRD)
NRAO........ Navy Regional Accounts Office
NRAP........ Naturally Radioactive Product (NRCH)
NRAS........ National Radio Astronomy Observatory [*Charlottesville, VA*] [*National Science Foundation*] (GRD)
NRAS........ Navy Readiness Analysis System
nras.......... No Risk after Shipment (MARI)
NRAS........ Nuclear Release Authentication System [*Seventh Army*] (AABC)
NRASF....... National Registry of Ambulatory Surgical Facilities (EA)
NRAT........ Nonrationed (AABC)
NRB.......... Mayport, FL [*Location identifier*] [*FAA*] (FAAL)
NRB.......... Nara [*Language symbol*] (ETLW)
NRB.......... National Religious Broadcasters (EA)
NRB.......... National Research Bureau [*Commercial firm*] (EA)
NRB.......... National Resources Board [*Terminated, 1935; functions transferred to National Resources Committee*]
NRB.......... National Roads Board (NADA)
NRB.......... Natural Rubber Bureau [*Later, MRB*] (EA)
NRB.......... Naval Reactor Branch (MUGU)
NRB.......... Naval Repair Base
NRB.......... Navy Recruiting Bureau
NRB.......... Navy Reservation Bureau
NRB.......... Nerve Root Block (MELL)
NRB.......... New Redundancy Benefit [*To reduce unemployment*] [*British*]
NRB.......... Nonconformance Review Board [*Nuclear Regulatory Commission*] (NRCH)
NRB.......... Nonrejoining Break [*Medicine*] (DMAA)
NRB.......... Non-Reportable Birth [*Medicine*] (MEDA)
NRB.......... Normalized Relative Backscatter (ARMP)
NRB.......... Northern Research Basins (SAUS)
NRB.......... Nuclear Reactors Branch [*AEC*]
NRB.......... Nuclear Resonance Broadening (SAUS)
NRB1CL..... Nuclear Reactor Operator, First-Class Badge [*Military decoration*] (GFGA)
NRB2CL..... Nuclear Reactor Operator, Second-Class Badge [*Military decoration*] (GFGA)
NRBA........ National Radio Broadcasters Association [*NAB*] [*Absorbed by*] (EA)
NRBA........ National Registered Builders Association [*British*] (DBA)
NRBBAS..... Nuclear Reactor Operator, Basic Badge [*Military decoration*] (GFGA)
NRBC........ National Rare Blood Club [*Later, NRBC/NYBC*] (EA)
NRBC........ Normal Red Blood Cell [*Medicine*] (DMAA)
NRBC........ Nucleated Red Blood Cell
NRBC/NYBC... National Rare Blood Club/New York Blood Center (EA)
NRBE........ Native Races of the British Empire [*A publication*]
NRBF........ Normalized Radial Basis Function (IDAI)
NRBF........ Number of Rounds between Failures [*Quality control*] (MCD)
NRBL........ Bausch & Lomb, Inc., Rochester, NY [*Library symbol*] [*Library of Congress*] (LCLS)
NRBL-S..... Bausch & Lomb, Inc., SOFLENS Division, Technical Information Center, Rochester, NY [*Library symbol*] [*Library of Congress*] (LCLS)
NRBP........ Natural Resource-Based Product
NRBP........ New Reports of Bosanquet and Puller [*A publication*] (DLA)
NRBQ........ New Rhythm and Blues Quartet [*Rock music group*]
NRBQ........ Nurses' Registration Board of Queensland [*Australia*]
NRBS........ Navy Recruiting Branch Station (DNAB)
NRBS........ Nonrebreathing System [*Medicine*] (DAVI)
NRBSUPV... Nuclear Reactor Operator, Shift Supervisor Badge [*Military decoration*] (GFGA)
NRC.......... Crows Landing, CA [*Location identifier*] [*FAA*] (FAAL)
NRC.......... NAC RE Corp. [*NYSE symbol*] (SAG)
NRC.......... National Racquetball Club (EA)
NRC.......... National Radio Club [*Defunct*] (EA)
NRC.......... National Radio Conference [*Broadcast regulations*] (NTCM)
NRC.......... National Railroad Construction and Maintenance Association, Inc. (EA)
NRC.......... National Ramah Commission (EA)
NRC.......... National Reading Conference (EA)
NRC.......... National Realty Club [*New York, NY*] (EA)
NRC.......... National Realty Committee [*Washington, DC*] (EA)
NRC.......... National Reconditioning Order [*National Weather Service*] (USDC)
NRC.......... National Recording Club [*Equine term*] (TED)
NRC.......... National Records Center
NRC.......... National Recycling Coalition (EA)
NRC.......... National Recycling Corp. (EFIS)
NRC.......... National Redemption Council [*Ghana*]
NRC.......... National Referral Center [*Defunct*] (EA)
NRC.......... National Register Criteria (COE)
NRC.......... National Rehabilitation Center (MELL)
NRC.......... National Remodelers Council [*Later, NAHB/RC*] (EA)
NRC.......... National Replacement Character (AGLO)
NRC.......... National Reprographic Centre for Documentation [*British*]
NRC.......... National Republican Club (EA)
NRC.......... National Republican Convention [*Nigeria*] [*Political party*]
NRC.......... National Research Center (NATG)
NRC.......... National Research Corp.
NRC.......... National Research Council [*National Academy of Sciences*] [*Washington, DC*]
NRC.......... National Research Council, Canada [*Research center*] (IRC)
NRC.......... National Research Council of Canada (IID)
NRC.......... National Resistance Committee (EA)
NRC.......... National Resource Center for Paraprofessionals in Special Education and Related Human Services (EA)
NRC.......... National Resources Committee [*Functions transferred to National Resources Planning Board*]
NRC.......... National Response Center [*Environmental Protection Agency*]
NRC.......... National Retreat Centre [*British*] (CB)
NRC.......... National Riding Committee [*Later, ANRC*] (EA)
NRC.......... National Rocket Club [*Later, NSC*]
NRC.......... National Rural Center (EA)
NRC.......... Natural Resources Center [*University of Alabama*] [*Research center*] (RCD)
NRC.......... Natural Resources Council of America (EA)
NRC.......... Natural Rights Center (EA)
NRC.......... Naval Radio Compass (IAA)
NRC.......... Naval Radiological Control (DNAB)
NRC.......... Naval Records Club [*Later, INRO*]
NRC.......... Naval Recreation Center (DNAB)
NRC.......... Naval Research Co. - Reserves
NRC.......... Naval Retraining Command
NRC.......... Navy Reconnaissance Center (MCD)
NRC.......... Navy Recruiting Command (DNAB)
NRC.......... Navy Reserve Centers (NVT)
NRC.......... Negative Resistance Characteristic [*Electrophysiology*]
NRC.......... Neotectonics Research Centre [*Brunel University*] [*United Kingdom*] (RCD)
NRC.......... Nerve Root Canal (MELL)
NRC.......... Nerve Root Compression (MELL)
NRC.......... Netherlands Red Cross
NRC.......... Net Replacement Cost [*Accounting*]
NRC.......... Networking Routing Center (MHDB)
NRC.......... Network Reliability Coordinator
NRC.......... Neuroscience Research Center [*University of Texas--Houston Health Science Center*] (RCD)
NRC.......... Neutron Radiation Capture
NRC.......... Newfoundland Safety Council (SAUS)
NRC.......... Newport Research Corp. (SAUS)
NRC.......... New Research Centers [*A publication*]
NRC.......... New Right Coalition (EA)
NRC.......... Newspaper Research Council (EA)
NRC.......... Nichols Research Corporation (ACAE)
NRC.......... Nigerian Railway Corp. (SAUS)
NRC.......... Nitrogen Consumption Rate (DB)
NRC.......... Noise-Rating Curve (OA)
NRC.......... Noise Reduction Circuitry (SAUS)
NRC.......... Noise Reduction Coefficient [*of insulation*]
NRC.......... Non-Railway Customer [*Indian Railway*] (TIR)
NRC.......... Nonrecurring Change (SAUS)
NRC.......... Nonrecurring Charge (SAUS)
NRC.......... Non-Recurring Charges (SAUS)
NRC.......... Nonrecurring Connection (SAUS)
NRC.......... Nonrecurring Costs [*Accounting*] (KSC)
NRC.......... Nonrecurring Recoupment Charge (ACAE)
NRC.......... Nonreusable Container (SAUS)
NRC.......... Non-Reusable Containers (GNE)
NRC.......... Non-unit-Related Cargo (DOMA)
NRC.......... Noranda Research Center (SAUS)
NRC.......... Norco Resources [*Vancouver Stock Exchange symbol*]
NRC.......... No Record [*Travel industry*] (TVEL)
NRC.......... Normal Rated Current (SAUS)
NRC.......... Normal Retinal Correspondence
NRC.......... North Carolina State University, Raleigh, NC [*OCLC symbol*] (OCLC)
NRC.......... Norwegian Refugee Council
NRC.......... Norwegian Research Council (SAUS)
NRC.......... Notch Root Contraction (OA)
NRC.......... Not Recommended for Children (ADA)
NRC.......... Not Routine Care [*Medicine*]
NRC.......... Nuclear Radiation Center [*Washington State University*] [*Research center*] (RCD)
NRC.......... Nuclear Reactor Control (SAUS)
NRC.......... Nuclear Recycling Consultants (EA)
NRC.......... Nuclear Regulatory Commission [*Washington, DC*]
NRC.......... Nuclear Reporting Cell (SAUS)
NRC.......... Nuclear Research Council
NRC.......... Nurses for the Rights of the Child (SAUS)
NRC.......... Nutrition-Related Complications [*Medicine*]
NRC.......... US National Research Council (SAUS)
NRCA........ National Reamer Collectors Association (EA)
NRCA........ National Rebel Class Association (EA)
NRCA........ National Recovery and Collection Association (EA)
NRCA........ National Redbone Coonhound Association (EA)
NRCA........ National Refrigeration Contractors Association (NTPA)
NRCA........ National Rehabilitation Counseling Association (EA)
NRCA........ National Resources Council of America
NRCA........ National Retail Credit Association [*Later, ICA*]
NRCA........ National Roofing Contractors Association (EA)
NRCA........ Nonconformance Reporting and Corrective Action (SAUS)
NRC-ACAC... National Research Council Army Countermine Advisory Committee
NRCAR...... Nuclear Regulatory Commission Acquisition Regulation (AAGC)
NRC BAST... National Research Council Board on Army Science and Technology
NRCC........ National Registry in Clinical Chemistry (EA)
NRCC........ National Registry of Clinical Chemists (SARE)
NRCC........ National Republican Coalition for Choice (EA)
NRCC........ National Republican Congressional Committee (EA)
NRCC........ National Research Council of Canada

NRCC .... National Resource for Computation in Chemistry [*Lawrence Berkeley Laboratory*] [*Terminated, 1981*]
NRCC .... Naval Regional Contracting Center (AAGC)
NRCC .... NORAD Region Combat Center [*Military*]
NRCC .... Northeast Regional Climate Center [*Cornell University*] (RCD)
NRCCL ...... Norwegian Research Centre for Computers and Law (NITA)
NRCCLS..... National Resource Center for Consumers of Legal Services (EA)
NRCCS ...... National Research Council Committee on Salmonella (EA)
NRCD........ National Redemption Council Decree [*Ghana*] [*A publication*] (DLA)
NRCd .... National Reprographic Centre for Documentation [*Hatfield Polytechnic Institute*] [*Hertfordshire, England*] [*Evaluation and information group*] [*Information service or system*]
NRCd .... National Reprographic Centre for Documentation Study (NITA)
NRCDA ...... North Region Cooperative Development Agency [*British*]
NRCDES..... National Research Council Division of Earth Sciences [*Marine science*] (OSRA)
NRC/DME ... National Research Council of Canada, Division of Mechanical Engineering [*Research center*] (RCD)
NRCE .... Natural Resource Conservation Education [*USDA Forest Service*] (ALAC)
NRCEP ...... Natural Resource Conservation Education Program [*USDA Forest Service*] (ALAC)
NRCF .... Not Reconfirmed [*Travel industry*] (TVEL)
NRC/GT ..... National Research Center on the Gifted and Talented (RCD)
NRCHB ...... Naval Reserve Cargo-Handling Battalion
NRCHMI..... National Resource Center on Homelessness and Mental Illness (EA)
NRCHTB..... Naval Reserve Cargo-Handling Training Battalion
NRCI......... National Radio Co., Inc. (IAA)
NRCI......... National Rainbow Coalition, Inc. (EA)
NRCI......... National Red Cherry Institute (EA)
NRCI......... Nuclear Regulatory Commission Issuances [*A publication*] (DLA)
NRCL......... National Research Council Library (DIT)
NRCL......... Nonrenal Clearance [*Medicine*] (DMAA)
NRCLS ...... National Resource Center for Consumers of Legal Services (DLA)
NRCLSE..... National Resource for Computers in Life Science Education (SAUS)
NRC-MAC... National Research Council - Mine Advisory Committee
NRC/MAI.... National Railroad Construction and Maintenance Association, Inc. (EA)
NRCMC...... National Resource Center for Minority Contractors (EA)
NRCMCA.... National Radiator Core Manufacturing Credit Association [*Later, NRMCA*] (EA)
NRCMF...... NRC Master File (NITA)
NRC-NAS ... National Research Council - National Academy of Sciences (AAG)
NRCP........ National Research Council for the Philippines (CARB)
NRCP........ Nonreinforced Concrete Pipe [*Technical drawings*]
NRCP........ Norcap Financial Corp. (SAUS)
NRC PAC.... National Railroad Construction and Maintenance Association PAC [*Washington, DC*] (PACS)
NRCPR ...... Nuclear Regulatory Commission Procurement Regulation (AAGC)
NRCPS ...... National Research Council on Peace Strategy (EA)
NRCR........ Colgate-Rochester Divinity School, Rochester, NY [*Library symbol*] [*Library of Congress*] (LCLS)
NRCR........ Northern Railway of Costa Rica (SAUS)
NR Crit...... Nuclear Rocket Critical (SAUS)
NRC RRC ... NRC Report Review Committee (SAUS)
NRCS........ National Resources Conservation Service (PA)
NRCS........ National Roller Canary Society [*British*] (BI)
NRCS........ Natural Resources Conservation Service
NRCS........ Normalized RADAR Cross Section
NRCS........ Normalized Radar Cross-Section (SAUS)
NRCS........ Nuclear Reactor Control System (SAUS)
NRCS........ United States Natural Resources Conservation Service
NRCSA ...... National Registration Center for Study Abroad (EA)
NRCSA ...... Neurological Resources Center of South Australia
NRCSE ...... National Research Center for Statistics and the Environment [*University of Washington*] (RCD)
NRCSL ...... National Research Center on Student Learning [*University of Pittsburgh*] [*Research center*] (RCD)
NRCSM...... Narcisism (ABBR)
NRCST ...... Narcisist (ABBR)
NRCST ...... National Referral Center for Science and Technology (MCD)
NRCT........ National Registry of Childhood Tumors [*British*]
NRCT........ National Rehabilitation Centers (EFIS)
NRCT........ National Research Council of Thailand (CARB)
NRCTK ...... Narcotic (ABBR)
NRC-TOX.... National Research Council - Committee on Toxicology
NRCV........ Consolidated Vacuum Corp., Rochester, NY [*Library symbol*] [*Library of Congress*] (LCLS)
NRCWA...... National Resource Center on Women and AIDS [*Acquired Immune Deficiency Syndrome*] (EA)
NRCX........ New Retail Concepts, Inc. (SAUS)
NRCX........ Nuclear Regulary Commission (EBF)
NRCY........ Not Received Yet (SAUS)
NRCYS ...... National Resource Center for Youth Services (EA)
NRCZ........ Northern Rail Car [*Federal Railroad Administration identification code*]
NRD .... Aeronardi SpA [*Italy*] [*ICAO designator*] (FAAC)
NRD .... National Range Division [*Air Force*]
NRD .... National Range Documentation (MUGU)
NRD .... National Registered Designer [*British*]
NRD .... Natural Resource Damage [*Environmental science*]
NRD .... Natural Resources Division [*An association*] (EAIO)
NRD .... Naval Radio Direction Finder (IAA)
NRD .... Naval Recruiting Department [*British military*] (DMA)
NRD .... Naval Research and Development (KSC)
NRD .... Navy Recruiting District (DNAB)
NRD .... Negative Resistance Diode
NRD .... Nerve Root Damage (MELL)
NRD .... Nominal Rim Diameter [*Automotive engineering*]
NRD .... Nonradiative Dielectric (SAUS)
NRD .... Nonrenal Death (MAE)
NRD .... Nonreplenishable Demand
NRD .... Norderney [*Germany*] [*Airport symbol*] (OAG)
NRD .... Nordlingen [*Federal Republic of Germany*] [*Seismograph station code, US Geological Survey*] [*Closed*] (SEIS)
NRD .... Nord Resources [*NYSE symbol*] (TTSB)
NRD .... Nord Resources Corp. [*NYSE symbol*] (SPSG)
NRD .... No Record of Destination [*Aviation*]
NRD .... Normal Retirement Date
NR/D......... Not Required, but Desired
NRD .... Nuclear Radiation Detector
NRD .... Nucleus Raphe Dorsalis [*Neuroanatomy*]
NRD .... Office of Naval Research and Development
NRDA........ Natural Resource Damage Assessment [*USDA Forest Service*] (ALAC)
NRDA........ Nevada Research and Development Area (SAUS)
NRDB........ National Residue Database
NRDB........ Nonreversing, Dynamic Braking (IAA)
NRDC........ N-Arginine Dibasic Convertase [*An enzyme*]
NRDC........ Natick Research and Development Center [*Army*] (INF)
NRDC........ National Research & Development Corp. [*Later, BTG*] [*British*]
NRDC........ National Resources Defence Council (ECON)
NRDC........ National Respiratory Disease Conference (DAVI)
NRDC........ National Retail Distribution Certificate [*British*]
NRDC........ National Running Data Center, Inc. [*Defunct*] (EA)
NRDC........ Natural Resources Defense Council (EA)
NRDC........ Navy Relief Society, Washington, DC, Auxiliary
NRDC........ Navy Research and Development Committee
NRDCA...... National Roof Deck Contractors Association (EA)
NRDEC ...... Natick Research Development and Engineering Center [*Army*] (INF)
NRDF........ Non-Recursive Digital File (NITA)
NRDF........ Nonrecursive Digital Filter [*Navy*]
NRDFS ...... Naval Radio Direction Finder Service
NRDI......... National Rural Development Institute (EA)
NRDL........ Naval Radiological Defense Laboratory
NRDL........ Navy Radiological Defense Laboratory (DNAB)
NRDLS ...... National Rural Development Leaders School (OICC)
NRDM .... NRD Mining Ltd. (SAUS)
NRDM .... Nuclear Weapons Reconnaissance Data Manual (COE)
NRDO........ National Research and Development Organization (WDAA)
NRDO........ Navy Radio (NOAA)
NRDP........ National Rural Development Partnership
NRDR........ Consolidated NRD Resources Ltd. (SAUS)
NRDR........ Non-Resetting Data Reconstruction (PDAA)
NRDR-CF... Non-Resetting Data Reconstruction with Continuous Feedback (PDAA)
NRDR-CF... Non-Resetting Data Reconstructor with Continuous Feedback (SAUS)
NRDR-DF... Non-Resetting Data Reconstruction with Digital Feedback (SAUS)
NRDR-DF... Non-Resetting Data Reconstruction with Discrete Feedback (PDAA)
NRDR-DF... Non-Resetting Data Reconstructor with Digital Feedback (SAUS)
NRDS........ Neonatal Respiratory Distress Syndrome [*Medicine*] (MELL)
NRDS........ Nuclear Rocket Detection System [*NASA*]
NRDS........ Nuclear Rocket Development Station
NRDSCG .... Naval Research and Development Satellite Communications Group (SAA)
NRDU-V..... Navy Research and Development Unit - Vietnam (MCD)
NRDX........ Nordic Warehouse [*Private rail car owner code*]
NRE.......... Aviones Are, SA de CV [*Mexico*] [*FAA designator*] (FAAC)
NRE.......... Eastman Kodak Co., Rochester, NY [*Library symbol*] [*Library of Congress*] (LCLS)
NRE.......... National Real Estate Corp. [*NYSE symbol*] (SPSG)
NRE.......... National Resource Explorations Ltd. [*Toronto Stock Exchange symbol*] [*Vancouver Stock Exchange symbol*]
NRE.......... Natl Re Corp. [*NYSE symbol*] (TTSB)
NRE.......... Natural Resources and Environment
NRE.......... Naval Research Establishment
NRE.......... Negative Regulatory Element [*Genetics*]
NRE.......... Negative Resistance Effect
NRE.......... Negative Resistance Element [*Electronics*] (IAA)
NRE.......... New and Renewable Energy (PDAA)
NRE.......... New York Revised Laws [*A publication*] (DLA)
NRE.......... Nonrecurring Engineering (AAEL)
NRE.......... Nonrecurring Engineering Expense
NRE.......... Non Recurring Expense (ACAE)
NRE.......... Nonrotating Earth (NATG)
NRE.......... Not Receiving Additional Irrigation [*Agriculture*]
NRE.......... Nuclear Receptor Element [*Biochemistry*]
NRE.......... Nuclear Rocket Engine (AAG)
NRe.......... [*Reynolds*] Number [*Aerodynamics*] (BARN)
NRE.......... Point Mugu, CA [*Location identifier*] [*FAA*] (FAAL)
NRE-A .... Eastman Kodak Co., Apparatus Division, Rochester, NY [*Library symbol*] [*Library of Congress*] (LCLS)
NREA .... National Rural Education Association (EA)
NREAN ...... Northern Rivers Energy Action Network [*Australia*]
NRE-B .... Kodak (Near East) Ltd., Beirut, Lebanon [*Library symbol*] [*Library of Congress*] (LCLS)
NREB .... Naval Reserve Evaluation Board (DNAB)
NREB .... Northern Empire Bancshares [*NASDAQ symbol*]

NREBX ...... Mgn. Stanley D. Witter Natural Resources Cl.B [*Mutual fund ticker symbol*] (SG)
NREC .... NAC Re Corp. (EFIS)
NREC .... National Reconnaissance Executive Committee (LAIN)
NREC .... National Resources Evaluation Center [*of OEP*] [*Nuclear effects*]
NREC .... Natural Resources and Environment Committee [*Victoria, Australia*]
NREC .... Navy Recruiting Exhibit Center (ACAE)
NRECA ...... National Rural Electric Cooperative Association (EA)
NREd .... Eastman Dental Center, Basil G. Bibby Library, Rochester, NY [*Library symbol*] [*Library of Congress*] (LCLS)
NRed .... Red Hook Public Library, Red Hook, NY [*Library symbol*] [*Library of Congress*] (LCLS)
NREDC ...... National Rocket Engine Development Complex (SAUS)
NRedL....... Red Hook Public Library, Red Hook, NY [*Library symbol*] [*Library of Congress*] (LCLS)
NRE-E .... Eastman Kodak Co., Engineering Division, Rochester, NY [*Library symbol*] [*Library of Congress*] (LCLS)
NREEC....... Natural Resources and Environmental Education Center [*Oklahoma State University*] [*Research center*] (RCD)
NREF .... North Russia Expeditionary Force [*World War I*] [*Canada*]
NREFA....... National Real Estate Fliers Association [*Later, Real Estate Aviation Chapter*] (EA)
NREH........ Normal Renin Essential Hypertension [*Medicine*] (DMAA)
NREH........ Nuclear Radiation Effects Handbook (SAA)
NREL .... CSIRO News Releases (SAUS)
NRE-L .... Kodak Ltd., Recordak Division, London, United Kingdom [*Library symbol*] [*Library of Congress*] (LCLS)
NREL .... National Renewable Energy Laboratory [*Department of Energy*]
NRE-M .... Eastman Kodak Co., Health and Safety Laboratory, Rochester, NY [*Library symbol*] [*Library of Congress*] (LCLS)
nREM........ Nonrapid Eye Movement (DIPS)
NREM .... Nonrapid Eye Movement [*Type of sleep*]
NREMS...... Nonrapid Eye Movement Sleep [*Neurology*] (DAVI)
NREMT...... National Registry of Emergency Medical Technicians (EA)
NREMT-P ... National Registry of Emergency Medical Technicians - Paramedics (DAVI)
NREN........ National Research and Education Network [*Federal government*]
NRenSA..... Saint Anthony-On-Hudson Theological Seminary, Rensselaer, NY [*Library symbol*] [*Library of Congress*] (LCLS)
NRenSW .... Sterling-Winthrop Research Institute, Rensselaer, NY [*Library symbol*] [*Library of Congress*] (LCLS)
NRE-P .... Eastman Kodak Co., Photographic Technology Library, Rochester, NY [*Library symbol*] [*Library of Congress*] (LCLS)
NREP .... Name Removed from End-Paper [*Antiquarian book trade*]
NREP .... National Registry of Environmental Professionals (EA)
NREP .... National Reliability Evaluation Program [*Nuclear Regulatory Commission*]
NREP .... Neutron Resonance Escape Probability [*Nuclear energy*] (NRCH)
NREPHC..... Northeast Regional Environmental Public Health Center [*University of Massachusetts at Amherst*] (RCD)
NRE-R .... Eastman Kodak Co., Research Laboratories, Rochester, NY [*Library symbol*] [*Library of Congress*] (LCLS)
NRER........ Non-Rejected Earth Radiance (SAUS)
NRERC ...... National Rural Education Research Consortium [*Defunct*] (EA)
NRES .... Natural Resources, Energy, and Environment [*Office of Management and Budget*]
NRES .... Naval Receiving Station
NRES .... Nichols Research [*NASDAQ symbol*] (TTSB)
NRES .... Nichols Research Corp. [*NASDAQ symbol*] (NQ)
NRETN ...... Nonreturn
NREVSS..... National Respiratory and Enteric Virus Surveillance System
NRF.......... National Republican Foundation (EA)
NRF.......... National Research Foundation [*Research center*] (RCD)
NRF.......... National Retail Federation (EA)
NRF.......... National Roofing Foundation (EA)
NRF.......... National Rowing Foundation (EA)
NRF.......... National Rural Fellows (EA)
NRF.......... Naval Reactor Facility
NRF.......... Naval Repair Facility
NRF.......... Naval Reserve Fleet [*or Force*]
NRF.......... Network Routing Facility [*IBM's SNA*] [*Communications term*] (DCT)
NRF.......... Neurite Retraction Factor [*Biochemistry*]
NRF.......... Neurosciences Research Foundation (DAVI)
NRF.......... Never Removed from Box [*Doll collecting*]
NRF.......... Newport Restoration Foundation (EA)
NRF.......... Nightingale Research Foundation [*Canada*] (EAIO)
NRF.......... Nitrogen Rejection Facility [*Process engineering*]
NRF.......... No Redeeming Features
NRF.......... No Reflight
NRF.......... No Reinforcement [*Psychology*]
NRF.......... Normal Renal Function [*Medicine*] (DMAA)
NRF.......... Not Running at the Finish [*Automobile racing term*]
NRF.......... Nuclear Reactor Fuel (SAUS)
NRF.......... Nuclear Resonance Fluorescence (IAA)
NRF.......... Nutrition Research Foundation [*Australia*]
NRF.......... R. T. French Co., Rochester, NY [*Library symbol*] [*Library of Congress*] (LCLS)
NRFA........ National Retail Florists Association [*Defunct*]
NRFA........ National Retail Furniture Association [*Later, NHFA*] (EA)
NRFA........ National Rural Fire Authority (SAUS)
NRFB........ Never Removed from Box [*Doll collecting*]
NRFBS ...... National Research Foundation for Business Statistics (EA)
NRFC........ National Railroad Freight Committee (EA)
NRFC........ Navy Regional Finance Center
NRFC........ Nonrosette-forming Cell [*Medicine*] (EDAA)
NRFC-B ..... Navy Regional Finance Center, Brooklyn [*New York*] (DNAB)
NRFC-GL.... Navy Regional Finance Center, Great Lakes (DNAB)
NRFC-N ...... Navy Regional Finance Center, Norfolk [*Virginia*] (DNAB)
NRFC-PH.... Navy Regional Finance Center, Pearl Harbor [*Hawaii*] (DNAB)
NRFC-SD.... Navy Regional Finance Center, San Diego [*California*] (DNAB)
NRFC-SF.... Navy Regional Finance Center, San Francisco [*California*] (DNAB)
NRFD........ Not Ready for Data
NRFEA....... National Retail Farm Equipment Association [*Later, NFPEDA*]
NRFF .... National Research Foundation for Fertility [*Inactive*] (EA)
NRFI .... National Rail Freight Initiative [*Australia*]
NRFI .... Nonrecurring Finished Intelligence (MCD)
NRFI .... Not Ready for Issue
NRFL .... National Rugby Football League (NADA)
NRFLK....... Camden Heights, VA [*American Association of Railroads railroad junction routing code*]
NRFMAU.... Naval Reserve Fleet Management Assistance Unit (DNAB)
NRFO .... Navy Regional Finance Office
NRFO .... Nonrecovergent Fan-Out (SAUS)
NRFS .... Naval Reserve Force Study Group (DNAB)
NRFS .... Nichols Research Corp. (SAUS)
NRFSA ...... Navy Radio Frequency Spectrum Activity
NRFSEA.... National Reciprocal and Family Support Enforcement Association [*Later, NCSEA*] (EA)
NRFU .... Nonresponse Follow-Up [*Bureau of the Census*] (GFGA)
NRG .... California Energy Co. [*AMEX symbol*] (COMM)
NRG .... Energy (ABBR)
NRG .... Mark West Hydrocarbon, Inc. [*AMEX symbol*] (NASQ)
NRG .... Nautical Research Guild (EA)
NRG .... Naval Research Group
NRG .... Northern Rhodesia Gazette [*A publication*] (DLA)
NRG .... Ross Aviation, Inc. [*ICAO designator*] (FAAC)
NRG .... Tri-Lite, Inc. [*AMEX symbol*] (SPSG)
NRGA........ National Rice Growers Association [*Defunct*] (EA)
NRGas....... Rochester Gas & Electric Corp., Technical Information Center, Rochester, NY [*Library symbol*] [*Library of Congress*] (LCLS)
NRGC........ Nucleus Reticularis Gigantocellularis [*Neuroanatomy*]
NRGD-SC... Stromberg-Carlson Corp., Rochester, NY [*Library symbol*] [*Library of Congress*] (LCLS)
NRGE........ George Eastman House, Rochester, NY [*Library symbol*] [*Library of Congress*] (LCLS)
NRGI......... National Energy Group [*NASDAQ symbol*] (SAG)
NRGI......... NRG [*Federal Railroad Administration identification code*]
NRGIS....... Natural Resources Geographic Information Systems Laboratory [*University of Minnesota, Duluth*] (RCD)
NRGM .... National Responsibility Group Minute (HEAS)
NRGN........ Neurogen Corp. [*NASDAQ symbol*] (NQ)
NRG PAC.... NRG Energy PAC [*Minneapolis, MN*] (PACS)
NRGR........ General Railway Signal Co., Rochester, NY [*Library symbol*] [*Library of Congress*] (LCLS)
NRGS........ Church of Jesus Christ of Latter-Day Saints, Genealogical Society Library, Rochester Branch, Rochester, NY [*Library symbol*] [*Library of Congress*] (LCLS)
NRH .... Natural Rate Hypothesis [*Economics*]
NRH .... Nodular Regenerative Hyperplasia [*of liver*] [*Medicine*]
NRH .... Nonready Hours
NRH .... No Reply Heard [*ICAO designator*] (FAAC)
NRHA........ National Radio Heritage Association (EA)
NRHA........ National Reining Horse Association (EA)
NRHA........ National Retail Hardware Association (EA)
NRHA........ National Roller Hockey Association of Great Britain (BI)
NRHA........ National Rural Health Association (EA)
NRHA........ Northern Rivers Hydrophonic Association [*Australia*]
NRhbA....... Astor Home for Children, Rhinebeck, NY [*Library symbol*] [*Library of Congress*] (LCLS)
NRHC........ National Rental Housing Council [*Later, NMHC*] (EA)
NRHC........ National Rivers and Harbors Congress [*Later, WRC*]
NRHC........ National Rural Housing Coalition (EA)
NRHCA ...... National Rural Health Care Association [*Formerly, NRPCA*] (EA)
NRhDH ...... Long Island Doctors' Hospital, Roslyn Heights, NY [*Library symbol*] [*Library of Congress*] (LCLS)
NRHE........ Nonregenerative Heat Exchanger [*Nuclear energy*] (NRCH)
NRHGC ...... National Republican Heritage Groups (Nationalities) Council (EA)
NRHi......... Rochester Historical Society, Rochester, NY [*Library symbol*] [*Library of Congress*] (LCLS)
NRHN........ National Rural Health Network (SAUS)
NRHP........ National Register of Historic Places [*A publication*]
NRHP........ National Register of Hypnotherapists and Psychotherapists [*British*] (DBA)
NRHP........ National River Health Program (SAUS)
NRHPI....... National Register of Historic Places Index [*Database*] (GDD)
NRHQ........ Northern Region Headquarters (SAUS)
NRHS........ National Railway Historical Society (EA)
NRHS........ New Royal Horticultural Society [*British*]
NRHSA ...... National Retail Hobby Store Association (NTPA)
NRHU........ National Rural Health Unit [*Australia*]
NRHX........ Nonregenerative Heat Exchanger [*Nuclear energy*] (NRCH)
NRI .... National Radio Institute
NRI .... National Rehabilitation Institute [*Medicine*] (EDAA)
NRI .... National Research Initiative
NRI .... National Research Institute [*Audience research organization*] (NTCM)
NRI .... National Research Inventory (SAUS)
NRI .... National Resource Inventory [*US database on erosion*]
NRI .... National Resources Institute (ODA)
NRI .... National Rivers Inventory (GNE)
NRI .... Nationsrent, Inc. [*NYSE symbol*] (SG)

NRI .... Natural Resources Institute [*University of Greenwich*] [*British*]
NRI .... Natural Resources International
NRI .... Nebkota Railway [*Federal Railroad Administration identification code*]
NRI .... Nerve Root Involvement (SAUS)
NRI .... Nerve Root Irritation (SAUS)
NRI .... Net Radio Interface [*Telecommunications*] (TEL)
NRI .... Neurological and Related Intervention [*Medicine*]
NRI .... Neutral Regular Insulin
NRI .... New Records, Inc. [*Record label*]
NRI .... New Ring Index [*of chemical compounds*] [*A publication*]
NRI .... Nomura Research Institute (NITA)
NRI .... Nonrecurring Installation Charge [*Telecommunications*] (TEL)
NRI .... Nonrecurring Investment (NASA)
NRI .... Nonrepairable Item (MCD)
NRI .... Nonresident Instruction (MCD)
NRI .... Non-Respiratory Infection [*Medicine*] (DMAA)
NRI .... Non-Roster Invitee [*Baseball term*] (NDBD)
NRI .... Noril'sk [*Former USSR*] [*Seismograph station code, US Geological Survey*] (SEIS)
NRI .... Novagold Resources, Inc. [*Toronto Stock Exchange symbol*]
NRI .... Number of Records Ignored (SAA)
NRI .... Nutrition Reports International [*Medicine*] [*Journal*] (EDAA)
NRIA......... Narrow Resonance Infinite Absorber (PDAA)
NRIA......... National Railroad Intermodal Association [*Defunct*] (EA)
NRIAD....... National Register of Industrial Art Designers [*British*] (DAS)
NRIC......... National Rehabilitation Information Center [*Catholic University of America*] [*Bibliographic Database*] [*Washington, DC*]
NRIC......... National Resource and Information Center [*Association*] (EA)
NRIC......... Natural Resources Information Council [*Association*] (EA)
NRIC......... Negative Return in Cartridge [*Advanced photo system*]
NRIC......... Non-Reciprocal Impedance Converter (PDAA)
NRIC......... Nuclear Research Information Center [*American Nuclear Center*] [*Information service or system*] (IID)
NRICGP ..... National Research Initiative Competitive Grants Program (SAUS)
NRICH....... National Resource Institute on Children and Youth with Handicaps [*Defunct*] (EA)
NRID......... National Registry [*NASDAQ symbol*] (SAG)
NRID......... National Registry of Interpreters for the Deaf (SAUS)
NRiding Sch Libr Guild Bull... North Riding School Library. Guild Bulletin (SAUS)
NRIFSD ..... Non-Recoverable In-Flight Shut-Down (ACAE)
NRIIA........ National Republican Institute for International Affairs (EA)
NRIM........ Narrow Resonance Infinite Mass [*Nuclear energy*] (NRCH)
NRIM........ Northrim Bank [*NASDAQ symbol*] (SAG)
NRIMS ...... National Research Institute for Mathematical Sciences [*South Africa*]
NRIP......... Navy Reserve Intelligence Program (MCD)
NRIP......... Number of Rejected Initial Pickups
NRIPMVLIC... Nonresident Interprovince Motor Vehicle Liability Insurance Card [*For travel in Canada*]
NRIS......... Natural Resource Information System [*Department of the Interior*]
NRIS......... New Mexico Natural Resources Information System [*New Mexico State Department of Natural Resources*] [*Santa Fe*] (IID)
NRIS......... Non-resident Indians
NRIS......... Nursing Research Initiative for Scotland (SAUS)
NRITL .... Northeastern Regional Instructional Television Library (SAUS)
NRITL .... Northeastern Regional Instructional Television Library, Cambridge (SAUS)
NRIU......... National Refrigerants [*Intermodal shipping container symbol*] (TVRC)
NRIUW...... Naval Reserve Inshore Undersea Warfare (DNAB)
NRJ.......... Natural Resources Journal [*A publication*] (BRI)
NRJ.......... Non-Reciprocal Junction (PDAA)
NRK.......... Newark (ABBR)
NRK.......... Normal Rat Kidney
NRK.......... Normotensive Rat Kidney
NRK.......... Norrkoping [*Sweden*] [*Airport symbol*] (OAG)
NRK.......... Norsk Rikskringkasting [*Norwegian Broadcasting Corporation*]
NRK.......... Nurek [*Former USSR*] [*Seismograph station code, US Geological Survey*] [*Closed*] (SEIS)
NRKF........ Normal Rat Kidney Fibroblast [*Cytology*]
NRkpJH..... Rocky Point Junior-Senior High School, Rocky Point, NY [*Library symbol*] [*Library of Congress*] (LCLS)
NRL.......... Naneco Resources Ltd. [*Vancouver Stock Exchange symbol*]
NRL.......... National Reference Library [*British*] (NUCP)
NRL.......... National Registry for Librarians (EA)
NRL.......... National Research Laboratory
NRL.......... National Research Library [*Canada*] (DIT)
NRL.......... National Resources Library
NRL.......... Naval Research Laboratory [*Washington, DC*] [*Seismograph station code, US Geological Survey*] [*Closed*] (SEIS)
NRL.......... Naval Research Laboratory, Washington, DC [*OCLC symbol*] (OCLC)
NRL.......... Nerve Root Lesion [*Medicine*] (EDAA)
NRL.......... Network Restructuring Language
NRL.......... New York Revised Laws [*A publication*] (DLA)
NRL.......... Night Ration Locker (MSA)
NRL.......... Normal Rated Load
NRL.......... Normal Response Level
NRL.......... Normal Running Load (SAUS)
NRL.......... Norrell Corp. [*NYSE symbol*] (SAG)
NRL.......... Norske Reindriftsamers Lansforbund [*Norway*]
NRL.......... North Ronaldsay [*Scotland*] [*Airport symbol*] (OAG)
NRL.......... Nuclear Reactor Laboratory [*Massachusetts Institute of Technology*] [*Research center*] (RCD)
NRL.......... Nuclear Referral List (SAUS)
NRL.......... Nuclear Weapons Reconnaissance List (COE)
NRL.......... Nucleus Reticularis Lateralis (DB)
NRL.......... Nutrition Research Laboratory (SAUS)
NRLA........ Network Repair Level Analysis
NRLA........ Northeastern Retail Lumbermen's Association (EA)
NRLC........ National Railway Labor Conference (EA)
NRLC........ National Right to Life Committee (EA)
NRLCA...... National Rural Letter Carriers' Association (EA)
NRLCHESBAYDET... Naval Research Laboratory, Chesapeake Bay Detachment (DNAB)
NRLD........ Norland Medical Systems [*NASDAQ symbol*] (TTSB)
NRLD........ Norland Medical Systems, Inc. [*NASDAQ symbol*] (SAG)
NRLDA...... National Retail Lumber Dealers Association [*Later, NLBMDA*]
NRL/EOTPO... Naval Research Laboratory Electro-Optical Technology Program Office [*Washington, DC*]
NRLETF..... National Right to Life Educational Trust Fund (EA)
NRLF........ Lincoln First Bank of Rochester, Rochester, NY [*Library symbol*] [*Library of Congress*] (LCLS)
NRLFLTSUPPDET... Naval Research Laboratory, Flight Support Detachment (DNAB)
NRLGY...... Neurology
NRLM....... National Research Lab of Metrology [*Japan*]
NRLN........ Northern Regional Legal Notice [*1954-61*] [*Nigeria*] [*A publication*] (DLA)
NRLP........ National Railway Labor Panel [*World War II*]
NRLR........ Northern Rhodesia Law Reports [*A publication*] (DLA)
NRLREP..... Naval Research Laboratory Representative (DNAB)
NRLSI....... National Reference Library of Science and Invention [*of the British Museum*]
NRLSITEDET... Naval Research Laboratory, Field Site Detachment (DNAB)
NRLSPECPROJDET... Naval Research Laboratory, Special Projects Detachment (DNAB)
NRL/SVIC... Naval Research Laboratory Shock and Vibration Information Center [*ONR*]
NRLUWSREFDET... Naval Research Laboratory, Underwater Sound Reference Detachment (DNAB)
NRLX........ Nichols Rock Line Railroad [*Federal Railroad Administration identification code*]
NRLX........ Norail [*Private rail car owner code*]
NRM......... Nara [*Mali*] [*Airport symbol*] (OAG)
NRM......... National Railway Museum (WDAA)
NRM......... National Railways of Mexico [*Federal Railroad Administration identification code*]
NRM......... National Registry of Microbiologists (DAVI)
NRM......... National Resistance Movement [*Uganda*] (PD)
NRM......... National Revolutionary Movement [*France*]
NRM......... Natural Remanent Magnetism [*or Magnetization*]
NRM......... Natural Remanent Magnetization (SAUS)
NRM......... Natural Resource Management
NRM......... Naval Reserve Medal
NRM......... Neurochem [*Toronto Stock Exchange symbol*] [*Canada*]
NRM......... Next to Reading Matter [*Advertising*] (WDMC)
NRM......... Nonrecurring Maintenance [*NASA*] (KSC)
NRM......... Non-Routine Maintenance (SAUS)
NRM......... Normalize (DEN)
NRM......... Normal Range of Motion (MELL)
NRM......... Normal Response Mode
NRM......... Normal Retinal Movement (SAUS)
NRM......... Norm-Referenced Measurement [*Education*]
NRM......... Northair Mines Ltd. [*Toronto Stock Exchange symbol*] [*Vancouver Stock Exchange symbol*]
NRM......... Northern Rocky Mountains
NRM......... Northern Roller Mills (SAUS)
NRM......... North Rainier Mesa [*Nevada*] [*Seismograph station code, US Geological Survey*] (SEIS)
NRM......... NRM Energy Co. Ltd. (SAUS)
NRM......... Nuclear Radiation Monitor (SAUS)
NRM......... Nucleus Reticularis Magnocellularis (DB)
NRM......... Numeral Reading Machine (SAUS)
NRM......... Rochester Museum and Science Center, Rochester, NY [*Library symbol*] [*Library of Congress*] (LCLS)
NRMA....... National Reloading Manufacturers Association (EA)
NRMA....... National Retail Merchants Association [*New York, NY*] (EA)
NRMA....... Nuclear Records Management Association (EA)
NRMADI..... Non Recedet Malum a Domo Ingrati [*Evil Shall Not Depart from the House of theUngrateful*] [*(After Prov., XVII. 13) Motto of Julius, Duke of Braunschweig-Wolfenbuttel (1529-89)*] [*Latin*]
NRMB....... News of Russian Medicine and Biochemistry [*Medicine*] (EDAA)
NRMC....... Monroe Community College, Rochester, NY [*Library symbol*] [*Library of Congress*] (LCLS)
NRMC....... National Records Management Council (EA)
NRMC....... National Resources Management Corp.
NRMC....... Naval Records Management Center
NRMC....... Naval Regional Medical Center (NVT)
NRMC....... Naval Reserve Manpower Center
NRMC....... Northeast Rat and Mouse Club (EA)
NRMCA..... National Radiator Manufacturing Credit Association (EA)
NRMCA..... National Ready Mixed Concrete Association (EA)
NRMCEN.... Naval Records Management Center
NRMCI...... Northeast Rat and Mouse Club (EA)
NRME....... Notched, Returned, and Mitred Ends [*Construction*]
NRMEC..... North American Rockwell Microelectronics Co. [*Obsolete*]
NRMF....... New Road Map Foundation (EA)
NRMI........ National Record Mart, Inc. [*NASDAQ symbol*] (SAG)
NRMI........ National Registry of Myocardial Infarction
NRMI........ Natl Record Mart [*NASDAQ symbol*] (TTSB)
NRMI........ Naval Medical Research Unit (SAUS)

NRMIUW.... Naval Reserve Mobile Inshore Undersea Warfare (DNAB)
NRML....... Monroe County Library System, Rochester, NY [*Library symbol*] [*Library of Congress*] (LCLS)
NRML....... Normal (WGA)
NRMLC...... Normalcy (ABBR)
NRMLT...... Normality (ABBR)
NRMLY...... Normally (ABBR)
NRMLZ...... Normalize (ABBR)
NRMLZD.... Normalized (ABBR)
NRMLZG.... Normalizing (ABBR)
NRMLZN.... Normalization (ABBR)
NRMLZR.... Normalizer (ABBR)
NRMM....... National Register of Microform Masters [*Library of Congress*]
NRMM....... NATO Reference Mobility Model
NRMOMAGU... Naval Reserve Mobile Mine Assembly Group (DNAB)
NRMP....... National Records Management Program (AEPA)
NRMP....... National Resident Matching Program (EA)
NRMRL...... National Risk Management Research Laboratory [*Environmental Protection Agency*] (AEPA)
NRMS....... National Registry of Medical Secretaries (EA)
NRMS....... Natural Resource Management System [*Army Corps of Engineers*] [*Database*]
NRMS....... Naval Reserve Midshipmen's School
NRMS....... Neutralization-Reionization Mass Spectrometry
NRMS....... Nominal Root Mean Square (IAA)
NRMS....... Norman Rockwell Memorial Society (EA)
NRMSC...... Northern Rocky Mountain Science Center [*US Geological Survey*] (RCD)
NRMS Value... Nominal Root Mean Square Value (SAUS)
NRMT....... Northern Rocky Mountain Trench [*Geology*]
NRMT....... Nuclear Resonance Magnetometer Tool (SAUS)
NRMTC...... Nordoff-Robbins Music Therapy Centre Ltd. [*British*] (CB)
NRMU....... National Railway Mazdoor Union [*Indian Railway*] (TIR)
NRMU....... Natural Resources Management [*Organization of Eastern Caribbean States*]
NRMU....... Northern Rhodesia European Mineworkers' Union
NRMV....... Normative (ABBR)
NRMVY...... Normatively (ABBR)
NRMW....... Margaret Woodbury Strong Museum, Rochester, NY [*Library symbol*] [*Library of Congress*] (LCLS)
NRM Wind Scale... Northern Rocky Mountains Wind Scale (SAUS)
NRMWRP... Northern Rocky Mountain Wolf Recovery Plan
NRMX....... Neurochem [*NASDAQ symbol*]
NRN......... Naryn [*Former USSR*] [*Seismograph station code, US Geological Survey*] (SEIS)
NRN......... National Research Network (SAUS)
NRN......... National Resource Network [*Commercial firm*] (EA)
NRN......... Natural Radioactive Nuclides
NRN......... Negative Run Number [*Computer science*] (OA)
NRN......... Neutron-Rich Nucleus (ODA)
NRN......... Noise Rating Number (SAUS)
NRN......... No Reply Necessary (SAUS)
NRN......... No Return Necessary [*Medicine*] (EDAA)
NRN......... Northern
NRN......... Novell Remote Network (SAUS)
NRN......... Royal Netherlands Navy [*ICAO designator*] (FAAC)
nRNA........ Ribonucleic Acid, Nuclear [*Biochemistry, genetics*]
NRNC........ Nazareth College of Rochester, Rochester, NY [*Library symbol*] [*Library of Congress*] (LCLS)
NRND........ Norand Corp. [*NASDAQ symbol*] (SAG)
NRNFC...... National Rick Nelson Fan Club (EA)
NRNHD...... Nixon, Hargrave, Devans & Doyle, Rochester, NY [*Library symbol*] [*Library of Congress*] (LCLS)
NRNLR...... Northern Region of Nigeria Law Reports [*A publication*] (DLA)
NRNP........ Nuclear Ribonucleoprotein [*Medicine*] (DMAA)
NRNR........ National Rotorcraft Noise Reduction [*Program to reduce noise of helicopters*]
NRNS........ Nearness (ABBR)
NRO......... National Range Operations (RDA)
NRO......... National Reconnaissance Office [*Air Force/CIA*]
NRO......... National Reconnaissance Organization [*CIA*]
NRO......... Naval Research Objectives
NRO......... Navy Retail Office (AFIT)
NRO......... Negative Resistance Oscillator [*Electronics*]
NRO......... Nobeyama Radio Observatory
NRO......... Nonresident-Owned Funds [*Investment term*]
NRO......... Non-Returnable Outer (SAUS)
NRO......... No Results Observed (SAUS)
NRock....... Rockville Centre Public Library, Rockville Centre, NY [*Library symbol*] [*Library of Congress*] (LCLS)
NRockH..... Mercy Hospital, Rockville Centre, NY [*Library symbol*] [*Library of Congress*] (LCLS)
NRockHE.... Hewett Elementary School, Rockville Centre, NY [*Library symbol*] [*Library of Congress*] (LCLS)
NRockL...... Lakeview Public Library, Rockville Centre, NY [*Library symbol*] [*Library of Congress*] (LCLS)
NRockM..... Molloy College, Rockville Centre, NY [*Library symbol*] [*Library of Congress*] (LCLS)
NRockRE.... Riverside School, Rockville Centre, NY [*Library symbol*] [*Library of Congress*] (LCLS)
NRockSMS... South Side Middle School, Rockville Centre, NY [*Library symbol*] [*Library of Congress*] (LCLS)
NRockSSH... South Side Senior High School, Rockville Centre, NY [*Library symbol*] [*Library of Congress*] (LCLS)
NRockWE... Wilson Elementary School, Rockville Centre, NY [*Library symbol*] [*Library of Congress*] (LCLS)
NRockWR... Woodfield Road School, Rockville Centre, NY [*Library symbol*] [*Library of Congress*] (LCLS)
NRockWS... Floyd B. Watson School, Rockville Centre, NY [*Library symbol*] [*Library of Congress*] (LCLS)
NROE........ Naval Reactor Organic Experiment
NROFF...... New Run-OFF (SAUS)
nroff......... Nontypesetting Runoff [*Computer science*] (CDE)
NROK........ Northern Rockies Intermontane Basins (SAUS)
NRom....... Jervis Library Association, Rome, NY [*Library symbol*] [*Library of Congress*] (LCLS)
NROM....... Noble Romns [*NASDAQ symbol*] (TTSB)
NROM....... Normal Range of Motion (SAUS)
NRomA...... Rome Air Development Center, Rome, NY [*Library symbol*] [*Library of Congress*] (LCLS)
NRomAF.... United States Air Force, Base Library, Griffiss Air Force Base, Rome, NY [*Library symbol*] [*Library of Congress*] (LCLS)
NRomAF-R... United States Air Force, Rome Air Development Center, Griffiss, NY [*Library symbol*] [*Library of Congress*] (LCLS)
NROMM..... Netherlands Register of Microform Masters (TELE)
NROO........ Naval Reactors Operations Office
NRoos....... Roosevelt Community Library, Roosevelt, NY [*Library symbol*] [*Library of Congress*] (LCLS)
NRoosCE.... Centennial Elementary School, Roosevelt, NY [*Library symbol*] [*Library of Congress*] (LCLS)
NRoosDP... Daniels Primary Center, Roosevelt, NY [*Library symbol*] [*Library of Congress*] (LCLS)
NRoosJH.... Roosevelt Junior-Senior High School, Roosevelt, NY [*Library symbol*] [*Library of Congress*] (LCLS)
NRoosPK.... Prekindergarten School, Roosevelt, NY [*Library symbol*] [*Library of Congress*] (LCLS)
NRoosRE.... Theadore Roosevelt Elementary School, Roosevelt, NY [*Library symbol*] [*Library of Congress*] (LCLS)
NRoosWE... Washington-Rose Elementary School, Roosevelt, NY [*Library symbol*] [*Library of Congress*] (LCLS)
NROPS...... New Riders of the Purple Sage [*Rock music group*]
NROS........ Naval Reserve Officer School
NRosl........ Bryant Library, Roslyn, NY [*Library symbol*] [*Library of Congress*] (LCLS)
NRoslH...... Saint Francis Hospital, Roslyn, NY [*Library symbol*] [*Library of Congress*] (LCLS)
NRoslhEI.... East Hills Intermediate School, Roslyn Heights, NY [*Library symbol*] [*Library of Congress*] (LCLS)
NRoslhHP... Heights Primary School, Roslyn Heights, NY [*Library symbol*] [*Library of Congress*] (LCLS)
NRoslhHS... Roslyn High School, Roslyn Heights, NY [*Library symbol*] [*Library of Congress*] (LCLS)
NRoslhJH... Roslyn Junior High School, Roslyn Heights, NY [*Library symbol*] [*Library of Congress*] (LCLS)
NRoslHS.... Roslyn High School, Roslyn, NY [*Library symbol*] [*Library of Congress*] (LCLS)
NRoslhWI... Willets Road Intermediate School, Roslyn Heights, NY [*Library symbol*] [*Library of Congress*] (LCLS)
NRoslJH.... Roslyn Junior High School, Roslyn, NY [*Library symbol*] [*Library of Congress*] (LCLS)
N-ROSS..... Naval Remote Ocean Sensing System (SAUS)
N-ROSS..... Naval Research Oceanographic Satellite System (SAUS)
NROSS...... Navy Remote Ocean Sensing System [*Proposed*]
NROTC...... Naval Reserve Officers' Training Corps
NROTCBA... National Reserve Officers' Training Corps Band Association (AEBS)
NROTCU.... Naval Reserve Officers' Training Corps Unit (DNAB)
NROTCUNAVADMINU... Naval Reserve Officers' Training Corps Unit and Administrative Unit (DNAB)
NROVA...... National Record of Vocational Achievement (AIE)
NRP.......... National Reconciliation Party (Gambia) [*Political party*] (PSAP)
NRP.......... National Register Publishing [*Reed Elsevier*] [*Reed Reference Group*] (IID)
NRP.......... National Religious Party [*Hamiflaga Hadatit Leumit*] [*Israel*] [*Political party*] (PPW)
NRP.......... National Religious Party (Israel) [*Political party*] (PSAP)
NRP.......... National Reporting Program [*National Institute of Mental Health*] [*Department of Health and Human Services*] (GFGA)
NRP.......... National Republican Party [*Guyana*] [*Political party*] (EY)
NRP.......... National Resistance Party [*Political party*] (BJA)
NRP.......... National Review Panel [*Work Incentive Program*] [*Department of Labor*]
NRP.......... National Route Program (GAVI)
N/RP......... Neoclassical/Rational Planning
NRP.......... Net Rating Point [*Advertising*] (DOAD)
NRP.......... Net Rating Points [*Media ratings*] (NTCM)
NRP.......... Network Resource Planning [*Computer science*] (CIST)
NRP.......... Neurosciences Research Program [*Massachusetts Institute of Technology*]
NRP.......... Nevis Reformation Party [*Political party*]
NRP.......... New Republic Party [*South Africa*] [*Political party*] (PPW)
NRP.......... New Rhodesia Party [*Political party*]
NRP.......... Nissan Revival Plan [*Automotive industry*]
NRP.......... Noise Review Program [*Navy*] (DNAB)
NRP.......... Nonregistered Publication
NRP.......... Nonreportable Property [*Military*]
NRP.......... Non-Revenue Passenger [*Travel industry*] (TRID)
NRP.......... Nonstationary Random Process
NRP.......... Non-unit Related Personnel [*Military*] (DOMA)
NRP.......... No Replacement Part (SAUS)
NRP.......... Normal Rated Power

NRP.......... Norwich Research Park [*United Kingdom*] (RCD)
NRP.......... Notice of Research Project
NRP.......... NRP, Inc. [*Associated Press*] (SAG)
NRP.......... Nuclear Reform Project (EA)
NRP.......... Nuclear Reprocessing Plant (ODA)
NRP.......... Nucleus Reticularis Parvocellularis (DB)
NRP.......... Null Reading Position (SAUS)
NRP.......... Nuwe Republiekparty [*New Republic Party*] [*Political party*] [*Afrikaans*]
NRP.......... People's Republican Party [*Turkey*] [*Political party*]
NRP.......... Pfaudler Technical Library, Rochester, NY [*Library symbol*] [*Library of Congress*] (LCLS)
NRpA........ Ayerst Science Laboratory, Rouses Point, NY [*Library symbol*] [*Library of Congress*] (LCLS)
NRPA........ National Recreation and Park Association (EA)
NRPA........ Non-Redundant Pinhole Array (PDAA)
NRPAC...... Naval Reserve Public Affairs Co.
NRPAI....... National Rifle and Pistol Association of Ireland (EAIO)
NRPAIN..... National Register of Prominent Americans and International Notables (EA)
NRPB........ National Radiological Protection Board [*British*]
NRPB........ National Research Planning Board
NRPB........ National Resources Planning Board [*Abolished, 1943*]
NRPB........ Naval Research Planning Board (DNAB)
NRPB........ Naval Reserve Policy Board (DNAB)
NRPB........ Nickerson RPB Ltd. [*British*] (IRUK)
NRPC........ National Railroad Passenger Corp. [*Government rail transportation*]
NRPC........ National Register Publishing Co. [*Information service or system*] (IID)
NRPC........ Naval Reserve Personnel Center (DNAB)
NRPC........ Nucleus Reticularis Pontis Caudalis (DB)
NRPCA...... National Rural Primary Care Association [*Later, NRHCA*] (EA)
NRPD........ National Radiological Protection Board [*British*]
NRPEO...... Naval Regional Plant Equipment Office [*or Officer*] (DNAB)
NRPF........ National Railroad Pension Forum [*Defunct*] (EA)
NRPF........ National Retinitis Pigmentosa Foundation [*Later, RPFFB*] (EA)
NRPG........ National Retinoblastoma Parents Group (EA)
NRPG........ Nucleus Reticularis Paragigantocellularis (DB)
NRPH........ Park Ridge Hospital, Medical Library, Rochester, NY [*Library symbol*] [*Library of Congress*] (LCLS)
NRPIO....... Naval Registered Publications Issuing Office
NRPJ........ Nezavisna Radnicka Partija Jugoslavije [*Independent Labor Party of Yugoslavia*] [*Political party*]
N-R PL...... Non-Reversible Plug (SAUS)
NRPlanP.... Planned Parenthood of Rochester and Monroe County, Rochester, NY [*Library symbol*] [*Library of Congress*] (LCLS)
NRPM....... Nonregistered Publications Memoranda
NRPM....... Nuclear Weapons Reconnaissance Planning Manual (COE)
NRPO........ Naval Regional Procurement Office
NRPP........ Pennwalt Corp., Pharmaceutical Division Research Library, Rochester, NY [*Library symbol*] [*Library of Congress*] (LCLS)
NRPRA...... Natural Rubber Producers' Research Association [*British*] (BI)
NRPS........ Naval Radiological Protection Service (PDAA)
NRPS........ New Riders of the Purple Sage [*Rock music group*]
NRPS........ Non-contact Rotary Position Sensor [*Automotive electronics*]
NRPS........ Non-Ribosomal Peptide Synthetase [*An enzyme*]
NRPSA...... National Retail Pet Supply Association [*Defunct*] (EA)
NRPSGA.... National Retail Pet Store and Groomers Association (EA)
NRPT........ National Register of Personal Trainers [*United Kingdom*] (EAIO)
NRPTC...... National Register of Potentially Toxic Chemicals (GNE)
NRR......... National Research Register (SAUS)
NRR......... Naval Research Reactor
NRR......... Naval Research Requirement
NRR......... Naval Reserve Requirement (MCD)
NRR......... Negative Radial Rake (IAA)
NRR......... Negative Resistance Repeater [*Electronics*] (IAA)
NRR......... Net Reproduction Rate [*Medicine*] (DMAA)
NRR......... Net Reproductive Rate
NRR......... Net Retail Requirements
NRR......... Nobles Rock Railroad [*Federal Railroad Administration identification code*]
NRR......... Noise Reduction Rating [*Audio technology*] (EG)
NRR......... Nonreactive Resistor (SAUS)
NRR......... No Response Required
NRR......... No Resume Required
NRR......... Northern Rhodesia Regiment
NRR......... North Reno [*Nevada*] [*Seismograph station code, US Geological Survey*] (SEIS)
NRR......... Note, Record, Report [*Medical records and nursing*] (DAVI)
NRR......... Nuclear Reactor Regulation (ABAC)
NRR......... Nuclear Reactor Research (SAUS)
NRR......... Nuclear Rocket Reactor
NRR......... Office of Nuclear Reactor Regulation [*Nuclear Regulatory Commission*]
NRR......... Roosevelt Roads, PR [*Location identifier*] [*FAA*] (FAAL)
NRRA........ National Rail Regulatory Authority [*Australia*]
NRRA........ National Resource Recovery Association (EA)
NRRA........ National Risk Retention Association (EA)
NRRA........ National Romany Rights Association (WDAA)
NRRA........ Northeast Resource Recovery Association (EARSL)
NRRAD...... Narrated (ABBR)
NRRAG...... Narrating (ABBR)
NRRAN...... Narration (ABBR)
NRR & C.... Russell and Chesley's Nova Scotia Reports [*A publication*] (DLA)
NRRAR...... Narrator (ABBR)
NRRAS...... Navy Readiness Reporting and Analysis System (MCD)
NRRAV...... Narrative (ABBR)
NRRB........ National Recovery Review Board [*Terminated, 1934*]
NRRC........ Narragansett Railway [*Federal Railroad Administration identification code*]
NRRC........ National Rex Rabbit Club (EA)
NRRC........ Naval Research Reserve Co.
NRRC........ Naval Reserve Readiness Command (ACAE)
NRRC........ Northern Regional Research Center [*Formerly, NRRL*] [*Peoria, IL*] [*Department of Agriculture*]
NRRC........ Northern Resources Research Centre [*University of Alberta*] [*Canada*] (RCD)
NRRC........ Nuclear Risk Reduction Center (DOMA)
NRRD........ Norstan, Inc. [*NASDAQ symbol*] (NQ)
NR Relay... Non-Reactive Relay (SAUS)
NRRF........ National Right to Read Foundation [*Association*] (EA)
NRRF........ Naval Radio Receiving Facility (DNAB)
NRRF........ Naval Reserve Readiness Facility (DNAB)
NRRF........ Northern Refrigerated Transportation [*Common carrier symbol*]
NRRFSS..... National Research and Resource Facility for Submicron Structures [*Cornell University*] [*Research center*] (RCD)
NRRI......... National Regulatory Research Institute [*Ohio State University*] [*Research center*] (RCD)
NRRI......... Natural Resources Research Institute [*Research center*] (RCD)
NRRI......... Rochester Institute of Technology, Rochester, NY [*Library symbol*] [*Library of Congress*] (LCLS)
NRRI-C...... Rochester Institute of Technology, Melbert B. Cary, Jr. Graphic Arts Collection,Rochester, NY [*Library symbol*] [*Library of Congress*] (LCLS)
NRRL........ Northern Regional Research Laboratory [*Later, NRRC*] [*Department of Agriculture*]
NRRM....... National Railroad Museum [*Federal Railroad Administration identification code*]
NRRO........ Naval Radio Research Observatory (IAA)
NRRO........ Nuclear Radiation-Resistant Oils (NRCH)
NRRP........ National Reservoir Research Program [*Department of the Interior*] (GRD)
NRRP........ Sybron Corp., Rochester, NY [*Library symbol*] [*Library of Congress*] (LCLS)
NRRPC...... National Rural and Resources Press Club [*Australia*]
NRRR........ Rochester Reference Research and Resources Council, Rochester, NY [*Library symbol*] [*Library of Congress*] (LCLS)
NRRS........ Naval Radio Research Station
NRRS........ Nebraska Reading Retrieval System (EDAC)
NRRS........ No Remaining Radiation Service [*Unit*] [*Military*]
NRS.......... Atlantic Richfield Co. [*ICAO designator*] (FAAC)
NRS.......... Imperial Beach, CA [*Location identifier*] [*FAA*] (FAAL)
NRS.......... Name Registration Scheme [*Telecommunications*] (OSI)
NRS.......... National Oil and Hazardous Substances Response System [*Emergency Management*] (EMA)
NRS.......... National Radio Station (IAA)
NRS.......... National Readership Survey [*British*]
NRS.......... National Real Estate Service [*Canada*]
NRS.......... National Reemployment Service
NRS.......... National Reporter System [*Database*] [*Maritime Law Book Co. Ltd.*] [*Information service or system*] (CRD)
NRS.......... National Reserves System (SAUS)
NRS.......... National Runaway Switchboard (EA)
NRS.......... Nationwide Refrigeration Supplies [*British*]
NRS.......... Naval Radio Station
NRS.......... Naval Receiving Station
NRS.......... Naval Recruiting Service [*British military*] (DMA)
NRS.......... Naval Recruiting Station
NRS.......... Naval Research Section [*Library of Congress*] (MCD)
NRS.......... Naval Rocket Society (IAA)
NRS.......... Navy Records Society [*British*] (DBA)
NRS.......... Navy Relief Society (EA)
NRS.......... Network Resource Server [*J & L Information Systems*]
NRS.......... Neurobehavioral Rating Scale [*Medicine*] (DMAA)
NRS.......... Nevada Revised Statutes [*A publication*]
NRS.......... Newborn Rights Society (EA)
NRS.......... New Reading System (SAUS)
NRS.......... New Red Sandstone
NRS.......... New Rural Society [*HUD project*]
NRS.......... Night Reconnaissance System
NRS.......... Night Rifle Sight [*Police and security equipment*]
NRS.......... Nitrogen Recharge Station
NRS.......... Noise-Reduction System (SAUS)
NRS.......... Nonconformance Reporting System (NASA)
NRS.......... Nonconforming Reporting System
NRS.......... Non-Rising Stem [*Valve*] (DICI)
NRS.......... No Rate Specified [*Travel industry*] (TRID)
NRS.......... Normal Rabbit Serum [*Culture medium*]
NRS.......... Normal Rake System (SAUS)
NRS.......... Normal Rat Serum [*Hematology*]
NRS.......... Normal Reference Serum (MAE)
NRS.......... North-Holland Research Series In Early Detection and Prevention of Behaviour Disorders (SAUS)
NRS.......... Novell Replication Services (SAUS)
NRS.......... Nuclear Radiation Shield
NRS.......... Nuclear Reaction Spectrometry (BARN)
NRS.......... Nuclear Rocket Shuttle (KSC)
NRS.......... Numerical Rating Scale (DMAA)
NRS.......... Numerical Rating System [*Insurance*]
NRS.......... Nurse (ABBR)
NRSA........ National Remote Sensing Agency [*India*]

NRSA National Rental Service Association (EA)

NRSA National Research Service Awards [*Department of Health and Human Services*]

NRSA National Rose Society of Australia

NRSA Natural Rubber Shippers Association (EA)

NRSA Northeast Rail Service Act [*1981*] [*Also, NERSA*]

NRSB Non-Returnable Steel Barrel [*Fuels and lubricants*]

NRSB Saint Bernard's Seminary and College, Rochester, NY [*Library symbol*] [*Library of Congress*] (LCLS)

NRSC National Radio Systems Committee

NRSC National Remote Sensing Centre [*Royal Aircraft Establishment Space Department*] [*British*] (CB)

NRSC National Republican Senatorial Committee (EA)

NRSC Naval Reserve Supply Company (DNAB)

NRSC Nordic Road Safety Council [*See also NTR*] [*Helsinki, Finland*] (EAIO)

NRSCC National Reference System in Clinical Chemistry (DAVI)

NRSCC National Registry System for Chemical Compounds (DIT)

NRSCO Navy Recruiting Station Commanding Officer

NRSD Non-Returnable Steel Drum [*Fuels and lubricants*]

NRSD Nursed (ABBR)

NRSDNC Nonresidence (ABBR)

NRSDNT Nonresident (ABBR)

NRSE Neuron-Restrictive Silencer Element [*Neurogenesis*]

NRSE Nurse (ABBR)

NRSe Sear-Brown Associates, PC, Rochester, NY [*Library symbol*] [*Library of Congress*] (LCLS)

NRSED Nursed (ABBR)

NRSEG Nursing (ABBR)

NRSEMD Nursemaid (ABBR)

NRSEP National Roster of Scientific and Engineering Personnel (IAA)

NRSF National Rehabilitation and Service Foundation (EA)

NRSF National Reye's Syndrome Foundation (EA)

NRSF Neuron-Restrictive Silencer Factor [*Neurogenesis*]

NRSFPS National Reporting System for Family Planning Services [*National Institutes of Health*]

NRSG Naval Reserve Security Group (DNAB)

NRSG Nursing

NRSH Nourish (ABBR)

NRSHD Nourished (ABBR)

NRSHG Nourishing (ABBR)

NRSHNT Nourishment (ABBR)

NRSI National Reading Styles Institute

NRSITD Near-Sighted (ABBR)

NRSITNS Near-Sightedness (ABBR)

NRSJ Saint John Fisher College, Rochester, NY [*Library symbol*] [*Library of Congress*] (LCLS)

N-R Skt Non-Reversible Socket (SAUS)

NRSL Navy Radio and Sound Laboratory (IAA)

NRSO Navy Resale Systems Office

NRSP National Remote Sensing Program [*Marine science*] (OSRA)

NRSP National Remote Sensing Programme (USDC)

NRSP Nonrestorative Sleep Pattern (MELL)

NRSP Non-Returnable Steel Pail [*Fuels and lubricants*]

NrSph Spring Hope Public Library (SAUS)

NRS(R) Naval Radio Station (Receiving) (DNAB)

NRSRO Nationally Recognised Statistical Rating Organisation

nrsry Nursery

NRS(S) Naval Radio Station (Sending) (DNAB)

NRSSC National Rural and Small Schools Consortium (EA)

NRSSFR Laser Nonresonant Superradiant Spin-Flip Raman Laser (SAUS)

NRSSG Nuclear Reactor Systems Safety Group [*Air Force*]

NRSSGP Nuclear Reactor Systems Safety Group [*Air Force*]

NRSSO Navy Resale and Services Support Office (DNAB)

NRST Nonractive Solute Transport (SAUS)

NRST Non-Resident Shareholders' Tax (SAFN)

NRSTCTV Nonrestrictive (ABBR)

NRSTK Narcisistic (ABBR)

NRSTP National Register of Scientific and Technical Personnel (IAA)

NRSU Nippon Riku-un Sangyo [*Intermodal shipping container symbol*] (TVRC)

NRSV Necrotic Ringspot Virus [*of prunes*]

NRSV New Revised Standard Version [*1989*] [*A publication*] (ODCC)

NRSW Nuclear River Service Water (IEEE)

NRSY Nordiska Forbundet for Studie- och Yrkesvagledning [*Nordic Association for Study and Vocational Guidance - NASVG*] (EAIO)

NRSY Nursery

NRT Burroughs Wellcome & Co., Research Triangle Park, NC [*OCLC symbol*] (OCLC)

nrt Narrator [*MARC relator code*] [*Library of Congress*] (LCCP)

NRT National Rally Terminology [*Automotive competition*]

NRT National Recreation Trail (COE)

NRT National Repertory Theatre Foundation [*Defunct*] (EA)

NRT National Resource Trustee (BCP)

NRT National Response Team [*RSPA*] (TAG)

NRT National Response Team for Oil and Hazardous Materials Spills [*Environmental Protection Agency*] [*Washington, DC*] (EGAO)

NRT National Responsibility Team (HEAS)

NRT Naval Revolutionary Technology Initiative (ACAE)

NRT Navy Reserve Training

NRT Near-Real Time

NRT Neighbours of the Roundtable (EA)

NRT Net Registered Tonnage

NRT Net Register Tons [*Shipping*]

NRT Network Readiness Test (KSC)

NRT Neuromuscular Re-Education Techniques (DAVI)

NRT Neutron Radiographic Testing (SAUS)

NRT Nicotine-Replacement Therapy [*Medicine*]

NRT Noise-Riding Threshold (SAUS)

NRT Nonradiating Target

NRT Nonreal Time

NRT Non-Requesting Terminal (SAUS)

NRT Nonrequestor Terminal (IAA)

NRT No Right Turn (SAUS)

NRT Normal Rated Thrust (AAG)

NRT Norm-Referenced Testing [*Education*]

NRT Nortel Inversora 10%'MEDS' [*NYSE symbol*] (TTSB)

NRT Nortel Inversora SA [*NYSE symbol*] (SAG)

NRT Northern Airlines, Inc. (SAUS)

NRT Northfield [*Vermont*] [*Seismograph station code, US Geological Survey*] [*Closed*] (SEIS)

NRT Norton Co. (SAUS)

NRT Notion Round Table (EA)

NRT Novogen Ltd. [*Australian Stock Exchange symbol*]

NRT Nucleus Reticularis Thalami [*Neuroanatomy*]

NRT Taylor Instrument Cos., Rochester (SAUS)

NRT Taylor Instrument Cos., Rochester, NY [*Library symbol*] [*Library of Congress*] (LCLS)

NRT Tokyo-Narita [*Japan*] [*Airport symbol*] (OAG)

NRTA National Retired Teachers Association, Division of AARP (EA)

NRTAC National Recreation Trails Advisory Committee (COE)

NRTAC National Road Trauma Advisory Council [*Australia*]

NRT & CMA National Retail Tea and Coffee Merchants Association

NRTB Naval Reserve Training Branch

nrtb No Risk until on Board (MARI)

NRTC National Retail Trade Centre (EAIO)

NRTC National Rotorcraft Technology Center

NRTC Naval Reserve Training Center

NRTC Nonreal-Time Conversion Subsystem [*Space Flight Operations Facility, NASA*]

NRTC Normalized Re-instrumented Terrain Computer (SAUS)

NRTC Northrop Research and Technology Center (ACAE)

NRTCOMD Naval Reserve Training Command

NRTC Subsystem Non Real Time Conversion Subsystem (SAUS)

NRT DAS Non-Real Time Data Automation System (SAUS)

NRTDAS Nonreal-Time Data Automation System [*NASA*] (IAA)

NRTEC National Rural Teacher Education Consortium [*National Rural Development Institute*] [*Later, NRSSC*] (EA)

NRTEM Near Real Time Exploitation Module (ACAE)

NRTF National Recreation Trails Fund (COE)

NRTF Naval Radio Transmitting Facility (DNAB)

NRTH North (ABBR)

NrthFce North Face, Inc. (The) [*Associated Press*] (SAG)

NRTHSD Northside

NRTHUM Northumberland [*County in England*] (ROG)

NRTI National Rehabilitation Training Institute [*Defunct*] (EA)

NRTI Nooney Realty Trust [*NASDAQ symbol*] (TTSB)

NRTI Nooney Realty Trust, Inc. [*NASDAQ symbol*] (NQ)

NRTI Nucleoside Revenue Transcript Inhibitor [*Biochemistry*]

NRTIPT Naval Reserve Training in Port (NVT)

NRTK Nonreceptor Tyrosine Kinase [*An enzyme*]

NRTL Nationally Recognized Testing Laboratory (COE)

NRTL Nonlinear Resistor Transistor Logic (SAUS)

NRTL Non-Random Two-Liquid [*Equation of state*]

NRTL Eq Non-Random Two-Liquid Equation (SAUS)

NRTM Near Real Time Module (ACAE)

NRTN Norton Enterprises, Inc. (SAUS)

NRTO National Remotivation Therapy Organization (EA)

NRTOB No Risk Till on Board (SAUS)

NRTOI National Range Technical Operating Instructions [*NASA*] (KSC)

NRTOR No Risk Till On Rail (SAUS)

NRTOR No Risk to Attach till on Rail (MARI)

nrtor No Risk until Waterborne (MARI)

NRTP Nucleus Reticularis Tegmenti Pontis [*Neuroanatomy*]

NRTR Near-Real-Time Reconnaissance (MCD)

NRTR Nurture (ABBR)

NRTRD Nurtured (ABBR)

NRTRG Nurturing (ABBR)

NRTS National Reactor Test Station [*INEL*] (NRCH)

NRTS Not Repairable This Ship [*Navy*] (AFIT)

NRTS Not Reparable This Station

NRTS Nuclear Reactor Testing Station (SAUS)

NRTSC Naval Reconnaissance and Technical Support Center

NRTSCPAC Naval Reconnaissance and Technical Support Center, Pacific (DNAB)

NRT-VBR Non Real-Time Variable Bit Rate (SAUS)

NRTW Northway Trailer [*NCIC trailer make code*]

NRTWB No Risk Till Water Borne (SAUS)

NRTWB No Risk to Attach till Waterborne (MARI)

NRTWC National Right to Work Committee (EA)

NRTWG Nutrient Reduction Targets Working Group (SAUS)

NRTWLDEF National Right to Work Legal Defense and Education Foundation [*Also, NRWLDF*] (EA)

NRTY Norton McNaughton [*NASDAQ symbol*] (TTSB)

NRTY Norton McNaughton, Inc. [*NASDAQ symbol*] (SAG)

NRU National Reactor Universal

NRU National Research Universal [*Nuclear reactor*] [*Canada*]

NRU National Rural Utilities Cooperative Finance Corp. [*NYSE symbol*] (SAG)

NRU .... Natural Resource Unit [*Environmental unit*]
NRU .... Nauru [*ANSI three-letter standard code*] (CNC)
NRU .... Network Resource Unit (MHDB)
NRU .... Neuropsychiatric Research Unit [*Navy*]
NRU .... Neutral Red Uptake (DMAA)
N Ru .... Nicolaus Rufulus [*Flourished, 13th century*] [*Authority cited in pre-1607 legal work*] (DSA)
NRU .... Nitrogen Rejection Unit [*Process engineering*]
NRU .... Nonreplaceable Unit (IAA)
NRU .... North Reference Unit (SAUS)
NRU .... Not Recently Used [*Replacement algorithm*] [*Computer science*] (BYTE)
NRU .... Nuclear Reactor Universal (SAUS)
NRU .... Nursing Effectiveness Utilization and Outcomes Research Unit [*Canada*] (RCD)
NRU .... Nursing Research Unit [*King's College London*] [*United Kingdom*] (RCD)
NRU .... University of Rochester, Rochester, NY [*Library symbol*] [*Library of Congress*] (LCLS)
NRU-A .... University of Rochester, Memorial Art Gallery, Rochester, NY [*Library symbol*] [*Library of Congress*] (LCLS)
NRUCFC ..... National Rural Utilities Cooperative Finance Corp. (EA)
NRU-M ...... University of Rochester, School of Medicine and Dentistry, Rochester, NY [*Library symbol*] [*Library of Congress*] (LCLS)
NRU-Mus ... University of Rochester, Eastman School of Music, Rochester, NY [*Library symbol*] [*Library of Congress*] (LCLS)
NRurU45 .... National Rural Utilities Cooperative Finance Corp. [*Associated Press*] (SAG)
NRUS .... Neighbors Are Us (PA)
NRUS .... Nonlinear Resonant Ultrasound Spectroscopy
NRU-W ...... University of Rochester, Women's College, Rochester, NY [*Library symbol*] [*Library of Congress*] (LCLS)
NRV .... Navarre Resources [*Vancouver Stock Exchange symbol*]
NRV .... Nerve (ABBR)
NRV .... Net Realizable Value
NRV .... Neubabylonische Rechts- und Verwaltungsurkunden [*A publication*] (BJA)
NRV .... Nodal Route Vector (SAUS)
NRV .... Non-Return Valve (SAUS)
NRV .... Nonrevenue [*Passengers or cargo*] [*Transportation*]
NRV .... Northamptonshire Rifle Volunteer Corps [*British military*] (DMA)
NRV .... North Carolina State University, School of Veterinary Medicine, Raleigh, NC [*OCLC symbol*] (OCLC)
NRV .... North Vancouver Airlines Ltd. [*Canada*] [*FAA designator*] (FAAC)
NRV .... Nucleus Reticularis Ventralis (DB)
NRVA .... Net Realizable Value Accounting (ADA)
NRVC .... National Religious Vocation Conference (EA)
NRvCH ...... Central Suffolk Hospital, Riverhead, NY [*Library symbol*] [*Library of Congress*] (LCLS)
NRVD .... Nerved (ABBR)
NRVG .... Nerving (ABBR)
NRVH .... National RV Holdings, Inc. [*NASDAQ symbol*] (SAG)
NRVH .... Natl R.V.Holding [*NASDAQ symbol*] (TTSB)
NRVI .... Nervy (ABBR)
NRVLS ...... Nerveless (ABBR)
NRVMA ...... National Roadside Vegetation Management Association (EA)
NRVOC ...... National RV [*Recreational Vehicle*] Owners Club (EA)
NRVR .... North River Homes [*NCIC trailer make code*]
NRvS .... Suffolk County Historical Society, Riverhead, NY [*Library symbol*] [*Library of Congress*] (LCLS)
NRVSBL ..... Nonreversible
NRvSL .... Supreme Court Law Library, Tenth Judical District, Riverhead, NY [*Library symbol*] [*Library of Congress*] (LCLS)
NRVU .... Nervous (ABBR)
NRVUNS .... Nervousness (ABBR)
NRVUS ...... Nervous (ABBR)
NRVUSNS ... Nervousness (ABBR)
NRVUSY .... Nervously (ABBR)
NRVUY ...... Nervously (ABBR)
NRVWRKG ... Nerve-Wracking (ABBR)
NRW .... NCL Holdings ADS [*NYSE symbol*] (SG)
NRW .... New Right Watch [*An association*] (EA)
NRW .... Nonradioactive Waste [*Nuclear energy*] (NRCH)
NRW .... Non-Reversed Word (SAUS)
NRW .... Nordrhein-Westfalen [*German license plate city code*]
NRW .... Norwegian (ABBR)
NRW .... Nuclear RADWASTE (IEEE)
NRW .... Number of Remaining Words
NR/WA ...... National Rep/Wholesaler Association (EA)
NRWA .... National Rural Water Association (EA)
NRWC .... National Right to Work Committee (EA)
NRWD .... Narrowed (ABBR)
NRWG .... Narrowing (ABBR)
NRWG .... Neutron Radiography Working Group [*EURATOM*]
NRW-KA ..... National Registry of Willys-Knight Automobiles [*Later, W-O-KR*]
NRWLDEF ... National Right to Work Legal Defense and Education Foundation [*Later, NRWLDF*] (EA)
NRWLDF .... National Right to Work Legal Defense Foundation (EA)
NRWMDD ... Narrow-Minded (ABBR)
NRWMDDNS ... Narrow-Mindedness (ABBR)
NRWN .... Norwin Trailer [*NCIC trailer make code*]
NRWO .... Nuclear RADWASTE [*Radioactive Waste*] Operator (IAA)
NRWT .... Non-Resident Withholding Tax (SAUS)
NRWV .... Nonradioactive Waste Vent [*Nuclear energy*] (NRCH)
NRX .... National Research Experiment [*Canadian reactor*]
NRX .... NERVA [*Nuclear Engine for Rocket Vehicle Application*] Reactor Experiment
NRX .... Nuclear Engine Reactor Experiment (NRCH)
NRX .... Nuclear Reactor Experiment (SAUS)
NRX .... Nuclear Reactor, Experimental
NRX .... Xerox Corp., Rochester, NY [*Library symbol*] [*Library of Congress*] (LCLS)
NRX(C) ...... Nonreturn-to-Zero (Change) Recording
NRX-CX ..... Nuclear Engine Reactor Critical Assembly (SAA)
NRX-EST .... NERVA [*Nuclear Engine for Rocket Vehicle Applications*] Reactor Experiment-EngineSystem Test (SAA)
NRY .... Nearly (ABBR)
Nry .... Newry (SAUS)
NRy .... Rye Free Reading Room, Rye, NY [*Library symbol*] [*Library of Congress*] (LCLS)
NRyHi .... Rye Historical Society, Rye, NY [*Library symbol*] [*Library of Congress*] (LCLS)
NRyS .... Sloan-Kettering Institute for Cancer Research, Rye, NY [*Library symbol*] [*Library of Congress*] (LCLS)
NRZ .... Nonreturn to Zero [*Data transmission*]
NRZ .... Not Return to Zero (SAUS)
NRZ .... Null Reception Zone
NRZ1 .... Nonreturn to Zero Change on One (BUR)
NRZ1 .... Non-Return-to-Zero-One (SAUS)
NRZC .... Nonreturn to Zero Change
NRZC .... Nonreturn-to-Zero Change Recording (SAUS)
NRZ Code ... Non-Returning-to-Zero Code (SAUS)
NRZ Code ... Non-Return-to-Zero Code (SAUS)
NRZI .... Non-Return to Zero Indicates (SAUS)
NRZI .... Nonreturn-to-Zero Indicator (SAUS)
NRZI .... Non-Return-to-Zero Indiscrete (SAUS)
NRZI .... Nonreturn to Zero Inverted [*Recording method*]
NRZI .... Nonreturn-to-Zero Inverted (SAUS)
NRZI .... NRZ Indicator (NITA)
NRZ-L .... Non Return to Zero Level (ACAE)
NRZL .... Nonreturn to Zero Level
NRZL .... Nonreturn-to-Zero Logic (MCD)
NRZL .... Nonreturn-to-Zero Logic (SAUS)
NRZM .... Nonreturn to Zero Mark
NRZR .... Non-Return-to-Zero Recording (SAUS)
NRZ-S .... Non-Return to Zero-Space (MCD)
N S .... Edward Henry Kraus Natural Science Building (SAUS)
NS .... Graduate of the Royal Naval Staff College, Greenwich [*British*]
NS .... Nachalnik Sektora [*Chief of Sector*] [*Soviet military rank*]
NS .... Name Server
NS .... Nano Second (AGLO)
ns .... Nanosecond [*One billionth of a second*] [*Also, nsec*]
NS .... Naram-Sin (BJA)
NS .... Narodna Stranka [*People's Party*] [*Montenegro*] [*Political party*] (EY)
NS .... Narodnye Sotsialisty [*Popular Socialists*] [*Former USSR*] [*Political party*] (PPE)
N-S .... Nassi-Schneiderman [*Computer science*]
NS .... National Savings [*British*]
NS .... National Scientific [*Vancouver Stock Exchange symbol*]
NS .... National Seashore (BARN)
NS .... National Security [*Emergency Management*] (EMA)
NS .... National Service [*in the armed forces*] [*British*]
NS .... National Society
NS .... National Sojourners (EA)
NS .... National Special [*Thread*]
NS .... National Standard (IEEE)
NS .... National Steel [*NYSE symbol*] (SPSG)
NS .... National Strategy
NS .... Natjonal Samling [*National Union*] [*Norway*] (PD)
NS .... Natl Steel 'B' [*NYSE symbol*] (TTSB)
NS .... NATO Secret (NATG)
NS .... NATO Surveillance (NATG)
NS .... Natural Sciences
NS .... Natural Stupidness (SAUS)
NS .... [*The*] Naturist Society (EA)
NS .... Naval School (MCD)
NS .... Naval Shipyard
NS .... Naval Station
NS .... Naval Stores [*British*]
NS .... Navigation Subsystem (OA)
NS .... NAVSHIPS [*Naval Ship Systems Command*] Publication
NS .... Near Side [*Technical drawings*]
NS .... Near Space
NS .... Nederlandse Spoorwegen [*Netherlands Railways*]
NS .... Neoplasm Staging [*Medicine*] (MELL)
NS .... Neo Sumerian (BJA)
N/S .... Neosynephrine (SAUS)
NS .... Nephrosclerosis [*Medicine*]
NS .... Nephrotic Syndrome [*Medicine*] (DAVI)
NS .... Nerine Society [*Defunct*] (EA)
NS .... Nerves (SAUS)
NS .... Nervous System
NS .... Net Sales (MHDW)
NS .... Net Surplus
NS .... Networked Systems [*Automotive engineering*]
NS .... Network Service [*Computer science*] (TNIG)
NS .... Neue Sachlichkeit [*New Objectivity*] [*Pre-World War II group of German artists*]
NS .... Neuroelectric Society [*Defunct*] (EA)
NS .... Neurologic Signs [*Medicine*] (CPH)

NS .... Neurologic Survey [*Medicine*] (MAE)
ns .... neuropsychiatric (SAUS)
NS .... Neurosecretory
NS .... Neurosurgery [*Medicine*]
NS .... Neuro-Syphilis [*Medicine*]
NS .... Neurotic Score [*Psychology*]
NS .... Neutral Solvent [*Petroleum engineering*]
NS .... Neutron Spectrometer (SAUS)
N/S .... Neutrons per Second
NS .... Neutron Star (SAUS)
NS .... Newport Steel Corp. (EFIS)
NS .... News [*A radio station format*] (WDMC)
NS .... New School
ns .... New Series (RION)
NS .... New Series [*Bibliography*]
NS .... New Side
NS .... New Signal (ELAL)
NS .... Newspaper Society [*British*]
n/s .... Newsstand [*Also N/S*] (WDMC)
N/S .... Newsstand
NS .... New Statesman [*A publication*] (BRI)
NS .... New Style
NS .... New Synchonization (SAUS)
NS .... New System [*Computer science*]
NS .... Next State (SAUS)
N/S .... Next Step (SPVS)
NS .... Next System [*Computer science*]
NS .... Nickel Silver [*Used in minting coins*]
NS .... Nickel Steel
NS .... Niederschlagstaub (SAUS)
Ns .... Nielsbohrium [*Proposed name and symbol for recently-discovered element*]
NS .... Nietzsche Society (EA)
NS .... Night Switch (SAUS)
NS .... Nilo-Saharan [*Linguistics*] (IEL)
NS .... Nimbostratus [*Cloud*] [*Meteorology*]
Ns .... Nimbostratus Cloud (WEAT)
NS .... Nippon Sanso Corporation (EFIS)
NS .... Nippon Steel Corporation (EFIS)
NS .... Nissan [*Society of Automotive Engineers auto manufacturer code for service information interchange*]
NS .... Nitrogen Supply
NS .... Nitrogen System
NS .... Nobelstiftelsen [*Nobel Foundation - NF*] (EAIO)
NS .... Nockian Society (EA)
NS .... Nodularia Spumigena (SAUS)
NS .... Nodular Sclerosis [*Medicine*] (AAMN)
NS .... Noise Sensitivity (IAA)
NS .... Noise Suppressor (SAUS)
NS .... Noise Supressor [*Radio*] (NTCM)
NS .... Nonscheduled
NS .... Nonschizophrenic [*Psychology*]
NS .... Nonsequenced (IAA)
NS .... Nonserviceable (MSA)
NS .... Nonshorting (IAA)
NS .... Nonskew (IAA)
NS .... Nonslip (ABBR)
NS .... Nonsmutted [*Plant pathology*]
NS .... Nonspecific (SAUS)
NS .... Nonspecified
NS .... Non-Staining (SAUS)
NS .... Nonstandard (AABC)
NS .... Nonstatus Candidates May Apply [*Civil Service*]
NS .... Nonstimulation
NS .... Nonstop [*Aviation*]
NS .... Non-Stored (SAUS)
NS .... Nonstructural [*Protein*] (DB)
NS .... Non Structure
NS .... Non-Sufficient Funds Fee [*Electric utility company*]
NS .... Nonsymptomatic [*Medicine*] (MAE)
NS .... Noonans Syndrome (SAUS)
NS .... Nordisk Speditorforbund [*Nordic Forwarding Agents Association - NFAA*] [*Defunct*] (EAIO)
NS .... Nordisk Svommeforbund [*Nordic Swimming Federations Association - NSFA*] (EAIO)
NS .... Norfolk Southern Corporation (EFIS)
NS .... Norfolk Southern Railway Co. [*AAR code*]
NS .... Normally Shut (NRCH)
N/S .... Normal Saline [*Medicine*] (AMHC)
NS .... Normal Saline [*Medicine*] (BCRP)
NS .... Normal Segment
NS .... Normal Serum
NS .... Normal Sodium (DB)
NS .... Normal State (SAUS)
NS .... North Sea (SAUS)
NS .... North Sea - Nonrigid Airship [*Royal Naval Air Service*] [*British*]
N/S .... North Side [*In outdoor advertising*] (WDMC)
NS .... North Somerset Imperial Yeomanry [*British military*] (DMA)
NS .... North-South
NS .... No Sample (MAE)
NS .... No Scramble (IAA)
NS .... Nose [*Horse racing*]
ns .... No Sequelae [*Aftereffects*] [*Medicine*] (MAE)
N/S .... No Service (SAUS)
N/S .... No Show (IDYL)
NS .... No Show (SAUS)
NS .... No Signal (SAUS)
NS .... No Smoking
NS .... No Sound [*Script notation*] (NTCM)
NS .... No Sparring (DS)
NS .... No Specimen [*Medicine*]
N/S .... No Stamp [*Deltiology*]
NS .... No Standard (SAUS)
NS .... No Stimulation [*Neurophysiology*]
NS .... No Stock (SAUS)
NS .... Nostro Signore [*Our Lord*]
NS .... No Surgery Performed
NS .... Notch Strength (SAUS)
NS .... Note Series (SAUS)
NS .... Note Statement (SAUS)
N/S .... Not in Stock (SAUS)
NS .... Notre Seigneur [*Our Lord*] [*French*]
N/S .... Not Scheduled (SAUS)
NS .... Not Seen
NS .... Not Signed (SAUS)
NS .... Not Significant
ns .... Not Specified (EBF)
NS .... Not Specified
NS .... Not Sprinklered [*Insurance*]
NS .... Not Stated
NS .... Not Stocked
NS .... Not Stung
n/s .... Not Sufficient (WDMC)
NS .... Not Sufficient
NS .... Not Suitable
NS .... Not Suppressed
NS .... Not Switchable (MCD)
NS .... Nougth State (SAUS)
NS .... Noun Substantive [*Grammar*] (ROG)
NS .... Nourishing Stout [*Brewing*] (ROG)
NS .... Nova Scotia [*Canadian province*] [*Postal code*]
NS .... Nova Scotia Power Inc. (EFIS)
NS .... Noxious Stimuli
NS .... Noxious Substances (COE)
NS .... Nuclear Safety (COE)
NS .... Nuclear Science
NS .... Nuclear Sclerosis [*Ophthalmology*]
NS .... Nuclear Ship
NS .... Nuclear Shuffle (SAUS)
NS .... Nuclear Shuttle (NASA)
NS .... Nuclear Spectroscopy (SAUS)
NS .... Nuclear Submarine
NS .... Nuclear Systems
NS .... Nuernberger [*ICAO designator*] (AD)
NS .... Null Statement (SAUS)
NS .... Number of Secondary Turns (IAA)
N_s .... Number of Secondary Turns (IDOE)
NS .... Number Series (SAUS)
NS .... Number System (SAUS)
NS .... Numerical Signal (SAUS)
NS .... Numismatic Society
NS .... Nursing Services
NS .... Nursing Sister [*Navy*] [*British*]
NS .... Nutation Synchronous (ACAE)
NS .... Nutrition Society [*British*] (EAIO)
NS .... Nylon Suture [*Medicine*]
NS .... Nzingha Society (EA)
ns .... Sodium Metasilicate [*CIPW classification*] [*Geology*]
Ns .... Surface Refractivity (CET)
NS4 .... Nuclear Steam Supply Shutoff System (SAUS)
NSa .... Bancroft Public Library, Salem, NY [*Library symbol*] [*Library of Congress*] (LCLS)
NSA .... Naphthalene Sulfonic Acid [*Organic chemistry*]
NSA .... Napoleonic Society of America (EA)
NSA .... National Safety Association (NADA)
NSA .... National Sawmilling Association [*British*] (BI)
NSA .... National Scrabble Association (EA)
NSA .... National Secretaries Association (International) [*Later, PSI*] (EA)
NSA .... National Security Act (AAG)
NSA .... National Security Agency [*Acronym is facetiously translated as No Such Agency or Never Say Anything because of staffers' reluctance to give interviews*] [*DoD*]
NSA .... National Security Agency, Fort George G. Meade, MD [*OCLC symbol*] (OCLC)
NSA .... National Security Archive
NSA .... National Security Area (COE)
NSA .... National Seniors' Association [*Australia*]
NSA .... National Service Acts [*British*]
NSA .... National Sheep Association [*British*] (DBA)
NSA .... National Shellfisheries Association (EA)
NSA .... National Sheriffs' Association (EA)
NSA .... National Shipping Authority [*Department of Commerce*]
NSA .... National Showmen's Association (EA)
NSA .... National Shuffleboard Association (EA)
NSA .... National Silo Association [*Later, ISA*] (EA)
NSA .... National Skating Association of Great Britain
NSA .... National Ski Association of America [*Later, United States Ski Association*]

NSA......... National Slag Association (EA)
NSA......... National Slate Association (EA)
NSA......... National Smokers Alliance
NSA......... National Snurfing Association (EA)
NSA......... National Society of Accountants (NTPA)
NSA......... National Society of Andersonville (EA)
NSA......... National Society of Artists (EA)
NSA......... National Society of Auctioneers [*Later, National Auctioneers Association*]
NSA......... National Softball Association (EA)
NSA......... National Sound Archive [*British Library*]
NSA......... National Speakers Association (EA)
NSA......... National Spiritual Alliance of the USA (EA)
NSA......... National Sports Association (EA)
NSA......... National Sprint Association [*British*] (DBA)
NSA......... National Sprouting Association (EA)
NSA......... National Standards Association (NADA)
NSA......... National Standards Association, Inc. [*Bethesda, MD*]
NSA......... National Steeplechase Association (EA)
NSA......... National Stereoscopic Association (EA)
NSA......... National Stone Association (EA)
NSA......... National Stroke Association (EA)
NSA......... National Student Association [*Later, USSA*]
NSA......... National Students Association (NADA)
NSA......... National Sunflower Association (EA)
NSA......... National Sunroom Association (EA)
NSA......... National System Architecture
NSA......... Nausea (KSC)
NSA......... Naval Stock Account
NSA......... Naval Supply Account
NSA......... Naval Support Activity [*Vietnam*]
NSA......... Navy Supply Annex (AFIT)
NSA......... Nebraska Statewide Arboretum
NSA......... Neighborhood Strategy Area [*Program*] [*HUD*]
NSA......... Nepal Studies Association (EA)
NSA......... Network Software Associates, Inc.
NSA......... Neurological Society of America (DAVI)
NSA......... Neurological Society of Australasia
NSA......... Neurosurgical Society of America (EA)
NSA......... New Sabina Resources Ltd. [*Vancouver Stock Exchange symbol*]
NSA......... New Shipborne Aircraft [*Canada*]
NSA......... New South Africa Fund [*NYSE symbol*] (SAG)
NSA......... Next Station Addressing (SAUS)
NSA......... Nichiren Shoshu Soka Gakkai of America [*Buddhist organization*] (EA)
NSA......... Night Sight Attachment [*Police and security equipment*]
NSA......... Nile Safaris Aviation [*Sudan*] [*ICAO designator*] (FAAC)
NSA......... Nitrosylsulfuric Acid [*Inorganic chemistry*]
NSA......... Node Switching Assembly (SSD)
NSA......... Noise Suppressor Assembly
NSA......... Nominal Stress Approach (PDAA)
NSA......... Nonenyl Succinic Anhydride (SAUS)
NSA......... Non-Self-Averaging (SAUS)
NSA......... Non-Sequenced Acknowledgement (SAUS)
NSA......... Nonsequenced Acknowledgment (IAA)
NSA......... Non-Sterling Area (PDAA)
NSA......... Non-surgical Sperm Aspiration (SAUS)
NSA......... Nonylsuccinic Acid [*Organic chemistry*]
NSA......... Noosa [*Australia*] [*Airport symbol*] (OAG)
NSA......... Normalised Site Attenuation (SAUS)
NSA......... Normal Serum Albumin [*Clinical chemistry*]
NSA......... Northeastern Saengerbund of America (EA)
NSA......... Northern Slope of Alaska (CARB)
NSA......... North Sea Assets [*Investment firm*] [*British*]
NSA......... North-South Acceleration
NSA......... North-South Alliance [*An association*] [*Civil War re-enactment group*]
NSA......... Norwegian Seamen's Association (EA)
nsa......... No Salt Added (DMAA)
NSA......... No Salt Added
NSA......... No Serious Abnormality (DAVI)
NSA......... No Significant Abnormalities [*Medicine*]
NSA......... No Significant Anomaly [*Medicine*] (DMAA)
NSA......... No Such Address [*Telegraphy*] (PCTE)
NSA......... No Suitable Applicant (SAUS)
NSA......... Not-For-Profit Services Association (EA)
NSA......... Not Seasonally Adjusted [*US Census terminology*]
NSA......... Nuclear Science Abstracts (ABAC)
NSA......... Nuclear Science Association (NADA)
NSA......... Nuclear Stock Association [*British*] (DBA)
NSA......... Nuclear Suppliers Association (EA)
NSA......... Nuclear Systems Analysis
NSA......... Null-Steering Antenna
NSA......... Number of Signals Averaged (DMAA)
NSA......... Nursery School Association [*British*] (BARN)
NSA......... Nurses Supply Association (SAUS)
NSA......... Sangtam Naga [*Language symbol*] (ETLW)
NSAA........ National Sales Achievement Award [*NALU*]
NSAA........ National Ski Areas Association (EA)
NSAA........ National Space and Aeronautics Agency (MCD)
NSAA........ National Sulphuric Acid Association [*British*] (DBA)
NSAA........ National Supply Association of America [*Later, NSDA*] (EA)
NSAA........ National Surgical Assistant Association (NTPA)
NSAA........ Norwegian Singers Association of America (EA)
NSAA........ Nova Scotia Association of Architecture (SAUS)
NSA/AAO.... North Slope of Alaska and Adjacent Arctic Ocean (SAUS)
NSA/AAO.... NSA/Adjacent Arctic Ocean (SAUS)
NSAAB...... National Security Agency Advisory Board [*Fort George G. Meade, MD*] (EGAO)
NSAAC...... Atlantic Co-Operator, Antigonish, Nova Scotia [*Library symbol*] [*National Library of Canada*] (NLC)
NSABA...... National Spiritual Assembly of Baha'is of Australia
NSABP...... National Surgical Adjuvant Breast and Bowel Project (DAVI)
NSABP...... National Surgical Adjuvant Breast Project
NSAC........ National Society for Autistic Children [*British*]
NSAC........ National Society of Accountants for Cooperatives (EA)
NSAC........ National Space Activities Council (ACAE)
NSAC........ National Spiritualist Association of Churches (EA)
NSAC........ National Sport Aviation Council [*Defunct*] (EA)
NSAC........ National Student Action Center (EA)
NSAC........ National Student Aid Coalition [*Defunct*] (EA)
NSAC........ Norwegian Society of Automatic Control (SAUS)
NSAC........ Nova Scotia Agricultural College
NSAC........ NSAC, the National Society for Children and Adults with Autism (EA)
NSAC........ Nuclear Safety Advisory Committee (NUCP)
NSAC........ Nuclear Safety Analysis Center [*Electric Power Research Institute*] (NRCH)
NSACA...... National School-Age Care Alliance [*Association*] (EA)
NSACG...... Nuclear Strike Alternate Control Group (NATG)
NSACS...... National Society for the Abolition of Cruel Sports [*British*] (BI)
NSACS...... Naval Ships Advanced Communications System (SAA)
NSACSS..... National Security Agency/Central Security Service (AABC)
NSAD........ National Society of Art Directors (EA)
NSAD........ Naval Support Activity, Da Nang [*Vietnam*] (VNW)
NSAD........ Naval Support Activity Detachment (DNAB)
NSAD........ No Sign of Acute Disease (MELL)
NSAD........ No Sign of Significant Disease (SAUS)
NSAD........ Nuclear Safety Analysis Document (KSC)
NSADN...... Daily News, Amherst, Nova Scotia [*Library symbol*] [*National Library of Canada*] (NLC)
NSAE........ National Society for Art Education [*British*]
NSAE........ National Society of Architectural Engineers (EA)
NSAE........ Nebraska Society of Association Executives (EARSL)
NSAF........ National Sanitation Foundation (IAA)
NSAF........ National Survey of America's Families
NSAF........ Naval Supply Account Fund
NSAFC...... National Service Armed Forces Act [*British*]
NSAFF...... National Society Against Factory Farming [*British*] (DBA)
NSAG........ Negative Channel Self-Aligned Gate (IAA)
NSAGT...... New South African Group Test [*Intelligence test*]
NSAH........ Heritage Association of Antigonish, Nova Scotia [*Library symbol*] [*National Library of Canada*] (NLC)
NSAI......... Nashville Songwriters Association, International (EA)
NSAI......... National Standards Authority of Ireland [*Irish Science and Technology Agency*] (IRC)
NSAI......... Need Satisfaction of Activity Interview
NSAI......... Neutropenia Support Association, Inc. (NRGU)
NSAI......... Nonsteroidal Anti-Inflammatory [*Pharmacochemistry*]
NSAI......... NSA International [*NASDAQ symbol*] (TTSB)
NSAI......... NSA International, Inc. [*NASDAQ symbol*] (SAG)
NSAIA....... Nonsteroidal Anti-Inflammatory Agent
NSAID....... Non Steroidal Anti Inflammatory Drug [*Medicine*] (STAH)
NSAID....... Non-Steroidal Anti-Inflammatory Drug [*Equine term*] (TED)
NSAIDS..... Non-Steroidal Anti-Inflammatory Drugs (SAUS)
NSAIE....... National Society for American Indian Elderly [*Association*] (EA)
NSAIN....... Indian and Northern Affairs Canada [*Affaires Indiennes et du Nord Canada*],Amherst, Nova Scotia [*Library symbol*] [*National Library of Canada*] (BIB)
NSAIN....... Indian and Northern Affairs Canada, Amherst, Nova Scotia (SAUS)
NSA Int...... NSA International, Inc. [*Associated Press*] (SAG)
NSAJ........ National Secretariat Australia Jaycees
NSAL........ National Society of Arts and Letters (EA)
NSALC...... Nonsmoking Attributable Lung Cancer
NSaIDH..... Salamanca District Hospital, Salamanca, NY [*Library symbol*] [*Library of Congress*] (LCLS)
NSA line eater... National Security Agency Line Eater [*Alleged NSA supercomputer that reads all Internet postings*] (NETL)
NSALO...... National Security Agency Liaison Officer
NSAM........ National Security Agency Memorandum
NSAM........ Naval School of Aviation Medicine
NSAM........ Norwegian Advanced Surface to Air Missile System
NSAMC...... Cumberland Regional Library, Amherst, Nova Scotia [*Library symbol*] [*National Library of Canada*] (NLC)
NS Am Law Register... American Law Register (SAUS)
NS Am Law Register... American Law Register (Reprint) [*Ohio*] [*A publication*] (DLA)
NSAMRMS... Maritime Resource Management Service [*Service d'Amenagement des Ressources des Maritimes*] Amherst, Nova Scotia [*Library symbol*] [*National Library of Canada*] (NLC)
NSAN........ Nissan Motor Co. Ltd. [*NASDAQ symbol*] (NQ)
NSan......... Sanborn-Pekin Free Library, Sanborn, NY [*Library symbol*] [*Library of Congress*] (LCLS)
NS & E...... New Systems and Enhancements (MCD)
NS & L...... NS & L Bancorp, Inc. [*Associated Press*] (SAG)
NS & S...... New Statesman & Society [*A publication*] (BRI)
NS & SO.... Nervous System and Sense Organs
NS & T...... National Status and Trends (GNE)
NS & T...... Naval Science and Tactics
NSanF....... National Sanitation Foundation
NSANL...... Non-Sectarian Anti-NAZI League (EA)

NSanO....... Orleans-Niagara Board of Cooperative Educational Services, Associates Special Educational Instruction Materials Center, Sanborn, NY [*Library symbol*] [*Library of Congress*] (LCLS)
NSanO-C.... Orleans-Niagara Board of Cooperative Educational Services, Educational Communications Center, Sanborn, NY [*Library symbol*] [*Library of Congress*] (LCLS)
NSanO-S.... Orleans-Niagara Board of Cooperative Educational Services, Sanborn, NY [*Library symbol*] [*Library of Congress*] (LCLS)
NSANY...... Nissan Motor Co. ADR [*NASDAQ symbol*] (TTSB)
NSAP........ Apia [*Western Samoa*] [*ICAO location identifier*] (ICLI)
NSAP........ National Socialist Action Party [*British*]
NSAP........ National Society for Animal Protection (EA)
NSAP........ National Strategic Acquisition Plan (SAUS)
NSAP........ Navy Science Assistance Program (CAAL)
NSAP........ Network Service Access Point [*Telecommunications*] (OSI)
NSAPAC..... National Security Agency Pacific (CINC)
NSAPEA..... Nordic Society Against Painful Experiments on Animals (EA)
NSAPI....... Netscape Server API [*All-Purpose Interface*] [*Computer science*]
NSAPI....... Netscape Server Application Programming Interface (DCOM)
NSA Publication... Nursery School Association Publication (SAUS)
NSAR........ Annapolis Valley Regional Library, Annapolis Royal, NS [*Library symbol*] [*National Library of Canada*] (NLC)
NSAR........ Nitrososarcosine [*Organic chemistry*]
NSARC....... Navy Systems Acquisition Review Council
NSARF...... Fort Anne Museum, Annapolis Royal, Nova Scotia [*Library symbol*] [*National Library of Canada*] (NLC)
NSAS........ National Society of Appraiser Specialists (NTPA)
NSAS........ Naval Support Activity, Saigon [*Vietnam*] (VNW)
NSAS........ Near Infrared Spectral Analysis Software
NSAS........ Nonscheduled Air Services (AAG)
NSAS........ Nonsystemic Antacid Suspension [*Medicine*] (MELL)
NSAS........ Nuclear Sealed Authentication System (AABC)
NSAS........ St. Francis Xavier University, Antigonish, Nova Scotia [*Library symbol*] [*National Library of Canada*] (NLC)
NSASAB..... National Security Agency Scientific Advisory Board [*Ft. George G. Meade, MD*] (EGAO)
NSASC...... Chemistry Department, St. Francis Xavier University, Antigonish, Nova Scotia [*Library symbol*] [*National Library of Canada*] (NLC)
NSAT........ NATO Small Arms Test (MCD)
NSAT........ NAVMAT [*Navy Material Command*] Special Assistance Team (DNAB)
NSAT........ NII Norsat International, Inc. [*NASDAQ symbol*] (SAG)
NSATE....... NII Norsat Intl. [*NASDAQ symbol*] (TTSB)
NSATS....... NAVMAT [*Navy Material Command*] Selected Acquisitions Tracking System (DNAB)
NSAU........ Asau [*Western Samoa*] [*ICAO location identifier*] (ICLI)
NSAU........ National Shipping of Saudi Arabia [*Common carrier symbol*]
NSau........ Saugerties Public Library, Saugerties, NY [*Library symbol*] [*Library of Congress*] (LCLS)
NSauF....... Ferroxcube Corp., Suagerties, NY [*Library symbol*] [*Library of Congress*] (LCLS)
NSA-US..... National Spiritual Assembly of the Baha'is of the US (EA)
NSAW....... National Society of Asphalt Workers [*A union*] [*British*]
NSAWI....... National Substance Abuse Web Index (SAUS)
NSay......... Sayville Library, Sayville, NY [*Library symbol*] [*Library of Congress*] (LCLS)
NSB.......... Bimini-North [*Bahamas*] [*Airport symbol*] (OAG)
NSB.......... Natal Shark Board (SAUS)
NSB.......... Nationaal-Socialistische Beweging [*National Socialist Movement*] [*Netherlands*] [*Political party*] (PPE)
NSB.......... National Savings Bank [*British*]
NSB.......... National Science Board [*National Science Foundation*]
NSB.......... National Small Business Association [*Later, NSBU*]
NSB.......... National Socialist Board [*Dutch National Socialist Party of 1931; later, Dutch NAZI Party*] [*Political party*]
NSB.......... NATO Security Board (NATG)
NSB.......... Naval Standardization Board
NSB.......... Naval Studies Board [*National Academy of Sciences*] (DOMA)
NSB.......... Naval Submarine Base
NSB.......... Near Surface Burst (MCD)
NSB.......... Network of Small Businesses [*Lyndhurst, OH*] (EA)
NSB.......... Newsprint Service Bureau [*Later, API*] (EA)
NSB.......... Nippon Short-wave Broadcasting (SAUS)
NSB.......... Nonspecific Binder
NSB.......... Non-Statutory Body
NSB.......... Nonsustained Breakdown (IAA)
NSB.......... Nordisk Sammanslutning for Barnavard [*Nordic Child and Youth Welfare Alliance - NCYWA*] (EA)
NSB.......... Nord-Sud [*Benin*] [*ICAO designator*] (FAAC)
NSB.......... Norges Statsbaner [*Norwegian State Railways*]
NSB.......... Northeast Federal (SAUS)
NSB.......... Northeast Savings F.A. [*NYSE symbol*] (COMM)
NSB.......... Northern Soviet Boundary
NSB.......... North Slope Borough (ARMP)
NSB.......... Not Separately Billed
NSB.......... Nuclear Standards Board (SAUS)
NSBA........ National Saanen Breeders Association (EA)
NSBA........ National Safe Boating Association (EA)
NSBA........ National Savings Bank of Albany [*NASDAQ symbol*] (COMM)
NSBA........ National School Band Association [*British*] (DBA)
NSBA........ National School Boards Association (EA)
NSBA........ National Semi-Professional Baseball Association (EA)
NSBA........ National Sheep Breeders' Association [*British*] (BI)
NSBA........ National Shrimp Breeders Association (EA)
NSBA........ National Small Business Association [*Later, NSBU*]
NSBA........ National Snaffle Bit Association (EA)
NSBA........ National Sugar Brokers Association (EA)
NSBB........ National Society for Business Budgeting [*Later, PEI*]
NSBBA...... National Small Business Benefits Association (EA)
NSBC........ National Safe Boating Council (EA)
NSBC........ National Safety Belt Coalition [*NHTSA*] (TAG)
NSBC........ National Shoeboard Conference (EA)
NSBC........ National Student Book Club
NSBC........ Natural Science Book Club
NSBC........ New South Bancorp, Inc. [*NASDAQ symbol*] (NASQ)
NS Bcp...... NS Bancorp, Inc. [*Associated Press*] (SAG)
NSBCSH..... Cape Sable Historical Society, Barrington, Nova Scotia [*Library symbol*] [*National Library of Canada*] (NLC)
NSBD........ Narrow Spectral Band Detection
NSBD........ National Society of Bank Directors [*Formerly, NABD*] [*Later, ASBD*] (EA)
NSBD........ NBG Radio Network, Inc. [*NASDAQ symbol*] (QUAN)
NSBD........ New Services Business Development (TIMI)
NSBDM...... DesBrisay Museum and National Exhibit Centre, Bridgewater, Nova Scotia [*Library symbol*] [*National Library of Canada*] (NLC)
NSBE........ National Society of Black Engineers (EA)
NSBEO....... National Sonic Boom Evaluation Office [*Air Force*] (MCD)
NSBET....... National Society of Biomedical Equipment Technicians (EA)
NSBF........ National Scientific Balloon Facility [*Palestine, TX*] [*NASA*]
NSBGCA..... National Small Business Government Contractors Association [*Defunct*] (EA)
NSBGW..... National Society of Brushmakers and General Workers [*A union*] [*British*] (DCTA)
NS/BH....... Neutron-Star/Black-Hole
NSBI......... NS Bancorp, Inc. [*NASDAQ symbol*] (SAG)
NSbIA....... Institute of Advanced Studies of World Religions, Stony Brook, NY [*Library symbol*] [*Library of Congress*] (LCLS)
NSBISS...... NATO Security Bureau Industrial Security Section (NATG)
NSBIU....... Nova Scotia Board of Insurance Underwriters (SAUS)
NSBJH....... James House, Bridgetown, Nova Scotia [*Library symbol*] [*National Library of Canada*] (NLC)
NSBK........ North Side Savings Bank [*NASDAQ symbol*] (NQ)
NSBL........ Lighthouse Publishing Ltd., Bridgewater, Nova Scotia [*Library symbol*] [*National Library of Canada*] (NLC)
NSBLE....... Leader, Berwick, Nova Scotia [*Library symbol*] [*National Library of Canada*] (NLC)
NSBM....... Monitor, Bridgetown, Nova Scotia [*Library symbol*] [*National Library of Canada*] (NLC)
NSBMA...... National Small Business Men's Association [*Later, NSBU*]
NSBNL...... Naval Submarine Base - New London (MCD)
NSBP........ National Society of Black Physicists (EA)
NSBPA....... National Shrimp Breeders and Processors Association (EA)
NSBPH...... National Library Service for the Blind and Physically Handicapped [*Library of Congress*] [*Washington, DC*] [*Library network*]
NSBR........ Register, Berwick, Nova Scotia [*Library symbol*] [*National Library of Canada*] (NLC)
NSBRH...... Bear River Historical Society, Nova Scotia [*Library symbol*] [*National Library of Canada*] (NLC)
NSBRI....... National Space Biomedical Research Institute (SAUS)
NSBRO...... National Service Board for Religious Objectors [*Later, NISBCO*] (EA)
NSBS........ South Shore Regional Library, Bridgewater, Nova Scotia [*Library symbol*] [*National Library of Canada*] (NLC)
NSbSM...... Suffolk Museum at Stony Brook, Stony Brook, NY [*Library symbol*] [*Library of Congress*] (LCLS)
NSBSSA..... National Strict Baptist Sunday School Association [*British*]
NSBSSN..... South Shore News, Bridgewater, Nova Scotia [*Library symbol*] [*National Library of Canada*] (NLC)
NSbSU...... State University of New York at Stony Brook, Stony Brook, NY [*Library symbol*] [*Library of Congress*] (LCLS)
NSbSU-H.... State University of New York at Stony Brook, Health Sciences Library, Stony Brook, NY [*Library symbol*] [*Library of Congress*] (LCLS)
NSBT........ National Swiss Battle Tank (MCD)
NSBT........ Not Series by Title (MCD)
NSBU........ National Center for Atmospheric Research [*Intermodal shipping container symbol*] (TVRC)
NSBU........ National Small Business United [*Washington, DC*] (EA)
NSBU PAC... National Small Business United Small Business Victory Fund [*Washington, DC*] (PACS)
NSBVCA..... Victoria County Archives and Museum, Baddeck, Nova Scotia [*Library symbol*] [*National Library of Canada*] (NLC)
NSBWC...... National Safe Boating Week Committee [*Later, NSBC*]
NSBWK...... Western King's Memorial Hospital, Berwick, Nova Scotia [*Library symbol*] [*National Library of Canada*] (NLC)
NSC.......... Arthur D. Little, Inc. [*Research code symbol*]
NSC.......... Bristol-Myers Co. [*Research code symbol*]
NSC.......... Hoffmann-La Roche, Inc. [*Research code symbol*]
NSC.......... NASCAR [*National Association for Stock Car Auto Racing*] Street Classics [*Later, WW*] (EA)
NSC.......... Nasdaq Small Cap (SG)
NSC.......... National Cancer Institute [*Research code symbol*]
NSC.......... National Safety Corp.
NSC.......... National Safety Council (NADA)
NSC.......... National Safflower Council [*Defunct*] (EA)
NSC.......... National Savings Certificates [*British*] (DAS)
NSC.......... National Savings Committee [*British*]
NSC.......... National Science Council [*Irish*] (MSC)
NSC.......... National Security Council
NSC.......... National Semiconductor Corp.
NSC.......... National Service Center
NSC.......... National Shrimp Congress (EA)

NSC......... National Simulation Capability (SAUS)
NSC......... National Simulation Council (SAA)
NSC......... National Slavic Convention (EA)
NSC......... National Smallgoods Council [*Australia*]
NSC......... National Snorkellers Club [*British*] (DBA)
NSC......... National Society of Chauffeurs [*A union*] [*British*]
NSC......... National Society of Computer/Genealogists [*Defunct*] (EA)
NSC......... National Society of Cwens (EA)
NSC......... National Space Club (EA)
NSC......... National Space Council
NSC......... National Spiritualist Church [*British*]
NSC......... National Staff Committee [*Nurses and midwives*] [*British*]
NSC......... National Standards Commission (NADA)
NSC......... National Stinson Club (EA)
NSC......... National Stinson Club - 108 Series (EA)
NSC......... National Supercomputer Center (CIST)
NSC......... National Supply Class [*Military*] (AFIT)
NSC......... National Surface Cleaning, Inc. (EFIS)
NSC......... National Survey of Children
NSC......... National Synthetics Collection [*Smithsonian Institution*]
NSC......... NATO [*North Atlantic Treaty Organization*] Science Committee (EAIO)
NSC......... NATO Steering Committee (NATG)
NSC......... NATO Supply Center (NATG)
NSC......... NATO Supply Classification
NSC......... Naval Coastal Systems Center [*Florida*]
NSC......... Naval Safety Center (MCD)
NSC......... Naval School Command
NSC......... Naval Sea Cadets
NSC......... Naval Space Command (MCD)
NSC......... Naval Staff College (DOMA)
NSC......... Naval Supply Center
NSC......... Navigation and Sensor Computer
NSC......... Navigation Star Catalogue
NSC......... Navy Service Center
NSC......... Net Sale Certificate (DGA)
NSC......... Network Service Center [*Telecommunications*]
NSC......... Network Support Committee (ACAE)
NSC......... Network Switching Center [*Telecommunications*] (TEL)
NSC......... Network Systems Corp. [*Brooklyn Park, MN*] [*Telecommunications*] (TSSD)
NSC......... Neuroscience Center (SAUS)
NSC......... Neurosecretory Cells
NSC......... Newark State College (SAUS)
NSC......... Newscope Resources Ltd. [*Toronto Stock Exchange symbol*]
NSC......... New Session Cases [*Scotland*] [*A publication*] (DLA)
NSC......... Newtex SS [*Steamship company*] [*AAR code*]
NSC......... Nicaragua Solidarity Campaign (EAIO)
NSC......... Nippon Steel Corp. [*Japan*]
NSC......... Nodal Switching Center
NSC......... Nodal Switching Center (or Centre) (SAUS)
NSC......... Noise Suppression Circuit (DEN)
NSC......... Nomenclature Sequence Code [*Navy*] (AFIT)
NSC......... Nominal Single Dose [*Pharmacology*] (DAVI)
NSC......... Non-Sequential Computer (VLIE)
NSC......... Non-Service-Connected
NSC......... Nonspecific Suppressor Cell [*Medicine*] (EDAA)
NSC......... Nordic Saami Council (SAUS)
NSC......... Norfolk Southern [*NYSE symbol*] (TTSB)
NSC......... Norfolk Southern Railway [*NYSE symbol*] (SPSG)
NSC......... Normal Short Child [*Medicine*] (EDAA)
NSC......... Northeastern State College [*Oklahoma*]
NSC......... North Sea Conference (SAUS)
NSC......... North Star Conference (PSS)
NSC......... North Stonington [*Connecticut*] [*Seismograph station code, US Geological Survey*] (SEIS)
NSC......... Norwegian Space Center (or Centre) (SAUS)
NSC......... No Significant Change [*Medicine*]
NSC......... No Significant Cloud [*Meteorology*] (FAAC)
NSC......... Nothing So Called [*Bookselling*]
NSC......... Notice of Schedule Change (SAUS)
NSC......... Not Service-Connected [*Medicine*] (MEDA)
nsc......... Nova Scotia [*MARC country of publication code*] [*Library of Congress*] (LCCP)
NSC......... NSC Corp. [*Associated Press*] (SAG)
NSC......... Nuclear Safety Concern (SAUS)
NSC......... Nuclear Safety Convention (SAUS)
NSC......... Nuclear Science Center [*Louisiana State University*] [*Research center*] (RCD)
NSC......... Nuclear Services Corporation (ABAC)
NSC......... Numerical Sequence Code
NSC......... Nursing Sentence Completions [*Nursing school test*]
NSC......... Nutrition Society of Canada (SAUS)
NSC......... Salem College, Winston-Salem, NC [*OCLC symbol*] (OCLC)
NSCA........ NASCOM [*NASA Communications Network*] Assembly
NSCA........ National institute for Supercomputing Applications (SAUS)
NSCA........ National Satellite Cable Association [*Defunct*] (EA)
NSCA........ National Scrip Collectors Association (EA)
NSCA........ National Senior Citizens Association [*Commercial firm*] (EA)
NSCA........ National Shiba Club of America [*Association*] (EA)
NSCA........ National Shrimp Canners Association
NSCA........ National Ski Credit Association (EA)
NSCA........ National Soccer Coaches Association of America (EA)
NSCA........ National Society for Clean Air [*British*] (DCTA)
NSCA........ National Society of Commercial Agents [*Australia*]
NSCA........ National Sound and Communications Association (EA)
NSCA........ National Spinal Cord Association (DHP)
NSCA........ National Sporting Clays Association
NSCA........ National Strength and Conditioning Association (EA)
NSCA........ National Subacute Care Association (EA)
NSCA........ National Systems Contractors Association (NTPA)
NSCA........ Natural Sausage Casings Association [*British*] (DBA)
NSCA........ Nevada State Council on the Arts (SAUS)
NSCA........ Northwest Salmon Canners Association (EA)
NSCA........ Nova Scotia College of Art
NSCA........ Nutrient Starch Cycloheximide Agar [*Microbiology*]
NSca........ Scarsdale Public Library, Scarsdale, NY [*Library symbol*] [*Library of Congress*] (LCLS)
NSCAA...... National Small College Athletic Association (EA)
NSCAA...... National Soccer Coaches Association of America (NTPA)
NSCAA...... [*The*] National Society for Children and Adults with Autism 2 [*Formerly, NSAC*] (EA)
NSCAA...... Nutrient Starch Cycloheximide Antibiotic Agar [*Microbiology*]
NSCAC...... National Society for Crippled Adults and Children [*Medicine*] (EDAA)
NSCAD...... Nova Scotia College of Art and Design (SAUS)
NSCAE...... National Standards Council of American Embroiderers [*Later, CAE*] (EA)
NSCAEU..... National Service Conference of the American Ethical Union (EA)
NSCAH...... National Student Campaign Against Hunger [*Later, NSCAHH*] (EA)
NSCAHH.... National Student Campaign Against Hunger and Homelessness (EA)
NSCAMP.... National Stock Control and Maintenance Point [*Army*] (AFIT)
NSC & MP... National Stock Control and Maintenance Point [*Army*] (AABC)
NSCAR...... National Society of the Children of the American Revolution (EA)
NSCAS...... Archelaus Smith Museum, Centreville (Shelburne Co.), Nova Scotia [*Library symbol*] [*National Library of Canada*] (NLC)
NSCAT...... NASA [*or NROSS*] Scatterometer [*Instrumentation*]
NSCAT...... NROSS Scatterometer (SAUS)
N-SCATT.... Navy Scatterometer (MCD)
NSCAV...... National Safety Council of Australia, Victoria Division
NSCB........ NBSC Corp. [*NASDAQ symbol*] (NQ)
NSCB........ Nordic Society for Cell Biology (EA)
NSCC........ National Securities Clearing Corp.
NSCC........ National Service Coordinating Committee [*Ministry of Labour and National Service*] [*British*] [*World War II*]
NSCC........ National Siamese Cat Club (EA)
NSCC........ National Social Conditioning Camps [*Later, NOC*] (EA)
NSCC........ National Society for Crippled Children (DAVI)
NSCC........ Naval Sea Cadet Corps (NVT)
NSCC........ Navy Sea Cargo Coordinator (DNAB)
NSCC........ New Sudan Council of Churches
NSCC........ North Shore Community College [*Beverly, MA*]
NSCC........ NSC Corp. [*NASDAQ symbol*] (SAG)
NSCC........ Nuclear Services Closed Cooling (IEEE)
NSCCA...... National Society for Crippled Children and Adults [*Later, NESS*] (EA)
NSCCA...... National Sports Car Club of America
NSCCA...... Nuclear Safety Cross-Check Analysis (DOMA)
NSCCF...... Canadian Forces Base, Cornwallis, Nova Scotia [*Library symbol*] [*National Library of Canada*] (NLC)
NSCCFE..... Ensign, Canadian Forces Base, Cornwallis, Nova Scotia [*Library symbol*] [*National Library of Canada*] (NLC)
NSCCLO..... Naval Sea Cadet Corps Liaison Officer (DNAB)
NSCCM...... Cumberland County Museum, Amherst, Nova Scotia [*Library symbol*] [*National Library of Canada*] (NLC)
NSCD........ National School Development Council (AEE)
NSCD........ Nonservice-Connected Disability (MAE)
NSCD........ Nuclear Service Control Date (DNAB)
NSCDA...... National Society of Colonial Dames of America (EA)
N Sc Dec... Nova Scotia Decisions [*A publication*] (DLA)
NSCDET..... Naval Supply Center Detachment (DNAB)
NSCDP...... Non-Sexist Child Development Project (EA)
NSCDRF..... National Sickle Cell Disease Research Foundation [*Defunct*] (EA)
NSCE........ NetSource Communications, Inc. [*NASDAQ symbol*] (SAG)
NSCEC...... National School Curriculum Center for Educational Computing [*Defunct*] (EA)
NSCEE...... National Schools Committee for Economic Education (EA)
NSCEO...... National Society of Chief Executive Officers [*Defunct*] (EA)
NSCF........ National Skin Cancer Foundation [*Later, SCF*] (EA)
NSCF........ National Student Christian Federation [*Later, UCM*] (EA)
NSCF........ Naval Small Craft Facilities
NSCF........ Northstar Computer Forms [*NASDAQ symbol*] (TTSB)
NSCF........ Northstar Computer Forms, Inc. [*NASDAQ symbol*] (SAG)
NSCFA...... National Support Center for Families of the Aging [*Defunct*] (EA)
NSCG........ Northeastern Spoon Collectors Guild (EA)
NSCH........ Canso Historical Society, Nova Scotia [*Library symbol*] [*National Library of Canada*] (NLC)
NSch......... Schenectady County Public Library, Schenectady, NY [*Library symbol*] [*Library of Congress*] (LCLS)
NSchC....... Schenectady County Community College, Schenectady, NY [*Library symbol*] [*Library of Congress*] (LCLS)
NSchE....... Ellis Hospital, Schenectady, NY [*Library symbol*] [*Library of Congress*] (LCLS)
NSCHE...... Non-Specific Cholinesterase (SAUS)
NSCHF...... National Sprint Car Hall of Fame [*Iowa*]
NSchGEKA.. General Electric Co., Knolls Atomic Laboratory, Technical Library, Schenectady, NY [*Library symbol*] [*Library of Congress*] (LCLS)
NSchGEM... General Electric Co., Main Library, Schenectady (SAUS)
NSchGEM... General Electric Co., Main Library, Schenectady, NY [*Library symbol*] [*Library of Congress*] (LCLS)
NSchGER... General Electric Co., Research Laboratory, Schenectady, NY [*Library symbol*] [*Library of Congress*] (LCLS)

NSchGERB .. General Electric Co., R and D Center, Branch Library, Schenectady, NY [*Library symbol*] [*Library of Congress*] (LCLS)
NSchHLC ..... Capital District Library Council, Schenectady, NY [*Library symbol*] [*Library of Congress*] (LCLS)
NSchM ...... Mohawk Valley Library Association, Schenectady, NY [*Library symbol*] [*Library of Congress*] (LCLS)
NSchoCHi... Schoharie County Historical Society, Schoharie, NY [*Library symbol*] [*Library of Congress*] (LCLS)
NSchSC ..... Schenectady Chemicals, Inc., Schenectady, NY [*Library symbol*] [*Library of Congress*] (LCLS)
N Sch Social Research... [*The*] New School for Social Research (GAGS)
NSchStC .... Saint Clare's Hospital, Physicians' Library, Schenectady, NY [*Library symbol*] [*Library of Congress*] (LCLS)
NSchU....... Union College, Schenectady, NY [*Library symbol*] [*Library of Congress*] (LCLS)
NSCI .... NASCOM System Control Interface [*NASA*] (MCD)
NSCI .... National Surgery Centers, Inc. [*NASDAQ symbol*] (SAG)
NSCI .... Natl Surgery Centers [*NASDAQ symbol*] (TTSB)
NSCI .... Neuroscience Citation Index [*Database*] (GDD)
NSCIA .... National Spinal Cord Injury Association (EA)
NSCIA .... National Supervisory Council for Intruder Alarms [*British*] (DBA)
NSCIC .... National Security Council Intelligence Committee [*Inactive*]
NSCIC .... National Soybean Crop Improvement Council
NSCID .... National Security Council Intelligence Directive [*Pronounced "nee-sid"*] (AFM)
NSCIF .... National Spinal Cord Injury Foundation [*Formerly, NPF*] [*Later, NSCIA*] (EA)
NSCIG .... National Security Council Interdepartmental Group (MCD)
NSCISC...... National Spinal Cord Injury Statistical Center [*University of Alabama at Birmingham*] [*Spine Rehabilitation Center*] (IID)
NSCISC...... National Spinal Cord Injury Statistical Center Database [*University of Alabama in Birmingham*] [*Information service or system*] (CRD)
NSCL .... National Superconducting Cyclotron Laboratory [*Michigan State University*] [*National Science Foundation*] [*Research center*] (RCD)
NSCLC....... National Senior Citizens Law Center (EA)
NSCLC....... Non-Small-Cell Lung Cancer [*Oncology*]
NSCLS....... Nevada School and Children's Library Section
NSCLS....... North State Cooperative Library System [*Library network*]
NSCM .... National Society of Cycle Makers [*A union*] [*British*]
NSCM .... NATO Supply Code for Manufacturing (MCD)
NSCM .... Non-Stockpile Chemical Materiel [*Military*] (RDA)
NSCMP...... Non-Stockpile Chemical Material Program [*Army*]
NSCN........ National Socialist Council of Nagaland [*India*] (PD)
NSCNC ...... Nascence (ABBR)
NSCNQH .... North Queens Heritage Society, Caledonia, Nova Scotia [*Library symbol*] [*National Library of Canada*] (NLC)
NSCNT ...... Nascent (ABBR)
NSCO......... National Scientific Committee on Oceanography
NSCO......... Naval Sea Cargo Coordinator (DNAB)
NSCO......... Naval Shipping Control Officer (SAUS)
NSCO......... Network Systems Corp. [*NASDAQ symbol*] (COMM)
NSCORT..... NASA Specialized Center for Research and Training
NSCP......... National Scalable Cluster Project [*Computer science*] (ITCA)
NSCP......... National Society of Compliance Professionals (EA)
NSCP......... National Soil Conservation Program [*Canada*]
NSCP......... Naval Stores Conservation Program
NSCP......... Navy Staffing Criteria Program
NSCP......... Netscape Communications [*NASDAQ symbol*] (TTSB)
NSCP......... Netscape Communications Corp. [*NASDAQ symbol*] (SAG)
NSCPA....... National Society of Certified Public Accountants (EA)
NSCPA....... Nevada Society of Certified Public Accountants (EARSL)
NSCPC ...... National Student Consumer Protection Council (EA)
NSCPS ...... Naval Supply Center, Puget Sound [*Bremerton, WA*] (DNAB)
NSCPT....... National Society for Cardiovascular and Pulmonary Technology (EA)
NSCR......... National Society for Cancer Relief [*British*]
NSCR......... National Sport Custom Registry (EA)
NSCR......... Non-Selective Catalytic Reduction [*Chemistry*]
NSCR......... Nuclear Science Center Reactor
NSCRC ...... National Stock Car Racing Commission
NSCRDFO... National Study Commission on Records and Documents of Federal Officials
NSCS .... National Scouting Collectors Society (EA)
NSCS .... National Security Council System (COE)
NSCS .... National Sisters Communications Service [*Later, CCM*] (EA)
NSCS .... National Small Craft School [*Red Cross*]
NSCS .... Naval Strategic Communications Simulator (MCD)
NSCS .... Navy Supply Corps School
NSCS .... Network Service Center System [*Computer science*] (VLIE)
NSCS .... Night Shift Call System (DMAA)
NSCS .... North Star Computer Society (EA)
NSCS .... Universite Sainte-Anne, Church Point, Nova Scotia [*Library symbol*] [*National Library of Canada*] (NLC)
NSCSA ...... Centre Acadien, Universite Sainte-Anne, Church Point, Nova Scotia [*Library symbol*] [*National Library of Canada*] (BIB)
NSCSC ...... National School Calendar Study Committee
NSCSCC.... National Standard for Common System Component Characteristics (MCD)
NSCSL....... National Center for Service Learning (EBF)
NSCSS ...... National Society of Consulting Soil Scientists
NSCSWD.... No Small Craft or Storm Warnings are Being Displayed [*Weather*]
NSCT .... National Students Center for Thailand
NSCT .... Niagara, St. Catharines & Toronto [*AAR code*]
NSCT .... North Staffordshire College of Technology (SAUS)
NSCTE....... National Society of College Teachers of Education [*Later, SPE*] (EA)
NSCTI .... National Society for Cardiopulmonary Technology, Inc. (DAVI)
NSCTRN...... Nonsectarian (ABBR)
NSCU......... Norfolk Southern Railway [*Intermodal shipping container symbol*] (TVRC)
NSCUFA..... Nova Scotia Council of University Faculty Associations (SAUS)
NSCVPT..... National Society for Cardiovascular and Pulmonary Technology (EA)
NSCVR....... National Student Campaign for Voter Registration (EA)
NSCW........ National Society of Cycle Workers [*A union*] [*British*]
NSCWS...... Nuclear Services Cooling Water System (SAUS)
NSCX......... National Steel [*Federal Railroad Administration identification code*]
NSCX......... National Steel Car [*Private rail car owner code*]
NSD.......... Dartmouth Regional Library, Dartmouth, Nova Scotia [*Library symbol*] [*National Library of Canada*] (NLC)
NSD.......... Ferrosan [*Denmark*] [*Research code symbol*]
NSD.......... Geldert and Oxley's Nova Scotia Decisions [*7-9 Nova Scotia Reports*] [*1866-75*] [*Canada*] [*A publication*] (DLA)
NSD.......... Nairobi Sheep Disease [*Medicine*] (DMAA)
NSD.......... NASA Standard Detonator (SAUS)
NSD.......... National Aeronautics and Space Administration Standard Detonator (NAKS)
NSD.......... National Security and Defense (ABAC)
NSD.......... National Security Directive (SAUS)
NSD.......... National Security Directorate [*Government term*]
NSD.......... National Security Division (ACAE)
NSD.......... National Silage Demonstration [*British*]
NSD.......... National Smooth Dancers (DICI)
NSD.......... National Standard Co. [*NYSE symbol*] (SAG)
NSD.......... Naval Stores Department [*British military*] (DMA)
NSD.......... Naval Supply Depot
NSD.......... Navy Support Date (NG)
NSD.......... Neonatal Staphylococcal Disease [*Medicine*] (DB)
NSD.......... Nervous System Disease [*Medicine*] (EDAA)
NSD.......... Networks and Services [*Lawrence Livermore National Laboratory*] (RCD)
NSD.......... Network Security Device (SAUS)
NSD.......... Network Status Display
NSD.......... Neurosecretory Dysfunction [*Medicine*] (EDAA)
NSD.......... New Spirit Research [*Vancouver Stock Exchange symbol*]
NSD.......... Next Most Significant Digit [*Computer science*]
NSD.......... Night Sleep Deprivation [*Medicine*] (DMAA)
NSD.......... Noise Suppression Device
NSD.......... Nominal Single Dose [*Medicine*] (DB)
NSD.......... Nominal Standard Dose [*Medicine*]
NSD.......... Nonlinear Sampled Data [*Computer science*] (VLIE)
NSD.......... Non-Self-Destroying
NSD.......... Non-Sequential Disc (or Disk) (SAUS)
NSD.......... Nonsequential Disk [*Computer science*] (IAA)
NSD.......... Nonsoapy Detergent (SAUS)
NSD.......... Non-Stored and Delayed (SAUS)
NSD.......... Norfolk Shipyard & Drydock [*Federal Railroad Administration identification code*]
NSD.......... Normal, Spontaneous Delivery [*Obstetrics*]
NSD.......... Normal Standard Dose [*Oncology radiation*]
NSD.......... Norsk Samfunnsvitenskapelig Datatjeneste [*Norwegian Social Science Data Services*] [*Information service or system*] (IID)
NSD.......... Northside Aviation Ltd. [*British*] [*ICAO designator*] (FAAC)
NSD.......... No Significant Defect (SAUS)
NSD.......... No Significant Defects [*or Deficiency*] [*Medicine*]
NSD.......... No Significant Deficiency (SAUS)
NSD.......... No Significant Deterioration (SAUS)
NSD.......... No Significant Deviation [*Medicine*]
NSD.......... No Significant Difference [*Medicine*]
NSD.......... No Significant Disease [*Medicine*]
NSD.......... No Structure Detected (EEVL)
NSD.......... United States Library of Congress, Washington, DC [*OCLC symbol*] (OCLC)
NSDA........ National Soft Drink Association (EA)
NSDA........ National Spasmodic Dysphonia Association (EA)
NSDA........ National Sprayer and Duster Association (EA)
NSDA........ National Supply Distributors Association [*Dayton, OH*] (EA)
NSDA........ National Surplus Dealers Association (EA)
NSDA........ Naval Supply Depot Annex
NSDA........ Nissan Safety Device Advisor [*Driver information system*]
NSDA........ Non-Self Deployment Aircraft (SAUS)
NSDA........ Non-Self Destruct Alternative [*Army*]
NSDA........ Nonsteroid Dependent Asthmatic [*Medicine*] (DAVI)
NSDAB ...... Non-Self-Deployable Aircraft and Boats (MCD)
NSDAP ...... Nationalsozialistische Deutsche Arbeiterpartei [*National Socialist German Workers' Party, 1919-45*] [*Political party*]
NSDAP-AO... NSDAP Auslands- und Aufbauorganisation (EA)
NSDAR ...... National Society, Daughters of the American Revolution (EA)
NSDAT....... Naval School of Dental Assisting and Technology (DNAB)
NSDAVNDEPT... Naval Supply Depot Aviation Department (DNAB)
NSDB........ Bedford Institute of Oceanography [*Institut Oceanographique de Bedford*] Dartmouth, Nova Scotia [*Library symbol*] [*National Library of Canada*] (NLC)
NSDB........ National Science Development Board
NSDB........ National Soil Database (SAUS)
NSDB........ NSD Bancorp [*NASDAQ symbol*] (SAG)
NSD Bc...... NSD Bancorp [*Associated Press*] (SAG)
NSDBE ...... National Society, Daughters of the British Empire (EA)
NSDBR ...... National Society, Daughters of the Barons of Runnemede (EA)
NSDC........ Courier, Digby, Nova Scotia [*Library symbol*] [*National Library of Canada*] (NLC)
NSDC........ National School Development Council (EA)

NSDC........ National Serials Data Centre [*British Library*] (PDAA)
NSDC........ National Space Development Center (ACAE)
NSDC........ National Square Dance Convention (EA)
NSDC........ National Staff Development Committee [*Australia*]
NSDC........ National Staff Development Council (EA)
NSDC........ Naval Special Devices Center (SAA)
NSDC........ Nonsuppurative Destructive Cholangitis [*Medicine*]
NSDC........ NORAD Sector Direction Center [*Military*]
NSDC........ Northern Shipowners' Defence Club [*See also NORDISK*] (EAIO)
NSDC........ Northern Shipowners Defense Council (SAUS)
NSDC........ Nova Scotia Design Craftsmen (SAUS)
NSDCM........ NORAD Sector Direction Center Manual [*Military*]
NSDD........ National Security Decision Directive
NSDDET..... Naval Supply Depot Detachment (DNAB)
NSDDS...... Dartmouth District School Board, Nova Scotia [*Library symbol*] [*National Library of Canada*] (NLC)
NSDE........ Environment Canada [*Environnement Canada*] Dartmouth, Nova Scotia [*Library symbol*] [*National Library of Canada*] (NLC)
NSDEA...... National Soda Dispensing Equipment Association (EA)
NS Dec...... Nova Scotia Decisions [*A publication*] (DLA)
NSDEQ...... National Society, Descendants of Early Quakers (EA)
NSDF........ National Student Drama Festival [*British*]
NSDF........ Navy Standard Distillate Fuel (NVT)
NSDG........ Digby General Hospital, Nova Scotia [*Library symbol*] [*National Library of Canada*] (NLC)
NSDGH...... Dartmouth General Hospital, Nova Scotia [*Library symbol*] [*National Library of Canada*] (NLC)
NSDGP...... Northern Sydey Division of General Practice (SAUS)
NSDH........ Hermes Electronics Ltd., Dartmouth, Novia Scotia [*Library symbol*] [*National Library of Canada*] (NLC)
NSDI........ National Sales Development Institute
NSDI........ National Spatial Data Infrastructure [*BTS*] (TAG)
NSDJA...... National Sash and Door Jobbers Association (EA)
NSDL........ National Science, Mathematics, Engineering and Technology Education Digital Library
NSDL........ National Soil Dynamics Laboratory [*Auburn, AL*] [*Department of Agriculture*] (GRD)
NSDL........ Navy Standard Distribution List (MCD)
NSDLANT/PAC... Naval Supply Depots, Atlantic/Pacific
NSDLMM... National Society of Descendants of Lords of the Maryland Manors (EA)
NSDM........ Mirror, Digby, Nova Scotia [*Library symbol*] [*National Library of Canada*] (NLC)
NSDM........ National Security Decision Memorandum [*Air Force*]
NSDM........ New School for Democratic Management [*Inactive*] (EA)
NSDM........ Nuclear Sediment Density Meter (PDAA)
NSDMM...... MacLaren Plansearch Ltd., Dartmouth, Nova Scotia [*Library symbol*] [*National Library of Canada*] (NLC)
NSDNHM.... North Highlands Museum, Dingwall, Nova Scotia [*Library symbol*] [*National Library of Canada*] (NLC)
NSDNSH.... Nova Scotia Hospital, Dartmouth, Nova Scotia [*Library symbol*] [*National Library of Canada*] (NLC)
NSDO........ National Seed and Development Organisation [*British*]
NSDP........ NASCOM System Development Plan
NSDP........ National Serials Data Program [*Library of Congress*] (EA)
NSDP........ National Society of Denture Prosthetists [*Later, ADP*]
NSDP........ Norfolk Sample Drug Program
NSDR........ National Ships Destination Room (NATG)
NSDR........ National Silver Dollar Roundtable (EA)
NSDR........ No-son Dependency Ratio [*Demographics*]
NSDRC...... National Standard Reference Data Center (VLIE)
NSDRV...... Dartmouth Regional Vocational School, Dartmouth, Nova Scotia [*Library symbol*] [*National Library of Canada*] (NLC)
NSDS........ Navy School, Diving and Salvage (NVT)
NSDS........ Neutron Spectrometer Digital System
NSDSA...... Naval Sea Data Support Activity (NVT)
NSDTA...... National Staff Development and Training Association (EA)
NSDU........ Network Service Data Unit [*Telecommunications*] (OSI)
NSDUP...... National Society, Daughters of Utah Pioneers (EA)
NSDV........ Netted Secure Digital Voice (MCD)
NSDW........ NSD Warehousing and Distribution Systems of California [*Common carrier symbol*]
NSDWR..... National Secondary Drinking Water Regualtions (GNE)
NSDX........ North San Diego County Transit Development Board [*Federal Railroad Administration identification code*]
NSE.......... Milton, FL [*Location identifier*] [*FAA*] (FAAL)
NSE.......... Nagoya Stock Exchange [*Japan*] (NUMA)
NSE.......... National Sales Executives
NSE.......... National Seafood Educators (EA)
NSE.......... National Society for Epilepsy [*British*]
NSE.......... National Stock Exchange [*Dissolved, 1975*]
NSE.......... National Student Exchange (EA)
NSE.......... National Support Elements [*British military*] (DMA)
NSE.......... Natural Space Environment
NSE.......... Naval Shore Establishment
NSE.......... Naval Support Element (DOMA)
NSE.......... Navier-Stokes Equation
NSE.......... Navigation Support Equipment
NSE.......... Net Sales Entered (TIMI)
NSE.......... Network Service Element [*Telecommunications*] (OSI)
NSE.......... Network Software Environment [*Computer science*] (VLIE)
NSE.......... Network SouthEast [*British Rail*] (ECON)
NSE.......... Network Support Encyclopedia (VLIE)
NSE.......... Network Systems Engineer (SSD)
NSE.......... Neuron-Specific Enolase [*Formerly, NSP*] [*An enzyme*]
NSE.......... Neuropsychological Status Examination [*Psychology*]
NSE.......... Neutral Stream Etch (AAEL)
NSE.......... New York Stock Exchange (EBF)
NSE.......... NiSource, Inc. [*NYSE symbol*]
NSE.......... Nitroguanidine Support Element (MCD)
NSE.......... Noise (ABBR)
NSE.......... Nonsecurity Exemption [*Military*]
NSE.......... Nonspecific Esterase [*An enzyme*]
NSE.......... Normal Saline Enema [*Medicine*] (MELL)
NSE.......... North Steaming Error (SAA)
NSE.......... Northwest Sports Enterprises Ltd. [*Vancouver Stock Exchange symbol*]
NSE.......... Nottingham Society of Engineers (SAUS)
NSE.......... Nuclear Science and Engineering [*A publication*]
NSE.......... Nuclear Statistical Equilibrium [*Physics*]
NSE.......... Nuclear Support Equipment
NSE.......... Nuclear Systems Engineering
NSE.......... Number of Simultaneous Engagements [*Military*]
NSE.......... Satena Servicios de Aeronavegacion A Territorios Nac [*Colombia*] [*ICAO designator*] (FAAC)
NSEA........ National Standards Educators Association (EA)
NSEA........ Naval Sea systems command headquarters (SAUS)
NSEA........ Nebraska State Education Association (EARSL)
NSea........ Seaford Public Library, Seaford, NY [*Library symbol*] [*Library of Congress*] (LCLS)
NSeacES.... Sea Cliff Elementary School, Sea Cliff, NY [*Library symbol*] [*Library of Congress*] (LCLS)
NSEAD...... National Society for Education in Art and Design (EAIO)
NSeaHE..... Seaford Harbor Elementary School, Seaford, NY [*Library symbol*] [*Library of Congress*] (LCLS)
NSeaME..... Seaford Manor Elementary School, Seaford, NY [*Library symbol*] [*Library of Congress*] (LCLS)
NSeaMH.... Massapequa General Hospital, Seaford, NY [*Library symbol*] [*Library of Congress*] (LCLS)
NSeaMS.... Seaford Middle School, Seaford, NY [*Library symbol*] [*Library of Congress*] (LCLS)
NSeaP....... Plainedge Public Library, Seaford, NY [*Library symbol*] [*Library of Congress*] (LCLS)
NSeaSH..... Seaford Senior High School, Seaford, NY [*Library symbol*] [*Library of Congress*] (LCLS)
NSeaTM..... Tackapausha Museum, Seaford, NY [*Library symbol*] [*Library of Congress*] (LCLS)
NSEC........ Nanoscale Science and Engineering Center for Integrated Nanopatterning and Detection Technologies [*Northwestern University*] (RCD)
nsec......... Nanosecond [*One billionth of a second*] [*Also, ns*]
NSEC........ National Security Group, Inc. [*NASDAQ symbol*] (SAG)
NSEC........ National Service Entertainments Council [*British*]
NSEC........ National Society of Environmental Consultants (EA)
NSEC........ National System for Emergency Coordination (EPAT)
NSEC........ Natl Security Group [*NASDAQ symbol*] (TTSB)
NSEC........ Naval Ship Engineering Center (MCD)
NSEC........ Nuclear Science and Engineering Corp. (SAUS)
NSecIn...... National Security Group, Inc. [*Associated Press*] (SAG)
NSECINST... Naval Ship Engineering Center Instruction
NSEDP...... National Sex Equity Demonstration Project (EDAC)
NSEE........ National Society for Experiential Education (NTPA)
NSEEC...... Naval Shore Electronics Engineering Center [*Terminated, 1966*] (MCD)
NSEF........ National SANE Education Fund (EA)
NSEF........ National Student Educational Fund (EA)
NSEF........ Navy Security Engineering Facility
NSEF........ New Society Educational Foundation (EA)
NSEH........ Neutron Scattering Experimental Hall (SAUS)
NSEI........ Norwegian Society for Electronic Information (SAUS)
NSEIP...... Norwegian Society for Electronic Information Processing (SAUS)
NSel......... Middle Country Public Library, Selden Branch, Selden, NY [*Library symbol*] [*Library of Congress*] (LCLS)
NSELA...... National Science Education Leadership Association (NTPA)
NSelC....... Suffolk County Community College, Selden, NY [*Library symbol*] [*Library of Congress*] (LCLS)
NSelC-E..... Suffolk County Community College, Eastern Campus, Riverhead, NY [*Library symbol*] [*Library of Congress*] (LCLS)
NSelC-W.... Suffolk County Community College, Western Campus, Brentwood, NY [*Library symbol*] [*Library of Congress*] (LCLS)
NSELH....... East Lake Ainslie Historical Society, Nova Scotia [*Library symbol*] [*National Library of Canada*] (BIB)
NSELS....... Noiseless (ABBR)
NSem........ National Semiconductor Corp. [*Associated Press*] (SAG)
NSEM........ Nederlandsche Standard Electric Maatschappij (NITA)
NSEMA...... National Spray Equipment Manufacturers Association (EA)
NSEN........ Network Simulations Engineer (SSD)
NSENS...... Noisiness (ABBR)
NSEP........ National Security and Emergency Preparedness
NSEP........ National Security Education Program [*The Academy for Educational Development*]
NS/EP....... National Security/Emergency Preparedness [*Emergency Management*] (EMA)
NSEP........ National System for Emergency Preparedness (EPAT)
NS/EQ....... New Source and Environmental Questionnaire [*Environmental Protection Agency*] (EG)
NSERC...... Natural Sciences and Engineering Research Council of Canada [*Research center*] (IRC)
NSERI....... National Solar Energy Research Institute [*Energy Research and Development Administration*]
NSES........ National Security Electronic Surveillance

NSES .... National Society of Electrotypers and Stereotypers [*British*] (BI)
NSESG ...... North Sea Environmental Study Group (SAUS)
NSetSP ...... Society for the Preservation of Long Island Antiquities, Setauket, NY [*Library symbol*] [*Library of Congress*] (LCLS)
NSewCH .... H.F. Carey High School, Sewanhaka, NY [*Library symbol*] [*Library of Congress*] (LCLS)
NSewEH ..... Elmont Memorial High School, Sewanhaka, NY [*Library symbol*] [*Library of Congress*] (LCLS)
NSewNH .... New Hyde Park Memorial High School, Sewanhaka, NY [*Library symbol*] [*Library of Congress*] (LCLS)
NSewSJ ..... Stanforth Junior High School, Sewanhaka, NY [*Library symbol*] [*Library of Congress*] (LCLS)
NSF .... Camp Springs, MD [*Location identifier*] [*FAA*] (FAAL)
NSF .... National Salvation Front [*Romania*] [*Political party*]
NSF .... National Sanitation Foundation (EA)
NSF .... National Schizophrenia Fellowship [*British*]
NSF .... National Science Foundation (EA)
NSF .... National Science Foundation, Washington, DC [*OCLC symbol*] (OCLC)
NSF .... National Scoliosis Foundation (EA)
NSF .... National Sex Forum [*Later, ET*] (EA)
NSF .... National Sharecroppers Fund (EA)
NSF .... National Ski Federation (BARN)
NSF .... National Sleep Foundation (MELL)
NSF .... National Soaring Foundation (EA)
NSF .... National Squash Federation [*British*] (DBA)
NSF .... National Stockbrokers Forum [*Later, CFC*] (EA)
NSF .... National Strike Force [*Marine science*] (MSC)
NSF .... National Support Facility (ACAE)
NSF .... Naval Stock Fund
NSF .... Naval Supersonic Facility
NSF .... Naval Supply Force
NSF .... Naval Support Force (MCD)
NSF .... Navy Security Force
NSF .... Navy Special Fuel
NSF .... Navy Stock Fund (DOMA)
NSF .... Negotiated Search Facility [*Information retrieval*]
NSF .... NEM [*N-Ethylmaleimide*]-Sensitive Fusion [*Biochemistry*]
NSF .... N-Ethylmaleimide-Sensitive Fusion (protein) [*Organic chemistry*]
NSF .... Net Square Feet (MCD)
NSF .... Neutron Scattering Facility [*Oak Ridge, TN*] [*Oak Ridge National Laboratory*] [*Department of Energy*] (GRD)
NSF .... Nightstick Fracture [*Medicine*] (MELL)
NSF .... Nitrogen Supply Flask
NSF .... Nodular Subepidermal Fibrosis [*Dermatology*] (DAVI)
NSF .... Noncancerous Skin Fibroblast [*Medicine*]
NSF .... Nonsaponifiable (SAUS)
NSF .... Non-Spin-Flip [*Solid state physics*]
NSF .... Non-Standard Facilities (SAUS)
NSF .... Non Standard Format (SAUS)
NSF .... Nonsterile Field Soil [*Agronomy*]
NSF .... Nonstock Fund
NSF .... Non-Sufficient Funds (SAUS)
NSF .... Nordiska Skattevetenskapliga Forskningradet [*Nordic Council for Tax Research - NCTR*] (EAIO)
NSF .... No Significant Findings (SAUS)
NSF .... Notes Storage File (SAUS)
nsf .... Not Sufficient Funds [*Banking*] (ODBW)
NSF .... Not Sufficient Funds [*Banking*]
NSF .... Nuclear Safety Facility
NSF .... Nuclear Science Foundation (IAA)
NSF .... Nuclear Structure Facility [*British*]
NSFA .... Faleolo/International [*Western Samoa*] [*ICAO location identifier*] (ICLI)
NSFA .... National Science Foundation Act [*1950*]
NSFA .... Naval Support Force, Antarctica (DNAB)
NSFA .... Nondeterministic Finite State Automaton (SAUS)
NSFA .... Nordic Swimming Federations Association (EA)
NSFAC .... National Student Financial Aid Council [*Later, NASFAA*] (EA)
NSFAR .... National Science Foundation Acquisition Regulation [*A publication*] (AAGC)
NSFB .... New School of Family Birthing (EA)
NSFC .... Nancy Sinatra Fan Club (EA)
NSFC .... National Small Flows Clearinghouse [*Environmental Protection Agency*] (AEPA)
NSFC .... National Society of Film Critics
NSFC .... Nat Stuckey Fan Club [*Defunct*] (EA)
NSFC .... Natural Science Foudation of China
NSFC .... Natural Science Foundation of China
NSFC .... Northern States Financial Corp. [*NASDAQ symbol*] (SAG)
NSFC .... Northern States Finl [*NASDAQ symbol*] (TTSB)
NSFCC .... National Strike Force Co-ordination Center (SAUS)
NSFCCDLR ... National Society of Fathers for Child Custody and Divorce Law Reform [*Later, FER*] (EA)
NSFD .... Notice of Structural and/or Functional Deficiency (SAUS)
NSFFC .... National Save the Family Farm Coalition (EA)
NSFFM ...... National Society - First Families of Minnesota [*Association*] (EA)
NSFG .... National Survey of Family Growth
NSFGA ...... Nova Scotia Fruit Growers Association (SAUS)
NSFGB ...... National Ski Federation of Great Britain (ODA)
NSFH .... North-South Fine, Hundreds
NSFI .... Fagali'I [*Western Samoa*] [*ICAO location identifier*] (ICLI)
NSF-I .... National Science Fair - International
NSF/IDOE ... National Science Foundation Office for the International Decade of Ocean Exploration
NSfK .... Nordiska Samarbetsradet for Kriminologi [*Scandinavian Research Council for Criminology - SRCC*] [*Finland*] (EAIO)
NSFL .... National Sanitation Foundation Laboratory
NSFL .... New Strip File (SAUS)
NSFL .... Nova Scotia Federation of Labour (SAUS)
NSFNET ..... National Science Foundation Network
NSFNet ...... National Science Foundation Network
NSFNet ...... NSF Network (SAUS)
NSFO .... Navy Special [*or Standard*] Fuel Oil
NSFORT ..... Non-Standard FORTRAN [*Computer science*] (PDAA)
NSFP .... Natural Suppressor Factor Protein (DB)
NSFP .... Non-Sodium Fire Protection [*Nuclear energy*] (NRCH)
NSFPA .... National Suppliers to Food Processors Association (EA)
NSFPR ...... National Science Foundation Procurement Regulation [*A publication*] (AAGC)
NSFR .... National Society of Fund Raisers [*Later, NSFRE*] (EA)
NSFR .... Nitroxide Stable Free Radical [*For tissue NMR*]
NSFRC ...... National Silver Fox Rabbit Club (EA)
NSFRE .... National Society of Fund Raising Executives (EA)
NSFRE Foundation ... National Society of Fund Raising Executives Foundation [*Formerly the National Society of Fund Raisers Institute of Continuing Education and the National Society of Fund Raising Executives*] (NFD)
NSFRE Institute ... Former name of the National Society of Fund Rainsing Executives Foundation (NFD)
NSFS .... National Society for Shut-Ins (EA)
NSFS .... Net Section Fracture Strength (PDAA)
NSfSC .... Sullivan County Community College, South Fallsburg, NY [*Library symbol*] [*Library of Congress*] (LCLS)
NSF/STAH ... National Science Foundation Program for Science and Technology Aid to the Handicapped
NSFT .... North-South Fine, Tens
NSFTD .... Normal, Spontaneous, Full Term Delivery [*Obstetrics*]
NSFTL .... National Sanitation Foundation Testing Laboratory, Inc. (MSA)
NSFU .... Needle Stampers' and Filers' Union [*British*]
NSFU .... North-South Fine, Units
NSF Univ ... Federal Support to Universities, Colleges and Nonprofit Institutions (SAUS)
NSG .... Aircompany Liana JSA [*Ukraine*] [*FAA designator*] (FAAC)
NSG .... National Society for Graphology (EA)
NSG .... National Steering Group (AIE)
NSG .... National Supply Group [*Military*] (AFIT)
NSG .... Natural Systems Group (SAUS)
NSG .... Naval Security Group
NSG .... Network Services Group (SAUS)
NSG .... Network Support Group (NITA)
NSG .... Neurosecretory Granules
NSG .... Neutron Scattering Group [*Medicine*] [*IOP*] (EDAA)
NSG .... Newspaper Systems Group (EA)
NSG .... Noise Signal Generator (SAUS)
NSG .... Non-Statutory Guidance [*British*] (DET)
NSG .... Non-Statutory Guidelines (WDAA)
NSG .... North Seeking Gyro
NSG .... Not So Good
NSG .... Nuclear Suppliers' Group [*Australia*] (ECON)
Nsg .... Nursing (AMHC)
nsg .... Nursing [*Therapy term*] (CTAA)
NSG .... Nursing
NSGA .... National Sand and Gravel Association [*Later, NAA*] (EA)
NSGA .... National Specialty Gift Association (EA)
NSGA .... National Sporting Goods Association (EA)
NSGA .... Naval Security Group Activity
NSGC .... National Self Government Committee (EA)
NSGC .... National Society of Genetic Counselors (EA)
NSGC .... National Swine Growers Council [*Later, NPPC*] (EA)
NSGC .... Naval Security Group Command (DNAB)
NSGC .... Nevada Space Grant Consortium (RCD)
NSGCC ...... Coastal Courier, Glace Bay, Nova Scotia [*Library symbol*] [*National Library of Canada*] (NLC)
NSGCFA ..... Aurora, Canadian Forces Base, Greenwood, Nova Scotia [*Library symbol*] [*National Library of Canada*] (NLC)
NSGCH .... Naval Security Group Command Headquarters
NSGCHQ .... Naval Security Group Command Headquarters (SAUS)
NSGCT ...... Nonsiminomatous Germ Cell Turmors [*Medicine*] (MEDA)
NSGCTT ..... Nonseminomatous Germ Cell Tumors of the Testes
NSGD .... National Sea Grant Depository [*National Oceanic and Atmospheric Administration*] [*Information service or system*] (IID)
NSGD .... National Support Group for Dermatomyositis (EA)
NSGD .... National Support Group for PM/DM [*Formerly, National Support Group for Dermatiomyositis*] (EA)
NS-GFW ..... Noise Substest of the Goldman-Fristoe-Woodcock Auditory Skills Test Battery (EDAC)
NSGI .... Nonspecific Genital Infection [*Medicine*] (EDAA)
NSGIB .... NAVSHIPS [*Naval Ship Systems Command*] General Information Book
NSGLS ...... Nordisk Sekretariat for Gartneri- Land-, og Skovarbejderforbund [*Nordic Secretariat for Agricultural and Horticultural Workers - NSAHW*] [*Denmark*] [*Defunct*] (EAIO)
NSGN .... Noise Generator (CET)
NSGOC ...... Naval Security Group Orientation Course (DNAB)
NSGOC ...... Old Court House Museum, Guysborough, Nova Scotia [*Library symbol*] [*National Library of Canada*] (NLC)
NSGP .... National Ship Corporation of the Philippines [*Common carrier symbol*]
NS Grp ...... NS Group, Inc. [*Associated Press*] (SAG)
Nsg Sta ..... Nursing Station (DAVI)

NSGT .... National Aeronautics and Space Administration Ground Terminal (NAKS)
NSGT .... Non-Self-Governing Territories [*United Nations*]
NSGTMEM... National Society of General Tool Makers, Engineers, and Machinists [*A union*] [*British*]
NSGTP ...... Naval Security Group Training Publication (DNAB)
NSGW .... National Society of Glass Workers [*A union*] [*British*]
NSGW .... Native Sons of the Golden West (EA)
NSH.......... Halifax City Regional Library, Nova Scotia [*Library symbol*] [*National Library of Canada*] (NLC)
NSh.......... John Jermain Memorial Public Library, Sag Harbor, NY [*Library symbol*] [*Library of Congress*] (LCLS)
NSH.......... Nashua Corp. [*NYSE symbol*] (SPSG)
NSH.......... Nashville [*Diocesan abbreviation*] [*Tennessee*] (TOCD)
NSH.......... National Society for Histotechnology (EA)
NSH.......... National Society of Hypnotherapists (EA)
NSH.......... National Surgical Hospitals (MHID)
NSH.......... Naval School of Health Sciences, Bethesda, MD [*OCLC symbol*] (OCLC)
NSH.......... New Search & rescue Helicopter (SAUS)
NSH.......... Nordisk Samarbeidskomite for Husstellundervisning [*Nordic Joint Committee for Domestic Education - NJCDE*] (EAIO)
NSH.......... Northern-Southern Hybrid [*Hemoglobin phenotype of Rana pipiens*]
NSH.......... Northville State Hospital (SAUS)
NSH.......... No Stock on Hand (SAUS)
NSH.......... Not So Hot [*Slang*]
NSH.......... Nutritional Secondary Hyperparathyroidism (SAUS)
NSHA........ National Smoking and Health Association [*Medicine*] [*Sweden*] (EDAA)
NSHA........ National Steeplechase and Hunt Association (EA)
NSHA........ National Stock Horse Association (EA)
NSHAC-FP... National Self-Help Action Center - Food Program (EA)
NSHAG ...... Art Gallery of Nova Scotia, Halifax, Nova Scotia [*Library symbol*] [*National Library of Canada*] (NLC)
NSHANSS... Synod Office, Diocese of Nova Scotia, Anglican Church of Canada, Halifax, Nova Scotia [*Library symbol*] [*National Library of Canada*] (NLC)
NSHAR ...... Algas Resources Ltd., Halifax, Nova Scotia [*Library symbol*] [*National Library of Canada*] (NLC)
NSHAVI...... [*The*] Atlantic Provinces Resource Centre for the Visually-Impaired, Halifax, Nova Scotia [*Library symbol*] [*National Library of Canada*] (NLC)
NSHAVI...... Atlantic Provinces Resource Centre for the Visually Impaired, Halifax, Nova Scotia (SAUS)
NSHBS ...... Nova Scotia Barristers Society, Halifax, Nova Scotia [*Library symbol*] [*National Library of Canada*] (NLC)
NSHC .... Cambridge Military Library, Halifax, Nova Scotia [*Library symbol*] [*National Library of Canada*] (NLC)
NSHC .... National Self-Help Clearinghouse (EA)
NSHC .... National Silver-Haired Congress (EA)
NSHC .... National Syrian Hamster Council [*British*] (DBA)
NSHC .... North Sea Hydrographic Commission [*of the International Hydrographic Organization*] [*Belgium*]
NSHC .... North Sea Hyperbaric Centre (SAUS)
NSHCA ...... Nova Scotia College of Art and Design, Halifax, Nova Scotia [*Library symbol*] [*National Library of Canada*] (NLC)
NSHCB ...... Music and Record Library, Canadian Broadcasting Corp. [*Musicotheque et Discotheque, Societe Radio-Canada*] Halifax, Nova Scotia [*Library symbol*] [*National Library of Canada*] (NLC)
NSHCBC..... Canadian British Consultants Ltd., Halifax, Nova Scotia [*Library symbol*] [*National Library of Canada*] (NLC)
NSHCBF..... Film Library, CBHT-TV, Halifax, Nova Scotia [*Library symbol*] [*National Library of Canada*] (NLC)
NSHCD ...... Law Library, Cox, Downie & Co., Halifax, Nova Scotia [*Library symbol*] [*National Library of Canada*] (NLC)
NSHCDD .... Nova Scotia Commission on Drug Dependency, Halifax, Nova Scotia [*Library symbol*] [*National Library of Canada*] (NLC)
NSHCFM .... Maritime Command Museum, Canadian Forces Base, Halifax, Nova Scotia [*Library symbol*] [*National Library of Canada*] (BIB)
NSHCH ...... Camp Hill Hospital, Halifax, Nova Scotia [*Library symbol*] [*National Library of Canada*] (NLC)
NSHCIC ..... National Solar Heating and Cooling Information Center [*Later, CAREIRS*]
NSHCIC ..... Nova Scotia Communications and Information Centre, Halifax, Nova Scotia [*Library symbol*] [*National Library of Canada*] (NLC)
NSHD........ Dalhousie University, Halifax, Nova Scotia [*Library symbol*] [*National Library of Canada*] (NLC)
NSHD........ Nodular Sclerosing Hodgkin's Disease [*Medicine*] (DMAA)
NSHDA...... Archives, Dalhousie University, Halifax, Nova Scotia [*Library symbol*] [*National Library of Canada*] (BIB)
NSHDAG .... Nova Scotia Department of the Attorney-General, Halifax, Nova Scotia [*Library symbol*] [*National Library of Canada*] (NLC)
NSHDCA .... Nova Scotia Department of Consumer Affairs, Halifax, Nova Scotia [*Library symbol*] [*National Library of Canada*] (NLC)
NSHDD ...... Nova Scotia Department of Industry, Trade, and Technology, Halifax, Nova Scotia [*Library symbol*] [*National Library of Canada*] (NLC)
NSHDE ...... Nova Scotia Department of the Environment, Halifax, Nova Scotia [*Library symbol*] [*National Library of Canada*] (NLC)
NSHDEA.... Resource Centre, Ecology Action Centre, Dalhousie University, Halifax, Nova Scotia [*Library symbol*] [*National Library of Canada*] (NLC)
NSHDF ...... Nova Scotia Department of Fisheries, Halifax, Nova Scotia [*Library symbol*] [*National Library of Canada*] (NLC)
NSHDH ...... Nova Scotia Department of Transportation, Halifax, Nova Scotia [*Library symbol*] [*National Library of Canada*] (NLC)
NSHDIP ..... Institute of Public Affairs, Dalhousie University, Halifax, Nova Scotia, [*Library symbol*] [*National Library of Canada*] (NLC)
NSHDIR ..... School of Resources and Environmental Studies, Dalhousie University, Halifax, Nova Scotia [*Library symbol*] [*National Library of Canada*] (NLC)
NSHDL ...... Law School, Dalhousie University, Halifax, Nova Scotia [*Library symbol*] [*National Library of Canada*] (NLC)
NSHDLS..... School of Library Service, Dalhousie University, Halifax, Nova Scotia [*Library symbol*] [*National Library of Canada*] (NLC)
NSHDM ..... W. K. Kellogg Health Sciences Library, Dalhousie University, Halifax, Nova Scotia [*Library symbol*] [*National Library of Canada*] (NLC)
NSHDMA.... Map Library, Dalhousie University, Halifax, Nova Scotia [*Library symbol*] [*National Library of Canada*] (NLC)
NSHDOL .... Nova Scotia Department of Labour and Manpower, Halifax, Nova Scotia [*Library symbol*] [*National Library of Canada*] (NLC)
NSHDOM.... Nova Scotia Department of Mines, Halifax, Nova Scotia [*Library symbol*] [*National Library of Canada*] (NLC)
NSHDOS .... Dalhousie Ocean Studies Programme, Dalhousie University, Halifax, Nova Scotia [*Library symbol*] [*National Library of Canada*] (NLC)
NSHDR ...... Cultural Affairs Library, Nova Scotia Department of Tourism and Culture, Halifa x, Nova Scotia [*Library symbol*] [*National Library of Canada*] (NLC)
NSHDS ...... MacDonald Science Library, Dalhousie University, Halifax, Nova Scotia [*Library symbol*] [*National Library of Canada*] (NLC)
NSHDS ...... National Society for Hebrew Day Schools (NTPA)
NSHE .... [*The*] New Schaff-Herzog Encyclopaedia of Religious Knowledge [*A publication*] (BJA)
NSHEB ...... North of Scotland Hydro-Electric Board (ECON)
NShei........ Shelter Island Public Library Society, Shelter Island, NY [*Library symbol*] [*Library of Congress*] (LCLS)
NSherb ...... Sherburne Public Library, Sherburne, NY [*Library symbol*] [*Library of Congress*] (LCLS)
NSHF .... Fisheries and Oceans Canada [*Peches et Oceans Canada*] Halifax, Nova Scotia [*Library symbol*] [*National Library of Canada*] (NLC)
NSHF .... Scotia-Fundy Regional Library, Fisheries and Oceans Canada [*Bibliotheque de la Region Scotia-Fundy, Peches et Oceans Canada*], Halifax, Nova Scotia [*Library symbol*] [*National Library of Canada*] (NLC)
NSHFIF...... Federal-Provincial Taxation and Fiscal Relations Library, Nova Scotia Departmentof Finance, Halifax, Nova Scotia [*Library symbol*] [*National Library of Canada*] (NLC)
NSHH........ Nova Scotia Department of Health, Halifax, Nova Scotia [*Library symbol*] [*National Library of Canada*] (NLC)
NSHHC ...... Halifax County Regional Library, Lower Sackville, Nova Scotia [*Library symbol*] [*National Library of Canada*] (NLC)
NSHHE ...... Halifax Herald Ltd., Nova Scotia [*Library symbol*] [*National Library of Canada*] (NLC)
NSHHI....... Health Services Library, Halifax Infirmary, Nova Scotia [*Library symbol*] [*National Library of Canada*] (NLC)
NSHHR ...... Nova Scotia Human Rights Commission, Halifax, Nova Scotia [*Library symbol*] [*National Library of Canada*] (NLC)
NSHHS ...... Hantsport and Area Historical Society, Nova Scotia [*Library symbol*] [*National Library of Canada*] (NLC)
NSHIAP ..... Atlantic Regional Library, Parks Canada [*Bibliotheque Regionale de l'Atlantique, Parcs Canada*] Halifax, Nova Scotia [*Library symbol*] [*National Library of Canada*] (NLC)
NSHIC .... International Centre for Ocean Development, Halifax, Nova Scotia [*Library symbol*] [*National Library of Canada*] (BIB)
NSHJ .... Canada Department of Justice [*Ministere de la Justice*] Halifax, Nova Scotia [*Library symbol*] [*National Library of Canada*] (NLC)
NSHK .... University of King's College, Halifax, Nova Scotia [*Library symbol*] [*National Library of Canada*] (NLC)
NSHKH ...... Izaak Walton Killam Hospital for Children, Halifax, Nova Scotia [*Library symbol*] [*National Library of Canada*] (NLC)
NSHKJ....... School of Journalism, University of King's College, Halifax, Nova Scotia [*Library symbol*] [*National Library of Canada*] (NLC)
NSHKMGM... Kitz, Matheson, Green & MacIsaac Law Firm, Halifax, Nova Scotia [*Library symbol*] [*National Library of Canada*] (NLC)
NSHL .... Legislative Library, Halifax, Nova Scotia [*Library symbol*] [*National Library of Canada*] (NLC)
NSHLA ...... Nova Scotia Legal Aid, Halifax, Nova Scotia [*Library symbol*] [*National Library of Canada*] (BIB)
NSHLP ...... Liberal Party of Nova Scotia, Halifax [*Library symbol*] [*National Library of Canada*] (BIB)
NSHM .... Atlantic Regional Laboratory, National Research Council [*Laboratoire Regionalde l'Atlantique, Conseil National de Recherches du Canada*] Halifax, Nova Sco tia [*Library symbol*] [*National Library of Canada*] (NLC)
NSHMA...... Nova Scotia Department of Municipal Affairs, Halifax, Nova Scotia [*Library symbol*] [*National Library of Canada*] (NLC)
NSHMBA.... National Society of Hispanic MBAs (EA)
NSHMC...... Maritime Conservatory of Music, Halifax, Nova Scotia [*Library symbol*] [*National Library of Canada*] (NLC)
NSHMCA.... Archives, Maritime Conference, United Church of Canada Halifax, Nova Scotia [*Library symbol*] [*National Conference of Commissioners on Uniform State Laws*] (BIB)
NSHMCR.... Law Library, McInnes, Cooper & Robertson, Halifax, Nova Scotia [*Library symbol*] [*National Library of Canada*] (NLC)
NSHML...... Martec Ltd., Halifax, Nova Scotia [*Library symbol*] [*National Library of Canada*] (NLC)
NSHMM..... Maritime Museum of the Atlantic, Halifax, Nova Scotia [*Library symbol*] [*National Library of Canada*] (NLC)
NSHMO ..... Mobil Oil Canada Ltd., Halifax, Nova Scotia [*Library symbol*] [*National Library of Canada*] (NLC)
NSHMS...... Nova Scotia Museum, Halifax, Nova Scotia [*Library symbol*] [*National Library of Canada*] (NLC)
NSHMT...... Regional Library, Canadian Coast Guard [*Bibliotheque Regionale, Garde CotiereCanadienne*] Dartmouth, Nova Scotia [*Library symbol*] [*National Library of Canada*] (NLC)

NSHMTT .... Information Resource Centre, Maritime Tel & Tel, Halifax, Nova Scotia [*Library symbol*] [*National Library of Canada*] (NLC)
NSHN .... Defence Research Establishment Atlantic, Canada Department of National Defence [*Centre de Recherches pour la Defense Atlantique, Ministere de la Defense Nationale*] Dartmouth, Nova Scotia [*Library symbol*] [*National Library of Canada*] (NLC)
NSHND ...... Reference and Recreational Library (Stadacona), Canada Department of National Defence [*Bibliotheque de Consultation et de Lecture (Stadacona), Ministere de la Defense Nationale*] Halifax, Nova Scotia [*Library symbol*] [*National Library of Canada*] (NLC)
NSHNF ...... National Film Board [*Office National du Film*], Halifax, Nova Scotia [*Library symbol*] [*National Library of Canada*] (NLC)
NSHNI .... Nova Scotia Nautical Institute, Halifax, Nova Scotia [*Library symbol*] [*National Library of Canada*] (NLC)
NSHNP ...... Nova Scotia Newspaper Project, Halifax [*Library symbol*] [*National Library of Canada*] (BIB)
NSHNS ...... Ships Recreational Library, Canadian Forces Base Halifax [*Bibliotheque Recreative, Base des Forces Canadiennes Halifax*], Nova Scotia [*Library symbol*] [*National Library of Canada*] (BIB)
NSHO .... Naval Service Headquarters, Ottawa (DNAB)
NShor .... Shoreham-Wading River Public Library, Shoreham, NY [*Library symbol*] [*Library of Congress*] (LCLS)
NShorHS .... Shoreham-Wading River High School, Shoreham, NY [*Library symbol*] [*Library of Congress*] (LCLS)
NSHP .... Nova Scotia Public Archives, Halifax, Nova Scotia [*Library symbol*] [*National Library of Canada*] (NLC)
NSHPC ...... Corporate Research and Information Centre, Nova Scotia Power Corp., Halifax, Nova Scotia [*Library symbol*] [*National Library of Canada*] (NLC)
NSHPH ...... Atlantic School of Theology, Halifax, Nova Scotia [*Library symbol*] [*National Library of Canada*] (NLC)
NSHPI .... Planning Information Office, City of Halifax, Nova Scotia [*Library symbol*] [*National Library of Canada*] (NLC)
NSHPL ...... Nova Scotia Union Catalogue, Nova Scotia Provincial Library, Halifax, Nova Scotia [*Library symbol*] [*National Library of Canada*] (NLC)
NSHPLX ..... Reference Services, Nova Scotia Provinicial Library, Halifax, Nova Scotia [*Library symbol*] [*National Library of Canada*] (NLC)
NSHPT ...... Neonatal Severe Hyperparathyroidism [*Medicine*] (DMAA)
NSHPW ..... Atlantic Regional Library, Public Works Canada [*Bibliotheque Regionale de l'Atlantique, Travaux Publics Canada*] Halifax, Nova Scotia [*Library symbol*] [*National Library of Canada*] (NLC)
NSHQ .... Naval Service Headquarters [*Canada*]
NSHQ .... Naval Staff Headquarters [*British military*] (DMA)
NShr .... John C. Hart Memorial Library, Shrub Oak, NY [*Library symbol*] [*Library of Congress*] (LCLS)
NSHR .... National Show Horse Registry (EA)
NSHR .... North Shore Railroad [*Federal Railroad Administration identification code*]
NSHR .... Nova Scotia Research Foundation, Dartmouth, Nova Scotia [*Library symbol*] [*National Library of Canada*] (NLC)
NSHRC ...... National Self-Help Resource Center [*Defunct*] (EA)
NSHRC ...... National Shared Housing Resource Center (EA)
NSHRC ...... Nova Scotia Rehabilitation Centre, Halifax, Nova Scotia [*Library symbol*] [*National Library of Canada*] (NLC)
NSHRCA .... Roman Catholic Archdiocesan Archives, Halifax, Nova Scotia [*Library symbol*] [*National Library of Canada*] (BIB)
NSHRL ...... Nova Scotia Regional Libraries, Halifax, Nova Scotia [*Library symbol*] [*National Library of Canada*] (NLC)
NSHRP ...... Photogrammetry Division, Nova Scotia Research Foundation, Halifax, Nova Scotia [*Library symbol*] [*Obsolete*] [*National Library of Canada*] (NLC)
NSHS .... National Slavic Honor Society (EA)
NSHS .... Naval School of Health Sciences [*Bethesda, MD*]
NSHS .... St. Mary's University, Halifax, Nova Scotia [*Library symbol*] [*National Library of Canada*] (NLC)
NSHSDET... Naval School of Health Sciences Detachment (DNAB)
NSHSG ...... Sable Gas Systems Ltd., Halifax, Nova Scotia [*Library symbol*] [*National Library of Canada*] (NLC)
NSHSMC .... Stewart, MacKeen & Covert Law Firm, Halifax, Nova Scotia [*Library symbol*] [*National Library of Canada*] (NLC)
NSHSP ...... Social Development Division Library, Social Planning Department, City of Halifax, Nova Scotia [*Library symbol*] [*National Library of Canada*] (NLC)
NSHSPT ..... Ferguson Library for Print Handicapped Students, Patrick Power Library, St. Mary's University, Halifax, Nova Scotia [*Library symbol*] [*National Library of Canada*] (NLC)
NSHSS ...... Nova Scotia Department of Community Services, Halifax, Nova Scotia [*Library symbol*] [*National Library of Canada*] (NLC)
NSHSW ..... Maritime School of Social Work, Halifax, Nova Scotia [*Library symbol*] [*National Library of Canada*] (NLC)
NSHT .... Technical University of Nova Scotia, Halifax, Nova Scotia [*Library symbol*] [*National Library of Canada*] (NLC)
NSHTI .... Nova Scotia Institute of Technology, Halifax, Nova Scotia [*Library symbol*] [*National Library of Canada*] (NLC)
NSHTU ...... Nova Scotia Teachers Union, Halifax, Nova Scotia [*Library symbol*] [*National Library of Canada*] (NLC)
NSHV .... Mount Saint Vincent University, Halifax, Nova Scotia [*Library symbol*] [*National Library of Canada*] (NLC)
NSHVA ...... Art Gallery, Mount Saint Vincent University, Halifax, Nova Scotia [*Library symbol*] [*National Library of Canada*] (NLC)
NSHVGH .... Health Sciences Library, Victoria General Hospital, Halifax, Nova Scotia [*Library symbol*] [*National Library of Canada*] (NLC)
NSHVH ...... Halifax Regional Vocational School, Nova Scotia [*Library symbol*] [*National Library of Canada*] (NLC)
NSHVL ...... Nashville, AR [*American Association of Railroads railroad junction routing code*]
NSHVTT ..... Nova Scotia Department of Advanced Education and Job Training, Halifax, Nova S cotia [*Library symbol*] [*National Library of Canada*] (NLC)
NSHW .... Atlantic Region, Atmospheric Environment Service, Environment Canada [*Bureau Regional de l'Atlantique, Service de l'Environnement Atmospherique, Environnement Canada*] Halifax, Nova Scotia [*Library symbol*] [*National Library of Canada*] (NLC)
NShW .... Sag Harbor Whaling and Historical Museum, Sag Harbor, NY [*Library symbol*] [*Library of Congress*] (LCLS)
NSI .... Handbook of North-Semitic Inscriptions [*A publication*] (BJA)
NSI .... Name Service Independent (SAUS)
NSI .... NASA Science Internet
NSI .... NASA [*National Aeronautical and Space Administration*] Standard Indicator
NSI .... NASA Standard Initiator (NASA)
NSI .... National environmental Satellite data and Information service (SAUS)
NSI .... National Security Index of the American Security Council [*A publication*] (DLA)
NSI .... National Security Information (NRCH)
NSI .... National Service Industries, Inc. [*NYSE symbol*] (SPSG)
NSI .... National Service [*Life*] Insurance
NSI .... National Shipbuilding Initiative [*MARAD*] (TAG)
NSI .... National Shoe Institute (EA)
NSI .... National Space Institute [*Later, NSS*] (EA)
NSI .... National Statistical Institute (EURO)
NSI .... National Supervisory Inspectorate [*British*] (EECA)
NSI .... Natl Service Indus [*NYSE symbol*] (TTSB)
NSI .... Naval Science Instructor (DNAB)
NSI .... Negative Self-Image [*Psychology*]
NSI .... Network Solutions
NSI .... Network Solutions, Inc.
NSI .... Network Strategies, Inc. [*Fairfax, VA*] [*Telecommunications*] (TSSD)
NSI .... Network Support, Inc.
NSI .... Neurosciences Institute (DAVI)
NSI .... Next Sequential Instruction
NSI .... Nielsen Station Index [*Nielsen Media Research*] [*Information service or system*]
NSI .... Nitrogen Solubility Index [*Analytical chemistry*]
NSI .... Noise Source Instrumentation
NSI .... Nonsatellite Identification
NSI .... Nonsequenced Information (IAA)
NSI .... Non-SNA Interconnect (SAUS)
NSI .... Non-Specific Illness (WDAA)
NSI .... Nonspecific Infection [*Medicine*] (MELL)
NSI .... Nonspecific Sexually Transmitted Infection [*Medicine*]
NSI .... Nonstandard Item
NSI .... Nonstocked Item
NSI .... Nonstreptococcal Infection [*Medicine*] (MELL)
NSI .... Non-Syncytium-Inducing [*Cytology*]
NSI .... Norsk Senter for Informatikk [*Norwegian Center for Informatics*] [*Information service or system*] (IID)
NSI .... North-South Institute [*Canada*] (EAIO)
NSI .... Norton Simon, Inc. (EFIS)
NSI .... No Sign of Infection (SAUS)
NSI .... No Sign of Inflammation (SAUS)
NSI .... No Signs of Infection [*Medicine*] (DMAA)
NSI .... Not Seriously Injured [*Environmental science*] (COE)
NSI .... Nuclear Safety Inspection (NVT)
NSI .... Nuclear Safety Institute
NSI .... Nuclear Services International
NSI .... Nuclear Status Indicator (DNAB)
NSI .... Nuclear Surety Inspection
NSI .... Numetic Signal Insignia (SAUS)
NSI .... Nusantara Systems International Inc. (EFIS)
NSI .... San Nicolas Island, CA [*Location identifier*] [*FAA*] (FAAL)
NSI-1 .... NASA [*National Aeronautics and Space Administration*] Standard Initiator -Type 1 [*Formerly, SMSI*] (NASA)
NSIA .... National Security and International Affairs [*Office of Management and Budget*]
NSIA .... National Security Industrial Association (EA)
NSIAC .... National Student Involvement Assistance Center [*Boston University*] [*Defunct*]
NSIAC .... Northern Sun Intercollegiate Athletic Conference (PSS)
NSIAD .... National Security and International Affairs Division (AAGC)
NSIC .... National Security Insurance Co. [*NASDAQ symbol*] (COMM)
NSIC .... National Spinal Injuries Centre [*Stoke Mandeville Hospital*] [*British*] (CB)
NSIC .... National Storage Industry Consortium
NSIC .... National Strategy Information Center (EA)
NSIC .... Naval Security and Investigative Command
NSIC .... Next Senior in Command [*Navy*]
NSIC .... Northern Sun Intercollegiate Conference (PSS)
NSIC .... Noster Salvator Iesus Christus [*Our Savior, Jesus Christ*] [*Latin*]
NSIC .... Nuclear Safety Information Center
NSIC .... Nuclear Strike Information Center
NSiC .... Staten Island Community College, Staten Island, NY [*Library symbol*] [*Library of Congress*] [*Obsolete*] (LCLS)
NSICC .... North Sea International Chart Commission [*Nautical term*] (HRNC)
NSiCS .... College of Staten Island, St. George Campus, Staten Island, NY [*Library symbol*] [*Library of Congress*] (LCLS)
NSICU .... Neurosurgical Intensive Care Unit [*Medicine*] (DMAA)
NSID .... National Society of Interior Designers [*Later, ASID*]
NSIDC .... National Snow and Ice Data Center [*National Oceanic and Atmospheric Administration*] (GFGA)

NSIDH .... National System of Interstate and Defense Highways (AFIT)
NSidHi ...... Sidney New York Historical Society, Sidney, NY [*Library symbol*] [*Library of Congress*] (LCLS)
NSidS .... Bendix Corp., Electrical Components Division, Engineering Library, Sidney, NY [*Library symbol*] [*Library of Congress*] (LCLS)
NSIDS .... National Shut-In Day Society (EA)
NSIDSC ..... National Sudden Infant Death Syndrome Clearinghouse (EA)
NSIDSF ...... National Sudden Infant Death Syndrome Foundation (EA)
NSIDSF ...... SIDS Alliance (EA)
NSIEE .... National Society for Internships and Experiential Education (EA)
NSIF .... National Swine Improvement Federation (EA)
NSIF .... Near Space Instrumentation Facility [*NASA*] (KSC)
NSIG .... North Sea Island Group (SAUS)
NSI-I .... NASA Standard Initiator-Type I (SAUS)
NSiIR .... New York State Department of Mental Hygiene, Institute for Basic Research in Mental Retardation, Staten Island, NY [*Library symbol*] [*Library of Congress*] (LCLS)
NSIL .... National Seafood Inspection Laboratory [*Pascagoula, MS*] [*Department of Commerce*] (GRD)
NSIL .... Nonsaturating Inverter Logic (IAA)
NSILA .... Nonsuppressible Insulin-Like Activity [*Cytochemistry*]
NSiIStC....... Saint Columban's Seminary, Silver Creek, NY [*Library symbol*] [*Library of Congress*] [*Obsolete*] (LCLS)
NSIME....... North Staffordshire Institute of Mining Engineers (SAUS)
NSiND .... Notre Dame College of Staten Island, Staten Island, NY [*Library symbol*] [*Library of Congress*] (LCLS)
N Sing....... Noun Singular (SAUS)
NSIO......... Nova Scotia Information Office (SAUS)
NSIP .... Nonlinear Signal and Image Processing (SAUS)
NSIP .... Nutrition Services Incentive Program
NSIPA .... National Society of Insurance Premium Auditors (EA)
NSIPS .... NRL [*Naval Research Laboratory*] Satellite Image Processing System [*Marine science*] (OSRA)
NSIR......... Nosier (ABBR)
NSIRC .... National Security Incident Response Center [*Emergency Management*] (EMA)
NSiRC .... Richmond College, Staten Island, NY [*Library symbol*] [*Library of Congress*] [*Obsolete*] (LCLS)
NSIS .... NASA Software Information System (SSD)
NSIS .... National Shut-In Society (EA)
NSIS .... National Survey of Instructional Staff [*Department of Education*] (GFGA)
NSIS .... New Submarine Intercept Sonar (SAUS)
NSIS .... Nova Scotian Institute of Science [*Canada*] (RCD)
NSISL .... New South Intercollegiate Swimming League (PSS)
NSiSV .... Saint Vincent's Medical Center of Richmond, Staten Island, NY [*Library symbol*] [*Library of Congress*] (LCLS)
NSIT .... Insight Enterprises, Inc. [*NASDAQ symbol*] (SAG)
NSIT .... Insiht Enterprises [*NASDAQ symbol*] (TTSB)
NSIT .... Not Safe in Taxis
NSIT .... Nova Scotia Institute of Technology (SAUS)
NSIT .... Trudeau Institute, Saranac Lake (SAUS)
N-SITE....... Near-Term System Integration Test and Evaluation (ACAE)
NSITF........ National Ship Installations Test Facility
NSIU .... Northland Services [*Intermodal shipping container symbol*] (TVRC)
NSIX......... Neuromedical Systems [*NASDAQ symbol*] (TTSB)
NSIX......... Neuromedical Systems, Inc. [*NASDAQ symbol*] (SAG)
NSIY......... North Somerset Imperial Yeomanry [*British military*] (DMA)
NSIZ .... NSP Industries [*Federal Railroad Administration identification code*]
NSJ .... Nova Scotia Judgments [*Database*] [*Canada*] (GDD)
NSJ .... Nuclear Society of Japan (SAUS)
NSJ .... Nuestro Senor Jesucristo [*Our Lord, Jesus Christ*] [*Spanish*]
NSJC .... National Society of Journeymen Curriers [*A union*] [*British*]
NSJC .... Noster Salvator Jesus Christus [*Our Savior, Jesus Christ*] [*Latin*]
NSJC .... Notre Seigneur Jesus Christ [*Our Lord, Jesus Christ*] [*French*]
NSK.......... Narrow Shift Keying [*Communications term*] (DCT)
NSK.......... New Skies Satellites ADS [*NYSE symbol*]
NSK.......... Nippon Seiko Kabushiki Kaisha [*Japan*]
NSK.......... Not Specified by Kind (MHDI)
NSKC .... National Safe Kids Campaign (EA)
NSKER ...... Efamol Research Institute, Kentville, Nova Scotia [*Library symbol*] [*National Library of Canada*] (NLC)
NSKIP .... Nordiska Samarbetskommitten for Internationell Politik [*Nordic Cooperation Committee for International Politics, Including Conflict and Peace Research*] (EAIO)
NSKKR ...... Kings Regional Vocational School, Kentville, Nova Scotia [*Library symbol*] [*National Library of Canada*] (NLC)
NSKL .... Wildlife Division, Nova Scotia Department of Lands and Forests, Kentville, Nova Scotia [*Library symbol*] [*National Library of Canada*] (NLC)
NSKOK ...... Old Kings Courthouse Heritage Museum, Kentville, Nova Scotia [*Library symbol*] [*National Library of Canada*] (NLC)
NSKR........ Research Station, Agriculture Canada [*Station de Recherches, Agriculture Canada*] Kentville, Nova Scotia [*Library symbol*] [*National Library of Canada*] (NLC)
NSKVH ...... Valley Health Services Association, Kentville, Nova Scotia [*Library symbol*] [*National Library of Canada*] (NLC)
NSKY .... New Sky Communications, Inc. (SAUS)
NSL.......... NanoStructures Laboratory [*Massachusetts Institute of Technology*] (RCD)
NSL.......... Nasal (ABBR)
NSL.......... Nasion-Sella Line [*Brain anatomy*]
NSL.......... National Science Laboratories (KSC)
NSL.......... National Science Library [*Later, Canada Institute for Scientific and Technical Information*] (DIT)
NSL.......... National Service League [*British military*] (DMA)
NSL.......... National Soccer League (EA)
NSL.......... National Standards Laboratory [*Formerly, IBS, IMR*] [*National Institute of Standards and Technology*]
NSL.......... National Story League (EA)
NSL.......... Naval Submarine League (EA)
NSL.......... Naval Supersonic Laboratory
NSL.......... Navigating Sub-Lieutenant [*Navy*] [*British*] (ROG)
NSL.......... Navy Standards Laboratory
NSL.......... Navy Stock List
NSL.......... Net Switching Loss [*Telecommunications*] (TEL)
NSL.......... New Simulation Language (SAUS)
NSL.......... New Special Libraries [*A publication*]
NSL.......... Next State List (SAUS)
NSL.......... Nonstandard Label [*Computer science*]
NSL.......... Nonstockage List
NSL.......... North Air Airlines (SAUS)
NSL.......... Northern Scientific Laboratory (SAUS)
NSL.......... Northrup Space Laboratories (KSC)
NSL.......... Norwood & St. Lawrence Railroad Co. [*AAR code*]
NSL.......... Not Stock Listed
NSL.......... Nuclear Safety Line
NSL.......... Numidian Support League (SAUS)
NSI........... Saranac Lake Free Library, Saranac Lake, NY [*Library symbol*] [*Library of Congress*] (LCLS)
NSLA .... Louisbourg Archives, Nova Scotia [*Library symbol*] [*National Library of Canada*] (NLC)
NSLA .... National Society of Literature and the Arts (EA)
NSLA .... National Staff Leasing Association (EA)
NSLA .... Nova Scotia Library Association
NSLAL....... Nova Scotia Land Survey Institute, Lawrencetown, Nova Scotia [*Library symbol*] [*National Library of Canada*] (NLC)
NSLB .... NS&L Bancorp [*NASDAQ symbol*] (TTSB)
NSLB .... NS & L Bancorp, Inc. [*NASDAQ symbol*] (SAG)
NSLC .... Naval Sea Logistics Center
NSLC .... Nuclear Safety and Licensing Commission
NSLF .... Fortress of Louisbourg, Canada National Historic Park [*Forteresse de Louisbourg, Parc Historique National*] Nova Scotia [*Library symbol*] [*National Library of Canada*] (NLC)
NSLF .... National Socialist Liberation Front (NADA)
NSLF .... Nonself
NSLFM ...... Fisheries Museum of the Atlantic, Lunenburg, Nova Scotia [*Library symbol*] [*National Library of Canada*] (NLC)
NSLFP....... Fort Point Museum, La Have, Nova Scotia [*Library symbol*] [*National Library of Canada*] (NLC)
NSlH......... General Hospital of Saranac Lake, Saranac Lake, NY [*Library symbol*] [*Library of Congress*] (LCLS)
NSLHS ...... Lunenburg Heritage Society, Nova Scotia [*Library symbol*] [*National Library of Canada*] (NLC)
NSLI .... National Service Life Insurance
NSLI .... National Street Law Institute (EA)
NSLIN .... Nonstandard Line Item Number [*Army*] (AABC)
NSLL .... National Save-a-Life League [*Defunct*] (EA)
NSLL .... National Savings and Loan League [*Formerly, NLISA*] (EA)
NSLL .... North Salt Lake Livestock [*Federal Railroad Administration identification code*]
NSLLS....... Lockeport Little School Museum, Nova Scotia [*Library symbol*] [*National Library of Canada*] (NLC)
NSLN .... NetSalon Corp. [*NASDAQ symbol*] (QUAN)
NSlNC .... North Country Community College, Saranac Lake, NY [*Library symbol*] [*Library of Congress*] (LCLS)
NSLookup... Name Server Lookup [*Computer science*] (DCOM)
NSLP .... National School Lunch Program [*Department of Agriculture*]
NSLPE....... Progress-Enterprise, Lunenburg, Nova Scotia [*Library symbol*] [*National Library of Canada*] (NLC)
NSLQCM .... Queens County Museum, Liverpool, Nova Scotia [*Library symbol*] [*National Library of Canada*] (NLC)
NSLR .... Nova Scotia Law Reports [*A publication*] (DLA)
NSLR .... Nuclear Spin-Lattice Relaxation (ODA)
NSLRB ...... National Steel Labor Relations Board [*New Deal*]
NSLRB ...... Nova Scotia Labour Relations Board (SAUS)
NSLRS ...... National School Labor Relations Service [*Later, LMRS*] (EA)
NSLS .... National Synchrotron Light Source [*Brookhaven National Laboratory*]
NSLS .... North Suburban Library System, Wheeling, IL [*Library network*]
NSLSA....... National Surf Life Saving Association of America [*Later, USLA*] (EA)
NSLSI .... Nova Scotia Land Survey Institute (SAUS)
NSLSRA..... National Society of Live Stock Record Associations (EA)
NSlT .... Trudeau Institute, Saranac Lake, NY [*Library symbol*] [*Library of Congress*] (LCLS)
N/S-LTI-G/T... National/State Leadership Training Institute on Gifted and Talented (EA)
NSLU .... Norasia Services [*Intermodal shipping container symbol*] (TVRC)
NSlW .... Will Rogers Memorial Fund, Saranac Lake, NY [*Library symbol*] [*Library of Congress*] (LCLS)
NSLX .... National Silicates [*Private rail car owner code*]
NSLY......... Nasally (ABBR)
NSLY......... Noisily (ABBR)
NSLZ .... Nestle Transportation [*Intermodal trailer symbol*]
NSM .... Narrow Band Sensor Monitor (ACAE)
NSM .... National Search and Rescue Manual (COE)
NSM .... National Security Management [*Military*]
NSM .... National Security Medal [*Military decoration*]
NSM .... National Selected Morticians (EA)
NSM .... National Semiconductor Corp. [*NYSE symbol*] (SPSG)
NSM .... National Serviceman [*British military*] (DMA)
NSM .... National Soaring Museum (DICI)

NSM .... National Socialist Movement (EA)
NSM .... National Student Marketing
NSM .... Natl Semiconductor [*NYSE symbol*] (TTSB)
NSM .... Naval School of Music
NSM .... Net-Shared Memory
NSM .... Network Security Module
NSM .... Network Space Monitor (SAA)
NSM .... Network Station Manager
NSM .... Network Status Monitor [*NASA*] (KSC)
NSM .... Network Storage Manager [*Computer science*] (GART)
NSM .... Network Support Manager (ACAE)
NSM .... Network/Systems Management (SAUS)
NSM .... Neurosecretory Material (MAE)
NSM .... Neurosecretory Motoneurons
NSM .... Nevada State Museum (SAUS)
NSM .... New Schools Movement [*Defunct*] (EA)
NSM .... New Smoking Material [*A wood cellulose-based tobacco substitute*]
NSM .... New Social Movement [*Theory*]
NSM .... Nice Safe Man [*Slang*]
NSM .... Nitsanim [*Israel*] [*Later, AMT*] [*Geomagnetic observatory code*]
NSM .... Noise Source Meter
NSM .... Nonantigenic Specific Mediator (DB)
NSM .... Nondeterministic Sequential Machine (IAA)
NSM .... Nonstipendiary Minister (ODA)
NSM .... Norseman [*Australia*] [*Airport symbol*] (OAG)
NSM .... Northern Student Movement [*Defunct*] (EA)
NSM .... North-South Map [*Via orbiter*]
NSM .... North Suburban Mass Transit [*Federal Railroad Administration identification code*]
NSM .... Nova Scotia Museum (SAUS)
NSM .... Nuclear Shell Modell (SAUS)
Nsm .... Number of similar matches (SAUS)
NSM .... Number System Matrix (SAUS)
NSM .... Nutrient Sporulation Medium [*Medicine*] (DMAA)
NSm .... Smithtown Public Library, Smithtown, NY [*Library symbol*] [*Library of Congress*] (LCLS)
N-S/M^2 ..... Newton Second per Square Meter (WDAA)
NSMA .... Maota [*Western Samoa*] [*ICAO location identifier*] (ICLI)
NSMA .... National Scale Men's Association (EA)
NSMA .... National Seasoning Manufacturers Association (EA)
NSMA .... National Second Mortgage Association [*Center Square, PA*] (EA)
NSMA .... National Shoe Manufacturers Association [*Later, FIA*] (EA)
NSMA .... National Soup Mix Association [*Defunct*] (EA)
NSMAPMAWOL... Not So Much a Programme, More a Way of Life [*British television program*]
NSMATCC... NATO Small Arms Test Control Commission (MCD)
NSMB .... Nuclear Standards Management Board (SAUS)
NSMC .... National Security Management Course [*National Defense University*] (GFGA)
NSMC .... National Student Marketing Corp.
NSMC .... Naval Submarine Medical Center
NSMCA...... National Shaving Mug Collectors Association (EA)
NSMCA...... National Spirit, Metropolitan Club of America (EA)
NSMCM ..... Naval Supplement, Manual for Courts-Martial [*United States*] [*A publication*] (DLA)
NSMDO ..... Naval Systems Management & Development Office (SAUS)
NSME........ Eastern Counties Regional Library, Mulgrave, Nova Scotia [*Library symbol*] [*National Library of Canada*] (NLC)
NSME........ Night Sight Maintenance Facility (TIMI)
NSME........ Nonstandard Measuring Equipment (SAUS)
NSMEX...... Examiner, Middleton, Nova Scotia [*Library symbol*] [*National Library of Canada*] (NLC)
NSMFA ...... North Sea Mine Force Association (EA)
NSMG ...... Naval School of Military Government
NSMG & A.. Naval School of Military Government and Administration
NSmGH ..... Smithtown General Hospital, Smithtown, NY [*Library symbol*] [*Library of Congress*] (LCLS)
NSMH .... Nuclear Systems Material Handbook (NRCH)
NSMHC...... National Society for Mentally Handicapped Children [*British*] (BI)
NSmHSE.... Smithtown High School East. Smithtown, NY [*Library symbol*] [*Library of Congress*] (LCLS)
NSmHSW.... Smithtown High School West, Smithtown, NY [*Library symbol*] [*Library of Congress*] (LCLS)
NSMI .... National Sports Medicine Institute (SAUS)
NSML........ Low-Sodium Meal [*Airline notation*] (ADA)
NSMM....... Macdonald Museum, Middleton, Nova Scotia [*Library symbol*] [*National Library of Canada*] (NLC)
NSMM....... National Society of Metal Mechanics [*A union*] [*British*] (DCTA)
NSMM....... National Sustainment Maintenance Management [*Army*]
NSMO .... NASTRAN [*NASA Structural Analysis*] Systems Management Office
NSMP .... National Society of Master Patternmakers [*British*] (BI)
NSMP .... National Society of Mural Painters (EA)
NSMP .... Navy Support and Mobilization Plan (NVT)
NSMPA...... National Screw Machine Products Association (EA)
NSMR .... National Society for Medical Research (EA)
NSMR .... Non-Store Marketing Report [*A publication*]
NSMRB...... National Society for Medical Research Bulletin [*Medicine*] (EDAA)
NSMRL...... Naval Submarine Medical Research Laboratory
NSMRSE.... National Study of Mathematics Requirements for Scientists and Engineers
NSMRTS.... Nuclear Submarine Maneuvering Room Training Simulator (PDAA)
NSMS .... National Safety Management Society (EA)
NSMS .... National Sheet Music Society (EA)
NSMS .... Network Server Management System [*Tylink Corp.*]
NSMS .... Soldiers Memorial Hospital, Middleton, Nova Scotia [*Library symbol*] [*National Library of Canada*] (NLC)
NSMSES .... Naval Ship Missile System Engineering Station
NSMSESDETLANT... Naval Ship Missile System Engineering Station Detachment, Atlantic (MUGU)
NSmSJH .... Saint John's Smithtown Hospital, Smithtown, NY [*Library symbol*] [*Library of Congress*] (LCLS)
NSMT........ National Society of Master Thatchers [*British*] (DBA)
NSMT........ National Society of Medical Technologists
NSMT........ Northwest Suburban Mass Transit [*Federal Railroad Administration identification code*]
NSMTD...... Northwest Suburban Mass Transit District (SAUS)
NSMU .... Nevada State Museum [*Federal Railroad Administration identification code*]
NSMV .... Valley Mirror, Middleton, Nova Scotia [*Library symbol*] [*National Library of Canada*] (NLC)
NSMW....... Naval Schools Mine Warfare
Ns/my .... Newton Second per Square Meter (SAUS)
NSMZ........ National Steel-Midwest [*Federal Railroad Administration identification code*]
NSN.......... Military Sealift Command, Washington, DC [*OCLC symbol*] (OCLC)
NSN.......... NASA Science Network [*Communications term*] (DCT)
NSN.......... National Sleep Network (SAUS)
NSN.......... National Stock Number (MCD)
NSN.......... NATO Stock Number (NATG)
NSN.......... Nelson [*New Zealand*] [*Airport symbol*] (OAG)
NSN.......... Nephrotoxic Serum Nephritis [*Medicine*] (DMAA)
NSN.......... New Substances Notification (SARE)
NSN.......... Nicotine-Stimulated Neurophysin [*Biochemistry*]
NSN.......... Northern Science Network (SAUS)
NSN.......... North Star Network [*Defunct*] (EA)
NSN.......... No Stock Number
Nsn .... Number of Similar Negative Matches
NSN.......... Nurses Support Network [*Later, NIT*] (EA)
NSNA........ National Socialist Nederlandse Arbeiders Partij [*Netherlands group favoring integration of the Netherlands into the German reich*] [*World War II*]
NSNA........ National Student Nurses' Association (EA)
NSNA........ Newcomen Society in North America (EA)
NSNA........ No Stock Number Assigned
NSNC........ National Society of Newspaper Columnists (NTPA)
NSNC........ Nova Scotia Normal College
NSNCE ...... Nuisance (ABBR)
NSNCL ...... Nonsensical (ABBR)
NSND........ Nonsymptomatic, Nondisabling (MAE)
NSND........ Normal Saline Nose Drops [*Pharmacology*] (DAVI)
NSNE........ Nappan Experimental Farm, Nova Scotia [*Library symbol*] [*National Library of Canada*] (NLC)
NSNEW...... National Society of New England Women (EA)
NSNF........ Nonstrategic Nuclear Forces (MCD)
NSnfG .... GTE Sylvania, Inc., Electronic Components Group, Seneca Falls, NY [*Library symbol*] [*Library of Congress*] (LCLS)
NSNG........ North Star Needlework Guild (EARSL)
NSNGA ...... Aberdeen Hospital, New Glasgow, Nova Scotia [*Library symbol*] [*National Library of Canada*] (NLC)
NSNGE ...... Evening News, New Glasgow, Nova Scotia [*Library symbol*] [*National Library of Canada*] (NLC)
NSNGH ...... New Glasgow Senior High School, Nova Scotia [*Library symbol*] [*National Library of Canada*] (BIB)
NSNGP ...... Pictou-Antigonish Regional Library, New Glasgow, Nova Scotia [*Library symbol*] [*National Library of Canada*] (NLC)
NSNHC ...... Cabot Archives, Neil's Harbour, Nova Scotia [*Library symbol*] [*National Library of Canada*] (NLC)
NSNMDR.... National Stock Number Master Data Records (MCD)
NSNMK...... Kentville Publishing, New Minas, Nova Scotia [*Library symbol*] [*National Library of Canada*] (NLC)
NSNN........ Northern Science Network Newsletter (SAUS)
NSNNF ...... National Special Needs Network Foundation [*Association*] (EA)
NSNP .... No Space, No Print [*Computer science*] (MHDI)
NSNRP ...... Nonstock Numbered Repair Parts
NSNS .... Nonsense (ABBR)
NSNSCLY... Nonsensically (ABBR)
NSNU........ Nam Sung Shipping [*Intermodal shipping container symbol*] (TVRC)
NSO.......... NASA Support Operation (KSC)
NSO.......... National Security Office [*or Officer*] (GFGA)
NSO.......... National Service Officer [*Ministry of Labour and National Service*] [*British*] [*World War II*]
NSO.......... National Solar Observatory [*Tucson, AZ*] [*National Science Foundation*] (GRD)
NSO.......... National Standardization Office [*US Army Materiel Command*]
NSO.......... National Symphony Orchestra
NSO.......... Naval Staff Officer
NSO.......... Naval Store Officer [*British*]
NSO.......... Navigation/Systems Operator (SAUS)
NSO.......... Navy Staff Offices (ACAE)
NSO.......... Navy Subsistence Office (DNAB)
NSO.......... Neighborhood Service Organization
NSO.......... Neosporin Ointment [*Medicine*] (CPH)
NSO.......... Network Server Option [*Computer science*] (GART)
NSO.......... Network Support Office [*NASA*]
NSO.......... New American Shoe Co., Inc. (SAUS)
NSO.......... Next Standing Order
NSO.......... Nitrogen, Sulfur, and Oxygen [*In chemical compounds*]
NSO.......... Nitrogen, Sulfur, Oxygen (SAUS)
NSO.......... Noise Suppression Oscillator (MCD)

NSO.......... Nonferrous Smelter Order [*Environmental Protection Agency*]
NSO.......... Norfolk Symphony Orchestra (SAUS)
NSO.......... Northern Sinfonia Orchestra (SAUS)
nso.......... Northern Sotho [*MARC language code*] [*Library of Congress*] (LCCP)
NSO.......... North State Cooperative Library System, Willows, CA [*OCLC symbol*] (OCLC)
NSO.......... No Spares Ordered (AAG)
NSO.......... nSTOR Technologies [*AMEX symbol*] (SG)
NSO.......... Nuclear Safety Office [*or Officer*] [*Air Force*] (AFM)
NSO.......... Nucleus Supraopticus (DMAA)
NSO.......... Numeric Stockage Objective [*Items*] [*DoD*]
nso.......... Nurses Service Organization
NSO.......... Scone [*Australia*] [*Airport symbol*] (OAG)
NSo.......... Somers Library, Somers, NY [*Library symbol*] [*Library of Congress*] (LCLS)
NSOA........ National School Orchestra Association (EA)
NSOA........ National Symphony Orchestra Association (EA)
NSOA........ Nuclear Safety Operational Analysis (NRCH)
NSoa........ Rogers Memorial Library, Southampton, NY [*Library symbol*] [*Library of Congress*] (LCLS)
NSoaH....... Southampton Hospital, Southampton, NY [*Library symbol*] [*Library of Congress*] (LCLS)
NSoaS....... Long Island University, Southampton College, Southampton, NY [*Library symbol*] [*Library of Congress*] (LCLS)
NSOB........ New Senate Office Building
NSOC........ National SIGINT [*Signal Intelligence*] Operations Center (MCD)
NSOC........ Navy Satellite Operations Center (NVT)
NSOC........ New South Conference (PSS)
NSOC........ Norbornene Spiroorthocarbonate [*Organic chemistry*]
NSOD........ Naval School of Ordnance Disposal
NSODCC.... North Sumatra Oil Development Corporation Co. (SAUS)
NSOEA...... National Stationery and Office Equipment Association [*Later, NOPA*] (EA)
NSOF........ Naval Status of Forces (MCD)
NSOF........ Navy Special Operations Force (AABC)
NSOG........ Navy Special Operations Group [*SEALS that operated in Vietnam*] (VNW)
NSOGA...... National Seniors' Open Golf Association (EA)
NSoHi....... Somers Historical Society, Somers, NY [*Library symbol*] [*Library of Congress*] (LCLS)
NSOHSC.... National Survey of Oral Health in School Children [*Department of Health and Human Services*] (GFGA)
NSOJ........ Journal, Oxford, Nova Scotia [*Library symbol*] [*National Library of Canada*] (NLC)
NSOL........ Network Solutions [*NASDAQ symbol*] (SG)
NSOM....... Near Field Scanning Optical Microscopy
NSoo........ Southold Free Library, Southold, NY [*Library symbol*] [*Library of Congress*] (LCLS)
NSOP........ National Second Opinion Program (EA)
NSOPCD.... National Society of Old Plymouth Colony Descendants (EA)
NSOPF...... National Survey of Postsecondary Faculty [*Department of Education*] (GFGA)
NSOR........ No Shop Order Required
NSORW..... National Stop on Red Week [*Auto safety*]
NSos......... South Salem Library, South Salem, NY [*Library symbol*] [*Library of Congress*] (LCLS)
NSOSG...... North Sea Oceanographical Study Group [*British*]
NSOW....... Naval Statement of Work (ACAE)
NSOW....... Norwegian Sea Overflow Water (SAUS)
NSP.......... NASA Support Plan (KSC)
NSP.......... National Salvation Party [*Milli Selamet Partisi*] [*Turkey*] [*Political party*] (PPW)
NSP.......... National Sea Products Ltd. [*Toronto Stock Exchange symbol*]
NSP.......... National Search and Rescue Plan (COE)
NSP.......... National Seoposengwe Party [*Bophuthatswana*] [*Political party*] (PPW)
NSP.......... National Service Provider [*Communications term*] (DCT)
NSP.......... National Services Program (SAUS)
NSP.......... National Ski Patrol System (EA)
NSP.......... National Socialist Party [*New Zealand*] [*Political party*] (PD)
NSP.......... National Society of Painters [*A union*] [*British*]
NSP.......... National Society of Professors [*Later, NEA Higher Education Council*] (EA)
NSP.......... National Solidarity Party (Singapore) [*Political party*] (PSAP)
NSP.......... National Space Program (AAG)
NSP.......... National Stolen Property
NSP.......... National Stuttering Project (EA)
NSP.......... Native Signal Processing [*Computer science*] (PCM)
NSP.......... Naval Special Projects (ACAE)
NSP.......... Navigational Satellite Program [*NASA*] (IAA)
NSP.......... Navy Safety Program (DNAB)
NSP.......... Navy Space Project
NSP.......... Navy Special Projects office (SAUS)
NSP.......... Navy Standard Part
NSP.......... Navy Support Plan
NSP.......... Neck and Shoulder Pain [*Medicine*] (EDAA)
NSP.......... Neighborhood Statistics Program [*Bureau of the Census*] (GFGA)
NSP.......... Nepalese Sign Language [*Language symbol*] (ETLW)
NSP.......... Net Social Profitability
NSP.......... Network Service Part [*Communications term*] (DCT)
NSP.......... Network Service Point (SAUS)
NSP.......... Network Service Provider [*Telecommunications*]
NSP.......... Network Services Protocol [*Digital Equipment Corp.*] [*Telecommunications*] (TEL)
NSP.......... Network Signal Processor (NASA)
NSP.......... Network Support Plan [*NASA*] (KSC)
NSP.......... Network Support Processor (NITA)
NSP.......... Neurological Shellfish Poisoning (USDC)
NSP.......... Neurological Society of Paris [*Medicine*] (EDAA)
NSP.......... Neuron-Specific Protein [*Later, NSE*] [*Biochemistry*]
NSP.......... Neurotoxic Shellfish Poisoning [*Medicine*]
NSP.......... Neutral Steer Point (SAUS)
NSP.......... New Species
NSP.......... Nominal Stagnation Point
NSP.......... Non-Self-Propelled
NSP.......... Nonseries Parallel (IAA)
NSP.......... Nonspecific Prostatitis [*Medicine*] (ADA)
NSP.......... Nonstandard Holding Pattern (SAUS)
NSP.......... Nonstandard Part
NSP.......... Nonstorage Protein [*Food technology*]
NSP.......... Nonstructural Protein (DMAA)
NSP.......... Non-Swelling and Paintable (SAUS)
NSP.......... Non-volatile, Serially Programmable (SAUS)
NSP.......... Nordiska Sjoforsakringspoolen [*Nordic Pool for Marine Insurance - NPMI*] (EA)
NSP.......... Normal Serum Pool
NSP.......... Normal Stage Punching (SAUS)
NSP.......... Normal Superphosphate [*Fertilizer*]
NSP.......... Northern States Power Co. [*NYSE symbol*] (SPSG)
NSP.......... Northern States Pwr [*NYSE symbol*] (TTSB)
NSP.......... North Solomons Province (SAUS)
NSP.......... No Separate Billing Price (MCD)
NSP.......... Nose Shipping Plug
NSP.......... No Smoking Please [*Medicine*] (EDAA)
NSP.......... Not Separately Priced (NG)
NSP.......... N-Succinylperimycin (DB)
NSP.......... Nuclear Strike Plan [*Army*] (AABC)
Nsp.......... Number of Similar Positive Matches
NSP.......... Numeric Space (SAUS)
NSP.......... Numeric Space Character [*Computer science*]
NSP.......... Numeric Subroutine Package [*Computer science*] (CIST)
NSP.......... Nutritional Support Panel [*Dietetics*] (DAVI)
nsp.......... Species Nova [*New Species*] [*Latin*] (EES)
NSP.......... St. Andrews Presbyterian College, Laurinburg, NC [*OCLC symbol*] (OCLC)
NSPA........ Advocate, Pictou, Nova Scotia [*Library symbol*] [*National Library of Canada*] (NLC)
NSPA........ National Scholastic Press Association (EA)
NSPA........ National Shrimp Processors Association (EA)
NSPA........ National Socialist Party of America (EA)
NSPA........ National Society of Public Accountants [*Alexandria, VA*] (EA)
NSPA........ National Soybean Processors Association [*Later, NOPA*] (EA)
NSPA........ National Split Pea Association [*Defunct*]
NSPA........ National Standard Parts Association [*Later, ASIA*]
NSPA........ National State Printing Association (EA)
NSPA........ National Stolen Property Act
NSPA........ Navy Shore Patrol Administration (WDAA)
NSPA........ Nova Scotia Pharmaceutical Association (SAUS)
NSPA........ Pictou Advocate, Nova Scotia [*Library symbol*] [*National Library of Canada*] (NLC)
NSPAC...... National Security Political Action Committee [*Defunct*] (EA)
NSPAR...... Nonstandard Part Approval Request
NSpaT....... Saint Thomas Aquinas College, Sparkill, NY [*Library symbol*] [*Library of Congress*] (LCLS)
NSPB........ National Society to Prevent Blindness (EA)
NSPB........ Prevent Blindness America [*Formerly, National Society to Prevent Blindness*] (EA)
NSPBB...... Burning Bush Museum, Pictou, Nova Scotia [*Library symbol*] [*National Library of Canada*] (BIB)
NSPB/PBA... National Society to Prevent Blindness/Prevent Blindness America (NTPA)
NSPC........ National Security Planning Commission
NSPC........ National Society of Painters in Casein (EA)
NSPC........ National Sound-Program Center [*Telecommunications*] (TEL)
NSPC........ National Standard Plumbing Code Committee (EA)
NSPC........ National Straight Pipe Threads in Pipe Couplings
NSPC........ Nova Scotia Power Corp. (SAUS)
NSPCA...... National Society for the Prevention of Cruelty to Animals
NSPCA...... National Society of Painters in Casein and Acrylic (EA)
NSPCB...... National Society for the Preservation of Covered Bridges (EA)
NSPCC...... National Society for the Prevention of Cruelty to Children
NSPCC...... Naval Ships Parts Control Center (MCD)
NSPCM...... National Society for Prevention of Cruelty to Mushrooms (EA)
NSPD........ Naval Shore Patrol Detachment
NSPE........ National Society of Professional Engineers (EA)
NSPE........ Navy Senior Procurement Executive (AAGC)
NSPE........ Nebraska Society of Professional Engineers (EARSL)
NSPE........ Network Services Procedure Error (ELAL)
NSPE........ Nuclear Superheat Performance Evaluation (SAUS)
NSPE........ Specimen Unobtainable [*Laboratory science*] (DAVI)
NSpeB....... Board of Cooperative Educational Services (BOCES), Spencerport, NY [*Library symbol*] [*Library of Congress*] (LCLS)
N-SPECS.... Navy Specifications (AAGC)
NSPE-PAC... National Society of Professional Engineers - PAC [*Alexandria, VA*] (PACS)
NSPF........ National Swimming Pool Foundation (EA)
nspf......... Not Specially Provided For (EBF)
NSPF........ Not Specifically Provided For
NSPFEA..... National Spray Painting and Finishing Equipment Association [*Later, NSEMA*] (EA)

NSPG........ National Security Planning Group
NSPH........ Neonatal Severe Hyperparathyroidism [*Medicine*] (DMAA)
NSPHM...... Port Hastings Museum and Archives, Nova Scotia [*Library symbol*] [*National Library of Canada*] (NLC)
NSPI......... National Society for Performance and Instruction (EA)
NSPI......... National Society for Programmed Instruction (IAA)
NSPI......... National Spa and Pool Institute (EA)
NSPI......... National Spatial Data Infrastructure [*BTS*] (TAG)
NSPI......... Nonstorage Protein Isolate [*Food technology*]
NSPIAE...... National Society of Professional Insurance Agency Executives (NTPA)
NSPIE....... National Society for the Promotion of Industrial Education [*Later, AVA*]
NSPII........ National Society of Professional Investigators [*Association*] (EA)
NSPK........ NetSpeak Corp. [*NASDAQ symbol*] (SG)
NSPKU...... National Society for Phenylketonuria and Allied Disorders [*British*] (DBA)
NSPL........ NASA Standard Parts List (SAUS)
NSPLO...... NATO Sidewinder Production and Logistics Organization [*Missiles*] (NATG)
NSPMH...... McCulloch House, Pictou, Nova Scotia [*Library symbol*] [*National Library of Canada*] (NLC)
NSPNC...... North Cumberland Historical Society, Pugwash, Nova Scotia [*Library symbol*] [*National Library of Canada*] (NLC)
NSPO........ NATO Sea Sparrow Project Office (MCD)
NSPO........ NATO Sidewinder Production Organization [*Missiles*] (NATG)
NSPO........ NATO Sidewinder Program Office [*Missiles*] (NATG)
NSPO........ Naval Ship Production Overseer [*British*]
NSPO........ Naval Space Projects Office
NSPO........ Navy Special Projects Office
NSPO........ Nuclear Systems Project Office [*Air Research and Development Command*] [*Air Force*] (AAG)
NS-POG..... NAVSHIPS [*Naval Ship Systems Command*] Propulsion Operating Guides
NSPOL...... Non-Scheduled Operations Policy (SAUS)
NSPP........ National Serials Pilot Project
NSPP........ Nuclear Safety Pilot Plant [*ORNL*]
NSPPrA..... Non'n St Pwr Minn,$3.60 Pfd [*NYSE symbol*] (TTSB)
NSPPrB..... No'n St Pwr Minn,$4.08 Pfd [*NYSE symbol*] (TTSB)
NSPPrC..... No'n Pwr Minn,$4.10 Pfd [*NYSE symbol*] (TTSB)
NSPPrE..... No's St Pwr Minn.$4.16 Pfd [*NYSE symbol*] (TTSB)
NSPPrG..... No'n St Pwr Minn,$4.56 Pfd [*NYSE symbol*] (TTSB)
NSPPrH..... No'n St Pwr Minn,$6.80 Pfd [*NYSE symbol*] (TTSB)
NSPPrI..... No'n St Pwr Minn,$7.00 Pfd [*NYSE symbol*] (TTSB)
NSPR........ INSpire Insurance Solutions [*NASDAQ symbol*] (SG)
NSPR........ National Society for Park Resources (EA)
NSPR........ National Society of Patient Representatives of the American Hospital Association (EA)
NSPR........ National Society of Pershing Rifles (EA)
NSPR........ Netscape Portable Runtime (SAUS)
NSPR........ Nonstandard Part Approval Request
NSPR........ Record, Parrsboro, Nova Scotia [*Library symbol*] [*National Library of Canada*] (NLC)
NSPRA...... National School Public Relations Association (EA)
NSPRCA..... National Society for Patient Representation and Consumer Affairs (NTPA)
NSPRCA..... National Society of Patient Representation and Consumer Affairs of the American Hospital Association (EA)
NSPrD....... No'n St Pwr Minn,$4.11 Pfd [*NYSE symbol*] (TTSB)
NSPRDS.... New Systems Personnel Requirements Data System [*Navy*]
NSPRI....... Nigeria Store Product Research Institute (SAUS)
NSPRM...... National Society of Professional Resident Managers (EA)
NSPRS...... Nigerian Society for Photogrammetry and Remote Sensing (SAUS)
NSPRT...... Nonsupport (ABBR)
NSPRV...... Pictou Regional Vocational School, Nova Scotia [*Library symbol*] [*National Library of Canada*] (NLC)
NSprvCH.... Bertrand Chaffee Hospital, Springville, NY [*Library symbol*] [*Library of Congress*] (LCLS)
NSPS........ National Ski Patrol System (EA)
NSPS........ National Society of Professional Sanitarians (EA)
NSPS........ National Society of Professional Surveyors (EA)
NSPS........ National Standards of Performance for Stationary Sources (ACII)
NSPS........ National Stockpile Purchase Specification [*for metals*]
NSPS........ National Sweet Pea Society [*British*] (BI)
NSPS........ New Source Performance Standards [*Environmental Protection Agency*] (AEPA)
NSPS........ Nonsynchronous Pulse Suppression (MCD)
NSPS........ Nuclear Safety Protection System (NRCH)
NSPS........ Nuclear Strike Planning System (MCD)
NSPSE....... National Society of Painters, Sculptors, and Engravers [*British*] (DI)
NSPSH...... Parrsboro Shore Historical Society, Parrsboro, Nova Scotia [*Library symbol*] [*National Library of Canada*] (BIB)
NSPSR...... New Source Performance Standard Review (SAUS)
NSPSS...... Scotia Sun, Port Hawkesbury, Nova Scotia [*Library symbol*] [*National Library of Canada*] (NLC)
NSPST....... National Society of Pharmaceutical Sales Trainers (EA)
NSPV........ Nandina Stem-Pitting Virus [*Plant pathology*]
NSPV........ Number of Scans per Vehicle (OA)
NSPVT....... Nonsustained Polymorphic Ventricular Tachycardia [*Cardiology*] (DAVI)
NSPw........ Northern States Power Co. [*Associated Press*] (SAG)
NSPWA...... National Society Patriotic Women of America
NSPZ........ Northern States Power [*Federal Railroad Administration identification code*]
NSQ.......... Neuroticism Scale Questionnaire [*Psychology*]
NSQ.......... Not Sufficient Quantity [*Clinical chemistry*]
NSQ.......... Nurse Satisfaction Questionnaire
NSQC........ National Society of Quality Circles [*British*] (DBA)
NSR.......... Mount Vernon, WA [*Location identifier*] [*FAA*] (FAAL)
NSR.......... Naphthenic SO2 (Sulfur Dioxide) Raffinate [*Petroleum engineering*]
NSR.......... Nasoseptal Reconstruction [*Otorhinolaryngology*] (DAVI)
NSR.......... Natinal Securities & Research Corp. (EFIS)
NSR.......... National Air Charter PT [*Indonesia*] [*ICAO designator*] (FAAC)
NSR.......... National Scenic Riverway
NSR.......... National Scientific Register
NSR.......... National Security Review (AAGC)
NSR.......... National Shipping Report [*NATO*]
NSR.......... National Shipping Representative (NATG)
NSR.......... National Shorthand Reporter [*A publication*]
NSR.......... National Singles Registry (EA)
NSR.......... National Slow Rate (NASA)
NSR.......... National Swine Registry (NTPA)
NSR.......... NATO Staff Requirements (MCD)
NSR.......... Naval Staff Requirement (SAUS)
NSR.......... Naval Supply Requirement (DNAB)
NSR.......... Net Survival Rate
NSR.......... Neutron Source Reactor
NSR.......... Newburgh & South Shore Railroad [*Federal Railroad Administration identification code*]
NSR.......... New Source Review [*A publication*] (EPA)
NSR.......... Night Sky Radiation
NSR.......... Nitrile Silicone Rubber [*Organic chemistry*]
NSR.......... Nizam's State Railway [*Indian Railway*] (TIR)
NSR.......... Noise-to-Signal Ratio (IAA)
NSR.......... Nominal Slow Rate [*NASA*] (KSC)
NSR.......... Non Sequential Recording (SAUS)
NSR.......... Non-Shared Resources (SAUS)
NSR.......... Non Significant Result [*Medicine*]
NSR.......... Non Slug Return (SAUS)
NSR.......... Non-Source Routed (SAUS)
NSR.......... Nonspecific Reaction [*Medicine*] (DMAA)
NSR.......... Non-Storage Resources (SAUS)
NSR.......... Norair Science Report (SAA)
NSR.......... Nordic Shooting Region (EAIO)
NSR.......... Nordiska Skidskolans Rad [*Nordic Council of Ski Schools - NCSS*] [*Finland*] (EAIO)
NSR.......... Nordiska Skogsarbetsstudiernas Rad [*Nordic Research Council on Forest Operations*] [*Sweden*] (EAIO)
NSR.......... Nordisk Skuespillerrad [*Nordic Actors' Council - NAC*] [*Sweden*] (EAIO)
NSR.......... Norfolk Southern Railway Co. [*NYSE symbol*] (SAG)
NSR.......... Normal Service Request (ELAL)
NSR.......... Normal Sinus Rhythm [*Medicine*] (DMAA)
NSR.......... Normal Slow Rate Maneuver (NASA)
NSR.......... Norske Samers Riksforbund [*Norway*]
NSR.......... Northern Sea Route (NATG)
NSR.......... North Staffordshire Railway [*British*] (ROG)
NSR.......... No Sign of Recurrence [*Medicine*] (DMAA)
NSR.......... No Slot Release (ELAL)
NSR.......... No Staff Responsibility [*Army*] (AABC)
NSR.......... Notch Strength Ratio (SAUS)
NSR.......... Notch Stress Rupture (SAUS)
NSR.......... Not Seen Regularly [*Medicine*] (DAVI)
NSR.......... Nova Scotia Provincial Library [*UTLAS symbol*]
NSR.......... Nova Scotia Regiment [*Canada*] (DMA)
NSR.......... NOx (Oxides of Nitrogen) Storage Reduction [*Automotive emissions*]
NSR.......... NSR Resources, Inc. [*Toronto Stock Exchange symbol*]
NSR.......... Nuclear Science References [*Database*] (GDD)
NSR.......... Nuclear Spin Relaxation [*Physics*]
NSR.......... Nuclear Structure References [*Brookhaven National Laboratory*] [*Information service or system*]
NSR.......... Nutrient Supply Rate [*Oceanography*]
NSR2........ Second Coelliptic Maneuver (SAUS)
NSRA........ National Scooter Riders Association [*British*] (DBA)
NSRA........ National Service Robot Association (EA)
NSRA........ National Shoe Retailers Association (EA)
NSRA........ National Shorthand Reporters Association (EA)
NSRA........ National Ski Retailers Association (EA)
NSRA........ National Smallbore Rifle Association [*British*]
NSRA........ National Society for Research into Allergy [*British*]
NSRA........ National Street Rod Association (EA)
NSRA........ National Swim and Recreation Association (EA)
NSRA........ North-South Reconstruction Advisors (SAUS)
NSRA........ Nuclear Safety Research Association [*See also GAKK*] [*Japan*] (NRCH)
NSRAA...... Northern Southeast Regional Aquaculture Association (ALAC)
NSRB........ National Security Resources Board [*Functions transferred to ODM, 1953*]
NSRB........ Nuclear Safety Review Board (NRCH)
NSRBD...... National Security Resources Board [*Functions transferred to ODM, 1953*] (GFGA)
NSRC........ National SIDS Resource Center (EA)
NSRC........ National Silver Rabbit Club (EA)
NSRC........ National Stereophonic Radio Committee
NSRC........ National Sudden Infant Death Syndrome Resource Center (NRGU)
NSRC........ NeoSynthesis Research Centre [*Sri Lanka*] (EAIO)
NSRC........ North Stratford Railroad Corp. [*AAR code*]
NSR Coch... Cochran's Nova Scotia Reports [*1859*] [*A publication*] (DLA)
NSR Coh.... Cohen's Nova Scotia Reports [*A publication*] (DLA)
NSRD........ National Security Resources Development
NSRD........ National Software Reuse Directory (SAUS)

NSRDB ...... National SIGINT [*Signal Intelligence*] Requirements Database (MCD)
NSRDB ...... National Solar Radiation Data Base (SAUS)
NSRDB ...... Nova Scotia Resources Development Board (SAUS)
NSRDC ...... National Standards Reference Data Center
NSRDC ...... [*David W. Taylor*] Naval Ship Research and Development Center (AAGC)
NSRDC/A.... Naval Ship Research and Development Center, Annapolis [*Maryland*] Division (DNAB)
NSRDC(AD)... Naval Ship Research and Development Center (Annapolis Division)
NSRDCANNADIV... Naval Ship Research and Development Center, Annapolis [*Maryland*] Division (DNAB)
NSRDF ...... Naval Supply Research and Development Facility
NSRDL ...... Naval Ship Research and Development Laboratory (MCD)
NSRDL/A.... Naval Ship Research and Development Laboratory, Annapolis [*Maryland*]
NSRDL/PC... Naval Ship Research and Development Laboratory, Panama City [*Florida*] [*Later, NCSC*]
NSRDS ...... National Standard Reference Data System [*Gaithersburg, MD*] [*National Institute of Standards and Technology*]
NSREA ...... National Society of Real Estate Appraisers (NTPA)
NSREC ...... National Society's Religious Education Centre (AIE)
NSREF....... National Society for Real Estate Finance [*Washington, DC*] (EA)
NS Rev Stat... Nova Scotia Revised Statutes [*Canada*] [*A publication*] (DLA)
NSRF........ National Stroke Recovery Foundation (EA)
NSRF........ Naval Ship Repair Facility (MCD)
NSRF........ Naval Strategic Reserve Fleet
NSRF........ Nova Scotia Research Foundation (SAUS)
NSRFC ...... Nova Scotia Research Foundation Corp. [*Crown Corp.*] [*Canada*] (IRC)
NSRG........ Northern Science Research Group (SAUS)
NSRG & O.. Nova Scotia Reports, by Geldert and Oxley [*A publication*] (DLA)
NSRG & R.. Nova Scotia Reports, by Geldert and Russell [*A publication*] (DLA)
NSRI......... National Soil Resources Institute [*Cranfield University*] [*United Kingdom*] (RCD)
NSRJ .... Nova Scotia Reports (James) [*A publication*] (DLA)
NSR (James)... Nova Scotia Reports (James) [*Canada*] [*A publication*] (DLA)
NSRL........ National SIGINT [*Signal Intelligence*] Requirements List (MCD)
NSRL........ Nuclear Structure Research Laboratory (NRCH)
NSRM....... National Strategy for Rangeland Management [*Australia*]
NSRM....... Nevada State Railroad Museum [*Federal Railroad Administration identification code*]
NSRMCA.... National Star Route Mail Contractors Association (EA)
NSRMP..... Net Survival Rate for Monocyclic Process
NSRN........ National School Resource Network [*Defunct*] (EA)
NSRO........ Navy Resale System Office (PDAA)
NSR Old .... Oldright's Nova Scotia Reports [*A publication*] (DLA)
NSRP........ National Search and Rescue Plan
NSRP........ National States Rights Party (EA)
NSRP........ Neutral Seat Reference Point (MCD)
NSRP........ Nonstandard Part Request
NSRP........ Nontechnical Support Real Property
NSRP........ Nordic Society for Radiation Protection [*See also NSFS*] [*Helsinki, Finland*] (EAIO)
NSRPIE...... Non-technical Support Real Property Installed Equipment (SAUS)
NSRPr....... NorfolkSo'nRy$2.60cmPfd [*NYSE symbol*] (TTSB)
NSR/PSD.... New Source Review and Prevention of Significant Deterioration Permitting (SAUS)
NSR PSU ... Non Self-Representing Primary Sampling Unit [*Bureau of the Census*] (GFGA)
NSRPT ...... Northern Southeast Alaska Regional Planning Team [*USDA Forest Service*] (ALAC)
NSRQCE..... National Symposium on Reliability and Quality Control in Electronics (MCD)
NSRR........ Normal Sinus Rate and Rhythm [*Cardiology*] (DAVI)
NSRR........ Nuclear Safety Research Reactors (NRCH)
NSRR & C.. Russell and Chesley's Nova Scotia Reports [*10-12 Nova Scotia Reports*] [*1875-79*] [*A publication*] (DLA)
NSRR & G.. Russell and Geldert's Nova Scotia Reports [*A publication*] (DLA)
NSRS........ NASA Safety Reporting System (SAUS)
NSRS........ National Scholarship Research Service [*Information service or system*] (IID)
NSRS........ National Shoreline Refuse Survey [*British*]
NSRS........ National Spatial Reference System [*Marine science*] (OSRA)
NSRS........ National Supply Radio Station (MCD)
NSRS........ Naval Supply Radio Station
NSRT........ Near-Surface Radiation Thermometer
NSRT........ Near Surface Reference Temperature [*Oceanography*]
NSRT........ North South Roundtable (EAIO)
NSR Thom... Thomson's Nova Scotia Reports [*A publication*] (DLA)
NSRU........ Nam Sung Shipping [*Intermodal shipping container symbol*] (TVRC)
NSRU........ North Star Universal [*NASDAQ symbol*] (TTSB)
NSRU........ North Star Universal, Inc. [*NASDAQ symbol*] (NQ)
NSrU........ Ulster County Community College, Stone Ridge, NY [*Library symbol*] [*Library of Congress*] (LCLS)
NSRW....... Nuclear Service Raw Water (IEEE)
NSR Wall... Wallace's Nova Scotia Reports [*6 Nova Scotia Reports*] [*1884-1907*] [*A publication*] (DLA)
NSRWP ..... Nuclear Service Raw Water Pump [*Electronics*] (IAA)
NSRX........ North Star Rail [*Federal Railroad Administration identification code*]
NSRy........ Norfolk Southern Railway Co. [*Associated Press*] (SAG)
NSS.......... Namespace Specific String (SAUS)
NSS.......... Name Switch Service (SAUS)
NSS.......... National Sample Survey (PDAA)
NSS.......... National Sculpture Society (EA)
NSS.......... National Search and Rescue Secretariat [*Canada*] (DA)
NSS.......... National Secular Society [*British*] (DBA)
NSS.......... National Seismic Stations
NSS.......... National Serigraph Society [*Defunct*]
NSS.......... National Service Secretariat (EA)
NSS.......... National Slovak Society of the USA
NSS.......... National Snapdragon Society (EA)
NSS.......... National Space Society (EA)
NSS.......... National Space Station [*NASA*] (IAA)
NSS.......... National Speleological Society (EA)
NSS.......... National Staff Side [*British*]
NSS.......... National Stockpile Site
NSS.......... National Study Service [*Defunct*] (EA)
NSS.......... National Supply System (MCD)
NSS.......... National Surveillance Scheme (WDAA)
NS/S......... Native Seeds/SEARCH [*Southwestern Endangered Arid-Land Resource Clearing House*] (EA)
NSS.......... Nature Society of Singapore [*Political party*] (PSAP)
NSS.......... Naval Sea Systems Command, Washington, DC [*OCLC symbol*] (OCLC)
NSS.......... Naval Security Station (NVT)
NSS.......... Naval Simulation System [*DoD*]
NSS.......... Naval Strategic Study
NSS.......... Naval Surveillance System [*Police and security equipment*]
NSS.......... Navigation Subsystem Switchboard
NSS.......... Navy Secondary Standards (MSA)
NSS.......... Navy Shore Station (IAA)
NSS.......... Navy Standard Score (DNAB)
NSS.......... Navy Strategic Study
NSS.......... Navy Supply System
NSS.......... Near-Source Simulation (SAUS)
NSS.......... Network Supervisor System
NSS.......... Network Support System [*Computer science*]
NSS.......... Network Synchronization Subsystem [*Telecommunications*] (TEL)
NSS.......... Network System Simulator (ACAE)
NSS.......... Neurological Soft Signs [*Occupational therapy*]
NSS.......... Neuropathy Symptom Score
NSS.......... Neutral Safety Switch [*Automotive engineering*]
NSS.......... Neutral Speed Stability (PDAA)
NSS.......... Neutron Scattering Society
NSS.......... Neutron Spectrometer System
NSS.......... [*The*] Newburgh & South Shore Railway Co. [*AAR code*]
NSS.......... New Shakespeare Society (SAUS)
NSS.......... New Simulation System (SAUS)
NSS.......... New Statesman and Society [*A publication*]
NSS.......... New Suppliers Service (SAUS)
NSS.......... New System Simulator (SAUS)
NSS.......... Nitrogen Supply Subsystem
NSS.......... Nitrogen Supply System [*or Subsystem*] (AAG)
NSS.......... NMIC [*National Military Information Center*] Support System (MCD)
NSS.......... Nodal Switching Subsystem (SAUS)
NSS.......... Nodding Subdish System
NSS.......... Noise Suppressor System (MCD)
NSS.......... Non-Salt Sensitive
NSS.......... Non-Sea Salt
nss........... Non-Sea-Salt (CARB)
NSS.......... Non-Seasalt Sulphate (QUAC)
NSS.......... Non-Self-Sustaining [*Container ship*] (MCD)
NSS.......... Nonspatial Statistics (SAUS)
NSS.......... Nonstandard Facilities Setup [*Computer science*]
NSS.......... Non Subscriber Site (ACAE)
NSS.......... Nordic Statistical Secretariat (SAUS)
NSS.......... Nordiska Kommitten for Samordning av Elektriska Sakerhetsfragor [*Nordic Committee for Coordination of Electrical Safety Matters*] (EAIO)
NSS.......... Nordiska Statistiska Sekretariatet [*Nordic Statistical Secretariat*] (EAIO)
NSS.......... Normal Saline Solution
NSS.......... Normal Size and Shape (SAUS)
NSS.......... Northstar Aviation, Inc. [*ICAO designator*] (FAAC)
NSS.......... Northwest Steam Society (EA)
NSS.......... Nortronics System Support
NSS.......... No Study Section (SAUS)
NSS.......... No Such Street [*Telegraphy*] (PCTE)
NSS.......... Not Statistically Significant (MAE)
NSS.......... NS Group [*NYSE symbol*] (SPSG)
NSS.......... Nuclear Science Symposium (PDAA)
NSS.......... Nuclear Steam System (NRCH)
NSS.......... Nuclear Support Services, Inc. (EFIS)
NSSA........ National Sanitary Supply Association [*Later, ISSA*] (EA)
NSSA........ National Scholastic Surfing Association (EA)
NSSA........ National Science Supervisors Association (EA)
NSSA........ National Senior Sports Association (EA)
NSSA........ National Sjogren's Syndrome Association (EA)
NSSA........ National Skeet Shooting Association (EA)
NSSA........ National Sportscasters and Sportswriters Association (EA)
NSSA........ National Suffolk Sheep Association (EA)
NSSA........ National Sunday School Association [*Defunct*] (EA)
NSSA........ National Swim School Association (EA)
NSSA........ Navy Space Systems Activity [*Los Angeles, CA*] (MCD)
NSSA........ Nebraska State Soccer Association (EARSL)
NSSA........ Nematological Society of Southern Africa (EAIO)
NSSA........ New York Skirt and Sportswear Association (EA)
N-SSA....... North-South Skirmish Association (EA)

NSSA .... Nova Scotia Salmon Association (SAUS)
NSSA .... Nova Scotia Society of Artists [*1922-72*] [*Canada*] (NGC)
NSSAB ...... National Selective Service Appeal Board [*of SSS*] [*Inactive since 1975*]
NSSAC ...... National Society, Sons of the American Colonists [*Defunct*] (EA)
NSS&FFA ... National Soft Serve and Fast Food Association (NTPA)
NSSAR ...... National Society, Sons of the American Revolution (EA)
NSSB .... National Society of Scabbard and Blade (EA)
NSSB .... Norwich Financial [*NASDAQ symbol*] (TTSB)
NSSB .... Norwich Financial Corp. [*NASDAQ symbol*] (NQ)
NSSC .... Cape Breton Regional Library, Sydney, Nova Scotia [*Library symbol*] [*National Library of Canada*] (NLC)
NSSC .... Napco Security Sys [*NASDAQ symbol*] (TTSB)
NSSC .... Napco Security Systems, Inc. [*NASDAQ symbol*] (NQ)
NSSC .... NASA Safety Standards Committee
NSSC .... National School Safety Center
NSSC .... National Science Strategy Committee (SAUS)
NSSC .... National Society for the Study of Communication [*Later, ICA*] (EA)
NSSC .... National Soil Survey Center [*Natural Resources Conservation Service*] (RCD)
NSSC .... National Soil Survey Committee [*Canada*]
NSSC .... National Space Science Center [*British*]
NSSC .... Naval Sea [*formerly, Ship*] Systems Command
NSSC .... Neutral Sulfite Semichemical [*Pulp*]
NSSC .... Neutral Sulfite Semimechanical Process (EDCT)
NSSC .... Nordic Symposium on Super Conductivity (SAUS)
NSSC .... Normal Size, Shape, and Consistency [*Medicine*] (MELL)
NSSC .... Nova Scotia Safety Council (SAUS)
NSSCB ...... Cape Breton Post, Sydney, Nova Scotia [*Library symbol*] [*National Library of Canada*] (NLC)
NSSCBD..... Cape Breton Development Corp., Sydney, Nova Scotia [*Library symbol*] [*National Library of Canada*] (NLC)
NSSCBH..... Cape Breton Hospital, Sydney, Nova Scotia [*Library symbol*] [*National Library of Canada*] (NLC)
NSSCC ...... National Space Surveillance Control Center
NSSCDS..... Naval Small Ship Combat Data System (SAA)
NSSCG ...... Canadian Coast Guard College [*College de la Garde Cotiere Canadienne*] Sydney, Nova Scotia [*Library symbol*] [*National Library of Canada*] (NLC)
NSSCM...... Shelburne County Museum, Nova Scotia [*Library symbol*] [*National Library of Canada*] (NLC)
NSSCO ...... Coast Guard, Shelburne, Nova Scotia [*Library symbol*] [*National Library of Canada*] (NLC)
NSS Co...... Northern Steam Ship Co. (SAUS)
NSSCS ...... Non-Self-Sustaining Containership [*Environmental science*] (COE)
NSSD .... National Security Study Directive (ACAE)
NSSD .... National Strategy for Sustainable Development [*Australia*]
NSSD .... North Shore Sanitary District, Lake County (SAUS)
NSSDC ...... National Space Science Data Center [*Greenbelt, MD*] [*NASA*] (MCD)
NSSDP ...... National Society of Sons and Daughters of the Pilgrims (EA)
NSSDU ...... Normal Data Session Service Data Unit (SAUS)
NSsE......... Empire State College, Saratoga Springs, NY [*Library symbol*] [*Library of Congress*] (LCLS)
NSSE .... National Society for the Study of Education (EA)
NSSE .... National Study of School Evaluation (EA)
NSSE .... Nordic Subarctic-Subalpine Ecology (SAUS)
NSSEA....... National School Supply and Equipment Association (EA)
NSSEB....... Non-Social Security Equivalent Benefit
NSSET....... National Symposium on Space Electronics and Telemetry [*IEEE*] (MCD)
NSSF .... National Shooting Sports Foundation (EA)
NSSF .... National Social Science Foundation [*Proposed in 1966*]
NSSF .... Near Surface Storage Facility (ABAC)
N/SSF .... Novice, Society of St. Francis
NSSFA....... National Single Service Food Association (EA)
NSSFC....... National Severe Storms Forecast Center [*National Oceanic and Atmospheric Administration*]
NSSFC....... National Society of Student Film Critics [*Defunct*] (EA)
NSSFFA ..... National Soft Serve and Fast Food Association (EA)
NSSFNS..... National Scholarship Service and Fund for Negro Students (EA)
NSSG .... National Ski Study Group [*Defunct*]
NSSGA ...... Nicherin Shoshu Soka Gakkai Academy (SAUS)
NSSHA ...... National Spotted Saddle Horse Association (EA)
NSSHA ...... National Student Speech and Hearing Association [*Later, NSSLHA*] (EA)
NSSHCF..... Canadian Forces Base Barrington, Stone Horse, Nova Scotia [*Library symbol*] [*National Library of Canada*] (NLC)
NSSHDC .... National Spanish Speaking Housing Development Corp.
NSSHET..... Newcomen Society for the Study of the History of Engineering and Technology [*British*] (EAIO)
NSSI......... Network 1 Security Solutions [*OTCBB symbol*]
NSSI......... Nuclear Sources & Services, Inc. (EFIS)
NSSI......... Nuclear Support Services, Inc. [*NASDAQ symbol*] (NQ)
NS-SIB ...... NAVSHIPS [*Naval Ship Systems Command*] Ship Information Booklets
NSSIC .... National Student Strike Information Center [*Brandeis University*]
NSSJD....... Community of the Nursing Sisters of St. John the Divine [*Anglican religious community*]
NSSK .... National Society of Student Keyboardists (EA)
NSSK .... North-South Station-Keeping (PDAA)
NSSL .... National Seed Storage Laboratory [*Department of Agriculture*] [*Fort Collins, CO*] (GRD)
NSSL .... National Service Star Legion (EA)
NSSL .... National Severe Storms Laboratory [*National Oceanic and Atmospheric Administration*] [*Research center*]
NSSL .... National Society of State Legislators [*Later, NCSL*]
NSSL .... National Survey of State Laws [*A publication*]
NSSLC....... National Social Science and Law Center (EA)
NSSLHA..... National Student Speech Language Hearing Association (EA)
NSSLP....... National Social Science and Law Project (EA)
NSSL PAC-WIS... North Shore Savings and Loan Association PAC [*Brookfield, WI*] (PACS)
NSSM .... National Security Study Memorandum [*Obsolete*]
NSSM .... Navy Spread Spectrum MODEM (MCD)
NSSMM ..... Memorial High School, Sydney Mines, Nova Scotia [*Library symbol*] [*National Library of Canada*] (NLC)
NSSMS...... NATO Sea Sparrow Missile System
NSSN........ National Speed Sport News [*A publication*]
NSSN........ National Standard Shipping Note (DS)
NSSN........ National Standards Systems Network
NSSN........ New Nuclear Attack Submarine [*Military*] (POLM)
NSSNF ...... Naval Strategic Systems Navigation Facility
NSSO........ National Second Surgical Opinion Program (MELL)
NSSO........ National Society of Student Organists [*Later, NSSK*] (EA)
NSSO........ National Solar Space Observatory [*NASA*]
NSSO........ Navy Ships' Store Office [*PX*]
NSSP .... National Severe Storms Project [*National Oceanic and Atmospheric Administration*]
NSSP .... National Shellfish Sanitation Program [*Food and Drug Administration*] (GFGA)
NSSP .... National Syrian Socialist Party [*Lebanon*] [*Political party*]
NSSP .... Nava Sama Samaja Party [*New Equal Society Party*] [*Sri Lanka*] [*Political party*] (PPW)
NSSP .... Neutralization Self-Solidification Process (PDAA)
NSSP .... Nonreporting Secondary Stock Point (AFIT)
NSSP .... Normal Size, Shape, and Position [*On examination*] [*Anatomy*] (DAVI)
NSSPAVAF... Normal Size, Shape, and Position Anteverted, and Anteflexed [*Uterus*] [*On examination*] [*Gynecology*] (DAVI)
NSSPO ...... Navy Strategic Systems Projects Office (ACAE)
NSSPS ...... New Space Signals Processing Stations (ACAE)
NSSR........ National Spotted Swine Record (EA)
NSSR........ New School for Social Research [*New York, NY*]
NSSR........ Nordic Cooperation for Sami and Reindeer Questions (SAUS)
NSSR........ Nordic Society of Space Research
NSSR........ North Shore Scenic Railroad [*Federal Railroad Administration identification code*]
NSSR........ Nuclear Science Series Report (SAUS)
NSSR........ Record, Springhill, Nova Scotia [*Library symbol*] [*National Library of Canada*] (NLC)
NSSRA ...... National Ski & Snowboard Retailers Association (NTPA)
NSSRI .... Nervous System Sports-Related Injury [*Medicine*]
NSSRM...... Soluth Rawdon Museum, Nova Scotia [*Library symbol*] [*National Library of Canada*] (NLC)
NSSS .... National Sewage Sludge Survey [*Environmental Protection Agency*]
NSSS .... National Space Surveillance System
NSSS .... Nuclear Steam Supply System [*Vendor*] (NRCH)
NSSS .... Nuclear Steam System Supply (SAUS)
NSsS .... Skidmore College, Saratoga Springs, NY [*Library symbol*] [*Library of Congress*] (LCLS)
NSsSA....... Southern Adirondack Library System, Saratoga Springs, NY [*Library symbol*] [*Library of Congress*] (LCLS)
NSsSC....... Supreme Court Library at Saratoga Springs, Saratoga Springs, NY [*Library symbol*] [*Library of Congress*] (LCLS)
NSSSE....... National Study of Secondary School Evaluation [*Later, NSSE*] (EA)
NSSSRH .... St. Rita's Hospital, Sydney, Nova Scotia [*Library symbol*] [*National Library of Canada*] (NLC)
NSSSS ...... Nuclear Steam Supply Shutoff System (NRCH)
NSST .... Non-Smoking Seat [*Travel industry*] (TRID)
NSST .... Nonspecific ST Segment Changes [*On electroencephalogram*] [*Cardiology*] (DAVI)
NSST .... Northwestern Syntax Screening Test [*Education*]
NSST .... No Smoking Seat [*Travel industry*] (TVEL)
NSSTA....... National Structured Settlements Trade Association (EA)
NS Stat...... Nova Scotia Statutes [*Canada*] [*A publication*] (DLA)
NSSTC....... National Small Shipments Traffic Conference (EA)
NSSTE....... National Society of Sales Training Executives [*Orlando, FL*] (EA)
NSS Test.... Neutral Salt Spray Test (SAUS)
NSSTT....... Nonspecific ST and T [*Wave on electrocardiogram*] [*Cardiology*] (DAVI)
NSSU........ Nam Sung Shipping [*Intermodal shipping container symbol*] (TVRC)
NSSU........ National Steam Service Union [*British*]
NSSU........ National Sunday School Union [*British*]
NSSUP ...... National Society of the Sons of Utah Pioneers (EA)
NSSX........ National Sanitary Supply Co. [*NASDAQ symbol*] (NQ)
NSSX........ Natl Sanitary Supply [*NASDAQ symbol*] (TTSB)
NSSX........ University College of Cape Breton, Sydney, Nova Scotia [*Library symbol*] [*National Library of Canada*] (NLC)
NSSXA ...... Archives and General Library, College of Cape Breton, Sydney, Nova Scotia [*Library symbol*] [*National Library of Canada*] (NLC)
NSSY........ Norwalk Savings Society [*NASDAQ symbol*] (SAG)
NSSYA....... National Small Sailing Yacht Association (EA)
NST.......... Aviacion Ejecutiva del Noroeste SA de CV [*Mexico*] [*ICAO designator*] (FAAC)
NST.......... Nasty (ABBR)
NST.......... National Scenic Trail
NST.......... National Security Technology (ABAC)
NST.......... National Skills Training
NST.......... National Standard Taper (IAA)
NST.......... National Starch [*Federal Railroad Administration identification code*]
NST.......... National Symposium on Telemetering (MCD)
NST.......... Navy Shipboard Terminal

NST .... Navy Standard Teleprinter (DOMA)
NST .... Nest (ABBR)
NST .... Nesting Module (MCD)
NST .... Network Support Team [*NASA*] (KSC)
NST .... Newfoundland Standard Time [*Aviation*] (AIA)
NST .... New Serial Titles [*A publication of Library of Congress*]
NST .... New Serial Titles, Library of Congress, Washington, DC [*OCLC symbol*] (OCLC)
NST .... New York Air (SAUS)
NST .... Nigata Sogo Television (SAUS)
NST .... Node Systems Trainer (SAUS)
NST .... Noise Source Tube
NST .... Noise, Spikes, and Transients (PDAA)
NST .... Nonshivering Thermogenesis [*Physiology*]
NST .... Nonslip Tread [*Technical drawings*]
NST .... Non Standard Transmission (SAUS)
NST .... Nonstress Test [*Gynecology*]
NST .... Normal Sphincter Tone [*Gastroenterology*] (DAVI)
NST .... North Solomon Trench [*Geoscience*]
NST .... North Sumatra Time (SAUS)
NST .... No Sales Tax (SAUS)
NST .... Not Sooner Than
NST .... NSTAR [*NYSE symbol*]
NST .... Nuclear and Space Talks (DOMA)
NST .... Nuclear Spin Tomography (DB)
NST .... Numerical Surface Techniques (SAUS)
NST .... Numerical Surveying Technique (PDAA)
NST .... Nutritional Support Team [*Dietetics*] (DAVI)
NSTA .... Anesta Corp. [*NASDAQ symbol*] (SAG)
NSTA .... National Safe Transit Association (EA)
NSTA .... National School Transportation Association (EA)
NSTA .... National Science Teachers Association (EA)
NSTA .... National Security Traders Association [*Later, STA*] (EA)
NSTA .... National Shoe Traveler's Association (EA)
NSTA .... National Spasmodic Torticollis Association (EA)
NSTA .... National Squash Tennis Association (EA)
NSTA .... Nova Scotia Agricultural College, Truro, Nova Scotia [*Library symbol*] [*National Library of Canada*] (NLC)
NS-TAB ...... NAVSHIPS [*Naval Ship Systems Command*] Training Aid Bulletins
NSTAC .... National Security Telecommunications Advisory Committee (NITA)
NSTAF .... National Solar Technical Audience File [*Solar Energy Research Institute*] [*Database*]
N Staff ...... North Staffordshire (SAUS)
NSTAG .... National Science and Technology Advisory Group [*Australia*]
NStand ...... National Standard Co. [*Associated Press*] (SAG)
NSTAP .... National Strategic Acquisition Plan (SAUS)
NSTAP .... National Strategic Targeting and Attack Policy (CINC)
NSTARS ..... Navy Standard Tracking and Retrieval System (MCD)
NStarU ...... North Star Universal, Inc. [*Associated Press*] (SAG)
NSTB .... Biblio-Tech Ltd., Three Fathom Harbor, Nova Scotia [*Library symbol*] [*National Library of Canada*] (NLC)
NSTB .... National Satellite Test Bed
NSTB .... National Science and Technology Board [*Singapore*]
NStBU .... St. Bonaventure University, St. Bonaventure, NY [*Library symbol*] [*Library of Congress*] (LCLS)
NSTC .... Colchester - East Hants Regional Library, Truro, Nova Scotia [*Library symbol*] [*National Library of Canada*] (NLC)
NSTC .... National Science and Technology Council [*Formerly, FCCSET*]
NSTC .... National Security Training Commission [*Expired, 1957*]
NSTC .... National Shade Tree Conference [*Later, ISA*]
NSTC .... National Spiritualist Teachers Club (EA)
NSTC .... Nineteenth Century Short Title Catalogue [*Avero Publications Ltd.*] [*Information service or system*] [*British*] (CRD)
NSTC .... Nonsmokers' Travel Club [*Defunct*] (EA)
NSTC .... Norwegian Save the Children (SAUS)
NSTC .... Not Subject to Call (MHDB)
NSTC .... Nova Scotia Teachers College [*Canada*]
NSTC .... Nova Scotia Technical College
NSTCH ...... Colchester Historical Society, Truro, Nova Scotia [*Library symbol*] [*National Library of Canada*] (BIB)
NST-D .... Navy Standard Transmission [*Dension hydraulics*] (CAAL)
NSTD .... Nested [*Packaging*]
NSTD .... Non-System Training Devices [*USA*]
NSTDB ...... National Strategic Target Data Base (CINC)
NSTDH ...... National STD [*Sexually Transmitted Disease*] Hotline (EA)
NSTDN ...... Daily News, Truro, Nova Scotia [*Library symbol*] [*National Library of Canada*] (NLC)
NSTDP ...... National Society of Tole and Decorative Painters (EA)
N-STDS ..... Navy Standards (AAGC)
NSTE .... National Society of Telephone Employees [*A union*] [*British*]
NSTEP .... National Spit Tobacco Education Program [*An initiative of Oral Health America*]
NSTEP .... Naval Scientist Training and Exchange Program (DNAB)
NSTF .... Fraser Culture Centre, Tatamagouche, Nova Scotia [*Library symbol*] [*National Library of Canada*] (NLC)
NSTF .... National Scholarship Trust Fund [*An affiliate of the Graphic Arts Technical Foundation*]
NSTF .... Near Surface Test Facility [*Nuclear energy*] (NUCP)
NSTF .... Neutron Sensor Testing Facility (IAA)
NSTF .... North Sea Task Force (SAUS)
NSTF .... Nuclear Science and Technology Facility [*State University of New York at Buffalo*] [*Research center*] (RCD)
NSTFI .... Nuveen Select Tax Free Income Portfolio [*Associated Press*] (SAG)
NSTFI2 ...... Nuveen Select Tax Free Income Portfolio 2 [*Associated Press*] (SAG)
NSTFI3 ...... Nuveen Select Tax Free Income Portfolio 3 [*Associated Press*] (SAG)
NSTG .... Nesting (ABBR)
NSTG .... Nuclear Strike Target Graphic (MCD)
NSTH .... Newstate Holdings [*OTCBB symbol*]
NSTI .... NASCOM [*NASA Communications Network*] Simulation Traffic Interface (SSD)
NSTI .... Norwalk State Technical Institute (SAUS)
NSTIC .... Naval Science and Technology Information Centre (NITA)
NSTIC .... Naval Scientific and Technical Information Centre [*Later, DRIC*] [*British*] (MCD)
NSTIC .... Navy Scientific and Technical Intelligence Center (IEEE)
NSTICLANT ... Naval Scientific and Technical Intelligence Center, Atlantic (DNAB)
NSTICPAC ... Naval Scientific and Technical Intelligence Center, Pacific (DNAB)
NSTIM .... Islands Museum and Tourist Bureau, Tiverton, Nova Scotia [*Library symbol*] [*National Library of Canada*] (NLC)
NStj .... Margaret Reaney Memorial Library, St. Johnsville, NY [*Library symbol*] [*Library of Congress*] (LCLS)
NSTK .... Nastech Pharmaceutical [*NASDAQ symbol*] (TTSB)
NSTK .... Nastech Pharmaceutical Co. [*NASDAQ symbol*]
NSTK .... Nastech Pharmaceuticals [*NASDAQ symbol*] (SAG)
NSTKW ..... Nastech Pharmaceutical Wrrt [*NASDAQ symbol*] (TTSB)
NSTL .... National Software-Testing Laboratories [*Computer science*]
NSTL .... National Space Technology Laboratories [*Formerly, MTF*] [*Mississippi*] [*NASA*]
NSTL .... National Strategic Target Line [*or List*] (AFM)
NSTL .... Nestled (ABBR)
NSTL .... Nuclear Services and Training Laboratory [*Ohio State University*] [*Research center*] (RCD)
NSTLG .... Nestling (ABBR)
NSTLG .... Nostalgia (ABBR)
NSTLGC ..... Nostalgic (ABBR)
NSTM .... Naval School Transportation Management
NSTM .... Navy Ship Technical Manual (CAAL)
NSTM .... Navy Standard Test Model (CAAL)
NSTM .... Nordiska Skeppstekniska Mote [*Joint Committee of Nordic Marine Technology - JCNMT*] (EAIO)
NS-TMI ...... NAVSHIPS [*Naval Ship Systems Command*] Technical Manual Index
NSTN .... Naval Shore Telecommunications Network (SAUS)
NSTN .... Nonstandard Telephone Number [*Telecommunications*] (TEL)
NSTN .... [*The*] Nova Scotia Technology Network [*Canada*] [*Computer science*] (TNIG)
NSTNS ...... Nastiness (ABBR)
NSTO .... New System Training Office [*Army*]
NSTO .... Non Statutory Training Organisation [*British*]
NSTOA ...... National Ski Touring Operators' Association (EA)
NSTP .... National Society of TV Producers (NTCM)
NSTP .... National Solar Terrestrial Program (SAUS)
NSTP .... Non-Stop (SAUS)
NSTP .... Northern Science Training Program (SAUS)
NSTP .... Northstar Transportation [*Common carrier symbol*]
NSTP .... Nuffield Science Teaching Project (SAUS)
NSTP .... Nuffield Service Teaching Project
NSTPC ...... Nova Scotia Tidal Power Corp. (SAUS)
NSTPS ...... Law Library, Patterson, Smith, Mathews & Grant, Truro, Nova Scotia [*Library symbol*] [*National Library of Canada*] (NLC)
NSTR .... Naval Sea Systems Command Technical Representative
NSTR .... Northstar Health Services, Inc. [*NASDAQ symbol*] (SAG)
NSTR .... Northstar Minerals (SAUS)
NSTR .... Record, Truro, Nova Scotia [*Library symbol*] [*National Library of Canada*] (NLC)
NSTRA ...... North Stratford, NH [*American Association of Railroads railroad junction routing code*]
NSTRE .... Northstar Health Svcs [*NASDAQ symbol*] (TTSB)
NSTRTU .... National Strategy to Reduce Tobacco Use (SAUS)
NSTS .... National Sea Training Schools [*British*]
NSTS .... National Secure Telephone System (SAUS)
NSTS .... National Securities Trading System
NSTS .... National Space Transportation System
NSTS .... National Student Traffic Safety Program [*National Commission on Safety Education*] [*Washington, DC*] (AEBS)
NST-S .... National Support Team-Sarajevo [*Military*]
NSTS .... Navy Stockpile to Target Sequence
NSTS .... NCC [*Navy Command Center*] Security Test System
NSTS .... Northwestern States Portland Cement Co. (SAUS)
NSTSPO .... National Space Transportation System Program Office (SSD)
NSTT .... National Sea Training Trusts [*British*] (DS)
NSTT .... Naval Strategy Think Tank (DOMA)
NSTT .... Nonseminomatous Testicular Tumor [*Medicine*] (DMAA)
NSTT .... Nova Scotia Teachers' College, Truro, Nova Scotia [*Library symbol*] [*National Library of Canada*] (NLC)
NSTTF .... National Solar Thermal Test Facility [*Sandia National Laboratories*]
NSTU .... Nuova Csti Line [*Intermodal shipping container symbol*] (TVRC)
NSTU .... Pago Pago/International, Tutuila Island [*American Samoa*] [*ICAO location identifier*] (ICLI)
NST-V .... Navy Standard Transmission [*Vickers hydraulics*] (CAAL)
NSTW .... National Science and Technology Week [*An annual outreach program begun in 1985 by the National Science Foundation*]
NSTX .... National Spherical Torus Experiment [*Plasma physics*]
NSTX .... North Star Steel [*Private rail car owner code*]
NSTY .... Nastily (ABBR)
NSU .... Naval Scout Unit
NSU .... Neckarsulm [*Location in Wuerttemberg, Germany, of NSU Werke, automobile manufacturer; initialism used as name of its cars*]
NSU .... Neighborhood Stabilization Unit (LAIN)
NSU .... Network Service Unit (NITA)
NSU .... Neurosurgical Unit [*Medicine*] (DMAA)

NSU.......... Nitrogen Supply Unit (AAG)
NSU.......... Nonspecific Urethritis [*Medicine*]
NSU.......... Non-Switching Unit (SAUS)
NSU.......... Norfolk State University (SAUS)
NSU.......... North Stansbury [*Utah*] [*Seismograph station code, US Geological Survey*] (SEIS)
NSU.......... NSU Prinz [*NCIC car make code*]
NSU.......... Nuova Sinistra Unita [*New United Left*] [*Italy*] [*Political party*] (PPE)
NSUA........ Nigerian Students Union in the Americas (EA)
NSUAA...... National Submetering and Utility Allocation Association (EA)
NSUB........ Neighbourhood Substitutability (SAUS)
NSUC........ North Staffordshire University College (SAUS)
NSU-COM... College of Osteopathic Medicine [*Nova Southeastern University*] (MHID)
NSUF........ NSU-Fiat [*NCIC car make code*]
NSuf......... Suffern Free Library, Suffern, NY [*Library symbol*] [*Library of Congress*] (LCLS)
NSufA....... Avon Products, Inc., Suffern, NY [*Library symbol*] [*Library of Congress*] (LCLS)
NSufR....... Rockland Community College, Suffern, NY [*Library symbol*] [*Library of Congress*] (LCLS)
NSUG........ Nihon Sun Users Group (SAUS)
NSUK........ Nichiren Shoshu of the UK [*Buddhist organization*] (DI)
N/Sun Sent... News/Sun-Sentinel (SAUS)
NSUP......... Naval Supply Systems Command Headquarters
N-Super..... Nuclear-powered Supercarrier (SAUS)
NSUPSC..... Naval Supply Systems Command [*Formerly, Bureau of Supplies and Accounts*] (MCD)
NSURG...... Neurosurgery [*Medicine*]
NSUS........ Newcomen Society of the United States (EA)
NSv.......... Finkelstein Memorial Library, Spring Valley, NY [*Library symbol*] [*Library of Congress*] (LCLS)
NSV.......... National Socialist Vanguard (EA)
NSV.......... Natl Equipment Svcs. [*NYSE symbol*] (SG)
NSV.......... Negative Supply Voltage
NSV.......... Net Sales Value (BUR)
NSV.......... Netted Secure Voice [*Military*] (CAAL)
NSV.......... Neurosecretory Vesicle [*Neuroanatomy*]
NSV.......... Noise, Shock, and Vibration (PDAA)
NSV.......... Nonautomatic Self-Verification [*Computer science*] (MDG)
NSV.......... Nonspecific Vaginitis [*Medicine*]
NSV.......... Nonspinning Vehicle
NSV.......... Nova Scotia Savings & Loans Co. [*Toronto Stock Exchange symbol*]
NSV.......... Nuclear Service Vessel
NSVA........ Navy Seabee Veterans of America (EA)
NSVA........ New South Wales Vigoro Association [*Australia*]
NSVC........ National Sisters Vocation Conference [*Later, NRVC*] (EA)
NSVD........ Normal Spontaneous Vaginal Delivery [*Obstetrics*] (DMAA)
NSVEA....... Natural-Source Vitamin E Association (EA)
NSVL........ NSL [*Common carrier symbol*]
NSVP........ National School Volunteer Program (EA)
NSVP........ National Student Volunteer Program [*Later, NCSL*] (EA)
NS/VPP..... Nuclear Survivability/ Vulnerability Program Plan (SAUS)
N/SVQ...... National/Scottish Vocational Qualification (WDAA)
NSVRA...... National Stenomask Verbatim Reporters Association (NTPA)
NSVT........ Nonsustained Ventricular Tachycardia [*Medicine*] (CPH)
NSW......... Ansett Airlines of New South Wales [*Australia*] [*ICAO designator*] (FAAC)
NSW......... Herbarium of New South Wales (SAUS)
NSW......... National Software Works
NSW......... Naval Special Warfare (NVT)
NSW......... Neutron Spin Wave (SAUS)
NSW......... New South Wales (WA)
NSW......... Northwestern Steel & Wire Co. (SAUS)
NSW......... NSP [*National Aeronautical and Space Administration Support Plan*] Status Word
NSWA....... Acadia University, Wolfville, Nova Scotia [*Library symbol*] [*National Library of Canada*] (NLC)
NSWA....... National Social Welfare Assembly [*Later, National Assembly of National Voluntary Health and Social Welfare Organizations*] (EA)
NSWA....... National Soft Wheat Association [*Later, MNF*] (EA)
NSWA....... National Stripper Well Association (EA)
NSWA....... North Shore Writers Alliance (EA)
NSW Adm.. New South Wales Reports, Admiralty [*A publication*] (DLA)
NSWAEM.... New South Wales Assemblies' Evangelic Mission [*Australia*]
NSWAG...... Department of Geography, Acadia University, Wolfville, Nova Scotia [*Library symbol*] [*Obsolete*] [*National Library of Canada*] (NLC)
NSWAGTC... New South Wales Association of Gifted and Talented Children [*Australia*]
NSWAHP.... New South Wales Association of Health Professions [*Australia*]
NSWAIP..... Australian Institute of Physics, NSW Branch (SAUS)
NSWALC.... New South Wales Adult Literacy Council [*Australia*]
NS Wales L... New South Wales Law [*A publication*] (DLA)
NS Wales LR Eq... New South Wales Law Reports, Equity [*A publication*] (DLA)
NSWAMH.... New South Waks Association for Mental Health (SAUS)
NSWAP...... National Socialist White American Party [*Political party*]
NSWAPA.... New South Wales Amateur Pistol Association [*Australia*]
NSWAR...... New South Wales Arbitration Reports [*A publication*] (DLA)
NSWAS...... New South Wales Association of Sephardim [*Australia*]
NSWAWL.... New South Wales Animal Welfare League [*Australia*]
NSWAWPA... New South Wales Amateur Water Polo Association [*Australia*]
NSWB....... New South Wales Bushmen [*British military*] (DMA)
NSWBA...... New South Wales Bar Association [*Australia*]
NSWBA...... New South Wales Basketball Association [*Australia*]
NSWBA...... New South Wales Bridge Association [*Australia*]
NSWBAC.... New South Wales Buying Advisory Center [*Australia*]
NSWBACE... New South Wales Board of Adult and Community Education [*Australia*]
NSWBBA.... New South Wales Bloodhorse Breeders' Association [*Australia*]
NSWBC...... Black Cultural Centre for Nova Scotia, Westphal [*Library symbol*] [*National Library of Canada*] (BIB)
NSWBCS.... New South Wales Bookmakers' Cooperative Society [*Australia*]
NSWBGA.... New South Wales Bowling Greenkeepers' Association [*Australia*]
NSWBIC..... New South Wales Banana Industry Committee [*Australia*]
NSWBJE.... New South Wales Board of Jewish Education [*Australia*]
NSW Bktcy Cas... New South Wales Reports, Bankruptcy Cases [*A publication*] (DLA)
NSWBL...... New South Wales Basketball League [*Australia*]
NSWBS...... New South Wales Board of Surveyors [*Australia*]
NSWBSA.... New South Wales Board Sailing Association [*Australia*]
NSWC....... Naval Surface Warfare [*or Weapons*] Center [*Dahlgren, VA*]
NSWC....... New South Wales Centre (SAUS)
NSWCA...... New South Wales Canoe Association [*Australia*]
NSWCA...... New South Wales Coal Association [*Australia*]
NSWCA...... New South Wales Council on the Aging [*Australia*]
NSW CAC Report... New South Wales Corporate Affairs Commission. Report [*Australia*] [*A publication*]
NSWCAF.... Naval Surface Weapons Center Acoustic Facility (GRD)
NSW Carpenters J... New South Wales Carpenters Journal (SAUS)
NSWCC...... New South Wales Canine Council [*Australia*]
NSWCC...... New South Wales Council of Churches [*Australia*]
NSWCCFT... New South Wales Council for Children's Films and Television [*Australia*]
NSWCCU.... New South Wales Churches Cricket Union [*Australia*]
NSWC/DL... Naval Surface Weapons Center, Dahlgren Laboratory
NSWC Eq... New South Wales Law Reports, Equity [*A publication*] (DLA)
NSWCF...... New South Wales Cycling Federation [*Australia*]
NSWCFA.... New South Wales Canning Fruitgrowers' Association [*Australia*]
NSWCFVI... New South Wales Chamber of Fruit and Vegetable Industries [*Australia*]
NSWCGA.... New South Wales Cane Growers' Association [*Australia*]
NSWCGA.... New South Wales Cherry Growers' Association [*Australia*]
NSWCGA.... New South Wales Chicken Growers' Association [*Australia*]
NSWCGC.... New South Wales Citrus Growers' Council [*Australia*]
NSWCHS.... New South Wales Cooperative Housing Society [*Australia*]
NSWCM..... New South Wales State Conservatorium of Music (SAUS)
NSWCMACA... New South Wales Chinese Martial Arts and Cultural Association [*Australia*]
NSWCMC... New South Wales Chicken Meat Council [*Australia*]
NSWCMOA... New South Wales Coal Mine Owners' Association [*Australia*]
NSWCOA.... New South Wales Colliery Officials' Association [*Australia*]
NSWCOHO... New South Wales Council of Heritage Organizations [*Australia*]
NSWCOTA... New South Wales Council on the Aging [*Australia*]
NSWCPA.... New South Wales Coal Proprietors' Association [*Australia*]
NSWCPC.... New South Wales Child Protection Council [*Australia*]
NSWCRL.... New South Wales Law Reports, Supreme Court [*A publication*] (DLA)
NSWCSA.... New South Wales Churches Soccer Association [*Australia*]
NSWCSA.... New South Wales Cold Storage Association [*Australia*]
NSWCTA.... New South Wales Council of Tourist Associations [*Australia*]
NSWCUA.... New South Wales Credit Unit Association [*Australia*]
NSWCUA.... New South Wales Cricket Umpires' Association [*Australia*]
NSWCUEA... New South Wales Credit Union Employers' Association [*Australia*]
NSWC/WOL... Naval Surface Weapons Center, White Oak Laboratory
NSWCYMCA... New South Wales Council of the Young Men's Christian Associations [*Australia*]
NSWDAA.... New South Wales Domestic Abattoirs Association [*Australia*]
NSWDAA.... New South Wales Drug and Alcohol Authority [*Australia*]
NSWDAHAC... National Society Women Descendants of the Ancient and Honorable Artillery Company (EA)
NSWDBA.... New South Wales Deer Breeders' Association [*Australia*]
NSW Dep Agric Dir Sci Serv Entomol Branch Insect Pest Leafl... New South Wales. Department of Agriculture. Division of Science Services. Entomology Branch. Insect Pest Leaflet (SAUS)
NSW Dep Mines Tech Rep... New South Wales. Department of Mines. Coalfields Branch. Technical Report (SAUS)
NSW Dept Forestry Bull... New South Wales. Department of Forestry. Bulletin [*Australia*] [*A publication*]
NSWDFA.... New South Wales Dairy Farmers' Association [*Australia*]
NSWDFA.... New South Wales Deer Farmers' Association [*Australia*]
NSWDFB.... New South Wales Dried Fruits Board [*Australia*]
NSWDIC..... New South Wales Dairy Industry Conference [*Australia*]
NSWDPA.... New South Wales Dairy Products Association [*Australia*]
NSWDSC.... New South Wales Dam Safety Committee [*Australia*]
NSWDU..... New South Wales Debating Union [*Australia*]
NSWEEU.... New South Wales Education Exports Unit [*Australia*]
NSWEK...... Eastern King's Memorial Hospital, Wolfville, Nova Scotia [*Library symbol*] [*National Library of Canada*] (NLC)
NSWEPA.... New South Wales Environment Protection Authority (SAUS)
NSWEPC.... New South Wales Egg Producers' Cooperative [*Australia*]
NSWEPOWA... New South Wales Ex-Prisoners of War Association [*Australia*]
NSW Eq Rep... New South Wales Law Reports, Equity [*A publication*] (DLA)
NSWETF.... New South Wales Education and Training Foundation [*Australia*]
NSWFA...... New South Wales Farmers' Association [*Australia*]
NSWFB...... New South Wales Fire Brigades [*Australia*]
NSWFBEU... New South Wales Fire Brigade Employee's Union [*Australia*]
NSWFC...... New South Wales Fitness Council [*Australia*]
NSWFC...... New South Wales Forestry Commission (SAUS)
NSWFCHA... New South Wales Farm and Country Holiday Association [*Australia*]

NSWFF...... New South Wales Folk Federation [*Australia*]
NSWFG...... New South Wales Furniture Guild [*Australia*]
NSWFGA.... New South Wales Flower Growers' Association [*Australia*]
NSWFGHC... New South Wales Free Growers' Horticultural Council [*Australia*]
NSWFHU.... New South Wales Friends of the Hebrew University [*Australia*]
NSWFIA..... New South Wales Farmers' Industrial Association [*Australia*]
NSWFIC..... New South Wales Fishing Industry Council [*Australia*]
NSWFITC ... New South Wales Food Industry Training Council [*Australia*]
NSWFITC... New South Wales Furniture Industry Training Council [*Australia*]
NSWFMC ... New South Wales Flour Millers' Council [*Australia*]
NSWFPA.... New South Wales Forest Products Association [*Australia*]
NSWFPCA... New South Wales Federation of Parents and Citizens' Associations [*Australia*]
NSWFS...... New South Wales Fabian Society [*Australia*]
NSWFTO.... New South Wales Film and Television Office [*Australia*]
NSWG....... Naval Special Warfare Group (NVT)
NSWG....... New South Wales Government (SAUS)
NSWG....... North Sea Working Group [*Advisory Committee on Pollution of the Sea*]
NSWG....... Nuclear Safety Working Group (CINC)
NSWGA..... New South Wales Golf Association [*Australia*]
NSWGB..... New South Wales Grains Board [*Australia*]
NSWGBOTA... New South Wales Greyhound Breeders, Owners and Trainers Association [*Australia*]
NSWGC..... New South Wales Gun Club [*Australia*]
NSWGCB.... New South Wales Guild of Craft Bookbinders [*Australia*]
NSWGCHS... New South Wales Group of Cooperative Housing Societies [*Australia*]
NSWGCSUA... New South Wales Glass and Ceramic Silica Users' Association [*Australia*]
NSW Geol Surv 1:250000 Geol Ser... New South Wales. Geological Survey. 1:250,000 Geological Series (SAUS)
NSW Geol Survey Mineral Resour... New South Wales. Geological Survey. Mineral Resources [*Australia*] [*A publication*]
NSWGFL.... New South Wales Gridiron Football League [*Australia*]
NSWGFM ... New South Wales Guild of Furniture Manufacturers [*Australia*]
NSWGIS..... New South Wales Government Information Service [*Australia*]
NSWGMA... New South Wales Girls' Marching Association [*Australia*]
NSWGMA... New South Wales Glass Merchants' Association [*Australia*]
NSWGR..... New South Wales Government Railways (SAUS)
NSWGTB.... New South Wales Government Tourist Bureau (SAUS)
NSWGTC.... New South Wales Government Travel Center [*Australia*]
NSWH....... Wolfville Historical Museum, Nova Scotia [*Library symbol*] [*National Library of Canada*] (NLC)
NSWHA..... New South Wales Hockey Association [*Australia*]
NSWHC..... New South Wales Health Commission (SAUS)
NSWHCA.... New South Wales Homeless Children's Association [*Australia*]
NSWHEA.... New South Wales Horticultural Exporters' Association [*Australia*]
NSWHGA.... New South Wales Hospital Group Apprentices Scheme [*Australia*]
NSWHJ...... Hants Journal, Windsor, Nova Scotia [*Library symbol*] [*National Library of Canada*] (NLC)
NSWHPAC... New South Wales Hospitals Planning Advisory Center [*Australia*]
NSWHRA.... New South Wales Hot Rod Association [*Australia*]
NSWHS..... New South Wales Humanist Society [*Australia*]
NSWHTA.... New South Wales Hardcourt Tennis Association [*Australia*]
NSWI........ National Safe Workplace Institute (EA)
NSWICCA... New South Wales Indo-China Chinese Association
NSWID...... New South Wales Institute of Dieticians [*Australia*]
NSWIG...... New South Wales Industrial Gazette [*Australia*] [*A publication*]
NSW Inc Acts... New South Wales Incorporated Acts [*A publication*] (DLA)
NSW Ind Arbtn... New South Wales Industrial Arbitration Cases [*A publication*] (DLA)
NSW Ind Arbtn Cas... New South Wales Industrial Arbitration Cases [*A publication*] (DLA)
NSW Indus Arb R... New South Wales Industrial Arbitration Reports [*A publication*] (DLA)
NSWIP...... New South Wales Institute of Physiotherapy [*Australia*]
NSWIP...... New South Wales Institute of Psychotherapy [*Australia*]
NSWJB...... New South Wales Judgements Bulletin [*Australia*] [*A publication*]
NSWJBD..... New South Wales Jewish Board of Deputies [*Australia*]
NSWJCU.... New South Wales Junior Cricket Union [*Australia*]
NSWJHS.... New South Wales Jersey Herd Society [*Australia*]
NSWJT...... Materials Laboratory Library, Nova Scotia Department of Transportation, Windsor Junction, Nova Scotia [*Library symbol*] [*National Library of Canada*] (NLC)
NSWJWM... New South Wales Jewish War Memorial [*Australia*]
NSWKE...... King's-Edgehill School, Windsor, Nova Scotia [*Library symbol*] [*National Library of Canada*] (NLC)
NSWL....... Naval Surface Warfare Laboratory
NSWL....... New South Wales Lotteries [*Australia*]
NSW Land App... New South Wales Land Appeal Court Cases [*A publication*] (DLA)
NSW Land App Cts... New South Wales Land Appeal Courts (DLA)
NSW Law Repts... New South Wales Law Reports [*A publication*]
NSWLC...... New South Wales Leagues Club [*Australia*]
NSWLHPB... New South Wales Ladies Highland Pipe Band [*Australia*]
NSW Local Gov't R... New South Wales Local Government Reports [*A publication*] (DLA)
NSWLR...... New South Wates Letters of Registration (SAUS)
NSWLRC.... New South Wales Law Reform Commission [*Australia*] (ILCA)
NSWLSEA... New South Wales Live Stock Exporters' Association [*Australia*]
NSWLVR.... New South Wales Land Valuation Reports (SAUS)
NSWMA..... National Soft Wheat Millers Association [*Later, MNF*] (EA)
NSWMA..... National Solid Wastes Management Association (EA)
NSWMA..... New South Wales Marching Association [*Australia*]
NSWMA..... New South Wales Midwives' Association [*Australia*]
NSWMB..... New South Wales Medical Board [*Australia*]
NSWMEA ... New South Wales Meat Exporters' Association [*Australia*]
NSWMEQB... New South Wales Migrant Employment and Qualifications Board [*Australia*]
NSWMH..... New South Wales Masonic Hospital [*Australia*]
NSWMIA.... New South Wales Meat Industry Authority [*Australia*]
NSWMSB ... New South Wales Maritime Services Board (SAUS)
NSWNA ..... New South Wales Netball Association [*Australia*]
NSWNA ..... New South Wales Nurses Association (SAUS)
NSWNCA.... New South Wales National Coursing Association [*Australia*]
NSWNGA.... New South Wales Nut Growers' Association [*Australia*]
NSWNPWS... New South Wales National Parks and Wildlife Service [*Australia*]
NSWNRB.... New South Wales Nurses' Registration Board [*Australia*]
NSWO....... Nuclear Surface Warfare Officer [*Navy*] (DOMA)
NSWODA.... New South Wales Oyster Distributors' Association [*Australia*]
NSWOTA.... New South Wales Occupational Therapy Association [*Australia*]
NSWOTA.... New South Wales Operating Theatre Association [*Australia*]
NSWOTA.... New South Wales Organic Traders' Association [*Australia*]
NSWP....... New South Wales Police (SAUS)
NSWP....... Non-Soviet Warsaw Pact (NATG)
NSWPA...... New South Wales Poker Association [*Australia*]
NSWPA...... New South Wales Polo Association [*Australia*]
NSWPACC... New South Wales Police Aero Club Company [*Australia*]
NSWPAG.... New South Wales Prisoners Action Group (SAUS)
NSWPBA.... New South Wales Pipe Band Association [*Australia*]
NSWPC...... New South Wales Parachute Council [*Australia*]
NSWPC...... New South Wales Parents' Council [*Australia*]
NSWPC...... New South Wales Prices Commission [*Australia*]
NSWPEA.... New South Wales Physical Education Association [*Australia*]
NSWPGA.... New South Wales Professional Golfers' Association [*Australia*]
NSWPL...... New South Wales Police Legacy [*Australia*]
NSWPMOA... New South Wales Public Medical Officers' Association [*Australia*]
NSWPOA.... New South Wales Property Owners' Association [*Australia*]
NSWPP...... National Socialist White People's Party [*Formerly, American NAZI Party*] (EA)
NSWPP...... New South Wales Parliamentary Papers [*A publication*]
NSWPR..... Newspaper
NSW Priv Com Papers... New South Wales Privacy Committee. Papers [*Australia*] [*A publication*]
NSWPSPOA... New South Wales Public Service Professional Officers' Association [*Australia*]
NSW Pub Acts... New South Wales Public Acts [*A publication*] (DLA)
NSW Pub Stat... New South Wales Public Statutes [*A publication*] (DLA)
NSWRA..... New South Wales Rifle Association [*Australia*]
NSWRA..... New South Wales Rowing Association [*Australia*]
NSWRAA.... New South Wales Rural Assistance Authority [*Australia*]
NSW Railway & Tramway Mag... New South Wales Railway and Tramway Magazine [*Australia*] [*A publication*]
NSWRCSA... New South Wales Registered Cereal Seedgrowers' Association [*Australia*]
NSWRDCU... New South Wales Rural Divisions Co-ordinating Unit (SAUS)
NSW Regs B&Ords... New South Wales Regulations, By-Laws and Ordinances (SAUS)
NSWRFAC... New South Wales Recreational Fishing Advisory Council [*Australia*]
NSWRFL.... New South Wales Rugby Football League [*Australia*]
NSWRFS.... New South Wales Rod Fishers' Society [*Australia*]
NSWRITC... New South Wales Rural Industry Training Committee [*Australia*]
NSWRLIFA... New South Wales Rugby League Insurance Finance Agency [*Australia*]
NSWRTA.... New South Wales Road Transport Association [*Australia*]
NSWRTEHF... New South Wales Railway and Transport Employees' Hospital Fund [*Australia*]
NSWRTLA... New South Wales Right to Life Association [*Australia*]
NSWRTM ... New South Wales Rail Transport Museum [*Australia*]
NSWRTTC... New South Wales Road Transport Training Council [*Australia*]
NSWS....... National Surface Water Survey (GNE)
NSWS....... Neutron Spin-Wave Scattering (SAUS)
NSWS....... Nondegenerate Series of Weighted Sum (SAUS)
NSWS....... Nuclear Service Water System (NRCH)
NSWSA...... New South Wales Ski Association [*Australia*]
NSWSA...... New South Wales Softball Association [*Australia*]
NSWSA...... New South Wales Swimming Association [*Australia*]
NSWSACW... New South Wales Standing Advisory Committee on Wheat [*Australia*]
NSWSBA.... New South Wales Sheepbreeders' Association [*Australia*]
NSWSCC.... New South Wales Society for Crippled Children [*Australia*]
NSWSCC.... New South Wales State Cancer Committee [*Australia*]
NSWSCR.... New South Wales Supreme Court Reports [*A publication*] (DLA)
NSW S Ct Cas... New South Wales Supreme Court Cases [*A publication*] (DLA)
NSW S Ct R... New South Wales Supreme Court Reports [*A publication*] (DLA)
NSWSDA.... New South Wales Soft Drink Association [*Australia*]
NSWSES.... Naval Ship Weapon Systems Engineering Station [*Port Hueneme, CA*]
NSWSF...... New South Wales Soccer Federation [*Australia*]
NSWSGA.... New South Wales Seed Growers' Association [*Australia*]
NSWSHS.... New South Wales School of Hypnotic Sciences [*Australia*]
NSWSJC.... New South Wales Show Jumping Council [*Australia*]
NSWSK...... New South Wales Shorinjiryu Karate-do Association [*Australia*]
NSWSMBA... New South Wales Stud Merino Breeders' Association [*Australia*]
NSWSO..... New South Wales Superannuation Office [*Australia*]
NSWSRCTG... New South Wales Sales Representatives and Commercial Travellers' Guild [*Australia*]

NSWSS ...... New South Wales Supply Service [*Australia*]
NSWSTC .... New South Wales Science and Technology Council [*Australia*]
NSWSTM ... New South Wales School of Therapeutic Massage [*Australia*]
NSWTA ...... National Senior Women's Tennis Association (EA)
NSWTA ...... New South Wales Transport Association (SAUS)
NSWTAFEC ... New South Wales Technical and Further Education Commission [*Australia*]
NSWTC ...... New South Wales Taxi Council [*Australia*]
NSWTC ...... New South Wales Tourism Commission [*Australia*]
NSWTC ...... New South Wales Travel Center [*Australia*]
NSWTEU .... New South Wales Theatrical Employees' Union [*Australia*]
NSWTF ...... New South Wales Teachers Federation (SAUS)
NSWTG ...... Naval Special Warfare Task Group (CAAL)
NSWTG-CENT ... Naval Special Warfare Task Group, Central Command (POLM)
NSWTITC ... New South Wales Timber Industry Training Council [*Australia*]
NSWTLMB ... New South Wales Tobacco Leaf Marketing Board [*Australia*]
NSWU .... Naval Special Warfare Unit (DOMA)
NSW Univ Sch Civ Eng UNICIV Rep Ser R ... New South Wales University. School of Civil Engineering. UNICIV Report. Series R (SAUS)
NSW Univ UNICIV Rep ... University of New South Wales. School of Civil Engineering UNICIV Report (SAUS)
NSWUT ...... New South Wales University of Technology (SAUS)
NSWVRA ..... New South Wales Video Retailers' Association [*Australia*]
NSWWA ..... New South Wales Wrestling Association [*Australia*]
NSWWA ..... North Shore Women Writers Alliance [*Later, NSWA*] (EA)
NSWWAC ... New South Wales Women's Advisory Council [*Australia*]
NSW Watt Conserv Irrig Comm Surv Thirty NSW River Valleys Re ... New South Wales. Water Conservation and Irrigation Commission. Survey of Thirty New South Wales River Valleys. Report (SAUS)
NSWWH ..... West Hants Historical Society Museum, Windsor, Nova Scotia [*Library symbol*] [*National Library of Canada*] (NLC)
NSWWJA ... New South Wales Women Justices' Association [*Australia*]
NSW Worker's Comp R ... New South Wales Worker's Compensation Reports [*A publication*] (DLA)
NSWWP ..... New South Wales Water Polo [*Australia*] [*An association*]
NSWWS ..... National Severe Weather Warning Service [*Emergency Management*] (EMA)
NSWWSA ... New South Wales Water Ski Association [*Australia*]
NSWWSBA ... New South Wales Wool Selling Brokers' Association [*Australia*]
NSWX .... Neversweat & Washoe Railroad [*Federal Railroad Administration identification code*]
NSX .... Neurosurgical Examination (MELL)
NSX .... Norfolk Southern [*Federal Railroad Administration identification code*]
NSX .... Northstar Energy Corp. [*Toronto Stock Exchange symbol*] [*Canada*]
NSXB .... Neutron Star X-Ray Binary [*Astrophysics*]
NSXZ .... Norfolk Southern Railway [*Intermodal trailer symbol*]
NSY .... Naval Shipyard
NSY .... New Scotland Yard
NSY .... Noisy (ABBR)
NSY .... North Salopian Yeomanry [*British military*] (DMA)
NSY .... North Somerset Yeomanry [*British military*] (DMA)
NSY .... Nursery (DAVI)
NSy .... Onondaga County Public Library, Syracuse, NY [*Library symbol*] [*Library of Congress*] (LCLS)
NSY .... Western Counties Regional Library, Yarmouth, Nova Scotia [*Library symbol*] [*National Library of Canada*] (NLC)
NSyA .... Allied Corp., Solvay Process Division, Syracuse, NY [*Library symbol*] [*Library of Congress*] (LCLS)
NSYA .... National School Yearbook Association [*Later, NSY/NA*]
NSyAF .... United States Air Force, Hancock Air Base Library, Syracuse, NY [*Library symbol*] [*Library of Congress*] (LCLS)
NSyAg .... Agway, Inc., Syracuse, NY [*Library symbol*] [*Library of Congress*] (LCLS)
NSyBL .... Bristol Laboratories, Syracuse, NY [*Library symbol*] [*Library of Congress*] (LCLS)
NSyC .... Carrier Corp., Syracuse, NY [*Library symbol*] [*Library of Congress*] (LCLS)
NSYC .... Courrier de la Nouvelle-Ecosse, Yarmouth, Nova Scotia [*Library symbol*] [*National Library of Canada*] (NLC)
NSyCA .... United States Court of Appeals, Syracuse, NY [*Library symbol*] [*Library of Congress*] (LCLS)
NSYCDA ..... Archives, Diocese of Yarmouth, Catholic Church, Nova Scotia [*Library symbol*] [*National Library of Canada*] (NLC)
NSyCH .... Crouse-Irving Hospital, Syracuse, NY [*Library symbol*] [*Library of Congress*] (LCLS)
NSYD .... Naval Shipyard
NSYDCN .... Diocese of Central New York, Syracuse, NY [*Library symbol*] [*Library of Congress*] (LCLS)
NSyEd .... Educational Opportunity Center, Syracuse, NY [*Library symbol*] [*Library of Congress*] (LCLS)
NSYF .... Natural Science for Youth Foundation (EA)
NSYFG ...... Fundy Group Publications, Yarmouth, Nova Scotia [*Library symbol*] [*National Library of Canada*] (NLC)
NSyGE .... General Electric Co., Syracuse, NY [*Library symbol*] [*Library of Congress*] (LCLS)
NSyGH ...... Community-General Hospital, Syracuse, NY [*Library symbol*] [*Library of Congress*] (LCLS)
NSYHM ...... Research Library, Yarmouth County Historical Society, Yarmouth, Nova Scotia [*Library symbol*] [*National Library of Canada*] (NLC)
NSyL .... LeMoyne College, Syracuse, NY [*Library symbol*] [*Library of Congress*] (LCLS)
NSyLG .... Loretto Geriatric Center, Educational Resource Center, Syracuse, NY [*Library symbol*] [*Library of Congress*] (LCLS)
NSyMR ...... Maria Regina College, Syracuse, NY [*Library symbol*] [*Library of Congress*] (LCLS)
NSyN .... City Normal School, Syracuse, NY [*Library symbol*] [*Library of Congress*] [*Obsolete*] (LCLS)
NSY/NA ..... National School Yearbook/Newspaper Association [*Defunct*] (EA)
NSyo .... Syosset Public Library, Syosset, NY [*Library symbol*] [*Library of Congress*] (LCLS)
NSyOB .... Onondaga-Courtland-Madison Board of Cooperative Education Service, Syracuse, NY [*Library symbol*] [*Library of Congress*] (LCLS)
NSyoBaE .... Baylis Elementary School, Syosset, NY [*Library symbol*] [*Library of Congress*] (LCLS)
NSyoBE ..... Berry Hill Elementary School, Syosset, NY [*Library symbol*] [*Library of Congress*] (LCLS)
NSyOC .... Onondaga Community College, Syracuse, NY [*Library symbol*] [*Library of Congress*] (LCLS)
NSyoF .... Fairchild Space and Defense System, Syosset, NY [*Library symbol*] [*Library of Congress*] (LCLS)
NSyoG .... United States Geological Survey, Water Resources Division, Syosset, NY [*Library symbol*] [*Library of Congress*] (LCLS)
NSyoH .... Syosset Hospital, Syosset, NY [*Library symbol*] [*Library of Congress*] (LCLS)
NSyOHi ...... Onondaga Historical Association, Syracuse, NY [*Library symbol*] [*Library of Congress*] (LCLS)
NSyOL .... Onondaga Library System, Syracuse, NY [*Library symbol*] [*Library of Congress*] (LCLS)
NSyoOL ..... Our Lady of Mercy Academy, Syosset, NY [*Library symbol*] [*Library of Congress*] (LCLS)
NSyoP .... PRD Electronics, Inc., Information Center Library, Syosset, NY [*Library symbol*] [*Library of Congress*] (LCLS)
NSyoRE ..... Robbins Elementary School, Syosset, NY [*Library symbol*] [*Library of Congress*] (LCLS)
NSyoSGE .... South Grove Elementary School, Syosset, NY [*Library symbol*] [*Library of Congress*] (LCLS)
NSyoSH ..... Syosset Senior High School, Syosset, NY [*Library symbol*] [*Library of Congress*] (LCLS)
NSyoSRE .... Split Rock Elementary School, Syosset, NY [*Library symbol*] [*Library of Congress*] (LCLS)
NSyoSwJ .... South Woods Junior High School, Syosset, NY [*Library symbol*] [*Library of Congress*] (LCLS)
NSyoTJ ...... Harry B. Thompson Junior High School, Syosset, NY [*Library symbol*] [*Library of Congress*] (LCLS)
NSyoVE ..... Village Elementary School, Syosset, NY [*Library symbol*] [*Library of Congress*] (LCLS)
NSyoWE ..... Willits Elementary School, Syosset, NY [*Library symbol*] [*Library of Congress*] (LCLS)
NSyoWhE ... Whitman Elementary School, Syosset, NY [*Library symbol*] [*Library of Congress*] (LCLS)
NSYR .... Medical Library, Yarmouth Regional Hospital, Nova Scotia [*Library symbol*] [*National Library of Canada*] (BIB)
NSyR .... Syracuse Research Corp., Syracuse, NY [*Library symbol*] [*Library of Congress*] (LCLS)
NSYS .... Nortech Systems [*NASDAQ symbol*] (TTSB)
NSYS .... Nortech Systems, Inc. [*NASDAQ symbol*] (SAG)
NSySC .... New York State Supreme Court Law Library, Syracuse, NY [*Library symbol*] [*Library of Congress*] (LCLS)
NSySJ .... Saint Joseph's Hospital, School of Nursing and Medical Library, Syracuse, NY [*Library symbol*] [*Library of Congress*] (LCLS)
NSYSP ...... National Summer Youth Sports Program
NSySU-F .... State University of New York, College of Environmental Sciences and Forestry at Syracuse University, Syracuse, NY [*Library symbol*] [*Library of Congress*] (LCLS)
NSySU-M ... State University of New York, Upstate Medical Center, Syracuse, NY [*Library symbol*] [*Library of Congress*] (LCLS)
NSyT .... Technology Club of Syracuse, Syracuse, NY [*Library symbol*] [*Library of Congress*] (LCLS)
NSyU .... Syracuse University, Syracuse, NY [*Library symbol*] [*Library of Congress*] (LCLS)
NSyU-CE .... Syracuse University, Library of Continuing Education at Syracuse, Syracuse, NY [*Library symbol*] [*Library of Congress*] (LCLS)
NSyU-G ..... Syracuse University, Educational Resources Center of the All-University Gerontology Center, Syracuse, NY [*Library symbol*] [*Library of Congress*] (LCLS)
NSyVA .... United States Veterans Administration Hospital, Syracuse, NY [*Library symbol*] [*Library of Congress*] (LCLS)
NSZ .... Norfolk Southern Railway [*Intermodal trailer symbol*]
NSZP .... Nemzeti Szabadelvu Part [*National Liberal Party*] [*Hungary*] [*Political party*] (PPE)
NT .... Iraq-Saudi Arabia Neutral Zone [*ANSI two-letter standard code*] (CNC)
NT .... Lake State Airways [*ICAO designator*] (AD)
N-T .... Nal-Tel [*Race of maize*]
nT .... Nanotesla
NT .... Narrower Term [*Indexing*]
NT .... Naso-Tracheal [*Medicine*]
NT .... National Taranesc [*National Peasant Party*] [*Romania*] [*Political party*] (PPE)
NT .... National Team
NT .... National Theatre [*Great Britain*]
NT .... National Trust (WDAA)
NT .... National Trust for Historic Preservation
NT .... Natty (ABBR)
NT .... Naturalization Test
NT .... Naval Training
NT .... Navy Type (MSA)
NT .... Neap Tide
NT .... Near Term
NT .... Neat [*Plain*] [*Bookbinding*] (ROG)
NT .... Neonatal Tetanus
NT .... Neotetrazolium

NT .... Nephrostomy Tube [*Nephrology*] (DAVI)
NT .... Nerve Treatment (SAUS)
NT .... Nested-Task [*Computer science*] (BYTE)
NT .... Net (WDAA)
NT .... Netilmicin-Ticarcillin [*Antibiotic combination*]
NT .... Nett [*Net*] [*British*] (ROG)
NT .... Net Tax [*IRS*]
N/t .... Net Terms [*Business term*] (DS)
NT .... Net Tons [*Shipping*]
NT .... Network Terminal (MCD)
NT .... Network Termination [*Telecommunications*]
NT .... Network Terminator (SAUS)
NT .... Neural Tube [*Anatomy*]
NT .... Neurologically Typical [*Psychology*]
NT .... Neurotensin [*Biochemistry*]
NT .... Neurotoxin [*Biochemistry*]
NT .... Neurotransmitter (SAUS)
NT .... Neurotrophin [*Neurobiology*]
NT .... Neuter (WGA)
NT .... Neutralization Test [*Chemistry*]
NT .... Neutralizing (MAE)
NT .... Neutral Zone [*Internet country code*]
NT .... Neutron Transmitter [*Nuclear energy*] (NRCH)
NT .... Nevada Territory [*Prior to statehood*]
NT .... Newfoundland Time (SAUS)
NT .... News/Talk [*Radio programming format*] (WDMC)
NT .... New Taiwan
NT .... New Technology [*Microsoft operating system*] [*Computer science*] (PCM)
N/T .... New Terms [*Business term*]
NT .... New Territories [*Hong Kong*]
NT .... New Testament (WDAA)
NT .... New Thailand Dollar [*Monetary unit*]
nt .... Newton (NASA)
NT .... Newton
NT .... Newtonian Telescope (SAUS)
NT .... New Towns [*British*]
NT .... New Translation (ODA)
NT .... New Trouble (SAUS)
NT .... New United Motor Manufacturing, Inc. [*Society of Automotive Engineers auto manufacturer code for service information interchange*]
Nt .... Nicotiana tabacum [*Tobacco*]
NT .... Night (ROG)
NT .... Night Telegram
NT .... Night Tracer (SAUS)
NT .... Night Trunk [*Business term*] (DCTA)
nt .... Nit [*Unit of luminance*]
NT .... Niton (ABBR)
Nt .... Nitron (SAUS)
NT .... Node Tracker [*Frye Computer Systems*] [*Telecommunications*] (PCM)
NT .... Node Type (SAUS)
NT .... Noise Temperature (ACAE)
NT .... Noise Thermometer (SAUS)
NT .... Nome Time (SAUS)
N/T .... None in Town [*Bookselling*]
N/T .... Nonmeasured Time
NT .... Non-T Cell [*Cytology*]
NT .... Nontender (DAVI)
NT .... Nontight (AAG)
NT .... Nontronite (SAUS)
NT .... Nontryptophan [*Protein-bound fluorescence*]
NT .... Nontumorous [*Medicine*] (DB)
NT .... Nontypeable (MAE)
NT .... Nordiska Transportarbetarefederationen [*Nordic Transportworkers' Federation - NTF*] (EAIO)
NT .... Nordisk Traebeskyttelsesrad [*Nordic Wood Preservation Council - NWPC*] (EAIO)
NT .... Norfolk Terminal [*Federal Railroad Administration identification code*]
NT .... Normalized and Tempered (MCD)
NT .... Normal Temperature (ADA)
NT .... Normal Threat (SAUS)
NT .... Normal Tour
NT .... Nortel Networks [*NYSE symbol*] (SG)
NT .... Nortel Networks Corp. [*NYSE symbol*]
NT .... North [*Telegraphy*] (PCTE)
NT .... Northern Air Taxis Ltd. (SAUS)
NT .... Northern Tablelands (SAUS)
NT .... Northern Telecom (SAUS)
NT .... Northern Territory (ACAE)
NT .... Northern Territory Herbarium International Acronym (SAUS)
NT .... Northwest Territories [*Postal code*] [*Canada*]
NT .... Nortriptyline [*Antidepressant drug*]
NT .... Nose Tackle (SAUS)
NT .... Note [*Online database field identifier*]
N/T .... No Terms [*Shipping*]
NT .... No Test
NT .... No Tested (SAUS)
N/T .... No Text [*E-mail lingo to state that the message contains no text*] (NETL)
NT .... No Tillage [*Agriculture*]
NT .... No Tone (SAUS)
NT .... No Tool (SAA)
NT .... No Trace [*Counterintelligence*]
NT .... No Transmission [*Telecommunications*]
NT .... No Trump [*in game of bridge*]
NT .... Not Technical (SAUS)
NT .... Not Tender (DAVI)
NT .... Not Tested
NT .... Not Titled [*Accounting*]
NT .... Not Typical
NT .... Novum Testamentum [*New Testament*] [*of the Bible*]
NT .... Nuclear Transfer
NT .... Nucleotidase [*An enzyme*] (DAVI)
nt .... Nucleotide [*Genetics*] (DOG)
NT .... Nuisance Tax (MHDW)
NT .... Numbering Transmitter
NT .... Number of Teams (SAUS)
NT .... Number of Teeth (SAUS)
NT .... Number of Tracks (SAUS)
NT .... Number Theory (SAUS)
NT .... Numerical Table (SAUS)
NT .... Nunavut [*Canada*] (FOTI)
NT .... Nurse Technician
NT .... Thermal Necrosis [*Roentgenology*]
NT .... Troy Public Library, Troy, NY [*Library symbol*] [*Library of Congress*] (LCLS)
NT-1 .... Network Terminator 1 [*Computer science*] (NETL)
NT-1 .... Network Terminator Type 1 (PCM)
NT-3 .... Neurotrophin-3 (SAUS)
NTA .... Anti-Imperialist Territorial Nuclei [*Government term*] (GA)
NTA .... Fujisawa Pharmaceutical Co. [*Japan*] [*Research code symbol*]
NTA .... Naphthoyltrifluoroacetone [*Organic chemistry*]
NTA .... Narcotics Treatment Administration [*Washington, DC*]
NTA .... National Tabletop Association (EA)
NTA .... National Tattoo Association (EA)
NTA .... National Tax Association [*Later, NTA-TIA*] (EA)
NTA .... National Tax Association-Tax Institute of America (NTPA)
NTA .... National Taxidermists Association [*Defunct*] (EA)
NTA .... National Taxpayers Alliance (EA)
NTA .... National Teachers Association (AEE)
NTA .... National Technical Association (EA)
NTA .... National Telecommunications Agency
NTA .... National Telefilm Associates, Inc. (NTCM)
NTA .... National Tennis Academy [*Commercial firm*] (EA)
NTA .... National Tennis Association [*Later, IRJA*] (EA)
NTA .... National Textile Association (EARSL)
NTA .... National Threshers Association (EA)
NTA .... National Tour Association (EA)
NTA .... National Tourism Administration [*China*] (EY)
NTA .... National Tourist Association (NADA)
NTA .... National Translator Association (EA)
NTA .... National Trappers Association (EA)
NTA .... National Triton Association (EA)
NTA .... National Trolleybus Association [*British*]
NTA .... National Troubleshooting Association (NTPA)
NTA .... National Tuberculosis Association [*Later, American Lung Association*] (EA)
NTA .... National Tutoring Association (NTPA)
NTA .... National Type Approval (PDAA)
NTA .... Natural Thymocytotoxic Autoantibody (DB)
NTA .... Naval Technical Assistants
NTA .... Navy Technical Assessment (MCD)
NTA .... Navy Technician Authorization (NG)
NTA .... Near-Terminal Area [*Airports*]
NTA .... Negotiated Testing Agreement (EEVL)
NTA .... Neher Tetrode Amplifier
NTA .... Net Tangible Assets [*Business term*] (ADA)
NTA .... Net Technical Assessment (MCD)
NTA .... Neutron Monitoring Film [*Medicine*] [*Kodak*] (EDAA)
NTA .... Nevada Test Site Array [*Nevada*] [*Seismograph station code, US Geological Survey*] (SEIS)
NTA .... New Territories Administration (SAUS)
NTA .... New Testament Abstracts [*A publication*]
NTA .... New Towns Act [*Town planning*] [*British*]
NTA .... New Transatlantic Agenda
NTA .... Nielsen Television Area (WDAA)
NTA .... Nitrilotriacetate (SAUS)
nta .... nitrilotriacetic (SAUS)
NTA .... Nitrilotriacetic Acid [*Organic chemistry*]
NTA .... Northern Textile Association (EA)
NTA .... Northern Thunderbird Air Ltd. [*Canada*] [*ICAO designator*] (FAAC)
NTA .... Northern Trade Association (SAUS)
NTA .... Northwest Territory Alliance (EA)
NTA .... Norwegian Telecommunications Administration [*or Agency*] [*Oslo*]
NTA .... Not in Target Area (SAUS)
NTA .... Nuclear Target Analysis (SAUS)
NTA .... Nuclear Test Aircraft
NTA .... Nurse Training Act
NTa .... Warner Library, Tarrytown, NY [*Library symbol*] [*Library of Congress*] (LCLS)
NTAA .... National Travelers Aid Association (EA)
NTAA .... Tahiti/FAAA [*French Polynesia*] [*ICAO location identifier*] (ICLI)
NTAB .... Nephrotoxic Antibody [*Medicine*] (EDAA)
NTAB .... Northern Territory Architects' Board [*Australia*]
NTAB .... Notable (ABBR)
NTAB .... Nuclear Technical Advisory Board [*American National Standards Institute*]

NTA Bul ..... Newfoundland Teachers Association. Bulletin (SAUS)
NTABY....... Notably (ABBR)
NTAC .... National Technical Assistance Center on Family Violence [*Defunct*] (EA)
NTAC .... National Threat Assessment Center [*United States Secret Service*] (RCD)
NTAC .... Naval Training Aids Center (DNAB)
NTAC .... New Technology Access Centre (AIE)
NTACF....... Northern Territory Anti-Cancer Foundation
NTACS....... National Truck Activity & Commodity Survey (SAUS)
NTACS....... Nationwide Truck Activity Survey [*BTS*] [*FHWA*] (TAG)
NTAF........ Naval Training Aids Facility (DNAB)
NTAG .... Network Technical Architecture Group [*Library of Congress*]
NTaGF .... General Foods Technical Center Library, Tarrytown, NY [*Library symbol*] [*Library of Congress*] (LCLS)
NTaHi........ Historical Society of the Tarrytowns, Tarrytown, NY [*Library symbol*] [*Library of Congress*] (LCLS)
NTAI .... Nam Tai Electronics, Inc. [*NASDAQ symbol*] (NQ)
NTaI.......... Washington Irving Home, Sleepy Hollow Restorations, Tarrytown, NY [*Library symbol*] [*Library of Congress*] [*Obsolete*] (LCLS)
NTAIDSC... Northern Territory AIDS [*Acquired Immune Deficiency Syndrome*] Council [*Australia*]
NTAIF........ Nam Tai Electronics [*NASDAQ symbol*] (TTSB)
NTAJ......... Newfoundland Teachers Association. Journal (SAUS)
NTaM........ Marymount College, Tarrytown, NY [*Library symbol*] [*Library of Congress*] (LCLS)
NTAM........ New Testament Archaeology Monographs [*A publication*] (BJA)
NTAMS...... Northern Territory Aerial Medical Service (SAUS)
NTAN .... Nitrilotriacetonitrile [*Organic chemistry*]
NT & SA .... National Trust & Savings Association (MHDB)
NTAOCH.... Notice to Air Operator Certificate Holders (SAUS)
NTAP .... National Targeting and Attack Policy (CINC)
NTAP .... National Track Analysis Program [*Aviation*] (FAAC)
NTAP .... Network Appliance [*NASDAQ symbol*] (TTSB)
NTAP .... Network Appliance Corp. [*NASDAQ symbol*] (SAG)
NTAP .... Notices to Airmen Publication [*A publication*] (FAAC)
NTap......... Tappan Free Library, Tappan, NY [*Library symbol*] [*Library of Congress*] (LCLS)
NTA Proceedings... National Tax Association. Proceedings [*A publication*] (DLA)
NTAR .... NetAir International Corp. [*NASDAQ symbol*] (COMM)
NTAR .... Nonviolent Techniques Against Rape [*An association*] (EA)
NTAR .... Rurutu [*French Polynesia*] [*ICAO location identifier*] (ICLI)
NTARH ...... National Teen Age Republican Headquarters (EA)
NTARS....... National Transportation Analysis Regions [*FHWA*] (TAG)
NTARY....... Notary (ABBR)
NTAS .... New Technology Advanced Server (SAUS)
NTAs......... Nielsen Television Areas (SAUS)
NTAS .... Northern Territory Archives Service [*Australia*]
NTAS .... Norwegian Tracking Adjunct System (ACAE)
NTAS .... NT Advamced Server (SAUS)
NTaS......... Sleepy Hollow Restorations, Tarrytown, NY [*Library symbol*] [*Library of Congress*] (LCLS)
NTAS .... Windows NT Advanced Server (SAUS)
NTAT........ Near-Term ACME Technology (SAUS)
NTAT........ Tubuai/Mataura [*French Polynesia*] [*ICAO location identifier*] (ICLI)
NTATB ...... Northwestern Truck Association and Tariff Bureau (SAUS)
NTATC ...... National Transportation Apprenticeship and Training Conference [*Bureau of Apprenticeship and Training*] [*Department of Labor*]
NTA-TIA..... National Tax Association - Tax Institute of America (EA)
NTATN....... Notation (ABBR)
NTATNL .... Notational (ABBR)
NTaUC....... Union Carbide Corp., Tarrytown Technical Center, Tarrytown, NY [*Library symbol*] [*Library of Congress*] (LCLS)
NtAust....... National Australia Bank [*Associated Press*] (SAG)
NTAVL ...... Not Available (NOAA)
NTB.......... National Target Base (MCD)
NTB.......... National Test Bed [*Military*] (SDI)
N-t-B......... Nitroso-tert-Butane (SAUS)
NTB.......... Non-selective Top-to-Bottom (SAUS)
NTB.......... Nontariff Barrier [*Kennedy Round*]
NTB.......... Nontumor-Bearing
NTB.......... Norsk Telegrambyra [*Norwegian News Agency*]
NTB.......... Northumbria Tourist Board [*British*] (DCTA)
NTB.......... Notable (ABBR)
NTB.......... No Talent Bum [*Slang*]
NTB.......... Not to Be (SAUS)
NTB.......... Nuclear Test Ban
NTBA .... Name to be Advised [*Travel industry*] (TVEL)
NTBA .... National Tour Brokers Association (EA)
NTBA .... National Tuberculosis Association [*Medicine*] (EDAA)
NTBA .... Network Terminator Basicrate Access (SAUS)
NTBA .... Northern Territory Bowls Association [*Australia*]
NTBB .... National Temporal Bone Banks Program of the DRF [*Deafness Research Foundation*] (EA)
N/TBC .... Nontuberculous [*Medicine*] (DAVI)
NTBIC .... National Test Bed Integration Contract (ACAE)
NTBIC .... Northern Territory Buffalo Industry Council [*Australia*]
NTBJPO ..... National Test Bed Joint Program Office (ACAE)
NTBK .... Net.Bank [*NASDAQ symbol*] (SG)
NTBK .... Notebook (ABBR)
Ntbk .... Notebook (DIAR)
NTBL .... Nuffield Talking Book Library (SAUS)
NTBM........ NU-Tech Bio-Med [*NASDAQ symbol*] (TTSB)
NTBM........ Nu-Tech Bio Med, Inc. [*NASDAQ symbol*] (SAG)
NTBP .... Normal Temperature and Blood Pressure (SAUS)
NTBPSC..... Nepal, Tibet, and Bhutan Philatelic Study Circle (EA)
NTBR .... National Temporal Bone Registry (EA)
NTBR .... Not to Be Resuscitated
NTBRB ...... Northern Territory Building Referees' Board [*Australia*]
NTBS .... Northern Territory Board of Studies [*Australia*]
NTBSIM ..... National Test Bed Simulation (ACAE)
NTBT .... Nuclear Test Ban Treaty (CCCA)
NT BUR STNDS... National Bureau of Standards [*Department of Commerce*] (WDAA)
NTBY .... Notably (ABBR)
NTC.......... Gibson Aviation [*ICAO designator*] (FAAC)
NTC.......... National Center for Transportation Management, Research, and Development [*Morgan State University*] (RCD)
NTC.......... National Tasking Center (MCD)
NTC.......... National Teachers Corps
NTC.......... National Team Championship [*Swimming*] [*British*] (ROG)
NTC.......... National Teen Challenge (EA)
NTC.......... National Telecommunications Conference [*IEEE*]
NTC.......... National Telemedia Council (EA)
NTC.......... National Teleregistration Center [*Emergency Management*] (EMA)
NTC.......... National Television Center [*Telecommunications*] (TEL)
NTC.......... National Territorial Command (MCD)
NTC.......... National Test Center (NATG)
NTC.......... National Textile Center (RCD)
NTC.......... National Thanksgiving Commission (EA)
NTC.......... National Theatre Conference (EA)
NTC.......... National Thrift Committee [*Defunct*] (EA)
NTC.......... National Timesharing Council (EA)
NTC.......... National Traditionalist Caucus (EA)
NTC.......... National Trails Council (EA)
NTC.......... National Training Center [*Military*] (INF)
NTC.......... National Training Center [*Red Cross*] [*Charlottesville, VA*]
NTC.......... National Transition Council (Algeria) [*Political party*] (PSAP)
NTC.......... National Translations Center [*John Crerar Library*] [*Information service or system*]
NTC.......... National Transportation Center [*Large city situated at a key junction of rail, air, and highway transportation*] [*Postal Service*]
NTC.......... National Travel Club [*Commercial firm*] (EA)
NTC.......... National Treatment Consortium for Alcohol and Other Drugs (EA)
NTC.......... National Troopers Coalition (EA)
NTC.......... National Tuberculosis Center (SAUS)
NTC.......... Naturally Occurring Top Component [*Virology*]
NTC.......... Nautical Training Corps [*British military*] (DMA)
NTC.......... Naval Training Center
NTC.......... Naval Training Command
NTC.......... Navy Test Controller (DNAB)
NTC.......... Negative Temperature Coefficient
NTC.......... Negative Thermal Coefficient (IAA)
NTC.......... Neotetrazolium Chloride [*A dye*]
NTC.......... Net Treating Cost [*Fuels and lubricants*]
NTC.......... Network Transmission Committee [*Video Transmission Engineering Committee*] (NTCM)
NTC.......... Neurotrauma Center [*Medicine*] (EDAA)
NTC.......... Nigerian Tobacco Co. (SAUS)
NTC.......... Nissan Technical Center [*Automobile manufacturing*]
NTC.......... Nonthermal Continuum (SAUS)
NTC.......... Noranda Technology Center (SAUS)
NTC.......... Nordic Temperance Council (EA)
NTC.......... Nordic Theater Committee [*Later, NTDC*] (EAIO)
NTC.......... Normal Tour of Duty Completed
NTC.......... Northern Telecommunications (SAUS)
NTC.......... Northern Telecommunication Station (SAUS)
NTC.......... Northern Transit [*Federal Railroad Administration identification code*]
ntc .... Northwest Territories [*MARC country of publication code*] [*Library of Congress*] (LCCP)
NTC.......... Norwegian Trade Council (EA)
NTC.......... Norwich Terrier Club [*Later, NNTC*] (EA)
NTC.......... Notice
NTC.......... No Traffic Reported [*Air Traffic Control*] (FAAC)
NTC.......... Nucleon Transport Code
NTC.......... Nu-Trans Cooperative (EA)
NTC.......... Nuveen Connecticut Premium Income Municipal Fund [*NYSE symbol*] (SPSG)
NTC.......... Nuveen CT Prem Inc. Muni [*NYSE symbol*] (TTSB)
NTC.......... Nylon Tire Cord [*Automotive engineering*]
NTCA .... National Telephone Cooperative Association (EA)
NTCA .... National Tile Contractors Association (EA)
NTCA .... National Town Class Association (EA)
NTCA .... National Tribal Chairman's Association [*Defunct*] (EA)
NTCA .... N-Nitrosothioazolidine Carboxylic Acid [*Organic chemistry*]
NTCA .... Non-Tutorial Computer Application (SAUS)
NTCA .... Northern Territory Cattlemens Association (SAUS)
NTCA .... Northern Territory Cricket Association [*Australia*]
NTCA .... North Texas Corvair Association (EARSL)
NtCapit...... National Capital Management Corp. [*Associated Press*] (SAG)
NTCAVAL... Notice of Availability
NTC/AW..... National Training Center / Air Warrior System (DWSG)
NTCB .... Network Trusted Computing Base [*Communications term*] (DCT)
NTCB .... (Nitro)thiocyanatobenzoic Acid [*Organic chemistry*]
NTCB .... Northern Territory Convention Bureau [*Australia*]
NTCB .... Noticeable (ABBR)
NTCBY....... Noticeably (ABBR)
NTCC .... National Type Culture Collection (MELL)
NTCC .... Naval Tactical Communications Center (MCD)

NTCC .... Naval Telecommunications Center (DOMA)
NTCC .... Neutron Transport Computer Code
NTCC .... Nimbus Technical Control Center
NTCC .... Northern Territory Conservation Commission [*Australia*]
NTCCDET... Naval Telecommunications Center Detachment (DNAB)
NTCCL....... Northern Territory Council for Civil Liberties (SAUS)
NTCCS....... Naval Tactical Command and Control System (PDAA)
NTCD .... Newark Transportation Control Depot (SAUS)
NTCD .... Nitro(thiocyano)benzoic Acid [*Organic chemistry*]
NTCD .... Noticed (ABBR)
NTCDC ...... Northern Territory Counter Disaster Council [*Australia*]
NTCF .... National Telemarketing Fulfillment Center
NTCF .... National Toxic Campaign Fund [*An association*]
NTCFA....... Northern Territory Commercial Fishermen's Association [*Australia*]
NTCFA....... Northern Territory Crab Fishermen's Association [*Australia*]
NTCG .... Noticing (ABBR)
NTCGA ...... Northern Territory Community Government Association [*Australia*]
Ntch .... Notch (SAUS)
NTCHA ...... National Taxi and Car Hire Association [*British*] (BI)
NTCHBA..... National Trust Closely Held Business Association (EA)
NTCI .... National Training Center - Phase I (MCD)
NTCKR ...... Nutcracker (ABBR)
NTCL .... Nautical
NTCLP....... Northern Territory Country Liberal Party [*Australia*] [*Political party*]
NTCMA...... National Traditional Country Music Association [*Later, NTMA*] (EA)
NtCmcBc.... National Commerce Bancorp [*Associated Press*] (SAG)
NTCMP...... Northern Territory Chamber of Mines and Petroleum [*Australia*]
NtCnv........ National Convenience Stores, Inc. [*Associated Press*] (SAG)
NTCOSS..... Northern Territory Council of Social Service [*Australia*]
NTCOTA..... Northern Territory Council on the Aging [*Australia*]
NTCP .... Near-Term Construction Permit [*Nuclear energy*] (NRCH)
NTCP .... Nightcap (ABBR)
NTCP .... Non-Traditional Casting Project (EA)
NTCP .... Nu-Trans Companies [*Common carrier symbol*]
NtCptr .... National Computer Systems, Inc. [*Associated Press*] (SAG)
NTCS .... Nonverbal Test of Cognitive Skills [*Intelligence test*]
NTCS-A...... Navy Tactical Command System Afloat (DOMA)
NTCS-A (DM)... Navy Tactical Command System Afloat-Database Management (POLM)
NTCS-A (SO)... Navy Tactical Command System Afloat-Staff Officer Course (POLM)
NTCSD ...... Naval Training Center, San Diego
NTCSOC..... Naval Telecommunications Command Satellite Operations Center (MCD)
NTCSS....... Navy Tactical Command and Support System (SAUS)
NTCT .... National Tennis Center Trust [*Australia*]
NTCT .... Naval Tactics & Command Trainer (SAUS)
NTCTA....... Northern Territory Clay Target Association [*Australia*]
NTCU .... Need to See You [*Online dialog*]
NTCU .... Northern Transportation [*Intermodal shipping container symbol*] (TVRC)
NTCZ .... Nello Teer [*Federal Railroad Administration identification code*]
NTD.......... Das Neue Testament Deutsch. Neues Goettinger Bibelwerk [*A publication*] (BJA)
NTD.......... NASA Test Director (MCD)
NTD.......... National Tap Dance Co. of Canada
NTD.......... National Technology Databank [*Singapore*] (DDC)
NTD.......... National Theatre of the Deaf (EA)
NTD.......... National Transit Database [*FTA*] (TAG)
NTD.......... Naval Training Department [*British military*] (DMA)
NTD.......... Negative to Date [*Medicine*] (MELL)
NTD.......... Neural Tube (Closure) Defect [*Medicine*]
NTD.......... Neutron Transmutation Doped [*Silicon for semiconductor use*]
NTD.......... Neutron Transmutation Doping (AAEL)
NTD.......... New Tyee Resources [*Vancouver Stock Exchange symbol*]
NTD.......... Nissan Torque Demand [*Automotive engineering*]
NTD.......... Nitroblue Tetrazolium Dye [*Test*] [*Laboratory science*] (DAVI)
NTD.......... Noise Tone Difference (DMAA)
NTD.......... Nontight Door
NTD.......... Noted (SAUS)
NTD.......... Not Top Drawer (ODA)
NTD.......... N-Tone International Ltd. [*Vancouver Stock Exchange symbol*]
NTD.......... Nuclear Test Directorate [*Air Force*]
NTD.......... Nuclear Training Division (SAUS)
NTD.......... Port Hueneme, CA [*Location identifier*] [*FAA*] (FAAL)
NTDA .... National Trade Development Association (WDAA)
NTDA .... National Trailer Dealers Association (EA)
NTDA .... National Tribal Development Association (EA)
NTDA .... National Tyre Distributors Association [*British*] (DBA)
NTDA .... Navy Tactical Doctrine Activity (NVT)
NTDAAM .... National Trust for the Development of African American Men (EA)
NTDAB ...... Northern Territory Drug and Alcohol Board [*Australia*]
NTDB .... National Trade Data Bank (EGAO)
NTDB .... National Trade Database (ACII)
NTDC .... NanoTechnology Development Corp.
NTDC .... Naval Training Devices Center [*Port Washington, LI*]
NTDC .... Nordic Theatre and Dance Committee (EAIO)
NTDDPA..... Navy Tactical Doctrine Development and Production Activity
NTDE .... North Dakota Tracer Experiment [*Marine science*] (OSRA)
NtDentex.... National Dentex Corp. [*Associated Press*] (SAG)
NTDG .... National Teaching Development Grant [*Australia*]
NTDI .... NATO Target Data Inventory (MCD)
NTDO .... Navy Technical Data Office [*of the Office of Naval Material*]
NTDP .... New Technology Demonstration Program (SAUS)
NTDPMA .... National Tool, Die, and Precision Machining Association [*Later, NTMA*] (EA)
NTDRA ...... National Tire Dealers and Retreaders Association (EA)
NTDRP ...... Northern Territory Drought Releif Policy (SAUS)
NTDS .... Naval Tactical Display System (ACAE)
NTDS .... Naval Technical Data System (IAA)
NTDS .... Navy Tactical Data System
NTDS .... Northern Telecom Data Systems (NITA)
NTDSC ...... Nondestructive Testing Data Support Center [*DoD*] (MCD)
NTDS/LBTS... Naval Tactical Data System / Land-Based Test Site (DNAB)
NTDT .... Non-Time Dependent Target (ACAE)
NTE .... Nantes [*France*] [*Airport symbol*] (OAG)
NTE .... National Teacher Examination
NTE .... National Transportation Exchange
NTE .... National Treasury Employees Union
NTE .... Navy Technical Evaluation (NG)
NTE .... Navy Teletypewriter Exchange [*Later, NTX*]
NTE .... Negative Thermal Expansion [*Physics*]
NTE .... Network Terminating Equipment [*Telecommunications*] (IAA)
NTE .... Neuropathy Target Esterase [*Medicine*] (DMAA)
NTE .... Neurotoxic Esterase [*Medicine*] (DMAA)
NTE .... Neutral Thermal Environment [*Medicine*] (MELL)
NTE .... Neutron Transient Effect
NTE .... Non-orthogonal Timing Error (SAUS)
NTE .... Nontactical Equipment
NTE .... Nontest Ear [*Medicine*] (EDAA)
NTE .... Non-Traditional Exports (SAUS)
NTE .... Northern Eagle Mines [*Vancouver Stock Exchange symbol*]
NTE .... Not to Exceed [*Aviation*]
NTE .... Nursing the Environment
NTEA .... National Tax Equality Association (EA)
NTEA .... National Telecommunications Electronics Administration
NTEA .... National Time Equipment Association (EA)
NTEA .... National Truck Equipment Association (EA)
NTeam....... National TechTeam, Inc. [*Associated Press*] (SAG)
NTEC .... National Telecommunications Education Committee [*North American Telecommunications Association*] [*Washington, DC*] [*Telecommunications service*] (TSSD)
NTEC .... National Traction Engine Club [*British*] (DBA)
NTEC .... Naval Training Equipment Center
NTEC .... Neose Technologies [*NASDAQ symbol*] (TTSB)
N-Tec........ Nuclear Technology (SAUS)
NTech........ National Technical Systems, Inc. [*Associated Press*] (SAG)
NTECPE ..... Naval Training Equipment Center, Project Engineer
NTEF......... National Tennis Educational Foundation [*Later, NTFHF*] (EA)
NTEFS .... NT Encrypted File System [*Information technology*]
NTEG .... Integ Inc. [*NASDAQ symbol*] (SAG)
NTEI .... New Technical Education Initiative (AIE)
NTE/IOTE... Navy Technical Evaluation/Initial Operational Test and Evaluation (MCD)
NTEL......... No-Toxic-Effect Level [*Toxicology*] (LDT)
NTelpd....... Northwest Teleproductions, Inc. [*Associated Press*] (SAG)
NTEO .... Northern Territory Electoral Office [*Australia*]
NTEP .... National Type Evaluation Program [*Environmental Protection Agency*]
NTEP .... New Technology Employment Program (SAUS)
NTEP .... Norwegian Terrestrial Ecosystem Profile (SAUS)
NTEP .... Not to Exceed Price (SAUS)
NTEPQ....... Not to Exceed Price Quoted (SAUS)
NTER .... Normalized Transmission Energy Requirement
N Terr .... Northern Territory
N Terr Austl Ord... Northern Territorial Ordinances [*Australia*] [*A publication*] (DLA)
NTES .... National Train Enquiry System [*Indian Railway*] (TIR)
NTES .... Northern Territory Emergency Service [*Australia*]
N-TEST...... Nuclear Testing (WDAA)
NTET......... National Traction Engine Trust [*British*] (DBA)
NTEU .... National Treasury Employees Union (EA)
NTEU CHAPTER 151... National Treasury Employees Union, CH 151, U.S. Customs Hawaii (EARSL)
NTEXIS...... North Texas Interconnected System (SAUS)
NTeZ......... North Temperate Zone [*Planet Jupiter*]
NTF .... National Tactical Force (NATG)
NTF .... National Tennis Foundation [*Formerly, NTEF*] [*Later, NTFHF*] (EA)
NTF .... National Test Facility [*Military*] (SDI)
NTF .... National Theater File [*Theater Sources, Inc.*] [*Information service or system*] [*Defunct*] (IID)
NTF .... National Tidal Facility [*Flinders University*] [*Australia*]
NTF .... National Trainers Federation [*British*] (DBA)
NTF .... National Transfer Format (VLIE)
NTF .... National Transonic Facility [*NASA*]
NTF .... National Transport Federation [*Australia*]
NTF .... National Turkey Federation (EA)
NTF .... Naval Task Force
NTF .... Navy Technological Forecast
NTF .... Network Transfer Function (ELAL)
NTF .... Neurotrophic Factor [*Medicine*] (DMAA)
NTF .... Neutral Transfer Format (SAUS)
NTF .... New Tactical Fighter (ACAE)
NTF .... Nigerian Trust Fund [*African Development Bank*]
NTF .... Nigeria Trust Fund (SAUS)
NTF .... Nitrofurantoin (SAUS)
NTF .... Nordic Transportworkers' Federation [*See also NT*] (EAIO)
NTF .... Nordisk Thoraxkirurgisk Forening [*Scandinavian Association for Thoracic and Cardiovascular Surgery - SATCS*] (EAIO)

NTF .... Normal Throat Flora [*Medicine*] (DMAA)
NTF .... Notify
NTF .... No Trouble Found
NTF .... No Trouble Fund (SAUS)
NTF .... Nuclear Test Facility
NTF .... Number Type Flag (SAUS)
NTFA......... National Teaching-Family Association (EA)
NTFA......... National Track and Field Association [*Superseded by ANG*] (EA)
NTFAO....... National Task Force on Autocratic Options (EA)
NTFC .... National Telemarketing Fulfillment Center
NTFC .... National Television Film Council (EA)
NTFC .... NATO Tactical Fighter Center
NTFC .... Nonlinear Transient Fuel Film Compsensation [*Automotive fuel system*]
NTFDC....... Non Theatrical Film Distributors Council (EA)
NTFEEG ..... National Task Force on Education for Economic Growth (EA)
NTFHF....... National Tennis Foundation and Hall of Fame [*Later, ITHOF*] (EA)
NTFI .... National Tackle Football Injury [*Medicine*] [*Surveillance project*] (EDAA)
NTFIC........ Northern Territory Fishing Industry Council [*Australia*]
NTFITC ...... Northern Territory Fishing Industry Training Committee [*Australia*]
NTFL......... National Touch Football Leagues (EA)
NTFNC....... Northern Territory Field Naturalists' Club [*Australia*]
NTFND ...... No Trouble Found [*Aviation*] (FAAC)
NTFP .... National Task Force on Prostitution (EA)
NTFS .... Network of Tropical Fisheries Scientists [*Marine science*] (OSRA)
NTFS .... New Technology File System [*Computer science*] (VLIE)
NTFS .... Northern Territory Fire Service [*Australia*]
NTFS .... NT File System [*Computer science*]
NTFSDOS... NT File System DOS [*Communications term*] (DCT)
NTFTA....... National Toy Fox Terrier Association (EA)
NTFWTC .... NATO Tactical Fighter Weapons Training Center
NTFY .... Notify (AFM)
NTFY .... Notify Technology Corp. [*OTCBB symbol*]
NTG.......... Natco Group 'A' [*NYSE symbol*] (SG)
NTG.......... Netzwerk und Telematic GmbH (EFIS)
NTG.......... Nitroglycerin [*Also, GTN, NG*] [*Explosive, vasodilator*]
Ntg........... Nitroglycerine [*Medicine*] (AMHC)
NTG.......... Nitrosoguanidine [*Organic chemistry*]
NTG.......... Nontactical Generator (RDA)
NTG.......... Non-Technical Generator [*Army*]
NTG.......... Nontoxic Goiter [*Medicine*]
NTG.......... Nontreatment Group [*Medical research*] (DAVI)
NTG.......... Normal Tension Glaucoma (SAUS)
NTG.......... Normal Triglyceridemic (DB)
NTG.......... Nothing [*Telegraphy*] (PCTE)
NTG.......... Not This Group [*Internet lingo*] (NETL)
NTG.......... Not Too Good (SAUS)
NTG.......... N-Tolylglycine [*Organic chemistry*]
NTG.......... Nuclear Test Gage [*Environmental science*] (COE)
NTGA .... Anaa [*French Polynesia*] [*ICAO location identifier*] (ICLI)
NTGA .... National Tabletop and Giftware Association (NTPA)
NTGA .... National Traveler's Gasoline Advisory (DICI)
NTGB .... Fangatau [*French Polynesia*] [*ICAO location identifier*] (ICLI)
NTGB .... North Thames Gas Board (SAUS)
NTGC .... Tikehau [*French Polynesia*] [*ICAO location identifier*] (ICLI)
NTGD........ Apataki [*French Polynesia*] [*ICAO location identifier*] (ICLI)
NTGDS ...... Non-Tritium Gas Delivery System (SAUS)
NTGE .... Reao [*French Polynesia*] [*ICAO location identifier*] (ICLI)
NTGF .... Fakarava [*French Polynesia*] [*ICAO location identifier*] (ICLI)
NTGH........ Hikueru [*French Polynesia*] [*ICAO location identifier*] (ICLI)
NTGI......... Manihi [*French Polynesia*] [*ICAO location identifier*] (ICLI)
NTGIS .... National Transit Geographic Information System [*FTA*] (TAG)
NTGJ .... Totegegie [*French Polynesia*] [*ICAO location identifier*] (ICLI)
NTGK .... Kaukura [*French Polynesia*] [*ICAO location identifier*] (ICLI)
NTGk .... New Testament Greek (BARN)
NTGL .... Fakahina [*French Polynesia*] [*ICAO location identifier*] (ICLI)
NTGM .... Makemo [*French Polynesia*] [*ICAO location identifier*] (ICLI)
NTGMA...... Northern Territory Girls' Marching Association [*Australia*]
NTGMB...... Northern Territory Grain Marketing Board [*Australia*]
NTGN .... Napuka [*French Polynesia*] [*ICAO location identifier*] (ICLI)
NTGO .... Nitroglycerine Ointment [*Pharmacy*]
NTGO .... Tatakoto [*French Polynesia*] [*ICAO location identifier*] (ICLI)
NTGP .... Northern Territory Government Publications [*Australia*]
NTGP .... Puka Puka [*French Polynesia*] [*ICAO location identifier*] (ICLI)
NTGPE....... Northern Territory Government Pipeline Executive [*Australia*]
NTGPO ...... Northern Territory Government Printing Office [*Australia*]
NTGQ .... Pukarua [*French Polynesia*] [*ICAO location identifier*] (ICLI)
NTGR .... Aratica [*French Polynesia*] [*ICAO location identifier*] (ICLI)
NTGR .... New Testament Greek (BJA)
NTGS .... National Technical Guidance Studies (EAGT)
NTGS .... Northwest Territory Genealogical Society (EA)
NTG SL...... Nitroglycerin Sublingual [*Pharmacology*] (DAVI)
NtGsO .... National Gas & Oil Corp. [*Associated Press*] (SAG)
NTGT .... Takapoto [*French Polynesia*] [*ICAO location identifier*] (ICLI)
NTGTS....... North Texas Global Telecommunications Society (EARSL)
NTGU .... Arutua [*French Polynesia*] [*ICAO location identifier*] (ICLI)
NTGV .... Mataiva [*French Polynesia*] [*ICAO location identifier*] (ICLI)
NTGW .... Nukutavake [*French Polynesia*] [*ICAO location identifier*] (ICLI)
NTGX .... net.Genesis Corp. [*NASDAQ symbol*] (SG)
NTGY .... Tureia [*French Polynesia*] [*ICAO location identifier*] (ICLI)
NTH.......... Hudson Valley Community College, Troy, NY [*Library symbol*] [*Library of Congress*] (LCLS)
NtH .... Natural Health Trends Corp. [*Associated Press*] (SAG)
NTH.......... New Testament Handbooks [*A publication*]
NTH.......... New Training Helicopter (SAUS)
NTH.......... Northern Platinum [*Vancouver Stock Exchange symbol*]
NTH.......... No Therapy Helpful (SAUS)
NTHA .... National Temple Hill Association (EA)
NTHA .... Northern Territory Hockey Association [*Australia*]
Nth BHH.... North Broken Hill Holdings (SAUS)
NTHC .... Northern Territory Housing Commission [*Australia*]
NTHCS ...... National Toothpick Holder Collector's Society (EA)
NthCsE ...... North Coast Energy [*Associated Press*] (SAG)
NthCst....... North Coast Energy, Inc. [*Associated Press*] (SAG)
NthCstE ..... North Coast Energy [*Associated Press*] (SAG)
NTHEST .... Northeast
NTHESTN... Northeastern
NTHEX....... Northeast Investors Tr. [*Mutual fund ticker symbol*] (SG)
NthfldLb..... Northfield Laboratories, Inc. [*Associated Press*] (SAG)
nthg.......... nothing (SAUS)
Nthgat....... Northgate Exploration Ltd. [*Associated Press*] (SAG)
NtHHlt....... National Home Health Care Corp. [*Associated Press*] (SAG)
NTHL .... National Treasure Hunters League [*Defunct*] (EA)
NthLily ...... North Lilly Mining Co. [*Associated Press*] (SAG)
NtHlt......... National Health Investors [*Associated Press*] (SAG)
NtHlthE...... National Health Enhancement Systems, Inc. [*Associated Press*] (SAG)
NtHltl .... National Health Investors [*Associated Press*] (SAG)
Nthmb .... Northumberland [*County in England*] (WGA)
NTHMF ...... Northair Mines Ltd. (SAUS)
Nthn .... Northern (TBD)
NTHN........ Northern
NthnTch ..... Northern Technologies International [*Associated Press*] (SAG)
NTHP .... National Trust for Historic Preservation (EA)
N-Threat .... Nuclear Threat (SAUS)
NTHRN ...... Northern
NthStat...... Northern States Financial Corp. [*Associated Press*] (SAG)
NthstCF ..... Northstar Computer Forms, Inc. [*Associated Press*] (SAG)
NthstrHl ..... Northstar Health Services, Inc. [*Associated Press*] (SAG)
NTHV .... Near-Term Hybrid Vehicle (PDAA)
NTHWST .... Northwest
NTHWSTN... Northwestern
NTHZ .... N-Nitrosothiazolidine [*Organic chemistry*]
NTI........... Bintuni [*Indonesia*] [*Airport symbol*] (OAG)
NTI........... Nadic-Terminated Imide [*Polymer technology*]
NTI........... National Tactical Interface (MCD)
NTI........... National Technology Initiative [*Program introduced by President Bush in February 1992*]
NTI........... National Television Index
NTI........... National Theatre Institute (EA)
NTI........... National Toxics Inventory [*Environmental science*] (EPAT)
NTI........... National Trade Index
NTI........... National Tune Index [*A publication*]
NTI........... Naval Travel Instructions
NTI........... Near Term Initiative (ACAE)
NTI........... Need Ticketing Information [*Travel industry*] (TRID)
NTI........... Nesbitt Thomson, Inc. [*Toronto Stock Exchange symbol*] [*Vancouver Stock Exchange symbol*]
NTI........... NeuROM Technology, Inc.
NTI........... Neuropsychiatric Interest Checklist
NTI........... Nielsen Television Index [*Nielsen Media Research*] [*Information service or system*]
NTI........... Noise Transmission Impairment [*Telecommunications*]
NTI........... Nonthyroidal Illness [*Medicine*]
NTI........... Nordman [*Idaho*] [*Seismograph station code, US Geological Survey*] [*Closed*] (SEIS)
NTI........... Northern Technology International [*AMEX symbol*] (SPSG)
NTI........... No Travel Involved [*Military*]
NTI........... Nuclear Threat Initiative [*Association*] (EA)
NTI........... Nursery and Tree Improvement [*USDA Forest Service*] (ALAC)
NTIA .... National Telecommunications and Information Administration [*Department of Commerce*] [*Washington, DC*]
NTIA .... Netia Holdings ADS [*NASDAQ symbol*] (SG)
NTIAC .... Nondestructive Testing Information Analysis Center [*Army Materials and Mechanics Research Center*] [*Watertown, MA*]
NTIB .... National Technology and Industrial Base (AAGC)
NTIC .... Immaculate Conception Seminary, College of Philosophy, Troy, NY [*Library symbol*] [*Library of Congress*] (LCLS)
NTIC .... National Training and Information Center (EA)
NTIC .... Naval Technical Intelligence Center [*Pronounced N-tech; Formerly, NISC, now NAVMIC*] (DOMA)
NTIC .... Nondestructive Testing Information Center [*Battelle Memorial Institute*] [*Databank*] [*Information service or system*] (IID)
NTICED...... National Training Institute for Community Economic Development (EA)
NTICL........ National Technical Information Centre and Library (NITA)
NTID .... National Technical Institute for the Deaf [*Rochester Institute of Technology*] [*Research center*]
NTIES........ National Treatment Improvement Evaluation Study [*Department of Health and Human Services*]
NTIEVA ...... North Texas Institute for Educators on the Visual Arts [*University of North Texas*] (RCD)
NTIF .... National Taxpayers' Investigative Fund (EA)
NTIF .... New Threat Intermediate Frequency (TIMI)
NTIG .... Nontreated Immunoglobulin [*Medicine*] (DMAA)
NTIH .... Normal Terminate Interrupt Handler (MCD)
NTII.......... Neurobiological Technologies, Inc. [*NASDAQ symbol*] (SAG)
NTIK .... Nontactical Instrumentation Kit [*Military*] (DWSG)

NTIM .... Not That It Matters (SAUS)
NTIMM ...... Not That It Matters Much (SAUS)
NTIMS .... Negative-Ion Thermal Ionization Mass Spectrometry
NTIOC .... No Travel Involved for Officer Concerned [*Military*]
N-TIP .... National Technology Investment Programme [*Canada*]
NTIP .... National Turkey Improvement Plan
NTIPP .... Navy Technical Information Presentation Program (MCD)
NTIPS .... Navy Technical Information Presentation System (MCD)
NTIPS .... Navy Technical Information Processing System (ACAE)
NTIQ .... NetIQ Corp. [*NASDAQ symbol*]
NTIR .... Nederlands Tijdschrift voor Internationaal Recht [*Netherlands*] [*A publication*] (ILCA)
NTIR .... Nontechnical Intelligence Report
NTIRA .... National Trucking Industrial Relations Association (EA)
NTIS .... National Technical Information Service [*Department of Commerce*] [*Springfield, VA*] [*Database producer and database*]
NTIS .... Navy Thermal Imaging System (SAUS)
NTIS .... NEC [*Nippon Electric Company*]-Toshiba Information Systems, Inc. [*Japan*]
NTIS .... Nippon Technical Information Service (SAUS)
NTIS .... NMOS Technical Information Services (SAUS)
NTIS .... Nondestructive Testing Information System (SAA)
NTISSC ...... National Telecommunications and Information System Security Committee (NITA)
NTITC .... National Tourism Industry Training Council [*Australia*]
NTITS .... Northern Territory Interpreter and Translator Service [*Australia*]
NTIU .... Germanishcher Lloyd [*Intermodal shipping container symbol*] (TVRC)
NTJ .... Nigeria Trade Journal [*A publication*]
NTJCAC ..... Northern Texas Junior College Athletic Conference (PSS)
NTK .... Ikoma [*Language symbol*] (ETLW)
NTK .... Need to Know (MCD)
NTK .... Newton Tool Kit [*Computer science*]
NTK .... New York Air (SAUS)
NTK .... Nontactical Kit [*Military*] (DWSG)
NTK .... Nordisk Teaterkomite [*Nordic Theater Committee - NTC*] (EAIO)
NTK .... Nortek, Inc. [*NYSE symbol*] (SPSG)
NTK .... Nunatak [*Alaska*] [*Seismograph station code, US Geological Survey*] (SEIS)
NTK .... Tustin, CA [*Location identifier*] [*FAA*] (FAAL)
NTKK .... Net2000 Communications [*NASDAQ symbol*] (SG)
NTKM .... Net Tonne-Kilometer [*Indian Railway*] (TIR)
NTKR .... Takaroa [*French Polynesia*] [*ICAO location identifier*] (ICLI)
NTKX .... VAE Nortrak North America [*Private rail car owner code*]
NTL .... Jacksonville, NC [*Location identifier*] [*FAA*] (FAAL)
NTL .... Narrow Track Longitudinal (GART)
ntL .... National (DD)
NTL .... National
NTL .... National Technology Ltd. (NITA)
NTL .... National Temperance League [*Later, ACAP*] (EA)
NTL .... National Tennis League
NTL .... National Testing Laboratories [*Australia*]
NTL .... National Training Laboratories [*Later, NTLI*] (EA)
NTL .... Natural Thermo Luminescence (IAA)
NTL .... Neon Test Light
NTL .... Nevertheless (SAUS)
NTL .... Newcastle [*Australia*] [*Airport symbol*] (OAG)
NTL .... Night Telegraph Letter
NTL .... Nonthreshold Logic (IAA)
NTL .... Nonuniform Transmission Line [*Computer science*] (IAA)
NTL .... Northair Aviation Ltd. [*British*] [*ICAO designator*] (FAAC)
NTL .... Northern Technol Intl. [*AMEX symbol*] (TTSB)
NTL .... Northern Telecom Ltd. [*Toronto Stock Exchange symbol*] [*Vancouver Stock Exchange symbol*]
NTL .... Northern Territory Library [*Australia*]
NTL .... No Time Lost [*Military*]
NTL .... NovAtel Communications Ltd. [*UTLAS symbol*]
NTL .... Novosti Tehnikskoi Literatury (NITA)
NTL .... Nuclear Technology Laboratory [*Stanford University*] (MCD)
NTL .... Nuclear Thermionics Laboratory
NTL .... Nuclear Transport Ltd. [*British*] (IRUK)
NTLA .... National Toy Libraries Association [*British*] (EAIO)
NTLA .... Nebraska Test of Learning Aptitude [*Education*]
NTLAM ...... New Technology Lunar Astronomy Mission (SAUS)
NTLAT ...... Northern Territory Land Acquisition Tribunal [*Australia*]
NTLB .... National Lumber & Supply, Inc. [*NASDAQ symbol*] (COMM)
NTLB .... Northern Territory Land Board [*Australia*]
NTLC .... National Tax-Limitation Committee (EA)
NTLC .... National Trades and Labour Congress [*Canada*]
NTLC .... National Traffic Law Center [*MHTSA*] (TAG)
NtlCity .... National City Corp. [*Associated Press*] (SAG)
NTLDO ...... Navy Terminal Leave Disbursing Office
NTLEN .... Nutlet Length [*Botany*]
NTLF .... National Taxpayers Legal Fund (EA)
NTLF .... Northern Troops and Landing Force
NTLG .... Novo Transportation Logistics [*Common carrier symbol*]
NTLGA .... Northern Territory Local Government Association [*Australia*]
NTLGGC ..... Northern Territory Local Government Grants Commission [*Australia*]
NTLI .... Neurotensin-Like Immunoreactivity
NTLI .... NTL, Inc. [*NASDAQ symbol*] (SG)
NTLI .... NTL Institute (EA)
NtlInco ...... National Income Realty Trust [*Associated Press*] (SAG)
NtlIns .... National Insurance Group [*Associated Press*] (SAG)
NTLIS .... Northern Territory Land Information System (SAUS)
NtlPict .... National Picture & Frame Co. [*Associated Press*] (SAG)
NTLPSS ..... Non-real-time Launch Processing Software System (SAUS)
NtlRlty .... National Realty Ltd. [*Associated Press*] (SAG)
NTLS .... National Truck Leasing System (EA)
NTLS .... Non-Transposed Loop Sensor (PDAA)
NTLSEA ..... Northern Territory Live Stock Exporters' Association [*Australia*]
NtlSecs ...... National Securities Corp. [*Associated Press*] (SAG)
NTLU .... Nantai Line Company [*Common carrier symbol*]
NTLU .... Navimport [*Intermodal shipping container symbol*] (TVRC)
NtlWire ...... National Wireless Holdings, Inc. [*Associated Press*] (SAG)
NtlWstA ..... National Westminster Bank Ltd. [*Associated Press*] (SAG)
NTM .... Narrowband Trunk Module [*Telecommunications*]
NTM .... National Technical Means [*For monitoring compliance with the provisions of an agreement*]
NTM .... NAVAIR Test Manual (MCD)
NTM .... Nazarene Theological Seminary, Kansas City, MO [*OCLC symbol*] (OCLC)
NTM .... Net Ton Mile [*Shipping*]
NTM .... Network Test Manager (ACAE)
NTM .... Network Traffic Management [*Computer science*] (VLIE)
NTM .... New to Market (JAGO)
NTM .... New Tribes Mission (EA)
NTM .... Night Message (MSA)
NTM .... Nondeterministic Turing Machine (RALS)
NTM .... Nontariff Measures
NTM .... Non-Transition Metal (MCD)
NTM .... Non-Tuberculous Mycobacteria [*Microbiology*]
NTM .... Normal Transmitting Male [*Genetics*]
NTM .... North American Airlines, Inc. [*Canada*] [*ICAO designator*] (FAAC)
NTM .... Northern Territory Art Gallery and Museum, Darwin (SAUS)
NtM .... Norton Micro Images, Inc., Trenton, NJ [*Library symbol*] [*Library of Congress*] (LCLS)
NTM .... Notice to Mariners
NTM .... Notice to Move (SAUS)
NTM .... Not to My Knowledge
NTM .... Nutmeg Industries, Inc. (SAUS)
NTMA .... National Tank Manufacturers Association [*Defunct*] (EA)
NTMA .... National Terrazzo and Mosaic Association (EA)
NTMA .... National Tooling and Machining Association (EA)
NTMA .... National Traditional Music Association (EA)
NTMB .... Nontuberculous Mycobacterium [*A bacterium*] (DAVI)
NTMD .... NetMed, Inc. [*NASDAQ symbol*] (QUAN)
NTMD .... Nuku Hiva [*French Polynesia*] [*ICAO location identifier*] (ICLI)
NTME .... Naval Technical Mission in Europe
NtMerc ...... National Mercantile Bancorp [*Associated Press*] (SAG)
NTMG .... Nutmeg Federal Savings & Loan Association [*NASDAQ symbol*] (SAG)
NTMG .... Nutmeg Fedl Svgs & Loan [*NASDAQ symbol*] (TTSB)
NTMI .... Net Ton of Molten Iron
NTMI .... Nontransmural Myocardial Infarction [*Cardiology*] (CPH)
NTMICP ..... National Topographic Map Inventory Control Point
NTMJ .... Naval Technical Mission to Japan
NTML .... National Tillage Machinery Laboratory [*Department of Agriculture*] [*Research center*] (GRD)
NTMN .... Hiva-Oa/Atuana [*French Polynesia*] [*ICAO location identifier*] (ICLI)
NTMN .... National Thrift and Mortgage News [*A publication*]
NTMNG ...... Nontoxic, Multinodular Goiter [*Medicine*] (DAVI)
NTMP .... Nike Target Measurements Program
NTMP .... Nitrate Motion Picture (VRA)
NTMP .... Nitrilo-Tris-Methylene Phosphoric Acid (SAUS)
NTMP .... Ua Pou [*French Polynesia*] [*ICAO location identifier*] (ICLI)
NTMPA ...... Northern Territory Marine and Ports Authority [*Australia*]
NTMS .... Northern Territory Medical Service (SAUS)
NTMT .... Navigation Tender Maintenance Training (DNAB)
NTMTAI ..... Nursing Touch and Massage Therapy Association International (EA)
NTMU .... Nederlandse Tanktrailervchuur [*Intermodal shipping container symbol*] (TVRC)
NTMU .... Ua Huka [*French Polynesia*] [*ICAO location identifier*] (ICLI)
NTMVSA .... National Traffic and Motor Vehicle Safety Act
NTMWG .... Nuclear Test Monitoring Working Group [*Military*]
NTN .... National Airways Corp. (Pty) Ltd. [*South Africa*] [*ICAO designator*] (FAAC)
NTN .... National TeleAccess Network [*Database of physician opportunities*]
NTN .... National Telecommunications Network [*Rockville, MD*] (TSSD)
NTN .... National Towing News [*A publication*] (EAAP)
NTN .... National Trends Network (EPA)
NTN .... Nephrotoxic Nephritis [*Medicine*]
NTN .... Network Terminal Number [*Telecommunications*]
NTN .... Network Termination Number [*Computer science*] (TNIG)
NTN .... Neutralized Twisted Nematic (VLIE)
NTN .... Neutral Twisted Nematic [*Computer science*] (PCM)
NTN .... Neutron [*A nuclear particle*] (MSA)
NTN .... Newton [*Diocesan abbreviation*] [*Melkite United States*] (TOCD)
NTN .... Newton College, Newton, MA [*Inactive*] [*OCLC symbol*] (OCLC)
NTN .... New Trade Names [*Later, NBTC*] [*A publication*]
NTN .... Normanton [*Australia*] [*Airport symbol*] (OAG)
NTN .... Northern [*Telegraphy*] (PCTE)
NTN .... Northern Territory News [*A publication*]
NTN .... Norton Co., Coated Abrasive Division, R and D Department, Troy, NY [*Library symbol*] [*Library of Congress*] (LCLS)
NTN .... NTN Canada, Inc. [*Associated Press*] (SAG)
NTN .... NTN Communications [*AMEX symbol*] (TTSB)
NTN .... NTN Communications, Inc. [*AMEX symbol*] (SPSG)
NTNA .... Northern Territory Nurserymen's Association [*Australia*]
NTNC .... Nippon Television Network Corp. (SAUS)

NTNC .... Non-Transient Non-Community [*Water system*] [*Environment term*] (EGA)
NTNC .... NTN Canada, Inc. [*NASDAQ symbol*] (SAG)
NTNC .... NTN Cda [*NASDAQ symbol*] (TTSB)
NTN Cda .... NTN Canada, Inc. [*Associated Press*] (SAG)
NTNCom .... NTN Communications, Inc. [*Associated Press*] (SAG)
NTNCW ...... Non-Transient Non-Community Water System (EEVL)
NTNCWS .... Non-Transient Non-Community Water System [*Environmental Protection Agency*]
NTND .... Not Tender, Not Distended [*Medicine*] (EDAA)
NTNF .... Norges Teknisk-Naturvitenskapelige Forskningsraad [*Online database*]
NTNG .... Nitrate Negative (VRA)
NTNI .... National Transaction Network, Inc. [*NASDAQ symbol*] (COMM)
NTNU .... National Container Network [*Intermodal shipping container symbol*] (TVRC)
NTNV .... Narcissus Tip Necrosis Virus [*Plant pathology*]
NTNVL .... Nortonville, KY [*American Association of Railroads railroad junction routing code*]
NTNX .... NTN Communications, Inc. (SAUS)
NTNYT .... Not the New York Times [*A publication*]
NTO .... Name To (AAG)
NTO .... National Tenants Organization [*Defunct*] (EA)
NTO .... National Tourist Office (TVEL)
NTO .... National Turnover [*Economics*]
NTO .... Natural Transition Orbitals [*Atomic physics*]
NTO .... Naval Technology Office [*Arlington, VA*] (GRD)
NTO .... Naval Transport Officer
NTO .... Network Terminal Operator
NTO .... Network Terminal Option [*Computer science*]
NTO .... New Technology Opportunities [*Program*] [*US government*]
NTO .... New Titles On-Line [*Database*] (GDD)
NTO .... Nitrogen Tetroxide [*Inorganic chemistry*]
NTO .... Nonorthogonal Timing Error (IAA)
NTO .... Non-Target Organism (EES)
NTO .... Nontraditional Occupations
NTO .... No Try On [*Purchaser did not have a fitting*] [*Merchandising slang*]
NTO .... Not Taken Out [*Insurance*]
NTO .... Not Tried On (SAUS)
NTO .... Nuclear Technologies Office (SAUS)
NTO .... Santo Antao [*Cape Verde Islands*] [*Airport symbol*] (OAG)
NTOC .... Naval Telecommunications Operations Center (DNAB)
NTOC .... Number to Character (SAUS)
NTOCDET... Naval Telecommunications Operations Center Detachment (DNAB)
NTOF .... National Traumatic Occupational Fatalities [*Surveillance system run by National Institute for Occupational Safety and Health*]
NTOFMS .... Neutral Time-of-Flight Mass Spectroscopy [*Aviation*]
NTOFMS .... Neutral Time-of-Flight Spectroscopy (SAUS)
NTOL .... Near-Term Operating License [*Nuclear energy*] (NRCH)
NTOL .... Normal Takeoff and Landing [*Aviation*] (MCD)
NTOMC ...... National Tung Oil Marketing Cooperative [*Defunct*] (EA)
NTonHi ...... Historical Society of the Tonawandas, Tonawanda, NY [*Library symbol*] [*Library of Congress*] (LCLS)
NTonL .... Union Carbide Corp., Linde Division, Tonawanda, NY [*Library symbol*] [*Library of Congress*] (LCLS)
NTonS .... Sheridan Park Hospital, Inc., Tonawanda, NY [*Library symbol*] [*Library of Congress*] (LCLS)
NTOP .... Net2Phone [*NASDAQ symbol*] (SG)
NTOP .... New Technology Opportunities Program [*US government*]
NTORS ...... Naval Torpedo Station
NTOS .... Natural Therapeutic and Osteopathic Society and Register [*British*] (DBA)
NTOTC .... National Training and Operational Technology Center [*Environmental Protection Agency*] (IID)
NTP .... Nathian [*Pakistan*] [*Seismograph station code, US Geological Survey*] (SEIS)
NTP .... National Tasking Plan [*Military*]
NTP .... National Toxicology Program [*Department of Health and Human Services*] [*Research Triangle Park, NC*]
NTP .... National Transportation Policy
NTP .... Naval Tactical Publication (NVT)
NTP .... Naval Telecommunications Procedures (NVT)
NTP .... Naval Telecommunications Publication (NVT)
NTP .... Naval Training Publication (POLM)
NTP .... Navy Technological Projections
NTP .... Navy Training Plan (NVT)
NTP .... Near Time Processing (IAA)
NTP .... Network Terminal Protocol
NTP .... Network Terminating Point [*Telecommunications*] (TEL)
NTP .... Network Termination Processor
NTP .... Network Test Panel [*NASA*] (KSC)
NTP .... Network Time Protocol
NTP .... Network Transaction Processing [*Computer science*] (VLIE)
NTP .... Neuronal Thread Protein [*Biology*]
NTP .... Nistransair [*Republic of Moldova*] [*FAA designator*] (FAAC)
NTP .... Nitrol Paste [*Pharmacology*] (DAVI)
NTP .... Nitroprusside [*A vasodilator*]
NTP .... Nontree Pollen (SAUS)
NTP .... Nonzero Temperature Plasma
ntp .... Normal Temperature and Pressure [*Construction term*] (MIST)
NTP .... Normal Temperature and Pressure [*Medicine*]
NTP .... Normal Temperature and Progress (SAUS)
NTP .... Notice to Proceed (KSC)
NTP .... No Title Page [*Bibliography*]
NTP .... Nuclear Non-Proliferation Treaty
NTP .... Nuclear Target Planning (SAUS)
NTP .... Nuclear Test Plant
NTP .... Nuclear Thermal Propulsion (COE)
NTP .... Nuclear Transportation Project (EA)
NTP .... Nucleoside Triphosphate [*Biochemistry*]
NTP .... Number of Theoretical Plates
NTP .... Numerical Tape Punch
NTP .... Sodium Nitroprusside [*An antihypertensive and reagent*] [*Pharmacology*] (DAVI)
NTPA .... National Tractor Pullers Association (EA)
NTPA .... National Trotting Pony Association [*Later, ITPA*]
NTPA .... Naval Technical Proficiency Assist (NVT)
NTPA .... Netopia, Inc. [*NASDAQ symbol*] (SG)
NTPA .... Northern Territory Planning Authority [*Australia*]
NTPA .... Northern Territory Police Association [*Australia*]
NTPAC .... Northern Territory Planning Appeals Committee [*Australia*]
NtPatnt ...... National Patent Development Corp. [*Associated Press*] (SAG)
NTPAW ...... National Transportation Public Affairs Workshop
NTPC .... National Technical Processing Center
NTPC .... National Temperance and Prohibition Council (EA)
NTPC .... Naval Training Publications Center
NTPC .... Navy Training Plan Conference
NTPCC ...... Northern Transvaal Peoples Coordinating Committee (SAUS)
NTPD .... Network Time Protocol Daemon [*Computer science*] (VLIE)
NTPD .... Normal Temperature and Pressure Dry (ACAE)
NTPD .... Normal Temperature, Pressure Differential (MCD)
NTPDLB ..... Northern Territory Plumbers and Drainers Licensing Board [*Australia*]
NTPE .... Non-Tactical Peripheral Equipment [*Military*]
NtPenn ...... National Penn Bancshares, Inc. [*Associated Press*] (SAG)
NTPF .... National Tile Promotion Federation [*Defunct*] (EA)
NTPF .... Near-Term Prepositioning Forces [*Navy*]
NTPF .... Number of Terminals per Failure [*Computer science*]
NTPG .... National Textile Processors Guild [*Defunct*] (EA)
NTPH .... Nucleosidetriphosphate Pyrophosphatase [*An enzyme*]
NTPHINB... National Trust for Places of Historic Interest or Natural Beauty [*British*] (EAIO)
NTPI .... Navy Technical Proficiency Inspection (NG)
NTPI .... Nuclear Training Proficiency Inspection [*Navy*] (DOMA)
NTP/IDCSP... Navy Test Plan for Initial Defense Communications Satellite Program (DNAB)
NTPL .... Navy Technical Proficiency List
NTPL .... Nut Plate (AAG)
NTPNC ...... Northern Territory Place Names Committee [*Australia*]
NTPO .... National Transuranic Waste Program Office [*Department of Energy*] (GAAI)
NTPO .... Nitrilotrimethylenephosphonic Acid [*Organic chemistry*]
NTPOC ...... Navy Technical Point of Contact (DOMA)
NTPP .... Normal through Patch Panel (MCD)
NTPR .... Nuclear Targeting Policy Review (MCD)
NTPR .... Nuclear Test Personnel Review Program (SAUS)
NtPrest ...... National Presto Industries, Inc. [*Associated Press*] (SAG)
NTPS .... Naval Test Pilot School
NTPS .... Near-Term Prepositioned Ships
NTPWA ...... Northern Territory Power and Water Authority [*Australia*]
NtPwADS ... National Power PLC [*Associated Press*] (SAG)
NtPwIntr .... National Power PLC [*Associated Press*] (SAG)
NTQ .... National Trust of Queensland [*Australia*]
NTQ .... Nebennieren, Thymus, Quotient [*Test*] [*Medicine*]
NTR .... Natchez Trace Railroad [*Federal Railroad Administration identification code*]
NTR .... National Tape Repository (EA)
NTR .... National Transcontinental Railway [*Canada*]
NTR .... Navigational Time Reference (AAG)
NTR .... Navy Technical Representative (MCD)
NTR .... Negative True Rake (IAA)
NTR .... Neither [*Telegraphy*] (PCTE)
NTR .... Nernst-Thomson Rule [*Physics*]
NTR .... Net-of-Tax Rate (ECON)
NTR .... Net Total Requirement (VLIE)
NTR .... Neutron Test Reactors (KSC)
NTR .... New Technology Report
NTR .... Next Task Register
NTR .... Nine Thousand Remote (ELAL)
NTR .... Noise Temperature Ratio (AAG)
NTR .... Non Tactical Radio (SAUS)
NTR .... Nonthermal Radiation (SAUS)
NTR .... Nontranslated Region [*Genetics*]
NTR .... Non-Typing Reperforator (SAUS)
NTR .... Nordiska Trafiksakerhetsradet [*Nordic Road Safety Council - NRSC*] [*Finland*] (EAIO)
NTR .... Nordisk Tolladministrativt Rad [*Nordic Customs Administrative Council - NCAC*] (EAIO)
NTR .... Northern Test Range (SAUS)
NTR .... No Texts Required [*Education*]
NTR .... Nothing to Report
NTR .... No Traffic Reported [*Aviation*]
NTR .... No Treatment Required [*Medicine*] (WDAA)
NTR .... Nuclear Test Reactor [*Also known as GETR*]
NTR .... Nuclear Thermal Rocket(ry) [*Astronomy term*]
NTR .... Nucledyne Training Reactor (SAUS)
NTR .... Nutrition
NTR .... Rensselaer Polytechnic Institute, Troy, NY [*Library symbol*] [*Library of Congress*] (LCLS)
NTRA .... National Television Rental Association [*British*]

NTRA .... National Trailer Rental Association (EA)
NTRA .... National Tumor Registrars Association (EA)
NTRA .... National Tyre Recycling Association [*British*] (DBA)
NTRA .... Northern Territory Rifle Association [*Australia*]
N Trans S Dec... National Transportation Safety Board Decisions [*A publication*] (DLA)
NTRAS ...... NT Remote Access Services (SAUS)
NTRB .... Northern Territory Reserve Board (SAUS)
NTRC .... National Tourism Review Commission
NTRC .... National Toxins Research Center (DMAA)
NTRC .... Natural Toxins Research Center [*Public Health Service*] (GRD)
NTRC .... Northern Territory Rural College [*Australia*]
NTRC .... Nuclear Threat Reduction Campaign [*Association*] (EA)
NTRDA ...... National Tuberculosis and Respiratory Diseases Association [*Later, American Lung Association*]
NT Rep...... New Term Reports, English Queen's Bench [*A publication*] (DLA)
NT Repts.... New Term Reports, English Queen's Bench [*A publication*] (DLA)
NTRG .... New Testament Reading Guide [*Collegeville, MN*] [*A publication*] (BJA)
NTRGLB..... Northern Territory Racing, Gaming and Liquor Board [*Australia*]
NTRI .... NCP Token-Ring Interconnection [*Communications term*] (DCT)
NTRI .... Network Token-Ring Interface [*Communications term*] (DCT)
NTRL .... NASA Technology Readiness Level (SSD)
NTRL .... Natural
NTRL .... Naval Training Research Laboratory (WDAA)
NTRL .... Neutral Posture Ergonomics, Inc. [*NASDAQ symbol*] (NASQ)
NtrlH......... Natural Health Trends Corp. [*Associated Press*] (SAG)
NTRLLy...... Naturally
NTRM .... Nitrogen-Tillage-Residue Management (GNE)
NTRMA...... National Tile Roofing Manufacturing Association (EA)
NTRN .... National Transaction Network [*OTCBB symbol*]
NTRP .... No Traffic Reported [*Aviation*] (FAAC)
NTRS .... National Therapeutic Recreation Society (EA)
NTRS .... Nationwide Trailer Rental System
NTRS .... Navy Tactical Reconnaissance System (ACAE)
NTRS .... Northern Trust [*NASDAQ symbol*] (TTSB)
NTRS .... Northern Trust Corp. [*NASDAQ symbol*] (NQ)
NTRS .... Russell Sage College, Troy, NY [*Library symbol*] [*Library of Congress*] (LCLS)
NTRU .... Northern Territory Rugby Union [*Australia*]
NTRX .... Netrix Corp. [*NASDAQ symbol*] (SAG)
NTRY .... Nimishillen & Tuscarawas Railway [*Federal Railroad Administration identification code*]
NTrZ .... North Tropical Zone [*Planet Jupiter*]
NTS .... Cirrus Air, Inc. [*ICAO designator*] (FAAC)
NTS .... Namens Trau- und Sterberegister der Judenschaft [*A publication*] (BJA)
NTS .... Narodno Trudovoi Soyuz [*People's Labor Union*] [*Frankfurt, Federal Republic of Germany*] (PD)
NTS .... NASA Test Support
NTS .... Nasotracheal Suction [*Medical procedure*] (DAVI)
NTS .... National Technical Systems
NTS .... National Technical Systems Inc. [*Commercial firm*]
NTS .... National Thespian Society [*Later, ITS*] (EA)
NTS .... National Traffic System [*Amateur radio*]
NTS .... National Transplant Society [*Association*] (EA)
NTS .... National Transportation Statistics [*or Survey*] [*Department of Transportation*]
NTS .... National Transportation System [*BTS*] (TAG)
NTS .... National Travel Survey [*Census Bureau*]
NTS .... National Trust for Scotland (DI)
NTS .... National Tulip Society [*Defunct*] (EA)
NTS .... Naval Target Subdivision [*G-2, SHAEF*]
NTS .... Naval Telecommunications System (NVT)
NTS .... Naval Torpedo Station
NTS .... Naval Training School
NTS .... Naval Training Station
NTS .... Naval Transportation Service [*Later, MSC*]
NTS .... Navigational Technology Satellite (MCD)
NTS .... Navigation Technology Satellite (PDAA)
NTS .... Navigation Technology System (IAA)
NTS .... Navigator Training Squadron [*Air Force*]
NTS .... Navy Technology Satellite
NTS .... Near Term Schedule (MCD)
NTS .... Negative Torque Signal (MSA)
NTS .... Netware Telephone Services [*Communications term*] (DCT)
NTS .... Network/TDRSS [*Tracking and Data Relay Satellite System*] [*NASA*] (MCD)
NTS .... Nevada Test Site [*Department of Energy*]
NTS .... Nevada Test Site, Mercury, Nevada (SAUS)
NTS .... New Tube Shelter [*British*]
NTS .... New Typesetting System (SAUS)
NTS .... Night Targeting System (SAUS)
NTS .... Nitroglycerin Transdermal System [*Pharmacy*]
NTS .... Nontariff Size
NTS .... Nontemporary Storage [*Personal property*]
NTS .... Non-Traffic Sensitive [*Costs*] [*Telecommunications*]
NTS .... Nontranscribed Spacer [*Genetics*]
NTS .... Nordiske Teleansattes Samarbeidsorgan [*Nordic Telecommunications Association*] (EAIO)
NTS .... Notch Tensile Strength (OA)
Nts .... Notes (EBF)
NTS .... Notes [*Finance*]
NTS .... Not to Scale [*Drafting*]
NTS .... No Turn Signal (SAUS)
NTS .... Nuclear Test Site (MCD)
NTS .... Nuclear Test Stage (AAG)
NTS .... Nucleus Tractus Solitarii [*Brain anatomy*]
NTS .... Number of Theoretical Stages [*Chemical engineering*]
NTS .... Nutrition Today Society [*Defunct*] (EA)
NTS .... Samaritan Hospital, Troy, NY [*Library symbol*] [*Library of Congress*] (LCLS)
NTSA .... National Tay-Sachs Association [*Later, NTSAD*] (EA)
NTSA .... National Technical Services Association (EA)
NTSA .... National Traffic Safety Agency [*Federal Highway Administration*]
NTSA .... National Trails System Act (COE)
NTSA .... National Training Systems Association (EA)
NTSA .... National Transportation Safety Association [*Defunct*] (EA)
NTSA .... National T-Shirt Association (EA)
NTSA .... National Tuberous Sclerosis Association (EA)
NTSA .... Naval Telecommunications System Architect (MCD)
NTSA .... Navy Tactical Support Activity (DNAB)
NTSA .... Northern Territory Softball Association [*Australia*]
NTSA .... Norway Technical Science Academy
NTSAD ...... National Tay-Sachs and Allied Diseases Association (EA)
NTSAI .... National Target Shooting Association of Ireland
NtSanit...... National Sanitary Supply Co. [*Associated Press*] (SAG)
NTSB .... National Traffic Safety Bureau
NTSB .... National Transportation Safety Board [*Independent government agency*] [*Washington, DC*]
NTSB .... Northern Territory Surveyor Board [*Australia*]
NTSC .... National Science and Technology Council (DDC)
NTSC .... National Tax Strike Coalition (EA)
NTSC .... National Technical Systems, Inc. [*NASDAQ symbol*] (NQ)
NTSC .... National Television Standard Code [*Video equipment*] (RDA)
NTSC .... National Television Standards Committee
NTSC .... National Television System Committee [*Formed in 1936*]
NTSC .... Natl Technical Sys [*NQS*] (TTSB)
NTSC .... Naval Training Systems Center [*Orlando, FL*]
NTSC .... Never The Same Color (SAUS)
NTSC .... Never Twice the Same Color (SAUS)
NTSC .... Nonextrusion Texturized Soy Concentrate
NTSC .... Northern Telecom Systems Corp. (SAUS)
NTSC .... North Texas State College [*Later, North Texas State University*]
NTSCH ...... Naval Training School
NTSC-TV... National Television Standards Committee Television
NTSD .... Light System Failing to Meet FAA Standards [*Aviation*] (PIPO)
NTSD .... Normal Theory Sampling Distribution (SAUS)
NTSDS ...... Near-Term Swimmer Defense System
NTSE .... Naval Telecommunications System Engineer (MCD)
NTSE .... Nontactical Support Equipment (MCD)
NTSEA....... National Trade Show Exhibitors Association [*Later, IEA*] (EA)
NTS EIS..... Nevada Test Site Environmental Impact Statement
NtSemi...... National Semiconductor Corp. [*Associated Press*] (SAG)
NTSF .... National Technical Scholarship Foundation (AEBS)
NTSF .... Nonextrusion Texturized Soy Flour
NTSH .... Near-Term Scout Helicopter [*Army*]
NTSI .... National Tire Svcs [*NASDAQ symbol*] (TTSB)
NTSI .... National Tribunal of Second Instance [*Catholic Church*] [*Australia*]
NTSI .... Nonextrusion Texturized Soy Isolate
NTSK .... Nordiska Tele-Satelit Kommitton [*Norway*]
NTSL .... NetSolve [*NASDAQ National Market symbol*]
NTSL .... Nonintegrated Two-Stage Liquid (ABAC)
NTSM........ Saint Mary's Hospital, Troy, NY [*Library symbol*] [*Library of Congress*] (LCLS)
Ntsmrt....... Netsmart Technologies, Inc. [*Associated Press*] (SAG)
NTSO .... NASA Test Support Office (KSC)
NTSP .... National Telecommunications Support Plan [*Emergency Management*] (EMA)
NTSR .... National Tunis Sheep Registry (EA)
NTSR .... NetStar, Inc. [*NASDAQ symbol*] (SAG)
NTSRI .... National Tunis Sheep Registry (NTPA)
NTSRP ...... Nontechnical Services Real Property
NTSRVA..... Nevada Test Site Radiation Victim Association (EA)
NTSSC....... Northern Territory School Sports Council [*Australia*]
NTSSO ...... Nevada Test Site Safety Office (SAUS)
NTST .... Netsmart Technologies, Inc. [*NASDAQ symbol*] (SAG)
NTSTN....... Naval Telecommunications System Test Node (CAAL)
NTSU .... Northern Transportation [*Intermodal shipping container symbol*] (TVRC)
NtSvIn....... National Service Industries, Inc. [*Associated Press*] (SAG)
NTT .... Nasotracheal Tube [*Medicine*] (DAVI)
NTT .... National Training Team [*Operated by the Helen Keller National Center for Deaf-Blind Youths and Adults (HKNC)*] (PAZ)
NTT .... National Tree Trust (WPI)
NTT .... Nearly Total Thyroidectomy [*Medicine*] (DMAA)
NTT .... New England Telephone and Telegraph Co. (SAUS)
NTT .... New Technology Telescopes [*Under development*]
NTT .... Nippon Tel & Tel ADS [*NYSE symbol*] (TTSB)
NTT .... Nippon Telegraph & Telephone Co. [*NYSE symbol*] (SAG)
NTT .... Nippon Telegraph & Telephone Corp. [*Telecommunications and videotex company*] [*Japan*]
NTT .... Nippon Telephone and Telegraph (SAUS)
NTT .... Non-Tactical Tape [*Military*]
NTT .... Nuiatoputapu [*Tonga*] [*Airport symbol*] (OAG)
NTT .... Numbered Test Trunk (SAUS)
NTT .... Number Theoretic Transform (MHDI)
NTTA......... National Tobacco Tax Association (EA)
NTTAB .... Northern Territory Totalizator Agency Board [*Australia*]

NTTAWWT... Not That Theres Anything Wrong With That (SAUS)
NTTB........ Bora Bora/Motu-Mute [*French Polynesia*] [*ICAO location identifier*] (ICLI)
NTTBR....... Nineteen Thirty-Two Buick Registry (EA)
NTTC........ National Tank Truck Carriers [*Alexandria, VA*] (EA)
NTTC........ National Technology Transfer Center [*NASA*]
NTTC........ Naval Technical Training Center
NTTC........ NAVFAC [*Naval Facilities Engineering Command*] Technical Training Center
NTTCIW..... National Technical Task Committee on Industrial Wastes
NTTE......... Non-Tactical Training Equipment [*Military*]
NTTE......... Tetiaroa [*French Polynesia*] [*ICAO location identifier*] (ICLI)
NTTF......... Networking and Telecommunications Task Force [*Computer science*] (TNIG)
NTTF......... Network Test and Training Facility [*Goddard Space Flight Center*]
NTTFX....... Hancock(J) Global Technology [*Mutual fund ticker symbol*] (SG)
NTTG........ Rangiroa [*French Polynesia*] [*ICAO location identifier*] (ICLI)
NTTH........ Huahine/Fare [*French Polynesia*] [*ICAO location identifier*] (ICLI)
NTT-IT....... Nippon Telegraph and Telephone-Intelligent Technology (SAUS)
NTTL......... Nettel Holdings [*OTCBB symbol*]
NTTLC....... Northern Territory Trades and Labor Council [*Australia*]
NTTM........ Moorea/Temae [*French Polynesia*] [*ICAO location identifier*] (ICLI)
NTTO........ Hao [*French Polynesia*] [*ICAO location identifier*] (ICLI)
NTTP........ Maupiti [*French Polynesia*] [*ICAO location identifier*] (ICLI)
NTTPC....... Nippon Telegraph & Telephone Public Corp. [*Telecommunications*] (IAA)
NTT Pupl Corp... Nippon Telegraph and Telephone Public Corp. (SAUS)
NTTR........ Naval Torpedo Testing Range
NTTR........ Nontactical Telecommunications Requirement [*Army*] (AABC)
NTTR........ Raiatea/Uturoa [*French Polynesia*] [*ICAO location identifier*] (ICLI)
NTTRL....... National Tissue Typing Reference Laboratory (PDAA)
NTTS........ National Technology Transfer Center
NTTS........ Northern Territory Teaching Service (SAUS)
NTTT......... Tahiti [*French Polynesia*] [*ICAO location identifier*] (ICLI)
NTTTTI...... National Truck Tank and Trailer Tank Institute [*Later, Tank Conference of the Truck Trailer Manufacturers Association*]
NTTX........ Mururoa [*French Polynesia*] [*ICAO location identifier*] (ICLI)
NTU.......... National Taxpayers Union (EA)
NTU.......... National Technological University [*Fort Collins, CO*]
NTU.......... National Tenants Union [*Defunct*] (EA)
NTU.......... National Turbidity Units [*Environment term*] (EGA)
NTU.......... Naval Training Unit
NTU.......... Navigation Training Unit (SAUS)
NTU.......... Navy Toxicology Unit
NTU.......... Nephelometric Turbidity Unit [*Analytical chemistry*]
NTU.......... Network Terminating [*or Termination*] Unit
NTU.......... New Threat Upgrade [*Military*] (CAAL)
NTU.......... Nishi Tokyo University (SAUS)
NTU.......... Nonimmune Transfer Utensil [*i.e., spoon*] [*Slang*]
NTU.......... Nordisk Trafikskoleunion [*Nordic Union of Motor Schools Associations - NUMSA*] [*Finland*] (EAIO)
NTU.......... Normal Trading Unit
NTU.......... Not Taken Up
NTU.......... Nuclear Training Unit (MCD)
NTU.......... Number of Transfer Units
NTU.......... Oceana, VA [*Location identifier*] [*FAA*] (FAAL)
NTUC........ National Trades Union Congress (NADA)
NTUC........ National Trade Union Congress [*Singapore*]
NTUC........ National Trade Union Council [*Hungary*]
NTUC........ National Trade Union Council for Human Rights (EA)
NTUC........ Nigerian Trade Union Congress
NTUC........ Nyasaland Trade Union Congress
NTuc......... Tuckahoe Public Library, Tuckahoe, NY [*Library symbol*] [*Library of Congress*] (LCLS)
NTucW....... Westchester County Historical Society, Tuckahoe, NY [*Library symbol*] [*Library of Congress*] (LCLS)
NTULC....... Negro Trade Union Leadership Council
NTuPSC..... Sunmount Development Center, Staff Library, Tupper Lake, NY [*Library symbol*] [*Library of Congress*] (LCLS)
NTUV........ Vahitahi [*French Polynesia*] [*ICAO location identifier*] (ICLI)
NTuxp........ Tuxedo Park Library, Tuxedo Park, NY [*Library symbol*] [*Library of Congress*] (LCLS)
NTuxpI....... International Paper Co., Corporate Research and Development Division, Technical Information Center, Tuxedo Park, NY [*Library symbol*] [*Library of Congress*] (LCLS)
NTV.......... Nerve Tissue Vaccine [*Medicine*] (DMAA)
NTV.......... Nervous Tissue Vaccine (AAMN)
NTV.......... Neurotransmitter Vesicle [*Medicine*] (MELL)
NTV.......... Nippon Television Network Corp. [*Japan*]
NTV.......... Nonlinear Thickness Variation (SAUS)
NTV.......... Nontactical Vehicle [*Army*]
NTV.......... NTV Oil Services Industries, Inc. [*Vancouver Stock Exchange symbol*]
NTVA........ Nondeterministic Time Variant Automation [*Mathematics*] (IAA)
NTVEI........ New Technical and Vocational Education Initiative (AIE)
NTVES....... Northern Territory Voluntary Euthanasia Society (SAUS)
NTVLRO..... National Television Licensing and Records Office [*British*]
NTVS........ Navy Television System
NTVT........ Non-Toxic Vinyl Tubing
NTVU........ National Trust Volunteer Unit [*British*] (EAIO)
NTW.......... Navigator Training Wing [*Military*]
NTW.......... Navy Theater Wide
NTW.......... Non-Pressure Thermit Welding (PDAA)
NTW.......... Normal Tool Wear (SAUS)
NTW.......... Nose, Tail, Waist [*Aviation*]
NTW.......... Not to Worry (SAUS)
NTWA........ National Trust of Western Australia
NTWA........ National Turf Writers Association (EA)
NtwExp...... Network Express, Inc. [*Associated Press*] (SAG)
NTWH........ National Theatre Workshop of the Handicapped (EA)
NTWISTDG... Notwithstanding (SAUS)
NTWK........ Network (MSA)
NTWK........ Network Long Distance [*NASDAQ symbol*] (TTSB)
NTWK........ Network Long Distance, Inc. [*NASDAQ symbol*] (SAG)
NtwkC........ Network Connection, Inc. [*Associated Press*] (SAG)
NtwkCn...... Network Connection, Inc. [*Associated Press*] (SAG)
NtwkEq...... Network Equipment Technologies, Inc. [*Associated Press*] (SAG)
NtwkG........ Network General Corp. [*Associated Press*] (SAG)
NtwkLng.... Network Long Distance, Inc. [*Associated Press*] (SAG)
NtwkPeri.... Network Periphrals, Inc. [*Associated Press*] (SAG)
NtwkSix..... Network Six, Inc. [*Associated Press*] (SAG)
NtWnLf...... National Western Life Insurance Co. [*Associated Press*] (SAG)
NTWR........ New Threat Warning Receiver (ACAE)
NTWRK...... Network
NTWRKNG... Networking
NTWS........ New Threat Warning System [*Military*]
NTWS........ Nontrack while Scan
NtWst........ National Westminster Bank Ltd. [*Associated Press*] (SAG)
NtWstmin... National Westminster Bank Ltd. [*Associated Press*] (SAG)
nt wt......... Net Weight (WDAA)
NT WT....... Net Weight
NTX.......... Naltrexone [*Medicine*] (MELL)
NTX.......... National Teletypewriter Exchange (IAA)
NTX.......... Naval Teletypewriter Exchange [*Formerly, NTE*]
NTX.......... Neonatal Thymectomy [*Medicine*]
NTX.......... Networking and Expansion [*Computer science*] (PCM)
NTX.......... Northern Air Service, Inc. [*ICAO designator*] (FAAC)
NTX.......... Notorious [*Telegraphy*] (PCTE)
NTX.......... Nuveen Texas Quality Income [*NYSE symbol*] (SPSG)
NTX.......... Nuveen TX Qual Income Muni [*NYSE symbol*] (TTSB)
NTXQI....... Nuveen Texas Quality Income [*Associated Press*] (SAG)
NTY.......... Northerly [*Telegraphy*] (PCTE)
NTY.......... Not This Year (SAUS)
NTY.......... Sun City [*South Africa*] [*Airport symbol*] (OAG)
N-type....... Jungian intuitive type (SAUS)
NT YT....... Not Yet (SAUS)
NTZ.......... Indstrie Natuzzi ADS [*NYSE symbol*] (TTSB)
NTZ.......... Industrie Natuzzi [*NYSE symbol*] (SPSG)
NTZ.......... Iraq-Saudi Arabia Neutral Zone [*ANSI three-letter standard code*] (CNC)
NTZ.......... National Taconite [*Federal Railroad Administration identification code*]
NTZ.......... Neuber, Teschen and Zimmer [*Auto parts*]
NTZ.......... Nitazoxanide [*Medicine*] (TAD)
NTZ.......... Normal Transformation Zone (DMAA)
NTZ.......... Northern Transgressive Zone [*Geology*]
NTZ.......... North Temperate Zone [*Planet Jupiter*]
NTZ.......... No Transgression Zone (SAUS)
NU........... Astronomy Department Library, Nanjing University (SAUS)
NU........... Lipnur [*Indonesia*] [*ICAO aircraft manufacturer identifier*] (ICAO)
NU........... Nachalnik Uprovlenia [*Chief of Directorate*] [*Soviet military rank*]
NU........... Name Unknown
nU........... Nanounit [*One billionth of a standard unit*]
NU........... National Union (EA)
NU........... National Unity Party [*British*] [*Political party*]
NU........... NATO Unclassified (NATG)
NU........... Natural Uranium (ODA)
nu........... Nauru [*MARC country of publication code*] [*Library of Congress*] (LCCP)
NU........... Nebraska University (MCD)
NU........... Nebraska Unofficial Reports [*A publication*] (DLA)
NU........... Neurologically Unique
NU........... Neurology (DAVI)
NU........... Neu-Ulm [*German license plate city code*]
NU........... New [*Telegraphy*] (PCTE)
NU........... New Ulm [*Diocesan abbreviation*] [*Minnesota*] (TOCD)
NU........... New Uses [*Research test*] [*Psychology*]
Nu........... Ngultrum [*Monetary unit*] [*Bhutan*] (BARN)
NU........... Nihon University (SAUS)
NU........... Niigata University (SAUS)
NU........... Niue [*ANSI two-letter standard code*] (CNC)
NU........... Nonuniform (SAUS)
NU........... Northeast Utilities [*NYSE symbol*] (SPSG)
NU........... Northern Union [*Rugby*] [*British*] (DAS)
NU........... Northrop Unit [*Of hydrolytic enzyme activity*]
NU........... North Up [*Automotive engineering*]
NU........... Norwich Union (WDAA)
NU........... Norwich University (SAUS)
NU........... Nose Up [*Aviation*]
NU........... Nothing Unsatisfactory (MHDB)
NU........... Not Used
NU........... No Umbra (SAUS)
Nu........... Nucleolus [*Cytology*]
Nu........... Nucleophile
nu........... Nude [*Mouse*] [*Medicine*] (DMAA)
NU........... Nu-Gro Corp. [*Toronto Stock Exchange symbol*]
NU........... Nullified Unpostable [*Computer science*]
Nu........... Numbers [*Old Testament book*] (BJA)
NU........... Number Unobtainable [*Telecommunications*]

Nu............ Nusselt Number [*IUPAC*]
NU............ Southwest Airlines [*ICAO designator*] (AD)
NU0B........ Numeric 0 Bit (SAUS)
NU1B........ Numeric 1 Bit (SAUS)
NUA.......... Nations Unies des Animaux [*United Animal Nations - UAN*] (EA)
NUA.......... Net Unrealized Appreciation Tax
NUA.......... Network User Address
NUA.......... Network Users Association [*Defunct*] (EA)
NUA.......... Nonylundecyladipat (SAUS)
NUA.......... Not Under the Act
NUA.......... Nuclear Agency [*Army*]
NUA.......... Nuna Air AS [*Denmark*] [*ICAO designator*] (FAAC)
NUAA........ NSW Users and AIDS Association (SAUS)
NUAAW...... National Union of Agricultural and Allied Workers [*British*]
NUABA...... National United Affiliated Beverage Association (EA)
NUAC........ National Urban Affairs Council (EA)
NUAC........ National Urban Agriculture Council [*Association*] (EA)
NUAD........ Nucleus Average Optical Density [*Microscopy*]
NUADC...... National Underwater Accident Data Center
NUAF Material... Non-Urea-Adduct-Forming Material (SAUS)
NUAH........ Nutrition and Health (SAUS)
NU AMERICA PAC... NU AMERICA PAC [*Washington, DC*] (PACS)
NUANS...... Newly Upgraded Automated Name Search (SAUS)
NUAT........ Nordisk Union for Alkoholfri Trafikk [*Scandinavian Union for Non-Alcoholic Traffic - SUNAT*] (EA)
NUATFAC... Nordiska Unionen for Arbetsledare, Tekniska Funktionarer och andra Chefer [*Nordic Confederation of Supervisors, Technicians and Other Managers*] (EAIO)
NUB.......... National Union of Busmen [*British*]
NUB.......... Navy Uniform Board (DNAB)
NUB.......... Net Units Billed (TIMI)
NUB.......... Northumberland Mines Ltd. [*Toronto Stock Exchange symbol*]
NUB.......... North University Building (SAUS)
Nub.......... Nubes [*Clouds*] [*of Aristophanes*] [*Classical studies*] (OCD)
nub.......... Nubian [*MARC language code*] [*Library of Congress*] (LCCP)
NUB.......... Nubira [*NCIC car model code*]
NUBA........ National UHF [*Ultrahigh Frequency*] Broadcasters Association (EA)
NUBC........ National Uniform-Billing Committee [*Insurance*] (DAVI)
NUBE........ National Union of Bank Employees [*Later, Banking, Insurance, and Finance Union*] (DCTA)
NUBF........ National Union of British Fishermen
NUBIC....... Nuclear Bunkered Instrumentation Center (MCD)
NUBICWOPS... Nuclear, Biological, and Chemical Warfare Operations [*Military*]
NUBLU...... New Basic Logic Unit [*Computer science*] (MHDI)
NUBOMCWKT... National Union of Blastfurnacemen, Ore Miners, Coke Workers, and Kindred Trades [*British*] (DCTA)
NUBS........ National Unemployment Benefit System [*Department of Health and Social Security*] [*British*]
NUBSO...... National Union of Boot and Shoe Operatives [*British*]
NUBTC...... National Union of Boot Top Cutters [*British*]
NUC.......... National Underseas Research Center (CARB)
NUC.......... National Unification Council [*Philippines*] [*Political party*] (FEA)
NUC.......... National Union Catalog: Pre-1956 Imprints [*A publication*]
NUC.......... National Union of Carriers [*British*]
NUC.......... National University Consortium for Telecommunications in Teaching (EA)
NUC.......... National Urban Coalition (EA)
NUC.......... Naval Undersea Center [*Later, NOSC*] (MCD)
NUC.......... Naval Undersea Research and Development Center [*Marine science*] (OSRA)
NUC.......... Navy Unit Commendation [*Military decoration*]
NUC.......... Neutral Unit of Construction (TVEL)
NUC.......... New University Conference
NUC.......... Nipissing University College (SAUS)
NUC.......... Nonspecific Ulcerative Colitis [*Medicine*] (MELL)
NUC.......... Non-Uniformity Compensation (ACAE)
NUC.......... Non-Uniformity Correction
NUC.......... Not Under Command (SAUS)
NUC.......... Not Under Control (SAUS)
nuc........... Nuclear (MILB)
NUC.......... Nuclear
NUC.......... Nucleated
Nuc........... [*A*] Nucleoside [*Also, N*]
NUC.......... Nucleus (WDAA)
NUC.......... Nucorr Petroleums Ltd. [*Toronto Stock Exchange symbol*]
NUC.......... Nulliparous Uterine Cervix [*Medicine*] (MELL)
NUC.......... Nuveen California Quality Income Municipal [*NYSE symbol*] (SPSG)
NUC.......... Nuveen CA Qual Income Muni [*NYSE symbol*] (TTSB)
NUC.......... San Clemente Island, CA [*Location identifier*] [*FAA*] (FAAL)
NUC.......... Sodium Urate Crystal [*Medicine*] (EDAA)
NUCA........ National Utility Contractors' Association (EA)
NUCAA...... National United Church Association of America (EA)
NUCAL...... National Union Catalog Author List
NUCAP...... Nuclear Cannon Projectile [*Army*]
NUCAP...... Nuclear Capabilities Data Base (SAUS)
NUCAP...... Nuclear Capability [*Military*]
NUCAP...... Nuclear Capability Report (CINC)
Nucaps...... National Union of Civil and Public Servants [*British*] (DBA)
Nu-car Prep... New-car Preparation (SAUS)
NUCAS...... Nuclear Authentication System
NUCAW...... National Union of Clerks and Administrative Workers [*British*]
NUCBO...... National Uniform Certification of Building Operators (EA)
NUCC........ North Up Cursor Centered [*Automotive engineering*]
NUCCA...... National Upper Cervical Chiropractic Association (EA)
NUCD........ National Union for Christian Democrats (Philippines) [*Political party*] (PSAP)
NUCD........ Nuclear Deployment (SAUS)
NUCDEF..... Nuclear Defense (AABC)
NUCDETS... Nuclear Detonation Detection and Reporting System (AABC)
NUCDSK.... New Cell Disk (SAUS)
Nuc E........ Nuclear Engineer
NUCEA...... National University Continuing Education Association (EA)
NUCEWA.... Nuclear Weapons Availability (SAUS)
NUCEX...... Nuclear Exercise [*Also, NUKEX*] (NVT)
NUCFO...... Nuclear Force Posture
NUCH........ Nucha [*Nape of the Neck*] [*Latin*] (ROG)
NUCIA....... National Union of Cooperative Insurance Agents [*British*]
NUCINT..... Nuclear Intelligence (MCD)
Nuci Sci Technol... Nuclear Science and Technology (SAUS)
NUCISE...... National Union of Cooperative Insurance Society Employees [*British*]
NUCL........ Nuclear
NUCL........ Nucleus
Nucl Austral Bull... Nuclear Australia Bulletin (SAUS)
Nuc L Bull... Nuclear Law Bulletin [*A publication*] (ILCA)
Nucl Data... Nuclear Data (SAUS)
NUCLE....... Nuclear
Nuclear Reg Rep (CCH)... Nuclear Regulation Reports (Commerce Clearing House) [*A publication*] (DLA)
Nucl Eng.... Nuclear Engineer [*A publication*] (CABS)
Nucl Eng Int... Nuclear Engineering International [*A publication*] (CABS)
Nucl Engng&Des... Nuclear Engineering and Design (SAUS)
NUCLENOR... Controles Nucleares del Norte, SA [*Spain*]
Nucl Eur.... Nuclear Europe (SAUS)
NUCLEX..... International Nuclear Industrial Fair and Technical Meeting (SAUS)
NUCLEX..... Nuclear Industries Exhibition
NUCLEX..... Nuclear Loadout Exercise [*Military*] (NVT)
Nucl Fusion... Nuclear Fusion [*A publication*] (CABS)
Nucl Fusion Plasma Phys... Nuclear Fusion and Plasma Physics (SAUS)
Nucl Instrum... Nuclear Instrumentation (SAUS)
Nucl Instrum Methods A... Nuclear Instruments and Methods A (SAUS)
Nucl Instrum Methods B... Nuclear Instruments and Methods B (SAUS)
Nucl Mater Manage... Nuclear Materials Management (SAUS)
Nucl News... Nuclear News (SAUS)
Nucl Phys... Nuclear Physics (MEC)
Nucl Prof... Nuclear Professional (SAUS)
Nucl Res Cent... Nuclear Research Center (SAUS)
Nucl Sci Appl B Phys Sci... Nuclear Science and Applications, Series B: Physical Sciences (SAUS)
Nucl Sci Appl Ser A... Nuclear Science and Applications. Series A. Biological Science (SAUS)
Nucl Sci Eng... Nuclear Science and Engineering [*A publication*] (CABS)
Nucl Tech... Nuclear Techniques (SAUS)
Nucl Technol... Nuclear Technology [*A publication*] (CABS)
Nucl Tracks Methods Instrum and Appl... Nuclear Tracks. Methods, Instruments and Applications (SAUS)
NUCM........ North Up Cursor Moving [*Automotive engineering*]
NUCM........ Nuclear Metals [*NASDAQ symbol*] (TTSB)
NUCM........ Nuclear Metals, Inc. [*NASDAQ symbol*] (NQ)
NUCMATTS... Nuclear Materials Transportation Tracking System (SAUS)
NUCMC...... National Union Catalog of Manuscript Collections [*Library of Congress*]
NucMet...... Nuclear Metals, Inc. [*Associated Press*] (SAG)
NUCMUN.... Nuclear Munitions (RDA)
NUCO........ National Union of Certified Officers [*British*]
NUCO........ NuCo2 Inc. [*NASDAQ symbol*] (TTSB)
NUCO........ Nucorp, Inc. (SAUS)
NUCO........ Numerical Code (NATG)
NUCO........ Numerical Coding (SAUS)
NuCo2....... NuCo2, Inc. [*Associated Press*] (SAG)
NUCOINS... Nutrition Consumer Information System (SAUS)
NUCOL...... Numerical Control Language [*Computer science*] (PDAA)
NUCOM..... Nuclear Effects on Joint Force Communications (MCD)
NUCOM..... Numerical Contouring Mechanism
NUCOR...... Nuclear Corporation (SAUS)
NUCOR...... Nuclear Development Corporation of South Africa (SAUS)
Nucor........ Nucor Corp. [*Associated Press*] (SAG)
NUCP........ National Union of Czechoslovak Protestants in America and Canada [*Defunct*] (EA)
NUCP........ New Century Entertainment Corp. (SAUS)
NUCP........ New Visions Entertainment Corp. [*NASDAQ symbol*] (COMM)
NUC PHY... Nuclear Physics (WDAA)
NUCPS...... National Union of Civil and Public Servants [*British*]
NUCPWR.... Nuclear Powered (NVT)
NucReaOpBasBad... Nuclear Reactor Operator, Basic Badge [*Military decoration*] (AABC)
NucReaOpFCBad... Nuclear Reactor Operator, First-Class Badge [*Military decoration*] (AABC)
NucReaOpSCBad... Nuclear Reactor Operator, Second-Class Badge [*Military decoration*] (AABC)
NucReaOpSftSupvBad... Nuclear Reactor Operator, Shift Supervisor Badge [*Military decoration*] (AABC)
Nuc Reg Com... Nuclear Regulatory Commission (SAUS)
NUCREP..... Nuclear Damage Report (AABC)
NUCS........ National Union of Christian Schools [*Later, CSI*] (EA)
NUCS........ National Union of Club Stewards [*British*] (DBA)
NUCSAM.... Nuclear Surface-to-Air Missile (NVT)
NucSciAb... Nuclear Science Abstracts (SAUS)
NUCSE...... National Union of Czechoslovak Students in Exile (EA)

NUCSEQ..... Nucleotide Sequencing Search System [*NIH/EPA Chemical Information System*] [*Database*]
NUCSTAT... Nuclear Operational Status (SAUS)
NUCSTAT... Nuclear Operational Status Report (NATG)
NUCUA...... National Union of Conservative and Unionists Associations (ODA)
NUCUAA.... National United Church Ushers Association of America (EA)
NUCURES... Northeastern University Center for Urban and Regional Economic Studies [*Research center*] (RCD)
NUCWA...... Nuclear Weapons Accounting (MCD)
NUCWAL.... Nuclear Weapons Allocation Logistics (SAUS)
NUCWAR.... Nuclear War
NUCWARN... Nuclear Warning Message [*Military*] (ADDR)
NUCWEP.... Nuclear Weapons (SAUS)
NUCWEPS... Nuclear Weapons Employment Course [*Military*] (POLM)
NUCWPN.... Nuclear Weapon (AABC)
NUCWPNSTRACEN... Nuclear Weapons Training Center
NUCX........ Nucor Steel [*Private rail car owner code*]
NUCY........ New Century Bank Corp. (SAUS)
NUD......... Adak, AK [*Location identifier*] [*FAA*] (FAAL)
NUD......... En Nahud [*Sudan*] [*Airport symbol*] (AD)
NUD......... National Union of the Deaf [*British*]
NUD......... Naval Unit Disseminator (RDA)
NUD......... Nebraska University Disease or N. Underdahl Disease [*A disease of swine named both for the place where it was originally identified and for the person who isolated the causative agent*]
NUD......... Ngala [*Language symbol*] (ETLW)
NUD......... Nonulcer Dyspepsia [*Gastroenterology*] (DAVI)
NUD......... Non-Update (SAUS)
nud.......... nudism (SAUS)
nud.......... nudist (SAUS)
NUDA & GO... National Union of Domestic Appliances and General Operatives [*British*] (DBA)
NUDAC...... Nuclear Data Center (IAA)
NUDAGMW... National Union of Domestic Appliance and General Metal-Workers [*British*] (DCTA)
NUDAGO.... National Union of Domestic Appliances & General Operatives (WDAA)
NUDAP...... Nuclear Detonating Data Points (MCD)
NUDAT...... Nuclear Data [*Database*] (GDD)
NUDAW...... National Union of Shop Distributive and Allied Workers [*British*]
NUDBTW.... National Union of Dyers, Bleachers, and Textile Workers [*British*] (DCTA)
NUDET...... Nuclear Detection (MCD)
NUDET...... Nuclear Detonation (COE)
NUDET...... Nuclear Detonation Evaluation Technique (MCD)
NUDET Rpt... Nuclear Detonation Report (SAUS)
NUDETS..... Nuclear Detection and Reporting System
NUDETS..... Nuclear Detection System (SAUS)
NUDETS..... Nuclear Detonation Detection and Reporting System
NUDETS..... Nuclear Detonation Reporting System (SAUS)
NUDIA....... Nutrio et Dieta. European Review of Nutrition and Dietetics (SAUS)
NUDO........ National United Democratic Organization [*Namibia*] [*Political party*] (PPW)
NUDOR...... Numerical Data Processor (SAUS)
NUDORE.... Nuclear Doctrine Organization and Equipment (MCD)
NUDWSS.... National Union of Docks, Wharves, and Shipping Staffs [*British*]
NUDYE...... ND Resources, Inc. [*NASDAQ symbol*] (COMM)
NUE.......... Net Units Entered (TIMI)
NUE.......... Nitrogen Utilization Efficiency [*Ecology*]
NUE.......... Niue [*Niue Island*] [*Seismograph station code, US Geological Survey*] (SEIS)
NUE.......... Nucor Corp. [*NYSE symbol*] (SPSG)
NUE.......... Nuremberg [*Germany*] [*Airport symbol*] (OAG)
NUEA........ National University Extension Association [*Later, NUCEA*] (EA)
NUEL........ Nuell Coach Corporation [*NCIC trailer make code*]
NUELA....... Nuevo Laredo, TM [*American Association of Railroads railroad junction routing code*]
NUERA...... Nuclear Extended Range Aircraft [*Proposed*] [*Air Force*]
NUESNA..... National Union of Eritrean Students - North America (EA)
NUET........ National Union of Elementary Teachers [*British*]
NuevEn...... Nuevo Energy Co. [*Associated Press*] (SAG)
NUEW........ National Union of Eritrean Women - North America (EA)
NUEXCO..... Nuclear Exchange Corp. (SAUS)
NUF.......... National Ulcer Foundation (EA)
NUF.......... National Unifying Force [*Zimbabwe*] [*Political party*] (PPW)
NUF.......... National Union of Firemen [*British*] (DAS)
NUF.......... National Unity Front [*Poland*] [*Political party*] (PPW)
NUF.......... National Urban Fellows (EA)
NUF.......... Natural Uranium Fuel
NUF.......... Noise Ulterior Flux (SAUS)
NUF.......... Nonwoven Unidirectional-glass Fibre (SAUS)
NUF.......... Nordisk Urologisk Forening [*Scandinavian Association of Urology - SAU*] (EAIO)
NUF.......... Nuveen Florida Quality Income Municipal [*NYSE symbol*] (SPSG)
NUF.......... Nuveen FL Qual Income Muni [*NYSE symbol*] (TTSB)
NUFAC....... Nuclear Weapons Planning Factors for Land Combat Forces (SAUS)
NUFAM....... Nuclear Fire Planning and Assessment Model (MCD)
NUFAS....... NATO UHF Frequency Assignment System (SAUS)
NUFCOR.... Nuclear Fuels Corp. (SAUS)
NUFCW...... National Union of Funeral and Cemetery Workers [*British*] (BI)
NUFD........ Naval Unit, Fort Detrick [*Maryland*]
NUFDC...... Northgate Universal Floppy Drive Controller [*Computer science*]
NUFGW..... National Union of Flint Glassworkers [*British*] (DBA)
NUFI......... National Unfinished Furniture Institute [*Defunct*] (EA)
Nufi.......... Nuffield College, Oxford (SAUS)
NUFLAT..... National Union of Footwear, Leather, and Allied Trades [*British*] (DCTA)
NUFLV....... National United Front for the Liberation of Vietnam (EA)
NUFO........ New Focus [*NASDAQ symbol*]
NUFON...... Northern UFO Network [*British*]
NUFP........ Not Used for Production (AAG)
NUFP........ Number of Uncorrected Flight Plans (SAA)
NUFRONLIV... National United Front for the Liberation of Vietnam (EA)
NUFS........ National United Front of Somalia [*Political party*] (EY)
NUFS........ National Utility Financial Statement Model [*Department of Energy*] (GFGA)
NUFSO...... National Union of Funeral Service Operatives [*British*] (DI)
NUFTIC...... Nuclear Fuels Technology Information Center (DIT)
NUFTO...... National Union of Furniture Trade Operatives [*British*]
NUFUCO.... Nuclear Fuel Cost (PDAA)
NUG......... Federation of NCR [*NCR Corp.*] User Groups (EA)
NUG......... National Union of Glovers [*British*]
NUG......... Necrotizing Ulcerative Gingivitis [*Dentistry*]
NUG......... Nonutility Generator
nug.......... nuggar (SAUS)
NUGATT..... Network Users Group AT&T [*Communications term*] (DCT)
NUGMW..... National Union of General and Municipal Workers [*British*]
NUGO........ Nugget Oil Corp. (SAUS)
NUGP........ Nominal Unit Ground Pressure (SAUS)
NUGS........ Nonutility Generating Source
NUGSAT..... National Union of Gold, Silver, and Allied Trades [*British*] (DCTA)
NUGT........ Nugget Exploration, Inc. (SAUS)
NUH......... National Union for the Homeless (EA)
NUH......... Nu Horizons Electronics Corp. [*AMEX symbol*] (COMM)
NUHADI..... Nuclear Helicopter Air Density Indicating [*System*] [*Army*]
NUHC........ Nu Horizons Electronics [*NASDAQ symbol*] (TTSB)
NUHC........ Nu-Horizons Electronics Corp. [*NASDAQ symbol*] (SAG)
NUHELI...... Nuclear Helicopter Lift Indicator (KSC)
NUHKW..... National Union of Hosiery and Knitwear Workers [*British*] (DCTA)
NuHoriz..... Nu-Horizons Electronics Corp. [*Associated Press*] (SAG)
NUHS........ New Utrecht High School (SAUS)
NUI.......... National University of Ireland
NUI.......... NetWare Users International
NUI.......... Networks Unlimited, Inc. [*Defunct*] (EA)
NUI.......... Network User Identifier [*or Identification*] [*Password*]
NUI.......... Norwegian Underwater Institute (SAUS)
NUI.......... Notebook User Interface [*Penpoint*] [*Computer science*]
NUI.......... Novell Users International [*Association*] (EA)
NUI.......... NUI Corp. [*NYSE symbol*] (SPSG)
NUI.......... Nuiqsut [*Alaska*] [*Airport symbol*] (OAG)
NUI.......... Number User Identification (DMAA)
NUI.......... Patuxent River, MD [*Location identifier*] [*FAA*] (FAAL)
NUIA........ National United Italian Associations (EA)
NUIC........ National Urban Indian Council (EA)
NUIR........ National Union for Independence and Revolution [*Chad*] [*Political party*]
NUIS........ National Union of Iraqi Students [*British*] (DI)
NUIS........ Navy Unit Identification System (NVT)
NUIU........ New University Industrial Unit [*New University of Ulster*] [*Research center*] [*British*]
NUIW........ National Union of Insurance Workers [*British*] (DCTA)
NUJ.......... National Union of Journalists [*British*]
NUJ.......... Nuveen New Jersey Quality Income Municipal (SAUS)
NUJMB...... Northern Universities Joint Matriculation Board (AIE)
NUK......... Nukutavake [*French Polynesia*] [*Airport symbol*] (OAG)
NUKE........ Nuclear
nuke leak... nuclear radioactive leak (SAUS)
NUKES...... Nuclear Explosives (SAUS)
NUKEX...... Nuclear Exercise [*Also, NUCEX*] (NVT)
NUKFAT..... National Union of Knitwear, Footwear & Apparel Trades (WDAA)
NUKO....... Nuko Information Sys [*NASDAQ symbol*] (TTSB)
NUKO....... Nuko Information Systems, Inc. [*NASDAQ symbol*] (SAG)
NukoInfo.... Nuko Information Systems Inc. [*Associated Press*] (SAG)
NuKote...... Nu-Kote Holding, Inc. [*Associated Press*] (SAG)
NUL.......... Dummy Device (SAUS)
NUL.......... National and University Library [*Israel*] (BJA)
NUL.......... National Union for Liberation [*Philippines*] [*Political party*] (PPW)
NUL.......... National Urban League (EA)
NUL.......... New Universal Library [*A publication*]
NUL.......... New Upper Lateral [*Botany*]
NUL.......... Nihon University [*UTLAS symbol*]
NUL.......... No Device (SAUS)
NUL.......... Non-GSE [*Ground Support Equipment*] Utilization List [*NASA*] (NASA)
NUL.......... Northwestern University Library (SAUS)
NUL.......... Nothing [*ACHII code*] [*Communications term*] [*Used as a fill character in some communications formats*] (DCT)
NUL.......... No Upper Limit (MHDW)
NUL.......... Nu-Lady Gold Mines [*Vancouver Stock Exchange symbol*]
NUL.......... Nulato [*Alaska*] [*Airport symbol*] (OAG)
NUL.......... Null (OSI)
NUL.......... Null Character [*Keyboard*] [*Computer science*]
NULAC...... Nuclear Liquid Air Cycle Engine
NULACE.... Nuclear Liquid Air Cycle Engine
NULBA...... National United Licensees Beverage Association [*Later, NUABA*] (EA)
NULC........ National Union of Liberal Clubs [*British*] (DBA)
NULCAIS... Northwestern University Library Computer-Assisted Information Service (OLDSS)

NULCW...... National Union of Lift and Crane Workers [*British*]
NULEOA...... National United Law Enforcement Officers Association (EA)
NULF........ National United Liberation Front [*Myanmar*] [*Political party*] (FEA)
NULF........ Nullify (SAUS)
NULFG...... Nullifying (SAUS)
NULFN...... Nullification (SAUS)
nullies....... nullifiers (SAUS)
nullip........ Nullipara [*obstetrics*] (DAVI)
NULMW..... National Union of Lock and Metal Workers [*British*] (DCTA)
NULO........ NASA Unmanned Launch Operations (MCD)
NULO........ National Union of Labour Organisers [*British*] (DBA)
NULOR...... Neuron Location and Ranging
NULS........ National Underwater Laboratory System [*Marine science*] (MSC)
NULS........ Net Unit-Load Size (MHDB)
NULU........ New Library Utility
NULU........ Uniline Naviera Universal [*Intermodal shipping container symbol*] (TVRC)
NUM......... Error in Use of Numbers [*Used in correcting manuscripts, etc.*]
NUM......... National Union of Mineworkers [*South Africa*]
NUM......... National Unity Movement [*Sierra Leone*] [*Political party*] (EY)
NUM......... New Ulster Movement (SAUS)
Num......... Numa [*of Plutarch*] [*Classical studies*] (OCD)
NUM......... Numadu [*Japan*] [*Seismograph station code, US Geological Survey*] [*Closed*] (SEIS)
NUM......... Number [*or Numerator, or Numeric*]
NUM......... Numbering (SAUS)
Num......... Numbers [*Old Testament book*]
num.......... Numeral (MIST)
NUM......... Numeral [*or Numerical*]
Num......... Numerator (SAUS)
NUM......... Numerics (SAUS)
NUM......... Numerologist (SAUS)
num.......... numerology (SAUS)
NUM......... Nurse Unit Manager
NUM......... Nuveen Michigan Quality Income Municipal [*NYSE symbol*] (SPSG)
NUM......... Nuveen MI Qual Income Muni [*NYSE symbol*] (TTSB)
NUMA....... National Underwater and Marine Agency (MCD)
NUMA....... Nonuniform - Memory - Access [*Computer science*]
NUMA....... Non Uniform Memory Address (SAUS)
NUMA....... Non-Uniform Memory Architecture (SAUS)
NUMA....... Nuclear Mitotic Apparatus [*Medicine*] (DMAA)
NUMAC...... Northumbrian Universities Multiple Access Computer (NITA)
Numac....... Numac Energy [*Associated Press*] (SAG)
NUMAC...... Numac Oil & Gas Ltd. (SAUS)
Num Adj.... Numeral Adjective (SAUS)
NUMAR..... Nuclear Magnetic Resonance [*Also, NMR*]
Numar....... Numar Corp. [*Associated Press*] (SAG)
NUMARC.... Nuclear Management and Resources Council (EA)
NUMARCOM... Nuclear Power for Marine Purposes Committee (MCD)
NUMAS...... Numerical Multifactor Assessment System (ADA)
NUMAST.... National Union of Marine Aviation and Shipping Transport [*British*]
NUMB....... Numbered
Numb........ Numbers [*Old Testament book*]
NUMBR..... Number (DAVI)
NUMC....... Newcastle University Mountaineering Club [*Australia*]
NUMD....... Numbered [*Telegraphy*] (PCTE)
NUMD....... Numed Home Health Care, Inc. [*NASDAQ symbol*] (SAG)
Numd........ Numed Home Health Care, Inc. [*Associated Press*] (SAG)
NUMD....... NuMED Home Hlth Care [*NASDAQ symbol*] (TTSB)
NUMDW..... NuMED Home Health Care Wrrt [*NASDAQ symbol*] (TTSB)
NUME....... Numerica Financial Corp. [*NASDAQ symbol*] (COMM)
NUME....... Numerical Methods in Engineering (SAUS)
NUMEC...... Nuclear Materials & Equipment Corp.
NUMEC...... Nuclear Uranium Materials and Equipment Corp. (GAAI)
Numed....... Numed Home Health Care, Inc. [*Associated Press*] (SAG)
NumedH..... Numed Home Health Care, Inc. [*Associated Press*] (SAG)
NUMEPS.... Numeric Meta Language Processing System (PDAA)
Numer....... Numerative (SAUS)
NUMERALS... Numerical Analysis System (BUR)
Numerex.... Numerex Corp. [*Associated Press*] (SAG)
Numer Heat Transf A... Numerical Heat Transfer A (SAUS)
Numer Heat Transf B... Numerical Heat Transfer B (SAUS)
NUMERIS... French ISDN Network (SAUS)
Numer Methods Partial Diff Equations... Numerical Methods for Partial Differential Equations (SAUS)
NUMETA.... Numerical Methods in Engineering-Theory and Applications (SAUS)
NUMG....... Numbering [*Telegraphy*] (PCTE)
NuMI........ Neutrinos at the Main Injector [*Fermilab*]
Numi........ Numismatic (DIAR)
Numid....... Numidian
NUMIS...... Navy Uniform Management Information System
NUMIS...... Northwestern University Multislice and Imaging System (SAUS)
Numis....... Numismatic (SAUS)
NUMIS...... Numismatics
NUMISM.... Numismatics
NumJ........ Numismatic Journal [*A publication*] (ABAR)
Num Lock... Numeric Lock [*Computer science*]
NUMM....... National Union of Masters and Mates [*British*]
NUMMA..... Nuclear Materials Management (SAUS)
NUMMI..... New United Motor Manufacturing, Inc. [*Joint venture of Toyota Motor Corp . and General Motors Corp.*]
NUMPES.... Numeric Meta-Language Processing System (SAUS)
NUMR....... Numar Corp. [*NASDAQ symbol*] (SAG)
NumR....... Numbers Rabbah
NUMR....... Numerex Corp. [*NASDAQ symbol*] (COMM)
NUMRUL.... Commonwealth Statutory Rules: Numbered (SAUS)
NUMS....... Northern University Medical School [*Medicine*] (EDAA)
NUMS....... Nuclear Materials Security (NRCH)
NUMS....... Numbers [*Telegraphy*] (PCTE)
NUMS....... Nu-Med, Inc. (EFIS)
NUMS....... Numerous (ROG)
NUMSA...... National Union of Metalworkers of South Africa
NUMW...... National Unemployed Workers' Movement [*British*]
NUN......... Network User Name [*Telecommunications*] (OSI)
NUN......... Nunasi-Central Airlines Ltd. [*Canada*] [*ICAO designator*] (FAAC)
NUN......... Nuveen New York Quality Income Municipal [*NYSE symbol*] (SPSG)
NUN......... Nuveen NY Qual Income Muni [*NYSE symbol*] (TTSB)
NUN......... Pensacola, FL [*Location identifier*] [*FAA*] (FAAL)
NUn.......... Uniondale Public Library, Uniondale, NY [*Library symbol*] [*Library of Congress*] (LCLS)
NUNA........ Not Used on Next Assembly (AAG)
nunc......... Now [*Medicine*] (BCRP)
NUnCCE..... Cornelius Court Elementary School, Uniondale, NY [*Library symbol*] [*Library of Congress*] (LCLS)
NUnCE....... California Elementary School, Uniondale, NY [*Library symbol*] [*Library of Congress*] (LCLS)
NUnH........ Uniondale High School, Uniondale, NY [*Library symbol*] [*Library of Congress*] (LCLS)
NUnLJ....... Lawrence Junior High School, Uniondale, NY [*Library symbol*] [*Library of Congress*] (LCLS)
NUnNE...... Northern Parkway Elementary School, Uniondale, NY [*Library symbol*] [*Library of Congress*] (LCLS)
NUnSE....... Smith Elementary School, Uniondale, NY [*Library symbol*] [*Library of Congress*] (LCLS)
NUnStA...... Saint Agnes Cathedral High School, Uniondale, NY [*Library symbol*] [*Library of Congress*] (LCLS)
NUnTHJ..... Turtle Hook Junior High School, Uniondale, NY [*Library symbol*] [*Library of Congress*] (LCLS)
NUnWE...... Walnut Elementary School, Uniondale, NY [*Library symbol*] [*Library of Congress*] (LCLS)
NUO......... Nugold Enterprises Corp. [*Vancouver Stock Exchange symbol*]
NUO......... Nuveen Ohio Quality Income Municipal [*NYSE symbol*] (SPSG)
NUO......... Nuveen OH Qual Incme Muni [*NYSE symbol*] (TTSB)
NUOL........ Naval Underwater Ordnance Laboratory (NOAA)
NUOM....... Northern Union of Operative Masons [*British*]
NUON........ Number One [*NCIC motorcycle make code*]
NUOR........ Nuclear Ordnance (SAUS)
NUOS........ Naval Underwater Ordnance Station
NUP.......... Nationalist Unionist Party [*Sudan*]
NUP.......... National Umma Party [*Sudan*] [*Political party*]
NUP.......... National Union of Protestants
NUP.......... National United Party [*Vanuatu*] [*Political party*] (EY)
NUP.......... National Unity Party [*British*] [*Political party*] (EA)
NUP.......... Negro Universities Press (AEBS)
NUP.......... Newspaper [*Telegraphy*] (PCTE)
NUP.......... New Union Party [*Later, IUP*] (EA)
NUP.......... Nonylundecylphthalat (SAUS)
NUP.......... Nunapitchuk [*Alaska*] [*Airport symbol*] (OAG)
NUP.......... Nupe-Nupe-Tako [*Language symbol*] (ETLW)
NUP.......... Nuveen Pennsylvania Quality Income Municipal (SAUS)
NUPAC...... Nuclear Packaging Inc (SAUS)
NUPAD...... Nuclear-Powered Active Detection System
NUPAD System... Nuclear-Powered Active Detection System (SAUS)
NUpB........ United States Brookhaven National Laboratory, Upton, NY [*Library symbol*] [*Library of Congress*] (LCLS)
NUPB & PW... National Union of Printing, Bookbinding, and Paperworkers [*British*] (DGA)
NUpB-MH... United States Brookhaven National Laboratory, Medical Research Center Hospital, Upton, NY [*Library symbol*] [*Library of Congress*] (LCLS)
NUPBP...... National Union of Printing, Bookbinding, and Paperworkers [*British*]
NUPC....... Nupec Resources (SAUS)
NUPD....... Non-Uniform Punched Document (SAUS)
NUPDTU.... National Union of Painters and Decorators Trade Union [*British*]
NUPE........ National Union of Public Employees [*British*]
NUPEC...... Nuclear Power Engineering Test Center (NRCH)
NUPGE...... National Union of Provincial Government Employees [*Canada*]
NUPI........ Norwegian Institute for International Affairs (SAUS)
NUPLEX..... Nuclear Complex
NUPOC...... Nuclear Power Candidate [*Navy*] (POLM)
NUPOC...... Nuclear Propulsion Officer Candidate [*Navy*]
NUPOC-S... Nuclear Propulsion Officer Candidate - Submarine (DNAB)
NUPPS...... Nonuniform Progressive Phase Shift (IAA)
NUPPSCO... Nuclear Power Plant Standards Committee (SAUS)
NUPRG...... New Ulster Political Research Group (Northern Ireland) [*Political party*] (PSAP)
NUPS........ Nordic Union of Private Schools (EA)
NUPT........ National Union of Press Telegraphists [*British*] (DGA)
NUPWR..... Nuclear Power [*or Powered*] (DNAB)
NUPWRU.... Nuclear Power Unit (DNAB)
NUPZ........ NU Pizza Holding Corp. [*OTCBB symbol*]
NUQ......... Mountain View, CA [*Location identifier*] [*FAA*] (FAAL)
NUR......... Natchez, Urania & Ruston Railway Co. [*AAR code*]
NUR......... National Union of Railwaymen [*British*]
NUR......... Net Unduplicated Research
Nur.......... Nitrosourea [*Biochemistry*]
NUR......... Nonuniformity Ratio
NUR......... Not Under Repair (MARI)

NUR .... Nurmijarvi [*Finland*] [*Seismograph station code, US Geological Survey*] (SEIS)
NUR .... Nurse (AABC)
NUR .... Nuspar Resources [*Vancouver Stock Exchange symbol*]
NURA .... National Union of Rate-Payers' Associations [*British*] (BI)
NURADS .... Netted Universal Radar System (ACAE)
NURAT ...... Newcastle University Root Analogue Tunneller (SAUS)
NuraTL ...... Nur Advanced Technologies Ltd. [*Associated Press*] (SAG)
NURB .... National Uniform Business Rate [*British*]
NURB .... Neville Upper Reservoir Buffer [*Medicine*] (DMAA)
NURBS ...... Nonuniform Rational B-Spline [*A type of spline*] [*Computer science*]
NURBS ...... Nonuniform Relational B-Spline [*Micro Cadam 3-D*] [*Computer science*]
NURC .... National Undersea Research Center [*Virgin Islands*]
NURC .... National Union of Railway Clerks [*British*]
NURC .... National Union of Retail Confectioners [*British*] (BI)
NURC/MAB ... National Undersea Research Center for the Middle Atlantic Bight Region (RCD)
NURDC ...... Naval Undersea Research and Development Center
NURE .... National Uranium Resource Evaluation [*Program*] [*Energy Research and Development Administration*]
NUREC ...... Nuclear Regulatory Commission (SAUS)
NURED ...... Nuclear Requirements Determination [*Military*]
NUREG ...... Criteria for Preparation and Evaluation of Radiological Regulations and Guides (SAUS)
NUREG ...... Nuclear Regulatory Commission
NUREG ...... U. S. Nuclear Regulatory Commission (SAUS)
NUREM ...... Nuclear Requirements Methodology [*Military*]
NUREP ...... New York University Resonance Escape Probability [*Code*] [*Nuclear energy*] (NRCH)
NUREP ...... Nuclear Reporting (SAUS)
NUREQ ...... Nuclear Requirements [*Military*]
NUREX ...... Nuclear Requirements Extrapolation [*Model*] (MCD)
NU/RF .... National Urban/Rural Fellows (EA)
NURF .... National Utility Reference File [*Department of Energy*]
NURF .... Nucleosome Remodeling Factor [*Analytical biochemistry*]
NURIG ...... Navy Utility Regulatory Intervention Group (DNAB)
NURO .... Neurotech Corp. (SAUS)
NUROC ...... Nuclear Rocket Project (SAA)
NURP .... National Undersea Research Program [*Department of Commerce*] (GRD)
NURP .... Nationwide Urban Runoff Program [*Water pollution*]
NURP .... NOAA [*National Oceanic and Atmospheric Administration*] Undersea Research Program [*Marine science*] (OSRA)
NURS .... International Nursing Services, Inc. [*NASDAQ symbol*] (SAG)
NURS .... International Nursing Svcs [*NASDAQ symbol*] (TTSB)
NURS .... Nursery
Nurs .... Nurses (AL)
Nurs .... Nursing (AL)
NURS .... Nursing
NURsc ...... New Jersey Resources [*Associated Press*] (SAG)
NURSE ...... Nurses Underrepresented in Social Equality (BABM)
NURSE ...... Nursing
NURSEDETS ... Nurse Detachments [*Army*]
Nurs Mirror ... Nursing Mirror and Midwives Journal (SAUS)
NURSW ..... International Nursing Wrrt [*NASDAQ symbol*] (TTSB)
NURSW ..... Nursing System-Wide
NURT .... National Union of Retail Tobacconists [*British*] (BI)
NURTE .... Nur Advanced Technologies Ltd. [*NASDAQ symbol*] (SAG)
NURX .... Nuclear Pharmacy, Inc. (SAUS)
NUS .... National Union of Scalemakers [*British*] (DCTA)
NUS .... National Union of Seamen [*British*]
NUS .... National Union of Students [*British*]
NUS .... National University of Singapore
NUS .... National Utility Services [*British*]
NUS .... News [*Telegraphy*] (PCTE)
NUS .... New Upper Stage [*NASA*] (KSC)
NUS .... Nominal Ultimate Strength (IAA)
NUS .... Nonuniformly Spaced (IAA)
NUS .... Norsup [*Vanuatu*] [*Airport symbol*] (OAG)
NUS .... No Upper Stage [*Space launch term*] (ISAK)
NUS .... Nuclear Upper Stage (SAUS)
NUS .... Nuclear Utility Services
NUS .... NUS Corp. (GAAI)
NUS .... Nu Skin Enterprises [*NYSE symbol*] [*Formerly, Nu Skin Asia Pacific*]
NUS .... Nu Skin Enterprises'A' [*NYSE symbol*] (SG)
NUS .... Nu-Start Resource Corp. [*Vancouver Stock Exchange symbol*]
n-us- .... United States [*MARC geographic area code*] [*Library of Congress*] (LCCP)
n-usa- .... Appalachian Area [*MARC geographic area code*] [*Library of Congress*] (LCCP)
NUSA .... NAMIC USA (EFIS)
NUSA .... National Union of Shop Assistants [*British*] (DAS)
N/USA .... National/United Service Agencies
NUSA .... Neighborhoods USA (EA)
NUSA .... Ninth United States Army
NUSAC ...... Nuclear Sciences Advisory Committee [*Department of Energy/National Science Foundation*]
NUSACC ..... National United States-Arab Chamber of Commerce (EA)
n-us-ak ...... Alaska [*MARC geographic area code*] [*Library of Congress*] (LCCP)
n-us-al ...... Alabama [*MARC geographic area code*] [*Library of Congress*] (LCCP)
n-us-ar ...... Arkansas [*MARC geographic area code*] [*Library of Congress*] (LCCP)
NUSAR ...... Nuclear Sweep and RADAR (IAA)
NUSAS ...... National Union of South African Students
NUSAS ...... Navy Underwater Swimmer Assault System (SAA)
NUSAT .... Northern Utah Satellite
NUSAT .... Nuclear Saturn (SAUS)
n-us-az ...... Arizona [*MARC geographic area code*] [*Library of Congress*] (LCCP)
NUSBA ...... Nuclear Science and Applications, Series B: Physical Sciences (SAUS)
NUSC .... Naval Undersea Systems Center (SAUS)
NUSC .... Naval Underwater Systems Center/Command (USDC)
n-usc- .... North Central States [*MARC geographic area code*] [*Library of Congress*] (LCCP)
n-us-ca ...... California [*MARC geographic area code*] [*Library of Congress*] (LCCP)
NUSCAT ..... New Airborne Scatterometer (MCD)
NUSCDET ... Naval Underwater Systems Center Detachment (DNAB)
NUSC/NL ... Naval Underwater Systems Center, New London [*Connecticut*]
NUSC/NPT ... Naval Underwater Systems Center, Newport [*Rhode Island*]
n-us-co ...... Colorado [*MARC geographic area code*] [*Library of Congress*] (LCCP)
NUSCOT ..... Nuclear Submarine Control Trainer (PDAA)
NUSCOT ..... Nuclear Submarine Simulator Complex (SAUS)
n-us-ct ...... Connecticut [*MARC geographic area code*] [*Library of Congress*] (LCCP)
NUSD .... Nucleus Sum Optical Density [*Microscopy*]
n-us-dc ...... District of Columbia [*MARC geographic area code*] [*Library of Congress*] (LCCP)
n-us-de ...... Delaware [*MARC geographic area code*] [*Library of Congress*] (LCCP)
n-use- .... Northeast (United States) [*MARC geographic area code*] [*Library of Congress*] (LCCP)
NUSEC ...... Naval Underwater Systems Engineering Center (MUGU)
NUSFDB ..... NUS [*National University of Singapore*] Financial Database [*Information service or system*] (IID)
n-us-fl .... Florida [*MARC geographic area code*] [*Library of Congress*] (LCCP)
n-us-ga ...... Georgia [*MARC geographic area code*] [*Library of Congress*] (LCCP)
NUSGGMW ... National Union of Stove Grate and General Metal Workers [*British*]
NUSGW ...... National Union of Stove and Grate Workers [*British*]
NUSH .... Nucleus Shape [*Microscopy*]
n-us-hi ...... Hawaii [*MARC geographic area code*] [*Library of Congress*] (LCCP)
n-us-ia ...... Iowa [*MARC geographic area code*] [*Library of Congress*] (LCCP)
n-us-id ...... Idaho [*MARC geographic area code*] [*Library of Congress*] (LCCP)
n-us-il ...... Illinois [*MARC geographic area code*] [*Library of Congress*] (LCCP)
n-us-in ...... Indiana [*MARC geographic area code*] [*Library of Congress*] (LCCP)
n-us-ks ...... Kansas [*MARC geographic area code*] [*Library of Congress*] (LCCP)
n-us-ky ...... Kentucky [*MARC geographic area code*] [*Library of Congress*] (LCCP)
n-usl- .... Middle Atlantic States [*MARC geographic area code*] [*Library of Congress*] (LCCP)
NUSL .... Naval Underwater Sound Laboratory [*Later, NUSC*]
n-us-la ...... Louisiana [*MARC geographic area code*] [*Library of Congress*] (LCCP)
NUSLUM .... Nuclear Detonation Summary (SAUS)
n-usm- ...... Mississippi River and Basin [*MARC geographic area code*] [*Library of Congress*] (LCCP)
n-us-ma ..... Massachusetts [*MARC geographic area code*] [*Library of Congress*] (LCCP)
n-us-md ..... Maryland [*MARC geographic area code*] [*Library of Congress*] (LCCP)
n-us-me ..... Maine [*MARC geographic area code*] [*Library of Congress*] (LCCP)
n-us-mi ..... Michigan [*MARC geographic area code*] [*Library of Congress*] (LCCP)
n-us-mn ..... Minnesota [*MARC geographic area code*] [*Library of Congress*] (LCCP)
n-us-mo ..... Missouri [*MARC geographic area code*] [*Library of Congress*] (LCCP)
n-us-ms ..... Mississippi [*MARC geographic area code*] [*Library of Congress*] (LCCP)
n-us-mt ..... Montana [*MARC geographic area code*] [*Library of Congress*] (LCCP)
NUSMWCHDE ... National Union of Sheet Metal Workers, Coppersmiths, Heating and Domestic Engineers [*British*] (DCTA)
n-usn- .... New England [*MARC geographic area code*] [*Library of Congress*] (LCCP)
n-us-nb ..... Nebraska [*MARC geographic area code*] [*Library of Congress*] (LCCP)
n-us-nc ..... North Carolina [*MARC geographic area code*] [*Library of Congress*] (LCCP)
n-us-nd ..... North Dakota [*MARC geographic area code*] [*Library of Congress*] (LCCP)
n-us-nh ..... New Hampshire [*MARC geographic area code*] [*Library of Congress*] (LCCP)
n-us-nj ..... New Jersey [*MARC geographic area code*] [*Library of Congress*] (LCCP)
n-us-nm ..... New Mexico [*MARC geographic area code*] [*Library of Congress*] (LCCP)
n-us-nv ..... Nevada [*MARC geographic area code*] [*Library of Congress*] (LCCP)
n-us-ny ..... New York [*MARC geographic area code*] [*Library of Congress*] (LCCP)
n-uso- .... Ohio River and Basin [*MARC geographic area code*] [*Library of Congress*] (LCCP)
n-us-oh ..... Ohio [*MARC geographic area code*] [*Library of Congress*] (LCCP)
n-us-ok ..... Oklahoma [*MARC geographic area code*] [*Library of Congress*] (LCCP)
n-us-or ..... Oregon [*MARC geographic area code*] [*Library of Congress*] (LCCP)
NUSOS ...... Nuclear Underwater Sound Source (NG)
n-usp- .... Pacific and Mountain States [*MARC geographic area code*] [*Library of Congress*] (LCCP)
n-us-pa ..... Pennsylvania [*MARC geographic area code*] [*Library of Congress*] (LCCP)

NUSPRAW... National Union of Storeworkers, Packers, Rubber and Allied Workers [*Australia*]
n-us-ri....... Rhode Island [*MARC geographic area code*] [*Library of Congress*] (LCCP)
NUSRL...... Navy Underwater Sound Reference Laboratory
n-uss-....... Missouri River and Basin [*MARC geographic area code*] [*Library of Congress*] (LCCP)
NUSS........ National Union of School Students [*British*] (DI)
NUSS........ Nuclear Safety Standard (PDAA)
n-us-sc...... South Carolina [*MARC geographic area code*] [*Library of Congress*] (LCCP)
n-us-sd...... South Dakota [*MARC geographic area code*] [*Library of Congress*] (LCCP)
NUSSE...... Nonuniform Simple Surface Evaporated Model (MCD)
NUST........ Nussbaum Trucking [*Common carrier symbol*]
n-ust-........ Southwest (United States) [*MARC geographic area code*] [*Library of Congress*] (LCCP)
n-us-tn...... Tennessee [*MARC geographic area code*] [*Library of Congress*] (LCCP)
n-us-tx...... Texas [*MARC geographic area code*] [*Library of Congress*] (LCCP)
NUSU........ Neptune Orient Lines [*Intermodal shipping container symbol*] (TVRC)
NUSU........ Nuclear Superheating (SAA)
n-usu-....... Southern States [*MARC geographic area code*] [*Library of Congress*] (LCCP)
NUSU-CX... Nuclear Superheat Critical Experiment (SAA)
NUSUM..... Nuclear Detonation Summary (NVT)
NUSUM..... Numerical Summary (SAUS)
NUSUM..... Numerical Summary Message (SAUS)
NUSUM..... Numerical Summary Report [*Military*] (AFM)
n-us-ut...... Utah [*MARC geographic area code*] [*Library of Congress*] (LCCP)
n-us-va...... Virginia [*MARC geographic area code*] [*Library of Congress*] (LCCP)
n-us-vt...... Vermont [*MARC geographic area code*] [*Library of Congress*] (LCCP)
n-usw-....... Northwest (United States) [*MARC geographic area code*] [*Library of Congress*] (LCCP)
n-us-wa..... Washington [*MARC geographic area code*] [*Library of Congress*] (LCCP)
n-us-wi...... Wisconsin [*MARC geographic area code*] [*Library of Congress*] (LCCP)
n-us-wv..... West Virginia [*MARC geographic area code*] [*Library of Congress*] (LCCP)
n-us-wy..... Wyoming [*MARC geographic area code*] [*Library of Congress*] (LCCP)
NUSZ........ Nucleus Size [*Microscopy*]
NUSZ........ Nucor Steel [*Federal Railroad Administration identification code*]
NUT.......... Mauna Loa Macadamia'A' [*NYSE symbol*] (TTSB)
NUT.......... Mauna Loa Macadamia Partners LP [*NYSE symbol*] (SPSG)
NUT.......... National Union of Teachers [*British*]
NUT.......... Nautilus Resources Ltd. [*Vancouver Stock Exchange symbol*]
N-U-T........ Newcastle-Upon-Tyne [*City in England*]
NUT.......... Nonobstructive Urinary Tract [*Medicine*] (MELL)
NUT.......... Northeast University of Technology (SAUS)
NUT.......... Number Unobtainable Tone [*Telecommunications*] (TEL)
NUT.......... Nutrient (SAUS)
NUt.......... Utica Public Library, Utica, NY [*Library symbol*] [*Library of Congress*] (LCLS)
NUTA........ Nagoya University Tandem Accelerator centre (SAUS)
NUTA........ National Used Truck Association
NUtC......... Utica College of Syracuse University, Utica, NY [*Library symbol*] [*Library of Congress*] (LCLS)
NUTEC....... Norwegian Underwater Technology Center (SAUS)
NU-TEC..... Nuclear Detection [*Radiation monitoring device*] (WDAA)
Nu-Tech..... Nu-Tech Bio Med, Inc. [*Associated Press*] (SAG)
NUTEK....... National Board for Industrial and Technical Development (SAUS)
NUTEK....... Swedish National Board for Industrial and Technical Development (SAUS)
NuTeV....... Neutrinos at the Tevatron
NUTEX....... Nuclear Tactical Exercise
NUTG........ National Union of Townswomen's Guilds [*British*]
NUtGE....... General Electric Co., Utica, NY [*Library symbol*] [*Library of Congress*] (LCLS)
NUTGW..... National Union of Tailors and Garments Workers [*British*]
NUtHi........ Oneida Historical Society, Utica, NY [*Library symbol*] [*Library of Congress*] (LCLS)
NUTI......... NASCOM User Traffic Interface [*NASA*] (MCD)
NUTI......... Northwestern University Traffic Institute (SAUS)
NUTIS....... Numerical and Textile Information System (PDAA)
NUTIS....... Numerical and Textual Information System (SAUS)
NUTK........ Nu Tech Industries (SAUS)
NUTL........ Nonuniform Transmission Line (IAA)
NUtM........ Munson-Williams-Proctor Institute, Utica, NY [*Library symbol*] [*Library of Congress*] (LCLS)
NUTM....... Nutmeg Industries, Inc. (MHDW)
NUTMAQ.... Nuclear Techniques in Mining and Quarrying (SAUS)
NutmgFd.... Nutmeg Federal Savings & Loan Association [*Associated Press*] (SAG)
NUtMI....... Utica Mutual Insurance Co., Utica, NY [*Library symbol*] [*Library of Congress*] (LCLS)
NUtMM...... Masonic Medical Research Laboratory, Utica, NY [*Library symbol*] [*Library of Congress*] (LCLS)
NUtMV...... Mohawk Valley Community College, Utica, NY [*Library symbol*] [*Library of Congress*] (LCLS)
NUtMVL..... Mohawk Valley Learning Resource Center, Utica Psychiatric Center, Utica, NY [*Library symbol*] [*Library of Congress*] (LCLS)
NUtMY...... Mid-York Library System, Utica, NY [*Library symbol*] [*Library of Congress*] (LCLS)
NUTN........ National Union of Trained Nurses [*British*] (DI)
NUTN........ National University Teleconference Network [*Stillwater, OK*] [*Telecommunications*] (TSSD)
NUTP........ National Uranium Tailings Program [*Canada*]
NUtP......... Utica Psychiatric Center, Utica, NY [*Library symbol*] [*Library of Congress*] (LCLS)
NUTPW...... National Union of Tin Plate Workers [*British*]
NUTR........ Nutrition (AABC)
NUTRAT..... Nuclear Uses Technology Reaction Analysis Team
Nutr Dieta... Nutrio et Dieta. European Review of Nutrition and Dietetics (SAUS)
NUTRI........ Nutrition
NUTRL...... Nutritional
NutrLf....... Nutrition For Life International, Inc. [*Associated Press*] (SAG)
NutrLfe...... Nutrition for Life International, Inc. [*Associated Press*] (SAG)
Nutrmax..... NutraMax Products, Inc. [*Associated Press*] (SAG)
NutrMg...... Nutrition Management [*Associated Press*] (SAG)
NutrMgt..... Nutrition Management [*Associated Press*] (SAG)
NUTS........ Newcastle University Teaching System (SAUS)
NUTS........ New Universal Terminology Subjects
NUTS........ Non-Used Trunk Scan [*Communications term*] (DCT)
NUTS........ Nuclear Utilization Target Selection (CARL)
NUTS........ Nuclear-Utilization Theories (SAUS)
NUTS........ Nutrition World, Inc. (SAUS)
NUtSC....... New York State Supreme Court Law Library, Utica, NY [*Library symbol*] [*Library of Congress*] (LCLS)
NUtSU....... State University of New York, College at Utica-Rome, Utica, NY [*Library symbol*] [*Library of Congress*] (LCLS)
NUTT........ National Union of Tobacco Trades [*British*]
NUTT........ Nuttall Trailers [*NCIC trailer make code*]
NUTTAB..... Nutrient Data Table
NUTX........ Nucleus Texture [*Microscopy*]
NUTX........ Nutraceutix [*OTCBB symbol*]
NUU......... New Universal Union (EA)
NUU......... New University of Ulster [*Ireland*] (DI)
NUUSFE..... National Union of United States Forces Employees [*South Korea*]
NUUT........ National Union of Uncertified Teachers [*British*]
NUV.......... Near Ultraviolet
NUV.......... Norges Unge Venstre [*Norway*]
NUV.......... Nuveen Municipal Value Fund, Inc. [*NYSE symbol*] (SPSG)
NUV.......... Nuveen Muni Value Fd [*NYSE symbol*] (TTSB)
NuvAZ....... Nuveen Arizona Premium Income [*Associated Press*] (SAG)
NUVB........ National Union of Vehicle Builders [*British*]
NuvCal...... Nuveen California Municipal Value Fund [*Associated Press*] (SAG)
NUVI......... NuVision, Inc. (SAUS)
NuvMu...... Nuveen Municipal Value Fund, Inc. [*Associated Press*] (SAG)
NuvPI........ Nuveen Premium Income Municipal Fund, Inc. [*Associated Press*] (SAG)
NuvPI2...... Nuveen Premium Income Municipal Fund 2 [*Associated Press*] (SAG)
NuvPI4...... Nuveen Premium Income Municipal Fund 4 [*Associated Press*] (SAG)
NuvPP....... Nuveen Performance Plus Municipal Fund [*Associated Press*] (SAG)
NuvQInc.... Nuveen Quality Income Municipal Fund [*Associated Press*] (SAG)
NuvSel...... Nuveen Select Quality [*Associated Press*] (SAG)
NUVW....... National Union of Vehicular Workers [*British*]
NuvWA...... Nuveen Washington Premium Income Municipal Fund [*Associated Press*] (SAG)
NUW......... National Universities Week [*Canada*]
NUW......... Nu-West Group Ltd. [*Toronto Stock Exchange symbol*]
NUW......... Whidbey Island, WA [*Location identifier*] [*FAA*] (FAAL)
NUWA....... National Unemployed Workers Association (NADA)
NUWA....... Nu-Wa Campers [*NCIC trailer make code*]
NUWAR..... Nuclear Warfare (SAUS)
NUWATI..... Nuclear Work Authorization Technical Instruction (DNAB)
NUWAX..... Nuclear Weapons Accident Exercises
NUWC....... Naval Undersea Warfare Center [*Later, NURDC*]
NUWDAT.... National Union of Wallcoverings, Decorative and Allied Trades [*British*] (DGA)
NUWE....... NuWay Mobile Home Manufacturing Company [*NCIC trailer make code*]
NUWEAMP... Nuclear Weapons Employment and Acquisition Master Plan (ACAE)
NUWEDS.... Nuclear Weapons Deniel System (SAUS)
NUWEDS.... Nuclear Weapons Emergency Destruction System (SAUS)
NUWEDS.... Nuclear Weapons Emergency Destruct System [*Navy*] (ANA)
NUWEP...... Nuclear Weapon Employment Policy (MCD)
NUWEP...... Nuclear Weapons Effect Planning
NUWEP...... Nuclear Weapons Employment Plan (SAUS)
NUWEP...... Nuclear Weapons Employment Policy (SAUS)
NUWEP...... Nuclear Weapons Employment Procedures (SAUS)
NUWES...... Naval Undersea Warfare Engineering Station (MCD)
NUWES...... Naval Underwater Weapons Evaluation Station
NUWH....... Nuwa Horizon Camper Trailer [*NCIC trailer make code*]
NUWMF..... Naval Undersea Warfare Museum Foundation (PDAA)
NUWPNSTRACEN... Nuclear Weapons Training Center (MCD)
NUWPNSUPANX... Nuclear Weapons Supply Annex
NUWPNTRACEN... Nuclear Weapons Training Center
NUWPNTRACENLANT... Nuclear Weapons Training Center, Atlantic
NUWPNTRACENPAC... Nuclear Weapons Training Center, Pacific
NUWRES.... Naval Underwater Weapons Research and Engineering Station
NUWS....... Naval Underwater Weapons Station (MCD)
NUWSAMBS... National United Women's Societies of the Adoration of the Most Blessed Sacrament (EA)
NUWSEC.... Naval Underwater Weapons Systems Engineering Center
NUWT....... National Union of Women Teachers [*British*] (DAS)
NUWT....... Northeast Utilities [*NASDAQ symbol*] (SAG)
NuWt........ Nu-West Industries, Inc. [*Associated Press*] (SAG)

NUWTW..... Northeast Utils Wrrt [*NASDAQ symbol*] (TTSB)
NUWW...... National Union of Women Workers (MHDB)
NUX.......... Numerous [*Telegraphy*] (PCTE)
NUYC........ Nordic Union of Young Conservatives (EA)
NV........... Naamloze Vennootschap [*Limited Company, Corporation*] [*Netherlands*] (GPO)
NV........... Naked Vision
nV........... Nanovolt [*One billionth of a volt*] (IEEE)
N/V.......... Nausea and Vomiting [*Medicine*] (AMHC)
NV........... Near Vertical [*Aerospace*]
NV........... Near Vision (MELL)
NV........... Needle Valve
NV........... Negative Variation [*Medicine*] (MAE)
NV........... Nerve and Vein [*Medicine*] (DAVI)
NV........... Net Value
NV........... Neurovascular [*Anatomy*]
NV........... Neutralization Value (IAA)
NV........... Nevada [*Postal code*]
Nv........... Nevada State Library, Carson City, NV [*Library symbol*] [*Library of Congress*] (LCLS)
NV........... Never [*Telegraphy*] (PCTE)
NV........... New Version [*of the Bible*]
NV........... Next Visit [*Medicine*]
NV........... Night Vision (SAUS)
NV........... Night Vision Device [*Optics*]
NV........... Nominal Value (SAUS)
NV........... Nonvaccinated
NV........... Non-Vegetarian [*Indian Railway*] (TIR)
NV........... Nonvenereal [*Medicine*]
NV........... Nonveteran
nv........... Non Vidi [*Not Seen*] [*Latin*]
NV........... Nonvintage [*Wine*]
NV........... Non-Virtual (AGLO)
nv........... Nonvirulent [*Pathology*]
nv........... Non Visus [*Not Seen*] [*Latin*] (EES)
NV........... Nonvolatile
NV........... Nonvoting [*Investment term*]
NV........... No Overflow (SAUS)
NV........... Nord-Viscount (SAUS)
NV........... Nord-Viscount Corp.
NV........... Normalized in Vacuum (SAUS)
NV........... Normalized Volume (SAUS)
NV........... Normal Value [*Clinical chemistry*]
NV........... Normal Vetting (SAUS)
NV........... Norske Veritas [*Norwegian ship classification society*] (DS)
NV........... North Anna [*Virginia*] [*Seismograph station code, US Geological Survey*] [*Closed*]
NV........... Northern Executive Aviation Ltd. (SAUS)
N-V.......... Northrop-Ventura (SAA)
NV........... Northwest Territorial Airways [*ICAO designator*] (AD)
NV........... Norwalk Virus [*Medicine*] (MELL)
NV........... Not Vaccinated [*Medicine*]
N/V.......... No Value [*Legal term*] (DLA)
NV........... Nozzle Vanes (AAG)
NV........... Nozzle Velocity (SAUS)
NV........... Nuclear Vessel (TVEL)
NV........... Nuclear Vitrification (SAUS)
NV........... Nuisance Value (MHDB)
N/V.......... Number of Engine Revolutions per Minute per Vehicle Miles per Hour [*Automotive engineering*]
NV........... Number of Variables (SAUS)
NVA.......... Nationale Volksarmee [*National Peoples' Army*] [*Germany*]
NVA.......... National Variety Artists [*Defunct*] (EA)
NVA.......... National Velthrow Association (EA)
NVA.......... National Veterans Association (EA)
NVA.......... National Viatical Association (ECON)
NVA.......... National Villa Association [*British*] (BI)
NVA.......... National Vista Alliance (EA)
NVA.......... National Vulvodynia Association [*Disseminate information about vulvar pain and establish support networks across the country*] [*Medicine*]
NVA.......... Native Vegetation Authority [*South Australia*]
NVA.......... Near Visual Acuity [*Medicine*]
NVA.......... Negative Vorticity Advection [*NWS*] (FAAC)
NVA.......... Neiva [*Colombia*] [*Airport symbol*] (OAG)
NVA.......... Nile Valley Aviation Co. [*Egypt*] [*ICAO designator*] (FAAC)
NVA.......... Non-Violent Alternatives [*An association*] (EA)
NvA.......... Normalized Volt-Ampere
NVA.......... North Vietnamese Army
Nva.......... Norvaline [*Biochemistry*]
Nva.......... Norvalyl (SAUS)
NVA.......... NOVA Corp.(Cda) [*NYSE symbol*] (TTSB)
NVA.......... Nova Corp. of Alberta [*Later, Nova Corp.*] [*NYSE symbol*] [*Toronto Stock Exchange symbol*] (SPSG)
NVA.......... No Voltage Amplification [*Electronics*] (IAA)
NVA.......... N-Vinylacetamide [*Organic chemistry*]
NVAC........ Natal Voluntary Ambulance Corps [*British military*] (DMA)
NVAC........ National Vaccine Advisory Committee [*Reports to Congress, Health and Human Services*]
NVAC........ North Vietnamese Army Captured
NVAC........ Sunny Von Bulow National Victim Advocacy Center [*Later, NVC*] (EA)
NVACP....... Neighborhoods, Voluntary Associations and Consumer Protection [*Environmental Protection Agency*] (ERG)
NVAE........ Non-viral Acute Encephalopathy [*Medicine*] (EDAA)
NVAF........ Nonvalvular Atrial Fibrillation [*Medicine*] (EDAA)
NVAF........ North Vietnamese Air Force
NVAFB....... North Vandenberg Air Force Base (NASA)
NVAL........ National Vision Associates [*NASDAQ symbol*] (SAG)
NVAL........ Natl Vision Associates [*NASDAQ symbol*] (TTSB)
Nval........ Norvaline (DB)
NVAL........ Not Available
NValHi...... Columbia County Historical Library, Valatie, NY [*Library symbol*] [*Library of Congress*] (LCLS)
NValhM..... Westchester Medical Center, Valhalla, NY [*Library symbol*] [*Library of Congress*] (LCLS)
NValhW..... Westchester Community College, Valhalla, NY [*Library symbol*] [*Library of Congress*] (LCLS)
NVAN........ Non-Violent Anarchist Network (EA)
NV & EOL... Night Vision and Electro-Optics Laboratory [*Army*] (RDA)
NV & H...... Nuclear Survivability and Hardening
NVAPI....... Nuveen Virginia Premium Income Municipal Fund [*Associated Press*] (SAG)
Nv-Ar........ Nevada State Library, Division of State Archives, Carson City, NV [*Library symbol*] [*Library of Congress*] (LCLS)
NVAR........ Normalized Variance (PDAA)
NVAS........ Night Vision Attack System
NVAS........ North Vietnamese Army Suspect
NVASD...... Night Vision Aerial Surveillance Device
NVASS...... Night Vision Airborne Surveillance System
NVATA...... National Vocational Agricultural Teachers' Association (EA)
NVB.......... Inco Ltd. [*NYSE symbol*] (SAG)
NVB.......... Napa Valley Bancorp (EFIS)
NVB.......... National Volunteer Brigade [*South African equivalent of the British Home Guard*]
NVB.......... Navigational Base (KSC)
NVB.......... Nederlandse Volksbeweging [*Dutch People's Movement*] [*Political party*] (PPE)
NVB.......... Neurovascular Bundle [*Medicine*] (DB)
NVB.......... Night Vision Binocular
NVB.......... Noise & Vibration Bulletin (SAUS)
Nvb.......... November (CDAI)
NVBA........ National Veteran Boxers Association (EA)
NvBc........ Boulder City Library, Boulder City, NV [*Library symbol*] [*Library of Congress*] (LCLS)
NVBC........ Napa Valley Bancorp [*NASDAQ symbol*] (COMM)
NvBcBM..... United States Bureau of Mines, Boulder City Metallurgy Research Laboratories, Boulder City, NV [*Library symbol*] [*Library of Congress*] (LCLS)
NvBcER..... United States Energy Research and Development Administration, Boulder City Metallurgy Research Laboratories, Boulder City, NV [*Library symbol*] [*Library of Congress*] (LCLS)
NVBF........ Nordic federation of Research Libraries (SAUS)
NVBF........ Nordisk Vetenskapliga Bibliotekarie-Forbundet [*Scandinavian Federation of Research Librarians*] (EA)
NvBL........ Lehman Caves National Monument, Baker, NV [*Library symbol*] [*Library of Congress*] (LCLS)
NVBR........ Nevada Basin and Range (SAUS)
NVB-SG..... Dutch Serials Group (SAUS)
NVC.......... National Victim Center (EA)
NVC.......... National Victims of Crime (EA)
NVC.......... National Video Clearinghouse [*Defunct*] (EA)
NVC.......... National Video Corp.
NVC.......... National Volunteer Center (EA)
NVC.......... Nonverbal Communication (ADA)
NVC.......... Noverco, Inc. [*Toronto Stock Exchange symbol*]
NVC.......... Nuriootpa Viticulture Center [*Australia*]
NVC.......... Nuveen California Select Quality Municipal [*NYSE symbol*] (SPSG)
NVC.......... Nuveen CA Select Qual Muni [*NYSE symbol*] (TTSB)
NvC.......... Ormsby Public Library, Carson City, NV [*Library symbol*] [*Library of Congress*] (LCLS)
NVCA........ National Valentine Collectors' Association (EA)
NVCA........ National Van Conversion Association (EA)
NVCA........ National Vehicle Conversion Association
NVCA........ National Venture Capital Association [*Arlington, VA*] (EA)
NVCAN...... National Victims' Constitutional Amendment Network [*Association*] (EA)
NvCAQI...... Nuveen California Quality Income Municipal [*Associated Press*] (SAG)
NVCASE..... National Voluntary Conformity Assessment System (SAUS)
NVCC........ Northern Virginia Community College
NVCF........ National Victims of Crime Foundation (EA)
NVCF........ Nova Container Freight Station [*Common carrier symbol*]
NVCH........ National Volunteer Clearinghouse for the Homeless [*Defunct*] (EA)
NvCIQ....... Nuveen California Investment Quality Municipal Fund [*Associated Press*] (SAG)
NV-CJD...... New Variant Creutzfeldt-Jakob Disease [*Medicine*]
NVCJD....... New Variant of Creutzfeldt-Jakob Disease (SAUS)
NvCMI....... Nuveen California Municipal Income Fund [*Associated Press*] (SAG)
NVCO........ Nodaway Valley Co. (SAUS)
NVCP........ Network Voice Conferencing Protocol (CCCA)
NVCPP...... Nuveen California Performance Plus Municipal Fund [*Associated Press*] (SAG)
NVCS........ Nissan Valve Control System [*Automotive engineering*]
NvCSQ....... Nuveen California Select Quality Municipal Fund [*Associated Press*] (SAG)
NVCT........ Nonverbal Classification Test
NVCU........ Naviera Consolidada [*Intermodal shipping container symbol*] (TVRC)
NVCX........ Nevada Cement [*Private rail car owner code*]
NVCZ........ N-Vinylcarbazole [*Organic chemistry*]
NVD.......... Nausea, Vomiting, Diarrhea [*Medicine*]

NVD......... Neck Vein Distention [*Medicine*]
NVD......... Neovascularization of the Disc [*Ophthalmology*] (DAVI)
NVD......... Neurovesicle Dysfunction [*Medicine*] (DMAA)
NVD......... Nevada, MO [*Location identifier*] [*FAA*] (FAAL)
NVD......... Newcastle Virus Disease [*Veterinary medicine*] (MAE)
NVD......... Nickel Vapor Deposition [*Metal treatment*]
NVD......... Night Viewing Device (SAUS)
NVD......... Night Vision Device [*Optics*]
NVD......... Nonvalvular Disease [*Medicine*] (DMAA)
NVD......... Nonvalvular Heart Disease (MAE)
NVD......... Normal Vaginal Delivery [*Medicine*] (DMAA)
NVD......... North Vancouver District Public Library [*UTLAS symbol*]
NVD......... No Value Declared [*Business term*] (DCTA)
NVD......... No Venereal Disease [*Medicine*] (EDAA)
NVD......... No Venous Distention [*Medicine*] (MEDA)
NVD......... Number of Vessels Diseased [*Medicine*] (DB)
NVDA........ National Vitamin Distributors Association (EA)
NVDA........ National Volunteer Defense Army (CARL)
NVDA........ NVIDIA Corp. [*NASDAQ symbol*] (NASQ)
N/V/D/C..... Nausea/Vomiting/Diarrhea/ Constipation (SAUS)
NVDC........ Navidec [*NASDAQ symbol*]
NV DISTRINAL... NV Distribution International (SAUS)
NVDM........ Network Virtual Data Manager [*Computer science*] (IAA)
NVDM........ Novadigm, Inc. [*NASDAQ symbol*] (SAG)
NVDML...... Network Virtual Data Management Language [*Telecommunications*] (OSI)
NVDU........ STR Group Netherlands [*Intermodal shipping container symbol*] (TVRC)
NVE......... Colvin Aviation, Inc. [*ICAO designator*] (FAAC)
NvE......... Elko County Library, Elko, NV [*Library symbol*] [*Library of Congress*] (LCLS)
NVE......... Native Valve Endocarditis [*Medicine*]
NVE......... Neovascular Edema [*Ophthalmology*] (DAVI)
NVE......... Neovascularization Elsewhere [*Cardiology*] (DAVI)
NVE......... Network-Visible Entity (DINT)
NVE......... New Vessels Elsewhere [*Medicine*] (AMHC)
NVE......... Night Vision Equipment (MCD)
NVE......... Nonvisual Eyepiece
NVe......... Vestal Public Library, Vestal, NY [*Library symbol*] [*Library of Congress*] (LCLS)
NVEB........ Non-Vacuum Electron Beam (SAUS)
NVEBW....... Non-Vacuum Electron Beam Welding (PDAA)
NVEC........ Night Vision Equipment Corp. (SAUS)
NVEE........ Non-Volatile Ether Extract (SAUS)
NVEF........ National Vocational Educational Foundation (EA)
NVeGS....... Church of Jesus Christ of Latter-Day Saints, Genealogical Society Library, Ithaca Branch, Vestal, NY [*Library symbol*] [*Library of Congress*] (LCLS)
NvEHi....... Northeastern Nevada Historical Society, Elko, NV [*Library symbol*] [*Library of Congress*] (LCLS)
NVEL........ Navel
NVeL........ Vestal Public Library, Vestal, NY [*Library symbol*] [*Library of Congress*] (LCLS)
NvEIGS...... Church of Jesus Christ of Latter-Day Saints, Genealogical Society Library, Ely Branch, Ely, NV [*Library symbol*] [*Library of Congress*] (LCLS)
NVEOC....... Night Vision and Electro-Optics Center [*Fort Belvoir, VA*] [*US Army Communications-Electronics Command*] (RDA)
NVEOD....... Night Vision and Electro Optics Directorate [*Army*] (RDA)
NVEOL....... Night Vision and Electro-Optics Laboratory [*Army*] (GRD)
NVEPDC...... National Vocational Educational Professional Development Consortium [*Later, NVEPDF*] (EA)
NVEPDF...... National Vocational Educational Professional Development Foundation [*Later, NVEF*] (EA)
NVERN....... North Vernon, IN [*American Association of Railroads railroad junction routing code*]
NVESD....... Night Vision and Electronic Sensors Directorate [*Army*] (RDA)
NVETS....... National Vocational Education and Training System [*Australia*]
NVEX........ Nevex Gold Co., Inc. (SAUS)
NVF......... Nasal Visual Field (DB)
NVF......... National Vitamin Foundation (EA)
NVF......... National Vitiligo Foundation (EA)
NVF......... National Volunteer Force (WDAA)
NVF......... Nordisk Vejteknisk Forbund [*Nordic Association of Road and Traffic Engineering*] (EAIO)
NVFC........ National Volunteer Fire Council (EA)
NVFC........ NVF Co [*OTCBB symbol*]
NVFEL....... National Vehicle and Fuel Emissions Laboratory
NVFET....... Non-Volatile Field-Effect-Transistor [*Electronics*]
NvFGS....... Church of Jesus Christ of Latter-Day Saints, Genealogical Society Library, Fallon Branch, Fallon, NV [*Library symbol*] [*Library of Congress*] (LCLS)
NVFI........ National Vitiligo Foundation (PAZ)
NvFL........ Nuveen Florida Investment Quality Municipal Fund [*Associated Press*] (SAG)
NVFR........ Night VFR (SAUS)
NVFR........ Night Visual Flight Rating
NVG......... National Trust Co. [*Toronto Stock Exchange symbol*]
NVG......... Neovascular Glaucoma (DAVI)
NVG......... Neoviridogrisein [*Antibacterial*]
NVG......... Night Vision Goggles
NVG......... Night Vision Group
NVG......... Nonventilated Group [*Medicine*] (EDAA)
NVG......... Null Voltage Generator (SAUS)
NVGA........ National Vocational Guidance Association (EA)
NVGC........ Night Vision Goggle Compatibiity (SAUS)
NVGGA....... Napa Valley Grape Growers Association (EA)
NVGI........ National Voluntary Groups Institute (EA)
NvGM........ Mormon Station State Park, Genoa, NV [*Library symbol*] [*Library of Congress*] (LCLS)
NVGS........ Night Vision Goggle Sensor (DWSG)
NVGTN....... Navigation
NvH......... Henderson District Public Library, Henderson, NV [*Library symbol*] [*Library of Congress*] (LCLS)
NVH......... Nasarian [*Language symbol*] (ETLW)
NVH......... National R.V. Holdings [*NYSE symbol*]
NVH......... Natl R.V.Holdings [*NYSE symbol*] (SG)
NVH......... Nitrogen Vent Header [*Nuclear energy*] (NRCH)
NVH......... Noise, Vibration, Harshness [*Automotive technology*]
NVHA........ National Voluntary Health Agencies (EA)
NvHi........ Nevada State Historical Society, Reno, NV [*Library symbol*] [*Library of Congress*] (LCLS)
NvHV-A...... United States Veterans Administration Hospital, Ambulatory Care Service, Henderson, NV [*Library symbol*] [*Library of Congress*] (LCLS)
NVI......... Near Vertical Incident (ACAE)
NVI......... Neovascularization of the Iris (SAUS)
NVI......... Night Vision Imaging (DWSG)
NVI......... Non-Value Indicator [*Type of postage stamp*] (ODBW)
NVI......... Nordic Volcanological Institute (SAUS)
NVI......... Normalized Vegetation Index [*Meteorology*]
NVI......... No Value Indicated [*Stamp collecting*]
NVIC........ National Vaccine Information Center
NVIC........ Navigational and Vessel Inspection Circular [*Coast Guard*] (GFGA)
NVIC........ N-Viro International [*NASDAQ symbol*] (TTSB)
NVIC........ N-Viro International Corp. [*NASDAQ symbol*] (SAG)
NVICP....... National Vaccine Injury Compensation Program (PAZ)
NVID........ NVID International [*OTCBB symbol*]
NVIEW....... NVIEW Corp. [*Associated Press*] (SAG)
NVII........ Navy Vocational Interest Inventory (NVT)
NvIMO....... Nuveen Insurance Municipal Opportunity Fund [*Associated Press*] (SAG)
NvInQI...... Nuveen Insured Quality Fund [*Associated Press*] (SAG)
NvIQI....... Nuveen Investment Quality Municipal Fund [*Associated Press*] (SAG)
N-ViroInt... N-Viro International Corp. [*Associated Press*] (SAG)
NVIS........ National Video, Inc. [*NASDAQ symbol*] (COMM)
NVIS........ Nearly Vertical Incident Skywave [*Propagation model*] (MCD)
NVIS........ Night Vision Imaging System
nVision..... N-Vision, Inc. [*Associated Press*] (SAG)
NVK......... Milton, FL [*Location identifier*] [*FAA*] (FAAL)
NVK......... Narvik [*Norway*] [*Airport symbol*] (OAG)
NVL......... Hunting Aviation Services Ltd. [*British*] [*ICAO designator*] (FAAC)
NvL......... Las Vegas Public Library, Las Vegas, NV [*Library symbol*] [*Library of Congress*] (LCLS)
NVL......... Nashville, TN [*Amtrak Busline code*]
NVL......... Nevertheless [*Telegraphy*] (PCTE)
NVL......... New Valley Corp. (EFIS)
NVL......... Night Vision Laboratory [*Army*]
NVL......... No Visible Lesion [*Medicine*] (MELL)
NVL......... Novolazarevskaya [*Antarctica*] [*Seismograph station code, US Geological Survey*] (SEIS)
NVLA........ National Vehicle Leasing Association (EA)
NVLA........ National Viewers' and Listeners' Association [*British*]
NVLAP....... National Association of Voluntary laboratory Accreditation Practices
NVLAP....... National Voluntary Laboratory Accreditation Program [*Gaithersburg, MD*] [*National Institute of Standards and Technology*]
NvLBM....... Basic Magnesium, Inc., Las Vegas, NV [*Library symbol*] [*Library of Congress*] [*Obsolete*] (LCLS)
NvLC........ Clark County Library, Las Vegas, NV [*Library symbol*] [*Library of Congress*] (LCLS)
NVLC........ National Veterans Law Center [*Defunct*] (EA)
NVLD........ Natural Vacuum Leak Detection [*Automotive testing*]
NVLD........ Non-Verbal Learning Disability
NvLGS....... Church of Jesus Christ of Latter-Day Saints, Genealogical Society Library, Las Vegas Branch, Las Vegas, NV [*Library symbol*] [*Library of Congress*] (LCLS)
NvLN........ University of Nevada, Las Vegas, NV [*Library symbol*] [*Library of Congress*] (LCLS)
NVLS........ Novellus Systems [*NASDAQ symbol*] (TTSB)
NVLS........ Novellus Systems, Inc. [*NASDAQ symbol*] (CTT)
NVLSP....... National Veterans Legal Services Program [*Association*] (EA)
NVLSPM...... Night Vision Laboratories Static Performance Model (SAUS)
NVM......... National Voter Mobilization [*Defunct*] (EA)
NVM......... Nativity of the Virgin Mary
NVM......... Nonvolatile Matter
NVM......... Nonvolatile Memory [*Computer science*] (HGAA)
NVM......... Non-Volatile Random Access Memory [*Computer science*]
NVM......... Non-Voltage Matter (SAUS)
NVM......... Nova Marketing Ltd. [*Vancouver Stock Exchange symbol*]
NVMA........ National Veterans Medical Association [*Medicine*] (EDAA)
NVMA........ National Veterinary Medical Association (WDAA)
NVMA........ Nebraska Veterinary Medical Association (GVA)
NVMA........ Nevada Mining Association (EARSL)
NVMA........ Noise and Vibration Monitor Analyzer [*Military*] (CAAL)
NvMAd....... Nuveen Municipal Advantage Fund [*Associated Press*] (SAG)
NvMAP....... Nuveen Massachusetts Premium Income Municipal Fund [*Associated Press*] (SAG)
NvMcK....... Kinnear Public Library, McGill, NV [*Library symbol*] [*Library of Congress*] (LCLS)

NvMiD........ Douglas County Library, Minden, NV [*Library symbol*] [*Library of Congress*] (LCLS)
NvMIPI...... Nuveen Michigan Premium Income Municipal [*Associated Press*] (SAG)
NvMO........ Nuveen Municipal Opportunity Fund [*Associated Press*] (SAG)
NVMS .... Night Visibility Measuring Set
NVMS .... Night Vision Modular System [*Police and security equipment*]
NVMS .... Noise and Vibration Monitoring System (SAUS)
Nvmt......... Novametrics Medical Systems [*Associated Press*] (SAG)
Nvmt......... Novametrix Medical Systems, Inc. [*Associated Press*] (SAG)
NvMul .... Nuveen Municipal Income Fund [*Associated Press*] (SAG)
NvMus....... Nevada State Museum, Capital Complex, Carson City, NV [*Library symbol*] [*Library of Congress*] (LCLS)
NVMV .... Nicotiana Velutina Mosaic Virus [*Plant pathology*]
NVN.......... Nirvana Industries Ltd. [*Vancouver Stock Exchange symbol*]
NVN.......... Non-Von Neumann
NVN.......... North Vietnam (VNW)
NVN.......... Noun-Verb-Noun [*Education of the hearing-impaired*]
NVN.......... Nuveen New York Select Quality Municipal [*NYSE symbol*] (SPSG)
NVN.......... Nuveen NY Selct Qual Muni [*NYSE symbol*] (TTSB)
NVNA........ Non-Volatile Nitrosamine [*Organic chemistry*]
NVNAD...... Nippon Volunteer Network Active in Disasters [*Emergency Management*] (EMA)
NVNAF ...... North Vietnamese Air Force
NvNJ......... Nuveen New Jersey Investment Quality Municipal Fund [*Associated Press*] (SAG)
NvNJPI...... Nuveen New Jersey Premium Income Municipal [*Associated Press*] (SAG)
NVNN........ North Vietnamese Navy
NvNoIC...... Clark County Community College, North Las Vegas, NV [*Library symbol*] [*Library of Congress*] (LCLS)
NVNTA....... Night Vision Net Technical Assessment (MCD)
NVNU........ Nova Natural Resources Corp. [*NASDAQ symbol*]
NVNW........ Novo Networks [*NASDAQ symbol*]
NvNYP....... Nuveen New York Performance Plus Municipal Fund [*Associated Press*] (SAG)
NvNYQI...... Nuveen New York Quality Income Municipal [*Associated Press*] (SAG)
NVO.......... Coalition of National Voluntary Organizations [*Also, National Voluntary Organizations*] (AC)
NVO.......... National Virtual Observatory
NVO.......... Nevada Operations Office [*Department of Energy*] (MCD)
NVO.......... New Vehicle Order
NVO.......... Nonverbal Operation
NVO.......... Nonvessel Operator [*Shipping*]
NVO.......... Non-Visual User Object (SAUS)
NVO.......... Nonvolatile Organic [*Residue of thermal processing*]
NVO.......... Novo Industri A/S [*NYSE symbol*] (COMM)
NVO.......... Novo Nordisk A/S ADR [*NYSE symbol*] (SPSG)
NVOAD...... National Voluntary Organizations Active in Disaster (EA)
NVOC........ Nitroveratryloxycarbonyl [*Organic radical*]
NVOC........ Nonvessel-Owning Carrier [*Shipping*] (DS)
NVOCC...... New Version Ocean Container Control (SAUS)
NVOCC...... New Version Overseas Container Control (SAUS)
NVOCC...... Non-Vehicle Owning/Operating Common Carrier [*Indian Railway*] (TIR)
NVOCC...... Nonvessel Operating Common Carrier [*Shipping*]
NVOCC...... Nonvessel-Owning Common Carrier [*Shipping*] (DS)
NVOCC...... Non-Volatile Ocean Container Control (SAUS)
NVOD........ Near Video on Demand (WDAA)
NvoFn....... Nuevo Financing I [*Associated Press*] (SAG)
NVOI......... National Voice of Iran [*Clandestine, Soviet-backed radio station*]
NVOILA...... National Voluntary Organizations for Independent Living for the Aging (EA)
NVOL........ Nonvolative (SAUS)
NVOO........ Nevada Operations Office [*Department of Energy*]
NVOP........ National Veteran's Outreach Program (EA)
NVORDCH... Naval Ordnance Chart
NVP.......... National Vaccine Program [*National Institutes of Health*]
NVP.......... Nausea and Vomiting in Pregnancy
NVP.......... Network Voice Protocol (CCCA)
NVP.......... Nevada Power Co. [*NYSE symbol*] (SPSG)
NVP.......... Nevirpine [*Organic chemistry*]
NVP.......... Night Visibility Plan (SAUS)
NVP.......... Night Vision Pocketscope [*Police and security equipment*]
NVP.......... Nominal Velocity of Propagation [*Electronics*] (PCM)
NVP.......... Nordvorpommern [*German license plate city code*]
NVP.......... N-Vinylpyrrolidone [*Organic chemistry*]
NVPA........ National Visual Presentation Association (EA)
NvPA......... Nuveen Pennsylvania Investment Quality Municipal Fund [*Associated Press*] (SAG)
NvPAP2..... Nuveen Pennsylvania Premium Income Municipal Fund [*Associated Press*] (SAG)
NvPIM........ Nuveen Premier Insured Municipal Income Fund [*Associated Press*] (SAG)
NvPMI........ Nuveen Premium Municipal Income Fund [*Associated Press*] (SAG)
NVPO........ Nuclear Vehicle Projects Office [*NASA*]
NVPOWG.... NASA/VAFB [*National Aeronautical and Space Administration/Vandenburg Air Force Base*] Payload Operations Working Group
NVPP........ National Vehicle Population Poll (COE)
NVPP........ National Vehicle Population Profile
NVPS........ Night Vision Pilotage Subsystem (SAUS)
NVPS........ Night Vision Pilotage System [*Military*]
NVPS........ Night Vision Pocket Scope [*Police and security equipment*]
NVP-U....... Nationale Volkspartij - Unie [*National United People's Party*] [*Netherlands Antilles*] [*Political party*] (PPW)
NVPX........ Nevada Power [*Private rail car owner code*]
NVQ.......... National Vocational Qualification (WDAA)
NVQ.......... National Vocation Qualification [*British*]
NVR.......... National Video Resources
NVR.......... Naval Vessel Register (MCD)
NVR.......... Nonvolatile Residue (NAKS)
NVR.......... Norfolk Volunteer Regiment [*British military*] (DMA)
NVR.......... Northern Vermont Railroad [*Federal Railroad Administration identification code*]
NVR.......... Not Very Relevant [*Internet lingo*] (NETL)
NVR.......... No Verification Required (NASA)
NVR.......... No Voltage Release [*Electronics*]
NVR.......... NVA [*North Vietnam Army*] Regulars (VNW)
NVR.......... NVR, Inc. [*AMEX symbol*] (SPSG)
NVR.......... NV Ryan L. P. [*AMEX symbol*] (COMM)
NVR.WS..... NVR Inc. Wrrt [*AMEX symbol*] (TTSB)
NVRA........ National Verbatim Reporters Association (EA)
NVRAM...... Non-Volatile Random Access Memory [*Automotive engineering*]
NVRAM...... Nonvolatile Random-Access Memory [*Computer science*]
NVRC........ National Retirees Volunteer Coalition [*An association*]
NVRC........ Northern Virginia Regional Commission (EARSL)
NvREr........ United States Energy Research Development Administration, Reno, NV [*Library symbol*] [*Library of Congress*] (LCLS)
NvRFM...... Grand Lodge of the Free and Accepted Masons of the State of Nevada, Reno, NV [*Library symbol*] [*Library of Congress*] (LCLS)
NvRGS...... Church of Jesus Christ of Latter-Day Saints, Genealogical Society Library, Reno Branch, Reno, NV [*Library symbol*] [*Library of Congress*] (LCLS)
NvRH......... Harrah's Automobile Collection and Pony Express Museum, Reno, NV [*Library symbol*] [*Library of Congress*] (LCLS)
NVRIA........ National Vision Research Institute of Australia
NvRNC...... National College of the State Judiciary, Law Library, Reno, NV [*Library symbol*] [*Library of Congress*] (LCLS)
NVROM..... Non-Volatile Read-Only Memory (SAUS)
NVRR........ Napa Valley Railroad [*Federal Railroad Administration identification code*]
NVRS........ National Vegetable Research Station [*Research center*] [*British*] (IRC)
NVRS........ Night Vision Reconnaissance System
NVRS........ Numerical Value Rating System [*Navy*]
NVRU........ Envirolease [*Intermodal shipping container symbol*] (TVRC)
NvRW........ Washoe County Library, Reno, NV [*Library symbol*] [*Library of Congress*] (LCLS)
NvRWL...... Washoe County Law Library, Reno, NV [*Library symbol*] [*Library of Congress*] (LCLS)
NVs.......... Henry Waldinger Memorial Library, Valley Stream, NY [*Library symbol*] [*Library of Congress*] (LCLS)
NVS.......... Narrowband Voice Security
NVS.......... National Vegetable Society [*British*] (DBA)
NVS.......... Neurological Vital Signs [*Medicine*]
NVS.......... Neutron Velocity Selector
NVS.......... Night Vision Safety [*Automotive rear-view mirrors*]
NVS.......... Night Vision Sight (ACAE)
NVS.......... Night Vision System
NVS.......... Nonvolatile Storage (SAUS)
NVS.......... Nonvoting Stock [*Investment term*]
NVS.......... Novosibirsk [*Former USSR*] [*Seismograph station code, US Geological Survey*] (SEIS)
NVS.......... Number of Video Samples
NVS.......... Southeastern Baptist Theological Seminary, Wake Forest, NC [*OCLC symbol*] (OCLC)
NVSA........ Ablow [*Vanuatu*] [*ICAO location identifier*] (ICLI)
NVSA........ Natuurbestuurvereniging van Suidelike Afrika [*Southern African Wildlife Management Association - SAWMA*] [*Pretoria, South Africa*] (EAIO)
NVSA........ Nematologiese Vereniging van Suidelike Afrika [*Nematological Society of Southern Africa*] (EAIO)
NVSA........ New Vehicle Security Assessment
NVsAE....... Alden Terrace Elementary School, Valley Stream, NY [*Library symbol*] [*Library of Congress*] (LCLS)
NVsBAE..... Brooklyn Avenue School, Valley Stream, NY [*Library symbol*] [*Library of Congress*] (LCLS)
NVsBE....... William L. Buck School, Valley Stream, NY [*Library symbol*] [*Library of Congress*] (LCLS)
NVSC........ Sola [*Vanuatu*] [*ICAO location identifier*] (ICLI)
NVsCE....... Robert W. Carbonaro School, Valley Stream, NY [*Library symbol*] [*Library of Congress*] (LCLS)
NVsCSE..... Clear Stream Avenue Elementary School, Valley Stream, NY [*Library symbol*] [*Library of Congress*] (LCLS)
NVsCSH..... Central Senior High School, Valley Stream, NY [*Library symbol*] [*Library of Congress*] (LCLS)
NVSD........ Lo-Linua [*Vanuatu*] [*ICAO location identifier*] (ICLI)
NVSD........ National Vital Statistics Division [*National Center for Health Statistics*] [*Obsolete*]
NVSD........ Night Vision System Development [*Military*]
NVsDE....... Devet Elementary School, Valley Stream, NY [*Library symbol*] [*Library of Congress*] (LCLS)
NVSDS...... New Vehicle Satisfaction with Dealer Service [*Quality research*]
NVSE........ Emae [*Vanuatu*] [*ICAO location identifier*] (ICLI)
NVSF........ Graig Cove [*Vanuatu*] [*ICAO location identifier*] (ICLI)
NVsFE....... Forest Elementary School, Valley Stream, NY [*Library symbol*] [*Library of Congress*] (LCLS)
NVsFH....... Franklin General Hospital, Valley Stream, NY [*Library symbol*] [*Library of Congress*] (LCLS)
NVSG........ Longana [*Vanuatu*] [*ICAO location identifier*] (ICLI)
NVSH........ Dutch Foundation for Sexual Reform

NVSH .... Nonvocal Severely Handicapped
NVSH .... Sara [*Vanuatu*] [*ICAO location identifier*] (ICLI)
NVsHE .... Howell Road School, Valley Stream, NY [*Library symbol*] [*Library of Congress*] (LCLS)
NVSI .... National Vision Services, Inc. [*NASDAQ symbol*] (COMM)
NVSIMM .... Non-Volatile Single Inline Memory Module (SAUS)
NVSL .... Lamap [*Vanuatu*] [*ICAO location identifier*] (ICLI)
NVSL .... National Veterinary Services Laboratory [*Ames, IA*] [*Department of Agriculture*] (GRD)
NVSM .... Lamen-Bay [*Vanuatu*] [*ICAO location identifier*] (ICLI)
NVSM .... Nonvolatile Semiconductor Memory (MCD)
NVSMD ...... Nonvolatile Semiconductor Memory Device (PDAA)
NVsMJH ..... Memorial Junior High School, Valley Stream, NY [*Library symbol*] [*Library of Congress*] (LCLS)
NvSMM ..... Nuveen Select Maturities Municipal Fund [*Associated Press*] (SAG)
NVSN .... Maewo-Naone [*Vanuatu*] [*ICAO location identifier*] (ICLI)
NVSN .... N-Vision, Inc. [*NASDAQ symbol*] (SAG)
NVSN .... N Vision Technology [*OTCBB symbol*]
NVsNSH ..... Valley Stream North High School, Valley Stream, NY [*Library symbol*] [*Library of Congress*] (LCLS)
NVSNW ..... n-Vision Inc. Wrrt [*NASDAQ symbol*] (TTSB)
NVSO .... Lonorore [*Vanuatu*] [*ICAO location identifier*] (ICLI)
NVsOE .... Ogden Elementary School, Valley Stream, NY [*Library symbol*] [*Library of Congress*] (LCLS)
N-VSOS ..... Non-Verbal Scale of Suffering [*Personality development test*] [*Psychology*]
NVSP .... Norsup [*Vanuatu*] [*ICAO location identifier*] (ICLI)
NVSR .... Redcliff [*Vanuatu*] [*ICAO location identifier*] (ICLI)
nvSRAM ..... Nonvolatile Static Random Access Memory (SAUS)
NVSRL ...... Northern Virginia Survey Research Laboratory [*George Mason University*] (RCD)
NVSS .... National Vital Statistics System [*Department of Health and Human Services*] (GFGA)
NVSS .... Nonvolatile Suspended Solids [*Environmental chemistry*]
NVSS .... Normal-Variant Short Stature [*Medicine*]
NVSS .... Santo/Pekoa [*Vanuatu*] [*ICAO location identifier*] (ICLI)
NVsSAE ..... Shaw Avenue Elementary School, Valley Stream, NY [*Library symbol*] [*Library of Congress*] (LCLS)
NVsSSH ..... South Senior High School, Valley Stream, NY [*Library symbol*] [*Library of Congress*] (LCLS)
NVST .... Tongoa [*Vanuatu*] [*ICAO location identifier*] (ICLI)
NVSU .... Ulei [*Vanuatu*] [*ICAO location identifier*] (ICLI)
NVSV .... Valesdir [*Vanuatu*] [*ICAO location identifier*] (ICLI)
NVSW .... Walaha [*Vanuatu*] [*ICAO location identifier*] (ICLI)
NVsWE .... Willow Elementary School, Valley Stream, NY [*Library symbol*] [*Library of Congress*] (LCLS)
NVsWhE ..... Wheeler Elementary School, Valley Stream, NY [*Library symbol*] [*Library of Congress*] (LCLS)
NVSX .... South West Bay [*Vanuatu*] [*ICAO location identifier*] (ICLI)
NVSZ .... North West Santo [*Vanuatu*] [*ICAO location identifier*] (ICLI)
NVT .... Navegantes [*Brazil*] [*Airport symbol*] (OAG)
NVT .... Nelson Vending Technology Ltd. [*Toronto Stock Exchange symbol*]
NVT .... Nerve, Vein, and Tendon (DAVI)
NVT .... Network Validation Testing [*Telecommunications*] (CIST)
NVT .... Network Virtual Terminal
NVT .... Neuton Velocity Time (IAA)
NVT .... Norton Villiers Triumph [*Automobile manufacturer*] [*British*]
NVT .... Novell Virtual Terminal [*Novell, Inc.*] [*Computer science*] (PCM)
NVT .... Nuisance Valve Tactics
NVTA .... National Visiting Teachers Association (EA)
NVTA .... NVT America [*NCIC motorcycle make code*]
NVTC .... Northern Virginia Transportation Commission [*Federal Railroad Administration identification code*]
NVTCS .... Nissan Valve Timing Control System
NVTG .... Norton Villiers Triumph Group [*Automobile manufacturer*] [*British*]
NVTHLSS ... Nevertheless (ROG)
NV-THS ...... National Vocational-Technical Honor Society (EA)
NVTI .... Napa Valley Trucking [*Common carrier symbol*]
NVTK .... Novatek International, Inc. [*NASDAQ symbol*] (SAG)
NVTOC ...... Nonvolatile Total Organic Carbon [*Environmental chemistry*]
NVTS .... National Vocational Training Service
NVTS .... Null Voltage Test Set (MCD)
NVTSY .... Novartis AG [*OTCBB symbol*]
NVTWUGBI ... National Vehicular Traffic Workers' Union of Great Britain and Ireland
NVU .... Dutch People's Union (Netherlands) [*Political party*] (PSAP)
nvu .... Nevada [*MARC country of publication code*] [*Library of Congress*] (LCCP)
NvU .... University of Nevada, Reno, NV [*Library symbol*] [*Library of Congress*] (LCLS)
NVUE .... NVIEW Corp. [*NASDAQ symbol*] (SAG)
NVVA .... Anatom [*Vanuatu*] [*ICAO location identifier*] (ICLI)
NVVA .... Napa Valley Vintners Association (EA)
NVVB .... Aniwa [*Vanuatu*] [*ICAO location identifier*] (ICLI)
NVVC .... National Vietnam Veterans Coalition (EA)
NV/VC .... North Vietnamese/Vietcong (SAUS)
NVVCCG ..... North Vietnamese and Viet Cong Collecting Group [*Defunct*] (EA)
NVVD .... Dillon's Bay [*Vanuatu*] [*ICAO location identifier*] (ICLI)
NVVF .... Futuna [*Vanuatu*] [*ICAO location identifier*] (ICLI)
NVVI .... Ipota [*Vanuatu*] [*ICAO location identifier*] (ICLI)
NVVJ .... Forari [*Vanuatu*] [*ICAO location identifier*] (ICLI)
NVVK .... Lenakel [*Vanuatu*] [*ICAO location identifier*] (ICLI)
NVVOAD .... Nevada Voluntary Organizations Active in Disaster [*Emergency Management*] (EMA)
NVVQ .... Quoin Hill [*Vanuatu*] [*ICAO location identifier*] (ICLI)
NVVRS ...... National Vietnam Veterans Readjustment Study [*Veterans Administration*]
NVVV .... Port-Vila/Bauerfield [*Vanuatu*] [*ICAO location identifier*] (ICLI)
NVWA .... National Volkswagen Association (EA)
NV Wine .... Nonvintage Wine (SAUS)
NVWLA ...... Napa Valley Wine Library Association (EA)
NVWSC ...... Nonvolatile Whole Smoke Condensate [*Environmental chemistry*] (AAMN)
NVWSM ..... Newfoundland Volunteers War Service Medal [*Canada*] (FOTI)
NVWT .... Napa Valley Wine Train [*Federal Railroad Administration identification code*]
NVX .... Nervous [*Telegraphy*] (PCTE)
NVX .... North American Vaccine [*AMEX symbol*] (TTSB)
NVX .... North American Vaccine, Inc. [*AMEX symbol*] (SAG)
NVY .... Royal Navy [*British*] [*ICAO designator*] (FAAC)
NW .... Chicago & North Western Railway (SAUS)
NW .... Naked Weight
NW .... Naked Wire (IAA)
nW .... Nanowatt [*One billionth of a watt*]
NW .... Narrow White [*Automotive tire design*]
NW .... Narrow Widths [*Construction*]
NW .... Nasal Wash [*Medicine*] (DMAA)
NW .... NASA Waiver (KSC)
NW .... Nasmyth Wilson [*Indian Railway*] [*Manchester*] (TIR)
NW .... National Westminster Bancorp, Inc. [*NYSE symbol*] (SPSG)
NW .... National Women's Conference Committee [*Formerly, CCNWC*] (EA)
NW .... Natl Westminster ADS [*NYSE symbol*] (TTSB)
NW .... Nat-War Alliance [*Defunct*] (EA)
NW .... Naval Air Systems Command
NW .... Net Weight
NW .... Network (NASA)
NW .... Network Cells [*Botany*]
NW .... Net Worth
NW .... Neustadt [*Weinstrasse*] [*German license plate city code*]
NW .... Neville and Winther's Acid
NW .... Neville-Winter (SAUS)
NW .... New
NW .... Newsweek [*A publication*] (BRI)
NW .... New Wave [*Style of music*]
NW .... New World [*Translation of the Holy Scriptures*] [*A publication*] (BJA)
NW .... Nominal Width (NATG)
NW .... Non-Weathering (SAUS)
NW .... Norfolk & Western Railway Co. [*AAR code*]
NW .... Normal Waste [*Nuclear energy*] (NRCH)
NW .... Norman-Wood Disease [*Medicine*] (DB)
NW .... Northern Wings Ltd (SAUS)
NW .... North Wales
NW .... North West (SAUS)
NW .... Northwest
NW .... North-Western (SAUS)
NW .... North-Western Provinces, High Court Reports [*India*] [*A publication*] (DLA)
NW .... North Western Reporter [*National Reporter System*] [*A publication*] (DLA)
NW .... Northwest Orient Airlines, Inc. [*ICAO designator*]
NW .... Nor-Weberine [*Biochemistry*]
NW .... Nose Wheel [*Aviation*] (MCD)
NW .... Not Waiverable (COE)
NW .... Now
NW .... No Wait [*Industrial engineering*]
NW .... No Wind [*Air*] Position [*Navigation*]
NW .... Nuclear Warfare
NW .... Nuclear Waste (SAUS)
NW .... Nuclear Weapon (NG)
NW .... Nuclear Weaponsman [*U.S. Navy enlisted rating*] (AUER)
NW .... Nucleonia Week (SAUS)
NW .... Number of Weeks (SAUS)
N-W .... Nu-West (EFIS)
nw--- .... West Indies [*MARC geographic area code*] [*Library of Congress*] (LCCP)
NW2 .... New River [*California*] [*Seismograph station code, US Geological Survey*] (SEIS)
NW 2d .... North Western Reporter, Second Series [*West*] [*A publication*] (AAGC)
NWA .... Moheli [*Comoro Islands*] [*Airport symbol*] (OAG)
NWA .... Narrogin [*Australia*] [*Seismograph station code, US Geological Survey*] (SEIS)
NWA .... National Water Alliance (EA)
NWA .... National Waterfowl Alliance, Waterfowl USA [*Later, WUSA*] (EA)
NWA .... National Watermelon Association (NTPA)
NWA .... National Water Well Association, Worthington, OH [*OCLC symbol*] (OCLC)
NWA .... National Weather Association (EA)
NWA .... National Welders Association [*A union*] [*British*]
NWA .... National Wellness Association (EA)
NWA .... National Wine Association [*Defunct*] (EA)
NWA .... National Wrestling Alliance (DAVI)
NWA .... National Writers Association (NTPA)
NWA .... Naval Warfare Analysis (MCD)
NWA .... Naval Weapons Annex
NWA .... Navy Wifeline Association (EA)
NWA .... New Work Authorized (MCD)
NWA .... New World Alliance [*Defunct*] (EA)
NWA .... Northumbrian Water Authority [*British*] (DCTA)
NWA .... North West Africa (SAUS)

NWA........ Northwest Airlines, Inc. [*ICAO designator*] (FAAC)
NWA........ Northwestern Australia (SAUS)
NWA........ Northwest Orient Airlines, Inc. (MCD)
NWA........ Nothin' Worth Askin' [*Rap recording group*]
NWA........ Nuclear Weapon Accident (SAUS)
NWA........ NWA, Inc. [*NYSE symbol*] (COMM)
NWAA....... National Wheelchair Athletic Association (EA)
NWAA....... National Women's Automotive Association [*Defunct*] (EA)
NWAACC.... Northwest Athletic Association of Community Colleges (PSS)
NWAAF...... Northwest African Air Forces [*World War II*]
NWAB....... National Women's Advisory Board [*on Sailing*] [*Nautical term*] (NTA)
NWAB....... Necks with Any Boy [*Slang*]
NWAC....... National Weather Analysis Center [*Air Force, Navy*]
NWAC....... National Wheelchair Athletic Committee
NWAC....... National Women's Advisory Council (NADA)
NWAC....... Native Women's Association of Canada
NWAC....... Northeast Women's Athletic Conference (PSS)
NWAC....... Northwest Airlines'A' [*NASDAQ symbol*] (TTSB)
NWAC....... Northwest Airlines Corp. [*NASDAQ symbol*] (SAG)
NWAC....... Northwestern Area Command (SAUS)
NWadd...... Hepburn Library, Waddington, NY [*Library symbol*] [*Library of Congress*] (LCLS)
NWAERP.... New World Association of Emigrants from Eastern Europe in Pennsylvania (EARSL)
NWAF....... New World Archeological Foundation (SAUS)
NWAFC...... Northwest and Alaska Fisheries Center [*National Marine Fisheries Service*] [*Department of Commerce*] [*Research center*] (RCD)
NWAG....... Naval Warfare Analysis Group
NWAHACA... National Warm Air Heating and Air Conditioning Association [*Later, ACCA*] (EA)
NWAI....... Nuclear Weapons Acceptance Inspection (NG)
NWAIB...... Nuclear Weapon Accident Investigation Board (AABC)
NWald...... Josephine-Louise Public Library, Walden, NY [*Library symbol*] [*Library of Congress*] (LCLS)
NWall....... Wallkill Public Library, Wallkill, NY [*Library symbol*] [*Library of Congress*] (LCLS)
NWan....... Wantagh Public Library, Wantagh, NY [*Library symbol*] [*Library of Congress*] (LCLS)
NWanE...... Wantagh Elementary School, Wantagh, NY [*Library symbol*] [*Library of Congress*] (LCLS)
NWanFLE... Forest Lake Elementary School, Wantagh, NY [*Library symbol*] [*Library of Congress*] (LCLS)
NWanJH..... Wantagh Junior High School, Wantagh, NY [*Library symbol*] [*Library of Congress*] (LCLS)
NWanJS..... Wantagh Junior-Senior High, Wantagh, NY [*Library symbol*] [*Library of Congress*] (LCLS)
NWanME.... Mandalay Elementary School, Wantagh, NY [*Library symbol*] [*Library of Congress*] (LCLS)
NWanSH.... Wantagh Senior High School, Wantagh, NY [*Library symbol*] [*Library of Congress*] (LCLS)
NWanSPE... Sunrise Park Elementary School, Wantagh, NY [*Library symbol*] [*Library of Congress*] (LCLS)
NWAO....... Narrogin [*Australia*] [*Seismograph station code, US Geological Survey*] (SEIS)
NWAP....... National White American Party (BJA)
NWapA...... Mount Alvernia Seminary, Wappingers Falls, NY [*Library symbol*] [*Library of Congress*] (LCLS)
NWAPP...... National Woman Abuse Prevention Project (EA)
nwaq-....... Antigua [*MARC geographic area code*] [*Library of Congress*] (LCCP)
NWAR....... New Air Flight, Inc. (SAUS)
N-War....... Nuclear Warfare (SAUS)
NWARC...... Navy Weapons Assessment Research Centre (SAUS)
NWARK...... Newark, NY [*American Association of Railroads railroad junction routing code*]
NWas....... Moffat Library Association, Washingtonville, NY [*Library symbol*] [*Library of Congress*] (LCLS)
NWAS....... Newton and Sons [*Common carrier symbol*]
NWASC...... Northwest Association of Schools and Colleges (DHP)
NWASI...... Northrop Worldwide Aircraft Services Inc. (SAUS)
N-Waste.... Nuclear Waste (SAUS)
NWAT....... Nuclear Weapon Assist Team (SAUS)
NWatfG...... General Electric Co., Silicone Products Department, Waterford, NY [*Library symbol*] [*Library of Congress*] (LCLS)
NWatt........ Roswell P. Flower Memorial Public Library, Watertown, NY [*Library symbol*] [*Library of Congress*] (LCLS)
NWattJ...... Jefferson Community College, Watertown, NY [*Library symbol*] [*Library of Congress*] (LCLS)
NWattJHi.... Jefferson County Historical Society, Watertown, NY [*Library symbol*] [*Library of Congress*] (LCLS)
NWattKH.... Samaritan Keep Nursing Home, Medical Library, Watertown, NY [*Library symbol*] [*Library of Congress*] (LCLS)
NWattMH... Mercy Hospital of Watertown, Watertown, NY [*Library symbol*] [*Library of Congress*] (LCLS)
NWattN...... North Country Library System, Watertown, NY [*Library symbol*] [*Library of Congress*] (LCLS)
NWatvlA..... Watervliet Arsenal Library, Watervliet, NY [*Library symbol*] [*Library of Congress*] (LCLS)
NWAVL...... Now Available (NOAA)
NWAX....... National Wax [*Private rail car owner code*]
NWB........ National Wiring Bureau [*Defunct*] (EA)
NWB........ Naval Weapons Bulletin
NWB........ Nederlandse Waterschapsbank NV [*Waterschaps Bank of the Netherlands*]
NWB........ New War Department Building [*Obsolete*]
NWB........ Next Working Block (SAUS)
NWB........ Non-Weight-Bearing [*Orthopedics and physical therapy*] (DAVI)
NWB........ Northwestbound [*ICAO designator*] (FAAC)
NWB........ North Western Bell (HGAA)
NWB........ Northwest Towboat Tariff Bureau, Inc., Seattle WA [*STAC*]
NWB........ No Weight-Bearing [*orthopedics*] (DAVI)
NWBA....... National Wheelchair Basketball Association (EA)
nwbb-....... Barbados [*MARC geographic area code*] [*Library of Congress*] (LCCP)
NWBB....... Noumea [*New Caledonia*] [*ICAO location identifier*] (ICLI)
NwbBc...... Newberry Bancorp, Inc. [*Associated Press*] (SAG)
nwbc-....... Barbuda [*MARC geographic area code*] [*Library of Congress*] (LCCP)
NWbC....... Cardion Electronics, Woodbury, NY [*Library symbol*] [*Library of Congress*] (LCLS)
NWBC....... National Women's Business Council
NWBC....... National Wooden Box Council [*Later, NWPCA*] (EA)
NWBD....... New World Brands [*OTCBB symbol*]
nwbf-....... Bahamas [*MARC geographic area code*] [*Library of Congress*] (LCCP)
NWBHI...... Nuclear Weapon Burst Height Indicator
NWbN....... Northwest by North
NWBR....... Nelson-Westerberg [*Common carrier symbol*]
NWBW....... National Women Bowling Writers Association (EA)
NWbW....... Northwest by West
NWbW....... Waldemar Medical Research Foundation, Woodbury, NY [*Library symbol*] [*Library of Congress*] (LCLS)
NWC........ National Waco Club (EA)
NWC........ National War College [*Later, UND*] [*DoD*]
NWC........ National Warning Center [*Civil Defense*]
NWC........ National Water Center (EA)
NWC........ National Water Commission [*Terminated, 1973*]
NWC........ National Water Council [*British*] (DCTA)
NWC........ National Waterfowl Council (EA)
NWC........ National Watershed Congress (EA)
NWC........ National Waterways Conference (EA)
NWC........ National Wetlands Coalition [*Association*] (EA)
NWC........ National Wildlife Centre (SAUS)
NWC........ National Wiretap Commission [*Department of Justice*]
NWC........ National Women's Coalition [*Defunct*] (EA)
NWC........ National Woodie Club (EA)
NWC........ National Writers Club (EA)
NWC........ Nationwide Cellular Service, Inc. (EFIS)
NWC........ Naval War College
NWC........ Naval Weapons Center
NWC........ Navy Widow's Certificate (GEAB)
NWC........ Net Working Capital
NWC........ Net Worth Certificate (EBF)
NWC........ New ACS Ltd. [*United Republic of Tanzania*] [*FAA designator*] (FAAC)
NWC........ New World Club (EA)
NWC........ New World Coalition (EA)
NWC........ Northwest Cape
NWC........ Northwest Caucasian [*Linguistics*] (IEL)
NWC........ Northwest College [*Washington*]
NWC........ North West Community College Library [*UTLAS symbol*]
NWC........ Nuclear War Capability (AAG)
NWC........ Nuclear Weapons Center (SAUS)
NWC........ Nuclear Weapons Complex (COE)
NWC........ Nuclear Weapons Control
NWC........ Nuclear Weapons Council (SAUS)
NWC........ Wingate College, Wingate, NC [*OCLC symbol*] (OCLC)
NWCA....... National Water Carriers Association
NWCA....... National Woodcarvers Association (EA)
NWCA....... National Wrestling Coaches Association (EA)
NWCA....... National Writing Centers Association (NTPA)
NWCA....... Native Writers' Circle of the Americas [*Association*] (EA)
NWCA....... Navy Wives Clubs of America (EA)
NWCA....... NewCare Health [*NASDAQ symbol*] (TTSB)
NWCA....... New Care Health Corp. [*NASDAQ symbol*] (SAG)
NWCA....... Northwest Cherry Briners Association
NWCAA...... National War College Alumni Association
NWCAEU.... National Women's Conference of the American Ethical Union (EA)
NWC/ARP... Naval War College Advanced Research Program [*Newport, RI*]
NWCC....... National Water Co. Conference [*Later, NAWC*]
NWCC....... National Women's Conference Committee (EA)
NWCC....... Neutron Well Coincidence Counter [*Nuclear energy*] (NRCH)
NWCC....... Northern Wyoming Community College (SAUS)
NWCC....... Northwest Christian College [*Oregon*]
NWCC....... Northwestern Weed Control Conference (SAUS)
NWCC....... Noumea/La Tontouta [*New Caledonia*] [*ICAO location identifier*] (ICLI)
NWCCA...... Naval Weapons Center, Corona Annex [*California*]
NWC/CAR... Naval War College Center for Advanced Research [*Newport, RI*]
NWCCL...... Naval Weapons Center, Corona Laboratories [*California*]
NWCCS...... Naval Worldwide Command and Control System (MCD)
NWCDC...... North West Cooperative Development Council [*British*]
NWCF....... New Waste Calcining Facility [*Nuclear energy*] (NUCP)
NWCF....... Northwest Citizens Forum (SAUS)
NWCG....... National Wildfire Coordinating Group (ALAC)
NWCG....... New World Communic Grp'A' [*NASDAQ symbol*] (TTSB)
NWCG....... New World Communictions Corp. [*NASDAQ symbol*] (SAG)
NWCG....... Northwest Cherry Growers [*Washington, Oregon, Idaho and Utah*] (EARSL)
NWCG....... Nuclear Weapons Coordinating Group
NWCHA..... Northwest Clearing House Association (TBD)
NWCI........ New World Coffee [*NASDAQ symbol*] (TTSB)
NWCI........ New World Coffee, Inc. [*NASDAQ symbol*] (SAG)
NWCI........ New World Coffee-Manhattan Bagel, Inc. [*NASDAQ symbol*] (NASQ)

NWCIEP..... Nation-Wide Committee on Import-Export Policy [*Defunct*] (EA)
nwcj-........ Cayman Islands [*MARC geographic area code*] [*Library of Congress*] (LCCP)
NWCM....... NewCom, Inc. [*NASDAQ symbol*] (NASQ)
NwCm........ News Communications, Inc. [*Associated Press*] (SAG)
NWCME..... National Winter Convention on Military Electronics [*IEEE*] (MCD)
NWC/NW.... Naval War College / Naval Warfare Course (DNAB)
nwco-........ Curacao Group [*MARC geographic area code*] [*Library of Congress*] (LCCP)
NWCO........ National Water Conservation Order (SAUS)
NWCOA..... National Wildlife Control Operators Association (EA)
NWCP....... National Wetlands Conservation Project [*Defunct*] (EA)
NWCP....... Navy Weight-Control Program (DNAB)
NWCP....... Noxious Weeds Control Program (SAUS)
NWCR....... National Weight Control Registry
NWCR....... Naval War College Review [*A publication*]
NWCR....... Nuclear Weapons Correction Report [*Army*] (AABC)
NWCRB..... Navy War Contracts Relief Board
NWCS....... NATO-Wide Communications System (NATG)
NWCS....... Netware Workstation Compatible Service (SAUS)
NWCS....... New Work Concept Sheet (HVTR)
NWCS....... Nuclear Weapons Control System
NWCT....... Northwest Custom Trailer [*NCIC trailer make code*]
NWCTU...... National Woman's Christian Temperance Union (WDAA)
nwcu......... Cuba [*MARC geographic area code*] [*Library of Congress*] (LCCP)
NWCX....... Northwest Container Services [*Private rail car owner code*]
NWD......... Naval Weapons Directory
NWD......... Navigation Weapon Delivery (ACAE)
NWD......... Network Wide Directory
NWD......... New World Dictionary [*A publication*]
NWD......... Normal Well Developed (MELL)
NWD......... Northwest Air Services Ltd. [*Nigeria*] [*ICAO designator*] (FAAC)
NWD......... Northwest Drug Co. Ltd. [*Toronto Stock Exchange symbol*]
NWD......... Nuclear Weapon Disposal (SAUS)
NWD......... Number of Words (MSA)
NWDA....... National Wholesale Druggists' Association (EA)
NWDA....... National Wine Distributors' Association (EA)
NwDay...... New Day Beverage, Inc. [*Associated Press*] (SAG)
NWDC....... National Wildlife Defence Council (USDC)
NWDC....... National Wildlife Defense Council [*Marine science*] (OSRA)
NWDC....... Navigation/Weapon Delivery Computer (PDAA)
NWDC....... Northwest Drama Conference (EA)
NWDC/S.... Navigation/Weapons Delivery Computer/System
NWDEN..... Number of Words per Entry (MSA)
NWDGA..... National Wholesale Dry Goods Association [*Later, NATAD*]
NWDL....... Modular Well-Differentiated Lymphocytic Lymphoma [*Medicine*] (MELL)
NWdmA..... Woodmere Academy, Woodmere, NY [*Library symbol*] [*Library of Congress*] (LCLS)
NWdmE..... No. 6 Elementary School, Woodmere, NY [*Library symbol*] [*Library of Congress*] (LCLS)
NWDO....... National Workforce Development Office (COE)
NWDP....... Nuclear Weapons Development Project (SAUS)
nwdq-....... Dominica [*MARC geographic area code*] [*Library of Congress*] (LCCP)
nwdr-........ Dominican Republic [*MARC geographic area code*] [*Library of Congress*] (LCCP)
NWDS....... National Water Data System [*US Geological Survey*] [*Reston, VA*]
NWDS....... Navigation/Weapons Delivery System
NWDS....... Network Wide Directory System (MHDI)
NWDS....... Noah Worcester Dermatological Society (EA)
NWDS....... Number of Words
NWDSEN.... Number of Words per Entry
NWE......... Narrow Width Effect (IAA)
NWE......... Newline Resources Ltd. [*Vancouver Stock Exchange symbol*]
NWE......... New World Entertainment Ltd. (SAUS)
NWE......... Northwest Aero Associates, Inc. [*FAA designator*] (FAAC)
NWE......... Nuclear Weapons Effects
NWe......... Westbury Memorial Public Library, Westbury, NY [*Library symbol*] [*Library of Congress*] (LCLS)
NWEA....... National Women's Economic Alliance [*Washington, DC*] (EA)
NWEA....... National Wood Energy Association (EA)
NWEA....... Nebraska Water Environment Association (EARSL)
NWEA....... Northwest Ecosystem Alliance [*Pacific Northwest and British Columbia*] (EARSL)
NWEA....... Northwest Evaluation Association
NWEAF...... National Women's Economic Alliance Foundation (NTPA)
NWEAMP... Nuclear Weapons Employment Acquisition Master Plan (CCCA)
NWEB....... Northwestern Electricity Board [*British*]
NWeBE...... Board of Cooperative Educational Services, Nassau Education Resource Center, Westbury, NY [*Library symbol*] [*Library of Congress*] (LCLS)
NWeBGE.... Bowling Green Elementary School, Westbury, NY [*Library symbol*] [*Library of Congress*] (LCLS)
NWebPH.... Pilgrim Hospital, West Brentwood, NY [*Library symbol*] [*Library of Congress*] (LCLS)
NWEC....... Nuclear Weapons Effects Course (MCD)
NWEC....... Nuclear Weapons Employment Course (SAUS)
NWeCJS..... W. Tresper Clarke Junior-Senior High School, Westbury, NY [*Library symbol*] [*Library of Congress*] (LCLS)
NWED....... Nuclear Weapon Effects Development
NWeDE...... Drexel Elementary School, Westbury, NY [*Library symbol*] [*Library of Congress*] (LCLS)
NWEE........ National Women's Employment and Education [*Defunct*] (EA)
NWEF........ National Women's Education Fund (EA)
NWEF........ Naval Weapons Evaluation Facility [*Kirtland Air Force Base, NM*]
NWEF........ New World Education Fund (EA)
NWEF........ North Western Expeditionary Force [*Norway*] [*World War II*]
NWEF........ Nuclear Weapons Education Fund (EA)
NWef........ Patterson Library, Westfield, NY [*Library symbol*] [*Library of Congress*] (LCLS)
NWefHi...... Chautauqua County Historical Society, Westfield, NY [*Library symbol*] [*Library of Congress*] (LCLS)
NWefMH.... Westfield Memorial Hospital, Inc., Westfield, NY [*Library symbol*] [*Library of Congress*] (LCLS)
NWehb...... Westhampton Free Library, Westhampton Beach, NY [*Library symbol*] [*Library of Congress*] (LCLS)
NWehbJH... Westhampton Beach Junior High School, Westhampton Beach, NY [*Library symbol*] [*Library of Congress*] (LCLS)
NWeJH...... Westbury Junior High School, Westbury, NY [*Library symbol*] [*Library of Congress*] (LCLS)
NWel........ David A. Howe Public Library, Wellsville, NY [*Library symbol*] [*Library of Congress*] (LCLS)
NWEL........ Nuclear Weapons Effects Laboratory
NWELF...... Nowsco Well Service Ltd. [*NASDAQ symbol*] (COMM)
NWelH....... Jones Memorial Hospital, Wellsville, NY [*Library symbol*] [*Library of Congress*] (LCLS)
NWeM....... Metco, Inc., Westbury, NY [*Library symbol*] [*Library of Congress*] (LCLS)
NWEN....... Northwest Engineering Co. (SAUS)
NWEO....... Nuclear Weapon Effects Office [*DoD*] (RDA)
NWEO....... Nuclear Weapon Employment Officer (AABC)
NWEP....... Nuclear Weapons Effects Panel
NWePLE..... Powell's Lane Elementary School, Westbury, NY [*Library symbol*] [*Library of Congress*] (LCLS)
NWePSE.... Park School Early Childhood Center, Westbury, NY [*Library symbol*] [*Library of Congress*] (LCLS)
NWEQ....... Northwest Equity Corp. [*NASDAQ symbol*] (TTSB)
NWER....... Nuclear Weapons Effects Research [*Army*]
NWER/T..... Nuclear Weapons Effects Research and Testing [*Army*] (RDA)
NWES....... Naval Weapons Engineering Support activity office (SAUS)
NWES....... New World Exploration Society (SAUS)
NWES....... Nuclear Weapons Electronic Specialist (AABC)
NWes........ Olive Free Library Association, West Shokan, NY [*Library symbol*] [*Library of Congress*] (LCLS)
NWESA...... Naval Weapons Engineering Support Activity (MCD)
NWesbHS... West Babylon High School, West Babylon, NY [*Library symbol*] [*Library of Congress*] (LCLS)
NWesbJH... West Babylon Junior High School, West Babylon, NY [*Library symbol*] [*Library of Congress*] (LCLS)
NWeSH...... Westbury Senior High School, Westbury, NY [*Library symbol*] [*Library of Congress*] (LCLS)
NWesyM.... Suffolk Marine Museum, West Sayville, NY [*Library symbol*] [*Library of Congress*] (LCLS)
NWET........ Nuclear Weapon Effects Test
nweu-....... Sint Eustatius [*MARC geographic area code*] [*Library of Congress*] (LCCP)
NWevNS.... West Valley Nuclear Services Co., West Valley, NY [*Library symbol*] [*Library of Congress*] (LCLS)
NWF......... International Women's Forum [*National Women's Forum*] [*Acronym is based on former name,*] (EA)
NWF......... National War Formulary
NWF......... National War Fund
NWF......... National Welfare Fund (WDAA)
NWF......... National Wildlife Federation (EA)
NWF......... Naval War College Foundation (POLM)
NWF......... Naval Weapons Factory [*Formerly, NGF*]
NWF......... Naval Working Fund [*Navy, Coast Guard*]
NWF......... New Wilderness Foundation (EA)
NWF......... New World Foundation (EA)
NWF......... Nuclear Waste Fund (NUCP)
NWF......... Numerical Weather Facility
NWFA........ National Wholesale Furniture Association (EA)
NWFA........ National Wood Flooring Association (EA)
NWFA........ Northwest Farm Managers Association (EA)
NWFA........ Northwest Fisheries Association (EA)
NWFAL...... Nation-Wide Fallout (SAA)
NWFC....... Nuclear Weapons Freeze Campaign (EA)
NWFF........ North West Frontier Fellowship (EA)
NWFI........ Non-Woven Fabrics Institute [*Defunct*] (EA)
NWFL........ Northwest Freight Lines [*Common carrier symbol*]
NWFM....... Northwest Farm Managers Association (EARSL)
NWFMA..... Northwest Farm Managers Association
NWFN....... Northwestern Financial (SAUS)
NWFP....... North-West Frontier Province [*Pakistan*] (PD)
NWFP....... Nuclear Weapons Fire Planning (MCD)
NWFP....... Rocky Flats/Nuclear Weapons Facilities Project [*Organization with goal of nuclear disarmament*] [*Defunct*] (EA)
NWF Pak.... North West Frontier, Pakistan (ILCA)
NWFS....... NetWare File System [*Computer science*]
NWFS....... NWS Capital Financing Trust [*Associated Press*] (SAG)
NWFSPCN... Nahanni National Park, Parks Canada [*Parc National Nahanni, Parcs Canada*] Fort Simpson, Northwest Territories [*Library symbol*] [*National Library of Canada*] (NLC)
NWFSPCW... Wood Buffalo National Park, Parks Canada [*Parc National Wood Buffalo, Parcs Canada*] Fort Smith, Northwest Territories [*Library symbol*] [*National Library of Canada*] (NLC)
NWFST...... Thebacha College Library, Fort Smith, Northwest Territories [*Library symbol*] [*National Library of Canada*] (NLC)
NWFWA..... Northwest Forest Workers Association [*Defunct*] (EA)
NWFZ........ Nuclear Weapons-Free Zone

NWG .... National Wire Gauge
NWG .... New Goliath Minerals Ltd. [*Toronto Stock Exchange symbol*] [*Vancouver Stock Exchange symbol*]
NWG .... North West Gold Corp. (SAUS)
NWG .... Notwithstanding [*Telegraphy*] (PCTE)
nwga- .... Greater Antilles [*MARC geographic area code*] [*Library of Congress*] (LCCP)
NWGA .... National Wool Growers Association [*Later, ASIA*] (EA)
NWGA .... Northwest Guides Association [*Defunct*]
NWGB .... Northwestern Gas Board (SAUS)
nwgd .... Grenada [*MARC geographic area code*] [*Library of Congress*] (LCCP)
NWGDE ..... Nordic Working Group on Development Education [*Nordic Council of Ministers*] [*Denmark*] (EAIO)
NWGN .... Newgen Results Corp. [*NASDAQ symbol*] (NASQ)
nwgp- .... Guadeloupe [*MARC geographic area code*] [*Library of Congress*] (LCCP)
NWGP .... Nuclear War Graphics Project [*Defunct*] (EA)
nwgs- .... Grenadines [*MARC geographic area code*] [*Library of Congress*] (LCCP)
NWGS .... Naval Warfare Gaming System
NWGS .... North Wall of the Gulf Stream (QUAC)
NWGSFW ... National Working Group on Screw Fly Worm [*Australia*]
NWGWU .... National Warehouse and General Workers' Union [*British*]
NWH .... Nawa Air Transport [*Hungary*] [*ICAO designator*] (FAAC)
NWH .... New Hombre Resources [*Vancouver Stock Exchange symbol*]
NWH .... Normal Working Hours
NWh .... West Hempstead Public Library, West Hempstead, NY [*Library symbol*] [*Library of Congress*] (LCLS)
NWHA .... National Wholesale Hardware Association (EA)
NWHC .... National Women's Health Coalition [*Later, IWHC*]
NWHC .... Naval Weapons Handling Center
NWhCE ...... Cornwell Avenue School, West Hempstead, NY [*Library symbol*] [*Library of Congress*] (LCLS)
NWHF .... National Wildlife Health Foundation (EA)
NWHF .... National Women's Hall of Fame (EA)
NWhh .... Whitehall Free Library, Whitehall, NY [*Library symbol*] [*Library of Congress*] (LCLS)
NWhHS ...... West Hempstead High School, West Hempstead, NY [*Library symbol*] [*Library of Congress*] (LCLS)
nwhi- .... Hispaniola [*MARC geographic area code*] [*Library of Congress*] (LCCP)
NWHI .... Northwestern Hawaiian Islands
NWHL .... National Wildlife Health Laboratory [*Department of the Interior*] (GRD)
NWHL .... Naval Weapons Handling Laboratory
NWhMS ..... West Hempstead Middle School, West Hempstead, NY [*Library symbol*] [*Library of Congress*] (LCLS)
NWHN .... National Women's Health Network (EA)
NWHP .... National Women's History Project (EA)
NWhp .... White Plains Public Library, White Plains, NY [*Library symbol*] [*Library of Congress*] (LCLS)
NWhpG ...... College of White Plains, White Plains, NY [*Library symbol*] [*Library of Congress*] (LCLS)
NWhpI .... IBM Library Processing Center, White Plains, NY [*Library symbol*] [*Library of Congress*] (LCLS)
NWhpNC .... Nynex Corp., White Plains, NY [*Library symbol*] [*Library of Congress*] (LCLS)
NWhpNH .... New York Hospital, Westchester Division, White Plains, NY [*Library symbol*] [*Library of Congress*] (LCLS)
NWhpSC .... New York State Supreme Court Law Library, White Plains, NY [*Library symbol*] [*Library of Congress*] (LCLS)
NWhpT ...... Texaco Inc., Corp. Library, White Plains, NY [*Library symbol*] [*Library of Congress*] (LCLS)
NWhpTI ..... Temple Israel Library, White Plains, NY [*Library symbol*] [*Library of Congress*] (LCLS)
NWhpW ..... Westchester Library System, White Plains, NY [*Library symbol*] [*Library of Congress*] (LCLS)
NWHRC ..... National Women's Health Resource Center (EA)
NWHRN ..... Northwest Territories Public Library Services, Hay River, Northwest Territories [*Library symbol*] [*National Library of Canada*] (NLC)
NWHSLC .... Northern Wisconsin Health Science Library Cooperative [*Library network*]
nwht- .... Haiti [*MARC geographic area code*] [*Library of Congress*] (LCCP)
NWhWE ..... George Washington School, West Hempstead, NY [*Library symbol*] [*Library of Congress*] (LCLS)
NWI .... National Wetlands Inventory
NWI .... National Wilderness Institute (RCD)
NWI .... Netherlands West Indies
NWI .... Networking and World Information [*Electronic information and communications exchange service*]
NWI .... New Work Item (RALS)
NWI .... Northwest Industries Ltd. (SAUS)
NWI .... Norwich [*England*] [*Airport symbol*] (OAG)
NWI .... Nuclear Weapons Inventory (SSD)
NWI .... Nuinsco Resources Ltd. [*Toronto Stock Exchange symbol*]
NWi .... West Islip Public Library, West Islip, NY [*Library symbol*] [*Library of Congress*] (LCLS)
NWIAC ...... Arctic College, Iqualuit, Northwest Territories [*Library symbol*] [*National Library of Canada*] (BIB)
NWIB .... National Westminster Investment Bank [*British*]
NWIB .... Northwest Illinois Bancorp, Inc. (SAUS)
NWIC .... National Water Information Clearinghouse [*Proposed*] [*US Geological Survey*]
NWIC .... National Women's Insurance Center (EA)
NWIC .... Northeast Women's Intercollegiate Association (PSS)
NWICO ...... New World Information and Communications Order [*UNESCO*]
NWIDA ...... North West Industrial Development Association (SAUS)
NWiH .... Good Samaritan Hospital, West Islip, NY [*Library symbol*] [*Library of Congress*] (LCLS)
NWII .... Inuvik Scientific Resource Centre, Indian and Northern Affairs Canada [*CentreScientifique de Ressources d'Inuvik, Affaires Indiennes et du Nord Canada*], Northwest Territories [*Library symbol*] [*National Library of Canada*] (NLC)
NWIIE .... Eastern Arctic Research Laboratory, Indian and Northern Affairs Canada [*Laboratoire de Recherches Arctique de l'Est, Affaires Indiennes et du Nord Canada*], Igloolik, Northwest Territories [*Library symbol*] [*National Library of Canada*] (BIB)
NWiIP .... Willard Psychiatric Center, Willard, NY [*Library symbol*] [*Library of Congress*] (LCLS)
NWils .... Wilson Free Library, Wilson, NY [*Library symbol*] [*Library of Congress*] (LCLS)
NWilsHi ..... Wilson Historical Society, Wilson, NY [*Library symbol*] [*Library of Congress*] (LCLS)
NwImag ..... New Image Industries, Inc. [*Associated Press*] (SAG)
NWin .... Windham Public Library, Windham, NY [*Library symbol*] [*Library of Congress*] (LCLS)
NWIO .... New World Information Order [*Term coined by the Nonaligned Countries at their Fifth Summit Meeting in 1976*]
NWIP .... Naval Warfare Information Publication
NWIP .... Naval Warfare Intercept Procedures (MCD)
NWIP .... Netware Internet Protocol (SAUS)
NWIP .... North Wales Independent Press
NWIR .... National Wireless Holdings, Inc. [*NASDAQ symbol*] (SAG)
NWIR .... Natl Wireless Hldgs [*NASDAQ symbol*] (TTSB)
NWIRP ...... Naval Weapons Industrial Reserve Plant (AFM)
NWIRP ...... Naval Weapons Integration Reserve Plant (TIMI)
NWIS .... National Water Information System [*Department of the Interior*] (GFGA)
NWIS .... Naval Weaponeering Information Sheet (MCD)
NWISO ...... Naval Weapons Industrial Support Office (DNAB)
NWIT .... Nuclear Waste Isolation Technology (NUCP)
NWIYRA ..... North West Intercollegiate Yacht Racing Association
NWJA .... National Wholesale Jewelers Association [*Later, AJDA*] (EA)
nwjm .... Jamaica [*MARC geographic area code*] [*Library of Congress*] (LCCP)
NWK .... Network Equipment Technologies, Inc. [*NYSE symbol*] (SPSG)
NWK .... Network Equip Tech [*NYSE symbol*] (TTSB)
NWK .... Newark, NJ [*Amtrak rail station code*]
NWK .... Norwalk Public Library, Norwalk, CT [*Inactive*] [*OCLC symbol*] (OCLC)
NWKC .... Network Commerce, Inc. [*NASDAQ symbol*] (QUAN)
NwkCmp .... Network Computing Devices, Inc. [*Associated Press*] (SAG)
NwkIm .... Network Imaging Corp. [*Associated Press*] (SAG)
NwkImg ..... Network Imaging Corp. [*Associated Press*] (SAG)
NWKLS ...... Northwest Kansas Library System [*Library network*]
NWL .... National Water Lift Co. (MCD)
NWL .... National Women's League of the United Synagogue of America [*Later, AWL*] (EA)
NWL .... Natural Wavelength
NWL .... Naval Weapons Laboratory [*Later, NSWC*]
NWL .... Newell Co. [*NYSE symbol*] (SPSG)
NWL .... Newell Rubbermaid
NWL .... Newline Development [*Vancouver Stock Exchange symbol*]
NWL .... Normal Water Leg [*Nuclear energy*] (NRCH)
NWL .... Normal Water Level (IAA)
NWL .... North Wright Air, Ltd. [*Canada*] [*FAA designator*] (FAAC)
nwla- .... Lesser Antilles [*MARC geographic area code*] [*Library of Congress*] (LCCP)
NWLA .... National Women and the Law Association (EA)
NWLA .... Northern Woods Logging Association (EA)
NW Law Rev ... Northwestern Law Review [*A publication*] (DLA)
NWLB .... National War Labor Board [*World War II*]
NWLC .... National Women's Law Center (EA)
NWL/D ...... Naval Weapons Laboratory / Dahlgren [*Virginia*] (DNAB)
NWldP .... New World Power Corp. (The) [*Associated Press*] (SAG)
NWldPwr .... [*The*] New World Power Corp. [*Associated Press*] (SAG)
NWLDYA .... National Wholesale Lumber Distributing Yard Association (EA)
NWLE .... Nuclear Weapons Logistical Element (SAUS)
NWLEE ...... Northwest Law Enforcement Equipment (SAUS)
NWLF .... National Watermen and Lightermen's Federation [*A union*] [*British*]
NWLF .... New World Liberation Front
nwli- .... Leeward Islands [*MARC geographic area code*] [*Library of Congress*] (LCCP)
NWLI .... National Western Life Insurance Co. [*NASDAQ symbol*] (NQ)
NWLIA .... Natl Western Life Ins'A' [*NASDAQ symbol*] (TTSB)
NWLISN ..... Northwest Land Information System Network (CARB)
NWL Rev ... North Western Law Review [*Chicago*] [*A publication*] (DLA)
NWLS .... Northwest Wisconsin Library System [*Library network*]
NWLSA ...... National Women Law Students Association (EA)
NWLSD ...... Northwest London Subdistrict (SAUS)
NWLU .... Norwegian American Line [*Intermodal shipping container symbol*] (TVRC)
NWly .... Northwesterly (SAUS)
NWM .... Morris County Free Library, Whippany, NJ [*OCLC symbol*] (OCLC)
NWM .... Newfields Minerals Ltd. [*Toronto Stock Exchange symbol*]
NWM .... New Ways Ministry (EA)
NWM .... New World Monkey
NWM .... Non-Woven Medium [*Automotive engineering*]
NWM .... Nordwestmecklenburg [*German license plate city code*]
NWM .... Northwest Monsoon
NWM .... Nuclear Waste Management (SAUS)
NWM .... Nuclear Waste Materials (SAUS)

NWM .... United States Military Academy, West Point, NY [*Library symbol*] [*Library of Congress*] (LCLS)
NWMA .... National Woodwork Manufacturers Association [*Formerly, NDMA*] [*Later, NWWDA*] (EA)
NWMA .... Northwest Mining Association (EA)
NWMAF ..... National Women's Martial Arts Federation (EA)
NWMC .... National Wool Marketing Corp. (EA)
NWMC .... New McGrath [*NCIC trailer make code*]
NWMC .... Northwest Michigan College
NWMCC ..... Nuclear Waste Materials Characterization Center (SAUS)
NWMF .... National Women's Music Festival (EA)
NWMF .... Nuclear Weapons Maintenance Foreman (AABC)
NWMI .... Newfields Minerals, Inc. (SAUS)
NwMilfd .... New Milford Bank & Trust Co. [*Associated Press*] (SAG)
nwmj- .... Montserrat [*MARC geographic area code*] [*Library of Congress*] (LCCP)
NWMKT ..... Newmarket [*Urban district in England*]
NWML .... National Women's Mailing List (EA)
N/Wmn ...... Night Watchman (SAUS)
NWMP .... North-West Mounted Police [*Later, RCMP*] [*Canada*]
NWMP .... Nuclear Weapons Master Plan (SAUS)
NWMPA ..... North Wales Master Printers Alliance (SAUS)
nwmq- .... Martinique [*MARC geographic area code*] [*Library of Congress*] (LCCP)
NWMRS ..... National Waste Minimization and Recycling Strategy [*Australia*]
NWMS .... Nazarene World Mission Society (EA)
NWMS .... Northwest Medical Service (SAUS)
NWMS .... Nuclear Weapons Maintenance Specialist (AABC)
NwmtG ...... Newmont Gold Co. [*Associated Press*] (SAG)
NWMTI ...... Northwest Medical Team International
NWN .... National Wireless Network (SAUS)
NWN .... National Workers Network [*Defunct*] (EA)
NWN .... Newcan Minerals [*Vancouver Stock Exchange symbol*]
NWN .... New Warrior Network [*An association*] (EA)
NWN .... Nonwhite Noise
NWN .... Northwestern
NWN .... Northwest Natural Gas Co. [*NYSE symbol*]
NWN .... Northwinds Northern Ltd. [*Canada*] [*ICAO designator*] (FAAC)
NWN .... Nuclear Waste News [*Business Publishers, Inc.*] [*No longer available online*] [*Information service or system*] (CRD)
nwna- .... Netherlands Antilles [*MARC geographic area code*] [*Library of Congress*] (LCCP)
NWNet ...... Northwestern States Network [*Computer science*] (TNIG)
NWnet .... North West Net (SAUS)
NWNG .... Northwest Natural Gas [*NASDAQ symbol*] (TTSB)
NWNG .... Northwest Natural Gas Co. [*NASDAQ symbol*] (NQ)
NWNGPAC ... Northwest Natural Gas PAC [*Portland, OR*] (PACS)
NWNL .... Northwestern National Life Insurance Co. (EFIS)
NWNSA ..... National Women's Neckwear and Scarf Association (EA)
NWNT .... North Wales Naturalists Trust (SAUS)
NW-NW ..... No Work - No Woo [*Slogan adopted by women war workers in Albina shipyards in Portland, Oregon, who agreed not to date men who were absent from work*] [*World War II*]
NWO .... Directory of National Women's Organizations [*A publication*]
NWO .... NASA Washington Office (KSC)
NWO .... Negation Weapons Officer (ACAE)
NWO .... Netherlands Organization for Scientific Research
NWO .... Network Outsourcing (GART)
NWO .... New Work Opportunities [*A publication*]
NWO .... New World Order [*Bush administration*]
NWO .... Nonwoven Oriented
NWO .... No World Order (SAUS)
NWOA .... National Woodland Owners Association (EA)
NWOA .... Nuclear Weapons Orientation Advanced Course (SAUS)
NWOBHM ... New Wave of British Heavy Metal [*Rock music type, 1979-81*]
NWOC .... Naval Weather and Oceanographic Center (DOMA)
NWOC .... New Way of Computing (SAUS)
NWOC .... New Woman On Campus (SAUS)
NWOFC ..... Numerical Weather and Oceanographic Forecasting Center [*Marine science*] (MSC)
NWOO .... NATO Wartime Oil Organization (NATG)
NWOR .... Neworld Bancorp, Inc. [*NASDAQ symbol*] (NQ)
n-word ...... nonce word (SAUS)
NWORG ..... North Western Operational Research Group (SAUS)
NWP .... National Water Project [*Later, RCAP*] (EA)
NWP .... National Woman's Party (EA)
NWP .... National Writing Project (EA)
NWP .... Nationwide Outdoor Recreation Plan [*Bureau of Outdoor Recreation*]
NWP .... Nationwide Permit [*Emergency Management*] (EMA)
NWP .... NATO and Warsaw Pact [*Projects*] (NATG)
NWP .... Naval Warfare Procedures (MCD)
NWP .... Naval Warfare Publications
NWP .... Naval Weapons Plant (AAG)
NWP .... Naval Weapons Publications
NWP .... Net Written Premiums [*Insurance*] (MARI)
NWP .... Northwestern Pacific Railroad Co. [*AAR code*]
NWP .... North-Western Provinces, High Court Reports [*India*] [*A publication*] (DLA)
NWP .... Northwest Passage (ROG)
NWP .... Northwest Plastics, Inc. (EFIS)
NWP .... North West Provinces (SAUS)
NWP .... Northwest Provinces
NWP .... Nuclear Waste Project [*Defunct*] (EA)
NWP .... Numerical Weather Prediction
NWP .... NWP Resources [*Vancouver Stock Exchange symbol*]
NWp .... Williston Park Public Library, Williston Park, NY [*Library symbol*] [*Library of Congress*] (LCLS)
NWPA .... Nuclear Waste Policy Act (NRCH)
NWPA .... Nuclear Waste Policy Act of 1982 (GAAI)
NWPAG ..... NATO Wartime Preliminary Analysis Group (NATG)
NwPar .... New Paradigm Software [*Associated Press*] (SAG)
NWPB .... National Watermelon Promotion Board
NWPC .... National Women's Political Caucus (EA)
NWPC .... National Women's Political Caucus Victory Fund [*Washington, DC*] (PACS)
NWPC .... [*The*] New World Power Corp. [*NASDAQ symbol*] (SAG)
NWPC .... Northwest Provinces Code [*India*] [*A publication*] (DLA)
NWPCA ..... National Wooden Pallet and Container Association (EA)
NWPCB ..... Naval Warfare Planning Chart Bases (MCD)
NWPCE ..... New World Power [*NASDAQ symbol*] (TTSB)
NWPCP ..... National Wetlands Priority Conservation Plan (COE)
NWpCsE .... Center Street Elementary School, Williston Park, NY [*Library symbol*] [*Library of Congress*] (LCLS)
NWPF .... National Water Purification Foundation
NWPF .... New Waste Processing Facility (SAUS)
NWPF .... Nonwoven Polyester Fabric
NWPFC ..... Northwest Pacific Fisheries Commission (SAUS)
NWPH .... Newport Pharmaceuticals International, Inc. (SAUS)
NWPHC ..... Northwest Provinces, High Court Reports [*India*] [*A publication*] (DLA)
NwpkRs .... Newpark Resources, Inc. [*Associated Press*] (SAG)
NWPL .... Naval Warfare Publications Library (NVT)
NWPM .... Numerical Weather Prediction Model (CARB)
NWPMA ..... National Wooden Pallet Manufacturers Association [*Later, NWPCA*] (EA)
NWPN .... Nordic Womens Peace Network (SAUS)
NWPO .... Northwest Pacific Oceanographers [*An association*] (NOAA)
NWPOG ..... Numerical Weather Prediction Operational Grid (SAA)
NWPP .... Nationwide Permit Program [*Army Corps of Engineers*] (GFGA)
NWPPCA .... Auyuittuq National Park, Parks Canada [*Parc National Auyuittuq, Parcs Canada*] Pangnirtung, Northwest Territories [*Library symbol*] [*National Library of Canada*] (NLC)
nwpr- .... Puerto Rico [*MARC geographic area code*] [*Library of Congress*] (LCCP)
NWPrA ...... Natl Westminister Pref'A'ADS [*NYSE symbol*] (TTSB)
NWPrB ...... Natl Westminster Pref'B'ADS [*NYSE symbol*] (TTSB)
NWPRT ...... Newport, WA [*American Association of Railroads railroad junction routing code*]
Nwprt News ... Newport News (SAUS)
NWPS .... National Wilderness Preservation System
NWPS .... Northwestern Public Service Co. [*Associated Press*] (SAG)
NWPS .... NWPS Capital Financing Tr PERCS [*Associated Press*] (SAG)
NWPSC ..... Nationwide Postal-Strike Contingency Plan (DNAB)
NWPSC ..... Northwestern Public Service Co. (SAUS)
NWPS EMPLOYEES' PAC ... Northwestern Public Service Company PAC [*Huron, SD*] (PACS)
NWPU .... Numerical Weather Prediction Unit (DNAB)
NWPW ...... Naval Weapons Plant, Washington, DC
NWPX .... Northwest Pipe [*NASDAQ symbol*] (TTSB)
NWPYVO ... National Working Party of Youth Volunteer Organisers (AIE)
NWPZ .... Niagara of Wisconsin Paper [*Federal Railroad Administration identification code*]
NWQ .... Northwest Digital Ltd. [*Toronto Stock Exchange symbol*]
NWQ .... Northwest Quadrant (SAUS)
NWQI .... National Water Quality Inventory [*Environmental Protection Agency*]
NWQL .... National Water Quality Laboratory
NWQS .... National Water Quality Standards [*Industrial hygiene term*] (OHS)
NWQSS ..... National Water Quality Surveillance System [*Dicontinued, 1981*] [*Environmental Protection Agency*]
NWR .... National Oceanic and Atmospheric Administration Weather Radio [*Emergency Management*] (EMA)
NWR .... National Welfare Rights (WDAA)
NWR .... National Wildlife Refuge (WDAA)
NWR .... National Women's Register [*British*] (DBA)
NWR .... Navy Weapons Requirement
NWR .... News Relationships (SAUS)
NWR .... Next Word Request
NWR .... Niwot Ridge (SAUS)
NWR .... Normotensive Wistar Rat (DB)
NWR .... North Western Railway [*India*]
NWR .... Northwestern Reporter [*Commonly cited NW*] [*A publication*] (DLA)
NWR .... Nuclear Weapons Report [*Army*] (AABC)
NWRA .... National Waterbed Retailers Association (EA)
NWRA .... National Water Resources Association (EA)
NWRA .... National Wheel and Rim Association (EA)
NWRA .... National Wildlife Refuge Association (EA)
NWRA .... National Wildlife Rehabilitators Association (EA)
NWRA .... National Women's Rowing Association [*Later, USRA*] (EA)
NWRA .... Nebraska Water Resources Association (EARSL)
NWRBBE .... Basin Planning Report. New York State Water Resources Commission. Series ENB (journ.) (SAUS)
NWRC .... National Weather Records Center [*Later, National Climatic Center*] [*National Oceanic and Atmospheric Administration*]
NWRC .... National Wildflower Research Center (EA)
NWRC .... Naval Warfare Research Center (MCD)
NWRC .... Nebraska Water Resources Center [*University of Nebraska - Lincoln*] [*Research center*] (RCD)
NWRC .... Northeast Watershed Research Center [*University Park, PA*] [*Department of Agriculture*] (GRD)
NWRE .... Neoware Systems, Inc. [*NASDAQ symbol*] (NASQ)

NWREL...... Northwest Regional Educational Laboratory [*Portland, OR*] [*Research center*]
NW Rep..... Northwestern Reporter [*Commonly cited NW*] [*A publication*] (DLA)
NWREP...... Nuclear Weapons Report (COE)
NW Repr.... North Western Reporter [*A publication*] (DLA)
NW Rev Ord... Northwest Territories Revised Ordinances [*Canada*] [*A publication*] (DLA)
NWRF....... Naval Weather Research Facility
NWRHB..... North West Regional Health Board [*Tasmania, Australia*]
NWRI........ National Water Research Institute [*Environment Canada*] [*Research center*] (RCD)
NWRI........ Norfolk & Western Rock Island Pullman [*Federal Railroad Administration identification code*]
NWRK....... Network Electronic Corp. [*NASDAQ symbol*] (COMM)
NWRL....... North Carolina's Northwestern Regional Library
NwrldCf..... New World Coffee, Inc. [*Associated Press*] (SAG)
NWRLF...... New World Radical Liberation Front (NADA)
NWRLS...... North Western Regional Library System (SAUS)
NWRN....... Northwestern (FAAC)
NWRO....... National Welfare Rights Organization [*Defunct*]
NWRP....... Nuclear Weapons Release Procedures (SAUS)
NWRS....... National Wildlife Refuge System (WDAA)
NWRS....... North-West Recording Society [*Record label*]
NWRS....... Nuclear Weapons Requirements Study (CINC)
NwRSA...... Northwest Region Spinners Association (EA)
NWRT....... National Wildlife Rescue Team (EA)
NWRWA..... North West Regional Water Authority [*Tasmania, Australia*]
NWRX....... Northwest Railroad [*Federal Railroad Administration identification code*]
NWS......... National Watercolor Society (EA)
NWS......... National Waterways Study [*Marine science*] (MSC)
NWS......... National Weather Service [*Formerly, US Weather Bureau*] [*Silver Spring, MD*] [*National Oceanic and Atmospheric Administration*]
NWS......... National Winter Sports [*Association*] [*Defunct*] (EA)
NWS......... Naval Weapons Station
NWS......... Navy Weather Service
NWS......... [*The*] News Corp. Ltd. [*NYSE symbol*] (SPSG)
NWS......... News Corp. Ltd ADS [*NYSE symbol*] (TTSB)
NWS......... New Workers Scheme (AIE)
NWS......... New World Society (EA)
NWS......... New World Symphony (SAUS)
NWS......... Nimbus Weather Satellite
NWS......... Non-Heatset Web Section (NTPA)
NWS......... Nonprogrammable Workstation (SAUS)
NWS......... Normal Water Surface (ADA)
NWS......... North Warning System (MCD)
NWS......... North-West Semitic (BJA)
NWS......... Northwest States (ROG)
NWS......... Norway Station [*South Africa*] [*Later, SNA*] [*Geomagnetic observatory code*]
NWS......... Nose Wheel Steering [*Aviation*]
NWS......... Nosewheel Steering (SAUS)
NWS......... Novell Web Server [*Computer science*] (HODG)
NWS......... Nowsco Well Service Ltd. [*Toronto Stock Exchange symbol*]
NWS......... Nuclear Weapon Site (CCCA)
NWS......... Nuclear Weapons State
NWS......... Nuclear Weapons Storage (SAUS)
NWS......... Nuclear Weapon Storage (ACAE)
NWS......... The News Corporation Ltd. [*NYSE symbol*]
NWS......... Weather radar system (SAUS)
NWSA....... National Water Slide Association (EA)
NWSA....... National Welding Supply Association (EA)
NWSA....... National Wheelchair Softball Association (EA)
NWSA....... National Winter Sports Association
NWSA....... National Women's Sailing Association (EA)
NWSA....... National Women's Studies Association (EA)
NWSA....... National Women's Suffrage Association (WDAA)
NWSA....... Naval Weapons Support Activity
NWSA....... Naval Weather Service Association (EA)
NWSA....... Nose Wheel Steering Actuator (SAUS)
NWSA....... Nose Wheel Steering Amplifier [*Aviation*] (MCD)
NWSA....... Nuclear Weapons Supply Annex
NWSA Jnl... NWSA Journal [*A publication*] (BRI)
NWSAP...... Naval Weapons Station Acceptance Program (MCD)
NWSB....... National Wage Stabilization Board [*Superseded NWLB, 1945; terminated, 1947*]
NWSB....... Northwest Savings Bank [*NASDAQ symbol*] (SAG)
NWSB....... Nuclear Warfare Status Branch (CINC)
nwsb-........ Saint-Barthelemy [*MARC geographic area code*] [*Library of Congress*] (LCCP)
NWSC....... National Water Safety Congress (EA)
NWSC....... National Weather Satellite Center [*Later, National Environmental Satellite Service*]
NWSC....... National Weather Service Center (MCD)
NWSC....... National Women's Student Coalition (EA)
NWSC....... Naval Weapons Support Center (MCD)
NWSC....... Naval Weather Service Command
NWSCA...... National Water and Soil Conservation Agency (BARN)
NWSCC...... Nuclear Weapons System Control Console (MCD)
NWSC/CR... Naval Weapons Support Center, Crane [*Indiana*]
Nwscop..... Newscope Resources Ltd. [*Associated Press*] (SAG)
NWS-CR.... National Weather Service-Central Region (PDAA)
NWSD....... Naval Weather Service Detachment [*or Division*]
nwsd-........ Saba [*MARC geographic area code*] [*Library of Congress*] (LCCP)
NWSDGP.... North West Slopes Division of General Practice (SAUS)
NWSED...... Naval Weather Service Environmental Detachment [*Navy*]
NWSEO...... National Weather Service Employees Organization (EA)
NWS-ER..... National Weather Service-Eastern Region (PDAA)
NWSF........ Northwest Sea Frontier
NWSF........ Nuclear Weapons Storage Facility [*Army*] (AABC)
NWSFO...... NEXRAD Weather Service Forecast Office (SAUS)
NWSFO...... NWS [*National Weather Service*] Forecast Office [*Marine science*] (OSRA)
NWSG........ Nuclear War Study Group (EA)
NWSG........ Nuclear Weapon Systems Surety Group [*Army*]
NWsH........ Houghton College, Buffalo Campus, West Seneca, NY [*Library symbol*] [*Library of Congress*] (LCLS)
NWSH........ National Weather Service Headquarters
NWsHeaC.... Health Care Plan Medical Center, West Seneca, NY [*Library symbol*] [*Library of Congress*] (LCLS)
NWSI......... New World Services, Inc.
NWSIA....... National Water Supply Improvement Association [*Later, IDA*] (EA)
NWSLF...... Nowsco WellService [*NASDAQ symbol*] (TTSB)
NWSLF...... Nowsco Well Services [*NASDAQ symbol*] (SAG)
NWSM....... Nuclear Weapons Stockpile Memorandum
NWSO........ Naval Weapons Services Office [*Also known as NAVWPNSERVO, WEPSO*]
NWSO........ Naval Weather Service Office
NWSP........ Nuclear Weapon Stockpile Plan (SAUS)
nwspa....... Newspaper (VRA)
NWSPr...... News Corp. Ltd Pfd ADS [*NYSE symbol*] (TTSB)
NWSPR...... Newsprint (SAUS)
NWSRFS.... National Weather Service River Forecast System (NOAA)
NWSRS..... National Wild and Scenic Rivers System
NWSS........ National Weather Satellite System (KSC)
NWSS........ National Women's Scuba Society (EA)
NWSS........ National Wool Sorters' Society [*A union*] [*British*] (DCTA)
NWSS........ Navy WWMCCS [*World-Wide Military Command and Control System*] Standardization Software
NWSS........ Network Six, Inc. [*NASDAQ symbol*] (SAG)
NWSS........ Nuclear Weapons Support Section [*Army*] (AABC)
NWsS......... West Seneca State School, West Seneca, NY [*Library symbol*] [*Library of Congress*] (LCLS)
NWSSC...... Nepal Water Supply and Sewerage Corp. (SAUS)
NWSSG..... Nuclear Weapons System Safety Group
NWSSG..... Nuclear Weapons System Satellite Group [*Military*] (IAA)
NWSSGP.... Nuclear Weapons System Safety Group
NWS-SR.... National Weather Service-Southern Region (PDAA)
NWST........ NewStar Media [*NASDAQ symbol*] [*Formerly, Dove Entertainment*]
nwst-......... St. Martin (Sint Maarten) [*MARC geographic area code*] [*Library of Congress*] (LCCP)
NwstAirl..... Northwest Airlines Corp. [*Associated Press*] (SAG)
NWSTC...... National Weather Service Telecommunications (SAUS)
NWSTC...... National Weather Service Training Center [*Emergency Management*] (EMA)
NwstEqty.... Northwest Equity Corp. [*Associated Press*] (SAG)
NWSTG...... National Weather Service Telecommunications Gateway
NWSTG...... NWS [*National Weather Service*] Telecommunications Gateway [*Marine science*] (OSRA)
NwStlWr.... Northwestern Steel & Wire Co. [*Associated Press*] (SAG)
NWSTR...... New Westminster, BC [*American Association of Railroads railroad junction routing code*]
NwstSBk.... Northwest Savings Bank [*Associated Press*] (SAG)
NWSTTC.... National Weather Service Technical Training Center
nwsv-........ Swan Islands [*MARC geographic area code*] [*Library of Congress*] (LCCP)
NWSW...... Northwestern Steel & Wire Co. [*NASDAQ symbol*] (SAG)
NWSW...... Nothwestern Steel & Wire [*NASDAQ symbol*] (TTSB)
NWS-WR.... National Weather Service-Western Region (PDAA)
NWSY....... Naval Weapons Station, Yorktown [*Virginia*]
NWSZ....... North West Steel & Wire [*Federal Railroad Administration identification code*]
N WT......... Net Weight
NWT......... Network 1 Security Solutions [*Boston Stock Exchange symbol*]
NWT......... New World Translation (of the Holy Scriptures) [*A publication*] (BJA)
NWT......... Non-Waste Technology (SAUS)
NWT......... Nonwatertight [*Packaging*] (AAG)
NWT......... Northwestern Terminal R. R. [*AAR code*]
NWT......... Northwestern Utilities Ltd. [*Toronto Stock Exchange symbol*]
NWT......... Northwest Territorial Airways [*Canada*] [*ICAO designator*] (FAAC)
NWT......... Northwest Territories [*Canada*]
NWT......... Nowata [*Papua New Guinea*] [*Airport symbol*] (OAG)
NWT......... Nylon Wire Tie
NWTA........ National Waterways Transport Association [*British*]
NWTA........ National Woman's Trucking Association [*Defunct*] (EA)
NWTA........ National Wool Trade Association [*Defunct*] (EA)
NWTA........ North West Territory Alliance (EA)
NWTB........ New Water-Tube Boiler (SAUS)
NWTB........ Northwestern Tariff Bureau
NWTB........ North West Tourist Board [*British*] (DCTA)
NWTC........ National Wetlands Technical Council (EA)
NWTC........ Naval Weapon Test Center [*China Lake, California*] [*Navy*]
NWTC........ Northern Warfare Training Center [*Army*] (MCD)
NWTC........ Nuclear Weapons Training Center
nwtc-......... Turks and Caicos Islands [*MARC geographic area code*] [*Library of Congress*] (LCCP)
NWTCL...... Nuclear Weapons Training Center, Atlantic (DNAB)
NWTCP...... Nuclear Weapons Training Center, Pacific (DNAB)
NWTD....... Nonwatertight Door (ADA)
NWTDB...... Naval Warfare Tactical Data Base (DOMA)

NWTDB ...... New Water-Tube Donkey Boiler (SAUS)
NWTEC ...... National Wool Textile Export Corp. [*British*] (BI)
NW Terr ..... Northwest Territories, Supreme Court Reports [*A publication*] (DLA)
NWTF .... National Wild Turkey Federation (EA)
NWTFL ...... Northwest Territories Federation of Labour (SAUS)
NWTG .... Nuclear Weapons Training Group (DNAB)
NWTGD ..... Northwest Gold Corp. (SAUS)
NWTGL ...... Nuclear Weapons Training Group, Atlantic (DNAB)
NWTGP ...... Nuclear Weapons Training Group, Pacific (DNAB)
NWTH .... Networth, Inc. [*NASDAQ symbol*] (SAG)
NWTI .... National Wood Tank Institute (EA)
NWTI .... Nuclear Weapons Technical Inspections
NWTK .... North West Token Kai [*An association*] (EA)
NWTL .... Northwest Teleprod'ns [*NASDAQ symbol*] (TTSB)
NWTL .... Northwest Teleproductions, Inc. [*NASDAQ symbol*] (NQ)
NWTLR ...... North West Territories Law Reports [*A publication*] (DLA)
NWTO .... Network for Work Time Options [*San Francisco, CA*] (EA)
NWT Ord .... Northwest Territories Ordinances [*Canada*] [*A publication*] (DLA)
NWTP .... Nationsway Transport Service [*Common carrier symbol*]
NWTP .... Naval Warfare Tactical Publication (DNAB)
NWTR .... North West Territories Reports [*1885-1907*] [*Canada*] [*A publication*] (DLA)
nwtr- .... Trinidad and Tobago [*MARC geographic area code*] [*Library of Congress*] (LCCP)
NWTRB ...... Nuclear Waste Technical Review Board [*Nuclear energy*] (EGAO)
NWTRCC .... National War Tax Resistance Coordinating Committee (EA)
NWT Rev Ord ... Northwest Territories Revised Ordinances [*Canada*] [*A publication*] (DLA)
NWTRNA .... Northwest Territories Registered Nurses Association (SAUS)
NWTS .... National Waste Terminal Storage [*For radioactive wastes*]
NWTS .... National Wilms' Tumor Study [*Oncology*]
NWTS .... Naval Weapons Test Station
NWT/S .... Nuclear Weapons Technician/Specialist (AAG)
NWTSBDC ... Northwest Texas Small Business Development Center (RCD)
NWTSG ...... National Wilms' Tumor Study Group [*Oncology*]
NWTS-RSP ... NWTS Repository Sealing Program (SAUS)
NWTZ .... NW Transport [*Intermodal trailer symbol*]
NWU .... National Workers Union (NADA)
NWU .... National Writers Union (EA)
NWU .... Nebraska Wesleyan University
NWU .... Northwestern University School of Law (DLA)
NWU .... Nose Wheel Up [*Aviation*]
NWUC .... National Works, United States Steel [*Federal Railroad Administration identification code*]
nwuc- .... United States Miscellaneous Caribbean Islands [*MARC geographic area code*] [*Library of Congress*] (LCCP)
NWUIS ...... Navy Work Unit Information System (DNAB)
NWUS .... Northwestern United States
NWV .... Newcoast Silver Mines [*Vancouver Stock Exchange symbol*]
NWV .... Norfolk, VA [*Location identifier*] [*FAA*] (FAAL)
nwvb- .... Virgin Islands, British [*MARC geographic area code*] [*Library of Congress*] (LCCP)
NWvH .... Millard Fillmore Suburban Hospital, Williamsville, NY [*Library symbol*] [*Library of Congress*] (LCLS)
nwvi- .... Virgin Islands of the US [*MARC geographic area code*] [*Library of Congress*] (LCCP)
NWVlz .... New Visions Entertainment Corp. (SAUS)
nwvr .... Virgin Islands [*MARC geographic area code*] [*Library of Congress*] (LCCP)
NWvS .... Sanders Associates, Inc., Williamsville, NY [*Library symbol*] [*Library of Congress*] (LCLS)
NWW .... Newgate Resources [*Vancouver Stock Exchange symbol*]
NWW .... New Ways to Work (EA)
NWW .... North West Airline [*Australia*] [*ICAO designator*] (FAAC)
NWW .... Nose Wheel Well [*Aviation*] (MCD)
NWWA .... National Water Well Association [*Database producer*] (EA)
NWWA .... North-West Water Authority [*British*] (DCTA)
NWWA .... Tiga, Iles Loyaute [*New Caledonia*] [*ICAO location identifier*] (ICLI)
NWWC ...... Ile Art/Wala, Iles Belep [*New Caledonia*] [*ICAO location identifier*] (ICLI)
NWWC ...... National White Wyandotte Club [*Defunct*] (EA)
NwWCof ...... New World Coffee, Inc. [*Associated Press*] (SAG)
NWWCSS ... Naval Worldwide Command Support System (MCD)
NWWD ...... Kone [*New Caledonia*] [*ICAO location identifier*] (ICLI)
NWWDA ..... National Wood Window and Door Association (EA)
NWWE .... Ile Des Pins/Moue [*New Caledonia*] [*ICAO location identifier*] (ICLI)
NwWEye .... New West Eyeworks, Inc. [*Associated Press*] (SAG)
NWWF .... Voh [*New Caledonia*] [*ICAO location identifier*] (ICLI)
NWWH ...... Houailou/Nesson [*New Caledonia*] [*ICAO location identifier*] (ICLI)
NWWI .... Hienghene/Henri Martinet [*New Caledonia*] [*ICAO location identifier*] (ICLI)
nwwi- .... Windward Islands [*MARC geographic area code*] [*Library of Congress*] (LCCP)
NWWIIGPA ... National World War II Glider Pilots Association (EA)
NWWJ .... Poum [*New Caledonia*] [*ICAO location identifier*] (ICLI)
NWWK ...... Koumac [*New Caledonia*] [*ICAO location identifier*] (ICLI)
NWWL .... Lifou/Ouanaham, Iles Loyaute [*New Caledonia*] [*ICAO location identifier*] (ICLI)
NWWM ...... Noumea/Magenta [*New Caledonia*] [*ICAO location identifier*] (ICLI)
NWWN ...... Noumea [*New Caledonia*] [*ICAO location identifier*] (ICLI)
NWWO ...... Ile Ouen/Edmond-Cane [*New Caledonia*] [*ICAO location identifier*] (ICLI)
NWWOX ..... Phoenix Aberdeen Worldwide Opportunities [*Mutual fund ticker symbol*] (SG)
NWWQ ...... Mueo/Nickel [*New Caledonia*] [*ICAO location identifier*] (ICLI)
NWWR ...... Mare/La Roche, Iles Loyaute [*New Caledonia*] [*ICAO location identifier*] (ICLI)
NWWS ...... NOAA [*National Oceanic and Atmospheric Administration*] Weather Wire Service (NOAA)
NWWS ...... Plaine Des Lacs [*New Caledonia*] [*ICAO location identifier*] (ICLI)
NWWU ...... Touho [*New Caledonia*] [*ICAO location identifier*] (ICLI)
NWWV ...... Ouvea/Ouloup, Iles Loyaute [*New Caledonia*] [*ICAO location identifier*] (ICLI)
NWWW ...... Noumea/La Tontouta [*New Caledonia*] [*ICAO location identifier*] (ICLI)
NWWY ...... Ouaco/Paquiepe [*New Caledonia*] [*ICAO location identifier*] (ICLI)
NWX .... National Westminster Bank PLC [*NYSE symbol*] (SAG)
NWX .... New Minex Resources Ltd. [*Vancouver Stock Exchange symbol*]
nwxi- .... St. Christopher-Nevis-Anguilla [*MARC geographic area code*] [*Library of Congress*] (LCCP)
nwxk- .... St. Lucia [*MARC geographic area code*] [*Library of Congress*] (LCCP)
nwxm .... St. Vincent [*MARC geographic area code*] [*Library of Congress*] (LCCP)
NWXPrA ..... Natl Westminster Bk Ex Cap Sec [*NYSE symbol*] (TTSB)
nwy .... newly (SAUS)
NWY .... New Penn Energy [*Vancouver Stock Exchange symbol*]
NWy .... Wyoming Free Public Library, Wyoming, NY [*Library symbol*] [*Library of Congress*] (LCLS)
NWY .... Yellowknife Public Library, Northwest Territories [*Library symbol*] [*National Library of Canada*] (NLC)
NWya .... Wyandanch Public Library, Wyandanch, NY [*Library symbol*] [*Library of Congress*] (LCLS)
NWyaHEC ... LaFrancis Hardiman Early Childhood Center, Wyandanch, NY [*Library symbol*] [*Library of Congress*] (LCLS)
NwyaHS ..... Wyandanch Memorial High School, Wyandanch, NY [*Library symbol*] [*Library of Congress*] (LCLS)
NWyaKE ..... Martin Luther King Elementary School, Wyandanch, NY [*Library symbol*] [*Library of Congress*] (LCLS)
NWyaOMS ... Milton Olive Middle School, Wyandanch, NY [*Library symbol*] [*Library of Congress*] (LCLS)
NWyaSE ..... Straightpath Elementary School, Wyandanch, NY [*Library symbol*] [*Library of Congress*] (LCLS)
NWYC .... Court Library, Department of Justice, Yellowknife, Northwest Territories [*Library symbol*] [*National Library of Canada*] (BIB)
NWYC .... National Write Your Congressman [*An association*] (EA)
NWYC .... Northway Carriers [*Common carrier symbol*]
NWYCC ...... National Write Your Congressman [*Also known as National Write Your Congressman Club*] (EA)
NWYCJ ...... Cooper-Johnson, Yellowknife, Northwest Territories [*Library symbol*] [*National Library of Canada*] (BIB)
NWYD .... Dene Nation, Yellowknife, Northwest Territories [*Library symbol*] [*National Library of Canada*] (BIB)
NWYECW ... Canadian Wildlife Service, Environment Canada [*Service Canadien de la Faune, Environnement Canada*] Yellowknife, Northwest Territories [*Library symbol*] [*National Library of Canada*] (NLC)
NWYEEP .... Assessment and Coordination Branch, Environmental Protection Service, Environment Canada [*Direction de l'Evaluation et de la Coordination, Service de la Protection de l'Environnement, Environnement Canada*] Yellowknife, Northwest Territories [*Library symbol*] [*National Library of Canada*] (NLC)
NWYGI ...... Government Library, Government of the Northwest Territories, Yellow kn ife, Northwest Territories [*Library symbol*] [*National Library of Canada*] (NLC)
NWYIN ...... Indian and Northern Affairs Canada [*Affaires Indiennes et du Nord Canada*] Yellowknife, Northwest Territories [*Library symbol*] [*National Library of Canada*] (NLC)
NWYND ..... Northern Region Information System (NORIS), Canada Department of National Defence [*Reseau d'Information de la Region du Nord (NORIS), Ministere de la DefenseNationale*] Yellowknife, Northwest Territories [*Library symbol*] [*National Library of Canada*] (NLC)
NWYOS ..... Dr. Otto Schaefer Health Resource Centre, Yellowknife, Northwest Territories [*Library symbol*] [*National Library of Canada*] (NLC)
NWYPC ...... Parks Canada [*Parcs Canada*] Yellowknife, Northwest Territories [*Library symbol*] [*National Library of Canada*] (NLC)
NWYPW ..... Technical Resource Centre, Department of Public Works and Highways, Government of the Northwest Territories, Yellowknife, Northwest Territories [*Library symbol*] [*National Library of Canada*] (BIB)
NWYRR ..... Renewable Resources Library, Government of the Northwest Territories, Yellowknife, Northwest Territories [*Library symbol*] [*National Library of Canada*] (NLC)
NWYWNH ... Prince of Wales Northern Heritage Centre, Government of the Northwest Territories, Yellowknife, Northwest Territories [*Library symbol*] [*National Library of Canada*] (NLC)
NWZ .... Niagara of Wisconsin [*Federal Railroad Administration identification code*]
NWZ .... Norfolk Southern Railway [*Intermodal trailer symbol*]
NX .... Entrance-Exit [*Indian Railway*] (TIR)
NX .... Naloxane [*Medicine*] (EDAA)
Nx .... Nephrectomy [*Medicine*] (MELL)
NX .... Net Exports
NX .... New Zealand Air Charter [*ICAO designator*] (AD)
NX .... Next [*Telegraphy*] (PCTE)
NX .... Nonexpendable (SAUS)
nx .... Norfolk Island [*MARC country of publication code*] [*Library of Congress*] (LCCP)
NX .... Normal to X-Axis (MCD)
NX .... Nose to X-Axis (MCD)
NX .... Not Exceeding
NX .... Not Expendable (MUGU)
NX .... Notice to Marines (SAUS)

nx........... Nourishment [*Dietetics*] (DAVI)
NX........... Quanex Corp. [*NYSE symbol*] (SPSG)
NXA.......... Nodal Exchange Area (MHDB)
NXA.......... Nolisair International, Inc. [*Canada*] [*ICAO designator*] (FAAC)
NXA.......... Norex America [*AMEX symbol*] (TTSB)
NXA.......... Norex America, Inc. [*AMEX symbol*] (SPSG)
NXA.......... Norex Industries [*AMEX symbol*] [*Formerly, Norex America*] (SG)
NXA.......... Siem Industries [*AMEX symbol*] [*Formerly, Norex Industries*]
NXA.......... Wake County Public Library, Raleigh, NC [*OCLC symbol*] (OCLC)
NXB.......... Neurotoxin B
NXB.......... Non-X-Ray Background
NX Button... Entrance-Exit Button (SAUS)
NXC.......... Nuveen Ins CA Sel Tax-Free Inc. [*NYSE symbol*] (TTSB)
NXC.......... Nuveen Insured California Select Tax-Free Income [*NYSE symbol*] (SPSG)
NXCD........ NextCard, Inc. [*NASDAQ symbol*] (SG)
NXCI........ National Xeriscape Council, Inc. [*An association*] (EA)
NXCO........ Neurex Corp. [*NASDAQ symbol*] (SAG)
NX Console... Entrance-Exit Console (SAUS)
NXD.......... Non-Executive Director (SAUS)
NXDO........ Nike-X Development Office [*Army*] (AABC)
NXG.......... Necrobiotic Xanthogranuloma [*Medicine*] (EDAA)
NXGN........ NexGen, Inc. [*NASDAQ symbol*] (SAG)
NXI.......... Oak Harbor, WA [*Location identifier*] [*FAA*] (FAAL)
NX Interlocking... Entrance-Exit Interlocking (SAUS)
NXK.......... Next Week [*Telegraphy*] (PCTE)
NXL.......... Napoleon Exploration [*Vancouver Stock Exchange symbol*]
NXL.......... New Plan Excel Realty Trust [*Formerly, New Plan Excel Realty*] [*NYSE symbol*]
NXL.......... South Nuaulu [*Language symbol*] (ETLW)
n-xl-......... St. Pierre and Miquelon [*MARC geographic area code*] [*Library of Congress*] (LCCP)
NXLK........ NEXTLINK Communications'A' [*NASDAQ symbol*] (SG)
NXLZ........ National Xpress Logistics [*Intermodal trailer symbol*]
NXM.......... Non-Existent Memory (MHDB)
NXM.......... Noramex Minerals [*Vancouver Stock Exchange symbol*]
NX Machine... Entrance-Exit Machine (SAUS)
NXMIS....... Nike-X Management Information System [*Army*]
NX MO....... Next Month (SAUS)
NXN.......... Milton, FL [*Location identifier*] [*FAA*] (FAAL)
NXN.......... No Christian Name
NXN.......... Nuveen Ins NY Sel Tax-Free Inc. [*NYSE symbol*] (TTSB)
NXN.......... Nuveen Insured New York Select Tax-Free Income [*NYSE symbol*] (SPSG)
NXON........ Nixon Trucking [*Common carrier symbol*]
NXP.......... Norberts XML Parser (SAUS)
NXP.......... Noxe Resources Corp. [*Vancouver Stock Exchange symbol*]
NXP.......... Nuveen Select Tax-Free Inc. [*NYSE symbol*] (TTSB)
NXP.......... Nuveen Select Tax-Free Income [*NYSE symbol*] (SPSG)
NXP.......... Twentynine Palms, CA [*Location identifier*] [*FAA*] (FAAL)
NX Panel... Entrance-Exit Panel (SAUS)
NXPM........ Nike-X Project Manager [*Army*] (AABC)
NXPO........ Nike-X Program [*or Project*] Office [*Army*]
NXPRG....... Nike-X Program Review Group [*Army*] (AABC)
NXQ.......... Nuveen Selct Tax-Free Inc. 2 [*NYSE symbol*] (TTSB)
NXQ.......... Nuveen Select Tax-Free Income 2 [*NYSE symbol*] (SPSG)
NXR.......... Noncrossing Rule
NXR.......... Nuveen Selct Tax-Free Inc. 3 [*NYSE symbol*] (TTSB)
NXR.......... Nuveen Select Tax-Free Income 3 [*NYSE symbol*] (SPSG)
NXRA........ Nextera Enterprises'A' [*NASDAQ symbol*] (SG)
NXRX........ National Sugar Refining [*Private rail car owner code*]
NXS.......... Nexus Resources Corp. [*Vancouver Stock Exchange symbol*] [*Toronto Stock Exchange symbol*]
NXSM........ Nike-X System Manager [*Army*] (AABC)
NXSMO....... Nike-X System Manager's Office [*Army*]
NXSO........ Nike-X Support Office [*Army*]
NXSPC....... Nexus Telecommunication Systems Ltd. [*NASDAQ symbol*] (SAG)
NXSR........ Non-Extraction Steam Rate (PDAA)
NX System... Entrance-Exit System (SAUS)
NXT.......... Next
NXTL........ Nextel Communications, Inc. [*NASDAQ symbol*] (NASQ)
NX Tower... Entrance-Exit Tower (SAUS)
NXTP........ Nextel Partners 'A' [*NASDAQ symbol*] (SG)
NXTR........ NeXstar Pharmaceutical [*NASDAQ symbol*] (SAG)
NXTR........ NeXstar Pharmaceuticals [*NASDAQ symbol*] (TTSB)
NXT SSN.... Next Season (SAUS)
NXUL........ Nexus Telecommunication Systems Ltd. [*NASDAQ symbol*] (SAG)
NXULF....... Nexus Telecomm Sys Wrrt [*NASDAQ symbol*] (TTSB)
NXUS........ Nexus Telecommunication Systems Ltd. [*NASDAQ symbol*] (SAG)
NXUSF....... Nexus Telecommns Sys Ltd [*NASDAQ symbol*] (TTSB)
NXUW........ Nexus Telecommunication Systems Ltd. [*NASDAQ symbol*] (SAG)
NXUWF....... Nexus Telecommuns Sys Wrrt'A' [*NASDAQ symbol*] (TTSB)
NXUZ........ Nexus Telecommunication Systems Ltd. [*NASDAQ symbol*] (SAG)
NXUZF....... Nexus Telecommuns Sys Wrrt'B' [*NASDAQ symbol*] (TTSB)
NXW.......... University of North Carolina, Wilmington, Wilmington, NC [*OCLC symbol*] (OCLC)
NX WK....... Next Week (SAUS)
NXWPC....... Nexus Telecommunication Systems Ltd. [*NASDAQ symbol*] (SAG)
NXX.......... End Office Code (CGWS)
NXX.......... Willow Grove, PA [*Location identifier*] [*FAA*] (FAAL)
NXXI........ Nutrition 21 [*NASDAQ symbol*]
NX YR....... Next Year (SAUS)
NXZPC....... Nexus Telecommunication Systems Ltd. [*NASDAQ symbol*] (SAG)
NY........... John Dewey [*Final letters of his first and last name used as a pseudonym*] [*American author, 1859-1952*]
NY........... Navy Yard
NY........... Nelen Yubu [*A publication*] (APTA)
NY........... Net Yield
NY........... New Year
NY........... New York [*City or state*] [*Postal code*]
NY........... New York [*Naval Shipyard*]
NY........... New York Airways, Inc. [*ICAO designator*]
NY........... New York Court of Appeals Reports [*A publication*] (DLA)
NY........... New Yorker [*A publication*] (BRI)
NY........... New Yorker (automobile) [*NCIC car model code*]
Ny........... Niles (SAUS)
NY........... Noorduyn Aviation Ltd. [*Canada*] [*ICAO aircraft manufacturer identifier*] (ICAO)
NY........... Normal to Y-Axis (MCD)
NY........... Northamptonshire Yeomanry [*British military*] (DMA)
NY........... Northumberland Yeomanry [*British military*] (DMA)
NY........... Nose to Y-Axis (NASA)
NY........... Not Yield (ELAL)
NY........... No Year [*of publication*] [*Bibliography*]
NY........... Nuclear Yellow [*A fluorescent dye*]
NY........... Nuclear Yield
NY........... Nyasaland (ROG)
Ny........... Nylan (SAUS)
NY........... Nylon [*Tire design*]
NY........... Yonkers Public Library, Yonkers, NY [*Library symbol*] [*Library of Congress*] (LCLS)
NY 2d....... New York Court of Appeals Reports, Second Series [*A publication*] (DLA)
NYA.......... National Yogurt Association (EA)
NYA.......... National Youth Administration [*Terminated, 1943*]
NYA.......... National Youth Alliance (EA)
NYA.......... Neighborhood Youth Administration (OICC)
NYA.......... New York Airways, Inc. [*Air carrier designation symbol*]
NYA.......... New York & Atlantic Railway [*Federal Railroad Administration identification code*]
NYA.......... New York Aquarium (SAUS)
NYA.......... Not Yet Answered
nya.......... Nyanja [*MARC language code*] [*Library of Congress*] (LCCP)
NYAB........ National Youth Advisory Board [*Environmental Protection Agency*]
NYAB........ New York Air Brake Co.
NYABIC...... New York Association for Brain Injured Children
NYAC........ National Youth Advocacy Coalition [*Association*] (EA)
NY Acad Sci Ann... New York Academy of Sciences, Annals (SAUS)
NYACH....... New York Automated Clearing House (TBD)
NYADC....... New York Air Defense Center (SAUS)
NY Admin Code... Official Compilation of Codes, Rules, and Regulations of the State of New York [*A publication*] (DLA)
NYADS....... New York Air Defense Sector (SAA)
NYAES-C.... New York Agricultural Experiment Station (Cornell University) [*Research center*] (RCD)
NYAHSA..... New York Association of Homes and Services for the Aging (EARSL)
NYAIC....... New York Association of Industrial Communicators [*Later, NY/IABC*] (EA)
NYAL........ National Yugoslav Army of Liberation [*World War II*]
NYAL........ New York Airlines (SAUS)
NYALR....... New Yorkers for Abortion Law Repeal (EA)
NYAM........ New York Academy of Medicine
NYAM........ New York Academy of Music
NYAMP....... New York Advertising Media Planners [*Defunct*] (EA)
NYANA....... New York Association for New Americans (EA)
NY & E...... New York & Erie Railroad
NY & NE.... New York & New England Railroad [*Nickname: Now You Are Nearing Eternity*]
NY & NH.... New York & New Haven Railroad
NYANG....... New York Air National Guard (MUSM)
NY Ann Ca... New York Annotated Cases [*A publication*] (DLA)
NY Ann Cas... New York Annotated Cases [*A publication*] (DLA)
NY Anno Cas... New York Annotated Cases [*A publication*] (DLA)
NY Anno Dig... New York Annotated Digest [*A publication*] (ILCA)
NY Annot Dig... New York Annotated Digest [*A publication*] (DLA)
NYAO........ New York Assay Office (SAUS)
NYap........ Middle Island Central Public Library, Yaphank, NY [*Library symbol*] [*Library of Congress*] (LCLS)
NYAP........ New York Assembly Program [*Computer science*]
NYAP........ New York Average Price per Share [*Stock market*]
NY App Dec... New York Court of Appeals Decisions [*A publication*] (DLA)
NY App Div... New York Supreme Court, Appellate Division Reports [*A publication*] (DLA)
NYARD....... North Yard, CO [*American Association of Railroads railroad junction routing code*]
NYARTCC... New York Air Route Traffic Control Center (SAUS)
NYAS........ New York Academy of Sciences (EA)
NYAS........ New York Asian Society (SAUS)
NYATI....... New York Agricultural and Technical Institute (SAUS)
NYATS FEDERAL PAC... New York Association of Temporary Services PAC [*Alexandria, VA*] (PACS)
NYAU........ Nippon Yusen Kaisha Line [*Intermodal shipping container symbol*] (TVRC)
NYAX........ New York Air Brake [*Federal Railroad Administration identification code*]
NYB.......... National Youth Bureau [*British*]
NYB.......... New American High Income Fund [*NYSE symbol*] (COMM)
NYB.......... New York Bancorp [*NYSE symbol*] (SAG)

NYB.......... New York Bancorp Inc. [*AMEX symbol*] (SPSG)
NYB.......... New York Bight [*Oceanography*] (MSC)
NYB.......... North York Board of Education [*UTLAS symbol*]
NYBA........ National Young Buddhist Association [*Defunct*] (EA)
NYBagel.... New York Bagel Enterprises, Inc. [*Associated Press*] (SAG)
NYB & M... New York, Boston & Montreal Railroad
NY Bank Law... New York Banking Law [*A publication*] (DLA)
NYBC........ National Yiddish Book Center (EA)
NYBC........ New York Bancorp, Inc. (SAUS)
NYBC........ New York Blood Center [*Medicine*] (EDAA)
NYBC........ New York Building Congress (EARSL)
NYBC........ New York Business Communicators [*Later, NY/IABC*] (EA)
NY Bcp...... New York Bancorp [*Associated Press*] (SAG)
NY Bcp...... New York Bancorp, Inc. [*Associated Press*] (SAG)
NYBE........ National Yiddish Book Exchange (EA)
NYBFU...... New York Board of Fire Underwriters (BARN)
NYBG........ New York Botanical Garden
NYBID....... New York interbank bid rate (SAUS)
NYBOR...... New York interbank offered rate (SAUS)
NYBOS...... Navy Yard, Boston, Massachusetts [*Obsolete*]
NYBOT...... New York Board of Trade
NYBP........ New York Bight Project (SAUS)
NYBPE....... New York Business Press Editors [*New York, NY*] (EA)
NYBS........ New York Bagel Enterprises, Inc. [*NASDAQ symbol*] (SAG)
NYBS........ New York Browning Society (EA)
NYBSBC..... New York Bureau of State Building Codes (BARN)
NYBT........ Boyce Thompson Institute for Plant Research, Yonkers, NY [*Library symbol*] [*Library of Congress*] (LCLS)
NYBT........ New York Board of Trade [*New York, NY*] (EA)
NYBTA....... New York Biology Teachers Association (EARSL)
NYBU........ Nippon Yusen Kaisha Line [*Intermodal shipping container symbol*] (TVRC)
NYC.......... Charley [*Nevada*] [*Seismograph station code, US Geological Survey*] [*Closed*] (SEIS)
NYC.......... Neighborhood Youth Corps [*Department of Labor*] [*Terminated*]
NYC.......... New York Central R. R. [*Later, Penn Central*] [*AAR code*]
NYC.......... New York Circus (EA)
NYC.......... New York City
NYC.......... New York, Motor Carrier Conference [*STAC*]
NYC.......... New York [*New York*]/Newark [*New Jersey*] [*Airport symbol*] (OAG)
NYC.......... New York, NY [*Location identifier*] [*FAA*] (FAAL)
NYCA........ New York City Affiliate (SAUS)
NYCA........ New York Court of Appeals Reports [*A publication*] (DLA)
NYCAC...... New York Collegiate Athletic Conference (PSS)
NYC & HR.. New York Central & Hudson River Railroad
NYC & HRR... New York Central & Hudson River Railroad (ROG)
NYC & SL... New York, Chicago and St. Louis Railroad Co. (IIA)
NYC & STL... New York, Chicago & St. Louis Railroad Co.
NY Cas Err... Caines' New York Cases in Error [*A publication*] (DLA)
NY Cas in Error... Caines' New York Cases in Error [*A publication*] (DLA)
NYCATC..... New York City Athletic Conference (PSS)
NYCB........ New York City Ballet
NYCB........ New York Community Bancorp [*Company symbol*]
NYCBA...... New York City Bar Association. Bulletin [*A publication*] (DLA)
NYCBA Bull... Bulletin. Association of the Bar of the City of New York [*A publication*] (DLA)
NYCBAN..... New York Center Beacon Alphanumerics [*FAA*]
NYCC........ New York Candy Club (EA)
NYCC........ New York City Commission for the United Nations, Consular Corps, and International Business (EA)
NYCC........ New York City Cycle [*Automotive emissions*]
NYCC........ New York Cultural Center (SAUS)
NYCCA...... New York Cocoa Clearing Association (EA)
NYCCC...... New York City Community College
NYCCD...... New York Current Court Decisions [*A publication*] (DLA)
NYCCH...... New York Advance Digest Service (Commerce Clearing House), Cited by Year [*A publication*] (DLA)
NYCCI....... New York Corset Club (EA)
NYCCIW.... New York City Correctional Institution for Women (SAUS)
NYCCOMP... New York City Composite [*Automotive emissions*]
NYCDC...... New York City Department of Correction (SAUS)
NYCDC...... New York Curtain and Drapery Club (EA)
NYCDH...... New York City Department of Health [*Medicine*] (EDAA)
NYC-DMDG... New York City Depression and Mood Disorder Group (EARSL)
NYCE........ New York Cash Exchange [*Automated teller machine network*]
NYCE........ New York Cocoa Exchange [*Later, CSCE*]
NYCE........ New York College of Education (SAUS)
NYCE........ New York, Commodities Exchange
NYCE........ New York Commodity Exchange (SAUS)
NYCE........ New York Cotton Exchange (EA)
NYCE........ New York Curb Exchange [*Later, AMEX*]
NYCEM...... New York Consortium for Earthquake Loss Mitigation [*Emergency Management*] (EMA)
NYCER...... New York Conference on Electronic Reliability (MCD)
NYCERS..... New York City Employees Retirement System (SAUS)
NYCFMA.... New York Credit and Financial Management Association [*New York, NY*] (EA)
NYCGA...... New York Cherry Growers Association (EARSL)
NY Ch....... Chancery Sentinel [*New York*] [*A publication*] (DLA)
NYCH........ National Youth Coalition on Housing [*Australia*]
NYCH........ New York Cross Harbor Railroad Terminal [*Federal Railroad Administration identification code*]
NYCHA...... New York City Housing Authority (SAUS)
NYCHA...... New York Clearing House Association [*New York, NY*] (EA)
NYCHARL... Navy Yard, Charleston, South Carolina
NY-CHI...... New York-Chicago (SAUS)
NY Ch Sent... New York Chancery Sentinel [*A publication*] (DLA)
NYCHVS..... New York City Housing and Vacancy Survey [*Database*] (GDD)
NYCI......... New York Carolina Express [*Common carrier symbol*]
NYCI......... New York City's First [*First beluga whale born at the New York Aquarium, 1981*] [*Pronounced "Nicky"*]
NY City Ct... New York City Court [*A publication*] (DLA)
NY City Ct Rep... New York City Court Reports [*A publication*] (DLA)
NY City Ct Supp... New York City Court Reports, Supplement [*A publication*] (DLA)
NY City Hall Rec... New York City Hall Recorder [*A publication*] (ILCA)
NY City H Rec... New York City Hall Recorder [*A publication*] (DLA)
NY Civ Prac Law & R... New York Civil Practice Law and Rules [*A publication*] (DLA)
NY Civ Pro... New York Civil Procedure [*A publication*] (DLA)
NY Civ Proc... New York Civil Procedure [*A publication*] (ILCA)
NY Civ Proc (NS)... New York Civil Procedure, New Series [*A publication*] (DLA)
NY Civ Proc R... New York Civil Procedure Reports [*A publication*] (DLA)
NY Civ Proc Rep... Civil Procedure Reports [*New York*] [*A publication*] (DLA)
NY Civ Proc R NS... New York Civil Procedure Reports, New Series [*A publication*] (DLA)
NY Civ Pro R... New York Civil Procedure Reports [*A publication*] (ILCA)
NY Civ Pro R NS... New York Civil Procedure Reports, New Series [*A publication*] (ILCA)
NY Civ Pr Rep... New York Civil Procedure Reports [*A publication*] (ILCA)
NYCJG....... Nikka Yuko Centennial Japanese Garden (SAUS)
NYCLA....... New York County Lawyers' Association (EARSL)
NYCM........ NYCOM Information Services, Inc. (SAUS)
NYCMA...... New York Clothing Manufacturers Association (EA)
NYCMD...... New York Contract Management District (SAA)
NYCME...... New York Clothing Manufacturers Exchange [*Later, NYCMA*] (EA)
NYCMSL.... New York County Medical Society Library (SAUS)
NYCN........ New York Connecting Railroad [*AAR code*]
NYCNHA.... New York City Nursing Home Association (SAUS)
NYCO........ New York City Opera
NYCO........ NYCOR, Inc. [*NASDAQ symbol*] (NQ)
NYCOA...... NYCOR Inc.'A' [*NASDAQ symbol*] (TTSB)
NY Code R... New York Code Reporter [*A publication*] (DLA)
NY Code Rep... New York Code Reporter [*A publication*] (DLA)
NY Code Rep NS... New York Code Reports, New Series [*A publication*] (DLA)
NY Code Report... New York Code Reporter [*A publication*] (DLA)
NY Code Report NS... New York Code Reporter, New Series [*A publication*] (DLA)
NY Code Reports NS... New York Code Reports, New Series [*A publication*] (DLA)
NY Code Reptr... New York Code Reporter [*A publication*] (DLA)
NY Code Reptr NS... New York Code Reporter, New Series [*A publication*] (DLA)
NY Code R NS... New York Code Reports, New Series [*A publication*] (DLA)
NYCOM...... New York College of Osteopathic Medicine [*New York Institute of Technology*] (MHID)
NYCOM...... New York Conference of Mayors and Municipal Officials (EARSL)
NY Cond.... New York Condensed Reports [*1881-82*] [*A publication*] (DLA)
Nycor........ NYCOR, Inc. [*Associated Press*] (SAG)
NY Co Rem... New York Code of Remedial Justice [*A publication*] (DLA)
NYCP........ Civil Procedure Reports [*New York*] [*A publication*] (DLA)
NYCPB....... New York Consumer Protection Board (SAUS)
NYCPD...... New York City Police Department (SAUS)
NYCPM...... New York City Police Museum (SAUS)
NY Cr........ New York Criminal Reports [*A publication*] (DLA)
NYCRC...... New York Civil Rights Coalition (SAUS)
NY Crim..... New York Criminal Reports [*A publication*] (DLA)
NY Crim R... New York Criminal Reports [*A publication*] (DLA)
NY Crim Rep... New York Criminal Reports [*A publication*] (DLA)
NYCRR...... New York Codes, Rules, and Regulations [*A publication*] (DLA)
NY Cr R..... New York Criminal Reports [*A publication*] (DLA)
NY Cr Rep... New York Criminal Reports [*A publication*] (DLA)
NYCS........ New York Chamber Symphony (SAUS)
NYCS........ New York Choral Society (SAUS)
NYCS........ New York Cipher Society (EA)
NYCS........ New York City Shoes, Inc. (SAUS)
NYCSA...... New York Coat and Suit Association (EA)
NYCSA...... New York College Stores Association
NYCSCE..... New York Coffee, Sugar, and Cocoa Exchange
NYCSE....... New York Coffee and Sugar Exchange [*Later, CSCE*] (EA)
NYCSG....... New York Constitution Study Group (EA)
NYCSLA..... New York City School Library Association
NYCSLS..... New York C. S. Lewis Society (EA)
NYCSMA.... National Young Christian Students' Movement of Australia
NYCT........ New York Community Trust (SAUS)
NYCTA....... New York Central Transit Authority (SAUS)
NYCTA....... New York City Transit Authority (SAUS)
NY Ct App... New York Court of Appeals (DLA)
NYCTC....... New York City Technical College
NYCTCG..... New York Cold Type Composition Group [*Later, TANY*] (EA)
NYCTN...... New York Cotton Exchange (EBF)
NYCTNCA... New York Cotton Exchange, Citrus Associates
NYCUC...... New York City Urban Corps (EA)
NYCWRU.... New York Cooperative Wildlife Research Unit (SAUS)
NYCX........ New York Commodity Exchange (SAUS)
NYD.......... Navy Yard
NYD.......... New York Datum (NRCH)
NYD.......... New York Dock Railway [*AAR code*]
NYD.......... Not Yet Dead (SAUS)
NYD.......... Not Yet Detected (SAUS)

NYD.......... Not Yet Determined (SAUS)
NYD.......... Not Yet Diagnosed [*Facetious translation: "Not Yet Dead"*] [*Medicine*]
NYD.......... Not Yet Discovered (DMAA)
NYD.......... Not Yet Dressed (SAUS)
NYD.......... Nycomed ASA ADS [*NYSE symbol*] (TTSB)
NY Daily L Gaz... New York Daily Law Gazette [*A publication*] (DLA)
NY Daily L Reg... New York Daily Law Register [*A publication*] (DLA)
NY Daily Reg... New York Daily Register [*A publication*] (DLA)
NY Daily Tr... New York Daily Transcript, Old and New Series [*A publication*] (DLA)
NYDCC ...... New York Disaster Counseling Coalition (EARSL)
NYDCC ...... New York Drama Critics Circle (EA)
NY Dep't R... New York Department Records [*A publication*] (DLA)
NYDF .... National Youth Development Foundation [*Defunct*] (EA)
NYDIC .... National Youth Development Information Center
NYDISS ..... New York Disposal Surveillance System [*U.S. Army Corps of Engineers*]
NYDLWC Dec... New York State Department of Labor. Court Decisions of Workmen's Compensation [*A publication*] (DLA)
NYDMC...... New York Downstate Medical Center (SAUS)
NYDO........ National Youth Development Officer (AIE)
NYDP........ Neighborhood Youth Development Program
NYD Poultry... New York Dressed Poultry (SAUS)
NYDR........ New York Department Reports [*A publication*] (DLA)
NYDR........ New York Dock Railway (SAUS)
NYDT .... New York Department of Transportation [*Federal Railroad Administration identification code*]
NYE.......... Nycomed Amersham ADS [*NYSE symbol*] (SG)
Nye .... Nye's Reports [*18-21 Utah*] [*A publication*] (DLA)
NYEC .... National Youth Employment Coalition (EA)
NYEEI........ New York Eye and Ear Institute [*Medicine*] (EDAA)
NYEG........ New York State Electric & Gas Corp. [*Associated Press*] (SAG)
NY El Cas... New York Election Cases [*A publication*] (DLA)
NY Elec Cas... New York Election Cases [*A publication*] (DLA)
NY Elect Cas... New York Election Cases [*A publication*] (DLA)
NYER........ Nyer Med Group [*NASDAQ symbol*] (TTSB)
NYER........ Nyer Medical Group [*NASDAQ symbol*] (SAG)
NyerMd ..... Nyer Medical Group [*Associated Press*] (SAG)
NYES .... Elizabeth Seton College, Yonkers, NY [*Library symbol*] [*Library of Congress*] (LCLS)
NYES .... New York Electrical Society (SAUS)
NYES .... New York Entomological Society (SAUS)
NYET LC .... Not Yet in Library of Congress [*Suggested name for the Library of Congress computer system*]
NYETR....... New York Estate Tax Reports [*Prentice-Hall, Inc.*] [*A publication*] (DLA)
NYEWW..... New York Exchange for Woman's Work [*New York, NY*] (EA)
NYF.......... National Yeomen F [*Defunct*] (EA)
NYF.......... National Youth Foundation [*Australia*]
NYF.......... New York Foundation
NYF.......... New York Futures Exchange
NY Farms&Markets Dept... New York State Department of Farms and Markets. Publications (SAUS)
NYFBT....... New York Film Board of Trade [*Defunct*] (EA)
NYFBX....... Mgn. Stanley D. Witter N.Y. Tax Free Cl.B [*Mutual fund ticker symbol*] (SG)
NYFC .... New York Film Critics (EA)
NYFCC....... New York Film Critics Circle (SAUS)
NYFCC....... New York Futures Clearing Corp. [*New York Futures Exchange*]
NYFD .... New York City Fire Department [*Emergency Management*] (EMA)
NYFD .... New York Fashion Designers [*Later, NYFDF*] (EA)
NYFDF....... New York Fashion Designers and Foundation [*Defunct*] (EA)
NYFDM...... New York Fire Department Museum (SAUS)
NYFE .... New York Futures Exchange [*Pronounced "knife"*]
NYFEA....... National Young Farmer Educational Association (EA)
NYFFFBA... New York Foreign Freight Forwarders and Brokers Association [*New York, NY*] (EA)
NYFH .... New York Foundling Hospital (SAUS)
NYFIRO ..... New York Fire Insurance Rating Organization (SAUS)
NY Food Life Sci Bull... New Yorks Food and Life Sciences Bulletin (SAUS)
NYFRF....... New York Fertility Research Foundation [*Later, FRF*] (EA)
NYFUO ...... New York Federation of Urban Organizations
NYFW .... New York Film Works, Inc. (SAUS)
NYFWA....... New York Financial Writers' Association (EA)
NYFX .... NYFIX [*NASDAQ symbol*]
NYG.......... Geigy Pharmaceuticals, Yonkers, NY [*Library symbol*] [*Library of Congress*] (LCLS)
NYG.......... New York Giants [*National Football League*] [*1925-present*] (NFLA)
NYG.......... New York State Library, Albany, NY [*OCLC symbol*] (OCLC)
NYG.......... Nyge Aero AB [*Sweden*] [*ICAO designator*] (FAAC)
NYG.......... Nyindu [*Language symbol*] (ETLW)
NYG.......... Quantico, VA [*Location identifier*] [*FAA*] (FAAL)
NYGB........ New York Genealogical and Biographical Society (SAUS)
NYGBR...... New York Genealogical and Biographical Society Record (SAUS)
NYGBS...... New York Genealogical and Biographical Society (EA)
NYGC....... New York Governor's Conference
NYGJB....... New York Guild for Jewish Blind [*Later, JGB*]
NYGL .... New York & Greenwood Lake Railway [*Federal Railroad Administration identification code*]
NYGS........ New York Graphic Society (SAUS)
NYH.......... New York Helicopter Corp. [*ICAO designator*] (FAAC)
NYH.......... New York Hospital (SAUS)
NYHA........ National Yacht Harbour Association [*British*] (BI)
NYHA........ New York Heart Association [*Classifications I, II, III, and IV*] [*Cardiology*] (DAVI)
NYHA........ New York Heart Associaton (MEDA)
NYHAFC..... New York Heart Association Functional Class [*Medicine*] (EDAA)
NYHC........ New York Health Care, Inc. [*NASDAQ symbol*] (SAG)
NYHD........ New York House of Detention (SAUS)
NYhI......... International Business Machines Corp., Thomas J. Watson Research Center, Yorktown Heights, NY [*Library symbol*] [*Library of Congress*] (LCLS)
NY Hist Soc... New York Historical Society (SAUS)
NYHlthC...... New York Health Care, Inc. [*Associated Press*] (SAG)
NYhP........ Putnam North Westchester S.L.S., Yorktown Heights, NY [*Library symbol*] [*Library of Congress*] (LCLS)
NYHS........ New York Herpetological Society (SAUS)
NYHS........ New York Historical Society (SAUS)
NYHSL...... New York Health and Safety Laboratory [*Energy Research and Development Administration*]
NYHT........ New York Herald Tribune [*Defunct newspaper*]
NYHTB...... New York Herald Tribune Books (SAUS)
NYHTBR..... New York Herald Tribune. Book Review (SAUS)
NYI.......... New York Institute (SAUS)
NYI.......... Not Yet Impacted (SAUS)
NYI.......... NSF Young Investigator (SAUS)
NYI.......... Sunyani [*Ghana*] [*Airport symbol*] (OAG)
NYIA........ New York Insurance Association (EARSL)
NYIA........ New York International Airport (SAUS)
NY/IABC..... New York/International Association of Business Communicators [*New York, NY*] (EA)
NYIAS....... New York Institute of the Aerospace Sciences (SAUS)
NYIBC....... New York International Ballet Competition
NYIBC....... New York Islanders Booster Club (EA)
NYIBS....... New York International Bible Society (EA)
NYIC........ New York Iroquois Conference (EA)
NYICD....... New York Institute for Child Development (EA)
NYICE....... New York Institute for Cultural Education
NYID........ Not-Yet-Invented Device (SAUS)
NYIDA....... New York Importers and Distillers Association (EA)
NYIE........ New York Insurance Exchange
NYIF........ New York Index - Finance [*Stock market*]
NYIF........ New York Institute of Finance (ECON)
NYIH........ New York Institute for the Humanities (SAUS)
NYII........ New York Index - Industrials [*Stock market*]
NYIL........ Netherlands Yearbook of International Law [*A publication*] (DLA)
NYIT........ New York Index - Transportation [*Stock market*]
NYIT........ New York Institute of Technology
NYIU........ New York Index - Utilities [*Stock market*]
NYJ.......... Joshua Tree [*Nevada*] [*Seismograph station code, US Geological Survey*] [*Closed*] (SEIS)
NYJ.......... National Young Judaea (EA)
NYJ.......... New York Jets [*National Football League*] [*1963-present*] (NFLA)
NYJM........ New York Journal of Mathematics (SAUS)
NYJO........ National Youth Jazz Orchestra [*British*]
NY Jud Rep... New York Judicial Repository [*A publication*] (DLA)
NY Jud Repos... New York Judicial Repository [*A publication*] (DLA)
NY Jur....... New York Jurisprudence [*A publication*] (DLA)
NY Jur....... New York Jurist [*A publication*] (DLA)
NYK.......... New York [*City*]
NYK.......... Nippon Yusen Kaisha Line (SAUS)
NYK.......... North York Public Library [*UTLAS symbol*]
NYKGRP .... New York Group [*Navy*]
NYKS........ Nippon Yusen Kaisha Line [*Common carrier symbol*]
NYKU........ Nippon Yusen Kaisha Line [*Intermodal shipping container symbol*] (TVRC)
NYKU........ NYK Lines [*Common carrier symbol*]
NYKZ........ NYK Line [*Intermodal trailer symbol*]
NYL.......... Neodymium YAG [*Yttrium Aluminum Garnet*] LASER
NYL.......... Nylon (MSA)
NYL.......... Yuma, AZ [*Location identifier*] [*FAA*] (FAAL)
NYLA........ New York Library Association
NYLA Bulletin... New York Library Association Bulletin (SAUS)
NY Law Bul... New York Monthly Law Bulletin [*A publication*] (DLA)
NY Law Gaz... New York Law Gazette [*A publication*] (DLA)
NY Law (McKinney)... McKinney's Consolidated Laws of New York [*A publication*] (DLA)
NY Law Sch... New York Law School (GAGS)
NY-LAX...... New York-Los Angeles (SAUS)
NYLB........ [*The*] New York & Long Branch Railroad Co. [*Absorbed into Consolidated Rail Corp.*] [*AAR code*]
NYLC........ National Young Life Campaign [*British*]
NYLC........ National Youth Leadership Council (EA)
NYLC Ann... New York Leading Cases, Annotated [*A publication*] (DLA)
NYL Cas.... New York Leading Cases [*A publication*] (DLA)
NYLCV....... New York League of Conservation Voters Education Fund Inc. - Federal Fund [*New York, NY*] (PACS)
NYLE........ New York & Lake Erie [*Federal Railroad Administration identification code*]
NYLE & W... New York, Lake Erie & Western Railroad [*Later, EL*] [*Nickname: Now You Lay Easy and Wait*]
NY Leg N... New York Legal News [*1880-82*] [*A publication*] (DLA)
NY Leg Obs... New York Legal Observer (Owen) [*A publication*] (DLA)
NY Leg Reg... New York Legal Register [*A publication*] (DLA)
NYLEX USA... New York Leather Exposition [*American European Trade and Exhibition Center*]
NYLFIN...... Nylon Finish (SAUS)

NYLG........ New York Law Group [*Later, BAHRGNY*] (EA)
NYL Gaz.... New York Law Gazette [*A publication*] (DLA)
NY Lib Assn Bul... New York Library Association Bulletin (SAUS)
NYLIC........ New York Library Instruction Clearinghouse (SAUS)
NY LIFE..... New York Life (EFIS)
NYLO........ New York Legal Observer [*A publication*] (DLA)
NYLON...... New York and London
NYLR........ Neodymium YAG [*Yttrium Aluminum Garnet*] LASER Range-Finder
Ny LR....... Nyasaland Law Reports [*South Africa*] [*A publication*] (DLA)
NYLRB...... New York State Labor Relations Board Decisions [*A publication*] (DLA)
NYLRB Dec... New York State Labor Relations Board Decisions and Orders [*A publication*] (DLA)
NYL Rec.... New York Law Record [*A publication*] (DLA)
NYLS........ New York Law School
NYLS........ New York State Longitudinal Study (EDAC)
NYLSMA.... New York Lamp and Shade Manufacturers Association (EA)
NYLS Stud L Rev... New York Law School. Student Law Review [*A publication*] (DLA)
NYLTI........ National Youth Leadership Training Institute
NYLU........ Japan Line [*Intermodal shipping container symbol*] (TVRC)
NYM......... Anonymous (SAUS)
NYM......... Climax Mine [*Nevada*] [*Seismograph station code, US Geological Survey*] [*Closed*] (SEIS)
NYM......... New York Mercantile Exchange
NYM......... New York Minute (SAUS)
NYM......... New York Movers Tariff Bureau, Inc. (SAUS)
NYM......... New York Movers Tariff Bureau, Inc., New York NY [*STAC*]
NYM......... Nigerian Youth Movement [*Political party*] (PSAP)
nym.......... Nyamwezi [*MARC language code*] [*Library of Congress*] (LCCP)
NYM......... NYMAGIC, Inc. [*Formerly, New York Marine & General Insurance Co.*] [*NYSE symbol*] (SPSG)
NYMA....... New York City Metropolitan Area
NYMA....... New York Metropolitan Area (SAUS)
NYMA....... New York Mounters Association [*New York, NY*] (EA)
NYMAGC.... NYMAGIC, Inc. [*Formerly, New York Marine & General Insurance Co.*] [*Associated Press*] (SAG)
NYM&S Brief... New York Medical and Surgical Brief (SAUS)
NYMC....... New York Maritime College (SAUS)
NYMC....... New York Medical College [*Valhalla, NY*]
NYME........ New York Mercantile Exchange (EA)
NY Med C.. New York Medicine College (GAGS)
NYMEX...... New York Mercantile Exchange (EA)
NYMHCA.... New York Mental Health Counselors Association (SEAT)
NYMI........ Navy Yard, Mare Island, California
NY-MIA...... New York-Miami (SAUS)
NY Misc..... New York Miscellaneous Reports [*A publication*] (DLA)
NY Misc 2d... New York Miscellaneous Reports. Second Series [*A publication*] (DLA)
NYMM....... New York Merchandise Mart
NYMNEX.... New York Mercantile Exchange
NYMO........ National Youth Ministry Organization (EA)
NY Mo Law Bul... New York Monthly Law Bulletin [*A publication*] (DLA)
NY Mo L Bul... New York Monthly Law Bulletin [*A publication*] (DLA)
NY Mo LR.. New York Monthly Law Reports [*A publication*] (DLA)
NY Mo L Rec... New York Monthly Law Record [*A publication*] (DLA)
NY Month L Bul... New York Monthly Law Bulletin [*A publication*] (DLA)
NY Month LR... New York Monthly Law Reports [*A publication*] (DLA)
NY Month L Rep... New York Monthly Law Reports [*A publication*] (DLA)
NY Monthly Law Bul... New York Monthly Law Bulletin [*A publication*] (DLA)
NYMPH...... Nymphomaniac (DSUE)
nymphm.... Nymphaeum (VRA)
NYMPHO.... Nymphomania (SAUS)
NYMPHO.... Nymphomaniac (DSUE)
NYMPHO.... Nymphomaniacal (SAUS)
NYMRRLA... New York Metropolitan Reference and Research Library Agency (SAUS)
NYMS........ New York Microscopical Society (EA)
NYMT........ New York Museum of Transportation [*Federal Railroad Administration identification code*]
NY Mun Gaz... New York Municipal Gazette [*A publication*] (DLA)
NYMX....... Nymox Pharmaceutical Corp. [*NASDAQ symbol*] (NASQ)
NYN.......... Non-Von Neumann (SAUS)
NYN.......... NYNEX Corp. [*NYSE symbol*] (SPSG)
NYN.......... Nyngan [*Australia*] [*Airport symbol*] (OAG)
NYNASHIPYD... New York Naval Shipyard (SAUS)
NYNCY...... NYNEX CableCommsGrpADS Unit [*NASDAQ symbol*] (TTSB)
NYNCY...... Nynex Cable Communications Group PLC [*NASDAQ symbol*] (SAG)
NYNEX...... New York New England Exchange [*Telecommunications*]
Nynex....... NYNEX Corp. [*Associated Press*] (SAG)
NYNH & H.. New York, New Haven & Hartford R. R.
NYNJDDA... New York and New Jersey Dry Dock Association [*Defunct*] (EA)
NY/NJ FFFBA... New York/New Jersey Foreign Freight Forwarders and Brokers Association (EARSL)
NYNMA...... New York New Media Association (IGQR)
NYNO........ NYK-NOS [*Common carrier symbol*]
NYNOR...... Navy Yard, Norfolk, Virginia
NYNP........ Northern Yukon National Park (SAUS)
NYNPA...... New York Newspaper Publishers Association (EARSL)
NYNR........ New York National Review (SAUS)
NYNS........ New York Naval Shipyards [*Obsolete*]
NYNS-ML... New York Naval Shipyard, Material Laboratory (MCD)
NynxCbl..... Nynex Cable Communications Group PLC [*Associated Press*] (SAG)
NYNYD...... New York Navy Yard (DNAB)
NYNYK...... Navy Yard, New York, New York
NYO.......... National Youth Orchestra [*British*] (DI)
NYO.......... New York Oils Ltd. [*Toronto Stock Exchange symbol*]
NYO.......... New York Operations [*AEC*] (MCD)
NYO.......... New York Operations Office (SAUS)
NYO.......... Not Yet Operating (DA)
NYO.......... Not Yet Out (SAUS)
nyo........... Nyoro [*MARC language code*] [*Library of Congress*] (LCCP)
NYo.......... Youngstown Free Library, Youngstown, NY [*Library symbol*] [*Library of Congress*] (LCLS)
NYO & W... New York, Ontario & Western Railway Co.
NYOC........ National Youth Orchestra Association of Canada (EAIO)
NYOC........ New York Opera Co. (SAUS)
NYOD........ New York Ordnance District [*Military*] (MUGU)
NY Off Dept R... New York Official Department Reports [*A publication*] (DLA)
NYOG........ New York & Ogdensburg Railway [*Federal Railroad Administration identification code*]
NYOHA...... New York Oil Heating Association (EARSL)
NYOL........ New York On-Line [*Information service or system*] (IID)
NYOL........ New York Opera Library (SAUS)
NYoOF....... Old Fort Niagara Association, Youngstown, NY [*Library symbol*] [*Library of Congress*] (LCLS)
NY Op Att Gen... Opinions of the Attorneys-General of New York [*A publication*] (DLA)
NY Ops Atty Gen... Opinions of the Attorney General of New York [*A publication*] (DLA)
NYork J Med... New York Journal of Medicine (SAUS)
NYORT...... New York Opera Repertory Theatre (SAUS)
NYOS........ National Youth Orchestra of Scotland (ODA)
NYOSL...... New York Ocean Science Laboratory
NYOTBC..... New York Off-Track Betting Corp. (SAUS)
NYP.......... New York-Pennsylvania League [*Baseball*]
NYP.......... New York-Pennsylvania Station, NY [*Amtrak rail station code*]
NYP.......... New York Port (SAUS)
NYP.......... New York Press (WDMC)
NYP.......... New York Public Library, Serials, New York, NY [*OCLC symbol*] (OCLC)
NYP.......... Not Yet Published
NYP.......... Not Your Problem (SAUS)
NYPA........ New York Port Authority
NYPA........ New York Press Association (EARSL)
NYPAA....... National Yellow Pages Agency Association [*Tucson, AZ*] (EA)
NYP & B.... New York, Providence & Boston Railroad
NYPC........ New York Pigment Club (EA)
NYPC........ New York Programming Center (SAUS)
NYPD........ New York Police Department [*Initialism also used as title of TV series*]
NYPD ESU K-9... New York Police Department Emergency Services Unit K-9 Team
NYPDis...... New York Procurement District (SAUS)
NYPE........ New York Port of Embarkation [*Military*]
NYPE........ New York Produce Exchange [*Defunct*] (EA)
NYPF........ National Young Professionals Forum (EA)
NYPF........ New York Planning Federation (EARSL)
NYPFO...... New York Air Force Procurement Field Office
NYPFO...... New York Procurement Field Office (SAUS)
NYPH........ Navy Yard, Pearl Harbor, Hawaii
NYPHIL...... Navy Yard, Philadelphia, Pennsylvania
NYPHR...... New York Physicians for Human Rights (SAUS)
NYPIRG..... New York Public Interest Research Group
NYPIUA..... New York Property Insurance Underwriting Association [*Emergency Management*] (EMA)
NYPL........ New York Public Library [*New York, NY*]
NYPLA....... New York Patent Law Association (SAUS)
NYPLC....... National Youth Pro-Life Coalition (EA)
NYPLR...... New York Prime Loan Rate [*Finance*] (DS)
NYPM....... National Yellow Pages Monitor (EFIS)
NYPM....... National Yokefellow Prison Ministry [*Later, YPM*] (EA)
NYPM....... Navy Youth Program Manager (MCD)
NYPM....... New York Pro Musica (SAUS)
NYPMA...... New York Paper Merchants Association (EA)
NYPMA Bulletin... New York Personnel Management Association Bulletin (SAUS)
NYPO........ New York Philharmonic Orchestra (SAUS)
NYPO........ New York Publicity Outlet [*A publication*] (WDMC)
NYPOE...... New York Port of Embarkation [*Military*]
NYPORT..... Navy Yard, Portsmouth, New Hampshire
NYPP........ New York Power Pool (SAUS)
NYPR........ New York Practice Reports [*A publication*] (DLA)
NYPR........ N-Nitrosopyrrolidine [*Also, NO-PYR*] [*Biochemistry, organic chemistry*]
NYPRPG.... New York Publishers Rights and Permissions Group (EA)
NY Pr Rep... New York Practice Reports [*A publication*] (DLA)
NYPS........ National Yellow Pages Service
NYPS........ Navy Yard, Puget Sound [*Bremerton*], Washington
NYPS........ New York Paleontological Society (SAUS)
NYPS........ New York Psychiatric Society (SAUS)
NYPS........ New York Publishing Society (SAUS)
NYP-SA..... National Yellow Pages Service Association (WDMC)
NYPSC....... New York Public Service Commission (SAUS)
NYPSO...... New York Philharmonic Symphony Orchestra
NYPSS...... New York Philharmonic-Symphony Society (SAUS)
NYPUM...... National Youth Project Using Minibikes [*Medicine*] (EDAA)
NYPYR...... Nitrosopyrrolidine [*Also, NPYR*] [*Organic chemistry*]
NYR.......... National Young Republicans (NADA)

NYR.......... Neodymium YAG [*Yttrium Aluminum Garnet*] Range-Finder
NYR.......... New York Court of Appeals Reports [*A publication*] (DLA)
NYR.......... Not Yet Reported [*Air Force*]
NYR.......... Not Yet Required (MUGU)
NYR.......... Not Yet Returned [*Military*]
NYR.......... Nuclear Yield Requirement (NATG)
NYR.......... Nyoro [*Language symbol*] (ETLW)
NYR.......... Receiver Site [*Nevada*] [*Seismograph station code, US Geological Survey*] [*Closed*] (SEIS)
NYRA........ New York Racing Association (SAUS)
NYRA........ New York Racing Authority [*Cable-television system*]
NYRAPG.... New York Rights and Permissions Group (EA)
NYRB........ New York Review of Books [*A publication*] (BRI)
NYRC........ New York Railroad Commission Reports [*A publication*] (DLA)
NY Rec...... New York Record [*A publication*] (DLA)
NY Reg...... New York Daily Register [*A publication*] (DLA)
NY Rep...... New York Court of Appeals Reports [*A publication*] (DLA)
NY Reps.... New York Court of Appeals Reports [*A publication*] (DLA)
NY Reptr.... New York Reporter [*A publication*] (ILCA)
NYRFC...... New York Rangers Fan Club (EA)
NYRG........ New York Recorder Guild (EARSL)
NYRG........ New York Rubber Group (SAUS)
NYRL........ New York Revised Laws [*A publication*] (DLA)
NYRM........ New York Reformatory for Men (SAUS)
NYRMA...... New York Raincoat Manufacturers Association (EA)
NYRRC...... New York Road Runners Club (EA)
NYRS........ New York Revised Statutes [*A publication*] (DLA)
NYRS........ New York Roentgen Society (SAUS)
NYRS........ New Youth Research Survey [*Religious education test*]
NYRW........ New York Reformatory for Women (SAUS)
NYS.......... New York Shavians (EA)
NYS.......... New York State
NYS.......... New York State Electric & Gas Corp. [*Associated Press*] (SAG)
NYS.......... New York State Reporter [*A publication*] (DLA)
NYS.......... New York State Union List, Albany, NY [*OCLC symbol*] (OCLC)
NYS.......... New York Supplement [*A publication*] (DLA)
NYS.......... Not Yet Specified
NYS.......... Syncline Ridge [*Nevada*] [*Seismograph station code, US Geological Survey*] [*Closed*] (SEIS)
NYS.......... Yonkers School System, Yonkers, NY [*Library symbol*] [*Library of Congress*] (LCLS)
NYS 2d...... New York Supplement, Second Series [*A publication*] (DLA)
NYSA........ New York Shipping Association (EA)
NYSA........ New York State Assembly (SAUS)
NYSAA...... New York State Archeological Association (SAUS)
NYSAA...... New York State Aviation Association (SAUS)
NYSAC...... New York State Athletic Commission (BARN)
NYSAES.... New York State Agricultural Experiment Station (SAUS)
NYSAEYC... New York State Association for the Education of Young Children (EARSL)
NYSAIS...... New York State Association of Independent Schools (SAUS)
NYSAJC.... New York State Association of Junior Colleges (SAUS)
NY-SAN...... New York-San Diego (SAUS)
NYSARC.... New York State Association of Retarded Citizens [*Not-for-profit*] (EARSL)
NYSASBO... New York State Association of School Business Officials (SAUS)
NYSASDA... New York State Atomic and Space Development Authority (SAUS)
NYSASS.... New York State Association of Service Stations [*Later, NYSASSRS*] (EA)
NYSASSRS... New York State Association of Service Stations and Repair Shops (EA)
NYSAVC.... New York State Audio-Visual Council (SAUS)
NYSBA...... New York State Bar Association (SAUS)
NYSBA Bull... New York State Bar Association. Bulletin [*A publication*] (DLA)
NYSBB...... New York State Banking Board (SAUS)
NY S B BULL... New York State Bar Bulletin [*A publication*] (LWAP)
NYSBC...... New York State Barge Canal (SAUS)
NYSBJ....... New York State Bar Journal (SAUS)
NYSC........ New York Shipbuilding Corp.
NYSC........ Thompson and Cook's New York Supreme Court Reports [*A publication*] (DLA)
NYSCA...... National Youth Sports Coaches Association (EA)
NYSCA...... New York State Council on the Arts [*An association*] [*New York, NY*]
NYSCAT..... New York State Union Catalog of Film and Video [*Mid-Hudson Library System*] [*Information service or system*] (IID)
NYSCATE... New York State Association for Computers and Technologies
NYSCC...... New York State College of Ceramics (SAUS)
NYSCC...... New York State Conservation Council (EARSL)
NYSCC...... New York State Crime Commission (SAUS)
NYSCCJ..... New York State Co-alition for Criminal Justice (SAUS)
NY Sch Indus Rel... New York State School of Industrial Relations (SAUS)
NYS/CLS.... New York State Society for Clinical Laboratory Science (EARSL)
NYSCOF..... New York State Coalition Opposed to Fluoridation (EARSL)
NYSCOPBA FEDERAL PAC... NYS Correctional Officers & PBA Inc. [*Albany, NY*] (PACS)
NYSCS...... New York State Colonization Society [*Defunct*] (EA)
NYSCSDA... New York State Council of School District Administrators (SAUS)
NYS Ct...... New York Superior Court Reports [*A publication*] (DLA)
NYSD........ New York Society for the Deaf [*Formerly, JSD*] (EA)
NYSDA...... New York Security Dealers Association (EA)
NYSDCS..... New York State Department of Correctional Services (SAUS)
NYSDEC..... New York State Department of Environmental Conservation
NYSDH...... New York State Department of Health (SAUS)
NYSDR...... New York State Department Reports [*A publication*] (DLA)
NYSE........ New York Stock Exchange [*New York, NY*] (EA)
NYSE........ New York Stock Exchange Guide [*Commerce Clearing House*] [*A publication*] (DLA)
NYSE........ New York Stock Exchange Inc. PAC [*Washington, DC*] (PACS)
NySEA....... New York Society of Enrolled Agents (SAUS)
NY Sea Grant L and Poly J... New York Sea Grant Law and Policy Journal (SAUS)
NYSEG...... New York State Electric & Gas Corp. [*Associated Press*] (SAG)
NYSEGPAC... New York State Electric & Gas Corporation PAC [*Binghamton, NY*] (PACS)
NYSEM...... New York Society of Electron Microscopy (SAUS)
NYSEMO.... New York State Emergency Management Office [*Emergency Management*] (EMA)
NY Sen J... New York Senate Journal [*A publication*] (DLA)
NYSERDA... New York State Energy Research and Development Authority
NYSERNET... New York State Educational and Research Network
NYSERNet.. New York State Education and Research Network, Inc. [*Telecommunications service*] (TSSD)
NYSES....... New York State Employment Service (SAUS)
NYSF........ National Youth Science Foundation
NYSF........ New York Shakespeare Festival (SAUS)
NY-SFO...... New York-San Francisco (SAUS)
NYSFOLA... New York State Federation of Lake Associations (EARSL)
NYSFTCA... New York State Fruit Testing Cooperative Association (EA)
NYSG........ New York State Grange (EARSL)
NYSGI....... New York Sea Grant Institute [*Albany, NY*] [*Department of Commerce*] (GRD)
NYSHESC... New York State Higher Education Service (SAUS)
NYSHFA..... New York State Health Facilities Association (EARSL)
NYSIIS...... New York State Identification and Intelligence System
NYSILL...... New York State Interlibrary Loan [*Network*]
NYSILL...... New York State Interlibrary Loan Program [*New York State Library*] (IID)
NYSILL...... New York State Inter-Library Loans System (NITA)
NYSILL Network... New York State Inter-Library Loan Network (SAUS)
NYSL........ New York Society Library (SAUS)
NYSL........ New York State Library (SAUS)
NYSLAA..... New York State Library Assistants Association
NYSM........ New York State Militia [*Civil War term*]
NYSM........ New York State Museum (SAUS)
NYSM........ New York State Volunteers [*Civil War term*]
NYSMA...... New York State Magistrates Association (EARSL)
NYSMM..... New York State Maritime Museum (SAUS)
NYSNA...... New York State Nurses Association (SAUS)
NYSNACC... New York State Narcotic Addiction Control Commission (SAUS)
NYSNC...... New York State Narcotics Commission (SAUS)
NYSNI....... New York State Nutrition Institute (SAUS)
NYSNY...... New York Naval Shipyard (New York)
NYSO........ New York String Orchestra (SAUS)
NYSOGA.... New York State Outdoor Guides Association (EARSL)
NYSP........ New York School of Printing (DGA)
NYSP........ New York State Police (SAUS)
NYSPA....... New York State Pharmaceutical Association (SAUS)
NYSPA....... New York State Power Authority (SAUS)
NYSPCC..... New York Society for the Prevention of Cruelty to Children
NY Spec Term R... Howard's New York Practice Reports [*A publication*] (DLA)
NY Spec Term Rep... Howard's New York Practice Reports [*A publication*] (DLA)
NYSPGA.... New York State Personnel and Guidance Association (SAUS)
NYSPI....... New York State Psychiatric Institute [*New York State Office of Mental Hygiene*] [*Research center*] (RCD)
NYSPIN..... New York State Police Intelligence Network (SAUS)
NYSPIN..... New York Statewide Police Information Network (SAUS)
NYSPMA.... New York State Podiatric Medical Association (EARSL)
NYSPTA..... New York State PTA (EARSL)
NYSR........ New York State Reporter [*A publication*] (DLA)
NYSRS...... New York State Radiological Society (SAUS)
NYSRTLC... New York State Right to Life Committee (EARSL)
NYSSA...... New York Skirt and Sportswear Association (EARSL)
NYSSA...... New York Society of Security Analysts [*New York, NY*] (EA)
NYSSA...... New York State Student Assembly (SAUS)
NYSSCPA... NY State Society of CPAs (SAUS)
NYSSDA..... New York State Safe Deposit Association [*New York, NY*] (EA)
NYSSF....... National Youth Sports Safety Foundation (EA)
NYSSILR... New York State School of Industrial and Labor Relations (SAUS)
NYSSIM..... New York State Society of Industrial Medicine (SAUS)
NYSSMA.... New York State School Music Association (SAUS)
NYSSOS..... New York State Society of Orthopaedic Surgeons (SAUS)
NYSSPE..... New York State Society of Professional Engineers (SAUS)
NYSSTF..... New York State Science and Technology Foundation (RDA)
NY St........ New York State Reporter [*A publication*] (DLA)
NYST........ Nystagmus [*Medicine*]
NYSTA....... New York State Teachers Association (SAUS)
NYSTA....... New York State Telecommunications Association (EARSL)
NYSTA....... New York State Thruway Authority (SAUS)
NY State R... New York State Reporter [*A publication*] (DLA)
NY State Rep... New York State Reporter [*A publication*] (DLA)
NY St Ba A... New York State Bar Association. Bulletin [*A publication*] (DLA)
NY St Bull... New York State Bulletin (AAGC)
NY St Dept Rep... New York State Department Reports [*A publication*] (DLA)
NYSTDL..... Agricultural Research. Seoul National University (journ.) (SAUS)
NYStJ........ Saint Joseph's Seminary, Dunwoodie, Yonkers, NY [*Library symbol*] [*Library of Congress*] (LCLS)
NY St R..... New York State Reporter [*A publication*] (DLA)
NY St Rep... New York State Reporter [*A publication*] (DLA)

NY St Repr... New York State Reporter [*A publication*] (DLA)
NYS TROOPERS PAC... NYS Troopers Police Benevolent Association PAC [*Albany, NY*] (PACS)
NYSU........ New York State University (SAUS)
NY Sup Ct... New York Supreme Court Reports [*A publication*] (DLA)
NY Sup Ct Rep... Thompson and Cook's New York Supreme Court Reports [*A publication*] (DLA)
NY Sup Ct (T & C)... Thompson and Cook's New York Supreme Court Reports [*A publication*] (DLA)
NY Super ... New York Superior Court Reports [*A publication*] (DLA)
NY Super Ct... New York Superior Court Reports [*Various reporters*] [*A publication*] (DLA)
NY Super Ct R... New York Superior Court Reports [*A publication*] (DLA)
NY Super Ct Rep... New York Superior Court Reports [*A publication*] (DLA)
NY Supl..... New York Supplement [*A publication*] (DLA)
NY Supp .... New York Supplement [*A publication*] (DLA)
NY Supp 2d... New York Supplement, Second Series [*A publication*] (DLA)
NY Suppl ... New York Supplement [*A publication*] (DLA)
NY Supr..... New York Superior Court Reports [*A publication*] (DLA)
NY Supr Ct... New York Superior Court Reports [*A publication*] (DLA)
NY Supr Ct R... New York Superior Court Reports [*A publication*] (DLA)
NY Supr Ct Rep... New York Superior Court Reports [*A publication*] (DLA)
NY Supr Ct Repts (T & C)... New York Supreme Court Reports, by Thompson and Cook [*A publication*] (DLA)
NY Suprm Ct... New York Supreme Court Reports [*A publication*] (DLA)
NYSUT........ New York State United Teachers (SAUS)
NYSV........ Narcissus Yellow Stripe Virus [*Plant pathology*]
NYSW........ New York, Susquehanna & Western Railroad Co. [*AAR code*]
NYSWAC.... New York State Women's Collegiate Athletic Conference (PSS)
NYSWGGI... New York State Wine Grape Growers, Inc. (EA)
NYSX........ New York State Electric and Gas [*Private rail car owner code*]
NYT.......... National Youth Theatre [*British*]
NYT.......... New Yiddish Theater (BJA)
NYT.......... New York Testing Laboratories, Inc.
NYT.......... New York Times [*Daily newspaper*]
NYT.......... [*The*] New York Times Co. [*AMEX symbol*] (SPSG)
NYT.......... New York Times Co. [*NYSE symbol*]
NYT.......... New York Titans [*National Football League*] [*1960-62*] (NFLA)
NYTA........ New York Theatre Annual [*A publication*]
NYTA........ New York Times Cl'A' [*AMEX symbol*] (TTSB)
NYTA........ New York Transit Authority (SAUS)
NY Tax Cas... New York Tax Cases [*Commerce Clearing House*] [*A publication*] (DLA)
NYTB........ New York Theatre Ballet
NYTBIO...... [*The*] New York Times Biographical File [*The New York Times Co.*] [*Information service or system*] (CRD)
NYTBR...... New York Times Book Review [*A publication*] (BRI)
NYTCL....... New York Temperance Civic League [*Later, AYE*] (EA)
NYTEE....... New York Times Electronic Edition [*Internet resource*]
NYTEI........ New York Tax Exempt Income Fund [*Associated Press*] (SAG)
NYTEMC.... New York Times Digital (IID)
Nytest....... NYTEST Environmental, Inc. [*Associated Press*] (SAG)
NY Them.... New York Themis [*New York City*] [*A publication*] (DLA)
NY Thru..... New York Thruway (SAUS)
NYT/IB....... New York Times Information Bank
NYTIC....... New York Technical Institute, Cincinnati (SAUS)
NY Tim....... [*The*] New York Times Co. [*Associated Press*] (SAG)
NYTIS....... New York Times Information Service, Inc. [*Mead Data Central*] [*Database originator and host*] (IID)
NYTLa....... New York Times (Late Edition) [*A publication*] (BRI)
NYTLC....... New York Taxi & Limousine Commission (WDAA)
NYTNS...... New York Times News Service
NY TOR..... New York-Toronto (SAUS)
NYTR........ New York Term Reports (Caines' Reports) [*A publication*] (DLA)
NY Trans.... New York Transcript [*Numbers 1-11*] [*1861*] [*New York City*] [*A publication*] (DLA)
NY Trans App... New York Transcript Appeals Reports [*A publication*] (DLA)
NY Trans NS... New York Transcript, New Series [*New York City*] [*A publication*] (DLA)
NY Trans Rep... New York Transcript Reports [*A publication*] (DLA)
NYT Rep.... Caines' Term Reports [*New York*] [*A publication*] (DLA)
NYTS........ New York Theological Seminary
NYTS........ Nytest Environmental [*NASDAQ symbol*] (TTSB)
NYTS........ NYTEST Environmental, Inc. [*NASDAQ symbol*] (NQ)
NYTTS....... New York Turtle and Tortoise Society (EA)
NYTU........ New York Theological Union (SAUS)
NYTU........ NYTA International [*Intermodal shipping container symbol*] (TVRC)
nyu........... New York [*MARC country of publication code*] [*Library of Congress*] (LCCP)
NYU.......... New York University
NYU.......... Nyaung-U [*Myanmar*] [*Airport symbol*] (OAG)
NYU Conf Charitable... New York University. Conference on Charitable Foundations. Proceedings [*A publication*] (DLA)
NYU Conf Charitable Fdn... New York University. Conference on Charitable Foundations. Proceedings [*A publication*] (DLA)
NYU Conf on Char Found Proc... Conference on Charitable Foundations. Proceedings. New York University [*A publication*] (DLA)
NYU Conf on Char Found Proc... Conference on Charitable Foundations. Proceedings. New York University (journ.) (SAUS)
NYUIMS..... New York University Institute of Mathematical Sciences (SAUS)
NYUIMS..... New York University-Institute of Mathematical Sciences (SAUS)
NYUL........ New York University Library (SAUS)
NYUL Center Bull... New York University. Law Center. Bulletin [*A publication*] (DLA)
NYULT....... New York University School of Continuing Education, Continuing Education in Law and Taxation [*A publication*] (DLA)
NYUMC...... New York University Medical Center (SAUS)
NYUMC...... New York Upstate Medical Center (SAUS)
NY Unconsol laws... New York Unconsolidated Laws (SAUS)
NY Unconsol Laws... New York Unconsolidated Laws (McKinney) [*A publication*] (DLA)
NYUP........ New York University Press (DGA)
NYU Rev L&Soc Change... New York University. Review of Law and Social Change (SAUS)
NYU Rev Law & Soc... New York University. Review of Law and Social Change [*A publication*] (DLA)
NYU Rev Law&Soc C... New York University. Review of Law and Social Change (SAUS)
NYUSM...... New York University School of Medicine (SAUS)
NYUTI....... New York University Tax Institute (DLA)
NYU/Ultra... New York Universitys Ultracomputer (SAUS)
NYV.......... Vern [*Nevada*] [*Seismograph station code, US Geological Survey*] [*Closed*] (SEIS)
NYVOAD.... New York Voluntary Organizations Active in Disaster [*Emergency Management*] (EMA)
NYVTX....... Davis New York Venture Cl.A [*Mutual fund ticker symbol*] (SG)
NYWA........ National Youth Work Alliance (EA)
NYWASH.... Navy Yard, Washington, DC [*Obsolete*]
NYWBA...... New York Women's Bar Association (EARSL)
NYWC....... New York Wine Council (EA)
NYWCC...... New York Water Color Club [*1890-1941*] (NGC)
NY Week Dig... New York Weekly Digest [*A publication*] (DLA)
NY Weekly Dig... New York Weekly Digest [*A publication*] (DLA)
NYWF....... New York World's Fair
NYWGF...... New York Wine/Grape Foundation (EA)
NYWIFT..... New York Women in Film & Television [*An association*] [*New York, NY*]
NY Wkly Dig... New York Weekly Digest [*A publication*] (DLA)
NYY.......... New York Yanks [*National Football League*] [*1950-51*] (NFLA)
NYYP........ New York Yellow Pages, Inc.
NYZP........ New York Zoological Park
NYZS........ New York Zoological Society
NYZZA3..... Journal. Japan Pharmaceutical Association (journ.) (SAUS)
NZ............ Air New Zealand Ltd. (Domestic Division) [*ICAO designator*] (ICDA)
Nz............ National Library of New Zealand, Wellington, New Zealand [*Library symbol*] [*Library of Congress*] (LCLS)
NZ............ Neutrality Zone
NZ............ New Mexico & Arizona Land Co. [*AMEX symbol*] (SPSG)
NZ............ New Mexico/Ariz Land [*AMEX symbol*] (TTSB)
NZ............ New Zealand [*ANSI two-letter standard code*] (CNC)
nz............ New Zealand [*MARC country of publication code*] [*Library of Congress*] (LCCP)
NZ............ New Zealand National Airways Corp. [*ICAO designator*]
NZ............ New Zealand Reports [*A publication*] (DLA)
N-Z........... Nike-Zeus [*Missiles*] (AAG)
NZ............ Non-Zero (VLIE)
NZ............ Normal Acceleration
NZ............ Normal load factor (SAUS)
NZ............ Normal to Z-Axis (MCD)
NZ............ Nose to Z-Axis (MCD)
NZ............ Not Zero (SAUS)
NZ............ No Zero (SAUS)
NZ............ Nuclear Zone
NZA.......... Niobium Zinc Alloy
NZAA........ Auckland/International [*New Zealand*] [*ICAO location identifier*] (ICLI)
NZAA........ New Zealand Antique Arms Association (SAUS)
NZAA........ New Zealand Auto Association (SAUS)
NZAB........ New Zealand Association of Bacteriologists (SAUS)
NZABC....... New Zealand Audit Bureau of Circulation (SAUS)
NZABM...... New Zealand Anglican Board of Missions (SAUS)
NZAC........ New Zealand Accommodation Council (SAUS)
NZAC........ New Zealand Alpine Club (SAUS)
NZACE....... New Zealand Association for Community Education (SAUS)
NZACT....... New Zealand Association of Chemistry Teachers (SAUS)
NZACU...... New Zealand Auto Cycle Union (SAUS)
NZADS...... New Zealand Association for Disabled Skiers (SAUS)
NZAF........ New Zealand Air Force (DAS)
NZAF........ New Zealand Authors Fund (SAUS)
NZAF........ New Zealand Aviation Federation (SAUS)
NZAFB....... New Zealand Air Force Base (SAUS)
NzAGS....... Church of Jesus Christ of Latter-Day Saints, Genealogical Society Library, Auckland Branch, Auckland, New Zealand [*Library symbol*] [*Library of Congress*] (LCLS)
NZAHBS..... New Zealand Arab Horse Breeders Society (SAUS)
NZAHPER... New Zealand Association of Health, Physical Education and Recreation (SAUS)
NZAI......... New Zealand Antarctic Institute (SAUS)
NZAK........ Auckland [*New Zealand*] [*ICAO location identifier*] (ICLI)
NZALO....... New Zealand Air Liaison Officer (SAUS)
NZALT....... New Zealand Association of Language Teachers (SAUS)
NZANN...... New Zealand Association of Neonatal Nurses (SAUS)
NZAP........ New Zealand Associated Press (BARN)
NZAP........ Taupo [*New Zealand*] [*ICAO location identifier*] (ICLI)
NZAPA....... New Zealand Airline Pilots Association (SAUS)
NZ App Rep... New Zealand Appeal Reports [*A publication*] (DLA)
NZAPS....... Nike-Zeus Automatic Programming System [*Missiles*]
NZAQ........ Auckland [*New Zealand*] [*ICAO location identifier*] (ICLI)
NZAR........ Ardmore [*New Zealand*] [*ICAO location identifier*] (ICLI)
NZAR........ New Zealand Administrative Reports [*A publication*] (SAFN)

NZARE .... New Zealand Association for Research on Education (SAUS)
NZARP ...... New Zealand Antarctic Research Programme (SAUS)
NZART .... New Zealand Amateur Radio Transmitters Association (SAUS)
NZAS .... New Zealand Aluminium Smelters (SAUS)
NZAS .... New Zealand Antarctic Society (SAUS)
NZAS .... New Zealand Arthritis Society (SAUS)
NZASA .... New Zealand Asian Studies Association (SAUS)
NZASC .... New Zealand Administrative Staff College (SAUS)
NZASC .... New Zealand Association of Soil Conservators (SAUS)
NZASF .... New Zealand Association of Small Farmers (SAUS)
NZASW ...... New Zealand Association of Social Workers (SAUS)
NZATD .... New Zealand Association of Training and Development (SAUS)
NzAU .... Auckland University, Auckland, New Zealand [*Library symbol*] [*Library of Congress*] (LCLS)
NZAWA ...... New Zealand Air Womens Association (SAUS)
NZ Awards... New Zealand Awards, Recommendations, Agreements, Etc. [*A publication*] (DLA)
NZB .... New Zealand Black [*Mice hybrids*]
NZB .... Nonzero Binary (NASA)
NZB .... Royal New Zealand Ballet
NZBA .... New Zealand Bankers Association (SAUS)
NZBA .... New Zealand Biotechnology Association (SAUS)
NZBA .... New Zealand Bowling Association (SAUS)
NZBC .... New Zealand Broadcasting Commission (WDAA)
NZBC .... New Zealand Broadcasting Corp.
NZBCSO ..... New Zealand Broadcasting Corporation Symphony Orchestra (SAUS)
NZBIE .... New Zealand Bureau of Importers and Exporters (SAUS)
NZB Mice ... New Zealand Black Mice (SAUS)
NZB Mouse... New Zealand Black Mouse (SAUS)
NZBS .... New Zealand Broadcasting Service
NZBTO .... New Zealand Book Trade Organisation (SAUS)
NZC .... Jacksonville, FL [*Location identifier*] [*FAA*] (FAAL)
NZC .... New Zealand Certificate (SAUS)
NZC .... New Zealand Chocolate [*Mouse*] (DMAA)
NZC .... New Zealand Cross (DAS)
NZC .... North Carolina School of the Arts, Winston-Salem (SAUS)
NZCA .... Campbell Island [*New Zealand*] [*ICAO location identifier*] (ICLI)
NZCA .... New Zealand Conservation Authority (SAUS)
NZCAR ...... New Zealand Civil Aviation Regulations (SAUS)
NZCAS .... New Zealand Clean Air Society (SAUS)
NZCAU ...... New Zealand Conservation Authority Unit (SAUS)
NZCC .... New Zealand Chamber of Commerce (SAUS)
NZCC .... New Zealand Conservation Corps (SAUS)
NZCD .... New Zealand Certificate in Draughting (SAUS)
NZCDC .... New Zealand Cooperative Dairy Co. (SAUS)
NZCE .... New Zealand Certificate in Engineering (SAUS)
NZCEA .... New Zealand Combined Educational Associations (SAUS)
NZCER .... New Zealand Council for Educational Research (WDAA)
NZCF .... New Zealand Cycling Federation (SAUS)
NZCG .... New Zealand Chemists Guild (SAUS)
NZCGF .... New Zealand Coast Guard Federation (SAUS)
NZCGP ...... New Zealand College of General Practitioners (SAUS)
NzCGS .... Church of Jesus Christ of Latter-Day Saints, Genealogical Society Library, Canterbury Branch, Christchurch, New Zealand [*Library symbol*] [*Library of Congress*] (LCLS)
NZCGS ...... New Zealand Standard Classification of all Goods and Services (SAUS)
NZCH .... Christchurch/International [*New Zealand*] [*ICAO location identifier*] (ICLI)
NZCH .... New Zealand Cement Holdings (SAUS)
NZCI .... Chatham Island/Tuuta [*New Zealand*] [*ICAO location identifier*] (ICLI)
NZCLA .... New Zealand Childrens Literature Association (SAUS)
NZCLS .... New Zealand Certificate of Land Surveying (SAUS)
NZCM .... McMurdo Sound, Antarctica [*New Zealand*] [*ICAO location identifier*] (ICLI)
NZCMA ...... New Zealand Cable Makers Association (SAUS)
NZCMA ...... New Zealand Concrete Masonry Association (SAUS)
NZCMF ...... New Zealand Coal Merchants Federation (SAUS)
NZCO .... Christchurch [*New Zealand*] [*ICAO location identifier*] (ICLI)
NZ Col LJ... New Zealand Colonial Law Journal [*A publication*] (DLA)
NZCPS .... New Zealand Coastal Policy Statement (SAUS)
NZCRA ...... New Zealand Coal Research Association (SAUS)
NZCRA ...... New Zealand Concrete Research Association (SAUS)
NZCRS ...... New Zealand Council for Recreation and Sports (SAUS)
NZCS .... New Zealand Certificate in Science (SAUS)
NZCS .... New Zealand Certificate in Statistics (SAUS)
NZCS .... New Zealand Computer Society (SAUS)
NzCSI-A ..... New Zealand Department of Scientific and Industrial Research, Antarctic Division, Christchurch, New Zealand [*Library symbol*] [*Library of Congress*] (LCLS)
NZ Ct App... New Zealand Court of Appeals (DLA)
NZ Ct Arb... New Zealand Court of Arbitration (DLA)
NZCTF .... New Zealand Cycle Traders Federation (SAUS)
NZCTOA ..... New Zealand Container Terminal Operators Association (SAUS)
NZCU .... P and O Containers [*Intermodal shipping container symbol*] (TVRC)
NZCU .... Shipping Corporation of New Zealand [*Intermodal trailer symbol*]
NZCUL .... New Zealand Credit Union League (SAUS)
NZD .... New Zealand Division (SAUS)
NZD .... New Zealand Dollar (SAUS)
NZD .... New Zoo Developments (SAUS)
NZD .... Nonzero Digit (ECII)
NZDA .... New Zealand Dairy Association (SAUS)
NZDA .... New Zealand Deerstalkers Association (SAUS)
NZDA .... New Zealand Department of Agriculture (SAUS)
NZDA .... New Zealand Dietetic Association (SAUS)
NZDCMBA... New Zealand Dairy Confectionary and Mixed Biscuits Association (SAUS)
NZDCS ...... New Zealand Department of Census and Statistics (SAUS)
NZDE .... New Zealand Department of Education (SAUS)
NZDF .... Christchurch/International [*New Zealand*] [*ICAO location identifier*] (ICLI)
NZDF .... New Zealand Defence Force (SAUS)
NZDF .... New Zealand Drug Foundation (SAUS)
NZDFA .... New Zealand Deer Farmers Association (SAUS)
NZDLS .... New Zealand Department of Lands and Survey (SAUS)
NZDN .... Dunedin [*New Zealand*] [*ICAO location identifier*] (ICLI)
NZDRI .... New Zealand Dairy Research Institute (SAUS)
NZDS .... New Zealand Drama School (SAUS)
NZDT .... New Zealand Daylight Time (SAUS)
NZDVA .... New Zealand Dunkirk Veterans Association (SAUS)
NZDXRA ..... New Zealand DX Radio Association (SAUS)
NZE .... Glenview, IL [*Location identifier*] [*FAA*] (FAAL)
NZE .... New Zealand Engineers (SAUS)
NZE .... New Zealand English (SAUS)
NZE .... North Zenith East
NZE .... Nzema [*Language symbol*] (ETLW)
NZE .... Nzerekore [*Guinea*] [*Airport symbol*] (AD)
N Zea .... New Zealand (VRA)
NZEA .... New Zealand Esperanto Association (SAUS)
NZEAS .... New Zealand East Asia Service (SAUS)
NZEAS .... New Zealand Educational Administration Society (SAUS)
NZEB .... New Zealand Electricity Board (SAUS)
NZEC .... New Zealand Electrotechnical Committee (AG)
NZECF .... New Zealand Electrical Contractors Federation (SAUS)
NZEF .... New Zealand Employees Federation (SAUS)
NZEF .... New Zealand Employers' Federation (ODBW)
NZEF .... New Zealand Expeditionary Force (WDAA)
NZEFIP ...... New Zealand Expeditionary Force in the Pacific (WDAA)
NZEI .... New Zealand Educational Institute (WDAA)
NZEI .... New Zealand Electronics Institute (SAUS)
NZERF .... New Zealand Engine Research Foundation (SAUS)
NZERF .... New Zealand Equine Research Foundation (SAUS)
NZES .... New Zealand Ecological Society (SAUS)
NZES .... New Zealand Employment Service (SAUS)
NZESA .... New Zealand Education Standards Association (SAUS)
NZESA .... New Zealand European Shipping Association (SAUS)
NZE System... North-Zenith-East System (SAUS)
NZF .... Near Zero Field
NZFB .... New Zealand Foundation for the Blind (SAUS)
NZFCA .... New Zealand Farmers Cooperative Association (SAUS)
NZFCA .... New Zealand Freezing Companies Association (SAUS)
NZFCDC ..... New Zealand Farmers Cooperative Distributing Co. (SAUS)
NZFCMA .... New Zealand Ferro Cement Marine Association (SAUS)
NZFF .... New Zealand Farmers Fertiliser (SAUS)
NZFF .... New Zealand Federated Farmers (SAUS)
NZFF .... New Zealand Fruitgrowers Federation (SAUS)
NZFFA .... New Zealand Federation of Freshwater Anglers (SAUS)
NZFG .... New Zealand Psychic Gazette (SAUS)
NZFGC .... New Zealand Fish and Game Council (SAUS)
NZFHA .... New Zealand Finance Houses Association (SAUS)
NZFKTA ..... New Zealand Free Kindergarten Teachers Association (SAUS)
NZFKU .... New Zealand Free Kindergarten Union (SAUS)
NZFL .... New Zealand Federation of Labor (ODBW)
NZFMA ...... New Zealand Ferrocement Marine Association (SAUS)
NZFMC ...... New Zealand Federation of Master Cleaners (SAUS)
NZFMRA .... New Zealand Fertiliser (or Fertilizer) Manufacturers Research Association (SAUS)
NZFOE .... New Zealand Futures and Options Exchange (NUMA)
NZFP .... New Zealand Family Physician (SAUS)
NZFPA .... New Zealand Family Planning Association (SAUS)
NZFRI .... New Zealand Forest Research Institute (SAUS)
NZFS .... New Zealand Film Service (SAUS)
NZFUW ...... New Zealand Federation of University Women (SAUS)
NZFWA ...... New Zealand Farm Workers Association (SAUS)
NZG .... Near Zero Gravity
NZG .... New Zealand Government (SAUS)
NZG .... North Carolina School of the Arts, Winston-Salem, NC [*OCLC symbol*] (OCLC)
NZGA .... New Zealand Gliding Association (SAUS)
NZ Gaz LR... New Zealand Gazette Law Reports [*A publication*] (DLA)
NZGBHTB... New Zealand Game Bird Habitat Trust board (SAUS)
NZGenS ..... New Zealand Genetical Society (SAUS)
NZGGA ...... New Zealand Geographer (SAUS)
NZGLR ...... New Zealand Gazette Law Reports [*A publication*] (DLA)
NZGR .... New Zealand Government Railways (SAUS)
NZGS .... Gisborne [*New Zealand*] [*ICAO location identifier*] (ICLI)
NZGS .... New Zealand Geological Survey (SAUS)
NZGTB .... New Zealand Government Tourist Bureau (SAUS)
NZGTC .... New Zealand Government Travel Commissioner (SAUS)
NZGTO ...... New Zealand Government Tourist Office (SAUS)
NZH .... New Zealand Helicopters (SAUS)
NZHC .... New Zealand High Commission (SAUS)
NZHF .... New Zealand Heart Foundation (SAUS)
NZHGA ...... New Zealand Hang Gliding Association (SAUS)
NZHI .... New Zealand Horological Institute (SAUS)
NZHK .... Hokitika [*New Zealand*] [*ICAO location identifier*] (ICLI)
NZHN .... Hamilton [*New Zealand*] [*ICAO location identifier*] (ICLI)
NZHO .... Wellington [*New Zealand*] [*ICAO location identifier*] (ICLI)

NZHPT....... New Zealand Historic Places Trust (SAUS)
NZHS........ New Zealand Horse Society (SAUS)
NZHTA....... New Zealand Health Technology Assessment (SAUS)
NZI.......... New Zealand Insulators (SAUS)
NZI.......... New Zealand Insurance (SAUS)
NZIA......... New Zealand Institute of Architects (SAUS)
NZIA......... New Zealand Institute of Architecture (SAUS)
NZIA......... New Zealand Irrigation Association (SAUS)
NZIA Journal... New Zealand Institute of Architecture Journal (SAUS)
NZIAS....... New Zealand Institute of Agricultural Science (SAUS)
NZIC......... New Zealand Institute of Chemistry
NZIC......... New Zealand Intelligence Council (SAUS)
NZICFM..... New Zealand Institute of Credit and Financial Management (SAUS)
NZICM....... New Zealand Institute of Credit Management (SAUS)
NZID......... New Zealand Institute of Draughtsmen (SAUS)
NZIDA....... New Zealand Invention Development Authority (SAUS)
NZIDC....... New Zealand Industrial Design Council (SAUS)
NZIE......... New Zealand Institute of Engineers (SAUS)
NZIELEC... New Zealand Institute of Electricians (SAUS)
NZIEPC...... New Zealand Indonesia Economic Promotion Council (SAUS)
NZIER....... New Zealand Institute of Economic Research
NZIET....... New Zealand Institute of Engineering Technicians (SAUS)
NZIF......... New Zealand Institute of Foresters (SAUS)
NZIG......... New Zealand Institute of Gases (SAUS)
NZIH......... New Zealand Institute of Horticulture (SAUS)
NZIHVE..... New Zealand Institute of Heating and Ventilation Engineers (SAUS)
NZIIS........ New Zealand Institute of Industial Safety (SAUS)
NZILA........ New Zealand Institute of Landscape Architects (SAUS)
NZIM........ New Zealand Institute of Mining (SAUS)
NZIME....... New Zealand Institute of Mechanical Engineers (SAUS)
NZIMP....... New Zealand Institute of Medical Photography (SAUS)
NZ Ind Arb... New Zealand Industrial Arbitration Awards [*A publication*] (DLA)
NZIP......... New Zealand Institute of Printing (SAUS)
NZIPA........ New Zealand Institute of Public Administration (SAUS)
NZIPE........ New Zealand Institution of Professional Engineers (SAUS)
NZIPM....... New Zealand Institute of Personnel Management (SAUS)
NZIPRA...... New Zealand Institute of Parks and Recreation Administration (SAUS)
NZIPS....... New Zealand Institute of Purchasing and Supply (SAUS)
NZIRE....... New Zealand Institute of Refrigeration Engineers (SAUS)
NZIS......... New Zealand Information Service (SAUS)
NZIS......... New Zealand Institute of Surveyors (SAUS)
NZISM....... New Zealand Institute of Safety Management (SAUS)
NZIT......... New Zealand Institute of Travel (SAUS)
NZIUW...... New Zealand Industrial Union of Workers (SAUS)
NZJ.......... Naze [*Ryukyu Islands*] [*Seismograph station code, US Geological Survey*] (SEIS)
NZJ.......... Santa Ana, CA [*Location identifier*] [*FAA*] (FAAL)
NZJHPER... New Zealand Journal of Health, Physical Education and Recreation (SAUS)
NZJP......... New Zealand Justice of the Peace [*1876-77*] [*A publication*] (DLA)
NZ J Phys Educ... New Zealand Journal of Health, Physical Education and Recreation (SAUS)
NZJU........ New Zealand Journalists Union (SAUS)
NZJU........ New Zealand Line [*Intermodal shipping container symbol*] (TVRC)
NZ Jur....... New Zealand Jurist [*1873-78*] [*A publication*] (DLA)
NZ Jur Mining Law... Jurist Reports, New Series, Cases in Mining Law [*New Zealand*] [*A publication*] (DLA)
NZ Jur NS... New Zealand Jurist, New Series [*A publication*] (DLA)
NZKB........ Wellington/Kilbirnie [*New Zealand*] [*ICAO location identifier*] (ICLI)
NZKI......... Kaikoura [*New Zealand*] [*ICAO location identifier*] (ICLI)
NZKL......... Wellington/Kelburn [*New Zealand*] [*ICAO location identifier*] (ICLI)
NZKMB...... New Zealand Kiwifruit Marketing Board
NZKT........ Kaitaia [*New Zealand*] [*ICAO location identifier*] (ICLI)
NZKVA....... New Zealand Korean Veterans Association (SAUS)
NZKX........ Kaitaia [*New Zealand*] [*ICAO location identifier*] (ICLI)
NZL.......... New Zealand [*ANSI three-letter standard code*] (CNC)
NZL.......... New Zealand Line (SAUS)
NZLA........ New Zealand Legal Association (SAUS)
NZLA........ New Zealand Loggers Association (SAUS)
NZ Law Soc N... New Zealand Law Society. Newsletter [*A publication*] (DLA)
NZLCC....... New Zealand Litter Control Council (SAUS)
NZLF......... New Zealand Literary Fund (SAUS)
NZLGR...... Local Government Reports [*New Zealand*] [*A publication*] (DLA)
NZLIRA..... New Zealand Logging Industry Research Association (SAUS)
NZLJ......... New Zealand Law Journal [*A publication*] (SAFN)
NZLJMC..... New Zealand Law Journal, Magistrates' Court Decisions [*A publication*] (DLA)
NZLL......... New Zealand Law Librarian (SAFN)
NZLL......... New Zealand Light Leathers (SAUS)
NZLO........ New Zealand Liaison Officer
NZLP........ New Zealand Labour Party [*Political party*] (PPW)
NZLR........ New Zealand Law Reports [*A publication*] (DLA)
NZLRCA..... New Zealand Law Reports, Court of Appeal [*A publication*] (DLA)
NZLS........ New Zealand Law Society (SAUS)
NZLS........ New Zealand Library School (SAUS)
NZLS........ New Zealand Library Service (SAUS)
NZLS........ New Zealand Securities (SAUS)
NZLT......... New Zealand Land Care Trust (SAUS)
NZLU........ New Zealand Line [*Intermodal shipping container symbol*] (TVRC)
NZM......... Mount Cook Airlines [*New Zealand*] [*ICAO designator*] (FAAC)
NZMA........ New Zealand Medical Association (SAUS)
NZMA........ New Zealand Modelling Association (SAUS)
NZMA........ New Zealand Motel Association (SAUS)
NZMAF...... New Zealand Ministry of Agriculture and Fisheries (SAUS)
NZM&WB... New Zealand Meat and Wool Board (SAUS)
NZMB........ New Zealand Meat Board (SAUS)
NZMBF....... New Zealand Master Builders Federation (SAUS)
NZMC........ New Zealand Maori Council (SAUS)
NZMCA...... New Zealand Motor Caravan Association (SAUS)
NZMEA...... New Zealand Mining and Exploration Association Inc. (SAUS)
NZMF........ Milford Sound [*New Zealand*] [*ICAO location identifier*] (ICLI)
NZMF........ New Zealand Manufacturers Federation (SAUS)
NZMF........ New Zealand Military Forces (SAUS)
NZMF........ New Zealand Motel Federation (SAUS)
NZMF........ New Zealand Music Federation (SAUS)
NZMFA...... New Zealand Master Floorcovering Association (SAUS)
NZMGA...... New Zealand Mountain Guides Association (SAUS)
NZMGC...... New Zealand Marriage Guidance Council (SAUS)
N-Z Missile... Nike-Zeus Missile (SAUS)
NZMN........ New Zealand Merchant Navy (DAS)
NZMOT...... New Zealand Ministry of Transport (SAUS)
NZMPH...... New Zealand Meat Packing House (SAUS)
NZMR........ New Zealand Mounted Rines (SAUS)
NZMRC...... New Zealand Medical Research Council (SAUS)
NZMS........ New Zealand Mapping Service (SAUS)
NZMS........ New Zealand Meteorological Service [*Marine science*] (OSRA)
NZMSC...... New Zealand Mountain Safety Council (SAUS)
NZMSS...... New Zealand Marine Sciences Society (SAUS)
NZMTCB.... New Zealand Motor Trade Certification Board (SAUS)
NZMTMA.... New Zealand Methods Time Measurement Association (SAUS)
NZ Mu Dep Fish Tech Rep... New Zealand Marine Department. Fisheries Technical Report (SAUS)
NZMWA..... New Zealand Maori Wardens Association (SAUS)
NZMWU..... New Zealand Meat Workers Union (SAUS)
NZN.......... Niedersachsischer Zeitschriftennachweis [*Deutsches Bibliotheksinstitut*] [*Germany*] [*Information service or system*] (CRD)
NZNA........ New Zealand Nurserymens Association (SAUS)
NZNA........ New Zealand Nurses Association (SAUS)
NZ Natl Radiat Lab Environ Radioact Annu Rep... New Zealand. National Radiation Laboratory. Environmental Radioactivity. Annual Report (SAUS)
NZNB........ New Zealand Naval Board [*Wellington*]
NZNCC...... New Zealand Nature Conservation Council (SAUS)
NZNEDA..... New Zealand National Electronics Development Association (SAUS)
NZNF........ New Zealand Neurological Foundation (SAUS)
NZNFC....... Norma Zimmer National Fan Club (EA)
NZNFU...... New Zealand National Film Unit (SAUS)
NZNO........ New Zealand Nurses Orgainisation (SAUS)
NZNP........ New Plymouth [*New Zealand*] [*ICAO location identifier*] (ICLI)
NZNPA....... New Zealand Newspaper Proprietors Association (SAUS)
NZNR........ Napier [*New Zealand*] [*ICAO location identifier*] (ICLI)
NZNRAC..... New Zealand National Research Advisory Council (SAUS)
NZNS........ Nelson [*New Zealand*] [*ICAO location identifier*] (ICLI)
NZNTA....... New Zealand National Travel Association (SAUS)
NZNV........ Invercargill [*New Zealand*] [*ICAO location identifier*] (ICLI)
NZNZ........ Nonzero-Nonzero (SAUS)
NZO.......... New Zealand Obese [*Mouse*] [*Medicine*] (DMAA)
NZOA........ New Zealand Optometrical Association (SAUS)
NZOC........ New Zealand Opera Co. (SAUS)
NZOH........ Ohakea [*New Zealand*] [*ICAO location identifier*] (ICLI)
NZOI......... New Zealand Oceanographic Institute
NZ Ords..... Ordinances of the Legislative Council of New Zealand [*A publication*] (DLA)
NZOU........ Oamaru [*New Zealand*] [*ICAO location identifier*] (ICLI)
NZP.......... National Zoological Park [*Smithsonian Institution*]
NZP.......... New Zealand Pacific (SAUS)
NZP.......... New Zealand Players (SAUS)
NZP.......... New Zealand Police (SAUS)
NZPA........ New Zealand Police Association (SAUS)
NZPA........ New Zealand Press Association
NZP&TC...... New Zealand Post and Telegraph Corps (SAUS)
NZPARS..... New Zealand Prisoners Aid and Rehabilitation Society (SAUS)
NZPB........ New Zealand Pony Breeders (SAUS)
NZPB........ New Zealand Potato Board (SAUS)
NZPBA....... New Zealand Power Boat Association (SAUS)
NZPBA....... New Zealand Publishers Association (SAUS)
NZPBR...... New Zealand Pony Breeders Register (SAUS)
NZPBS....... New Zealand Pony Breeders Society (SAUS)
NZPC........ New Zealand Peace Council (SAUS)
NZPC........ New Zealand Petroleum Company Ltd. (SAUS)
NZPC........ New Zealand Planning Council (SAUS)
NZPC........ New Zealand Press Council (SAUS)
NZPC........ New Zealand Print Council (SAUS)
NZPCA....... New Zealand Portland Cement Association (SAUS)
NZPCC....... New Zealand Privy Council Cases [*A publication*] (DLA)
NZPC Cas... New Zealand Privy Council Cases [*A publication*] (DLA)
NZPEA....... New Zealand Port Employers Association (SAUS)
NZPECC..... New Zealand Committee of the Pacific Economic Cooperation Council
NZPGMF.... New Zealand Post Graduate Medical Federation (SAUS)
NZPM........ New Zealand Paper Mills (SAUS)
NZPM........ Palmerston North [*New Zealand*] [*ICAO location identifier*] (ICLI)
NZPMS...... New Zealand Plumbers Merchants Society (SAUS)
NZPO........ New Zealand Post Office [*Telecommunications*]
NZPP........ Paraparaumu [*New Zealand*] [*ICAO location identifier*] (ICLI)
NZPPA....... New Zealand Professional Photographers Association (SAUS)
NZPPTA..... New Zealand Post Primary Teachers Association (SAUS)

NZPS .... New Zealand Park Service (SAUS)
NZPS .... New Zealand Police Service (SAUS)
NZPSA....... New Zealand Political Studies Association (SAUS)
NZPSA....... New Zealand Public Service Association (SAUS)
NZPTA....... New Zealand Parent Teachers Association (SAUS)
NZPTO....... New Zealand Public Trust Office (SAUS)
NZQHA ...... New Zealand Quarter Horse Association (SAUS)
NZQN........ Queenstown [*New Zealand*] [*ICAO location identifier*] (ICLI)
NZR.......... New Zealand Red [*Rabbit*] [*Medicine*] (DMAA)
NZR.......... Non-Zero Result (SAUS)
NZRA........ New Zealand Recreation Association (SAUS)
NZRC........ New Zealand Red Cross (SAUS)
NZ Rep...... New Zealand Reports, Court of Appeals [*A publication*] (DLA)
NZ Repr Stat... Reprint of the Statutes of New Zealand [*A publication*] (DLA)
NZRFU ...... New Zealand Rugby Football Union
NZRLS....... New Zealand Railway and Locomotive Society (SAUS)
NZRMA...... New Zealand Ready Mix Concrete Association (SAUS)
NZRMTA .... New Zealand Retail Motor Trade Association (SAUS)
NZRN........ New Zealand Registered Nurse (SAUS)
NZRN........ Raoul Island [*New Zealand*] [*ICAO location identifier*] (ICLI)
NZRNC ...... New Zealand Radio Navigation Chart (SAUS)
NZRO........ Rotorua [*New Zealand*] [*ICAO location identifier*] (ICLI)
NZRR........ New Zealand Rough Riders [*Military*] (ROG)
NZR Regs & B... Rules, Regulations, and By-Laws under New Zealand Statutes [*A publication*] (DLA)
NZRRS ...... New Zealand Railways Road Services (SAUS)
NZRTA....... New Zealand Road Transport Association (SAUS)
NZS.......... Near-Zero Stamping (VLIE)
NZS.......... New Zealand Ship (SAUS)
NZS.......... New Zealand Standard (SAUS)
NZS.......... Nonzero Sum [*Genetics*]
NZSB .... New Zealand Soil Bureau (SAUS)
NZSB .... New Zealand Speech Board (SAUS)
NZSB .... New Zealand Survey Board (SAUS)
NZSBG ...... New Zealand South British Group (SAUS)
NZSC .... New Zealand Sealers Club (SAUS)
NZSC .... New Zealand Securities Commission (SAUS)
NZSC .... New Zealand Squid Co. (SAUS)
NZSC .... New Zealand Standards Council (SAUS)
NZSC .... New Zealand Supreme Court [*A publication*] (DLA)
NZSCA....... New Zealand Sheep and Cattlemens Association (SAUS)
NZSCA....... New Zealand Society of Customs Agents (SAUS)
NZSCA....... New Zealand Soil Conservation Association (SAUS)
NZSCC....... New Zealand Standard Country Code (SAUS)
NZSCES ..... New Zealand Society of Certified Executive Secretaries (SAUS)
NZSCHA..... New Zealand Society of Custom House Agents (SAUS)
NZSCI .... New Zealand Standard Classification of Imports (SAUS)
NZS Co...... New Zealand Shipping Co. (SAUS)
NZSCO ...... New Zealand Standard Classification of Occupations (SAUS)
NZSCS....... New Zealand Senior Citizens Service (SAUS)
NZSDA ...... New Zealand Sign and Display Association (SAUS)
NZSDA ...... New Zealand Stamp Dealers Association (SAUS)
NZSE .... New Zealand Stock Exchange
NZSEAFRON... New Zealand Sea Frontier
NZSG........ Non-Zero-Sum Game (MHDW)
NZSI......... New Zealand Seismological Institute (SAUS)
NZSIA .... New Zealand Security Industry Association (SAUS)
NZSID .... New Zealand Society of Industrial Designers (SAUS)
NZSIS .... New Zealand Security Intelligence Service (CARL)
NZSK .... Sky Network Television, Ltd. [*NASDAQ symbol*] (NASQ)
NZSL .... New Zealand Shipping Line (SAUS)
NZSL .... New Zealand Steel Ltd. (SAUS)
NZSLO....... New Zealand Scientific Liaison Office (SAUS)
NZSNA ...... New Zealand Society of National Accounts (SAUS)
NZ Soc Earthquake Eng Bull... New Zealand Society for Earhtquake Engineering. Bulletin (SAUS)
NZSS .... New Zealand Social Security (SAUS)
NZSS .... New Zealand Speleological Society (SAUS)
NZ Stat...... Statutes of New Zealand [*A publication*] (DLA)
NZ Stat Regs... New Zealand Statutory Regulations [*A publication*] (DLA)
NZSU .... P and O Containers [*Intermodal shipping container symbol*] (TVRC)
NZSU .... Shipping Corporation of New Zealand [*Intermodal trailer symbol*]
NZSWWS ... New Zealand Spinning, Weaving and Woolcrafts Society (SAUS)
NZT.......... New Zealand Time (SAUS)
NZT.......... Nonzero Test (IAA)
NZT.......... Nonzero Transfer
NZT.......... Telecom Corp. New Zealand [*NYSE symbol*] (SPSG)
NZT.......... Telecom Corp. New Zealand ADS [*NYSE symbol*] (TTSB)
NZTB .... New Zealand Tourism Board (EA)
NZTBR....... New Zealand Taxation Board of Review Decisions [*A publication*] (DLA)
NZTC .... New Zealand Trade Commission (SAUS)
NZTCA....... New Zealand Teachers College Association (SAUS)
NZTCB....... New Zealand Trade Certification Board (SAUS)
NZTCI........ New Zealand Technical College Institute (SAUS)
NZTCI........ New Zealand Technical Correspondence Institute (SAUS)
NZTF......... New Zealand Theatre Federation (SAUS)
NZTG .... Tauranga [*New Zealand*] [*ICAO location identifier*] (ICLI)
NZTJWG .... Nike-Zeus Target Joint Working Group [*Missiles*] (MUGU)
NZTO .... New Zealand Tourism Office (EA)
NZTP .... New Zealand Tourist and Publicity Office [*Later, NZTO*] (EA)
NZTPA....... New Zealand Japan Parliamentary Association (SAUS)
NZTS .... New Zealand Treaty Series [*A publication*] (DLA)
NZTU .... Timaru [*New Zealand*] [*ICAO location identifier*] (ICLI)
NZTV .... Nike-Zeus Target Vehicle [*Missiles*] (IAA)
NzTvGS...... Church of Jesus Christ of Latter-Day Saints, Genealogical Society Library, Temple View Branch, Temple View, New Zealand [*Library symbol*] [*Library of Congress*] (LCLS)
NZUA........ New Zealand Underwater Association (SAUS)
NZUA........ New Zealand Underwriters Association (SAUS)
NZUE .... New Zealand Unit Express (SAUS)
NZUKCC..... New Zealand-United Kingdom Chamber of Commerce (SAUS)
NZUNINET... New Zealand University Network
NZUSUGI... New Zealand Unix System User Group, Inc. (SAUS)
NZV.......... New Zealand Victoria (SAUS)
NZVA .... New Zealand Veterinary Association (GVA)
NZW .... New Zealand White [*Mice hybrids*]
NZW .... South Weymouth, MA [*Location identifier*] [*FAA*] (FAAL)
NZWA........ Chatham Island/Waitangi [*New Zealand*] [*ICAO location identifier*] (ICLI)
NZWA........ New Zealand Woolbuyers Association (SAUS)
NZW&PCS... New Zealand Weed and Pest Control Society (SAUS)
NZWB .... New Zealand Wool Board (SAUS)
NZWB .... Woodbourne [*New Zealand*] [*ICAO location identifier*] (ICLI)
NZWCC...... New Zealand Weed Control Conference (SAUS)
NZWEA...... New Zealand Workers Educational Association (SAUS)
NZWG .... Wigram [*New Zealand*] [*ICAO location identifier*] (ICLI)
NzWGAL .... General Assembly Library, Wellington, New Zealand, [*Library symbol*] [*Library of Congress*] (LCLS)
NzWGS...... Church of Jesus Christ of Latter-Day Saints, Genealogical Society Library, Wellington Stake Branch, Wellington, New Zealand [*Library symbol*] [*Library of Congress*] (LCLS)
NZWK .... Whakatane [*New Zealand*] [*ICAO location identifier*] (ICLI)
NZW Mice.. New Zealand White Mice (SAUS)
NZW Mouse... New Zealand White Mouse (SAUS)
NzWMW..... New Zealand Ministry of Works and Development, Head Office Library, Wellington, New Zealand [*Library symbol*] [*Library of Congress*] (LCLS)
NZWN .... Wellington/International [*New Zealand*] [*ICAO location identifier*] (ICLI)
NzWNA...... National Archives, Wellington, New Zealand [*Library symbol*] [*Library of Congress*] (LCLS)
NZWP .... Whenuapai [*New Zealand*] [*ICAO location identifier*] (ICLI)
NZWQ .... Wellington [*New Zealand*] [*ICAO location identifier*] (ICLI)
NZWR .... Whangarei [*New Zealand*] [*ICAO location identifier*] (ICLI)
NZWRAC.... New Zealand Womens Royal Army Corps (SAUS)
NZWS .... New Zealand Wildlife Service (SAUS)
NZWS .... Westport [*New Zealand*] [*ICAO location identifier*] (ICLI)
NZWSC...... New Zealand Water Safety Council (SAUS)
NZWTA...... New Zealand Wool Testing Authority (SAUS)
NZWU .... Wanganui [*New Zealand*] [*ICAO location identifier*] (ICLI)
NZWWC..... New Zealand Working Womens Council (SAUS)
NZWWF..... New Zealand Waterside Workers Federation (SAUS)
NZY.......... San Diego, CA [*Location identifier*] [*FAA*] (FAAL)
NZYF .... New Zealand Yachting Federation (SAUS)
NZYHA ...... New Zealand Youth Hostels Association (SAUS)
NZYM........ Synthetech, Inc. [*NASDAQ symbol*] (NQ)
NZZA .... Auckland [*New Zealand*] [*ICAO location identifier*] (ICLI)
NZZC .... Christchurch [*New Zealand*] [*ICAO location identifier*] (ICLI)
NZZO .... Auckland [*New Zealand*] [*ICAO location identifier*] (ICLI)
NZZW........ Wellington [*New Zealand*] [*ICAO location identifier*] (ICLI)

O

By Acronym

O .... Absence of Sex Chromosome (DAVI)
O .... Angel (SAUS)
O .... An Oige [*The Irish Youth Hostels Association*] [*Founded in 1931*]
O .... Center of the Earth (SAUS)
O .... Cleared to the Outer Marker (SAUS)
o .... Deamino [*As substituent on nucleoside*] [*Biochemistry*]
O .... for those innocent souls (SAUS)
O .... Horizontal Opposed [*Aircraft engine*]
O .... Law Opinions [*A publication*] (DLA)
O .... New Orleans [*Louisiana*] [*Mint mark, when appearing on US coins*] [*Obsolete*]
O .... None (DAVI)
O .... Nonmotile [*Laboratory science*] (DAVI)
O .... Oasis
o .... Oath (GEAB)
O .... Oath
O .... Oberst [*Colonel*] [*German military - World War II*]
O .... Obiit [*He, or She, Died*] [*Latin*]
O .... Object
O .... Objective
O .... Oblast [*Governmental subdivision in USSR corresponding to a province or state*]
O .... Oboe [*Phonetic alphabet*] [*World War II*] (DSUE)
O .... Observation Aircraft [*Designation for all US military aircraft*]
O .... Observer
O .... Obsolescent (AFIT)
O .... Obstetrics [*Medicine*] (MAE)
O .... Obvious (STED)
O .... Occasional [*Concerning occurrence of species*]
O .... Occidental
O .... Occipital (STED)
O .... Occiput [*Medicine*]
O .... Occlusal [*Dentistry*]
O .... Occupation (ADA)
O .... Occurrence
O .... Ocean [*Maps and charts*]
O .... Oceanic (SAUS)
O .... Oceanic Steamship Company (SAUS)
O .... Octal [*Number system with a base of eight*] [*Computer science*] (BUR)
O .... Octarius [*Pint*] [*Pharmacy*]
O .... Octavo [*Book from 20 to 25 centimeters in height*] [*Bibliography*]
O .... October
O .... Octupole [*Physics*] (OA)
O .... Oculus [*Eye*] [*Latin*]
O .... Oddfellows (ODA)
O .... Odericus [*Flourished, 1166-1200*] [*Authority cited in pre-1607 legal work*] (DSA)
O .... Of [*Telegraphy*] (PCTE)
O .... Off
O .... Offered [*Stock exchange term*] (SPSG)
O .... Office [*or Officer*]
O .... Office of Operations [*Coast Guard*]
O .... Official [*Rate*] [*Value of the English pound*]
O .... Often (STED)
O .... Ohio
O .... Ohio Reports [*A publication*] (DLA)
O .... Ohio State Library, Columbus, OH [*Library symbol*] [*Library of Congress*] (LCLS)
O .... Ohm [*Electricity*]
O .... Ohne [*Antigen*] [*Immunology*]
o .... Oil (VRA)
O .... Oil
O .... Oklahoma (DLA)
O .... Old
O .... Olivine Subgroup [*Fayalite, forsterite*] [*CIPW classification*] [*Geology*]
O .... Oman (MILB)
O .... Omicron [*Fifteenth letter of the Greek alphabet*] (NASA)
O .... Omnipol Foreign Trade Corp. [*Former Czechoslovakia*] [*ICAO aircraft manufacturer identifier*] (ICAO)
O .... Omnivore
O .... Oncovin [*Leurocristine, Vincristine*] [*Also, LCR, V, VC, VCR*] [*Antineoplastic drug*]
O .... Ongoing
O .... Only
O .... Ontario (DLA)
O .... Ontario Reports [*A publication*] (DLA)
O .... Ontario Securities Commission [*Canada*]
O .... Opacity (MCD)
O .... Open [*Dancing position*]
O .... Open-Air Places [*Parks, pools, etc.*] [*Public-performance tariff class*] [*British*]
O .... Open Circuit
O .... Opening
O .... Operand [*Computer science*]
O .... Operating Room Attendant [*Ranking title*] [*British Royal Navy*]
O .... Operation
O .... Operator
O .... Operon [*Genetics*]
O .... Ophthalmology [*Medical Officer designation*] [*British*]
O .... Opium [*Slang*]
O .... Optimus [*Best*] [*Latin*]
O .... Optional Dishes [*School meals*] [*British*]
o .... Options [*Computer science*] [*Telecommunications*]
O .... Oral [*Medicine*]
O .... Orange [*Color*] [*Medicine*] (DMAA)
O .... Orange [*Phonetic alphabet*] [*Royal Navy*] [*World War I*] [*Pre-World War II*] (DSUE)
O .... Orange [*Maps and charts*]
O .... Orbit [*Medicine*] (DAVI)
O .... Orchid Flowering [*Horticulture*]
O .... Ordained
O .... Order
O .... Orderly [*Medicine*] (DAVI)
O .... Orders Group [*British military*] (DMA)
O .... Ordinance
O .... Ordinary
O .... Ordinary Level [*School graduating grade*] [*British*]
O .... Ordinary Ray [*Direction of*]
O .... Ordinate [*Mathematics*] (MSA)
O .... Ordinis [*By the Order Of*] [*Latin*]
O .... Ordnance
O .... Ordonnanzoffizier [*Special-Missions Staff Officer*] [*German military - World War II*]
O .... Ordovician [*Paleontology*] (QSUL)
O .... Oregon (ROG)
O .... Oregon Reports [*A publication*] (DLA)
O .... Organ
o .... Organ
O .... Organic [*Soil*]
O .... Organism [*Psychology*]
O .... Organization
O .... Organized Naval Reserve
O .... Orient [*Freemasonry*]
O .... Oriental
O .... Oriented (IDYL)
o .... Origin (IDOE)
O .... Origin
O .... Original
O .... Original Response (DIPS)
O .... Orotidine [*One-letter symbol; see Ord*]
o .... Ortho [*Chemistry*]
O .... Orthodox [*Judaism*]
O .... Orthopedic (STED)
O .... Os [*Bone*] [*Latin*]
O .... Oscar [*Phonetic alphabet*] [*International*] (DSUE)
O .... Oscillation or Fluctuation in Behavior [*Psychology*]
O .... Oscillators [*JETDS nomenclature*] [*Military*] (CET)
O .... Osphradium [*An organ in mollusks*]
O .... Osten [*East*] [*German*]
O .... Osteocyte (MELL)
O .... Ostiole [*Biology*]
o .... Other [*Therapy term*] (CTAA)
O .... Other
O .... Other Program (NTCM)
O .... Otto's United States Supreme Court Reports [*91-107 United States*] [*A publication*] (DLA)
O .... Ouest [*West*] [*French*]
o .... Out (VLIE)
O .... Out
O .... Outboard (DS)
O .... Outfield [*Baseball*]
O .... Outlay (GFGA)
O .... Outlet
O .... Output (BUR)
o .... Output (IDOE)

O .... Outside Cylinders [*Trains*] [*British*]
O .... Outside Edge [*Skating*]
O .... Outstanding (ADWA)
O .... Ovary
O .... Ovation (WGA)
O .... Oven
O .... Over
O .... Overall (IAA)
O .... Overall Rating [*Broadcasting*]
O .... Overcast
O .... Overflow (VLIE)
o .... Overruled [*Ruling in cited case expressly overruled*] [*Used in Shepard's Citations*] [*Legal term*] (DLA)
O .... Overseer
O .... Ovulation
O .... Ovule [*Botany*]
O .... Owner
O .... Oxford [*County borough in England*]
O .... Oxidative (STED)
O .... Oxygen [*Chemical element*]
O .... Oxygenium (SAUS)
O .... Realty Income Corp. [*NYSE symbol*] (SAG)
O .... Respirations [*on anesthesia chart*] (DAVI)
O .... Shoulder Season [*Airline fare code*]
O .... Solicitor's Opinion [*A publication*] (DLA)
O .... South African Law Reports, Orange Free State Provincial Division [*1910-46*] [*A publication*] (DLA)
O .... Without Film [*Bacteriology*] (DAVI)
O1 .... Ensign [*Navy*]
O1 .... Organized Naval Reserve Seagoing
O1 .... Second Lieutenant [*Air Force, Army, Marine Corps*]
O^2 .... Both Eyes [*Pharmacy*]
O2 .... First Lieutenant [*Air Force, Army, Marine Corps*]
O2 .... Lieutenant Junior Grade [*Navy*]
O2 .... molecular Oxygen (SAUS)
O2 .... Organized Naval Reserve Aviation
O_2 .... Oxygen (IDOE)
O-2A .... Oligodendrocytes and Type 2 Astrocytes [*Neurology*]
O_2 Cap .... Oxygen Capacity (MAE)
O2S .... Oxygen Sensor [*Automotive engineering*]
O_2sat .... Oxygen Saturation (MAE)
O_2V .... Oxygen Ventilation Equivalent [*Laboratory science*] (DAVI)
O3 .... Captain [*Air Force, Army, Marine Corps*]
O3 .... Lieutenant [*Navy*]
O_3 .... Ozone (PS)
O4 .... Lieutenant Commander [*Navy*]
O4 .... Major [*Air Force, Army, Marine Corps*]
O4O .... October 4th Organization (EA)
O5 .... Commander [*Navy*]
O5 .... Lieutenant Colonel [*Air Force, Army, Marine Corps*]
O-5-P Orotidine-5-Phosphate
O6 .... Captain [*Navy*]
O6 .... Colonel [*Air Force, Army, Marine Corps*]
O7 .... Brigadier General [*Air Force, Army, Marine Corps*]
O7 .... Commodore [*Navy*]
O8 .... Major General [*Air Force, Army, Marine Corps*]
O8 .... Rear Admiral [*Navy*]
O9 .... Lieutenant General [*Air Force, Army, Marine Corps*]
O9 .... Vice Admiral [*Navy*]
O10 .... Admiral [*Navy*]
O10 .... General [*Air Force, Army, Marine Corps*]
OA .... Almonte Public Library, Ontario [*Library symbol*] [*National Library of Canada*] (NLC)
OA .... Oberallgaeu [*German license plate city code*]
OA .... Object Adapter (SAUS)
OA .... Objective Analysis (ODA)
O-A .... Objective Analytic Batteries [*Personality development test*] [*Psychology*]
OA .... Objective Aperture [*Microscopy*]
OA .... Objective Area [*Military*]
OA .... Oblate Sisters of the Assumption [*Roman Catholic religious order*]
OA .... Obligation Authority [*Army*]
OA .... Obstacle Avoidance (MCD)
OA .... Obstructive Apnea [*Medicine*] (MELL)
OA .... Occipital Artery [*Anatomy*]
OA .... Occipito-Anterior (SAUS)
OA .... Occiput Anterior [*Medicine*]
OA .... Ocean Acre [*Marine science*] (MSC)
OA .... Oceanic Abstracts [*Database*] (GDD)
OA .... Ocular Albinism [*Medicine*] (MELL)
OA .... Odd Address (SAUS)
OA .... Of A [*Telegraphy*] (PCTE)
O/A .... Offer Accepted (ADA)
OA .... Office Address (WDAA)
OA .... Office Assistant (SAUS)
OA .... Office Audit [*IRS*]
OA .... Office Automation
OA .... Office for Accreditation [*American Library Association*]
OA .... Office of Administration [*NASA*]
OA .... Office of Applications [*NASA*]
OA .... Office of Audits (COE)
OA .... Office of Operations Analysis [*Arms Control and Disarmament Agency*] (GRD)
OA .... Office of the Administrator [*Environment term*] (EGA)
OA .... Officers Association [*British military*] (DMA)
OA .... Official Assignee (ROG)
OA .... Ohio Appellate Reports [*A publication*] (DLA)
OA .... Oil Analysis [*Fuels and lubricants*]
OA .... Oil-Immened Self-Cooled (SAUS)
OA .... Oil-immersed Air-cooled (SAUS)
OA .... Oil-Immersed Self-Cooled [*Transformer*] (IEEE)
OA .... Oil-to-Air (SAUS)
OA .... Old Account [*Banking*]
OA .... Old Age
OA .... Old Assyrian (BJA)
OA .... Oleic Acid [*Medicine*] (DMAA)
OA .... Olymbiaki Aeroporia [*Olympic Airlines*]
OA .... Olympic Airways [*Greece*] [*ICAO designator*] (OAG)
OA .... Omniaerial (SAUS)
OA .... Omniantenna
OA .... Omnirange Antenna (IAA)
oa .... On Acceptance (EBF)
OA .... On Acceptance [*Business term*]
OA .... On Account [*Business and trade*]
OA .... On Account Of
O/A .... On Application (NITA)
O/A .... On Approval [*Construction term*] (MIST)
OA .... On Arrival (ADA)
O/A .... On or About (WDAA)
o/a .... On or About (WDMC)
O/A .... Open Access [*Library shelves*] (DGA)
OA .... Open Account
OA .... Open Agility
OA .... Open Annealed [*Metal industry*]
OA .... Open Architecture [*Telecommunications*] (IAA)
OA .... Opera America [*An association*] (EA)
OA .... Operand Address (NITA)
OA .... Operand Address Register [*Computer science*]
OA .... Operating Agency
OA .... Operating Aircraft
OA .... Operating Assemblies [*JETDS nomenclature*] [*Military*] (CET)
OA .... Operating Authorization
OA .... Operational Advice
OA .... Operational Aft (MCD)
OA .... Operational Amplifier [*Telecommunications*] (TEL)
OA .... Operational [*or operations*] Analysis
OA .... Operational Architecture (SAUS)
OA .... Operational Area (SAUS)
OA .... Operational Assessment (SAUS)
OA .... Operationally Available (NATG)
OA .... Operation Analysis [*or Analyst*] (WDAA)
OA .... Operation Appreciation (EA)
O/A .... Operations/Administration (SSD)
OA .... Operations Advisor [*NASA*]
OA .... Operations Analysis (SAUS)
OA .... Operations Analyst (SAUS)
OA .... Operations Area
OA .... Operator Access (IAA)
OA .... Operator Assistance [*Telecommunications*] (VLIE)
OA .... Operator Availability (SAUS)
OA .... Ophthalmic Artery (SAUS)
OA .... Opiate Analgesia
OA .... Opioid Analgesics [*Medicine*] (MELL)
OA .... Optical Absorption (SAUS)
OA .... Optical Adjunct
OA .... Optical Augmentation (ACAE)
OA .... Optic Atrophy (CPH)
OA .... Optic Axis (SAUS)
OA .... Options Analysis [*Emergency Management*] (EMA)
OA .... Optoacoustic [*Cell*]
OA .... Oral Administration (MELL)
OA .... Oral Alimentation [*Gastroenterology*] (DAVI)
OA .... Oral Apparatus [*Zoology*]
OA .... Orbital Assembly (MCD)
OA .... Orbit Analysis
OA .... Orbit Analyst (MCD)
O/A .... Orbit/Attitude (ACAE)
OA .... Orbiter Access Arm [*NASA*]
OA .... Order Action (VLIE)
OA .... Order Address (SAUS)
OA .... Order Administration (SAUS)
O/A .... Order Authority (MCD)
OA .... Order of AHEPA [*Also known as American Hellenic Educational Progressive Association*] (EA)
OA .... Order of Australia (WDAA)
OA .... Order of the Alhambra (EA)
OA .... Order of the Arrow (EA)
O/A .... Ordnance Alteration (MCD)
OA .... Ordnance Artificer [*Obsolete*] [*Navy*] [*British*]
OA .... Organic Acid (AAEL)
OA .... Organizational Analysis
OA .... Organizational Assessment
O/A .... Original-Abfuellung [*On estate-bottled German wine labels*]
OA .... Original Address (SAUS)
OA .... Originating Agency (SAA)
OA .... Orlando Aerospace [*Martin Marietta*] (RDA)
OA .... Oro Americano [*American Gold*] [*Spanish*] [*Business term*]
OA .... Oronite Additives [*Fuels and lubricants*]

OA .... Osborne Association (EA)
OA .... Osteoarthritis [*Medicine*]
OA .... Osteogenesis Imperfecta [*Brittle bone disease*]
OA .... Other Appointments
OA .... Other Articles
OA .... Oudh Appeals [*India*] [*A publication*] (DLA)
O/A.......... Our Account [*Business term*]
OA .... Out-Agency [*Indian Railway*] (TIR)
OA .... Outdoor Air (LDOE)
O/A.......... Outer Anchorage [*Navigation*]
OA .... Outgoing Access (SAUS)
OA .... Output Acknowledge (SAUS)
OA .... Output Amplifier (SAUS)
OA .... Output Amplitude
OA .... Output Available (SAUS)
OA .... Output Axis
OA .... Outside Air (SAUS)
OA .... Ovalbumin [*Also, OV, OVA, OVAL*] [*Biochemistry*]
OA .... Overachievers Anonymous (EA)
OA .... Overaction (SAUS)
OA .... Over Aged (RIMS)
OA .... Overaging (SAUS)
oa........... Overall [*Ship length*] (POLM)
OA .... Overall [*Technical drawings*]
OA .... Overall noise level (SAUS)
OA .... Overeaters Anonymous (EA)
OA .... Overfire Airport [*Combustion technology*]
OA .... Overflow Area (SAUS)
OA .... Overhead Approach (SAUS)
OA .... Overtime Authorization (AAG)
OA .... Oxalic Acid [*Organic chemistry*] (AAMN)
OA .... Oxamic Acid (SAUS)
OA .... Oxygen Absorbed (SAUS)
OA .... Services to the Aged under the Older Americans Act [*Public human service program*] (PHSD)
OA 2d ...... Ohio Appellate Reports, Second Series [*A publication*] (DLA)
OA-37 ...... Dragonfly [*Ground support aircraft*] [*Air Force*] (POLM)
OA-37B...... Dragonfly (SAUS)
OAA.......... Argentine Accreditation Body (SAUS)
OAA.......... Hereditary Order of Armigerous Augustans (EA)
OAA.......... Nora, AK [*Location identifier*] [*FAA*] (FAAL)
OAA.......... o-Aminoacetanilide [*Organic chemistry*]
OAA.......... Obstetric Anaesthetists Association [*British*] (DBA)
OAA.......... Office of Academic Affairs
OAA.......... Office of Administrative Appeals [*U.S. Department of Labor*] (BARN)
OaA.......... Office of Aging (SAUS)
OAA.......... Office of Air Accidents (SAUS)
OAA.......... Office of Assessment and Assurance (SAUS)
OAA.......... Office of Aviation Affairs [*Army*]
OAA.......... Oglethorpe Astronomical Association [*Savannah, Georgia*]
OAA.......... Ohio Apartment Association (EARSL)
OAA.......... Old-Age Assistance [*Superseded by SSI*] [*HEW*]
OAA.......... Older Americans Act [*1965*]
OAA.......... Older Americans Almanac [*A publication*]
OAA.......... Ontario Association of Architects [*1890*] [*Canada*] (NGC)
OAA.......... Open Agent Architecture (SAUS)
OAA.......... Open Arcade Architecture (SAUS)
OAA.......... Optical Acquisition Aid [*Deep Space Instrumentation Facility, NASA*]
OAA.......... Opticians Association of America (EA)
OAA.......... Orbiter Access Arm [*NASA*] (NASA)
OAA.......... Orbiter Alternate Airfield [*NASA*] (MCD)
OAA.......... Order of Australia Association
OAA.......... Organic Acidemia Association (EA)
OAA.......... Organisation des Nations Unies pour l'Alimentation et l'Agriculture [*Food and Agriculture Organization of the United Nations*]
OAA.......... Organization of Athletic Administrators [*Defunct*] (EA)
OAA.......... Orient Airlines Association (EA)
OAA.......... Other Acronymic Agencies
OAA.......... Outdoor Advertising Association (BARN)
OAA.......... Outdoor Advertising Association of Great Britain (BUAC)
OAA.......... Oxalacetic Acid (SAUS)
OAA.......... Oxaloacetate (SAUS)
OAA.......... Oxaloacetic [*or Oxalacetic*] Acid [*Organic chemistry*]
OAA.......... Oxley Aviation [*Australia*] [*ICAO designator*] (FAAC)
OAAA .... Oceania Amateur Athletic Association (EAIO)
OAAA .... Order of Americans of Armorial Ancestry (EA)
OAAA .... Outdoor Advertising Association of America [*Washington, DC*] (EA)
OAAA .... Outdoor Advertising Association of Australia, Inc. (BUAC)
OAAB .... Austrian Association of Workers and Employees [*Political party*] (PSAP)
OAAB .... Objective-Analytic Anxiety Battery [*Psychology*]
OAAC .... Ocean Affairs Advisory Committee [*Department of State*] (MSC)
OAAC .... Older Americans Advocacy Commission [*HEW*]
OAAC .... Outdoor Advertising Association of Canada (BUAC)
OAAD .... Amdar [*Afghanistan*] [*ICAO location identifier*] (ICLI)
OAAD .... Ovarian Ascorbic Acid Depletion [*Test*]
OAADM...... Ovarian Ascorbic Acid Depletion Material
OAAD Test... Ovarian Ascorbic Acid Depletion Test (SAUS)
OAAI .... Office of Air Accidents Investigation (SAUS)
OAAIS ...... Office of Administrative Analysis, Information, and Statistics [*Red Cross*]
OAAK .... Andkhoi [*Afghanistan*] [*ICAO location identifier*] (ICLI)
OAAM .... Oahu Amakihi [*North American bird banding code*] (BIBA)
OA & C...... Ohio Circuit Court Decisions [*A publication*] (DLA)
OA&M....... Operations Administration & Maintainance (SAUS)
OA & M..... Operations, Administration, and Maintenance [*Telecommunications*]
OA&M....... Operations Administration & Management (SAUS)
OA & MS ... Office of Administration and Management Services [*Employment and Training Administration*] [*Department of Labor*]
OA&R........ Office of Air and Radiation (EAGT)
OA & S...... Other Arms and Services [*Military*]
OAAPS ...... Organization for Afro-Asian Peoples Solidarity
OAARD ...... Office of the Assistant Administrator for Research and Development [*HEW*]
OAAS .... Asmar [*Afghanistan*] [*ICAO location identifier*] (ICLI)
OAA/S .... Observer's Assessment of Alertness / Sedation Scale [*Medicine*]
OAAS .... Office of the Administrative Assistant to the Secretary of the Army (SAUS)
OAAS .... Omnibus Army Aircraft Survivability Study (SAUS)
OAAS .... Ontario Association of Agricultural Societies [*Canada*] (BUAC)
OAAS .... Organization of the Armed Arab Struggle (CARL)
OAASA ...... Office of the Administrative Assistant to the Secretary of the Army
OAASN ...... Office of the Administrative Assistant to the Secretary of the Navy (SAUS)
OAAT .... Ortho-Aminoazotoluene [*A dye*] [*Organic chemistry*]
OAATM ...... Office of the Assistant for Automation (SAUS)
OAAU .... Organization of Afro-American Unity
OAAU .... Orthogonal Array Arithmetic Unit [*Computer science*]
OAAV .... Organization of African-American Veterans (EA)
OAB.......... ABO Blood Group [*Medicine*] (EDAA)
OAB.......... Attawapiskat Band Library, Ontario [*Library symbol*] [*National Library of Canada*] (BIB)
OAB.......... Moab, UT [*Location identifier*] [*FAA*] (FAAL)
OAB.......... Oakland [*California*] Army Base (VNW)
OAB.......... Ocean Affairs Board [*National Academy of Sciences*] (MSC)
OAB.......... Ohio Association of Broadcasters (EARSL)
OAB.......... Old-Age Benefits
OAB.......... Olive Advisory Board [*Defunct*] (EA)
OAB.......... One-to-All Broadcast (SAUS)
OAB.......... Ordnance Assembly Building (MUGU)
OAB.......... Organisation Africaine du Bois [*African Timber Organization*] (EAIO)
OAB.......... Outer Air Battle [*Navy*] (ANA)
OAB.......... Overseas Affairs Branch [*Army*]
OAB.......... Overseas Appointments Bureau [*Christian Education Movement*] [*British*] (AEBS)
OAB.......... Owners Abroad Aviation Ltd. [*British*] [*ICAO designator*] (FAAC)
OAB.......... Oxford Annotated Bible [*New York*] [*A publication*] (BJA)
OABA .... Burleigh-Anstruther and Chandos Union Public Library, Apsley, Ontario [*Library symbol*] [*National Library of Canada*] (BIB)
OABA .... Outdoor Amusement Business Association (EA)
OABD .... Behsood [*Afghanistan*] [*ICAO location identifier*] (ICLI)
OABETA ..... Office Appliance and Business Equipment Trades Association (HGAA)
OABG .... Baghlan [*Afghanistan*] [*ICAO location identifier*] (ICLI)
OABK .... Bandkamalkhan [*Afghanistan*] [*ICAO location identifier*] (ICLI)
OABM .... Outer Air Battle Missile (ACAE)
OABN .... Bamyan [*Afghanistan*] [*ICAO location identifier*] (ICLI)
OABP .... Organic Anion Binding Protein [*Biochemistry*]
OABR .... Bamar [*Afghanistan*] [*ICAO location identifier*] (ICLI)
OABS .... Sarday [*Afghanistan*] [*ICAO location identifier*] (ICLI)
OABT .... Bost [*Afghanistan*] [*ICAO location identifier*] (ICLI)
OABT .... Ortho-Aminobenzenethiol [*Organic chemistry*]
OAC.......... Acton Public Library, Ontario [*Library symbol*] [*National Library of Canada*] (NLC)
OAC.......... Cleveland Institute of Art, Cleveland, OH [*OCLC symbol*] (OCLC)
OAC.......... Oceanic Affairs Committee (BUAC)
OAC.......... Oceanic Area Control [*Aviation*] (FAAC)
OAC.......... Oceanographic Advisory Committee [*Navy Oceanographer*] (USDC)
OAC.......... Ocwen Asset Investment Corp. [*NYSE symbol*]
OAC.......... Office of Academic Computing [*Research center*] (RCD)
OAC.......... Office of Antiboycott Compliance
OAC.......... Officer Advanced Course [*Army*] (INF)
OAC.......... Officers Advanced Course (SAUS)
OAC.......... Official Acceptance of Construction (SAUS)
OAC.......... Officials Antarctic Committee (SAUS)
OAC.......... Ohio Administrative Code [*A publication*] (AAGC)
OAC.......... Ohio Arts Council (EARSL)
OAC.......... Ohio Athletic Conference (PSS)
Oac........... On Approval of Credit
OAC.......... On Approved Credit
OAC.......... One-Address Code (SAUS)
OAC.......... One-Address Computer (SAUS)
OAC.......... Ontario Academic Course (SAUS)
OAC.......... Ontario Agricultural College [*Canada*]
OAC.......... Ontario Appeal Cases [*Database*] [*Maritime Law Book Co. Ltd.*] [*Information service or system*] (CRD)
OAC.......... Ontario Arts Council
OAC.......... Open Air Campaigners, US (EA)
OAC.......... Operating Agency Code (AFM)
OAC.......... Operation Anti-Christ (EA)
OAC.......... Operation of Aircraft Costs (DNAB)
OAC.......... Operations Advisory Committee (SAUS)
OAC.......... Operations Analysis Center
OAC.......... Operations Analysis Chief [*Air Force*]
OAC.......... Operator Access Console (SAUS)
OAC.......... Optical Absorption Coefficient (AAEL)
OAC.......... Optical Acceleration Cancellation [*Vision*]
OAC.......... Optical Area Correlator
OAC.......... Optimal Automatic Control

OAC......... Optimally Adaptive Control (SAUS)
OAC......... Optimized Aftercooled [*Truck engineering*]
OAC......... Optimum Approach Course [*Navy*] (NVT)
OAC......... Oral AIDS Center [*University of California, San Francisco*] (RCD)
OAC......... Ordnance Ammunition Command [*Merged with Munitions Command*] [*Army*]
OAC......... Ordo ab Chao [*Order Out of Chaos*] [*Freemasonry*] [*Latin*]
OAC......... Oregon Administrative Code [*A publication*] (AAGC)
OAC......... Oregon Agriculture College (SAUS)
OAC......... Organo-Aluminium (ODA)
OAC......... Oriental Airlines Ltd. [*Nigeria*] [*ICAO designator*] (FAAC)
OAC......... Original Acquisition Cost (AAGC)
OAC......... Original Air Conditioning (IIA)
OAC......... Orleans Area Command (SAUS)
OAC......... Outdoor Advertising Council (BUAC)
OAC......... Outer Approach Channel
OAC......... Overseas Automotive Club (EA)
OACA........ Ontario Arms Collectors Association (SAUS)
OACB........ Charburjak [*Afghanistan*] [*ICAO location identifier*] (ICLI)
OACB........ Output Area Control Block (SAUS)
OACC........ Chakhcharan [*Afghanistan*] [*ICAO location identifier*] (ICLI)
OACC........ Oceanic Area Control Centre
OACC........ Older Americans Consumer Cooperative [*Washington, DC*] (EA)
OACC........ Organic Agriculture Centre of Canada [*Nova Scotia Agricultural College*] [*Canada*] (RCD)
OACD........ Office of Agricultural and Chemical Development [*of TVA*]
OACDT...... Order Acknowledge Date (SAUS)
OACDT...... Outback Areas Community Developmnent Trust [*Australia*]
OA Cell...... Opto-Acoustic Cell (SAUS)
OACES....... Ocean-Atmosphere Carbon Exchange Study [*Marine science*] (OSRA)
OACES....... Oregon Association for Counselor Education and Supervision (SEAT)
OACETT..... Ontario Association of Certified Engineering Technicians and Technologists (SAUS)
OACG........ Office of the Assistant Comptroller General (AAGC)
OACH........ Acton High School, Ontario [*Library symbol*] [*National Library of Canada*] (NLC)
OACI......... Ontario Academic Courses Institute (SAUS)
OACI......... Optical Automatic Car Identification
OACI......... Organisation de l'Aviation Civile Internationale [*International Civil Aviation Organization*] [*French*] [*United Nations*]
OACI......... Organizacion de Aviacion Civil Internacional [*International Civil Aviation Organization*] [*Spanish*] [*United Nations*] (DUND)
OACII........ Operational Approved Configuration Identification Index (SAA)
OACIS....... Ocean-Atmospheric Climatic Interaction Studies
OACIS....... Oregon Advanced Computing Institute [*Research center*] (RCD)
OACJC....... Oklahoma Association of Community and Junior Colleges (SAUS)
OACLD...... Ontario Association for Children with Learning Disabilities (SAUS)
OACM........ Offensive Air Combat Manoeuvre (SAUS)
OACO........ Operation and Checkout [*NASA*] (IAA)
OAC of S.... Office of the Assistant Chief of Staff [*Military*]
OACP........ Canada Publishing Corp., Agincourt, Ontario [*Library symbol*] [*National Library of Canada*] (BIB)
OACP........ Operational Analysis Code Package (PDAA)
OACR........ Oahu Creeper [*North American bird banding code*] (BIBA)
OACR........ Office of the Admiral Commanding Reserves [*Navy*] [*British*]
OACS........ Office of the Assistant Chief of Staff [*Military*] (AAG)
OACSA...... Office of the Assistant Chief of Staff for Automation and Communications [*Military*] (MCD)
OACSAC..... Office of the Assistant Chief of Staff for Automation and Communications [*Military*]
OACSC-E.... Office of the Assistant Chief of Staff for Communications-Electronics (AABC)
OACSEA..... Older American Community Service Employment Act [*1975*]
OACSFOR... Office of the Assistant Chief of Staff for Force Development [*Army*]
OACSI....... Office of the Assistant Chief of Staff for Intelligence [*Army*]
OACSIM..... Office of the Assistant Chief of Staff for Information Management [*Military*]
OACSIM..... Office of the Assistant Chief of Staff for Installation Management
OACSU...... Off-Air Call Set-Up (SAUS)
OACT........ Office of Advanced Concepts and Technology (SAUS)
OACT........ Office of the Actuary [*Department of Health and Human Services*] (GFGA)
OACT........ Officer, Airman, Civilian, and Total (MCD)
OACT........ Ohio Association of Classroom Teachers (SAUS)
OACT........ Organisation Africaine de Cartographie et de Teledetection [*Algeria*] (EAIO)
OACT........ Ormone Adrenocorticotropina [*Italian*] [*Medicine*]
OACTA....... Ohio Association of Civil Trial Attorneys (EARSL)
OACUL...... Ontario Association of College and University Libraries (SAUS)
OAD.......... Adria Laboratories, Inc., Columbus, OH [*OCLC symbol*] (OCLC)
OAD.......... Obsessive Acronym Disorder
OAD.......... Obstructive Airway Disease [*Medicine*]
OAD.......... Obstructive Arterial Disease [*Medicine*] (MELL)
OAD.......... Occlusive Arterial Disease (SAUS)
OAD.......... Office of Administration
OAD.......... Officers' Accounts Division [*Navy*]
OAD.......... Officers' Assignment Division, The Adjutant General's Office [*Army*]
OAD.......... Open Architecture Driver (SAUS)
OAD.......... Opening of Anterior Digestive [*Gland*]
OAD.......... Operational Active Data [*Navy*]
OAD.......... Operational Analysis Division [*Air Force*]
OAD.......... Operational Availability Data [*Military*]
OAD.......... Operational Availability Data (or Date) (SAUS)
OAD.......... Operational Availability Date [*Nuclear Regulatory Commission*] (GFGA)
OAD.......... Operations Analysis Division (SAUS)
OAD.......... Operator Aiding Demonstrator (SAUS)
OAD.......... Optical Activity Detection
OAD.......... Optoacoustic Device (SAUS)
OAD.......... Orbiter Atmospheric Drag [*NASA*]
OAD.......... Ordered, Adjudged, and Decreed (WDAA)
OAD.......... Ordered to Active Duty (AABC)
OAD.......... Ordering and Distributing (IAA)
OAD.......... Oregon Association of the Deaf (SAUS)
OAD.......... Organic Anionic Dye [*Medicine*] (DMAA)
OAD.......... Organization Address (SAUS)
OAD.......... Organizations and Agencies Directories Series [*A publication*]
OAD.......... Original Air Date [*of program's first telecast*]
OAD.......... Overall Absolute Deviation [*Mathematics*]
OAD.......... Overall Density (SAUS)
OAD.......... Overall Depth (WDAA)
OAD.......... Overall Dimensions (IAA)
OAD.......... Overlay Area Description (TIMI)
OAD.......... Oxford American Dictionary [*A publication*]
OAD.......... Special Audit Division (AAGC)
OADAB...... Office of the Assistant Director of the Army Budget
OADAP...... Office of Alcoholism and Drug Abuse Prevention [*Department of Health and Human Services*]
OADARS.... Optical Aids to Detection and Ranging Systems (SAUS)
OADC........ Oleate-Albumin-Dextrose-Catalase [*Medium*] (DMAA)
OADC........ Oleic Acid, Albumin, Dextrose, Catalase
OADC........ Oregon Aging and Alzheimer's Disease Center [*Oregon Health and Science University*] (RCD)
OADCE...... Open Architecture Distribution Computing Environment (TIMI)
OADD........ Dawlatabad [*Afghanistan*] [*ICAO location identifier*] (ICLI)
OA/DDP..... Office Automation / Distributed Data Processing (MHDI)
OADEMQA... Office of Acid Deposition, Environmental Monitoring, and Quality Assurance [*Environmental Protection Agency*] (GFGA)
OADF........ Darra-I-Soof [*Afghanistan*] [*ICAO location identifier*] (ICLI)
OA-DG....... Occupational Area Defense Grouping (DNAB)
OADG........ Open Architecture Development Group [*IBM Corp.*] (CDE)
OAD Gland... Opening of Anterior Digestive Gland (SAUS)
OADH........ One-Arm Dove Hunt Association (EA)
OADH........ Organization of Advanced Disabled Hobbyists (EA)
OADM........ Optical Add Drop Multiplexer (DINT)
OADMS....... Office of Automated Data Management Services [*General Services Administration*]
OADMT...... Oliphant Auditory Discrimination Memory Test [*Medicine*] (STED)
OAdN........ Ohio Northern University, Ada, OH [*Library symbol*] [*Library of Congress*] (LCLS)
OADP........ Organisation de l'Action Democratique et Populaire [*Morocco*]
OADPM....... Office of ADP Management (SAUS)
OADPS...... Office of Automatic Data Processing Services (AAGC)
OADR........ Office of Agricultural Defense Relations [*New Deal*]
OADR........ Originating Agency Determination Required (MCD)
OADS........ Omnidirectional Air Data System
OADSS...... Office Assignment Decision Support System (SAUS)
OADV........ Devar [*Afghanistan*] [*ICAO location identifier*] (ICLI)
OADW........ Wazakhwa [*Afghanistan*] [*ICAO location identifier*] (ICLI)
OADZ........ Darwaz [*Afghanistan*] [*ICAO location identifier*] (ICLI)
OAE.......... NOAA [*National Oceanic and Atmospheric Administration*]-LISD Seattle Center, Seattle, WA [*OCLC symbol*] (OCLC)
OAE.......... Occupational and Adult Education [*Office of Education*] (OICC)
OAE.......... Oceanic Anoxic Event
OAE.......... Office of Analysis and Evaluation [*Environmental Protection Agency*] (EPA)
OAE.......... Office of Applied Economics [*National Institute of Standards and Technology*] (RCD)
OAE.......... Officer of Arms Extraordinary [*College of Arms/Heralds' College*] [*British*]
OAE.......... Old Antarctic Explorer
OAE.......... Operational Analysis and Exercises (SAUS)
OAE.......... Operational Area Evaluation [*Environmental science*] (COE)
OAE.......... Optical Alignment Equipment
OAE.......... Optima Energy Corp. [*Vancouver Stock Exchange symbol*]
OAE.......... Orbiting Astronomical Explorer [*NASA*] (IIA)
OAE.......... Orchestra of the Age of Enlightenment [*British*]
OAE.......... Organization of Architectural Employees
OAE.......... Orzeck Aphasia Evaluation [*Psychology*]
OAE.......... Oscillating-Analyzer Ellipsometer (PDAA)
OAE.......... Otoacoustic Emission [*Audiology*]
OAEAO...... Ontario Association of Education Administration Officials (SAUS)
OAEC........ Essa Centennial Library, Angus, Ontario [*Library symbol*] [*National Library of Canada*] (BIB)
OAEC........ Organization for Asian Economic Cooperation (SAUS)
OAECC....... Operational Area Emergency Communications Committee [*Emergency Management*] (EMA)
OAEFI........ Astorville Branch, East Ferris Township Public Library, Ontario (SAUS)
OAEFT....... Astorville Branch, East Ferris Township Public Library, Ontario [*Library symbol*] [*National Library of Canada*] (NLC)
OAEK........ Keshm [*Afghanistan*] [*ICAO location identifier*] (ICLI)
OAEM........ Eshkashem [*Afghanistan*] [*ICAO location identifier*] (ICLI)
OAEM........ Ontario Approved Educational Microcomputers (SAUS)
OAEQ........ Islam Qala [*Afghanistan*] [*ICAO location identifier*] (ICLI)
OAES........ Ohio Agricultural Experimental Station (SAUS)
OAESA....... Ohio Association of Elementary School Administrators (SAUS)

OAET .... Elma Township Public Library, Atwood, Ontario [*Library symbol*] [*National Library of Canada*] (NLC)
OAET .... Office of Aeronautics, Exploration, and Technology (SAUS)
OAEYC .... Oregon Association for the Education of Young Children (EARSL)
OAF .... Austrian Air Ambulance [*ICAO designator*] (FAAC)
OAF .... Occidentale Afrique Francaise [*French West Africa*]
OAF .... Off-Axis Factor (RAWO)
OAF .... Office of Alcohol Fuels [*Department of Energy*]
OAF .... Officer Assignment Folder [*Military*] (AFM)
OAF .... Ontario Ministry of Agriculture and Food [*UTLAS symbol*]
OAF .... Open Air Factor
OAF .... Optimum Array Filter (SAUS)
OAF .... Options for Animals Foundation (EA)
OAF .... Orbital Antenna Farm (PDAA)
OAF .... Origin Address Field [*Computer science*] (IBMDP)
OAF .... Origination Address Field (SAUS)
OAF .... Orthodox and Anglican Fellowship (EA)
OAF .... Osteoclast Activating Factor [*Endocrinology*]
OAF .... Overhaul Attrition Factor (SAUS)
OAF .... Oxygen Alternate Fill
OA/FA .... Oil-immersed Air-cooled/Forced-Air-cooled (SAUS)
OAFB .... Offutt Air Force Base [*Nebraska*] (AAG)
OAFC .... Arden Branch, Frontenac County Library, Ontario [*Library symbol*] [*National Library of Canada*] (BIB)
OAFC .... Occupational Analysis Field Center
OAFC .... Office of Air Force Chaplains
OAFC .... Official Aerrage Fan Club [*Defunct*] (EA)
OAFCCD ..... Ontario Association for Families of Children with Communication Disorders (SAUS)
OAFD .... Orbiter Air Flight Deck [*NASA*] (MCD)
OAFG .... Khost-O-Fering [*Afghanistan*] [*ICAO location identifier*] (ICLI)
OA/FI .... Operational Assurance/Fault Isolation (MCD)
OAFIE .... Office of Armed Forces Information and Education
OAFL .... O and A Tex-Pack Express [*Common carrier symbol*]
OAFM .... On or After Full Moon [*Freemasonry*] (ROG)
OAFR .... Farah [*Afghanistan*] [*ICAO location identifier*] (ICLI)
OAFSC .... Other Air Force Speciality Code (SAUS)
OAFT .... Official Air Freight Tariffs
OAFTO .... Orbiter Atmospheric Flight Test Office [*NASA*] (NASA)
OAFU .... Observers Advanced Flying Unit (SAUS)
OAFZ .... Faizabad [*Afghanistan*] [*ICAO location identifier*] (ICLI)
OAG .... Oblique Anterior Gauche [*Left Anterior Oblique Position*] [*Medicine*]
OAG .... Office of the Adjutant General [*Military*] (MCD)
OAG .... Office of the Attorney-General
OAG .... Official Airline Guide, Inc. [*ICAO designator*] (FAAC)
OAG .... Official Airline Guides, Inc. [*Information service or system*] (IID)
OAG .... Oleoyl(acetyl)glycerol [*Organic chemistry*]
OAG .... Online Air Guide (SAUS)
OAG .... Online Airlines Guide [*A publication*]
OAG .... Open Angle Glaucoma [*Ophthalmology*]
OAG .... Open Application Group (SAUS)
OAG .... Open Applications Group [*An association*] (NTPA)
OAG .... Operand Address Generator (SAUS)
OAG .... Operations Advisory Group (CARL)
OAG .... Opinions of the Attorney General
OAG .... Optical Alignment Group
OAG .... Orange [*Australia*] [*Airport symbol*] (OAG)
OAG .... Ostriches Ambling Gracefully
OAGA .... Ghaziabad [*Afghanistan*] [*ICAO location identifier*] (ICLI)
OAGB .... Osteopathic Association of Great Britain
OAGCM .... Ocean-Atmosphere General Circulation Model [*Oceanography*]
OAGD .... Gader [*Afghanistan*] [*ICAO location identifier*] (ICLI)
OAG-EE ...... Official Airline Guide-Electronic Edition [*Official Airline Guides, Inc.*] [*Database*]
OAGG .... Gage Educational Publishing Ltd., Agincourt, Ontario [*Library symbol*] [*National Library of Canada*] (NLC)
OAGL .... Gulistan [*Afghanistan*] [*ICAO location identifier*] (ICLI)
OAGM .... Ghelmeen [*Afghanistan*] [*ICAO location identifier*] (ICLI)
OAG Massachusetts ... Massachusetts Attorney General Reports [*A publication*] (DLA)
OAGN .... Ghazni [*Afghanistan*] [*ICAO location identifier*] (ICLI)
OAGS .... Gasar [*Afghanistan*] [*ICAO location identifier*] (ICLI)
OAG West Virginia ... West Virginia Attorney General Reports [*A publication*] (DLA)
OAGZ .... Gardez [*Afghanistan*] [*ICAO location identifier*] (ICLI)
OAH .... Ancaster High and Vocational School, Ontario [*Library symbol*] [*National Library of Canada*] (NLC)
OAH .... Office of Aboriginal Health [*Australia*]
OAH .... Office of Administrative Hearings (SAUS)
OAH .... Organization of American Historians (EA)
OAH .... Outstanding American Handgunner (GOBB)
OAH .... Ovarian Androgenic Hyperfunction [*Medicine*] (DMAA)
oah .... Overall Height (ODA)
OAH .... Overall Height [*Automotive specifications*]
OAH .... Overhead Air Hoist
OAHE .... Hazrat Eman [*Afghanistan*] [*ICAO location identifier*] (ICLI)
OAHE .... Ohio Association for Higher Education (SAUS)
OAHJ .... Hajigak [*Afghanistan*] [*ICAO location identifier*] (ICLI)
OAHN .... Khwahan [*Afghanistan*] [*ICAO location identifier*] (ICLI)
OAHPERD ... Ohio Association for Health, Physical Education, Recreation and Dance (EARSL)
OAHR .... Herat [*Afghanistan*] [*ICAO location identifier*] (ICLI)
OAHS .... O-Acetylhomoserine (thiol)-lyase [*An enzyme*]
OAHSM ...... Ohio Association of Historical Societies and Museums (EARSL)
OAI .... Office Appliance Institute (SAUS)
OAI .... Office of Aeronautical Intelligence (SAUS)
OAI .... Office of Analysis and Inspections [*Department of Health and Human Services*] (GFGA)
OAI .... Office of Audit and Inspection [*Energy Research and Development Administration*]
OAI .... Office of Audit and Investigation [*United States Geological Survey*]
OAI .... Ohio Aerospace Institute
OAI .... One-Address Instruction (SAUS)
OAI .... Open Application Interface
OAI .... Opera America, Inc. (SAUS)
OAI .... Optical Associates Inc. (NITA)
OAI .... OR Accumulators to Indicators (SAUS)
OAI .... Or-and-Invert (SAUS)
OAI .... Organization of African Immigrants (SAUS)
OAI .... Osborne Association, Inc. (SAUS)
OAI .... Outside Air Intake (NRCH)
OAIAC .... Operational Area Industry Advisory Committee [*Civil Defense*]
OAIB .... Old-Age Insurance Benefit (MHDB)
OAICU .... Oklahoma Association of Independent Colleges and Universities (SAUS)
OAID .... Older Americans Information Directory [*A publication*]
OAIDE .... Operational Assistance and Instructive Data Equipment
OAII .... Oasis Resorts Intl, Inc. [*NASDAQ symbol*] (QUAN)
OAII .... Ocean-Atmosphere-Ice Interactions Program (SAUS)
OAIM .... Office of Aviation Information Management [*Department of Transportation*] [*Information service or system*] (IID)
OAINN .... Ohio Aerospace Institute Neural Networks (HGEN)
OAIP .... Ontario Assessment Instrument Pool [*Educational test*] [*Canada*]
OAIP .... Organic Ablative Insulative Plastic
OAI-PMH .... Open Archives Initiative Protocol for Metadata Harvesting [*Computer science*]
OAIS .... Online Administrative Information System (SAUS)
OAIS .... Opinion, Attitude, and Interest Survey [*Psychology*]
OAISN .... OJCS Automated Information System Network (SAUS)
OAIT .... Office of American Indian Trust
OAIW .... International Waxes Ltd., Agincourt, Ontario [*Library symbol*] [*National Library of Canada*] (NLC)
OAJ .... Ajax Public Library, Ontario [*Library symbol*] [*National Library of Canada*] (NLC)
OAJ .... Jacksonville [*North Carolina*] [*Airport symbol*] (OAG)
OAJ .... Jacksonville, NC [*Location identifier*] [*FAA*] (FAAL)
OAJ .... Open Apophyseal Joint (DB)
OAJ .... Opening Altitude Judgement [*Parachuting*] (DICI)
OAJL .... Jalalabad [*Afghanistan*] [*ICAO location identifier*] (ICLI)
OAJS .... Jabul Saraj [*Afghanistan*] [*ICAO location identifier*] (ICLI)
OAJW .... Jawand [*Afghanistan*] [*ICAO location identifier*] (ICLI)
OAk .... Akron Public Library, Akron, OH [*Library symbol*] [*Library of Congress*] (LCLS)
OAK .... Oakfield [*New York*] [*Seismograph station code, US Geological Survey*] [*Closed*] (SEIS)
OAK .... Oak Industries, Inc. [*NYSE symbol*] (SPSG)
OAK .... Oakland [*California*] [*Airport symbol*]
OAK .... Oakland Operations Office (DOGT)
Oak .... Oakland Raiders [*National Football League*] [*1960-81*] (NFLA)
OAK .... Oakwood College, Huntsville, AL [*OCLC symbol*] (OCLC)
OAK .... Oakwood Petroleums Ltd. [*Toronto Stock Exchange symbol*]
OAK .... Object Application Kernel (SAUS)
OAK .... Oklahoma-Arkansas-Kansas League [*Old baseball league*]
OAK .... Older Americans Corps [*Proposed*]
OAK .... Optical Alignment Kit (MCD)
OAK .... Organization for the Advancement of Knowledge (EA)
OAK .... Overhaul Alignment Kit (MCD)
OAK .... San Francisco [*California*] Oakland [*Airport symbol*] (OAG)
OAKA .... Koban [*Afghanistan*] [*ICAO location identifier*] (ICLI)
OAKB .... Kabul Ad [*Afghanistan*] [*ICAO location identifier*] (ICLI)
OAKC .... Oak Coach Company [*NCIC trailer make code*]
OAKC .... Oakhurst Capital, Inc. [*NASDAQ symbol*] (SAG)
OAKC .... Oakhurst Co. [*NASDAQ symbol*] (TTSB)
OAKC .... Oakhurst Co., Inc. [*NASDAQ symbol*] (SAG)
OAkCh .... Akron Child Guidance Center, Akron, OH [*Library symbol*] [*Library of Congress*] (LCLS)
OAKCY ...... Oakland City, IN [*American Association of Railroads railroad junction routing code*]
OAKD .... Kamdesh [*Afghanistan*] [*ICAO location identifier*] (ICLI)
OAKDA ...... Oakdale, CA [*American Association of Railroads railroad junction routing code*]
OAKDL ...... Oakesdale, WA [*American Association of Railroads railroad junction routing code*]
OAKE .... Organization of American Kodaly Educators (EA)
OAKES .... Oakes, ND [*American Association of Railroads railroad junction routing code*]
OAkF .... Firestone Tire & Rubber Co., Akron, OH [*Library symbol*] [*Library of Congress*] (LCLS)
OAKF .... Oak Hill Financial, Inc. [*NASDAQ symbol*] (SAG)
OAKG .... Khojaghar [*Afghanistan*] [*ICAO location identifier*] (ICLI)
OAkGr .... B. F. Goodrich Co., Akron, OH [*Library symbol*] [*Library of Congress*] (LCLS)
OAkGy .... Goodyear Tire & Rubber Co., Akron, OH [*Library symbol*] [*Library of Congress*] (LCLS)
OAKH .... Oak Harbor Freight Lines [*Common carrier symbol*]
OakHill ...... Oak Hill Financial, Inc. [*Associated Press*] (SAG)
OakHill ...... Oak Hill Sportswear Corp. [*Associated Press*] (SAG)
OakHillF .... Oak Hill Financial, Inc. [*Associated Press*] (SAG)
Oakhurst .... Oakhurst Capital, Inc. [*Associated Press*] (SAG)
Oakhurst .... Oakhurst Co., Inc. [*Associated Press*] (SAG)

OakInds ..... Oak Industries, Inc. [*Associated Press*] (SAG)
OAKIX .... Oakmark International Fund [*Mutual fund ticker symbol*] (SG)
OAKJ .... Kajaki [*Afghanistan*] [*ICAO location identifier*] (ICLI)
OAKJC .... Oakwood Junction, MI [*American Association of Railroads railroad junction routing code*]
OAkk .... Old Akkadian (BJA)
OAKL .... Konjak-I-Logar [*Afghanistan*] [*ICAO location identifier*] (ICLI)
OAKL .... Oakland [*NCIC car make code*]
OAKL .... Oaks Lumber and Hardware [*Common carrier symbol*]
OAKLA .... Oakland, CA [*American Association of Railroads railroad junction routing code*]
Oakland U ... Oakland University (GAGS)
OAKLD ...... Oakland, IL [*American Association of Railroads railroad junction routing code*]
Oakly .... Oakly, Inc. [*Associated Press*] (SAG)
OAKM .... Kamar [*Afghanistan*] [*ICAO location identifier*] (ICLI)
OAKMX ...... Oakmark Fund [*Mutual fund ticker symbol*] (SG)
OAKN .... Kandahar [*Afghanistan*] [*ICAO location identifier*] (ICLI)
OAKR .... Kaldar [*Afghanistan*] [*ICAO location identifier*] (ICLI)
OAKR .... Oakridge Energy, Inc. (SAUS)
Oak Ridge Natl Lab Met Ceram Tech Rep ... Oak Ridge National Laboratory Metals and Ceramics Technical Report (SAUS)
OAKS .... Khost [*Afghanistan*] [*ICAO location identifier*] (ICLI)
OAKS .... River Oaks Furniture [*NASDAQ symbol*] (TTSB)
OAKS .... River Oaks Furniture, Inc. [*NASDAQ symbol*] (SAG)
Oak Sym .... Oakland Symphony (SAUS)
OAKT .... Kalat [*Afghanistan*] [*ICAO location identifier*] (ICLI)
OAKT .... Oak Technology [*NASDAQ symbol*] (TTSB)
OAKT .... Oak Technology, Inc. [*NASDAQ symbol*] (SAG)
OakTch ...... Oak Technology, Inc. [*Associated Press*] (SAG)
OAKU .... Oakshott [*Intermodal shipping container symbol*] (TVRC)
OAkU .... University of Akron, Akron, OH [*Library symbol*] [*Library of Congress*] (LCLS)
OAkU-L ...... University of Akron, School of Law, Akron, Ohio [*Library symbol*] [*Library of Congress*] (LCLS)
Oakwood .... Oakwood Homes Corp. [*Associated Press*] (SAG)
OAKX .... Kabul [*Afghanistan*] [*ICAO location identifier*] (ICLI)
OAKZ .... Karez-I-Mir [*Afghanistan*] [*ICAO location identifier*] (ICLI)
OAL .... Alliston Memorial Public Library, Ontario [*Library symbol*] [*National Library of Canada*] (BIB)
OAL .... Audit Liaison Division (AAGC)
OAL .... Coaldale, NV [*Location identifier*] [*FAA*] (FAAL)
OAL .... National Oceanic and Atmospheric Administration, Miami Branch, Miami, FL [*OCLC symbol*] (OCLC)
OAL .... Ocean Acoustics Laboratory [*Woods Hole Oceanographic Institution*] (RCD)
OAL .... Office of Administrative Law (SAUS)
OAL .... Office of Arts and Libraries [*British*]
OAL .... Olympic Airways SA [*Greece*] [*ICAO designator*] (FAAC)
OAL .... Operational Applications Laboratory [*Air Force*]
OAL .... Operations and Logistics (IAA)
OAL .... Order Action List [*Military*] (DNAB)
OAL .... Order of Ancient Lights
OAL .... Ordnance Aerophysics Laboratory
OAL .... Ostallgaeu [*German license plate city code*]
OAL .... Overall Length [*Automotive specifications*]
OAL .... Overall Level (NASA)
OALAC .... Amherstview Branch, Lennox and Addington County Public Library, Ontario [*Library symbol*] [*National Library of Canada*] (NLC)
OALAC .... Older Americans' Legal Action Center (DICI)
OAIB .... Babcock & Wilcox Co., Alliance, OH [*Library symbol*] [*Library of Congress*] (LCLS)
OALC .... Ogden Air Logistics Center (MCD)
OALDCE ...... Oxford Advanced Learner's Dictionary of Current English
OALF .... Organic Acid Labile Fluoride [*Chemistry*] (AAMN)
OALF .... Oromo Abo Liberation Front [*Ethiopia*] [*Political party*] (EY)
OALG .... Logar [*Afghanistan*] [*ICAO location identifier*] (ICLI)
OALJ .... Office of Administrative Law Judges [*Department of Agriculture*] (GFGA)
OALL .... Allenford Branch, Bruce County Public Library, Ontario [*Library symbol*] [*National Library of Canada*] (NLC)
OALL .... Lal [*Afghanistan*] [*ICAO location identifier*] (ICLI)
OALL .... Ossification of Anterior Longitudinal Ligament [*Medicine*] (STED)
OAIM .... Mount Union College, Alliance, OH [*Library symbol*] [*Library of Congress*] (LCLS)
OALM .... Of a Like Mind [*An association*] (EA)
OALM .... Optical Address Light Modulator [*Instrumentation*]
OALMA ...... Orthopedic Appliance and Limb Manufacturers Association [*Later, AOPA*]
OALN .... Laghman [*Afghanistan*] [*ICAO location identifier*] (ICLI)
OALOS ...... Office for Ocean Affairs and the Law of the Sea [*United Nations*] (GNE)
OALS .... Observer Air Lock System (OA)
OALS .... Office of Arid Lands Studies [*University of Arizona*] [*Research center*] (RCD)
OALS .... Orbiter Automatic Landing System (MCD)
OALT .... Ontario Association of Library Technicians (SAUS)
OALT .... Operational Acceptable Level of Traffic [*FAA*] (TAG)
O ALT HOR ... Omnibus Alternis Horis [*Every Other Hour*] [*Pharmacy*] (ROG)
OAM .... Medal of the Order of Australia (ODA)
OAM .... Oamaru [*New Zealand*] [*Airport symbol*] (OAG)
OAM .... Object Access Method (SAUS)
OAM .... Oblique Abdominal Muscle [*Medicine*] (MELL)
OAM .... Office Administration Manual (SAUS)
OAM .... Office of Administration and Management [*Employment and Training Administration*] [*Department of Labor*]
OAM .... Office of Aerospace Medicine [*NASA*] (MCD)
OAM .... Office of Alternative Medicine [*National Institutes of Health*]
OAM .... Office of Automation and Manpower [*Department of Labor*] [*See also OMAT*]
OAM .... Office of Aviation Medicine [*FAA*]
OAM .... Once-A-Month [*Communications term*] (DCT)
OAM .... One Australian Movement [*Political party*]
OAM .... Ontario Agricultural Museum (SAUS)
OAM .... Onze Alma Mater (BJA)
OAM .... Open-Air Mission
OAM .... Operand Addressing Mode (SAUS)
OAM .... Operation, Administration, Maintenance (SAUS)
OAM .... Operational, Administrative and Maintenance (SAUS)
OAM .... Operation and Maintenance (SAUS)
OAM .... Operations, Administration, and Maintenance (CIST)
OAM .... Operations and Management (MCD)
OAM .... Operator Assistance Menu (SAUS)
OAM .... Optimum Artillery Mix (SAA)
OAM .... Orbit Adjust Module [*Space launch term*] (ISAK)
OAM .... Orbital Assembly Module (MCD)
OAM .... Order of Ancient Maccabees (BJA)
OAM .... Order of Australia Medal (SAUS)
OAM .... Organization and Methods [*Military*] (AFIT)
OAM .... Orthopedic Appliance Mechanic [*Navy*]
OAM .... Oscillator Activity Monitor [*Telecommunications*] (TEL)
OAM .... Outer Acrosomal Membrane [*Medicine*] (DMAA)
OAMA .... Office Automation Management Association (EA)
OAMA .... Ogden Air Material Area [*AFLC*]
OAMA .... Oil Appliance Manufacturers' Association [*British*] (BI)
OAMAC ...... Oceanic and Atmospheric Management Advisory Committee [*National Oceanic and Atmospheric Administration*] (EGAO)
OAM&P ..... Operations, Administration, Maintenance and Provisioning (SAUS)
OAMB PAC ... Ohio Association of Mortgage Brokers PAC [*North Canton, OH*] (PACS)
OAMCE ...... Optical Alignment, Monitoring, and Calibration Equipment
OAMDG ..... Omnia ad Majorem Dei Gloriam [*All to the Greater Glory of God*] [*Latin*]
OAMES ...... Ohio Association of Medical Equipment Services (EARSL)
OAMEX ...... Ocean-Atmosphere Exchange Processes [*Marine science*] (MSC)
OAMEX ...... Ocean-Atmosphere Materials Exchange (SAUS)
OAMF .... Fort Malden National Historic Park, Amherstburg, Ontario [*Library symbol*] [*National Library of Canada*] (NLC)
OAMF .... Ohio Association of Metal Finishers (EARSL)
OAMHS ...... Ameliasburgh Historical Society, Ontario [*Library symbol*] [*National Library of Canada*] (BIB)
OAMK .... Mukur [*Afghanistan*] [*ICAO location identifier*] (ICLI)
OAML .... Oceanographic and Atmospheric Master Library (SAUS)
OAML .... Ontario Association of Medical Laboratories (SAUS)
OAMN .... Maimama [*Afghanistan*] [*ICAO location identifier*] (ICLI)
OAMN .... Operations and Maintenance, Navy (AFIT)
OAMP .... Optical Airborne Measurement Platform (SAUS)
OAMP .... Optical Analog Matrix Processing
OAMRT ...... Ontario Association of Medical Radiation Technologists (SAUS)
OAMS .... Mazar-I-Sharif [*Afghanistan*] [*ICAO location identifier*] (ICLI)
OAMS .... Office of Administrative and Management Systems [*Social Security Administration*]
OAMS .... Optical Angular Motion Sensor
OAMS .... Orbital Altitude and Maneuvering System (IAA)
OAMS .... Orbital Attitude and Maneuvering System [*NASA*]
OAMS .... Orbit Attitude and Maneuvering System (SAUS)
OAMS .... Organic and Atmospheric Mass Spectrometer (KSC)
OAMT .... Munta [*Afghanistan*] [*ICAO location identifier*] (ICLI)
OAN .... Curriculum Resources Centre, Niagara South Board of Education, Allanburg, Ontario [*Library symbol*] [*National Library of Canada*] (BIB)
OAN .... NMFS [*National Marine Fisheries Service*] Southeast Fisheries Center, Beaufort Laboratory, Beaufort, NC [*OCLC symbol*] (OCLC)
OAN .... Ocean Aids to Navigation [*Coast Guard*]
OAN .... Omega Arts Network (EA)
OAN .... Optical Access Networking [*Computer science*] (VLIE)
OANA .... Organisation of Asian News Agencies (BUAC)
OANA .... Organization of Asia-Pacific News Agencies [*Malaysia*] (EY)
OANC .... Orbiter Ancillary (SAUS)
OAND .... Origin and Destination (NITA)
O & A .... Observation and Assessment [*Medicine*]
O & A .... October and April [*Denotes semiannual payments of interest or dividends in these months*] [*Business term*]
O&A .... Odontectomy and Alveolectomy (SAUS)
O&A .... Odontectomy and Alveoplasty [*Medicine*] (EDAA)
O&A .... Orbit and Attitude (ACAE)
O & A (Date) ... Oath and Acceptance Date [*Date from which a military officer's commissioned service runs*]
O & B .... Opium and Belladonna [*Pharmacy*] (MAE)
o & c .... Onset and Course [*Medicine*] (AD)
O&C .... Onset and Course (SAUS)
O & C .... Onset and Course [*of a disease*] [*Medicine*]
O & C .... Operation and Checkout [*NASA*]
O&C .... Operations and Checkout (SAUS)
O&C .... Operations and Control (NAKS)
O & C .... Oxford and Cambridge Schools Examination Board [*British*] (DCTA)
O & CC ...... Order and Change Control (AAG)
o & cc .... Order and Change Control (AD)

O & CM..... Organist and Choir Master (ROG)
O&CO........ Operational and Checkout (SAUS)
O & C/O..... Operation and Checkout [*O & C is preferred*] [*NASA*] (KSC)
O&D........ Ordering and Distribution (SAUS)
O&D........ Organization & Deployment (SAUS)
o & d........ Origin and Destination (AD)
O & D....... Origin and Destination [*Aviation*]
O&E.......... Errors and Omissions (LDOE)
O & E....... Observation and Evaluation [*Medicine*] (DAVI)
O & E....... Observation and Examination [*Medicine*]
O&E.......... Officers and Employees (SAUS)
O and E..... Officers and Employers (SAUS)
o & e........ Operations and Engineering (AD)
O&E.......... Operations and Engineering (SAUS)
O & E....... Operations and Engineering
O&EP........ Occupational and Environmental Protection (SAUS)
O & F....... Organizations and Functions (MCD)
O & FN...... Ordnance and Facilities - Navy
O&FN........ Ordnance and Facilities-Navy (SAUS)
O & FS...... Operations and Flight Support [*NASA*] (NASA)
O&G......... Obstetrics and Gynecology (DMAA)
O&G......... Oil and Gas (EEVL)
O&G......... Oil and Grease (EEVL)
O& G Jour... Oil and Gas Journal. Forecast/Review (SAUS)
O & G/PF... Oil and Gas/Pipeline Facilities
O&H......... Oxygen and Hydrogen (SAUS)
O & I....... Operations and Intelligence [*Section*] [*Army*] (INF)
o & i........ Organizational and Intermediate (AD)
O & I........ Outline and Installation (MCD)
O&IA........ Operations and Integration Agreement (SAUS)
O & IR...... Operation and Inspection Record (KSC)
O & K....... Orenstein & Koppel (AD)
O&L.......... Osteoporosis and Leukemia [*Medicine*] (MELL)
O & LS...... Ocean and Lake Surveys [*Budget appropriation title*] [*Navy*]
O & M....... Ogilvy & Mather [*Advertising agency*]
O & M....... Ohio & Morenci Railroad (IIA)
O&M......... Operating and Maintenance [*USCG*] (TAG)
O & M....... Operation and Maintenance (DOMA)
O&M......... Operation and Maintenance
O&M......... Operations and Maintenance (CIST)
O & M....... Operations and Management
O & M....... Organization and Management
O & M....... Organization and Methods (AABC)
O & M....... Orientation and Mobility [*for the blind*]
O&M......... Outline and Mounting (ACAE)
O&M......... Region 4 O&M Municipal Inventory (SAUS)
O & MA..... Operation and Maintenance Activities (AAG)
O&MA....... Operation and Maintenance, Army (AAGC)
O and MA... Operations and Maintenance-Army (SAUS)
O & M-DA.. Operation and Maintenance, Defense Agencies [*DoD*]
O&M-DA.... Operation and Maintenanee, Defense Agencies (SAUS)
O & MF..... Operation and Maintenance Facilities (MUGU)
O & MFH... Operation and Maintenance, Family Housing [*Army*] (AABC)
O & MMC... Operations and Maintenance, Marine Corps
O & MN..... Operation and Maintenance, Navy
O&MN....... Operations and Maintenance, Navy (SAUS)
O & MN..... Overhaul and Maintenance, Navy (MCD)
O & MNR... Operation and Maintenance, Naval Reserve (NVT)
O&M Service... Operation and Maintenance Service (SAUS)
O&N......... Old and New (SAUS)
O & N....... Oregon & Northwestern Railroad Co. (IIA)
O&O......... On and Off (DMAA)
O & O....... One and Only (IIA)
o-and-o..... one-and-only (SAUS)
O & O....... Operational and Organizational (RDA)
O & O....... Organization and Operation
O&O......... Oriental and Occidental Steamship Company (ODA)
O & O....... Owned and Operated
O & OP...... Organizational and Operational Plan [*Army*]
O & OS...... Ordnance and Ordnance Stores [*Navy*]
OANDOS.... Ordnance and Ordnance Stores [*Coast Guard*]
O&P......... Objectives and Policies (TIMI)
O & P....... Operations and Procedures (KSC)
O&P......... Organization & Procedures (SAUS)
O & P....... Ova and Parasites [*Medicine*]
O & PC...... Owl and the Pussy Cat [*Poem by Edward Lear, 1871*]
o&r.......... Ocean and Rail (EBF)
O&R......... Ocean and Rail (SAUS)
O & R....... Ocean and Rail [*Shipping*]
OANDR...... Operation and Regulation
O&R......... Operations and Robotics (SPST)
O and R..... Optimal and Right (SAUS)
O&R......... Orange & Rockland Utilities, Inc. (EFIS)
O & R....... Overhaul and Repair
O&RR........ Oudh and Rohilkhund Railway [*Indian Railway*] (TIR)
O & S....... Operation and Support Funds [*DoD*] (RDA)
O&S......... Operation & Sustainment (SAUS)
O&S......... Operations and Service (CCCA)
O & S....... Operations and Support (MCD)
O&S......... Operations and Sustainment
O & S....... Optics and Sensors Program
O&S......... Over and Short (SAUS)
O & S....... Over and Short Account [*Business term*]
O & SCMIS... Operating and Support Costs Management Information System
O & S HA... Operating and Support Hazard Analysis
O & ST...... Order and Shipping Time [*Military*] (MCD)
O & T........ Operations and Training [*Military*]
O & T........ Organization and Training [*Military*]
OANDT...... Organization and Training Division [*Supreme Headquarters Allied Powers Europe*] (NATG)
O & T........ Oyer and Terminer [*Hear and Determine*] [*Legal term*] (DLA)
O&U......... Over and Under (SAUS)
O & W....... Oldest and Wisest [*Nickname for President Ronald Reagan*]
O & W....... Oneida & Western Railroad (IIA)
O & W....... Ontario & Western Railroad [*Nickname: Old and Weary*]
O and W.... Optimal and Wrong (SAUS)
O & W Dig... Oldham and White's Digest of Laws [*Texas*] [*A publication*] (DLA)
O & Y....... Olympia & York [*Commercial firm*] [*Canada*] (ECON)
OANFE....... Operational Aircraft Not Fully Equipped (NG)
OANI......... Office of the Administrator of Norfolk Island [*Australia*]
OANM....... On or After New Moon [*Freemasonry*] (ROG)
OANR........ Nawor [*Afghanistan*] [*ICAO location identifier*] (ICLI)
OANR........ Office of Air, Noise, and Radiation [*Environmental Protection Agency*] (ERG)
OANS........ Occupied Area News Service [*Military*] (IAA)
OANS........ Salang-I-Shamali [*Afghanistan*] [*ICAO location identifier*] (ICLI)
OANT........ Normanby Township Community and School Library, Ayton, Ontario [*Library symbol*] [*National Library of Canada*] (NLC)
OA/NWOB... Open Allotments/Navy-Wide Operating Budgets (MCD)
OAO.......... Arkhangelsk 2 Aviation Division [*Former USSR*] [*FAA designator*] (FAAC)
OAO.......... National Oceanic and Atmospheric Administration, Miami, Miami, FL [*OCLC symbol*] (OCLC)
OAO.......... Off and On (SAUS)
OAO.......... Office of Aircraft Operations [*Miami, FL*] [*National Oceanic and Atmospheric Administration*] (GRD)
OAO.......... On Account Of [*Telegraphy*] (PCTE)
OAO.......... One and Only [*A favorite girl or boy friend*]
OAO.......... Ontario Association of Orthodontists (SAUS)
OAO.......... Operational and Organizational (MCD)
OAO.......... Orbited Assembly Operation
OAO.......... Orbiting Astronomical Observatory [*Astronomy term*]
OAO.......... Orthogonalized Atomic Orbital (OA)
OAO.......... Outdoor Adventure Online [*America Online*]
OAO.......... Over and Out (VLIE)
OAO 3....... Orbiting Astronomical Observatory (SAUS)
OAOAF...... Operations Analysis Office, Air Force (MCD)
OAOAFLC... Operations Analysis Office, Air Force Logistics Command (MCD)
OAOB........ Obeh [*Afghanistan*] [*ICAO location identifier*] (ICLI)
OAOCR...... Oxygen Adsorption, Outgassing and Chemical Reduction (SAUS)
OAOG........ Urgoon [*Afghanistan*] [*ICAO location identifier*] (ICLI)
OAOI......... On and Off Instruments [*Aviation*]
OAOO........ Deshoo [*Afghanistan*] [*ICAO location identifier*] (ICLI)
OAOP........ Older Adult Offender Project [*of the Alston Wilkes Society*] (EA)
OAOR........ Oxygen Adsorption, Out-gassing, and Chemical Reduction (PDAA)
OAOT........ OAO Technology Solutions, Inc. [*NASDAQ symbol*] (NASQ)
OAP.......... NMFS [*National Marine Fisheries Service*] Northeast Fisheries Center, WoodsHole, MA [*OCLC symbol*] (OCLC)
OAP.......... Observation Amphibian Plane [*Coast Guard*]
OAP.......... Occupational Ability Patterns [*Psychologic test*] (STED)
OAP.......... Occupational Aptitude Pattern [*US Employment Service*] [*Department of Labor*]
OAP.......... Oceanic Automation Program [*FAA*] (TAG)
OAP.......... Office of Adolescent Pregnancy [*Medicine*] (BABM)
OAP.......... Office of Aerial Phenomena [*Air Force*]
OAP.......... Office of Aircraft Production [*World War II*]
OAP.......... Office of Air Programs [*Obsolete*] [*Environmental Protection Agency*]
OAP.......... Office of Alien Property [*World War II*] (DLA)
OAP.......... Office of Antarctic Programs [*National Science Foundation*] [*Later, Division of Polar Programs*]
OAP.......... Office of Atomic Programs [*DoD*]
OAP.......... Office of the Assistant to the President (SAUS)
OAP.......... Office of the Director of Aerospace Programs [*Air Force*]
OAP.......... Offset Aiming Point (AFM)
OAP.......... Oil Analysis Program [*Military*] (AFIT)
OAP.......... Old-Age Pension [*or Pensioner*]
OAP.......... Old Age Pensioner (SAUS)
OAP.......... On-Axis Pointing (PDAA)
OAP.......... Oncovin [*Vincristine*], Ara-C, Prednisone [*Antineoplastic drug regimen*]
OAP.......... Ontario Apprenticeship Program (SAUS)
OAP.......... Operating and Assurance Program (SAUS)
OAP.......... Operation Angel Plane (EA)
OAP.......... Operations and Procedures (IAA)
OAP.......... Ophthalmic Arterial Pressure [*Medicine*]
OAP.......... Ophthalmic Artery Pressure [*Medicine*] (STED)
OAP.......... Optical Adjunct Program (ACAE)
OAP.......... Optical Augmentation Project
OAP.......... Optical Axial Plane (SAUS)
OAP.......... Optically Active Polymer
OAP.......... Ordinary Alterations Plan [*Navy*] (OAG)
OAP.......... Organic Ablative Plastic
OAP.......... Organizational Assessment Package (ACAE)
OAP.......... Ortho-Aminoacelophenone (SAUS)
OAP.......... Ortho-Aminoacetophenone [*Organic chemistry*]
OAP.......... Ortho-Amino-Phenols [*Medicine*] (MELL)
OAP.......... Orthogonal Array Processor [*Computer*]
OAP.......... Orthosorb Absorbable Pin [*Medicine*] (MELL)
OAP.......... Osteoarthropathy [*Medicine*] (MAE)

OAP.......... Outlet Absolute Pressure
OAP.......... Outline Acquisition Plan [*Army*]
OAP.......... Overall Average Percentage (DNAB)
OAP.......... Over Anxious Person (BB)
OAP.......... Over Fire Air Port
OAP.......... Overlapping Atomic Potential (SAUS)
OAP.......... Oxygen at Atmospheric Pressure
OAPBC ...... Office for Advancement of Public Black Colleges [*of the National Association of State Universities and Land Grant Colleges*] (EA)
OAP-BLEO... Oncovin [*Vincristine*] ARA-C [*Cytarabine or cytosine arabinoside*] Prednisone, Bleomycin [*Antineoplastic drug regimen*] (DAVI)
OAPC........ Office of Alien Property Custodian [*World War II*]
OAPC........ Office of the Alien Property Custodian (SAUS)
OAPCA ...... Organotin Antifouling Paint Control Act (SAUS)
OAPCA ...... Organotin Antifouling Paint Control Act of 1988
OAPCB ...... Old-Age-Pensioner CBer [*Experienced citizens band radio operator*]
OAPCC ...... Ortho Abnormal Plasma Coagulation Control [*Medicine*] (EDAA)
OAPEC....... Organization of Arab Oil Exporting Countries (SAUS)
OAPEC....... Organization of Arab Petroleum Exporting Countries [*See also OPAEP*] [*OPEC*] [*Kuwait*] [*Absorbed by*]
OAPEP....... Organisation Arabe des Pays Exportateurs de Petrole [*Organization of Arab Petroleum Exporting Countries*]
OAPG........ Paghman [*Afghanistan*] [*ICAO location identifier*] (ICLI)
OAPJ .... Pan Jao [*Afghanistan*] [*ICAO location identifier*] (ICLI)
OAPM .... Optimal Amplitude and Phase Modulation
OAPNA ...... Organization of Asian-Pacific News Agencies (BUAC)
OAPO........ Eastern Pacific Tuna Fishing Organization [*Marine science*] (OSRA)
OAPP........ Office of Adolescent Pregnancy Programs [*HEW*]
O App .... Ohio Appellate Reports [*A publication*] (DLA)
O App 2d ... Ohio Appellate Reports, Second Series [*A publication*] (DLA)
OAPQ........ Office of Assistance Program Quality (SAUS)
OAPS........ Orbit Adjust Propulsion Subsystem [*NASA*]
OAPU........ Old Age Pension Union (SAUS)
OAPU........ Overseas Air Preparation Unit [*British military*] (DMA)
OAPWL....... Overall Power Watt Level (PDAA)
OAQ.......... National Climatic Center, Ashville, NC [*OCLC symbol*] (OCLC)
OAQ.......... Observatorio Astronomico de Quito [*Ecuador*] [*Seismograph station code, US Geological Survey*] (SEIS)
OAQ.......... Order of Architects of Quebec [*1974, founded 1890 as PQAA*] [*Canada*] (NGC)
OAQD........ Qades [*Afghanistan*] [*ICAO location identifier*] (ICLI)
OAQK........ Qala-I-Nyazkhan [*Afghanistan*] [*ICAO location identifier*] (ICLI)
OAQM........ Kron Monjan [*Afghanistan*] [*ICAO location identifier*] (ICLI)
OAQN........ Qala-I-Naw [*Afghanistan*] [*ICAO location identifier*] (ICLI)
OAQPS ...... Office of Air Quality Planning and Standards [*Environmental Protection Agency*]
OAQPS ...... US EPA Office of Air Quality Planning and Standards (SAUS)
OAQPSTTN... Office of Air Quality Planning and Standards Technology Transfer Network [*Environmental Protection Agency*] (AEPA)
OAQQ........ Qarqin [*Afghanistan*] [*ICAO location identifier*] (ICLI)
OAQR........ Qaisar [*Afghanistan*] [*ICAO location identifier*] (ICLI)
OAQS........ Online Associative Query System (NITA)
OAR.......... Arnprior Public Library, Ontario [*Library symbol*] [*National Library of Canada*] (NLC)
OAR.......... Augustinian Recollect Sisters (TOCD)
OAR.......... Monterey/Fort Ord, CA [*Location identifier*] [*FAA*] (FAAL)
OaR.......... Oakland Raiders [*National Football League*] [*1995-present*] (NFLA)
OAR.......... Object Address Register (SAUS)
OAR.......... Oceanic and Atmospheric Research (SAUS)
OAR.......... Off-Axis Ratio (RAWO)
OAR.......... Offender Aid and Restoration (EA)
OAR.......... Office of Aerospace Research [*Air Force*]
OAR.......... Office of AIDS Research [*National Institute of Health*]
OAR.......... Office of Air and Radiation [*Environmental Protection Agency*] (GFGA)
OAR.......... Office of Analysis and Review [*Army, Navy*]
OAR.......... Office of Atmospheric Research (SAUS)
OAR.......... Office of Oceanic and Atmospheric Research [*National Oceanic and Atmospheric Administration*]
OAR.......... Ohio Appellate Reports [*A publication*] (DLA)
OAR.......... Ohio Art [*AMEX symbol*] (TTSB)
OAR.......... [*The*] Ohio Art Co. [*AMEX symbol*] (SPSG)
O-Ar .... Ohio State Archives, Columbus, OH [*Library symbol*] [*Library of Congress*] (LCLS)
O Ar .... Old Arabic (SAUS)
OAR.......... Old Augusta Railroad [*Federal Railroad Administration identification code*]
OAR.......... Ontario Appeal Reports [*A publication*] (DLA)
OAR.......... Open Air Range
OAR.......... Open Architecture Receiver [*Telecommunications*]
OAR.......... Operand Address Register [*Computer science*] (IAA)
OAR.......... Operational Address Register [*Computer science*] (IAA)
OAR.......... Operational Analysis Research (SAUS)
OAR.......... Operational Availability and Reliability [*Military*]
OAR.......... Operation Assessment and Readiness [*Environmental science*] (COE)
OAR.......... Operations Activity Recorder (VLIE)
OAR.......... Operations Analysis Report
OAR.......... Operations and Regulations (IAA)
OAR.......... Operator Authorization Record [*Computer science*] (IBMDP)
OAR.......... Optical Angle Readout
OAR.......... Optical Automatic Ranging
OAR.......... Optional Address Register (VLIE)
OAR.......... ORDALT [*Ordnance Alterations*] Accomplishment Requirement (NG)
OAR.......... Ordering as Required (MHDB)
OAR.......... Order of the Augustinian Recollects [*Roman Catholic men's religious order*]
OAR.......... Ordnance Accomplishment Requirement (SAUS)
OAR.......... Ordnance Allowance Report [*Navy*]
OAR.......... Ordnance Alteration Reporting
OAR.......... Ordnance Alteration Requirement (NG)
OAR.......... Oregon Administrative Rules (SARE)
OAR.......... Organized Air Reserve
OAR.......... Orientation/Alertness Remediation (STED)
OAR.......... Original Action Record
OAR.......... Other Administrative Reasons [*Medicine*] (MAE)
OAR.......... Ottawa Ankle Rules
OAR.......... Over All Rate [*Real estate*] (DICI)
OAR.......... Overall Rate of Capitalization
OAR.......... Overall Rate of Return [*Business term*]
OAR.......... Overhaul and Repair
OAR.......... Overtime Authorization Request (MCD)
OAR.......... Oxford Applied Research [*Software manufacturer*] [*British*]
OARAC ...... Office of Aerospace Research Automatic Computer (SAUS)
OARAC ...... Office of Air Research Automatic Computer
OARB........ Azilda Branch, Rayside-Balfour Public Library, Ontario [*Library symbol*] [*National Library of Canada*] (NLC)
OARB........ Oakland Army Base [*California*] (AABC)
OARBC ...... Boeing of Canada Ltd., Arnprior, Ontario [*Library symbol*] [*National Library of Canada*] (BIB)
OARC........ Office of Air Research Automatic Calculator (SAUS)
OARC........ Ordinary Administrative Radio Conference
OARD........ Arthur District High School, Arthur, Ontario [*Library symbol*] [*National Library of Canada*] (NLC)
OARDC...... Ohio Agricultural Research and Development Center [*Ohio State University*] [*Research center*] (RCD)
OARE........ Orbital Acceleration Research Experiment (SAUS)
OARG........ Uruzgan [*Afghanistan*] [*ICAO location identifier*] (ICLI)
OARM .... Dilaram [*Afghanistan*] [*ICAO location identifier*] (ICLI)
OARM .... Middlesex County Public Library, Arva, Ontario [*Library symbol*] [*National Library of Canada*] (NLC)
OARM .... Office of Administration and Resources Management [*Environmental Protection Agency*] (GFGA)
OARMS...... Armstrong Community Library, Ontario [*Library symbol*] [*National Library of Canada*] (NLC)
OAR-N....... Office of Analysis and Review, Navy (MUGU)
OARnet...... Ohio Academic Research Network
OARnet...... [*The*] Ohio Academic Resources Network [*Computer science*] (TNIG)
OARP........ Office of Advanced Research Programs [*Later, OART*] [*NASA*]
OARP........ Old Age Revolving Pensions (SAUS)
OARP........ Operator Accelerated Retraining Program [*Nuclear energy*] (NRCH)
OARP........ Rimpa [*Afghanistan*] [*ICAO location identifier*] (ICLI)
OARS........ Ocean Area Reconnaissance Satellite [*Antisubmarine warfare*]
OARS........ Ocean Atmosphere Response Studies [*Marine science*] (MSC)
OARS........ Ocean Reconnaissance Submarine [*NATO*] (LAIN)
OARS........ Offenders Aid Rehabilitation Services (SAUS)
OARS........ Office Automation Reporting Service (NITA)
OARS........ On-Line Automated Reference Service [*Library science*]
OARS........ Ontario Association for Remote Sensing (SAUS)
OARS........ Opening Automated Report Service [*NYSE*]
OARSI ...... OsteoArthritis Research Society International [*Association*] (EA)
OART .... Oakland Army Terminal [*California*]
OART .... Office of Advanced Research and Technology [*Later, OAST*] [*NASA*]
OARTS....... Oceanic Air Roule Tracking System (SAUS)
OAR/USA.... Offender Aid and Restoration USA [*An association*] (EA)
OAS.......... O-Acetylserine (thiol)-lyase [*An enzyme*]
OAS.......... Oasis [*Board on Geographic Names*]
OAS.......... Oasis [*NCIC car model code*]
OAS.......... Oasis Residential [*NYSE symbol*] (SPSG)
OAS.......... Obstacle Assessment Surface [*Aviation*] (DA)
OAS.......... Occupational Aspiration Scale [*Education*]
OAS.......... Occupied Areas Section [*Military government*]
OAS.......... Offensive Air Support (MCD)
OAS.......... Offensive Attack System (DOMA)
OAS.......... Offensive Avionics System
OAS.......... Office Automation System (NASA)
OAS.......... Office for Advanced Studies (AAG)
OAS.......... Office of Administrative Systems [*Department of Agriculture*] (GFGA)
OAS.......... Office of Advanced Studies (SAUS)
OAS.......... Office of Aircraft Services [*Emergency Management*] (EMA)
OAS.......... Office of Airline Statistics [*U.S. Department of Transportation*] (BARN)
OAS.......... Office of Appalachian Studies (SAUS)
OAS.......... Office of Oceanic and Atmospheric Services [*National Oceanic and Atmospheric Administration*] (MSC)
OAS.......... Office of the Assistant for Study Support [*Air Force*]
OAS.......... Office of the Assistant Secretary [*Defense*] [*Navy*]
OAS.......... Ohio Academy of Science (EARSL)
OAS.......... Oklahoma Academy of Science (BUAC)
OAS.......... Old Age and Survivors' Insurance (IAA)
OAS.......... Old-Age Security
OAS.......... Olley Air Service Ltd.
OAS.......... Oman Aviation Services Co. [*ICAO designator*] (FAAC)
OAS.......... On Active Service
OAS.......... One-Address-System (SAUS)
OAS.......... One-to-All Scatter (VLIE)
OAS.......... Ontario Archaeological Association (SAUS)
OAS.......... Open-Health Acid Steel (SAUS)
OAS.......... Open-Hearth Acid Steel
OAS.......... Operational Announcing System (IAA)
OAS.......... Ophthalmic Anesthesia Society (SAUS)

OAS.......... Opiate Abstinence Syndrome [*Medicine*] (MELL)
OAS.......... Optical Alignment Sights [*NASA*]
OAS.......... Optical Array Spectrometer
OAS.......... Optical Augmentation System
OAS.......... Optics and Sensors [*Program*] (MCD)
OAS.......... Option Adjusted Spread
OAS.......... Optoacoustic Spectrometry [*Also, PAS*]
OAS.......... Optoacoustic Spectroscopy (SAUS)
OAS.......... Oracle Application Server [*Computer science*] (VLIE)
OAS.......... Oral Allergy Syndrome [*Medicine*] (DMAA)
OAS.......... Orbit Adjust Subsystem (SAUS)
OAS.......... Orbiter Aeroflight Simulator [*NASA*] (NASA)
OAS.......... Orbiter Atmospheric Simulator [*NASA*] (MCD)
OAS.......... Orbiter Avionia System (SAUS)
OAS.......... Orbiter Avionics System [*NASA*] (NASA)
OAS.......... Orbitor Avionics Simulator [*NASA*]
OAS.......... Order Allocation System (VLIE)
OAS.......... Order Automation System (TIMI)
OAS.......... Ordinary Ammunition Storage (SAUS)
OAS.......... Ordinary Ammunition Stowage (SAUS)
OAS.......... Organisation de l'Armee Secrete [*Secret Army Organization*] [*France*] (PD)
OAS.......... Organizational Accounting Structure (IAA)
OAS.......... Organization of American States (EA)
OAS.......... Organization of Arab Students in the USA and Canada (EA)
OAS.......... Oriental and African Studies
OAS.......... Origin-of-Assembly Sequence [*Genetics*]
OAS.......... Orthopedic Appliance Service
OAS.......... Osmotically Active Substance [*Medicine*] (DMAA)
OAS.......... Other Active Military Service (DNAB)
OAS.......... Other Approved Studies (ADA)
OAS.......... Output Amplitude Stability
OAS.......... Oxygen Activated Sludge (DICI)
OAS.......... Secret Army Organisation [*Algeria*] (BUAC)
OAS[2].......... Officer Accession/Separation System (MCD)
OASAA ...... Other Arms NCOs Skill At Arms (SAUS)
OASAALT... Office of the Assistant Secretary of the Army for Acquisition, Logistics and Technology
OASAF....... Office of Assistant Secretary of Air Force
OASAF....... Optical Active Surface Approach Fuze
OASA (FM)... Office of the Assistant Secretary of the Army (Financial Management) (MUGU)
OASA (I & L)... Office of the Assistant Secretary of the Army (Installations and Logistics) (MUGU)
OASAM...... Office of the Assistant Secretary for Administration and Management (SAUS)
OASA(M & RA)... Office of the Assistant Secretary of the Army (Manpower and Reserve Affairs)
OASA (R & D)... Office of the Assistant Secretary of the Army (Research and Development) (MUGU)
OASARDA... Office of the Assistant Secretary of the Army (Research, Development and Aquisition) (RDA)
OASAS ...... Office of Alcoholism and Substance Abuse Services [*U.S. Department of Health and Human Services*] (BARN)
OASB .... Sarobi [*Afghanistan*] [*ICAO location identifier*] (ICLI)
OASBO ...... Office of Asbestos and Small Business Ombudsman [*Environmental Protection Agency*]
OASBO ...... Ohio Association of School Business Officials (SAUS)
OASBO ...... Oregon Association of School Business Officials (SAUS)
OAsC .... Ashland College, Ashland, OH [*Library symbol*] [*Library of Congress*] (LCLS)
OASC .... Office Automation Steering Committee (SAUS)
OASC .... Office Automation Support Center (SAUS)
OASC .... Office of Advanced Scientific Computing [*National Science Foundation*]
OASC .... Officer & Aircrew Selection Center (or Centre) (SAUS)
OASCB .... Orbiter Avionics Software Control Board [*NASA*] (NASA)
OASCMIS... Operating and Support Costs Management Information System (MCD)
OASD .... Ocular Albinism-Sensorineural Deafness [*Medicine*] [*Syndrome*] (EDAA)
OASD .... Office of the Assistant Secretary of Defense
OASD .... Shindand [*Afghanistan*] [*ICAO location identifier*] (ICLI)
OASD-AE... Office of the Assistant Secretary of Defense, Application in Engineering (SAUS)
OASD(AE)... Office of the Assistant Secretary of Defense (Applications Engineer) (MCD)
OASD-C ..... Office of the Assistant Secretary of Defense - Comptroller
OASDG ...... Alexandria Branch, Stormount, Dundas, and Glengarry County Public Library, Ontario [*Library symbol*] [*National Library of Canada*] (NLC)
OASD(HA) .. Office of the Assisant Secretary of Defense (Health Affairs) (DNAB)
OASDHI ..... Old-Age, Survivors, Disability, and Health Insurance [*Program*] [*Social Security Administration*]
OASDI .... Old-Age, Survivors, and Disability Insurance [*Program*] [*Social Security Administration*]
OASD/IL..... Office of the Assistant Secretary of Defense/Installations and Logistics (SAUS)
OASDI Program... Old-Age and Survivors Disability Insurance Program (SAUS)
OASD/ISA... Office of the Assistant Secretary of Defense/International Security Affairs (SAUS)
OASD/ISP... Office of the Assistant Secretary of Defense for International Security Policy (SAUS)
OASDITF... Old-Age, Survivors, and Disability Insurance Trust Fund [*Medicine*] [*Social Security Administration*] (EDAA)
OASD(MRA)... Office of the Assistant Secretary of Defense (Manpower and Reserve Affairs)
OASD (MRA & L)... Office of Assistant Secretary of Defense (Manpower-Reserve Affairs and Logistics) (MCD)
OASD(PA)... Office of the Assistant Secretary of Defense (Public Affairs) (NTCM)
OASD-R&D... Office Assistant Secretary of Defense, Research and Development (SAUS)
OASD(R & D)... Office of the Assistant Secretary of Defense (Research and Development) (MCD)
OASD(SA)... Office of the Assistant Secretary of Defense (Systems Analysis) (CINC)
OASD-S&L.. Office Assistant Seeretary of Defense, Supply and Logistics (SAUS)
OASD(S & L)... Office of the Assistant Secretary of Defense (Supply and Logistics) [*Obsolete*] (MCD)
OASD SO/LIC... Office of the Assistant Secretary of Defense for Special Operations and Low Intensity Conflict (POLM)
OASD(T) .... Office of the Assistant Secretary of Defense (Telecommunications)
OASE .... Offensive Aircraft Survivability Equipment
OASE .... Office Automation Services (SAUS)
OAS/EOM ... Organization of American States Electoral Observation Mission
OASES....... Oceanic Applied Sciences and Environmental Solutions (RCD)
OASES....... Open Access Satellite Education Services (EDAC)
OASES....... Organization for American-Soviet Exchanges (EA)
OASES....... Oxygen-Activated Sludge Environmental System (SAUS)
OASET....... Office of the Assistant Secretary for Employment and Training [*Department of Labor*]
OASF .... Office Automation System Facility (SAUS)
OASF .... Orbital Astronomy Support Facility (SAUS)
OASF .... Orbiting Astronomical Support Facility (MCD)
OASFP....... Old Alliance Society of French Polishers [*A union*] [*British*]
OASG .... Office Automation Specialist Group (NITA)
OASG .... Sheberghan [*Afghanistan*] [*ICAO location identifier*] (ICLI)
OASH .... Obstructive Asymmetrical Septal Hypertrophy [*Medicine*] (CPH)
OASH .... Office of the Assistant Secretary for Health [*Department of Health and Human Services*]
OASH .... Office of the Assistant Secretary for Housing (SAUS)
OASHA ...... Operating and Support Hazard Analysis (MCD)
OASHDI ..... Old Age Survivors Health and Disability Program [*Health insurance*] (GHCT)
OASHDS .... Office of the Assistant Secretary for Human Development Services (SAUS)
OAsht........ Ashtabula County District Library, Ashtabula, OH [*Library symbol*] [*Library of Congress*] (LCLS)
OAshtK...... Kent State University, Ashtabula Regional Campus, Ashtabula, OH [*Library symbol*] [*Library of Congress*] (LCLS)
OASI .... Oasis Travel Trailer [*NCIC trailer make code*]
OASI .... Office Automation Society International (EA)
OASI .... Old-Age and Survivors Insurance [*Program*] [*Social Security Administration*]
OASI .... Old America Stores [*NASDAQ symbol*] (TTSB)
OASI .... Old Americia Stores, Inc. [*NASDAQ symbol*] (SAG)
OASIA .... Office of the Assistant Secretary for International Affairs [*Department of the Treasury*]
OASIS .... Observation, Analysis and Simulation of Interacting Systems (SAUS)
OASIS .... Observation at Several Interacting Scales (SAUS)
OASIS .... Observations At Several Interacting Scales (SAUS)
OASIS .... Obstetric Anesthesia Safety Improvement Study (SAUS)
OASIS .... Occupational Aptitude Survey and Interest Schedule
OASIS .... Ocean All-Source Information System
OASIS .... Ocean Atmospheric Surveillance and Information System (SAUS)
OASIS .... Oceanic and Atmospheric Satellite Imaging System (SAUS)
OASIS .... Oceanic and Atmospheric Scientific Information System [*National Oceanic and Atmospheric Administration*] (MCD)
OASIS .... Oceanic Area System Improvement Study (SAUS)
OASIS .... Oceanographic and Atmospheric Support and Information System (SAUS)
OASIS .... Office Administration Simulation Study
OASIS .... Office Automation Secure Information System (SAUS)
OASIS .... Office Automation Services and Information Systems (SAUS)
OASIS .... Office for Academic Support in Service (SAUS)
OASIS .... Office of Academic Support Instructional Services (SAUS)
OASIS .... Ohio of the American Society for Information Science (SAUS)
OASIS .... Older Adult Service and Information System (SAUS)
OASIS .... Older Adult Singles in Support (SAUS)
OASIS .... Onboard at Site Invoicing System [*IBM Computer Program*]
OASIS .... Online Administrative Information System [*Computer science*] (IAA)
OASIS .... Online Application System Interactive Software (SAUS)
OASIS .... On-line Asperger Syndrome Information and Support (SAUS)
OASIS .... On-line Automotive Service Information System [*Automotive engineering*]
OASIS .... Open Access Same-Time Information Service [*Joint venture from IBM and TradeWave Corp.*]
OASIS .... Open and Secure Information Systems (SAUS)
OASIS .... Operational Analysis and System Interface System
OASIS .... Operational Analysis Strategic Interaction Simulator (SAUS)
OASIS .... Operational and Supportability Implementation System [*FAA*] (TAG)
OASIS .... Operational Applications of Special Intelligence System (MCD)
OASIS .... Operational Area Satellite Information System [*Emergency Management*] (EMA)
OASIS .... Operational Automated Ships Information System (SAUS)
OASIS .... Operational Automatic Scheduling Information System (MUGU)
OASIS .... Operation Analysis Strategic Interaction Simulator [*Nuclear war games*]
OASIS .... Optimized Air-to-Surface Infrared Seeker
OASIS .... Orbiter Experiments Program Autonomous Supporting Instrumentation System (SAUS)

OASIS .... Order, Accounting, Stock, Invoicing and Statistics (MHDB)
OASIS .... Order and Schedules Input System (MCD)
OASIS .... Organisation for Article Standards in Science (SAUS)
OASIS .... Organization for Applied Science in Society
OASIS .... Organization for the Advancement of Structured Information Standards [*Computer term*]
OASIS .... Organized Adoption Search Information Services (EA)
OASIS .... Outcome and Assessment Information Set
OASIS .... Outlook and Situation Information System [*Department of Agriculture*] [*Defunct*] (IID)
OASIS .... Outpatient Appointment Scheduling and Information System
OASIS .... Overseas Access Service for Information Systems (SAUS)
OASIS .... Over-the-Horizon Airborne Sensor Information System [*Navy*] (DOMA)
OASIS .... Overweight & Seeking Infertility Support (SAUS)
OASIS .... Ownership Accountability of Selected Secondary Items Stocked
OASIS .... OzonAction Strategic Information System
OASIS-AS... Occupational Aptitude Survey and Interest Schedule - Aptitude Survey [*Vocational guidance test*]
OASIS-IS... Occupational Aptitude Survey and Interest Schedule - Interest Schedule [*Vocational guidance test*]
OasisR ...... Oasis Residential, Inc. [*Associated Press*] (SAG)
OasisRsd ... Oasis Residential, Inc. [*Associated Press*] (SAG)
OASK .... Serka [*Afghanistan*] [*ICAO location identifier*] (ICLI)
OASL .... Salam [*Afghanistan*] [*ICAO location identifier*] (ICLI)
OASM .... Office of Aerospace Medicine [*NASA*] (KSC)
OASM .... Ohm-Ampere-Second Meter [*System of units*]
OASM .... Samangan [*Afghanistan*] [*ICAO location identifier*] (ICLI)
OASMA...... Offensive Air Support Mission Analysis (MCD)
OASMS...... Ordnance Ammunition Surveillance and Maintenance School [*Army*]
OASN .... Office of the Assistant Secretary of the Navy
OASN .... Sheghnan [*Afghanistan*] [*ICAO location identifier*] (ICLI)
OASN(FM) .. Office of the Assistant Secretary of the Navy for Financial Management
OASN(I & L)... Office of the Assistant Secretary of the Navy for Installations and Logistics
OASN(M/RA)... Office of the Assistant Secretary of the Navy (Manpower and Reserve Affairs)
OASN(M/RA/L)... Office of the Assistant Secretary of the Navy (Manpower, Reserve Affairs, and Logistics)
OASN(P & RF)... Office of the Assistant Secretary of the Navy for Personnel and Reserve Force
OASN(R & D)... Office of the Assistant Secretary of the Navy for Research and Development
OASO......... Overactive Superior Oblique [*Medicine*] (EDAA)
OAS-OGN ... Organization of American States-Observer Group in Nicaragua
OASP .... Organic Acid Soluble Phosphorus
OASP .... Over-All Sound Pressure (PDAA)
OASP .... Sare Pul [*Afghanistan*] [*ICAO location identifier*] (ICLI)
OASPL........ Overall Sound Pressure Level
OASPrA ..... Oasis Residential $2.25'A' Pfd [*NYSE symbol*] (TTSB)
OASR......... Office of Aeronautical and Space Research [*Later, OART*] [*NASA*]
OASR......... Overactive Superior Rectus [*Medicine*] (EDAA)
OASR......... Sabar [*Afghanistan*] [*ICAO location identifier*] (ICLI)
OAss.......... Old Assyrian (BJA)
OASS .... Salang-I-Junubi [*Afghanistan*] [*ICAO location identifier*] (ICLI)
OASSA ...... Ohio Association of Secondary School Administrators (EARSL)
OASSO ...... Operational Applications of Satellite Snowcover Observations [*NASA*]
OAsT......... Ashland Theological Seminary, Ashland, OH [*Library symbol*] [*Library of Congress*] (LCLS)
OAST .... Office of Aeronautical and Space Technology [*Formerly, OART*] [*NASA*]
OAST .... Order and Shipping Time [*Military*] (AFIT)
OAST .... Overland Air Superiority Training [*Navy*] (DOMA)
OAST .... Shur Tepa [*Afghanistan*] [*ICAO location identifier*] (ICLI)
OASTP....... Office of the Assistant Secretary for Technology Policy [*U.S. Department of Commerce*] (BARN)
OASU .... Oceanographic Air Survey Unit
OASV .... Orbital Assembly Support Vehicle
OASW .... Office of the Assistant Secretary of War [*World War II*]
OASy .... Officer Accession/Separation System (SAUS)
OASYS ..... Obstacle Avoidance System [*Army*] (RDA)
OASYS ..... Office Automation System
OASYS ..... Order Allocation System
OAT .... Atikokan Public Library, Ontario [*Library symbol*] [*National Library of Canada*] (NLC)
OAT .... Ocean Acoustic Tomography
OAT .... Office Automation Tools (TIMI)
OAT .... Office for Advanced Technology [*Air Force*]
OAT .... Office for the Advancement of Telehealth (SAUS)
OAT .... Office of Advanced Technology (SAUS)
OAT .... On-Air Test [*Telecommunications*] (DOAD)
OAT .... One at a Time
OAT .... Open-Air Theater
OAT .... Operating Acceptance Test (SAUS)
OAT .... Operating Ambient Temperature
OAT .... Operational Acceptance Test
OAT .... Operational Air Traffic (NATG)
OAT .... Optical Adaptive Technique
OAT .... Optional Application Tapes (SAUS)
OAT .... Optometry Admissions Test (GAGS)
OAT .... Organic Acid Technology [*Automotive cooling systems*]
OAT .... Ornithineaminotransferase [*An enzyme*]
OAT .... Ornithine keto-acid Aminotransferase (SAUS)
OAT .... Outer Atmospheric Temperature (IAA)
OAT .... Outside Air Temperature [*Aviation*]
OAT .... Overall Test
OAT .... Overseas Airways Transmission (SAUS)
OAT .... Oxide-Aligned Transistor [*Electronics*] (PDAA)
OAT .... Oxoacid Aminotransferase Inhibition (DB)
OAT .... Quaker Oats Co. [*NYSE symbol*] [*Toronto Stock Exchange symbol*] (SPSG)
OAT .... Sogervair/Transoceanic Aviation [*France*] [*ICAO designator*] (FAAC)
OATA......... Optical Acquisition and Tracking Aid Assembly
OATA Assembly... Optical Acquisition and Tracking Aid Assembly (SAUS)
OATC .... Oceanic Air Traffic Center
OATC .... Oceanic Air Traffic Control (SAUS)
OATC .... Officers Advanced Training Course (SAUS)
OATC .... Overseas Air Traffic Control
OATCD....... Ohio Association of Tobacco and Candy Distributors (EARSL)
OATD .... Toorghondi [*Afghanistan*] [*ICAO location identifier*] (ICLI)
OATG .... Tashkurghan [*Afghanistan*] [*ICAO location identifier*] (ICLI)
OATH .... Atikokan High School, Ontario [*Library symbol*] [*National Library of Canada*] (NLC)
OATH .... Olympic Advocates Together Honourably [*Canada*] (EAIO)
OATHS....... One-in-a-Thousand Society (EA)
OATI .... Oak Titmouse [*North American bird banding code*] (BIBA)
OATK .... Kotal [*Afghanistan*] [*ICAO location identifier*] (ICLI)
OATM........ Atikokan Centennial Museum, Ontario [*Library symbol*] [*National Library of Canada*] (BIB)
OATM........ Operations Analysis Technical Memorandum (SAUS)
OATM........ Orbiter Antenna Test Model [*NASA*]
OATMEAL... Optimum Allocation of Test and Equipment Manpower Against Logistics
OATN .... Tereen [*Afghanistan*] [*ICAO location identifier*] (ICLI)
OATP .... On-Aircraft Test Procedure (MCD)
OATP .... Operational Acceptance Test Procedure (NRCH)
OATQ .... Taluqan [*Afghanistan*] [*ICAO location identifier*] (ICLI)
OATRU ...... Organic and Associated Terrain Research Unit (SAUS)
OATS .... Office Automation Technology Services [*AT&T*] (CIST)
OATS .... Office of Air Transportation Security [*FAA*]
OATS .... Old-Age Theatre Society (SAUS)
OATS .... On-Board Acoustic Tracking System [*Navy*] (CAAL)
OATS .... Open Architecture Test System (MCD)
OATS .... Operational Air Training School (SAUS)
OATS .... Optical Attitude Transfer System (SSD)
OATS .... Optical Augmentation Target Screen (ACAE)
OATS .... Optimum Aerial Target Sensor
OATS .... Orbit and Attitude Tracking (GAVI)
OATS .... Organisation of Adult Trades and Services
OATS .... Original Article Tear Sheets
OATS .... Original Article Tearsheet Service (NITA)
OATS .... Original Article Text Service
OATS .... Outdoor Advertising Total System (PDAA)
OATS .... Overall Test Set
OATS .... Over Armor Technology Synthesis (RDA)
OATS .... Oxford Air Training School [*British*] (PIAV)
OATS .... Wild Oats Markets, Inc. [*NASDAQ symbol*] (SAG)
OATT......... Officials at the Track [*Motorsports*]
OATU .... Orey Antunes Transportes e Navegacao [*Intermodal shipping container symbol*] (TVRC)
OATUS....... On a Totally Unrelated Subject (ADWA)
OATUU ...... Organisation of African Trade Union Unity [*Formerly, AATUF, ATUC*] [*See also OUSA*] [*Accra, Ghana*] (EAIO)
OATW........ Tewara [*Afghanistan*] [*ICAO location identifier*] (ICLI)
OATZ......... Tesak [*Afghanistan*] [*ICAO location identifier*] (ICLI)
OAU.......... Aurora Public Library, Ontario [*Library symbol*] [*National Library of Canada*] (NLC)
OAU.......... Ohio University, Athens, OH [*Library symbol*] [*Library of Congress*] (LCLS)
OAU.......... Operator Assistance Unit (NITA)
OAU.......... Optical Alignment Unit
OAU.......... Organization for African Unity (NADA)
OAU.......... Organization of African Unity
OAU.......... Original Sixteen To One Mine [*PC, exchange symbol*] (TTSB)
OAU.......... Oriol Avia [*Russian Federation*] [*ICAO designator*] (FAAC)
OAUDC ...... Ohlone Area United Democratic Campaign [*San Leandro, CA*] (PACS)
OAUG........ Oracle Applications Users Group [*Association*] (EA)
OAUH........ Aurora Historical Society, Ontario [*Library symbol*] [*National Library of Canada*] (NLC)
OAUHS ...... PRECIS Project, Aurora High School, Ontario [*Library symbol*] [*National Library of Canada*] (NLC)
OAULC ...... OAU [*Organization of African Unity*] Liberation Committee [*Addis Ababa, Ethiopia*] (EAIO)
OAUM .... Aurora Museum, Ontario [*Library symbol*] [*National Library of Canada*] (BIB)
OAUS........ On an Unrelated Subject (ADWA)
OAUS........ Sterling Drug Ltd., Aurora, Ontario [*Library symbol*] [*National Library of Canada*] (BIB)
OAU/STRC... Organization of African Unity Scientific and Technical Research Commission [*Marine science*] (MSC)
OAUYCE..... York County Board of Education, Aurora, Ontario [*Library symbol*] [*National Library of Canada*] (NLC)
OAUZ .... Kunduz [*Afghanistan*] [*ICAO location identifier*] (ICLI)
O-A-V........ Object-Attribute-Value
oav........... oculoauriculovertebral (SAUS)
OAV.......... Oculoauriculovertebral Dysplasia [*Medicine*] (MAE)
OAV.......... Omni-Aviacao e Tecnologia Lda. [*Portugal*] [*ICAO designator*] (FAAC)

OAV .... Operational Aerospace Vehicle
OAV .... Original Animation Video (SAUS)
OAVC of SA... Office of the Assistant Vice Chief of Staff, Army [*Later, OAVCSA*] (AABC)
OAVCSA..... Office of the Assistant Vice Chief of Staff, Army [*Formerly, OAVC of SA*] (AABC)
OAVD .... Oculoauriculovertebral Dysplasia [*Medicine*] (MEDA)
OAVE .... Occupational, Adult, and Vocational Education (OICC)
OAvG .... B. F. Goodrich Chemical Co. [*of B. F. Goodrich Co.*], Development Center Library, Avon Lake, OH [*Library symbol*] [*Library of Congress*] (LCLS)
OAVP .... Older Americans Volunteer Program [*ACTION*]
OAVSDG..... Avonmore Branch, Stormont, Dundas, and Glengarry County Public Library, Ontario [*Library symbol*] [*National Library of Canada*] (BIB)
OAVTME..... Office of Adult, Vocational, Technical, and Manpower Education [*Office of Education*]
OAW .... Old Abandoned Well (WDAA)
OAW .... Optically Assisted Winchester [*Computer science*]
OAW .... Oral Airways (MELL)
OAW .... Overall Width
OAW .... Oxyacetylene Welding
OAWC .... Overseas Air Weapons Control (SAUS)
OAWCS....... Overseas Air Weapons Control System
OAWM....... Office of Air and Water Measurement [*National Institute of Standards and Technology*]
OAWO .... Opening Abductory Wedge Osteotomy [*Medicine*] (MELL)
OAWOP...... Ontario Police College, Aylmer West, Ontario [*Library symbol*] [*National Library of Canada*] (NLC)
OAWP .... Office of Air and Water Programs (OICC)
OAWP .... Operations Analysis Working Paper [*NASA*] (KSC)
OAWR .... Office of Agricultural War Relations [*World War II*]
OAWR .... Office of Atmospheric Water Resources [*Bureau of Reclamation*]
OAWRMR... Other Acquisition War Reserve Material Requirements (MCD)
OAWU .... Wurtach [*Afghanistan*] [*ICAO location identifier*] (ICLI)
OAWZ........ Wazirabad [*Afghanistan*] [*ICAO location identifier*] (ICLI)
OAX.......... Oaxaca [*Mexico*] [*Airport symbol*] (OAG)
OAX.......... Oaxaca [*Mexico*] [*Seismograph station code, US Geological Survey*] (SEIS)
OAX.......... Operational Aviation Services - Australia [*ICAO designator*] (FAAC)
OAXTC....... Ocean Atmosphere Exchange of Trace Compounds (SAUS)
OAY.......... Moses Point, AK [*Location identifier*] [*FAA*] (FAAL)
OAY.......... NOAA [*National Oceanic and Atmospheric Administration*] Geophysical Fluid Dynamics Laboratory, Princeton, NJ [*OCLC symbol*] (OCLC)
OAY.......... Outstanding Airmen of the Year (SAUS)
OAYM........ Aylmer District Museum, Ontario [*Library symbol*] [*National Library of Canada*] (BIB)
OAYQ .... Yangi Qala [*Afghanistan*] [*ICAO location identifier*] (ICLI)
OAYR .... Outstanding Airman of the Year Ribbon [*Military decoration*] (AFM)
OAZB .... Zebak [*Afghanistan*] [*ICAO location identifier*] (ICLI)
OAZG .... Zaranj [*Afghanistan*] [*ICAO location identifier*] (ICLI)
OB .... Austrian Airtransport (SAUS)
OB .... Brockville Public Library, Ontario [*Library symbol*] [*National Library of Canada*] (NLC)
OB .... Brought Over (ROG)
Ob............ Obadiah [*Old Testament book*]
OB .... Oberhausen [*Rheinland*] [*German license plate city code*]
OB .... Oberlerchner [*Joseph Oberlerchner Holzindustrie*] [*Austria*] [*ICAO aircraft manufacturer identifier*] (ICAO)
OB .... Obese [*Medicine*] (EDAA)
ob............ Obese
OB .... Obeum [*Nickname for toilets at Cambridge University*] [*Slang*] [*British*] (DSUE)
OB .... Obidiah [*Old Testament*]
OB .... Obiit [*He, or She, Died*] [*Latin*]
ob............ Obiter [*Incidentally*] [*Latin*] (GPO)
OB .... Obituary Notice (DSUE)
OB .... Objection (ROG)
OB .... Objective [*Microscopy*]
OB .... Objective Benefit (MAE)
OB .... Obligation (ROG)
OB .... Obligation Bond
OB .... Obligatory
OB .... Obliteration
OB .... Obliterative Bronchiolitis [*Medicine*] (MELL)
ob............ Oblong [*Bookbinding*] (WDMC)
OB .... Oblong
ob............ Oboe (WDAA)
OB .... Oboe
OB .... Obolus [*Coin*] [*Latin*] (ADA)
OB .... O'Brien Energy & Resources Ltd. [*Toronto Stock Exchange symbol*]
OB .... Obscure (KSC)
OB .... Observation (WGA)
OB .... Observation Balloon (SAUS)
OB .... Observed Bearing [*Navigation*]
OB .... Obsolete (AABC)
OB .... Obstetrician
ob............ Obstetrics (SHCU)
OB .... Obstetrics [*Medicine*]
OB .... Obtain [*Telegraphy*] (PCTE)
OB .... Obtuse Bisectrix [*Crystallography*]
ob............ Obvious (ADWA)
OB .... Occult Bleeding [*Medicine*]
OB +......... Occult Blood Positive [*Medicine*] (DAVI)
OB .... Occupational Behavior
OB .... Ocean Beach (SAUS)
OB .... Ocean Bottom
OB .... Octagon Barrel [*Gunnery*]
OB .... Octal-to-Binary [*Computer science*] (BUR)
OB .... Octave Band
O-B .... Oerlikon-Buehrle [*Switzerland*]
OB .... Off-Broadway (WGA)
OB .... Offensive Back [*Football*]
OB .... Official Board of Ballroom Dancing [*British*] (BI)
OB .... Official Bulletin (SAUS)
OB .... Official Bulletin. International Commission for Air Navigation [*A publication*] (DLA)
OB .... Official Business (ELAL)
O-B .... Ohio Brass Co. (EFIS)
OB .... Oil Base (SAUS)
OB .... Oil Bearing (DCTA)
OB .... Oil Bomb
OB .... Oil-Break (SAUS)
OB .... Old Babylonian (BJA)
OB .... [*The*] Old Bailey [*London court*]
OB .... Old Bonded [*Whiskey*] (ROG)
OB .... Old Boy [*Communications operators' colloquialism*]
OB .... Old Buildings [*British Admiralty*]
OB .... Olecranon Bursitis [*Medicine*] (MELL)
OB .... Oligoclonal Band [*Analytical biochemistry*]
OB .... Ombudsman for Business [*Department of Commerce*]
OB .... On Base [*Baseball*] (GOBB)
OB .... On Being: the Servant's Servant [*A publication*] (APTA)
OB .... On Board
O/B........... Onboard (NAKS)
OB .... One-Bearing (SAUS)
OB .... Opal Air [*ICAO designator*] (AD)
OB .... Opening of Books
ob............ Opera Buffa [*Music*] (GROV)
OB .... Operating Base [*Navy*]
OB .... Operating Budget (AFM)
OB .... Operational Base [*Navy*]
OB .... Operation Brotherhood
OB .... Operations Branch (HEAS)
OB .... Optical Bench (SAUS)
OB .... Optometrists' Board [*Australian Capital Territory*]
OB .... Or Better [*Business term*]
OB .... Ordered Back
OB .... Order of Battle [*Military*]
OB .... Order of Burma [*British military*] (DMA)
OB .... Order of the Bath
OB .... Order of the Boer People (SAUS)
OB .... Order of the Boer State (SAUS)
OB .... Ordnance Battalion [*Navy*]
OB .... Ordnance Board [*Navy*]
OB .... Oregon Ballet
OB .... Organization Blocks (SAUS)
OB .... Organized Baseball (NDBD)
OB .... Orgelbuechlein [*Little Organ Book*] [*Bach*] [*Music*]
OB .... Orientalische Bibliographie [*A publication*] (BJA)
OB .... Orthodontic Bulletin [*Medicine*] [*Journal*] (EDAA)
OB .... Ortsbatterie [*Local Battery*] [*German military - World War II*]
OB .... Outboard
ob............ Outboard Buffer (SAUS)
OB .... Outbound (WDAA)
OB .... Out of Bounds [*Sports*] (GOBB)
OB .... Out-of-Business (OICC)
OB .... Output Block (SAUS)
OB .... Output Buffer [*Computer science*]
OB .... Output Bus [*Computer science*]
OB .... Outside Broadcast (EY)
OB .... Outside Bugs [*Nonresident staff at a school*] [*British*] (DSUE)
OB .... Outward Bound (EA)
OB .... Over Bath [*Classified advertising*] (ADA)
OB .... Overboard (AAG)
OB .... Over Bought (SAUS)
OB .... Overburden (SAUS)
OB .... Overseas Brats [*Commercial firm*] (EA)
OB .... Overseas Broadcast [*or Broadcasting*] (IAA)
OB .... Owena Bank [*Nigeria*]
OB .... Own Brand (MHDB)
OB .... Oxford Biographies [*A publication*]
OB .... Peru [*International civil aircraft marking*] (ODBW)
OB1KB....... Order of Battle Version 1 Knowledge Based (SAUS)
OBA.......... Barrie Public Library, Ontario [*Library symbol*] [*National Library of Canada*] (NLC)
OBA.......... Oasis Bungera [*Antarctica*] [*Seismograph station code, US Geological Survey*] [*Closed*] (SEIS)
OBA.......... Oba, ON [*American Association of Railroads railroad junction routing code*]
OBA.......... Oberhasli Breeders of America (EA)
OBA.......... Object Behavior Analysis [*Computer science*]
OBA.......... Octave Band Analyzer
OBA.......... Off Boresight Angle (MCD)
OBA.......... Office of Business Administration [*Later, Office of Administration*] [*NASA*]
OBA.......... Office of Business Affairs [*Northern Territory, Australia*]
OBA.......... Office of Business Analysis [*Information service or system*] (IID)

OBA Oil Burning Apparatus (SAUS)
OBA On-Base Average [*Baseball term*] (NDBD)
OBA Online Banking Association (SAUS)
OBA Open Broadcasting Authority [*Noncommercial TV channel*] [*British*]
OBA Operating Basis Accident [*Environmental science*] (COE)
OBA Operating Budget Authority (MCD)
OBA Optical Barrel Assembly (ACAE)
OBA Optical Base Assembly (KSC)
OBA Optical Bleaching Agent (SAUS)
OBA Optical Brightening Agents
OBA Ornithyl-Beta-Alanine [*Biochemistry*]
OBA Outward Bound Australia
OBA Over Burner Air
OBA Oxygen Breathing Apparatus
OBAA Oil Burning Apparatus Association (BUAC)
OBAALA Organisation for Black Arts Advancement and Learning Activities [*British*]
OBAC One Bit Adder Computer (SAUS)
Obad Obadiah [*Old Testament book*]
OBAD Object Average Optical Density [*Microscopy*]
OBAD Operating Budget Authority Document [*Military*] (AFIT)
OBADRS Octave Band Automatic Data Reduction System
OBAG Georgian Bay Regional Library, Barrie, Ontario [*Library symbol*] [*National Library of Canada*] (NLC)
OBAGC Georgian College of Applied Arts and Technology, Barrie, Ontario [*Library symbol*] [*National Library of Canada*] (NLC)
OBAL Balmertown Public Library, Ontario [*Library symbol*] [*National Library of Canada*] (NLC)
OBAN Bancroft Public Library, Ontario [*Library symbol*] [*National Library of Canada*] (NLC)
OBAN Operating Budget Account Number [*Air Force*]
OBAN United Public Library, Carlow, Dungannon and Mayo Townships, Bancroft, Ontario (SAUS)
OB & F Ollivier, Bell, and Fitzgerald's Court of Appeal Reports [*1878-80*] [*New Zealand*] [*A publication*] (DLA)
OB & F (CA) Ollivier, Bell, and Fitzgerald's Court of Appeal Reports [*1878-80*] [*New Zealand*] [*A publication*] (DLA)
OB & FNZ Ollivier, Bell, and Fitzgerald's New Zealand Reports [*A publication*] (DLA)
OB & F (SC) Ollivier, Bell, and Fitzgerald's Supreme Court Reports [*New Zealand*] [*A publication*] (DLA)
OB & PA Office of Budget and Program Analysis [*Department of Agriculture*] (GFGA)
Ob&Sol Objection and Solution (SAUS)
OBANU United Public Library, Carlow, Dungannon, and Mayo Townships, Bancroft, Ontario [*Library symbol*] [*National Library of Canada*] (BIB)
OBAP Organization of Black Airline Pilots (EA)
OBAR Ohio Bar (NITA)
OBAR Ohio Bar Automated Research (SAUS)
OBarb Barberton Public Library, Barberton, OH [*Library symbol*] [*Library of Congress*] (LCLS)
OBarn Barnesville Public Library, Barnesville, OH [*Library symbol*] [*Library of Congress*] (LCLS)
OBAS Optibase, Ltd. [*NASDAQ symbol*] (NASQ)
OBAS Organ Builders' Amalgamated Society [*A union*] [*British*]
OBAS Simcoe County Co-Op, Barrie, Ontario [*Library symbol*] [*National Library of Canada*] (NLC)
OBAT Augusta Township Public Library, Brockville, Ontario [*Library symbol*] [*National Library of Canada*] (NLC)
OBat Clermont County Public Library, Batavia, OH [*Library symbol*] [*Library of Congress*] (LCLS)
OBAT Olympic International Bank & Trust Co. (SAUS)
OBATA Ontario Biological Aeration Tillage Association (SAUS)
OBatC Clermont General and Technical College, Batavia, OH [*Library symbol*] [*Library of Congress*] (LCLS)
OBatH Clermont Mercy Hospital, Batavia, OH [*Library symbol*] [*Library of Congress*] (LCLS)
OBAWS On-Board Aircraft Weighing System (MCD)
OBB Austrian Farmer's Association [*Political party*] (PSAP)
OBB Barry's Bay Public Library, Ontario [*Library symbol*] [*National Library of Canada*] (NLC)
OBB Obbligato [*Essential*] [*Music*]
OBB Obsidian Butte [*California*] [*Seismograph station code, US Geological Survey*] (SEIS)
OBB Oesterreichische Bundesbahnen [*Austrian Federal Railways*]
OBB Old Battleship [*Navy*]
OBB On-Board Buffer (CIST)
OBB One Button Boy (SAUS)
OBB Operation Better Block
OBB Own Bed Bath [*Medicine*] (DMAA)
OBB Oxybisbenzene [*Organic chemistry*]
OBBB Bahrain [*Bahrain*] [*ICAO location identifier*] (ICLI)
OBBD Official Board of Ballroom Dancing [*British*]
OBBFC Official Betty Boop Fan Club (EA)
OBBI Bahrain/International [*Bahrain*] [*ICAO location identifier*] (ICLI)
Obbl Obbligato [*Essential*] [*Music*]
OBBM Brant County Historical Museum, Brantford, Ontario [*Library symbol*] [*National Library of Canada*] (NLC)
Obbmo Obbligatissimo [*Your Obedient Servant*] [*Italian*]
OBBMV Madawaska Valley District High School, Barry's Bay, Ontario [*Library symbol*] [*National Library of Canada*] (NLC)
OBBO Observation Balloon
OBC Barwick Community Library, Ontario [*Library symbol*] [*National Library of Canada*] (BIB)
OBC Obedience [*Telegraphy*] (PCTE)
OBC Obock [*Djibouti*] [*Airport symbol*] (OAG)
OBC Oceania Basketball Confederation [*Australia*] (EA)
OBC Off Boresight Correction [*Military*] (CAAL)
OBC Officer Basic Course [*Military*]
OBC Ohio Bell Communications, Inc. [*Cleveland*] [*Telecommunications*] (TSSD)
OBC Old Bottle Club of Great Britain (BUAC)
OBC Old Boys' Corps [*Military*] [*British*]
OBC On-Board Checkout [*Aircraft*]
OBC On-Board Computer (MCD)
OBC On-Board Controller [*Telecommunications*]
OBC One Big Computer [*Proposed model for automation of the New York and American stock exchanges*]
OBC Optical Bar Camera [*NASA*] (LAIN)
OBC Optical Bar Code (SAUS)
OBC Optical Barrel Camera (SAUS)
OBC Order of British Columbia [*Canada*] (DD)
OBC Order of Merit of British Columbia [*Canada*] (FOTI)
OBC Ore Bulk Carrier (SAUS)
OBC Osaka Broadcasting Corporation (SAUS)
OBC Ouachita Baptist College [*Arkadelphia, AR*] [*Later, OBU*]
OBC Outboard Boating Club of America [*Defunct*] (EA)
OBC Outer Back Cover (SAUS)
OBC Outside Back Cover [*Publishing*] (WDMC)
OBC Oversea Broadcasting (SAUS)
OBC Overseas Bankers' Club [*British*]
OBC Overseas Book Centre
OBC Oxide-Coated Brush Cathode
OBCA Office of Bank Customer Affairs [*FDIC*]
OBCAB Albion-Bolton Branch, Town of Caledon Public Libraries, Bolton, Ontario [*Library symbol*] [*National Library of Canada*] (NLC)
OBCC Olympic Broadcasting Corporation (SAUS)
OBCC Ore Bulk Car Container (SAUS)
OBC Carrier Ore Bulk Container Carrier (SAUS)
OBCCC Olympic Broadcasting Corp. [*NASDAQ symbol*] (COMM)
OBCC Carrier Ore Bulk Car Container Carrier (SAUS)
OBCCL Canada Cement Lafarge Ltd., Belleville, Ontario [*Library symbol*] [*National Library of Canada*] (NLC)
OBCE On-Board Checkout Equipment (MCD)
OBCE Operational Baseline Cost Estimate [*Army*]
OBCG O'Brien Cartage Company [*Common carrier symbol*]
OBCGEH Housewares and Home Entertainment Department, Canada General Electric Co. Ltd., Barrie, Ontario [*Library symbol*] [*National Library of Canada*] (NLC)
OBCH Overseas Booksellers' Clearing House (DGA)
OBCI Ocean Bio-Chem [*NASDAQ symbol*] (TTSB)
OBCI Ocean Bio-Chem, Inc. [*NASDAQ symbol*] (NQ)
OBCI On-Board Controller Interface [*Telecommunications*]
OBCIEP Ontario Breast Cancer Information Exchange Partnership (SAUS)
OBCO On-Board Checkout [*NASA*] (KSC)
OBCOOP Observation Control Optimization (SAUS)
OB/CP Observation/Command Post (DNAB)
OBCP Ortho-Benzyl-para-chlorophenol [*Disinfectant*]
OBCR Optical Bar Code Reader (NITA)
OBCs Backward Castes (India) [*Political party*] (PSAP)
OBCS Chromatographic Specialties Ltd., Brockville, Ontario [*Library symbol*] [*National Library of Canada*] (NLC)
OBCS On-Board Checkout Subsystem [*NASA*] (NASA)
OBCS On-Board Checkout [*Instrumentation*] System
OBCT Objective Brigade Combat Team
OBCU Orbicon [*Intermodal shipping container symbol*] (TVRC)
Obd Obadiah [*Old Testament book*] (BJA)
OBD Obtained [*Telegraphy*] (PCTE)
OBD Odorant-Binding Protein (DB)
OBD Off Board Drone (ACAE)
OBD Office of Business Development [*Economic Development Administration*]
o/bd Oil on Board (VRA)
OBD Omnibearing Distance
OBD On-Board Diagnostics [*Chrysler Corp.'s computer system*]
OBD Online Bugs Database (SAUS)
OBD Open Blade Damper (OA)
OBD Operational Base Development (AAG)
OBD Operation Buckle Down [*NHTSA*] (TAG)
OBD Optical Beam Deflection
OBD Ordnance Base Depot (SAUS)
OBD Organic Brain Disease
OBD Organization for Black Designers
OBDB On-Board Data Bank (DNAB)
OBDC On-Board Diagnostics Class
OBDC Open Database Connectivity [*Computer science*]
OBDC Otago Business Development Centre (SAUS)
OBDD Ordered Bicontinuous Double Diamond [*Phase structure*]
OBDD Ordered Binary Decision Diagram [*Computer science*] (VLIE)
OBDE Dollman Electronics Canada Ltd., Brampton, Ontario [*Library symbol*] [*National Library of Canada*] (NLC)
OBDH On Board Data Handling (ACAE)
OBDH On-Board Data Handling (SAUS)
OBDICS Order Backlog Delivery and Installation Control System (VLIE)
OBDIF Order of Battle Data Interchange Format (SAUS)
OBD-II On-Board Diagnostics, Second Generation [*Automotive engineering*]
OBDII On-oard Diagnostics-Second Generation
OB DK Observation Deck (WDAA)
OBDM On-Board Data Management (SAUS)

OBDO........ Oceanographic, Boarding, and Diving Officer [*Navy*] [*British*]
OBDT........ Obedient
Obdt-Srvt... Obedient Servant. [*Polite way to sign a letter*] [*Civil War term*]
OBDU........ Old Bushmills Distillery [*Intermodal shipping container symbol*] (TVRC)
OBDV........ Oat Blue Dwarf Virus [*Plant pathology*]
OBE.......... Belleville Public Library, Ontario [*Library symbol*] [*National Library of Canada*] (NLC)
OBE.......... Oberlin College, Oberlin, OH [*OCLC symbol*] (OCLC)
OBE.......... Offboard Expendables (SAUS)
OBE.......... Office of Biological Education (DAVI)
OBE.......... Office of Business Economics [*Later, Office of Economic Analysis*] [*Department of Commerce*]
OBE.......... Officer of the British Empire (SAUS)
OBE.......... Officer of the Most Excellent Order of the British Empire (WDAA)
OBE.......... Officer of the Order of the British Empire (NGC)
OBE.......... Okeechobee, FL [*Location identifier*] [*FAA*] (FAAL)
OBE.......... Onboard Electronics Operating Basis Earthquake (SAUS)
OBE.......... On-Board Equipment
OBE.......... One-Boson Exchange [*Physics*] (OA)
OBE.......... Online Banking Excellence (SAUS)
OBE.......... Open Both Ends (SAUS)
OBE.......... Operating Basis Earthquake [*Nuclear reactor*] (NRCH)
OBE.......... Operating Basis Event (IEEE)
OBE.......... Order of the British Empire [*Facetious translations: Old Boiled Egg, Other Buggers' Efforts*]
OBE.......... Other Buggers Efforts (SAUS)
OBE.......... Ottawa Board of Education, Library Services Centre [*UTLAS symbol*]
OBE.......... Outcome-Based Education [*School reform*]
OBE.......... Outerback End
OBE.......... Out-of-Body Experience [*Parapsychology*]
OBE.......... Output Buffer Empty [*Computer science*] (VLIE)
OBE.......... Overcome [*or Overtaken*] by Events
OBE.......... Overtaken by Events (SAUS)
OBEA........ Ontario Business Education Association (SAUS)
OBEA........ Oregon Business Education Association (EDAC)
OBEAB....... Beaverton Branch, Brock Township Public Library, Ontario [*Library symbol*] [*National Library of Canada*] (BIB)
OBEAR...... Beardmore Public Library, Ontario [*Library symbol*] [*National Library of Canada*] (NLC)
OBEATE..... Beaverton-Thorah Eldon Historical Society, Inc., Ontario [*Library symbol*] [*National Library of Canada*] (NLC)
OBEC........ Organization for Economic Cooperation and Development (EBF)
OBECO...... Outboard Engine Cutoff [*NASA*] (KSC)
OBED........ Beamsville District Secondary School, Ontario [*Library symbol*] [*National Library of Canada*] (NLC)
OBed........ Bedford Public Library, Bedford, OH [*Library symbol*] [*Library of Congress*] (LCLS)
OBedF....... Ferro Corp., Chemical Library, Bedford, OH [*Library symbol*] [*Library of Congress*] (LCLS)
OBEDS...... Deloro Stellite Co., Belleville, Ontario [*Library symbol*] [*National Library of Canada*] (BIB)
OBEE........ Beeton Public Library, Ontario [*Library symbol*] [*National Library of Canada*] (BIB)
OBEGOSC... Organizational Effectiveness General Officer Steering Committee (MCD)
OBEH........ Hastings County Historical Society, Belleville, Ontario [*Library symbol*] [*National Library of Canada*] (BIB)
OBEHP...... Hastings and Prince Edward County Health Unit, Belleville, Ontario [*Library symbol*] [*National Library of Canada*] (BIB)
OBEL........ Loyalist College of Applied Arts and Technology, Belleville, Ontario [*Library symbol*] [*National Library of Canada*] (NLC)
Obel......... Obelisk (SAUS)
OBELF....... Fleming Branch, Lincoln Public Library, Beamsville, Ontario [*Library symbol*] [*National Library of Canada*] (BIB)
OBEM........ Beachville Ye Olde Museum, Ontario [*Library symbol*] [*National Library of Canada*] (BIB)
OBEM........ Object-Based Equipment Model (AAEL)
OBEM........ On-Board Emissions Measurement [*Automotive engineering*]
OBEM........ One-Boson Exchange Model
OBEM........ Operational Battery Effectiveness Model (MCD)
OBEMLA.... Office of Bilingual Education and Minority Language Affairs [*Department of Education*] (GFGA)
O Ben....... Old Benloe's Reports, English Common Pleas [*1486-1580*] [*A publication*] (DLA)
OBENFX..... Olive Branch Entry Fix (SAUS)
O Benl...... Old Benloe's Reports, English Common Pleas [*1486-1580*] [*A publication*] (DLA)
OBEP........ One-Boson Exchange Potential
OBER........ Oberlin Trailers [*NCIC trailer make code*]
OBEr......... OB [*Out-of-the-Body*] Experient [*Parapsychology*]
OBER........ Office of Biological and Environmental Research (HGEN)
OBerB....... Baldwin-Wallace College, Berea, OH [*Library symbol*] [*Library of Congress*] (LCLS)
OBERS...... Office of Business Economics Research Service (NRCH)
OBERST..... Oberstimme [*Upper Part*] [*Music*]
OBERW...... Oberwerk [*Upper Work*] [*Music*]
OBES........ Office of Basic Energy Sciences (COE)
OBES........ Office of Basic Energy Services [*Department of Energy*]
OBES........ Office of Basic Engineering Sciences (SAUS)
OBES........ Ohio Bureau of Employment Services (SAUS)
OBES........ Orthonormal Basis of an Error Space [*Statistics*]
OBESA....... Stephens-Adamson, Belleville, Ontario [*Library symbol*] [*National Library of Canada*] (NLC)
OBESG...... Office of Basic Energy Science/Geosciences [*Department of Energy*]
Obesity&Bariatric Med... Obesity and Bariatric Medicine (SAUS)
OBESSI...... Organizing Bureau of European School Student Unions (SAUS)
OBESSU..... Organising Bureau of European School Student Unions (EAIO)
OBEV........ Oxford Book of English Verse (SAUS)
OBEWS...... On-Board Electronic Warfare Simulation [*Air Force*]
OBEWS...... On-Board Electronic Warfare System [*Military*] (POLM)
OBEX........ Object Exchange [*Computer science*] (PCM)
OBEXFX.... Olive Branch Exit Fix (SAUS)
OBF.......... Octave Band Filter
OBF.......... One-Bar Function (OA)
OBF.......... Open Book Fracture [*Medicine*] (MELL)
OBF.......... Operating Basis Flood (SAUS)
OBF.......... Operational Base Facility
OBF.......... Organ Blood Flow [*Physiology*]
OBF.......... Ottawa Board of Education, Library Services Centre (Films) [*UTLAS symbol*]
OBF.......... Output Buffer Full [*Computer science*] (IAA)
OBFAR....... Burks Falls, Armour, and Ryerson Union Library, Burks Falls, Ontario [*Library symbol*] [*National Library of Canada*] (NLC)
OBFC........ Barriefield Branch, Frontenac County Library, Ontario [*Library symbol*] [*National Library of Canada*] (BIB)
OBFC........ O'Leary Brothers Fan Club (EA)
OBFCS...... On Board Fire Control System (SAUS)
OBFM........ Octagon Barrel Full Magazine [*Gunnery*]
OBFM........ Offensive Basic Flight Manoeuvres (SAUS)
OBFM........ On or Before Full Moon [*Freemasonry*] (ROG)
OBFNO...... Northern Ontario Public School Principals' Association, Burks Falls, Ontario [*Library symbol*] [*National Library of Canada*] (NLC)
OBFS........ Octave Band Filter Set
OBFS........ Office of Basic Energy Services (SAUS)
OBFS........ Offshore Bulk Fuel System
OBFS........ Organization of Biological Field Stations (EA)
OBFS........ Overseas Base Facilities Summary [*Navy*]
OBFSSU..... Organising Bureau of European School Student Unions (SAUS)
obfusc....... obfuscated (SAUS)
Ob G......... Obergericht [*Court of Appeal*] [*German*] (DLA)
OBG.......... Oberg Industries Ltd. [*Vancouver Stock Exchange symbol*]
OBG.......... Obigarm [*Former USSR*] [*Seismograph station code, US Geological Survey*] [*Closed*] (SEIS)
OBG.......... O'Brien & Gere Limited (EFIS)
OBG.......... Obstetrics-Gynecology [*Medicine*]
OBG.......... Obtaining [*Telegraphy*] (PCTE)
OBG.......... Oldie but Goodie [*Music*]
OBGA........ Office of Block Grant Assistance (SAUS)
OBgCE....... Conneaut Elementary School, Bowling Green, OH [*Library symbol*] [*Library of Congress*] (LCLS)
OBgCrE...... Crim Elementary School, Bowling Green, OH [*Library symbol*] [*Library of Congress*] (LCLS)
ob gene..... Obese Gene [*Medicine*] (MELL)
OBGI......... Orion Broadcasting Group, Inc. (SAUS)
OBgJH....... Bowling Green Junior High School, Bowling Green, OH [*Library symbol*] [*Library of Congress*] (LCLS)
OBgKE....... Kenwood Elementary School, Bowling Green, OH [*Library symbol*] [*Library of Congress*] (LCLS)
OBgRE....... Ridge Elementary School, Bowling Green, OH [*Library symbol*] [*Library of Congress*] (LCLS)
OBGS........ On-Board Gunnery Simulator (PDAA)
OBGS........ Orbital Bombardment Guidance System
OBgSH....... Bowling Green Senior High School, Bowling Green, OH [*Library symbol*] [*Library of Congress*] (LCLS)
OBgSME.... South Main Elementary School, Bowling Green, OH [*Library symbol*] [*Library of Congress*] (LCLS)
OBGT........ Old Babylonian Grammatical Texts [*A publication*] (BJA)
OBgU........ Bowling Green State University, Bowling Green, OH [*Library symbol*] [*Library of Congress*] (LCLS)
OBgU-C..... Bowling Green State University, Center for Archival Collections, Bowling Green, OH [*Library symbol*] [*Library of Congress*] (LCLS)
OB-GYN..... Obstetrical-Gynecological (SAUS)
OB-GYN..... Obstetrician-Gynecologist (PAZ)
OB-GYN..... Obstetrics-Gynecology [*Medicine*]
ob-gyn...... Obstetrics/Gynecology (SHCU)
OBH.......... Office Busy Hour [*Telecommunications*] (TEL)
OBH.......... Oil Bath Heater
OBH.......... Old Berkeley Hunt [*British*]
OBH.......... Old Berkshire Hounds [*British*]
OBH.......... Old Highland Blend [*Whisky*] (ROG)
OBH.......... Operational Biomedical Harness
OBH.......... Wolbach, NE [*Location identifier*] [*FAA*] (FAAL)
OBHFC...... Official Bobby Hart Fan Club (EA)
OBHT........ Tecumseh Township Public Library, Bond Head, Ontario [*Library symbol*] [*National Library of Canada*] (BIB)
OBI........... Obidos [*Brazil*] [*Airport symbol*] (AD)
obi........... obiectum (SAUS)
OBI........... Obihiro [*Japan*] [*Seismograph station code, US Geological Survey*] (SEIS)
OBI........... Obligated Involuntary Officer [*Military*]
OBI........... Obliterate (SAUS)
OBI........... Office du Baccalaureat International [*International Baccalaureate Office - IBO*] (EAIO)
OBI........... Office of Basic Instrumentation [*National Bureau of Standards*]
OBI........... Old Babylonian Inscriptions [*A publication*] (BJA)
OBI........... Omnibearing Indicator [*Radio*]
OBI........... Online Book Initiative [*Trademark name*] [*Internet*]
OBI........... Open-Back Inclinable
OBI........... Open-Back Inclinable Press [*Manufacturing term*]

OBI.......... Open Buying on the Internet [*Computer science*]
OBI.......... Operation Blessing International [*An association*]
OBI.......... Optical-Beam-Induced (SAUS)
OBI.......... Order of British India
OBI.......... Organisation du Baccalaureat International [*International Baccalaureate Organisation - IBO*] (EAIO)
OBI.......... Osaka Bioscience Institute [*Japan*]
OBIA......... Ontario Brain Injury Association (SAUS)
OBIC......... Optical Beam Induced Contrast (SAUS)
OBIC......... Optical Beam Induced Current [*Electronics*] (AAEL)
OBIC......... Optical-Beam-Induced Current (SAUS)
O BID........ Omni Bidus [*Every Two Days*] [*Pharmacy*] (ROG)
OBIE......... Obie Media Corp. [*NASDAQ symbol*] (SAG)
ObieMed.... Obie Media Corp. [*Associated Press*] (SAG)
OBIFC....... Osmond Boys International Fan Club (EA)
OBIFCO...... On-Board In-Flight Checkout (MCD)
OBIG......... Oesterreichisches Bundesinstitut fuer Gesundheitswesen [*Austrian National Institute for Public Health*] [*Information service or system*] (IID)
OBIGGS..... On-Board Inert Gas Generator System [*Aviation*] (MCD)
O BIH........ Omni Bihora [*Every Two Hours*] [*Pharmacy*] (ROG)
OBINXTO... Obiit in Christo [*Died in Christ*] [*Latin*]
OBIP......... Ontario Business Incentive Program (SAUS)
OBI Press... Open Back Inclinable Press (SAUS)
OBIPS....... Optical Band Imager and Photometer System [*Aerospace*]
OBIRCH..... Optical-Beam-Induced Resistance Change (SAUS)
OBIS......... Optical Backplane Interconnect System programme (SAUS)
OBIS......... Optimum Burn-In Screening
OBIS......... Outdoor Biology Instructional Strategies [*National Science Foundation project*]
OBIT......... Obiit [*He, or She, Died*] [*Latin*]
Obit......... Obiter [*A publication*]
OBIT......... Obituary (GOBB)
obit......... Obituary [*Journalism*] [*Also, ob*] (WDMC)
OBIT......... Obituary Notice (DSUE)
OBIU......... On-Board Interface Unit (DWSG)
OBIWR...... Whitefish River Band Public Library, Birch Island, Ontario [*Library symbol*] [*National Library of Canada*] (NLC)
OBJ.......... Intermediate Object Code File [*Computer science*]
OBJ.......... Object (AAG)
obj.......... Object (VRA)
OBJ.......... Object File (SAUS)
OBJ.......... Objection (WDAA)
obj.......... Objection (WDAA)
Obj.......... Objective (AMHC)
OBJ.......... Oklahoma Bar Association. Journal [*A publication*] (DLA)
OBJ.......... Operation Buster-Jangle [*Atomic weapons testing*]
OBJ.......... Orthodox Black Jews (BJA)
OBJ.......... Query Object Systems [*AMEX symbol*]
ObjDes...... Object Design, Inc. [*Associated Press*] (SAG)
OBJN......... Objection
OBJS......... ObjectShare [*NASDAQ symbol*]
OBJS......... Object Share, Inc. [*NASDAQ symbol*] (NASQ)
ObjSoft...... ObjectSoft Corp. [*Associated Press*] (SAG)
ObjSys...... Objective Systems Integrators, Inc. [*Associated Press*] (SAG)
OBJV......... Objective (MSA)
OBK.......... Northbrook, IL [*Location identifier*] [*FAA*] (FAAL)
OBK.......... Open Breaker Keying (SAUS)
OBK.......... Organisation pour l'Amenagement et le Developpement du Bassin de la Riviere Kagera [*Organization for the Management and Development of the Kagera River Basin - KBO*] (EAIO)
OBL.......... League of Off-Broadway Theatres and Producers (EA)
OBL.......... Object-Based Language (AAEL)
OBL.......... Oblast [*Governmental subdivision in USSR corresponding to a province or state*]
OBL.......... Obligation (ADA)
OBL.......... Obligato [*Obbligato*] [*Music*] (ROG)
OBL.......... Oblique (AABC)
obl.......... Oblique (STED)
obl.......... Oblong [*Bookbinding*] (WDMC)
OBL.......... Oblong
obl.......... obloquy (SAUS)
OBL.......... Ocean Beach Library (SAUS)
OBL.......... Oceanic Boundary Layer
OBL.......... Office of Business Liaison
OBL.......... Office of Business Loans [*Economic Development Administration*]
OBL.......... Ohio Barge Line (SAUS)
OBL.......... Older Bill of Lading (SAUS)
OBL.......... One Block Look-Ahead [*Computer science*]
obl.......... Opera-Ballet [*Music*] (GROV)
OBL.......... Operational Base Launch [*Air Force*]
OBL.......... Order Bill of Lading [*Shipping*]
OBL.......... Order of the Brave Librarian (SAUS)
OBL.......... Osama Bin Laden
OBL.......... Outlined Black Letters [*Tire design*]
OBL.......... Outside of the Battery Limits [*Engineering economics*]
OBL.......... Outstanding Balance List [*IRS*]
OBla......... Blanchester Public Library, Blanchester, OH [*Library symbol*] [*Library of Congress*] (LCLS)
OBLAC....... Bath Branch, Lennox and Addington County Public Library, Ontario [*Library symbol*] [*National Library of Canada*] (NLC)
OBLACS..... Sandburst Branch, Lennox and Addington County Public Library, Bath, Ontario [*Library symbol*] [*National Library of Canada*] (BIB)
OBLAT....... Oblatum [*Cachet*] [*Pharmacy*]
OBLAUTH... Obligation Authority [*Army*] (AABC)
OBIC......... Bluffton College, Bluffton, OH [*Library symbol*] [*Library of Congress*] (LCLS)
OBIC-M...... Bluffton College, Mennonite Historical Library, Bluffton, OH [*Library symbol*] [*Library of Congress*] (LCLS)
OBLG........ Obligate (AABC)
OBLH........ Bloomfield-Hallowell Union Library, Bloomfield, Ontario [*Library symbol*] [*National Library of Canada*] (BIB)
OBLI......... Oxford and Bucks Light Infantry [*Military unit*] [*British*]
Oblig........ Obligation (TBD)
OBLIGN..... Obligation (ROG)
OBLISERV... Obligated Services of [*numbers of months indicated*] Required [*Navy*]
OBLISERVNATRA... Obligated to Serve Three and One-Half Years Following Date of Completion of Training within the Naval Air Training Command (SAUS)
OBLISERVONEASIX... Obligated to Serve on Active Duty One Year for Each Six Months Schooling or Fraction Thereof [*Navy*]
OBLISERVTHREETIME... Obligated to Serve on Active Duty a Period Three Times the Length of Period of Education [*Navy*]
OBLISERVTWOYR... Obligated to Serve on Active Duty a Period of Two Years [*Navy*]
OBLN........ Obligation (AFM)
OBLR........ Blind River Public Library, Ontario [*Library symbol*] [*National Library of Canada*] (NLC)
Obl Serv.... Obligation Service (SAUS)
OBLu........ Old Babylonian Version of Lu [*A publication*] (BJA)
OBlv......... Bliss Memorial Public Library, Bloomville, OH [*Library symbol*] [*Library of Congress*] (LCLS)
OBM......... Aviaobshemash [*Former USSR*] [*FAA designator*] (FAAC)
OBM......... Morobe [*Papua New Guinea*] [*Airport symbol*] (OAG)
OBM......... Oberlin College, Conservatory of Music, Library, Oberlin, OH [*OCLC symbol*] (OCLC)
OBM......... Ocean Biogeochemical Model
OBM......... Ogilvy Benson & Mather Ltd. (EFIS)
OBM......... Oil-Base Mud (SAUS)
OBM......... Ontario Basic Mapping (SAUS)
OBM......... Optical Business Machines, Inc. (SAUS)
OBM......... Optimal Body Mass [*Ecology*]
OBM......... Ordnance Bench Mark (IAA)
OBM......... Oriental Boat Mission [*Later, International Missions*] (EA)
OBM......... Oxygen-Bottom Blown Maxhutte (SAUS)
OBM......... Ulan Bator [*Mongolia*] [*Seismograph station code, US Geological Survey*] [*Closed*] (SEIS)
OBMA....... Outboard Boat Manufacturers Association [*Later, NMMA*] (EA)
OBMC....... Officers' Basic Military Corps [*Air Force*]
OBMC....... Outbound Midcourse Correction [*NASA*] (KSC)
Ob MOK..... Oberbefehlshaber der Marine-Oberkommandos (SAUS)
OBMP....... Bruce Mines and Plummer Additional Union Public Library, Bruce Mines, Ontario [*Library symbol*] [*National Library of Canada*] (NLC)
OBMPH..... Observed Miles per Hour [*Automotive emissions*]
OBMS....... Objectives-Based Management System (ADA)
OBMZ....... Old Ben #21 Mine [*Federal Railroad Administration identification code*]
OBN.......... Oban [*Scotland*] [*Airport symbol*] (OAG)
OBN.......... Obninsk [*Former USSR*] [*Seismograph station code, US Geological Survey*] (SEIS)
OBN.......... Occult Blood Negative [*Medicine*] (DAVI)
OBN.......... Office Balancing Network [*Telecommunications*] (TEL)
OBN.......... Office of Biochemical Nomenclature [*NAS-NRC*]
OBN.......... On-Board Navigation
OBN.......... Open Library Network (SAUS)
OBN.......... Optical Broadband Network (SAUS)
OBN.......... Out-of-Band Noise
OBNA........ Only But Not All (NITA)
OBNE........ Department 9911, Northern Telecom Ltd., Belleville, Ontario [*Library symbol*] [*National Library of Canada*] [*Obsolete*] (NLC)
OBNM....... On or Before New Moon [*Freemasonry*] (ROG)
OBNQ........ Oborn Transfer and Storage Company [*Common carrier symbol*]
OBNR........ Oil Burner Route (SAUS)
OBNR........ Olive Branch Route (SAUS)
OBNREN Point... Oil Burner Entry Point (SAUS)
OBNREX Point... Oil Burner Exit Point (SAUS)
OBNTC...... Old Boys Network Turtle Club (EA)
OBO.......... Obihiro [*Japan*] [*Airport symbol*] (OAG)
OBO.......... Obock [*Djibouti*] [*Seismograph station code, US Geological Survey*] (SEIS)
OBO.......... Official Business Only (AFM)
OBO.......... Oil/Bulk/On Carrier (SAUS)
OBO.......... Oil/Bulk/Ore (SAUS)
OBO.......... Oil/Bulk/Ore Carrier [*Multipurpose bulk carrier*] (DS)
OBO.......... On Behalf Of [*Telegraphy*] (PCTE)
obo.......... Or Best Offer (SHCU)
OBO.......... Or Best Offer [*Classified advertising*]
OBO.......... Orbital Bomber (IAA)
OBO.......... Order Book Official [*Investment term*]
OBO.......... Order by Order
O/B/O....... Ore/Bulk/Oil [*Bulk carrier vessel*]
OBO.......... Ore/Bulk/Oil carrier (SAUS)
OBO.......... Organization of Bricklin Owners (EA)
OBO.......... Output Back-Off (SAUS)
OBOA........ Ontario Building Officials Association [*Canada*] (AAGC)
OBOC........ Ore/Bulk/Oil Carrier (SAUS)
OBO Carrier... Oil/Bulk/Oil Carrier (SAUS)
OBO Carrier... Oil/Bulk/Ore Carrier (SAUS)

OB/OD .... Open Burning/Open Detonation [*Military*]
OBOE .... Observed Bombing of Enemy
OBOE .... Offensive Built Operational Environment (ACAE)
OBOE .... Offensive Burst Operating Environment
OBOE .... Offshore Buoy-Observing Equipment (PDAA)
OBOE .... Offshore Buoy Observing System (SAUS)
OBOE Radar... Observed Bombing of Enemy Radar (SAUS)
OBOF .... Old Buffer over Forty [*Elderly recruits*] [*World War I*] [*British*]
OBOG .... On-Board Oxygen-Generation [*For military aviation*]
OBOGS ...... On-Board Oxygen Generating System [*Navy*] (CAAL)
OBOLC ...... Caledon Public Libraries, Bolton, Ontario [*Library symbol*] [*National Library of Canada*] (NLC)
OBOM .... Bowmanville Museum, Ontario [*Library symbol*] [*National Library of Canada*] (BIB)
OBON .... Newcastle Public Library Board, Bowmanville, Ontario [*Library symbol*] [*National Library of Canada*] (NLC)
OBONF ...... Bonfield Public Library, Ontario [*Library symbol*] [*National Library of Canada*] (NLC)
OBOP .... Observatory Operations Group [*National Oceanic and Atmospheric Administration*] (RCD)
OBOS .... Ore/Bulk/Oil Ship (SAUS)
OBOS .... Our Bodies Ourselves [*A publication*]
OBP .... Occult Blood Positive [*Medicine*] (DAVI)
OBP .... Occupational Back Pain
OBP .... Octyl Benzyl Phthalate (EDCT)
OBP .... Odorant-Binding Protein [*Biochemistry*]
OBP .... Offensive Beating Posture (SAUS)
OBP .... Offshore Biological Programme (SAUS)
OBP .... Oil Breather Pressure
OBP .... On-Base Percentage [*Baseball*]
OBP .... On-Board Processing (SAUS)
OBP .... On-Board Processor
OBP .... On-Line Benefits Processing
OBP .... Open Break Position [*Dancing*]
OBP .... Ordinary Bulb Plate (SAUS)
OBP .... Osteoporosis and Back Pain [*Medicine*] (MELL)
OBP .... Outer (Edge of) Basal Piece
OBP .... Ova, Blood, and Parasites [*Medicine*] (MAE)
obp .... Oxygen at High Pressure (AD)
OBPA .... Office of Budget and Program Analysis
OBPA .... Ogdensburg Bridge & Port Authority [*Federal Railroad Administration identification code*]
OBPA .... Outer Banks Protection Act (AAGC)
OBPA .... Oxybisphenoxarsine [*Organic chemistry*]
OBPC .... Optical Bar Panoramic Camera (SAUS)
OB PH .... Oblique Photography (WDAA)
OBPH .... People Helping People, Inc., Brantford, Ontario [*Library symbol*] [*National Library of Canada*] (NLC)
OBPI .... Otisville BioPharm, Inc. (SAUS)
OBPOE ...... L'Ordre de Bienfaisance et de Protection de l'Ordre des Elans [*Association*] [*Canada*] (EAIO)
OBQ .... Obscure [*Telegraphy*] (PCTE)
OBQ .... Optometrists' Board of Queensland
OBQD .... Obscured [*Telegraphy*] (PCTE)
OBQG .... Obscuring [*Telegraphy*] (PCTE)
OBQY .... Obscurity [*Telegraphy*] (PCTE)
OBR .... Bradford Public Library, Ontario [*Library symbol*] [*National Library of Canada*] (NLC)
OBR .... Office of Budget and Reports
OBR .... Ohio Board of Regents (SAUS)
OBR .... One-Button-Recording [*Video technology*]
OBR .... Optical Bar Code
OBR .... Optical Bar Code Reader (MHDB)
OBR .... Optical Bar Recognition [*Commonly known as a bar code*] (WDMC)
OBR .... Optical Beam Riding (SAUS)
OBR .... Origin of Bidirectional Replication [*Genetics*]
OBR .... Osteoporosis from Bed Rest [*Medicine*] (MELL)
OBR .... Outboard Recorder [*Computer science*] (BUR)
OBR .... Outboard Recording (SAUS)
OBR .... Outbound Record [*Communications term*] (DCT)
OBR .... Owens, B. R., Montebello CA [*STAC*]
OBRA .... Brampton Public Library, Ontario [*Library symbol*] [*National Library of Canada*] (NLC)
OBRA .... Office of Business Research and Analysis [*Department of Commerce*]
OBRA .... Omnibus Budget Reconciliation Act [*1987*]
OBRA .... Omnibus Budget Reconciliation Act of 1990 (COE)
OBRA .... Overseas Broadcasting Representatives Association (IAA)
OBRAC ...... Bracebridge Public Library, Ontario [*Library symbol*] [*National Library of Canada*] (NLC)
OBRAD ...... Oblate Radial (PDAA)
OBRAM ...... Chinguacousy Township Public Library, Bramalea, Ontario [*Library symbol*] [*National Library of Canada*] (NLC)
OBRAMB .... Bell Northern Research, Bramalea, Ontario [*Library symbol*] [*National Library of Canada*] (NLC)
OBRANT ..... Northern Telecom, Brampton, Ontario [*Library symbol*] [*National Library of Canada*] (NLC)
OBRAPA ..... Archives, Region of Peel, Brampton, Ontario [*Library symbol*] [*National Library of Canada*] (BIB)
OBRASC ..... Brampton Campus, Sheridan College, Brampton, Ontario [*Library symbol*] [*National Library of Canada*] (BIB)
OBRC .... Operating Budget Review Committee [*Military*]
OBRER ...... Blind River Refinery, Eldorado Resources Ltd., Ontario [*Library symbol*] [*National Library of Canada*] (NLC)
OBRET .... Old Breton [*Language, etc.*]
OBrG .... B. F. Goodrich Co., Technical Library, Brecksville, OH [*Library symbol*] [*Library of Congress*] (LCLS)
OBRH .... Home Care Program, Brockville, Ontario [*Library symbol*] [*National Library of Canada*] (BIB)
OBRI .... Belle River Public Library, Ontario [*Library symbol*] [*National Library of Canada*] (NLC)
OBRI .... Obrect Trailer [*NCIC trailer make code*]
O Bridg ...... Orlando Bridgman's English Common Pleas Reports [*A publication*] (DLA)
O Bridg (Eng)... Orlando Bridgman's English Common Pleas Reports [*A publication*] (DLA)
O Bridgm ... Orlando Bridgman's English Common Pleas Reports [*A publication*] (DLA)
O'Brien ...... O'Brien's Upper Canada Reports [*A publication*] (DLA)
OBRIG .... Brighton Public Library, Ontario [*Library symbol*] [*National Library of Canada*] (BIB)
O'Bri Lawy... O'Brien's Lawyer's Rule of Holy Life [*A publication*] (DLA)
O'Bri ML .... O'Brien's Military Law [*A publication*] (DLA)
OBRIS .... Smith Township Public Library, Bridgenorth, Ontario [*Library symbol*] [*National Library of Canada*] (BIB)
OBRIT .... Britt Area Community Library, Britt, Ontario [*Library symbol*] [*National Library of Canada*] (NLC)
OBRIT .... Old British [*Language, etc.*]
OBRM .... W. Ross MacDonald School, Brantford, Ontario [*Library symbol*] [*National Library of Canada*] (NLC)
OBRMR ..... Mississauga Reserve Library, Blind River, Ontario [*Library symbol*] [*National Library of Canada*] (NLC)
OBRN .... O'Brien and Nye Cartage Company [*Common carrier symbol*]
OBRNR ...... Oil Burner
OBRO .... Or Best Reasonable Offer
OBRO .... Oxford-On-Rideau Township Public Library, Burritt's Rapids, Ontario [*Library symbol*] [*National Library of Canada*] (BIB)
OBROW ..... Ochotnicza Brygada Robotnicza Obrony Warszawy [*A publication*] (BJA)
OBRP .... On-Board Repair Parts [*Navy*]
OBRP .... Pauline Johnson College, Brantford, Ontario [*Library symbol*] [*National Library of Canada*] (NLC)
OBRPH ...... Library Resources & Information Centre, Brockville Psychiatric Hospital, Ontario [*Library symbol*] [*National Library of Canada*] (NLC)
OBRR .... Obstetric Recovery Room (STED)
OBRT .... Brantford Public Library, Ontario [*Library symbol*] [*National Library of Canada*] (NLC)
OBrV .... United States Veterans Administration Hospital, Brecksville, OH [*Library symbol*] [*Library of Congress*] (LCLS)
OBRWI ...... [*The*] Woodland Indian Cultural Educational Centre, Brantford, Ontario [*Library symbol*] [*National Library of Canada*] (NLC)
OBS .... Aubenas [*France*] [*Airport symbol*] (OAG)
OBS .... Obesity [*Medicine*] (DMAA)
OBS .... Obligations (ROG)
OBS .... O'Brien Energy Systems, Inc. [*AMEX symbol*] (COMM)
OBS .... O'Brien Environmental Energy (EFIS)
obs .... Obscene (SHCU)
Obs .... Obscene [*Legal term*]
obs .... Obscura (VRA)
OBS .... Obscurant
OBS .... Obscure (ADA)
obs .... Observation (MILB)
OBS .... Observation (ROG)
OBS .... Observation Balloon System (SAUS)
OBS .... Observatory
OBS .... Observe
Obs .... Observer (London) [*A publication*] (BRI)
OBS .... Obsolescence (SAUS)
OBS .... Obsolete (AAG)
obs .... Obsolete (STED)
OBS .... Obstacle (AABC)
Obs .... Obstacle Light [*Aviation*] (DA)
OBS .... Obstetrical Service [*Medicine*] (MAE)
OBS .... Obstetrics [*Medicine*]
obs .... Obstruction [*Baseball term*] (NDBD)
OBS .... Obstruction (WGA)
OBS .... Obtains [*Telegraphy*] (PCTE)
OBS .... Ocean Bottom Seismometer [*California*] [*Seismograph station code, US Geological Survey*] [*Closed*] (SEIS)
OBS .... Ocean Bottom Station
OBS .... Ocean Bottom Suspension (SAUS)
OBS .... Office of Biological Service [*Marine science*] (MSC)
OBS .... Office of Boating Safety [*Coast Guard*]
OBS .... Official Bulletin Station [*Amateur radio*]
OBS .... Oita Broadcasting Service (SAUS)
OBS .... Old Babylonian Sumerian (BJA)
OBS .... Old Bailey's Sessions Papers [*A publication*] (DLA)
OBS .... Omnibearing Selector [*Radio*]
OBS .... Onboard Shuttle (ACAE)
OBS .... On-Board Spares [*Army*]
OBS .... On-Board System [*Navy*] (CAAL)
OBS .... Online BookStore [*Commercial firm*]
OBS .... Online Business Systems (SAUS)
OBS .... On-Line Business Systems, Inc. [*Information service or system*] (IID)
OBS .... Open-Back Stationary Press [*Manufacturing term*]
OBS .... Open Back Strike [*Construction term*] (MIST)
OBS .... Open Bidding Service (SAUS)
OBS .... Open-Hearth Basic Steel
OBS .... Opera Ballet School (DICI)
OBS .... Operand Buffering System [*Computer science*] (IAA)

OBS......... Operational Bioinstrumentation System [*NASA*]
OBS......... Operational Biomedical Sensors (NASA)
OBS......... Operational Biomedical Systems (KSC)
OBS......... Optical Beam Scanner
OBS......... Optical Beam Steering
OBS......... Optimum Blending System (VLIE)
OBS......... Orange Badge Scheme [*Disabled parking permit*] [*British*]
OBS......... Orbital Bombardment System
OBS......... Organic Brain Syndrome [*Psychiatry*]
OBS......... Organizational Breakdown Structure (SAUS)
OBS......... Organization Breakdown Structure [*Computer science*] (PCM)
OBS......... Organized Behavioral System (WDMC)
OBS......... Oriental and Biblical Studies [*A publication*] (BJA)
OBS......... OSIS [*Ocean Surveillance Information System*] Baseline System [*Navy*]
OBS......... Ottawa Board of Education, Library Services Centre (Software) [*UTLAS symbol*]
OBS......... Outlined Black Letters on One Side [*Tire design*]
OBS......... Output Buffer Storage (SAUS)
OBS......... Output Buffer Store (SAUS)
OBS......... Oxford Bibliographical Society (DGA)
OBS......... Sidney Township Public Library, Batawa, Ontario [*Library symbol*] [*National Library of Canada*] (BIB)
OBSC........ Obscure
OBSC........ Obscured Light [*Navigation signal*]
OBSC........ Obscuring (SAUS)
Obscd....... Obscured [*Nautical term*] (HRNC)
OBSCD....... Obscured [*Weather codes - aviation*] (PIPO)
obscen...... obscenity (SAUS)
OBSCIS...... Offender Based State Corrections Information System (OICC)
OBSD........ Object Sum Optical Density [*Microscopy*]
obsd........ Observed (STED)
OBSD........ Observed
OBSD........ Optical Beam Steering Device
OBSE........ Observer Transportation Company [*Common carrier symbol*]
OBSERV...... Observatory
OBSET....... Observation Set (SAUS)
OBSH........ Object Shape [*Microscopy*]
OBSH........ Oxybis(benzenesulfonylhydrazine) [*Organic chemistry*]
Obs Handb Can... Observers Handbook. Royal Astronomical Society of Canada (SAUS)
OBSHT....... Obstacle Height
OBSL........ St. Lawrence College [*College Saint-Laurent*], Brockville, Ontario [*Library symbol*] [*National Library of Canada*] (NLC)
Obs Lt....... Observer Lieutenant [*British military*] (DMA)
Obs Mer Alt... Observed Meridian Altitude (SAUS)
OBSN........ Observation (AAG)
OBSN FL.... Observation Flash (SAUS)
OBSNFL..... Observation Flight (IAA)
OBSN L..... Observation Line (SAUS)
OBSOL...... Obsolescent
Obsoles..... Obsolescent
OBSP........ Obiit sine Prole [*Died without Issue*] [*Latin*]
OBSP........ Old Bailey's Sessions Papers [*Legal term*] [*British*]
OBS PAT.... Observation Patrol (SAUS)
OBS PL...... Observation Plane (SAUS)
OBSPL....... Octave Band Sound Pressure Level
OBSPM...... Obiit sine Prole Masculus [*He, or She, Died without Male Issue*] [*Latin*]
OBSR........ Observation
OBSRON.... Observation Squadron
OBSRVTRY... Observatory
OBSS........ Ocean Bottom Scanning SONAR
OBSS........ Off Board Sensor Systems (ACAE)
OBSS........ Operations Briefing Support System (ACAE)
Obs Spot.... Observation Spot [*Control point*] [*Nautical charts*]
OBS Station... Ocean Bottom Seismographic Station (SAUS)
OBST........ Object Management System of STONE (SAUS)
obst......... Oboist (ODA)
OBST........ Obstacle (AFM)
OBST........ Obstetric
Obst......... Obstetrician (STED)
OBST........ Obstetrics [*Medicine*]
obst......... Obstipation (STED)
OBST........ Obstruction (AFM)
obst......... Obstruction (PIAV)
OBST CL.... Obstacle Clearing (SAUS)
obstet....... Obstetric (STED)
OBSTET..... Obstetrics [*Medicine*]
Obst Gynec... Obstetria and Gynecology (SAUS)
Obst J Gr Brit... Obstetrical Journal of Great Britain and Ireland (SAUS)
obstl......... Obstruction Light (AD)
OBSTN...... Obstruction (MSA)
OBSTR...... Obstruct (SAUS)
obstr......... Obstruction (AD)
Obstr......... Obstruction
OBSTRN..... Obstetrician [*Medicine*]
OBSTRUCT... Obstructive (SAUS)
OBSUED..... Oberbefehlshaber Suedost [*Headquarters, Commander-in-Chief, South*] [*Southern Germany and several army groups on the Eastern Front*] [*German military - World War II*]
OBSUM...... Order of Battle Summary [*Military*] (MCD)
obsv......... Observation (AD)
OBSV........ Observation (IAA)
obsv......... Observatory (AD)
OBSV........ Observatory (IAA)
obsv......... Observer (AD)
OBSV........ Observer
OBSVE....... Observe (ROG)
OBSY........ Observatory (AABC)
ob syn....... Organic Brain Syndrome [*Medicine*] (AD)
OBSZ........ Object Size [*Microscopy*]
obt........... Obedient (AD)
OBT.......... Obedient
OBT.......... Obiit [*He, or She, Died*] [*Latin*]
OBT.......... Observer Training [*Army*]
OBT.......... Obtain [*Motor vehicle violation code used in state of Maryland*] (MVRD)
obt........... Obtained (STED)
OBT.......... Office of Building Technologies (SAUS)
OBT.......... Officers Basic Training (ACAE)
OBT.......... On-Board Trainer [*Navy*] (CAAL)
OBT.......... One Billion Trees program (SAUS)
OBT.......... Oriental Bank & Trust [*NYSE symbol*] (TTSB)
OBT.......... Overseas Branch Transfer (AD)
OBT.......... Sisters Oblates to the Blessed Trinity (TOCD)
OBTA........ Oak Bark Tanners' Association (AD)
OBTAINDORSETRANS... Obtain Endorsement to Transport (DNAB)
obtd.......... Obtained (AD)
OBTD........ Obtained
OBTEX....... Offboard Targeting Experiments (GAVI)
OBTG........ Obtaining (ROG)
OBTN........ Obtain (ROG)
obts.......... Offender-Based Transaction Statistics (AD)
OBTS........ Offender Base Transaction Statistical System [*Department of Justice*] [*Database*] [*Information service or system*] (IID)
OBTS........ On-Board Test Set (SAUS)
OBTS........ Organizational Behavior Teaching Society (EA)
OBTVR...... Office for Battlefield Technical Vulnerability Reduction [*Army*] (RDA)
OBTW........ Oh, By the Way [*Computer hacker terminology*] (NHD)
OBTX........ Object Texture [*Microscopy*]
OBU.......... Burlington Public Library, Ontario [*Library symbol*] [*National Library of Canada*] (NLC)
OBU.......... Kobuk [*Alaska*] [*Airport symbol*] (OAG)
OBU.......... Kobuk, AK [*Location identifier*] [*FAA*] (FAAL)
OBU.......... Ocean Information System Baseline Upgrade (SAUS)
OBU.......... Ocean Surveillance Information System Baseline Upgrade [*Military*] (POLM)
OBU.......... Offshore Banking Unit
OBU.......... Oklahoma Baptist University
OBU.......... One Big Union [*A reference to Canada*]
OBU.......... Operational Base Unit [*British military*] (DMA)
OBU.......... Operative Bootmakers Union (AD)
OBU.......... Operative Builders' Union [*British*]
OBU.......... OSIS [*Ocean Surveillance Information System*] Baseline Upgrade [*Navy*]
OBU.......... Ouachita Baptist University [*Arkadelphia, AR*] [*Formerly, OBC*]
OBUA........ Operating in Built-Up-Areas (SAUS)
OBUAA...... Oklahoma Baptist University Alumni Association (EA)
OBUAA...... Ouachita Baptist University Alumni Association (EA)
OBUC........ Canada Centre for Inland Waters [*Centre Canadien des Eaux Interieures*], Burlington, Ontario [*Library symbol*] [*National Library of Canada*] (NLC)
OBUCC...... Canadian Canners Ltd., Burlington, Ontario [*Library symbol*] [*National Library of Canada*] (NLC)
OBUFBL..... Bayfield Laboratory, Ocean Science and Surveys, Fisheries and Oceans Canada [*Laboratoire Bayfield, Science et Leves Oceaniques, Peches et Oceans Canada*] Burlington, Ontario [*Library symbol*] [*National Library of Canada*] (NLC)
OBUJB....... Joseph Brant Memorial Hospital, Burlington, Ontario [*Library symbol*] [*National Library of Canada*] (BIB)
OBUL........ Lord Elgin High School, Burlington, Ontario [*Library symbol*] [*National Library of Canada*] (NLC)
O Bul........ Old Bulgarian (AD)
OBulg........ Old Bulgarian [*Language*] (BARN)
OBUR........ Burford Public Library, Ontario [*Library symbol*] [*National Library of Canada*] (BIB)
OBur......... Burton Public Library, Burton, OH [*Library symbol*] [*Library of Congress*] (LCLS)
o/bur......... Oil on Burlap (VRA)
OB-US....... Obstetrical Ultrasound (STED)
OBUS........ Obstetric Ultrasound [*Microcomputer system dealing with results of obstetric ultrasound examinations*]
OBUTS...... Organ Builders' United Trade Society [*A union*] [*British*]
OBUV........ Operative Bakers' Union of Victoria [*Australia*]
OBv.......... Bellevue Public Library, Bellevue, OH [*Library symbol*] [*Library of Congress*] (LCLS)
OBV.......... Bobcaygeon Branch, Victoria County Public Library, Ontario [*Library symbol*] [*National Library of Canada*] (BIB)
OBV.......... Obligated Volunteer Officer [*Military*]
OBV.......... Observe (SAUS)
OBV.......... Obstacle Breaching Vehicle [*Military*]
obv........... Obverse (AD)
OBV.......... Obverse
obv........... Obvious (AD)
obv........... Ocean Boarding Vessel (AD)
OBV.......... Ocean Boarding Vessel
obv........... Octane Blending Value (AD)
OBV.......... Octane Blending Value (PDAA)

OBV .... On-Balance Volume [*Measurement devised by stock market technician Joseph Granville*]
OBV .... Operation Big Vote (EA)
OBV .... Outside Broadcasting Van (SAUS)
OBV .... Oxidizer Bleed Valve (NASA)
OBVA .... Orthoptic and Binocular Vision Association [*United Kingdom*] (EAIO)
OBVACT .... On-Board Visual Aimer Continuation Trainer (SAUS)
OBVP .... Obiit Vita Patris [*He, or She, Died in the Lifetime of His, or Her, Father*] [*Latin*]
OBVR .... On-Board Vapor Recovery [*Automotive engineering*]
obvy .... Obviously (AD)
OBW .... Oberwerk [*Upper Work*] [*Music*]
Obw .... Oberwerk [*Highest Organ Bank*] [*German*] (AD)
obw .... Observation Window (AD)
OBW .... Observation Window
OBW .... Oxford Bible Warehouse [*British*] (ROG)
OBWC .... Westinghouse Canada, Inc., Burlington, Ontario [*Library symbol*] [*National Library of Canada*] (NLC)
OBWO .... O-Type Backward-Wave Oscillator (IDOE)
O-BWO .... Type-O Backward Wave Oscillator (SAUS)
OBX .... Oslo Stock Exchange [*Norway*] (NUMA)
OBy .... Old Byblian (BJA)
OBZ .... Outer Border Zone [*Geology*]
OC .... Air California [*Air carrier designation symbol*] (AD)
OC .... Cornwall Public Library, Ontario [*Library symbol*] [*National Library of Canada*] (NLC)
OC .... Degrees Celsius
OC .... Jersey. Ordres du Conseil [*A publication*] (DLA)
OC .... Oakwood College (SAUS)
OC .... Obayashi Corporation (EFIS)
OC .... Oberlin College (AD)
OC .... Object Class [*Military*]
O/C .... Object Classification (NG)
OC .... Object Computer (SAUS)
OC .... Objective Capability
OC .... Oblate College (AD)
OC .... Observation Car [*British*]
OC .... Observer Computer (SAUS)
OC .... Observer-Controller [*Army*] (INF)
OC .... Observer Corps [*Became ROC, 1941*] [*British*]
OC .... Obsessive Compulsive (PAZ)
OC .... Obstacle Clearance (PDAA)
oc .... Obstetrical Conjugate [*Medicine*] (AD)
OC .... Obstetric Conjugate [*Pelvic measurement*] [*Gynecology*]
OC .... Obstruction Chart
OC .... Occidental
OC .... Occidental College (AD)
OC .... Occipital Cortex [*Brain anatomy*]
OC .... Occlusocervical [*Dentistry*]
OC .... Occulentum [*Medicine*] (CPH)
Oc .... Occulting Light [*Navigation signal*]
OC .... Occupied [*International telex abbreviation*] (WDMC)
OC .... Occurs (MDG)
Oc .... Ocean (AD)
OC .... Ocean
oc .... Ocean (AD)
OC .... Oceanographic Devices [*JETDS nomenclature*] [*Military*] (CET)
O/C .... O'Clock (ROG)
OC .... O'clock [*Telegraphy*] (PCTE)
Oc .... Octahedral [*Molecular geometry*]
OC .... Octal Code (SAUS)
OC .... Octane Control [*Automotive engineering*]
OC .... October (ADA)
Oc .... Octyl [*Biochemistry*]
OC .... Ocular [*Microscopy*]
OC .... Oculentum [*Eye Ointment*] [*Pharmacy*]
OC .... Odessa College (AD)
oc .... Odor Control (AD)
OC .... Odor Control
OC .... Oedipus Coloneus [*of Sophocles*] [*Classical studies*] (OCD)
OC .... Of Course
OC .... Off-Camera [*Film*] (WDMC)
OC .... Off Center (WGA)
OC .... Off Cover (SAUS)
OC .... Offensive Center [*Football*]
OC .... Office Call [*Medicine*]
OC .... Office Consultation (AD)
OC .... Office Copy
OC .... Office of Censorship [*Terminated, 1945*] [*Military*]
OC .... Office of Compliance [*U.S. Food and Drug Administration*]
OC .... Office of the Commissioner [*Office of Education*]
OC .... Office of the Comptroller
O/C .... Officer Cadet [*British military*] (DMA)
OC .... Officer Candidate [*Military*]
OC .... Officer Commanding [*Military*]
OC .... Officer in Charge (AD)
OC .... Officer, Order of Canada [*Decoration*] (CMD)
OC .... Officers' Cook
OC .... Official Circular [*Poor Law Board, etc.*] [*A publication*] (DLA)
OC .... Official Classification
OC .... Official Communication (SAUS)
OC .... Off-Machine Coated [*Paper*] (DGA)
OC .... Ohio College (AD)
OC .... Oil Consumption [*Fuels and lubricants*]
OC .... Oil Cooler
OC .... Oiler Contact (SAUS)
o/c .... Oil on Canvas (VRA)
OC .... Okolona College (AD)
OC .... Old Carthusian
OC .... Old Category Code (NITA)
OC .... Old Catholic
OC .... Old Chap [*Amateur radio shorthand*] (WDAA)
O/C .... Old Charter [*Business and trade*]
OC .... Old Cheltonian [*British*] (ROG)
OC .... Old Code [*Louisiana Code of 1808*] [*A publication*] (DLA)
OC .... Old Crop
OC .... Oleoresin Capsicum (BARN)
OC .... Olin [*Federal Railroad Administration identification code*]
OC .... Olivet College (AD)
OC .... Olympic College (AD)
OC .... On Call (BUR)
oc .... On Camera (AD)
OC .... On Camera (WDMC)
OC .... On Cards
oc .... On Center (AD)
OC .... On Center [*Technical drawings*]
O/C .... On Completion (SAUS)
oc .... On-Condition (NAKS)
OC .... On-Condition (NASA)
OC .... On Consignment (MHDB)
OC .... On Course [*Navigation*]
OC .... Online Chronicle (NITA)
OC .... Only Child
OC .... Ope Consilio [*By Aid and Counsel*] [*Latin*] [*Legal term*] (DLA)
OC .... Open Channel (SAUS)
oc .... Open Charter (AD)
OC .... Open Charter [*Business term*]
OC .... Open Chock [*Shipfitting*]
oc .... Open Circuit (NAKS)
OC .... Open Circuit
OC .... Open Circuited (SAUS)
OC .... Open Circular [*Configuration of DNA*] [*Microbiology*]
O/C .... Open/Closed [*Mouth*] [*Doll collecting*]
OC .... Open Cockpit (SAUS)
OC .... Open Coil (SAUS)
OC .... Open Collector (IAA)
OC .... Open College (AIE)
OC .... Open Commitment (SAUS)
OC .... Open Contract
OC .... Open Control (SAUS)
o/c .... Open Cover (AD)
O/C .... Open Cover [*Shipping*]
OC .... Open Crossing (HEAS)
oc .... Open Cup (AD)
OC .... Open Cup [*Electronics*]
oc .... Opera Comique [*Music*] (GROV)
OC .... Opera-Comique [*Comic Opera*] [*French*] (AD)
OC .... Opera Company (AD)
OC .... Operand Channel (SAUS)
OC .... Operating Characteristic
OC .... Operating Coil (IAA)
OC .... Operating Company
OC .... Operating Contractor (SAUS)
OC .... Operating Control (SAUS)
OC .... Operating Curve (NRCH)
OC .... Operational Calculus (SAUS)
OC .... Operational Capability (AAG)
OC .... Operational Characteristic (SAUS)
OC .... Operational Check (MCD)
OC .... Operational Circular (HEAS)
OC .... Operational Command (SAUS)
OC .... Operational Computer (IEEE)
OC .... Operational Concept (SAUS)
OC .... Operational Condition (SAUS)
OC .... Operational Control (SAUS)
OC .... Operation Code (IAA)
OC .... Operation CORK [*Joan B. Kroc Foundation*] [*CORK is derived from the foundation name*] [*Defunct*] (EA)
OC .... Operation Crossroads [*Atomic weapons testing*]
OC .... Operations Center [*Military*]
OC .... Operations Chief [*Deep Space Network, NASA*]
OC .... Operations Commence (SAUS)
OC .... Operations Communications (SAUS)
OC .... Operations Conductor (MUGU)
OC .... Operations Contract (SAUS)
OC .... Operations Control
OC .... Operations Controller (SAUS)
OC .... Operations Coordinator (SAUS)
O/C .... Operations Critical (MCD)
OC .... Operator Call (SAUS)
OC .... Operator Centralization (VLIE)
OC .... Operator Circuit [*Telecommunications*] (IAA)
OC .... Operator Command (NITA)
OC .... Opere Citato [*In the Work Cited*] [*Latin*] (WDAA)
OC .... Opportunity Cost (MHDB)
OC .... Optical Carrier
OC .... Optical Cavity [*LASER technology*] (EECA)
OC .... Optical Center (SAUS)

OC .... Optical Channel (SAUS)
OC .... Optical Communication (ELAL)
OC .... Optical Computer (SAUS)
OC .... Optical Coupler (SAUS)
OC .... Optic Chiasm [*Anatomy*]
OC .... Optimal Control (SAUS)
OC .... Optimizing Control (SAUS)
OC .... Optometric Corp. (AD)
OC .... Oral Care [*Denistry*] (DAVI)
oc .... Oral Contraceptive [*Medicine*] (AD)
OC .... Oral Contraceptive [*Endocrinology*]
OC .... Orbital Check (MCD)
oc .... Orbital Check [*NASA*] (NAKS)
OC .... Order Canceled
OC .... Order Card
OC .... Order Code (SAUS)
OC .... Order Confirmation (SAUS)
OC .... Order in Council [*A publication*] (DLA)
OC .... Orderly Corporal [*British*]
OC .... Order of Canada (SAUS)
OC .... Order of Cistercians [*Roman Catholic religious order*]
OC .... Ordinary Capital Account [*Inter-American Development Bank*]
OC .... Ordinary Chondrite [*A type of meteorite*]
OC .... Ordinary Colourless (SAUS)
OC .... Ordnance Chart (MCD)
OC .... Ordnance College [*Military*] [*British*] (ROG)
OC .... Ordo Charitatis [*Fathers of the Order of Charity*] [*Roman Catholic religious order*]
OC .... Organic Carbon
OC .... Organic Chemistry (SAUS)
OC .... Organizational Chart
o/c .... Organized Crime (AD)
OC .... Organochlorine [*Also, OCL*] [*Organic chemistry*]
OC .... Organo Corale [*Choir Organ*] [*Latin*] (AD)
OC .... Organ of Consultation
OC .... Oriel College (AD)
OC .... Oriens Christianus [*A publication*] (ODCC)
OC .... Orienteering Club (ODA)
OC .... Original Claim (MAE)
OC .... Original Cosmopolitans [*Defunct*] (EA)
OC .... Original Cover
OC .... Orion Capital Corp. [*NYSE symbol*] (SPSG)
OC .... Orlando College (AD)
OC .... Orphans' Court (DLA)
OC .... Oscillating Current (SAUS)
OC .... Osteocalcin [*Biochemistry*]
OC .... Osteochondritis (DB)
OC .... Osteocyte (SAUS)
OC .... Otero College (AD)
OC .... Otter Controls Ltd. (SAUS)
OC .... Oudh Cases [*India*] [*A publication*] (DLA)
OC .... Out Cold [*Slang*]
OC .... Outer Canthus (DB)
OC .... Outflow Channels [*A filamentary mark on Mars*]
OC .... Outing Club
OC .... Outlet Contact
O/C .... Out of Charge [*Customs*]
O/C .... Out-of-Country [*Motor vehicle violation code used in state of Maryland*] (MVRD)
OC .... Output Card (SAUS)
OC .... Output Class (SAUS)
OC .... Output Code (SAUS)
OC .... Output Computer
OC .... Output Controller (VLIE)
OC .... Outside Circumference (MSA)
OC .... Outsiders Club (EAIO)
OC .... Over Center (SAUS)
o/c .... Overcharge (AD)
O/C .... Overcharge
O/C .... Overcharging (SAUS)
OC .... Over-Compounded (SAUS)
OC .... Overcorrected (SAUS)
oc .... Overcurrent (NAKS)
OC .... Overcurrent
oc .... Overdraft Charge [*Banking*] (AD)
OC .... Overhaul Cycle (SAUS)
OC .... Overseas Chinese (AD)
OC .... Overseas Commands [*Air Force*]
OC .... Overseas Country (ODBW)
O/C .... Over-the-Counter [*Also, OTC*] [*Stock exchange term*]
OC .... Over-the-Horizon Compressed (MCD)
OC .... Oxidation Catalyst [*Automotive engineering*]
OC .... Oxide Cathode (SAUS)
OC .... Oxygen Chemisorption (SAUS)
OC .... Oxygen Consumed
OC .... Oxygen Cutting [*Welding*]
OC .... Public Library of Cincinnati and Hamilton County, Cincinnati, OH [*Library symbol*] [*Library of Congress*] (LCLS)
OC-5 .... Organizing Committee for a Fifth Estate (AD)
OCA .... Aeroservicios Carabobo CA (ASERCA) [*Venzuela*] [*ICAO designator*] (FAAC)
OCA .... Campbellford Branch, Northumberland County Public Library, Ontario [*Library symbol*] [*National Library of Canada*] (NLC)
OCA .... Carmelite Vietnamese of Our Lady of Mt. Carmel (TOCD)
OCA .... Cincinnati Art Museum, Cincinnati, OH [*Library symbol*] [*Library of Congress*] (LCLS)
OCA .... Creighton University, Alumni Library, Omaha, NE [*OCLC symbol*] (OCLC)
OCA .... Observatoire de la Cote d'Azur [*France*]
OCA .... Obsessive-Compulsive Anonymous (EA)
OCA .... Obstacle Clearance Altitude [*Aviation*] (DA)
OCA .... Ocaina [*Language symbol*] (ETLW)
OCA .... Ocala, FL [*Amtrak rail station code*]
oca .... Ocarina (AD)
OCA .... Occasion [*Telegraphy*] (PCTE)
OCA .... Ocean Control Authority
OCA .... Oceanic Control Area [*ICAO*]
OCA .... Ocean Reef Club [*Florida*] [*Airport symbol*] (OAG)
OCA .... Oceans and Coastal Areas
OCA .... Oculocutaneous Albinism [*Medicine*] (DAVI)
OCA .... Offensive Counterair [*Army*] (ADDR)
OCA .... Office, Comptroller of the Army
OCA .... Office of Competitive Assessment [*Department of Commerce*]
OCA .... Office of Computing Activities [*Later, DCR*] [*National Science Foundation*]
OCA .... Office of Congressional Affairs [*Energy Research and Development Administration*]
OCA .... Office of Consumer Advisor [*USDA*]
OCA .... Office of Consumer Affairs [*US Postal Service ombudsman*]
OCA .... Office of the City Attorney (AD)
OCA .... Office of the Community Advocate [*Australian Capital Territory*]
OCA .... Officers' Caterer [*Navy*] [*British*]
OCA .... Off-Site Consequence Analysis [*Emergency Management*] (EMA)
OCA .... Ohio College Association (AD)
OCA .... Ohio Courts of Appeals Reports [*A publication*] (DLA)
OCA .... Oil Company of Australia (AD)
OCA .... Old Comrades Association [*British military*] (DMA)
OCA .... Oldsmobile Club of America (EA)
OCA .... Olivopontocerebellar Atrophy [*Medicine*] (DMAA)
OCA .... Olympic Council of Asia [*Hawalli, Kuwait*] (EAIO)
OCA .... Oncovin [*Vincristine*] Cyclophosphamide, Adriamycin [*Doxorubicin*] [*Antineoplastic drug regimen*] (DAVI)
OCA .... Ontario Chiropractic Association (SAUS)
OCA .... Ontario College of Agriculture
OCA .... Ontario College of Art
OCA .... Opencast Coal Act [*Town planning*] [*British*]
OCA .... Open College of Arts [*British*]
OCA .... Open Communication Architecture (CIST)
OCA .... Open Component Architecture (SAUS)
OCA .... Operational Control Authority [*NATO*]
OCA .... Operation Crossroads Africa (EA)
OCA .... Operation of Combined Arms (SAUS)
OCA .... Operations of Combined Arms (SAUS)
OCA .... Oral Contraceptive Agent [*Endocrinology*]
OCA .... Orbital Carrier Aircraft [*Space launch term*] (ISAK)
OCA .... Order of the Crown in America [*Later, TOCA*] (EA)
OCA .... Oregon Corrections Association (AD)
OCA .... Oregon Counseling Association (SEAT)
OCA .... Organisation Combat Anarchiste [*Anarchist Combat Organization*] [*France*] [*Political party*] (PPW)
OCA .... Organizacion de las Cooperativas de America [*Organization of the Cooperatives of America - OCA*] (EAIO)
OCA .... Organization of Chinese Americans (EA)
OCA .... Organization of the Cooperatives of America (SAUS)
OCA .... Original Classification Authority (SAUS)
OCA .... Orthodontic Centers of America [*NYSE symbol*]
OCA .... [*The*] Orthodox Church of America
OCA .... Osteopathic Cranial Association [*Later, CA*]
OCA .... Other Competitive Action (SAUS)
OCA .... Otterhound Club of America (EA)
OCA .... Output Communications Adapter (SAUS)
OCA .... Outstanding Claims Advance [*Insurance*] (AIA)
OCa .... Ovarian Cancer [*Medicine*] (EDAA)
OCa .... Ovarian Carcinoma [*Medicine*] (EDAA)
OCA .... Owner Controlled Area (SAUS)
OCA .... Oxychloride Cement Association [*Defunct*]
OCAA .... Oklahoma City-Ada-Atoka Railway Co. [*AAR code*]
OCAA .... Organization of Central American Armies (AD)
OCAAF .... Order of the Chief of the Army Air Forces
OCAAR .... Occupational Accidents Analysis and Reporting
OCAB .... Cannington Branch, Brock Township Public Library, Ontario [*Library symbol*] [*National Library of Canada*] (BIB)
OCAB .... Overseas Correspondents Association Bangladesh (BUAC)
OCAC .... Ocean Acre Project [*Marine science*] (MSC)
OCAC .... Office of the Chief of Air Corps [*World War II*]
OCAC .... Officer Commanding Administrative Centre [*World War I*] [*British*]
OCAC .... Open-Circuit After-Charge [*Automotive engineering*]
OCAC .... Operations, Control, and Analysis Center (DOMA)
OCACV .... Open-Circuit After-Charge Voltage [*Automotive engineering*]
OCad .... Cadiz Public Library, Cadiz, OH [*Library symbol*] [*Library of Congress*] (LCLS)
OCAD .... Occlusive Cartoid Artery Disease [*Medicine*] (DMAA)
OCAD .... Occupational and Career Analysis Development (SAUS)
OCAD .... Optical Character and Detect (SAUS)
OCAD .... Orcad, Inc. [*NASDAQ symbol*] (SAG)
OCADA .... Office of the Chief, Air Defense Artillery
OCADS .... Oklahoma City Air Defense Sector (SAA)
OCAE .... United States Army Engineer Division, Ohio River, Technical Library, Cincinnati,OH [*Library symbol*] [*Library of Congress*] (LCLS)

OCAF .... Office, Chief of Aerospace (SAA)
OCAF .... Oklahomans for Children and Families
OCAFF .... Office, Chief of Army Field Forces
OCAHO ...... Office of the Chief Administrative Hearing Officer (SAUS)
OCAI .... Orthodontic Centers of Amer [*NASDAQ symbol*] (TTSB)
OCAI .... Orthodontic Centers of America, Inc. [*NASDAQ symbol*] (SAG)
OCAJ .... American Jewish Periodical Center, Cincinnati, OH [*Library symbol*] [*Library of Congress*] (LCLS)
OCAJA .... American Jewish Archives, Cincinnati, OH [*Library symbol*] [*Library of Congress*] (LCLS)
OCal .... Caldwell Public Library, Caldwell, OH [*Library symbol*] [*Library of Congress*] (LCLS)
OCAL .... Ocal, Inc. [*NASDAQ symbol*] (SAG)
Ocal .... Octo Archives, Inc., Laurel, MD [*Library symbol*] [*Library of Congress*] (LCLS)
ocal .... On-Line Cryptanalytic Aid Language [*Computer science*] (AD)
OCAL .... Online Cryptanalytic Aid Language [*Computer science*]
OCAL .... Organization of Communist Action in Lebanon (PD)
OCAL .... Overseas Containers Australia Ltd (SAUS)
OCAL .... Overseas Containers of Australia, Ltd. (AD)
OCAL .... [*The*] Oxford Companion to American Literature [*A publication*]
OCALA .... Open Common Annotation Language (SAUS)
OCALC .... Oklahoma City Air Logistic Center [*Formerly, OCAMA*] (MCD)
O'Callaghan New Neth... O'Callaghan's History of New Netherland [*A publication*] (DLA)
OCAM .... Afro-Malagasy Common Organization (SAUS)
OCAM .... Common Organization of African, Malagasy, and Mauritian States (EBF)
OCAM .... Office, Computing, and Accounting Machinery
OCAM .... Ontario Center for Advanced Manufacturing (SAUS)
OCAM .... Organisation Commune Africaine et Mauricienne [*African and Mauritian Common Organization*] [*Formerly, Organisation Commune Africaine et Malgache*]
OCAMA ...... Oklahoma City Air Materiel Area [*Later, OCALC*]
OCAMA-SED... Oklahoma City Air Materiel Area [*later, OCALC*] Service Engineering Division
OCamd ...... Preble County District Library, Camden Branch, Camden, OH [*Library symbol*] [*Library of Congress*] (LCLS)
OCAMM ..... Organisation Commune Africaine, Malgache, et Mauricienne [*African, Malagasy, and Mauritian Common Organization*] [*Formerly, Organisation Commune Africaine et Malgache*] [*Later, OCAM*]
OCAMPR .... Orthodox Christian Association of Medicine, Psychology and Religion (EA)
OCan .... Canton Public Library Association, Canton, OH [*Library symbol*] [*Library of Congress*] (LCLS)
OCAN .... Officer Candidate Airman
OC & E ...... Oregon, California, and Eastern Railroad (AD)
OC & R ...... Operations, Commitments, and Requirements [*Military*]
OC & S ...... Ordnance Center and School [*Army*] (RDA)
OC&T .... Office of Certification and Training (SAUS)
OCanK .... Kent State University, Stark County Regional Campus, Canton, OH [*Library symbol*] [*Library of Congress*] (LCLS)
OCanM ...... Malone College, Canton, OH [*Library symbol*] [*Library of Congress*] (LCLS)
OCanS .... Stark County District Library, Canton, OH [*Library symbol*] [*Library of Congress*] (LCLS)
OCanW ...... Walsh College, Canton, OH [*Library symbol*] [*Library of Congress*] (LCLS)
OCAO .... Athenaeum of Ohio, Eugene H. Maly Library, Cincinnati, OH [*Library symbol*] [*Library of Congress*] (LCLS)
OCAP .... Capreol Public Library, Ontario [*Library symbol*] [*National Library of Canada*] (NLC)
OCAP .... Oceans and Coastal Areas Programme (SAUS)
OCAP .... Ontario Career Action Program (SAUS)
OCAP .... Open Channel Air Preheater [*Heat exchanger*]
OCAP .... Operating Criteria and Procedures (SAUS)
OCA/PAC .... Oceans and Coastal Areas Programme Activity Centre (SAUS)
OCAPO ...... Office of Compliance Analysis and Program Operations [*Environmental Protection Agency*] (GFGA)
OCAPT .... Ontario Center for Automotive Parts Technology (SAUS)
OCAQ .... Ordre de Comptables Agrees du Quebec [*Canada*] (DD)
OCAR .... Cargill Branch, Bruce County Public Library, Ontario [*Library symbol*] [*National Library of Canada*] (NLC)
OCAR .... Office of the Chief, Army Reserve (AABC)
OCARD ...... Cardinal Public Library, Ontario [*Library symbol*] [*National Library of Canada*] (BIB)
OCareyS .... Our Lady of Carey Seminary, Carey, OH [*Library symbol*] [*Library of Congress*] (LCLS)
OCARINA... Ocean, Atmosphere, Research and Investigation with Acoustic Techniques (SAUS)
OCarm .... Calced Carmelites (TOCD)
OCarm .... Carmelite Fathers and Brothers (TOCD)
ocarm .... Carmelite Fathers and Brothers (TOCD)
OCarm .... Carmelite Nuns of the Ancient Observance (TOCD)
OCarm .... Carmelite Sisters (Corpus Christi) (TOCD)
OCarm .... Carmelite Sisters for Aged and Infirm (TOCD)
OCarm .... Congregation of Our Lady of Mount Carmel (TOCD)
OCarm .... Institute of the Sisters of Our Lady of Mt. Carmel (TOCD)
OCARM ...... Order of Brothers of the Blessed Virgin Mary of Mount Carmel [*Rome, Italy*] (EAIO)
O Carm ...... Order of Carmelites (ODA)
OCART .... Cartier Public Library, Ontario [*Library symbol*] [*National Library of Canada*] (NLC)
ocart .... Order of Carthusians (TOCD)
OCart .... Order of Carthusians [*Roman Catholic religious order*]
OCartSC ..... Saint Charles Seminary, Carthagena, OH [*Library symbol*] [*Library of Congress*] (LCLS)
OCAS .... Office, Coordinator of Army Studies (AABC)
OCAS .... Office of Carrier Accounts and Statistics [*of CAB*]
OCAS .... Office of Civil Aviation Security (AD)
OCAS .... Office of the Chief of Air Service [*World War II*]
OCAS .... Officer-in-Charge of Armament Supply
OCAS .... Ohio Casualty Corp. [*NASDAQ symbol*] (NQ)
OCAS .... Ohio College of Applied Science
OCAS .... Online Cryptanalytic Aid System [*Computer science*] (IEEE)
OCAS .... Ordnance Configuration Accounting System [*Navy*]
OCAS .... Organization of Central American States [*See also ODECA*] [*San Salvador, El Salvador*] (EAIO)
OCAS .... Out of Controlled Airspace [*Aviation*] (FAAC)
OCASA ...... Overseas Chinese Association of South Australia
OCASCO ..... Ohio Casualty Corporation (EFIS)
OCASP ...... Olivetti Complete Accounting and Stock Package (SAUS)
Ocass Pap Fla State Collect Arthropods... Occasional Papers. Florida State Collection of Arthropods (SAUS)
O Cat .... Old Catalan (AD)
OCAT .... Optometric College Aptitude Test (WDAA)
OCAT .... Optometry College Admissions Test (WDAA)
OCATE .... Oregon Center for Advanced Technology Education (SAUS)
OCATOUR... Office National Centrafricain du Tourisme (EY)
OCAU .... Observation, Classification, and Allocation Unit (WDAA)
OCAW .... Oil, Chemical, and Atomic Workers International Union (EA)
OCAW .... Organization of Chinese American Women (EA)
OCAWU ..... Oil, Chemical, and Atomic Workers Union [*Medicine*] (EDAA)
OCB .... Cache Bay Public Library, Ontario [*Library symbol*] [*National Library of Canada*] (NLC)
OCB .... Cincinnati Bible Seminary, Cincinnati, OH [*Library symbol*] [*Library of Congress*] (LCLS)
OCB .... Obsessive-Compulsive Behavior (MELL)
OCB .... Ocean Crust Boundary (SAUS)
OCB .... Officer Career Brief [*Resume*] [*Military*]
OCB .... Officers' Cadet Battalion [*British*]
OCB .... Off-Machine Coated Board [*Paper*] (DGA)
OCB .... Offshore Certification Bureau [*British*] (CB)
OCB .... Oil [*Operated*] Circuit Breaker
ocb .... Oil Circuit Breaker (AD)
OCB .... Oil Collection Basin (NRCH)
OCB .... Oil Control Board [*British*]
OCB .... Oil-Cooled Disc Brake [*Automotive engineering*]
OCB .... Oil-operated Circuit Breaker (SAUS)
OCB .... Olivocochlear Bundle (SAUS)
OCB .... Operated Circuit Breaker (SAUS)
OCB .... Operations Center Building (SAUS)
OCB .... Operations Coordinating Board [*Terminated, 1961*] [*National Security Council*]
OCB .... Outer Core Barrel (SAUS)
OCB .... Outgoing Calls Barred [*Telecommunications*] (TEL)
OCB .... Output Current Booster
OCB .... Override Control BITS [*Binary Digits*] [*Computer science*]
OCB .... Over-the-Counter Batch [*Stock exchange term*] (MHDW)
OCBA .... Ortho-Chlorobenzoic Acid [*Organic chemistry*]
OCBB .... Operating Cost Board Budget (ACAE)
OCBC .... Ortho-Chlorobenzyl Chloride [*Organic chemistry*]
OCBC .... Overseas Chinese Banking Corp. (AD)
OCBF .... Outer Cortical Blood-Flow [*Medicine*] (DB)
OCBH .... Bethesda Base Hospital, Information Resource Center, Cincinnati, OH [*Library symbol*] [*Library of Congress*] (LCLS)
oc b/l .... Ocean Bill of Lading (AD)
OC/B/L .... Ocean Bill of Lading [*Shipping*]
OCBN .... Ortho-Chlorobenzonitrile [*Organic chemistry*]
OCBOA ...... Other Comprehensive Bases of Accounting (ADA)
OCBP .... Output Control Block Pointer (SAUS)
OCBR .... Other than Cost Base Review [*DoD*]
OCBR .... Output Channel Buffer Register [*Computer science*] (IAA)
OCB(S) ...... Oil Control Board, Supply [*British*]
OCBSD ...... Officer Commanding, Base Supply Depot (SAUS)
OCBU .... Ocean Container [*Intermodal shipping container symbol*] (TVRC)
OCC .... CARSTAB Corp., Research Library, Cincinnati, OH [*Library symbol*] [*Library of Congress*] (LCLS)
OCC .... Coca [*Ecuador*] [*Airport symbol*] (OAG)
OCC .... Object-Centered Coordinate (DMAA)
OCC .... Object Class Code [*Military*] (AFM)
OCC .... Obus a Charge Creuse (SAUS)
occ .... Occasional
occ .... Occasionally (AD)
OCC .... Occasionally
occ .... Occidental (SHCU)
occ .... Occipital [*or Occiput*] [*Anatomy*] (MAE)
OCC .... Occiput (SAUS)
OCC .... Occluded Corrosion Cell (PDAA)
OCC .... Occlusion
OCC .... Occultation [*Astronomy*]
Occ .... Occulting (AD)
OCC .... Occulting Light [*Navigation signal*]
occ .... Occupation (AD)
OCC .... Occupation (AFM)
OCC .... Occupied (IAA)
OCC .... Occupied Command Center [*Military*]
OCC .... Occurrence
Occ .... Occurs (ILCA)

OCC......... Ocean City College [*Maryland*]
OCC......... Ocean Coordinating Committee [*IEEE*] (MSC)
OCC......... Ocean Cruising Club [*British*] (DI)
OCC......... Oceanic Control Center (OA)
OCC......... OCLC [*Online Computer Library Center*] Library, Columbus, OH [*OCLC symbol*] (OCLC)
OCC......... Octagon Car Club [*Later, MOCC*] (EAIO)
OCC......... Octal Correction Cards [*Computer science*]
OCC......... Ocutech Canada [*Vancouver Stock Exchange symbol*]
OCC......... Office Communications Cabinet (SAUS)
OCC......... Office of Cancer Communications [*Department of Health and Human Services*] (GFGA)
OCC......... Office of Chemical Control (COE)
occ......... Office of Contract Compliance (NAKS)
OCC......... Office of Contract Compliance [*NASA*] (NASA)
OCC......... Office of the Chief Counsel [*U.S. Food and Drug Administration*]
OCC......... Office of the Comptroller of the Currency [*Department of the Treasury*]
OCC......... Office of the Director of Command, Control, and Communications [*Air Force*]
OCC......... Officer Candidate Class (SAUS)
OCC......... Officer Commanding, Camp (SAUS)
OCC......... Officers' Chief Cook
OCC......... Official Custodian of Charities [*British*]
OCC......... Offset Course Computer (SAUS)
OCC......... Offshore Construction Council (BUAC)
OCC......... Offshore Craft Conference (BUAC)
OCC......... Offsite Coordination Center [*Environmental science*] (COE)
OCC......... Ohio Circuit Reports [*or Decisions*] [*A publication*] (DLA)
OCC......... Ohio College of Chiropody
OCC......... Ohio Conservation Consortium [*Library network*]
OCC......... Oklahoma Crime Commission (AD)
OCC......... Old Corrugated Container [*Paper recycling*]
OCC......... Olney Communication College (AD)
OCC......... Olney Community College (SAUS)
OCC......... Olympic Committee Congress
OCC......... Omnibus Crime Control and Safe Streets Act [*1968*]
OCC......... Onondaga Community College (AD)
OCC......... Onsite Construction Contractor (SAUS)
OCC......... Open Channel Cooperative
OCC......... Open Circuit Characteristic (IAA)
OCC......... Open-Circuit Characteristic (SAUS)
OCC......... Open, Cooperative Computing (SAUS)
OCC......... Operating Characteristics Curve
OCC......... Operational Computer Complex (KSC)
OCC......... Operational Control Center (or Centre) (SAUS)
OCC......... Operations Command Center (ACAE)
OCC......... Operations Control Center [*or Console*] (AFM)
occ......... Operations Control Center (NAKS)
OCC......... Operations Control Console (SAUS)
OCC......... Operations Coordination Center [*Emergency Management*] (EMA)
OCC......... Operator Control Command (BUR)
OCC......... Operator Control Console [*Canadian Navy*]
OCC......... Operator's Computer Console
OCC......... Oppenheimer Capital Ltd. [*NYSE symbol*] (SPSG)
OCC......... Oppenheimer Cap L.P. [*NYSE symbol*] (TTSB)
OCC......... Opportunity Cost of Capital (GART)
OCC......... Opposition Coordinating Committee (SAUS)
OCC......... Optical Circuit and Component (NITA)
OCC......... Option Clearing Corp.
OCC......... Oral Cholecystography [*Medicine*] (DMAA)
OCC......... Oral Contraceptive Council [*Defunct*] (EA)
OCC......... Orange Carpet Crowd [*An association*]
OCC......... Orange Coast College [*Formerly, OCJC*] [*Costa Mesa, CA*]
OCC......... Order Control Card (VLIE)
OCC......... Order of Calced Carmelites [*Roman Catholic religious order*] (DICI)
OCC......... Ordnance Command Converter [*Military*] (IAA)
OCC......... Ordo Carmelitarum Calceatorum [*Carmelites*] [*Roman Catholic religious order*]
OCC......... Organic Carbon Cycle
OCC......... Organic Consultative Committee [*Victoria, Australia*]
OCC......... Organisation Combat Communiste [*Communist Combat Organization*] [*France*] [*Political party*] (PPW)
OCC......... Organization Chart and Charter (SAUS)
OCC......... Osborne Computer Corporation (NITA)
OCC......... Osteopathic Centre for Children [*United Kingdom*] (RCD)
OCC......... Other Common Carrier [*Telecommunications*]
OCC......... Other Communications Company
OCC......... Outer Critics Circle (EA)
OCC......... Output Circuit Check [*Electronics*]
OCC......... Output Code Converter (SAUS)
OCC......... Output Control Character (SAUS)
OCC......... Owens Community College in Ohio (SAUS)
OCCA........ Ocean Cargo Clearance Authority (DOMA)
OCCA........ Office, Chief of Civil Affairs
OCCA........ Office of Compliance and Consumer Assistance (SAUS)
OCCA........ Officer-in-Charge of Civilian Affairs [*in newly occupied countries*] [*Army*] [*World War II*]
OCCA........ Oil and Colour Chemists' Association
OCCA........ Omnibus Crime Control Act of 1970 (OICC)
OCCA........ Ontario Control Contractors Association [*Canada*]
OCCA........ Open, Cooperative Computing Architecture (SAUS)
OCCA........ Organized Crime Control Act of 1970
OCCA........ Overseas Communications Cooperation Association (SAUS)
OCCABA..... Open Circuit Compressed Air Breathing Apparatus (SAUS)
OCCAC...... Ohio Community College Athletic Conference (PSS)
OCCAM...... Ocean Circulation and Climate Advanced Modelling
OCCAM...... Office of Cancer Complementary and Alternative Medicine [*National Cancer Institute*] (RCD)
occas........ Occasional (AD)
Occas........ Occasional (DIAR)
OCCAS...... Occasional
Occas........ Occasional Light [*Navigation signal*]
occas........ Occasionally (NTIO)
OCCASL..... Occasional
Occas Pap Inst Min Metall... Occasional Papers Institution of Mining and Metallurgy (SAUS)
Occas Pap R Coll Gen Pract... Occasional Paper/Royal College of General Practitioners (SAUS)
Occas Pap San Diego Soc Nat Hist... Occasional Papers. San Diego Society of Natural History (SAUS)
OCCB........ Operational Configuration Control Board (AFM)
OCCB........ Organized Crime Control Bureau (LAIN)
OCC-BL...... Occult Blood [*Medicine*] (DAVI)
OCCBP...... Organization for Collectors of Covered Bridge Postcards (EA)
OCCC........ Obfuscated C Code Contest (SAUS)
OCCC........ Oil Control Coordination Committee (AD)
OCCC........ Ontario Crippled Children's Center [*Medicine*] [*Canada*] (EDAA)
OCCC........ Oocyte-Corona-Cumulus Complex
OCCC........ Open Chest Cardiac Compression [*Cardiology*] (DAVI)
OCCC........ Orange County Community College (AD)
OCCC........ Organized Crime-Control Commission [*California*] (AD)
OCCCA...... Office of Congressional, Community, and Consumer Affairs
OCCCE....... Organization for Coordination and Cooperation in the Control of Major Endemic Diseases
OCCCF....... Operator Communication and Control Facility (SAUS)
Oc C Cm O... Office of the Chief Chemical Officer (AD)
OCCD........ Com Dev Ltd., Cambridge, Ontario [*Library symbol*] [*National Library of Canada*] (NLC)
occd......... Occupied (AD)
OCCDC...... Oregon Coastal Conservation and Development Commission (AD)
OCC-E....... Office of the Chief of Communications-Electronics [*Army*] (AABC)
OCCE........ Oklahoma Citizen's Commission on Education (EDAC)
OCCE........ Operational Clothing and Combat Equipment (SAUS)
OCCEDCA... Organization for Co-Ordination in Control of Endemic Diseases in Central Africa (EA)
OCCF........ Oklahoma City Community Foundation (AD)
OCCF........ Operator Communication and Control Facility [*IBM Corp.*]
OCCF........ Optical Cable [*NASDAQ symbol*] (TTSB)
OCCF........ Optical Cable Corp. [*NASDAQ symbol*] (SAG)
OCCGE...... Organisation de Coordination et de Cooperation pour la Lutte Contre les Grandes Endemies [*Organization for Co-Ordination and Co-Operation in the Control of Major Endemic Diseases*] (EAIO)
OCCGERMDL... Army of Occupation of Germany Medal [*Military decoration*]
OCCH........ Childrens Hospital Research Foundation, Research Library, Cincinnati (SAUS)
OCCH........ Children's Hospital Research Foundation, Research Library, Cincinnati, OH [*Library symbol*] [*Library of Congress*] (LCLS)
OCCH........ Office, Chief of Chaplains [*Formerly, OC of Ch*] [*Army*] (AABC)
Occ Heal ANZ... Occupational Health Australia and New Zealand [*A publication*]
Occ Health&Sfty... Occupational Health and Safety (SAUS)
OCCI......... Optical Coincidence Coordinate Indexing (PDAA)
Occident.... Occidental (DIAR)
Occidental C... Occidental College (GAGS)
OCCIM....... Christ Hospital Institute of Medical Research, Research Library, Cincinnati, OH [*Library symbol*] [*Library of Congress*] (LCLS)
OCCIN....... Process Technology Department, Inco Ltd., Copper Cliff, Ontario [*Library symbol*] [*National Library of Canada*] (BIB)
occip........ Occipital (AD)
OCCIP....... Occiput [*Anatomy*] (WDAA)
OcciPet...... Occidental Petroleum Corp. [*Associated Press*] (SAG)
OcciPt....... Occidental Petroleum Corp. [*Associated Press*] (SAG)
OCCIS....... Operational Command and Control Intelligence System [*Army*] (AABC)
OCCIS....... Operations Command and Control Information System [*Military*]
occl.......... Occlude (AD)
OCCL........ Occluded (SAUS)
OCCL........ Occluding (SAUS)
OCCL........ Occlusal (SAUS)
OCCL........ Occupational License [*Vehicle license type used in state of Wisconsin*] (MVRD)
OCCL........ Ontario Community College Librarians [*Canada*] (AD)
OCCM........ Ocean Carbon Cycle Model (SAUS)
OCCM........ Office of Commercial Communications Management (AFM)
OCCM........ Open Chest Cardiac Massage [*Cardiology*] (DAVI)
OCCM........ Optical Counter-Countermeasures
OCCMDL.... Army of Occupation Medal [*Military decoration*]
OCCMDL.... Occupation Medal (SAUS)
OCCMED.... Occupational Medicine (AABC)
OCCMH...... Cambridge Memorial Hospital, Ontario [*Library symbol*] [*National Library of Canada*] (BIB)
OCCMLC.... Office, Chief, Chemical Corps [*Army*]
OCCMLO.... Office of the Chief Chemical Officer [*Military*]
OCCMS...... Occupational Measurement Squadron [*Air Force*]
OCCN........ Occasion
OCCN........ Occasionally (SAUS)
Occ N........ Occasional Notes, Canada Law Times [*A publication*] (DLA)
OCCN........ Occidental Nebraska Federal Savings Bank (SAUS)

Occ Newsl... Occasional Newsletter [*American Bar Association, Committee on Environmental Law*] [*A publication*] (ILCA)
OCC/NIBS... Ohio Consultive Council of the National Institute of Building Sciences (SAUS)
OCC NS..... Ohio Circuit Court Reports, New Series [*A publication*] (DLA)
OCCO........ Office Canadien de Commercialisation des Oeufs
OCCO........ Office of the Chief Chemical Officer [*Military*] (AAG)
OCCP........ Octachlorocyclopentene [*Organic chemistry*]
OCCP........ Outside Communications Cable Plant (CET)
Occ Pap Univ NSW... University of New South Wales. Occasional Papers [*A publication*]
OCCPR...... Open-Chest Cardiopulmonary Resuscitation
OCCR........ Cramahe Township Public Library, Castleton, Ontario [*Library symbol*] [*National Library of Canada*] (BIB)
OCCR........ Overseas Custody (Child Removal)
OCCS........ Oce Copy Control System (NITA)
OCCS........ Office of Combined Chiefs of Staff [*World War II*]
OCCS........ Office of Computer and Communication Systems (NITA)
OCCS........ Officer Career Counseling System [*Army*] (RDA)
OCCS........ Operational Command and Control System [*Army*] (AABC)
OCCS........ Optical Contrast Contour Seeker
OCCS........ Ordnance and Chemical Center and School [*Army*] (MCD)
OCCSA...... Ohio Correctional and Court Services Association (AD)
OCCSLY..... Occasionally (SAUS)
OCCSPEC... Occupational Specialities [*A publication*] (DNAB)
OCCT........ Collingwood Township Public Library, Clarksburg, Ontario [*Library symbol*] [*National Library of Canada*] (NLC)
OccTh....... Occupational Therapist (SAUS)
occ th....... Occupational Therapy (AD)
OccTh....... Occupational Therapy [*or Therapist*] (DAVI)
OCCU........ Trans-Ocean Container [*Intermodal shipping container symbol*] (TVRC)
OccuHlt..... Occupational Health & Rehabilitation, Inc. [*Associated Press*] (SAG)
OCCULT..... Optical Coven Communications Using Laser Transceivers (SAUS)
OCCULT..... Optical Covert Communications Using LASER Transceivers (MCD)
OCCULT..... Ordered Computer Collation of Unprepared Literary Texts
OCCULT..... Orser Complete Conversational User-Language Translator (SAUS)
occup........ Occupation (AD)
OCCUP...... Occupational
OCCUPNTS... Occupants [*National Highway Traffic Safety Administration Fatal Accident Recording System code*]
OCCUPON... Occupation (ROG)
OCCUPTN... Occupation
OCCUPTNL... Occupational
OccuSys..... OccuSystems, Inc. [*Associated Press*] (SAG)
OCCWC...... Office of Chief of Counsel, War Crimes [*Allied German Occupation Forces*]
OCCX........ Occidental Chemical [*Private rail car owner code*]
OC Cycle.... Open-Close Cycle (SAUS)
OCCZ........ Occidental Chemical [*Federal Railroad Administration identification code*]
OCD.......... Carmelitas del Sagrado Corazon (TOCD)
OCD.......... Carmelite Sisters of the Most Sacred Heart of Los Angeles (TOCD)
OCD.......... Central Office for General Defense (SAUS)
OCD.......... Discalced Carmelite Fathers (TOCD)
ocd.......... Discalced Carmelite Friars (TOCD)
OCD.......... Discalced Carmelite Nuns (TOCD)
ocd.......... Obsessive Compulsive Disorder [*Medicine*] (AD)
OCD.......... Obsessive-Compulsive Disorder [*Psychology*]
OCD.......... Occasioned [*Telegraphy*] (PCTE)
OCD.......... Occupation Centres for Defectives [*British*]
OCD.......... Ocean Chemistry Division [*Atlantic Oceanographic and Meteorological Laboratory*] (USDC)
OCD.......... Off Chip Driver (VLIE)
OCD.......... Office of Child Development [*HEW*]
OCD.......... Office of Civil Defense
OCD.......... Office of Civilian Defense [*Within Office of Emergency Management*] [*World War II*]
OCD.......... Office of Collection and Dissemination (SAUS)
OCD.......... Office of Community Development [*HUD*]
OCD.......... Office of the Center Director [*U.S. Food and Drug Admistration*]
OCD.......... Offshore and Coastal Dispersion (GNE)
OCD.......... Offshore and Coastal Dispersion Model (EAGT)
OCD.......... Ohio Circuit Court Decisions [*A publication*] (DLA)
OCD.......... Online Communications Drive [*or Driver*] [*Computer science*] (WDAA)
ocd.......... On-Line Communications Driver [*Computer science*] (AD)
OCD.......... Operational Capability Date (AAG)
ocd.......... Operational Capability Date (AD)
OCD.......... Operational Capability Demonstration (AAGC)
OCD.......... Operational Capability Development
OCD.......... Operational Concept Demonstration (SAUS)
OCD.......... Operational Concept Document
OCD.......... Operations Concept Document
OCD.......... Optical Car Detection
ocd.......... Optical Character Definition [*Computer science*] (AD)
OCD.......... Orbis Computer Deutschland (SAUS)
OCD.......... Ordnance Classification of Defects [*Navy*]
OCD.......... Ordo Carmelitarum Discalceatorum [*Order of Discalced, or Barefoot, Carmelites*] [*Roman Catholic religious order*]
OCD.......... Organ-Confined Disease [*Medicine*] (MELL)
OCD.......... Osteochondritis Dissecans [*Medicine*]
OC/D......... Other Cargo Damage (SAUS)
OCD.......... Other Checkable Deposits [*Federal Reserve system*] (GFGA)
OCD.......... Outer Canthal Distance [*Medicine*] (MELL)
O/C/D........ Out of Collector's District [*Bookselling*] (ROG)
OCD.......... Output-only Console Device (SAUS)
ocd.......... Ovarian Cholesterol Depletion [*Medicine*] (AD)
OCD.......... Ovarian Cholesterol Depletion [*Test*]
OCD.......... Overhaul Consumption Data
OCD.......... [*The*] Oxford Classical Dictionary [*A publication*] (ODCC)
OCD.......... Oxygen Cost Diagram (DMAA)
OCDA........ Officer Commanding, Divisional Artillery (SAUS)
OCDA........ Ordnance Corps Detroit Arsenal (SAUS)
OCDA........ Oregon Career Development Association (SEAT)
o/cdbd....... Oil on Cardboard (VRA)
OCDD........ Octachlorodibenzodioxin [*Organic chemistry*]
OCDD........ On-Line Call Detail Delivery [*AT&T*] (CIST)
OCDE........ Officer Commanding, Divisional Engineers (SAUS)
OCDE........ Organisation de Cooperation et de Developpement Economiques [*Organization for Economic Cooperation and Development - OECD*] [*France*] (EAIO)
OCDE........ Organizacion de Cooperacion y Desarrollo Economicos [*Organization for Economic Cooperation and Development - OECD*] [*Spain*] (MSC)
OCDETF..... Organized Crime Drug Enforcement Task Force
OCDF........ Operations Control and Display Facility [*Military*] (RDA)
OCDM........ Office of Civil and Defense Mobilization [*Merged with Office of Emergency Planning*]
OCDM........ Offshore and Coastal Dispersion Model [*Environmental science*] (COE)
OCDMS...... On-Board Checkout and Data Management System (MCD)
OCDN........ Order for Correction of Defect of Nonconformance
OCDP........ Officer Career Development Program (SAUS)
OCDQ........ Organizational Climate Description Questionnaire
OCDr......... Drackett Co., Research and Development Library, Cincinnati, OH [*Library symbol*] [*Library of Congress*] (LCLS)
OCDR........ Office of Collateral Development Responsibility (AFM)
OCDR........ Officer Control Distribution Report
OCDR........ Orbiter Critical Design Review [*NASA*] (NASA)
OCDRE...... Organic-Cooled Deuterium Reactor Experiment [*Nuclear energy*]
OCDS........ Officer Commanding, Divisional Signals (SAUS)
OCDS........ Offline Control Data Set (SAUS)
OCDS........ Output Command Data Set [*Computer science*] (ELAL)
OCDS........ Overseas College of Defence Studies [*British*]
OCDS........ Secular Order of Discalced Carmelites [*Rome, Italy*] (EAIO)
O/CDT....... Officer Cadet [*Military*] (WDAA)
O/Cdt........ Officer-Cadet (AD)
OCdt......... Officer-Commandant (SAUS)
OCD Test.... Ovarian Cholestrol Depletion Test (SAUS)
OCDU........ Optics Coupling Data [*or Display*] Unit [*Guidance and navigation*] (KSC)
OCDU........ Optics Coupling Display Unit (SAUS)
OCDW........ Ocean Climate Data Workshop (SAUS)
OCE.......... Edgecliff College, Cincinnati, OH [*Library symbol*] [*Library of Congress*] (LCLS)
OCE.......... Helicocean [*France*] [*ICAO designator*] (FAAC)
OCE.......... Ocean City [*Maryland*] [*Airport symbol*] (OAG)
OCE.......... Ocean Color Experiment [*NASA*]
OCE.......... Ocean Covered Earth (OA)
Oce.......... Oceanic [*Record label*]
OCE.......... Odessa Commodity Exchange [*Ukraine*] (EY)
OCE.......... Office, Chief of Engineers [*Army*]
OCE.......... Office of Career Education [*Office of Education*]
OCE.......... Office of Coastal Environment [*National Oceanic and Atmospheric Administration*]
OCE.......... Office of Criminal Enforcement [*Environmental Protection Agency*] (EPA)
OCE.......... Office of Cultural Exchange [*Department of State*]
OCE.......... Office of the Chief Economist (AAGC)
OCE.......... Office of the Director of Civil Engineering [*Air Force*]
OCE.......... Officer Commanding Exercises [*Military*]
OCE.......... Officer Conducting the Exercise [*Navy, Coast Guard*] [*Military*]
OCE.......... Officer Corps Engineers
OCE.......... Omega Chi Epsilon [*Honor society*] (EA)
OCE.......... OMGUS [*Office of Military Government, United States*] Civilian Employees Association [*Post-World War II, Germany*]
OCE.......... Ontario College of Education
OCE.......... Open Collaborative Environment [*Apple Computer, Inc.*]
oce.......... Operational Control Equipment (AD)
OCE.......... Optical Control Electronics (SAUS)
OCE.......... Orbital Computations Engineer (ACAE)
OCE.......... Oregon, California & Eastern Railway Co. [*AAR code*]
OCE.......... Oregon College of Education
OCE.......... Organizational Climate Exercise II [*Test*] (TMMY)
OCE.......... Oscillating Current Element
OCE.......... Other Common carrier channel Equipment (SAUS)
OCE.......... Other Controllable Expenses (MEDA)
OCE.......... Unesco Division of Marine Sciences (SAUS)
OCEA........ Outstanding Civil Engineering Achievement [*Award*] [*American Society of Civil Engineers*]
OCEA Award... Outstanding Civil Engineering Achievement Award (SAUS)
OCEAC....... Organisation de Coordination pour la Lutte Contre les Endemies en Afrique Centrale [*Organization for Co-Ordination in Control of Endemic Diseases in Central Africa - OCCEDCA*] (EAIO)
OCEAN...... Ocean Color Environment Archive Network (SAUS)
OCEAN...... Ocean Colour European Archive Network (SAUS)
Ocean....... Oceania (DIAR)
OCEAN...... Oceanographic Coordination, Evaluation, and Analysis Network
Ocean....... Ocean Transport and Trading Ltd. (SAUS)

OCEAN ...... Organisation de la Communaute Europeenne des Avitailleurs des Navires [*Ship Suppliers' Organization of the European Community - SSOEC*] [*Hague, Netherlands*] (EAIO)
Ocean&Shoreline Manage... Ocean and Shoreline Management (SAUS)
OCEANAV... Naval Oceanography Command [*Marine science*] (MSC)
OCEANAV... Oceanographer of the Navy
OCEANAVINST... Naval Oceanographic Office Instruction
OceanB...... Ocean Bio-Chem, Inc. [*Associated Press*] (SAG)
OCEANDEVRON... Oceanographic Development Squadron [*Navy*] (DNAB)
Ocean E..... Ocean Engineer (PGP)
Oceaner..... Oceaneering International, Inc. [*Associated Press*] (SAG)
OceanF...... Ocean Financial Corp. [*Associated Press*] (SAG)
OCEANIC... Ocean Information Center (SAUS)
OCEANIC... Ocean Network Information Center [*Information service or system*] (IID)
Ocean Inst... Oceanografiska Institute [*Oceanographic Institute*] [*Goeteborg, Sweden*] (AD)
OCEANLANT... Ocean Subarea (Atlantic) [*NATO*] (NATG)
Ocean Man... Ocean Management [*A publication*] (ILCA)
OCEANO..... Oceanic Fluxes of NO and NOx (SAUS)
oceano ...... Oceanologist (AD)
oceanog..... Oceanography (AD)
OCEANOG... Oceanography
OCEANOGR... Oceanographer (SAUS)
OCEANOGR... Oceanographic (SAUS)
Oceanogr Mar Biol Annu Rev... Oceanography and Marine Biology: Annual Review (SAUS)
Oceanogr Mar Biol Annu Rev... Oceanogrraphy and Marine Biology Annual Review (SAUS)
OceanOpt... Ocean Optique Distributors, Inc. [*Associated Press*] (SAG)
OCEAN-PC... Ocean Personal Computer Project (SAUS)
OCEANS..... Offshore and Civil Engineering Analysis System (SAUS)
OCEANS..... Omnibus Conference on Experimental Aspects of NMR [*Nuclear Magnetic Resonance*] Spectroscopy (MUGU)
OCEANSAT... Ocean Studies Satellite (SAUS)
OCEANSYSLANT... Ocean Systems, Atlantic
OCEANSYSPAC... Ocean Systems, Pacific
OCEB .... Ocean Beach Transfer and Storage [*Common carrier symbol*]
OCEC .... Officials Committee on Expenditure Control (SAUS)
OCED .... Office of Comprehensive Employment Development [*Department of Labor*]
OCED .... Organization for Economic Co-Operation and Development (WPI)
OCedC....... Cedarville College, Cedarville, OH [*Library symbol*] [*Library of Congress*] (LCLS)
OCEFT....... Corbeil Branch, East Ferris Township Public Library, Ontario [*Library symbol*] [*National Library of Canada*] (NLC)
OCEI .... Ocean Construction Equipment Inventory (DNAB)
OCel .... Dwyer-Mercer County District Library, Celina, OH [*Library symbol*] [*Library of Congress*] (LCLS)
OCEL .... Optical Coating Evaluation Laboratory (AD)
OCEL .... Oxford Companion to English Literature [*A publication*] (AD)
OCELAC ..... Camden East Branch, Lennox and Addington County Library, Ontario [*Library symbol*] [*National Library of Canada*] (NLC)
OCEleC...... Cincinnati Electronics Corporation, Cincinnati, OH [*Library symbol*] [*Library of Congress*] (LCLS)
O Celt .... Old Celtic (AD)
OCEM........ Office of Cooperative Environmental Management (SAUS)
OCEM........ Oklahoma Certified Emergency Manager [*Emergency Management*] (EMA)
OCEmI....... Emery Industries, Inc., Research Library, Cincinnati, OH [*Library symbol*] [*Library of Congress*] (LCLS)
OCEN .... Oce-Van der Grinten NV [*Netherlands*] [*NASDAQ symbol*]
OCEN .... Oce-van N.V. [*NASDAQ symbol*] (NASQ)
OCENY ...... Oce-van der Grinten ADR [*NASDAQ symbol*] (TTSB)
Oce-NY...... Oce-Van der Grinten NV [*Associated Press*] (SAG)
OCEO .... Office of the Commissioner for Equal Opportunity [*Australia*]
OCEO .... Open Change Engineering Orders (SAUS)
OCEP .... Office of Community Employment Programs [*Department of Labor*]
OCEP .... Officials Committee on Energy Policy (SAUS)
OCEPA....... Office of Communications, Education, and Public Affairs (AUEG)
OCEPA....... United States Environmental Protection Agency, Cincinnati, OH [*Library symbol*] [*Library of Congress*] (LCLS)
OCE Potential... Open Circuit Electrode Potential (SAUS)
OCER........ Oceaneering International, Inc. [*NASDAQ symbol*] (COMM)
OCESD ...... Organisation Canadienne pour l'Education au Service du Developpement [*Association*] [*Canada*] (EAIO)
OCESL....... Office of Criminal Enforcement and Special Litigation (COE)
OCET .... Ocean Terminals [*Common carrier symbol*]
OCEX .... Oceanic Exploration Co. [*OTCBB symbol*]
OCEX .... Oregon Coastline Express [*Federal Railroad Administration identification code*]
OCf........... Chagrin Falls Public Library, Chagrin Falls, OH [*Library symbol*] [*Library of Congress*] (LCLS)
OCF.......... Objects Components Framework (VLIE)
OCF.......... Obsessive Compulsive Foundation (EA)
OCF.......... Ocala [*Florida*] [*Airport symbol*] (OAG)
OCF.......... Office of the Chief of Finance [*Military*]
OCF.......... Officers' Christian Fellowship of the USA (EA)
OCF.......... Officiating Chaplain to the Forces [*Military*] [*British*]
OCF.......... On-Board Computational Facility [*NASA*] (NASA)
OCF.......... Ontario Cancer Foundation (SAUS)
OCF.......... Open Channel Flow
OCF.......... Open Computing Facility
OCF.......... Operational Control Facility (SAA)
OCF.......... Operation Code Field (SAUS)
OCF.......... Operator Console Facility [*Computer science*] (IBMDP)
OCF.......... Orbiter Computational Facility [*NASA*] (NASA)
OCF.......... Organic Crystal Growth Facility (SAUS)
OCF.......... Orientation Correlation Function (SAUS)
ocf .... Originally Cultured Formulation (AD)
OCF.......... Ossining Correctional Facility [*Sing Sing*] (AD)
OCF.......... Osteopathy in the Cranial Field (SAUS)
OCF.......... Output Characteristic Function (SAUS)
OCF.......... Owens-Corning Fiberglas Corp. [*NYSE symbol*] (SPSG)
OCF.......... Owner Control File (TIMI)
OCF.......... Ozenji Critical Facility [*Nuclear reactor*] [*Japan*]
OCFA .... Overseas Christian Fellowship Australia
OCF & A .... Office, Chief of Finance and Accounting [*Army*] (AABC)
OCFC .... Cloyne Branch, Frontenac County Library, Ontario [*Library symbol*] [*National Library of Canada*] (BIB)
OCFC .... Ocean Financial Corp. [*NASDAQ symbol*] (SAG)
OCFC .... Overseas Combined Federal Campaign [*Red Cross*]
OCFDA ...... United States Food and Drug Administration, Cincinnati, OH [*Library symbol*] [*Library of Congress*] (LCLS)
OCFIBRAS... Owens-Corning Fiberglas Corporation (EFIS)
OCFMFP .... Ontario Centre for Farm Machinery and Food Processing Technology, Chatham, Ontario [*Library symbol*] [*National Library of Canada*] (NLC)
OCFMFPT... Ontario Center for Farm Machinery and Food Processing Technologies (SAUS)
OCF-ML ..... Organisation Communiste de France - Marxiste-Leniniste [*Communist Organization of France - Marxist-Leninist*] (PPW)
OCFNT....... Occluded Front (SAUS)
OCFNT....... Occuluded Front [*NWS*] (FAAC)
OCFP .... Office of Commercial and Financial Policy [*Department of Commerce*]
OCFP .... Operator Command Function Processor [*Computer science*] (MHDI)
OCFR .... Oxford Committee for Family Relief [*British*] (AD)
OCFR .... Oxford Committee for Famine Relief [*British*] (DI)
OCFT .... Office of Curriculum Frameworks and Textbooks (AD)
OCFX .... Owens Corning Fiberglas [*Private rail car owner code*]
OCG.......... Cincinnati General Hospital, Medical Library, Cincinnati, OH [*Library symbol*] [*Library of Congress*] (LCLS)
OCG.......... Occasioning [*Telegraphy*] (PCTE)
OCG.......... Occupational Changes in a Generation [*Socioeconomics*]
OCG.......... OCG Technology, Inc. [*Associated Press*] (SAG)
OCG.......... Oesterreichische Computer Gesellscahft [*Austrian Computer Society*] [*German*] (AD)
OCG.......... Office of Challenge Grants [*National Endowment for the Humanities*] (BARN)
OCG.......... Office of the Commanding General [*Army*]
OCG.......... Office of the Comptroller General (AAGC)
OCG.......... Official Cruise Guide (TVEL)
OCG.......... Olin Corporation (EFIS)
ocg........... Omnicardiogram [*Medicine*] (AD)
OCG.......... Omnicardiogram [*Medicine*] (DMAA)
OCG.......... Operations Control Group (SAUS)
OCG.......... Optimal Code Generation
OCG.......... Oral Cholecystogram (SAUS)
OCG.......... Oral Cholecystography [*or Cholecystogram*] [*Radiology*]
OCG.......... Orbital Curve of Growth [*Mathematics*]
OCG.......... Osborne & Chappel Goldfields US [*Toronto Stock Exchange symbol*]
OCG.......... Overall Conflict Graph (VLIE)
OCG.......... Oxygen Consumption Gauge
OCGA........ Official Code of Georgia, Annotated [*A publication*] (DLA)
OCGAPAC... Ohio Corn Growers Association PAC [*Marion, OH*] (PACS)
OCGF .... Organic Crystal Growth Facility (SAUS)
OCGF .... Organic Crystal Growth Laboratory Facility (SAUS)
OCGH........ Cornwall General Hospital, Ontario [*Library symbol*] [*National Library of Canada*] (NLC)
OCGI......... Omni Capital Group (EFIS)
OCGM .... Office of Cabinet and Government Management [*Australia*]
OCGS........ Church of Jesus Christ of Latter-Day Saints, Genealogical Society Library, Cincinnati Branch, Cincinnati, OH [*Library symbol*] [*Library of Congress*] (LCLS)
OCGS........ Ontario Council on Graduate Studies (SAUS)
OCGSH ...... Good Samaritan Hospital, Medical Library, Cincinnati, OH [*Library symbol*] [*Library of Congress*] (LCLS)
OCGT .... OCG Technology [*NASDAQ symbol*] (TTSB)
OCGT .... OCG Technology, Inc. [*NASDAQ symbol*] (NQ)
OCGT........ Open-Cycle Gas Turbine (PDAA)
OCH.......... Chesley Branch, Bruce County Public Library, Ontario [*Library symbol*] [*National Library of Canada*] (NLC)
OCh.......... Chillicothe and Ross County Public Library, Chillicothe, OH [*Library symbol*] [*Library of Congress*] (LCLS)
OCH.......... Hebrew Union College - Jewish Institute of Religion, Cincinnati, OH [*Library symbol*] [*Library of Congress*] (LCLS)
OCH.......... Nacogdoches, TX [*Location identifier*] [*FAA*] (FAAL)
OCH.......... Obedience Champion [*Dog show term*]
OCH.......... Obstacle Clearance Height [*Aviation*] (FAAC)
och........... Ochre (AD)
OCH.......... Ochre [*Philately*] (ROG)
OCH.......... Office for Communication in the Humanities (NITA)
OCH.......... Oral Contraceptive Hormone (DB)
OCH.......... Orbiter Common Hardware [*NASA*] (NASA)
OCH.......... Order of the Compassionate Heart (EA)
OCH.......... Organ Clearing House (EA)
OCH.......... Outpatient Clinic (Hospital) [*Veterans Administration*]
OCHA........ Chatham Public Library, Ontario [*Library symbol*] [*National Library of Canada*] (NLC)

OCHA........ Office for the Coordination of Humanitarian Affairs [*United Nations*]
OCHA........ Office of Consumer Health Affairs [*Medicine*] (EDAA)
OCHA........ Oregon Clearing House Association (TBD)
OChaG....... Geauga County Public Library, Chardon, OH [*Library symbol*] [*Library of Congress*] (LCLS)
OCHAH...... Chatham Public General Hospital, Ontario [*Library symbol*] [*National Library of Canada*] (NLC)
OCHAK...... Chatham-Kent Museum, Chatham, Ontario [*Library symbol*] [*National Library of Canada*] (NLC)
OCHAKC..... Kent County Public Library, Chatham, Ontario [*Library symbol*] [*National Library of Canada*] (NLC)
OCHAMPUS... Office for the Civilian Health and Medical Program of the Uniformed Services (AABC)
OCHAMPUS... Office of Civilian Health and Medical Program of the Uniformed Services (USGC)
OCHAMPUSEUR... Office of the Civilian Health and Medical Program of the Uniformed Services in Europe (DNAB)
OCHAP...... Chapleau Public Library, Ontario [*Library symbol*] [*National Library of Canada*] (NLC)
OCharlys.... OCharleys, Inc. [*Associated Press*] (SAG)
OCHAT....... Thames Arts Centre, Chatham, Ontario [*Library symbol*] [*National Library of Canada*] (NLC)
OCHC........ Ohio Council for Home Care (EARSL)
OCHC........ Operator Call Handling Center [*Telecommunications*] (TEL)
OCHCB...... Huron County Board of Education, Clinton, Ontario [*Library symbol*] [*National Library of Canada*] (NLC)
OCHDC...... Hilton Davis Chemical Co., Cincinnati, OH [*Library symbol*] [*Library of Congress*] (LCLS)
OCHERB..... Chelmsford Branch, Rayside-Balfour Public Library, Chelmsford, Ontario [*Library symbol*] [*National Library of Canada*] (NLC)
OCHIN....... Norton Co. Electric, Chippewa, Ontario [*Library symbol*] [*National Library of Canada*] (NLC)
OC-HLTHLB... Occupational Health Labels [*Army*]
OCHM....... Haldimand County Museum Board, Cayuga, Ontario [*Library symbol*] [*National Library of Canada*] (NLC)
OCHP........ Cincinnati Historical Society, Cincinnati, OH [*Library symbol*] [*Library of Congress*] (LCLS)
OCHR........ Oil Catcher
OCHRE...... Optical Character Recognition Engine (PDAA)
OCHS........ Office of Cooperative Health Statistics [*Medicine*] (EDAA)
OCHS........ Old Colony Historical Society (AD)
OCHSDG.... Chesterville Branch, Stormont, Dundas, and Glengarry County Public Library, Ontario [*Library symbol*] [*National Library of Canada*] (BIB)
OChU........ Ohio University, Chillicothe Branch Campus, Chillicothe, OH [*Library symbol*] [*Library of Congress*] (LCLS)
OCHWL...... Wollaston and Limerick Public Library, Coe Hill, Ontario [*Library symbol*] [*National Library of Canada*] (BIB)
OCHZ........ Oil City Historical Society [*Federal Railroad Administration identification code*]
OCI........... Integrated Revolutionary Organizations [*Cuba*] (PPW)
OCI........... Object Code Insertion (SAUS)
OCI........... Occlude (DA)
OCI........... Ocean Color Imager [*Meteorology*] [*NASA*]
OCI........... Ocean Industry (SAUS)
OCI........... O.C. International [*Formerly, Orient Crusades Gospel Outreach*] (EA)
OCI........... Office of Community Investment [*Federal Home Loan Bank Board*]
OCI........... Office of Computer Information [*Department of Commerce*] [*Originator and database*]
OCI........... Office of Corollary Interest [*DoD*]
OCI........... Office of Criminal Investigation [*Environmental Protection Agency*] (EPA)
OCI........... Office of Current Intelligence (MCD)
OCI........... Office of the Coordinator of Information (AD)
OCI........... Old Canada Investment Corp. Ltd. [*Toronto Stock Exchange symbol*]
OCI........... Olympic Council of Ireland (EAIO)
OCI........... Ontario Cancer Institute [*UTLAS symbol*]
OCI........... Open Circuit Inductance (IAA)
OCI........... Operational Checkout Instruction (AD)
OCI........... Operation Child Identification [*Defunct*] (EA)
OCI........... Operator Control Interface (OA)
OCI........... Optically-Coupled Insulator (IAA)
OCI........... Optically Coupled Isolator
OCI........... Oracle Call-Level Interface [*Computer science*] (GART)
OCI........... Oregon Cancer Institute [*Oregon Health and Science University*] (RCD)
OCI........... Organisation Communiste Internationaliste [*Internationalist Communist Organization*] [*France*] [*Political party*] (PPW)
OCI........... Organisation de la Conference Islamique [*Organization of the Islamic Conference - OIC*] [*Jeddah, Saudi Arabia*] (EAIO)
OCI........... Organizational Climate Index [*Test*]
OCI........... Organizational Conflict of Interest (AAGC)
OCI........... Organization City (SAUS)
oci........... Organization Conflict of Interest (AD)
OCI........... Organization of CANDU Industries [*Canada*] (EAIO)
OCI........... Organized Crime Intelligence Unit [*Law Enforcement Assistance Administration*]
OCI........... Oryzacystatins I [*Biochemistry*]
OCI........... Other Cooperating Institutions (SAUS)
OCI........... Outer Compass Locator (LDOE)
OCI........... Out of City Indicator
OCI........... Outpatient Clinic (Independent) [*Veterans Administration*]
OCI........... Oxide Control and Indication (NRCH)
OCIA......... Organic Crop Improvement Association (EA)
OCIAA....... Office of Coordinator of Inter-American Affairs [*World War II*]
OCIB......... Beausoleil Indian Band Library, Christian Island, Ontario [*Library symbol*] [*National Library of Canada*] (BIB)
OCIB......... Organized Crime Intelligence Bureau (AD)
OCIC......... Officer Commanding in Charge [*Facetious acronym*] [*Army*] [*British*] (DSUE)
OCIC......... Organisation Catholique Internationale du Cinema et de l'Audiovisuel [*International Catholic Organization for Cinema and Audiovisual*] (EAIO)
OCID......... Dyke College, Cleveland (SAUS)
OCID......... Organized Crime Intelligence Division (SAUS)
OCIE......... Organizational Clothing and Individual Equipment [*Military*]
OCIEP....... Office of the Commissioners of Inquiry for Environment and Planning [*Australia*]
OCIF......... Out Card in File
OCII.......... Oryzacystatins II [*Biochemistry*]
OCIL......... Ocilla Industries, Inc. (SAUS)
OCIL......... Office of Community and Intergovernmental Liaison [*Environmental Protection Agency*] (GFGA)
OCIL......... Overdrive Cancel Indicator Light [*Automotive engineering*]
OCIM........ Osher Center for Integrative Medicine [*University of California, San Francisco*] (RCD)
OCIMF....... Oil Companies International Marine Forum [*British*] (EAIO)
OCINFO..... Office of the Chief of Information [*Military*]
OCIR......... Office of Community and Intergovernmental Relations (COE)
OCIR......... Operational Capability Inprovement Request Out of Commission, In Reserve [*Vesselstatus*] (DNAB)
OCIR......... Out of Commission in Reserve (SAUS)
OCirP........ Pickaway County District Public Library, Circleville, OH [*Library symbol*] [*Library of Congress*] (LCLS)
OCIS......... Oacis Healthcare Holdings Corp. [*NASDAQ symbol*] (SAG)
OCIS......... Office for Church in Society (EA)
OCIS......... Office of Computing and Information Services [*University of Georgia*] [*Research center*] (RCD)
OCIS......... Oncology Center Information System (MELL)
OCIS......... On-line Chemical Information System (SAUS)
OCIS......... Operational Control Information System [*Computer science*] (VLIE)
OCIS......... Organized Crime Information System [*Federal Bureau of Investigation*] [*Information service or system*] (IID)
OCIS......... OSHA [*Occupational Safety and Health Administration*] Computerized Information System [*Environmental science*]
OCIS......... Oxford Centre for Islamic Studies [*British*]
OcisHlth..... Oacis Healthcare Holdings Corp. [*Associated Press*] (SAG)
OCist......... Cistercian Fathers (TOCD)
ocist......... Cistercian Fathers (TOCD)
OCist......... Cisterdan Nuns (TOCD)
O CIST...... Ordinis Cisterciensis [*Cistercian Order*] (ROG)
OCIT......... Office of Combat Identification Technology [*Military*] (POLM)
OCITA........ Office of the Chemical Industry Trade Advisor
OCIU......... Chemprox Chimie [*Intermodal shipping container symbol*] (TVRC)
OCIU......... Optical Cable Interface Unit (MCD)
OCIX......... OCI Chemical [*Private rail car owner code*]
OCIZ......... Oneida County Industrial Development Agency [*Federal Railroad Administration identification code*]
OCJ.......... Ocho Rios [*Jamaica*] [*Airport symbol*] (OAG)
OCJ.......... Oklahoma City Junction Railway [*Federal Railroad Administration identification code*]
OCJ.......... Optional Construction Joint
OCJA........ Oklahoma Criminal Justice Association (AD)
OCJC........ Orange Coast Junior College [*California*] [*Later, OCC*]
OCJCS....... Office of the Chairman, Joint Chiefs of Staff (MCD)
OCJH........ Jewish Hospital, Medical Library, Cincinnati, OH [*Library symbol*] [*Library of Congress*] (LCLS)
OCJH-N..... Jewish Hospital, School of Nursing, Cincinnati, OH [*Library symbol*] [*Library of Congress*] (LCLS)
OCJP........ Office of Criminal Justice Planning (AD)
OCJP........ Office of Criminal Justice Program (OICC)
OCK.......... Chalk River Public Library, Ontario [*Library symbol*] [*National Library of Canada*] (BIB)
OCK.......... Kent State University, Stark County Regional Campus, Canton, OH [*OCLC symbol*] (OCLC)
OCK.......... Operation Control Key [*Computer science*] (IAA)
OCKA........ Atomic Energy of Canada [*L'Energie Atomique du Canada*] Chalk River, Ontario [*Library symbol*] [*National Library of Canada*] (NLC)
OCKE........ Petawawa National Forestry Institute, Canadian Forestry Service, Environment Canada [*Institut Forestier National Petawawa, Service Canadien des Forets, Environnement Canada*] Chalk River, Ontario [*Library symbol*] [*National Library of Canada*] (NLC)
Ocl.......... Cleveland Public Library (SAUS)
OCl.......... Cleveland Public Library, Cleveland, OH [*Library symbol*] [*Library of Congress*] (LCLS)
OCL.......... Object Constraint Language (VLIE)
OCL.......... Obstacle Clearance Limit (SAUS)
OCL.......... Obstruction Clearance Limit [*Aviation*] (PIPO)
OCL.......... Occasional [*Telegraphy*] (PCTE)
OCL.......... Ocean Cargo Line (AD)
OCL.......... Ocellus
OCL.......... Office of Congressional Liaison [*Environmental Protection Agency*] (GFGA)
OCL.......... Offshore Commercial Loan
OCL.......... Oil City Lubricants Ltd. [*Vancouver Stock Exchange symbol*]
OCL.......... Old Light Cruiser [*Navy symbol*]
OCL.......... Operating Control Language [*Computer science*] (VLIE)
OCL.......... Operational Check List (MUGU)
OCL.......... Operational Control Level

OCL .... Operation Control Language [*Computer programming*]
ocl .... Operator Control Language (AD)
OCL .... Operators Control Language [*Computer science*] (BUR)
ocl .... Optical Communications Linkage (AD)
OCL .... Oral Colonic Lavage [*Medicine*] (RAWO)
OCL .... Ordnance Circular Letter
OCL .... Organochlorine [*Also, OC*] [*Organic chemistry*]
OCL .... Orthopedic Casting Laboratory (DAVI)
OCL .... OS/2 inside Class Library (SAUS)
OCL .... Other Carrier Liability [*Insurance*] (MHCS)
OCL .... Ottumwa Connecting Line [*Federal Railroad Administration identification code*]
OCL .... Outer Compass Locator [*Aviation*] (LDOE)
OCL .... Outgoing Correspondence Log (AAG)
OCL .... Output Capacitorless (SAUS)
OCL .... Output Capacity Loading [*Computer science*] (ELAL)
OCL .... Overall Cartridge Length (SAUS)
OCL .... Overall Connection Loss [*Telecommunications*] (TEL)
OCL .... Overcorrected Lens (SAUS)
OCL .... Overhaul Cycle Limit
OCL .... Over-Night Cargo Ltd. [*Nigeria*] [*ICAO designator*] (FAAC)
OCL .... Overseas Container Line (AD)
OCL .... Overseas Containers Ltd. (AD)
OCL .... Overseas Currency Loan
OCIA .... Alcan Aluminum Co., Cleveland, OH [*Library symbol*] [*Library of Congress*] (LCLS)
OCLA .... Office of Congressional and Legislative Affairs [*U.S. Department of Interior*] (BARN)
OCLA .... Oregon Compiled Laws Annotated [*A publication*]
OCL/ACT .... Overseas Container Lines and Associated Container Transport (AD)
OCLAE .... Organizacion Continental Latinoamericana de Estudiantes [*Latin American Continental Students' Organization*] (EAIO)
OCIAM .... Arthur G. McKee & Co., Cleveland, OH [*Library symbol*] [*Library of Congress*] (LCLS)
OCLaw .... Cincinnati Law Library Association, Cincinnati, OH [*Library symbol*] [*Library of Congress*] (LCLS)
OCLB .... Office Club, Inc. (SAUS)
OCIBE .... Board of Education, Cleveland, OH [*Library symbol*] [*Library of Congress*] (LCLS)
OCIBHS ..... Benedictine High School, Cleveland, OH [*Library symbol*] [*Library of Congress*] (LCLS)
OCI-BPH .... Ohio Regional Library, Braille and Talking Books Division, Cleveland Public Library, Cleveland, OH [*Library symbol*] [*Library of Congress*] (LCLS)
OCIBS .... Blessed Sacrament Seminary, Cleveland, OH [*Library symbol*] [*Library of Congress*] (LCLS)
OCIC .... Cleveland Clinic Educational Foundation, Cleveland, OH [*Library symbol*] [*Library of Congress*] (LCLS)
OCLC .... Ohio College Library Center (BARN)
OCLC .... Online Computer Library Center [*Formerly, Ohio College Library Center. Initialism used in reference to cataloging system it developed*] [*Information service or system*]
OCICC .... Cuyahoga Community College, Cleveland, OH [*Library symbol*] [*Library of Congress*] (LCLS)
OCICh .... Christian Science Reading Room, Cleveland, OH [*Library symbol*] [*Library of Congress*] (LCLS)
OCICIM .... Cleveland Institute of Music, Cleveland, OH [*Library symbol*] [*Library of Congress*] (LCLS)
OCICo .... Cuyahoga County Public Library, Cleveland, OH [*Library symbol*] [*Library of Congress*] (LCLS)
OCID .... Dyke College, Cleveland, OH [*Library symbol*] [*Library of Congress*] (LCLS)
OCLD .... Occlude (SAUS)
OCLD .... Oil-Cooled
OCIDe .... Deaconess Hospital, Medical Library, Cleveland, OH [*Library symbol*] [*Library of Congress*] (LCLS)
OCLDP-K ... Open Court Language Development Program: Kindergarten (EDAC)
OCLE .... Continuing Legal Education, University of Oklahoma Law Center (DLA)
OCIFRB .... Federal Reserve Bank of Cleveland, Cleveland, OH [*Library symbol*] [*Library of Congress*] (LCLS)
OCIG .... Glidden Co. Research Library, Cleveland, OH [*Library symbol*] [*Library of Congress*] (LCLS)
OCIGC .... Garden Center of Greater Cleveland, Cleveland, OH [*Library symbol*] [*Library of Congress*] (LCLS)
OCIGI .... Gould, Incorporated, Gould Information Center, Cleveland, OH [*Library symbol*] [*Library of Congress*] (LCLS)
OCIh .... Cleveland Heights-University Heights Public Library, Cleveland Heights, OH [*Library symbol*] [*Library of Congress*] (LCLS)
OCLI .... Curve Lake Indian Band Library, Ontario [*Library symbol*] [*National Library of Canada*] (BIB)
OCLI .... Optical Coating Lab [*NASDAQ symbol*] (TTSB)
OCLI .... Optical Coating Laboratories, Inc. (PCM)
OCLI .... Optical Coating Laboratory, Inc. [*NASDAQ symbol*] (NQ)
OCLID .... Outgoing Called Line Identification [*Communications term*] (DCT)
OCLife .... Orthodox Christians for Life [*Association*] (EA)
OCLIPS .... Operational Climate Prediction and Services [*Marine science*] (OSRA)
OCIJC .... John Carroll University, Cleveland, OH [*Library symbol*] [*Library of Congress*] (LCLS)
OCIL .... General Electric Co., Light Research Laboratory, Cleveland, OH [*Library symbol*] [*Library of Congress*] (LCLS)
OCLL .... Office, Chief of Legislative Liaison [*Military*]
OCILH .... Lakeside Hospital, Cleveland, OH [*Library symbol*] [*Library of Congress*] (LCLS)
OCLloyd .... Lloyd Library and Museum, Cincinnati, OH [*Library symbol*] [*Library of Congress*] (LCLS)
OCIMA .... Cleveland Museum of Art, Cleveland, OH [*Library symbol*] [*Library of Congress*] (LCLS)
OCIMGH ..... Cleveland Metropolitan General Hospital, Cleveland, OH [*Library symbol*] [*Library of Congress*] (LCLS)
OCIMN .... Cleveland Museum of Natural History, Cleveland, OH [*Library symbol*] [*Library of Congress*] (LCLS)
OCIMt .... Mount Sinai Hospital, Cleveland, OH [*Library symbol*] [*Library of Congress*] (LCLS)
OCLN .... Occlusion [*Weather codes - aviation*] (PIPO)
OCINASA .... National Aeronautics and Space Administration, Lewis Research Center, Cleveland,OH [*Library symbol*] [*Library of Congress*] (LCLS)
OCIND .... Notre Dame College, Cleveland, OH [*Library symbol*] [*Library of Congress*] (LCLS)
OCLNR .... Oil Cleaner
OCIO .... Chlorine Dioxide (SAUS)
OCIP .... Park Synagogue, Cleveland, OH [*Library symbol*] [*Library of Congress*] (LCLS)
OCLR .... Ocular Sciences, Inc. [*NASDAQ symbol*] (NASQ)
OCLR .... Oil Cooler
OCIRC .... Rowfant Club, Cleveland, OH [*Library symbol*] [*Library of Congress*] (LCLS)
OCISA .... Cleveland Institute of Art, Cleveland, OH [*Library symbol*] [*Library of Congress*] (LCLS)
OCISS .... Saint Stanislaus Seminary, Cleveland, OH [*Library symbol*] [*Library of Congress*] (LCLS)
OCIStJ .... Saint John College of Cleveland, Cleveland, OH [*Library symbol*] [*Library of Congress*] (LCLS)
OCIStM .... Saint Mary's Seminary, Cleveland, OH [*Library symbol*] [*Library of Congress*] (LCLS)
OCITem .... Temple Library, Tiffereth Israel Congregation, Cleveland, OH [*Library symbol*] [*Library of Congress*] (LCLS)
OCIU .... Cleveland State University, Cleveland, OH [*Library symbol*] [*Library of Congress*] (LCLS)
OCLU .... Overseas Container Line Unit (AD)
OCLU .... Overseas Containers [*Intermodal shipping container symbol*] (TVRC)
O CLUB ..... Officers Club [*Military*] (GOBB)
OCIU-L .... Cleveland-Marshall College of Law, Cleveland State University, Cleveland, OH [*Library symbol*] [*Library of Congress*] (LCLS)
OCIUr .... Ursuline College, Pepper Pike, OH [*Library symbol*] [*Library of Congress*] (LCLS)
OCLUS .... Outside Continental Limits of United States [*Military*]
OCIV .... United States Veterans Administration Hospital, Cleveland, OH [*Library symbol*] [*Library of Congress*] (LCLS)
OCIW .... Case Western Reserve University, Cleveland, OH [*Library symbol*] [*Library of Congress*] (LCLS)
OCIW-H ..... Case Western Reserve University, Cleveland Health Sciences Library, Cleveland, OH [*Library symbol*] [*Library of Congress*] (LCLS)
OCIWHi ..... Western Reserve Historical Society, Cleveland, OH [*Library symbol*] [*Library of Congress*] (LCLS)
OCIWHi-AM ... Western Reserve Historical Society, Frederick C. Crawford Auto-Aviation Museum, Cleveland, OH [*Library symbol*] [*Library of Congress*] (LCLS)
OCIW-L .... Case Western Reserve University, Law Library, Cleveland, OH [*Library symbol*] [*Library of Congress*] (LCLS)
OCIW-LS .... Case Western Reserve University, School of Library Science, Cleveland, OH [*Library symbol*] [*Library of Congress*] (LCLS)
OCIW-S .... Case Western Reserve University, Sears Library, Cleveland, OH [*Library symbol*] [*Library of Congress*] (LCLS)
OCIW-SS .... Case Western Reserve University, School of Applied Social Science, Cleveland, OH [*Library symbol*] [*Library of Congress*] (LCLS)
OCM .... Cincinnati Masonic Temple, Cincinnati, OH [*Library symbol*] [*Library of Congress*] (LCLS)
OCM .... Creighton University, Health Sciences Library, Omaha, NE [*OCLC symbol*] (OCLC)
OCM .... Matchedash Public Library, Coldwater, Ontario [*Library symbol*] [*National Library of Canada*] (BIB)
OCM .... Mentor Plus [*Database*] [*United Kingdom*] (GDD)
OCM .... Ocean Circulation Model (QUAC)
OCM .... Ocean Color Monitor (ACAE)
OCM .... Ocean Colour Monitor (SAUS)
OCM .... Ocular Connection Machine (VLIE)
OCM .... Office of Compliance Monitoring [*Environmental Protection Agency*] (GFGA)
OCM .... Office of Country Marketing [*Department of Commerce*] (IMH)
OCM .... Office of the Commission [*Nuclear energy*] (NRCH)
OCM .... Ohm Centimeter (IAA)
o-cm .... Ohm-Centimetre (SAUS)
ocm .... Oil Content Monitor (AD)
OCM .... Oil Content Monitor [*Navy*] (CAAL)
OCM .... On-Camera Meteorologist
OCM .... On-Condition Maintenance (AABC)
OCM .... One-Channel Map [*Computer science*] [*NASA*]
OCM .... One Chip Module (SAUS)
OCM .... Ontario Center for Microelectronics (SAUS)
OCM .... Operator Console Module (TIMI)
OCM .... Operator Console Monitor
OCM .... Operator's Control Module
OCM .... Optical Contour Maximization [*Chemistry*]
OCM .... Optical Countermeasures
OCM .... Ordnance Committee Meeting (AAG)
OCM .... Ordnance Committee Minutes [*Military*]
OCM .... Ordo Constantini Magni [*International Constantinian Order*] (EA)
ocm .... Organic Content Monitor (NAKS)
OCM .... Organic Content Monitor (NASA)
OCM .... Origin of Columellar Muscle

OCM .... Oscillator and Clock Module
OCM .... Outline of Cultural Materials [*Human Relations Area Files*] [*Information retrieval*]
OCM .... Oxford Companion to Music [*A publication*] (AD)
OCM .... Oxidative Coupling of Methane [*Chemistry*]
OCMA .... Oil Companies' Materials Association [*British*] (BI)
OCMCEN .... Occupational Measurement Center [*Air Force*]
OCMCU ...... One-Chip Microcomputer Unit (SAUS)
OCME .... Oceanographic Community Modeling Effort (SAUS)
OCMH .... Madonna House Library, Combermere, Ontario [*Library symbol*] [*National Library of Canada*] (NLC)
OCMH .... Office of the Chief of Military History [*Army*]
OCMH .... Oklahoma Children's Memorial Hospital [*Medicine*] (EDAA)
OCMI .... Officer-in-Charge, Marine Inspection Office [*Coast Guard*]
OCMil .... Cincinnati Milacron, Inc., Research Library, Cincinnati, OH [*Library symbol*] [*Library of Congress*] (LCLS)
OCMilC ...... Cincinnati Milacron, Inc., Corporate Information Center, Cincinnati, OH [*Library symbol*] [*Library of Congress*] (LCLS)
OCMil-T ..... Cincinnati Milacron, Inc., Technical Information Center, Cincinnati, OH [*Library symbol*] [*Library of Congress*] (LCLS)
OCMIP .... Ocean Carbon-Cycle Model Intercomparison Project (SAUS)
OCM-LP ..... Organizacao Comunista Marxista-Leninista Portuguesa [*Portuguese Communist Organization, Marxist-Leninist*] [*Political party*] (PPE)
OCMLR ...... Organisation Communiste Marxiste-Leniniste de la Reunion [*Reunionese Communist Organization, Marxist-Leninist*] [*Political party*] (PPW)
OCMM .... Office of Civilian Manpower Management [*Later, Office of Civilian Personnel*] [*Navy*]
OCMMINST ... Office of Civilian Manpower Management Instruction [*Navy*]
OCMM-N .... Office of Civilian Manpower Management - Navy
OCMN .... Merrell-National Laboratories, Cincinnati, OH [*Library symbol*] [*Library of Congress*] (LCLS)
OCMODL .... Operating Cost Model
OCMR .... On-Condition Maintenance Rate (MCD)
OCMR .... Ontario Centre for Materials Research [*Canada*] [*Research center*] (RCD)
OCMR .... Organic-Cooled and Moderated Reactor (SAUS)
OCMS .... Onboard and Checkout Monitoring System (SAUS)
OCMS .... On-Board Checkout and Monitoring System [*NASA*] (KSC)
OCMS .... On-Chip test and Maintenance System (SAUS)
OCMS .... Operative Crate Makers' Society [*A union*] [*British*]
OCMS .... Optional Calling Measured Service [*Telecommunications*] (TEL)
OCMS .... Ordnance Command Management System
OCMS .... Ordnance Committee Meeting Standards (AAG)
OCMSq ...... Occupational Measurement Squadron [*Air Force*]
OCMTC ...... Officer Commanding Motor Transport Company (SAUS)
OCMU .... Ocmulgee National Monument
OCN .... Canadian Park Service, Environment Canada [*Service Canadien des Parcs, Environnement Canada*], Cornwall, Ontario [*Library symbol*] [*National Library of Canada*] (NLC)
ocn .... Ocean (BEE)
OCN .... Ocean
OCN .... Oceanair-Transportes Aeroes Regional SA [*Portugal*] [*ICAO designator*] (FAAC)
OCN .... Ocean Airways, Inc. (SAUS)
OCN .... Oceania (CARB)
OCN .... Oceanside, CA [*Location identifier*] [*FAA*] (FAAL)
OCN .... Oculomotor Nucleus [*Eye anatomy*]
OCN .... Office of the Commissioner of Namibia (BUAC)
OC-N .... Office of the Comptroller of the Navy
OCN .... Olde Colony & New Port [*Federal Railroad Administration identification code*]
OCN .... Oncology Certified Nurse (NUJO)
OCN .... Open College Network (AIE)
OCN .... Operational Carrier Number (SAUS)
OCN .... Operation Completion Notice (AAG)
OC-n .... Optical Carrier-n (SAUS)
OCN .... Optimal Channel Network [*Physics*]
OCN .... Optimal Climate Normals [*Climatology*]
OCN .... Orcana Resources Ltd. [*Vancouver Stock Exchange symbol*]
OCN .... Order Control Number (NASA)
OCN .... Organization Change Notice
OCN .... Organized Crime Narcotics Program [*Department of Justice*]
OCN .... Over Castle Rock [*New York*] [*Seismograph station code, US Geological Survey*] (SEIS)
OCNA .... Ovarian Cancer National Alliance
OCNAUD .... Oficina del Coordinador de las Naciones Unidas para la Ayuda en los Desastres [*Office of the Coordinator of the United Nations for Help in Disasters*] [*Spanish*] (AD)
OCNAV ...... Office of the Oceanographer of the Navy
Ocn Bch ..... Ocean Beach (AD)
OCNC .... Coniston Branch, Nickel Centre Public Library, Ontario [*Library symbol*] [*National Library of Canada*] (NLC)
OCNE .... Off Colour, Not Eating (SPVS)
OCNew ...... New Church Library, Cincinnati, OH [*Library symbol*] [*Library of Congress*] [*Obsolete*] (LCLS)
OCnf .... Canal Fulton Public Library, Canal Fulton, OH [*Library symbol*] [*Library of Congress*] (LCLS)
OCNFT .... Ocean Front (TVEL)
OCNGA ...... Officer-in-Charge of National Guard Affairs
OCNGH ...... Garden Hill Branch, Northumberland County Public Library, Campbellcroft, Ontario [*Library symbol*] [*National Library of Canada*] (BIB)
OCNGS ...... Oyster Creek Nuclear Generating Station (NRCH)
OCNHT ...... North Himsworth Township Public Library, Callander, Ontario [*Library symbol*] [*National Library of Canada*] (NLC)
OCNI .... Optimal Communications, Navigation and Identification (ACAE)
OCNIOS ..... National Institute for Occupational Safety and Health, Cincinnati, OH [*Library symbol*] [*Library of Congress*] (LCLS)
OCNJ .... First Occupational Center of New Jersey (EARSL)
ocnl .... Occasional (AD)
OCNL .... Occasional
OCNLY .... Occasionally
OCNM .... Oregon Caves National Monument (AD)
OCNM .... Organization of the Crimean Tatar National Movement (BUAC)
OCNMAP .... Ocean Map [*Marine science*] (OSRA)
OCNO .... Office of the Chief of Naval Operations
OCNPP ...... Oyster Creek Nuclear Power Plant (NRCH)
OCNPR ...... Operation and Conservation of Naval Petroleum Reserves [*Budget appropriation title*]
OCNR .... Office of the Chief of Naval Research (SAUS)
OCNS .... Oklahoma City NORAD [*North American Air Defense*] Sector (SAA)
OCNSW ..... Outdoor Club of New South Wales [*Australia*]
OCNU .... Ocean Lines [*Intermodal shipping container symbol*] (TVRC)
OCNVW ..... Ocean View (TRID)
OCNWU ..... Organizing Committee for a National Writers Union (EA)
OCO .... Cobourg Public Library, Ontario [*Library symbol*] [*National Library of Canada*] (NLC)
Oco .... Columbus Public Library (SAUS)
OCo .... Columbus Public Library, Columbus, OH [*Library symbol*] [*Library of Congress*] (LCLS)
OCO .... Object Code Only (HGAA)
OCO .... Office, Chief of Ordnance [*Army*]
OCO .... Office of Central Operations [*Bureau of Health Insurance*]
OCO .... Office of Civil Operations [*Coordinated US civilian pacification efforts in Vietnam*] (VNW)
OCO .... Off-Load Control Officer [*Navy*] (ANA)
OCO .... Oil/Coal/Ore (SAUS)
OCO .... Old Cornish [*Language, etc.*]
OCO .... OMS [*Orbital Maneuvering Subsystem*] Cutoff [*NASA*] (NASA)
OCO .... One-Cancels-the-Other Order [*Business term*]
OCO .... Ontario College of Ophthalmology [*Canada*] (AD)
oco .... Open-Close-Open (AD)
OCO .... Open-Close-Open [*Technical drawings*]
OCO .... Operating Capital Outlay (WPI)
OCO .... Operational Capabilities Objectives (SAUS)
OCO .... Operational Capability Objective [*Army*]
OCO .... Operational Checkout (AAG)
OCO .... Operations Console Operator (MUGU)
OCO .... Optically-Coupled Oscillator [*Instrumentation*]
OCO .... Ordnance Corps Order (AAG)
OCO .... Oregon Center for Optics [*University of Oregon*] (RCD)
OCO .... Public Library of Columbus and Franklin County, Columbus, OH [*OCLC symbol*] (OCLC)
OCOA .... Art Gallery of Cobourg, Ontario [*Library symbol*] [*National Library of Canada*] (NLC)
OCoa .... Columbiana Public Library, Columbiana, OH [*Library symbol*] [*Library of Congress*] (LCLS)
OCOA .... Organismo Coordinador de Operaciones Antisubversivas [*Coordinating Organism of Antisubversive Operations*] [*Uruguay*] (AD)
OCoAC .... American Ceramic Society, Columbus, OH [*Library symbol*] [*Library of Congress*] (LCLS)
OCOAP ...... Oscillating-Compensator Oscillating-Analyzer Polarimeter (PDAA)
OCoB .... Battelle-Columbus Laboratories, Columbus, OH [*Library symbol*] [*Library of Congress*] (LCLS)
OCOB .... Cobalt Public Library, Ontario [*Library symbol*] [*National Library of Canada*] (BIB)
OCOBD ...... Cobden Public Library, Ontario [*Library symbol*] [*National Library of Canada*] (BIB)
OCoBex ..... Bexley Public Library, Columbus, OH [*Library symbol*] [*Library of Congress*] (LCLS)
OCoC .... Capital University, Columbus, OH [*Library symbol*] [*Library of Congress*] (LCLS)
OCOC .... Cochrane Public Library, Ontario [*Library symbol*] [*National Library of Canada*] (NLC)
OCOCC ...... Ontario CAD/CAM Centre, Cambridge, Ontario [*Library symbol*] [*National Library of Canada*] (NLC)
OCoC-L ...... Capital University, School of Law, Columbus, OH [*Library symbol*] [*Library of Congress*] (LCLS)
OCoCT .... Columbus Technical Institute, Columbus, OH [*Library symbol*] [*Library of Congress*] (LCLS)
OCoCU ...... Capital University, Columbus, OH [*Library symbol*] [*Library of Congress*] (LCLS)
OCO Cycle ... Open-Close-Open Cycle (SAUS)
OCoD .... Ohio Dominican College, Columbus, OH [*Library symbol*] [*Library of Congress*] (LCLS)
OCOD .... Organization for Cooperation in Overseas Development [*Canada*] (EAIO)
OCoE .... Evangelical Lutheran Theological Seminary, Columbus, OH [*Library symbol*] [*Library of Congress*] (LCLS)
OCOE .... Office of the Chief of Engineers [*Army*] (RDA)
OCoF .... Franklin University, Columbus, OH [*Library symbol*] [*Library of Congress*] (LCLS)
OC of AC .... Office of the Chief of Air Corps [*World War II*]
OC of AS .... Office of the Chief of Air Staff [*World War II*]
OC of Ch .... Office, Chief of Chaplains [*Later, OCCH*] [*Army*] (AABC)
OC of F ...... Office of the Chief of Finance [*Military*]
OC of ORD ... Office, Chief of Ordnance [*Army*]
OC of SA .... Office, Chief of Staff, Army (AABC)
OC of SptS ... Office of the Chief of Support Services [*Army*] (AABC)
OC of T ...... Office, Chief of Transportation [*Army*]

OCoG .... Grandview Heights Library, Columbus, OH [*Library symbol*] [*Library of Congress*] (LCLS)
OCOGC ...... Official Centennial Olympic Games Club (EA)
OCOGF ...... General Foods Ltd., Cobourg, Ontario [*Library symbol*] [*National Library of Canada*] (NLC)
OCoGS ...... Church of Jesus Christ of Latter-Day Saints, Genealogical Society Library, Columbus Branch, Columbus, OH [*Library symbol*] [*Library of Congress*] (LCLS)
OCOKA ...... Observation and Fields of Fire, Cover, and Concealment, Obstacles and Movement, Key Terrain, and Avenues of Approach [*Military*]
OCOKA ...... Observation and Fields of Fire, Cover and Concealment, Obstacles, Key Terrain, Avenues of Approach (MCD)
OCOKA ...... Observation and Fire, Concealment and Cover, Obstacles, Key Terrain, Avenues of Approach [*Military*]
OCOL .... Collingwood Public Library, Ontario [*Library symbol*] [*National Library of Canada*] (NLC)
OCOLB ...... Colborne Public Library, Ontario [*Library symbol*] [*National Library of Canada*] (BIB)
OCoLC .... OCLC Online Computer Library Center, Dublin, OH [*Library symbol*] [*Library of Congress*] (LCLS)
OCoLC .... Ohio College Library Center, Columbus, OH [*Library symbol*] [*Library of Congress*] (LCLS)
OCOLD ...... Coldwater Memorial Public Library, Ontario [*Library symbol*] [*National Library of Canada*] (BIB)
OCOM .... Oficina Central de Organizacion y Metodos [*Central Office of Organization and Methods*] [*Spain*] (AD)
OCOM .... Outlet Communications, Inc. [*NASDAQ symbol*] (NQ)
OComS ...... Office of Community Services (AD)
OCOMS ...... Office of Community Services [*Military*]
OCON .... Northumberland and Newcastle Board of Education, Cobourg, Ontario [*Library symbol*] [*National Library of Canada*] (NLC)
OCON .... Orders for Correction of Nonconformance [*Navy*] (NG)
OCoNC ...... National Center on Educational Media and Materials for the Handicapped, Columbus, OH [*Library symbol*] [*Library of Congress*] (LCLS)
OConCL ..... Carnegie Public Library, Conneaut, OH [*Library symbol*] [*Library of Congress*] (LCLS)
OCONT ...... Oil Control
OCONUS .... Outside Contiguous United States (ALAC)
OConUS .... Outside Continental Limits of the United States (AD)
OCONUS .... Outside Continental United States [*Military*]
OCOO .... Cookstown Public Library, Ontario [*Library symbol*] [*National Library of Canada*] (BIB)
OCoO .... Ohioana Library, Columbus, OH [*Library symbol*] [*Library of Congress*] (LCLS)
OCOO .... Osteopathic College of Ophthalmology and Otorhinolaryngology (EA)
OCOO .... Osteopathic Colleges of Ophthalmology and Otolaryngology-Head and Neck Surgery (EA)
OC Ooutput... Open Collector Output (SAUS)
OCOP .... Outline Contingency Operation Plan (COE)
OCoR .... Riverside Methodist Hospital, Columbus, OH [*Library symbol*] [*Library of Congress*] (LCLS)
OCORD ...... Office, Chief of Ordnance [*Army*]
O Corn ...... Old Cornish (AD)
OCOS .... Ocean Climate Observing System (SAUS)
OCoSH ...... Columbus State Hospital, Columbus, OH [*Library symbol*] [*Library of Congress*] (LCLS)
OCOT .... Office, Chief of Transportation [*Army*]
OCoV .... Center for Vocational and Technical Education, Ohio State University, Columbus, OH [*Library symbol*] [*Library of Congress*] (LCLS)
OCoY .... Young Men's Christian Association, Columbus, OH [*Library symbol*] [*Library of Congress*] (LCLS)
OCOZ .... Owens-Corning [*Federal Railroad Administration identification code*]
OCP .... Carleton Place Public Library, Ontario [*Library symbol*] [*National Library of Canada*] (NLC)
OCP .... Obstacle [*or Obstruction*] Clearance Panel [*Aviation*] (OA)
OCP .... Occupational Cluster Program (OICC)
OCP .... Ocean Culture Product
OCP .... Ocean Surveillance Product (SAUS)
OCP .... Octacalcium Phosphate [*Inorganic chemistry*]
OCP .... Ocular Cicatricial Pemphigoid [*Ophthalmology*]
OCP .... Oerlikon-Contraves Pyrotec AG (SAUS)
OCP .... Office of Civilian Personnel [*Military*]
OCP .... Office of Commercial Programs [*NASA*]
OCP .... Office of Consumer Protection (AD)
OCP .... Office of Cultural Presentations (AD)
OCP .... Office of the Chief of Protocol [*US Department of State*] (AD)
OCP .... Officer Candidate Programme [*British military*] (DMA)
OCP .... Official Crude Prices [*Petroleum Intelligence Weekly*] [*Information service or system*] (CRD)
OCP .... Oficina Central de Personal [*Central Personnel Office*] [*Spain*] (AD)
OCP .... Olefin Co-Polymer [*Lubricants*]
OCP .... Onchocerciasis Chemotherapy Project [*WHO*]
OCP .... Onchocerciasis Control Program [*World Health Organization*] (BUAC)
OCP .... One-Component Plasma
OCP .... Ontario College of Pharmacy
OCP .... Open Circuit Potential (PDAA)
OCP .... Operating [*or Operational*] Control Procedure (MSA)
OCP .... Operational Capability Plan [*Army*]
OCP .... Operational Checkout Procedure [*NASA*] (KSC)
OCP .... Operational Communications Plan (MCD)
OCP .... Operational Computer Program (ACAE)
OCP .... Operational Configuration Processing (COE)
OCP .... Operational Control Panel
OCP .... Operation Control Panel (SAUS)
OCP .... Operations Control Plan (AAG)
OCP .... Operator Command Processor (TIMI)
OCP .... Operators Control Panel (SAUS)
OCP .... Optical Character Printing
OCP .... Oral Contraceptive Pill [*Gynecology*] [*Pharmacology*] (DAVI)
OCP .... Orbital Combustion Process (PDAA)
OCP .... Orbital Control Program (SAA)
OCP .... Orbital Correction Program [*NASA*] (KSC)
OCP .... Order Code Processor [*International Computers Ltd.*]
OCP .... Organic Conducing Polymer (ODA)
OCP .... Organizational Competitiveness Program [*Motivational program*]
OCP .... Organization of Czech Palynologists (SAUS)
OCP .... Orientalia Christiana Periodica [*A publication*] (ODCC)
OCP .... Ortho-Chlorophenol [*Organic chemistry*]
OCP .... Ostacalcium Phosphate [*A fertilizer*]
OCP .... Out of Commission for Parts (AFM)
OCP .... Output Control Program
OCP .... Output Control Pulse (NASA)
ocp .... Output Control Pulses (AD)
OCP .... Ova, Cysts, Parasites [*Gastroenterology*] (DAVI)
OCP .... Overcharge Protection (ACAE)
OCP .... Overhead Control Panel [*Automotive engineering*]
OCP .... Overland Common Point [*Imported item*] [*Business term*]
ocp .... Overland Common Points (AD)
OCP .... Overload Control Process [*Telecommunications*] (TEL)
OCP .... Overseas Common Point [*Exported item*] [*Business term*]
OCP .... Overseas Communications Project (SAUS)
OCP .... Owners and Contractors Protective [*Insurance*]
OCP .... Oxford Concordance Project (NITA)
OCP .... Public Library of Cincinnati and Hamilton County, Cincinnati, OH [*OCLC symbol*] (OCLC)
OCPA .... O-Chlorophenylacetic Acid (SAUS)
OCPA .... Office, Chief of Public Affairs [*Army*]
OCPA .... Office of Congressional and Public Affairs [*FCC*] (TSSD)
OCPA .... Office of Governmental and Public Affairs (SAUS)
OCPA .... Oklahoma Council of Public Affairs (RCD)
OCPA .... Ornamental Concrete Producers' Association (EA)
OCPA .... Ortho-Chlorophenoxyacetic Acid [*Organic chemistry*]
OCPA .... Ortho-Chlorophenylacetic Acid [*Organic chemistry*]
OCPAC .... Orange County Performing Arts Center, Segerstrom Hall, Costa Mesa (SAUS)
OCPCA ...... Oil and Chemical Plant Constructors' Association [*British*]
OCPCJR ..... Office of Crime Prevention and Criminal Justice Research (AD)
OCPCSB ..... Operational Computer Program Configuration Sub-Board (SAUS)
OCPD .... Coastal Protection Division [*Environmental Protection Agency*] (RCD)
OCPD .... Obsessive-Compulsive Personality Disorder (MELL)
OCPD .... Occult Constrictive Pericardial Disease [*Cardiology*] (CPH)
OCPD .... Officer Commanding Police Division (SAUS)
OCPD .... Officer-in-Charge Police District (AD)
OCPDB ...... Organic Chemical Producers Data Base (NITA)
OCPED ...... Office de Commercialisation du Poisson d'Eau Douce [*Freshwater Fish Marketing Corp. - FFMC*]
OCPG .... Goodwood Data Systems Ltd., Carleton Place, Ontario [*Library symbol*] [*National Library of Canada*] (NLC)
OCPG .... Procter & Gamble Co., Cincinnati, OH [*Library symbol*] [*Library of Congress*] (LCLS)
OCPG-H ..... Procter and Gamble Co., Health and Beauty Library, Cincinnati, OH [*Library symbol*] [*Library of Congress*] (LCLS)
OCPG-I ...... Procter & Gamble Co., Ivorydale Technical Center, Cincinnati, OH [*Library symbol*] [*Library of Congress*] (LCLS)
OCPG-Mv ... Procter & Gamble Co., Miami Valley Laboratories, Cincinnati, OH [*Library symbol*] [*Library of Congress*] (LCLS)
OCPG-Sw ... Procter & Gamble Co., Sharon Woods Technical Center, Technical Library, Cincinnati, OH [*Library symbol*] [*Library of Congress*] (LCLS)
OCPG-Wh ... Procter & Gamble Co., Winton Hill Technical Center, Cincinnati, OH [*Library symbol*] [*Library of Congress*] (LCLS)
OCPH .... Providence Hospital, Medical Library, Cincinnati, OH [*Library symbol*] [*Library of Congress*] (LCLS)
OCPI .... Ohio Cancer Pain Initiative (SAUS)
OCPI .... Optical Communic. Prod 'A' [*NASDAQ symbol*]
OCPINST ... Office of Civilian Personnel Instruction [*Navy*] (MCD)
OCPL .... Leigh Instruments Ltd., Carleton Place, Ontario [*Library symbol*] [*National Library of Canada*] (NLC)
OCPL .... Oklahoma City Public Library (AD)
OCPL .... Onondaga Library System [*Library network*]
OCPL .... Optical Computing and Processing Laboratory [*University of Arizona*] (RCD)
OCPL .... Orange County Public Library [*Florida*]
OCPLACS ... Ontario Cooperative Program in Latin American and Caribbean Studies [*Research center*] (RCD)
OCPM .... Optically Connected Parallel Machines [*Computer science*]
OCPNA ...... Ortho-Chloro-para-nitroaniline [*Organic chemistry*]
OCPO .... Office of Civilian Personnel Operations [*Air Force*]
OCPO .... Office of Computer Processing Operations [*Social Security Administration*]
OCPO .... Operations Cargo Passenger Office (DNAB)
OCPP .... Orbiter Cloud Photopolarimeter [*NASA*]
OCPP .... Oregon Center for Public Policy (RCD)
OCPP .... (Ortho-Chlorophenoxy)propionic Acid [*Organic chemistry*]
OCPR .... Office of Claims and Payments Requirements [*Social Security Administration*]
OCPR .... Office of Collateral Policy Responsibility (AFM)
OCPR .... Operation and Conversion of Naval Petroleum Reserves (DNAB)

OCPS .... I. P. Sharp Associates Ltd., Carleton Place, Ontario [*Library symbol*] [*National Library of Canada*] (NLC)
OCPS .... Office Canadien du Poisson Sale [*Canadian Saltfish Corporation*]
OCPS .... Office of Census and Population Studies [*British*]
OCPS .... Officer Candidate Preparatory School (DNAB)
OC/PS .... Open Connect/Presentation Services [*Computer science*] (HODG)
OCPS .... Orbiter Camera Payload System (SAUS)
OCPS .... Oxygen Cabin Pressurization Section [*NASA*] (KSC)
OCPSF .... Organic Chemical, Plastic, and Synthetic Fiber
OCPU .... P and O Containers [*Intermodal shipping container symbol*] (TVRC)
OCPV .... Open Circuit Photovoltage (SAUS)
OCPW .... Office of Chief of Psychological Warfare (LAIN)
OCQ .... Membre de l'Ordre des Chimistes du Quebec [*Canada*] (DD)
OCQ .... Oconto, WI [*Location identifier*] [*FAA*] (FAAL)
OCQ .... Oneida Ltd. [*NYSE symbol*] (SPSG)
OCQM .... Office of Chief Quartermaster [*Military*]
OCR .... Creemore Public Library, Ontario [*Library symbol*] [*National Library of Canada*] (BIB)
OCR .... Norcross, GA [*Location identifier*] [*FAA*] (FAAL)
OCR .... Occupational Safety and Health Control Report [*Navy*]
OCR .... Occurrence (SAUS)
OCR .... Ocean Colour Radiometer (SAUS)
OCR .... O'Connell Ranch [*California*] [*Seismograph station code, US Geological Survey*] (SEIS)
OCR .... Oculocardiac Reflex [*Physiology*]
OCR .... Off-Center Ratio (RAWO)
OCR .... Office for Civil Rights [*Department of Education*]
OCR .... Office of Civilian Requirements [*Division of War Production Board*] [*World War II*]
OCR .... Office of Civil Rights [*Environmental Protection Agency*] (GFGA)
OCR .... Office of Coal Research [*Energy Research and Development Administration*]
OCR .... Office of Collateral Responsibility (AFM)
OCR .... Office of Community Relations (COE)
OCR .... Office of Coordinating Responsibility [*Air Force*]
OCR .... Office of Corollary Responsibility (ACAE)
OCR .... Office of the County Recorder (AD)
OCR .... Oil Circuit Recloser
OCR .... Oil Control Ring [*Automotive engineering*]
OCR .... Oklahoma Central Railroad [*Federal Railroad Administration identification code*]
O Cr .... Oklahoma Criminal Reports [*A publication*] (DLA)
OCR .... Omnicare, Inc. [*NYSE symbol*] (SPSG)
OCR .... Operational Capability Release
OCR .... Operational Capability Requirement (SAUS)
OCR .... Operational Change Report [*Military*] (NVT)
OCR .... Operational Concept Review (ACAE)
OCR .... Operational Control Record [*Nuclear energy*] (NRCH)
OCR .... Operations Capability Reference (SSD)
OCR .... Operations Control Room [*Military*] (CAAL)
OCR .... Optical Card Reader (SAUS)
ocr .... Optical Character Reader [*Computer science*] (AD)
OCR .... Optical Character Reader [*Computer science*]
OCR .... Optical Character Recognition [*Computer science*]
OCR .... Optical Character Resolution [*Ligature Co.*] (PCM)
OCR .... Optical Code Reader (or Reading) (SAUS)
OCR .... Optical Curve Recognition (SAUS)
OCR .... Opticat Character Recognition (SAUS)
OCR .... Optimum Change Regulator (SAUS)
OCR .... Optimum Charge Regulator
OCR .... Optional Character Reader [*Computer science*] (DA)
OCR .... Oracle Resources [*Vancouver Stock Exchange symbol*]
OCR .... Order Change Record (SAUS)
OCR .... Order Control Record (SAA)
OCR .... Order of Corporate Reunion [*British*]
OCR .... Order of the Crown of Rumania
OCR .... Ordo Reformatorum Cisterciensium [*Cistercians, Trappists*] [*Roman Catholic men's religious order*]
OCR .... Organic-Cooled Reactor [*Nuclear energy*] (OA)
OCR .... Organisation for the Collaboration of Railways [*See also OSShD*] [*Warsaw, Poland*] (EAIO)
OCR .... Organization Change Request
OCR .... Organization of work Camps of the Revolution (SAUS)
OCR .... Organized Crime and Racketeering Section [*Department of Justice*] (DLA)
OCR .... Output Control Register
OCR .... Over Consolidated Ratio [*Nuclear energy*] (NUCP)
OCR .... Overcurrent Relay (MSA)
OCR .... Overhaul Component Requirement [*NASA*] (KSC)
OCR .... Overhead Component Requirement (IAA)
OCR .... Oxidizable Carbon Ratio
OCRA .... Office Communications Research Association (SAUS)
OCRA .... Officer Commanding, Royal Artillery (SAUS)
OCRA .... Optical Character Recognition - ANSI Standard (Font A) [*Computer science*]
OCR-A .... Optical Character Recognition-Font A (SAUS)
OCR-A .... Optical Character Recognition Type A (SAUS)
OCRA .... Organisation Clandestine de la Revolution Algerienne [*Secret Organization of the Algerian Revolution*] [*France*] (AD)
OCRA .... Overseas Company Registration Agents Ltd. (ECON)
OCRASC ..... Officer Commanding, Royal Army Service Corps (SAUS)
OCRB .... Optical Character Recognition - ANSI Standard (Font B) [*Computer science*]
OCRB .... Optical Character Recognition Bar [*Computer science*] (IAA)
OCR-B .... Optical Character Recognition-Font B (SAUS)
OCR-B .... Optical Character Recognition Type B (SAUS)
OCRBI .... Organization for Cooperation in the Roller Bearings Industry [*Warsaw, Poland*] (EAIO)
OCRC .... Ocean Climate Research Committee (SAUS)
O Cr C .... Oudh Criminal Cases [*India*] [*A publication*] (DLA)
OCRCWA .... Outcare Civil Rehabilitation Council of Western Australia
OCRD .... Ocean Climate Research Division [*Pacific Marine Environmental Laboratory*] (USDC)
OCRD .... Oculocerebrorenal Disease [*Medicine*] (MELL)
OCRD .... Office, Chief of Research and Development [*Army*]
OCRD .... Office of Crystalline Repository Development (SAUS)
OCRE .... Office of Conservation and Renewable Energy (COE)
OCRE .... Officer Commanding, Royal Engineers (SAUS)
OCRE .... Optical Character Reader Equipment (CCCA)
OCRE .... Optical Character Recognition Equipment [*Computer science*] (AABC)
ocre .... Optical Character Recognition Equipment [*Computer science*] (AD)
OCRE .... Organizations Concerned about Rural Education (AD)
oCRF .... Ovine Corticotrophin Releasing Factor [*Endocrinology*]
OCRHA ...... Overseas Command Records Holding Area [*Army*]
OCRI .... Office Canadien pour un Renouveau Industriel [*Canadian Office for Industrial Revival*]
OCRI .... Ottawa-Carleton Research Institute (SAUS)
OCRIE .... Ocean Resources, Inc. [*NASDAQ symbol*] (QUAN)
OCRIT .... Office of Combat Indentification Technology [*Army*]
OCRIT .... Optical Character Recognizing Intelligent Terminal [*Computer science*] (IAA)
ocrit .... Optical Character-Recognizing Intelligent Terminal [*Computer science*] (AD)
OCRM .... Ocean and Coastal Resource Management (GNE)
OCRM .... Office of Coastal Resource Management (USDC)
OCRM .... Officer Commanding Royal Marines [*British military*] (DMA)
OCRM .... Orbiter Crash and Rescue Manuals [*NASA*]
OCRM .... Outer Core Restraint Module (SAUS)
OCRMI ...... Officer Commanding Royal Marines (SAUS)
OCRO .... Office of Central Records Operations (SAUS)
OCRR .... Office of the Coordinator, Regulatory Reform [*Canada*]
OCRR .... Ottawa Central Railway [*Federal Railroad Administration identification code*]
OCRS .... Oculocerebrorenal Syndrome [*Medicine*] (DMAA)
OCRS .... Online Computing Reviews Service (RALS)
OCRS .... Ontario Centre for Remote Sensing [*Canada*]
OCRS .... Operational Change Reporting System (SAUS)
OCRS .... Optical Character Recognition System (NITA)
OCRS .... Organisation Commune des Regions Sahariennes [*Common Organization of the Saharan Regions*]
OCRS .... Organized Crime and Racketeering Section [*Department of Justice*]
OCRSDG .... Crysler Branch, Stormont, Dundas, and Glengarry County Library, Ontario [*Library symbol*] [*National Library of Canada*] (BIB)
OCRSF ...... Organized Crime and Racketeering Strike Force (AD)
OcrstLb ..... Ocurest Laboratories, Inc. [*Associated Press*] (SAG)
OCRT .... Ontario Consultants on Religious Tolerance
OCRU .... Office of Communication and Research Utilization (AD)
OCRUA ...... Optical Character Recognition Users Association [*Later, RTUA*] (EA)
OCRW .... Raymond Walters General and Technical College, Cincinnati, OH [*Library symbol*] [*Library of Congress*] (LCLS)
OCR WAND ... Optical Character Reader Wand (SAUS)
OCRWM ..... Office of Civilian Radioactive Waste Management [*Oak Ridge National Laboratory*]
OCRX .... OncoRx, Inc. [*NASDAQ symbol*] (SAG)
OCS .... Cities Service Co., Technical Center - Energy Resources Group, Research Library,Tulsa, OK [*OCLC symbol*] (OCLC)
OCS .... Object Compatibility Standard (SAUS)
OCS .... Obsessive Compulsive Scale [*Psychology*] (EDAC)
ocs .... Obstacle Clearance Surface (AD)
OCS .... Obstruction Clearance Surface (SAUS)
OCS .... O-Carbonyl Sulfide (SAUS)
OCS .... Occipital Condyle Syndrome [*Medicine*] (MELL)
OCS .... Occult Congenital Syphilis [*Medicine*] (MELL)
OCS .... Ocean Color Scanner (PDAA)
OCS .... Ocean Culture System
OCS .... Octachlorostyrene [*Organic chemistry*]
OCS .... Octopine Synthase [*An enzyme*]
OCS .... Office, Chief of Staff [*Army*]
OCS .... Office Cleaning Service [*Commercial firm*] [*British*]
OCS .... Office Communications System (SAUS)
OCS .... Office Computer System (IAA)
OCS .... Office for Consumer Services [*HEW*]
OCS .... Office of Civilian Supply [*Division of War Production Board*]
OCS .... Office of Commercial Services [*Department of Commerce*]
OCS .... Office of Commodity Standards (SAUS)
OCS .... Office of Communication Systems [*Air Force*]
OCS .... Office of Community Services [*Family Support Administration*] [*Department of Health and Human Services*] (GFGA)
OCS .... Office of Community Services [*Bureau of Indian Affairs*]
OCS .... Office of Computing Services [*Georgia Institute of Technology*] [*Research center*] (RCD)
OCS .... Office of Contact Settlement (SAUS)
OCS .... Office of Contract Settlement [*Functions transferred to GSA, 1949; now obsolete*]
OCS .... Office of the Chief Scientist
OCS .... Office of the Chief Surgeon [*Military*]
OCS .... Officer Cadet School (SAUS)
OCS .... Officer Candidate School [*Military*]
OCS .... Officers' Chief Steward [*Navy*]

OCS.......... Officers Command School (SAUS)
OCS.......... Oil Conditioning System [*Automotive lubricants*]
OCS.......... Oklahoma Climatological Society (SAUS)
OCS.......... Old Church Slavonic [*Language, etc.*]
OCS.......... On-Board Checkout System [*NASA*]
ocs.......... Onboard Checkout System [*NASA*] (NAKS)
OCS.......... On Call System (SAUS)
OCS.......... On-Card Sequencer (VLIE)
ocs.......... On Company Service (AD)
OCS.......... One-Control Switch (SAUS)
OCS.......... Open Cabling System (SAUS)
OCS.......... Open Canalicular System [*Hematology*]
OCS.......... Open-Circuit-Stable
OCS.......... Operating Control System [*Computer science*] (VLIE)
OCS.......... Operational Call Sign (IAA)
OCS.......... Operational Characteristics (NATG)
OCS.......... Operational Computer Software (VLIE)
OCS.......... Operational Control Segment (SSD)
OCS.......... Operational Control System (SAUS)
OCS.......... Operations Control System
OCS.......... Operator Communications Software (SAUS)
OCS.......... Operator Console Services (VLIE)
OCS.......... Operator Control Station (SAUS)
OCS.......... Operator's Connection Set (IAA)
OCS.......... Optical Character Scanner [*Computer science*]
OCS.......... Optical Communications System (SAUS)
OCS.......... Optical Communication System (SAUS)
OCS.......... Optical Communicator System (MCD)
OCS.......... Optical Computer System (IAA)
OCS.......... Optical Contact Sensor
OCS.......... Optical Contrasting Seeker (MCD)
OCS.......... Optimizing Control System (SAUS)
OCS.......... Optimum Coordinated Shipboard [*or Shorebased*] Allowance List (DNAB)
OCS.......... Oral Contraceptive Steroid [*Medicine*] (MELL)
OCS.......... Orbit Computation System (MCD)
OCS.......... Orbit Correction Subsystem (NOAA)
OCS.......... Order Communications System (SAUS)
OCS.......... Order Communications Systems (VLIE)
OCS.......... Order Control System (SAUS)
OCS.......... Order of the Cross Society (EA)
OCS.......... Organe de Controle des Stupefiants [*Narcotic Drug Control Organization*] [*France*] (AD)
OCS.......... Organocyclosiloxane (SAUS)
OCS.......... Oriel Computer Services Ltd. (NITA)
OCS.......... Oriental Ceramic Society (EA)
OCS.......... Oriental Chair of Solomon [*Freemasonry*]
OCS.......... Oriented Cellular Structure
OCS.......... Orifice of Coronary Sinus [*Medicine*] (MELL)
OCS.......... Original Combat System (SAUS)
OCS.......... Ornithodoros Coriaceus Spirochete [*Entomology*]
OCS.......... Oronite Customer Service [*Fuels and lubricants*]
OCS.......... Outer Continental Shelf
ocs.......... Outler Continental Shelf (AD)
OCS.......... Outpatient Clinic Substation [*Veterans Administration*]
OCS.......... Output Control Subsystem
OCS.......... Output Control System (SAUS)
OCS.......... Outside Chip Storage (SAUS)
OCS.......... Overdrive Cancel Switch [*Automotive engineering*]
OCS.......... Overload Control Subsystem [*Telecommunications*] (TEL)
OCS.......... Overload Control System (SAUS)
OCS.......... Overseas Citizens Services (IID)
OCS.......... Overseas Civil Servants (AD)
OCS.......... Overseas Communication Service [*India*] (BUAC)
OCS.......... Overseas Courier Service (AD)
OCS.......... Overspeed Control System (AAG)
OCS.......... Saint Thomas Institute, Cincinnati, OH [*Library symbol*] [*Library of Congress*] (LCLS)
OCSA........ Office, Chief of Staff, Army
OCSA........ Ohio Collegiate Soccer Association (PSS)
OCSA........ Ontario Council of Safety Associations (SAUS)
OCSA........ Orchid Society of South Australia
OCSA........ Outstanding Civilian Service Award
OCSAA...... Official Committee on Service Attaches and Advisers [*British*]
OCSAB...... Office of Contract Settlement Appeal Board [*Abolished, 1952*]
OCSAB...... Outer Continental Shelf Advisory Board [*Marine science*] (MSC)
OCSAN...... Organisation pour la Conservation du Saumon de l'Atlantique Nord [*North Atlantic Salmon Conservation Organization*] [*Scotland*] (EAIO)
OCSAPB..... Outer Continental Shelf Environmental Assessment Program. Arctic Project Bulletin (SAUS)
OCSAPSB... Outer Continental Shelf Environmental Assessment Program. Arctic Project Special Bulletin (SAUS)
OCSB........ Outer Continental Shelf Environmental Assessment Program. Bering Sea-Gulf of Alaska Newsletter (SAUS)
OCSC........ Outer Continental Shelf Committee [*Congressional committee*] (MSC)
OCSD........ Obsessive Compulsive Spectrum Disorder [*Psychology*]
OCSD........ Oculocraniosomatic Disease [*Medicine*] (DMAA)
OCSDG...... Stormont, Dundas, and Glengarry County Public Library, Cornwall, Ontario [*Library symbol*] [*National Library of Canada*] (NLC)
OCSDGL..... Stormont, Dundas, and Glengarry Law Association, Cornwall, Ontario [*Library symbol*] [*National Library of Canada*] (BIB)
OCSE........ Office of Child Support Enforcement [*Department of Health and Human Services*]
OCSEA....... Outer Continental Shelf Environmental Assessment [*Marine science*] (MSC)
OCSEAC..... Outer Continental Shelf Environmental Studies Advisory Commission [*Department of the Interior*] (MSC)
OCSEAP..... Outer Continental Shelf Environmental Assessment Program [*Department of Commerce, Department of the Interior*]
OCSEF....... Outer Continental Shelf Events File [*Department of the Interior*] (MSC)
OCSEP....... Outer Continental Shelf Energy Program [*Marine science*] (MSC)
ocsf.......... Office Contents Special Form [*Inventor*] (AD)
OCSF........ Office Contents Special Form [*Insurance*]
OCSIGO..... Office of the Chief Signal Officer
OCSL........ Oriel Computer Services Limited (NITA)
OCSL........ St. Lawrence College [*College Saint-Laurent*], Cornwall, Ontario [*Library symbol*] [*National Library of Canada*] (NLC)
OCSLA....... Outer Continental Shelf Lands Act
OCSLAA..... Outer Continental Shelf Lands Act Amendments of 1978 (COE)
OCSM........ Organization of Canadian Symphony Musicians [*See also OMOSC*]
OCSM........ Outer Continental Shelf Oil and Gas Supply Model [*Department of Energy*] (GFGA)
ocsn......... Occasion (AD)
ocsnl........ Occasional (AD)
ocsnly....... Occasionally (AD)
ocso......... [*The*] Cistercians Order of the Strict Observance, Trappists (TOCD)
OCSO........ Office of the Chief Signal Officer
OCSO........ Order of Cistercian Nuns of the Strict Observance [*Roman Catholic religious order*]
OCSO........ Order of Cistercians of the Strict Observance [*Trappists*] [*Roman Catholic men's religious order*]
OCSOT...... Overall Combat Systems Operability Test (NVT)
OCSP........ Office of Cued Speech Programs [*Gallaudet College*] [*Research center*] (RCD)
OCSP........ On-Line Certificate Status Protocol [*Computer science*] (VLIE)
OCSP........ Out of Commission, Special [*Vessel status*] (DNAB)
OCSPC...... Outer Continental Shelf Policy Committee [*California*] (AD)
OCSPWAR... Office of the Chief of Special Warfare [*Army*]
OCSR........ Optical Cable Signal Repeater (MCD)
OCSR........ Serpent River Band Public Library, Cutler, Ontario [*Library symbol*] [*National Library of Canada*] (NLC)
OCSS........ Office of the Chief of Support Services [*Army*]
OCST........ Office of Cable Signal Theft [*National Cable Television Association*] (NTCM)
OCST........ Office of Commercial Space Transportation [*Astronomy term*]
OCST........ Overcast (AABC)
ocst......... Overcast (AD)
OC Stage... Open Collector Stage (SAUS)
OCStFH...... Saint Francis/Saint George Hospital, Cincinnati, OH [*Library symbol*] [*Library of Congress*] (LCLS)
OCStG....... Saint Gregory Seminary, Cincinnati, OH [*Library symbol*] [*Library of Congress*] (LCLS)
OCSTL....... On-Board Checkout System Test Language [*NASA*] (KSC)
OCSU........ Scripps Institute of Oceanography [*Intermodal shipping container symbol*] (TVRC)
OCSW....... Objective Crew-Served Weapon
OCT.......... Cincinnati Technical College, Cincinnati, OH [*Library symbol*] [*Library of Congress*] [*OCLC symbol*] (LCLS)
OCT.......... Object Classification Test (DMAA)
OCT.......... Object Code Translator (SAUS)
OCT.......... O-Chlorotoluene (SAUS)
OCT.......... Octagon (AAG)
oct.......... Octagon (AD)
OCT.......... Octahedral [*Molecular geometry*] (IAA)
oct.......... Octal (AD)
OCT.......... Octal [*Number system with a base of eight*] [*Computer science*] (CET)
OCT.......... Octane (AAG)
oct.......... Octane (AD)
OCT.......... Octanol [*Organic chemistry*]
Oct.......... Octans [*Constellation*] (WDAA)
Oct.......... Octanus [*Constellation*]
OCT.......... Octarius [*Pint*] [*Pharmacy*]
oct.......... Octave (AD)
OCT.......... Octave (ADA)
Oct.......... Octavius (AD)
oct.......... Octavo (AD)
OCT.......... Octavo [*Book from 20 to 25 centimeters in height*] [*Bibliography*]
oct.......... Octet (AD)
OCT.......... Octet (GOBB)
Oct.......... October (AD)
OCT.......... October (EY)
oct.......... Octobre [*October*] [*French*] (ASC)
OCT.......... Octoraro Railway [*Federal Railroad Administration identification code*]
OCT.......... Octuple (MSA)
OCT.......... Office, Chief of Transportation [*Army*]
OCT.......... Office of Critical Tables [*NAS-NRC*]
OCT.......... Office of the Chief of Transportation (SAUS)
OCT.......... Officer Candidate Test [*Army*]
OCT.......... Officer Classification Test
OCT.......... Operational Climatic Testing (MCD)
OCT.......... Operational Cycle Time
OCT.......... Operations Control Team [*Deep Space Network, NASA*]
OCT.......... Operator Control Table (SAUS)
OCT.......... Optical Coherence Tomography [*Medicine*]
OCT.......... Optical Contract Seeker (MCD)
OCT.......... Optimal Control Theory

OCT .... Optimal Cutting Temperature [*Material for tissue fixation*]
OCT .... Optimized Compensation Transactions (SAUS)
OCT .... Oral Contraceptive Therapy [*Endocrinology*] (AAMN)
OCT .... Orbital Circularization Technique
OCT .... Organisation Communiste des Travailleurs [*Communist Organization of Workers*] [*France*] [*Political party*] (PPW)
OCT .... Ornithin-Carbonyl-Transferase (SAUS)
OCT .... Ornithine Carbamoyltransferase [*Also, OTC*] [*An enzyme*]
OCT .... Ortho-Chlorotoluene [*Organic chemistry*]
OCT .... Orthotopic Cardiac Transplantation [*Medicine*] (DMAA)
OCT .... Output Clock Trigger (IAA)
OCT .... Overseas Container Transportation (SAUS)
OCT .... Overseas Countries and Territories [*Common Market*]
OCT .... Oxford Classical Texts [*A publication*] (OCD)
OCT .... Oxytocin Challenge Test [*Medicine*]
OCTA .... Oceanic Control Area [*Aviation*] (DA)
OCTA .... Octanucleotide [*Biochemistry*]
OCTA .... Octapentadiene [*Toxic chemical*]
OCTA .... Office of the Chemical Industry Trade Advisor (SAUS)
OCTA .... On-Line Corporation Tax Assessment [*British*]
OCTA .... Oregon-California Trails Association (EA)
OCTA .... Ortho-Cyclohexanediaminetetraacetic Acid [*Also, DCTA*] [*Organic chemistry*]
OCTA .... Outsized Cargo Tanker Aircraft
OCTADJ ..... Octane Adjust [*Automotive electronics*]
OCTAHDR... Octahedral
OCTAHDR... Octahedron (SAUS)
OCTANE ..... Operations Control Technique for Actuals Number Extraction (MCD)
OCTAP .... Of Concern to Air Passengers [*Group affiliated with PATCO*] (EA)
OCTB .... Oxford Church Textbooks [*A publication*]
OCTC .... O-Chlorobenzotrichloride (SAUS)
OCTC .... Operators Console Transfer Channel (SAUS)
OCTC .... Operator's Control Transfer Channel [*Electronics*] (ECII)
OCTD .... Observation, Conclusion, Temporary Data (SAUS)
OCTD .... Orange County Transit District (SAUS)
OCTD .... Ornithine Carbamoyltransferase Deficiency [*Medicine*]
OCTD .... Other Connective Tissue Diseases [*Medicine*]
OCTD .... Overlap Connective Tissue Disease [*Medicine*] (DMAA)
octe .... Optical Component Testing and Evaluation (AD)
Octel .... Octel Communications [*Associated Press*] (SAG)
Octember ... October and November (SAUS)
OCTFCU EMPLOYEES PAC... Orange County Teachers Federal Credit Union Employees PAC [*Santa Ana, CA*] (PACS)
OCTG .... Oil Country Tubular Goods [*Metal industry*]
OCTG .... Oil Country Tubular Goods [*Energy industry*]
OCTH .... Town of Haldimand Public Libraries, Caledonia, Ontario [*Library symbol*] [*National Library of Canada*] (NLC)
OCTHB ...... Office, Chief of Transportation, Historical Branch [*Army*]
OCTI .... Office Central des Transports Internationaux par Chemins de Fer [*Central Office for International Railway Transport*] (EAIO)
OCTI .... Ordnance Corps Technical Instruction
OCTL .... Octel Communications Corp. [*NASDAQ symbol*] (NQ)
OCTL .... Oil Creek & Titusville Lines [*Federal Railroad Administration identification code*]
OCTL .... One-Channel-to-Line (SAUS)
OCTL .... Open-Circuited Terminating Line (IAA)
OCTL .... Open-Circuited Transmission Line
OCTLA....... Out of Control Area (SAUS)
OCTM........ Organization Concepts for Top Management (SAUS)
Octn .... Octanus [*Constellation*]
OCTO .... October Oil Co. (SAUS)
OCTOPUS... Ocean Colour Techniques for Observation, Processing and Utilization Systems (SAUS)
oct pars..... Octava Pars [*Eighth Part*] [*Latin*] (AD)
OCTR .... Octoraro Railway, Inc. [*AAR code*]
O/CTR .... Over Center [*Automotive engineering*]
OCTRF....... Ontario Cancer Treatment and Research Foundation [*Canada*] (BUAC)
octr prot... Octrooi Protectie [*Patent Protected*] [*Dutch*] (AD)
OCT/RR ..... Off Course Target/Remote Reference Display (NG)
OCT/RR Display... Off-Course Target/Remote Reference Display (SAUS)
OCTS .... Japanese Ocean Color Temperature Scanner (SAUS)
OCTS .... Occupational Carpal-Tunnel Syndrome (SAUS)
OCTS .... Ocean Color and Temperature Scanner (SAUS)
OCTS .... Ocean Color and Temperature Sensor (ACAE)
OCTS .... Ocean Color and Temperature Sounder (SAUS)
OCTS .... Ocean Colour and Temperature Sensor (SAUS)
OCTS .... Ocean Colour and Thermal Scanner (SAUS)
OCTS .... Open Cooperative Test System [*Trademark of NCR Corp.*]
OCTS .... Optical Cable Transmission System (MCD)
OC/TS Output... Open Collector/Tri-State Output (SAUS)
Oct Str ...... Octavo Strange [*Strange's Select Cases on Evidence*] [*A publication*] (DLA)
OCTU .... Officer Cadet Training Unit [*Military*] [*British*]
octup .... Octuplus [*Eightfold*] [*Latin*] (MAE)
octupl .... Octuplicate (AD)
octv .... Open-Circuit Television (AD)
OCTV .... Open-Circuit Television
OCTW .... Optical Communications Through the shuttle Window (SAUS)
OCU.......... Observation Care Unit [*Medicine*] (DAVI)
OCU.......... Occur [*Telegraphy*] (PCTE)
OCU.......... Oceanroutes, Inc., Palo Alto, CA [*OCLC symbol*] (OCLC)
OCU.......... Office Channel Unit (IAA)
OCU.......... Oklahoma City University
OCU.......... Ontario Council of Universities (SAUS)
OCU.......... Operational Capability Upgrade (ACAE)
OCU.......... Operational Control Unit
ocu........... Operational Conversion Unit (AD)
OCU.......... Operational Conversion Unit (NATG)
OCU.......... Order of Christian Unity [*British*]
OCU.......... Orderwire Operator Control Unit (MCD)
OCU.......... Osaka City University (SAUS)
OCU.......... Oscillator Clock Unit (SAUS)
OCU.......... Over-the-Counter Control Unit [*Stock exchange term*] (MHDW)
OCU.......... University of Cincinnati, Cincinnati, OH [*Library symbol*] [*Library of Congress*] (LCLS)
OCUA .... Ontario Council on University Affairs [*Canada*] (AD)
OCUAO ...... Oklahoma City University Alumni Office [*Association*] (EA)
OCUB .... Osmium Collidine Uranylenbloc (SAUS)
OCU-B .... University of Cincinnati, Biology Library, Cincinnati, OH [*Library symbol*] [*Library of Congress*] (LCLS)
OCUC .... Oxford and Cambridge Universities Club [*British*] (DAS)
OCUD .... Occurred [*Telegraphy*] (PCTE)
OCU-DA ..... University of Cincinnati, Design, Architecture, and Art Library, Cincinnati, OH [*Library symbol*] [*Library of Congress*] (LCLS)
OCU-E .... University of Cincinnati, Engineering Library, Cincinnati, OH [*Library symbol*] [*Library of Congress*] (LCLS)
OCUFA....... Ontario Confederation of University Facility Associations [*Canada*] (AD)
OCUG .... Occurring [*Telegraphy*] (PCTE)
OCUG .... Union Gas Ltd., Chatham, Ontario [*Library symbol*] [*National Library of Canada*] (NLC)
OCUG .... Union Graduate School, Cincinnati, OH [*Library symbol*] [*Library of Congress*] (LCLS)
OCU-Geo.... University of Cincinnati, Geology-Geography Library, Cincinnati, OH [*Library symbol*] [*Library of Congress*] (LCLS)
ocul .... Oculis [*To the Eyes*] [*Latin*] (AD)
OCUL .... Oculo [*To the Eye*] [*Pharmacy*]
OCUL .... Ocurest Laboratories, Inc. [*NASDAQ symbol*] (SAG)
OCUL .... Ontario Council on University Libraries (SAUS)
OCU-L .... University of Cincinnati, Law Library, Cincinnati, OH [*Library symbol*] [*Library of Congress*] (LCLS)
OCULA ...... Ontario College and University Library Association (SAUS)
OCULENT... Oculentum [*Eye Ointment*] [*Pharmacy*]
oculent ...... Oculentum [*Eye Ointment*] [*Latin*] (AD)
OCU-M ...... University of Cincinnati, School of Medicine, Cincinnati, OH [*Library symbol*] [*Library of Congress*] (LCLS)
OCU-Math... University of Cincinnati, Mathematics Library, Cincinnati, OH [*Library symbol*] [*Library of Congress*] (LCLS)
OCuME ...... Milton Elementary School, Custar, OH [*Library symbol*] [*Library of Congress*] (LCLS)
OCU-Mu..... University of Cincinnati, College Conservatory of Music, Cincinnati, OH [*Library symbol*] [*Library of Congress*] (LCLS)
OCU-N....... University of Cincinnati, College of Nursing, Cincinnati, OH [*Library symbol*] [*Library of Congress*] (LCLS)
OCU-Ph ..... University of Cincinnati, Physics Library, Cincinnati, OH [*Library symbol*] [*Library of Congress*] (LCLS)
OCUS .... Oblate Conference of the United States (EA)
OCUSI .... United States Industrial Chemicals Co., Research Center Library, Cincinnati, OH [*Library symbol*] [*Library of Congress*] (LCLS)
OCV.......... Bering Sea, AK [*Location identifier*] [*FAA*] (FAAL)
OCV.......... Consultative Committee for Exploratory Studies (SAUS)
OCV.......... Ocana [*Colombia*] [*Airport symbol*] (OAG)
OCV.......... Oil Check Valve
OCV.......... Old Aircraft Carrier [*Navy symbol*]
OCV.......... Onsite Calibration Van (SAUS)
ocv........... Open-Circuit Voltage (AD)
OCV.......... Open-Circuit Voltage
OCV.......... Operational Compliance Value (SAUS)
OCV.......... Opimian California Vineyards Corp. [*Toronto Stock Exchange symbol*]
OCV.......... Ordinary Conversational Voice [*Medicine*]
OCV.......... Ordre des Chevaliers du Verseau [*Knights of Aquarius Order*] (EAIO)
OCV.......... Other Coaching Vehicle [*Indian Railway*] (TIR)
OCV.......... Overriding Cam Valve
OCV.......... Overseas Cooperation Volunteers (SAUS)
OCV.......... United States Veterans Administration Hospital, Cincinnati, OH [*Library symbol*] [*Library of Congress*] (LCLS)
OCVD .... Open-Circuit Voltage Decay [*In silicon devices*]
OCV-L .... Oil Control Valve - Low-Speed
OCVM .... Occult Cerebral Vascular Malformation [*Medicine*] (RAWO)
OCVR .... Open Circuit Voltage Response (SAUS)
OCVRA ...... Overseas Citizens Voting Rights Act
oc vu .... Ocean View (AD)
OCW.......... Ocean City Western Railroad [*Federal Railroad Administration identification code*]
OCW.......... Oklahoma College for Women
OCW.......... Old Cars Weekly [*A publication*]
OCW.......... Operation Command Word [*Computer science*] (VLIE)
OCW.......... Orange Cyan Wideband (IAA)
OCW.......... Washington, NC [*Location identifier*] [*FAA*] (FAAL)
OCW.......... Waterloo Regional Library, Waterloo, Ontario [*Library symbol*] [*National Library of Canada*] (NLC)
OCWA .... Orange-Crowned Warbler [*North American bird banding code*] (BIBA)
OCWCIB..... Organizing Committee of the World Congress on Implantology and Bio-Materials [*See also COCMIB*] [*Rouen, France*] (EAIO)
OCWCT..... West Carleton Township Public Library, Carp, Ontario [*Library symbol*] [*National Library of Canada*] (BIB)
OCWFLU .... Operative Coachmakers' and Wheelwrights' Federal Labour Union [*British*]

OCWG Ocean Color Working Group (SAUS)
OCWN Ocwen Financial Corp. [*NASDAQ symbol*] (SAG)
OcwnFin Ocwen Financial Corp. [*Associated Press*] (SAG)
OCWP Operational Control Work Post (SAUS)
OCX Object Linking and Embedding Control Extension [*Computer science*] (IGQR)
OCX OLE Control Extensions (SAUS)
OCX OLE Custom Control (SAUS)
OCX Onex Corp. [*Toronto Stock Exchange symbol*]
OCX Open Compact Exchange (VLIE)
OCX Xavier University, Cincinnati, OH [*Library symbol*] [*Library of Congress*] (LCLS)
OCXO Oven-Controlled Crystal Oscillator
OCXO Ovenized Crystal Oscillator [*Electronics*]
OCXO Oven-temperature Controlled Crystal Oscillator (SAUS)
OCY Occasionally [*Telegraphy*] (PCTE)
OCY Organization Country (SAUS)
OCY Young Men's Mercantile Library Association, Cincinnati, OH [*Library symbol*] [*Library of Congress*] (LCLS)
OCYF Office for Children, Youth & Families (SAUS)
OCZ Lincoln, NE [*Location identifier*] [*FAA*] (FAAL)
OCZ Ocean Container Zebrugge (AD)
OCZ Operational Control Zone (MCD)
OCZM Office of Coastal Zone Management [*National Oceanic and Atmospheric Administration*]
OD Aerovias Condor de Colombia Ltda. (AEROCONDOR) [*Colombia*] [*ICAO designator*] (ICDA)
OD Delaware County District Library, Delaware, OH [*Library symbol*] [*Library of Congress*] (LCLS)
OD Doctor of Ophthalmology (WDAA)
OD Doctor of Optometry
OD Doctor of Osteopathy (WDAA)
OD Drug Overdose [*Emergency Medicine*] (DAVI)
OD Dundas Public Library, Ontario [*Library symbol*] [*National Library of Canada*] (NLC)
OD Emerald Airlines [*ICAO designator*] (AD)
OD Lebanon [*Civil aircraft markings - international*] (PIPO)
OD Obiter Dicta [*Legal term*] [*Latin*] (DLA)
OD Object Data (SAUS)
OD Observable Difference
OD Observation Data (SAUS)
OD Observed Drift
O-D Obstacle-Dominance [*Medicine*] (DMAA)
OD Obtained Absorbance [*Medicine*] (EDAA)
OD Occipital Dysplasia [*Medicine*] (EDAA)
OD Occupational Disease
OD Oceanographic Data (SAUS)
OD Oceanographic Datastation [*Telecommunications*] (TEL)
od Och Dylika [*And the Like*] [*Swedish*] (AD)
OD Octal-to-Decimal [*Computer science*] (BUR)
OD Ocular Density [*Ophthalmology*]
OD Ocular Dominance [*Opthalmology*]
OD Oculus Dexter [*Right Eye*] [*Ophthalmology*]
od Oculus Dexter [*Right Eye*] [*Latin*] (AD)
Od Odeon [*Record label*] [*Europe, etc.*]
Od Odericus [*Flourished, 1166-1200*] [*Authority cited in pre-1607 legal work*] (DSA)
Od Odofredus [*Deceased, 1265*] [*Authority cited in pre-1607 legal work*] (DSA)
od Odur [*or*] [*German*] (AD)
Od Odyssey [*of Homer*] [*Classical studies*] (OCD)
OD Office Decision [*United States Internal Revenue Bureau*] [*A publication*] (DLA)
OD Office of Disability [*Department of Health and Human Services*] (GFGA)
OD Office of the Director
OD Officer of the Day [*or Deck*] [*Also, OOD*] [*Navy*]
OD Ohio Decisions [*A publication*] (DLA)
OD Oil Desurger
OD Oil Distribution (DNAB)
OD Oil Drainage
OD Oildroplet (SAUS)
OD Oktal Dump (SAUS)
OD Old Dutch [*Language, etc.*]
OD Oldesloe [*German license plate city code*]
OD Oldest Dryas (SAUS)
od Olive Drab (WDAA)
OD Olive Drab [*Color often used for military clothing and equipment*]
OD Ollier Disease [*Medicine*] (EDAA)
OD Omnes Dies [*Every Day*] [*Pharmacy*]
OD Once a Day [*or Daily*] (DAVI)
OD Once Daily (SAUS)
O/D On Deck (KSC)
od On Demand (AD)
OD On Demand [*Business term*]
O/D On Dock (MCD)
OD On Duty
OD One Day (SAA)
od Only Daughter (WDAA)
OD Onrechtmatige Daad [*Tort or Tortious Act*] [*Netherlands*] (ILCA)
OD Opendoc, Open Document (SAUS)
OD Open Drain (IAA)
OD Open Drop
OD Operational Data (SAUS)
OD Operational Decoder (SAUS)
OD Operational Demonstration (SAUS)
O/D Operational Difficulty (ACAE)
OD Operational Directive (SAUS)
OD Operational Downlink (SAUS)
OD Operational Downlink/Downlist (NASA)
OD Operational DownList
OD Operation Description
OD Operations Directive [*or Director*]
OD Operations Director (SAUS)
OD Operations Division
OD Ophthalmic Dispenser [*Medicine*] (EDAA)
OD Opioid Dependence [*Medicine*] (MELL)
od Optical Density (AD)
OD Optical Density
OD Optical Detection (ABAC)
OD Optical Disc (SAUS)
OD Optical Disk [*Computer science*] (TELE)
OD Optimal Dose [*Medicine*] (EDAA)
OD Opus Dei (EA)
OD Orbit Determination
OD Orbiter (Operational) Downlink [*NASA*]
OD Order [*Telegraphy*] (PCTE)
OD Order Dienst [*Netherlands first organized resistance group, 1940*] [*World War II*]
OD Order of Daedalians (EA)
OD Order of Death (SAUS)
OD Order of DeMolay (EA)
O/D Order of Deportation
OD Order of the Day (SAUS)
OD Ordinary (SAUS)
OD Ordinary Seaman [*British*] (DMA)
OD Ordnance (ACAE)
OD Ordnance Corps [*Army*] (GFGA)
OD Ordnance Data [*Inspection and test data*]
OD Ordnance Delivery (SAUS)
OD Ordnance Department [*or Division*]
OD Ordnance Depot (SAUS)
OD Ordnance Disposal (SAUS)
OD Ordnance Document [*Navy*]
OD Ordnance Drawing
OD Ordnungsdienst [*Military Police Service*] [*German military - World War II*]
od Organizational Development (AD)
OD Organization Development [*Human resources*] (WYGK)
OD Original Data (SAUS)
od Original Design (AD)
OD Original Design
OD Original Dirac [*Vacuum model*] [*Physics*]
OD Originally Derived
OD Origin and Destination [*Aviation*] (AFM)
OD Orphan Drug [*Medicine*] (MELL)
OD Osseous Defect [*Medicine*]
OD Other Denomination [*British military*] (DMA)
OD Out Diffusion (SAUS)
OD Outer Detector
od Outer Diameter (SHCU)
OD Outer Diameter [*Mechanical engineering*]
OD Out-of-Date
OD Output Data (IEEE)
OD Output Diode (SAUS)
OD Output Disable
OD Output Display [*Computer science*] (IAA)
od Outside Diameter (AD)
OD Outside Diameter (EAGT)
OD Outside Dimension
OD Outstanding Debt [*Finance*] (MHDB)
od Oven Dried (AD)
OD Oven Dry
OD Overall Depth [*Typography*] (DGA)
OD Overburden Drill (PDAA)
od Overdose (AD)
OD Overdose [*of narcotics*]
OD Overdraft [*or Overdrawn*] [*Banking*]
OD Overdrawn [*Banking*] (WDAA)
OD Overdrive (AAG)
od Overdrive (AD)
Od Overdue
OD Overload Detection [*Telecommunications*] (TEL)
OD Overtly Diabetic [*Medicine*]
OD Oxford Dictionary (SAUS)
OD Oxygen Demand [*Medicine*] (EDAA)
OD Oxygen Drain (MCD)
O-D Zero Dimensional (AAEL)
OD3 Operational Data Dictionary/Directory (SAUS)
OD3 Optical Digital Data Disk
ODA Civic Democratic Alliance [*Czech Republic*] [*Political party*] (BUAC)
ODa Dayton and Montgomery County Public Library, Dayton, OH [*Library symbol*] [*Library of Congress*] (LCLS)
ODA Iso-Octyldecyladipinat (SAUS)
oda Occipito-Dextra Anterior (AD)
ODA Occipitodextra Anterior [*A fetal position*] [*Medicine*] (AAMN)
ODA Octadecylamine (SAUS)
ODA Octal Debugging Aid [*Computer science*]
ODA Octyldecyladipat (SAUS)

Oda .... Odessa (AD)
ODA.......... Offa's Dyke Association [*British*] (DBA)
ODA.......... Office Data Architecture (SAUS)
ODA.......... Office Document Architecture [*Telecommunications*] (TSSD)
ODA.......... Office of Debt [*or Depreciation*] Analysis [*Department of the Treasury*]
ODA.......... Office of Drug Abuse (AD)
ODA.......... Office of the Defense Attache [*Foreign Service*]
ODA.......... Office of the Deputy Administrator (COE)
ODA.......... Office of the District Administrator (AD)
ODA.......... Office of the District Attorney (AD)
ODA.......... Official Development Aid [*or Assistance*]
ODA.......... Ohio Dental Association (SAUS)
ODA.......... Oklahoma Dental Association (SAUS)
ODa.......... Old Danish (AD)
ODA.......... Omni Deployment Actuator (ACAE)
ODA.......... Omnidirectional Aerial (SAUS)
ODA.......... Omnidirectional Antenna
ODA.......... One-Digit Adder (SAUS)
ODA.......... Online Delivery Acknowledgement (SAUS)
ODA.......... Ontario Dental Association [*Canada*] (BUAC)
ODA.......... Open Document Architecture (SAUS)
ODA.......... Operational Data Analysis
ODA.......... Operational Design and Analysis (IEEE)
ODA.......... Optical Diffraction Analyser (SAUS)
ODA.......... Optical Diffraction Analyses (SAUS)
ODA.......... Optical Diffraction Analysis [*Microscopy*]
ODA.......... Oronite Diesel Additive [*Fuels and lubricants*]
ODA.......... Oronite Fuel Additive (SAUS)
ODA.......... Orphan Drug Ace [*1983*] (BARN)
ODA.......... Oscillating Doublet Antenna
ODA.......... Oscillator/Doubler/Amplifier
ODA.......... Osmotic Driving Agent [*Medicine*] (EDAA)
ODA.......... Other Design Activity (MSA)
ODA.......... Ouadda [*Central African Republic*] [*Airport symbol*] (AD)
ODA.......... Output Data Acknowledge (SAUS)
ODA.......... Overseas Development Administration [*British*] (EAIO)
ODA.......... Overseas Development Agency [*British*]
ODA.......... Overseas Development Aid
ODA.......... Overseas Development Assistance (AD)
ODA.......... Overseas Doctors Association in the United Kingdom [*British*]
ODA.......... Oxydianiline [*Organic chemistry*]
ODAA........ Aden/International [*People's Democratic Republic of Yemen*] [*ICAO location identifier*] (ICLI)
ODaA........ Dayton Art Institute, Dayton, OH [*Library symbol*] [*Library of Congress*] (LCLS)
ODAA........ Office of Dependent Area Affairs [*Department of State*]
ODAB........ Beihan [*People's Democratic Republic of Yemen*] [*ICAO location identifier*] (ICLI)
ODAC........ Oil Depletion Analysis Center (STAH)
ODAC........ Old Dominion Athletic Conference (PSS)
ODAC........ On Demand Analyzer Computer
ODAC........ Open Document Architecture Consortium (SAUS)
ODAC........ Operations Distribution Administration Center (SAUS)
ODACA...... Original Doll Artists Council of America (EA)
ODaCox..... Cox Coronary Heart Institute, Dayton, OH [*Library symbol*] [*Library of Congress*] (LCLS)
ODADAS.... Ohio Department of Alcohol and Drug Addiction Services
ODADC...... Omnidirectional Air Data Computer (MCD)
ODaE........ Engineers' Club of Dayton, Dayton, OH [*Library symbol*] [*Library of Congress*] (LCLS)
ODAF........ Aden [*People's Democratic Republic of Yemen*] [*ICAO location identifier*] (ICLI)
ODAG........ Al-Gheida [*People's Democratic Republic of Yemen*] [*ICAO location identifier*] (ICLI)
ODaGH...... Grandview Hospital, Dayton, OH [*Library symbol*] [*Library of Congress*] (LCLS)
ODaGL...... Church of Jesus Christ of Latter-Day Saints, Genealogical Society Library, Dayton Ohio Branch, Dayton, OH [*Library symbol*] [*Library of Congress*] (LCLS)
ODaGMI..... General Motors Corp., Inland Manufacturing Division, Engineering Library, Dayton, OH [*Library symbol*] [*Library of Congress*] (LCLS)
ODaGMI..... General Motors Corp., Inland Manufacturing Division, Engineering Library, Dayton (SAUS)
ODaGS...... Good Samaritan Hospital, Dayton, OH [*Library symbol*] [*Library of Congress*] (LCLS)
ODAI......... Origin/Destination Address Assignor Indicator (SAUS)
ODAI......... Origin-Destination Assignor Identifier (SAUS)
ODAL........ Octadecenal (SAUS)
ODALC...... Ogden Air Logistics Center (MCD)
ODALE....... Office of Drug Abuse Law Enforcement [*Later, Drug Enforcement Administration*] [*Department of Justice*]
ODALS...... Omnidirectional Approach Lighting System [*Aviation*] (FAAC)
ODAM....... Mukeiras [*People's Democratic Republic of Yemen*] [*ICAO location identifier*] (ICLI)
ODAM....... Open Distributed Application Model (SAUS)
ODaMC...... Barney Children's Medical Center, Dayton, OH [*Library symbol*] [*Library of Congress*] (LCLS)
ODaMCo.... Mead Corp., Dayton, OH [*Library symbol*] [*Library of Congress*] (LCLS)
ODaMNH.... Dayton Museum of Natural History, Dayton, OH [*Library symbol*] [*Library of Congress*] (LCLS)
ODaMR...... Monsanto Research Corp., Dayton Laboratory, Dayton, OH [*Library symbol*] [*Library of Congress*] (LCLS)
ODAMS...... Open Water Disposal Area Management Simulation [*US Army Corps of Engineers*]
ODaMVH.... Miami Valley Hospital, Dayton, OH [*Library symbol*] [*Library of Congress*] (LCLS)
ODAN........ Kamaran [*People's Democratic Republic of Yemen*] [*ICAO location identifier*] (ICLI)
ODaN........ National Cash Register Co., NCR Library, Dayton, OH [*Library symbol*] [*Library of Congress*] (LCLS)
ODan........ Old Danish (BEE)
ODAN........ Old Danish [*Language, etc.*]
O'D & Br Eq Dig... O'Donnell and Brady's Irish Equity Digest [*A publication*] (DLA)
OD and MC... Operational Direction and Management Control (NATG)
OD & RD.... Overseas Discharge and Replacement Depot
ODaNR...... North Research Stillwater Pioneers, Dayton, OH [*Library symbol*] [*Library of Congress*] (LCLS)
ODaNT...... National Cash Register Co., Technical Library, Dayton, OH [*Library symbol*] [*Library of Congress*] (LCLS)
ODA/ODIF... Office Document Architecture/Office Document Interchange Format (DOMA)
ODAP........ Office of Drug and Alcohol Programs (SAUS)
O-DAP....... Oncovin [*Vincristine*], Dianhydrogalactitol, Adriamycin, Platinol [*Cisplatin*] [*Antineoplastic drug regimen*]
ODAP........ Operation Data Analysis Program (IAA)
ODAP........ Perim [*People's Democratic Republic of Yemen*] [*ICAO location identifier*] (ICLI)
ODAPI....... Omnidirectional Approach Path Indicator (SAUS)
ODAPI....... Open Database Applications Program Interface [*Microsoft Corp.*]
ODAPS...... Oceanic Display and Planning System [*Air traffic control*]
ODAPS...... Operational OGE [*Operational Ground Equipment*] Data Acquisition and Patch Subsystem (GAVI)
ODAQ........ Qishn [*People's Democratic Republic of Yemen*] [*ICAO location identifier*] (ICLI)
ODAR........ Omnidirectional Airborne Radar (SAUS)
ODAR........ Optical Detection and Ranging (DNAB)
ODAR........ Riyan [*People's Democratic Republic of Yemen*] [*ICAO location identifier*] (ICLI)
ODAS........ OCA-DLR Asteroid Survey (SAUS)
ODAS........ Ocean Data Acquisition System [*Nautical term*] (NTA)
ODAS........ Ocean Data Acquisition Systems, Aids and Devices [*Marine science*] (OSRA)
ODAS........ Ocean Dynamics Advisory Subcommittee [*NASA*] (MSC)
ODAS........ Oceanic Data Assimilation System (SAUS)
ODAS........ Offshore Data Acquisition System (SAUS)
ODAS........ Oral Deaf Adults Section [*Later, OHIS*] (EA)
ODAS........ Socotra [*People's Democratic Republic of Yemen*] [*ICAO location identifier*] (ICLI)
ODaSC...... Sinclair Community College, Dayton, OH [*Library symbol*] [*Library of Congress*] (LCLS)
ODASD...... Office of the Deputy Assistant Secretary of Defense
ODaSR...... Standard Register Co., Engineering and Research Library, Dayton, OH [*Library symbol*] [*Library of Congress*] (LCLS)
ODaStE...... Saint Elizabeth Hospital, Dayton, OH [*Library symbol*] [*Library of Congress*] (LCLS)
ODaStL...... Saint Leonard College, Dayton, OH [*Library symbol*] [*Library of Congress*] (LCLS)
ODAT........ Ataq [*People's Democratic Republic of Yemen*] [*ICAO location identifier*] (ICLI)
odat.......... One Day at a Time (AD)
ODATS....... Office Director Assignment Tracking System (SAUS)
ODaTS....... United Theological Seminary, Dayton, OH [*Library symbol*] [*Library of Congress*] (LCLS)
ODaU........ University of Dayton, Dayton, OH [*Library symbol*] [*Library of Congress*] (LCLS)
ODaU-L..... University of Dayton, Law Library, Dayton, OH [*Library symbol*] [*Library of Congress*] (LCLS)
ODaUM...... United Methodist Church, Commission on Archives and History, Dayton, OH [*Library symbol*] [*Library of Congress*] (LCLS)
ODaU-M..... University of Dayton, Marian Library, Dayton, OH [*Library symbol*] [*Library of Congress*] (LCLS)
ODaV........ United States Veterans Administration Center, Library Services, Dayton, OH [*Library symbol*] [*Library of Congress*] (LCLS)
ODaWU..... Wright State University, Dayton, OH [*Library symbol*] [*Library of Congress*] (LCLS)
ODaWU-H... Wright State University, School of Medicine, Fordham Library, Dayton, OH [*Library symbol*] [*Library of Congress*] (LCLS)
ODaWU-W... Wright State University, Western Ohio Branch Campus, Celina, OH [*Library symbol*] [*Library of Congress*] (LCLS)
O Day....... Organization Day (SAUS)
ODB.......... Air Service [*Mali*] [*ICAO designator*] (FAAC)
ODB.......... Cordoba [*Spain*] [*Airport symbol*] (OAG)
ODB.......... Ocean Data Buoy [*Marine science*] (MSC)
ODB.......... O-Dichlorobenzene (SAUS)
ODB.......... Odontoblast
ODB.......... Office of Dependency Benefits
ODB.......... Oil-Degrading Bacteria
ODB.......... Operational Database (SSD)
ODB.......... Operational Data Book [*NASA*] (NAKS)
odb.......... Opiate-Directed Behavior (AD)
ODB.......... Opiate-Directed Behavior
ODB.......... Orbit Determination Beacon (SAUS)
ODB.......... Output Data Buffer
ODB.......... Output Data Bulk (SAUS)
ODB.......... Output Display Branch [*Computer science*] (IAA)
odb.......... Output to Display Buffer [*Computer science*] (AD)
ODB.......... Output to Display Buffer [*Computer science*]

ODB.......... Oven Dry Basis
ODB.......... Overseas Development Bank [*Investors' Overseas Services*]
ODB.......... Oxydibenzil [*Organic chemistry*]
ODBA........ Ocean Dumping Ban Act [*1988*]
ODBA........ Oregon Dairy Breeders Association (BUAC)
ODBC........ Object-Oriented Database Connectivity (SAUS)
ODBC........ Official Doctor of Broken Computers
ODBC........ Open Database Connectivity [*Computer science*]
ODBMS...... Object Database Management System (SAUS)
ODBMS...... Object-Oriented Database Management System
ODBMS...... On-Board Database Management System (SSD)
OD Boat..... One-Design Boat (SAUS)
ODBR........ Output Data Buffer Register (SAUS)
ODB/Server... Open Database/Server [*Computer science*] (HODG)
ODBTS ...... United Theological Seminary, Dayton (SAUS)
ODBZ........ Old Ben #24 Mine [*Federal Railroad Administration identification code*]
ODC.......... Ocean Dynamics and Climate (SAUS)
ODC.......... Oceanographic Data Center (MCD)
ODC.......... Odometer Data Computer [*Developed by Mileage Validator, Inc.*]
ODC.......... Office of Defense Cooperation (DOMA)
ODC.......... Office of Defense Co-ordination (SAUS)
ODC.......... Office of Deputy Chief of Staff Programs and Resources [*Air Force*]
ODC.......... Officer Data Card
ODC.......... Ohio Dominican College, Columbus, OH [*OCLC symbol*] (OCLC)
ODC.......... Oil-Dri Corp. of America [*NYSE symbol*] (SPSG)
ODC.......... Old Dominion College (SAUS)
ODC.......... Oligodendrocyte [*Also, OLG*] [*Cytology*]
ODC.......... One-Directional Control [*Engineering*]
ODC.......... Online Data Capture
ODC.......... Ontario Development Corporation (SAUS)
ODC.......... Operational Data Center [*Deep Space Network, NASA*]
ODC.......... Operational Document Control
ODC.......... Operation Desert Capture [*DoD*]
ODC.......... Operation Design Criteria (MCD)
ODC.......... Operation Digital Chalkboard
ODC.......... Optical Data Collecting (SAUS)
ODC.......... Optical Disc Controller (NITA)
ODC.......... Optical Disc Corporation (SAUS)
ODC.......... Orbital Data Collector
ODC.......... Order of Discalced Carmelites [*Roman Catholic religious order*]
ODC.......... Ordinary Decent Criminal [*British prison slang for other than a political prisoner*]
ODC.......... Organization Development Council [*Defunct*] (EA)
ODC.......... Original Design Cutoff (AAG)
ODC.......... Oritidine Decarboxylase (DMAA)
ODC.......... Ornithine Decarboxylase [*An enzyme*]
ODC.......... Orotidylate Decarboxylase (SAUS)
ODC.......... Oscilloscope Digital Control
ODC.......... Other Data Center (SAUS)
ODC.......... Other Direct Charge (ACAE)
odc.......... Other Direct Costs (AD)
ODC.......... Other Direct Costs [*Accounting*]
odc.......... Outer Dead Center (AD)
ODC.......... Outer Dead Center (DNAB)
ODC.......... Outpatient Diagnostic Center (STED)
ODC.......... Output Data Carrier (SAUS)
ODC.......... Output Data Control
ODC.......... Overseas Development Corporation (NADA)
ODC.......... Overseas Development Council (EA)
ODC.......... Overseas Diplomacy Coordinator (DNAB)
ODC.......... Oxford Decimal Classification
ODC.......... Oxygen Dissociation Curve [*Medicine*] (DMAA)
ODC.......... Oxyhaemoglobin Dissociation Curve (PDAA)
ODC.......... Ozone Depleting Chemical (LDOE)
ODC.......... Ozone-Depleting Chemicals (LDOE)
ODC.......... Ozone-Depleting Compound [*Environmental chemistry*]
ODCA........ Ocean Dumping Control Act [*Canada*] (MSC)
ODCA........ Opened Dull, but Closed Active [*Telegraphy*] (PCTE)
ODCA........ Organizacion Democrata Cristiana de America [*Christian Democratic Organization of America - CDOA*] [*Caracas, Venezuela*]
ODCARP .... Operational Data Collection, Analysis and Reporting Program (ACAE)
ODCBA ...... Oxford and District Cattle Breeders Association (SAUS)
ODCC........ Ohio Decisions, Circuit Court [*Properly cited Ohio Circuit Decisions*] [*A publication*] (DLA)
ODCC........ On-Board Digital Computer Control
ODCC........ One-Design Class Council (EA)
ODCC........ Oxford Dictionary of the Christian Church
ODCC........ United States One-Design Class Council (EA)
ODCCP ...... United Nations Office for Drug Control and Crime Prevention (SAUS)
ODCDR...... Orbiter Delta CDR [*NASA*] (GFGA)
ODCEM...... Oklahoma Department of Civil Emergency Management [*Emergency Management*] (EMA)
ODCF........ One-Dimensional Compressible Flow (SAUS)
ODCH........ Ordinary Disease of Childhood (STED)
OD Class.... One-Design Class (SAUS)
ODCM .... Office of Defense and Civilian Mobilization [*See also OCDM*] (MUGU)
ODCM .... Office of the Director of Civilian Marksmanship (ACAE)
ODCM .... Off-Site Dose Calculation Manual [*Nuclear energy*] (NRCH)
ODC of S.... Office of the Deputy Chief of Staff [*World War II*]
ODCOPS .... Office of the Deputy Chief of Staff for Operations & Plans (SAUS)
ODCP........ Office of the Deputy Commissioner for Programs (SAUS)
ODCP........ One-Digit Code Point [*Telecommunications*] (TEL)
ODCPC ...... Order of Descendants of Colonial Physicians and Chirurgiens [*Defunct*] (EA)
ODCR........ Officer Distribution Control Report [*Navy*] (NG)
ODCR........ Operations Deputies Conference Room (SAUS)
ODCS........ Office of the Deputy Chief of Staff [*World War II*]
ODCS........ Online Data Compression System (PDAA)
ODCS........ Open Distributed Computing Structure (SAUS)
ODCS........ Operational Data Collection System (SAUS)
ODCSCD .... Office of the Deputy Chief of Staff, Combat Developments [*Army*]
ODCSI .... Office of the Deputy Chief of Staff for Intelligence
ODCSLOG... Office of the Deputy Chief of Staff for Logistics [*Army*] (AABC)
ODCSO ...... Office of Data Collection and Survey Operations [*Bureau of Labor Statistics*]
ODCSOPS... Office of the Deputy Chief of Staff for Operations and Plans [*Army*]
ODCSPER... Office of the Deputy Chief of Staff for Personnel [*Army*]
ODCSRDA... Office of the Deputy Chief of Staff for Research, Development, and Acquisition [*Army*] (AABC)
ODCTI ...... Old Dominion College Technical Institute (AD)
ODD .... Obsessive-Deductive Disorder [*Facetious term for a malady affecting some taxpayers*]
ODD .... Obstacle Detection Device
ODD .... Ocean Disposal Database [*US Army Corps of Engineers*]
odd .... oculodentodigital (SAUS)
ODD .... Oculodentodigital Dysplasia [*Medicine*] (MAE)
ODD .... Offboard Deception Device [*Navy*] (CAAL)
ODD .... Office Channel Unit [*Communications term*] (DCT)
ODD .... Old Destroyer [*Navy symbol*]
ODD .... Oodnadatta [*Australia*] [*Airport symbol*] (OAG)
ODD .... Open Data Desktop (SAUS)
ODD .... Operational Detachment Delta [*Antiterrorist unit*] [*Military*] (LAIN)
odd .... Operator Distance Dialing (AD)
ODD .... Operator Distance Dialing
ODD .... Oppositional Defiant Disorder
ODD .... Oppositional Developmental Disorder (SAUS)
ODD .... Optical Data Digitizer [*Computer science*]
ODD .... Optical Data Disc (NITA)
ODD .... Optical Digital Data Disk
ODD .... Optical Digital Disc (NITA)
ODD .... Optical Disk Drive (GART)
ODD .... Optical Downconverter Demultiplexer (ACAE)
ODD .... Order and Dispatch Desk for SAR data products (SAUS)
ODD .... Ordered [*Telegraphy*] (PCTE)
ODD .... Organizing District Delegate [*British labor*]
ODD .... Ouchterlony Double Diffusion Test [*Immunogel assay*]
ODD .... Outside Design and Development
ODD .... Overdetermined Dual-Doppler (SAUS)
ODD .... Overseas Deployment Data [*Military*]
ODD .... Oxalate Deposition Disease [*Medicine*] (MELL)
ODDA........ Office of Deputy Director for Administration [*Marshall Space Flight Center*] (KSC)
ODDD........ Operator Direct Distance Dialing (SAUS)
ODDD........ Optical Digital Data Disk
ODDDR & R... Office of the Deputy Director of Defense Research and Engineering (RDA)
ODDH........ On-Board Digital Data Handling
ODDJ........ Odd Job Stores [*OTCBB symbol*]
ODDL........ Onboard Digital Data Load (ACAE)
ODDO........ Operation Description Distribution Order
ODDP........ Office of the Director of Development Planning [*Air Force*] (MCD)
ODDR & E... Office of the Director of Defense Research and Engineering [*Later, Office of the Under Secretary of Defense for Research and Engineering*] [*Army*]
ODDRD...... Office of Deputy Director for Research and Development [*Marshall Space Flight Center*] (KSC)
ODDRE ...... Office of the Director of Defense Research and Engineering [*Later, Office of the Under Secretary of Defense for Research and Engineering*] [*Army*]
ODDS........ Oceanographic Digital Data System [*Navy*]
ODDS........ Online Data Entry and Display System [*Job Service*] (OICC)
ODDS........ Operational Data Delivery Services (MCD)
ODDS........ Optical Disk Data System (NITA)
ODDS........ Optional Delivery Dispenser System (MCD)
ODE.......... Delhi Public Library, Ontario [*Library symbol*] [*National Library of Canada*] (NLC)
ODE.......... Odense [*Denmark*] [*Airport symbol*] (OAG)
ODE.......... O-Desmethylencainide (STED)
ODE.......... Odessa [*Former USSR*] [*Geomagnetic observatory code*]
ODE.......... Odessa, TX [*Amtrak Busline code*]
ODE.......... Office 97 Developer Edition [*Microsoft*]
ODE.......... Office of Device Evaluation [*U.S. Food and Drug Administration*]
ODE.......... Oil Drilling and Exploration (AD)
ODE.......... Old-Dog Encephalitis (SAUS)
ODE.......... Omicron Delta Epsilon [*Fraternity*]
ODE.......... One Day Event [*Horse-riding*] [*British*] (DI)
ode .... One-Day Event (AD)
ODE.......... One-Dimensional Equilibrium (MCD)
ODE.......... Online Data Entry (ADA)
ODE.......... Open Distributed Environment [*Information technology*]
ODE.......... Optical Designation Evaluation (MCD)
ODE.......... Optimally Designed Experiments
ODE.......... Orbit Data Editor Assembly [*Space Flight Operations Facility, NASA*]
ODE.......... Ordinary Differential Equation [*Mathematics*]
ODE.......... Ordnance Development & Engineering (SAUS)
ODE.......... Ortho-Demethylencainide [*Biochemistry*]

ODE.......... OSF Development Environment (SAUS)
ODE.......... Oxford Dictionary of the English Language (SAUS)
ODE.......... Oxygen Defect Electron (SAUS)
ODEA........ Oxygen Enriched Air (ACAE)
ODEAG...... Research Station, Agriculture Canada [*Station de Recherches, Agriculture Canada*] Delhi, Ontario [*Library symbol*] [*National Library of Canada*] (NLC)
O'Dea Med Exp... O'Dea's Medical Experts [*A publication*] (DLA)
ODE Assembly... Orbit Data Editor Assembly (SAUS)
ODEC........ Ocean Data Equipment Corporation (SAUS)
ODEC........ Ocean Design Engineering Corp. (AD)
ODEC........ Overdrive Engagement Control [*Automotive engineering*]
ODECA...... Organizacion de los Estados Centroamericanos [*Organization of Central American States - OCAS*] [*San Salvador, El Salvador*] (EAIO)
ODECO...... Ocean Drilling & Exploration Company, New Orleans (SAUS)
O Dec Rep... Ohio Decisions Reprint [*A publication*] (DLA)
ODEE........ [*The*] Oxford Dictionary of English Etymology [*A publication*]
ODef........ Defiance Public Library, Defiance, OH [*Library symbol*] [*Library of Congress*] (LCLS)
ODefC....... Defiance College, Defiance, OH [*Library symbol*] [*Library of Congress*] (LCLS)
ODelp....... Delphos Public Library, Delphos, OH [*Library symbol*] [*Library of Congress*] (LCLS)
OdeM........ Order of Our Lady of Mercy (TOCD)
odem........ Order of Our Lady of Mercy (TOCD)
ODEND...... OR Optical Detected ENDOR (SAUS)
ODENDOR... Optical Detected Electron Nuclear Double Resonance (AAEL)
OD-ENDOR... Optically Detected Electron Nuclear Double Resonance [*Spectroscopy*]
Odeneal..... Odeneal's Reports [*9-11 Oregon*] [*A publication*] (DLA)
ODEP........ Office Depot, Inc. [*NASDAQ symbol*] (COMM)
ODEP........ Oxford Dictionary of English Proverbs (SAUS)
ODEPA....... Organizacion Deportiva Panamericana [*Pan American Sports Organization - PASO*] [*Mexico City, Mexico*] (EAIO)
ODEPA....... Oxapentamethylenediethylenephosphoramide [*Pharmacology*]
ODEPLAN... Oficina de Planificacion Nacional [*Office of National Planning*] [*Spain*] (AD)
ODEPR...... Optical Detected Electron Paramagnetic Resonance (AAEL)
O Dep Rep... Ohio Department Reports [*A publication*] (DLA)
ODEQ........ Oklahoma Department of Environmental Quality (SAUS)
Oderi........ Odericus [*Flourished, 1166-1200*] [*Authority cited in pre-1607 legal work*] (DSA)
ODES........ Deseronto Public Library, Ontario [*Library symbol*] [*National Library of Canada*] (NLC)
ODES........ Ocean Data Evaluation System [*Environmental Protection Agency*] (AEPA)
ODES........ Optical Discrimination Evaluation Study [*NASA*] (NASA)
OD-ESR..... Optically Detected Electron Spin Resonance [*Spectroscopy*]
ODESSA..... Ocean Data Environmental Science Services Acquisition [*Buoy*]
ODESSA..... Oceanographic Data & Environmental Satellite System Application (SAUS)
ODESSA..... Oceanographic Data for the Environmental Science Services Administration (GFGA)
ODESSA..... Organisation der Ehemaligen Schutzstaffel Angehoeriggen [*Organization of Former Members of the Elite Guard*] [*Founded after World War II to smuggle war criminals out of Germany and provide them with false identities*]
Odes Sol.... Odes of Solomon [*Biblical*] (RION)
ODESUR.... Organizacion Deportiva Sudamericana [*An association*] (EAIO)
ODESY...... Online Data Entry System [*Burroughs Corp.*]
ODET........ Odetics, Inc. [*NASDAQ symbol*] (SAG)
ODETA....... Odetics,Inc.'A' [*NASDAQ symbol*] (TTSB)
ODETB....... Odetics,Inc.'B' [*NASDAQ symbol*] (TTSB)
Odetics...... Odetics, Inc. [*Associated Press*] (SAG)
ODETTE..... Organisation for Data Exchange by Tele-Transmission in Europe (SAUS)
ODEX........ Optical Dynamics Experiment (SAUS)
ODF.......... Object Definition Facility [*Computer science*] (HODG)
ODF.......... Oceanographic Data Facility (SAUS)
Odf.......... Odofredus [*Deceased, 1265*] [*Authority cited in pre-1607 legal work*] (DSA)
ODF.......... Official Development Finance
ODF.......... Old Dominion Foundation (AD)
ODF.......... One-Dimension Flow
ODF.......... Opacity Distribution Function [*Spectroscopy*]
ODF.......... Opendoc Development Framework (SAUS)
ODF.......... Opendoc Part Framework (SAUS)
ODF.......... Operational Deployment Force (AD)
ODF.......... Operations Data File (SAUS)
ODF.......... Optimal Decision Function
ODF.......... Optoelectronic Data Filter (SAUS)
ODF.......... Orbit Determination Facility (MCD)
ODF.......... Orientation Distribution Function
ODF.......... Original Data File (NITA)
ODF.......... Output Data File
odfc.......... Outside Diameter of Female Coupling (AD)
ODFFU...... Organization for Defense of Four Freedoms for Ukraine (EA)
ODFI......... Open Die Forging Institute (EA)
ODFI......... Originating Depository Financial Institute
ODFL........ Old Dominion Freight Line [*Common carrier symbol*]
ODFL........ Old Dominion Freight Lines, Inc. [*NASDAQ symbol*] (SPSG)
ODFR........ Oxygen-Derived Free Radicals [*Biochemistry*]
OD-FSR..... Optically Detected Electron Spin Resonance (SAUS)
ODFT........ Odd Discrete Fourier Transform (MCD)
ODFW....... Oregon Department of Fish and Wildlife Research and Development Section [*Oregon State University*] [*Research center*] (RCD)
ODG......... Enid, OK [*Location identifier*] [*FAA*] (FAAL)
ODG......... Offline Data Generator
ODG......... Ontario Drive & Gear Ltd (SAUS)
ODG......... Operational Data Group (MCD)
ODG......... Operational Design Group
ODG......... Orbit Data Generator [*NASA*]
ODG......... Ordering [*Telegraphy*] (PCTE)
Odgers...... Odgers on Libel and Slander [*A publication*] (DLA)
ODGF........ Osteosarcoma-Derived Growth Factor [*Biochemistry*]
Odg Lib..... Odgers on Libel and Slander [*A publication*] (DLA)
ODGP........ Osborne Division of General Practice (SAUS)
Odg Pl....... Odgers on Principles of Pleading [*20th ed.*] [*1975*] [*A publication*] (DLA)
ODGRT...... Oman Directorate General of Radio and Television (SAUS)
ODGSE...... Operational Development Ground Support Equipment (AAG)
ODGSO...... Office of Domestic Gold and Silver Operations [*Department of the Treasury*]
ODH......... Highland Secondary School, Dundas, Ontario [*Library symbol*] [*National Library of Canada*] (NLC)
ODH......... Octanol Dehydrogenase [*An enzyme*]
ODH......... Octopine Dehydrogenase [*An enzyme*]
ODH......... Ontario Department of Health [*Canada*] (AD)
ODH......... Operations Directive Handbook (SAUS)
ODHS........ Dundas Historical Society Museum, Ontario [*Library symbol*] [*National Library of Canada*] (BIB)
ODHT........ Hagerman Township Public Library, Ontario [*Library symbol*] [*National Library of Canada*] (NLC)
ODHWS..... Office of Defense Health and Welfare Services [*World War II*]
ODI.......... Nodine, MN [*Location identifier*] [*FAA*] (FAAL)
ODI.......... Odin Industry Ltd. [*Vancouver Stock Exchange symbol*]
ODI.......... Office Document Index
ODI.......... Office of Defense Investigation (SAUS)
ODI.......... Office of Director of Intelligence [*Military*]
ODI.......... Oil Drain Interval
ODI.......... Open Datalink Interface [*Computer science*]
ODI.......... Open Device Interconnect (SAUS)
ODI.......... Open-Door International [*An association*] (AD)
ODI.......... Open Door International for the Economic Emancipation of the Woman Worker [*Brussels, Belgium*] (EAIO)
ODI.......... Open Driver Interface [*Computer science*] (CIST)
ODI.......... Operational Development Inspection (SAA)
ODI.......... Optical Digital Image (SAUS)
ODI.......... Optical Digital Imagery
ODI.......... Optonics Devices Incorporated
ODI.......... Organization Development Institute (SAUS)
ODI.......... Overseas Development Institute (EA)
ODI.......... Oxygen Desaturation Index [*Medicine*]
O Dia........ Outer Diameter (SAUS)
ODIC......... Oceanographic Data and Information Centre (SAUS)
ODIC......... Office of the Director of Information Control (SAUS)
ODIC......... Outside Diameter of Inner Conductor
ODID......... Office of the Director of Industrial Demobilization
ODID......... Operational Display and Input Development (SAUS)
ODIF......... Office Document Interchange Format (HGAA)
ODIF......... Open Document Interchange Format (SAUS)
ODIFF....... Oil Differential
ODIHR....... Office for Democratic Institutions & Human Rights [*British*] (WDAA)
ODIL......... Overseas Development Institute Ltd. (AD)
ODIMS....... Open Distributed Information Management System (SAUS)
ODIN......... Ocean Data and Information Network (SAUS)
ODIN......... Odin, IL [*American Association of Railroads railroad junction routing code*]
ODIN......... Onboard Data Interfaces and Network [*NASA*] (SPST)
ODIN......... Online Dakota Information Network [*Information service or system*] (IID)
ODIN......... On-line Documentation and Information Network (SAUS)
ODIN......... Online Dokumentations- und Informationsverbund [*Online Documentation and Information Affiliation*]
ODIN......... Operational Data Interface (SAUS)
ODIN......... Operational Display Information Network (MCD)
ODIN......... Optical Design Integration (SAUS)
ODIN......... Optimal [*or Orbital*] Design Integration [*Computer program*]
ODIN......... Orbital Design Integration [*NASA*] (NAKS)
ODINEA..... Ocean Data and Information Network for Eastern Africa (SAUS)
Oding........ Overdosing (SAUS)
OD Input.... Output Disable Input (SAUS)
OD Institu... Organization Development Institute (NTPA)
Odinsup..... ODI-NDIS Supplementary Driver (SAUS)
ODINSUP... Open Data link Interface-Network driver interface specification Support (SAUS)
ODIRP....... Office, Director of Personnel [*Air Force*]
ODIS......... Object Design, Inc. [*NASDAQ symbol*] (SAG)
ODIS......... Ocean Dynamics Information System [*Marine science*] (MSC)
ODIS......... Oceanographic Data Information System (SAUS)
ODIS......... Online Data Information System (SAUS)
ODIS......... Onsite Discharge Information System (SAUS)
ODIS......... Optical Disk Interface System [*Computer science*]
ODIS......... Orbital Design Integration System
ODIS......... Origin Destination Information System [*US Postal Service*]
ODISC4...... Office of the Director of Informantion Systems for Command, Control, Communications, and Computers [*Army*]
ODISS....... Optical Digital Image Storage System (ACAE)
ODISTA..... Oceanographic Data in Subtrial Areas

O Div........ Ontario Division (SAUS)
ODJ......... Ouanda Djalle [*Central African Republic*] [*Airport symbol*] (AD)
ODJB........ Original Dixieland Jazz Band
ODJS........ Office of the Director, Joint Staff (MCD)
ODK......... Kodiak, AK [*Location identifier*] [*FAA*] (FAAL)
ODK......... Office Develoment Kit (SAUS)
ODK......... Omicron Delta Kappa [*Fraternity*]
ODK......... One-Dimensional Kinetics [*Computer program*] (MCD)
ODK......... Orlop Deck (SAUS)
ODKCNV.... Old Dominion Kennel Club of Northern Virginia (EARSL)
ODKG........ O'Daniel Trucking Company [*Common carrier symbol*]
ODL......... Cordillo Downs [*South Australia*] [*Airport symbol*] (AD)
ODL......... Object Definition Language [*Computer science*]
ODL......... Object Description Language (SAUS)
ODL......... Object Design Language (SAUS)
ODL......... Occupational Driver's License [*Motor vehicle term used in state of Washington*] (MVRD)
ODL......... Oceanic Data Link [*FAA*] (TAG)
ODL......... Office Document Language [*Telecommunications*]
ODL......... Office of Defense Lending [*Department of the Treasury*]
ODL......... Office of the Duchy of Lancaster [*British*]
ODL......... Officer Deficiency Letter [*Navy*] (NVT)
ODL......... Oklahoma Department of Libraries
ODL......... Open and Distance Learning (AIE)
ODL......... Open Discrepancy List (ACAE)
ODL......... Open Document Language (SAUS)
ODL......... Optical Disc Library (SAUS)
ODL......... Ostwald Dilution Law [*Chemistry*]
ODL......... Overseas Drilling Ltd. (SAUS)
ODL......... University of Dayton, Law Library, Dayton, OH [*OCLC symbol*] (OCLC)
ODLAMP.... One-Dimensional LASER and Mixing Program
ODLB........ Dwight Branch, Lake Of Bays Township Public Library, Ontario [*Library symbol*] [*National Library of Canada*] (BIB)
ODLB........ Optical Dispensers' Licensing Board [*New South Wales, Australia*]
ODLC........ Outboard Data Link Control (SAUS)
ODLI........ Open Data Link Interface [*Computer science*]
ODLIS....... Online Dictionary of Library and Information Science
ODLRO...... Off-Diagonal Long-Range Order [*Physics*]
odlsq........ Odalisque (VRA)
ODLY........ Orderly (WGA)
ODM......... Methodist Theological School in Ohio, Delaware, OH [*Library symbol*] [*Library of Congress*] (LCLS)
ODM......... Object Database Manager (SAUS)
ODM......... Object Data Manager (SAUS)
ODM......... Odiham FTU [*British*] [*ICAO designator*] (FAAC)
ODM......... Office of Defense Mobilization [*Transferred to Office of Defense and Civilian Mobilization, 1958*]
ODM......... Oil Debris Monitor
ODM......... One Day Mission [*NASA*] (KSC)
ODM......... Open Document Management [*Computer science*] (GART)
ODM......... Operational Data Management (KSC)
ODM......... Operational Development Memorandum (AAG)
ODM......... Operational Development Model (ACAE)
ODM......... Operations Data Message (MCD)
odm.......... Ophthalmodynamometry [*Ophthalmology*] (AD)
ODM......... Ophthalmodynamometry [*Ophthalmology*] (MAE)
ODM......... Optical Diffractogram
ODM......... Optical Disk Memory
ODM......... Optical Display Memory [*Computer science*]
ODM......... Optical Driver Modem (SAUS)
ODM......... Optimized Delivery Model [*Compaq*] [*Computer science*]
ODM......... Optimized Distribution Model [*Compaq Computer Corp.*] [*Computer science*]
ODM......... Orbital Determination Module
ODM......... Order of De Molay (AD)
ODM......... Original Design Manufacturer (AGLO)
ODM......... Outboard Data Manager [*Computer science*] (BUR)
ODM......... Overseas Development Ministry [*British*]
ODMA....... Office of the Director of Military Assistance [*Air Force*] (AFM)
ODMA....... Open Document Management API [*Application Programming Interface*] [*Computer science*]
ODMA....... Optical Disc Manufacturing Association (IGQR)
ODMA....... Optical Distributors and Manufacturers Association (AD)
ODMC....... Office for Dependents' Medical Care [*Army*] (AABC)
odmc........ Outside Diameter of Male Coupling (AD)
ODMD....... Delcan, Don Mills, Ontario [*Library symbol*] [*National Library of Canada*] (NLC)
ODMF....... Ortho-Demethylfortimicin [*Biochemistry*]
ODMG....... Object Database Management Group [*Computer science*] (CDE)
ODMG....... Object Data Management Group [*Computer science*] (HODG)
ODMH....... Ohio Department of Mental Health
ODMHSAS... Oklahoma Department of Mental Health and Substance Abuse Services (MHID)
ODMIBM..... IBM Canada Ltd., Don Mills, Ontario [*Library symbol*] [*National Library of Canada*] (NLC)
ODMII....... Optical Detected Microwave Induced Impact Ionization (AAEL)
ODMN....... National Research Council, Don Mills, Ontario [*Library symbol*] [*National Library of Canada*] (NLC)
ODMO....... Office of Defense Management and Organization [*Military*]
ODMR....... Optical Detection of Magnetic Resonance (SAUS)
ODMR....... Optical Double Magnetic Resonance (SAUS)
ODMR....... Optically Deflected Magnetic Resonance (SAUS)
ODMR....... Optically Detected Magnetic Resonance [*Spectroscopy*]
ODMRJ...... Rolf Jensen & Associates Ltd., Don Mills, Ontario [*Library symbol*] [*National Library of Canada*] (NLC)
ODMS....... Odesta Document Management System (SAUS)
ODMS....... Operational Data Management System [*FAA*] (TAG)
ODMT....... Office of the Director of Military Training
ODMWS..... Wyda Systems Canada, Inc., Don Mills, Ontario [*Library symbol*] [*National Library of Canada*] (NLC)
ODN......... Company of Mary [*Roman Catholic women's religious order*]
ODN......... Dalton-Dalton-Newport, Cleveland, OH [*OCLC symbol*] (OCLC)
ODN......... Long Seridan [*Malaysia*] [*Airport symbol*] (OAG)
ODN......... Obligation Document Number (SAUS)
ODN......... Octadecennitril (SAUS)
Odn.......... Odense (AD)
Odn.......... Odin (AD)
ODN......... Oligodeoxynucleotide [*Biochemistry*]
ODN......... Ophthalmodynamometry [*Ophthalmology*]
ODN......... Optical Data Network (SAUS)
ODN......... Organization Development Network (EA)
ODN......... Out Dial Notification (SAUS)
ODN......... Overseas Development Network (EA)
odn.......... Own Doppler Nullifer (AD)
ODN......... Own Doppler Nullifier
ODN......... Oxbridge Directory of Newsletters [*A publication*]
ODNA........ Operational Data and Notices to Airmen [*FAA*]
ODNMR..... Optically-Detected Nuclear Magnetic Resonance [*Spectroscopy*]
ODNP........ Ohio Decisions [*A publication*] (DLA)
ODNR........ Ohio Department of Natural Resources (SAUS)
ODNR........ Oxford Dictionary of Nursery Rhymes [*A publication*]
ODNRI....... Overseas Development Natural Resources Institute [*British*] [*Information service or system*] (IID)
ODNS........ Operations Division of Naval Staff [*British*]
Odo.......... Odofredus [*Deceased, 1265*] [*Authority cited in pre-1607 legal work*] (DSA)
ODO......... Odometer [*Automotive engineering*]
ODO......... Offensive Duty Officer (SAUS)
ODO......... Office of Disability Operations [*Social Security Administration*] [*Began in 1979*] (OICC)
ODO......... Opeongo High School, Douglas, Ontario [*Library symbol*] [*National Library of Canada*] (NLC)
ODO......... Operations Duty Officer (MUGU)
ODO......... Outdoor Officer [*Customs*] [*British*]
ODOB........ Dobie Public Library, Ontario [*Library symbol*] [*National Library of Canada*] (BIB)
ODOD........ Oculodento-Osseous Dysplasia (STED)
ODOE........ Oregon Department of Energy (AD)
OD/OE....... Organizational Development/Organizational Effectiveness (MCD)
ODOF........ Dowling Branch, Onaping Falls Public Library, Ontario [*Library symbol*] [*National Library of Canada*] (NLC)
Odof......... Odofredus [*Deceased, 1265*] [*Authority cited in pre-1607 legal work*] (DSA)
Odofr........ Odofredus [*Deceased, 1265*] [*Authority cited in pre-1607 legal work*] (DSA)
Odofre....... Odofredus [*Deceased, 1265*] [*Authority cited in pre-1607 legal work*] (DSA)
ODOM....... Odom Boyd Trailer Manufacturing Company [*NCIC trailer make code*]
ODOM....... Odometer (AAG)
odom........ Odometer (AD)
Odonel Mercandil... Odonellus Mercandilis [*Authority cited in pre-1607 legal work*] (DSA)
odont........ Odontogenic (STED)
odont........ Odontology (AD)
Odont........ Odontology (STED)
ODONT...... Odontology
ODOO........ Overdrive On-Off [*Automotive engineering*]
OdoorS...... Outdoor Systems, Inc. [*Associated Press*] (SAG)
odop......... Offset Doppler (AD)
ODOP........ Offset Doppler
ODOP........ Orbital Doppler (IAA)
ODOPA...... Publications. Dominion Observatory (SAUS)
ODOP System... Orbital Doppler System (SAUS)
ODOR........ Dorion Public Library, Ontario [*Library symbol*] [*National Library of Canada*] (NLC)
odoram...... Odoramentum [*Perfume*] [*Latin*] (MAE)
odorat....... Odoratus [*Odorous*] [*Latin*] (MAE)
odorl......... Odorless (AD)
ODOT........ Oklahoma Department of Transportation [*Federal Railroad Administration identification code*]
ODOT........ Oregon Department of Transportation
ODOTS...... One-Day One-Trial System (AD)
ODOU........ Douro Public Library, Ontario [*Library symbol*] [*National Library of Canada*] (BIB)
ODOW....... Ohio Division of Wildlife
O'Dowd Sh... O'Dowd's Merchant Shipping Act [*A publication*] (DLA)
ODP......... Iso-Octyldecylphthalat (SAUS)
odp.......... Occipito-Dextra Posterior (AD)
ODP......... Occipitodextra Posterior [*A fetal position*] [*Medicine*] (AAMN)
ODP......... Ocean Drilling Program [*Texas A & M University*] [*Research center*] (RCD)
ODP......... Octyldecylphthalat (SAUS)
ODP......... Octyl Isodecyl Phthalate [*Organic chemistry*]
ODP......... Oekologisch-Demokratische Partei [*Ecological Democratic Party*] [*Germany*] [*Political party*] (PPW)
ODP......... Office Data Processing (TIMI)
ODP......... Office Depot, Inc. [*NYSE symbol*] (SPSG)
ODP......... Office Development Permit (SAUS)

ODP.......... Office of Defense Planning [*of FRS*]
ODP.......... Office of Disability Programs [*Social Security Administration*] (OICC)
ODP.......... Office of Disaster Preparedness (AD)
ODP.......... Office of Disclosure Policy (SAUS)
ODP.......... Office of Domestic Preparedness
ODP.......... Officer Distribution Plan [*Army*]
ODP.......... Official Development Planning (SAUS)
ODP.......... Offshore Drilling Platform
ODP.......... Offspring of Diabetic Parent [*Medicine*] (MELL)
ODP.......... Onboard Data Processor (SAUS)
ODP.......... On-Demand Publishing (SAUS)
ODP.......... Open Data Path (MCD)
ODP.......... Open Distributed Processing [*Telecommunications*] (OSI)
ODP.......... Open Door Policy
ODP.......... Open Dripproof
ODP.......... Operational Development Phase (SAUS)
ODP.......... Operational Development Plan [*or Program*]
ODP.......... Operational Development Program (SAUS)
ODP.......... Operational Display Procedure [*NASA*] (NAKS)
ODP.......... Optical Data Processing
ODP.......... Optical Data Processor (SAUS)
ODP.......... Orbit Determination Program
ODP.......... Order Despatched (SAUS)
odp.......... Order-Despatched (AD)
ODP.......... Orderly Departure Program [*for Vietnamese refugees*] [*United Nations*]
ODP.......... Order of the Sons of Divine Providence
ODP.......... Organic Development Problem (SAA)
ODP.......... Organization Department (SAUS)
ODP.......... Organized Reservists in Drill Pay Status [*Military*]
ODP.......... Original Departure Point
ODP.......... Original Document Processing
O/DP.......... Originating/Destination Point (SAUS)
ODP.......... Originator Detection Pattern [*Communications term*] (DCT)
ODP.......... Outline Development Plan [*Army*] (AFIT)
ODP.......... Output-to-Display Parity Error [*Computer science*] (SAA)
ODP.......... Overall Development Planning (SAUS)
ODP.......... Overall Documentation Plan [*NATO*] (NATG)
ODP.......... Overdrive Processor (SAUS)
ODP.......... Overlay Demonstration Program [*Military*]
ODP.......... Oviposition-Determining Pheromone
ODP.......... Ozone-Depleting [*or Depletion*] Potential [*Environmental science*]
ODP.......... Ozone Depletion Potential [*Meteorology*]
ODPA.......... Octylated Diphenyl Amine (SAUS)
ODPA.......... Organization of Democratic and Popular Action [*Morocco*] [*Political party*] (BUAC)
OD (PA & E)... Office of the Director (Program Analysis and Evaluation) (MCD)
ODPC.......... ODP Council (SAUS)
ODPCS.......... Oceanographic Data Processing and Control System (OA)
ODPEX.......... Offshore Drilling and Production Exhibition (PDAA)
ODPHP.......... Office of Disease Prevention and Health Promotion [*US Public Health Service*] [*Information service or system*] (IID)
ODPI.......... Office of Director Public Information [*Military*]
ODP/MT.......... Organisation pour la Democratie Populaire/Mouvement du Travail [*Burkina Faso*] [*Political party*] (EY)
ODPN.......... Oxydipropionitrile (SAUS)
ODPP.......... Office of the Director of Public Prosecutions [*Australia*]
ODPP.......... Open Dripproof Protected
ODPPP.......... Operating Division Project Product Policy (SAUS)
ODPR.......... Office of the Data Protection Registrar (BUAC)
ODPR.......... OverDrive Processor Replacement (SAUS)
O'D Pr & Acc... O'Dedy's Principal and Accessory [*1812*] [*A publication*] (DLA)
ODPRF.......... Operating Documents Preliminary Review Form (SAUS)
ODPS.......... Operational Data Processing Squadron
ODPSK.......... Oil Dipstick
ODQ.......... On Direct Questioning (DMAA)
ODQ.......... Opponens Digiti Quinti [*Muscle*] [*Anatomy*] (DAVI)
ODQ.......... [*The*] Oxford Dictionary of Quotations [*A publication*]
ODQM.......... Office of the Division Quartermaster
ODR.......... Dryden Public Library, Ontario [*Library symbol*] [*National Library of Canada*] (NLC)
ODR.......... Ocean Drilling & Exploration Co. (SAUS)
ODR.......... Oculomotor Delayed Response [*Performance test task*]
ODR.......... Office of Defense Representative (COE)
ODR.......... Office of Defense Resources [*Civil Defense*]
ODR.......... Office of Dissemination and Resources [*HEW*]
ODR.......... Officer of Defense Resources (SAUS)
ODR.......... Official Discount Rate [*Finance*] (ECON)
ODR.......... Oil Droplet Reflex [*Medicine*] (MELL)
ODR.......... Omnidirectional Range
ODR.......... Omnidirection Range (SAUS)
ODR.......... On Display Racks [*Freight*]
ODR.......... Ontrack Data Recovery (SAUS)
ODR.......... Operational Design Resolution (SAA)
ODR.......... Operator Data Register [*Telecommunications*] (TEL)
ODR.......... Optical Data Recognition [*Computer science*]
ODR.......... Optical Digital Reference (SAUS)
ODR.......... Optical Double Resonance (SAUS)
ODR.......... Optically-Detected Resonance (SAUS)
ODR.......... Optimized Dynamic Routing (SAUS)
ODR.......... ORDALT [*Ordnance Alterations*] Deficiency Review (MCD)
odr.......... Order (AD)
ODR.......... Ordnance Difficulty Report (MCD)
ODR.......... Original Data Record
ODR.......... Oscillating Disk Rheometer (AAEL)
ODR.......... Output Data Redundancy (MCD)
ODR.......... Output Data Request (SAUS)
ODR.......... Output Definition Register
ODR.......... Overland Downlook Radar (SAUS)
ODR.......... Oxygen Diffusion Rate (OA)
ODR.......... Roanoke, VA [*Location identifier*] [*FAA*] (FAAL)
ODRAN.......... Operational Drawing Revision Advance Notice (NASA)
ODRC.......... Office of Disaster Relief Coordinator [*United Nations*] (WDAA)
ODRC.......... Orbiter Data Reduction Center [*NASA*] (MCD)
OD Re.......... Ohio Decisions Reprint [*A publication*] (DLA)
OD Rep.......... Ohio Decisions Reprint [*A publication*] (DLA)
ODRES.......... Old Dominion Real Estate (SAUS)
ODRI.......... Deep River Public Library, Ontario [*Library symbol*] [*National Library of Canada*] (NLC)
ODRI.......... Office of United States Defense Representative, India [*Army*] (AABC)
ODRL.......... Delta Branch, Rideau Lakes Union Library, Ontario [*Library symbol*] [*National Library of Canada*] (BIB)
ODRM.......... Operations Design Reference Mission (MCD)
ODRN.......... Orbiting Data Relay Network
ODRP.......... Office of Defense Representative, Pakistan [*Army*]
ODRP.......... Office of Defense Representative-Pakistan (POLM)
ODRS.......... Orbiting Data Relay System (MCD)
ODRS.......... Ore Deposits Research Section [*Pennsylvania State University*] [*Research center*] (RCD)
ODRSS.......... Orbiting Data Relay Satellite System (MCD)
O/DRV.......... Over Drive [*Automotive engineering*]
ODS.......... Civic Democratic Party (Czech Rep.) [*Political party*] (PSAP)
ODS.......... Obstacle Detection System
ODS.......... Occupational Demand Schedule (ADA)
ODS.......... Ocean Data Station [*Marine science*] (MSC)
ODS.......... Octadecylsilane [*Organic chemistry*]
ODS.......... Octadecyltrimethyloxysilane (SAUS)
ODS.......... Octadeyl(dimethyl)chlorosilane [*Organic chemistry*]
ODS.......... Odessa [*Ukraine*] [*Airport symbol*] (OAG)
ODS.......... Odessa [*Washington*] [*Seismograph station code, US Geological Survey*] (SEIS)
ODS.......... Odessa Explorations Ltd. [*Vancouver Stock Exchange symbol*]
ODS.......... Odometer Disclosure Statement
ODS.......... Office Dialog System [*Computer science*]
ODS.......... Office for Domestic Shipping [*Department of Commerce*]
ODS.......... Office of Defender Services (AD)
ODS.......... Office of Dietary Supplements (SAUS)
ODS.......... Office of Disability Services (SAUS)
ODs.......... Oildroplets (SAUS)
ODS.......... Old Dominion Speedway [*Auto racing*]
ODS.......... One Digit Subtractor (SAUS)
ODS.......... Open Database Server [*Computer science*]
ODS.......... Open Data Service [*Electronics systems testing*]
ODS.......... Open Data Services (SAUS)
ODS.......... Open Distributed System (RALS)
ODS.......... Operating-Differential Subsidy [*Authorized by Merchant Marine Act of 1936*]
ODS.......... Operational Data Store [*Computer science*] (ITCA)
ODS.......... Operational Data Summary (AAG)
ODS.......... Operational Display System (SAUS)
ODS.......... Operation Desert Storm [*Military*] (RDA)
ODS.......... Operations Directorate Station (SAA)
ODS.......... Optical Data Systems (SAUS)
ODS.......... Optical Design System [*Automotive lighting*]
ODS.......... Optical Discrimination System (SAUS)
ODS.......... Optical Disk Storage (SAUS)
ODS.......... Optical Disk System (SAUS)
ODS.......... Optical Display System (SAUS)
ODS.......... Optical Docking System
ODS.......... Optical Document Sorter (SAUS)
ODS.......... Optimal Decisions System
ODS.......... Orbiter Docking System [*NASA*]
ODS.......... Orbiter Dynamic Simulator [*NASA*]
ODS.......... Orders [*Telegraphy*] (PCTE)
ODS.......... Ordnance Delivery Schedule [*Navy*] (NG)
ODS.......... Orton Dyslexia Society (EA)
ODS.......... Osric Dining Society (EA)
ODS.......... Output Data Set (SAUS)
ODS.......... Output Data Store [*Computer science*] (TIMI)
ODS.......... Output Data Strobe
ODS.......... Overall Distance Standard [*for golf balls*] [*Adopted by the United States Golf Association in 1976*]
ODS.......... Overdrive Disable Switch [*Automotive engineering*]
ODS.......... Overhead Data Stream (SAUS)
ODS.......... Oxidative-Desulfurization [*Fuel technology*]
ods.......... Oxide Dispersion Strengthened (AD)
ODS.......... Oxide Dispersion Strengthened [*Ferrous metallurgy*]
ODS.......... Oxide Dispersion Strengthening (ODA)
ODS.......... Oxygen Depletion Sensor
ODS.......... Oxygen Dispersion Strengthening (SAUS)
ODS.......... Ozone-Depleting Substance (AAGC)
ODSA.......... Oil-Dri Corp. of America (EFIS)
ODSA.......... Open Distributed Systems Architecture [*British*]
ODSA.......... Operating Deflection Shape Analysis
ODSA.......... Operating-Differential Subsidy Agreement [*MARAD*] (TAG)
ODSA.......... Original Doctors' Shorthand Acronym (BB)
ODSA.......... Overseas Development Service Association (BUAC)
ODSAS.......... Officer Dual Specialty Allocation System

ODSB .... Ocean Data Station Buoy
ODSBA ...... Oxford Down Sheep Breeders Association [*British*] (DBA)
ODSD .... Oversea Duty Selection Date [*Air Force*]
odsd .... Overseas Duty Selection Date (AD)
ODSDG ...... Dalkeith Branch, Stormont, Dundas, and Glengarry County Library, Ontario [*Library symbol*] [*National Library of Canada*] (BIB)
ODSE .... Open Door Student Exchange (EA)
ODS/FRODS... Observable Differences/Functionally Related Observable Differences (MCD)
ODSG .... Ophthalmic Doppler Sonogram [*Medicine*] (MELL)
ODSI .... Ocean Data Systems, Inc. [*Information service or system*] (IID)
ODSI .... ODS Networks [*NASDAQ symbol*] (SG)
ODSI .... Old Dominion Systems, Inc. (SAUS)
ODSI .... Open Directory Service Interfaces [*Computer science*] (HODG)
ODSI .... Open Directory Services Interface [*Microsoft*] (GART)
ODSI .... Optical Data Systems, Inc. [*NASDAQ symbol*] (SAG)
ODSR .... Office of the Director of Scientific Research (AD)
ODSRS ...... Orbiting Deep Space Relay Station (MCD)
ODSS .... Ocean Dumping Surveillance System [*Coast Guard*] (MSC)
ODSS .... Odyssey [*NCIC motorcycle make code*]
ODSS .... Order Delivery Schedule Summary (MCD)
ODST .... Online Depression Screening Test (SAUS)
OD Structure... Order-Disorder Structure (SAUS)
ODSY .... Sayun [*People's Democratic Republic of Yemen*] [*ICAO location identifier*] (ICLI)
ODT .... Occipitodextra Transversa [*A fetal position*] [*Medicine*] (AAMN)
odt .... Occipito-Dextra Transverse (AD)
ODT .... Ocean Data Transmitter
odt .... Octal Debugging Technique (AD)
ODT .... Octal Debugging Technique [*Computer science*] (IEEE)
odt .... Odor Detection Threshold (AD)
ODT .... Odor Detection Threshold (PDAA)
ODT .... Office of Defense Transportation [*Within Office for Emergency Management*] [*World War II*]
ODT .... Oklahoma Department of Transportation
ODT .... Omnidirection Transmission (NVT)
ODT .... On Demand Technologies (SAUS)
odt .... One-Day Trials (AD)
odt .... On-Line Debugging Technique [*Computer science*] (AD)
ODT .... Online Debugging Technique
ODT .... Open Desktop (SAUS)
ODT .... Operational Demand Time [*Military*] (CAAL)
ODT .... Operational Demonstration Test
ODT .... Operational Development Team (IAA)
ODT .... Operator Display Terminal (SAUS)
ODT .... Optical Data Transmission
ODT .... Order-Disorder Transformation
ODT .... Order-Disorder Transition
ODT .... Otago Daily Times [*A publication*] (AD)
ODT .... Outdoor Trainer (SAUS)
ODT .... Outside Diameter Tube (MSA)
ODT .... Overseas Deployment Training [*Army*]
ODTAA .... One Damn Thing After Another [*Title of book by John Masefield*]
ODTACCS... Office of the Director, Telecommunications, and Command and Control Systems [*DoD*] (PDAA)
ODTC .... Office of Defense Trade Controls (AAGC)
ODTC .... Optic Display Test Chamber
ODTF .... Operational Development Test Facility (AAG)
ODTM .... n-Octyldecyltrimellitat (SAUS)
ODTM .... Optical Time Division Multiplexing (SAUS)
ODTM .... Orbiter Dynamic Test Model [*NASA*]
ODTS .... Offset Doppler Tracking System (KSC)
ODTS .... Operational Development Test Site (AAG)
ODTS .... Optical Data Transmission System
ODTS .... Optical Discrimination and Tracking System [*Army*]
ODTS .... Organic Dust Toxic Syndrome [*Medicine*]
ODTUG ...... Oracle Development Tools User Group [*Association*] (EA)
ODTW .... Oppositely-Directed Travelling Wave (PDAA)
ODTX .... Oil-Dri [*Private rail car owner code*]
ODU .... Civic Democratic Union (Slovakia) [*Political party*] (PSAP)
ODU .... Dunnville Public Library, Ontario [*Library symbol*] [*National Library of Canada*] (NLC)
ODU .... Old Dominion University [*Virginia*]
ODU .... Old Dutch [*Language, etc.*]
ODU .... Optical Density Unit
ODU .... Optical Display Unit [*Computer science*] (MCD)
ODU .... Output Display Unit [*Computer science*]
ODUB .... Bibliotheque Publique de Dubreuilville, Ontario [*Library symbol*] [*National Library of Canada*] (NLC)
ODUC .... Ohio Data Users Center [*Columbus*] [*Information service or system*] (IID)
ODUM .... Association of American Youth of Ukrainian Descent (EA)
ODUMP ..... Ocean Dumping Permits [*Database*] [*Environment Canada*] [*Information service or system*] (CRD)
ODUN .... Dundalk Public Library, Ontario [*Library symbol*] [*National Library of Canada*] (NLC)
od units ..... Optical-Density Units (AD)
ODUR .... Durham Public Library, Ontario [*Library symbol*] [*National Library of Canada*] (NLC)
ODURF ...... Old Dominion University Research Foundation [*Old Dominion University*] [*Research center*] (RCD)
ODUSD(ES)... Office of the Deputy Under Secretary of Defense (Environmental Security) [*DoD*] (RDA)
ODUSD (R & AT)... Office of the Deputy Under Secretary of Defense for Research and Advanced Technology [*DoD*] (RDA)
ODUSM ..... Office, Deputy Under Secretary for Manpower [*Navy*]
ODUSN ...... Office, Deputy Under Secretary of the Navy
ODV .... Eau-de-Vie [*Taken from the French pronunciation and used to refer to brandy*]
ODVA .... Open DeviceNet Vendors Association (ACII)
ODVAR ...... Orbit Determination and Vehicle Attitude Reference
ODVP .... Optimal Digital Voice Processor (MCD)
ODW .... Oak Harbor [*Washington*] [*Airport symbol*] (OAG)
ODW .... Office of Drinking Water [*Environmental Protection Agency*]
ODW .... Ohio Wesleyan University, Delaware, OH [*Library symbol*] [*Library of Congress*] (LCLS)
ODW .... Omega Dropwindsonde [*Meteorology*]
ODW .... Oregon Draymen & Warehousemen's Association, Portland OR [*STAC*]
ODW .... Organic Dry Weight
ODW .... Our Developing World [*An association*] (EA)
ODW .... Output Discrete Word (MCD)
ODW .... Oven-Dried Weight
ODW .... Workers Health and Safety Centre, Don Mills, Ontario [*Library symbol*] [*National Library of Canada*] (BIB)
ODWA .... Odwalla, Inc. [*NASDAQ symbol*] (SAG)
Odwalla ..... Odwalla, Inc. [*Associated Press*] (SAG)
ODWC .... West Carleton Secondary School, Dunrobin, Ontario [*Library symbol*] [*National Library of Canada*] (BIB)
ODWG .... Offset Drilling Working Group (SAUS)
ODWIN ...... Opening Doors Wider in Nursing [*Project*]
ODWSA ..... Office of the Directorate of Weapon Systems Analysis [*Army*] (AABC)
O'Dwyer..... Jack O'Dwyer's Newsletter [*A publication*] [*New York, NY*] (WDMC)
ODX .... Ord, NE [*Location identifier*] [*FAA*] (FAAL)
ODXT .... Omnidentix Systems (SAUS)
ODY .... Odyssey [*NCIC car model code*]
ODY .... Odyssey Industries, Inc. [*Toronto Stock Exchange symbol*]
ODY .... Odyssey International [*Canada*] [*ICAO designator*] (FAAC)
ODY .... Orderly [*Telegraphy*] (PCTE)
ODYE .... Odyssea Ship Line [*Common carrier symbol*]
ODYS .... Odyssey Trailer Company [*NCIC trailer make code*]
ODYY .... Odyssey Entertainment Ltd. (SAUS)
ODZ .... Outer Defense Zone
OE .... Austria [*International civil aircraft marking*] (ODBW)
OE .... Exeter Public Library, Ontario [*Library symbol*] [*National Library of Canada*] (NLC)
O/E .... Observed versus Expected
OE .... Occupied by Enemy (SAUS)
OE .... Oceanic Engineering (SAUS)
OE .... OE, Inc. [*Toronto Stock Exchange symbol*]
oe .... Oersted (AD)
Oe .... Oersted [*Unit of magnetizing intensity*]
OE .... Offensive End [*Football*]
OE .... Office Equipment
OE .... Office of Education [*HEW*]
OE .... Office of Emergency Planning and Operations (SAUS)
OE .... Office of Energy [*Department of Agriculture*] (GFGA)
OE .... Office of Enforcement [*Environmental Protection Agency*] (GFGA)
OE .... Oil Emulsion [*Microbiology*]
OE .... Oil Equivalent
OE .... Old England (GEAB)
OE .... Old English [*Typeface*] (WDMC)
OE .... Old English [*Language, etc.*] [*i.e., before 1150 or 1200*]
OE .... Old Etonian [*British*]
OE .... Olpe [*German license plate city code*]
OE .... Omission Excepted (IAA)
oe .... Omissions Excepted (WDAA)
oe .... Omissions Expected (AD)
OE .... One Edge (SAUS)
o/e .... On Examination (AD)
OE .... On Examination [*Medicine*]
OE .... Opened Edges [*Publishing*] (DGA)
OE .... Open Edition (SAUS)
oe .... Open End (AD)
OE .... Open End (MSA)
OE .... Operating Engineer (NRCH)
OE .... Operating Environment (CTAS)
OE .... Operating Expense
OE .... Operational Efficiency (SAUS)
OE .... Operational Evaluation [*Army*]
OE .... Operation Enterprise [*Hamilton, NY*] (EA)
OE .... Operation Enterprise Newsletter [*A publication*]
OE .... Operations Engineering (AAG)
OE .... Opportunity Evaluation (SAUS)
OE .... Optical/Electrical Conversion [*Telecommunications*]
OE .... Optical Emission (MCD)
OE .... Optical Engineering
O/E .... Optical-to-Electrical (SAUS)
OE .... Optoelectronics (SAUS)
OE .... Orbital Engine ADS [*NYSE symbol*] (SPSG)
OE .... Order Entry (DMAA)
O/E .... Order/Entry System [*Computer science*] (DHSM)
OE .... Ordnance Electrician [*British military*] (DMA)
OE .... Ordnance Engineer [*British military*] (DMA)
OE .... Oregon Electric Railway Co. [*AAR code*]
oe .... Organizational Effectiveness (AD)
OE .... Organizational Effectiveness
OE .... Organizational Entity
OE .... Organizational Error [*Engineering*]

OE .... Organo Espressivo [*Swell Organ*] [*Music*]
oe .... Organo Espressivo [*Swell Organ*] [*Italian*] (AD)
OE .... Orientalium Ecclesiarum [*Decree on the Eastern Catholic Churches*] [*Vatican II document*]
OE .... Original Entry [*Computer science*]
OE .... Original Equipment [*Automobile industry*]
OE .... Original Error [*Navigation*]
OE .... Originating Exchange (SAUS)
OE .... Orion Express [*Federal Railroad Administration identification code*]
OE .... Orthoenstatite [*Mineral*]
OE .... Orthopedic Examination (SAUS)
OE .... Other Essays [*Literature*] (ROG)
o/e .... Otitis Externa (AD)
OE .... Otitis Externa [*Medicine*] (DMAA)
oe .... Outdoor Education (AD)
OE .... Out Island Airways (OAG)
OE .... Outlook Express [*Computer science*] (PCM)
O/E .... Output Electronics (SAUS)
OE .... Output Enable [*Semiconductor memory*] (IEEE)
OE .... Overrun Error (SAUS)
OE .... Over-the-Horizon Expanded (MCD)
OE .... Own Exchange [*Telecommunications*] (TEL)
OE .... Oxide Electrode (SAUS)
OE .... Samoan [*ICAO designator*] (AD)
OEA .... Archives, City of Etobicoke, Ontario [*Library symbol*] [*National Library of Canada*] (BIB)
OEA .... Eastern Oklahoma District Library, Muskogee, OK [*OCLC symbol*] (OCLC)
OEA .... Oahu Education Association [*Hawaii*] (AD)
OEA .... Oblate Education Association [*Defunct*] (EA)
OEA .... OEA, Inc. [*NYSE symbol*] (SPSG)
OEA .... Office Education Association (EA)
OEA .... Office Executives Association (AD)
OEA .... Office of Economic Adjustment [*Air Force*] (AFM)
OEA .... Office of Economic Analysis [*Formerly, Office of Business Economics*] [*Department of Commerce*]
OEA .... Office of Environmental Affairs (AD)
OEA .... Office of Environmental Analysis [*Oak Ridge National Laboratory*]
OEA .... Office of Ethnic Affairs [*Victoria, Australia*]
OEA .... Office of European Associations in Higher Education [*Belgium*] (BUAC)
OEA .... Office of Export Administration [*Formerly, OEC*] [*Department of Commerce*]
OEA .... Office of External Affairs [*Environmental Protection Agency*] (GFGA)
OEA .... Ohio Education Association (AD)
OEA .... Ohio Environmental Agency (SAUS)
OEA .... Operational Effectiveness Analysis (MCD)
OEA .... Operator Error Analysis
OEA .... Ophthalmic Exhibitors' Association [*British*] (DBA)
OEA .... Optometric Editors Association (EA)
OEA .... Orchestral Employers' Association [*British*] (BI)
OEA .... Ordnance Electrical Artificer [*British military*] (DMA)
OEA .... Oregon Education Association (AD)
OEA .... Organisation of Europe Aluminium-Smelters (BUAC)
OEA .... Organizacion de los Estados Americanos [*Organization of American States - OAS*] [*Spanish*]
OEA .... Organizational Expense Accounts [*Army*]
OEA .... Original Equipment Assembler [*Automotive engineering*]
OEA .... Outdoor Education Association (EA)
OEA .... Overseas Education Association (EA)
OEA .... Oxygen Enriched Atmosphere (SAUS)
OEA .... Vincennes, IN [*Location identifier*] [*FAA*] (FAAL)
OEAA .... Oil Engineering Apprentices Association (AD)
OEAB .... Abha [*Saudi Arabia*] [*ICAO location identifier*] (ICLI)
OEac .... East Cleveland Public Library, East Cleveland, OH [*Library symbol*] [*Library of Congress*] (LCLS)
OEAH .... Al-Ahsa [*Saudi Arabia*] [*ICAO location identifier*] (ICLI)
OEal .... East Liverpool Carnegie Public Library, East Liverpool, OH [*Library symbol*] [*Library of Congress*] (LCLS)
OEALC .... Oficina Regional de Educacion para America Latina y el Caribe [*Regional Office for Education in Latin America and the Caribbean-Chile*] (IID)
OEalK .... Kent State University, East Liverpool Regional Campus, East Liverpool, OH [*Library symbol*] [*Library of Congress*] (LCLS)
OE & TB .... Officer Education and Training Branch [*BUPERS*]
OEAP .... Operational Error Analysis Program
OEAQ .... Outdoor Educators' Association of Queensland [*Australia*]
OEAS .... Orbital Emergency Arresting System [*NASA*] (NASA)
OEAS .... Organisation Europaischer Aluminium Schmelzhutten [*Organization of European Aluminium Foundries*] (PDAA)
OEAS .... Oxygen Enriched Air System (MCD)
OEASA .... Outdoor Educators Association of South Australia (SAUS)
OEB .... Officers' Organization for Economic Benefits [*Commercial firm*] (EA)
OEB .... Ontario Energy Board (SAUS)
OEB .... Open Electronic Book (SAUS)
OEB .... Oregon Educational Broadcasting (AD)
OEB .... Organic Electrolyte Battery
OEBA .... El-Baha [*Saudi Arabia*] [*ICAO location identifier*] (ICLI)
OEBA .... Office for Economic and Business Affairs [*Department of State*]
OeBF .... Open eBook Forum
OEBH .... Bisha [*Saudi Arabia*] [*ICAO location identifier*] (ICLI)
OE-BR .... Oil Extended Butadiene Rubber (SAUS)
OEBR .... Optical Edge Bead Removal (AAEL)
OEBS .... Office of Employee Benefits Security [*Department of Labor*]
OEBS .... Organic Electrolyte Battery System
OEBU .... Oesterreichische Bundesbahnen [*Intermodal shipping container symbol*] (TVRC)
OEC .... Electro-Optical Center (EFIS)
OEC .... Observed Effect Concentration [*Environmental science*] (ERG)
OEC .... Odd-Even Check
Oec .... Oeconomica [*of Aristotle*] [*Classical studies*] (OCD)
Oec .... Oeconomicus [*of Xenophon*] [*Classical studies*] (OCD)
OEC .... Oesterreichischer Aero-Club [*Austrian Aero Club*] [*German*] (AD)
OEC .... Office of Electronics and Control (SAUS)
OEC .... Office of Emergency Communications [*FCC*] (NTCM)
OEC .... Office of Energy Conservation [*Functions transferred to Federal Energy Administration*]
OEC .... Office of Environmental Compliance (SAUS)
OEC .... Office of Export Control [*Later, OEA*] [*World War II*]
OEC .... Office on Educational Credit [*Later, OECC*] (EA)
OEC .... Ohio Edison Co. [*NYSE symbol*] (SPSG)
OEC .... Ohio Edison Financing Trust [*NYSE symbol*] (SAG)
OEC .... Oil Exporting Countries (AD)
OEC .... Ontario Economic Council (SAUS)
OEC .... Ontario Election Decisions [*A publication*] (DLA)
OEC .... Ontario Energy Corporation (SAUS)
OEC .... Open-End Company [*Business term*] (MHDW)
OEC .... Open-End Credit [*Business term*] (MHDW)
OEC .... Open Enterprise Computing [*Computer science*] (GART)
OEC .... Open Environment Corporation (SAUS)
OEC .... Operational Employment Concept [*Army*] (AABC)
OEC .... Operational Evaluation Command [*Army*] (DOMA)
OEC .... Optical Effect Code
OEC .... Optic-Electronic Corp. (RDA)
OEC .... Opto-Electronics Center (MCD)
OEC .... Orange Empire Conference (PSS)
OEC .... Orbital Electron Capture
OEC .... Orbiting Experimental Capsule
OEC .... Ordnance Equipment Chart
OEC .... Organizational Effectiveness Consultants (INF)
oec .... Organizational Entity Code (AD)
OEC .... Organizational Entity Code
OEC .... Oribital Engine Corporation (SAUS)
OEC .... Other Early Capability (ACAE)
OEC .... Output Edge Control (SAUS)
OEC .... Overpaid Entry Certificate (DS)
OEC .... Overseas Employment Corp. [*Pakistan*] (BUAC)
OEC .... Oxygen Equilibrium Curve (DB)
OEC .... Oxygen-Evolving Complex [*Photosynthesis*]
OECA .... Office of Enforcement and Compliance Assurance [*Environmental Protection Agency*] (AEPA)
OECA .... Ontario Educational Communications Authority [*Canada*]
OEC & S .... Organizational Effectiveness Center and School [*Army*]
OECC .... Office on Educational Credit and Credentials (EA)
OECC .... Oregon Educational Computing Consortium (EDAC)
OECCNU .... Organizacion para la Educacion la Ciencia, y la Cultura [*Organization for Education, Science, and Culture*] [*United Nations*] (AD)
OECD .... Organisation for Economic Co-Operation and Development (IID)
OECD .... Organization for Economic Cooperation and Development [*Formerly, OEEC*]
OECD .... Organization for European Community Development (SAUS)
OECD/ENC ... Organization for Economic Cooperation and Development/ Environment Committee [*Marine science*] (MSC)
OECD/MEI ... OECD Main Economics Indicators (NITA)
OECD/NIA ... OECD National Income Accounts (NITA)
OECD/SIDS ... Organization for Economic Cooperation and Developments Screening Information Data [*Environment term*] (EGA)
OECE .... Organisation Europeenne de Cooperation Economique [*Organization for European Economic Cooperation - OEEC*] [*Later, OECD*] [*See also OCDE*] [*France*] (MSC)
OECE .... Organizacion Europea de Cooperacion Economica [*Organization for European Economic Cooperation - OEEC*] [*Later, OECD*] [*Spain*]
OECF .... Overseas Economic Cooperation Fund (AD)
OECF .... Overseas Economic Cooperation Fund of Japan (BUAC)
OECIC .... Open-End Contract Information Circulars (AAGC)
OECM .... Office of Enforcement and Compliance Monitoring [*Environmental Protection Agency*] (GFGA)
OEC Md .... OEC Medical [*Associated Press*] (SAG)
oeco .... Outboard Engine Cutoff (AD)
OECO .... Outboard Engine Cutoff [*NASA*]
OECO .... Oxygen Enrichment Company Ltd. (SAUS)
OECON .... Offshore Engineering Conference (MCD)
OECON .... Offshore Exploration Conference
OECOS .... Organizational Engineering for Communications and Organizational Systems (SAUS)
OECPrA .... Ohio Edison 3.90% Pfd [*NYSE symbol*] (TTSB)
OECPrB .... Ohio Edison, 4.40% Pfd [*NYSE symbol*] (TTSB)
OECPrC .... Ohio Edison 4.44% Pfd [*NYSE symbol*] (TTSB)
OECPrT .... Ohio Edison Fin Tr 9.00% Pfd [*NYSE symbol*] (TTSB)
OECQ .... Organisation Europeene pour la Controle de la Qualite GG1European Quality-Control OrganizationGG2 [*France*] (AD)
OECQ .... Organisation Europeenne pour la Qualite [*European Organization for Quality -EOQC*] [*Switzerland*]
OECS .... Optics of Excitons in Confined Systems (SAUS)
OECS .... Optoelectronics Circuits and Systems Laboratory [*University of California, Los Angeles*] (RCD)
OECS .... Organisation of Eastern Caribbean States (EAIO)
OECS .... Organization for the Enforcement of Child Support (EA)

OECSEAS... Organisation of Eastern Caribbean States, Economic Affairs Secretariat [*St. Johns, Antigua*] (EAIO)
OECT........ European Association of the Textile Wholesale Trade [*EC*] (ECED)
OECT........ Oxford Editions of Cuneiform Texts [*A publication*] (BJA)
oecu......... Outboard Engine Cutoff (AD)
OED.......... Ocean Engineering Division [*Coast Guard*]
OED.......... Office Equipment Division (SAUS)
OED.......... Office of Economic Development [*Bureau of Indian Affairs*]
OED.......... Operational Engineering Detachment (MCD)
OED.......... Operational Engineering Division [*Central Electricity Generating Board*] [*British*] (IRUK)
OED.......... Operational Evaluation Demonstration (MCD)
OED.......... Operation Effectiveness Demonstration (RDA)
OED.......... Optoelectronic Device (SAUS)
OED.......... Opto Electronic Display [*Computer science*] (ELAL)
OED.......... Orbiting Energy Depot
OED.......... Oscillating Electron Discharge (SAUS)
OED.......... Otto Erich Deutsch [*Music cataloger*]
OED.......... Oxford English Dictionary [*Information service or system*] [*A publication*]
OED.......... Oxidation-Enhanced Diffusion (SAUS)
OEDA........ Office of Energy Data and Analysis [*Functions transferred to Federal Energy Administration*]
OEDC........ Office of Engineering Design and Construction [*Tennessee Valley Authority*]
OEDC........ Offshore Energy Development Corp. [*NASDAQ symbol*] (SAG)
OEDC........ Ontario Engineering Design Competition (SAUS)
OEDC........ Organization for Economic Cooperation and Development (AG)
OEDIPUS... Oxford English Dictionary Inputting, Proofing, and Updating Service
OEDIT....... Octal Editor [*Computer science*] (MHDI)
OEDO........ Ordnance Engineering Duty Officer
OEDP........ Office of Employment Development Programs (AD)
OEDP........ Overall Economic Development Program [*Bureau of Indian Affairs*]
OEDR........ Dhahran/International [*Saudi Arabia*] [*ICAO location identifier*] (ICLI)
OEDRC...... Optico-Electronic Device for Registering Coincidences (PDAA)
OEDSF...... On-Board Experimental Data Support Facility
OEDX........ Ohio Edison [*Private rail car owner code*]
OEE.......... Ernst & Whinney, Cleveland, OH [*OCLC symbol*] (OCLC)
OEE.......... Essex County Public Library, Essex, Ontario [*Library symbol*] [*National Library of Canada*] (NLC)
OEE.......... Odd-Even Effect (SAUS)
OEE.......... Office of Educational Exchange [*Department of State*]
OEE.......... Office of the Assistant Secretary for Export Enforcement [*Department of Commerce*] (GFGA)
OEE.......... Ordre de l'Etoile de l'Europe [*Huy, Belgium*] (EAIO)
oee.......... Outer Enamel Epithelium (AD)
OEE.......... Outer Enamel Epithelium [*Dentistry*]
OEE.......... Overall Equipment Effectiveness (AAEL)
OEEC........ Organization for European Economic Cooperation [*Later, OECD*]
OEED........ Oxford Encyclopedic English Dictionary [*A publication*]
OEEO........ Office of Equal Educational Opportunities [*Office of Education*]
OEEO........ Office of Equal Employment Opportunity [*Department of Labor*] (OICC)
OE-EPDM... Oil Extended Ethylene-Propylene Diene Monomer (SAUS)
OEEPE...... Organisation Europeenne d'Etudes Photogrammetriques Experimentales [*European Organisation for Experimental Photogrammetric Research*] [*Research Center*] [*Netherlands*] (PDAA)
OEER........ Oceanographic Equipment Evaluation Range (NOAA)
OEES........ Interagency Committee on Ocean Exploration and Environmental Services [*Terminated, 1971*] (EGAO)
OEES........ Office of Emergency and Energy Services [*Emergency Management*] (EMA)
OEES........ Organization for Equal Education of the Sexes (EA)
OE-E-SBR... Oil Extended Emulsion Styrene Butadiene Rubber (SAUS)
OEET........ Office of Environmental Engineering and Technology [*Environmental Protection Agency*] (EPA)
OEETD...... Office of Environmental Engineering and Technology Demonstration [*Washington, DC*] [*Environmental Protection Agency*] (GRD)
OEF.......... Ear Falls Public Library, Ontario [*Library symbol*] [*National Library of Canada*] (NLC)
OEF.......... Oceanic Educational Foundation (EA)
OEF.......... Officeholders Expense Funds [*Slush money*]
OEF.......... Oil Emersion Field [*Biochemistry*] (DAVI)
OEF.......... Online Education Facility [*Computer science*] (VLIE)
OEF.......... Open-End Funds [*Investment term*]
OEF.......... Operational Efficiency Factor (SAUS)
OEF.......... Operation Enduring Freedom [*Government term*] (GA)
OEF.......... Optical Evaluation Facility (RDA)
OEF.......... Order Entry Form (TIMI)
OEF.......... Organization of Employers Federations (SAUS)
OEF.......... Origin Element Field [*Computer science*] (ELAL)
OEF.......... Osteopathic Educational Foundation (AD)
OEF.......... Overseas Education Fund [*Later, OEFI*] (EA)
OEF.......... Oxford Economic Forecasting (BUAC)
OEF.......... Oxygen Extraction Fraction [*Medicine*] (DMAA)
OEFD........ Orbiter Electric Field Detector [*NASA*]
OEFE........ Flos-Elmvale Public Library, Elmvale, Ontario [*Library symbol*] [*National Library of Canada*] (BIB)
OEFFA...... Ohio Ecological Food and Farm Association (EARSL)
OEFI........ OEF [*Overseas Educational Fund*] International (EA)
OEFS........ Interagency Committee on Ocean Exploration and Environmental Services (SAUS)
OEFS........ Organisation for Equal Education of the Sexes (SAUS)
OEG.......... Eganville Public Library, Ontario [*Library symbol*] [*National Library of Canada*] (NLC)
OEG.......... Occluded Eye Gunsight [*Military*] (INF)
Oeg.......... Oestrogene (SAUS)
OEG.......... Office of Environmental Guidance (SAUS)
OEG.......... Open-End Guide (SAUS)
OEG.......... Operational Exposure Guidance [*Military*] (INF)
OEG.......... Operational Exposure Guide
OEG.......... Operations Evaluation Group [*Military*]
OEG.......... Organization and Equipment Guide [*Army*] (AABC)
OEG.......... Outdoor Ethics Guild (EA)
OEG.......... Public Library of Enid and Garfield County, Enid, OK [*OCLC symbol*] (OCLC)
OEGCA...... Old English Game Club of America (EA)
OEGCMJ.... Officer Exercising General Court-Martial Jurisdiction
OEGN........ Gizan [*Saudi Arabia*] [*ICAO location identifier*] (ICLI)
OEGS........ Gassim [*Saudi Arabia*] [*ICAO location identifier*] (ICLI)
OEGT........ Guriat [*Saudi Arabia*] [*ICAO location identifier*] (ICLI)
oegt.......... Observable Evidence of Good Teaching (AD)
OEGT........ Observable Evidences of Good Teaching
OEGT........ Office of Education for the Gifted and Talented [*HEW*]
OEH.......... Baltimore, MD [*Location identifier*] [*FAA*] (FAAL)
OEH.......... Occupational & Environmental Health Library (SAUS)
OEH.......... Orient Express Hotels (EFIS)
OEHA........ Office of Environmental and Health Affairs [*World Bank*] (BUAC)
OEHL........ Hail [*Saudi Arabia*] [*ICAO location identifier*] (ICLI)
OEHL........ Hoffman-La Roche Ltd., Etobicoke, Ontario [*Library symbol*] [*National Library of Canada*] (NLC)
OEHL........ Occupational and Environmental Health Laboratory [*Brooks Air Force Base, TX*] [*Air Force*]
OEHMO...... Open-Ended Health Maintenance Organization [*Insurance*] (WYGK)
OEHS........ Office of Environmental Health & Safety (SAUS)
OEI........... Ocean Energy [*NYSE symbol*] [*Formerly, Flores & Rucks*] (SG)
OEI........... Officers Efficiency Index (SAUS)
OEI........... Official Establishment Inventory
OEI........... Offshore Ecology Investigation [*Oil study*]
OEI........... Oficina de Educacion Iberoamericana [*Ibero-American Bureau of Education - IABE*] [*Madrid, Spain*] (EAIO)
OEI........... One Engine Inoperative [*Aviation*]
OEI........... One Essential Ingredient (SAUS)
OEI........... Open Enterprise Infrastructure (TIMI)
OEI........... Options Exchange Index
OEI........... Optoelectronic Isolator
OEI........... Order and Equipment Installed (VLIE)
OEI........... Organizacion de Estados Iberoamericanos para la Educacion, la Ciencia, y la Cultura [*Organization of Ibero-American States for Education, Science, and Culture*] (EAIO)
oei........... Organizational Entity Identity (AD)
OEI........... Organizational Entity Identity
OEI........... Overall Efficiency Index
OEI........... Own Equipment Inventory (VLIE)
OEIAA...... Office Equipment Industry Association of Australia
OEIC........ Ocean Engineering Information Centre [*Memorial University of Newfoundland*] [*Information service or system*] (IID)
OEIC........ Open-End Investment Co. [*Investment term*]
OEIC........ Optoelectronic Integrated Circuit [*Computer science*]
OEIC........ Opto-Electronic Integrated Circuits
OEIC........ Overseas Economic Intelligence Committee [*Military*]
OEID........ Office of Engineering Infrastructure Development [*Washington, DC*] [*National Science Foundation*] (GRD)
OEII.......... O'Neill Educational Ideologies Inventory (EDAC)
OEII.......... Operation Everest II [*Army*] (RDA)
OEIMC...... Oklahoma Environmental Information and Media Center (SAUS)
OEIO........ Odds and Ends Input/Output (MCD)
OEIPS...... Office of Engineering and Information Processing Standards [*National Bureau of Standards*]
OEIS........ Office of Energy Information Services [*Department of Energy*] (IID)
OEIS........ Offshore Engineering Information Service [*Heriot-Watt University Library*] (IID)
OEIS........ Orbiter Electrical Interface Simulator [*NASA*]
OEIT........ Open-End Investment Trust [*Investment term*]
OEITFL...... Organisation Europeenne des Industries Transformatrices de Fruits et Legumes [*European Organization of Fruit and Vegetable Processing Industries*] [*Common Market*] [*Belgium*]
OEIU........ Office Employes International Union [*Later, OPEIU*]
OEJ.......... Office of Environmental Justice [*Environmental Protection Agency*] (AEPA)
OEJB........ Jubail [*Saudi Arabia*] [*ICAO location identifier*] (ICLI)
OEJD........ Jeddah [*Saudi Arabia*] [*ICAO location identifier*] (ICLI)
OEJH........ Office of Environmental Justice Hotline [*Environmental Protection Agency*] (AEPA)
OEJN........ Jeddah/King Abdul Aziz International [*Saudi Arabia*] [*ICAO location identifier*] (ICLI)
OEKJ........ Al-Kharj [*Saudi Arabia*] [*ICAO location identifier*] (ICLI)
OEKM........ Khamis Mushait [*Saudi Arabia*] [*ICAO location identifier*] (ICLI)
OEL.......... Elliot Lake Public Library, Ontario [*Library symbol*] [*National Library of Canada*] (NLC)
OEL.......... Eugene Public Library, Eugene, OR [*OCLC symbol*] (OCLC)
OEL.......... Oakley, KS [*Location identifier*] [*FAA*] (FAAL)
OEL.......... Occupational Exposure Limit
OEL.......... Ontario Electrical League (SAUS)
OEL.......... Ontario Express Ltd. [*Canada*] [*ICAO designator*] (FAAC)
OEL.......... Ordered Edge List (SAUS)
OEL.......... Ordnance Engineering Laboratory
OEL.......... Ordnance Equipment List [*Navy*] (NG)
OEL.......... Organic Electroluminescent (AEBE)
OEL.......... Organizational Equipment List [*Army*]

OE LASE.... Optics, Electro-Optics and Laser Applications in Science and Engineering (SAUS)
OELB........ Oertlicher Landwirtschaftsbetrieb [*Local Agricultural Enterprise*] [*German*]
OELD........ Office of the Executive Legal Director [*Nuclear Regulatory Commission*] (GFGA)
OELF........ Fort Hope Band Library, Eabamet Lake, Ontario [*Library symbol*] [*National Library of Canada*] (BIB)
OELK........ Elk Lake Public Library, Ontario [*Library symbol*] [*National Library of Canada*] (BIB)
OELM........ Elmwood Branch, Bruce County Public Library, Ontario [*Library symbol*] [*National Library of Canada*] (NLC)
OELMA...... Ohio Educational Library Media Association (EDAC)
OEL/MA...... Ohio Educational Library/Media Association (SAUS)
OELMN(A)... Ordnance Electrical Mechanician (Air) [*British military*] (DMA)
OELR........ Oelrich Manufacturing Company [*NCIC trailer make code*]
OELRR...... Office of Economic Liaison and Regulatory Review [*Western Australia*]
OELS........ Elliot Lake Secondary School, Ontario [*Library symbol*] [*National Library of Canada*] (NLC)
OELS........ Operationally Efficient Launch Site Study (SAUS)
OELX........ Linsin [*Private rail car owner code*]
OEly........ Elyria Library, Elyria, OH [*Library symbol*] [*Library of Congress*] (LCLS)
OElyL........ Lorain County Community College, Elyria, OH [*Library symbol*] [*Library of Congress*] (LCLS)
OEM........ Emo Public Library, Ontario [*Library symbol*] [*National Library of Canada*] (NLC)
OEM........ Occupational and Environmental Medicine
OEM........ Odd Even Merge (SAUS)
OEM........ Office & Electronic Machines Ltd.d (SAUS)
OEM........ Office Equipment Maintenance
OEM........ Office for Emergency Management [*World War II*]
OEM........ Office of Electronic Machines [*Commercial firm*] [*British*]
OEM........ Office of Emergency Management (New York City Mayor's Office) [*Emergency Management*] (EMA)
OEM........ Office of Environmental Mediation
OEM........ Office of Executive Management
oem........ Oil-Emulsion Mud (AD)
OEM........ On Equipment Materiel [*Army*] (AABC)
OEM........ Open-End Marriage
OEM........ Optical Electronic Microscope (WDAA)
oem........ Optical Electron Microscope (AD)
OEM........ Optical Electron Microscope (PDAA)
OEM........ Ordnance Electrical Mechanic [*British military*] (DMA)
OEM........ Oregon Emergency Management Division [*Emergency Management*] (EMA)
OEM........ Organizational Element Model
oem........ Original Equipment Manufacturer (AD)
OEM........ Original Equipment Manufacturer
OEM........ Original Equipment Manufacturing (SAUS)
OEM........ Original Equipment Market (SAUS)
OEM........ Other Equipment Manufacturer (IAA)
OEM........ Other Equipment Manufacturers (CMD)
OEM........ Own Equipment Material
OEMA........ Madinah [*Saudi Arabia*] [*ICAO location identifier*] (ICLI)
OEMA........ Office Equipment Manufacturers Association (AD)
OEMA........ Office of Educational and Manpower Assistance (OICC)
OEMA........ Office of Export Marketing Assistance [*Department of Commerce*]
OEMA........ Oregon Educational Media Association
OEMA........ Oregon Emergency Management Association [*Emergency Management*] (EMA)
oemcp....... Optical Effects Module Electronic Controller and Processor (AD)
OEMCP...... Optical Effects Module Electronic Controller and Processor [*NASA*]
OEMI........ Office Equipment Manufacturers Institute [*Later, CBEMA*]
OEMI........ Office of Energy, Minerals, and Industry [*Environmental Protection Agency*]
OEMI........ Original Equipment Manufacture Interface (SAUS)
OEMI........ Original Equipment Manufacturers Information (VLIE)
OEMI........ Other Equipment Manufacturer's Information (IAA)
OEMM........ Operational Experiment on Mesoscale Meteorology (SAUS)
OEMN........ Ordnance Electrical Mechanician [*British military*] (DMA)
OEMO........ One-Electron Molecular Orbital (DB)
OEMP........ Office of Emergency Medical Preparedness [*Emergency Management*] (EMA)
OEMP........ Office of Environmental Monitoring and Prediction [*Marine science*] (OSRA)
OEMP........ Operational Environmental Monitoring Program (SAUS)
OEMP........ Oral Evaluation of Mechanical Proficiency (SAUS)
OEMS........ Office of Emergency Medical Services (Virginia) [*Emergency Management*] (EMA)
OEMS........ Optical Emission under Mechanical Stress (SAUS)
OEMSA...... Optical Equipment Manufacturers and Suppliers Association (BUAC)
OEMT........ Operational Emergency Management Team [*Environmental science*] (COE)
OEN........ Ennismore Township Public Library, Ontario [*Library symbol*] [*National Library of Canada*] (BIB)
OEN........ Odd-Even Nuclei
oen........ Oenanthic (AD)
oen........ Oenanthyl (AD)
oen........ oenological (SAUS)
oen........ oenologist (SAUS)
OEN........ Oenology (SAUS)
oen........ oenolyn (SAUS)
oen........ oenomancy (AD)
oen........ oenomel (AD)
oen........ oenometer (AD)
oen........ oenophilist (AD)
oen........ oenophobist (AD)
oen........ oenopoetic (AD)
OEN........ Ohio Environmental Protection Agency Library, Columbus, OH [*OCLC symbol*] (OCLC)
OEN........ Operating Environment (SAUS)
OEN........ Organizational Entity Name
OEN........ Oxford Energy Co. (SAUS)
OENCO...... Organizational Effectiveness Noncommissioned Officer [*Military*]
OENG........ Englehart Public Library, Ontario [*Library symbol*] [*National Library of Canada*] (BIB)
OENG........ Nejran [*Saudi Arabia*] [*ICAO location identifier*] (ICLI)
OENLA....... Enterprise Branch, Lennox and Addington County Library, Ontario [*Library symbol*] [*National Library of Canada*] (NLC)
OENR........ Oil-Extended Natural Rubber
OE-NR....... Oil Extended Nitrile Rubber (SAUS)
OENR........ Organization for European Nuclear Research
OEO........ Office of Economic Opportunity [*Functions transferred to other federal agencies, 1973-75*]
OEO........ Office of Equal Opportunity [*NASA*]
oeo........ Officer's Eyes Only (AD)
OEO........ Officers' Eyes Only [*Military*] (NVT)
OEO........ Operating Expense Objective
OEO........ Operational Equipment Objective (VLIE)
OEO........ Ordnance Engineer Overseer (AD)
OEO........ Ordnance Executive Officer [*Military*] [*British*]
OEO........ Osceola, WI [*Location identifier*] [*FAA*] (FAAL)
OEO........ Oversea Employment Office [*Air Force*] (AFM)
OEOA........ Office for Emergency Operations in Africa [*United Nations*] (EY)
OEOB........ Old Executive Office Building [*Washington, DC*]
OE/OE....... Open Entry/Open Exit (OICC)
OE/OEM..... Original Equipment/Original Equipment Manufacturer (SAUS)
OEP........ Occupational Education Project
OEP........ Occupational Exploration Program (OICC)
OEP........ Ocean Education Project (EA)
OEP........ Octaethylporphine (SAUS)
OEP........ Octaethyl Porphyrin (SAUS)
OEP........ Odd-Even Predominance [*Organic chemistry*]
OEP........ Office of Economic Planning (SAUS)
OEP........ Office of Economic Policy (SAUS)
OEP........ Office of Economic Programs [*of BDSA*]
OEP........ Office of Emergency Planning (AD)
OEP........ Office of Emergency Preparedness [*formerly, Planning*] [*Terminated, 1973*]
OEP........ Office of Energy Planning (COE)
OEP........ Office of Energy Programs [*NASA*]
OEP........ Office of Enforcement Policy (SAUS)
OEP........ Office of Environmental Policy [*White House*] [*Marine science*] (OSRA)
OEP........ Office of External Programs [*Environmental Protection Agency*] (GFGA)
OEP........ Office of Extramural Programs (MELL)
OEP........ Officer Education Program (SAUS)
OEP........ Oil-Extended Polymer (IAA)
OEP........ Open-Ended Plan [*Human resources*] (WYGK)
OEP........ Operand Execution Pipeline [*Computer science*]
OEP........ Operational Employment Plan [*Army*]
OEP........ Optional Educational Programs (AD)
OEP........ Optoelectronic Packaging (SAUS)
OEP........ Organization, Education and Personnel (SAUS)
OEP........ Original Element Processor (MHDB)
OEP........ Outside Engineering Personnel (MCD)
OEP........ Overall Economic Perspective (SAUS)
OEP........ Overseas Employment Program [*DoD*]
OEP........ Owen Electric Pictures [*Telecommunications service*] (TSSD)
OEP........ Preble County District Library, Eaton, OH [*Library symbol*] [*Library of Congress*] (LCLS)
OEP........ United States Environmental Protection Agency, Cincinnati (SAUS)
OEPA........ Hafr Al-Batin Airport [*Saudi Arabia*] [*ICAO location identifier*] (ICLI)
OEPA........ Ohio Environmental Protection Agency
OEPA........ Vincristine, Etoposide, Prednisone, and Doxorubicin [*Medicine*]
OEPAC....... Office of the Economic Planning Advisory Council [*Australia*]
OEP&GR.... Office of Employment Policy and Grievance Review (ACAE)
OEPER....... Office of Environmental Processes and Effects Research [*Environmental Protection Agency*] [*Washington, DC*] (GRD)
OEPF........ Optometric Extension Program Foundation (EA)
OEPFC....... Official Elvis Presley Fan Club (EAIO)
OEP Off Equip Prod... OEP Office Equipment and Products (SAUS)
OEPP........ Organisation Europeenne et Mediterraneenne pour la Protection des Plantes [*European and Mediterranean Plant Protection Organization - EPPO*] (EAIO)
OEPR........ Office of Environmental Project Review [*Department of the Interior*]
OEPR........ Office of Extramural Program Review [*Department of Health and Human Services*] (GRD)
OEPS........ Office of Educational Programs and Services [*NASA*]
OEPSS....... Operationally Efficient Propulsion System Study (SAUS)
OEPT........ Perry Township Public Library Emsdale, Ontario [*Library symbol*] [*National Library of Canada*] (NLC)
OEQ........ Order of Engineers of Quebec [*Canada*] (PDAA)
OEQ........ Organisation Europeenne pour la Qualite [*Switzerland*] (EAIO)
OEQC........ Office of Environmental Quality Control (AD)
OER........ National Institutes of Health [*Department of Health and Human Services*] (IID)
OER........ Odd-Even Rule

OER......... Oersted [*Unit of magnetizing intensity*]
OER......... Offensive Efficiency Ratio [*Basketball*]
OER......... Office of Aerospace Research [*Air Force*] (AD)
OER......... Office of Economic Research [*Department of Commerce*]
OER......... Office of Energy Research [*Department of Energy*] [*Washington, DC*] (GRD)
OER......... Office of Energy Research [*University of Illinois*] [*Research center*] (RCD)
OER......... Office of Environmental Restoration (AUEG)
OER......... Office of Evaluation Research [*University of Illinois at Chicago*] [*Research center*] (RCD)
OER......... Office of Exploratory Research [*Environmental Protection Agency*] [*Washington, DC*] (GRD)
OER......... Officer Effectiveness Report [*Air Force*] (AFM)
OER......... Officer Efficiency Report [*Military*]
OER......... Officer Engineering Reserve (AD)
OER......... Officer Evaluation Report [*Military*] (INF)
OER......... Officer Evaluation Reports
OER......... Officers Effectiveness Report (SAUS)
OER......... Officers Efficiency Report (SAUS)
OER......... Officers' Emergency Reserve [*British*]
OER......... Officers Evaluation Report (SAUS)
OER......... Oil Extended Rubber (EDCT)
OER......... Operating Equipment Requirements (VLIE)
OER......... Operational Effectiveness Rate (SAUS)
OER......... Operational ELINT Requirements (MCD)
OER......... Operational Equipment Requirement (AAG)
OER......... Operations Engineering Report (AAG)
OER......... Oregon Electric Railway [*Federal Railroad Administration identification code*]
OER......... Organization for European Research (AD)
oer......... Original Equipment Replacement (AD)
OER......... Original Equipment Request (AAG)
OER......... Ornskoldsvik [*Sweden*] [*Airport symbol*] (OAG)
OER......... Osmotic Erythrocyte Resistance
O'ER......... Over (ROG)
OER......... Overhead Expenditure Request
OER......... Oxygen Enhancement Ratio
OER......... Oxygen Evolution Reaction (PDAA)
OER......... Oxygen Extraction Rate [*Medicine*] (RAWO)
OERA........ Omnibus Education Reconciliation Act of 1981
OERAHA..... Organisation Europeenne pour des Recherches Astronomiques dans l'Hemisphere Austral [*European Southern Observatory - ESO*] (EAIO)
OERC........ Ocean Engineering Research Centre [*Memorial University of Newfoundland*] [*Canada*] (RCD)
OERC........ Ontario Educational Research Council [*Canada*] (EDAC)
OERC........ Optimum Earth Reentry Corridor [*Aerospace*]
oerc......... Optimum Earth-Reentry Corridor (AD)
OERCPrD.... Ohio Edison 4.56% Pfd [*NYSE symbol*] (TTSB)
OERD........ Erin District High School, Erin, Ontario [*Library symbol*] [*National Library of Canada*] (NLC)
OERD........ Ocean Environment Research Division [*Formerly, MARD, Marine Assessment Research Division and MRRD, Marine Resources Research Division*] [*Marine science*] (OSRA)
OERD........ Office of Economic and Regional Development (SAUS)
OERD........ Office of Energy Research and Development (SAUS)
OERF........ Orthodontic Education and Research Foundation (EA)
OERF........ Rafha [*Saudi Arabia*] [*ICAO location identifier*] (ICLI)
OERI........ Office of Educational Research and Improvement [*Department of Education*] [*Washington, DC*]
OERI........ Office of Energy-Related Inventions [*Gaithersburg, MD*] [*National Institute of Standards and Technology*]
OERK........ Riyadh/King Khalid International [*Saudi Arabia*] [*ICAO location identifier*] (ICLI)
OERL........ Elgin Branch, Rideau Lakes Union Library, Ontario [*Library symbol*] [*National Library of Canada*] (NLC)
OERL........ Officer Education Research Laboratory [*Air Force*]
OERL........ Overall Echo Return Loss
OERP........ Office of Education and Regional Programming [*Medicine*] (EDAA)
OERP........ Overseas Expenditure Reduction Program [*Military*] (AFM)
OERPA....... Office of Exploratory Research and Problem Assessment [*National Science Foundation*] (AD)
OERR........ Arar [*Saudi Arabia*] [*ICAO location identifier*] (ICLI)
OERR........ Office of Emergency and Remedial Response [*Environmental Protection Agency*] (GFGA)
OERR........ Office of Environmental Regulatory Research (SAUS)
OERS........ Officer Evaluation Reporting System [*Army*]
OERS........ Operational Earth Resources System (SAUS)
OERS........ Organisation Europeenne de Recherches Spatiales
OERT........ Succursale d'Embrun, Bibliotheque Publique du Canton de Russell [*Embrun Branch, Russell Township Public Library*] Ontario [*Library symbol*] [*National Library of Canada*] (BIB)
OERWM..... Office of Environmental Restoration and Waste Management [*U.S. Department of Energy*] (BARN)
OERY........ Orange Empire Railway Museum [*Federal Railroad Administration identification code*]
OERY........ Riyadh [*Saudi Arabia*] [*ICAO location identifier*] (ICLI)
OES......... Bureau of Oceans and International Environmental and Scientific Affairs [*Department of State*]
OES......... Espanola Public Library, Ontario [*Library symbol*] [*National Library of Canada*] (NLC)
OES......... Occupational Employment Statistics [*Department of Labor*]
OES......... Occupational Exposure Standard [*Environmental chemistry*]
OES......... Oceanic Engineering Society (SAUS)
OES......... Odd Even Sort (SAUS)
OES......... Office Evaluation System (SAUS)
OES......... Office of Earthquake Studies (SAUS)
OES......... Office of Economic Stabilization [*World War II*]
OES......... Office of Emergency Service [*Federal disaster planning*]
OES......... Office of Emergency Services (California Governor's Office) [*Emergency Management*] (EMA)
OES......... Office of Emergency Services (Los Angeles) [*Emergency Management*] (EMA)
OES......... Office of Employment Security [*Department of Labor*]
OES......... Office of Endangered Species [*Department of the Interior*]
OES......... Office of Examinations and Supervision [*Federal Home Loan Bank Board*]
OES......... Office of Executive Support [*Environmental Protection Agency*] (GFGA)
OES......... Officer Education System [*Army*] (RDA)
OES......... Officer Evaluation System (SAUS)
OES......... Official Experimental Station [*Amateur radio*]
OES......... Offshore Engineering Society (BUAC)
OES......... Ohio Edison Company (EFIS)
OES......... Old English Sheepdog (SPVS)
OES......... Olympus Endoscopy System [*Gastroenterology*] (DAVI)
OES......... Open-Ended Spinning [*Textile industry*]
OES......... Open-Ended System [*Computer science*]
OES......... Operations and Engineering Squadron
OES......... Operations and Equipment Section (SAA)
OES......... Optical Emission Spectroscopy [*Laboratory science*] (DAVI)
OES......... Oral Esophageal Stethoscope [*Medicine*] (EDAA)
OES......... Orange Environmental Services, Inc. (EFIS)
OES......... Orbital-Escape System [*NASA*]
OES......... Orbiter Emergency Site [*NASA*] (NASA)
OES......... Order Entry System (SAUS)
OES......... Order/Entry System [*Computer science*] (OA)
OES......... Order of the Eastern Star [*Freemasonry*] (EA)
OES......... Organisation Europeenne des Scieries [*European Sawmills Organization*] [*EC*] (ECED)
OES......... Organizacion de Estados Americanos [*Organization of American States*] [*Spain*] (AD)
OES......... Organization of European Saw-Mills (BUAC)
OES......... Organization of European States (AD)
OES......... Ostrich Eggshell [*Archeological material*]
OES......... Outgoing Echo Suppressor [*Telecommunications*] (TEL)
OES......... Output Enable Serial [*Computer science*] (VLIE)
OES......... Overseas Educational Service [*Defunct*]
OES......... San Antonio Oeste [*Argentina*] [*Airport symbol*] (OAG)
OESA........ Office of Earth Sciences Applications [*Department of the Interior*] (GRD)
OESA........ Office of Employment Service Administration [*US Employment Service*] [*Department of Labor*]
OESBR...... Oil Extended Styrene Butadiene Rubber (PDAA)
oesbr........ Oil-Extended Styrene-Butadiene Rubber (AD)
OESC........ Open-Ended Systems Corp.
OESCA....... Old English Sheepdog Club of America (EA)
OESCAND... Old East Scandinavian [*Language, etc.*]
OESD........ Ocean Engineering System Development
OESD........ Opto-Electronic Semiconductor Device (SAUS)
OESE........ Office of Elementary and Secondary Education [*Department of Education*]
OES/E........ Office of the Environment (US Department of) State/Environment, Health and Natural Resources (GNE)
OES/EGC.... Office of the Environment (US Department of) State/Office of Global Change (GNE)
OES/EHC.... Office of the Environment (US Department of) State/Office of Ecology, Health and Conservation (GNE)
OES/ENP.... Bureau of Oceans and International Environmental and Scientific Affairs/Environmental and Population Affairs [*Department of State*] (MSC)
OES/ENV.... Office of the Environment (US Department of) State/Office of Environmental Protection (GNE)
OESH........ Office of Environment, Safety, and Health (COE)
OESH........ Shared Library Services, South Huron Hospital, Exeter, Ontario [*Library symbol*] [*National Library of Canada*] (BIB)
OESH........ Sharurah [*Saudi Arabia*] [*ICAO location identifier*] (ICLI)
OESK........ Al-Jouf [*Saudi Arabia*] [*ICAO location identifier*] (ICLI)
OESK........ Osteuropeiska Solidaritetskommitten [*East European Solidarity Committee*] (EAIO)
OESL........ Oceanographic and Environmental Service Laboratory [*Raytheon Co.*]
OESL........ Sulayel [*Saudi Arabia*] [*ICAO location identifier*] (ICLI)
OESLA....... Office of Engineering Standards Liaison and Analysis [*National Bureau of Standards*] (IAA)
OESM........ Occupational and Environmental Safety Management
OES/N....... Office of the Environment (US Department of) State/Nuclear Energy and Energy Technology Affairs (GNE)
OES/NED.... Office of the Environment (US Department of) State/Office of Export and Import Control (GNE)
OES/NEP.... Office of the Environment (US Department of) State/Office of Non-Proliferation and Export Policy (GNE)
OES/NTS.... Office of the Environment (US Department of) State/Office of Nuclear Technology and Safeguards (GNE)
OES/O....... Office of the Environment (US Department of) State/Oceans and Fisheries Affairs (GNE)
OESO........ Organisation Internationale d'Etudes Statistiques pour les Maladies de l'Oesophage [*International Organization for Statistical Studies on Diseases of the Esophagus*] (EAIO)
OESO........ Organizational Effectiveness Staff Officer [*Military*]
OESOC...... Organizational Effectiveness Staff Officer Course [*Army*]

OES/OFA .... Bureau of Oceans and International Environmental and Scientific Affairs/Ocean and Fishery Affairs [*Department of State*] (MSC)
OES/OFA .... Office of the Environment (US Department of) State/Office of Fisheries Affairs (GNE)
OES/OLP .... Office of the Environment (US Department of) State/Office of Ocean Law and Policy (GNE)
oesoph ...... Oesophagus (AD)
OESOPH..... Oesophagus
OES/OSP.... Office of the Environment (US Department of) State/Office of Marine Science and Polar Affairs (GNE)
OESP .... O Estado de Sao Paulo [*State of Sao Paulo*] [*Brazil*] [*A publication*] (AD)
OESP .... Ontario Export Support Programme (SAUS)
OESPCMJ... Officer Exercising Special Court-Martial Jurisdiction
OE Spinning... Open End Spinning (SAUS)
OESR .... Oil Extended Synthetic Rubber (PDAA)
OESS .... O/ET [*Orbiter/External Tank*] Separation System [*NASA*] (MCD)
OESS .... Office of Engineering Standards Services [*National Bureau of Standards*]
OES/S .... Office of the Environment (US Department of) State/Science and Technology Affairs (GNE)
OESS .... Organizational Effectiveness Survey System [*Army*]
OES/SAT .... Office of the Environment (US Department of) State/Office of Advanced Technology (GNE)
OES/SCI..... Bureau of Oceans and International Enviromental and Scientific Affairs/Scientific and Technological Affairs [*Department of State*] (MSC)
OES/SCT .... Office of Environment (US Department of) State/Office of Cooperative Science and Technology Programs (GNE)
OEST .... Outline European Staff Target (SAUS)
OET .... Objective End Time
OET .... Office of Economic Transition (SAUS)
OET .... Office of Education and Training (AD)
OET .... Office of Emergency Transportation [*FAA*]
OET .... Office of Employment Training (SAUS)
OET .... Office of Engineering and Technology [*Washington, DC*] [*FCC*] (GRD)
OET .... Official English Title
OET .... Official Establishments Trust [*Australia*]
OET .... Oldest English Texts
OET .... On Equipment Training (MCD)
OET .... Open Epicutaneous Test (SAUS)
OET .... Optic-Electronic Transducer (SAUS)
OET .... Oral Esophageal Tube [*Medicine*] (MELL)
O/ET .... Orbiter/External Tank [*NASA*] (NASA)
OET .... Organ Extract Therapy [*Medicine*] (MELL)
OET .... Organizacion para Estudios Tropicales [*Organization for Tropical Studies*] (EAIO)
OET .... Organizational Effectiveness Team (TIMI)
OET .... Overseas Exchange Transactions (AD)
OETA......... Occupied Enemy Territory Administration [*World War II*]
OETA......... Original Estimated Time of Arrival (CTAS)
OETA......... Township of Armstrong Public Library [*Bibliotheque Publique Canton Armstrong*], Earlton, Ontario [*Library symbol*] [*National Library of Canada*] (BIB)
OET & E..... Operational Employment Testing and Evaluation (AFM)
OETB .... Ocean Economics and Technology Branch [*United Nations*] (MSC)
OETB .... Offshore Energy Technology Board [*British*]
OETB .... Tabuk [*Saudi Arabia*] [*ICAO location identifier*] (ICLI)
OETB .... United Nations Ocean Economics and Technology Branch (SAUS)
OETC .... Optoelectronics Technology Consortium [*Sponsored by the Department of Defense*]
OETC .... Oregon Educational Technology Consortium
OETC .... Organizational Effectiveness Training Center [*Army*] (MCD)
OETC .... Oronite European Technical Center [*Fuels and lubricants*]
OETF......... Taif [*Saudi Arabia*] [*ICAO location identifier*] (ICLI)
OETLC....... Office of Economic Trends and Labor Conditions [*Department of Labor*]
OETO .... United Nations Ocean Economics and Technology Office (SAUS)
OETP .... Operations Experimental Test Plan (IAA)
OETP .... Orbiter Electron Temperature Probe [*NASA*]
OETR .... Turaif [*Saudi Arabia*] [*ICAO location identifier*] (ICLI)
OETT......... Oral Endotracheal Tube [*Medicine*] (STED)
OEu .... Euclid Public Library, Euclid, OH [*Library symbol*] [*Library of Congress*] (LCLS)
OEU .... Operational Evaluation Unit (SAUS)
OEU .... Operation Eyesight Universal [*Canada*] (EAIO)
OEUNAH .... Econometrics and Operations Research (journ.) (SAUS)
OEVE .... Office of Earthquakes, Volcanoes, and Engineering [*US Geological Survey*] (AD)
OEW .... Offensive Electronic Warfare (SAUS)
OEW .... Office of Economic Warfare [*World War II*]
OEW .... Old English White [*Automobile classified advertising*]
OEW .... Open-End Wrench
OEW .... Operating Empty Weight (SAUS)
OEW .... Operational Empty Weight [*Aviation*]
OEW .... Ordinary Electromagnetic Wave
OEW .... Ordnance and Explosive Waste [*Military*]
OEWG .... Open-Ended Working Group (NATG)
OEWG .... Open-End Waveguide (SAUS)
OEWG .... Operation, Evaluation Wartime Group (NATG)
OEWGP...... Operational Experiments Working Group (SAUS)
OEWJ........ Wejh [*Saudi Arabia*] [*ICAO location identifier*] (ICLI)
OEX.......... Office of Educational Exchange [*Department of State*]
OEX.......... Oklahoma City, OK [*Location identifier*] [*FAA*] (FAAL)
OEX.......... Options Exchange [*Finance*]
OEX.......... Orbiter Experiments [*NASA*] (MCD)
OEX.......... Standard & Poor's 100 Stock Index (DFIT)
OEXP .... Office of Exploration [*NASA*]
OEYN .... Yenbo [*Saudi Arabia*] [*ICAO location identifier*] (ICLI)
OEZ .... Osteuropaeische Zeit [*East European Time*] [*German*] (AD)
OF............ Degrees Fahrenheit
OF............ Fast Airways BV [*Netherlands*] [*ICAO designator*] (ICDA)
OF............ Fitted for Oil Fuel [*Ships*]
OF............ Frankford Public Library, Ontario [*Library symbol*] [*National Library of Canada*] (BIB)
OF............ Noosa Air [*ICAO designator*] (AD)
OF............ Objective Force
OF............ Occipitalfrontal [*Diameter of skull*]
OF............ Occupations Finder [*A publication*] (DHP)
OF............ Oceanographic Facility
OF............ Odd Fellows [*An association*]
OF............ Off Course (SAUS)
OF............ Offenbach [*Main*] [*German license plate city code*]
O/F........... Off Food (SPVS)
Of .... Official (DAVI)
of............. Official (ELAL)
OF............ Official Files
Of .... Offizier (SAUS)
OF............ Offset Printing Program [*Association of Independent Colleges and Schools specialization code*]
OF............ Offshore Funds [*Investment term*]
OF............ Offshore Oil International (SAUS)
OF............ Oil Facility [*International Monetary Fund*]
OF............ Oil-Filled (IAA)
OF............ Oil Fired (ADA)
OF............ Oil Fuel [*British military*] (DMA)
of............. Old Face (AD)
OF............ Old Face [*Typography*]
OF............ Old Field [*Botany*]
OF............ Old French [*Language, etc.*]
OF............ One of the Finn (SAUS)
OF............ One of the Firm [*Telecommunications*] (TEL)
O/F........... On File (SAUS)
OF............ Open Forum [*An association*] (EA)
OF............ Open Fracture [*Medicine*] (MELL)
OF............ Open Full [*Container*] (DCTA)
OF............ Operand Field (SAUS)
OF............ Operating Forces [*Navy*]
OF............ Operational Fixed
OF............ Operational Functionality (SAUS)
OF............ Operation Friendship (BUAC)
OF............ Operations and Food Analysis
OF............ Operations Following (MCD)
OF............ Ophthalmological Foundation [*Later, NSPB*]
OF............ Optical Fibre (EECA)
OF............ Optical Flat (SAUS)
OF............ Optical Fluorescence (SAUS)
OF............ Optical Frequency
OF............ Optic Fundi (STED)
OF............ Optimal Feedback (SAUS)
OF............ Optimal Filtering (SAUS)
OF............ Optional Feature (IAA)
OF............ Optional File (SAUS)
of............. Optional Form (AD)
OF............ Optional Form
OF............ Orbital Facilities (SAUS)
OF............ Orbital Facility (IAA)
O/F........... Orbital Flight [*NASA*] (KSC)
OF............ Orbitofrontal
OF............ Order of the Founder [*Salvation Army*]
OF............ Ordnance Factory (SAUS)
OF............ Oriented Film (SAUS)
OF............ Orphan Foundation [*Later, OFA*] (EA)
OF............ Orthochromatic Film [*Photography*] (DGA)
OF............ Oscillator Frequency [*Telecommunications*] (IAA)
OF............ Osfriends (EA)
Of .... Osmond Tape Exchange [*An association*] (EA)
OF............ Osmotic Fragility Test
OF............ Osseointegration Foundation (SAUS)
OF............ Osteitis Fibrosa [*Medicine*] (MAE)
OF............ Osteopathic Foundation [*Later, NOF*]
OF............ Ostrum-Furst [*Syndrome*] [*Medicine*] (STED)
OF............ Other Medical/Surgical Facility (MEDA)
OF............ Outer Flame (SAUS)
OF............ Outfield [*Baseball*]
OF............ Outfielder [*Baseball term*] (NDBD)
O/F........... Outfit [*Doll collecting*]
OF............ Output Factor [*Computer science*] (IEEE)
OF............ Output File (SAUS)
of............. Outside Face (AD)
OF............ Outside Face [*Technical drawings*]
Of .... Ovenstone Factor (AD)
OF............ Ovenstone Factor [*Medicine*] (MAE)
of............. Overflow (ELAL)
OF............ Overflow
OF............ Overflow Flag (SAUS)
OF............ Overfrequency (MSA)
OF............ Oxbow Falls (AD)
OF............ Oxenstierna Foundation (AD)

OF .... Oxford Foundation (AD)
O-F .... Oxidation-Fermentation [*Growth medium*]
o/f .... Oxidation/Fermentation (AD)
OF .... Oxide Film (SAUS)
O/F .... Oxidizer-to-Fuel [*Ratio*]
o/f .... Oxidizer to Fuel Ratio (AD)
of .... Oxidizing Flame (AD)
OF .... Oxidizing Flame
OF .... Oxydizer-to-Fuel [*Ratio*]
OF .... Oxygen Fill (NASA)
OF .... Oxygen-Free (ACAE)
OF/2 .... Operator Facility/2 (SAUS)
OFA .... Fairfield County District Library, Lancaster, OH [*OCLC symbol*] (OCLC)
OFA .... Object Free Area [*FAA*] (TAG)
OFA .... Odell Family Association (EA)
OFA .... Office for the Aging (BARN)
OFA .... Office of Family Assistance [*Department of Health and Human Services*] (GFGA)
OFA .... Office of Federal Activities [*Environmental Protection Agency*] (GFGA)
OFA .... Office of Financial Analysis [*Department of the Treasury*]
OFA .... Office of Flight Assurance (SAUS)
OFA .... Oficina Alemania [*Chile*] [*Seismograph station code, US Geological Survey*] (SEIS)
OFA .... O'Hare Family Association (EA)
OFA .... Ohio Florists' Association (EARSL)
OFA .... Oil-Immersed Forced-Air-Cooled [*Transformer*] (IEEE)
OFA .... Oklahoma Forestry Association (WPI)
OFA .... Old Farmers Almanac (SAUS)
OFA .... Old Folks Association (AD)
OFA .... Omnite Fuel Additive (SAUS)
OFA .... Oncofetal Antigen [*Immunology*]
OFA .... Ontario Federation of Agriculture [*Canada*]
OFA .... Ontario Film Association [*Canada*] (BUAC)
OFA .... Optimal Flexible Architecture (SAUS)
OFA .... Optimized Fuel Assembly [*Nuclear energy*] (NRCH)
OFA .... Order for Assignment [*Military*] (CAAL)
OFA .... Organic Food Alliance (EA)
OFA .... Organization of Flying Adjusters (NTPA)
OFA .... Organized Flying Adjusters (EA)
OFA .... Orienteering Federation of Australia
OFA .... Oronite Fuel Additive
OFA .... Orphan Foundation of America (EA)
OFA .... Orthopedic Foundation for Animals (EA)
OFA .... Other Federal Agencies (ABAC)
OFA .... Over Fifties Association [*Australia*]
OFA .... Over Fire Air [*Combustion technology*]
OFA .... Overseas Family Allowance [*British military*] (DMA)
OFA .... Owen Family Association (EA)
OFA .... Oxygenated Fuels Association (EA)
OFAA .... Oyster Farmers' Association of Australia
OFAAP .... Ontario Farm Adjustment Assistance Program (SAUS)
OFAB .... Fort Albany Band Library, Ontario [*Library symbol*] [*National Library of Canada*] (BIB)
OFAC .... Office of Foreign Assets Control [*Government term*] (GA)
OFAC .... Owens Fine Arts Center (SAUS)
OFACS .... Overseas-Foreign Aeronautical Communications Station (MUGU)
O Factor .... Oscillation Factor (ODA)
OFAD .... Ocean Floor Analysis Division [*Later, Sea Floor Division*] [*NORDA*] (EA)
OFAED .... Organization Forecast Authorization Equipment Data [*Military*] (AFIT)
OFAES .... Oriental Fine Arts Exchange Society [*China*] (BUAC)
OFAF .... Metallurgical Research Library, Falconbridge Nickel Mines Ltd., Falconbridge, Ontario [*Library symbol*] [*National Library of Canada*] (NLC)
OFAGE .... Orthogonal-Field-Alternation Gel Electrophoresis [*Analytical biochemistry*]
OFALF .... Omega First Amendment Legal Fund (EA)
OFALL .... O'Fallon, IL [*American Association of Railroads railroad junction routing code*]
OFAM .... Office of Financial and Administrative Management [*Department of Labor*]
OFANC .... Falconbridge Branch, Nickel Centre Public Library, Ontario [*Library symbol*] [*National Library of Canada*] (NLC)
OFANSW .... Oyster Farmers' Association of New South Wales [*Australia*]
OFAP .... Observing Facilities Advisory Panel (SAUS)
OFAR .... Office of Foreign Agricultural Relations [*Department of Agriculture*]
OFARS .... Overseas-Foreign Aeronautical Receiver Station
OFAS .... Overseas Flight Assistance Service
OFATS .... Overseas-Foreign Aeronautical Transmitter Station
OFAV .... Opened Firm, Advanced [*Telegraphy*] (PCTE)
OFavp .... Fairview Park Regional Library, Fairview Park, OH [*Library symbol*] [*Library of Congress*] (LCLS)
OFB .... Oil Forced Blast (IAA)
OFB .... Operational Facilities Branch [*NASA*] (MCD)
OFB .... Output Feedback (NITA)
OFBCD ...... Opened Firm, but Closing Dull [*Telegraphy*] (PCTE)
OFBF-AGGPAC ... Ohio Farm Bureau Federation Inc. Agriculture for Good Government PAC [*Columbus, OH*] (PACS)
OFBM .... Oxidation-Fermentation Basal Medium (STED)
OFC .... Conference on Optical Fiber Communication [*Optical Society of America*] [*Washington, DC*] (TSSD)
OFC .... Corporate Office Properties Trust [*NYSE symbol*]
OFC .... Corporate Office Prop Tr SBI [*NYSE symbol*] (SG)
OFC .... Foleyet Community Library, Ontario [*Library symbol*] [*National Library of Canada*] (NLC)
OFC .... High Court Reports, Orange Free State [*A publication*] (DLA)
OFC .... Occipitofrontal Circumference [*Anatomy*]
OFC .... Oceania Football Confederation
OFC .... Oceanography and Fisheries Committee (ASF)
ofc .... Office (AD)
OFC .... Office [*or Officer*] (AFM)
Ofc .... Office (TBD)
OFC .... Office of Fishery Coordination [*World War II*]
OFC .... Officer [*Telegraphy*] (PCTE)
OFC .... Oil-Filled Cable (SAUS)
OFC .... Oil Free Compressor
OFC .... Oldest Finest Canadian [*Whiskey*] (IIA)
OFC .... Old Fired Copper [*Initialism once used as brand name for bourbon*]
OFC .... Old French Canadian [*Initialism used in Schenley brand of Canadian whisky*]
OFC .... One Flow Cascade Cycle (IAA)
OFC .... Open Financial Connectivity [*Microsoft Computer Software*] [*Computer Science*]
OFC .... Operational Flight Control [*NASA*]
OFC .... Opposing Force Component (MCD)
OFC .... Optical Fiber Communication (CIST)
OFC .... Optical Fiber Control (DCDG)
OFC .... Optical Fibre Cable [*Indian Railway*] (TIR)
OFC .... Optical File Cabinet [*Computer science*]
OFC .... Optical Formatter Controller (NITA)
OFC .... Optical Frequency Conversion
OFC .... Orbitofacial Cleft [*Medicine*] (STED)
OFC .... Orthonormal Function Coding (SAUS)
OFC .... Oscillation Frequency Control (CIST)
OFC .... Osteitis Fibrosa Cystica [*Medicine*] (DMAA)
OFC .... Outside Front Cover [*Publishing*] (NTCM)
OFC .... Overflow Card (SAUS)
OFC .... Overflow Control (SAUS)
OFC .... Overhead Foxhole Cover (SAUS)
OFC .... Overseas Food Corp. (AD)
OFC .... Oxford First Corporation (SAUS)
OFC .... Oxyfuel-Gas Cutting [*Welding*]
OFC .... Oxygen-Free Copper (SAUS)
OFCA .... Ontario Federation of Construction Associations [*Canada*] (AD)
OFCA .... Organisation des Fabricants de Produits Cellulosiques Alimentaires de la CEE [*Organization of Manufacturers of Cellulose Products for Foodstuffs in the European Economic Community*]
OFC-A .... Oxyfuel-Gas Cutting - Acetylene [*Welding*]
OFCAPPDE ... Office Application Descriptons (SAUS)
OFCAPPE ... Office Application Entries (SAUS)
OFCATS ..... Optical Fiber Cable Assembly Automatic Test System (ACAE)
OFCC .... Office of Federal Contract Compliance [*Later, OFCCP*] [*Department of Labor*]
OFCCP ...... Office of Federal Contract Compliance Programs [*Formerly, OFCC*] [*Department of Labor*]
OFCCP Fed Cont Compl Man ... OFCCP Federal Contract Compliance Manual [*A publication*] (AAGC)
OFCE .... Office [*or Officer*]
OFCF .... Overseas Farmers Co-Operative Federation Ltd. (BUAC)
OFC-H .... Oxyfuel-Gas Cutting - Hydrogen [*Welding*]
Ofcl .... Official (TBD)
OFCL .... Official
Of Cl Pac ... Officium Clerici Pacis [*A publication*] (DLA)
OFCM .... Office of the Federal Coordinator for Meteorological Services and Research
OFCM .... Office of the Federal Coordinator for Meteorology (SAUS)
OFCN .... Organization for Community Networks (IGQR)
OFC-N .... Oxyfuel Cutting - Natural Gas [*Welding*]
OFC-N .... Oxynatural Gas Cutting (SAUS)
OFCO .... Offensive Counterintelligence Operations (MCD)
OFCO .... Office of the Federal Coordinating Officer (SAUS)
OFCOFASSTSECNAV ... Office of the Assistant Secretary of the Navy (DNAB)
OFCOFASSTSECNAV(FINMGMT) ... Office of the Assistant Secretary of the Navy (Financial Management) (DNAB)
OFCOFASSTSECNAV(INSTALLOG) ... Office of the Assistant Secretary of the Navy (Installations and Logistics) (DNAB)
OFCOFASSTSECNAV(PERSRESFOR) ... Office of the Assistant Secretary of the Navy (Personnel and Reserve Force) (DNAB)
OFCOFASSTSECNAV(RSCHDEV) ... Office of the Assistant Secretary of the Navy (Research and Development) (DNAB)
OFCOFINFO ... Office of Information (DNAB)
OFCP .... Ontario Federation for Cerebral Palsy [*Canada*] (NRGU)
OFCP .... Ottawa Financial [*NASDAQ symbol*] (TTSB)
OFCP .... Ottawa Financial Corp. [*NASDAQ symbol*] (SAG)
OFC-P .... Oxyfuel-Gas Cutting - Propane [*Welding*]
OFC-P .... Oxypropane Cutting (SAUS)
OFCR .... Officer
OFCS .... Office of Foreign Commercial Services [*Abolished 1970, functions transferred to Bureau of International Commerce*]
OFCS .... Operational Flight Control System [*NASA*] (KSC)
OFCSAV .... Orchardists and Fruit Cool Stores Association of Victoria [*Australia*]
OFCT .... Order Fulfillment Cycle Time (TIMI)
OFCTAD ..... Occipito-facio-cervico-thoraco-abdomino-digital [*Medicine*] [*Dysplasia*] (EDAA)
OFD .... Object Film Distance [*Optics*]
OFD .... Objective Force Designator (MCD)
OFD .... Occipitofrontal Diameter [*of the skull*]
OFD .... Ocean Floor Drilling

OFD.......... Ocean Freight Differential [*MARAD*] (TAG)
OFD.......... Offered [*Telegraphy*] (PCTE)
Ofd.......... Offered [*Stock exchange term*]
OFD.......... Ohio Federal Decisions [*A publication*] (DLA)
ofd.......... One-Function Diagram (AD)
OFD.......... One-Function Diagram
OFD.......... Open-Face Dectector [*Instrumentation*]
ofd.......... Optical Fire Detector (AD)
OFD.......... Optical Fire Director (SAUS)
OFD.......... Optical Frequency Division Demultiplexer (or Demultiplexing) (SAUS)
OFD.......... Optical Gun Fire Director [*Military*] (PDAA)
OFD.......... Oral-Facial-Digital [*Genetics*] (DAVI)
OFD.......... Ordnance Field Depot (SAUS)
OFD.......... Orofacial Dyskinesia (DIPS)
OFD.......... Oro-Facio-Digital [*Syndrome*] [*Medicine*]
OFD.......... Oued Fodda [*Algeria*] [*Seismograph station code, US Geological Survey*] (SEIS)
OFD.......... Overflow Data (SAUS)
OFDA........ Office Foreign Disaster Assistance (SAUS)
OFDA........ Office Furniture Distribution Association (EA)
OFDA........ Office of Foreign Disaster Assistance (COE)
OFDA........ Office of United States Foreign Disaster Assistance [*Agency for International Development*]
OFDAP...... Office of the Field Directorate of Ammunition Plants
OFDC........ Official First Day Cover [*Canada Post Corp.*]
OFDC........ Ontario Film Development Corp. [*Canada*]
OFDG........ Operator Fractionation Decision Guide [*Process control*]
OFDI......... Office of Foreign Direct Investments [*Department of Commerce*]
OFDM....... Orthogonal Frequency Division Modulation (SAUS)
OFDM....... Orthogonal Frequency Division Multiplex (SAUS)
OFDR........ Off-Frequency Decoupling Resonance [*Physical chemistry*]
OFDS........ Optimal Financial Decision Strategy (MHDI)
OFDS........ Orbiter Flight Dynamics Simulator [*NASA*] (NASA)
OFDS........ Oxygen Fluid Distribution System [*NASA*] (NASA)
OFE.......... Odds for Effectiveness [*Navy*]
OFE.......... Office of Federal Elections [*Later, FEC*]
OFE.......... Office of Fossil Energy (COE)
OFE.......... Office of Fuels and Engergy (AD)
OFE.......... Office of Fusion Energy [*Oak Ridge National Laboratory*]
OFE.......... Open Finance Exchange (SAUS)
OFE.......... Operative Functional Element (SAUS)
OFE.......... Optical Flight Evaluation
OFE.......... Order for Engagement [*Military*] (CAAL)
OFE.......... Osteogenic Factor Extract (DB)
OFE.......... Other Further Education
OFE.......... Ottawa Fundraising Executives [*Ontario, Canada*]
OFE.......... Overall Factory Effectiveness (SAUS)
OFEA........ Office of Foreign Economic Administration [*Lend-Lease*] [*World War II*]
OFEA........ Officer Front End Analysis (MCD)
OFEC........ Office of Federal Employees Compensation [*Department of Labor*]
OFEC........ Office of Foreign Economic Coordination [*World War II*]
OFEC........ Wellington County Museum, Fergus, Ontario [*Library symbol*] [*National Library of Canada*] (BIB)
OFEHM...... Fort Erie Historical Museum, Ontario [*Library symbol*] [*National Library of Canada*] (BIB)
OFEMA...... Office Francais d'Exportation de Materiel Aeronautique [*French Office for theExportation of Aeronautical Materiel*] (AD)
OFEP........ Fort Erie Public Library, Ontario [*Library symbol*] [*National Library of Canada*] (NLC)
OFER........ Fergus Public Library, Ontario [*Library symbol*] [*National Library of Canada*] (NLC)
OFER........ Ohio Ferro-Alloys Corp. (SAUS)
OFERC....... Centre Wellington District High School, Fergus, Ontario [*Library symbol*] [*National Library of Canada*] (NLC)
OFERRA..... Office of Foreign Economic Relief and Rehabilitation Administration
OFERW...... Wellington County Public Library, Fergus, Ontario [*Library symbol*] [*National Library of Canada*] (NLC)
OFERWM... Wellington County Museum and Archives, Fergus, Ontario [*Library symbol*] [*National Library of Canada*] (BIB)
OFF.......... Challenge Air Transport, Inc. [*ICAO designator*] (FAAC)
Off.......... De Officiis [*of Cicero*] [*Classical studies*] (OCD)
OFF.......... Fort Frances Public Library, Ontario [*Library symbol*] [*National Library of Canada*] (NLC)
OFF.......... Offensive
OFF.......... Offer
off.......... Offertory (GROV)
OFF.......... Offertory
OFF.......... Office [*or Officer*] (AFM)
off.......... Office (DD)
OFF.......... Office for Families (DICI)
OFF.......... Office of Facts and Figures [*Later, Office of War Information*] [*Military*]
Off.......... Officer (AD)
off.......... Officer (SHCU)
OFF.......... Officers' Family Fund
off.......... Official (MILB)
Off.......... Official (STED)
OFF.......... Official
OFF.......... Offretite [*A zeolite*]
OFF.......... Omaha, NE [*Location identifier*] [*FAA*] (FAAL)
OFF.......... Organization for Femininity
OFF.......... State of Being Powered Down (SAUS)
OFFA........ One Fund for All [*An association*] (BUAC)
Off Abr...... Official Abbreviation (SAUS)
Off&WO..... Officers and Warrant Officers (SAUS)
OFFAR....... Office of Fuel and Fuel Additive Registration [*Environmental Protection Agency*]
Off Br........ Officina Brevium [*1679*] [*A publication*] (DLA)
Off Brev..... Officina Brevium [*1679*] [*A publication*] (DLA)
OFF BUS ONLY... Official Business Only (DNAB)
OFFC........ Office
OFFC........ Office Master [*NCIC trailer make code*]
OFFC........ Offshore Crane and Service Company [*Common carrier symbol*]
OffcDpt...... Office Depot [*Associated Press*] (SAG)
OFFEE....... Offeree [*Legal shorthand*] (LWAP)
OFFEG....... Offshore Fossil-Fueled Electric Generators
OFFEN....... Offensive [*Ammunition*] (AAG)
offen........ Offensive (AD)
OFFENS..... Offensive
Off Environ... Office Environment (SAUS)
offeq......... Office Equipment (AD)
Off Equip Index... Office Equipment Index (SAUS)
Off Equip Methods... Office Equipment and Methods (SAUS)
Off Equip News... Office Equipment News (SAUS)
offer......... Offertories (AD)
Offer......... Office of Electricity Regulation [*British*] (WA)
OFFER....... Office of Electricity Regulation [*British*]
Off Ex........ Wentworth's Office of Executors [*A publication*] (DLA)
Off Exec..... Wentworth's Office of Executors [*A publication*] (DLA)
offg.......... Offering (AD)
OFFG........ Officiating
Off Gaz Pat Office... Official Gazette. United States Patent and Trademark Office [*A publication*] (DLA)
Off Home... Office at Home (SAUS)
OFFI......... Officer [*NCIC trailer make code*]
OFFI......... Official
OFFI......... Old Fashion Foods, Inc. (SAUS)
offic.......... Official (AD)
OFFIC........ Official
OFFIC........ Officiate
Office A&A... Office Administration and Automation (SAUS)
Office Adm&Automation... Office Administration and Automation (SAUS)
Office Pubns... Office Publications (AD)
Officer....... Officer's Reports [*1-9 Minnesota*] [*A publication*] (DLA)
Official J Ind Comm Prop... Official Journal of Industrial and Commercial Property [*Eire*] [*A publication*] (DLA)
Official Rep Ill Courts Commission... Official Reports, Illinois Courts Commission [*A publication*] (DLA)
Officmx...... Officemax, Inc. [*Associated Press*] (SAG)
Off Inf Manage Int... Office and Information Management International (SAUS)
OFFINTAC... Offshore Installations Technical Advisory Committee (BUAC)
Off J Eur Communities Inf Not... Official Journal of the European Communities. Information and Notices (SAUS)
OFFL......... Official (AFM)
OFFLIN...... Off-Line [*Communications term*] (DCT)
OFFM........ Fort Frances Museum and Cultural Centre, Ontario [*Library symbol*] [*National Library of Canada*] (BIB)
Off Mag..... Office Magazine (SAUS)
OFFMAUTSYS... Officer Master File Automated System (DNAB)
OFFNAVHIST... Office of Naval History [*Also, ONH*]
OFFNAVWEASERV... Office of Naval Weather Service
Off Nom..... Official Nomenclature (SAUS)
OFFOR...... Offeror [*Legal shorthand*] (LWAP)
OFFP........ Fenelon Falls Public Library, Ontario [*Library symbol*] [*National Library of Canada*] (BIB)
OFFP........ Ovarian Follicular Fluid Peptide [*Endocrinology*]
OFF PREM... Off Premises (SAUS)
Off Prod News... Office Products News (SAUS)
OFFPROMSYS... Officer Promotion System (DNAB)
Off Publ Assoc Am Plant Food Control Off... Official Publication Association of American Plant Food Control Officials (SAUS)
Offr.......... Officer (AL)
OFFR........ Officer
Off Rep...... Official Reports of the High Court of the Transvaal [*A publication*] (DLA)
OFFS........ Optical Fiber Field Sensor (ACAE)
Offset Print Reprogr... Offset Printing and Reprographics (SAUS)
OffshEnr..... Offshore Energy Development Corp. [*Associated Press*] (SAG)
OFFSHR..... Offshore (NVT)
OffsLog...... Offshore Logistics, Inc. [*Associated Press*] (SAG)
OFF STA..... Officer Status (DNAB)
off-st pkg... Off-Street Parking (AD)
Off Syst Res J... Office Systems Research Journal (SAUS)
OFFV........ Order of First Families of Virginia, 1607-1624/5 (EA)
Off World News... Office World News (SAUS)
OFG.......... Offering [*Telegraphy*] (PCTE)
OFG.......... Opferfuersorgegesetz (BJA)
OFG.......... Optical Frequency Generator
OFG.......... Ordnance Field Guide (SAUS)
OFG.......... Organic Farmers and Growers Ltd. (BUAC)
OFG.......... Organic Functional Group (SAUS)
OFG.......... Oriental Financial Group [*NYSE symbol*]
OFGA........ Oxyacetylene Cutting (SAUS)
OFGAS...... Office of Gas Service [*Government body*] [*British*]
Ofgas........ Office of Gas Supply [*British*] (WA)
Ofgem....... Office of Gas and Electricity Markets [*United Kingdom*] [*Gas and Electricity Markets Authority*]
OFGH........ Oxyhydrogen Cutting (SAUS)

OFGR .... Objective Force Gross Requirement [*Army*] (AABC)
OFGSA ...... Organic Farming and Gardening Society of Australia
OFGST .... Organic Farming and Gardening Society of Tasmania [*Australia*]
OFH .... Odd Fellows Hall (ROG)
OFH .... Oil Field Haulers Association Inc., Austin TX [*STAC*]
OFH .... Rutherford B. Hayes Library, Fremont, OH [*Library symbol*] [*Library of Congress*] (LCLS)
OFHA .... Occipitofrontal Headache [*Medicine*] (DMAA)
OFHA .... Oil Field Haulers Association (EA)
OFHA .... Oilfield Haulers Association (SAUS)
OFHC .... Oxygen Free Hard Copper (IAA)
ofhc .... Oxygen-Free High-Carbon (AD)
ofhc .... Oxygen-Free High Conductivity (AD)
OFHC .... Oxygen-Free, High-Conductivity [*Copper*]
OFHC .... Oxygen-Free High-Conductivity Copper [*Electronics*] (AAEL)
OFHC Copper ... Oxygen-Free High Conductivity Copper (SAUS)
OFHEO ...... Office of Federal Housing Enterprise Oversight (SAUS)
OFHIC .... Oxygen-Free High Conductivity Copper (SAUS)
OFHR .... Office of Federal Health Relations [*Medicine*] (EDAA)
OFi .... Findlay-Hancock County District Public Library, Findlay, OH [*Library symbol*] [*Library of Congress*] (LCLS)
OFI .... Office of Foreign Investment [*Department of Commerce*]
OFI .... Office of the Federal Inspector (AD)
OFI .... Omni Films International, Inc. (EFIS)
OFI .... On-Line Free Form Input [*Computer science*] (MHDI)
OFI .... Operational Flight Instrumentation [*NASA*] (NASA)
OFI .... Opportunity for Improvement (ACAE)
OFI .... Optical Fiber Identifier (SAUS)
OFI .... Orangutan Foundation International (SAUS)
OFI .... Orbital Flight Instrumentation (SAUS)
OFI .... Ornamental Fish International (EAIO)
OFI .... Overflow Incontinence [*Medicine*] (MELL)
OFI .... Overflow Indicator (SAUS)
OFI .... Oxford Forestry Institute [*University of Oxford*] [*British*] (IRUK)
OFIA .... Ontario Forest Industries Association (SAUS)
OFIA .... Optical Frame Importers' Association [*British*] (DBA)
OFiC .... Findlay College, Findlay, OH [*Library symbol*] [*Library of Congress*] (LCLS)
ofic .... Oficial [*Official*] [*Spanish*] (AD)
OFIC .... Ohio Foundation of Independent Colleges (AD)
OFID .... OPEC [*Organization of Petroleum Exporting Countries*] Fund for International Development (EAIO)
OFID .... Optical Free Induction Decay (SAUS)
O-FID .... Oxygen-Flame Ionization Detector
OFIG .... Operational Forces Interface Group [*US Army Natick Research, Development, and Engineering Center*] [*Natick, MA*] (RDA)
OFII .... Omni Films International, Inc. (SAUS)
OFII .... Organization for International Investment (NTPA)
OFII .... Otto Fuel II [*Military*] (DNAB)
OFINDMAN ... Office of Industrial Management [*Navy*] (DNAB)
OFINTAC ... Offshore Installations Technical Advisory Committee [*British*] [*Marine science*] (MSC)
OFIR .... Oceanic Flight Information Region (IAA)
OFIS .... Office Information System (NITA)
OFIS .... Office of Transportation Security (SAUS)
OFIS .... Operational Flight Information Service [*ICAO*] (DA)
OFIS .... US Office Products Co. [*NASDAQ symbol*] (SAG)
OFIX .... Office of the Future Information Exchange (NITA)
OFIX .... Orthofix International [*NASDAQ symbol*] (SAG)
OFIX .... Orthofix International N.V. [*NASDAQ symbol*] (NASQ)
OFIXF .... Orthofix International [*NASDAQ symbol*] (TTSB)
OFJ .... Olafsfjordur [*Iceland*] [*Airport symbol*] (OAG)
OFK .... Norfolk [*Nebraska*] [*Airport symbol*] (OAG)
OFK .... Norfolk, NE [*Location identifier*] [*FAA*] (FAAL)
OFK .... Oberfeldkommandantur [*Military government area headquarters*] [*German military - World War II*]
OFK .... Official Flight Kit [*NASA*] (NASA)
OFK .... Optical Flight Kit (NASA)
OFKX .... Koch Tank Line [*Private rail car owner code*]
OFL .... Flesherton Public Library, Ontario [*Library symbol*] [*National Library of Canada*] (NLC)
OFL .... Official (AABC)
ofl .... Official (AD)
OFL .... Ontario Federation of Labour (SAUS)
OFL .... Open Fault Locater
OFL .... Optical Fault Locator (SAUS)
OFL .... Optic Fiber Layer
OFL .... Overflow [*Computer science*]
OFL .... Own Front Line (SAUS)
OFL .... Oxidizer Fill Line (AAG)
Oflag .... Offizierlager [*Officer's Prison Camp*] [*German*] (AD)
OFLAG .... Offizierslager [*Permanent Prison Camp for Captured Officers*] [*German military - World War II*]
OFLC .... Office of Foreign Liquidation Commission
OFLD .... Off-Load (NVT)
OFLDF .... Officeland, Inc. [*NASDAQ symbol*] (COMM)
OFlem .... Old Flemish [*Language, etc.*] (BARN)
OFLIC .... Office of Foreign Liquidation Commission
OFLINPS ... Open Frame Linear Power Supply [*Electronics*] (EECA)
OFLOT .... Office of the National Lottery (BUAC)
OFLP .... Oxygen-Free Low-Phosphorus (SAUS)
OFLPC .... Oxygen-Free Low-Phosphorus Copper (SAUS)
OFLT .... Office of Foreign Labor and Trade [*Department of Labor*]
OFLTR .... Oil Filter
OFLUSE ..... For Official Use Only [*Army*]
OFLW .... Overflow (SAUS)
Ofly .... Offaly (AD)
ofm .... Conventual Franciscans, Friars Minor (TOCD)
OFM .... Franciscan Friars (TOCD)
ofm .... Franciscan Friars, Order of Friars Minor (TOCD)
OFM .... Observation File Maintenance
OFM .... Office of Finance and Management [*Department of Agriculture*] (GFGA)
OFM .... Office of Financial Management [*Bureau of the Budget; later, OMB*]
OFM .... Office of Flight Missions [*NASA*] (MCD)
OFM .... Office of Foreign Missions [*Department of State*]
OFM .... Open Face Mask [*Medicine*] (MELL)
OFM .... Open Frame Motor
OFM .... Optical Frequency Division Multiplexer (or Multiplexing) (SAUS)
OFM .... Optofiber Metric Switch
OFM .... Order of Friars Minor (ODA)
OFM .... Ordnance Field Manual [*Military*]
OFM .... Ordo Fratrum Minorum [*Order of Friars Minor*] [*Observant Franciscans*] [*Roman Catholic religious order*] (EA)
OFM .... Organization Field Maintenance
OFM .... Oriental Fruit Moth [*Entomology*]
OFM .... Original Equipment Manufacturer (SAUS)
OFM .... Orofacial Malformation
OFM .... Otto Fuel Monitor (SAUS)
OFM .... Our First Men [*Slang*]
OFM .... Out for Maintenance [*Aviation*] (FAAC)
OFM .... Outlet Feature Model (SAUS)
OFM .... Oxygen Fill to Missile (AAG)
OFMC .... Operational Fixed Microwave Council (IAA)
OFMC .... Order of Friars Minor Conventual [*Conventuals*] [*Roman Catholic religious order*]
OFMCap ..... [*The*] Capuchin Friars (TOCD)
ofmcap ...... [*The*] Capuchin Friars, Franciscan Fathers (TOCD)
OFM Cap .... Order of Friars Minor Capuchin [*Capuchins*] [*Roman Catholic religious order*]
OFMConv ... Conventual Franciscans (TOCD)
OFM Conv .. Order of Friars Minor Conventual [*Conventuals*] [*Roman Catholic religious order*]
OFMConv ... Ordo Fratrum Minorum Conventualium (SAUS)
OFMIS .... Office of Financial and Management Information Systems (OICC)
OFMP .... Organization of Facility Managers and Planners [*Later, OMERF*] (EA)
OFMS .... Office of Financial and Management Services [*Department of Labor*]
OFMS .... Organic-Functionalized Molecular Sieve [*Organic chemistry*]
OFM Switch ... Opto-Fibre Metric Switch (SAUS)
OFMT .... Output Format (SAUS)
OFN .... Often [*Telegraphy*] (PCTE)
OFN .... Open File Number (SAUS)
OFN .... Organization for Flora Neotropica (EA)
OFN .... Ottawa Fundraisers Network [*Ontario, Canada*]
OFN .... Overfull Employment [*Economics*]
OFNCS ...... Orange Field Naturalist and Conservation Society [*Australia*]
OFNPS ...... Outstate Facility Network Planning System [*Telecommunications*] (TEL)
OFNS .... Observer Foreign News Service (AD)
OFO .... Office of Field Operations [*Employment and Training Administration*] [*Department of Labor*]
OFO .... Office of Flight Operations [*NASA*]
OFO .... Orbiting Frog Otolith [*NASA experimental spacecraft*]
Ofo .... Orfeo [*Record label*]
OFOBA .... Oils, Fats, and Oilseeds Brokers Association [*Netherlands*] (BUAC)
OFOC .... Old Free Order of Chaldeans [*Freemasonry*] (ROG)
OFOD .... On-Flight Origin and Destination [*International Civil Aviation Organization*] [*Information service or system*] (DUND)
OFOFLEGAFFAIRS ... Office of Legal Affairs [*Navy*] (DNAB)
OFOM .... Operational Figure of Merit [*Military*] (CAAL)
OFOS .... Opening Filled Other State [*Employment*]
OFOX .... Residco [*Private rail car owner code*]
OFP .... Ashland, VA [*Location identifier*] [*FAA*] (FAAL)
OFP .... Occluded Frontal Passage (SAUS)
OFP .... Offensive Firepower (SAUS)
OFP .... Office of Family Planning (SAUS)
OFP .... Office of Federal Policy (COE)
OFP .... Offshore Pipelines (SAUS)
OFP .... Oil Filter Pack
OFP .... On-the-Fly Printer
OFP .... Open Fireplace [*Classified advertising*] (ADA)
OFP .... Operating Force Plan
OFP .... Operational Flight Profile [*NASA*] (NASA)
OFP .... Operational Flight Profit
OFP .... Operational Flight Program [*NASA*] (NASA)
OFP .... Operational Format Program [*NASA*] (KSC)
OFP .... Operations Funded Project (SAUS)
OFP .... Operative Federal Plasterers [*A union*] [*British*]
OFP .... Optical Fiber Patch Cable [*Communications term*] (DCT)
OFP .... Orbiter Flight Program [*NASA*] (NASA)
OFP .... Order of Friars Preachers [*Dominicans*] (ADA)
OFP .... Ordnance Field Park [*British*]
OFP .... Organizations, Functions, and Programs [*IRS*]
OFP .... Original Flight Plan
OFP .... Oscilloscope Face Plane
OFP .... Ozone Forming Potential [*Exhaust emissions*] [*Automotive engineering*]
OFPA .... Federal Office of Armament Production (SAUS)
OFPA .... Ontario Food Protection Association (SAUS)

OFPA .... Orange-Fronted Parakeet [*North American bird banding code*] (BIBA)
OFPA .... Order of the Founders and Patriots of America (EA)
OFPA .... Organic Foods Production Act
OFPANA ..... Organic Foods Production Association of North America (EA)
OFPC .... Office Federal de la Protection Civile [*Emergency Management*] (EMA)
OFPCP .... Organization of Fitness and Personal Care Professionals [*Defunct*] (EA)
OFPF .... Optical Fiber-Pulling Facility (SSD)
OFPM .... Office of Fiscal Plans and Management [*Bureau of Indian Affairs*]
OFP-MIR .... Ozone-Forming Potential-Maximum Incremental Reactivity [*Exhaust emissions*] [*Automotive engineering*]
OFPP .... Office of Federal Procurement Policy [*Executive Office of the President*] (MCD)
OFPP .... Office of Procurement & Policy (SAUS)
OFPPA .... Office of Federal Procurement Policy Act (COE)
OFPPL .... Office of Federal Procurement Policy Letters (SAUS)
OFPS .... Office of Field Project Support (SAUS)
OFPS .... Open Frame Power Supply [*Electronics*] (EECA)
OFPSD ...... Office of Financial Policy and Systems Design (SAUS)
OFPTA .... Oregon Forest Products Transportation Association (EARSL)
OFPU .... Optical Fiber Production Unit
OFr .... Franklin Public Library, Franklin, OH [*Library symbol*] [*Library of Congress*] (LCLS)
OFR .... Ocean Freight Reimbursement (SAUS)
OFR .... Ocular Following Reflex [*Ophthalmology*]
OFR .... Offer
ofr .... Off Frequency Rejection (AD)
OFR .... Off Frequency Rejection [*Radio communications*]
OFR .... Office for Recruitment [*American Library Association*]
OfR .... Office for Research (AD)
OFR .... Office for Research [*American Library Association*]
OFR .... Office of the Federal Register
Ofr .... Officer (PHSD)
OFR .... Officer Fitness Report [*Navy*] (NVT)
OFR .... Official Failure Rate [*Military*] (AFIT)
OFR .... Oil-Filled Resistor
OFR .... Oil-Resistant, Flame-Retardant (SAUS)
O Fr .... Old French (AD)
OFR .... Old French [*Language, etc.*]
OFR .... On-Frequency Repeater (IEEE)
OFR .... Open Failure Report [*NASA*] (KSC)
OFR .... Open File Report (MCD)
OFR .... Operational Failure Report (IAA)
OFR .... Operational Fleet Requirements (MCD)
OFR .... Optical Film Reader (SAUS)
OFR .... Ordering Function Register
OFR .... Order of the Federal Republic of Nigeria (ODA)
OFR .... Over-Flow Register (SAUS)
OFR .... Over Frequency Relay
OFR .... Overfrequency Relay (SAUS)
OFR .... Overseas Fuel Region (AFIT)
OFR .... Oxidation-Fluorination Ratio (MCD)
OFR .... Oxygen Free Radical (SAUS)
OFR .... United Front of Workers (BUAC)
OFRA .... O'Dochartaigh Family Research Association (EA)
OFRAC ...... On Farm Research Advisory Committee [*Australia*]
OFR-ALA .... Office of Recruitment-American Library Association (AD)
O/F Ratio ... Oxidant/Fuel Ratio (SAUS)
OFRF .... Organic Farming Research Foundation
OFRF .... Overland Flow Research Facility [*Army*]
OFRID .... Outline of Factors Relating to Industry Development (SAUS)
OFris .... Old Frisian (AD)
OFRIS .... Old Frisian [*Language, etc.*]
O Frk .... Old Frankish (AD)
OFRP .... Overseas Family Residence Program [*Military*] (NVT)
OFRPTR ..... IBM 8219 Optical Fiber Repeater [*Communications term*] (DCT)
OFRR .... Office of Foreign Relief and Rehabilitation [*Obsolete*]
OFRRO ...... Office of Foreign Relief and Rehabilitation Operation [*Obsolete*]
OFrS .... Franklin City Schools, Franklin, OH [*Library symbol*] [*Library of Congress*] (LCLS)
OFRW .... Oklahoma Federation of Republican Women
OFS .... Fauquier-Strickland Public Library, Fauquier, Ontario [*Library symbol*] [*National Library of Canada*] (BIB)
OFS .... Object File System [*Computer science*] (VLIE)
OFS .... Octave Filter Set
OFS .... Office [*Telegraphy*] (PCTE)
OFS .... Office of Field Service [*OSRD*] [*World War II*]
OFS .... Office of Field Services [*Later, Bureau of Domestic Commerce*] [*Department of Commerce*]
OFS .... Office of Oceanographic Facilities and Support [*National Science Foundation*] (USDC)
OFS .... Office of the Foreign Secretary (SAUS)
OFS .... Offset (MSA)
OFS .... Oil from Sludge
OFS .... One Finger Salute (SAUS)
ofs .... One-Function Sketch (AD)
OFS .... One-Function Sketch
OFS .... Ontario Federation of Students [*Canada*] (AD)
OFS .... Operating Functional Summary (VLIE)
OFS .... Operational Fixed-microwave Service (SAUS)
OFS .... Operational Fixed Service (SAUS)
OFS .... Operational Flight Simulator (SAUS)
OFS .... Operational Flight Software (ACAE)
OFS .... Operational Flying School (SAUS)
OFS .... Operations Fixed Service [*Microwave service*] (NTCM)
OFS .... Optical Fiber Sensor
OFS .... Optical Fuzing System
OFS .... Orange Free State (ODA)
OFS .... Orange Free State Reports, High Court [*1879-83*] [*South Africa*] [*A publication*] (DLA)
OFS .... Orbital [*or Orbiter*] Flight System [*NASA*] (MCD)
OFS .... Orbiter Flight System (SAUS)
OFS .... Orbiter Functional Simulator (NASA)
OFS .... Order of Free State (SAUS)
OFS .... Organofunctional Silanes (SAUS)
OFS .... Output Field Separator [*Computer science*] (VLIE)
OFS .... Output Format Specification (SAUS)
OFS .... Oxygen-Free with Silver (SAUS)
OFSA .... Optical Fire Sensor Assembly (SAUS)
OFSA .... Ordo Fratrum Sancti Augustini [*Order of St. Augustine - OSA*] [*Rome, Italy*] (EAIO)
OFSB .... Fort Severn Band Library, Ontario [*Library symbol*] [*National Library of Canada*] (BIB)
OFSB .... Ordnance Field Service Bulletin [*Military*]
OFSB .... Oriental Federal Savings Bank (EFIS)
OFSC .... Ordnance Field Service Circular [*Military*]
OFSC .... Organization and Finance Subcommittee
OFSCC .... Orbiter Functional Simulator Control Center (MCD)
OFSD .... Operating Flight Strength Diagram
OFSDG ...... Finch Branch, Stormont, Dundas, and Glengarry County Public Library, Ontario [*Library symbol*] [*National Library of Canada*] (BIB)
OFSE .... Operating Forces Support Equipment (DNAB)
OFSH .... Ovine Follicle Stimulation Hormone (SAUS)
OFSH .... Shared Library Services, South Huron Hospital, Exeter, Ontario (SAUS)
OFSI .... OESI Power (SAUS)
OFSI .... Of Service Transportation [*Common carrier symbol*]
OFSL .... Orange Free State Investment Ltd. (SAUS)
OFSLY .... Orange Free State Investments Ltd. [*NASDAQ symbol*] (COMM)
OFSM .... Operational Flight Safety Monitor (SAA)
OFSMPS .... Open Frame Switch Mode Power Supply [*Electronics*] (EECA)
OFSO .... Oracle Field Sales Online [*Computer science*] (VLIE)
OFSO .... Overfill Shutoff Sensor (KSC)
OFSOC ...... Organizational Effectiveness Staff Officer Course (SAUS)
OFS/OFA .... Bureau of Oceans and International Environmental and Scientific Affairs/ Ocean and Fishery Affairs (SAUS)
OFSP .... Office of Federal Statistical Policy [*Later, OFSPS*] [*Department of Commerce*]
OFSPCMJ ... Officer Exercising Special Court-Martial Jurisdiction (SAUS)
OFSPS .... Office of Federal Statistical Policy and Standards [*Formerly, OFSP*] [*Department of Commerce*]
OFSR .... Office of Food Safety and Recall [*Canadian Food Inspection Agency*] [*Canada*] (RCD)
OFSS .... Optical Fiber Strain Sensing [*Mechanical engineering*]
OFSSA .... Orange Free State, South Africa (ILCA)
OFST .... Lateral Offset Active Light (GAVI)
OFST .... Office of the Secretary of the Air Force (AD)
ofst .... Offset (VRA)
OFST .... Operational Flight Simulator Trainer (SAUS)
Ofsted .... Office for Standards in Education [*British*] (WA)
OFSTED ..... Office for Standards in Education [*British*] (WDAA)
OFSTNO ..... Offset Switch Number (SAUS)
OFSYF .... Offshore Systems International Ltd. [*OTCBB symbol*]
OFT .... Field Township Public Library, Ontario [*Library symbol*] [*National Library of Canada*] (NLC)
OFT .... Observed Fire Trainer [*Army*] (RDA)
OFT .... Office of Fair Trade (SAUS)
OFT .... Office of Fair Trading [*British*]
oft .... Often (GEAB)
OFT .... Often
OFT .... Ohio Federation of Teachers (AD)
OFT .... Operational Feasibility Testing (MCD)
OFT .... Operational Flight Trainer
OFT .... Optical Fiber Thermometry [*Instrumentation*]
OFT .... Optical Fiber Tube
OFT .... Optical Fibre Technology
OFT .... Optical Fourier Transform
OFT .... Optimal Foraging Theory [*Animal behavior*]
OFT .... Orbital Flight Test [*NASA*] (NASA)
OFT .... Orbiter Flight Test (SAUS)
OFT .... Outer Fix Time [*FAA*] (TAG)
OFT .... Outfit (MSA)
OFT .... Outline Feasibility Test [*Army*]
OFTA .... Office for the Aged [*Australia*]
OFTA .... Office of the Telecommunications Authority (SAUS)
OFTA .... Operational Flight Transfer Airframe
OFTB .... Offshore Technology Board [*British*]
OFTC .... Overseas Finance and Trade Corporation (SAUS)
OFTD .... Oxygen Furnace Tilt Drive
OFTDA ...... Office of Flight Tracking and Data Acquisition [*NASA*]
OFTDA ...... Office of Right Tracking and Data Acquisition (SAUS)
OFTDS ...... Orbital Flight Test Data System [*NASA*] (MCD)
OFTEC ...... Oil Firing Technical Association for the Petroleum Industry (BUAC)
OFTEL ...... Office of Director General of Telecommunications (SAUS)
Oftel .... Office of Telecommunications [*British*] (WDAA)
OFTEL ...... Office of Telecommunications [*Independent government agency*] [*British*]
OFTF .... Objective Force Task Force

OFTF......... Optical Fibre Transfer Function (EECA)
OFTM........ On-Orbit Flight Technique Meeting [*NASA*] (MCD)
OFTMS...... Output Format Table Modification Submodule
OFTP........ Odette File Transfer Protocol (SAUS)
OFTR........ Orbital Flight Test Requirement [*NASA*] (NASA)
OFTS........ Office of Technical Services (AD)
OFTS........ Office of Transportation Security (AD)
OFTS........ Officers Training School (AD)
OFTS........ Operational Flight and Tactics Simulator (MCD)
OFTS........ Optical Fibre Transmission System (NITA)
OFTS........ Overseas Fixed Telecommunications System (AD)
OFTT......... Federal Office of Transport Troops (SAUS)
OFTT......... Operational Flight and Tactics Trainer (MCD)
OFTT......... Organic Failure to Thrive [*Medicine*] (MEDA)
OF Type..... Old Face Type (SAUS)
OFU.......... Floating Units Division [*Coast Guard*]
OFU.......... Franklin University, Columbus, OH [*OCLC symbol*] (OCLC)
OFU.......... Ofu Island [*American Samoa*] [*Airport symbol*] (OAG)
OFU.......... Ofunato [*Japan*] [*Seismograph station code, US Geological Survey*] (SEIS)
OFUS........ Orbit Frequency Utilization Simulation (SAUS)
OFUS-M..... Orbit Frequency Utilization Simulation-Mobile (SAUS)
OFV.......... Opposing Forces Vehicle [*Military*]
OFV.......... Optical Fiber Vibrometer [*Automotive engineering*]
OFV.......... Orchid Fleck Virus [*Plant pathology*]
OFV.......... Overflow Valve (SAUS)
OFW.......... Objective Family of Weapons
OFW.......... Off Watch [*Aviation*] (FAAC)
OFW.......... Operation Fish Watch [*National Oceanic and Atmospheric Administration*] (MSC)
OFW.......... Opportunities for Women (BUAC)
OFW.......... Oxyfuel-Gas Welding
Ofwat........ Office of Water Services [*British*] (WDAA)
OFWAT...... Office of Water Services [*British*]
OFWN........ Ontario Library Service - Nipigon, Thunder Bay, Ontario [*Library symbol*] [*National Library of Canada*] (NLC)
OF/WST..... Operational Flight/Weapons System Trainer (NG)
OFX.......... Open Financial Exchange [*Computer science*]
OFX.......... Outer Fix (CTAS)
OFXLP....... Oxygen-Free Extra-Low-Phosphorus (SAUS)
OFXLPC..... Oxygen-Free Extra-Low-Phosphorus Copper (SAUS)
OFXT......... Outer Fix Time [*Aviation*] (FAAC)
OFY.......... Officially [*Telegraphy*] (PCTE)
OFY.......... Operation Feed Yourself [*Ghana*] (BUAC)
OFY.......... Opportunities for Youth [*Canada*] (AD)
OFY.......... Opportunities for Youth Program [*Canada*]
OFZ.......... Fort Sill, OK [*Location identifier*] [*FAA*] (FAAL)
OFZ.......... Obstacle Free Zone
OG........... Air Guadeloupe [*ICAO designator*] (AD)
OG........... Guelph Public Library, Ontario [*Library symbol*] [*National Library of Canada*] (NLC)
OG........... Obergericht [*Court of Appeal*] [*German*] (DLA)
OG........... Oberstes Gericht [*Supreme Court*] [*German*]
OG........... Object Glass (MSA)
OG........... Obscure Glass
OG........... Observation Group (SAUS)
OG........... Obstetrics-Gynecology [*Medicine*]
OG........... Occlusogingival [*Dentistry*]
OG........... Ocean Going (SAUS)
OG........... Octyl Glucoside [*Organic chemistry*]
OG........... Oesterreichische Galerie [*Austrian Gallery*] (AD)
OG........... Offenburg [*German license plate city code*]
OG........... Offensive Guard [*Football*]
OG........... Off-Gas [*Nuclear energy*] (NRCH)
OG........... Office of Geography [*Functions transferred to Geographic Names Division of Army Topographic Command*] [*Department of the Interior*]
OG........... Officer of the Guard [*Army*]
OG........... Official Gazette [*PTO*] [*A publication*] (AAGC)
OG........... Ogasawara Trench
OG........... Ogden Corp. [*NYSE symbol*] (SPSG)
OG........... Ogdensburg [*Diocesan abbreviation*] [*New York*] (TOCD)
og............ Ogee [*Construction term*] (MIST)
OG........... Ogee [*A molding*] [*Architecture*] (ROG)
og............ Oh Gee (AD)
OG........... Oil Gauge
og............ Oil Gland (AD)
OG........... Oil Glands [*In propeller shaft*]
OG........... Old Gaelic (AD)
OG........... Old Georgian [*Linguistics*] (IEL)
OG........... Old German [*Language, etc.*]
og............ Old Girl (AD)
OG........... Old Girl [*A wife*] [*Slang*]
OG........... Old Greasybeard: Tales from the Cumberland Gap [*A publication*]
OG........... Old Greek (SAUS)
OG........... Old Growth [*USDA Forest Service*] (ALAC)
OG........... Oligodendrocyte (DMAA)
OG........... Olive Green [*Army*] (ADDR)
OG........... Olympic Games
OG........... Ongoing (ADA)
OG........... On Grade (DAC)
og............ On Ground (AD)
OG........... On Ground [*Aviation*]
og............ On Guard (AD)
OG........... Openly Gay [*An association*] (BUAC)
OG........... Operational Group [*World War II*]
OG........... Operation Greenhouse [*Atomic weapons testing*]
OG........... Operations Guide (VLIE)
OG........... Optical Generation (SAUS)
OG........... Optical Glass (SAUS)
OG........... Optic Ganglion
o/g........... Opto-Graphic (AD)
O/G........... Opto/Graphic (AD)
OG........... Orange Green [*Stain*] [*Medicine*]
o-g........... Orange-Green (AD)
OG........... Ordinary Goods (SAUS)
OG........... Organic Gardening [*A publication*]
OG........... Organic Geochemistry (SAUS)
OG........... Organisation Gestosis [*Basel, Switzerland*] (EAIO)
OG........... Organize [*Telegraphy*] (PCTE)
OG........... OR Gate [*Electronics*] (ECII)
OG........... Orientation Group [*Air Force*]
OG........... Original Gangster (ODA)
OG........... Original Gravity (BARN)
og............ Original Gum (AD)
OG........... Original Gum [*Philately*]
OG........... Orogastric [*Feeding*] [*Gastroenterology*] (DAVI)
OG........... Outdoor Girl [*Max Factor cosmetic line*]
OG........... Outer Gimbal
o/g........... Outgoing (AD)
OG........... Outgoing (VLIE)
O/G........... Outgoing [*Computer science*]
OG........... Outguard (SAUS)
OG........... Output Gate [*Computer science*] (IAA)
OG........... Outside Guard
OG........... Outside Guardian [*Freemasonry*] (ROG)
OG........... Oxygen Gage (NAKS)
OG........... Oxygen Gas Process (SAUS)
OG........... Oxygen Gauge (NASA)
OG........... Zero Gravity
OGA.......... Obergurgl [*Austria*] [*Seismograph station code, US Geological Survey*] (SEIS)
OGA.......... Oculogyric Attack [*Medicine*] (EDAA)
OGA.......... Oesterreichische Gesellschaft fur Akupunktur [*Austrian Society of Acupuncture and Auricular Therapy*] (EAIO)
OGA.......... Office of Government Affairs (SAUS)
OGA.......... Ogallala, NE [*Location identifier*] [*FAA*] (FAAL)
O/GA......... Oil Gauge [*Automotive engineering*]
OGA.......... Omega Ltd. [*Ukraine*] [*FAA designator*] (FAAC)
OGA.......... Option Generation Aid (SAUS)
OGA.......... Organic Growers Association [*British*] (DBA)
OGA.......... Ornamental Growers Association (EA)
OGA.......... Orogastric Aspirate [*Medicine*] (AAMN)
OGA.......... Orogastric Gonococcal Aspirates [*Medicine*] (EDAA)
OGA.......... Oronite Gasoline Additive [*Fuels and lubricants*]
OGA.......... Other Government Agencies (COE)
OGA.......... Outer Gimbal Angle (NASA)
OGA.......... Outer Gimbal Assembly (NASA)
OGA.......... Outer Gimbal Axis [*NASA*] (IAA)
OGAC........ Galt Collegiate Institute, Cambridge, Ontario [*Library symbol*] [*National Library of Canada*] (NLC)
OGAC........ Organizational Governance Advisory Committee [*NERComP*]
OGAE........ Oklahoma Gas and Electric, Co. (SAUS)
O Gael...... Old Gaelic (AD)
OGalG....... Gallia County District Library, Gallipolis (SAUS)
OGAL........ Cambridge Public Library, Ontario [*Library symbol*] [*National Library of Canada*] (NLC)
OGalG....... Gallia County District Library, Gallipolis, OH [*Library symbol*] [*Library of Congress*] (LCLS)
OGALL....... Cavendish Public Library (G. Galloway), Ontario [*Library symbol*] [*National Library of Canada*] (BIB)
OGAMA...... Ogden Air Material Area [*AFLC*]
OGAMM..... Optical Glass and Macromolecular Materials [*Imaging*]
OGAN........ Gananoque Public Library, Ontario [*Library symbol*] [*National Library of Canada*] (NLC)
OGANSW.... Organic Growers' Association of New South Wales [*Australia*]
OGAR........ O'Gara Co. [*NASDAQ symbol*]
OGAR........ OGara Co. (The) [*NASDAQ symbol*] (SAG)
OGaraCo.... OGara Co. (The) [*Associated Press*] (SAG)
OGAWA...... Organic Growers' Association of Western Australia [*Australia*]
OGB.......... Beriault Branch, Gloucester Public Library, Ontario [*Library symbol*] [*National Library of Canada*] (NLC)
OGB.......... Oesterreichischer Gewerkschaftsbund [*Austrian Trade Union Federation*] [*German*] (AD)
OGB.......... Old Government Buildings (SAUS)
OGB.......... Orangeburg, SC [*Location identifier*] [*FAA*] (FAAL)
OGB.......... Overseas Golden Bar (SAUS)
OGBA........ Organic Growers and Buyers Association (EA)
OGBD........ Orbiter Gamma Burst Detecter [*NASA*]
OGBG........ Official Gazette Reports, British Guiana [*A publication*] (DLA)
OGBH........ Blackburn Hamlet Branch, Gloucester Public Library, Ontario [*Library symbol*] [*National Library of Canada*] (NLC)
OGBKT...... Blessed Kateri Tekakwitha School, Gloucester, Ontario [*Library symbol*] [*National Library of Canada*] (NLC)
OGBU........ Gore Bay Union Public Library, Ontario [*Library symbol*] [*National Library of Canada*] (NLC)
OGC.......... Centennial Collegiate Vocational Institute, Guelph, Ontario [*Library symbol*] [*National Library of Canada*] (NLC)
OGC.......... Grove City Public Library (SAUS)

OGc......... Grove City Public Library, Grove City, OH [*Library symbol*] [*Library of Congress*] (LCLS)
OGC......... Oculogyric Crisis [*Medicine*] (DMAA)
OGC......... Office of General Counsel
OGC......... Office of the General Counsel (SAUS)
OGC......... Omnibus-Gebrauchtwagen-Centrum [*Used Coach Vehicle Center*] [*Automotive industry*]
OGC......... On-Going Care [*Medicine*] (MELL)
OGC......... Open GIS Consortium (SAUS)
OGC......... Open GIS (Geographic Information System) Consortium
OGC......... Order of the Golden Chain (EA)
OGC......... Oregon Graduate Center for Study and Research [*Research center*] (RCD)
OGC......... Ore Grain Carrier (SAUS)
OGC......... Other Government Costs (ACAE)
OGC......... Outgoing Trunk Circuit (SAUS)
OGCA........ Ohio Gun Collectors Association
OGCA........ Ontario General Contractors Association (SAUS)
OGCB........ O-G Cab Company [*Common carrier symbol*]
OGCF........ Canadian Farm Management Data System, Agriculture Canada [*Systeme Canadien deDonnees sur la Gestion Agricole, Agriculture Canada*] Guelph, Ontario [*Library symbol*] [*National Library of Canada*] (NLC)
OGCH........ College Heights Secondary School, Guelph, Ontario [*Library symbol*] [*National Library of Canada*] (NLC)
OGCM....... Ocean General Circulation Model [*Atmospheric science*]
OGCM....... Oceanic General Circulation Model (SAUS)
OGCM....... Oceanic General Climate Model
OGCMD..... Ogden Contract Management District (SAA)
OGC-N....... Office of General Counsel - NASA
OGCV........ Guelph Collegiate Vocational Institute, Ontario [*Library symbol*] [*National Library of Canada*] (NLC)
OGCW....... Cairine Wilson Secondary School, Gloucester, Ontario [*Library symbol*] [*National Library of Canada*] (BIB)
OGCWS..... Office of Government Contract Wage Standards (AAGC)
OGCZ........ Overland Grain [*Federal Railroad Administration identification code*]
OGD......... Oesophogogastroduodenoscopy [*Medicine*] (WDAA)
OGD......... Ogden [*Utah*] [*Airport symbol*] (AD)
Ogd.......... Ogdensburg (AD)
OGD......... Ogdensburg [*New Jersey*] [*Seismograph station code, US Geological Survey*] (SEIS)
Ogd.......... Ogden's Reports [*12-15 Louisiana*] [*A publication*] (DLA)
OGD......... Ogden, UT [*Location identifier*] [*FAA*] (FAAL)
OGD......... Old Granulomatus Disease (DAVI)
OGD......... Omega Gamma Delta [*Fraternity*] (EA)
OGD......... Open Government Document (PDAA)
OGD......... Organized [*Telegraphy*] (PCTE)
OGD......... Other Government Departments (HEAS)
OGDA........ Oregon Gasoline Dealers Association (EARSL)
OGDA........ Oyster Growers and Dealers Association (EA)
OGDC........ Office of Geographic Data Coordination (SAUS)
OGDC........ Oil and Gas Development Corp. (AD)
OGDD........ Outgoing/Delay Dial [*Telecommunications*] (TEL)
Ogden....... Ogden Corp. [*Associated Press*] (SAG)
Ogden....... Ogden's Reports [*12-15 Louisiana*] [*A publication*] (DLA)
OGDEN...... Ogden, UT [*American Association of Railroads railroad junction routing code*]
OGDH........ Oxoglutarate Dehydrogenase [*An enzyme*]
Ogdn......... Ogden Corp. [*Associated Press*] (SAG)
OGDN........ Ogden, TX [*American Association of Railroads railroad junction routing code*]
OGDR........ Uniroyal Research Laboratories, Guelph, Ontario [*Library symbol*] [*National Library of Canada*] (NLC)
OGE.......... Entomological Society of Ontario, Guelph, Ontario [*Library symbol*] [*National Library of Canada*] (NLC)
OGE.......... Objective Grating Electronics (SPST)
OGE.......... Observer Group Egypt [*UN Truce Supervisor Organization*]
OGE.......... Office of Genome Ethics [*National Human Genome Research Institute*] (RCD)
OGE.......... Office of Government Ethics
OGE.......... OGE Energy Corp. [*NYSE symbol*] (SAG)
OGE.......... Oklahoma Gas & Electric Co. [*NYSE symbol*] (SPSG)
OGE.......... Omaha Grain Exchange [*Defunct*] (EA)
OGE.......... On-Gimbal Electronics (ACAE)
OGE.......... Operating [*or Operational*] Ground Equipment
oge........... Operational Ground Equipment (AD)
OGE.......... Optional Ground Equipment (AAGC)
OGE.......... Optogalvanic Effect (MCD)
OGE.......... Oregon Graduate Center, Beaverton, OR [*OCLC symbol*] (OCLC)
OGE.......... Oregon Great Eastern [*Federal Railroad Administration identification code*]
OGE.......... Osaka Grain Exchange [*Japan*] (NUMA)
OGE.......... Out-of-Ground Effect
OGEC........ Organization of Gas Exporting Countries [*Proposed gas cartel*]
OGEDJ....... E. D. Jones Branch, Gloucester Public Library, Ontario [*Library symbol*] [*National Library of Canada*] (NLC)
OGEE........ Ogeechee Railway [*Federal Railroad Administration identification code*]
OGE Engy... OGE Energy Corp. [*Associated Press*] (SAG)
OGEG........ Georgetown District High School, Ontario [*Library symbol*] [*National Library of Canada*] (NLC)
OGEH........ Georgetown Branch, Halton Hills Public Libraries, Ontario [*Library symbol*] [*National Library of Canada*] (BIB)
OGELR...... Ecole Secondaire Louis-Riel, Gloucester, Ontario [*Library symbol*] [*National Library of Canada*] (BIB)
OGELS....... Observer Group in El Salvador
OGEN........ Ogden Express [*Common carrier symbol*]
OGEO........ Georgetown Public Library, Ontario [*Library symbol*] [*National Library of Canada*] (NLC)
OGeo........ Mary P. Shelton Library, Georgetown, OH [*Library symbol*] [*Library of Congress*] (LCLS)
OGEPrA..... Okla Gas & Elec,4% Pfd [*NYSE symbol*] (TTSB)
OGER........ Geraldton Public Library, Ontario [*Library symbol*] [*National Library of Canada*] (NLC)
OGer......... Germantown Public Library, Germantown, OH [*Library symbol*] [*Library of Congress*] (LCLS)
OGE/RPIE... Operating Ground Equipment/Real Property Installed Equipment (AFM)
OGES........ Operating Ground Equipment Specification [*Italian*] (AD)
OGEV........ Varian Canada, Inc., Georgetown, Ontario [*Library symbol*] [*National Library of Canada*] (NLC)
OGEZ........ Ogden Elevator [*Federal Railroad Administration identification code*]
OGF.......... Omnium Gestion Financiere (EFIS)
ogf........... Option Growth Fund (AD)
OGF.......... Orogastric Feeding [*Gastroenterology*] (DAVI)
OGF.......... Ovarian Growth Factor [*Medicine*]
OGF.......... Oxygen Gain Factor [*Medicine*] (DMAA)
OGFC........ Official Gumby Fan Club (EA)
OGFP........ Obtaining Goods by False Pretense
OGFS........ Oil and Gas Field Study [*Department of the Interior*]
OGG......... GasTOPS Ltd., Gloucester, Ontario [*Library symbol*] [*National Library of Canada*] (NLC)
OGG......... Kahului, HI [*Location identifier*] [*FAA*] (FAAL)
ogg.......... Oggetto [*Object*] [*Italian*] (AD)
OGG......... Orchard Grubbing Grant (SAUS)
OGG......... Organic Geochemistry Group
OGG......... Organizing [*Telegraphy*] (PCTE)
OGGI......... Old Guard Group, Inc. [*NASDAQ symbol*] (NASQ)
OGH......... Opera-Glass Hand (MELL)
OGH......... Ovine Growth Hormone (DB)
OGHC........ Hart Chemicals Ltd., Guelph, Ontario [*Library symbol*] [*National Library of Canada*] (NLC)
OGHS........ Gloucester High School, Ontario [*Library symbol*] [*National Library of Canada*] (BIB)
OGHS........ Orbit Gas Co. (SAUS)
OGI.......... Gould Information Center, Cleveland, OH [*OCLC symbol*] (OCLC)
OGI.......... Oceanic Gamefish Investigations [*National Oceanic and Atmospheric Administration*] (MSC)
OGI.......... Oculogyral Illusion [*NASA*]
OGI.......... Oesterreichische Gesseleschaft fuer Informatik [*Austrian Society for Information Processing*] [*German*] (AD)
OGI.......... Off-Gas Isolation [*Nuclear energy*] (NRCH)
OGI.......... Ontario Government Information [*Database*] [*Ministry of Culture and Communications*] [*Information service or system*] (CRD)
OGI.......... Opera Guilds International (AD)
OGI.......... Oregon Graduate Institute (SAUS)
OGI.......... Orientis Graeci Inscriptiones Selectae [*A publication*] (OCD)
OGI.......... Outer Grid Injection
OGI.......... Oxygen-Glucose Index [*Medicine*] (DMAA)
OGIB......... Occult Gastrointestinal Bleeding [*Medicine*]
OGIC......... Omnium de Gestion des Valeurs Industrielles et Commerciales (EFIS)
OGICSE...... Oregon Graduate Institute Computer Science and Engineering (SAUS)
OGID......... Outgoing/Immediate Dial [*Telecommunications*] (TEL)
OGIFC....... Original Gilligan's Island Fan Club (EA)
OGIL......... Ogilvy Group, Inc. [*NASDAQ symbol*] (COMM)
OGIL......... Open General Import Licence [*British*] (DS)
Ogilvie Dict... Ogilvie's Imperial Dictionary of the English Language [*A publication*] (DLA)
OGIP......... Office of Guest Investigator Programs (SAUS)
OGIP......... Original Gas in Place [*Natural resources*]
OGIRS....... Oklahoma Geographic Information Retrieval System (SAUS)
OGIS......... Open Geodata Interoperability Specification (SAUS)
OGIS......... Open Geographic Information System
OGJ.......... Oil and Gas Journal [*A publication*] (AD)
OGJ.......... Outgoing Junction [*Telecommunications*] (TEL)
OGJFR....... John F. Ross Collegiate Vocational Institute, Guelph, Ontario [*Library symbol*] [*National Library of Canada*] (NLC)
OGK.......... Kenyon College, Gambier, OH [*Library symbol*] [*Library of Congress*] (LCLS)
OGL.......... Obscure Glass (AAG)
ogl........... Obscure Glass (AD)
OGL.......... Open General License [*Import license*] (DS)
OGL.......... Oral Glucose Loading [*Endocrinology*]
OGL.......... Original [*Telegraphy*] (PCTE)
OGL.......... Outgoing Line
OGLA........ Officer Grade Limitations Act of 1954
OGLA........ Officers Grade Limitation Action (SAUS)
Oglbay...... Oglebay Norton Co. [*Associated Press*] (SAG)
OGLE........ Ogle [*NCIC car make code*]
OGLE........ Oglebay Norton [*NASDAQ symbol*] (TTSB)
OGLE........ Oglebay Norton Co. [*NASDAQ symbol*] (NQ)
OGLE........ Optical Gravitational Lens Experiment [*Astronomy*]
OGLE........ Optical Gravitational Lensing Experiment
OGLE........ Organization for Getting Legs Exposed [*Group opposing below-the-knee fashions introduced in 1970*]
OGLET....... Oglethorpe, GA [*American Association of Railroads railroad junction routing code*]
Oglethorpe U... Oglethorpe University (GAGS)
OGLPFC..... Official Gary Lewis and the Playboys Fan Club (EA)

OGM .... Office of Grants Management [*Public Health Service*]
OGM .... Office of Guided Missile (IAA)
OGM .... Ontonagon, MI [*Location identifier*] [*FAA*] (FAAL)
OGM .... Optimum Gradient Method
OGM .... Ordinary General Meeting
OGM .... Organic Gaseous Mercury [*Environmental chemistry*]
OGM .... Outgoing Message [*Telecommunications*]
OGM .... Outgrowth Medium [*Microbiology*] (DAVI)
OGM .... Outside Gage Marks (SAA)
OGMB .... Mattagami Band Public Library, Gogama, Ontario [*Library symbol*] [*National Library of Canada*] (NLC)
OGMC .... Ordnance Guided Missile Center (MCD)
OGMH .... Morrison Hershfield Ltd., Guelph, Ontario [*Library symbol*] [*National Library of Canada*] (NLC)
OGMS .... Ordnance Guided Missile School
OGMSD ..... Glen Morris Branch, South Dumfries Township Public Library, Ontario [*Library symbol*] [*National Library of Canada*] (BIB)
OGMT .... Orbiter Greenwich Mean Time [*NASA*] (MCD)
OGN .... Obstetric, Gynecologic, and Neonatal
OGN .... Organization [*Telegraphy*] (PCTE)
OGN .... Yonagunijima [*Japan*] [*Airport symbol*] (OAG)
OGNB .... Orange National Bancorp [*NASDAQ symbol*] (SAG)
OGNB .... Orange Natl Bancorp [*NASDAQ symbol*] (TTSB)
OGNC .... Garson Branch, Nickel Centre Public Library, Ontario [*Library symbol*] [*National Library of Canada*] (NLC)
OGNC .... Organic, Inc. [*NASDAQ symbol*] (SG)
OGNP .... Obstetrical Gynecological Nurse Practitioner (NUJO)
OGNR .... Oribi Gorge Nature Reserve [*South Africa*] (AD)
OGO .... Abengourou [*Ivory Coast*] [*Airport symbol*] (OAG)
OGO .... City Hall Branch, Gloucester Public Library, Ontario [*Library symbol*] [*National Library of Canada*] (NLC)
OGO .... Gould, Inc., Ocean Systems Information Center, Cleveland, OH [*OCLC symbol*] (OCLC)
OGO .... Officer Grade Objectives
OGO .... Oliver Gold Corp. [*Vancouver Stock Exchange symbol*]
OGO .... Orbiting Geophysical Observatory [*NASA*]
OG/OB .... Office Group/Office Branch [*IRS*]
OGOD .... One Gene One Disorder [*Hypothesis*]
OGOG .... Gogama Community Library, Ontario [*Library symbol*] [*National Library of Canada*] (NLC)
OGOH .... Huron County Public Library, Goderich, Ontario [*Library symbol*] [*National Library of Canada*] (NLC)
OGOHC ...... Huron County Pioneer Museum, Goderich, Ontario [*Library symbol*] [*National Library of Canada*] (BIB)
OGOR .... Goulais River Community Library, Ontario [*Library symbol*] [*National Library of Canada*] (NLC)
OGOS .... Outward Grade of Service (DNAB)
OGP .... Office of Global Programs [*National Oceanic and Atmospheric Administration*] (USDC)
OGP .... Oncogenic Potential (MELL)
OGP .... Original Gross Premium [*Insurance*] (AIA)
OGP .... Outgoing Message Process [*Telecommunications*] (TEL)
OGPA .... Office of Governmental and Public Affairs [*Department of Agriculture*] (GFGA)
OGPA .... Office of the General Purchasing Agent [*Military*]
OGPI .... Optical Glide Path Indicator
OGPr .... Ogden Corp. $1.875 cm Cv Pfd [*NYSE symbol*] (TTSB)
OGPS .... Office of Grants and Program Systems [*Department of Agriculture*]
OGPU .... Obiedinennoye Gosudartsvennoye Politicheskoye Upravlenie [*United State Political Administration*] [*Russian*] (AD)
OGPU .... Otdelenie Gosudarstvenni Politcheskoi Upravi [*Special Government Political Administration*] [*Former Soviet secret service organization, also known as GPU*] [*Later, KGB*]
OGPW .... Outer Garment Protective Waistcoat [*Police and security equipment*]
OGR .... B. F. Goodrich Co., Information Center, Brecksville, OH [*OCLC symbol*] (OCLC)
OGr .... Greenville Public Library, Greenville, OH [*Library symbol*] [*Library of Congress*] (LCLS)
OGR .... Grimsby Public Library and Art Gallery, Ontario [*Library symbol*] [*National Library of Canada*] (NLC)
OGR .... Oak Ridge Graphite Reactor (SAUS)
OGR .... Office of Geologic Repositories (SAUS)
OGR .... Office of Government Relations [*Environmental Protection Agency*] (GFGA)
OGR .... Office of Government Reports [*New Deal*]
OGR .... Officer Grade Requirements (ACAE)
OGR .... Official Guide of the Railways [*A publication*] (AD)
OGR .... Oil and Grease Resistant [*Automotive service*]
OGR .... Old Garden Rose [*Pre-1870*] [*Horticulture*]
OGR .... Ontario Government Railway [*Canada*] (AD)
OGR .... Operation Grass Roots [*Small communities employment service*]
OGR .... Order of the Golden Rule (EA)
OGR .... Ordnance, Gunnery, and Readiness Division [*Coast Guard*]
OGR .... Original Gross Rate [*Insurance*] (AIA)
OGR .... ORNL [*Oak Ridge National Laboratory*] Graphite Reactor
OGR .... Outgoing Repeater
OGR .... Oxygen-Gas Recovery System (SAUS)
OGRA .... Gravenhurst Public Library, Ontario [*Library symbol*] [*National Library of Canada*] (NLC)
OGraD .... Denison University, Granville, OH [*Library symbol*] [*Library of Congress*] (LCLS)
OGRAN ...... Open Gate-Router Access Node (SAUS)
OGraO .... Owens-Corning Fiberglas Corp., Granville, OH [*Library symbol*] [*Library of Congress*] (LCLS)
OGRC .... Office of Grants and Research Contracts [*NASA*]
OGRE .... Greely Public Library, Ontario [*Library symbol*] [*National Library of Canada*] (NLC)
OGRE .... Optical Grating Reflectance Evaluator (PDAA)
OGRE .... Organization of Generally Rotten Enterprises [*Evil organization in television cartoon series "The Drak Pack"*]
OGRL .... Outgoing Rural Line [*Telecommunications*] (IAA)
OGRM .... Grimsby Museum, Ontario [*Library symbol*] [*National Library of Canada*] (BIB)
OGRS .... Outgoing Relay Set [*Telecommunications*] (IAA)
OGRS .... Outgoing Rural Selector [*Telecommunications*] (IAA)
OGRV .... Grand Valley Public Library, Ontario [*Library symbol*] [*National Library of Canada*] (NLC)
OGS .... Oakland Growth Study [*1932-1964*] [*Sociology*]
OGS .... Obsolete General Supplies [*Military*]
OGS .... Obstetrical and Gynecological Survey [*Medicine*] (EDAA)
OGS .... Off-Gas System [*Nuclear energy*] (NRCH)
OGS .... Ogdensburg [*New York*] [*Airport symbol*] (OAG)
OGS .... Ogdensburg, NY [*Location identifier*] [*FAA*] (FAAL)
OGS .... Ohio Genealogical Society (EA)
OGS .... Ontario Geological Survey [*Ontario Ministry of Northern Development and Mines*] [*Canada*] (IRC)
OGS .... Ontario Graduate Scholarship (SAUS)
OGS .... Operative Glovers' Society [*A union*] [*British*]
O-GS .... Operator-to-General Support [*Maintenance*] (MCD)
OGS .... Optical Grating Spectrometer (SAUS)
OGS .... Optical Guidance System
OGS .... Oratory of the Good Shepherd [*British*]
OGS .... Organizes [*Telegraphy*] (PCTE)
OGS .... Original Ground Surface
OGS .... Osteogenic Sarcoma (MELL)
OGS .... Osteogenic Scoliosis (MELL)
OGS .... Other Government Securities (SAUS)
OGS .... Outer Glidescope
OGS .... Outer Glide Slope [*Aviation*] (NASA)
OGS .... Outgoing Secondary Switch (IAA)
OGS .... Outgoing Secondary Switches (SAA)
OGS .... Overseas Geological Survey (SAUS)
OGS .... Overseas Ground Station (MCD)
OGS .... Oxford GlycoSciences
OGS .... Oxogenic Steroid (MAE)
OGS .... Oxygen Generation System (NASA)
OGSA .... Open Grid Services Architecture [*Computer science*]
OGSE .... Operational Ground Support Equipment (AAG)
ogse .... Operational Ground-Support Equipment (AD)
OGSEL .... Operational Ground Support Equipment List (AAG)
OGSESS ..... Operational Ground Support Equipment Systems Specification (SAA)
OGSGS ...... Orangeburgh German Swiss Genealogical Society (EA)
OGSI .... Ongard Sys [*NASDAQ symbol*] (TTSB)
OGSI .... On Gard Systems [*NASDAQ symbol*] (SAG)
OGSM .... Office of the General Sales Manager [*Department of Agriculture*]
OGSM .... Stone Shop Museum, Grimsby, Ontario [*Library symbol*] [*National Library of Canada*] (NLC)
Ogs Med Jur ... Ogston's Medical Jurisprudence [*1878*] [*A publication*] (DLA)
OGSO .... O-Anon General Service Office [*An association*] (EA)
OGSO .... Obvious Goal Scoring Opportunity [*Soccer*]
OGSR .... Office of Graduate Studies and Research (AD)
OGST .... Overthread Guide Sleeve Tool [*Nuclear energy*] (NRCH)
o-g stain ... Orange-Green Stain (AD)
OGSTM ...... St. Matthew High School, Gloucester, Ontario [*Library symbol*] [*National Library of Canada*] (BIB)
OGSX .... IES Utilities [*Private rail car owner code*]
OGT .... MIS Division, Turnelle Productions Ltd., Gloucester, Ontario [*Library symbol*] [*National Library of Canada*] (BIB)
OGT .... Office for Gifted and Talented [*Education*]
ogt .... On-Going Thing (AD)
OGT .... On the Ground That [*Telegraphy*] (PCTE)
OGT .... Oppenheimer Multi-Government Trust [*NYSE symbol*] (SPSG)
OGT .... Outgoing Toll (SAUS)
OGT .... Outgoing Trunk
ogt .... Outlet Gas Temperature (AD)
OGT .... Outlet Gas Temperature (MSA)
OGTC .... Outgoing Toll Center [*Telecommunications*] (IAA)
OGTC .... Outgoing Toll Circuit [*Telecommunications*] (IAA)
OGTC .... Tudor and Cashel Public Library, Gilmour, Ontario [*Library symbol*] [*National Library of Canada*] (BIB)
OGTM .... Official Gazette. United States Patent and Trademark Office [*A publication*] (DLA)
OGTT .... Oral Glucose Tolerance Test [*Medicine*]
OGU .... Occupational Guidance Unit [*Department of Employment*] [*British*]
OGU .... Ogbronuagum [*Language symbol*] (ETLW)
OGU .... Ogden Bay [*Utah*] [*Seismograph station code, US Geological Survey*] (SEIS)
OGU .... Orogenital Ulceration [*Medicine*] (DB)
OGU .... Outgoing Unit [*Telecommunications*] (IAA)
OGU .... Outgoing Unit [*Military*]
OGU .... University of Guelph, Ontario [*Library symbol*] [*National Library of Canada*] (NLC)
ogv .... Outlet Guide Vane (AD)
OGV .... Outlet Guide Vane
OGV .... Oxygen Gauge Valve (NASA)
OGW .... Overhead Ground Wire
OGW .... Overload Gross Weight (NG)
OGWE .... Education Library, Wellington County Board of Education, Guelph, Ontario [*Library symbol*] [*National Library of Canada*] (NLC)
OGWMN ..... Operational Groundwater Monitoring Network (SAUS)

OGWP .... Office of Ground Water Protection [*Environmental Protection Agency*] (GFGA)
OGWS .... Outgoing/Wink Start [*Telecommunications*] (TEL)
OGX......... Ouargla [*Algeria*] [*Airport symbol*] (OAG)
OGY......... O'Gyalla [*Later, HRB*] [*Czechoslovakia*] [*Geomagnetic observatory code*]
OGY......... OGY Petroleum [*Vancouver Stock Exchange symbol*]
OGY......... Originally [*Telegraphy*] (PCTE)
OH.......... Comair [*ICAO designator*] (AD)
OH.......... Finland [*International civil aircraft marking*] (ODBW)
OH.......... Hamilton Public Library, Ontario [*Library symbol*] [*National Library of Canada*] (NLC)
oh.......... Hospitaller Brothers of St. John of God (TOCD)
OH.......... Hospitaller Order of St. John of God [*Roman Catholic men's religious order*]
OH.......... Hydroxy [*As substituent on nucleoside*] [*Also, HO*] [*Biochemistry*]
OH.......... Hydroxycorticosteroid [*Endocrinology*] (DAVI)
OH.......... Hydroxyl (SAUS)
OH.......... Hydroxyl ion of water (SAUS)
OH.......... Hydroxyl Radical (AD)
OH.......... Oakwood Homes Corp. [*NYSE symbol*] (SPSG)
OH.......... Observation Helicopter
OH.......... Obstructive Hypopnea (DMAA)
OH.......... Occipital Horn [*Brain anatomy*]
OH.......... Occupational Health
OH.......... Occupational History [*Medicine*]
O-H......... Octal-to-Hexadecimal [*Computer science*] (IEEE)
OH.......... Ocular Herpes [*Medicine*] (AD)
OH.......... Ocular Hypertension (MELL)
OH.......... Off Hook [*Computer science*]
oh.......... Office Hours (AD)
OH.......... Office Hours
OH.......... Office of Hydrology (SAUS)
OH.......... Office of the Handicapped
OH.......... Official Hostess (BARN)
OH.......... Ohio [*Postal code*]
Oh.......... Ohio Courts of Appeals Reports [*A publication*] (DLA)
OH.......... Ohio Field Office (SAUS)
OH.......... Ohmic Heating
Oh.......... Oholoth (BJA)
OH.......... Oil Hardened (SAUS)
OH.......... Oil Hardening (SAUS)
OH.......... Old Harrovian (WDAA)
OH.......... Olduvai Hominid [*Paleoanthropology*]
OH.......... Oligomer Hybridization (DMAA)
OH.......... Omega House (AD)
OH.......... Omni Hora [*Every Hour*] [*Pharmacy*]
oh.......... Omni Hora [*Hourly*] [*Latin*] (AD)
oh.......... On Hand (AD)
OH.......... On Hand
o-H......... On-Hudson (AD)
OH.......... Ontario Hydro (SAUS)
OH.......... Ontario Hydroelectric [*Canada*]
oh.......... Open Hearth (AD)
OH.......... Open Hearth
OH.......... Open Heart Surgery [*Medicine*]
OH.......... Opera House (AD)
OH.......... Operand Holen (SAUS)
OH.......... Operating Hours (MCD)
OH.......... Operational Handbook [*Marine Corps*] (INF)
OH.......... Operational Hardware (KSC)
OH.......... Operator's Handbook
OH.......... Opposite Hand (OA)
OH.......... Optical Harness (SAUS)
OH.......... Orah Hayyim Shulhan 'Arukh (BJA)
OH.......... Oral Hygiene [*Dentistry*] (DAVI)
OH.......... Originating Hospital [*Aeromedical evacuation*]
OH.......... Orthohydrogen (SAUS)
OH.......... Orthostatic Hypotension [*Medicine*]
OH.......... Osteopathic Hospital (DAVI)
OH.......... Ostholstein [*German license plate city code*]
OH.......... Otago Hussars [*British military*] (DMA)
OH.......... Outer Housing (COE)
oh.......... Out Home (AD)
OH.......... Out Home [*Men's lacrosse position*]
OH.......... Outlaw HAWK [*Naval Air Development Center*]
OH.......... Out of Hospital (DMAA)
OH.......... Outpatient Hospital [*Medicine*]
oh.......... Oval Head (AD)
OH.......... Overall Height [*of the Vehicle*] [*TII*] (TAG)
o/h......... Overhaul (AD)
OH.......... Overhaul
oh.......... Overhead (AD)
O/H......... Overhead (MIST)
OH.......... Overhead
O/H......... Over-the-Horizon Transmission
O/H......... Overzuche Handels Maatschappij [*Foreign Trade Company*] [*Dutch*] (ILCA)
O/h......... Ovulation-producing Hormone (SAUS)
OH.......... Ozar Hatorah (EA)
OH.......... San Francisco and Oakland Helicopter Airlines (SAUS)
OH.......... SFO [*San Francisco and Oakland*] Helicopter Airlines, Inc. [*ICAO designator*] (OAG)
OH-6........ Cayuse Hughes [*Liaison helicopter*] [*Military*] (POLM)
OHA......... Chicago, IL [*Location identifier*] [*FAA*] (FAAL)
OHA......... Havelock Public Library, Ontario [*Library symbol*] [*National Library of Canada*] (BIB)
OHA......... Hydroxyandrostenedione [*Antineoplastic drug*] (CDI)
OHa......... Lane Public Library, Hamilton, OH [*Library symbol*] [*Library of Congress*] (LCLS)
OHA......... Occupational Health Administration (AD)
OHA......... Office of Health Affairs [*U.S. Food and Drug Administration*]
OHA......... Office of Hearings and Appeals [*In various federal departments*]
OHA......... Officers' Home Advance (ADA)
OHA......... Off-station Housing Allowance (DOMA)
Oha......... Ohaloth (BJA)
OHA......... OH Aviationa [*France*] [*ICAO designator*] (FAAC)
Oh A........ Ohio Appellate Reports [*A publication*] (DLA)
OHA......... Ohio Hospital Association (EARSL)
OHA......... Ontario Homeopathic Association (SAUS)
OHA......... Ontario Horticultural Association (SAUS)
OHA......... Ontario Hospital Association (SAUS)
OHA......... Operational Hazard Analysis (NASA)
OHA......... Oral History Association (EA)
OHA......... Oral Hypoglycemic Agent [*Medicine*] (CPH)
OHA......... Oral Hypoglycemic Agents [*Medicine*] (DMAA)
OHA......... Orbital Height Adjustment Maneuver (MCD)
OHA......... Oriental Herb Association (AD)
OHA......... Oscillator Housing Assembly
OHA......... Osterode am Harz [*German license plate city code*]
oha......... Outside Helix Angle (AD)
OHA......... Outside Helix Angle
OHA......... Overseas Housing Allowance
OHA......... Owner Handler Association of America (EA)
OHA......... Oxygen Hemoglobin Affinity (OA)
Oh A 2d..... Ohio Appellate Reports, Second Series [*A publication*] (DLA)
OHaBHi...... Butler County Historical Society, Hamilton, OH [*Library symbol*] [*Library of Congress*] (LCLS)
OHAD........ Dysart Branch, Haliburton County Public Library, Ontario [*Library symbol*] [*National Library of Canada*] (BIB)
OHADOE...... Office of Hearings and Appeals, Department of Energy (SAUS)
OHADOI...... Office of Hearings and Appeals, Department of the Interior (SAUS)
OHAG........ Art Gallery of Hamilton, Ontario [*Library symbol*] [*National Library of Canada*] (NLC)
OHAI........ Haileybury Public Library, Ontario [*Library symbol*] [*National Library of Canada*] (NLC)
OHAINC...... Haileybury School of Mines Campus, Northern College of Applied Arts and Technology, Ontario [*Library symbol*] [*National Library of Canada*] (BIB)
OHAL........ Haliburton County Public Library, Ontario [*Library symbol*] [*National Library of Canada*] (NLC)
OHALM....... Haliburton Highlands Museum, Haliburton, Ontario [*Library symbol*] [*National Library of Canada*] (BIB)
OHaMH....... Mercy Hospital, Health Science Library, Hamilton, OH [*Library symbol*] [*Library of Congress*] (LCLS)
OHAN........ Hanover Public Library, Ontario [*Library symbol*] [*National Library of Canada*] (NLC)
OH&LA....... Ohio Hotel and Lodging Association (EARSL)
OH&S........ Occupational Health and Safety [*Industrial hygiene term*] (OHS)
OH&T........ Oil Hardened and Tempered (SAUS)
Oh Ap....... Ohio Appellate Reports [*A publication*] (DLA)
OHAPT....... Orleans-Hanna Algebra Prognosis Test (EDAC)
OHARAG...... Research Station, Agriculture Canada [*Station de Recherches, Agriculture Canada*] Harrow, Ontario [*Library symbol*] [*National Library of Canada*] (NLC)
OhArt....... [*The*] Ohio Art Co. [*Associated Press*] (SAG)
OHAS........ Occupational Health and Safety
OHaU........ Miami University, Hamilton Campus, Hamilton, OH [*Library symbol*] [*Library of Congress*] (LCLS)
OHAV........ O'Hare Van Lines [*Common carrier symbol*]
OHB......... L'Equilibre Biologique [*France*] [*Research code symbol*]
OH-B........ Ocean Hill-Brownsville (AD)
OHB......... O-Hydroxybenzamide (SAUS)
OHB......... Orleans Homebuilders [*Montreal Stock Exchange*] [*Formerly, FPA Corp.*]
OHBA........ Ontario Home Builders' Association [*Canada*]
OHBC........ Ohio Bancorp (SAUS)
OHBC........ Oregon Highland Bentgrass Commission (EA)
OHBES....... Schools, Hamilton Board of Education, Ontario [*Library symbol*] [*National Library of Canada*] (NLC)
OHBFS....... Schools, Hamilton Board of Education, Ontario (SAUS)
OHBHU....... Hilton Union Public Library, Hilton Beach, Ontario [*Library symbol*] [*National Library of Canada*] (NLC)
OHBMS....... On His [*or Her*] Britannic Majesty's Service
OHBP........ Pic Heron Bay Band Public Library, Heron Bay, Ontario [*Library symbol*] [*National Library of Canada*] (BIB)
OHC......... Hydroxycholecalciferol [*A form of vitamin D*] (DAVI)
OHC......... Occupational Health Center (KSC)
OHC......... Ocean Heat Convergence
OHC......... Office of Humanities Communication (AD)
OHC......... Office of HUMINT [*Human Intelligence*] Collection [*Military*]
OHC......... O'Higgins [*Antarctica*] [*Seismograph station code, US Geological Survey*] (SEIS)
OHC......... On Board Hard Copier (NASA)
OHC......... Ontario Housing Corporation (SAUS)
OHC......... Optics Hand Controller (KSC)
OHC......... Oral History Collection (SAUS)
OHC......... Order of the Holy Cross [*Episcopalian religious order*]
OHC......... Organization for the History of Canada (EAIO)
OHC......... Oriole Homes Convertible (EFIS)

OHC......... Oriole Homes Corporation (SAUS)
OHC......... Other Hanford Contractor (SAUS)
OHC......... Ottumwa Heights College [*Iowa*]
ohc......... Outer Hair Cells (AD)
OHC......... Outer Hair Cells [*of cochlea*] [*Anatomy*]
OHC......... Over-Head-Cam [*TII*] (TAG)
ohc......... Overhead Cam (AD)
OHC......... Overhead Camshaft [*Automotive term*]
OHC......... Overhead Cupboards [*Classified advertising*] (ADA)
OHC......... Overseas Hotel Corp. (AD)
OHC......... Oxygen Hole Centers (SAUS)
OHC.A....... Oriole HomesCv'A' [*AMEX symbol*] (TTSB)
OHC.B....... Oriole Homes 'B' [*AMEX symbol*] (TTSB)
OHCA........ Otter Hound Club of America [*Later, OCA*] (EA)
OHCA........ Out-of-Hospital Cardiac Arrest [*Medicine*] (DMAA)
OH-Cbl...... Hydroxycobalamin [*Medicine*] (BABM)
OHCC........ Ordinary High Current Configuration [*Magnetic field*]
OHCEN...... Ontario Health Care Evaluation Network (SAUS)
OHCI......... Open Host Controller Interface (SAUS)
Oh Cir Ct... Ohio Circuit Court Reports [*A publication*] (DLA)
Oh Cir Ct NS... Ohio Circuit Court Reports, New Series [*A publication*] (DLA)
Oh Cir Dec... Ohio Circuit Decisions [*A publication*] (DLA)
OHC-OHP... Overhead Camshaft-Overhead Pushrod [*Automotive engines*]
OHCR........ Ohio Central Railroad [*Federal Railroad Administration identification code*]
OHCS........ Hydroxycorticosteroid [*Endocrinology*] (AAMN)
OHCS........ Office of Home Care Services (AD)
OHCU........ College Universitaire de Hearst, Ontario [*Library symbol*] [*National Library of Canada*] (NLC)
OHD......... Hydroxycholecalciferol (STED)
OHD......... Hydroxyvitamin D (DMAA)
OHD......... Occupational Health Division (COE)
OHD......... Office of Human Development [*Later, OHDS*] [*HEW*]
OHD......... Ohrid [*Former Yugoslavia*] [*Airport symbol*] (OAG)
OHD......... Old Hickory Dam [*TVA*]
OHD......... Ondine-Hirschprung Disease [*Medicine*] (DMAA)
OHD......... One-Hour Duty (IAA)
OHD......... Optical Heterodyne Detection
OHD......... Ordinary Hydrodynamic
ohd......... Organic Hearing Disease [*Medicine*] (AD)
ohd......... Organic Heart Disease [*Medicine*] (AD)
OHD......... Organic Heart Disease [*Medicine*]
OHD......... Overhead Display
OHD......... Overhead Door Corp. (EFIS)
OHD......... Overhead Drive (SAUS)
OHD......... Over-the-Horizon Detector [*RADAR*]
OHDA........ Hydroxydopamine [*Also, HDA, HDM*] [*Biochemistry*]
OH/D&D-G.. Ontario Hydro/Design and Development Division-Generation (SAUS)
OHD & W... Outer Harbor Dock and Wharf (AD)
OHD-B....... Over-the-Horizon Detection RADAR-Backscatter (MCD)
OHDDD....... Ontario Hydro Design and Development Division (SAUS)
Oh Dec...... Ohio Decisions [*A publication*] (DLA)
Oh Dec Rep... Ohio Decisions Reprint [*A publication*] (DLA)
OHDET...... Over-the-Horizon Detection [*RADAR*] (SAA)
OHDETS..... Over-the-Horizon Detection System [*RADAR*]
OHDF........ Dofasco, Inc., Hamilton, Ontario [*Library symbol*] [*National Library of Canada*] (NLC)
OHDFR...... Research Information Center, DOFASCO, Inc., Hamilton, Ontario [*Library symbol*] [*National Library of Canada*] (NLC)
OHDMS..... Operational Hydromet Data Management System (PDAA)
OH-DOC...... Hydroxydeoxycorticosterone [*Endocrinology*] (DAVI)
OHDS........ Office of Human Development Services [*Formerly, OHD*] [*Department of Health and Human Services*]
OHDU........ Other Hybrid Duck [*North American bird banding code*] (BIBA)
OHE......... Hearst Public Library, Ontario [*Library symbol*] [*National Library of Canada*] (NLC)
OHE......... Office of Hanford Environment (SAUS)
OHE......... Office of Health Economics [*British*]
OHE......... Office of the Housing Expediter [*Terminated, 1951*] (GPO)
OHE......... Overhead Equipment [*Indian Railway*] (TIR)
OHE......... Oxidizer Heat Exchange (MCD)
OHEA........ Office of Health and Environmental Assessment [*Environmental Protection Agency*] (GFGA)
OHEA........ Office of Health Effects Assessment (SAUS)
oheat........ Overheat (AD)
OHEAT....... Overheat
OHEC........ Dr. Harry Paikin Library, Hamilton Board of Education, Ontario [*Library symbol*] [*National Library of Canada*] (NLC)
OHEC........ Hamilton Education Centre, Ontario [*Library symbol*] [*National Library of Canada*] (NLC)
OhEd......... Ohio Edison Co. [*Associated Press*] (SAG)
OhEd......... Ohio Edison Financing Trust [*Associated Press*] (SAG)
OHEF........ Oral Health Education Foundation (SAUS)
OHEP........ Hepworth Branch, Bruce County Public Library, Ontario [*Library symbol*] [*National Library of Canada*] (NLC)
OHER........ Office of Health and Environmental Research [*Department of Energy*] [*Washington, DC*]
OHESC...... Ontario Library Service - Escarpment, Hamilton, Ontario [*Library symbol*] [*National Library of Canada*] (NLC)
OHET........ Erin Township Public Library, Hillsburgh, Ontario [*Library symbol*] [*National Library of Canada*] (NLC)
OHF......... Occupational Health Facility [*NASA*] (KSC)
OHF......... Old Hydrofracture Facility (SAUS)
ohf......... Omsk Hemorrhagic Fever (AD)
OHF......... Omsk Hemorrhagic Fever [*Medicine*]
OHF......... O'Neill Hull Form (ACAE)
OHF......... Ordnance Historical Files [*Military*]
ohf......... Overhaul Factor (AD)
OHF......... Overhead Fire (MCD)
OHF......... Overhead Frame (MEDA)
OHF......... Oxalosis and Hyperoxaluria Foundation (EA)
OHFA........ Hydroxy Fatty Acid [*Biochemistry*] (AAMN)
OHFC........ Hartington Branch, Frontenac County Library, Hartington, Ontario [*Library symbol*] [*National Library of Canada*] (BIB)
OHFC........ Owen Hart Fan Club (EA)
Oh F Dec... Ohio Federal Decisions [*A publication*] (DLA)
OH/FH....... Operating Hour/Flight Hour [*Ratio*]
OHFR........ Objective High Frequency Radio (ACAE)
OHFS........ Optimized Hartree-Fock-Slater (SAUS)
OHFT........ Overhead Frame Trapeze (STED)
OHFX........ Fluor Daniel Fernald [*Private rail car owner code*]
OHG......... Banco OHiggins [*NYSE symbol*] (SAG)
OHG......... Banco O'Higgins ADS [*NYSE symbol*] (TTSB)
OHG......... Offene Handelsgesellschaft [*General Partnership*] [*German*]
OHG......... Official Hotel Guide (TRID)
OHG......... Old High German [*Language, etc.*]
OHG......... Oral Hypoglycemic [*Endocrinology*] (DAVI)
OHGI......... Over the Hill Gang, International (EA)
OHGO........ Other Hybrid Goose [*North American bird banding code*] (BIBA)
OHGS........ Omega Hyperbolic Grid System
OHGVT...... Orbital Horizontal Ground Vibration Test [*NASA*] (NASA)
OHH......... Herrold Hall Learning Resource Center, Zanesville (SAUS)
OHH......... Ohio Household Goods Carriers Bureau Inc., Warren OH [*STAC*]
OHH......... Orthopedia Head Halter (MELL)
OHH......... Owen Harrison Harding [*of the James W. Ellison novel, "I'm Owen Harrison Harding"*]
OHHA........ Occupational Health Hazard Assessment
OHI......... HUNA International (EA)
OHI......... Occupational Health Institute [*Defunct*] (EA)
ohi......... Ocular Hypertension Indicator (AD)
OHI......... Ocular Hypertension Indicator
OHI......... Office for Handicapped Individuals [*Medicine*] (EDAA)
OHi......... Ohio Historical Society, Columbus, OH [*Library symbol*] [*Library of Congress*] (LCLS)
OHI......... Oil-Heat Institute of America [*Later, PMAA*]
OHI......... Omega Healthcare Investors [*NYSE symbol*] (SPSG)
OHI......... Open Head Injury [*Medicine*] (PAZ)
OHI......... Oral Hygiene Index (STED)
OHI......... Oral Hygiene Instruction [*Medicine*] (EDAA)
OHI......... Ordnance Handling Instructions
OHI......... Organisation Hydrographique Internationale [*International Hydrographic Organization - IHO*] [*Monte Carlo, Monaco*]
OHI......... Other Health Impaired [*Education*]
OHI......... State Library of Ohio, Columbus, OH [*OCLC symbol*] (OCLC)
OHIA......... Oil-Heat Institute of America [*Later, PMAA*] (KSC)
OHIAA....... Hydroxyindolacetic Acid [*Oncology*] (DAVI)
OH-IAA...... Hydroxyindoleacetic Acid (STED)
OHIC......... ODPHP Health Information Center (EA)
OHIC......... Ohi-Rail [*Federal Railroad Administration identification code*]
OHICU....... Open Heart Intensive Care Unit (NUJO)
OHICY....... Ohio City, OH [*American Association of Railroads railroad junction routing code*]
OHilH........ Highland County District Library, Hillsboro, OH [*Library symbol*] [*Library of Congress*] (LCLS)
OHilS........ South Hillsboro City Schools, Hillsboro, OH [*Library symbol*] [*Library of Congress*] (LCLS)
OHIMA...... Ohio Health Information Management Association (SAUS)
Ohio......... College Library Center (SAUS)
OHIO......... Ohio Body Manufacturing Company [*NCIC trailer make code*]
Ohio......... Ohio Supreme Court Reports [*1821-51*] [*A publication*] (DLA)
OHIO......... Over the Hill in October [*Used prior to the bombing of Pearl Harbor to typify a recruit's view of US Army life*]
Ohio Abs.... Ohio Law Abstract [*A publication*] (DLA)
Ohio Abstract... Ohio Law Abstract [*A publication*] (DLA)
Ohio Admin Code... Ohio Administrative Code [*Official compilation published by Banks-Baldwin*] [*A publication*] (DLA)
Ohio Ag Exp... Ohio. Agricultural Experimental Station. Publications (SAUS)
Ohio Agric Exp Stn Res Bull... Ohio. Agricultural Experimental Station. Research Bulletin (SAUS)
Ohio Agric Exp Stn Res Circ... Ohio. Agricultural Experimental Station. Research Circular (SAUS)
Ohio Agric Exp Stn Spec Circ... Ohio. Agricultural Experimental Station. Special Circular (SAUS)
Ohio App.... Ohio Appellate Reports [*A publication*] (DLA)
Ohio App 2d... Ohio Appellate Reports, Second Series [*A publication*] (DLA)
Ohio Apps... Ohio Appellate Reports [*A publication*] (DLA)
OHIO BANKPAC - FED... Ohio Bankers Association PAC [*Columbus, OH*] (PACS)
Ohio BTA.... Ohio Board of Tax Appeals Reports [*A publication*] (DLA)
OhioCa...... Ohio Casualty Corp. [*Associated Press*] (SAG)
Ohio CA..... Ohio Courts of Appeals Reports [*A publication*] (DLA)
OhioCas..... Ohio Casualty Corp. [*Associated Press*] (SAG)
Ohio CC..... Ohio Circuit Court Reports [*A publication*] (DLA)
Ohio CC Dec... Ohio Circuit Court Decisions [*A publication*] (DLA)
Ohio CC NS... Ohio Circuit Court Reports, New Series [*A publication*] (DLA)
Ohio CCR... Ohio Circuit Court Reports [*A publication*] (DLA)
Ohio CCR NS... Ohio Circuit Court Reports, New Series [*A publication*] (DLA)
Ohio CD..... Ohio Circuit Decisions [*A publication*] (DLA)
Ohio C Dec... Ohio Circuit Decisions [*A publication*] (DLA)
Ohio Circ Dec... Ohio Circuit Decisions [*A publication*] (DLA)
Ohio Cir Ct... Ohio Circuit Court Decisions [*A publication*] (DLA)

Ohio Cir Ct (NS)... Ohio Circuit Court Reports, New Series [*A publication*] (DLA)
Ohio Cir Ct R... Ohio Circuit Court Reports [*A publication*] (DLA)
Ohio Cir Ct R NS... Ohio Circuit Court Reports, New Series [*A publication*] (DLA)
Ohio Circuits... Ohio Circuit Court Decisions [*A publication*] (DLA)
Ohio Cir Dec... Ohio Circuit Decisions [*A publication*] (DLA)
Ohio Cond... Wilcox's Condensed Ohio Reports [*A publication*] (DLA)
Ohio Cond R... Wilcox's Condensed Ohio Reports [*A publication*] (DLA)
Ohio Ct App... Ohio Courts of Appeals Reports [*A publication*] (DLA)
Ohio Dec.... Ohio Decisions [*A publication*] (DLA)
Ohio Dec NP... Ohio Decisions Nisi Prius [*A publication*] (DLA)
Ohio Dec R... Ohio Decisions Reprint [*A publication*] (DLA)
Ohio Dec Re... Ohio Decisions Reprint [*A publication*] (DLA)
Ohio Dec Rep... Ohio Decisions Reprint [*A publication*] (DLA)
Ohio Dec Repr... Ohio Decisions Reprint [*A publication*] (DLA)
Ohio Dep't... Ohio Department Reports [*A publication*] (DLA)
Ohio Div WaterTech Rep... Ohio. Division of Water. Technical Report (SAUS)
OhioEd...... Ohio Edison Co. [*Associated Press*] (SAG)
Ohio FD..... Ohio Federal Decisions [*A publication*] (DLA)
Ohio F Dec... Ohio Federal Decisions [*A publication*] (DLA)
Ohio Fed Dec... Ohio Federal Decisions [*A publication*] (DLA)
Ohio Gov't... Ohio Government Reports [*A publication*] (DLA)
Ohio GSB... Ohio. Geological Survey. Bulletin (SAUS)
Ohio Jur.... Ohio Jurisprudence [*A publication*] (DLA)
Ohio Jur 2d... Ohio Jurisprudence, Second Series [*A publication*] (DLA)
Ohio L Abs... Ohio Law Abstract [*A publication*] (DLA)
Ohio Law Abs... Ohio Law Abstract [*A publication*] (DLA)
Ohio Law Abst... Ohio Law Abstract [*A publication*] (DLA)
Ohio Law Bull... Weekly Law Bulletin [*Ohio*] [*A publication*] (DLA)
Ohio Law J... Ohio Law Journal [*A publication*] (DLA)
Ohio Law R... Ohio Law Reporter [*A publication*] (DLA)
Ohio Law Rep... Ohio Law Reporter [*A publication*] (DLA)
Ohio Law Repr... Ohio Law Reporter [*A publication*] (DLA)
Ohio Laws... State of Ohio: Legislative Acts Passed and Joint Resolutions Adopted [*A publication*] (DLA)
Ohio LB..... Weekly Law Bulletin [*Ohio*] [*A publication*] (DLA)
Ohio L Bull... Ohio Law Bulletin [*A publication*] (DLA)
Ohio Legal N... Ohio Legal News [*A publication*] (DLA)
Ohio Legis Bull... Ohio Legislative Bulletin (Anderson) [*A publication*] (DLA)
Ohio Legis Serv... Ohio Legislative Service [*A publication*] (DLA)
Ohio Leg N... Ohio Legal News [*A publication*] (DLA)
Ohio Leg News... Ohio Legal News [*A publication*] (DLA)
OhioLINK... Ohio Library and Information Network
Ohio LJ..... Ohio Law Journal [*A publication*] (DLA)
Ohio Low Dec... Ohio Lower Court Decisions [*A publication*] (DLA)
Ohio Lower Dec... Ohio Lower Court Decisions [*A publication*] (DLA)
Ohio LR..... Ohio Law Reporter [*A publication*] (DLA)
Ohio LR & Wk Bul... Ohio Law Reporter and Weekly Bulletin [*A publication*] (DLA)
Ohio L Rep... Ohio Law Reporter [*A publication*] (DLA)
OHIO M..... Ohio Magazine [*A publication*] (ROG)
Ohio Misc... Ohio Miscellaneous Reports [*A publication*] (DLA)
Ohio Misc 2d... Ohio Miscellaneous Reports, Second Series [*A publication*] (DLA)
Ohio Misc 3d... Ohio Miscellaneous Reports, Third Series [*A publication*] (DLA)
Ohio Misc Dec... Ohio Miscellaneous Decisions [*A publication*] (DLA)
Ohio Monthly Rec... Ohio Monthly Record [*A publication*] (DLA)
Ohio Nat.... Ohio Naturalist (SAUS)
OHIONET... Ohio Network (NITA)
Ohio (New Series)... Ohio State Reports, New Series [*A publication*] (DLA)
Ohio Nisi Prius... Ohio Nisi Prius Reports [*A publication*] (DLA)
Ohio Nisi Prius (NS)... Ohio Nisi Prius Reports, New Series [*A publication*] (DLA)
Ohio No U... Ohio Northern University (GAGS)
Ohio NP..... Ohio Nisi Prius Reports [*A publication*] (DLA)
Ohio NP NS... Ohio Nisi Prius Reports, New Series [*A publication*] (DLA)
Ohio NS..... Ohio State Reports, New Series [*A publication*] (DLA)
Ohio O...... Ohio Opinions [*A publication*] (DLA)
Ohio O...... Ohio Opinions, Annotated [*A publication*] (DLA)
Ohio O 2d... Ohio Opinions, Second Series [*A publication*] (DLA)
Ohio Op..... Ohio Opinions [*A publication*] (DLA)
Ohio Op 2d... Ohio Opinions, Second Series [*A publication*] (DLA)
Ohio Op 3d... Ohio Opinions, Third Series [*A publication*] (DLA)
Ohio Ops.... Ohio Opinions [*A publication*] (DLA)
Ohio Prob... Ohio Probate Reports, by Goebel [*A publication*] (DLA)
Ohio Prob Ct... Goebel's Probate Reports [*Ohio*] [*A publication*] (DLA)
Ohio R...... Ohio Report [*A publication*] (DLA)
Ohio R Cond... Ohio Reports Condensed [*A publication*] (DLA)
Ohio Rep Res Develop... Ohio Report on Research and Development. Ohio Agricultural Experiment Station (SAUS)
Ohio Rev Code Ann... Ohio Revised Code, Annotated [*A publication*] (DLA)
Ohio Rev Code Ann (Anderson)... Ohio Revised Code, Annotated (Anderson) [*A publication*] (DLA)
Ohio Rev Code Ann (Baldwin)... Ohio Revised Code, Annotated (Baldwin) [*A publication*] (DLA)
Ohio Rev Code Ann (Page)... Ohio Revised Code, Annotated (Page) [*A publication*] (DLA)
Ohio S....... Ohio State Reports [*A publication*] (DLA)
Ohio S & CP... Ohio Superior and Common Pleas Decisions [*A publication*] (DLA)
Ohio S & CP Dec... Ohio Superior and Common Pleas Decisions [*A publication*] (DLA)
Ohio SBA Bull... Ohio State Bar Association. Bulletin [*A publication*] (DLA)
Ohio SR..... Ohio State Reports [*A publication*] (DLA)
Ohio S Rep... Ohio State Reports [*A publication*] (DLA)
Ohio St...... Ohio State Reports [*A publication*] (DLA)
Ohio St 2d... Ohio State Reports, Second Series [*A publication*] (DLA)
Ohio St 3d... Ohio State Reports, Third Series [*A publication*] (DLA)
Ohio State... Ohio State Reports [*A publication*] (DLA)
Ohio State Rep... Ohio State Reports [*A publication*] (DLA)
Ohio State R (NS)... Ohio State Reports, New Series [*A publication*] (DLA)
Ohio State U Bull Bus Res... Ohio State University Bulletin of Business Research [*A publication*] (JLIT)
Ohio St R... Ohio State Reports [*A publication*] (DLA)
Ohio St Rep... Ohio State Reports [*A publication*] (DLA)
Ohio St Report... Ohio State Reports [*A publication*] (DLA)
Ohio St R (NS)... Ohio State Reports, New Series [*A publication*] (DLA)
Ohio St U... [*The*] Ohio State University (GAGS)
Ohio SU..... Ohio Supreme Court Decisions, Unreported Cases [*A publication*] (DLA)
Ohio Sup & CP Dec... Ohio Superior and Common Pleas Decisions [*A publication*] (DLA)
Ohio Supp... Ohio Supplement [*A publication*] (DLA)
Ohio Turn... Ohio Turnpike (AD)
Ohio U...... Ohio University (GAGS)
Ohio Unrep... Ohio Supreme Court Decisions, Unreported Cases [*A publication*] (DLA)
Ohio Unrep Jud Dec... Pollack's Ohio Unreported Judicial Decisions Prior to 1823 [*A publication*] (DLA)
Ohio Unrept Cas... Ohio Supreme Court Decisions, Unreported Cases [*A publication*] (DLA)
Ohio U Pr... Ohio University Press (AD)
OhioVal..... Ohio Valley Banc Corp. [*Associated Press*] (SAG)
OHIP......... Office of Health and Industry Programs [*U.S. Food and Drug Administration*]
OHIP......... Ontario Health Insurance Plan [*Canada*] (CMD)
OHIP......... Ontario Hospital Insurance Plan [*Canada*] (AD)
OHIR......... Operating House of Ill Repute
OHirC........ Hiram College, Hiram, OH [*Library symbol*] [*Library of Congress*] (LCLS)
OHirP........ Portage County District Library, Hiram, OH [*Library symbol*] [*Library of Congress*] (LCLS)
OHIS......... Oral Hearing-Impaired Section [*of the Alexander Graham Bell Association for the Deaf*] (EA)
OHI-S........ Oral Hygiene Index-Simplified
OHI-S........ Oral Hygiene Instruction-Simplified [*Medicine*] (EDAA)
OHJ.......... Old-House Journal [*A publication*]
OHJD........ John Deere Ltd., Hamilton, Ontario [*Library symbol*] [*National Library of Canada*] (NLC)
Oh Jur....... Ohio Jurisprudence [*A publication*] (DLA)
OHK.......... Hawkesbury Public Library, Ontario [*Library symbol*] [*National Library of Canada*] (NLC)
OHKAC...... Resource Centre, Algonquin College of Applied Arts and Technology [*Centre de Documentation, College Algonquin des Arts Appliques et de la Technologie*], Hawkesbury, Ontario [*Library symbol*] [*National Library of Canada*] (BIB)
OHKC........ CIP Research Ltd., Hawkesbury, Ontario [*Library symbol*] [*National Library of Canada*] (NLC)
OHKGH...... Hawkesbury General Hospital, Ontario [*Library symbol*] [*National Library of Canada*] (BIB)
OHKU........ Ohka American [*Intermodal shipping container symbol*] (TVRC)
OHL.......... Oberste Herresleitung [*Supreme Headquarters*] [*German*] (AD)
OHL.......... Occupational Health Laboratory (SAUS)
OHL.......... Occupational Hygiene Laboratory (SAUS)
OHL.......... Officer Hand Launcher [*Police and security equipment*]
OHL.......... Ontario Hydro Library [*UTLAS symbol*]
OHL.......... Oral Hairy Leukoplakia [*Medicine*]
OHL.......... Overhaul
OHL.......... Oxford Higher Local Examination [*British*] (ROG)
OHLA........ Anthony Pape Memorial Law Library, Hamilton Law Association, Ontario [*Library symbol*] [*National Library of Canada*] (BIB)
OHLA........ Over-Hung Load Adapter [*Hydraulic equipment*]
Oh L Bul.... Ohio Law Bulletin [*A publication*] (DLA)
Oh L Ct D... Ohio Lower Court Decisions [*A publication*] (DLA)
OHLEG...... East Gwillimbury Public Libraries, Holland Landing, Ontario [*Library symbol*] [*National Library of Canada*] (NLC)
Oh Leg N... Ohio Legal News [*A publication*] (DLA)
OHLH........ Overhead Heavy Load Handling [*Nuclear energy*] (NRCH)
Ohlinger Fed Practice... Ohlinger's Federal Practice [*A publication*] (DLA)
Oh LJ........ Ohio Law Journal [*A publication*] (DLA)
Oh L Rep... Ohio Law Reporter [*A publication*] (DLA)
OHM......... McMaster University, Hamilton, Ontario [*Library symbol*] [*National Library of Canada*] (NLC)
OHM......... Miami University, Hamilton Campus, Hamilton, OH [*OCLC symbol*] (OCLC)
OHM......... Office of Hazardous Materials [*Department of Transportation*]
OHM......... O.H. Materials Corp. (EFIS)
OHM......... OHM Corp. [*NYSE symbol*] (SPSG)
OHM......... Ohmmeter [*Engineering*] (AAG)
ohm.......... Ohmmeter (AD)
OHM......... Oil and Hazardous Materials (SAUS)
OHM......... Oil and Hazardous Materials Incidence
OHMA....... Archives and Special Collections Division, McMaster University, Hamilton, Ontario [*Library symbol*] [*National Library of Canada*] (NLC)
OHMA....... Office of Health and Medical Affairs (GHCT)
OHMAH..... Department of Art and Art History, McMaster University, Hamilton, Ontario [*Library symbol*] [*National Library of Canada*] (NLC)
OHMAR..... Oral History in the Mid-Atlantic Region [*An association*]
OHMB....... Health Sciences Library, McMaster University, Hamilton, Ontario [*Library symbol*] [*National Library of Canada*] (NLC)
OHMC....... Mohawk College of Applied Arts and Technology, Hamilton, Ontario [*Library symbol*] [*National Library of Canada*] (NLC)

OHMcGF .... Odyssey House McGrath Foundation [*Australia*]
OHMCI ...... Office of Her Majesty's Chief Inspector of Schools [*British*] (DET)
OHMCL...... Library Technician Program, Mohawk College of Applied Arts & Technology, Hamilton, Ontario [*Library symbol*] [*National Library of Canada*] (NLC)
OHM-CM.... Ohm-Centimeter (AAG)
ohm-cm ..... Ohm-Centimeter (AD)
OHM Cp..... OHM Corp. [*Associated Press*] (SAG)
OHMDBA.... Canadian Baptist Archives, McMaster Divinity College, McMaster University, Hamilton, Ontario [*Library symbol*] [*National Library of Canada*] (NLC)
OHMEA...... Office of Hazardous Materials Exemptions and Approvals [*RSPA*] (TAG)
OHMES...... Occupational Health Monitoring and Evaluation System (PDAA)
OHMIS ...... Occupational Health Management Information System [*Military*] (GFGA)
Oh Misc..... Ohio Miscellaneous Reports [*A publication*] (DLA)
OHMM....... Map Library, McMaster University, Hamilton, Ontario [*Library symbol*] [*National Library of Canada*] (NLC)
OHMM....... Ohmmeter [*Engineering*]
ohm/m ...... Resistence per Meter
OHMO .... Office of Hazardous Materials Operations [*Department of Transportation*] (DLA)
OHMO .... Office of Health Maintenance Organization [*Insurance*] (DHSM)
OHMP .... Occupational Health Maintenance Program (SARE)
OHMP .... Oral Health Maintenance Program [*Army*] (AABC)
OHMP .... United States Army Oral Health Maintenance Program (SAUS)
OHMR .... Office of Hazardous Materials Regulation [*Department of Transportation*] (OICC)
OHMS .... Office of Hazardous Materials Safety (SAUS)
OHMS .... Office of Hazardous Materials Standards [*RSPA*] (TAG)
OHMS .... Onboard Health Monitoring System (AD)
OHMS .... On His [*or Her*] Majesty's Service
OHMS .... Our Helpless Millions Saved [*Title of early film*]
OHMS .... Overhead Machine Screw [*Technical drawings*]
OHMSB...... Oil and Hazardous Materials Spills Branch [*Environmental Protection Agency*] (GRD)
OHMSETT... Oil and Hazardous Materials Simulated Environmental Test Tank [*Leonardo, NJ*] [*Environmental Protection Agency*]
OHMT .... Office of Hazardous Materials Transportation [*Department of Transportation*] (GFGA)
OHM-TADS... Oil and Hazardous Materials Technical Assistance Data System [*Databank*] [*Environmental Protection Agency*] (IID)
OHMTADS... Oil and Hazardous Material Technical Assistance Data System [*Environmental Protection Agency*] (AEPA)
OHMVR ..... Off-Highway Motor Vehicle Recreation (SAUS)
OHN .... Hastings Branch, Northumberland County Public Library, Ontario [*Library symbol*] [*National Library of Canada*] (BIB)
OHN .... Memphis, TN [*Location identifier*] [*FAA*] (FAAL)
OHN .... Occupational Health Nurse [*Government classification*]
OHN .... Occupational Health Nursing [*Medicine*] [*AAIN journal*] (EDAA)
OHN .... OHIONET, Columbus, OH [*OCLC symbol*] (OCLC)
OHNC........ Occupational Health Nursing Certificate [*British*]
OH/NMMD .. Ontario Hydro/Nuclear Materials Management Department (SAUS)
OHNN........ Otorhinolaryngology and Head/Neck Nurses (EA)
OHNO........ Occupational Health Nursing Officer (AD)
OHNP........ Ohio Natural Heritage Program [*Ohio State Department of Natural Resources*] [*Division of Natural Areas and Preserves*] (IID)
Oh NP .... Ohio Nisi Prius Reports [*A publication*] (DLA)
OHNP........ Ohio State Department of Natural Resources (IID)
Oh NP (NS)... Ohio Nisi Prius Reports, New Series [*A publication*] (DLA)
OHNS........ Occupational Health Nursing Sister (AD)
Oh NU Intra LR... Ohio Northern University. Intramural Law Review [*A publication*] (DLA)
OHO .... Ohio Hospice Organization (SAUS)
OHO .... Ohio Resources Corp. [*Vancouver Stock Exchange symbol*]
Oho .... Oholoth (BJA)
OHO .... Order Holding Office
OHO .... Ordnance Handling Officer [*Navy*] (DOMA)
oho .... Out-of-House Operation (AD)
OHOB........ O'Neill House Office Building [*U.S. House of Representatives*] [*Washington, D.C.*]
OHOC........ Oregon Hanford Oversight Committee (SAUS)
OHOHS...... Canadian Centre for Occupational Health and Safety [*Centre Canadien d'Hygieneet de Securite au Travail*] Hamilton, Ontario [*Library symbol*] [*National Library of Canada*] (NLC)
Ohol .... Oholoth (BJA)
OHOX........ U.S. Department of Energy [*Private rail car owner code*]
OHP.......... Hydroxyprogesterone [*Medicine*] (EDAA)
OHP.......... Hydroxypyroline [*Biochemistry*] (AAMN)
OHP.......... Oban-Heliport [*Scotland*] [*Airport symbol*] (OAG)
OHP.......... Occupational Health Physician (SAUS)
OHP.......... Ocean History Panel (SAUS)
OHP.......... Office of Health Physics [*U.S. Food and Drug Administration*]
OHP.......... Open Hypertext Protocol (RALS)
OHP.......... Operational Health Physics (SAUS)
OHP.......... Operational Hit Probabilities (SAUS)
OHP.......... Operational Hydrology Program [*World Meteorological Organization*] (GFGA)
OHP.......... Order of the Holy Paraclete [*Anglican religious community*]
OHP.......... Orthogonal-Hole Test Pattern (RAWO)
OHP.......... Outer Helmholtz Plane [*Physics*]
ohp .... Overhead Projection (AD)
OHP.......... Overhead Projector (ADA)
OHP.......... Overhead Transparency Panel (SAUS)
OHP.......... Oxygen at High Pressure [*Also, HBO, HPO*] (MCD)
OHP.......... Oxygen under Hyperbaric Pressure [*For hyperbaric oxygen therapy*] [*Medicine*] (DAVI)
OhP25....... Ohio Power Co. [*Associated Press*] (SAG)
OHPA........ Ohio & Pennsylvania Railroad [*Federal Railroad Administration identification code*]
OH PED ..... Ohne Pedal [*Without Pedal*] [*Music*]
oh Ped ...... Ohne Pedale [*Without Pedals*] [*German*] (AD)
OHPELRA... Ohio Public Employer Labor Relations Association (EARSL)
OHPO........ Organization Health Program Officer (AFM)
OHPR........ Outstanding Hardware Problem Report (MCD)
Oh Prob..... Ohio Probate [*A publication*] (DLA)
OHPS........ Oil Hydraulic Power Switch
OHPSS ...... Operational Health Physics Site Surveillance (SAUS)
OHQ .... Originating Headquarters (SAUS)
OHQ .... Overseas Headquarters [*British military*] (DMA)
OHR .... Office of Health Research [*Environmental Protection Agency*] [*Washington, DC*] (GRD)
OHR .... Office of Human Resources (SAUS)
OHR .... Office of the High Representative
OHR .... Of Human Rights (EA)
OHR .... O'Hara Resources Ltd. [*Vancouver Stock Exchange symbol*]
OHR .... Ohrid [*Yugoslavia*] [*Seismograph station code, US Geological Survey*] (SEIS)
OHR .... Ontario Hydro-Research (SAUS)
OHR .... Operating House of Ill Repute (SAUS)
OHR .... Operational Hazard Report [*Air Force*] (AFM)
OHR .... Our Home Is Russia [*Political party*] (PSAP)
OHR .... Over-the-Horizon RADAR
OHRB........ Royal Botanical Gardens, Hamilton, Ontario [*Library symbol*] [*National Library of Canada*] (NLC)
OHRC........ Redeemer College, Ancaster, Ontario [*Library symbol*] [*National Library of Canada*] (NLC)
OHRD........ Ontario Hydro Research Division (SAUS)
OHRDP...... Ontario Health Resources Development Program (SAUS)
OHRD/TSTA... Ontario Hydro Research Division/Tritium Systems Test Assembly (SAUS)
OHRE........ Department of Energy, Office of Human Radiation Experiments (SAUS)
OHRE........ Office of Human Radiation Experiments. Department of Energy (SAUS)
ohrf .... Overhaul Replacement Factor (AD)
OHRG........ Official Hotel and Resort Guide [*A publication*] (AD)
OHRI......... Occupational Health and Rehabilitation [*OTCBB symbol*]
OHRI......... Occupational Health & Rehabilitation, Inc. [*NASDAQ symbol*] (SAG)
OHRI......... Oral Health Research Institute [*Indiana University*] [*Research center*] (RCD)
OHRI......... Ottawa Health Research Institute [*Canada*] (RCD)
OHRI......... Overhaul Recurrent Item (CINC)
OHRI......... Overhaul Removal Interval [*Military*] (AFIT)
OHRI......... Overhaul Removal Item (CINC)
OHRIM ...... Office of Human Resource Information Management [*Department of Health and Human Services*] (GFGA)
OHRM .... Office of Human Resources Management [*Environmental Protection Agency*] (GFGA)
OHRR........ Institute for Labor Studies and Research [*West Virginia University*] (IID)
OHRR........ Open Heart Recovery Room [*Cardiology*] (DAVI)
OHRS........ Overflow Heat Removal System [*Nuclear energy*] (NRCH)
OHRU........ JJ Ohrem Spedition [*Intermodal shipping container symbol*] (TVRC)
OHRY........ Owego & Hartford Railway [*Federal Railroad Administration identification code*]
OHS.......... Hamilton Spectator, Ontario [*Library symbol*] [*National Library of Canada*] (NLC)
OHS.......... Hydroxy-Steroids (SAUS)
OHS.......... Obesity Hypoventilation Syndrome
OHS.......... Occupational Health and Safety
OHS.......... Occupational Health Services, Inc. [*Secaucus, NJ*] [*Medical databank originator*] [*Information service or system*]
OHS.......... Occupational Hearing Service
OHS.......... Oceanography & Hydrographic Ship (SAUS)
OHS.......... Octadecylhydrogensuccinate (SAUS)
OHS.......... Ocular Histoplasmosis Syndrome (SAUS)
OHS.......... Ocular Hypofusion Syndrome (MELL)
OHS.......... Off-Hook Service [*Telecommunications*] (TEL)
OHS.......... Office of Highway Safety [*of BPR*]
OHS.......... Ohio Historical Society (IID)
OHS.......... Oil Hydraulic Assembly (SAUS)
OHS.......... Ontario Historical Society (SAUS)
OHS.......... Ontario Humane Society [*Canada*] (AD)
OHS.......... Open-Health Steel (SAUS)
ohs........... Open-Hearth Steel (AD)
OHS.......... Open-Hearth Steel
OHS.......... Open Heart Surgery [*Medicine*]
OHS.......... Optometric Historical Society (EA)
OHS.......... Oral History Society [*United Kingdom*] (EAIO)
OHS.......... Oral Hygiene Service (AD)
OHS.......... Oral Hygiene Society (NADA)
OHS.......... Oregon Historical Society (SAUS)
OHS.......... Organ Historical Society (EA)
OHS.......... Organization Health Survey [*Test*]
OHS.......... Organization of Historical Studies (EA)
OHS.......... Oval-Headed Screw (DAC)
OHS.......... Ovarian Hyperstimulation Syndrome [*Medicine*] (DMAA)
OHS.......... Overland Highway Society (SAUS)

OHS.......... Oxford High School (SAUS)
OHS.......... Oxford Historical Society [*British*] (ODCC)
OHS.......... University of Oregon, Health Sciences Library, Portland, OR [*OCLC symbol*] (OCLC)
OHSA........ Occupational Health and Safety Act (SAUS)
OHSA........ Occupational Health and Safety Authority [*Victoria, Australia*]
Oh S & CP... Ohio Superior and Common Pleas Decisions [*A publication*] (DLA)
OHSB........ Occupational Health and Safety Branch (SAUS)
OHSC........ Oak Hill Sportswear Corp. [*NASDAQ symbol*] (NQ)
OHSC........ Occupational Health and Safety Commission (SAUS)
OHSCC...... Steel Company of Canada, Hamilton, Ontario [*Library symbol*] [*National Library of Canada*] (NLC)
Oh SCD..... Ohio Supreme Court Decisions, Unreported Cases [*A publication*] (DLA)
OH Screw... Oval Head Screw (SAUS)
OHSCSA..... Occupational Health and Safety Commission of South Australia
OHSD........ Hydroxysteroid Dehydrogenase [*Medicine*] (EDAA)
OHSD........ Occupational Health and Safety Division (SAUS)
OhSEA....... Ohio Society of Enrolled Agents (SAUS)
OHSGT...... Office of High-Speed Ground Transportation [*Department of Transportation*]
OHSI......... Omega Health Systems [*NASDAQ symbol*] (TTSB)
OHSI......... Omega Health Systems, Inc. [*NASDAQ symbol*] (SAG)
OHSI......... Oral Health Status Index [*Dentistry*]
OHSIP....... Ontario Health-Services Insurances Plan [*Canada*] (AD)
OHSL......... OHSL Financial Corp. [*NASDAQ symbol*] (SAG)
OHSL Fn.... OHSL Financial Corp. [*Associated Press*] (SAG)
OHS MSDS... Occupational Health Services Material Safety Data Sheets [*Database*]
OHSPAC..... Occupational Health-Safety-Programs Accreditation Commission (AD)
OHSPC...... Oil and Hazardous Substance Pollution Contingency (SAUS)
OHSRC...... Occupational Health Safety and Rehabilitation Council [*New South Wales, Australia*]
OHSS........ Occupational Health and Safety Staff [*Environmental Protection Agency*] (GFGA)
OHSS........ Occupation Health and Safety Staff (SAUS)
OHSS........ Ovarian Hyperstimulation Syndrome [*Medicine*] (DMAA)
OHST........ Occupational Health & Safety Technicians (SAUS)
OHST........ Occupational Health and Safety Technologist
Oh St........ Ohio State Reports [*A publication*] (DLA)
OHST........ Overhead Storage Tank [*Nuclear energy*] (NRCH)
OHSU........ Oregon Health Sciences University (IID)
OHT.......... Hornepayne Township Public Library, Ontario [*Library symbol*] [*National Library of Canada*] (NLC)
OHT.......... Occupational Health Technician [*Medicine*] (EDAA)
OHT.......... Ocean Heat Transport
OHT.......... Ocular Hypertensive [*Ophthalmology*]
OHT.......... Office of Housing Technology [*National Bureau of Standards*]
OHT.......... Ohio Historical Society, Columbus, OH [*OCLC symbol*] (OCLC)
OHT.......... Ohio Tank Truck Carriers Bureau, Worthington OH [*STAC*]
OHT.......... Ought [*Telegraphy*] (PCTE)
oht........... Overheating Temperature (AD)
OHT.......... Overheating Temperature (PDAA)
OHT.......... Oxygen at High Temperature (OA)
OHTA........ Office of Health Technology Assessment [*HHS*]
OHTA........ Ohta [*NCIC car make code*]
OHTA........ Organ Historical Trust of Australia
OHTA........ Ozark Heritage-Tourism Association [*Missouri*] (EARSL)
OHTB........ Ontario Highway and Transport Board (SAUS)
OHTCS...... Outer Head Temperature Control System [*Nuclear energy*] (NRCH)
OHTDC...... Ontario Hydro Tritium Dispersion Code (SAUS)
OHTE........ Ohmically-Heated Toroidal Experiment (SAUS)
OHTE........ Ohmic Heating Toroidal Experiment [*Nuclear fusion device*]
OHTEX....... Ocean Heat Transport Experiment [*Japan*] [*Marine science*] (OSRA)
OHTR........ Theological College of the Canadian Reformed Churches, Hamilton, Ontario [*Library symbol*] [*National Library of Canada*] (NLC)
O/H Transmission... Over-the-Horizon Transmission (SAUS)
OHTS........ Oil-Hardened Tool Steel
OHu.......... Hubbard Public Library, Hubbard, OH [*Library symbol*] [*Library of Congress*] (LCLS)
OHU.......... Huntsville Public Library, Ontario [*Library symbol*] [*National Library of Canada*] (NLC)
ohu........... Ohio [*MARC country of publication code*] [*Library of Congress*] (LCCP)
OHU.......... Optical Head Unit (SAUS)
OHU.......... Overseas Homeported Units [*Navy*] (NVT)
OHUM....... Muskoka Pioneer Village, Huntsville, Ontario [*Library symbol*] [*National Library of Canada*] (BIB)
OHur......... Huron Public Library, Huron, OH [*Library symbol*] [*Library of Congress*] (LCLS)
OHV.......... Oberhavel [*German license plate city code*]
OHV.......... Off-Highway Vehicle
ohv........... Overhead Valve (AD)
OHV.......... Overhead Valve
OHV.......... Overhead Valve Engine (SAUS)
OHV.......... Overhead Vent (WDAA)
OHVE........ Hanmer Branch, Valley East Public Library [*Succursale Hanmer, Bibliotheque Publique de Valley-East*], Ontario [*Library symbol*] [*National Library of Canada*] (NLC)
OHVT........ Office of Heavy Vehicle Technology [*Federal agency department*]
OHW.......... Electronic Systems Library, Westinghouse Canada Ltd., Burlington, Ontario [*Library symbol*] [*National Library of Canada*] (NLC)
OHW.......... Oak Harbor [*Washington*] [*Seismograph station code, US Geological Survey*] (SEIS)
OHW.......... Oxygen-Hydrogen Welding (SAUS)
OHW.......... Oxyhydrogen Welding
OHWL........ Wentworth Public Library, Hamilton, Ontario [*Library symbol*] [*National Library of Canada*] (NLC)
OHWM....... Office of Hazardous Waste Management (SAUS)
OHWM....... Open Heart World Mission (EA)
OHWM....... Ordinary High Water Mark (SAUS)
OHWS........ Offensive Handgun Weapon System (SAUS)
OHWS........ Overhead Wood Screw [*Technical drawings*]
OHY.......... Onur Hava Tasimacilik AWMS [*Turkey*] [*ICAO designator*] (FAAC)
OHZ.......... Osterholz [*German license plate city code*]
OI............ Ingersoll Public Library, Ontario [*Library symbol*] [*National Library of Canada*] (NLC)
OI............ Object Interface (SAUS)
OI............ Obturator Internus [*Muscle*] (MELL)
OI............ Occipito Iliacus (SAUS)
OI............ Occult Injury (MELL)
OI............ Ockenden International - England [*United Kingdom*] (EAIO)
OI............ Odyssey Institute [*Later, OIC*] (EA)
OI............ Office Information (SAUS)
OI............ Office Instruction (AFM)
OI............ Office of Information (AFM)
OI............ Office of Investigations [*Environmental Protection Agency*] (GFGA)
OI............ Ohashi Institute (EA)
oi............ Oil-Immersed (AD)
OI............ Oil-Immersed
OI............ Oil Immersion (SAUS)
OI............ Oil-Insulated
OI............ Oil Insulation (SAUS)
OI............ Old Icelandic [*Language*] (BARN)
OI............ Old Iranian [*Linguistics*] (IEL)
OI............ Omega Inertial (SAUS)
OI............ ONE, Inc. (EA)
OI............ On Instruments [*Aviation*]
OI............ Opener Inhibitor
OI............ Opening of Intestine
OI............ Open Issue (SAUS)
OI............ Operating Income [*Accounting*]
OI............ Operating Instructions
OI............ Operational Instrumentation (NASA)
OI............ Operational Intelligence
OI............ Operational Issue [*Military*]
OI............ Operation Identity (EA)
OI............ Operation Interface (SAUS)
OI............ Operations Instruction (SAUS)
OI............ Operations Intelligence (SAUS)
OI............ Operations Interface (MCD)
OI............ Operator Input
OI............ Operator Interface (ACII)
OI............ Opportunistic Illness (MELL)
OI............ Opportunistic Infection [*Medicine*]
OI............ Opportunity International-USA [*Association*] (EA)
OI............ Opsconic Index [*Laboratory science*] (DAVI)
o/i........... Opsonic Index (AD)
OI............ Opsonic Index [*Medicine*]
OI............ Optical Isolator [*Nuclear energy*] (NRCH)
O/I........... Optimal Interpolation (SAUS)
OI............ Optimist International (EA)
OI............ Optimum Interpolation [*Marine science*] (OSRA)
OI............ Opto Isolator (AAEL)
OI............ Orbiter Instrumentation [*NASA*] (NASA)
OI............ Orbit [*or Orbital*] Insertion
OI............ Ordinary Interest [*Banking*]
OI............ Organizational/Intermediate (MCD)
OI............ Organization Integration [*Military*]
o-i........... Orgasmic Impairment (AD)
OI............ Orgasmic Impairment [*Medicine*]
OI............ Oriental Institute (AD)
OI............ Orientation Inventory [*Psychology*]
OI............ Orthopedically Impaired
OI............ Osteogenesis Imperfecta [*Medicine*]
OI............ Ote Iwapo [*All That Is Must Be Considered*] [*of OI Committee International, a third-world lobby opposing systematic birth control*] [*Swahili*]
OI............ Otitis Interna [*Medicine*] (MELL)
OI............ Ours, Inc. (EA)
O-I........... Outer and Inner (DMAA)
OI............ Output Impedance
O/I........... Output/Input (SAUS)
OI............ Ovarian Insufficiency [*Medicine*] (MELL)
OI............ Overdrive Inhibit [*Automotive engineering*]
O/I........... Overseas Investment [*Economics*]
OI............ Owens-Illinois, Inc. [*NYSE symbol*] (SPSG)
OI............ Oxide Isolated (TIMI)
OI............ Oxygen Income [*or Intake*] [*Medicine*]
OI............ Oxygen Index [*Medicine*] (DAVI)
OI............ Oxygen Intact [*Medicine*] (DAVI)
OI............ Oxygen Intake (SAUS)
OIA.......... Municipal Income Opportunity Trust [*Formerly, Allstate Municipal Income Opportunities Trust*] [*NYSE symbol*] (SPSG)
OIA.......... Ocean Industries Association (AD)
OIA.......... Office Information Architecture (SAUS)
OIA.......... Office of Impact Analysis [*Environmental Protection Agency*] (BARN)
OIA.......... Office of Industrial Associates (AD)

OIA.......... Office of Inspector and Auditor [*Nuclear Regulatory Commission*] (NRCH)
OIA.......... Office of International Activities [*American Chemical Society*]
OIA.......... Office of International Administration [*Department of State*]
OIA.......... Office of International Affairs [*NASA, HUD*]
OIA.......... Official Information Act (SAUS)
OIA.......... Oil Import Administration [*Later, Office of Oil and Gas*] [*Department of the Interior*]
OIA.......... Oil Insurance Association [*Later, Industrial Risk Insurance*] (EA)
OIA.......... Oishiyama A [*Japan*] [*Seismograph station code, US Geological Survey*] (SEIS)
OIA.......... Old Indo-Aryan [*Linguistics*] (IEL)
OIA.......... Operations Intelligence Automation (SAUS)
OIA.......... Operative Ironmoulders' Association [*A union*] [*British*]
OIA.......... Operator Information Area (SAUS)
OIA.......... Optical Immunoassay [*Clinical chemistry*]
OIA.......... Optics Inertial Analyzer (SAA)
OIA.......... Orbiter Interface Adapter [*NASA*] (NASA)
OIA.......... Organizacion Internacional del Azucar [*International Sugar Organization - ISO*] (EAIO)
OIA.......... Outboard Industry Association [*Later, NMMA*] (EA)
OIAA........ Abadan/International [*Iran*] [*ICAO location identifier*] (ICLI)
OIAA........ Office of Inter-American Affairs [*Later, BIAA*]
OIAA........ Office of International Aviation Affairs [*FAA*]
OIA & TU... Office of Industry Affairs and Technology Utilization [*NASA*]
OIAB........ Boostan [*Iran*] [*ICAO location identifier*] (ICLI)
OIAB........ Oil Import Appeals Board (AD)
OIAC........ Organizacion Internacional de la Aviacion Civil [*International Civil AviationOrganization*] [*Spanish*] (AD)
OIAD........ Dezful [*Iran*] [*ICAO location identifier*] (ICLI)
OIADA...... Oregon Independent Automobile Dealers Association (EARSL)
OIAF........ Office of Information for the Armed Forces (DNAB)
OIAG........ Aghajari [*Iran*] [*ICAO location identifier*] (ICLI)
OIAH........ Gachsaran [*Iran*] [*ICAO location identifier*] (ICLI)
OIAI........ Masjed Soleiman [*Iran*] [*ICAO location identifier*] (ICLI)
OIAI........ OIA, Inc. (SAUS)
OIAJ........ Office for Improvements in the Administration of Justice (AD)
OIAJ........ Omidyeh [*Iran*] [*ICAO location identifier*] (ICLI)
OIAK........ Haft-Gel [*Iran*] [*ICAO location identifier*] (ICLI)
OIAL........ Lali [*Iran*] [*ICAO location identifier*] (ICLI)
OIAM........ Bandar Mahshahr [*Iran*] [*ICAO location identifier*] (ICLI)
OIAN........ Andimeshk [*Iran*] [*ICAO location identifier*] (ICLI)
OI & C...... Office of Investigation and Compliance [*Employment and Training Administration*] [*Department of Labor*]
OI & I....... Office of Invention and Innovation [*Disbanded*] [*National Institute of Standards and Technology*]
OIAO........ Ogaden Islamic Alliance Organization (SAUS)
OIAS........ Observer Impression Assessment Scale
OIAS........ Occupational Information Access System (WDAA)
OIAT........ Abadan [*Iran*] [*ICAO location identifier*] (ICLI)
OIAT........ Osteopathic Institute of Applied Technique (SAUS)
OIATU...... Office of Industry Affairs and Technology Utilization [*NASA*]
OIAW........ Ahwaz [*Iran*] [*ICAO location identifier*] (ICLI)
OIB.......... Briggs-Lawrence County Public Library, Ironton, OH [*Library symbol*] [*Library of Congress*] (LCLS)
OIB.......... Iron Bridge Public Library, Ontario [*Library symbol*] [*National Library of Canada*] (NLC)
OIB.......... Municipal Income Opportunity Trust [*Formerly, Allstate Municipal Income Opportunities Trust*] [*NYSE symbol*] (SPSG)
OIB.......... Oceanic Island Basalt [*Geology*]
OIB.......... Official Information Base
OIB.......... Ohio Inspection Bureau (AD)
OIB.......... Oishiyama B [*Japan*] [*Seismograph station code, US Geological Survey*] (SEIS)
OIB.......... Oklahoma Inspection Bureau (AD)
OIB.......... Oligoclonal Immunoglobulin Bands [*Clinical chemistry*]
OIB.......... Olympic Installations Board
OIB.......... Operating Impedance Bridge (IAA)
OIB.......... Operation Instruction Block (NITA)
OIB.......... Operation Instruction Book (SAUS)
OIB.......... Operations Integration Branch [*NASA*] (KSC)
OIB.......... Operations Intelligence Branch (SAUS)
OIB.......... Orbiter Interface Box [*NASA*] (NASA)
OIB.......... Ortho-Iodobenzoic (Acid) [*Biochemistry*]
OIBA........ Abumusa Island [*Iran*] [*ICAO location identifier*] (ICLI)
OIBA........ Office of Industrial Base Assessment (DOMA)
OIBB........ Bushehr/Bushehr [*Iran*] [*ICAO location identifier*] (ICLI)
OIBD........ Bandar Deylam [*Iran*] [*ICAO location identifier*] (ICLI)
OIBF........ Forouz Island [*Iran*] [*ICAO location identifier*] (ICLI)
OIBG........ Ganaveh [*Iran*] [*ICAO location identifier*] (ICLI)
OIBH........ Bastak [*Iran*] [*ICAO location identifier*] (ICLI)
OIBI........ Golbandi [*Iran*] [*ICAO location identifier*] (ICLI)
OIBK........ Kish Island [*Iran*] [*ICAO location identifier*] (ICLI)
OIBL........ Bandar Lengeh [*Iran*] [*ICAO location identifier*] (ICLI)
OIBN........ Borazjan [*Iran*] [*ICAO location identifier*] (ICLI)
OIBQ........ Khark Island [*Iran*] [*ICAO location identifier*] (ICLI)
OIBS........ Siri Island [*Iran*] [*ICAO location identifier*] (ICLI)
OIBT........ Bushehr [*Iran*] [*ICAO location identifier*] (ICLI)
OIBV........ Lavan Island [*Iran*] [*ICAO location identifier*] (ICLI)
OIBX........ Tonb Island [*Iran*] [*ICAO location identifier*] (ICLI)
OIC.......... Municipal Income Opportunity Trust [*Formerly, Allstate Municipal Income Opportunities Trust*] [*NYSE symbol*] (SPSG)
OIC.......... Norwich, NY [*Location identifier*] [*FAA*] (FAAL)
OIC.......... Objective Individual Combat Weapon
OIC.......... Ocean Information Center (SAUS)
OIC.......... Oceanographic Instrumentation Center [*Navy*]
OIC.......... Oceans Institute of Canada (IRC)
OIC.......... Octyl Isocyanate [*Organic chemistry*]
OIC.......... Odyssey Institute Corp. (EA)
OIC.......... Offer in Compromise [*IRS*]
OIC.......... Office of Independent Counsel [*U.S. Department of Justice*] (BARN)
OIC.......... Office of Industrial Cooperation [*AEC*]
OIC.......... Office of International Conferences [*Department of State*]
OIC.......... Office of International Cooperation [*in CAA*]
OIC.......... Office of the Independent Counsel (SAUS)
OIC.......... Office of the Insurance Commissioner (AD)
Oic.......... Officer-in-Charge (WDAA)
OIC.......... Officer-in-Charge
OIC.......... Ohio Improved Chesters [*Initialism itself now used as name of breed of swine*]
OIC.......... Oh, I See [*Online dialogue*] (IGQR)
OIC.......... Oil Cooler (SAUS)
OIC.......... Oil Industry Commission (AD)
OIC.......... Oil Information Committee (SAUS)
OIC.......... Oil-Insulated Cable (SAUS)
OIC.......... Oishiyama C [*Japan*] [*Seismograph station code, US Geological Survey*] (SEIS)
OIC.......... Okinawa Interboard Committee [*Absorbed by Interboard Committee for Christian Work in Japan*] (EA)
OIC.......... Oklahoma Intercollegiate Conference (PSS)
OIC.......... On-line Instrument and Control (SAUS)
OIC.......... Online Instrument and Control Program [*Computer science*] (NRCH)
OIC.......... On-line Instrumentation Coordinator (SAUS)
OIC.......... Only-in-Chain (ELAL)
OIC.......... Ontario International Corporation (SAUS)
OIC.......... Operational Intelligence Centre [*British military*] (DMA)
OIC.......... Operations Instrumentation Coordinator [*NASA*] (KSC)
OIC.......... Operator's Instruction Chart
OIC.......... Opportunities Industrialization Center (OICC)
OIC.......... Optical Integrated Circuit (IEEE)
OIC.......... Optimized Image Compression (PCM)
oic.......... Orbiter Integrated Checkout [*NASA*] (NAKS)
OIC.......... Orbiter Integrated Checkout [*NASA*] (NASA)
O-I-C........ Order-in-Council [*Canada*]
OIC.......... Order of the Imitation of Christ (TOCD)
oic.......... Order of the Imitation of Christ (TOCD)
O-I-C........ Organisation Interafricaine du Cafe [*Inter-African Coffee Organization*] [*French*] (AD)
OIC.......... Organisation Internationale Catholique
OIC.......... Organisation Internationale du Commerce [*International Organization for Commerce*] [*France*]
OIC.......... Organization for International Cooperation (EA)
OIC.......... Organization of Islamic Countries [*Intergovernmental group*]
OIC.......... Organization of the Islamic Conference [*See also OCI*] [*Jeddah, Saudi Arabia*] (EAIO)
OIC.......... Oriental Institute Communications [*A publication*] (ABAR)
OIC.......... Overseas Investment Commission (AD)
OICA........ Azna [*Iran*] [*ICAO location identifier*] (ICLI)
OICA........ Ontario Institute of Chartered Accountants [*Canada*] (DD)
OICA........ OPLAN Implementation Capabilities Report (SAUS)
OIC/A........ Opportunities Industrialization Centers of America (EA)
OICA........ Oregon Independent Colleges Association (SAUS)
OICA........ Organisation Internationale des Constructeurs d'Automobiles (EAIO)
OICAP...... Ocean Industries Capital Assistance Program (SAUS)
OICB........ Baneh [*Iran*] [*ICAO location identifier*] (ICLI)
OICC........ Bakhtaran [*Iran*] [*ICAO location identifier*] (ICLI)
OICC........ Officer-in-Charge of Construction [*Navy*]
OICC........ Ontario Institute of Chartered Cartographers (SAUS)
OICC........ Operational Intelligence Coordination Center (COE)
OICC........ Operational Intelligence Crisis Center [*Defense Intelligence Agency*] (DOMA)
OICC........ Operations Interface Control Chart (KSC)
OICC........ Organization of Islamic Capitals and Cities (EA)
OICCD...... Oblique Imaging Charged Couple Device (ACAE)
OICCFE..... Officer-in-Charge of Construction, Far East [*Navy*]
OICCSOWESPAC... Officer-in-Charge of Construction, South Western Pacific (DNAB)
OICCSW..... Objective Individual Combat & Crew Served Weapon (SAUS)
OICD........ Abdanan [*Iran*] [*ICAO location identifier*] (ICLI)
OICD........ Office of International Cooperation and Development [*Department of Agriculture*]
OICD........ On-Board Information Compression Device [*Aerospace*]
OICE........ Bijar [*Iran*] [*ICAO location identifier*] (ICLI)
O ICE........ Old Icelandic [*Language, etc.*] (ROG)
OIcel........ Old Icelandic [*Language*] (BARN)
OICETS...... Optical Inter-Orbit Communications Engineering Test Satellite [*Sponsored by European Space Agency and Japan Space Agency*]
OICF........ Naft-E-Shah [*Iran*] [*ICAO location identifier*] (ICLI)
OICF........ Oklahoma Independent College Foundation (AD)
OICF........ Oregon Independent College Foundation (AD)
OICG........ Ghasre-Shirin [*Iran*] [*ICAO location identifier*] (ICLI)
OICH........ Islam Abad [*Iran*] [*ICAO location identifier*] (ICLI)
OICI........ Ilam [*Iran*] [*ICAO location identifier*] (ICLI)
OICI........ Oficina Internacional Catolica de la Infancia [*International Catholic Child Bureau*]
OICI........ Opportunities Industrialization Centers International [*Association*] (EA)
OICI........ Organizacion Ibero-Americana de Cooperacion Intermunicipal [*Ibero-American Municipal Organization*] (EAIO)

OICI.......... Organizacion Interamericana de Cooperacion [*Inter-American Cooperation Organ ization*] [*Spanish*] (AD)
OICI.......... Organizacion Interamericana de Cooperacion Intermunicipal [*Inter-american Municipal Organization*]
OICJ......... Boroujerd [*Iran*] [*ICAO location identifier*] (ICLI)
OICJ......... Office of International Criminal Justice (AD)
OICK......... Khorram Abad [*Iran*] [*ICAO location identifier*] (ICLI)
OICL......... Sare Pole Zahab [*Iran*] [*ICAO location identifier*] (ICLI)
OICM........ Mehran [*Iran*] [*ICAO location identifier*] (ICLI)
OICM........ Organisation Internationale pour la Cooperation Medicale [*International Organization for Medical Cooperation*]
OICMA....... Organisation Internationale Contre le Criquet Migrateur Africain [*International African Migratory Locust Organization*] (EAIO)
OICMATU... Officer-in-Charge, Marine Air Traffic Control Unit (DNAB)
OICMILDEPT... Officer-in-Charge, Military Department (DNAB)
OICNA....... Overseas Indian Congress of North America [*Defunct*] (EA)
OICO......... Office of Integration and Checkout
OICO......... OI Corp. [*NASDAQ symbol*] (NQ)
OICO......... OI Corporation (SAUS)
OICO......... Songhor [*Iran*] [*ICAO location identifier*] (ICLI)
OI Corp...... OI Corp. [*Associated Press*] (SAG)
OICP......... Office of International Communications Policy (NITA)
OICP......... Paveh [*Iran*] [*ICAO location identifier*] (ICLI)
OICQ......... Takab [*Iran*] [*ICAO location identifier*] (ICLI)
OICR......... Dehloran [*Iran*] [*ICAO location identifier*] (ICLI)
OICR......... Office of International Commercial Relations [*Department of State*]
OICR......... Ontario Institute for Computer Research (SAUS)
OICR......... Operational Intelligence Collection Requirement (SAUS)
OICR......... Operation, Implementation, Capabilities Report (SAUS)
OICS......... Office of Interoceanic Canal Studies [*National Oceanic and Atmospheric Administration*] (NOAA)
OICS......... Operational Intelligence Collection System
OICS......... Organe International de Controle des Stupefiants [*International Narcotics Control Board*] (EAIO)
OICS......... Sanandaj [*Iran*] [*ICAO location identifier*] (ICLI)
OICT......... Bakhtaran [*Iran*] [*ICAO location identifier*] (ICLI)
OICTP........ Outline Individual and Collective Training Plan [*Army*]
OICW........ Objective Individual Combat Weapon [*Army*] (INF)
OICW........ Opportunities Industrial Center West (SAUS)
OICY......... Malavi [*Iran*] [*ICAO location identifier*] (ICLI)
OICZ......... Aligoodarz [*Iran*] [*ICAO location identifier*] (ICLI)
OID.......... Object Identification (AAEL)
OID.......... Object Identifier [*Computer science*]
OID.......... Object Interaction Diagram (AAEL)
OID.......... Octal Identifier [*Computer science*] (KSC)
OID.......... Ofensiva de Izquierda Democratica [*Offensive of the Democratic Left*] [*Bolivia*] (PPW)
OID.......... Operator Instruction Document (TIMI)
OID.......... Optoelectronic Imaging Device
OID.......... Order Initiated Distribution
OID.......... Organism Identification Number [*Microbiology*] (DAVI)
oid........... Original Issue Discount (AD)
OID.......... Original Issue Discount [*Business term*]
OID.......... Original Issue Discount Obligations (TDOB)
OID.......... Outline and Installation Drawing
OID.......... Ovine Interdigital Dermatitis (SAUS)
OIDA......... Optoelectronics Industry Development Association (SAUS)
OIDA......... Ordnance Industrial Data Agency
OIDA......... Original Image Data Array (SAUS)
OIDC......... Object Identifier Component (SAUS)
OIDC......... Oil Importing and Developing Country
OIDC......... Ontario Industrial Development Council (SAUS)
OIDI.......... Optically Isolated Digital Input
OI DIV....... Operations/Combat Information Center Division (DNAB)
OIDL......... Object Interface Definition Language [*Computer science*]
OIDMM...... Office Internationale de Documentation de Medecine Militaire [*International Office of Documentation on Military Medicine - IO-DMM*] (EAIO)
OIDO......... Ocean Industries Development Office (SAUS)
OIDO......... Original Issue Discount Obligations (EBF)
OIDP......... Oracle Internet Development Pack (SAUS)
OIDP......... Oversea Internal Defense Policy [*Army*] (AABC)
OIDPS....... Oversea Intelligence Data Processing System
OIDT......... Operator Interactive Display Terminal (SAUS)
OIDZ......... Oil-Dri [*Federal Railroad Administration identification code*]
OIE........... Central Library, Albright & Wilson Americas, Islington, Ontario [*Library symbol*] [*National Library of Canada*] (NLC)
OIE........... Office International des Epizooties [*International Office of Epizootics*] [*Research center*] [*France*] (IRC)
OIE........... Office of Indian Education [*Department of Education*] (GFGA)
OIE........... Office of Inspection and Enforcement [*Nuclear Regulatory Commission*]
OIE........... Office of International Epizootics (AD)
O/I/E......... Offsites/Infrastructure/Establishment [*Engineering*]
OIE........... Operational Independent Evaluator
OIE........... Optical Incremental Encoder
OIE........... Optical Infrared Equipment
OIE........... Organisation Internationale des Employeurs [*International Organization of Employers*]
OIE........... Overseas Investment Exchange (NUMA)
OIEA......... Office of Integrated Environmental Analysis (SAUS)
OIEA......... Organismo Internacional de Energia Atomica [*International Atomic Energy Agency*] [*Spanish*] [*United Nations*] (DUND)
OIEC......... Office International de l'Enseignement Catholique [*Catholic International Education Office - CIEO*] (EAIO)
OIEO......... Ocean Instrumentation Engineering Office [*National Oceanic and Atmospheric Administration*] (MSC)
OIEO......... Offers in Excess of (ODA)
OIER......... Office of International Economic Research (AD)
OIER......... Official Intermodal Equipment Register [*Intermodal Publishing Co.*] [*Information service or system*] (IID)
OIER......... Operational Information Exchange Requirement (SAUS)
OIES......... Office of Interdisciplinary Earth Studies (SAUS)
OIES......... Oxford Institute for Energy Studies [*British*]
OIESA....... Office of International Economic and Social Affairs [*Department of State*]
OIF........... American Opportunity Income [*NYSE symbol*] (SPSG)
OIF........... Amer Opportunity Income [*NYSE symbol*] (TTSB)
OIF........... Iroquois Falls Public Library, Ontario [*Library symbol*] [*National Library of Canada*] (NLC)
OIF........... Observed Intrinsic Frequency [*Medicine*] (DMAA)
OIF........... Office for Intellectual Freedom [*American Library Association*]
OIF........... Office Interconnect Facility [*Computer science*] (BTTJ)
OIF........... Office of International Finance [*Department of the Treasury*]
OIF........... Oil Immersion Field (MAE)
OIF........... Optical Internetworking Forum [*Association*] (EA)
OIF........... Optimum Index Factor (SAUS)
OIF........... Option Institute and Fellowship (EA)
OIF........... Osteogenesis Imperfecta Foundation (EA)
OIF........... Osteoinductive Factor [*Biochemistry*]
OIF........... Other Intelligence File (MCD)
OIFB......... Boroujen [*Iran*] [*ICAO location identifier*] (ICLI)
OIFC......... Ghamsar [*Iran*] [*ICAO location identifier*] (ICLI)
OIFC......... Oil-Insulated, Fan-Cooled
OIFC......... Osmonds International Fan Club (EA)
OIFD......... Ardestan [*Iran*] [*ICAO location identifier*] (ICLI)
OIFE......... Outside-In Flow Element [*Automotive engineering*]
OIFF......... Soffeh [*Iran*] [*ICAO location identifier*] (ICLI)
OIFG......... Golpaygan [*Iran*] [*ICAO location identifier*] (ICLI)
OIFH......... Esfahan [*Iran*] [*ICAO location identifier*] (ICLI)
OIFI.......... Semirom [*Iran*] [*ICAO location identifier*] (ICLI)
OIFIG........ Official Irish FORTH [*Programming language*] Interest Group (EAIO)
OIFJ......... Najaf Abad [*Iran*] [*ICAO location identifier*] (ICLI)
OIFK......... Kashan [*Iran*] [*ICAO location identifier*] (ICLI)
OIFL......... Felavarjan [*Iran*] [*ICAO location identifier*] (ICLI)
OIFM......... Esfahan [*Iran*] [*ICAO location identifier*] (ICLI)
OIFN......... Naein [*Iran*] [*ICAO location identifier*] (ICLI)
OIFO......... Khomeini Shahr [*Iran*] [*ICAO location identifier*] (ICLI)
OIFOC....... Oil-Immersed, Forced-Oil-Cooled (SAUS)
OIFR......... Ghomsheh [*Iran*] [*ICAO location identifier*] (ICLI)
OIFS......... Shahrekord [*Iran*] [*ICAO location identifier*] (ICLI)
OIFT......... Esfahan [*Iran*] [*ICAO location identifier*] (ICLI)
OIFU......... Fereidan [*Iran*] [*ICAO location identifier*] (ICLI)
OIFW........ Khomein [*Iran*] [*ICAO location identifier*] (ICLI)
OIFY......... Meymeh [*Iran*] [*ICAO location identifier*] (ICLI)
OIFZ......... Natanz [*Iran*] [*ICAO location identifier*] (ICLI)
OIG.......... Ignace Public Library, Ontario [*Library symbol*] [*National Library of Canada*] (NLC)
OIG.......... Office of the Inspector General [*Army*]
OIG.......... Operations Interface Group (SAUS)
OIG.......... Optically Isolated Gate (IEEE)
OIG.......... Organisation Intergouvernementale [*Inter-Governmental Organization*] [*French*] (AD)
OIGA......... Astara [*Iran*] [*ICAO location identifier*] (ICLI)
OIGF......... Fouman [*Iran*] [*ICAO location identifier*] (ICLI)
OIGG......... Rasht [*Iran*] [*ICAO location identifier*] (ICLI)
OIGH......... Hashtpar [*Iran*] [*ICAO location identifier*] (ICLI)
OIGIS........ Office of the Inspector-General of Intelligence and Security [*Australia*]
OIGK......... Khailkhal [*Iran*] [*ICAO location identifier*] (ICLI)
OIGL......... Langerood [*Iran*] [*ICAO location identifier*] (ICLI)
OIGM......... Manjil [*Iran*] [*ICAO location identifier*] (ICLI)
OIGN......... Lahijan [*Iran*] [*ICAO location identifier*] (ICLI)
OIGP......... Bandar Anzali [*Iran*] [*ICAO location identifier*] (ICLI)
OIGR......... Office of Industrial Growth and Research [*of BDSA*]
OIGR......... Office of Intergovernmental Relations [*US Congress*] [*Washington, DC*] (GRD)
OIGR......... Roodsar [*Iran*] [*ICAO location identifier*] (ICLI)
OIGS......... On Indian Government Service (SAUS)
OIGT......... Rasht [*Iran*] [*ICAO location identifier*] (ICLI)
OIGU......... Roodbar [*Iran*] [*ICAO location identifier*] (ICLI)
OIH.......... Oceanic Institute of Hawaii
OIH.......... Oceanographic Institute of Hawaii (SAUS)
OIH.......... Office of International Health [*Department of Health and Human Services*]
OIH.......... Oil in Hole (SAUS)
OIH.......... Ortho-Iodohippurate [*Clinical chemistry*] (AAMN)
OIH.......... Ovulation-Inducing Hormone [*Endocrinology*]
OIH.......... Ovulation-Producing Hormone [*Medicine*] (AD)
OIHA......... Orthoiodohippuric Acid [*Clinical chemistry*] (DAVI)
OIHA......... Takestan [*Iran*] [*ICAO location identifier*] (ICLI)
OIHB......... Asad Abad [*Iran*] [*ICAO location identifier*] (ICLI)
OIHD......... Shahzand [*Iran*] [*ICAO location identifier*] (ICLI)
OIHF......... Tafresh [*Iran*] [*ICAO location identifier*] (ICLI)
OIHG......... Kharaghan [*Iran*] [*ICAO location identifier*] (ICLI)
OIHH......... Hamadan [*Iran*] [*ICAO location identifier*] (ICLI)
OIHJ......... Avaj [*Iran*] [*ICAO location identifier*] (ICLI)
OIHM......... Malayer [*Iran*] [*ICAO location identifier*] (ICLI)
OIHN......... Nahavand [*Iran*] [*ICAO location identifier*] (ICLI)
OIHP......... Office International d'Hygiene Publique [*United Nations*]

OIHQ......... Kangavar [*Iran*] [*ICAO location identifier*] (ICLI)
OIHR......... Arak [*Iran*] [*ICAO location identifier*] (ICLI)
OIHS......... Hamadan [*Iran*] [*ICAO location identifier*] (ICLI)
OIHT......... Hamadan [*Iran*] [*ICAO location identifier*] (ICLI)
OIHU......... Tooyserkan [*Iran*] [*ICAO location identifier*] (ICLI)
OII........... Occupational Injury/Illness (SAUS)
OII........... Oceaneering International, Inc. [*NYSE symbol*] (SPSG)
OII........... Office of International Investment [*Department of Commerce*]
OII........... Office of Invention and Innovation (AD)
OII........... Oil Investment Institute [*Washington, DC*] (EA)
OII........... Open Information Interchange (SAUS)
OII........... Operations Integration Instruction [*NASA*] (NASA)
OII........... Operations-Intelligence Interface (SAUS)
OII........... Optical Imaging Instrument (SAUS)
OII........... Ourobourus Institute (EA)
OII........... Oxford Internet Institute
OIIA.......... Abe-Ali [*Iran*] [*ICAO location identifier*] (ICLI)
OIIC.......... Kushke Nosrat [*Iran*] [*ICAO location identifier*] (ICLI)
OIIC.......... Oil Industry Industrial Committee [*Australia*]
OIIC.......... Oil Industry Information Committee (SAUS)
OIID.......... Tehran/Doshan Tappeh [*Iran*] [*ICAO location identifier*] (ICLI)
OIIE.......... Abyek [*Iran*] [*ICAO location identifier*] (ICLI)
OIIF.......... Firouzkouh [*Iran*] [*ICAO location identifier*] (ICLI)
OIIFDRES... Oficina Internacional de Informacion del Frente Democratico Revolucionario de ElSalvador [*International Information Office of the Democratic Revolutionary Front of El Salvador - IIODRFES*] [*San Jose, Costa Rica*] (EAIO)
OIIG.......... Tehran/Ghaleh Morghi [*Iran*] [*ICAO location identifier*] (ICLI)
OIIH.......... Mahallat [*Iran*] [*ICAO location identifier*] (ICLI)
OIII.......... Tehran/Mehrabad International [*Iran*] [*ICAO location identifier*] (ICLI)
OIIJ.......... Karaj [*Iran*] [*ICAO location identifier*] (ICLI)
OIIK.......... Ghazvin [*Iran*] [*ICAO location identifier*] (ICLI)
OIIM.......... Khoram Dareh [*Iran*] [*ICAO location identifier*] (ICLI)
OIIM.......... Overseas Issues Identification Meeting (DNAB)
OIIN.......... Delijan [*Iran*] [*ICAO location identifier*] (ICLI)
OIIQ.......... Ghom [*Iran*] [*ICAO location identifier*] (ICLI)
OIIR.......... Garmsar [*Iran*] [*ICAO location identifier*] (ICLI)
OIIS.......... Semnan [*Iran*] [*ICAO location identifier*] (ICLI)
OIIT.......... Tehran [*Iran*] [*ICAO location identifier*] (ICLI)
OIIU.......... Damghan [*Iran*] [*ICAO location identifier*] (ICLI)
OIIV.......... Seveh [*Iran*] [*ICAO location identifier*] (ICLI)
OIIW.......... Varamin [*Iran*] [*ICAO location identifier*] (ICLI)
OIIX.......... Tehran [*Iran*] [*ICAO location identifier*] (ICLI)
OIJ........... Octarius Duos [*Two Pints*] [*Pharmacy*] (ROG)
OIJ........... Organisation Internationale des Journalistes [*International Organization of Journalists - IOJ*] (EAIO)
OIJSS........ Octarios Duobus cum Semisse [*Two and a Half Pints*] [*Pharmacy*] (ROG)
OIK........... Ocean City, MD [*Location identifier*] [*FAA*] (FAAL)
OIKA......... Shahre Babak [*Iran*] [*ICAO location identifier*] (ICLI)
OIKB......... Bandar Abbas [*Iran*] [*ICAO location identifier*] (ICLI)
OIKD......... Darband/Ravar [*Iran*] [*ICAO location identifier*] (ICLI)
OIKE......... Anar [*Iran*] [*ICAO location identifier*] (ICLI)
OIKF......... Baft [*Iran*] [*ICAO location identifier*] (ICLI)
OIKI......... Bandar Khamir [*Iran*] [*ICAO location identifier*] (ICLI)
OIKJ......... Jiroft [*Iran*] [*ICAO location identifier*] (ICLI)
OIKK......... Kerman [*Iran*] [*ICAO location identifier*] (ICLI)
OIKM......... Bam [*Iran*] [*ICAO location identifier*] (ICLI)
OIKN......... Narmashir [*Iran*] [*ICAO location identifier*] (ICLI)
OIKO......... Minab [*Iran*] [*ICAO location identifier*] (ICLI)
OIKQ......... Gheshm Island [*Iran*] [*ICAO location identifier*] (ICLI)
OIKR......... Rafsanjan [*Iran*] [*ICAO location identifier*] (ICLI)
OIKS......... Shahdad [*Iran*] [*ICAO location identifier*] (ICLI)
OIKT......... Kerman [*Iran*] [*ICAO location identifier*] (ICLI)
OIKU......... Hengam Island [*Iran*] [*ICAO location identifier*] (ICLI)
OIKW......... Kahnooj [*Iran*] [*ICAO location identifier*] (ICLI)
OIKX......... Hormoz Island [*Iran*] [*ICAO location identifier*] (ICLI)
OIKY......... Sirjan [*Iran*] [*ICAO location identifier*] (ICLI)
OIKZ......... Zarand [*Iran*] [*ICAO location identifier*] (ICLI)
OIL........... Ocelot Industries Ltd. [*Toronto Stock Exchange symbol*]
OIL........... Office of Intergovernmental Liaison [*Environmental Protection Agency*] (GFGA)
OIL........... Oil City, PA [*Location identifier*] [*FAA*] (FAAL)
OIL........... Oklahoma Information Lines [*Oklahoma State Department of Libraries*] [*Oklahoma City*] [*Information service or system*] (IID)
OIL........... Only Input Line (MHDI)
OIL........... Open Individual License (SAUS)
OIL........... Operation Inspection Log (AAG)
OIL........... Operator Identification Language (SAUS)
OIL........... Orange Indicating Lamp (SAUS)
OIL........... Orange Indicating Light (MSA)
OIL........... Orbital International Laboratory
OIL........... Ordnance Investigation Laboratory
OIL........... Outside Independent Laboratory (SAUS)
OIL........... Triton Energy Corp. [*NYSE symbol*] (SPSG)
OILA......... Office of International Labor Affairs [*Department of Labor*]
Oil & Gas... Oil and Gas Reporter [*A publication*] (DLA)
Oil & Gas LR... Oil and Gas Law Review [*A publication*] (DLA)
Oil & Gas Reptr... Oil and Gas Reporter [*A publication*] (DLA)
Oil & Gas Rptr... Oil and Gas Reporter [*A publication*] (DLA)
OILB......... Organisation Internationale de Lutte Biologique Contre les Animaux et les Plantes Nuisibles [*International Organization for Biological Control of Noxious Animals and Plants - IOBC*] (EAIO)
OILC......... Oil-Dri Corporation of America (SAUS)
Oil Colour Chemist Assoc J... Oil and Colour Chemists Association. Journal (SAUS)
OILCOM..... Oil Company of Malawi (SAUS)
OILD......... Occupational Immunologic Lung Disease (MELL)
OILD......... Occupationally Induced Lung Disease
OilDri........ Oil-Dri Corp. of America [*Associated Press*] (SAG)
OILF......... Oromo Islamic Liberation Front (SAUS)
Oil Gas Compact Bull... Interstate Oil and Gas Compact Commission. Committee Bulletin (journ.) (SAUS)
Oil Gas Petrochem Equip... Oil, Gas and Petrochem Equipment (SAUS)
Oilgear...... [*The*] Oilgear Co. [*Associated Press*] (SAG)
OILHM....... Oil and Hazardous Material Information System (SAUS)
Oilman Wkly Newsl... Oilman Weekly Newsletter (SAUS)
OILN......... Oil International Ltd. (SAUS)
oiloff......... Oil Ripoff (AD)
Oil Paint Drug Rep... Oil, Paint and Drug Reporter (SAUS)
OILPOL...... Convention for the Prevention of Pollution of the Sea by Oil (SAUS)
OILPOL...... Convention for the Provention of Pollution of the Sea by Oil (SAUS)
OILPOL...... International Convention for the Prevention of Pollution of the Sea by Oil (SAUS)
OILREC...... Oil Recovery (RIMS)
OILS......... Oil Securities, Inc. (SAUS)
OILSAR...... Ocean-Ice-Land Synthetic Aperture Radar (SAUS)
OILSR....... Office of Interstate Land Sales Registration (AD)
OILT.......... Oiltight (SAUS)
OIL TURP... Oil of Turpentine (SAUS)
OIM.......... Office of Industrial Managers [*Navy*]
OIM.......... Office of Industrial Mobilization [*of BDSA*]
OIM.......... Office of Intergovernmental Management (OICC)
OIM.......... Offshore-Installation Manager [*Oil well drilling*]
OIM.......... On Its Merits [*British*] (ROG)
OIM.......... Open Information Model (VLIE)
OIM.......... Open systems interconnections Internet Management (SAUS)
OIM.......... Optical Index Modulation (VLIE)
OIM.......... Orbit Insertion Maneuver
OIM.......... Organic Insulating Material
OIM.......... Organizational Intermediate Maintenance [*Military*] (AFIT)
OIM.......... Oriental Institute Museum [*University of Chicago*] (AD)
OIM.......... Orientational Imaging Microscopy (AAEL)
OIM.......... Oshima Island [*Japan*] [*Airport symbol*] (OAG)
OIMA........ Torbat-E-Jam [*Iran*] [*ICAO location identifier*] (ICLI)
OIMB........ Birjand [*Iran*] [*ICAO location identifier*] (ICLI)
OIMC........ Office of Information Services (AAGC)
OIMC........ Sarakhs [*Iran*] [*ICAO location identifier*] (ICLI)
OIMD........ Goonabad [*Iran*] [*ICAO location identifier*] (ICLI)
OIME........ Esfarayen [*Iran*] [*ICAO location identifier*] (ICLI)
OIMF........ Ferdous [*Iran*] [*ICAO location identifier*] (ICLI)
OIMG........ Ghaen [*Iran*] [*ICAO location identifier*] (ICLI)
OIMH........ Torbat-E-Heidarieh [*Iran*] [*ICAO location identifier*] (ICLI)
OIMJ........ Emam Shahr [*Iran*] [*ICAO location identifier*] (ICLI)
OIMK........ Nehbandan [*Iran*] [*ICAO location identifier*] (ICLI)
OIML........ Janat Abad [*Iran*] [*ICAO location identifier*] (ICLI)
OIML........ Organisation Internationale de Metrologie Legale [*International Organization of Legal Metrology*] (EAIO)
OIMM........ Mashhad [*Iran*] [*ICAO location identifier*] (ICLI)
OIMN........ Bojnord [*Iran*] [*ICAO location identifier*] (ICLI)
OIMO........ Ghoochan [*Iran*] [*ICAO location identifier*] (ICLI)
OIMP........ Taybad [*Iran*] [*ICAO location identifier*] (ICLI)
OIMQ........ Kashmar [*Iran*] [*ICAO location identifier*] (ICLI)
OIMR........ Fariman [*Iran*] [*ICAO location identifier*] (ICLI)
OIMS........ Orbiter Ion Mass Spectrometer [*NASA*]
OIMS........ Oscillator Instability Measurement System
OIMS........ Sabzevar [*Iran*] [*ICAO location identifier*] (ICLI)
OIMSJ....... Micropower/St. Joseph's High School, Islington, Ontario [*Library symbol*] [*National Library of Canada*] (NLC)
OIMT........ Tabas [*Iran*] [*ICAO location identifier*] (ICLI)
OIMV........ Mashhad [*Iran*] [*ICAO location identifier*] (ICLI)
OIMW........ Shirvan [*Iran*] [*ICAO location identifier*] (ICLI)
OIMX........ Shahr Abad [*Iran*] [*ICAO location identifier*] (ICLI)
OIMY........ Neishaboor [*Iran*] [*ICAO location identifier*] (ICLI)
OIMYFC..... Official International Michael York Fan Club (EA)
OIN.......... Oberlin, KS [*Location identifier*] [*FAA*] (FAAL)
OI-N......... Office of Information, Navy
OIN.......... Ointment (SAUS)
OIN.......... Organisation Internationale de Normalisation [*International Organization for Standardization*]
OIN.......... Organization of International Numismatists
OIN.......... Osrodek Informacji Naukowej [*Scientific Information Center*] [*Polish Academy of Sciences*] [*Warsaw*] [*Information service or system*] (IID)
OINA......... Amol [*Iran*] [*ICAO location identifier*] (ICLI)
OINA......... Oyster Institute of North America [*Later, SINA*] (EA)
OINB......... Babolsar [*Iran*] [*ICAO location identifier*] (ICLI)
OINC......... Chalous [*Iran*] [*ICAO location identifier*] (ICLI)
O in C....... Officer-in-Charge
OINC......... Officer-in-Charge [*Navy*]
OINCABCCTC... Officer-in-Charge, Advanced Base Combat Communication Training Center [*Pearl Harbor*] [*Navy*]
OIND......... Minoo Dasht [*Iran*] [*ICAO location identifier*] (ICLI)
OINE......... Kalaleh [*Iran*] [*ICAO location identifier*] (ICLI)
OInF......... Ferro Corp., Independence, OH [*Library symbol*] [*Library of Congress*] (LCLS)
OING......... Gorgan [*Iran*] [*ICAO location identifier*] (ICLI)

OING......... Organisation Internationale Non-Gouvernementale [*Non-Governmental International Organization*] [*French*] (AD)
OINH......... Behshahr [*Iran*] [*ICAO location identifier*] (ICLI)
OINI......... Ghaem Shahr [*Iran*] [*ICAO location identifier*] (ICLI)
OINK......... Gonbad Ghabous [*Iran*] [*ICAO location identifier*] (ICLI)
Oink......... One Income, No Kids [*Lifestyle classification*]
OINL......... Alamdeh [*Iran*] [*ICAO location identifier*] (ICLI)
OINM......... Mahmood Abad [*Iran*] [*ICAO location identifier*] (ICLI)
OINN......... Noshahr [*Iran*] [*ICAO location identifier*] (ICLI)
OINO......... Noor [*Iran*] [*ICAO location identifier*] (ICLI)
OINP......... Azad Shahr [*Iran*] [*ICAO location identifier*] (ICLI)
OINQ......... Kelardasht [*Iran*] [*ICAO location identifier*] (ICLI)
OINR......... Ramsar [*Iran*] [*ICAO location identifier*] (ICLI)
OINS......... Sari [*Iran*] [*ICAO location identifier*] (ICLI)
oint......... Ointment (AD)
OINT......... Ointment
OINT......... Omni-Intersection (SAUS)
OINV......... Tonkabon [*Iran*] [*ICAO location identifier*] (ICLI)
OINY......... Bandar Torkaman [*Iran*] [*ICAO location identifier*] (ICLI)
OINZ......... Dasht-E-Naz [*Iran*] [*ICAO location identifier*] (ICLI)
OIO......... Obligated Involuntary Officers [*Used in movie "Spies Like Us"*]
OIO......... Office of International Operations [*of IRS*]
OIO......... Oklahomans for Indian Opportunity (AD)
OIO......... Operations Integration Officer [*NASA*] (MCD)
OIOPSWL... Old Input/Output Program Status Word Location [*Computer science*] (MHDB)
OIP......... Eastland, TX [*Location identifier*] [*FAA*] (FAAL)
OIP......... Offical Index Period (SAUS)
OIP......... Office for Information Programs (SAUS)
OIP......... Office of Import Programs [*Functions transferred to Domestic and International Business Administration*] [*Department of Commerce*]
OIP......... Office of Industrial Programs [*Department of Energy*]
OIP......... Office of International Programs [*National Science Foundation*]
oip......... Oil in Place (AD)
OIP......... Oil-in-Place
OIP......... Ontario Institute of Painters, Toronto [*1958*] [*Canada*] (NGC)
OIP......... Operating Internal Pressure [*Nuclear energy*] (NRCH)
OIP......... Operational Improvement Plan [*or Program*] [*Navy*]
OIP......... Operational Improvement Program (SAUS)
OIP......... Operational Instruction Pamphlet
OIP......... Operations Improvement Program (SAUS)
OIP......... Operations Interface Procedure (SAUS)
OIP......... Optical Image Processing (SAUS)
OIP......... Optical Image Processor
OIP......... Optical Improvement Program [*Army*]
OIP......... Orbital Improvement Program
OIP......... Ordnance Installation Plan (MCD)
OIP......... Organic Insulative Plastic
OIP......... Organisation Internationale de la Paleobotanique [*International Organization of Paleobotany*]
OIP......... Organisation Internationale de Psychophysiologie [*International Organization of Psychophysiology - IOP*] (EAIO)
OIP......... Organisation Internationale pour le Progres [*Austria*] (EAIO)
OIP......... Organizacion Iberoamericana de Pilotos [*Ibero-American Organization of Pilots - IOP*] [*Mexico City, Mexico*] (EAIO)
OIP......... Organizing Interstitial Pneumonia [*Medicine*]
OIP......... Oriental Institute Publications [*A publication*] (ABAR)
oip......... Oxford India Paper (AD)
OIPA......... Ortho-Isopropylaniline [*Organic chemistry*]
OIPAAR...... Office of Industrial Personnel Access Authorization Review [*Army*] (AABC)
OIPC......... Organisation Internationale de Police Criminelle [*International Criminal Police Organization*] [*French*] (AD)
OIPC......... Organisation Internationale de Protection Civile [*International Civil Defense Organization - ICDO*] (EAIO)
OIPCFC...... Official International Peter Coyote Fan Club (EA)
OIPD......... Operations Interface Procedure Document (ACAE)
OIPEEC...... Organisation Internationale pour l'Etude de l'Endurance des Cables [*International Organization for the Study of the Endurance of Wire Ropes - IOSEWR*] (EAIO)
OIPH......... Office of International Public Health (AD)
Oipi......... One Income plus Inheritance [*Lifestyle classification*]
OIPMT....... Optimum Insect Pest Management Trial [*Department of Agriculture*]
OIPO......... Optimum Installation Position Only (MCD)
OIPR......... Office of Information, Publications, and Reports [*Department of Labor*]
OIPR......... Office of Intelligence Policy and Review [*U.S. Department of Justice*] (BARN)
OIPRC....... Oxford Intellectual Property Research Centre [*St. Peter's College*] [*United Kingdom*] (RCD)
OIPS......... Optical Image Processing System
OIPT......... Overarching Integrated Product Team [*Army*]
OIQ......... Ordre des Ingenieurs du Quebec [*Canada*] (DD)
OIQ......... Sioux City, IA [*Location identifier*] [*FAA*] (FAAL)
OIR......... Iroquois Public Library, Ontario [*Library symbol*] [*National Library of Canada*] (BIB)
OIR......... Office of Indian Rights [*Department of Justice*]
OIR......... Office of Industrial Relations [*Superseded, 1966, by Office of Civilian Manpower*] [*Navy*]
OIR......... Office of Industrial Research [*University of Manitoba*] [*Canada*] [*Research center*] (RCD)
OIR......... Office of Industry Relations (SAUS)
OIR......... Office of Institutional Relations [*Energy Research and Development Administration*]
OIR......... Office of Institutional Research [*Concordia University (Montreal, QC, Canada)*] [*Canada*] (RCD)
OIR......... Office of Inter-American Radio (AD)
OIR......... Office of Intergovernmental Relations
OIR......... Office of International Research [*National Institutes of Health*]
OIR......... Office of International Resources [*Department of State*]
OIR......... Official Information Request (SAUS)
OIR......... Okushiri [*Japan*] [*Airport symbol*] (OAG)
OIr......... Old Irish (AD)
OIR......... Old Irish [*Language, etc.*]
OIR......... Online Information Retrieval Ltd. [*Information service or system*] [*Defunct*] (IID)
OIR......... Open Item Review (KSC)
OIR......... Operational and Information Requirements (SAUS)
OIR......... Operations Integration Review (NASA)
OIR......... Orbiter Infrared Radiometer [*NASA*]
OIR......... Organisation Internationale de Radiodiffusion [*International Radio Organization*] [*Later, OIRT*]
OIR......... Other Intelligence Requirements [*Army*] (MCD)
OIR......... Slov-Air [*Slovakia*] [*ICAO designator*] (FAAC)
OIRA......... Office of Industrial Resource Administration (AAGC)
OIRA......... Office of Information and Regulatory Affairs [*Office of Management and Budget*]
OIRA......... Officials of the Irish Republican Army [*Northern Ireland*]
OIran........ Old Iranian (SAUS)
OIRB......... Oregon Insurance Rating Bureau (AD)
OIRCA....... Ontario Industrial Roofing Contractors Association (SAUS)
OIRD......... Object-to-Image Receptor Distance [*Radiology*] (DAVI)
OIRE......... Optical Infrared Equipment
OIRM......... Office and Industrial Records Management (AD)
OIRM......... Office of Information Resources Management [*General Services Administration*]
OIR-N........ Office of Industrial Relations, Navy [*Superseded, 1966, by Office of Civilian Manpower*]
OIRS......... Occupational Interest Rating Scale [*Vocational guidance test*]
OIRS......... Operation and Inspection Route Sheet (DNAB)
OIRSA....... Organismo Internacional Regional de Sanidad Agropecuaria [*Regional International Organization of Plant Protection and Animal Health*] [*El Salvador*]
OIRT......... Organisation Internationale de Radiodiffusion et Television [*International Radio and Television Organization*] [*Formerly, OIR*] (EAIO)
OIRTD....... Office of Industrial Relations and Technology Development (SAUS)
OIS......... Obstacle Identification Surface [*Aviation*] (DA)
OIS......... Occupational Information System [*Department of Labor*]
OIS......... Occupational Interest Survey [*Aptitude test*]
OIS......... Office of Industrial Security [*DoD*]
OIS......... Office of Information Services [*Council of State Governments*] [*Lexington, KY*]
OIS......... Office of Information Systems [*Social and Rehabilitation Service, HEW*]
OIS......... Office of International Services [*Red Cross*]
OIS......... Office of Investigatory Services (SAUS)
OIS......... Officer of Information Service (SAUS)
OIS......... Oishiyama [*Japan*] [*Seismograph station code, US Geological Survey*] (SEIS)
OIS......... OIS Optical Imaging Systems, Inc. [*Associated Press*] (SAG)
OIS......... Oncology Information Service [*University of Leeds*] [*England*] [*Information service or system*] (IID)
OIS......... Operating Information System [*Army*]
OIS......... Operational Information Service (SAUS)
OIS......... Operational Insertion System
OIS......... Operational Instruction Sheet (ACAE)
OIS......... Operational Instrumentation System
OIS......... Operational Intercommunication System [*NASA*] (KSC)
ois......... Operational Intercommunication System (NAKS)
OIS......... Ophthalmic Imaging Systems [*Boston Stock Exchange symbol*]
OIS......... Opium Investigation Service (SAUS)
OIS......... Optical Image Sensor
OIS......... Optical Image Stabilizer
OIS......... Optical Imaging Systems (RDA)
OIS......... Optical Information Storage (SAUS)
OIS......... Optical Information System [*Computer science*]
OIS......... Orbiter Insertion Stage (SAUS)
ois......... Orbiter Instrumentation System [*NASA*] (NAKS)
OIS......... Orbiter Instrumentation Systems [*NASA*] (MCD)
OIS......... Orbit Injection System (ACAE)
OIS......... Osteopathic Information Service (SAUS)
OIS......... Ounce-Inches per Second (IAA)
OIS......... Output Information Signal (SAUS)
OIS......... Overseas Investors Services (AD)
OIS......... Oxford Institute of Statistics (SAUS)
OIS......... Oxygen Isotope Stage (QUAC)
OIS......... WWW Operational Information Service (SAUS)
OISA......... Abadeh [*Iran*] [*ICAO location identifier*] (ICLI)
OISA......... Office of International Science Activities [*National Science Foundation*]
OISA......... Office of International Scientific Affairs (AD)
OIS & T..... Office of Information Systems and Telecommunications [*Veterans Administration*] (TSSD)
OISB......... Bavanat [*Iran*] [*ICAO location identifier*] (ICLI)
OISC......... Ardakan-E-Fars [*Iran*] [*ICAO location identifier*] (ICLI)
OISC......... Oil-Insulated, Self-Cooling
OISCA....... Organization for Industrial, Spiritual and Cultural Advancement (SAUS)

OISCA .... Organization for Industrial, Spiritual, and Cultural Advancement International [*Tokyo, Japan*] (EAIO)
OISD .... Darab [*Iran*] [*ICAO location identifier*] (ICLI)
OISDG .... Ingleside Branch, Stormont, Dundas, and Glengarry County Library, Ontario [*Library symbol*] [*National Library of Canada*] (BIB)
OISE .... Estahbanat [*Iran*] [*ICAO location identifier*] (ICLI)
OISE .... Office Information System Equipment (SAUS)
OISE .... Office of Industrial Security, Europe [*DoD*]
OISE .... Ontario Institute for Studies in Education [*University of Toronto*] [*Research center*] (RCD)
OISF .... Fasa [*Iran*] [*ICAO location identifier*] (ICLI)
OISH .... Farashband [*Iran*] [*ICAO location identifier*] (ICLI)
OISI .... Dehbid [*Iran*] [*ICAO location identifier*] (ICLI)
OISI .... Office of Industrial Security, International [*DoD*] (MCD)
OISI .... Ophthalmic Imaging Sys [*NASDAQ symbol*] (TTSB)
OISI .... Ophthalmic Imaging Systems, Inc. [*NASDAQ symbol*] (SAG)
OIS/IGP ..... Office Information System Intelligent Gateway Processor (SAUS)
OISILGR... Office of Industry and State and Local Government Relations (SAUS)
OISJ .... Jahrom [*Iran*] [*ICAO location identifier*] (ICLI)
OISK .... Kazeroun [*Iran*] [*ICAO location identifier*] (ICLI)
OISL .... Lar [*Iran*] [*ICAO location identifier*] (ICLI)
OISLGR ..... Office of Industry and State and Local Government Relations [*Energy Research and Development Administration*]
OISM .... Mamassani [*Iran*] [*ICAO location identifier*] (ICLI)
OISN .... Neiriz [*Iran*] [*ICAO location identifier*] (ICLI)
OISP .... Overseas Internal Security Program [*Army*]
OISP .... Persepolis/Marvdasht [*Iran*] [*ICAO location identifier*] (ICLI)
OISQ .... Ghir/Karzin [*Iran*] [*ICAO location identifier*] (ICLI)
OISR .... Lamerd [*Iran*] [*ICAO location identifier*] (ICLI)
OISR .... Office of Interstate Sales Registration [*HUD*]
OISR .... Open Item Status Report (NASA)
OISRU .... Office of Intergovernmental Science and Research Utilization [*National Science Foundation*]
OISS .... Office of Information Systems and Services (AAGC)
OISS .... Online Information Search Service [*Computer science*] (AD)
OISS .... Operational Intelligence Support System (MCD)
OISS .... Organizacion Iberoamericana de Seguridad Social [*Ibero-American Social Security Organization*]
OISS .... Shiraz/International [*Iran*] [*ICAO location identifier*] (ICLI)
OISSP .... Office of Interim Space Station Program [*NASA*]
OIST .... Operator Integration Shakedown Test
OIST .... Shiraz [*Iran*] [*ICAO location identifier*] (ICLI)
OISTV .... Organisation Internationale pour la Science et la Technique du Vide [*International Organization for Vacuum Science and Technology*] [*French*] (AD)
OISU .... Abarghou [*Iran*] [*ICAO location identifier*] (ICLI)
OISW .... Kohkiloyeh [*Iran*] [*ICAO location identifier*] (ICLI)
OISX .... Khonj [*Iran*] [*ICAO location identifier*] (ICLI)
OISY .... Yasouj [*Iran*] [*ICAO location identifier*] (ICLI)
OISZ .... Firouzabad [*Iran*] [*ICAO location identifier*] (ICLI)
OIT .... Object Identification Test
OIT .... Object Identifier Tree (SAUS)
OIT .... Oblique-Incidence Transmission
OIT .... Office of Industrial Technologies (SAUS)
OIT .... Office of International Trade [*Department of Commerce*]
O i T .... Officer in Training (AD)
OIT .... Office Software Development & Information Technology (SAUS)
OIT .... Oil Immersion Test (MELL)
OIT .... Oil Interceptor Trap
OIT .... Oita [*Japan*] [*Airport symbol*] (OAG)
OIT .... Oita [*Japan*] [*Seismograph station code, US Geological Survey*] (SEIS)
O It .... Old Italian (AD)
O IT .... Old Italian [*Language, etc.*] (ROG)
OIT .... Ontario Ministry of Industry, Trade, and Technology [*UTLAS symbol*]
OIT .... Operational Instruction Title (ACAE)
OIT .... Operator Interface Terminal (MCD)
OIT .... Optical Image Terminal [*Computer science*] (VLIE)
OIT .... Optical Information Transfer (SAUS)
OIT .... Optimum Insulation Thickness (DICI)
OIT .... Orbiter Integrated Test [*NASA*] (NASA)
OIT .... Oregon Institute of Technology, Klamath Falls, OR [*OCLC symbol*] (OCLC)
OIT .... Organic Integrity Test [*Psychology*]
OIT .... Organisation Internationale du Travail [*International Labor Organization*] [*French United Nations*] (EAIO)
OIT .... Organizacion Internacional del Trabajo [*International Labor Organization*] [*Spanish*] [*United Nations*] (DUND)
OIT .... Organization Iberoamericaine de Television (NTCM)
OITA .... Office of International Tax Affairs [*Department of the Treasury*]
OITA .... Sarab [*Iran*] [*ICAO location identifier*] (ICLI)
OITAF-NACS... Organizzazione Internazionale dei Trasporti a Fune [*International Organization for Transportation by Rope*] - North American Continental Section (EA)
OITB .... Mahabad [*Iran*] [*ICAO location identifier*] (ICLI)
OITC .... Officer-in-Tactical Command (SAUS)
OITC .... Sardasht [*Iran*] [*ICAO location identifier*] (ICLI)
OITD .... Marand [*Iran*] [*ICAO location identifier*] (ICLI)
OITDA .... Optoelectronic Industry and Technology Development Association [*Japan*]
OITDS .... Operations and Intelligence Tactical Data Systems (MCD)
OITF .... Office of International Trade and Finance [*Department of State*]
OITF .... Office of International Trade Fairs [*Department of Commerce*]
OITF .... Organisation Intergouvernementale pour les Transports Internationaux Ferroviaires [*Intergovernmental Organization for International Carriage by Rail*] (EAIO)
OITG .... Naghadeh [*Iran*] [*ICAO location identifier*] (ICLI)
OITH .... Khaneh/Piranshahr [*Iran*] [*ICAO location identifier*] (ICLI)
OITI .... Mianeh [*Iran*] [*ICAO location identifier*] (ICLI)
OITJ .... Julfa [*Iran*] [*ICAO location identifier*] (ICLI)
OITK .... Khoy [*Iran*] [*ICAO location identifier*] (ICLI)
OITL .... Outdoor-Indoor Transmission Loss (SAUS)
OITM .... Maragheh [*Iran*] [*ICAO location identifier*] (ICLI)
OITN .... Meshgin Shahr [*Iran*] [*ICAO location identifier*] (ICLI)
OITO .... Mian Do Ab [*Iran*] [*ICAO location identifier*] (ICLI)
OITP .... Office for Information Technology Policy [*American Library Association*]
OITP .... Office of International Trade Promotion [*Department of State*]
OITP .... Ohio Industrial Training Program
OITP .... Parsabad/Moghan [*Iran*] [*ICAO location identifier*] (ICLI)
OITQ .... Ahar [*Iran*] [*ICAO location identifier*] (ICLI)
OITR .... Uromiyeh [*Iran*] [*ICAO location identifier*] (ICLI)
OITS .... Saghez [*Iran*] [*ICAO location identifier*] (ICLI)
OITT .... Outpulser, Identifier, Trunk Test
OITT .... Tabriz [*Iran*] [*ICAO location identifier*] (ICLI)
OITT Frame... Outpulse Identifier Trunk Test Frame (SAUS)
OITU .... Makou [*Iran*] [*ICAO location identifier*] (ICLI)
OITV .... Tabriz [*Iran*] [*ICAO location identifier*] (ICLI)
OITW .... Azar Shahr [*Iran*] [*ICAO location identifier*] (ICLI)
OITX .... Sareskand [*Iran*] [*ICAO location identifier*] (ICLI)
OITY .... Marivan [*Iran*] [*ICAO location identifier*] (ICLI)
OITZ .... Zanjan [*Iran*] [*ICAO location identifier*] (ICLI)
OIU .... Office Interface Unit [*Computer science*] (VLIE)
OIU .... Ogaden Islamic Union (SAUS)
OIU .... Operator Interface Unit [*Computer science*]
OIU .... Optical Image Unit [*Computer science*] (VLIE)
OIUC .... Optical Infrared Ultraviolet Communications (ACAE)
OIUC .... Oriental Institute of the University of Chicago (SAUS)
OIUCSAOC... Oriental Institute. University of Chicago. Studies in Ancient Oriental Civilization (SAUS)
OIUS .... Optical Infrared Ultraviolet Surveillance (ACAE)
OIV .... Object Idenitfier Value (SAUS)
OIV .... Octarios Quatior [*Four Pints*] [*Pharmacy*] (ROG)
OIV .... Office International de la Vigne et du Vin [*International Vine and Wine Office*] (EAIO)
OIV .... Overhead Inlet Valve [*Automotive engineering*]
OIV .... Oxidizer Isolation Valve (MCD)
oiv .... Oxidizer Isolation Valve (NAKS)
OIVA .... 127th Infantry Veterans Association (EA)
oivs .... Orbiter Interface Verification Set [*NASA*] (NAKS)
OIVS .... Orbiter Interface Verification Set [*NASA*] (NASA)
OIVV .... Office Internationale de la Vigne et du Vin [*International Office of Vines and Wines*] [*French*] (AD)
OIW .... Oceanographic Institute of Washington [*Marine science*] (MSC)
OIW .... Oceanographic Institute Wellington New Zealand (AD)
OIW .... Office of Indigenous Women [*Australia*]
OIW .... Oiwake [*Japan*] [*Seismograph station code, US Geological Survey*] [*Closed*] (SEIS)
OIW .... Open Information Warehouse (SAUS)
OIW .... Open systems environment Implementors Workshop (SAUS)
OIW .... Order of the Indian Wars (EA)
OIW .... OSI Implementors Workshop (SAUS)
OIWC .... Oil-Immersed, Water-Cooled (SAUS)
OIWC .... Oil-Insulated, Water-Cooled
OIWG .... Operations-Intelligence Working Group (SAUS)
OIWG .... Operations Interface Working Group (ACAE)
OIWP .... Oil Industry Working Party (AD)
OIWR .... Office of Indian Water Rights [*Bureau of Indian Affairs*]
OIX .... Ottawa, IL [*Location identifier*] [*FAA*] (FAAL)
OIYA .... Ardakan-E-Yazd [*Iran*] [*ICAO location identifier*] (ICLI)
OIYB .... Bafgh [*Iran*] [*ICAO location identifier*] (ICLI)
OIYD .... Dehshir [*Iran*] [*ICAO location identifier*] (ICLI)
OIYF .... Taft [*Iran*] [*ICAO location identifier*] (ICLI)
OIYK .... Khor/Jandagh [*Iran*] [*ICAO location identifier*] (ICLI)
OIYM .... Mehriz [*Iran*] [*ICAO location identifier*] (ICLI)
OIYN .... Khore Beyabanak [*Iran*] [*ICAO location identifier*] (ICLI)
OIYQ .... Khezr Abad [*Iran*] [*ICAO location identifier*] (ICLI)
OIYT .... Yazd [*Iran*] [*ICAO location identifier*] (ICLI)
OIYY .... Yazd [*Iran*] [*ICAO location identifier*] (ICLI)
OIYZ .... Ashkezar [*Iran*] [*ICAO location identifier*] (ICLI)
OIZA .... Jalagh [*Iran*] [*ICAO location identifier*] (ICLI)
OIZB .... Zabol [*Iran*] [*ICAO location identifier*] (ICLI)
OIZC .... Chah Bahar/Konarak [*Iran*] [*ICAO location identifier*] (ICLI)
OIZD .... Dashtyari [*Iran*] [*ICAO location identifier*] (ICLI)
OIZG .... Ghasre Ghand [*Iran*] [*ICAO location identifier*] (ICLI)
OIZH .... Zahedan [*Iran*] [*ICAO location identifier*] (ICLI)
OIZI .... Iran Shahr [*Iran*] [*ICAO location identifier*] (ICLI)
OIZJ .... Jask [*Iran*] [*ICAO location identifier*] (ICLI)
OIZK .... Khash [*Iran*] [*ICAO location identifier*] (ICLI)
OIZL .... Zabolee [*Iran*] [*ICAO location identifier*] (ICLI)
OIZM .... Mirjaveh [*Iran*] [*ICAO location identifier*] (ICLI)
OIZN .... Bazman [*Iran*] [*ICAO location identifier*] (ICLI)
OIZO .... Sarbaz [*Iran*] [*ICAO location identifier*] (ICLI)
OIZP .... Bampoor [*Iran*] [*ICAO location identifier*] (ICLI)
OIZR .... Bask [*Iran*] [*ICAO location identifier*] (ICLI)
OIZS .... Saravan [*Iran*] [*ICAO location identifier*] (ICLI)
OIZT .... Zahedan [*Iran*] [*ICAO location identifier*] (ICLI)

OIZY......... Nik-Shahr [*Iran*] [*ICAO location identifier*] (ICLI)
OJ........... Air Texana [*ICAO designator*] (AD)
OJ........... Jackson Public Library, Jackson, OH [*Library symbol*] [*Library of Congress*] (LCLS)
OJ........... Object [*Telegraphy*] (PCTE)
OJ........... Obstructive Jaundice [*Medicine*] (MELL)
OJ........... Official Journal (HEAS)
OJ........... Ohne Jahr [*Without Date of Publication*] [*Bibliography*] [*German*]
oJ........... Ohne Jahr [*Without Year*] [*German*] (AD)
OJ........... Ontario Judgments [*Database*] [*Canada*] (GDD)
OJ........... Open Joint (SAUS)
oj........... Open-Joint (AD)
OJ........... Open-Joisted [*Technical drawings*]
OJ........... Open Web Joist [*Technical drawings*]
OJ........... Operation Joshua (EA)
OJ........... Opium Joint [*Slang*]
OJ........... Orange Co. [*NYSE symbol*] (SPSG)
oj........... Orange Juice (AD)
OJ........... Orange Juice
OJ........... Order of Jamaica
OJ........... Orenthal James [*Given names of football player O. J. Simpson*]
OJ........... Oriental Pearl Airways Ltd. (SAUS)
OJ........... Originating Junctor [*Telecommunications*] (TEL)
OJ........... Orthomode Junction [*Electronics*]
OJ........... Orthoplast Jacket [*Orthopedics*] (DAVI)
OJ........... Outer Jacket
OJ........... Outgoing Junctor (SAUS)
OJA.......... Onklos-Jonathan Aramaic (BJA)
OJA.......... Oriental Pearl Airways Ltd. [*British*] [*ICAO designator*] (FAAC)
OJA.......... Oxford Journal of Archaeology [*A publication*] (ABAR)
OJA.......... Weatherford, OK [*Location identifier*] [*FAA*] (FAAL)
OJAC......... Amman [*Jordan*] [*ICAO location identifier*] (ICLI)
OJ Act....... Ontario Judicature Act [*A publication*] (DLA)
OJAF......... Amman [*Jordan*] [*ICAO location identifier*] (ICLI)
OJA-G........ Office of the Judge Advocate General [*British*]
OJAI......... Amman/Queen Alia [*Jordan*] [*ICAO location identifier*] (ICLI)
OJAI......... Ojai Van Lines [*Common carrier symbol*]
OJAJ......... October, January, April, and July [*Denotes quarterly payments of interest or dividends in these months*] [*Business term*]
OJAM......... Amman/Marka [*Jordan*] [*ICAO location identifier*] (ICLI)
OJapan....... Order of Japan (DD)
OJAQ......... Aqaba [*Jordan*] [*ICAO location identifier*] (ICLI)
OJARS........ Office of Justice Assistance, Research, and Statistics [*Department of Justice*]
OJAY......... Orange Julius International, Inc. (SAUS)
OJBD......... Irbid [*Jordan*] [*ICAO location identifier*] (ICLI)
OJC.......... North Central Regional Library, Ojibway Cree Project [*UTLAS symbol*]
OJC.......... Occupied Japan Club (EA)
OJC.......... Office of Job Corps [*Department of Labor*]
OJC.......... Olathe, KS [*Location identifier*] [*FAA*] (FAAL)
OJC.......... Operation Job Card (TIMI)
OJC.......... Order of Jacques-Cartier [*Canada*] (BARN)
OJC.......... Organisation Juive de Combat [*Jewish Combat Organization*] [*French*] (AD)
OJC.......... Orlando Junior College [*Florida*]
OJC.......... Otero Junior College [*La Junta, CO*]
OJC.......... Overseas Jazz Club (EA)
OJCAC........ Ohio Junior College Athletic Conference (PSS)
OJCCT........ On-Line Journal of Current Clinical Trends (TELE)
OJCCT........ Online Journal of Current Clinical Trials [*A publication*]
OJCE......... Orchestre des Jeunes de la Communaute Europeenne [*European Community Youth Orchestra - ECYO*] (EAIO)
OJCN......... Jarvis Branch, City of Nanticoke Public Library, Ontario [*Library symbol*] [*National Library of Canada*] (BIB)
OJCS......... Office of the Joint Chiefs of Staff (AFM)
OJCS......... Organization of the Joint Chiefs of Staff
OJCT......... OJ Commercial Transport [*Common carrier symbol*]
OJD.......... Objected [*Telegraphy*] (PCTE)
OJD.......... Order of Job's Daughters
OJDYD........ Office of Juvenile Delinquency and Youth Development [*Later, Youth Development Bureau*] [*HEW*]
OJE.......... Okumenischer Jugendrat in Europa [*Ecumenical Youth Council in Europe - EYCE*] (EAIO)
OJE.......... On-the-Job Education
OJE.......... On-the-Job Evaluation (OICC)
OJE.......... On-the-Job Evaluator (SAUS)
OJE.......... On-the-Job Experience
OJE.......... Operation Joint Endeavor [*Army*]
OJE.......... Orthodox Job Enrichment (PDAA)
OJEC......... Official Journal of the European Communities [*A publication*] (AD)
OJG.......... Objecting [*Telegraphy*] (PCTE)
OJG.......... Operation Joint Guard [*Army*]
OJG.......... Ordnance Job Guide
OJHF......... Hotel Five [*Jordan*] [*ICAO location identifier*] (ICLI)
OJHR......... Hotel Four [*Jordan*] [*ICAO location identifier*] (ICLI)
oji.......... Ojibwa [*MARC language code*] [*Library of Congress*] (LCCP)
oji.......... On-the-Job Injuries (AD)
OJI.......... On-the-Job Injuries
OJIN......... Online Journal of Issues in Nursing (SAUS)
OJJ.......... Office of Juvenile Justice (AD)
OJJDP........ Office of Juvenile Justice and Delinquency Prevention [*Department of Just ice*] [*Washington, DC*]
OJJO......... Jericho [*Jordan*] [*ICAO location identifier*] (ICLI)
OJJR......... Jerusalem [*Jordan*] [*ICAO location identifier*] (ICLI)
OJKSN........ Online Journal of Knowledge Synthesis for Nursing (SAUS)
OJL.......... Josephine County Library System, Grants Pass, OR [*OCLC symbol*] (OCLC)
OJL.......... Objectionable [*Telegraphy*] (PCTE)
OJL.......... Office Journal (SAUS)
OJL.......... Oronite Japan Limited [*Fuels and lubricants*]
OJLS......... Oxford Journal of Legal Studies [*A publication*] (SAFN)
OJMF......... Mafraq [*Jordan*] [*ICAO location identifier*] (ICLI)
OJN.......... Objection [*Telegraphy*] (PCTE)
OJNI......... On-line Journal of Nursing Informatics (SAUS)
OJNRF........ O. J. Noer Research Foundation (EA)
OJOP......... Olympic Job Opportunities Program
OJP.......... Office of Justice Programs [*Department of Justice*]
OJP.......... Ontong Java Plateau [*Geology*]
OJP.......... Orlando, FL [*Location identifier*] [*FAA*] (FAAL)
OJPR......... Office for Jewish Population Research [*Defunct*] (EA)
OJQ.......... Objective Judgment Quotient
oJr.......... Old Jamaica Rum (AD)
OJR.......... Old Jamaica Rum (ROG)
OJRL......... Optoelectronics Joint Research Laboratory [*Japan*]
OJRO......... Optical Journal and Review of Optometry [*Medicine*] (EDAA)
OJS.......... Las Oblatas de Jesus Sacerdote [*Oblates of Jesus the Priest*] [*Roman Catholic women's religious order*]
OJS.......... Objects [*Telegraphy*] (PCTE)
OJS.......... Optical Jammer Source
OJS.......... Organization Jointly Shared (SAUS)
OJS.......... Output Job Stream [*Computer science*] (VLIE)
OJSA......... Orthomode Junction and Switching Assembly [*Electronics*]
ojt.......... On-the-Job Training (AD)
OJT.......... On-the-Job Training
OJT.......... Over-Water Jet Transport (MCD)
OJTA......... Officer Job/Task Analysis [*Military*]
OJTC......... Outgoing Junctor Test Circuit (SAUS)
O Jur........ Ohio Jurisprudence [*A publication*] (DLA)
OJV.......... Objective [*Telegraphy*] (PCTE)
OJVR......... Online Journal of Veterinary Research (SAUS)
OJW.......... Otjiwarongo [*South-West Africa*] [*Airport symbol*] (AD)
OJY.......... Florida Air, Inc. [*ICAO designator*] (FAAC)
OJZ.......... White Plains, NY [*Location identifier*] [*FAA*] (FAAL)
OJZZ......... Amman [*Jordan*] [*ICAO location identifier*] (ICLI)
ok........... all correct (SAUS)
OK........... All Right [*From Oll Korrect; or from Old Kinderhook, a political club that supported the 1840 presidential campaign of Martin Van Buren*]
OK........... Approved (EBF)
OK........... Correct (EBF)
OK........... Czechia [*Civil aircraft markings - international*] (PIPO)
OK........... Czechoslovak Airlines [*ICAO designator*] (AD)
OK........... Kingston Public Library, Ontario [*Library symbol*] [*National Library of Canada*] (NLC)
O-K.......... Object-Kowal [*Object in the solar system*]
OK........... Odorless Kerosene
OK........... Ohne Kosten [*Without Cost*] [*German*]
ok........... Ohne Kosten [*Without Cost*] [*German*] (AD)
OK........... Ohrekreis [*German license plate city code*]
OK........... Okay [*International telex abbreviation*] (WDMC)
OK........... Okinawa [*Japan*]
OK........... Oklahoma [*Postal code*]
Ok........... Oklahoma Department of Libraries, Oklahoma City, OK [*Library symbol*] [*Library of Congress*] (LCLS)
OK........... Okonite (IAA)
OK........... Oktal (IAA)
OK........... Ola Kala [*All Is Well*] [*Greek*]
ok........... Ola Kala [*All is Fine*] [*Greek*] (AD)
OK........... Old Kent Financial [*NYSE symbol*]
OK........... Old Khmer [*Linguistics*] (IEL)
OK........... Old Kinderhook (IIA)
OK........... Old Kingdom [*Egyptology*] (ROG)
ok........... Optical Klystron (AD)
OK........... Optical Klystron (PDAA)
OK........... Order of Knights (ADA)
OK........... Oskar Kokoschka [*Austrian painter*] [*1886-1980*]
OK........... Our King (SAUS)
ok........... Outer Keel (AD)
OK........... Outer Keel
OKA.......... Bethany Nazarene College, Bethany, OK [*OCLC symbol*] (OCLC)
OKA.......... Kingston Laboratories, Alcan International Ltd., Ontario [*Library symbol*] [*National Library of Canada*] (NLC)
OKA.......... Okayama [*Japan*] [*Seismograph station code, US Geological Survey*] (SEIS)
OKA.......... Okinawa [*Japan*] [*Airport symbol*] (OAG)
oka.......... Otherwise Known As (AD)
OKA.......... Otherwise Known As
OKA.......... Out-of-Kilter Algorithm [*Mathematics*]
OKAA......... Kuwait Directorate General of Civil Aviation [*Kuwait*] [*ICAO location identifier*] (ICLI)
OKAAN........ Optokinetic After-After-Nystagmus [*Ophthalmology*]
OKAB......... Beaverbrook Branch, Kanata Public Library, Ontario [*Library symbol*] [*National Library of Canada*] (NLC)
OKAC......... Kuwait [*Kuwait*] [*ICAO location identifier*] (ICLI)
OkAd......... Ada Public Library, Ada, OK [*Library symbol*] [*Library of Congress*] (LCLS)
OkAdE........ East Central State College [*Later, East Central Oklahoma State University*], Ada, OK [*Library symbol*] [*Library of Congress*] (LCLS)

OKAER ...... Radiochemical Co., Atomic Energy of Canada Ltd., [*Societe Radiochimique, L'Energie Atomique du Canada Ltee.*], Kanata, Ontario [*Library symbol*] [*National Library of Canada*] (NLC)
OKAF .... Kuwait Air Force [*Kuwait*] [*ICAO location identifier*] (ICLI)
OKAH .... Hazeldean Branch, Kanata Public Library, Ontario [*Library symbol*] [*National Library of Canada*] (NLC)
OKAI .... Research & Technology Centre, AMCA International Ltd., Kanata, Ontario [*Library symbol*] [*National Library of Canada*] (NLC)
OKAKS ...... Synod Office, Diocese of Keewatin, Anglican Church of Canada, Kenora, Ontario [*Library symbol*] [*National Library of Canada*] (NLC)
OkAl .... Altus Library, Altus, OK [*Library symbol*] [*Library of Congress*] (LCLS)
OKAL .... Aluminum Co. of Canada Ltd., Kingston, Ontario [*Library symbol*] [*National Library of Canada*] (NLC)
OkAlS .... Southern Prairie Library System, Altus, OK [*Library symbol*] [*Library of Congress*] (LCLS)
OkAlvN ...... Northwestern State College, Alva, OK [*Library symbol*] [*Library of Congress*] (LCLS)
OKAMA ...... Okinawa Air Materiel Area (SAUS)
OKAN .... Kanata Public Library, Ontario [*Library symbol*] [*National Library of Canada*] (BIB)
OKAN .... Optokinetic After-Nystagmus [*Ophthalmology*]
OKANA ...... Arctec Canada Ltd., Kanata, Ontario [*Library symbol*] [*National Library of Canada*] (NLC)
OKAOS ...... Synod Office, Diocese of Ontario, Anglican Church of Canada, Kingston, Ontario [*Library symbol*] [*National Library of Canada*] (NLC)
OKAP .... Kapuskasing Public Library, Ontario [*Library symbol*] [*National Library of Canada*] (NLC)
OkArC .... Chickasaw Library System, Ardmore, OK [*Library symbol*] [*Library of Congress*] (LCLS)
OKASG ...... St. George's Cathedral, Anglican Church of Canada, Kingston, Ontario [*Library symbol*] [*National Library of Canada*] (NLC)
OKAT .... Oka Transfer Company [*Common carrier symbol*]
Okayama Univ Inst Therm Spring Res Pap... Okayama University. Institue for Thermal Spring Research. Papers (SAUS)
OKAYJ .... A. Y. Jackson High School, Kanata, Ontario [*Library symbol*] [*National Library of Canada*] (BIB)
OkB .... Bartlesville Public Library, Bartlesville, OK [*Library symbol*] [*Library of Congress*] (LCLS)
OKB .... Design Bureau (SAUS)
OKB .... Kashechewan Band Library, Ontario [*Library symbol*] [*National Library of Canada*] (BIB)
OKB .... Missile design bureau (SAUS)
OKB .... Oklahoma Baptist University, Shawnee, OK [*OCLC symbol*] (OCLC)
OKB .... Orchid Beach [*Australia*] [*Airport symbol*]
OkBERDA ... United States Energy Research Development Administration, Energy Research Center, Bartlesville, OK [*Library symbol*] [*Library of Congress*] (LCLS)
OkBetC ...... Bethany Nazarene College, Bethany, OK [*Library symbol*] [*Library of Congress*] (LCLS)
OKBK .... Kuwait/International [*Kuwait*] [*ICAO location identifier*] (ICLI)
OkBP .... Phillips Petroleum Co., Research and Development Department, Bartlesville, OK [*Library symbol*] [*Library of Congress*] (LCLS)
OkBP-NR .... Philips Petroleum Co., Exploration and Production Library, Bartlesville, OK [*Library symbol*] [*Library of Congress*] (LCLS)
OkBr .... Bristow Public Library, Bristow, OK [*Library symbol*] [*Library of Congress*] (LCLS)
OKBT .... Billings Township Public Library, Kagawong, Ontario [*Library symbol*] [*National Library of Canada*] (NLC)
OkBUSM .... United States Bureau of Mines, Petroleum Research Center, Bartlesville, OK [*Library symbol*] [*Library of Congress*] [*Obsolete*] (LCLS)
OKC .... Cameron University, Lawton, OK [*OCLC symbol*] (OCLC)
OKC .... Canadian Forces School of Communications and Electronics, Kingston, Ontario [*Library symbol*] [*National Library of Canada*] (BIB)
OKC .... Odontogenic Keratocyst [*Medicine*] (DMAA)
OKC .... Okanagan College Learning Resources Centre [*UTLAS symbol*]
OKC .... Oklahoma Cement Co. (EFIS)
OKC .... Oklahoma City [*Oklahoma*] [*Airport symbol*] (OAG)
OKC .... Will Rogers World Airport [*FAA*] (TAG)
OKCAA ...... Archives, Archdiocese of Kingston, Catholic Church, Ontario [*Library symbol*] [*National Library of Canada*] (NLC)
OKCE .... Okarche Central Railroad [*Federal Railroad Administration identification code*]
OkChicW .... Oklahoma College of Liberal Arts, Chickasha, OK [*Library symbol*] [*Library of Congress*] (LCLS)
OKCHN ...... Pan-National Congress of the Chechen People [*Russian Federation*]
OKCK .... Oak Creek Homes [*NCIC trailer make code*]
OKCKT .... King Township Public Library, King City, Ontario [*Library symbol*] [*National Library of Canada*] (NLC)
OkCl .... Clinton Public Library, Clinton, OK [*Library symbol*] [*Library of Congress*] (LCLS)
OkClaW ..... Will Rogers Library, Claremore, OH [*Library symbol*] [*Library of Congress*] (LCLS)
OkClW .... Western Plains Library System, Clinton, OK [*Library symbol*] [*Library of Congress*] (LCLS)
OKCM .... Canadian Marconi Co., Kanata, Ontario [*Library symbol*] [*National Library of Canada*] (NLC)
OKCO .... Oakbrook Consolidated (SAUS)
OKCS .... Oklahoma Climatological Survey (SAUS)
OKCT .... Okarcke Central Railway [*Federal Railroad Administration identification code*]
OKD .... Oklahoma Department of Libraries, Oklahoma City, OK [*OCLC symbol*] (OCLC)
OKD .... Research Centre Library, Du Pont Canada, Inc., Kingston, Ontario [*Library symbol*] [*National Library of Canada*] (NLC)
OKD .... Sapporo/Okadama [*Japan*] [*Airport symbol*] (OAG)
OKDAL ...... Oakdale, LA [*American Association of Railroads railroad junction routing code*]
OKDBMS .... Operations Knowledge Data Base Management System [*NASA*]
OKDC .... Du Pont Canada, Inc., Kingston, Ontario [*Library symbol*] [*National Library of Canada*] (NLC)
OkDurS ...... Southeastern State College, Durant, OK [*Library symbol*] [*Library of Congress*] (LCLS)
OKE .... Kenora Public Library, Ontario [*Library symbol*] [*National Library of Canada*] (NLC)
OKE .... Metropolitan Library System, Capitol Hill Branch, Oklahoma City, OK [*OCLC symbol*] (OCLC)
OKE .... Okeechobee, FL [*Amtrak rail station code*]
OKE .... Okino Erabu [*Japan*] [*Airport symbol*] (OAG)
OKE .... Okpe [*Language symbol*] (ETLW)
OKE .... ONEOK, Inc. [*NYSE symbol*] (SPSG)
OKE .... Optical Kerr Effect [*Birefringence induced in an electrical field*]
OkE .... Public Library of Enid and Garfield County, Enid, OK [*Library symbol*] [*Library of Congress*] (LCLS)
OKEA .... Kearney and Area Public Library, Kearney, Ontario [*Library symbol*] [*National Library of Canada*] (NLC)
OKED .... Okinawa Engineer District (SAUS)
OkEdT .... Central State University, Edmond, OK [*Library symbol*] [*Library of Congress*] (LCLS)
OKEE .... Keewatin Public Library, Ontario [*Library symbol*] [*National Library of Canada*] (NLC)
OKEE .... Oklahoma Kids in Environmental Education (EARSL)
O'Keefe Ord... O'Keefe's Order in Chancery [*Ireland*] [*A publication*] (DLA)
OKEEN .... Okeene, OK [*American Association of Railroads railroad junction routing code*]
Oke Fish L... Oke. Fisher Laws [*4th ed.*] [*1924*] [*A publication*] (DLA)
OkEG .... Phillips University, Graduate Seminary, Enid, OK [*Library symbol*] [*Library of Congress*] (LCLS)
Oke Game L... Oke. Game Laws [*5th ed.*] [*1912*] [*A publication*] (DLA)
OKEH .... Okehampton [*England*]
OKEM .... Kemptville Public Library, Ontario [*Library symbol*] [*National Library of Canada*] (NLC)
OKEMAF .... Ontario Ministry of Agriculture and Food, Kemptville, Ontario [*Library symbol*] [*National Library of Canada*] (NLC)
Oke Mag Form... Oke. Magisterial Formulist [*19th ed.*] [*1978*] [*A publication*] (DLA)
Oke Mag Syn... Oke. Magisterial Synopsis [*14th ed.*] [*1893*] [*A publication*] (DLA)
OKEMC ...... Kemptville College of Agricultural Technology, Ontario [*Library symbol*] [*National Library of Canada*] (BIB)
OKEMS ...... Earl of March Secondary School, Kanata, Ontario [*Library symbol*] [*National Library of Canada*] (NLC)
OKEN .... Old Kent Financial Corp. [*NASDAQ symbol*] (NQ)
OKEN .... Old Kent Finl [*NASDAQ symbol*] (TTSB)
OKentU ...... Kent State University, Kent, OH [*Library symbol*] [*Library of Congress*] (LCLS)
OkEP .... Phillips University, Enid, OK [*Library symbol*] [*Library of Congress*] (LCLS)
OkErC .... El Reno Junior College Learning Resource Center, El Reno, OK [*Library symbol*] [*Library of Congress*] (LCLS)
OKES .... Georgina Township Public Library, Keswick, Ontario [*Library symbol*] [*National Library of Canada*] (NLC)
OKET .... Euphrasia Township Public Library, Kimberley, Ontario [*Library symbol*] [*National Library of Canada*] (NLC)
OKetBD ...... BDM International, Information Service Center, Kettering, OH [*Library symbol*] [*Library of Congress*] (LCLS)
OKetH .... Kettering Memorial Hospital, Kettering, OH [*Library symbol*] [*Library of Congress*] (LCLS)
OKetK .... Charles F. Kettering Foundation, Kettering, OH [*Library symbol*] [*Library of Congress*] (LCLS)
Oke Turn .... Oke. Turnpike Laws [*2nd ed.*] [*1861*] [*A publication*] (DLA)
OKF .... Fort Frontenac Library, Canada Department of National Defence [*Bibliotheque Fort Frontenac, Ministere de la Defense Nationale*] Kingston, Ontario [*Library symbol*] [*National Library of Canada*] (NLC)
OKFC .... Frontenac County Library, Kingston, Ontario [*Library symbol*] [*National Library of Canada*] (NLC)
OKFCSM .... Frontenac County Schools Museum Association, Kingston, Ontario [*Library symbol*] [*National Library of Canada*] (BIB)
OKFI .... Siltronics Ltd., Kanata, Ontario [*Library symbol*] [*National Library of Canada*] (NLC)
OkFsAGM ... United States Army, Artillery and Guided Missile School, Fort Sill, OK [*Library symbol*] [*Library of Congress*] (LCLS)
OKG .... Oak Grove [*Tennessee*] [*Seismograph station code, US Geological Survey*] (SEIS)
OKG .... Okoyo [*Congo*] [*Airport symbol*] (OAG)
OKG .... Phillips University, Graduate Seminary Library, Enid, OK [*OCLC symbol*] (OCLC)
OKGE .... Oklahoma General Electric [*Federal Railroad Administration identification code*]
OKGH .... Kingston General Hospital, Ontario [*Library symbol*] [*National Library of Canada*] (NLC)
OkGoP .... Panhandle State College, Goodwell, OK [*Library symbol*] [*Library of Congress*] (LCLS)
OkGuC .... Catholic College of Oklahoma for Women, Guthrie, OK [*Library symbol*] [*Library of Congress*] [*Obsolete*] (LCLS)
OkGuy .... Guymon City Library, Guymon, OK [*Library symbol*] [*Library of Congress*] (LCLS)
OKH .... Oberkommando des Heeres [*Army High Command*] [*German military - World War II*]
OKH .... Okha [*Former USSR*] [*Seismograph station code, US Geological Survey*] (SEIS)
OKH .... University of Oklahoma, Health Science Center Library, Oklahoma City, OK [*OCLC symbol*] (OCLC)

OKHD........ Hotel-Dieu Hospital, Kingston, Ontario [*Library symbol*] [*National Library of Canada*] (NLC)
OkHenn..... Hennessey Public Library, Hennessey, OK [*Library symbol*] [*Library of Congress*] (LCLS)
OkHi......... Oklahoma Historical Society, Oklahoma City, OK [*Library symbol*] [*Library of Congress*] (LCLS)
OKHT........ OK Horse Trailer [*NCIC trailer make code*]
OKI........... Choctaw Nation Multi-County Library, McAlester, OK [*OCLC symbol*] (OCLC)
OKI........... Kincardine Branch, Bruce County Public Library, Ontario [*Library symbol*] [*National Library of Canada*] (NLC)
OKI........... Ohio-Kentucky-Indiana Regional Planning Authority
OKI........... Oki Island [*Japan*] [*Airport symbol*] (OAG)
OKI........... Okijuku [*Japan*] [*Seismograph station code, US Geological Survey*] [*Closed*] (SEIS)
OKI........... Oko Electric Industry Company (SAUS)
OKIESMO... Oklahoma Machismo [*Term coined by author Mark Singer*]
OKIL......... Killaloe Public Library, Ontario [*Library symbol*] [*National Library of Canada*] (NLC)
OkIM......... McUrtain County High Education Program, Idabel, OK [*Library symbol*] [*Library of Congress*] (LCLS)
Okin......... Okinawa (AD)
OKIT......... Kitchener Public Library, Ontario [*Library symbol*] [*National Library of Canada*] (NLC)
OKI-TAC..... Oki Transistorized Computer (SAUS)
OKITAI....... Okinawa-Taiwan Submarine Cable (SAUS)
OKITC....... Learning Resource Centre, Conestoga College of Applied Arts and Technology, Kitchener, Ontario [*Library symbol*] [*National Library of Canada*] (NLC)
OKITD....... Doon Pioneer Village, Kitchener, Ontario [*Library symbol*] [*National Library of Canada*] (BIB)
Oki Tech Rev... Oki Technical Review (SAUS)
OKITM....... Ontario Library Service - Saugeen, Kitchener, Ontario [*Library symbol*] [*National Library of Canada*] (NLC)
OKITW....... Kitchener-Waterloo Record, Kitchener, Ontario [*Library symbol*] [*National Library of Canada*] (NLC)
OKITWC..... Waterloo County Board of Education, Kitchener, Ontario [*Library symbol*] [*National Library of Canada*] (NLC)
OKJ.......... Oakland, CA [*Amtrak rail station code*]
OKJ.......... Okada Airlines Ltd. [*Nigeria*] [*ICAO designator*] (FAAC)
OKJ.......... Okayama [*Japan*] [*Airport symbol*] (OAG)
OKJ.......... Oklahoma City Community College, Oklahoma City, OK [*OCLC symbol*] (OCLC)
OKK.......... Charles F. Kettering Foundation, Dayton, OH [*OCLC symbol*] (OCLC)
OKK.......... Kokomo [*Indiana*] [*Airport symbol*] (OAG)
OKK.......... Kokomo, IN [*Location identifier*] [*FAA*] (FAAL)
OKKBWP.... One Kind Kiss Before We Part [*Slang*]
OKL.......... Lake Ontario Regional Library System, Kingston, Ontario [*Library symbol*] [*Obsolete*] [*National Library of Canada*] (NLC)
OkL.......... Lawton Public Library, Lawton, OK [*Library symbol*] [*Library of Congress*] (LCLS)
OKL.......... Oakville, Ontario, Canada [*Amtrak rail station code*]
OKL.......... Oberkommando der Luftwaffe [*Air Force High Command*] [*German military - World War II*]
Okl.......... Oklahoma (DLA)
OKL.......... Oklahoma City [*Diocesan abbreviation*] [*Oklahoma*] (TOCD)
Okl.......... Oklahoma Reports [*A publication*] (DLA)
OKL.......... On Key Label (SAUS)
OKL.......... University of Oklahoma, Law Library, Norman, OK [*OCLC symbol*] (OCLC)
Okla......... Oklahoma (AD)
OKLA........ Oklahoma (AFM)
Okla......... Oklahoma Criminal Reports [*A publication*] (DLA)
OKLA........ Oklahoma Horse Trailer [*NCIC trailer make code*]
Okla......... Oklahoma Supreme Court Reports [*A publication*] (DLA)
OklaAgric Exp Stn Prog Rep... Oklahoma. Agricultural Experiment Station. Progress Report (SAUS)
Okla Ap Ct Rep... Oklahoma Appellate Court Reporter [*A publication*] (DLA)
OklaC........ Oklahoma City (AD)
OklaChronicles... Chronicles of Oklahoma (journ.) (SAUS)
Okla City U... Oklahoma City University (GAGS)
Okla Cr...... Oklahoma Criminal Reports [*A publication*] (DLA)
Okla Crim... Oklahoma Criminal Reports [*A publication*] (DLA)
Okla CULR... Oklahoma City University. Law Review [*A publication*] (DLA)
OklaG........ Oklahoma Gas & Electric Co. [*Associated Press*] (SAG)
Okla Gaz.... Oklahoma Gazette [*A publication*] (DLA)
OklaGE...... Oklahoma Gas & Electric Co. [*Associated Press*] (SAG)
Okla GS..... Oklahoma. Geological Survey (SAUS)
Oklahoma... Oklahoma Reports [*A publication*] (DLA)
Okla ICR.... Oklahoma Industrial Commission Reports [*A publication*] (DLA)
Okla Lawy... Oklahoma Lawyer [*A publication*] (DLA)
Okla LJ...... Oklahoma Law Journal [*A publication*] (DLA)
Okla LRev... Oklahoma Law Review [*A publication*] (SAFN)
Okla Mil Dist... Oklahoma Military District (SAUS)
Okl App..... Oklahoma Court of Appeals (DLA)
Okla SBJ.... Oklahoma State Bar Journal [*A publication*] (DLA)
Okla Sess Laws... Oklahoma Session Laws [*A publication*] (DLA)
Okla Sess Law Serv... Oklahoma Session Law Service (SAUS)
Okla Sess Law Serv... Oklahoma Session Law Service (West) [*A publication*] (DLA)
Okla Stat... Oklahoma Statutes [*A publication*] (DLA)
Okla Stat Ann (West)... Oklahoma Statutes, Annotated (West) [*A publication*] (DLA)
Okla St U... Oklahoma State University (GAGS)
OkLaU....... Langston University, Langston, OK [*Library symbol*] [*Library of Congress*] (LCLS)
OkLC......... Cameron University, Lawton, OK [*Library symbol*] [*Library of Congress*] (LCLS)
Okl City UL Rev... Oklahoma City University. Law Review [*A publication*] (DLA)
OkLC-M..... Cameron College, Medical Library Resource Center, Lawton, OK [*Library symbol*] [*Library of Congress*] (LCLS)
Okl Cr....... Oklahoma Criminal Reports [*A publication*] (DLA)
Okl Cr R.... Oklahoma Criminal Reports [*A publication*] (DLA)
OKLCY....... Oklahoma City, OK [*American Association of Railroads railroad junction routing code*]
OKLEM...... McMichael Canadian Collection, Kleinburg, Ontario [*Library symbol*] [*National Library of Canada*] (NLC)
OKLFC....... Official Kate Linder Fan Club (EA)
OKLN........ Northeastern Regional Library, Kirkland Lake, Ontario [*Library symbol*] [*National Library of Canada*] (NLC)
OKLN........ Ontario Library Service - James Bay, Kirkland Lake, Ontario [*Library symbol*] [*National Library of Canada*] (NLC)
OKLNC...... Kirkland Lake Campus, Northern College, Ontario [*Library symbol*] [*National Library of Canada*] (NLC)
Okl St Ann... Oklahoma Statutes, Annotated [*A publication*] (DLA)
OKLT......... Teck Centennial Public Library, Kirkland Lake, Ontario [*Library symbol*] [*National Library of Canada*] (NLC)
OKLU........ Lumonics, Inc., Kanata, Ontario [*Library symbol*] [*National Library of Canada*] (NLC)
OKLZ........ Oklahoma Feed [*Federal Railroad Administration identification code*]
OKM......... Mitel Corp., Kanata, Ontario [*Library symbol*] [*National Library of Canada*] (NLC)
OKM......... Oberkommando der Kriegsmarine [*Navy High Command*] [*German military - World War II*]
OKM......... Oklahoma Mesonet (SAUS)
OKM......... Okmulgee, OK [*Location identifier*] [*FAA*] (FAAL)
OKM......... Pioneer Multi-County Library, Norman, OK [*OCLC symbol*] (OCLC)
OKMC....... Miller Communications Systems Ltd., Kanata, Ontario [*Library symbol*] [*National Library of Canada*] (NLC)
OkMcC...... Choctaw Nation Multi-County Library, McAlester, OK [*Library symbol*] [*Library of Congress*] (LCLS)
OkMcO...... Oscar Rose Junior College, Midwest City, OK [*Library symbol*] [*Library of Congress*] (LCLS)
OKMD....... Digital Equipment of Canada Ltd., Kanata, Ontario [*Library symbol*] [*National Library of Canada*] (NLC)
OKME........ Metro Canada Ltd., Kingston, Ontario [*Library symbol*] [*National Library of Canada*] (NLC)
OKMM....... Marine Museum of the Great Lakes at Kingston, Ontario [*Library symbol*] [*National Library of Canada*] (NLC)
OkMu........ Muskogee Public Library, Muskogee, OK [*Library symbol*] [*Library of Congress*] (LCLS)
OkMuE...... Eastern Oklahoma District Library, Muskogee, OK [*Library symbol*] [*Library of Congress*] (LCLS)
OkMuV...... United States Veterans Administration Hospital, Muskogee, OK [*Library symbol*] [*Library of Congress*] (LCLS)
OKMV....... Okra Mosaic Virus [*Plant pathology*]
OKN.......... Northeastern Oklahoma State University, Tahlequah, OK [*OCLC symbol*] (OCLC)
OKN.......... Okmulgee Northern Railway Co. [*AAR code*]
OKN.......... Okondja [*Gabon*] [*Airport symbol*] (OAG)
OKN.......... Optokinetic Nystagmus [*Ophthalmology*]
OkN.......... Pioneer Multi-County Library, Norman, OK [*Library symbol*] [*Library of Congress*] (LCLS)
OKNC........ Newbridge Communication Network Corp., Kanata, Ontario [*Library symbol*] [*National Library of Canada*] (BIB)
OKNeoAC... Neo-American Church, the Original Kleptonian [*An association*] (EA)
OkNNS...... National Severe Storms Laboratory, Norman, OK [*Library symbol*] [*Library of Congress*] (LCLS)
OKNO........ Kuwait International NOTAM Office [*Kuwait*] [*ICAO location identifier*] (ICLI)
OKO.......... Of Course [*Telegraphy*] (PCTE)
OKO.......... Oral Roberts University, Tulsa, OK [*OCLC symbol*] (OCLC)
OKOH........ Penrose Division, Ongwanada Hospital, Kingston, Ontario [*Library symbol*] [*National Library of Canada*] (NLC)
OkOk......... Oklahoma County Libraries, Oklahoma City, OK [*Library symbol*] [*Library of Congress*] (LCLS)
OKOK........ Oklahoma Energy Corp. [*OTCBB symbol*]
OkOkB....... Oklahoma Library for the Blind and Physically Handicapped, Oklahoma City, OK [*Library symbol*] [*Library of Congress*] (LCLS)
OkOkC....... Oklahoma Christian College, Oklahoma City, OK [*Library symbol*] [*Library of Congress*] (LCLS)
OkOkCGS... Oklahoma City Geological Survey, Inc., Oklahoma City, OK [*Library symbol*] [*Library of Congress*] (LCLS)
OkOkD....... Deaconess Hospital, Oklahoma City, OK [*Library symbol*] [*Library of Congress*] (LCLS)
OkOke....... Okemah Public Library, Okemah, OK [*Library symbol*] [*Library of Congress*] (LCLS)
OkOkFA..... United States Federal Aviation Administration, Civil Aeromedical Institute, Oklahoma City, OK [*Library symbol*] [*Library of Congress*] (LCLS)
OkOkGS..... Church of Jesus Christ of Latter-Day Saints, Genealogical Society Library, Oklahoma City Branch, Oklahoma City, OK [*Library symbol*] [*Library of Congress*] (LCLS)
OkOkK....... Kerr-McGee Corp., Oklahoma City, OK [*Library symbol*] [*Library of Congress*] (LCLS)
OkOkM...... Mid-America Bible College, Oklahoma City, OK [*Library symbol*] [*Library of Congress*] (LCLS)
OkOkSO..... Oklahoma City Community College, Learning Resources Center, Oklahoma City, OK [*Library symbol*] [*Library of Congress*] (LCLS)
OkOkU...... Oklahoma City University, Oklahoma City, OK [*Library symbol*] [*Library of Congress*] (LCLS)
OkOkU-L.... Oklahoma City University, Law Library, Oklahoma City, OK [*Library symbol*] [*Library of Congress*] (LCLS)

OkOkV .... United States Veterans Administration Hospital, Oklahoma City, OK [*Library symbol*] [*Library of Congress*] (LCLS)
OKOT .... Otonabee Township Library, Keen, Ontario [*Library symbol*] [*National Library of Canada*] (NLC)
OKP .... Citizens' Parliamentary Club [*Poland*] [*Political party*]
OKP .... Oksapmin [*Papua New Guinea*] [*Airport symbol*] (OAG)
OKP .... O'Okiep Copper Co. Ltd. [*AMEX symbol*] (SPSG)
OKP .... Optimized Kill Probability
OKP .... Southern Prairie Library System, Altus, OK [*OCLC symbol*] (OCLC)
OkPo .... Ponca City Public Library, Ponca City, OK [*Library symbol*] [*Library of Congress*] (LCLS)
OkPoC .... Continental Oil Co., R and D Technical Information Service, Ponca City, OK [*Library symbol*] [*Library of Congress*] (LCLS)
OkPot .... Buckley Public Library, Poteau, OK [*Library symbol*] [*Library of Congress*] (LCLS)
OKQ .... Okaba [*Indonesia*] [*Airport symbol*] (OAG)
OKQ .... Queen's University, Kingston, Ontario [*Library symbol*] [*National Library of Canada*] (NLC)
OKQA .... Agnes Etherington Art Centre, Queen's University, Kingston, Ontario [*Library symbol*] [*National Library of Canada*] (NLC)
OKQAR ...... Archives, Queen's University, Kingston, Ontario [*Library symbol*] [*National Library of Canada*] (NLC)
OKQCI .... Canadian Institute of Guided Ground Transport, Queen's University, Kingston, Ontario [*Library symbol*] [*National Library of Canada*] (NLC)
OKQG .... Department of Geography, Queen's University, Kingston, Ontario [*Library symbol*] [*National Library of Canada*] (NLC)
OKQGS ...... Department of Geological Sciences, Queen's University, Kingston, Ontario [*Library symbol*] [*National Library of Canada*] (NLC)
OKQH .... Bracken Library, Queen's University, Kingston, Ontario [*Library symbol*] [*National Library of Canada*] (NLC)
OKQL .... Law Library, Queen's University, Kingston, Ontario [*Library symbol*] [*National Library of Canada*] (NLC)
OKQM .... McArthur College of Education, Queen's University, Kingston, Ontario [*Library symbol*] [*National Library of Canada*] (NLC)
OKQMA ...... Map Collection, Douglas Library, Queen's University, Kingston, Ontario [*Library symbol*] [*National Library of Canada*] (NLC)
OKR .... Optical Key Reader [*Automotive engineering*]
OKR .... Royal Military College of Canada, Kingston, Ontario [*Library symbol*] [*National Library of Canada*] (NLC)
OKRASA ..... Oettinger Kraftfahrttechnische Spezial Anstalt [*Oettinger Automotive Special Institute*] [*Automotive parts*]
OKRC .... Regiopolis - Notre Dame High School, Kingston, Ontario [*Library symbol*] [*National Library of Canada*] (NLC)
Ok Reg ...... Oklahoma Register [*A publication*] (AAGC)
OKRGI .... Rutherford and George Island Township Public Library, Killarney, Ontario [*Library symbol*] [*National Library of Canada*] (NLC)
OKRS .... Science Engineering Library, Royal Military College of Canada, Kingston, Ontario [*Library symbol*] [*National Library of Canada*] (BIB)
OKS .... Ohio Kache Systems Corp.
OKS .... Okanagan Skeena Group Ltd. [*Vancouver Stock Exchange symbol*] [*Toronto Stock Exchange symbol*]
OkS .... Oklahoma State University, Stillwater, OK [*Library symbol*] [*Library of Congress*] (LCLS)
OKS .... Old King's Scholars Association [*Canterbury, England*]
OKS .... Oshkosh, NE [*Location identifier*] [*FAA*] (FAAL)
OKSB .... Southwest Bancorp [*NASDAQ symbol*] (SAG)
OKSBP ...... Southwest Bcp 9.2% cm 'A'Pfd [*NASDAQ symbol*] (TTSB)
OkSEA ...... Oklahoma Society of Enrolled Agents (SAUS)
OkShB .... Oklahoma Baptist University, Shawnee, OK [*Library symbol*] [*Library of Congress*] (LCLS)
OKSL .... St. Lawrence College of Applied Arts and Technology, Kingston, Ontario [*Library symbol*] [*National Library of Canada*] (NLC)
OKSMG ...... Gibson Medical Library, St. Mary's of the Lake Hospital, Kingston, Ontario [*Library symbol*] [*National Library of Canada*] (NLC)
OkS-T .... Oklahoma State University Technical Institute Library, Oklahoma City, OK [*Library symbol*] [*Library of Congress*] (LCLS)
OkSt .... Stillwater Public Library, Stillwater, OK [*Library symbol*] [*Library of Congress*] (LCLS)
OkS-TBO .... Oklahoma State University Technical Branch, Okmulgee, OK [*Library symbol*] [*Library of Congress*] (LCLS)
OKT .... Oakite Products, Inc. (SAUS)
OKT .... [*The*] Oakland Terminal Railway [*Later, OTR*] [*AAR code*]
OKT .... Oklahoma Kansas & Texas Railroad [*Federal Railroad Administration identification code*]
okt .... Oktober [*October*] [*GRM*] (AD)
okt .... Oktyab [*October*] [*Russian*] (AD)
OKT .... Ollier-Klippel-Trenaunay [*Syndrome*] [*Medicine*] (DB)
OKT .... Oslo Kommune Tunnelbanekontoret [*Oslo Subway System*] (AD)
OkT .... Tulsa City-County Library System, Tulsa, OK [*Library symbol*] [*Library of Congress*] (LCLS)
OKT .... University of Tulsa, Tulsa, OK [*OCLC symbol*] (OCLC)
OKT .... Yoakum, TX [*Location identifier*] [*FAA*] (FAAL)
OkTA .... American Association of Petroleum Geologists, Energy Resources Library, Tulsa, OK [*Library symbol*] [*Library of Congress*] (LCLS)
OkTahN ...... Northeastern State College, Tahlequah, OK [*Library symbol*] [*Library of Congress*] (LCLS)
OkTAm ...... AMOCO Production Co., Research Center Geology Library, Tulsa, OK [*Library symbol*] [*Library of Congress*] (LCLS)
OkTC .... Ceja Corp., Tulsa, OK [*Library symbol*] [*Library of Congress*] (LCLS)
OKTc .... Ortho-Kung T-cell (SAUS)
OkTCS .... Cities Service Co., Energy Resources Group, E & P Library, Tulsa, OK [*Library symbol*] [*Library of Congress*] (LCLS)
OkTG .... Thomas Gilcrease Institute of American History and Art, Tulsa, OK [*Library symbol*] [*Library of Congress*] (LCLS)
OkTGS .... Church of Jesus Christ of Latter-Day Saints, Genealogical Society Library, TulsaBranch, Tulsa, OK [*Library symbol*] [*Library of Congress*] (LCLS)
OkTo .... Tonkawa Public Library, Tonkawa, OK [*Library symbol*] [*Library of Congress*] (LCLS)
OkTOR .... Oral Roberts University, Learning Resources Center, Tulsa, OK [*Library symbol*] [*Library of Congress*] (LCLS)
OkTPA .... Pan American Oil Corp., Research Library, Tulsa, OK [*Library symbol*] [*Library of Congress*] (LCLS)
OkTPh .... Philbrook Art Center, Tulsa, OK [*Library symbol*] [*Library of Congress*] (LCLS)
Oktronics ... Oklahoma Electronics (AD)
OkTU .... University of Tulsa, Tulsa, OK [*Library symbol*] [*Library of Congress*] (LCLS)
OkTU-L ...... University of Tulsa, College of Law, Tulsa, OK [*Library symbol*] [*Library of Congress*] (LCLS)
oku .... Oklahoma [*MARC country of publication code*] [*Library of Congress*] (LCCP)
OKU .... Omicron Kappa Upsilon [*Fraternity*]
OkU .... University of Oklahoma, Norman, OK [*Library symbol*] [*Library of Congress*] (LCLS)
OkU-C .... University of Oklahoma, Communication Department, Political Communications Center, Political Commercial Archives, Norman, OK [*Library symbol*] [*Library of Congress*] (LCLS)
OkU-L .... University of Oklahoma, Law School, Norman, OK [*Library symbol*] [*Library of Congress*] (LCLS)
OkU-M .... University of Oklahoma, Health Sciences Center, Oklahoma City, OK [*Library symbol*] [*Library of Congress*] (LCLS)
OkU-P .... University of Oklahoma, College of Pharmacy, Norman, OK [*Library symbol*] [*Library of Congress*] (LCLS)
OKUTD ...... Urban Transportation Development Corp., Kingston, Ontario [*Library symbol*] [*National Library of Canada*] (NLC)
OkU-TM ..... University of Oklahoma, Tulsa Medical College, Tulsa, OK [*Library symbol*] [*Library of Congress*] (LCLS)
OkU-W ...... University of Oklahoma, Western History Collections, Norman, OK [*Library symbol*] [*Library of Congress*] (LCLS)
OKV .... University of Oklahoma, Library School, Norman, OK [*OCLC symbol*] (OCLC)
OKVOAD .... Oklahoma Voluntary Organizations Active in Disaster [*Emergency Management*] (EMA)
OKW .... Brookwood, AL [*Location identifier*] [*FAA*] (FAAL)
OKW .... Oberkommando der Wehrmacht [*Armed Forces High Command*] [*German military - World War II*]
OKW .... University of Tulsa, College of Law, Tulsa, OK [*OCLC symbol*] (OCLC)
OK W/C ..... Okay Except for [*with*] the Corrections [*Proofreading*] (WDMC)
OkWeaT ..... Southwestern State College, Weatherford, OK [*Library symbol*] [*Library of Congress*] (LCLS)
OkWo .... Woodward Carnegie Library, Woodward, OK [*Library symbol*] [*Library of Congress*] (LCLS)
OKX .... Central State University, Edmond, OK [*OCLC symbol*] (OCLC)
OKXS .... Xenotech Systems, Inc., Kitchener, Ontario [*Library symbol*] [*National Library of Canada*] (NLC)
OKY .... Oakey [*Queensland*] [*Airport symbol*] (AD)
OKY .... Oklahoma City University, Law Library, Oklahoma City, OK [*OCLC symbol*] (OCLC)
OKZ .... Phillips University, Zollars Memorial Library, Enid, OK [*OCLC symbol*] (OCLC)
OKZ .... Sandersville, GA [*Location identifier*] [*FAA*] (FAAL)
OL .... London Public Library, Ontario [*Library symbol*] [*National Library of Canada*] (NLC)
OL .... Object Language (SAUS)
OL .... Object Lifecycles [*Computer science*] (HODG)
O/L .... Observation/Losing [*Army*] (ADDR)
OL .... Observer, Left (SAUS)
OL .... Occupational Level
OL .... Ocean Letter
OL .... October League (AD)
OL .... Oculus Laevus [*Left Eye*] [*Ophthalmology*]
ol .... Oculus Laevus [*Left Eye*] [*Latin*] (AD)
OL .... Odd Lot [*Stock exchange term*]
OL .... Offering Line (SAUS)
OL .... Office Lady [*Japan*] (ECON)
OL .... Office of Labor (SAUS)
OL .... Officer of the Order of Leopold
OL .... Official Liquidator [*British*] (ROG)
OL .... Ohio Laws [*A publication*] (DLA)
ol .... Oil [*Pharmacy*] (CPH)
OL .... Oil Level (AAG)
ol .... Oil Level (AD)
OL .... Oil Lighter [*Shipping*] [*British*]
OL .... Oiseau-Lyre [*Record label*] [*France*]
OL .... Oldenburg [*German license plate city code*]
OL .... Oldham [*Postcode*] (ODBW)
OL .... Old Latin [*Language, etc.*]
OL .... Old Leysian (WDAA)
Ol .... Oldradus da Ponte de Laude [*Deceased, 1335*] [*Authority cited in pre-1607 legal work*] (DSA)
OL .... Oleum [*Oil*] [*Pharmacy*]
ol .... Oleum [*Oil*] [*Latin*] (AD)
OL .... Oligoblastic Leukemia [*Oncology*]
OL .... Olivary [*Neurology*]
Ol .... Olive [*Political party*] (AD)
ol .... Olive [*Philately*]
OL .... Oliver [*Tire retread brand*]
ol .... Olivine [*CIPW classification*] [*Geology*]
OL .... Olsen Line (AD)

Ol .... Olympian [*of Pindar*] [*Classical studies*] (OCD)
OL .... Olympic
OL .... Olympic Lift [*Sports*]
OL .... Online
OL .... Only Loadable [*Computer science*] (IAA)
OL .... Open Learning (AIE)
OL .... Open Light (SAUS)
OL .... Open Loop
OL .... Operating Level (IEEE)
ol .... Operating License (AD)
OL .... Operating License
OL .... Operating Limit (COE)
OL .... Operating Location [*Army*]
OL .... Operating Log
OL .... Operating Loss
OL .... Operational Left [*NASA*] (NAKS)
OL .... Operational Left DSC or MDM (SAUS)
OL .... Operational Semantics (SAUS)
OL .... Operation Liftoff (EA)
OL .... Operation Limits (SAUS)
O/L .... Operations and Logistics (SAUS)
o/l .... Operations/Logistics (AD)
OL .... Optical Limiter (SAUS)
OL .... Orbital Launch
OL .... Ordered List (SAUS)
OL .... Order of Lafayette (EA)
OL .... Ordinary Leave [*Military*] (AFM)
OL .... Ordinary Letter (WDAA)
OL .... Ordnance Lieutenant [*Navy*] [*British*]
OL .... Organization List (MCD)
OL .... Organizing Language (SAUS)
OL .... Original Learning [*Psychometrics*]
ol .... Or Less (AD)
OL .... Or Less
OL .... Oscillating Limiter (IAA)
OL .... Ostfriesische Lufttransport GmbH [*Germany*] [*ICAO designator*] (ICDA)
OL .... Other Line [*Telecommunications*] (TEL)
OL .... Outgoing Letter
o/l .... Outlook (AD)
OL .... Output Latch
OL .... Output List (SAUS)
OL .... Output Logic (SAUS)
OL .... Outside Left [*Soccer position*]
OL .... Overflow Level
OL .... Overhead Line
OL .... Overlap
OL .... Overlay (NASA)
OL .... Overload
OLA .... Fetal Presentation (Occiput Toward Left Acetabulum) [*Medicine*] (BCRP)
OLA .... Lakefield Public Library, Ontario [*Library symbol*] [*National Library of Canada*] (NLC)
OLA .... National Oceanic and Atmospheric Administration, Rockville, MD [*OCLC symbol*] (OCLC)
OLA .... Oaklahoma Lumbermen's Association (WPI)
ola .... Occipito-Laeva Anterior (AD)
OLA .... Occipitolaeva Anterior [*A fetal position*] [*Medicine*] (AAMN)
OLA .... Occupiers' Liability Act [*1957*] [*British*] (DCTA)
OLA .... Office of Legislative Affairs
OLA .... Office of Legislative Analysis [*Environmental Protection Agency*] (GFGA)
OLA .... Official Languages Act [*Canada*]
OLA .... Ohio Law Abstract [*A publication*] (DLA)
OLA .... Ohio Library Association (AD)
OLA .... Ohio Lumbermen's Association (EARSL)
OLA .... Oklahoma Library Association (AD)
OLA .... Oklahoma Lupus Association (EARSL)
OLA .... Oligonucleotide Ligation Assay [*Analytical biochemistry*]
OLA .... Ollier-Klippel-Trenaunay [*Syndromes*] [*Medicine*] (QSUL)
OLA .... On-Line AUTODIN (SAUS)
OLA .... Ontario Library Association [*Canada*] (AD)
OL-A .... Operating Location-A (SAUS)
OLA .... Optical Laboratories Association (EA)
OLA .... Optical Link in the Atmosphere (PDAA)
OLA .... Optimally Localized Averages [*Mathematics*]
OLA .... Orbital Lock Assembly
OLA .... Oregon Lodging Association (EARSL)
OLA .... Original Language (SAUS)
OLA .... Orland [*Norway*] [*Airport symbol*] (OAG)
OLA .... Osteopathic Libraries Association [*Defunct*] (EA)
OLA .... Overview Latin America (EA)
OLA .... Walungge [*Language symbol*] (ETLW)
OLAA .... Office of Legal Aid Administration
OLABS .... Offshore Labrador Biological Studies (SAUS)
OL Abs .... Ohio Law Abstract [*A publication*] (DLA)
OLA Bulletin... Ohio Library Association. Bulletin (SAUS)
OLAC .... Offline Adaptive Computer [*Computer science*]
OLAC .... On-Line Accelerated Cooling (SAUS)
OLAC .... Online Audiovisual Catalogers [*An association*] (EA)
OLAD .... Operating Location Alert Detachment (SAUS)
OLADE .... Organizacion Latin-Americana de Energia [*Latin American Energy Organization*] [*Spanish*] (AD)
OLAF .... Operand Lattice File (SAUS)
OLAFL .... Front of Leeds and Lansdowne Public Library, Lansdowne, Ontario [*Library symbol*] [*National Library of Canada*] (NLC)
OLAFS .... Office of Legal Aid and Family Services
OLAFS .... Orbiting and Launch Approach Flight Simulator
OLAG .... London Research Center, Agriculture Canada [*Centre de Recherches de London, Agriculture Canada*] London, Ontario [*Library symbol*] [*National Library of Canada*] (NLC)
OLAG .... Oesterreichische Luftverkehrs Aktiengesellschaft [*Austrian Airlines*]
O-Lager .... Ortslager (SAUS)
OLak .... Lakewood Public Library, Lakewood, OH [*Library symbol*] [*Library of Congress*] (LCLS)
OLakB .... Lakewood Board of Education, Lakewood, OH [*Library symbol*] [*Library of Congress*] (LCLS)
OLAL .... Bibliotheque Publique du Canton d'Alfred [*Alfred Township Public Library*],Lefaivre, Ontario [*Library symbol*] [*National Library of Canada*] (BIB)
OLAM .... Online Alpha Monitor (SAUS)
OLAMINE... Ethanolamine [*Also, EA, Etn*] [*USAN*] [*Organic chemistry*]
OLAN .... Landsdowne Public Library, Ontario [*Library symbol*] [*National Library of Canada*] (BIB)
OLA-N .... Office of Legislative Affairs, Navy (MUGU)
OLAN .... On-Board Local Area Network [*Aviation*]
O/LAND .... Overland
O/LANDED... Overlanded
ol & t .... Owners, Landlords, and Tenants (AD)
OL & T .... Owners, Landlords, and Tenants [*Liability insurance*]
OL&T .... Owners, Landlords, and Tenants [*Insurance*]
OLanF .... Fairfield County District Library, Lancaster, OH [*Library symbol*] [*Library of Congress*] (LCLS)
OLanU .... Ohio University, Lancaster Branch Campus, Lancaster, OH [*Library symbol*] [*Library of Congress*] (LCLS)
OLAP .... Online Analytical Processing [*Computer science*] (CDE)
OLAPEC .... Organization of Latin American Petroleum Exporting Countries (AD)
OLAR .... On-Line Analytical Processing [*Computer science*]
OLAS .... Office of Arid Land Studies [*University of Arizona*] (AD)
OLAS .... On-Line Acquisitions Systems [*Brodart, Inc.*] [*Book acquisition system*] [*Information service or system*] (IID)
OLAS .... Organizacion Latino-Americana de Solidaridad [*Latin American Solidarity Organization*] [*Spanish*] (AD)
OLAS .... Organization of Latin American Students (AD)
OLATH .... Olathe, KS [*American Association of Railroads railroad junction routing code*]
OLATN .... Township of Norfolk Public Library, Langton, Ontario [*Library symbol*] [*National Library of Canada*] (NLC)
OLAU .... Lanark Union Public Library, Lanark, Ontario [*Library symbol*] [*National Library of Canada*] (BIB)
OLAU .... Occidental Chemical [*Intermodal shipping container symbol*] (TVRC)
Olav Tryg... Olav Trygvason (AD)
OLAW .... Office of Laboratory Animal Welfare
OLB .... London Board of Education, Ontario [*Library symbol*] [*National Library of Canada*] (NLC)
OLB .... Odd-Lot Broker [*Finance*] (MHDW)
OLB .... Oertlicher Landwirtschaftsbetrieb [*Local Agricultural Enterprise*] [*German*]
OLB .... Official Log Book [*Ship's diary*] (DS)
OLB .... Ohio Law Bulletin [*A publication*] (DLA)
OLB .... Olbia [*Italy*] [*Airport symbol*] (OAG)
OLB .... Olfactory Bulb [*Medicine*] (EDAA)
OLB .... Omaha, Lincoln & Beatrice Railway Co. [*AAR code*]
OLB .... Online Batch (NITA)
OLB .... Open Liver Biopsy [*Medicine*] (DMAA)
OLB .... Open-Loop Bandwidth [*Also, OLBW*]
OLB .... Open Lung Biopsy
OLB .... Outer Lead Bond [*Integrated circuit technology*]
OLB .... Outside Linebacker [*Football*]
OLBA .... Beirut/International [*Lebanon*] [*ICAO location identifier*] (ICLI)
OLBA .... Ohio Licensed Beverage Association (EARSL)
OLBANK PAC... Old National Bank in Evansville PAC [*Evansville, IN*] (PACS)
OLBGFC .... Official Lane Brody Global Fan Club (EA)
OLBIEN .... Olsen's Biomass Energy [*G. V. Olsen Associates*] [*Information service or system*] (CRD)
OLBK .... Old Line Bank [*NASDAQ symbol*] (QUAN)
olbm .... Orbital Launched Balistic Missile (AD)
OLBM .... Orbital Launched Ballistic Missile [*Military*] (WDAA)
OLBM .... Overlay Battle Manager
OLBR .... Brescia College, London, Ontario [*Library symbol*] [*National Library of Canada*] (NLC)
OlBr .... Olive Brown (AD)
OLBR .... Operational LASER Beam Recorder
OLBS .... OnLine Bookstore
OLBV .... Beirut [*Lebanon*] [*ICAO location identifier*] (ICLI)
OLBW .... Open-Loop Bandwidth [*Also, OLB*]
OLBZ .... Old Ben #25 Mine [*Federal Railroad Administration identification code*]
olc .... Brothers of Our Lady of Providence (TOCD)
OLC .... Catholic Central High School, London, Ontario [*Library symbol*] [*National Library of Canada*] (NLC)
OLC .... Linfield College, McMinnville, OR [*OCLC symbol*] (OCLC)
OLC .... Oak Leaf Cluster [*Military decoration*]
OLC .... Occupation Level Crossing (HEAS)
OLC .... Office of Legal Counsel [*Department of Justice*]
Ol C .... Oil Cable (SAUS)
Olc .... Olcott's United States District Court Reports, Admiralty [*A publication*] (DLA)

OLC .... Olema [*California*] [*Seismograph station code, US Geological Survey*] (SEIS)
OLC .... Oneida, TN [*Location identifier*] [*FAA*] (FAAL)
OLC .... One Level Code (SAUS)
OLC .... On-Line Classifier (SAUS)
olc .... On-Line Computer (AD)
OLC .... Online Computer [*System*] [*Computer science*]
OLC .... Ontario Ladies College
OLC .... Ontario Land Corporation (SAUS)
OLC .... Ontario Library Co-Operative [*UTLAS symbol*]
OLC .... Ontario Library Council (SAUS)
OLC .... Open-Loop Control (CIST)
OLC .... Operating Location Clerk (SAUS)
OLC .... Operational Logical Circuit (SAUS)
OLC .... Operation Load Code (MCD)
OLC .... Operator-Level Chan (SAUS)
OLC .... Operator-Level Chart (AFIT)
OLC .... Optical Link Card (SAUS)
OLC .... Optical Loop Carrier (SAUS)
OLC .... Order Location and Control (MCD)
OLC .... Oubain-Like Compound [*Biochemistry*]
OLC .... Outgoing Line Circuit
OLC .... Overload Class (CGWS)
OLC .... Overseas Liaison Committee [*of the American Council on Education*] [*Later, Division of International Educational Relations of the American Council on Education*] (EA)
OLC .... Sisters of Our Lady of Charity (TOCD)
OLCA .... Office of Legislation and Congressional Affairs (SAUS)
OLCA .... Online Circuit Analysis [*System*] [*Computer science*]
OLCA .... Orifice of Left Coronary Artery [*Medicine*] (MELL)
Olc Adm .... Olcott's United States District Court Reports, Admiralty [*A publication*] (DLA)
OLCAO ...... Orthogonalized Linear Combination of Atomic Orbitals [*Optics*]
OLCA System... One-Line Circuit Analysis System (SAUS)
OLCA System... On-Line Circuit Analysis System (SAUS)
OLCC .... Olympus Capital Corp. (SAUS)
OLCC .... On-Line Card Catalog (SAUS)
OLCC .... Ontario Cancer Clinic, London, Ontario [*Library symbol*] [*National Library of Canada*] (NLC)
OLCC .... Optimum Life Cycle Costing (PDAA)
olcc .... Optimum Life-Cycle Costing (AD)
OLCC .... Ordinary Low Current Configuration [*Magnetic field*]
OLCC .... Our Lady of Cincinnati College [*Ohio*]
OLCC .... Overseas Labour Consultative Committee [*British*] (DCTA)
OLCD .... Overseas Liaison and Consultancy Department (NITA)
OLCG .... Clarkson Gordon, London, Ontario [*Library symbol*] [*National Library of Canada*] (BIB)
OLCM .... Olicom AS [*NASDAQ symbol*] (SAG)
OLCMF ...... Olicom A/S [*NASDAQ symbol*] (TTSB)
OLCMS ...... On-Line Cargo Movement System (SAUS)
Ol Conv ..... Oliver's Conveyancing [*A publication*] (DLA)
Olcott .... Olcott's United States District Court Reports, Admiralty [*A publication*] (DLA)
Olcott Adm (F)... Olcott's United States District Court Reports, Admiralty [*A publication*] (DLA)
Olcott's Adm... Olcott's United States District Court Reports, Admiralty [*A publication*] (DLA)
OLCP .... Oil City Petroleum, Inc. (SAUS)
OLCP .... Online Complex Processing [*Computer science*] (CDE)
OLCP .... Open-Loop Conjugate Point (SAUS)
OLCPR ...... Canadian Peace Research Institute, London, Ontario [*Library symbol*] [*National Library of Canada*] (NLC)
OLCR .... Clark Road Secondary School, London, Ontario [*Library symbol*] [*National Library of Canada*] (NLC)
OLCR .... On-Line Character Recognition (SAUS)
O L Cr .... Ordinance Lieutenent-Commander (AD)
OLCR .... Ordnance Lieutenant-Commander [*Navy*] [*British*]
OLCR .... Sisters of Our Lady of Charity of Refuge [*Roman Catholic religious order*]
OLCS .... On-Line Computer System (AD)
OLCS .... On-Line Cover System (SAUS)
OLCSSCP... Children's Psychiatric Research Institute, Ontario Ministry of Community and Social Services, London, Ontario [*Library symbol*] [*National Library of Canada*] (NLC)
OLC System... One-Line Computer System (SAUS)
OLCT .... Tax Services, Canada Trust Co., London, Ontario [*Library symbol*] [*National Library of Canada*] (BIB)
OLCV .... Century Village, Lang, Ontario [*Library symbol*] [*National Library of Canada*] (BIB)
OLCV PAC... Oregon League of Conservation Voters PAC [*Portland, OR*] (PACS)
OLD .... Obstructive Lung Disease [*Medicine*] (DMAA)
OLD .... Odd Lot Dealer
OLD .... Office of Legislative Development [*Bureau of Indian Affairs*]
OLD .... Ohio Lower Court Decisions [*A publication*] (DLA)
Old .... Oldradus da Ponte de Laude [*Deceased, 1335*] [*Authority cited in pre-1607 legal work*] (DSA)
Old .... Oldright's Nova Scotia Reports [*A publication*] (DLA)
OLD .... Old Town, ME [*Location identifier*] [*FAA*] (FAAL)
OLD .... Online Debug [*Computer science*] (IAA)
OLD .... On-Line Tests and Diagnostics [*Environmental science*] (COE)
OLD .... Onsite Licensing Office (SAUS)
OLD .... Open-Loop Damping
OLD .... Open Loop Drive (SAUS)
OLD .... Operating Level Days
OLD .... Operations and Liquidations Division [*Federal Savings and Loans Insurance Corporation*]
OLD .... Oral Lethal Dose [*Medicine*]
OLD .... Orthochromatic Leukodystrophy [*Medicine*] (DMAA)
OLD .... Ototoxic Labyrinthine Damage [*Medicine*] (EDAA)
OLD .... Our Lady of Deliverance Syriac, Union City [*Diocesan abbreviation*] [*New Jersey*] (TOCD)
OLD .... Oxford Latin Dictionary [*A publication*]
OldAmer .... Old America Stores, Inc. [*Associated Press*] (SAG)
OLDAP ...... Online Data Processor (PDAA)
OLDB .... Old Natl Bancorp(Ind) [*NASDAQ symbol*] (TTSB)
OLDB .... On-Line Data Bank [*NASA*] (NAKS)
OLDB .... Online Database [*or Data Bank*]
Old Bailey... London's Central Criminal Court [*England*] (AD)
Old Bailey Chr... Old Bailey Chronicle [*A publication*] (DLA)
Old Ben ..... Benloe in Benloe and Dalison's English Common Pleas Reports [*A publication*] (DLA)
Old Benloe... Benloe in Benloe and Dalison's English Common Pleas Reports [*A publication*] (DLA)
OLDC .... Off-Line Data Collection (SAUS)
OLDC .... One-Line Data Collecting (SAUS)
OLDC .... Online Data Collection [*Computer science*] (MCD)
OLDD .... Beirut [*Lebanon*] [*ICAO location identifier*] (ICLI)
OldDom ..... Old Dominion Freight Lines, Inc. [*Associated Press*] (SAG)
Old Dom U... Old Dominion University (GAGS)
OLD ECC.... Ordinary Linear Differential Equations with Constant Coefficients [*Mathematics*]
Old Ent ...... Rastell's Old Entries [*A publication*] (DLA)
OLDERT ..... On-Line Executive for Real-Time [*Computer science*] (MHDB)
old-fash ..... Old Fashioned (AD)
Oldfos .... Old Established Forces (AD)
OLDFOS ..... Old Established Forces [*Military*] (CINC)
OldGBl ...... Oldenburgisches Gesetzblatt (SAUS)
OLDHM ...... Oldham [*City in England*]
OLDI .... On-Line Data Input (SAUS)
OLDI .... Online Data Interchange (DA)
OLDIV .... Operations/Lookout and Recognition Division (DNAB)
OldKent ..... Old Kent Financial Corp. [*Associated Press*] (SAG)
Old Maid's... Old Maid's Day [*June 4*] (AD)
Old Nat Brev... Old Natura Brevium [*A publication*] (DLA)
OldNB .... Old National Bancorp Industries [*Associated Press*] (SAG)
Oldn Pr ...... Oldnall's Sessions Practice [*A publication*] (DLA)
OLDO .... On-Line Data Output (SAUS)
OLDP .... Off-Line Data Processing (SAUS)
Oldr .... Oldradus da Ponte de Laude [*Deceased, 1335*] [*Authority cited in pre-1607 legal work*] (DSA)
OLDR .... Old Republic International Corp. [*NASDAQ symbol*] (COMM)
Oldr .... Oldright's Nova Scotia Reports [*A publication*] (DLA)
OLDR .... On-Line Data Reduction (SAUS)
OLDR .... On-Time Data Reduction (SAUS)
OLDR .... Quick Look Data Reference [*NASA*] (NAKS)
Oldra .... Oldradus da Ponte de Laude [*Deceased, 1335*] [*Authority cited in pre-1607 legal work*] (DSA)
Oldra de Lau... Oldradus da Ponte de Laude [*Deceased, 1335*] [*Authority cited in pre-1607 legal work*] (DSA)
old rep ...... Old Repertory (AD)
OldRep ...... Old Republic International Corp. [*Associated Press*] (SAG)
Oldr NS ..... Oldright's Nova Scotia Reports [*A publication*] (DLA)
OldRp .... Old Republic International Corp. [*Associated Press*] (SAG)
OLDS .... Off-Axis LASER Detection System (MCD)
OLDS .... Offshore Lease Data System [*Department of the Interior*] [*Information service or system*] (IID)
Olds .... Oldsmobile (AD)
OLDS .... Oldsmobile [*Automotive engineering*]
OLDS .... Oldsmobile [*NCIC car make code*]
OLDS .... Oldsmobile (trucks) [*NCIC truck make code*]
OLDS .... On-Line Detection System [*Nuclear energy*]
OLDS .... Online Display System [*Computer science*]
OLDS .... Open Loop Drive System (SAUS)
OLDS .... Ozone Level Depleting Substances (LDOE)
OLDSA ...... Old Saybrook, CT [*American Association of Railroads railroad junction routing code*]
Old SC ...... Old Select Cases [*Oudh, India*] [*A publication*] (DLA)
OldSecBc ... Old Second Bancorp, Inc. [*Associated Press*] (SAG)
OLDSS .... Online Database Search Services Directory [*A publication*]
OLDT .... Oklahoma Trailer OKLH Trails Trailer [*NCIC trailer make code*]
Old Territorial... Old Territorial Penitentiary (SAUS)
Old Test..... Old Testament (AD)
OLDU .... On-Line Distillation Unit (SAUS)
Old Vetern... Caring for the Older Veteran (journ.) (SAUS)
OLE .... Lane Community College, Eugene, OR [*OCLC symbol*] (OCLC)
OLE .... Leamington Public Library, Ontario [*Library symbol*] [*National Library of Canada*] (NLC)
OLe .... Lebanon Public Library, Lebanon, OH [*Library symbol*] [*Library of Congress*] (LCLS)
OLE .... Object-Linked Environment (SAUS)
OLE .... Object Linking and Embedding [*Windows*] [*Computer science*]
OLE .... Office for Library Education [*American Library Association*]
OLE .... Olean [*New York*] [*Airport symbol*] (AD)
OLE .... Olean, NY [*Location identifier*] [*FAA*] (FAAL)
OLE .... On-Line Edit (SAUS)
OLE .... On-Line Encyclopedia [*Hypergraphics Corp.*]
OLE .... Online Enquiry [*System*]
OLE .... On-Line Equipment (SAUS)

OLE .... Ontario Land Economist [*Canada*] (DD)
OLE .... Optical Logic Etalon (ACAE)
OLE .... Oral Language Evaluation [*English and Spanish test*]
OLE .... Organisational Learning in Enterprises (EURO)
OLE .... Organizational Leadership for Executives [*Military*] (RDA)
OLE .... Oriole Communication [*Vancouver Stock Exchange symbol*]
OLE .... Outside Location Engineer (MCD)
OLEA .... Office of Law Enforcement Assistance (AD)
OLEASS ..... Organic Long Endurance Airborne Area Surveillance System (ACAE)
OLeC .... Lebanon Correctional Institution Library, Lebanon, OH [*Library symbol*] [*Library of Congress*] (LCLS)
OLEC .... Other Local Exchange Carrier (SAUS)
Oleck Corporations... Oleck's Modern Corporation Law [*A publication*] (DLA)
OLED .... Organic Light Emitting Device (SAUS)
OLED .... Organic Light-Emitting Device [*Photonics*]
OLED .... Organic Light Emitting Diode [*Electronics*]
OLED .... Organic Light Emitting Display (SAUS)
OLE DB ..... OLE Database [*Computer science*]
OLEDS ..... Object Linking and Embedding Directory Services (SAUS)
OLEG .... On-Line English Grammar [*Internet resource*]
O Legal News... Ohio Legal News [*A publication*] (DLA)
OLEI .... Point Pelee National Park, Parks Canada [*Parc National de la Pointe-Pelee, Parcs Canada*] Leamington, Ontario [*Library symbol*] [*National Library of Canada*] (NLC)
OLELB .... Lyn Branch, Elizabethtown Township Public Library, Ontario [*Library symbol*] [*National Library of Canada*] (BIB)
OLEM .... Other Loans Especially Mentioned (EBF)
oleo .... Oleomargarine [*Dietetics*] (DAVI)
oleo .... Oleoresins (AD)
OLEO .... Open Linking and Embedding of Objects (SAUS)
OLEO .... Orbiting Large Engineering Observatory (SAUS)
OLEP .... Office of Law Enforcement and Planning (AD)
OLEP .... Office of Law Enforcement Programs [*Federal government*]
OLEP .... Office of Legal Enforcement Policy [*Environmental Protection Agency*] (EPA)
OLEP .... Organization for the Lifelong Establishment of Paternity (EA)
OLEP .... Osculating Lunar Elements Program (SAUS)
OLER .... Olericulture
olericult... Olericulture (AD)
OLERT .... Online Executive for Real Time [*Computer science*] (IEEE)
OLES .... Online Editorial System [*Computer science*] (DGA)
OLESS .... Open Learning Electronic Support Services [*Australia*]
OLETC .... Office of Law Enforcement Technology [*National Institute of Justice*]
OLETC .... Office of Law Enforcement Technology Commercialization (SAUS)
O level ...... Ordinary Level (ODBW)
O-level ...... Ordinary Level Examination [*Education*] (WDAA)
O-levels ..... Ordinary Levels [*of educational tests*] (AD)
OLEW .... Open Learning Experimental Workshop (EURO)
OLeWHi ..... Warren County Historical Society, Lebanon, OH [*Library symbol*] [*Library of Congress*] (LCLS)
OLEX .... Ontario Livestock Exchange (SAUS)
OLF .... A Perceived Air Quality Term that Attempts to Quantify the Level of Odorous Pollutants in OLFS [*Industrial hygiene term*] (OHS)
OLF .... Ohio Library Foundation (AD)
OLF .... Old Low Franconian [*Language, etc.*]
olf .... Olfactory [*Medicine*] (DAVI)
OLF .... One Hundred Linear Feet (SAUS)
olf .... On-Line Filing (AD)
OLF .... Online Filing [*Computer science*] (PDAA)
OLF .... Only Living Father [*of Newfoundland's confederation with Canada in 1949*] [*Epithet for Joseph R. Smallwood*]
OLF .... Open Learning Federation [*British*] (DI)
OLF .... Open-Loop Feedback (SAUS)
OLF .... Orbital Launch Facility
OLF .... Orbiter Landing Facility [*NASA*] (NASA)
OLF .... Organ Literature Foundation (EA)
OLF .... Oromo Liberation Front [*Ethiopia*] [*Political party*] (PD)
OLF .... Outline Font [*Computer science*] (PCM)
OLF .... Outlying Field [*Army*]
OLF .... Overland Flow (SAUS)
OLF .... Wolf Point [*Montana*] [*Airport symbol*] (OAG)
OLF .... Wolf Point, MT [*Location identifier*] [*FAA*] (FAAL)
OLFC .... Fanshawe College of Applied Arts and Technology, London, Ontario [*Library symbol*] [*National Library of Canada*] (NLC)
OLFDEMO... Outline Font Demonstration [*Computer science*]
OLFO .... Open-Loop Feedback Optimal (PDAA)
OLFR .... Olfactory Receptor [*Medicine*] (DMAA)
OLFZ .... Olympic Foundry [*Federal Railroad Administration identification code*]
OLG .... Nordmaling [*Sweden*] [*Airport symbol*] (AD)
OLG .... Oberlandesgericht [*District Court of Appeal*] [*German*] (DLA)
OLG .... Ohio Legislative Service Commission, Columbus, OH [*OCLC symbol*] (OCLC)
OLG .... Old Low German [*Language, etc.*]
OLG .... Oligodendrocyte [*Also, ODC*] [*Cytology*]
OlG .... Olive Green (AD)
OLG .... Open Level Generation (SAUS)
OLG .... Open-Loop Gain
OLG .... Operation Landing Ground (SAUS)
OLG .... Sisters of Guadalupe [*Roman Catholic religious order*]
OLG .... Sisters of Our Lady of the Garden [*Roman Catholic religious order*]
OLGA .... On-line Guitar Archive [*Internet site*]
OLGC .... Orthologic Corp. [*NASDAQ symbol*] (SAG)
OLGE .... Olgen Manufacturing Company [*NCIC trailer make code*]
OIGI .... TIGR [*The Institute of Genomic Research*] Oryzias latipes Gene Index [*Database*] (GDD)
OLGR .... [*The*] Oilgear Co. [*NASDAQ symbol*] (NQ)
OLH .... Huron College, London, Ontario [*Library symbol*] [*National Library of Canada*] (NLC)
OLH .... Old Harbor [*Alaska*] [*Airport symbol*] (OAG)
OLH .... Old Harbor, AK [*Location identifier*] [*FAA*] (FAAL)
OLH .... Orpen's Light Horse [*British military*] (DMA)
OLH .... Ovine Lactogenic Hormone [*Endocrinology*] (MAE)
OLH .... Ovine Luteinizing Hormone [*Endocrinology*]
OLH .... Oxfordshire Light Horse [*British military*] (DMA)
OLHC .... Old Lyme Holding Corp. [*NASDAQ symbol*] (SAG)
OLHI .... Ovine Luteinizing Hormone (SAUS)
OLHM .... London Historical Museums, Ontario [*Library symbol*] [*National Library of Canada*] (BIB)
OLHMIS ..... On-Line Hospital Management Information System [*Computer science*]
Ol Horse .... Oliphant's Law of Horses [*6th ed.*] [*1908*] [*A publication*] (DLA)
OLI .... Lindsay Public Library, Ontario [*Library symbol*] [*National Library of Canada*] (NLC)
OLI .... Ocean Living Institute [*Defunct*] (EA)
OLI .... Olafsvik [*Iceland*] [*Airport symbol*] (OAG)
Oli .... Oligocene (ODA)
OLI .... Oliktok, AK [*Location identifier*] [*FAA*] (FAAL)
Oli .... Oliver (AD)
OLI .... Online Information
OLI .... On-Line Input (SAUS)
OLI .... Open Learning Institute [*UTLAS symbol*]
OLI .... Open Link Interface (TNIG)
OLI .... Operation Lifesaver [*An association*] (EA)
OLI .... Optical Line Interface (SAUS)
OLI .... Optical Phone Line Interface (SAUS)
OLI .... Originating Line Information (SAUS)
OLI .... Out-of-Line Igniter [*Military*] (CAAL)
OLI .... Out-of-Line Interrupter (MCD)
OLI .... Out-of-Lock Indicator (SAUS)
OLI .... Overlay Interceptor
OLI .... Oxfordshire Light Infantry [*Military unit*] [*British*]
OLiC .... Columbiana County Court House, Lisbon, OH [*Library symbol*] [*Library of Congress*] (LCLS)
OLIC .... Online Information Centre (NITA)
OLIC .... On-Line Inspection Centre [*British Gas*] (WDAA)
OL-IC .... Operating Location-Iceland (DNAB)
O-Licence... Operators Licence (SAUS)
O-license... Operator's License (AD)
Olicom ..... Olicom AS [*Associated Press*] (SAG)
OLICU .... Little Current Public Library, Ontario [*Library symbol*] [*National Library of Canada*] (NLC)
OLICUS ..... Sucker Creek Indian Band Public Library, Little Current, Ontario [*Library symbol*] [*National Library of Canada*] (NLC)
OLID .... On-Line Identification (SAUS)
OLIDS .... Open Loop Insulin Delivery System [*Medicine*] (DMAA)
OLIF .... Orbiter Landing Instrumentation Facilities [*NASA*] (NASA)
OLIFLM ..... Online Image Forming Light Modulator
Olig .... Oligocene (AD)
OLIH .... Lion's Head Branch, Bruce County Public Library, Ontario [*Library symbol*] [*National Library of Canada*] (NLC)
OLI/HMD .... Online Images from the History of Medicine Division (SAUS)
OLIM .... Olimpiadas [*Ministerio de Cultura*] [*Spain*] [*Information service or system*] (CRD)
OLima .... Lima Public Library, Lima, OH [*Library symbol*] [*Library of Congress*] (LCLS)
OLimaAL .... Allen County Law Library, Lima, OH [*Library symbol*] [*Library of Congress*] (LCLS)
OLIMCH ..... Open Learning Information and Materials Clearing House [*Australia*]
OLIN .... Oklahoma Library Information Network (SAUS)
Olin .... Olin Corp. [*Associated Press*] (SAG)
OLIP .... Online Instrument Package [*Computer science*] (NRCH)
OLIPaC ..... Office of Land Information Policy and Coordination (SAUS)
OLIPAC ..... Oligotrophic Pacific (SAUS)
Oliph Hor... Oliphant's Law of Horses [*6th ed.*] [*1908*] [*A publication*] (DLA)
OLIPS .... Open Literature Information Processing System (ACAE)
OLIPSE ..... Optizon Liquid Phase Sintering Experiment [*NASA*] (SPST)
OLIS .... Listowel Public Library, Ontario [*Library symbol*] [*National Library of Canada*] (NLC)
OLIS .... Online Information Services [*Mercer County Community College Library*] (OLDSS)
OLIS .... On-Line Information System (SAUS)
OLIS .... Oregon Legislative Information System [*Information service or system*]
OLIS .... Oxford Library Information System (TNIG)
OLIS .... Oxford Library Integrated System [*British*] (TELE)
OLIS .... Oxide Layer Isolation Structure
OLISF .... Frost Campus Library, Sir Sandford Fleming College, Lindsay, Ontario [*Library symbol*] [*National Library of Canada*] (NLC)
OLIT .... Open Look Interface Toolkit (SAUS)
OLIT .... OPEN LOOK Intrinsic Toolkit
OLitW .... Wagnalls Memorial Library, Lithopolis, OH [*Library symbol*] [*Library of Congress*] (LCLS)
OLIV .... Oleum Olivae [*Olive Oil*] [*Pharmacy*] (ROG)
OLIV .... Victoria County Public Library, Lindsay, Ontario [*Library symbol*] [*National Library of Canada*] (NLC)
Oliv B & L... Oliver, Beavan, and Lefroy's English Railway and Canal Cases [*A publication*] (DLA)
Oliv Conv... Oliver's Conveyancing [*A publication*] (DLA)

Olive......... Olivera (AD)
OLIVER...... Online Instrumentation via Energetic Radioisotopes [*Computer science*] (PDAA)
OLIVER...... Online Interactive Variable Editing Reporter [*Computer science*] (IAA)
Olivet Naz U... Olivet Nazarene University (GAGS)
Oliv Prec... Oliver's Precedents [*A publication*] (DLA)
OLIVR....... Online Interactive Virtual Reality (SAUS)
OLIVW....... Walden Public Library, Lively, Ontario [*Library symbol*] [*National Library of Canada*] (BIB)
OLIW........ Olive-Capped Warbler [*North American bird banding code*] (BIBA)
OLJ.......... Ohio Law Journal [*A publication*] (DLA)
OLJ.......... Order of St. Lazarus of Jerusalem [*British*]
OLJ.......... Oudh Law Journal [*India*] [*A publication*] (DLA)
OLJ.......... Spokane, WA [*Location identifier*] [*FAA*] (FAAL)
OLJOD....... Only Limited Jobbing Demand [*Telegraphy*] (PCTE)
OL Jour..... Ohio Law Journal [*A publication*] (DLA)
OL Jour..... Oudh Law Journal [*India*] [*A publication*] (DLA)
OLK.......... King's College, London, Ontario [*Library symbol*] [*National Library of Canada*] (NLC)
OLK.......... Salomon, Inc. [*AMEX symbol*] (SPSG)
OLK.......... Salomon Inc, 7.25% ORCL'ELKS' [*AMEX symbol*] (TTSB)
OLK.......... Wolf Lake, IN [*Location identifier*] [*FAA*] (FAAL)
OLKK........ Tripoli [*Lebanon*] [*ICAO location identifier*] (ICLI)
OLKV........ Tripoli [*Lebanon*] [*ICAO location identifier*] (ICLI)
OLL.......... Larder Lake Public Library, Ontario [*Library symbol*] [*National Library of Canada*] (BIB)
OLL.......... Oceaneering International, Inc. (SAUS)
OLL.......... Office of Legislative Liaison (AD)
OLL.......... Ollague [*Chile*] [*Seismograph station code, US Geological Survey*] [*Closed*] (SEIS)
OLL.......... Online Learning (GART)
OLL.......... Open-Loop Loss (SAUS)
OLL.......... Organic Liquid LASER
OLL.......... Our Lady of Lebanon of Los Angeles [*Diocesan abbreviation*] [*California*] (TOCD)
OLL.......... Output Logic Level
OLLA........ Office of Lend-Lease Administration [*World War II*]
OLLA........ Oil Lands Leasing Act
Oll B & F... Ollivier, Bell, and Fitzgerald's New Zealand Reports [*A publication*] (DLA)
OLLC........ Office of the Liquor Licensing Commissioner [*South Australia*]
OLLC........ Our Lady of the Lake College [*Texas*]
OLLCR....... Labatt's Central Research Library, London, Ontario [*Library symbol*] [*National Library of Canada*] (NLC)
OLLE......... Lake Erie Regional Library System, London, Ontario [*Library symbol*] [*National Library of Canada*] (NLC)
OLLE......... Ontario Library Service - Thames, London, Ontario [*Library symbol*] [*National Library of Canada*] (NLC)
OLLFSC..... Open-Loop Leader-Follower Speed Control [*Hydraulics*]
OLLI......... Online Library Index [*Western Michigan University*]
OLLI......... Online Library Information (SAUS)
OLLIE........ Operation Last Laugh Independence Expenditure [*Political Action Committee opposed to Oliver North's candidacy for United States Senator of Virginia*]
OL LINI SI... Oleum Lini sine Igne [*Cold-Drawn Linseed Oil*] [*Pharmacy*] (ROG)
Olliv B & F... Ollivier, Bell, and Fitzgerald's New Zealand Reports [*A publication*] (DLA)
OLLL......... Beirut [*Lebanon*] [*ICAO location identifier*] (ICLI)
OLLS........ Online Logical Simulation System [*Computer science*] (KSC)
OLLS........ Operational Logistics Support Summary (SAUS)
OLLS........ Optical Locator Laser Station (SAUS)
OLLT........ Office of Libraries and Learning Technologies (NITA)
OLLU........ Ocean Leasing [*Intermodal shipping container symbol*] (TVRC)
OLLU........ Our Lady of the Lake University [*Texas*]
OLM......... Lloyd Library and Museum, Cincinnati, OH [*OCLC symbol*] (OCLC)
OLM......... Office for Laboratory Management [*DoD*] (MCD)
OLM......... Oil Life Monitor [*Automotive engineering*]
OLM......... Olympia [*Washington*] [*Airport symbol*] (AD)
OLM......... Olympia, WA [*Location identifier*] [*FAA*] (FAAL)
OLM......... Olympic Financial Ltd [*NYSE symbol*] (TTSB)
OLM......... On-Line Measurement (SAUS)
OLM......... Online Monitor [*Computer science*]
OLM......... Optical Light Microscopy (SAUS)
OLM......... Optical Link Modul (SAUS)
OLM......... Organic Leach Model [*Landfill technology*]
OLM......... Sisters of Charity of Our Lady of Mercy [*Roman Catholic religious order*]
OLMA........ Ontario Lumber Manufacturers Association (SAUS)
OLMAT...... Otis Lennon Mental Ability Test (EDAC)
OLMC........ Olivier Management Corporation (SAUS)
OLMC........ On-Line Machine Control (SAUS)
OLMC........ Output Logic Macrocell [*Computer science*]
OLMCPR.... Operating Limit of MCPR (SAUS)
OLMR....... Office of Labor Management Relations (AD)
OLMR....... Organic Liquid Moderated Reactor
olmr......... Organic Liquid-Moderator Reactor (AD)
Olms......... Decisions of the Judicial Committee of the Privy Council re the British North American Act, 1867, and the Canadian Constitution [*A publication*] (DLA)
OLMS........ Office of Labor-Management Standards [*Department of Labor*]
OLMS........ Osborn Laboratories of Marine Sciences [*New York Zoological Society*] [*Research center*] (RCD)
OLMSA...... Office of Life & Microgravity Sciences & Applications [*NASA*]
Olmsted..... Olmsted's Privy Council Decisions [*1867-1954*] [*A publication*] (DLA)
OLMT........ Organizational Level Maintenance Timer
OLMUG...... Online Librarian's Microcomputer User Group [*Teleconferencing system*]
OLMWPR... Office of Labor-Management and Welfare-Pension Reports [*Department of Labor*]
OLN.......... Colonia Sarmiento [*Argentina*] [*Airport symbol*] (AD)
OLN.......... Lane Public Library, Hamilton, OH [*OCLC symbol*] (OCLC)
OLN.......... Ohio Legal News [*A publication*] (DLA)
OLN.......... Old Man, AK [*Location identifier*] [*FAA*] (FAAL)
OLN.......... Oleylnitril (SAUS)
OLN.......... Olin Corp. [*NYSE symbol*] (TTSB)
OLN.......... Online News (NITA)
OLN.......... Operators Drivers License Number
OLN.......... Operator's License Number (SARE)
OLNEY....... Olney, IL [*American Association of Railroads railroad junction routing code*]
OLO.......... Longlac Public Library, Ontario [*Library symbol*] [*National Library of Canada*] (NLC)
OLO.......... Off-Line Operation (SAUS)
OLO.......... Olomouc [*Czechoslovakia*] [*Airport symbol*] (AD)
OLO.......... Olotillo [*Race of maize*]
OLO.......... Online Operation [*Computer science*]
OLO.......... On-Line Output (SAUS)
OLO.......... Oologah [*Oklahoma*] [*Seismograph station code, US Geological Survey*] [*Closed*] (SEIS)
OLO.......... Operations Launch Order (MUGU)
OLO.......... Orbital Launch Operation
OLOA........ Oronite Lubricating Oil Additive [*Fuels and lubricants*]
OLOC........ Old Lesbians Organizing for Change [*An association*] (EA)
OLOE........ Online Order Entry
OLOF........ Levack Branch, Onaping Falls Public Library, Ontario [*Library symbol*] [*National Library of Canada*] (NLC)
Olofson...... Olofsson Corp. [*Associated Press*] (SAG)
OLOFV....... Olofsson Corp. [*NASDAQ symbol*] (SAG)
OLOG........ Offshore Logistics [*NASDAQ symbol*] (TTSB)
OLOG........ Offshore Logistics, Inc. [*NASDAQ symbol*] (NQ)
OLogC....... Logan-Hocking County District Library, Logan, OH [*Library symbol*] [*Library of Congress*] (LCLS)
OLOGP...... Offshore Logistics, Inc. [*NASDAQ symbol*] (COMM)
OLOGS...... Open-Loop Oxygen-Generating System [*Air Force*]
ol ol......... Olive Oil (AD)
ol oliv....... Oleum Olivae [*Olive Oil*] [*Pharmacy*]
OLOM....... Orbiter Lift-Off Mass [*NASA*] (KSC)
OLor......... Lorain Public Library, Lorain, OH [*Library symbol*] [*Library of Congress*] (LCLS)
OLOS........ Oakridge Secondary School, London, Ontario [*Library symbol*] [*National Library of Canada*] (NLC)
OLOS........ Observer Line of Sight (SAUS)
OLOS........ Office for Library Outreach Service [*American Library Association*]
OLOS........ Office for Literacy and Outreach Services (AL)
OLOS........ Operational Land Observation System (SAUS)
olos.......... Out of Line of Sight (AD)
OLOS........ Out of Line of Sight (NATG)
OLou......... Loudonville Public Library, Loudonville, OH [*Library symbol*] [*Library of Congress*] (LCLS)
OLOW....... Orbiter Lift-Off Weight [*NASA*]
olow......... Orbiter Liftoff Weight (AD)
O Lower D... Ohio Lower Court Decisions [*A publication*] (DLA)
OLP.......... Brothers of Our Lady of Providence (TOCD)
OLP.......... Lewis and Clark College, Portland, OR [*OCLC symbol*] (OCLC)
OLP.......... Missionaries of the Third Order of St. Francis of Our Lady of the Prairies [*Roman Catholic women's religious order*]
OLP.......... Objective Lens Power Supply (SAUS)
OLP.......... Observation Landplane [*Coast Guard*]
olp........... Occipito-Laeva Posterior (AD)
OLP.......... Occipitolaeva Posterior [*A fetal position*] [*Medicine*] (AAMN)
OLP.......... Office of Labor Production [*WPB*] [*World War II*]
OLP.......... Officially Licensed Product
OLP.......... Off-Line Processing (SAUS)
OLP.......... Off-Line Program [*Computer science*]
OLP.......... Olympic Dam [*Australia*] [*Airport symbol*] (OAG)
OLP.......... One Liberty Properties, Inc. [*AMEX symbol*] (SPSG)
OLP.......... On-Line Processing (SAUS)
OLP.......... Online Processor (TEL)
OLP.......... Online Programming
OLP.......... Open Learning Programme (AIE)
OLP.......... Optical Line Pair
OLP.......... Oral Lichen Plannus [*Medicine*]
OLP.......... Order Load Print (SAUS)
OLP.......... Organizacion para la Liberacion Palestina [*Palestinian Liberation Organization*] [*Spanish*] [*Political party*] (AD)
olp........... Original List Price (AD)
OLP.......... Outside Left Position [*Dancing*]
OLP.......... Oxygen at Low Pressure (KSC)
OLP.......... Oxygen Lance Powder (IAA)
OLP.......... Oxygen Lime Powder [*Steelmaking process*]
OLP.......... Oxygen Low Pressure (SAUS)
OLP.......... Sisters of Our Lady of Providence [*Roman Catholic religious order*]
olpar......... Other Large Phased-Array RADAR (AD)
OLPARS..... Online Pattern Analysis and Recognition System [*Computer science*] (MCD)
OLPBAR..... On-Line Patient Billing and Accounts Receivable (SAUS)
OL/PBAR.... Online Patient Billing and Accounts Receivable System [*Computer science*] (PDAA)
OLPBAR System... On-Line Patient Billing and Accounts Receivable System (SAUS)

OLPH .... London Psychiatric Hospital, Ontario [*Library symbol*] [*National Library of Canada*] (NLC)
OLPHS ...... Parkwood Hospital Services, London, Ontario [*Library symbol*] [*National Library of Canada*] (BIB)
OLPP .... One Liberty Prop $1.60 Cv Pfd [*AMEX symbol*] (TTSB)
OLP Process... Oxygen Lime Powder Process (SAUS)
OLPR .... Office of Library Personnel Resources [*American Library Association*]
Ol Prec...... Oliver's Precedents [*A publication*] (DLA)
OLPS .... Online Programming System [*Computer science*]
OLPT .... Oxford Library of Practical Theology [*A publication*]
OLPT .... Pinchas Troester Library, Congregation B'Nai Israel, London, Ontario [*Library symbol*] [*National Library of Canada*] (NLC)
OLQ.......... Biloxi, MS [*Location identifier*] [*FAA*] (FAAL)
olq........... Officer-Like Qualities (AD)
OLQ.......... Officer-Like Qualities [*British military*] (DMA)
OLQ.......... Olsobip [*Papua New Guinea*] [*Airport symbol*] (OAG)
OLQ.......... On-Line Query (SAUS)
OLR.......... Oak-Leaf Roller [*Moth*] [*Entomology*]
OLR.......... Objective Loudness Rating [*of telephone connections*] (IEEE)
OLR.......... Objective Loudness Ratio (SAUS)
OLR.......... Office Loop Regenerator (ACAE)
OLR.......... Office Loop Repeater (MHDB)
OLR.......... Office of Labor Racketeering [*Department of Labor*]
OLR.......... Office of Legislative Reference [*Bureau of the Budget; later, OMB*]
OLR.......... Offline Reader [*Bulletin board*]
OLR.......... Offline Recovery [*Telecommunications*] (TEL)
OLR.......... Off Load Route [*Aviation*] (DA)
OLR.......... Off Load Routes (SAUS)
OLR.......... Ohio Law Reporter [*A publication*] (DLA)
O-LR......... Ohio Legislative Reference Bureau, Columbus, OH [*Library symbol*] [*Library of Congress*] (LCLS)
OLR.......... On-Line Research, Inc. [*Information service or system*] (IID)
OLR.......... On Location Repair (MCD)
OLR.......... Ontario Law Reporter [*A publication*] (DLA)
OLR.......... Ontario Law Reports [*A publication*] (DLA)
OLR.......... Open-Loop Receiver [*or Response*]
OLR.......... Open Loop Response (CIST)
OLR.......... Operator's Local Representative (AIA)
OLR.......... Organisation pour la Liberation du Rwanda [*Organization for the Liberation of Rwanda*]
OLR.......... Otology, Laryngology, and Rhinology [*Medicine*] (EDAA)
OLR.......... Oudh Law Reports [*India*] [*A publication*] (DLA)
OLR.......... Outer Lindblad Resonance [*Planetary science*]
OLR.......... Outgoing Long-Wave Radiation [*Satellite sensed*]
OLR.......... Overall Loudness Rating (SAUS)
olr........... Overload Relay (AD)
OLR.......... Overload Relay
OLR.......... Robarts School Library, London, Ontario [*Library symbol*] [*National Library of Canada*] (BIB)
OLRA .... Ontario Labour Relations Act (SAUS)
OLRAG ...... London Regional Art Gallery, Ontario [*Library symbol*] [*National Library of Canada*] (NLC)
OLRB .... Ontario Labor Relations Board [*Canada*] (AD)
OLRB .... Ontario Labour Relations Board Monthly Report [*A publication*] (DLA)
O/L-RC ...... Overload-Reverse Current (NASA)
OL Rep...... Ohio Law Reporter [*A publication*] (DLA)
ol res........ Oleoresin (AD)
Ol Res....... Oleoresin [*Also, OR*] [*Pharmacy*]
OLRI .... Office & Factory, Rochevert Industrie, Inc., Lindsay, Ontario [*Library symbol*] [*National Library of Canada*] (NLC)
OL RIC ...... Oleum Ricine (SAUS)
OL RIC ...... Oleum Ricini [*Castor Oil*] [*Pharmacy*] (ROG)
OLRL .... Lyndhurst Branch, Rideau Lakes Union Library, Ontario [*Library symbol*] [*National Library of Canada*] (BIB)
OLRM .... Medical Library, Ross Memorial Hospital, Lindsay, Ontario [*Library symbol*] [*National Library of Canada*] (BIB)
OLRP .... On-Line Report Processor (SAUS)
OLRS .... Optical LASER Ranging System
olrt........... On-Line Real Time [*Computer science*] (AD)
OLRT .... Online Real Time [*Computer science*]
OLRT Computer... On-Line Real Time Computer (SAUS)
OLRV .... Olive Latent Ringspot Virus [*Plant pathology*]
OLS.......... Nogales, AZ [*Location identifier*] [*FAA*] (FAAL)
OLS.......... Oceanographic Lidar System (SAUS)
OLS.......... Office of Legal Services [*of Office of Economic Opportunity*]
OLS.......... Office of Library Services (AAGC)
OLS.......... Off-Line Storage (SAUS)
OLS.......... OLS Asia Holdings Ltd. [*Associated Press*] (SAG)
OLS.......... Olsten Corp. [*NYSE symbol*] (SAG)
OLS.......... Online Library System (AEPA)
OLS.......... Online Scan [*Computer science*] (CAAL)
OLS.......... Online Search (NITA)
OLS.......... Online Services (GART)
OLS.......... Online System [*Computer science*]
OLS.......... Ontario Land Surveyor [*Canada*] (ASC)
OLS.......... Open-Loop System [*Chemical engineering*]
OLS.......... Operational Launch Station (AAG)
OLS.......... Operational License Stage (CARB)
OLS.......... Operational Line Scanner (CARB)
OLS.......... Operational Linescan System [*Navy*] (ANA)
OLS.......... Operational Lines of Succession [*Defense readiness*]
OLS.......... Operation Lifeline Sudan
OLS.......... Operation...Life Support [*Online lobbying for the television show "My So-Called Life"*]
OLS.......... Operation Line Scanner (SAUS)
OLS.......... Optical Landing System
OLS.......... Optical Line Scanner (EOSA)
OLS.......... Orbiting Lunar Station [*NASA*]
OLS.......... Ordinary Least Squares [*Statistics*]
OLS.......... Original Line of Sight
OLS.......... Overlap Shear
OLS.......... Sisters of Our Lady of Sorrows [*Roman Catholic religious order*]
OLS.......... Spartan of Canada Ltd., London, Ontario [*Library symbol*] [*National Library of Canada*] (NLC)
OLSA .... Off-Line Selectric Analyser [*Computer science*] (IAA)
OLSA .... OLS Asia Holdings Ltd. [*NASDAQ symbol*] (SAG)
OLSA .... Orbiter Logistics Support Plan [*NASA*]
OLSA .... Orbiter/LPS [*Launch Processing System*] Signal Adapter [*NASA*] (NASA)
OLS AH ..... OLS Asia Holdings Ltd. [*Associated Press*] (SAG)
OL'SAM ..... Online Database Search Assistance Machine [*Franklin Institute*] [*Information service or system*] [*Defunct*] (IID)
OL'SAM ..... Online Search Assistance Machine (NITA)
OLSASS..... Online System Availability and Service Simulation [*Computer science*] (PDAA)
OLSA-T...... Off-Line Selectric Analyzer-Transistorized (SAUS)
OLSAT .... Otis-Lennon School Ability Test [*Education*]
OLSAY....... OLS Asia Hlds ADS [*NASDAQ symbol*] (TTSB)
olsc........... On-Line Scientific Computer (AD)
OLSC .... Online Scientific Computer [*Computer science*]
OLSCA....... Orientation Linkage for a Solar Cell Array
OLSCG ...... Latchford Senior Citizens Group, Ontario [*Library symbol*] [*National Library of Canada*] (BIB)
OLSD .... Office for Library Service to the Disadvantaged [*American Library Association*]
OLSDG ...... Lancaster Branch, Stormont, Dundas, and Glengarry County Library, Ontario [*Library symbol*] [*National Library of Canada*] (BIB)
OLSDMS .... On-Line Strain and Damage Measurement System (SAUS)
OLSE .... Ordinary Least-Squares Estimators [*Statistics*]
OLSF .... Olson Farms, Inc. (SAUS)
OLSF .... Online Subsystem Facility [*Computer science*] (MCD)
OLSG .... Gary Olson Trucking [*Common carrier symbol*]
OLSH .... Our Lady of the Sacred Heart (ADA)
OLSIDI-F.... Oral Language Sentence Imitation Diagnostic Inventory Format Revised (SAUS)
OLSILC...... On the Lighter Side, International Lighter Collectors (EA)
OLSIST-F.... Oral Language Sentence Imitation Screening Test - Format Revised [*Educational test*]
OLSJ......... St. Joseph's Hospital, London, Ontario [*Library symbol*] [*National Library of Canada*] (NLC)
OLSN .... Olson Industries, Inc. (SAUS)
OLSNA ...... Orthopaedic Laser Society of North America (SAUS)
OLSO .... Olson [*NCIC trailer make code*]
OLSOR ...... Object Location and Small Object Recovery [*Military*] (DNAB)
OLSP .... Office of Life Science Programs [*Obsolete*] [*NASA*]
OLSP .... Olive Sparrow [*North American bird banding code*] (BIBA)
OLSP .... Operational Logistic Support Plan
OLSP .... Orbiter Logistics Support Plan [*NASA*] (NASA)
OLSP .... St. Peter's Seminary, London, Ontario [*Library symbol*] [*National Library of Canada*] (NLC)
OLSS .... On-Line Sodium Sampling (SAUS)
OLSS .... Online Software System [*Computer science*] (IEEE)
OLSS .... On-Line Support Software (SAUS)
OLSS .... Operational Logistic Support Summary [*Military*] (CAAL)
OLSS .... Overseas Limited Storage Site [*Army*]
OLSSDG..... Long Sault Branch, Stormont, Dundas, and Glengarry County Public Library, Ontario [*Library symbol*] [*National Library of Canada*] (BIB)
Olsten .... Olsten Corp. [*Associated Press*] (SAG)
OLSUS ...... Online System Use Statistics (NITA)
OLSWF...... OLS Asia HLDS ADS Wrrt [*NASDAQ symbol*] (TTSB)
OLT .... Occipitolaeva Transversa [*A fetal position*] [*Medicine*] (AAMN)
olt............ Occipito-Laeva Transverse (AD)
OLT .... Oddity-Learning Task [*Psychology*]
OLT .... Official Latin Title
OLT .... Off-Line Transmission (SAUS)
Olt .... Old Italian (AD)
OLT .... On-Line Teller (SAUS)
OLT .... Online Test [*Computer science*]
OLT .... On-Line Testing (SAUS)
OLT .... On-Line Transmission (SAUS)
OLT .... Optical Line Termination (SAUS)
OLT .... Orange Light
OLT .... Orthotopic Liver Transplantation [*Medicine*]
OLT .... Osteochondral Lesion of the Talus [*Medicine*] (RAWO)
OLT .... Ostfriesische Lufttransport GmbH [*Germany*] [*ICAO designator*] (FAAC)
OLT .... Oxford Library of Translations [*A publication*]
OLT .... United Lodge of Theosophists, London, Ontario [*Library symbol*] [*National Library of Canada*] (NLC)
OLTC......... On-Load Tap Changer (SAUS)
OLTE......... Online Test (NITA)
OLTE......... On-Line Test Equipment (SAUS)
OLTE......... Online Test Executive Program [*Computer science*] (PDAA)
OLTE......... Optical Line Terminating Equipment (SAUS)
OLTE......... Organizational Level Test Equipment (MCD)
OLTEP ...... On-Line Test Executive Program [*IBM Corp.*] [*Computer science*]
OLTG......... Oliver Trucking Corporation [*Common carrier symbol*]
OLTL......... One Life to Live [*Television program*]

OLTM .... Optical Line Terminating Multiplexer (SAUS)
OLTMC ...... Technical Information Centre, 3M Canada, Inc., London, Ontario [*Library symbol*] [*National Library of Canada*] (NLC)
OLTP .... Off-Line Tape Preparation (SAUS)
OLTP .... On-Line Transaction Processing [*Tandem Computers*]
OLTP .... On-Line Transaction Processor (SAUS)
OLTS .... On-Line Mainframe Testing System [*Computer science*] (IAA)
OLTS .... On-Line Tape System [*Computer science*] (VLIE)
OLTS .... On-Line Testing System (SAUS)
OLTS .... Online Test Section (NITA)
OLTS .... Online Test System [*Computer science*] (BUR)
OLTS .... Online Time Share [*Computer science*]
OLTS .... On Line Tracking System (SAUS)
OLTS .... On-Line Tracking System [*Environmental Protection Agency*] (EPAT)
OLTS .... Online Transaction System [*Computer science*] (IAA)
OLTSEP ...... On-Line Test Stand-Alone Executive Program [*Computer science*] (VLIE)
oltt .... On-Line Teller Terminal [*Computer science*] (AD)
OLTT .... Online Teller Terminal
OLTT .... Online Terminal Test [*Computer science*] (IBMDP)
OLTU .... Oceans Leasing and Logistics [*Intermodal shipping container symbol*] (TVRC)
OLTU .... Optical Line Terminating Unit (SAUS)
OLU .... Columbus [*Nebraska*] [*Airport symbol*] (OAG)
OLU .... On-Line Unit (SAUS)
OLU .... Origin Logical Unit [*IBM's SNA*] [*Communications term*] (DCT)
OLU .... Outdoing Line Unit (IAA)
OLU .... Outgoing Line Unit (SAUS)
OLU .... University of Western Ontario, London, Ontario [*Library symbol*] [*National Library of Canada*] (NLC)
OLUC .... Lucknow Branch, Bruce County Public Library, Ontario [*Library symbol*] [*National Library of Canada*] (NLC)
OLUC .... Office of Land Use Coordination [*Abolished, 1944*] [*Department of Agriculture*]
OLUC .... Online Union Catalog [*Online Computer Library Center, Inc.*] [*Information service or system*] (CRD)
OLuCF .... Southern Ohio Correctional Facility, Lucasville, OH [*Library symbol*] [*Library of Congress*] (LCLS)
OLUD .... Online Update (TEL)
OLUE .... Engineering Library, University of Western Ontario, London, Ontario [*Library symbol*] [*National Library of Canada*] (BIB)
OLUG .... Department of Geography, University of Western Ontario, London, Ontario [*Library symbol*] [*National Library of Canada*] (NLC)
OLUG .... Office Landscape Users Group [*Later, OPUG*] (EA)
OLUH .... University Hospital, London, Ontario [*Library symbol*] [*National Library of Canada*] (NLC)
OLUHO ...... Okinawa-Luzon-Hong Kong Submarine Cable (SAUS)
OLUIT .... Object Oriented Librarian User Interface Tool (TELE)
OLUL .... Law Library, University of Western Ontario, London, Ontario [*Library symbol*] [*National Library of Canada*] (NLC)
OLUM .... Online Update Control Module (TEL)
OLUM .... Sciences Library, Natural Sciences Centre, University of Western Ontario, London, Ontario [*Library symbol*] [*National Library of Canada*] (NLC)
OLUMG ...... MacIntosh Gallery, University of Western Ontario, London, Ontario [*Library symbol*] [*National Library of Canada*] (NLC)
OLUNO ...... Northern Outreach Library Service, University of Western Ontario, London, Ontario [*Library symbol*] [*National Library of Canada*] (BIB)
OLURC ...... London Urban Resource Centre, Ontario [*Library symbol*] [*National Library of Canada*] (NLC)
OLUS .... Online Update System (RDA)
OLUS .... On-Line User Services (SAUS)
OLUS .... School of Library and Information Science, University of Western Ontario, London, Ontario [*Library symbol*] [*National Library of Canada*] (NLC)
OLuS .... Scioto Technical College, Lucasville, OH [*Library symbol*] [*Library of Congress*] [*Obsolete*] (LCLS)
OLUVA .... Visual Arts Department, University of Western Ontario, London, Ontario [*Library symbol*] [*National Library of Canada*] (NLC)
OLUWP ...... Office of Land Use and Water Planning [*Abolished, 1976*] [*Department of the Interior*]
olv .... Olivaceous (AD)
olv .... Olive (AD)
OLV .... Olive Branch, MS [*Location identifier*] [*FAA*] (FAAL)
OLV .... Oliver Resources [*Vancouver Stock Exchange symbol*]
OLV .... One-Lung Ventilation [*Medicine*]
olv .... On-Line Validation [*Computer science*] (AD)
OLV .... Onze Lieve Vrouw [*Our Lady*] [*Dutch*] (AD)
OLV .... Open-Frame Low Voltage (IEEE)
OLV .... Orbital Launch Vehicle
OLVG .... Open-Loop Voltage Gain
OLVH .... Medical Library, South Street Campus, Victoria Hospital Corp., London, Ontario [*Library symbol*] [*National Library of Canada*] (NLC)
OLVIMS ..... On-Line Vehicle Interactive Management System (SAUS)
OLVL .... Oil Level
O-LVL .... Organizational Level (MCD)
OLVM .... Our Lady of Victory Missionary Sisters [*Roman Catholic religious order*]
olvn .... Olivine [*Philately*]
OLVP .... Office of Launch Vehicle Programs [*Obsolete*] [*NASA*]
OLVP .... Office of Launch Vehicles and Propulsion (SAUS)
OLVWM ..... Open Look Virtual Window Manager [*Computer science*] (VLIE)
OLW .... Olympia, WA [*Amtrak rail station code*]
OLWA .... Olive Warbler [*North American bird banding code*] (BIBA)
OLWI .... Organic Liquid Waste Incinerator (SAUS)
Olwine's LJ (PA) ... Olwine's Law Journal [*Pennsylvania*] [*A publication*] (DLA)
OLWM .... Open Look Window Manager (VLIE)
OLWM .... Open-Look Window Manager (SAUS)
OLWM .... Ordinary Low Water Mark (SAUS)
OLX .... Linn-Benton Community College, Albany, OR [*OCLC symbol*] (OCLC)
OLX .... Off-Line Express [*Mustang Software, Inc.*] (PCM)
OLX .... On-Line Executive [*Computer science*] (MHDB)
OLY .... Olney-Noble, IL [*Location identifier*] [*FAA*] (FAAL)
Oly .... Olympia (AD)
OLY .... Olympia [*NCIC car model code*]
Oly .... Olympic (AD)
OLY .... Olympic Aviation SA [*Greece*] [*ICAO designator*] (FAAC)
OLY .... Olympic Cascade Financial Corp. [*AMEX symbol*]
OLY .... Olympic Cascade Finl. [*AMEX symbol*]
Olym .... Olympia (AD)
OLYM .... Olympiad
OLYM .... Olympia (trucks) [*NCIC truck make code*]
OLYM .... Olympic Financial Ltd. [*NASDAQ symbol*] (NQ)
OLYM .... Olympic National Park
OlymF .... Olympic Financial Ltd. [*Associated Press*] (SAG)
OlymFn ...... Olympic Financial Ltd. [*Associated Press*] (SAG)
OLYMP ...... Olympia, WA [*American Association of Railroads railroad junction routing code*]
Olymp .... Olympic (DIAR)
OLYMP ...... Olympic Finl Cv Exch Pfd [*NASDAQ symbol*] (TTSB)
Olympic ..... Olympic National Park, Washington (AD)
OlympStl .... Olympic Steel, Inc. [*Associated Press*] (SAG)
OLYR .... Olympic Railroad [*Federal Railroad Administration identification code*]
OLYU .... Olympic Container [*Intermodal shipping container symbol*] (TVRC)
OLYZ .... Showa Line [*Intermodal trailer symbol*]
OLZ .... Oelwein, IA [*Location identifier*] [*FAA*] (FAAL)
OLZ .... Ontario Locomotive [*Federal Railroad Administration identification code*]
OM .... Air Mongol [*ICAO designator*] (AD)
Om .... Book of Omni (AD)
OM .... Member of the Order of Merit [*Canada*] (DD)
OM .... Minim Fathers (TOCD)
om .... Minim Fathers (TOCD)
OM .... Mississauga Public Library, Ontario [*Library symbol*] [*National Library of Canada*] (NLC)
OM .... Obermanual [*Upper Manual*] [*Music*]
OM .... Object Machine (SAUS)
OM .... Object Management (AG)
OM .... Object Manager (SAUS)
OM .... Object Marker [*Linguistics*] (IEL)
OM .... Object Module (SAUS)
OM .... Observer's Mate [*British military*] (DMA)
OM .... Obtuse Marginal [*Medicine*] (MAE)
OM .... Occipitomental [*Diameter of skull*]
OM .... Occupational Medal [*as used with special reference to Germany or Japan*] [*Military decoration*]
OM .... Occupational Medicine
OM .... Ocean Mapping (SAUS)
OM .... Oceanographic and Meteorological (SAUS)
OM .... Oceanography and Meteorology
OM .... Ochsner-Mahorner [*Echocardiogram*] (DAVI)
OM .... Oculomotor (DB)
OM .... Oduma Magazine [*A publication*]
OM .... Odyssey of the Mind
OM .... Oesterreichische Monatsschrift fuer den Orient (BJA)
OM .... Office Management (SAUS)
OM .... Office Manager
OM .... Office Master (ELAL)
OM .... Office Messenger [*Military*]
OM .... Office Model (SAUS)
OM .... Office of Meteorology [*Emergency Management*] (EMA)
OM .... Officer Messenger (SAUS)
OM .... Officine Meccaniche [*Italian auto manufacturer*]
om .... Old Man (AD)
om .... Old Measurement (AD)
OM .... Old Measurement
OM .... Olympus Mons [*A filamentary mark on Mars*]
OM .... Omaha [*Diocesan abbreviation*] [*Nebraska*] (TOCD)
Om .... Oman (AD)
OM .... Oman [*IYRU nationality code*] [*ANSI two-letter standard code*] (CNC)
OM .... Omit [*Telegraphy*] (PCTE)
om .... Omit
OM .... Omni Mane [*Every Morning*] [*Pharmacy*]
om .... Omni Mane [*Every Morning*] [*Latin*] (AD)
OM .... On Margin [*Investment term*]
OM .... Opaque Media [*X-ray microscopy*]
OM .... Open Market
OM .... Open Matching [*Parapsychology*]
OM .... Open Mouth [*Doll collecting*]
OM .... Opera di Maria [*Work of Mary*] [*An association*] (EAIO)
OM .... Opera Mundi [*Book-packaging firm based in Paris*]
OM .... Operand Manipulation (SAUS)
OM .... Operating Memorandum
OM .... Operating Memory (KSC)
OM .... Operating Method (COE)
OM .... Operational Maintenance (SAUS)
OM .... Operational Management [*Computer science*] (IAA)

OM.......... Operational Mid DSC or MDM (SAUS)
OM.......... Operational Modeling (AAEL)
om.......... Operational Monitor (AD)
OM.......... Operational Monitor (IAA)
OM.......... Operation and Maintenance [*Electric utility company*]
OM.......... Operation and Management (ALAC)
OM.......... Operation Mainstream (OICC)
OM.......... Operation Memorandum (SAUS)
OM.......... Operation Minute (HEAS)
OM.......... Operation Mobilisation [*Religious movement*] [*British*]
OM.......... Operation Monkees (EA)
O/M.......... Operations and Maintenance (SAUS)
OM.......... Operations Maintenance
OM.......... Operations Manager
OM.......... Operations Manual (NITA)
OM.......... Operations Memorandum [*Department of Agriculture*] (GFGA)
OM.......... Operations Module (SAUS)
OM.......... Operator's Manual
OM.......... Optical Man (SAUS)
OM.......... Opticalman [*Navy*] (DAVI)
OM.......... Optical Master (KSC)
OM.......... Optical Media [*Computer graphics*]
OM.......... Optical Metallography (SAUS)
OM.......... Optical Microscope (ECII)
OM.......... Optical Microscopy
OM.......... Optical Modulation (SAUS)
OM.......... Optical Modulator (VLIE)
OM.......... Optimal Mismatch (SAUS)
OM.......... Optimus Maximus [*Greatest and Best*] [*Latin*]
OM.......... Options for Men [*A publication*]
OM.......... Options Market [*Finance*]
OM.......... Oral Motor (IDYL)
OM.......... Orbital Maneuvering Engine [*NASA*] (NAKS)
OM.......... Orbiter Main Engine [*NASA*] (NAKS)
OM.......... Orbit Modification (IAA)
OM.......... Order of Merit
Om.......... Ordinance Map (AD)
OM.......... Ordnance Map (SAUS)
OM.......... Ordnance Mission (AAG)
OM.......... Ordo [*Fratrum*] Minimorum [*Minims of St. Francis of Paul*] [*Roman Catholic men's religious order*]
om.......... Organic Matter (AD)
OM.......... Organic Matter
OM.......... Organizational Maintenance (MCD)
OM.......... Organized Militia (GEAB)
OM.......... Organo Metallic (ACAE)
OM.......... Organometallic
OM.......... Orifice Meter (SAUS)
OM.......... Orthogonal Memory (MHDB)
OM.......... Osborne Mendel Rat [*Medicine*] (DMAA)
OM.......... Osmiophilic Layer [*Botany*]
OM.......... Osteomalacia [*Medicine*] (MAE)
OM.......... Osteomyelitis [*Medicine*]
OM.......... Osteopathic Manipulation (SAUS)
OM.......... Ostmark [*Monetary unit*] [*Germany*]
OM.......... Otitis Media [*Medicine*]
OM.......... Otolitic Membrane [*Otology*]
om.......... Our Memo (AD)
OM.......... Our Message
OM.......... Outboard Marine [*NYSE symbol*] (TTSB)
om.......... Outer Marker (AD)
OM.......... Outer Marker [*Part of an instrument landing system*] [*Aviation*]
OM.......... Outer Membrane [*Biochemistry*]
OM.......... Out for Maintenance (SAUS)
OM.......... Out of Memory [*Computer science*] (VLIE)
OM.......... Output Machine (SAUS)
OM.......... Output Memory (SAUS)
OM.......... Output Module
OM.......... Outside Manufacturing
O/M.......... Outside of Metal (MSA)
OM.......... Overall Modernity [*Sociological scale*]
OM.......... Overhaul Manual (MCD)
OM.......... Overland Monthly [*A publication*] (ROG)
OM.......... Overseas Mail [*British*]
OM.......... Overseas Minister [*World War I*] [*Canada*]
OM.......... Overt Meditation
OM.......... Overturning Moment
OM.......... Ovulation Method [*Birth control*]
OM.......... Owners Manual
O/M.......... Oxygen-to-Metal [*Ratio*] (NRCH)
OM.......... Slovakia [*Civil aircraft markings - international*] (PIPO)
OM1.......... Open MPEG consortium 1 (SAUS)
OM1.......... Opticalman, First Class [*Navy rating*]
OM2.......... Opticalman, Second Class [*Navy rating*]
OM3.......... Opticalman, Third Class [*Navy rating*]
OMA.......... Eppley Airfield [*FAA*] (TAG)
OMA.......... Markham Public Library, Ontario [*Library symbol*] [*National Library of Canada*] (NLC)
OMA.......... Object Management Architecture [*Computer science*] (CDE)
OMA.......... Ocean Mining Administration (AD)
OMA.......... Oceanography and Marine Assessment [*Marine science*] (OSRA)
OMA.......... Ocular Motor Apraxia
OMA.......... Office of Management and Administration [*Social Security Administration*] (OICC)
OMA.......... Office of Maritime Administration [*Navy*]
OMA.......... Office of Maritime Affairs (AD)
OMA.......... Office of Military Affairs
OMA.......... Office of Military Applications [*Department of Energy*]
OMA.......... Office of Military Assistance
OMA.......... Office of Mine Awareness (SAUS)
OMA.......... Office of Minority Affairs [*Department of Agriculture*] (GFGA)
OMA.......... Oilskin Manufacturers' Association of Great Britain Ltd. (BI)
OMA.......... Oklahoma Military Academy
OMA.......... Omaezaki [*Japan*] [*Seismograph station code, US Geological Survey*] (SEIS)
OMA.......... Omaha [*Nebraska*] [*Airport symbol*]
Oma.......... Omaha, Nebraska (AD)
OMA.......... Ontario Medical Association [*Canada*] (AD)
OMA.......... Ontario Mining Act (SAUS)
OMA.......... Ontario Mining Association (SAUS)
OMA.......... Ontario Ministry of Agriculture (SAUS)
OMA.......... Ontario Museums Association (SAUS)
OMA.......... Open Management Architecture (SAUS)
OMA.......... Operational Maintenance Activity (NVT)
OMA.......... Operation and Maintenance, Army (SAUS)
OMA.......... Operation Medicare Alert
OMA.......... Operations and Maintenance Appopriation [*Army*]
OMA.......... Operations and Maintenance, Army
OMA.......... Operations Maintenance Area (NASA)
OMA.......... Operations Management Application (SSD)
OMA.......... Operations Management Society (NTPA)
OMA.......... Operations Monitor Alarm
OMA.......... Optical Manufacturers Association (EA)
OMA.......... Optical-Mechanical Assembly [*Apollo*] [*NASA*]
OMA.......... Optical Multichannel Analyzer [*Spectrometry*]
OMA.......... Orbiter Maintenance Area [*NASA*] (MCD)
OMA.......... Orderly Marketing Agreement
oma.......... Orderly Marketing Arrangement (AD)
OMA.......... Oregon Medical Association [*Medicine*] (EDAA)
OMA.......... Organizational Maintenance Activity
OMA.......... Oriental Merchants Association [*Defunct*] (EA)
OMA.......... Outlook Mobile Access
OMA.......... Output Message Area (SAUS)
OMA.......... Outstanding Merchandising Achievement Award
OMA.......... Outstanding Merchandising Awards (SAUS)
OMA.......... Overall Manufacturers' Association (AD)
OMA.......... Overall Manufacturers' Association of Great Britain (BI)
OMA.......... Overseas Mining Association (SAUS)
OMAA.......... Abu Dhabi/International [*United Arab Emirates*] [*ICAO location identifier*] (ICLI)
OMAA.......... Occupational Medical Administrators' Association (EA)
OMAA.......... Office of Management Analysis and Audit [*Civil Service Commission*]
OMAAEEC... Organisation Mondiale des Anciens et Anciennes Eleves de l'Enseignement Catholique [*World Organization of Former Pupils of Catholic Schools*] (EAIO)
OMAB.......... Buhasa [*United Arab Emirates*] [*ICAO location identifier*] (ICLI)
OMABP...... Abitibi-Price, Inc., Mississauga, Ontario [*Library symbol*] [*National Library of Canada*] (NLC)
OMAC.......... Alkaril Chemicals Ltd., Mississauga, Ontario [*Library symbol*] [*National Library of Canada*] (NLC)
OMAC.......... Asab [*United Arab Emirates*] [*ICAO location identifier*] (ICLI)
OMAC.......... Occupational Medical Association of Canada (SAUS)
OMAC.......... Old Man's Aircraft Company (ACAE)
OMAC.......... Online Manufacturing, Accounting, and Control System
OMAC.......... Online Manufacturing Control (NITA)
OMAC.......... Open Modular Architecture Controller (ACII)
OMAC.......... Operator Measures and Criteria (MCD)
OMAC.......... Otitis Media, Acute Catarrhal [*Medicine*] (MELL)
OMA CCD... Optical Multichannel Analyzer Charge-Coupled Device (SAUS)
OMACON.... Optimized Magnetohydrodynamic Conversion
OMACS...... Online Manufacturing and Control System [*Computer science*] (PDAA)
OMAD.......... Abu Dhabi/Bateen [*United Arab Emirates*] [*ICAO location identifier*] (ICLI)
OMAD.......... Madoc Public Library, Ontario [*Library symbol*] [*National Library of Canada*] (BIB)
OMAD.......... Oncovin [*Vincristine*], Methotrexate, Adriamycin, Dactinomycin [*Actinomycin D*] [*Antineoplastic drug regimen*]
OMAD.......... Optical Mark and Automatic Dialing [*Facsimile transmission*] (DGA)
OMADA...... Airway Centre, AES Data Ltd., Mississauga, Ontario [*Library symbol*] [*National Library of Canada*] (NLC)
OMAE.......... Emirates Flight Information Region [*United Arab Emirates*] [*ICAO location identifier*] (ICLI)
OMAE.......... Offshore Mechanics and Arctic Engineering (SAUS)
OMAECL.... AECL International, Mississauga, Ontario [*Library symbol*] [*National Library of Canada*] (NLC)
OMAF.......... Ontario Ministry of Agriculture and Food [*Canada*]
OMAF.......... Operations and Maintenance, Air Force
OMAFRA..... Ontario Ministry of Agriculture, Food and Rural Affairs
OMAG.......... Geac Computers International, Markham, Ontario [*Library symbol*] [*National Library of Canada*] (NLC)
OMAG.......... Orbiter Magnetometer [*NASA*]
OMAH.......... Al Hamra [*United Arab Emirates*] [*ICAO location identifier*] (ICLI)
OMAH.......... Markham High School, Ontario [*Library symbol*] [*National Library of Canada*] (NLC)
OMAH.......... Omaha Standard Flatbed Trailer [*NCIC trailer make code*]
OMAHA...... Omaha, NE [*American Association of Railroads railroad junction routing code*]
Omaha System... Omaha System for Community Health Nursing (SAUS)

OMAHM ..... Markham District Historical Museum, Ontario [*Library symbol*] [*National Library of Canada*] (BIB)
OMAI .... Allelix, Inc., Mississauga, Ontario [*Library symbol*] [*National Library of Canada*] (NLC)
OMAI .... Organisation Mondiale Agudath Israel [*Agudas Israel World Organization - AIWO*] (EAIO)
OMAJ .... Jebel Dhana [*United Arab Emirates*] [*ICAO location identifier*] (ICLI)
OMAL .... Al Ain [*United Arab Emirates*] [*ICAO location identifier*] (ICLI)
OM-AI .... Organic Monomeric Aluminum (SAUS)
O'Mal & H... O'Malley and Hardcastle's Election Cases [*England*] [*A publication*] (DLA)
OMAM .... Abu Dhabi/Al Dhafra [*United Arab Emirates*] [*ICAO location identifier*] (ICLI)
OMAN .... Manitouwadge Public Library, Ontario [*Library symbol*] [*National Library of Canada*] (NLC)
O-MAN ...... Overhead Manipulator [*For handling loads in a nuclear environment*]
OM/A/N/AF/M... Operation and Maintenance, Army/Navy/ Air Force/USMC (SAUS)
OMancAH... Alfred Holbrook College, Manchester, OH [*Library symbol*] [*Library of Congress*] [*Obsolete*] (LCLS)
OMancO..... Ohio Valley Local District Free Public Library, Manchester, OH [*Library symbol*] [*Library of Congress*] (LCLS)
OM&F .... Organization, Mission and Functions Manual (SAUS)
OM&GA ..... West Virginia Oil Marketers and Grocers Association (EARSL)
O'M & H .... O'Malley and Hardcastle's Election Cases [*England*] [*A publication*] (DLA)
O'M & H El Cas... O'Malley and Hardcastle's Election Cases [*England*] [*A publication*] (DLA)
OM & MG... Organizational Manual and Management Guide
OM & S ..... Osteopathic Medicine and Surgery
OMANO ..... Manotick Public Library, Ontario [*Library symbol*] [*National Library of Canada*] (NLC)
OMans ...... Mansfield Public Library, Mansfield, OH [*Library symbol*] [*Library of Congress*] (LCLS)
OMansK..... Kingwood Center Library, Mansfield, OH [*Library symbol*] [*Library of Congress*] (LCLS)
OMansU..... Ohio State University, Mansfield Regional Campus, Mansfield, OH [*Library symbol*] [*Library of Congress*] (LCLS)
OMAP .... Object Module Assembly Program
OMAP .... Oceanic Monitoring, Assessment and Prediction (SAUS)
OMAP .... Office of Military Assistance Programs (SAUS)
OMAP .... Operations and Maintenance Application Pan (SAUS)
OMAP .... Operations and Maintenance Application Part [*Telecommunications*]
OMAP .... Operations, Maintenance and Administration Part (SAUS)
OMAP .... Vaughan Public Library, Maple, Ontario [*Library symbol*] [*National Library of Canada*] (NLC)
OMAPC ...... Astra Pharmaceuticals Canada Ltd., Mississauga, Ontario [*Library symbol*] [*National Library of Canada*] (NLC)
OMAPFW ... Ontario Ministry of Natural Resources, Maple, Ontario [*Library symbol*] [*National Library of Canada*] (NLC)
OMAQ .... Quarmain [*United Arab Emirates*] [*ICAO location identifier*] (ICLI)
OMAR .... Arzana [*United Arab Emirates*] [*ICAO location identifier*] (ICLI)
OMar .... Congregation of Maronite Monks (TOCD)
omar .... Congregation of Maronite Monks (TOCD)
OMAR .... Marathon Public Library, Ontario [*Library symbol*] [*National Library of Canada*] (NLC)
OMAR .... Office of Medical Applications of Research [*Bethesda, MD*] [*Department of Health and Human Services*] [*National Institutes of Health*]
OMAR .... Operations and Maintenance, Army Reserve (AABC)
OMAR .... Optical Mark Reader [*Computer science*]
OMAR .... Order Maintenance Analysis Report (VLIE)
OMAR .... Order Management and Routing (VLIE)
OMAR .... Ozone Monitoring and Research (ACAE)
omarb .... Omarbetad [*Revised*] [*Swedish*] (AD)
OMarion .... Marion Carnegie Public Library, Marion, OH [*Library symbol*] [*Library of Congress*] (LCLS)
OMarionU... Ohio State University, Marion Campus, Marion, OH [*Library symbol*] [*Library of Congress*] (LCLS)
OMARK...... Markdale Public Library, Ontario [*Library symbol*] [*National Library of Canada*] (NLC)
OMARNG.... Operation and Maintenance, Army National Guard (AABC)
OMARS...... Outstanding Media Advertising by Restaurants (AD)
OMAS .... Assiginack Public Library, Manitowaning, Ontario [*Library symbol*] [*National Library of Canada*] (NLC)
OMAS .... Das Island [*United Arab Emirates*] [*ICAO location identifier*] (ICLI)
OMas .... Massillon Public Library, Massillon, OH [*Library symbol*] [*Library of Congress*] (LCLS)
OMAS .... Occupational Maladjustment Syndrome [*Medicine*] (EDAA)
OMAS .... Off-Magic-Angle-Spinning [*Spectroscopy*]
OMAS .... One-Man Atmospheric Submersible (PDAA)
OMAS .... Operational Miscellaneous Audio Subsystem
OMAS .... Otitis Media, Acute, Suppurating [*Medicine*] (EDAA)
OMASD...... Office of Management Appraisal and Systems Development (SAUS)
OMAST...... Massey and Township Public Library, Ontario [*Library symbol*] [*Library network*] (NLC)
OMAT........ Matheson Public Library, Ontario [*Library symbol*] [*National Library of Canada*] (NLC)
OMAT........ Ocean Measurement and Array Technology [*Navy*] (CAAL)
OMAT........ Office of Manpower, Automation, and Training [*See also OAM*] [*Department of Labor*]
OMAT........ Optimal Modified Adaptive Test (SAUS)
OMATT ...... Mattawa Public Library, Ontario [*Library symbol*] [*National Library of Canada*] (NLC)
OMAU .... Magnetawan Area Union Public Library, Magnetawan, Ontario [*Library symbol*] [*National Library of Canada*] (NLC)
OMAU .... Ocean Marine Line [*Intermodal shipping container symbol*] (TVRC)
OMAZ........ Zirku [*United Arab Emirates*] [*ICAO location identifier*] (ICLI)
OMB .... Midhurst Branch Library, Ontario [*Library symbol*] [*National Library of Canada*] (NLC)
OMB .... Object Management Architecture [*Computer science*]
OMB .... Obtuse Marginal Branch (RAWO)
OMB .... Office of Management and Budget [*Executive Office of the President*] [*Formerly, Bureau of the Budget*] [*Washington, DC*]
OMB .... Office of Money and Banking (WPI)
OMB .... Omboue [*Gabon*] [*Airport symbol*] (OAG)
Omb .... Ombudsman (AD)
OMB .... Ombudsperson-Faculty (SAUS)
OMB .... Ombudsperson-Student (SAUS)
OMB .... Ontario Municipal Board (SAUS)
OMB .... Operational Maintenance Battalion [*Army*] (DOMA)
OMB .... Ordnance Maintenance Bulletin
OMB .... Outboard Motorboat
OMB .... Outer Marker Beacon [*Part of an instrument landing system*] [*Aviation*]
OMB .... Out-of-Home Measurement Bureau [*Later, TABMM*] (EA)
OMBA .... Oklahoma Malt Beverage Association (EARSL)
OMBAC...... Old Mission Beach Athletic Club (AD)
OMBC .... Beak Consultants, Mississauga, Ontario [*Library symbol*] [*National Library of Canada*] (NLC)
OMB Circular... Office of Management and Budget Circular (AAGC)
OMBE........ Office of Minority Business Enterprise [*Later, MBDA*] [*Department of Commerce*]
OMBE........ Oxford Mission Brotherhood of the Epiphany [*Anglican religious community*]
OMBFC...... Official Michael Biehn Fan Club [*Association*] (EA)
OMB/FPPO... Office of Management and Budget/Federal Procurement Policy Office (OICC)
OMBI .... Observation-Measurement-Balancing and Installation [*Production analysis*]
OMBI .... Overcoming Mobility Barriers International (EA)
om bid ...... Omnibus Bidendis [*Every Two Days*] [*Latin*] (AD)
OMBK .... OmniBank of Connecticut, Inc. (SAUS)
OMBO .... One man Bridge Operation (SAUS)
OMBR .... Ontario Municipal Board Reports [*A publication*] (DLA)
OMBS .... Ouachita Mountains Biological Station (RCD)
OMBUU ..... Orbiter Midbody Umbilical Unit [*NASA*] (NASA)
OMBVT...... Minesing Branch, Vespra Township Public Library, Ontario [*Library symbol*] [*National Library of Canada*] (BIB)
OMBW....... Bangor, Wicklow, McClure, and Monteagle Union Public Library, Maynooth, Ontario [*Library symbol*] [*National Library of Canada*] (BIB)
OMBW....... OMB [*Office of Management and Budget*] Watch (EA)
OMC .... Chief Opticalman [*Navy rating*]
OMc .... Herbert Wescoat Memorial Library, McArthur, OH [*Library symbol*] [*Library of Congress*] (LCLS)
OMC .... Marietta College, Marietta, OH [*Library symbol*] [*Library of Congress*] (LCLS)
OMC .... Mayo Clinic Library, Rochester, MN [*OCLC symbol*] (OCLC)
OMC .... Occupational Measurement Center (SAUS)
OMC .... Occupational Medical Center (EFIS)
OMC .... Office of Military Cooperation [*Foreign Service*]
OMC .... Office of Motor Carriers [*FHWA*] [*NHSTA*] [*RSPA*] (TAG)
OMC .... Office of Munitions Control [*Department of State*]
OMC .... Official Mail Center [*Air Force*] (AFM)
OMC .... Off-Machine Coated [*Paper*] (DGA)
OMC .... Omnicom Group, Inc. [*NYSE symbol*] (SPSG)
OMC .... One-Man Control (DNAB)
OMC .... Opel Motorsport Club AG (EA)
OMC .... Open Magnetic Circuit [*Computer science*] (ELAL)
OMC .... Open Market Committee [*Also, FOMC*] [*Federal Reserve System*]
OMC .... Open Mutual Commissurotomy [*Medicine*] (EDAA)
OMC .... Operating and Maintenance Costs
OMC .... Operation and Maintenance Center (VLIE)
OMC .... Operations and Maintenance Center (SAUS)
OMC .... Operations Management Consultant [*Department of Emergency Management*] (DEMM)
OMC .... Operations Monitoring Computer
OMC .... Opticalman, Chief [*Navy rating*] (DNAB)
OMC .... Optical Memory Card [*Computer science*] (CIST)
OMC .... Optimum Moisture Content (SAUS)
omc.......... Orbiter Maintenance and Checkout [*NASA*] (NAKS)
OMC .... Orbiter Maintenance and Checkout [*NASA*] (NASA)
OMC .... Ordnance Missile Command [*Later, Missile Command*]
OMC .... Ordo Minorum Cappucinorum [*Capuchins*] [*Roman Catholic men's religious order*]
OMC .... Ordo Minorum Conventualium [*Conventual Franciscans*] [*Roman Catholic men's religious order*]
OMC .... Organic Matrix Composite (SAUS)
OMC .... Organic Molecular Crystal
OMC .... Organizational Member Council (of ANSI) (AG)
OMC .... Organometallic Chemistry (SAUS)
OMC .... Organometallic Compound (SAUS)
OMC .... Orion Molecular Cloud [*Astronomy*]
OMC .... Outboard Marine Corp.
OMC .... Oxford Military College (ROG)
OMC .... Oxford Mission to Calcutta [*British*] (ROG)
OMC .... Oxidized Microcrystalline (SAUS)
OMC .... Oxidized Microcrystalline Waxes (EDCT)
OMC .... TOGA XBT Operations and Management Committee (SAUS)
OMC1........ Orion Molecular Cloud 1 [*Astronomy*]
OMCA .... Occupational Medical Corp. of America, Inc. (SAUS)
OMCA .... Ontario Motor Coach Association

OMCA .... Open Manage Client Administrator [*Computer science*]
OMCA .... Organic-Moderated Critical Assembly [*Nuclear energy*] (NRCH)
OMCA .... Otitis Media, Catarrhal, Acute [*Medicine*] (MAE)
OMCB .... Off-Machine Coated Board [*Paper*] (DGA)
OMCC .... Open Minded Comics Club [*Defunct*] (EA)
OMCC .... Otitis Media, Catarrhalis, Chronic [*Medicine*] (EDAA)
OMCE........ Organization of New York State Management Confidential Employees (EARSL)
OMCF........ Operations and Maintenance Control File [*NASA*] (NASA)
OMCF........ Orbiter Maintenance and Checkout Facility [*NASA*] (NASA)
OMCFP...... Optimized MAC Computer Flight Plan (SAUS)
OMCG .... Ciba/Geigy Canada Ltd., Mississauga, Ontario [*Library symbol*] [*National Library of Canada*] (NLC)
OMCHE...... Organic Material Hydrocarbon Equivalent [*Materials science*]
OMChS...... Otitis Media, Chronic, Suppurating [*Medicine*] (STED)
OMCI .... Organisation Maritime Consultatif Intergouvernementale [*Intergovernmental Maritime Consultative Organization*]
OMCILCR... Chemical Research Laboratory, CIL, Inc., Mississauga, Ontario [*Library symbol*] [*National Library of Canada*] (NLC)
OMCJ........ OMC Johnson [*NCIC trailer make code*]
OMcL........ Herbert Wescoat Memorial Library, McArthur, OH [*Library symbol*] [*Library of Congress*] (LCLS)
OMCL........ Online Medieval & Classical Library [*Database*] (GDD)
OMCM....... Master Chief Opticalman [*Navy rating*]
OMCM....... Omnicom Group, Inc. (MHDW)
OMCO .... Official Mail Control Officer (MCD)
OMCO .... Overmyer Corporation (SAUS)
OMCP .... Orion Marine Corporation [*Common carrier symbol*]
OMCPAC .... Outboard Marine Corporation PAC [*Waukegan, IL*] (PACS)
OMCR .... Chippewa Resource Centre, Muncey, Ontario [*Library symbol*] [*National Library of Canada*] (NLC)
OMC-R ...... Operation and Maintenance Center Radio (SAUS)
OMCR .... Organic-Moderated Cooled Reactor
OMCR .... Organized Marine Corps Reserve
OMCS .... Office of Motor Carrier Standards [*Federal Highway Administration*]
OMCS .... Office of the Minister for the Civil Service (ODA)
OMC-S ...... Operation and Maintenance Center Switch (SAUS)
OMCS .... Operations and Maintenance Communications System (ACAE)
OMCS .... Ozone Monitor Comparison System (CARB)
OMCS .... Senior Chief Opticalman [*Navy rating*]
OMCS .... Sheridan Park Research Community, Cominco Ltd., Mississauga, Ontario [*Library symbol*] [*National Library of Canada*] (NLC)
OMCSDG.... Moose Creek Branch, Stormount, Dundas, and Glengarry County Public Library, Ontario [*Library symbol*] [*National Library of Canada*] (NLC)
OMCSG...... Canada Systems Group, Mississauga, Ontario [*Library symbol*] [*National Library of Canada*] (NLC)
OMCT........ Carnarvon Township Public Library, Mindemoya, Ontario [*Library symbol*] [*National Library of Canada*] (NLC)
OMCT........ Office of Motor Carrier Transportation [*Federal Highway Administration*]
OMCT........ Organisation Mondiale Contre la Torture [*World Organization Against Torture*] [*Switzerland*] (EAIO)
OMCT........ Orientation-Memory-Concentration Test [*Medicine*] (EDAA)
OMCTS...... Octamethylcyclotetrasiloxane [*Organic chemistry*]
OMCT/SOST... Organisation Mondiale Contre la Torture/SOS-Torture [*World Organization Against Torture/SOS-Torture*] [*Geneva, Switzerland*] (EAIO)
OMCU .... Ontario Ministry of Colleges and Universities (SAUS)
OMCU .... Outstation Monitoring and Control Unit [*Traffic operations*]
OM-CVD..... Organometallic Chemical Vapor Deposition [*Also, OM-VPE, MO-CVD, MO-VPE*] [*Semiconductor technology*]
OMCVD...... Organo-Metallic Chemical Vapour Deposition (SAUS)
OMCVD...... OrganoMetallic CVD (SAUS)
OMCVH...... Credit Valley Hospital, Mississauga, Ontario [*Library symbol*] [*National Library of Canada*] (NLC)
OMC Wax... Oxidized Microcrystalline Wax (SAUS)
OMCZ........ O'Keene Milling [*Federal Railroad Administration identification code*]
OMD .... Doctor of Oriental Medicine
OMD .... Du Pont Canada, Inc., Maitland, Ontario [*Library symbol*] [*National Library of Canada*] (NLC)
OMD .... Ocean Margin Drilling [*Program*] [*National Science Foundation*]
OMD .... Ocean Movement Designator
OMD .... Ocular Muscle Dystrophy [*Ophthalmology*] (MAE)
OMD .... Oculoman Dibulodyscephaly (STED)
OMD .... Office of Management Development [*Later, OMPR*] [*NASA*]
omd.......... Off-Market Date (AD)
OMD .... Oldsmobile Motor Division [*General Motors Corp.*]
OMD .... O-Methyldopa [*Biochemistry*]
OMD .... Omitted [*Telegraphy*] (PCTE)
OMD .... Online Medical Dictionary (MHID)
OMD .... Open Macrodefinition
OMD .... Operations and Maintainer Decision
OMD .... Operations and Maintenance Documentation [*NASA*] (NASA)
OM/D .... Orbital Mode/Data (SAUS)
OMD .... Orbiter Mating Device [*NASA*]
OMD .... Orchestral Manoeuvres in the Dark [*Pop music group*]
OMD .... Ordnance Medical Department [*British military*] (DMA)
OMD .... Organic Mental Disorder [*Neurology*] (CPH)
OMD .... Oriental Medicine Doctor [*Medicine*]
OMD .... Ormand Industries, Inc. (SAUS)
OMD .... Oromandibular Dystonia [*Medicine*] (EDAA)
OMDB .... Dubai [*United Arab Emirates*] [*ICAO location identifier*] (ICLI)
OMDB .... Over My Dead Body
OMDC .... Du Pont Canada, Inc., Mississauga, Ontario [*Library symbol*] [*National Library of Canada*] (NLC)
OMDCPL .... Patent & Legal Library, DuPont Canada, Inc., Mississauga, Ontario [*Library symbol*] [*National Library of Canada*] (NLC)
OMDEAC .... Dearborn Chemical Co. Ltd., Mississauga, Ontario [*Library symbol*] [*National Library of Canada*] (NLC)
OMDG .... Dominion Glass Co. Ltd., Mississauga, Ontario [*Library symbol*] [*National Library of Canada*] (NLC)
OMDIR ...... Research Library, Duracell, Inc., Mississauga, Ontario [*Library symbol*] [*Obsolete*] [*National Library of Canada*] (NLC)
OMDL .... Marmora, Deloro, and Lake Union Public Library, Marmora, Ontario [*Library symbol*] [*National Library of Canada*] (BIB)
OMDM....... Optomechanical Display Module
OMDO .... Corporate Library, Domglas, Inc., Mississauga, Ontario [*Library symbol*] [*National Library of Canada*] (NLC)
OMDP .... Ocean Margin Drilling Program [*National Science Foundation*]
OMDP .... Orbiter Maintenance Down Period (SAUS)
OMDR .... Dunlop Research Centre, Sheridan Park, Mississauga, Ontario [*Library symbol*] [*National Library of Canada*] (NLC)
omdr......... Off-Market Date Received (AD)
OMDR .... Operation and Maintainability Data Record
OMDR .... Operation and Maintenance Deficiency Report (SAUS)
OMDR .... Operations and Maintenance Data Record [*NASA*] (KSC)
OMDR .... Optical Memory Disk Recorder Animation System (SAUS)
OMDR .... Optic Memory Disk Recorder
OMDR1...... Operations and Maintainability Data Record (SAUS)
OMDS .... Delphax Systems, Mississauga, Ontario [*Library symbol*] [*National Library of Canada*] (NLC)
OMDS .... Online Diver Monitoring System
OMDS .... Optical Mass Data Storage (SAUS)
OMDW ...... Diversey Wyandotte, Inc., Mississauga, Ontario, [*Library symbol*] [*National Library of Canada*] (NLC)
OME .... Erindale College, University of Toronto, Mississauga, Ontario [*Library symbol*] [*National Library of Canada*] (NLC)
OME .... Nome [*Alaska*] [*Airport symbol*] (OAG)
OME .... Object Management Extension
OME .... Office of Management Engineer
OME .... Office of Manpower Economics [*Department of Employment*] [*British*]
OME .... Office of Minerals Exploration [*Functions transferred to Geological Survey*] [*Department of the Interior*]
OME .... Office of the Medical Examiner (DAVI)
OME .... Omega [*NCIC car model code*]
Ome .... Omega [*Record label*] [*Belgium, etc.*]
OME .... Omega Protein [*NYSE symbol*] (SG)
OME .... Ometepe [*Nicaragua*] [*Seismograph station code, US Geological Survey*] (SEIS)
O-Me .... O-Methyl Diisopropyl (SAUS)
OME .... On-board Modul Extension (SAUS)
OME .... One-Meson Exchange (SAUS)
OME .... Ontario Ministry of Education (SAUS)
OME .... Ontario Ministry of Energy (SAUS)
OME .... Ontario Ministry of the Environment (SAUS)
OME .... Open Messaging Environment [*Computer science*] (CDE)
OME .... Operational Mission Environment (MCD)
OME .... Optimum Mineral Extraction (SAUS)
OME .... Orbital [*or Orbiter*] Main Engine [*NASA*] (NASA)
OME .... Orbital Maneuvering Engine [*NASA*] (KSC)
OME .... Ordnance Mechanical Engineer [*British military*] (DMA)
OME .... Oregon Microcomputer Engineering (SAUS)
OME .... Organisation Mondiale de l'Emballage [*World Packaging Organization - WPO*] (EAIO)
OME .... Organizational Maintenance Equipment (SAUS)
OME .... Ormont Explorations Ltd. [*Vancouver Stock Exchange symbol*]
OME .... Otitis Media with Effusion [*Medicine*]
OMEA........ Meaford Public Library, Ontario [*Library symbol*] [*National Library of Canada*] (NLC)
OMEA........ Office of Multicultural and Ethnic Affairs [*Australia*]
OMEA........ Ontario Municipal Electric Association (SAUS)
OMEC........ Online Medical Employment Center (SAUS)
OMEC........ Optimized Microminiature Electronic Circuit
OMEC........ Organization of Mineral Exporting Countries [*Proposed*]
OMED .... Oxboro Medical International, Inc. [*NASDAQ symbol*] (SAG)
OMED .... Oxboro Med Intl. [*NASDAQ symbol*] (TTSB)
OMEE........ Ontario Ministry of Environment and Energy [*Canada*]
OMEF........ Office Machines and Equipment Federation [*British*] (DIT)
OMEF........ Omega Financial [*NASDAQ symbol*] (TTSB)
OMEF........ Omega Financial Corp. [*NASDAQ symbol*] (SAG)
OMEG .... Omega [*NCIC motorcycle make code*]
OMEG .... Omega [*NCIC car make code*]
OMEG .... Omega Environmental [*NASDAQ symbol*] (SPSG)
OMEG .... Omega Optical Co. (SAUS)
OMEGA...... A navigation system which electronically determines position
OMEGA...... Observing and Modelling of Eddy Scale Geostrophic and Ageostrophic Circulation (SAUS)
OMEGA...... Octanoyl-N-Methylglucamide (SAUS)
OMEGA...... Off-Road Mobility Evaluation and Generalized Analysis [*Army*]
OMEGA...... Ohio Mid-Eastern Governments Association (EARSL)
OMEGA...... Operation Model Evaluation Group, Air Force (MCD)
OMEGA...... Optimal Missile Engagement Guidance Algorithm (AD)
OmegaEn ... Omega Environmental, Inc. [*Associated Press*] (SAG)
Omega-Int J... Omega-The International Journal of Management Science (SAUS)
Omega Rho... Operations Research Honor Society (SAUS)
OmegFn..... Omega Financial Corp. [*Associated Press*] (SAG)
OmegHlt .... Omega Healthcare Investors [*Associated Press*] (SAG)

OMeH .... Holden Arboretum, Mento, OH [*Library symbol*] [*Library of Congress*] (LCLS)
OM/EH....... Occupational Medicine/Environmental Health Evaluation Center [*Emory University*]
OMEI .... Office of Minority Economic Impact [*Department of Energy*]
OMEI .... Other Major End Item [*Military*] (AFIT)
OMEI .... Other Major Equipment Items (SAUS)
OMEL........ Orient Mid-East Lines (AD)
OMEM....... Other Major Engine Manufacturer [*Automotive engineering*]
OMEN .... Ohio Medical Education Network [*Ohio State University*] [*Columbus*] (TSSD)
OMEN .... Orthogonal Mini-Embedment (MHDI)
OMEP........ Office of Marine and Estuarine Protection [*Environmental Protection Agency*] (EPA)
OMEP........ One-Meson Exchange Potential (SAUS)
OMEP........ Ontario Mineral Exploration Program (SAUS)
OMEP........ Organisation Mondiale pour l'Education Prescolaire [*World Organization for Early Childhood Education*] (EAIO)
OMER .... Merrickville Public Library, Ontario [*Library symbol*] [*National Library of Canada*] (NLC)
OMER .... Operations Management Education and Research Foundation (EA)
OMERAD.... Office of Medical Education Research and Development [*Michigan State University*] [*Research center*] (RCD)
OMerc....... Order of Mercedarians [*Also, MMB*] [*Roman Catholic women's religious order*]
OME-RESA... Ohios Mid-Eastern Regional Education Services Agency (SAUS)
OMERF...... Operations Management Education and Research Foundation [*Formerly, OFMP*] (EA)
O-Mess...... Officer's Mess [*Military*] (AD)
OMET........ Orbiter Mission Elapsed Time [*NASA*] (MCD)
OMET........ Ordnance Middle East Tasks [*Military*]
OMET........ Organization Manning Equipment Table (MCD)
OMET........ Orthomet, Inc. [*NASDAQ symbol*] (COMM)
OMETA...... Ordnance Management Engineering Training Agency [*Army*]
OMEU .... Odom Maritime Enterprises [*Intermodal shipping container symbol*] (TVRC)
OMEW....... Office of Missile Electronic Warfare [*Army*] (RDA)
OMEWG..... Orbiter Maintenance Engineering Working Group [*NASA*] (NASA)
OMEX........ Ocean Margin Exchanges (CARB)
OMEX........ Odyssey Marine Exploration [*OTCBB symbol*]
OMF .... Moose Factory Library, Ontario [*Library symbol*] [*National Library of Canada*] (BIB)
OMF .... Object Management Facility [*Computer science*]
OMF .... Object Management Framework (SAUS)
OMF .... Object Module File [*Computer science*] (IAA)
OMF .... Object Module Format
OMF .... Office of Management and Finance (AD)
OMF .... Office of Marketing Facilities (SAUS)
OMF .... Officer Master File [*Army*] (INF)
OMF .... Old Master File
OMF .... Omniflys SA de CV [*Mexico*] [*ICAO designator*] (FAAC)
OMF .... Open Media Framework (DOM)
OMF .... Open Message Format (SAUS)
OMF .... Open Modeling Forum (SAUS)
OMF .... Operational Mission Failure (MCD)
OMF .... Operation and Maintenance of Facilities [*Army*]
OMF .... Operations Management Forum (HEAS)
OMF .... Optical Matched Filter
OMF .... Order Materials For
OMF .... Organizational Master File [*Army*]
OMF .... Organization Master File (SAUS)
OMF .... Oscillatory Magnetic Field
OMF .... Osteomyelofibrose (SAUS)
OMF .... Overseas Missionary Fellowship, USA Headquarters (EA)
OMFBAA.... Operation and Maintenance of Facilities Budget Activity Account [*Army*] (AABC)
OMFBR...... Organic-Moderated Fluidized Bed Reactor
OMFC........ Overseas Military Forces of Canada [*World War I*]
OMFCA...... Operation and Maintenance of Facilities Cost Account [*Army*] (AABC)
OMFCU...... Outboard Message Format Conventional Unit (SAUS)
OMFCU...... Outboard Message Format Conversion Unit (MCD)
OMFD .... Mount Forest District High School, Mount Forest, Ontario [*Library symbol*] [*National Library of Canada*] (NLC)
OMFE........ Front of Escott Public Library, Mallorytown, Ontario [*Library symbol*] [*National Library of Canada*] (NLC)
OMFG .... Official Meeting Facilities Guide (TVEL)
OMFG .... Optimum Manufacturing, Inc. (SAUS)
OMFI .... Open Media Framework Interchange (SAUS)
OMFJ........ Fujeirah/International [*United Arab Emirates*] [*ICAO location identifier*] (ICLI)
OMFP........ Obtaining Money by False Pretense
omfp......... Obtaining Money by False Pretenses (AD)
OMFP........ Ortho-Methylfluorescein Phosphate [*Biochemistry*]
OMFS........ Office Master Frequency Supply [*Telecommunications*] (TEL)
OMFS........ Optimum Metric Fastener System
OMFSCA.... Operation and Maintenance of Facilities Summary Cost Account [*Army*] (AABC)
OMFT........ Optical Matched Filter Technique
OMFTS...... Operational Maneuver from the Sea [*Marine Corps*] (DOMA)
OMFUG...... Other Music for Urban Gormandizers [*Acronym used as subtitle to the New York City nightclub name, CBGB*]
OMFY........ Front of Yonge Township Public Library, Mallorytown, Ontario [*Library symbol*] [*National Library of Canada*] (BIB)
OMG......... Aeromega Ltd. [*British*] [*ICAO designator*] (FAAC)
OMG......... Object Management Group [*Computer science*]
OMG......... Ocean Mapping Group (SAUS)
OMG......... Office Machines Group [*Business Equipment Manufacturers Association*]
OMG......... Office of Marine Geology [*United States Geological Survey*]
OMG......... Office of Military Government
OMG......... Older Metamorphic Group [*Geology*]
OMG......... Oligodendrocyte-Myelin Glycoprotein (DMAA)
OMG......... Omega [*Namibia*] [*Airport symbol*] (OAG)
OMG......... Omitting [*Telegraphy*] (PCTE)
OMG......... Omni Multimedia Group, Inc. [*AMEX symbol*] (SAG)
OMG......... Open Management Group (SAUS)
OMG......... Operational-Maneuver Group [*Military*]
OMG......... Opthalmology Medical Group (AD)
OMG......... Osteopathic Medical School Graduate (DMAA)
OMG......... Outlaw Motorcycle Gang
OMG......... Outokumpu Mooney Group [*Automotive industry*]
OMGA .... Golder Associates, Mississauga, Ontario [*Library symbol*] [*National Library of Canada*] (NLC)
OMGA .... Omega Research, Inc. [*NASDAQ symbol*] (NASQ)
OMGA .... Operations Management Ground Application (SSD)
OmgaHl..... Omega Health Systems, Inc. [*Associated Press*] (SAG)
OMGB .... Georgian Bay Township Public Library, Mactier, Ontario [*Library symbol*] [*National Library of Canada*] (BIB)
OMGB .... Office of Military Government for Bavaria [*US Military Government, Germany*]
OMGBS...... Office of Military Government for Berlin Sector [*US Military Government, Germany*]
OMGCR ..... Research & Development, Gulf Canada Ltd., Mississauga, Ontario [*Library symbol*] [*National Library of Canada*] (NLC)
OMGCR ..... Technical Library, Petro-Canada Products, Mississauga, Ontario [*Library symbol*] [*National Library of Canada*] (NLC)
OMGE .... Organisation Mondiale de Gastroenterologie [*World Organization of Gastroenterology - WOG*] [*Edinburgh, Scotland*] (EAIO)
OMGH....... Office of Military Government for Hesse [*US Military Government, Germany*]
OMGI........ OM Group [*NASDAQ symbol*] (TTSB)
OMGI........ OM Group, Inc. [*NASDAQ symbol*] (SAG)
OMGL .... Gartner Lee Associates Ltd., Markham, Ontario [*Library symbol*] [*National Library of Canada*] (NLC)
OMGR....... Omni Insurance Group [*NASDAQ symbol*] (TTSB)
OMGR....... Omni Insurance Group, Inc. [*NASDAQ symbol*] (SAG)
OM Grp ..... OM Group, Inc. [*Associated Press*] (SAG)
OMGT .... Overall Missile Guidance Tests (MCD)
OMGUS ..... Office of Military Government, United States
OMGWB..... Office of Military Government for Wuerttemberg-Baden [*US Military Government, Germany*]
OMH......... Health Sciences Library, Mississauga Hospital, Ontario [*Library symbol*] [*National Library of Canada*] (BIB)
OMH......... Office of Mental Health (DMAA)
OMH......... Office of Minority Health (SAUS)
OMH......... Omaha Aviation, Inc. (SAUS)
OMH......... Omega Hydrocarbons Ltd. [*Toronto Stock Exchange symbol*]
OMH......... Omohyoid [*Muscle*] (MELL)
OMH......... Ontario Ministry of Health (SAUS)
OMH......... Orumieh [*Iran*] [*Airport symbol*] [*Obsolete*] (OAG)
OMHA .... Ohio Manufactured Homes Association (EARSL)
OMHCE...... Organic Material Hydrocarbon Equivalent [*Automotive emissions control*]
OMHE .... America Council on Education, Office of Minorities in Higher Education [*Association*] (EA)
OMHE .... Office of Minorities in Higher Education [*Association*] (EA)
OMHL .... Occupational Medicine and Hygiene Laboratory [*British*] (IRUK)
OMH-RC .... Office of Minority Health Resource Center
OMHSA...... Ontario Municipal Health and Safety Association (SAUS)
OMHT .... Hagar Township Public Library, Markstay, Ontario [*Library symbol*] [*National Library of Canada*] (NLC)
OMI.......... Middletown Public Library, Middletown, OH [*OCLC symbol*] (OCLC)
OMI.......... Midland Public Library, Ontario [*Library symbol*] [*National Library of Canada*] (NLC)
OMI.......... Oblate of Mary Immaculate (SAUS)
OMI.......... Oblates of Mary Immaculate (TOCD)
omi.......... Oblates of Mary Immaculate (TOCD)
OMI.......... Oblats de Marie Immaculee [*Oblates of Mary Immaculate*] [*Rome, Italy*] (EAIO)
OMI.......... Office of Management Improvement [*Department of Agriculture*]
OMI.......... Office of Management Information [*Military*] (AFIT)
OMI.......... Office of Medical Investigator (DMAA)
OMI.......... Office of Multicultural Interests [*Western Australia*]
OMI.......... Ogilvy & Mather International, Inc. (EFIS)
OMI.......... Ohio Mechanics Institute
OMI.......... Old Myocardial Infarction [*Medicine*]
OMI.......... Olympic Media Information (AD)
OMI.......... OMI Corp. [*Associated Press*] (SAG)
OMI.......... Omni [*NCIC car model code*]
OMI.......... Omni-bearing Magnetic Indicator (SAUS)
OMI.......... Omnibus Computer Graphics, Inc. [*Toronto Stock Exchange symbol*]
OMI.......... Oocyte Maturation Inhibitor [*Endocrinology*]
OMI.......... Open Market, Inc. (IGQR)
OMI.......... Open Messaging Interface [*Lotus Development Corp.*] (PCM)
OMI.......... Open Microprocessor (SAUS)
OMI.......... Open Microprocessor Initiative (SAUS)
OMI.......... Open Microprocessorsystems Initiative (SAUS)
OMI.......... Open Modelling Interface (SAUS)
OMI.......... Operating Memorandum - Information
OMI.......... Operational Maintenance Instruction (AAG)
OMI.......... Operation Move-In [*New York City*]

omi .... Operations and Maintenance Instruction (NAKS)
OMI .... Operator Message Input (SAUS)
OMI .... Opinions about Mental Illness [*A questionnaire*]
OMI .... Optical Mapping Instrument (SAUS)
OMI .... Optical Measurement Instrument (SAA)
OMI .... Optical Mode Interference (SAUS)
OMI .... Opto Mechanik Inc. (SAUS)
OMI .... Ordnance Modifications Instructions
OMI .... Organisation Maritime Internationale [*International Maritime Organization - IMO*] (EAIO)
OMI .... Organisation Meteorologique Internationale
OMI .... Organizacion Maritima Internacional [*International Maritime Organization*] [*Spanish*] [*United Nations*] (DUND)
OMI .... Organization for Microinformation
OMI .... Organizations Master Index [*A publication*]
OMI .... Other Manufacturing Industries [*Department of Employment*] [*British*]
OMI .... Our Main Interest (LAIN)
OMI .... Owens & Minor, Inc. [*NYSE symbol*] (SPSG)
OMI .... Ozone Monitoring Instrument (SAUS)
OMI .... Systems Initiative (SAUS)
OMIA .... Online Mendelian Inheritance in Animals (SAUS)
OMIA .... Operating, Maintenance, Interest, and Adaptability
OMIAA .... Orientation and Mobility Instructors Association of Australasia (SAUS)
OMiabM ..... Monsanto Research Corp., Mound Laboratory, Miamisburg, OH [*Library symbol*] [*Library of Congress*] (LCLS)
OMiabMI .... Mead Imaging, Miamisburg, OH [*Library symbol*] [*Library of Congress*] (LCLS)
OMiabMM ... Monarch Marking Systems, Pitney Bowes, Chemical Research and Development Library, Miamisburg, OH [*Library symbol*] [*Library of Congress*] (LCLS)
OMIBAC ..... Ordinal Memory Inspecting Binary Automatic Calculator (RALS)
OMIBAC ..... Ordinal Memory Inspecting Binary Automatic Computer (IEEE)
OMIBM ...... IBM Canada Ltd., Markham, Ontario [*Library symbol*] [*National Library of Canada*] (NLC)
OMIC .... OMI Corp. [*NASDAQ symbol*] (COMM)
OMICA .... Organized Migrants in Community Action [*Florida*] [*Defunct*]
OMid .... Middletown Public Library, Middletown, OH [*Library symbol*] [*Library of Congress*] (LCLS)
OMID .... Ontario Midland Railroad [*Federal Railroad Administration identification code*]
OMidAR ..... Armco, Inc., Research Center, Technical Library, Middletown, OH [*Library symbol*] [*Library of Congress*] (LCLS)
OMidH .... Middletown Hospital Association, Ada Leonard Memorial Library, Middletown, OH [*Library symbol*] [*Library of Congress*] (LCLS)
OMidU .... Miami University, Middletown Campus, Middletown, OH [*Library symbol*] [*Library of Congress*] (LCLS)
OMIH .... Huronia Historical Park, Midland, Ontario [*Library symbol*] [*National Library of Canada*] (NLC)
OMIHM ...... Halton Region Museum, Milton, Ontario [*Library symbol*] [*National Library of Canada*] (BIB)
OMIHS ...... Institute for Hydrogen Systems, Mississauga, Ontario [*Library symbol*] [*National Library of Canada*] (NLC)
OMII .... Oxy Metal Industries International (AD)
OMIKK .... Orszagos Muszaki Informacios Kozpont es Konyvtar [*National Technical Information Center and Library*] [*Information service or system*] (IID)
OMIL .... Milton Public Library, Ontario [*Library symbol*] [*National Library of Canada*] (NLC)
OMILD .... Mildmay Branch, Bruce County Public Library, Ontario [*Library symbol*] [*National Library of Canada*] (NLC)
OMill .... Holmes County Public Library, Millersburg, OH [*Library symbol*] [*Library of Congress*] (LCLS)
OMILL .... Millbrook Public Library, Ontario [*Library symbol*] [*National Library of Canada*] (BIB)
OMILV .... Milverton Public Library, Ontario [*Library symbol*] [*National Library of Canada*] (NLC)
OMiM .... Megis Local School District Public Library, Middleport Branch, Middleport, OH [*Library symbol*] [*Library of Congress*] (LCLS)
OMIM .... Online Mendelian Inheritance in Man [*Genetics*]
OMiM .... Outer Mitochondrial Membrane [*Also, OMM*] [*Cytology*]
OMIN .... Inco Ltd., Mississauga, Ontario [*Library symbol*] [*National Library of Canada*] (NLC)
OMIOM ...... Original Meaning Is the Only Meaning [*Writing term*]
omiom ...... Original Meaning is the Only Meaning (AD)
OMIP .... Ocean Model Intercomparison Project (SAUS)
OMIP .... Office of Minority Institutions Program [*U.S. Department of the Interior*] (BARN)
OMIS .... Office, Management Information System (SAUS)
OMIS .... Office of Management Information Systems [*Office of Administration and Management*] [*Department of Labor*]
OMIS .... Office of Media and Information Services (SAUS)
OMIS .... Omission (AAG)
OMiS .... Operational Management Information System [*NASA*] (NAKS)
OMIS .... Operational Multi-Spectral Imager Suite (ACAE)
OMIS .... Operations Management Information System (SAUS)
OMIS .... Optical Microscope Inspection System (SAUS)
O Misc ...... Ohio Miscellaneous Reports [*A publication*] (DLA)
OMiSS .... Operation and Maintenance Instruction Summary Sheet [*NASA*] (NAKS)
OMISTN ..... Optical Mode Interface Super Twisted Nematic (SAUS)
OMIT .... Mitchell Public Library, Ontario [*Library symbol*] [*National Library of Canada*] (NLC)
OMIT .... Orienthine-decarboxylase, Motility, Indole, Tryptophandeaminase (SAUS)
omit .... Orinthine-Decarboxylase, Motility, Indole, Trytophandeaminase (AD)
OMIT .... Orinthine-decarboxylase, Motility, Indole, Trytophandeandeaminase (SAUS)
OMITT .... Omittatur [*Let It Be Omitted*] [*Pharmacy*] (ROG)
OMJ .... Ohmine [*Japan*] [*Seismograph station code, US Geological Survey*] (SEIS)
OMJ .... Orthomode Junction [*Electronics*]
OMJ .... Osler Medical Journal (SAUS)
OMJAT ...... J. A. Turner Professional Library, H. J. A. Brown Education Centre, Mississauga,Ontario [*Library symbol*] [*National Library of Canada*] (NLC)
OMK .... Omak, WA [*Location identifier*] [*FAA*] (FAAL)
OMK .... Owl Monkey Kidney [*Cell line*]
omkr .... Omdring [*About*] [*Norwegian*] (AD)
OMKR .... Outer Marker [*Part of an instrument landing system*] [*Aviation*]
OMKT .... Open Market [*NASDAQ symbol*] (TTSB)
OMKT .... Open Market, Inc. [*NASDAQ symbol*] (SAG)
OML .... Object Manipulation Language (SAUS)
OML .... Object Module Library [*Computer science*] (VLIE)
OML .... Ocean Mixed Layer (SAUS)
OML .... One-conductor Many-turn Loop (SAUS)
OML .... One-Man-LAN [*Linked Access Network*] [*PC Interconnect, Inc.*] [*Telecommunications*] (PCM)
OML .... Ontario Ministry of Labour (SAUS)
OML .... Ontario Ministry of Labour Library [*UTLAS symbol*]
OML .... Ontario Motor League [*Canada*] (AD)
OML .... Ontology Markup Language (IDAI)
OML .... Open Modelling Language [*Computer science*] (VLIE)
OML .... Operations Manual Letter [*National Weather Service*] (NOAA)
OML .... Orbiter Mold Line [*NASA*] (NASA)
OML .... Orbiting Military Laboratory (AAG)
OML .... Orbitomeatal Line (STED)
OML .... Orbitomental Line (DMAA)
OML .... Order of Merit List [*Army*] (AABC)
OML .... Ordnance Material Letter (SAA)
OML .... Ordnance Missile Laboratories (KSC)
OML .... Ordnance Muzzle Loading [*British military*] (DMA)
OML .... Organic Materials Laboratory [*Watertown, MA*] [*Army*] (GRD)
OML .... Organizational Maintenance Level (NVT)
OML .... Outer Mold Line (NASA)
OML .... Outgoing Matching Loss [*Telecommunications*] (TEL)
oml .... Outside Mold Line (AD)
OML .... Outside Mold Line [*Technical drawings*]
OML .... University of Cincinnati, Marx Law Library, Cincinnati, OH [*OCLC symbol*] (OCLC)
OMLA .... Organizational Maintenance Level Activity (MCD)
OMLAC ...... Oxfordshire Modern Languages Achievement Certificate [*British*] (AIE)
OMLCSA .... Old Mine Lamp Collectors Society of America (EA)
OMLE .... Organization of Spanish Marxist-Leninists (PD)
OMLET ...... Ocean Mixed Layer Experiment (SAUS)
OMLF .... Oromo Muslim Liberation Front (SAUS)
OMLIT .... One-Man Live Interception Test (SAA)
OMLJ .... Officer of Merit, Order of St. Lazarus of Jerusalem (DD)
OMLP .... Ohio Midland Light & Power [*AAR code*]
OMLRS ...... Operations, Maintenance and Logistics Resources Simulation (SAUS)
OMLS .... Office of Management Information Systems (SAUS)
OMLT .... [*The*] Learning Tree, Mississauga, Ontario [*Library symbol*] [*National Library of Canada*] (NLC)
OMLTA .... Ohio Modern Language Teachers Association (EDAC)
OMLX .... London Securities and Derivatives Exchange (SAUS)
OMLX .... Omnitrax Leasing [*Private rail car owner code*]
OMM .... Miami University, Middletown Campus, Middletown, OH [*OCLC symbol*] (OCLC)
OMM .... Office of Marine Minerals
OMM .... Office of Minerals Mobilization [*Later, OMSF*] [*Department of the Interior*]
OMM .... Officer Message Mail [*Military*]
OMM .... Officer Messenger Mail (SAUS)
OMM .... Officer of the Order of Military Merit [*Canada*] (DD)
OMM .... Offshore Minerals Management Program
OMM .... Oil Market Module [*Department of Energy*] (GFGA)
OMM .... OMI Corp. [*NYSE symbol*] (TTSB)
OMM .... Ommatidium [*Arthropod eye anatomy*]
OMM .... Operation and Maintenance Manual
omm .... ophchalmomandibulomelic (SAUS)
OMM .... Ophthalmomandibulomelic [*Dysplasia Syndrome*] [*Medicine*] (STED)
OMM .... Orbicular Muscle of Mouth (MELL)
OMM .... Orbital Maintenance Mission [*NASA*] (SSD)
OMM .... Organisation Meteorologique Mondiale [*World Meteorological Organization - WMO*] (EAIO)
OMM .... Organizacion Meteorologica Mundial [*World Meteorological Organization - WMO*] [*Spanish*]
OMM .... Organometallic Material
OMM .... Outer Mitochondrial Membrane [*Also, OMiM*] [*Cytology*]
OMM .... Output Message Manual [*Computer science*] (VLIE)
OMM .... Oxford Medical Manuals [*A publication*]
OMMA .... Outboard Motor Manufacturers Association [*Later, MEMA*] (EA)
OMMB .... Information Centre, Molson Breweries of Canada Ltd., Mississauga, Ontario [*Library symbol*] [*National Library of Canada*] (NLC)
OMMB .... Ontario Milk Marketing Board (SAUS)
OMMC .... Officer Message Mail Center [*Military*]
OMMC .... Officer Messenger Mail Center (SAUS)
OMMCS ..... Ordnance Missile and Munitions Center and School [*Army*]
Om Mer Sh ... Omond's Merchant Shipping Acts [*1877*] [*A publication*] (DLA)

OMMH....... Orbiter Maintenance Man-Hours [*NASA*] (NASA)
OMMI........ Magna International, Inc., Markham, Ontario [*Library symbol*] [*National Library of Canada*] (BIB)
OMMI........ Oblate Missionaries of Mary Immaculate (TOCD)
OMMIC...... Ordnance Maintenance Management Information Center [*Navy*]
OMMLT...... Murchison Lyell Township Community Library, Madawaska, Ontario [*Library symbol*] [*National Library of Canada*] (NLC)
OMMM...... Moore Museum, Mooretown, Ontario [*Library symbol*] [*National Library of Canada*] (BIB)
OMMMSA... Oil Mill Machinery Manufacturers and Supply Association (EA)
OMMS....... Office of Merchant Marine Safety [*Coast Guard*]
OMMS....... Organizational Missile Maintenance Squadron [*Air Force*]
OMMS....... Oxygen Mask-Mounted Sight (SAUS)
OMM(S)C... Officer Messenger Mail (Sub) Center [*Navy*]
OMMSC..... Officer Messenger Mail Sub-Center (SAUS)
OMMSQA... Office of Modeling, Monitoring Systems, and Quality Assurance [*Environmental Protection Agency*]
OMN......... Mansfield-Richland County Public Library, Mansfield, OH [*OCLC symbol*] (OCLC)
OMN......... Octamethylnaphthalene [*Organic chemistry*]
OMN......... Oculomotor Nerve [*Medicine*] (STED)
OMN......... Oman [*ANSI three-letter standard code*] (CNC)
OMN......... Omission [*Telegraphy*] (PCTE)
OMN......... Omnivorous
OMN......... Omnova Solutions [*NYSE symbol*]
OMN......... Ormond Beach, FL [*Location identifier*] [*FAA*] (FAAL)
OMN......... Orthomin
omn 2 hor... Omni Secunda Hora [*Every Two Hours*] [*Latin*] [*Pharmacy*] (DAVI)
OMN BID.... Omni Bidus [*Every Two Days*] [*Pharmacy*] (ROG)
OMN BIH.... Omni Bihora [*Every Two Hours*] [*Pharmacy*]
omn bih..... Omni Bihora [*Every Two Hours*] [*Latin*] (AD)
Omncre..... Omnicare, Inc. [*Associated Press*] (SAG)
OMNCS...... Office of the Manager National Communications System [*GSA*]
OMNDM..... Ontario Ministry of Northern Development and Mines (SAUS)
OMNET...... Organizational Maintenance New Equipment Training [*Army*] (INF)
OMNG....... Operations and Maintenance, National Guard [*Army*]
OMN H....... Omni Hora [*Every Hour*] [*Pharmacy*]
OMN HOR... Omni Hora [*Every Hour*] [*Pharmacy*]
omni......... Omnidirectional [*Microphone*] (WDMC)
OMNI......... Omnidirectional
OMNI......... OMNI Energy Services Corp. [*NASDAQ symbol*] (NASQ)
Omni......... Omni Multimedia Group, Inc. [*Associated Press*] (SAG)
OMNI......... Omni-Range (NAKS)
omni......... Omnirange (AD)
omni......... Omnivisual (AD)
omni......... Onmidirectional (AD)
OMNI......... On-Site Multiple Network Installation [*Thomas & Betts Corp.*]
OMNI......... Optical Microwave Networks, Inc. (EFIS)
OMNI......... Optimum Management with Necessary Information (SAUS)
OMNI......... Organization for Minnesota Nanotechnology Initiatives [*University of Minnesota*] (RCD)
OMNI......... Organizing Medical Networked Information [*British*] (TELE)
Omnicm..... Omnicom Group, Inc. [*Associated Press*] (SAG)
OmniIns..... Omni Insurance Group, Inc. [*Associated Press*] (SAG)
OmniMult... Omni Multimedia Group, Inc. [*Associated Press*] (SAG)
OMNIPoint... Open Management Interoperability Point (GART)
Omnipt...... Omnipoint Corp. [*Associated Press*] (SAG)
OMNIRANGE... Omnidirectional Radio Range (MSA)
OMNITAB... Omnibus Program with Tabular Numerical Functions [*Programming language*] [*1965*] (CSR)
OMNITENNA... Omnirange Antenna
OmniUSA... Omni USA, Inc. [*Associated Press*] (SAG)
OMNIX...... Onyx Microcomputer Unix (SAUS)
OMN MAN.. Omni Mane [*Every Morning*] [*Pharmacy*]
omn man... Omni Mane [*Every Morning*] [*Latin*] (AD)
OMNMHCE... Organic Material Non-Methane Hydrocarbon Equivalent (EEVL)
OMNMPS... Operative Machine Needle Makers' Protection Society [*A union*] [*British*]
OMN NOCT... Omni Nocte [*Every Night*] [*Pharmacy*]
omn noct... Omni Nocte [*Every Night*] [*Latin*] (AD)
omn quad hor... Omni Quadrante Hora [*Every quarter of An Hour*] [*Latin*] [*Pharmacy*] (DAVI)
OMN QUADR HOR... Omni Quadrante Horae [*Every Quarter of an Hour*] [*Pharmacy*] (ROG)
OMNR....... Ontario Ministry of Natural Resources [*Canada*]
OMNRF...... Omni Resources, Inc. (SAUS)
OMNS....... OMNIS Technology Corp. [*OTCBB symbol*]
OMNS....... Open Network Management System [*Computer science*] (VLIE)
OMNT....... Northern Telecom, Mississauga, Ontario [*Library symbol*] [*National Library of Canada*] (NLC)
OMNTS...... Over Mountains (WEAT)
OMNU....... Orthomolecular Nutrition Institute (SAUS)
OMNX....... Omni Exploration, Inc. (SAUS)
OMNY....... Omni Sky Corp. [*NASDAQ symbol*]
OMO......... Moonbeam Public Library, Ontario [*Library symbol*] [*National Library of Canada*] (BIB)
OMO......... Mostar [*Yugoslavia*] [*Airport symbol*] (AD)
OMO......... Oblates of the Mother of Orphans (TOCD)
OMO......... Occupational Medicine Office (SAUS)
OMO......... Office of Management and Organization (SAUS)
OMO......... Office of Marine Operations [*Marine science*] (OSRA)
OMO......... Office of Meteorological Observations (SAUS)
OMO......... Office of the Director of Manpower and Organization [*Air Force*]
OMO......... Old Man's Out [*Facetious translation of Omo, a brand of detergent*] [*British*]
OMO......... Omoco Holdings [*Vancouver Stock Exchange symbol*]
OMO......... One-Man Operated (SAUS)
OMO......... One-Man-Operated Bus [*London, England*]
OMO......... One Man Operation [*Railroad*] [*British*]
OMO......... On Motion Of [*Telegraphy*] (PCTE)
OMO......... Open Market Operations [*Economics*]
OMO......... Operator Message Output (SAUS)
OMO......... Oral Malodor [*Medicine*] (MELL)
OMO......... Orbiting Meteorological Observatory (SAUS)
OMO......... Ordinary Money Order
OMO......... Singly-Occupied Molecular Orbital [*Physical chemistry*]
OMO......... Utarmbung [*Language symbol*] (ETLW)
OMOAM..... Ontario Agricultural Museum, Milton, Ontario [*Library symbol*] [*National Library of Canada*] (NLC)
OMOB....... Offensive Missile Order of Battle (MCD)
OMODE...... Ordinary Mode (MCD)
OMOL....... Oliver Township Public Library, Murillo, Ontario [*Library symbol*] [*National Library of Canada*] (BIB)
OMOO....... Moosonee Public Library, Ontario [*Library symbol*] [*National Library of Canada*] (BIB)
omor......... One Man, One Responsibility (AD)
OMorS....... Salem Township Public Library, Morrow, OH [*Library symbol*] [*Library of Congress*] (LCLS)
OMORSDG... Morewood Branch, Stormont, Dundas, and Glengarry County Public Library, Ontario [*Library symbol*] [*National Library of Canada*] (BIB)
OMOSC...... Organisation des Musiciens d'Orchestres Symphoniques du Canada [*Organization of Canadian Symphony Musicans - OCSM*]
OMOSDG.... Morrisburg Branch, Stormont, Dundas, and Glengarry County Public Library, Ontario [*Library symbol*] [*National Library of Canada*] (NLC)
OMOT....... Metcalfe Branch, Osgoode Township Library, Ontario [*Library symbol*] [*National Library of Canada*] (BIB)
OMOTH...... Osgoode Township High School Library, Metcalfe, Ontario [*Library symbol*] [*National Library of Canada*] (BIB)
OMOV....... One Member, One Vote [*System to select parliamentary candidates*] [*British*]
OMP......... Espe [*Germany*] [*Research code symbol*]
OMP......... Marion Public Library, Marion, OH [*OCLC symbol*] (OCLC)
OMP......... Obstetrical Measuring Plate [*Medicine*] (MELL)
OMP......... Ocean Margins Program (SAUS)
OMP......... Ocean Microwave Package (SSD)
OMP......... Office of Metric Programs [*Department of Commerce*]
OMP......... Olfactory Marker Protein [*Biochemistry*]
OMP......... Oligo-N-methylmorpholinopropylene Oxide [*Pharmacology*]
OMP......... OM Group, Inc. [*NYSE symbol*] (SAG)
OMP......... Operating Maintenance Panel (IAA)
OMP......... Operating Maintenance Procedure (IAA)
OMP......... Operating Memorandum - Policy
OMP......... Operations and Maintenance Plan [*NASA*] (NASA)
OMP......... Optical Mark Printer (NITA)
omp......... Organo-Metallic Polymer (AD)
OMP......... Organometallic Polymer (CAAL)
OMP......... Ormetoprim [*Potentiator for antibacterials*] [*Veterinary medicine*]
OMP......... Ornithine Monophosphate (DMAA)
OMP......... Orotidine Monophosphate [*Organic chemistry*]
Omp......... Outer Membrane Protein [*Biochemistry*] (QSUL)
OMP......... Outer Membrane Protein [*Biochemistry*]
OMP......... Output Makeup
OMP......... Overseas Manpower [*British*]
OMP......... Oxford Medical Publications [*A publication*]
OMpA........ American Society for Metals Library, Metals Park, OH [*Library symbol*] [*Library of Congress*] (LCLS)
OMPA........ Octamethylpyrophosphoramide [*Insecticide*]
OMPA........ Octamethylpyrophosphoramide, Schradan (EDCT)
OMPA........ Office of Marine Pollution Assessment [*National Oceanic and Atmospheric Administration*] (ASF)
ompa........ One-Man Pension Arrangement (AD)
OMPA........ One-Man Pension Arrangement [*Management*]
OMPA........ Operating Memorandum - Personnel Assignment
OMPA........ Otitis Media, Purulent, Acute [*Medicine*]
OMPA........ Outer Membrane Protein A [*Biochemistry*]
OMPAC...... Ohio Medical PAC [*Hillard, OH*] (PACS)
OMPC....... Office of Municipal Pollution Control [*Environmental Protection Agency*] (GFGA)
OMPC....... Overseas Military Personnel Charter (MCD)
OMPD....... Office of Mineral Policy Development [*Department of the Interior*]
OMPE....... Office of Management Planning and Evaluation [*Environmental Protection Agency*] (EPA)
OMPE & R... Office of Manpower Policy, Evaluation, and Research [*Department of Labor*]
OMPEC...... Offshore Mechanics and Polar Engineering Council
OMPER...... Office of Manpower Policy, Evaluation, and Research [*Department of Labor*]
OMPF........ Official Military Personnel File [*Army*] (AABC)
OMPF........ Official Military Police File (SAUS)
ompf......... Omphaloskepsis (AD)
OMPF........ Operation and Maintenance Processor Frame [*Computer science*] (VLIE)
OMPI........ Ordnance Master Publication Index (MCD)
OMPI........ Organisation Mondiale de la Propriete Intellectuelle [*World Intellectual Property Organization - WIPO*] [*Information service or system*] (IID)

OMPI .... Organizacion Mundial de la Propiedad Intelectual [*World Intellectual Property Organization*] [*Spanish*] [*United Nations*] (DUND)
OMPI .... Ottawa Medical Physics Institute [*Carleton University*] [*Canada*] (RCD)
OMPI .... Oxo(mercaptoethyl)(phenyl)imidazolidine [*Biochemistry*]
OMPLA ...... Outer Membrane Phospholipase A
OMPO .... Oahu Metropolitan Planning Organization [*Hawaii*] (AD)
OMPR .... Office of Management Planning and Review [*Formerly, OMD*] [*NASA*]
OMPR .... Operational Maintainability Problem Reporting (NASA)
OMPR .... Optical Mark Page Reader [*Computer science*] (AABC)
ompr .... Optical Mark Page Reader (AD)
OMPR .... Optical Mark Printer (CIST)
OMPR .... Optimal Multiple Point Reassignment (SAUS)
OMPRA ...... Office of Minerals Policy and Research Analysis (AD)
OMPRA ...... One-Man Propulsion Research Apparatus [*NASA*]
OMPS .... On-orbit Maneuvering Propulsion System (SAUS)
OMPS .... Orbit Maneuvering Propulsion System [*NASA*] (KSC)
OMPSA ...... Organisation Mondiale pour le Promotion Sociale des Aveugles [*World Council for the Welfare of the Blind - WCWB*] (EAIO)
OMPT .... Observed Man [*or Mass*] Point Trajectory [*NASA*] (KSC)
OMPT .... Omnipoint Corp. [*NASDAQ symbol*] (TTSB)
OMPU .... Oficina Municipale de Planeamiento Urbano [*Municipal Office of Urban Planning*] [*Spain*] (AD)
OMPUS ...... Official Munitions Production United States
OMPW .... Pratt & Whitney Aircraft Ltd., Mississauga, Ontario [*Library symbol*] [*National Library of Canada*] (NLC)
OMPX .... OCLC Microcomputer Program Exchange (NITA)
OMQP .... Omni Quip International, Inc. [*NASDAQ symbol*] (NASQ)
OM QUAR HOR ... Omni Quarta Hora [*Every Quarter of An Hour*] [*Latin*] [*Pharmacy*] (DAVI)
OMR .... Midland-Ross Corp., Library, Cleveland, OH [*OCLC symbol*] (OCLC)
omr .... Office Methods Research (AD)
OMR .... Office Methods Research
OMR .... Office of Marine Resources [*Department of the Interior*] (NOAA)
OMR .... Officer Master Record [*Air Force*] (AFM)
OMR .... Offsite Methods Retrieval (SAUS)
OMR .... Oligomycin-Resistant (DMAA)
OMR .... Online Medical Record (HCT)
OMR .... Operational Microwave Receiver (SAUS)
OMR .... Operational Modification Report (IAA)
OMR .... Operation Management Room [*NASA*] (KSC)
OMR .... Operations and Maintenance Requirements (NASA)
OMR .... Operations Management Room [*NASA*]
OMR .... Operations Manager's Report
OMR .... Operative Morality Rate [*Statistics*] [*Medicine*] (DAVI)
OMR .... Optical Mark and Read (SAUS)
OMR .... Optical Mark Read (SAUS)
omr .... Optical Mark Reader (AD)
OMR .... Optical Mark Reader [*Computer science*]
OMR .... Optical Mark Reading (SAUS)
omr .... Optical Mark Recognition (AD)
OMR .... Optical Mark Recognition [*Computer science*] (MCD)
OMR .... Optical Meter Relay
OMR .... Orad [*Romania*] [*Airport symbol*] (OAG)
OMR .... Orbiter Management Review [*NASA*] (NASA)
OMR .... Organic Magnetic Resonance
OMR .... Organic-Moderated Reactor [*Nuclear energy*]
OMR .... Our Material Returned (AAG)
OMR .... Output Message Report (SAUS)
OMR .... Overhaul, Maintenance, and Repair (MCD)
OMR .... Overhead Materials Requirement [*Manufacturing*]
OMRA .... 135th Medical Regiment Association (EA)
OMRAS ...... Online Music Recognition and Searching
OMRB .... Operating Material Review Board [*NASA*] (NASA)
OMRB .... Outstanding National Resource Waters (SAUS)
OMRC .... Operational Maintenance Requirements Catalog [*NASA*] (MCD)
OMRC .... Optical Mark Reader Card [*Computer science*] (MHDI)
OMRCA ...... Organic-Moderated Reactor Critical Assembly [*Nuclear energy*]
OMRD .... Office of Manpower Research and Development [*National Academy of Sciences*]
OMRD .... Overseas Mineral Resource Development (AD)
OMRE .... Organic-Moderated Reactor Experiment [*Nuclear energy*]
OMRF .... Oklahoma Medical Research Foundation [*University of Oklahoma*] [*Research center*]
OMRF .... Orbiter Maintenance and Refurbishment Facility (SAUS)
OMRF .... Orbiter Modification and Refurbishment Facility [*NASA*] (NAKS)
OMRI .... Oklahoma Medical Research Institute
OMRI .... Open Media Research Institute [*Non-profit news and analysis organization covering Eastern Europe and the former Soviet Union*] (ECON)
OMRK .... Ras Al Khaimah/International [*United Arab Emirates*] [*ICAO location identifier*] (ICLI)
OMRM .... Manitou Library (Ojibway of Manitou Rapids Indian Band), Manitou Rapids, Ontario [*Library symbol*] [*National Library of Canada*] (BIB)
OMRO .... Ordnance Materials Research Office [*Later, AMMRC*] [*Army*] (MCD)
OMR/P ...... Operations and Maintenance Requirements/Plan [*NASA*] (NASA)
OMRR .... Ordnance Material Research Reactor [*Nuclear energy*]
OMRS .... Onsite Management Records System (SAUS)
OMRS .... Operations and Maintenance Requirements Specifications (NASA)
OMRS .... Optical Mark Reader Sheet [*Computer science*] (MHDI)
OMRS .... Orders and Medals Research Society (EA)
OMRSD ..... O&M Requirements and Specification Documentation (SAUS)
OMRSD ..... Operational Maintainability Reporting Systems Document [*NASA*] (NASA)
OMRSD ..... Operational Maintenance Requirements and Specifications Document [*NASA*] (NASA)
OMRSD ..... Operations and Maintenance Requirements and Specification Documentation (NASA)
OMRSD ..... Operations and Maintenance Requirements and Specifications Documentation
OMRSP ...... Operations and Maintenance Requirements and Specification Document (SAUS)
OMRV .... Operational Maneuvering Reentry Vehicle (MCD)
OMRW ...... Optical MASER [*Microwave Amplification by Stimulated Emission of Radiation*] Radiation Weapon (AAG)
OMS .... Margin System on OMLX (SAUS)
OMS .... Object Management Services (SAUS)
OMS .... Object Management System [*Computer science*] (VLIE)
OMS .... Ocean Minesweeper
OMS .... Octahedral Molecular Sieve [*Inorganic chemistry*]
OMS .... Office Mail System [*Computer science*] (VLIE)
OMS .... Office Management System [*Computer science*] (IAA)
OMS .... Office of Management Services [*Department of Agriculture*]
OMS .... Office of Management Studies (EA)
OMS .... Office of Management Support [*Environmental Protection Agency*] (EPA)
OMS .... Office of Marketing Services [*of BDSA*]
OMS .... Office of Mobile Sources [*Environmental Protection Agency*] (GFGA)
OMS .... Off-Line Management System (SAUS)
OMS .... Oil Market Simulation Model [*Department of Energy*] (GFGA)
OMS .... Omits [*Telegraphy*] (PCTE)
OMS .... Omsk [*Former USSR*] [*Airport symbol*] (OAG)
OMS .... On-Board Maintenance System [*Aviation*]
OMS .... One-Minute Superstar [*Actor whose bit part in a television series results in instant stardom*]
OMS .... Opcode MIDI [*Musical Instrument Digital Interface*] System
OMS .... Open Mail System [*Raindrop Software Co.*] (PCM)
OMS .... Open Management System [*Vitalink Communicatons Corp.*]
OMS .... Open Measurement Solution
OMS .... Open Music System (SAUS)
OMS .... Operational Maintenance System
OMS .... Operational Meteorological Satellite [*NASA*]
OMS .... Operational Mission Summary [*Army*]
OMS .... Operational Mode Summary
OMS .... Operational Monitoring System (MCD)
OMS .... Operation and Maintenance Subsystem (SAUS)
OMS .... Operations Management System (SSD)
OMS .... Opocode MIDI System (SAUS)
OMS .... Oppenheimer Multi-Sector Income Trust [*NYSE symbol*] (SPSG)
OMS .... Opportunity Management System (GART)
OMS .... Opsocionus-Myoclonus Support Network, Inc. (NRGU)
OMS .... Opsocionus-Myoclonus Syndrome [*Medicine*] (MELL)
OMS .... Optical MASER [*Microwave Amplification by Stimulated Emission of Radiation*] System
OMS .... Optical Mass Spectroscopy (AAEL)
OMS .... Optical Modulation System
OMS .... Optimum Mode Selector (CAAL)
OMS .... Optoelectronic Measuring System (SAUS)
OMS .... Optronic Mast Sensor (SAUS)
OMS .... Oral and Maxillofacial Surgery
OMS .... Oral Morphine Sulfate [*Medicine*] (MELL)
oms .... Orbital Maneuvering Subsystem [*NASA*] (NAKS)
OMS .... Orbital Maneuvering System [*or Subsystem*] [*NASA*]
OMS .... Orbital Mapping System (SAUS)
OMS .... Orbital Multifunction Satellite
OMS .... Orbit Mode Software (ACAE)
OMS .... Order Management System [*Computer science*] (GART)
OMS .... Ordnance Machine Shop
OMS .... Ordnance Management System (SAUS)
OMS .... Ordnance Mounting System (SAUS)
OMS .... Organic Mass Spectroscope (SAUS)
OMS .... Organic Mass Spectroscopy
OMS .... Organic Mental Syndrome [*Medicine*] (DMAA)
OMS .... Organisation Mondiale de la Sante [*World Health Organization - WHO*] [*Switzerland*]
OMS .... Organizacion Mundial de la Salud [*World Health Organization*] [*Spanish*] [*United Nations*] (DUND)
OMS .... Organizational Maintenance Shop [*Army*]
OMS .... Organizational Maintenance Squadron [*Air Force*] (MCD)
OMS .... Organizational Maintenance Support
OMS .... Oriental Missionary Society [*Later, OMS International*] (EA)
OMS .... Oscillation Monitoring System [*Indian Railway*] (TIR)
OMS .... Other Members Score (SAUS)
OMS .... Otomandibular Syndrome [*Medicine*] (DMAA)
OMS .... Outcomes Management System (AMHC)
OMS .... Outdoor Microphone System
OMS .... Output Multiplex Synchronizer
oms .... Output per Man Shift (AD)
OMS .... Output per Man Shift
OMS .... Overnight Message Service [*Diversified Data Processing and Consulting, Inc.*] [*Oak Park, MI*] [*Telecommunications*] (TSSD)
OMS .... Overseas Mission Society [*Defunct*] (EA)
OMS .... Ovonic Memory Switch (PDAA)
OMS .... Spectravac Power Conversion Systems, Inc., Mississauga, Ontario [*Library symbol*] [*National Library of Canada*] (NLC)
OMSA .... Offshore Marine Service Association [*New Orleans, LA*] (EA)
OMSA .... Ohio Middle School Association (EARSL)

OMSA .... Ontario Medical Secretaries Association (SAUS)
OMSA .... Orders and Medals Society of America (EA)
OMSA .... Ordnance Missile Support Agency (SAA)
OMSA .... Otitis Media, Suppurative, Acute [*Medicine*]
OMSA .... Seaman Apprentice, Opticalman, Striker [*Navy rating*]
OMSA .... Simcoe County Archives, Minesing, Ontario [*Library symbol*] [*National Library of Canada*] (NLC)
OMS&A ..... Office of Mission Safety and Assurance (SAUS)
OMSAP ...... Occupational Medicine Self-Assessment Program (SAUS)
OMSAPC .... Office of Mobile Source Air Pollution Control [*Environmental Protection Agency*]
OMSB .... Outcomes Management System Information Board
OMSC .... Organisation Mondiale pour la Systemique et la Cybernetique [*World Organization of Systems and Cybernetics*] (EAIO)
OMSC .... Otitis Media, Secretory, Chronic [*Medicine*] (DAVI)
OMSC .... Otitis Media, Suppurative, Chronic [*Medicine*]
OMSCh ...... Otitis Media, Secretory Chronic [*Medicine*] (EDAA)
OMSD .... Organization and Management Services Division (SAUS)
OMSDG ..... Maxville Branch, Stormount, Dundas, and Glengarry County Public Library, Ontario [*Library symbol*] [*National Library of Canada*] (NLC)
OMSE .... Office of Management Systems and Evaluation [*Environmental Protection Agency*] (GFGA)
Om Sea ..... Omond's Law of the Sea [*1916*] [*A publication*] (DLA)
OMSF .... Office of Manned Space Flight [*NASA*]
OMSF .... Office of Minerals and Solid Fuels [*Formerly, OMM*] [*Abolished, 1971*] [*Department of the Interior*]
OMSG .... Official Mail Study Group [*Defunct*] (EA)
OMSG .... Our Message [*Aviation*] (FAAC)
OMSI .... Oregon Museum of Science and Industry
OMSIP .... Ontario Medical Surgical Insurance Plan [*Canada*] (AD)
OMSITE ..... Oral and Maxillofacial Surgery In-Training Examination
OMSJ .... Sharjah/International [*United Arab Emirates*] [*ICAO location identifier*] (ICLI)
OMSJB ...... St. Jean Bosco Library, Matachewan, Ontario [*Library symbol*] [*National Library of Canada*] (BIB)
OMSK .... Smith, Kline & French Canada Ltd., Mississauga, Ontario [*Library symbol*] [*National Library of Canada*] (NLC)
OMSLMSq ... Organizational Missile Maintenance Squadron [*Air Force*]
OMSM .... Medical Library, Syntex, Inc., Mississauga, Ontario [*Library symbol*] [*National Library of Canada*] (NLC)
OMS/MP .... Operational Mode Summary/Mission Profiles (MCD)
OMS/MP .... Opmode Summary/Mission Profile (SAUS)
OMSMT ..... South Marysburgh Township Public Library, Milford, Ontario [*Library symbol*] [*National Library of Canada*] (BIB)
OMsn .... Mason Public Library, Mason, OH [*Library symbol*] [*Library of Congress*] (LCLS)
OMSN .... Seaman, Opticalman, Striker [*Navy rating*]
OMSP .... Operational Maintenance Support Plan [*NASA*] (MCD)
OMSPAC .... American Association of Oral & Maxillofacial Surgeons PAC [*Rosemont, IL*] (PACS)
OMSq .... Organizational Maintenance Squadron [*Air Force*] (AFM)
OMSQA ...... Office of Monitoring Systems and Quality Assurance [*Environmental Protection Agency*] (EPA)
OMSRADS ... Optimum Mix of Short Range Air Defense Systems
OMSS .... Operational Meteorological Satellite System (SAUS)
OMST .... Object Manipulation Speed Test
OMSWG ..... Operations and Maintenance Security Working Group (SSD)
OMT .... McKellar Township Public Library, Ontario [*Library symbol*] [*National Library of Canada*] (NLC)
OMT .... Metropolitan Toronto Library, Multilanguage Service [*UTLAS symbol*]
OMT .... Object Management Technique (SAUS)
OMT .... Object Modeling Technique (AAEL)
OMT .... Object Modeling Technology [*Ungermann-Bass, Inc.*]
OMT .... Object Model Template (SAUS)
OMT .... Ocean Marine Technology [*Vancouver Stock Exchange symbol*]
OMT .... Oceanography and Marine Technology [*Defunct*] (USDC)
OMT .... Office of Manufacturing Technology [*DARCOM*] [*Army*] (RDA)
OMT .... Officiating Minister to the Troops [*British*]
OMT .... Ohio Mattress Co. (EFIS)
OMT .... Old Merchant Taylors [*School*] [*British*] (ROG)
OMT .... Oleoyl Methyl Taurate [*Organic chemistry*]
OMT .... O-Methylthreonine [*Biochemistry*]
OMT .... O-Methyl Transferase [*An enzyme*]
OMT .... Ophthalmic Medical Assistant (DAVI)
OMT .... Ophthalmic Medical Technician [*or Technologist*] (HCT)
OMT .... Oral Mucosal Transudate [*Clinical chemistry*]
OMT .... Ordnance Maintenance Truck [*British*]
OMT .... Organizational Maintenance Technician [*Army*] (AABC)
OMT .... Organizational Maintenance Trainer (MCD)
OMT .... Oriental Movement Therapy (MELL)
OMT .... Orthogonal Mode Transducer (IAA)
omt .... Orthomode Transducer (AD)
OMT .... Orthomode Transducer [*Electronics*]
OMT .... Ortho-Mycaminosyltylonolide [*Antibacterial compound*]
OMT .... Orthotropic Multicell Tank
OMT .... Osteopathic Manipulative Therapy (CPH)
OMT .... Other Military Target
OMTA .... Office of Management and Technical Assessment [*Environmental Protection Agency*] (GFGA)
OMTA .... Ovulation Method Teachers Association (EA)
OMTBP ...... Octamethyltetrabenzporphyrin [*Organic chemistry*]
OMTC .... Ontario Ministry of Transportation and Communications [*Downsview, ON*] [*Telecommunications*] (TSSD)
OMTD .... Omitted (SAUS)
OMTD .... Operator/Maintenance Task Description (DNAB)
OMTE .... Organizational Maintenance Test Equipment (SAUS)
OMTF .... Officers Master Tape File (SAUS)
OMTF .... Optical Modulation Transfer Function (ACAE)
OMTF .... Overall Missile Test Facility (SAUS)
OMTL .... Omtool, Ltd. [*NASDAQ symbol*] (NASQ)
OMTL .... Optical Mechanical Tube Length (SAUS)
OMTN .... Other Military Teletypewriter Network (CET)
OMTNS ...... Over Mountains [*NWS*] (FAAC)
OMTR .... Officer Master Tape Record [*Army*] (AABC)
OMTR .... Officer Master Tape Recorder (SAUS)
OMTS .... Organizational Maintenance Test Station [*Army*]
OMtsjC ...... College of Mount St. Joseph-On-The-Ohio, Mount St. Joseph, OH [*Library symbol*] [*Library of Congress*] (LCLS)
OMTSS ...... Ordnance Multiple-Purpose Tactical Satellite System
OMTU .... Organizational Maintenance Trainer Unit (ACAE)
OMtv .... Mount Vernon Public Library, Mount Vernon, OH [*Library symbol*] [*Library of Congress*] (LCLS)
OMtvN .... Mount Vernon Nazarene College, Mount Vernon, OH [*Library symbol*] [*Library of Congress*] (LCLS)
OMU .... Operational Mock-Up
OMU .... Operative Mechanics' Union [*British*]
OMU .... Optical Measuring Unit (KSC)
omu .... Optical Measuring Unit (NAKS)
OMU .... Optical Memory Unit (SAUS)
OMU .... Orbital Maneuvering Unit (ACAE)
OMUA .... Office Machinery Users Association (SAUS)
OMUC .... Upper Canada Village, Morrisburg, Ontario [*Library symbol*] [*National Library of Canada*] (NLC)
OMUG .... Organizations for the Exploitation of the Gambia River (Guinea-Bissau) [*Political party*] (PSAP)
OMUP .... Operating and Maintenance User Part (SAUS)
OMUP .... Organization and Management User Parts [*Telecommunications*] (OSI)
OMUS .... Organizations for the Exploitation of the Senegal River (Guinea-Bissau) [*Political party*] (PSAP)
OMV .... Oat Mosaic Virus [*Plant pathology*]
OMV .... Oblates of the Virgin Mary (TOCD)
omv .... Oblates of the Virgin Mary (TOCD)
OMV .... Office Machines Vocabulary (SAUS)
OMV .... Orbital Maneuvering Vehicle [*NASA*]
OMV .... Ornskoldsviks Mekaniska Verkstad (EFIS)
OMV .... Overseas Media Visitor
omv .... Oxygen Manual Valve (NAKS)
OMV .... Oxygen Manual Valve (NASA)
OMVC .... Mattice-Val Cote Public Library, Mattice, Ontario [*Library symbol*] [*National Library of Canada*] (BIB)
OMVC .... Open Mitral Valve Commissurotomy [*Medicine*]
OMVCC ...... Orbital Maneuvering Vehicle Control Center [*NASA*] (SSD)
OMVD .... Operator Multi-Valued Dependency (SAUS)
OMVG .... Gambia River Development Organization (SAUS)
OMVG .... Organisation pour la Mise en Valeur du Fleuve Gambie [*Gambia River Basin Organisation*] (EAIO)
OMVI .... Operating a Motor Vehicle Intoxicated (MEDA)
OMVPE ...... Organo-Metallic Vapor-Phase Epitaxy (SAUS)
OM-VPE ..... Organometallic Vapor Phase Epitaxy [*Also, OM-CVD, MO-CVD, MO-VPE*] [*Semiconductor technology*]
OMVPE ...... Organometallic Vapour Phase Epitaxy (AAEL)
OMVS .... Senegal River Development Organization (SAUS)
OMVTO ...... Office Motor Vehicle Transportation Officer [*Army*] (AABC)
OMVUIL ..... Operating Motor Vehicle under the Influence of Liquor [*Traffic offense charge*]
OMVWI ...... Operating Motor Vehicle while Intoxicated [*Traffic offense charge*]
OMW .... Office of the Mining Warden [*Victoria, Australia*]
OMW .... Olds Motor Works [*Precursor of Oldsmobile Division of General Motors*]
OMW .... Omak [*Washington*] [*Seismograph station code, US Geological Survey*] (SEIS)
OMW .... Ordnance Mobile Workshop (SAUS)
OMWG ...... Object Model Working Group
OMWIL ...... Operating Motor Vehicle under the Influence of Liquor (SAUS)
OMWM ...... Open Marsh Water Managed [*Ecology*]
OMWOG ..... Ocean-based Measurements Working Group (SAUS)
OMWOG ..... Oceans-based Measurements Working Group (SAUS)
OMX .... Officemax, Inc. [*NYSE symbol*] (SAG)
OMX .... Option Market Index [*Sweden*] (NUMA)
OMX .... Xerox Research Centre of Canada, Mississauga, Ontario [*Library symbol*] [*National Library of Canada*] (NLC)
OMXP .... Orleans Motor Express [*Common carrier symbol*]
OMY .... Output per Man-Year (SAUS)
OMZ .... Oamaru [*New Zealand*] [*Seismograph station code, US Geological Survey*] (SEIS)
OMZ .... Omack Mill [*Federal Railroad Administration identification code*]
OMZ .... Oxygen-Minimum Zone [*Oceanography*]
OMZ .... Oxymorphonazine [*An analgesic*]
ON .... Air Nauru [*ICAO designator*] (AD)
ON .... Central Branch, Nepean Public Library, Ontario [*Library symbol*] [*National Library of Canada*] (NLC)
ON .... McKinley Memorial Library, Niles, OH [*Library symbol*] [*Library of Congress*] (LCLS)
ON .... New Order [*Revolutionary group*] [*Italy*]
ON .... Obsessional Neurosis [*Medicine*] (EDAA)
ON .... Obstructive Nephropathy [*Medicine*] (MELL)
ON .... Occipitonuchal [*Medicine*] (EDAA)
ON .... Occupational Nursing (SAUS)

on Octane Number (AD)
ON Octane Number [*Fuel terminology*]
ON Oculonasal [*Anatomy*]
ON Office Nurse
ON Officer's Name (NITA)
ON Official Number (DS)
ON Off Normal
ON Ogden Nash (AD)
ON Oil-Immersed Natural-Colled Transformer (IAA)
ON Oil-immersed Natural-cooled (or cooling) (SAUS)
ON Old Norse [*Language, etc.*]
ON Olfactory Nerve [*Neuroanatomy*]
ON Oligonucleotide [*Chemistry*]
ON Omega Navigation (PDAA)
ON Omega Neuron [*Neuroanatomy*]
ON Omni Nocte [*Every Night*] [*Pharmacy*]
on Omni Nocte [*Every Night*] [*Latin*] (AD)
ON Oncology [*Medical specialty*] (DHSM)
ON Oncor [*Tire retread brand*]
ON Onions (ROG)
on Onomastikon [*Lexicon*] [*Greek*] (AD)
ON Onorevole [*Honorable*] (EY)
On Onorevole [*Honorable*] [*Italian*] (AD)
On Onsdag [*Wednesday*] [*Danish*] (AD)
on Onstage [*Theater*] (WDMC)
ON Ontario [*Canadian province*] [*Postal code*]
ON Ontario Northland Railway [*Canada*] (AD)
ON OnX Enterprise Solutions [*Toronto Stock Exchange symbol*] [*Canada*]
ON Opera News [*A publication*] (BRI)
ON Operation Notice (AAG)
ON Operation Number (ELAL)
ON Optic Nerve [*Anatomy*]
ON Optic Neuritis (SAUS)
ON Optic Neuropathy (SAUS)
O/N Order Notify [*Bill of lading*] [*Shipping*]
ON Order Number (NITA)
ON Ordre Nouveau [*New Order*] [*France*] [*Political party*] (WDAA)
ON Oregon [*Obsolete*] (ROG)
ON Original Negative (MCD)
ON Oronasal [*Medicine*] (EDAA)
ON Ortho-Novum [*A contraceptive*] [*Ortho Pharmaceutical Corp.*] (DAVI)
ON Orthopedic Nurse
ON Osteonecrosis [*Medicine*] (EDAA)
ON Other Networks (SAUS)
ON Our Neighbours [*A publication*]
ON Overnighter (SAUS)
o/n Own Name (AD)
O/N Own Name
ON Oxidation Number (IAA)
O/N Oxygen-to-Nitrogen ratio (SAUS)
ONA Nakina Public Library, Ontario [*Library symbol*] [*National Library of Canada*] (BIB)
ONA Office of National Assessments [*Australia*]
ONA Ohio Nurses Association (SAUS)
ONA Oklahoma Nurses Association (SAUS)
ONA Onahama [*Japan*] [*Seismograph station code, US Geological Survey*] (SEIS)
ONA Oneita Industries [*NYSE symbol*] (SAG)
ONA O-Nitroaniline (SAUS)
ONA Online News Association (EA)
ONA Ontario, CA [*Amtrak rail station code*]
ONA Ontario Nurses Association (SAUS)
ONA Open Network Architecture [*Computer science*]
ONA Optical Navigation Attachment (WDAA)
ONA Oregon Nurses Association (SAUS)
ONA Orthonitroaniline (DICI)
ONA Overseas National Airways [*Belgium*] [*ICAO designator*] (FAAC)
ONA Overseas National Airways, Inc.
ONA Overseas News Agency
ONA Oxides of Nitrogen Analysis [*Automotive emissions*]
ONA Winona [*Minnesota*] [*Airport symbol*] (AD)
ONA Winona, MN [*Location identifier*] [*FAA*] (FAAL)
ONAC Office of Noise Abatement and Control [*Environmental Protection Agency*]
On a/c On Account (EBF)
ONAC Operating Network Advisory Committee [*NERComP*]
ONAC Operations Network Administration Center (SAUS)
ONAC Oregon Newspaper Publishers Association (EARSL)
ONADE Office of New Animal Drug Evaluation [*Food and Drug Administration*] (RCD)
ONAIS Organization of North American Indian Students [*Defunct*] (EA)
ONA J Orthopedic Nurses Association. Journal (SAUS)
ONA-JPU Uruguayan National Organization of Retirees' and Pensioner's Associations [*Political party*] (PSAP)
ONAL Off-Net Access Line [*Telecommunications*] (TEL)
ONAP Orbit Navigation Analysis Program
ONAP Organisation Nationale d'Anti-Pauvrete [*Canada*]
ON APPROV On Approval (SAUS)
ONARP Occurrence Notification and Report Program (SAUS)
ONAS Office of Naval Acquisition Support (SAUS)
ONAS Outpatient Nonavailability Statement [*DoD*]
OnAssign On Assignment, Inc. [*Associated Press*] (SAG)
ONAT Off-Network Access Trunk (SAUS)
on av on average (SAUS)
O-NAV On-Board Navigation (MCD)
ONAX Overseas National Airways, Inc. [*Air carrier designation symbol*]
ONB Monkey Bay [*Malawi*] [*Airport symbol*] (AD)
ONb New Breman Public Library, New Breman, OH [*Library symbol*] [*Library of Congress*] (LCLS)
ONB North Bay Public Library, Ontario [*Library symbol*] [*National Library of Canada*] (NLC)
ONB Obturator Nerve Block [*Medicine*] (MELL)
ONB Octane Number Barrel [*Fuel terminology*]
ONB Old Natura Brevium [*A publication*] (DLA)
ONB O-Nitrobiphenyl (SAUS)
ONB Ortho-Nitrobiphenyl [*Organic chemistry*]
ONBA Centre de Ressources, Ecole Secondaire Algonquin, North Bay, Ontario [*Library symbol*] [*National Library of Canada*] (NLC)
ONBC Ouachita National Bancshares (SAUS)
ONBCC Canadore College, North Bay, Ontario [*Library symbol*] [*National Library of Canada*] (NLC)
Onbcp ONBANcorp, Inc. [*Associated Press*] (SAG)
ONBD On Board (NASA)
ONBK Onbancorp, Inc. [*NASDAQ symbol*] (NQ)
ONBKP ONBANCorp 6.75% Cv 'B' Pfd [*NASDAQ symbol*] (TTSB)
ONBM Belmont and Methuen Township Public Library, Nephton, Ontario [*Library symbol*] [*National Library of Canada*] (BIB)
ONBNU Nipissing University College, North Bay, Ontario [*Library symbol*] [*National Library of Canada*] (NLC)
O-N Border Oder-Neisse Border (SAUS)
ONBOSUB On Board a Submarine [*Navy*]
ONBOWCOM Duty on Board that Vessel when Placed in Commission [*Navy*]
ONBOWSERV Duty on Board that Vessel when Placed in Service [*Navy*]
ONBP Staff Library, North Bay Psychiatric Hospital, Ontario [*Library symbol*] [*National Library of Canada*] (NLC)
ONBT Orbiter Neutral Buoyancy Trainer [*NASA*] (MCD)
ONBT Ownby Trucking [*Common carrier symbol*]
ONBT Regroupement des Organisations Nationales Benevoles [*Also, National Voluntary Organizations*] (AC)
ONBWF West Ferris Secondary School, North Bay, Ontario [*Library symbol*] [*National Library of Canada*] (NLC)
ONC Confederation High School, Nepean, Ontario [*Library symbol*] [*National Library of Canada*] (NLC)
ONC Occurrence Notification Center (SAUS)
ONC Office of Narcotics Coordinator [*Later, NARCOG*] [*CIA*]
ONC Office of New Careers [*HEW*]
ONC Olivet Nazarene College [*Kankakee, IL*]
ONC Oncology (DAVI)
ONC Oncor, Inc. [*AMEX symbol*] (SAG)
ONC On-Site Container (DOMA)
onc Ontario [*MARC country of publication code*] [*Library of Congress*] (LCCP)
ONC Open Network Computing [*Computer science*] (PCM)
ONC+ Open Network Computing Plus [*Computer science*] (PCM)
ONC Open Network Connectivity [*Computer science*] (GART)
ONC Open Networking Consortium (SAUS)
ONC Operational Navigation Charts [*Air Force*]
ONC Optimists National Corps [*British military*] (DMA)
ONC Ordinary National Certificate [*British*]
ONC Oregon-Nevada-California [*Truck line*] (IIA)
ONC Organization of Nigerian Citizens
ONC Orthopaedic Nurse Certified (NUJO)
ONC Orthopedic Nursing Certificate
ONC Overall NATO Command (NATG)
ONC Over-the-needle Catheter [*Medicine*] (EDAA)
ONCB Centennial Branch, Nepean Public Library, Ontario [*Library symbol*] [*National Library of Canada*] (NLC)
ONCB Office of the Narcotics Control Board, Thailand (SAUS)
ONCC Oncology Nursing Certification Corporation (SAUS)
ONC/D Ordinary National Certificate/Diploma (ACII)
ONCE Office of National Cost Estimates [*Department of Health and Human Services*] (GFGA)
ONCF Office National des Chemins de Fer [*Moroccan Railways*]
ONCFM Office National des Chemins de Fer du Maroc [*Moroccan Railways*] (DCTA)
ONCG-A Oncogenic Virus Battery - Acute [*Oncology*] (DAVI)
ONCLA Nursing Committee for Leprosy Control [*Medicine*] [*Brazil*] (EDAA)
ONcM Muskingum College, New Concord, OH [*Library symbol*] [*Library of Congress*] (LCLS)
ONCMM Cosby, Mason, and Martland Public Library, Noelville, Ontario [*Library symbol*] [*National Library of Canada*] (NLC)
ONCN [*An*] O'Neill Concordance [*A publication*]
ONCO Office of NOAA [*National Oceanic and Atmospheric Administration*] Corps Operations [*Marine science*] (OSRA)
ONCO Oglebay Norton Company (EFIS)
ONCO On Command Corp. [*NASDAQ symbol*] (SAG)
OnCo On Command Corp. [*Associated Press*] (SAG)
Onco OncoRx, Inc. [*Associated Press*] (SAG)
ONCO Operations Non-Commissioned Officer (SAUS)
Oncogn Oncogene Science, Inc. [*Associated Press*] (SAG)
oncol oncologic (SAUS)
ONCOL Oncologist
Oncol Oncology [*Medicine*] (IDYL)
oncol oncolysis (SAUS)
OnCom On Command Corp. [*Associated Press*] (SAG)
OnComm On Command Corp. [*Associated Press*] (SAG)
Oncor Oncor, Inc. [*Associated Press*] (SAG)
ONCORE On-Command Restartable (MCD)

Oncormd.... OncorMed, Inc. [*Associated Press*] (SAG)
OncoRx...... OncoRx, Inc. [*Associated Press*] (SAG)
ONCR........ Oncor [*OTCBB symbol*]
ONCRC...... Central Resource Centre, Carleton Roman Catholic School Board, Nepean, Ontario [*Library symbol*] [*National Library of Canada*] (NLC)
ONCS........ Oncogene Science [*NASDAQ symbol*] (TTSB)
ONCS........ Oncogene Science, Inc. [*NASDAQ symbol*] (NQ)
ONCT........ Ontario Central Railroad [*Federal Railroad Administration identification code*]
ONCU........ Cumberland Township Library, Navan, Ontario [*Library symbol*] [*National Library of Canada*] (BIB)
ONCU........ OnCure Technologies Corp. [*NASDAQ symbol*] (QUAN)
ONCXDR.... Open Network Computing External Data Representation (SAUS)
ONCZ........ Owens/Negs [*Federal Railroad Administration identification code*]
OND......... Office for Network Development [*Ottawa, ON*] [*National Library of Canada*] [*Telecommunications service*] (TSSD)
OND......... Office of Neighborhood Development (OICC)
OND......... Office of the Nominal Defendant [*Australia*]
OND......... Ondangua [*Namibia*] [*Airport symbol*] (OAG)
OND......... Operator Need Dale (SAUS)
OND......... Operator Need Date (NASA)
OND......... Ophthalmic Nursing Diploma
OND......... Optical Neural Device (SAUS)
OND......... Ordinary National Diploma [*British*]
OND......... Organic Nervous Disease [*Medicine*] (MELL)
OND......... Orthopaedic Nursing Diploma [*British*]
OND......... Other Neurological Disorders
OND......... Owned [*Telegraphy*] (PCTE)
OND......... Own Number Dialing [*Telecommunications*] (OA)
ONDA........ Norwich and District Archives, Norwich, Ontario [*Library symbol*] [*National Library of Canada*] (BIB)
ONDC........ Office of National Drug Control (SAUS)
ONDCP...... Office of National Drug Control Policy [*Executive Office of the President*]
ONDE........ Office of Naval Disability Evaluation (NVT)
OnderstJ V... Onderstepoort Journal of Veterinary Research (SAUS)
ONDI........ Ontrack Data International, Inc. [*NASDAQ symbol*] (SAG)
ONDO........ ODP Nankai Downhole Observatory (SAUS)
ONDS........ Dipix Systems Ltd., Nepean, Ontario [*Library symbol*] [*National Library of Canada*] (NLC)
ONDS........ Open Network Distribution Services (SAUS)
ONDS........ Optic Nerve Decompression Surgery
ONDS........ Oriental Nocturnal Death Syndrome [*Neurology*] (DAVI)
ONE.......... Bank One Corp. [*NYSE symbol*] (SG)
ONE.......... Current Tech [*Vancouver Stock Exchange symbol*]
ONE.......... Current Technology [*VS, exchange symbol*] (TTSB)
ONe.......... Nelsonville Public Library, Nelsonville, OH [*Library symbol*] [*Library of Congress*] (LCLS)
ONE.......... Newmarket Public Library, Ontario [*Library symbol*] [*National Library of Canada*] (NLC)
ONE.......... Northeastern Ohio University, College of Medicine, Rootstown, OH [*OCLC symbol*] (OCLC)
ONE.......... Office National de l'Energie [*National Energy Board - NEB*] [*Canada*]
ONE.......... Office Network Exchange [*Honeywell, Inc.*]
ONE.......... Office of National Estimates (SAUS)
ONE.......... Onepusu [*Solomon Islands*] [*Airport symbol*] [*Obsolete*] (OAG)
ONE.......... Onerahi [*Whangarei*] [*New Zealand*] [*Seismograph station code, US Geological Survey*] (SEIS)
ONE.......... OPAC Network in Europe (SAUS)
ONE.......... Open Network Environment [*Netscape network*] [*Computer science*]
ONE.......... Optimum Network Executive (SAUS)
ONE.......... Optimum Nutritional Effectiveness [*Brand name of dog food*] [*Ralston Purina Co.*]
ONE.......... Organization for Nutrition Education [*Canada*] (EAIO)
ONE.......... Organization Number of Employees (SAUS)
ONeA........ Newark Public Library, Newark (SAUS)
O'Neal Neg L... O'Neal's Negro Law of South Carolina [*A publication*] (DLA)
ONEB........ Office of National Environmental Board (SAUS)
ONEC........ OneComm Corp. [*NASDAQ symbol*] (SAG)
OneCm...... OneComm Corp. [*Associated Press*] (SAG)
ONEG........ O Negative [*Blood type*] [*Hematology and laboratory*] (DAVI)
ONeH........ Hocking Technical College, Nelsonville, OH [*Library symbol*] [*Library of Congress*] (LCLS)
ONEI......... Oneida Coach Manufacturing [*NCIC trailer make code*]
ONEID....... Oneida, TN [*American Association of Railroads railroad junction routing code*]
Oneida...... Oneida Ltd. [*Associated Press*] (SAG)
ONEIL....... O'Neill, NE [*American Association of Railroads railroad junction routing code*]
Oneita....... Oneita Industries [*Associated Press*] (SAG)
ONELAC..... Newburgh Branch, Lennox and Addington County, Ontario [*Library symbol*] [*National Library of Canada*] (BIB)
OneLb....... One Liberty Properties, Inc. [*Associated Press*] (SAG)
Onelibt...... One Liberty Properties, Inc. [*Associated Press*] (SAG)
ONEM........ OneMain.com, Inc. [*NASDAQ symbol*] (NASQ)
ONEMI....... National Emergency Office of the Ministry of the Interior [*Emergency Management*] (EMA)
ONEMRCM... BCC Library, CANMET, Energy, Mines, and Resources Canada [*Bibliotheque du CBC, CANMET, Energie, Mines, et Ressources Canada*], Nepean, Ontario [*Library symbol*] [*National Library of Canada*] (NLC)
ONEO........ Office of Navajo Economic Opportunity
ONEOK...... Oklahoma Natural Gas Company (EFIS)
ONEOK...... ONEOK, Inc. [*Associated Press*] (SAG)
ONEP........ Office National d'Edition et de Presse [*News agency*] [*Niger*] (EY)
ONEP........ Pickering College, Newmarket, Ontario [*Library symbol*] [*National Library of Canada*] (NLC)
ONEPI....... Office National d'Edition, de Presse, et d'Imprimerie [*Publisher*] [*Benin*] (EY)
OnePrice.... One Price Clothing Stores, Inc. [*Associated Press*] (SAG)
ONER........ Oceanic Navigational Error Report [*Aviation*] (FAAC)
ONE-R....... One Time and Revisions as Required (ACAE)
ONER........ Ontario Eastern Railroad [*Federal Railroad Administration identification code*]
ONES........ OneSource Information Services, Inc. [*NASDAQ symbol*] (NASQ)
ONet......... Ontario Network [*Canada*]
Onet......... Ontario Regional Network [*Canada*] [*Computer science*] (TNIG)
ONEU........ Neustadt Village Public Library, Ontario [*Library symbol*] [*National Library of Canada*] (NLC)
OneVall..... One Valley Bancorp of West Virginia, Inc. [*Associated Press*] (SAG)
ONew........ Newark Public Library, Newark, OH [*Library symbol*] [*Library of Congress*] (LCLS)
ONewU...... Ohio State University, Newark Campus, Newark, OH [*Library symbol*] [*Library of Congress*] (LCLS)
OneWve..... OneWave, Inc. [*Associated Press*] (SAG)
ONF.......... Niagara Falls Public Library, Ontario [*Library symbol*] [*National Library of Canada*] (NLC)
ONF.......... Offensive Nuclear Forces (SAUS)
ONF.......... Office National du Film du Canada [*National Film Board of Canada - NFB*]
ONF.......... Old Norman French [*Language, etc.*]
ONF.......... Old Northern French [*Language, etc.*]
ONF.......... Oncology Nursing Forum (SAUS)
ONF.......... Oncology Nursing Foundation
ONF.......... On File (SAUS)
ONF.......... Optic Nerve Fiber [*Anatomy*]
ONFA........ Acres Consulting Services Ltd., Niagara Falls, Ontario [*Library symbol*] [*National Library of Canada*] (NLC)
ONFCY...... Cyanamid, Niagara Falls, Ontario [*Library symbol*] [*National Library of Canada*] (NLC)
ONFJC....... John Coutts Library Services Ltd., Niagara Falls, Ontario [*Library symbol*] [*National Library of Canada*] (NLC)
ONFLC....... Lanmer Consultants Ltd., Niagara Falls, Ontario [*Library symbol*] [*National Library of Canada*] (NLC)
ONFM........ On Nearest Full Moon (SAUS)
ONFM........ On or Nearest Full Moon [*Freemasonry*] (ROG)
ONFR........ Old Northern French [*Language, etc.*]
ONFWM..... Willoughby Historical Museum, Niagara Falls, Ontario [*Library symbol*] [*National Library of Canada*] (BIB)
ONFWPL.... W. P. London & Associates, Niagara Falls, Ontario [*Library symbol*] [*National Library of Canada*] (NLC)
ONG......... Donalsonville, GA [*Location identifier*] [*FAA*] (FAAL)
ONG......... Mornington Island [*Australia*] [*Airport symbol*] (OAG)
ONG......... Oklahoma Natural Gas Company (EFIS)
ONG......... Old North German (SAUS)
ONG......... Oneok, Inc. (EFIS)
ONG......... Ongar [*England*]
ONG......... Ongoro [*Peru*] [*Seismograph station code, US Geological Survey*] [*Closed*] (SEIS)
ONG......... Osteopathic and Naturopathic Guild [*British*] (DBA)
ONGA........ Overseas Number Group Analysis [*Telecommunications*] (TEL)
ONGC........ Office des Normes Generales du Canada
ONGC........ Oil & Natural Gas Commission (SAUS)
OnGrd....... On Gard Systems [*Associated Press*] (SAG)
OnGrdSy.... On Gard Systems [*Associated Press*] (SAG)
ONGRT...... North Gower Branch, Rideau Township Library, Ontario [*Library symbol*] [*National Library of Canada*] (BIB)
ONGS........ Office of National Geodetic Survey [*National Ocean Survey*]
ONH......... Office of Naval History [*Also, OFFNAVHIST*]
ONH......... Oneonta [*New York*] [*Airport symbol*] (OAG)
ON/H........ On the Hatch Cover [*Stowage*] (DNAB)
ONHA........ Office of Nursing Home Affairs [*Medicine*] (EDAA)
ONHI......... Niagara Historical Society, Niagara-On-The-Lake, Ontario [*Library symbol*] [*National Library of Canada*] (NLC)
ONHIC....... ODPHP [*Office of Disease Prevention and Health Promotion*] National Health Information Center (IID)
ONHN........ OnHealth Network [*NASDAQ symbol*] (SG)
ONHN........ OnHealth Network Co. [*NASDAQ symbol*]
ONI.......... Moanamani [*Indonesia*] [*Airport symbol*] (OAG)
ONI.......... Nipigon Public Library, Ontario [*Library symbol*] [*National Library of Canada*] (NLC)
ONI.......... Office of National Waste Terminal Storage Integration (SAUS)
ONI.......... Office of Naval Intelligence
ONI.......... Office of NWTS Integration (SAUS)
ONI.......... Oficina Nacional de Informacion [*National Information Office*] [*Press agency*] [*Peru*]
ONI.......... Oni [*Former USSR*] [*Seismograph station code, US Geological Survey*] (SEIS)
ONI.......... Operator Number Identification [*Bell System*]
ONI.......... Optical Network Interface [*Telecommunications*] (DCDG)
ONI.......... Optical Networks, Inc.
ONI.......... Ottaway Newspapers (IID)
ONIN......... Online Innovation [*OTCBB symbol*]
ONIO......... Office of Naval Inspectors of Ordnance
ONIP......... Office of National Industry Promotion [*Bureau of Apprenticeship and Training*] [*Department of Labor*]
ONIP......... Perry County District Library, New Lexington (SAUS)
ONIS......... ONI Systems [*NASDAQ symbol*]
OnIssues.... On the Issues [*A publication*] (BRI)
ONIX......... Online Information Exchange [*Association of American Publishers*]
ONJ.......... Olivia Newton-John [*Singer*]

ONJSW...... J. S. Woodsworth Secondary School, Nepean, Ontario [*Library symbol*] [*National Library of Canada*] (NLC)
Onk.......... Targum Onkelos (BJA)
ONL.......... New Liskeard Public Library, Ontario [*Library symbol*] [*National Library of Canada*] (NLC)
ONL.......... Office of Naval Liaison [*NASA*] (KSC)
ONL.......... Ohio Northern University, Law Library, Ada, OH [*OCLC symbol*] (OCLC)
ONL.......... O'Neill, NE [*Location identifier*] [*FAA*] (FAAL)
ONL.......... On-Line (SAUS)
ONL.......... Outer Nuclear Layer [*Anatomy*]
ONL.......... Overnight Loan (ADA)
ONLAC ...... Lennox and Addington Counties Public Library, Napanee, Ontario [*Library symbol*] [*National Library of Canada*] (NLC)
ONLAH ...... Lennox and Addington Historical Society, Napanee, Ontario [*Library symbol*] [*National Library of Canada*] (BIB)
ONLAM...... Lennox and Addington Museum, Napanee, Ontario [*Library symbol*] [*National Library of Canada*] (NLC)
ONLAS ...... Optical Night Landing Approach System [*Aviation*] (PDAA)
ONLEXCRT... Online Exercise Critique System (SAUS)
ONLF .... Ogaden National Liberation Front [*Ethiopia*]
ONLICATS... Online Shared Cataloging System [*Computer science*]
ONLIN .... On-Line [*Communications term*] (DCT)
Online Bus Inf... Online Business Information (SAUS)
Online Libr Microcomput... Online Libraries and Microcomputers (SAUS)
ONLI-PAC... Ohio National Life Insurance Company PAC [*Cincinnati, OH*] (PACS)
ONLP .... On-Line Program Development [*Computer science*] (MHDB)
ONlP......... Perry County District Library, New Lexington, OH [*Library symbol*] [*Library of Congress*] (LCLS)
ONLS .... Sunnidale Township Public Library, New Lowell, Ontario [*Library symbol*] [*National Library of Canada*] (BIB)
ONLU .... United Arab Shipping [*Intermodal shipping container symbol*] (TVRC)
ONLY .... Online Yield [*Computer science*]
ONM......... Condamine [*Queensland*] [*Airport symbol*] (AD)
ONM......... National Organization of Veterans (Algeria) [*Political party*] (PSAP)
ONM......... Ocmulgee National Monument (SAUS)
ONM......... Office of Naval Material [*Later, NMCOM*]
ONM......... OncorMed, Inc. [*AMEX symbol*] (SAG)
ONM......... Open Network Management (SAUS)
ONM......... Organization Name (SAUS)
ONM......... Outer Nuclear Membrane [*Cell biology*] (QSUL)
ONM......... Socorro, NM [*Location identifier*] [*FAA*] (FAAL)
ONMB .... Merivale Road Branch, Nepean Public Library, Ontario [*Library symbol*] [*National Library of Canada*] (BIB)
ONMINST... Office of Naval Material Publication Type Instruction
ONMM....... On-Board Microwave MODEM [*Telecommunications*] (LAIN)
ONMO .... O'Neil Moving Systems [*Common carrier symbol*]
ONMP .... Office of Nuclear Materials Processing (SAUS)
ONMPC...... Office of Naval Material - Permanent Cadre
ONMS .... Open Network Management System (SAUS)
ONMS .... Orbiter Neutral Mass Spectrometer [*NASA*]
ONMSS...... Office of Nuclear Materials Safety and Safeguards [*Nuclear Regulatory Commission*]
ONN .... Enkabe Contact (journ.) (SAUS)
ONN .... Fort Meade, MD [*Location identifier*] [*FAA*] (FAAL)
ONN .... National Standardisation Office (SAUS)
ONN .... Onobasulu [*Language symbol*] (ETLW)
ONN .... O'Nyong-Nyong Virus
ONN .... Open Network Node (SAUS)
ONNA........ Oh No, Not Again! [*Computer hacker terminology*]
ONNI......... Office of National Narcotics Intelligence [*Later, Drug Enforcement Administration*] [*Department of Justice*]
ONNM .... On or Nearest New Moon [*Freemasonry*] (ROG)
ONNN........ ON Semiconductor [*Company symbol*]
ONNN........ SCG Holdings [*NASDAQ symbol*] (SG)
ONO .... Norwood Public Library, Ontario [*Library symbol*] [*National Library of Canada*] (BIB)
ONO .... Office of Naval Operations
ONO .... Ontario [*Oregon*] [*Airport symbol*] (AD)
ONO .... Ontario, OR [*Location identifier*] [*FAA*] (FAAL)
ONO .... Organization of News Ombudsmen (EA)
ONO .... Or Nearest [*or Near*] Offer [*Business term*] (ADA)
ONO .... Oxide-Nitride-Oxide (SAUS)
ONOC........ Oceania National Olympic Committee [*Australia*]
ONocHE ..... Hoover Co., Engineering Division, North Canton, OH [*Library symbol*] [*Library of Congress*] (LCLS)
ON-OFF ..... Oscillatory, Nonoscillatory Flip-Flop [*Computer science*]
ONOI......... Ono [*NCIC trailer make code*]
ONOL........ Niagara-On-The-Lake Public Library, Ontario [*Library symbol*] [*National Library of Canada*] (BIB)
Onom........ Onomasticon [*of Eusebius*] (BJA)
onomast .... onomastics (SAUS)
onomast .... onomatologist (SAUS)
onomat...... onomatology (SAUS)
onomat...... onomatopeic (ODA)
onomat...... Onomatopoeia (ODA)
ONOMAT.... Onomatopoeia (ROG)
onomat...... onomatopoeical (SAUS)
ONOO........ Outline NATO Operational Objective (MCD)
ONOP........ Office of Naval Officer Procurement
ONOP........ Officer-in-Charge, Branch Office of Naval Officer Procurement (DNAB)
O Norw...... Old Norwegian (SAUS)
ONowdM.... Athenaeum of Ohio, Norwood, OH [*Library symbol*] [*Library of Congress*] (LCLS)
ONOZ........ Oil Nozzle
ONP......... Newport [*Oregon*] [*Airport symbol*] [*Obsolete*] (OAG)
ONP......... Office of National Programs [*Employment and Training Administration*] [*Department of Labor*]
ONP......... Ohio Nisi Prius Reports [*A publication*] (DLA)
ONP......... Old Newspaper [*Recycling*]
ONP......... Olympic National Park (SAUS)
ONP......... Onex Packaging, Inc. [*Toronto Stock Exchange symbol*]
ONP......... Open Networking Platform (SAUS)
ONP......... Open Network Provision
ONP......... Operating Nursing Procedure
ONP......... Optical Nuclear Polarization (AAEL)
ONP......... Original Net Premium [*Insurance*] (AIA)
ONP......... Ortho-Nitrophenol [*Organic chemistry*]
ONPA........ Office of National Projects Administration [*Department of Labor*]
ONPG........ O-Nitrophenyl-a-D-Galactoside (SAUS)
ONPG........ O-Nitrophenyl-beta-D-galactopyranoside [*Test*] [*Microbiology*]
ONPG........ O-Nitrophenyl Galactoside (DOG)
ONPG........ Operational Nuclear Planning Group [*Military*]
ONPG........ Operations Nuclear Planning Group (SAUS)
ONPG........ Ortho-Nitrophenyl-a-D-Galactopyranoside (SAUS)
ONP-GAL.... Ortho-Nitrophenyl-B-Galactosidase [*Organic chemistry*] (MAE)
ONPI......... Office of News and Public Information (SAUS)
ONpK........ Kent State University, Tuscarawas County Regional Campus, New Philadelphia, OH [*Library symbol*] [*Library of Congress*] (LCLS)
ONPNS ...... Ohio Nisi Prius Reports, New Series [*1903-13*] [*A publication*] (DLA)
OnPointT.... On-Point Technology Systems, Inc. [*Associated Press*] (SAG)
ONPOSR .... Office of Naval Petroleum and Oil Shale Reserves
ONPPL ...... Optical Networking and Parallel Processing Laboratory [*University of Arizona*] (RCD)
ONPR........ Office of New Production Reactors [*U.S. Department of Energy*] (BARN)
ONPR........ One Price Clothing Stores, Inc. [*NASDAQ symbol*] (NASQ)
ONPR........ One Price Clothing Strs [*NASDAQ symbol*] (TTSB)
ONPT .... On-Point Technology Systems, Inc. [*NASDAQ symbol*] (NASQ)
ONQ .... Order of Nurses of Quebec (SAUS)
ONR .... Monkira [*Queensland*] [*Airport symbol*] (AD)
ONR .... Oboz Narodowo-Radykalny [*Radical Nationalist Camp*] [*Poland*] [*Political party*] (PPE)
ONR .... Octane Number Requirement [*Automotive engineering*]
ONR .... Office of Naval Research [*Arlington, VA*]
ONR .... Official Naval Reporter [*British*]
ONR .... Ontario Northland Railway
ONR .... Operational NonRADAR Directed Flights (NATG)
ONR .... Organization for National Reconstruction (Trinidad and Tobago) [*Political party*] (PSAP)
ONR .... Original Net Rate [*Insurance*] (AIA)
ONR .... Owner [*Telegraphy*] (PCTE)
ONR .... Phillips Petroleum Co., Exploration and Product Library, Bartlesville, OK [*OCLC symbol*] (OCLC)
ONRARO .... Office of Naval Research, Area Research Office (DNAB)
ONR/BO .... Office of Naval Research/Branch Office (SAUS)
ONR BR..... Branch Office, Office of Naval Research
ONRBRO .... Office of Naval Research Branch Research Office
ONRC........ Office of Naval Research, Chicago
ONRC ACTION FEDERAL PAC... Oregon Natural Resources Council Action Federal PAC [*Portland, OR*] (PACS)
ONRDB...... Ruth E. Dickinson Branch, Nepean Public Library, Ontario [*Library symbol*] [*National Library of Canada*] (BIB)
ONRDET..... Office of Naval Research Detachment (DNAB)
ONREAST... Office of Naval Research, East Coast Regional Office (DNAB)
ONRFE ...... Office of Naval Research, Far East Regional Office (DNAB)
ONRI......... Octane Number Requirement Increase [*Automotive engineering*]
ONRL........ Office of Naval Records and Library (SAUS)
ONRL........ Office of Naval Research, London
ONRO........ ODA Natural Resources Office
ONRR........ Office of Nuclear Regulatory Research (SAUS)
ONRRR...... Office of Naval Research Resident Representative
ONRS........ Oceanic Navigation Research Society (EA)
ONRS........ Office of National Range Support (SAA)
ONRT........ Office of Naval Research, Tokyo
ONRT........ Online Real Time [*Computer science*] (ADA)
ONRW........ Outstanding National Resource Waters (EEVL)
ONRWEST... Office of Naval Research, West Coast Regional Office (DNAB)
ONRY........ Ogdensburg Bridge & Port Authority [*AAR code*]
ONS.......... Northwestern School of Law, Lewis and Clark College, Portland, OR [*OCLC symbol*] (OCLC)
ONS.......... Oconee Nuclear Station (NRCH)
ONS.......... Office for National Statistics [*British*]
ONS.......... Office of National Statistics (SAUS)
ONS.......... Office of Nuclear Systems (SAA)
ONS.......... Off-Normal Switch
ONS.......... Oklahoma National Stockyards [*Federal Railroad Administration identification code*]
ONS.......... Omega Navigation System
ONS.......... Oncology Nursing Society (EA)
ONS.......... One Night Stand (SAUS)
ONS.......... Onslow [*Australia*] [*Airport symbol*] [*Obsolete*] (OAG)
ONS.......... Open Network Server [*Tylink Corp.*]
ONS.......... Operational Needs Statement [*Army*]
ONS.......... Oriental Numismatic Society [*Reading, Berkshire, England*] (EAIO)
ONS.......... Overseas News Service (SAUS)
ONSA........ Organization for Nucleotide Sequencing and Analysis
ONSAM...... Onsala Atmospheric Measurements (SAUS)
ONSD........ Optic Nerve Sheath Decompression (SAUS)

ONSDG...... Newington Branch, Stormont, Dundas, and Glengarry County Library, Ontario [*Library symbol*] [*National Library of Canada*] (BIB)
ONSE........ Onsite Energy Corp. [*OTCBB symbol*]
On Serv..... On Service [*A publication*]
ONSHR...... On Shore [*NWS*] (FAAC)
ONSI......... Orion Network Systems [*NASDAQ symbol*] (TTSB)
ONSI......... Orion Network Systems, Inc. [*NASDAQ symbol*] (SAG)
ONSIDIV... On-Sight Surveys Division
OnSiteS..... On-Site Sourcing, Inc. [*Associated Press*] (SAG)
ONSL........ ONSALE, Inc. [*NASDAQ symbol*] (NASQ)
Onsl NP..... Onslow's Nisi Prius [*A publication*] (DLA)
ONSOD...... Omega Navigation System Operations Detail
ONSPS...... Office of Nuclear Safety Policy and Standards (SAUS)
ONSR........ Ozark National Scenic Riverways (SAUS)
ONSR........ Sir Robert Borden High School, Nepean, Ontario [*Library symbol*] [*National Library of Canada*] (BIB)
ONSS........ On-Site Sourcing, Inc. [*NASDAQ symbol*] (SAG)
ONST........ Office of National Security Technology (SAUS)
ONST........ On Stage Entertainment [*NASDAQ symbol*] (SG)
ONST........ Outline NATO Staff Target
On Sta....... On Station (SAUS)
ONSX........ Oglebay Norton Industrial Sands [*Private rail car owner code*]
ONT.......... Air Ontario Ltd. [*Canada*] [*ICAO designator*] (FAAC)
ONT.......... Office Nationale du Tourisme [*Algeria*] (EY)
ONT.......... Office of Naval Technology (MCD)
ONT.......... Ombudsman of the Northern Territory [*Australia*]
ONT.......... On2 Technologies [*AMEX symbol*]
ONT.......... O-Nitrotoluene (SAUS)
Ont........... Ontario [*Canada*] (DD)
ONT.......... Ontario [*Canadian province*]
ONT.......... Ontario [*California*] [*Airport symbol*]
ONT.......... Ontario City Library, Ontario, CA [*OCLC symbol*] (OCLC)
ONT.......... Ontario Northland Railway [*AAR code*]
ONT.......... Ontario, OR [*Amtrak Busline code*]
Ont........... Ontological (SAUS)
Ont........... Ontologist (SAUS)
Ont........... Ontology (SAUS)
ONT.......... Ordinary Neap Tide (WDAA)
ONT.......... Orthogonal Noise Tuning (SAUS)
ONT.......... Our New Thread [*Clark thread designation*]
Ont 2d....... Ontario Reports, Second Series [*Canada*] [*A publication*] (DLA)
Ont A........ Ontario Appeals [*A publication*] (DLA)
ONTAP....... Online Training and Practice (NITA)
ONTAP....... On-Line Training and Practice File [*Lockheed*] [*Computer science*]
Ont App..... Ontario Appeal Reports [*A publication*] (DLA)
ONTAQ...... Oneita Industries [*OTCBB symbol*]
Ontario Cons Reg... Ontario Consolidated Regulations [*Canada*] [*A publication*] (DLA)
Ontario Technol... Ontario Technologist (SAUS)
ONTC........ O'Neill Transfer Company [*Common carrier symbol*]
ONTC........ Ontario Northland Transportation Commission (SAUS)
ONTC........ ON Technology Corp. [*NASDAQ symbol*] (SAG)
ON Tch...... ON Technology Corp. [*Associated Press*] (SAG)
Ont Dig...... Digest of Ontario Case Law [*A publication*] (DLA)
Ont Dig...... Digest of Ontario Case Law (journ.) (SAUS)
Ont Div Mines Missc Pap... Ontario. Division of Mines. Miscellaneous Paper (SAUS)
Ont El Cas... Ontario Election Cases [*1884-1900*] [*Canada*] [*A publication*] (DLA)
Ont Elec..... Ontario Election Cases [*1884-1900*] [*Canada*] [*A publication*] (DLA)
Ont Elec C... Ontario Election Cases [*1884-1900*] [*Canada*] [*A publication*] (DLA)
Ont Elect... Ontario Election Cases [*1884-1900*] [*Canada*] [*A publication*] (DLA)
ONTERIS... Ontario Educational Research Information System (SAUS)
ONTERIS... Ontario Education Resources Information System [*Ontario Ministry of Education*] [*Toronto*] [*Information service or system*] (IID)
ONTG........ Oral Nitroglycerine [*Medicine*]
ONTK........ OnTrak Systems [*NASDAQ symbol*] (TTSB)
ONTK........ On Trak Systems, Inc. [*NASDAQ symbol*] (SAG)
Ont L........ Ontario Law Reports [*A publication*] (DLA)
Ont LJ....... Ontario Law Journal [*A publication*] (DLA)
Ont LJ (NS)... Ontario Law Journal, New Series [*A publication*] (DLA)
Ont LR...... Ontario Reports [*A publication*] (DLA)
Ont L Rep... Ontario Law Reports [*A publication*] (DLA)
ONTN........ One Transportation Service [*Common carrier symbol*]
ONTOLT..... Onion, Tomato, or Lettuce [*Notation on restaurant checks*]
Ont Pen..... Ontario Penitentiary (SAUS)
Ont Pr....... Ontario Practice [*A publication*] (DLA)
Ont PR...... Ontario Practice Reports [*A publication*] (DLA)
Ont Pr Rep... Ontario Practice Reports [*A publication*] (DLA)
Ont R........ Ontario Reports [*A publication*] (DLA)
ONTR........ Ontario (trucks) [*NCIC truck make code*]
ONTR........ Orders Not to Resuscitate [*Medicine*]
OnTrak....... OnTrak Systems, Inc. [*Associated Press*] (SAG)
Ont R & WN... Ontario Reports and Ontario Weekly Notes [*Canada*] [*A publication*] (DLA)
OntrDta...... Ontrack Data International, Inc. [*Associated Press*] (SAG)
Ont Reg..... Ontario Regulations [*Canada*] [*A publication*] (DLA)
Ont Regs.... Ontario Regulations [*Canada*] [*A publication*] (DLA)
Ont Rev Regs... Ontario Revised Regulations [*Canada*] [*A publication*] (DLA)
Ont Rev Stat... Ontario Revised Statutes [*Canada*] [*A publication*] (DLA)
Ont Rgt...... Ontario Regiment [*Canada*] (DMA)
Ont Sci Cen... Ontario Science Center (SAUS)
Ont Stat..... Ontario Statutes [*Canada*] [*A publication*] (DLA)
Ont Tax Rep (CCH)... Ontario Tax Reporter (Commerce Clearing House) [*A publication*] (DLA)
ONTV........ On Time Messenger Service [*Common carrier symbol*]
ONTV........ ONTV, Inc. [*NASDAQ symbol*] (QUAN)
Ont Week N... Ontario Weekly Notes [*A publication*] (DLA)
Ont Week R... Ontario Weekly Reporter [*A publication*] (DLA)
Ont Wkly N... Ontario Weekly Notes [*A publication*] (DLA)
Ont Wkly Rep... Ontario Weekly Reporter [*A publication*] (DLA)
Ont WN..... Ontario Weekly Notes [*A publication*] (DLA)
Ont WR..... Ontario Weekly Reporter [*A publication*] (DLA)
Ont WR Op... Ontario Weekly Reporter. Opinions of United States Attorneys General [*A publication*] (DLA)
ONU......... Kongoussi [*Upper Volta*] [*Airport symbol*] (AD)
ONU......... Ohio Northern University [*Ada, OH*]
ONU......... Ohio Northern University, Ada, OH [*OCLC symbol*] (OCLC)
ONU......... Ono-I-Lau [*Fiji*] [*Airport symbol*] [*Obsolete*] (OAG)
ONU......... Optical Network Unit [*Telecommunications*]
ONU......... Organisation des Nations Unies [*United Nations*] [*French*]
ONU......... Organizacion de las Naciones Unidas [*United Nations*] [*Spanish*] (DUND)
ONU......... Organizzazione Nazioni Unite [*United Nations*] [*Italian*]
ONUC........ Organisation des Nations Unies au Congo [*United Nations Organization in the Congo*]
ONUDI....... Organisation des Nations Unies pour le Developpement Industriel [*United Nations Industrial Development Organization*]
ONUDI....... Organizacion de las Naciones Unidas para el Desarrollo Industrial [*United Nations Industrial Development Organization*] [*Spanish*] (DUND)
ONU Intra LR... Ohio Northern University. Intramural Law Review [*A publication*] (DLA)
ONULP...... Ontario New Universities Library Project
Onuphr De Interp Voc Eccles... Onuphrius. De Interpretatione Vocum Ecclesiae [*A publication*] (DLA)
ONUSAL..... United Nations Observer Mission in El Salvador [*Political party*] (PSAP)
ONV.......... Organisations Nationales Volontaires [*Canada*]
ON-VA....... Operator Network Validation Area (SAUS)
ONVI......... Onvia.com, Inc. [*NASDAQ symbol*] (SG)
ONVL........ Over-the-Nose Vision Line (PDAA)
ONW......... Office of Naval Weapons
ONW......... Onwards (RIMS)
ONW......... On Watch
ONW......... Oregon & Northwestern Railroad Co. [*AAR code*]
ONWARD.... Organization of Northwest Authorities for Rationalized Design (SAUS)
ONWB....... Oregon Nuclear Waste Board (SAUS)
ONWI........ Office of Nuclear Waste Isolation (MCD)
ONWL........ Whitefish Lake Band Public Library, Naughton, Ontario [*Library symbol*] [*National Library of Canada*] (NLC)
ONWM...... Office of Nuclear Waste Management (SAUS)
ONWR....... Okefinokee National Wildlife Refuge (SAUS)
ONWR....... Ottawa National Wildlife Refuge (SAUS)
ONWR....... Ouray National Wildlife Refuge (SAUS)
ONWS....... Office of Naval Weather Service
ONX.......... Colon [*Panama*] [*Airport symbol*] (OAG)
ONX.......... Mount Olive, NC [*Location identifier*] [*FAA*] (FAAL)
ONX.......... ONIX Systems, Inc. [*AMEX symbol*] (NASQ)
onx........... Onyx (VRA)
ONX.......... Onyx Petroleum Exploration Co. Ltd. [*Toronto Stock Exchange symbol*]
ONXS........ ONYX Software Corp. [*NASDAQ symbol*] (NASQ)
ONXX........ ONYX Pharmaceuticals [*NASDAQ symbol*] (TTSB)
ONXX........ Onyx Pharmaceuticals, Inc. [*NASDAQ symbol*] (SAG)
ONY.......... Olney, TX [*Location identifier*] [*FAA*] (FAAL)
ony........... onymous (SAUS)
ONYX........ Onyx Acceptance [*NASDAQ symbol*] (TTSB)
ONYX........ Onyx Acceptance Corp. [*NASDAQ symbol*] (SAG)
OnyxAcc..... Onyx Acceptance Corp. [*Associated Press*] (SAG)
OnyxPh...... Onyx Pharmaceuticals, Inc. [*Associated Press*] (SAG)
OO........... Belgium [*International civil aircraft marking*] (ODBW)
OO........... Naval Oceanographic Office [*Also known as NOO; formerly, HO, NHO, USNHO*]
OO........... Oakly, Inc. [*NYSE symbol*] (SAG)
OO........... Oberlin College, Oberlin, OH [*Library symbol*] [*Library of Congress*] (LCLS)
OO........... Object-Oriented (BYTE)
OO........... Observation Officer [*Military*]
OO........... Oceanic Operators (SAUS)
OO........... Oceanographic Office
OO........... Ocean Outlook (EA)
O/O.......... Office of Oceanography (SAUS)
OO........... Office of Operations [*Department of Agriculture*] (GFGA)
O/O.......... Office of Origin (AFM)
OO........... Office of Outreach
O/O.......... Off Ocean (SAA)
OO........... Ohio Opinions [*A publication*] (DLA)
OO........... Ohne Ort [*Without Place of Publication*] [*Bibliography*] [*German*]
O/O.......... Oil/Ore [*Ship*] (DS)
OO........... Old Orkney [*Whisky*] (ROG)
OO........... Once Over [*To examine cursorily*] [*Slang*]
o-o........... Once-Over [*Theater*] [*Slang*] (WDMC)
O/O.......... Only to Order (DGA)
O/O.......... On Orbit (MCD)
OO........... On Order
OO........... Oophorectomized [*Gynecology*]
OO........... Open Order

OO .... Operation Office (SAUS)
OO .... Operation Order [*Military*]
OO .... Operations Office [*Environmental Protection Agency*] (GFGA)
OO .... Operations Officer [*Navy*] [*British*]
OO .... Optical Orientation (SAUS)
OO .... Oral Order (SAUS)
OO .... Orbiting Observatory (SAUS)
OO .... Orderly Officer [*British*]
O/O .... Order Of [*Business term*]
O/o .... Order of (EBF)
o/o .... Order of (EBF)
OO .... Ordnance Office [*or Officer*]
O/O .... Ore/Oil (SAUS)
OO .... Orthopaedics Overseas (EA)
OO .... Osobyi Otdel [*Counterintelligence surveillance unit in military formation until 1943*] [*Former USSR*]
O/O .... Owner/Operator
O/O .... Owner or Operator (COE)
OO .... Owner's Option (RIMS)
OO .... Own Occupation [*Banking*]
OO .... Skywest Airlines (SAUS)
OO .... Sunaire Lines [*ICAO designator*] (AD)
OO 2d .... Ohio Opinions, Second Series [*A publication*] (DLA)
OO4GL ...... Object-Oriented Fourth-Generation Language [*Computer science*] (GART)
OOA.......... Object of Affections [*Slang*]
OOA.......... Object-Oriented Analysis [*Computer science*]
OOA.......... Office of Ocean Affairs [*Navy*]
OOA.......... Office of the Americas [*An association*] (EA)
OOA.......... Olive Oil Association (EA)
OOA.......... On or About (WDAA)
OOA.......... Open Ocean Area (SAA)
OOA.......... Optimum Orbital Altitude (AAG)
OOA.......... Optimum Orbital Attitude (SAUS)
OOA.......... Oskaloosa, IA [*Location identifier*] [*FAA*] (FAAL)
OOA.......... Outer Otic Anlage (DMAA)
OOA.......... Out of Action (MCD)
OOA.......... Out of Area (NVT)
OOA.......... Owner Operators of America [*Boston, NY*] (EA)
OOA.......... Public Archives [*Archives Publiques*] Ottawa, Ontario [*Library symbol*] [*National Library of Canada*] (NLC)
OOAA .... Olive Oil Association of America [*Later, OOA*] (EA)
OOAC .... Algonquin College of Applied Arts and Technology, Ottawa, Ontario [*Library symbol*] [*National Library of Canada*] (NLC)
OOACC ...... Colonel By Campus, Algonquin College of Applied Arts and Technology, Ottawa, On tario [*Library symbol*] [*National Library of Canada*] (NLC)
OOACF ...... Alta Vista Branch, Ontario Cancer Foundation, Ottawa, Ontario [*Library symbol*] [*National Library of Canada*] (NLC)
OOACH ...... Heron Park Campus, Algonquin College of Applied Arts and Technology, Ottawa, Ontario [*Library symbol*] [*National Library of Canada*] (BIB)
OOACL ...... Library Technician Program, Algonquin College of Applied Arts & Technology, Ottawa, Ontario [*Library symbol*] [*National Library of Canada*] (NLC)
OOACR ...... Rideau Campus, Algonquin College of Applied Arts and Technology, Ottawa, On tario, [*Library symbol*] [*National Library of Canada*] (NLC)
OOAD........ Object-Oriented Analysis & Design [*Computer science*] (CDE)
OOAD........ Object Oriented Application Design (SAUS)
OOAD........ Object Oriented Application Development (SAUS)
OOADE ...... Archives Deschatelets (Oblats de Marie-Immaculee), Ottawa, Ontario [*Library symbol*] [*National Library of Canada*] (NLC)
OOAEA ...... Ethnic Archives of Canada, Public Archives [*Archives Ethniques du Canada, Archives Publiques*] Ottawa, Ontario [*Library symbol*] [*National Library of Canada*] (NLC)
OOAECB..... Atomic Energy Control Board [*Commission de Controle de l'Energie Atomique*]Ottawa, Ontario [*Library symbol*] [*National Library of Canada*] (NLC)
OOAER ...... Research Co., Atomic Energy of Canada Ltd. [*Societe de Recherches, L'Energie Atomique du Canada Ltee*] Ottawa, Ontario [*Library symbol*] [*National Library of Canada*] (NLC)
OOAF .... Bibliotheque de l'Ambassade de France, Ottawa, Ontario [*Library symbol*] [*National Library of Canada*] (BIB)
OOAFN ...... Assembly of First Nations, Ottawa, Ontario [*Library symbol*] [*National Library of Canada*] (NLC)
OOAG........ Libraries Division, Agriculture Canada [*Division des Bibliotheques, Agriculture Canada*] Ottawa, Ontario [*Library symbol*] [*National Library of Canada*] (NLC)
OOAGA ...... Animal Diseases Research Institute, Agriculture Canada [*Institut de Recherches Veterinaires, Agriculture Canada*] Ottawa, Ontario [*Library symbol*] [*National Library of Canada*] (NLC)
OOAGAR .... Animal Research Institute, Agriculture Canada [*Institut de Recherches Zootechniques, Agriculture Canada*] Ottawa, Ontario [*Library symbol*] [*National Library of Canada*] (NLC)
OOAGB ...... Plant Research Library, Biosystematics Research Institute, Agriculture Canada [*Bibliotheque de Recherches sur les Vegetaux, Institut de Recherches Biosystematiques, Agriculture Canada*] Ottawa, Ontario [*Library symbol*] [*National Library of Canada*] (NLC)
OOAGCH .... Neatby Library, Agriculture Canada [*Bibliotheque Neatby, Agriculture Canada*] Ottawa, Ontario [*Library symbol*] [*National Library of Canada*] (NLC)
OOAGE ...... Entomology Research Library, Biosystematics Research Institute, Agriculture Canada [*Bibliotheque de Recherches Entomologiques, Institut de Recherches Biosytematiques, Agriculture Canada*] Ottawa, Ontario [*Library symbol*] [*National Library of Canada*] (NLC)
OOAGER .... Engineering and Statistical Research Centre, Agriculture Canada [*Centre de Recherche Technique et de Statistique, Agriculture Canada*] Ottawa, Ontario [*Library symbol*] [*National Library of Canada*] (NLC)
OOAGFP..... Laboratory Services Section, Food Production and Marketing Branch, Agriculture Canada [*Section des Services d'Analyse, Direction de la Production et de la Commercialisation des Aliments, Agriculture Canada*] Ottawa, Ontario [*Library symbol*] [*National Library of Canada*] (NLC)
OOAGFR .... Food Research Centre, Agriculture Canada [*Centre de Recherches sur les Aliments,Agriculture Canada*], Ottawa, Ontario [*Library symbol*] [*National Library of Canada*] (BIB)
OOAGO ...... Research Station, Agriculture Canada [*Station de Recherches, Agriculture Canada*] Ottawa, Ontario [*Library symbol*] [*National Library of Canada*] (NLC)
OOAGSR .... Soil Research Institute, Agriculture Canada [*Institut de Recherches sur les Sols, Agriculture Canada*] Ottawa, Ontario [*Library symbol*] [*National Library of Canada*] (NLC)
OOAI .... AMCA International Ltd., Ottawa, Ontario [*Library symbol*] [*National Library of Canada*] (NLC)
OOAK .... Oakville Public Library, Ontario [*Library symbol*] [*National Library of Canada*] (NLC)
OOAKA ...... Appleby College, Oakville, Ontario [*Library symbol*] [*National Library of Canada*] (NLC)
OOAKG ...... G. D. Searle Co. of Canada Ltd., Oakville, Ontario [*Library symbol*] [*National Library of Canada*] (BIB)
OOAKM ...... Oakville Museums, Ontario [*Library symbol*] [*National Library of Canada*] (BIB)
OOAKS ...... Shell Research Centre, Oakville, Ontario [*Library symbol*] [*National Library of Canada*] (NLC)
OOAKSC..... Sheridan College, Oakville, Ontario [*Library symbol*] [*National Library of Canada*] (NLC)
OOAKSCL... Library Techniques, Sheridan College, Oakville, Ontario [*Library symbol*] [*National Library of Canada*] (NLC)
OOAMA...... National Map Collection, Public Archives [*Collection Nationale des Cartes et Plans, Archives Publiques*] Ottawa, Ontario [*Library symbol*] [*National Library of Canada*] (NLC)
OOAMA...... Office, Ogden Air Material Area [*AFLC*]
OOAM & S.. On-Orbit Assembly, Maintenance, and Service [*NASA*] (SSD)
OOAMS...... Manuscript Division, Public Archives [*Division des Manuscrits, Archives Publiques*] Ottawa, Ontario [*Library symbol*] [*National Library of Canada*] (NLC)
OOANF ...... National Film Archives, Public Archives [*Archives Nationales du Film, Archives Publiques*] Ottawa, Ontario [*Library symbol*] [*National Library of Canada*] (NLC)
OOAOA ...... Archives, Diocese of Ottawa, Anglican Church of Canada, Ontario [*Library symbol*] [*National Library of Canada*] (NLC)
OOA/OOD ... Object-Oriented Analysis/Object-Oriented Design [*Computer science*] (HODG)
OOAR........ Canadian Broadcasting Corp. [*Societe Radio-Canada*] Ottawa, Ontario [*Library symbol*] [*National Library of Canada*] (NLC)
OOASH ...... Ashbury College, Ottawa, Ontario [*Library symbol*] [*National Library of Canada*] (NLC)
OOB.......... Bank of Canada [*Banque du Canada*] Ottawa, Ontario [*Library symbol*] [*National Library of Canada*] (NLC)
OOB.......... Offensive Operations Branch (SAUS)
OOB.......... Off-Off Broadway [*Theater*]
OOB.......... Off Our Backs [*A publication*] (BRI)
OOB.......... Old Orchard Beach (SAUS)
OOB.......... Opening of Business (MCD)
OOB.......... Operations Operating Budget [*Military*] (AFIT)
OOB.......... Order of Battle [*Military*] (NVT)
OOB.......... Ordnance Office Bulletin [*Military*]
OOB.......... Out of Balance (SAUS)
OOB.......... Out of Band [*Telecommunications*] (TEL)
OOB.......... Out-of-Band Signal (DCOM)
oob .... Out of Bed [*Therapy term*] (CTAA)
OOB.......... Out of Bed [*Medicine*]
OOB.......... Out of Body [*Parapsychology*]
OOB.......... Out of Bounds (IIA)
OOB.......... Outs on Base (SAUS)
OOBA........ Brewers Association of Canada, [*Association des Brasseurs du Canada*], Ott awa, Ontario [*Library symbol*] [*National Library of Canada*] (NLC)
OOBA........ Off Off Broadway Alliance [*Later, ART/NY*]
OOBBRP .... Out of Bed with Bathroom Privileges [*Medicine*] (DAVI)
OOBC........ Bowmar Canada Ltd., Ottawa, Ontario [*Library symbol*] [*National Library of Canada*] (NLC)
OOBE .... Ottawa Board of Education, Ontario [*Library symbol*] [*National Library of Canada*] (NLC)
OOBE .... Out-of-Body Experience [*Parapsychology*]
OOBE .... Out-Of-Box Experience [*Computer hacker's terminology*] (PCM)
OOBH........ Information Library, British High Commission, Ottawa, Ontario [*Library symbol*] [*National Library of Canada*] (BIB)
OOBLA ...... Onset of Blood Lactose Accumulation [*Metabolism*]
OOBM .... Bartonian Metaphysical Society, Ottawa, Ontario [*Library symbol*] [*National Library of Canada*] (NLC)
OOBMC...... Bureau of Management Consulting, Department of Supply and Services [*Bureau des Conseillers en Gestion, Ministere des Approvisionnements et Services*] Ottawa, Ontario [*Library symbol*] [*National Library of Canada*] (NLC)

OOBMI ...... Bell Canada Market Information Centre, Ottawa, Ontario [*Library symbol*] [*National Library of Canada*] (NLC)
OOBMM ..... Medical Library, Bristol-Myers Pharmaceutical Group, Ottawa, Ontario [*Library symbol*] [*National Library of Canada*] (NLC)
OOBP .... Opponents on-base Percentage (SAUS)
OOBR .... Buraimi [*Oman*] [*ICAO location identifier*] (ICLI)
OOC .... Junior Optimist Octagon International [*Formerly, Optimist Octagon Clubs*] (EA)
OOC .... Oberlin College, Conservatory of Music, Oberlin, OH [*Library symbol*] [*Library of Congress*] (LCLS)
OOC .... OEC Compression [*AMEX symbol*] (SG)
OOC .... Office of Censorship [*Terminated, 1945*] [*Military*]
OOC .... Office of Corrections [*Victoria, Australia*]
OOC .... Office of Olympic Coordination [*New South Wales, Australia*]
OOC .... Off-On Control
OOC .... On-Off Control (SAUS)
OOC .... Operating Vehicle without Owner's Consent [*Traffic offense charge*]
OOC .... Operating without Owners Consent (SAUS)
OOC .... Operational Oceanography Center (USDC)
OOC .... Operation Oceanography Center [*Marine science*] (OSRA)
OOC .... Ore/Oil Carrier (SAUS)
OOC .... Organized Occupational Curricula
OOC .... Ottawa Public Library [*Bibliotheque Publique d'Ottawa*] Ontario [*Library symbol*] [*National Library of Canada*] (NLC)
OOC .... Out of Character [*Internet lingo*] (NETL)
OOC .... Out of Characters (SAUS)
OOC .... Out of Commission (NVT)
OOC .... Out of Control
OOC .... Over-Ocean Communications
OOC .... Overseas Operating Committee [*World War II*]
OOCAA ...... Canadian Astronautics, Ottawa, Ontario [*Library symbol*] [*National Library of Canada*] (NLC)
OOCAAS ..... Canadian Automobile Association, Ottawa, Ontario [*Library symbol*] [*National Library of Canada*] (BIB)
OOCAB ...... Canadian Association of Broadcasters [*Association Canadienne des Radiodiffuseurs*] Ottawa, Ontario [*Library symbol*] [*National Library of Canada*] (NLC)
OOCAC ...... Canada Council [*Conseil des Arts du Canada*] Ottawa, Ontario [*Library symbol*] [*National Library of Canada*] (NLC)
OOCACR .... Research and Evaluation Section, Canada Council [*Service de Recherche et d'Evaluation, Conseil des Arts du Canada*], Ottawa, Ontario [*Library symbol*] [*National Library of Canada*] (BIB)
OOCACSW ... Documentation Centre, Canadian Advisory Council on the Status of Women [*Centre de Documentation, Conseil Consultatif Canadien de la Situation de la Femme*]Ottawa, Ontario [*Library symbol*] [*National Library of Canada*] (NLC)
OOCAM ...... Canadian Association of Medical Radiation Technologists, Ottawa, Ontario [*Library symbol*] [*National Library of Canada*] (BIB)
OOCANM .... Canadian Museum Association [*Association des Musees Canadiens*], Ottawa, Ontario [*Library symbol*] [*National Library of Canada*] (NLC)
OOCAR ...... Canadian Arctic Resources Committee, Ottawa, Ontario [*Library symbol*] [*National Library of Canada*] (NLC)
OOCARE ..... Care Canada, Ottawa, Ontario [*Library symbol*] [*National Library of Canada*] (BIB)
O/O Carrier ... Ore/Oil Carrier (SAUS)
OOCAS ...... Children's Aid Society of Ottawa-Carleton, Ottawa, Ontario [*Library symbol*] [*National Library of Canada*] (NLC)
OOCB .... Colonel By Secondary School, Ottawa, Ontario [*Library symbol*] [*National Library of Canada*] (NLC)
OOCBC ...... Conference Board of Canada, Ottawa, Ontario [*Library symbol*] [*National Library of Canada*] (NLC)
OOCBE ...... Carleton Board of Education, Ottawa, Ontario [*Library symbol*] [*National Library of Canada*] (NLC)
OOCBH ...... Human Resources Department, Canadian Broadcasting Corp. [*Departement des Ressources Humaines, Societe Radio-Canada*], Ottawa, Ontario [*Library symbol*] [*National Library of Canada*] (BIB)
OOCC .... Carleton University, Ottawa, Ontario [*Library symbol*] [*National Library of Canada*] (NLC)
OOCCAH .... Department of Art History, Carleton University, Ottawa, Ontario [*Library symbol*] [*Obsolete*] [*National Library of Canada*] (NLC)
OOCCFA ..... Canadian Centre for Films on Art [*Centre Canadien du Film sur l'Art*] Ottawa, Ontario [*Library symbol*] [*National Library of Canada*] (NLC)
OOCCG ...... Geography Department, Carleton University, Ottawa, Ontario [*Library symbol*] [*Obsolete*] [*National Library of Canada*] (NLC)
OOCCJ .... Church Council on Justice and Correction [*Conseil des Eglises pour la Justiceet la Criminologie*], Ottawa, Ontario [*Library symbol*] [*National Library of Canada*] (BIB)
OOCCL ...... County of Carleton Law Library, Ottawa, Ontario [*Library symbol*] [*National Library of Canada*] (NLC)
OOCCR ...... Canada Centre for Remote Sensing, Energy, Mines and Resources Canada [*Centre Canadien de Teledetection, Energie, Mines et Ressources Canada*] Ottawa, Ontario [*Library symbol*] [*National Library of Canada*] (NLC)
OOCCU ...... Canadian Commission for UNESCO, Ottawa, Ontario [*Library symbol*] [*National Library of Canada*] (BIB)
OOCD .... Canadian International Development Agency [*Agence Canadienne de DeveloppementInternational*] Ottawa, Ontario [*Library symbol*] [*National Library of Canada*] (NLC)
OOCDA ...... Canadian Dental Association, Ottawa, Ontario [*Library symbol*] [*National Library of Canada*] (NLC)
OOCDC ...... Computing Devices of Canada, Ottawa, Ontario [*Library symbol*] [*National Library of Canada*] (NLC)
OOCDP ...... College Dominicain de Philosophie et de Theologie, Ottawa, Ontario [*Library symbol*] [*National Library of Canada*] (NLC)
OOCEEC ..... Delegation of the Commission of the European Communities [*Delegation de la C ommission des Communautes Europeennes*], Ottawa, Ontario [*Library symbol*] [*National Library of Canada*] (BIB)
OOCES ...... Combustion Engineering Superheater Ltd., Ottawa, Ontario [*Library symbol*] [*National Library of Canada*] (NLC)
OOCESC ..... Centre d'Animation Pedagogique, Conseil des Ecoles Separees Catholiques d'Ottawa, Ontario [*Library symbol*] [*National Library of Canada*] (BIB)
OOCF .... Canadian Film Institute [*Institut Canadien du Film*] Ottawa, Ontario [*Library symbol*] [*National Library of Canada*] (NLC)
OOCFB ...... Canadian Forces Base, Ottawa, Ontario [*Library symbol*] [*National Library of Canada*] (BIB)
OOCFS ...... Combustion Engineering Superheater Ltd., Ottawa, Ontario (SAUS)
OOCH .... Orient Overseas Container Holdings (SAUS)
OOCHA ...... Canadian Hospital Association [*Association des Hopitaux du Canada*] Ottawa,Ontario [*Library symbol*] [*National Library of Canada*] (NLC)
OOCHAC .... Catholic Health Association of Canada [*Association Catholique Canadienne de la Sante*], Ottawa, Ontario [*Library symbol*] [*National Library of Canada*] (NLC)
OOCHC ...... Canadian Horticultural Council [*Conseil Canadien de l'Horticulture*], Ottawa, Ontario [*Library symbol*] [*National Library of Canada*] (BIB)
OOCHEO .... Children's Hospital of Eastern Ontario [*Hopital pour Enfants de l'Est de l'Ontario*] Ottawa, Ontario [*Library symbol*] [*National Library of Canada*] (NLC)
OOCHI .... Chreod International, Ottawa, Ontario [*Library symbol*] [*National Library of Canada*] (NLC)
OOCHP ...... Common Heritage Programme, Ottawa, Ontario [*Library symbol*] [*National Library of Canada*] (BIB)
OOCHR ...... Canadian Human Rights Commission [*Commission Canadienne des Droits de la Personne*] Ottawa, Ontario [*Library symbol*] [*National Library of Canada*] (NLC)
OOCI .... Department of Consumer and Corporate Affairs [*Ministere de la Consommation etdes Corporations*] Ottawa, Ontario [*Library symbol*] [*National Library of Canada*] (NLC)
OOCIC .... Documentation Centre, Canadian Intergovernmental Conference Secretariat [*Centre de Documentation, Secretariat des Conferences Intergouvernementales Canadiennes*], Ottawa, Ontario [*Library symbol*] [*National Library of Canada*] (NLC)
OOCIFE ...... Field Exploration Library, Inco Ltd., Copper Cliff, Ontario [*Library symbol*] [*National Library of Canada*] (NLC)
OOCIHM ..... Canadian Institute for Historical Microreproductions [*Institut Canadien de Microreproductions Historiques*] Ottawa, Ontario [*Library symbol*] [*National Library of Canada*] (NLC)
OOCIIPS ..... Canadian Institute for International Peace and Security [*Institut Canadien pour la Paix et la Securite Mondiales*] Ottawa, Ontario [*Library symbol*] [*National Library of Canada*] (NLC)
OOCIRS ..... Canadian Institute for Radiation Safety, Ottawa, Ontario [*Library symbol*] [*National Library of Canada*] (NLC)
OOCITT ...... Canadian International Trade Tribunal [*Tribunal Canadien du Commerce Exterieur*], Ontario [*Library symbol*] [*National Library of Canada*] (BIB)
OOCL .... Capital Library Wholesale, Ottawa, Ontario [*Library symbol*] [*National Library of Canada*] (NLC)
OOCLA ...... Canadian Library Association, Ottawa, Ontario [*Library symbol*] [*National Library of Canada*] (BIB)
OOCLC ...... Canadian Labour Congress [*Congres du Travail du Canada*] Ottawa, Ontario [*Library symbol*] [*National Library of Canada*] (NLC)
OOCLCG ..... Coopers & Lybrand Consulting Group, Ottawa, Ontario [*Library symbol*] [*National Library of Canada*] (BIB)
OOCLM ...... Canadian Labour Market and Productivity Centre [*Centre Canadien du Marche du Travail et de la Productivite*], Ottawa, Ontario [*Library symbol*] [*National Library of Canada*] (NLC)
OOCM .... Canadian Housing Information Centre, Canada Mortgage and Housing Corp. [*Centre Canadien de Documentation sur l'Habitation, Societe Canadienne d'Hypotheques et de Logement*] Ottawa, Ontario [*Library symbol*] [*National Library of Canada*] (NLC)
OOCMA ...... Canadian Medical Association, Ottawa, Ontario [*Library symbol*] [*National Library of Canada*] (NLC)
OOCMC ...... Children's Environments Advisory Service, Canada Mortgage and Housing Corp. [*Service Consultatif sur l'Environnement de l'Enfant, Societe Canadienne d'Hypotheques et de Logement*] Ottawa, Ontario [*Library symbol*] [*National Library of Canada*] (NLC)
OOCMF ...... Office of the Commissioner for Federal Judicial Affairs [*Bureau du Commissaire a la Magistrature Federale*], Ottawa, Ontario [*Library symbol*] [*National Library of Canada*] (BIB)
OOCN .... Canadian Nurses' Association [*Association Canadienne des Infirmieres*] Ottawa, Ontario [*Library symbol*] [*National Library of Canada*] (NLC)
OOCNET ..... Office of Corrections Network
OOCNP ...... CNP Resource Centre, Energy, Mines, and Resources Canada [*Centre d'Information EESP, Energie, Mines, et Ressources Canada*] Ottawa, Ontario [*Library symbol*] [*National Library of Canada*] (NLC)
OOCO .... Department of Communications [*Ministere des Communications*] Ottawa, Ontario [*Library symbol*] [*National Library of Canada*] (NLC)
OOCOAC .... Consumer's Association of Canada, Ottawa, Ontario [*Library symbol*] [*National Library of Canada*] (BIB)
OOCOG ...... COGLA [*Canada Oil and Gas Lands Administration*] Ocean Mining Resource Centre , Ottawa, Ontario [*Centre de Ressources sur l'Extraction de Minerais Oceaniques, Administration du Petrole et du Gaz des Terres du Canada*] [*Library symbol*] [*National Library of Canada*] (NLC)

OOCOI .... Cognos, Inc., Ottawa, Ontario [*Library symbol*] [*National Library of Canada*] (BIB)
OOCOL ...... Commissioner of Official Languages [*Commissaire aux Langues Officielles*] Ottawa, Ontario [*Library symbol*] [*National Library of Canada*] (NLC)
OOCOT ...... Competition Tribunal [*Tribunal de la Concurrence*], Ottawa, Ontario [*Library symbol*] [*National Library of Canada*] (BIB)
OOCOW ..... Cowater International, Inc., Ottawa, Ontario [*Library symbol*] [*National Library of Canada*] (BIB)
OOCP .... Community Planning Association of Canada [*Association Canadienne d'Urbanisme*] Ottawa, Ontario [*Library symbol*] [*National Library of Canada*] (NLC)
OOCPA ...... Canadian Payments Association, Ottawa, Ontario [*Library symbol*] [*National Library of Canada*] (BIB)
OOCPB ...... Planning and Development Library, City of Ottawa, Ontario [*Library symbol*] [*National Library of Canada*] (BIB)
OOCPR ...... Canadian Public Relations Society [*Societe Canadienne des Relations Publiques*], Ottawa, Ontario [*Library symbol*] [*National Library of Canada*] (BIB)
OOCRC ...... Canadian Red Cross Society [*Societe Canadienne de la Croix-Rouge*] Ottawa, Ontario [*Library symbol*] [*National Library of Canada*] (NLC)
OOCRI .... Canadian Research Institute for the Avancement of Women [*Institut Canadien deRecherches sur les Femmes*] Ottawa, Ontario [*Library symbol*] [*National Library of Canada*] (NLC)
OOCRLF ..... Canadian Rights and Liberties Federation, Ottawa, Ontario [*Library symbol*] [*National Library of Canada*] (NLC)
OOCRM ..... Canadian Royal Mint [*Monnaie Royale Canadienne*] Ottawa, Ontario [*Library symbol*] [*National Library of Canada*] (NLC)
OOCS .... Public Service Commission [*Commission de la Fonction Publique*] Ottawa, Ontario [*Library symbol*] [*National Library of Canada*] (NLC)
OOCSC ...... Canada Safety Council [*Conseil Canadien de la Securite*] Ottawa, Ontario [*Library symbol*] [*National Library of Canada*] (NLC)
OOCT .... Canadian Teachers Federation, Ottawa, Ontario [*Library symbol*] [*National Library of Canada*] (NLC)
OOCTG ...... Object Orientated COBOL Task Group (SAUS)
OOCTI .... Canadian Textiles Institute [*Institut Canadien des Textiles*], Ottawa, Ontario [*Library symbol*] [*National Library of Canada*] (BIB)
OOCU .... Association of Universities and Colleges of Canada [*Association des Universites et Colleges du Canada*], Ottawa, Ontario [*Library symbol*] [*National Library of Canada*] (NLC)
OOCUI .... Canadian Unity Information Office [*Centre d'Information sur l'Unite Canadienne*] Ottawa, Ontario [*Library symbol*] [*National Library of Canada*] (NLC)
OOCUS ...... CUSO [*Canadian University Service Overseas*], Ottawa, Ontario [*Library symbol*] [*National Library of Canada*] (NLC)
OOCVB ...... Central Volunteer Bureau of Ottawa-Carleton [*Bureau Central des Benevoles d'Ottawa-Carleton*] Ottawa, Ontario [*Library symbol*] [*National Library of Canada*] (BIB)
OOCW .... Canadian Council on Social Development [*Conseil Canadien de Developpement Social*] Ottawa, Ontario [*Library symbol*] [*National Library of Canada*] (NLC)
OOCWC ..... Canadian Wood Council [*Conseil Canadien du Bois*] Ottawa, Ontario [*Library symbol*] [*National Library of Canada*] (NLC)
OOCZ .... Orient Overseas Line [*Intermodal trailer symbol*]
OOCZ .... Ottawa Citizen, Ontario [*Library symbol*] [*National Library of Canada*] (NLC)
OOD .... Object-Oriented Design [*Computer science*]
OOD .... Object Oriented Development (SAUS)
OOD .... Office of Disability [*Australia*]
OOD .... Office Operations Department
OOD .... Officer of the Day [*or Deck*] [*Also, OD*] [*Navy*]
OOD .... Operations Orientation Director [*NASA*]
OOD .... Opposite Oriented Diffusion (SAUS)
OOD .... Orbiter on Dock [*NASA*] (KSC)
OOD .... Woodstown, NJ [*Location identifier*] [*FAA*] (FAAL)
OODA .... Observation, Orientation, Decision, Action
OODB .... Dominion Bridge Co. Ltd., Ottawa, Ontario [*Library symbol*] [*National Library of Canada*] (NLC)
OODB .... Object-Oriented Database [*Computer science*] (CDE)
OODBMS .... Object-Oriented Database Management System [*Objectivity, Inc.*] [*Computer science*]
OODBS ...... DOBIS (Dortmunder Bibliothekssystem), Ottawa, Ontario [*Library symbol*] [*National Library of Canada*] (NLC)
OODBS ...... Object-Oriented Database System (SAUS)
OODCH ...... DCH Consultants, Inc., Ottawa, Ontario [*Library symbol*] [*National Library of Canada*] (NLC)
OODE .... Office of Overseas Dependent Education [*Military*]
OODEP ...... Owner, Officer, Director, or Executive Personnel (MCD)
OODF .... Officer-of-the-Deck (Fleet Task Force Operations) [*Navy*] (DNAB)
OODI .... Officer-of-the-Deck (Independent) [*Navy*] (DNAB)
OODL .... Object-Oriented Dynamic Language [*Computer science*] (PCM)
OODLAC ..... Odessa Branch, Lennox and Addington County Library, Ontario [*Library symbol*] [*National Library of Canada*] (NLC)
OODLC ...... Library Education Services, Data Logic Canada, Ottawa, Ontario [*Library symbol*] [*National Library of Canada*] (NLC)
OODM .... Dali Management [*Gestion Dali*], Ottawa, Ontario [*Library symbol*] [*National Library of Canada*] (BIB)
OODMR ..... DMR Group, Inc., Ottawa, Ontario [*Library symbol*] [*National Library of Canada*] (BIB)
OODMS ..... Object Oriented Database Management System [*Computer science*] (VLIE)
OODP .... Department of Supply and Services [*Ministere des Approvisionnements et Services*] Ottawa, Ontario [*Library symbol*] [*National Library of Canada*] (NLC)
OODP .... Out-of-Detent Pitch [*Aviation*] (MCD)
OODPS ...... Superannuation Division, Compensation Services Branch, Department of Supply and Services [*Division des Pensions de Retraite, Direction des Services de Renumeration, Ministere des Approvisionnements et Services*] Ottawa, Ontario [*Library symbol*] [*National Library of Canada*] (NLC)
OODQ .... Oliver Organization Description Questionnaire [*Test*]
OODR .... Out-of-Detent Roll [*Aviation*] (MCD)
OODRC ...... Defence Research Establishment Ottawa, Department of National Defence [*Centrede Recherches pour la Defense Ottawa, Ministere de la Defense Nationale*] Ont ario [*Library symbol*] [*National Library of Canada*] (NLC)
OODR-MPI ... Optical-Optical Double Resonance Multiphonton Ionization [*Spectrocopy*]
OODSIS ..... Directorate of Scientific Information Services, Department of National Defence [*Services d'Information Scientifique, Ministere de la Defense Nationale*] Ottawa, Ontario [*Library symbol*] [*National Library of Canada*] (NLC)
OODV .... Orbit-on-Demand Vehicle
OOD/W ...... Officer of the Day/Watch (SAUS)
OOE .... Department of External Affairs [*Ministere des Affaires Exerieures*] Ottawa,Ontario [*Library symbol*] [*National Library of Canada*] (NLC)
OOE .... Odd-Odd Effect (SAUS)
OOE .... Office of Employment [*Victoria, Australia*]
OOE .... Office of Energy [*New South Wales, Australia*]
OOE .... Office of Ocean Engineering [*National Oceanic and Atmospheric Administration*] (MSC)
OOE .... Opening of Oesophagus
OOE .... Out-of-Ecliptic Mission [*NASA*] (EGAO)
OOE .... Out-of-Order Execution (GART)
OOEA .... Embassy of Argentina, Ottawa, Ontario [*Library symbol*] [*National Library of Canada*] (BIB)
OOEAB ...... Archaeological Research, Environment Canada [*Recherches Archeologiques, Environnement Canada*] Ottawa, Ontario [*Library symbol*] [*National Library of Canada*] (NLC)
OOEAPT ..... River Road Environmental Technology Centre, Environment Canada [*Centre de Techologie Environnementale de River Road, Environnement Canada*] Ottawa, Ontario [*Library symbol*] [*National Library of Canada*] (NLC)
OOEB .... Elisabeth Bruyere Health Center [*Centre de Sante Elisabeth Bruyere*] Ottawa, Ontario [*Library symbol*] [*National Library of Canada*] (NLC)
OOEC .... Economic Council of Canada [*Conseil Economique du Canada*] Ottawa, Ontario [*Library symbol*] [*National Library of Canada*] (NLC)
OOEC .... Oxford Orthopaedic Engineering Centre [*British*] (IRUK)
OOECS ...... ECS [*Energy Conversion Systems*] Power Systems, Inc., Ottawa, Ontario [*Library symbol*] [*National Library of Canada*] (NLC)
OOECW ...... Canadian Wildlife Service, Environment Canada [*Service Canadien de la Faune, Environnement Canada*] Ottawa, Ontario [*Library symbol*] [*National Library of Canada*] (NLC)
OOECWN .... National Wildlife Research Centre, Canadian Wildlife Service, Environment Canada[*Centre National de Recherche sur la Faune, Service Canadien de la Faune, En vironnement Canada*] Ottawa, Ontario [*Library symbol*] [*National Library of Canada*] (NLC)
OOEDC ...... Export Development Corp. [*Societe pour l'Expansion des Exportations*] Ottawa, Ontario [*Library symbol*] [*National Library of Canada*] (NLC)
OOEE .... Engineering and Economic Research Technologies, Inc., Ottawa, Ontario [*Library symbol*] [*National Library of Canada*] (BIB)
OOEIB .... Interpretation Division, Environment Canada - Parks [*Direction de l'Interpretation, Environnement Canada - Parcs*], Ottawa, Ontario [*Library symbol*] [*National Library of Canada*] (NLC)
OOEK .... Embassy of Korea, Ottawa, Ontario [*Library symbol*] [*National Library of Canada*] (BIB)
OOELB .... Legal Branch, Department of External Affairs [*Direction des Operations Juridiques, Ministere des Affaires Exterieures*] Ottawa, Ontario [*Library symbol*] [*National Library of Canada*] (NLC)
OOELC .... Elections Canada, Ottawa, Ontario [*Library symbol*] [*National Library of Canada*] (BIB)
OOELS .... Legal Services, Environment Canada [*Services Juridiques, Environnement Canada*] Ottawa, Ontario [*Library symbol*] [*National Library of Canada*] (NLC)
OOEMB ...... Embassy of Brazil, Ottawa, Ontario [*Library symbol*] [*National Library of Canada*] (BIB)
OOEN .... Cameco Research Center, Ottawa, Ontario [*Library symbol*] [*National Library of Canada*] (NLC)
OOEO .... Eastern Ontario Regional Library, Ottawa, Ontario [*Library symbol*] [*National Library of Canada*] (NLC)
OOEO .... Ontario Library Service - Rideau, Ottawa, Ontario [*Library symbol*] [*National Library of Canada*] (NLC)
OOEOB ...... Conservation Division, Environment Canada [*Division de la Conservation, Environnement Canada*] Ottawa, Ontario [*Library symbol*] [*National Library of Canada*] (NLC)
OOEPC ...... Emergency Planning Canada [*Planification d'Urgence Canada*] Ottawa, Ontario [*Library symbol*] [*National Library of Canada*] (NLC)
OOEPSE ..... Socio-Economic Research Division, Parks Canada Program, Environment Canada [*Division de la Recherche Socio-Economique, Programme Parcs Canada, Environnement Canada*] Ottawa, Ontario [*Library symbol*] [*National Library of Canada*] (NLC)
OOESC ...... Ecole Secondaire Champlain, Ottawa, Ontario [*Library symbol*] [*National Library of Canada*] (NLC)
OOEU .... Euroline, Ottawa, Ontario [*Library symbol*] [*National Library of Canada*] (BIB)

OOEY........ Eyretechnics Ltd., Ottawa, Ontario [*Library symbol*] [*National Library of Canada*] (NLC)
OOF........ Department of Finance [*Ministere des Finances*] Ottawa, Ontario [*Library symbol*] [*National Library of Canada*] (NLC)
OOF........ Offense Only Fighter (MCD)
OoF........ Office of Facilitation (SAUS)
OOF........ Office of Fisheries [*National Oceanic and Atmospheric Administration*] (GFGA)
OOF........ Office of the Family [*Western Australia*]
OOF........ Office of the Future (IAA)
OOF........ Open Order File (TIMI)
OOF........ Orbiting Quarantine Facility [*A proposed Earth-orbiting laboratory*]
OOF........ Other Official Flows (ADWA)
OOF........ Out of Frame [*Telecommunications*] (ITD)
OOFA........ Documentation Centre, Family Action [*Centre de Documentation, Action Famille*], Ottawa, Ontario [*Library symbol*] [*National Library of Canada*] (NLC)
OOFA........ Oblinger/Oplinger Family Association (EA)
O of A........ Office of Administration (SAUS)
O of A........ Order of Amaranth (EA)
O of B........ Order of Battle (SAUS)
OOFC........ Federal Court of Canada [*Cour Federale du Canada*] Ottawa, Ontario [*Library symbol*] [*National Library of Canada*] (NLC)
O of C........ Order of the Chief (SAUS)
O of C........ Order of the Coif (SAUS)
OOFCC........ Farm Credit Corp., Ottawa, Ontario [*Library symbol*] [*Obsolete*] [*National Library of Canada*] (NLC)
OOFD........ Fahud [*Oman*] [*ICAO location identifier*] (ICLI)
OOFE........ Federal Environmental Assessment Review Office [*Bureau Federal d'Examen des Evaluations Environnementales*], Ottawa, Ontario [*Library symbol*] [*National Library of Canada*] (BIB)
OOFF........ Departmental Library, Environment Canada [*Bibliotheque du Ministere, Environnemet Canada*] Ottawa, Ontario [*Library symbol*] [*National Library of Canada*] (NLC)
O Offr........ Orderly Officer (SAUS)
OOFI........ Fisheries and Oceans Canada [*Peches et Oceans Canada*] Ottawa, Ontario [*Library symbol*] [*National Library of Canada*] (NLC)
OOFL........ Federal Liberal Agency of Canada, Ottawa, Ontario [*Library symbol*] [*National Library of Canada*] (NLC)
OOFM........ Mining Library, Falconbridge Ltd., Onaping, Ontario [*Library symbol*] [*National Library of Canada*] (NLC)
O of O........ Order of Owls (SAUS)
OOFP........ Forintek Canada Corp., Ottawa, Ontario [*Library symbol*] [*National Library of Canada*] (NLC)
OOFQ........ Firq [*Oman*] [*ICAO location identifier*] (ICLI)
O of R........ Office for Research (SAUS)
OOFS........ Sport Information Resource Centre [*Centre de Documentation de Reference pour le Sport*] Ottawa, Ontario [*Library symbol*] [*National Library of Canada*] (NLC)
O of SC........ Order of Scottish Clans (SAUS)
OOG........ Geological Survey of Canada [*Commission Geologique du Canada*] Ottawa, Ontario [*Library symbol*] [*National Library of Canada*] (NLC)
OOG........ Office of Gambling [*Victoria, Australia*]
OOG........ Office of Oil and Gas [*Functions transferred to Energy Research and Development Administration*] [*Department of the Interior*]
OOG........ Officer of the Guard [*Navy*] [*British*]
OOG........ Olive Oil Group [*Later, OOA*] (EA)
OOG........ Oscillating Output Geneva
OOG........ Out of Gauge [*Shipping*] (DCTA)
OOGB........ Ghaba Central [*Oman*] [*ICAO location identifier*] (ICLI)
OOGDC........ Gandalf Data Ltd., Ottawa, Ontario [*Library symbol*] [*National Library of Canada*] (NLC)
OOGE........ Canadian Government Expositions Centre, Department of Supply and Services [*Centre des Expositions du Gouvernement Canadien, Ministere des Approvisionnements et Services*] Ottawa, Ontario [*Library symbol*] [*National Library of Canada*] (NLC)
OOGG........ Documentation Centre, Goss, Gilroy & Associates, Ottawa, Ontario [*Library symbol*] [*National Library of Canada*] (BIB)
OOGGH........ Grace General Hospital, Ottawa, Ontario [*Library symbol*] [*National Library of Canada*] (NLC)
OOGH........ Reference Library, Government House [*Salle de Reference, Residence du Gouverneur-General*] Ottawa, Ontario [*Library symbol*] [*National Library of Canada*] (NLC)
OOGKS........ Gottlieb Kaylor & Stocks, Ottawa, Ontario [*Library symbol*] [*National Library of Canada*] (BIB)
OOGOH........ Gowling & Henderson, Ottawa, Ontario [*Library symbol*] [*National Library of Canada*] (NLC)
OOGUI........ Object-Oriented Graphical User Interface [*Computer science*]
OOH........ Heraldry Society of Canada [*Societe Heraldique du Canada*], Ottawa, Ontario [*Library symbol*] [*National Library of Canada*] (BIB)
OOH........ Occupational Outlook Handbook [*A publication*] (OICC)
OOH........ Other Overhead (TIMI)
OOH........ Out-of-Hospital (DMAA)
OOH........ Out of Hours (SPVS)
OOHA........ Haima [*Oman*] [*ICAO location identifier*] (ICLI)
OOHA........ Operation Oil Heat Associates (SAUS)
OOHC........ Heritage Canada Foundation [*Fondation Canadienne pour la Protection du Patrimoine*] Ottawa, Ontario [*Library symbol*] [*National Library of Canada*] (NLC)
OOHG........ Ottawa General Hospital [*Hopital General d'Ottawa*] Ontario [*Library symbol*] [*National Library of Canada*] (NLC)
OOHI........ Historical Society of Ottawa Library and the Bytown Historical Museum, Ontario [*Library symbol*] [*National Library of Canada*] (NLC)
OOH-OOH... On the One Hand, On the Other Hand
OOHUR........ Huronia Regional Centre, Orillia, Ontario [*Library symbol*] [*National Library of Canada*] (NLC)
OOI........ Informetrica Ltd., Ottawa, Ontario [*Library symbol*] [*National Library of Canada*] (NLC)
OOI........ Memphis, TN [*Location identifier*] [*FAA*] (FAAL)
OOI........ Object Oriented Implementation (SAUS)
OOI........ Out of Interest (ADWA)
OOI........ Oxygen/Ozone Indicator
OOIA........ Ibra [*Oman*] [*ICAO location identifier*] (ICLI)
OOIB........ Imperial Ballet of Canada, Ottawa, Ontario [*Library symbol*] [*National Library of Canada*] (NLC)
OOIC........ Information Centre, Investment Canada [*Centre d'Information, Investissement Canada*] Ottawa, Ontario [*Library symbol*] [*National Library of Canada*] (NLC)
OOICC........ Indian Claims Commission [*Commission d'Etude des Revendications des Indiens*] Ottawa, Ontario [*Library symbol*] [*National Library of Canada*] (NLC)
OOICCS........ International Council for Canadian Studies [*Conseil International d'Etudes Canadiennes*], Ottawa, Ontario [*Library symbol*] [*National Library of Canada*] (BIB)
OOICP........ Phototheque, National Film Board [*Phototheque, Office National du Film*] Ottawa, Ontario [*Library symbol*] [*National Library of Canada*] (NLC)
OOID........ International Development Research Centre [*Centre de Recherches pour le Developpement International*] Ottawa, Ontario [*Library symbol*] [*National Library of Canada*] (NLC)
OOIDA........ Owner-Operator Independent Drivers Association
OOIDA-PAC... Owner-Operator Independent Drivers Association Inc. PAC [*Washington, DC*] (PACS)
OOIHC........ India High Commission, Ottawa, Ontario [*Library symbol*] [*National Library of Canada*] (BIB)
OOII........ Ibri [*Oman*] [*ICAO location identifier*] (ICLI)
OOIJC........ International Joint Commission [*Commission Mixte Internationale*], Ottawa, Ontario [*Library symbol*] [*National Library of Canada*] (NLC)
OOIL........ Osage Energy, Inc. (SAUS)
OOIN........ Office of the Superintendent of Financial Institutions Canada [*Bureau du Surintendant des Institutions Financieres Canada*] Ottawa, Ontario [*Library symbol*] [*National Library of Canada*] (NLC)
OOIP........ Original Oil in Place [*Petroleum*]
OOIPC........ Offices of the Information and Privacy Commissioners of Canada [*Bureaux des Commissaires a l'Information et a la Protection de la Vie Privee du Canada*] Ottawa, Ontario [*Library symbol*] [*National Library of Canada*] (NLC)
OOIRB........ Immigration and Refugee Board [*Commission d'Immigration et du Status de Refugie*], Ottawa, Ontario [*Library symbol*] [*National Library of Canada*] (BIB)
OOIRP........ Institute for Research on Public Policy [*Institut de Recherches Politiques*], Ottawa, Ontario [*Library symbol*] [*National Library of Canada*] (NLC)
OOIRS........ Irving R. Silver Associates Library [*IRSA*], Ottawa, Ontario [*Library symbol*] [*National Library of Canada*] (NLC)
OOIT........ Inuit Tapirisat of Canada, Ottawa, Ontario [*Library symbol*] [*National Library of Canada*] (NLC)
OOIZ........ Izki [*Oman*] [*ICAO location identifier*] (ICLI)
OOJ........ Department of Justice [*Ministere de la Justice*] Ottawa, Ontario [*Library symbol*] [*National Library of Canada*] (NLC)
OOJ........ Obstruction of Justice
OOJN........ Jarf North [*Oman*] [*ICAO location identifier*] (ICLI)
OOK........ On-Off Keying [*Computer science*] (IEEE)
OOK........ Toksook [*Alaska*] [*Airport symbol*] (OAG)
OOKB........ Khasab [*Oman*] [*ICAO location identifier*] (ICLI)
OOkiep........ O'Okiep Copper Co. Ltd. [*Associated Press*] (SAG)
OOL........ Coolangatta [*Queensland*] [*Airport symbol*] (AD)
OOL........ Gold Coast [*Australia*] [*Airport symbol*] (OAG)
OOL........ Labour Canada [*Travail Canada*] Ottawa, Ontario [*Library symbol*] [*National Library of Canada*] (NLC)
OOL........ Oberlin Public Library, Oberlin, OH [*Library symbol*] [*Library of Congress*] (LCLS)
OOL........ Object-Oriented Language [*Computer science*] (BYTE)
OOL........ Odessa Ocean Line (SAUS)
OOL........ Office of Oceanography and Limnology [*Smithsonian Institution*] (MCD)
Ool........ Oology (SAUS)
OOL........ Open Objects Library (SAUS)
OOL........ Operator-Oriented Language [*Computer science*]
OOL........ Optimized Optical Link
OOL........ Out of Lock (SAUS)
OOL........ Out of Orbit Launch [*NASA*] (LAIN)
OOLAP........ Occupational Safety and Health Branch, Labour Canada [*Direction de la Securite et de l'Hygiene, Travail Canada*] Ottawa, Ontario [*Library symbol*] [*National Library of Canada*] (NLC)
OOLC........ Labour College of Canada, Ottawa, Ontario [*Library symbol*] [*National Library of Canada*] (NLC)
OOLHMD........ Optimized Optical Link Helmet-Mounted Display
OOLK........ Lekhwair [*Oman*] [*ICAO location identifier*] (ICLI)
OOLM........ Computing Department, Loeb's MIS, Ottawa, Ontario [*Library symbol*] [*National Library of Canada*] (BIB)
OOLML........ Lang, Michener, Lash & Johnston, Ottawa, Ontario [*Library symbol*] [*National Library of Canada*] (BIB)
Oologists Rec... Oologists Record (SAUS)
OOLP........ Object-Oriented Literate Programming (SAUS)
OOLR........ Law Reform Commission [*Commission de Reforme du Droit*] Ottawa, Ontario [*Library symbol*] [*National Library of Canada*] (NLC)
OOLR........ Ophthalmology, Otology, Laryngology, Rhinology

OOLR........ Overall Objective Loudness Rating [*of telephone connections*] (IEEE)
OOLRB...... Canada Labour Relations Board [*Conseil Canadien des Relations de Travail*] Ottawa, Ontario [*Library symbol*] [*National Library of Canada*] (NLC)
OOLRS...... Research Library, LRS Trimark Ltd., Ottawa, Ontario [*Library symbol*] [*National Library of Canada*] (BIB)
OOLU........ Orient Overseas Container Line [*Common carrier symbol*]
OOLU........ Orient Overseas Line [*Intermodal shipping container symbol*] (TVRC)
OOLUG...... Oklahoma On Line Users Group (NITA)
OOLWB...... Women's Bureau, Labour Canada [*Bureau de la Main-d'Oeuvre Feminine, Travail Canada*] Ottawa, Ontario [*Library symbol*] [*National Library of Canada*] (NLC)
OOM......... CANMET [*Canada Centre for Mineral and Energy Technology*] Library, Energy, Mines, and Resources Canada , Ottawa, Ontario [*Bibliotheque CANMET, Energie, Mines, et Ressources Canada*] [*Library symbol*] [*National Library of Canada*] (NLC)
OOM......... Cooma [*Australia*] [*Airport symbol*] (OAG)
OOM......... Object-Oriented Methodology (SAUS)
OOM......... Office of Ocean Management [*Marine science*] (MSC)
OOM......... Office of Organization and Management [*NASA*]
OOM......... Officers' Open Mess [*Military*] (AFM)
OOM......... Oomiya [*Japan*] [*Seismograph station code, US Geological Survey*] [*Closed*] (SEIS)
OOM......... Open Ocean Mining
OOM......... Open Order Master (MCD)
OOM......... Order of March (SAUS)
OOM......... Organized Organic Monolayer [*Organic chemistry*]
OOM......... Original Online Module [*Computer science*] (PDAA)
OOM......... Outside Office Memo (SAUS)
OOMA....... Masirah [*Oman*] [*ICAO location identifier*] (ICLI)
OOMAD..... Michael A. Dagg Associates [*Michael A. Dagg Associes*], Ottawa, Ontario [*Library symbol*] [*National Library of Canada*] (NLC)
OOMB....... Out of My Box [*Internet lingo*] (NETL)
OOMFC...... Ompah Branch, Frontenac County Library, Ontario [*Library symbol*] [*National Library of Canada*] (BIB)
OOMHC..... Malaysia High Commission, Ottawa, Ontario [*Library symbol*] [*National Library of Canada*] (NLC)
OOMHS..... Merivale High School, Ottawa, Ontario [*Library symbol*] [*National Library of Canada*] (NLC)
OOMI........ Employment and Immigration Canada [*Emploi et Immigration Canada*] Ottawa, Ontario [*Library symbol*] [*National Library of Canada*] (NLC)
OOMIL....... MIL Systems Engineering, Inc., Ottawa, Ontario [*Library symbol*] [*National Library of Canada*] (BIB)
OOMJ........ Macera & Jarzyna, Ottawa, Ontario [*Library symbol*] [*National Library of Canada*] (BIB)
OOML....... Metropolitan Life Insurance Co., Ottawa, Ontario [*Library symbol*] [*National Library of Canada*] (NLC)
OOMM....... Muscat [*Oman*] [*ICAO location identifier*] (ICLI)
oomm....... Organizational Operations and Maintenance Manual (NAKS)
OOMM....... Organizational Operations and Maintenance Manual (NASA)
OOMNA..... National Air Photo Library, Energy, Mines, and Resources Canada [*BibliothequePhotographie Aerienne Nationale, Energie, Mines, et Ressources Canada*], Otta wa, Ontario [*Library symbol*] [*National Library of Canada*] (BIB)
OOMO....... Oxford Mills Branch, Oxford-On-Rideau Township Public Library [*Library symbol*] [*National Library of Canada*] (BIB)
OOMP....... Physical Metallurgy Division, Energy, Mines and Resources Canada [*Division dela Metallurgie Physique, Energie, Mines et Ressources Canada*] Ottawa, Ontari o [*Library symbol*] [*National Library of Canada*] (NLC)
OOMPR..... Microtel Pacific Research Ltd., Ottawa, Ontario [*Library symbol*] [*National Library of Canada*] (NLC)
OOMR....... Headquarters Library, Energy, Mines and Resources Canada [*Bibliotheque Centrale, Energie, Mines et Ressources Canada*] Ottawa, Ontario [*Library symbol*] [*National Library of Canada*] (NLC)
OOMS....... Muscat/Seeb International [*Oman*] [*ICAO location identifier*] (ICLI)
OOMS....... On-Orbit Maintenance/Servicing (ACAE)
OOMSD..... Ministry of State for Social Development [*Ministere d'Etat au Developpement Social*] Ottawa, Ontario [*Library symbol*] [*National Library of Canada*] (NLC)
OOMSS...... Ministry of State for Science and Technology [*Ministere d'Etat pour les Sciences et la Technologie*], Ottawa, Ontario [*Library symbol*] [*National Library of Canada*] (NLC)
OON......... Canada Institute for Scientific and Technical Information, National Research Council (CISTI) [*Institut Canadien de l'Information Scientifique et Technique, Conseil National de Recherches (ICIST)*] Ottawa, Ontario [*Library symbol*] [*National Library of Canada*] (NLC)
OON......... Object Oriented Nonsens (SAUS)
OON......... Odd-Odd Nuclei
OON......... Officer of the Order of Niger
OON......... Out-of-Network (SAUS)
OONAB...... Administration Building Library, Canada Institute for Scientific and Technical Information [*Bibliotheque de l'Edifice de l'Administration, Institut Canadien de l'Information Scientifique et Technique*] Ottawa, Ontario [*Library symbol*] [*National Library of Canada*] (NLC)
OONAM..... Aeronautical and Mechanical Engineering Branch, Canada Institute for Scientific and Technical Information [*Division du Genie Aeronautique et Mecanique, Institut Canadien de l'Information Scientifique et Technique*] Ottawa, Ontario [*Library symbol*] [*National Library of Canada*] (NLC)
OONAMC.... NABU Manufacturing Corp., Ottawa, Ontario [*Library symbol*] [*National Library of Canada*] (NLC)
OONBR...... IRC [*Institute for Research in Construction*] Library, National Research Council Canada Ottawa, Ontario [*Bibliotheque IRC (Institut de Recherche en Construction), Conseil National de Recherches Canada*] [*Library symbol*] [*National Library of Canada*] (NLC)
OONC........ Chemistry Library, Canada Institute for Scientific and Technical Information [*Division de Chimie, Institut Canadien de l'Information Scientifique et Technique*] Ottawa, Ontario [*Library symbol*] [*National Library of Canada*] (NLC)
OONCC...... National Capital Commission [*Commission de la Capitale Nationale*] Ottawa, Ontario [*Library symbol*] [*National Library of Canada*] (NLC)
OOND........ Department of National Defence [*Ministere de la Defense Nationale*] Ottawa,Ontario [*Library symbol*] [*National Library of Canada*] (NLC)
OONDAT..... Air Technical Library, Department of National Defence [*Bibliotheque Techniquede l'Aviation, Ministere de la Defense Nationale*] Ottawa, Ontario [*Library symbol*] [*National Library of Canada*] (NLC)
OONDC...... Communications and Electronics Engineering Library, Department of National Defence [*Bibliotheque du Genie Electronique et des Communications, Ministere de laDefense National*] Ottawa, Ontario [*Library symbol*] [*National Library of Canada*] (NLC)
OONDCP.... Chief, Construction and Properties, Library, Department of National Defence [*Bibliotheque, Chef - Construction et Immeubles, Ministere de le Defense Nationale*] Ottawa, Ontario [*Library symbol*] [*National Library of Canada*] (NLC)
OONDCS.... Communications Security Establishment, Department of National Defence [*Centrede la Securite des Telecommunications, Ministere de la Defense Nationale*] Ot tawa, Ontario [*Library symbol*] [*National Library of Canada*] (NLC)
OONDH...... Directorate of History, Department of National Defence [*Bureau du Service Historique, Ministere de la Defense Nationale*] Ottawa, Ontario [*Library symbol*] [*National Library of Canada*] (NLC)
OONDIS..... Directorate of Information Services, Department of National Defence [*Servicesd'Information, Ministere de la Defense Nationale*] Ottawa, Ontario [*Library symbol*] [*National Library of Canada*] (NLC)
OONDJ...... Judge Advocate General, Department of National Defence [*Jugeavocat General, Ministere de la Defense Nationale*] Ottawa, Ontario [*Library symbol*] [*National Library of Canada*] (NLC)
OONDLT..... Land Technical Library, Department of National Defence [*Bibliotheque Technique (Terre), Ministere de la Defense Nationale*] Ottawa, Ontario [*Library symbol*] [*National Library of Canada*] (NLC)
OONDM..... National Defence Medical Centre, Department of National Defence [*Centre Medical de la Nationale, Ministere de la Defense Nationale*] Ottawa, Ontario [*Library symbol*] [*National Library of Canada*] (NLC)
OONDMC.... Mapping and Charting Establishment, Department of National Defence [*Service de la Cartographie, Ministere de la Defense Nationale*] Ottawa, Ontario [*Library symbol*] [*National Library of Canada*] (NLC)
OONDMT.... Maritime Technical Library, Department of National Defence [*Bibliotheque Technique (Mer), Ministere de la Defense Nationale*] Ottawa, Ontario [*Library symbol*] [*National Library of Canada*] (NLC)
OONDORAE... Operational Research and Analysis Establishment, Department of National Defence [*Centre d'Analyse et de Recherche Operationnelle, Ministere de la Defense Nationale*] Ottawa, Ontario [*Library symbol*] [*National Library of Canada*] (NLC)
OONDT...... Secretary of State Library at National Defence [*Bibliotheque du Secretariat d'Etat a la Defense Nationale*], Ottawa, Ontario [*Library symbol*] [*National Library of Canada*] (NLC)
OONE........ National Energy Board [*Office National de l'Energie*] Ottawa, Ontario [*Library symbol*] [*National Library of Canada*] (NLC)
OONFP...... National Farm Products Marketing Council [*Conseil National de Commercialisation des Produits Agricoles*], Ottawa, Ontario [*Library symbol*] [*National Library of Canada*] (BIB)
OONG........ National Gallery of Canada [*Galerie Nationale du Canada*] Ottawa, Ontario [*Library symbol*] [*National Library of Canada*] (NLC)
OONH........ Department of National Health and Welfare [*Ministere de la Sante Nationale etdu Bien-Etre Social*] Ottawa, Ontario [*Library symbol*] [*Obsolete*] [*National Library of Canada*] (NLC)
OONHAC.... Federal Centre for AIDS [*Acquired Immune Deficiency Syndrome*], Health Protection Branch, Health and Welfare Canada , Ottawa, Ontario [*Centre Federal du SIDA, Direction Generale de la Protection de la Sante, Sante et Bien-Etre Social Canada*] [*Library symbol*] [*National Library of Canada*] (BIB)
OONHBR.... Banting Research Centre Library, Department of National Health and Welfare [*Bibliotheque du Centre de Recherches Banting, Ministere de la Sante Nationale et du Bien-Etre Social*] Ottawa, Ontario [*Library symbol*] [*National Library of Canada*] (NLC)
OONHFV.... National Clearinghouse on Family Violence, Health and Welfare Canada [*Centre National d'Information sur la Violence dans la Famille, Sante et Bien-Etre Social Canada*], Ottawa, Ontario [*Library symbol*] [*National Library of Canada*] (BIB)
OONHHP.... Library Services Division, Health Protection Branch, Health and Welfare Canada [*Service de Bibliotheque, Direction Generale de la Protection de la Sante, Sante et Bien-Etre Social Canada*] Ottawa, Ontario [*Library symbol*] [*National Library of Canada*] (NLC)
OONHHS.... Health Services and Promotion Branch, Department of National Health and Welfare [*Direction Generale des Services et de la Promotion de la Sante, Ministere dela Sante Nationale et du Bien-Etre Social*] Ottawa, Ontario [*Library symbol*] [*National Library of Canada*] (NLC)

OONHP ...... Vanier Reading Room, Place Vanier, Health Protection Branch, Health and Welfare Canada [*Salle de Lecture de Vanier, Place Vanier, Direction Generale de la Protection de la Sante, Sante et Bien-Etre Social Canada*], Ottawa, Ontario [*Library symbol*] [*National Library of Canada*] (NLC)
OONHPP .... Library Services, Policy, Communications, and Information Branch, Health and Welfare Canada [*Services de Bibliotheque, Direction Generale de la Politique, des Communications, et de l'Information, Sante et Bien-Etre Social Canada*] Ottawa, Ontario [*Library symbol*] [*National Library of Canada*] (NLC)
OONIN .... National Institute of Nutrition [*Institut National de la Nutrition*], Ottawa, Ontario [*Library symbol*] [*National Library of Canada*] (BIB)
OONL .... National Library of Canada [*Bibliotheque Nationale du Canada*] Ottawa, Ontario [*Library symbol*] [*National Library of Canada*] (NLC)
OONLB ...... Union Catalogue of Books, National Library of Canada [*Catalogue Collectif desLivres, Bibliotheque Nationale du Canada*] Ottawa, Ontario [*Library symbol*] [*National Library of Canada*] (NLC)
OONLC ...... Canadiana Acquisitions, National Library of Canada [*Acquisitions pour Canadiana, Bibliotheque Nationale du Canada*] Ottawa, Ontario [*Library symbol*] [*National Library of Canada*] (NLC)
OONLD ...... Information Technology Services, National Library of Canada [*Services de Technologie de l'Information, Bibliotheque Nationale de Canada*], Ottawa, Ontario [*Library symbol*] [*National Library of Canada*] (NLC)
OONLD ...... Library Systems Centre, National Library of Canada [*Centre des Systemes de Bibliotheque, Bibliotheque Nationale du Canada*] Ottawa, Ontario [*Library symbol*] [*National Library of Canada*] (NLC)
OONLG ...... Official Publications, National Library of Canada [*Publications Officielles, Bibliotheque Nationale du Canada*] Ottawa, Ontario [*Library symbol*] [*National Library of Canada*] (NLC)
OONLI .... ISDS Canada, National Library of Canada [*ISDS Canada, Bibliotheque Nationale du Canada*], Ottawa, Ontario [*Library symbol*] [*National Library of Canada*] (BIB)
OONLMBS... Multilingual Biblioservice, National Library of Canada [*Biblioservice Multilingue, Bibliotheque Nationale du Canada*] Ottawa, Ontario [*Library symbol*] [*National Library of Canada*] (NLC)
OONLN ...... Newspaper Division, National Library of Canada [*Division des Journaux Bibliotheque Nationale du Canada*] Ottawa, Ontario [*Library symbol*] [*National Library of Canada*] (NLC)
OONLP ...... Serials Record, National Library of Canada [*Enregistrement des Publications en Serie, Bibliotheque Nationale du Canada*] Ottawa, Ontario [*Library symbol*] [*National Library of Canada*] (NLC)
OONLR ...... Retrospective Bibliography, National Library of Canada [*Bibliographie Retrospective, Bibliotheque Nationale du Canada*] Ottawa, Ontario [*Library symbol*] [*National Library of Canada*] (NLC)
OONLS ...... Union Catalogue of Serials, National Library of Canada [*Catalogue Collectif des Periodiques, Bibliotheque Nationale du Canada*] Ottawa, Ontario [*Library symbol*] [*National Library of Canada*] (NLC)
OONM .... National Museums of Canada [*Musees Nationaux du Canada*] Ottawa, Ontario [*Library symbol*] [*National Library of Canada*] (NLC)
OONMA ..... National Aviation Museum [*Musee National de l'Aviation*], Ottawa, Ontario [*Library symbol*] [*National Library of Canada*] (NLC)
OONMC ..... Canadian War Museum [*Musee de Guerre du Canada*] Ottawa, Ontario [*Library symbol*] [*National Library of Canada*] (NLC)
OONMCC.... Canadian Conservation Institute, National Museums of Canada [*Institut Canadien de Conservation, Musees Nationaux du Canada*] Ottawa, Ontario [*Library symbol*] [*National Library of Canada*] (NLC)
OONMM..... Canadian Museum of Civilization, National Museums of Canada [*Musee Canadien des Civilisations, Musees Nationaux du Canada*] Ottawa, Ontario [*Library symbol*] [*National Library of Canada*] (NLC)
OONMNS.... National Museum of Natural Sciences [*Musee National des Sciences Naturelles*], Ottawa, Ontario [*Library symbol*] [*National Library of Canada*] (NLC)
OONMS ..... National Museum of Science and Technology [*Musee National des Sciences et de la Technologie*] Ottawa, Ontario [*Library symbol*] [*National Library of Canada*] (NLC)
OONORE .... Bell Northern Research, Ottawa, Ontario [*Library symbol*] [*National Library of Canada*] (NLC)
OONP........ Division of Physics, Canada Institute for Scientific and Technical Information [*Division de Physique, Institute Canadien de l'Information Scientifique et Technique*] Ottawa, Ontario [*Library symbol*] [*National Library of Canada*] (NLC)
OONR........ Customs and Excise Division, Department of National Revenue [*Division des Douanes et de l'Accise, Ministere du Revenu National*] Ottawa, Ontario [*Library symbol*] [*National Library of Canada*] (NLC)
OONR........ Marmul/Nasir [*Oman*] [*ICAO location identifier*] (ICLI)
OONRE ...... Electrical Engineering Division, Canada Institute for Scientific and Technical Information [*Division de Genie Electrique, Institut Canadien de l'Information Scientifique et Technique*] Ottawa, Ontario [*Library symbol*] [*National Library of Canada*] (NLC)
OONRT ...... Taxation Division, Department of National Revenue [*Division de l'Impot, Ministere du Revenu National*] Ottawa, Ontario [*Library symbol*] [*National Library of Canada*] (NLC)
OONRTC..... Centre for Career Development, Revenue Canada - Taxation [*Centre de Developpement Professionnel, Revenu Canada - Impot*] Ottawa, Ontario [*Library symbol*] [*National Library of Canada*] (NLC)
OONS........ Sussex Library, Canada Institute for Scientific and Technical Information [*Bibliotheque Sussex, Institut Canadien de l'Information Scientifique et Technique*] Ottawa, Ontario [*Library symbol*] [*National Library of Canada*] (NLC)
OONSE ...... Natural Sciences and Engineering Research Council of Canada [*Conseil de Recherches en Sciences Naturelles et en Genie du Canada*], Ottawa, Ontario [*Library symbol*] [*National Library of Canada*] (NLC)
OONSF ...... National Science Film Library [*Cinematheque Nationale Scientifique*] Ottawa, Ontario [*Library symbol*] [*National Library of Canada*] (NLC)
OONSI....... North-South Institute [*L'Institut Nord-Sud*], Ottawa, Ontario [*Library symbol*] [*National Library of Canada*] (NLC)
OOnt......... Ontario Order of Merit [*Canada*] (FOTI)
OOnt......... Order of Ontario [*Decoration*] [*Canada*] (CMD)
OONU........ Uplands Library, Canada Institute for Scientific and Technical Information [*Bibliotheque d'Uplands, Institut Canadien de l'Information Scientifique et Technique*] Ottawa, Ontario [*Library symbol*] [*National Library of Canada*] (NLC)
OONUL ...... Union List of Scientific Serials in Canadian Libraries [*Catalogue Collectif des Publications Scientifiques dans les Bibliotheques Canadiennes*] Ottawa, Ontario [*Library symbol*] [*National Library of Canada*] (NLC)
OONVRC .... National Victims Resource Centre [*Centre National de la Documentation sur lesVictimes*] Ottawa, Ontario [*Library symbol*] [*National Library of Canada*] (NLC)
OONY........ Opera Orchestra of New York
OONZ........ Nizwa [*Oman*] [*ICAO location identifier*] (ICLI)
OOO .... Earth Physics Branch, Energy, Mines and Resources Canada [*Direction de la Physique du Globe, Energie, Mines et Resources Canada*] Ottawa, Ontario [*Library symbol*] [*National Library of Canada*] (NLC)
OOO .... Geophysics Collection, Geological Survey of Canada [*Collection de la Geophysique, Commission Geologique du Canada*], Ottawa, Ontario [*Library symbol*] [*National Library of Canada*] (NLC)
OOO .... Grants Pass, OR [*Location identifier*] [*FAA*] (FAAL)
OOO .... Oath of Office [*Telegraphy*] (PCTE)
OOO .... Office of the Ombudsman
OOO .... Oleum Olivae Optimum [*Best Olive Oil*] [*Pharmacy*] (ROG)
OOO .... Order of Owls (EA)
OOO .... O Sapientia, O Radix, O Adonai [*Three anthems sung in Roman Catholic churches before Christmas*] (ROG)
OOO .... Out of Office [*Internet lingo*] (NETL)
OOO .... Out of Order [*Telecommunications*] (TEL)
OOOA........ City of Ottawa Archives, Ontario [*Library symbol*] [*National Library of Canada*] (NLC)
OOOAG...... Office of the Auditor General [*Bureau du Verificateur General*] Ottawa, Ontario [*Library symbol*] [*National Library of Canada*] (NLC)
OOOCF ...... Ottawa Clinic, Ontario Cancer Foundation, Ontario [*Library symbol*] [*National Library of Canada*] (NLC)
OOOCH...... Ottawa Civic Hospital, Ontario [*Library symbol*] [*National Library of Canada*] (NLC)
OOOCM ..... Information Services, Ontario Centre for Microelectronics, Nepean, Ontario [*Library symbol*] [*National Library of Canada*] (NLC)
OOOF........ Onaping Branch, Onaping Falls Public Library, Ontario [*Library symbol*] [*National Library of Canada*] (NLC)
OOOI......... Out-Off-On-In [*Telecommunications*]
OOOL........ Optotek Ltd., Ottawa, Ontario [*Library symbol*] [*National Library of Canada*] (NLC)
OOOS........ Object-Oriented Operating System [*Computer science*] (CDE)
OOOTQFUE... Omnipotent Overseer of the Quest for Unsurpassable Excellence [*Rank in the Junior Woodchucks organization mentioned in Donald Duck comic by Carl Barks*]
OOP.......... Library of Parliament [*Bibliotheque du Parlement*] Ottawa, Ontario [*Library symbol*] [*National Library of Canada*] (NLC)
OOP.......... Object Oriented Pleasure (SAUS)
OOP.......... Object-Oriented Programming [*Computer science*] (NETL)
OOP.......... Oceanographic Observations of the Pacific
OOP.......... Office of Organization Planning
OOP.......... Offline Orthophoto Printer [*Computer science*] (PDAA)
OOP.......... Optimum Optical Pump
OOP.......... Ounce of Prevention [*A publication*]
OOP.......... Out of Pelvis [*Obstetrics*] (DAVI)
OOP.......... Out-of-Phase [*Gynecology*]
OOP.......... Out of Plane
OOP.......... Out of Plant
OOP.......... Out of Plaster [*Orthopedics*] (DAVI)
OOP.......... Out Of Pocket (SAUS)
OOP.......... Out of Pocket Cost
OOP.......... Out of Pocket Expense
OOP.......... Out of Position (MCD)
OOP.......... Out of Position [*Automotive safety*]
OOP.......... Out of Print [*Also, OP*] [*Publishing*]
OOP.......... Out on Pass (DAVI)
OOPA........ National Arts Centre [*Centre National des Arts*] Ottawa, Ontario [*Library symbol*] [*National Library of Canada*] (NLC)
OOPA........ One and Only Parents Association (EA)
OOPAC ...... Chaudiere Branch, Departmental Library, Environment Canada [*Succursale Chaudiere, Bibliotheque du Ministere, Environnement Canada*] Ottawa, Ontario [*Library symbol*] [*National Library of Canada*] (NLC)
OOPART..... Out of Place Artifact [*Archeology*]
OOPC........ Management Information Centre, Privy Council Office [*Regie Interne de l'Information, Bureau du Conseil Prive*] Ottawa, Ontario [*Library symbol*] [*National Library of Canada*] (NLC)
OOPC........ Ocean Observations Panel for Climate (SAUS)

OOPC........ Office of Operational Planning and Control [*Social Security Administration*]
OOPC........ Owners & Officers of Private Companies [*A publication*]
OOPCF...... Parliamentary Centre for Foreign Affairs and Foreign Trade [*Centre Parlementaire pour les Affaires Etrangeres et le Commerce Exterieur*], Ottawa, Ontario [*Library symbol*] [*National Library of Canada*] (NLC)
OOPEC...... Office for Official Publications of the European Communities (ECED)
OOPEC...... Petro-Canada, Ottawa, Ontario [*Library symbol*] [*National Library of Canada*] (NLC)
OOPED...... Pylon Electronic Development Co. Ltd., Ottawa, Ontario [*Library symbol*] [*National Library of Canada*] (NLC)
OOPF........ Resource Centre, Ottawa Police Force, Ontario [*Library symbol*] [*National Library of Canada*] (BIB)
OOPH........ Perley Hospital, Ottawa, Ontario [*Library symbol*] [*National Library of Canada*] (NLC)
OOPI........ Petroleum Incentives Program, Energy, Mines and Resources Canada [*Programmes d'Encouragement Petrolier, Energie, Mines et Ressources Canada*] Ottawa, Ontario [*Library symbol*] [*National Library of Canada*] (NLC)
OOPIP....... Professional Institute of the Public Service of Canada [*Institut Professionnel de la Fonction Publique du Canada*], Ottawa, Ontario [*Library symbol*] [*National Library of Canada*] (BIB)
OOPL........ Object-Oriented Programming Language [*Computer science*] (PCM)
OOPLFC & A... Only Official Peggy Lee Fan Club and Archives (EA)
OOPM........ National Postal Museum [*Musee National des Postes*] Ottawa, Ontario [*Library symbol*] [*National Library of Canada*] (NLC)
OOPMF...... Marten Falls Band Library, Ogoki Post, Ontario [*Library symbol*] [*National Library of Canada*] (BIB)
OOPMP...... Peat, Marwick & Partners, Ottawa, Ontario [*Library symbol*] [*National Library of Canada*] (NLC)
O Opns...... Overseas Operations (SAUS)
OOPO........ Canada Post [*Postes Canada*] Ottawa, Ontario [*Library symbol*] [*National Library of Canada*] (NLC)
OOPO........ Out of Position Occupant [*Automotive safety*]
OOPOM..... Meriline Branch, Canada Post [*Postes Canada*], Ottawa, Ontario [*Library symbol*] [*National Library of Canada*] (BIB)
OOPOR...... Ports Canada, Ottawa, Ontario [*Library symbol*] [*National Library of Canada*] (NLC)
OOPS........ Object-Oriented Pieces of Something [*Computer science*]
OOPS........ Object-Oriented Programming (BYTE)
OOPS........ Object-Oriented Programming Software (SAUS)
OOPS........ Object-Oriented Programming System (AAEL)
OOPS........ Object Oriented Program Support (SAUS)
OOPS........ O'Brien's Oil Pollution Service of New Orleans [*Oil spill cleanup service*]
OOPS........ Office for Operations in Political Systems
OOPS........ Off-Line Operating Simulator [*Computer science*]
OOPS........ Offshore Oil Pollution Sleeve (SAUS)
OOPS........ Online Object Patching System [*Computer science*] (PDAA)
OOPS........ Operational Ozone Processing System (SAUS)
OOPS........ Operational Ozone Product System (SAUS)
OOPS........ Operator Oriented Problem Source (VLIE)
OOPS........ Organization of Oil Producing States (SAUS)
OOPS........ Originals on Permanent Sale
OOPs........ Out-of-Pocket Expense (MHCS)
OOPS........ Public Service Staff Relations Board [*Commission des Relations de Travail dans la Fonction Publique*] Ottawa, Ontario [*Library symbol*] [*National Library of Canada*] (NLC)
OOPSAC..... Public Service Alliance of Canada [*Alliance de la Fonction Publique du Canada*] Ottawa, Ontario [*Library symbol*] [*National Library of Canada*] (NLC)
OOPSLA..... Object-Oriented Programming Systems, Languages, and Applications [*Computer conference*]
OOPSTAD... Object Orientated Programming for Small Talk Application Development association (SAUS)
OOPSTAD... Object Oriented Programming for Smalltalk Application Developers Association (SAUS)
OOPW....... Public Works Canada [*Travaux Publics Canada*] Ottawa, Ontario [*Library symbol*] [*National Library of Canada*] (NLC)
OOPWC..... Capital Region Library, Public Works Canada [*Bibliotheque de la Region de la Capitale, Travaux Publics Canada*] Ottawa, Ontario [*Library symbol*] [*National Library of Canada*] (NLC)
OOPWR..... Research and Development Laboratories, Public Works Canada [*Laboratoires de Recherche et de Developpement, Travaux Publics Canada*] Ottawa, Ontario [*Library symbol*] [*Obsolete*] [*National Library of Canada*] (NLC)
OOQ......... Officer of the Quarters
OOQ......... Original Order Quantity (SAUS)
OOQA........ Director-General, Quality Assurance Library, Department of National Defence [*Bibliotheque du Directeur General-Assurance de la Qualite, Ministere de la Defense Nationale*], Ottawa, Ontario [*Library symbol*] [*National Library of Canada*] (NLC)
OOQC........ Queensway-Carleton Hospital, Ottawa, Ontario [*Library symbol*] [*National Library of Canada*] (NLC)
OOQM........ Queen Mary Street School, Ottawa, Ontario [*Library symbol*] [*National Library of Canada*] (BIB)
OOR......... Mooraberrie [*Queensland*] [*Airport symbol*] (AD)
OOR......... Office for Ordnance Research [*Later, Army Research Office*]
OOR......... Office of Ordnance Research (SAUS)
OOR......... Open Ocean Release
OOR......... Operator Override [*Telecommunications*] (TEL)
OOR......... Out of Range (VLIE)
OOR......... Out of Room (DAVI)
OOR......... Out-of-Roundness [*Manufacturing term*]
OOR......... Oxygen/Ozone Recorder
OOR......... RCMP Headquarters [*Direction Generale de la GRC*] Ottawa, Ontario [*Library symbol*] [*National Library of Canada*] (NLC)
OOR......... RCMP [*Royal Canadian Mounted Police*] Law Enforcement Reference Centre , Ottawa, Ontario [*Centre de Documentation Policiere, Gendarmerie Royale du Canada*] [*Library symbol*] [*National Library of Canada*] (NLC)
OORA........ Oligoarticular Onset Rheumatoid Arthritis [*Medicine*] (MELL)
OORA........ Orangeville Public Library, Ontario [*Library symbol*] [*National Library of Canada*] (NLC)
OORASS.... Object Oriented Role Analysis, Synthesis and Structuring (SAUS)
OORCS...... Ottawa Roman Catholic Separate School Board, Ontario [*Library symbol*] [*National Library of Canada*] (NLC)
OORD........ Indian and Northern Affairs Canada [*Affaires Indiennes et du Nord Canada*] Ottawa, Ontario [*Library symbol*] [*National Library of Canada*] (NLC)
OORDBMS... Object-Oriented Relational Database Management System (SAUS)
OORH........ Riverside Hospital, Ottawa, Ontario [*Library symbol*] [*National Library of Canada*] (NLC)
OORI......... Orillia Public Library, Ontario [*Library symbol*] [*National Library of Canada*] (NLC)
OORIA....... J. L. Richard & Associates Ltd., Ottawa, Ontario [*Library symbol*] [*National Library of Canada*] (NLC)
OORIGC..... Learning Resources Centre, Georgian College of Applied Arts and Technology, Orillia, Ontario [*Library symbol*] [*National Library of Canada*] (NLC)
OORIMT..... Mara Township Public Library, Orillia, Ontario [*Library symbol*] [*National Library of Canada*] (BIB)
OORISMH... OSMH Health Sciences Library, Orillia Soldiers' Memorial Hospital, Ontario [*Library symbol*] [*National Library of Canada*] (NLC)
OORM....... Planning Department Library, Regional Municipality of Ottawa-Carleton, Ottawa, Ontario [*Library symbol*] [*National Library of Canada*] (NLC)
OORM....... Rima [*Oman*] [*ICAO location identifier*] (ICLI)
OORMT...... Transportation-Works Department, Regional Municipality of Ottawa-Carleton, Ottawa, Ontario [*Library symbol*] [*National Library of Canada*] (NLC)
OORO........ Royal Ottawa Hospital, Ontario [*Library symbol*] [*National Library of Canada*] (NLC)
OORORR.... Royal Ottawa Regional Rehabilitation Centre, Royal Ottawa Hospital, Ontario [*Library symbol*] [*National Library of Canada*] (NLC)
OORP........ Rockliffe Park Public Library, Ottawa, Ontario [*Library symbol*] [*National Library of Canada*] (BIB)
OORPL...... Communications Research Centre, Department of Communications [*Centre de Recherches sur les Communications, Ministere des Communications*] Ottawa, Ontario [*Library symbol*] [*National Library of Canada*] (NLC)
OORQ........ Rostaq [*Oman*] [*ICAO location identifier*] (ICLI)
OORR........ Regional Realty Ltd., Ottawa, Ontario [*Library symbol*] [*National Library of Canada*] (BIB)
OOrrW....... Wayne General and Technical College, Orrville, OH [*Library symbol*] [*Library of Congress*] (LCLS)
OORS........ RCMP Scientific Information Centre [*Centre d'Information Scientifique de la GRC*] Ottawa, Ontario [*Library symbol*] [*National Library of Canada*] (NLC)
OORSFC..... Only Official Rolling Stones Fan Club (EAIO)
OORSS...... CSIS [*Canadian Security Intelligence Service*] Open Information Centre Ontario [*Bibliotheque du SCRS (Service Canadien du Renseignement de Securite), Ottawa*] [*Library symbol*] [*National Library of Canada*] (NLC)
OORT........ Canadian Radio-Television and Telecommunications Commission [*Conseil de la Radiodiffusion et des Telecommunications Canadiennes*] Ottawa, Ontario [*Library symbol*] [*National Library of Canada*] (NLC)
OORTA....... Roads and Transportation Association of Canada [*Association des Routes et Transports du Canada*] Ottawa, Ontario [*Library symbol*] [*National Library of Canada*] (NLC)
OOS.......... Object Oriented Software [*Computer science*] (VLIE)
OOS.......... Object-Oriented Systems (SAUS)
OOS.......... Occupational Overuse Syndrome
OOS.......... Ocean Observing System [*Marine science*] (OSRA)
OOS.......... Office of Operations Support [*Law Enforcement Assistance Administration*]
OOS.......... Off-Line Operating Simulator [*Computer science*] (VLIE)
oos.......... On-Orbit Station [*NASA*] (NAKS)
OOS.......... On-Orbit Station [*NASA*] (NASA)
OOS.......... On-Orbit Support
OOS.......... Operational Operating System [*Telecommunications*] (TEL)
oos.......... Orbit-to-Orbit Shuttle [*NASA*] (NAKS)
OOS.......... Orbit-to-Orbit Shuttle [*NASA*]
oos.......... Orbit-to-Orbit Stage [*NASA*] (NAKS)
OOS.......... Orbit-to-Orbit Stage [*NASA*] (NASA)
OOS.......... Orbit to Orbit Unmanned System (ACAE)
OOS.......... Ore/Oil Ship (SAUS)
OOS.......... Out of School (OICC)
OOS.......... Out of Sequence (NRCH)
OOS.......... Out of Service (NRCH)
OOS.......... Out-of-Shot [*Photography*] (ADA)
OOS.......... Out-of-Sight (SAUS)
OOS.......... Out of Stock
OOS.......... Statistics Canada [*Statistique Canada*] Ottawa Ontario [*Library symbol*] [*National Library of Canada*] (NLC)
OOSA........ National Social Services Consultant and Government Relations Officer, Salvation Army Library, Ottawa, Ontario [*Library symbol*] [*National Library of Canada*] (BIB)
OOSA........ Object Orientated System Analysis (SAUS)
OOSA........ Object-Oriented Software Architecture (SAUS)

OOSA........ Object-Oriented Structured Analysis [*Computer science*] (HODG)
OOSA........ Salalah [*Oman*] [*ICAO location identifier*] (ICLI)
OOSAR...... Government Relations Office, Spar Aerospace Ltd., Ottawa, Ontario [*Library symbol*] [*National Library of Canada*] (BIB)
OOSB........ Smart & Biggar, Ottawa, Ontario [*Library symbol*] [*National Library of Canada*] (BIB)
OOSC........ Olfactronics and Odor Sciences Center (SAUS)
OOSC........ Out-of-Sight Control (MUGU)
OOSC........ Supreme Court of Canada [*Cour Supreme du Canada*] Ottawa, Ontario [*Library symbol*] [*National Library of Canada*] (NLC)
OOSCA...... Archives des Soeurs de la Charite d'Ottawa, Ontario [*Library symbol*] [*National Library of Canada*] (NLC)
OOSCAC..... Scanada Consultants Ltd., Ottawa, Ontario [*Library symbol*] [*National Library of Canada*] (NLC)
OOSCC...... Out-of-Site Control Center (SAA)
OOSCC...... Science Council of Canada [*Conseil des Sciences du Canada*] Ottawa, Ontario [*Library symbol*] [*National Library of Canada*] (NLC)
OOSCL...... Census Library, Statistics Canada [*Bibliotheque du Recensement, Statistique Canada*] Ottawa, Ontario [*Library symbol*] [*National Library of Canada*] (NLC)
OOSCM...... Census Map Library, Statistics Canada [*Cartotheque du Recensement, Statistique Canada*] Ottawa, Ontario [*Library symbol*] [*National Library of Canada*] (NLC)
OOSD........ Object Oriented Structured Design [*Computer science*]
OOSD........ Object-Oriented System Development [*Computer science*] (HODG)
OOSDG...... Ontario Secondary School Graduation Diploma (SAUS)
OOSDP...... On-Orbit Station Distribution Panel [*NASA*] (MCD)
OOSE........ Object-Oriented Software Engineering (SAUS)
OOSE........ Object-Oriented System Engineering [*Computer science*] (HODG)
OOSG........ Ministry of the Solicitor General [*Ministere du Solliciteur General*] Ottawa, Ontario [*Library symbol*] [*National Library of Canada*] (NLC)
OOSGO...... Osgoode Public Library, Ontario [*Library symbol*] [*National Library of Canada*] (BIB)
OOSH........ Object Oriented Shell (SAUS)
OOSH........ Oshawa Public Library, Ontario [*Library symbol*] [*National Library of Canada*] (NLC)
OOSH........ Out of School Hours
OOSH........ Sohar [*Oman*] [*ICAO location identifier*] (ICLI)
OOSHD...... Durham College of Applied Arts and Technology, Oshawa, Ontario [*Library symbol*] [*National Library of Canada*] (NLC)
OOSHH...... Education Resource Centre, Oshawa General Hospital, Ontario [*Library symbol*] [*National Library of Canada*] (BIB)
OOSHR...... Robert McLaughlin Gallery, Oshawa, Ontario [*Library symbol*] [*National Library of Canada*] (NLC)
OOSHT...... Technical Library, Systemhouse Ltd., Ottawa, Ontario [*Library symbol*] [*National Library of Canada*] (NLC)
OOSJ........ La Bibliotheque Deschatelets Peres Oblats [*Closed to the public*] Ottawa, Ontario [*Library symbol*] [*National Library of Canada*] (NLC)
OOSLM...... Montfort Hospital [*Hopital Montfort*] Ottawa, Ontario [*Library symbol*] [*National Library of Canada*] (NLC)
OOSLR...... S. L. Ross Environmental Research, Ottawa, Ontario [*Library symbol*] [*National Library of Canada*] (BIB)
OOSM........ Sahma [*Oman*] [*ICAO location identifier*] (ICLI)
OOSMM..... Map Library, Energy, Mines and Resources Canada [*Cartotheque, Energie, Mines et Ressources Canada*] Ottawa, Ontario [*Library symbol*] [*National Library of Canada*] (NLC)
OOSN........ Six Nations Public Library, Ohsweken, Ontario [*Library symbol*] [*National Library of Canada*] (BIB)
OOSP........ Patent and Copyright Office, Department of Consumer and Corporate Affairs [*Bureau des Brevets et du Droit d'Auteur, Ministere de la Consommation et des Corporations*] Ottawa, Ontario [*Library symbol*] [*National Library of Canada*] (NLC)
OOSPD...... Ocean Observing System Development Panel [*Marine science*] (OSRA)
OOSPX...... St.-Pius X High School, Ottawa, Ontario [*Library symbol*] [*National Library of Canada*] (BIB)
OOSQ........ Saiq [*Oman*] [*ICAO location identifier*] (ICLI)
OOSR........ Sur [*Oman*] [*ICAO location identifier*] (ICLI)
OOSS........ Department of the Secretary of State [*Secretariat d'Etat*] Ottawa, Ontario [*Library symbol*] [*National Library of Canada*] (NLC)
OOSS........ Outpatient Ophthalmic Surgery Society (EA)
OOSS........ Overseas Operational Storage Site [*Army*]
OOSSHRC... Social Sciences and Humanities Research Council of Canada [*Conseil de Recherches en Sciences Humaines du Canada*] Ottawa, Ontario [*Library symbol*] [*National Library of Canada*] (NLC)
OOSS PAC... Outpatient Ophthalmic Surgery Society PAC [*Washington, DC*] (PACS)
OOSSTE..... Terminology and Documentation Branch, Translation Bureau, Department of the Secretary of State [*Direction generale de la Terminologie et de la Documentation,Bureau des Traductions, Secretariat d'Etat*] Ottawa, Ontario [*Library symbol*] [*National Library of Canada*] (NLC)
OOSSTE..... Terminology Library, Information Resource Services Directorate, Secretary of State [*Bibliotheque de la Terminologie, Direction Info-Ressources, Secretariat d'Etat*], Ottawa, Ontario [*Library symbol*] [*National Library of Canada*] (NLC)
OOSSTM.... Multilingual Services Directorate, Translation Bureau, Department of the Secretary of State [*Direction des Services Multilingues, Bureau des Traductions, Secretariat d'Etat*] Ottawa, Ontario [*Library symbol*] [*National Library of Canada*] (NLC)
OOSSTR..... Translation Services Branch, Translation Bureau, Department of the Secretary of State [*Direction Generale des Services de Traduction, Bureau des Traductions,Secretariat d'Etat*] Ottawa, Ontario [*Library symbol*] [*National Library of Canada*] (NLC)
OOST........ Engle-Oostdyk [*Common carrier symbol*]
OOST........ Standards Council of Canada, Ottawa, Ontario [*Library symbol*] [*National Library of Canada*] (BIB)
OOSTM...... Careerware Reference Centre, STM Systems Corp., Ottawa, Ontario [*Library symbol*] [*National Library of Canada*] (BIB)
OOSU........ St. Paul University [*Universite St-Paul*] Ottawa, Ontario [*Library symbol*] [*National Library of Canada*] (NLC)
OOSUA...... Archives, St. Paul University [*Archives, Universite St-Paul*] Ottawa, Ontario [*Library symbol*] [*National Library of Canada*] (NLC)
OOSV........ St. Vincent Hospital [*Hopital St-Vincent*] Ottawa, Ontario [*Library symbol*] [*National Library of Canada*] (NLC)
OOSW........ Status of Women Canada [*Condition Feminine Canada*] Ottawa, Ontario [*Library symbol*] [*National Library of Canada*] (NLC)
OOSWH..... Soloway, Wright & Houston Law Firm, Ottawa, Ontario [*Library symbol*] [*National Library of Canada*] (BIB)
OOT.......... Object-Oriented Technology [*Computer science*] (CDE)
OOT.......... Office of Operational Testing (SAUS)
OOT.......... Oil Out Temperature
OOT.......... Onotoa [*Kiribati*] [*Airport symbol*] (OAG)
OOT.......... Ootomari [*Former USSR*] [*Seismograph station code, US Geological Survey*] [*Closed*] (SEIS)
OOT.......... Out of Oxygen Tent
OOT.......... Out of Territory (VLIE)
OOT.......... Out of Tolerance (FAAC)
OOT.......... Out-of-Town [*Word processing*]
OOT.......... Transport Canada [*Transports Canada*] Ottawa, Ontario [*Library symbol*] [*National Library of Canada*] (NLC)
OOTA........ Airworthiness Library, Transport Canada [*Bibliotheque de la Navigabilite Aerienne, Transports Canada*], Ottawa, Ontario [*Library symbol*] [*National Library of Canada*] (NLC)
OOTAC....... Airports and Construction Services, Transport Canada [*Service des Aeroports et de la Construction, Transports Canada*] Ottawa, Ontario [*Library symbol*] [*National Library of Canada*] (NLC)
OOTAS....... Canadian Aviation Safety Board [*Bureau Canadien de la Securite Aerienne*] Ottawa, Ontario [*Library symbol*] [*National Library of Canada*] (NLC)
OOTB........ Out of the Blue [*Internet lingo*] (NETL)
OOTB........ Out of the Box (ADWA)
OOTB........ Tourism Reference and Documentation, Regional Industrial Expansion [*Centre deReference et de Documentation Touristique, Expansion Industrielle Regionale*] , Ottawa, Ontario [*Library symbol*] [*National Library of Canada*] (NLC)
OOTC........ Department of Regional Industrial Expansion [*Ministere de l'Expansion Industrielle Regionale*] Ottawa, Ontario [*Library symbol*] [*National Library of Canada*] (NLC)
OOTC........ Obligatory On-Topic Comment [*Computer hacker terminology*]
OOTC........ Oceania Olympic Training Center [*Australia*]
OOTC........ Old Old Timers Club (EA)
OOTCI....... Documentation Centre, Communications and Informatics, Transport Canada [*Centre de Documentation, Communications et Informatique, Transports Canada*], Ottawa, Ontario [*Library symbol*] [*National Library of Canada*] (BIB)
OOTCO...... Telecommunications Library, Transport Canada [*Bibliotheque de Telecommunications, Transports Canada*], Ottawa, Ontario [*Library symbol*] [*National Library of Canada*] (NLC)
OOTCT....... TransCanada Telephone System, Ottawa, Ontario [*Library symbol*] [*National Library of Canada*] (NLC)
OOTE........ Out-of Town Executive (SAUS)
OOTE........ Out-of-Town Executive
OOTEL....... Telesat Canada, Ottawa, Ontario [*Library symbol*] [*National Library of Canada*] (NLC)
OOTFS....... Technical Library AAFBAA, Flight Services Directorate, Transport Canada [*Bibliotheque Technique AAFBAA, Direction Generale du Service des Vols, Transports Canada*], Ottawa, Ontario [*Library symbol*] [*National Library of Canada*] (NLC)
OOTG........ One of the Greats (SAUS)
OOTH........ Thumrait [*Oman*] [*ICAO location identifier*] (ICLI)
OOTI......... Technical Information Centre, Transport Canada Training Institute [*Centre d'Information Technique, Institut de Formation Transports Canada*], Cornwall, Ontario [*Library symbol*] [*National Library of Canada*] (NLC)
OOTIR....... Traffic Injury Research Foundation of Canada [*Fondation de Recherches sur lesBlessures de la Route au Canada*] Ottawa, Ontario [*Library symbol*] [*National Library of Canada*] (NLC)
OOTN........ Trade Negotiations Office, External Affairs Canada [*Affaires Exterieures Canada*] Ottawa, Ontario [*Library symbol*] [*National Library of Canada*] (NLC)
OOTR........ Tax Court of Canada [*Cour Canadienne de l'Impot*] Ottawa, Ontario [*Library symbol*] [*National Library of Canada*] (NLC)
OOTRAT..... Les Traductions Tessier SCC (Division de Multiscript International), Ottawa, Ontario [*Library symbol*] [*National Library of Canada*] (BIB)
OOTRS....... Road Safety and Motor Vehicle Regulation Branch, Transport Canada [*Direction de la Securite Routiere et de la Reglementation Automobile, Transports Canada*], Ottawa, Ontario [*Library symbol*] [*National Library of Canada*] (NLC)
OOTRT....... Railway Transportation Directorate, Transport Canada [*Direction du Transport Ferroviaire, Transports Canada*] Ottawa, Ontario [*Library symbol*] [*National Library of Canada*] (NLC)
OOTSSA..... St. Lawrence Seaway Authority, Transport Canada [*Administration de la Voie Maritime du Saint-Laurent, Transports Canada*] Ottawa, Ontario [*Library symbol*] [*National Library of Canada*] (NLC)
OOTT........ National Transportation Agency of Canada [*Office National des Transports du Canada*], Ottawa, Ontario [*Library symbol*] [*National Library of Canada*] (NLC)

OOTTD ...... Technical Data Resource Centre, Transport Canada [*Centre de la Documentation Technique, Transports Canada*], Ottawa, Ontario [*Library symbol*] [*National Library of Canada*] (NLC)
OOTTE....... Telecommunications and Electronics Directorate, Transport Canada [*Direction des Telecommunications et de l'Electronique, Transports Canada*] Ottawa, Ontario [*Library symbol*] [*Obsolete*] [*National Library of Canada*] (NLC)
OOTW .... Operations Other Than War [*Army*] (INF)
Ooty .... Ootacamund Madras (SAUS)
OOU .... Out of Use (IAA)
OOU .... University of Ottawa [*Universite d'Ottawa*] Ontario [*Library symbol*] [*National Library of Canada*] (NLC)
OOUA........ Archives, Universite d'Ottawa [*Archives, University of Ottawa*], Ontario [*Library symbol*] [*National Library of Canada*] (BIB)
OOUC........ Department of Criminology, University of Ottawa [*Departement de Criminologie,Universite d'Ottawa*] Ontario [*Library symbol*] [*National Library of Canada*] (NLC)
OOUD........ Faculty of Civil Law, University of Ottawa [*Faculte de Droit Civil, Universite d'Ottawa*] Ontario [*Library symbol*] [*National Library of Canada*] (NLC)
OOUG........ Oregon Online User Group (NITA)
OOUH........ Health Sciences Library, University of Ottawa [*Bibliotheque des Sciences de la Sante, Universite d'Ottawa*] Ontario [*Library symbol*] [*National Library of Canada*] (NLC)
OOUI......... Object-Oriented User Interface [*Computer science*]
OOUIC .... Institute of International Cooperation, University of Ottawa [*Institut de Cooperation Internationale, Universite d'Ottawa*] Ontario [*Library symbol*] [*National Library of Canada*] (NLC)
OOUM .... Vanier Library, University of Ottawa [*Bibliotheque Vanier, Universite d'Ottawa*] Ontario [*Library symbol*] [*National Library of Canada*] (NLC)
OOUMA ..... Map Library, University of Ottawa [*Cartotheque, Universite d'Ottawa*] Ontario [*Library symbol*] [*National Library of Canada*] (NLC)
OOURC ...... Centre de Recherche en Civilisation Canadienne-Francaise, Universite d'Ottawa [*Centre for Research on French Canadian Culture, University of Ottawa*], Ontario [*Library symbol*] [*National Library of Canada*] (BIB)
OOUSA ...... United States Information Service, Ottawa, Ontario [*Library symbol*] [*National Library of Canada*] (NLC)
OOUSC ...... Unitarian Service Committee of Canada, Ottawa, Ontario [*Library symbol*] [*National Library of Canada*] (BIB)
OOUU........ Orient Overseas Line [*Intermodal shipping container symbol*] (TVRC)
OOV.......... Objects of Verification [*Arms control*] (DOMA)
OOV.......... Orbit-to-Orbit Vehicle (MCD)
OOV.......... Out of View
OOV.......... Out of Vision [*Films, television, etc.*]
OOVIF .... Vanier Institute of the Family [*Institut Vanier de la Famille*] Ottawa, Ontario [*Library symbol*] [*National Library of Canada*] (NLC)
OOVV .... Versatile Vickers Systems, Inc., Ottawa, Ontario [*Library symbol*] [*National Library of Canada*] (NLC)
OOW......... Officer of the Watch [*Navigation*]
OOW......... Out-of-Warranty (TIMI)
OOW......... Out of Wedlock (MELL)
OOW......... Owen Sound Public Library, Ontario [*Library symbol*] [*National Library of Canada*] (NLC)
OOW......... Versatile Vickers Systems, Inc., Ottawa, Ontario (SAUS)
OOWC .... Wordcount, Creative Writing Services, Inc., Ottawa, Ontario [*Library symbol*] [*National Library of Canada*] (NLC)
OOWD .... Western Diversification [*Diversification de l'Ouest*], Ottawa, Ontario [*Library symbol*] [*National Library of Canada*] (BIB)
OOWGC ..... Georgian College Resource Centre, Owen Sound, Ontario [*Library symbol*] [*National Library of Canada*] (NLC)
OOWGM..... Health Sciences Library, General & Marine Hospital, Owen Sound, Ontario [*Library symbol*] [*National Library of Canada*] (NLC)
OOWGM..... Health Sciences Library, Grey Bruce Regional Health Centre, Owen Sound, Ontario [*Library symbol*] [*National Library of Canada*] (NLC)
OOWIC ...... West Island College of Ontario, Ottawa [*Library symbol*] [*National Library of Canada*] (BIB)
OOWLS...... Sir Wilfrid Laurier High School Library, Carleton Board of Education, Ottawa, Ontario [*Library symbol*] [*National Library of Canada*] (BIB)
OOWM ...... Owen Sound Museum, County of Grey, Ontario [*Library symbol*] [*National Library of Canada*] (BIB)
OOWSRA.... Omnibus Oregon Wild and Scenic Rivers Act of 1988 (COE)
OOWT .... Tom Thomson Memorial Gallery, Owen Sound, Ontario [*Library symbol*] [*National Library of Canada*] (NLC)
OOWU .... Briefing Centre, World University Services of Canada [*Centre de Ressources, Entraide Universitaire Mondiale du Canada*], Ottawa, Ontario [*Library symbol*] [*National Library of Canada*] (NLC)
OOX.......... XIOS Research Corp., Ottawa, Ontario [*Library symbol*] [*National Library of Canada*] (BIB)
OOXL .... Ontario-Ohio Express [*Common carrier symbol*]
OOxM........ Miami University, Oxford, OH [*Library symbol*] [*Library of Congress*] (LCLS)
OOxM-S..... Miami University, Scripps Foundation for Research in Population Problems, Oxford, OH [*Library symbol*] [*Library of Congress*] (LCLS)
OOYB........ Yibal [*Oman*] [*ICAO location identifier*] (ICLI)
OOZ.......... Open Ocean Zone [*Oceanography*]
OOZE........ Object-Oriented Z Environment [*Computer science*]
OP .... Air Panama Internacional [*ICAO designator*] (AD)
Op............ De Opficio Mundi [*Philo*] (BJA)
OP .... Dominican Contemplative Nuns (Cloistered) (TOCD)
OP .... Dominican Rural Missionaries (TOCD)
OP .... Dominican Sisters (Adrian, MI) (TOCD)
OP .... Dominican Sisters (Akron, OH) (TOCD)
OP .... Dominican Sisters (Amityville, NY) (TOCD)
OP .... Dominican Sisters (Blauvelt, NY) (TOCD)
OP .... Dominican Sisters (Caldwell, PA) (TOCD)
OP .... Dominican Sisters (Colombia) (TOCD)
OP .... Dominican Sisters (Columbus, OH) (TOCD)
OP .... Dominican Sisters (Ecuador) (TOCD)
OP .... Dominican Sisters (Edmonds, WA) (TOCD)
OP .... Dominican Sisters (Fall River, MA) (TOCD)
OP .... Dominican Sisters (Grand Rapid, MI) (TOCD)
OP .... Dominican Sisters (Great Bend, KS) (TOCD)
OP .... Dominican Sisters (Hawthorne, NY) (TOCD)
OP .... Dominican Sisters (Houston, TX) (TOCD)
OP .... Dominican Sisters (Justice, IL) (TOCD)
OP .... Dominican Sisters (Kenosha, WI) (TOCD)
OP .... Dominican Sisters (Media, PA) (TOCD)
OP .... Dominican Sisters (Nashville, TN) (TOCD)
OP .... Dominican Sisters (Newburgh, NY) (TOCD)
OP .... Dominican Sisters (New Orleans, LA) (TOCD)
OP .... Dominican Sisters of Carondelet (TOCD)
OP .... Dominican Sisters of Charity of the Presentation of the Blessed Virgin (TOCD)
OP .... Dominican Sisters of Mt. Thabor (TOCD)
OP .... Dominican Sisters of Our Lady of the Most Holy Rosary (TOCD)
OP .... Dominican Sisters of Our Lady of the Rosary and of Saint Catherine of Siena, Cabra (TOCD)
OP .... Dominican Sisters of the Roman Congregation (TOCD)
OP .... Dominican Sisters (Ossining, NY) (TOCD)
OP .... Dominican Sisters (Oxford, MI) (TOCD)
OP .... Dominican Sisters (Oxford, South Africa) (TOCD)
OP .... Dominican Sisters (Racine, WI) (TOCD)
OP .... Dominican Sisters (San Jose, CA) (TOCD)
OP .... Dominican Sisters (San Rafael, CA) (TOCD)
OP .... Dominican Sisters (Sinsinawa, WI) (TOCD)
OP .... Dominican Sisters (Sparkill, NY) (TOCD)
OP .... Dominican Sisters (Spokane, WA) (TOCD)
OP .... Dominican Sisters (Springfield, IL) (TOCD)
OP .... Dominican Sisters (St. Catherine, KY) (TOCD)
OP .... Dominican Sisters (Tacoma, WA) (TOCD)
OP .... Dominican Sisters (Vietnam) (TOCD)
OP .... Eucharistic Missionaries of St. Dominic (TOCD)
OP .... Hermanas Dominicanas de la Doctrine Cristiana (TOCD)
OP .... Marian Society of Dominican Catechists (TOCD)
OP .... Null Operator [*Linguistics*] (IEL)
OP .... Object Program (IAA)
OP .... Obligated Position [*Civil Service*]
OP .... Observation Patrol (SAUS)
OP .... Observation Plane
OP .... Observation Point [*or Post*]
OP .... Observation Post [*Military*]
OP .... Observed Position [*Navigation*]
OP .... Obstructive Pancreatitis [*Medicine*] (MELL)
OP .... Occasional Paper
OP .... Occipitoparietal [*Medicine*] (AAMN)
OP .... Occiput Posterior [*Medicine*]
OP .... Occupational Psychologist
OP .... Oceanus Procellarum [*Lunar area*]
OP .... Octapeptide [*Biochemistry*]
OP .... Offering Price
OP .... Office of Personnel [*Department of Agriculture*] (GFGA)
OP .... Office of Pesticides [*Public Health Service*]
OP .... Office of Planning (SAUS)
OP .... Office of Policy [*NASA*]
OP .... Office of Preparedness (DNAB)
OP .... Office of Protocol (SAUS)
OP .... Office of the president (SAUS)
OP .... Office Pass (AAG)
OP .... Office Power (SAUS)
OP .... Office Printer (SAUS)
OP .... Office Processor (SAUS)
OP .... Office Product (IAA)
OP .... Officer Program [*Military*] (DNAB)
OP .... Official Publication (ADA)
O/P........... Off Peak (WDAA)
O-P .... Off-Price [*A retail outlet selling discounted merchandise*]
o/p .... Oil on Panel (VRA)
OP .... Oilpalm [*Soil biology*] [*Human-introduced crops*] (QSUL)
OP .... Oil Pressure
OP .... Oilproof
OP .... Oil Pump
OP .... Old Particular [*Marsala*]
OP .... Old [*Previously seen*] Patient
OP .... Old Pattern [*British military*] (DMA)
OP .... Old Persean (WDAA)
OP .... Old Persian [*Language, etc.*]
OP .... Old Portuguese [*Linguistics*] (IEL)
OP .... Old Price [*Riots*] [*Occurred for 67 nights, beginning December 30, 1808, opening night of rebuilt Covent Garden Theatre, London, because of new and higher prices*]
OP .... Old Process (SAUS)
OP .... Old Prussian [*Linguistics*] (IEL)
OP .... Olfactory Peduncle [*Medicine*] (DMAA)
OP .... Omega Project (EA)
O/P........... On Proof [*Publishing*] (DGA)
OP .... Opaque [*Envelopes*]

OP .... Open [*Stock exchange term*]
OP .... Opening Pressure [*Medicine*]
OP .... Opening Price [*Stock exchange term*]
OP .... Opening Purchase [*Stock exchange term*]
OP .... Open Pit (SAUS)
OP .... Open Policy
OP .... Open Position [*Dancing*]
OP .... Opera
op .... Opera [*Works*] [*Italian*]
Op .... Opera et Dies [*of Hesiod*] [*Classical studies*] (OCD)
OP .... Operand [*Computer science*]
op .... Operate (IDOE)
OP .... Operate
OP .... Operating [*Motor vehicle violation code used in state of Maryland*] (MVRD)
OP .... Operating Plan
OP .... Operating Point (IAA)
OP .... Operating Policy [*Military*]
OP .... Operating Potential (SAUS)
OP .... Operating Procedure [*Management term*] (KSC)
OP .... Operating Profit [*DoD*]
OP .... Operation (AFM)
op .... Operation (ELAL)
OP .... Operational (CAAL)
op .... Operational (IDOE)
OP .... Operational Performance (SAUS)
OP .... Operational Priority
OP .... Operational Procedure (MCD)
OP .... Operational Process (SAUS)
OP .... Operational Project [*Army*] (AABC)
OP .... Operation Overlord Preparations [*World War II*]
OP .... Operation Part (SAUS)
OP .... Operation Plans
OP .... Operations (KSC)
OP .... Operations Order (MCD)
OP .... Operations Plan (IAA)
op .... Operative [*Therapy term*] (CTAA)
OP .... Operative Procedure
op .... Operator (IDOE)
OP .... Operator [*Computer science*]
OP .... Operator Panel (SAUS)
OP .... Operator Performance (SAUS)
OP .... Operator Position (SAUS)
OP .... Operator Precedence (SAUS)
OP .... Ophthalmology
OP .... Opinion (ADA)
OP .... Opium (SAUS)
O-P .... Oppenheimer-Phillips [*Process*]
OP .... Opportunity [*Telegraphy*] (PCTE)
OP .... Opposed (NVT)
op .... Opposite (WDMC)
OP .... Opposite
OP .... Opposite Prompt [*i.e., the left side*] [*A stage direction*]
OP .... Optical Probe (AAG)
OP .... Optical Properties (SAUS)
OP .... Optical Technician Program [*Association of Independent Colleges and Schools specialization code*]
OP .... Optime [*Best*] [*Latin*] (ROG)
OP .... Optimum Programming (SAUS)
op .... Optional (ELAL)
OP .... Optional
OP .... Optional Flag [*Navy*] [*British*]
op .... Opus (WDMC)
OP .... Opus [*Work*] [*Latin*]
Op .... Opus
OP .... Orange Pekoe [*Tea*]
OP .... Orbital Period (AAG)
OP .... Orbital Probe [*NASA*]
OP .... Ordering Possibility (SAUS)
op .... Order of Preachers, Dominican Fathers (TOCD)
OP .... Order of Preachers (Dominicans) (TOCD)
OP .... Order of Preceptors
OP .... Order Parameter (SAUS)
OP .... Order Policy [*Insurance*]
OP .... Ordinary Pay (SAUS)
OP .... Ordinis Praedicatorum [*Of the Order of Preachers, or Dominicans*] [*Latin*]
OP .... Ordnance Pamphlets
OP .... Ordnance Personnel
OP .... Ordnance Publications [*Navy*] (MCD)
OP .... Ordo Praedicatorum [*Order of Preachers*] [*Dominicans*] [*Roman Catholic religious order*]
Op .... Oregon pine (SAUS)
OP .... Organic Phosphates (GNE)
OP .... Organization Problem (SAUS)
OP .... Organophoshate (LDT)
OP .... Organophosphorus [*Organic chemistry*]
OP .... Oriented Polymer (SAUS)
OP .... Orient Press [*Press agency*] [*South Korea*]
OP .... Original Pack (DB)
OP .... Original Policy (ADA)
OP .... Original Premium [*Insurance*]
OP .... Orthogonal Polynomial (OA)
OP .... Orthogonal Processor (SAUS)
OP .... Orthomat Plot (MCD)
OP .... Ortho-Phosphate (SAUS)
OP .... Oscillatory Potentials (SAUS)
OP .... Osmotic Pressure
OP .... Osteopoetin [*Biochemistry*]
OP .... Osteoporosis [*Orthopedics*] (DAVI)
OP .... Osterogenic Protein
OP .... Other Papers (ROG)
OP .... Other People's [*Borrowed money, cigarettes, etc.*] [*Slang*]
OP .... Other Person (TRID)
OP .... Other Procurement
OP .... Other than Psychotic
OP .... Outer Panel (AAG)
OP .... Out-of-Press [*Recordings*]
op .... Out of Print [*Publishing*] (WDMC)
OP .... Out of Print [*Also, OOP*] [*Publishing*]
OP .... Outpatient [*Medicine*]
op .... Outport (SAUS)
OP .... Outpost
OP .... Out Primary (SAUS)
OP .... Output (AAG)
o/p .... Output
OP .... Output Point (SAUS)
OP .... Output Port (CCCA)
O/P .... Output Power (ACAE)
OP .... Output Primary [*Electronics*]
OP .... Output Printer (SAUS)
OP .... Output Processor (SAUS)
OP .... Output Puncher (SAUS)
OP .... Outside Production
OP .... Overall Position [*Tertiary entrance*]
OP .... Overflow Position (ELAL)
OP .... Overpotential (SAUS)
OP .... Over Pressure (AAG)
OP .... Overpressure (SAUS)
O/P .... Overpriced (WDAA)
op .... Overprint [*Journalism*] (WDMC)
OP .... Overprint
OP .... Over Proof (SAUS)
OP .... Overproof [*Distilling*]
OP .... Overprune (SAUS)
OP .... Overpuff (SAUS)
OP .... Overseas Post (ADA)
OP .... Overtime Pay (MHDB)
OP .... Ovine Prolactin [*Endocrinology*]
O/P .... Ownership Purpose Code [*Army*] (AABC)
OP .... Own Protection (WDAA)
OP .... Oxazolinylphenoxy [*Organic radical*]
OP .... Oxygen Point (SAUS)
OP .... Oxygen Pressure Process [*Ore leach process*]
OP .... Oxygen Purge [*NASA*] (NASA)
OP .... Ozone Protection [*Environmental science*] (COE)
OP .... Paulding County Carnegie Public Library, Paulding, OH [*Library symbol*] [*Library of Congress*] (LCLS)
OP .... Perth Public Library, Ontario [*Library symbol*] [*National Library of Canada*] (NLC)
OP .... Religious Missionaries of St. Dominic (Spanish Prov.) (TOCD)
OPA .... Isopropyl Alcohol (SAUS)
OPA .... Kopasker [*Iceland*] [*Airport symbol*] (OAG)
OPa .... Morley Library, Painesville, OH [*Library symbol*] [*Library of Congress*] (LCLS)
OPA .... Obscene Publications Act [*British*]
OPA .... Obstetrical Physician's Assistant [*Medicine*] (EDAA)
OPA .... Occupational Personality Assessment [*Test*] (TMMY)
OPA .... Office of Performance Assessment (SAUS)
OPA .... Office of Petroleum Allocation [*Federal Energy Administration*]
OPA .... Office of Planning and Analysis (SAUS)
OPA .... Office of Policy Analysis [*Environmental Protection Agency*] (GFGA)
OPA .... Office of Population Affairs [*HEW*]
OPA .... Office of Population Affairs Clearinghouse (EA)
OPA .... Office of Price Administration [*World War II*]
OPA .... Office of Producer Affairs [*Federal Telecommunications Commission*]
OPA .... Office of Program Analysis [*Department of Energy*] [*Washington, DC*]
OPA .... Office of Program Appraisal [*Navy*]
OPA .... Office of Public Affairs [*in various government agencies*]
OPA .... Office of Public Assistance (SAUS)
OPA .... Office of the Pardon Attorney [*Department of Justice*]
OPA .... Officer Personnel Act
o/pa .... Oil on Paper (VRA)
OPA .... Oil Pollution Act of 1990 [*MARAD*] (TAG)
OPA .... Onafhankelijke Partij [*Independent Party*] [*Netherlands*] [*Political party*] (PPW)
OPA .... One-Photon Absorption (SAUS)
OPA .... Online Privacy Alliance [*Association*] (EA)
OPA .... Online Publishers Association
OPA .... Ontario Paramedic Association (SAUS)
OPA .... Ontario Pharmacists Association (SAUS)
OPA .... Ontario Physiotherapists Association (SAUS)
OPA .... Opal Air Pty Ltd. [*Australia*] [*FAA designator*] (FAAC)
OPA .... Opana [*Hawaii*] [*Seismograph station code, US Geological Survey*] (SEIS)
OPA .... Opaque [*Type of ice formation*]
OPA .... Open Protocol Architecture (SAUS)

OPA .... Open Publishing Architecture (SAUS)
Opa .... Opera of the Month Club [*Record label*]
OPA .... Operations Planning Analysis [*NASA*] (MCD)
OPA .... Operator Priority Access (NITA)
OPA .... O-Phthalaldehyde
OPA .... Optical Parametric Amplifier (SAUS)
OPA .... Optical Parametric Oscillator [*Physics*]
OPA .... Optical Plotting Attachment (WDAA)
OPA .... Optical Publishing Association (EA)
OPA .... Optoelectric Pulse Amplifier (SAUS)
OPA .... Optoelectronic Pulse Amplifier
OPA .... Oral Pharyngeal Airway [*Medicine*] (EDAA)
OPA .... Orbiter Plasma Analyzer [*NASA*]
OPA .... Organophosphorous Acid [*Organic chemistry*]
OPA .... Organ Procurement Agency [*Department of Health and Human Services*] (GFGA)
OPA .... Oropharyngeal Airway (SAUS)
OPA .... Ortho-Phthaldehyde [*Organic chemistry*]
OPA .... Ortho-Propylaniline
OPA .... Other Procurement, Army (AABC)
OPA .... Outpatient Anesthesia [*Medicine*] (EDAA)
OPA .... Output and Performance Analysis (HEAS)
OPA .... Output Plate Assembly (MCD)
OPA .... Ovarian Papillary Adenocarcinoma [*Oncology*]
OPA .... Overall Paid Attendance [*Sports*] (GOBB)
OPA .... Overall Pavments Agreement (SAUS)
OPA .... Overall Probability of Attack (DNAB)
OPA .... Overhead Precautionary Approach
OPA .... Overview Pac Attribute (SAUS)
OPAA .... Organophosphorous Acid Anhydrase [*An enzyme*]
OPAAER ..... Archaeological Survey of Alberta. Occasional Papers (journ.) (SAUS)
OPAAS ...... Optimum Aircraft Armament System (SAUS)
OPAAW ...... Organization of Pan Asian-American Women (EA)
OPAB .... Abbottabad [*Pakistan*] [*ICAO location identifier*] (ICLI)
OPAC .... Omnova Solutions Inc. PAC [*Fairlawn, OH*] (PACS)
OPAC .... On-line Payment and Collection System [*Emergency Management*] (EMA)
OPAC .... Online Public Access Catalog [*Silicon Valley Information Center - SVIC*] [*San Jose, CA*] [*Information service or system*] (IID)
Op A/C ...... Operational Aircraft (SAUS)
OPAC .... Operation of Aircrafts (SAUS)
OPAC .... Operations Planning Advisory Committee (SAUS)
OPAC .... Optimized Policies for Adaptive Control [*Traffic management*]
OPAC .... Overall Performance Appraisal Certification [*Environmental Protection Agency*] (GFGA)
OPAC .... Resource Centre, School of Lanark County, Algonquin College of Applied Arts & Technology, Perth, Ontario [*Library symbol*] [*National Library of Canada*] (NLC)
OPACK .... Operation Acknowledge [*Computer science*] (MHDI)
OPACS .... Office of Price Administration and Civilian Supply [*Name changed to Office of Price Administration*] [*World War II*]
OPACS .... Order Planning and Control System (MCD)
OPACT .... Organization of Professional Acting Coaches and Teachers (EA)
OPaD .... Diamond Shamrock Corp., Research Library, Painesville, OH [*Library symbol*] [*Library of Congress*] (LCLS)
OPADEC ..... Optical Partial Decoy (IAA)
OPADEC ..... Optical Particle Decoy
OPADR ...... Operand Address [*Computer science*] (IAA)
OPAE .... Office of Program Analysis and Evaluation [*DoD*]
OPAEP .... Organisation des Pays Arabes Exportateurs de Petrole [*Organization of Arab Petroleum Exporting Countries*] (EAIO)
OPAFD7 ..... Allan Hancock Foundation. Occasional Papers (journ.) (SAUS)
OPA/FMOCCl ... Orthophthalaldehyde/Fluorenylmethoxycarbonyl Chloride (SAUS)
OPAG .... Operations and Planning Group (SAUS)
Op AG .... Opinions of the Attorney General [*A publication*] (DLA)
OPAGREE ... Operational Agreement (DNAB)
OPAGY ...... Operating Agency [*Military*]
OPAH .... Oil Pump Assembly Housing (MCD)
OPAI .... Paisley Branch, Bruce County Public Library, Ontario [*Library symbol*] [*National Library of Canada*] (NLC)
OPAIT .... Ontario Program for the Advancement of Industrial Technology (SAUS)
OPaL .... Lake Erie College, Painesville, OH [*Library symbol*] [*Library of Congress*] (LCLS)
OPAL .... Lakehead University, Thunder Bay, Ontario [*Library symbol*] [*National Library of Canada*] (NLC)
OPAL .... Ocean Process Analysis Laboratory [*University of New Hampshire*] [*Research center*] (RCD)
OPAL .... Older People with Active Lifestyles [*Lifestyle classification*]
OPAL .... Omni Purpose Apparatus for LEP (SAUS)
OPAL .... Oncovin [*Vincristine*], Prednisolone, Adriamycin, L-Asparaginase [*Antineoplastic drug regimen*]
OPAL .... One People of Australia League (SAUS)
OPAL .... Opal, Inc. [*NASDAQ symbol*] (SAG)
Opal .... Open Advisors Ltd. (IID)
OPAL .... Operation Alert [*Designed to test ability to recover from an enemy attack*]
OPAL .... Operational Performance Analysis Language [*Computer science*]
OPAL .... Operation Plan Analysis Logic [*Search technology*]
OPAL .... Optical Platform Alignment Linkage
OPAL .... Order Processing Automated Line (SAUS)
OPAL .... Orientation Program in American Law [*of AALS*]
OPALE .... Faculty of Education, Lakehead University, Thunder Bay, Ontario [*Library symbol*] [*National Library of Canada*] (NLC)
OPALE .... French bibliographic database (SAUS)
OPALG .... Department of Geography, Lakehead University, Thunder Bay, Ontario [*Library symbol*] [*National Library of Canada*] (NLC)
OPALs .... Older People with Active Lifestyles [*Lifestyle classification*]
Opals .... Older People with an Active Lifestyle [*Lifestyle classification*]
OPALS .... Optical Parallel Array Logic System (SAUS)
OpAmp ...... Operational Amplifier (AAEL)
op amp ...... Operational Amplifier (IDOE)
OP AMP ..... Operational Amplifier [*Computer science*]
OP/A/N/AF ... Other Procurement, Army/Navy/Air Force (SAUS)
OPANAL ..... Agency for the Prohibition of Nuclear Weapons in Latin America and the Caribbean (SAUS)
OPANAL ..... Operations Analysis [*Navy*] (NG)
OPANAL ..... Organismo para la Proscripcion de las Armas Nucleares en la America Latina [*Agency for the Prohibition of Nuclear Weapons in Latin America*] (EAIO)
OP&C .... Operations Planning and Control (SAUS)
OP&CMIA ... Operative Plasterers and Cement Masons International Association
OP & I .... Office of Patents and Inventions
OP & I .... Office of Publications and Information [*Department of Commerce*]
OP & PB .... Oceanographic Plans and Policy Board (SAA)
OP & R ...... Offset Printing and Reprographics [*A publication*] (DGA)
OPAP .... Operational Performance Acceptance Procedures (SAUS)
OPAPE .... Organisation Pan-Africaine de la Profession Enseignante [*All Africa Teachers' Organization*] (EAIO)
OPAQ .... Offer Parent-Adolescent Questionnaire [*Personality development test*] [*Psychology*]
OPAQUE ..... Optical Atmospheric Quality in Europe (MCD)
OPAR .... Office of Policy Analysis and Review [*Environmental Protection Agency*] (GFGA)
OPAR .... Operation Plans Assessment Report [*Environmental science*] (COE)
OPAR .... Paris Public Library, Ontario [*Library symbol*] [*National Library of Canada*] (NLC)
Op Arch ..... Opuscula Archaeologica [*A publication*] (OCD)
OPAREA ..... Operating Area (CAAL)
OPARI .... Occasional Publications. African and Afro-American Research Institute. University of Texas, Austin (SAUS)
OPARS ...... Optimum Path Aircraft Routing System (SAUS)
op art .... Optical Art (ODBW)
OPAS .... Occupation Pensions Advisory Service (WDAA)
OPAS .... Off-Power Assisted Steering [*Automotive engineering*]
OPAS .... Operational Assignment (DA)
OPAS .... Operational Assistance [*United Nations Development Program*]
OPAS .... Operational Public Address System
OPAS .... Overpass [*Postal Service standard*] (OPSA)
OPASTCO ... Organization for the Promotion and Advancement of Small Telephone Companies (CGWS)
OPASTCO ... Organization for the Protection and Advancement of Small Telephone Companies (EA)
OPat .... Pataskala Public Library, Pataskala, OH [*Library symbol*] [*Library of Congress*] (LCLS)
OPATSS ..... Offshore Product Acceptance Tests Specification System (TIMI)
Op Att Gen ... Opinions of the Attorneys-General [*United States*] [*A publication*] (DLA)
OPATTI ...... Office de Promotion et d'Animation Touristique de Tahiti et ses Iles (EY)
Op Att'y Gen ... Opinions of the Attorney General [*A publication*] (DLA)
Op Attys Gen ... Opinions of the Attorneys-General [*United States*] [*A publication*] (DLA)
OPB .... Observation Preparation Branch (SAUS)
OPB .... Occupational Pensions Board [*British*] (DCTA)
OPB .... Office of Plans and Budget (SAUS)
OPB .... Office of the Publication Board [*Department of Commerce*]
OPB .... Open Bay [*Papua New Guinea*] [*Airport symbol*] (OAG)
OPB .... Ophthalmic Pathology Branch [*Medicine*] [*AFIP*] (EDAA)
OPB .... Oregon Public Broadcasting (SAUS)
OPB .... Other People's Butts [*Cigarette butts garnered from ash trays*] [*Slang*]
OPB .... Outpatient Basis [*Medicine*]
OPB .... Oxidizer Preburner (KSC)
OPB .... Pikangikum Band Library, Ontario [*Library symbol*] [*National Library of Canada*] (BIB)
OPBA .... Ontario Public Buyers Association (SAUS)
OPBAT .... Operation Bahamas, Antilles, and Turks [*Air Force*]
OPBCT .... Providence Bay Branch, Carnarvon Township Public Library, Ontario [*Library symbol*] [*National Library of Canada*] (NLC)
OPBDR ...... Office of Program and Budget Development and Review [*Bureau of Apprenticeship and Training*] [*Department of Labor*]
OPBE .... Office of Planning, Budgeting, and Evaluation [*National Institute of Education*]
OPBG .... Bhagtanwala [*Pakistan*] [*ICAO location identifier*] (ICLI)
OPBL .... Bela [*Pakistan*] [*ICAO location identifier*] (ICLI)
Opble .... Operable (SAUS)
OPBMA ...... Ocean Pearl Button Manufacturers Association [*Defunct*]
OPBN .... Bannu [*Pakistan*] [*ICAO location identifier*] (ICLI)
OPBOV ...... Oxidizer Preburner Oxidizer Valve (NASA)
OPBR .... Bahawalnagar [*Pakistan*] [*ICAO location identifier*] (ICLI)
OPBU .... Operating Budget
OPBW .... Bahawalpur [*Pakistan*] [*ICAO location identifier*] (ICLI)
OPC .... Committee on Ocean Processes and Climate (SAUS)
OPC .... Occult Papillary Carcinoma [*Oncology*]
OPC .... Ocean Policy Committee [*Marine science*] (MSC)
OPC .... Ocean Products Center [*Marine science*] (OSRA)
OPC .... Oculopalatocerebral [*Syndrome*] [*Medicine*] (DMAA)
OPC .... Odd Parity Check (SAUS)
OPC .... Office de la Protection du Consommateur [*Quebec, PQ*]

OPC.......... Office of Peoples Counsel (SAUS)
OPC.......... Office of Policy Coordination (LAIN)
OPC.......... Office of Price Control [*World War II*]
OPC.......... Office of Primary Concern [*DoD*]
OPC.......... Office of Private Cooperation [*Department of State*]
OPC.......... Office of Procurement and Contracts [*Department of Housing and Urban Development*] (GFGA)
OPC.......... Office of Program Coordination (SAUS)
OPC.......... Office of Public Communication (SAUS)
OPC.......... Office of the Parliamentary Counsel (SAUS)
OPC.......... Office of the Protective Commissioner [*Australia*]
OPC.......... Office Percentage (SAUS)
OPC.......... Ogren, Paul C., South Bend IN [*STAC*]
OPC.......... Ohio Power Co. (SAUS)
OPC.......... Oil Policy Committee [*Office of Emergency Preparedness*] [*Obsolete*]
OPC.......... Oil Process Company (EFIS)
OPC.......... Old People's Center (GOBB)
OPC.......... Oldsmobile Performance Chapter (EA)
OPC.......... OLE [*Object Linking and Embedding*] for Process Control (ACII)
OPC.......... Oligonucleotide Purification Cartridge [*Chromatography*]
OPC.......... Olivetti Personal Computers
OPC.......... One Pound Charge (MCD)
OPC.......... Online Plotter Controller [*California Computer Products, Inc.*]
OPC.......... Ontario Press Council (SAUS)
OPC.......... Ontario Prevention Clearinghouse (SAUS)
OPC.......... Open GL performance Characterization (SAUS)
OPC.......... Open Printed Circuit (IAA)
OPC.......... Open Promoter Complex [*Genetics*]
OPC.......... Operated Preference Controls
OPC.......... Operating Center (SAUS)
OPC.......... Operation Code
Op C.......... Operation Complete (SAUS)
OPC.......... Operation Planning and Control (SAUS)
OPC.......... Operations Code [*Army*] (IAA)
OPC.......... Operations Control (IAA)
OPC.......... Operator Position Controller [*Telecommunications*]
OPC.......... Optical Particle Counter (PDAA)
OPC.......... Optical Phase Conjugator [*LASER-aiming device*]
OPC.......... Optical Photoconductor (PCM)
OPC.......... Optical Photo Coupler
OPC.......... Optical Propagation Conference (SAUS)
OPC.......... Optical Proximity Correct (AAEL)
OPC.......... Optional Calling (SAUS)
OPC.......... Optional Calling Plans [*Telecommunications*] (TEL)
OPC.......... Orange Pigment Cell
OPC.......... Ordinary Portland Cement
OPC.......... Ordnance Procurement Center [*Army*]
OPC.......... Organic Photoconducting Cartridge (RALS)
OPC.......... Organic Photoconductor
OPC.......... Organizational Point of Contact (SAUS)
OPC.......... Organization Postcode (SAUS)
OPC.......... Origination Point Code (SAUS)
OPC.......... Orion Pictures Corporation (SAUS)
OPC.......... Other Parks Corrector (SAUS)
OPC.......... Other Project Costs (ABAC)
OPC.......... Outer Passenger Cabin
OPC.......... Outer Proliferative Center [*Brain anatomy*]
opc.......... Out of Print and Cancelled [*Publishing*] (WDMC)
OPC.......... Out of Print, Canceled [*Publishing*]
OPC.......... Outpatient Care [*Medicine*] (EDAA)
OPC.......... Outpatient Catheterization [*Medicine*] (MELL)
OPC.......... Outpatient Clinic [*Medicine*]
OPC.......... Outpatient Psychiatric Care [*Health insurance*] (GHCT)
OPC.......... Output Control (SAUS)
OPC.......... Output Punched Card (SAUS)
OPC.......... Ovamboland Peoples Congress (SAUS)
OPC.......... Overall Performance Category
OPC.......... Overseas Press Club of America (EA)
OPC.......... Ownership Purpose and Condition Code [*Navy*] (DNAB)
OPC.......... Oxford Pocket Classics [*A publication*] (ROG)
OPC.......... Oxypneumocardiogram [*Cardiology*] (DAVI)
OPC.......... Perth Courier, Ontario [*Library symbol*] [*National Library of Canada*] (NLC)
OPC.......... QC Optics [*AMEX symbol*] (SAG)
OPCA.......... Occupational Program Consultants Association (EA)
OPCA.......... Olivopontocerebellar Atrophy [*Neurology*]
OPCA.......... Opium Poppy Control Act of 1942
OPCA.......... Ornamental Plant Collection Association (SAUS)
OPCA.......... Ornamental Plant Collectors Association (SAUS)
OPCA.......... Overseas Press Club of America (WDAA)
OP-CAL.......... Operation California (EA)
Op Cal Att'y Gen... Opinions of the Attorney General of California [*A publication*] (DLA)
OPCC.......... Office of Preschool and Child Care [*Victoria, Australia*]
OPCC.......... Offutt Air Force Base Processing and Correlation Center (MCD)
OPCC.......... Offutt Processing and Correlation Center (SAUS)
OPCC.......... Optical Product Code Council (EA)
OPCC.......... Outpatient Psychiatric Care Coverage
Op CCCG.... Opinion, Chief Counsel, United States Coast Guard [*A publication*] (DLA)
OP-CCK..... Octapeptide of Cholecystokinin (SAUS)
OPCD.......... Olivopontocerebellar Degeneration [*Medicine*] (RAWO)
OPCD.......... Operational Planning and Coordination Directorate (SAUS)
OPCE.......... Operator Control Element [*Computer science*] (IBMDP)
OPCEN...... Operations Center [*INTELSAT*]
OPC/ESA.... Operations, Planning & Control/ESA (SAUS)
OPCG.......... Organic Polymer Crystal Growth (SAUS)
OPCG.......... Original Print Collectors Group (EA)
OPCGE...... Organic/Polymer Crystal Growth Experiment (SSD)
OPCGF...... Organic/Polymer Crystal Growth Facility (SSD)
OPCH.......... Chitral [*Pakistan*] [*ICAO location identifier*] (ICLI)
op cit........ Opere Citato [*In the work cited*] [*Latin*] (WDMC)
OP CIT...... Opere Citato [*In the Work Cited*] [*Latin*]
OPCIT........ Opus Citatum (IAA)
OPCL.......... Chilas [*Pakistan*] [*ICAO location identifier*] (ICLI)
OPCM.......... Operative Plasterers and Cement Masons International Association of the US and Canada
OPC/MCA... Optical Particle Counter/Multi-Channel Analyzer (SAUS)
OPCMIA..... Operative Plasterers and Cement Masons International Association of US and Canada (EA)
OPCML...... Township of Muskoka Lakes Public Library Board, Port Carling, Ontario [*Library symbol*] [*National Library of Canada*] (BIB)
OPCNM...... Organ Pipe Cactus National Monument (SAUS)
OPCO.......... Operating Company (SAUS)
OPCO.......... Operating Plan Change Orders [*Coast Guard publication*]
OPCO.......... Outside Production Consignment Order
OPCOCM Symposium... Symposium on the Occurrence, Prediction and Control of Outbursts in Coal Mines (SAUS)
OP-COD..... Operating Code [*Computer science*]
Opcode...... Operating Code [*Computer science*] (ITCA)
OPCODE..... Operational Code (SAUS)
op code..... Operation Code (IDOE)
OPCODE..... Operations Code [*Army*] (AABC)
O/P Code... Ownership Purpose Code (SAUS)
OP-COM..... Opera-Comique [*Comic Opera*] [*Music*]
OPCOM..... Operational Command [*Military*] (MCD)
OP-COM..... Operations-Communications
OPCOM..... Operator Communications (SAUS)
op-com...... Optical Communication (MED)
OPCOM..... Optical Communications (ACAE)
OPCOMCTR... Operational Command Center [*Navy*] (NVT)
OPCOM System... Operator Communication System (SAUS)
OPCON...... Operational Control [*Army*] (NVT)
OPCON...... Operation and Control (SAUS)
OPCON...... Operation Control [*Military*] (VNW)
OPCON...... Operations and Control System (IAA)
OPCON...... Operator's Console
OPCON...... Optimizing Control [*Military*]
OPCONCEN... Operational Control Center [*Navy*]
OPCONCTR... Operational Control Center [*Navy*] (NVT)
OPCONCTR... Operations Control Center (SAUS)
OPCON System... Operation and Control System (SAUS)
OPCOSAL... Optimum Coordinated Shipboard [*or Shorebased*] Allowance List
OPCPL....... Port Colborne Public Library, Ontario [*Library symbol*] [*National Library of Canada*] (NLC)
OPCR.......... Chachro [*Pakistan*] [*ICAO location identifier*] (ICLI)
OPCR.......... One-Pass Cold-Rolled [*Steel sheets*]
OPCR.......... Original Program Clock Reference (SAUS)
OPCS.......... Office of Population Census and Surveys [*British*] (ECON)
OPCS.......... Office of Population Censuses and Surveys [*Department of Employment*] [*British*]
OPCS.......... Operational Planning and Control System [*Department of Labor*] (OICC)
OPCT.......... Chirat [*Pakistan*] [*ICAO location identifier*] (ICLI)
OPCTR...... Operation Counter (IAA)
OPCTR...... Operations Center [*Military*]
OPCV.......... Office of Planning, Control, and Validation [*Social Security Administration*]
OPCW.......... Office of Petroleum Coordination for War [*New Deal*]
OPCW.......... Organization for the Prohibition of Chemical Weapons [*Proposed, 1992*]
OPD.......... Audit Programs Division (AAGC)
OPD.......... Chemical Marketing Reporter (journ.) (SAUS)
OPD.......... Delayed Opening
OPD.......... Observed Position Data
OPD.......... Obstetric Prediabetic [*Medicine*] (DMAA)
OPD.......... Obstructive Pulmonary Disease [*Medicine*] (RAWO)
OPD.......... Office of Policy Development [*Executive Office of the President*]
OPD.......... Office of Program Development [*Environmental Protection Agency*] (GFGA)
OPD.......... Office of Public Defender (SAUS)
OPD.......... Office Product Division (ELAL)
OPD.......... Office Products Division (SAUS)
OPD.......... Officer Personnel Directorate [*Army*]
OPD.......... Officer Professional Development [*Military*] (INF)
OPD.......... Ohio College of Podiatric Medicine, Cleveland, OH [*OCLC symbol*] (OCLC)
OPD.......... One Per Desk (NITA)
OPD.......... Open Distributed Processing [*Computer science*] (TELE)
OPD.......... Opened [*Telegraphy*] (PCTE)
OPD.......... Opened [*Stock exchange term*] (SPSG)
OPD.......... Opening Delayed (SAUS)
OPD.......... Opening Posterior Digestive [*Gland*]
OPD.......... Operand [*Computer science*]
OPD.......... Operational Programming Department [*Telecommunications*] (TEL)
OPD.......... Operations Division [*War Department General Staff*] [*World War II*]
OPD.......... Operations Planning Division [*Manned Spacecraft Center*]
OPD.......... O-Phenylenediamine (SAUS)

OPD.......... Optical Particle Detector [*for evaluating film quality*]
OPD.......... Optical Path Difference (MCD)
OPD.......... Optical Phase Distortion (PDAA)
OPD.......... Optical Proximity Detector
OPD.......... Oral and Pharyngeal Development [*Section*] [*National Institute of Dental Research*]
OPD.......... Orbiting Propellant Depot [*NASA*]
OPD.......... Original Pack Dispensing [*For drugs*] [*Packaging*]
OPD.......... Original Point of Distribution (SAUS)
OPD.......... Originator Detection Pattern [*Communications term*] (DCT)
OPD.......... Ortho-Phenylenediamine [*Organic chemistry*]
OPD.......... 'Osef Piskei Din shel ha-Rabanut ha-Rashit le-'Erets Yisrael (BJA)
OPD.......... Oto-Palato-Digital [*Syndrome*]
OPD.......... Outpatient Department [*or Dispensary*] [*Medicine*]
OPD.......... Outpatient Diagnostic Rider [*Insurance*] (MHCS)
OPD.......... Outpatient Dispensary [*Medicine*] (DMAA)
OPD.......... Output Driver (SAUS)
OPD.......... Overall Program Design (OICC)
OPD.......... Overcurrent Protective Device (ELAL)
O/PD......... Overpaid (ROG)
OPD.......... Over Pin Diameter (SAUS)
OPD.......... Overseas Policy Defence Committee [*British*]
OPD.......... Oxford Paperback Dictionary [*A publication*]
OPD.......... Port Dover Centennial Public Library, Ontario [*Library symbol*] [*National Library of Canada*] (NLC)
OPDAC...... Optical Data Converter (NOAA)
OPDAG...... Original Paper Doll Artists Guild (EA)
OPDAR...... Optical Detection and Ranging
OPDAR...... Optical Direction and Ranging (SAUS)
OPDAR...... Optical Radar (SAUS)
OPDARS.... Optical Detection and Ranging System (IAA)
OPDAT....... Office of Professional Development and Training (SAUS)
OPDATS..... Operational Performance Data System
OPDB........ Dalbandin [*Pakistan*] [*ICAO location identifier*] (ICLI)
OPDC........ Overseas Policy Defence Committee [*British*] (DI)
OPDD........ Dadu [*Pakistan*] [*ICAO location identifier*] (ICLI)
OPDD........ Operational Plan Data Document [*Military*] (AFM)
OPDD........ Overall Plant Design Description (SAUS)
O,p-DDD.... Ortho, Para-Dichloro-Diphenyldichlorethane [*Mitotane*] [*Antineoplastic drug regimen*] (DAVI)
OPDEC...... Operational Deception [*Navy*] (NVT)
OPDEC PL... Operational Deception Planner [*Military*] (POLM)
OPDEF....... Operational Defect (SAUS)
OPDEFSYS... Operational Defects System (SAUS)
OPDEM...... Operational Demand (SAUS)
OpDent...... Operative Dentistry (BABM)
Opdent...... Operative Dentistry (DAVI)
OPDESC..... Operation Description (SAUS)
OPDET....... Operational Detachment (MCD)
OPDEVFOR... Operational Development Forces
OPDF........ Omo Peoples Democratic Front (SAUS)
OPDF........ Output Data Funnel (SAUS)
OPDG........ Dera Ghazi Khan [*Pakistan*] [*ICAO location identifier*] (ICLI)
OPDG........ Ocular Plethysmodynamography (DB)
OPD Gland... Opening of Posterior Digestive Gland (SAUS)
OPDI......... Dera Ismail Khan [*Pakistan*] [*ICAO location identifier*] (ICLI)
OPDI......... Operator Please Deliver Immediately
OP DIAP.... Open Diapason [*Organ stop*] [*Music*]
OPDIF....... Operational Planning Identification File [*Military*]
OPDIN....... Ocean Pollution Data and Information Network [*Washington, DC*] [*Department of Commerce*] (GRD)
OPDIN....... Ocean Pollution Data Center [*Marine science*] (OSRA)
OPDIR....... Operational Directive (SAUS)
OP DIV...... Operations/Air Intelligence Photography Division (DNAB)
OPDK........ Daharki [*Pakistan*] [*ICAO location identifier*] (ICLI)
OPDL........ Office of Production and Defense Lending [*Department of the Treasury*]
OPDO........ Oromo People's Democratic Organization [*Ethiopia*] [*Political party*] (EY)
OPDOC...... Operational Documentation [*Military*]
OPDP........ Officer Professional Development Program [*Pronounced "opey-dopey"*] [*Canadian Navy*]
OPDPE...... Office of Policy Development Planning and Evaluation [*Pronounced "opey dopey"*] [*NIMH*]
OPDR........ Office of Primary Development Responsibility (AFM)
OPDS........ Occupant Position Detection System [*Automotive safety systems*]
OPDS........ Office Professional Development System (MCD)
OPDS........ Officer Professional Development Seminar (SAUS)
OPDS........ Offshore Petroleum Distribution System
OPDS........ Overall Plant Design Specification (SAUS)
OPD Syndrome... Oto-Palato-Digital Syndrome (SAUS)
OPDU........ Operation Protocol Data Unit [*Telecommunications*] (OSI)
OPDU........ Powassan and District Union Public Library, Powassan, Ontario [*Library symbol*] [*National Library of Canada*] (NLC)
OPDUA...... Operative Painters amd Decorators' Union of Australia
OPD WDGS... Operations Division, War Department General Staff [*World War II*]
OPDZ........ Omaha Power District [*Federal Railroad Administration identification code*]
OPE.......... Eldorado Nuclear Ltd., Port Hope, Ontario [*Library symbol*] [*National Library of Canada*] (NLC)
OPE.......... Office of Planning and Environment (ABAC)
OPE.......... Office of Planning and Evaluation [*Office of Personnel Management*] (GRD)
OPE.......... Office of Policy Evaluation [*Nuclear energy*] (NRCH)
OPE.......... Office of Postsecondary Education [*Department of Education*] (GFGA)
OPE.......... Office of Program Eligibility (AAGC)
OPE.......... Office of Program Evaluation [*Office of Policy, Evaluation, and Research*] [*Department of Labor*]
OPE.......... Olivetti Peripheral Equipment (SAUS)
OPE.......... One-Particle Exchange (SAUS)
OPE.......... One-Pion Exchange [*Nuclear energy*]
OPE.......... Open Point Expanding [*Bullet*] (DICI)
OPE.......... Operational Planning Estimate
OPE.......... Operational Proficiency Examination (SAUS)
OPE.......... Operations Project Engineer [*NASA*] (KSC)
OPE.......... Optical Pointing Error
OPE.......... Optical-Probe Experiment [*Giotto probe of Halley's comet*] [*European Space Agency*]
OPE.......... Optimized Processing Element
OPE.......... Oral Proficiency Examination (SAUS)
OPE.......... Orbiting Primate Experiment (MCD)
OPE.......... Oregon, Pacific & Eastern Railway Co. [*AAR code*]
OPE.......... Other Plant Equipment [*DoD*]
OPE.......... Other Project Element (NASA)
OPE.......... Outer Planets Explorer [*NASA*]
OPE.......... Oxygen Plasma Etching (SAUS)
OPE.......... Societe 3S Aviation (Aerope) [*France*] [*ICAO designator*] (FAAC)
OPE.......... Topeka, KS [*Location identifier*] [*FAA*] (FAAL)
OPEAA....... Outdoor Power Equipment Aftermarket Association (EA)
OPEB........ Bruce County Public Library, Port Elgin, Ontario [*Library symbol*] [*National Library of Canada*] (NLC)
OPEC........ Oil Producers' Economic Cartel (NADA)
OPEC........ Oil Producers Equipment (SAUS)
OPEC........ One-Pion Exchange Contribution (SAUS)
Opec......... Organisation of Petroleum Exporting Countries (SAUS)
OPEC........ Organization of Petroleum Exporting Countries (NADA)
OPECNA..... OPEC [*Organization of Petroleum Exporting Countries*] News Agency [*See also APOPEC*] [*Vienna, Austria*] (EAIO)
OPECNA..... Organization of Petroleum Exporting Countries News Agency (SAUS)
OPECO...... Operations Coordinator [*Marine science*] (MSC)
OP-ED....... Opinion-Editorial (SAUS)
OP-ED....... Opposite Editorial Page [*in a newspaper*] [*Usually consists of opinion columns by various guest writers or syndicated columnists*]
Op-Ed........ Opposite the Editorial (ADWA)
op ed........ Opposite - the Editorial Page [*Newspapers*] (WDMC)
OPED........ Other Pay Entry Date [*Army*] (AABC)
OPED........ Point Edward Public Library, Ontario [*Library symbol*] [*National Library of Canada*] (NLC)
OPEDA...... Organization of Professional Employees of the United States Department of Agriculture (EA)
OPEDA...... Outdoor Power Equipment Distributors Association (EA)
OPEDC...... Overseas Private Enterprise Development Corp. [*Proposed successor to Agency for International Development*]
OPeeO........ Ohio Valley Local District Free Public Library, Peebles Branch, Peebles, OH [*Library symbol*] [*Library of Congress*] (LCLS)
OPEF........ Overall Plume Enhancement Factor [*Space Shuttle*] [*NASA*]
OPEG........ Oregon Pacific & Eastern Railway [*Federal Railroad Administration identification code*]
OPEI......... Office of Public Education and Information [*NASA*]
OPEI......... Outdoor Power Equipment Institute (EA)
OPEI......... Outdoor Power Equipment Institute, Inc.
OPEIU....... Office and Professional Employees International Union (EA)
OPEL........ Opel [*NCIC car make code*]
OPE Language... Office Procedures by Example Language (SAUS)
OPELI........ Opelika, AL [*American Association of Railroads railroad junction routing code*]
OPELO....... Opelousas, LA [*American Association of Railroads railroad junction routing code*]
OPEM........ One-Pion Exchange Model [*Nuclear energy*]
OPEM........ Pembroke Public Library, Ontario [*Library symbol*] [*National Library of Canada*] (NLC)
OPEMA...... Oilfield Production Equipment Manufacturers Association [*Defunct*] (EA)
OPEMAC.... Upper Ottawa Valley Campus Resource Centre, Algonquin College, Pembroke, Ontario [*Library symbol*] [*National Library of Canada*] (NLC)
OPEMO...... Ottawa Valley Historical Society, Pembroke, Ontario [*Library symbol*] [*National Library of Canada*] (BIB)
OPEN........ Fund for an Open Society (EA)
OPEN........ Ocean Production Enhancement Network (SAUS)
OPen......... Olympic Peninsula (SAUS)
OPEN........ Oncovin, Prednisone, Etopside, Mitoxantrone [*Antineoplastic drug*] (CDI)
OPEN........ Online Public Education Network
OPEN........ Open Environment Corp. [*NASDAQ symbol*] (SAG)
OPEN........ Opening (SAUS)
OPEN........ Open Protocol Enhanced Network [*Northern Telecom communications network*] [*Canada*]
OPEN........ Open Road [*NCIC truck make code*]
OPEN........ Open ROUTE Network [*NASDAQ symbol*] [*Formerly, Proteon, Inc.*]
OPEN........ Optical Pan-European Network (SAUS)
OPEN........ Organisation des Producteurs d'Energie Nucleaire [*Paris, France*] (EAIO)
OPEN........ Organization of Pakistani Entrepreneurs of North America [*Association*] (EA)
OPEN........ Origins of Plasma in the Earth's Neighborhood [*Ad Hoc Advisory Committee terminated, 1981*]

OPEN .... Penetanguishene Public Library, Ontario [*Library symbol*] [*National Library of Canada*] (BIB)
OPENAH..... Operational Evaluation of Armed Helicopters (MCD)
OPENE....... Ecole Secondaire le Caron, Penetanguishene, Ontario [*Library symbol*] [*National Library of Canada*] (BIB)
Open Economies Rev... Open Economies Review [*A publication*] (JLIT)
OPENGL..... Open Graphics Language (SAUS)
OPENHCI... Open Host Controller Interface (SAUS)
OPENM...... Mental Health Centre, Penetanguishene, Ontario [*Library symbol*] [*National Library of Canada*] (NLC)
OpenMkt.... Open Market, Inc. [*Associated Press*] (SAG)
OpenPln..... Open Plan Systems, Inc. [*Associated Press*] (SAG)
Open Syst Softw... Open Systems and Software (SAUS)
OpenTxt..... Open Text Corp. [*Associated Press*] (SAG)
OpenVis...... OpenVision Technologies, Inc. [*Associated Press*] (SAG)
OpenVMS... Open Virtual Memory System (SAUS)
OPEO .... Oakland-Pontiac Enthusiast Organization (EA)
OPEO .... Octylphenol Polyethoxylate [*Organic chemistry*]
OPEOS ...... Outside Plant Planning, Engineering, and Construction Operations System (MCD)
OPEP .... One-Pion Exchange Potential (SAUS)
OPEP .... Orbital-Plane Experiment Package [*NASA*]
OPEPB....... Eastern Pentecostal Bible College, Peterborough, Ontario [*Library symbol*] [*National Library of Canada*] (NLC)
OPER .... Coin Phones, Inc. (SAUS)
OPER .... Office of Policy and Economic Research [*Federal Home Loan Bank Board*] [*Washington, DC*] (GRD)
OPER .... Office of Policy, Evaluation, and Research [*Employment and Training Administration*] [*Department of Labor*]
OPer .... Old Persian [*Language*] (BARN)
OPER .... Open Roadsters [*NCIC car make code*]
OPER .... Operating [*Automotive engineering*]
oper .... Operation (DD)
OPER .... Operation [*or Operational*] (KSC)
Oper .... Operation (TBD)
OPER .... Operations, Operate, Operator (SAUS)
OPER .... Operator
OPERA ...... Operational Analysis (IAA)
OPERA ...... Ordnance Pulses Experimental Research Assembly [*Nuclear reactor*]
OPERA ...... Out-of-Pile Expulsion and Reentry Apparatus [*Nuclear energy*]
OPERA ...... Outpatient Endometrial Resection and Ablation [*Medicine*]
OPERATORS... Optimization Program for Economical Remote Trunk Arrangement and TSPS [*Traffic Service Positions System*] Operator Arrangements [*Telecommunications*] (TEL)
OPERG ...... Operating (MDG)
Oper Geogr... Operational Geographer (SAUS)
Oper Manage Rev... Operations Management Review (SAUS)
Oper Off..... Operations Officer (TBD)
O-PERS ..... Officer Personnel Office (DNAB)
OPers........ Old Persian [*Language*] (BARN)
OPERSCRS... Officer Personnel Course [*Air Force*]
OPersLex ... Old Persian Grammar Texts Lexicon [*A publication*] (BJA)
OPERSUN... Operation Planning and Execution System for Railway Unified Network (SAUS)
Oper Syst Netw... Operating Systems and Networks (SAUS)
OPERUN .... Operation Planning and Execution System for Railway Unified Network (PDAA)
OPES .... Centre de Documentation, Ecole Secondaire de Plantagenet [*Documentation Centre, Plantagenet Secondary School*], Ontario [*Library symbol*] [*National Library of Canada*] (BIB)
OPEST....... Oil Protection of Emissions System Test [*Lubricants*]
OPEST....... Oil Protection of Emission Systems Test [*Automotive lubricants*]
OPET .... Organization, Personnel Equipment and Training [*Group*]
OPET .... Oriented Polyester (SAUS)
OPET .... Oriented Polyethylene Terephthalate [*Organic chemistry*]
OPET .... Trent University, Peterborough, Ontario [*Library symbol*] [*National Library of Canada*] (NLC)
OPETA....... Trent University Archives, Peterborough, Ontario [*Library symbol*] [*National Library of Canada*] (NLC)
OPETAL ..... Trent Audio Library Services, Trent University, Peterborough, Ontario [*Library symbol*] [*National Library of Canada*] (NLC)
OPETC....... Trent Canal Office, Peterborough, Ontario [*Library symbol*] [*National Library of Canada*] (BIB)
OPETCG..... Canadian General Electric Co. Ltd., Peterborough, Ontario [*Library symbol*] [*National Library of Canada*] (NLC)
OPETCM .... Peterborough Centennial Museum and Archives, Ontario [*Library symbol*] [*National Library of Canada*] (BIB)
OPETHS..... Hutchison House Museum, Peterborough Historical Society, Ontario [*Library symbol*] [*National Library of Canada*] (BIB)
OPETM ...... Map Library, Trent University, Peterborough, Ontario [*Library symbol*] [*National Library of Canada*] (NLC)
OPETP....... Peterborough Public Library, Ontario [*Library symbol*] [*National Library of Canada*] (NLC)
OPETSF ..... Brealy Library, Sir Sandford Fleming College, Peterborough, Ontario [*Library symbol*] [*National Library of Canada*] (NLC)
OPETSFD... Daniel Library, Sir Sandford Fleming College, Peterborough, Ontario [*Library symbol*] [*National Library of Canada*] (BIB)
OPEV .... Petawawa Village and Township Union Public Library, Ontario [*Library symbol*] [*National Library of Canada*] (NLC)
OPEVAL ..... Operational Evaluation [*Navy*] (NG)
OPEX .... Operational and Executive (SAUS)
OPEX .... Operational Executive (CIST)
OPEX .... Operational, Executive, and Administrative Personnel Program [*United Nations*]
OPEX .... Operational Experience (SAUS)
OPEX .... Operational Extension
OPF.......... Miami, FL [*Location identifier*] [*FAA*] (FAAL)
OPf........... Office of Promotion and Tourism (SAUS)
OPF.......... Official Personnel File (MCD)
OPF.......... Official Personnel Folder [*Military*]
OPF.......... One-Piece Folder [*Publishing*] (WDMC)
OPF.......... Open-Pore Foam [*Plastic*]
OPF.......... Operations Flight [*Military*]
OPF.......... Optical Propagation Facility
OPF.......... Orbiter Processing Facility [*NASA*] (NASA)
OPF.......... Osmium Potassium Ferrocyanide (SAUS)
OPF.......... Output Filter (SAUS)
OPF.......... Overseas Project Fund [*British Overseas Trade Board*] (DS)
OPFA .... Faisalabad [*Pakistan*] [*ICAO location identifier*] (ICLI)
OPFAC....... Operating Facilities [*Coast Guard publication*]
OPFAC....... Operational Facility (RDA)
OPFAD....... Outer-Perimeter Fleet Air Defense
OPFAEI ...... Freshwater Biological Association. Occasional Publication (journ.) (SAUS)
OPFC .... Hinchinbrooke Public Library, Frontenac County Library, Parkham, Ontario [*Library symbol*] [*National Library of Canada*] (BIB)
OPFC .... Orbiter Preflight Checklist [*NASA*] (MCD)
OPFCA....... Ornamental Pool and Fountain Constructors Association [*British*] (DBA)
OPFCDIN... Great Britain. Forestry Commission. Occasional Paper (journ.) (SAUS)
OPFCO ...... Operational Program Functional Checkout (MCD)
OPFET....... Optical Field-Effect Transistor (SAUS)
OPFI......... Office of Program and Fiscal Integrity (USGC)
OPFM........ Outlet Plenum Feature Model [*Nuclear energy*] (NRCH)
OPFOR ...... Opportunity to Confront the Best Opposing Force [*Army*] (INF)
OPFOR ...... Opposing Force [*Military*] (INF)
OpFor........ Opposing Force
OPFOR ...... Opposing Force Program (SAUS)
OPFOR ...... Opposition Force (SAUS)
OPFRC ...... Clarendon-Miller Branch, Frontenac County Library, Plevna, Ontario [*Library symbol*] [*National Library of Canada*] (NLC)
OPFT .... Other than Permanent Full-Time (GFGA)
OPFTE....... Other than Permanent Full-Time Equivalent (GFGA)
OPG.......... Ocular Pneumoplethysmography [*Medicine*] (RAWO)
OPG.......... Oculoplethysmograph [*Instrumentation*]
OPG.......... Office Of Global Programs [*Marine science*] (OSRA)
OPG.......... Office of the Postmaster General [*Obsolete*]
OPG.......... Official Parliamentary Group (Pakistan) [*Political party*] (PSAP)
O Pg .... Old Portuguese (SAUS)
OPG.......... Opening
OPG.......... Operating
OPG.......... Operational Performance Goals
OPG.......... Operational Planning Grant (OICC)
OPG.......... Operations Planning Group [*Military*]
OPG.......... Original Proof Gallon
OPG.......... Orthopantomogram (ODA)
OPG.......... Outside Production Group
OPG.......... Overseas Products Group [*Department of Trade*] [*British*]
OPG.......... Overseas Project Group (SAUS)
OPG.......... Oxalate, Peroxide and Gluconic Acid (SAUS)
OPG.......... Oxypolygelatin [*Plasma extender*]
OPGA........ Ohio Personnel and Guidance Association (SAUS)
OPGA........ Oregon Personnel and Guidance Association (SAUS)
OPGA........ Outpatient General Anesthesia (MELL)
Op GA Att'y Gen... Opinions of the Attorney General of Georgia [*A publication*] (DLA)
OPG/CPA.... Oculoplethysmography/Carotid Phonoangiography [*Medicine*] (DAVI)
Op GCT...... Opinion, General Counsel, United States Treasury Department [*A publication*] (DLA)
OPGD........ Gwadar [*Pakistan*] [*ICAO location identifier*] (ICLI)
OPGE........ OEEC [*Organization for European Economic Cooperation*] Petroleum Industry Emergency Group (NATG)
OPGEN ...... Operation Plan Generation (SAUS)
OPGEN ...... Operations General Message (SAUS)
OP/GSA ..... Office of Preparedness, General Services Administration [*Later, Federal Preparedness Agency*]
OPGSX ...... Oppenheimer Gold & Spl. Minerals [*Mutual fund ticker symbol*] (SG)
OPGT........ Gilgit [*Pakistan*] [*ICAO location identifier*] (ICLI)
OPGT........ Outer Planets Grand Tour [*NASA*]
OPGUID ..... Optimum Guidance [*Technique*] (NASA)
OPGW .... Optical Groundwire [*Telecommunications*] (TSSD)
OPH.......... Obliterative Pulmonary Hypertension [*Medicine*]
OPH.......... Office Phone (SAUS)
OPH.......... Old Parliamentary Hand [*Political*] [*British*]
OPh.......... Old Phoenician (BJA)
OPH.......... Operational Propellant Handling [*NASA*] (AAG)
oph .... Ophicleide (WDAA)
OPH.......... Ophicleide [*Musical instrument*]
Oph .... Ophiuchus [*Constellation*]
OPH.......... Ophthalmodynamometry [*Ophthalmology*]
OPH.......... Ophthalmolgist
OPH.......... Ophthalmology [*or Ophthalmoscopy*]
OPH.......... [*The*] Ophthalmoscope [*London*] [*A publication*] (ROG)
Oph .... Ophthalmoscope [*or Ophthalmoscopic*] [*Ophthalmology*] (DAVI)
OPH.......... Ophthalmoscopic (SAUS)
OPH.......... Opposite Hand [*Technical drawings*]
OPH.......... Organophosphorus Hydrolase [*An enzyme*]
OPH.......... Public Library, Port Hope, Ontario [*Library symbol*] [*National Library of Canada*] (NLC)
OPHA........ Ontario Public Health Association (SAUS)

OPHC........ Office of Prepaid Health Care [*Department of Health and Human Services*] (GFGA)
Oph D....... Doctor of Ophthalmology
OPHELIOS... Optronic Passive Highly-sensitive Light IR Optical Sensor (SAUS)
OPHF........ Orbital Polarized Hartree-Fock [*Atomic physics*]
Ophi......... Ophiuchus [*Constellation*]
ophidiol..... ophidiologist (SAUS)
ophidiol..... ophtdiology (SAUS)
OPHIR........ Organic Power and Heat Industrial Reactor
OPHM........ OraPharma, Inc. [*NASDAQ symbol*] (SG)
Ophn......... Orpheon [*Record label*] [*Poland*]
OPHQ........ Karachi [*Pakistan*] [*ICAO location identifier*] (ICLI)
OPHR........ Olympic Project for Human Rights
Op Hrs...... Operation Hours (DA)
OPHS........ Office of Public Health and Science
OPHS........ Operational Propellant Handling System [*NASA*] (AAG)
OPHT........ Ophthalmic
OPHTH...... Ophthalmology (AABC)
OPHTHAL... Ophthalmology
Ophthal..... Ophthalmoloscope (SAUS)
OPHTHPAC... American Academy of Ophthalmology Inc. Political Committee [*San Francisco, CA*] (PACS)
OphtImg.... Ophthalmic Imaging Systems [*Associated Press*] (SAG)
OPHTS...... Operational Propellant Handling Test Site [*NASA*] (AAG)
OPHWA...... Nuclear Products Department, Westinghouse Canada, Inc., Port Hope, Ontario [*Library symbol*] [*National Library of Canada*] (NLC)
OPi........... Flesh Public Library, Piqua, OH [*Library symbol*] [*Library of Congress*] (LCLS)
OPI........... Oculoparalytic Illusion [*Ophthalmology*]
OPI........... Office of Planning and Integration (ABAC)
OPI........... Office of Primary Interest
OPI........... Office of Programs Integration [*Energy Research and Development Administration*]
OPI........... Office of Protective Intelligence (SAUS)
OPI........... Office of Public Information [*UNESCO*]
OPI........... Office of Public Inquiry (SAUS)
OPI........... Off-Site Production Inspection (AAG)
OPI........... Ogden Projects (SAUS)
OPI........... Oil Patch Group, Inc. [*Toronto Stock Exchange symbol*]
OPI........... Oil Pressure Indicator
OPI........... Omnibus Personality Inventory [*Psychology*]
OPI........... One Person's Impact [*An association*] (EA)
OPI........... Open for Public Inspection [*Patent applications*]
OPI........... Open Information Interchange (SAUS)
OPI........... Open Prepress Interface [*Computer science*] (PCM)
OPI........... Open Prepress Standard (SAUS)
OPI........... Open Protocol Interface [*Telecommunications*]
OPI........... Operator Interface (SAUS)
OPI........... Opinion Research Corp. [*AMEX symbol*] (NASQ)
OPI........... Optical Publishing, Inc. [*Information service or system*] (IID)
OPI........... Orbital Position Indicator
OPI........... Orbiter Payload Interface (ACAE)
OPI........... Orbiter Payload Interrogator [*NASA*] (MCD)
OPI........... Ordnance Procedure Instrumentations (AAG)
OPI........... Ordnance Procurement Instructions [*Army*]
OPI........... Organophosphate Insecticide
OPI........... Other Party Identifier (SAUS)
OPI........... Output Productivity Index
OPI........... Outside Procurement [*or Purchase*] Inspection (AAG)
OPI........... Outside Production Inspection (SAUS)
OPI........... Outside Purchase Inspection (SAUS)
OPI........... Overall Performance Index [*Finance*]
OPI........... Picton Public Library, Ontario [*Library symbol*] [*National Library of Canada*] (NLC)
OPIA......... Ontario Plumbing Inspectors Association [*Canada*]
OPIA......... Optical Imaging Association (EA)
OPIA......... Opto-Precision Instruments Association (NTPA)
OPIAT....... Opiates [*Chemical dependency*] [*Pharmacology*] (DAVI)
OPIC......... Oficina Permanente Internacional de la Carne [*Permanent International Meat Office*] (EAIO)
OPIC......... Open Programmable Interrupt Controller (SAUS)
OPIC......... Organization of Professional Immigration Consultants [*Canada*] (EAIO)
OPIC......... Overseas Petroleum Investment Group (EFIS)
OPIC......... Overseas Private Investment Corp. [*US International Development Cooperatio n Agency*] [*Washington, DC*]
OPIC......... Overseas Processing and Interpretation Center (SAUS)
OPIC......... Pickering Public Library, Ontario [*Library symbol*] [*National Library of Canada*] (NLC)
OPID......... Operational Procedures Interface Document (MCD)
OPIDF....... Operational Planning Identification File (MCD)
OPIDN....... Organophosphate Induced Delayed Neural Toxicity
OPiE......... Edison State Community College, Piqua, OH [*Library symbol*] [*Library of Congress*] (LCLS)
OPIE......... Ohio Program of Intensive English (EDAC)
OPIET........ Eco-Tec Ltd., Pickering, Ontario [*Library symbol*] [*National Library of Canada*] (NLC)
OPIEW....... Older People in Europe Week (WDAA)
OPIG......... Picton Gazette, Ontario [*Library symbol*] [*National Library of Canada*] (NLC)
OPIL......... Opalescent Indicating Light
Op Ill Att'y Gen... Illinois Attorney General's Opinion [*A publication*] (DLA)
Op Ill Atty Gen... Illinois Attorney Generals Opinion (journ.) (SAUS)
OPIM........ Operations & Information Management (SAUS)
OPIM........ Order Processing and Inventory Monitoring [*Computer science*]
OPIM........ Other Potentially Infectious Material (AMHC)
Opin......... Opinions of the Attorneys-General [*United States*] [*A publication*] (DLA)
Opinc........ Options Income (BARN)
OPINDOC... Operational Indoctrination (ACAE)
OPINE....... Operations in a Nuclear Environment [*DoD*]
Opine........ Option Income [*Business term*]
OP INIT..... Operator Initials [*Communications term*] (DCT)
OPINM...... North Marysburgh Museum, Picton, Ontario [*Library symbol*] [*National Library of Canada*] (BIB)
OpinRsh..... Opinion Research Corp. [*Associated Press*] (SAG)
OPINS....... Oakland Planning Information System (SAUS)
OPINT....... Optical Intelligence
OPINTEL... Operational Intelligence
OPIO......... Office of Policy, Integration and Outreach (SAUS)
OPIR......... Office of Program and Integrity Reviews (SAUS)
OPIRI........ Osaka Prefectural Industrial Research Institute (SAUS)
OPIRL....... Operator Interface Rolling Loop
OPIS......... Operational Priority Indicating System (NATG)
opis.......... opisometer (SAUS)
OPIS......... Orbiter Prime Item Specification [*NASA*] (NASA)
OPIS......... Pelee Island Public Library, Ontario [*Library symbol*] [*National Library of Canada*] (NLC)
OP(IT)....... Operation Overlord Preparations, Inland Transport [*World War II*]
OPIT......... Operator Interface Table (MCD)
OPIT......... Oxide-Powder-in-Tube
OPIVITA... Outpatient Intravenous Infusion Therapy Association (NTPA)
OP I WDW TNT... Operating with Illegal Window Tinting [*Conviction term used in state of Oregon*] (MVRD)
OPiWU...... Wright State University, Piqua Branch Campus, Piqua, OH [*Library symbol*] [*Library of Congress*] (LCLS)
OPIX.OB.... Odyssey Pictures Corp. [*OTCBB symbol*]
OPJ.......... Ohio Power 8.16% Jr Sub Debs [*NYSE symbol*] (TTSB)
OPJA........ Jacobabad [*Pakistan*] [*ICAO location identifier*] (ICLI)
Op JAGAF... Opinion, Judge Advocate General, United States Air Force [*A publication*] (DLA)
Op JAGN.... Opinion, Judge Advocate General, United States Navy [*A publication*] (DLA)
OPJC........ Jacobabad [*Pakistan*] [*ICAO location identifier*] (ICLI)
OPJI......... Jiwani [*Pakistan*] [*ICAO location identifier*] (ICLI)
Op Judge Adv Gen... Opinion of the Judge Advocate General (AAGC)
OPK.......... Kopkaka [*Language symbol*] (ETLW)
OPK.......... Operative Personenkontrolle [*Operational Person Control*] [*German*]
OPK.......... Optokinetic
OPK.......... Ovulation Prediction Kit
OPK.......... Ovulation Predictor Kit
OPKA........ Cape Monze [*Pakistan*] [*ICAO location identifier*] (ICLI)
Op Kan Att'y Gen... Opinions of the Attorney General of Kansas [*A publication*] (DLA)
OPKC........ Karachi/International [*Pakistan*] [*ICAO location identifier*] (ICLI)
OPKD........ Hyderabad [*Pakistan*] [*ICAO location identifier*] (ICLI)
OPKE........ Chore [*Pakistan*] [*ICAO location identifier*] (ICLI)
OPKE........ Knudsen Engineering Ltd., Perth, Ontario [*Library symbol*] [*National Library of Canada*] (BIB)
OPKF........ Gharo [*Pakistan*] [*ICAO location identifier*] (ICLI)
OPKH........ Khuzdhar [*Pakistan*] [*ICAO location identifier*] (ICLI)
OPKK........ Karachi/Korangi Creek [*Pakistan*] [*ICAO location identifier*] (ICLI)
OPKL........ Kalat [*Pakistan*] [*ICAO location identifier*] (ICLI)
OPKN........ Kharan [*Pakistan*] [*ICAO location identifier*] (ICLI)
OPKO........ Kohat [*Pakistan*] [*ICAO location identifier*] (ICLI)
OPKR........ Karachi [*Pakistan*] [*ICAO location identifier*] (ICLI)
OPKT........ Kohat [*Pakistan*] [*ICAO location identifier*] (ICLI)
Op KY Att'y Gen... Opinion of Attorney General, State of Kentucky [*A publication*] (DLA)
OPL.......... Air Cote d'Opale [*France*] [*ICAO designator*] (FAAC)
OPL.......... Lavalas Political Organization (Haiti) [*Political party*] (PSAP)
OPL.......... Oberlin Public Library, Oberlin, OH [*OCLC symbol*] (OCLC)
OPL.......... Obvious Panty Line (SAUS)
OPL.......... Ocean Physics Laboratory [*University of California, Santa Barbara*] (RCD)
OPL.......... Ocean Pressure Laboratory
OPL.......... Office of Presidential Libraries [*National Archives*] (BARN)
OPL.......... Official Publications Library [*The British Library*]
OPL.......... Old Product Line (IAA)
OPL.......... Omaha Public Library (SAUS)
OPL.......... One-Person Library
OPL.......... Opel [*NCIC motorcycle make code*]
OPL.......... Opelousas, LA [*Location identifier*] [*FAA*] (FAAL)
OPL.......... Open Problem List (NASA)
OPL.......... Open Publication License
OPL.......... Operational (AFM)
OPL.......... Operations Plan (KSC)
OPL.......... Optically Pumped LASER (AAEL)
OPL.......... Optical Path Length
OPL.......... Organization of the Struggling People (Haiti) [*Political party*] (PSAP)
OPL.......... Organizer Programming Language [*Computer science*]
OPL.......... Orient-Pacific Line [*Shipping*] (ROG)
OPL.......... Orlando Public Library (SAUS)
OPL.......... Other Party Liability [*Insurance*] (DMAA)
OPL.......... Ottawa Public Library [*UTLAS symbol*]
OPL.......... Outer Plexiform Layer [*Retina*]
OPL.......... Out-of-Phase Loading
OPL.......... Outpost Line
OPL.......... Overpaid Last Account

OPL .... Ovine Placental Lactogen [*Medicine*] (DMAA)
OPLA .... Lahore [*Pakistan*] [*ICAO location identifier*] (ICLI)
OPLA .... Offshore Pollution Liability Agreement (SAUS)
OPLA .... Ontario Public Library Association (SAUS)
Op LA Att'y Gen... Opinions of the Attorney General of Louisiana [*A publication*] (DLA)
OPLAC....... Argyle Community Library, Port Loring, Ontario [*Library symbol*] [*National Library of Canada*] (NLC)
OPLAC....... Ontario Public Libraries Advisory Committee (SAUS)
OPLAN ...... Operation Plan [*Army*]
OPLAN REV... Operation Plan Review (SAUS)
OPLANS..... Operations Plans (ACAE)
OPLAN SEA... Operation Plan, Southeast Asia [*Military*]
OPLAW...... Operational Law (COE)
OPLB .... Ontario Public Libraries Board (SAUS)
OPLC .... Ontario Provincial Libraries Council (SAUS)
OPLC .... Organizacion para la Liberacion de Cuba [*Organization for the Liberation of Cuba*] (PD)
OPLC .... Overpressure Layer Chromatography
OPLE .... Omega Position Location Equipment (SAUS)
OPLE .... Omega Position Location Experiment [*NASA*]
OP LEAK LD... Operating with a Sifting or Leaking Load [*Conviction term used in state of Oregon*] (MVRD)
Op Let....... Opinion Letter [*A publication*] (DLA)
OPLF .... Orbiter Processing and Landing Facility [*NASA*] (MCD)
OPLF .... Oromo Peoples Liberation Front (SAUS)
OPLG .... Oil Plug
OPLH .... Lahore/Walton [*Pakistan*] [*ICAO location identifier*] (ICLI)
OP/LIM...... Operational Limitation (SAUS)
OPLIN .... Ohio Public Library Information Network
OPLIN .... Ontario Public Libraries Information Network (SAUS)
OPLK .... Oplink Communications [*NASDAQ symbol*]
OPLL .... Loralai [*Pakistan*] [*ICAO location identifier*] (ICLI)
OPLL .... Optical Phase-Locked Loop (SAUS)
OPLL .... Ossification of Posterior Longitudinal Ligament [*Orthopedics*] (DAVI)
OPLO .... Oromo Peoples Liberation Organization (SAUS)
OPLP .... Office of Program and Legislative Planning (SAUS)
OPLP .... Pickle Pat Public Library, Pickle Lake, Ontario [*Library symbol*] [*National Library of Canada*] (NLC)
OPLR .... Lahore [*Pakistan*] [*ICAO location identifier*] (ICLI)
OPLR .... Outpost Line of Resistance
OPLSS....... Optimized Portable Life-Support System [*NASA*]
OPLX .... Oregon Pacific Line [*Federal Railroad Administration identification code*]
OPM .... Free Papua Movement [*Government term*] (GA)
OPM .... Object Properties Manager
OPM .... Occult Primary Malignancy [*Oncology*]
OPM .... Office of Personnel Management [*Supersedes Civil Service Commission*]
OPM .... Office of Planning and Management [*DoD*]
OPM .... Office of Policy and Management [*Environmental Protection Agency*] (GFGA)
OPM .... Office of Procurement and Materiel [*Army*]
OPM .... Office of Production Management [*Superseded by WPB, 1942*]
OPM .... Office of Program Management [*Environmental Protection Agency*] (GFGA)
OPM .... Office of Program Management [*Unemployment Insurance Service*] [*Department of Labor*]
OPM .... Office of the Program Manager (SAUS)
OPM .... Office, Personnel Manager [*Army*] (MUGU)
OPM .... Open Pit Mining (SAUS)
OPM .... Operating Plane Months [*Navy*] (NG)
OPM .... Operating Procedure for Ministers
OPM .... Operations Message (SSD)
OPM .... Operations per Minute [*Performance measure*]
OPM .... Operator Master (SAUS)
OPM .... Operator Programming Method [*Computer science*]
OPM .... Ophthalmodynamometry [*Ophthalmology*]
OPM .... Ophthalmoplegic Migraine [*Medicine*] (DB)
OPM .... Optically Projected Map
OPM .... Optical Power Meter
OPM .... Options Pricing Model
OPM .... Orbits per Minute (SAUS)
OPM .... Orders per Thousand
OPM .... Ordnance Proof Manual (SAA)
OPM .... Organisasi Papua Merdeka [*Papua Independent Organization*] [*Indonesia*] (PD)
OPM .... Organisation Papua Merduka (SAUS)
OPM .... Organizacion Politico-Militar [*Politico-Military Organization*] [*Paraguay*] (PD)
OPM .... Organization & Procedures Manual (SAUS)
OPM .... Original Program Model (SAUS)
OPM .... Orthophoto Map (SAUS)
OPM .... Oscillating Pressure Method
OPM .... Other People's Money
OPM .... Outer Planet Mission
OPM .... Out-Patient Medical [*Medicine*] (BCRP)
OPM .... Output and Performance Measures (HEAS)
OPM .... Output per Man (ODBW)
OPM .... Output Position Map [*Computer science*] (OA)
OPM .... Output Processor Module (MCD)
OPM .... Outside Plant Module (SAUS)
OPM .... Owner President Management Program (DD)
OPM .... Oxford Policy Management [*British*]
OPM .... Perth Museum, Ontario [*Library symbol*] [*National Library of Canada*] (NLC)
OPMA .... Mangla [*Pakistan*] [*ICAO location identifier*] (ICLI)
OPMA .... Office Products Manufacturers Association (EA)
OPMA .... Open Pit Mining Association (EA)
OPMA .... Ophthalmic Prescription Manufacturers Association [*British*] (DBA)
OPMA .... Overseas Press and Media Association [*British*] (EAIO)
OPMAC ..... Operations for Military Assistance to the Community (PDAA)
OPMACC .... Operation Military Aid to the Civil Community [*British military*] (DMA)
OPMARV.... Operational Maneuvering Reentry Vehicle (MCD)
OPMC .... Office of Professional Medical Conduct (SAUS)
OPMC .... One Player Median Competitive (PDAA)
OPMC .... OptimumCare Corp. [*NASDAQ symbol*] (QUAN)
OPMCS...... Otto Pre-Marital Counseling Schedules [*Psychology*]
OPMD .... Officer Personnel Management Directorate [*Military*]
OPME........ Office of Personnel Management Evaluation (DNAB)
OPME........ Office of Program Management and Evaluation [*Environmental Protection Agency*] (GFGA)
OPMEM ..... Operand Memory (SAUS)
OPMET ...... Operational Meteorological Information [*ICAO*] (FAAC)
OPMF........ Muzaffarabad [*Pakistan*] [*ICAO location identifier*] (ICLI)
OPMG .... Office of the Provost Marshal General [*Army*]
OpMG .... Oppenheimer Multi-Government Trust [*Associated Press*] (SAG)
OPMH .... Occupations for Patients in Mental Hospitals [*British*]
OPMI .... Mianwali [*Pakistan*] [*ICAO location identifier*] (ICLI)
OPMI .... Open Perfusion Micro-Incubator
OPMI .... Operation Microscope [*Surgery*]
Op Minn Att'y Gen... Opinions of the Attorney General of Minnesota [*A publication*] (DLA)
OPMIS....... Optical Propulsion Management Interface System
OPMJ........ Moenjodaro [*Pakistan*] [*ICAO location identifier*] (ICLI)
OPMK .... Mir Pur Khas [*Pakistan*] [*ICAO location identifier*] (ICLI)
OPMK .... Optimark Data Systems, Inc. [*NASDAQ symbol*] (QUAN)
OPMN .... Miranshah [*Pakistan*] [*ICAO location identifier*] (ICLI)
OPMN .... Port McNicoll Public Library, Ontario [*Library symbol*] [*National Library of Canada*] (NLC)
OPMO .... Office of Program Management Operations [*Environmental Protection Agency*] (GFGA)
OPMOPLAN... Operation Missouri Plan [*Program for five-day state funeral planned several years in advance for ex-President Harry Truman*] [*Army*]
OPMOR ..... Operations Materiel and Organization Review (SAUS)
OPMPR...... Office of Personnel Management Procurement Regulations [*A publication*] (AAGC)
OP MP SW/TR... Operation of a Moped on a Sidewalk or Bicycle Trail [*Conviction term used in state of Oregon*] (MVRD)
OPMR .... Karachi/Masroor [*Pakistan*] [*ICAO location identifier*] (ICLI)
OPMR .... Optimal Robotics Corp. [*NASDAQ symbol*] (SAG)
OPMS .... Miranshah [*Pakistan*] [*ICAO location identifier*] (ICLI)
OPMS .... Office of Physical Measurement Services [*Gaithersburg, MD*] [*National Institute of Standards and Technology*] (GRD)
OPMS .... Office of Program Management and Support [*Environmental Protection Agency*] (GFGA)
OPMS .... Officer Personnel Management System [*Army*]
OPMS .... On-the-machine Probe Measuring System (SAUS)
OPMS .... Outplant Procurement Manufacturing Specification (SAA)
OPM-SANG... Office of the Program Manager, Saudi Arabian National Guard
OPMSO...... Outside Production Material Sales Order
OPMT........ Multan [*Pakistan*] [*ICAO location identifier*] (ICLI)
OPMT........ Office of Program Management and Technology (SAUS)
OP MV BYC TR... Operation of a Motor Vehicle on a Bicycle Trail [*Conviction term used in state of Oregon*] (MVRD)
OPMW....... Mianwali [*Pakistan*] [*ICAO location identifier*] (ICLI)
OPMX .... Optimax Industries, Inc. [*NASDAQ symbol*] (SAG)
OPMX .... Otimax Industries [*NASDAQ symbol*] (TTSB)
OPMXZ...... Optimax Inds Wrrt'BB' [*NQS*] (TTSB)
OPN.......... Norwell District Secondary School, Palmerston, Ontario [*Library symbol*] [*National Library of Canada*] (NLC)
OPN.......... Office of the Chief of Naval Operations
OPN.......... Office Productivity Network [*Computer science*]
OPN.......... Oil Pan
OPN.......... One-Port Network (SAUS)
OPN.......... Open (AAG)
opn .... Open
OPN.......... Operation
OPN.......... Opercular Nerve
OPN.......... Ophthalmic Nurse (DAVI)
OPN.......... Opinion (ROG)
OPN.......... Optimised-Profile Navigation (SAUS)
OPN.......... Option (ADA)
OPN.......... Ora pro Nobis [*Pray for Us*] [*Latin*]
OPN.......... Organ Pipe National Monument (SAUS)
OPN.......... Osteopontin (DMAA)
OPN.......... Other Procurement, Navy
OPNAV ...... Chief of Naval Operations (AAGC)
OPNAV ...... Office of the Chief of Naval Operations
OPNAVCOMMO... Office of the Chief of Naval Operations, Communications Office (DNAB)
OPNAVINST... Office of the Chief of Naval Operations Instruction
OPNAVINST... OPNAV Instruction (SAUS)
OPNAVO..... Office of the Chief of Naval Operations
OPNAVSUPPACT... Office of the Chief of Naval Operations, Support Activity (DNAB)
OPNAVSUPPACTDET... Office of the Chief of Naval Operations, Support Activity Detachment (DNAB)

OPNAVSUPPACT FIG... Office of the Chief of Naval Operations, Support Activity Flight Information Group (DNAB)
OPNAVSUPPACT TCC... Office of the Chief of Naval Operations, Support Activity Telecommunications Center (DNAB)
OPNAVSUPPACT WWMCCS DP... Office of the Chief of Naval Operations, Support Activity, Worldwide Military Command Control System, Data Processing (DNAB)
OPNAVSUPPACT WWMCCS EMPSKED... Office of the Chief of Naval Operations, Support Activity, Worldwide Military Command Control System, Employment Schedule (DNAB)
OPNAVSUPPACT WWMCCS FORSTAT... Office of the Chief of Naval Operations, Support Activity, Worldwide Military Command Control System, Force Status (DNAB)
OPNAVSUPPACT WWMCCS MOVREP... Office of the Chief of Naval Operations, Support Activity, Worldwide Military Command Control System, Movement Reports (DNAB)
OPNAVTCC... Ofice of the Chief of Naval Operations, Telecommunications Center (DNAB)
OP N BRK LT... Operation without Required Brake Lights [*Conviction term used in state of Oregon*] (MVRD)
OPN CEN.... Operation Center (SAUS)
OP N CL LT... Operation without Required Clearance Lighting [*Conviction term used in state of Oregon*] (MVRD)
Op N Cplt... Operation Not Complete (SAUS)
OPND........ Operand (ECII)
Op ND Att'y Gen... Opinions of the Attorney General of North Dakota [*A publication*] (DLA)
OpnEnv...... Open Environment Corp. [*Associated Press*] (SAG)
OPNET....... Operator's Training New Equipment Training [*Army*] (INF)
OPNET....... WWMCCS Operational Network (SAUS)
Op Nev Att'y Gen... Official Opinions of the Attorney General of Nevada [*A publication*] (DLA)
OP N EXH SYS... Operation without Proper Exhaust System [*Conviction term used in state of Oregon*] (MVRD)
OPNG........ Opening (AAG)
OPNH........ Nawabshah [*Pakistan*] [*ICAO location identifier*] (ICLI)
OP N HBM IND... Operation without Required High Beam Indicators [*Conviction term used in state of Oregon*] (MVRD)
OpnhCa..... Oppenheimer Capital Ltd. [*Associated Press*] (SAG)
OP N HD LT... Operation without Required Headlights [*Conviction term used in state of Oregon*] (MVRD)
OP N ID LT... Operating without Front and Rear Identification Lights [*Conviction term used in state of Oregon*] (MVRD)
OPNJC....... Ora pro Nobis Jesu Christe [*Pray for Us, Jesus Christ*] [*Motto of Ernst, Duke of Bavaria (1554-1612)*] [*Latin*]
OPNK........ Naushki [*Pakistan*] [*ICAO location identifier*] (ICLI)
opnl.......... Operational (ELAL)
OPNL........ Operational
OPNL........ Osaka Prefectural Nakanoshima Library (SAUS)
OPNL RPTS... Operational Reports (SAUS)
OPNML...... Operations Normal (FAAC)
OPNMR..... Optically Pumped Nuclear Magnetic Resonance [*Physics*]
Op no........ Opus number (SAUS)
OPNO........ Originating Public Network Operator (SAUS)
OPNOTE..... Operational Note (MCD)
OPNR........ Open Road Campers [*NCIC trailer make code*]
OPNS........ Operational Phase [*NASA*] (NAKS)
OPNS........ Operations (NASA)
OPNSEVAL & TNGSq... Operational Evaluation and Training Squadron [*Air Force*]
OP Nurse... Ophthalmic Nurse (SAUS)
opnwndo.... Open Window
Op NY Atty Gen... Opinions of the Attorneys-General of New York [*A publication*] (DLA)
OPo.......... Megis Local School District Public Library, Pomeroy, OH [*Library symbol*] [*Library of Congress*] (LCLS)
OPO.......... Office of Personnel Operations [*Army*]
OPO.......... Officer of the Post Office [*British*]
OPO.......... Oil Pressure Out
OPO.......... One-Person Operation [*Slang*] [*Business term*] (DCTA)
OPO.......... One Point Operation (VLIE)
OPO.......... One Price Only (WDAA)
OPO.......... Online Process Optimization [*Computer science*] (VLIE)
OPO.......... Operational Performance Objectives (SAUS)
OPO.......... Oporto [*Portugal*] [*Airport symbol*] (OAG)
OPO.......... Optical Parametric Oscillator [*Tunable LASER device*]
OPO.......... Orbiter Project Office [*NASA*] (MCD)
OPO.......... Orbiting Planetary Observatory
OPO.......... Ordnance Personnel Office [*Army*]
OPO.......... Organ Procurement Organization [*Generic term*] [*Medicine*]
OPO.......... Oropharyngeal Candidiasis [*Medicine*] (MELL)
OPO.......... Other Programmed Operations (IAA)
OPO.......... Outside Production Order (SAA)
OPO.......... Outside Purchase Order (SAA)
OPO.......... Ovamboland Peoples Organization (SAUS)
OPO.......... Overseas Press Club (NADA)
OPOA........ Office Products of America, Inc. (SAUS)
OPOC........ On-Board Pilot-Observer Camera (SAA)
OPOCX...... Oppenheimer Discovery [*Mutual fund ticker symbol*] (SG)
OPOEB...... Port Elgin Branch, Bruce County Public Library, Ontario [*Library symbol*] [*National Library of Canada*] (NLC)
Op Off Legal Counsel... Opinions of the Office of Legal Counsel [*A publication*] (DLA)
Op Offr...... Operations Officer (SAUS)
Op Ohio Att'y Gen... Opinions of the Attorney General of Ohio [*A publication*] (DLA)
OPOK........ Okara [*Pakistan*] [*ICAO location identifier*] (ICLI)
Op Okla Att'y Gen... Opinions of the Attorney General of Oklahoma [*A publication*] (DLA)
OPOL........ Offshore Pollution Liability Association Ltd. (EA)
O Pol........ Old Polish (SAUS)
OPOL........ Optimization-Oriented Language
OPOL Agreement... Offshore Pollution Liability Agreement (SAUS)
OPOMP...... Overall Planning and Optimization and Machining Process (MHDI)
OPON........ Opinion (ROG)
OPOP........ Operation (SAUS)
op/ops....... Operational/Operations (MILB)
OPOR........ Office of Public Opinion Research (SAUS)
OPOR........ Ormara [*Pakistan*] [*ICAO location identifier*] (ICLI)
Op Or Att'y Gen... Opinions of the Attorney General of Oregon [*A publication*] (DLA)
OPORC...... Port Carling Public Library, Ontario [*Library symbol*] [*National Library of Canada*] (BIB)
OPORD...... Operations Order [*Army*]
OPORPL..... Opposed Replenishment (SAUS)
OPORPL..... Oppose Replenishment [*Navy*] (NVT)
O Port....... Old Portuguese (SAUS)
OPOS........ Optical Property of Orbiting Satellite [*NASA*] (PDAA)
OPOS........ Outside Production Operation Sheet (MCD)
O-POS....... Oxygen-Dope Polysilicon (PDAA)
OPOSENT... Opposed Entry (SAUS)
OPOSENT... Oppose Entry [*Navy*] (NVT)
OPOS-Film... Oxygen-doped Polysilicon Film (SAUS)
OPosm...... Portsmouth Public Library, Portsmouth, OH [*Library symbol*] [*Library of Congress*] (LCLS)
OPosmG.... Goodyear Atomic Corp., Portsmouth, OH [*Library symbol*] [*Library of Congress*] (LCLS)
OPosmS..... Shawnee State College, Portsmouth, OH [*Library symbol*] [*Library of Congress*] (LCLS)
OPosmU.... Ohio University, Portsmouth Branch Campus, Portsmouth, OH [*Library symbol*] [*Library of Congress*] [*Obsolete*] (LCLS)
OPOSORT... Oppose Sortie [*Navy*] (NVT)
OPOSS...... Office of Personnel Operations Standards and Systems Office [*Army*]
OPOSSMS... Options to Purchase or Sell Specific Mortgage-Backed Securities [*Merrill Lynch & Co.*] [*Finance*]
OPOSTOR... Oppose Sortie [*Navy*] (ANA)
OPOU........ Oldenburg-Portligiesische Dampfschiffs-Reederei [*Intermodal shipping container symbol*] (TVRC)
OPOV........ Oxidizer Preburner Oxidizer Valve (MCD)
OPOVA...... Oxidizer Preburner Oxidizer Valve Actuator (SAUS)
OPowS...... Scioto Village High School, Powell, OH [*Library symbol*] [*Library of Congress*] (LCLS)
OPP.......... Occiput Posterior Position (DAVI)
OPP.......... Octal Print Punch [*Computer science*]
OPP.......... Office of Pesticide Programs [*Environmental Protection Agency*]
OPP.......... Office of Plans and Policy (LAIN)
OPP.......... Office of Polar Programs [*Later, Division of Polar Programs*] [*National Science Foundation*]
OPP.......... Office of Policy and Planning [*Office of Policy, Evaluation, and Research*] [*Department of Labor*]
OPP.......... Office of Productivity Programs [*Office of Personnel Management*] (GRD)
OPP.......... Office of Program Planning (AAGC)
OPP.......... Office of Public Programs [*National Archives*] (BARN)
OPP.......... Office of Public Prosecutions [*Northern Territory, Australia*]
OPP.......... Off-Load Preparation Party [*Navy*] (ANA)
OPP.......... Off-Peak Power (SAUS)
OPP.......... Oncovin [*Vincristine*], Procarbazine, Prednisone [*Antineoplastic drug regimen*]
OPP.......... Ontario Provincial Police [*UTLAS symbol*]
OPP.......... Open Pore (SAUS)
OPP.......... Open-Pore Polyurethan [*Plastic*]
OPP.......... Operator Preparation Program (IAA)
OPP.......... Opponent
OPP.......... Opportunity (ADA)
opp.......... Opposed (DAVI)
OPP.......... Opposed To
OPP.......... Opposing (GOBB)
OPP.......... Opposite (AAG)
opp.......... Opposite (WDMC)
OPP.......... Oppure [*Otherwise*] [*Music*]
OPP.......... Optical Precipitate Profiler (SAUS)
OPP.......... Optical Printer Projector (VLIE)
OPP.......... Order Processing Pipeline (AGLO)
OPP.......... Organizational Project Plan [*Civil Defense*]
OPP.......... Organization and Personnel Plan [*Army*]
OPP.......... [*The*] Organization of Plastics Processors
OPP.......... Organ of People's Power (Cuba) [*Political party*] (PSAP)
OPP.......... Organophosphorous Poisoning [*Medicine*] (MELL)
OPP.......... Oriented Polypropylene [*Plastics technology*]
OPP.......... Ortho-Phenylphenol [*Disinfectant*]
OPP.......... Osmotic Pressure of Plasma [*Medicine*] (EDAA)
OPP.......... Otago Press and Produce (SAUS)
OPP.......... Other Physical Principles [*Defense system*]
OPP.......... Other Programme Participation (SAUS)
OPP.......... Outer Planet Project
opp.......... Out of Print at Present [*Publishing*] (WDMC)
OPP.......... Out of Print at Present [*Publishing*]
OPP.......... Oxidative Pentose Phosphate (PDAA)
OPP.......... Oxygen Partial Pressure

OPPA .... Octylphenyl Phosphoric Acid (EDCT)
OPPA .... Octylpyrophosphoric Acid [*Organic chemistry*]
OPPA .... Office of Publications and Public Affairs [*National Endowment for the Humanities*] (BARN)
OPPA .... Operation Plan Package Appraisal (AFM)
Op PA Att'y Gen... Opinions of the Attorney General of Pennsylvania [*A publication*] (DLA)
OPPAR ...... Orbiter Project Parts Authorization Request [*NASA*] (NASA)
OPPAS....... OPP Administrative Support Systems (SAUS)
OPPAX....... Oppenheimer Global Cl.A [*Mutual fund ticker symbol*] (SG)
OPPC .... Optima Petroleum Corp. [*NASDAQ symbol*] (SAG)
OPPC .... Outpatient Professional Psychiatric Clinic [*Health insurance*] (GHCT)
OPPC .... Parachinar [*Pakistan*] [*ICAO location identifier*] (ICLI)
OPPCE....... Opposite Commutator End (IEEE)
OPPCF....... Optima Petroleum [*NASDAQ symbol*] (TTSB)
OPPD .... Omaha Public Power District
OPPE .... Office of Plans and Program Evaluation (SAA)
OPPE .... Office of Policy, Planning, and Evaluation [*Environmental Protection Agency*] (GFGA)
OPPE .... Office of Programming, Planning and Evaluation (SAUS)
OPPE .... Office of Program Planning and Evaluation [*National Institutes of Health*]
OPPE .... Operational Propulsion Plant Examination [*Navy*] (NVT)
OPPE .... Operations Planning Project Engineer [*Deep Space Instrumentation Facility, NASA*]
OPPE .... Organic and Polymer Processing Experiment (SAUS)
OPPEX....... Oppenheimer Equity Inc. Cl.A [*Mutual fund ticker symbol*] (SG)
OPPF .... Operation of Property and Pressurization Facility (SAUS)
OPP Film ... Orientated Polypropylen Film (SAUS)
OPPG .... Oculopneumoplethysmography (DAVI)
OPPG .... Office of Propulsion and Power Generation (SAA)
OPPG .... Panjgur [*Pakistan*] [*ICAO location identifier*] (ICLI)
OPP HND ... Opposite Hand (MSA)
OPPHX ...... Oppenheimer High Yield Cl.A [*Mutual fund ticker symbol*] (SG)
OPPI .... Office of Policy, Planning, and Information [*Environmental Protection Agency*] (GFGA)
OPPI .... Organization of Pharmaceutical Producers of India (SAUS)
OPPI .... Pasni [*Pakistan*] [*ICAO location identifier*] (ICLI)
oppies....... Older Professional Parents (ADWA)
Opp Int L... Oppenheim's International Law [*A publication*] (DLA)
OPPL .... Orbiter Project Parts List [*NASA*] (NASA)
OPPLAN..... Operations Plan (KSC)
OPPM .... Office of Policy and Program Management [*Environmental Protection Agency*] (GFGA)
OPPM .... Outside Principal Period of Maintenance (SAUS)
OppMS ...... Oppenheimer Multi-Sector Income Trust [*Associated Press*] (SAG)
OPPMSA .... Ontario Pulp and Paper Makers Safety Association (SAUS)
OPPN .... Pishin [*Pakistan*] [*ICAO location identifier*] (ICLI)
OPPOR ...... Opportunity (AABC)
OPPORT..... Opportunity (ADA)
OPPOSIT... Optimization of a Production Process by an Ordered Simulation and Iteration Technique (IEEE)
OPPOSSMS... Options to Purchase or Sell Specified Mortgage-Backed Securities (EBF)
OPPP .... Office of Program Policy and Planning [*Social Security Administration*] (OICC)
OPPP .... Order Point and Peak Point (VLIE)
OPPP .... Port Perry High School, Ontario [*Library symbol*] [*National Library of Canada*] (NLC)
OPP PE...... Opposite Pulley End (SAUS)
OPPR .... Office of Priority Populations Research [*Agency for Healthcare Research and Quality*] (RCD)
OPPR .... Offset Printing Press
OPPR .... Oil Pollution Preparedness and Response (SAUS)
OPPR .... Operating Program
OPPRC ...... International Convention on Oil Pollution, Preparedness, Response and Cooperation (SAUS)
OPPROC .... Operation Procedures (TIMI)
O-P Process... Oppenheimer-Phillips Process (SAUS)
OPPS .... Office of Planning and Program Services [*Office of Field Operations*] [*Department of Labor*]
OPPS .... Overpressurization Protection Switch (IEEE)
OPPS .... Overpressurization Protection System (IEEE)
OPPS .... Oxygen Partial Pressure Sensor
OPPS .... Peshawar [*Pakistan*] [*ICAO location identifier*] (ICLI)
OPPSD ...... Organic Peroxide Producers Safety Division (SAUS)
OPPSL....... Office of Private and Public Sector Liaison [*Environmental Protection Agency*] (GFGA)
OPPSX ...... Oppenheimer Growth Cl.A [*Mutual fund ticker symbol*] (SG)
OPPT .... Office of Pollution Prevention and Toxics [*Environmental Protection Agency*] (AEPA)
OPPTS....... EPA Office of Prevention, Pesticides and Toxic Substances (SAUS)
OPPTS....... Office of Prevention, Pesticides, and Toxic Substances [*Environmental Protection Agency*] (AEPA)
OPPWFA .... Operative Plasteres amd Plaster Workers' Federation of Australia
OPPY .... Opportunity (ROG)
OPPZ .... Osage Power Plant [*Federal Railroad Administration identification code*]
OPQ.......... Occupational Personality Questionnaires [*Employment test*]
OPQ.......... Occupying Public Quarters [*Military*]
OPQ.......... Opaque (SAUS)
OPQC .... Office Professional Quality Council (SAUS)
OPQS .... Qasim [*Pakistan*] [*ICAO location identifier*] (ICLI)
OPQT .... Quetta/Samungli [*Pakistan*] [*ICAO location identifier*] (ICLI)
OPR.......... Lifts Operating [*Skiing*]
OPR.......... Office of Planning and Research [*International Trade Administration*] (GRD)
OPR.......... Office of Population Research (SAUS)
OPR.......... Office of Pre-Claims Requirements [*Social Security Administration*]
OPR.......... Office of Primary Responsibility [*Air Force*]
OPR.......... Office of Private Resources [*Department of State*]
OPR.......... Office of Professional Responsibility [*Department of Justice*]
OPR.......... Office of Public Relations [*Later, PUBINFO*] [*Navy*]
OPR.......... Offsite Procurement Request (IEEE)
OPR.......... Oil Production Rate (SAUS)
OPR.......... Old Prussian [*Language, etc.*]
OPR.......... Olympic Practice Regatta [*Nautical term*] (NTA)
OPR.......... Ontario Practice Reports [*A publication*] (DLA)
OPR.......... Opener (MSA)
OPR.......... Open Pool Reactor [*Nuclear energy*] (NRCH)
OPR.......... Operand [*Computer science*]
OPR.......... Operate [*or Operator*] (AAG)
OPR.......... Operated (SAUS)
OPR.......... Operating (SAUS)
OPR.......... Operational Preference (DA)
OPR.......... Operational Project Requirements (AABC)
OPR.......... Operation Planning Report (SAUS)
OPR.......... Operations Planning Review (NASA)
OPR.......... Operations Procedure (MUGU)
OPR.......... Operative (SAUS)
OPR.......... Operator
OPR.......... Operator Request (SAUS)
OPR.......... OP Resources Ltd. [*Vancouver Stock Exchange symbol*]
OPR.......... Optical Page Reader [*Computer science*]
OPR.......... Optical Page Reading (SAUS)
OPR.......... Optical Pattern Recognition
OPR.......... Optimized Palette Reduction [*Algorithm*] [*Computer Presentations, Inc.*] (PCM)
OPR.......... Optional Parts Request (SAA)
OPR.......... Orbit/Payload Recorder [*NASA*] (MCD)
OPR.......... Order Point Recognition (ADA)
OPR.......... Ordnance Property Regulations (SAUS)
OPR.......... Oregon Pacific Railroad [*Federal Railroad Administration identification code*]
OPR.......... Ostprignitz-Ruppin [*German license plate city code*]
OPR.......... Outpatient Rate [*Medicine*] (AFM)
OPR.......... Outstanding Performance Rating [*Military*] (RDA)
OPR.......... Overall Pressure Ratio
OPR.......... Over-Pressure Relief [*Automotive emissions*]
OPR.......... Oxygen Pressure Regulator (MCD)
OPR.......... Oxygen Production Rate [*Biochemistry*]
OPR.......... Port Rowan Public Library, Ontario [*Library symbol*] [*National Library of Canada*] (NLC)
OPR.......... Santander Overseas Bank [*NYSE symbol*] (SPSG)
OPRA........ Observation Post Royal Artillery [*British military*] (DMA)
OPRA........ Office Products Representatives Association (SAUS)
OPRA........ Ohio Penal Racing Association (EA)
OPRA........ Options Price Reporting Authority [*Information service or system*] (IID)
OPRAD ...... Operations Research and Development Management (PDAA)
OPraem ..... Canons Regular of Premontre (TOCD)
opraem..... Canons Regular of Premontre, Premonstratensians, Norbetines (TOCD)
OPraem ..... Ordo Canonicorum Regularium Praemonstatenstium [*Order of the Canons Regular of Premontre*] [*Norbertines*] [*Roman Catholic men's religious order*]
OPRAF ...... Office of Passenger Rail Franchising [*British*] (ECON)
OPRC........ International Convention for Oil Pollution Preparedness, Response and Cooperation (SAUS)
OPRC .... Oil Pollution Preparedness, Response and Co-operation (SAUS)
OPRC........ Oil Pollution Preparedness, Response and Cooperation Convention (SAUS)
OPRD........ Office of Production Research and Development
OPRD........ Organic Process Research & Development [*A publication*]
OPRDY ...... Operationally Ready [*Army*] (AABC)
OPRE........ Prescott Public Library, Ontario [*Library symbol*] [*National Library of Canada*] (NLC)
OPRED ...... Operations Reduction [*Government term*]
OPREDS..... Operational Performance Recording and Evaluation Data System [*Military*] (CAAL)
OPREG ...... Operation Register (IAA)
OPrem....... Ordre de Premontre [*Order of the Canons Regular of Premontre*] [*Rome, Italy*] (EAIO)
OPREP ...... Operational Report (POLM)
OPREP ...... Operational Reporting [*Army*]
OPREPS..... Operational Reporting System [*Military*]
OPREQ ...... Operation Request [*Computer science*] (MHDI)
OPRES ...... Operations Research (ACAE)
OPREX ...... Operational Exercise [*NATO*] (NATG)
OPRFLT ..... Operator Fault (AAG)
oprg .... Operating (STED)
OPRG........ Oxygenated Fuels Program Reformulated Gasoline
OPRI......... Office de la Propriete Industrielle [*Department of Industrial Property*] [*Ministry of Economic Affairs*] (IID)
OPRI......... Office de Protection contre les Rayonnements Ionisants [*France*]
OPRIC....... Operator in Charge (IAA)
Opr i/C ...... Operator-in-Charge (SAUS)
OPRIS .... Ohio Project for Research in Information Service (NITA)
OPRK........ Opiate Receptor Kappa (DMAA)
OPRK........ Rahimyarkhan [*Pakistan*] [*ICAO location identifier*] (ICLI)

OPRL........ Ovine Prolactin [*Endocrinology*]
OPRL........ Portland Branch, Rideau Lakes Union Library, Ontario [*Library symbol*] [*National Library of Canada*] (BIB)
OPRLFT..... Operator Fault [*Computer science*] (MHDI)
OPRN........ Islamabad/Chaklala [*Pakistan*] [*ICAO location identifier*] (ICLI)
OPRN........ Operation
Opr N Compl... Operation Not Complete (SAUS)
OPRND...... Operand (VLIE)
OPRNL...... Operational (AAG)
OPRNTL..... Operational
OPRO........ Operations Order (SAUS)
OPRO........ Output Processing (SAUS)
Opro........ Oxyprolin (SAUS)
OpRobt...... Optimal Robotics Corp. [*Associated Press*] (SAG)
OPROM..... Optical Programmable Read-Only Memory [*Disk*] (BYTE)
OProv........ Old Provencal [*Language*] (BARN)
OPRPrC..... Santander Overseas Bk'C'Pfd [*NYSE symbol*] (TTSB)
OPRPrD..... Santander Overseas Bk 'D'Pfd [*NYSE symbol*] (TTSB)
OPRQ........ Shorekote/Rafiqui [*Pakistan*] [*ICAO location identifier*] (ICLI)
OPRR........ Office for Protection from Research Risks [*Bethesda, MD*] [*National Institutes of Health*] (GRD)
OPRR........ Outside Production Requirement Record (SAA)
OPRRA...... Ohio Petroleum Retailers & Repair Association PAC [*Gahanna, OH*] (PACS)
OPRRB...... Officer Personnel Record Review Board [*Air Force*] (AFM)
OPRRE...... Office of Public Roads and Rural Engineering [*Later, Bureau of Public Roads*]
OPRS........ Office of Professional Research Services [*American Occupational Therapy Association*]
OPRS........ Oil Pressure
OPRS........ Operational Planning and Review Systems [*Employment and Training Administration*] [*Department of Labor*]
OPRS........ Risalpur [*Pakistan*] [*ICAO location identifier*] (ICLI)
OpRsch...... Operations Research (SAUS)
OPRT........ Operator Table
OPRT........ Orotate Phosphoribosyltransferase (STED)
OPRT........ Rawalakot [*Pakistan*] [*ICAO location identifier*] (ICLI)
OPRTNTY... Opportunity
OPRU........ Oil Pollution Research Unit [*British*] (ARC)
OPruss...... Old Prussian [*Language*] (BARN)
OPRV........ Oxygen Pressure Relief Valve (MCD)
OPS.......... Oblique Photo Sketcher
OPS.......... Obscene Publications Squad [*British*] (DI)
OPS.......... Obstacle Planner Software (RDA)
OPS.......... Occupational Preparation Scheme (AIE)
OPS.......... Ocean Patrol Ship (SAUS)
OPS.......... Ocean Platform Station [*National Data Buoy Office*] (NOAA)
OPS.......... Office of Pipeline Safety [*Department of Transportation*]
OPS.......... Office of Population Surveys [*British*]
OPS.......... Office of Price Stabilization [*Terminated, 1953*]
OPS.......... Office of Products Safety [*FDA*]
OPS.......... Office of Product Standards [*Department of Commerce*] (WDAA)
OPS.......... Office of Programmatic Systems [*Social Security Administration*]
OPS.......... Office of Program Services [*US Employment Service*] [*Department of Labor*]
OPS.......... Office of Public Service [*British*] (WA)
OPS.......... Office of Publishing Services (AAGC)
OPS.......... Office Procedure Specification (VLIE)
OPS.......... Official Phone Station [*Amateur radio*]
OPS.......... Official Production System [*Production-system language*]
OPS.......... Official Public Service Reports [*New York*] [*A publication*] (DLA)
OPS.......... Off-Premise Station [*Telecommunications*] (TEL)
OPS.......... Offshore Power Systems, Inc. (SAUS)
OPS.......... Oil Pressure Switch
OPS.......... Oil Production Stock
OPS.......... Omnidirectional Point Source (PDAA)
OPS.......... On-Line Process Synthesis [*Computer science*]
OPS.......... On-line Process Synthesizer (SAUS)
OPS.......... Online Programming and Simulation (SAUS)
OPS.......... On-Site Inspection Agency [*DoD*] [*ICAO designator*] (FAAC)
OPS.......... Open Pan Sulphitation [*Sugar production*]
OPS.......... Open Price System (SAUS)
OPS.......... Open Profiling Standard [*Internet privacy standard*] (NETL)
OPS.......... Operating hours (SAUS)
OPS.......... Operating Plans Summary (VLIE)
OPS.......... Operating System (SAUS)
OPS.......... Operational Paging System [*NASA*] (KSC)
OPS.......... Operational Performance Standard [*Aviation*] (DA)
OPS.......... Operational Power Supply
OPS.......... Operational Protection System [*Nuclear energy*] (NRCH)
OPS.......... Operational Sequence [*NASA*] (NAKS)
OPS.......... Operational Station (SAA)
OPS.......... Operational Support (MCD)
OPS.......... Operation and Support (MCD)
ops.......... Operations (ELAL)
OPS.......... Operations (MCD)
OPS.......... Operations Division [*NATO*] (NATG)
OPS.......... Operations Group (SAUS)
OPS.......... Operations Officer (SAUS)
OPS.......... Operations per Second (IAA)
ops.......... Operations per Second (VLIE)
OPS.......... Operations Planning System (VLIE)
OPS.......... Operations Processing System (SAUS)
OPS.......... Operations Sequence [*NASA*] (MCD)
OPS.......... Operations Squadron
OPS.......... Operations Staff [*Military*] [*British*]
OPS.......... Operator's Subsystem [*Telecommunications*] (TEL)
OPS.......... Operator System Program [*Manufacturing engineering*] [*Computer science*]
OPS.......... Ophthalmic Photographers' Society (EA)
Ops.......... Opinions [*Legal term*] (DLA)
OPS.......... Opportunities [*Telegraphy*] (PCTE)
OPS.......... Opposite Prompters' Side [*i.e., the left side*] [*Stage direction*] (ROG)
OPS.......... Opposite Surface [*Technical drawings*]
OPS.......... OPSEC [*Operations Security*] Professional Society (EA)
OPS.......... Optical Power Spectrum (PDAA)
OPS.......... Optical Processing System
OPS.......... Optical Propagation Study (SAUS)
OPS.......... Optical Proximity Connection (GART)
OPS.......... Optical Sensor (EOSA)
OPS.......... Oracle Parallel Server [*Computer science*]
OPS.......... Orbiter Project Schedules [*NASA*] (NASA)
OPS.......... Orbiting Primate Spacecraft (MCD)
OPS.......... Organisation Panamericaine de la Sante [*Pan American Health Organization*] (MSC)
OPS.......... Oriented Polystyrene [*Plastics technology*]
OPS.......... Ortho-Phosphoserine [*Biochemistry*]
O-Ps.......... Ortho-Positronium (SAUS)
OPS.......... Other Personal Services
OPS.......... Outlet Pipe Space (SAUS)
ops.......... Out of Print and Searching [*Publishing*] (WDMC)
OPS.......... Out of Print, Searching [*Publishing*]
OPS.......... Out of Production Spares (MCD)
OPS.......... Outpatient Section (DAVI)
OPS.......... Outpatient Service [*Medicine*]
OPS.......... Outpatient Supervision [*Medicine*] (DHP)
OPS.......... Outpatient Surgery [*Health insurance*] (GHCT)
OPS.......... Outside Production Service (SAA)
OPS.......... Overhead Positioning System [*AEC*]
OPS.......... Overpressure [*or Overpressurization*] Protection System [*Nuclear energy*] (NRCH)
OPS.......... Oxidized Porous Silicon [*Materials science*]
OPS.......... Oxidizer Particle Size
OPS.......... Oxygen Purge Subsystem (SAUS)
OPS.......... Oxygen Purge System [*or Subsystem*] [*NASA*]
OPS.......... Parry Sound Public Library, Ontario [*Library symbol*] [*National Library of Canada*] (NLC)
OPS.......... Phillips Petroleum Co., Research and Development Department, Bartlesville, OK [*OCLC symbol*] (OCLC)
OPS.......... P-Octylphenylsalicylat (SAUS)
OpS.......... Specialist in Optical Science (GAGS)
OPSA........ Algonquin Regional Library, Parry Sound, Ontario [*Library symbol*] [*Obsolete*] [*National Library of Canada*] (NLC)
OPSA........ Optimal Pneumatic Systems Analysis (PDAA)
OPSA........ Ovarian Papillary Serous Adenocarcinoma [*Medicine*] (DMAA)
Ops AAG POD... United States Post Office Department. Official Opinions of the Solicitor [*A publication*] (DLA)
OPSADT..... Optically Programmable Semi-Automatic Direct-current Tester (SAUS)
Ops AG...... Opinions of the Attorney General [*A publication*] (DLA)
OPSAM...... Optical Storage Access Method [*Computer science*] (PDAA)
OPSAN...... Operations Analysis System (SAUS)
Ops Analysis... Operations Analysis (SAUS)
OP(S)ARMYJAG... Opinion(s) of the Army Judge Advocate General
OPSAS...... Office of Program Support and Advanced Systems (SAA)
OPSATCOM... Optical Satellite Communications (MCD)
Ops Atts Gen... Opinions of the Attorneys-General of the United States (SAUS)
Ops Atty Gen... Opinions of the Attorney General [*A publication*] (DLA)
Ops Atty Gen Wisc... Wisconsin Attorney General Reports [*A publication*] (DLA)
OPSB........ Orbiter Processing Support Building [*NASA*] (NASA)
OPSB........ Sibi [*Pakistan*] [*ICAO location identifier*] (ICLI)
OPSC........ Office of Planning Standards and Coordination [*HUD*]
OPSC........ Office of the Public Service Commissioner [*Australia*]
OPSC........ Optical Security Group [*NASDAQ symbol*] (TTSB)
OPSC........ Optical Security Group, Inc. [*NASDAQ symbol*] (SAG)
OPSC........ Osteopathic Physicians and Surgeons of California [*Medicine*] (EDAA)
OpScan...... Optical Scanning [*Medicine*] (STED)
OPSCAN..... Optical Scanning [*Computer science*] (WDAA)
OPSCO...... Operations Co-ordinator (SAUS)
OPSCOM.... Operational Secure Communications (SAUS)
OPSCOMM... Operational Communications (SAUS)
OPSCOMM... Operations Communications (MCD)
Ops Comms... Opinions of the Commissioners (SAUS)
OPSCON.... Operations Control [*NASA*] (KSC)
OPSCOP..... Operations Control [*Monitor*] Program
OPSCT....... Christie Township Public Library, Parry Sound, Ontario [*Library symbol*] [*National Library of Canada*] (NLC)
OPSD........ Office of Placement Support and Development [*US Employment Service*] [*Department of Labor*]
OPSD........ Openside
OPSD........ O Products and Services Division (SAUS)
OPSD........ Skardu [*Pakistan*] [*ICAO location identifier*] (ICLI)
OPSDEP..... Operations Deputy [*In JCS system*] [*Military*]
OPSDEPS... Operations Deputies (SAUS)
OPS DIV.... Operations Division (SAUS)
OPSE........ Optically Pumped Stimulated Emission (AAEL)
OPSEC....... Open Platform for Secure Enterprise Connectivity (SAUS)
OPSEC....... Operational Security

OPSEC....... Operations per Second (IAA)
OPSEC....... Operations security (SAUS)
OPSEC....... Operations Security Program (AAGC)
OPSEC....... OPSEC Professionals Society [*Later, OPS*] (EA)
Opsec/CI.... Operational Security/Counterintelligence (CARL)
OPSEC M&A... Operations Security Management and Analysis Section (SAUS)
OPSER...... Operator Service (CIST)
OPSET....... Operation Set (SAUS)
OPSET....... Optimal Set [*of Parameters*] [*Hydrology*]
OPSET....... Optional Set (SAUS)
OPSF....... Karachi/Shara-E-Faisal [*Pakistan*] [*ICAO location identifier*] (ICLI)
OP SF....... Office of Preparedness, General Services Administration [*later, Federal Preparedness Agency*], Special Facility
OPSF....... Orbital Propellant Storage Facility (MCD)
OPSG....... Operation Plans Steering Group (DOMA)
OPSHT...... Humphrey Township Public Library, Parry Sound, Ontario [*Library symbol*] [*National Library of Canada*] (NLC)
OPSI......... Optical Sensors, Inc. [*NASDAQ symbol*] (SAG)
OPSI......... Ordnance Publications for Supply Index [*Military*]
OPSI......... Overwhelming Post-Splenectomy Infection [*Medicine*]
OPSIM....... Officer Planning and Simulation Model (ACAE)
OPSIM....... Operational Simulator [*Coast Guard*]
OPSIMS..... Operational Simulation Subsystem (MCD)
OPSIX....... Oppenheimer Strategic Inc. Cl.A [*Mutual fund ticker symbol*] (SG)
Ops JAG.... Opinions of the Judge Advocate General, United States Army [*A publication*] (DLA)
OPSK........ Optimum Phase-Shif Keying (SAUS)
OPSK........ Sukkur [*Pakistan*] [*ICAO location identifier*] (ICLI)
OPSKIP...... Optional Skip (SAUS)
OPSKS...... Optimum Phase Shift Keyed Signals [*Telecommunications*]
OPSM....... Office of Public Sector Management [*Australian Capital Territory*]
OPSM....... Optical Prescriptions Spectacle Makers (SAUS)
OPSM....... Outside Plant Subscriber Module (SAUS)
OPSMB...... Organization of Progressive Socialists of the Mediterranean Basin
OPSMOD.... Operations Planning Module (SAUS)
OPSNET..... Operations System Network (SAUS)
OPSNOTE... Operations Note (SAUS)
OPSO........ Office of Pipeline Safety Operations [*Department of Transportation*] (DLA)
OPS O....... Operations Officer [*Navy*] (DOMA)
Op Sol Dept... Opinions of the Solicitor for the Department of Labor [*United States*] [*A publication*] (DLA)
Op Sol Dept Labor... Opinions of the Solicitor for the Department of Labor Dealing with Workmen's Compensation [*A publication*] (DLA)
Op Solic PO Dep't... Official Opinions of the Solicitor for the Post Office Department [*A publication*] (DLA)
Op Sol POD... Opinions of the Solicitor for the Post Office Department [*United States*] [*A publication*] (DLA)
OPSORD.... Operations Order (SAUS)
OPSP........ Office of Product Standards Policy [*Gaithersburg, MD*] [*Department of Commerce*] (GRD)
OPSP........ Online Privacy-Seal Program [*Computer science*] (GART)
OPSP........ Operations Panel [*ICAO*] (DA)
OPSP........ Shekhupura [*Pakistan*] [*ICAO location identifier*] (ICLI)
OPSPA....... Oleandomycin-Polymyxin-Sulphadiazine-Perfringens Agar (SAUS)
OPSR........ Office of Pipeline Safety Regulation [*Department of Transportation*] (OICC)
OPSR........ Office of Professional Standards Review [*Medicare and Medicaid*] [*HEW*]
OPSR........ Operations Supervisor [*NASA*] (MCD)
OPSR........ Ordnance Provision System Regulations (SAUS)
OPSR........ Sargodha [*Pakistan*] [*ICAO location identifier*] (ICLI)
OPSRDY.... Operations Readiness (MCD)
OPSREP..... Operations Report [*NATO*] (NATG)
OPSRO...... Office of Professional Standards Review [*Medicare and Medicaid*] Organization [*HEW*]
OPSS........ Intelligent Occupant Position and Sensing System [*Automotive safety*]
OPSS........ Office of Principal Staff Support (SAUS)
OPSS........ Orbital Propellant Storage Subsystem (MCD)
OPSS........ Overweight & Pregnant Support (SAUS)
OPSS........ Saidu Sharif [*Pakistan*] [*ICAO location identifier*] (ICLI)
OP(ST)...... Operation Overlord Preparations, Service Leave and Travel [*World War II*]
OPST........ Out-of-Pile Systems Test [*Nuclear energy*] (NRCH)
OPSTACOM... Optical Satellite Communications
OPSTAT..... Operational Status [*Navy*] (NVT)
OPSTATUSREP... Operations Status Report (NATG)
OPST-BQA... Office of Professional Standards Review-Bureau of Quality Assurance (STED)
OPSTOP..... Optional Stop (SAUS)
OPSTR...... Operating Strength [*Army*] (AABC)
OPSU........ Sui [*Pakistan*] [*ICAO location identifier*] (ICLI)
OPSUB...... Operational SUBPAY (DNAB)
OPSUM...... Operational Summary [*Navy*] (NVT)
OPSUPPFAC... Operational Support Facility (MCD)
OPSW....... Opsware Inc [*Stock exchange symbol*] [*Formerly Loudcloud Inc*]
OPSW....... Sahiwal [*Pakistan*] [*ICAO location identifier*] (ICLI)
OPSWL...... Old Program Status Word Location
OPS-X....... Operational Teletype Message
OPSY........ Optical Systems, Inc. [*NASDAQ symbol*] (QUAN)
OPSYS...... Operating System [*Computer science*]
OPT.......... International Finance Corp. [*NYSE symbol*] (SAG)
OPT.......... Office of the Public Trustee [*Australian Capital Territory*]
OPT.......... Oil Point [*Alaska*] [*Seismograph station code, US Geological Survey*] (SEIS)
OPT.......... Oil Pressure Transmitter
OPT.......... Open Pneumothorax [*Medicine*] (MELL)
OPT.......... Open Protocol Technology [*Computer science*] (AGLO)
OPT.......... Operability Testing [*Military*] (CAAL)
OPT.......... Operate (WGA)
OPT.......... Operational Pressure Transducer (MCD)
OPT.......... Operation Prime Time [*Television*]
OPT.......... Operations and Telling (SAA)
OPT.......... Operations Planning Team [*Air Force*] (DOMA)
OPT.......... Opponent [*Telegraphy*] (PCTE)
OPT.......... Opportunities for Professional Transition [*An association*] (EA)
OPT.......... Optative [*Grammar*]
OPT.......... Optic (IAA)
OPT.......... Optical (AAG)
opt........... Optical (NTIO)
OPT.......... Optical Point Transfer
OPT.......... Optician
OPT.......... Optics
OPT.......... Optima [*NCIC car model code*]
opt........... optimal (SAUS)
OPT.......... Optimization (SAUS)
OPT.......... Optimization Study [*Nuclear energy*] (NRCH)
OPT.......... Optimization Under Uncertainty Project (SAUS)
OPT.......... Optimized Production Technology
OPT.......... Optimizer (SAUS)
OPT.......... Optimum (AAG)
OPT.......... Optimus [*Best*] [*Latin*]
Opt........... Option (EBF)
OPT.......... Option [*Shares*]
OPT.......... Optional (AAG)
Opt........... Optional (EBF)
opt........... Optional (IDOE)
OPT.......... Options (SAUS)
Opt........... Optometrist (STED)
OPT.......... Orange Port Terminal Railway [*Federal Railroad Administration identification code*]
OPT.......... Ortho-Phthaladehyde (DB)
OPT.......... Other People's Tobacco [*Slang*]
OPT.......... Outpatient [*Medicine*] (AAMN)
OPT.......... Outpatient Physical Therapy [*Health insurance*] (GHCT)
OPT.......... Outpatient Therapy (DAVI)
OPT.......... Outpatient Treatment [*Medicine*]
OPT.......... Output Position Transducer [*Electronics*]
OPT.......... Output Punched Tape (SAUS)
OPT.......... Output Transformer (IAA)
OPT.......... Overhead Projection Transparency (MCD)
OPT.......... Ovulation Predictor Test (SAUS)
OPT.......... Pakenham Township Public Library, Ontario [*Library symbol*] [*National Library of Canada*] (BIB)
OPT.......... Payne Theological Seminary, Wilberforce, OH [*OCLC symbol*] (OCLC)
Opta......... Opta Food Ingredients, Inc. [*Associated Press*] (SAG)
OPTA........ Optimal Performance Theoretically Attainable (IEEE)
OPTA........ Optimum Performance Theoretically Obtainable (SAUS)
OPTA........ Organ and Piano Teachers Association [*Defunct*] (EA)
OPTA........ Terbela [*Pakistan*] [*ICAO location identifier*] (ICLI)
OPTAC....... Optical Target Acquisition and Cueing (ACAE)
OPTACON... Optical-to-Tactile Converter [*Electronic reader for the blind*]
OPTADS..... Operations Tactical Data Systems [*Army*] (RDA)
OPTAG....... Optical Aimpoint Guidance System [*Weaponry*]
OPTAG....... Optical Pickoff Two-Axis Gyroscope (SAA)
OPTAL....... Olivetti Press Tool Automation Language (SAUS)
OPTAN....... Operations Target Analysis [*of strike missions in North Vietnam*]
OPTAR....... Operating Target
OPTAR....... Optical Automatic Ranging
OPTARE..... Office of Planning, Technical Assistance, Research, and Evaluation [*Washington, DC*] [*Department of Commerce*] (GRD)
OPTASK..... Operational Tasking (DOMA)
OPTAX....... Oppenheimer Municipal Bond Cl.A [*Mutual fund ticker symbol*] (SG)
OPT AX..... Optical Axis (SAUS)
OPTB........ Operational Program Time Base [*NASA*] (MCD)
OPTC........ Optelecom, Inc. [*NASDAQ symbol*] (NQ)
OptCble..... Optical Cable Corp. [*Associated Press*] (SAG)
OptclData... Optical Data Systems [*Associated Press*] (SAG)
OptclDt...... Optical Data Systems, Inc. [*Associated Press*] (SAG)
Opt Clm..... Optional Claiming Race (WGA)
OPTCN...... Optician
Opt Commun... Optical Communication (SAUS)
Opt Comput Process... Optical Computing Processing [*A publication*] (CABS)
Opt County Gov't... Optional County Government [*A publication*] (DLA)
Opt D........ Doctor of Optometry
OPT'D....... Optioned [*Automotive advertising*]
OPTE........ Operational Proficiency Training Equipment [*Roland International Corp.*] (MCD)
OPTEC....... Operational Test and Evaluation Command [*Army*] (RDA)
OPTEC....... Optical Properties Technical Evaluation Center
OpTeC....... Optical Technology Center [*Montana State University-Bozeman*] (RCD)
Opt Electron Microsc... Optical and Electron Microscopy (SAUS)
OPTEMPO... Operational Tempo [*Military*]
OPTEMPO... Tempo of Operations (MCD)
Opt Eng Rep... Optical Engineering Report (SAUS)

Op Tenn Att'y Gen... Opinions of the Attorney General of Tennessee [*A publication*] (DLA)
OPTEV....... Operational Test and Evaluation [*Military*]
OPTEVFOR... Operational Test and Evaluation Force [*Norfolk, VA*] [*Navy*]
OPTEVFORDET... Operational Test and Evaluation Force Detachment (DNAB)
OPTEVG..... Operational Test and Evaluation Group (SAUS)
OPTEX....... Optical Exploder (TIMI)
OptEx....... Optional Exchange [*Dietetics*]
Op Tex Att'y Gen... Opinions of the Attorney General of Texas [*A publication*] (DLA)
OPTG........ Operating (SAUS)
OPTH........ Ophthalmic (ROG)
OPTH........ Ophthalmology [*Medicine*] (IDYL)
OPTH........ Talhar [*Pakistan*] [*ICAO location identifier*] (ICLI)
OPTHD...... Optimal Hemodialysis [*Medicine*] (EDAA)
OPTI......... Office of Productivity, Technology, and Innovation [*Department of Commerce*]
OPTI......... OPTI, Inc. [*NASDAQ symbol*] (SAG)
OPTI......... Optimize (SAUS)
OPTI......... Optimum Holding Corp. (SAUS)
OPTIC....... Ophthalmological Products Trade and Industry Conference [*British*] (DBA)
OPTIC....... Optical
OPTIC....... Optical Procedural Task Instruction Compiler
optic........ opticociliary (SAUS)
optic........ opticopupillary (SAUS)
OPTIC....... Oryx Pecos Test Inquiry and Control System (NITA)
Opticam..... Optics Automation and Management (RDA)
OpticC....... Optical Coating Laboratory, Inc. [*Associated Press*] (SAG)
OPTICIMP... Optimization of Computer Integrated Materials Processing (SAUS)
OPTICON... Optical Tactical Converter (SAUS)
OPTIM....... Occupational Projections and Training Information for Michigan [*Information service or system*] (IID)
OPTIM....... Order Point Technique for Inventory Management (BUR)
Optima...... Optima Petroleum Corp. [*Associated Press*] (SAG)
OPTIMA..... Optimization of Policies for Transport Integration in Metropolitan Areas
OPTIMA..... Organization for the Phyto-Taxonomic Investigation of the Mediterranean Area [*Berlin, Federal Republic of Germany*] (EAIO)
OptImag..... Optika Imaging Systems, Inc. [*Associated Press*] (SAG)
Optimax..... Optimax Industries, Inc. [*Associated Press*] (SAG)
OPTIMOS... Optimized Metal Oxide Semiconductor (SAUS)
OPTIMUM... Obtain Increased Productivity through Improved Modernization of Facilities and Updating Maintenance Tools, Equipment, and Methods [*Military*]
OPTIMUM... Optimum Product Time Innovation Market Understanding Motivation [*Management*]
OPTIMUS... Office of Public Trustee Information Management User System [*Canada*]
Opt Inf Syst... Optical Information Systems (SAUS)
OPTINT...... Optical Intelligence (MCD)
OPTIPARES... Optical Processing of Airborne Remote Sensing (SAUS)
OPTIR....... Optical Infrared (ACAE)
OPTIS....... Oxfordshire Project for the Training of Instructors and Supervisors [*British*] (AIE)
OptiSG...... Optical Security Group, Inc. [*Associated Press*] (SAG)
OPTK........ Optika Imaging Systems, Inc. [*NASDAQ symbol*] (SAG)
OPTK........ Optika, Inc. [*NASDAQ symbol*] (NASQ)
OPTL........ Optional (MSA)
OPTL........ OptiSystems Solutions, Ltd. [*NASDAQ symbol*] (NASQ)
Opt Lasers Eng... Optics and Lasers in Engineering [*A publication*] (CABS)
OPTLC....... Overpressurized Thin-Layer Chromatography
Optlcm...... Optelecom, Inc. [*Associated Press*] (SAG)
OPTM........ Optometry
Opt Mater... Optical Materials (SAUS)
Opt Min..... Optical Mineralogy (SAUS)
OPTMRST... Optometrist (SAUS)
OPTMTRC... Optometric
Optmx....... Optimax Industries, Inc. [*Associated Press*] (SAG)
OPTN........ [*The*] National Organ Procurement and Transplantation Network [*Information service or system*] (IID)
OPTN........ Optician (SAUS)
OPTN........ Option [*Legal shorthand*] (LWAP)
OPTN........ Option Care, Inc. [*NASDAQ symbol*] (SAG)
OptnCr....... Option Care, Inc. [*Associated Press*] (SAG)
OPTNET..... Optimum Private Trunk Network Embodying Tandems (PDAA)
Opt News... Optical News (SAUS)
OPT-NSC.... Outpatient Treatment/Nonservice-Connected [*Veterans Administration*] (DAVI)
OPTO........ Opto Mechanik, Inc. [*NASDAQ symbol*] (COMM)
OPTO........ Optometry Library (SAUS)
OPTOEL..... Optoelectronics (SAUS)
Optoelectron Instrum Data Process... Optoelectronics, Instrumentation and Data Processing (SAUS)
OPTOL....... Optimized Test-Oriented Language [*Computer science*] (PDAA)
OPTOM...... Optometer (SAUS)
OPTOM...... Optometrist
Optom....... Optometry
OPTOM...... Optomyometer (SAUS)
OPTOMA.... Ocean Prediction through Observation, Modeling, and Analysis [*Experimental program*]
OPT/OSP.... Outpatient Physical Therapy/Outpatient Speech Pathology Services [*Department of Health and Human Services*] (GFGA)
OPTQ........ Ocean Optique Distributors, Inc. [*NASDAQ symbol*] (SAG)
OPTQ........ Ocean Optique Dstr [*NASDAQ symbol*] (TTSB)
Opt Quantum Electron... Optical and Quantum Electronics [*A publication*] (CABS)
OPTR........ Optical Punched Tape Reader (SAUS)
O/P Tr....... Output Transformer (SAUS)
OPTRA...... Operational Training (DNAB)
OPTRAK..... Optical Tracking and Ranging Kit (PDAA)
OPTRAN..... Operational Transit (GAAI)
OPTRAN..... Optical Transmission (SAUS)
OPTRARON... Operational Training Squadron (DNAB)
OPTRONICS... Optical Electronics (SAUS)
OPTRX...... Oppenheimer Total Return Cl.A [*Mutual fund ticker symbol*] (SG)
OPTS........ Office of Pesticides and Toxic Substances [*Environmental Protection Agency*]
OPTS........ Office of Program and Technical Services [*Employment and Training Administration*] [*Department of Labor*]
OPTS........ Online Peripheral Test System
OPTS........ Online Program Testing System [*Computer science*] (IAA)
OPTS........ Operations (SAUS)
OPTS........ Opta Food Ingredients, Inc. [*NASDAQ symbol*] (SAG)
Opt S........ Optical Sight (SAUS)
OPTS........ Organization of Parents through Surrogacy (EA)
OPT-SC...... Outpatient Treatment/Service Connected [*Veterans Administration*] (DAVI)
OptSens..... Optical Sensors, Inc. [*Associated Press*] (SAG)
OPTS RTS... OPTS Regulation Tracking System (SAUS)
OPTT........ Optek Technology [*NASDAQ symbol*] (TTSB)
OPTT........ Taftan [*Pakistan*] [*ICAO location identifier*] (ICLI)
OPTU........ Turbat [*Pakistan*] [*ICAO location identifier*] (ICLI)
OPTUL....... Optical Pulse Transmitter Using LASER
OPTV........ OpenTV Corp. [*NASDAQ symbol*]
OPTV........ Operative
OPTX........ Optek Technology, Inc. (SAUS)
OPTX........ Optex Biomedical [*NASDAQ symbol*] (TTSB)
OPTYP....... Opalotype (VRA)
OPTZU....... Optical-Pan-Tilt-Zoom Unit (SAA)
OPU.......... Balimo [*Papua New Guinea*] [*Airport symbol*] (OAG)
OPU.......... Operational Performance Unit (ADA)
OPU.......... Operations Priority Unit
OPU.......... Operator Processing Unit (SAUS)
OPU.......... Opportune [*Telegraphy*] (PCTE)
OPU.......... Out-Plant Usage (VLIE)
OPU.......... Overseas Plexiglas Unit
OPU.......... Pacific University, Forest Grove, OR [*OCLC symbol*] (OCLC)
OPU.......... Unemployed Peoples Union (NADA)
OP/UCOP.... Office of the President/UC Office of the President (SAUS)
OPUG........ Office Planners and Users Group (NTPA)
OPUR........ Object Program Utility Routine
OPURD7..... Institute of Arctic and Alpine Research. University of Colorado. Occasional Paper (journ.) (SAUS)
OPUS........ Obvious Password Utility System [*Computer science*] (VLIE)
OPUS........ Octal Program Updating System [*Computer science*]
OPUS........ Officer Planning Utilization System (SAUS)
OPUS........ Offshore Persistent Upwelling Structure
OPUS........ Older People United for Service (SAUS)
OPUS........ Open University System (SAUS)
OPUS........ Operating Utility System (SAUS)
OPUS........ Optical Prism Uniformity System
OPUS........ Opus 360 Corp. [*NASDAQ symbol*] (SG)
OPUS........ Opus Computer Products, Inc. (SAUS)
OPUS........ Organisation of Professional Users of Statistics
OPUS........ Organization for Promoting the Understanding of Society (SAUS)
OPUS........ Organization of Persistant Upwelling Structure (SAUS)
OPUS........ Organization of Professional Users of Statistics (SAUS)
OPUSA...... Operation U.S.A. [*An association*] (EA)
OPUSC...... Opuscula [*Minor Works*] [*Latin*] (ROG)
OPV.......... Bedarfsfluguntemehmen Dr. L. Polsterer [*Austria*] [*ICAO designator*] (FAAC)
OPV.......... Observation Post Vehicle (SAUS)
OPV.......... Offshore Patrol Vessel (DOMA)
OPV.......... Ohms per Volt
OPV.......... Optical Path-Length Variation (PDAA)
OPV.......... Optionally Piloted Vehicle (SAUS)
OPV.......... Oral Polio Vaccine [*Also, Sabin vaccine*] (PAZ)
OPV.......... Oral Poliovirus [*Infectious diseases*] (DAVI)
OPV.......... Oral Polio Virus Vaccine
OPV.......... Organic PhotoVoltaic (SAUS)
Op VA Att'y Gen... Opinions of the Attorney General and Report to the Governor of Virginia [*A publication*] (DLA)
OPVN........ OpenVision Technologies, Inc. [*NASDAQ symbol*] (SAG)
OPVN........ Open Vision Technology [*NASDAQ symbol*] (TTSB)
OPW......... Objective Personal Weapon
OPW......... Oboz Polski Walczacej [*A publication*] (BJA)
OPW......... Office of Public Works (WDAA)
OPW......... Opawica Explorations, Inc. [*Toronto Stock Exchange symbol*]
OPW......... Open Pilot Warranty [*Insurance*] (AIA)
OPW......... Operating Weight [*Air Force*]
OPW......... Optical Window
OPW......... Opuwa [*Namibia*] [*Airport symbol*] (OAG)
OPW......... Orthogonalized Plane Wave
OPW......... Orthogonal Plane Wave (SAUS)
OPW......... Porter Public Library, Westlake, OH [*OCLC symbol*] (OCLC)
OPW......... Whitney Public Library, Porcupine, Ontario [*Library symbol*] [*National Library of Canada*] (NLC)
OPWA....... Office Products Wholesalers Association (NTPA)

Op Wash Att'y Gen... Office of the Attorney General (State of Washington) Opinions [*A publication*] (DLA)
OPWC....... Old Peoples Welfare Centre (SAUS)
OPWI........ Opiate Withdrawal [*Medicine*] (DMAA)
Op Wis Att'y Gen... Opinions of the Attorney General of Wisconsin [*A publication*] (DLA)
OpWldBd.... Oppenheimer World Bond Fund [*Associated Press*] (SAG)
OPWN....... Wana [*Pakistan*] [*ICAO location identifier*] (ICLI)
OPWS....... Occupant Position and Weight Sensor [*Automotive safety*]
OPWS....... Orbiter Payload Work Station (MCD)
OPWSA...... Ontario Prader-Willi Syndrome Association (SAUS)
Op Wyo Att'y Gen... Opinions of the Attorney General of Wyoming [*A publication*] (DLA)
OPX.......... Off-Premise Exchange Operation (AGLO)
OPX.......... Off-Premise Extension [*Nuclear energy*] (NRCH)
OPX.......... Online Performance Monitor Destination (SAUS)
OPX.......... Orthopyroxene [*A silicate mineral*]
OPY.......... Oppenheimer Holdings [*NYSE symbol*]
OPY.......... Salomon, Inc. [*AMEX symbol*] (SAG)
OP Year..... Original Production Year (EEVL)
OPZ.......... Opsonized Zymosan [*Biochemistry*]
OPZB........ Zhob [*Pakistan*] [*ICAO location identifier*] (ICLI)
OPZONE..... Operation Zone (COE)
OQ........... Occupy [*Telegraphy*] (PCTE)
OQ........... Officers' Quarters [*Military*]
OQ........... Officier de l'Ordre du Quebec [*French*] (CPGU)
OQ........... Oil Quench (IAA)
OQ........... Oil Quenching (SAUS)
OQ........... Operational Qualification (ACII)
OQ........... Optical Quality
OQ........... Order Quantity (DNAB)
OQ........... Ordre du Quebec [*Order of Quebec*] [*Canada*] (DD)
OQ........... Output Quantity (SAUS)
OQ........... Output Queue [*Computer science*] (VLIE)
oq............ overmation quotient (SAUS)
OQ........... Royale Airlines [*ICAO designator*] (AD)
OQ........... Tropical Air Services (SAUS)
OQA.......... Operations Quality Assurance [*Nuclear energy*] (NRCH)
OQA.......... Optical Quantum Amplifier (PDAA)
OQA.......... Reidsville, NC [*Location identifier*] [*FAA*] (FAAL)
OQ&A........ Oil Quenched and Annealed (SAUS)
OQAP........ Oil Quality Assessment Program [*Society of Automotive Engineers, Inc.*]
O-QAR....... Optical Quick Access Recorder (GAVI)
OQC.......... Office of Quality Control [*Social and Rehabilitation Service, HEW*]
OQC.......... Officers Qualification Card (SAUS)
OQC.......... Operator Quality Control [*RADAR*]
OQC.......... Outgoing Quality Control (SAUS)
OQC.......... Outside Quality Control (KSC)
OQD......... Occupied [*Telegraphy*] (PCTE)
OQD......... Optical Quantum Detector
OQE.......... Objective Quality Evidence (MCD)
OQG......... Occupying [*Telegraphy*] (PCTE)
OQG......... Optical Quantum Generator
OQI.......... Oil Quantity Indicator
OQL.......... Oberserved Quality Level (SAUS)
OQL.......... Object Query Language [*Computer science*] (VLIE)
OQL.......... Observed Quality Level
OQL.......... Online Query Language
OQL.......... Outgoing Quality Level
OQL.......... Outgoing Quality Limit
OQM......... Office of the Quartermaster [*Military*]
OQMG....... Office of the Quartermaster General [*Military*]
OQN......... Occupation [*Telegraphy*] (PCTE)
OQP.......... Optimum Qualification Procedure
OQPSK...... Offset Quadrature Phase Shift Keying (SAUS)
O-QPSK..... Offset Quaternary Phase Shift Keying (SAUS)
OQQ......... Officer Qualification Questionnaire [*Navy*] (DOMA)
OQR......... Officer's Qualification Record [*Army*]
OQS.......... Occupies [*Telegraphy*] (PCTE)
OQS.......... Offsite Quality Surveillance (SAUS)
OQSMAT.... Otis Quick Scoring Mental Abilities Tests [*Psychology*] (DAVI)
OQT.......... Occupant [*Telegraphy*] (PCTE)
OQT.......... Officer Qualification Test
OQTD........ Operational Qualifications Test Deficiency [*Air Force*]
OQU......... North Kingstown, RI [*Location identifier*] [*FAA*] (FAAL)
OQUAT...... Operation Quality Assurance Team [*Traffic control*]
OQW......... Maquoketa, IA [*Location identifier*] [*FAA*] (FAAL)
OQY.......... Occupancy [*Telegraphy*] (PCTE)
OQZ.......... Union City, TN [*Location identifier*] [*FAA*] (FAAL)
OR........... Air Comores [*ICAO designator*] (AD)
OR........... Beginning of Record (SAUS)
Or............ Indian Law Reports, Orissa Series [*A publication*] (DLA)
OR........... Oahu Railway [*Federal Railroad Administration identification code*]
OR........... Oak Ridge Complex [*Department of Energy*] [*Oak Ridge National Laboratory*] (GAAI)
OR........... Oak Ridge Operations Office (DOGT)
OR........... Objective Reliability (MCD)
OR........... Object-Relational (GART)
OR........... Object Routine (SAUS)
OR........... Observed Ratio (MCD)
OR........... Observer, Right (SAUS)
OR........... Occurrence Report (ABAC)
OR........... Octane Rating [*Automotive engineering*]
OR........... Octane Requirement [*Fuels and lubricants*]
OR........... Odds Ratio [*Statistics*]
O/R.......... Office of Record (AFM)
OR........... Officer of Reserve (SAUS)
OR........... Officer Records [*Military*] (AFM)
OR........... Official Receiver
OR........... Official Records
OR........... Official Records [*Of the War of the Rebellion*] [*Civil War term*]
OR........... Official Referee
OR........... Official Reports, South Africa [*A publication*] (DLA)
OR........... Official Requirement (SAUS)
OR........... Off-Radial (RDA)
OR........... Off-Route [*Telecommunications*] (OTD)
OR........... Ohms, Resistance (SAUS)
OR........... Oil Rehabilitation Committee [*British*]
OR........... Oil Resistance (SAUS)
OR........... Oil Retention [*Enema*] [*Medicine*]
OR........... Oil Ring (MSA)
OR........... Oldenburg Registry [*Association*] (EA)
OR........... Old Roman (ADA)
OR........... Oleoresin [*Also, Ol Res*] [*Pharmacy*]
OR........... Oleoresinous (SAUS)
OR........... Olfactory Receptor [*Biochemistry*]
OR........... Oligomer Restriction [*Genetics*]
OR........... Olympic Range (SAUS)
OR........... Olympic Record (SAUS)
OR........... Omega Rho (SAUS)
OR........... Omnidirectional Radio Range (MCD)
OR........... On Rail (SAUS)
o/r............ On Request (PIAV)
O/R.......... On Request
OR........... On Return
OR........... Ontario Reports [*A publication*] (DLA)
OR........... Open Reduction [*Orthopedics*] (DAVI)
OR........... Open Registry [*Flag of convenience*] [*Shipping*] (DS)
OR........... Open Routine (SAUS)
OR........... Operand Register (VLIE)
OR........... Operating Reactor [*Nuclear energy*] (NRCH)
OR........... Operating Resources (AFM)
OR........... Operating Revenue (SAUS)
OR........... Operating Room [*Medicine*]
OR........... Operational Equipment Requirement (IAA)
OR........... Operationally Ready (MCD)
or............ Operationally Risky (ODA)
OR........... Operational Readiness [*Army*]
OR........... Operational Recorder (SAUS)
OR........... Operational Reliability [*Army*] (AABC)
OR........... Operational Report (AAG)
OR........... Operational Requirement
OR........... Operational Research
OR........... Operational Right
OR........... Operational Right DSC or MDM (SAUS)
OR........... Operation Rate (SAUS)
OR........... Operation Reach-Out [*Department of Labor*]
OR........... Operation Record
OR........... Operation Rescue (EA)
OR........... Operation Research (SAUS)
OR........... Operations and Regulations (SAUS)
OR........... Operations Request [*Military*]
OR........... Operations Requirements
OR........... Operations Research [*Computer science*]
OR........... Operations Review [*NASA*] (MCD)
OR........... Operations Room
OR........... Operator (IAA)
OR........... Operator Register (SAUS)
OR........... Operator Routine (SAUS)
OR........... Operculum Ridge
OR........... Ophthalmic Rete [*Bird anatomy*]
OR........... Opponents' Runs [*Baseball*]
OR........... Optical Reader [*Computer science*] (BUR)
OR........... Optical Receiver (SAUS)
OR........... Optic Radiation (DB)
O+R.......... Optiram, St. Helier, Jersey, Channel Islands, United Kingdom [*Library symbol*] [*Library of Congress*] (LCLS)
OR........... Oral Rehydration [*Medicine*] (MELL)
OR........... Orange
Or............ Oratio [*A publication*] (OCD)
Or............ Orationes [*of Julian*] [*Classical studies*] (OCD)
Or............ Orationes [*of Dio Chrysostomus*] [*Classical studies*] (OCD)
OR........... Oratorians
OR........... Orbital Rhabdomyosarcoma [*Medicine*] (EDAA)
OR........... Ordered Recorded
OR........... Ordering Register (IAA)
OR........... Orderly Room
OR........... Order of the Road [*British*] (DBA)
OR........... Order Pennant [*Navy*] [*British*]
OR........... Order [*or Ordering*] Register (SAA)
OR........... Order Release (SAUS)
OR........... Ordinance Report (SAUS)
OR........... Ordnance Requirement
Or............ Oregon (NTIO)
OR........... Oregon [*Postal code*]
Or............ Oregon State Library, Salem, OR [*Library symbol*] [*Library of Congress*] (LCLS)

Or .... Oregon Supreme Court Reports [*A publication*] (DLA)
OR .... Ore Reserve (SAUS)
Or .... Orestes [*of Euripides*] [*Classical studies*] (OCD)
OR .... Organizational Representative (SAUS)
OR .... Organizational Research (SAUS)
OR .... Organized Reserves [*Military*]
OR .... Organ Recovery (EA)
OR .... OR Gate (SAUS)
Or .... Oriel College, Oxford (ODA)
OR .... Orient
OR .... Oriental (ROG)
OR .... Orientation Ratio (VLIE)
OR .... Orientation Response (SAUS)
OR .... Oriented (SAUS)
OR .... Orienting Reflex [*Medicine*] (MELL)
OR .... Orienting Response [*Psychology*]
Or .... Origen [*Deceased circa 254*] [*Authority cited in pre-1607 legal work*] (DSA)
OR .... Origin (VLIE)
OR .... Original (ADA)
OR .... Originating Register (VLIE)
O/R .... Originator or Recipient [*Telecommunications*] (OSI)
OR .... O-Ring [*Automotive engineering*]
'Or .... 'Orlah (BJA)
OR .... Orosomucoid [*Biochemistry*]
or .... Orthoclase [*CIPW classification*] [*Geology*]
Or .... Orthoclase Feldspar
OR .... Orthopaedic Review [*Medicine*] [*Journal*] (EDAA)
OR .... Orthopedic
OR .... Orthopedic Research [*Medicine*]
OR .... Orthophthalic Resin [*Plastics*]
OR .... Oswestry Rangers [*British military*] (DMA)
OR .... Other (ROG)
OR .... Other Ranks [*Ranks other than officers*] [*Military*]
OR .... Outer Roll [*Aviation*] (MCD)
OR .... Out of Range
OR .... Output Record (SAUS)
OR .... Output Register (MSA)
OR .... Output Routine (SAUS)
OR .... Outside Radius [*Technical drawings*]
OR .... Outside Right [*Soccer position*]
OR .... Overall Report
OR .... Overall Resistance (IAA)
OR .... Overflow Register (SAUS)
OR .... Overhaul and Repair
OR .... Overload Relay (KSC)
O/R .... Overrange [*System or element*] (IEEE)
O/R .... Override (KSC)
OR .... Over Run (MHDW)
OR .... Overrun (SAUS)
OR .... Oversea Requisition (SAUS)
OR .... Overseas Replacement [*Military*]
OR .... Owasco River [*AAR code*]
or .... Owner's Risk (WDAA)
OR .... Owner's Risk [*Shipping*]
OR .... Own Recognizance [*Legal term*]
O-R .... Oxidation-Reduction
OR .... Oxidation Resistance (SAUS)
OR .... Oxide Removal (SAUS)
OR .... Oxygen Enchancement Ratio (IAA)
OR .... Oxygen Relief (NASA)
OR .... Renfrew Public Library, Ontario [*Library symbol*] [*National Library of Canada*] (NLC)
OR2000 ..... Ocean Rescue 2000 (SAUS)
ORA .... Montauk Caribbean Airways, Inc. [*ICAO designator*] (FAAC)
ORA .... Occultation Radiometer (SAUS)
ORA .... Office of Records Administration [*National Archives*] (BARN)
ORA .... Office of Redress Administration [*Department of Justice*]
ORA .... Office of Regulatory Affairs [*U.S. Food and Drug Administration*]
ORA .... Office of Regulatory Analysis [*Federal Energy Regulatory Commission*]
ORA .... Office of Research Administration [*University of Hawaii*] [*Research center*] (RCD)
ORA .... Office of Research Administration [*University of Pennsylvania*] [*Research center*] (RCD)
ORA .... Office of Research Administration [*North Carolina A & T State University*] [*Research center*] (RCD)
ORA .... Office of Research Administration [*St. Louis University*] [*Research center*] (RCD)
ORA .... Office of Research Analysis [*Air Force*]
ORA .... Office of Research and Applications (SAUS)
ORA .... Office of Rural Affairs [*Victoria, Australia*]
ORA .... Official Records of the Admiralty (SAUS)
ORA .... Oil Refiners Association (NADA)
ORA .... Operating Room Attendant [*British military*] (DMA)
ORA .... Operational RADAR Directed Flights (NATG)
ORA .... Operational Readiness Assessment
ORA .... Operational Requirements Analysis (SPST)
ORA .... Operation Response Area (MCD)
ORA .... Operations Research Analyst [*Army*] (AABC)
ORA .... Operations Research Appreciation (SAUS)
ORA .... Opiate Receptor Agonist [*Medicine*] (MELL)
ORA .... Opportunities for Rural Areas (EURO)
ORA .... Opportunity Resources for the Arts (EA)
ORA .... Optical Reference Axis
ORA .... Option Revision Agreement (VLIE)
ORA .... Oran [*Argentina*] [*Airport symbol*] (AD)
ORA .... Order for Reinforced Alert (NATG)
Or A .... Oregon Court of Appeals Reports [*A publication*] (DLA)
ORA .... Organisation de Resistance de l'Armee [*France*]
ORA .... Organisation Revolutionnaire Anarchiste [*Revolutionary Anarchist Organization*] [*France*] [*Political party*] (PPE)
ORA .... Organizacao Revolucionaria Armada [*Terrorist group*] [*Portugal*] (EY)
ORA .... Organizational Role Analysis (PDAA)
ORA .... Orifice Rod Assembly [*Nuclear energy*] (NRCH)
ORA .... Ormet Railroad [*Federal Railroad Administration identification code*]
ORA .... Oromo Relief Association [*Ethiopia*]
ORA .... Oronite Refinery Additive [*Fuels and lubricants*]
ORA .... Orthopaedic Rehabilitation Association (SAUS)
ORA .... OR to Accumulator (SAUS)
ORA .... Output Reference Axis (IAA)
ORA .... Output Register Address
ORA .... Ramore Library, Ontario [*Library symbol*] [*National Library of Canada*] (BIB)
ORA .... Ross Laboratory Library, Columbus, OH [*OCLC symbol*] (OCLC)
ORAAP ...... Outstanding Reserve Airman Appointment Program
ORAC .... Optical Reference for Azimuth Correction (SAUS)
ORAC .... Oxygen Radical Absorbance Capacity [*Analytical Chemistry*]
ORACBA ..... Office of Risk Assessment and Cost-Benefit Analysis
ORACLE ..... Oak Ridge Automatic Computer and Logical Engine
ORACLE ..... Observational Research and Classroom Learning Evaluation [*British*] (DET)
ORACLE ..... On-Line Retrieval and Computational Language for Economists [*Computer science*]
ORACLE ..... Operational Research and Critical Link Evaluation (SAUS)
ORACLE ..... Operations Research and Critical Link Evaluator (SAUS)
ORACLE ..... Optical Reception of Announcements by Coded Line Electronics
ORACLE ..... Optimized Reliability and Component Life Estimate
ORACLE ..... Optimum Record Automation for Court and Law Enforcement
ORACLE ..... Optional Reception of Announcements by Coded Line Electronics [*Independent Television "newspaper"*] [*British*] (DI)
ORACLE ..... Optional Recovery of Announcements by Coded Line Electronics (NITA)
Oracle .... Oracle Systems Corp. [*Associated Press*] (SAG)
ORACLE ..... Ordnance Rapid Area Clearance [*Military*] (CAAL)
ORACLE ..... Organic Rankine Cycle
ORACLE ..... Oversight of Resources and Capability for Logistics Effectiveness (PDAA)
ORACT ...... Operational Readiness and Confidence Test
OrAd .... Adams Public Library, Adams, OR [*Library symbol*] [*Library of Congress*] (LCLS)
ORAD .... Office of Rural Areas Development [*Later, Rural Community Development Service*] [*Department of Agriculture*]
ORad .... Officer Radar (SAUS)
ORAD .... Orbiter RADAR [*NASA*]
ORAD .... Outbound Radian (SAUS)
ORAD .... Outhound Radial (SAUS)
Or Admin R... Oregon Administrative Rules [*A publication*] (DLA)
Or Admin R Bull... Oregon Administrative Rules Bulletin [*A publication*] (DLA)
ORADS .... Optical Ranging and Detection System
Or Ad Sh.... Supreme Court of the State of Oregon Advance Sheets [*A publication*] (DLA)
ORAE .... Aerospace Industries Association of Canada (SAUS)
ORAE .... Office de Repartition des Approvisionnements d'Energie [*Canada*]
ORAE .... Operational Research and Analysis Establishment (MCD)
OrAg .... Agness Community Library, Agness, OR [*Library symbol*] [*Library of Congress*] (LCLS)
ORaH .... Robinson Memorial Hospital, Ravenna, OH [*Library symbol*] [*Library of Congress*] (LCLS)
OrAh .... Washington County Cooperative Library Services, Aloha, OR [*Library symbol*] [*Library of Congress*] (LCLS)
ORAIS .... Opportunities and Risks of Artificial Intelligent Systems (SAUS)
OrAl .... Albany Public Library, Albany, OR [*Library symbol*] [*Library of Congress*] (LCLS)
ORAL .... Oral Access to Library
ORAL .... OrthAlliance, Inc. [*NASDAQ symbol*] (NASQ)
OrAlBM...... United States Bureau of Mines, Education and Training Center, Albany, OR [*Library symbol*] [*Library of Congress*] (LCLS)
OrAlC .... Linn-Benton Community College, Albany, OR [*Library symbol*] [*Library of Congress*] (LCLS)
ORALFORE... Opposed Rates of Advance of Large Forces in Europe (SAUS)
OrAlH .... Albany General Hospital, Albany, OR [*Library symbol*] [*Library of Congress*] (LCLS)
ORALL....... Ohio Regional Association of Law Libraries (EARSL)
Oral Roberts U... Oral Roberts University (GAGS)
Oral Surg Oral Med Oral Pathol... Oral Surgery, Oral Medicine and Oral Pathology (SAUS)
OrAlT .... Teledyne-Wah Chang Albany, Albany, OR (LCLS)
ORALTOX... Acute Oral Toxicity for Birds, Mice, Rats (SAUS)
OrAm .... Amity Public Library, Amity, OR [*Library symbol*] [*Library of Congress*] (LCLS)
ORAM .... Office for Research in Academic Methods (SAUS)
ORAM .... Orbital Repair and Maintenance (SAUS)
ORAN .... Orange [*Laboratory science*] (DAVI)
ORAN .... Orangequit [*North American bird banding code*] (BIBA)
ORAN .... Orange Terminal [*Federal Railroad Administration identification code*]
ORAN .... Orbital Analysis
ORAN .... Organisation Regionale Africaine de Normalisation [*African Regional Organization for Standardization - AROS*] (EAIO)
OR&E .... Office of Research and Engineering (SAUS)

OR&F........ Open Reduction and Fixation (DMAA)
OR&F........ Operations, Research and Facilities [*Marine science*] (OSRA)
OR&IE........ Operations Research and Industrial Engineering (SAUS)
OR & N..... Oregon Railroad & Navigation Co.
OR & SP.... Office of Research and Sponsored Programs [*Research center*] (RCD)
ORANG...... Orange, TX [*American Association of Railroads railroad junction routing code*]
ORANG...... Oregon Air National Guard (MUSM)
Orange...... Orange PLC [*Associated Press*] (SAG)
Orange Cty Dent Soc Bull... Orange County Dental Society. Bulletin (SAUS)
Orange Light... Change Approaching (SAUS)
OrangN...... Orange National Bancorp [*Associated Press*] (SAG)
OranRk...... Orange & Rockland Utilities, Inc. [*Associated Press*] (SAG)
ORANS...... Oak Ridge Analytical System(s) [*Medicine*] (EDAA)
ORAP........ Originator/Recipient Address Prefix (VLIE)
ORAPA....... Ontario Retail Accident Prevention Association (SAUS)
Or App...... Oregon Reports, Court of Appeal [*A publication*] (DLA)
ORAQI........ Oak Ridge Air Quality Index (SAUS)
OrAr......... Arlington Public Library, Arlington, OR [*Library symbol*] [*Library of Congress*] (LCLS)
Or-Ar......... Oregon State Archives, Salem, OR [*Library symbol*] [*Library of Congress*] (LCLS)
ORAR........ Rainy River Public Library, Ontario [*Library symbol*] [*National Library of Canada*] (NLC)
ORAS........ Oil Recovery and Separation Technology [*Jastram Werke*]
ORASA...... Operational Research and Systems Analysis (PDAA)
OrAshS...... Southern Oregon College, Ashland, OR [*Library symbol*] [*Library of Congress*] (LCLS)
ORASS...... Offender Risk Assessment Scoring System (SAUS)
OrAst........ Astor Library, Astoria, OR [*Library symbol*] [*Library of Congress*] (LCLS)
OrAstC....... Clatsop Community College, Astoria, OR [*Library symbol*] [*Library of Congress*] (LCLS)
OrAstM...... Columbia River Maritime Museum, Astoria, OR [*Library symbol*] [*Library of Congress*] (LCLS)
ORAT........ Oralorical (SAUS)
Orat.......... Oration [*or Orator or Oratorio*]
Orat.......... Orator ad M. Brutum [*of Cicero*] [*Classical studies*] (OCD)
ORAT........ Oratorical
Orat.......... Oratorio (SAUS)
Orat.......... Oratory (SAUS)
ORATE....... Ordered Random Access Talking Equipment
ORATMS.... Off-Route Antitank Mine System (MCD)
ORATOS..... Orbit & Attitude Operations System (SAUS)
ORATS....... Operational Readiness Assessment and Training System (MCD)
ORAU........ Oak Ridge Associated Universities (EA)
OraVax...... OraVax, Inc. [*Associated Press*] (SAG)
ORAW....... Oil Remaining after Waterflooding [*Petroleum technology*]
ORAW....... Orange-Cheeked Waxbill [*North American bird banding code*] (BIBA)
OrB.......... Beaverton City Library, Beaverton, OR [*Library symbol*] [*Library of Congress*] (LCLS)
ORB.......... Object Request Broker [*Computer science*]
ORB.......... Oceanic Ridge Basalts
ORB.......... Oceanographic Research Buoy
ORB.......... Ocean Research Buoy (IAA)
ORB.......... Offenders' Review Board [*New South Wales, Australia*]
ORB.......... Office Repeater Bay (SAUS)
ORB.......... Officer Record Brief [*Army*] (AABC)
ORB.......... Offsets Review Board [*New South Wales, Australia*]
ORB.......... Omnidirectional Radio Beacon
ORB.......... Omnidirectional Research Beacon (SAUS)
ORB.......... Online Reference Book for Medieval Studies [*Internet resource*]
ORB.......... Operational Research Branch [*Canada*]
ORB.......... Operational Review Board (ACAE)
ORB.......... Operation Request Block [*Computer science*] (MWOL)
ORB.......... Operations Record Book [*Air Ministry*] [*British*] [*World War II*]
ORB.......... Optometrists' Registration Board [*Victoria, Australia*]
ORB.......... Orbe [*Switzerland*] [*Seismograph station code, US Geological Survey*] [*Closed*] (SEIS)
Orb.......... Orbis [*Record label*] [*Germany, etc.*]
ORB.......... Orbit
ORB.......... Orbital (KSC)
ORB.......... Orbital Sciences Corp. [*NYSE symbol*]
ORB.......... Orbiter [*NASA*] (NASA)
ORB.......... Orbit Oil & Gas Ltd. [*Toronto Stock Exchange symbol*]
ORB.......... Order
ORB.......... Orebro [*Sweden*] [*Airport symbol*] (OAG)
ORB.......... Organitzational Records Branch (SAUS)
ORB.......... Organizational Records Branch [*Army*]
ORB.......... Orr, MN [*Location identifier*] [*FAA*] (FAAL)
ORB.......... Outcomes Research Branch [*National Cancer Institute*] (RCD)
ORB.......... Outer Radiation Belt
ORB.......... Outside Reactor Building [*Nuclear energy*] (NRCH)
orb.......... Owner's Risk of Breakage (ODA)
Orb.......... Owners Risk of Breakage (EBF)
ORB.......... Owners Risk of Breakage (or Breaking) (SAUS)
ORB 1-G.... Orbiter One-G Trainer [*NASA*] (NASA)
OrBa......... Banks Community Library, Banks, OR [*Library symbol*] [*Library of Congress*] (LCLS)
ORBA........ Erbil [*Iraq*] [*ICAO location identifier*] (ICLI)
ORBA........ Ontario Road Builders Association (SAUS)
ORBACT..... Optometrists' Registration Board of the Australian Capital Territory
OrBak........ Baker County Public Library, Baker, OR [*Library symbol*] [*Library of Congress*] (LCLS)
OrBakSE.... Saint Elizabeth Hospital, Baker, OR [*Library symbol*] [*Library of Congress*] (LCLS)
OrBan....... Bandon Public Library, Bandon, OR [*Library symbol*] [*Library of Congress*] (LCLS)
ORBANCO... Oregon Bank (EFIS)
Or Bar Bull... Oregon Bar Bulletin [*A publication*] (DLA)
ORBAT....... Order of Battle (SAUS)
ORBAT....... Order of Battle Report [*Military*] (NATG)
ORBATREP... Order of Battle Report (SAUS)
ORBATTOA... Order of Battle-Transfer of Authority (SAUS)
ORBB........ Sirsenk/Bamarni [*Iraq*] [*ICAO location identifier*] (ICLI)
ORBC........ Baghdad/Soica Headquarters [*Iraq*] [*ICAO location identifier*] (ICLI)
ORBC........ Ox Red Blood Cell [*Medicine*] (DMAA)
ORBD........ Object Relational Database (SAUS)
ORBD-NRC... Osteoporosis and Related Bone Diseases-National Resource Center (SAUS)
OrBe......... Deschutes County Library, Bend, OR [*Library symbol*] [*Library of Congress*] (LCLS)
ORBE........ Open Reciprocating Brayton Engine (PDAA)
OrBeBR..... Bend Research, Inc., Bend, OR [*Library symbol*] [*Library of Congress*] (LCLS)
OrBeC....... Central Oregon Community College, Bend, OR [*Library symbol*] [*Library of Congress*] (LCLS)
OrBeCJ...... Cascade Junior High School, Bend, OR [*Library symbol*] [*Library of Congress*] (LCLS)
OrBeHS..... Bend Senior High School, Bend, OR [*Library symbol*] [*Library of Congress*] (LCLS)
OrBeMC..... Saint Charles Medical Center, Medical Library, Bend, OR [*Library symbol*] [*Library of Congress*] (LCLS)
OrBeMH..... Mountain View High School, Bend, OR [*Library symbol*] [*Library of Congress*] (LCLS)
OrbEng...... Orbital Engine Corp. Ltd. [*Associated Press*] (SAG)
OrBeOHM... Oregon High Desert Museum, Bend, OR [*Library symbol*] [*Library of Congress*] (LCLS)
OrBePJ...... Pilot Butte Junior High School, Bend, OR [*Library symbol*] [*Library of Congress*] (LCLS)
ORBF........ Ordinary Radial Basis Function (IDAI)
OrBFP....... Floating Point Systems, Inc., Beaverton, OR [*Library symbol*] [*Library of Congress*] (LCLS)
OrBG......... Oregon Graduate Center, Beaverton, OR [*Library symbol*] [*Library of Congress*] (LCLS)
OrBGS....... Church of Jesus Christ of Latter-Day Saints, Genealogical Society Library, Beaverton Branch, Beaverton, OR [*Library symbol*] [*Library of Congress*] (LCLS)
ORBI......... Orange Bishop [*North American bird banding code*] (BIBA)
ORBI......... Orbital Sciences Corp. [*NASDAQ symbol*] (SAG)
ORBI......... Orbit Industries [*NCIC trailer make code*]
ORBI......... Rocky Band No. 1 Indian Band Library, Ontario [*Library symbol*] [*National Library of Canada*] (BIB)
orbic......... orbicular (SAUS)
orbic......... orbicularis (SAUS)
ORBID....... On-line Retrieval of Bibliographic Data (SAUS)
ORBIFC...... Oak Ridge Boys International Fan Club (EA)
ORBIS....... Orbiting Radio Beacon Ionospheric Satellite [*NASA*]
ORBIS....... Ordering and Billing System
ORBIS....... Oregon Business Information System [*Oregon State Economic Development Department*] [*Information service or system*] [*Defunct*] (IID)
ORBIS CAL... Orbiting Radio Beacon Ionosphere Satellite for Calibration [*NASA*] (PDAA)
ORBISCAL... Orbiting Radio Beacon Ionospheric Satellite for Calibration (SAUS)
Orbis Econ... Orbis Economicus [*A publication*] (JLIT)
ORBIT....... Oak Ridge Binary Internal-Translator
ORBIT....... Objectives-Referenced Bank of Items and Tests (TES)
ORBIT....... Office Research into Buildings and IT (NITA)
ORBIT....... On-Line, Real-Time, Branch Information Transmission [*IBM Corp.*] [*Computer science*]
ORBIT....... On-Line Reduced Bandwidth Information Transfer [*Computer science*]
ORBIT....... On-line Retrieval of Bibliographic Information Timeshared (SAUS)
ORBIT....... On-Line Retrieval of Bibliographic Text [*Search system*] [*Computer science*]
ORBIT....... ORACLE Binary Internal Translator [*Algebraic programming system*]
ORBIT....... Orbit, Ballistic Impact, and Trajectory [*Computer*] (MUGU)
Orbit........ Orbit International Corp. [*Associated Press*] (SAG)
ORBIT....... Order Billing Inventory Technique (PDAA)
ORBITSIM... Orbit Simulation (ACAE)
ORBK........ Orbotech Ltd. [*Formerly, Optrotech Ltd.*] [*NASDAQ symbol*] (SPSG)
ORBKF....... Orbotech Ltd Ord [*NASDAQ symbol*] (TTSB)
ORBL........ Outline Raised Black Letter [*Tire design*]
ORBM........ Mosul [*Iraq*] [*ICAO location identifier*] (ICLI)
ORBN........ Orbanco Financial Services Corp. (SAUS)
OrBo......... Boardman Public Library, Boardman, OR [*Library symbol*] [*Library of Congress*] (LCLS)
Orbotch..... Orbotech [*Associated Press*] (SAG)
OrBP......... Oregon Regional Primate Research Center, Beaverton, OR [*Library symbol*] [*Library of Congress*] (LCLS)
ORBPAC..... The PAC of Orbital Sciences [*Dulles, VA*] (PACS)
Or-BPH...... Oregon State Library, Services for the Blind and Physically Handicapped, Salem, OR [*Library symbol*] [*Library of Congress*] (LCLS)
ORBR........ Baghdad/Rasheed [*Iraq*] [*ICAO location identifier*] (ICLI)
OrBroo...... Chetco Community Public Library, Brookings, OR [*Library symbol*] [*Library of Congress*] (LCLS)
ORBS........ Baghdad/Saddam International [*Iraq*] [*ICAO location identifier*] (ICLI)
ORBS........ Off Reservation Boarding School (EDAC)

ORBS........ Orbital Rendezvous Base System
ORBS........ Orbiting Rendezvous Base System (SAUS)
OrbSci....... Orbital Sciences Corp. [*Associated Press*] (SAG)
ORBT........ Orbit International Corp. [*NASDAQ symbol*] (NQ)
OrBT......... Tektronix, Inc., Beaverton, OR [*Library symbol*] [*Library of Congress*] (LCLS)
OrbtSemi... Orbit Semiconductor Co. [*Associated Press*] (SAG)
ORBU........ Enterprise Container Lines [*Intermodal shipping container symbol*] (TVRC)
Or Bull...... Oregon Bulletin [*A publication*] (AAGC)
ORBV........ Optometrists' Registration Board of Victoria [*Australia*]
ORBW........ Baghdad/Muthenna [*Iraq*] [*ICAO location identifier*] (ICLI)
ORBWA...... Optometrists' Registration Board of Western Australia
ORBZ........ Ain Zalah [*Iraq*] [*ICAO location identifier*] (ICLI)
OrC.......... Corvallis Public Library, Corvallis, OR [*Library symbol*] [*Library of Congress*] (LCLS)
ORC.......... Occupational Research Centre [*Hatfield Polytechnic*] [*British*] (CB)
ORC.......... Oculo-Reno-Cerebellar [*Syndrome*] [*Medicine*] (DMAA)
ORC.......... Office of Regional Counsel [*Environmental Protection Agency*] (GFGA)
ORC.......... Office of Reserve Components [*Army*]
ORC.......... Office of the Regional Commissioner [*Social Security Administration*] (OICC)
ORC.......... Officers' Reserve Corps [*Later, Army Reserve*]
ORC.......... Offshore Racing Council
ORC.......... Oil Ring Clogging [*Fuels and lubricants*]
ORC.......... Oilseeds Research Council [*Australia*]
ORC.......... Oklahoma Religious Coalition for Reproductive Choice (EARSL)
ORC.......... On-Line Reactivity Computer [*Nuclear energy*] (NRCH)
ORC.......... On-Road Costs [*Motor vehicles*]
ORC.......... Operarios del Reina de Cristo (TOCD)
orc........... Operarios del Reina de Cristo (TOCD)
ORC.......... Operational Readiness Check
ORC.......... Operational Reports Control [*Military*] (AFM)
ORC.......... Operational Requirements Committee [*Ministry of Defence*] [*British*]
ORC.......... Operational Research Committee (SAUS)
ORC.......... Operations Research Center [*Massachusetts Institute of Technology*] [*Research center*] (KSC)
ORC.......... Operations Review Committee (COE)
ORC.......... Opinion Research Center
ORC.......... Opinion Research Corp. (SAUS)
ORC.......... Optical Radiation Corp.
ORC.......... Optical Recording Corp.
ORC.......... Optical Recording Corporation (SAUS)
ORC.......... Orange City, IA [*Location identifier*] [*FAA*] (FAAL)
ORC.......... Orange River Colony [*Later, Orange Free State*] [*South Africa*]
ORC.......... Orbital Research Centrifuge [*NASA*] (KSC)
ORC.......... Orcadas Del Sur [*Argentina*] [*Geomagnetic observatory code*]
ORC.......... Orcatech, Inc. [*Toronto Stock Exchange symbol*]
ORC.......... Orderly Room Corporal [*British*]
ORC.......... Order of the Red Cross
ORC.......... Ordnance Rocket Center (KSC)
ORC.......... Organic Rankine Cycle [*for power generation*] (PDAA)
ORC.......... Organization Requirements Clerk [*Defense Supply Agency*]
ORC.......... Organization Resources Counselors (MCD)
ORC.......... Organized Reserve Corps [*Later, Army Reserve*]
ORC.......... Origin Recognition Complex [*Genetics*]
ORC.......... Orthogonal Row Computer
ORC.......... Orthopedic Rehabilitation Center [*Medicine*] (EDAA)
ORC.......... Osteoporosis Research Center [*Creighton University*] (RCD)
ORC.......... Outbound RADAR Control
ORC.......... Overrun Clutch
ORC.......... Over-Running Clutch [*Automotive engineering*]
ORC.......... Overseas Reconstruction Committee [*British*] [*World War II*]
ORC.......... Overseas Replacement Center (SAUS)
ORC.......... Overseas Research Center [*Wake Forest University*] [*Research center*] (RCD)
ORC.......... Overseas Research Council (SAUS)
ORC.......... Owner's Risk of Chafing [*Shipping*]
ORC.......... Oxidation Reduction Converter [*Automotive term*] (HAWK)
ORC.......... Oxidation-Reduction Converter [*Automotive engineering*]
ORC.......... Oxidation Reduction Cycle (SAUS)
ORC.......... Oxidation-Resistant Coating
ORC.......... Oxidized Regenerated Cellulose [*Hemostatic*] [*Organic chemistry*]
ORC.......... Ozarks Regional Commission [*Department of Commerce*]
ORC.......... Reed College, Portland, OR [*OCLC symbol*] (OCLC)
ORC.......... Reports of the High Court of the Orange River Colony [*South Africa*] [*A publication*] (DLA)
ORCA........ Ocean Resource Coordination and Assessment [*National Oceanic and Atmospheric Administration*]
ORCA........ Ocean Resources Conservation Association [*British*]
ORCA........ Official Receiver under the Companies Act (SAUS)
ORCA........ Oldtime Radio-Show Collector's Association (EA)
ORCA........ Online Resource Control Aid [*Computer science*] (HGAA)
ORCA........ Ontario Royal Commission on Asbestos (SAUS)
ORCA........ Operations Requirements Continuity Assessment (SAUS)
ORCA........ Orcas Island Freight Lines [*Common carrier symbol*]
ORCA........ Oregon Caves National Monument
ORCA........ Organisme Europeen de Recherche sur la Carie [*European Organization for Caries Research*] (EAIO)
ORCA........ Organization of Regulatory and Clinical Associates [*Association*] (EA)
ORCA........ Organized Resistance to Capture in Alaska [*Defunct*] (EA)
ORCA........ Regional Office for Central America (SAUS)
Orcad........ Orcad, Inc. [*Associated Press*] (SAG)
ORCAL...... Orange County Manufacturing and Metalworking Conference and Exposition (SAUS)
ORCALMIS... Ordnance Calibration Management Information System [*Navy*] (DNAB)
OrCan....... Canby Public Library, Canby, OR [*Library symbol*] [*Library of Congress*] (LCLS)
OrCanHS.... Canby Union High School, Canby, OR [*Library symbol*] [*Library of Congress*] (LCLS)
ORCATS..... Oldtime Radio Collectors and Traders Society (EA)
OrCb......... Coos Bay Public Library, Coos Bay, OR [*Library symbol*] [*Library of Congress*] (LCLS)
ORCB........ Order of Railway Conductors and Brakemen [*Later, United Transportation Union*] (EA)
OrCbS....... Southwestern Oregon Community College, Coos Bay, OR [*Library symbol*] [*Library of Congress*] (LCLS)
OrCC......... Corvallis Clinic, Corvallis, OR [*Library symbol*] [*Library of Congress*] (LCLS)
ORCC........ Ohio Regional Campus Conference (PSS)
ORCC........ Online Resources Communications Co.
ORCC........ Operational Requirements Committee (SAUS)
ORCC........ Orangutan Research and Conservation Center (SAUS)
ORCC........ Outward-Rectifying Chloride Channel [*Biochemistry*]
ORCCA...... Open Road Camper Clubs of America [*Later, ORSAC*] (EA)
ORCEF...... Oak Ridge Critical Experimental Facility (SAUS)
ORCEMS.... Oregon Certified Emergency Management Specialist [*Emergency Management*] (EMA)
ORCEN...... Overseas Records Center [*Military*]
OrCEPA...... United States Environmental Protection Agency, Corvallis Environmental Research Laboratory, Corvallis, OR [*Library symbol*] [*Library of Congress*] (LCLS)
OrCg......... W. A. Woodward Memorial Library, Cottage Grove, OR [*Library symbol*] [*Library of Congress*] (LCLS)
OrCGS....... Church of Jesus Christ of Latter-Day Saints, Genealogical Society Library, Corvallis Branch, Corvallis, OR [*Library symbol*] [*Library of Congress*] (LCLS)
OrCGSH..... Good Samaritan Hospital, Corvallis, OR [*Library symbol*] [*Library of Congress*] (LCLS)
ORCH........ Orchard
orch.......... Orchestra (WDAA)
ORCH........ Orchestra
Orch.......... Orchestra
orch.......... Orchestral (GROV)
ORCH........ Orchiectomy [*Medicine*] (MELL)
ORCHARD... Orchard [*Commonly used*] (OPSA)
Orch Circ... Orchestra Circle (SAUS)
orchd........ Orchestrated (GROV)
ORCHD...... Orchestrated (By) [*Music*]
Orch H...... Orchestra Hall (SAUS)
ORCHIS..... Oak Ridge Computerized Hierarchical Information System [*AEC*] (IID)
ORCHL...... Orchestral [*Music*]
ORCHRD.... Orchard [*Commonly used*] (OPSA)
OrchSHw.... Orchard Supply Hardware Stores Corp. [*Associated Press*] (SAG)
ORCI......... Office for the Research and Collection of Information (SAUS)
ORCI......... Opinion Research [*NASDAQ symbol*] (TTSB)
ORCI......... Opinion Research Corp. [*NASDAQ symbol*]
ORCID....... Optical Readout Cherenkov Imaging Detector [*Computer science*] (PDAA)
OrckitCo..... Orckit Communications Ltd. [*Associated Press*] (SAG)
ORCL........ Oracle Corp. [*NASDAQ symbol*] (NASQ)
ORCL........ Oracle Systems Corp. [*NASDAQ symbol*] (NQ)
OrCIS........ Sunnyside Medical Library, Clackamas, OR [*Library symbol*] [*Library of Congress*] (LCLS)
ORCMD...... Orlando Contract Management District (SAA)
OrCMG...... Mid-Valley Genealogical Society, Corvallis, OR [*Library symbol*] [*Library of Congress*] (LCLS)
ORCO........ Central Ontario Regional Library, Richmond Hill, Ontario [*Library symbol*] [*National Library of Canada*] (NLC)
OrCo......... Coquille Public Library, Coquille, OR [*Library symbol*] [*Library of Congress*] (LCLS)
ORCO........ Ontario Library Service - Trent, Richmond Hill, Ontario [*Library symbol*] [*National Library of Canada*] (NLC)
ORCO........ Optical Radiation Corporation (SAUS)
ORCO........ Orcon Industries [*NCIC trailer make code*]
ORCO........ Organization Committee (SAUS)
ORCODO.... Annual Research Reviews. Oral Contraceptives (journ.) (SAUS)
OrColHS..... Colton High School, Colton, OR [*Library symbol*] [*Library of Congress*] (LCLS)
OrCon....... Condon Public Library, Condon, OR [*Library symbol*] [*Library of Congress*] (LCLS)
ORCON...... Observation Report Conversion [*Program*]
ORCON...... Organic Control
ORCON...... Originator Controlled [*Information dissemination*]
ORCON...... Originator Control of Information Release (SAUS)
ORCON Program... Observation Report Conversion Program (SAUS)
OrCor........ Cornelius Public Library, Cornelius, OR [*Library symbol*] [*Library of Congress*] (LCLS)
ORCP........ Ocean Ridge Crest Processes (SAUS)
ORCP........ Optical Reader Card Punch (SAUS)
ORCS........ Omnitronics Research Corporation (SAUS)
ORCS........ On-line Remote Compile System (SAUS)
OrCS......... Oregon State University, Corvallis, OR [*Library symbol*] [*Library of Congress*] (LCLS)
ORCS........ Organic Rankine Cycle System [*For power generation*]
ORCS........ Organic Reactions Catalysis Society (EA)
ORCSA...... Orange River Colony, South Africa (ILCA)

OrCS-Ar ..... Oregon State University Archives, Corvallis, OR [*Library symbol*] [*Library of Congress*] (LCLS)
OrCS-MB .... Oregon State University, Institute of Marine Biology, Coos Bay, OR [*Library symbol*] [*Library of Congress*] (LCLS)
OrCS-MSC .. Oregon State University, Hatfield Marine Science Center, Newport, OR [*Library symbol*] [*Library of Congress*] (LCLS)
ORCT .... Orckit Communications Ltd. [*NASDAQ symbol*] (SAG)
ORCU .... BSL Transport [*Intermodal shipping container symbol*] (TVRC)
OrCuHS ..... Culver Senior High School, Culver, OR [*Library symbol*] [*Library of Congress*] (LCLS)
ORCUP ...... Ontario Region Canadian University Press (SAUS)
ORCUS ...... Operational Research Co., Universal Systems
ORCV .... Outdoor Recreation Center Victoria [*Australia*]
ORCV .... Overriding Cam Valve
ORC youth... Opinion Research Corporation Youth (NITA)
ORCZ .... Ohio River [*Federal Railroad Administration identification code*]
ORD .... CAP PA Gutierrez [*Hernando R.*] Ordonez [*Mexico*] [*ICAO designator*] (FAAC)
ORD .... Chicago [*Illinois*] O'Hare Airport [*Derived from former name: Orchard Field*] [*Airport symbol*]
ORD .... Observed Range Deviation [*Navigation systems*]
ORD .... Octane Requirement Decrease [*Fuels and lubricants*]
ORD .... Office for Research and Development [*American Library Association*] (AEBS)
ORD .... Office of Rare Diseases, National Institutes of Health (SAUS)
ORD .... Office of Regional Development [*Organization of American States*]
ORD .... Office of Research and Development [*National Oceanic and Atmospheric Administration*] (GFGA)
ORD .... Office of Research and Development [*Washington, DC*] [*Environmental Protection Agency*] (GRD)
ORD .... Office of Research Development [*Office of Policy, Evaluation, and Research*] [*Department of Labor*]
ORD .... Office of Rubber Director [*WPB*] [*World War II*]
ORD .... Officers Replacement Depot (SAUS)
ORD .... Off-Range Distance (MCD)
ORD .... Ohio River Division [*Army Corps of Engineers*]
ORD .... Once-Run Distillate (PDAA)
ORD .... Operational Readiness Date
ORD .... Operational Readiness Demonstration [*FAA*] (TAG)
ORD .... Operational Ready [*or Readiness*] Data [*NASA*] (GFGA)
ORD .... Operational Ready Data (or Date) (SAUS)
ORD .... Operational Requirements Document (COE)
ORD .... Operational Research Division [*Department of National Defence*] [*Canada*]
ORD .... Operational Suitability (SAUS)
ORD .... Operation Readiness Demonstration (SAUS)
ORD .... Operations [*or Operational*] Requirement Document
ORD .... Optical Reference Device
ORD .... Optical Rotary Dispersion
ORD .... Oral Radiation Death (MELL)
ORD .... Orbital Requirements Document
ord .... Ordained (GEAB)
ORD .... Ordained
Ord .... Order (EBF)
ord .... Order (WDAA)
ORD .... Order
ORD .... Orderly
ord .... Ordinal (NTIO)
ORD .... Ordinal
ord .... Ordinance (WDAA)
ORD .... Ordinance
Ord .... Ordinary (EBF)
ord .... Ordinary (ELAL)
ORD .... Ordinary (MSA)
ORD .... Ordinary Seaman [*British*]
ORD .... Ordinary Share (SAUS)
Ord .... Ordinate (SAUS)
ORD .... Ordnance (AAG)
ORD .... Ordovician [*Period, era, or system*] [*Geology*]
Ord .... Orotidine [*Also, O*] [*A nucleoside*]
ORD .... Overseas Replacement Depot [*Military*]
ORD .... Owner's Risk of Damage [*Shipping*]
ORD .... Oxidation-Reduced Diffusion (SAUS)
ORDA .... NIH Office of Recombinant DNA Activities (SAUS)
ORDA .... Ober Ramstadt Depot Activity [*Germany*] [*Army*]
ORDA .... Oceanographic Research for Defense Application (SAUS)
ORDA .... Office of Recombinant DNA Activities [*Bethesda, MD*] [*National Institute of Allergy and Infectious Diseases*]
ORDA .... Office of Research Development Administration (SAUS)
ORDAC ...... Overrange Detection and Correction [*Analytical chemistry*]
OrDal .... Dallas Public Library, Dallas, OR [*Library symbol*] [*Library of Congress*] (LCLS)
ORDAL ...... Operations Research Direct Access Language (SAUS)
ORD-ALA .... Office of Research and Development-American Library Association (SAUS)
ORDALT ..... Ordnance Alterations
Ord Amst ... Ordinance of Amsterdam [*A publication*] (DLA)
Ord Antw ... Ordinance of Antwerp [*A publication*] (DLA)
Ord Austl Cap Terr... Ordinances of the Australian Capital Territory (SAUS)
ORDB .... Olfactory Receptor Database (GDD)
ORDB .... Open Relay Database [*Computer science*]
ORD BBS ... Office of Research and Development Electronic Bulletin Board System [*Environmental Protection Agency*] (AEPA)
ORD BD ..... Ordnance Board [*Military*] (WDAA)
Ord Bilb ..... Ordinance of Bilboa [*A publication*] (DLA)
ORDBMS .... Object-Relational Database Mangement System (SAUS)
ORDBN ...... Ordnance Battalion
OrdBrd ...... Ordnance Board [*British*]
ORDC .... Orbiter Data Reduction Center [*NASA*]
ORDC .... Ordnance Corps [*Army*]
ORDC .... Ordnance Research and Development Center [*Aberdeen Proving Ground, Maryland*] [*Navy*]
ORDCAL ..... Ordnance Calibration [*Navy*] (NVT)
ORDCAN .... Orders Canceled [*Air Force*]
ORDCIT ..... Ordnance Department and California Institute of Technology [*Army*] (RDA)
ORDCONCAN... Orders Considered Canceled [*Air Force*]
ORDCONTECH... Ordnance Control Technician (DNAB)
Ord Copen... Ordinance of Copenhagen [*A publication*] (DLA)
ORDCOR .... Orders Corrected [*Air Force*]
ORDCORPS... Ordnance Corps [*Army*]
ORDCU ...... Occupational Research and Development Coordinating Unit
ORDD .... Office of Research, Development, and Demonstrations [*Federal Railroad Administration*]
ORDD .... Ordered (ROG)
OrdDep .... Ordnance Depot (SAUS)
ORD DEPT... Ordnance Department [*Military*] (WDAA)
ORDDIS ..... Ordinary Discharge [*Military*]
ORDDIST... Ordnance District (SAUS)
ORDEAL ..... Oak Ridge Data Evaluation and Analysis Language [*Department of Energy*] (PDAA)
ORDEAL ..... Orbital Rate Drive Electronics for Apollo and LM [*NASA*]
ORDEAL ..... Orbit Rate Display - Earth and Lunar [*NASA*]
ORDEF ...... Ontario Research Development Foundation (SAUS)
ORDEM ...... Orbital Debris Engineering Model
OrdEng ...... Ordnance Engineer (SAUS)
ORDENG .... Ordnance Engineering
ORDER ...... On-Line Order Entry System [*Computer science*] (MHDB)
ORDER ...... Organization and Retrieval of Data for Efficient Research (SAUS)
ORDER ...... Outstanding Requisitions Defeat Endurance Readiness (DNAB)
ORDET ...... Orbit Determination Group
ORDet .... Owner's Risk of Deterioration [*Shipping*]
ORDFAC ..... Ordnance Facility
ORDFC ...... Official Red Dwarf Fan Club [*Association*] (EA)
OrdFdPk ..... Ordnance Field Park (SAUS)
ORDFIAC... Ordnance Fiscal and Inventory Automatic Computer (SAUS)
ORDFIN ..... Ordinary Finish (SAUS)
Ord Flor ..... Ordinance of Florence [*A publication*] (DLA)
OrdFuzeLab... Ordnance Fuze Laboratory (SAUS)
Ord Gen ..... Ordinance of Genoa [*A publication*] (DLA)
ORDHAC .... Ordnance Systems Command Hydroballistics Advisory Committee [*Obsolete*] [*Navy*]
Ord Hamb .. Ordinance of Hamburg [*A publication*] (DLA)
ORD/HWERL... Office of Research and Development/ Hazardous Waste Environmental Research Laboratory (SAUS)
OrdInsp ..... Ordnance Inspector (SAUS)
ORDINST... Ordnance Instruction
ORDIP .... Ordnance Alteration Installation Plan [*Navy*]
ORDIR .... Omnirange Digital RADAR
ORDIS .... Office of Research and Development Information Systems (SAUS)
ORDIS .... Optical Reading Direct Input System (IAA)
ORDIS .... Ordnance Discharge (DNAB)
Ord Konigs... Ordinance of Konigsberg [*A publication*] (DLA)
ORDL .... Ohio River Division Laboratory [*Army Corps of Engineers*] (KSC)
ORDL-EC ... Ohio River Division Laboratory, Engineer Corps [*Army*] (MCD)
Ord Leg ..... Ordinance of Leghorn [*A publication*] (DLA)
ORDLIS ..... Ordnance Logistics Information System [*Navy*]
ORDLIX ..... Organized Design for Line and Crew System (SAUS)
ORDM .... Ordnance Corps Manual (AAG)
ORDMAINTCO... Ordnance Maintenance Company [*Navy*] (DNAB)
Ord Man .... Ordnance Manual (SAUS)
Ord Med Jur... Ordronaux's Medical Jurisprudence [*A publication*] (DLA)
ORDMOD ... Orders Modified [*Navy*]
OrdMslComd... Ordnance Missile Command (SAUS)
ordn .... Ordinance (WDAA)
ORDN .... Ordnance (KSC)
ORDNA ...... Organismes de Radiodiffusion des Pays NonAlignes [*Broadcasting Organizations of Non-Aligned Countries - BONAC*] (EAIO)
ORDNG ...... Ordering
Ordn Surv... Ordnance Survey (SAUS)
ORDNTR .... Ordinator
ORDO .... Ordinario [*Ordinarily*] [*Music*] (ROG)
OrdO .... Ordnance Officer (SAUS)
Ordo Nob Urb... Ordo Nobilium Urbium [*of Ausonius*] [*Classical studies*] (OCD)
ORDP .... Office of Rural Development Policy [*Department of Agriculture*]
ORDP .... Ordnance Corps Pamphlet [*Army*] (MCD)
ORDPDS .... Offender Rehabilitation Division of the Public Defender Service (EA)
OrdPG .... Ordnance Proving Ground (SAUS)
Ord Port ..... Ordinance of Portugal [*A publication*] (DLA)
OrdProcDist... Ordnance Procurement District (SAUS)
Ord Prus ..... Ordinance of Prussia [*A publication*] (DLA)
ORDR .... Order
ORDRAT ..... Ordnance Dial Reader and Translator
OrdRepSh... Ordnance Repair Shop (SAUS)
ORDREV .... Ordnance Procedures Review [*Military*] (NVT)
Ordr Jud Ins... Ordronaux on Judicial Aspects of Insanity [*A publication*] (DLA)
Ordr Med Jur... Ordronaux's Medical Jurisprudence [*A publication*] (DLA)
Ord Rott ..... Ordinance of Rotterdam [*A publication*] (DLA)

ORDRPT.... Ordnance Report
ORDS........ Observation Requirements Data Sheet (IAA)
ORDS........ Office of Research, Demonstrations, and Statistics [*Health Care Financing Administration*]
ORDS........ Ordinary Shares (WDAA)
OrdSch...... Ordnance School (SAUS)
ORDSER.... Ordnance Support Element Review (NVT)
Ord Sgt...... Ordnance Sergeant [*Military*] (DMA)
Ords NZ..... Ordinances of the Legislative Council of New Zealand [*A publication*] (DLA)
OrdSpActv... Ordnance Special Activity (SAUS)
ORDSTA..... Ordnance Station
OrdSupDep... Ordnance Supply Depot (SAUS)
Ord Swe.... Ordinance of Sweden [*A publication*] (DLA)
ORDSYSCOM... Ordnance Systems Command [*Formerly, Bureau of Naval Weapons; later, Naval Sea Systems Command*]
ORDT........ Office of Research, Demonstrations, and Training [*Social and Rehabilitation Service, HEW*]
OrdTestSta... Ordnance Test Station (SAUS)
OrdTTC...... Ordnance Technical Training Center (SAUS)
Ord Us....... Ord on Usury [*A publication*] (DLA)
ORDVAC..... Ordinance Variable Automatic Computer (RALS)
OrdVAC...... Ordnance Variable Automatic Computer (SAUS)
OrdWpnComd... Ordnance Weapons Command (SAUS)
ORDY........ Ordinary (AABC)
Ordy......... Ordinary [*Stopping passenger*] [*Indian Railway*] (TIR)
OrE........... Eugene Public Library, Eugene, OR [*Library symbol*] [*Library of Congress*] (LCLS)
ORE.......... Greendale Aviation Co. [*Nigeria*] [*FAA designator*] (FAAC)
ORE.......... Greenfield [*Massachusetts*] [*Airport symbol*] (AD)
ORE.......... Obtained Radiation Emittance
ORE.......... Occupational Radiation Exposure (NRCH)
ORE.......... Oceanographic Research Equipment
ORE.......... Ocean Research Equipment (SAUS)
ORE.......... Ocean Resources Engineering (SAUS)
ORE.......... Office of Regional Economics [*Department of Commerce*]
ORE.......... Office of Research and Evaluation [*Bureau of Labor Statistics*] (GRD)
ORE.......... Officer Responsible for the Exercise [*Navy*] (NVT)
ORE.......... Oil Retention Enema [*Medicine*] (BCRP)
ORE.......... On-Orbit Repair Experiment [*NASA*] (NASA)
ORE.......... Operational Readiness [*Navy*] (NG)
ORE.......... Operational Readiness Evaluation [*Army*]
ORE.......... Operational Readiness Exercise (MCD)
ORE.......... Operational Research Establishment (SAUS)
ORE.......... Operational Research Executive (SAUS)
ORE.......... Optimum Resource Extraction (PDAA)
ORE.......... Orange, MA [*Location identifier*] [*FAA*] (FAAL)
ORE.......... Oregon (AAG)
Ore........... Oregon (ODBW)
ORE.......... Oregon Resources Corp. [*Vancouver Stock Exchange symbol*]
ORE.......... Oregon State University, Corvallis, Corvallis, OR [*OCLC symbol*] (OCLC)
ORE.......... Organization Region (SAUS)
ORE.......... Ornitologia Rondo Esperantlingva [*Esperantist Ornithologists' Association*] (EAIO)
ORE.......... Orthophoto Resolution Enhancer [*Army*]
ORE.......... Output Register Empty (MHDB)
ORE.......... Overall Reference Equivalent (NITA)
ORE.......... Overhaul, Rebuild, and Exchange (MCD)
ORE.......... Overtraining Reversal Effect
OREA........ Office of Russian and European Analysis [*Central Intelligence Agency*] (RCD)
OREALC..... Regional Office for Education in Latin America and the Caribbean [*UNESCO*] [*Acronym is based on foreign phrase*]
Ore App..... Oregon Court of Appeals Reports [*A publication*] (DLA)
OrEc......... Echo Public Library, Echo, OR [*Library symbol*] [*Library of Congress*] (LCLS)
OREC........ Eramosa Community Library, Rockwood, Ontario [*Library symbol*] [*National Library of Canada*] (NLC)
OREC........ Optimises Rectangles [*AERE Harwell*] [*Software package*] (NCC)
OREC........ Oxidation-Resistant Elemental Carbon [*Chemistry*]
ORECA...... Organisation et Exploitation Courses Automobiles [*Racing Car Design and Development*] [*Motorsports*]
ORECHL..... Centre Hospitalier Le Gardeur, Repentigny, Quebec [*Library symbol*] [*National Library of Canada*] (NLC)
OrECoAr..... Lane County Archives, Eugene, OR [*Library symbol*] [*Library of Congress*] (LCLS)
OrECoL...... Lane County Law Library, Eugene, OR [*Library symbol*] [*Library of Congress*] (LCLS)
ORECY...... Oregon City, OR [*American Association of Railroads railroad junction routing code*]
ORE/ERO.... Organisation Regionale de la Federation Internationale Dentaire pour l'Europe [*European Regional Organization of the International Dental Federation*] (EAIO)
OREF........ Orthopedic Research and Education Foundation [*Medicine*] (DMAA)
OREG........ Operation Register (IAA)
OREG........ Ordinary Multiple Regression [*Statistics*]
OREG........ Oregon (AFM)
Oreg......... Oregon (ODBW)
OREG........ Oregon Manufacturing Company [*NCIC trailer make code*]
Oreg Fish Comm Contrib... Oregon Fish Commission Contributions (SAUS)
Oreg Fish Comm Res Briefs... Oregon Fish Commission Research Briefs (SAUS)
OregMt...... Oregon Metallurgical Corp. [*Associated Press*] (SAG)
Oregon...... Oregon Reports [*A publication*] (DLA)
Oregon Bus Rev... Oregon Business Review [*A publication*] (JLIT)
Oreg Rev Stat... Oregon Revised Statutes [*A publication*] (DLA)
OrEGS....... Church of Jesus Christ of Latter-Day Saints, Genealogical Society Library, Eugene Branch, Eugene, OR [*Library symbol*] [*Library of Congress*] (LCLS)
Oreg SB Bull... Oregon State Bar Bulletin [*A publication*] (DLA)
Ore Health Sci U... Oregon Health Sciences University (GAGS)
OreHSocQuar... Oregon Historical Society Quarterly (SAUS)
Ore-Ida pots... Oregon-Idaho potatoes (SAUS)
OReilyAu.... O'Reilly Automotive [*Associated Press*] (SAG)
OrEL......... Lane Community College, Eugene, OR [*Library symbol*] [*Library of Congress*] (LCLS)
OREL........ Ocean Research and Engineering Laboratory (SAA)
ORELA....... Oak Ridge Electron Linear Accelerator [*Oak Ridge, TN*] [*Department of Energy*]
OREM....... Objective Reference Equivalent Measurement (IAA)
OREM....... Objective Reference Equivalent Meter (SAUS)
OREM....... Office of Research and Evaluation Methods [*National Institute of Justice*] (GRD)
OREM....... Oregon Metallurgical Corp. [*NASDAQ symbol*] (NQ)
OREM....... Overall Reference Equivalence Measurement (SAUS)
OREM-B...... Overall Reference Equivalance Measurement, Method B (SAUS)
OREN........ Orthorhombic Enstatite [*Geology*]
OrENC....... Northwest Christian College, Eugene, OR [*Library symbol*] [*Library of Congress*] (LCLS)
OrEnW....... Wallowa County Library, Enterprise, OR [*Library symbol*] [*Library of Congress*] (LCLS)
OrEnWM.... Wallowa Memorial Hospital, Burton Carlock Memorial Library, Enterprise, OR [*Library symbol*] [*Library of Congress*] (LCLS)
OREO........ Operations Response Engineering Order (SAUS)
OREO........ Orbiting Radio Emission Observatory [*Satellite*]
OREO........ Other Real Estate Owned (EBF)
O Rep....... Ohio Reports [*A publication*] (DLA)
OREP........ Optical Repeater Equipment (SAUS)
OrEPM....... Lane County Museum [*Formerly, Lane County Pioneer Museum*], Eugene, OR [*Library symbol*] [*Library of Congress*] (LCLS)
OREPS...... Operational Research in Electrical Power Systems (PDAA)
ORER........ Official Railway Equipment Register [*National Railway Publication Co.*] [*Information service or system*] (IID)
ORE RES.... Ore Reserve (SAUS)
Ore Rev Stat... Oregon Revised Statutes [*A publication*] (DLA)
ORERP...... Off-Site Radiation Exposure Review Project [*Department of Energy*]
OrEs......... Estacada Public Library, Estacada, OR [*Library symbol*] [*Library of Congress*] (LCLS)
ORES........ Office of Research and Engineering Services (SAUS)
ORESCO.... Overseas Research Council (SAUS)
OrESH....... Sacred Heart General Hospital, Eugene, OR [*Library symbol*] [*Library of Congress*] (LCLS)
OrEsHS...... Estacada High School, Estacada, OR [*Library symbol*] [*Library of Congress*] (LCLS)
Ore St B Bull... Oregon State Bar Bulletin [*A publication*] (DLA)
OreStl....... Oregon Steel Mills [*Associated Press*] (SAG)
Ore St U.... Oregon State University (GAGS)
ORET........ Oregon Transfer Company [*Common carrier symbol*]
Ore Tax Ct... Oregon Tax Court Reports [*A publication*] (DLA)
ORETF....... Outdoor Residential Exposure Task Force [*A consortium of pesticide manufacturers*]
OREX........ Isolyser Co. [*NASDAQ symbol*] (TTSB)
OREX........ Isolyser Company, Inc. [*NASDAQ symbol*] (SAG)
OREX........ Orbital Reentry Vehicle [*Space launch term*] (ISAK)
ORF.......... Norfolk/Virginia Beach [*Virginia*] [*Airport symbol*] (OAG)
ORF.......... Obesity Research Foundation [*British*] (DI)
ORF.......... Oceanic Research Foundation [*Australia*]
ORF.......... Ocean Racing Fleet [*Nautical term*] (NTA)
ORF.......... Oesterreichischer Rundfunk [*Radio and television network*] [*Austria*]
ORF.......... Officers' Recreation Facility
ORF.......... Olfactory Research Fund
ORF.......... Oman Royal Flight [*ICAO designator*] (FAAC)
ORF.......... Ontario Research Foundation [*Canada*] [*Research center*] (RCD)
ORF.......... Open Reading Frame [*Genetics*]
ORF.......... Operational Readiness Fleet (SAUS)
ORF.......... Operational Readiness Float (AABC)
ORF.......... Optical Rangefinder (SAUS)
ORF.......... Oral Rehydration Fluid
ORF.......... Oratorum Romanorum Fragmenta [*A publication*] (OCD)
Orf........... Orfeo [*Record label*]
ORF.......... Orifice (NASA)
ORF.......... Ortho Pharmaceutical Corp. [*Research code symbol*]
ORF.......... Overhaul Replacement Factor (MCD)
ORF.......... Owner's Risk of Fire [*Shipping*]
ORF.......... Owner's Risk of Freezing [*Shipping*]
OrF........... Rogers City Public Library, Forest Grove, OR [*Library symbol*] [*Library of Congress*] (LCLS)
ORFA........ ORFA Corp. of America [*NASDAQ symbol*] (COMM)
OrFc......... Falls City Public Library, Falls City, OR [*Library symbol*] [*Library of Congress*] (LCLS)
ORFC........ Orifice (AAG)
ORFCOM.... Oak Ridge Facility Comparison Study (SAUS)
ORFEUS.... Orbiting and Retrievable Far and Extreme Ultraviolet Spectrometer
ORFEUS.... Orbiting Far and Extreme Ultraviolet Spectrometer [*Telescope*]
OrFFM....... Oregon Masonic Grand Lodge, Forest Grove, OR [*Library symbol*] [*Library of Congress*] (LCLS)
OrFl.......... Florence Public Library, Florence, OR [*Library symbol*] [*Library of Congress*] (LCLS)
ORFLS....... Oak Ridge Full Matrix Least Squares
ORFM........ Outlet Region Feature Model [*Nuclear energy*] (NRCH)

Orf ML ...... Orfila's Medecine Legale [*A publication*] (DLA)
OrFP .... Pacific University, Forest Grove, OR [*Library symbol*] [*Library of Congress*] (LCLS)
ORFR .... ORBIT/FR, Inc. [*NASDAQ symbol*] (NASQ)
OrFS .... Orange Free State (DAS)
ORFS .... Origin Rail Freight [*MARAD*] (TAG)
ORG .... Glen Robertson Branch, Stormont, Dundas, and Glengarry County Public Library, Ontario [*Library symbol*] [*National Library of Canada*] (BIB)
org .... Nonprofit Organization
ORG .... Office of Racing and Gaming [*Western Australia*]
ORG .... Official Recreation Guide (TRID)
ORG .... Olympics Research Group [*University of Calgary*] [*Canada*] [*Research center*] (RCD)
ORG .... Operations Research Group
ORG .... Orange [*Diocesan abbreviation*] [*California*] (TOCD)
org .... Orange [*Philately*]
ORG .... Orange, TX [*Location identifier*] [*FAA*] (FAAL)
org .... Organ (WDAA)
ORG .... Organ
org .... Organic (NTIO)
ORG .... Organic
ORG .... Organism (ADA)
ORG .... Organization [*or Organizational*] (AAG)
Org .... Organization (AAGC)
org .... Organization (GEAB)
Org .... Organizational (AL)
ORG .... Organize (SAUS)
Org .... Organizer (SAUS)
ORG .... Organogenesis, Inc. [*AMEX symbol*] (SPSG)
ORG .... Organon [*Netherlands*] [*Research code symbol*]
ORG .... Oriental Airlines (Gambia) Ltd. [*ICAO designator*] (FAAC)
ORG .... Origin (MDG)
ORG .... Original [*Motor vehicle violation code used in state of Maryland*] (MVRD)
Org .... Original (TBD)
ORG .... Original New York Seltzer of Canada Ltd. [*Vancouver Stock Exchange symbol*]
ORG .... Origination (SAUS)
org .... Originator [*MARC relator code*] [*Library of Congress*] (LCCP)
ORG .... Paramaribo [*Surinam*] Zorg En Hoop Airport [*Airport symbol*] (OAG)
ORGA .... Organizacion Regional Gallega Autonoma [*Regional Galician Autonomy Organization*] [*Spain*] [*Political party*] (PPE)
ORGALIME ... Liaison Group of the European Mechanical, Electrical, Electronic and Metal Working Industries (SAUS)
ORGALIME ... Organisme de Liaison des Industries Metalliques Europeennes [*Liaison Group for the European Engineering Industries*] [*Brussels, Belgium*] (EAIO)
ORGAN ...... Organisation Regionale Africaine de Normalisation [*African Regional Organization for Standardization - AROS*] (EA)
ORGAN ...... Organization
Organ Am Stats Ann ... Organization of American States. Annals (SAUS)
Organ Environ ... Organization and Environment [*A publication*] (JLIT)
Organik ..... Organik Technologies, Inc. [*Associated Press*] (SAG)
organiz ...... Organization [*or Organizational*] (DAVI)
ORGANONPAC ... Organon Inc. PAC [*West Orange, NJ*] (PACS)
OrGb .... Curry Public Library, Gold Beach, OR [*Library symbol*] [*Library of Congress*] (LCLS)
OrgBehav ... Organizational Behaviour (DD)
ORGBG ...... Orangeburg, SC [*American Association of Railroads railroad junction routing code*]
Orgburo ..... Organizational Bureau of the Central Committee (SAUS)
ORgC .... Rio Grande College, Rio Grande, OH [*Library symbol*] [*Library of Congress*] (LCLS)
Org Chem ... Organic Chemistry (SAUS)
ORGD .... Organized
ORGDP ...... Oak Ridge Gaseous Diffusion Plant [*Department of Energy*]
ORGEL ...... Organique et Eau Lourde [*Organic liquid and heavy water nuclear reactor*]
Org Exp ..... Organo Espressivo [*Swell Organ*] [*Music*]
OrGH .... Josephine Memorial Hospital, Grants Pass, OR [*Library symbol*] [*Library of Congress*] (LCLS)
ORGK .... Organik Technologies [*NASDAQ symbol*] (TTSB)
ORGK .... Organik Technologies, Inc. [*NASDAQ symbol*] (SAG)
ORGKL ...... Organik Tech Wrrt [*NASDAQ symbol*] (TTSB)
ORGKW ..... Organik Technologies Wrrt'A' [*NASDAQ symbol*] (TTSB)
ORGKZ ...... Organik Technologies Wrrt'B' [*NASDAQ symbol*] (TTSB)
OrGl .... Gladstone Public Library, Gladstone, OR [*Library symbol*] [*Library of Congress*] (LCLS)
ORGL .... Organizational (AFM)
ORGL .... Overall Reading Grade Level (MCD)
OrGlHS ...... Gladstone High School, Gladstone, OR [*Library symbol*] [*Library of Congress*] (LCLS)
ORGM .... Outdoor Recreation Grants-in-Aid Manual
Org-Man .... Organization Man (SAUS)
ORGN .... Organization (AFM)
Orgngn ...... Organogenesis, Inc. [*Associated Press*] (SAG)
Orgnik .... Organik Technologies, Inc. [*Associated Press*] (SAG)
ORGNL ...... Organizational
Org No ...... Originators Number (SAUS)
ORGO .... Organo [*Organ*] [*Music*] (ROG)
ORGR .... Oriental Greenfinch [*North American bird banding code*] (BIBA)
OrGR .... Rogue Community College, Grants Pass, OR [*Library symbol*] [*Library of Congress*] (LCLS)
OrGrC .... Mount Hood Community College, Gresham, OR [*Library symbol*] [*Library of Congress*] (LCLS)
Org React ... Organic Reactivity (SAUS)
OrGrGS ...... Church of Jesus Christ of Latter-Day Saints, Genealogical Society Library, Gresham Branch, Gresham, OR [*Library symbol*] [*Library of Congress*] (LCLS)
ORGS .... Operational Research Group of Scotland (SAUS)
ORGSBS .... Oak Ridge Graduate School of Biomedical Sciences [*Tennessee*]
ORGSC ...... Oregon Ryegrass Growers Seed Commission (EA)
Orgst .... Organist (SAUS)
ORGSYN .... Organic Syntheses Database [*Database*] (GDD)
ORGT .... Organist
ORGY .... Organization for the Rational Guidance of Youth [*Fictitious organization in film, "The Man from ORGY"*]
ORH .... Occupational Role History [*Psychology*]
ORH .... Odyssey Re Holdings Corp. [*NYSE symbol*]
ORH .... Office of Rural Health (MEDA)
ORH .... Operational Requirements Handbook
ORH .... Orchard Supply Hardware Strs [*NYSE symbol*] (TTSB)
o-rh .... Orthorhombic [*Crystallography*]
ORH .... Richmond Hill Public Library, Ontario [*Library symbol*] [*National Library of Canada*] (NLC)
ORH .... Worcester [*Massachusetts*] [*Airport symbol*] (OAG)
OrHe .... Hermiston Public Library, Hermiston, OR [*Library symbol*] [*Library of Congress*] (LCLS)
OrHeGS ..... Good Shepherd Hospital, Hermiston, OR [*Library symbol*] [*Library of Congress*] (LCLS)
OrHep .... Heppner Public Library, Heppner, OR [*Library symbol*] [*Library of Congress*] (LCLS)
OrHepPM ... Pioneer Memorial Hospital, Heppner, OR [*Library symbol*] [*Library of Congress*] (LCLS)
ORHFC ...... Official Rocky Horror Fan Club (EA)
OrHi .... Oregon Historical Society, Portland, OR [*Library symbol*] [*Library of Congress*] (LCLS)
OrHil .... Hillsboro Public Library, Hillsboro, OR [*Library symbol*] [*Library of Congress*] (LCLS)
OrHilHI ...... Tuality Health Information Resource Center, Hillsboro, OR [*Library symbol*] [*Library of Congress*] (LCLS)
OrHilT .... Tuality Community Hospital, Hillsboro, OR [*Library symbol*] [*Library of Congress*] (LCLS)
OrHilW ...... Washington County Law Library, Hillsboro, OR [*Library symbol*] [*Library of Congress*] (LCLS)
ORHP .... Office of Rural Health Policy
OrHr .... Hood River County Library, Hood River, OR [*Library symbol*] [*Library of Congress*] (LCLS)
OrHx .... Helix Pubic Library, Helix, OR [*Library symbol*] [*Library of Congress*] (LCLS)
ORHX .... Howard Tank Line [*Private rail car owner code*]
ORHZ .... Oreville Heritage Railroad Committee [*Federal Railroad Administration identification code*]
OrI .... Independence Public Library, Independence, OR [*Library symbol*] [*Library of Congress*] (LCLS)
ORI .... Occurrence of Reinforcing Information (SAUS)
ORI .... Ocean Research Institute (WDAA)
ORI .... Ocean Resources Institute (COE)
ORI .... Octane Requirement Increase [*Fuels and lubricants*]
ORI .... Ocurrence of Reinforcing Information (PDAA)
ORI .... Office of Research and Inventions
ORI .... Office of Research Integrity [*Department of Health and Human Services*]
ORI .... Office of Road Inquiry [*Later, Bureau of Public Roads*]
ORI .... Office Research Institute (NADA)
ORI .... Old Republic International Corp. [*NYSE symbol*] (SPSG)
ORI .... Omni Resources, Inc. [*Vancouver Stock Exchange symbol*]
ORI .... Online Retrieval Interface (SAUS)
ORI .... Operating and Repair Instruction
ORI .... Operational Readiness Inspection [*Army*]
ORI .... Operational Readiness Instruction [*Military*]
ORI .... Operations Research and Industrial Engineering (SAUS)
ORI .... Operations Research and Information Systems (SAUS)
ORI .... Operations Research, Inc. [*Information service or system*]
ORI .... Ophthalmic Research Institute (EA)
ORI .... Orders and Requests for Information (SAUS)
ORI .... Oregon Research Institute
ORI .... Orient Air Ltd. [*British*] [*ICAO designator*] (FAAC)
ORI .... Orientation Inventory [*Vocational guidance test*]
ORI .... Originating Body (SAUS)
Ori .... Oriole [*Record label*] [*Great Britain*]
Ori .... Orion [*Constellation*]
ori .... Oriya [*MARC language code*] [*Library of Congress*] (LCCP)
ORI .... Outdoor Recreation Institute (EA)
ORI .... Overhaul and Repair Instruction
ORI .... Overriding Royalty Interest (SAUS)
ORI .... Port Lions [*Alaska*] [*Airport symbol*] (OAG)
ORIA .... Office of Radiation and Indoor Air [*US Environmental Protection Agency*] (RCD)
ORIA .... Office of Regulatory and Information Affairs (SAUS)
ORIA .... Oriental Rug Importers Association of America (EA)
ORIAC .... CERN Accounting System (SAUS)
ORIADOC ... Orientation and Access to Information and Documentation Sources in France [*Commission de Coordination de la Documentation Administrative*] [*Database*]
ORIC .... Oak Ridge Isochronous Cyclotron [*Department of Energy*]
ORIC .... Operational Readiness Inspection Committee [*NASA*]
ORICAT ...... Original Cataloguing System (NITA)
ORICS .... Optical Ranging, Identification, and Communications System (ACAE)

ORICS .... Optical Ranging Identification Friend or Foe Communication System (ACAE)
ORIDE .... Override (KSC)
ORIE .... Operational Radiation Instrumentation Equipment (SAA)
ORIEL .... Oriel College,Oxford (SAUS)
ORIEN .... Orientation (AABC)
ORIENT ...... Orient Airways (SAUS)
Orient .... Oriental (DIAR)
ORIENT ...... Orientation
Oriental J Chem ... Oriental Journal of Chemistry [*A publication*] (PABS)
OrientB ...... Oriental Bank & Trust [*Associated Press*] (SAG)
Ori Exp ...... Orient Express (SAUS)
ORIF .... Open Reduction with Internal Fixation [*Medicine*]
Orig .... Origen [*Deceased circa 254*] [*Authority cited in pre-1607 legal work*] (DSA)
ORIG .... Origin [*or Original*] (AAG)
orig .... Origin (VRA)
orig .... Original (BEE)
Orig .... Original
orig .... Originally (NTIO)
Orig .... Originally (SAUS)
ORIG .... Originated (TVEL)
ORIG .... Originator (MSA)
ORIGAN ..... Origanum [*Marjoram*] [*Pharmacology*] (ROG)
ORIG BDS ... Original Boards [*Graphic arts*] (DGA)
Orig Ed ...... Original Edition (SAUS)
ORIGEN2 .... Oak Ridge Isotope Generation and Depletion Code [*Department of Energy*] (GAAI)
Orig Enl ..... Original Enlistment (SAUS)
ORIGINATG ... Originating (ROG)
ORIGINS ... Oklahoma Resources Integrated General Information Network System
ORIGL .... Original (ROG)
Orig Publ ... Original Publication (SAUS)
Orig Publ ... Original Publisher (SAUS)
ORILL .... Orillia, ON [*American Association of Railroads railroad junction routing code*]
ORIN .... Orin, WY [*American Association of Railroads railroad junction routing code*]
ORIN .... Orleans Installation (SAUS)
O Ring ...... O-shaped Ring (SAUS)
ORINS .... Oak Ridge Institute of Nuclear Studies [*Later, ORAU*] (EA)
ORINT .... Oriented Integrator (SAUS)
ORIO .... Oak Ridge Regional Inspections Office (SAUS)
ORIO .... Oriole Trailer Manufacturing Company [*NCIC trailer make code*]
Orio .... Orion [*Constellation*]
OriolH .... Oriole Homes Corp. [*Associated Press*] (SAG)
ORION .... Online Retrieval of Information over a Network
ORION .... Operational Radio Interferometry Observing Network (MCD)
OrionCap .... Orion Capital Corp. [*Associated Press*] (SAG)
OrionNS ..... Orion Network Systems, Inc. [*Associated Press*] (SAG)
ORIP .... Ripley Branch, Bruce County Public Library, Ontario [*Library symbol*] [*National Library of Canada*] (NLC)
ORIPrH ...... Old Republic Int 8.75% Pfd'H' [*NYSE symbol*] (TTSB)
ORIR .... Orion Research, Inc. [*NASDAQ symbol*] (COMM)
Oris .... All India Reporter, Orissa [*A publication*] (DLA)
ORIS .... Object Recognition and Identification System (VLIE)
ORIS .... Office of Regulatory Information Systems [*Energy Regulatory Commission*] (IID)
ORIS .... Officeworker Reader Information Services [*British*]
oris .... orismological (SAUS)
Oris .... Orismologist (SAUS)
Oris .... Orismology (SAUS)
ORIS .... Overlapped Rank-Intervals Set (VLIE)
ORIS .... South Carleton High School, Richmond, Ontario [*Library symbol*] [*National Library of Canada*] (NLC)
ORISE .... Oak Ridge Institute for Science and Education [*Oak Ridge Associated Universities*] [*Research center*] (RCD)
Orissa .... All India Reporter, Orissa [*A publication*] (DLA)
ORIT .... Operational Readiness Inspection Team [*Air Force*]
ORIT .... Operational Readiness Inspection Test [*Air Force*]
ORIT .... Organization Regional Interamericana de Trabdjadores [*Inter-American Labor Organization*] [*Spanish*] (BARN)
ORITE .... Ohio Research Institute for Transportation and the Environment [*Ohio University*] (RCD)
ORJ .... Corry, PA [*Location identifier*] [*FAA*] (FAAL)
ORJ .... Ohio Power Co. [*NYSE symbol*] (SAG)
ORJ .... Oneida Resources, Inc. [*Vancouver Stock Exchange symbol*]
OrJ .... Orange Juice
ORJ .... Orinduik [*Guyana*] [*Airport symbol*] (OAG)
OrJc .... Junction City Public Library, Junction City, OR [*Library symbol*] [*Library of Congress*] (LCLS)
OrJe .... Jefferson Public Library, Jefferson, OR [*Library symbol*] [*Library of Congress*] (LCLS)
ORJETS ..... On-Line Remote Job Entry Terminal System [*Computer science*]
OrJM .... Jacksonville Museum, Jacksonville, OR [*Library symbol*] [*Library of Congress*] (LCLS)
ORJU .... Oregon Junco [*North American bird banding code*] (BIBA)
OrJvHS ...... Jordan Valley High School, Jordan Valley, OR [*Library symbol*] [*Library of Congress*] (LCLS)
ORK .... Air Orkney [*British*] [*ICAO designator*] (FAAC)
ORK .... Cork [*Ireland*] [*Airport symbol*] (OAG)
OrK .... Klamath County Library, Klamath Falls, OR [*Library symbol*] [*Library of Congress*] (LCLS)
ORK .... Office Resource Kit (SAUS)
ORK .... Orkney [*County in Scotland*] (ROG)
ORKID .... Open Real-Time Kernel Interface Definition [*Computer science*] (VLIE)
ORKID .... Orientation Determination from Kikuchi Diagrams (SAUS)
OrKM .... Merle West Medical Center Library, Klamath Falls, OR [*Library symbol*] [*Library of Congress*] (LCLS)
OrKT .... Oregon Technical Institute, Klamath Falls, OR [*Library symbol*] [*Library of Congress*] (LCLS)
ORL .... Journal for Oto-Rhino-Laryngology and its related specialties (SAUS)
ORL .... Observed Range Limit
ORL .... Olivetti Research Laboratory Ltd. [*British*] (IRUK)
ORL .... On Air Ltd. [*Canada*] [*ICAO designator*] (FAAC)
ORL .... Optimum Repair Level Analysis
ORL .... Orbital Research Laboratory [*NASA*]
ORL .... Orbiting Research Laboratory (SAUS)
ORL .... Ordnance Research Laboratory [*Later, Applied Research Laboratory*] [*Pennsylvania State University*] (MCD)
ORL .... Orion Resources Ltd. [*Vancouver Stock Exchange symbol*]
'Orl .... 'Orlah (BJA)
ORL .... Orlando [*Florida*] [*Airport symbol*] (OAG)
ORL .... Orlando Public Library, Orlando, FL [*OCLC symbol*] (OCLC)
ORL .... Otorhinolaryngologist (SAUS)
ORL .... Otorhinolaryngology [*Medicine*]
ORL .... Outlook on Research Libraries (SAUS)
ORL .... Overrun Lights (SAUS)
ORL .... Owner's Risk of Leakage [*Shipping*]
ORL .... Red Lake Public Library, Ontario [*Library symbol*] [*National Library of Canada*] (NLC)
ORLA .... Optical Remote Sensing of the Land (SAUS)
ORLA .... Optimum Repair Level Analysis [*Air Force*]
ORLA .... Optimum Repair Level Authorization (MCD)
ORLA .... Optimum Report Level Analysis [*Military*]
Orla .... Orde Lama (SAUS)
ORLA .... Orlando Boar Company [*NCIC trailer make code*]
OrLak .... Lake County Library, Lakeview, OR [*Library symbol*] [*Library of Congress*] (LCLS)
OrLan .... Langlois Public Library, Langlois, OR [*Library symbol*] [*Library of Congress*] (LCLS)
Or Laws ..... Oregon Laws and Resolutions [*A publication*] (DLA)
Or Laws Adv Sh ... Oregon Laws Advance Sheets [*A publication*] (DLA)
Or Laws Spec Sess ... Oregon Laws and Resolutions [*A publication*] (DLA)
Orl Bridg ... Orlando Bridgman's English Common Pleas Reports [*A publication*] (DLA)
Orl Bridgman ... Orlando Bridgman's English Common Pleas Reports [*A publication*] (DLA)
Orleans App ... Orleans Court of Appeals [*Louisiana*] (DLA)
Orleans TR ... Orleans Term Reports [*1, 2 Martin*] [*Louisiana*] [*A publication*] (DLA)
OrLeH .... Lebanon Community Hospital, Lebanon, OR [*Library symbol*] [*Library of Congress*] (LCLS)
ORLF .... Oil Ring Land Face [*Fuels and lubricants*]
OrLg .... La Grande Public Library, La Grande, OR [*Library symbol*] [*Library of Congress*] (LCLS)
OrLgE .... Eastern Oregon College, La Grande, OR [*Library symbol*] [*Library of Congress*] (LCLS)
OrLgFS ...... United States Forest Service, Range and Wildlife Habitat Laboratory, La Grande, OR [*Library symbol*] [*Library of Congress*] (LCLS)
OrLgGRH .... Grande Ronde Hospital, LaGrande, OR [*Library symbol*] [*Library of Congress*] (LCLS)
OrLgGS ...... Church of Jesus Christ of Latter-Day Saints, Genealogical Society Library, La Grande Branch, La Grande, OR [*Library symbol*] [*Library of Congress*] (LCLS)
ORLIS .... Orts-, Regional-, und Landesplanung Literaturinformationssystem [*Literature Information System for Town and Regional Planning*] [*1974-1978*] [*Database*]
ORLL .... Operational Reports - Lessons Learned [*Army*] (AABC)
OrLo .... Lake Oswego Public Library, Lake Oswego, OR [*Library symbol*] [*Library of Congress*] (LCLS)
OrLoHS ...... Lake Oswego High School, Lake Oswego, OR [*Library symbol*] [*Library of Congress*] (LCLS)
OrLoJS ...... Lake Oswego Junior High School, Lake Oswego, OR [*Library symbol*] [*Library of Congress*] (LCLS)
OrLoLHS .... Lakeridge High School, Lake Oswego, OR [*Library symbol*] [*Library of Congress*] (LCLS)
OrLpHS ...... La Pine Senior High School, La Pine, OR [*Library symbol*] [*Library of Congress*] (LCLS)
OrlPID .... Industrial Design Corp., Portland, OR [*Library symbol*] [*Library of Congress*] (LCLS)
ORLPP ...... Office of Research, Legislation, and Program Policies [*Unemployment Insurance Service*] [*Department of Labor*]
ORLRAPS ... Online Remedial Action Progress System (SAUS)
ORLS .... Selco Mining Corp., Red Lake, Ontario [*Library symbol*] [*National Library of Canada*] (NLC)
Or LSJ .... Oregon Law School Journal [*1902-03*] [*A publication*] (DLA)
ORLSTJ ..... St. Joseph Township Public Library, Richards Landing, Ontario [*Library symbol*] [*National Library of Canada*] (NLC)
Orl TR .... Orleans Term Reports [*1, 2 Martin*] [*Louisiana*] [*A publication*] (DLA)
ORLY .... O'Reilly Automotive [*NASDAQ symbol*] (SAG)
ORLY .... Overload Relay (IEEE)
ORM .... Bine [*Language symbol*] (ETLW)
ORM .... Northampton [*England*] [*Airport symbol*] (AD)
ORM .... Object Role Modeling (SAUS)
ORM .... Object Role Modelling (VLIE)
ORM .... Office of Recycled Materials [*National Bureau of Standards*]
ORM .... Office of Regional Management [*Employment and Training Administration*]

ORM .... Office of Regulated Material [*Environmental Protection Agency*] (GFGA)
ORM .... Office of Resource Management (SAUS)
ORM .... Off-Road Mobility
ORM .... Off-Route Mine
ORM .... Ohio Reformatory for Men (SAUS)
ORM .... On Request from Manufacturer (SAUS)
ORM .... Operational Resource Management (GART)
ORM .... Operators Reference Manual (IAA)
ORM .... Optically Remote Module [*Communications term*] (DCT)
ORM .... Optically Remote switching Module (SAUS)
ORM .... Optical Reference Manual
ORM .... Optical Remote Module [*Computer science*] (VLIE)
ORM .... Optimal Replacement Method (SAUS)
ORM .... Opytnyi Reaktivnyi Motor [*Experimental Reaction Motor*] [*Former USSR*]
orm .... Ormolu (VRA)
ORM .... OSHA Reference Method [*Industrial hygiene term*] (OHS)
ORM .... Other Regulated Material
ORM .... Outside Rearview Mirror [*Automotive engineering*]
ORM .... Overhaul and Repair Manual
ORM .... Overlapping Resolution Mapping [*Computer science*]
ORMA .... Office of Refugee and Migration Affairs [*Department of State*]
ORMA .... Regional Office for Meso-America (SAUS)
OrMaC....... Marylhurst College, Marylhurst, OR [*Library symbol*] [*Library of Congress*] (LCLS)
ORMAC...... Oral Response Machine (VLIE)
OrMad....... Jefferson County Library, Madras, OR [*Library symbol*] [*Library of Congress*] (LCLS)
OrMadHS ... Madras High School, Madras, OR [*Library symbol*] [*Library of Congress*] (LCLS)
OrMadJH.... Madras Junior High School, Madras, OR [*Library symbol*] [*Library of Congress*] (LCLS)
ORMAK...... Oak Ridge TOKAMAK [*Energy Research and Development Administration*]
ORMAS...... Operational Resource Management Assessment Plan (SAUS)
ORMAS...... Operational Resource Management Assessment System [*Military*]
OrMc .... McMinnville Public Library, McMinnville, OR [*Library symbol*] [*Library of Congress*] (LCLS)
ORMC .... Off-Route [*Smart*] Mine Clearance [*Military*]
OR/MC ...... Operational Requirements/Military Characteristics (NG)
OrMcL....... Linfield College, McMinnville, OR [*Library symbol*] [*Library of Congress*] (LCLS)
OrMeGS..... Church of Jesus Christ of Latter-Day Saints, Genealogical Society Library, Medford Branch, Medford, OR [*Library symbol*] [*Library of Congress*] (LCLS)
OrMeJ .... Jackson County Library System, Medford, OR [*Library symbol*] [*Library of Congress*] (LCLS)
OrMePH..... Providence Hospital, Medford, OR [*Library symbol*] [*Library of Congress*] (LCLS)
OrMeRM .... Rogue Valley Medical Center, Medford, OR [*Library symbol*] [*Library of Congress*] (LCLS)
OrMf......... Milton-Freewater Public Library, Milton-Freewater, OR [*Library symbol*] [*Library of Congress*] (LCLS)
ORMH .... Office of Research on Minority Health (SAUS)
OrMi......... Milwaukie Public Library, Milwaukie, OR [*Library symbol*] [*Library of Congress*] (LCLS)
ORMI........ Oak Ridge Military Institute
OrMiCHS.... Clackamas High School, Media Center, Milwaukie, OR [*Library symbol*] [*Library of Congress*] (LCLS)
OrMiD .... Dwyer Community Hospital, Medical Library, Milwaukie, OR [*Library symbol*] [*Library of Congress*] (LCLS)
OrMiHS ..... Milwaukie High School, Milwaukie, OR [*Library symbol*] [*Library of Congress*] (LCLS)
OrMiLHS.... La Salle High School, Milwaukie, OR [*Library symbol*] [*Library of Congress*] (LCLS)
OrMiPHS.... Rex Putnam High School, Milwaukie, OR [*Library symbol*] [*Library of Congress*] (LCLS)
ORML .... Oriental Meal (TVEL)
ORMM....... Basrah/Magal [*Iraq*] [*ICAO location identifier*] (ICLI)
ORMOA ..... Office for Relations with Military and Occupation Authorities
OrMol .... Molalla Public Library, Molalla, OR [*Library symbol*] [*Library of Congress*] (LCLS)
OrMolHS.... Molalla Senior High School, Molalla, OR [*Library symbol*] [*Library of Congress*] (LCLS)
OrMolMS ... Molalla Mid-High School, Molalla, OR [*Library symbol*] [*Library of Congress*] (LCLS)
OrMon....... Monmouth Library, Monmouth, OR [*Library symbol*] [*Library of Congress*] (LCLS)
Ormond ..... Ormond's Reports [*19-107 Alabama*] [*A publication*] (DLA)
OrMonO .... Oregon College of Education, Monmouth, OR [*Library symbol*] [*Library of Congress*] (LCLS)
ORMONS.... Operational Readiness Monitoring System (MCD)
OrMonW .... Western Oregon State College, Monmouth, OR [*Library symbol*] [*Library of Congress*] (LCLS)
OrMp .... Myrtle Point Public Library (Flora M. Laird Library), Myrtle Point, OR [*Library symbol*] [*Library of Congress*] (LCLS)
ORMS .... Basrah/Shaibah [*Iraq*] [*ICAO location identifier*] (ICLI)
ORMS .... Office Resources Management System (SAUS)
ORMS .... On-Line Report Management System [*Computer science*] (HODG)
ORMS .... Operating Resource Management System (VLIE)
ORMS .... Operational Readiness Management System
OR/MS ...... Operational Research/Management Systems (SAUS)
OR/MS ...... Operations Research or Management Science
ORMS .... Operative Roller Makers' Society [*A union*] [*British*]
ORMS .... Other Regulated Materials (GNE)
ORMSS...... Ohio River Main Stem Study (SAUS)
OrMta .... Mount Angel Public Library, Mount Angel, OR [*Library symbol*] [*Library of Congress*] (LCLS)
OrMtaC..... Mount Angel College [*Later, Cesar Chavez College*], Mount Angel, OR [*Library symbol*] [*Library of Congress*] (LCLS)
ORMU .... Orbital Remote Maneuvering Unit
ORMU .... Orval [*Intermodal shipping container symbol*] (TVRC)
ORMWH.... Office of Research on Minority and Womens Health (SAUS)
ORMX .... DL Orme [*Private rail car owner code*]
ORMX .... Operating Resource Management Exchange (GART)
OrN .... Newberg Library Association, Newberg, OR [*Library symbol*] [*Library of Congress*] (LCLS)
ORN .... Oak Ridge National Laboratory, Oak Ridge, TN [*OCLC symbol*] (OCLC)
ORN .... Olfactory Receptor Neuron [*Biochemistry*]
ORN .... Operating Room Nurse [*Medicine*]
ORN .... Oran [*Algeria*] [*Airport symbol*] (OAG)
ORN .... Orange (AAG)
ORN .... Organization of Revolutionaries of the North [*Lebanon*] (PD)
ORN .... Orient Airways [*Pakistan*] [*ICAO designator*] (FAAC)
ORN .... Orion Power Hldgs. [*NYSE symbol*]
ORN .... Ornament (MSA)
orn .... ornamental (SAUS)
ORN .... Ornamentation (SAUS)
ORN .... OrNda Healthcorp [*NYSE symbol*] (TTSB)
ORN .... Ornithine (DB)
Orn........... Ornithine [*Same as DAV*] [*An amino acid*]
ORN .... Ornithology
Orn........... Ornithyl (SAUS)
ORN .... Oronite Reference Number [*Fuels and lubricants*]
ORN .... Orthopedic Nurse
ORN .... Osteoradionecrosis [*Medicine*] (MELL)
ORN .... Output Reconfiguration Network (SAUS)
ORNAC ...... Operating Room Nurses Association of Canada (SAUS)
ornam .... Ornament (VRA)
ORNAM ..... Ornamental
ORNAME.... Originator/Recipient Name (VLIE)
Ornam/Misc Met Fabr... Ornamental/Miscellaneous Metal Fabricator (SAUS)
OrNb......... North Bend Public Library, North Bend, OR [*Library symbol*] [*Library of Congress*] (LCLS)
OrNbGS ..... Church of Jesus Christ of Latter-Day Saints, Genealogical Society Library, Coos Bay Stake Branch, North Bend, OR [*Library symbol*] [*Library of Congress*] (LCLS)
ORND........ Ornda Healthcorp [*Formerly, Republic Health Corp.*] [*NASDAQ symbol*] (SPSG)
Ornda........ Ornda Healthcorp [*Associated Press*] (SAG)
OrNep .... Newport Public Library, Newport, OR [*Library symbol*] [*Library of Congress*] (LCLS)
OrNepH ..... Pacific Communities Hospital Library, Newport, OR [*Library symbol*] [*Library of Congress*] (LCLS)
ORNG........ Orange
ORNG........ Orange PLC [*NASDAQ symbol*] (SAG)
OrngCo ...... Orange-Co., Inc. [*Associated Press*] (SAG)
ORNGE ...... Orange, VA [*American Association of Railroads railroad junction routing code*]
OrNGF....... George Fox College, Newberg, OR [*Library symbol*] [*Library of Congress*] (LCLS)
ORNGY...... Orange PLC ADR [*NASDAQ symbol*] (TTSB)
ornith........ ornithological (SAUS)
ornith........ Ornithology (NTIO)
ORNITH ..... Ornithology
ornithol ..... ornithologic (SAUS)
ornithol ..... Ornithology (BEE)
ORNITHOL... Ornithology
ORNL......... Oak Ridge National Laboratory [*Oak Ridge, TN*] [*Department of Energy*]
ORNL......... Ordnance Navy Laboratory (SAUS)
ORNL-CF ... Oak Ridge National Laboratory Critical Facility (SAUS)
ORNL/DAAC... Oak Ridge National Laboratory Distributed Active Archive Center for Biogeochemical Dynamics (SAUS)
ORNLL ...... Oak Ridge National Laboratory Library (SAUS)
ORNL-PCA... Oak Ridge National Laboratory Pool Critical Assembly (SAA)
ORNLY-NDP... Oak Ridge National Laboratory Nuclear Data Project [*Database producer*]
ORNMT...... Ornament
ORNTL ...... Ornamental
OrNyGS ..... Church of Jesus Christ of Latter-Day Saints, Genealogical Society Library, NyssaBranch, Nyssa, OR [*Library symbol*] [*Library of Congress*] (LCLS)
OrNyMH..... Malheur Memorial Hospital, J. J. Sarazin Memorial Library, Nyssa, OR [*Library symbol*] [*Library of Congress*] (LCLS)
ORO .... Oak Ridge Operations Office (MCD)
ORO .... Office of Regional Operations [*Environmental Protection Agency*] (GFGA)
ORO .... Office of Regional Operations [*Office of Field Operations*] [*Department of Labor*]
ORO .... Official Receiver's Office [*Australia*]
ORO .... Oil Red O [*A stain*]
ORO .... Operations Research Office
ORO .... Orapouche [*An arbovirus*] [*Laboratory science*] (DAVI)
OrO .... Oregon City Public Library, Oregon City, OR [*Library symbol*] [*Library of Congress*] (LCLS)
ORO .... Orofino Resources Ltd. [*Toronto Stock Exchange symbol*] [*Vancouver Stock Exchange symbol*]
ORO .... Oropa [*Italy*] [*Seismograph station code, US Geological Survey*] [*Closed*] (SEIS)

ORO .... Oropouche [*An arbovirus*]
Oro.......... Orotate [*Biochemistry*]
Oro.......... Orotic Acid [*Biochemistry*]
ORO .... Orthicon Read-Out
ORO .... Porto Seguro [*Brazil*] [*Airport symbol*] (AD)
ORO .... Rockland Public Library, Ontario [*Library symbol*] [*National Library of Canada*] (NLC)
OrOa......... Oakridge Public Library, Oakridge, OR [*Library symbol*] [*Library of Congress*] (LCLS)
OROA........ Oroamerica, Inc. [*NASDAQ symbol*] (SAG)
Oroamer .... Oroamerica, Inc. [*Associated Press*] (SAG)
OROAP ...... Organizacion Regional del Oriente para la Administracion Publica [*Eastern Regional Organization for Public Administration*] (EAIO)
OrOC......... Clackamas County Public Library, Oregon City, OR [*Library symbol*] [*Library of Congress*] (LCLS)
OrOCC .... Clackamas Community College, Oregon City, OR [*Library symbol*] [*Library of Congress*] (LCLS)
OROCS ...... Optical Recognition of Chemical Structures Program [*IBM Almaden Research Center*] [*San Jose, CA*]
OR/OD....... Operations requirements/Operations Directive (SAUS)
Orog .... Orographer (SAUS)
Orog .... Orography (SAUS)
OrOgCL...... Cooperative Library Network of Clackamas County, Oak Grove, OR [*Library symbol*] [*Library of Congress*] (LCLS)
OrOHS .... Oregon City Senior High School, Oregon City, OR [*Library symbol*] [*Library of Congress*] (LCLS)
OROM .... Optical Read-Only Memory [*Computer science*]
OrOn......... Malheur County Library, Ontario, OR [*Library symbol*] [*Library of Congress*] (LCLS)
OrOnHR ..... Holy Rosary Hospital, Weise-Biggs Memorial Medical Library, Ontario, OR [*Library symbol*] [*Library of Congress*] (LCLS)
OrOnT .... Treasure Valley Community College, Ontario, OR [*Library symbol*] [*Library of Congress*] (LCLS)
ORootN...... Northeastern Ohio Universities, College of Medicine, Basic Medical Sciences Library, Rootstown, OH [*Library symbol*] [*Library of Congress*] (LCLS)
OROR........ Orchard Oriole [*North American bird banding code*] (BIBA)
OROR........ O'Rourke Cartage Company [*Common carrier symbol*]
OROS........ Optical Read-Only Storage [*Computer science*]
OROS........ Oral Osmotic [*System for delivering drugs into the bloodstream*] [*Alza Corp. trademark*]
OROS........ Ostomotic Release Oral System [*Medicine*] (EDAA)
OROS........ Rosseau Public Library, Ontario [*Library symbol*] [*National Library of Canada*] (NLC)
OROSS ...... Operational Readiness-Oriented Supply System [*Army*] (PDAA)
OROVL ...... Oroville, CA [*American Association of Railroads railroad junction routing code*]
OrOWH...... Willamette Falls Community Hospital, Oregon City, OR [*Library symbol*] [*Library of Congress*] (LCLS)
OrP .... Library Association of Portland [*Public Library for Portland and Multnomah County*], Portland, OR [*Library symbol*] [*Library of Congress*] (LCLS)
ORP.......... Objective Rallying Point (SAUS)
ORP.......... Objective Rally [*or Rallying*] Point [*Military*]
ORP.......... Objective Release Point [*Army*] (INF)
ORP.......... Occiput Right Posterior Fetal position [*Medicine*] (STED)
ORP.......... Occurrence Reporting Program (SAUS)
ORP.......... Office of Radiation Programs [*Environmental Protection Agency*]
ORP.......... Office of Regulatory Programs [*Federal Energy Administration*] [*Obsolete*]
ORP.......... Officer Requirements Plan (DNAB)
ORP.......... OFS [*Orbital Flight System*] Retransmission Processor [*NASA*] (GFGA)
ORP.......... OFS [*Orbiter Functional Simulator*] Retransmission Processor [*NASA*]
ORP.......... Ontario Reports Plus [*Database*] [*Canada*] (GDD)
ORP.......... Operational Readiness Panel
ORP.......... Operational Readiness Platform [*Aviation*] (DA)
ORP.......... Operational Readiness Program (SAUS)
ORP.......... Opioid-Resistant Pain [*Medicine*] (MELL)
ORP.......... Optical Response Poll (SAUS)
ORP.......... Optical Rotary Power
ORP.......... Optional Response Poll (VLIE)
ORP.......... Optional Retirement Program (SAUS)
ORP.......... Oranje River Project (SAUS)
ORP.......... Orapa [*Botswana*] [*Airport symbol*] [*Obsolete*] (OAG)
ORP.......... Orbital Radiation Program (ACAE)
ORP.......... Orbital Rendezvous Procedure (AAG)
ORP.......... Ordinary, Reasonable, and Prudent [*Legal term*] (BARN)
ORP.......... Organ Recovery Program (EA)
ORP.......... Ormara [*Pakistan*] [*Airport symbol*] (AD)
ORP.......... Outside Right Position [*Dancing*]
ORP.......... Oxidation-Reduction Potential
ORP.......... Oxidation-Reduction Probe (SAUS)
ORP.......... Oxygen-Regulated Protein [*Biochemistry*]
ORP.......... Phelps Community Library, Redbridge, Ontario [*Library symbol*] [*National Library of Canada*] (NLC)
ORPA........ Armed People's Organization (Guatemala) [*Political party*] (PSAP)
ORPA........ Office of Regional and Political Affairs (SAUS)
ORPA........ Orbiter Retarding Potential Analyzer [*NASA*]
ORPA........ Organizacion Revolucionaria del Pueblo en Armas [*Revolutionary Organization of the People in Arms*] [*Guatemala*] [*Political party*] (PD)
OrP-A........ Portland City Archives, Portland, OR [*Library symbol*] [*Library of Congress*] (LCLS)
OrPAA .... Arthur Anderson & Co., Portland, OR [*Library symbol*] [*Library of Congress*] (LCLS)
OrPAB .... Academic Book Center, Portland, OR [*Library symbol*] [*Library of Congress*] (LCLS)
ORP Amp ... Oxidation-Reduction Potential Amplifier (SAUS)
OrPB......... Bonneville Power Administration, Portland, OR [*Library symbol*] [*Library of Congress*] (LCLS)
OrPBC .... Blue Cross/Blue Shield of Oregon, Portland, OR [*Library symbol*] [*Library of Congress*] (LCLS)
OrPBK .... Bess Kaiser Foundation Hospital, Medical Library, Portland, OR [*Library symbol*] [*Library of Congress*] (LCLS)
OrPC......... Cascade College, Portland, OR [*Library symbol*] [*Library of Congress*] (LCLS)
ORPC........ Office of Rail Public Counsel [*Terminated, 1979*] [*Affiliated with Interstate Commerce Commission*]
ORPC........ Old Radio Program Collectors Club (EA)
OrPCA .... Roman Catholic Archdiocese of Portland in Oregon, Chancery Office, Portland, OR [*Library symbol*] [*Library of Congress*] (LCLS)
OrPCC .... Concordia College, Portland, OR [*Library symbol*] [*Library of Congress*] (LCLS)
OrPCM ...... Cedar Mill Community Library, Portland, OR [*Library symbol*] [*Library of Congress*] (LCLS)
OrPCNM.... National College of Naturopathic Medicine, Portland, OR [*Library symbol*] [*Library of Congress*] (LCLS)
OrPCol ...... Columbia Christian College, Portland, OR [*Library symbol*] [*Library of Congress*] (LCLS)
OrPD......... Protestant Episcopal Church, Diocesan Library, Portland, OR [*Library symbol*] [*Library of Congress*] (LCLS)
ORPE........ Oleum Ricine Polyoxyaethylat (SAUS)
OrPeB .... Blue Mountain Community College, Pendleton, OR [*Library symbol*] [*Library of Congress*] (LCLS)
OrPeCH ..... Pendleton Community Hospital, Pendleton, OR [*Library symbol*] [*Library of Congress*] (LCLS)
OrPEH .... Emanuel Hospital, Portland, OR [*Library symbol*] [*Library of Congress*] (LCLS)
OrPeSA...... Saint Anthony Hospital, Pendleton, OR [*Library symbol*] [*Library of Congress*] (LCLS)
OrPeU .... Umatilla County Library, Pendleton, OR [*Library symbol*] [*Library of Congress*] (LCLS)
OrPFW ...... United States Fish and Wildlife Service, Portland, OR [*Library symbol*] [*Library of Congress*] (LCLS)
OrPGE .... Portland General Electric Co., Portland, OR [*Library symbol*] [*Library of Congress*] (LCLS)
OrPGF .... Genealogical Forum of Portland, Portland, OR [*Library symbol*] [*Library of Congress*] (LCLS)
OrPGH....... Good Samaritan Hospital and Medical Center, Portland, OR [*Library symbol*] [*Library of Congress*] (LCLS)
OrPGS .... Church of Jesus Christ of Latter-Day Saints, Genealogical Society Library, Portland Branch, Portland, OR [*Library symbol*] [*Library of Congress*] (LCLS)
OrPGSE ..... Church of Jesus Christ of Latter-Day Saints, Genealogical Society Library, Portland East Branch, Portland, OR [*Library symbol*] [*Library of Congress*] (LCLS)
ORPH........ Orphan [*or Orphanage*]
orph .... orphanage (SAUS)
orph .... orphaned (SAUS)
ORPH........ Orphan Medical, Inc. [*NASDAQ symbol*] (SAG)
orph .... orphans (SAUS)
OrphanM.... Orphan Medical, Inc. [*Associated Press*] (SAG)
Orph Frag... Orphica Fragmenta [*A publication*] (OCD)
ORPHIC ..... Organized Projected Hypotheses for Innovations in Curriculum [*Educational planning*]
OrPHP....... Holladay Park Hospital, Medical Library, Portland, OR [*Library symbol*] [*Library of Congress*] (LCLS)
OrPHS-D .... Oregon Health Sciences University, Dental Library, Portland, OR [*Library symbol*] [*Library of Congress*] (LCLS)
ORPI......... Organ Pipe Cactus National Monument
ORPICS ..... Orbital Rendezvous Positioning, Indexing, and Coupling System
OrPK......... Bess Kaiser Foundation Hospital, Medical Library, Portland, OR [*Library symbol*] [*Library of Congress*] (LCLS)
OrPKF .... Kaiser Foundation Hospitals, Health Services Research Center, Portland, OR [*Library symbol*] [*Library of Congress*] (LCLS)
OrPL......... Lewis and Clark College, Portland, OR [*Library symbol*] [*Library of Congress*] (LCLS)
ORPL .... Office de Protection contre les Rayonnements Ionisants [*Office for Protecti on Against Ionizing Radiation*] [*France*]
ORPL .... Overseas Replacement [*Military*]
OrPL-L ...... Northwestern School of Law, Lewis and Clark College, Portland, OR [*Library symbol*] [*Library of Congress*] (LCLS)
ORPM .... Office of Research Program Management [*Environmental Protection Agency*] (GFGA)
ORPM .... Orthorhythmic Pacemaker [*Medicine*] (STED)
OrPMB ...... Multnomah School of the Bible, Portland, OR [*Library symbol*] [*Library of Congress*] (LCLS)
OrPML....... Multnomah County Law Library, Portland, OR [*Library symbol*] [*Library of Congress*] (LCLS)
OrPNA....... Northwest Association of Private Colleges and Universities, Microform Center, Portland, OR [*Library symbol*] [*Library of Congress*] (LCLS)
OrPNR....... Northwest Regional Educational Laboratory, Information Center Library, Portland,OR [*Library symbol*] [*Library of Congress*] (LCLS)
OrPO......... Oregonian Publishing Co. Library, Portland, OR [*Library symbol*] [*Library of Congress*] (LCLS)
OrPOF .... Oregon Odd Fellows Grand Lodge, Portland, OR [*Library symbol*] [*Library of Congress*] (LCLS)
OrPOj........ Oregon Daily Journal, Portland, OR [*Library symbol*] [*Library of Congress*] (LCLS)

OrPoL .... Hazel M. Lewis Library (Powers Public Library), Powers, OR [*Library symbol*] [*Library of Congress*] (LCLS)
ORPOS ...... Office of Regulatory Policy, Oversight, and Supervision [*Federal Home Loan Bank Board*]
OrPP......... Port of Portland Library, Portland, OR [*Library symbol*] [*Library of Congress*] (LCLS)
OrPPC .... Portland Community College, Portland, OR [*Library symbol*] [*Library of Congress*] (LCLS)
OrPPCP ..... Precision Cast Parts, Portland, OR [*Library symbol*] [*Library of Congress*] (LCLS)
OrPPL .... Pacific Power & Light Co., Portland, OR [*Library symbol*] [*Library of Congress*] (LCLS)
OrPPM ...... Providence Medical Center, Portland, OR [*Library symbol*] [*Library of Congress*] (LCLS)
OrPPS .... Portland Public School District, Portland, OR [*Library symbol*] [*Library of Congress*] (LCLS)
OrPr .... Crook County Library, Prineville, OR [*Library symbol*] [*Library of Congress*] (LCLS)
OrPR......... Reed College, Portland, OR [*Library symbol*] [*Library of Congress*] (LCLS)
OrPRAM..... Oregon Royal Arch Masons Grand Chapter Archives, Portland, OR [*Library symbol*] [*Library of Congress*] (LCLS)
OrPrC........ Crook County Library, Prineville, OR [*Library symbol*] [*Library of Congress*] (LCLS)
OrPrH........ Pioneer Memorial Hospital Library, Prineville, OR [*Library symbol*] [*Library of Congress*] (LCLS)
OrPrK........ Pilot Rock Public Library, Pilot Rock, OR [*Library symbol*] [*Library of Congress*] (LCLS)
OrPRP .... Riverside Psychiatric Hospital, Portland, OR [*Library symbol*] [*Library of Congress*] (LCLS)
ORPS .... Occurrence Reporting and Processing System [*Environmental science*] (COE)
ORPS .... Overseas Return Placement System [*Military*]
OrPS......... Portland State University, Portland, OR [*Library symbol*] [*Library of Congress*] (LCLS)
OrPSMA..... Saint Mary's Academy, Portland, OR [*Library symbol*] [*Library of Congress*] (LCLS)
OrPS-MI..... Metropolitan Instructional Support Laboratory, Portland State University, Portland, OR [*Library symbol*] [*Library of Congress*] (LCLS)
OrPStV ...... Saint Vincent Hospital and Medical Center, Portland, OR [*Library symbol*] [*Library of Congress*] (LCLS)
ORPSU ...... Organized Reserve Port Security Unit [*Military*]
OrPT......... Temple Beth Israel, Portland, OR [*Library symbol*] [*Library of Congress*] (LCLS)
OrPTC .... Town Center Library at Tanasbourne, Portland, OR [*Library symbol*] [*Library of Congress*] (LCLS)
OrPto .... Port Orford Public Library, Port Orford, OR [*Library symbol*] [*Library of Congress*] (LCLS)
OrPU......... University of Portland, Portland, OR [*Library symbol*] [*Library of Congress*] (LCLS)
OrPUCA ..... United States Court of Appeals, Portland, OR [*Library symbol*] [*Library of Congress*] (LCLS)
Or PUC Ops... Oregon Office of the Public Utilities Commissioner. Opinions and Decisions [*A publication*] (DLA)
OrPUDC ..... United States District Court, Central Library, Portland, OR [*Library symbol*] [*Library of Congress*] (LCLS)
OrPV......... United States Veterans Administration Hospital, Portland, OR [*Library symbol*] [*Library of Congress*] (LCLS)
OrPW........ Western Evangelical Seminary, Portland, OR [*Library symbol*] [*Library of Congress*] (LCLS)
OrPWB ...... Western Conservative Baptist Theological Seminary, Portland, OR [*Library symbol*] [*Library of Congress*] (LCLS)
OrPWP ...... Warner Pacific College, Portland, OR [*Library symbol*] [*Library of Congress*] (LCLS)
OrPWS ...... Western States Chiropractic College, Portland, OR [*Library symbol*] [*Library of Congress*] (LCLS)
OrPWsC..... West Slope Community Library, Portland, OR [*Library symbol*] [*Library of Congress*] (LCLS)
ORQ .... Norwalk, CT [*Location identifier*] [*FAA*] (FAAL)
ORQ .... Outstanding Performance Rating with Quality Step Increase [*Military*] (DNAB)
ORQMC ..... Orderly Room Quartermaster-Corporal [*British military*] (DMA)
ORQMS ..... Orderly Room Quartermaster-Sergeant [*British military*] (DMA)
ORR .... Oak Ridge Reactor (SAUS)
ORR .... Oak Ridge Research Reactor [*ORNL*] (NRCH)
ORR .... Oak Ridge Reservation
ORR .... Office of Ready Reserve [*Army*]
ORR .... Office of Refugee Relief [*Department of Health and Human Services*]
ORR .... Office of Refugee Resettlement (USGC)
ORR .... Office of the Rail Regulator [*British*] (WA)
ORR .... Omnidirectional RADAR Range (IAA)
ORR .... Omnidirectional Radio Range (IAA)
ORR .... Onsager Reciprocal Relations [*Thermodynamics*]
ORR .... Operational Radar Replacement (SAUS)
ORR .... Operational Readiness Report (SAUS)
ORR .... Operational Readiness Reporting
ORR .... Operational Readiness Review (NASA)
ORR .... Operational Ready Rate (MCD)
ORR .... Operational Research Research (SAUS)
ORR .... Operations Requirements Review (NASA)
ORR .... Operations Research Research (SAUS)
ORR .... Optical Ratio Reflector
ORR .... Orbital Rendezvous RADAR (AAG)
ORR .... Orroval Valley, Australia, Tracking Station [*NASA*] (NASA)
ORR .... Orthographic RADAR Restitutor
ORR .... Osage Railroad [*Federal Railroad Administration identification code*]
ORR .... Oudh and Rohilkand Railway Rifles [*British military*] (DMA)
ORR .... Overhaul Replacement Rate
ORR .... Overseas Research Reports (SAUS)
ORR .... Owner's Risk Rates [*Shipping*]
ORR .... Red Rock Public Library, Ontario [*Library symbol*] [*National Library of Canada*] (NLC)
ORR .... Rogue Community College Library, Grants Pass, OR [*OCLC symbol*] (OCLC)
ORRA........ Orbit Semiconductor [*NASDAQ symbol*] (SAG)
ORRA........ Oriental Rug Retailers of America (EA)
ORRAS ...... Optical Research Radiometrical Analysis System (IEEE)
ORRB........ Organic Radio Review Board (SAUS)
ORRCAT..... Ridgetown College of Agricultural Technology, Ontario [*Library symbol*] [*National Library of Canada*] (NLC)
OrRed .... Redmond Public Library, Redmond, OR [*Library symbol*] [*Library of Congress*] (LCLS)
OrRedDH.... Central Oregon District Hospital, Medical Library, Redmond, OR [*Library symbol*] [*Library of Congress*] (LCLS)
OrRedHS.... Redmond Senior High School, Redmond, OR [*Library symbol*] [*Library of Congress*] (LCLS)
OrRedOJ .... Obsidian Junior High School, Redmond, OR [*Library symbol*] [*Library of Congress*] (LCLS)
OrRedTE .... John Tuck Elementary School, Redmond, OR [*Library symbol*] [*Library of Congress*] (LCLS)
O-R Release... Own-Recognizance Release (SAUS)
Or Rep ...... Oregon Reports [*A publication*] (DLA)
Or Rev Stat... Oregon Revised Statutes [*A publication*] (DLA)
ORRIO....... Oak Ridge Regional Investigation Office (SAUS)
ORRMIS..... Oak Ridge Regional Modeling Information System
OrRoD .... Douglas County Library, Roseburg, OR [*Library symbol*] [*Library of Congress*] (LCLS)
OrRoM ...... Douglas County Museum, Roseburg, OR [*Library symbol*] [*Library of Congress*] (LCLS)
OrRoMM .... Mercy Medical Center, Roseburg, OR [*Library symbol*] [*Library of Congress*] (LCLS)
OrRoU .... Umpqua Community College, Roseburg, OR [*Library symbol*] [*Library of Congress*] (LCLS)
OrRoV .... United States Veterans Administration Hospital, Roseburg, OR [*Library symbol*] [*Library of Congress*] (LCLS)
ORRPB ...... Ottawa River Regulation Planning Board (SAUS)
ORRR........ Oak Ridge Research Reactor [*Department of Energy*] (NRCH)
ORRRC ...... Outdoor Recreation Resources Review Commission [*Terminated, 1962*] [*Department of the Interior*]
ORRS........ Outer Radial Reflector Surveillance (SAUS)
ORRSR ...... Onsite Routine Radioactive Shipment Record (SAUS)
ORRT........ Operational Readiness and Reliability Test
ORRTA....... Office of the Registrar of Restrictive Trading Agreements (PDAA)
ORRV........ Off-Road Recreation Vehicle
ORS.......... Object Recognition Systems (SAUS)
ORS.......... Obligated Reserve Section [*Air Force*] (AFM)
ORS.......... Oceanographic Research Ship
ORS.......... Octahedral Research Satellite [*NASA*]
ORS.......... Offensive Radar System (ACAE)
ORS.......... Office for Research & Statistics [*American Library Association*]
ORS.......... Office of Radiation Standards [*AEC*]
ORS.......... Office of Refugee Settlement (SAUS)
ORS.......... Office of Regulatory Support [*Environmental Protection Agency*] (GFGA)
ORS.......... Office of Rent Stabilization [*Functions transferred to Office of Defense Mobilization, 1953*]
ORS.......... Office of Research and Statistics [*Social Security Administration*]
ORS.......... Office of Research, Evaluation, and Statistics [*US Social Security Administration*] (IID)
ORS.......... Office of Research Safety [*Medicine*] [*NCI*] (EDAA)
ORS.......... Office of Research Services (SAUS)
ORS.......... Office of Revenue Sharing [*Department of the Treasury*]
ORS.......... Official Rate Standard (SAUS)
ORS.......... Official Relay Station [*Amateur radio*]
ORS.......... Off-Site Repair and Support (MCD)
ORS.......... Oil Recovery System
ORS.......... Old Red Sandstone
ORS.......... Olfactory Reference Syndrome [*Medicine*] (DMAA)
ORS.......... Omnidirectional Range Station (SAUS)
ORS.......... Online Reference Service [*Thunder Bay Public Library*] [*Canada*] (OLDSS)
ORS.......... Online Research Systems [*Information service or system*] (IID)
ORS.......... On-Line Retrieval System [*Computer science*] (TELE)
ORS.......... On-Site Reclamation System (SAUS)
ORS.......... Operating Review System (SAUS)
ORS.......... Operational Reactor Safeguards (DNAB)
ORS.......... Operational Reports Section (SAUS)
ORS.......... Operational Research Society [*British*]
ORS.......... Operational Research Station [*Air Ministry*] [*British*] [*World War II*]
ORS.......... Operations Research Society (SAUS)
ORS.......... Optical Rendezvous System (ACAE)
ORS.......... Optimal Real Storage (CMD)
ORS.......... Optional Remittance Scheme (SAUS)
ORS.......... Oral Electrolyte Solution [*Nutrition*]
ORS.......... Oral Rehydration Salts [*or Solution*]
ORS.......... Oral Rehydration Solution (SAUS)
ORS.......... Oral Surgeon
ORS.......... Orbital Refueling System [*NASA*] (NASA)
ORS.......... Orbiter Refueling System [*NASA*]
ORS.......... Orbiter Relay Simulator [*NASA*]
ORS.......... Orbiting Research Satellite [*NASA*]

ORS......... Orderly Room Sergeant [*British*]
ORS......... Ordnance Repair Shop (SAUS)
ORS......... Oregon Radiological Society (SAUS)
ORS......... Oregon Revised Statutes [*A publication*] (AAGC)
ORS......... Organization Rating Scale
ORS......... Originating Register Sender
ORS......... O-Ring Seal (SAUS)
ORS......... Oronite Report System [*Fuels and lubricants*]
ORS......... Orphan Boy Resources [*Toronto Stock Exchange symbol*] [*Canada*]
ORS......... Orpheus Island [*Australia*] [*Airport symbol*]
ORS......... Orsett [*England*]
ORS......... Orsina Resources [*Vancouver Stock Exchange symbol*]
ORS......... Orthopedic Research Society (EA)
ORS......... Orthopedic Surgeon
ORS......... Orthopedic Surgery (STED)
ORS......... OR to Storage (SAUS)
ORS......... Oscillographic Recording System
ORS......... Others
ORS......... Outboard Rotating Shield
ORS......... Outdoor Research Surveys (SAUS)
ORS......... Output Record Separator (SAUS)
ORS......... Outstanding Requisition System (DNAB)
ORS......... Oval Ring Seal
ORS......... Ovarian Remnant Syndrome [*Medicine*] (MELL)
ORS......... Overlay Reproducer System
ORS......... Over Range Station (SAUS)
ORS......... Overrange Station (SAUS)
ORS......... Ownership Reporting System [*Securities and Exchange Commission*] (GFGA)
ORS......... Owner's Risk of Shifting [*Shipping*]
ORS......... Oxfordshire Record Society [*British*] (DBA)
ORS......... Oxygen Radical Scavengers [*Medicine*] (EDAA)
ORS......... Research and Development Library, Shaw Industries, Rexdale, Ontario [*Library symbol*] [*National Library of Canada*] (BIB)
ORSA........ Oceanic Remote Sensing Assembly (SAUS)
ORSA........ Ogive Recovery System Assembly (SAUS)
ORSA........ Operational Research System Analysts
ORSA........ Operations Research Society of America (EA)
OR/SA....... Operations Research/Systems Analysis [*Army*]
ORSA........ Order of Recollects of St. Augustine
ORSA........ Oregon Revised Statutes Annotated [*A publication*]
ORSA........ Osteoclast Resorption Stimulating Activity (DMAA)
OrSa........ Salem Public Library, Salem, OR [*Library symbol*] [*Library of Congress*] (LCLS)
OrSaC....... Chemeketa Community College, Salem, OR [*Library symbol*] [*Library of Congress*] (LCLS)
ORSAC....... Oak Ridge Systems Analysis Code
ORSAC....... Open Road "See America" Club [*Defunct*] (EA)
OR/SAEC.... Operations Research/Systems Analysis Executive Course [*Army*]
OrSaGS..... Church of Jesus Christ of Latter-Day Saints, Genealogical Society Library, SalemBranch, Salem, OR [*Library symbol*] [*Library of Congress*] (LCLS)
OrSaH....... Salem Hospital, Salem, OR [*Library symbol*] [*Library of Congress*] (LCLS)
OrSaMHi.... Marion County Historical Society, Salem, OR [*Library symbol*] [*Library of Congress*] (LCLS)
OrSan....... Sandy Public Library, Sandy, OR [*Library symbol*] [*Library of Congress*] (LCLS)
ORSANCO... Ohio River Valley Water Sanitation Commission
OrSanHS.... Sandy Union High School, Sandy, OR [*Library symbol*] [*Library of Congress*] (LCLS)
ORSAR....... Official Reports, South African Republic [*A publication*] (DLA)
OrSaSH..... Oregon State Hospital, Medical Library, Salem, OR [*Library symbol*] [*Library of Congress*] (LCLS)
OrSaT....... Oregon Department of Transportation, Salem, OR [*Library symbol*] [*Library of Congress*] (LCLS)
OrSaW...... Willamette University, Salem, OR [*Library symbol*] [*Library of Congress*] (LCLS)
OrSaWB..... Western Baptist Bible College, Salem, OR [*Library symbol*] [*Library of Congress*] (LCLS)
OrSaW-L.... Willamette University, Law Library, Salem, OR [*Library symbol*] [*Library of Congress*] (LCLS)
Or SB Bull... Oregon State Bar. Bulletin [*A publication*] (ILCA)
ORS(BC).... Operational Research Section (Bomber Command) [*British*] [*World War II*]
ORS-BR..... O-Ring Seal, Braze Type (SAUS)
ORS-BT..... O-Ring Seal, Bite Type (SAUS)
Or-SC....... Oregon Supreme Court, Salem, OR [*Library symbol*] [*Library of Congress*] (LCLS)
ORSDI....... Oak Ridge Selective Dissemination of Information [*Department of Energy*] (NASA)
ORSE........ Operational Reactor Safeguard Examination (NVT)
ORSE........ Otherwise
OrSEA....... Oregon Society of Enrolled Agents (SAUS)
ORSEP...... Operational Reentry Systems Evaluation Program (SAA)
ORSEP...... Organic Separation (SAUS)
ORSER...... Office for Remote Sensing of Earth Resources [*Pennsylvania State University*] [*Research center*]
OrSh........ Sherwood Public Library, Sherwood, OR [*Library symbol*] [*Library of Congress*] (LCLS)
OrShe....... Sheridan Public Library, Sheridan, OR [*Library symbol*] [*Library of Congress*] (LCLS)
ORSI......... Office of Retirement and Survivors Insurance (SAUS)
ORSI......... Operations Research Society of India (SAUS)
OrSi......... Sisters Public Library, Sisters, OR [*Library symbol*] [*Library of Congress*] (LCLS)
OrSibyll..... Sibylline Oracles (Pseudepigrapha) (BJA)
OrSil......... Silverton Public Library, Silverton, OR [*Library symbol*] [*Library of Congress*] (LCLS)
ORSIP....... Office of Research, Statistics, and International Policy [*Later, ORS*] [*Social Security Administration*] (IID)
ORSIS....... Oak Ridge Sector Isotope Separator (SAUS)
ORSL........ Order of the Republic of Sierra Leone
ORSoc....... Operational Research Society [*British*] (DBA)
ORSociety... Operational Research Society (ACII)
ORSON...... Orient, Spell Out, Nail Down [*Method for organizing and communicating information, proposed by Barry Tarshis in his book "How to Write without Pain"*]
ORSORT..... Oak Ridge School of Reactor Technology [*Department of Energy*]
ORSP........ Office of Research and Sponsored Programs [*South Dakota State University*] (RCD)
OrSp......... Springfield Public Library, Springfield, OR [*Library symbol*] [*Library of Congress*] (LCLS)
ORSR........ Offsite Radioactive Shipment Record (SAUS)
ORSR........ Onsite Radioactive Shipment Record (SAUS)
ORS(S)...... Operational Research Section (Singapore) [*Military*]
ORSSA...... Office of Regulatory Support and Scientific Analysis [*Environmental science*] (COE)
ORSST...... Operating Review System Support Team (SAUS)
OrSt.......... Stayton Public Library, Stayton, OR [*Library symbol*] [*Library of Congress*] (LCLS)
OR St B..... Operation Rescue Saint Bernard [*Test given to Junior Woodchucks in Donald Duck comic by Carl Barks*]
Or St B Bull... Oregon State Bar Bulletin [*A publication*] (DLA)
OrStbM...... Mount Angel College, Mount Angel Abbey, St. Benedict, OR [*Library symbol*] [*Library of Congress*] (LCLS)
OrStf......... Stanfield Public Library, Stanfield, OR [*Library symbol*] [*Library of Congress*] (LCLS)
OrSthDH.... Columbia District Hospital, Medical Library, St. Helens, OR [*Library symbol*] [*Library of Congress*] (LCLS)
ORSTOM.... Office de la Recherche Scientifique et Technique Outre-Mer (USDC)
ORSV........ Odontoglossum Ringspot Virus [*Plant pathology*]
O-R system... Oxidation Reduction System (ADWA)
ORT.......... Northway, AK [*Location identifier*] [*FAA*] (FAAL)
ORT.......... Oak Ridge [*Tennessee*] [*Seismograph station code, US Geological Survey*] (SEIS)
ORT.......... Object Relations Technique [*Psychology*]
ORT.......... Ocular Radiation Therapy [*Medicine*] (RAWO)
ORT.......... Odor Recognition Threshold (SAUS)
ORT.......... Ongoing Reliability Test (SAUS)
ORT.......... Ooty Radio Telescope [*India*]
ORT.......... Open Radiator Tank [*Automotive engineering*]
ORT.......... Operating Room Technician [*Medicine*]
ORT.......... Operationally Ready Time
ORT.......... Operational Readiness Test
ORT.......... Operational Readiness Training [*Army*]
ORT.......... Operational Reliability Test joint (SAUS)
ORT.......... Optical Relay Tube (MCD)
ORT.......... Optical Rotary Table
ORT.......... Optimum Resolution Technique
ORT.......... Oral Rehydration Therapy
ORT.......... Orbital Rendezvous Technique (AAG)
ORT.......... Orbit Readiness Test [*NASA*] (NASA)
ORT.......... Order of Railroad Telegraphers [*Later, Transportation-Communication Employees Union*] (EA)
ORT.......... Ordnance Repair Truck [*British*]
ORT.......... Organization for Rehabilitation through Training [*Acronym is used in names of several Jewish social welfare organizations*]
ORT.......... Orient-Avia [*Former USSR*] [*FAA designator*] (FAAC)
ORT.......... Original Running Time [*Movies*] (CDAI)
Ort........... Ortho Diagnostics
ORT.......... Overage Retirement Training (SAUS)
ORT.......... Overhaul RADAR Technology
ORT.......... Overland RADAR Technology (MCD)
ORT.......... Owner Requirements Table (HLLA)
ORT.......... Registered Occupational Therapist (STED)
ORTA........ Office of Research and Technology Applications [*Gaithersburg, MD*] [*National Institute of Standards and Technology*] (GRD)
ORTA........ Office of Research and Technology Applications [*Berkeley, CA*] [*Lawrence Berkeley Laboratory*] [*Department of Energy*] (GRD)
ORTA........ Office of Research and Technology Applications [*Army*] (RDA)
ORTA........ Optical Relay Tube Assembly (MCD)
ORTAG...... Operations Research Technical Assistance Group [*Army*] (PDAA)
ORTAI....... Orbit-to-Air Intercept (IAA)
ORTC........ Organized Reserve Training Center [*Military*]
ORTC........ Ortec International, Inc. [*NASDAQ symbol*] (SAG)
ORTC........ Ortec Intl. [*NASDAQ symbol*] (TTSB)
ORTC........ Ortec Intl. Wrrt'B' [*NASDAQ symbol*] (TTSB)
ORT/CTL.... Operational Readiness Training - Combat Training Launch [*Military*] (SAA)
ORTCW...... Ortec Intl. Wrrt'A' [*NASDAQ symbol*] (TTSB)
ORTE........ Operational Readiness Training Equipment [*Military*] (SAA)
ORTEC...... Oak Ridge Technical Enterprises Corp.
ORTECH..... Ontario Research and Technology Foundation (SAUS)
OR tech..... Operating Room Technician (DAVI)
Ortecint..... Ortec International, Inc. [*Associated Press*] (SAG)
Ortel......... Ortel Corp. [*Associated Press*] (SAG)
ORTEP...... Oak Ridge Thermal Ellipsoid Program (SAUS)
ORTF........ Office de la Radio et de la Television Francaise [*State-owned radio and television network*] [*France*]
ORTF........ Office de Radiodiffusion-Television Francaise [*National Broadcasting Organization*] [*France*] (NTCM)

ORTF .... Organization Radio Television France (IAA)
Orth .... Orthodox (WDAA)
ORTH .... Orthodox
ORTH .... Orthography
orth .... Orthopedic (NTIO)
ORTH .... Orthopedic
ORTH .... Orthopedic Technology, Inc. [*NASDAQ symbol*] (SAG)
Orthdx .... Orthodox (DIAR)
Orthfx .... Orthofix International [*Associated Press*] (SAG)
orthg .... Orthogonals (VRA)
Ort Hist ..... Ortolan's History of the Roman Law [*A publication*] (DLA)
Orthlog ...... Orghologic Corp. [*Associated Press*] (SAG)
ORTHO ...... American Orthopsychiatric Association (EA)
ORTHO ...... Orthochromatic [*Photography*] (ROG)
ortho .... orthographical (SAUS)
ORTHO ...... Orthopedic
Ortho .... Orthopedics [*Medicine*] (AMHC)
Orthodon .... Orthodontic Centers of America, Inc. [*Associated Press*] (SAG)
ORTHOG .... Orthagonal
ORTHOG .... Orthogonal (NASA)
ortho-k ...... orthokeratologist (SAUS)
Ortho-K ...... Orthokeratology [*Medicine*]
orthokera ... orthokeratologist (SAUS)
orthokera ... orthokeratology (SAUS)
orthomol .... orthomolecular (SAUS)
ORTHOMOL ... Orthomolecularologist (SAUS)
ORTHOMOL ... Orthomolecularology (SAUS)
orthop .... Orthopnea [*Medicine*] (DAVI)
ORTHOPHOS ... Orthophosphoric acid (SAUS)
orthopod .... Orthopedist [*Orthopedic Physician*] (DAVI)
OrthopT ..... Orthopedic Technology, Inc. [*Associated Press*] (SAG)
orthor .... orthorhombic (SAUS)
OrTig .... Tigard Public Library, Tigard, OR [*Library symbol*] [*Library of Congress*] (LCLS)
Ort Inst ...... Ortolan's Justinian's Institutes [*A publication*] (DLA)
OrtInt .... Ortec International, Inc. [*Associated Press*] (SAG)
ORTL .... Ortel Corp. [*NASDAQ symbol*] (SAG)
ORTM .... On-orbit Right Technique Meeting (SAUS)
ORTN .... Officie Radiodiffusion Television du Niger [*Radio and television network*] [*Niger*]
ORTO .... Occupational Rehabilitation Training for Overseas (SAUS)
ORTO .... Olympics Radio and Television Organization [*Organisme de Radio-Television des Olympiques*] [*Canada*]
ORTP .... Operational Readiness Training Program [*Military*] (AABC)
ORTPA .... Oven-Ready Turkey Producers Association (SAUS)
Or TR .... Oregon Tax Reporter [*A publication*] (DLA)
Or T Rep .... Oregon Tax Reporter [*A publication*] (ILCA)
Or T Rep .... Orleans Term Reports [*1, 2 Martin*] [*Louisiana*] [*A publication*] (DLA)
Ort Rom Law ... Ortolan's History of the Roman Law [*A publication*] (DLA)
ORTS .... Occurrence Reporting and Tracking System (SAUS)
ORTS .... Operational Readiness Test System [*Military*] (CAAL)
ORTS .... Operational Test and Readiness System (SAUS)
ORTS .... Optional Residence (or Residential) Telephone Service (SAUS)
ORTS .... Optional Residential Telephone Service [*Telecommunications*] (TEL)
ORTT .... Operational Readiness Training Test [*Army*] (AABC)
ORTT .... Overreaching Transfer Trip (IAA)
ORTU .... Organized Reserve Training Unit [*Military*]
ORTU .... Other Ranks Training Unit (SAUS)
OrTua .... Tualatin Public Library, Tualatin, OR [*Library symbol*] [*Library of Congress*] (LCLS)
ORTUAG ..... Organized Reserve Training Unit, Vessel Augmentation [*Military*]
OrTuaM ...... Meridian Park Hospital, Medical Library, Tualatin, OR [*Library symbol*] [*Library of Congress*] (LCLS)
ORTUAM .... Organized Reserve Training Unit, Administration of Mobilization [*Military*]
ORTUAV ..... Organized Reserve Training Unit, Aviation Support [*Military*]
ORTUEL ..... Organized Reserve Training Unit, Electronics [*Military*]
ORTUF .... Organized Reserve Training Unit, Coastal Force [*Military*]
ORTUPS ..... Organized Reserve Training Unit, Port Security [*Military*]
ORTUPS(O) ... Organized Reserve Training Unit, Port Security (Operational) [*Military*]
ORTUR ...... Organized Reserve Training Unit, Rescue Coordination Center [*Military*]
OrTW .... Wasco County Library, The Dalles, OR [*Library symbol*] [*Library of Congress*] (LCLS)
ORTX .... Ohio River Terminal [*Federal Railroad Administration identification code*]
ORTX .... Ortner Air Service [*Air carrier designation symbol*]
ORTZ .... Oregon Trunk [*Federal Railroad Administration identification code*]
ORU .... On-Line Replacement Unit [*Computer science*] (MCD)
ORU .... Operational Readiness Unit
ORU .... Operational Research Unit (SAUS)
ORU .... Operator Radio Unit (SAUS)
ORU .... Optical Reference Unit
ORU .... Optimal Replaceable Unit (IAA)
ORU .... Oral Roberts University [*Oklahoma*]
ORU .... Orange & Rockland Utilities, Inc. [*NYSE symbol*] (SPSG)
ORU .... Orbital Replaceable Unit (SSD)
ORU .... Orbit Replaceable Unit (SAUS)
oru .... Oregon [*MARC country of publication code*] [*Library of Congress*] (LCCP)
ORU .... Organization for Rebirth of Ukraine (EA)
ORU .... Organized Research Unit (SAUS)
ORU .... Oruro [*Bolivia*] [*Airport symbol*] (AD)
ORU .... Other than Ship or Squadron Reinforcement Unit [*Naval Reserve*] (DNAB)
ORU .... Russell Branch, Russell Township Public Library, Ontario [*Library symbol*] [*National Library of Canada*] (BIB)
OrU .... University of Oregon, Eugene, OR [*Library symbol*] [*Library of Congress*] (LCLS)
ORU .... University of Oregon Library, Eugene, OR [*OCLC symbol*] (OCLC)
ORUC .... Orbital Replacement Unit Carrier (SAUS)
OrU-C .... University of Oregon, Computing Center, Eugene, OR [*Library symbol*] [*Library of Congress*] (LCLS)
OrU-D .... University of Oregon, Dental School, Portland, OR [*Library symbol*] [*Library of Congress*] (LCLS)
ORUEF ...... Oral Roberts University Educational Fellowship (EA)
ORUFE ...... Operational Research Unit, Far East
OrUk .... Ukiah Public Library, Ukiah, OR [*Library symbol*] [*Library of Congress*] (LCLS)
OrU-L .... University of Oregon, Law Library, Portland, OR [*Library symbol*] [*Library of Congress*] (LCLS)
OrU-M .... University of Oregon, Medical School, Portland, OR [*Library symbol*] [*Library of Congress*] (LCLS)
OrUma ...... Umatilla Public Library, Umatilla, OR [*Library symbol*] [*Library of Congress*] (LCLS)
OrUmaH ..... Umatilla Hospital, Umatilla, OR [*Library symbol*] [*Library of Congress*] (LCLS)
OrUmH ...... Umatilla Hospital, Umatilla, OR [*Library symbol*] [*Library of Congress*] (LCLS)
OrUn .... Carnegie Public Library, Union, OR [*Library symbol*] [*Library of Congress*] (LCLS)
O/RUNN ..... Overrunning [*Automotive engineering*]
OrU-O .... University of Oregon, Ocean and Coastal Law Center, Eugene, OR [*Library symbol*] [*Library of Congress*] (LCLS)
OrU-Or ...... University of Oregon, Oriental Museum, Portland, OR [*Library symbol*] [*Library of Congress*] (LCLS)
ORUP .... Ocean Resource Utilization Program (ASF)
ORUS .... Official Register of the United States
ORUS .... Orbital Replacement Units (SAUS)
OrU-S .... University of Oregon, Science Division Library, Eugene, OR [*Library symbol*] [*Library of Congress*] (LCLS)
ORuss .... Old Russian [*Language*] (BARN)
ORUZ .... Orlando Utilities Commission [*Federal Railroad Administration identification code*]
OrV .... Fern Ridge Community Library, Veneta, OR [*Library symbol*] [*Library of Congress*] (LCLS)
ORV .... Noorvik [*Alaska*] [*Airport symbol*] (OAG)
ORV .... Oceanographic Research Vessel
ORV .... Ocean Range Vessel [*Air Force*]
ORV .... Off-Road Vehicle
ORV .... Operational Range Vessels (ACAE)
ORV .... Orbital Reentry Vehicle [*NASA*] (IAA)
ORV .... Orbital Rescue Vehicle [*NASA*] (KSC)
ORV .... Orbital Return Vehicle [*NASA*] (IAA)
ORV .... Oroville [*California*] [*Seismograph station code, US Geological Survey*] (SEIS)
ORV .... Oroville, CA [*Amtrak Busline code*]
ORVAT .... Organizational Vehicle Automatic Tester
ORVC .... River Valley Community Library, Ontario [*Library symbol*] [*National Library of Canada*] (NLC)
ORVID .... Online X-ray Evaluation over Video-Display Including Documentation (PDAA)
ORVLL .... Orrville, OH [*American Association of Railroads railroad junction routing code*]
ORVM .... Outside Rear-View Mirror [*Automotive systems*]
ORVR .... On-Board Refueling Vapor Recovery [*Automotive engineering*]
ORVX .... OraVax, Inc. [*NASDAQ symbol*] (SAG)
ORW .... Norwich, CT [*Location identifier*] [*FAA*] (FAAL)
ORW .... Ohio Reformatory for Women (SAUS)
ORW .... Orange Walk [*British Honduras*] [*Airport symbol*] (AD)
ORW .... Orwell Resources Ltd. [*Vancouver Stock Exchange symbol*]
ORW .... Orwex [*Poland*] [*ICAO designator*] (FAAC)
ORW .... Outstanding Resource Waters [*Water quality standards*] [*Environmental Protection Agency*]
ORW .... Owner's Risk of Becoming Wet [*Shipping*]
ORW .... Raymond Walters General and Technical College, Blue Ash, OH [*OCLC symbol*] (OCLC)
OrWe .... Weston Public Library, Weston, OR [*Library symbol*] [*Library of Congress*] (LCLS)
OrWel .... West Linn Public Library, West Linn, OR [*Library symbol*] [*Library of Congress*] (LCLS)
OrWelH ..... West Linn High School, West Linn, OR [*Library symbol*] [*Library of Congress*] (LCLS)
ORWG .... Operational Requirements Working Group (DOMA)
ORWH .... Office of Research on Women's Health [*National Institutes of Health*]
OrWi .... Willamina Public Library, Willamina, OR [*Library symbol*] [*Library of Congress*] (LCLS)
ORWISE ..... Otherwise (ROG)
ORWL .... Outline Raised White Letter [*Tire design*]
OrWo .... Woodburn Public Library, Woodburn, OR [*Library symbol*] [*Library of Congress*] (LCLS)
ORWP .... Optical Radiation Weapon Program (AAG)
ORX .... Oriximina [*Brazil*] [*Airport symbol*] (AD)
ORX .... Oryx Aviation [*South Africa*] [*ICAO designator*] (FAAC)
ORX .... Oryx Energy Co. [*NYSE symbol*] (SPSG)
ORY .... Ohio Railway Museum [*Federal Railroad Administration identification code*]
ORY .... Ordinary [*Telegraphy*] (PCTE)
ORY .... Paris [*France*] Orly Airport [*Airport symbol*] (OAG)
Oryx .... Oryx Energy Co. [*Associated Press*] (SAG)

ORYX .... Oryx Technology [*NASDAQ symbol*] (TTSB)
ORYX .... Oryx Technology Corp. [*NASDAQ symbol*] (SAG)
OryxTc .... Oryx Technology Corp. [*Associated Press*] (SAG)
ORYXW ...... Oryx Technology Wrrt [*NASDAQ symbol*] (TTSB)
ORZ .... Omnirange Zero (IAA)
ORZ .... Omnirange Zone
ORZ .... Orange Walk [*Belize*] [*Airport symbol*] [*Obsolete*] (OAG)
ORZ .... Outer Radiation Zone
OS .... Austrian Airlines [*ICAO designator*] (AD)
OS .... By Mouth [*Pharmacy*] (DAVI)
os .... Left Eye [*Therapy term*] (CTAA)
os .... Mouth [*Medicine*] (BCRP)
Os .... Oberseminar (SAUS)
OS .... Obese Strain [*White leghorn*]
OS .... Object-Subject [*Education of the hearing-impaired*]
OS .... Oblique Sounding [*Telecommunications*] (OA)
OS .... Observation-Scouting Plane [*When first two letters in Navy designation*]
OS .... Observation Squadron (SAUS)
OS .... Observation Station (SAUS)
OS .... Observer School (SAUS)
OS .... Observing Station [*Marine science*] (MSC)
OS .... Occipitosacral [*Medicine*] (EDAA)
OS .... Occupational Safety (DAVI)
OS .... Oceanic Society (EA)
OS .... Oceanography Section (SAUS)
os .... Ocean Station (ODA)
OS .... Ocean Station [*Maps and charts*]
OS .... Ocean Surveillance (ACAE)
OS .... Octane Switch [*Automotive engineering*]
OS .... Octavian Society (EA)
OS .... Oculus Sinister [*Left Eye*] [*Ophthalmology*]
OS .... Odd Symmetric
OS .... Offensive Support (SAUS)
OS .... Office of Supply (SAUS)
OS .... Office of Systems [*NASA*] (KSC)
OS .... Office of the Secretary
OS .... Officer of the Sword [*Civil War term*]
OS .... Officers' Steward [*Ranking title*] [*British Women's Royal Naval Service*]
OS .... Office Surgery (SAUS)
OS .... Office System
OS .... Official Scorer [*Baseball term*] (NDBD)
OS .... Official Station
OS .... Off Scale (IAA)
OS .... Off Screen [*or Stage*]
OS .... Offset
OS .... Off Stage (SAUS)
OS .... Ohio State (SAUS)
OS .... Ohio State Reports [*A publication*] (DLA)
OS .... Oil Sand (SAUS)
OS .... Oil Shale (SAUS)
OS .... Oil Solenoid
OS .... Oil Solubility (SAUS)
OS .... Oil-Soluble (SAUS)
OS .... Oil Solvent (SAUS)
OS .... Oil Switch
OS .... Old Saxon [*Language, etc.*]
OS .... Old School
os .... Old Series [*Linguistics*] (IEL)
OS .... Old Series
OS .... Old Side
OS .... Old Standard [*Currency*] (ROG)
OS .... Old Style [*Printing*] (NTCM)
OS .... Old Style [*Calendar, previous to 1752*]
OS .... Old Style date (SAUS)
OS .... Omega Society [*Defunct*] (EA)
OS .... Omenn Syndrome [*Medicine*] (EDAA)
OS .... Omnibus Society [*British*]
OS .... One Shot
OS .... One Side
OS .... One-Stop [*Aviation*]
os .... Only Son (WDAA)
OS .... Only Son
OS .... On-Orbit Station [*NASA*] (MCD)
os .... On-Orbit Station [*NASA*] (NAKS)
OS .... On Sale
OS .... On Sample
OS .... On Schedule
O/S .... On Sea [*In place names*] [*British*] (ROG)
o-S .... on-Sea (SAUS)
OS .... On Sheet (WGA)
OS .... On Side
OS .... On-Site
OS .... On Spot (ROG)
OS .... On Station [*Military*]
OS .... On Switch
OS .... Opening Snaps [*Cardiology*]
OS .... Open Shop (SAUS)
OS .... Open Side (SAUS)
OS .... Open Statement (SAUS)
OS .... Open Subroutine (SAUS)
OS .... Open System (SAUS)
os .... Opera Seria [*Music*] (GROV)
OS .... Operating Schedule [*Field stations*] (MCD)
OS .... Operating Software (MCD)
OS .... Operating System [*Computer science*] (BUR)
O/S .... Operational Assist Project/Shipborne Application
OS .... Operational Sequence (KSC)
OS .... Operational Sheets
OS .... Operational Software (SAUS)
OS .... Operational Specialist [*Navy*]
OS .... Operational Suitability
OS .... Operational Supplements [*Air Force*] (MCD)
OS .... Operation Sandstone [*Atomic weapons testing*]
O/S .... Operations and Support (SAUS)
O/S .... Operations and Support Phase (POLM)
OS .... Operation Sheet (SAUS)
OS .... Operation Smile (EA)
OS .... Operation Snapper [*Atomic weapons testing*]
OS .... Operations Specialist [*Navy*] (DNAB)
OS .... Operations Superintendent (SAUS)
OS .... Operations Support [*Office of U.S. Foreign Disaster Assistance*]
OS .... Operations System (SAUS)
OS .... Operation Suburbia [*Defunct*] (EA)
OS .... Operator Service (SAUS)
OS .... Operator's Set
OS .... Oppose [*Telegraphy*] (PCTE)
OS .... Optical Scanner (SAUS)
OS .... Optical Scanning [*Computer science*]
OS .... Optical Society (NADA)
OS .... Optical Spectroscopy (SAUS)
OS .... Optical System (SAUS)
OS .... Optics Subsystem
OS .... Optimum Size (ELAL)
OS .... Option Spreading [*Investment term*]
OS .... Oral Surgery
OS .... Oral Suspension [*Pharmacy*]
OS .... Orbital Servicing (SAUS)
OS .... Orbiter CEI [*Contract End Item*] Specification [*NASA*] (NASA)
OS .... Orderly Sergeant (SAUS)
OS .... Order of Servites
OS .... Order Sheet
OS .... Ordinary Seaman [*British*]
OS .... Ordnance School [*Army*] (MCD)
OS .... Ordnance Server (SAUS)
OS .... Ordnance Services [*Military*] [*British*]
OS .... Ordnance Specifications [*Navy*]
OS .... Ordnance Survey
OS .... Oregon State (SAUS)
OS .... Oregon Steel Mills [*NYSE symbol*] (SPSG)
OS .... Organic Solvent (SAUS)
OS .... Organic Synthesis (SAUS)
OS .... Organizational Source [*Online database field identifier*] [*Computer science*]
OS .... Organizational Support (SAUS)
OS .... Organizations System (IAA)
OS .... Organization System (SAUS)
OS .... Organosilicon (SAUS)
OS .... Original Series
OS .... Ornamental Stitching (DNAB)
OS .... Oro Sellado [*Standard Gold*] [*Business term*] [*Spanish*]
OS .... Orthogonal System (SAUS)
O/S .... Orthopaedic Surgery [*Medical Officer designation*] [*British*]
OS .... Orthopedics (DAVI)
OS .... Orthopedic Surgery (DAVI)
OS .... Orton Society [*Later, ODS*] (EA)
Os .... Oscan [*Linguistics*] (IEL)
OS .... Osgood-Schlatter's Disease [*Medicine*]
Os .... Osmium [*Chemical element*]
OS .... Osmotic Shock
OS .... Osnabrueck [*German license plate city code*]
OS .... Osteogenic Sarcoma [*Medicine*]
OS .... Osteosarcoma [*Oncology*]
OS .... Osteosclerosis [*Medicine*] (DAVI)
OS .... Oszillator im Sender (SAUS)
OS .... Other Side [*A publication*] (BRI)
OS .... Other Sources
OS .... Otherwise Specified (MSA)
OS .... Outer Segment
OS .... Outer Sheath [*Botany*]
OS .... Outer Space (SAUS)
OS .... Outlaw Shark [*RADAR surveillance*] [*Naval Electronic Systems Command*]
OS .... Outline Square Condition [*Vision*]
O/S .... Out of Service (AFM)
O/S .... Out-of-Shot [*Photography*]
O/S .... Out of State (SAUS)
OS .... Out of Stock (NTCM)
OS .... Output Secondary [*Electronics*]
OS .... Output Signal (SAUS)
OS .... Output Source (SAUS)
OS .... Output Specification (SAUS)
OS .... Output Store (SAUS)
OS .... Output System (SAUS)
OS .... Out Secondary (SAUS)
OS .... Outside
OS .... Outside Sales (TRID)

OS .... Outside Sentinel
OS .... Outsize [*Of clothes*]
os .... Outstanding (ELAL)
O/S .... Outstanding
OS .... Outstate (SAUS)
OS .... Outstation (MCD)
OS .... Out Stealing [*Baseball*]
OS .... Overall Size (SAUS)
OS .... Overall Survival [*Medicine*]
OS .... Overlong Sentence [*Used in correcting manuscripts, etc.*]
OS .... Overscene [*Films, television, etc.*]
OS .... Oversea [*Military*]
OS .... Overseas Service (SAUS)
O/S .... Overshipped (MCD)
OS .... Overshoot (SAUS)
OS .... Oversize (AAG)
O/S .... Oversize [*Automotive engineering*]
OS .... Overspecificity [*Psychometrics*]
OS .... Overstressing (SAUS)
OS .... Over-the-Horizon Targeting System (MCD)
OS .... Over-the-Shoulder Cinematography (NTCM)
OS .... Over the State [*Regarding distribution*]
OS .... Own Ship [*Navy*] (CAAL)
OS .... Oxygen Saturation (DB)
OS .... Oxygen Sensor [*Automotive engineering*]
OS .... Oxygen Service (DNAB)
OS .... Sarnia Public Library, Ontario [*Library symbol*] [*National Library of Canada*] (NLC)
OS .... Shell Development Co. [*Research code symbol*]
OS .... Test Oscilloscope [*JETDS nomenclature*] [*Military*] (CET)
OS .... Warder Public Library of Springfield and Clark County, Springfield, OH [*Library symbol*] [*Library of Congress*] (LCLS)
OS/2 .... IBMs Operating System (SAUS)
OS/2 .... Operating System 2 [*Computer science*]
OS 2d .... Ohio State Reports, Second Series [*A publication*] (DLA)
OS9 .... Operating System-9 (SAUS)
OS/390 .... Open Server/390 (SAUS)
OS/400 .... Operationg System/400 (SAUS)
OS/400 .... Optimized Server for AS/400 computers (SAUS)
OSA .... Aero Astra [*Mexico*] [*ICAO designator*] (FAAC)
OSA .... Augustinian Nuns of Contemplative Life (TOCD)
OSA .... [*The*] Augustinians (TOCD)
OSA .... Augustinian Sisters of Our Lady of Consolation (TOCD)
OSA .... Congregation of Augustinian Sisters Servants of Jesus and Mary (TOCD)
OSA .... Object System Adaptor (SAUS)
OSA .... Obstructive Sleep Apnea [*Medicine*]
OSA .... Occupational Safety Aid
OSA .... Ocean Shipping Act (SAUS)
OSA .... Office of Safety Assessment (ABAC)
OSA .... Office of Savings Associations [*Formerly, FHLIC*]
OSA .... Office of Services to the Aging (DAVI)
OSA .... Office of Special Activities (CINC)
OSA .... Office of Special Applications (SAUS)
OSA .... Office of State Administration [*Australia*]
OSA .... Office of Student Affairs (SAUS)
OSA .... Office of Student Aid (SAUS)
OSA .... Office of the Secretary of the Army
OSA .... Office of the Special Assistant to the Ambassador
OSA .... Office Systems Administrator (SAUS)
OSA .... Office Systems Architecture (SAUS)
OSA .... Official Secrets Act [*British*]
OSA .... Offshore Acquisition [*Army*] (AABC)
OSA .... Oil-Soluble Acid (SAUS)
OSA .... Oklahoma Statutes Annotated [*A publication*] (DLA)
OSA .... Old South Arabic (BJA)
OSA .... Old Style Antique [*British*]
OSA .... Olefin-Modified Styrene-Acrylonitrile (SAUS)
OSA .... Omnibus Society of America (EA)
OSA .... On-Stream Analysis (SAUS)
OSA .... Ontario Society of Artists [*Canada*] (BARN)
OSA .... Open Scripting Architecture (SAUS)
OSA .... Open Solutions Architecture (SAUS)
OSA .... Open Storage Architecture (SAUS)
OSA .... Open System Adapter (SAUS)
OSA .... Open Systems Architecture [*Computer science*]
OSA .... Operational Safety Analysis (SAUS)
OSA .... Operational Safety Assessment (SAUS)
OSA .... Operational Support Agreement (GART)
OSA .... Operational Support Aircraft [*or Airlift*]
OSA .... Operational Support Airlift [*Air Force*] (DOMA)
OSA .... Operational Support Area
OSA .... Operation Sciences Appliquees [*Quebec*]
OSA .... Optical Society of America (EA)
OSA .... Optimization by Simulated Annealing [*Mathematics*]
OSA .... Order for Simple Alert (NATG)
OSA .... Order of St. Anne [*Anglican religious community*]
OSA .... Order of St. Augustine [*See also OFSA*] [*Rome, Italy*] (EAIO)
OSA .... Order-Sorting Aperture [*Instrumentation*]
OSA .... Organic Soil Association (SAUS)
OSA .... Organisation for Strategic Labour Markets (SAUS)
OSA .... Ormec Serro Analyst (NITA)
OSA .... Orthodox Society of America
OSA .... Osage [*Language symbol*] (ETLW)
osa .... Osage [*MARC language code*] [*Library of Congress*] (LCCP)
OSA .... Oscilloquartz SA (SAUS)
OSA .... Ossa Resources, Inc. [*Vancouver Stock Exchange symbol*]
OSA .... Osteosarcoma (SAUS)
OSA .... Other States Accepted
OSA .... Outfit Supply Activity (MCD)
OSA .... Ovarian Sectional Area [*Medicine*] (DMAA)
OSA .... Overall System Attenuation (SAUS)
OSA .... Overseas Sterling Area (SAUS)
OSA .... Overseas Supply Agency [*Military*]
OSA .... Overspenders Anonymous (EA)
OSA .... Oyster Shell Association (SAUS)
OSa .... Sabina Public Library, Sabina, OH [*Library symbol*] [*Library of Congress*] (LCLS)
OSA .... Sisters of St. Augustine (TOCD)
OSA .... Sisters of St. Rita (TOCD)
OSAA .... Ocean State Aquaculture Association [*Rhode Island*] (EARSL)
OSAA .... Operational Satellite Active Archive [*Marine science*] (OSRA)
OSA (ABCMR) ... Office, Secretary of the Army (Army Board for Correction of Military Records)
OSAC .... Open Space Action Committee (SAUS)
OSAC .... Operator Services Assistance Center (SAUS)
OSAC .... Orifice Spark Advance Control [*Valve*] [*Automotive technology*]
OSAC .... Overseas Schools Advisory Council [*Department of State*] [*Washington, DC*] (EGAO)
OSAC .... Overseas Security Advisory Council [*Department of State*] [*Washington, DC*] (EGAO)
OSAC .... Oxford System of Automated Cartography (SAUS)
OSACA .... Open System Architecture for Controls within Automation systems (SAUS)
OSACI .... Ecumenical Study and Action Centre on Investment [*Netherlands*]
OSACY .... Osage City, KS [*American Association of Railroads railroad junction routing code*]
OSAD .... Outer Space Affairs Division (SAUS)
OSAD A & L ... Office of the Secretary of the Army for Development / Acquisition and Logistics
OSADBU .... Office of Small and Disadvantaged Business Utilization (AAGC)
OS/AEL .... Operating Space/Allowance Equipage List
OSAF .... Office of the Secretary of the Air Force
OSAF .... Origin Subarea Address Field (SAUS)
OSAF .... Origin Subarea Field (SAUS)
OSAFO .... Office of the Special Assistant for Field Operations [*Formerly, CORDS*] (VNW)
OSAFU .... Oromo Students Association of Finfine University [*Ethiopia*]
OSAG .... Osage Trailer Manufacturing Company [*NCIC trailer make code*]
OSAH .... Health Sciences Library, Sudbury Algoma Hospital, Sudbury, Ontario [*Library symbol*] [*National Library of Canada*] (NLC)
OSAHRC .... Occupational Safety and Health Review Commission [*Department of Labor*]
OSAI .... Office of Systems Analysis and Information [*Department of Transportation*]
OSAIS .... Oil Spillage Analytical and Identification Service [*Laboratory of the Government Chemist*] (PDAA)
OSAIS .... Oil Spillage Analytical Information Service (NITA)
OSAK .... Open Systems Application Kernel (SAUS)
OSAK .... OSI [*Open Systems Interconnection*] Applications Kernel [*Computer science*] (TNIG)
Osaka Pref Bull ... Osaka Prefecture. University. Bulletin [*A publication*] (DLA)
Osaka ULR ... Osaka University. Law Review [*A publication*] (DLA)
Osaka UL Rev ... Osaka University. Law Review [*A publication*] (DLA)
Osaka Univ L Rev ... Osaka University. Law Review [*Osaka, Japan*] [*A publication*] (DLA)
OSAL .... Opening of Salivary [*Gland*]
OSal .... Salem Public Library, Salem, OH [*Library symbol*] [*Library of Congress*] (LCLS)
OSALC .... Savant Lake Community Library, Ontario [*Library symbol*] [*National Library of Canada*] (NLC)
OSalK .... Kent State University, Columbiana Regional Campus, Salem, OH [*Library symbol*] [*Library of Congress*] (LCLS)
OSALSAA ... Office, Special Assistant for Logistical Support of Army Aircraft (AABC)
OSALSTC ... Office, Special Assistant for Logistical Support of Tactical Communications (AABC)
OSAM .... Online Systems Activity Monitor [*Computer science*] (HODG)
OSAM .... Overflow Sequential Access Method [*Computer science*]
OSAMM .... Optimum Supply and Maintenance Model [*Army*] (RDA)
OSAMS .... Synod Office, Diocese of Moosonee, Anglican Church of Canada, Schumacher, Ontario [*Library symbol*] [*National Library of Canada*] (NLC)
OSand .... Sandusky Library Association, Sandusky, OH [*Library symbol*] [*Library of Congress*] (LCLS)
OS & CP Dec ... Ohio Superior and Common Pleas Decisions [*A publication*] (DLA)
OS & D .... Over, Short, and Damaged [*Report*] [*Shipping*] (MSA)
OS&D .... Over, Short and Damage Report (SAUS)
OS & DR .... Over, Short, and Damaged Report [*Shipping*]
OS and D Report ... Over, Short and Damaged Report (SAUS)
OS&E .... Ocean Science and Engineering (SAUS)
OS&ER .... Operational Safety and Engineering Research [*Minerals Management Service*] (RCD)
OS & FM .... Office of Systems and Financial Management [*DoD*]
OS&M .... Operational Support and Maintenance (SAUS)
OS & RP .... On-Board Spares and Repair Parts [*Navy*] (DNAB)
OS & TD .... Ocean Science and Technology Division [*Office of Naval Research*] (DNAB)
OS&W .... Oak, Sunk and Weathered (ODA)

OS & W..... Oak, Sunk, and Weathered [*Construction*]
OS & Y...... Outside Screw and Yoke
OS&Y........ Outside Screw and Yolk (SAUS)
OSAP........ Aleppo/Neirab [*Syria*] [*ICAO location identifier*] (ICLI)
OSAP........ Ocean Surveillance Air Patrol (CINC)
OSAP........ Ocean Survey Advisory Panel [*Marine science*] (MSC)
OSAP........ Office of Scientific and Academic Publications (SAUS)
OSAP........ Office of Substance Abuse Prevention [*Department of Agriculture*] (EGAO)
OSAP........ Office Space Allocation Plan (MCD)
OSAP........ Ontario Student Assistance Program (SAUS)
OSAP........ Ontario Student Awards Program (SAUS)
OSAP........ Organization for Safety and Asepsis Procedures [*Association*] (EA)
OSAPI....... Operating System/Application Program Interface [*Computer science*]
OSAR........ Office of Substance Abuse Research [*James Madison University*] (RCD)
OSAR........ Operational Safety Analysis Report (ABAC)
OSAR........ Operations Suitability Assessment Report (SSD)
OSAR........ Optical Storage and Retrieval [*Computer science*]
OSAR........ Overhead Systems Apprearance Research (IAA)
OSarS....... Southern State Community College, Sardinia, OH [*Library symbol*] [*Library of Congress*] (LCLS)
OSART....... Operational Safety Review Team [*International Atomic Energy Agency*]
OSAS........ Obstructive Sleep Apnea Syndrome [*Medicine*] (DMAA)
OSAS........ Office of Substance Abuse Studies [*University of Maryland at Baltimore*] (RCD)
OSAS........ Ohio Social Acceptance Scale (EDAC)
OSAS........ Open Systems Accounting Software [*Computer science*]
OSAS........ Overseas Service Aid Scheme
OSASA...... Obstructive Sleep Apnea Sydrome (SAUS)
OSASF....... Overseas Supply Agency, San Francisco [*Military*] (CINC)
OSASN...... Office of Special Assistant, Secretary of the Navy
OSAT........ Office for the Study of Automotive Transportation [*Department of Transportation*]
OSAT........ Office of the Special Assistant for Training [*Army*] (RDA)
OSAT........ Optical Sensor and Tracker
OSAT........ Optimized Sustained Action Technology (DB)
OSATA....... Order of Saint Andrew the Apostle (EA)
OSATRMS... Operational Resource Tracking and Management System (SAUS)
OSA-UCS.... Optical Society of America Uniform Color Scales (SAUS)
OSAWA...... Osawatomie, KS [*American Association of Railroads railroad junction routing code*]
OSAY........ Outside Screw and Yoke (IAA)
OSB.......... Benedictine Congregation of Our Lady of Monte (TOCD)
OSB.......... Benedictine Monks (TOCD)
osb........... Benedictine Monks, Olivetan Benedictines, Sylvestrine Benedictines (TOCD)
OSB.......... Benedictine Nuns (TOCD)
OSB.......... Benedictine Nuns of the Congregation of Solesmes (TOCD)
OSB.......... Benedictine Nuns of the Primitive Observance (TOCD)
OSB.......... Benedictine Sisters (TOCD)
OSB.......... Benedictine Sisters of Liberty (TOCD)
OSB.......... Benedictine Sisters of Pontifical Jurisdiction (TOCD)
OSB.......... Benedictine Sisters of Sacred Heart (TOCD)
OSB.......... Congregation of Jesus Crucified (TOCD)
OSB.......... Congregation of the Benedictine Sisters of Perpetual Adoration of Pontifical Jurisdiction (TOCD)
OSB.......... Congregation of the Benedictine Sisters of the Sacred Heart (TOCD)
OSB.......... Contemplative Sisters of St. Benedict (TOCD)
OSB.......... Missionary Benedictine Sisters (TOCD)
OSB.......... Occupational Safety Bulletin (SAUS)
OSB.......... Ocean Sciences Board [*NASA*] (MSC)
OSB.......... Ocean Studies Board (SAUS)
OSB.......... Office of Savings Bonds [*Navy*]
OSB.......... Office of Surveillance and Biometrics [*U.S. Food and Drug Administration*]
OSB.......... Officer Selection Battery [*Military*]
OSB.......... Officer Selection Board
OSB.......... Officer Selection Brief (SAUS)
OSB.......... Old Saybrook, CT [*Amtrak rail station code*]
OSB.......... Olivetan Benedictine Sisters (TOCD)
OSB.......... One-Statement Banking (MHDB)
OSB.......... Operational Stations Book (SAUS)
OSB.......... Operational Status BIT [*Binary Digit*]
OSB.......... Operations and Services Building (SAUS)
OSB.......... Operations Software Branch (SAUS)
OSB.......... Operations Stations Book [*Navy*]
OSB.......... Operations Support Building [*NASA*] (KSC)
OSB.......... Operation Support Building (SAUS)
OSB.......... Operative Society of Bricklayers [*A union*] [*British*]
OSB.......... Orangeburg [*South Carolina*] [*Seismograph station code, US Geological Survey*] (SEIS)
OSB.......... Orbital Solar Observation (IAA)
OSB.......... Order of Saint Benedict (SAUS)
OSB.......... Order of Shepherds of Bethlehem (EA)
OSB.......... Order of St. Benedict (SAUS)
OSB.......... Order of the Stars and Bars [*Later, MOSB*] (EA)
OSB.......... Ordinis Sancti Bernardi [*Order of St. Bernard*] [*Latin*] (ROG)
OSB.......... Ordnance Supply Bulletin
OSB.......... Ordo Sancti Benedicti [*Order of St. Benedict*] [*Roman Catholic religious order*]
OSB.......... Oregon State Bar (EARSL)
OSB.......... Oriented-Strand Board [*A plywood panel composition*]
OSB.......... Orthopedic Seat Backrest [*Automotive engineering*]
OSB.......... Osage Beach [*Missouri*] [*Airport symbol*] [*Obsolete*] (OAG)
OSB.......... Output Signal Balance (SAUS)
OSB.......... Overseas Brats
OSB.......... Overseas Service Bureau (SAUS)
OSB.......... Sauble Beach Branch, Bruce County Public Library, Ontario [*Library symbol*] [*National Library of Canada*] (NLC)
OSBA........ Ohio School Boards Association (SAUS)
OSBA........ Oregon School Boards Association (SAUS)
OSBA........ Outlet and Switch Box Association [*Defunct*] (EA)
OSBA Bull... Ohio State Bar Association. Bulletin [*A publication*] (DLA)
OSBC........ Old Second Bancorp [*NASDAQ symbol*] (TTSB)
OSBC........ Old Second Bancorp, Inc. [*NASDAQ symbol*] (SAG)
OSBCam.... Camaldolese Benedictine Sisters (TOCD)
OSBCam.... Camaldolese Hermits (TOCD)
osbcam..... Camaldolese Hermits (TOCD)
OSBE........ Organization of State Broadcasting Executives (SAUS)
OSBF........ Damascus [*Syria*] [*ICAO location identifier*] (ICLI)
OSBF........ OSB Financial [*NASDAQ symbol*] (SAG)
OSBF........ OSB Finl Corp. [*NASDAQ symbol*] (TTSB)
OSB Fn...... OSB Financial [*Associated Press*] (SAG)
OSBK........ Orange Savings Bank [*NASDAQ symbol*] (COMM)
OSBL........ Outside Battery Limits [*Chemical engineering*]
OSB Loss... Output Signal Balance Loss (SAUS)
OSBM........ Morrison Library Outpost, Severn Bridge, Ontario [*Library symbol*] [*National Library of Canada*] (NLC)
OSBM........ Office of Space Biology and Medicine [*Proposed for NASA*]
osbm......... Order of St. Basil the Great (TOCD)
OSBM........ Ordo Sancti Basil Magni [*Order of St. Basil the Great*] [*Roman Catholic religious order*]
OSBM........ Sisters of the Order of St. Basil the Great (TOCD)
OSBN........ Osborn Communications [*NASDAQ symbol*] (TTSB)
OSBN........ Osborn Communications Corp. [*NASDAQ symbol*] (NQ)
OSBO........ Osborn & Company [*NCIC trailer make code*]
OSBOR...... Osborn, IN [*American Association of Railroads railroad junction routing code*]
Osborn...... Osborn Communications [*Associated Press*] (SAG)
Osborn...... Osborne Communications Corp. [*Associated Press*] (SAG)
OSBP........ Office of Small Business Programs
OSBP........ Ontario Special Bursary Plan (SAUS)
OSBR........ Seeley's Bay Branch, Rideau Lakes Union Library, Ontario [*Library symbol*] [*National Library of Canada*] (BIB)
OSBRB...... Overhead/Support Budget Review Board (SAUS)
OSBRD...... Office of Small Business Research and Development [*National Science Foundation*] (GRD)
OSBRN...... Osborne, KS [*American Association of Railroads railroad junction routing code*]
OSBS........ Oblate Sisters of the Blessed Sacrament [*Roman Catholic religious order*]
OSBT........ Officer Selection Battery Test [*Military*]
OSBW........ Olympic Savings Bank [*NASDAQ symbol*] (COMM)
OSC.......... Canonici Regulares Ordinis Sanctae Crucis [*Canons Regular of the Order of the Holy Cross*] [*Crosier Fathers*] [*Roman Catholic religious order*]
osc........... Canons Regular of the Order of the Holy Cross, Crosier Fathers (TOCD)
OSC.......... Clan Grant No. 17, Order of Scottish Clans (EA)
OSC.......... Clark County Technical Institute, Springfield, OH [*Library symbol*] [*Library of Congress*] (LCLS)
OSC.......... Complete Operational Software [*Telecommunications*] (TEL)
OSC.......... Oak Satellite Corp. (NITA)
OSC.......... Obedience Stewards Club (EA)
OSC.......... Objective Supply Capability [*Army*] (RDA)
OSC.......... Oblate of Saint Charles (SAUS)
OSC.......... Oblate Spherical Coordinates
OSC.......... Oblati Sancti Caroli [*Oblate Fathers of St. Charles*] [*Roman Catholic religious order*]
OSC.......... Occupational Standards Council (AIE)
OSC.......... Ocean Science Committee [*National Academy of Sciences/Ocean Affairs Board*] (NOAA)
OSC.......... Ocean Sciences Center [*Memorial University of Newfoundland*] [*Canada*]
OSC.......... Offence against Sine Condition (SAUS)
OSC.......... Office of Scientific Computing (SAUS)
OSC.......... Office of Space Communications [*NASA*] (BARN)
OSC.......... Office of Special Counsel [*Federal agency*]
OSC.......... Office of the Security Council
OSC.......... Officer Specialty Code [*Army*] (INF)
OSC.......... Offshore Survival Centre [*Robert Gordon's Institute of Technology*] [*British*] (CB)
OSC.......... Ogden [*Utah*] Service Center [*IRS*]
OSC.......... Ohio Soybean Council (SAUS)
OSC.......... Ohio Supercomputer Center (SAUS)
O-SC.......... Ohio Supreme Court, Columbus, OH [*Library symbol*] [*Library of Congress*] (LCLS)
OSC.......... Oil Screen Clogging [*Fuels and lubricants*]
OSC.......... One Shoe Crew [*An association*] (EA)
OSC.......... Online Scenario Controller (SAUS)
OSC.......... On-Scene Commander [*Navy*] (NVT)
OSC.......... On-Scene Coordinator [*Environmental Protection Agency*] (FFDE)
OSC.......... On-Site Safety Committee (IAA)
OSC.......... Ontario Citator Service [*Database*] [*Canada*] (GDD)
OSC.......... Ontario Science Center (SAUS)
OSC.......... Ontario Securities Commission (HGAA)
OSC.......... Open System Center (SAUS)
OSC.......... Operating Switching Cabinet (SAUS)

OSC .... Operating System Command (SAUS)
OSC .... Operating System Control (VLIE)
OSC .... Operational Simulator Console
OSC .... Operational Summary Console
OSC .... Operational Support Center (NRCH)
OSC .... Operational Support Chart [*Nuclear energy*] (NUCP)
OSC .... Operational Switching Cabinet
OSC .... Operational System Control (SAUS)
OSC .... Operations Sequence Chart (MCD)
OSC .... Operations Support Center (SAUS)
OSC .... Operation Switching Cabinet (SAUS)
OSC .... Operator Services Center (VLIE)
OSC .... Operator Services Complex [*Telecommunications*] (TEL)
OSC .... Optically Sensitive Controller (SAUS)
OSC .... Optical Sciences Center [*University of Arizona*] [*Research center*] (RCD)
OSC .... Optical Signature Code
OSC .... Optical String Switch Controller (NITA)
OSC .... Options Selection Committee (COE)
OSC .... Orangeburg [*South Carolina*] [*Seismograph station code, US Geological Survey*] [*Closed*] (SEIS)
OSC .... Orbital Sciences Corporation (SAUS)
OSC .... Orbit Shift Coil
OSC .... Orbit-Spin Coupling (SAUS)
OSC .... Order of St. Clare [*Roman Catholic women's religious order*]
OSC .... Order to Show Cause
OSC .... Order to Show Cause and Notice of Hearing (SAUS)
OSC .... Ordnance Store Corps [*British military*] (DMA)
OSC .... Ordnance Systems Command [*Formerly, Bureau of Naval Weapons; later, Naval Sea Systems Command*]
OSC .... Oregon State College [*Later, OSU*]
OSC .... Organic Solderability Coating [*Electronics*] (AAEL)
OSC .... Organic Sulfur Compound [*Organic chemistry*]
OSC .... Organizational Structure Code [*Air Force*] (AFIT)
OSC .... Organizational Supply Code [*Army*] (AABC)
OSC .... Organosilicon Compound (SAUS)
OSC .... Orthosubstitution Compound (SAUS)
OSC .... Osceola, IA [*Amtrak rail station code*]
OSC .... Oscillate [*or Oscillation, Oscillator, Oscillograph, Oscilloscope*] (KSC)
OSC .... Oscillation (SAUS)
OSC .... Oscillator (ACAE)
osc .... Oscillator (IDOE)
OSC .... Oscoda, MI [*Location identifier*] [*FAA*] (FAAL)
OSC .... Osmotically Sensitive Cell
OSC .... Outer Space Committee (SAUS)
OSC .... Outer Space Contact
OSC .... Out of Stock, Canceled [*Business term*]
OSC .... Output State Check [*Electronics*]
OSC .... Output State Control [*Automotive engineering*]
OSC .... Out, See Copy [*Proofreader's note*]
OSC .... Overlapping Spreading Centers [*Geology*]
OSC .... Overlap Slotted Container [*Packaging*]
OSC .... Overseas Settlement Committee [*World War I*] [*British*]
OSC .... Overseas Shipping Company (SAUS)
OSC .... Overseas Staff College [*British*]
OSC .... Overseas Supply Committee [*World War II*]
OSC .... Own Ship's Course [*Navy*]
OSC .... Oxidatively Solubilized Coal [*Fuel technology*]
OSC .... Oxygenated Sterol Compound [*Biochemistry*]
OSC .... Oxygen Storage Capacity [*Automotive emissions control*]
OSC .... Royal Clan, Order of Scottish Clans [*Later, Independent Order of Foresters*] (EA)
OSC .... Scugog Public Library, Ontario [*Library symbol*] [*National Library of Canada*] (NLC)
OSC .... Sisters of St. Clare (TOCD)
OSC .... Southern State Community College, Wilmington, OH [*OCLC symbol*] (OCLC)
OSCA .... Office of Saver and Consumer Affairs [*Federal Reserve Board*]
OSCA .... Office of Senior Citizens Affairs (NADA)
OSCA .... Office of State Corporate Affairs [*Western Australia*]
OSCA .... Operations Systems Computing Architecture (SAUS)
OSCA .... Optical Sensors Collaborative Association [*British*] (DBA)
OSCA .... OSCA [*NCIC car make code*]
OSCA .... OSCA, Inc. [*NASDAQ symbol*]
OSCA .... Out-of-School Childcare Association (WDAA)
OSCAA ...... Oil Spill Control Association of America [*Later, SCAA*] (EA)
OSCAD ...... Office of the Scientific Advisor (SAUS)
oscam .... Camillian Fathers and Brothers (TOCD)
OS Cam ..... Order of St. Camillus [*Camillians*] [*Roman Catholic religious order*]
OScan .... Old Scandinavian (ODA)
OSCAND .... Old Scandinavian [*Language, etc.*]
OSCAP ...... Operating System Communication Application Program [*Computer science*]
OSCAR ...... Observation Schedule and Records
OSCAR ...... Oil Spill Computer Aided Response (SAUS)
OSCAR ...... Omnium System Car [*Research vehicle*]
OSCAR ...... Online Serials Control at Ratcliffe (NITA)
OSCAR ...... Online System for Controlling Activities and Resources (SAUS)
OSCAR ...... OnScreen Configuration & Activity Reporting (SAUS)
OSCAR ...... On-Site Computer Assisted Research [*Oscar, Inc.*] [*Information service or system*] (IID)
OSCAR ...... Operating Sequence Control Array [*NASA*]
OSCAR ...... Operational System Characteristics
OSCAR ...... Operations, Scheduling, Control, and Reporting (MCD)
OSCAR ...... Optically Scanned Character Automatic Reader [*Computer science*] (DIT)
OSCAR ...... Optical Submarine Communications by Aerospace Relay
OSCAR ...... Optimum Survival Containment and Recovery (AAG)
OSCAR ...... Optimum System for the Control of Aircraft Retardation
OSCAR ...... Optimum Systems Covariance Analysis Results (IEEE)
oscar .... Orbital-Satellite-Carrying Amateur Radio (SAUS)
OSCAR ...... Orbiting Satellite Carrying Amateur Radio [*Telecommunications*] (TEL)
OSCAR ...... Order Status Control and Reporting [*Telecommunications*] (TEL)
OSCAR ...... Oregon State Conversational Aid to Research [*Computer science*] (CSR)
OSCAR ...... Organisation for Sickle Cell Anemia Research [*British*]
OSCAR ...... Organization for Scientific Coordination in AIDS [*Acquired Immune Deficiency Syndrome*] Research, Inc. [*New York, NY*]
OSCAR ...... Oscillogram Scan and Recorder System (PDAA)
OSCAR ...... Outside Cable Rehabilitation (SAUS)
OSCAR ...... Overnight Statewide Customer Accounting Reporting (IAA)
OSCAR ...... Oxidant-Scavenging Characteristics of April Rains (SAUS)
OSCAR ...... Oxygen Steelmaking Computer and Recorder (SAUS)
OSCAR II ... Outside Cable Rehabilitation II [*Army*] (RDA)
OSCARS ..... One-way Synchronous Collision Avoidance and Ranging System (SAUS)
OSCARS ..... Order Status Control and Reporting System [*Telecommunications*]
OSCAS ...... Office of Statistical Coordination and Standards (SAUS)
OSCB .... College Bibliocentre, Scarborough, Ontario [*Library symbol*] [*National Library of Canada*] (BIB)
OSCCap ..... Capuchin Poor Clares (TOCD)
OSCCB ...... On-Site Change Control Board [*Military*] (CAAL)
OSCCJA ..... Casimir, Jennings, and Appleby Public Library, St. Charles, Ontario [*Library symbol*] [*National Library of Canada*] (NLC)
OSCD .... Ohio Supreme Court Decisions, Unreported Cases [*A publication*] (DLA)
OSCD .... Ontario Securities Commission Decisions [*QL Systems Ltd.*] [*Information service or system*] [*Canada*] (CRD)
OSCD .... Operations Support Computing Division (ACAE)
OSCE .... Objective Structured Clinical Exam [*Medicine*] (EDAA)
OSCE .... Office of Child Support Enforcement (USGC)
OSCE .... Office Statistique des Communautes Europeennes [*Statistical Office of the European Communities - EUROSTAT*] [*Commission of the European Communities*]
OSCE .... Organisation for Security and Co-Operation in Europe (ECON)
OSCE .... Organization on Security and Cooperation in Europe (SAUS)
OSCER ...... Offshore Survival Craft Emergency Radiotelephone [*Telecommunications*] (PDAA)
OSCF .... Oligomycin-sensitivity-conferring Factor [*Medicine*] (EDAA)
OSCF .... Operations Support Computing Facility (MCD)
OSCG .... Information Resource Centre, Consumers Gas, Scarborough, Ontario [*Library symbol*] [*National Library of Canada*] (NLC)
OSCG .... Oscillating
OSCG .... Oscillograph, String
OSCGRM .... Oscillogram [*Engineering*]
OSCH .... Schreiber Public Library, Ontario [*Library symbol*] [*National Library of Canada*] (NLC)
OSCIA .... Ontario Soil and Crop Association [*Canada*]
OSCILAB ... Ocean Science Laboratory [*Oceanography*]
OSCILLOSC ... Oscilloscope (IAA)
OSCL .... Operating System Control Language (NITA)
OSCL .... Own Ship's Centerline [*Navy*]
OSCMF ...... Oxygen Scavenging Cell Membrane Fragment [*Biochemistry*]
OSCMIS ..... Operating and Support Costs Management Information System (MCD)
OS/CMP ..... Operational Support/Configuration Management Plan (SAUS)
OSC-MULT ... Oscillator-Multiplier [*Telecommunications*] (TEL)
OSCN .... Ocean Star Container Line [*Common carrier symbol*]
OSCO .... Oil & Solvent Process Co. (EFIS)
OSCO .... Oil Service Company (EFIS)
OSCO .... Oil Shipment Corp. (SAUS)
OSCO .... Organizational Source Code (NITA)
OSCOE ...... Objective Structured Clinical and Oral Examination [*Medicine*] (EDAA)
OSCOM ...... Oslo Commission (EAIO)
OSCOM ...... Oslo Commission for the Prevention of Marine Pollution by Dumping from Ships and Aircraft (SAUS)
OSCON/M ... Oslo Convention/Commission (SAUS)
OSCOT ...... Overall Systems Combat Operability Test [*Navy*] (ANA)
OSCP .... Ocean Sediment Coring Program [*National Science Foundation*]
OSCP .... Off Shore Centrally Procured (SAUS)
OSCP .... Oligomycin-Sensitivity-Conferring Protein [*Biochemistry*] (QSUL)
OSCP .... On-Site Computer Programmer (SAUS)
OSCP .... Oscilloscope (AAG)
OSCP .... Oscilloscope Panel
OSCPS ...... Oxygen Supply and Cabin Pressurization Section [*Apollo*] [*NASA*]
OSCR .... Ocean Surface Current RADAR
OSCR .... Off Standard Condition Report (SAUS)
OSCR .... Online Service Center Response [*Computer science*] (VLIE)
OSCR .... Operating and Support Cost Reduction [*Army*]
OSCR .... Operations and Sustainment Cost Reduction Strategy (RDA)
OSCRL ...... Operating System Command and Response Language
OSCRN ...... Oil Screen
OSCRO ...... Oglala Sioux Civil Rights Organization [*South Dakota*]
OSCRS ...... Orbital Spacecraft Consumables Resupply System (SAUS)
OSCT .... Office of Scholarly Communication and Technology (SAUS)
OSCUT ...... Oil Spill Clean-Up Technology (ASF)
OSCZ .... Intermodal Service [*Intermodal trailer symbol*]

OSD.......... Dow Chemical Co., Sarnia, Ontario [*Library symbol*] [*National Library of Canada*] (NLC)
OSD.......... Oceanside, CA [*Amtrak rail station code*]
OSD.......... Office of Standards Development [*Abolished*] [*Nuclear Regulatory Commission*]
OSD.......... Office of Student Detachment [*Navy*]
OSD.......... Office of Systems Development [*Social Security Administration*]
OSD.......... Office of the Secretary of Defense
OSD.......... Officer on Special Duty [*Indian Railway*] (TIR)
OSD.......... Officer Service Date [*Air Force*] (AFM)
OSD.......... Officers Service Dress [*British military*] (DMA)
OSD.......... Office Systems Design (SAUS)
OSD.......... One Stop Data Ltd.
OSD.......... On-line System Driver (SAUS)
OSD.......... Online System Drivers [*NCR Corp.*]
OSD.......... Online Systems Driver (SAUS)
OSD.......... On-Screen Digital (SAUS)
OSD.......... On Screen Display [*Computer science*] (AAEL)
OSD.......... Open Shelter Deck [*Shipping*] (DS)
OSD.......... Open Software Description [*Computer science*]
OSD.......... Open Software Description standard (SAUS)
OSD.......... Open Software Distribution [*Computer science*] (VLIE)
OSD.......... Open System Direction (SAUS)
OSD.......... Operating Safety Document (SAUS)
OSD.......... Operating Specification Document (SAUS)
OSD.......... Operational Sea Vehicle Diagram (MCD)
OSD.......... Operational Sequence Diagram (IEEE)
OSD.......... Operational Service Date (VLIE)
OSD.......... Operational Specification Document (SAUS)
OSD.......... Operational Support Directive [*Military*] (AFM)
OSD.......... Operational System Diagram (SAUS)
OSD.......... Operational Systems Development (MCD)
OSD.......... Operations Subdirective
OSD.......... Opposed [*Telegraphy*] (PCTE)
OSD.......... Optical Scanning Device [*Computer science*]
OSD.......... Ordinis Sancti Dominici [*Order of St. Dominic*] [*Latin*] (ROG)
OSD.......... Ordnance Safing Device
OSD.......... Ordnance Store Department [*British*] (ROG)
OSD.......... Ordnance Sub-Depot (SAUS)
OSD.......... Ordnance Supply Depot
OSD.......... Organization Subject Details (SAUS)
OSD.......... Organosilicon Device (SAUS)
OSD.......... Original Sponsoring Distributor (SAUS)
OSD.......... Osgood-Schlatter Disease
OSD.......... Osgood Semantic Differential [*Occupational therapy*]
OSD.......... Ostersund [*Sweden*] [*Airport symbol*] (OAG)
OSD.......... Outer Sleeve and Dome (SAUS)
OSD.......... Out-of-Station Designation (SAUS)
OSD.......... Out of Stock for the Duration [*Business term*] (DGA)
OSD.......... Overseas Duty
OSD.......... Overseas Settlement Department [*World War I*] [*British*]
OSD.......... Overseas Shipping Directive (SAUS)
OSD.......... Overseas Standards Digest [*A publication*] (ADA)
OSD.......... Overseas Supply Division [*Military*]
OSD.......... Over, Short, and Damaged [*Report*] [*Shipping*] (MCD)
OSD.......... Overside Drainage [*Medicine*] (DAVI)
OSD.......... Own Ship's Distance [*Navy*] (MCD)
OSD.......... Oxygen Selective Detector [*Chromatography*]
OSDA........ Oceanic System Development and Support [*FAA*] (TAG)
OSDA........ Onsite Sewage Disposal Act (SAUS)
OSDA........ Original Subimage Data Array (SAUS)
OSDB........ Ocean Surveillance Data Base (SAUS)
OSDBMC.... Office of the Secretary of Defense, Ballistic Missile Committee
OSDBU...... Office of Small and Disadvantaged Business Utilization [*See also SDBU/CR*] [*Agency for International Development*]
OSDC........ Oklahoma State Data Center [*Oklahoma State Department of Commerce*] (IID)
OSD/CSD.... Open Shelter Deck/Closed Shelter Deck [*Shipping*] (DS)
OSD/DSAA... Office of the Secretary of Defense, Defense Security Assistance Agency (MCD)
OSDH........ Oklahoma State Department of Health (SAUS)
OSDH........ Optical Shubnikhov-de Haas [*Effect*] (AAEL)
OSDH........ Orbiter System Definition Handbook [*NASA*] (NASA)
OSDI......... Damascus/International [*Syria*] [*ICAO location identifier*] (ICLI)
OSDI......... Own Ships Data Interface (SAUS)
OSDIDBAD... Office of the Secretary of Defense Identification Badge [*Military decoration*] (GFGA)
OSDIdentBad... Office of the Secretary of Defense Identification Badge (AABC)
OSD/ISA..... Office of the Secretary of Defense for International Security Affairs
OSDIT....... Office of Software Development and Information Technology [*General Services Administration*]
OSDIU....... Over-the-Horizon Targeting System Digital Interface Unit
OSDM....... Optical Space-Division Multiplexing (EECA)
OSDMT...... Organization for the Support of Democratic Movement of Taiwan (EA)
OSDNRL.... Ocean Science Division-Naval Research Laboratory (SAUS)
OSDOC...... Offshore Discharge of Container-Ships (RDA)
OSDOC...... Over-the-Shore Discharge of Cargo [*Navy*] (CAAL)
OSDOCS.... Over-the-Shore Discharge of Container Ships (SAUS)
OSDOC Ship... Offshore Discharge of Container Ship (SAUS)
OSDOC Ship... Over-the-Store Discharge of Container Ship (SAUS)
OS/DOS..... Operating System/Disk Operating System [*Software*]
OSDP........ On-Site Data Processing [*or Processor*] [*NASA*]
OSDP........ On-Site Data Processor (SAUS)
OSDP........ Operational System Development Program
OSDP........ Operations System Development Program [*Marine science*] (OSRA)
OSD(PA & E)... Office of the Secretary of Defense for Program Analysis and Evaluation (MCD)
OSDPD...... Office of Satellite Data Processing and Distribution (SAUS)
OSDPT...... Optimization of Systems for Data Processing and Transmission (PDAA)
OSDR........ Oil Slick Detection RADAR
OS/D Report... Over, Short and Damaged Report (SAUS)
OSDS........ Operating System for Distributed Switching [*Computer science*] (VLIE)
OSD-SA..... Office of the Secretary of Defense - Systems Analysis
OSDSA...... Office of the Secretary of Defense Systems Analysis (SAUS)
OSDSAC..... Office of the Secretary of Defense, Scientific Advisory Committee
OSDS-M..... Operating System for Distributed Switching in the Switching Module [*Communications term*] (DCT)
OSDT........ Damascus [*Syria*] [*ICAO location identifier*] (ICLI)
OSDU........ Output Signal Distribution Unit (MCD)
OSDV........ Oat Sterile Dwarf Virus [*Plant pathology*]
OSDZ........ Deir Ez Zor [*Syria*] [*ICAO location identifier*] (ICLI)
OSE.......... Bethel, AK [*Location identifier*] [*FAA*] (FAAL)
OSE.......... Edwardsburg Township Public Library, Spencerville, Ontario [*Library symbol*] [*National Library of Canada*] (BIB)
OSE.......... Oblique Seismic Experiment (SAUS)
OSE.......... Occupational Supplies and Equipment [*Red Cross*]
OSE.......... Ocean and Science Engineering Inc.
OSE.......... Oceanic Society Expeditions (EA)
OSE.......... Ocean Shipping and Enterprises (SAUS)
OSE.......... Office of Science Education (SAUS)
OSE.......... Office of Sex Equity (SAUS)
OSE.......... Office of Systems Engineering [*Social Security Administration*]
OSE.......... Officer Scheduling the Exercise [*Navy*] (NVT)
OSE.......... Office Server Extension
OSE.......... Olefin Strain Energy [*Organic chemistry*]
OSE.......... Omniforce Spatial Environment (AAG)
OSE.......... On Scene Endurance [*Environmental science*] (COE)
OSE.......... Open Software Environment (SAUS)
OSE.......... Open Systems Environment [*Computer science*] (CIST)
OS/E......... Operating System/Environment [*Computer science*] (BYTE)
OSE.......... Operational Security Evaluation (MCD)
OSE.......... Operational Support Equipment
OSE.......... Operations Simulations Engineer (ADWA)
OSE.......... Operation Status Equipment
OSE.......... Operation Support Equipment (SAUS)
OSE.......... Optical Science and Engineering (SAUS)
OSE.......... Orbital Sequence of Events [*NASA*] (IAA)
OSE.......... Orbiter Support Equipment [*NASA*] (NASA)
OSE.......... Order of the Star in the East [*A theosophical organization*]
OSE.......... Organizational Support Equipment [*Army*]
OSE.......... Osage Systems Group [*AMEX symbol*] (SG)
OSE.......... Osaka Securities Exchange (SAUS)
OSE.......... Osaka Stock Exchange [*Japan*]
OSE.......... Osec Petroleum [*Vancouver Stock Exchange symbol*]
OSE.......... Overall System Effectiveness (IAA)
OSE.......... Overseas Security Eligibility [*DoD*]
OSE.......... Salem Public Library, Salem, OR [*OCLC symbol*] (OCLC)
OSE.......... Union Mondiale pour la Protection de la Sante des Populations Juives et Oeuvres de Secours aux Enfants
OSEA........ Oregon School Employees Association
OSEAP....... Oil Shale Environmental Advisory Panel [*Department of the Interior*]
OSEAS....... Ocean Sampling and Environmental Analysis System (PDAA)
O/SEAS...... Overseas
OSEC........ Office of the Secretary
OSEC........ Office Systems Education and Counseling (HGAA)
OSECCA..... Old Sleepy Eye Collectors' Club of America (EA)
OSECY....... Office of the Secretary to the Staff [*NATO*] (NATG)
OSEDA....... Office of Social and Economic Data Analysis (VLIE)
OSEDS....... Operational Support Equipment Design Specification
OSEE........ Optically Stimulated Electron Emission [*Also, PEE*] [*Physics*]
OSEE........ Optically Stimulated Exoelectron Emission (SAUS)
O/SEER...... Overseer
OSEH........ Order of St. Elizabeth of Hungary [*Anglican religious community*]
OSEIA....... Open System Environment profile for Imminent Acquisitions (SAUS)
OSEM........ Office of Systems Engineering Management [*Department of Transportation*]
OSEOS....... Operational Synchronous Earth Observatory Satellite [*Telecommunications*] (TEL)
OSEP........ Office of Scientific and Engineering Personnel [*National Academy of Sciences*] [*Information service or system*] (IID)
OSEP........ Office of Special Education Programs [*Also, SEP*] [*Department of Education*]
OSER........ Virginia Tech Applied Biosciences Center [*Virginia Polytechnic Institute and State University*] (RCD)
OSERA....... Ohio Scientific Education and Research Association (EARSL)
O Serb....... Old Serbian (SAUS)
OSERP....... Oil Sands Environmental Research Program (SAUS)
OSERS....... Office of Special Education and Rehabilitative Services [*Department of Education*]
OSES........ Office of Solar Energy Studies [*Medicine*] (EDAA)
OSES........ Operations Systems Engineering Support (MCD)
OSESG....... Oil Sands Environmental Study Group [*Canada*]
OSETI........ Optical Search for Extraterrestrial Intelligence (SAUS)
OSETNO..... Offset Number (SAUS)
OSEXT....... Operating System Extensions [*Computer science*] (VLIE)
OSF.......... Bernardine Sisters of the Third Order of St. Francis (TOCD)

OSF.......... Congregation of the Religious Brothers of the Third Order Regular of St. Francis (TOCD)
OSF.......... Congregation of the Sisters of the Third Order of St. Francis Oldenburg, IN (TOCD)
OSF.......... Congregation of the Third Order of St. Francis of Mary Immaculate, Joliet IL (TOCD)
OSF.......... Franciscan Brothers of Christ the King (TOCD)
osf.......... Franciscan Brothers of Christ the King (TOCD)
osf.......... Franciscan Brothers of the Third Order Regular (TOCD)
OSF.......... Franciscan Missionaries of Our Lady (TOCD)
OSF.......... Franciscan Missionary Brothers of the Sacred Heart of Jesus (TOCD)
osf.......... Franciscan Missionary Brothers of the Sacred Heart of Jesus (TOCD)
OSF.......... Franciscan Missionary Sisters for Africa (TOCD)
OSF.......... Franciscan Missionary Sisters of Our Lady of Sorrows (TOCD)
OSF.......... Franciscan Missionary Sisters of the Immaculate Conception (TOCD)
OSF.......... Franciscan Sister, Daughters of the Sacred Hearts of Jesus and Mary (TOCD)
OSF.......... Franciscan Sisters of Allegany, New York (TOCD)
OSF.......... [*The*] Franciscan Sisters of Baltimore (TOCD)
OSF.......... Franciscan Sisters of Chicago (TOCD)
OSF.......... Franciscan Sisters of Christian Charity (TOCD)
OSF.......... Franciscan Sisters of Christ the Divine Teacher (TOCD)
OSF.......... Franciscan Sisters of Little Falls, Minnesota (TOCD)
OSF.......... Franciscan Sisters of Our Lady of Perpetual Help (TOCD)
OSF.......... Franciscan Sisters of St. Paul (TOCD)
OSF.......... Franciscan Sisters of the Immaculate Conception and St. Joseph for the Dying (TOCD)
OSF.......... Franciscan Sisters of the Sacred Heart (TOCD)
OSF.......... Fransciscan Brothers of the Third Order Regular (TOCD)
OSF.......... Hospital Sisters of the Third Order of St. Francis (TOCD)
OSF.......... Missionary Franciscan Sisters of the Immaculate Conception (TOCD)
OSF.......... Obtain Service From [*Navy*] (NVT)
OSF.......... Ocean Simulation Facility [*Naval Coastal Systems Laboratory*] (DNAB)
OSF.......... Odd Side Flat
OSF.......... Office of Space Flight [*NASA*] [*Washington, DC*] (NASA)
OSF.......... Office Systems Family (HGAA)
OSF.......... Official Statistics for Finland (SAUS)
OSF.......... One Hundred Square Feet (SAUS)
OSF.......... Open Software Foundation [*An association*] [*Commission*] (NETL)
OSF.......... Open Systems Foundation
OSF.......... Operational Service Fee (WDAA)
OSF.......... Operations System Function (SAUS)
OSF.......... Operations Systems Function Block (SAUS)
OSF.......... Operation Support Facility [*National Weather Service*] (USDC)
OSF.......... Oppose Sun Forever (SAUS)
OSF.......... Optically-Shaped Film
OSF.......... Optronic Sector System (SAUS)
OSF.......... Order of St. Francis [*Franciscans*] [*Roman Catholic religious order*]
OSF.......... Ordinary Shareholders Fund (WDAA)
OSF.......... Ordnance Storage Facility (KSC)
OSF.......... Organic Storage Facility (SAUS)
OSF.......... Organizational Status File (SAUS)
OSF.......... Organ System Failure [*Medicine*]
OSF.......... Osaka Stock Futures [*Japan*] (ECON)
OSF.......... Outer Spiral Fibers [*Ear anatomy*]
OSF.......... Out of Stock, To Follow [*Business term*]
OSF.......... Overgrowth Stimulating Factor [*Cancer cause*]
OSF.......... Oxidation-Induced Stacking Fault (PDAA)
osf.......... Religious Brothers of the Third Order Regular of St. Francis (TOCD)
OSF.......... School Sisters of St. Francis (TOCD)
OSF.......... School Sisters of the Third Order of St. Francis (Bethlehem, PA) (TOCD)
OSF.......... School Sisters of the Third Order of St. Francis (Panhandle, TX) (TOCD)
OSF.......... School Sisters of the Third Order of St. Francis (Pittsburgh, PA) (TOCD)
OSF.......... Servants of the Holy Infancy of Jesus (TOCD)
OSF.......... Sisters of Saint Francis, Clinton, Iowa (TOCD)
OSF.......... Sisters of Saint Francis of Milvale, Pennsylvania (TOCD)
OSF.......... Sisters of Saint Francis of the Providence of God (TOCD)
OSF.......... Sisters of St. Francis (TOCD)
OSF.......... Sisters of St. Francis of Christ the King (TOCD)
OSF.......... Sisters of St. Francis of Penance and Christian Charity (TOCD)
OSF.......... Sisters of St. Francis of Perpetual Adoration (TOCD)
OSF.......... Sisters of St. Francis of Savannah, MO (TOCD)
OSF.......... Sisters of St. Francis of the Congregation of Our Lady of Lourdes, Sylvania, Ohio (TOCD)
OSF.......... Sisters of St. Francis of the Holy Cross (TOCD)
OSF.......... Sisters of St. Francis of the Holy Eucharist (TOCD)
OSF.......... Sisters of St. Francis of the Holy Family (TOCD)
OSF.......... Sisters of St. Francis of the Immaculate Conception (TOCD)
OSF.......... Sisters of St. Francis of the Immaculate Heart of Mary (Hankinson, North Dakota) (TOCD)
OSF.......... Sisters of St. Francis of the Martyr St. George (TOCD)
OSF.......... Sisters of St. Francis of the Third Order Regular (Williamsville, New York) (TOCD)
OSF.......... Sisters of the Third Franciscan Order (TOCD)
OSF.......... Sisters of the Third Order of St. Francis of Penance and Charity (TOCD)
OSF.......... Sisters of the Third Order of St. Francis (Peoria, IL) (TOCD)
OSF.......... Sisters of the Third Order Regular of St. Francis of the Congregation of Our Lady of Lourdes (TOCD)
OSF.......... St. Francis Mission Community (TOCD)
OSF.......... [*The*] Sisters of St. Francis of Assisi (TOCD)
OSF.......... [*The*] Sisters of St. Francis of Philadelphia (TOCD)
OSFA........ Office of Student Financial Assistance [*Department of Education*] (GFGA)
OSFA........ Offshore Shrimp Fisheries Act of 1973
OSFAR....... Sturgeon Falls Branch of the Algonquin Regional Library System, Ontario [*Library symbol*] [*National Library of Canada*] (NLC)
OSFAS....... Overseas Students Fee Awards Scheme (SAUS)
OSFC........ Fiberglas Canada, Inc., Sarnia, Ontario [*Library symbol*] [*National Library of Canada*] (NLC)
OSFC........ Ordinis Sancti Francisci Capuccini [*Franciscan Capuchins*] [*Roman Catholic men's religious order*]
OSFCO...... Office of Solid Fuels Coordinator [*Military*] (DNAB)
OSFCSR..... Rideau Regional Centre, Ministry of Community and Social Services, Smiths Falls,Ontario [*Library symbol*] [*National Library of Canada*] (NLC)
OSFCW...... Office of Solid Fuels Coordinator for War [*World War II*]
OSFD........ Office of Space Flight Development [*Obsolete*] [*NASA*]
OSF/DCF.... Open Software Foundation/Distributed Computing Environment [*Computer science*] (AGLO)
OSF/DME... Operation System Function/Distributed Management Environment (SAUS)
OSFET....... Oxide Semiconductor Field Effect Transistor (SAUS)
OSFI......... Le Bureau du Surintendant des Institutions Financieres (IID)
OSFI......... Office of the Superintendent of Financial Institutions [*Department of Insurance*] [*Ottawa, ON*] [*Information service or system*] (IID)
OSFI......... Open Steel Flooring Institute [*Defunct*]
OSFL........ Olive-Sided Flycatcher [*North American bird banding code*] (BIBA)
OSFM........ Office of Spacecraft and Flight Missions [*NASA*]
OSFM........ Office of Surplus Facility Management (SAUS)
OSFP........ Office of Space Flight Programs [*Obsolete*] [*NASA*]
OSFS........ Oblate of Saint Francis of Sales (SAUS)
OSFS........ Oblates of St. Francis de Sales (TOCD)
osfs.......... Oblates of St. Francis de Sales (TOCD)
OSFS........ Oblati Sancti Francisci Salesii [*Oblate Fathers or Sisters of St. Francis of Sales*] [*Roman Catholic religious orders*]
OSFT........ ObjectSoft Corp. [*NASDAQ symbol*] (SAG)
OSFT........ Outstretched Fingertip(s) [*Medicine*] (EDAA)
OSG.......... Occupations Study Group [*British*]
OSG.......... Office of Sea Grant [*National Oceanic and Atmospheric Administration*]
OSG.......... Office of the Secretary General [*United Nations*]
OSG.......... Office of the Solicitor General [*Department of Justice*]
OSG.......... Office of the Surgeon General [*of Public Health Service; later, absorbed by office of Assistant Secretary for Health and Scientific Affairs*]
OSG.......... Official Steamship Guide (SAUS)
OSG.......... Open Service Gateway (RALS)
OSG.......... Operand Select Gate [*Computer science*]
OSG.......... Operations Support Group [*Nuclear energy*] (NRCH)
OSG.......... Opposing [*Telegraphy*] (PCTE)
OSG.......... Organization and Staffing Guide [*Department of Labor*] (OICC)
OSG.......... Osphradial Ganglion [*In mollusks*]
OSG.......... Otosclerosis Study Group (EA)
OSG.......... Overseas Shipholding Group, Inc. [*NYSE symbol*] (SPSG)
OSG.......... Overspeed Generator (SAUS)
OSG.......... South Gillies Library, Ontario [*Library symbol*] [*National Library of Canada*] (BIB)
OSGB........ Orchid Society of Great Britain (EAIO)
OSGC........ Ohio Space Grant Consortium (RCD)
OSGD........ Office of Sea Grant Development [*National Oceanic and Atmospheric Administration*] (MSC)
OSGI......... Open-Service Gateway Interface
OSGI......... Open Systems Gateway Initiative [*Communications*]
OsGI......... TIGR [*The Institute of Genomic Research*] Rice Gene Index [*Database*] (GDD)
OSGLI....... Office of Servicemen's Group Life Insurance
OSGOO...... Osgood, PA [*American Association of Railroads railroad junction routing code*]
OSGP........ Office of Sea Grant Programs [*National Oceanic and Atmospheric Administration*]
OSGP........ Ontario Study Grant Plant (SAUS)
OSGP........ Operations Support Group Prototype (SAUS)
OSGR........ Oscillator Single Gain Region (PDAA)
OSGS........ Office of the Secretary of the General Staff
OSGS........ On Sudan Government Service (SAUS)
OSGS........ Stittsville Branch, Goulbourn Township Public Library, Ontario [*Library symbol*] [*National Library of Canada*] (NLC)
OSH.......... Community Hospital of Springfield, Springfield, OH [*Library symbol*] [*Library of Congress*] (LCLS)
OSH.......... National Institute for Occupational Safety and Health, Cincinnati, OH [*OCLC symbol*] (OCLC)
OSH.......... Occupational Safety and Health [*Department of Labor*]
OSH.......... Office on Smoking and Health Database [*Centers for Disease Control*] [*Information service or system*] (CRD)
OSH.......... Oil Search Ltd. [*Australian Stock Exchange symbol*]
OSH.......... Omni Singula Hora [*Every Hour*] [*Pharmacy*]
OSH.......... Ordo Sancti Hieronymi [*Hieronymites*]
OSH.......... Oshawa Group Ltd. [*Toronto Stock Exchange symbol*]
OSH.......... Oshima [*Japan*] [*Seismograph station code, US Geological Survey*] (SEIS)
OSH.......... Oshkosh [*Wisconsin*] [*Airport symbol*] (OAG)
OSH.......... Oshman's Sporting Goods, Inc. [*AMEX symbol*] (SAG)
OSH.......... Own Ship's Heading [*Navy*]
OSh.......... Shaker Heights Public Library, Shaker Heights, OH [*Library symbol*] [*Library of Congress*] (LCLS)

OSH......... Shelburne Public Library, Ontario [*Library symbol*] [*National Library of Canada*] (NLC)
OSHA........ Occupational Safety and Health Act [*1970*]
OSHA........ Occupational Safety and Health Administration [*Department of Labor*] [*Washington, DC*]
OSHA........ Occupational Safety Hazards Act (AAEL)
OSHA........ Office of Special Housing Assistance [*HUD*]
OSHAct...... Occupational Safety and Health Act (EEVL)
Oshap....... OSHAP Technologies Ltd. [*Associated Press*] (SAG)
OSHAW...... Oshawa, ON [*American Association of Railroads railroad junction routing code*]
OSHB........ One-Sided Height Balanced [*Telecommunications*]
OshB......... Oshkosh B'Gosh, Inc. [*Associated Press*] (SAG)
OSHB........ Sheshegwaning Band Public Library, Ontario [*Library symbol*] [*National Library of Canada*] (NLC)
OSHC........ Orchard Supply Hardware Stores Corp. [*NASDAQ symbol*] (SAG)
OSHC........ Outside School Hours Care
OSHC........ Overseas Student Health Coverage
OSH Cas.... Occupational Safety and Health Cases [*A publication*] (DLA)
OSHD........ Occupational Safety and Health Decisions [*A publication*] (DLA)
OSH Dec.... Occupational Safety and Health Decisions [*A publication*] (DLA)
o/sheep..... odd sheep (SAUS)
OShelS...... Sacred Heart Seminary, Shelby, OH [*Library symbol*] [*Library of Congress*] (LCLS)
OSHI......... Occupational, Safety, and Health Institute [*University of Houston*] [*Research center*] (RCD)
OSHI......... Office of Special Health Issues (SAUS)
O/SHIP...... Ownership (SAUS)
OSHJ......... Oblate Sisters of the Sacred Heart of Jesus [*Roman Catholic religious order*]
OSHK........ Oshkosh [*NCIC truck make code*]
OSHKO...... Oshkosh, WI [*American Association of Railroads railroad junction routing code*]
OshkT....... Oshkosh Truck Corp. [*Associated Press*] (SAG)
OShL........ Shaker Heights Public Library, Shaker Heights, OH [*Library symbol*] [*Library of Congress*] (LCLS)
OSHM....... Oshman's Sporting Goods, Inc. [*NASDAQ symbol*] (COMM)
Oshmn...... Oshman's Sporting Goods, Inc. [*Associated Press*] (SAG)
OSHPD...... Office of Statewide Health Planning and Development [*California Health and Human Services Agency*] (MHID)
OSHR........ Occupational Safety and heal Review Commission (EBF)
OSHRC...... Occupational Safety and Health Review Commission [*Department of Labor*]
OSHS........ Occupational Safety and Health Scheme (SAUS)
OSHS........ Occupational Safety and Health Statistics [*Bureau of Labor Statistics*] (GFGA)
OSHS........ OSHAP Technologies Ltd. [*NASDAQ symbol*] (NQ)
OShS........ Shaker Heights City School District, Shaker Heights, OH [*Library symbol*] [*Library of Congress*] (LCLS)
OSHSA...... Occupational Safety and Health Standards Act (SAUS)
OSHSF...... Oshap Technologies Ltd. [*NASDAQ symbol*] (TTSB)
OSHT........ Grand Lodge Order of the Sons of Hermann in Texas [*San Antonio, TX*] (EA)
OSHT........ Sharon Temple, Sharon, Ontario [*Library symbol*] [*National Library of Canada*] (NLC)
OSI........... Aerosi SA de CV [*Mexico*] [*ICAO designator*] (FAAC)
OSI........... National Institute for Occupational Safety and Health, Rockville, MD [*OCLC symbol*] (OCLC)
OSI........... Office of Samoa Information [*Press agency*]
OSI........... Office of Scientific Information [*National Science Foundation*] (MCD)
OSI........... Office of Scientific Integrity [*National Institutes of Health*]
OSI........... Office of Scientific Intelligence [*Fictitious government agency on TV series "The Six Million Dollar Man"*]
OSI........... Office of Seniors' Interests [*Australia*]
OSI........... Office of Special Investigation [*Air Force*]
OSI........... Office of Strategic Information [*DoD*]
OSI........... Office of Strategic Intelligence [*Air Force*] (INF)
OSI........... Office of Systems Integration [*Social Security Administration*]
OSI........... Officer Skill Identifiers [*Army*]
OSI........... Office Systems Interconnection [*Telecommunications*] (TSSD)
OSI........... Offshore Islands (CINC)
OSI........... Offshore Systems International Ltd. [*Toronto Stock Exchange symbol*] [*Canada*]
OSI........... Off Site Instruction (SAUS)
OSI........... Ohio Scientific Inc. (SAUS)
OSI........... Olivetti e Segre Industria [*Automobile manufacturer*] [*Defunct*]
OSI........... Online Software International (SAUS)
OSI........... On-Site Inspection
OSI........... Opening Shock Inhibitor (SAUS)
OSI........... Open Society Institute [*Russia*]
OSI........... Open Source Initiative [*Computer science*] (FOTI)
OSI........... Open Space Institute (EA)
OSI........... Open Standards Interconnection [*International Standards Organisation*]
OSI........... Open System Interconnect [*Automotive engineering*]
OSI........... Open System Interconnections [*Networking technique*]
OSI........... Open System Interface (SAUS)
OSI........... Open Systems Interconnect
OSI........... Open Systems Interface (SAUS)
OSI........... Operating Space Item [*Military*] (CAAL)
OSI........... Operating System Interface
OSI........... Operating Systems, Inc. (MCD)
OSI........... Operational Status Indicator (MUGU)
OSI........... Operation Smile International (EA)
OSI........... Optical Sciences Institute (SAUS)
OSI........... Optical Society of India (SAUS)
OSI........... Optical Surface Imaging (RAWO)
OSI........... Optimum Scale Integration (SAUS)
OSI........... Optional Stop Instruction (SAUS)
OSI........... ORDALT [*Ordnance Alterations*]/SHIPALT Inspector [*Ship Alteration*] (MCD)
OSI........... Organic Sign Index [*Psychology*]
OSI........... Oriental Shorthairs International (EA)
OSI........... OR Storage to Indicators (SAUS)
OSI........... OSI [*NCIC car make code*]
OSI........... Osijek [*Former Yugoslavia*] [*Airport symbol*] (OAG)
OSI........... Other Service Information (TRID)
OSI........... Other Service Investigation (SAUS)
OSI........... Other Support Items
OSI........... Otto-Suhr-Institut (SAUS)
OSI........... Outback Steakhouse [*NYSE symbol*]
OSI........... Out of Stock, Indefinite [*Business term*]
OSI........... Out of Stock Indefinitely (ADWA)
OSI........... Overhead Supply Inventory (MCD)
OSI........... Owner Satisfaction Index (SAUS)
OSI........... Oyster Shell Institute (EA)
OSI........... Ozark Society (EA)
OSI........... Research Technical Information Centre, ESSO Petroleum Canada, Sarnia, Ontario [*Library symbol*] [*National Library of Canada*] (NLC)
OSI........... Woodside, CA [*Location identifier*] [*FAA*] (FAAL)
OSIA......... Office, Services and Information Agency [*Military*] (AABC)
OSIA......... On-Site Inspection Agency [*DoD*]
OSIA......... Open Systems Interconnection Association (SAUS)
OSIA......... Open Systems Interconnections Architecture (SAUS)
OSIA......... Order Sons of Italy in America (EA)
OSIA......... Outdoor Systems, Inc. [*NASDAQ symbol*] (SAG)
OSIASL...... Order Sons of Italy in America Supreme Lodge [*Later, OSIA*] (EA)
OSIC......... Ocean Science Information Center [*University of Hawaii*] (NOAA)
OSIC......... Offshore Suppliers Information Centre (SAUS)
OSIC......... Oil Spill Information Center [*Santa Barbara, CA*]
OSIC......... Optimization of Subcarrier Information Capacity
OSIC......... Osicom Technologies, Inc. [*NASDAQ symbol*] (COMM)
OSICOM..... Open Systems Interconnections Division [*Now Open Systems Interconnection Division*] (ACII)
Osicom...... Osicom Technologies, Inc. [*Associated Press*] (SAG)
OSICS....... Commission Scolaire de Sept-Iles, Quebec [*Library symbol*] [*National Library of Canada*] (NLC)
OSI/CS...... Open Systems Interconnection/Communications Subsystem (SAUS)
OSI/CS...... OSI/Communications Subsystem (SAUS)
OSICS....... OSI Communication Systems (SAUS)
OSID......... Open Systems Interconnection Division (ACII)
OSID......... Operational System Interface Document (MCD)
OSID......... Origination Signaling Identifier (SAUS)
OSIDM...... Eva Brook Donly Museum, Simcoe, Ontario [*Library symbol*] [*National Library of Canada*] (NLC)
OSIE......... Office of Software Improvement and Engineering [*Social Security Administration*]
OSIE......... Open Systems Interconnection Environment [*Telecommunications*] (OSI)
OSIE......... Operational Support Integration Engineering
OS/IES...... On-Site Integrated Energy System
OSIFA....... Operational Sequence and Information Flow Analysis (SAUS)
OSI/FS...... OSI File Services (SAUS)
OSIGA....... Ohio State Inventory of Guidance Awareness
OSIGO....... Office of the Chief Signal Officer
OSIGO....... Office of the Signal Officer (SAUS)
OSII.......... Objective Sys Integrators [*NASDAQ symbol*] (TTSB)
OSII.......... Objective Systems Integrators, Inc. [*NASDAQ symbol*] (SAG)
OSIL......... Lynwood Arts Centre, Simcoe, Ontario [*Library symbol*] [*National Library of Canada*] (NLC)
OSIL......... Operating System Implementation Language
OSINET...... Open System Interconnection Network (SAUS)
OSINET...... Open Systems Interconnection Network (SAUS)
OSInet....... OSI Network (SAUS)
OSINH....... Norfolk Historical Society, Simcoe, Ontario [*Library symbol*] [*National Library of Canada*] (NLC)
OSINLCP... OSI Network Layer Control Protocol (SAUS)
OSI/NMF.... Open Systems Interconnect Network Management Forum [*Computer science*] (BTTJ)
OSI/NMF.... OSI Network Management Forum (SAUS)
OSINT....... Open Source Intelligence (SAUS)
OSIP......... Operational and Safety Improvement Program (NVT)
OSIP......... Operational Satellite Improvement Program (ACAE)
OSIP......... Operational Suitability Improvement Program [*Aviation*]
OSIP......... OSI Pharmaceuticals [*NASDAQ symbol*] [*Formerly, Oncogene Science*] (SG)
OSIP......... Simcoe Public Library, Ontario [*Library symbol*] [*National Library of Canada*] (NLC)
OS/IPC...... Operating System/Inter-Process Communications (DOMA)
OSIQ......... Offer Self-Image Questionnaire
OSIQA....... Offer Self-Image Questionnaire for Adolescents (EDAC)
OSIR......... Office of Scientific Integrity Review [*US Secretary of Health*]
OSIR......... Oil Spill Intelligence Report
Os-Ir......... Osmiridium (IDOE)
OSIR......... Out of Service in Reserve [*Military*] (CINC)
OSIRIS...... Online Search Information Retrieval Information Storage [*Computer science*] (PDAA)
OSIRIS...... Online Serials Information Registration and Inquiry System (SAUS)
OSIRIS...... Optical Simulation for Imaging Reconnaissance and Intelligence Sensors (SAUS)

OSI/RM...... Open System Interconnection/Reference Model (SAUS)
OSIRM ...... Open Systems Interconnection Reference Model (SAUS)
OSI/RM...... OSI Reference Model (SAUS)
OSIS......... Ocean Surveillance Information System [*Navy*] (MCD)
OSIS......... Office of Science Information Service [*National Science Foundation*]
OSIS......... On-Site Inspection System (SAUS)
OSIS......... Operating-System-Independent Server (GART)
OSIS......... Operating Systems Installation Support (SAUS)
OSIS......... Organization Structure Information System (SAUS)
OSITOP...... Open Systems Interconnection Technical and Office Protocols [*Telecommunications*] (OSI)
OSIX......... Optical Specialties, Inc. [*NASDAQ symbol*] (COMM)
OSIX......... Peavey Corp. [*NASDAQ symbol*]
osj........... Oblates of St. Joseph (TOCD)
OSJ.......... Oblates of St. Joseph [*Roman Catholic religious order*]
OSJ.......... Office of Supervisory Jurisdiction [*Investment term*]
OSJ.......... Sovereign Order of Saint John of Jerusalem (EA)
OSJD........ Ordinis Sancti Joannis de Deo [*Order of St. John of God*]
OS-JTF...... Open Systems Joint Task Force (SAUS)
OSK.......... Occasional Swimmer's Kit [*Police and security equipment*]
OSK.......... Osaka [*Takayasuyama*] [*Japan*] [*Seismograph station code, US Geological Survey*] (SEIS)
OSK.......... Oshkosh Truck Corp. [*NYSE symbol*]
OSK.......... Oskarshamn [*Sweden*] [*Airport symbol*] (OAG)
OSKAR...... Outstanding Superior Kitchen All-Rounder [*Trademark of Sunbeam Corp.*]
OSKL........ Kamishly [*Syria*] [*ICAO location identifier*] (ICLI)
OSKL........ Swastika Branch, Kirkland Lake Public Library, Ontario [*Library symbol*] [*National Library of Canada*] (BIB)
OSKNC...... Skead Branch, Nickel Centre Public Library, Ontario [*Library symbol*] [*National Library of Canada*] (NLC)
OSKY........ Mahaska Investment [*NASDAQ symbol*] (TTSB)
OSKY........ Mahaska Investment Co. [*NASDAQ symbol*] (SAG)
OSL.......... International Order of Saint Luke the Physician (EA)
OSL.......... Oberspreewald-Lausitz [*German license plate city code*]
OSL.......... Object Script Language (SAUS)
OSL.......... Observed Significance Level (SAUS)
OSL.......... Office of the Secretary of Labor (SAUS)
OSL.......... Oil Seal
OSL.......... Old [*Church*] Slavonic [*Language, etc.*]
OSL.......... Old Style Latin (ADA)
OSL.......... Ontario Safety League (SAUS)
OSL.......... Open/Short Locator
OSL.......... Operand Specification List (SAUS)
OSL.......... Operating Safety Limit (SAUS)
OSL.......... Operating System Language
OSL.......... Operational Safety Limit (SAUS)
OSL.......... Operator Set Loop [*Electronics*] (ECII)
OSL.......... Optically Stimulated Luminescence [*Analytical Chemistry*]
OSL.......... Optical Storage Ltd.
OSL.......... Optimization Subroutine Library [*Computer science*] (HODG)
OSL.......... Orbital Space Laboratory (SAUS)
OSL.......... Orbiting Solar Laboratory (SAUS)
OSL.......... Orbiting Space Laboratory
OSL.......... Order of St. Luke the Physician of America (EA)
OSL.......... Ordnance Sub-Lieutenant [*British military*] (DMA)
OSL.......... Oregon Short Line Railroad [*of Union Pacific Railroad Co.*]
OSL.......... Organic Semiconductor LASER [*Materials science*]
OSL.......... Osgood-Schlatter Lesion [*Medicine*] (STED)
OSL.......... Osler Resources, Inc. [*Vancouver Stock Exchange symbol*]
OSL.......... Oslo [*Norway*] [*Airport symbol*] (OAG)
OSL.......... O'Sullivan Corp. [*AMEX symbol*] (SPSG)
OSL.......... Outer Structured Layer (SAUS)
OSL.......... Outstanding Leg [*NASA*] (KSC)
OSL.......... Seitel [*Toronto Stock Exchange symbol*] [*Canada*]
OSL.......... Sioux Lookout Public Library, Ontario [*Library symbol*] [*National Library of Canada*] (NLC)
OSL.......... University of Oregon, School of Librarianship, Eugene, OR [*OCLC symbol*] (OCLC)
OSLA........ Ontario Association of Speech-Language Pathologists and Audiologists (SAUS)
OSLA........ Stella Branch, Lennox and Addington County Library, Ontario [*Library symbol*] [*National Library of Canada*] (NLC)
OS Language... Old Saxon Language (SAUS)
O Slav....... Old [*Church*] Slavic [*Language*] (BARN)
OSLB........ Operational Search Lower Bound [*RADAR*]
OSLC........ Lambton College of Applied Arts and Technology, Sarnia, Ontaria [*Library symbol*] [*National Library of Canada*] (NLC)
OSLDPS..... Office of State and Local Domestic Preparedness Support [*Emergency Management*] (EMA)
OSLEAS..... Association Sectorielle de Fabrication d'Equipement de Transport et de Machines,St.-Leonard, Quebec [*Library symbol*] [*National Library of Canada*] (NLC)
OSLFC....... Sharbot Lake Branch, Frontenac County Library, Ontario [*Library symbol*] [*National Library of Canada*] (BIB)
OSLI......... Office of Servicemen's Life Insurance (OICC)
OSLJ......... Law Journal. Student Bar Association. Ohio State University [*A publication*] (DLA)
OSLK........ Latakia/Latakia [*Syria*] [*ICAO location identifier*] (ICLI)
OSLM........ Operations Shop/Laboratory Manager [*NASA*] (MCD)
O-SLM....... Optically addressed Spatial Light Modulator (SAUS)
OSLO........ Other Six Leases Operation (SAUS)
OSLP........ Ontario Student Loans Plan (SAUS)
OSLR........ Intergovernmental Committee for Ocean Science and Living Resources [*Marine science*] (OSRA)
OSLR........ Ocean Sciences and Living Resources (SAUS)
OSLT........ On-Site Logistics Team (MCD)
OSLU........ Ocean Star Line [*Intermodal shipping container symbol*] (TVRC)
OSM......... Mantellate Sisters, Servants of Mary of Blue Island (TOCD)
OSM......... Mental Health Services for Clark County, Springfield, OH [*Library symbol*] [*Library of Congress*] (LCLS)
OSM......... Mosul [*Iraq*] [*Airport symbol*] (AD)
OSM......... Oblates of St. Martha (TOCD)
OSM......... Office of Sample Management (SAUS)
OSM......... Office of Spectrum Management [*US National Telecommunications and Information Administration*] (TSSD)
OSM......... Office of Surface Mining (EAGT)
OSM......... Office of Surface Mining Reclamation and Enforcement [*Department of the Interior*]
OSM......... Office Service Manual (SAUS)
OSM......... Off-Screen Model [*Computer science*]
OSM......... Oil-Sands Mining (SAUS)
OSM......... Omnispectra Miniature
OSM......... Oncostatin [*Antibiotic*]
OSM......... One of the Swinish Multitude (SAUS)
OSM......... On-Screen Manager [*Computer science*]
OSM......... On Screen Menue (SAUS)
OSM......... On-Site Maintenance
OSM......... On Station Mode
OSM......... Open System Module (SAUS)
OSM......... Operating Service Month
OSM......... Operating System Manual (MCD)
OSM......... Operating System Monitor
OSM......... Operating System Service Module (SAUS)
OSM......... Operating System Specific Module (SAUS)
OSM......... Operational Space Medicine Program [*Canadian Space Agency*] (RCD)
OSM......... Operations Sampling Management (SAUS)
OSM......... Operations Systems Manager (SAUS)
OSM......... Operator's Service Manual
OSM......... Opisu Struktur Mikroprogramownych [*Programming language*] (CSR)
OSM......... Optical Section Microscope
OSM......... Optical Storage Manager (SAUS)
OSM......... Optical Support Measures (SAUS)
OSM......... Option Select Mode [*Computer science*] (OA)
OSM......... Orbital Service Module [*NASA*] (MCD)
osm.......... Orbital Service Module [*NASA*] (NAKS)
OSM......... Ordnance Safety Manual [*Military*]
OSM......... Ordnance Supply Manual (SAUS)
OSM......... Ordo Servorum Mariae [*Order of Servants of Mary*] [*Servites*] [*Roman Catholic religious order*]
OSM......... Organization Structure Model (TIMI)
OSM......... Orr-Schelen-Mayeron & Associates (EFIS)
OSM......... Oscillating Secondary Mirror [*Telescope*]
Osm......... Osmania (SAUS)
OSM......... Osmol (SAUS)
osM.......... Osmolar [*Chemistry*] (DAVI)
OSM......... Osmolarity (STED)
Osm......... Osmole [*Physical chemistry*]
OSM......... Osmonics, Inc. [*NYSE symbol*] (SPSG)
OSM......... Osmosis (SAUS)
osm.......... Osmotic (STED)
OSM......... Osmotic
OSM......... Output Switch Module [*Automotive engineering*]
OSM......... Outside Mail (AFM)
OSM......... Outside of Metal
OSM......... Ovine Submaxillary Mucin [*Medicine*] (DMAA)
OSM......... Oxygen Saturation Meter (MAE)
OSM......... Oxygen Steel Making
OSM......... Schumacher Memorial Library, Ontario [*Library symbol*] [*National Library of Canada*] (BIB)
OSM......... Servants of Mary (TOCD)
osm.......... Servite Fathers (TOCD)
OSM......... Servites (TOCD)
OSMA....... Occidental Society of Metempiric Analysis (EA)
OSMA....... Office of Small Manufacturers Assistance [*FDA*]
OSMA....... Oklahoma State Medical Association (EARSL)
OSMA....... Optical Spectrometric Multichannel Analyzer [*Instrumentation*]
OSMA....... Orthopedic Surgical Manufacturers Association (EA)
OSMA....... Otago-Southland Manufacturers Association (SAUS)
OSMA....... Overseas Sales and Marketing Association of America [*Lake Bluff, IL*] (EA)
OSMA/CD... Optical Sense Multiple Access with Collision Detection (SAUS)
OSMAS...... Oil Spill Modelling for the Antarctic Seas (SAUS)
OSMC....... Object Storage Management Component (SAUS)
OSM Connector... Omni Spectra Miniature Connector (SAUS)
OSM Connector... Omnispectra Miniature Connector (SAUS)
OSME........ Open Systems Message Exchange [*Computer science*] (CIST)
OSME........ Oral Speech Mechanism Screening Examination [*Educational test*]
OSME........ Ornithological Society of the Middle East (EAIO)
OSMED...... Otospondylomegaepiphyseal Dystrophy [*Medicine*] (DAVI)
OSMF........ O'Fahey SDS Motor Freight [*Common carrier symbol*]
OSMF........ Oral Submucous Fibrosis [*Medicine*] (STED)
OSMF........ Smith Falls Public Library, Ontario [*Library symbol*] [*National Library of Canada*] (NLC)
OS/MFT..... Operating System/Multiprogramming Fixed Task (NITA)
OS/MFT..... Operating System/Multiprogramming with a Fixed Number of Tasks [*IBM Corp.*] [*Computer science*]
OSML........ McNeil Laboratories (Canada) Ltd., Stouffville, Ontario [*Library symbol*] [*National Library of Canada*] (NLC)

OSML........ Operating System Machine Level (VLIE)
OSMM....... Mercy Medical Center, Springfield, OH [*Library symbol*] [*Library of Congress*] (LCLS)
OSMM....... Office of Safeguards and Materials Management [*AEC*]
OSMM....... Optimum Supply and Maintenance Model
osmo........ Osmolality [*Chemistry*]
OSMO........ Osmonics, Inc. [*NASDAQ symbol*] (COMM)
osmol....... Osmole [*Measurement*] (DAVI)
Osmonic.... Osmonics, Inc. [*Associated Press*] (SAG)
OSMOS...... Own Ship's Motion Simulator [*Navy*]
OSMOS...... Own Ship's Motion System [*Navy*]
OSMP........ Operational Support Maintenance Plan [*NASA*] (MCD)
OSMR........ Office of Systems Modernization Requirements [*Social Security Administration*]
OSMRE...... Office of Surface Mining Reclamation and Enforcement [*Also, OSM*] [*Department of the Interior*]
OSMS........ Organizational Supply Management System [*Army*] (INF)
OSM S....... Osmolarity Serum [*Biochemistry*] (DAVI)
OSMSE-R... Oral Speech Mechanism Screening Examination-Revised [*St. Louis and Ruscello*] (TES)
OSMU........ Oesterreichische Schuhmusterschau [*Austrian Footwear Exhibition*] [*Wiener Messen und Kongress GmbH*] (TSPED)
OSM U....... Osmolarity Urine [*Biochemistry*] (DAVI)
OSMV........ Oat Striate Mosaic Virus [*Plant pathology*]
OSMV........ One Shot Multivibrator (MSA)
OS/MVS..... Operating System/Multiprogramming with Virtual Storage [*Computer science*]
OS/MVT..... Operating System/Multiprogramming with a Variable Number of Tasks [*Computer science*]
OSN.......... Ocean Science News [*Marine science*] (OSRA)
OSN.......... Ocean Seismic Network (SAUS)
OSN.......... Ocular Surgery News (SAUS)
OSN.......... Office of the Secretary of the Navy
OSN.......... Office Systems Node (VLIE)
OSN.......... Off Service Note [*Medicine*] (DAVI)
OSN.......... Open Systems Network [*Computer science*] (VLIE)
OSN.......... Operations System Network [*Communications term*] (DCT)
OSN.......... Opposition [*Telegraphy*] (PCTE)
OSN.......... Orient Group Satellite Networks Technology
OSN.......... Osphradial Nerve [*In mollusks*]
OSN.......... Output Sequence Number
OSN.......... Sioux Narrows Public Library, Ontario [*Library symbol*] [*National Library of Canada*] (NLC)
OSNA........ Ornithological Societies of North America Database [*Database*] (GDD)
OSNAP...... Object Snap [*Auto CAD*] [*Computer science*]
OSNC........ Orient Steam Navigation Company (SAUS)
OSNC........ Sarnia Northern Collegiate, Ontario [*Library symbol*] [*National Library of Canada*] (NLC)
OSNI......... Ordinance Survey of Northern Island (SAUS)
OSNLR...... Ocean Science in Relation to Non-Living Resources [*Marine science*] (OSRA)
OSNS........ Open Systems Network Support [*Computer science*] (VLIE)
OSNS........ Shedden Public Library, Spanish, Ontario [*Library symbol*] [*National Library of Canada*] (NLC)
OSNSW..... Office of the Sheriff of New South Wales [*Australia*]
OSNY........ Oratorio Society of New York (SAUS)
OSNZ........ Ornithological Society of New Zealand (SAUS)
OSO.......... Objective and Strategies Overview (SAUS)
oso........... Ocean Systems Operation [*NASA*] (NAKS)
OSO.......... Ocean Systems Operation [*NASA*]
OSO.......... Offensive System Operator (ACAE)
OSO.......... Offensive Systems Operator (SAUS)
OSO.......... Office of Satellite Operations (SAUS)
OSO.......... Office of Space Operations (ACAE)
OSO.......... Office of Systems Operations [*Social Security Administration*]
OSO.......... Officer Selection Office (DNAB)
OSO.......... Offshore Suppliers Office [*British*]
OSO.......... Offshore Supply Office (SAUS)
OSO.......... Omaha Symphony Orchestra (SAUS)
OSO.......... One-Shot Operation (SAUS)
OSO.......... One Side Only (SAUS)
OSO.......... Onsala Space Observatory [*Sweden*]
OSO.......... Onsite Office (SAUS)
OSO.......... Open Server Offering [*IBM*] (GART)
OSO.......... Operations Scheduling Office (SSD)
OSO.......... Orbital Solar Observation (SAUS)
OSO.......... Orbital Solar Observatory (SAUS)
OSO.......... Orbiting Satellite Observer (IEEE)
OSO.......... Orbiting Scientific Observatory (IAA)
OSO.......... Orbiting Solar Observatory [*A satellite*]
OSO.......... Ordnance Supply Office
OSO.......... Oregon State Library, Salem, OR [*OCLC symbol*] (OCLC)
OSO.......... Oregon Symphony Orchestra (SAUS)
O/S/O........ Ore/Slurry/Oil [*Supertanker*]
OSO.......... Originating Screening Office (SAUS)
OSO.......... Originating Signaling Office (SAUS)
OSO.......... Originating Signalling Office (VLIE)
OSO.......... Origination Screening Office [*Telecommunications*] (TEL)
OSO.......... Overscan Operation (SAUS)
OSO.......... Overseas Security Operations (SAUS)
OSO.......... Southampton Branch, Bruce County Public Library, Ontario [*Library symbol*] [*National Library of Canada*] (NLC)
OSO 1-8..... Orbiting Solar Observatories 1-8 (SAUS)
OSOB........ Old Senate Office Building [*Also, RSOB*] [*Washington, DC*] (DLA)
OSOC........ Off-Site Originated Change (AAG)
OSOCC...... On-Site Operations Coordination Center
OSODS...... Office of Strategic Offensive and Defensive Systems [*Navy*]
OSOG........ Office Systems Owners Group (HGAA)
OSOIPB..... Ordnance Supply Office Illustrated Parts Breakdown [*Navy*]
OSol......... Odes of Solomon (BJA)
OSOL........ Office of the Solicitor [*Department of Labor*]
OS/OLM..... On-Site/On-Line Maintenance
OSOM........ Bruce County Museum, Southampton, Ontario [*Library symbol*] [*National Library of Canada*] (BIB)
OSOP........ Off-Site Operations Plan (SSD)
OSOP........ Orbiter Systems Operating Procedures [*NASA*] (NASA)
OSOR........ Operational Standoff Range (NVT)
OSOS........ Ore/Slurry/Oil Ship (SAUS)
OSOS........ Oxide Silicon Oxide Semiconductor (SAUS)
OSoSJ....... Saint Joseph's Priory, Somerset, OH [*Library symbol*] [*Library of Congress*] (LCLS)
OSOT........ Oakland Township Public Library, Scotland, Ontario [*Library symbol*] [*National Library of Canada*] (BIB)
OSOTM...... Sombra Township Museum, Ontario [*Library symbol*] [*National Library of Canada*] (BIB)
OSP.......... Obiit sine Prole [*Died without Issue*] [*Latin*]
OSP.......... Objective and Strategies Plan (SAUS)
OSP.......... Oblate Sisters of Providence [*Roman Catholic religious order*]
OSP.......... Occupational Safety Programs Branch (SAUS)
OSP.......... Ocean Surveillance Product (DOMA)
OSP.......... Ocean Survey Plan [*or Program*] [*Navy*]
OSP.......... Ocean Survey Program (SAUS)
OSP.......... Office of Science Policy [*National Science Foundation*]
OSP.......... Office of Scientific Personnel [*NAS-NRC*]
OSP.......... Office of Special Projects (COE)
OSP.......... Office of Special Technology [*Formerly, Office of Special Projects*] [*Washington, DC*] [*Department of Energy*] (GRD)
OSP.......... Office of Sponsored Projects (SAUS)
OSP.......... Office of Staffing Policy [*Office of Personnel Management*] [*Washington, DC*] (GRD)
OSP.......... Office of Statistical Policy (SAUS)
OSP.......... Office of Surplus Property [*Superseded by War Assets Corporation*] [*World War II*]
OSP.......... Office of the Special Prosecutor [*Queensland, Australia*]
OSP.......... Offshore Patrol (SAUS)
OSP.......... Off-Shore Procedure (SAUS)
OSP.......... Offshore Procurement [*Army*]
O-SP......... Off-Street Parking (WDAA)
OSP.......... Oficina Sanitaria Panamericana [*Pan-American Sanitary Bureau - PASB*] [*Washington, DC*]
OSP.......... Ohio State Highway Patrol
OSP.......... Oil Suction Pump (MSA)
OSp.......... Old Spanish (BEE)
OSP.......... OLE-DB Simple Provider (SAUS)
OSP.......... Online Service Provider
OSP.......... On-Screen Programming (SAUS)
OSP.......... On-Site Programmer (SAUS)
OSP.......... On-Site Service Provider [*Computer science*] (VLIE)
OSP.......... On Station Position (MUGU)
OSP.......... Open-Space Program (SAUS)
OSP.......... Operating Steam Pressure (MSA)
OSP.......... Operating System Plan (SAA)
OS/P......... Operating Systems for People (SAUS)
OSP.......... Operational Safety Procedures (COE)
OSP.......... Operational Surveillance Program [*Nuclear Regulatory Commission*] (NRCH)
OSP.......... Operational Survival Plan [*Civil Defense*]
OSP.......... Operations Special Procedures (SAUS)
OSP.......... Operations Support Plan [*Navy*] (NG)
OSP.......... Operator Service Provider (SAUS)
OSP.......... Operator Station Processor [*Computer science*] (VLIE)
OSP.......... Optical Signal Processing (SAUS)
OSP.......... Optical Signature Program [*Military*] (CAAL)
OSP.......... Optical Storage Processor [*Computer science*] (VLIE)
OSP.......... Optical Surveillance Platform (SAUS)
OSP.......... Optimum Sustainable Population [*Marine science*] (MSC)
OSP.......... Optoelectronic Systems Programme [*British*]
OSP.......... Orbital Space Plane [*NASA*]
OSP.......... Orbital/Suborbital Program [*Space launch term*] (ISAK)
OSP.......... Orbital Support Plan (MCD)
OSP.......... Orbiting Standards Platform (ACAE)
OSP.......... Order of St. Paul [*Anglican religious community*]
OSP.......... Order of St. Paul the First Hermit [*Pauline Fathers*] [*Roman Catholic religious order*]
OSP.......... Ordinary Superphosphate (EDCT)
OSP.......... Organic Solderability Perservative [*Electronics*] (AAEL)
OSP.......... Original Set Pattern [*Ice dancing*]
OSP.......... Outer Surface Protein [*Cytology*]
OSP.......... Outfitting Stock Point
OSP.......... Outside Plant [*Telecommunications*] (TEL)
OSP.......... Outside Procured Stores (AAG)
OSP.......... Outside Purchase (WDAA)
OSP.......... Own Ship's Position [*Navy*] (MCD)
OSP.......... Polysar Ltd., Sarnia, Ontario [*Library symbol*] [*National Library of Canada*] (NLC)
OSP.......... Slupsk [*Poland*] [*Airport symbol*] (OAG)
OSPA........ Ohio School Psychologists Association (EARSL)
OSPA........ Open Signal Coprocessing Architecture [*Computer science*]
OSPA........ Operator Service Providers of America [*Communications term*] (DCT)

OSPA .... Oregon State Pharmacists Association (EARSL)
OSPAAAL ... Organization of Solidarity of the Peoples of Africa, Asia, and Latin America
OSPAR ...... Oslo and Paris Convention for Protection of the Marine Environment of the North-East Atlantic (SAUS)
OSPARCOM... Oslo-Paris Commission
OSPC .... Off-Site Property Control (SAUS)
OSPC .... Options Service of Project Concern [*An association*] (EA)
OSPCS ...... Charles M. Shields Centennial Library, South Porcupine, Ontario [*Library symbol*] [*National Library of Canada*] (BIB)
OSPD .... Office of Sponsored Program Development [*State University of New York at Binghamton*] [*Research center*] (RCD)
OSPD .... Official Scrabble Players Dictionary [*A publication*]
OSPDS ...... Ocean Surveillance Product Dissemination Service (SAUS)
OSPE .... Organizational Spare Parts and Equipment [*Army*]
OSPENEA... Conventions for the protection of the marine environment of the North-East Atlantic (SAUS)
OSPES....... Outer Shell Photoelectron Spectroscopy
OSPF .... Internes Routingprotokoll (SAUS)
OSPF .... Open Shortest Path First [*Communications routing protocol*]
OSPG .... Original Society of Painters and Glaziers [*A union*] [*British*]
OSPI .... Office of Strategic Planning and Integration (SAUS)
OSPI .... Office of Superintendent of Public Instruction
OSPI .... Operating System Programming Interface (SAUS)
OSPIC .... Oil Spill Public Information Center (SAUS)
OSPIC .... Overseas Patent Information Center (SAUS)
OS-PIF ...... Office of the Secretary of Defense Productivity Investment Funding
OSPIRG ..... Oregon State Public Interest Research Group [*Research center*] (RCD)
OSPJ .... Offshore Procurement, Japan
OSpM........ Mental Health Services for Clark County, Springfield, OH [*Library symbol*] [*Library of Congress*] (LCLS)
OSPM .... Operating System directed Power Management (SAUS)
OSPNC ...... Porcupine Campus, Northern College of Applied Arts and Technology, South Porcupine, Ontario [*Library symbol*] [*National Library of Canada*] (NLC)
OSPPE....... Pauline Fathers (TOCD)
osppe........ Pauline Fathers (TOCD)
OSPR .... Office for Social Policy Research [*Northern Illinois University*] (RCD)
OSPR .... Office of Oil Spill Prevention and Response
OSPR .... Osprey [*North American bird banding code*] (BIBA)
OSPR .... Palmyra [*Syria*] [*ICAO location identifier*] (ICLI)
OSPRC ...... Office for the Study of the Psychological Rights of the Child (RCD)
OSPRDS .... Oblate Spheroid (PDAA)
OSPREY..... Ocean Swell Powered Renewable Energy [*United Kingdom*]
OSPRO ...... Ocean Shipping Procedures
OSPS .... Operator Service Position System (SAUS)
OSPS .... Operator Services Position System (SAUS)
OSPTM...... Timmins Museum, South Porcupine, Ontario [*Library symbol*] [*National Library of Canada*] (BIB)
OSQ.......... Officer Separation Questionnaire (DNAB)
OSQ.......... Officer Student Quarters (DNAB)
OS Q......... Operating System Q (SAUS)
OSQ.......... San Antonio, TX [*Location identifier*] [*FAA*] (FAAL)
OSQL .... Object Structured Query Language (SAUS)
OSR.......... Occupational Survey Report
OSR.......... Oceanographic Survey Recorder (SAUS)
OSR.......... OEM Service Release (SAUS)
OSR.......... Offender Status Register (SAUS)
OSR.......... Office for Scientific Research (SAUS)
OSR.......... Office of Scientific Research [*AFSC*]
OSR.......... Office of Security Review [*Obsolete*] [*DoD*]
OSR.......... Office of Sponsored Research (SAUS)
OSR.......... Office of Sport and Recreation [*Australian Capital Territory*]
OSR.......... Office of Standards and Regulations [*Environmental Protection Agency*] (GFGA)
OSR.......... Office of Strategic Research (SAUS)
OSR.......... Office of Systems Requirements [*Social Security Administration*]
OSR.......... Official Visitors Spot Report (SAUS)
OSR.......... Ohio State Reports [*A publication*] (DLA)
OSR.......... Oil Shale Reserves (SAUS)
OSR.......... Oil/Steam Ratio (SAUS)
OSR.......... Old Style Roman (ADA)
OSR.......... Onsite Review [*Military*]
OSR.......... Open System Recognition [*Computer communications*]
OSR.......... Operand Storage Register [*Computer science*]
OSR.......... Operating Safety Requirements (SAUS)
OSR.......... Operational Safety Requirements (COE)
OSR.......... Operational Scanning Recognition
OSR.......... Operational Status Release [*Navy*] (NG)
OSR.......... Operational Support Readiness
OSR.......... Operational Support Requirement [*Military*]
OSR.......... Operations Safety Requirement (SAUS)
OSR.......... Operations Support Room [*NASA*]
OSR.......... Optical Scanner Reader (SAUS)
OSR.......... Optical Scanning Recognition [*Computer science*]
OSR.......... Optical Solar Reflector
OSR.......... Optical Sound Recorder
OSR.......... Optical Spectral Reflector (SAUS)
OSR.......... Optical Still Recorder [*LASER-disc technology*]
OSR.......... Optical Surface Reflector (SAUS)
OSR.......... Optimum Ship Routing [*Obsolete*]
OSR.......... Ordnance Status Report (NG)
OSR.......... Original Stock Requisition (TIMI)
OSR.......... Originators Status Report [*Army*]
OSR.......... OR with Switch Register (SAUS)
OSR.......... Oscar Resources Ltd. [*Vancouver Stock Exchange symbol*]
OSR.......... Ostrava [*Former Czechoslovakia*] [*Airport symbol*] (OAG)
OSR.......... Output Shift Register
OSR.......... Output Signal Range
OSR.......... Output Status Register
OSR.......... Oversea Returnee [*Military*]
OSR.......... Overseas Service Ribbon [*Military decoration*]
OSR.......... Over-the-Shoulder Rating
OSR.......... Own Ship's Roll [*Navy*]
OSR.......... Oxide-Stable Resin
OSRA........ Office Systems Research Association [*Cleveland, OH*] (EA)
OSRA........ Oil Spill Risk Analysis (SAUS)
OSRA........ Operational Software Release Approval (SAUS)
OSRA........ Overseas Shipping Representatives Association (SAUS)
OSRAC ...... Ocean Shipping Requirements and Capabilities
OSRADP .... Oil Spill Research and Development Program [*Louisiana*]
Osram....... Osmium und Wolfram (SAUS)
OSRAP ...... Optimum Stockage Requirements Analysis Program
OSRB........ Overseas Service Resettlement Bureau (SAUS)
OSRC........ Oil Sands Research Centre [*Alberta*]
OSRD........ Office of Scientific Research and Development [*World War II*]
OSRD........ Office of Standard Reference Data [*Gaithersburg, MD*] [*National Institute of Standards and Technology*]
OSRDB ...... Office of Standard Reference Data Bibliography [*National Institute of Standards and Technology*]
OS Rep...... Ohio State Reports [*A publication*] (DLA)
OSREPL..... Oversea Replacement [*Army*]
OSRET....... Oversea Returnee [*Army*]
OSRF .... Smooth Rock Falls Public Library, Ontario [*Library symbol*] [*National Library of Canada*] (NLC)
OSRI......... Originating Station Routing Identifier
OSRI......... Originating Station Routing Indicator (SAUS)
OSRL .... Oregon Survey Research Laboratory [*University of Oregon*] (RCD)
OSRL .... Organizations and Systems Research Laboratory [*Army*] (RDA)
OSRM .... Office of Standard Reference Materials [*Gaithersburg, MD*] [*National Institute of Standards and Technology*] (GRD)
OSRM .... South River-Machar Union Public Library, South River, Ontario [*Library symbol*] [*National Library of Canada*] (NLC)
OSRMD ..... Office of Scientific Research, Mechanics Division (SAUS)
OSRMS...... Ocean Surface Roughness Measurement System (SAUS)
OSRO........ Office for the Sahelian Relief Operation [*UN Food and Agriculture Organization*]
OSRO........ Operations Support Requirements Office [*NASA*] (KSC)
OSROK...... Office of Supply Republic of Korea (SAUS)
OSRP........ Occupant Safety Research Partnership
OSRP........ Occupant Safety Research Project (SAUS)
OSRP........ Oil Spill Response Plan [*Pollution prevention*]
OSRPA ...... Offices, Shops, and Railway Premises Act [*1963*] [*British*]
OSRR........ Ohio Southern Railroad [*Federal Railroad Administration identification code*]
OSRR........ Oil Spill Response Research Program [*Minerals Management Service*] (RCD)
OSRR........ Spanish River Reserve Band Public Library, Ontario [*Library symbol*] [*National Library of Canada*] (NLC)
OSRS........ Oceanic Satellites and Remote Sensing (SAUS)
OSRS........ Operational Status Recording Subsystem
OSRS........ Organization of Senegal River States (SAUS)
OSRS........ Subgroup on Ocean Satellites and Remote Sensing (SAUS)
OSRTN ...... Office of the Special Representative for Trade Negotiations [*Later, Office of the United States Trade Representative*] [*Executive Office of the President*]
OSRU........ Optical Sensors Research Unit (NITA)
OSRV........ Oil Spill Response Vehicle
OSRV........ Outside Rear View [*Mirrors*] [*Automotive features*]
OSRX........ Ontario Southland Railway [*Private rail car owner code*]
OSS.......... Los Angeles, CA [*Location identifier*] [*FAA*] (FAAL)
OSS.......... Objective Supply System [*Army*]
OSS.......... Object Services Standard (AAEL)
OSS.......... Object Sorting Scales [*Psychology*]
OSS.......... Observatory of the Sahara and the Sahel (SAUS)
OSS.......... Observing Simulation System (USDC)
OSS.......... Observing Stimulation System [*Marine science*] (OSRA)
OSS.......... Occupant Sensing System [*Automotive safety systems*]
OSS.......... Occupational Superannuation Standard
OSS.......... Oceanic Scanning Spectrophotometer
OSS.......... Oceanic Space Subcommittee [*Congressional committee*] (MSC)
OSS.......... Ocean Science and Surveys (SAUS)
OSS.......... Ocean Surveillance Satellite (MCD)
OSS.......... Ocean Surveillance System [*Navy*] (SAA)
OSS.......... Ocean Survey Ship (NOAA)
OSS.......... OEX [*Orbiter Experiments*] Support System [*NASA*]
OSS.......... Office of Safeguards and Security [*Department of Energy*] [*Washington, DC*] (GRD)
OSS.......... Office of Secret Services (SAUS)
OSS.......... Office of Senate Security [*Congress*]
oss........... Office of Space Science [*NASA*] (NAKS)
OSS.......... Office of Space Science [*NASA*]
OSS.......... Office of Space Station (ACAE)
OSS.......... Office of Space Systems [*Air Force*]
OSS.......... Office of Statistical Standards [*Bureau of the Budget; later, OMB*]
OSS.......... Office of Strategic Services [*Facetiously translated as "Oh So Social" because some of its staff were socially prominent*] [*World War II*]
OSS.......... Office of Support Services [*Army*]

OSS.......... Office of Systems Operations [*National Weather Service*] (USDC)
OSS.......... Office of the Space Station (SAUS)
OSS.......... Office Skills Series [*Test*] (TMMY)
OSS.......... Office Support System (SAUS)
OSS.......... Offshore Surveillance System
OSS.......... Oh So Social
OSS.......... Old Submarine [*Navy symbol*]
OSS.......... One Stop Shop [*Small business advice*] [*British*] (ECON)
OSS.......... Online Service System (SAUS)
OSS.......... Online Support System von SAP (SAUS)
OSS.......... Ontario Secondary School Teachers' Federation [*UTLAS symbol*]
OSS.......... Open Sound System (SAUS)
OSS.......... Open Source Software (SAUS)
OSS.......... Open Source Solution (SAUS)
OSS.......... Open-Source Spectrometer (SAUS)
oss.......... Opera Semiseria [*Music*] (GROV)
oSS.......... operates Saturday and Sunday (SAUS)
OSS.......... Operating Supply Specification (SAUS)
OSS.......... Operating System Software [*Personal computers*]
OSS.......... Operating System Supervisor
OSS.......... Operating System Support (NITA)
OSS.......... Operational Storage Site [*Army*]
OSS.......... Operational Support Squadron (SAUS)
OSS.......... Operational Support System [*Computer science*]
OSS.......... Operation Safe Streets (SAUS)
OSS.......... Operations Support Services (SAUS)
OSS.......... Operations Support Squadron (SAUS)
OSS.......... Operations Support System (DOMA)
OSS.......... Operator Service Switch (SAUS)
OSS.......... Operator Service System (SAUS)
OSS.......... Operator Support System (SAUS)
OSS.......... Opposes [*Telegraphy*] (PCTE)
OSS.......... Optical Sensor Subsystem [*Military*] (CAAL)
OSS.......... Optical Sight System
OSS.......... Optical Subsystem (KSC)
OSS.......... Optical Surveillance System (AAG)
OSS.......... Optics Subsystems (SAUS)
OSS.......... Optimized Systems Software [*San Jose, CA*]
OSS.......... Orbital Space Station Study [*NASA*] (IAA)
OSS.......... Orbital Stabilization System (MCD)
oss.......... Orbiting Space Station [*NASA*] (NAKS)
OSS.......... Orbiting Space Station [*NASA*]
OSS.......... Order Short Shipped (SAUS)
OSS.......... Ordnance Safety Switch [*Military*] (IAA)
OSS.......... Organised Science Series [*A publication*]
OSS.......... Organization for Cooperation of Socialist Countries in the Domain of Posts and Telecommunications [*Defunct*] (EAIO)
OSS.......... Orient Shipping Services (SAUS)
OSS.......... Osisko Lake Mines Ltd. [*Toronto Stock Exchange symbol*]
oss.......... Ossetic [*MARC language code*] [*Library of Congress*] (LCCP)
OSS.......... Ossory [*Ireland*] (ROG)
OSS.......... Outer Solar System
OSS.......... Output Shaft Speed [*Automotive engineering*]
OSS.......... Overhead Speaker System [*Automotive engineering*]
OSS.......... Overseas Shipping Services (SAUS)
OSS.......... Overseas Switch [*Military*]
OSS.......... Over-the-Shoulder Shot [*Photography*] (WDMC)
OSS.......... Over-the-Shoulder Strap (DMAA)
OSS.......... Own Ship's Speed [*Navy*]
OSS.......... Oxygen Sleep Starvation
OSS.......... Religious of the Order of the Blessed Sacrament and Our Lady [*Sacramentine Nuns*] [*Roman Catholic religious order*]
OSS.......... Sacramentine Nuns (TOCD)
OSS.......... Sahara and Sahel Observatory (SAUS)
OSS.......... Shawnee State Community College, Portsmouth, OH [*OCLC symbol*] (OCLC)
OSSA........ Office of Space Science and Applications [*Washington, DC*] [*NASA*]
OSSA........ Order Scheduled Shipment Analysis (MCD)
OSSA........ Order Secular of St. Augustine [*See also ASAS*] [*Rome, Italy*] (EAIO)
OSSBA...... Oklahoma State School Boards Association (SAUS)
OSSC........ Oblati Sacratissimi Cordis [*Oblate Fathers of the Sacred Heart*] [*Roman Catholic religious order*]
OSSC........ Office of Stationary Source Compliance (COE)
OSSC........ Ordnance Storage and Shipment Chart [*Army*] (MCD)
OSSC........ Oregon School Study Council (SAUS)
OSSD........ Office of Space Systems Development [*NASA*]
OSSD........ Off-Site Surveillance Data [*Military*]
OSSD........ Ontario Secondary School Diploma (SAUS)
OSSE........ Object/Surface/Special Effect
OSSE........ Observation Simulation System Experiments (SAUS)
OSSE........ Observation System Simulation Experiments (SAUS)
OSSE........ Observing System Sensitivity Experiments (SAUS)
OSSE........ Observing Systems Simulation Experiments [*National Center for Atmospheric Research*]
OSSE........ Oriented Scintillation Spectrometer Experiment [*Instrumentation in Gamma Ray Observatory*] [*NASA*]
OSSEs....... Observing Systems Simulation Experiments (SAUS)
OSSF........ Operating System Storage Facility (SAUS)
OSSF........ Operating System Support Facility (MHDI)
OSSF........ Other Services Stock Fund (ACAE)
OSSF........ Overseas Services Storage Facility
OSShD...... Organisation fur die Zusammenarbeit der Eisenbahnen [*Organisation for the Collaboration of Railways - OCR*] (EAIO)
OSSHE...... Oregon State System of Higher Education (SAUS)
OSSHGD.... Ontario Secondary School Honour Graduation Diploma (SAUS)
OSSI......... Office of Supplemental Security Income (SAUS)
OSSI......... Open Storage Systems Interconnection (RALS)
OSSI......... Outback Steakhouse, Inc. [*NASDAQ symbol*] (SPSG)
OSSJ........ St. Joseph's Hospital, Sarnia, Ontario [*Library symbol*] [*National Library of Canada*] (BIB)
OSSKC...... Operative Society of Spring Knife Cutlers [*A union*] [*British*]
OSSL........ Operating Systems Simulation Language (SAUS)
OSSM....... Office of Safety Surface Mining [*Department of the Interior*] (COE)
OSSM....... Oil Spill Simulation Model
OSSM....... Optimum Shipboard Spares Model (SAUS)
OSSM Connector... Omnispectra Subminiature Connector (SAUS)
OSSMJ...... Order of the Societies of Mary and Joseph (ROG)
OSSN........ Operational Specialist Supervisor, Night [*Navy*]
OSSN........ Originating Station Serial Number (SAUS)
OSSN........ Other Specialty Serial Numbers [*Air Force*]
OSSN........ Outside Sales Support Network Association (TVEL)
OSSNSS..... Ordnance Supply Segment of the Navy Supply System
OSSO........ Office of State Systems Operations [*Social and Rehabilitation Service, HEW*]
OSSO........ Open Source Solutions Operation (SAUS)
OSSO........ Southwest Seismological Observatory [*Emergency Management*] (EMA)
OSSP........ Operational Supply Support Plan (MCD)
OSSP........ Oregon Small Schools Program (SAUS)
OSSP........ Outer Solar System Probe
OS-SPT...... Osmolality Urin-Spot [*Test*] [*Biochemistry*] (DAVI)
OSSR........ Oblates [*or Order*] of the Most Holy Redeemer [*Roman Catholic women's religious order*]
OSSR........ Order of the Most Holy Redeemer (TOCD)
OSSR........ Own Ship's Speed Repeater [*Navy*]
OSSRH...... Orbiter Subsystem Requirements Handbook [*NASA*] (NASA)
OSSRS...... Optimum Step Size Random Search [*Computer science*] (IAA)
osss......... Brigittine Monks (TOCD)
OSSS........ Damascus [*Syria*] [*ICAO location identifier*] (ICLI)
OSSS........ Optical Space Surveillance Subsystem (AAG)
OSSS........ Optical Space Surveillance System [*or Subsystem*] (IAA)
OSSS........ Orbital Space Station Studies (or Study) (SAUS)
OSSS........ Orbital Space Station Study
OSSS........ Orbital Space Station System [*of NASA*]
OSSS........ Orbiting Space Station Study (SAUS)
OSSS........ Order of the Most Holy Savior [*Bridgettine Sisters*] [*Roman Catholic religious order*]
OSSS........ The Brigittine Sisters (TOCD)
OSST........ Ocean Ship Surveillance Training
OSST........ Official Summary of Security Transactions and Holdings
OSST........ Offshore Storage Tank
OSST........ Operating System Symbol Table (SAUS)
OSST........ Operational Site System Test (SAUS)
OSST........ Order of the Holy Trinity (TOCD)
osst.......... Order of the Most Holy Trinity, Trinitarian Fathers (TOCD)
OSsT......... Ordo Sanctissimae Trinitatis Redemptionis Captivorum [*Order of the Most Holy Trinity*] [*Trinitarians*] [*Roman Catholic religious order*]
OSST........ Sisters of the Most Holy Trinity (TOCD)
OSSTF....... Ontario Secondary School Teachers Federation (SAUS)
OSSU........ Operator Services Switching Unit [*Telecommunications*] (TEL)
OSSU........ Ossborn [*Intermodal shipping container symbol*] (TVRC)
OSSU........ Sundridge & Strong Union Public Library, Sundridge, Ontario [*Library symbol*] [*National Library of Canada*] (NLC)
OSSup....... Overseas Supply (SAUS)
OS Supp.... Oklahoma Statutes, Supplement [*A publication*] (DLA)
OST.......... Austria Fund [*NYSE symbol*] (SPSG)
OST.......... Objectives, Strategy, and Tactics [*Management system*]
OST.......... Objective Start Time
OST.......... Object Sorting Test [*Psychology*]
OST.......... Observation Skills Test
OST.......... Observatoire des Sciences et des Techniques [*France*]
OST.......... Occlusal Splint Therapy [*Medicine*] (MELL)
OST.......... Ocean Surface Temperature [*Marine science*] (OSRA)
OST.......... Office of Science and Technology [*Terminated 1973, functions transferred to National Science Foundation*] [*Later, CSTD*]
OST.......... Office of Strategic Trade (SAUS)
OST.......... Office of Systems Operations [*Marine science*] (OSRA)
OST.......... Office of the Secretary of Transportation [*Department of Transportation*]
OST.......... Office of the Special Trustee
OST.......... Offline Store [*Computer science*] (GART)
OST.......... Offshore Storage and Treatment (SAUS)
O St.......... Ohio State Reports [*A publication*] (DLA)
OST.......... Oilfield Service Trucking & Crane, Inc. (EFIS)
OST.......... Old Spanish Trail (SAUS)
OST.......... One-Station Training
OST.......... On Same Terms (WDAA)
OST.......... On-Shift Test (IEEE)
OST.......... On-Site Test (IAA)
OST.......... Operating System Toolbox (SAUS)
OST.......... Operating System Trap (SAUS)
OST.......... Operational Sea Training (SAUS)
OST.......... Operational Suitability Test [*Aviation*]
OST.......... Operational System Test (KSC)
OST.......... Operations Support Team [*NASA*] (MCD)
OST.......... Operator Station Task (ELAL)
OST.......... Opposite [*Telegraphy*] (PCTE)
OST.......... Optical Sensing Trigger
OST.......... Optical Star Tracker

OST .... Optic Support Table
OST .... Orbiter Support Trolley [*NASA*] (NASA)
OST .... Orbit Stay Time
OST .... Order Shipping Time (SAUS)
OST .... Order Ship Time [*DoD*]
OST .... Ordinary Spring Tides
OST .... Ordnance Shock Test [*Military*]
OST .... Ordnance Special Training (AAG)
OST .... Ordnance Suitability Test
OST .... Organisation Socialiste des Travailleurs [*Socialist Workers' Organization*] [*Senegal*] [*Political party*] (PPW)
OST .... Organizacion Socialista de los Trabajadores [*Socialist Workers' Organization*] [*Bolivia*] [*Political party*] (PPW)
OST .... Organizacion Socialista de los Trabajadores [*Socialist Workers' Organization*] [*Costa Rica*] [*Political party*] (PPW)
OST .... Originating Station Treatment [*Telecommunications*] (TEL)
OST .... Ostend [*Belgium*] [*Airport symbol*] (OAG)
OST .... Osteopathic (WGA)
Ost .... Osteotomy [*Orthopedics*] (DAVI)
OST .... Osterhout Free Library, Wilkes-Barre, PA [*OCLC symbol*] (OCLC)
OST .... Outer Space Treaty (SAUS)
OST .... Out of Stock, Temporary [*Business term*]
OST .... Output Stage Tube (SAUS)
OST .... Overseas Students Trust [*British*] (AEBS)
OST .... Over Stress Testing
OST .... Oxford Superconductive Technology [*Manufacturing company*] [*British*]
OST .... Stratford Public Library, Ontario [*Library symbol*] [*National Library of Canada*] (NLC)
OSTA .... Office of Space and Terrestrial Applications [*NASA*] (GRD)
OSTA .... Optical Storage Technology Association (CDE)
OSTA .... Stayner Public Library, Ontario [*Library symbol*] [*National Library of Canada*] (NLC)
OSTAC .... Bibliotheque Publique Cambridge-St.-Albert, St.-Albert, Ontario [*Library symbol*] [*National Library of Canada*] (NLC)
OSTAC .... Ocean Science Technology Advisory Committee [*Terminated, 1976*] [*National Security Industrial Association*] (MSC)
OSTAG .... Gallery Stratford, Ontario [*Library symbol*] [*National Library of Canada*] (NLC)
OSTAR .... Observer Single-Handed Transatlantic Race [*Sailing*]
OSTARE ..... Old Scientific Technical Aerospace Reports Extended
OSTARS ..... Orbiting Surveillance and Target Acquisition Relay [*Army*] (RDA)
OSTASDG ... St. Andrews Branch, Stormount, Dundas, and Glengarry County Library, Ontario [*Library symbol*] [*National Library of Canada*] (BIB)
O State ...... Ohio State Reports [*A publication*] (DLA)
OSTB .... Office of the State Training Board [*Australia*]
OSTB .... Organs and Systems Toxicology Branch [*National Institute of Environmental Health Sciences*] (RCD)
OSTC .... Office for Scientific, Technical and Cultural affairs (SAUS)
OSTC .... Open Systems Testing Consortium (TELE)
OSTC .... St. Catharines Public Library, Ontario [*Library symbol*] [*National Library of Canada*] (NLC)
OStcB .... Belmont Technical Institute, St. Clairsville, OH [*Library symbol*] [*Library of Congress*] (LCLS)
OSTCB .... Brock University, St. Catharines, Ontario [*Library symbol*] [*National Library of Canada*] (NLC)
OSTCBG ..... Department of Geography, Brock University, St. Catharines, Ontario [*Library symbol*] [*National Library of Canada*] (NLC)
OSTCG ...... Grantham High School, St. Catharines, Ontario [*Library symbol*] [*National Library of Canada*] (NLC)
OSTCGL ..... Genaire Ltd., St. Catharines, Ontario [*Library symbol*] [*National Library of Canada*] (NLC)
OSTCH ...... Hotel-Dieu Hospital, St. Catharines, Ontario [*Library symbol*] [*National Library of Canada*] (BIB)
OSTCM ...... St. Catharines Historical Museum, Ontario [*Library symbol*] [*National Library of Canada*] (BIB)
OSTCMEC ... Monenco Consultants Ltd., St. Catharines, Ontario [*Library symbol*] [*National Library of Canada*] (NLC)
OSTCOOP ... Office of the Secretary of Transportation Continuity of Operations Plan
OSTCT .... St. Catharines Teachers' College, Ontario [*Library symbol*] [*National Library of Canada*] (NLC)
OSTCTR ..... St. Catharines Teachers' Reference Library, Ontario [*Library symbol*] [*National Library of Canada*] (NLC)
OStcU .... Ohio University, Belmont County Branch Campus, St. Clairsville, OH [*Library symbol*] [*Library of Congress*] (LCLS)
OSTD .... Office of Supersonic Transport Development [*Department of Transportation*] [*Obsolete*]
OSTD .... Off-Site Technical Director (MHDI)
OSTD .... Ontario Society for Training and Development [*Canada*] (EDAC)
OSTD .... Ordnance Standards
OSTD .... Ordnance Standard Technical Directives [*Obsolete*]
OSTD .... Oshkosh Trailer Division [*NCIC trailer make code*]
OSTDS ...... Office of Space Tracking and Data Systems [*NASA*] (NASA)
OSTE .... Osteotech, Inc. [*NASDAQ symbol*] (SAG)
OSte .... Public Library of Steubenville and Jefferson County, Steubenville, OH [*Library symbol*] [*Library of Congress*] (LCLS)
OSteC .... College of Steubenville, Steubenville, OH [*Library symbol*] [*Library of Congress*] (LCLS)
OSTEMS .... Overseas Technology Missions
osteo .... Osteoarthritis [*Medicine*]
Osteo .... Osteomyelitis [*Orthopedics*] (DAVI)
OSTEO .... Osteomyelitis [*Medicine*]
OSTEO .... Osteopathic
osteoart ..... osteoarthritic (SAUS)
Osteoart ..... Osteoarthritis (SAUS)
Osteoarthritis Cartilage ... Osteoarthritis and Cartilage (SAUS)
OSTEOL ..... Osteology (SAUS)
OSTEOPORO ... Osteoporosus (SAUS)
OSTEOPTH ... Osteopath
Osteotch .... Osteotech, Inc. [*Associated Press*] (SAG)
OSTEST ..... Operating System Test [*Telecommunications*] (TEL)
Ostex .... Ostex International, Inc. [*Associated Press*] (SAG)
OSTF .... Off-Site Test Facility (SAUS)
OSTF .... Operational Silo Test Facility
OSTF .... Operational Suitability Test Facility [*Aviation*]
OSTF .... Operational System Test Facility [*Air Force*]
OSTF .... Optical, Sensor, Test, Facilities (ACAE)
OSTF .... Ordnance Survey Transfer Format (SAUS)
OSTFC .... Storrington Branch, Frontenac County Library, Ontario [*Library symbol*] [*National Library of Canada*] (BIB)
OSTG .... Ocean Science and Technology Group [*Navy*] (MCD)
OSTG .... St. Georges Branch, South Dumfries Public Library, Ontario [*Library symbol*] [*National Library of Canada*] (BIB)
OSTI .... Bibliotheque Publique de St.-Isidore, Ontario [*Library symbol*] [*National Library of Canada*] (NLC)
OSTI .... Office of Science and Technology
OSTI .... Office of Scientific and Technical Information [*Later, BLR & DD*] [*British Library*]
OSTI .... Office of Scientific and Technical Information [*Department of Energy*] [*Information service or system*] (IID)
OSTI .... Organization for Social and Technical Innovation
OSTI .... Organization for Social and Technological Innovation (SAUS)
OSTIR .... Stirling Public Library, Ontario [*Library symbol*] [*National Library of Canada*] (BIB)
OSTIV .... Organisation Scientifique et Technique Internationale du Vol a Voile [*International Technical and Scientific Organization for Soaring Flight*]
OStJ .... Officer of the Order of Saint John of Jerusalem (SAUS)
OStJ .... Officer of the Order of St. John of Jerusalem [*British*]
OStJ .... Officer, Venerable Order of St. John of Jerusalem [*Decoration*] (CMD)
ostk .... Oilstick (VRA)
OSTL .... Operating System Table Loader [*Telecommunications*] (TEL)
OSTL .... Ovary Style Length [*Botany*]
OSTM .... Open System Transaction Management (SAUS)
OSTM .... Sault Ste. Marie Public Library, Ontario [*Library symbol*] [*National Library of Canada*] (NLC)
OSTMA ...... Algoma College, Sault Ste. Marie, Ontario [*Library symbol*] [*National Library of Canada*] (NLC)
OSTMAAS ... Synod Office, Diocese of Algoma, Anglican Church of Canada, Sault Ste. Marie, Ontario [*Library symbol*] [*National Library of Canada*] (NLC)
OStmaC ..... Chatfield College, St. Martin, OH [*Library symbol*] [*Library of Congress*] (LCLS)
OSTMAS .... Research Library, Algoma Steel Corp. Ltd., Sault Ste. Marie, Ontario [*Library symbol*] [*National Library of Canada*] (NLC)
OSTMB ...... Batchewana Indian Band, Sault Ste. Marie, Ontario [*Library symbol*] [*National Library of Canada*] (NLC)
OSTMEF ..... Sea Lamprey Control Centre, Fisheries and Oceans Canada [*Centre de Controle des Lamproies de Mer, Peches et Oceans Canada*] Sault Ste. Marie, Ontario [*Library symbol*] [*National Library of Canada*] (NLC)
OSTMF ...... Great Lakes Forest Research Centre, Canadian Forestry Service [*Centre de Recherches Forestieres des Grands Lacs, Service Canadien des Forets*] Sault Ste. Marie, Ontario [*Library symbol*] [*National Library of Canada*] (NLC)
OSTMFF ..... Forest Pest Management Institute, Canadian Forestry Service [*Institut pour laRepression des Ravageurs Forestiers, Service Canadien des Forets*], Sault-Ste .-Marie, Ontario [*Library symbol*] [*National Library of Canada*] (NLC)
OSTMGH .... General Hospital, Sault Ste. Marie, Ontario [*Library symbol*] [*National Library of Canada*] (NLC)
OSTMH ...... Sault Ste. Marie and 49th (SSM) Field Regiment RCA Historical Society, Ontario [*Library symbol*] [*National Library of Canada*] (NLC)
OSTMM ..... Strathroy Middlesex Museum, Strathroy, Ontario [*Library symbol*] [*National Library of Canada*] (BIB)
OSTMNA .... Aviation and Fire Management Centre, Ontario Ministry of Natural Resources, Sault Ste. Marie [*Library symbol*] [*National Library of Canada*] (BIB)
OSTMPH .... Plummer Public Hospital, Sault Ste. Marie, Ontario [*Library symbol*] [*National Library of Canada*] (NLC)
OSTMSC .... Sault College of Applied Arts and Technology, Sault Ste. Marie, Ontario [*Library symbol*] [*National Library of Canada*] (NLC)
OSTMY ...... St. Mary's Public Library, Ontario [*Library symbol*] [*National Library of Canada*] (NLC)
OSTMYM .... St. Mary's District Museum, St. Mary's, Ontario [*Library symbol*] [*National Library of Canada*] (BIB)
OSTN .... Old Stone Corp. [*NASDAQ symbol*] (COMM)
OSTNPS ..... Operator Services Traffic Network Planning System (SAUS)
OSTO .... Office of Space Transportation Operations [*NASA*] (NASA)
OST-ONA .... Office of the Secretary of Transportation Office of Noise Abatement
OSTP .... Office of Science and Technology Policy [*Executive Office of the Presiden t*] [*Washington, DC*]
OSTP .... Office of Scientific and Technical Personnel (SAUS)
OSTP .... Onboard Short Term Plan [*NASA*] (SPST)
OSTP .... On-Site Test Procedure
OSTP .... Orbiting System Test Plan [*NASA*] (NASA)
OSTP .... Strathroy Public Library, Ontario [*Library symbol*] [*National Library of Canada*] (NLC)

OSTPA....... Stratford-Perth Archives Board, Ontario [*Library symbol*] [*National Library of Canada*] (BIB)
O St R....... Ohio State Reports [*A publication*] (DLA)
OSTR........ Oregon State Triga Reactor (SAUS)
OSTR........ Streetsville Public Library, Ontario [*Library symbol*] [*National Library of Canada*] (NLC)
OSTRE....... Objective Sidetone Reference Equivalent (SAUS)
O St Rep.... Ohio State Reports [*A publication*] (DLA)
OSTRO...... Stroud Branch, Township of Innisfil Public Library, Ontario [*Library symbol*] [*National Library of Canada*] (NLC)
OSTS........ Office of Space Transportation System [*NASA*]
OSTS........ Office of Space Transportation Systems [*NASA*] (GRD)
OSTS........ Office of State Technical Services [*Also, STS*] [*Abolished, 1970*] [*Department of Commerce*]
OSTS........ Official Seed Testing Station (WDAA)
OSTS........ Operational Suitability Test Site [*Aviation*] (AAG)
OST/SS...... Open Systems Transport/Session Support (SAUS)
OST System... Objectives-Strategy-Tactics System (SAUS)
OSTT........ Damascus [*Syria*] [*ICAO location identifier*] (ICLI)
OSTT........ Open Systems Technology Transfer Programme [*British*]
OSTT........ Ost Trucking [*Common carrier symbol*]
OSTT........ St. Thomas Public Library, Ontario [*Library symbol*] [*National Library of Canada*] (NLC)
OSTTE....... Elgin County Public Library, St. Thomas, Ontario [*Library symbol*] [*National Library of Canada*] (NLC)
OSTTP....... St. Thomas Psychiatric Hospital, Ontario [*Library symbol*] [*National Library of Canada*] (NLC)
OSTU........ Oestab Sonderabfallentsorgun [*Intermodal shipping container symbol*] (TVRC)
OSTV........ Operational Support Television [*Military*] (AFM)
OSTX........ Ostex International, Inc. [*NASDAQ symbol*] (SAG)
OSTX........ Ostex Intl. [*NASDAQ symbol*] (TTSB)
OSU.......... Columbus, OH [*Location identifier*] [*FAA*] (FAAL)
OSU.......... Irish Ursuline Union (TOCD)
OSU.......... Officially Sanctioned User (SAUS)
OSU.......... Ohio State University, Columbus, OH [*OCLC symbol*] (OCLC)
O Su......... Ohio Supplement [*A publication*] (DLA)
OSU.......... Ohio Supreme Court Decisions, Unreported Cases [*A publication*] (DLA)
OSU.......... Oklahoma State University
OSU.......... Older-Worker Service Unit [*US Employment Service*] [*Department of Labor*]
OSU.......... Omega VLF Sensor Unit (SAUS)
OSU.......... Open Systems Unit [*British*]
OSU.......... Operational Strategy Unit (HEAS)
OSU.......... Operational Switching Unit
OSU.......... Operation Sisters United (EA)
OSU.......... Optical Scanning Unit (DNAB)
OSU.......... Optical Service Unit [*Telecommunications*]
OSU.......... Order of St. Ursula [*Roman Catholic women's religious order*]
OSU.......... Ordnance Support Unit (SAUS)
OSU.......... Oregon State University [*Formerly, OSC*]
OSU.......... Osaka Sangyo University (SAUS)
OSU.......... O'Sullivan Industries Holding [*NYSE symbol*] (SPSG)
OSU.......... Own Ship's Use [*Navy*] (DNAB)
OSU.......... Sudbury Public Library, Ontario [*Library symbol*] [*National Library of Canada*] (NLC)
OSU.......... Ursuline Nuns of the Congregation of Paris (Cincinnati, OH) (TOCD)
OSU.......... Ursuline Nuns of the Congregation of Paris (Cleveland, OH) (TOCD)
OSU.......... Ursuline Nuns of the Congregation of Paris (Kansas City, KS) (TOCD)
OSU.......... Ursuline Nuns of the Congregation of Paris (Louisville, KY) (TOCD)
OSU.......... Ursuline Nuns of the Congregation of Paris (Owensboro, KY) (TOCD)
OSU.......... Ursuline Nuns of the Congregation of Paris (St. Martin, OH) (TOCD)
OSU.......... Ursuline Nuns of the Congregation of Paris (Toledo, OH) (TOCD)
OSU.......... Ursuline Nuns of the Congregation of Paris (Youngstown, OH) (TOCD)
OSU.......... Ursuline Sisters of Belleville (TOCD)
OSU.......... Ursuline Sisters of the Congregation of Tildonk, Belgium (TOCD)
OSUAS...... Ohio State University Administrative Science (SAUS)
OSUBE...... Educational Media Centre, Sudbury Board of Education, Ontario [*Library symbol*] [*National Library of Canada*] (NLC)
OSUC........ Cambrian College, Sudbury, Ontario [*Library symbol*] [*National Library of Canada*] (NLC)
OSU-CISRC... Ohio State University-Computer and Information Science Research Center (SAUS)
OSUCOM.... Center for Health Sciences [*Oklahoma State University*] (MHID)
OSUCS...... Civic Square, Information and Reference, Sudbury Public Library, Ontario [*Library symbol*] [*National Library of Canada*] (NLC)
OSUE........ On-Site User Evaluation (MCD)
OSUGH...... Sudbury General Hospital, Ontario [*Library symbol*] [*National Library of Canada*] (NLC)
OSUHRF.... Ohio State University Heat Release Calorimeter (SAUS)
OSUK........ Ophthalmological Society of the United Kingdom
OSUL........ Laurentian University [*Universite Laurentienne*] Sudbury, Ontario [*Library symbol*] [*National Library of Canada*] (NLC)
OSUL........ Ohio State University Libraries (NITA)
OSUL........ Oklahoma State University Library (SAUS)
OSUL........ Oregon State University Library (SAUS)
OSULH...... Medical Library, Laurentian Hospital, Sudbury, Ontario [*Library symbol*] [*National Library of Canada*] (BIB)
OSullvnC.... O'Sullivan Corp. [*Associated Press*] (SAG)
OSULP...... O'Sullivan Industries Holdings [*OTCBB symbol*]
OSulvInd.... O'Sullivan Industries Holdings [*Associated Press*] (SAG)
OSUM....... Ohio State University Museum of Zoology [*Research center*] (RCD)
OSUME...... Ontario Ministry of Education, Sudbury, Ontario [*Library symbol*] [*National Library of Canada*] (BIB)
OSUN........ North Central Regional Library, Sudbury, Ontario [*Library symbol*] [*National Library of Canada*] (NLC)
OSUN........ Ontario Library Service - Voyageur, Sudbury, Ontario [*Library symbol*] [*National Library of Canada*] (NLC)
OSUNB...... Brock Township Public Library, Sunderland, Ontario [*Library symbol*] [*National Library of Canada*] (NLC)
OSUOP...... Northeastern Ontario Oncology Program [*Programme d'Oncologie du Nord-Est de l'Ontario*], Sudbury, Ontario [*Library symbol*] [*National Library of Canada*] (NLC)
OSUP........ Ohio State University Press (DGA)
OSUPE...... Ohio State University Psychological Exam (EDAC)
O Supp...... Ohio Supplement [*A publication*] (DLA)
OSUR........ Ohio State University Reactor
OSUREP..... Overseas Unit Replacement System [*Military*] (AFIT)
OSU Research Review... Ohio State University Research Review (SAUS)
OSURF...... Ohio State University Research Foundation
OSURO...... Ohio State University Radio Observatory
OSUS........ Ocean Surveillance (SAUS)
OSUT........ One-Station-Unit Training [*Army*]
OSUT........ On-Site User Test
OSUT........ On-Site User Training
OSUT........ Ordinary Seamen Under Training [*Canadian Navy*]
OSUTCB..... Ohio State University Theatre Collection Bulletin (SAUS)
OSUT-COFT... One-Station-Unit Training - Conduct of Fire Trainer [*Army*] (MCD)
OSUU........ University of Subury [*Universite de Sudbury*] Ontario [*Library symbol*] [*National Library of Canada*] (NLC)
OSV.......... Object-Subject-Verb (ADWA)
OSV.......... Ocean Station Vessel
OSV.......... Office of Space Vehicles
OSV.......... Offscreen Voice [*Films, television, etc.*]
OSV.......... Offset Scan Voting (AAEL)
OSV.......... Offshore Supply Vessel [*Coast Guard*] (GFGA)
OSV.......... Offshore Support Vessel (SAUS)
OSV.......... On-Site Vendor (TIMI)
OSV.......... On-Site Verification (SAUS)
OSV.......... On Station Vehicle (MCD)
OSV.......... OPFOR Surrogate Vehicle (SAUS)
OSV.......... Orbital Servicing Vehicle (ACAE)
OSV.......... Orbital Support Vehicle
OSV.......... Orbiting Servicing Vehicle (SAUS)
OSV.......... Order of St. Vincent (EA)
OSV.......... Ordnance Spare Vehicle (SAUS)
OSV.......... Oriented Space Vehicle
OSV.......... Output Serving Voltage
OSV.......... Over-Sand Vehicle
OSVA........ Off-Site Vital Area (MCD)
OSVC........ Outgoing Switched Virtual Circuit (SAUS)
OS/VS....... Operating Schedule/Virtual System
OS/VS....... Operating System/Virtual Storage [*Computer science*] (MDG)
OS/VS1...... Operating System/Virtual Storage 1 [*Computer science*] (ITCA)
OS/VS2...... Operating System/Virtual Storage 2 [*Computer science*] (ITCA)
OSW.......... Oblique Shock Wave
OSW.......... Office of Saline Water [*Later, OWRT*] [*Department of the Interior*]
OSW.......... Office of Secretary of War [*Obsolete*]
OSW.......... Office of Solid Waste [*Environmental Protection Agency*] (EPA)
OSW.......... Office Saline Water (SAUS)
OSW.......... Old Swedish [*Language, etc.*]
OSW.......... Olique Shock Wave (SAUS)
OSW.......... Operational Switching Unit
OSW.......... Operations Support Wing [*NASA*]
OSW.......... Orbital Weapon System (SAUS)
OSW.......... Order of the Sacred Word [*Affiliate of the magical society, Aurum Solis*]
OSW.......... Ordnance Weapon Systems (SAUS)
OSW.......... Oswego, KS [*Location identifier*] [*FAA*] (FAAL)
OSW.......... Oswestry [*British depot code*]
OSW.......... Wittenberg University, Springfield, OH [*Library symbol*] [*Library of Congress*] (LCLS)
OSWA........ Off-Shift Work Authorization (AAG)
OSWA........ Orchid Society of Western Australia
OSWA........ Organ Society of Western Australia
OSWAC...... Ordnance Special Weapons Ammunition Command [*Later, Weapons Command*]
OSWC........ Ordnance Special Weapons Command [*Merged with Missile Command*] [*Army*]
OSWD........ Office of Special Weapons Development [*Army*]
OSWEP...... Overseas Student Welfare Expansion Programme (SAUS)
OSWER...... Office of Solid Waste and Emergency Response [*Environmental Protection Agency*] [*Washington, DC*]
OSWER BBS... OSWER [*Office of Solid Waste and Emergency Response*] Electronic Bulletin Board System [*Environment term*] (EGA)
OSWG........ Optical Systems Working Group (MUGU)
OSWI........ Old Spaghetti Warehouse, Inc. (MHDW)
OSWMP..... Office of Solid Waste Management Programs [*Environmental Protection Agency*]
OSWO........ Oh Shoot! We're Out!
OSWR........ Office of Solid Waste Research (SAUS)
OSWS........ Operating System Workstation [*Computer science*]
OSWS........ Whitchurch-Stouffville Public Library, Stouffville, Ontario [*Library symbol*] [*National Library of Canada*] (NLC)
OSWV........ Osteryoung Square Wave Voltammogram [*Electrochemistry*]
OSX.......... Kosciusko, MS [*Location identifier*] [*FAA*] (FAAL)
OS X......... Operating System X [*Apple's UNIX-based operating system*] (NETL)

OSY.......... Namsos [*Norway*] [*Airport symbol*] (OAG)
OSY.......... National Institute for Occupational Safety and Health, Morgantown, WV [*OCLC symbol*] (OCLC)
OSY.......... Odyssey Resources Ltd. [*Vancouver Stock Exchange symbol*]
OSY.......... Optimum Sustainable Yield (SAUS)
OSYC........ Officer Supervising Yardcraft [*Canadian Navy*]
OSYFC....... Sydenham Branch, Frontenac County Library, Ontario [*Library symbol*] [*National Library of Canada*] (BIB)
OSYS........ OccuSystems, Inc. [*NASDAQ symbol*] (SAG)
OSyS........ Sylvania Schools, Sylvania, OH [*Library symbol*] [*Library of Congress*] (LCLS)
OSZ.......... Koszalin [*Poland*] [*Airport symbol*] (OAG)
OSZ.......... Offshore Surf Zone
OSZ.......... Ottawa Silica [*Federal Railroad Administration identification code*]
OSZ.......... Washington, DC [*Location identifier*] [*FAA*] (FAAL)
OSzK......... Orszagos Szechenyi Konyvtar [*National Szechenyi Library*] [*Information service or system*] (IID)
OT............ Evergreen Helicopters of Alaska [*ICAO designator*] (AD)
OT............ Objective Test [*Psychology*]
OT............ Object Technology [*Computer science*] (CDE)
OT............ Object Track (ACAE)
OT............ Oblique Talus [*Medicine*] (EDAA)
OT............ Observer Target [*Army*]
OT............ Occipitotransverse [*Obstetrics*]
OT............ Occlusion Time (MAE)
OT............ Occupational Therapist [*or Therapy*] [*Medicine*]
OT............ Occupational Therapy (SAUS)
OT............ Occupational Therapy Technician [*Navy*]
OT............ Occupational Training (AIE)
OT............ Occupied Territories (BJA)
OT............ Ocean Systems Technician [*Navy*] (DNAB)
OT............ Ocean Transportation [*Military*]
OT............ Ocular Tension [*Medicine*]
OT............ Oedipus Tyrannus [*of Sophocles*] [*Classical studies*] (OCD)
OT............ Oesterreicher-Turner [*Syndrome*] [*Medicine*] (DB)
OT............ Offensive Tackle [*Football*]
OT............ Offensive Threat (ACAE)
OT............ Office of Telecommunications [*Department of Commerce*]
OT............ Office of Territories [*Department of the Interior*]
OT............ Office of Transportation [*Department of Agriculture*]
OT............ Off Time (WDAA)
OT............ Off Topic (SAUS)
OT............ Off-Topic [*Astronomy term*]
OT............ Oil Tanker (SAUS)
OT............ Oil Temperature [*Automotive engineering*]
OT............ Oil-Tempered (IAA)
OT............ Oil-Tight
OT............ Old Term
OT............ Old Terminology
OT............ Old Testament [*of the Bible*]
OT............ Old Timer [*Communications operators' colloquialism*]
OT............ Old Tom [*British slang term for gin*] (ROG)
OT............ Old Top [*Communications operators' colloquialism*]
OT............ Old [*or Original*] Tuberculin [*Also, TO*] [*Medicine*]
OT............ Olfactory Threshold
OT............ Olfactory Tubercle [*Neuroanatomy*]
OT............ On a Track [*Rail*] [*Shipping*] (DCTA)
OT............ Once-Through [*Nuclear reactor technology*]
OT............ One Time
OT............ On Target [*Military*] (CAAL)
O/T........... On Thames [*In place names*] [*British*] (ROG)
o-T........... on-Thames (SAUS)
OT............ On Time
OT............ Ontological Theory (VLIE)
OT............ On Track (VLIE)
OT............ On Trajectory (ACAE)
O/T........... On Trent [*In place names*] [*British*] (ROG)
OT............ On Truck [*Shipping*]
OT............ Onward Transfer (SAUS)
OT............ Opening Time (SAUS)
OT............ Open Topped [*Container*] [*Packaging*] (DCTA)
OT............ Open Transport [*Computer science*]
OT............ Operability Test (SAUS)
OT............ Operating Temperature [*Nuclear energy*]
OT............ Operating Theater
OT............ Operating Thetan (SAUS)
OT............ Operating Time
OT............ Operational instrumentation MDM-Tank (SAUS)
OT............ Operational Instrumentation Tank [*NASA*] (NAKS)
OT............ Operational Technology [*Nuclear energy*] (NRCH)
OT............ Operational Test (AFM)
OT............ Operational Testing (SAUS)
OT............ Operational Training (MCD)
OT............ Operational Trajectory [*Aerospace*] (KSC)
OT............ Operations Team (MCD)
OT............ Operation Time (SAUS)
OT............ Opisthotonus [*Medicine*] (EDAA)
OT............ Opportunity Target (SAUS)
OT............ Optatam Totius [*Decree on Priestly Formation*] [*Vatican II document*]
OT............ Optical Techniques group (SAUS)
OT............ Optical Technology (SAUS)
OT............ Optical Thickness (ADWA)
OT............ Optical Tool
OT............ Optical Tracker [*NASA*] (NAKS)
OT............ Optical Tracking [*NASA*] (KSC)
OT............ Optical-Transient [*Astronomy*]
OT............ Optic Tectum [*Anatomy*]
OT............ Optimality Theory [*Linguistics*] (IEL)
O/T........... Oral Temperature (DAVI)
OT............ Oral Testimony (BJA)
OT............ Oral Thrush [*Medicine*] (MEDA)
OT............ Ordering Table (SAUS)
OT............ Oregon Territory [*Prior to statehood*]
OT............ Oregon Trunk Railway [*AAR code*]
OT............ Organizational Table
OT............ Organization Table
OT............ Organization Theory (SAUS)
OT............ Orienteering Tasmania [*Australia*] [*An association*]
OT............ Orifice Tube [*Automobile air conditioning system*]
OT............ Original Transposed (SAUS)
OT............ Original Tuberculin [*Medicine*] (DMAA)
OT............ Orotracheal [*Medicine*]
OT............ Orthite (SAUS)
OT............ Orthogonal Trees (SAUS)
O-T........... Orthohombic-Tetragonal [*Temperature transition*]
OT............ Ortho Tolidine (PDAA)
OT............ Oscillation Transformer [*Radio*]
OT............ Osmium Tetroxide [*Inorganic chemistry*]
OT............ Other (VLIE)
OT............ Other Than
OT............ Other Time
o/t........... Other Times (PIAV)
O/T........... Other Times (PIPO)
OT............ Otis Elevator (SAUS)
OT............ Otis Test [*Psychiatry*] (DAVI)
Ot............ Otolaryngologist (SAUS)
OT............ Otolaryngology [*Medicine*]
OT............ Otology [*Medicine*]
OT............ O'Toole's Group, Inc. [*Toronto Stock Exchange symbol*]
Ot............ Otto Papiensis [*Flourished, 12th century*] [*Authority cited in pre-1607 legal work*] (DSA)
Ot............ Otto's United States Supreme Court Reports [*91-107 United States*] [*A publication*] (DLA)
OT............ Ought (ROG)
OT............ Outer Table (MCD)
OT............ Outer Tube
OT............ Outfit
OT............ Out of Territory (VLIE)
OT............ Out of Tolerance
OT............ Out of Town (GOBB)
OT............ Output [*Computer science*] (IAA)
OT............ Output Tape (SAUS)
OT............ Output Terminal
OT............ Outside Test (SAUS)
OT............ Out Temperature (MCD)
OT............ Overall Test (KSC)
OT............ Overhead Transparencies
OT............ Overlap Technician
OT............ Overlap Telling (MCD)
OT............ Overseas Tankship (SAUS)
OT............ Overseas Territories (MCD)
OT............ Overseas Trade
OT............ Overseas Trading [*A publication*]
OT............ Overseas Transportation (SAUS)
O/T........... Overtemperature (KSC)
OT............ Over There (ADA)
OT............ Overtime
OT............ Overtone
OT............ Ovotransferrin [*Biochemistry*]
OT............ Ovum Transfer (SAUS)
OT............ Owing To [*Telegraphy*] (PCTE)
OT............ Oxygen Therapy (MELL)
OT............ Oxytocin [*Endocrinology*]
OT............ Stations Open Exclusively to Operational Traffic of the Services Concerned [*ITU designation*] (CET)
OT............ Tara Branch, Bruce County Public Library, Ontario [*Library symbol*] [*National Library of Canada*] (NLC)
OT............ Toledo-Lucas County Public Library, Toledo, OH [*Library symbol*] [*Library of Congress*] (LCLS)
OT1H......... On The One Hand (SAUS)
OTA.......... Academy of Medicine, Toronto, Ontario [*Library symbol*] [*National Library of Canada*] (NLC)
OTA.......... Congressional Office of Technology Assessment (SAUS)
OTA.......... Mota [*Ethiopia*] [*Airport symbol*] (AD)
OTA.......... Occupational Therapists Association (NADA)
OTA.......... Occupational Therapy Assistant (IDYL)
OTA.......... Occupied Territory Administration [*World War II*]
OTA.......... Office of Tax Analysis [*Department of the Treasury*]
OTA.......... Office of Technical Assistance (USGC)
OTA.......... Office of Technology Assessment [*Congressional study group*] [*Washington, DC*]
OTA.......... Office of Technology Assistance [*General Services Administration*]
OTA.......... Office of Telecommunications Applications [*US National Telecommunications and Information Administration*] (TSSD)
OTA.......... Office of Territorial Affairs (SAUS)
OTA.......... Officer Training Allowance [*Naval Reserve*]
OTA.......... Official Test Aerosol (SAUS)
OTA.......... Off-the-Air Record Club [*Record label*]
OTA.......... Oil Trades Association of New York (EA)

OTA .... Old Testament Abstracts [*A publication*] (BJA)
OTA .... Omnidirectional Transmitter Antenna
OTA .... Ontario Trucking Association (SAUS)
OTA .... Open Terminal Architecture (RALS)
OTA .... Open Test Assembly [*Nuclear energy*] (NRCH)
OTA .... Operational Test Agency (DOMA)
OTA .... Operational Transconductance Amplifier (IEEE)
OTA .... Operational Transconductance Array (SAUS)
OTA .... Operation Town Affiliations [*An association*] (EA)
OTA .... Operation-Triggered Architecture [*Computer science*]
OTA .... Optical Telescope Assembly [*NASA*]
OTA .... Optical Tracking Aid [*Deep Space Instrumentation Facility, NASA*]
OTA .... Organic Trade Association
OTA .... Organisation Mondiale du Tourisme et de l'Automobile [*World Touring and Automobile Organization*]
OTA .... Ornithine Transaminase (DB)
OTA .... Orthodontic Technicians Association [*British*] (DBA)
OTA .... Orthopaedic Trauma Association (SAUS)
OTA .... Ortho-Tolidine Arsenite [*Organic chemistry*]
OTA .... Other Talk Address (IAA)
OTA .... Other than Air (CINC)
ota .... Ottoman Turkish [*MARC language code*] [*Library of Congress*] (LCCP)
OTA .... Outer Transport Area
OTA .... Output Transformerless Amplifier (DICI)
OTA .... Outside-Wheel Turning Angle [*Automotive engineering*]
OTA .... Ovarian Tumor-Associated Antigen [*Medicine*] (MELL)
OTA .... Overflight Top Attack (SAUS)
OTA .... Over-the-air [*Television technology*]
OTA .... U. S. Congress Office of Technology Assessment (SAUS)
OTAA .... AASTRA Aerospace, Inc., Downsview, Ontario [*Library symbol*] [*National Library of Canada*] (BIB)
OTAA .... Office of Trade Adjustment Assistance [*Department of Labor*]
OTABN .... Ortho-Tolueno-Azo-Beta-Naphthol [*Medicine*] (MELL)
OTAC .... Acres Consulting Services Ltd., Toronto, Ontario [*Library symbol*] [*National Library of Canada*] (NLC)
OTAC .... Oceanic Trade Alliance Council International
OTAC .... Ordnance Tank-Automotive Command [*Merged with Weapons and Mobility Command*] [*Army*]
OTACS .... Old Timer Assay Commissioners Society [*Defunct*] (EA)
OTAD .... Addiction Research Foundation, Toronto, Ontario [*Library symbol*] [*National Library of Canada*] (NLC)
OTAD .... Office of Tributary Area Development [*Tennessee Valley Authority*]
OTAD .... Oversea Terminal Arrival Date [*Army*] (AABC)
OTADA .... Office of Tracking and Data Acquisition [*NASA*]
OTADL .... Outer Target Azimuth Datum Line
OTAE .... Atomic Energy of Canada [*L'Energie Atomique du Canada*] Toronto, Ontario [*Library symbol*] [*National Library of Canada*] (NLC)
OTAE .... [*The*] Old Testament in the Light of the Ancient East [*A publication*] (BJA)
OTAF .... Office of Technology Assessment and Forecast [*Patent and Trademark Office*] [*Washington, DC*]
OTAF .... Ontario Ministry of Agriculture and Food, Toronto, Ontario [*Library symbol*] [*National Library of Canada*] (NLC)
OTAF .... Operating Time at Failure (MCD)
OTAF Data Base ... Office of Technology Assessment and Forecasts Data Base (NITA)
OTAG .... Art Gallery of Ontario, Toronto, Ontario [*Library symbol*] [*National Library of Canada*] (NLC)
OTAG .... Office of the Adjutant General [*Military*]
OTAG .... Operations & Training Analysis Group (SAUS)
OTAG .... Ozone Transport Assessment Group
OTAGAV ..... Audiovisual Library, Art Gallery of Ontario, Toronto, Ontario [*Library symbol*] [*National Library of Canada*] (NLC)
Otago Pol Gaz ... Otago Police Gazette [*1861-64*] [*New Zealand*] [*A publication*] (DLA)
OTAJ .... James Ota Trucking [*Common carrier symbol*]
OTAL .... Arts and Letters Club, Toronto, Ontario [*Library symbol*] [*National Library of Canada*] (NLC)
OTAN .... Organisation du Traite de l'Atlantique Nord [*North Atlantic Treaty Organization - NATO*] [*Brussels, Belgium*]
OTAN .... Organizacao do Tratado do Atlantico Norte [*North Atlantic Treaty Organization*] [*Portuguese*]
OT&A .... Operational Test and Acceptance (SAUS)
OT & E ...... Operational Test and Evaluation [*Military*] (AFM)
OT&E .... Operational Testing and Evaluation (USDC)
OTANS .... Offshore Trade Association of Nova Scotia (SAUS)
OTANY .... Oil Trades Association of New York (EA)
OTANZ .... Output Tape Analyzer [*Computer science*] (VLIE)
OTAP .... Alternative Press Centre, Toronto, Ontario [*Library symbol*] [*National Library of Canada*] (NLC)
OTAQ .... Offer Therapist-Adolescent Questionnaire [*Personality development test*] [*Psychology*]
OTAR .... Archives of Ontario, Toronto, Ontario [*Library symbol*] [*National Library of Canada*] (NLC)
OTAR .... Overseas Tariffs and Regulations (DS)
OTAR .... Over-the-Air Rekey (SAUS)
OTARC .... Centennial College of Applied Arts and Technology, Scarborough, Ontario [*Library symbol*] [*National Library of Canada*] (NLC)
OTAS .... Observers Target Acquisition System (SAUS)
OTAS .... Observer Target Acquisition Subsystem (MCD)
OTAS .... On Top and Smooth [*NWS*] (FAAC)
OTASO .... Organizacao do Tratado da Asia Sul-Oriental [*South-East Asia Treaty Organization*] [*Portuguese*]
OTAT .... Office of Technical Assistance and Training (SAUS)
OTATO .... One Trip Air Travel Orders (SAUS)
OTAU .... OT Africa Line [*Intermodal shipping container symbol*] (TVRC)
O T AUTIC ... Other than Automatic [*Freight*]
OTAWA ...... Occupational Therapy Association of Western Australia
OTAWA ...... Ottawa, KS [*American Association of Railroads railroad junction routing code*]
O-TAWCS ... Okinawa-Tactical Air Weapons Control System (SAUS)
Otb .... October (CDAI)
OTB .... Office Track Betting (SAUS)
OTB .... Off the Board [*Investment term*]
OTB .... Off Track Betting (EFIS)
OTB .... Off-Track Betting
OTB .... Old Tired Broads
OTB .... On the Bow [*Nautical*]
OTB .... Open to Buy
OTB .... Operations Training Branch (SAUS)
OTB .... Orbiting Tanker Base [*NASA*] (NASA)
OTB .... Ordnance and Terminal Ballistics
OTB .... Ortho-Toluidine Boric Acid [*Organic chemistry*]
OTB .... Oval Fat Body (SAUS)
OTB .... Overseas Trust Bank [*Hong Kong*]
OTB .... Oxide Titanium Bronze (ODA)
OTB .... Waverly Resource Library, Thunder Bay Public Library, Ontario [*Library symbol*] [*National Library of Canada*] (NLC)
OTBA .... Ocean Thermal Boundary Analysis Charts [*Marine science*] (MSC)
OTBA .... Oregon Thoroughbred Breeding Association (EARSL)
OTBA .... Owners, Traders, Breeders Association (NADA)
OTBA .... Terrace Bay Public Library, Ontario [*Library symbol*] [*National Library of Canada*] (NLC)
OTBBR ...... Brodie Resource Library, Thunder Bay, Ontario [*Library symbol*] [*National Library of Canada*] (NLC)
OTBC .... Canadian Broadcasting Corp. [*Societe Radio-Canada*] Toronto, Ontario [*Library symbol*] [*National Library of Canada*] (NLC)
OTBCC .... Confederation College, Thunder Bay, Ontario [*Library symbol*] [*National Library of Canada*] (NLC)
OTBCG ...... Blake, Cassels & Graydon, Toronto, Ontario [*Library symbol*] [*National Library of Canada*] (NLC)
OTBCGC ..... Staff Library, Baycrest Centre for Geriatric Care, Toronto, Ontario [*Library symbol*] [*National Library of Canada*] (BIB)
OTBCIR ...... Bell Canada Information Resource Centre, Toronto, Ontario [*Library symbol*] [*National Library of Canada*] (NLC)
OTBCO ...... Technical Information Facility, Canadien Imperial Bank of Commerce, Toronto, Ontario [*Library symbol*] [*National Library of Canada*] (NLC)
OTBCP .... Program Archives, Canadian Broadcasting Corp. [*Archives des Emissions, Societe Radio-Canada*] Toronto, Ontario [*Library symbol*] [*National Library of Canada*] (NLC)
OTBD .... Doha/International [*Qatar*] [*ICAO location identifier*] (ICLI)
OTBD .... Outboard (ADA)
OTBDHC ..... Thunder Bay District Health Council, Thunder Bay, Ontario [*Library symbol*] [*National Library of Canada*] (NLC)
OTBE .... Ontario Ministry of Education, Thunder Bay, Ontario [*Library symbol*] [*National Library of Canada*] (NLC)
OTBE .... Out of the Body Experiences [*Parapsychology*] (ECON)
OTBE .... Overtaken by Events [*Military*]
OTBGH ...... General Hospital of Port Arthur, Thunder Bay, Ontario [*Library symbol*] [*National Library of Canada*] (NLC)
OTBH .... Thunder Bay Historical Museum Society, Ontario [*Library symbol*] [*National Library of Canada*] (NLC)
OTBhd .... Oil-Tight Bulkhead (SAUS)
OTBHS ...... Hammarskjold High School, Thunder Bay, Ontario [*Library symbol*] [*National Library of Canada*] (NLC)
OTBLA .... Audio Library Services of Northwestern Ontario, Lakehead University, Thunder Bay, Ontario [*Library symbol*] [*National Library of Canada*] (NLC)
OTBLL .... School of Library Technology, Lakehead University, Thunder Bay, Ontario [*Library symbol*] [*National Library of Canada*] (NLC)
OTBLP .... Staff Library, Lakehead Psychiatric Hospital, Thunder Bay, Ontario [*Library symbol*] [*National Library of Canada*] (NLC)
OTBM .... Technical Information Centre, Bank of Montreal, Willowdale, Ontario [*Library symbol*] [*National Library of Canada*] (NLC)
OTBMB ...... Mary J. L. Black Library, Thunder Bay, Ontario [*Library symbol*] [*National Library of Canada*] (NLC)
OTBMBI ..... Business Information Centre, Bank of Montreal, Toronto, Ontario [*Library symbol*] [*National Library of Canada*] (BIB)
OTBMC ...... Medical Library, McKellar General Hospital, Thunder Bay, Ontario [*Library symbol*] [*National Library of Canada*] (NLC)
OTBML ...... Music Library, Canadian National Institute for the Blind, Toronto, Ontario [*Library symbol*] [*National Library of Canada*] (BIB)
OTBNL .... National Library Division, Canadian National Institute for the Blind, Toronto, Ontario [*Library symbol*] [*National Library of Canada*] (NLC)
OTBNR ...... Learning Resource Centre, BNR Ltd., Toronto, Ontario [*Library symbol*] [*National Library of Canada*] (NLC)
OTBNS ...... Bell Northern Software Research, Toronto, Ontario [*Library symbol*] [*National Library of Canada*] (NLC)
OTBOC ...... Ontario Cancer Treatment and Research Foundation, Thunder Bay, Ontario [*Library symbol*] [*National Library of Canada*] (NLC)
OTBP .... Blaney, Pasternak, Smela, Eagleson & Watson, Toronto, Ontario [*Library symbol*] [*National Library of Canada*] (NLC)
OTBQ .... Occupational Therapists' Board of Queensland [*Australia*]
OTBR .... Barringer Research Ltd., Rexdale, Ontario [*Library symbol*] [*National Library of Canada*] (NLC)
OTBS .... One True Bracketing Style (VLIE)
OTBS .... On-the-Bottom Sonobuoy (MCD)
OTBSL .... Bassel, Sullivan & Leake, Toronto, Ontario [*Library symbol*] [*National Library of Canada*] (NLC)
OTBSSC ..... Over Thirty but Still Swinging Club

OTBV .... Oxidizer Turbine Bypass Valve (KSC)
OTBV .... Victoriaville Branch, Thunder Bay Public Library, Ontario [*Library symbol*] [*National Library of Canada*] (BIB)
OTC .... Bol [*Chad*] [*Airport symbol*] (AD)
OTC .... Faculty of Education, University of Toronto, Ontario [*Library symbol*] [*National Library of Canada*] (NLC)
OTC .... Objective, Time, and Cost
OTC .... Ocean Transshipment Cargo (SAUS)
OTC .... Office of Technical Cooperation [*United Nations*]
OTC .... Office of Telecommunications (SAUS)
OTC .... Office of Temporary Controls
OTC .... Office of Transport and Communications (SAUS)
OTC .... Officer in Tactical Command [*Air Force*]
OTC .... Officers' Training Camp [*World War I*]
OTC .... Officers' Training Corps
OTC .... Officers Transit Camp [*British military*] (DMA)
OTC .... Officer Training Center [*Navy*]
OTC .... Office Telecommunication Commission (SAUS)
OTC .... Offshore Technology Conference
OTC .... Ohio Motor Freight Tariff Committee Inc., Columbus OH [*STAC*]
OTC .... Old Testament Commentary [*A publication*] (BJA)
OTC .... Old Timers' Club (EA)
OTC .... Once-Through Cooling [*Nuclear energy*] (NRCH)
OTC .... One-Stop Charter (SAUS)
OTC .... One-Stop Tour Charter [*Airline fare*]
OTC .... One-Time Carbon [*Paper*] (PDAA)
OTC .... One-Time Charge (VLIE)
OTC .... One Touch Changeover
OTC .... Online Training Center (MELL)
OTC .... On-Tape Catalog (MWOL)
OTC .... Open Tubular Column [*For gas chromatography*]
OTC .... Operado de Terminal de Contenedores [*Container Terminal Operator*] [*Shipping*] [*Spanish*]
OTC .... Operador de Transporte Combinado [*Combined Transport Operator*] [*Spanish*] [*Business term*]
OTC .... Operating Telephone Company (SAUS)
OTC .... Operational Techniques Conference
OTC .... Operational Test Center [*NASA*] (KSC)
OTC .... Operational Test Command [*Army*]
OTC .... Operational Test Coordinator [*Military*] (CAAL)
OTC .... Operational Training Capability [*Air Force*] (AFM)
OTC .... Operational Training Centre (SAUS)
OTC .... Operational Training Command (MCD)
OTC .... Operational Training Course (SAUS)
OTC .... Operatore di Trasporto Combinato [*Combined Transport Operator*] [*Italian*] [*Business term*]
OTC .... Orbiter Test Conductor [*NASA*] (NASA)
OTC .... Orbiting Trajectory Computations
OTC .... Order of Three Crusades (EA)
OTC .... Ordnance Technical Committee [*Military*] (MUGU)
OTC .... Ordnance Training Command [*Army*]
OTC .... Oregon Technical Council (SAUS)
OTC .... Organization for Trade Cooperation [*GATT*]
OTC .... Organize Training Center (EA)
OTC .... Organotin Compound [*Organic chemistry*]
OTC .... Orginating Toll Center (SAUS)
OTC .... Orginating Toll Circuit (SAUS)
OTC .... Orginating Trunk Center (SAUS)
OTC .... Original Trenton Cracker Co. [*Maker of Chowder & Oyster Crackers, claimed by some to be the oldest continuously manufactured American food product*]
OTC .... Originating Toll Center [*Telecommunications*] (TEL)
OTC .... Originating Toll Circuit [*Telecommunications*] (IAA)
OTC .... Originating Trunk Center [*Telecommunications*] (IAA)
OTC .... Ornithine Transcarbamoylase [*Also, OCT*] [*An enzyme*]
OTC .... Orthogonal Transform Coding (CCCA)
OTC .... Orthogonal Tree Cycles (SAUS)
OTC .... Osaka Transformer Co. Ltd. (SAUS)
OTC .... Oshkosh Truck Corp.
OTC .... Ottawa Transit Commission (SAUS)
OTC .... Otterbein College, Westerville, OH [*OCLC symbol*] (OCLC)
OTC .... Outcrop (SAUS)
OTC .... Outer Tube Centerline
OTC .... Output Technology Corporation (VLIE)
OTC .... Oval Target Cell (DMAA)
OTC .... Overhead Travelling Crane (SAUS)
OTC .... Overhead Trip Computer [*Automotive engineering*]
OTC .... Overseas Telecommunications Commission (NITA)
OTC .... Overseas Telecommunications Commission of Australia (BARN)
OTC .... Overseas Telecommunications Corporation (SAUS)
OTC .... Over-the-Calf [*Women's fashions*] (IIA)
OTC .... Over-the-Capacitor [*Sockets*]
OTC .... Over-the-Counter [*Pharmacy*]
OTC .... Over-the-Counter [*Also, O/C*] [*Stock exchange term*]
OTC .... Over-the-Counter Drug [*Medicine*] (MHCS)
OTC .... Ownership Transfer Corporation (SAUS)
OTC .... Oxygen Transfer Compressor
OTC .... Oxytetracycline [*Antibiotic*]
OTC .... Ozone Transport Commission [*State environmental agencies*]
OTCA .... Olson 30 Class Association (EA)
OTCA .... Omnibus Trade and Competitiveness Act of 1988 (JAGO)
OTCA .... Ontario College of Art, Toronto, Ontario [*Library symbol*] [*National Library of Canada*] (NLC)
OTCA .... Oxothiazolidinecarboxylic Acid [*Biochemistry*]
OTCAG ...... Canada Arctic Gas Study Ltd., Toronto, Ontario [*Library symbol*] [*National Library of Canada*] (NLC)
OTCAS .... Canadian Association in Support of the Native Peoples, Toronto, Ontario [*Library symbol*] [*National Library of Canada*] (NLC)
OTCAX .... MFS Mid-Cap Growth
OTCBS .... Central Baptist Seminary and Bible College, Toronto, Ontario [*Library symbol*] [*National Library of Canada*] (NLC)
OTCC .... Operator Test Control Console (MCD)
OTCC .... Organic Thermal Control Coating
OTCC .... United Church of Canada Archives, Toronto, Ontario [*Library symbol*] [*National Library of Canada*] (NLC)
OTCCC .... Cross Cultural Communication Centre, Toronto, Ontario [*Library symbol*] [*National Library of Canada*] (NLC)
OTCCC .... Open Type Control Circuit Contacts (MSA)
OTCCL .... Currie, Coopers & Lybrand Ltd., Toronto, Ontario [*Library symbol*] [*National Library of Canada*] (NLC)
OTCCP .... Canadian Centre for Philanthropy, Toronto, Ontario [*Library symbol*] [*National Library of Canada*] (NLC)
OTCCRT ..... Technical Standards Division, Ontario Ministry of Consumer and Commercial Relations, Toronto, Ontario [*Library symbol*] [*National Library of Canada*] (NLC)
OTCD .... Ornithine Carbomoyltransferase Deficiency (DMAA)
OTCD .... Over-the-Counter-Drug (MEDA)
OTCE .... Central Library, North York, Ontario [*Library symbol*] [*National Library of Canada*] (NLC)
OTCEA .... [*The*] Canadian Education Association [*L'Association Canadienne d'Education*] Toronto, Ontario [*Library symbol*] [*National Library of Canada*] (NLC)
OTCEPAC ... Oshkosh Truck Corporation Employees PAC [*Oshkosh, WI*] (PACS)
OTCF .... H. Ward Smith Library, Centre of Forensic Sciences, Toronto, Ontario [*Library symbol*] [*National Library of Canada*] (NLC)
OTCFA .... Occupational Therapy Comprehensive Functional Assessment
OTCFX .... Price T. Rowe: Small-Cap Stock [*Mutual fund ticker symbol*] (SG)
OTCGL .... Campbell, Godfrey & Lewtas, Toronto, Ontario [*Library symbol*] [*National Library of Canada*] (NLC)
OTCGR ...... Canadian Gas Research Institute, Don Mills, Ontario [*Library symbol*] [*National Library of Canada*] (NLC)
OTCGW ...... Clarkson, Gordon, Woods, Gordon, Toronto, Ontario [*Library symbol*] [*National Library of Canada*] (NLC)
OTCH .... Anglican Church House, Toronto, Ontario [*Library symbol*] [*National Library of Canada*] (NLC)
OTCH .... Obedience Trial Champion [*Dog training*]
OTCh .... Obedience Trial Champion [*Prefix*]
OTCHA ...... Canadian Hospital Association [*Association des Hopitaux du Canada*] Toronto, Ontario [*Library symbol*] [*National Library of Canada*] (NLC)
OTCHAR ..... Anglican Church of Canada Archives, Toronto, Ontario [*Library symbol*] [*National Library of Canada*] (NLC)
OTCI .... OTC [*Overseas Telecommunications Commission*] International Ltd. [*Australia*] [*Telecommunications service*] (TSSD)
OTCIA .... Canadian Institute of International Affairs [*Institut Canadien des Affaires Internationales*] Toronto, Ontario [*Library symbol*] [*National Library of Canada*] (NLC)
OTCIB .... Canadian Imperial Bank of Commerce, Toronto, Ontario [*Library symbol*] [*National Library of Canada*] (NLC)
OTCIL .... Central Library, C-I-L, Inc., North York, Ontario [*Library symbol*] [*National Library of Canada*] (NLC)
OTCILL ...... Law Library, C-I-L, Inc., North York, Ontario [*Library symbol*] [*National Library of Canada*] (NLC)
OTCIXS ...... Officer in Tactical Command Information Exchange Subsystem [*Navy*] (ANA)
OTCJC .... Genealogical Society Library, Church of Jesus Christ of Latter-Day Saints, Etobicoke, Ontario [*Library symbol*] [*National Library of Canada*] (NLC)
OTCL .... Connaught Laboratories Ltd., Willowdale, Ontario [*Library symbol*] [*National Library of Canada*] (NLC)
OTCLA .... Confederation Life Association, Toronto, Ontario [*Library symbol*] [*National Library of Canada*] (NLC)
OTCLANT ... Fleet Operational Training Command, Atlantic [*Usually, COTCLANT*]
OTCLEV ..... Ozone Transport Commission Low-Emissions Vehicle
OTCLH .... Research and Information Library, Canadian Life and Health Insurance Association, Toronto, Ontario [*Library symbol*] [*National Library of Canada*] (BIB)
OTCM .... Canadian School of Missions and Ecumenical Institute, Toronto, Ontario [*Library symbol*] [*National Library of Canada*] (NLC)
OTCM .... Ocean Systems Technician, Master Chief [*Navy rating*] (DNAB)
OTCM .... Orbiter Thermal Control Model [*NASA*]
OTCM .... Ordnance Technical Committee Minutes [*Military*]
OTCM .... Royce Micro-Cap Tr [*NASDAQ symbol*] (TTSB)
OTCM .... Royce OTC [*Over the Counter*] Micro Capital Fund [*NASDAQ symbol*] (SAG)
OTCMC ...... Canadian Memorial Chiropractic College, Toronto, Ontario [*Library symbol*] [*National Library of Canada*] (NLC)
OTCMCC .... Old Time Country Music Club of Canada (EA)
OTCMH ...... Saul A. Silverman Library, C. M. Hincks Treatment Centre, Toronto, Ontario [*Library symbol*] [*National Library of Canada*] (BIB)
OTCMHA .... Canadian Mental Health Association, Toronto, Ontario [*Library symbol*] [*National Library of Canada*] (BIB)
OTCMLA .... Canadian Music Library Association [*Association Canadienne des Bibliotheques Musicales*] Toronto, Ontario [*Library symbol*] [*National Library of Canada*] (NLC)
OTCMS ...... Operations Training Certification Management System [*NASA*]
OTCO .... Owensville Terminal [*Federal Railroad Administration identification code*]
OTCOM ...... Cominco Ltd., Toronto, Ontario [*Library symbol*] [*National Library of Canada*] (NLC)
OTCOP ...... Olympic Training Center Outreach Program

OTCOS ...... Concord Scientific Corp., Downsview, Ontario [*Library symbol*] [*National Library of Canada*] (NLC)
OTCOU ...... Council of Ontario Universities, Toronto, Ontario [*Library symbol*] [*National Library of Canada*] (NLC)
OTCP .... Canada Packers Ltd., Toronto, Ontario [*Library symbol*] [*National Library of Canada*] (NLC)
OTCPAC ..... Fleet Operational Training Command, Pacific [*Usually, COTCPAC*]
OTC Paper... One-Time Carbon Paper (SAUS)
OTCPB....... Toronto City Planning Board Library, Ontario, [*Library symbol*] [*National Library of Canada*] (NLC)
OTCQ .... Osborne Trucking Company [*Common carrier symbol*]
OTCQM...... Office of the Theater Chief Quartermaster [*World War II*]
OTCR .... Office of Technical Cooperation and Research [*Department of State*]
OTCR .... Ontario Ministry of Culture and Communications, Toronto, Ontario [*Library symbol*] [*National Library of Canada*] (NLC)
OTCRC ...... National Office Library, Canadian Red Cross Society [*Bibliotheque du Siege Social, Societe Canadienne de la Croix-Rouge*] Toronto, Ontario [*Library symbol*] [*National Library of Canada*] (NLC)
OTCRx....... Over-the-Counter Drug (MEDA)
OTCS .... Ocean Systems Technician, Senior Chief [*Navy rating*] (DNAB)
OTCS .... Ontario Ministry of Correctional Services, Toronto, Ontario [*Library symbol*] [*National Library of Canada*] (NLC)
OTCS .... Operational Teletype Communications Subsystem
OTCS .... Optical Transient Current Spectroscopy
OTCSA....... Canadian Standards Association, Rexdale, Ontario [*Library symbol*] [*National Library of Canada*] (NLC)
OTCSAO..... Construction Safety Association of Ontario, Toronto, Ontario [*Library symbol*] [*National Library of Canada*] (NLC)
OTCSC....... Civil Service Commission of Ontario, Toronto, Ontario [*Library symbol*] [*National Library of Canada*] (NLC)
OTCSE....... Canadian Selection, Toronto, Ontario [*Library symbol*] [*National Library of Canada*] (NLC)
OTCSS....... CANEBSCO Subscription Service Ltd., Toronto, Ontario [*Library symbol*] [*National Library of Canada*] (NLC)
OTCT .... Canadian Tax Foundation [*Association Canadienne d'Etudes Fiscales*] Toronto, Ontario [*Library symbol*] [*National Library of Canada*] (NLC)
OTCTA....... Canadian Telebook Agency, Toronto, Ontario [*Library symbol*] [*National Library of Canada*] (NLC)
OTCTAR ..... Division of Records and Archives, City of Toronto (NLC)
OTCTH....... Town Hall, Collins Canada, Toronto, Ontario [*Library symbol*] [*National Library of Canada*] (NLC)
OTCTVN ..... CTV News Research Library, CTV Television Network, Toronto, Ontario [*Library symbol*] [*National Library of Canada*] (NLC)
OTCW .... Canada Wire & Cable Co. Ltd., Toronto, Ontario [*Library symbol*] [*National Library of Canada*] (NLC)
OTCWB...... Welding Institute of Canada, Oakville, Ontario [*Library symbol*] [*National Library of Canada*] (NLC)
OTCWT...... Canadian Waste Technology, Inc., Toronto, Ontario [*Library symbol*] [*National Library of Canada*] (NLC)
OTD.......... Contadora [*Panama*] [*Airport symbol*] (OAG)
OTD.......... Doctor of Occupational Therapy (PGP)
OTD.......... Observer Time Difference [*Navigation systems*]
OTD.......... Ocean Technology Division (SAUS)
OTD.......... Ocean Travel Development (DS)
OTD.......... Oculotrichodysplasia (DMAA)
OTD.......... Office of Technology Development (COE)
OTD.......... Official Table of Distances (AFM)
OTD.......... Official Tour Directory (TRID)
OTD.......... Offset, Tilted Dipole [*Model of Uranus' magnetic field*]
OTD.......... Oil Turbine Dose [*Medicine*] [*Centrifuge*] (EDAA)
OTD.......... Oil Turbine Drive
OTD.......... Old Total Depth (SAUS)
OTD.......... On the Deck
OTD.......... On-Time Delivery (SAUS)
OTD.......... Operational Technical Documentation [*NASA*] (NASA)
OTD.......... Operational Test Director [*Navy*]
OTD.......... Operations and Technical Data [*Engineering*]
OTD.......... Operator Training Device (SAUS)
OTD.......... Optical Technology Development (ACAE)
OTD.......... Optical Time Division (SAUS)
OTD.......... Optical Time Domain (EECA)
OTD.......... Optical Tracking Device
OTD.......... Optical Transient Detector
OTD.......... Optimal Terminal Descent (PDAA)
OTD.......... Oral Temperature Device (MCD)
OTD.......... Orbital Test Direction (SAUS)
OTD.......... Orbital Test Directive (SAUS)
OTD.......... Orbiter Test Director [*NASA*] (NASA)
OTD.......... Orbit Test Direction [*or Directive*] (IAA)
OTD.......... Order to Delivery [*Automotive manufacturing*]
OTD.......... Organ Tolerance Dose [*Medicine*] (DMAA)
OTD.......... Original Transmission Density (OA)
OTD.......... Ortho-Toluenediamine [*Organic chemistry*]
OTD.......... Out the Door (DAVI)
OTD.......... Overseas-Trained Doctors
OTDA .... DSMA Acton Ltd., Toronto, Ontario [*Library symbol*] [*National Library of Canada*] (NLC)
OTDA .... Office of Tracking and Data Acquisition [*NASA*]
OTDA .... Other-Than-Defined Adult (SAUS)
OTD&C ...... Offshore Technology Development & Consulting (EFIS)
OTD&SP .... Office of Technical Data and Standardization Policy (SAUS)
OTDAR ...... Alexander Raxlen Memorial Library, Doctors Hospital, Toronto, Ontario [*Library symbol*] [*National Library of Canada*] (NLC)
OTDB .... Operations Tasking Data Base (SAUS)
OTDC .... Dominion Colour Ltd., Toronto, Ontario [*Library symbol*] [*National Library of Canada*] (NLC)
OTDC .... Observational Test and Development Center [*National Weather Service*] (NOAA)
OTDC .... Optical Target Designation Computer
OTDCB ...... Dictionary of Canadian Biography, Toronto, Ontario [*Library symbol*] [*National Library of Canada*] (BIB)
OTDD .... Optical Target Detecting Device
OTDE .... Ontario Ministry of Education, Toronto, Ontario [*Library symbol*] [*National Library of Canada*] (NLC)
OTDH .... Ontario Ministry of Health, Toronto, Ontario [*Library symbol*] [*National Library of Canada*] (NLC)
OTDHA ...... De Havilland Aircraft of Canada Ltd., Downsview, Ontario [*Library symbol*] [*National Library of Canada*] (NLC)
OTDHC ...... Oceanographic Technical Data Handling Committee
OTDHL ...... Laboratory Services, Ontario Ministry of Health, Toronto, Ontario [*Library symbol*] [*National Library of Canada*] (NLC)
OTDL .... Ontario Ministry of Labour, Toronto, Ontario [*Library symbol*] [*National Library of Canada*] (NLC)
OTDM .... Mines Library, Ontario Ministry of Natural Resources, Toronto, Ontario [*Library symbol*] [*National Library of Canada*] (NLC)
OTDM .... Optical Time Division Multiplexer (SAUS)
OTDM .... Optical Time Division Multiplexing (SAUS)
OTDO........ Donwood Institute, Toronto, Ontario [*Library symbol*] [*National Library of Canada*] (BIB)
OTDR........ Optical Fiber Time-Domain Reflectometer [*Computer science*]
OTDR........ Optical Test Data Receiver (SAUS)
OTDR........ Optical Time Domain Reflectometer (NITA)
OTDR........ Optical Time Domain Reflectometry (SAUS)
OTDR........ Outdoor
OTDRE ...... Ontario Ministry of Treasury and Economics, Toronto, Ontario [*Library symbol*] [*National Library of Canada*] (NLC)
OTDT .... Ontario Ministry of Transportation and Communications, Toronto, Ontario [*Library symbol*] [*National Library of Canada*] (NLC)
OTDT .... Operational Test, Development Test
OTDT .... Operations Training Development Team [*Air Force*]
OTDT .... Over Temperature Delta T (SAUS)
OTDU........ Ontario Ministry of Colleges and Universities, Toronto, Ontario [*Library symbol*] [*National Library of Canada*] (NLC)
OTDW .... Day-Wilson-Campbell, Toronto, Ontario [*Library symbol*] [*National Library of Canada*] (BIB)
OTDX........ O-T-D [*Private rail car owner code*]
OTE .... Emmanuel College, Victoria University, Toronto, Ontario [*Library symbol*] [*National Library of Canada*] (NLC)
OTE .... Odd Transversal Electrical (SAUS)
OTE .... On-Target Earnings [*Sales industry*] (ODBW)
OTE .... Ontario Ministry of Treasury and Economics Library [*UTLAS symbol*]
OTE .... Operational Test and Evaluation [*Army*] (AABC)
OTE .... Operational Test Equipment [*NASA*] (KSC)
OTE .... Operator Training Equipment (SAUS)
OTE .... Optically Transparent Electrode
OTE .... Optical Tracking Electronics
OTE .... Organismos Tilepikoinonion Ellados [*Hellenic Telecommunications Organization*] [*Greek*]
OTE .... Other Technical Effort
OTE .... Outer Tube Equipment
OTE .... Overtaken by Events [*US Congress*]
OTE .... Oxalyl Thiolester [*Biochemistry*]
OTEA .... Office of Trade & Economic Analysis [*U.S. Department of Commerce*] [*Internet resource*]
OTEA .... Operational Test and Evaluation Agency [*Army*]
OTEA .... Oval Track Equipment Association (EA)
OTEAOW .... Atmospheric Environment Service (ODIT Ontario Weather Centre), Environment Canada [*Service de l'Environnement Atmospherique (Centre Meteorologique de l'Ontario), Environnement Canada*] Toronto, Ontario [*Library symbol*] [*National Library of Canada*] (NLC)
OTEBE....... Resource Library, Board of Education for the City of Etobicoke, Ontario [*Library symbol*] [*National Library of Canada*] (NLC)
OTEC .... Education Centre, Toronto Board of Education, Ontario [*Library symbol*] [*National Library of Canada*] (NLC)
OTEC .... Ocean Thermal Energy Conservation (SAUS)
OTEC .... Ocean Thermal Energy Conversion
OTEC .... Ontario Teacher Education Colleges (SAUS)
OTEC .... Operational Test and Evaluation Center (SAUS)
OTEC .... Operational Test and Evaluation Command [*Army*] (AAGC)
OTEC .... Oriental Telephone and Electric Company (SAUS)
OTEC .... Osage Tribal Education Committee [*Department of the Interior*] [*Muskogee, OK*] (EGAO)
OTECA....... Ocean Thermal Energy Conversion Act of 1980
OTECH....... Oceaneering Technology Integration (ABAC)
OTEC R&D.. Ocean Thermal Energy Conversion Research and Development (SAUS)
OTECS....... Ocean Thermal Energy Conversion Systems [*Department of Energy*]
OTECU....... Colleges and Universitites, Ontario Ministry of Education, Toronto, Ontario [*Library symbol*] [*National Library of Canada*] (NLC)
OTEE......... Teeswater Branch, Bruce County Public Library, Ontario [*Library symbol*] [*National Library of Canada*] (NLC)
OTEF......... Operational Test and Evaluation Facility (ACAE)
OTEF......... Operational Training and Evaluation Facility
OTEF......... Overseas Troop Entertainment Fund (SAUS)
OTEM........ ESSO [*Standard Oil*] Minerals of Canada, Toronto, Ontario [*Library symbol*] [*National Library of Canada*] (NLC)
OTEMAC .... Temagami Community Library, Ontario [*Library symbol*] [*National Library of Canada*] (NLC)
OTEMAS .... Osaka International Textile Machinery Show

OTEMC ...... Elizabeth McRae Associates, Toronto, Ontario [*Library symbol*] [*Obsolete*] [*National Library of Canada*] (NLC)
OTEMP ...... Overtemperature (NASA)
OTEMPO .... Operating Temporaries
OTEMR ...... Conservation and Renewable Energy Office, Energy, Mines, and Resources Canada [*Bureau de la Conservation de l'Energie et de l'Energie Renouvelable, Energie, Mines, et Ressources Canada*] Toronto, Ontario [*Library symbol*] [*National Library of Canada*] (NLC)
OTEP .... Office of Transportation Energy Policy [*Department of Transportation*]
OTEP .... Operational Test and Evaluation Plan [*Military*] (AFM)
OTEPL .... Etobicoke Public Library, Ontario [*Library symbol*] [*National Library of Canada*] (NLC)
OTEPS .... Environmental Protection Service, Environment Canada [*Service de la Protection de l'Environnement, Environnement Canada*] Toronto, Ontario [*Library symbol*] [*National Library of Canada*] (NLC)
OTEPSE ..... Environmental Emergency Library, Environmental Protection Service, Environment Canada [*Bibliotheque des Incidences Environnementales, Service de la Protection de l'Environnement, Environnement Canada*] Toronto, Ontario [*Library symbol*] [*National Library of Canada*] (NLC)
OTER .... Ontario Institute for Studies in Education, Toronto, Ontario [*Library symbol*] [*National Library of Canada*] (NLC)
OTES .... Operational Test and Evaluation Squadron [*Military*]
OTES .... Optical Technology Experiment Study (SAUS)
OTES .... Optical Technology Experiment System
OTES .... Orbiter Thermal Effects Simulator [*NASA*]
OTET .... Ontario Educational Communications Authority, Toronto, Ontario [*Library symbol*] [*National Library of Canada*] (NLC)
OTET .... TVOntario, Toronto, Ontario [*Library symbol*] [*National Library of Canada*] (NLC)
OTEU .... Consent Equipment [*Intermodal shipping container symbol*] (TVRC)
OTEU .... Office and Technical Employees (International) Union
OTeut .... Old Teutonic (ODA)
O TEUT ...... Old Teutonic [*Language, etc.*] (ROG)
OTEVFOR ... Operational Test & Evaluation for Operational Requirements (SAUS)
OTEX .... Open Text Corp. [*NASDAQ symbol*] (SAG)
OTEXA .... Office of Textiles and Apparel [*Department of Commerce*] (GFGA)
OTEXF .... Open Text [*NASDAQ symbol*] (TTSB)
OTEY .... East York Public Library, Toronto, Ontario [*Library symbol*] [*National Library of Canada*] (NLC)
OTEYBE ..... Professional Library, Board of Education for the Borough of East York, Toronto, Ontario [*Library symbol*] [*National Library of Canada*] (NLC)
OTF .... Institute of Environment Studies, University of Toronto, Ontario [*Library symbol*] [*National Library of Canada*] (NLC)
OTF .... Ocean Test Fixture (SAUS)
OTF .... Octamer Transcription Factor [*Genetics*]
OTF .... Off the Film (ODA)
OTF .... Off-the-Film [*Photography*] (WDMC)
OTF .... Off-the-Film Metering [*Olympus cameras*]
OTF .... Ontario Teachers Federation (AEBS)
OTF .... Ontario Technology Fund (SAUS)
OTF .... On the Floor [*Computer language*] [*Computer science*]
OTF .... On-the-Fly [*Computer compression program*] (PCM)
OTF .... Open Telematics Framework [*Automotive engineering*]
OTF .... Open Token Foundation (BTTJ)
OTF .... Operational Test Flight (ACAE)
OTF .... Optical Transfer Function
OTF .... Optimum Traffic Condition [*Radio*] (IAA)
OTF .... Optimum Traffic Frequency [*Radio*]
OTF .... Oral Transfer Factor [*Virology*]
OTF .... Orbital Test Flight (MCD)
OTF .... Ordered Triangular Factorization (SAUS)
OTF .... Order to Fire (SAUS)
OTF .... Organ Transplant Fund (SAUS)
OTF .... Other than Flat [*Freight*]
OTF .... Oxford Tax Exempt Fund II, L.P. [*AMEX symbol*] (NASQ)
OTFA .... Office of Technical Financial Assistance (ABAC)
OTFC .... Official 3 Stooges Fan Club [*Defunct*] (EA)
OTFC .... Ontario Ministry of Consumer and Commercial Relations, Toronto, Ontario [*Library symbol*] [*National Library of Canada*] (NLC)
OTFC .... Oregon Trail Financial Corp. [*NASDAQ symbol*] (NASQ)
OTFC .... Overflight Traffic [*Aviation*] (FAAC)
OTFCS .... On-Target Fire Control System (MCD)
OTFDC .... One-and Two-Family Dwelling Code [*Emergency Management*] (EMA)
OTFE .... Optical Terminal Flight Evaluation
OTFE .... Oscillatory Thermocapillary Flow Experiment (SAUS)
OTFEC .... Fenco Consultants Ltd., Toronto, Ontario [*Library symbol*] [*National Library of Canada*] (NLC)
OTFH .... Forest Hill Public Library, Toronto, Ontario [*Library symbol*] [*National Library of Canada*] (NLC)
OTFM .... Fire Marshal of Ontario, Toronto, Ontario [*Library symbol*] [*National Library of Canada*] (NLC)
OTFN .... Information Centre, Falconbridge Nickel Mines Ltd., Toronto, Ontario [*Library symbol*] [*National Library of Canada*] (NLC)
OT/FOT ...... Operational Test/Follow-On Operational Test
OTFP .... Fisons Corp. Ltd., Markham, Ontario [*Library symbol*] [*National Library of Canada*] (NLC)
OTFP .... Octylthio(trifluoro)propanone [*Biochemistry*]
OTFP .... Operational Traffic Flow Planning (GAVI)
OTFP .... Other than Full Paid [*IRS*]
OTFR .... Overall Transfer Function Response
OTF Reporter ... Ontario Teachers Federation Reporter (SAUS)
OTFT .... Financial Times, Don Mills, Ontario [*Library symbol*] [*National Library of Canada*] (NLC)
OTFT .... Observer Tit for Tat [*Gene theory*]
OT/FT .... Operational Test/Follow-On Test [*Missiles*] (DOMA)
OTFTS .... Outfits
OTG .... Information Centre, Glaxo Canada, Inc., Toronto, Ontario [*Library symbol*] [*National Library of Canada*] (BIB)
OTG .... Objective Transmission Grating (SAUS)
OTG .... Oil Temperature Gauge (MSA)
OTG .... OPTEVFOR [*Operational Test and Evaluation Force*] Tactics Guide [*Navy*] (CAAL)
OTG .... Option Table Generator
OTG .... Otolith Test Goggles [*NASA*] (KSC)
OTG .... Outrage [*Telegraphy*] (PCTE)
OTG .... Outside Temperature Gauge (ODA)
OTG .... Worthington [*Minnesota*] [*Airport symbol*] (OAG)
OTGA .... Information Centre, Giffels Associates Ltd., Rexdale, Ontario [*Library symbol*] [*National Library of Canada*] (NLC)
OTGAR ...... Engineering Library, Garrett Canada, Rexdale, Ontario [*Library symbol*] [*National Library of Canada*] (BIB)
OTGB .... Library and Audio-Visual Services, George Brown College of Applied Arts and Technology, Toronto, Ontario [*Library symbol*] [*National Library of Canada*] (BIB)
OTGFM ...... Management Science Department, General Foods, Inc., Don Mills, Ontario [*Library symbol*] [*National Library of Canada*] (NLC)
OTGG .... Goodman & Goodman, Toronto, Ontario [*Library symbol*] [*National Library of Canada*] (BIB)
OTGH .... Fudger Medical Library, Toronto General Hospital, Ontario [*Library symbol*] [*National Library of Canada*] (NLC)
OTGHPP ..... Ocean Thermal Gradient Hydraulic Power Plant
OTGM .... Globe and Mail, Toronto, Ontario [*Library symbol*] [*National Library of Canada*] (NLC)
OTGMC ...... Gulf Minerals Canada Ltd., Toronto, Ontario [*Library symbol*] [*National Library of Canada*] (NLC)
OTGOH ...... Gowling & Henderson, Toronto, Ontario [*Library symbol*] [*National Library of Canada*] (NLC)
OTGS .... Gore & Storrie Ltd., Toronto, Ontario [*Library symbol*] [*National Library of Canada*] (NLC)
OTGS .... Ocean Thermal Gradient System [*National Science Foundation*]
OTGS .... OTG Software [*NASDAQ symbol*] (SG)
OTGSB ...... Bibliographic Centre, Ontario Ministry of Government Services, Toronto, Ontario [*Library symbol*] [*National Library of Canada*] (NLC)
OTGSI .... CTS Information Resource Centre, Ontario Ministry of Government Services, Toronto [*Library symbol*] [*National Library of Canada*] (BIB)
OTGX .... Outrageous [*Telegraphy*] (PCTE)
OTH .... Independent Institute, NAD, Dublin, OH [*OCLC symbol*] (OCLC)
OTH .... North Bend [*Oregon*] [*Airport symbol*] (OAG)
OTH .... Oil-Tight Hatch [*Shipfitting*]
OTH .... Ontario Hydro, Toronto, Ontario [*Library symbol*] [*National Library of Canada*] (NLC)
OTH .... Optical Time History (MCD)
OTH .... Othello [*Washington*] [*Seismograph station code, US Geological Survey*] (SEIS)
Oth .... Othello [*Shakespearean work*]
OTH .... Other (DAVI)
oth .... Other (VRA)
OTH .... Other than Hand [*Freight*]
OTH .... Other than Honorable Conditions [*Military*] (AABC)
OTH .... Over-the-Horizon [*RADAR*]
OTHA .... Hatch Associates Ltd., Toronto, Ontario [*Library symbol*] [*National Library of Canada*] (NLC)
OTHB .... Over-the-Horizon Back-Scatter [*RADAR*]
OTH-B .... Over-the-Horizon Backscatter [*RADAR*] (POLM)
OTHB .... Toronto Historical Society, Ontario [*Library symbol*] [*National Library of Canada*] (BIB)
OTHB Radar ... Over-the-Horizon Backscatter Radar (SAUS)
OTH-B WCRS ... Over-the-Horizon Backscatter West Coast Radar System (SAUS)
OTHC .... Humber College of Applied Arts and Technology, Rexdale, Ontario [*Library symbol*] [*National Library of Canada*] (NLC)
OTH/DA ..... Over-the-Horizon/Damage Assessment [*Navy*] (CAAL)
OTHDC & T ... Over-the-Horizon Detection, Classification, and Targeting (NVT)
OTH-DC&T .. Over-the-Horizon Detection, Classification and Tracking (SAUS)
OTHDT ...... Over-The-Horizon Detection & Targeting (SAUS)
OTH-E .... Over-the-Horizon - Expanded
OTHE .... Thessalon Union Public Library, Ontario [*Library symbol*] [*National Library of Canada*] (NLC)
OTHER ...... Open Tubular Heterogeneous Enzyme Reactor [*Biochemical engineering*]
OTHF .... Over the Horizon Forwardscatter (SAUS)
OTH-F .... Over-the-Horizon - Forward Scatter
OTHG .... Over the Hill Gang, International (EA)
OTHL .... Advanced Technology Centre, Honeywell Ltd., Willowdale, Ontario [*Library symbol*] [*National Library of Canada*] (NLC)
OTHMC ...... Information Resources, Hay Management Consultants, Toronto, Ontario [*Library symbol*] [*National Library of Canada*] (NLC)
OTHMH ...... Humber Memorial Hospital, Weston, Ontario [*Library symbol*] [*National Library of Canada*] (NLC)
OTHO .... Thornbury Public Library, Ontario [*Library symbol*] [*National Library of Canada*] (NLC)
OTHOP ...... Quebec & Ontario Paper Co. Ltd., Thorold, Ontario [*Library symbol*] [*National Library of Canada*] (NLC)
OTHOR ...... Thornhill Public Library, Ontario [*Library symbol*] [*National Library of Canada*] (NLC)
OTHORF ..... Metallurgical Laboratory, Falconbridge Nickel Mines Ltd., Thornhill, Ontario [*Library symbol*] [*National Library of Canada*] (NLC)

OTHORO .... Thorold Public Library, Ontario [*Library symbol*] [*National Library of Canada*] (BIB)
OTHR .... Ontario Hydro Research, Toronto, Ontario [*Library symbol*] [*National Library of Canada*] (NLC)
OTHR .... Over-the-Horizon RADAR (MCD)
OTHS .... Other Services (TVEL)
OTHSA ...... Orphan Train Heritage Society of America (EA)
OTHSC ...... Hospital for Sick Children, Toronto, Ontario [*Library symbol*] [*National Library of Canada*] (NLC)
OTHSSM .... Over-the-Horizon Ship-to-Ship Missile
OTH-SW ..... Over-The-Horizon, Surface Wave (SAUS)
OTH-T .... Over the Horizon-Targeting (ACAE)
OTHT .... Over-the-Horizon Targeting (NVT)
OTH-T .... Over-the-Horizon-Targeting (SAUS)
OTHT-G ...... Over the Horizon Targeting Gold (SAUS)
OTHU .... Huntec Ltd., Toronto, Ontario [*Library symbol*] [*National Library of Canada*] (NLC)
OTI .... Morotai Island [*Indonesia*] [*Airport symbol*] (OAG)
OTI .... Newport, RI [*Location identifier*] [*FAA*] (FAAL)
OTI .... Office of Technical Information (MUGU)
OTI .... Office of Technology Integration (ABAC)
OTI .... Office of Trade and Investment [*Victoria, Australia*]
OTI .... Office of Transition Initiative (SAUS)
OTI .... Office of Transnational Issues [*Central Intelligence Agency*] (RCD)
OTI .... Office of Treatment Improvement [*U.S. Public Health Service*] (BARN)
OTI .... Official Test Insecticide
OTI .... Open Technology Interface (SAUS)
OTI .... Optimum Time Invariant (IAA)
OTI .... Ordnance Technical Instructions [*Navy*]
OTI .... Oregon Technical Institute
OTI .... Original Title [*Online database field identifier*]
OTI .... Original Transmitter Identification (SAUS)
OTI .... Otiai [*Former USSR*] [*Seismograph station code, US Geological Survey*] [*Closed*] (SEIS)
OTI .... OT Industries, Inc. [*Vancouver Stock Exchange symbol*]
OTI .... Ovomucoid Trypsin Inhibitor [*Medicine*] (DMAA)
OTI .... Oxide Throat Insert
OTI .... Timmins Public Library, Ontario [*Library symbol*] [*National Library of Canada*] (NLC)
OTIA .... Office of Technical Information Agency [*Army*] (MCD)
OTIA .... Ohio Telecom Association (EARSL)
OTIA .... Ordnance Technical Intelligence Agency (AAG)
OTIAP .... IAPA [*Industrial Accident Prevention Association*] Library, Toronto, Ontario [*Library symbol*] [*National Library of Canada*] (NLC)
OTIBI .... IBI Group, Toronto, Ontario [*Library symbol*] [*National Library of Canada*] (BIB)
OTIC .... Idea Corp., Toronto, Ontario [*Library symbol*] [*National Library of Canada*] (NLC)
OTIC .... Innovation Ontario Corp., Toronto, Ontario [*Library symbol*] [*National Library of Canada*] (NLC)
OTICA .... Institute of Chartered Accountants of Ontario, Toronto, Ontario [*Library symbol*] [*National Library of Canada*] (NLC)
OTICS .... Offset Target Indicator System (SAUS)
OTID .... Industrial Disease Standards Panel, Toronto, Ontario [*Library symbol*] [*National Library of Canada*] (BIB)
OTID .... Office of Talented Identification and Development [*Johns Hopkins University*] (EDAC)
OTID .... Office of Talented Indentification and Development [*Johns Hopkins Institute*] (WDAA)
OTIEP .... Office of Technical Information and Educational Programs [*Terminated*] [*NASA*]
OTIF .... Organisation Intergouvernementale pour les Transports Internationaux Ferrovaires [*Intergovernmental Organization for International Carriage by Rail*] (EAIO)
OTif .... Tiffin Seneca Public Library, Tiffin, OH [*Library symbol*] [*Library of Congress*] (LCLS)
OTifH .... Heidelberg College, Tiffin, OH [*Library symbol*] [*Library of Congress*] (LCLS)
OTI Filtering... Optimum Time-Invariant Filtering (SAUS)
OTIG .... Office of the Inspector General [*Army*] (AABC)
OTIHM .... Tillsonburg and District Historical Museum Society, Tillsonburg, Ontario [*Library symbol*] [*National Library of Canada*] (NLC)
OTII .... Our Torah Institutions of Israel (EA)
OTIL .... Tilbury Public Library, Ontario [*Library symbol*] [*National Library of Canada*] (NLC)
OTIM .... Pontifical Institute of Mediaeval Studies, University of Toronto, Ontario [*Library symbol*] [*National Library of Canada*] (NLC)
OTIME .... One Time (ACAE)
OTIN .... International Nickel Co. of Canada Ltd., Toronto, Ontario [*Library symbol*] [*National Library of Canada*] (NLC)
OTINF .... Infomart, Toronto, Ontario [*Library symbol*] [*National Library of Canada*] (NLC)
OTINP .... Information Plus Library, Toronto, Ontario [*Library symbol*] [*National Library of Canada*] (BIB)
OTIO .... United Kingdom Information Office, Toronto, Ontario [*Library symbol*] [*National Library of Canada*] (NLC)
OTIOL .... Imperial Oil Ltd., Toronto, Ontario [*Library symbol*] [*National Library of Canada*] (NLC)
OTIP .... Occupational Therapist in Independent Practice
OTIP .... Offense Technology Interaction Program (ACAE)
OTIP .... Ontario Training Incentive Program (SAUS)
OTIP .... Tillsonburg Public Library, Ontario [*Library symbol*] [*National Library of Canada*] (NLC)
OTIR .... Operational Test Incident Report (MCD)
OTIS .... Observer's Thermal Imaging System (PDAA)
OTIS .... Occupational Training Information System
OTIS .... Offset Target Indicator System (MCD)
OTIS .... Oklahoma Telecommunications Interlibrary System (AUEG)
OTIS .... Oklahoma Teletype Interlibrary System [*Library network*]
OTIS .... Once-Through Integral System [*Nuclear energy*] (NRCH)
OTIS .... One Term In-Service Course (AIE)
OTIS .... Online Telecommunications Information Service [*Connections Telecommunications, Inc.*] [*West Bridgewater, MA*] [*Telecommunications service*] (TSSD)
OTIS .... Operational Test Instrumentation Ship [*Navy*]
OTIS .... Operation, Transport, Inspection, Storage (MHDB)
OTIS .... Optimum Thermal Interpolation System (SAUS)
OTIS .... Order Trend Information System (SAUS)
OTIS .... Ordnance Telemetry Instrumentation Station [*Army*] (AABC)
OTIS .... Oregon Total Information System [*Eugene*] [*Information service or system*] (IID)
OTIS .... Other than Iron or Steel [*Freight*]
OTIS .... Overhead Travel Information System [*Automotive electronics*]
OTIS .... Overstayer Tracing and Intelligence System [*British*]
Otis Art Inst... Otis Art Institute of Parsons School of Design (GAGS)
OT/ITS .... Office of Telecommunications Institute for Telecommunication Sciences [*Boulder, CO*] [*Department of Commerce*]
OT/ITSRR... Office of Telecommunications/Institute for Telecommunications Sciences Research (SAUS)
OTIU .... Overseas Technical Information Unit [*Department of Trade*] [*British*]
OTIV .... Tiverton Branch, Bruce County Public Library, Ontario [*Library symbol*] [*National Library of Canada*] (NLC)
OTJ .... Off-the-Job
OTJ .... On the Job
OTJ .... Overt Tactical Jacket [*Police and security equipment*]
OTJ .... Toronto Regional Office, Department of Justice Canada [*Bureau Regional de Toronto, Ministere de la Justice du Canada*] Toronto, Ontario [*Library symbol*] [*National Library of Canada*] (NLC)
OTJAE .... John Arpin Enterprises, Inc., Toronto, Ontario [*Library symbol*] [*National Library of Canada*] (NLC)
OTJAG .... Office of the Judge Advocate General [*Army*] (AABC)
OTJFM ...... James F. MacLaren Ltd., Willowdale, Ontario [*Library symbol*] [*National Library of Canada*] (NLC)
OTJL .... Judges Library, Ontario Ministry of the Attorney General, Toronto, Ontario [*Library symbol*] [*National Library of Canada*] (NLC)
OTJPS .... Sands Pharmaceutical Division, Jerram Pharmaceuticals Ltd., Toronto, Ontario [*Library symbol*] [*National Library of Canada*] (NLC)
OTJT .... On the Job Training
OTJWT ...... Information Centre, J. Walter Thompson Co. Ltd., Toronto, Ontario [*Library symbol*] [*National Library of Canada*] (NLC)
OTK .... Knox College, University of Toronto, Ontario [*Library symbol*] [*National Library of Canada*] (NLC)
OTK .... Oil Tank
OTK .... Old Tuberculin Koch (SAUS)
OTK .... One-Time Key (SAUS)
OTK .... Over the Knee (SAUS)
OTK .... Oxidizer Tank (MCD)
OTKC .... Kidd Creek Mines Ltd., Toronto, Ontario [*Library symbol*] [*National Library of Canada*] (NLC)
OTKDF .... Other than Knocked Down Flat [*Freight*]
OTKE .... Kilborn Engineering Ltd., Toronto, Ontario [*Library symbol*] [*National Library of Canada*] (NLC)
OTL .... Boutilimit [*Mauritania*] [*Airport symbol*] (AD)
OTL .... Legislative Library of Ontario, Toronto, Ontario [*Library symbol*] [*National Library of Canada*] (NLC)
OTL .... Libbey-Owens-Ford Glass Co., Technical Library, Toledo, OH [*Library symbol*] [*Library of Congress*] (LCLS)
OTL .... Observer Target Line (NVT)
OTL .... Office Technology Ltd. (NITA)
OTL .... Ogden Technology Laboratories [*NASA*] (KSC)
OTL .... Ohio Theological Librarians [*Library network*]
OTL .... Oil-Tight Light
OTL .... [*The*] Old Testament Library [*A publication*] (BJA)
OTL .... Online Task Loader
OTL .... Operating Temperature Limit
OTL .... Operating Time Log (AAG)
OTL .... Opportunity to Learn
OTL .... Oracle Teletext Ltd. (NITA)
OTL .... Order Trunk Line [*Telecommunications*] (OA)
OTL .... Ordnance Test Laboratory (NASA)
OTL .... OSI Testing Liaison Group (SAUS)
OTL .... Outer Tube Limit [*Chemical engineering*]
OTL .... Outland Resources [*Vancouver Stock Exchange symbol*]
OTL .... Output-Transformerless (SAA)
OTL .... Out to Lunch
OTL .... Over the Line (WDAA)
OTL .... Ovine Testicular Lymph [*Endocrinology*]
OTL .... Oxidizer Tapping Line (SAUS)
OTL .... Oxidizer Topping Line (AAG)
OTL .... Tilapa Otomi [*Language symbol*] (ETLW)
OTLAC .... Tamworth Branch, Lennox and Addington County Library, Ontario [*Library symbol*] [*National Library of Canada*] (BIB)
OTLAMR .... Ocean Temperature Large Antenna Microwave Radiometer (SAUS)
OTLC .... Information Section, Ontario Ministry of Natural Resources, Toronto, Ontario [*Library symbol*] [*National Library of Canada*] (NLC)
OTLC .... Open Tubular Liquid Chromatography
OTLC .... Orbiter Timeline Constraints [*NASA*] (NASA)
OTLCC .... Lummus Co. Canada Ltd., Willowdale, Ontario [*Library symbol*] [*National Library of Canada*] (NLC)
OTLF .... Natural Resources Library, Ontario Ministry of Natural Resources, Toronto, Ontario [*Library symbol*] [*National Library of Canada*] (NLC)

OTLF One-Time License Fee (SAUS)
OTLH Laventhol & Horwath, Toronto, Ontario, [*Library symbol*] [*National Library of Canada*] (BIB)
OTLK Outlook [*NWS*] (FAAC)
OTLMO Orde des Technologistes de Laboratoire Medical de l'Ontario (AC)
OTLN Outline (SAUS)
OTLO Libbey-Owens-Ford Glass Co., Corporate Library, Toledo, OH [*Library symbol*] [*Library of Congress*] (LCLS)
OTLP Ledbury Park Junior High School, Toronto, Ontario [*Library symbol*] [*National Library of Canada*] (NLC)
OTLR Research Branch, Ontario Ministry of Natural Resources, Toronto, Ontario [*Library symbol*] [*National Library of Canada*] (NLC)
OTLS Law Society of Upper Canada, Toronto, Ontario [*Library symbol*] [*National Library of Canada*] (NLC)
OTLSC Litton Systems Canada Ltd., Rexdale, Ontario [*Library symbol*] [*National Library of Canada*] (NLC)
OTLT Outlet (SAUS)
OTLU Orient Tainers [*Intermodal shipping container symbol*] (TVRC)
OTM Atmospheric Environment Service, Environment Canada [*Service de l'Environnement Atmospherique, Environnement Canada*] Downsview, Ontario [*Library symbol*] [*National Library of Canada*] (NLC)
OTM Centre for Research in Operations and Technology [*London Business School*] [*United Kingdom*] (RCD)
OTM Object Transaction Monitor [*Computer science*] (GART)
OTM Office of Telecommunications Management [*Later, OTP*] [*FCC*]
OTM Office of Transportation Materials (SAUS)
OTM Office Technology Management Association (SAUS)
OTM Old Turkey Mill (SAUS)
OTM Once-through-Methanol [*Fuel technology*]
OTM One Time Measure [*Training term*] (LPT)
OTM On the Mark - Mark Hamill Fan Club (EA)
OTM On-the-Move (SAUS)
OTM On-Time Marker [*Computer science*]
OTM Operational Test Models (SAUS)
OTM Optical Tool Master (MCD)
OTM Orbit Trim Maneuver (ACAE)
OTM Organo-Transition-Metal (PDAA)
OTM Original Turkey Mill [*Paper*] (DGA)
OTM Ortho-Tolidine Manganese Sulphate
OTM Other than Mexican [*Term applied by US Border Patrol to certain illegal immigrants*]
otm other track material (SAUS)
OTM Ottumwa [*Iowa*] [*Airport symbol*] (OAG)
OTM Out of the Money [*Options*] [*Investment term*] (NUMA)
OTM Overseas Trade Mission (JAGO)
OTM Timken Co., Research Library, Canton, OH [*OCLC symbol*] (OCLC)
OTM Toledo Museum of Art, Toledo, OH [*Library symbol*] [*Library of Congress*] (LCLS)
OTMA Office Technology Management Association [*Defunct*] (EA)
OTMA Oilfield Tank Manufacturers Association (EA)
OTMAG Ontario Ministry of the Attorney General [*Ministere du Procureur-General*],Toronto [*Library symbol*] [*National Library of Canada*] (BIB)
OTMB McMillan, Binch, Toronto, Ontario [*Library symbol*] [*National Library of Canada*] (NLC)
OTMC Massey College, Toronto, Ontario [*Library symbol*] [*National Library of Canada*] (NLC)
OTMC Medical College of Ohio at Toledo, Toledo, OH [*Library symbol*] [*Library of Congress*] (LCLS)
OTMCL Metropolitan Toronto Library, Ontario [*Library symbol*] [*National Library of Canada*] (NLC)
OTME Ontario Ministry of Energy, Toronto, Ontario [*Library symbol*] [*National Library of Canada*] (NLC)
OTMEN Ontario Ministry of the Environment, Toronto, Ontario [*Library symbol*] [*National Library of Canada*] (NLC)
OTMENL Laboratory, Ontario Ministry of the Environment, Rexdale, Ontario [*Library symbol*] [*National Library of Canada*] (NLC)
OTMF McIntyre-Falconbridge Library, Toronto, Ontario [*Library symbol*] [*National Library of Canada*] (NLC)
OTMH Financial Post, Toronto, Ontario [*Library symbol*] [*National Library of Canada*] (NLC)
OTMI Royal Canadian Military Institute, Toronto, Ontario [*Library symbol*] [*National Library of Canada*] (NLC)
OTMIO Employment and Immigration Canada [*Emploi et Immigration Canada*] Toronto, Ontario [*Library symbol*] [*National Library of Canada*] (NLC)
OTMIO Ontario Region Library, Employment and Immigration Canada [*Bibliotheque de laRegion de l'Ontario, Emploi et Immigration Canada*], North York, Ontario [*Library symbol*] [*National Library of Canada*] (NLC)
OTMIP One-Time Mortgage Insurance Premium (GFGA)
OTMIR Office of Tropical Medicine and International Research (SAUS)
OTMIS Medical Information Services, Toronto, Ontario [*Library symbol*] [*National Library of Canada*] (BIB)
OTMJ Outgoing Trunk Message Junction [*Telecommunications*] (OA)
OTML Law Library, Manufacturers Life Insurance Co., Toronto, Ontario [*Library symbol*] [*National Library of Canada*] (BIB)
OTML Oatmeal [*Freight*]
OTMM Mary Manse College, Toledo, OH [*Library symbol*] [*Library of Congress*] (LCLS)
OTMM McCarthy & McCarthy, Barristers & Solicitors, Toronto, Ontario [*Library symbol*] [*National Library of Canada*] (NLC)
OTMMB Ontario Milks Marketing Board, Toronto, Ontario [*Library symbol*] [*National Library of Canada*] (NLC)
OTMML Micromedia Ltd., Toronto, Ontario [*Library symbol*] [*National Library of Canada*] (NLC)
OTMMM Marshall-Macklin-Monaghan Library, Don Mills, Ontario [*Library symbol*] [*National Library of Canada*] (NLC)
OTMN Oxotremorine [*Cholinergic agent*]
OTMO Monopros Ltd., Toronto, Ontario [*Library symbol*] [*National Library of Canada*] (BIB)
OTMOF MacDonald Ophthalmic Foundation, Toronto, Ontario [*Library symbol*] [*National Library of Canada*] (NLC)
OTMS Mount Sinai Hospital, Toronto, Ontario [*Library symbol*] [*National Library of Canada*] (NLC)
OTMS [*The*] Old Testament and Modern Study [*A publication*] (BJA)
OTMS Operational Technical Managerial System (NVT)
OTMS Over Thirty Months Slaughter scheme (SAUS)
OTMSM Management Services Department Library, Municipality of Metropolitan Toronto, Ontario [*Library symbol*] [*National Library of Canada*] (BIB)
OTMSS Professional Library, Metropolitan Separate School Board, Willowdale, Ontario [*Library symbol*] [*National Library of Canada*] (NLC)
OTM Sulphate Orthotolidine Manganese Sulphate (SAUS)
OTMT Monetary Times, Toronto, Ontario [*Library symbol*] [*National Library of Canada*] (NLC)
OTMTC Economic Development Division, Metro Toronto Chairman's Office, Toronto, Ontario [*Library symbol*] [*National Library of Canada*] (BIB)
OTMTS Metropolitan Toronto School Board, Ontario [*Library symbol*] [*National Library of Canada*] (NLC)
OTMTSS Secondary Schools, Metropolitan Toronto School Board, Ontario [*Library symbol*] [*National Library of Canada*] (NLC)
OTMW Department of Works, Municipality of Metropolitan Toronto, Ontario [*Library symbol*] [*National Library of Canada*] (BIB)
OTN Lastp-Linhas Aereas de Sao Tome e Principe [*ICAO designator*] (FAAC)
OTN Newtonbrook Secondary School, Willowdale, Ontario [*Library symbol*] [*National Library of Canada*] (NLC)
OTN Oaktown, IN [*Location identifier*] [*FAA*] (FAAL)
OTN Octal Track Number [*Computer science*]
OTN Operational Teletype Network
OTN Operational Test, Non-Major Systems (MCD)
OtN Order to Negotiate (SAUS)
OTN Orthogonal Tree Network (SAUS)
OTN Over the Nose [*Aviation*]
OTN Own-the-Night [*Technology*] [*Army*] (INF)
OTNA Ontario Ministry of Northern Development and Mines, Toronto, Ontario [*Library symbol*] [*National Library of Canada*] (NLC)
OTNC International Council for Adult Education, Toronto, Ontario [*Library symbol*] [*National Library of Canada*] (BIB)
OTNG Observer Training [*Army*] (AABC)
OTNGH Health Sciences Library, Northwestern General Hospital, Toronto, Ontario [*Library symbol*] [*National Library of Canada*] (BIB)
OTNH National Heritage Ltd., Toronto, Ontario [*Library symbol*] [*National Library of Canada*] (NLC)
OTNHH Health Protection Branch, Canada Department of National Health and Welfare [*Direction Generale de la Protection de la Sante, Ministere de la Sante Nationale et du Bien-Etre Social*] Toronto, Ontario [*Library symbol*] [*National Library of Canada*] (NLC)
OTNI Industrial Development Office, National Research Council Canada [*Bureau du Developpement Industriel, Conseil National de Recherches Canada*], Scarborough, Ontario [*Library symbol*] [*National Library of Canada*] (NLC)
OTNIMR G. Allan Roeher Institute, Downsview, Ontario [*Library symbol*] [*National Library of Canada*] (NLC)
OTNIMR National Institute on Mental Retardation [*Institut National pour la Deficience Mentale*] Toronto, Ontario [*Library symbol*] [*National Library of Canada*] (NLC)
OTNM Northern Mines, Toronto, Ontario [*Library symbol*] [*National Library of Canada*] (NLC)
OTNM Over-Thirty-Never-Married [*Lifestyle classification*]
OTNO Our Telegram Number (SAUS)
OTNP Other than New Procurement [*Navy*] (DNAB)
OTNR Survey Records Branch, Ontario Ministry of Natural Resources, Toronto, Ontario [*Library symbol*] [*National Library of Canada*] (BIB)
OTNS Bank of Nova Scotia [*Banque de Nouvelle-Ecosse*], Toronto, Ontario [*Library symbol*] [*National Library of Canada*] (NLC)
OTNY North York Public Library, Willowdale, Ontario [*Library symbol*] [*National Library of Canada*] (NLC)
OTNYE F. W. Minkler Library, North York Board of Education, Willowdale, Ontario [*Library symbol*] [*National Library of Canada*] (NLC)
OTO Oblique Takeoff (SAUS)
OTO Oil Temperature Out
OTO One-Time-Only
OTO Operational Testing Office (SAUS)
OTO Operator-to-Operator [*Military*] (CAAL)
OTO Optical Tracker Operator (MUGU)
OTO Ordo Templi Orientis [*Order of the Oriental Templars*] [*A mystical lodge*] [*Latin*] (ADA)
Oto Otolaryngology [*Medicine*]
Oto Otology [*Medicine*] (AMHC)
OTO Otology [*Medicine*]
oto Otomian [*MARC language code*] [*Library of Congress*] (LCCP)
OTO Otorhinolaryngologist (SAUS)
OTO Otorhinolaryngology [*Medicine*] (DHSM)
OTO Otto, NM [*Location identifier*] [*FAA*] (FAAL)
OTO Out-to-Out (AAG)
OTO Owens-Illinois, Inc., Technical Information Service-NTC, Toledo, OH [*Library symbol*] [*Library of Congress*] (LCLS)
OTO Oxford Textbook of Oncology [*Database*] [*United Kingdom*] (GDD)
OTO Tottenham Public Library, Ontario [*Library symbol*] [*National Library of Canada*] (NLC)

OTOB .... Tobermory Branch, Bruce County Public Library, Ontario [*Library symbol*] [*National Library of Canada*] (NLC)
OTOC .... Ontario Cancer Institute, Toronto, Ontario [*Library symbol*] [*National Library of Canada*] (NLC)
OTOCTA ..... Optimum Technical Operational Concept to Accomplish
OTOD .... Organization of Teachers of Oral Diagnosis (EA)
OTOE .... Omnispace Environments Ltd., Toronto, Ontario [*Library symbol*] [*National Library of Canada*] (NLC)
OTOEB .... Ontario Energy Board, Toronto, Ontario [*Library symbol*] [*National Library of Canada*] (NLC)
OTO EPROM ... One-Time-Only Erasable Read-Only Memory [*Computer science*] (MED)
OTOGR ...... Canadian Geriatrics Research Society, Toronto, Ontario [*Library symbol*] [*National Library of Canada*] (NLC)
OTOH .... Ontario Ministry of Municipal Affairs and Housing, Toronto, Ontario [*Library symbol*] [*National Library of Canada*] (NLC)
OTOH .... On The One Hand (SAUS)
OTOH .... On the Other Hand [*Internet language*] [*Computer science*]
OTOHCR .... Central Records, Ontario Hydro, Toronto, Ontario [*Library symbol*] [*National Library of Canada*] (NLC)
OTOL .... Ontario Lottery Corporation, Toronto, Ontario [*Library symbol*] [*National Library of Canada*] (BIB)
otol .... otological (SAUS)
Otol .... Otologist (STED)
OTOL .... Otology [*Medicine*]
Otolar .... Otolaryngology [*Medicine*] (DAVI)
Otolaryngol Head Neck Surg... Otolaryngology-Head and Neck Surgery (SAUS)
OTOLR ...... Ontario Labour Relations Board [*Commission des Relations de Travail de l'Ontario*], Toronto, Ontario [*Library symbol*] [*National Library of Canada*] (NLC)
OTOLRC ..... Ontario Law Reform Commission, Toronto, Ontario [*Library symbol*] [*National Library of Canada*] (BIB)
OTOMA ...... Ontario Medical Association, Toronto, Ontario [*Library symbol*] [*National Library of Canada*] (NLC)
OTOME ...... Information Resource Centre, Ontario Municipal Employees Retirement Board, Toronto [*Library symbol*] [*National Library of Canada*] (BIB)
OTOMR ...... Ontario Ministry of Revenue, Toronto, Ontario [*Library symbol*] [*National Library of Canada*] (NLC)
OTONA ...... Ontario Nurses Association, Toronto, Ontario [*Library symbol*] [*National Library of Canada*] (NLC)
OTO NAVSUPPACT... Overseas Transportation Office, Naval Support Activity (DNAB)
OTO/Neth ... Only to Order from Netherlands (SAUS)
O to O .... Out to Out [*Technical drawings*]
O to O .... Out-to-Out (SAUS)
OTOPC ...... Ortho Pharmaceutical Canada Ltd., Don Mills, Ontario [*Library symbol*] [*National Library of Canada*] (NLC)
OTOPCT ..... Planning and Research Library, Technical Services Branch, Ontario Police Commission, Toronto, Ontario [*Library symbol*] [*National Library of Canada*] (NLC)
OTORHINOL... Otorhinolaryngology (SAUS)
Otorhinol... Otorhinology (SAUS)
OTOS .... Orbit-to-Orbit Stage [*NASA*] (MCD)
OTOS .... Otosan [*NCIC car make code*]
OTOSC ...... Ontario Securities Commission, Toronto, Ontario [*Library symbol*] [*National Library of Canada*] (NLC)
OTOSS ...... Ontario Secondary School Teachers Federation, Toronto, Ontario [*Library symbol*] [*National Library of Canada*] (NLC)
OTOW .... Resource Centre, Ontario Women's Directorate [*Library symbol*] [*National Library of Canada*] (BIB)
OTP .... Obstacle to Progress (SAUS)
OTP .... Ocean Test Platform [*Marine science*] (MSC)
OTP .... Office of Telecommunications Policy [*Terminated, 1978*] [*Executive Office of the President*]
OTP .... Office of Territorial Programs (COE)
OTP .... Office of Terrorism Preparedness [*Emergency Management*] (EMA)
OTP .... Office of Trade Promotion [*Department of Commerce*]
OTP .... Office Technology Plus [*General Services Administration*]
OTP .... Off True Position (SAUS)
OTP .... Of This Parish
OTP .... Of True Position (MSA)
OTP .... One-Time Pad [*Navy*] [*British*]
OTP .... One Time Password (SAUS)
OTP .... One-Time Process (SAUS)
OTP .... One-Time Programmable [*Computer science*]
OTP .... One-Time Programmable [*Automotive electronics*]
OTP .... On Top [*Aviation*]
OTP .... On Top Position (SAUS)
OTP .... Open Top [*Freight*]
OTP .... Open Trade Protocol (SAUS)
OTP .... Operational Test Plan
OTP .... Operational Test Procedure (KSC)
OTP .... Operations Turnaround Plan (NASA)
OTP .... Order to Plan (SAUS)
OTP .... Oscillation Test Point [*British military*] (DMA)
OTP .... Otepa [*Tuamotu Archipelago*] [*Seismograph station code, US Geological Survey*] (SEIS)
OTP .... Other than Portable [*Freight*]
Ot P .... Otto Papiensis [*Flourished, 12th century*] [*Authority cited in pre-1607 legal work*] (DSA)
OTP .... Outline Test Plan [*Army*]
OTP .... Overhead Trickle Purification (PDAA)
OTP .... Overtemperature Protection (SAUS)
OTP .... Overtime Premium (MCD)
OTP .... Ovine Trophoblast Protein [*Biochemistry*]
OTP .... Oxidizer Tanking Panel (AAG)
OTP .... Oxygen Tanking Panel (SAUS)
OTP .... Ozone Trends Panel [*NASA*]
OTP .... Toronto Public Libraries, Ontario [*Library symbol*] [*National Library of Canada*] (NLC)
OTPA .... Institute of Public Administration of Canada [*Institut d'Administration Publique du Canada*] Toronto, Ontario [*Library symbol*] [*National Library of Canada*] (NLC)
OTPAL .... PAL Reading Service, Toronto, Ontario [*Library symbol*] [*National Library of Canada*] (NLC)
OTPEC .... Officer Training Program Examining Center [*Air Force*]
OTP-EPROM... One-Time Programmable-Electrically Programmable Read-Only Memory (SAUS)
OTPFA .... Fine Arts Library, Northern District, Toronto Public Libraries, Ontario [*Library symbol*] [*National Library of Canada*] (NLC)
OTPG .... Polar Gas Library, Toronto, Ontario [*Library symbol*] [*National Library of Canada*] (NLC)
OTPH .... History Section, Metropolitan Toronto Library, Ontario [*Library symbol*] [*National Library of Canada*] (NLC)
OTPHC ...... Prentice Hall Canada, Inc., Scarborough, Ontario [*Library symbol*] [*National Library of Canada*] (NLC)
OTPHR ...... Resource Centre, Department of Public Health, City of Toronto, Ontario [*Library symbol*] [*National Library of Canada*] (BIB)
OTPI .... Olive Tree-Pipit [*North American bird banding code*] (BIBA)
OTPI .... On Top Position Indicator [*Navy*] (NG)
OTPI .... Operational Test Program Instruction (MCD)
OTPM .... Peat, Marwick & Partners, Toronto, Ontario [*Library symbol*] [*National Library of Canada*] (NLC)
OTPMG ...... Office of the Provost Marshal General [*Army*]
OTPNL .... Outer Pane [*Aerospace*] (IAA)
OTPNL .... Outer Panel (SAUS)
OTPP .... Ocean Thermal Power Plant
OTPP .... Office of Transport, Policy and Planning [*South Australia*]
OTPP .... Ontario Provincial Police, Toronto, Ontario [*Library symbol*] [*National Library of Canada*] (NLC)
OTPP .... Operational Transfer Point Plan (SAUS)
Ot Pp .... Otto Papiensis [*Flourished, 12th century*] [*Authority cited in pre-1607 legal work*] (DSA)
OTPPC .... Ontario Provincial Police College, Toronto, Ontario [*Library symbol*] [*National Library of Canada*] (NLC)
OTPPP .... Open Transport/Point-to-Point Protocol (SAUS)
OTPR .... Proctor & Redfern Group, Don Mills, Ontario [*Library symbol*] [*National Library of Canada*] (NLC)
OTPROM .... One-Time Programmable Read Only Memory [*Computer science*]
OTP/RS ..... Outline Test Plan/Resume Sheet (MCD)
OTPRW ...... National Office Library, Price Waterhouse & Co., Toronto, Ontario [*Library symbol*] [*National Library of Canada*] (BIB)
OTPS .... Oceanic Traffic Planning System [*FAA*] (TAG)
OTPS .... One-Time Process System (SAUS)
OTPS .... Operational Test Program Set (MCD)
OTPT .... Operational Test Program Tape (MCD)
OTPT .... Output (KSC)
O-TPV .... Olefinic Thermoplastic Vulcanizate (SAUS)
OTPV2 .... Operational Test Perspective View and Visualization (SAUS)
OTPW .... Ontario Ministry of Community and Social Services, Toronto, Ontario [*Library symbol*] [*National Library of Canada*] (NLC)
OTPWC ...... Ontario Regional Library, Public Works Canada [*Bibliotheque Regionale de l'Ontario, Travaux Publics Canada*] Toronto, Ontario [*Library symbol*] [*National Library of Canada*] (NLC)
OTQ .... On the Quarter
OTQE .... Queen Elizabeth Hospital, Toronto, Ontario [*Library symbol*] [*National Library of Canada*] (NLC)
OTQL .... Quaere Legal Resources Ltd., Toronto, Ontario [*Library symbol*] [*National Library of Canada*] (NLC)
OTQRM ...... [*The*] Queen's Own Rifles of Canada Regimental Museum, Toronto, Ontario [*Library symbol*] [*National Library of Canada*] (NLC)
OTQSM ...... Queen Street Mental Health Centre, Toronto, Ontario [*Library symbol*] [*National Library of Canada*] (NLC)
OTR .... Coto 47 [*Costa Rica*] [*Airport symbol*] (OAG)
OTR .... [*The*] Oakland Terminal Railway [*Formerly, OKT*] [*AAR code*]
OTR .... Observed Temperature Rise
OTR .... Occupational Therapist, Registered
OTR .... Oceanic Transition Route [*FAA*] (TAG)
OTR .... Office of Technical Resources
OTR .... Office of Testing and Research [*Drug evalution*]
OTR .... Off-the-Road
OTR .... Old Time Radio
OTR .... One Touch Recording
OTR .... On The Rag (SAUS)
OTR .... Open-Tubular Reactor
OTR .... Operating Temperature Range
OTR .... Operating Time Record (SAUS)
OTR .... Operational Time Record (AAG)
OTR .... Operational Turn-Round (SAUS)
OTR .... Optical Tracking [*NASA*] (KSC)
OTR .... Optical Transition Radiation [*Physics*]
OTR .... Oregon Tax Reports [*A publication*] (DLA)
OTR .... Organic Test Reactor [*Nuclear energy*]
OTR .... Organ Transplant Rejection [*Medicine*] (MELL)
OTR .... Orotek Resources Corp. [*Vancouver Stock Exchange symbol*]
OTR .... Other [*Telegraphy*] (PCTE)
OTR .... Other-Total Ratio [*B. Mullen*] (DIPS)
OTR .... Oudh and Tirhut Railway [*Indian Railway*] (TIR)
OTR .... Outer (MSA)
OTR .... Out-Turn Report (SAUS)
OTR .... Ovarian Tumor Registry [*Medicine*]

OTR......... Overload Time Relay (SAUS)
OTR......... Over the Road
OTR......... Over-the-Road [*Automotive engineering*]
OTR......... Owning-the-Realty (SAUS)
OTR......... Oxygen Transfer Rate [*Chemical engineering*]
OTR......... Oxygen Transmission Rate (SAUS)
OTR......... Oxytocin Receptor [*Endocrinology*]
OTR......... Ozone Transport Region [*Environmental Protection Agency*] (EPAT)
OTR......... Registered Occupational Therapist (SAUS)
OTR......... Ryerson Polytechnical Institute, Toronto, Ontario [*Library symbol*] [*National Library of Canada*] (NLC)
OTr......... Troy-Miami County Public Library, Troy, OH [*Library symbol*] [*Library of Congress*] (LCLS)
OTRA........ Other than Regular Army (AABC)
OTRA........ Oversea Theater Requisitioning Authority [*Military*]
OTRA........ Royal Astronomical Society [*Societe Royale d'Astronomie*] Toronto, Ontario [*Library symbol*] [*National Library of Canada*] (NLC)
OTRAC...... Oscillogram Trace Reader [*Non-Linear Systems, Inc.*] [*Computer science*]
OTRAG...... Orbital Transport and Rocket AG (SAUS)
OTRAG...... Orbital Transport- und Raketen-Aktiengesellschaft [*Rocket company*] [*Germany*]
OTRAL....... Rio Algom Ltd., Toronto, Ontario [*Library symbol*] [*National Library of Canada*] (NLC)
OTRAN...... Ocean Testing Ranges and Instrumentation Conference
OTRAN...... Ocean Test Range and Instrumentation (SAUS)
O/Trans...... Output Transformer (SAUS)
OTRAR...... Other than Regular Army
OTRAT....... Overseas Tour Renewal Agreement Travel [*USDA Forest Service*] (ALAC)
OTRBI....... Information Resources, Royal Bank of Canada, Toronto, Ontario [*Library symbol*] [*National Library of Canada*] (NLC)
OTRBSA..... Occupational Therapists' Registration Board of South Australia
OTRC........ Canadian Forces College, Toronto, Ontario [*Library symbol*] [*National Library of Canada*] (NLC)
OTRC........ Old Time Radio Club [*Association*] (EA)
OTRCF....... Royal Commission on the Future of the Toronto Waterfront, Toronto, Ontario [*Library symbol*] [*National Library of Canada*] (BIB)
OTRCL....... Reichhold Chemicals Ltd., Weston, Ontario [*Library symbol*] [*National Library of Canada*] (NLC)
OTRCR...... Trout Creek Community Library, Ontario [*Library symbol*] [*National Library of Canada*] (NLC)
OTRCS...... Canadian Forces Staff School, Canada Department of National Defence [*College d'Etat-Major des Forces Canadiennes, Ministere de la Defense Nationale*] Toronto, Ontario [*Library symbol*] [*National Library of Canada*] (NLC)
OTRDA...... Ontario Tuberculosis and Respiratory Disease Association [*Medicine*] [*Canada*] (EDAA)
OTRE........ Trenton Public Library, Ontario [*Library symbol*] [*National Library of Canada*] (NLC)
OTREC....... Regis College, Toronto, Ontario [*Library symbol*] [*National Library of Canada*] (NLC)
OTReg....... Occupational Therapist Registered [*Canada*] (DAVI)
OTREN...... Northumberland County Public Library, Warkworth, Ontario [*Library symbol*] [*National Library of Canada*] (NLC)
OTREX....... Canada Department of Regional Industrial Expansion [*Ministere de l'Expansion Industrielle Regionale*] Toronto, Ontario [*Library symbol*] [*National Library of Canada*] (NLC)
OTR Ex...... OTR Express, Inc. [*Associated Press*] (SAG)
OTRF........ Ontario Research Foundation, Sheridan Park, Mississauga, Ontario [*Library symbol*] [*National Library of Canada*] (NLC)
OTRG........ Office Technology Research Group [*Defunct*] (EA)
OTRG........ Old Testament Reading Guide [*Collegeville, MN*] [*A publication*] (BJA)
OTRHNLRGYNGY... Otorhinolaryngology
OTRIC....... Collins Canada Division, Rockwell International, Toronto, Ontario [*Library symbol*] [*National Library of Canada*] (NLC)
OTRK........ Oshkosh Truck Corp. [*Oshkosh, WI*] [*NASDAQ symbol*] (NQ)
OTRKB....... Oshkosh Truck'B' [*NASDAQ symbol*] (TTSB)
OTR/L....... Occupational Therapist Registered/Licensed (IDYL)
OTRL........ Reed Ltd., Toronto, Ontario [*Library symbol*] [*National Library of Canada*] (NLC)
OTrL......... Troy-Miami County Public Library, Troy, OH [*Library symbol*] [*Library of Congress*] (LCLS)
OTRM....... Royal Ontario Museum, Toronto, Ontario [*Library symbol*] [*National Library of Canada*] (NLC)
OTRMC...... Canadiana Department, Royal Ontario Museum, Toronto, Ontario [*Library symbol*] [*National Library of Canada*] (NLC)
OTRMF...... Far Eastern Department, Royal Ontario Museum, Toronto, Ontario [*Library symbol*] [*National Library of Canada*] (NLC)
OTRO........ Overhaul Test Requirement Outline
OTROT...... Corporate Information Centre, Royal Trust, Toronto, Ontario [*Library symbol*] [*National Library of Canada*] (BIB)
OTRPM...... Rothmans of Pall Mall Ltd., Don Mills, Ontario [*Library symbol*] [*National Library of Canada*] (NLC)
OTRR........ Operation Test Readiness Review [*Army*]
OTRR........ Organisation for the Total Redemption of Rwandese (SAUS)
OTRS........ Operational Test Readiness Statement
OTRS........ Oxford Tobacco Research Station [*North Carolina Department of Agriculture and Consumer Services*] (RCD)
OT/RT........ Occupational Therapy/Recreational Therapy (STED)
OTRT........ Operating Time Record Tag (AAG)
OTRT........ Rose Technology Group Ltd., Toronto, Ontario [*Library symbol*] [*National Library of Canada*] (NLC)
OTRX........ On-Track Railway Services [*Private rail car owner code*]
OTRX........ OTR Express [*NASDAQ symbol*] (TTSB)
OTRX........ OTR Express, Inc. [*NASDAQ symbol*] (SAG)
OTS.......... Oakhanger Tracking Station (ACAE)
OTS.......... Object Time System (MHDB)
OTS.......... Object Transaction Service (VLIE)
OTS.......... Occipital Temporal Sulcus [*Medicine*] (DMAA)
OTS.......... Octadecyltrichlorosilane [*Organic chemistry*]
OTS.......... Office of Technical Services [*Later, CFSTI, NTIS*] [*National Institute of Standards and Technology*]
OTS.......... Office of Technical Support [*US Employment Service*] [*Department of Labor*]
OTS.......... Office of Technological Services (SAUS)
OTS.......... Office of Thrift Supervision [*Department of the Treasury*] [*Superseded Federal Home Loan Bank Board, 1989*]
OTS.......... Office of Toxic Substances [*Environmental Protection Agency*]
OTS.......... Office of Traffic Safety (SAUS)
OTS.......... Office of Transportation Security [*Department of Transportation*]
OTS.......... Office of Treaty Settlements (SAUS)
OTS.......... Officers' Tactical School [*Navy*] (NVT)
OTS.......... Officers' Training School
OTS.......... Officer Training School (SAUS)
OTS.......... Office TeleSystem (SAUS)
OTS.......... Off the Shelf
OTS.......... Ohio Carriers Tariff Service Inc., Cleveland OH [*STAC*]
OTS.......... Omega Tau Sigma [*An association*] (NTPA)
OTS.......... Omologato Turismo Sport [*Touring Sport Homologated*] [*Automobile model designation*]
OTS.......... One-man operated Ticketing System (SAUS)
OTS.......... One-Time Source (MCD)
OTS.......... On-Line Terminal System [*Computer science*] (MHDB)
OTS.......... On the Spot (VLIE)
OTS.......... Open Two Seater [*Style of automobile*]
OTS.......... Operational Test Site (AAG)
OTS.......... Operational Time Synchronization (VLIE)
OTS.......... Operational Training Squadron (MCD)
OTS.......... Operational Training System [*HAWK*]
OTS.......... Operator Telephone System (SAUS)
OTS.......... Opportunities to See [*Business term*]
OTS.......... Optical Technology Satellite
OTS.......... Optical Tracking Satellite [*NASA*] (IAA)
OTS.......... Optical Tracking System (SAUS)
OTS.......... Optical Transport Systems (IEEE)
OTS.......... Orbital Technical Satellite (SAUS)
OTS.......... Orbital Technology Satellite (SAUS)
OTS.......... Orbital Test Satellite [*Communications satellite*] [*European Space Agency*]
OTS.......... Orbital Transport Systems (MCD)
OTS.......... Orbiter Test Conductor (SAUS)
OTS.......... Organization for Tropical Studies (EA)
OTS.......... Organized Track Structure (SAUS)
OTS.......... Organized Track System [*Aviation*]
OTS.......... Orotracheal Suction [*Medicine*] (DAVI)
OTS.......... Ortho-Toluenesulfonamide [*Used in manufacture of saccharin*]
OTS.......... Other-than-Serious Violation (LDOE)
OTS.......... O-Toluenesulfonamide (SAUS)
OTS.......... Out-of-house Time Sharing (SAUS)
OTS.......... Out of Service (PIPO)
OTS.......... Outside Temperature Sensor [*Automotive engineering*]
OTS.......... Overlap Technician Supervisor (SAA)
OTS.......... Overlap Telling and Surveillance (SAA)
OTS.......... Overseas Telecommunications Services (SAUS)
OTS.......... Overseas Telephone Services (DAS)
OTS.......... Over-the-Shoulder [*Cinematography*]
OTS.......... Over-the-Side [*Navy*] (CAAL)
OTS.......... Ovionic Threshold Switch (SAUS)
OTS.......... Ovonic Threshold Switch
OTS.......... Own Time Switch [*Connection or call*] [*Telecommunications*] (TEL)
OTS.......... Oxford Text System (NITA)
OTS.......... Oxygen Test Stand (KSC)
OTS.......... Statistics Canada [*Statistique Canada*] Toronto, Ontario [*Library symbol*] [*National Library of Canada*] (NLC)
OTSA........ Ocean Systems Technician, Seaman Apprentice [*Navy rating*] (DNAB)
OTSA........ Orthodox Theological Society in America (EA)
OTSA........ Salvation Army, Toronto, Ontario [*Library symbol*] [*National Library of Canada*] (NLC)
OTSAA....... Officer Training School Alumni Association (EA)
OTSAC....... Sanco Consultants Ltd., Toronto, Ontario [*Library symbol*] [*National Library of Canada*] (NLC)
OTS-AES.... Optical Technology Satellite - Apollo Extension System (DNAB)
OTSAP....... Spar Aerospace Products, Toronto, Ontario [*Library symbol*] [*National Library of Canada*] (NLC)
OTSC........ Officials Treaty Strategy Committee (SAUS)
O/TSC....... Other than Special Consultants [*Military*]
OTSC........ Seneca College, Willowdale, Ontario [*Library symbol*] [*National Library of Canada*] (NLC)
OTSCC....... Scarborough College, Ontario [*Library symbol*] [*National Library of Canada*] (NLC)
OTSCI....... Sulzer Canada, Inc., Toronto, Ontario [*Library symbol*] [*National Library of Canada*] (NLC)
OTSCL....... Shell Canada Ltd., Toronto, Ontario [*Library symbol*] [*National Library of Canada*] (NLC)
OTSCLT...... Library Techniques, Seneca College of Applied Arts and Technology, Willowdale, Ontario [*Library symbol*] [*National Library of Canada*] (NLC)
OTSD........ Operational Test Supportability Demonstration
OTSDG...... Outstanding (SAUS)

OTSE .... Toronto Stock Exchange Library, Ontario [*Library symbol*] [*National Library of Canada*] (BIB)
OTS/ECS .... Orbital Test Satellite/European Communications Satellite (SAUS)
OTSED....... Scarborough Borough Board of Education, Toronto, Ontario [*Library symbol*] [*National Library of Canada*] (NLC)
OTSF .... Open Telephony Server Forum [*Computer science*] (VLIE)
OTSG .... Office of the Surgeon General [*Public Health Service*]
OTSG .... Once-Through Steam Generator [*Nuclear energy*]
OTSGS ...... Once-Through Steam Generating System [*Nuclear energy*] (IEEE)
OTSI .... Over-The-Shoulder Inspection (SAUS)
OTSLI........ Sun Life of Canada, Toronto, Ontario [*Library symbol*] [*National Library of Canada*] (NLC)
OTSM........ St. Michael's Hospital, Toronto, Ontario [*Library symbol*] [*National Library of Canada*] (NLC)
OTSMC...... Sunnybrook Medical Centre, Toronto, Ontario [*Library symbol*] [*National Library of Canada*] (NLC)
OTSMG...... St. Mary's General Hospital, Timmins, Ontario [*Library symbol*] [*National Library of Canada*] (NLC)
OTSML ...... Selco Mining Corp., Toronto, Ontario [*Library symbol*] [*National Library of Canada*] (NLC)
OTS MTS ... OTS Milestone Tracking System (SAUS)
OTSN .... Ocean Systems Technician, Seaman [*Navy rating*] (DNAB)
OTSO .... Office of Telecommunications Systems Operations [*Social Security Administration*]
OTSOA ...... Overseas Telegraph Superintending Officers' Association [*A union*] [*British*]
OTSOG ...... On the Shoulders of Giants [*Literature*]
OTSP .... Office of Technology Support Programs [*Washington, DC*] [*Department of Energy*] (GRD)
OTSP .... Office of Transportation Systems and Planning [*Battelle Memorial Institut e*] [*Department of Energy*] [*Also, an information service or system*] (IID)
OTSP .... Scarborough Public Library, Ontario [*Library symbol*] [*National Library of Canada*] (NLC)
OTSPA....... Albert Campbell Branch, Scarborough Public Library, Ontario [*Library symbol*] [*National Library of Canada*] (NLC)
OTSPC....... Cedarbrae Branch, Scarborough Public Library, Ontario [*Library symbol*] [*National Library of Canada*] (NLC)
OTS-PST.... Orbiting Transition State-Phase Space Theory [*Physical chemistry*]
OTSQ .... Offer Teacher-Student Questionnaire [*Personality development test*] [*Psychology*]
OTSR .... Once-Through Superheat Reactor [*Nuclear energy*]
OTSR .... Optics Technology for Stand-Off Reconnaissance (ACAE)
OTSR .... Optimum Track Ship Routing [*Navy*] (NVT)
OTSS .... Office of Technical and Special Services [*Office of Field Operations*] [*Department of Labor*]
OTSS .... Off-the-Shelf System [*Bell System*]
OTSS .... Omologato Turismo Super Sport [*Touring Super Sport Homologated*] [*Automobile model designation*]
OTSS .... Ontario Regional Library, Secretary of State Canada [*Bibliotheque Regionale de l'Ontario, Secretariat d'Etat*], Toronto, Ontario [*Library symbol*] [*National Library of Canada*] (NLC)
OTSS .... Open Systems Transport and Session Support [*Computer science*] (VLIE)
OTSS .... Open Transport and Session Support (NITA)
OTSS .... Operational Telecommunications Switching System (SAUS)
OTSS .... Operational Test Support System
OTSS .... Optical Tracking Servo
OTS SB...... Office of Technical Service, Selective Bibliographies [*US government*]
OTS SB...... Office of Technical Service, Selective Biographies (SAUS)
OTST .... Ontario Science Centre, Toronto, Ontario [*Library symbol*] [*National Library of Canada*] (NLC)
OTSTA....... St. Augustine's Seminary, Toronto, Ontario [*Library symbol*] [*National Library of Canada*] (NLC)
OTSTB....... St. Basil's Seminary [*Collection transferred to OTSTM*] Ontario [*Library symbol*] [*National Library of Canada*] (NLC)
OTSTF....... Ontario Film Institute, Ontario Science Centre Library, Don Mills, Ontario [*Library symbol*] [*National Library of Canada*] (NLC)
OTSTG....... St. George's College, Toronto, Ontario [*Library symbol*] [*National Library of Canada*] (NLC)
OTSTJ .... George Pennal Library, St. Joseph's Health Centre, Toronto, Ontario [*Library symbol*] [*National Library of Canada*] (BIB)
OTSTM ...... University of Saint Michael's College, Toronto, Ontario [*Library symbol*] [*National Library of Canada*] (NLC)
OTSU .... Open Technology Support Unit (HEAS)
OTSZH....... Other than Steel or Zinc Heads [*Freight*]
OTT .... Nottingham, MD [*Location identifier*] [*FAA*] (FAAL)
OTT .... Ocean Transport and Trading [*British*]
OTT .... Oesophageal Transit Test (ODA)
OTT .... Office of Technology Transfer [*University of Illinois*]
OTT .... Office of Traffic and Transportation (SAUS)
OTT .... Office of Transportation Technologies
OTT .... One Terminal per Task (SAUS)
OTT .... One-Time Tape
OTT .... Operational Training Test (NVT)
OTT .... Operations Team Trainer (SAUS)
OTT .... Operator Tactics Trainer [*Patriot air defense system*] (MCD)
OTT .... Optional Team Targeting (MCD)
OTT .... Oral Trade Tests [*Department of Labor*]
OTT .... Orotracheal Tube [*Medicine*] (DAVI)
OTT .... Ottava [*Octave*] [*Music*]
OTT .... Ottawa [*Ontario*] [*Seismograph station code, US Geological Survey*] (SEIS)
OTT .... Ottery Saint Mary [*Urban district in England*]
Ott .... Ottoman (DIAR)
Ott .... Otto's United States Supreme Court Reports [*91-107 United States*] [*A publication*] (DLA)
OTT .... Ottumwa Terminal Railroad [*Federal Railroad Administration identification code*]
OTT .... Outgoing Teletype
OTT .... Outgoing Trunk Terminal [*Telecommunications*] (IAA)
OTT .... Outlet Tank Temperature [*Automotive engineering*]
OTT .... Outside Trim Template (MSA)
OTT .... Overall Treatment Time [*Medicine*] (RAWO)
OTT .... Over the Top [*British*] [*Slang*]
OTT .... Over-the-Top [*Marshall-MacIntosh knee operation*]
OTT .... Over the Transom (ADWA)
OTT .... Oxygen Tolerance Test
OTT .... Teledyne CAE Engineering Library, Toledo, OH [*Library symbol*] [*Library of Congress*] (LCLS)
OTT .... Toronto Transit Commission, Ontario [*Library symbol*] [*National Library of Canada*] (NLC)
OTT .... University of Ottawa Library [*UTLAS symbol*]
OTT&E....... Operational Test Training & Evaluation (SAUS)
OTTAW ...... Ottawa-Walkley Road, ON [*American Association of Railroads railroad junction routing code*]
OttawFn..... Ottawa Financial Corp. [*Associated Press*] (SAG)
OTTB .... Optically-Thin Thermal Bremsstrahlung [*Astrophysics*]
OTTB .... Owner to Take Back (SAUS)
OTTC .... University of Trinity College, Toronto, Ontario [*Library symbol*] [*National Library of Canada*] (NLC)
OTTCA....... University of Trinity College Archives, Toronto, Ontario [*Library symbol*] [*National Library of Canada*] (NLC)
OTTDB....... Toronto-Dominion Bank, Toronto, Ontario [*Library symbol*] [*National Library of Canada*] (NLC)
OTTE......... Operational Testing, Training, and Evaluation
OTTE......... Otterbacher Manufacturing [*NCIC trailer make code*]
OTTEC....... Toronto Teachers' College, Ontario [*Library symbol*] [*National Library of Canada*] (NLC)
OTTER....... Operational Training, Test, and Evaluation RADAR
OTTER....... Oregon Transect Ecosystem Research (SAUS)
OTTER....... Organized Techniques for Theorem-Proving and Effective Research (RALS)
OTTEX....... Texaco Canada, Inc., Don Mills, Ontario [*Library symbol*] [*National Library of Canada*] (NLC)
OTTFC....... Official Tim Topper Fan Club [*Defunct*] (EA)
OTTH .... On the Third Hand (ADWA)
OTTI .... Ontario Ministry of Industry and Trade, Toronto, Ontario [*Library symbol*] [*National Library of Canada*] (NLC)
OTTLE....... Optically Transparent Thin-Layer Electrode
OTTO .... Olympic Technology Trailer Operations
OTTO .... Once Through, Then Out [*Fuel management system*]
OTTO .... Optical-to-Optical (IAA)
Otto .... Otto's United States Supreme Court Reports [*91-107 United States*] [*A publication*] (DLA)
OTTOA....... Ontario Region, Canadian Air Transportation Administration, Transport Canada [*Region de l'Ontario, Administration Canadienne des Transports Aeriens, Transports Canada*] Toronto, Ontario [*Library symbol*] [*National Library of Canada*] (NLC)
OTTOMH.... Off the Top of My Head (VLIE)
OTTR .... Otter Tail Power [*NASDAQ symbol*] (TTSB)
OTTR .... Otter Tail Power Co. [*NASDAQ symbol*] (NQ)
OTTR .... Thomson, Rogers, Barristers & Solicitors, Toronto, Ontario [*Library symbol*] [*National Library of Canada*] (NLC)
OTTRAC..... Travelers Canada, Toronto, Ontario [*Library symbol*] [*National Library of Canada*] (BIB)
OTTRC....... Thistletown Regional Centre for Children and Adolescents, Rexdale, Ontario [*Library symbol*] [*National Library of Canada*] (NLC)
OTTRC....... Touche Ross & Co., Toronto, Ontario [*Library symbol*] [*National Library of Canada*] (NLC)
OttrTP .... Otter Tail Power Co. [*Associated Press*] (SAG)
OTTS .... Operations Training and Technical Services [*Nuclear Regulatory Commission*] (NRCH)
OTTS .... Organisation of Teachers of Transport Studies [*British*]
OTTS .... Outgoing Trunk Testing System [*Telecommunications*] (TEL)
OTTST....... Toronto School of Theology, Toronto, Ontario [*Library symbol*] [*National Library of Canada*] (NLC)
OTTSU....... Open Tech Training Support Unit (AIE)
Ott's US Sup Ct R... Otto's United States Supreme Court Reports [*91-107 United States*] [*A publication*] (DLA)
OTTT......... Tory, Tory, DesLauriers & Binnington, Toronto, Ontario [*Library symbol*] [*National Library of Canada*] (BIB)
OTTUM...... Ottumwa, IA [*American Association of Railroads railroad junction routing code*]
OTTW........ Optical Telescope Technology Workshop [*NASA*] (PDAA)
OTTWA...... Ottawa, IL [*American Association of Railroads railroad junction routing code*]
OTTWH...... Health Sciences Library, Toronto Western Hospital, Ontario [*Library symbol*] [*National Library of Canada*] (NLC)
OTU.......... Odometer Transducer Unit (SAUS)
OTU.......... Office of Technology Utilization [*NASA*]
OTU.......... Officers' Training Unit [*Air Force*] [*British*]
OTU.......... Ogden Test Unit (SAA)
OTU.......... Olfactory Tubercle (STED)
OTU.......... One-Time Use
OTU.......... Operating Time Update
OTU.......... Operational Taxonometric Unit (SAUS)
OTU.......... Operational Taxonomic Unit [*Numerical taxonomy*]
OTU.......... Operational Test Unit (KSC)
OTU.......... Operational Training Unit [*Military*]

OTU.......... Opetus-ja Tutkimusalan Unioni [*Teaching and Research Employees Union*] [*Finalnd*] (EY)
OTU.......... Organization Turnover (SAUS)
OTU.......... Orthopedic Transcription Unit
OTU.......... Otu [*Colombia*] [*Airport symbol*] (OAG)
OTU.......... Output Terminal Unit (SSD)
OTU.......... Oxygen Toxicity Unit (SAUS)
OTU.......... University of Toledo, Toledo, OH [*Library symbol*] [*Library of Congress*] (LCLS)
OTUA........ Institute for Aerospace Studies, University of Toronto, Ontario [*Library symbol*] [*National Library of Canada*] (NLC)
OTUAN...... Department of Anatomy, University of Toronto, Ontario [*Library symbol*] [*National Library of Canada*] (NLC)
OTUAP...... Department of Applied Physics, University of Toronto, Ontario [*Library symbol*] [*National Library of Canada*] (NLC)
OTUAR...... University of Toronto Archives, Ontario [*Library symbol*] [*National Library of Canada*] (NLC)
OTUAV....... Audio-Visual Library, University of Toronto, Ontario [*Library symbol*] [*National Library of Canada*] (NLC)
OTUB........ Department of Biochemistry, University of Toronto, Ontario [*Library symbol*] [*National Library of Canada*] (NLC)
OTUBP...... Banting-Best Physiology Library, University of Toronto, Ontario [*Library symbol*] [*National Library of Canada*] (NLC)
OTUC........ Department of Chemistry, University of Toronto, Ontario [*Library symbol*] [*National Library of Canada*] (NLC)
OTUCC...... Institute of Computer Science, University of Toronto, Ontario [*Library symbol*] [*National Library of Canada*] (NLC)
OTUCE....... Department of Chemical Engineering and Applied Chemistry, University of Toronto,Ontario [*Library symbol*] [*National Library of Canada*] (NLC)
OTUCI........ Department of Civil Engineering, University of Toronto, Ontario [*Library symbol*] [*National Library of Canada*] (NLC)
OTUCR...... Centre of Criminology, University of Toronto, Ontario [*Library symbol*] [*National Library of Canada*] (NLC)
OTUCS...... Institute of Child Study, University of Toronto, Ontario [*Library symbol*] [*National Library of Canada*] (NLC)
OTUD........ David Dunlap Observatory, University of Toronto, Ontario [*Library symbol*] [*National Library of Canada*] (NLC)
OTUDB....... Department of Botany, University of Toronto, Ontario [*Library symbol*] [*National Library of Canada*] (NLC)
OTUDM...... Department of Mathematics, University of Toronto, Ontario [*Library symbol*] [*National Library of Canada*] (NLC)
OTUDP...... Clarke Institute of Psychiatry, University of Toronto, Ontario [*Library symbol*] [*National Library of Canada*] (NLC)
OTUE........ Engineering Library, University of Toronto, Ontario [*Library symbol*] [*National Library of Canada*] (NLC)
OTUEE....... Department of Electrical Engineering, University of Toronto, Ontario [*Library symbol*] [*National Library of Canada*] (NLC)
OTUFA....... Department of Fine Art, University of Toronto, Ontario [*Library symbol*] [*National Library of Canada*] (NLC)
OTUFD...... Faculty of Dentistry, University of Toronto, Ontario [*Library symbol*] [*National Library of Canada*] (NLC)
OTUFM...... Faculty of Music, University of Toronto, Ontario [*Library symbol*] [*National Library of Canada*] (NLC)
OTUFP....... Faculty of Pharmacy, University of Toronto, Ontario [*Library symbol*] [*National Library of Canada*] (NLC)
OTUG........ Department of Geological Sciences, University of Toronto, Ontario [*Library symbol*] [*National Library of Canada*] (NLC)
OTUGL...... Geophysics Laboratory, University of Toronto, Ontario [*Library symbol*] [*National Library of Canada*] (NLC)
OTUH........ Operational Training Unit, Helicopter (SAUS)
OTUH........ Science and Medicine Library, University of Toronto, Ontario [*Library symbol*] [*National Library of Canada*] (NLC)
OTUHO...... Occupational & Environment Health Unit, Science and Medicine Library, Universityof Toronto, Ontario [*Library symbol*] [*National Library of Canada*] (NLC)
OTUINC..... Innis College, University of Toronto, Ontario [*Library symbol*] [*National Library of Canada*] (NLC)
OTUIRN..... [*The*] Jean and Dorothy Newman Industrial Relations Library, Center for Industrial Relations, University of Toronto, Ontario [*Library symbol*] [*National Library of Canada*] (NLC)
OTUL........ Faculty of Law, University of Toronto, Ontario [*Library symbol*] [*National Library of Canada*] (NLC)
OTU-L....... University of Toledo, Law Library, Toledo, OH [*Library symbol*] [*Library of Congress*] (LCLS)
OTULAS..... UTLAS [*University of Toronto Library Automation System*] International Canada, Toronto, Ontario [*Library symbol*] [*National Library of Canada*] (NLC)
OTULS....... Faculty of Library Science, University of Toronto, Ontario [*Library symbol*] [*National Library of Canada*] (NLC)
OTUM....... Department of Mechanical Engineering, University of Toronto, Ontario [*Library symbol*] [*National Library of Canada*] (NLC)
OTUM....... Ottumwa Connecting Railroad [*Federal Railroad Administration identification code*]
OTUMA....... Map Library, University of Toronto, Ontario [*Library symbol*] [*National Library of Canada*] (NLC)
OTUME...... Department of Metallurgical Engineering, University of Toronto, Ontario [*Library symbol*] [*National Library of Canada*] (NLC)
OTUMI....... Department of Mining Engineering, University of Toronto, Ontario [*Library symbol*] [*National Library of Canada*] (NLC)
OTUMS...... Faculty of Management Studies, University of Toronto, Ontario [*Library symbol*] [*National Library of Canada*] (NLC)
OTUN........ Faculty of Nursing, University of Toronto, Ontario [*Library symbol*] [*National Library of Canada*] (NLC)
OTUNC...... Union Carbide Canada Ltd., Toronto, Ontario [*Library symbol*] [*National Library of Canada*] (NLC)
OTUNWC.... New College, University of Toronto, Ontario [*Library symbol*] [*National Library of Canada*] (NLC)
OTUP........ Department of Physics, University of Toronto, Ontario [*Library symbol*] [*National Library of Canada*] (NLC)
OTUPA....... Department of Pathology, Banting-Best Institute, University of Toronto, Ontario [*Library symbol*] [*National Library of Canada*] (NLC)
OTUPG...... Information Centre, Programme in Gerontology, University of Toronto, Ontario [*Library symbol*] [*National Library of Canada*] (NLC)
O Turk....... Old Turkish (SAUS)
OTUS........ Office of the Treasurer of the United States
OTUSA...... School of Architecture, University of Toronto, Ontario [*Library symbol*] [*National Library of Canada*] (NLC)
OTUSP...... School of Physical and Health Education (Women), University of Toronto, Ontario [*Library symbol*] [*National Library of Canada*] (NLC)
OTUSW...... School of Social Work, University of Toronto, Ontario [*Library symbol*] [*National Library of Canada*] (NLC)
OTUTD...... Urban Transportation Development Corp., Toronto, Ontario [*Library symbol*] [*National Library of Canada*] (NLC)
OTUTF....... Thomas Fisher Rare Book Library, University of Toronto, Ontario [*Library symbol*] [*National Library of Canada*] (NLC)
OTUTP....... University of Toronto Press, Ontario [*Library symbol*] [*National Library of Canada*] (NLC)
OTUUC...... University College, University of Toronto, Ontario [*Library symbol*] [*National Library of Canada*] (NLC)
OTUZ........ Department of Zoology, University of Toronto, Ontario [*Library symbol*] [*National Library of Canada*] (NLC)
OTV.......... Operational Television (KSC)
OTV.......... Operational Test Vehicle (IAA)
OTV.......... Optimum Time Varying (IAA)
OTV.......... Orbiter Transfer Vehicle [*NASA*]
OTV.......... Otavi [*South-West Africa*] [*Airport symbol*] (AD)
OTV.......... Outer Television (SAUS)
OTV.......... Victoria University, Toronto, Ontario [*Library symbol*] [*National Library of Canada*] (NLC)
OTVC........ Open Top Vapor Cleaner [*Engineering*]
OTVCT....... Outer Tube Vertical Centerline Target
OTVL........ V & L Enterprises, Downsview, Ontario [*Library symbol*] [*National Library of Canada*] (NLC)
OTVR........ Otter Tail Valley Railroad [*Federal Railroad Administration identification code*]
OTV System... Operational Television System (SAUS)
OTW.......... Off the Wall [*Slang*]
OTW.......... On the Whole (VLIE)
OTW.......... Over the Wing [*Aircraft*]
OTW.......... Owner's Tank Wagons [*Shipping*]
OTW.......... Owning the Weather [*Army*] (RDA)
OTW.......... Wycliffe College, Toronto, Ontario [*Library symbol*] [*National Library of Canada*] (NLC)
OTWA........ Ottawa Transport [*Common carrier symbol*]
OTWC........ Ontario Workmen's Compensation Board, Toronto, Ontario [*Library symbol*] [*National Library of Canada*] (NLC)
OTWCA...... Ontario Workers' Compensation Appeals Tribunal, Toronto, Ontario [*Library symbol*] [*National Library of Canada*] (NLC)
OTWCH...... Medical Library, Women's College Hospital, Toronto, Ontario [*Library symbol*] [*National Library of Canada*] (NLC)
OTWD........ Out-The-Window Display (SAUS)
OTWE........ Tweed Public Library, Ontario [*Library symbol*] [*National Library of Canada*] (BIB)
OTWEN...... Ontario Ministry of Northern Development and Mines, Tweed [*Library symbol*] [*National Library of Canada*] (BIB)
OTWFC...... Old Time Western Film Club (EA)
OTWG........ Operational Test Working Group (SAUS)
OTWH........ Wellesley Hospital, Toronto, Ontario [*Library symbol*] [*National Library of Canada*] (NLC)
OTWL........ William Lyon Mackenzie Collegiate Institute, Downsview, Ontario [*Library symbol*] [*National Library of Canada*] (NLC)
OTWLC...... Warner-Lambert Canada Ltd., Scarborough, Ontario [*Library symbol*] [*National Library of Canada*] (NLC)
OTWM....... William M. Mercer Ltd., Toronto, Ontario [*Library symbol*] [*National Library of Canada*] (NLC)
OTWR........ Oblique Tape Wound Refrasil
OTWRC...... Weston Research Centre, Toronto, Ontario [*Library symbol*] [*National Library of Canada*] (NLC)
OTWY........ Medical Library, Wyeth Ltd., Downsview, Ontario [*Library symbol*] [*National Library of Canada*] (BIB)
OTX.......... Oiltex International Ltd. [*Toronto Stock Exchange symbol*]
OTXRA...... X-Ray Assay Laboratories Ltd., Don Mills, Ontario [*Library symbol*] [*National Library of Canada*] (NLC)
OTY.......... Organization Type (SAUS)
OTY.......... Oria [*Papua New Guinea*] [*Airport symbol*] [*Obsolete*] (OAG)
OTY.......... York University, Toronto, Ontario [*Library symbol*] [*National Library of Canada*] (NLC)
OTYA........ York University Archives, Toronto, Ontario [*Library symbol*] [*National Library of Canada*] (NLC)
OTYBE....... Professional Library, Board of Education for the City of York, Toronto, Ontario [*Library symbol*] [*National Library of Canada*] (NLC)
OTYBE....... York Borough Board of Education, Toronto, Ontario [*Library symbol*] [*National Library of Canada*] (NLC)
OTYBES..... Schools, Board of Education for the City of York, Toronto, Ontario [*Library symbol*] [*National Library of Canada*] (NLC)
OTYF........ Hospital Library, York-Finch General Hospital, Downsview, Ontario [*Library symbol*] [*National Library of Canada*] (BIB)
OTYL........ Law Library, York University, Toronto, Ontario [*Library symbol*] [*National Library of Canada*] (NLC)
OTYLR....... Listening Room, York University, Toronto, Ontario [*Library symbol*] [*National Library of Canada*] (NLC)
OTYP........ City of York Public Library, Toronto, Ontario [*Library symbol*] [*National Library of Canada*] (NLC)

OTZ.......... Kotzebue [*Alaska*] [*Airport symbol*] (OAG)
OTZ.......... Ortiz [*New Mexico*] [*Seismograph station code, US Geological Survey*] (SEIS)
OTZ.......... Oxothiazolidine [*Biochemistry*]
ou.......... Both Eyes [*Therapy term*] (CTAA)
OU.......... Both Eyes Together [*Medicine*] (EDAA)
OU.......... City Express [*ICAO designator*] (AD)
OU.......... Each Eye [*Medicine*] (EDAA)
OU.......... Oat Unit (SAUS)
OU.......... Object Unit (NITA)
OU.......... Observation Unit
OU.......... Observation Unknown (SAUS)
OU.......... Oculi Unitas [*Both Eyes Together*] [*Ophthalmology*]
OU.......... Oculus Uterque [*Each Eye*] [*Ophthalmology*]
OU.......... Odense University (SAUS)
OU.......... Odor Unit [*Air pollution*]
OU.......... Official Use (WDAA)
OU.......... Oglethorpe University (SAUS)
OU.......... Ohio State University, Columbus, OH [*Library symbol*] [*Library of Congress*] (LCLS)
OU.......... Ohio University [*Athens*]
OU.......... Okayama University (SAUS)
OU.......... Oklahoma University
OU.......... Open University [*British*]
OU.......... Operable Unit (BCP)
OU.......... Operation Unit
OU.......... Oppenheim-Urbach [*Disease*] [*Medicine*] (DB)
OU.......... Opposition Unie [*United Opposition*] [*The Comoros*] [*Political party*] (EY)
OU.......... Organizational Unit (MWOL)
OU.......... Osaka University (SAUS)
OU.......... Otago University (SAUS)
OU.......... Otonabee Airways [*ICAO designator*] (AD)
OU.......... Ottawa University (SAUS)
OU.......... Otterbein University (SAUS)
ou.......... Ounce [*Unit of weight*] (CDAI)
OU.......... Our [*Telegraphy*] (PCTE)
OU.......... Outlook Unusual (VLIE)
OU.......... Output Unit [*Computer science*] (IAA)
O/U.......... Over and Under (GOBB)
OU.......... Owen University (SAUS)
OU.......... Owosso University (SAUS)
OU.......... Oxford University [*England*]
OU.......... University of Oklahoma (SAUS)
OU.......... University of Oklahoma, Norman [*USA*] [*Marine science*] (OSRA)
OUA.......... Office of University Affairs [*NASA*]
OUA.......... Order of United Americans (NADA)
OUA.......... Organisation de l'Unite Africaine [*Organization of African Unity - OAU*] (EAIO)
OUA.......... Ouagadougou [*Burkina Faso*] [*Airport symbol*] (OAG)
OUA.......... Ouanaham [*Loyalty Islands*] [*Seismograph station code, US Geological Survey*] (SEIS)
OUa.......... Upper Arlington Public Library, Upper Arlington, OH [*Library symbol*] [*Library of Congress*] (LCLS)
OUAA.......... Ontario Universities Athletic Association (SAUS)
OUAC.......... Ontario University Application Center (SAUS)
OUAC.......... Oxford University Appointments Committee (SAUS)
OUADP.......... Operational Utility of ADP (SAUS)
OUAM.......... Order of United American Mechanics
OUAS.......... Oxford University Air Squadron [*British*] (DI)
OUASS.......... Omega Upper Atmospheric Sounding Systems (SAUS)
OUAT.......... Once upon a Time (The Prisoner Fan Club) (EA)
OUB.......... Glio-Oubi [*Language symbol*] (ETLW)
OUB.......... Occasional-Use Bands (SAUS)
OUBD.......... Outbound [*ICAO designator*] (FAAC)
OU-BP.......... Ohio State University, Byrd Polar Research Center, Goldthwait Polar Library, Columbus, OH [*Library symbol*] [*Library of Congress*] (LCLS)
OUBS.......... Open University Business School [*British*]
OUC.......... Ocracoke, NC [*Location identifier*] [*FAA*] (FAAL)
OUC.......... Ohio University, Chillicothe Branch Campus, Chillicothe, OH [*OCLC symbol*] (OCLC)
OUCA.......... Chemical Abstracts, Ohio State University, Columbus, OH [*Library symbol*] [*Library of Congress*] (LCLS)
OUCA.......... Ontario University Council on Admissions (SAUS)
OUCC.......... Ohio University Cartographic Center [*Research center*] (RCD)
OUCC.......... Oxford University Cricket Club (ODA)
OUCD.......... Operations Utilization and Capability Development (SAUS)
OUCH.......... Occupational-Urgent Care Health Systems, Inc. [*NASDAQ symbol*] (COMM)
OUCH.......... Off-Line Universal Command History [*Computer science*] (KSC)
OUCH.......... Organised Unitary Content Hypothesis (SAUS)
OUCH.......... Ouachita Railroad [*Federal Railroad Administration identification code*]
OUCL.......... Oxford University Computing Laboratory (SAUS)
OUCOM.......... College of Osteopathic Medicine [*Ohio University*] (MHID)
OUCTA.......... Order of United Commercial Travelers of America (EA)
OUCZ.......... Ozark Utilities [*Federal Railroad Administration identification code*]
OUD.......... AMOCO Production Co., Library, Tulsa, OK [*OCLC symbol*] (OCLC)
OUD.......... Operational Use Data
OUD.......... Oujda [*Morocco*] [*Airport symbol*] (OAG)
Oud C.......... Oudh Code [*India*] [*A publication*] (DLA)
Oudh C.......... Oudh Code [*India*] [*A publication*] (DLA)
Oudh LJ.......... Oudh Law Journal [*India*] [*A publication*] (DLA)
Oudh LR.......... Oudh Law Reports [*India*] [*A publication*] (DLA)
Oudh Rev Sel Cas... Revised Collection of Selected Cases Issued by Chief Commissioner and Financial Commissioner of Oudh [*A publication*] (DLA)
Oudh Wkly N... Oudh Weekly Notes [*India*] [*A publication*] (DLA)
Oudh WN... Oudh Weekly Notes [*India*] [*A publication*] (DLA)
OUDP.......... Officer Undergraduate Degree Program [*Army*] (AABC)
OUDS.......... Oxford University Dramatic Society [*British*] (AIE)
OUE.......... National Oceanic and Atmospheric Administration, National Severe Storms Laboratories, Norman, OK [*OCLC symbol*] (OCLC)
OUE.......... Operational Utility Evaluation
OUE.......... Orbital Uncertainty Estimate
OUE.......... Ouesso [*Congo*] [*Airport symbol*] (OAG)
OUE.......... Ouvriers Unis de l'Electricite, de la Radio, et de la Machinerie d'Amerique [*United Electrical, Radio, and Machine Workers of America - UE*]
OUEL.......... Oxford University Engineering Laboratory (SAUS)
OUEQ.......... Lucien Ouellette Cartage [*Common carrier symbol*]
OUF.......... Northwestern Oklahoma State University, Library, Alva, OK [*OCLC symbol*] (OCLC)
OUF.......... Optimum Usable (or Usual) Frequency (SAUS)
OUF.......... Optimum Usual Frequency Radio (IAA)
OUF.......... Order of Use File (MCD)
OUF.......... Oxygen Utilization Factor
OUG.......... Occam User Group (SAUS)
OUG.......... Oklahoma Children's Memorial Hospital, Library, Oklahoma City, OK [*OCLC symbol*] (OCLC)
OUG.......... On-line Users Group (SAUS)
OUG.......... Organisation de l'Unite Guineenne [*Organization of Guinean Unity*] (PD)
OUG.......... Ouahigouya [*Upper Volta*] [*Airport symbol*] (AD)
Ought.......... Oughton's Ordo Judiciorum [*Order of Judgments*] [*A publication*] (DLA)
OUG/I.......... Online Users' Group/Ireland (EAIO)
OU-H.......... Ohio State University, Health Sciences Library, Columbus, OH [*Library symbol*] [*Library of Congress*] (LCLS)
OUH.......... Oklahoma College of Osteopathic Medicine and Surgery, Library, Tulsa, OK [*OCLC symbol*] (OCLC)
OUH.......... Oudtshoorn [*South Africa*] [*Airport symbol*] (OAG)
OUHK.......... Open University of Hong Kong
OUHS.......... Oxford University Historical Society (SAUS)
OUHSC.......... Oklahoma University Health Sciences Center
OUI.......... Ban Houei Sai [*Laos*] [*Airport symbol*] (AD)
OUI.......... Office of Unemployment Insurance [*Employment and Training Administration*] [*Department of Labor*]
OUI.......... Oklahoma Osteopathic Hospital, Library, Tulsa, OK [*OCLC symbol*] (OCLC)
OUI.......... Operating under the Influence (GOBB)
OUI.......... Organisation Universitaire Interamericaine [*Inter-American Organization for Higher Education*] (EAIO)
OUI.......... Organizationally Unique Identifier (SAUS)
OUI.......... Organizational Unit Identifier (SAUS)
OUI.......... Outdoors Unlimited (EA)
OUI.......... Outer Integument [*Botany*]
OUIC.......... Operational Unit Identification Code (SAUS)
OUIL.......... Operating a Vehicle while under the Influence of Liquor [*Traffic offense charge*]
OUJ.......... Oklahoma State University, Technical Institute Library, Oklahoma City, OK [*OCLC symbol*] (OCLC)
OUK.......... Operation Upshot-Knothole [*Atomic weapons testing*]
OUK.......... Oscar Rose Junior College Library, Midwest City, OK [*OCLC symbol*] (OCLC)
OUL.......... Air Atonabee Ltd. [*Canada*] [*ICAO designator*] (FAAC)
OU-L.......... Ohio State University, College of Law, Columbus, OH [*Library symbol*] [*Library of Congress*] (LCLS)
OUL.......... Ohio University, Lancaster Branch Campus, Lancaster, OH [*OCLC symbol*] (OCLC)
OUL.......... Orbital Utility Light
OUL.......... Oulu [*Finland*] [*Airport symbol*] (OAG)
OUL.......... Oulu [*Finland*] [*Seismograph station code, US Geological Survey*] (SEIS)
OULC.......... Oxford University Lacrosse Club (SAUS)
OULCS.......... Ontario University Libraries Cooperative System (NITA)
OULQ.......... Outer Upper Left Quadrant [*Medicine*] [*Breast*] (EDAA)
Oult Ind.......... Oulton's Index to Irish Statutes [*A publication*] (DLA)
Oult Laws Ir... Oulton's Laws of Ireland [*A publication*] (DLA)
OUM.......... Oxford University Mission (SAUS)
OUM.......... Philbrook Art Center Library, Tulsa, OK [*OCLC symbol*] (OCLC)
OUMC.......... Otago University Medical Corps [*British military*] (DMA)
OUN.......... Norman, OK [*Location identifier*] [*FAA*] (FAAL)
OUN.......... Ohio University, Athens, OH [*OCLC symbol*] (OCLC)
OUN.......... Organization of Ukrainian Nationalists (CARL)
OUNPSA.......... Office of United Nations Political and Security Affairs [*Department of State*]
OUNS.......... Office of Urban Neighborhood Services [*HUD*]
OUNSAF.......... Office of the Under Secretary of the Air Force
OUNSPI.......... Ontario Universities Non Salary Price Index (SAUS)
OUO.......... Official Use Only
OUO.......... United States Army, Morris Swett Library, Fort Sill, OK [*OCLC symbol*] (OCLC)
OUP.......... Official Unionist Party [*Northern Ireland*] (PPW)
OUP.......... OFS [*Orbiter Functional Simulator*] Uplink Processor [*NASA*]
OU-P.......... Ohio State University, Pharmacy and Bacteriology Library, Columbus, OH [*Library symbol*] [*Library of Congress*] (LCLS)
OUP.......... Operative United Painters [*A union*] [*British*]
OUP.......... Operative United Plumbers [*A union*] [*British*]
OUP.......... Oxford University Press, Inc. [*New York, NY*]

OUP .... University of Portland, Portland, OR [*OCLC symbol*] (OCLC)
OUPID .... Ontario Universities Program for Instructional Development (SAUS)
OUPID .... Ontario University Program for Instructional Development (SAUS)
OUPT .... Output (AAG)
OUPV .... Operator of Uninspected Passenger Vessels [*Nautical term*] (NTA)
OUQ .... Ocean University of Qingdao (SAUS)
OUQ .... United States Army, Nye Library, Fort Sill, OK [*OCLC symbol*] (OCLC)
OUR .... Batouri [*Cameroon*] [*Airport symbol*] (OAG)
OUR .... Office of the University Registrar (SAUS)
OUR .... Office of University Research (SAUS)
OUR .... Organizacion de Unidad Revolucionaria [*Organization of Revolutionary Unity*] [*Bolivia*] [*Political party*] (PPW)
OUR .... Our Msg Date [*Telegraphy*] (PCTE)
OUR .... Oxygen Uptake Rate [*Biochemistry*]
OUR .... Oxygen Utilization Rate [*Photosynthesis*]
OUR .... United States Federal Aviation Administration, Aeronautical Center Library, Oklahoma City, OK [*OCLC symbol*] (OCLC)
OURAD ...... Our Radiogram (SAUS)
OUrC .... Urbana College, Urbana, OH [*Library symbol*] [*Library of Congress*] (LCLS)
OURD .... [*The*] Ogden Union Railway & Depot Co. [*AAR code*]
OURD .... Operated Unilateral Renovascular Disease [*Medicine*] (EDAA)
OURD Co ... Overseas Uranium Resources Development Company (SAUS)
OURI .... Oklahoma University Research Institute
Our Lady Lake U ... Our Lady of the Lake University (GAGS)
OURQ .... Outer Upper Right Quadrant [*Anatomy*]
OURS .... Open Users Recommended Solutions (SAUS)
OURS .... Orangutan Recovery Service [*Later, IUCN*]
OURS .... Organization for United Response [*Later, AFA (Adoptive Families of America)*] (PAZ)
OURT .... Order of the United Republic of Tanzania (ODA)
OURTEL ..... Our Telegram (NATG)
OURY .... Ogdensburg Bridge & Port Authority [*Federal Railroad Administration identification code*]
OUS .... Oculo Urethro Synovite (SAUS)
OUS .... Ogden Union Stockyards [*Federal Railroad Administration identification code*]
OUS .... Okayama University of Science (SAUS)
OUS .... Oklahoma Union List of Serials Project, Stillwater, OK [*OCLC symbol*] (OCLC)
OUS .... Ourinhos [*Brazil*] [*Airport symbol*] (OAG)
OUS .... Outdoor Unit Substation
O/US .... Over-Under Shotgun (SAUS)
OUS .... Overuse Syndrome [*Medicine*] (EDAA)
OUS .... Oxford Union Society (SAUS)
OUSA .... Office of the Under Secretary of the Army
OUSA .... Omni USA, Inc. [*NASDAQ symbol*] (SAG)
OUSA .... Open University Students' Association [*British*]
OUSA .... Operation USA [*An association*] (EA)
OUSA .... Organisation de l'Unite Syndicale Africaine [*Organisation of African Trade Union Unity - OATUU*] [*Accra, Ghana*] (EAIO)
OUSAF ...... Office of the Under Secretary of the Air Force
OUSAIRA ... Office of the United States Air Attache (CINC)
OUSARMA ... Office of the United States Army Attache
OUSCS ...... Office of Urban Studies and Clearinghouse Services [*HUD*]
OUSD .... Office of the Under Secretary of Defense (MCD)
OUSDA ...... Office of the Under Secretary of Defense for Acquisition
OUSD(A & T) ... Office of the Under Secretary of Defense (Acquisition and Technology) (RDA)
OUSD(P) .... Office of the Under Secretary of Defense (Policy) (MCD)
OUSDRE .... Office of the Under Secretary of Defense for Research and Engineering
OUSF .... Oxford University School of Forestry (SAUS)
OUSH .... Uxbridge-Scott Historical Society, Uxbridge, Ontario [*Library symbol*] [*National Library of Canada*] (BIB)
OUSL .... Office of the Undersecretary of Labor (SAUS)
OUSN .... Office of the Under Secretary of the Navy
OUSOFA ..... Office of the Under Secretary of the Army
OUST .... Office of Underground Storage Tanks [*Environmental Protection Agency*]
OUSW .... Office of the Under Secretary of War [*Obsolete*]
OUT .... Bousso [*Chad*] [*Airport symbol*] (AD)
OUT .... Check-Out Date (TVEL)
OUT .... Operational Utilization Test (ACAE)
OUT .... Orbiter Utilities Tray [*NASA*] (NASA)
OUT .... Organizacao Unida de Trabalhadores [*United Organization of Workers*] [*Portugal*] [*Political party*] (PPE)
OUT .... Organization for Unemployed Teachers
OUT .... Organization for Use of the Telephone (EA)
Out .... Outerbridge's State Reports [*97, 98 Pennsylvania*] [*A publication*] (DLA)
out .... Outgoing (ELAL)
OUT .... Outgoing
OUT .... Outing (ROG)
OUT .... Outlet [*Hawaii*] [*Seismograph station code, US Geological Survey*] (SEIS)
OUT .... Outlines (SAUS)
OUT .... Output (NASA)
OUT .... Outsize Cargo (COE)
OUT .... United States Federal Aviation Administration, CAMI Library, Oklahoma City, OK [*OCLC symbol*] (OCLC)
OUT .... Uxbridge Township Public Library, Uxbridge, Ontario [*Library symbol*] [*National Library of Canada*] (NLC)
OUTA .... Ontario Urban Transit Association (SAUS)
OUTA .... Ouvriers Unis des Textiles d'Amerique [*United Textile Workers of America - UTWA*]
Out Aer ...... Outdoor Aerial (SAUS)
Out Ant ...... Outdoor Antenna (SAUS)
OUTBD ...... Outboard
OUTBD ...... Outbound
OutbdM ..... Outboard Marine Corp. [*Associated Press*] (SAG)
OUTBGS ..... Outbuildings (ROG)
OutbkStk .... Outback Steakhouse, Inc. [*Associated Press*] (SAG)
OUTC .... Ordnance Unit Training Center [*Military*]
OUTC .... Outbound Cargo (SAUS)
OUTCONUS ... Outside Continental Limits of the United States [*Military*] (DNAB)
OUTD .... Outdoor Equipment [*NCIC trailer make code*]
OUTDA ...... Ontario Urban Transportation Development Agency (SAUS)
OUTG .... Outage (KSC)
OUTHO ...... Outhouse (ROG)
OUTL .... Outlet
outl .... Outline (VRA)
OUTL .... Outlook Group Corp [*NASDAQ symbol*] (SPSG)
Outlet .... Outlet Communications, Inc. [*Associated Press*] (SAG)
OUTLIM ..... Output Limiting (SAUS)
OUTLIM ..... Output Limiting Facility [*Computer science*] (MDG)
OUTLIM Facility ... Output Limiting Facility (SAUS)
OutlkGrp .... Outlook Group Corp. [*Associated Press*] (SAG)
Outlook Res Libr ... Outlook on Research Libraries (SAUS)
OUTLT .... Outlet
Out of Sync ... Out of Synchronization (SAUS)
OUTPUTM ... Output Measures for Public Libraries [*Clarion University of Pennsylvania*] [*Information service or system*] (IID)
OUTRAN .... Outlet
OUTRAN .... Output
OUTRAN .... Output Translator [*IBM Corp.*]
OUTRE ...... Outremont, MJ [*American Association of Railroads railroad junction routing code*]
OUTREG ..... Output Register (IAA)
OUTS .... Operational Unit Transportable System (MCD)
OUTS .... Output String (SAUS)
Outstdg ...... Outstanding (EBF)
OUTSTDG ... Outstanding [*Business term*]
outstg .... Outstanding [*Business term*] (MHDW)
OUTUS ...... Outside the United States
OUTWATS ... Outgoing Wide-Area Telephone Service [*Telecommunications*] (TEL)
OUTWATS ... Outward Wide Area Telephone Service (SAUS)
OUTWD ..... Outward (ROG)
OUTXLTR ... Output Translator [*IBM Corp.*] (MSA)
OUU .... University of Oklahoma, Tulsa Medical College Library, Tulsa, OK [*OCLC symbol*] (OCLC)
OUUI .... Decisions Given by the Office of the Umpire (Unemployment Insurance) Respecting Claims to Out-of-Work Donation [*England*] (DLA)
OUUIBD ..... Benefit Decisions of the British Umpire [*A publication*] (DLA)
OUUID .... Umpire Decisions, Benefit Claims [*England*] [*A publication*] (DLA)
OUUISD ..... Benefit and Donation Claims, Selected Decisions of Umpire [*England*] [*A publication*] (DLA)
OUV .... University of Science and Arts of Oklahoma Libraries, Chickasha, OK [*OCLC symbol*] (OCLC)
OUVB .... Oxford University Volunteer Battalion [*British military*] (DMA)
OUVS .... Orbiter Ultraviolet Spectrometer [*NASA*]
OUW .... Elkins, WV [*Location identifier*] [*FAA*] (FAAL)
OUW .... Western Oklahoma State College, Library, Altus, OK [*OCLC symbol*] (OCLC)
OUZ .... Zouerate [*Mauritania*] [*Airport symbol*] (OAG)
OV .... Observed Vehicle (WDAA)
OV .... Observed Velocity (SAUS)
OV .... Obvious (AAMN)
OV .... Offense Variable [*Criminal sentencing*]
OV .... Office of Volunteers [*Red Cross*]
OV .... Office Visit [*Medicine*]
OV .... Ohio Valley
OV .... Oil of Vitriol
OV .... Olivine (SAUS)
OV .... One Village [*An association*] (EAIO)
OV .... One Voice: a Magazine about Church Music [*A publication*] (APTA)
OV .... Open Valve [*Automotive fuel systems*]
OV .... Open Ventilated (MSA)
OV .... Open Visit (WDAA)
OV .... Operational Verification (SAUS)
OV .... Operation Venus (EA)
OV .... Optimum Value (SAUS)
OV .... Orange Volunteers [*Government term*] (GA)
OV .... Orbital [*or Orbiter*] Vehicle [*NASA*]
ov .... Orbiter Vehicle [*NASA*] (NAKS)
OV .... Orbiting Vehicle (ACAE)
OV .... Organic Variable (DIPS)
OV .... Organismic Variable (DIPS)
OV .... Orientation Visit (SAUS)
OV .... Orphan Voyage (EA)
OV .... Osler-Vaquez [*Disease*] [*Medicine*] (DB)
OV .... Output Voltage
OV .... Oval
OV .... Oval [*Auto racing*]
OV .... Ovalbumin [*Also, OA, OVA, OVAL*] [*Biochemistry*]
OV .... Ovarian Volume [*Gynecology*]
OV .... Ovary (ADA)

OV .... Oven [*Refers to the open space below the stage in a theater*] [*Slang*] (DSUE)
OV .... Over (AAG)
ov .... Over (VRA)
OV .... Overflow
OV .... Overruled [*Legal shorthand*] (LWAP)
OV .... Overseas National Airways (GAVI)
ov .... Overture (GROV)
OV .... Overture (ROG)
OV .... Overventilation [*Medicine*]
OV .... Overvoltage
OV .... Ovid [*Roman poet, 43BC-17AD*] [*Classical studies*] (ROG)
OV .... Ovulate [*Gynecology*] (DAVI)
OV .... Ovum [*Egg*] [*Latin*]
OV .... Owner's Vans [*Shipping*]
ov .... Oxygen Vent (NAKS)
OV .... Oxygen Vent (NASA)
OVA .... Bekily [*Madagascar*] [*Airport symbol*] (OAG)
OVA .... Office of Veterans' Affairs
OVA .... Offshore Valve Association (EA)
OVA .... Ontario Veterinary Association (SAUS)
OVA .... Operational Voltage-controlled Amplifier (SAUS)
OVA .... Optical Visual Analysis (SAUS)
OVA .... Organic Vapor Analyzer [*Chromatography*]
OVA .... Original Video Animation (SAUS)
OVA .... Ottava [*Octave*] [*Music*]
OVA .... Ovalbumin [*Also, OA, OV, OVAL*] [*Biochemistry*]
OVA .... Ovation [*Telegraphy*] (PCTE)
OVA .... Overhead Value Analysis (ADA)
OVAB .... Orbiting Vehicle Assembly Building [*Later, OVSB*]
OVAC .... Organisation Value Analysis Chart (PDAA)
OVAC .... Overseas Visual Aids Centre [*British*]
OVAE .... Office of Vocational and Adult Education [*Department of Education*] (OICC)
OVAG .... Horticultural Research Institute of Ontario Ministry of Agriculture and Food, Vineland Station, Ontario [*Library symbol*] [*National Library of Canada*] (NLC)
OVAGR .... Research Station, Agriculture Canada [*Station de Recherches, Agriculture Canada*] Vineland Station, Ontario [*Library symbol*] [*National Library of Canada*] (NLC)
Ovako Steel Tech Rep... Ovako Steel Technical Report (SAUS)
OVAL .... Object-Based Virtual Application Language (SAUS)
OVAL .... Oval [*Postal Service standard*] (OPSA)
OVAL .... Ovalbumin [*Also, OA, OV, OVA*]
OVAL .... Ovalocytes [*Laboratory science*] (DAVI)
OVAL .... Overalls [*Freight*]
OVALO .... Ovalocytosis [*Laboratory science*] (DAVI)
OVAM .... Orbital Vehicle Assembly Mode [*NASA*]
OVAMS .... Office of Vulnerability Assessment and Management Services [*Department of Commerce*]
OVAN .... Vanier Public Library, Ontario [*Library symbol*] [*National Library of Canada*] (NLC)
OVAR .... Off Vertical Axis Rotation (SAUS)
OVAS .... Offshore Vessels Availability System [*Alpha Asia Systems Pte. Ltd.*] [*Defunct*] [*Information service or system*] (CRD)
OVATE .... Okumenische Vereinigung der Akademien und Tagungzentren in Europa [*Ecumenical Association of Laity Centres and Academies in Europe - EALCAE*] [*Bad Boll, Federal Republic of Germany*] (EAIO)
OVAX .... Ovariectomized [*Gynecology*]
OVB .... Novosibirsk [*Former USSR*] [*Airport symbol*] (OAG)
OVB .... Overboard [*Telegraphy*] (PCTE)
OVB .... Overseas Visitors Bureau [*Department of Trade*] [*British*]
OVBC .... Ohio Valley Banc Corp. [*NASDAQ symbol*] (SAG)
OVBD .... Overboard (AAG)
OVC .... Occupational Violent Crime (HEAS)
OVC .... Office for Victims of Crime [*Department of Justice*]
OVC .... Ohio Valley Conference [*Collegiate sports*]
OVC .... Ontario Veterinary College
OVC .... Optimized Valence Configuration [*Air Force*]
ovc .... Other Valuable Considerations [*Commerce*] (BARN)
OVC .... Ovarian Cancer (MELL)
OVC .... Overcast
OVC .... Oxidizer Vent Control
OVC .... Valley East Public Library, Val Caron, Ontario [*Library symbol*] [*National Library of Canada*] (NLC)
OVCA .... Ovarian Carcinoma [*Oncology*]
OVCO .... Operational Voice Communication Office [*NASA*] (MCD)
ovco .... Operational Voice Communication Office [*NASA*] (NAKS)
OVCP .... Orbiting Vehicle Checkout Procedure
OVCQ .... Overland Transportation System [*Common carrier symbol*]
OVCS .... Operational Voice Communication Subsystem
OVCSEL .... Organic Vertical-Cavity Surface-Emitting LASER [*Materials science*]
OVCST .... Overcast (AFM)
OVCT .... Caldwell Township Public Library, Verner, Ontario [*Library symbol*] [*National Library of Canada*] (NLC)
OVCU .... Overseas Containers [*Intermodal shipping container symbol*] (TVRC)
OVD .... Occlusal Vertical Dimension [*Dentistry*]
OVD .... Occlusive Vascular Disease [*Medicine*] (EDAA)
OV/D .... Operational Verification/Demonstration
OVD .... Optically Variable Device
OVD .... Optical Video Disk
OVD .... Optimum Velocity Distribution (SAUS)
OVD .... Outer Vapor Phase Deposition [*Coating technology*]
OVD .... Outside Vapor Deposition [*Coating technology*]
OVD .... Overdue (ACAE)
OVD .... Oviedo [*Spain*] [*Airport symbol*] (OAG)
OVDED .... Overdeduction
OVDF .... Official Visitors to Departmental Facilities [*New South Wales, Australia*]
OvDF .... Ovarian Dysfunction [*Medicine*] (EDAA)
OVDP .... Outside Vapor-Deposition Process (SAUS)
OVDR .... Observed Vertical Detection Range
OVE .... Ohio Valley Electric Railroad
OVE .... On Vehicle Equipment
OVE .... Optimum Value Engineered (Home)
OVE .... Orator Verbis Electric (IAA)
OVE .... Oroville, CA [*Location identifier*] [*FAA*] (FAAL)
OVE .... Overton [*Nevada*] [*Seismograph station code, US Geological Survey*] [*Closed*] (SEIS)
OVE .... Owen Vapor Engine
OVEA .... Overland Western International [*Common carrier symbol*]
OVEATP .... Ohio Vocational Education Achievement Test Program (EDAC)
OVEC .... Ohio Valley Electric Corporation (SAUS)
OVEL .... Overland [*NCIC truck make code*]
OVEL .... Overland Manufacturing Company [*NCIC trailer make code*]
OVEN .... Italian Oven [*NASDAQ symbol*] (TTSB)
OVEN .... [*The*] Italian Oven, Inc. [*NASDAQ symbol*] (SAG)
OVER .... Optimum Vehicle for Effective Reconnaissance [*Air Force*] (PDAA)
OVER .... Overland [*NCIC car make code*]
OVER .... Oversize (SAUS)
OVER .... Oversize Cargo (COE)
Over .... Overtone [*Record label*]
Over .... Overton's Tennessee Supreme Court Reports [*1791-1816*] [*A publication*] (DLA)
Overl .... Overland [*A publication*]
OVERMATION... Over-Instrumentation (SAUS)
OVERPASS... Overpass [*Commonly used*] (OPSA)
Overr .... Overruled In [*or Overruling*] [*Legal term*] (DLA)
OVERS .... Orbital Vehicle Reentry Simulator [*NASA*]
OVERS .... Overplus (DGA)
Overs .... Overshoes (SAUS)
Overseas Devt Nat Resourc Inst Newsl... Overseas Development Natural Resources Institute Newsletter (SAUS)
Overseas Trade Stat... Overseas Trade Statistics (SAUS)
Overt .... Overton's Tennessee Supreme Court Reports [*1791-1816*] [*A publication*] (DLA)
Overt Pr .... Overton's Iowa and Wisconsin Practice [*A publication*] (DLA)
OVF .... Overfill (NASA)
OVF .... Overflow [*Computer science*]
OVF .... Overhead Fire (SAUS)
OVF .... Overvoltage Factor (IAA)
OVF .... Oxygen Vent Fill
OVF Bit .... Overflow Bit (SAUS)
OVFF .... Orbital Valence Force Field (SAUS)
OVFL .... Overflow (AAG)
ovflo .... Overflow (HGAA)
OVG .... Oberverwaltungsgericht [*Provincial Administrative Court of Appeal*] [*German*] (DLA)
OVG .... Office of the Valuer-General [*Northern Territory, Australia*]
OvGI .... TIGR [*The Institute of Genomic Research*] Onchocerca volvulus Gene Index [*Database*] (GDD)
OVGWU .... Orange Vaal General Workers Union (SAUS)
OVH .... Vankleek Hill Public Library, Ontario [*Library symbol*] [*National Library of Canada*] (NLC)
OVHD .... Oval Head
OVHD .... Overhead (AAG)
OVHDLD .... Overhandled [*Freight*]
OVHD PWR CAB... Overhead Power Cable [*Nautical charts*]
OVHG .... Overhanging
OVHL .... Overhaul (AAG)
OVHT .... Overheat (NASA)
OVHT .... Tay-Victoria Harbour Union Library, Victoria Harbour, Ontario [*Library symbol*] [*National Library of Canada*] (BIB)
OVI .... Ocean Voice International [*Canada*] (EAIO)
OVI .... Office of Volunteerism Initiatives (BARN)
OVI .... Ohio Volunteer Infantry [*US Federal troops*] [*Civil War term*]
OVI .... Open Verilog International (SAUS)
OVI .... Operational Validation Inspection (MCD)
ovi .... Operational Validation Inspection (NAKS)
OVIC .... Orbiting Vehicle Integrating Contractor
OVID .... Object, View, and Interaction Design (SAUS)
OVID .... On-line Visual Display (SAUS)
OVID .... Optical Visible and near Infrared Detector (SAUS)
OVID .... Ovid Technologies [*NASDAQ symbol*] (SAG)
OvidTec .... Ovid Technoloiges [*Associated Press*] (SAG)
OVIFT .... Ohio Valley Institute of Food Technology (SAUS)
OVIR .... Office of Visas and Registrations [*Former USSR*]
OVIS .... Ohio Vocational Interest Survey [*Vocational guidance test*]
OVK .... Overkill (SAUS)
OVKOT .... On Various Kinds of Thinking (SAUS)
OVL .... Office of Volunteer Liaison [*ACTION*]
OVL .... Optically Void Liquid
OVL .... Oval [*Commonly used*] (OPSA)
OVL .... Overhead Line (SAUS)
OVL .... Overlap (IAA)
OVL .... Overlay (IAA)
OVL .... Overlay File [*Computer science*]
OVL .... Program Overlay (SAUS)

OVLA .... Oblique Vein of Left Atrium [*Medicine*] (MELL)
OVLA .... Optical Very Large Array (SAUS)
OVLAY .... Overlay
OVLBI .... Orbital Very-Long Baseline Interferometer [*Communications satellite*] [*Telecommunications*] (IEEE)
OVLD .... Overload (AAG)
ovld .... Overload (ELAL)
OVLMA ...... Orbiting Vehicle Limited Maintenance Area
OVLO .... Over-Voltage Lock-Out (CIST)
OVLP .... Overvoltage Load Protection
OVLT .... Organum Vasculosum of the Lamina Terminalis [*Medicine*]
OVM .... Congregation of the Oblates of the Virgin Mary [*Rome, Italy*] (EAIO)
OVM .... Department of Computational Mathematics, Academy of Sciences, Moscow (SAUS)
OVM .... McGarry Public Library, Virginiatown, Ontario [*Library symbol*] [*National Library of Canada*] (BIB)
OVM .... Ohio Volunteer Militia [*Ohio state militia troops*] [*Civil War term*]
OVM .... Online Vacation Mall [*Computer site*]
OVM .... On Vehicle Materiel [*Military*]
OVM .... Operator-Valued Measure (SAUS)
OVM .... Orbiting Velocity Meter
OVM .... Overwhelm [*Telegraphy*] (PCTE)
OVMD .... Overwhelmed [*Telegraphy*] (PCTE)
OVMG .... Overwhelming [*Telegraphy*] (PCTE)
OVMS .... Overwhelms [*Telegraphy*] (PCTE)
OVN .... Oxygen Ventilation Network (SAUS)
OVNGT ...... Overnight (FAAC)
ovno .... Or Very Near Offer (ODA)
OVNO .... Or Very Near Offer [*Automotive classified advertising*]
OVNT .... Overnite Transportation Company [*Common carrier symbol*]
OVNZ .... Overnite Transportation [*Intermodal trailer symbol*]
OVO .... North Vernon, IN [*Location identifier*] [*FAA*] (FAAL)
OVO .... Orbiting Volcanological Observatory (ACAE)
Ovolactos... Ovolactovegetarians (SAUS)
OVON .... OIS Optical Imaging Sys [*NASDAQ symbol*] (TTSB)
OVON .... OIS Optical Imaging Systems, Inc. [*NASDAQ symbol*] (SAG)
OVONIC ..... Ovshinsky and Electronic [*Excitation processing term formed by combining name of Stanford Ovshinsky, energy researcher, and "electronic"*]
Ovos .... Ovovegetarians (SAUS)
OVOT .... Vernon Branch, Osgoode Township Library, Ontario [*Library symbol*] [*National Library of Canada*] (NLC)
OVP .... Oesterreichische Volkspartei [*Austrian People's Party*] [*Political party*] (PPW)
OVP .... Office of the Vice-President
OVP .... Oil-Vapor Pump
OVP .... Ostvorpommern [*German license plate city code*]
OVP .... Outside Vendor Personnel
OVP .... Oval Paint
OVP .... Ovarian Vein Plasma [*Endocrinology*]
OVP .... Overplay (SAUS)
OVP .... Overseas Private Investment Corp., Washington, DC [*OCLC symbol*] (OCLC)
OVP .... Overvoltage Protection
OVPC .... Ovary Pubescence - Curly [*Botany*]
OVPD .... Overpaid (AFM)
OVPG .... Ovary Pubescence, Glandular [*Botany*]
OVPLOT ..... Over Plot (SAUS)
OVPO .... Outside Vapor Phase Oxidation [*Glass technology*]
OVPR .... Over-Voltage Protection Relay [*Electrical engineering*]
OVPRESS... Overpressurized
OVPRT .... Overprinted (SAUS)
OVPT .... Overprint (SAUS)
OVPU .... Over-Voltage Protection Unit [*Computer science*] (EECA)
OVPUS ...... Office of the Vice President of the United States (BARN)
OVPWR ..... Overpower
OVR .... Office of Vocational Rehabilitation [*Later, Vocational Rehabilitation Administration*] [*HEW*]
OVR .... Operable Vehicle Rate (SAUS)
OVR .... Orbiting Vehicle Requirements
OVR .... Oudtshoorn Volunteer Rifles [*British military*] (DMA)
OVR .... Overlay File [*Computer science*]
OVR .... Oversized Cargo [*Air Force*] (POLM)
OVR .... Overvoltage Relay
OVR .... Program Overlay (SAUS)
OVRA .... Organizzazione Vigilanza Repressione Antifascismo [*Italian Organisation for Vigilance & Repression of Anti-Fascism*] [*Political party*] (WDAA)
OVRC .... Opposing Viewpoints Resource Center [*Database*] (GDD)
OVRD .... Override (AAG)
OVRH .... Val Rita-Harty Public Library, Val Rita, Ontario [*Library symbol*] [*National Library of Canada*] (BIB)
OVRHD ...... Overhead
OVRL .... Over-Lowe Company [*NCIC trailer make code*]
OVRMP ...... Ohio Valley Regional Medical Program (SAUS)
OVRN .... Overrun (AFM)
OVRN .... Overrun Standard Approach Lighting System [*Aviation*] (DA)
OVRNG ...... Overrunning (DA)
OVRO .... Owens Valley Radio Observatory [*California Institute of Technology*] [*Research center*] (RCD)
OVRO Millimeter Array... Owens Valley Radio Observatory Millimeter Array (SAUS)
OVRP .... Organizacion de Voluntarios para la Revolucion Puertorriquena [*Organization of Volunteers for the Puerto Rican Revolution*] (PD)
OVRR .... Office of Veterans Reemployment Rights [*Department of Labor*]
OVRS .... Operational Voice Recording Subsystem
OVRSGHT... Oversight
OVRSTK ..... Overstrike (SAUS)
OVRVTG ..... Overvoltage [*Automotive engineering*]
OVRWGT .... Overweight (SAUS)
OVS .... Object-Verb-Subject (ADWA)
OVS .... Official Visitors' Scheme
OVS .... Online Version Storage [*Computer science*] (PDAA)
OVS .... Operational Voice System (MCD)
ovs .... Operational Voice System (NAKS)
OVS .... Optical Viewing System
OVS .... Orbiting Vehicle System
OVS .... Ovarian Vein Serum [*Endocrinology*]
OVS .... Overhaul Specification (NG)
OVS .... Oversize
OVS .... Overvoltage Sensing (MCD)
OVSB .... Orbiting Vehicle Support Building [*Formerly, OVAB*]
OVSC .... Office of Vehicle Safety Compliance [*Automotive safety*]
OVSEA .... Overseas [*Aviation*] (FAAC)
OvShip ...... Overseas Shipholding Group, Inc. [*Associated Press*] (SAG)
OVSL .... Overslow (SAUS)
OVSP .... Overspeed (AAG)
OVSR .... Office of Vehicle Systems Research [*Later, Safety System Laboratory*] [*National Institute of Standards and Technology*]
OVSTFD ..... Overstuffed [*Freight*]
OVT .... Occupational-Vocational-Technical Training
OVT .... Oceonics Vehicle Technology (SAUS)
OVT .... Operational Validation Test (SAUS)
OVT .... Operational Verification Test
OVT .... Optical Van Trailer
OVTK .... Overtake (FAAC)
OVTR .... Operational Video Tape Recorder [*Air Force*] (MCD)
OVTR .... Overtravel
OVTS .... On-Vehicle Test System [*Automotive engineering*]
OVTU .... Comptoir Occitant des Viandes [*Intermodal shipping container symbol*] (TVRC)
OVUIL .... Operating Vehicle under Influence of Liquor or Narcotic Drugs [*FBI standardized term*]
OVUREP ..... Overseas Unit Replacement [*System*] [*Army*]
OVUREP ..... Oversea Unit Replacement System (SAUS)
OVUREP System... Overseas Units Replacement System (SAUS)
O/V-U/V ..... Over Voltage - Under Voltage (MCD)
OVV .... Optically Violently Variable [*QUASAR*]
ovv .... Overvoltage (NAKS)
OVV .... Overvoltage
OVV .... Ovvero [*Otherwise*] [*Music*]
OVW .... Open-View Windows (SAUS)
OVWA .... On-Line Voltammetric Wastewater Analyzer [*Biochemistry*]
OVWD .... Operating Vehicle while Drunk [*Traffic offense charge*]
OVWV .... One Valley Bancorp [*NASDAQ symbol*] (TTSB)
OVWV .... One Valley Bancorp of West Virginia, Inc. [*NASDAQ symbol*] (NQ)
OVX .... Ovariectomized [*Gynecology*] (DAVI)
OVX .... Ovariectomy [*Medicine*] (MELL)
OVXO .... Oven-controlled, Voltage-controlled Crystal Oscillator (SAUS)
OW .... Obere Winkelgruppe [*Angles above 45*] [*German military - World War II*]
OW .... Observation Ward [*British*]
OW .... Ocellus Width
OW .... Offer Wanted
OW .... Office of Water [*Environmental Protection Agency*] (GFGA)
OW .... Officer's Writer [*British military*] (DMA)
OW .... Off White (SAUS)
OW .... Ohne Wert [*Without Value*] [*German*]
O/W .... Oil-dispersed-in-Water [*Emulsion*]
OW .... Oil-Immersed Water-Cooled [*Transformer*] (IEEE)
O/W .... Oil in Water
O/W .... Oil-Water [*Ratio*] [*Laboratory science*] (DAVI)
OW .... Older Worker
OW .... Old Well (SAUS)
OW .... Old Wellingtonian [*Wellington College*] [*British*]
OW .... Old Welsh [*Language, etc.*]
OW .... Old Woman [*A wife*] [*Slang*]
OW .... One Way [*Fare*]
OW .... On Which [*Telegraphy*] (PCTE)
OW .... Open Web (SAUS)
OW .... Open Wedge [*Osteotomy*] [*Orthopedics*] (DAVI)
OW .... Open Wheel [*A publication*]
OW .... Open-Window (SAUS)
OW .... Open Wire (NATG)
OW .... Open Work (SAUS)
OW .... Open Wound (SAUS)
OW .... Operand Word (SAUS)
ow .... Optical Window (NAKS)
OW .... Optical Window (NASA)
OW .... Optical World [*Medicine*] [*Journal*] [*United Kingdom*] (EDAA)
O/W .... Optional With [*Automotive engineering*]
OW .... Optional Word (SAUS)
OW .... Options for Women [*Later, Options*] (EA)
OW .... Optometric World [*Medicine*] [*Journal*] (EDAA)
OW .... Order Wire [*Military*] (AABC)
OW .... Order Writing (IAA)
OW .... Ordinary Warfare
O-W .... Ordinary Wave (MCD)

OW........ Ordinary Welfare (BABM)
OW........ Ordnance Workshop (SAUS)
OW........ Outer Wing
OW........ Out of Wedlock
OW........ Oval Window (MELL)
OW........ Over-Achieving Women
OW........ Overall Width [*of the Vehicle*] [*TII*] (TAG)
OW........ Overseas Writers (EA)
OW........ Over Water (WDAA)
OW........ Over Write (SAUS)
Ow........ Owen's English Common Pleas Reports [*A publication*] (DLA)
Ow........ Owen's English King's Bench Reports [*1556-1615*] [*A publication*] (DLA)
OW........ Owners (RIMS)
OW........ Owner's Wagons [*Shipping*]
OW........ Trans Mountain Airlines [*ICAO designator*] (AD)
OW........ Warren Public Library, Warren, OH [*Library symbol*] [*Library of Congress*] (LCLS)
OW........ Windsor Public Library, Ontario [*Library symbol*] [*National Library of Canada*] (NLC)
OWA........ Optical Wholesalers Association [*Later, OLA*] (EA)
OWA........ Oregon Winegrowers Association (EARSL)
OWA........ Organics-in-Water Analyzer [*Instrumentation*]
OWA........ Other Weird Arrangements (AMHC)
OWA........ Outlook Web Access [*Computer science*] (VLIE)
OWA........ Owase [*Japan*] [*Seismograph station code, US Geological Survey*] (SEIS)
OWA........ Owatonna, MN [*Location identifier*] [*FAA*] (FAAL)
OWA........ University of Windsor, Ontario [*Library symbol*] [*National Library of Canada*] (NLC)
OWAA........ Anderson Associates Ltd., Willowdale, Ontario [*Library symbol*] [*National Library of Canada*] (NLC)
OWAA........ Outdoor Writers Association of America (EA)
OWAAD........ Organisation of Women of Asian and African Descent [*British*] (DI)
OWAB........ Wasaga Beach Public Library, Ontario [*Library symbol*] [*National Library of Canada*] (BIB)
OWAEC........ Organization for West African Economic Co-operation
OWAG........ Art Gallery of Windsor, Ontario [*Library symbol*] [*National Library of Canada*] (NLC)
OWAIT........ Airy Township Public Library, Whitney, Ontario [*Library symbol*] [*National Library of Canada*] (NLC)
OWAL........ Law Library, University of Windsor, Ontario [*Library symbol*] [*National Library of Canada*] (NLC)
OWALK........ Walkerton Branch, Bruce County Public Library, Ontario [*Library symbol*] [*National Library of Canada*] (NLC)
OWALL........ Wallaceburg Public Library, Ontario [*Library symbol*] [*National Library of Canada*] (NLC)
OWAN........ Old World Archaeology Newsletter [*A publication*] (ABAR)
OWAP........ Overhead Warning Annunciator Panel (MCD)
OWaP........ Pike County Free Public Library, Waverly, OH [*Library symbol*] [*Library of Congress*] (LCLS)
OWAP........ Waterford Public Library, Ontario [*Library symbol*] [*National Library of Canada*] (NLC)
OWAR........ Warkworth Public Library, Ontario [*Library symbol*] [*National Library of Canada*] (NLC)
OWARNP........ Percy Township Branch, Northumberland County Public Library, Warkworth, Ontario [*Library symbol*] [*National Library of Canada*] (BIB)
OWas........ Carnegie Public Library, Washington Court House, OH [*Library symbol*] [*Library of Congress*] (LCLS)
OWASU........ Old World Archaeological Study Unit (EA)
OWAT........ Wainfleet Township Library, Ontario [*Library symbol*] [*National Library of Canada*] (NLC)
OWATO........ Owatonna, MN [*American Association of Railroads railroad junction routing code*]
OWAV........ OneWave, Inc. [*NASDAQ symbol*] (SAG)
OWAVE........ Ordinary Wave (MSA)
OWay........ Mary L. Cook Public Library, Waynesville, OH [*Library symbol*] [*Library of Congress*] (LCLS)
OWB........ Austrian Economic Association [*Political party*] (PSAP)
OWB........ Oppenheimer World Bond Fund [*NYSE symbol*] (SAG)
OWB........ Oscillating Waterbed (MELL)
OWB........ Owensboro [*Kentucky*] [*Airport symbol*] (AD)
OWB........ West Bay Public Library, Ontario [*Library symbol*] [*National Library of Canada*] (NLC)
OWBA........ Office of Women's Business Ownership (EBF)
OW Bailey Chr... Old Bailey Chronicle (SAUS)
OWBC........ Health Sciences Library, Bloorview Children's Hospital, Willowdale, Ontario [*Library symbol*] [*National Library of Canada*] (BIB)
OWBE........ Office of Women's Business Enterprise [*Federal government*]
OWBE........ Windsor Board of Education, Ontario [*Library symbol*] [*National Library of Canada*] (NLC)
OWBL........ Beaver Lake Branch, Walden Public Library, Ontario [*Library symbol*] [*National Library of Canada*] (NLC)
OWBL........ Office of Work-Based Learning [*U.S. Department of Labor*] (BARN)
OWBMS........ Manitoulin Secondary School Library, West Bay, Ontario [*Library symbol*] [*National Library of Canada*] (BIB)
OWBO........ Office of Women's Business Ownership [*Small Business Administration*]
OWBPA........ Older Workers Benefit Protection Act of 1990 (WYGK)
OWBR........ Bartlet & Richardes, Windsor, Ontario [*Library symbol*] [*National Library of Canada*] (BIB)
OWC........ Centennial Secondary School, Windsor, Ontario [*Library symbol*] [*National Library of Canada*] (NLC)
OWC........ Officers' Wives Club [*Military*]
OWC........ Oil Well Cement (SAUS)
OwC........ Omniwest Corporation, Salt Lake City, UT [*Library symbol*] [*Library of Congress*] (LCLS)
OWC........ One Way Communication (ELAL)
OWC........ Ontario Workers' Compensation Appeals Tribunal [*UTLAS symbol*]
OWC........ Order of Woodcraft Chivalry [*British*] (DBA)
OWC........ Ordinary Wave Component
OWC........ Ordnance Weapons Command [*Later, Weapons Command*]
OWC........ Outline of World Cultures [*Human Relations Area Files*] [*Information retrieval*]
OWC........ Owner Will Carry [*Banking*]
OWC........ Owning Work Center [*Military*] (AFIT)
OWC........ Wood County District Public Library, Bowling Green, OH [*OCLC symbol*] (OCLC)
OWCA........ Canadian Automobile Workers Union, Willowdale, Ontario [*Library symbol*] [*National Library of Canada*] (BIB)
OWCC........ Cape Croker Public Library, Wiarton, Ontario [*Library symbol*] [*National Library of Canada*] (NLC)
OWCF........ Canadian Federation of Independent Business, Willowdale, Ontario [*Library symbol*] [*National Library of Canada*] (BIB)
OWCL........ Octane Weekly Cost Ledger (MCD)
OWCL........ Old World Cutaneous Leishmaniasis [*Medicine*] (MELL)
OWCP........ Office of Workers' [*formerly, Workmen's*] Compensation Programs [*Formerly, Bureau of Employees' Compensation*] [*Department of Labor*]
OWCS........ Outer Wing Canted Station (MCD)
OWCSC........ Old Water Colour Society's Club (EA)
OWCZ........ Omack Wood [*Federal Railroad Administration identification code*]
OWD........ Norwood, MA [*Location identifier*] [*FAA*] (FAAL)
OWD........ Oil-in-Water Dispersion [*Pollution*]
OWD........ One-Way Doppler (MCD)
OWD........ On-Line Wholesale Distribution System [*Computer science*] (BUR)
OWD........ Owed [*Telegraphy*] (PCTE)
OWDC........ Office of Water Data Coordination [*US Geological Survey*] [*Reston, VA*]
OWDD........ Old Well Drilling Deeper (SAUS)
OWDE........ One-Way Doppler Extraction
OWDM........ Original Water Depth Mine (SAUS)
OWE........ Eagle, CO [*Location identifier*] [*FAA*] (FAAL)
OWE........ Office of Water Enforcement [*Environmental Protection Agency*] (ERG)
OWE........ Operating Weight Empty [*of space shuttle*] [*NASA*]
OWE........ Optimum Working Efficiency
OWE........ Outer Window Envelope [*Business stationery*]
OWE........ Welland Public Library, Ontario [*Library symbol*] [*National Library of Canada*] (NLC)
OWE........ Western Plains Library System, Clinton, OK [*OCLC symbol*] (OCLC)
OWe........ Westerville Public Library, Westerville, OH [*Library symbol*] [*Library of Congress*] (LCLS)
OWEB........ Webbwood Public Library, Ontario [*Library symbol*] [*National Library of Canada*] (NLC)
OWEC........ Centennial Secondary School, Welland, Ontario [*Library symbol*] [*National Library of Canada*] (NLC)
OWEGO........ Owego, NY [*American Association of Railroads railroad junction routing code*]
OWel........ Sylvester Memorial Wellston Public Library, Wellston, OH [*Library symbol*] [*Library of Congress*] (LCLS)
OWEL........ Wellington Public Library, Ontario [*Library symbol*] [*National Library of Canada*] (BIB)
OWelsh........ Old Welsh (ADWA)
O/W Emulsion... Oil/Water Emulsion (SAUS)
OWEN........ Niagara College of Applied Arts and Technology, Welland, Ontario [*Library symbol*] [*National Library of Canada*] (NLC)
OWEN........ Owen Healthcare, Inc. [*NASDAQ symbol*] (SAG)
Owen........ Owen's English King's Bench Reports [*1556-1615*] [*A publication*] (DLA)
OWEN........ Science & Engineering Library (SAUS)
Owen Bankr... Owen on Bankruptcy [*A publication*] (DLA)
OwenC........ Owens-Corning Fiberglas Corp. [*Associated Press*] (SAG)
OWENC........ Westport-North Crosby Public Library, Westport, Ontario [*Library symbol*] [*National Library of Canada*] (NLC)
OwenHlt........ Owen Healthcare, Inc. [*Associated Press*] (SAG)
OWENL........ Library Technician Program, Niagara College of Applied Arts & Technology, Welland, Ontario [*Library symbol*] [*National Library of Canada*] (NLC)
OWENS........ Owensboro, KY [*American Association of Railroads railroad junction routing code*]
OwensIll........ Owens Illinois [*Associated Press*] (SAG)
OwensM........ Owens & Minor Inc. Holding Co. [*Associated Press*] (SAG)
OWeO........ Otterbein College, Westerville, OH [*Library symbol*] [*Library of Congress*] (LCLS)
OWEP........ Office of Water Enforcement and Permits [*Environmental Protection Agency*] (GFGA)
OWEP........ Oily Waste Extraction Program (SAUS)
OWERP........ Open Window Early Retirement Plans
OWES........ Owens-Classic [*NCIC trailer make code*]
OWESBC........ Borden Chemical, Westhill, Ontario [*Library symbol*] [*National Library of Canada*] (NLC)
OWESO........ Owen Sound, ON [*American Association of Railroads railroad junction routing code*]
OWEST........ Asphodel Township Public Library, Westwood, Ontario [*Library symbol*] [*National Library of Canada*] (BIB)
OWF........ Object World Frankfurt (SAUS)
OWF........ Oceania Weightlifting Federation [*Australia*] (EA)
OWF........ One-Way Function (VLIE)
OWF........ On Weight of Fiber
OWF........ Optimal Work Function (SAUS)

OWF .... Optimum Working Facility (NITA)
OWF .... Optimum Working Frequency [*Telecommunications*]
OWF .... Orbital, Weightless Flight (IAA)
OWF .... Overwing Fairing (SAUS)
OWFEA ...... Ontario Wholesale Farm Equipment Association (SAUS)
OWFS .... Optical WORM File System (SAUS)
OWFU .... Zim Israel Navigation [*Intermodal shipping container symbol*] (TVRC)
OWG .... Oil, Water, Gas
OWG .... Open Waveguide (SAUS)
OWG .... Optical Waveguide (SAUS)
OWG .... Owing [*Telegraphy*] (PCTE)
OWG .... Washington, DC [*Location identifier*] [*FAA*] (FAAL)
OWGL .... Obscure Wire Glass
OWH .... CDCs Office of Womens Health (SAUS)
OWH .... Herman Collegiate Institute, Windsor, Ontario [*Library symbol*] [*National Library of Canada*] (NLC)
OWH .... Office of the War on Hunger (SAUS)
OWH .... Ordinary Working Hours (SAUS)
OWH .... Warren General Hospital, Warren, OH [*Library symbol*] [*Library of Congress*] (LCLS)
OWHA .... Oliver Wendell Holmes Association
OWHA .... Outerwear Hard Armor [*Police and security equipment*]
OWHD .... Medical Library, Hotel-Dieu of St. Joseph Hospital, Windsor, Ontario [*Library symbol*] [*National Library of Canada*] (NLC)
OWHM ...... Hiram Walker Historical Museum, Windsor, Ontario [*Library symbol*] [*National Library of Canada*] (BIB)
CWHM ...... Office of Water and Hazardous Materials (OICC)
OWHN ...... One Word Host Name (SAUS)
OWHP .... Whitby Public Library, Ontario [*Library symbol*] [*National Library of Canada*] (NLC)
OWHU .... Hacklin [*Intermodal shipping container symbol*] (TVRC)
OWI .... Ocellus Width Index
OWI .... Office of War Information [*World War II*]
OWI .... Office of Waste Isolation [*Department of Energy*]
OWI .... OneWorld Internet [*Global Village Communication*] [*Internet gateway service*]
OWI .... Open Work Items (KSC)
OWI .... Operating Vehicle while Intoxicated [*Traffic offense charge*]
OWI .... Operating While Intoxicated (SAUS)
OWI .... Ottawa, KS [*Location identifier*] [*FAA*] (FAAL)
OWI .... Owens-Illinois, Inc., Technical and Business Information Services, Toledo, OH [*OCLC symbol*] (OCLC)
OWI .... Wiarton Branch, Bruce County Public Library, Ontario [*Library symbol*] [*National Library of Canada*] (NLC)
OWIB .... Wikwemikong Band Public Library, Ontario [*Library symbol*] [*National Library of Canada*] (NLC)
OWibfC ...... Central State University, Wilberforce, OH [*Library symbol*] [*Library of Congress*] (LCLS)
OWibfP ...... Payne Theological Seminary, Wilberforce, OH [*Library symbol*] [*Library of Congress*] (LCLS)
OWibfU ...... Wilberforce University, Wilberforce, OH [*Library symbol*] [*Library of Congress*] (LCLS)
OWicB .... Borromeo Seminary of Ohio, Wickliffe, OH [*Library symbol*] [*Library of Congress*] (LCLS)
OWIFC .... Wolfe Island Branch, Frontenac County Public Library, Ontario [*Library symbol*] [*National Library of Canada*] (NLC)
OWIJC .... International Joint Commission [*Commission Mixte Internationale*] Windsor, Ontario [*Library symbol*] [*National Library of Canada*] (NLC)
OWil .... Willard Memorial Library, Willard, OH [*Library symbol*] [*Library of Congress*] (LCLS)
OWillo .... Willoughby-Eastlake Public Library, Willowick, OH [*Library symbol*] [*Library of Congress*] (LCLS)
OWilm .... Wilmington Public Library, Wilmington, OH [*Library symbol*] [*Library of Congress*] (LCLS)
OWilmC ..... Wilmington College, Wilmington, OH [*Library symbol*] [*Library of Congress*] (LCLS)
OWilmH ..... Clinton Memorial Hospital, Health Resource Center, Wilmington, OH [*Library symbol*] [*Library of Congress*] (LCLS)
OWilm-O .... Southwestern Ohio Rural Library, Wilmington, OH [*Library symbol*] [*Library of Congress*] (LCLS)
OWilmS ..... Southern State Community College, Wilmington, OH [*Library symbol*] [*Library of Congress*] (LCLS)
OWin .... Adams-Brown County Bookmobile, Winchester, OH [*Library symbol*] [*Library of Congress*] (LCLS)
OWIN .... Office of Work Incentive Program [*Office of Comprehensive Employment Development*] [*Department of Labor*]
OWINF ...... F. E. Madill Secondary School, Wingham, Ontario [*Library symbol*] [*National Library of Canada*] (NLC)
OWISDG .... Williamstown Branch, Stormount, Dundas, and Glengarry County Library, Ontario [*Library symbol*] [*National Library of Canada*] (NLC)
owise .... otherwise (SAUS)
OWIT .... Organization of Women in International Trade (NTPA)
OWIU .... Oil Workers International Union [*Later, OCAW*]
OWJ .... Orthodontics Web Journal (SAUS)
OWK .... Kent State University, Trumbull Regional Campus, Warren, OH [*Library symbol*] [*Library of Congress*] [*OCLC symbol*] (LCLS)
OWK .... Norridgewock, ME [*Location identifier*] [*FAA*] (FAAL)
OWKG .... William Olson Trucking [*Common carrier symbol*]
OWL .... Lowe Technical School, Windsor, Ontario [*Library symbol*] [*National Library of Canada*] (NLC)
OWL .... Maui Airlines, Inc. [*ICAO designator*] (FAAC)
OWL .... National Order of Women Legislators (EA)
OWL .... Object Windows Library [*Borland International*] [*Computer science*] (PCM)
OWL .... Ocotillo Water League (SAUS)
OWL .... Office Workstations Ltd. (NITA)
OWL .... Older Women's League (EA)
OWL .... Older Women's Liberation [*Feminist group*] [*Defunct*]
OWL .... Olympic-Wallowa Lineament [*Geology*]
OWL .... One Watt Linear (ACAE)
OWL .... On-line Without Limitation (SAUS)
OWL .... Online without Limits
OWL .... Online Writing Lab [*Purdue University*] [*Computer science*]
OWL .... Open Windows Library [*Computer science*] (VLIE)
OWL .... Optimal Waste Loading (ABAC)
OWL .... Orbiting Wide-Angle Light Collectors (SAUS)
OWL .... Order of Women Legislators (SAUS)
OWL .... Orthopaedic Web Links (SAUS)
OWL .... Other Woman Limited [*An association*]
OWL .... Outlined-White Letter (SAUS)
OWL .... Outlined White Letters [*Tire design*]
OWL .... Overland Western Limited (SAUS)
OWL .... Over Water Line (SAUS)
OWL .... Overwhelmingly Large (SAUS)
OWL .... Westerville Public Library, Westerville, OH [*OCLC symbol*] (OCLC)
OWLA .... Organization of Women for Legal Awareness (EA)
OWLaw ..... Trumbull County Law Library, Warren, OH [*Library symbol*] [*Library of Congress*] (LCLS)
OWLB .... Wunnummin Lake Band Library, Ontario [*Library symbol*] [*National Library of Canada*] (BIB)
OWLD .... OneWorld Systems [*NASDAQ symbol*]
OWL/D ..... Optical Warning Locator/Detector (MCD)
OWLEF ..... Older Women's League Educational Fund (EA)
OWIGS ..... Church Jesus Christ of Latter-Day Saints, Genealogical Society Library, Cleveland Branch, Westlake, OH [*Library symbol*] [*Library of Congress*] (LCLS)
OWIGS ..... Church of Jesus Christ of Latter-Day Saints, Genealogical Society Library, Cleveland Branch, Westlake, OH [*Library symbol*] [*Library of Congress*] (LCLS)
OWLI .... Lively Branch, Walden Public Library, Ontario [*Library symbol*] [*National Library of Canada*] (NLC)
OWLS .... Office Workers Link Shift [*After-hours production workers*] [*World War II*]
OWLS .... Operation Work Load Scheduling (MCD)
OWLS .... Outagamie-Waupaca Counties Federated Library System [*Library network*]
OWLS .... Overseas Weapons, Logistically Supported (MCD)
OWLS .... Owl Transfer and Storage Company [*Common carrier symbol*]
OWLS .... Oxford Word and Language Service [*A service of the Oxford English Dictionary group*]
OWLT .... One-Way Light Time
OWLU .... Ocean World Lines [*Common carrier symbol*]
OWM .... Office of War Mobilization [*Succeeded by OWMR, 1944*]
OWM .... Office of Weights and Measures [*National Institute of Standards and Technology*]
OWM .... Office Work Measurement (CIST)
OWM .... Optical Waveguide Microscopy (SAUS)
OWM .... Over Without Marks (SAUS)
OWMA .... Oscar Wells Museum of Art (SAUS)
OWMC .... Ontario Waste Management Corporation (SAUS)
OWML .... Occoquan Watershed Monitoring Laboratory [*Virginia Polytechnic Institute and State University*] (RCD)
OWMMD .... M. M. Dillon Ltd., Willowdale, Ontario [*Library symbol*] [*National Library of Canada*] (NLC)
OWMR ...... Office of War Mobilization and Reconversion [*Succeeded OWM, 1944; became part of Office of Temporary Controls, 1946*]
OWMR ...... Other War Materiel Requirements [*Army*]
OWMT .... Michipicoten Township Public Library, Wawa, Ontario [*Library symbol*] [*National Library of Canada*] (NLC)
OWN .... Naughton Branch, Walden Public Library, Ontario [*Library symbol*] [*National Library of Canada*] (NLC)
OWN .... Ontario Weekly Notes [*A publication*] (DLA)
OWN .... Oudh Weekly Notes [*India*] [*A publication*] (DLA)
OWN .... Overwintered Nest [*Ornithology*]
OWN .... Owen Healthcare [*NYSE symbol*] (TTSB)
OWN .... Owensboro [*Diocesan abbreviation*] [*Kentucky*] (TOCD)
OWN .... Owens Group Ltd. [*New Zealand*] [*ICAO designator*] (FAAC)
OWN .... Owen Ventures Ltd. [*Vancouver Stock Exchange symbol*]
OWN .... Owner (MCD)
OWN .... Sunterra Corp. [*NYSE symbol*] [*Formerly, Signature Resorts*]
OWN .... Wise, VA [*Location identifier*] [*FAA*] (FAAL)
OWNA .... Ownahome [*NCIC trailer make code*]
OWNR .... Owner
OWNS .... Owens Manufacturing Company [*NCIC trailer make code*]
OWO .... On Work Order [*Military*] (AFIT)
OWO .... OWI Washington Office (SAUS)
OWo .... Wayne County Public Library, Wooster, OH [*Library symbol*] [*Library of Congress*] (LCLS)
OWO .... Woodstock Public Library, Ontario [*Library symbol*] [*National Library of Canada*] (NLC)
OWoA .... Ohio Agricultural Research and Development Center, Wooster, OH [*Library symbol*] [*Library of Congress*] (LCLS)
OWOBC ..... J. William Horsey Library, Ontario Bible College, Ontario Theological College, Willowdale, Ontario [*Library symbol*] [*National Library of Canada*] (NLC)
OWoC .... College of Wooster, Wooster, OH [*Library symbol*] [*Library of Congress*] (LCLS)
OWOH .... Huron Park Secondary School, Woodstock, Ontario [*Library symbol*] [*National Library of Canada*] (NLC)
OWoH .... Wooster Community Hospital, Wooster, OH [*Library symbol*] [*Library of Congress*] (LCLS)

OWOL .... Ontario Library Co-Operative, Wyoming, Ontario [*Library symbol*] [*National Library of Canada*] (NLC)
OWOM ...... Woodstock Museum, Ontario [*Library symbol*] [*National Library of Canada*] (BIB)
OWOO .... Oxford County Public Library, Woodstock, Ontario [*Library symbol*] [*National Library of Canada*] (NLC)
OWor .... Worthington Public Library, Worthington, OH [*Library symbol*] [*Library of Congress*] (LCLS)
OWorNW .... National Water Wall Association, Ground Water Library/Information Center, Worthington, OH [*Library symbol*] [*Library of Congress*] (LCLS)
OWorP .... Pontifical College Josephinum, Worthington, OH [*Library symbol*] [*Library of Congress*] (LCLS)
OWOS .... Owosso Corp. [*NASDAQ symbol*] (SAG)
OWOSS ..... Owosso, MI [*American Association of Railroads railroad junction routing code*]
Owosso ..... Owosso Corp. [*Associated Press*] (SAG)
OWOW ...... Office of Wetlands, Oceans, and Watersheds (WPI)
OWoWCL .... Wayne County Law Library, Wooster, OH [*Library symbol*] [*Library of Congress*] (LCLS)
OWP .... Oboz Wielkiej Polski [*Camp of Great Poland*] (PPE)
OWP .... Office of Water Policy [*Department of the Interior*]
OWP .... Office of Water Programs [*Abolished*] [*Environmental Protection Agency*]
OWP .... Office of Wetlands Protection [*Office of Water*] (COE)
OWP .... Oil Well Pumper (SAUS)
OWP .... One-Way Polar [*Telegraph*]
OWP .... One-Write Plus [*Computer software*]
OWP .... Operations Work Procedure [*Nuclear energy*] (NRCH)
OWP .... Orange Washed Pulp [*Citrus processing*]
OWP .... Organization of Wildlife Planners (EA)
OWP .... Outer Wing Panel
OWP .... Overall Work Programs (EEVL)
OWP .... Warner Pacific College, Portland, OR [*OCLC symbol*] (OCLC)
OWpAR ...... United States Air Force, Aerospace Research Laboratories, Wright-Patterson Air Force Base, OH [*Library symbol*] [*Library of Congress*] (LCLS)
OWPB .... Old Well Plugging Back (SAUS)
OWPD .... Office of Waste Programs Enforcement [*Environment term*] (EGA)
OWpDI ...... United States Air Force, Defense Institute of Security Administration Management, Wright-Patterson Air Force Base, OH [*Library symbol*] [*Library of Congress*] (LCLS)
OWPE .... Office of Waste Programs Enforcement [*Environmental Protection Agency*] (EPA)
OWPH .... Whitby Psychiatric Hospital, Ontario [*Library symbol*] [*National Library of Canada*] (NLC)
OWpIT .... United States Air Force Institute of Technology, Wright-Patterson Air Force Base, OH [*Library symbol*] [*Library of Congress*] (LCLS)
OWpL .... United States Air Force, Air Force Logistics Command, Wright-Patterson Air ForceBase, OH [*Library symbol*] [*Library of Congress*] (LCLS)
OWpM .... United States Air Force, Medical Center Library, SGEL, Wright Patterson AFB, OH [*Library symbol*] [*Library of Congress*] (LCLS)
OWPO .... Office of Water Program Operations [*Environmental Protection Agency*] (EPA)
OWPP .... Office of Welfare and Pension Plans [*Department of Labor*]
OWPR .... Ocean Wave Profile Recorder (IEEE)
OWPS .... Offshore Windpower System [*Proposed system to generate electricity by wind turbines mounted on offshore platforms*]
OWPT .... Overpaid Windfall Profits Tax (SAUS)
OWpT .... United States Air Force, Wright-Patterson Technical Library, Wright-Patterson Air Force Base, OH [*Library symbol*] [*Library of Congress*] (LCLS)
OWQ .... Output Work Queue (SAUS)
OWR .... Obligated War Reserves [*Army*] (AABC)
OWR .... Office of Worship Resources [*Later, WRO*] (EA)
OWR .... Old World Realm (SAUS)
OWR .... Omega West Reactor [*Los Alamos, NM*] [*Department of Energy*]
OWR .... Ontario Weekly Reporter [*A publication*] (DLA)
OWR .... Open Workgroup Repository [*Computer science*] (GART)
OWR .... Order of the White Rose of Finland (DD)
OWR .... Ouse Washes Reserve (SAUS)
OWR .... Riverside Secondary School, Windsor, Ontario [*Library symbol*] [*National Library of Canada*] (NLC)
OWR .... Worthington Public Library, Worthington, OH [*OCLC symbol*] (OCLC)
OWRAP ..... Office of Worker Retraining and Adjustment Programs [*U.S. Department of Labor*] (BARN)
OWRB .... RC Reid-Bicknell Eng. Ltd., Woodbridge, Ontario [*Library symbol*] [*National Library of Canada*] (NLC)
OWRC .... Office of Water Resource Center [*Environmental Protection Agency*] (AEPA)
OWRC .... Old West Regional Commission [*Department of Commerce*]
OWRC .... Ontario Water Resources Commission (SAUS)
OWRC .... White River Community Library, Ontario [*Library symbol*] [*National Library of Canada*] (NLC)
OWRD .... Ratter and Dunnet Public Library, Warren, Ontario [*Library symbol*] [*National Library of Canada*] (NLC)
OWRHS ..... Ontario and Western Railroad Historical Society (EA)
OWRL .... One-Way Radio Link [*Telecommunications*] (LAIN)
OWRM ...... Office of Weather Research and Modification [*National Oceanic and Atmospheric Administration*] (GRD)
OWRM ...... Other War Reserve Materiel
OWRMR ..... Other War Reserve Materiel Requirement (AFIT)
OWRMS ..... Other War Reserve Materiel Stocks [*Army*] (AABC)
OWRR .... Office of Water Resources Research [*Later, OWRT*] [*Department of the Interior*]
OWRRI ...... Oklahoma Water Resources Research Institute [*Stillwater, OK*] [*Department of the Interior*] (GRD)
OWRS .... Office of Water Regulations and Standards [*Environmental Protection Agency*] (GFGA)
OWRT .... Office of Water Research and Technology [*Formerly, OSW, OWRR*] [*Abolished, 1982*] [*Department of the Interior*]
OWRTS ...... Open-Wire Radio Transmission System (VLIE)
OWS .... Cargosur [*Spain*] [*ICAO designator*] (FAAC)
OWS .... Obstacle Warning System (SAUS)
OWS .... Occupational Wage Survey
OWS .... Ocean Weather Service (SAUS)
OWS .... Ocean Weather Ship
OWS .... Ocean Weather Station (MCD)
OWS .... Oil Water Separator [*Navy*] (CAAL)
OWS .... Old West Saxon [*Language, etc.*] (ROG)
OWS .... Oliphant Washington Service [*Information service or system*] (IID)
OWS .... One-Way Simultaneous (VLIE)
OWS .... Operational Weapon Satellite (SAUS)
OWS .... Operational Weather Support
OWS .... Operations Weather Support (SAUS)
OWS .... Operators Workstation (SAUS)
OWS .... Optical Witness Sample (SAUS)
OWS .... Orbital Weapon System (AAG)
OWS .... Orbital Workshop [*NASA*]
OWS .... Ordnance Weapon Systems [*Army*]
OWS .... Oscar Wilde Society [*United Kingdom*] (EAIO)
OWS .... Outerwear Syndrome [*Medicine*] (DMAA)
OWS .... Outer Wing Station (MCD)
OWS .... Overhead Weapon Station (SAUS)
OWS .... Overload Warning System (MCD)
OWS .... Overwear Syndrome [*Of contact lens*]
OWS .... Southwestern Regional Library, Windsor, Ontario [*Library symbol*] [*Obsolete*] [*National Library of Canada*] (NLC)
OWS .... Willamette University, Salem, OR [*OCLC symbol*] (OCLC)
OWSA .... Spar Aerospace Ltd., Weston, Ontario [*Library symbol*] [*National Library of Canada*] (NLC)
OWSAH ..... Salvation Army Grace Hospital, Windsor, Ontario [*Library symbol*] [*National Library of Canada*] (BIB)
OWSC .... Old West Scandinavian [*Language, etc.*]
OWSC .... St. Clair College, Windsor, Ontario [*Library symbol*] [*National Library of Canada*] (NLC)
OWSCC ...... Simon-Carves of Canada Ltd., Willowdale, Ontario [*Library symbol*] [*National Library of Canada*] (NLC)
OWSCL ...... Senes Consultants Ltd., Willowdale, Ontario [*Library symbol*] [*National Library of Canada*] (NLC)
OWSDG ..... Winchester Branch, Stormount, Dundas, and Glengarry County Public Library, Ontario [*Library symbol*] [*National Library of Canada*] (NLC)
OWSE .... Otherwise
OWSG .... Older Worker Specialists Group
OWSJ .... Off the Wall Street Journal [*Parody of the Wall Street Journal*]
OWSM .... Seagram Museum, Waterloo, Ontario [*Library symbol*] [*National Library of Canada*] (BIB)
OWS Meteorological Summary ... Ocean Weather Ship Meteorological Summary (SAUS)
OWSP .... One Word Storage Programmer (SAUS)
OWSS .... Ocean Weather Ship Service (SAUS)
OWT .... Organic Weather Team
OWT .... Waterloo Public Library, Ontario [*Library symbol*] [*National Library of Canada*] (NLC)
OWT .... Willamette University, Law Library, Salem, OR [*OCLC symbol*] (OCLC)
OWTA .... Kitchener-Waterloo Academy of Medicine, Kitchener, Ontario [*Library symbol*] [*National Library of Canada*] (NLC)
OWTAI .... Airworthiness Library, Ontario Region, Transport Canada [*Bibliotheque de la Navigabilite Aerienne, Region de l'Ontario, Transports Canada*], Willowdale, Ontario [*Library symbol*] [*National Library of Canada*] (NLC)
OWTD .... Office of Waste Technology Development (SAUS)
OWTG .... Kitchener-Waterloo Hospital, Kitchener, Ontario [*Library symbol*] [*National Library of Canada*] (NLC)
OWTL .... Open-Wire Transmission Line [*Telecommunications*] (VLIE)
OWTL .... Wilfrid Laurier University [*Formerly, Waterloo Lutheran University*] Waterloo, Ontario [*Library symbol*] [*National Library of Canada*] (NLC)
OWTM .... Legal Reference Centre, Manufacturers' Life Insurance Co., Waterloo, Ontario [*Library symbol*] [*National Library of Canada*] (BIB)
OWTML ..... Corporate Library, Mutual Life of Canada, Waterloo, Ontario [*Library symbol*] [*National Library of Canada*] (BIB)
OWTO .... Ontario Library Services Center, Waterloo, Ontario [*Library symbol*] [*National Library of Canada*] (NLC)
OWTS .... St. Mary's General Hospital, Kitchener, Ontario [*Library symbol*] [*National Library of Canada*] (NLC)
OWTTE ...... Or Words to That Effect (VLIE)
OWTU .... Oilfields Workers Trade Union (SAUS)
OWTU .... University of Waterloo, Ontario [*Library symbol*] [*National Library of Canada*] (NLC)
OWTUE ...... Environmental Studies Library, University of Waterloo, Ontario [*Library symbol*] [*National Library of Canada*] (NLC)
O/W Type ... Oil/Water Type (SAUS)
OWU .... Office of War Utilities [*War Production Board*]
OWU .... Office Workers Union (SAUS)
OWU .... Ohio Wesleyan University, Delaware, OH [*OCLC symbol*] (OCLC)
OWU .... Open-Window Unit (MSA)
OWU .... Overload Warning Unit (MCD)

OWU......... Woodward, OK [*Location identifier*] [*FAA*] (FAAL)
OW-USS..... Our World-Underwater Scholarship Society (EA)
OWV......... Ocean Weather Vessel [*Shipping*] (AIA)
OWVL....... One-Way Voice Link (GOBB)
OWVM....... Vincent Massey Secondary School, Windsor, Ontario [*Library symbol*] [*National Library of Canada*] (NLC)
OWW........ Organic Wash Waste (ABAC)
OWW........ Walkerville Collegiate Institute, Windsor, Ontario [*Library symbol*] [*National Library of Canada*] (NLC)
OWWA....... Waters Branch, Walden Public Library, Ontario [*Library symbol*] [*National Library of Canada*] (NLC)
OWWH...... OW Office Warehouse (EFIS)
OWWH...... Whitefish Branch, Walden Public Library, Ontario [*Library symbol*] [*National Library of Canada*] (NLC)
OWWI....... Omega Worldwide, Inc. [*NASDAQ symbol*] (NASQ)
OWWM...... Office of Water and Waste Management (ERG)
OWWS...... Office of World Weather Systems (SAUS)
OWX......... Office of the Assistant for Weather [*Air Force*]
OWX......... Ottawa, OH [*Location identifier*] [*FAA*] (FAAL)
OWY......... Owyhee, NV [*Location identifier*] [*FAA*] (FAAL)
OWYL....... Lambton County Public Library, Wyoming, Ontario [*Library symbol*] [*National Library of Canada*] (NLC)
OW/YM...... Older Woman / Younger Man (WDAA)
OWZ......... Otherwise [*Telegraphy*] (PCTE)
OX........... Air Atlantic Airlines [*ICAO designator*] (AD)
Ox........... Odd Oxygen (SAUS)
OX........... Optic Chiasm (STED)
OX........... Optic Chiasma [*Medicine*] (MELL)
OX........... Order Crossover (VLIE)
OX........... Orthopedic Examination (STED)
OX........... Ottawa Exchange (SAUS)
OX........... Overnight eXpress (SAUS)
OX........... Oxacillin [*Medicine*] (MELL)
OX........... Oxford [*England*]
Ox........... Oxford [*Record label*]
OX........... Oxidant [*Photochemical*] (ERG)
OX........... Oxidation (EEVL)
OX........... Oxide [*or Oxidizer*] (AAG)
ox........... Oxides (VRA)
ox........... Oxidizer (NAKS)
OX........... Oxygen [*Chemical element*] (IAA)
ox........... Oxygen (IDOE)
Ox........... Oxygen (STED)
OX........... Oxymel [*Syrup of vinegar and honey*] [*Pharmacy*]
OX........... Oxytocin [*Medicine*] (MELL)
Ox........... Total Oxidants (SAUS)
OX1......... High Pressure Oxygen [*Aviation*] (PIPO)
OX2......... Low Pressure Oxygen [*Aviation*] (PIPO)
OXA......... Oxalic Acid [*Organic chemistry*]
OXA......... Oxaprotiline (DMAA)
OXAL....... Oxalate (SAUS)
OXB......... Baldwin-Wallace College, Berea, OH [*OCLC symbol*] (OCLC)
OxboroM.... Oxboro Medical International, Inc. [*Associated Press*] (SAG)
Oxbridge.... Oxford and Cambridge Universities (NTIO)
OXBRIDGE... Oxford/Cambridge [*England*]
OXC......... Oxford, CT [*Location identifier*] [*FAA*] (FAAL)
OXC......... Oxidizing Catalyst [*Automotive engineering*]
OXC......... Waterbury [*Connecticut*] [*Airport symbol*] (AD)
OXCI........ Oxford Consolidated, Inc. [*NASDAQ symbol*] (NQ)
OXD......... Oxford [*England*] [*Seismograph station code, US Geological Survey*] [*Closed*] (SEIS)
OXD......... Oxidation (SAUS)
O-X-D....... Oxidative Dehydrogenation (SAUS)
OXD......... Oxide (NAKS)
OXD......... Oxidized (MSA)
OXDZR...... Oxidizer (NASA)
OXe......... Greene County District Library, Xenia, OH [*Library symbol*] [*Library of Congress*] (LCLS)
OXE......... OEC Medical Sys [*NYSE symbol*] (TTSB)
OXE......... OEC Medical Systems [*Formerly, Diasonics, Inc.*] [*NYSE symbol*] (SPSG)
OXE......... Oxaero [*British*] [*FAA designator*] (FAAC)
OXEA....... Ox Erythrocyte Antibody [*Medicine*] (STED)
OXeGH...... Greene Memorial Hospital, Health Resource Library, Xenia, OH [*Library symbol*] [*Library of Congress*] (LCLS)
OXERA...... Oxford Economic Research Associates Ltd
OXF......... Open Exchange Format (SAUS)
OXF......... Oxford [*England*] [*Airport symbol*] (AD)
OXF......... Oxford [*Mississippi*] [*Seismograph station code, US Geological Survey*] [*Closed*] (SEIS)
OXF......... Oxford [*British depot code*]
OXF......... Oxford [*NCIC car model code*]
OXF......... Oxford Properties Canada Ltd. [*Toronto Stock Exchange symbol*]
OXFAM...... Oxford Committee for Family Relief (SAUS)
OXFAM...... Oxford Committee for Famine Relief [*Acronym is now organization's official name*] [*British*] (EA)
Oxfam....... Oxford Committee for Famine Relief (NTIO)
OXFD........ Oxford Resources Cl'A' [*NASDAQ symbol*] (TTSB)
OXFD........ Oxford Resources Corp. [*NASDAQ symbol*] (SAG)
OxfdHlt..... Oxford Health Plans, Inc. [*Associated Press*] (SAG)
OxfdRsc..... Oxford Resources Corp. [*Associated Press*] (SAG)
Oxf Lawy.... Oxford Lawyer [*1958-61*] [*A publication*] (DLA)
Oxford....... Oxford Industries, Inc. [*Associated Press*] (SAG)
Oxford Bull Econ Statist... Oxford Bulletin of Economics and Statistics [*A publication*] (JLIT)
Oxford Devel Stud... Oxford Development Studies [*A publication*] (JLIT)
Oxford Econ Pap... Oxford Economic Papers [*A publication*] (JLIT)
Oxford Law... Oxford Lawyer [*1958-61*] [*A publication*] (DLA)
Oxford Rev Econ Pol... Oxford Review of Economic Policy [*A publication*] (JLIT)
OxfrdC....... Oxford Consolidated, Inc. [*Associated Press*] (SAG)
OXGN........ Oxigene, Inc. [*NASDAQ symbol*] (SAG)
OXGNW..... OXIGENE Inc. Wrrt [*NASDAQ symbol*] (TTSB)
OXH......... Oxygen Heat Exchanger (KSC)
OXHP........ Oxford Health Plans [*NASDAQ symbol*] (SPSG)
OXI.......... Knox, IN [*Location identifier*] [*FAA*] (FAAL)
OXI.......... Orbex Industries, Inc. [*Vancouver Stock Exchange symbol*]
Oxi.......... Oximeter (STED)
OXID........ Oxidizer (AAG)
OXID........ Oxidyne Group, Inc. [*NASDAQ symbol*] (COMM)
OXIDN...... Oxidation
Oxigene..... Oxigene, Inc. [*Associated Press*] (SAG)
Oxign........ Oxigene, Inc. [*Associated Press*] (SAG)
OXIL........ Oxid Insulated (or Insulation) Logic (SAUS)
OXIM........ Oxide-Isolated Mask (SAUS)
OXIM........ Oxide-Isolated Monolith
OXIM Technology... Oxide-Isolated Monolithic Technology (SAUS)
OXINE...... Oxyquinoline [*Organic chemistry*]
OXIRM...... Oxford Institute of Retail Management [*University of Oxford*] [*United Kingdom*] (RCD)
OXIS........ Oxide Insulation (SAUS)
OXIS........ Oxide Isolated (NITA)
OXIS........ Oxide Isolation (IAA)
OXIS........ Oxis International, Inc. [*NASDAQ symbol*] (SAG)
OXK......... Belleville, IL [*Location identifier*] [*FAA*] (FAAL)
OXLAT...... Oxalate [*Laboratory science*] (DAVI)
Oxley....... Oxley's Railway Cases [*1897-1903*] [*A publication*] (DLA)
Oxley....... Young's Nova Scotia Vice-Admiralty Decisions, Edited by Oxley [*A publication*] (DLA)
OXM........ Oxford Indus [*NYSE symbol*] (TTSB)
OXM........ Oxford Industries, Inc. [*NYSE symbol*] (SPSG)
OXM........ Oxtotitlan [*Mexico*] [*Seismograph station code, US Geological Survey*] (SEIS)
Ox M OUP.. Oxford Medical Oxford University Press (SAUS)
OXN......... Oxin Industries Ltd. [*Vancouver Stock Exchange symbol*]
OXN......... Oxnard, CA [*Amtrak rail station code*]
OXNAR...... Oxnard, CA [*American Association of Railroads railroad junction routing code*]
OXO......... Million Air, Inc. [*ICAO designator*] (FAAC)
OXO......... Orbiting X-Ray Observatory [*NASA*]
OXO......... Orientos [*Queensland*] [*Airport symbol*] (AD)
OXOCO...... Offshore Exploration Oil Company (SAUS)
Oxon........ Oxfordshire (DIAR)
OXON....... Oxfordshire [*County in England*]
Oxon........ Oxoiensis [*Academic degree*] (WDAA)
OXON....... Oxonia [*Oxford University*] [*Latin*]
OXON....... Oxoniensis [*Of Oxford University*] [*Latin*]
OXP......... Oxford Poets [*A publication*]
OXP......... Oxprenolol [*Vasodilator*]
OXP......... Oxypressin [*Medicine*] (MELL)
OXPHOS.... Oxidative Phosphorylation [*Medicine*]
OXR......... Oxidizer (SAUS)
OXR......... Oxnard [*California*] [*Airport symbol*] (OAG)
OXRB........ Oxygen Replacement Bottles
OXRO........ Orbiting X-Ray Observatory (ACAE)
OXS......... Objective X-ray Crystal Spectrometer (SAUS)
OXS......... Oxygen Sensor (ACAE)
OXSOME.... Oxford County Soil Moisture Experiment (SAUS)
OXT......... Oxytocin [*Medicine*] (MELL)
OXV......... Knoxville, IA [*Location identifier*] [*FAA*] (FAAL)
OXWLD...... Oxyacetylene Weld (SAUS)
Oxy......... Occidental College (SAUS)
OXY......... Occidental Petroleum Corp. [*NYSE symbol*]
Oxy......... Occidental Petroleum Corporation (SAUS)
OXY......... Oxley [*British depot code*]
OXY......... Oxygen [*Chemical element*] [*Symbol is O*] (AAG)
OXY......... Oxytocin [*Endocrinology*]
oxycephs.... oxycephalics (SAUS)
OXYCOD.... Oxycodone Hydrochloride (SAUS)
OXYCOD TER... Oxycodone Terephthalate (SAUS)
OXYG........ Oxygen [*Chemical element*] [*Symbol is O*]
OXYG........ Oxygon (SAUS)
OXYM........ Oxymel [*Syrup of vinegar and honey*] [*Pharmacy*] (ROG)
OXYPAR..... Occidental Petroleum Corporation (EFIS)
OXYPrA..... Occidental Petr $3 Cv Pfd [*NYSE symbol*] (TTSB)
OXYU........ Eurotainer United States [*Intermodal shipping container symbol*] (TVRC)
OXZ......... Oxazepam [*Medicine*] (MELL)
Oy........... Both Eyes (SAUS)
OY........... Denmark [*International civil aircraft marking*] (ODBW)
OY........... New Jersey Airways [*ICAO designator*] (AD)
OY........... Operating Year (COE)
OY........... Optimum Yield
OY........... Orange Yellow
Oy........... Osakeyhtioe [*Limited Company*] [*Finland*]
Oy........... Oyster (SAUS)
OY........... Public Library of Youngstown and Mahoning County, Youngstown, OH [*Library symbol*] [*Library of Congress*] (LCLS)
OYA......... Goya [*Argentina*] [*Airport symbol*] (OAG)
OYA......... Orthodox Youth of America [*Later, SOYO*]

Oya Cur ..... Oyashio Current (SAUS)
OYAK .... Army Mutual Assistance Foundation (Turkey) [*Political party*] (PSAP)
OYAP .... Outstanding Young American Pianist
OYAS .... Abbs [*Yemen*] [*ICAO location identifier*] (ICLI)
OYBI .... Al-Beida [*Yemen*] [*ICAO location identifier*] (ICLI)
OYBO .... Al-Bough [*Yemen*] [*ICAO location identifier*] (ICLI)
OYBT .... Barat [*Yemen*] [*ICAO location identifier*] (ICLI)
OYC .... Conair AS [*Denmark*] [*ICAO designator*] (FAAC)
OYC .... Corpus Christi, TX [*Location identifier*] [*FAA*] (FAAL)
OYC .... Out Year Costs (MCD)
OYCV .... Optimum Yaw Control Vertical (SAA)
OYD .... Office of Youth Development (SAUS)
OYD .... Rome, GA [*Location identifier*] [*FAA*] (FAAL)
OYDV .... Onion Yellow Dwarf Virus [*Plant pathology*]
OYE .... Old Yellow Enzyme [*Biochemistry*]
OYE .... Oyem [*Gabon*] [*Airport symbol*] (OAG)
OYesA .... Antioch College, Yellow Springs, OH [*Library symbol*] [*Library of Congress*] (LCLS)
OYesF .... Fels Research Institute, Yellow Springs, OH [*Library symbol*] [*Library of Congress*] (LCLS)
OYesK .... Charles F. Kettering Foundation, Research Laboratory Library, Yellow Springs, OH [*Library symbol*] [*Library of Congress*] (LCLS)
OYG .... Operating Year Guidance (GFGA)
OYHD .... Hodeidah [*Yemen*] [*ICAO location identifier*] (ICLI)
OYHFS ...... Optimist Youth and Family Services (MHID)
OYK .... Oiapoque [*Brazil*] [*Airport symbol*] (AD)
OYKM .... Kamaran [*Yemen*] [*ICAO location identifier*] (ICLI)
OYLU .... Taylor Minster Leasing [*Intermodal shipping container symbol*] (TVRC)
OYM .... Outstanding Young Man (DICI)
OYM .... Oyama [*Japan*] [*Seismograph station code, US Geological Survey*] (SEIS)
OYM .... St. Mary's, PA [*Location identifier*] [*FAA*] (FAAL)
OYMB .... Marib [*Yemen*] [*ICAO location identifier*] (ICLI)
OYMC .... Mokha [*Yemen*] [*ICAO location identifier*] (ICLI)
OYMHi ...... Mahoning Valley Historical Society, Arms Museum, Youngstown, OH [*Library symbol*] [*Library of Congress*] (LCLS)
OYMV .... Ononis Yellow Mosaic Virus [*Plant pathology*]
OYO .... Own Your Own (SAUS)
OYO .... Tres Arroyos [*Argentina*] [*Airport symbol*] (OAG)
OYOC .... One-Year-On-Campus (SAUS)
OYOG .... OYO Geospace Corp. [*NASDAQ symbol*] (SAG)
OYOGeo ..... OYO Geospace Corp. [*Associated Press*] (SAG)
OYP .... O and Y Properties Corp. [*Toronto Stock Exchange symbol*] [*Canada*]
OYP .... Office of Youth Programs [*Department of Labor*]
OYP .... Opportunities for Youth Program [*Canada*]
OYS .... Otsar Yehude Sefarad (BJA)
OYS .... Outstanding Young Singaporeans (SAUS)
Oys .... Oysters [*Quality of the bottom*] [*Nautical charts*]
OYS .... Yosemite National Park [*California*] [*Airport symbol*] [*Obsolete*] (OAG)
OYSH .... Saada [*Yemen*] [*ICAO location identifier*] (ICLI)
OYSN .... Sanaa/International [*Yemen*] [*ICAO location identifier*] (ICLI)
OYSREA ..... Office of Youth, Sport, Recreation and Ethnic Affairs [*Northern Territory, Australia*]
OYSTER ..... Optical Yardsticks Toward Error Reduction (ACAE)
OYTS .... Ocean Youth Trust Scotland [*United Kingdom*] (EAIO)
OYTZ .... Taiz/Ganad [*Yemen*] [*ICAO location identifier*] (ICLI)
OYU .... Youngstown State University, Youngstown, OH [*Library symbol*] [*Library of Congress*] (LCLS)
OYWS .... Own Your Wagon Scheme [*Indian Railway*] (TIR)
OYY .... Columbus, OH [*Location identifier*] [*FAA*] (FAAL)
OYZM .... Al-Hazm [*Yemen*] [*ICAO location identifier*] (ICLI)
OZ .... Oldsmobile [*Federal Railroad Administration identification code*]
Oz .... Ooze [*Quality of the bottom*] [*Nautical charts*]
OZ .... Ounce [*Unit of weight*] (AAG)
oz .... Ounce (IDOE)
OZ .... Outer Zone (HEAS)
OZ .... Ozark Airlines, Inc. [*ICAO designator*] (OAG)
OZ .... Ozonation (SAUS)
oz .... Ozone (IDOE)
OZ .... Ozone
OZA .... Ozark (MCD)
OZA .... Ozark Airlines (MHDB)
OZA .... Ozona, TX [*Location identifier*] [*FAA*] (FAAL)
OZ AP .... Apothecaries' Ounce (WDAA)
oz ap .... ounze, apothecaries (SAUS)
oz apoth .... Apothecaries Ounce (BARN)
OZAR .... Ozark National Scenic Riverways [*National Park Service designation*]
OZAR .... Ozark Trailer & Mobile Homes [*NCIC trailer make code*]
OZAR .... Ozark Transfer [*Common carrier symbol*]
OZARC ...... Ozone ARCAS [*All-Purpose Rocket for Collecting Atmospheric Soundings*] [*Navy*]
OZav .... John McIntire Public Library, Zanesville, OH [*Library symbol*] [*Library of Congress*] (LCLS)
OZavU .... Ohio University, Zanesville Branch Campus, Zanesville, OH [*Library symbol*] [*Library of Congress*] (LCLS)
OZC .... Cleveland Heights-University Heights Public Library, Cleveland Heights, OH [*OCLC symbol*] (OCLC)
OZC .... Ozamis City [*Philippines*] [*Airport symbol*] (OAG)
OZ-CCA ...... Danmark-Cross-Country Award (SAUS)
OZCX .... Ozark-Mahoning [*Private rail car owner code*]
OZD .... Observed Zenith Distance [*Navigation*]
OZE .... Outer Zone Electron
OZEM .... OzMail Ltd. [*NASDAQ symbol*] (SAG)
OzEmail ..... OZEmail Ltd. [*Associated Press*] (SAG)
OZEMY ...... OzEmail Ltd ADR [*NASDAQ symbol*] (TTSB)
OZEP .... Outer Zone Electron Precipitation
ozf .... ounce-force (SAUS)
oz ff .... Fluid Ounce (SAUS)
ozf-in .... ounce-force-inch (SAUS)
oz fl .... ounze, fluid ounce (SAUS)
OZFLUX ..... Australian Flux Measurement Network (SAUS)
OZ-FT .... Ounce Foot (AAG)
oz ft .... ounce-foot (SAUS)
OZ/FT^2 .... Ounces per Square Foot
OZ/GAL ...... Ounces per Gallon
OZH .... Zaporozh'ye [*Former USSR*] [*Airport symbol*] [*Obsolete*] (OAG)
OZ-IN .... Ounce Inch (AAG)
oz-in .... Ounce-Inch (IDOE)
oz-in .... Ounce-Inches (IDOE)
OZ/IN^2 .... Ounces per Square Inch
OZ/IN^3 .... Ounces per Cubic Inch
OZIPP .... Ozone Isopleth Plotting Package (GFGA)
OZIPPM ..... Ozone Isopleth Plotting Package, Modified (GFGA)
OZN .... St. George, UT [*Location identifier*] [*FAA*] (FAAL)
OZO .... Orbiting Zoological Observatory to Track Animals
OZON .... Cyclc3PSS Corp. [*NASDAQ symbol*] (SAG)
OZON .... Cyclopss Corp. [*NASDAQ symbol*] (TTSB)
Ozone Sci Eng... Ozone Science and Engineering (SAUS)
OZ/PT .... Ounces per Pint
OZR .... Ozark, Fort Rucker, AL [*Location identifier*] [*FAA*] (FAAL)
OZRF .... Opposed Zone Reheating Furnace (PDAA)
OZRK .... Ozark Plateaus (SAUS)
oz/t .... ounces per ton (SAUS)
OZT .... Ounces Troy [*Unit of weight*]
oz t .... ounce troy (SAUS)
OZ TR .... Ounce Troy (GOBB)
oz tr .... ounze,troy (SAUS)
OZTS .... Ozinga Transportation Systems [*Common carrier symbol*]
ozws .... otherwise (SAUS)
OZWV .... Ozone and Water Vapor Group [*National Oceanic and Atmospheric Administration*] (RCD)
OZX .... Oneonta, NY [*Location identifier*] [*FAA*] (FAAL)
Ozy .... Ozzie (SAUS)
OZ/YD^2 ...... Ounces per Square Yard
OZZ .... Ouarzazate [*Morocco*] [*Airport symbol*] (OAG)
OZZ .... Ozark, AR [*Location identifier*] [*FAA*] (FAAL)

P
By Acronym

P .... Aircraft [*Wind triangle problems*]
P .... All India Reporter, Patna [*A publication*] (DLA)
P .... Armour Pharmaceutical Co. [*Research code symbol*]
P .... Assistant in Private Practice [*Chiropody*] [*British*]
P .... Asta Werke AG [*Germany*] [*Research code symbol*]
P .... Bristol Laboratories [*Research code symbol*]
P .... cis-Platinum [*Cisplatin*] [*Also, cis-DDP, CDDP, CPDD, CPT, DDP*] [*Antineoplastic drug*]
P .... Dainippon Pharmaceutical Co. [*Japan*] [*Research code symbol*]
P .... Democratic People's Republic of Korea [*Aircraft nationality and registration mark*] (FAAC)
p .... Density [*Heat transmission symbol*]
P .... Departure
p .... Difficulty [*of a test item*] [*Psychology*]
p .... Druck (SAUS)
P .... Electric Dipole Moment (BARN)
P .... Farbenfabriken Bayer [*Germany*] [*Research code symbol*]
P .... Farmitalia [*Italy*] [*Research code symbol*]
P .... Faulty Punctuation [*Used in correcting manuscripts, etc.*]
P .... first class premium (SAUS)
p .... fluid density (SAUS)
P .... Force of Concentrated Load
P .... Games [*or Matches*] Played [*Sports statistics*]
P .... gas pressure in blood (SAUS)
P .... Hole P-Type Semiconductor Material
P .... Indian Law Reports, Patna Series [*A publication*] (DLA)
P .... Law Reports, Probate, Divorce, and Admiralty [*Since 1890*] [*England*] [*A publication*] (DLA)
P .... Lepetit [*Italy*] [*Research code symbol*]
P .... Mainsail Hoist Lenght [*IOR*]
p .... Momentum [*Symbol*] [*IUPAC*]
P .... North Korea [*Civil aircraft markings - international*] (PIPO)
P .... Office of Personnel [*Coast Guard*]
p .... On Probation [*Navy*] [*British*]
P .... Orbital Period [*of a comet*] [*In years*]
P .... Overpressure [*Emergency Management*] (EMA)
P .... Pacer
P .... Pacific Coast Stock Exchange [*Later, PSE*]
p---- .... Pacific Ocean [*MARC geographic area code*] [*Library of Congress*] (LCCP)
P .... Pacific Reporter [*A publication*] (DLA)
P .... Pacific Stock Exchange (SG)
P .... Pack [*JETDS*]
P .... Packed Lunches [*School meals*] [*British*]
P .... Pad (SAA)
P .... Paddington Railway Station (ROG)
P .... Paddle (DS)
P .... Page
P .... Paid This Year [*In stock listings of newspapers*]
P .... Pain [*Medicine*]
P .... Pair (IAA)
P .... Paired [*for or against*] [*Votes in Congress*]
P .... Paise [*Monetary unit*] [*India*]
P .... Palace (ROG)
P .... Pale (ADA)
p .... Pallet (NAKS)
P .... Pallet [*Spacelab*] [*NASA*] (NASA)
P .... Pamphlet
P .... Panama Line (SAUS)
P .... Pancreas (MELL)
P .... Pancuronium [*A muscle relaxant*]
P .... Pandects [*A publication*] [*Authority cited in pre-1607 legal work*] (DSA)
P .... Panel (NFPA)
P .... Papa [*Phonetic alphabet*] [*International*] (DSUE)
P .... Papa [*Pope*] [*Latin*]
P .... Paper
P .... Paperback (WGA)
P .... Papilla [*Optic*] [*Medicine*]
P .... Papillate [*A type of seed*] [*Botany*]
P .... Para [*Monetary unit*] [*Former Yugoslavia*]
p .... Para [*Chemistry*]
P .... Parabellum (GOBB)
P .... Parachutist [*Army skill qualification identifier*] (INF)
P .... Paragraph (ADA)
P .... Paralegal Program [*Association of Independent Colleges and Schools specialization code*]
P .... Parallax
P .... Parallel
P .... Paramecin [*A protozoan toxin*]
P .... Parashah (BJA)
P .... Pardon (ADA)
P .... Parenchyma [*Botany*]
P .... Parent (CPH)
P .... Parental
P .... Parental Generation (ODA)
P .... Parentalgeneration (SAUS)
P .... Parietal Electrode Placement in Electroencephalography [*Medicine*] (DMAA)
P .... Parish (ROG)
P .... Parity [*Obstetrics*] (DAVI)
P .... Parity [*Atomic physics*]
P .... Park
P .... Parking Place [*Traffic sign*] [*British*]
P .... Parlophone [*Record label*] [*Great Britain, Italy, Australia, etc.*]
P .... Parous (STED)
P .... Parson
p .... Part (WDMC)
P .... Part
P .... Parthian [*Language, etc.*]
P .... Partial [*Astronomy*]
P .... Partial Agonist [*Pharmacology*] (QSUL)
P .... Partial Pressure (MAE)
P .... Partial Tension [*Medicine*] (DAVI)
p .... Participle (NTIO)
P .... Participle [*Grammar*]
P .... Partim [*In Part*]
P .... Partnership
P .... Party
P .... Parve [*or Pareve*] [*In food labeling, indicates food is kosher and can be used with either meat or dairy products*]
P .... Pass (SAUS)
P .... Passable (SAUS)
P .... Passed [*Examination*]
P .... Passenger [*Automotive tire designation*]
p .... Passing Showers (ODA)
P .... Passing Showers [*Meteorology*]
p .... Past (WDMC)
P .... Past
P .... Paste
P .... Pasteboard (DGA)
P .... Pasteurella [*Genus of bacteria*]
P .... Pastor
P .... Patella (MELL)
P .... Patent
P .... Pater [*Father*] [*Latin*]
P .... Paternal (STED)
P .... Paternally Contributing [*Genetics*] (DAVI)
P .... Patient
P .... Patrol [*Designation for all US military aircraft*]
P .... Patrol Service Gunnery Instructor [*Officer's rating*] [*British Royal Navy*]
P .... Patron
P .... Pattern
P .... Paulus de Liazaris [*Deceased, 1356*] [*Authority cited in pre-1607 legal work*] (DSA)
P .... Paused Program [*Computer science*]
P .... Paved Surface [*Aviation*] (DA)
P .... Pavilion (ROG)
P .... Pawn [*Chess*]
P .... Pax [*Peace*] [*Latin*]
P .... Pay
P .... Payee
P .... Paymaster [*Military*] (ROG)
p .... P-Doped Semiconductor [*Photovoltaic energy systems*]
P .... Peak
P .... Pear (SAUS)
P .... Peat (ROG)
P .... Pebbles [*Quality of the bottom*] [*Nautical charts*]
P .... Pectoral [*Anatomy*] (ROG)
p .... Peculiar [*Astronomy*]
P .... Pedal (WDAA)
P .... Pedestrian (WDAA)
P .... Pedicle [*Medicine*] (EDAA)
P .... Pediculus [*Medicine*] (EDAA)
P .... Peg [*Telecommunications*] (IAA)

P .... Pelagius [*Deceased, 1232*] [*Authority cited in pre-1607 legal work*] (DSA)
P .... Pellagra [*Medicine*] (MELL)
P .... Pelvis (STED)
P .... Pen [*Sports*]
p .... Pence [*Monetary unit*] [*British*]
P .... Pencil Tube (MDG)
P .... Pengo [*Monetary unit in Hungary until 1946*]
P .... Penicillin
p .... Penni(a) [*Penny or Pence*] [*Monetary unit*] [*Finland*] (GPO)
P .... Pennsylvania (DLA)
P .... Pennsylvania State Library, Harrisburg, PA [*Library symbol*] [*Library of Congress*] (LCLS)
p .... Penny (ODBW)
P .... Penny
P .... Pennzoil (SAUS)
P .... Pentachlorophenol [*Also, PCP*] [*Wood preservative*] [*Organic chemistry*] (TEL)
P .... Pentode [*Electronics*] (OA)
P .... Peony [*Horticulture*]
P .... People
P .... Pepper (DICI)
p .... Per (WDMC)
P .... Per
P .... Percent (STED)
P .... Percentile
P .... Perceptual
P .... Perceptual Speed [*A factor ability*] [*Psychology*]
P .... Perch
P .... Perchloroethylene [*Also, TCE*] [*Dry cleaning*]
p .... Percussion (ODA)
P .... Percussion
P .... Pere [*Father*] [*French*]
P .... Perforateur Honeywell Bull (IAA)
P .... Perforating (SAUS)
P .... Perforation
P .... Performance [*Army*] (INF)
P .... Performer
P .... Perfusionist [*Medicine*] (DAVI)
P .... Perianth
P .... Pericardium [*Medicine*]
P .... Perimeter
p .... Period (NAKS)
P .... Period
P .... Peripheral (DAVI)
P .... Periphery (SAUS)
P .... Perishable
P .... Peritoneum [*Medicine*] (MELL)
P .... Permanent [*Inks*] (DGA)
P .... Permanent Stay [*in hospital*] [*British*]
P .... Permeability (STED)
P .... Permeance (IDOE)
P .... Permian [*Paleontology*] (QSUL)
P .... Permutation (NITA)
P .... Perpetuus [*Uninterrupted*] [*Latin*]
p .... Perseverate [*Psychology*]
P .... Persian (DLA)
P .... Persimmon
P .... Persistence [*Medicine*]
P .... Person
P .... Personal (DA)
P .... Personality Organization and Stability [*Eysenck*] [*Psychology*]
P .... Personnel
P .... Person to Person [*Telecommunications*] (TEL)
P .... Perstetur [*Continue*] [*Pharmacy*] (ROG)
P .... Persuasion [*Novel by Jane Austen*]
P .... Peseta [*Monetary unit*] [*Spain and Latin America*]
P .... Pesewa [*Monetary unit*] [*Ghana*]
P .... Pesher (BJA)
P .... Peshitta (BJA)
p .... Peso (NTIO)
P .... Peso [*Monetary unit*] [*Spain and Latin America*]
P .... Peta [*A prefix meaning multiplied by* 10^{15}] [*SI symbol*]
p .... Peta, 1 E15 [*Industrial hygiene term*] (OHS)
P .... Peter [*Phonetic alphabet*] [*World War II*] (DSUE)
P .... Peter [*New Testament book*]
P .... Peters' United States Supreme Court Reports [*26-41 United States*] [*A publication*] (DLA)
P .... Petiole [*Botany*]
P .... Petite (WGA)
P .... Petrol [*British Waterways Board sign*]
P .... Petrus Hispanus [*Authority cited in pre-1607 legal work*] (DSA)
P .... Peyote
P .... Pfizer, Inc. [*Research code symbol*]
P .... Pharmacopoeia
P .... Pharmacy (WDAA)
P .... Pharynx (MELL)
P .... Phenacetin (STED)
P .... Phencyclidine [*An anesthetic*]
P .... Phenolphthalein [*Chemical indicator*]
P .... Phenylalanine [*Medicine*] (EDAA)
P .... Philadelphia [*Pennsylvania*] [*Mint mark, when appearing on US coins*]
P .... Philadelphia Stock Exchange, Inc.
P .... Phillips Petroleum [*NYSE symbol*] (TTSB)
P .... Phillips Petroleum Co. [*NYSE symbol*] (SPSG)
P .... Phoenician (BJA)
P .... Phon [*Unit of loudness level*]
P .... Phone (IAA)
p .... Phosphate [*One-letter symbol*] [*Biochemistry*]
P .... Phosphorescence (SAUS)
p .... Phosphoric Residue [*As substituent on nucleoside*] [*Biochemistry*]
P .... Phosphorus [*Chemical element*]
P .... Photographic Reconnaissance Capability [*When suffix to Navy aircraft designation*]
P .... Phototropism [*Botany*]
P .... Phrase [*Linguistics*] (IEL)
P .... Phrase Structure Rule [*Linguistics*]
P .... Physics [*Secondary school course*] [*British*]
P .... Physiology [*Medical Officer designation*] [*British*]
P .... Phytophthora [*A fungus*]
P .... Piaggio Rinaldo [*Industria Aeronautiche & Meccaniche SpA*] [*Italy*] [*ICAO aircraft manufacturer identifier*] (ICAO)
P .... Pianissimo [*Very Softly*] [*Music*]
P .... Piano [*Softly*] [*Music*]
P .... Piaster [*Monetary unit*] [*Spain, Republic of Vietnam, and some Middle Eastern countries*]
p .... Pica [*Typography*] [*Also, P*] (WDMC)
P .... Pick (IAA)
P .... Pickering's Massachusetts Reports [*18-41 Massachusetts*] [*A publication*] (DLA)
P .... Pico
p .... Pico [*A prefix meaning divided by one trillion*] [*SI symbol*]
P .... Picot [*Crochet*] (ROG)
P .... Pie
P .... Pied [*Foot*] [*French*]
P .... Pierced [*Quilting*]
P .... Pigs (ROG)
P .... Pilaster [*Technical drawings*]
P .... Pillar [*Buoy*]
P .... Pilot
P .... Pilotage (SAUS)
P .... Pilotless (SAUS)
P .... Pincherle Catalogue [*Vivaldi*] (GROV)
P .... Pink
P .... Pinnule
P .... Pint
P .... Pip [*Phonetic alphabet*] [*Pre-World War II*] (DSUE)
P .... Pipe
P .... Pipe Rolls [*British*]
P .... Pique; Inclusions [*Diamond clarity grade*]
p .... Pitch (NAKS)
P .... Pitch [*or Pitcher*] [*Baseball*]
P .... Pitch [*Technical drawings*]
P .... Pitcher (NTIO)
P .... Pith [*Botany*]
P .... Pitman Examination Institute [*British*]
P .... Pitman-Moore Co. [*Research code symbol*]
P .... Pius [*Dutiful*] [*Latin*]
P .... Placebo [*Medicine*]
P .... Placentinus [*Deceased, 1192*] [*Authority cited in pre-1607 legal work*] (DSA)
P .... Placitum [*or Placita*] [*Agreeable, Agreed Upon*] [*Latin*] [*Legal term*] (DLA)
P .... Plaintiff [*Legal shorthand*] (LWAP)
P .... Plan (CPH)
P .... Planed
P .... Planning
p .... Plasma [*Medicine*] (QSUL)
P .... Plasma
P .... Plasmodium [*Biology*] (MAE)
P .... Plastid [*Botany*]
P .... Plate [*Electron tube*] [*Technical drawings*]
P .... Platform (DCTA)
P .... Players League [*Major league in baseball, 1890*]
P .... Pleasant
P .... Pleinsbachian [*Geology*]
P .... Pleyel (SAUS)
P .... Plotter [*British military*] (DMA)
P .... Plug
P .... Plus [*More*]
P .... Pneumocystis [*Medicine*] (EDAA)
P .... Poco [*Somewhat*] [*Music*]
P .... Point [*Lacrosse position*]
P .... Point-to-Point Radio [*FAA designator*] (CET)
P .... Poise [*Unit of dynamic viscosity*]
P .... Poison
P .... Polar Distance [*Navigation*]
P .... Polarizability (SAUS)
P .... Polarization
p .... Pole (NAKS)
P .... Pole
P .... Political Division [*Geography*]
P .... Polka [*Music*]
P .... Pollen [*Botany*]
P .... Pollicis (MELL)
P .... Poll rate (SAUS)
P .... Polymorphic [*Biology*]

P .... Polymyxin [*An antibiotic*] (DAVI)
P .... Polyneuropathy [*Medicine*]
P .... Polynomial Time (IAA)
P .... Polyphagous [*Biology*]
P .... Polytechnic (AIE)
P .... Pond [*Maps and charts*]
P .... Pondere [*By Weight*] [*Latin*]
p .... Pondus [*Weight*] [*Latin*] (MAE)
P .... Ponendum [*To Be Placed*] [*Latin*]
P .... Pontifex [*Bishop*] [*Latin*]
P .... Pool
P .... Poop [*Portion of a ship*]
P .... Poorly Organized, Unstable Personality [*Eysenck*] [*Psychology*]
P .... Poor Skiing Conditions
P .... Pope
P .... Popular Response [*Rorschach*] [*Psychology*]
P .... Population
p .... Populus (GEAB)
P .... Populus [*People*] [*Latin*]
P .... Porcelain
P .... Porphyrin [*Medicine*] (DAVI)
P .... Port [*Maps and charts*]
P .... Portable [*JETDS nomenclature*]
P .... Portion
P .... Portland [*Diocesan abbreviation*] [*Oregon*] (TOCD)
P .... Portugal [*IYRU nationality code*]
P .... Position
P .... Positive (IAA)
p .... Positive [*Crystal*]
P .... Positive Conducting [*Electronics*] (IAA)
P .... Post [*After*] [*Latin*]
P .... Post [*Surgery laboratory work*] (DAVI)
p .... Post, After [*Therapy term*] (CTAA)
P .... Postage
P .... Posten [*Sentry*] [*German military*]
P .... Posterior
P .... Postpartum [*Medicine*]
P .... Potsdam [*German license plate city code*]
P .... Pott's Shunt [*Medicine*] (EDAA)
P .... Pouce [*Inch*] [*French*]
P .... Pound (IDOE)
P .... Pounds [*As measurement of total stress*] [*Aerospace*] (AAG)
P .... Pour [*For*] [*French*]
p .... Power (MIST)
P .... Power [*Symbol*] [*IUPAC*]
P .... Poynting Vector [*Electromagnetism*] (DEN)
P .... Practical
p .... Practical Intelligence (DIPS)
P .... Practical Intelligence
P .... Pre-1920 [*Deltiology*]
P .... Preceding
p .... pre-cell (SAUS)
P .... Precipitation Static
P .... Precise Code [*Computer science*] (RDA)
P .... Precision (SAUS)
P .... Precursor (MELL)
P .... Predators Present [*Ecology*]
P .... Predicate
P .... Predictor [*British military*] (DMA)
P .... Prednisolone [*Endocrinology*]
P .... Prednisone [*Also, PDN, Pr, Pred, Pro*] [*Endocrinology*] [*Antineoplastic drug*]
P .... Preferred
P .... Prefix [*Indicating a private radiotelegram*]
P .... P-Register [*Computer science*]
P .... Preliminary
P .... Premolar [*Dentistry*]
P .... Preposition [*Linguistics*] (IEL)
P .... Presbyopia [*Ophthalmology*]
P .... Presbyterian
P .... Prescribing
P .... Present
P .... Present BIT [*Binary Digit*] [*Computer science*]
P .... Preset
P .... President
P .... Press [*Publishing*]
p .... Pressure (NAKS)
P .... Pressure [*or p*] [*Symbol*] [*IUPAC*]
P .... Pressurized Tank [*Liquid gas carriers*]
P .... Preview
P .... Prey [*Zoology*]
P .... Price [*Economics*]
P .... Pridie [*The Day Before*] [*Latin*]
P .... Priest
P .... Priestly (SAUS)
P .... Priestly Source [*Biblical scholarship*]
P .... Prilled
p .... Primary (NAKS)
P .... Primary
P .... Primary [*or Push*] Wave [*Earthquakes*]
p .... Prime (NAKS)
P .... Prime
P .... Primipara [*Woman bearing first child*] [*Medicine*] (MAE)
P .... Primitive
P .... Primus [*First*] [*Latin*]
P .... Prince
P .... Princeps [*First Edition*] [*French*]
P .... Princess (ROG)
P .... Principal
P .... Print
P .... Printer [*Communications term*] (DCT)
P .... Prions [*Medicine*] (MELL)
P .... Priority [*Telecommunications*] (TEL)
P .... Priority Precedence (SAUS)
P .... Priory
P .... Prismatic Joint (IAA)
P .... Prisoner [*Military*]
P .... Private
P .... Private Trust [*Includes testamentary, investment, life insurance, holding title, etc.*] [*Legal term*] (DLA)
P .... Private Venture
P .... Privy (ROG)
P .... Pro [*For*] [*Latin*]
p .... Probability (DIPS)
P .... Probability [*or Probability Ratio*] [*Statistics*]
P .... Probate
P .... Probe (MSA)
P .... Probucol [*Anticholesteremic*]
P .... Procarbazine [*Also, PC, PCB, Pr*] [*Antineoplastic drug*]
P .... Procedure
P .... Proceedings (IAA)
P .... Processor [*Computer science*]
P .... Proconsul
P .... Producer [*Films, television, etc.*]
P .... Product
P .... Production [*of Energy*]
P .... Profession
P .... Professional [*Civil Service employees designation*]
P .... Professor
P .... Proficiency
P .... Profit
P .... Progesterone [*A hormone*]
P .... Program (KSC)
P .... Programmable
P .... Progressive
P .... Prohibited Area [*Followed by identification*]
P .... Prolactin (MELL)
P .... Proliferation [*Biology*]
P .... Proline [*One-letter symbol; see Pro*]
P .... Promoter [*Genetics*]
P .... Prompt [*i.e., the right side*] [*A stage direction*]
P .... Proof [*Philately*]
P .... Prop (DS)
P .... Propagation Distribution [*Broadcasting*]
P .... Propionic [*Bacteriology*] (DAVI)
P .... Proportional (IAA)
P .... Proportion in a Specific Class
P .... Propulsion (AAG)
P .... Protected [*Communications term*] (DCT)
P .... Protein
P .... Proteinuria [*Clinical chemistry*]
P .... Protestant
P .... Protet [*Protest*] [*French*]
P .... Proteus [*Genus of bacteria*] (MAE)
P .... Proto [*Linguistics*]
p .... Proton [*A nuclear particle*]
P .... Protoplasmic [*Freeze etching in microscopy*]
P .... Prototroch
P .... Prototype (AAG)
P .... Provisional
P .... Proximal [*Medicine*] (EDAA)
p .... Proximum [*Near*] [*Latin*] (MAE)
P .... Pseudomonas [*Medicine*] (EDAA)
P .... Psychiatry
P .... Psychometrist [*Psychology*]
P .... Public (AL)
P .... Publications
P .... Public Houses [*Public-performance tariff class*] [*British*]
P .... Public Safety [*FCC*] (NTCM)
P .... Pudding [*Phonetic alphabet*] [*Royal Navy*] [*World War I*] (DSUE)
P .... Pugillus [*A Handful*] [*Pharmacy*] (ROG)
P .... Pula [*Monetary unit*] (ODBW)
P .... Pull (NFPA)
P .... Pulled Up [*Horse racing*]
P .... Pulmonary (MELL)
P .... Pulse
P .... Pump (AAG)
P .... Punch
P .... Punic (BJA)
P .... Punkt [*Point*] [*German military*]
P .... Punter [*Football*]
P .... Pupil
P .... Purchased (AAG)
P .... Purified [*Animal breeding*]
P .... Purinethol [*Mercaptopurine*] [*Also, M, MP*] [*Antineoplastic drug*]
P .... Purkinje Cell [*Neuroanatomy*]
P .... Purl [*Knitting*]
P .... Purple

P .... Purpure [*Purple*] [*Heraldry*]

P .... Pursuit [*Airplane designation*]

P .... Put [*In options listings of newspapers*]

P .... Pya [*Monetary unit*] [*Myanmar*]

P .... Pylon (SAUS)

p .... Pyranose [*One-letter symbol*] [*Biochemistry*]

P .... Pyroxene Subgroup [*Acmite, sodium metasilicate, potassium metasilicate, diopside, wollastonite, hypersthene*] [*CIPW classification*] [*Geology*]

P .... RADAR [*JETDS nomenclature*]

P .... Rank Correlation (DIPS)

P .... Reproducing [*JETDS nomenclature*]

P .... Rippled Lipid Phase [*Biochemistry*] (QSUL)

P .... Roll Rate

P .... Single Paper [*Wire insulation*] (AAG)

P .... Soft Pad [*Missile launch environment symbol*]

P .... Warner-Lambert Pharmaceutical Co. [*Research code symbol*]

P00 .... Program Zero-Zero (SAUS)

P1 .... Form to arrange payment to an outside body (SAUS)

P_1 .... Inorganic Phosphate [*Chemistry*] (DAVI)

p-1 .... Page 1 [*Also, P-1*] (WDMC)

P-1 .... Page One [*Broadcasting*] (WDMC)

p1 .... Para 1 [*Unipara - having borne one child*] (DAVI)

P_1 .... Parental Generation (MAE)

P1 .... Pershing 1 [*Missile*] (GFGA)

P_1 .... Pulmonic First Heart Sound [*Medicine*] (DAVI)

P_1 .... Pulmonic First Sound [*Medicine*] (MEDA)

P1 .... Pump, Smallest

P1a .... Pershing 1a [*Missile*] (GFGA)

P1E .... Planed One Edge [*Technical drawings*] (DAC)

P1MG .... P1 [*Code*] for Multigroup [*Method*] [*Nuclear energy*] (NRCH)

P1S .... Planed One Side [*Technical drawings*] (DAC)

P1S2E .... Planed One Side and Two Edges [*Technical drawings*] (DAC)

P2 .... Papua New Guinea [*Aircraft nationality and registration mark*] (FAAC)

P2 .... Pollution Prevention

P-2 .... Propaganda Due [*Secret Italian Masonic organization, allegedly tied to the Roman Catholic church*]

P_2 .... Pulmonic Second Sound [*Medicine*]

P2 .... Pump, Next to Smallest

P2 .... Second Parental Generation (EES)

P2 .... Second Pilot [*Aviation*] (AIA)

P2C4I .... Power Projection C4I (SAUS)

P2d .... Pacific Reporter, Second Series [*West*] [*A publication*] (AAGC)

P2I .... Planned Product Improvement

P2(L)(R) .... 2 Papi Lights (Left or Right Side off Runway) [*Aviation*] (PIPO)

P^{2NBC2} .... Physiological and Psychological Effects of NBC [*Nuclear, Biological, and Chemical Warfare*] and Extended Operations [*Army study project*] (INF)

P2P .... Peer-to-Peer

P2P .... Person to Person [*Communications term*] (DCT)

P2S .... Panoramic Periscope System (SAUS)

P-3 .... Fixed wing ASW aircraft (SAUS)

P3 .... Industry Composites and Polymer Processing Program [*Massachusetts Institute of Technology*] [*Research center*] (RCD)

P-3 .... Orion [*Maritime patrol/anti-submarine aircraft*] [*Navy*] (POLM)

P3 .... Pacific Project Phoenix

P3 .... Panoz [*Society of Automotive Engineers auto manufacturer code for service information interchange*]

P3 .... Phillips Post Processor

P3 .... Platform for Privacy Preferences (SAUS)

P3 .... Polluter-Pays-Principle (SAUS)

P3 .... Portable Plotting Package [*Nuclear energy*] (NRCH)

P/3 .... Proximal Third [*of bone*] [*Orthopedics*] (DAVI)

P3FE .... Polytrifluoroethylene (EDCT)

P_3I .... Planned Program Product Improvement [*Army*]

P3I .... Precision Plan Position Indication (SAUS)

P3I .... Precision Plan Position Indicator (SAUS)

P^3I .... Preplanned Product Improvement [*DoD*]

P3P .... Platform for Privacy Preferences

P3P .... Platform for Privacy Preferences Project [*Computer science*]

P3RDB .... Prelaunch/Postlanding Processing Requirements Data Base (SAUS)

P4 .... Aruba [*Aircraft nationality and registration mark*] (FAAC)

P4 .... Production Process Prove-Out Program

P 4 CAST Model... Probabilistic Forecasting Model (SAUS)

P4(L)(R) .... 4 Papi Lights (Left or Right Side of Runway) [*Aviation*] (PIPO)

P4MEP ...... Pray for Me Please [*Internet lingo*] (NETL)

P4P .... Pagans for Peace Network [*Canada*] (EAIO)

P4PS .... Partnership for Patient Safety [*Association*] (EA)

P4S .... Planed Four Sides [*Technical drawings*] (DAC)

P4SR .... Predicted Four Hour Sweat Rate (PDAA)

P6ROC ...... P6 Rover Owners Club (EAIO)

P08 .... German marking denoting the so-called luger service pistol (SAUS)

P 14 .... Pattern 14 Rifle [*Made in the US for Great Britain, beginning in 1914*]

P31 .... Pre-Planned Product Improvement [*Training term*] (LPT)

P 32 .... Radioactive Phosphorus (DAVI)

p35 .... Protein of 35 kDa Molar Mass [*Molecular biology*] (QSUL)

P38 .... German 9mm service pistol (SAUS)

P_{50} .... Partial pressure of oxygen at 50% hemoglobin saturation [*Medicine*]

P53 .... IARC Somatic P53 Mutation Database (MHID)

P-55 .... Hydroxypregnanedione [*Endocrinology*] (DAVI)

P-88/ARA ... Project '88: Americans for the Reagan Agenda [*Defunct*] (EA)

P450 .... P450-Aromatase (SAUS)

P680 .... Pigments Absorbing Light at 680 nm [*Biochemistry*] (QSUL)

P700 .... Pigments Absorbing Light at 700 nm [*Biochemistry*] (QSUL)

P_A .... Alveolar Pressure [*Medicine*] (DAVI)

PA .... B. F. Jones Memorial Library, Aliquippa, PA [*Library symbol*] [*Library of Congress*] (LCLS)

PA .... Office of Public Affairs [*DoD*]

P-A .... Pacific-Atlantic Line (SAUS)

PA .... Package Application (SAUS)

PA .... Pack Area (SAUS)

PA .... Packet Adapter [*Telecommunications*] (IAA)

PA .... Pad Abort [*NASA*] (KSC)

PA .... Paging Algorithm (SAUS)

PA .... Paging and Area Warning (MCD)

P/A .... Paid Annually (SAUS)

Pa .... Paine's United States Circuit Court Reports [*A publication*] (DLA)

PA .... Paintmakers Association [*British*] (DBA)

PA .... Paired Associates [*Psychometrics*]

PA .... Pakistan Army

PA .... Palaeontology Association (SAUS)

PA .... Paleopathology Association

PA .... Palestine Affairs [*New York*] [*A publication*] (BJA)

PA .... Palestinian (SAUS)

PA .... Palestinian Authority [*Political movement*] (ECON)

PA .... Palladium [*Chemical element*] (ROG)

PA .... Panama [*ANSI two-letter standard code*] (CNC)

PA .... Panama Area (SAUS)

PA .... Pan American (SAUS)

PA .... Pan American World Airways, Inc. [*See also PAA, PAN-AM, PN*] [*ICAO designator*] (MCD)

P-A .... Pan-Atlantic Line (SAUS)

P-A .... Pan-Atlantic Steamship Corp. (MHDW)

PA .... Panatlas Energy, Inc. [*Toronto Stock Exchange symbol*]

PA .... pancreatic Ascites [*Medicine*] (MELL)

PA .... Panel Absorber (SAUS)

PA .... Panic Alarm (SAUS)

PA .... Panic Attack [*Medicine*] (MEDA)

PA .... Panniculus Adiposus [*Medicine*] (MELL)

PA .... Pantothenic Acid [*Biochemistry*] (DB)

pa .... Paper (VRA)

PA .... Paper (WGA)

PA .... Paper Advance (BUR)

PA .... Para-Amps (EA)

Pa .... Parachutist [*British military*] (DMA)

PA .... Parallel Access (SAUS)

PA .... Parallel Adder (SAUS)

PA .... Parallel Algorithm (SAUS)

PA .... Paralysis Agitans

PA .... Parameter Address (SAUS)

PA .... Parametric Amplifier

PA .... Par Amitie [*By Favor*] [*French*]

Pa .... Paranoia [*Psychology*]

PA .... Parapsychological Association (EA)

PA .... Parasitic Antenna (SAUS)

PA .... Parathion (LDT)

PA .... Par Autorite [*By Authority*] [*French*]

PA .... Parental Advisory (WDMC)

PA .... Parent Atom (ODA)

PA .... Parenteral Alimentation [*Medicine*] (MELL)

PA .... Parents Anonymous (EA)

PA .... Parents' Association

PA .... Parish

Pa .... Paris Stock Exchange [*France*]

PA .... Parti Affectae [*To the Affected Part*] [*Pharmacy*]

PA .... Partial Application [*Military*] (AFIT)

P_A .... Partial Pressure in Arterial Blood [*Medicine*] (DAVI)

PA .... Participating Activity [*Responsible for standardization efforts*] [*DoD*]

PA .... Participial Adjective [*Grammar*]

PA .... Particle Accelerator (SAUS)

PA .... Particular Average

PA .... Parti de l'Action [*Party of Action*] [*Morocco*] [*Political party*] (PPW)

PA .... Partido Andalucista [*Spain*] [*Political party*] (ECED)

PA .... Partido Arnulfista [*Panama*] [*Political party*] (EY)

PA .... Partners of the Americas (EA)

PA .... Pascal [*Unit of measure*]

Pa .... Pascal [*Symbol*] [*SI unit of pressure*]

PA .... Passau [*German license plate city code*]

PA .... Passenger Address System [*Aviation*] (DA)

PA .... Passenger Agent

PA .... Passenger Ship

PA .... Passive Aggressive (DMAA)

pa .... Past (ODA)

PA .... Patent Assignee (NITA)

PA .... Patents (NITA)

PA .... Pathfinder Association (EAIO)

PA .... Pathologist [*Medicine*] (EDAA)

PA .... Pathology [*Medicine*] (EDAA)

PA .... Patient

PA .... Patient's Advocate [*Medicine*] (DMAA)

PA .... Patrol Aircraft (NATG)

PA .... Pattern Analysis [*Test*]

PA .... Pay and Allowances

PA .... Paying Agent [*Legal term*] (DLA)

PA .... Payload Accommodations (SAUS)

PA .... Payment Appropriations (EURO)

P/A .... Payment Authority [*Business term*]

PA........... Peak-Aged (SAUS)
PA........... Peak Amplitude [*Medicine*] (DMAA)
P-A........... Peak-to-Average (SAUS)
PA........... Pedestrians Association [*British*] (DBA)
PA........... Pending Availability
PA........... Pendulous Axis [*Accelerometer*] (IEEE)
Pa........... Pennsylvania (ODBW)
PA........... Pennsylvania [*Postal code*]
PA........... Pennsylvania Railroad Co. (SAUS)
Pa........... Pennsylvania Reports [*A publication*] (AAGC)
PA........... Pennsylvania Supreme Court Reports [*1845-date*] [*A publication*] (DLA)
PA........... People's Alliance [*Althydubandalag*] [*Iceland*] [*Political party*] (PPW)
PA........... Peptide Absorption
PA........... Per Abdomen
PA........... Per Adresse [*Care Of*] [*German*]
PA........... Per Annum [*By the Year*] [*Latin*]
pa........... Per annum (EBF)
PA........... Per Auguri [*Used on visiting cards to express congratulations, birthday wishes, etc.*] [*Italian*]
PA........... Percentage Activity [*Measurement*] (DAVI)
PA........... Performance Alertness (AEBS)
PA........... Performance Analysis
PA........... Performance Analysts (SAUS)
PA........... Performance Appraisal
PA........... Performance Appraisal Required [*Civil Service*]
PA........... Performance Assessment (DOGT)
PA........... Performing Arts [*US Copyright Office class*]
PA........... Periapical [*Anatomy*] (DAVI)
PA........... Periarteritis [*Medicine*] (DMAA)
PA........... Peridural Artery [*Medicine*] (DMAA)
PA........... Periodic Acid [*Inorganic chemistry*]
PA........... Periodontal Abscess [*Medicine*] (MELL)
pA........... Periplanone A [*Biochemistry*]
PA........... Peritoneal Adhesions [*Medicine*] (MELL)
PA........... Permanent Abeyance [*FDA*]
PA........... Permanent Address (ROG)
PA........... Permanent Appointment
PA........... Permanently Assigned (ACAE)
PA........... Permanently Associated [*Telecommunications*] (TEL)
PA........... Pernicious Anemia [*Hematology*]
PA........... Personal Accident [*Insurance*] (AIA)
P/A........... Personal Account (WDAA)
PA........... Personal Adjutant (SAUS)
PA........... Personal Affairs (AFM)
pa........... Personal Appearance (ODA)
PA........... Personal Appearance
PA........... Personal Assistant [*British*]
PA........... Personal Audit [*Psychological testing*]
PA........... Personality Accentuation [*Medicine*] (EDAA)
PA........... Personnel Administrator [*American Society for Personnel Administration*] [*A publication*] [*Information service or system*]
PA........... Personnel Area (NRCH)
PA........... Personnel Assistant
PA........... Personnel Association
PA........... Perturbation Analysis (SAUS)
PA........... Petroleum Abstracts [*A Publication*] (IID)
PA........... Petroleum Association (SAUS)
PA........... Pfizer, Inc. [*Research code symbol*]
PA........... Phakic-Aphakic [*Ophthalmology*] (MAE)
PA........... Pharmacology, Clinical [*Medical specialty*] (DHSM)
PA........... Phase Angle (IAA)
PA........... Phased Array (SAUS)
PA........... Phenol Alcohol [*Chemistry*] (DAVI)
PA........... Phentolamine [*Antiadrenergic*]
PA........... Phenylalanine (SAUS)
PA........... Phenylalkylamine [*Medicine*] (EDAA)
PA........... Philippine Army
PA........... Philippine Association (EA)
PA........... Phobics Anonymous (MELL)
PA........... Phonocardiogram Amplifier [*Cardiology*]
PA........... Phosphatidic Acid [*Biochemistry*]
PA........... Phosphoarginine [*Biochemistry*]
PA........... Phosphoric Acid (ECON)
PA........... Photoallergenic [*Response*] [*Medicine*]
PA........... Photodiode Amplifier
PA........... Photoinduced Anisotropy [*Physics*]
PA........... Phthalic Anhydride [*Organic chemistry*]
PA........... Physical Activity (MCD)
PA........... Physical Address (SAUS)
P/A........... Physical Asymmetric (GART)
PA........... Physician Advisor (HCT)
PA........... Physician's Assistant
PA........... Physics Abstracts [*Institution of Electrical Engineers*] [*Information service or system*] [*A publication*] (CRD)
PA........... Phytoalexin [*Plant pathology*]
PA........... Piaster [*Monetary unit*] [*Spain, Republic of Vietnam, and some Middle Eastern countries*]
PA........... Picatinny Arsenal [*New Jersey*] [*Later, Armament Development Center*] [*Army*]
pA........... Picoampere [*One trillionth of an ampere*]
PA........... Pierre Allain [*Lightweight rock-climbing boot named after its designer*]
PA........... Pierre Arpels [*Jewelry designer*]
PA........... Pilgrim Adventure [*United Kingdom*] (EAIO)
PA........... Pills Anonymous [*Later, DA*] [*An association*] (EA)
PA........... Pilot Amplifier (SAUS)
PA........... Pilot Approval [*Automotive project management*]
PA........... Pilotless Aircraft
PA........... PIMCO Advisors'A' [*NYSE symbol*] (TTSB)
PA........... Pimco Advisors Ltd. [*NYSE symbol*] (SAG)
PA........... Pipeline Authority [*Australia*]
PA........... Piper Aircraft Corp. [*ICAO aircraft manufacturer identifier*] (ICAO)
PA........... Pirke Avot (BJA)
PA........... Pitch Angle
PA........... Pituitary-Adrenal [*Endocrinology*] (DAVI)
PA........... Placenta Accreta [*Medicine*] (MELL)
P/A........... Planetary Atmosphere (SAA)
PA........... Planning Assistance (EA)
PA........... Planning Authority (HEAS)
PA........... Plant Association (ALAC)
PA........... Plasma Adsorption [*Medicine*] (DMAA)
PA........... Plasma Aldosterone [*Endocrinology*]
PA........... Plasma-Arc (SAUS)
PA........... Plasminogen Activator [*Biochemistry*]
PA........... Plate Appearance [*Baseball term*] (NDBD)
PA........... Platelet Adhesiveness [*Hematology*]
PA........... Platelet-Associated (DB)
PA........... Platform Assembly (MCD)
PA........... Play Aid (SAUS)
PA........... Podiatry Association [*British*] (DBA)
PA........... Point of Aim [*Military*]
PA........... Points Against [*Football*]
PA........... Polar Atlantic [*American air mass*]
PA........... Polarization Approximation [*Physical chemistry*]
PA........... Polarographic Analyzer
PA........... Polar to Analog
PA........... Police Academy
PA........... Police Agent (WDAA)
PA........... Policy Analyst (GNE)
PA........... Polled Angus (SAUS)
PA........... Polyacetal [*Organic chemistry*]
PA........... Polyacrylate (EDCT)
PA........... Polyacrylic [*Organic chemistry*]
PA........... Polyallomer (SAUS)
PA........... Polyamide [*Organic chemistry*]
PA........... Polyanhydride [*Organic chemistry*]
PA........... Polyarteritis [*Medicine*]
PA........... Polyarthritis [*Medicine*] (DMAA)
PA........... Polyarylate (SAUS)
PA........... Polymer Adhesive
PA........... Port Agency [*Army*]
PA........... Port Authority [*Western Australia*]
PA........... Port of Arrival (SAUS)
PA........... Position Accuracy
PA........... Position Angle [*Astronomy*]
PA........... Position Approximate [*Nautical charts*]
P/A........... Positioner/Actuator (SAUS)
PA........... Position of Assembly (SAUS)
PA........... Positive Addiction [*Self-improvement method developed by William Glasser, MD*]
PA........... Positive Attitude
PA........... Postacceleration (SAUS)
PA........... Post Adjutant
PA........... Postal Assistant (DCTA)
PA........... Post Amplifier
PA........... Post-Aural [*Medicine*] (DMAA)
PA........... Post Award Contract [*Department of Defense*]
PA........... Posterior Anterior [*Medicine*]
PA........... Posterior Aorta
PA........... Postero-Anterior (SAUS)
PA........... Postmortem Aging [*of meat*]
PA........... Post-Secondary Accreditation (SAUS)
PA........... Potato Agar [*Microbiology*]
PA........... Potsmokers Anonymous (EA)
PA........... Poverty Alliance [*United Kingdom*] (EAIO)
PA........... Power Alarm (SAUS)
PA........... Power Amplification (SAUS)
PA........... Power Amplifier
PA........... Power Antenna [*Automotive term*]
PA........... Power Approach [*Aerospace*]
PA........... Power of Attorney
P/A........... Power of Authority
PA........... Practice Amendment (AAG)
PA........... Preacceleration (SAUS)
PA........... Prealbumin [*Biochemistry*]
PA........... Prealloying (SAUS)
PA........... Preamble (SAUS)
PA........... Preamplifier
PA........... Preapproved
PA........... Prearm
PA........... Preavailability
PA........... Precision-Acrobatics (DOMA)
PA........... Precision Angle (IAA)
PA........... Precision Approach (SAUS)
PA........... Precision Architecture [*Hewlett-Packard Co.*] [*Computer science*]
PA........... Precomputed Altitude
PA........... Predictive Accuracy [*Medicine*] (DMAA)

PA............ Predictive Analyzer [*Computer science*] (DIT)
PA............ Prefect-Apostolic [*Roman Catholic*]
PA............ Preferential Adsorption (SAUS)
PA............ Pregnancy-Associated [*Gynecology*] (MAE)
PA............ Preliminary Acceptance (KSC)
PA............ Preliminary Amplifier (IAA)
PA............ Preliminary Assessment (ERG)
PA............ Preliminary Award (SAUS)
PA............ Preparing Activity [*Responsible for Federal document and study projects*]
PA............ Preplaced Aggregate (SAUS)
P/A............ Presence or Absence
PA............ Present Again (ADA)
PA............ Presentation Architecture (SAUS)
PA............ Preservation Action (EA)
PA............ Presidents Association [*New York, NY*] (EA)
PA............ Press Agency (WDAA)
PA............ Press Agent
PA............ Press Association Ltd. (IID)
PA............ Pressure Actuated [*Switch*]
PA............ Pressure Alarm [*Nuclear energy*] (NRCH)
PA............ Pressure Altitude [*Aviation*]
PA............ Pressure Angle (MSA)
PA............ Pressure Anomaly (SAUS)
PA............ Pressure Area [*Medicine*]
PA............ Presumptive Address (SAUS)
PA............ Price Analyst
PA............ Price Availability (SAUS)
PA............ Primary Aerospace Vehicle [*or Aircraft*]
PA............ Primary Amenorrhea [*Gynecology*] (MAE)
PA............ Primary Anemia [*Medicine*]
PA............ Prince Albert (ACAE)
PA............ Prince Albert Coat [*Slang*]
PA............ Principal Applicant (SAUS)
PA............ Principal Assistant (NOAA)
PA............ Principal Axes
PA............ Principle of Adding [*New math*]
PA............ Priority A (MCD)
PA............ Priority Aggregate
PA............ Prior to Admission [*Medicine*]
PA............ Prison Auxiliary (WDAA)
PA............ Privacy Act
PA............ Privacy Act of 1974 (COE)
PA............ Private Account [*Banking*]
PA............ Private Architect [*British*]
Pa............ Proactinium (IDOE)
PA............ Proactivator [*Medicine*]
PA............ Pro Anno [*For the Year*] [*Latin*]
PA............ Proanthocyanidin (Assay) [*Analytical chemistry*]
PA............ Pro Applicatione [*To Be Applied*] [*Pharmacy*] (ROG)
PA............ Probability of Acceptance (KSC)
PA............ Probability of Acquisition [*Military*]
PA............ Probability of Arrival (SAUS)
PA............ Problem Analysis
PA............ Problem Area (ACAE)
PA............ Probleme der Agyptologie [*A publication*] (BJA)
PA............ Procainamide [*Cardiac depressant*]
PA............ Procedure Administrator (SAUS)
PA............ Process Alert (SAUS)
PA............ Process Allocator [*Telecommunications*] (TEL)
PA............ Process Automation (CMD)
PA............ Procurement Agency (MCD)
PA............ Procurement Appropriations [*Army*] (AABC)
PA............ Procurement, Army
PA............ Procurement Authorization
PA............ Procuring Activity [*Military*]
PA............ Product Acceptance [*Automotive engineering*]
PA............ Product Administration (HCT)
PA............ Product Analysis (IEEE)
PA............ Product Analyst (SAUS)
PA............ Product Assortment (MHDB)
PA............ Product Assurance (NASA)
PA............ Product Attention (ELAL)
PA............ Production Adjustment
PA............ Production Agency (COE)
PA............ Production Analysis (SAUS)
PA............ Production Approval [*Automotive engineering*]
PA............ Production Assistant
PA............ Professional Administrator [*Australia*] [*A publication*]
PA............ Professional Agent [*Professional Insurance Agents*] [*A publication*]
PA............ Professional Archeologist (SAUS)
PA............ Professional Association [*Telecommunications*]
PA............ Profile Analysis [*Medicine*]
PA............ Profile Angle (MSA)
PA............ Program Access
PA............ Program Account (NG)
PA............ Program Action (SAUS)
PA............ Program Address
PA............ Program Administrator (MCD)
PA............ Program Agent (OICC)
PA............ Program Aid [*A publication*]
PA............ Program Amount (NITA)
PA............ Program Analysis [*Computer science*]
PA............ Program Announcement
PA............ Program Application (SAUS)
PA............ Program Application Instructions [*Telecommunications*] (TEL)
PA............ Program Assessment (MCD)
PA............ Program Attention [*Computer science*] (IAA)
PA............ Program Attention Key [*Computer science*]
PA............ Program Authorization (AFM)
PA............ Program for the Aging (OICC)
PA............ Programmable Automation
PA............ Programmatic Agreement (SAUS)
PA............ Programmed Addressing (SAUS)
PA............ Programmed Algorithm (SAUS)
PA............ Programmed Arithmetic (IAA)
P/A............ Programmer/Analyst [*Computer science*] (VLIE)
PA............ Programming Address (SAUS)
PA............ Programming Aid (SAUS)
PA............ Progressive Alliance [*Defunct*] (EA)
PA............ Prohibited Area (SAUS)
PA............ Project Accounting (GART)
PA............ Project Administration (MCD)
PA............ Project Analysis (MHDB)
PA............ Project Authorization
PA............ Proliferating Angioendotheliomatosis
PA............ Prologue Auditor (ACAE)
PA............ Prolonged-Action [*Pharmacy*]
PA............ Prolotherapy Association (EA)
PA............ Propane Asphalt [*Petroleum engineering*]
PA............ Property Administrator [*DoD*]
PA............ Prophylactic Antibiotic
PA............ Propionic Acid (DMAA)
PA............ Proponent Agency [*Army*]
PA............ Proportional Action (AAG)
PA............ Proposal Authorization
PA............ Proposed Algorithm (SAUS)
PA............ [*The*] Proprietary Association [*Later, NDMA*] (EA)
PA............ Propulsion Assistance (DS)
PA............ Propulsion Assisted (SAUS)
P/A............ Propulsion/Avionics (SAUS)
PA............ Prosecuting Attorney
PA............ Prospecting Authority [*Australia*]
PA............ Prostitutes Anonymous (EA)
PA............ Protactinium
Pa............ Protactinium [*or Protoactinium*] [*Chemical element*]
PA............ Protected Area [*Nuclear energy*] (NRCH)
PA............ Protective Action (COE)
PA............ Protective Agent (SAUS)
PA............ Protective Antigen
PA............ Proteolytic Action [*Medicine*] (EDAA)
PA............ Protestant Alliance [*British*] (DBA)
PA............ Prothonotary Apostolic
PA............ Proto-Australian [*Linguistics*] (IEL)
PA............ Protocol Adapter [*Communications*]
PA............ Proton Affinity [*Surface ionization*]
PA............ Protrusio Acetabuli [*Medicine*] (DMAA)
PA............ Provisional Acceptance (SAUS)
PA............ Provisional Allowance
PA............ Pseudo Address (SAUS)
PA............ Pseudoaneurysm [*Medicine*]
PA............ Pseudo-Astronomy
PA............ Pseudomonas aeruginosa [*Bacterium*]
PA............ Psoriasis Association [*Australia*]
PA............ Psoriatic Arthritis
PA............ Psychiatric Aide (DAVI)
PA............ Psychoacoustics (SAUS)
PA............ Psychoanalyst
PA............ Psychogenic Aspermia [*Medicine*]
PA............ Psychological Age
PA............ Public Accountant
PA............ Public Act
PA............ Public Address [*Amplification equipment*] [*Communications*]
PA............ Public Address System (WDMC)
PA............ Public Administration
PA............ Public Advocate (EA)
PA............ Public Affairs
PA............ Public Affairs Specialist [*Military*] (POLM)
PA............ Public Agent (WDAA)
PA............ Public Archives [*of Canada*]
PA............ Public Art (SAUS)
PA............ Public Assistance
PA............ Publication Announcement
PA............ Public Awareness (SAUS)
PA............ Publicity Agent (WDAA)
PA............ Published Author (CPGU)
PA............ Publishers' Alliance [*Defunct*] (EA)
PA............ Publishers' Association [*London, England*] (DIT)
PA............ Pull and Adjust [*Brace*] [*Medicine*]
PA............ Pulmonary Angiography [*Medicine*]
pa............ Pulmonary Artery [*Medicine*] (ADWA)
PA............ Pulmonary Artery [*Medicine*]
PA............ Pulmonary Atresia [*Medicine*]
PA............ Pulpoaxial [*Dentistry*]
PA............ Pulsating Arc (IAA)
PA............ Pulse Amplifier
PA............ Pulse Analyzer (SAUS)
PA............ Puppeteers of America (EA)

PA.......... Purchase Agreement (VLIE)
PA.......... Purchasing Agent
PA.......... Purge Alarm [*Nuclear energy*] (NRCH)
PA.......... Puromycin Aminonucleoside [*Biochemistry*] (OA)
PA.......... Purpose and Activities (NITA)
PA.......... Put Away [*Papers*] [*British*]
PA.......... Puumala [*Vole virus*]
PA.......... Pyro Ammonia (ROG)
PA.......... Pyrrolizidine Alkaloid [*Toxicology*]
PA.......... Pyruvic Acid [*Medicine*] (EDAA)
PA.......... Pythium aphanidermatum [*A fungus*]
PAO_2.......... Arterial Oxygen Pressure (MAE)
PAA.......... Pa-An [*Myanmar*] [*Airport symbol*] (OAG)
PAA.......... Pacific Alaska Airways (SAUS)
PAA.......... Pacific Arts Association (EA)
PAA.......... Pan Am Corp. [*AMEX symbol*] (SAG)
PAA.......... Pan American Minerals Corp. [*Toronto Stock Exchange symbol*] [*Vancouver Stock Exchange symbol*]
PAA.......... Pan American Silver Corp. [*Toronto Stock Exchange symbol*] [*Canada*]
PAA.......... Pan American World Airways, Inc. [*See also PA, PAN-AM, PN*]
PAA.......... Pancretan Association of America (EA)
PAA.......... Pancyprian Association of America [*Defunct*] (EA)
PAA.......... Panguna [*Solomon Islands*] [*Seismograph station code, US Geological Survey*] (SEIS)
PAA.......... Paper Agents Association [*British*] (DBA)
paa.......... Papuan-Australian [*MARC language code*] [*Library of Congress*] (LCCP)
PAA.......... Para-Azoxyanisole [*Organic chemistry*]
PAA.......... Parke, Davis & Co. [*Research code symbol*]
PAA.......... Parti Affectae Applicandus [*Apply to the Affected Part*] [*Pharmacy*]
PAA.......... Partial Agonist Activity (DB)
PAa.......... Passive Acoustic Analysis (ACAE)
PAA.......... Patriot Airlines, Inc. [*ICAO designator*] (FAAC)
PAA.......... Pattern Analysis and Applications [*Database*] [*United Kingdom*] (GDD)
PAA.......... Pay Adjustment Authorization
PAA.......... Payload Attach Assembly [*Space launch term*] (ISAK)
PAA.......... P-azoxyanisole (SAUS)
PAA.......... Peer Access Approval (VLIE)
PAA.......... Pennsylvania Automotive Association (EARSL)
PAA.......... Per Acetic Acid (SAUS)
PAA.......... Peracetic Acid [*Organic chemistry*]
PAA.......... Peri-Appendicular Abscess [*Medicine*] (MELL)
PAA.......... Peroxyacetic Acid (SAUS)
PAA.......... Peruvian American Association (EA)
PAA.......... Petroleum Administration Act [*Canada*]
PAA.......... Phase Antenna Array (SAUS)
PAA.......... Phased Array Aerial (or Antenna) (SAUS)
PAA.......... Phased Array Antenna
PAA.......... Phenanthrene Amino Alcohol [*Organic chemistry*]
PAA.......... Phenanthrylacetamide [*Organic chemistry*]
PAA.......... Phenylacetic Acid [*Organic chemistry*]
PAA.......... Phonetic Alphabet Association (DGA)
PAA.......... Phosphonoacetic Acid [*Antiviral compound*]
PAA.......... Phosphoric Acid Aluminum Treatment (SAUS)
PAA.......... Photographers Association of America [*Later, Professional Photographers of America*]
PAA.......... Photon Activation Analysis
PAA.......... Physiological Amino Acid (SAUS)
PAA.......... Pi Alpha Alpha (EA)
PAA.......... Pill Addicts Anonymous (EA)
PAA.......... Plains All American Pipeline LP [*NYSE symbol*]
PAA.......... Plains All Amer Pipeline [*NYSE symbol*] (SG)
PAA.......... Planar Array Aerial (or Antenna) (SAUS)
PAA.......... Planar Array Antenna
PAA.......... Plasma Amino Acid (SAUS)
PAa.......... Plasma Angiotensinase Activity [*Medicine*] (MELL)
PAA.......... Plasminogen Activator Activity [*Biochemistry*]
PAA.......... Platelet Associated Activity [*Pharmacology*]
PAA.......... Polish Association of America [*Later, NFLI*] (EA)
PAA.......... Polocrosse Association of Australia
PAA.......... Poly Acetic Acid (SAUS)
PAA.......... Polyacrylamide [*Also, PAAM, PAM*] [*Organic chemistry*]
PAA.......... Polyacrylic Acid [*Organic chemistry*]
PAA.......... Polyammino Acid [*Medicine*] (MELL)
PAA.......... Polyaspartic Acid [*Biochemistry*]
PAA.......... Polycyclic Aromatic Amine [*Organic chemistry*]
PAA.......... Population Association of America (EA)
PAA.......... Port Autonome d'Abidjan [*The Ivory Coast*] (EY)
PAA.......... Post Award Action
PAA.......... Potato Association of America (EA)
PAA.......... Power Amplifier Assembly
PAA.......... Pre-Apprenticeship Allowance
PAA.......... Pre-arrangement Association of America (SAUS)
PAA.......... Primary Aircraft Assigned (ACAE)
PAA.......... Primary Aircraft Authorized [*Air Force*]
PAA.......... Primary Aromatic Amine (ABAC)
PAA.......... Primary Authorized Aircraft (SAUS)
PAA.......... Primary Auxiliary Area [*Nuclear energy*] (NRCH)
PAA.......... Print Advertising Association [*Defunct*] (EA)
PAA.......... Priority Abatement Areas [*Environment*] (GNE)
PAA.......... Priority Problem Areas
PAA.......... Prisoners Aid Association (SAUS)
PAA.......... Procurement Appropriation, Army (MCD)
PAA.......... Procurement of Ammunition, Army (AABC)
PAA.......... Professional Apparel Association
PAA.......... Professional Archers Association (EA)
PAA.......... Program Assistant Administrator (SAUS)
PAA.......... Programme d'Aide aux Athletes [*Athlete Assistance Program*] [*Canada*]
PAA.......... Provincial Archives of Alberta (SAUS)
PAA.......... Psoriatic Arthropathy Alliance [*United Kingdom*] (EAIO)
PAA.......... Pulse-Amplitude Analyzer (SAUS)
PAA.......... Purchasing Agents Association (NADA)
PAA.......... Pyridineacetic Acid [*Organic chemistry*]
P/AA3.......... Probationary Aircraft Artificer 3rd Class [*British military*] (DMA)
PAAA.......... Pan-American Aerobiology Association (EA)
PAAA.......... Polyaminoamido Acid (SAUS)
PAAA.......... Premium Advertising Association of America [*Later, PMAA*] (EA)
PAAA.......... Price Anderson Amendments Act (SAUS)
P/AAA2.......... Probationary Aircraft Artificer, Acting, 2nd Class [*British military*] (DMA)
PAAAC.......... Pan-American Agricultural Aviation Center (SAUS)
PAAAEL.......... Pennsylvania Association of Accredited Environmental Laboratories (EARSL)
PAAAR.......... Pioneers Across America for Alzheimer's Research [*An association*]
PAAAS.......... Proceedings of the American Academy of Arts and Sciences (SAUS)
PAAB.......... PERSCOM [*Personnel Command*] Acquisition Accession Board [*Army*] (INF)
PAAB.......... Public Arts Advisory Board (SAUS)
PAABA.......... P-Acetamidobenzoic Acid (SAUS)
PAABA.......... Para-Acetamidobenzoic Acid [*Biochemistry*]
PAABS.......... PanAmerican Association of Biochemical Societies (EA)
PAAC.......... Pacific and Asian Affairs Council
PAAC.......... Payments and Administrative Communication Corp. (SAUS)
PAAC.......... Pennsylvania Athletic Conference (PSS)
PAAC.......... Port Authority of Alleghany County [*Federal Railroad Administration identification code*]
PAAC.......... Product Assurance Action Center (SAUS)
PAAC.......... Program Analysis Adaptable Control [*Computer science*]
PAAC.......... Public Arts Advisory Council (SAUS)
PAACE.......... Precision Aircraft Armament Control Experiment (RDA)
PAACS.......... Prior Active Army Commissioned Service
PAACT.......... Patient Advocates for Advanced Cancer Treatments
PAAD.......... Private Automatic Answering Device [*Telecommunications*] (VLIE)
PAAD.......... Program Assistance Approval Document (SAUS)
PAAD.......... Project Army Aviation Data (SAUS)
PAADAR.......... Passive Airborne Detection and Ranging (MSA)
PAADC.......... Principal Air Aide-de-Camp [*RAF*] [*British*]
PA Admin Bull... Pennsylvania Bulletin [*A publication*] (DLA)
PA Admin Code... Pennsylvania Administrative Code [*A publication*] (DLA)
PAAE.......... Pennsylvania Association for Adult Education (SAUS)
PAAECI.......... Pan American Association of Educational Credit Institutions [*See also APICE*] (EAIO)
PAAES.......... Prior Active Army Enlisted Service
PAAES.......... Publications. American Archaeological Expedition to Syria [*A publication*] (BJA)
PAAF.......... Professional Actors Association of Florida (SAUS)
PAAFB.......... Patrick Auxiliary Air Force Base [*Florida*] (SAA)
PAAFCS.......... Prior Active Air Force Commissioned Service
PAAFES.......... Prior Active Air Force Enlisted Service
PAAG.......... Portable Airfield Arrestor Gear (SAUS)
PAAGE.......... Panel on Alternate Approaches to Graduate Education (EA)
PAAGE.......... Polyacryl-Amide Gel Electrophoresis (SAUS)
PAAH.......... Polyacrylamide-Hydrazide [*Organic chemistry*]
PAAHA.......... Para-Acetamidohippuric Acid [*Biochemistry*]
PAAJR.......... Proceedings of the American Academy for Jewish Research (SAUS)
PAAJR.......... Proceedings of the American Academy of Jewish Research (SAUS)
PAAL.......... Paleolimnology of Alpine-Adriatic Lakes (SAUS)
PAAM.......... Physicians Association for Anthroposophical Medicine (EA)
PAAM.......... Polyacrylamide [*Also, PAA, PAM*] [*Organic chemistry*]
PAAM.......... Projective Assessment of Aging Method [*Personality development test*] [*Psychology*]
P/AAMHRC. Pacific/Asian American Mental Health Research Center [*University of Illinois at Chicago*] [*Research center*] (RCD)
PAAMS.......... Principal Anti-Air Missile System (MILB)
PAAN.......... Physician Assistant AIDS Network (SAUS)
PAAN.......... Product Assurance Alert Notice (MCD)
PA/A/N/AF... Procurement of Ammunition, Army/Navy/Air Force (SAUS)
PA&C.......... Plessey Avionics & Communications (SAUS)
PA&D.......... Purchase Authorization and Directive (SAUS)
PA & E.......... Program Analysis and Evaluation
PA & F.......... Percussion, Auscultation, and Fremitus [*Medicine*]
PA & I.......... Planning, Analysis, and Integration
PA&I.......... Project Analysis and Integration (SAUS)
PA and SP... Positioner Antenna and Solar Panel (SAUS)
PA & T.......... Product Assurance and Test
PAANG.......... Pennsylvania Air National Guard (MUSM)
PAANS.......... Pan African Association of Neurological Sciences (EAIO)
PAANSW.......... Prisoners' Aid Association of New South Wales [*Australia*]
PAAO.......... Pan-American Association of Ophthalmology (EA)
$P(A\text{-}a)O^2$.......... Alveolar-Arterial Pressure Difference [*For $A\text{-}aDO_2$*] [*Medicine*] (DAVI)
PAAORLBE... Pan-American Association of Oto-Rhino-Laryngology and Broncho-Esophagology [*Mexico City, Mexico*] (EAIO)
PAAP.......... Peaceful Alternatives to the Atlantic Pact
PAAP.......... Plastic Area Array (SAUS)
PAAP.......... Provisional Algal Assay Procedure [*Test measuring impact of chemicals on algal growth*]

PAA-PS ...... Polyacrylic Acid-Polysulfone (SAUS)
PAAQ .... Palmer [*Alaska*] [*ICAO location identifier*] (ICLI)
PAAR .... American Academy in Rome. Papers and Monographs [*A publication*] (ABAR)
PAAR .... Pioneers Across America for Alzheimer's Research [*An association*]
PAAR .... Precision Approach Airfield RADAR [*Aviation*] (IAA)
PAAR .... Product Assurance Analysis Report (SAUS)
PAARC........ Pittsburgh Adolescent Alcohol Research Center (RCD)
PAAS .... Pakistan Association for the Advancement of Science (SAUS)
PAAS .... Pan American Allergy Society (EA)
PAAS .... Pan American Silver Corp. [*NASDAQ symbol*] (NASQ)
PAAS .... Passive Active All Weather System (ACAE)
PAAS .... Passive-Active Attack System (ACAE)
PAAS .... Performance Assessment and Appraisal System
PAAS .... Phased Array Aerial (or Antenna) System (SAUS)
PAAS .... Phased Array Analysis System
PAAS .... Phased Array Antenna System
PAAS .... Proceedings of the American Antiquarian Society (SAUS)
PAAS .... Region 10 External Affairs Labels System (SAUS)
PAASF....... Pan American Silver Corp. [*NASDAQ symbol*] (SAG)
PAASF....... Pan Amer Silver [*NASDAQ symbol*] (TTSB)
PAAT......... Parent as a Teacher Inventory [*Psychology*]
PAAT......... Passive Acoustics Analysis Trainer (SAUS)
PAAT......... Personnel and Administrative Assistance Team [*Navy*] (NVT)
PAAT......... Personnel Assistance and Audit Team [*Military*]
PAAT......... Professional Association of Alexander Teachers [*British*] (DBA)
PAAT......... Programmer Analyst Aptitude Test
PAAT......... Public Affairs Assist Team [*Hazardous substance emergency response*]
PAATI........ Phased Array Antenna Technology Investigation
PAATLANT... Personnel and Administration Assistance Team, Atlantic [*Navy*] (DNAB)
PAATPAC ... Personnel and Administration Assistance Team, Pacific [*Navy*] (DNAB)
PAATS....... Precision Approach Area Tracking System (ACAE)
PAAWA...... Pakistan Australia Association of Western Australia
PAAWA...... Progressive Axemen's Association of Western Australia
P(A-awo).... Pressure Gradient from Alveolus to Airway Opening [*Medicine*] (DAVI)
PAAWS...... Precision Advanced All Weather Strike (ACAE)
PAAWS...... Principal Anit-Air Warfare System (SAUS)
PAAWWW... Pacific Asian American Women Writers West (EA)
PAAXOP..... Pan-Dodecanesian Association of America "Xanthos O Philikos" (EA)
PAb .... Abington Free Library, Abington, PA [*Library symbol*] [*Library of Congress*] (LCLS)
PAB .... Cabrini College, Library, Radnor, PA [*OCLC symbol*] (OCLC)
PAB .... PAB Bankshares, Inc. [*AMEX symbol*] (SAG)
PAB .... Pacific Air Boats Ltd. [*Canada*] [*ICAO designator*] (FAAC)
PAB .... Panair do Brasil, SA
PAB .... Para-Aminobenzoate (DB)
PAB .... Para-Aminobenzoic Acid [*Also, PABA*] [*Biochemistry*]
PAB .... Para-Aminobenzyl (SAUS)
PAB .... Paramaribo [*Suriname*] [*Geomagnetic observatory code*]
PAB .... Parti des Paysans, Artisans, et Bourgeois [*Farmers', Artisans', and Burghers' Party*] [*Switzerland*] [*Political party*] (PPE)
PAB .... Passed a Bill [*Telegraphy*] (PCTE)
PAB .... Passenger Air Bag [*Automotive safety systems*]
PAB .... Patent Abstracts Bibliography [*NASA*]
PAB .... Patrick Air Force Base [*Florida*]
PAB .... Peanut Advisory Board (EA)
PAB .... Pedro Afonso [*Brazil*] [*Airport symbol*] (AD)
PAB .... Pension Appeals Board [*Canada*]
pab .... per acre bonus (SAUS)
PAB .... Performance Assesment Battery [*Medicine*] (DMAA)
PAB .... Personal Address Book [*MAPI - Mail Applications Program Interface*] [*Microsoft Corp.*] [*Computer science*]
PAB .... Pes Anserinus Bursa [*Medicine*] (MELL)
PAB .... Petroleum Administrative Board [*Terminated, 1936*]
PAB .... Pharmaceutical Affairs Branch (HVTR)
PAB .... Pharmacologic Autonomic Block [*Medicine*] (DMAA)
PAB .... Plastic Assault Boat [*Navy*]
PAB .... Plumbing Advisory Board [*South Australia*]
PAB .... Police Administration Building
PAB .... Police Appeal Board [*South Australia*]
PAB .... Policies Allotment Board [*Navy*] (DNAB)
PAB .... Policy Advisory Body (SAUS)
PAB .... Polyclonal Antibody [*Immunochemistry*]
PAB .... Polymer Alloys and Blends (SAUS)
P/AB .... Port Side Abreast (DNAB)
PAB .... Potter & Brumfield, Inc. (IAA)
PAB .... Poultry Advisory Board [*Queensland, Australia*]
PAB .... Power-Assisted Brakes
PAB .... Prealbumin [*Biochemistry*]
PAB .... Precision Aneroid Barometer (DNAB)
PAB .... Preliminary As-Built [*Nuclear energy*] (NRCH)
PAB .... Premature Anti-Berninghausenite (SAUS)
PAB .... Premature Atrial Beat [*Cardiology*] (AAMN)
PAB .... Price Adjustment Board
PAB .... Price Agreement Bulletin
PAB .... Primary Application Block [*Computer science*] (ELAL)
PAB .... Primary Auxiliary Building [*Nuclear energy*] (NRCH)
PAB .... Priorities Allotment Board
PAB .... Priority Assignment Base (MCD)
PAB .... Private Activity Bond (AAGC)
PAB .... Problems Analysis Branch of the CIA (SAUS)
PAB .... Process Anchor Block [*IBM's SNA*] [*Communications term*] (DCT)
PAB .... Product Application Bulletins [*A publication*] (EAAP)
PAB .... Program Advisory Board (MCD)
PAB .... Programmer Aptitude Battery [*Terence R. Taylor*] (TES)
PAB .... Promotions Appeal Board [*Victoria, Australia*]
PAB .... Psychiatric Attitudes Battery [*Psychology*]
PAB .... Psychology of Addictive Behaviors [*An association*] (EA)
PAB .... Public Affairs Bureau (SAUS)
PAB .... Pulmonary Artery Banding [*Cardiology*]
PAB .... Pulsed Adsorption Bed [*Process*]
PAB .... Pulsed Air Blast
PAB .... Purple Agar Base [*Media*] [*Microbiology*]
PABA .... Barter Island [*Alaska*] [*ICAO location identifier*] (ICLI)
PABA .... Para-Aminobenzoic Acid [*Also, PAB*] [*Biochemistry*]
PA BA .... Pennsylvania Bar Association. Reports [*A publication*] (DLA)
PABA .... Pro-Am Bowfishing Association
PABA .... Progressive Angus Breeders Association
PAB Bk...... PAB Bankshares, Inc. [*Associated Press*] (SAG)
PA B Brief... Pennsylvania Bar Brief [*A publication*] (DLA)
PABC .... Pacific Bancorp (EFIS)
PABC .... Pan American Basketball Confederation [*See also CPB*] (EAIO)
PABC .... Physiotherapy Association of British Columbia (SAUS)
PABD .... Post-anoxic Brain Damage [*Medicine*] (EDAA)
PABD .... Precise Access Block Diagram
PABD .... Predeposited Autologous Blood Donation [*Medicine*] (MELL)
PABE......... Bethel [*Alaska*] [*ICAO location identifier*] (ICLI)
PABE......... Program and Budget Estimate (MCD)
PABF......... Precision Air-Bearing Floor (SSD)
PABFSA..... Pediatric Association of Black French-Speaking Africa (EAIO)
PABG .... Big Delta [*Alaska*] [*ICAO location identifier*] (ICLI)
PABI .... Delta Junction/Allen Army Air Field [*Alaska*] [*ICAO location identifier*] (ICLI)
PA Bk Cas... Pennsylvania Bank Cases [*A publication*] (DLA)
PABLA....... Problem Analysis by Logical Approach
PABLE........ Payable (ROG)
PABLI........ Pages Bleues Informatisees [*Commission of the European Communities*] [*Information service or system*] (CRD)
PABLOS..... Program to Analyse the Block System [*Computer science*] (PDAA)
PABM........ Big Mountain Air Force Station [*Alaska*] [*ICAO location identifier*] (ICLI)
PABMI....... Performing Arts Biography Master Index [*A publication*]
PABN .... Pacific Capital Bancorp [*NASDAQ symbol*] (SAG)
PABP .... Poly(A)-Binding Protein
PABP .... Pulmonary Artery Ballon Pump [*Medicine*] (DMAA)
PAB Process... Pulsed Adsorption Bed Process (SAUS)
PAB-PTC .... Promotion Appeal Board, Postal and Telecommunications Commission [*Australia*]
PAB(Q) ...... Poultry Advisory Board (Queensland) [*Australia*]
PABR .... Barrow [*Alaska*] [*ICAO location identifier*] (ICLI)
PABR .... Planning Appeals Board. Reports [*A publication*]
P Abr .... Pulton's Abridgment of the Statutes [*A publication*] (DLA)
PA Browne (PA)... Browne's Reports (Pennsylvania) [*A publication*] (DLA)
PA Browne R... Browne's Reports [*Pennsylvania*] [*A publication*] (DLA)
PABRX....... Phoenix-Engemann Balanced Return Cl.A [*Mutual fund ticker symbol*] (SG)
PABS .... Pan-American Biodeterioration Society (EA)
PABS .... Para-Aminobenzensulfonamide [*Antibiotic*]
PABST....... Primary Adhesively Bonded Structural Technology [*Aviation*]
PABST....... Primary Adhesively Bonded Structure Techniques
PABT......... Bettles [*Alaska*] [*ICAO location identifier*] (ICLI)
PABU .... Painted Bunting [*North American bird banding code*] (BIBA)
PABV .... Percutaneous Aortic Balloon Valvuloplasty [*Medicine*] (HCT)
PABV .... Pyroactuated Ball Valve
PABX .... Private Access Branch Exchange (SAUS)
PABX .... Private Automatic Branch Exchange [*Telecommunications*] (DEN)
PABX .... Public-Area Branch Exchange (AEBE)
PAC .... cis-Platinum [*Cisplatin*], Adriamycin, Cyclophosphamide [*Antineoplastic drug regimen*]
PAC .... Civilian Self-Defense Patrol (Guatemala) [*Political party*] (PSAP)
PAC .... P1 Artificial Chromosome (SAUS)
PAC .... Pacemaker [*NCIC car model code*]
PAC .... Pacer [*NCIC car model code*]
pac........... Pachytene (QSUL)
PAC .... Pacific (AFM)
Pac .... Pacific [*Record label*] [*France*]
Pac .... Pacifica: Australian Theological Studies [*A publication*] (APTA)
PAC .... Pacific Accreditation Cooperation (SAUS)
PAC .... Pacific Aerospace Corp. Ltd. (SAUS)
PAC .... Pacific Air Command [*Air Force*]
PAC .... Pacific Airmotive Corporation
PAC .... Pacific Automotive Corp. (SAUS)
PAC .... Pacific Command [*Military*] (GFGA)
PAC .... Pacific Health Corp. (MHID)
PAC .... Pacific Ocean
PAC .... Pacific Region [*USTTA*] (TAG)
Pac .... Pacific Reporter [*A publication*] (DLA)
PAC .... Pacific Telesis Group [*NYSE symbol*] (SPSG)
PAC .... Pacific Telesis Group Financing I [*NYSE symbol*] (SAG)
PAC .... Pacific Telesis Group Financing II [*NYSE symbol*] (SAG)
PAC .... Package Assembly Circuit (SAUS)
PAC .... Package Attitude Control [*NASA*]
PAC .... Packaged Assembly Circuit
PAC .... Packaged Attitude Control (SAUS)
PAC .... Packaging Association of Canada (SAUS)

PAC .... Packard Automobile Classics (EA)
PAC .... Packard Club [*Association*] (EA)
PAC .... Packed Memory [*Computer science*] (IAA)
PAC .... Packet Autopiloted Cruiseway
PAC .... Pacoh [*Language symbol*] (ETLW)
PAC .... Pacto de Alianza de Centro [*Chile*] [*Political party*] (EY)
PAC .... Pad Air Conditioner (SAUS)
PAC .... Paging Area Controller (VLIE)
PAC .... Pakistan Aeronautical Complex (SAUS)
PAC .... Pak-Man Resources, Inc. [*Vancouver Stock Exchange symbol*]
PAC .... Palestine Affairs Center (EA)
PAC .... Palo Alto - Branner [*California*] [*Seismograph station code, US Geological Survey*] [*Closed*] (SEIS)
PAC .... Palo Alto Clinic (SAUS)
PAC .... Pan African Congress (SAUS)
PAC .... Pan-Africanist Congress [*South Africa*]
PAC .... Panama City [*Panama*] Paitilla Airport [*Airport symbol*] (OAG)
PAC .... Pan American College [*Texas*]
PAC .... Pan-American Congress
PAC .... Papular Acrodermatitis of Childhood
PAC .... Para-Aminoclonidine [*Biochemistry*]
PAC .... Para-Aminosalicylic Acid Calcium Salt [*Pharmacology*]
PAC .... Parachute and Cable (SAUS)
PAC .... Parachute and Cable Defence [*British military*]
PAC .... Parallel Alternate Curriculum (EDAC)
PAC .... Parametric Amplifier Converter
P-A-C .... Parent-Adult-Child [*Transactional analysis*]
PAC .... Parent Advisory Committee [*Migrant education*] (AEE)
PAC .... Parent Advisory Council (EDAC)
PAC .... Parker Aircraft Corp. (MCD)
PAC .... Partido Autentico Constitucional [*Authentic Constitutional Party*] [*El Salvador*] [*Political party*]
PAC .... Parts Allocation Chart (MCD)
PAC .... Pascagoula, MS [*Location identifier*] [*FAA*] (FAAL)
PAC .... Passed the Final Examination of the Advanced Class [*Military College of Science*] [*British*]
PAC .... Passive Acoustic Classification (NVT)
PAC .... Passive Air Cycle (ODA)
PAC .... Patents Advisory Committee [*British*]
PAC .... Patient Airlift Center [*Aeromedical evacuation*]
PAC .... Patriot Advanced Capability [*Missile technology*] [*Military*] (PS)
PAC .... Patriot Antimissile Capability [*Army*]
PAC .... Patriot ATM Capability (SAUS)
PAC .... Payment after Closing [*Insurance*]
PAC .... Peace Action Center [*Defunct*] (EA)
PAC .... Pedagogic Automatic Computer (IEEE)
PAC .... Pediatric AIDS [*Acquired Immune Deficiency Syndrome*] Coalition (EA)
PAC .... Penal Affairs Consortium (WDAA)
PAC .... Penalty Assessment Criteria [*Environmental Protection Agency*]
PAC .... Penetration Aid Carrier (SAUS)
PAC .... Penetration Aids Deployment Concept (SAA)
PA C .... Pennsylvania Commonwealth Court Reports [*A publication*] (DLA)
PAC .... People Against Cancer
PAC .... People's Army Congress
PAC .... Peptide Acid [*Organic chemistry*]
PAC .... Perceptual Audio Coding (VLIE)
PAC .... Performance Analysis and Control
PAC .... Performance Assured Certification
PAC .... Performing Arts Center (SAUS)
PAC .... Periapical Cyst [*Medicine*] (MELL)
PAC .... Peripheral Autonomous Control (NITA)
PAC .... Permanent Accomodation Complex (SAUS)
PAC .... Permanent Agricultural Committee (SAUS)
PAC .... Personal Access Code
PAC .... Personal Accident Coverage [*Travel industry*] (TRID)
PAC .... Personal Analog Computer
PAC .... Personal Authentication Code (VLIE)
PAC .... Personal Authenticator Card (SAUS)
PAC .... Person in Addition to Crew [*Sailing*]
PAC .... Personnel Action Center [*Army*] (INF)
PAC .... Personnel Action Code
PAC .... Personnel Administration Center [*Army*]
PAC .... Personnel Administrative Center
PAC .... Personnel and Administration Center [*Army*] (AABC)
PAC .... Personnel Assistance Center [*Military*] (INF)
PAC .... Perturbation Angular Correlation (SAUS)
PAC .... Perturbed Angular Correlation
PAC .... Pesticides Advisory Committee [*Tasmania, Australia*]
PAC .... Petroleum Advisory Committee [*of Organization for Economic Cooperation and Development*] [*Terminated, 1976*] (EGAO)
PAC .... Pharmaceutical Advertising Council [*New York, NY*] (EA)
PAC .... Phenacetin [*Acetophenetidin*], Aspirin, Caffeine [*Pharmacology*]
PAC .... Phenacetin-Aspirin-Caffeine (SAUS)
PAC .... Phenacetin, Aspirin, Coffeine (SAUS)
PAC .... Philbrook Art Center (SAUS)
PAC .... Photoacoustic [*Spectroscopy*]
PAC .... Photoactive Compound [*Chemistry*]
PAC .... Photo Aperture Card (SAA)
PAC .... Phototypesetting Automatic Controller (DGA)
PA-C .... Physician's Assistant-Certified (WGA)
PAC .... Pilotless Aircraft [*Navy*] (IAA)
PAC .... Piper Aircraft Corp.
PAC .... Pittsburgh Activated Carbon (SAUS)
PAC .... Place Complement of Address in Index Register (SAA)
PAC .... Planned Amortization Class [*Investment term*] (DFIT)
PAC .... Planned-Amortization-Class Bond [*Investment term*]
PAC .... Planned Amortization Credit [*Investment term*] (ECON)
PAC .... Planned Availability Concept (MHDI)
PAC .... Planning Advisory Committee (OICC)
PAC .... Plasma Aldosterone Concentration [*Hematology*] (DMAA)
PAC .... Plasma Arc Chamber
PAC .... Plasma Arc Cutting [*Welding*]
PAC .... Platelet-Associated Complement [*Medicine*] (DMAA)
PAC .... Platinol [*Cisplatin*], Adriamycin, Cyclophosphamide [*Antineoplastic drug regimen*]
PAC .... Player Access Control (SAUS)
PAC .... Plowshare Advisory Committee [*AEC*]
PAC .... Pneumatic Analog Computer
PAC .... Pneumatic Auxiliary Console (AAG)
PAC .... Pod Air Conditioner (AAG)
PAC .... Poisons Advisory Committee [*Australia*]
PAC .... Polar Air Cargo, Inc. [*FAA designator*] (FAAC)
PAC .... Polar Atmospheric Chemistry (CARB)
PAC .... Policy Advisory Center
PAC .... Policy Advisory Committee [*National Cancer Institute*] [*Department of Health and Human Services*] (GFGA)
PAC .... Policy Advisory Committee [*Office of Economic Opportunity*]
PAC .... Policy Analysis Center [*George Mason University*] (RCD)
PAC .... Polish American Congress (EA)
PAC .... Political Action Caucus [*Superseded by LPAC*] (EA)
PAC .... Political Action Club [*Federal political committee terminology*] (PACS)
PAC .... Political Action Committee [*Generic term*]
PAC .... Political Assistance Committee [*Federal political committee terminology*] (PACS)
PAC .... Polled Access Circuit
PAC .... Pollution Abatement and Control
PAC .... Pollution Abatement Control (SAUS)
PAC .... Polyacrylat (SAUS)
PAC .... Polyalkene Carbonate (SAUS)
PAC .... Polyaluminum Chloride [*Inorganic chemistry*]
PAC .... Polyanionic Cellulose [*Organic chemistry*]
PAC .... Polycyclic Aromatic Compound [*Organic chemistry*]
PAC .... Polymer-Asphalt Composite (ODA)
PAC .... Population Action Council (EA)
PAC .... Portable Air Compressor (SAUS)
PAC .... Porterfield Airplane Club (EA)
PAC .... Post-Adoption Centre [*British*] (CB)
PAC .... Post Award Conference (MCD)
PAC .... Post Award Contract
PAC .... Potentially Adverse Condition (SAUS)
PAC .... Powder Air Conveyor (SAUS)
PAC .... Powdered Activated Carbon [*Adsorbent*]
PAC .... Pre-Action Calibration [*Gunnery*] (NVT)
PAC .... Pre-Admission Certification [*Medicine*] (MEDA)
PAC .... Prearrival Confirmation (SAUS)
PAC .... Preauthorized Checking (SAUS)
PAC .... Preauthorized Check Plan [*Insurance*]
PAC .... Preauthorized Check System
PAC .... Pre-Authorized Chequing [*Canada*]
PAC .... Premature Atrial Contraction [*Medicine*]
PAC .... Premature Auricular Contraction [*Cardiology*] (AAMN)
PAC .... Premium Acoustics Concept [*Automotive engineering*]
PAC .... Prepared Advisory Council [*Automobile competition*]
PAC .... Preservation and Conservation [*IFLA Core Program*]
PAC .... President of the Air Council (SAUS)
PAC .... President's Advisor for Science
PAC .... Presidents Advisory Council (SAUS)
PAC .... Presidents' Athletic Conference (PSS)
PAC .... Pressure Alpha Center (MCD)
PAC .... Primary Address Code (AFM)
PAC .... Prime [*or Principal*] Associate Contractor (MCD)
PAC .... Principal Associate Contractor (MCD)
PAC .... Printing Accountants Club (EA)
PAC .... Printing Automatic Calculator (SAUS)
PAC .... Priority Area Children (AIE)
PAC .... Privacy Act Coordinator [*Navy*] (DNAB)
PAC .... Privilege Access Certificate (SAUS)
PAC .... Privilege Attribute Certificate (SAUS)
PAC .... Probably Approximately Correct (IDAI)
PAC .... Probe Aerodynamic Center [*NASA*]
PAC .... Problem Action Center [*NASA*] (NASA)
PAC .... Problem Assessment Center (SAUS)
PAC .... Process Analytical Chemistry
PAC .... Process Automation Computer (SAUS)
PAC .... Procurement and Contract (IAA)
PAC .... Production Acceleration Capacity [*Manufacturing*]
PAC .... Product of Ambulatory Care [*Medicine*] (HCT)
PAC .... Professional Activities Committee (SAUS)
PAC .... Professional Activities Survey [*Medicine*]
PAC .... Professional Advisory Committee (DIPS)
PAC .... Program Acquisition Cost (MCD)
PAC .... Program Address Counter [*Computer science*] (EECA)
PAC .... Program Adjustment Committee
PAC .... Program Administration and Control (SAUS)
PAC .... Program Advisory Committee
PAC .... Program Allocation Checker
PAC .... Program Application Code (DNAB)

PAC .... Program Assembly Card (NITA)
PAC .... Program Authorized Credentials [*Computer science*]
PAC .... Programmable Analogical Controller (NITA)
PAC .... Programmable Armament Control (SAUS)
PAC .... Programmable Automatic Comparator
PAC .... Programmable Automotive Controller (SAUS)
PAC .... Programme Activity Center [*Advisory Committee on Pollution of the Sea*]
PAC .... Progress Assessment Chart [*Psychology*]
PAC .... Project Advisory Committee (EGAO)
PAC .... Project Analysis and Control (IAA)
PAC .... Promoting Achievement through Communications [*Education*]
PAC .... Protect America's Children [*An association*] (EA)
PAC .... Protection Against Aircraft (SAUS)
PAC .... Protection Auxiliary Cabinet [*Nuclear energy*] (NRCH)
PAC .... Prudential Assurance Co. Ltd. [*Australia*]
PAC .... Public Access Catalogue (ADA)
PAC .... Public Access Control
PAC .... Public Accounts Committee [*British government*]
PAC .... Public Affairs Committee [*Defunct*] (EA)
PAC .... Public Affairs Coordinator [*Nuclear energy*] (NRCH)
PAC .... Public Affairs Council (EA)
PAC .... Public Archives of Canada
PAC .... Public Assistance Cooperative (SAUS)
PAC .... Public Authority Contribution [*Australia*]
PAC .... Public Awareness Committee [*American Library Association*]
PAC .... Publishers' Ad Club [*New York, NY*] (EA)
PAC .... Pulmonary Artery Catheter [*Medicine*]
PAC .... Pulse Aperture Correlation [*Communications*]
PAC .... Purchasing and Contracting [*Army*] (IAA)
PAC .... Pure and Applied Chemistry [*IUPAC*]
p A c .... pure Argentinian cocaine (SAUS)
PAC .... Pursuant to Authority Contained (SAUS)
PAC .... Pursuant to Authority Contained In [*Army*]
PAC .... Put and Call [*Stock exchange term*]
Pac 2d .... Pacific Reporter, Second Series [*A publication*] (DLA)
PAC-3 .... Patriot Advanced Capability-3 [*Army*]
PAC-4-PYRO ... Americans Supporting the Pyrotechnics Industry [*Bethesda, MD*] (PACS)
PAC-10 .... Pacific 10 Conference (EA)
PAC 67 .... Corridor 67, Inc. PAC [*Jacksonville, IL*] (PACS)
Pac A .... Pacific Affairs [*A publication*] (BRI)
PACA .... Pennsylvania Aggregates and Concrete Association (EARSL)
PACA .... Perishable Agricultural Commodities Act, 1930
PACA .... Physics and Chemistry of the Atmosphere (SAUS)
PACA .... Picture Agency Council of America (EA)
PACA .... Polyamide Carboxylic Acid (SAUS)
PACA .... Principal Assistant County Architect [*British*]
PACA .... Proceedings of the African Classical Association (SAUS)
PACA .... Propulsion and Control Assembly
PACA .... Proyecto Ambiental para Centro America [*Environmental Project for Central America*] [*Spanish*] (ECON)
PACAACS ... Pacific Area Airways and Air Communications (IAA)
PACAACS ... Pacific Area Airways and Air Communications Service (SAUS)
PacA & E ... Pacific Aerospace & Electronics, Inc. [*Associated Press*] (SAG)
PACAB .... Port-Access Coronary Artery Bypass [*Medicine*] (EDAA)
PACADIV ... Pacific Fleet Advance Headquarters Division (DNAB)
PACADV .... Pacific Fleet Advance Headquarters [*Guam*]
PACAF .... Pacific Air Command Air Forces (SAUS)
PACAF .... Pacific Air Forces
PACAFBASECOM ... Pacific Air Forces Base Command
PACAF-OA ... Pacific Air Forces Operations Analysis
PACAF-OA ... Pacific Air Forces Operations Analysis Office [*Hickam Air Force Base, HI*]
PACAH .... Pitch Attitude Command/Attitude Hold [*Aviation*] (MCD)
PACAMS .... Pacific Aircrew Management System (SAUS)
PacAni .... Pacific Animated Imaging Corp. [*Associated Press*] (SAG)
PACAP .... Pituitary Adenylate Cyclase Activating Polypeptide [*Biochemistry*]
PACAP .... Pituitary Adenylyl Cyclase-Activating Polypeptide [*Endocrinology*]
PACAP .... Sandra Ann Morsilli Pacific-Basin Capital Markets Research Center [*University of Rhode Island*] (RCD)
Pacar .... PACCAR, Inc. [*Associated Press*] (SAG)
PAC Area ... Pacific Area (SAUS)
PacAS .... Pacific American Income Shares, Inc. [*Associated Press*] (SAG)
PACAS .... Patient Care System [*Army*] (AABC)
PA Cas .... Pennsylvania Supreme Court Cases (Sadler) [*A publication*] (DLA)
PACAS .... Personnel Access Control Accountability System [*NASA*] (MCD)
PACAS .... Psychological Abstracts Current Awareness Service (IID)
PA CASA .... Pennsylvania Court Appointed Special Advocate Association (EARSL)
PACB .... Pacemaker Boat Trailer [*NCIC trailer make code*]
PACB .... Pacific Bulk Transportation Company [*Common carrier symbol*]
PACB .... Pan-American Coffee Bureau [*Defunct*] (EA)
PACB .... Pennsylvania Association of Community Bankers (TBD)
PACB .... Poppy Advisory and Control Board [*Tasmania, Australia*]
PACBA .... Pan-African Christian Broadcast Associaton (SAUS)
PACBAR .... Pacific Barrier RADAR (MCD)
PacBB .... Pacific Basin Bulk Shippers Ltd. [*Associated Press*] (SAG)
PacBBS .... Pacific Basin Bulk Shippers Ltd. [*Associated Press*] (SAG)
Pac Bch .... Pacific Beach (SAUS)
Pac Bell .... Pacific Bell (SAUS)
PacBio .... Pacific Biometrics, Inc. [*Associated Press*] (SAG)
PacBiom .... Pacific Biometrics, Inc. [*Associated Press*] (SAG)
PACC .... Pacemaker Mobile Homes & Travel [*NCIC trailer make code*]
PACC .... Pacific Airlift Control Center (ACAE)
PACC .... Pacific Coach [*NCIC truck make code*]
PACC .... Pacific Coast [*Railroad*] (MHDB)
PA CC .... Pennsylvania County Court Reports [*A publication*] (DLA)
PACC .... PERT [*Program Evaluation and Review Technique*] Associated Cost Control [*Computer science*] (IAA)
PACC .... Portable Arm Control Console (KSC)
PACC .... Primary Alternative Command Centre (SAUS)
PACC .... Primary Ambulatory Care Center [*Medicine*] (DMAA)
P(ACC) .... Probability of Acceptance
PACC .... Problem Action Control Center [*NASA*] (NASA)
PACC .... Product Administration and Contract Control (IAA)
PACC .... Professional Association of Custom Clothiers (EA)
PACC .... Programmable Array Combinatorial Circuit (NITA)
PACC .... Project Administration Contact Control (SAUS)
PACC .... Promoting Aphasics' Communicative Competence [*Medicine*] (DMAA)
PACC .... Propulsion and Auxiliary Control Console [*NASA*] (DNAB)
PACC .... Protected Air-Cooled Condenser [*Nuclear energy*] (NRCH)
PACC .... Protein A Immobilized in Collodion Charcoal (DAVI)
PACC .... Provident Life & Accident Insurance Co. [*NASDAQ symbol*] (COMM)
PACC .... Public Arts Advisory Council (NADA)
PACCA .... Airfield Capabilities Application (SAUS)
PACCA .... Policy Alternatives for the Caribbean and Central America (EA)
PACCALL ... Pacific Fleet Calls [*Radio call signs*]
PacCapB .... Pacific Capital Bancorp [*Associated Press*] (SAG)
PACCAR .... Pacific Car and Foundry
PACCAT .... Pacific Area Command & Control AUTODIN Terminal (SAUS)
PACCE .... Providing Professional Development, Assessment, and Coordination of Competency-Based Education Project [*Illinois*] (EDAC)
PACCIOS ... Pan American Council of International Committee of Scientific Management
PACCO .... Cisplatin, Adriamycin, Cyclophosphamide, CCNU [*Lomustine*], Oncovin [*Vincristine*] [*Antineoplastic drug regimen*]
Pac Coast Int ... Pacific Coast International [*A publication*] (ILCA)
Pac Coast LJ ... Pacific Coast Law Journal [*A publication*] (DLA)
PACCOM .... Pacific Command [*Military*]
PACCOM .... Pacific Communications Network [*Computer science*] (TNIG)
PACCOM .... Pacific Computer Communications
PACCOM .... Pacific Fleet Communications Instructions
PACCOMMAREA ... Pacific Communications Area (SAUS)
PACCOMOPCONCEN ... Pacific Fleet Command Operational Control Center (DNAB)
PA CCR .... Pennsylvania County Court Reports [*A publication*] (DLA)
PA CC Reps ... Pennsylvania County Court Reports [*A publication*] (DLA)
PacCrst .... Pacific Crest Capital [*Associated Press*] (SAG)
PACCS .... Pan American Cancer Cytology Society [*Defunct*] (EA)
PACCS .... Post-Attack Command and Control System [*Military*]
PACCS .... Product Administration and Contract Control System (SAUS)
PACCS/ADA ... Post-Attack Command and Control System/Airborne Data Automation [*Military*]
PACCSq .... Post-Attack Command Control Squadron [*Air Force*]
PACCT .... PERT [*Program Evaluation and Review Technique*] and Cost Correlation Technique
PACCT .... Political Action Committee for Cable Television (NTCM)
PACD .... Cold Bay [*Alaska*] [*ICAO location identifier*] (ICLI)
PACD .... Pacific Division [*Military*]
PACD .... Parachute and Cable Defence [*British military*] (DMA)
PACD .... Pennsylvania Association of Conservation Districts (EARSL)
PACD .... Plan of Action to Combat Desertification (SAUS)
PACDA .... Personnel and Administration, Combat Development Activity [*Army*] (AABC)
PA C Dec WCC ... Pennsylvania Courts, Decisions in Workmen's Compensation Cases [*A publication*] (DLA)
PACDIGS ... Pacific Digital Graphics System (SAUS)
PACDIV .... Pacific Division [*Military*]
PacDunl .... Pacific Dunlop Ltd. [*Associated Press*] (SAG)
PACE .... Ampace Corp. [*NASDAQ symbol*] (SAG)
PACE .... Ashland Inc. PAC for Employees [*Covington, KY*] (PACS)
PACE .... Coors Brewing Company - Political Action Coors Employees [*Washington, DC*] (PACS)
PACE .... Pacemaker [*NCIC motorcycle make code*]
PACE .... Pacific Agricultural Cooperative for Export [*Corte Madera, CA*] (EA)
PACE .... Pacific Airlift Center (SAUS)
PACE .... Pacific Alternate Command Element (CINC)
PACE .... Pacific America Container Express (MHDB)
PACE .... Pacific Atoll Cratering Experiment [*Military*] (DNAB)
PACE .... Pacing and Clinical Electrophysiology (SAUS)
PACE .... Packaged CRAM [*Card Random-Access Memory*] Executive [*NCR Corp.*] [*Computer science*]
PACE .... Package for Architectural Computer Evaluation (PDAA)
PACE .... Packet of Accelerated Christian Education [*Educational material marketed by fundamentalist company, Accelerated Christian Education*]
PACE .... PAC of Employees of the Dow Chemical Company [*Detroit, MI*] (PACS)
PACE .... Paging Access Control Equipment (SAUS)
PACE .... Paper, Allied-Industrial, Chemical and Energy Workers International
PACE .... Parent Aid for Curriculum Enrichment (EARSL)
PACE .... Parental Alliance for Choice in Education (AIE)
PACE .... Parents and Children's Equality [*An association*] (PAZ)
PACE .... Parts Automated Control through Electronics (SAUS)
PACE .... Passive Attitude Control Experimental [*Satellite*]
PACE .... Patient Advise and Consent Encounter
PACE .... Patrol Airship Concept Evaluation
PACE .... Peninsula Alliance for Creative Empowerment (EARSL)
PACE .... People with Arthritis Can Exercise [*Medical program*]

PACE......... Performance Advantage with Cummins Electronics [*Automotive engineering*]
PACE......... Performance and Cost Evaluation
PACE......... Performing Arts, Culture, and Entertainment [*Proposed cable television system*]
PACE......... Perigee Augmentation Control Electronics (ACAE)
PACE......... Peripheral Automatic Channel Emulator [*Computer science*]
PACE......... Permafrost and Climate in Europe (SAUS)
PACE......... Personal Assessment for Continuing Education [*Medicine*] (EDAA)
PACE......... Personal Audio Computer Editing (SAUS)
PACE......... Personalized Aerobics for Cardiovascular Enhancement
PACE......... Petroleum Association for Conservation of the Canadian Environment
PACE......... Phased Array Control Electronics
PACE......... Philippine Association of Civil Engineers (SAUS)
PACE......... Physics and Chemistry Experiment
PACE......... Planetary Association for Clean Energy (EA)
PACE......... Plan for Action by Citizens in Education
PACE......... Planned Action with Constant Evaluation [*Computer science*]
PACE......... Planning and Control Made Easy (PDAA)
PACE......... Plant Acquisition and Construction Equipment [*Nuclear energy*] (NRCH)
PACE......... Plant and Capital Equipment (MCD)
PACE......... Plasma-Assisted Chemical Etching [*Metallurgy*]
PACE......... Platinol [*Cis-Platinum*] [*Antineoplastic drug regimen*] (DAVI)
PACE......... Plessey Adaptive Compass Equipment (SAUS)
PACE......... Polar Anglo-American Conjugate Experiment (SAUS)
PACE......... Police and Criminal Evidence Act [*1964*] [*British*]
PACE......... Policy Analysis for California Education [*Research center*] (RCD)
PACE......... Political Action Committee for Employees [*Federal political committee terminology*] (PACS)
PACE......... Political Action for Candidate Election [*National Association*]
PACE......... Pollution Abatement Capital Expense (EDCT)
PACE......... Portable Acoustic Collection Equipment (MCD)
PACE......... Portable Applications and Containerized Engineering [*Motor generators*]
PACE......... Power at Combined Efficiency (SAUS)
PACE......... Precipitation Augmentation for Crops Experiment (SAUS)
PACE......... Precision Analog Computing Equipment
PACE......... Preflight Acceptance Checkout Equipment
PACE......... Preflight Automatic Checkout Equipment (SAUS)
PACE......... Prelaunch Automatic Checkout Equipment [*NASA*]
PACE......... Premier Automotive Supplier Contribution to Excellence
PACE......... Priority Access Control Enabled [*Telecommunications*]
PACE......... Priority Activities in Cancer Education
PACE......... Prisoners Accelerated Creative Exposure [*An association*]
PACE......... Procedural Approach to the Composition of Essays [*In book title*]
PACE......... Process and Assembly Computerized Environment (SAUS)
PACE......... Process Automation and Control Extecutive (SAUS)
PACE......... Processing and Classification of Enlistees (SAUS)
PACE......... Processing and Control Element [*Computer science*] (IAA)
PACE......... Processing Control Element (SAUS)
PACE......... Producers of Associated Components for Electronics (IAA)
PACE......... Producible Alternative to Cadmium telluride for Epitaxy (SAUS)
PACE......... Product Assurance Confidence Evaluator (SAUS)
PACE......... Professional Activities Committees for Engineers (SAUS)
PACE......... Professional Activities for Continuing Education [*AEC*]
PACE......... Professional and Administrative Career Examination [*Formerly, FSEE*] [*Civil Service*]
PACE......... Professional and Career Education for Early Childhood
PACE......... Professional Application Creation Environment (NITA)
PACE......... Professional Association of Christian Educators (EA)
PACE......... Professional Association of Consulting Engineers
PACE......... Professional Athletes Career Enterprises (SAUS)
PACE......... Professional Automotive Career Education [*Automotive industry training*]
PACE......... Program Acquisition Cost Estimate (SAUS)
PACE......... Program Analysis Control and Evaluation [*Computer science*] (IAA)
PACE......... Program for Acquiring Competence in Entrepreneurship (EDAC)
PACE......... Program for Afloat College Education [*Navy*] (NVT)
PACE......... Program for Arrangement of Cables and Equipment (SAUS)
PACE......... Programmable Aerospace Checkout Equipment (ACAE)
PACE......... Programmable Autonomously-Controlled Electrode [*Instrumentation*]
PACE......... Programmed Automatic Communications Equipment
PACE......... Programmed Automatic Customer Engineer (SAUS)
PACE......... Programming Analysis Consulting Education (IEEE)
PACE......... Program of Adult College Education (SAUS)
PACE......... Program of All-Inclusive Care for the Elderly
PACE......... Programs Advancing Citizenship Education [*Institute*]
PACE......... Program to Advance Creativity in Education (SAUS)
PACE......... Progressive Aerobic Circuit Exercise [*Fitness training*]
PACE......... Project for the Advancement of Church Education
PACE......... Projects to Advance Creativity in Education [*HEW*]
PACE......... Promoting Aphasics Communicative Effectiveness [*Australia*]
PACE......... Providing Avenues for Continuing Encouragement [*Scholarship awarded by Fraternity of Recording Executives*]
PACE......... Proving & Adjustment for Communications Efficiency (SAUS)
PACE......... Provisioning Action Control Evaluation [*Military*] (AFIT)
PACE......... Public Access Cabletelevision by and for the Elders (SAUS)
PACE......... Public Affairs Council for Education [*Canada*]
PACE......... Public Awareness Communication Exchange (SAUS)
PACE......... Pulmonary Angiotensin I Converting Enzyme [*Medicine*] (EDAA)
PACE......... Pulsed Analog-to-Digital Converter and Encoder (SAUS)
PACE......... Pulse-Synthesized Advanced Conversion Equipment
P/ACEA2 .... Probationary Control Electrical Artificer, Acting, 2nd Class [*British military*] (DMA)
PACECO..... Pacific Coast Engineering Co. (SAUS)
PACED....... Program for Advanced Concepts in Electronic Design
PACEE....... Propulsion and Auxiliary Control Electronic Enclosure (DNAB)
PACEG COMMITTEE... PAC for Effective Government [*Ruan Corporation*] [*Des Moines, IA*] (PACS)
PaceHlt ..... Pace Health Management Systems, Inc. [*Associated Press*] (SAG)
PACE LOCAL 8-5 COPE... Paper Allied-Industrial, Chemical & Chemical Workers International Union, Local 8-5 Committee on Political Education [*Martinez, CA*] (PACS)
PACE-LV ... Preflight Acceptance Checkout Equipment-Launch Vehicle [*NASA*]
PACEM ...... Physics and Chemistry of Earth Materials (SAUS)
PACEMAKER... Public Agency Career Employment Maker [*OEO project*]
PACEN....... Public Affairs Center [*Navy*] (DNAB)
PACENLANT... Public Affairs Center, Atlantic [*Navy*] (DNAB)
PACENPAC... Public Affairs Center, Pacific [*Navy*] (DNAB)
PACENS..... Patient Census
PacEnt....... Pacific Enterprises [*Associated Press*] (SAG)
PACEO....... Professional Application Creation Environment (HGAA)
PACER....... Parent Advocacy Coalition for Educational Rights [*Minnesota*] (EDAC)
PACER....... Part and Component Evaluation Report [*NASA*]
PACER....... Planning and Control of Engineering Resources (SAUS)
PACER....... Planning Automation and Control for Evaluating Requirements
PACER....... Portable Aircraft Condition Evaluation Recorder (SAUS)
PACER....... Portable Aircraft Condition Evaluator Recorder
PACER....... Portfolio Analysis, Control, Evaluation and Reporting (SAUS)
PACER....... Postadoption Center for Education and Research
PACER....... Post-Operational Analysis and Exercise Review [*Program*]
PACER....... Postoperational Analysis Critique and Exercise Report [*Military*] (CAAL)
PACER....... Prescriptive Analysis for Curriculum Evaluation [*Vocational guidance*]
PACER....... Prescriptive Analysis for Curriculum Evaluation and Review (SAUS)
PACER....... Priority for Allocation/Application of COMSEC Equipment Resources (MCD)
PACER....... Private Access to Court Electronic Records (AAGC)
PACER....... Process Assembly Case Evaluator Routine [*Computer science*]
PACER....... Professional Association of Comics Entertainment Retailers (NTPA)
PACER....... Program-Assisted Console Evaluation and Review [*Air Force*]
PACER....... Program for the Acceleration of Commercial Energy Research (SAUS)
PACER....... Programmed Automatic Circuit Evaluator and Recorder
PACER....... Programmed Automatic Communications Equipment Requirements
PACER....... Program of Active Cooling Effects and Requirements
PACER....... Purpose, Agenda, Code of Conduct, Expectations/Introductions and Roles (SAUS)
PACER ACQUIRE... AFLC Management System Acquisition (SAUS)
PACERS..... Pacing and Cardiac Electrophysiology Retrieval System [*Intermedics, Inc.*] [*Information service or system*] (IID)
PACES....... Pan-American Center for Earth and Environmental Studies [*University of Texas at El Paso*] (RCD)
PACES....... Parent Attitude Toward Child Experssiveness Scale (EDAC)
PACES....... Patient as Customer Evaluation Survey
PACES....... Political Action Committee for Engineers and Scientists
PACE-S/C... Preflight Acceptance Checkout Equipment for Spacecraft
PACESETTER-PAC... Kansas-National Education Association Pacesetter PAC [*Topeka, KS*] (PACS)
Pace U...... Pace University (GAGS)
PAC-EX...... Canadian National Packaging Exposition [*Packaging Association of Canada*] (TSPED)
PACEX....... Pacific Exchange [*System*] [*Military*] (AFM)
PACEX System... Pacific Exchange System (SAUS)
PACF......... Pacific
Pacf......... PacifiCorp [*Associated Press*] (SAG)
PACF......... Partial Autocorrelation Function [*Statistics*]
PACF......... Periodic Autocorrelation Function (SAUS)
PACF......... Polish Arts and Culture Foundation [*Association*] (EA)
PAC-FACS... Programmed Appropriation Commitments-Fixed Asset Control System (SAUS)
PACFAST ... Pacific Forward Area Support Team (DNAB)
PACFASTDET... Pacific Forward Area Support Team Detachment (DNAB)
PACFASTREP... Pacific Forward Area Support Team Representative (DNAB)
PACFI........ Pennsylvania Cystic Fibrosis (EARSL)
PacFIN ...... Pacific Fishery Information Network [*Database*] [*National Marine Fisheries Service*]
PACFLAP ... Pacific Fleet Augmentation Plan [*Navy*] (NVT)
PACFLT...... Pacific Fleet
PACFLTCOM... Pacific Fleet Command
PACFLTMOPHOTOU... Pacific Fleet Mobile Photographic Unit (MUGU)
PACFLTPROPEXAMBD... Pacific Fleet Propulsion Examining Board (DNAB)
PACFORNET... Pacific Coast Forest Research Information Network [*Later, WESTFORNET*] [*Forest Service*] (IID)
PACFW ...... President's Advisory Committee for Women [*Terminated, 1980*] (EGAO)
Pac Gas&El... Pacific Gas and Electric (SAUS)
PacGate..... Pacific Gateway Properties [*Associated Press*] (SAG)
PACGCS..... Prior Active Coast Guard Commissioned Service
PacGE....... Pacific Gas & Electric Co. [*Associated Press*] (SAG)
PACGEEIA... Pacific Area Ground Environment Electronic Installation Agency (CINC)
PACGES..... Prior Active Coast Guard Enlisted Service
PACGO ...... President's Advisory Committee on Government Organization [*Abolished, 1961*]

PACGSR..... Pan American Center for Geographical Studies and Research [*See also CEPEIGE*] (EAIO)
PacGul...... Pacific Gulf Properties, Inc. [*Associated Press*] (SAG)
PacGulf..... Pacific Gulf Properties [*Associated Press*] (SAG)
PACH........ Performing Arts Center for Health [*New York University/Bellevue Hospital, New York, NY*] [*Superseded by Center for Dance Medicine -CDM*]
PACH........ Pipers to After Coming Head [*Obstetrics*] (DAVI)
PACH........ Public Administration Clearing House [*1931-1956*]
PACH........ Publishers' Accounts Clearing House [*British*] (BI)
PACHACH... Partizanim-Chayalim-Chalutzim (BJA)
PACHEDPEARL... Pacific Headquarters, Pearl Harbor, Hawaii [*Navy*]
PACHEM.... Point Area Chemical Effects Model (ACAE)
PACHG...... Program Advisory Committee on the Human Genome (HGEN)
PACI......... Pacific Campers [*NCIC trailer make code*]
PACI......... Partnerships for Advanced Computational Infrastructure [*National Science Foundation*]
PACIA........ Angolan Party of African Identity Conservative [*Political party*] (PSAP)
PACIA........ Particle Counting Immunoassay
PACICOM... Pacific Coastal Marine Productivity [*Marine science*] (OSRA)
Pacif......... Pacific (NTIO)
PACIF........ Pacific
PACIF........ Pacific, MO [*American Association of Railroads railroad junction routing code*]
Pacif......... PacifiCorp [*Associated Press*] (SAG)
PacifBnk.... Pacific Bank NA [*Associated Press*] (SAG)
PacifC....... PacifiCare Health Systems, Inc. [*Associated Press*] (SAG)
PacifCp...... PacifiCorp [*Associated Press*] (SAG)
Pacif Defence Reporter... Pacific Defence Reporter [*A publication*]
PACIFIC.... Peripheral Audio Chip for Improved Features in Cellular Phones (TIMI)
PACIFIC.... Planning, Accounting and Control Information for use in Construction (SAUS)
Pacific Asian J Energy... Pacific and Asian Journal of Energy [*A publication*] (JLIT)
Pacific Basin Countries... Australia, China, Hong Kong, Indonesia, Japan, Malaysia, New Zealand, Philippines, Singapore, South Korea, Taiwan, Thail (SAUS)
Pacific-Basin Finance J... Pacific-Basin Finance Journal [*A publication*] (JLIT)
Pacific CLJ... Pacific Coast Law Journal [*San Francisco*] [*A publication*] (DLA)
Pacific Econ Bull... Pacific Economic Bulletin [*A publication*] (JLIT)
Pacific Econ Rev... Pacific Economic Review [*A publication*] (JLIT)
Pacific Law Mag... Pacific Law Magazine [*A publication*] (DLA)
Pacific Rep... Pacific Reporter [*A publication*] (DLA)
Pacif Is Mon... Pacific Islands Monthly [*A publication*]
Pacif Rep... Pacific Reporter [*A publication*] (DLA)
PACIFY...... Parents and Alumni Committee Involved for Youth [*Brown University*]
PAC II....... CCSC Project Management System (SAUS)
PACIMS..... Passive Chemical Ionization Mass Spectrometry
PACINTCEN... Pacific Intelligence Center (DNAB)
PacIntl...... Pacific International Services Corp. [*Associated Press*] (SAG)
PAC IO...... Planned Amortization Class Interest-Only (SAUS)
PACIR....... Practical Approach to Chemical Information Retrieval
PACIR....... Propulsion, Aerodynamics, Control, Integration, Research (SAUS)
PACIS........ Pilot Aid & Close-In Surveillance (SAUS)
PACIT........ Passive and Active Interface Test [*Electronic warfare*]
PACIT........ Process Automation for Cable Interface Tape (VLIE)
Pac J Math... Pacific Journal of Mathematics (SAUS)
PACK........ Gibraltar Packaging Group, Inc. [*NASDAQ symbol*] (SAG)
PACK........ Packard [*NCIC car make code*]
pack......... Packed
PACK........ Packing (SAUS)
PACK........ Packing and Allocation for a COMPOOL [*Communications Pool*] Kaleidoscope (SAA)
PACK........ Parents and Cataract Kids [*An association*] (PAZ)
PACK........ Pontoon Air Cushion Kit [*Army*] (RDA)
PACKAGE... Planned Aids for Cross-Culture Knowledge, Action and Growth in Effectiveness
PACKE....... Packerton Junction, PA [*American Association of Railroads railroad junction routing code*]
PackRs...... Packaging Research Corp. [*Associated Press*] (SAG)
PackRsh.... Packaging Research Corp. [*Associated Press*] (SAG)
PACKS....... Parametric Composite Knowledge System [*Plastics engineering*]
PACKT....... Packton, LA [*American Association of Railroads railroad junction routing code*]
PACL......... Clear [*Alaska*] [*ICAO location identifier*] (ICLI)
Pac Law Mag... Pacific Law Magazine [*A publication*] (DLA)
Pac Law Reptr... Pacific Law Reporter [*San Francisco*] [*A publication*] (DLA)
Pac Leg N... Pacific Legal News [*A publication*] (DLA)
Pac Luth U... Pacific Lutheran University (GAGS)
PACM........ Parts and Components Manual (SAUS)
PACM........ Passive Access Control Module (SAUS)
PACM........ Passive Countermeasures (MSA)
PACM........ Presumptive Asbestos-Containing Material (LDOE)
PACM........ Pulse Amplitude Code Modulation [*Electronics*]
PAC-Man.... Center for Polymer-Assisted Ceramic Manufacturing [*Alfred University*] (RCD)
PACMAR.... Pacific Management Resources (SAUS)
Pac Mar Fish Comm Bull/Annu Rep... Pacific Marine Fisheries Commission Bulletin/Annual Report (SAUS)
PACMD...... Philadelphia Contract Management District (SAA)
PACMEDS... Pacific Meteorological Distribution Systems (SAUS)
PACMETNET... Pacific Meteorological Network (AAG)
PACMI....... President's Advisory Committee on Management Improvement [*Terminated, 1973*]
PACMISCEN... Pacific Missile Center [*Marine science*] (DNAB)
PACMISRAN... Pacific Missile Range [*Later, WTR*] (MUGU)
PACMISRANFAC... Pacific Missile Range Facility [*Obsolete*]
PACMISRANFACDET... Pacific Missile Range Facility Detachment [*Obsolete*] (DNAB)
PACMISRANFACREP... Pacific Missile Range Facility Representative [*Obsolete*] (DNAB)
PACMISTESTCEN... Pacific Missile Test Center [*Navy*]
PACMISTESTCEN LO... Pacific Missile Test Center Liaison Office [*Navy*] (DNAB)
PACMS...... Pacific Crisis Management System (SAUS)
PACMS...... Psycho-Acoustical Measuring System (PDAA)
PA Cmwlth... Pennsylvania Commonwealth Court Reports [*A publication*] (DLA)
PACN........ Pacific Area Communicatios Network (SAA)
PACN........ Pacification [*Telegraphy*] (PCTE)
PACN........ Pacific Nuclear Systems (EFIS)
PACNAVCONSTFOR... Pacific Naval Construction Force (DNAB)
PACNAVFACENGCOM... Pacific Division Naval Facilities Engineering Command
PACNCF...... Pacific Naval Construction Force (DNAB)
PACNCO..... Personnel Assistance Center Noncommissioned Officer (INF)
PACNET..... OCLC Pacific Network [*Claremont, CA*] [*Information service or system*] (IID)
PACNET..... Pacific Network [*Communications term*] (DCT)
PacNET...... Pacific Public Health Surveillance Network
PACNET..... Plymouth Audioconferencing Network [*Plymouth Polytechnic*] [*Plymouth, England*] [*Telecommunications*] (TSSD)
PACNET..... POCC [*Payload Operations Control Center*] Automated Computer Network
PacNoRGG.. Pacific Northwest Regional Genetics Group (SAUS)
PACNY....... Pawnbrokers' Association of the City of New York (EA)
PACO........ Accounting Policy Division (AAGC)
PacO......... Pacific Ocean
PACO........ Peak Aboriginal Community Organisation [*Australia*]
PACO........ Pivot Ambulating Crutchless Orthosis [*Medicine*]
PACO........ Polaris Accelerated Change Operation [*Missiles*]
PACO........ Primary Administrative Contracting Officer [*Military*] (AFIT)
PACO........ Principal Administrative Contracting Officer (AAGC)
PA_{CO2}........ Alveolar Carbon Dioxide Pressure [*in blood gases*] [*Medicine*] (DAVI)
PaCO2....... Arterial Carbon Dioxide Pressure (SAUS)
$Paco_2$........ Arterial Carbon Dioxide Pressure, Tension [*Medicine*] (MAE)
PaCO2....... Pressure of Carbon Dioxide (SAUS)
PACOB....... Propulsion Auxiliary Control Box (AAG)
Pac Ocean Terr... Pacific Ocean Territories (SAUS)
PA Co Ct.... Pennsylvania County Court Reports [*A publication*] (DLA)
PA Co Ct R... Pennsylvania County Court Reports [*A publication*] (DLA)
PACOM...... Pacific Command [*Military*]
PACOM...... Pacific Communications Group
PACOMBPO... Pacific Command Blood Program Office [*Military*] (DNAB)
PACOMDET... Pacific Command Detachment [*Military*] (DNAB)
PACOMEP... Pacific Command Emergency Procedures (CINC)
PACOMEW... Pacific Command Electronic Warfare (CINC)
PACOMINTS... Pacific Command Intelligence School (CINC)
PACOMJRO... Pacific Command Joint Medical Regulating Office (DNAB)
PA Commw... Pennsylvania Commonwealth Court Reports [*A publication*] (DLA)
Pa Commw... Pennsylvania Commonwealth Reports [*A publication*] (AAGC)
PA Commw Ct... Pennsylvania Commonwealth Court Reports [*A publication*] (DLA)
PA Com Pl... Pennsylvania Common Pleas Reporter [*A publication*] (DLA)
PA Cons Stat... Pennsylvania Consolidated Statutes [*A publication*] (DLA)
PA Cons Stat Ann... Pennsylvania Consolidated Statutes, Annotated [*A publication*] (DLA)
PA Cons Stat Ann (Purdon)... Pennsylvania Consolidated Statutes, Annotated (Purdon) [*A publication*] (DLA)
PACOPS..... Pacific Air Combat Operations Staff
PACOPS..... Pacific Air Force Operations (MCD)
PACOR...... Packet Processor (ADWA)
PACOR...... Passive Correlation and Ranging
PACOR...... Passive Correlation and Ranging Station (IAA)
PACORE..... Parabolic Corner Reflector
PACORNALOG... Pacific Coast Coordinator of Naval Logistics
PA Corp..... Pennsylvania Corp. Reporter [*A publication*] (DLA)
PA Corp R... Pennsylvania Corp. Reporter [*A publication*] (DLA)
PA Corp Rep... Pennsylvania Corp. Reporter [*A publication*] (DLA)
PACOS....... Package Operating System (PDAA)
PACOS....... Procedure for Automatic Computing Steps (SAUS)
PACOS....... Process Automation Control Operating System (VLIE)
PACOSS...... Passive and Active Control of Space Structure (ACAE)
PA County Ct... Pennsylvania County Court Reports [*A publication*] (DLA)
PA CP........ Pennsylvania Common Pleas Reporter [*A publication*] (DLA)
PACP........ Photo Aperture Card Program (SAA)
PACP........ Propulsion Auxiliary Control Panel [*NASA*] (KSC)
PACP........ Pulmonary Alveolar-Capillary Permeability [*Medicine*] (MELL)
PACP........ Pulmonary Artery Counter-Pulsation [*Cardiology*] (MAE)
PacPhy...... Pacific Physician Services, Inc. [*Associated Press*] (SAG)
PACPIP...... Public Advocate - Coalition of Public Interest Professionals (EA)
PACPrT...... Pac Telesis Fin I 7.56%'TOPrS' [*NYSE symbol*] (TTSB)
PACQI....... Probability of Acquisition [*Military*]
Pac R......... Pacific Reporter [*Commonly cited as P*] [*A publication*] (DLA)
PA CR....... Pennsylvania County Court Reports [*A publication*] (DLA)
PACR........ Performance and Compatibility Requirements
PACR........ Perimeter Acquisition RADAR (MSA)
PACRAD..... Practical Absolute Cavity Radiometer (PDAA)
PacR & E... Pacific Research & Engineering Corp. [*Associated Press*] (SAG)
PACRAO..... Pacific Association of Collegiate Registrars and Admission Officers

PACRED..... Pacific Area Cooperative Renewable Energy Development [*University of Hawaii*]
PacRehab... Pacific Rehabilitation & Sports Medicine, Inc. [*Associated Press*] (SAG)
Pac Rep..... Pacific Reporter [*Commonly cited as P*] [*A publication*] (DLA)
PACREP..... Port Activities Report [*Navy*]
PACREPCOMNAVSURFRES... Pacific Representative for Commander Naval Surface Reserve Force (DNAB)
PACREPNAVRES... Pacific Representative of the Chief of Naval Reserve (DNAB)
Pac Repr.... Pacific Reporter [*A publication*] (DLA)
PACRESFLT... Pacific Reserve Fleet
PacRim..... Pac Rim Holding Corp. [*Associated Press*] (SAG)
PACRNB..... Presidents Advisory Commission on Recreation and Natural Beauty (SAUS)
PACS........ Cape Sarichef Air Force Station [*Alaska*] [*ICAO location identifier*] (ICLI)
PACS........ Pacesetter [*NCIC truck make code*]
PACS........ Pacesetter [*NCIC motorcycle make code*]
PACS........ Pacesetter [*NCIC trailer make code*]
PACS........ Pacific Area Communications Service (SAUS)
PACS........ Pacific Area Communications System (MCD)
PACS........ Pacific Storage Company [*Common carrier symbol*]
Pac S........ Pacific Studies [*A publication*] (BRI)
PACS........ Pan America Climate Studies [*Marine science*] (OSRA)
PACS........ Pan American Climate Studies (SAUS)
PACS........ Particle Analysis Cameras for the Shuttle [*NASA*]
PACS........ Passenger Automated Check-In System (SAUS)
PACS........ Patient Accounting, Census, and Statistics
PACS........ Patient Care and Services (DMAA)
PACS........ Payload Actuation and Control System (SAUS)
PACS........ Payroll Accounting and Cost System (SAUS)
PACS........ Peace and Common Security [*Defunct*] (EA)
PACS........ Pentagon Automated Communications System (SAUS)
PACS........ Personal Access Communications System (VLIE)
PACS........ Photo Aperture Card System (SAA)
PACS........ Physics and Astronomy Classification Scheme
PACS........ Physics and Chemistry Classification Scheme (SAUS)
PACS........ Picture Archival and Communication System
PACS........ Picture Archiving and Communication System (ADWA)
PACS........ Pitch Augmentation Control System (PDAA)
PACS........ Plant Automation Communication System [*IBM Corp.*]
PACS........ Pointing and Attitude Control System [*Aerospace*] (NASA)
PACS........ Pointing and Control System (SAUS)
PACS........ Polar Acquisition and Control Subsystem (SAUS)
PACS........ Post-Attack Communication System
PACS........ Press and Automation Control System [*Metal Stamping*]
PACS........ Principal Appreciation Conversion Security [*Finance*]
PACS........ Process Accounting and Chargeback System [*Computer science*] (HODG)
PACS........ Process Automation & Computer Systems
PACS........ Program Authorization Control System (MCD)
PACS........ Programmable Armament Control Set (DOMA)
PACS........ Provisional Army of the Confederate States [*Civil War term*]
PACS........ Proximity Access Control System [*Police and security equipment*]
PACS........ Public-Access Computing Systems (SAUS)
Pa CSA...... Pennsylvania Consolidated Statutes, Annotated [*A publication*] (DLA)
PACSAT..... Packet Satellite [*Telecommunications*]
PACSAT..... Passive Communications Satellite
PACSBB..... Phased Array Concept Study and Brass Board (ACAE)
PA/CSC...... Payload Accommodation/Carrier Support Center [*NASA*] (SSD)
PACSC...... Pesticides and Agricultural Chemicals Standing Committee (SAUS)
PACSCAT... Pacific Ionospheric Scatter (CINC)
Pac Sci...... Pacific Science (SAUS)
PacSci....... Pacific Scientific Co. [*Associated Press*] (SAG)
PACS DB.... Picture Archiving and Communication System Data Base (DMAA)
PacSen....... Pacific Sentinel Gold Corp. [*Associated Press*] (SAG)
PACSICOM... Pan African Conference on Sustainable Integrated Coastal Management (SAUS)
PACSIM..... Performance Achievement Computer Model for Waste Package (SAUS)
PACS-L...... Public Access Computers in Libraries-Listservice (SAUS)
PACS-L...... Public Access Computer Systems List (VLIE)
PACS Review... Public-Access Computer Systems Review [*A publication*]
PACSRO..... Picture Archiving and Communications Systems in Radiation Oncology (RAWO)
PACSUBDSEC... Pacific Submarine Direct Support Element Coordinator (DNAB)
PacSun...... Pacific Sunwear of California, Inc. [*Associated Press*] (SAG)
Pac Sym.... Pacific Symphony (SAUS)
PacT......... Pacific Telesis Group Financing I [*Associated Press*] (SAG)
PacT......... Pacific Telesis Group Financing II [*Associated Press*] (SAG)
PACT......... Pan American Commission of Tampa (EA)
PACT......... Pandick Computerized Typesetting (NITA)
PACT......... Papillary Carninoma of Thyroid [*Medicine*] (DMAA)
PACT......... Parents, Children, and Teachers (AIE)
PACT......... Participating and Assertive Consumer Training [*Health education*]
PACT......... Partnership for Capacity Building in Africa
PACT......... Partnership in Advanced Computing Technologies (SAUS)
PACT......... Passive Active Correlation Techniques (ACAE)
PACT......... Paved Concrete Track [*Railways*]
PACT......... Pay Actual Computer Time
PACT......... Performing Arts for Crisis Training [*In association name, PACT Training*] (EA)
PACT......... Personal Air Communications Technology (CGWS)
PACT......... Perturbed-Anisotropic-Chain Theory [*Chemistry*]
PACT......... Phased Control Technique (PDAA)
PACT......... Philadelphia Association for Clinical Trials (DAVI)
PACT......... Philco Automatic Circuit Tester
PACT......... Plan of Action for Challenging Times (EA)
PACT......... Plasma Arc Centrifugal Treatment
PACT......... Portable Aircraft Calibration Tracker [*NASA*]
PACT......... Portable Automatic Calibration Tracker (ACAE)
PACT......... Poseidon Automatic Cable Tester [*Missiles*] (DNAB)
PACT......... Powdered Activated Carbon Treatment [*For wastewater*] [*E. I. Du Pont De Nemours & Co., Inc.*]
PACT......... Precision Aircraft Control Technology (MCD)
PACT......... Precordial Acceleration Tracing [*Medicine*] (DMAA)
PACT......... Predictive Analysis and Crash Testing [*Automotive safety research*]
PACT......... Prefix Access Code Translator (VLIE)
PACT......... Prepaid Accountable Care Term [*Medicine*] (DMAA)
PACT......... Print Active Computer Tables (SAA)
PACT......... Prisoners and Community Working Together [*Institute*]
PACT......... Private Agencies Collaborating Together (EA)
PACT......... Processing and Communications Terminal (MCD)
PACT......... Producers Alliance for Cinema & Television
PACT......... Production Action Control Technique (SAA)
PACT......... Production Analysis Control Technique [*Navy*]
PACT......... Professional Association of Canadian Theatres
PACT......... Program for Advancement of Commercial Technology (SAUS)
PACT......... Program for Automatic Coding Techniques [*Computer science*]
PACT......... Programmable Asynchronous Clustered Teleprocessing
PACT......... Programmable Automatic Continuity Tester (SAUS)
PACT......... Programmed All-purpose Communications Terminal (SAUS)
PACT......... Programmed Analysis Computer Transfer (KSC)
PACT......... Programmed Automatic Circuit Tester
PACT......... Progress in Advanced Circuit Technology (SAUS)
PACT......... Progress in Advanced Component Technology (IAA)
PACT......... Project Accounting by Cost and Time (SAUS)
PACT......... Project Analysis and Control Technique (SAUS)
PACT......... Project for the Advancement of Coding Techniques
PACT......... Prorated from Actual Read [*Electric utility company*]
PACT......... Protective Action for Children's Television (NTCM)
PACT......... Provide Addict Care Today [*Later, NADAP*]
PACT......... Public Access Cordless Telephony (VLIE)
PACT......... Public Action Coalition on Toys [*Opposes sexist toys*]
PACTA....... Packed Tape Assembly
PACTAIS..... Pacific Theater Air Intelligence System (SAUS)
PACTCU..... Pacific Area Communications Message Traffic Control Unit (IAA)
PacTec...... Pacer Technology [*Associated Press*] (SAG)
Pac Tel...... Pacific Telephone (SAUS)
PACTEL...... Pacific Telesis (NITA)
PacTel....... Pacific Telesis Group [*Associated Press*] (SAG)
PACTEL...... PA Computers & Telecommunications [*Information service or system*] (IID)
PACTEL...... Planning Associates for Computers and Telecommunications (NITA)
PACTEX..... Pacific-Texas [*Pipeline*]
PACTG....... Pediatric AIDS Clinical Trials Group (SAUS)
PACTIDS... Pacific TAC Intelligence Data System (SAUS)
PACTIV...... Principos Activos [*Ministerio de Sanidad y Consumo*] [*Spain*] [*Information service or system*] (CRD)
PACTO....... Professional, Administrative, Clerical, Technical, and Other (BARN)
PACTOA..... Pacific Technical Operations Area [*Military*]
PacTOP..... Pacific Tsunami Observation Program [*Marine science*] (OSRA)
PACTS....... Parents, Administrators, Community, Teachers, and Students [*School-community groups*]
PACTS....... Programmer Aptitude Competence Test System
PACTS....... Public Access Cordless Telephone Service [*Australia*]
PACTT....... Planning the Australian Capital Territory Together
PACTVN..... Private Agencies Collaborating Together [*Association*] (EA)
PACU........ Pacific America Container Express [*Intermodal shipping container symbol*] (TVRC)
Pac U........ Pacific University (GAGS)
PACU........ Pennsylvania Association of Colleges and Universities (SAUS)
PACU........ Post-Anesthesia Care Unit (MEDA)
PACUIT..... Packet + Circuit (MHDI)
Pac Union C... Pacific Union College (GAGS)
PACUSA..... Pacific Air Command, United States Army
PACV........ Cordova [*Alaska*] [*ICAO location identifier*] (ICLI)
PACV........ Patrol Air-Cushion Vehicle [*Also called Hovercraft*] [*Navy*]
PACV........ Personnel Air-Cushion Vehicle
PACV........ Post-Accident Containment Venting [*Nuclear energy*] (NRCH)
PACVD....... Plasma-Assisted Chemical Vapor Deposition [*Coating technology*]
PACVIS...... Pathological Cardiovascular Ischemic States [*Medicine*] (DB)
PACWP....... Pulmonary Arterial Capillary Wedge Pressure [*Medicine*] (DMAA)
PACX........ Private Automatic Computer Exchange [*Telecommunications*]
PACY........ Prairie Central Railway [*Federal Railroad Administration identification code*]
PACZ......... Calmenson Paper [*Federal Railroad Administration identification code*]
PACZ......... Cape Romanzof Air Force Station [*Alaska*] [*ICAO location identifier*] (ICLI)
PAD.......... Accounting Policy Division (AAGC)
PAD.......... Anthropology of Development Programme [*McGill University*] [*Canada*] [*Research center*] (RCD)
PAD.......... Packet Assembler/Disassembler [*Switching technique*] [*Computer science*]
PAD.......... Packet Assembly Disassembly (NITA)
PAD.......... Padder [*Capacitor*] [*Electronics*]
PAD.......... Padding (SAUS)
PAD.......... Paddling (SAUS)
PAD.......... Paderborn [*Germany*] [*Airport symbol*] (OAG)

PAD .... Padlock (SAUS)
PAD .... Padova [*Italy*] [*Seismograph station code, US Geological Survey*] (SEIS)
PAD .... Padstow [*Town in England*]
PAD .... Paducah Gaseous Diffusion Plant [*Department of Energy*] [*Paducah, KY*] (GAAI)
PAD .... Palestine Arab Delegation (EA)
PAD .... Panama Air Depot (SAUS)
PAD .... Panama District (SAUS)
PAD .... Panoz Automotive Development [*Automobile manufacturing*]
PAD .... Para-Amino Benzoic Acid (SAUS)
PAD .... Partido Accion Democratica [*Democratic Action Party*] [*El Salvador*] [*Political party*] (PPW)
PAD .... Partido de Accion Democrata [*Democratic Action Party*] [*Spain*] [*Political party*] (PPW)
PAD .... Passenger Airbag Disable
PAD .... Passive Acoustic Detection [*Military*] (CAAL)
PAD .... Passive Air Defense [*British*]
PAD .... Patient Accounts Department (SAUS)
PAD .... Patriot Arm Decoy [*Weaponry*] (DWSG)
PAD .... Payable after Death [*Insurance*] (ADA)
PAD .... Pedagogischer Austauschdienst [*Pedagogical Exchange Service*] [*German*]
PAD .... Penetration Aids Deployment [*Weaponry*] (DWSG)
PAD .... People Against Displacement (NADA)
PAD .... People's Party for Democracy and Development (Ghana) [*Political party*] (PSAP)
PAD .... Percutaneous Abscess Drainage [*Surgery*] (DAVI)
PAD .... Percutaneous Automated Diskectomy [*Neurology*] (DAVI)
PAD .... Percutaneous Device (SAUS)
PAD .... Performance Analysis and Design [*Nuclear energy*] (NRCH)
PAD .... Performance Analysis Department (SAUS)
PAD .... Performing Arts Directory [*A publication*]
PAD .... Peripheral Adaptor (SAUS)
PAD .... Peripheral Arterial Disease [*Medicine*]
PAD .... Permissible Accumulated Dose
PAD .... Personal Articulation Device [*Facetious term for pre-word-processing equipment*]
PAD .... Personnel Armoured Devices (SAUS)
PAD .... Perturbed Angular Distribution [*Nuclear physics*]
PAD .... Peters' United States District Court Reports, Admiralty Decisions [*A publication*] (DLA)
PAD .... Petroleum Administration for Defense [*Abolished, 1954*]
PAD .... Phenacetin [*Acetophenetidin*], Aspirin, Deoxyephedrine [*Pharmacology*]
PAD .... Phenacetin, Aspirin, Desoxyephedrine (SAUS)
PAD .... Phi Alpha Delta [*An association*] (NTPA)
PAD .... Phonological Acquisition Device (DAVI)
PAD .... Photon Absorption Densitometry [*Medicine*] (DMAA)
pad .... Photoshop File [*Computer science*]
PAD .... Physical Acoustics/Dunnegan (SAUS)
PAD .... Physician-Assisted Death (MELL)
PAD .... Pilotless Aircraft Division [*Navy*]
PAD .... Pitch Angle Distribution
PAD .... Pitch Axis Definition
PAD .... Pitless Adapter Division
PAD .... Pitless Adapter Division of Water Systems Council (EA)
PAD .... Pixel Access Definition (SAUS)
PAD .... Planning Action Directive [*Military*] (AFIT)
PAD .... Planning Analysis Document (SAUS)
PAD .... Planning and Analysis Division [*Environmental Protection Agency*] (GFGA)
PAD .... Plant Apparatus Division (SAUS)
PAD .... Plastics Analysis Division (SAUS)
PAD .... Player Assessment Device
PAD .... Pododermatitis Aseptica Diffusa (SAUS)
PAD .... Point Air Defence (SAUS)
PAD .... Polar and Auroral Dynamics [*Meteorology*]
PAD .... Polyaperture Device [*NASA*] (KSC)
PAD .... Pontoon Assembly Depot (NVT)
PAD .... Pontoon Assembly Detachment
PAD .... Poor Acquisition Data (AAG)
PAD .... Port Air Defense (SAUS)
PAD .... Port of Aerial Debarkation [*Air Force*]
PAD .... Positioning Arm Disk
PAD .... Post-Activation Diffusion (IEEE)
PAD .... Post Alloy Diffused (SAUS)
PAD .... Post Alloy Diffusion (IAA)
PAD .... Potential Area of Danger [*Navigation*]
PAD .... Power Amplifier Device [*or Driver*]
PAD .... Power Amplifier Driver (SAUS)
PAD .... Preadvisory Data (KSC)
PAD .... Pre Aid to the Disabled [*Medicine*] (EDAA)
PAD .... Pre-Authorized Debit (EBF)
PAD .... Precise Access Diagram
PAD .... Preferential Adaptive Defense (ACAE)
PAD .... Preferred Arrival Date (AFM)
PAD .... Preliminary Advisory Data (MCD)
PAD .... Preliminary Analysis Document (SAUS)
PAD .... Presence and Amplitude Detector
PAD .... Pressure Alarm Detector (SAUS)
PAD .... Pressure Anomaly Difference (PDAA)
PAD .... Preventive Aggressive Device [*Restraint*] [*Medicine*]
PAD .... Primary Aeronautical Designation (DNAB)
PAD .... Primary Affective Disorder [*Psychiatry*] (DAVI)
PAD .... Primary Afferent Depolarization [*Electrophysiology*]
PAD .... Prime Contractor Address (SAUS)
PAD .... Principal Associate Director (SAUS)
PAD .... Procurement Acquisition Directive
PAD .... Product Assembly Document
PAD .... Product Assembly Drawing [*Automotive project management*]
PAD .... Product Assurance Directorate [*Armament, Munitions, and Chemical Command*] [*Army*]
PAD .... Professional Administrative Development [*Medicine*]
PAD .... Professional Express Courier Service, Inc. [*ICAO designator*] (FAAC)
PAD .... Program Action Directive (AFM)
PAD .... Program Analysis Division (AAGC)
PAD .... Program Analysis for Documentation [*Computer science*]
PAD .... Program and Acquisition Division (ACAE)
PAD .... Program Approval Document [*NASA*] (KSC)
PAD .... Programmable Algorithm for Drafting (SAUS)
PAD .... Project Approval Document [*NASA*]
PAD .... Propellant Acquisition Device (NASA)
PAD .... Propellant-Actuated Device
PAD .... Property Accountability Document (ACAE)
PAD .... Protective Action Decision [*Emergency Management*] (EMA)
PAD .... Provisional Acceptance Date (NATG)
PAD .... Provisional Air Division (SAUS)
PAD .... Provisional Assembly Date (SAUS)
PAD .... Pseudoachondroplastic Spondyloepiphysial Dysplasia (DIPS)
PAD .... Psychoaffective Disorder [*Psychiatry*] (DAVI)
PAD .... Public Access Device (VLIE)
PAD .... Public Affairs Department (SAUS)
PAD .... Public Affairs Detachment
PAD .... Public Affairs Division [*Military*] (AABC)
PAD .... Public Assistance Director [*Federal disaster planning*]
PAD .... Pueblo Army Depot [*Colorado*]
PAD .... Pulmonary Artery Diastolic [*Pressure*] [*Cardiology*]
PAD .... Pulsatile Assist Device [*Cardiology*]
PAD .... Pulse amplifier discriminator (SAUS)
PAD .... Pulse Amplitude Density (SAUS)
PAD .... Pulse Averaging Discriminator
PAD .... Pulsed Activation Doppler (MCD)
PAD .... Pulsed Amperometric Detection [*Electroanalytical chemistry*]
PADA .... Panda [*NCIC truck make code*]
PADA .... Payroll Automation for Department of Agriculture
PADA .... Pennsylvania Dietetic Association (EARSL)
PADA .... Pharmacists Against Drug Abuse (EA)
PADA .... Poly(adipicanhydride) [*Organic chemistry*]
PADA .... Prespin Automatic Dynamic Alignment
PADA .... Private Art Dealers Association (EA)
PADA .... Public Address Assembly [*Ground Communications Facility, NASA*]
PADA .... Pyridine-2-Azo-P-Dimethylaniline (SAUS)
PADA .... (Pyridylazo)dimethylaniline [*Organic chemistry*]
PADAC .... Professional Art Dealers Association of Canada
PADAF .... Pacific Command Air Defense Analysis Facility (CINC)
PADAL .... Pattern for Analysis, Decision, Action, and Learning
PA D & C ... Pennsylvania District and County Reports [*A publication*] (DLA)
PA D & C 2d ... Pennsylvania District and County Reports, Second Series [*A publication*] (DLA)
PA D & C 3d ... Pennsylvania District and County Reports, Third Series [*A publication*] (DLA)
PA D & C Rep ... Pennsylvania District and County Reports [*A publication*] (DLA)
PADAR ...... Passive Airborne Detection and Ranging
PADAR ...... Passive Detection and Ranging [*Electronics*] (IAA)
PADAR ...... Photoacoustic Detection and Ranging (SAUS)
PADAR ...... Program Approval Disposal and Redistribution [*Army*] (AABC)
PADAT .... Psychological Abstracts Direct Access Terminal
PADAT .... Psychological Abstracts Direct Action Terminal (SAUS)
PADC .... Pennsylvania Avenue Development Corp. [*Washington, DC*] [*Federal corporatio n*]
PADC .... Piccole Apostole della Carita [*Ponte Lambro, Italy*] (EAIO)
PADCO ...... Pan American Development Corp. (SAUS)
PADCO ...... Planning and Development Collaboratives International [*Association*] (EA)
PADCP .... Paul Andrew Dawkins Children's Project (EA)
PADD .... Passive Antidrown Device (DWSG)
PADD .... Pedestrians Against Dangerous Drivers (SAUS)
PADD .... Pedestrians Against Drunken Drivers (SAUS)
PADD .... Personal Access Display Device (VLIE)
PADD .... Petroleum Administration for Defense District [*Department of Energy*]
PADD .... Planned Active Duty Date [*Military*]
PADD .... Political Art Documentation and Distribution (SAUS)
PADD .... Portable Acoustic Doppler Detector
PADD .... Positive Alternatives to Dangerous and Destructive Decisions (EARSL)
PADDLERS ... Paddling Athletes Defying Disabilities Limitations Enjoying Recreational Sport (EARSL)
PADDS ...... Procurement Automated Data Document System [*Military*] (RDA)
PADE .... Pad Automatic Data Equipment (PDAA)
PADEL .... Pattern Description Language
PA Dep L & I Dec ... Pennsylvania Department of Labor and Industry Decisions [*A publication*] (DLA)
PA Dep Rep ... Pennsylvania Department Reports [*A publication*] (DLA)
PADER .... Pennsylvania Department of Environmental Resources
PADF .... Driftwood Bay Air Force Station [*Alaska*] [*ICAO location identifier*] (ICLI)
PADF .... Pan American Development Foundation (EA)
PAD Facility ... Packet Assembly/Disassembly Facility (SAUS)

PAD Facility... Paket Assembly/Disassembly Facility (SAUS)
PADFAR..... Program for Air Defense Forward Area (SAUS)
PADGEM.... Platelet Activation-Dependent Granulocyte External Membrane Protein [*Biochemistry*]
PADGERC... PACOM [*Pacific Command*] Air Defense Ground Environment Requirements Committee (CINC)
PADGT....... Past Assistant Deputy Grand Treasurer [*Freemasonry*]
PADI......... Parti pour l'Avancement de la Democratie en Ituri [*Party for Democratic Advancement in Ituri*] [*Political party*]
PADI......... Personal Alarm Dose Integrator (SAUS)
PADI......... Professional Association of Diving Instructors (EA)
PADIA....... Patrol Diagnosis (NITA)
PADIE........ Prevention and Detection of Illegal Entry [*Military*] (DNAB)
PADIL........ Patriot Air Defense Information Language [*Army*]
Padin........ Partido de Integracion Nacional [*National Integration Party*] [*Peru*] [*Political party*] (PPW)
PADIRT...... Platform for Atmospheric Data in Real-Time (SAUS)
PADIS....... Pan African Development and Information System (SAUS)
PADIS....... Pan-African Documentation and Information System [*Economic Commission for Africa*] [*United Nations*] (IID)
PA Dist...... Pennsylvania District Reporter [*A publication*] (DLA)
PA Dist & Co R... Pennsylvania District and County Reports [*A publication*] (DLA)
PA Dist & Co Repts... Pennsylvania District and County Reports [*A publication*] (DLA)
PA Dist & C Rep... Pennsylvania District and County Reports [*A publication*] (DLA)
PA Dist R... Pennsylvania District Reporter [*A publication*] (DLA)
PA Dist Rep... Pennsylvania District Reports [*A publication*] (DLA)
PADK........ Adak/Davis [*Alaska*] [*ICAO location identifier*] (ICLI)
PADL........ Dillingham [*Alaska*] [*ICAO location identifier*] (ICLI)
PADL........ Part and Assembly Description Language [*Computer science*]
PADL........ Parts and Design Language (NITA)
PADL........ Parts Application Data List (SAUS)
PaDL........ Pattern Development Language (SAUS)
PADL........ Performing and Captive Animals Defence League [*British*] (BI)
PADL........ Personal Activities of Daily Living (DMAA)
PADL........ Pilotless Aircraft Development Laboratory [*Navy*]
PADL........ Polycell and Device Library (SAUS)
PADLA....... Programmable Asynchronous Dual Line Adapter
PADLOC..... Passive Active Detection and Location (IEEE)
PADLOC..... Passive Detection and Location [*Air Force*] (IAA)
PADLOC..... Passive Detection and Location of Countermeasures [*Air Force*]
PADLOCC... Passive Active Detection and Location Countermeasures (SAUS)
PADLOCC... Passive Detection and Location of Countermeasures [*Air Force*] (IAA)
PADM........ Product Assurance Directives Manual (ACAE)
PAdm........ Professional Administrator (DD)
PADMIS..... Patient Administration Information System [*Army*] (AABC)
PADO........ Passive Air Defence Officer (SAUS)
PADO........ Proposed Advanced Development Objective [*Army*] (AABC)
PADOC...... Pay Adjustment Document [*Army*]
PADP........ Physicians Against the Death Penalty (EA)
PADP........ Proposal for Advanced Development Program
PADP........ Pulmonary Artery Diastolic Pressure [*Cardiology*] (AAMN)
PADPAO..... Philippine Agency Detective Protective Association (SAUS)
PADQ........ Kodiak [*Alaska*] [*ICAO location identifier*] (ICLI)
PADR........ Parts and Data Record System (MCD)
PaDR........ Payload Design Review (SAUS)
PA DR....... Pennsylvania District Reports [*A publication*] (DLA)
PADR........ Portable Automatic Data Recorder [*Traffic management*]
PADR........ Product Assurance Discrepancy Report
PADR........ Production Administration Deficiency Report [*DoD*]
PADRA...... Pass to Air Defense RADAR [*Aviation*] (FAAC)
PADRE....... Packaging Administration & Inventory Services (SAUS)
PADRE....... Particle Analysis and Data Reduction [*Environmental Protection Agency*] (GFGA)
PADRE....... Particulate Data Reduction (EPA)
PADRE....... Patient Automatic Data Recording Equipment (IEEE)
PADRE....... Pilot Automatic Dead-Reckoning Equipment (SAUS)
PADRE....... Portable Automatic Data Recording Equipment
PADS........ Parametric Array Doppler SONAR (PDAA)
PADS........ Passive-Active Data Simulation
PADS........ Passive Advanced Sonobuoy
PADS........ Pen Application Development System [*Computer software*] [*Slate Corp.*] (PCM)
PADS........ Penetration Aid Deployment System (SAUS)
PADS........ People Against Dioxins in Sanitary Products [*An association*] [*Australia*]
PADS........ Performance Analysis and Design Synthesis [*Computer program*] [*NASA*]
PADS........ Performance Analysis Display System (NITA)
PADS........ Peroxylaminedisulfonate [*Organic chemistry*]
PADS........ Personnel Automated Data System [*TIMMS*] [*Navy*]
PADS........ Planned Arrival and Departure System [*FAA*] (TAG)
PADS........ Plant Alarm and Display System [*Nuclear energy*] (NRCH)
PADS........ Point Air Defense System
PADS........ Port and Airport Development Strategy (SAUS)
PADS........ Position and Azimuth Determining System [*Aviation*]
PADS........ Position Attack Defence System (SAUS)
PADS........ Positioning Azimuth Determining System
PADS........ Precision Aerial Delivery System
PADS........ Precision Aerial Display System
PADS........ Precision Antenna Display System (IAA)
PADS........ Precision Azimuth Determination System (SAUS)
PADS........ Product Assurance Data System (SPST)
PADS........ Professional Application Development System [*Slate*] [*Computer science*]
PADS........ Program Allocator to Drum Storage (VLIE)
PADS........ Programmer Advanced Debugging System [*Computer science*]
PADS........ Programming Advanced Debugging System [*Computer science*] (HODG)
PADS........ Publications of the American Dialect Society (SAUS)
PADS........ Punch and Drill System (SAUS)
PADS System... Parametric Array Doppler Sonar System (SAUS)
PADT........ Point Air Defence Trainer (SAUS)
PADT........ Post Allow Diffused Transistor (VLIE)
PADT........ Postalloy Diffusion Technique (IAA)
PADT........ Postalloy Diffusion Transistor
PADT........ Preliminary Aircraft Design Technology (ACAE)
PADU........ Dutch Harbour [*Alaska*] [*ICAO location identifier*] (ICLI)
PADU........ Protected Areas Data Unit (SAUS)
PADU........ Reederei Transatlantic [*Intermodal shipping container symbol*] (TVRC)
PADUA...... Pennsylvania Analysis of Decompression for Undersea and Aerospace (SAUS)
PADUA...... Progressive Augmentation by Dilating the Urethra Anterior [*Medicine*] (DMAA)
PADUC...... Paducah, KY [*American Association of Railroads railroad junction routing code*]
PADUD...... Program of Advanced Professional Development, University of Denver College of Law (DLA)
PADWSS.... Pulsed Acoustic Doppler Wind Shear Sensing System (PDAA)
PAE.......... Everett, WA [*Location identifier*] [*FAA*] (FAAL)
PAE.......... Paea [*Society Islands*] [*Seismograph station code, US Geological Survey*] (SEIS)
PAE.......... Paisajes Espanoles SA [*Spain*] [*ICAO designator*] (FAAC)
PAE.......... Parachutust Adjustable Equipment Bag [*Army*] (VNW)
PAE.......... Park Air Electronics Ltd. (SAUS)
P AE......... Partes Aequales [*Equal Parts*] [*Pharmacy*]
PAE.......... Passed Assistant Engineer [*British*]
PAE.......... Payload Accomodations Equipment [*NASA*] (SSD)
PAE.......... Payload Attach Equipment [*NASA*] (SSD)
PAE.......... Peace Arch Entertainment'B' [*AMEX symbol*] (SG)
PAE.......... Peoria & Eastern Railway [*Absorbed into Consolidated Rail Corp.*] [*AAR code*]
PAE.......... Personal Arms and Equipment [*Army*] (ADDR)
PAE.......... Phase Angle Error
PAE.......... Photo-Anodic Engraving (PDAA)
PAE.......... Phthalic Acid Esters [*Organic chemistry*]
PAE.......... Physical Aptitude Examination (AFM)
PAE.......... Pioneer Systems, Inc. [*AMEX symbol*] (COMM)
PAE.......... Planning and Estimating (IAA)
PAE.......... Polyarylene Ether (SAUS)
PAE.......... Polyarylene Ethylene (SAUS)
PAE.......... Polyaryl Ether (SAUS)
PAE.......... Polyarylether [*Organic chemistry*]
PAE.......... Polyaspartic Ester [*Organic chemistry*]
PAE.......... Port of Aerial Embarkation [*Air Force*]
PAE.......... Positive Affect Enhancement (MELL)
PAE.......... Post-Accident Environment [*Nuclear energy*] (IEEE)
PAE.......... Postantibiotic Effect [*Medicine*] (MELL)
PAE.......... Power-Added Efficiency (SAUS)
PAE.......... Precision Attack Enhancement (ACAE)
PAE.......... Preliminary Airworthiness Evaluations
PAE.......... Preliminary Army Evaluation (MCD)
PAE.......... Preventive Action Engineer (NASA)
PAE.......... Problem Assessment Engineer (SAUS)
PAE.......... Problem Assessment Engineering (NASA)
PAE.......... Products-Activities-End Products (SAUS)
PAE.......... Progress Aerospace Enterprises (SAUS)
PAE.......... Project Assurance Engineer (SAUS)
PAE.......... Projets pour une Agriculture Ecologique [*Ecological Agriculture Projects - EAP*] [*Sainte Anne De Bellevue, PQ*] (EAIO)
PAE.......... Proto-Athabaskan-Eyak [*Linguistics*] (IEL)
PAE.......... Public Affairs Event (NVT)
PAEA........ Pakistan Atomic Energy Authority (SAUS)
PAEAC....... Parliamentary Association for Euro-Arab Cooperation (EA)
PAEB........ Pan American EDIFACT Board (SAUS)
PAEC........ Pakistan Army Education Corps [*British military*] (DMA)
PAEC........ Pakistan Atomic Energy Commission (or Council) (SAUS)
PAEC........ Philippine Atomic Energy Commission (SAUS)
PAECI........ Pan American Association of Educational Credit Institutions [*Bogota, Colombia*] (EAIO)
PAECT....... Pollution Abatement and Environmental Control Technology [*Army*] (AABC)
PAED........ Anchorage/Elmendorf Air Force Base [*Alaska*] [*ICAO location identifier*] (ICLI)
PAED........ Paediatric [*or Paediatrics*]
PAED........ Plans, Analysis, and Evaluation Division [*Army*] (MCD)
PAEDP....... Pulmonary Artery End-Diastolic Pressure [*Cardiology*]
PAEF........ Peace Action Education Fund (EA)
PAEG........ Prueba de Admisiones para Estudios Graduados (GAGS)
PAEH........ Cape Newenham Air Force Station [*Alaska*] [*ICAO location identifier*] (ICLI)
PAEI......... Fairbanks/Eielson Air Force Base [*Alaska*] [*ICAO location identifier*] (ICLI)
PAEI......... Periscope Azimuth Error Indicator
PAEI......... Plane Avionic Enterprises Inc. (SAUS)
PAEI......... Purchasing Agents of the Electronic Industry [*Rosedale, NY*] (EA)
PAEK........ Polyarylether Ketone (SAUS)

PAEK Polyaryletherketone [*Organic chemistry*]
PAEL Anthony Pacheco [*Common carrier symbol*]
PAEL Preliminary Allowance Equipage List [*Military*] (CAAL)
PAEM Program Analysis and Evaluation Model (IEEE)
PAEMST Presidential Awards for Excellence in Math and Science Teaching
PAEN Kenai [*Alaska*] [*ICAO location identifier*] (ICLI)
PAEN Performance Analysis of Electrical Networks (SAUS)
PAEP Preliminary Annual Engineering Plan [*Military*] (AFIT)
P AEQ Partes Aequales [*Equal Parts*] [*Pharmacy*]
PAES Phenyl(aminoethyl)sulfide [*Biochemistry*]
PAES Planning Analysis Evaluation System
PAES Positron annihilation Auger Electron Spectroscopy (SAUS)
PAESP Pennsylvania Association of Elementary School Principals (SAUS)
PAET Planetary Atmosphere Experimental [*or Experiments*] Test [*NASA*]
PAETS Product Assurance Estimating Techniques System (ACAE)
PAET Vehicle Planetary Atmosphere Experiments Test Vehicle (SAUS)
PAEW Personnel and Equipment Working [*Aviation*] (FAAC)
PAEWCC Peace Activists East and West Coordinating Committee (EA)
PAEZ Palmyra Elevator [*Federal Railroad Administration identification code*]
PAF Pacific Air Forces
PAF Pacific Aqua Foods Ltd. [*Toronto Stock Exchange symbol*]
PAF Page Address Field
PAF Pakistan Air Force
PAF Panaf Airways Ltd. [*Gambia*] [*ICAO designator*] (FAAC)
PAF Pan American Foundation [*Defunct*] (EA)
PAF Paraburdoo [*Western Australia*] [*Airport symbol*] (AD)
PAF Paroxysmal Atrial [*or Auricular*] Fibrillation [*Medicine*] (MAE)
PAF Particle and Field Package (SAUS)
PAF Partitive Analytical Forecasting (PDAA)
PAF Payload Attach Fitting (SAUS)
PAF Payload Attachment Fitting [*NASA*]
PAF Peak Annual Funding (NASA)
PAF Pediatric AIDS Foundation (PAZ)
PAF Performing Arts Foundation (EA)
PAF Peripheral Address Field
PAF Peripheral Airfield (SAUS)
PAF Permanent Air Force [*Australia*]
PAF Peroxisome Assembly Factor [*Biochemistry*]
PAF Personal Achievement Formula [*Test*] (TES)
PAF Personal Ancestry File [*Computer science*] (PCM)
PAF Personal Article Floater [*Air baggage insurance*]
PAF Personnel Action Form (SAUS)
PAF Pet Assistance Foundation (SAUS)
PAF Pfaffenhofen an der Ilm [*German license plate city code*]
PAF Philippine Air Force
PAF Phosphodiesterase-Activating Factor [*Medicine*] (DMAA)
PAF Photoactivated Fluorescence Molecules [*Analytical biochemistry*]
PAF Picric Acid Formaldehyde (SAUS)
PAF Pilotage Aerodynamique Fort (SAUS)
PAF Pilots Active File (SAUS)
PAF Platelet-Activating Factor [*Hematology*]
PAF Platelet Aggregation Factor [*Hematology*]
PAF Polaris Accelerated Flight [*Chamber*] [*Missiles*]
PAF Polish Air Force (SAUS)
PAF Political Action Fund [*Federal political committee terminology*] (PACS)
PAF Pollen Adherence Factor [*Immunology*] (DMAA)
PAF Portable Arc Furnace
PAF Port-Aux-Francais [*Kerguelen Islands*] [*Seismograph station code, US Geological Survey*] [*Closed*] (SEIS)
PAF Ports Authority of Fiji (SAUS)
PAF Portuguese Air Force
PAF Postcode Address File [*Computer science*] (TELE)
PAF Posterior Auditory Field
PAF Preadmission Assessment Form [*Health Care Financing Administration*]
PAF Prearranged Fire
PAF Preatomized Fuel [*Trademark*] [*Petroferm product*]
PAF Premature Anti-Fascist [*World War II designation used by Army Counterintelligence Department*]
PAF Preprocessing and Archiving Facility (ACAE)
PAF Price Analysis File (AFIT)
PAF Printed and Fired (SAUS)
PAF Printed and Fired Circuit
PAF Pro-American Forum [*Defunct*] (EA)
PAF Processing and Archiving Facility (SAUS)
PAF Processor Availability Facility (SAUS)
PAF Production Assembly Facility [*Manufacturing*]
PAF Pseudoamniotic Fluid [*Gynecology*]
PAF Pseudo-Archaic Forgery
PAF Psychoanalytic Assistance Fund (EA)
PAF Public Agenda Foundation (EA)
PAF Public Art Fund (EA)
PAF Publication Authority Form (AAG)
PAF Pulmonary Arteriovenous Fistula [*Medicine*]
PAF Pulse-Air Feeder [*Automotive engineering*]
PAF Punishment and Fine (SAUS)
PAFA Fairbanks/International [*Alaska*] [*ICAO location identifier*] (ICLI)
PAFA Pakistan Australia Friendship Association [*Australia*]
PAFA Pan-American Festival Association (EA)
PAFA Pennsylvania Academy of the Fine Arts
PAFA Presidential Academic Fitness Award [*Department of Education*] (GFGA)
PAFA Priority Based Assessment of Foot Additives [*Medicine*] (DMAA)
PAFAC Plastic and Failure Analysis of Composites (SAUS)
PAFAM Performance and Failure Assessment Monitor (MCD)
PAFAMS Pan American Federation of Associations of Medical Schools [*See also FEPAFEM*] [*Caracas, Venezuela*] (EAIO)
PAFATU Pan-African Federation of Agricultural Trade Unions (EA)
PAFB Fairbanks/Wainwright Army Air Field [*Alaska*] [*ICAO location identifier*] (ICLI)
PAFB Patrick Air Force Base [*Florida*]
PAFC Paul Anka Fan Club (EA)
PAFC Phase-Locked Automatic Frequency Control [*Telecommunications*]
PAFC Philippine-American Financial Commission (SAUS)
PAFC Phosphoric Acid Fuel Cell [*Automotive engineering*]
PAFC Phosphoric-Acid Fuel Cell (SAUS)
PAFC Public Affairs Field Center (SAUS)
PAFCO Pacific Fishing Co. (SAUS)
PAFCOMNET Pacific Air Forces Communications Network (SAA)
PAFCS Prior Active Foreign Commissioned Service
PAFD Percutaneous Abscess and Fluid Drainage [*Medicine*] (DMAA)
PAFDEFNET Pacific Air Forces Defense Network (SAA)
PAFE Place Accepted for Enlistment
PAFEC Program for Automatic Finite Element Calculation (IAA)
PAFES Prior Active Foreign Enlisted Service (DNAB)
PAFI Platelet-Aggregation Factor Inhibitor [*Medicine*] (DMAA)
PAFIB Paroxysmal Atrial [*or Auricular*] Fibrillation [*Medicine*] (MAE)
PA Fid Pennsylvania Fiduciary Reporter [*A publication*] (DLA)
PA Fiduc Pennsylvania Fiduciary Reporter [*A publication*] (DLA)
PAFL Padre Freight Lines [*Common carrier symbol*]
PA Flow Pulmonary Artery Flow (SAUS)
PAFLU Philippine Association of Free Labour Unions (SAUS)
PAFMECA Pan-African Freedom Movement of East and Central Africa (SAUS)
PAFMECSA Pan African Freedom Movement for East, Central, and Southern Africa [*Superseded in 1963 by the liberation committee of the Organization of African Unity*] (PD)
PA FOOD PAC Pennsylvania Food PAC [*Wormleysburg, PA*] (PACS)
PAFP Photochemical Aerosol-Forming Potential of Polluted Air [*Environmental chemistry*]
PAFP Pre-Achilles Fat Pad [*Medicine*] (DMAA)
PAFR Fort Richardson/Bryant Army Air Field [*Alaska*] [*ICAO location identifier*] (ICLI)
PAF Resistor Printed and Fired Resistor (SAUS)
PAFS Primary Air Force Specialty
PAFS Publication of the American Folklore Society (SAUS)
PAFSC Primary Air Force Specialty Code
PAFSO Professional Association of Foreign Service Officers [*Canada*] (EAIO)
PAFT Polish American Folk Theatre
PAFT Programme for Alternative Fluorocarbon Toxicity Testing [*British*]
PAFTA Pacific Free Trade Area
PAFTA Pacifiic Area Free Trade Association (SAUS)
PAFTAD Pacific Trade and Development Conference
PA-FTIR Photoacoustic Fourier Transform Infrared Spectroscopy (AAEL)
PAFTT Program for Alternative Fluorocarbon Toxicity Testing [*Environmental science*]
PAFU Patriot Arm Fire Unit [*Weaponry*] (MCD)
PAFU Propulsion Arming and Firing Unit [*Military*]
PAFVA Polish Air Force Veterans Association (EA)
PAFW Farewell [*Alaska*] [*ICAO location identifier*] (ICLI)
PAG I Pagliacci [*Opera*] (DSUE)
PAG Pacific Gulf Properties, Inc. [*AMEX symbol*] (SAG)
PAG Pagadian [*Philippines*] [*Airport symbol*] (OAG)
Pag Page's Three Early Assize Rolls, County of Northumberland [*Surtees Society Publications, Vol. 88*] [*A publication*] (ILCA)
PAG Paget Resources Ltd. [*Vancouver Stock Exchange symbol*]
PAG Paging (SAUS)
Pag Pagoda
PAG Pamphlet Antigas (SAUS)
PAG Panagjuriste [*Bulgaria*] [*Geomagnetic observatory code*]
PAG Panjim [*India*] [*Airport symbol*] (AD)
PAG Pariaqueductal Grey Matter [*Neurology*] (DAVI)
PAG Parts Acquisition Group
PAG Party for the Autonomy of Gibraltar [*Political party*] (PPW)
PAG Pascagoula, MS [*Amtrak rail station code*]
PAG Paying [*Telegraphy*] (PCTE)
PAG Pentaacetylglucose [*Laundry bleach activator*]
PAG Periaqueductal Gray Matter [*Brain anatomy*]
PAG Perimeter Aviation Ltd. [*Canada*] [*ICAO designator*] (FAAC)
PAG Pesticide Assessment Guideline [*Environmental Protection Agency*]
PAG Photoacid Generator
Pag Piper [*Airplane code*]
PAG Planning Advisory Group (SAUS)
PAG Plant Advisory Group (SAUS)
PAG Plasma-Arc-Based Gasifier (SAUS)
PAG Pneumatic Antishock Garment (MELL)
PAG Polyacrylamide Gel [*Analytical chemistry*]
PAG Polyalkylene Glycol [*Organic chemistry*]
PAg Poultry-Related Antigens [*Immunology*]
PAG Poverty Advisory Group
PAG Prealbumin Globulin [*Biochemistry*] (OA)
PAG Precision Alignment Gyrocompass
PAG Precursor Active Galaxies
PAG Pregnancy-Associated alpha-Glycoprotein [*Gynecology*]
PAG Pregnancy-Associated Globulin [*Medicine*] (MELL)
PAG Preliminary Analysis Group (NATG)
PAG Premier Automotive Group [*Automotive corporate organization*]
PAG Primary Analysis Group (SAUS)

PAG .... Prince Albert's Guard [*British military*] (DMA)
PAG .... Prior Austenite Grain (SAUS)
PAG .... Priorities Analysis Group
PAG .... Professional Activities Group
PAg .... Professional Agrologist (DD)
PAG .... Professional Auto Group, Inc.
PAG .... Program Advisory Group
PAG .... Program Assessment Guide [*Department of Labor*] (OICC)
PAG .... Progress Analysis Group [*Navy*] (MCD)
PAG .... Project Advisory Group [*Army*]
PAG .... Property Advisory Group [*British*] (DCTA)
PAG .... Protection Against Gas (SAUS)
PAG .... Protection Anti-Gas (SAUS)
PAG .... Protective Action Guide [*Nuclear energy*]
PAG .... Protein A colloidal Gold (SAUS)
PAG .... Protein Advisory Group [*United Nations*]
pAg .... Protein A-Gold Technique [*Medicine*] (DMAA)
PAG .... Public Affairs Guidance [*Environmental science*] (COE)
PAG .... Spring Garden College, Philadelphia, PA [*OCLC symbol*] (OCLC)
PAGA .... Galena [*Alaska*] [*ICAO location identifier*] (ICLI)
PAGA .... Pan American Grace Airways, Inc. [*Also, PANAGRA*]
PAGA .... Prematurely Appropriate for Gestational Age [*Medicine*] (EDAA)
PAGA .... Proliferation-Associated Gene A (DMAA)
PAGAD ...... People Against Gangsterism and Drugs [*South Africa*]
PAGAN ...... Pattern Generation Language [*Computer science*]
PAGAN ...... People Against Goodness & Normalcy (WDAA)
PAGB .... Poultry and Egg Producers Association of Great Britain (SAUS)
PAGB .... Proprietary Association of Great Britain
PAGB Yearbook... Poultry Association of Great Britain Yearbook (SAUS)
PAGCH ...... Paging and Access Grant Channel (CGWS)
PAGDC ...... Past Assistant Grand Director of Ceremonies [*Freemasonry*] (ROG)
PAGE .... Page Generation [*or Generator*] (PDAA)
Page .... Page's Three Early Assize Rolls, County of Northumberland [*Surtees Society Publications, Vol. 88*] [*A publication*] (DLA)
PAGE .... Page Trailer [*NCIC trailer make code*]
PAGE .... Paging Network [*NASDAQ symbol*] (SPSG)
PAGE .... Permanent Automatic Ground Environment (SAUS)
PAGE .... PERT [*Program Evaluation and Review Technique*] Automated Graphical Extension (KSC)
PAGE .... Philatelic Association of Government Employees
PAGE .... Piston Arrestment Gas Entrapment System [*SPRINT launch cell*] [*Army*] (AABC)
PAGE .... Polyacrylamide Gel Electrophoresis [*Analytical chemistry*]
PAGE .... Preliminary Automated Ground Environment
PAGE .... Preview and Graphics Editing [*Computer science*] (MHDI)
PAGE .... Program for Automated Gated Evaluation [*Cardiology*] (DAVI)
PAGE .... Programmable Aerospace Ground Equipment (SAUS)
PAGE .... Publish Australia Group Enterprise
PageAm..... Page America Group, Inc. [*Associated Press*] (SAG)
Page Contr... Page on Contracts [*A publication*] (DLA)
Page Div.... Page on Divorce [*A publication*] (DLA)
PAGEL .... Priced Aerospace Ground Equipment List
PAGEN....... Pattern Generation (SAUS)
PAGEN....... Pattern Generator (SAUS)
PAGEN Language... Pattern Generation Language (SAUS)
PAGEOS..... Passive Geodetic Earth-Orbiting Satellite [*NASA*]
PAGER....... Pediatric/Adolescent Gastroesophageal Reflux Association, Inc. (NRGU)
Pa Ger Soc... Pennsylvania German Society (SAUS)
Pages .... Pages, Inc. [*Associated Press*] (SAG)
PAGES....... Past Global Changes [*Marine science*] (OSRA)
PAGES....... Past Global Environmental Changes (SAUS)
PAGES....... Print and Graphics Express Station (ACAE)
PAGES....... Program Affinity Grouping and Evaluation System
PAGES/CPO... PAGES/Core Project Office (SAUS)
PAGES-EXCOMM... PAGES Executive Committee (SAUS)
PAGES-SSC... PAGES Scientific Steering Committee (SAUS)
PAGE System... Pharmacia Gel Electrophoresis System (SAUS)
PAGE System... Piston Arrestment Gas Entropment System (SAUS)
PAGi .... Parent Advisory Group for the Internet
PAGI .... Pemco Aviation Group [*NASDAQ symbol*]
PAGI .... Penn America Group [*NASDAQ symbol*] (SAG)
PAGICEP ... Petroleum and Gas Industry Communications Emergency Plan [*FCC*]
PAGIF........ Polyacrylamide Gel Isoelectric Focusing (DB)
Paging ...... Paging Network, Inc. [*Associated Press*] (SAG)
Paging ...... Paging Partners Corp. [*Associated Press*] (SAG)
PagingN..... Paging Network Inc. [*Associated Press*] (SAG)
PagingP..... Paging Partners Corp. [*Associated Press*] (SAG)
PAGIS .... Participatory GPS (Global Positioning System) [*Navigation systems*]
PAGIS .... Pastoral and Agricultural Geographic Information System (SAUS)
PAGIS .... Performance Assessment of Geological Isolation System [*Nuclear energy*] (NUCP)
Pag Jud Puz... Paget's Judicial Puzzles [*A publication*] (DLA)
PAGK .... Gulkana [*Alaska*] [*ICAO location identifier*] (ICLI)
PAGL .... Pulsed Argon Gas LASER
PAGM........ Permit Applicants Guidance Manual (COE)
PAGMK...... Primary African Green Monkey Kidney [*Cells*]
PAGN .... Pagnall [*England*]
PAGOS ...... Program for the Analysis of General Optical Systems (SAUS)
PAGP .... Pacific Golden-Plover [*North American bird banding code*] (BIBA)
PAGP .... Pennsylvania Academy of General Practice [*Medicine*] (EDAA)
PAgP......... Port Aggregation Protocol [*Computer science*] (DINT)
PAGS .... Parti de l'Avant-Garde Socialiste [*Socialist Vanguard Party*] [*Algeria*] [*Political party*] (PD)
PAGS .... Polish-American Guardian Society (EA)
PAGS .... Prior Austenite Grain Size (SAUS)
PAGSE....... Partnership Group for Science and Engineering (SAUS)
PAGT .... Port Authority Grain Terminal (SAUS)
PAGT .... Provincial Association of Geography Teachers (SAUS)
PAGTU....... Pan-American Ground Training Unit
PAGU .... Paganella [*Intermodal shipping container symbol*] (TVRC)
PAGX .... Planta Almacenadora de Gas [*Private rail car owner code*]
PAGZ .... Pages, Inc. [*NASDAQ symbol*] (SAG)
PAH.......... Paducah [*Kentucky*] [*Airport symbol*] (OAG)
PAH.......... Pahoa [*Hawaii*] [*Seismograph station code, US Geological Survey*] [*Closed*] (SEIS)
PAH.......... Pan American Highway (SAUS)
PAH.......... Panorama Air Tour, Inc. [*ICAO designator*] (FAAC)
PAH.......... Para-Aminohippurate [*Clearance Test*] [*Urology*] (DAVI)
PAH.......... Para-Aminohippuric [*Biochemistry*]
PAH.......... Para-Aminohippuric Acid (SAUS)
PAH.......... Para-Amino-Hyppurate (SAUS)
PAH.......... Parts Application Handbook
PAH.......... Pathtechnics Ltd. [*Vancouver Stock Exchange symbol*]
PAH.......... Patriot American Hospitality, Inc. [*NYSE symbol*] (SAG)
PAH.......... Payload Accommodations Handbook [*NASA*] (NASA)
PAH.......... Phase Adjusting Hub
PAH.......... Phenylalanine Hydroxylase [*An enzyme*]
Pah .... Piper Pressurised Prop-Jet [*Airplane code*]
PAH.......... Pitch Attitude Hold [*Aviation*] (MCD)
PAH.......... Polyaromatic Hydrocarbon (EDCT)
PAH.......... Polycyclic [*or Polynuclear*] Aromatic Hydrocarbon [*Organic chemistry*]
PAH.......... Polycyclic Aromatic Hydrocarbons [*Automotive emissions*] [*Organic chemistry*]
PAH.......... Polynuclear Aromatic Hydrocarbon (EEVL)
PAH.......... Pulmonary Artery Hypertension [*Medicine*]
PAH.......... Pulmonary Artery Hypotension [*Cardiology*] (DAVI)
PAH.......... Push and Hold [*Push button*]
PAHA .... P-Aminohippuric Acid (SAUS)
PAHA .... Para-Aminohippuric Acid
PAHA .... Polish American Historical Association (EA)
PAHA .... Procainamide-Hydroxylamine (DMAA)
PAHBAH..... Para-Hydroxybenzoic Acid Hydrazide [*Organic chemistry*]
PAHC .... HC Parrish Truck Service [*Common carrier symbol*]
PAHC .... Pan American Highway Congresses (EA)
PAHC .... Pioneer American Holding Co. [*NASDAQ symbol*] (COMM)
PAHC .... Pontifical Association of the Holy Childhood (EA)
PAHCOM.... Professional Association of Health Care Office Managers
PAHdb .... Phenylalanine Hydroxylase Locus Knowledgebase [*Database*] [*Canada*] (GDD)
PAHEF....... Pan American Health and Education Foundation (EA)
PAHEL....... Pay Records and Health Records
PAHEO....... Particle Accelerators in High Earth Orbit [*Proposed*]
PAHEP....... Plasma and High Energy Physics (IAA)
PAHF .... Pan American Hockey Federation [*Winnipeg, MB*] (EAIO)
PAHHA ...... Pennsylvania Association of Home Health Agencies (EARSL)
PAHL .... Pressure Alarm, High-Limit [*Nuclear energy*] (NRCH)
PAHO .... Homer [*Alaska*] [*ICAO location identifier*] (ICLI)
PAHO .... Pan American Health Organization (EA)
PAHOCENDES... Pan-American Health Organization Center for Development Studies (SAUS)
PAHR .... Post-Accident Heat Removal [*Nuclear energy*]
PAHRI .... Pakistan Animal Husbandry Research Institute (SAUS)
PAHS .... Passive Annual Heat Storage [*Housing technology*]
PAHVC....... Pulmonary Alveolar Hypoxic Vasoconstriction [*Medicine*] (STED)
PAHVC....... Pulmonary Alveolar Hypoxic Vasoconstrictor [*Medicine*] (MELL)
PAHZ .... Panzer Abwewp Hubschrauber [*Attack Helicopter*]
PAI........... Angolan Independent Party [*Political party*] (PSAP)
PAI........... Kitty Hawk Aircargo, Inc. [*ICAO designator*] (FAAC)
PAI........... Pacific Aerospace Index (DIT)
PAI........... Pacific American Income Shares, Inc. [*NYSE symbol*] (SPSG)
PAI........... Pacific American Institute (EA)
PAI........... Pacoima, CA [*Location identifier*] [*FAA*] (FAAL)
Pai .... Paige's New York Chancery Reports [*A publication*] (DLA)
Pai .... Paine's United States Circuit Court Reports [*A publication*] (DLA)
PAI........... Pair Attraction Inventory [*Premarital, marital, and family counseling test*] [*Psychology*]
PAI........... Panama Airways Inc. (SAUS)
PAI........... Parachute Association of Ireland (EAIO)
PAI........... Paradise Airways, Inc. [*FAA designator*] (FAAC)
PAI........... Parti Africain de l'Independance [*African Independence Party*] [*Senegal*] [*Political party*] (PPW)
PAI........... Partido Aragones Independiente [*Spain*] [*Political party*] (EY)
PAI........... Parts Application Information [*Manufacturing*]
PAI........... Passive-Aggressive Index [*Psychology*]
PAI........... Patient Assesment Instrument [*Medicine*] (DMAA)
PAI........... Percent Adherence Index
PAI........... Performance Audit Inspection [*Environmental Protection Agency*] (GFGA)
PAI........... Personal Accident Insurance
PAI........... Personal Adjustment Inventory [*Psychology*]
PAI........... Personnel Accreditation Institute (EA)
PAI........... Pesticide Active Ingredient (EEVL)
PAI........... Phosphate Adsorption Index [*Analytical chemistry*]
PAI........... Photographic Administrators, Inc. (EA)
PAI........... Piedmont Aviation, Inc. [*Air carrier designation symbol*]

PAI.......... Pilot Attack Instructor (SAUS)
PAI.......... Piping and Instrumentation [*Nuclear energy*] (IAA)
PAI.......... Pirchei Agudath Israel (EA)
PAI.......... Place Accumulator in Indicators (IAA)
PAI.......... Plasminogen-Activator Inhibitor [*Biochemistry*]
PAI.......... Platelet Accumulation Index [*Medicine*] (MELL)
PAI.......... Please Airmail Immediately (SAUS)
PAI.......... Plunger Actuated Indexer
PAI.......... Poale Agudath Israel of America (EA)
PAI.......... Polar Area Index [*Palynology*] (QUAC)
PAI.......... Polish Assistance, Inc. (EA)
PAI.......... Polyamide-Imide [*Organic chemistry*]
PAI.......... Population Action International (SAUS)
PAI.......... Post-operative Adynamic Ileus [*Medicine*] (EDAA)
PAI.......... Prearrival Inspection
PAI.......... Precise Angle Indicator
PAI.......... Primary Aerospace Vehicle [*or Aircraft*] Inventory
PAI.......... Primary Aircraft Inventory (SAUS)
PAI.......... Process After Input (SAUS)
PAI.......... Process Analytical Instrument
PAI.......... Process Analytical Instrumentation (SAUS)
PAI.......... Process Automation Interface (IAA)
PAI.......... Processed Apples Institute (EA)
PAI.......... Product Assurance Instruction (ACAE)
PAI.......... Production Acceptance Inspection (IAA)
PAI.......... Production Adjustment Index [*Word processing*]
PAI.......... Professional Athletes International [*Later, NFLPA*] (EA)
PAI.......... Programmer Appraisal Instrument [*Computer science*] (IEEE)
PAI.......... Project Assignment Instruction (MCD)
PAI.......... Property Agents International
PAI.......... Protected Area Information (SAUS)
PAI.......... Protocol Addressing Information [*Telecommunications*] (OSI)
PAI.......... Provisional Acceptance Inspection (SAUS)
PAI.......... Public Affairs Information, Inc. [*Sacramento, CA*] [*Database producer*] [*Information service or system*]
PAI.......... Public Affairs Institute [*Defunct*] (EA)
PAI.......... Public Assistance Information [*A publication*]
PAI.......... Pure Active Ingredient (EEVL)
PAI.......... Pure Active Ingredient compound (SAUS)
PAIA........ Pan American Implant Association (EA)
PAIA........ Parents of Apneic Infants Association [*Medicine*] (EDAA)
PAIAW....... Philadelphia Association of Intercollegiate Athletics for Women (PSS)
PAIB........ Polish-American Information Bureau [*Later, PATIB*] (EA)
PAIC........ Center for Improvement of Family Life (EARSL)
PAIC........ Persia and Iraq Command [*World War II*]
PAIC........ Personal Attribute Inventory for Children (EDAC)
PAIC........ Procedures, Alternatives, Indications, and Complications [*Medicine*] (DMAA)
PAIC........ Public Address Intercom System (NRCH)
PAICC....... Professional Association of the Interstate Commerce Commission
Pai Ch....... Paige's New York Chancery Reports [*A publication*] (DLA)
PAICR....... Professional Association for Investment Communications (EA)
PAICV....... African Party for the Independence of Cape Verde [*Political party*] (PSAP)
PAID........ Pacific Animated Imaging [*NASDAQ symbol*] (TTSB)
PAID........ Pacific Animated Imaging Corp. [*NASDAQ symbol*] (SAG)
PAID........ Pan African Institute for Development (EAIO)
PAID........ Parked Aircraft Intrusion Detector (PDAA)
PAID........ People Against Impaired Driving [*Canada*] (EAIO)
PAID........ Personnel and Accounting Integrated Data [*System*] [*Veterans Administration*]
PAID........ Piping and Instrumentation Diagram [*or Design*] [*Nuclear energy*] (IAA)
PAID........ Piping and Instrumentation Drawing (SAUS)
PAID........ Plutonium Air Inhalation Dose (SAUS)
PAID........ Price and Item Display [*British*]
PAID........ Problem Areas in Diabetes [*Scale*] [*Medicine*] (DMAA)
PAID........ Programmers Aid in Debugging [*Computer science*] (MHDI)
PAIDS....... Paralyzed Academic Investigator's Disease Syndrome [*Medicine*] (DMAA)
PAIDS....... Pediatric Acquired Immune Deficiency Syndrome [*Medicine*]
PAIDS....... Pediatric Acquired Immunodeficiency Syndrome [*Medicine*] (STED)
PAID System... Personnel and Accounting Integrated Data System (SAUS)
PAIE........ Pam's Delivery Service [*Common carrier symbol*]
PAIF........ Persia and Iraq Force [*World War II*]
PAIFORCE... Persia and Iraq Force [*World War II*] (DMA)
PAIg........ Platelet-Associated Immunoglobulin [*Hematology*]
PAIGC....... Partido Africano da Independencia da Guine e do Cabo Verde [*African Party for the Independence of Guinea and Cape Verde*] [*Political party*] (PPW)
Paige........ Paige's New York Chancery Reports [*A publication*] (DLA)
PAIGE........ Patient Instruction Generator (ADWA)
Paige Ch.... Paige's New York Chancery Reports [*1828-45*] [*A publication*] (DLA)
Paige Ch Rep... Paige's New York Chancery Reports [*A publication*] (DLA)
Paige's Ch... Paige's New York Chancery Reports [*A publication*] (DLA)
PAIgG........ Platelet-Associated Immunoglobulin G [*Hematology*]
PAIGH....... Pan American Institute of Geography and History [*Research center*] [*Mexico*] (IRC)
PAIH........ Public-Access Internet Host [*Computer science*] (VLIE)
PAII........ Professional Association of Innkeepers International (NTPA)
PAIL........ Iliamna [*Alaska*] [*ICAO location identifier*] (ICLI)
PAIL........ Post-Attack Intercontinental Link
PAIL........ Procedural Aspects of International Law Institute (SAUS)
PAILS....... Projectile Airburst and Impact Location System
PAILS....... Projectile and Impact Location System (SAUS)
PAILS....... Publication Automated Information Locator System [*Army*]
PAIM........ Indian Mountain Air Force Station [*Alaska*] [*ICAO location identifier*] (ICLI)
PAIM........ Parti Africain pour l'Independance des Masses [*African Party for the Independence of the Masses*] [*Senegal*] [*Political party*] (PPW)
PAIM........ Primary Air Inlet Muffler (MCD)
PAIMEG..... Pan American Institute of Mining, Engineering, and Geology [*Defunct*]
PAIN........ Paccar [*NCIC trailer make code*]
PAIN........ Pain Suppresion Labs, Inc. [*NASDAQ symbol*] (COMM)
PAIN........ Pan American Institute of Neurology (SAUS)
PAIN........ Parents Against Injustice (WDAA)
PAIN........ Prisoners' Advice & Information Network (WDAA)
Paine........ Paine's United States Circuit Court Reports [*A publication*] (DLA)
Paine & D Pr... Paine and Duer's Practice [*A publication*] (DLA)
Paine CC.... Paine's United States Circuit Court Reports [*A publication*] (DLA)
Paine CCR... Paine's United States Circuit Court Reports [*A publication*] (DLA)
Paine Cir Ct R... Paine's United States Circuit Court Reports [*A publication*] (DLA)
PAINS....... Patient Information System (SAUS)
PAINT........ Painter (SAUS)
PAINT........ Painting (ROG)
PAINT........ Post-Attack Intelligence
Painters Union... International Brotherhood of Painters and Allied Trades of the United States and Canada (SAUS)
Paint Resin... Paint and Resin (SAUS)
PainWeb.... PaineWebber Group, Inc. [*Associated Press*] (SAG)
PainWP..... Paine Webber Premier Tax Free Income [*Associated Press*] (SAG)
PAIP........ Preverbal Assessment-Intervention Profile [*Test*]
PAIP........ Production Acceleration Insurance Program
PAIP........ Public Affairs and Information Program [*Atomic Industrial Forum*] (NRCH)
PAIR........ Pairgain Technologies [*NASDAQ symbol*] (SAG)
PAIR........ Performance Accountability and Improvement Report
PAIR........ Performance and Improved Reliability
PAIR........ Performance and Integration Retrofit
PAIR........ Performance Assessment in Reading [*Educational test*]
PAIR........ Personal Assessment of Intimacy in Relationships (STED)
PAIR........ Personnel Administration and Industrial Relations
PAIR........ Polarization-Agile Instrumentation Radar (SAUS)
PAIR........ Precision Approach Interferometer RADAR (MCD)
PAIR........ Preliminary Assessment Information Rule [*Environmental Protection Agency*]
PAIR........ Procurement Automated Integrated Requirements (MCD)
PAIR........ Product Analysis Incident Report (VLIE)
PAIR........ Product Analysis Information Report (SAUS)
PAIR........ Psychological Audit for Interpersonal Relations [*Psychology*]
PAIR........ Pulse-Air Injection Reactor [*Automotive engineering*]
PAIRC....... Planning and Architecture Internet Resource Center [*Now called Cyburbia*] [*Internet resource*]
PAIRC....... Polish American Immigration and Relief Committee (EA)
PAIRMEM... Paired Word Memory Task (TES)
PAIRO....... Professional Association of Interns and Residents (SAUS)
PAIRS....... Pain and Impairment Relationship Scale (MELL)
PAIRS....... Parent Assisted Instruction in Reading and Spelling (AIE)
PAIRS....... Practical Application of Intimate Relationship Skills
PAIRS....... Private Aircraft Inspection Reporting System (PDAA)
PAIRS....... Product Assurance Information Retrieval System [*Boeing*]
PAIRS....... Program for the Analysis of Infrared Spectra [*Computer program*] [*Analytical chemistry*]
PAIRS....... Pushbroom Airborne Infrared Remote Sensor (SAUS)
PairTch...... Pairgain Technologies [*Associated Press*] (SAG)
PAIS........ Open Politics for the Social Country (Argentina) [*Political party*] (PSAP)
PAIS........ Padre Island National Seashore [*National Park Service designation*]
PAIS........ PAIS International in Print
PAIS........ Paris [*NCIC motorcycle make code*]
PAIS........ Partial Androgen Insensitivity Syndrome [*Medicine*] (EDAA)
PAIS........ Partido Amplio de Izquierda Socialista [*Chile*] [*Political party*] (EY)
PAIS........ Partido Autentico Institucional Salvadoreno [*Salvadoran Authentic Institutional Party*] [*Political party*] (PPW)
PAIS........ Pennsylvania Association of Independent Schools (SAUS)
PAIS........ Personnel Authentication Identification System (MCD)
PAIS........ Petroleum Abstracts Information Services [*University of Tulsa*] [*Oklahoma*] [*Information service or system*] (IID)
PAIS........ Phosphoribosylaminoimidazole Synthetase [*Medicine*] (EDAA)
PAIS........ Project Analysis Information System [*Agency for International Development*]
PAIS........ Prototype Advanced Indicator System (MCD)
PAIS........ Psychological Abstracts Information Services [*American Psychological Association*]
PAIS........ Psychosocial Adjustment to Illness Scale [*Personality development test*] [*Psychology*]
PAIS........ Public-Access Internet Site [*Computer science*] (VLIE)
PAIS........ Public Affairs Information Service [*Environment term*] (EGA)
PAISA....... Paisano, TX [*American Association of Railroads railroad junction routing code*]
PAISA....... Partido Autentico Institucional Salvadoreno [*Salvadoran Authentic Institutional Party*] [*Political party*] (EY)
PAIS FLI.... PAIS Foreign Language Index (NITA)
PAIS FLI... Public Affairs Information Service-Foreign Language Index (SAUS)
PAIT........ Pait, IL [*American Association of Railroads railroad junction routing code*]
PAIT........ Passive Adoptive Immunotherapy [*Medicine*] (MELL)
PAIT........ Program for Advancement of Industrial Technology [*Canada*]
PAIV........ Power as an Integral Variable

PAIVL .... Painesville, OH [*American Association of Railroads railroad junction routing code*]
PAIVM .... Passive Accessory InterVertebral Movement (SAUS)
PAIVS .... Pulmonary Atresia with Intact Ventricular Septum [*Cardiology*] (DAVI)
PAIX .... Pacific Alaska Airlines [*Air carrier designation symbol*]
PAJ .... Kansas City, MO [*Location identifier*] [*FAA*] (FAAL)
PAJ .... Paralysis Agitans Juvenilis [*Medicine*] (DMAA)
PAJ .... Performing Arts Journal [*A publication*]
PAJ .... Petroleum Association of Japan (SAUS)
PAJA .... Parachute Jumping Activities [*Aviation*] (FAAC)
PAJA .... Parasitic Jaeger [*North American bird banding code*] (BIBA)
PAJAR .... Parti Rakyat Jati Sarawak [*Sarawak Native People's Party*] [*Malaysia*] [*Political party*] (PPW)
PAJES .... Parents of Adult Jewish Singles
PAJHS .... Publications of the American Jewish Historical Society (SAUS)
PAJN .... Juneau [*Alaska*] [*ICAO location identifier*] (ICLI)
PAJOCA ..... Party of the Alliance for Youth, Workers, and Farmers of Angola [*Political party*] (PSAP)
PAK .... Hanapepe, HI [*Location identifier*] [*FAA*] (FAAL)
PAK .... Pacific Alaska Airlines [*ICAO designator*] (FAAC)
PAK .... Packed (SAUS)
PAK .... Packet (SAUS)
PAK .... Pakistan [*ANSI three-letter standard code*] (CNC)
Pak .... Pakistan (VRA)
PAK .... Palatka, FL [*Amtrak rail station code*]
PAK .... Panzer Abwehr Kanone [*Cannon Against Armor*] [*German antitank gun*]
PAK .... Performance Advantage Kit [*Personal computers*]
PAK .... Polycyclic Aromatic Ketone [*Organic chemistry*]
PAK .... Polyester Alkyd (SAUS)
PAK .... Power Amplifier Klystron
PAK .... Product Authorization Key (VLIE)
PAK .... Program Attention Key [*Computer science*] (BUR)
PAK .... Projector Alignment Kit (SAUS)
PAK .... Pseudomonas Aeruginosa Strain K (DB)
Pak Bar J ... Pakistan Bar Journal [*A publication*] (DLA)
Pak Crim LJ... Pakistan Criminal Law Journal [*A publication*] (DLA)
PakE .... Pakistani English (SAUS)
Pakete .... Daten-Pakete (SAUS)
PAKEX .... International Packaging Exhibition [*British*] (ITD)
PA KEY ...... Program Extension Key [*Computer science*] (ITCA)
PAKH .... Pacific Alaska Transport [*Common carrier symbol*]
PAKH .... Parkhurst Manufacturing Company [*NCIC trailer make code*]
PakisInv ..... Pakistan Investment Fund, Inc. [*Associated Press*] (SAG)
Pak J Sci... Pakistan Journal of Science (SAUS)
Pak J Sci Res... Pakistan Journal of Scientific Research (SAUS)
PakLibrAssQJ... Pakistan Library Association Quarterly Journal (SAUS)
PakLibrRev... Pakistan Library Review (SAUS)
Pak LR ...... Pakistan Law Reports [*India*] [*A publication*] (DLA)
Pak L Rev... Pakistan Law Review [*A publication*] (DLA)
PAKM .... Pak-Mor Manufacturing Company [*NCIC trailer make code*]
PAKN .... King Salmon [*Alaska*] [*ICAO location identifier*] (ICLI)
PAKOMIN... Pakistan Oxygen Minimum (SAUS)
PAK-PAC .... Pakistani American Public Affairs Committee [*Laurel, MD*] (PACS)
PAKSI .... Pakistan Standards Institute (SAUS)
Pak Sup Ct Q... Pakistan Supreme Court Law Quarterly [*Lahore, Pakistan*] [*A publication*] (DLA)
PAKT .... Ketchikan [*Alaska*] [*ICAO location identifier*] (ICLI)
PAKU .... Pacorini [*Intermodal shipping container symbol*] (TVRC)
PAL .... Allegheny County Law Library, Pittsburgh, PA [*OCLC symbol*] (OCLC)
PAL .... Angolan Liberal Party [*Political party*] (PSAP)
PAL+ .... Enhanced-fidelity PAL (SAUS)
PAL .... North Amer. Palladium [*AMEX symbol*]
PAL .... Pacific Aeronautical Library
PAL .... Pacific Aerospace Library (SAUS)
PAL .... Pacific Air Lines
PAL .... Pacific Aluminium (SAUS)
PAL .... Packet Access Line [*Communications term*] (DCT)
PAL .... Paducah & Louisville Railway [*Federal Railroad Administration identification code*]
pal .... Pahlavi [*MARC language code*] [*Library of Congress*] (LCCP)
PAL .... Paired-Associates Learning [*Task*] [*Psychology*]
PAL .... Pakistan Airlines (SAUS)
PAL .... Palace
Pal .... Palamedes [*of Gorgias*] [*Classical studies*] (OCD)
pal .... Palate (DMAA)
PAL .... Palatine [*or Palatinate*] [*Genealogy*]
PAL .... Paleography (ROG)
PAL .... Paleontology
PAL .... Paleozoic [*Period, era, or system*] [*Geology*]
Pal .... Palestine (NTIO)
PAL .... Palestine
pal .... Palette (VRA)
PAL .... Palinuro [*NCIC car model code*]
PAL .... Palisades [*New York*] [*Seismograph station code, US Geological Survey*] (SEIS)
PAL .... Pallet (VLIE)
PAL .... Pallor (KSC)
Pal .... Palmer's Assizes at Cambridge [*England*] [*A publication*] (DLA)
Pal .... Palmer's English King's Bench Reports [*1619-29*] [*A publication*] (DLA)
Pal .... Palmer's Reports [*53-60 Vermont*] [*A publication*] (DLA)
PAL .... Paloma Petroleum Ltd. [*Toronto Stock Exchange symbol*]
PAL .... Pan Asia Line (SAUS)
PAL .... Paradox Application Language [*ANSA*] [*Computer science*]
PAL .... Parcel Air Lift [*US Postal Service*]
PAL .... Parents Anonymous Lifeline [*British*] (DI)
PAL .... Parser Assembly Language [*Computer science*]
PAL .... Partition Allocation Utility (SAUS)
PAL .... Parts and Assemblies Locator [*ADP/CES*]
PAL .... Parts Authorization List (KSC)
PAL .... Passive Activity Loss [*Investment term*] (DFIT)
PAL .... Patent Associated Literature
PAL .... Pathology Laboratory [*Test*]
PAL .... Pectin Acid Lyase [*An enzyme*]
PAL .... Pedagogic Algorithmic Language [*Computer science*]
PAL .... Pensioners Advancement League (SAUS)
PAL .... People Against Chlordane (EA)
PAL .... People-Animals-Love (EA)
PAL .... People for Animals League (EARSL)
PAL .... Peptidyl-Alpha-Hydroxyglycine Alpha-Amidating Lysine Phase Alteration Plane [*Medicine*] (DMAA)
PAL .... Perceptual Alternatives Laboratory [*University of Louisville*] [*Research center*] (RCD)
PAL .... Performance Assessment Logic
PAL .... Peripheral Access Lattices
PAL .... Permanent Artificial Lighting (IEEE)
PAL .... Permissive Action Link [*Army*]
PAL .... Permissive Arming Line [*or Link*]
PAL .... Peroxide Assisted Leach [*Ore processing*]
PAL .... Personal Answer Line [*Telecommunications*] (VLIE)
PAL .... Personal Assets Line
PAL .... Personnel Accounting Level [*Air Force*] (AFM)
PAL .... Personnel Address Listing (SAA)
PAL .... Personnel Airlock [*Nuclear energy*] (NRCH)
PAL .... Personnel Augmentation List [*Military*]
PAL .... Phase Alternate Line (NITA)
PAL .... Phase Alternating Line [*Telecommunications*] (MLOA)
PAL .... Phase Alternating Loop (SAUS)
PAL .... Phase Alternation Line [*West German color television system*]
PAL .... Phase Alternation Standard (SAUS)
PAL .... Phase-Alternation System [*A color TV format*] [*Also, phase alternate each line*] (WDMC)
PAL .... Phase Attenation by Line (SAUS)
PAL .... Phenylalanine Ammonia-Lyase [*An enzyme*]
PAL .... Philippine Air Lines
PAL .... Philippine Air Lines, Inc. [*ICAO designator*] (FAAC)
PAL .... Philips Air Liquefier (SAUS)
PAL .... Philips Assembler Language (IAA)
PAL .... Physical Activity Level (WDAA)
PAL .... Pipe Analysis Log [*Gas well*]
PAL .... Plasma Ammonia Level [*Medicine*] (MELL)
PAL .... Platform Abstraction Layer (VLIE)
PAL .... Podiatry Arts Laboratory (SAUS)
PAL .... Point, Area, and Line Source Air Quality Model [*Environmental Protection Agency*] (GFGA)
PAL .... Police Athletic League
PAL .... Police Attendance Line
PAL .... Poligono de Actividades Logisticas (EFIS)
PAL .... Polyacrylnitril (SAUS)
PAL .... Polyaniline (SAUS)
PAL .... Poly-DL-alanine Poly-L-lysine [*Biochemical analysis*]
PAL .... Polynesian Airlines Ltd. (SAUS)
PAL .... Portable, Accurate, Lightweight (SAUS)
PAL .... Portable Advanced Laser (SAUS)
PAL .... Positive Arming Link [*Military*] (DNAB)
PAL .... Postal Answer Line [*US Postal Service automated telephone information service*]
PAL .... Posterior Axillary Line [*Medicine*]
PAL .... Power and Light (IAA)
PAL .... Power Assist Lathe
PAL .... Pre-Academic Learning Inventory [*Child development test*]
PAL .... Preapproved Loan [*Business term*]
PAL .... Precision Artwork Language [*Computer science*]
PAL .... Preliminary Allowance List [*Military*] (DNAB)
PAL .... Premier Automobiles Ltd. [*India*]
PAL .... Prescribed Action Link [*DoD*]
PAL .... Present Atmospheric Level
PAL .... Prevent-a-Litter of Cats (EARSL)
PAL .... Price and Availability List (CINC)
PAL .... Princeton Accelerator Laboratory
PAL .... Princeton Air Link
PAL .... Prison Atheist League (SAUS)
PAL .... Prisoner-at-Large
PAL .... Privileged Architecture Library (SAUS)
PAL .... Privileged Architecture Library Code
PAL .... Problem Action Log (AAG)
PAL .... Process Assembler Language
PAL .... Process Assembly Languages
PAL .... Process Asset Library
PAL .... Process Audit List (MCD)
PAL .... Process Automation Language [*Computer science*] (AAEL)
PAL .... Processing and Analytical Laboratories (SAUS)
PAL .... Production and Application of Light (MCD)
PAL .... Product of Activated Lymphocytes [*Medicine*] (DMAA)
PAL .... Products and Area Locator (SAUS)
PAL .... Professional Adjustable Ladder (SAUS)

PAL .... Profile Automobile League (EA)
PAL .... Profile of Aptitude for Leadership [*Test*] (TMMY)
PAL .... Program Array Logic (SAUS)
PAL .... Program Assembler (or Assembly) Language (SAUS)
PAL .... Programmable Algorithm Machine Assembly Language [*Computer science*]
PAL .... Programmable Array Logic [*Computer science*] (IEEE)
PAL .... Programmable Automation Laboratory [*University of Southern California*] (RCD)
PAL .... Programmed Application Library [*IBM Corp.*]
PAL .... Programmed Array Logic (SAUS)
PAL .... Programmed Audit Library
PAL .... Programmer Assistance and Liaison [*Computer science*] (NRCH)
PAL .... Programming Application Language (SAUS)
PAL .... Programming Assembly Language (SAUS)
PAL .... Progressive Alliance of Liberia [*Political party*] (PPW)
PAL .... Prototype Application Loop [*Nuclear energy*] (NRCH)
PAL .... Protuberance Aerodynamic Load (SAUS)
PAL .... Psycho-Acoustic Laboratory [*Harvard University*] (MCD)
PAL .... Public Archives Library (SAUS)
PAL .... Public Archives of Canada Library [*UTLAS symbol*]
PAL .... Publication Applicability List [*Navy*]
PAL .... Publications Allowance List [*Military*] (CAAL)
PAL .... Pulmonary Air Leak [*Medicine*] (DB)
PAL .... Pulsed Argon LASER
PAL .... Push and Latch [*Push button*]
PAL .... Pyogenic Abscess of the Liver [*Medicine*] (DMAA)
PALA......... N-(Phosphoacetyl)-L-aspartate [*Biochemistry*]
pala.......... Palace (VRA)
pala.......... Palazzo (VRA)
Pala .... Partido Laborista [*Labor Party*] [*Panama*] [*Political party*] (PPW)
PALA......... Partition Affinity Ligand Assay [*Analytical microbiology*]
PALA......... Passenger Acceptance and Load Accumulation [*Aviation*]
PaLA......... Pennsylvania Library Associaton
PALA......... Phosphonoacetyl-L-Aspartate [*Biochemistry*]
PALA......... Poetics and Linguistics Association [*United Kingdom*] (EAIO)
PALA......... Polish American Librarians Association (EA)
PALA......... Prison Atheist League of America (EA)
PALAAS ..... Property and Liability Agency Accounting System (SAUS)
PALACE ..... Profiling ALACE [*Autonomous Lagrangian Circulation Explorer*] [*Marine science*] (OSRA)
palaeob ..... Palaeobotanical (SAUS)
palaeob ..... Palaeobotany (ODA)
PALAEOB... Palaeobotany
palaeog ..... palaeographical (SAUS)
PALAEOG ... Palaeography
Palaeogeogr Palaeoclimatol Palaeoecol... Palaeogeography Palaeoclimatology Palaeoecology (SAUS)
Palaeo III ... Palaeogeography, Palaeoclimatology, Palaeoecology (SAUS)
PALAEONT... Palaeontology
Palaeontol... Palaeontological (DIAR)
Pal Ag........ Paley on Principal and Agent [*3rd ed.*] [*1833*] [*A publication*] (DLA)
PAL APA .... Indonesian Communications Satellite (SAUS)
PALASM..... Programmable Array Logic Assembler [*Computer science*] (IEEE)
Palat.......... Palatinate (SAUS)
PALAT .... Palatka, FL [*American Association of Railroads railroad junction routing code*]
PA Law J ... Pennsylvania Law Journal [*A publication*] (DLA)
PA Law Jour... Pennsylvania Law Journal [*Philadelphia*] [*A publication*] (DLA)
PA Laws .... Laws of the General Assembly of the Commonwealth of Pennsylvania [*A publication*] (DLA)
PA Law Ser... Pennsylvania Law Series [*A publication*] (DLA)
PALB......... Pallas's Bunting [*North American bird banding code*] (BIBA)
PALC......... Palace
PALC......... Pal Manufacturing Company [*NCIC trailer make code*]
PALC......... Passenger Acceptance and Load Control [*Aviation*]
PALC......... Plasma-Addressed Liquid Crystal (SAUS)
PALC......... Point Arguello Launch Complex
PALC......... Precastable Autoclaved Lightweight Concrete [*Residential construction*]
PAL-C........ Profile of Adaptation to Life - Clinical [*Personality development test*] [*Psychology*]
PALCD....... Plasma Addressable Liquid Crystal Display (SAUS)
PALCO....... Pacific Lumber Co. (EFIS)
PALCO....... Pan American Liaison Committee of Women's Organizations (EA)
PALCON..... Pallet-Size Container (MCD)
Pal Conv.... Paley on Summary Convictions [*10th ed.*] [*1953*] [*A publication*] (DLA)
PALCR....... Propulsion Auxiliaries Local Control Rack (DNAB)
PALCRU..... Pay and Allowances Accrue From [*Air Force*]
PALCS....... Permissive Action Link Cypher System (MCD)
PALC System... Passenger Acceptance and Load Control System (SAUS)
PALCTS ..... Processing Analytical Laboratories Commitment Tracking System (SAUS)
PALCUS ..... Portuguese American Leadership Council of the United States [*Association*] (EA)
PALD .... Phase Alternation Line Delay
PALDS....... Point, Area, and Line Source with Deposition and Settling of Pollutants [*Air quality model*] [*Environmental Protection Agency*] (GFGA)
PALE......... Palace Corporation [*NCIC trailer make code*]
PALE......... Palaeoclimate from Arctic Lakes and Estuaries (SAUS)
Pale .... Palestine (VRA)
PALE......... Pelvis and Legs Elevating [*Pilot seat*]
PALE......... People Against Landfill Expansion (EARSL)
PALE......... Popular Army for the Liberation of Eritrea (SAUS)
PA Leg Gaz... Legal Gazette (Pennsylvania) [*A publication*] (DLA)
PA Leg Gaz... Legal Gazette Reports (Campbell) [*Pennsylvania*] [*A publication*] (DLA)
PA Legis Serv... Pennsylvania Legislative Service (Purdon) [*A publication*] (DLA)
Paleo......... Paleolithic (SAUS)
paleob....... Paleobotany (BARN)
Paleoclim Res... Paleoclimate Research (SAUS)
PALEOECOL... Paleoecologic
paleog....... Paleography
PALEOGEOG... Paleogeographic
Paleol .... Paleolithic (VRA)
paleon....... Paleontology
PALEONT ... Paleontologic
PALEONT ... Paleontological (SAUS)
PALEO NT... Paleontologist (SAUS)
Paleontol ... Paleontology (BEE)
PALE Seat... Pelvis and Legs Elevating Seat (SAUS)
Palest .... Palestinian (DIAR)
PALEX .... Pacific Armies Look Exercise
Paley Ag .... Paley on Principal and Agent [*A publication*] (DLA)
Paley Princ & Ag... Paley on Principal and Agent [*3rd ed.*] [*1833*] [*A publication*] (DLA)
PALF......... Palestinian Arab Liberation Front (CARL)
Palfed .... PALFED, Inc. [*Associated Press*] (SAG)
PAL format... Phase Alternation Line Video Format (MWOL)
PA LG .... Legal Gazette (Pennsylvania) [*A publication*] (DLA)
PA LG .... Legal Gazette Reports (Campbell) [*Pennsylvania*] [*A publication*] (DLA)
Palg Ch ..... Palgrave's Proceedings in Chancery [*A publication*] (DLA)
Palgrave .... Palgrave's Proceedings in Chancery [*A publication*] (DLA)
Palgrave .... Palgrave's Rise and Progress of the English Commonwealth [*A publication*] (DLA)
Palg Rise & Prog... Palgrave's Rise and Progress of the English Commonwealth [*1832*] [*A publication*] (DLA)
Palg Rise Etc... Palgrave's Rise and Progress of the English Commonwealth [*A publication*] (DLA)
PAL-H .... Profile of Adaptation to Life - Holistic [*Personality development test*] [*Psychology*]
PALI .... Pacific and Asian Linguistics Institute [*University of Hawaii*]
PALI .... Palila [*North American bird banding code*] (BIBA)
Pali .... Partido Liberal [*Nicaragua*] [*Political party*] (EY)
PALI .... Prince Albert's Light Infantry [*Military unit*] [*British*]
PALIC PAC... Pan-American Life Insurance Company PAC [*New Orleans, LA*] (PACS)
PALIKA...... Parti de Liberation Kanak [*New Caledonia*] [*Political party*] (EY)
palin......... palindromic (SAUS)
PA line...... Pulmonary Artery Line [*Medicine*] (BCRP)
PALINET..... Pennsylvania Area Library Network
PALINET..... Philadelphia Area Library Network (SAUS)
PALINET/ULC... PALINET and Union Library Catalogue of Pennsylvania [*Philadelphia, PA*] [*Library network*]
PALIPEHUTU... Party for the Liberation of the Hutu People (Burundi) [*Political party*] (PSAP)
PALIS........ Polarized Airborne Laser Imaging Sensor (SAUS)
PALIS........ Programmable Adapter Logic Sequence (SAUS)
PALIS........ Property and Liability Information System
PA LJ......... Pennsylvania Law Journal [*A publication*] (DLA)
PA LJ......... Pennsylvania Law Journal Reports [*1842-52*] [*A publication*] (DLA)
PA LJR ...... Clark's Pennsylvania Law Journal Reports [*A publication*] (DLA)
PALL......... Pallet [*Freight*]
PALL......... Palliser [*NCIC car make code*]
Pall .... Pallium (SAUS)
PALLA .... Pallas, UT [*American Association of Railroads railroad junction routing code*]
PallCp....... Pall Corp. [*Associated Press*] (SAG)
PALLNIC .... Palladium-Nickel (EECA)
PALM........ PALFED, Inc. [*NASDAQ symbol*] (NQ)
PALM........ Palm [*Company symbol*]
Palm......... Palmer's Assizes at Cambridge [*England*] [*A publication*] (DLA)
Palm......... Palmer's English King's Bench Reports [*1619-29*] [*A publication*] (DLA)
Palm......... Palmer's Reports [*53-60 Vermont*] [*A publication*] (DLA)
PALM........ Palm, Inc. [*NASDAQ symbol*] (SG)
PALM........ Palmistry (ADA)
PALM........ Palm Trailers [*NCIC trailer make code*]
Palm......... Palmyrene (BJA)
PALM........ Personalized Automated Life Management (SAUS)
PALM........ Philips Automated Laboratory Management (SAUS)
PALM........ Philips Automated Laboratory Management System (NITA)
PALM........ Precision Altitude and Landing Monitor [*Aircraft location*]
PALM........ Pro Audio, Light & Music (SAUS)
Palma .... Palma de Mallorca (SAUS)
Palm Comp L... Palmer's Company Law [*22nd ed.*] [*1976*] [*A publication*] (DLA)
Palm Comp Prec... Palmer's Company Precedents [*17th ed.*] [*1956-60*] [*A publication*] (DLA)
Palmer ...... Palmer's Assizes at Cambridge [*England*] [*A publication*] (DLA)
Palmer ...... Palmer's English King's Bench Reports [*A publication*] (DLA)
Palmer ...... Palmer's Reports [*53-60 Vermont*] [*A publication*] (DLA)
Palmer Co Prec... Palmer's Company Precedents [*16 eds.*] [*1877-1952*] [*A publication*] (DLA)
PALMER FLD... Palmer Field (SAUS)
Palmer Pr Comp... Palmer's Private Companies [*41st ed.*] [*1950*] [*A publication*] (DLA)

PALMES..... Pulsed Appendage Large Mobile Electromagnetic-Pulse Simulator (PDAA)
PalmHH..... Palm Harbor Homes, Inc. [*Associated Press*] (SAG)
PALMNET... Protocol for Automotive Local Area Network
Palm Pr Lords... Palmer's Practice in the House of Lords [*1830*] [*A publication*] (DLA)
PALMR...... Palmer, MA [*American Association of Railroads railroad junction routing code*]
PalmrMd.... Palomar Medical Technologies [*Associated Press*] (SAG)
PALMS...... Pennsylvania Lake Management Society (EARSL)
PALMS...... Propulsion Alarm and Monitoring System (PDAA)
PALMS...... Provisioning Automated Logistics Material System (MCD)
Palm Sh.... Palmer's Shareholders [*34th ed.*] [*1936*] [*A publication*] (DLA)
Palm Wr.... Palmer's Law of Wreck [*1843*] [*A publication*] (DLA)
PALN........ Palmetto Sales of Laurens [*NCIC trailer make code*]
PALN........ Para-Aortic Lymph Node [*Anatomy*] (DAVI)
PALNI........ Private Academic Library Network of Indiana
PALO........ Pacific Loon [*North American bird banding code*] (BIBA)
PALO........ Palamino Camping Trailer [*NCIC trailer make code*]
PALO........ Phosphonoacetyl-L-Ornithine [*Biochemistry*]
PALO........ Port Amenities Liaison Officer [*British*] (DSUE)
Pal Obs..... Palomar Observatory (SAUS)
PALOS....... Pacific Logistic Operations - Streamline [*Army*]
PA Loudspeaker... Public Address Loudspeaker (SAUS)
PALP......... Palm Express [*Common carrier symbol*]
PALP......... Palpable [*Medicine*]
palp......... Palpitation [*Cardiology*] (DAVI)
PALP......... Protected Areas and Landscapes Programme (SAUS)
PALP......... Pyridoxal Phosphate [*Also, PLP*] [*Biochemistry*]
PALPI........ Palpitation [*Medicine*]
palpit........ Palpitation [*Medicine*]
PALR........ Permissive Action Link Report [*Army*] (AABC)
PA L Rec.... Pennsylvania Law Record [*A publication*] (DLA)
PALS......... Paedriatic Advanced Life Support [*Medicine*] (WDAA)
PALS......... Paired Associate Learning Subtest [*Speech and language therapy*] (DAVI)
PALS......... Parents and Loyal Supporters of Gymnastics (EARSL)
PALS......... Patient Advocacy Legal Service [*An association*] [*Defunct*] (EA)
PALS......... Pediatric Advanced Life Support [*Medicine*] (ADWA)
PA LS......... Pennsylvania Law Series [*A publication*] (DLA)
PALS......... People Against Lenient Sentences [*An association*] [*Australia*]
PALS......... People Against Loneliness [*British*] (DI)
PALS......... Periarteriolar Lymphocyte Sheath (AAMN)
PALS......... Permissive Action Link System [*Army*]
PALS......... Phase Alternation Line Simple [*TV decoding system*]
PAL-S......... Phase Alternation Line-Simple (SAUS)
PALS......... Photo Area and Location System (NASA)
PALS......... Photographic Area and Location System
PALS......... Point Arguello Launch Site (AAG)
PALS......... Portable Airfield Lighting System (SAUS)
PALS......... Portable Airfield Light Set (SAUS)
PALS......... Positioning and Locating System [*Aviation*] (PDAA)
PALS......... Pre-Announcement Level System (SAUS)
PALS......... Precision Approach and Landing System (NASA)
PALS......... Precision Approach Lighting System [*Aviation*] (FAAC)
PALS......... Preliminary Award Letter System
PALS......... Prestaged Ammunition Loading System [*Army*] (RDA)
PALS......... Principle of the Alphabet Literacy System [*Software*] [*IBM Corp.*]
PALS......... Principles of Adult Learning Scale (EDAC)
PALS......... Prison-Acquired Lymphoproliferative Syndrome [*Medicine*] (DMAA)
PALS......... Program for Address List Supplementation (SAUS)
PALS......... Protection Against Limited Strikes [*Military defence system*]
PALS......... Public Access Library System (SAUS)
PA L Ser.... Pennsylvania Law Series [*A publication*] (DLA)
PALS-G...... Passive Artillery Locating System - Ground Based (MCD)
PALSG....... Personnel and Logistics Systems Group [*Army*] (AABC)
PA-LS-ID.... Pernicious Anemia-Like Syndrome and Immunoglobulin Deficiency [*Hematology*] (AAMN)
PALST....... Picture Articulation and Screening Test
PAL System... Phase Alternating (or Alternation) Line System (SAUS)
PAlt.......... Altoona Area Public Library, Altoona, PA [*Library symbol*] [*Library of Congress*] (LCLS)
PALT......... Procurement Acquisition Lead Times (SAUS)
PALT......... Procurement Administrative Lead Time
PALTC....... Pacific Asian and Latino Training Center (SAUS)
PAL test..... Pathology Laboratory Test [*Medicine*] (EDAA)
PALU........ Cape Lisburne Air Force Station [*Alaska*] [*ICAO location identifier*] (ICLI)
PALU........ Progressive Arbeiders- en Landbouwersunie [*Progressive Workers' and Farm Laborers' Union*] [*Surinam*] [*Political party*] (PPW)
PALU........ United Lumumbist Party (D. Rep. Congo) [*Political party*] (PSAP)
Palud........ Paludonus [*Pierre de la Palu*] [*Deceased, 1342*] [*Authority cited in pre-1607 legal work*] (DSA)
PALUP....... Patterned-prepreg Lay-Up Process [*Automotive electronics*]
PALV......... Passiflora Latent Virus [*Plant pathology*]
PALW......... Palmer's Machine Works [*NCIC trailer make code*]
PALW......... Plasma Arc-augmented Laser Welding
PALX......... PalEx, Inc. [*NASDAQ symbol*] (NASQ)
PALX......... Private Automatic Loudspeaking Exchange [*Telecommunications*] (IAA)
PAM......... Pacific Armies Management
PAM......... Pacific CMA [*AMEX symbol*]
PAM......... Package for Analogue Modeling (SAUS)
PAM......... Page Allocation Map (SAUS)
PAM......... Paging Area Memory (SAUS)
PAM......... Palermo [*California*] [*Seismograph station code, US Geological Survey*] (SEIS)
PAM......... Pamida Holdings Corp. [*AMEX symbol*] (SPSG)
PAM......... Pamour, Inc. [*Toronto Stock Exchange symbol*]
Pam......... Pampa [*Record label*] [*Brazil*]
PAM......... Pamphlet (AFM)
pam......... Pamphlet (WDMC)
PAM......... PAM Transportation Services, Inc. [*Associated Press*] (SAG)
PAM......... Pan Africanist Movement (SAUS)
PAM......... Panama City, FL [*Location identifier*] [*FAA*] (FAAL)
PAM......... Panel Monitor (MHDI)
PAM......... Panoramic
PAM......... Panvalet Access Method (IAA)
PAM......... Parallel Associative Memory (SAUS)
PAM......... Parameter Adjusting Mechanism
PAM......... Parametric Amplifier (NATG)
PAM......... Parents Against Molesters (EA)
PAM......... Parititioned Access Method (SAUS)
PAM......... Partial Mobilization Expansion Plan [*Army*] (GFGA)
PAM......... Particle Anticoincidence Mantle (SAUS)
PAM......... Partitioned Access Method [*Computer science*]
PAM......... Pasadena Art Museum (SAUS)
PAM......... Payload Accommodation Manager (SAUS)
PAM......... Payload Assist Module [*NASA*] (MCD)
PAM......... Peachtree Accounting-Macintosh (SAUS)
PAM......... Peer-A-Med [*Database*] (GDD)
PAM......... Penetration Augmented Munition
PAM......... Penicillin Aluminum Monostearate [*Antibiotic*]
PAM......... People's Action Movement [*Nevis*] [*Political party*] (PPW)
PAM......... People's Anti-War Mobilization (EA)
PAM......... Performance Analysis Model (MCD)
PAM......... Performance Assessment Matrix (SARE)
PAM......... Performance Assessment Monitoring (MCD)
PAM......... Performing Arts Medicine
PAM......... Perigee Assist Motor (ACAE)
PAM......... Peripheral Adapter Module
PAM......... Personal Accounting Management
PAM......... Personal Application Monitor (SAUS)
PAM......... Personal Applications Manager [*Hewlett-Packard Co.*]
PAM......... Personnel Action Memorandum [*Military*]
PAM......... Personnel Availability Model (PDAA)
PAM......... Pesticide Analytical Manual (EEVL)
PAM......... Phase-Amplitude Modulation
PAM......... Phased Array Module
PAM......... Phenylacetamidomethyl (SAUS)
PAM......... Phenylalanine Mustard (AAMN)
PAM......... Philosophies, Ancient and Modern [*A publication*]
PAM......... Phoenix Airborne Missile
PAM......... Phoenix Air Service GmbH [*Germany*] [*ICAO designator*] (FAAC)
PAM......... Phone Activities Manager (SAUS)
PAM......... Phono Amplifier (SAUS)
PAM......... Photoacoustic Microscopy (SAUS)
PAM......... Pittsburgh, Allegheny & McKees Rocks Railroad Co. [*AAR code*]
PAM......... Plan-Applier Mechanism (SAUS)
PAM......... Planning, Activation, Modification [*Army reorganization*]
PAM......... Plant Available Moisture (SAUS)
PAM......... Plasma-Arc Machining [*Manufacturing term*]
PAM......... Pledged Account Mortgage
PAM......... Pluggable Authentication Module (RALS)
PAM......... Pole Amplitude Modulation (IEEE)
PAM......... Policies and Measures (SAUS)
PAM......... Polyacrylamide [*Also, PAA, PAAM*] [*Organic chemistry*]
PAM......... Portable Activity Monitor (SAUS)
PAM......... Portable Alpha Meter (SAUS)
PAM......... Portable Alpha Monitor
PAM......... Portable Automated Mesonet [*Meteorology*]
PAM......... Portland Art Museum (SAUS)
PAM......... Position and Altitude Monitor (MCD)
PAM......... Post-Accident Monitoring [*Nuclear energy*] (NRCH)
PAM......... Postauricular Myogenic [*Medicine*] (DMAA)
PAM......... Potential Acuity Meter [*Instrumentation*]
PAM......... Potential Available Market (TIMI)
PAM......... Power Assist Module [*NASA*]
PAM......... Pozzolan Aggregate Mixture (OA)
PAM......... Pralidoxime [*Pharmacology*] (DAVI)
PAM......... Pralidoxime Chloride [*Pharmacology*] (DAVI)
PAM......... Pralidoxime Methiodide [*Biochemistry*]
PAM......... Precision Angular Mover (SAUS)
PAM......... Preliminary Aerosol Monitor (SAUS)
PAM......... Presbyterian Association of Musicians (EA)
PAM......... Pressure-Acoustic-Magnetic [*Minesweeping system*] (DNAB)
PAM......... Primary Access Method [*Sperry UNIVAC*]
PAM......... Primary Acquired Melanosis [*Oncology*]
PAM......... Primary Amoebic Meningitis [*or Meningoencephalitis*] [*Medicine*]
PAM......... Primary Amoebic Meningoencephalitis (SAUS)
PAM......... Primary Auxiliary Memory [*Unit*] [*Computer science*] (MCD)
PAM......... Printer Authorization Matrix (VLIE)
PAM......... Priorities and Allocations Manual [*Army*] (AABC)
PAM......... Process Application Module (AAEL)
PAM......... Process Automatic Monitor (SAUS)
PAM......... Process Automation Monitor [*Texas Instruments, Inc.*]
PAM......... Processor and Memory [*Computer science*]
PAM......... Procurement Aids Man [*Marine Corps*]
PAM......... Procurement Aircraft and Missiles (SAUS)

PAM .... Procurement and Acquisition Management (SAUS)
PAM .... Procurement of Aircraft and Missiles
PAM .... Product Assurance Manager (ACAE)
PAM .... Profit Analysis Model (MHDI)
PAM .... Program Analysis Memorandum (MCD)
PA-M .... Program Authorization - Map [*Military*] (AFIT)
PAM .... Program Automated Method [*Computer science*]
PAM .... Programmable Active Memory [*Computer science*] (VLIE)
PAM .... Programmable Algorithmic Machine (SAUS)
PAM .... Programmable Algorithm Machine [*Computer science*]
PAM .... Programmed Accounting Machine (SAUS)
PAM .... Programmed Associative Memory [*Computer science*] (VLIE)
PAM .... Project Assurance Manager (SAUS)
PAM .... Project Assurance Manual (SAUS)
PAM .... Propulsion Assistance Module (MCD)
PAM .... Protopan Chloride [*Medicine*] (BARN)
PAM .... Provincial Archives of Manitoba (SAUS)
PAM .... Pulmonary Alveolar Macrophage [*Attacks inhaled particles*]
PAM .... Pulmonary Alveolar Microlithiasis [*Medicine*] (MAE)
PAM .... Pulmonary Artery Mean Pressure [*Medicine*] (RAWO)
PAM .... Pulse Amplification Modulation (SAUS)
PAM .... Pulse Amplified Modulation (SAUS)
PAM .... Pulse Amplifier Modulation (NAKS)
PAM .... Pulse Amplitude Modulated (SAUS)
PAM .... Pulse Amplitude Modulation [*Electronics*]
PAM .... Pulse Amplitude Modulator (SAUS)
PAM .... Pyridine Aldoxime Methiodide [*Biochemistry*]
PAM .... Pyridine Aldoxime Methyl [*Pharmacology*]
PAM .... Pyridine-Aldoxime-N-Methyliodide (SAUS)
PAM .... University of Pennsylvania, School of Medicine, Philadelphia, PA [*OCLC symbol*] (OCLC)
PAm .... Wissahickon Valley Public Library, Ambler, PA [*Library symbol*] [*Library of Congress*] (LCLS)
PAM 250.... Accepted Point Mutation 250 (SAUS)
PAMA........ Pama Camper [*NCIC truck make code*]
PAM-A....... PAM [*Payload Assist Module*] Atlas-Centaur Class Spacecraft (NASA)
PAMA........ Pan American Medical Association [*Also known as Association Medica Pan Americana*] (EA)
PAMA........ Para-Dimethylaminophenylazopyridine [*An indicator*] [*Chemistry*]
PAM-A....... Payload Assist Module - Atlas Class Spacecraft (MCD)
PAMA........ Philippines Air Materiel Area (SAUS)
PAMA........ Polish Alma Mater of America (EA)
PAMA........ Polyalkylmethacrylate (IAA)
PAMA........ Pre-Assigned Multiple Access [*Telecommunications*] (LAIN)
PAMA........ Preferred Acquisition Method of Analysis (SAUS)
PAMA........ Press Advertisement Managers' Association (DGA)
PAMA........ Processing Algorithm for Maintenance Actions (SAUS)
PAMA........ Professional Aviation Maintenance Association (EA)
PAMA........ Publishers Advertising and Marketing Association (SAUS)
PAMA........ Pulse-Address Multiple Access [*Satellite communications*]
PAMAC....... Parts and Materials Accountability Control
PAMAD....... Parents Against Middle-Aged Discrimination [*British*] (DI)
PAMAI....... Program of Action for Mediation, Arbitration, and Inquiry [*American Library Association*]
PAMAM ..... Polyamidoamine [*Organic chemistry*]
PAMARS .... Program Accounting Management Attainment Reporting System [*USDA Forest Service*] (ALAC)
PAMB........ Pressure Ambient (NASA)
PAMBA....... Para-Aminomethylbenzoic Acid (SAUS)
PAmbT ...... Trinity Episcopal School, Ambridge, PA [*Library symbol*] [*Library of Congress*] (LCLS)
PAMBU....... Pacific Manuscripts Bureau (SAUS)
PAMC........ McGrath [*Alaska*] [*ICAO location identifier*] (ICLI)
PAMC........ Pakistan Army Medical Corps
PAMC........ Pamco Trailer [*NCIC trailer make code*]
PAMC........ Pan-American Container Corporation [*Common carrier symbol*]
PAMC........ Progressive Aircraft Maintenance Concept (SAUS)
PAMC........ Provident American Corp. [*Norristown, PA*] [*NASDAQ symbol*] (NQ)
PAMC........ Provisional Acceptable Means of Compliance (MCD)
PAMC........ Pterygoarthromyodysplasia Congenital [*Medicine*] (DMAA)
PAmC........ Temple University, Ambler Campus, Ambler, PA [*Library symbol*] [*Library of Congress*] (LCLS)
PAMCCS .... Prior Active Marine Corps Commissioned Service
PAMCES..... Prior Active Marine Corps Enlisted Service
PAMCI....... Pyridinealdoxime Methochloride [*Organic chemistry*]
PAMCO....... Pacific Annuity Marketing Co. (SAUS)
PAMCO....... Progressive Assembly Machine Co., Inc. (EFIS)
PAMCS ...... Panel on Air Space Management & Control System (SAUS)
PAMCS ...... Phoenix Airborne Missile Control System
PAM-D....... PAM [*Payload Assist Module*] Delta Class Spacecraft (NASA)
PAMD........ Pan-American Independent Line [*Common carrier symbol*]
PAMD........ Parallel Access Multiple Distribution (PDAA)
PAM-D....... Payload Assist Module - Delta Class Spacecraft (MCD)
PAMD........ Periodic Acid Mixed Diamine (OA)
PAMD........ Prelingually Acquired Meningitic Deafness [*Medicine*] (MELL)
PAMD........ Price and Management Data
PAMD........ Primary Adrenocortical Micronodular Dysplasia [*Medicine*] (DMAA)
PAM/D....... Process Automation Monitor/Disc Version (NITA)
PAMD........ Process Automation Monitor/Disk Version [*Texas Instruments, Inc.*]
PAMD........ Public Access Machine Readable Documents (NITA)
PAM-DII..... Payload Assist Module-Delta Class 2 (SAUS)
PAMDS...... Price and Management Data Section [*of a stock list*] [*Navy*]
PAME........ Pandemokratiki Agrotikon Metapon Ellados [*Pan-Democratic Agrarian Front of Greece*] [*Political party*] (PPE)
PAME........ Primary Amoebic Meningoencephalitis [*Medicine*]
P/AMEA2.... Probationary Marine Engineering Artificer, Acting, 2nd Class [*British military*] (DMA)
Pa Med ..... Pennsylvania Medicine (SAUS)
PAMEE ...... Philippine Association of Mechanical and Electrical Engineers (SAUS)
PAMELA..... Patient Automatic Monitoring Endless Loop Attachment (SAUS)
PAMELA..... Plan-Applier Mechanism for English Language Analysis (SAUS)
PAMELA..... Process Abstraction Method for Embedded Large Applications (SAUS)
PAMETON... Paracetamol and Methionine [*Pain-relief drug*]
PAMETRADA... Parsons Marine Experimental Turbine Research and Development Association (SAUS)
PAMEX ...... Pancho's Mexican Buffet, Inc. (EFIS)
PAMF........ Parker Motor Freight [*Common carrier symbol*]
PAMF........ Portable Arc Melting Furnace
PAMF........ Programmable Analogue Matched Filter (PDAA)
PAM FILE ... Pamphlet File (SAUS)
PAM/FM..... Pulse Amplitude Modulated-Frequency Modulated (SAUS)
PAM-FM..... Pulse Amplitude Modulation - Frequency Modulation [*Electronics*]
PAmh........ Amherst Papyri [*A publication*] (OCD)
PamHld ..... Pamida Holdings Corp. [*Associated Press*] (SAG)
PAMI......... Performing Arts Management Institute (SAUS)
PAMI......... Personnel Accounting Machine Installation
PAMI......... Prairie Agricultural Machinery Institute [*Canada*]
PAMI......... Primary Angioplasty in Myocardial Infarction [*Cardiology study*]
PAMI......... Professional Arts Management Institute (EA)
PAMIC....... Pennsylvania Association of Mutual Insurance Companies (EARSL)
PAMICONUS... Personnel Accounting Machine Installation, Continental United States (SAUS)
PA Microphone... Public Address Microphone (SAUS)
PAMIE....... Physical and Mental Impairment of Function Evaluation [*Medicine*] (DMAA)
PAMIF....... Physical and Mental Impairment-of-Function [*Scale*] [*Medicine*] (DB)
PAMII....... Protection and Advocacy for Mentally Ill Individuals Act [*1986*]
PAMIPAC ... Personnel Accounting Machine Installation Pacific Fleet (SAUS)
PAMIR....... Passive Airborne Modular Infra-Red (SAUS)
PAMIR....... Passive and Active Microwave and Infrared Radiometer (SAUS)
PAMIRASAT... Passive Microwave Radiometer Satellite (PDAA)
PAMIRASAT... Primary Afferent Depolarization (PDAA)
PAMIS....... Processing and Manufacturing in Space [*European Space Agency*]
PAMIS....... Psychological Operations Automated Management Information System (MCD)
PAMIS....... PSYOP Automated Manpower Information System (SAUS)
PA Misc..... Pennsylvania Miscellaneous Reports [*A publication*] (DLA)
PAML........ Pan American Mail Line (SAUS)
PAML........ Program Authorized Materials List (SAUS)
PAML........ Publicly Accessible Mailing Lists (SAUS)
PAMLPU .... Pianoforte Action Makers' Labour Protection Union [*British*]
PAMM....... Payload and Mission Model (SAUS)
PAMM....... Precision Automatic Measuring Machine (VLIE)
PAMM....... Procurement, Accounts payable and Materials Management (SAUS)
PAMM....... Program Against Micronutrient Malnutrition (SAUS)
PAMN........ Procurement Aircraft and Missiles, Navy [*An appropriation*]
PAMN........ Propiono Atropine Methyl Nitrate (SAUS)
PAMNET..... Public Affairs Management Network [*Air Force*]
PAMO........ Pacific Airlift Management Office [*Military*]
PAMO........ Port Air Materiel Office
PAMP........ Pampero [*River Plate gale*] [*Nautical term*] (DSUE)
PAMP........ Plasma-Assisted Materials Processing (SAUS)
PAMP........ Precision-Aimed Mortar Projectile (SAUS)
PAMP........ Public Art Master Plan (SAUS)
PAMP........ Pulmonary Artery Mean Pressure [*Medicine*] (MEDA)
PAMP........ Pulmonary Artery Medium Pressure (SAUS)
PAMPA....... Pacific Area Movement Priority Agency [*Military*]
PAMPA....... Precision Aerobatics Model Pilots Association (EA)
PamPAC..... Pamela's Political Action Committee [*Nickname of "Democrats for the '80's," a committee founded by Pamela Harriman*]
PAM-PDM... Product and Machine Performance (SAUS)
PAM-PDM... Pulse Amplitude Modulation-Pulse Duration Modulation (SAUS)
PAMPER .... Practical Application of Mid-Points for Exponential Regression
PAMPH...... Pamphlet [*Freight*]
Pamph Laws... Pamphlet Laws, Acts [*A publication*] (DLA)
Pamphl Laws... Pamphlet Laws, Acts [*A publication*] (DLA)
PAMPS...... Poly(Acrylamidomethyl Propane) Sulphonic Acid [*Organic chemistry*]
PAMPUS .... Photons for Atomic and Molecular Processes and Universal Studies [*Physics*]
PAMR........ Anchorage/Merrill Field [*Alaska*] [*ICAO location identifier*] (ICLI)
PAMR........ Pace American [*NCIC trailer make code*]
PAMR........ Public Access Mobile Radio (VLIE)
Pamrapo.... Pamrapo Bancorp, Inc. [*Associated Press*] (SAG)
PAMRF...... Palo Alto Medical Research Foundation [*Research center*] (RCD)
PAMRI....... Peripheral Adapter Module Replacement Item (CTAS)
PAMRS...... Parameter Adaptive Model Reference System
PAMS........ Pacific Advanced Media Studies [*Australia*]
PAMS........ Pacific Armies Management Seminar
PAMS........ Pacific AUTODIN Multiplex System (SAUS)
PAMS........ Pad Abort Measuring System [*NASA*] (KSC)
PAMS........ Paging Area Memory Space [*Computer science*] (IAA)
PAMS........ Parallel Application Management System (SAUS)
PAMS........ Parents Advocating Morality Standards [*Medicine*] (EDAA)
PAMS........ Parts Management System
PAMS........ Passive Multifrequency Microwave Scanner Radiometer (SAUS)
PAMS........ Pentax Analytical Measurement System (SAUS)

PAMS........ Photo and Audio/visual Management System (SAUS)
PAMS........ Photochemical Assessment Monitoring Station (EEVL)
PAMS........ Photogrammetric Analytical Measurement System (SAUS)
PAMS........ Plan Analysis and Modeling System (MHDB)
PAMS........ Point Anti-Missile System (SAUS)
PAMS........ Portable Acoustic Monitoring System
PAMS........ Post-Accident Monitoring System [*Nuclear energy*] (NRCH)
PAMS........ Predictive Aircraft Maintenance System
PAMS........ Preselected Alternate Master-Slave [*Telecommunications*] (TEL)
PAMS........ Printing Advisory and Management Service (DGA)
PAMS........ Proceedings of the American Mathematical Society [*A publication*]
PAMS........ Procurement Action Management System (MCD)
PAMS........ Public Access Message System
PAM SCAD... Program of Action To Mitigate the Social Cost of Adjustment (SAUS)
PAM Signal... Pulse-Amplitude-Modulated Signal (SAUS)
PAMT........ Payment [*Electric utility company*]
PAMT........ Port Authority Marine Terminal (SAUS)
PAMTGG.... Pan Am Makes the Going Great [*Title of ballet choreographed by George Balanchine, taken from Pan American World Airways' slogan*] [*Pronounced "pam-ti-guh-guh"*]
PAMU........ Pan Atlantic Lines [*Intermodal shipping container symbol*] (TVRC)
PAMUSA.... Post-Attack Mobilization of the United States Army
PAMUX...... Parallel Addressable Multiplexer [*Telecommunications*] (IAA)
PAMV........ Petunia Asteroid Mosaic Virus [*Plant pathology*]
PAMWA..... Pan American Medical Women's Alliance (EA)
PAMX........ Pancho's Mexican Buffet [*NASDAQ symbol*] (TTSB)
PAMX........ Pancho's Mexican Buffet, Inc. [*NASDAQ symbol*] (NQ)
PAN.......... Film Producers Association of Newfoundland [*An association*] [*Canada*]
PAN.......... National Action Party [*Mexico*] [*Political party*] (PD)
PAN.......... National Advancement Party (Guatemala) [*Political party*] (PSAP)
PAN.......... Pagans Against Nukes [*British*] (DI)
PAN.......... Paladin Fuel Technology [*Vancouver Stock Exchange symbol*]
PAN.......... Pan African Congress (SAUS)
PAN.......... Panama [*ANSI three-letter standard code*] (CNC)
Pan.......... Panama (VRA)
PAN.......... Pan American Navigation (SAUS)
PAN.......... Panartriitis Nodosa (SAUS)
PAN.......... Panchromatic (DEN)
pan.......... Panchromatic [*Photography*] (WDMC)
pan.......... Pancreas (STED)
Pan.......... Panegyricus [*of Pliny the Younger*] [*Classical studies*] (OCD)
pan.......... Panel (MIST)
PAN.......... Panel (SAUS)
PAN.......... Paneled (WGA)
PAN.......... Pangseng [*Language symbol*] (ETLW)
PAN.......... Panimavida [*Chile*] [*Seismograph station code, US Geological Survey*] [*Closed*] (SEIS)
PAN.......... Panis [*Bread*] [*Pharmacy*] (ROG)
pan.......... Panjabi [*MARC language code*] [*Library of Congress*] (LCCP)
pan.......... Panorama
PAN.......... Panoramic (MSA)
Pan.......... Panormitanus [*Nicholas de Tudeschis*] [*Deceased, 1445*] [*Authority cited in pre-1607 legal work*] (DSA)
Pan.......... Pantheon [*Record label*] [*France, etc.*]
pan.......... Pantomime (GROV)
PAN.......... Pantry (MSA)
PAN.......... Parents Against Narcotics (SAUS)
PAN.......... Partido de Accion Nacional [*Nicaragua*] [*Political party*] (EY)
PAN.......... Pattani [*Thailand*] [*Airport symbol*] (OAG)
PAN.......... Peace Action Network (EA)
PAN.......... Pennsylvania Animal Network [*Coalition operated by Trans-Species Unlimited*]
PAN.......... Pennsylvania Association of Notaries (EA)
PAN.......... Percussion Actuated Nonelectric [*An explosive disrupter*]
PAN.......... Performing Artists Network [*Electronic network*]
PAN.......... Periaortic Nodes [*Medicine*] (MELL)
PAN.......... Periarteritis Nodosa [*Also, PN*] [*Medicine*]
PAN.......... Periodic Alternating Nystagmus [*Ophthalmology*]
PAN.......... Peripheral Area Network (VLIE)
PAN.......... Peroxyacetyl Nitrate [*Lacrimator*]
PAN.......... Peroxyacetylnitrate (SAUS)
PAN.......... Personal Account Number (VLIE)
PAN.......... Personal Area Network [*Computer science*]
PAN.......... Personnel Advice Notes (HEAS)
PAN.......... Pesticides Action Network (EA)
PAN.......... Pfarrkirchen [*German license plate city code*]
PAN.......... Phase Advance Network [*Computer science*] (VLIE)
PAN.......... Physical Association Number (SAUS)
PAN.......... Polled Access Network
PAN.......... Pollution Abatement Notice [*Environmental science*] (COE)
PAN.......... Polska Akademia Nauk [*Polish Academy of Sciences*] [*Also, an information service or system*] (IID)
PAN.......... Polyacrylonitrile [*Organic chemistry*]
PAN.......... Polyarteritis Nodosa [*Medicine*]
PAN.......... Porte-Avion Nucleaire
PAN.......... Positional Alcohol Nystagmus [*Physiology*]
PAN.......... Practical Active Network [*Computer science*] (VLIE)
PAN.......... Preauricular Node (SAUS)
PAN.......... Primary Access Network [*Computer science*] (VLIE)
PAN.......... Primary Account Number [*Business term*]
PAN.......... Primary Alerting Network (SAUS)
PAN.......... Project Authorization Notice (MCD)
PAN.......... Propodial Anlage [*Zoology*]
PAn.......... Proto-Anatolian [*Linguistics*] (IEL)
PAN.......... Proto-Austronesian [*Linguistics*] (IEL)
PAN.......... Publications Account Number [*DoD*]
PAN.......... Puromycin Aminonucleoside [*Medicine*] (DMAA)
PAN.......... Pyridineazohydroxynaphthalene (SAUS)
PAN.......... Pyridylazonaphthol [*An indicator*] [*Chemistry*]
PAN.......... Switchboard Panel [*Telecommunications*] (TEL)
PA$_{N2O}$... Mean Alveolar Nitrous Oxide Tension [*Medicine*] (DAVI)
PANA........ Panaco, Inc. [*NASDAQ symbol*] (SAG)
PANA........ PanAfrican News Agency (EAIO)
PANA........ Pan-African Press Agency (SAUS)
PANA........ Pana, IL [*American Association of Railroads railroad junction routing code*]
PANA........ Panama Transfer [*Common carrier symbol*]
PANA........ Pan American Mobile Homes [*NCIC trailer make code*]
PANA........ Pan-Asia News Agency Ltd. [*Also, PANASIA*] [*Hong Kong*]
PANA........ Pan-Asia Newspaper Alliance (SAUS)
PANA........ Pan-Asian Newspaper Alliance [*Also, PANANEWS*] (NADA)
PANA........ Panorama (VRA)
PANA........ Polish-American Numismatic Association (EA)
PANABANK... Banco Panamericano [*Panama*] (EY)
PanaBev.... Panamerican Beverages [*Commercial firm*] [*Associated Press*] (SAG)
PANACEA... Package for Analysis of Networks of Asynchronous Computers with Extended Asymptotics (SAUS)
Panaco...... Panaco, Inc. [*Associated Press*] (SAG)
PANAFTEL... Pan-African Telecommunications (BARN)
PANAFTEL... Pan-African Telecommunications Network (TELE)
PANAFTEL Network... Pan-African Telecommunications Network (SAUS)
PANAFU..... Pan African Union (SAUS)
PANAGRA... Pan American Grace Airways, Inc. [*Also, PAGA*]
PANAIR...... Panama Air Lines
PANAL...... Papuan National Alliance [*Political party*] (PPW)
PANALU..... Parti National Lumumba [*Lumumba National Party*] [*Political party*]
PANALYZER... Peroxyacetyl Nitrate Analyzer (SAUS)
PANAM...... Panama, OK [*American Association of Railroads railroad junction routing code*]
Pan-Am..... Pan American (SAUS)
PANAM...... Pan American World Airways (SAUS)
PAN-AM..... Pan American World Airways, Inc. [*See also PA, PAA, PN*]
PANAMAC... Pan American World Airways Communications System
PANAMAC System... Pan-American Airways Communications System (SAUS)
PanAmC..... Pan Am Corp. [*Associated Press*] (SAG)
PANAMIN... Presidential Arm for National Minorities (SAUS)
PanAmSat.. Pan American Satellite [*Greenwich, CT*] [*Telecommunications service*] (TSSD)
Pan-Am TS... Pan-American Treaty Series [*A publication*] (DLA)
PANANEWS... Pan-Asia Newspaper Alliance (SAUS)
PANANEWS... Pan-Asian Newspaper Alliance [*Also, PANA*] (NADA)
PANAR...... Panoramic RADAR
PANASH..... Palaeoclimates of the Northern and Southern Hemispheres (SAUS)
PANASH..... Paleoclimates of the Northern and Southern Hemisphere (SAUS)
PANASIA... Organization of Pan Asian American Women (EA)
PANASIA... Pan-Asia News Agency Ltd. [*Also, PANA*] [*Hong Kong*]
PanASlv..... Pan American Silver Corp. [*Associated Press*] (SAG)
Panax....... Panax Pharmaceutical Co. Ltd. [*Associated Press*] (SAG)
PanaxP...... Panax Pharmaceutical Co. Ltd. [*Associated Press*] (SAG)
PANB........ Panic Bolt
PANC........ Anchorage/International [*Alaska*] [*ICAO location identifier*] (ICLI)
panc........ pancreas (SAUS)
PANC........ Power Amplifier Neutralizing Capacitor (DEN)
P-ANCA..... Perinuclear Anti-Neutrophilic Cytoplasmic Antibody [*Medicine*] (DMAA)
PANCAN..... [*The*] Panama Canal
PANCANCO... Panama Canal Co. [*Superseded by Panama Canal Commission*]
PANCAP..... Practical Annual Capacity [*FAA*]
panchr....... Panchromatic (VRA)
PancMx..... Pancho's Mexican Buffet, Inc. [*Associated Press*] (SAG)
PANCO...... Procurement Aids Noncommissioned Officer [*Marine Corps*]
Pand........ [*The*] Pandects [*A publication*] (DLA)
PAND........ Pandering [*FBI standardized term*]
PAND........ Passive Air Navigation Device
PAND........ Performing Artists for Nuclear Disarmament (EA)
PAND........ Primary Adrenocortical Nodular Dysplasia [*Endocrinology*] (DMAA)
P & A........ Page and Adams' Code [*1912*] [*A publication*] (DLA)
P & A........ Pay and Allowances
P & A........ Pennsylvania & Atlantic Railroad Co. (IIA)
P&A......... Percussion and Auscultation [*Medicine*] (AMHC)
P and A..... Percussion and Auscultation (SAUS)
P & A........ Percussion and Auscultation [*Medicine*]
PANDA...... Performance and Demand Analyser (PDAA)
P & A........ Personnel and Administration [*Army*] (AABC)
P and A..... Personnel and Administration (SAUS)
P and A..... Pioneer and Ammunition (SAUS)
P & A........ Pioneer and Ammunition
P&A......... Planning and Analysis (ABAC)
P & A........ Plans and Analysis
PANDA...... Portable Array for Numerical Data Acquisition [*Instrumentation*]
PANDA...... Portable Atmospheric Noise Data Acquisition (SAUS)

P&A......... Precision and Accuracy (COE)
P and A..... Prediction and Allocation (SAUS)
P & A........ Prediction and Allocation
PANDA...... Prestel Advanced Network Design Architecture
PANDA...... Prevent Abuse and Neglect Dental Awareness (SAUS)
P and A..... Price and Availability (SAUS)
P & A........ Price and Availability
P & A........ Pricing and Acceptability Claims Processing System [*Health insurance*] (GHCT)
P & A........ Print and Advertising [*Marketing*] (ECON)
P & A........ Priorities and Allocations (MUGU)
P&A......... Prizes and Awards Committee (ACII)
P & A........ Procedures and Analysis
P and A..... Procurement and Assignment (SAUS)
P & A........ Procurement and Assignment
P & A........ Professional and Administrative (AAG)
P and A..... Professional and Administrative (SAUS)
P&A......... Program and Acquisition (ACAE)
PANDA...... Programmers Analysis and Development Aid (SAUS)
P&A......... Programming and Analysis (SAUS)
P & A........ Protection and Advocacy [*System*] [*To protect the rights of developmentally disabled persons*]
PANDAPAC... Panda Energy International Inc. PAC [*Dallas, TX*] (PACS)
PandaPrj.... [*The*] Panda Project, Inc. [*Associated Press*] (SAG)
P & AR...... Pacific & Arctic Railway (MHDB)
P & AW..... Paging and Area Warning
P&B......... Pain & Burning [*Medicine*] (DMAA)
P & B........ Phenobarbital and Belladonna [*A drug regimen*]
P & B........ Planning and Budgeting [*Military*] (AFIT)
P & B........ Price and Budgeting (MCD)
P & B........ Printing and Binding [*Publishing*]
P & B........ Pugsley and Burbridge's New Brunswick Reports [*A publication*] (DLA)
P&C......... Parents and Citizens Association (SAUS)
P & C........ Parge and Core [*Construction*]
P & C........ Performance and Control (SSD)
P & C........ Physical and Chemical (AAG)
P&C......... Precautions and Contraindications [*Medicine*] (MELL)
P & C........ Prideaux and Cole's English Reports [*4 New Sessions Cases*] [*A publication*] (DLA)
P & C........ Prism and Cover (Test) [*Ophthalmology*]
P & C........ Procurement and Contracting (AFM)
P&C......... Procurement and Contracting (or Contracts) (SAUS)
P&C......... Property and Casualty [*Insurance*]
P&C......... Property or Casualty
P and C..... Purchases and Contracts (SAUS)
P & C........ Purchasing and Contracting
P & C........ Put and Call [*Stock exchange term*]
P & CA...... Paying and Collecting Area (AFM)
P&CG....... Planning and Coordination Group (SAUS)
P & CO...... Plans and Combat Operations
P & CP...... Plate and Cylinder Production (DGA)
P & CR...... Performance and Compatibility Requirements
P & CR...... Planning and Compensation Reports [*British*]
P & CR...... Property and Compensation Reports [*A publication*] (DLA)
P & CYC.... Police and Citizens' Youth Club [*Australia*]
P & D........ Law Reports, Probate and Divorce [*England*] [*A publication*] (DLA)
P&D......... Performance and Demonstration
P & D........ Perry and Davison's English Queen's Bench Reports [*1834-44*] [*A publication*] (DLA)
P & D........ Pick Up and Delivery [*Business term*]
P and D..... Pickup and Delivery (SAUS)
P&D......... Pick Ups and Deliveries [*Of freight*] (LDOE)
P & D........ Pioneer and Demolition Section [*Army*]
P&D......... Plug and Display [*Computer science*]
P & D........ Pressing and Distribution (WDMC)
P&D......... Price and Delivery (SAUS)
P & D........ Probate and Divorce [*Legal*] [*British*]
P & D........ Procurement and Distribution [*Military*]
P&D......... Production and Deployment
P & D........ Promote and Develop Fishery Products Pertaining to American Fisheries Account [*National Oceanic and Atmospheric Administration*] (GFGA)
P & DD...... Plumbing and Deck Drain (MSA)
P & DR...... Price and Delivery Request
P & DSEC... Pioneer and Demolition Section [*Army*]
P & E........ Pike and Eel [*A pub at Cambridge University*] [*British*] (DSUE)
P & E........ Planning and Estimating (AAG)
P&E......... Planning and Evaluation (ACAE)
P&E......... Pneumonia and Empyema (MELL)
P & E........ Privileges and Elections Subcommittee [*US Senate*]
P & E........ Procurement and Expedition
P & E........ Propellants and Explosives [*Military*] (AABC)
P & E........ Pyrotechnical and Explosive [*NASA*] (KSC)
Pandect Flor... Pandectae Florentinae [*A publication*] (DSA)
P & EE...... Proof and Experimental Establishments (RDA)
P & EML.... Personnel and Equipment Modification List [*Air Force*]
P & ESI..... Physical and Engineering Sciences Division [*Army Research Office*]
P & F........ P & F Industries, Inc. [*Associated Press*] (SAG)
P & F........ Petroleum and Fuel
P & F........ Pike and Fischer's Administrative Law [*A publication*] (DLA)
P & F........ Pike and Fischer's Federal Rules Service [*A publication*] (DLA)
P & F........ Pike and Fischer's OPA Price Service [*A publication*] (DLA)
P & F........ Planning and Forecasting (MCD)
P & F........ Plant and Facilities
P&F......... Program and Financial Plan (SAUS)
P&FA....... Program and File Analysis [*Computer science*] (CIST)
P & F chart... Point-and-Figure Chart (ODA)
Pand Flo.... Pandectae Florentinae [*A publication*] (DSA)
P & FM..... Programs and Financial Management [*Navy*]
P & F Radio Reg... Pike and Fischer's Radio Regulation Reporter [*A publication*] (DLA)
P & FS...... Particles and Fields Subsatellite [*NASA*] (KSC)
P & G....... Post and Girder [*Lumber*] (DAC)
P & G....... Procter & Gamble Co.
P & G News... Plants and Gardens News [*A publication*]
P&G PAC.... Proctor & Gamble Company Good Government Committee [*Cincinnati, OH*] (PACS)
P & H....... Patton, Jr., and Heath's Reports [*Virginia Special Court of Appeals*] [*A publication*] (DLA)
P&H........ Pawling and Harnischfeger [*Off-Highway equipment*]
p&h......... Postage and Handling (NTIO)
P&H........ Postage and Handling (WDMC)
P&HEP...... Plasma and High Energy Physics (SAUS)
P&HTGR.... Peach Bottom High-Temperature Gas-Cooled Reactor (SAUS)
P & I........ Passenger and Immigration Lists [*A publication*]
P & I........ Performance and Interface [*Specification*] [*NASA*] (NASA)
P&I......... Physics & Irradiation (SAUS)
P & I........ Piping and Instrumentation [*Nuclear energy*] (NRCH)
P&I......... Planning & Integration (SAUS)
P & I........ Pneumonia and Influenza (MELL)
P & I........ Postage and Insurance
P&I......... Principal and Interest [*Finance*] (DFIT)
P and I...... Principal and Interest (SAUS)
p&i......... Principal and Interest (SHCU)
P & I........ Privileges and Immunities [*Legal shorthand*] (LWAP)
P&I......... Probe and Irrigate (SAUS)
P & I........ Properties and Installations
P & I........ Protection and Indemnity [*Insurance*]
P&I......... Protection and Indemnity [*Insurance*]
P and I club... Protection and Indemnity club (SAUS)
P&ID........ Piping and Instrumentation Design (SAUS)
P & ID...... Piping and Instrumentation Diagram [*or Design or Drawing*] [*Calcomp Ltd.*] [*Software package*] [*Nuclear energy*] (NRCH)
P&ID........ Piping and Instrumentation Drawing (LDOE)
P & ID...... Process and Instrumentation Diagram [*Engineering*] (NRCH)
P&II......... Personalization and Identification Institute (NTPA)
P&IM Rev.. Production Inventory Management Reviews (SAUS)
PANDIT...... Produce an Adjusted Nuclear Data Input Tape (SAUS)
P & J........ Plaza y Janes [*Publisher*] [*Spain*]
P&J......... Protection and Indemnity (EBF)
P & K........ Perry and Knapp's English Election Cases [*1833*] [*A publication*] (DLA)
P&KI........ Promisel and Korn (IID)
P & KI...... Promisel & Korn, Inc. [*Information service or system*] (IID)
P & L........ Paul and Lisa (EA)
P&L......... Pioneer & Labour (SAUS)
P & L........ Points and Lines [*Military*] (CAAL)
P&L......... Power and Light (SAUS)
P & L........ Power and Lighting (MSA)
P & L........ Pratt & Lambert, Inc.
P & L........ Profit and Loss [*Accounting*]
P&L......... Profit and Loss Statement [*Finance*] (DFIT)
P&L......... Projects and Logistics (SAUS)
PANDLCHAR... Pay and Allowances Chargeable
P & L Dig Laws... Pepper and Lewis' Digest of Laws [*Pennsylvania*] [*A publication*] (DLA)
P&L DISTR... Power and Lighting Distribution (SAUS)
P & LERR... [*The*] Pittsburgh & Lake Erie Railroad Co.
P & L Laws... Private and Local Laws [*A publication*] (DLA)
P & M....... Law Reports, Probate and Matrimonial Cases [*England*] [*A publication*] (DLA)
P&M........ Performance Monitor (SAUS)
P&M........ Phase Modulated (or Modulation) (SAUS)
P&M........ Planetary Mission (SAUS)
P & M....... Pollock and Maitland's History of English Common Law [*A publication*] (DLA)
P & M....... Probate and Matrimonial [*Legal*] [*British*]
P & M....... Processes and Materials (NASA)
P&M........ Program Milestone (SAUS)
P&M........ Protection and Maintenance (ALAC)
P&MC....... Procurement and Material Control (SAUS)
P & MHEL.. Pollock and Maitland's History of English Common Law [*A publication*] (DLA)
P & MP..... Paris & Mount Pleasant Railroad (IIA)
P & N....... Piedmont and Northern Railroad (AD)
p & n....... Psychiatry and Neurology (AD)
P&N........ Psychiatry and Neurology (SAUS)
P & N....... Psychiatry and Neurology
p & o....... Paints and Oil (AD)
P & O....... Paints and Oil
P & O....... Parasites and Ova [*Gastroenterology*] (DAVI)
P & O....... Peninsular & Occidental Steamship Co. (AD)
P&O........ Peninsular & Oriental Line (SAUS)
P & O....... Peninsular & Oriental Steam Navigation Co. [*Steamship line*]
P & O....... Performance and Operational [*Test or reports*]
p & o....... Pickled and Oiled (AD)
P&O........ Pickled and Oiled (SAUS)

P & O .... Pickled and Oiled
P&O .... Pipe and Operating (SAUS)
P & O .... Planning and Operations
P & O .... Planning and Organization
P & O .... Plans and Operations Division [*War Department*] [*World War II*]
P & O .... Portland & Ogdensburgh Railroad
P & O .... Positioning and Orientation
P&O .... Prosthetic and Orthotic [*Health insurance*] (GHCT)
P & OC....... Peninsular & Oriental (Steam Navigation) Co. Ltd. (ROG)
P & O Div... Planning and Operations Division [*Military*]
p & oo ...... Pianistic and Orchestral Orgasm [*Music*] (AD)
PANDORA... Passive and Active Signal Digital Correlator Analyzer (MCD)
PANDORA... Preserving and Accessing Networked Documentary Resources of Australia (SAUS)
PANDORA... Prototyping a Navigation Database of Road Network Attributes (SAUS)
P & OSCC .. Plans and Operations for the Safeguard Communications Command [*Army*] (RDA)
P & OSNCo... Peninsular & Oriental Steam Navigation Co. [*Steamship line*]
P&OT........ Physical & Occupational Therapy (CMD)
P & P........ Packing and Preservation
P & P........ Pam and Peter Fisher [*Commercial firm*] [*British*]
P&P.......... Parrots and People [*Association*] (EA)
p & p......... Parsimonious and Penurious (AD)
P&P.......... Past and Present (SAUS)
P&P.......... Pay & Privileges (WDAA)
p&p.......... Payments and Progress (AD)
P and P ..... Payments and Progress Committee [*NATO*] (NATG)
P & P........ Peace and Prosperity Issue [*Politics*]
P & P........ Pins and Plaster [*Orthopedics*] (DAVI)
P&P.......... Planning and Programming (SAUS)
P & P........ Plans and Policies
P & P........ Plans and Programs
P&P.......... Policy and Procedure Statements (SAUS)
p&p.......... Postage & Packing (WDAA)
P & P........ Postage and Packing [*Shipping*]
P&P.......... Preservation and Packing
P & P........ Pride and Prejudice [*Novel by Jane Austen*]
P & P........ Procurement and Production [*Military*]
P & P........ Production and Procurement [*Military*]
P & P/CT.... Prothrombin and Proconvertin Control [*Hematology*] (DAVI)
P & PD...... Percussion and Postural Drainage
P&P Intnl... Pulp and Paper International Annual Review (SAUS)
P&P Jrl ..... Pulp and Paper Journal (SAUS)
P & PM ..... Packing and Packaging Manual (MCD)
p & pp ..... Pull and Push Plate (AD)
P & PP...... Pull and Push Plate
P&P Qtly.... Pulp and Paper Quarterly Statistics (SAUS)
P&PR........ Psychoanalysis and the Psychoanalytic Review (SAUS)
P and Ps.... Practices and Procedures [*Industrial hygiene term*] (OHS)
P & PU...... Peoria and Pekin Union [*Railroad*] (AD)
P & PW ..... Publicity and Psychological Warfare
p & q........ Peace and Quiet (AD)
P & Q .... Peace and Quiet
P and Q ..... Prime Quality [*Slang*]
p & r .... Parallax and Refraction (AD)
P&R.......... Parks & Recreation [*A publication*] (BRI)
P & R .... Pelvic and Rectal [*Medicine*]
P & R .... Performance and Resources (NASA)
P & R .... Philadelphia & Reading Railway
P & R .... Picture and Resume [*Theatre slang*]
P & R .... Pigott and Rodwell's Reports in Common Pleas [*1843-45*] [*A publication*] (DLA)
P&R .... Planning & Research Ltd. (SAUS)
P & R .... Planning and Review (MCD)
P&R .... Plans and Requirements (SAUS)
P & R .... Post and Rail
P & R .... Pulse and Respiration [*Medicine*]
P and RD ... Decisions of the Department of the Interior, Pension and Retirement Claims [*United States*] [*A publication*] (DLA)
P&RF........ Personnel and Reserve Force (ACAE)
P&RP........ Production and Research Property [*Department of Defense*]
P & RT...... Physical and Recreational Training [*Navy*] [*British*]
P & S........ Packers and Stockyards
P & S........ Pain and Suffering (DAVI)
P&S.......... Panel and Shelf
P & S........ Paracentesis and Suction [*Medicine*]
P & S........ Pay and Supply [*Coast Guard*]
P & S........ Perkins & Squier [*Paper manufacturer*]
P&S.......... Permanent and Stationary (SAUS)
P&S.......... Personnel and Security (SAUS)
P & S........ Physicians and Surgeons (DAVI)
P & S........ [*The*] Pittsburg & Shawmut Railroad Co.
P & S........ Planking and Strutting [*Construction*]
P&S.......... Planning and Scheduling (CIST)
P and S ..... Plugged and Suspended (SAUS)
P & S........ Port and Starboard
PANDS ...... Print and Search Processor [*Computer science*]
P & S........ Purchase and Sale [*Business term*]
P & SA...... Packers and Stockyards Administration [*Department of Agriculture*]
P&SA........ Payload and Servicing Accommodations [*NASA*] (SPST)
P&SA........ Program and Systems Analysis (SAUS)
P&SB........ Portland & South Bend (SAUS)
P & SF...... Panhandle & Santa Fe Railway Co.
P & SI....... Pay and Supply Instruction [*Coast Guard*]
P & SM ..... Procurement and Subcontract Management [*NASA*] (NASA)
P & SNP.... Pay and Subsistence of Naval Personnel [*Budget appropriation title*]
P&SS........ Provost & Security Services (SAUS)
P&T.......... Packaging and Transportation (SAUS)
P & T........ Permanent and Total [*Disability*] [*Medicine*]
P & T........ Personnel and Training [*Military*] (MUGU)
P & T........ Pharmacy and Therapeutics
P & T........ Plans and Training [*Military*] (IIA)
P&T.......... Pointing and Tracking (ACAE)
P&T.......... Pope and Talbot (SAUS)
P & T........ Posts and Timbers [*Technical drawings*]
P&T.......... Privilege & Tenure Committee (SAUS)
P & T........ Professional and Technology [*Category*] [*British*]
P & T........ Pugsley and Trueman's New Brunswick Reports [*A publication*] (DLA)
P & T........ Purge-and-Trap [*Technique*] [*Environmental Protection Agency*]
P & TD....... Parts and Tool Disposition (SAA)
P & T Div... Plans and Training Division [*Military*]
P&U .... Pharmacia & Upjohn AB [*Commercial firm*] [*Sweden*]
P & V........ Percuss and Vibrate [*Medicine*] (DAVI)
P&V.......... Pressure and Velocity (SAUS)
P & V........ Pyloroplasty and Vagotomy [*Medicine*]
P&V.......... Pyloroplasty and Vagtomy (SAUS)
P & VE ...... Propulsion and Vehicle Engineering [*A Marshall Space Flight Center laboratory*] (MCD)
P & VE-ADM... Propulsion and Vehicle Engineering - Administrative [*Marshall Space Flight Center Laboratory*] (SAA)
P & VE-DIR... Propulsion and Vehicle Engineering - Director [*Marshall Space Flight Center Laboratory*] (SAA)
P & VE-E.... Propulsion and Vehicle Engineering - Vehicle Engineering [*Marshall Space Flight Center Laboratory*] (SAA)
P & VE-F.... Propulsion and Vehicle Engineering - Advanced Flight Systems [*Marshall Space Flight Center Laboratory*] (SAA)
P & VE-M... Propulsion and Vehicle Engineering - Engineering Materials [*Marshall Space Flight Center Laboratory*] (SAA)
P & VE-N ... Propulsion and Vehicle Engineering - Nuclear Vehicle Projects [*Marshall Space Flight Center Laboratory*] (SAA)
P & VE-P ... Propulsion and Vehicle Engineering - Propulsion and Mechanics [*Marshall Space Flight Center Laboratory*] (SAA)
P & VE-PC... Propulsion and Vehicle Engineering - Program Coordination [*Marshall Space FlightCenter Laboratory*] (SAA)
P & VE-REL... Propulsion and Vehicle Engineering - Reliability [*Marshall Space Flight Center Laboratory*] (SAA)
P & VE-S ... Propulsion and Vehicle Engineering - Structures [*Marshall Space Flight Center Laboratory*] (SAA)
P & VE-TS... Propulsion and Vehicle Engineering - Technical and Scientific Staff [*Marshall Space Flight Center Laboratory*] (SAA)
P & VE-V ... Propulsion and Vehicle Engineering - Vehicle Systems Integration [*Marshall Space Flight Center Laboratory*] (SAA)
P&VIR....... Pure and Vulcanized India Rubber (SAUS)
P & VIR..... Pure and Vulcanized Rubber Insulation
P&VR........ Pure and Vulcanized Rubber (SAUS)
P&W......... Particles and Waves (SPST)
P & W....... Penrose and Watts' Pennsylvania Reports [*1829-32*] [*A publication*] (DLA)
P & W....... Pension and Welfare (WDMC)
P & W....... Post and Wire (ADA)
P & W....... Pratt & Whitney [*Aircraft*]
P&W......... Pratt and Whitney Aircraft Division, United Aircraft Corp. (SAUS)
P & WA ..... Pratt & Whitney Aircraft (KSC)
P&W I....... Poets and Writers Inc. (SAUS)
P&WV....... Pittsburgh & West Virginia (SAUS)
P & WV .... Pittsburgh & West Virginia Railroad
P&Y.......... Pitch and Yaw
P&Z.......... Planning and Zoning (PA)
PANE .... Panther [*NCIC car make code*]
PANE .... People Against Nuclear Energy [*Medicine*] (EDAA)
PANE .... Performance Analysis of Networks, Electrical
PanEC .... Panhandle Eastern Corp. [*Associated Press*] (SAG)
PANEC....... Performance Analysis of Electrical Circuits (SAUS)
PANEES ..... Professional Association of Naval Electronics Engineers and Scientists (SAUS)
Paneg .... Panegyricus [*of Isocrates*] [*Classical studies*] (OCD)
panendo .... Panendoscopy [*Medicine*]
PANES....... Prior Active Navy Enlisted Service
PANES....... Program for Analysis of Nonlinear Equilibrium and Stability [*NASA*]
PANESS ..... Physical and Neurologic Examination for Soft Signs [*Medicine*] (MELL)
PA News Letter... Physical Anthropology News Letter (SAUS)
PANF .... Plan Account Number File [*IRS*]
PANFERT ... Pregnancy After Infertility [*Medicine*]
PANFI........ Precision Automatic Noise Figure Indicator
PANFX....... Phoenix-Engemann Nifty Fifty Cl.A [*Mutual fund ticker symbol*] (SG)
PANGAEA ... Paleo-Network for Geological and Environmental Data (SAUS)
PANGCS..... Prior Active National Guard Commissioned Service
PANGES..... Prior Active National Guard Enlisted Service
PANGIS...... Pan-African Network for a Geological Information System [*UNESCO*] (DUND)
PANGLOSS... Parallel Architecture for Networking Gateways Linking OSI Systems (NITA)
PAngV .... Preisangabenverordnung (SAUS)
PANH .... Panhandling [*FBI standardized term*]
PANH .... Panhard [*NCIC car make code*]
PANH .... Picolinaldehyde Nicotinoylhydrazone [*Reagent*]

PANH Polycyclic Aromatic Nitrogen Heterocyclic (ODA)
Pan-Hd Pan Head (SAUS)
PANHONLIB Panama, Honduras, and Liberia [*Acronym used to refer to merchant ships operating under "flags of convenience"*]
PANI Patriarch Athenagoras National Institute (EA)
PAni Polyaniline (SAUS)
PANIC Parameter Analysis of Integrated Circuits (SAUS)
PANIC Planned Attack on Nine Inner Cities [*to build education parks*]
PANIC Potential and Needs, Investments and Capabilities (SAUS)
Panj C Panjab Code [*India*] [*A publication*] (DLA)
Pank Jur Pankhurst's Jurisprudence [*A publication*] (DLA)
PAnL Lebanon Valley College, Annville, PA [*Library symbol*] [*Library of Congress*] (LCLS)
PANL Universal Display [*NASDAQ symbol*] (TTSB)
PANL Universal Display Corp. [*NASDAQ symbol*] (SAG)
PANLAR PanAmerican League Against Rheumatism [*Canada*] (EAIO)
PANLIBHON Panama, Liberia, and Honduras [*Acronym used to refer to merchant ships operating under "flags of convenience"*]
PANLIBHONCO Panama-Liberia-Honduras-Costa Rica
PANLW Universal Display Wrrt [*NASDAQ symbol*] (TTSB)
Pan Met Pan American Meteorological Station (SAUS)
PANMV Panicum Mosaic Virus [*Plant pathology*]
PANN Pannonia [*NCIC motorcycle make code*]
PANN Professional Association of Nursery Nurses [*British*] (DBA)
PAN NA Pesticides Action Network, North America (GNE)
PANNAP Panavia New Aircraft Project (MCD)
PANNA RC Pesticide Action Network North America Regional Center (EA)
PANNDA Precedent Analysis by Nearest Neighbor Discriminant Analysis
PANNR Previous Applicants Need Not Reapply [*Civil Service*]
PANO Panorama Homes [*NCIC trailer make code*]
pano Panoramic (ADWA)
PANO Pennsylvania Association of Nonprofit Organizations (EARSL)
panograms panoramas (SAUS)
Panol Panology (SAUS)
PANOPO Pacific to Atlantic via North Pole (SAUS)
PANOR Panoramic (IAA)
Panor Panormitanus [*Nicholas de Tudeschis*] [*Deceased, 1445*] [*Authority cited in pre-1607 legal work*] (DSA)
PANOS Panos Institute [*An association*] (EA)
PA NP Brightly's Pennsylvania Nisi Prius Reports [*A publication*] (DLA)
PANPA Pacific Area Newspaper Publishers Association (EAIO)
PAN-PAN International Distress Signal [*Aviation*] (PIPO)
Pan Phot Panoramic Photograph (SAUS)
PANPRA Parti Nationaliste Progressiste Revolutionnaire [*Haiti*] [*Political party*] (EY)
PANPUB Panel Publishers (DLA)
PANR Panhandle Royalty Co. [*NASDAQ symbol*] (SAG)
PANRA Panhandle Rty [*NASDAQ symbol*] (TTSB)
PanRoyl Panhandle Royalty Co. [*Associated Press*] (SAG)
PANS Peripheral Autonomic Nervous System [*Medicine*] (MELL)
PANS Personal-Area Networks
PANS Pest Articles News Summaries [*Commonwealth Mycological Institute*] [*Kew, England*] [*A publication*]
PANS Position and Navigation System (SAUS)
PANS Positioning and Navigation System
PANS Potentially Attractive New Services (SAUS)
PANS Pretty Advanced New Stuff (SAUS)
PANS Pretty Amazing New Services (NITA)
PANS Pretty Amazing New Stuff (SAUS)
PANS Pretty Awesome New Stuff [*Internet chat term*] (NETL)
PANS Priority Admission to Nursery Schools (AIE)
PANS Procedures for Air Navigation Services [*ICAO*]
PANS Programmable Augmented Noise Source [*Military*] (CAAL)
PANS Public Archives of Nova Scotia (SAUS)
PANS Puromycin Aminonucleoside [*Biochemistry*]
PANSDOC Pakistan National Scientific and Documentation Center [*Later, PASTIC*]
PANSDOC Pakistan National Scientific and Technology Documentation Centre (NITA)
PANSEAFRON Panama Sea Frontier
PANSIP Propulsion and Airframe Structural Integration Program (SAUS)
PANSMET Procedures for Air Navigation Services - Meteorology (IEEE)
PANS/OPS Procedures for Air Navigation Services/ Aircraft Operations (SAUS)
PANS/RAC Procedures for Air Navigation Services/ Rules of the Air Traffic Services (SAUS)
PANSS Positive and Negative Syndrome Scale [*Medicine*] (DMAA)
PANSW Playgroup Association of New South Wales [*Australia*]
PANSW Police Association of New South Wales [*Australia*]
PANSY Program Analysis System (PDAA)
PANT Annette Island [*Alaska*] [*ICAO location identifier*] (ICLI)
PANT Pantera's Corp. [*NASDAQ symbol*] (COMM)
PANT Pantex Plant [*Department of Energy*] [*Amarillo, TX*] (GAAI)
PANT Panther [*NCIC motorcycle make code*]
PANT Pantograph (KSC)
pant Pantomine
PANT Police Association of the Northern Territory [*Australia*]
Pantch Panatech Research & Development Corp. [*Associated Press*] (SAG)
Pantes Panel Tester (SAUS)
Pantex Pantex Site
Pantex EIS Pantex Site Environmental Impact Statement
panth pantheism (SAUS)
panth pantheist (SAUS)
PANTHEON Public Access by New Technology to Highly Elaborate Online Networks [*Computer science*] (PDAA)
PANTIES Passive Automatic Nighttime Tracking Investigation and Evaluation Studies [*DoD*]
PAntin [*The*] Antinoe Papyrus of Theocritus [*Classical studies*] (OCD)
PAntinoop Antinoopolis Papyri [*A publication*] (OCD)
PantiP Peroxidase-Antiperoxidase [*Immunochemistry*]
Panto Pantographic (SAUS)
panto Pantomime [*British*] [*Slang*] (WDMC)
PANTO Pantomime
panto pantomimic (SAUS)
Pan trog Pan troglodytes (SAUS)
pantrop Pantropical [*Botany*]
PANTS Pantaloons (DSUE)
PANTS Public Acceptance of New Technologies (SAUS)
PANVALET Direct Access Library Maintenance Package [*Pansophic Systems*]
PANX Dorchester Gas [*Private rail car owner code*]
PANX Panax Pharmaceutical [*NASDAQ symbol*] (TTSB)
PANX Panax Pharmaceutical Company Ltd. [*NASDAQ symbol*] (SAG)
PANXU Panax Pharmaceutical Unit [*NASDAQ symbol*] (TTSB)
PANXW Panax Pharmaceutical Wrrt [*NASDAQ symbol*] (TTSB)
PANY Platinumsmiths Association of New York (EA)
PANY Port Authority of New York [*Later, PANYNJ*]
PANYNJ Port Authority of New York and New Jersey [*Formerly, PANY*]
PANZ Panoz [*NCIC car make code*]
PANZ Public Access New Zealand (SAUS)
PAo Airway Opening Pressure [*Medicine*] (EDAA)
Pao Ascending Aortic Pressure [*Medicine*] (STED)
PAO Palo Alto, CA [*Location identifier*] [*FAA*] (FAAL)
PAO Paoli, PA [*Amtrak rail station code*]
PAO Paotow [*Republic of China*] [*Seismograph station code, US Geological Survey*] (SEIS)
PAO Paragon Group [*NYSE symbol*] (TTSB)
PAO Paragon Group, Inc. [*NYSE symbol*] (SAG)
PAO Paramount Resources, Inc. [*Vancouver Stock Exchange symbol*]
PaO Paranoia Obvious [*Psychology*]
PAO Parts Assembly Order (IAA)
PAO Peacetime Acquisition Objective [*DoD*] (AFIT)
PAO Peak Acid Output [*Physiology*]
PAO Pediatric Assessment Online (SAUS)
PAO Penalty Appeals Officer [*IRS*]
PAO Performance Assessment and Oversight (SAUS)
PA/O Performing Arts/Omaha [*Nebraska*]
PAO Peripheral Airway Obstruction [*Medicine*] (DMAA)
PAO Personnel Administration Office (SAUS)
PAO Phenylarsine Oxide
PAO Pinellas Area Office [*Energy Research and Development Administration*]
PAO Plasma Amine Oxidase [*Hematology*] (DMAA)
PAO Polyalkaline Oxide (SAUS)
PAO Polyalkyleneoxide [*Organic chemistry*]
PAO Polyalpha Olefin [*Fuels and lubricants*]
PAO Polyalphaolefin [*Organic chemistry*]
PAO Polyamine Oxidase (STED)
PAO Polynesian Airline Operations Ltd. [*Western Samoa*] [*ICAO designator*] (FAAC)
PAO Poultry Advisory Officer (SAUS)
PAO Primary Action Office [*or Officer*] [*Army*]
PAO Prince Albert's Own [*Military unit*] [*British*]
PAO Princeton Area Office (SAUS)
PAO Principal Administrative Officer
PAO Pro Athletes Outreach (EA)
PAO Procurement Assistance Office (AAGC)
PAO Product Activity/Operational Code (MCD)
PAO Product Assurance Operations [*Army*]
PAO Program Action Officer [*Navy*] (CAAL)
PAO Project Action Officer [*Air Force*] (AFIT)
PAO Project Administration Officer [*Military*] (AFIT)
PAO Property Accountable Officer (SAUS)
PAO Property Accounting Office (SAUS)
PAO Property Action Order
PAO Psychiatric Admitting Office [*Medicine*] (EDAA)
PAO Public Affairs Office [*NASA*]
PAO Public Affairs Officer [*Embassies*]
PAO Public Assistance Officer (DEMM)
PAO Pulmonary Artery Occlusion [*Medicine*] (DMAA)
PAo Pulmonary Artery Occlusion Pressure [*Medicine*] (EDAA)
PAO Pulsed Avalanche Diode Oscillator [*Telecommunications*] (IEEE)
PAO Pustulotic Arthroosteitis [*Medicine*] (DMAA)
PAO2 Alveolar Oxygen Pressure (WDAA)
PAO2 Arterial Oxygen Pressure (WDAA)
PaO_2 Arterial Partial Pressure of Oxygen [*Medicine*] (DAVI)
pAO_2 Oxygen Pressure on Room Air [*Medicine*] (DAVI)
PAOA Pan American Odontological Association (EA)
PAOC Pacific Air Operations Center (SAUS)
PAOC Pakistan Army Ordnance Corps [*British military*] (DMA)
PAOC Pan-African Ornithological Congress
PAOC Pentacostal Assemblies of Canada
PAOC Pollution Abatement Operations Center (MCD)
PAOC Post Award Orientation Conference (ACAE)
PAOC Principal Administrative Officers Committee [*Chiefs of Staff*] [*World War II*]
PAOCCS 2 Portuguese Air Command & Control Systems 2 (SAUS)
PAOD Peripheral Arterial Occlusive Disease [*Medicine*] (MELL)
PAOD Peripheral Arteriosclerotic Occlusive Disease [*Medicine*] (MAE)
PAOD Plant and Animal Products Department (SAUS)

PAODAP..... Presidents Action Office for Drug Abuse Prevention (SAUS)
P/AOEA2.... Probationary Ordnance Electrical Artificer, Acting, 2nd Class [*British military*] (DMA)
PA of W..... Pentecostal Assemblies of the World (EA)
PAOI......... Peak Acid Output Insulin-Induced (STED)
PAOL........ Poly-alpha-olefin [*Organic chemistry*]
PAOLA....... Paola, KS [*American Association of Railroads railroad junction routing code*]
PAOM........ Nome [*Alaska*] [*ICAO location identifier*] (ICLI)
PAOO........ Pennsylvania Academy of Ophthalmology and Otolaryngology [*Medicine*] (EDAA)
PAOP........ Pulmonary Artery Occlusion Pressure [*Cardiology*]
PAOR........ Northway [*Alaska*] [*ICAO location identifier*] (ICLI)
PAOS........ Physician Assistants in Orthopaedic Surgery (SAUS)
PAOS........ Proceedings of American Oriental Society (SAUS)
PAOT........ Kotzebue [*Alaska*] [*ICAO location identifier*] (ICLI)
PAOT........ Persons at One Time
PAOTS....... Power and Ordnance Test Set (ACAE)
PAP.......... Asia Pulp & Paper ADS [*NYSE symbol*] (TTSB)
PAP.......... Asia Pulp and Paper Co. Ltd. [*NYSE symbol*] (SAG)
PAP.......... Langtry Flying Group Ltd. [*British*] [*FAA designator*] (FAAC)
PAP.......... Meiklejohn-Eaton-Liu Virus [*Medicine*] (EDAA)
PAP.......... Pacific Automation Products (IAA)
PAP.......... Packet-level Procedure (SAUS)
P/AP......... Painter/Apprentice Painter (AAG)
PAP.......... Pancreatitis-Associated Protein [*Medicine*] (DMAA)
PAP.......... Papain [*An enzyme*]
pap.......... papal (SAUS)
PAP.......... Papanicolaou [*Diagnosis, smear, stain, or test*] [*Medicine*]
Pap.......... Papanicolaou Smear [*Medicine*] (BCRP)
Pap.......... Paper (DIAR)
PAP.......... Paper (DSUE)
PAP.......... Paper Bound [*Books*] (ROG)
pap.......... Papilla [*Medicine*]
Pap.......... Papist (SAUS)
Pap.......... Pappie (SAUS)
Pap.......... Papua [*New Guinea*] (BARN)
Pap.......... Papyrus (BJA)
pap.......... Papyrus (VRA)
PAP.......... Para-Aminophenol [*Organic chemistry*]
PAP.......... Parallel Applications Programme [*British*]
PAP.......... Participatory Anthropic Principle [*Term coined by authors John Barrow and Frank Tipler in their book, "The Anthropic Cosmological Principle"*]
PAP.......... Parti d'Action Paysanne [*Farmers Actions Party*] [*Burkina Faso*] [*Political party*]
PAP.......... Partido Accion Popular [*Popular Action Party*] [*Peru*] [*Political party*]
PAP.......... Partido Accion Popular [*Popular Action Party*] [*Ecuador*] [*Political party*]
PAP.......... Password Authentication Protocol [*Computer science*] (PCM)
PAP.......... Patient Assesment Program [*Medicine*] (DMAA)
PAP.......... Patrol Amphibian Plane
PAP.......... Paulin [*H.*] & Co. Ltd. [*Toronto Stock Exchange symbol*]
PAP.......... Payload Activity Planner [*NASA*]
PAP.......... Peak Airway Pressure [*Physiology*]
PAP.......... Pension Administration Plan [*Insurance*]
PAP.......... Pentyl-alpha-pyrone [*Organic chemistry*]
PAP.......... People's Action Party [*Papua New Guinea*] [*Political party*] (EY)
PAP.......... People's Action Party [*Singapore*] [*Political party*] (PPW)
PAP.......... People's Action Party [*Malaya*] [*Political party*]
PAP.......... People's Alliance Party [*Solomon Islands*] [*Political party*] (PPW)
PAP.......... People's Armed Police (CARL)
PAP.......... Performance Assessment Plan (SAUS)
PAP.......... Periphery Access Processor [*Computer science*] (IAA)
PAP.......... Peroxidase-Antibody to Peroxidase (DB)
PAP.......... Peroxidase-Antiperoxidase [*Immunochemistry*]
PAP.......... Personal Auto Policy [*Insurance*]
PAP.......... Personnel Allocation Plan [*Navy*]
PAP.......... Personnel Assistance Point [*Army*] (AABC)
PAP.......... Phase Advance Pulse
PAP.......... Phenolphthalein in Paraffin [*Emulsion*]
PAP.......... Phenyl Acid Phosphate [*Organic chemistry*]
PAP.......... Philippine Aid Plan
PAP.......... Phosphoadenosine Phosphate [*Biochemistry*]
PAP.......... Photodiode Array Processing (MCD)
PAP.......... Photon-Assisted Processing (SAUS)
PAP.......... Photonic Array Processor [*Device for manipulating light beams in an optical computer*]
PAP.......... Physics and Astronomy (SAUS)
PAP.......... Physics and Astronomy Programs [*NASA*]
PAP.......... Phytolacca Americana Protein (DB)
PAP.......... Pierced Aluminum Plank [*Technical drawings*]
PAP.......... Pilotless Aircraft Program (NG)
PAP.......... Placental Alkaline Phosphatase (DB)
PAP.......... Plans Activation Party (SAUS)
PAP.......... Plant Acquisition Plan (SAUS)
PAP.......... Plant Air Package (IAA)
PAP.......... Plasma-Assisted Processing (SAUS)
PAP.......... Platelet Aggregation Profiler [*Hematology*]
PAP.......... Platelet Alkaline Phosphatase [*An enzyme*]
P a P........ Poco a Poco [*Little by Little*] [*Music*]
PAP.......... Point Authorization Protocol (SAUS)
PAP.......... Pokeweed Antiviral Protein [*Immunochemistry*]
PAP.......... Political Asylum Project [*Defunct*] (EA)
PAP.......... Politiki Aneksartitos Parataksis [*Independent Political Front*] [*Greek*] [*Political party*] (PPE)
PAP.......... Polska Agencja Prasowa [*Polish Press Agency*]
PAP.......... Poly(acryloylpyrrolidine) [*Organic chemistry*]
PAP.......... Poly-a-polymerase [*An enzyme*]
PAP.......... Popular Alliance Party (SAUS)
PAP.......... Port-Au-Prince [*Haiti*] [*Airport symbol*] (OAG)
PAP.......... Positive Airway Pressure (MAE)
PAP.......... Post Apollo Program (SAUS)
PAP.......... Pouchou and Pichoir (SAUS)
PAP.......... Prealloyed Powder (SAUS)
PAP.......... Preapproved Payment (SAUS)
PAP.......... Pre-Approved Procedures (SAUS)
PAP.......... Prearranged Payments [*Business term*]
PAP.......... Preauthorized Payment (SAUS)
pAP.......... Presynaptic Action Potential [*Neurochemistry*]
PAP.......... Primary Atypical Pneumonia [*Medicine*]
PAP.......... Printer Access Protocol (BYTE)
PAP.......... Priority Action Programme (SAUS)
PAP.......... Prison-Ashram Project (EA)
PAP.......... Process/Application Protocol (SAUS)
PAP.......... Procurement and Production (AFIT)
PAP.......... Product Assurance Plan [*Army*] (AABC)
PAP.......... Production Allocation Program
PAP.......... Production Assurance Program (SAUS)
PAP.......... Program Advanced Planning (SAUS)
PAP.......... Project Aerospace Plane (AAG)
PAP.......... Projected Average Progress (NG)
PAP.......... Propagation Analysis Package (SAUS)
PAP.......... Prostatic Acid Phosphatase [*An enzyme*]
PAP.......... Proton Attenuation Procedure
PAP.......... Public Access Profile (SAUS)
PAP.......... Public Affairs Program [*of the American Friends Service Committee*] (EA)
PAP.......... Public Assistance Program
PAP.......... Public Awareness Program
PAP.......... Pulmonary Alveolar Proteinosis [*Medicine*]
PAP.......... Pulmonary Arterial [*or Artery*] Pressure [*Medicine*]
PAP.......... Purple Acid Phosphatase [*An enzyme*]
PAPA......... Back Bay Restaurant Group, Inc. [*NASDAQ symbol*] (SAG)
PAPA......... Parallax Aircraft Parking Aid (PDAA)
PAPA......... Parents and Professionals and Autism Northern Ireland [*United Kingdom*] (EAIO)
PAPA......... Parents As Partners Associated (SAUS)
PAPA......... Pesticide Applicators Professional Association (SAUS)
PAPA......... Philippines Alien Property Administration
PAPA......... Pizza and Pasta Association [*British*] (DBA)
PAPA......... Pollution Abatement and Prevention Analysis [*Environmental science*] (BCP)
PAPA......... Polyazelaic Polyanhydride (EDCT)
PAPA......... Probabilistic Automatic Pattern Analyzer [*Computer science*]
PAPA......... Programmer and Probability Analyzer [*Computer science*] (IEEE)
PAPA......... Psychiatrists Against Psychiatric Abuse [*Canada*] (EAIO)
PAPABILES... Projet Autoroutier Pilote Aubonne-Belmont pour une Initiative Lausannoise [*Aubonne-Belmont Pilot Plan for Telematics in the Lausanne area*]
PapaJohn... Papa Johns International, Inc. [*Associated Press*] (SAG)
Pap & Disc Vic Inst Eng... Papers and Discussions. Victorian Institute of Engineers [*Australia*] [*A publication*]
Pap & Proc Roy Soc Tas... Papers and Proceedings. Royal Society of Tasmania [*A publication*]
PAPAS....... Pennsylvania Association of Private Academic Schools (SAUS)
PAPAS....... Pin and Pellet Assay System [*Nuclear energy*] (NRCH)
Papav....... Papaverine (SAUS)
PAPAV....... Papaver Poppy [*Botany*] (ROG)
PAPB........ Point Barrow [*Alaska*] [*ICAO location identifier*] (ICLI)
PAPC........ Presidents Accident Prevention Council (SAUS)
PAPC........ Processed Apple and Pear Committee [*Victoria, Austria*]
PAPCA....... Pan-American Progressive Consumers Alliance [*Later, NPCA*] (EA)
PAPCAPS... Publicly Available Price Cap Agreements (AAGC)
PapclS...... Paperclip Imaging Software, Inc. [*Associated Press*] (SAG)
PAPCNY....... Portuguese American Progressive Club of New York (EA)
PAPD........ Passive-Agressive Personality Disorder (MELL)
PAPD........ Periodate Dimethylphenylenediamine (SAUS)
Pap Diag.... Papanicolaou Diagnosis (SAUS)
PAPE......... Photoactive Pigment Electrophotography (IEEE)
PAPER....... People and Physical Environmental Research (SAUS)
PAPER....... Prairie Association of Publishers Education Representatives [*Canada*]
Paperboard Packag... Paperboard Packaging (SAUS)
PAPERCHEM... Paper Chemistry [*Institute of Paper Chemistry*] [*Appleton, WI*] [*Bibliographic database*]
Paper Conserv News... Paper Conservation News (SAUS)
PAPERMAN... Payroll and Accounting, Personnel Management, Manpower Utilization [*Air Force*]
Paper Technol... Paper Technology (SAUS)
Paper Twine J... Paper and Twine Journal (SAUS)
Paper Yearb... Paper Yearbook (SAUS)
PAPF......... Platelet Adhesiveness Plasma [*Hematology*] (DMAA)
PAPH........ (Pyridinealdehyde)pyridylhydrazone [*Organic chemistry*]
PAPHCC..... Pennsylvania Association of Plumbing-Heating-Cooling Contractors (EARSL)
PAPI......... Pacific Pigeon [*North American bird banding code*] (BIBA)
Papi......... Papi [*Aemilius*] Papinianus [*Deceased, 212*] [*Authority cited in pre-1607 legal work*] (DSA)

Papi .... Papirius Justus [*Flourished, 2nd century*] [*Authority cited in pre-1607 legal work*] (DSA)
PAPI .... Polymethylene Polyphenyl Isocyanate (EDCT)
PAPI .... Precision Approach Path Indicator [*FAA*] (TAG)
PAPI .... Professional Association of Pet Industries (EA)
Papil .... Papilla (SAUS)
Pap Inf ...... Papal Infallability (SAUS)
PapJohn .... Papa Johns International, Inc. [*Associated Press*] (SAG)
PaPL .... Pennsylvania Power & Light Co. [*Associated Press*] (SAG)
PAPL .... Preliminary Allowance Parts List [*Military*] (CAAL)
PaPL .... W. and F. Pascoe Proprietory Ltd., Milsons Point, NSW, Australia [*Library symbol*] [*Library of Congress*] (LCLS)
Pap Lab Tree Ring Res... Papers of the Laboratory of Tree Ring Research (SAUS)
Pap Lib ..... Paperback Library (SAUS)
PAPM .... Pall Aircraft Porous Media
PAPM .... Passed Assistant Paymaster [*British*]
PAPM .... Port Moller Air Force Station [*Alaska*] [*ICAO location identifier*] (ICLI)
PAPM .... Pulse Amplitude and Phase Modulation (PDAA)
Pap Mich Acad Sci Arts Lett... Papers of the Michigan Academy of Science, Arts and Letters (SAUS)
PAPMOP .... Product Assurance Program Management Operations Plan (MCD)
PAPMV ...... Papaya Mosaic Virus [*Plant pathology*]
Pap Non-Market Dec Making... Papers on Non-Market Decision Making [*A publication*] (JLIT)
Papo .... Partido de Accion Popular [*Popular Action Party*] [*Panama*] [*Political party*] (PPW)
PAPOC .... Parents' Alliance to Protect Our Children (EA)
PAPOILA .... Pacis Amico, Persecutionis Osore, Joanne Lockio Anglo [*Pseudonym used by John Locke*]
PAPOVA ..... Papilloma Virus, Polyoma Virus, Vacuolating Virus
PAPP .... Pappenheimer Bodies [*Hematology*] (DAVI)
PAPP .... Para-Aminopropiophenone [*Pharmacology*]
PAPP .... Parametric Aircraft Performance Program (MCD)
PAPP .... Pre-Approved Payment Plan (SAUS)
PAPP .... Pregnancy-Associated Plasma Protein
PAPP .... Product Assurance Program Plan (ACAE)
PAPP .... Pull and Push Plate (IAA)
PAPPA .... Pulp and Paper Prepackaging Association [*Later, SSI*] (EA)
PAPPGM .... Preliminary Army Planning and Program Guidance Memorandum (MCD)
Pa Pple ..... Passive Participle (SAUS)
Pa Pple ..... Past Participle (SAUS)
PAPR .... Powered Air Purifying Respirator (ERG)
PAP/RAC .... Priority Action Programme/Regional Activity Centre (SAUS)
PA Prac ..... Standard Pennsylvania Practice [*A publication*] (DLA)
Pap Reg Sci... Papers in Regional Science [*A publication*] (JLIT)
PAPRICAN... Pulp and Paper Research Institute of Canada [*McGill University*] [*Research center*] (RCD)
PA Projection... Posterior Anterior Projection (SAUS)
PAPROS ..... Parallel Processing System (SAUS)
PAPS .... Papers [*Telegraphy*] (PCTE)
Paps .... Papillomas [*Medicine*] (DMAA)
PAPS .... Performance Analysis and Prediction Study (PDAA)
PAPS .... Periodic Acid Phenylhydrazine Schiff (SAUS)
PAPS .... Periodic Acid-Schiff with Phenylhydrazine Interposition [*A stain*]
PAPS .... Periodic Armaments Planning System (MCD)
PAPS .... Periodic Arrays of Pinning Sites [*Solid state physics*]
PAPS .... Permissive Arming and Protection System [*AEC*]
PAPS .... Phased Armaments Programme Systems (SAUS)
PAPS .... Phosphoadenosine Diphosphosulfate [*Phosphoadenosyl-Phosphosulfate*] [*Biochemistry*] (DAVI)
PAPS .... Phosphoadenosine Phosphosulfate [*Also, APPS*] [*Biochemistry*]
PAPS .... Phosphoadenylyl Sulfate [*Biochemistry*]
PAPS .... Physics Auxiliary Publication Service (SAUS)
PAPS .... Portable Ada Programming System (SAUS)
PAPS .... Proceedings of the American Philosophical Society [*A publication*] (ABAR)
PAPS .... Procurement and Production Status System
PAPS .... Public Assistance Processing System
PA/PS .... Pulmonary Atresia/Pulmonary Stenosis [*Cardiology*] (DAVI)
PAPSA .... Pennsylvania Association of Private School Administrators (EARSL)
PAPSB .... Patent Attorneys' Professional Standards Body [*Australia*]
PA PSC ...... Pennsylvania Public Service Commission Annual Report [*A publication*] (DLA)
PA PSC Dec... Pennsylvania Public Service Commission Decisions [*A publication*] (DLA)
PAPSI .... Pregnancy-Associated Prostaglandin Synthetase Inhibitor [*Endocrinology*]
Pap smear... Papanicolaou smear (SAUS)
Papsom ..... Papaver somniferum (SAUS)
PAPSS .... Procurement and Production Status System (SAUS)
Pap Sta ..... Papal States (SAUS)
PAPT .... Palladium Print (VRA)
PAPTC .... Pakistan Army Physical Training Corps [*British military*] (DMA)
PAPTC .... Paper Tape Controller (NITA)
PAPTE .... President's Advisory Panel on Timber and the Environment
Pap Ter ...... Papua Territory (SAUS)
Pap Test .... Papanicolaou Test (SAUS)
PAPUFA ..... Physiologically Active Polyunsaturated Fatty Acid [*Nutrition*]
Pa-Pv .... Pulmonary Arterial Pressure-Pulmonary Venous Pressure [*Medicine*] (STED)
PAPVC .... Partial Anomalous Pulmonary Venous Connection (MAE)
PAPVR .... Partial Anomalous Pulmonary Venous Return
PAPW .... Papworth [*England*]
PAPW .... Posterior Aspect of the Pharyngeal Wall [*Medicine*] (STED)
PAPX .... Pennsylvania Pullmans [*Private rail car owner code*]
Papy .... Papy's Reports [*5-8 Florida*] [*A publication*] (DLA)
PAQ .... Palmer, AK [*Location identifier*] [*FAA*] (FAAL)
PAQ .... Partially Allocated Quotas [*Ocean fishery management*]
PAQ .... Passive Asynchronous Quenching (SAUS)
PAQ .... Pending Action Queue (SAUS)
PAQ .... Personal Attributes Questionnaire
PAQ .... Port Authorities Queensland [*Australia*]
PAQ .... Position Analysis Questionnaire
PAQ .... Preliminary Allowance Quantity [*Military*] (CAAL)
PAQ .... Process Average Quality
PAQ .... Production, Accounting, Quality (SAUS)
PAQAB .... President's Air Quality Advisory Board [*Environmental Protection Agency*]
PAQR .... Polyacene Quinone Radical (SAUS)
PAQR .... Polyacenequinone Radical [*Organic chemistry*]
PAQS .... Pacific Association of Quantity Surveyors [*Australia*]
PAQSS .... Pennsylvania Air Quality Surveillance System (SAUS)
PAR .... Coastcast Corp. [*NYSE symbol*] (SPSG)
Par .... Guiraudus Pargues [*Authority cited in pre-1607 legal work*] (DSA)
PAR .... Pacific-Antarctic Ridge [*Geology*]
PAR .... Page Address Register
PAR .... Panama Canal Commission Acquisition Regulation (AAGC)
PAR .... Parabolic Aluminized Reflector [*Lamp*]
PAR .... Paracel Islands [*ANSI three-letter standard code*] (CNC)
PAR .... Parachute
par .... Paraffin [*Chemistry*] (DAVI)
PAR .... Paraffin (STED)
PAR .... Paragon Resources Ltd. [*Vancouver Stock Exchange symbol*]
PAR .... Paragraph (AAG)
par .... Paragraph (WDMC)
Par .... Paraguay
Par .... Parah (BJA)
PAR .... Paralipomenon [*Old Testament book*] [*Douay version*]
PAR .... Parallax
PAR .... Parallax and Refraction (IAA)
Par .... Parallaxe (SAUS)
PAR .... Parallel (KSC)
par .... Parallel (WDMC)
PAR .... Parallelogram [*Geometry*] (ADA)
PAR .... Parameter
PAR .... Parameter Request (SAUS)
PAR .... Parametric Amplifier
Par .... Paranoid [*Psychiatry*] (DAVI)
par .... Parapet (MIST)
PAR .... Paraphrase (ADA)
PAR .... Parcel
PAR .... Parcel Service [*Indian Railway*] (TIR)
Par .... Parenchesis (SAUS)
PAR .... Parent [*Motor vehicle violation code used in state of Maryland*] (MVRD)
PAR .... Parental Awareness and Responsibility (SAUS)
par .... Parenthesis (WDMC)
PAR .... Parenthesis
Par .... Parents Magazine [*A publication*] (BRI)
PAR .... Parimeter Array Radar
PAR .... Paris [*France*] [*Airport symbol*] (OAG)
par .... Parish (GEAB)
PAR .... Parish
PAR .... Parisienne [*NCIC car model code*]
PAR .... Paris - Parc St. Maur [*France*] [*Seismograph station code, US Geological Survey*] (SEIS)
PAR .... Parity (ADA)
Par .... Parker's English Exchequer Reports [*A publication*] (DLA)
Par .... Parker's New York Criminal Reports [*A publication*] (DLA)
PAR .... Parklane [*NCIC car model code*]
PAR .... Parkwood [*NCIC car model code*]
PAR .... Parochial
PAR .... Parole Assessment Report (WDAA)
PAR .... Parole Services for Adults [*Public human service program*] (PHSD)
Par .... Parsons' Reports [*65-66 New Hampshire*] [*A publication*] (DLA)
par .... Part (BARN)
PAR .... Partheite [*A zeolite*]
Par .... Participating (AMHC)
PAR .... Participating [*Health insurance*] (GHCT)
PAR .... Participating Provider [*Health insurance*] (DMAA)
PAR .... Participation-Achievement-Reward (PDAA)
PAR .... Partido Aragones Regionalista [*Aragonese Regional Party*] [*Spain*] [*Political party*] (PPW)
PAR .... Partition [*Construction term*] (MIST)
PAR .... Partito Anti-Reformista [*Anti-Reform Party*] [*Malta*] [*Political party*] (PPE)
PAR .... Parts Approval Request (MCD)
PAR .... Passive Avoidance Reaction [*Medicine*] (DMAA)
PAR .... Payload Accommodations Requirements (SAUS)
PAR .... Payload Adapter Ring
PAR .... [*The*] Payment Analysis Report [*Dun & Bradstreet Credit Services*] [*Information service or system*] (CRD)
PAR .... Peacetime Airborne Reconnaissance (AFM)
PAR .... Peak Accelerometer Recorder (IEEE)
PAR .... Peak Area Ratio [*Chromatographic analysis*]
PAR .... Peak Average Rectified (SAUS)
PAR .... Peak-to-Average Ratio [*Telecommunications*]

PAR.......... Peak-to-Average Reading (SAUS)
PAR.......... Pennsylvania Advanced Reactor
PAR.......... Pennsylvania Association of Realtors (EARSL)
PAR.......... Pennsylvania Association of Resources for People with Mental Retardation (EARSL)
PAR.......... People Against Racism [*Civil rights organization*]
PAR.......... People Against Rape (EA)
PAR.......... Per Acre Rental (WDAA)
PAR.......... Perennial Allergic Rhinitis [*Medicine*]
PAR.......... Performance Analysis and Review
PAR.......... Performance Analysis Report
PAR.......... Performance Analysis Routine [*Computer science*]
PAR.......... Performance and Availability Report (SAUS)
PAR.......... Performance Appraisal Report [*Nuclear energy*] (NRCH)
PAR.......... Performance Assessment Report [*Small Cities Community Development Block Grant*] [*Department of Housing and Urban Development*] (GFGA)
PAR.......... Performance Augmentation Ring (MCD)
PAR.......... Perimeter Acquisition RADAR [*Army*]
PAR.......... Perimeter Array RADAR (MCD)
PAR.......... Peripheral Arterial Resistance [*Medicine*] (EDAA)
PAR.......... Personal Animation Recorder (SAUS)
PAR.......... Personnel Accountability Report [*Emergency Management*] (EMA)
PAR.......... Personnel Activity Report [*Office of Management and Budget*]
PAR.......... Personnel Activity Request
PAR.......... Personnel Advancement Requirement [*Navy*] (NVT)
PAR.......... Personnel At Risk (SAUS)
PAR.......... PERT [*Program Evaluation and Review Technique*] Analysis Report (KSC)
PAR.......... Phased Array RADAR
PAR.......... Phosphoric Acid-Resistant
PAR.......... Photosynthetically Active Radiation
PAR.......... Photosynthetically Active Radiometer
PAR.......... Photosynthetically Active Range
PAR.......... Photosynthetically Available Radiation (CARB)
PAR.......... Physical Activity Ratio (WDAA)
PAR.......... Physiological Aging Rate
PAR.......... Pilot Action Request
PAR.......... Plain Abdominal Radiograph [*Medicine*] (DMAA)
PAR.......... Planed All Around (SAUS)
PAR.......... Planed All Round (DAC)
Par.......... Planed All Round [*Construction term*] (MIST)
PAR.......... Planning Action Request [*NASA*] (MCD)
PAR.......... Planning Activity Report
PAR.......... Planning and Allocation of Resources (SAUS)
PAR.......... Plasma-Arc Reduction (SAUS)
PAR.......... Plasma-Arc Remelting (SAUS)
PAR.......... Platelet Aggregate Ratio [*Hematology*]
PAR.......... Point Address Register (SAUS)
PAR.......... Police Accident Report [*NHTSA*] (TAG)
PAR.......... Policy and Administrative Reform (SAUS)
PAR.......... Pollen Accumulation Rate [*Botany*]
PAr.......... Polyarteritis (STED)
PAR.......... Polyarylate [*Resin*]
PAR.......... Population at Risk (FFDE)
PAR.......... Positive Acknowledgment and Retransmission [*Telecommunications*] (IAA)
PAR.......... Positive Attitudinal Reinforcement [*In George Lee Walker novel "The Chronicles of Doodah"*]
PAR.......... Post Adjudicative Review [*Social Security Administration*] (OICC)
PAR.......... Postanesthesia [*or Postanesthetic*] Room [*Medicine*]
PAR.......... Postanesthetic Recovery [*Medicine*]
PAR.......... Post Attach Requirements (AAG)
PAR.......... Potassium-Adsorption-Ratio
PAR.......... Power Analyser & Recorder (SAUS)
PAR.......... Power Analysis Report [*Automobile testing*]
PAR.......... Practical Accounts Receivable (SAUS)
PAR.......... Preadmission Review (WYGK)
PAR.......... Precedent, Action, and Result
PAR.......... Precision Aerotech (EFIS)
PAR.......... Precision Aircraft Reference
PAR.......... Precision Approach RADAR [*Aviation*]
PAR.......... Preferential Arrival Route [*Aviation*] (DA)
PAR.......... Preferred Arrival Route (CTAS)
PAR.......... Preliminary Analysis Review (SAUS)
PAR.......... Preparedness Assessment Report [*Environmental science*] (COE)
PAR.......... Price-Adjusted Rate Preferred [*Investment term*] (MHDW)
PAR.......... Prime Assets Ratio
PAR.......... Princeton Applied Research Corp. [*Princeton University*]
PAR.......... Print Area Reader (DGA)
PAR.......... Priority Action Report (AAG)
PAR.......... Priority Action Request (AAG)
PAR.......... Probabilistic Analysis of Risk (KSC)
PAR.......... Probable Allergic Rhinitis [*Medicine*] (DAVI)
PAR.......... Problem Accountability Record (NASA)
PAR.......... Problem Action Record (KSC)
PAR.......... Problem Action Request (NASA)
PAR.......... Problem Analysis and Resolution
PAR.......... Problem Analysis and Response (SAUS)
PAR.......... Problem Analysis and Response Program (IAA)
PAR.......... Problem Analysis Report (MCD)
PAR.......... Process Action Request
PAR.......... Processor Address Register (SAUS)
PAR.......... Procurement Advisory Release (SAUS)
PAR.......... Product Acceptance & Research [*Commercial firm*] (WDMC)
PAR.......... Product Acceptance Review (NASA)
PAR.......... Product Analytical Review [*Medicine*] (EDAA)
PAR.......... Product Assurance Requirements (ACAE)
PAR.......... Production Acceptance Review
PAR.......... Production Action Request (MCD)
PAR.......... Production Analysis Report
PAR.......... Production, Augmentation, and Reliability (NG)
PAR.......... Production Automated Riveting
PAR.......... Product of Antigenic Recognition [*Immunochemistry*]
PAR.......... Professional Abstracts Registries [*Database Innovations, Inc.*]
PAR.......... Profile of Average Reflectivity
PAR.......... Program Acquisition Request (SAUS)
PAR.......... Program Acquisition Review (ACAE)
PAR.......... Program Action Request (SSD)
PAR.......... Program Activity Recording [*Computer science*] (IAA)
PAR.......... Program Address Register
PAR.......... Program Adjustment Request [*Navy*]
PAR.......... Program Administrator's [*Progress*] Report [*DoD*]
PAR.......... Program-Aid Routine [*Computer science*]
PAR.......... Program Allocation and Reimbursements (AFIT)
PAR.......... Program Analysis and Review
PAR.......... Program Analysis Report
PAR.......... Program Appraisal and Review (IEEE)
PAR.......... Program Appraisal Report
PAR.......... Program Assessment Report [*or Review*] (MCD)
PAR.......... Program Audience Rating
PAR.......... Program for Alcohol(ic) Recovery [*Medicine*] (EDAA)
PAR.......... Program for Alcohol Recovery
PAR.......... Programmed and Remote (SAUS)
PAR.......... Progressive Aircraft Repair [*or Rework*]
PAR.......... Progressive Airframe Rework
PAR.......... Project Activity Report (SAUS)
PAR.......... Project Analysis and Reporting system (SAUS)
PAR.......... Project Anthorization Request (SAUS)
PAR.......... Project Appraisal Report (SAUS)
PAR.......... Project Approval Review (SAUS)
PAR.......... Project Audit Report
PAR.......... Project Authorization Request (IAA)
PAR.......... Projected Automation Requirement
PAR.......... Proposal Analysis Report (AAGC)
PAR.......... Propulsion and Aeroballistics Research (SAA)
PAR.......... Protease-Activated Receptor [*Hematology*]
PAR.......... Protect Abortion Rights (SAUS)
PAR.......... Protection Action Recommendation [*Department of Emergency Management*] (DEMM)
PAR.......... Protective Action Recommendation (COE)
PAR.......... Provisioning Allowance Record (SAUS)
PAR.......... Proximal Absolute Reabsorption [*Medicine*] (EDAA)
PAR.......... Proximal Alveolar Region [*Medicine*] (DMAA)
PAR.......... Pseudoautosomal Region [*Genetics*]
PAR.......... Psychological Assessment Resources, Inc. (DHP)
PAR.......... Public Accounting Report (SAUS)
PAR.......... Public Administration Review [*A publication*] (BRI)
PAR.......... Public Affairs Research Council [*Research center*] (RCD)
PAR.......... Publication Analysis Report (SAA)
PAR.......... Pulmonary Arteriolar Resistance [*Medicine*] (MAE)
PAR.......... Pulse Acquisition RADAR [*Military*] (NG)
PAR.......... Pulse Address Register (VLIE)
PAR.......... Punch Address Register (SAUS)
PAr.......... Punta Arenas (SAUS)
PAR.......... Purchasing Approval Request (NRCH)
PAR.......... Push and Release [*Push button*]
PAR.......... Pyridinazo-Resorcin (SAUS)
PAR.......... (Pyridylazo)resorcinol [*Organic chemistry*]
PAR.......... Spair [*Russian Federation*] [*ICAO designator*] (FAAC)
Para.......... Number of Pregnancies [*Therapy term*] (CTAA)
PARA.......... Parabellum (GOBB)
PARA.......... Parabolic (IAA)
para.......... Paracentesis [*Medicine*] (MAE)
PARA.......... Parachute
PARA.......... Parachutist (SAUS)
PARA.......... Paragraph (AFM)
para.......... Paragraph (DIAR)
PARA.......... Paraguay
PARA.......... Parallel (WDAA)
PARA.......... Paramagnetic (SAUS)
PARA.......... Paramedic (SAUS)
PARA.......... Paramount Financial [*NASDAQ symbol*] (TTSB)
PARA.......... Paramount Financial Corp. [*NASDAQ symbol*] (SAG)
para.......... Paraphrase (BARN)
para.......... Paraplegic
PARA.......... Parasite (SAUS)
para.......... Parathy Roidectomy [*Medicine*] (DMAA)
para.......... Paratroop (MILB)
PARA.......... Paratrooper (GOBB)
para.......... Parity [*Gynecology and obstetrics*] (DAVI)
para.......... Parquet (BARN)
PARA.......... Particle Aiding Replication of Adenovirus [*Virology*]
PARA.......... Perceiving and Recognition Automation (SAUS)
PARA.......... Policy Analysis and Resource Allocation [*Department of State*]
PARA.......... Polyarylamid [*Organic chemistry*]
PARA.......... Problem Analysis and Recommended Action (IAA)
PARA.......... Professional Audiovideo Retailers Association (EA)

PARA .... Program for At-Risk Addicts (SAUS)
Para 1 .... Unipara [*Having borne one child*] [*Gynecology and obstetrics*] (DAVI)
Para-A .... Paratyphoid A [*Medicine*] (DAVI)
PARAB .... Parabola [*Mathematics*] (IAA)
parab .... Parabola (ODA)
Para-B .... Paratyphoid B [*Medicine*] (DAVI)
PARABAT ... Parachute Battalion [*Army*]
PARABOL... Parabolic (IAA)
PARABOLA... Portable Apparatus for Rapid Acquisition of Bidirectional Observations of Land and Atmosphere (SAUS)
Para-C .... Paratyphoid C [*Medicine*] (DAVI)
Paracels .... Paracelsus Healthcare Corp. [*Associated Press*] (SAG)
paracent .... Paracentesis [*Medicine*]
PARACOMPT... Parameter Analysis of Respiration Agents Considering Operations Motivation Protection and Time Model (MCD)
PARACS ..... Perimeter Acquisition RADAR Attack Characterization System (MCD)
PARAD ...... Paradichlorobenzene (SAUS)
parad .... paradisal (SAUS)
parad .... paradise (SAUS)
parad .... paradoxicalness (SAUS)
PARADA ..... Preparatory Academy for the Royal Academy of Dramatic Art [*British*] (BI)
PARADE ..... Passive-Active Range Determination
Paradl .... Paradise, Inc. [*Associated Press*] (SAG)
PARADISE... Centre for Parallel and Distributed Computing [*Carleton University*] [*Canada*] (RCD)
PARADISE... Phased Array RADAR and Divers Integrated Semiconductor Elements (PDAA)
Par Adm .... Parsons on the Law of Shipping and Admiralty [*A publication*] (DLA)
PARADROP... Parachute Airdrop (SAUS)
PAR AFF .... Pars Affecta [*The Part Affected*] [*Pharmacy*]
PARAFRAG... Parachute Fragmentation Bomb [*Air Force*]
PARAFRAG Bomb... Parachute Fragmentation Bomb (SAUS)
PARAG ...... Paragould, AR [*American Association of Railroads railroad junction routing code*]
PARAG ...... Paraguay [*or Paraguayan*] (WDAA)
Parag .... Paraguayan (DIAR)
ParagGg .... Paragon Group, Inc. [*Associated Press*] (SAG)
ParagGp .... Paragon Group, Inc. [*Associated Press*] (SAG)
PARAGON... Processing and Archiving of Radar and Gauge Data Off-Line and in Near Real Time (SAUS)
ParagTr ...... Paragon Trade Brands [*Associated Press*] (SAG)
Para II .... Bipara [*Having borne two children*] [*Gynecology and Obstetrics*] (DAVI)
Para III ...... Tripara [*having borne three children*] [*Gynecology and obstetrics*] (DAVI)
PARAKU ..... Pasokan Rakyat Kalimantan Utara [*North Kalimantan People's Forces*] [*Malaya*]
Parallel Comput... Parallel Computing (SAUS)
PARAM ...... Parameter (KSC)
PARAM ...... Parametric (SAUS)
ParaMed .... Paradigm Medical Industries, Inc. [*Associated Press*] (SAG)
Parameters... Parameters: US Army War College Quarterly [*A publication*] (BRI)
PARAMI ..... Parsons Active Ring-Around Miss Indicator
PARAMIS... Parsons Passive Miss Distance Indicating System (SAA)
Par Am Law... Parsons' Commentaries on American Law [*A publication*] (DLA)
Par Am Law Comm... Parsons' Commentaries on American Law [*A publication*] (DLA)
Paramnt ..... Paramount Financial Corp. [*Associated Press*] (SAG)
PARAMP .... Parametric Amplifier
paramp ...... Parametric Amplifier (VLIE)
ParamrkE .... Paramark Enterprises, Inc. [*Associated Press*] (SAG)
Paramt ...... Paramount Financial Corp. [*Associated Press*] (SAG)
PARAN ...... Perimeter Array Antenna (PDAA)
Par & Fonb Med Jur... Paris and Fonblanque's Medical Jurisprudence [*A publication*] (DLA)
Par Ant ...... Parochial Antiquities [*A publication*] (DLA)
PARAP .... Polarized Absorption Recovery After Photobleaching [*Biophysics*] [*Biochemistry*] (QSUL)
Parapsy ..... Parasychologist (SAUS)
PARAPSYCH... Parapsychologist (SAUS)
PARAPSYCH... Parapsychology
PARAQUAD... Paraplegic and Quadriplegic Association of New South Wales [*Australia*]
ParaQuad NSW... Paraplegic and Quadriplegic Association of NSW (SAUS)
PARARESCUE... Rescue by Individuals Parachuted to Distressed Persons [*Air Force*]
PARAS .... Parasitic (IAA)
Paras .... Parasitism (SAUS)
PARAS .... Pye Automatic Roadside Alarm System (SAUS)
PARASAIL... Parachute Sail (SAUS)
PARASEV ... Paraglider Research Vehicle [*NASA*]
parasit ...... Parasitology [*Medicine*] (DMAA)
PARASITOL... Parasitologic (SAUS)
Parasitol... Parasitologist (SAUS)
PARASITOL... Parasitology
parasym .... Parasympathetic [*Division of autonomic nervous system*] [*Neurolgoy*] (DAVI)
parasym div... Parasympathetic Division [*of autonomic nervous system*] [*Neurology*] (DAVI)
PARASYN... Parametric Synthesis [*Computer science*]
PARATHORMONE... Parathyroid Hormone [*Endocrinology*]
PARATROOPS... Parachute Infantry [*Military*]
para VIII... Octipara [*Having borne eight children*] [*Gynecology and obstetrics*] (DAVI)

Paravnt ...... Paravant Computer Systems, Inc. [*Associated Press*] (SAG)
PARAW ...... Paramount Financial Wrrt [*NASDAQ symbol*] (TTSB)
PARB .... Perimeter Acquisition RADAR Building [*Army*] (AABC)
PARB .... Permanent Automatic Road Barrier [*Police and security equipment*]
PARB .... Public Accountants Registration Board [*Australia*]
Parbhani AgricCollMag... Parbhani Agricultural College Magazine (SAUS)
PARBICA ...... Pacific Regional Branch of the International Council on Archives ...... (EAIO)
Par Bills & N... Parsons on Bills and Notes [*A publication*] (DLA)
PARC .... Pacific Agri-Food Research Centre, Agassiz [*Agriculture and Agri-Food Canada*] [*Canada*] (RCD)
PARC .... Pacific Air Rescue Center [*or Command*] (CINC)
PARC .... Pacific-Asia Resources Center [*Japan*] (EAIO)
PARC .... Palo Alto Research Center [*Xerox Corp.*]
PARC .... Pan-African Resource Center (EA)
PARC .... Pan-African Rinderpest Campaign [*Organization of African Unity*]
PARC .... Parallel Algorithm and Architectures Research Centre [*Loughborough University*] [*United Kingdom*] (RCD)
PARC .... Parcelas
parc .... Parchment (VRA)
PARC .... Paris Trailer Company [*NCIC trailer make code*]
PARC .... Park Communications, Inc. [*NASDAQ symbol*] (COMM)
PARC .... Partners in Amphibian and Reptile Conservation [*An association*]
PARC .... Pennsylvania Association for Retarded Children (EDAC)
PARC .... Performing Arts Research Center (SAUS)
PARC .... Pericardial Fluid [*Cardiology*] (DAVI)
PARC .... Periodic Aircraft Reconditioning Cycle (DNAB)
PARC .... Polarimetric Active Radar Calibrator (SAUS)
PARC .... Portland Alcohol Research Center [*Oregon Health and Science University*] (RCD)
PARC .... Predator and Rodent Control [*US Fish and Wildlife Service*] (IIA)
PARC .... President's Appalachian Regional Commission
PARC .... Princeton Applied Research Corp.
PARC .... Principal Assistant Responsible for Contracting [*Army*]
PARC .... Prison Activist Resource Center (SAUS)
PARC .... Profile Analysis and Recording Control (PDAA)
PARC .... Program on the Analysis & Resolution of Conflicts (SAUS)
PARC .... Progressive Aircraft Reconditioning [*or Repair*] Cycle
PARC .... Progressive Aircraft Repair Cycle (SAUS)
PARC .... Protected Area Resource Centres (SAUS)
PARC .... Public Affairs Research Council (SAUS)
PARC .... Public Archives Records Centre (SAUS)
PARCA .... Pan American Railway Congress Association
PARCA .... Patient Access to Responsible Care Act
PARCAC ..... Polar Amateur Radio Club of Alaska Certificate (SAUS)
Par Car Ret... Partial Carriage Return (SAUS)
PARCC .... Precision, Accuracy, Representativeness, Completeness, Comparability (SAUS)
PARCH ...... Parchment (ADA)
Par Ch ...... Parents' Choice [*A publication*]
PARCHM .... Parchment (ROG)
PARCHT ..... Parchment
PaRCL .... Parsec Research Control Language [*Pronounced "parkul"*] [*Parsec Reseach*] [*Robotics*]
Parcls .... Paracelsian, Inc. [*Associated Press*] (SAG)
Parclsn ...... Paracelsian, Inc. [*Associated Press*] (SAG)
PARCO ...... Parker Drilling Company (EFIS)
PARCO ...... Portland Asbestos Removal Co. (EFIS)
PARCOM .... Paris Commission [*See also CP*] (EAIO)
PARCOM .... Paris Commission for the Environmental Protection of the North East Atlantic (SAUS)
Par Cont .... Parsons on Contracts [*A publication*] (DLA)
PARCOR ..... Partial Correlation (SAUS)
Par Costs ... Parsons on Costs [*A publication*] (DLA)
PARCP .... PEMARS [*Procurement of Equipment and Missiles, Army Management and AccountingReporting System*] Accounting and Reporting Control Point [*Army*]
ParcPplce... Parcplace Systems, Inc. [*Associated Press*] (SAG)
PARCS .... Parking and Revenue Control System (SAUS)
PARCS .... Perimeter Acquisition RADAR Attack Characterization System [*Army*]
PARCS .... Pesticide Analysis Retrieval and Control System (NITA)
PARC System... Profile Analysis and Recording Control System (SAUS)
PARD .... Pardonnet Manufacturing Company [*NCIC trailer make code*]
PARD .... Parts Application Reliability Data (IEEE)
PARD .... Periodic and Random Deviation
PARD .... Personal Alarm Radiation Dose (SAUS)
PARD .... Personnel Actions and Records Directorate [*Military Personnel Center*] (AABC)
PARD .... Phased Array Radar Detection/Track (SAUS)
PARD .... Pilot Airborne Recovery Device [*A balloon-parachute*]
PARD .... Pilotless Aircraft Research Division [*Later, Applied Materials and Physics Division*] [*Langley Research Center*]
PARD .... Post-Accident Radioactivity Depletion [*Nuclear energy*] (NRCH)
PARD .... Precision Annotated Retrieval Display [*System*] [*Computer science*]
PARD .... Project Activities Relationship Diagram (PDAA)
PARD .... Protect as Restricted Data
PARDAC ..... Parallel Digital-to-Analog Converter
Par Dec ..... Parsons' Decisions [*2-7 Massachusetts*] [*A publication*] (DLA)
PARDEM .... Participatory Democracy (SAUS)
PARDENTL... Paradental
Pardgm ..... Paradigm Technology, Inc. [*Associated Press*] (SAG)
Pard Lois Mar... Pardessus' Lois Maritimes [*A publication*] (DLA)

PARDON .... Pastors' Anonymous Recovery-Directed Order for Newness [*Rehabilitation program for troubled clergymen*] [*Defunct*]
PARDOP..... Passive Ranging Doppler
PARDP ...... Perimeter Acquisition RADAR Data Processor [*Army*] (AABC)
PARDPS..... PAR Data Processing System (SAUS)
PARDRIL ... Parker Drilling Company (EFIS)
PARDS ...... Phased Array RADAR Detection System (PDAA)
Pard Serv... Pardessus' Traites des Servitudes [*A publication*] (DLA)
PARE .... Painted Redstart [*North American bird banding code*] (BIBA)
PARE .... Park Estates Homes [*NCIC trailer make code*]
PARE .... People Against Racism in Education
PARE .... Physical Ability Requirement Evaluation (SAUS)
PARE .... Physiological and Anatomical Rodent Experiment (SAUS)
PARE .... Price Adjusted Rates of Exchange [*Monetary conversion rate*] (ECON)
PARE .... Program Analysis and Resouces Evaluation (IAA)
PARE .... Program for Analytical Reliability Estimation (VLIE)
P/AREA...... Probationary Acting Radio Electrical Artificer [*British military*] (DMA)
PAREC....... Pay Record
PA Rec ...... Pennsylvania Record [*A publication*] (DLA)
paren........ Parenterally [*Medicine*] (BCRP)
PAREN....... Parenthesis [*or Parentheses*] (AFM)
paren........ Parenthesis (WDMC)
PAREN....... Progressive Aircraft Engine Repair
PARENA..... Party for National Renewal (Mali) [*Political party*] (PSAP)
PARENS..... Parentheses (NTCM)
parent....... parentally (SAUS)
PARENT..... Parenteral
PARENTS ... People of America Responding to Educational Needs of Today's Society (EA)
Parents Cit Guide... Parents and Citizens Guide [*A publication*]
PARENTS FLAG... Parents and Friends of Lesbians and Gays [*An association*]
PARENTSQ... Parent Squadron Base [*Military*] (NVT)
PA Rep...... Pennsylvania Reports [*A publication*] (DLA)
Par Eq Cas... Parsons' Select Equity Cases [*1842-51*] [*Pennsylvania*] [*A publication*] (DLA)
Par Eq Cases... Parsons' Select Equity Cases [*Pennsylvania*] [*A publication*] (DLA)
pares........ paresthesia (SAUS)
PARES....... Passive Radar ESM System (SAUS)
PARES....... Preprocessing of Airborne Remote Sensing Data (SAUS)
PARESEV... Paraglider Research Vehicle [*NASA*] (MCD)
Par Ess...... Parsons' Essays on Legal Topics [*A publication*] (DLA)
PARET....... Parallel Architecture Research and Evaluation Tool [*Computer science*]
PARET....... Program for the Analysis of Reactor Transients (SAUS)
PAREX....... Programmed Accounts Receivable Extra Service [*Computer science*]
Parexel...... Parexel International Corp. [*Associated Press*] (SAG)
PARF .... Paradise, Inc. [*NASDAQ symbol*] (SAG)
PARF .... Pennsylvania Association of Rehabilitation Facilities (EARSL)
PARF .... Polymorphic Amplifiable Restriction (Endonuclease) Fragment [*Genetics*]
PARF .... Post-anesthetic Respiratory Failure [*Medicine*] (EDAA)
PARF .... Practical Allergy Research Foundation (EA)
PARFAS ..... Passive Radio Frequency Acquisition System
PARFC....... Power Amplifier Radio Frequency Coil (SAUS)
par for....... par for the course (SAUS)
PARFORCE... Parallel Formal Computing Environment (VLIE)
PARFOX..... Parapet Foxhole
PARFR....... Program for Applied Research on Fertility Regulation [*Northwestern University*] [*Research center*]
Parg .... Parguay (SAUS)
PARG .... Polytechnic Academic Registrars' Group (AIE)
Pargs......... Guiraudus Pargues [*Authority cited in pre-1607 legal work*] (DSA)
PARGS ...... Parks and Recreation Girls Service
PARH........ Park Homes [*NCIC trailer make code*]
PARI .... Parent Attitude Research Instrument [*A questionnaire*]
pari .... parietal (SAUS)
PARI .... Parilla [*NCIC motorcycle make code*]
PARI .... Pre-Columbian Art Research Institute
PARIET...... Parietal Cell Antibody [*Immunology*] (DAVI)
PARIF........ Program for Automatic Retrieval Improvement by Feedback (SAUS)
PARIF........ Program for Automation Retrieval Improvement by Feedback (NITA)
PARIK .... Paris, KY [*American Association of Railroads railroad junction routing code*]
PARIMPS... Professional Association of Residents in the Maritime Provinces (SAUS)
PARIS .... Paris, IL [*American Association of Railroads railroad junction routing code*]
PARIS .... Passenger Routing and Information System [*FTA*] (TAG)
PARIS .... Passive Active Ranging & Intercept System (SAUS)
PARIS .... Passive/Activity Radar Identification System (ACAE)
PARIS .... Persantin/Aspirin Reinfarction Study [*Medicine*] (DB)
PARIS .... Pictorial and Artifact Retrieval and Information System [*Canadian Heritage Information Network*] [*Information service or system*]
PARIS .... Planning Aid for Retail Information System [*IBM Corp.*]
PARIS .... Polarized Angle-Resolved Infrared Spectroscopy (SAUS)
PARIS .... Portable Automated Remote Inspection System [*Failure Analysis Associates*] (RDA)
PARIS .... Postal Address Reader Indexer System (PDAA)
PARIS .... Pour l'Amenagement et le Renouveau Institutionel et Social [*France*] [*Political party*]
PARIS .... Pulse Analysis-Recording Information System
ParisBu ..... Paris Business Forms, Inc. [*Associated Press*] (SAG)
PA-RISC... Precision Architecture-Reduced Instruction Set Computing (SAUS)
Paris O...... Paris Opera Computing (SAUS)
PARIT........ Paris (Betner), TX [*American Association of Railroads railroad junction routing code*]
PARK .... Park [*Postal Service standard*] (OPSA)
PARK .... Parkerized [*Metallurgy*] [*Tradename*]
Park .... Parker's English Exchequer Reports [*1743-67*] [*A publication*] (DLA)
Park .... Parker's New Hampshire Reports [*A publication*] (DLA)
Park .... Parker's New York Criminal Cases [*1823-68*] [*A publication*] (DLA)
PARK .... Parking
PARK .... Park Lane Mobile Homes [*NCIC trailer make code*]
PARK .... Photorefractive Astigmatic Keratectomy (SAUS)
PARK .... Premier Parks, Inc. [*NASDAQ symbol*] (SAG)
PARKA....... Pacific Acoustic Research (SAUS)
PARKA....... Pacific Acoustic Research Kaneohe-Alaska [*Navy*]
Park Arb .... Parker on Arbitration [*1820*] [*A publication*] (DLA)
Park Ch ..... Parker's Practice in Chancery [*A publication*] (DLA)
Park CR ..... Parker's New York Criminal Reports [*A publication*] (DLA)
Park Cr Cas... Parker's New York Criminal Cases [*A publication*] (DLA)
Park Crim L... Parker's New York Criminal Reports [*A publication*] (DLA)
Park Crim (NY)... Parker's New York Criminal Cases [*A publication*] (DLA)
Park Crim R... Parker's New York Criminal Reports [*A publication*] (DLA)
Park Crim Rep... Parker's New York Criminal Reports [*A publication*] (DLA)
Park Cr Rep... Parker's New York Criminal Reports [*A publication*] (DLA)
PARKD ...... Parkdale, ON [*American Association of Railroads railroad junction routing code*]
Park Dig .... Parker's California Digest [*A publication*] (DLA)
Park Dow ... Park. Dower [*1819*] [*A publication*] (DLA)
ParkDrl...... Parker Drilling Co. [*Associated Press*] (SAG)
ParkEl .... Park Electrochemical Corp. [*Associated Press*] (SAG)
Parker....... Parker on the Laws of Shipping and Insurance [*England*] [*A publication*] (DLA)
Parker....... Parker's English Exchequer Reports [*A publication*] (DLA)
Parker....... Parker's New Hampshire Reports [*A publication*] (DLA)
Parker....... Parker's New York Criminal Reports [*6 vols.*] [*A publication*] (DLA)
Parker Cr Cas... Parker's New York Criminal Reports [*A publication*] (ILCA)
Parker Cr Cas (NY)... Parker's New York Criminal Reports [*A publication*] (ILCA)
Parker Cr R... Parker's New York Criminal Reports [*A publication*] (ILCA)
Parker Cr R (NY)... Parker's New York Criminal Reports [*A publication*] (ILCA)
PARKER PAC... Parker-Hannifin Corporation PAC [*Cleveland, OH*] (PACS)
Parker's Crim R... Parker's New York Criminal Reports [*A publication*] (DLA)
Parker's Crim Rep (NY)... Parker's New York Criminal Reports [*A publication*] (DLA)
Parker's Cr R... Parker's New York Criminal Reports [*A publication*] (DLA)
Park Exch... Parker's English Exchequer Reports [*1743-67*] [*A publication*] (DLA)
Park Hist Ch... Parkes' History of Court of Chancery [*1828*] [*A publication*] (DLA)
ParkHn ...... Parker-Hannifin Corp. [*Associated Press*] (SAG)
Park Ins..... Parker's Insurance [*8 eds.*] [*1787-1842*] [*England*] [*A publication*] (DLA)
ParkMed .... Park Meditech, Inc. [*Associated Press*] (SAG)
ParkNatl .... Park National Corp. [*Associated Press*] (SAG)
Park NH..... Parker's New Hampshire Reports [*A publication*] (DLA)
ParkOh ...... Park Ohio Industries [*Associated Press*] (SAG)
ParkOh ...... Park-Ohio Industries, Inc. [*Associated Press*] (SAG)
ParkPar ..... Parker & Parsley Petroleum [*Associated Press*] (SAG)
Park Pr Ch... Parker's Practice in Chancery [*A publication*] (DLA)
Park Rev Cas... Parker's English Exchequer Reports (Revenue Cases) [*A publication*] (DLA)
Parkrvsn .... Parkervision, Inc. [*Associated Press*] (SAG)
PARKS....... Parks [*Commonly used*] (OPSA)
Parks&Rec... Parks and Recreation (SAUS)
ParkvF....... Parkvale Financial Corp. [*Associated Press*] (SAG)
PARKWAY... Parkway [*Commonly used*] (OPSA)
PARKWAYS... Parkways [*Commonly used*] (OPSA)
PARKWY .... Parkway [*Commonly used*] (OPSA)
Parkwy ...... [*The*] Parkway Co. [*Associated Press*] (SAG)
PARL .... Palo Alto Research Laboratory (SAUS)
PARL .... Parallel
PARL .... Parallel Architecture Research Laboratory [*Clemson University*] (RCD)
PARL .... Park Royal [*NCIC trailer make code*]
Parl.......... Parliament (DIAR)
parl .... Parliament (NTIO)
PARL .... Parliament
PARL .... Parliamentary (SAUS)
PARL .... Parlux Fragrances, Inc. [*NASDAQ symbol*] (NQ)
Par L .... Parsons' Law by Hughes [*A publication*] (DLA)
PARL .... Preferential Arrival Route [*Aviation*] (PIPO)
PARL .... Prince Albert RADAR Laboratory
Parlacen .... Central American Parliament (SAUS)
Parl Agt..... Parliamentary Agent (SAUS)
PARLARS... Particulars
PARLATINO... Latin American Parliament [*Emergency Management*] (EMA)
Par Laws Bus... Parsons' Laws of Business [*A publication*] (DLA)
PARLB....... Parliamentary Borough
Parl Cas .... Parliamentary Cases [*House of Lords Reports*] [*A publication*] (DLA)
Parl Const... Parliamentary Constituency (SAUS)
PARLE....... Parallel Architectures and Languages Europe (SAUS)
Parlex........ Parlex Corp. [*Associated Press*] (SAG)
Parl Hist Eng... Parliamentary History of England [*Pre-1803*] [*A publication*] (DLA)
PARLIGAES... Parliamentary Liaison Group for Alternative Energy Strategies [*British*]
PAR Light... Parabolic Aluminized Reflector Lamp (SAUS)
PARLIKDER... Partiya Litsom k Derevne [*The Party Face to Face with the Countryside*] [*Given name popular in Russia after the Bolshevik Revolution*]

PARLIQ...... Phase Partitioning in Liquids (SAUS)
PARLO....... Parlando [*Music*] (ROG)
parl proc... Parliamentary Procedure [*British*] (WDAA)
Parl Reg.... Parliamentary Register [*England*] [*A publication*] (DLA)
PARLT....... Parliament
PARLTY..... Parliamentary
Parlux....... Parlux Fragrances, Inc. [*Associated Press*] (SAG)
PARLV....... Parsley Latent Virus [*Plant pathology*]
PARLY....... Parliamentary
PARM........ Parallelogram [*Geometry*] (ROG)
parm......... Parameter (ELAL)
PARM........ Parameter [*Computer science*]
PARM........ Parmiter & Sons [*NCIC trailer make code*]
PARM........ Participating Manager
PARM........ Partido Autentico de la Revolucion Mexicana [*Authentic Party of the Mexican Revolution*] [*Political party*] (PPW)
PARM........ Persistent Antiradiation Missile (MCD)
PARM........ Post-Attack Resource Management System (MCD)
PARM........ Precision Anti-Radiation Missile [*Military*] (PDAA)
PARM........ Primary Alignment Reference Mirror (ACAE)
PARM........ Program Analysis for Resource Management
PARMA...... Program for Analysis, Reporting, and Maintenance [*Computer science*]
PARMA...... Public Agency Risk Managers Association [*San Jose, CA*] (EA)
Par Mar Ins... Parsons on Marine Insurance and General Average [*A publication*] (DLA)
Par Mar L... Parsons on Maritime Law [*A publication*] (DLA)
ParMd....... Paradigm Medical Industries, Inc. [*Associated Press*] (SAG)
PARMEDL... Paramedical
Par Merc Law... Parsons on Mercantile Law [*A publication*] (DLA)
PARMIS..... Planning and Resource Management Information System (SAUS)
PARMLIB... Parameter Library (VLIE)
PARMOD.... Progressive Aircraft Rework Modification (SAUS)
ParmTch.... Parametric Technology Corp. [*Associated Press*] (SAG)
PARMV...... Parsnip Mosaic Virus [*Plant pathology*]
PARN........ Pacific & Arctic Railroad & Navigation [*Federal Railroad Administration identification code*]
Par N & B... Parsons' Notes and Bills [*A publication*] (DLA)
Parnassus... Parnassus: Poetry in Review [*A publication*] (BRI)
PARNE....... Parnell, KS [*American Association of Railroads railroad junction routing code*]
PARO........ Pace Arrow [*NCIC truck make code*]
PARO........ Patent Royalties (AAGC)
Paroch...... Parochial (DIAR)
PAROCH..... Parochial (ROG)
Paroch Ant... Kennett's Parochial Antiquities [*A publication*] (DLA)
Parod Epic Gr Rel... Parodorum Epicorum Graecorum Reliquiae [*A publication*] (OCD)
PAROM...... Passive Assistance Range of Motion [*Medicine*] (EDAA)
PAROS...... Passive Ranging on Submarines [*Navy*]
PAROS...... Programmed Automated Replenishment Ordering System (IAA)
PAROSS..... Passive/Active Reporting Ocean Surveillance System [*Navy*] (NVT)
parot......... parotid (SAUS)
PAROX...... Paroxysmal [*Medicine*]
PARP........ Park Trailer Corporation [*NCIC trailer make code*]
PARP........ Partially Acidulated Rock Phosphate (OA)
PARP........ Pre-Engineered AUTOVON Restoral Plan Pacific (SAUS)
PARP........ Procyclic Acidic Repetitive Protein [*Biochemistry*]
PARP........ Production Assistance Report to Pricing [*DoD*]
Par Part..... Parsons on Partnership [*1889*] [*A publication*] (DLA)
ParPet...... Parallel Petroleum Corp. [*Associated Press*] (SAG)
ParPf2....... Partners Preferred Yield II [*Associated Press*] (SAG)
ParPf3....... Partners Perferred Yield III [*Associated Press*] (SAG)
ParPfd....... Partners Preferred Yield [*Associated Press*] (SAG)
PARPRO..... Peacetime Aerial Reconnaissance Program [*Military*] (NVT)
PARPRO..... Peacetime Airborne Reconnaissance Program
PAR Program... Problem Analysis and Response Program (SAUS)
PARQ........ ParcPlace-Digitalk [*NASDAQ symbol*] [*Formerly, ParcPlace Systems*] (SG)
PARQ........ Parcplace Systems, Inc. [*NASDAQ symbol*] (SAG)
PARQ........ Parental Acceptance-Rejection Questionnaire [*Psychology*]
parq......... parquet (SAUS)
PAR-Q........ Physical Activity Readiness Questionnaire
PARR........ Bullet Sports International, Inc. [*NASDAQ symbol*] (SAG)
PARR........ Pakistan Atomic Research Reactor
PARR........ Parker [*NCIC trailer make code*]
Par R........ Parsons' Select Equity Cases [*Pennsylvania*] [*A publication*] (DLA)
PARR........ Performance Analysis Reliability Reporting (DNAB)
PARR........ Post-Accident Radioactivity Removal [*Nuclear energy*] (NRCH)
PARR........ Postanesthesia Recovery Room [*Medicine*] (DAVI)
PARR........ Procurement Authorization and Receiving Report [*NASA*] (KSC)
PARR........ Program Analysis and Resources Review
PARR........ Program Assessment Review Report [*Military*] (GFGA)
PARRAS..... Prototype Army Rapid Reprogramming System (SAUS)
PARRC...... Pacific Aerospace Rescue and Recovery Center [*Air Force*]
Parres plot... Partial Residual Plot
PARREV..... Paraglider Research Vehicle
Par Rights Cit... Parsons on the Rights of a Citizen of the United States [*A publication*] (DLA)
PAR Room.. Postanesthetic Recovery Room (SAUS)
PARROT..... Position Adjustable Radar Range and Orientation Transponder (ACAE)
PARRS...... Postal Analysis Response and Reporting System [*Computer system designed to track mail through the US Postal Service*] [*R. R. Donnelley & Sons Co.*]
PARRS...... Psychological Abstracts Reference Retrieval System [*Syracuse University*]
PARS........ Paging and Radiotelephone Service [*Telecommunications*] (OTD)
PARS........ Parachute Altitude Recognition System (MCD)
pars.......... Paragraphs (SAFN)
PARS........ Parkmaster [*NCIC trailer make code*]
Pars......... Parsons' Select Equity Cases [*1842-51*] [*Pennsylvania*] [*A publication*] (DLA)
PARS........ Passenger Airlines Reservation System
PARS........ Patrol Analysis Recording System [*British*]
PARS........ Pedestrians Association for Road Safety [*British*] (DI)
PARS........ Performance Analysis and Reporting System (VLIE)
PARS........ Performance Analysis Reports System (SAUS)
PARS........ Perimeter Acquisition RADAR [*Characterization*] System (MCD)
PARS........ Pershing Audio Reproduction System (PDAA)
PARS........ Personal Adjustment and Role Skills Scale [*Medicine*] (DMAA)
PARS........ Pharmos Corp. [*NASDAQ symbol*] (SAG)
PARS........ Photoacoustic Raman Spectroscopy
PARS........ Pilotless Aircraft Research Station [*NASA*]
PARS........ Portable Analyzer for Residual Stresses (SAUS)
PARS........ Precision and Accuracy Reporting System [*Environmental Protection Agency*] (GFGA)
PARS........ Primary Attitude Reference Systems (SAUS)
PARS........ Prisoner Aid and Rehabilitation Society (NADA)
PARS........ Private Advanced Radio Service (SAUS)
PARS........ Private Aircraft Reporting System [*FAA*] (PDAA)
PARS........ Procurement Accounting and Reporting System [*Navy*] (NVT)
PARS........ Procurement Action Reporting System (ACAE)
PARS........ Program Analysis and Review System (EDAC)
PARS........ Programmed Airline Reservation System
PARS........ Project Analysis Reporting System (SAUS)
PARS........ Property Accountability Record System (NASA)
PARS........ Provincial Archives and Records Service [*Canada*]
PARSA....... Parasitological Society of Southern Africa (EAIO)
PARSA....... Postgraduate and Research Students' Association [*Australian National University*]
PARSAC..... Particle Size Analog Computer (IAA)
Pars Ans.... Parsons' Answer to the Fifth Part of Coke's Reports [*A publication*] (DLA)
PARSAVAL... Pattern Recognition System Application Evaluation (IAA)
Pars Bills & N... Parsons on Bills and Notes [*A publication*] (DLA)
Pars Cont... Parsons on Contracts [*A publication*] (DLA)
Pars Dec.... Parsons' Decisions [*2-7 Massachusetts*] [*A publication*] (DLA)
parsec....... Parallax Second (SHCU)
PARSEC..... Parallax Second [*Unit of interstellar-space measure*]
PARSEC..... Parallel State Event Condition (VLIE)
PARSEC..... Parliament Secretariat (SAUS)
PARSEC..... Parser and Extensible Compiler [*Programming language*] (CSR)
PARSECS... Program for Astronomical Research and Scientific Experiments Concerning Space
Pars Eq Cas... Parsons' Select Equity Cases [*1842-51*] [*Pennsylvania*] [*A publication*] (DLA)
PARSET..... Precision Askania Range System of Electronic Timing (MUGU)
PARSEV..... Paraglider Research Vehicle [*NASA*] (KSC)
PARS-F...... Programmed Airlines Reservation System-Financial (SAUS)
Par Sh & Adm... Parsons on the Law of Shipping and Admiralty [*A publication*] (DLA)
PARSIM..... Perimeter Acquisition RADAR Simulation [*Missile system evaluation*] (RDA)
PARSIM..... Plant Appropriation Request Simulation (IAA)
PARSIP...... Point Arguello Range Safety Impact Predictor (MUGU)
PARSL....... Parsley, PQ [*American Association of Railroads railroad junction routing code*]
Pars Mar Ins... Parsons on Marine Insurance [*A publication*] (DLA)
Pars Mar Law... Parsons on Maritime Law [*A publication*] (DLA)
Pars Merc Law... Parsons on Mercantile Law [*A publication*] (DLA)
PARSO...... Parsons, KS [*American Association of Railroads railroad junction routing code*]
Parsons'.... Parsons' Select Equity Cases [*Pennsylvania*] [*A publication*] (DLA)
PARSQ...... Pararescue
Pars Sel Eq Cas (PA)... Parsons' Select Equity Cases [*Pennsylvania*] [*A publication*] (DLA)
Pars S Eq Cas... Parsons' Select Equity Cases [*Pennsylvania*] [*A publication*] (DLA)
Pars Shipp & Adm... Parsons on Shipping and Admiralty [*A publication*] (DLA)
PARSYM.... Partial Symmetry
PARSYN.... Parametric Synthesis [*Computer science*]
part.......... palticiple (SAUS)
PART........ Pan American Round Tables in the USA [*Defunct*] (EA)
PART........ Part Allocation Requirements Technic (SAUS)
Part.......... Parterre (SAUS)
PART........ Partial (MSA)
part.......... Partial (VRA)
PART........ Participate (AABC)
Part.......... Participating (EBF)
part.......... Participle (NTIO)
PART........ Participle [*Grammar*]
PART........ Particle (IAA)
PART........ Particular
PART........ Partis [*A Part*] [*Pharmacy*]
part.......... Partition [*Construction term*] (MIST)
PART........ Partition [*Ballistics*]

PART .... Partner (ADA)
PART .... Partnership (SAUS)
PART .... Parts Allocation Requirements Technique
PART .... People Against Racist Terror (EA)
PART .... Performing Arts Repertory Theater
PART .... Pressure Altitude Reporting Transponder (SAUS)
PART .... Production Allocation and Requirements Technique (MHDB)
PART .... Professional Audit Review Team (AAGC)
PARTAC ..... Precision Askania Range Target Acquisition and Control (MUGU)
Part Adj ..... Participle Adjective (SAUS)
PART AEQ... Partes Aequales [*Equal Parts*] [*Pharmacy*]
PART AEQUAL... Partes Aequales [*Equal Parts*] [*Pharmacy*] (ROG)
Part An....... De Partibus Animalium [*of Aristotle*] [*Classical studies*] (OCD)
PARTAN ..... Parallel Tangents (SAUS)
PARTAN/SD... Parallel Tangents and Steepest Descent (SAUS)
PARTAS ..... Precision Asrania Range Target Acquisition and Control
ParTch....... PAR Technology Corp. [*Associated Press*] (SAG)
Part Charact... Particle Characterization (SAUS)
PART DOLENT... Partes Dolentes [*Painful Parts*] [*Pharmacy*]
PARTEI ...... Purchasing Agents of the Radio, Television, and Electronics Industries [*An association*] (IAA)
PARTEQ ..... Partners in Technology at Queens (SAUS)
PARTES ..... Piece-Wise Application of Radiation through the Electromagnetic-Pulse Simulator (PDAA)
Parth .... Parthenius [*First century BC*] [*Classical studies*] (OCD)
Parth .... Parthenogenesis (SAUS)
PARTIAL .... Participation in Architectural Layout (PDAA)
parti bd ..... Particle Board (VRA)
Partic........ Participating [*or Participation*] (DLA)
PARTIC ...... Participial [*Grammar*]
PARTIC ...... Particle
PARTIC ...... Particular
PARTIC EXH... Particulate Exhaust (SAUS)
PARTICO... Parti d'Interets Congolais [*Party for Congolese Interests*] [*Political party*]
PARTIC PHYS... Particle Physics (SAUS)
Partidas..... Moreau-Lislet and Carleton's Laws of Las Siete Partidas in Force in Louisiana [*A publication*] (DLA)
PARTIE ...... People's Alliance to Reform, Transform and Improve Everything (EA)
Partit .... Partitive (SAUS)
PARTN....... Partnership (ADA)
PARTNER ... Proof of Analog Results through a Numerical Equivalent Routine [*Computer science*]
PartnerR .... PartnerRe Ltd. [*Associated Press*] (SAG)
PARTNERS... Partners Task Force for Gay and Lesbian Couples [*Association*] (EA)
PARTNO..... Part Number (SAUS)
Part Or ...... Partitiones Oratoriae [*of Cicero*] [*Classical studies*] (OCD)
Part Part Syst Charact... Particle and Particle Systems Characterization (SAUS)
PARTR....... Particular (ROG)
PARTS....... Parts Analysis and Review Technique for Spares (SAUS)
PARTS....... Parts Assembly and Reuse Tool Set [*Computer software*] [*Digitalk, Inc.*] (PCM)
PARTS....... Parts Automated Repairable Tracking System (SAUS)
PARTS....... Pennsylvania Automotive Recycling Trade Society (EARSL)
PARTS....... Performing Arts Research and Training Studios (EURO)
PARTS....... Precision Approach RADAR Training System (MCD)
PARTS....... Price Analysis and Review Technique for Spares
Part Sci Technol... Particulate Science and Technology (SAUS)
PARTSHIP... Partnership [*Legal shorthand*] (LWAP)
PartsS .... Parts Source, Inc. (The) [*Associated Press*] (SAG)
PART VIC... Partitis Vicibus [*In Divided Parts*] [*Pharmacy*]
Part World... Particle World (SAUS)
PARU........ Parkway Manufacturing Company [*NCIC trailer make code*]
PARU........ Personnel Applied Research Unit [*Canadian military*]
PARU........ Photographic and Reproduction Unit
PARU........ Police Aerial Reinforcement [*or Resupply*] Unit [*Thailand*] (CINC)
PARU........ Postanesthetic Recovery Unit [*Medicine*]
Par Uni...... Party Unity (SAUS)
PARV........ Paravane [*Anti-moored-mine device*] (KSC)
PARV........ Parvus [*Small*] [*Pharmacy*]
PARV3....... Parsnip Virus 3 [*Plant pathology*]
ParVec ...... Purdue Center for Parallel and Vector Computing [*Purdue University*] [*Research center*] (RCD)
Parvnt....... Paravant Computer Systems, Inc. [*Associated Press*] (SAG)
PARVO ...... Professional and Academic Regional Visits Organization (SAUS)
PARVSTRCRA... Paravane and Stores Crane [*Engineering*]
PARW .... Parkwood Homes [*NCIC trailer make code*]
PARW .... Professional Association of Resume Writers (EA)
Par WC...... Parish Will Case [*A publication*] (DLA)
Par Wills... Parsons on Wills [*1854*] [*A publication*] (DLA)
PARX........ Palouse River Railroad [*Federal Railroad Administration identification code*]
PARX........ Parkwood Mobile Homes of Florida [*NCIC trailer make code*]
PARY .... Prairie Trunk Railway [*Federal Railroad Administration identification code*]
PARZ .... Park Industries [*Federal Railroad Administration identification code*]
PAS......... National Postsecondary Agriculture Student Organization (EA)
PAS......... Pakistan Academy of Sciences (SAUS)
PAS......... Palestine Aid Society of America (EA)
PAS......... P-Aminosalicylic Acid (SAUS)
PAS......... Para-Aminosalicylic [*Acid*] [*Organic chemistry*]
PAS......... Parallel Assignment Statement (SAUS)
PAS......... Parametric Amplifier System
PaS......... Paranoia Subtle [*Psychology*]
PAS......... Parent Attitude Scale
PAS......... Paros [*Greece*] [*Airport symbol*] (OAG)
PAS......... Partido de Accion Socialista [*Socialist Action Party*] [*Costa Rica*] [*Political party*] (PPW)
PAS......... Parti Islam se Malaysia [*Islamic Party of Malaysia*] [*Political party*] (PPW)
PAS......... Partition Alternate Sector (SAUS)
PAS......... Partito de Azione de Sardegna [*Sardinian Action Party*] [*Italy*] [*Political party*] (PPW)
PAS......... Pasadena [*California*] [*Seismograph station code, US Geological Survey*] (SEIS)
PA S......... Pascal Second
PAS......... PASCAL source code (SAUS)
PAS......... Pascal Source File [*Computer science*]
PAS......... Paseo [*NCIC car model code*]
PAS......... Passage (AABC)
PAS......... Passat [*NCIC car model code*]
PAS......... Passed to the Adjacent Sector
PAS......... Passing Aid System (IAA)
Pas......... Passipoverus [*Flourished, 13th century*] [*Authority cited in pre-1607 legal work*] (DSA)
pas......... Passive (IDYL)
PAS......... Passive (WDAA)
PAS......... Passive Alcohol Sensor (SAUS)
PAS......... Passport (automobile) [*NCIC car model code*]
PAS......... Patent Applicant Service (NITA)
PAS......... Patient Administration System [*British*]
PAS......... Patient Appointments and Scheduling [*Medicine*] (DMAA)
PAS......... Patients' Aid Society
PAS......... Pattern Analysis System (SAUS)
PAS......... Payload Accommodations Studies [*NASA*] (NASA)
PAS......... Payload Analysis Section (SAUS)
PAS......... Payload Assist Stage (ACAE)
PAS......... Payload Assist System (SAUS)
PAS......... Payload Attach Structure (SAUS)
PAS......... Pelita Air Service PT [*Indonesia*] [*ICAO designator*] (FAAC)
PAS......... Penetration Aids System (ACAE)
PA S......... Pennsylvania Superior Court Reports [*A publication*] (DLA)
PAS......... Pepsiamericas [*Company symbol*]
PAS......... Perceptual Aberration Scale (SAUS)
PAS......... Percussive Arts Society (EA)
PAS......... Performance Abatement Services, Inc. (EFIS)
PAS......... Performance Advisory System (SAUS)
PAS......... Performance Analysis and Systems development (SAUS)
PAS......... Performance Assessment System (ACAE)
PAS......... Perigee-Apogee Satellite [*Aerospace*]
PAS......... Perigee-Apogee Stage [*Aerospace*]
PAS......... Perigee-Apogee System [*Aerospace*]
PAS......... Periodic Acid Schiff (SAUS)
PA/S......... Periodic Acid/Schiff [*A stain*]
PAS......... Peripheral Anterior Synechia [*Ophthalmology*]
PAS......... Persistent Atrial Standstill [*Medicine*] (DMAA)
PAS......... Personal Acquaintance Service
PAS......... Personal Attitude Survey (EDAC)
PAS......... Personnel Accounting Symbol [*Air Force*] (AFM)
PAS......... Personnel Accounting System [*Marine Corps*]
PAS......... Personnel Activity Sequence (AAG)
PAS......... Personnel Administration Section [*Library Administration Division of ALA*]
PAS......... Personnel Assignment Survey (MCD)
PAS......... Phase Address System
PAS......... Phase Array System
PAS......... Philanthropic Advisory Service
PAS......... Phosphatase Acid Serum [*Medicine*] (MELL)
PAS......... Phosphoric Acid-Sensitive
PAS......... Photoabsorption Spectroscopy [*Chemistry*]
PAS......... Photoacoustic Spectrometry [*Also, OAS*]
PAS......... Physician-Assisted Suicide
PAS......... Physicians for Automotive Safety [*Defunct*] (EA)
PAS......... Pierce-Arrow Society (EA)
PAS......... Pilots Advisory Service
PAS......... Pilot's Attack Sight [*British*]
PAS......... Pioneer Aerodynamic Systems
PAS......... Pioneer Air System (SAUS)
PAS......... Pioneer America Society (EA)
PAS......... Planning Advisory Service (GNE)
PAS......... Planning and Scheduling (SAUS)
PAS......... Plant Alarms Sum (ECII)
PAS......... Plasma Arc Spraying (SAUS)
PAS......... Plasma Arc System
PAS......... Plessey Assessment Services (NITA)
PAS......... Pneumatic Actuation System (ACAE)
PAS......... Pneumatic Air Saw
PAS......... Police Aviation Services Ltd (SAUS)
PAS......... Policy Analysis Staff [*Environmental Protection Agency*] (GFGA)
PAS......... Polish Academy of Sciences
PAS......... Polish Astronautical Society [*See also PTA*]
PAS......... Pollution Abatement Seminar (SAUS)
PAS......... Poly(alkyl Sulfone) [*Organic chemistry*]
PAS......... Polyaminosiloxane [*Organic chemistry*]
PAS......... Polyarylsulfone [*Organic chemistry*]
PAS......... Pontifical Academy of Science (SAUS)
PAS......... Positron Annihilation Spectroscopy (MCD)

PAS .... Post Abortion Syndrome
PAS .... Postacoustic Spectroscopy
PAS .... Posterior Airway Space [*Medicine*] (DMAA)
PAS .... Posterior Area of [*Loose*] Skin
PAS .... Postponed Accounting System [*Banking*]
PAS .... Power Apparatus and Systems (MCD)
pas.......... Power-Assisted Steering (ODA)
PAS .... Power-Assisted Steering [*Automotive feature*]
PAS .... Power-Assist System [*Motorcycle steering*]
PAS .... Power Available Shaft (SAUS)
PAS .... Pre-Admission Screening [*Medicine*] (MEDA)
PAS .... Preaward Survey [*To determine a contractor's capability*] [*DoD*]
PAS .... Precategorical Acoustic Storage (DIPS)
PAS .... Precise Acquisition System
PAS .... Precision Acquisition System
PAS .... Preconscious Activity Scale (EDAC)
PAS .... Preferred Argument Structure [*Linguistics*] (IEL)
PAS .... Pregnancy Advisory Service [*British*]
PAS .... Premature Atrial Stimulus [*Medicine*] (DMAA)
PAS .... Premorbid Adjustment Scale (SAUS)
PAS .... Presidential Appointee Subject
PAS .... President's Advisor for Science
PAS .... Pressure Alarm Switch (SAUS)
PAS .... Pressure-Assisted Sintering [*Forging*] [*Automotive engineering*]
PAS .... Pressurized Air Subsystem
PAS .... Price Analysis Sheet
PAS .... Primary Alerting System
PAS .... Primary Ascent System [*Aerospace*] (NASA)
PAS .... Princeton Aqua Science, New Brunswick (SAUS)
PAS .... Principal Assistant Secretary
PAS .... Prisoners' Advice Service (WDAA)
PAS .... Prisoners' Aid Society [*Australia*]
PAS .... Privacy Act Statement (NRCH)
PAS .... Probation and Aftercare Service (SAUS)
PAS .... Problem Appraisal Scales [*Personality development test*] [*Psychology*]
PAS .... Problem Assessment System (SAUS)
PAS .... Process Analysis Services (SAUS)
PAS .... Process Automation System (SAUS)
PAS .... Processed Array Signal
PAS .... Procurement Action System (MCD)
PAS .... Procurement Appropriation, Secondary (MCD)
PAS .... Product Acceptance Standard [*Automotive engineering*]
PAS .... Product Acceptance Test Specification (SAUS)
PAS .... Product Assurance Survey
PAS .... Product Availability Search (MCD)
PAS .... Professional Activity Study [*Later, CPHA*]
PAS .... Professional Advancement Series [*National Court Reporters Association*]
PAS .... Professor of Aerospace Studies [*Air Force*] (AFIT)
PAS .... Professor of Air Science [*Air Force*]
PAS .... Program Activity Structure
PAS .... Program Address Storage (IEEE)
PAS .... Program Allowance Schedule
PAS .... Program Alternative Simulation (IAA)
PAS .... Programmable Audio Synthesiser (SAUS)
PAS .... Program of Advanced Studies
PAS .... Progressive Accumulated Stress [*Psychiatry*]
PAS .... Propellant Acquisition System (ISAK)
PAS .... Propulsion and Auxiliary Systems Department [*David W. Taylor Naval Ship Research and Development Center*]
PAS .... Protocol Analysis System (ABAC)
PAS .... Pseudo Aircraft Simulation (CTAS)
PAS .... Psychiatric Assessment Scale (SAUS)
PAS .... Psychopathological Assessment Scale (DB)
PAS .... Public Address System
PAS .... Public Administration Service (EA)
PAS .... Public Affairs Specialist
PAS .... Public Announcement Service (SAUS)
PAS .... Public Automobile System (SAUS)
PAS .... Publicly Available Specification (RALS)
PAS .... Publishers Association of the South (EARSL)
PAS .... Pulmonary Artery Stenosis [*Medicine*]
PAS .... Pulmonary Artery Systolic Pressure [*Medicine*] (RAWO)
PAS .... Pulmonary Aspiration Syndrome [*Medicine*] (MELL)
PAS .... Pulsating Air System [*Automotive engineering*]
PAS .... Pulse Analysis System (SAUS)
PAS .... Pulsed Air Solenoid [*Automotive engineering*]
PAS .... Pump Actuator Set
PAS .... Pyrotechnics Arming Switch
Pas .... Terminus Paschae [*Easter Term*] [*Latin*] [*Legal term*] (DLA)
PASA .... Pacific American Steamship Association [*Later, AIMS*]
PASA .... Para-Aminosalicylic Acid [*Organic chemistry*]
PASA .... Participating Agency Service Agreement (GNE)
PASA .... PCR [*Polymerase Chain Reaction*] Amplification of Specific Alleles [*Genetics*]
PASA .... Pennsylvania Association of School and Administrators (SAUS)
PASA .... Personnel Administrative Services Agency [*Army*]
PASA .... Pioneers' Association of South Australia
PASA .... Pipelines Authority of South Australia
PASA .... Playgroup Association of South Australia
PASA .... Police Association of South Australia
PASA .... Polymerase Chain Reaction Amplification of specific alleles (SAUS)
PASA .... Primary Acquired Sideroblastic Anemia [*Medicine*]
PASA .... Proximal Articular Set Angle [*Orthopedics*] (DAVI)
PASA .... Quepass.com, Inc. [*NASDAQ symbol*]
PAS&T....... Particle Accelerator Science and Technology (SAUS)
PASAR....... Philippine Associated Smelting and Refining (SAUS)
PASAR....... Psychological Abstracts Search and Retrieval
PASARR..... Preadmission Screening and Annual Resident Review [*Medicare*]
PASARS..... Podded Advanced Synthetic Aperture Radar System (SAUS)
PASARU..... All Wales Purchasing and Supply Applied Research Unit [*University of Glamorgan*] [*United Kingdom*] (RCD)
PASAT .... Paced Auditory Serial Addition Task [*Medicine*] (EDAA)
PASAT .... Particle Accelerator Science and Technology (IAA)
PASAT .... Poppleton-Allen Sales Aptitude Test
PASB .... Pan American Sanitary Bureau
PASB .... Perpetual Savings Bank FSB (MHDW)
PASb......... Predneaziatskii Sbornik Voprosy Khattologii i Khurritologii [*A publication*] (BJA)
PASB .... Proceedings of the Anthropological Society of Bombay (SAUS)
PASB .... Proceedings of the Asiatic Society of Bengal (SAUS)
P-as-B...... Program as Broadcast [*Radio*] (DEN)
PASB .... Public Authorities Superannuation Board [*New South Wales, Australia*]
PASBA....... Procurement and Supply Chain Benchmarking Association (EA)
PASBI....... Palo Alto Social Background Inventory [*Psychology*]
PASBO....... Pennsylvania Association of School Business Officials (SAUS)
PASC .... Deadhorse [*Alaska*] [*ICAO location identifier*] (ICLI)
PASC .... Pacific Air Service Command (SAUS)
PASC .... Pacific Area Standards Congress [*American National Standards Institute*]
PASC .... Palestine Armed Struggle Command (PD)
PASC .... Panama Area Service Command (SAUS)
PASC .... Pan American Sanitary Conference
PASC .... Pan-American Standardization Conference (SAUS)
PASC .... Pan American Standards Commission [*See also COPANT*] (EAIO)
PASC .... Pan American Standards Committee
PAS-C .... Para-Aminosalicylic Acid Crystallized with Ascorbic Acid [*Organic chemistry*] (MAE)
Pasc .... Paschal [*Easter Term*] [*Legal term*] (DLA)
Pasc .... Paschal's Reports [*25, 28-31 Texas*] [*A publication*] (DLA)
PASC .... Petroleum Accounting Society of Canada (AG)
PASC .... Planning Advisory Subcommittee (SAUS)
PASC .... Polar Air and Snow Chemistry Programme (SAUS)
PASC .... Polar Atmospheric and Snow Chemistry (CARB)
PASC .... Portable Application Standards Committee (SAUS)
PASC .... Port Authority of Shelby County [*Federal Railroad Administration identification code*]
PASC .... Precision Adaptive Sub-Band Coding [*Electronics*]
PASC .... Primitive Art Society of Chicago (EA)
PASCA....... Pascagoula, MS [*American Association of Railroads railroad junction routing code*]
PASCA....... Positron Annihilation Spectroscopy for Chemical Analysis
PASCAL ..... Philips Automatic Sequence Calculator
PASCAL ..... Program Applique a la Selection et a la Compilation Automatique de la Litterature [*Centre National de la Recherche Scientifique-Informascience*] [*Bibliographic database*]
PASCALS ... Projected Antisubmarine Classification and Location System (DNAB)
PASCH....... Pascha [*Easter*] [*Church calendars*] (ROG)
Pasch........ Paschal [*Easter Term*] [*Legal term*] (DLA)
Paschal ..... Paschal's Reports [*28-31 Texas*] [*Supplement to Vol. 25*] [*A publication*] (DLA)
Paschal's Ann Const... Paschal's United States Constitution, Annotated [*A publication*] (DLA)
Pasch Dig... Paschal's Texas Digest of Decisions [*A publication*] (DLA)
PASCO....... Pan American Sulfur Corp. (SAUS)
PASCO....... Professional Asbestos Services Corp. (EFIS)
PASCOSS... Passive and Active Control of Space Structures
PASCT....... Pan American Society for Chemotherapy of Tuberculosis [*See also SAQT*] [*Buenos Aires, Argentina*] (EAIO)
PASD .... After Diastase Digestion [*Biochemistry*] (DAVI)
p'ase .... Alkaline Phosphatase [*Biochemistry*] (DAVI)
PASE......... Passive Start and Entry [*Automotive engineering*]
PASE......... Passive Start and Entry System
PASE......... Polar Air-Snow Experiment (CARB)
PASE......... Post-Apollo Space Electrophoresis [*European Space Agency*]
PASE......... Power-Assisted Storage Equipment (IEEE)
PASE......... Product Acceptance Exceptions
PASE......... Programs in the Arts for Special Education Project (EDAC)
PaSEA....... Pennsylvania Society of Enrolled Agents (SAUS)
PASEAFRON... Panama Sea Frontier [*Nautical term*] (NTA)
PASECT ..... Panama Sector (SAUS)
PASEM ..... Program of Assistance to Solar Equipment Manufacturers (SAUS)
PASEM System... Partial Analysis by Scanning Electron Microscopy System (SAUS)
PASEP....... Passed Separately [*Military*]
PASEP....... Pass Separately
PASES....... Performance Assessment of Syntax: Elicited and Spontaneous [*Educational test*]
Pas Ex....... Passive Exercise [*Physical Therapy*] (DAVI)
PASEX....... Polar Atmosphere Snow Experiment (SAUS)
PASF......... Photographic Art and Science Foundation (EA)
PASFIS ...... Philippines Aquatic Sciences and Fisheries Information System [*Marine science*] (OSRA)
PASG .... Patent Abstracts Section, Official Gazette [*Federal government*] [*A publication*]
PASG .... Pneumatic Antishock Garment [*Roentgenology*]
PASG .... Programs Activities and Services Guide (SAUS)

PASG .... Pulse Amplifier/Symbol Generator
PASG .... Pulse Analyzer Signal Generator
PASGAP ..... Pacific Sea Grant Advisory Program (SAUS)
PASGT .... Personnel Armor System for Ground Troops (RDA)
PASGX .... Phoenix-Engemann Growth Cl.A [*Mutual fund ticker symbol*] (SG)
PASH .... Palaeoclimates of the Southern Hemisphere (SAUS)
PASH .... Periodic Acid-Schiff Hematoxylin [*Medicine*] (EDAA)
PASH .... Polynuclear Aromatic Sulphur Heterocyclic (ODA)
PASH .... Pseudoangiomatous Stromal Hyperplasia [*Medicine*] (RAWO)
PASI .... Pacific Silver Corp. [*NASDAQ symbol*] (COMM)
PASI .... Pikunas Adult Stress Inventory [*Psychology*]
PA/SI .... Preliminary Assessment and Site Inspection [*Environmental Protection Agency*] (FFDE)
PA/SI .... Preliminary Assessment/Site Investigation (SAUS)
PASI .... Professional Associate, Chartered Surveyors' Institution [*Later, ARICS*]
PASI .... Psoriasis Area and Severity Index [*Medicine*]
PASI .... Sitka [*Alaska*] [*ICAO location identifier*] (ICLI)
PASIC........ Percussive Arts Society International Convention [*Percussive Arts Society*]
PasifSat..... Pasifik Satelit Nusantara (PT) [*Associated Press*] (SAG)
pasim .... paimological (SAUS)
Pasim .... Pasimologist (SAUS)
PASIM .... Pasimology (SAUS)
PASIN .... Particle-Matter Airborne Sampling Inlet Experiment (SAUS)
PAS-INAH ... Para-Aminosalicylic Acid and Isonicotinic Acid Hydrazide (BARN)
PASIPS...... Parallel Signal and Image Processing System (SAUS)
PASITAM ... Program of Advanced Studies of Institution Building and Technical Assistance Methodologies [*MUCIA*]
PASJ......... Publications of the Astronomical Society of Japan (SAUS)
PASJC .... Passaic Junction, NJ [*American Association of Railroads railroad junction routing code*]
PASL......... Physical Activity Sciences Laboratory (SAUS)
PASL......... Polish Americans for the Statue of Liberty [*Defunct*] (EA)
PASLA....... Programmable Asynchronous Line Adapter
PASLIB ...... Pakistan Association of Special Libraries (NITA)
Pas Lux ..... Pasicrisie Luxembourgeoise [*Luxembourg Law Reports*] [*A publication*] (ILCA)
PASM........ Partitionable SIMD/MIMD [*Single Instruction, Multiple Data/Multiple Instruction, Multiple Data*] (MCD)
PASM........ Periodic Acid - Silver Methenamine [*Biological stain*]
PA-SM........ Periodic Acid-Silver Methenamine (SAUS)
PASM........ Preaward Survey Monitor [*DoD*]
PASMA ...... Prefabricated Aluminium Scaffold Manufacturers Association [*British*] (DBA)
PASN .... St. Paul Island [*Alaska*] [*ICAO location identifier*] (ICLI)
PASNAP-PAC... Pennsylvania Association of Staff Nurses and Allied Professionals [*Conshohocken, PA*] (PACS)
PASO .... Pan Africanist Students Organization (SAUS)
PASO .... Pan American Sanitary Organization
PASO .... Pan American Sports Organization [*See also ODEPA*] [*Mexico City, Mexico*] (EAIO)
PA/SO .... Port Antisubmarine Officer [*Navy*]
PASO .... Principal Armament Supply Officer [*British military*] (DMA)
PASOC....... Partido de Accion Socialista [*Party of Socialist Action*] [*Spain*] [*Political party*] (PPW)
PASOCO..... Parti Socialiste des Comores [*Socialist Party of Comoros*] [*Political party*] (EY)
PASOH ...... Partido de Accion Socialista de Honduras [*Political party*] (EY)
PASOH ...... Partido Socialista de Honduras [*Honduran Socialist Party*] [*Political party*]
PASOK....... Panellinion Sosialistikon Kinema [*Pan-Hellenic Socialist Movement*] [*Greek*] [*Political party*] (PPE)
PASOK....... Pan-Hellenic Socialist Commune (SAUS)
PASOLS ..... Pacific Area Senior Officer Logistics Seminar (MCD)
PASOS....... Paperless Shop-Order System (SAUS)
PASP .... Pancreas-Specific Protein [*Medicine*] (DMAA)
PASP .... Port Autonome de San Pedro [*The Ivory Coast*] (EY)
PA/SP........ Positioner Antenna and Solar Panel [*NASA*]
PASP .... Price Adjusting Sampling Plan (PDAA)
PASP .... Program in Aegean Scripts and Prehistory (SAUS)
PASP .... Publications of the Astronomical Society of the Pacific (SAUS)
PASP .... Pulmonary Artery Systolic Pressure [*Medicine*] (DMAA)
PASPAC ..... El Paso Corporation PAC [*Washington, DC*] (PACS)
PAS(PR)..... Principal Assistant Secretary (Priority)
PAS procedure... Periodic Acid Schiff Procedure (DOG)
P-as-R........ Program as Recorded [*Radio*] (DEN)
PASR .... Project Authorization Status Report (SAUS)
PASRB....... Preaward Survey Review Board [*DoD*]
PAS Reaction... Periodic Acid Schiff Reaction (SAUS)
PASS .... Panic Attack Sufferers' Support Groups (EA)
PASS .... Parameterization of Subgrid Scale (SAUS)
PASS .... Parents Against Secondhand Smoke (SAUS)
PASS .... Parents Against Subliminal Seduction [*Defunct*] (EA)
PASS .... Parked Aircraft Security System (PDAA)
PASS .... Partnership for Achieving Successful Schools
PASS .... Parts Analysis Summary Sheet
PASS .... Pass [*Postal Service standard*] (OPSA)
Pass......... Passage (DD)
PASS .... Passage [*Maps and charts*] (KSC)
PASS .... Passenger (KSC)
PASS .... Passenger Automated Selection System (ADA)
PASS .... Passim [*Everywhere*] [*Latin*]
PASS .... Passitive (SAUS)
PASS .... Passivate [*Metallurgy*] (IAA)
PASS .... Passivated (SAUS)
pass......... Passive (NTIO)
PASS .... Passive
PASS .... Passive Acquisiton Surveillance System (SAUS)
PASS .... Passive-Active Surveillance System (MCD)
PASS .... Passive Aircraft Surveillance System
PASS .... Passive & Active Sensor Subsystem (SAUS)
Pass......... Passover (BARN)
PASS .... Passport (SAUS)
PASS .... Passport [*NCIC car make code*]
PASS .... Patrol Advanced Surveillance System (MCD)
PASS .... Pay/Personnel Administrative Support System (NVT)
PASS .... Penetration Aids/Strike System (NG)
PASS .... Performance Analysis Software System (SAUS)
PASS .... Performance Analysis Subsystem [*Military*] (CAAL)
PASS .... Performance Assessment Scientific Support (ABAC)
PASS .... Personal Access Satellite System [*NASA*] (CIST)
PASS .... Personalized Automotive Security System [*In product name, PASS-Key*] [*Delco Electronics*] [*Automotive engineering*]
PASS .... Personnel Accounting & Skills System (SAUS)
PASS .... Petroleum Abstracts Search Service [*Online information service*]
PASS .... Petroleum Abstracts Search System (SAUS)
PASS .... Phased Array Sector Scanner [*Instrument for measuring ultrasound*] [*Trademark of General Electric Co.*]
PASS .... Phoenix Ability Survey System [*Test*]
PASS .... Photo-Access Security System (SAUS)
PASS .... Photogrammetric Archival Storage System (SAUS)
PASS .... Pilot Aerial Survival System (PDAA)
PASS .... Pirelli Active Safety System
PASS .... Planning and Scheduling Session
PASS .... Planning and Scheduling System (NASA)
PASS .... Planning and Specification Software (SAUS)
PASS .... Policyowner Attitude Survey Service [*LIMRA*]
PASS .... Polish Assembler (SAUS)
PASS .... Polymeric Aluminum Silicate Sulfate [*Inorganic chemistry*]
PASS .... Pooled Analytical Stereoplotter System (PDAA)
PASS .... Portable Analysis/Synthesis System (TIMI)
PASS .... Portable Analyze/Synthesize System (SAUS)
PASS .... Portable Assisted Study Sequence Program [*California*] (EDAC)
PASS .... Position and Surveyance System (SAUS)
PASS .... Positioning and Surveying System (MCD)
PASS .... Post-Accident Sampling Systems [*Nuclear energy*]
PASS .... Precision Angulation and Support System (SAUS)
PASS .... Precision Autocollimating Solar Sensor
PASS .... Prenotification Analysis Support System (SAUS)
PASS .... Pressurized Air Starter System (MCD)
PASS .... Price Adjusted Single Sampling (PDAA)
PASS .... Primary Academic Sentiment Scale [*Child development test*]
PASS .... Primary Avionics Software System (NASA)
PASS .... Prince Albert Satellite Station (SAUS)
PASS .... Priority Academic Student Skills
PASS .... Private Alarm Signalling System
PASS .... Private Automatic Switching System [*Telecommunications*]
PASS .... Procurement Aging and Staging System [*Army*] (AABC)
PASS .... Procurement and Acquisition Support System (SAUS)
PASS .... Procurement Automated Source System [*Small Business Administration*] [*Washington, DC*] [*Information service or system*] (IID)
PASS .... Production Automated Scheduling System (IEEE)
PASS .... Professional Accounting System for Schools (AIE)
PASS .... Professional Airways Systems Specialists (EA)
PASS .... Professional Airways Systems Specialists Division [*An association*] (EA)
PASS .... Professional Amateur Sports Systems [*Cable-television network*]
PASS .... Professional Association for SQL Server (EA)
PASS .... Professional Association of Secretarial Services [*Later, NASS*] (EA)
PASS .... Program Aid Software Systems [*Computer science*] (IEEE)
PASS .... Program Alternative Simulation System (KSC)
PASS .... Program Analysis of Service Systems [*Procedure to evaluate human service programs*]
PASS .... Programmed Access/Security System [*Card Key Systems*]
PASS .... Programming Aid Software System (SAUS)
PASS .... Project Activating Signal System (SAUS)
PASS .... Prototype Artillery Sub-System (SAUS)
PASS .... Purchasing Activities Support System (SAUS)
PASS .... Pure Acoustic Sounder (SAUS)
PASSA....... Pacific American Steamship Association [*Later, AIMS*] (EA)
PASSAGE... Passage [*Commonly used*] (OPSA)
PASSAT ..... PASCAL Subset for Application in Test Computers (NITA)
PASSCAL... Program for Array Seismic Studies of the Continental Lithosphere (SAUS)
PASSEX ..... Passing Exercise (DOMA)
PASSIM ..... President's Advisory Staff on Scientific Information Management
PASS-IN-REVIEW... Priority Aircraft Subsystem Suitability Intensive Review (MCD)
PASSION... Program for Algebraic Sequences Specifically of Input-Output Nature [*Computer science*]
PASSMAN... Pay/Personnel Administrative Support System Manual (DNAB)
PAssn........ Postassistentin (SAUS)
PASSP....... Pennsylvania Association of Secondary School Principals (SAUS)
PASSR....... Passenger (DCTA)
Pass Tr...... Passenger Train (SAUS)
PASSWD.... Password [*Computer science*]
PAST......... Pacific/Asian Strategy for Tomorrow (SAUS)
PAST......... Pasteurella [*Genus of bacteria*]

PAST......... Pastillus [*A Lozenge, Troch, Pastil*] [*Pharmacy*] (ROG)
PAST......... Pastime Manufacturing Company [*NCIC trailer make code*]
Past......... Pastoral Epistles (BJA)
PAST......... Pastorate
PA St........ Pennsylvania State Reports [*A publication*] (DLA)
PAST......... Periodic Acid-Schiff Technique [*Medicine*] (DMAA)
PAST......... Portable Arming System Trainer (MCD)
PAST......... Process Accessible Segment Table
PAST......... Professor of Air Science and Tactics
PAST......... Propulsion and Associated Systems Test (MCD)
PASTA....... Polarity-Altered Spectral-Selective Acquisition (RAWO)
PA Stat Ann... Pennsylvania Statutes, Annotated [*A publication*] (DLA)
PA Stat Ann (Purdon)... Pennsylvania Statutes, Annotated (Purdon) [*A publication*] (DLA)
PA State.... Pennsylvania State Reports [*A publication*] (DLA)
PA State R... Pennsylvania State Reports [*A publication*] (DLA)
PASTIC...... Pakistan Scientific and Technological Information Center [*Formerly, PANSDOC*] [*Quaid-I-Azan University Campus*] [*Islamabad, Pakistan*]
PAstO........ Our Lady of Angels College, Aston, PA [*Library symbol*] [*Library of Congress*] (LCLS)
PA St R..... Pennsylvania State Reports [*A publication*] (DLA)
PASTRAM... Passenger Traffic Management System (SAUS)
PASTRAM... Passenger Traffic Management System [*Army*]
PASTRAM System... Passenger Traffic Management System (SAUS)
PA St Tr..... Pennsylvania State Trials (Hogan) [*A publication*] (DLA)
PASU........ Anagra Sentana Gas Indonesia [*Intermodal shipping container symbol*] (TVRC)
PASU........ Pan-African Socialist Union [*Southern Rhodesia*]
PASU........ Patrol Aircraft Service Unit
PASU........ Performing Arts Study Unit (EA)
PASU........ Polyarylsulfone [*Organic chemistry*]
PASU........ Preliminary Approval for Service Use [*Military*]
PASU........ Provisional Approval for Service Use [*Navy*] (NVT)
PA Summary... Summary of Pennsylvania Jurisprudence [*A publication*] (DLA)
PA Super.... Pennsylvania Superior Court Reports [*A publication*] (DLA)
PA Super Ct... Pennsylvania Superior Court Reports [*A publication*] (DLA)
PA Superior Ct... Pennsylvania Superior Court Reports [*A publication*] (DLA)
PASUS....... Pan American Society of the United States (EA)
PASV........ Pangola Stunt Virus [*Plant pathology*]
PASV........ Sparrevohn Air Force Station [*Alaska*] [*ICAO location identifier*] (ICLI)
PASVR....... Pulmonary Anomalous Superior Venous Return [*Medicine*] (EDAA)
PASW........ Personal Assistance Service Worker [*Medicine*] (DMAA)
PASW........ Pure Atria [*NASDAQ symbol*] [*Formerly, Pure Software*] (SG)
PASW........ Pure Atria Corp. [*NASDAQ symbol*] (SAG)
PASWEPS... Passive Antisubmarine Warfare Environmental Protection System [*Navy*] (NATG)
PASX........ Passumpsic Railroad [*Federal Railroad Administration identification code*]
PASY........ Shemya Air Force Base [*Alaska*] [*ICAO location identifier*] (ICLI)
PAt.......... Allentown Public Library, Allentown, PA [*Library symbol*] [*Library of Congress*] (LCLS)
Pat.......... All India Reporter, Patna Series [*A publication*] (ILCA)
PAT.......... Athenaeum of Philadelphia (EA)
PAT.......... Athenaeum of Philadelphia, Philadelphia, PA [*OCLC symbol*] (OCLC)
Pat.......... Indian Law Reports, Patna Series [*A publication*] (DLA)
Pat.......... Indian Rulings, Patna Series [*A publication*] (DLA)
PAT.......... International Brotherhood of Painters and Allied Trades
PAT.......... International Union of Painters & Allied Trades Political Action Together Political Committee [*Washington, DC*] (PACS)
PAT.......... National Patents Appeal Tribunal [*England*] (DLA)
PAT.......... Pacific Air Transport (SAUS)
PAT.......... Pacific Automobile Train (SAUS)
PAT.......... Packed Tower Aeration (EEVL)
PAT.......... Pain Apperception Test [*Medicine*] (EDAA)
PAT.......... Palleted Automated Transport (PDAA)
PAT.......... Parametric Artificial Talker
PaT.......... Parents as Teachers (SAUS)
PAT.......... Paroxysmal Atrial [*or Auricular*] Tachycardia [*Medicine*]
PAT.......... Parts Accountability Technique (MCD)
PAT.......... Passive Acoustic Target [*Military*]
PAT.......... Passive Acoustic Torpedo [*Military*]
PAT.......... Passive Acting Tracking (SAUS)
PAT.......... Passive Angle Attack
PAT.......... Passive Angle Track (NVT)
pa t.......... Past Tense [*Grammar*] (BARN)
PAT.......... Patch (SAUS)
PAT.......... Patelet Aggregation Test (SAUS)
pat.......... Patella (STED)
Pat.......... Patent (AAGC)
pat.......... Patent (STED)
PAT.......... Patent (KSC)
PAT.......... Patent Rolls [*British*]
Pat.......... Paternal (SAUS)
pat.......... Paternal Origin [*Medicine*] (DMAA)
PAT.......... Paterson [*Diocesan abbreviation*] [*New Jersey*] (TOCD)
PAT.......... Patersons [*Publisher*]
Pat.......... Paterson's Scotch Appeals, House of Lords [*A publication*] (DLA)
Pat.......... Pathe [*Record label*] [*France*]
pat.......... Patient [*Medicine*] (BCRP)
PAT.......... Patient
pat.......... Patient [*Linguistics*] (IEL)
pat.......... Patina (VRA)
PAT.......... Patio
PAT.......... Patna [*India*] [*Airport symbol*] (OAG)
Pat.......... Paton's Scotch Appeal Cases, House of Lords [*A publication*] (DLA)
PAT.......... Patras [*Greece*] [*Seismograph station code, US Geological Survey*] (SEIS)
PAT.......... Patriarch [*Greek Church*] (ROG)
PAT.......... Patrician [*NCIC car model code*]
PAT.......... Patrick Air Force Base [*Florida*] (KSC)
PAT.......... Patrol
PAT.......... Patten Corp. [*NYSE symbol*] (SPSG)
Pat.......... Pattern (MIST)
PAT.......... Pattern
PAT.......... Pattern Analysis Test [*Army*]
PAT.......... Peninsulator Air Transport (SAUS)
PAT.......... People's Action Team [*South Vietnam*]
PAT.......... Performance Acceptance Test (SAA)
PAT.......... Performance Alignment Tester (SAUS)
PAT.......... Performance Appraisal Team [*Nuclear energy*] (NRCH)
PAT.......... Performance Assessment Team (SAUS)
PAT.......... Peripheral Allocation Table (NITA)
PAT.......... Peripheral Assignment Table (CMD)
PAT.......... Permit Assistance Team [*Environmental Protection Agency*] (GFGA)
PAT.......... Person Activity Tracker (VLIE)
PAT.......... Personalized Array Translator (IEEE)
PAT.......... Personnel Assistance Team [*Military*]
PAT.......... Personnel Authorization Table [*Air Force*]
PAT.......... Pesticide Applicator Training [*Environmental Protection Agency*] (AEPA)
PAT.......... Pets as Therapy (WDAA)
PAT.......... Phenylaminotetrazole [*Psychology*]
PAT.......... Phenylazotriphenylmethane (SAUS)
PAT.......... Philippine Aerial Taxi (SAUS)
PAT.......... Phosphinothricin Acetyl Transferase [*An enzyme*]
PAT.......... Photo Articulation Test
PAT.......... Physical Abilities Test [*Medicine*] (EDAA)
PAT.......... Physics Achievement Test
PAT.......... Picric Acid Turbidity Test
PAT.......... Picture Arrangement Test
PAT.......... Planar Assembly and Test System (VLIE)
PAT.......... Plasma Arc Tunnel
PAT.......... Plastic Apply Template (MCD)
PAT.......... Platelet Aggregation Test [*Medicine*] (MELL)
PAT.......... Platoon Anti-Tank (SAA)
PAT.......... Plenum Air Tread [*Army amphibian vehicle*]
PAT.......... Plutonium Air Transportable [*Nuclear energy*] (NRCH)
PAT.......... Point after Touchdown [*Football*]
PAT.......... Point-After Try (SAUS)
PAT.......... Polar Adjectives Test (AEBS)
PAT.......... Polar Auxin Transport [*Botany*]
PAT.......... Polaris Acceleration Test [*Military*] (SAA)
PAT.......... Police Association of Tasmania [*Australia*]
PAT.......... Political Action Teams
PAT.......... Polyamine Acetyltransferase (DB)
PAT.......... Polyaminotriazole [*Organic chemistry*]
PAT.......... Polyarlterephthalate [*Organic chemistry*]
PAT.......... Population, Affluence and Technology (SAUS)
PAT.......... Portable Audio Terminal (VLIE)
PAT.......... Port Address Translation [*Computer science*] (VLIE)
PAT.......... Port and Address Translation (SAUS)
PAT.......... Port Authority Transit (SAUS)
PAT.......... Position Adjusting Type
PAT.......... Postavailability Trials
PAT.......... Power Alarm Test (SAUS)
PAT.......... Power Ascension Testing (IEEE)
PAT.......... Power-Assisted Traverse (SAUS)
PAT.......... Practical, Available Technology (SAUS)
PAT.......... Preadmission Screening and Assessment Team [*Medicine*] (DB)
PAT.......... Preadmission Testing
PAT.......... Prearranged Transfers
PAT.......... Pre-Authorized Transfer (SAUS)
PAT.......... Precision Aim Technique [*for helicopters*] [*Army*] (RDA)
PAT.......... Prediction Analysis Techniques
PAT.......... Predictive Ability Test [*Medicine*] (EDAA)
PAT.......... Pregnancy at Term [*Gynecology*]
PAT.......... Preliminary Acceptance Tests
PAT.......... Preliminary Acceptance Trials [*Navy*]
PAT.......... Prescription Athletic Turf [*Trademark for an artificial turf*]
PAT.......... Pressure Assembled Thyristor
PAT.......... Printer Action Table [*Computer science*] (HGAA)
PAT.......... Prioirty Access Timer [*Telecommunications*] (OSI)
PAT.......... Priority Air Transport [*Army*] (FAAC)
PAT.......... Priority Air Travel [*Army*]
PAT.......... Prism Adaptation Test [*Ophthalmology*]
PAT.......... Problem Action Team [*NASA*] (NASA)
PAT.......... Procedure for Automatic Testing (IAA)
PAT.......... Procedures Authorized Task (MCD)
PAT.......... Process Action Team [*Army*] (RDA)
PAT.......... Process-Activation Table [*Computer science*]
PAT.......... Process Analysis Team
PAT.......... Product Acceptance Test [*Advertising*] (DOAD)
PAT.......... Product Adaption Tool (VLIE)
PAT.......... Production Acceptance Test [*NASA*] (KSC)
PAT.......... Production Acceptance Testing (SAUS)
PAT.......... Production Assessment (SAUS)
PAT.......... Production Assessment Test

PAT .... Professional, Administrative, and Technical (OICC)
PAT .... Professional Association of Teachers [*British*]
PAT .... Proficiency Analytical Testing [*National Institute on Occupational Safety and Health*]
PAT .... Profit After Tax (SAUS)
PAT .... Profit After Taxes
PAT .... Program Activity Transmission
PAT .... Program Analysis Table (VLIE)
PAT .... Program Analysis Team (KSC)
PAT .... Program Analyzer Tool (VLIE)
PAT .... Program Attitude Test (IEEE)
PAT .... Programmable Actuator-Transducer [*Automotive engineering*]
PAT .... Programmable Automatic Tester (SAUS)
PAT .... Programmed Activity Transmission (MCD)
PAT .... Programmer Aptitude Test
PAT .... Progressive Achievement Test of Listening Comprehension (TMMY)
PAT .... Project Action Team [*Acquisition Reform*] (AAGC)
PAT .... Property and Accounting Technician [*Navy*]
PAT .... Proportional to Absolute Temperature (IAA)
PAT .... Prototype Adaptation Toolkit (CTAS)
PAT .... Pseudoadder Tree [*Computer science*]
PAT .... Psychoacoustic Testing
PAT .... PSYOP [*Psychological Operation*] Automated Terminal (RDA)
PAT .... Public Access Terminal (SAUS)
PAT .... Public Administration Times [*A publication*] (EAAP)
PAT .... Public Affairs Team (COE)
PAT .... Pulsed Amplifier Tube
PAT .... Pump Algebra Tutor [*Computer program*]
PaT .... Purge-and-Trap [*Technique*] [*Environmental Protection Agency*]
PAtA .... Air Products & Chemicals, Inc., Allentown, PA [*Library symbol*] [*Library of Congress*] (LCLS)
PATA .... Pacific American Tankship Association [*Defunct*] (EA)
PATA .... Pacific Area Travel Association [*San Francisco, CA*]
PATA .... Pacific Asia Travel Association (EA)
PATA .... Patagonia [*Region of South America*] (ROG)
PATA .... Pensions Appeal Tribunals Act (SAUS)
PATA .... Plenum Air Tread, Amphibious [*Army vehicle*]
PATA .... Pneumatic All-Terrain Amphibian (IEEE)
PATA .... Professional Aeromedical Transport Association (EA)
PATA .... Proprietary Articles Trade Association [*British*] (BI)
PATA .... Tanana [*Alaska*] [*ICAO location identifier*] (ICLI)
Pat Abr...... Paterson's Abridgment of Poor Law Cases [*1857-63*] [*A publication*] (DLA)
PATAFIL ..... Policies of Author Affiliation Listing (SAUS)
PAT & E...... Product Acceptance Testing and Evaluation [*Marketing*] (MCD)
PAT&E........ Product Assurance Test and Evaluation
PAT&E........ Production Acceptance Test and Evaluation
Pat & H ..... Patton, Jr., and Heath's Reports [*Virginia Special Court of Appeals*] [*A publication*] (DLA)
Pat & Mr.... Paterson and Murray's Reports [*1870-71*] [*New South Wales*] [*A publication*] (DLA)
Pat App ..... Craigie, Stewart, and Paton's House of Lords Appeals from Scotland [*1726-1857*] [*A publication*] (DLA)
Pat App Cas... Paterson's Scotch Appeal Cases [*A publication*] (DLA)
Pat App Cas... Paton's Scotch Appeal Cases [*Craigie, Stewart, and Paton*] [*A publication*] (DLA)
PAT/ARM.... Passive Angle Tracking/Anti-Radiation Missile system (SAUS)
PATAS .... Portable Air-Launched Missile Telemetry Acquisition System (MCD)
PATAs........ Provincially Administered Tribal Areas (Pakistan) [*Political party*] (PSAP)
PATAS .... Publications Automated Task Analysis System (SAUS)
PATASWDEVGRU... Patrol Antisubmarine Warfare Development Group
PATBOMRON... Patrol-Bombing Squadron
PatBt .... Patrol Boat (SAUS)
PATBX .... Private Automatic Telegraph Branch Exchange [*Telecommunications*]
PATBX .... Private Automatic Telex Branch Exchange (NITA)
PAtC .... Cedar Crest College, Allentown, PA [*Library symbol*] [*Library of Congress*] (LCLS)
PATC......... Page Address Translation Cache (SAUS)
PATC......... Pain-Anxiety-Tension Cycle (MELL)
PATC......... Paroxysmal Atrial [*or Auricular*] Tachycardia [*Medicine*]
PATC......... PATCLASS [*Pergamon ORBIT InfoLine, Inc.*] [*No longer available online*] [*Information service or system*] (CRD)
PATC......... Pioneer Automobile Touring Club (EA)
PATC......... Port Authority Transit Commission [*Federal Railroad Administration identification code*]
PAT-C........ Position, Attitude, Trajectory-Control [*Aerospace*] (AAG)
PATC......... Potomac Appalachian Trail Club (EA)
PATC......... Professional, Administrative, Technical, and Clerical [*Bureau of Labor Statistics survey*]
PATC......... Professional Air Traffic Controller (SAUS)
PATC......... Tin City Air Force Station [*Alaska*] [*ICAO location identifier*] (ICLI)
PATCA .... Panama Air Traffic Control Area
PATCA .... Phase Lock Automatic Tuned Circuit Adjustment [*Telecommunications*]
PATCA .... Printing and Allied Trades Christian Association (DGA)
PATCA .... Professional and Technical Consultants Association (EA)
Pat Cas ..... Reports of Patent, Design, and Trade Mark Cases [*England, Scotland, Ireland*] [*A publication*] (DLA)
PATCENT... Patching Central [*Army*] (AABC)
PATCH .... People Against Toxic Chemical Hazards [*An association*] [*Australia*]
PATCH .... Planned Approach to Community Health
PATCH .... Precision Approach To Coupled Hover (SAUS)
PA-TCH-SP... Periodic Acid-Thiocarbohydrazide-Silver Proteinate [*Test*] [*Cytology*]
PATCO .... Port Authority Transit Corp. (SAUS)
PATCO .... Prednisone, ara-C [*Cytarabine*], Thioguanine, Cyclophosphamide, Oncovin [*Vincristine*] [*Antineoplastic drug regimen*]
PATCO .... Professional, Administrative, Technical, Clerical, and Other [*Bureau of Labor Statistics survey*] (DNAB)
PATCO .... Professional Air Traffic Controllers Association (SAUS)
PATCO .... Professional Air Traffic Controllers Organization [*Defunct*] (EA)
PATCOM..... Patriot Communications Model (MCD)
Pat Comp... Paterson's Compendium of English and Scotch Law [*A publication*] (DLA)
PATCRA ..... Papua New Guinea Australia Trade and Commercial Relations Agreement (SAUS)
PATD......... Parts and Tool Disposition (IAA)
patd.......... Patented (NTIO)
PATD......... Patented
PATD......... Pathfinder Trucking [*Common carrier symbol*]
Pat Dec ..... Decisions of the Commissioner of Patents [*A publication*] (DLA)
Pat Des & TM Rev... Patent, Design, and Trade Mark Review [*India*] [*A publication*] (DLA)
PAT Device... Parametric Artificial Talking Device (SAUS)
Pat Dig...... Pattison's Missouri Digest [*A publication*] (DLA)
PATDPA ..... Deutsche Patent Datenbank [*German Patent Database*] [*German Patent Office*] [*Information service or system*] (IID)
PATE......... Philippine Association of Technological Education (SAUS)
PATE......... Pointing and Tracking Experiment (SAUS)
PATE......... Production Acceptance Test and Evaluation
PATE......... Programmed Automatic Telemetry Evaluator
PATE......... Programmed Automatic Test Equipment
PATE......... Psychodynamics and Therapeutic Education
PATE......... Pulmonary Artery Thromboembolectomy [*Cardiology*] (DAVI)
Pate .... Pulmonary Artery Thromboembolism [*Medicine*] (STED)
PATEC .... Pacific Technica Corp. (EFIS)
PATEFA News... Printing and Allied Trades Employers' Federation. News [*A publication*]
PATELL...... Psychological Abstracts Tape Edition Lease or Licensing
PatEng ...... Patterson Energy, Inc. [*Associated Press*] (SAG)
Pater .... Paterson's New South Wales Reports [*A publication*] (DLA)
Pater .... Paterson's Scotch Appeal Cases [*A publication*] (DLA)
Pater Ap Cas... Paterson's Scotch Appeal Cases [*A publication*] (DLA)
Pater App... Paterson's Scotch Appeal Cases [*A publication*] (DLA)
Paters App... Paterson's Appeal Cases [*A publication*] (ILCA)
Paters Comp... Paterson's Compendium of English and Scotch Law [*A publication*] (DLA)
Paterson .... Paterson on the Game Laws [*A publication*] (DLA)
Paterson .... Paterson on the Liberty of the Subject [*A publication*] (DLA)
Paterson .... Paterson's Compendium of English and Scotch Law [*A publication*] (DLA)
Paterson .... Paterson's Law and Usages of the Stock Exchange [*A publication*] (DLA)
Paterson .... Paterson's Scotch Appeal Cases [*A publication*] (DLA)
Paterson Sc App Cas... Paterson's Scotch Appeal Cases [*A publication*] (DLA)
PATF......... Program Activation Task Force [*Military*] (AFIT)
PATF......... Property Accountability Task Force [*Army*] (MCD)
PATFOR ..... Patrol Force
Pat Game L... Paterson on the Game Laws [*1861*] [*A publication*] (DLA)
PATGC .... Purge-and-Trap Gas Chromatography [*Environmental Protection Agency*]
PATH......... AmeriPath, Inc. [*NASDAQ symbol*] (NASQ)
PATH......... Partnership Approach to Health (MEDA)
PATH......... Path [*Postal Service standard*] (OPSA)
PATH......... Pathfinder Mobile Homes [*NCIC trailer make code*]
path.......... Pathogen (STED)
Path .... Pathological [*Medicine*] (BCRP)
PATH......... Pathological (GOBB)
path.......... Pathologist (IDYL)
PATH......... Pathology (AABC)
path.......... Pathology (STED)
PATH......... Peer Attitudes Toward the Handicapped Scale [*Psychology*] (EDAC)
PATH......... Performance Analysis and Test Histories (KSC)
PATH......... Performing Arts Theater of the Handicapped (SAUS)
PATH......... Physicians at Teaching Hospitals [*Program*]
PATH......... Pituitary Adrenotrophic Hormone [*Endocrinology*]
PATH......... Port Authority Trans-Hudson [*New York*]
PATH......... Postflight Attitude and Trajectory History (SAUS)
PATH......... Preserve American Patriotic Holidays Committee (EA)
PATH......... Prevention of Abuse in the Home (MHID)
PATH......... Professional Association of Traditional Healers (SAUS)
PATH......... Program for Appropriate Technology in Health (EA)
PATH......... Program on Advanced Technology for the Highway
PATH......... Prospectors and Treasure Hunters Guild (EA)
PATH......... Providing Access to Help (MHID)
PATHAT...... Precision Aim-Technique Heliborne Antitank [*Gun system concept*] [*Ballistic Research Laboratory*] (RDA)
PATHE .... Positive Action Through Holistic Evaluation Program (EDAC)
PATHFINDER... Pathological Element Finder (SAUS)
Pat HL Sc... Paterson's Scotch Appeal Cases [*A publication*] (DLA)
Pat HL Sc... Paton's Scotch Appeal Cases [*A publication*] (DLA)
PathoG ...... PathoGenesis Corp. [*Associated Press*] (SAG)
PATHOGEN... Pathogenic (SAUS)
PATHOL ..... Pathologic (SAUS)
PATHOL ..... Pathological (MSA)
PATHOL ..... Pathologically (SAUS)
Pathol Int... Pathology International (SAUS)
Pathol Res Pract... Pathology, Research and Practice (SAUS)
PATHOMORPH... Pathomorphologic (SAUS)
PATHOMORPH... Pathomorphologist (SAUS)

PATHOMORPH... Pathomorphology (SAUS)
PATHS....... Pacific Transport of Heat and Salt [*Canada-Japan-USA*] [*Marine science*] (OSRA)
PATHS....... Path [*Commonly used*] (OPSA)
PATHS....... Peer Attitudes Toward the Handicapped Scale [*Educational testing*]
PATHS....... Precursor above the Horizon Sensor [*Strategic Defense Initiative*]
PATI.......... Passive Airborne Time-Difference Intercept [*Navy*]
PATI.......... Patient Infosystems, Inc. [*NASDAQ symbol*] (SAG)
PATI.......... Penetrating Abdominal Trauma Index (MELL)
PATI.......... Phoenix Advanced Technology, Inc. [*NASDAQ symbol*] (COMM)
PATIA......... Pacific Area Trading and Investment Area
Patiala...... Indian Law Reports, Patiala Series [*A publication*] (DLA)
PATIB......... Polish-American Travel Information Bureau (EA)
PATIE......... Pointing and Tracking Integrated Experiment (SAUS)
PATINA...... Potomac Antique Tools and Industries Association (EA)
PatInfo...... Patient Infosystems, Inc. [*Associated Press*] (SAG)
Pat Ins...... Paton on Insurance [*1962*] [*A publication*] (DLA)
PATIO......... Program Addressable Table Index Operation [*Computer science*] (VLIE)
Pat J......... Patent Journal, Including Trademarks and Models [*South Africa*] [*A publication*] (DLA)
PATK......... Patrick Indus [*NASDAQ symbol*] (TTSB)
PATK......... Patrick Industries, Inc. [*NASDAQ symbol*] (NQ)
PATK......... Talkeetna [*Alaska*] [*ICAO location identifier*] (ICLI)
PAtL......... Lehigh County Historical Society, Allentown, PA [*Library symbol*] [*Library of Congress*] (LCLS)
PATL......... Tatalina Air Force Station [*Alaska*] [*ICAO location identifier*] (ICLI)
PATLAW..... Patent Law (NITA)
Pat Law Rev... Patent Law Review [*A publication*] (DLA)
PATLC....... Progessive Achievement Tests of Listening Comprehension (STED)
Patlex....... Patlex Corp. [*Associated Press*] (SAG)
Pat Licens... Paterson's Licensing Acts Annual [*A publication*] (DLA)
Pat LJ....... Patna Law Journal [*India*] [*A publication*] (DLA)
Pat LR....... Patent Law Review [*A publication*] (DLA)
Pat LR....... Patna Law Reports [*India*] [*A publication*] (DLA)
Pat L Reptr... Patna Law Reporter [*India*] [*A publication*] (DLA)
Pat L Rev... Patent Law Review [*A publication*] (DLA)
Pat LT....... Patna Law Times [*India*] [*A publication*] (DLA)
Pat LW...... Patna Law Weekly [*A publication*] (DLA)
PAtM......... Muhlenberg College, Allentown, PA [*Library symbol*] [*Library of Congress*] (LCLS)
pat med..... Patent Medicine (STED)
PAT MED.... Patent Medicine (WDAA)
PATMI....... Powder Actuated Tool Manufacturers' Institute (EA)
PATMI....... Power Actuated Tool Manufacturers Institute (SAUS)
PATMKG..... Patternmaking (WGA)
PATMO...... Patent and Trademark Office (SAUS)
Pat Mort.... Patch on Mortgages [*1821*] [*A publication*] (DLA)
PATMRG.... PACOM [*Pacific Command*] Air Target Materials Review Group (CINC)
PATN......... Pattern (MDG)
PATN......... Pattern Analysis Package (SAUS)
PATN......... Promotional Port Access Telephone Number (SAUS)
PATNT....... Patent
PATNT....... Playgroup Association of the Northern Territory [*Australia*]
PATO......... Pacific-Asian Treaty Organization (NADA)
PATO......... Partial Acceptance and Takeover Date [*Telecommunications*] (TEL)
PATO......... Pattetico [*Pathetically*] [*Music*] (ROG)
PATO......... Principal Ammunition Technical Officer [*British military*] (DMA)
Pat Off...... Patent Office (DLA)
Pat Off J.... Patent Office Journal [*India*] [*A publication*] (DLA)
Pat Off Rec... Patent Office Record (SAUS)
Pat Off Rep... Patent Office Reports [*A publication*] (DLA)
PATOLIS....... Patent Online Information System [*Database*] [*Japan*]
Paton......... Craigie, Stewart, and Paton's Scotch Appeal Cases [*1726-1821*] [*A publication*] (DLA)
Paton App Cas... Paton's Scotch Appeal Cases [*A publication*] (DLA)
Paton Sc App Cas... Paton's Scotch Appeal Cases [*A publication*] (DLA)
PATOOMB... Phage and the Origins of Molecular Biology
PATOS....... Patent-Online-System [*Bertelsmann Datenbankdienste GmbH*] [*Database*]
PATOS....... Payment at Time of Service (ADWA)
PATOUSA... Police and Traffic Officers Union of South Africa (SAUS)
PATP......... Poets and the Pub [*Programme*] [*Australia*]
PATP......... Preliminary Authority to Proceed (NASA)
PATP......... Production Acceptance Test Procedure (MCD)
PATP......... (Pyridylcarbonylamino)tetrahydropyridine [*Biochemistry*]
PATPAC...... Preserving America's Traditions [*Alexandria, VA*] (PACS)
Pat Pend.... Patent Pending (SAUS)
patpend..... Patent Pending (SHCU)
PATPEND... Patent Pending
PAT Personnel... Professional-Administrative-Technical Personnel (SAUS)
PAT-PTR..... US Patent Data Base - Patent Technology Reports [*Patent and Trademark Office*] [*Database*]
patr.......... Patriarch (RION)
PATR......... Patriarch
PATR......... Patriotic (ROG)
Patr.......... Patrol (SAUS)
PATR......... Patron
PATR......... Production Acceptance Test Requirement (MCD)
PATRA....... Packaging and Allied Trades Research Association (SAUS)
PATRA....... Printing, Packaging, and Allied Trades Research Association
PATRA....... Professional and Technical Role Analyses [*Occupational therapy*]
PatrAH...... Patriot American Hospitality, Inc. [*Associated Press*] (SAG)
Patra Journal... Printing, Packaging and Allied Trades Research Association Journal (SAUS)
PATRAM..... Packaging and Transport of Radioactive Materials (HEAS)
PATRDL..... Pan American Tung Research and Development League [*Defunct*] (EA)
Patr Elect Cas... Patrick's Election Cases [*1824-49*] [*Upper Canada*] [*A publication*] (DLA)
Patriarch... Patriarchate (DIAR)
PATRIC...... Pattern Recognition and Information Correlations [*Police crime-detection computer*]
PATRIC...... Pattern Recognition Interpretation and Correlation (CET)
PATRIC...... Position and Time-Resolved Ion Counting [*Detector*]
PATRICIA... Practical Algorithm to Receive Information Coded in Alphanumeric [*Information retrieval*]
Patrick El Cas... Patrick's Election Cases [*Canada*] [*A publication*] (DLA)
PATRIC System... Pattern Recognition, Information and Correlation System (SAUS)
Patrida Seybolds Off Comput Res... Partricia Seybolds Office Computing Report (SAUS)
Patriot....... Patriotic (DIAR)
PATRIOT.... Pesticide Assessment Tool for Rating Investigations for Transport [*Environmental Protection Agency*] (AEPA)
PATRIOT...... Phased Array Tracking to Intercept of Target [*Air defense system unit*] [*Army*] (RDA)
PatriotB..... Patriot Bank Corp. (PA) [*Associated Press*] (SAG)
PATRIOT ICC... Patriot Information Control Center
Patrklnd..... Patrick Industries, Inc. [*Associated Press*] (SAG)
Patrm........ Patrimony (DIAR)
PatrNBk..... Patriot National Bank CT [*Associated Press*] (SAG)
PATROL..... Program for Administrative Traffic Reports On-Line [*Computer program*] [*Bell System*]
PatrolGr..... Patrologia Graeca (BJA)
PatrolLat... Patrologia Latina (BJA)
PATRON..... Patrol Squadron
PATS......... Pacific Animal Therapy Society (SAUS)
PATS......... Parameterized Abstract Test Suite (VLIE)
PATS......... Parametrized Abstract Test Suite (SAUS)
PATS......... Parents Against Teen Suicide (EARSL)
PATS......... Passive Angle Tracking System (SEWL)
PATS......... Passive Auto Theft System [*Automotive security*]
PATS......... Payload Avionics Test Station [*NASA*] (SSD)
PATS......... Payment and Telecommunication Services Corp. [*New York, NY*] [*Telecommunications*] [*Defunct*] (TSSD)
PATS......... People Against Tobacco Smoke (EA)
PATS......... Personnel Assistance Teams [*Military*]
PATS......... Personnel in an Awaiting Training Status [*Air Force*] (AFM)
PATS......... Pesticide Action Tracking System (EEVL)
PATS......... Pesticides Analytical Transport Solution (EEVL)
PATS......... Plant Action Tracking System [*Environmental science*] (COE)
PATS......... Portable Acoustic Tracking System for Divers (MCD)
PATS......... Preacademic Training Student [*Military*]
PATS......... Preauthorized Automatic Transfer Scheme [*Banking*]
PATS......... Precise Automated Tracking System (PDAA)
PATS......... Precision Aircraft Tracking System (SAUS)
PATS......... Precision Altimeter Techniques Study
PATS......... Precision Automated Tracking System [*FAA*] (TAG)
PATS......... Predicasts Abstract Terminal System [*Computer science*]
PATS......... Primary Aircraft Training System (MCD)
PATS......... Priority Activity Tracking System (DB)
PATS......... Product Acceptance Test Specification (TIMI)
PATS......... Program for Analysis of Time Series (NASA)
PATS......... Programmable Automatic Test System (SAUS)
PATS......... Programmatic and Technical Support [*Army*]
PATS......... Programming and Testing System [*Computer science*] (HODG)
PATS......... Program on Agricultural Technology Studies [*University of Wisconsin--Madison*] (RCD)
PATS......... Proliferation of Antitank Systems (SAUS)
PATS......... Proof and Transit System (SAUS)
PATS......... Propulsion Analysis Trajectory Simulation [*Computer program*] [*NASA*]
PATS......... Prototype Automated Telecommunications System (SAUS)
PATS......... Prototype Automatic Target Screener (SAUS)
PATS Corporation... Payment and Telecommunication Services Corp. (SAUS)
PATSEARCH... Patent Search [*Computer science*]
PATSEARCH... Patent Search System (NITA)
PAT-SED..... Pseudoachondroplastic Dysplasia [*Medicine*] (EDAA)
Pat Ser...... Indian Law Reports, Patna Series [*A publication*] (DLA)
PA-T-SP..... Periodic Acid-Thiocarbohydrazide-Silver Proteinate (STED)
Pat St Tr... Paton on Stoppage in Transitu [*1859*] [*A publication*] (DLA)
PATSU....... Patrol Aircraft Service Unit
PATSY....... Parametric Test Synthesis [*Computer science*]
PATSY....... Picture Animal Top Star of the Year [*or Performing Animal Television Star of the Year*] [*American Humane Association award*]
PATSY....... Programmed Automatic Testing System (SAUS)
PATSY....... Programmer's Automatic Testing System
PATSY....... Pulse-Amplitude Transmission System (PDAA)
PAT System... Planar Assembly and Test System (SAUS)
PATT......... Partial Automatic Translation Technique
pat T......... Patellar Tenderness [*Medicine*] (STED)
PATT......... Patent (ROG)
PATT......... Pattern (AAG)
patt.......... Pattern (ELAL)
PATT......... Programmable Automatic Transistor Tester (PDAA)
PATT......... Project for the Analysis of Technology Transfer [*NASA*]

Patt & H .... Patton, Jr., and Heath's Reports [*Virginia*] [*A publication*] (DLA)
Patt & Heath R... Patton, Jr., and Heath's Reports [*Virginia*] [*A publication*] (DLA)
Patt & H (VA)... Patton, Jr., and Heath's Reports [*Virginia*] [*A publication*] (DLA)
PattDntl ..... Patterson Dental Co. [*Associated Press*] (SAG)
Patten .... Patten Corp. [*Associated Press*] (SAG)
PATTERN... Planning Assistance Through Technical Evaluation of Relevance Numbers [*RAND Corp.*]
Pattern Recognit... Pattern Recognition (SAUS)
Pattern Recognit Lett... Pattern Recognition Letters (SAUS)
PAT Test .... Picric Acid Turbidity Test (SAUS)
PATTH .... People Against Telephone Terrorism and Harassment (EA)
PATTI .... Pneumatic Adhesion Tensile Testing Instrument (SAUS)
PATTI .... Precise and Accurate Time and Time Interval [*An experiment aboard the Spacelab*] [*NASA*] (PDAA)
PATTI .... Prompt Action to Telephone Inquiries (SAA)
PAT/TM...... Patient's Time (DAVI)
Pat TM & Copyr J of R & Educ... Patent, Trademark, and Copyright Journal of Research and Education [*A publication*] (DLA)
Patton & H... Patton, Jr., and Heath's Reports [*Virginia Special Court of Appeals*] [*A publication*] (DLA)
Patton & Heath... Patton, Jr., and Heath's Reports [*Virginia*] [*A publication*] (DLA)
Patton & H (VA)... Patton, Jr., and Heath's Reports [*Virginia Special Court of Appeals*] [*A publication*] (DLA)
Pat Trademark & Copyright J (BNA)... Patent, Trademark, and Copyright Journal (Bureau of National Affairs) [*A publication*] (DLA)
PATTS .... Programmed Auto Trim/Test System (SAUS)
PATU......... PanAfrican Telecommunications Union (EAIO)
PATU......... Pan American Taekwondo Union (EA)
PATWA .... Playgroup Association of Western Australia
PATWA ...... Professional and Technical Workers Aliyah [*British*] (BI)
PATWAS..... Pilots Automatic Telephone Weather Answering Service
PATWING ... Patrol Wing [*Later, Fleet Air Wing*]
PATWINGDET... Patrol Wing [*Later, Fleet Air Wing*] Detachment (DNAB)
PATWINGLANTFLT... Patrol Wing [*later, Fleet Air Wing*] Atlantic Fleet
PATWINGSCOFOR... Patrol Wing [*later, Fleet Air Wing*] Scouting Force
PATX......... Private Automatic Telegraph Exchange (PDAA)
PATX......... Private Automatic Telex Exchange (NITA)
PATY......... Private Annuity for Term of Years (SAUS)
PAU......... Pacific Command Frequency Allocation and Uses (CINC)
PAU......... Pan American Union [*Central organ and permanent secretariat of the OAS*]
PAU......... Pan American University (SAUS)
PAU......... Parallel Arithmetic Unit (SAUS)
PAU......... Pattern Articulation Unit [*Computer science*]
PAU......... Pauk [*Myanmar*] [*Airport symbol*] (OAG)
PAU......... Paulingite [*A zeolite*]
Pau......... Paulus de Liazaris [*Deceased, 1356*] [*Authority cited in pre-1607 legal work*] (DSA)
PAU......... Pause [*Telegraphy*] (PCTE)
PAU......... Pauzhetka [*Former USSR*] [*Seismograph station code, US Geological Survey*] (SEIS)
pau......... Pennsylvania [*MARC country of publication code*] [*Library of Congress*] (LCCP)
PAU......... Phenol-Acetic Acid-Urea [*Medicine*] (DMAA)
PAU......... Pilotless Aircraft Unit
PAU......... Police Airborne Unit (SAUS)
PAU......... Portable Annotation Unit [*Military*] (CAAL)
PAU......... Position Analog Unit [*Manufacturing term*]
PAU......... Power and Alarm Unit (SAUS)
PAU......... Present Address Unknown
PAU......... Probe Aerodynamic Upper [*NASA*] (MCD)
PAU......... Production Assurance Unit (MCD)
PAU......... Programmes Analysis Unit [*British*] (MCD)
PAU......... Public Awareness Unit (SAUS)
PAU......... University of Pennsylvania, Philadelphia, PA [*OCLC symbol*] (OCLC)
PAUB .... Platform Access Under Bridge (SAUS)
PAUBM....... Pan American Union of Baptist Men [*Defunct*] (EA)
PAUC .... Program Acquisition Unit Cost (AAGC)
PAUCA....... Providence Association of Ukrainian Catholics in America (EA)
Pau de Cast... Paulus de Castro [*Deceased, 1441*] [*Authority cited in pre-1607 legal work*] (DSA)
Pau de La... Paulus de Liazaris [*Deceased, 1356*] [*Authority cited in pre-1607 legal work*] (DSA)
Pau de Montep... Paulus Ruinus de Montepico [*Flourished, 15th century*] [*Authority cited in pre-1607 legal work*] (DSA)
PAUDGET... Photometer, Automated Universal Distribution Gonielectric Type
PAUG .... Paughco [*NCIC motorcycle make code*]
PAUH .... Harris [*Paul*] Stores [*NASDAQ symbol*] (SAG)
PAUH .... Paul Harris Stores [*NASDAQ symbol*] (SAG)
Pau Hunga... Paulus Hungarus [*Deceased, 1242*] [*Authority cited in pre-1607 legal work*] (DSA)
Pau Hungar... Paulus Hungarus [*Deceased, 1242*] [*Authority cited in pre-1607 legal work*] (DSA)
PAUKO ...... Pan-American Union of Karatedo Organizations [*Later, PUKO*] (EA)
PAUL .... Parallel-Axis Ultraprecision Lathe (SAUS)
PAUL .... Pauli Cooling Systems [*NCIC trailer make code*]
PAUL .... Paullum [*A Little*] [*Pharmacy*]
PAULA....... Port, Audio, Uart and Logic (SAUS)
Paul de Cast... Paulus de Castro [*Deceased, 1441*] [*Authority cited in pre-1607 legal work*] (DSA)
Paul de Castr... Paulus de Castro [*Deceased, 1441*] [*Authority cited in pre-1607 legal work*] (DSA)
Pau Leon ... Paulus Leonius [*Flourished, 16th century*] [*Authority cited in pre-1607 legal work*] (DSA)
Paul Liaz... Paulus de Liazaris [*Deceased, 1356*] [*Authority cited in pre-1607 legal work*] (DSA)
PAULS....... Pennsylvania Union List of Serials
Paulson ..... Paulson Capital Corp. [*Associated Press*] (SAG)
PaulSon..... Paul-Son Gaming Corp. [*Associated Press*] (SAG)
Paulus....... Julius Paulus. Sententiae Receptae [*A publication*] (DLA)
PAU Message... Pause Message (SAUS)
PAUMV...... Potato Aucuba Mosaic Virus [*Plant pathology*]
PAUN .... Peoples Assembly for the United Nations (EA)
PAUN .... Unalakleet [*Alaska*] [*ICAO location identifier*] (ICLI)
PAUP .... Phylogenic Analysis Using Parsimony [*Biology*]
PAUR .... Pauraque [*North American bird banding code*] (BIBA)
PAUS .... Pale Amber Unsmoked Sheet (SAUS)
Paus......... Pausanias [*Second century AD*] [*Classical studies*] (OCD)
PAUS .... Piedmontese Association of the United States (EA)
PAUS .... Planning and Analysis for Uncertain Situations (MHDI)
PAUS .... Public Advocate of the United States (EA)
PAUSE....... Parents Against Unauthorized Sex Education [*Medicine*] (EDAA)
PAUSE....... People Against Unconstitutional Sex Education
PAUT .... Pennsylvania & Atlantic Railroad Co. [*Absorbed into Consolidated Rail Corp.*] [*AAR code*]
PAUT .... Profit After Ultimate Tax (TIMI)
PAUX .... Pauxillum [*A Little*] [*Pharmacy*]
P/AV .... Particular Average
PaV.......... Pathe-Vox [*Record label*] [*France*]
PAV.......... Paulo Afonso [*Brazil*] [*Airport symbol*] (OAG)
PAV.......... Pavia [*Italy*] [*Seismograph station code, US Geological Survey*] (SEIS)
Pav.......... Pavilion (DIAR)
PAV.......... Pavilion
Pav.......... Pavillon (SAUS)
Pav.......... Pavo [*Constellation*]
PAV.......... Pay Adjustment Voucher [*Military*]
PAV.......... Personnel Allotment Voucher [*Army*]
PAV.......... Phase Angle Voltmeter
PAV.......... Pneumatic Actuated Valve (SAUS)
PA(V)........ Police Association (Victoria) [*Australia*]
PAV.......... Position and Velocity
PAV.......... Position and Velocity Tracking (IAA)
PAV.......... Poste-Avion [*Airmail*] [*French*]
PAV.......... Potential Acquisition Valuation Method [*Management*]
PAV.......... Potential AIDS [*Acquired Immune Deficiency Syndrome*] Victim
PAV.......... Pressure Actuated Valve (SAUS)
PAV.......... Pressure-Actuated Valve (NASA)
PAV.......... Pressure Ageing Vessel (ABAC)
PAV.......... Pressure Altitude Variation [*Aviation*]
PAV.......... Program Activation Vector [*Computer science*] (ELAL)
PAV.......... Propellant-Actuated Valve
PAV.......... Prototype Availability (SAUS)
PAV.......... Public Access Videotex
PAV.......... Public Against Violence [*Former Czechoslovakia*] [*Political party*]
PAV.......... Puella Americana Vallensis [*Valley Girl*] [*Teenaged girl who follows the fads, fashions, and slang originated among teenagers in California's San Fernando Valley*]
PAV.......... Pyrotechnically Activated Venting [*Automotive safety systems*]
PAV.......... Stock Pavilion (SAUS)
PAVA......... Polish Army Veterans Association of America (EA)
PAVAS........ Performing and Visual Arts Society (EA)
PAVD .... Valdez [*Alaska*] [*ICAO location identifier*] (ICLI)
PAVE......... Parents Active for Vision Education [*An association*] (EA)
PAVE......... Paving
PAVE......... People Against Violent Environments (MHID)
PAVE......... Performance-Based Adult Vocational Education (EDAC)
PAVE......... Philippine Association for Vocational Education (SAUS)
PAVE......... Position and Velocity Extraction
PAVE......... Precision Acquisition Vehicle Entry (SEWL)
PAVE......... Preparing for AIDS/HIV Vaccine Evaluation [*National Institutes of Health project*]
PAVE......... Primary Auditory Visual Experience [*National Visitor Center*]
PAVE......... Principles and Applications of Value Engineering
PAVe......... Procarbazine, Alanine Nitrogen Mustard [*L-Phenylanine mustard, L-PAM*], Velban [*Vinblastine*] [*Antineoplastic drug regimen*]
PAVE......... Professional Audiovisual Education Study
PAVE......... Programmed Analysis for Value Engineering (or Engineers) (SAUS)
PAVE......... Programmed Analysis for Value Engineers
PAVE......... Programmed Assistance to Vocational Education (SAUS)
PAVE-PAWS... Phased-Array Radars (SAUS)
PAVE-PAWS... Precision Acquisition of Vehicle Entry and Phased Array Warning System
PAVE PAWS... Precision Acquisition of Vehicle Entry Phased Array Warning System
PAVE Study... Professional Audiovisual Education Study (SAUS)
PAVF......... Pulmonary Arteriovenous Fistula [*Medicine*]
PAVFC........ Princeton Azimuthally-Varying-Field Cyclotron
PAVG .... Prince Albert's Volunteer Guards [*British military*] (DMA)
PAVGX....... One Group: Value Growth Cl.A [*Mutual fund ticker symbol*] (SG)
pavl.......... Pavilion (VRA)
PAVL......... Protected Areas Virtual Library (SAUS)
PAVLA....... Papal Volunteers for Latin America [*Defunct*]
PAVM........ Patrons of the Arts in the Vatican Museum (EA)
PAVM........ Phase Angle Voltmeter
PAVM........ Potential Acquisition Valuation Method (SAUS)
PAVM........ Proximity Automatic Vehicle Monitoring (PDAA)
PAVM........ Pulmonary Arteriovenous Malformation [*Medicine*] (DMAA)

PAVMT ...... Pavement
PAVN .... People's Army of Vietnam
PAVO .... Prince Albert Victor's Own [*British military*] (DMA)
PAVOC .... Prince Albert Victor's Own Cavalry [*British military*] (DMA)
PA/VR .... Public Assistance/Vocational Rehabilitation
PAVR Insulation... Pure and Vulvanized Rubber Insulation (SAUS)
PAVS .... Passive Aided Visual Sensor (ACAE)
PAVS .... Pulmonary Arterial Vasconstrictor Substance [*Medicine*]
PA/VSI .... Preliminary Assessment and Visual Site Inspection [*Environmental science*] (BCP)
PAVT .... Position and Velocity Tracking
PAVUS .... Post Attack Viability of the US (SAUS)
PAW .... Florida Panthers Hlds [*NYSE symbol*] (SG)
PAW .... Pambwa [*Papua New Guinea*] [*Airport symbol*] (OAG)
PAW .... Panel of American Women (EA)
PAW .... Parents Are Watching [*Internet lingo*] (NETL)
PAW .... Peachtree Accounting for Windows (SAUS)
PAW .... Peak Airway Pressure [*Medicine*] (DAVI)
PAW .... Pentanol Acedic-acid Water (SAUS)
PAW .... Pentecostal Assemblies of the World (EA)
PAW .... People for the American Way (EA)
PAW .... Percussive Arc Welder
PAW .... Performance Analysis Workstation [*Computer science*]
PAW .... Performance Automotive Warehouse (SAUS)
PAW .... Peripheral Airways [*Medicine*] (DMAA)
PAW .... Petroleum Administration for War [*World War II*]
PAW .... Pets and Wildlife (SAUS)
PAW .... Physics Around the World (SAUS)
PAW .... Plant-Available Water [*Botany*]
PAW .... Plasma Arc Welding
PAW .... Poetic Allusion Watch
PAW .... Portable Auxiliary Workroom (SAUS)
PAW .... Port Angeles Western Railroad (IIA)
PAW .... Powered All the Way
Paw .... Pressure in the Airway [*level to be specified*] (DAVI)
PAW .... Primary Affective Witzelsucht [*Medicine*] (CPH)
PAW .... Princeton Alumni Weekly (SAUS)
PAW .... Programmed Automatic Welding (SAUS)
PAW .... Protect Appalachian Wilderness [*An association*] (WPI)
PAW .... Public Administered Whipping [*Slang*]
PAW .... Pulmonary Artery Wedge [*Pressure*] [*Cardiology*] (DAVI)
PAW .... Pulmonary Artery Wedge Pressure [*Cardiology*]
PAWA .... Pan American Women's Association (EA)
PAWA .... Pan-American World Airways (NADA)
PAWA .... Power and Water Authority [*Northern Territory, Australia*]
PAWAF ...... Polish American Workmen's Aid Fund (EA)
PAWBP ...... Pension and Welfare Benefit Programs [*Labor-Managment Services Administration*] (IAA)
PAWC .... Pacific West Conference (PSS)
PAWC .... Pan-African Womens Conference (SAUS)
PAWC .... Pan-American Weightlifting Confederation (EA)
PA WC Bd Dec... Pennsylvania Workmen's Compensation Board Decisions [*A publication*] (DLA)
PA WC Bd Dec Dig... Digest of Decisions, Pennsylvania Workmen's Compensation Board [*A publication*] (DLA)
PA WC Bd (Dep Rep Sup)... Workmen's Compensation Supplement to Department Reports of Pennsylvania [*A publication*] (DLA)
PAWD .... Kodiak/Municipal [*Alaska*] [*ICAO location identifier*] (ICLI)
PAWE .... Program for Analysis of the World Ecosystem
PAWES .... Performance Assessment and Workload Evaluation (GAVI)
PAWLC ...... Pan-American Weightlifting Confederation (EA)
PAWLS ...... Passive Artillery Weapons Locating System (ACAE)
PAWN .... First Cash [*NASDAQ symbol*] (TTSB)
PAWN .... First Cash, Inc. [*NASDAQ symbol*] (SAG)
PAWN .... Pawnee Transfer [*Common carrier symbol*]
PAWN .... Photon Adjoint with Neutron (PDAA)
PAWN .... Poole, Aberley, Worthington, and Nolen [*Four early residents of Pawn, Oregon. The city derives its name from the initial letters of their surnames*]
PAWNE ...... Pawnee, OK [*American Association of Railroads railroad junction routing code*]
PAWNW ..... First Cash Wrrt [*NASDAQ symbol*] (TTSB)
PAWO .... Pan-African Women's Organization [*Commercial firm*] (NADA)
Pawo .... Pressure at the Airway Opening [*Medicine*] (DAVI)
PAWOB ...... Passenger Arriving Without Baggage
PAWOS ...... Portable Automatic Weather Observing Station (MCD)
PAWP .... Pulmonary Artery Wedge Pressure [*Medicine*]
PAWRS ...... Private Aviation Weather Research Station (SAUS)
PAWS .... Parachute Altitude Wind Sensor
PAWS .... Passive Airborne Warning System [*Military*] (SEWL)
PAWS .... Performing Animal Welfare Society (EA)
PAWS .... Pet Animal Welfare Scheme [*British*] (DI)
PAWS .... Pets Abandoned Wanting Support (EARSL)
PAWS .... Pets Are Worth Safeguarding [*An association*]
PAWS .... Phased Array Warning System
PAWS .... Polar Automatic Weather Station (NG)
PAWS .... Portable Acoustic Wave Sensor (AAEL)
PAWS .... Portable AN/UYS-1 Work Station (SAUS)
PAWS .... Portable ASAS/ENSCE Work Station (SAUS)
PAWS .... Portable Automatic Weather Station (MUGU)
PAWS .... Pro-Active Wind Suspension [*Automotive engineering*]
PAWS .... Program for Avionics & Weapon Systems (SAUS)
PAWS .... Programmed Automatic Welding System
PAWS .... Progressive Animal Welfare Society (GNE)
PAWS .... Protection Against Wrapped Sequence numbers (SAUS)
PAWS .... Prototype Analyst Work Station (SAUS)
PAWS .... Psychological Abuse Warriors and Survivors (SAUS)
PAWS .... Psychological, Atmospheric, and Weather Sciences (SAUS)
PAWT .... Wainwright [*Alaska*] [*ICAO location identifier*] (ICLI)
PAWW .... Wildwood [*Alaska*] [*ICAO location identifier*] (ICLI)
PAX .... OPTEVFOR [*Operational Test and Evaluation Force*] Detachment, Patuxent River, MD [*Navy*] (CAAL)
PAX .... Pan Air, Inc. [*ICAO designator*] (FAAC)
PAX .... Pan Central Explorations Ltd. [*Toronto Stock Exchange symbol*]
PAX .... Parallel Architecture Extended [*Computer science*]
PAX .... Passenger (AFM)
PAX .... Passenger Aircraft (SAUS)
pax .... Passengers (PIAV)
PAX .... Passengers
PAX .... Patuxent River [*Maryland*] (MCD)
PAX .... Patuxent River Office Field Support (SAUS)
PAX .... Paxson [*Alaska*] [*Seismograph station code, US Geological Survey*] (SEIS)
PAX .... Paxson Communications 'A' [*AMEX symbol*] (SG)
Pax .... Paxton [*Record label*] [*Great Britain*]
PAX .... Person-to-Person Accelerated Xerography [*Office technology*] [*British*]
PAX .... Photoemission of Adsorbed Xenon [*Physics*]
PAX .... Physical Address Extension
PAX .... Pixel Addressing Extension (SAUS)
PAX .... Place Address in Index (SAUS)
PAX .... Place Address in Index Register (SAA)
PAX .... Portable Archive Exchange (SAUS)
PAX .... Private Area Exchange (SAUS)
PAX .... Private Automatic Exchange [*Telecommunications*]
PAX6 .... Human PAX6 Allelic Variant Database [*United Kingdom*] (GDD)
Paxar .... Paxar Corp. [*Associated Press*] (SAG)
PAXCON ..... Passenger Airlift Contract [*Military*]
PAX DOC .... Passenger Documentation (SAUS)
PAXL .... Pac-Ex Services [*Common carrier symbol*]
PAX PAC .... Paxson Communications Corporation PAC [*West Palm Beach, FL*] (PACS)
PAXR .... Pacific Apparel Xpress [*Common carrier symbol*]
PAX Register... Place Address in Index Register (SAUS)
PaxsnC ...... Paxson Communications Corp. [*Associated Press*] (SAG)
PAXTA .... Frank Paxton Co. (Class A) [*NASDAQ symbol*] (COMM)
PAXTO .... Paxton, IL [*American Association of Railroads railroad junction routing code*]
PAXWX ...... Pax World Fund [*Mutual fund ticker symbol*] (SG)
PAY .... Pamol [*Malaysia*] [*Airport symbol*] (OAG)
PAY .... Payment [*Motor vehicle violation code used in state of Maryland*] (MVRD)
PAY .... Pech [*Language symbol*] (ETLW)
PAY .... Prison Awareness for Youth (EARSL)
PAY .... SPS Transaction Services [*NYSE symbol*] (SAG)
PAYA .... Yakutat [*Alaska*] [*ICAO location identifier*] (ICLI)
PAYABL ...... Payable
Pay & Iv Carr... Payne and Ivamy's Carriage by Sea [*10th ed.*] [*1976*] [*A publication*] (DLA)
PAYC .... Payco American Corp. [*NASDAQ symbol*] (NQ)
Paychx .... Paychex, Inc. [*Associated Press*] (SAG)
Pay Cmdr... Paymaster Commander (SAUS)
Payco .... Payco American Corp. [*Associated Press*] (SAG)
PAYCOM .... Payload Command [*NASA*] (MCD)
PayCsh ...... Payless Cashways, Inc. [*Associated Press*] (SAG)
PAYDAT ..... Payload Data [*NASA*] (MCD)
PAYE .... Pay As You Earn
PAYE .... Pay As You Enter
PAYE .... Pitch and Yaw Engine (MCD)
PAYERS ..... Program Accomplishment Year to Date Evaluation Reviews
PAYES .... Program for Assessing Youth Employment Skills [*Vocational guidance test*]
PAYG .... Pay-As-You-Go
PAYGO ...... Pay-As-You-Go
PAYLD .... Payload
PAYLL .... Payroll (SAUS)
PaylSh ...... Payless ShoeSource, Inc. [*Associated Press*] (SAG)
PAYM .... Pan-African Youth Movement (BUAC)
PAYM .... Paymaster [*Military*] [*British*] (ROG)
PAYMARCORPS... Paymaster, Marine Corps
PAYMR ...... Paymaster
PAYMT ...... Payment
PAYMTR .... Paymaster [*Military*] [*British*] (ROG)
PAYN .... Pay'n Save, Inc. [*NASDAQ symbol*] (COMM)
PAYNE ...... Paynesville, MN [*American Association of Railroads railroad junction routing code*]
PAYR .... Paymaster (WGA)
PAYS .... Patriotic American Youth Society
PAYSOP .... Payroll-Based Stock Option Plan [*Human resources*] (WYGK)
PAYSOP .... Payroll/Stock Ownership Plan
PAYSU ...... P'Eylim-American Yeshiva Student Union (EA)
Payt .... Payment (EBF)
payt .... Payment (WDAA)
PAYT .... Payment
Paytel .... Pay Television (SAUS)
PAY-TV ..... Pay-Television (SAUS)
PAYX .... Paychex, Inc. [*NASDAQ symbol*] (NQ)
PAZ .... Palaeozoic Axial Zone [*Geophysics*]
PAZ .... Partial Annealing Zone [*Geology*]

PAZ.......... PM Air, Inc. [*ICAO designator*] (FAAC)
PAZ.......... Pollen Assemblage Zone (QUAC)
PAZ.......... Poza Rica [*Mexico*] [*Airport symbol*] (OAG)
PAZA........ Anchorage [*Alaska*] [*ICAO location identifier*] (ICLI)
PAZA........ Pan American Zebu Association [*Later, IZBA*] (EA)
PAZA........ Press Association of Zambia (BUAC)
PAZF........ Fairbanks [*Alaska*] [*ICAO location identifier*] (ICLI)
PB............ Air Burundi [*ICAO designator*] (AD)
PB............ Bachelor of Philosophy (WDAA)
PB............ Barometric Pressure [*Medicine*] (STED)
PB............ Bethlehem Public Library, Bethlehem, PA [*Library symbol*] [*Library of Congress*] (LCLS)
PB............ Dr. Karl Thomae GmbH [*Germany*] [*Research code symbol*]
PB............ Lead [*BTS*] (TAG)
Pb............ Lead
PB............ Pacific Beach (SAUS)
PB............ Packard Bell (SAUS)
P/B.......... Pad and Boom [*Refueling*] [*Aerospace*] (MSA)
PB............ Paderborn [*German license plate city code*]
PB............ Page Buffer (NITA)
PB............ Painted Base (AAG)
PB............ Panama Basin
PB............ Panamco [*NYSE symbol*]
PB............ Panamerican Beverages [*NYSE symbol*] (SPSG)
PB............ Panamerican Beverages 'A' [*NYSE symbol*] (TTSB)
PB............ Panic Bar [*Technical drawings*]
PB............ Paperback (CDAI)
PB............ Paper Base (MSA)
PB............ Paperboard Industries Corp. [*Toronto Stock Exchange symbol*]
PB............ Papua Besena [*Papua New Guinea*] [*Political party*] (FEA)
PB............ Parabellum (GOBB)
PB............ Paraffin Bath [*Medicine*]
PB............ Parallel Binary (ACAE)
PB............ Paris Bourse [*The French stock exchange*]
PB............ Parity BIT [*Binary Digit*] [*Data communications*] (IAA)
PB............ Parke-Bernet [*Later, SPB*] [*Manhattan art auction house*]
PB............ Parliamentary Bill [*British*] (ROG)
PB............ Parole Board [*Australian Capital Territory*]
PB............ Particle Beam
PB............ Particle-Beam Weapon
PB............ Parts Breakdown
PB............ Passband (SAUS)
P/B.......... Pass Book (SAUS)
PB............ Passbook [*Banking*]
PB............ Passed Ball
PB............ Patch Bay (SAUS)
PB............ Patrol Base [*Army*] (VNW)
PB............ Patrol Boat [*Navy symbol*]
PB............ Patrol Bomber
PB............ Paul-Bunnell [*Test*] [*Immunology*] (AAMN)
PB............ Pawnbroker
PB............ Pay Board
PB............ Peaceful Beginnings (EA)
PB............ Peach Bottom (SAUS)
P/B.......... Peak-to-Background (SAUS)
PB............ Peanut Butter [*Brand name of the Red Wing Co.*]
PB............ Pending Bid (TIMI)
PB............ Pennsylvania Ballet
PB............ Pentaborane [*Rocket fuel*]
PB............ Pentobarbital [*Organic chemistry*]
PB............ Peribrachialis [*Anatomy*]
PB............ Period Breathing [*Therapy term*] (CTAA)
PB............ Peripheral Blood [*Medicine*] (AAMN)
PB............ Peripheral Buffer
PB............ Permanent Ballast (DS)
PB............ Permanent Base (SAUS)
PB............ Permanent Bunkers
PB............ Permanently Blind
PB............ Permian Basis (SAUS)
PB............ Peroneus Brevis [*Muscle*] [*orthopedics*] (DAVI)
PB............ Personnel Board (SAUS)
PB............ Petabyte (SAUS)
PB............ Petrus Brito [*Flourished, 13th century*] [*Authority cited in pre-1607 legal work*] (DSA)
PB............ Phalangeal Bracket [*i.e., cup handle*] [*Slang*]
PB............ Pharmacopoeia Britannica [*British Pharmacopoeia*]
PB............ Phase Boundary (SAUS)
Pb............ Phenobarbital (STED)
PB............ Phenobarbital [*A drug*]
PB............ Philosophiae Baccalaureus [*Bachelor of Philosophy*]
PB............ Phonetically Balanced [*With reference to word lists*]
PB............ Phosphate Buffer
PB............ Phosphoribosyl
PB............ Photon Barrier [*Astrophysics*]
PB............ Physics Briefs [*Physikalische Berichte*] [*American Institute of Physics*] [*Database*] [*Information service or system*] (IID)
PB............ Physiotherapists Board [*Australian Capital Territory*]
PB............ Picket Boat [*Navy*]
PB............ Piebald
P/B.......... Piggy Back (SAUS)
PB............ Piggyback (IAA)
PB............ Pilot Balloon (SAUS)
PB............ Pilotless Bomber [*Air Force*]
PB............ Pinchbeck [*Jewelry*] (ROG)
PB............ Pinch Biopsy [*Medicine*] (MEDA)
PB............ Pine Bark
PB............ Pink Bollworm [*Cotton pest*]
PB............ Pipe Break [*Nuclear energy*] (NRCH)
PB............ Pipeline Burst (SAUS)
PB............ Piperonyl Butoxide [*Organic chemistry*]
PB............ Pit Border [*Paleobotany*]
PB............ Pitney-Bowes, Inc.
PB............ Planning Board
PB............ Plasma reactor, Barrel type (SAUS)
PB............ Plasminogen Binding [*Hematology*]
PB............ Plastic Banded (SAUS)
PB............ Plate Block [*Philately*]
PB............ Playback (KSC)
PB............ Plot Board (KSC)
PB............ Plotboard (SAUS)
PB............ Plotting Board (SAUS)
PB............ Plugboard
PB............ Plugged Back (SAUS)
PB............ Plugging Back [*Computer science*] (IAA)
Pb............ Plumbum [*Lead*] [*Chemical element*]
PB............ Plymouth Brethren (ROG)
PB............ Pocket Book
PB............ Police Band (SAUS)
PB............ Police Boat (SAUS)
PB............ Police Burgh
PB............ Policy Board (OICC)
PB............ Polished Buckram (DGA)
PB............ Pollen Body [*Botany*]
PB............ Polybenzene [*Organic chemistry*]
PB............ Polybutadiene (SAUS)
PB............ Polybutylene [*Organic chemistry*]
PB............ Polymer Blend (SAUS)
PB............ Polymyxin B [*An antibiotic*]
PB............ Polystyrene Base (DGA)
PB............ Pony Baseball (EA)
PB............ Pony Baseball/Softball [*An association*] (EA)
PB............ Poop and Bridge [*of a ship*] (DS)
PB............ Poor Box
PB............ Population Biology
PB............ Portable (SAUS)
PB............ Ports and Beaches (NATG)
PB............ Post Bag (SAUS)
PB............ Post Boost (ACAE)
PB............ Powder Bed (DAVI)
PB............ Powder Board (DAVI)
PB............ Power Boiler
PB............ Power Box (IAA)
PB............ Power Brakes [*Automotive engineering*]
PB............ Power Builder [*Computer software*] (CDE)
PB............ Prayer Book
PB............ Pre-Boreal (SAUS)
PB............ Preburner [*NASA*] (NASA)
PB............ Precipitation Body (SAUS)
PB............ Preliminary Breakdown
PB............ Premature Beat [*Medicine*] (CPH)
PB............ Premium Bond (ODBW)
Pb............ Presbyopia [*Ophthalmology*]
PB............ Presentation Brothers [*See also FPM*] (EAIO)
PB............ Presidents Budget (SAUS)
PB............ Presiding Bishop [*Episcopal Church*]
PB............ Pressure-Barometer [*Automotive emissions*]
PB............ Pressure Breathing
PB............ Primary Buffer [*Chemistry*]
PB............ Primary Bus [*Computer science*] (CAAL)
PB............ Primitive Baptist
PB............ Printed Board (AAEL)
PB............ Prisoners' Barracks (ADA)
PB............ Private Bus (SAUS)
PB............ Private Business [*Slang*] [*British*]
PB............ Privately Bonded
Pb............ Probability (PCM)
PB............ Probable [*Telegraphy*] (PCTE)
Pb............ Probenecid (STED)
PB............ Process Basic (ECII)
PB............ Process Bulletin
PB............ Procurement Board (SAUS)
PB............ Product Baseline (SAUS)
PB............ Product Bulletin (SAUS)
PB............ Production Base (MCD)
pB............ product of polarization and brightness (SAUS)
PB............ Professional Books Ltd. (ILCA)
PB............ Profile Block (MCD)
PB............ Program Base [*Computer science*] (ELAL)
PB............ Program Baseline (DOMA)
PB............ Program Block (IAA)
PB............ Program Breakdown
PB............ Program Budgeting (ADA)
PB............ Programming Block (SAUS)
PB............ Property Book [*Army*] (AABC)
PB............ Proportional Band
PB............ Protein-Binding (MAE)
PB............ Protein-Bound [*Clinical chemistry*] (DAVI)
PB............ Provisional Battalion [*Military*] [*A publication*] (ROG)

PB........... Pseudo Boolean (SAUS)
PB........... Pseudoterminal Bud [*Botany*]
PB........... Ptychodiscus brevis [*An alga, the cause of the red tide*]
PB........... Public (DSUE)
PB........... Publication Bulletin (SAUS)
PB........... Publications (NITA)
PB........... Publications Board [*Later, CFSTI, NTIS*]
PB........... Publications Bulletin
PB........... Public Buildings (SAUS)
PB........... Publisher (NITA)
PB........... Publishers' Binding (DGA)
PB........... Publisher's Name [*Online database field identifier*]
PB........... Pull Back (NTCM)
PB........... Pull Box (AAG)
PB........... Pulse Beacon (KSC)
PB........... Pulse Bonded (SAUS)
PB........... Punch Buffer (SAUS)
PB........... Punching Block (SAUS)
PB........... Pure Binary (SAUS)
PB........... Purl into Back of Stitch [*Knitting*] (WDAA)
PB........... Purplish Blue
PB........... Push Button
PB4.......... Plate Block of Four [*Philately*]
PBa.......... Academy of the New Church, Bryn Athyn, PA [*Library symbol*] [*Library of Congress*] (LCLS)
Pba.......... Brachial Arterial Pressure [*Medicine*] (MAE)
PBA.......... Pacific Broadcasting Association (EAIO)
PBA.......... Paid by Agent [*Business term*] (DCTA)
PBA.......... Partial-Birth Abortion (MELL)
PBA.......... Partido Barrientista Autentico [*Bolivia*] [*Political party*] (PPW)
PBA.......... Patrol Boat, Air Cushion (MCD)
PBA.......... Patrolmen's Benevolent Association
PBA.......... Pencil Beam Aerial (or Antenna) (SAUS)
PBA.......... Pencil Beam Antenna
PBA.......... Percutaneous Bladder Aspiration [*Urology*] (DAVI)
PBA.......... Permanent Budget Account
PBA.......... Personal Body Armor [*Police and security equipment*]
PBA.......... Phenylboronate Agarose [*Biochemistry*] (DAVI)
PBA.......... Phenylboronic Acid [*Organic chemistry*]
PBA.......... Phenylbutyric Acid [*Organic chemistry*]
PBA.......... Philadelphia Bar Association (SAUS)
PBA.......... Physical Block Address (SAUS)
PBA.......... Physical Blowing Agent [*Plastics technology*]
PBA.......... Pill Box Aerial (or Antenna) (SAUS)
PBA.......... Pill Box Antenna
PBA.......... Pine Bluff Arsenal [*Army*] (AABC)
PBA.......... Plant Breeding Abstracts [*A publication*]
PbA.......... Plasmodium Berghei Anka [*Bacteriology*]
PBA.......... Plastic Bag Association (EA)
PBA.......... Polar Bear Association (EA)
PBA.......... Polish Beneficial Association (EA)
PBA.......... Polybenzamide [*Organic chemistry*]
PBA.......... Polybutene Amine [*Fuels and lubricants*]
PBA.......... Polybutyl Acrylate [*Organic chemistry*]
PBA.......... Polyclonal B Cell Activator [*Hematology*]
PBA.......... Port Blair [*Andaman Islands*] [*Seismograph station code, US Geological Survey*] (SEIS)
PBA.......... Port of Brisbane Authority (SAUS)
PBA.......... Port of Bristol Authority [*British*]
PBA.......... Poultry Bowling Association
PBA.......... Poultry Breeders of America (EA)
PBA.......... Power-Book Army [*Computer science*]
PBA.......... Powered Battle Armor [*A computer game*] (PCM)
PBA.......... Preliminary Benefit Analysis [*Environmental Protection Agency*] (EPAT)
PBA.......... Prescott Builders Association (EA)
PBA.......... President of the British Academy
PBA.......... Pressure Breathing Assister [*Medicine*] (STED)
PBA.......... Pressure Breathing Assistor [*Medicine*]
PBA.......... Principal Business Activity (GFGA)
PBA.......... Printed Board Assembly (IAA)
PBA.......... Printing Brokerage Association (EA)
PBA.......... Probation Boards' Association [*United Kingdom*] (EAIO)
PBA.......... Production Base Analysis (MCD)
PBA.......... Production Business Application (GART)
PBA.......... Professional Bookmen of America [*Later, Pi Beta Alpha*] (EA)
PBA.......... Professional Bowlers Association of America (EA)
PBA.......... Prolactin-Binding Assay (STED)
PBA.......... Proportional Band Adjustment (SAUS)
PBA.......... Provincetown-Boston Airlines, Inc.
PBA.......... Prune Belly Anomaly [*Medicine*] (DMAA)
PBA.......... Public Buildings Administration [*Functions transferred to PBS, 1949*]
PBA.......... Published by Arrangement (SAUS)
PBA.......... Pudendal Block Anesthesia [*Medicine*] (MELL)
PBA.......... Pulpobuccoaxial [*Dentistry*]
PBA.......... Pyrene Butyric Acid (SAUS)
PBA.......... Pyrenebutyric Acid [*Organic chemistry*]
PBAA........ Periodical and Book Association of America (EA)
PBAA........ Polybatadieneacrylic Acid (SAUS)
PBAA........ Poly(butadiene-acrylic Acid) [*Organic chemistry*]
PBAA........ Polybutadiene Acrylic Acid (SAUS)
PBAA........ Polybutadiene Acrylic Acid Copolymer (EDCT)
PBAA........ Private Businesses Association of Australia
PBAAC....... Polybutadiene Acrylic Acid Copolymer (SAUS)
PBAC........ Pacific Bantam Austin Club (EA)
PBAC........ Peach Belt Athletic Conference (PSS)
PBAC........ Program Budget Advisory Committee [*Army*]
PB-AESRS... Property Book - Army Equipment Status Reporting System (AABC)
PBAFB....... Palm Beach Air Force Base (SAUS)
P Bag........ Paper Bag (SAUS)
PBAL........ Protected Bronchoalveolar Lavage [*Medicine*] (DMAA)
PBAM........ Problem Billing Analysis Module (VLIE)
P-BAMS..... Programming-Budgeting and Accounting Management System (SAUS)
PBAN........ Pheromone Biosynthesis-Activating Neuropeptide [*Biochemistry*]
PBAN........ Poly(butadiene-acrylonitrile) [*Organic chemistry*]
PBAN........ Polybutadiene Acrylonitrile Copolymer (EDCT)
P-BAND..... 225-390 Megacycles per Second
PB&D........ Piano, Bass & Drums (WDAA)
PB and J.... Peanut Butter and Jelly
PB-AP....... Plastic Banded, Armour Piercing (SAUS)
PBA Package... Public Budgeting and Accounting Package (SAUS)
PB-APDS... Plastic Banded, Armour Piercing, Discarding Sabot (SAUS)
PBAPRS..... Program/Budget Accounting and Progress Reporting System [*Proposed*] [*Navy*]
PBAPS....... Peach Bottom Atomic Power Station (NRCH)
PBAPS....... Pipe Break Air Piping System (IEEE)
PBAPS....... Pipe Break Automatic Protective System (IEEE)
PBAR........ Baker Island Army Air Field [*Baker Island*] [*ICAO location identifier*] (ICLI)
PBAR........ Post-Balloon Angioplasty Restenosis [*Medicine*] (MELL)
PBAR........ Print Buffer Address Register [*Computer science*] (VLIE)
PBAR........ Programming, Budgeting, Accounting and Reporting (SAUS)
PBAS........ Program Budget Accounting System [*Military*] (GFGA)
PBASCO..... Puritan-Bennett Aero Systems Co. (SAUS)
PBAT......... Pyro Battery (KSC)
PBATS....... Portable Battlefield Attack System (SAUS)
PBATS....... Professional Baseball Athletic Trainers Society (EA)
PBAU........ Acugreen [*Intermodal shipping container symbol*] (TVRC)
PBAV........ Percutaneous Balloon Aortic Valvuloplasty [*Cardiology*] (CPH)
PBAV........ Power Boat Association of Victoria [*Australia*]
PBAX........ Private Automatic Branch Exchange [*Computer science*] (ITCA)
PBB.......... Bloomsburg State College, Bloomsburg, PA [*OCLC symbol*] (OCLC)
PBB.......... Parallel by Bit
PBB.......... Paranaiba [*Brazil*] [*Airport symbol*] (OAG)
PBB.......... Parti Pesaka Bumiputera Bersatu Sarawak [*United Bumiputra Party*] [*Malaysia*] [*Political party*] (FEA)
PBB.......... Please Be Brief [*Internet dialog*]
PBB.......... Polybrominated Biphenyl [*Flame retardant, toxic chemical*]
PBB.......... Posterior Basal Body [*Botany*]
PBB.......... Private Boxes and Bags
PBB.......... Program Plan Budgeting (TDOB)
PBB.......... Project Blue Book [*An association*] (EA)
PBB.......... Push-Button Banking (SAUS)
PBBA........ Printing Brokerage Buyers Association (NTPA)
PBBA........ Pro-Bessarabia and Bukovina Association [*Romania*] (BUAC)
PBBATU..... Pastrycooks, Bakers, Biscuitmakers, and Allied Trades Union [*Australia*]
PBBCAS..... Program-Based Budget Classification and Analysis System [*Pronounced "pib-kaz"*] [*Office of Management and Budget*]
PBbCHi...... Columbia County Historical Society, Bloomsburg, PA [*Library symbol*] [*Library of Congress*] (LCLS)
PBBFI........ Pearl S. Buck Birthplace Foundation, Inc. (EA)
PBBH........ Peter Bent Brigham Hospital [*Boston*]
PBBI......... Polybutadiene Bisimide (SAUS)
PBBL........ Project Budget Baseline Log (SAUS)
PBBO........ Phenylbiphenylylbenzoxazole (SAUS)
PBBP........ Passive Beamformer Broadband Processor (ACAE)
PBbS........ Bloomsburg State College, Bloomsburg, PA [*Library symbol*] [*Library of Congress*] (LCLS)
PBBS........ Pertubuhan Bumiputera Bersatu Sarawak [*United Sarawak National Association*] [*Malaysia*] [*Political party*] (FEA)
PBBS........ Physical Baseline Build Standard (SAUS)
PBBs......... Polybromated Biphenyls [*Organic chemistry*] (DAVI)
PBBS........ Public Bulletin Board System (ACAE)
PBBSF....... Pacific Basin Bulk [*NASDAQ symbol*] (TTSB)
PBBSF....... Pacific Basin Bulk Shippers Ltd. [*NASDAQ symbol*] (SAG)
PBBT........ Performance-Based Brake Tester [*Automotive engineering*]
PBBWF....... Pacific Basin Blk Shipng Wrrt [*NASDAQ symbol*] (TTSB)
PBBWF....... Pacific Basin Bulk Shippers Ltd. [*NASDAQ symbol*] (SAG)
PBC.......... Columbia/Mt. Pleasant, TN [*Location identifier*] [*FAA*] (FAAL)
PBC.......... Pacific Basin Conference (EEVL)
PBC.......... Pacific Bible College [*California*]
PBC.......... Packed Bed Condenser (EEVL)
PBC.......... Packed by Carrier
PBC.......... Pakistan Broadcasting Corp. (IMH)
PBC.......... Panamerican Badminton Confederation (EAIO)
PBC.......... Parallel by Character
PBC.......... Parent Behavior Checklist [*Test*] (TMMY)
PBC.......... Patrol Boat, Coastal [*Navy designation*] (POLM)
PBC.......... Pedal Branch of Columellar [*Muscle*]
PBC.......... Pen and Brush Club (EA)
PBC.......... People's Bank of China (ECON)
PBC.......... People's Bicentennial [*later, Business*] Commission
PBC.......... Period Batch Control [*Computer science*] (VLIE)
PBC.......... Periodic Binary Convolutional [*Computer science*] (VLIE)
PBC.......... Periodic Bond Chain (IAA)
PBC.......... Periodic Boundary Conditions (SAUS)

PBC......... Peripheral Blood Cells [*Medicine*]
PBC......... Peripheral Board Controller (SAUS)
PBC......... Peripheral Buffer Computer (SAUS)
PBC......... Peripheral Bus Computer [*Bell System*]
PBC......... Personal Business Computer (VLIE)
PBC......... Personnel/Burden Carrier Manufacturers Association [*Defunct*] (EA)
PBC......... Philadelphia Blood Clinic (SAUS)
PBC......... Philadelphia Book Clinic (SAUS)
PBC......... Plain Bond Copier [*Pitney Bowes*]
PBC......... Planning and the Black Community (EA)
PBC......... Point of Basal Convergence
PBC......... Practice Bomb Carrier (SAUS)
PBC......... Practice Bomb Contained (NG)
PBC......... Practice Bomb Container (SAUS)
PBC......... Prebed Care [*Medicine*] (MAE)
PBC......... Prefix Block Code (SAUS)
PBC......... Pregnancy and Birth Complications (STED)
PBC......... Presbyterians for Biblical Concerns (EA)
PBC......... Primary Biliary Cirrhosis [*Medicine*]
PBC......... Processor Bus Controller [*Computer science*] (VLIE)
PBC......... Produce Buying Co. (SAUS)
PBC......... Progestin-Binding Complement (STED)
PBC......... Program Booking Center [*Telecommunications*] (TEL)
PBC......... Program Breakdown Code (ACAE)
PBC......... Program Budget Committee [*Military*]
PBC......... Psychometric Behavior Checklist [*Psychology*]
PBC......... Public Broadcasting Corp. (SAUS)
PBC......... Public Buildings Commission [*Functions transferred to PBA, 1939*]
PBC......... Pure Binary Code [*Computer science*] (VLIE)
pBc......... pure Bolivian cocaine (SAUS)
PBCA........ Pacific Bible College of Azusa [*California*]
PBCA........ Paperboard Butter Chip Association
PBCA........ Professional Business Colleges of Australia
PBCB........ Pierce-Blank Die (Class B) (MCD)
PBCB........ Plugboard Circuit Breaker (SAUS)
PBCB........ Professional Boxing Control Board [*Victoria, Australia*]
PBCC........ Packard Bell Computer Corp. (IAA)
PBCC........ Palm Beach Computer Consultants (SAUS)
PBCC........ Peabody Coal [*Federal Railroad Administration identification code*]
PBCC........ Pigmented Basal Cell Carcinoma [*Medicine*] (MELL)
PBCC........ Pitney Bowes Credit Corp.
PBCC........ Pro Beach Cat Challenge [*Nautical term*] (NTA)
PBCCH...... Pentabromochlorocyclohexane [*Flame retardant*] [*Organic chemistry*]
PBCD........ Packed Binary Coded Decimal [*Computer science*] (VLIE)
PBCE........ Pine Bluff Cotton Exchange [*Defunct*] (EA)
PBCF........ Prudential-Bache Capital Funding
PBCFIA...... President's Board of Consultants for Foreign Intelligence Activities (CARL)
PBCH........ Primitive Bose Chaudhuri-Hocquenghem (SAUS)
PBCI........ Pamrapo Bancorp [*NASDAQ symbol*] (TTSB)
PBCI........ Pamrapo Bancorp, Inc. [*NASDAQ symbol*] (NQ)
PBCLS....... Palm Beach County Library System [*Florida*]
PBCMO...... Poly(bis(chloromethyl)oxetane) [*Organic chemistry*]
PBCO........ Praseodymium Barium Copper Oxide [*Inorganic chemistry*]
PB/COC...... Plymouth Barracuda/Cuda Owners Club (EA)
PbCoNA..... Publishing Co. of North America, Inc. (The) [*Associated Press*] (SAG)
PBCP........ Political Bureau of the Communist Party (BUAC)
PBCS........ Persian Bicolor and Calico Society (EA)
PBCS........ Post Boost Control System [*Aerospace*]
PBCT........ People's Bank [*Bridgeport, CT*] [*NASDAQ symbol*] (NQ)
PBCT........ Polybutadiene Carboxyl-Terminated (SAUS)
PBCT........ Proposed Boundary Crossing Time [*Aviation*]
PBCTP....... People's Bank 8.5% Cv 'A' Pfd [*NASDAQ symbol*] (TTSB)
PBCU........ Predominately Black Colleges and Universities
PBCU........ Puritan Bennett-Gas Products [*Intermodal shipping container symbol*] (TVRC)
PBC-USA.... Polar Bear Club - USA (EA)
PBC Vector... Periodic Bond Chain Vector (SAUS)
PBC-WS..... Polar Bear Club - Winter Swimmers [*Later, PBC-USA*] (EA)
PBD......... Pacific Basin Development Corp. [*Vancouver Stock Exchange symbol*]
PBD......... Pacific Bell Directory (SAUS)
PBD......... Paperboard (MSA)
PBD......... Parallel Blade Damper (OA)
PBD......... Particle Board [*Technical drawings*]
PBD......... Paul-Bunnell-Davidsohn [*Test*] [*Immunology*]
PBD......... Payload Bay Door [*NASA*] (NASA)
PBD......... Percutaneous Biliary Drainage [*Gastroenterology*] (DAVI)
PBD......... Performance Based Design [*Emergency Management*] (EMA)
PBD......... Phenylbiphenylyloxadiazole [*Analytical biochemistry*]
PBD......... Pierce-Blank Die (MCD)
PBD......... Pigeon Breeder's Disease [*Medicine*] (MELL)
PBD......... Place Bearing/Distance [*Way point*] (GAVI)
PBD......... Plans and Budget Division (SAUS)
PBD......... Plasterboard
PBD......... Plenum Bleed Duct [*Hovercraft*]
PBD......... Point Ball Dead [*Football*]
PBD......... Polybutadiene [*Organic chemistry*]
PBD......... Porbandar [*India*] [*Airport symbol*] (OAG)
PBD......... Postburn Day [*Medicine*] (DMAA)
PBD......... Power Building (NATG)
PBD......... Prayer Book Dictionary [*A publication*] (ODCC)
PBD......... Precise Block Diagram
PBD......... Pressboard (MSA)
PBD......... Primary Blistering Disorder [*Medicine*] (MELL)
PBD......... Production Buy Decision (SAUS)
PBD......... Professional Building Designer [*Accreditation from the American Institute of Building Designers*]
PBD......... Program Budget Decision [*DoD*]
PBD......... Program Budget Directive (MCD)
PBD......... Program Budget Document (MCD)
PBD......... Programmer Brain Damage [*Computer hacker terminology*] (NHD)
PBD......... Proliferative Breast Disease [*Medicine*]
PBD......... Public Buildings Department (SAUS)
PBDB........ Provisional Base Defense Battalion [*Marine Corps*] (VNW)
PBDBM...... Peripheral Backup Detailed Billing Control Element (SAUS)
PBDC........ Pacific Basin Development Council (EA)
PBDE........ Polybrominated Diphenyl Ether [*Flame retardant*]
PBDF........ Payload Bay Door Forward [*NASA*] (MCD)
PBDG........ Push-Button Data Generator (IEEE)
PBDI........ Position Bearing and Distance Indicator (MCD)
PBDIS....... Planning & Budgeting Distributed Information System [*USDA Forest Service*] (ALAC)
PBDM........ Payload Bay Door Mechanism [*NASA*] (NASA)
PBDMA...... Poly(butadiene-malic Acid) [*A polymer*]
PBDNDB.... Perceived Barking Dog Noise Decibels (SAUS)
PBDP........ Protective Barrier Development Program (SAUS)
Pbd Pkg.... Paperboard Packaging (SAUS)
PBDR........ Push Button Dialing Receiver (SAUS)
PBDS........ Parti Bansa Dayak Sarawak [*Malaysia*] [*Political party*] (FEA)
PBDS........ Photothermal Beam Deflection Spectroscopy (SAUS)
PBDU........ Pancreaticobiliary Ductal Union [*Anatomy*]
PBDU........ Protocol Bridge Data Unit (SAUS)
PBe......... Beaver Memorial Library, Beaver, PA [*Library symbol*] [*Library of Congress*] (LCLS)
PBE......... Paint, Body, and Equipment [*Automotive engineering*]
PBE......... Partial Breech Extraction [*Medicine*] (EDAA)
PBE......... Paschen-Back Effect [*Spectroscopy*]
PBE......... Pemberton Exploration [*Vancouver Stock Exchange symbol*]
PBE......... Perlsucht Bacillary Emulsion [*Medicine*]
PBE......... Piggyback Experiment
PBE......... Plain Both Ends (SAUS)
PBE......... Poison-Boltzmann Equation [*Physical chemistry*]
PBE......... Polybutene [*Organic chemistry*]
PBE......... Pool Boiling Experiment (SAUS)
PBE......... Present-Barrel-Equivalent
PBE......... Probability of Bit Error (CCCA)
PBE......... Prompt Burst Experiments [*Nuclear energy*] (NRCH)
PBE......... Prompt-by-Example [*Computer science*]
PBE......... Proton Balance Equation
PBE......... Proton Binding Energy
PBE......... Puerto Berrio [*Colombia*] [*Airport symbol*] (OAG)
PBE......... Pulsed Bridge Element [*Telecommunications*] (OA)
PBEA........ Paint, Body, and Equipment Association (EA)
PBEB........ Pentabromoethylbenzene [*Flame retardant*] [*Organic chemistry*]
PBeC........ Beaver County Court House, Beaver, PA [*Library symbol*] [*Library of Congress*] (LCLS)
PBEC........ Pacific Basin Economic Committee (or Council) (SAUS)
PBEC........ Pacific Basin Economic Council (FEA)
PBEC........ Public Broadcasting Environment Center [*Corporation for Public Broadcasting*]
PBECCC..... Pacific Basin Economic Council - Canadian Committee [*Canada*] (EAIO)
PBECL....... Performance-Based Exposure Control Limit [*Environmental science*]
PBECS....... Pacific Basin Extended Climate Study (SAUS)
PBEI........ Performance-Based Evaluation Instrument (EDAC)
PBEIC....... Point Beach Energy Information Center (SAUS)
PBEIST...... Planning Board European Inland Surface Transport [*Army*] (AABC)
PBel........ Centre County Library, Bellefonte, PA [*Library symbol*] [*Library of Congress*] (LCLS)
PBelC....... Centre County Court House, Bellefonte, PA [*Library symbol*] [*Library of Congress*] (LCLS)
PBEM........ Play by Electronic Mail [*Computer science*]
PBEN........ Puritan-Bennett Corp. [*NASDAQ symbol*] (COMM)
PBER........ Program Budget Execution Review [*Army*]
PBerol....... Berlin Papyri [*A publication*] (OCD)
PBET........ Performance-Based Equipment Training (AAEL)
PBf......... Carnegie Free Library, Beaver Falls, PA [*Library symbol*] [*Library of Congress*] (LCLS)
PBF......... Fast Patrol Boat [*Ship symbol*] [*NATO*] (NATG)
PBF......... Patriotic Burmese Forces [*World War II*]
PBF......... Patrol Boat, Fast [*British military*] (DMA)
PBF......... Peribronchial Fibrosis [*Medicine*]
PBF......... Permalloy-Bar File (SAUS)
PBF......... Pilot Briefing Facility (SAUS)
PBF......... Pilot Bypass Filter (IAA)
PBF......... Pine Bluff [*Arkansas*] [*Airport symbol*] [*Obsolete*] (OAG)
PBF......... Plastic Bottle Feeder
PBF......... Plates for Beam Forming (DEN)
PBF......... Poop, Bridge, and Forecastle [*of a ship*] (DS)
PBF......... Poplar Bluff, MO [*Amtrak rail station code*]
PBF......... Portal Blood Flow [*Physiology*]
PBF......... Potential Benefit Factor (OA)
PBF......... Power Burst Facility [*Nuclear energy*]
PBF......... Pulmonary Blood Flow [*Medicine*]
PBFA........ Particle Beam Fusion Accelerator
PBFA........ Provincial Booksellers' Fairs Association [*British*] (DI)
PBFC........ Peter Breck Fan Club (EA)
PBFC........ Pierce Brosnan Fan Club (EA)

PBFC .... Portland Blast-Furnace Cement (SAUS)
PBFD .... Pierce Bland and Form Die (MSA)
PBFD .... Psittacine beak and feather disease (SAUS)
PBFE......... Peroxisomal Bifunctional Enzyme (DMAA)
PB-Fe......... Protein-Bound Iron (MAE)
PBfG .... Geneva College, Beaver Falls, PA [*Library symbol*] [*Library of Congress*] (LCLS)
PBFG .... Guided Missile Fast Patrol Boat [*Ship symbol*] (NATG)
PBFG .... Patrol Boat, Fast, Guided Weapon [*British military*] (DMA)
PBFI .... Paris Business Forms, Inc. [*Burlington, NJ*] [*NASDAQ symbol*] (NQ)
PBFI .... Paris Corp. [*NASDAQ symbol*] (TTSB)
PBFL......... Planning for Better Family Living [*UN Food and Agriculture Organization*]
PBFP .... Provisioning Budget Forecast Procedure (MCD)
PBF/WR..... Presiding Bishop's Fund for World Relief (EA)
PBG.......... Pepsi Bottling Group [*Company symbol*]
PBG.......... Phenylbiguanide [*Biochemistry*]
PBG.......... Phorphobilinogen (SAUS)
PBG.......... Photonic Bandgap [*Physics*]
PBG.......... Pittsburgh [*Telegraphy*] (PCTE)
PBG.......... Plattsburgh, NY [*Location identifier*] [*FAA*] (FAAL)
PBG.......... Poly(benzyl Glutamate) [*Organic chemistry*]
PBG.......... Porphobilinogen [*Clinical chemistry*]
PBG.......... Powszechny Bank Gospodarczy [*Poland*]
PBG.......... Program and Budget Guidance [*Army*]
PBGA........ Plastic Ball Grid Arrays
PBGC........ Pension Benefit Guaranty Corp. [*Government agency*]
PBGCH...... Palm Beach Gardens Community Hospital (EFIS)
PBG-D....... Porphobilinogen Deaminase [*Medicine*] (EDAA)
PBGD........ Porphobilinogen Deaminase [*An enzyme*]
PBGI......... Piedmont BankGroup, Inc. [*NASDAQ symbol*] (NQ)
PbGI......... TIGR [*The Institute of Genomic Research*] Plasmodium berghei Gene Index [*Database*] (GDD)
PBGM........ Brazilian Marine Geology Programme (SAUS)
PBG-QN..... Porphobilinogen - Quantitative [*Genetics*] (DAVI)
PBGR........ Pied-Billed Grebe [*North American bird banding code*] (BIBA)
PBG-S....... Porphobilinogen Synthase [*Medicine*] (DMAA)
PBH.......... Partial Bulkhead (DS)
PBH.......... Patrol Boat, Hydrofoil (MCD)
PBH.......... Phillips, WI [*Location identifier*] [*FAA*] (FAAL)
PBH.......... Planar-Buried Heterostructure (SAUS)
PBH.......... Point Ball Held [*Football*]
PBH.......... Post Biblical Hebrew [*Language, etc.*] (BJA)
PBH.......... Primary Borehole (SAUS)
PBH.......... Primordial Black Hole [*Astrophysics*]
PBH.......... Pulling Boat Hands (DMAA)
PBHB........ Poly-Beta-Hydroxybutyrate (DMAA)
PBHC........ Pilgrim Basset Hound Club [*New England*] (EARSL)
PB-HEPI.... Plastic Banded, High Explosive, Penetrating Incendiary (SAUS)
PBHF........ President Benjamin Harrison Foundation (EA)
PBHGX...... PBHG Growth Fund [*Mutual fund ticker symbol*] (SG)
PBHLX....... PBHG Large-Cap Growth
PBHP........ Pounds per Brake Horsepower
PB-HTGR... Peach Bottom High-Temperature Gas-Cooled Reactor
PBI........... Pacific Bell Internet (SAUS)
PBI........... Palm Beach International Airport [*FAA*] (TAG)
PBI........... Paper Bag Institute (EA)
PBI........... Parental Bonding Index (SAUS)
PBI........... Parental Bonding Instrument
PBI........... Partial Background Investigation [*Army*]
PBI........... Partial Bony Impaction [*Orthopedics*] (DAVI)
PBI........... Paving Block Institute (SAUS)
PBI........... Paving Brick Institute
PBI........... Peace Brigades International (EA)
PBI........... Pen and Brush, Inc. (EA)
PBI........... Penile-Brachial Index [*Medicine*] (DAVI)
PBI........... Peterson Builders Inc. (SAUS)
PBI........... Phenformin [*An oral hypoglycemic*] [*Obsolete*] (DAVI)
PBI........... Philadelphia Bible Institute [*Pennsylvania*]
PBI........... Phillips Business Information, Inc. (IID)
PBI........... Phone Based Interface (SAUS)
PBI........... Pitch Boundary Indicator (MCD)
PBI........... Pitney-Bowes, Inc. [*NYSE symbol*] (SPSG)
PBI........... Plant Biological Institute [*University of Saskatchewan*] [*Canada*]
PBI........... Plant Biotechnology Institute [*National Research Council of Canada*] [*Research center*] (RCD)
PBI........... Plant Breeding Institute [*British*]
PBI........... Plastic Bottle Institute (EA)
PBI........... Please Book Immediately (SAUS)
PBI........... Plumbing Brass Institute [*Later, PMI*] (EA)
PBI........... Polybenzimidazole [*Organic chemistry*] (NATG)
PBI........... Poly(phenylenebibenzimidazole) [*Organic chemistry*]
PBI........... Poor Bloody Infantry [*British military slang*]
PBI........... Post-Bonding Inspection (VLIE)
PBI........... Post Boost Intercept (ACAE)
PBI........... Post, Buckley International
PBI........... Power Base Inventory [*Test*] (TMMY)
PBI........... Prime Bank Instrument
PBI........... Process Branch Indicator
PBI........... Program Baseline Integration (SAUS)
PBI........... Programme Biologique Internationale [*International Biological Program - IBP*] (MSC)
PBI........... Projected Books, Inc. [*Defunct*] (EA)
PBI........... Prophylactic Brain Irradiation [*Oncology*]
PBI........... Protein-Bound Iodine [*Clinical chemistry*]
PBI........... Public Benevolent Institution [*Australia*]
PBI........... Pupil Behavior Inventory [*Psychology*]
PBI........... Push Button Indicator (NAKS)
PBI........... Puzzle Buffs International (EA)
PBI........... West Palm Beach [*Florida*] [*Airport symbol*]
PBIA......... Pacific Brain Injury Association (SAUS)
PBiB......... Paperback Books in Print (SAUS)
PBIB......... Partially-Balanced Incomplete Block (PDAA)
PBIB Design... Partially Balanced Incomplete Block Design (SAUS)
PBIC......... Plant Breeding International Cambridge (BUAC)
PBIC......... Poly(butyl Isocyanate) [*Organic chemistry*]
PBIC......... Polybutylisocyanate (SAUS)
PBIC......... Programmable Buffer Interface Card [*Computer science*] (NASA)
PBICSGH... Permanent Bureau of International Congresses for the Sciences of Genealogy and Heraldry (EA)
PBIF......... Pacific Bible Institute of Fresno [*California*]
PBIF......... Plastics and Board Industries Federation [*United Kingdom*] (EAIO)
PBIL......... Polybenzimidazolone [*Organic chemistry*]
PBIM........ Programmable Buffer Interface Module (MCD)
PBIMR....... Push Broom Imaging Microwave Radiometer (SAUS)
PBIO......... PerSeptive Biosystems [*NASDAQ symbol*] (TTSB)
PBIO......... PerSeptive Biosystems, Inc. [*NASDAQ symbol*] (SAG)
PBIOZ........ PerSeptive Biosystems Wrrt [*NASDAQ symbol*] (TTSB)
PBIP......... Paperbound Books in Print [*A publication*]
PBIP......... Pulse Beacon Impact Predictor (AAG)
PBIPr........ Pitney Bowes $2.12 Cv Pref [*NYSE symbol*] (TTSB)
PBIS......... Peachtree Business Internet Suit (SAUS)
PBIS......... Performance-Based Incentive System (AAGC)
PBISTP...... Peter Burwash International Special Tennis Programs (EA)
PBIT......... Parity BIT [*Binary Digit*] [*Data communications*]
PBIU......... Palm Beach International Shipping [*Intermodal shipping container symbol*] (TVRC)
PBI-USA..... Peace Brigades International-United States of America (EA)
PB/IWT...... Ports and Beaches and Inland Waterways Transports [*Military*] (NATG)
PBIX......... Patriot Bank [*NASDAQ symbol*] (TTSB)
PBIX......... Patriot Bank Corp. (PA) [*NASDAQ symbol*] (SAG)
PBJ.......... Paper-Braided Jute (IAA)
PBJ.......... Partial-Band Jammer (SAUS)
PBJ.......... Peanut Butter and Jelly
PBJ.......... Peanut Butter and Jelly Sandwich (TAG)
PBJ.......... Presa Benito Juarez [*Mexico*] [*Seismograph station code, US Geological Survey*] (SEIS)
PBJ.......... Probation before Judgment [*Motor vehicle violation code used in state of Maryland*] (MVRD)
PBJC......... Palm Beach Junior College [*Lakeworth, FL*]
PBJ Cable... Paper, Braided Jute Cable (SAUS)
PBK.......... Palm Beach, Inc. (EFIS)
PBK.......... Paperback
PBK.......... Payload Bay Kit [*NASA*] (NASA)
PBK.......... Phi Beta Kappa [*Honorary society*]
PB (k)....... Phonetically Balanced (Kindergarten) [*Speech and language therapy*] (DAVI)
PBK.......... Phosphorylase B Kinase [*An enzyme*] (MAE)
PBK.......... Poncebank [*NYSE symbol*] (SAG)
PBK.......... Pseudophakic Bullous Keratopathy (SAUS)
PBKAL....... Paris, Brussels, Koln [*Cologne*], Amsterdam, London [*High-speed rail network*] (ECON)
PBKB........ Peoples Bancshares, Inc. [*NASDAQ symbol*] (SAG)
PBKB........ People's Savings Bank of Brockton [*Brockton, MA*] [*NASDAQ symbol*] (NQ)
PBKC........ Premier Bankshares [*NASDAQ symbol*] (TTSB)
PBKC........ Premier Bankshares Corp. [*NASDAQ symbol*] (NQ)
PBKS........ Provident Bankshares [*NASDAQ symbol*] (TTSB)
PBKS........ Provident Bankshares Corp. [*NASDAQ symbol*] (NQ)
PBKTOA..... Printing, Bookbinding and Kindred Trades Overseers Association (SAUS)
PBL.......... Bethlehem Public Library, Bethlehem, PA [*OCLC symbol*] (OCLC)
PBl.......... Blairsville Public Library, Blairsville, PA [*Library symbol*] [*Library of Congress*] (LCLS)
PBL.......... Lehigh University, Bethlehem, PA [*Library symbol*] [*Library of Congress*] (LCLS)
PBL.......... Pacific Beach Library (SAUS)
PBL.......... Parachute-Braked Landing [*Military*] (IAA)
PBL.......... Patrol Boat, Light [*Navy designation*] (POLM)
PBL.......... Payload Bay Liner [*NASA*] (MCD)
PBL.......... Performance Based Logistics
PBL.......... Peripheral Blood Leukocyte [*or Lymphocyte*] [*Hematology*]
PBL.......... Peripheral Blood Lymphocyte [*Medicine*] (MELL)
PBL.......... Pharmacokinetics/Biopharmaceutics Laboratory [*University of Maryland*] (RCD)
PBL.......... [*The*] Philadelphia Belt Line Railroad Co. [*AAR code*]
PBL.......... Photo Butt Line (MSA)
PBL.......... Pigeon Breeder's Lung [*Medicine*] (MELL)
PBL.......... Planetary Boundary Layer [*Aerospace*]
PBL.......... Plateau Black-Bladed Letters [*Tire design*]
PBL.......... Poly-Buffered Local Oxidation of Silicon (AAEL)
PBL.......... Potential Binding Level [*Of natural waters for metal ions*]
PBL.......... Problem Based Learning [*Education*]
PBL.......... Product Baseline (MCD)
PBL.......... Prune Brownline [*Plant pathology*]
PBL.......... Public Broadcasting Laboratory (NTCM)
PBL.......... Public Broadcast Laboratory
pbl.......... Publisher [*MARC relator code*] [*Library of Congress*] (LCCP)

PBL......... Pueblo [*Diocesan abbreviation*] [*Colombia*] (TOCD)
PBL......... Puerto Cabello [*Venezuela*] [*Airport symbol*] (OAG)
PBlbM....... Montgomery County Community College, Blue Bell, PA [*Library symbol*] [*Library of Congress*] (LCLS)
PBLC........ Peripheral Blood Lymphocyte Count [*Medicine*] (EDAA)
PBLD........ Progressive Base Line Dimensioning (SAA)
PBLG........ Polybenzyl-L-glutamate [*Biochemistry*]
PBLI........ Premature Birth, Live Infant [*neonatology*] (DAVI)
PBIP........ Blairsville Public Library, Blairsville, PA [*Library symbol*] [*Library of Congress*] (LCLS)
PBLS........ Production Baseline Set (MCD)
pblsh....... publish (SAUS)
PBLSHNG... Publishing
PBLT........ Peripheral Blood Lymphocyte Count Transformation [*Medicine*] (EDAA)
PBLU........ Containers and Pressure Vessels [*Intermodal shipping container symbol*] (TVRC)
PBm......... Bryn Mawr College, Bryn Mawr, PA [*Library symbol*] [*Library of Congress*] (LCLS)
PBM......... Paramaribo [*Surinam*] [*Airport symbol*] (OAG)
PBM......... Parrot Beak-Micromelia (SAUS)
PBM......... Patrol Boat Multi-Mission (ACAE)
PBM......... Patrol Search Plane [*Navy designation for Mariner aircraft*]
PBM......... Pay By Mail (SAUS)
PBM......... Peak Bone Mass [*Medicine*] (DMAA)
PBM......... Performance-Based Management (AAGC)
PBM......... Performance Based Method [*Environmental Protection Agency*] [*Analytical chemistry*]
PBM......... Peribacteriod Membrane (CARB)
PBM......... Peripheral Basement Membrane [*Medicine*] (DMAA)
PBM......... Peripheral Blood Mononuclear [*Cells*] [*Hematology*]
PBM......... Permanent Bench Mark
PBM......... Pharmaceutical Benefit Manager [*or Management*] [*Managed health care*]
PBM......... Pharmacy Benefit Managers (ECON)
PBM......... Pipelined Burst Mode (SAUS)
PBM......... PIXEL Block Mode [*Computer science*] (BYTE)
PBM......... Placental Basement Membrane [*Medicine*] (DMAA)
PBM......... Play By Mail (SAUS)
PBM......... Portable BIT [*Binary Digit*] Map [*Computer science*]
PBM......... Port Bypass Module (SAUS)
PBM......... Poskanzer Portable Bitmap (SAUS)
PBM......... Potential Barrier Method (IAA)
PBM......... Power Balance Model (SAUS)
PBM......... Prescription Benefit Manager (ADWA)
PBM......... Pressure Bias Modulation (MCD)
PBM......... Principal Beach Master [*RAF*] [*British*]
PBM......... Probability Based-Matched [*Database search techniques*]
PBM......... Problem [*Telegraphy*] (PCTE)
PBM......... Production Base Modernization (MCD)
PBM......... Production Bill of Material (SAUS)
PBM......... Program Budget Manager (MCD)
PBM......... Program Business Management (NASA)
PBM......... Pulse Burst Modulation (IAA)
PBmA........ American College of Life Underwriters, Bryn Mawr, PA [*Library symbol*] [*Library of Congress*] (LCLS)
PBMA........ Peanut Butter Manufacturers Association [*Later, PBNPA*] (EA)
PBMA........ Plastic Bath Manufacturers Association [*British*] (DI)
PBMA........ Plumbers and Builders Merchants Association [*Australia*]
PBMA........ Polybutyl Methacrylate [*Organic chemistry*]
PBMA........ Pressed Brick Makers' Association Ltd. [*British*] (BI)
PBMA........ Public Broadcasting Management Association (SAUS)
PBMASA.... Paper Bag Manufacturers' Association of South Australia
PBMC........ Moravian College and Theological Seminary, Bethlehem, PA [*Library symbol*] [*Library of Congress*] (LCLS)
PBMC........ Peripheral Blood Mononuclear Cells [*Hematology*]
PBMCA...... Archives of the Moravian Church, Bethlehem, PA [*Library symbol*] [*Library of Congress*] (LCLS)
PBMCHRC... Pacific Basin Maternal and Child Health Resource Center [*Guam*] (BUAC)
PBMD-Bull... PBMD-Bulletin (SAUS)
PBME........ Physiology and Biomedical Engineering [*Program*] (DAVI)
PBME........ Physiology and Biomedical Engineering Program (BABM)
PBMI........ Pacific Biometrics, Inc. [*NASDAQ symbol*] (SAG)
PBMI........ Polybismaleinimid (SAUS)
PBMI........ Program Budget Management Information [*USDA Forest Service*] (ALAC)
PBMI........ Purchase Base Machine Inventory (SAUS)
PBmL........ Ludington Public Library, Bryn Mawr, PA [*Library symbol*] [*Library of Congress*] (LCLS)
PBMNC...... Peripheral Blood Monomuclear Cell [*Hematology*] (DAVI)
PBMR........ Pennsylvania Bureau of Municipal Research (MCD)
PBMR........ Provisional Basic Military Requirements (NATG)
PBMR........ Push Broom Microwave Radiometer (SAUS)
PBMR........ Pushbroom Microwave Radiometer (SAUS)
PBMS........ Pacific Bell Mobile Services (SAUS)
PBMS........ Parcel Business Machine System (NITA)
PBMS........ Performance-Based Measurement System [*Environmental Protection Agency*]
PBMS........ Photonburst Mass Spectrometry
PBMS........ Pitney Bowes Management Services
PBM/STIRS... Probability Based Matching and Self-Trained Interpretive and Retrieval Systems [*Database*] [*John Wiley & Sons, Inc.*] [*Information service or system*] (CRD)
PBMV........ Percutaneous Balloon Mitral Valvoplasty [*Medicine*] (MELL)
PBMV........ Pulmonary Blood Mixing Volume [*Medicine*] (EDAA)
PBMW........ Moravian College, Bethlehem, PA [*Library symbol*] [*Library of Congress*] (LCLS)
PBN......... Kpasam [*Language symbol*] (ETLW)
PBN......... Northampton County Area Community College, Bethlehem, PA [*Library symbol*] [*Library of Congress*] (LCLS)
PBN......... Paralytic Brachial Neuritis [*Medicine*] (MAE)
PBN......... PE Ben Oilfield Services Ltd. [*Toronto Stock Exchange symbol*]
PBN......... Peribrachialis Nuclei [*Neurology*]
PBN......... Peripheral Benign Neoplasm [*Medicine*] (EDAA)
PBN......... Peroxybutryl Nitride (SAUS)
PBN......... Phenyl(butyl)nitrone [*Organic chemistry*]
PBN......... Physical Block Number
PBN......... Pilatus Britten-Norman Ltd. [*British*] [*ICAO designator*] (FAAC)
PBN......... PointCast Business Network
PBN......... Policy-Based Networking (GART)
PBN......... Polybutylene Napthalate (SAUS)
PBN......... Polymixin-B Sulfate/Bacitracin/Neomycin [*Antibacterial regime*]
PBN......... Porto Amboin [*Angola*] [*Airport symbol*] (OAG)
PBN......... Posteriobuccal Nerve (SAUS)
PBN......... Primary Block Number [*Computer science*]
PBN......... Provisional Buy Notice (SAUS)
PBN......... Pyrolytic Boron Nitride [*Inorganic chemistry*]
PBNA........ Partial Body Neutron Activation [*Radiology*]
PBNA........ Phenyl-beta-naphthylamine [*Organic chemistry*]
PBNB........ Peoples Savings Bank of New Britain (Connecticut) [*NASDAQ symbol*] (COMM)
PBNB........ People's Savings Financial Corp. [*Formerly, People's Savings Bank New Britain*] [*NASDAQ symbol*] (NQ)
PBNB........ Peoples Svgs Finl [*NASDAQ symbol*] (TTSB)
PBNB PAC FED... Pine Bluff National Bank PAC Federal [*Pine Bluff, AR*] (PACS)
PBND........ Pollybeak Nasal Deformity [*Medicine*] (MELL)
PBNE........ Philadelphia, Bethlehem & New England Railroad Co. [*AAR code*]
PBNI........ PacBell Networking Integration
PBNK........ Prime Bancorp, Inc. [*NASDAQ symbol*] (NASQ)
PBNM........ Parallel Bar Noise Maker [*Antiacoustic torpedo device*]
PBNP........ Phipps Bend Nuclear Plant (NRCH)
PBNP........ Point Beach Nuclear Plant (NRCH)
PBNP........ Porcine Brain Natriuretic Peptide [*Biochemistry*]
PBNPA....... Peanut Butter and Nut Processors Association (EA)
PBNS........ Proceedings of the Bristol Naturalists Society (SAUS)
PBNSC....... Peripheral Backup NSC Control Element (SAUS)
PBNSW...... Pharmacy Board of New South Wales [*Australia*]
PBNSW...... Police Board of New South Wales [*Australia*]
PBNT........ Parole Board of the Northern Territory [*Australia*]
PBO......... Packed by Owner
PBO......... Paleobioclimatic Operator
PBO......... Paraburdoo [*Australia*] [*Airport symbol*] (OAG)
PBO......... Pauling Bond Order [*Physical chemistry*]
PBO......... Penicillin in Beeswax [*Medicine*] (DMAA)
PBO......... Penicillin in Beeswax and Oil [*Medicine*] (DMAA)
PBO......... Performance-Based Organization
PBO......... Personal Banking Officer (TBD)
P Bo......... Petrus Boaterius [*Flourished, 1285-1321*] [*Authority cited in pre-1607 legal work*] (DSA)
PBO......... Piperonylbutoxid (SAUS)
pbo......... Placebo [*Medicine*]
PBO......... Plotting Board Operator (MUGU)
PBO......... Polite Brush-Off (SAUS)
PBO......... Poly(p-phenylene Benzobisoxazole) (RDA)
PBO......... Poor Bloody Observer [*British World War I military slang*] (DSUE)
PBO......... Print Business Opportunities [*A publication*] (EAAP)
PBO......... Priority Back Order (TIMI)
PBO......... Process Before Output (SAUS)
PBO......... Projected Benefit Obligation (TDOB)
PBO......... Property Book Officer [*Army*] (AABC)
PBO......... Push-Button Operation
PBoC........ People's Bank of China
PBOCST..... Poly(butoxycarbonyloxystyrene) [*Organic chemistry*]
PBOD........ Phytoplankton Biochemical Oxygen Demand [*Oceanography*]
PBOI........ Public Board of Inquiry
PBOIP....... Preliminary Basis of Issue Plan [*Military*] (MCD)
PBOK........ Pawnbroker.com, Inc. [*NASDAQ symbol*] (QUAN)
p-book....... Printed Book [*Internet lingo*] (NETL)
PBOS........ Planning Board for Ocean Shipping [*Army*] [*NATO*]
PBOT........ Philadelphia Board of Trade (NUMA)
PBP......... Packet Burst Protocol (SAUS)
PBP......... [*The*] Paper Bag Players (EA)
PBP......... Para-(Benzyloxy)phenol [*Organic chemistry*]
PB/P........ Particleboard/Plywood
PBP......... Pay-Back Period [*Finance*]
PBP......... Pay by Phone [*Business term*]
PBP......... Payrole, Budgeting, Personnel-System (SAUS)
PBP......... Peak Blood Pressure [*Cardiology*] (DAVI)
PBP......... Pellin-Broca Prism [*Physics*]
PBP......... Penicillin-Binding Protein [*Biochemistry*]
PBP......... Performance-Based Pay
PBP......... Periplasmic Binding Protein [*Biochemistry*]
PBP......... Person Before Place [*Library cataloguing*] (DGA)
PBP......... Pheromonebinding Proteins [*Biochemistry*]
PBP......... Phosphate-Binding Protein [*Biochemistry*]
PBP......... Picnic Basket Porphyrin [*Organic chemistry*]
PBP......... Picture-by-Picture [*Television technology*] (PS)
PBP......... Play-by-Play (WDMC)

PBP.......... Plotting Board Plot (MUGU)
PBP.......... Point by Point
PBP.......... Porphyrin Biosynthetic Pathway [*Biochemistry*] (AAMN)
PBP.......... Post Boost Phase (ACAE)
PBP.......... Postural Back Pain (MELL)
PBP.......... Power Bias Panel
PBP.......... Preburner Pump (SAUS)
PBP.......... Pregnenolone Binding Protein [*Endocrinology*]
PBP.......... Private Brand Proneness [*Marketing*]
PBP.......... Production Base Plan (MCD)
PBP.......... Program and Budget Planning
PBP.......... Program Board Panel
PBP.......... Progressive Bulbar Palsy [*Medicine*] (MEDA)
PBP.......... Provider Based Physician
PBP.......... Pulse Burst Period (PDAA)
PBP.......... Purified Brucella Protein [*Biochemistry*] (DAVI)
PBP.......... Push-Button Panel
PBPA........ Pharmaceutical Benefits Pricing Authority [*Australia*]
PBPB........ Para-bromophenacyl Bromide [*Organic chemistry*]
PBPB........ Performance Based Program Budgeting [*Emergency Management*] (EMA)
PBPB........ Pyridinium Bromide Perbromide [*Inorganic chemistry*]
PBPC........ Passenger and Baggage Processing Committee [*IATA*] (DS)
PBPC........ Phantom Blue Phan Club [*Association*] (EA)
PBPE........ Population Biology/Physiological Ecology [*Program*] [*National Science Foundation*]
PBPI......... Penile-Brachial Pressure Index [*Medicine*] (RAWO)
PBPITMT... Production Base Productivity Improvement through Manufacturing Technology (MCD)
PBPK........ Physiologically Based Pharmacokinetics [*Biochemistry*]
PBPM........ Poultry Byproduct Meal
PBP-PAC.... Peanut Buying Point PAC [*Tifton, GA*] (PACS)
PBPS........ Painting Brushmakers' Provident Society [*A union*] [*British*]
PBPS........ Paulist Bible Pamphlet Series [*Glen Rock, NJ*] [*A publication*] (BJA)
PBPS........ Performance-Based Payment System
PBPS........ Post-Boost Propulsion System [*Aerospace*]
PB/PS....... Power Brakes/Power Steering (SAUS)
PBPS........ Program Budgeting and Planning System (SAUS)
PBPTC....... Palm Beach Psychotherapy Training Center (EA)
PBPV........ Percutaneous Balloon Pulmonary Valvuloplasty [*Medicine*] (DMAA)
PBPZ........ Pittsburgh Paints [*Federal Railroad Administration identification code*]
PBQ.......... Pharmacy Board of Queensland [*Australia*]
PBQ.......... Physiotherapists' Board of Queensland [*Australia*]
PBQ.......... Podiatrists' Board of Queensland [*Australia*]
PBQ.......... Poste De La Baleine [*Quebec*] [*Seismograph station code, US Geological Survey*] (SEIS)
PBQ.......... Preschool Behavior Questionnaire
PBr........... Carnegie Public Library, Bradford, PA [*Library symbol*] [*Library of Congress*] (LCLS)
PBR.......... Pabst Blue Ribbon [*Beer*]
PBR.......... Packed Bed Reactor
PBR.......... Particle Bed Reactor [*Department of Energy*]
PBR.......... Patapsco & Back Rivers Railroad Co. [*AAR code*]
PBR.......... Patient's Bill of Rights (MELL)
PBR.......... Patrol Boat, River [*Navy symbol*]
PBR.......... Patrol Boat Roadstead [*Navy*]
PBR.......... Payment by Results [*Payment system*]
PBR.......... Pebble-Bed Reactor [*Nuclear energy*]
PBR.......... Pembroke, NH [*Location identifier*] [*FAA*] (FAAL)
PBR.......... Pencil Beam RADAR
PBR.......... Performance-Based Regulation (SAUS)
PBR.......... Permit by Rule [*Pollution control*]
PBR.......... Photobioreactor (ADWA)
PBR.......... Pigment-Binder Ratio [*Weight*]
PBR.......... Pittsburgh Byzantine [*Diocesan abbreviation*] [*Pennsylvania*] (TOCD)
PBR.......... Plant Breeders' Rights
PBR.......... Plum Brook Reactor [*Nuclear energy*]
PBR.......... Polar Biomedical Research (SAUS)
PBR.......... Pole Broken [*Telecommunications*] (TEL)
PBR.......... Polished-Bore Receptacle (SAUS)
PBR.......... Power Breeder Reactor (AAG)
PBR.......... Precision Bombing Range [*Army*]
PBR.......... Pressurized Ballistic Range [*NASA*]
PBR.......... Price-to-Book Value Ratio [*Investment term*] (DFIT)
PBR.......... Procedure Base Register (IAA)
PBR.......... Procion Brilliant Red (DB)
PBR.......... Professional Bull Riders [*An association*]
PBR.......... Program Budgetary Review (SAUS)
PBR.......... Program Business Representative (SAUS)
PBR.......... Puerto Barrios [*Guatemala*] [*Airport symbol*] (AD)
PBR.......... Pyridine-Butadiene Rubber
PBR.......... River Patrol Craft [*Navy designation*] (POLM)
PBR.......... Vinylpyridine-Butadiene Rubber (SAUS)
PBra......... Carnegie Free Library, Braddock, PA [*Library symbol*] [*Library of Congress*] (LCLS)
PBRA........ Practical Bomb Rack Adapter (NG)
PBRA........ Professional Bicycle Racers Association [*Defunct*] (EA)
PBracAL..... Allegheny International, Inc., Brackenridge, PA [*Library symbol*] [*Library of Congress*] (LCLS)
Pb-RBC...... Lead Red Blood Count [*For lead poisoning*] [*Medicine*] (DAVI)
PBR Beer... Pabst Blue Ribbon Beer (SAUS)
PBRC........ Permian Basin Railroad [*Federal Railroad Administration identification code*]
PBRC........ Program Budget Review Committee (SAUS)
PBRE........ Pebble-Bed Reactor Experiment [*Nuclear energy*]
PB Report... Publications Board Report (SAUS)
PBRERP..... Permanent Board for Review of the Enlisted Retention Program
PBRERS..... Permanent Board for Review of the Enlisted Rating Structure
PBRESD..... Polar Branch, Research Environmental Science Division [*Army*]
PBRF........ Plant Breeding Research Forum [*Defunct*] (EA)
PBRF........ Plum Brook Reactor Facility [*Lewis Research Center*]
PBriR........ Rohm & Haas Co., Bristol, PA [*Library symbol*] [*Library of Congress*] (LCLS)
P/BRK....... Power Brake [*Automotive engineering*]
PBRNs....... Primary Care Practice-Based Research Networks [*Agency for Healthcare Research and Quality*] (RCD)
PBroGS...... Church of Jesus Christ of Latter-Day Saints, Genealogical Society Library, Philadelphia Branch, Broomall, PA [*Library symbol*] [*Library of Congress*] (LCLS)
PBRR........ Pine Belt Southern Railroad [*Federal Railroad Administration identification code*]
PBRS........ Polybromostyrene [*Organic chemistry*]
PBRS........ Prison Behavior Rating Scale
PBRS........ Pupil Behavior Rating Scale [*Psychology*]
PBRS........ Push-Button Rotary Switch
PBRT........ Pedro's Biomolecular Research Tools
PBRV........ Potato Black Ringspot Virus [*Plant pathology*]
PBS.......... Bethlehem Steel Corp., Charles H. Herty, Jr., Memorial Library, Bethlehem, PA [*Library symbol*] [*Library of Congress*] (LCLS)
PbS.......... Lead Sulphide (SAUS)
PBS.......... Pacific Biological Station [*Department of Fisheries and Oceans*] [*Canada*] [*Research center*] (RCD)
PBS.......... Packed Bed Scrubber (EEVL)
PBS.......... Paginated By Sections (SAUS)
PBS.......... Palestine Broadcasting Service (BJA)
PBS.......... Panama Bureau of Shipping (SAUS)
PBs.......... Paperback Books (SAUS)
PBS.......... Parenchymatous Bundle Sheath [*Botany*]
PBS.......... Parimutuel Betting System
PBS.......... Parti Bersatu Sabah [*Malaysia*] [*Political party*] (ECON)
PBS.......... Particulate Biogenic Silica [*Environmental science*]
PBS.......... Parts Breakdown Structure
PBS.......... Path Between the Seas (SAUS)
PBS.......... Peninsular Base Section [*Military*]
PBS.......... Percent Bone Solids (SAUS)
PBS.......... Periscope Bombsight Stabilizer
PBS.......... Permanent Building Societies (SAUS)
PBS.......... Personal Bibliographic Software, Inc. [*Information service or system*] (IID)
PBS.......... Peterborough Board of Education [*UTLAS symbol*]
PBS.......... Philippine Broadcasting Service (NADA)
PBS.......... Philips Business Systems (NITA)
PBS.......... Phosphate-Buffered Saline
PBS.......... Phosphate-Buffered Sodium (MAE)
PBS.......... Photon Backscattering (AAEL)
PBS.......... Phycobilisome [*Biochemistry*]
PBS.......... Picture Building System (NITA)
PBS.......... Pigeon Bay [*South Carolina*] [*Seismograph station code, US Geological Survey*] (SEIS)
PBS.......... Pilgrim Amer Bk & Thrift [*NYSE symbol*] (TTSB)
PBS.......... Pilgrim American Bank & Thrift Fund, Inc. [*NYSE symbol*] (SAG)
PBS.......... Pilgrim Regional BankShares [*NYSE symbol*]
PBS.......... Pilgrim Regional Bank Shares, Inc. [*NYSE symbol*] (SPSG)
PBS.......... Place Before Subject [*Library cataloguing*] (DGA)
PBS.......... Plant Breeding Station (SAUS)
PBS.......... Plettenberg Bay [*South Africa*] [*Airport symbol*] (AD)
PBS.......... Podiatry Bibliographical Society [*Defunct*] (EA)
PBS.......... Polarization Beam Splitter
PBS.......... Polarizing Beamsplitter (SAUS)
PBS.......... Polybutadiene Styrene (SAUS)
PBS.......... Polybutene Succinimide [*Fuels and lubricants*]
PBS.......... Poly(butenesulfone) [*Organic chemistry*]
PBS.......... Polysteel Building Systems Ltd. [*Toronto Stock Exchange symbol*]
PBS.......... Portable Base Station (SAUS)
PBS.......... Portable Batch System (SAUS)
PBS.......... Potere Battericida del Sangue [*Bactericidal Property of the Blood*] [*Medicine*]
PBS.......... Poverty Budget Share [*Bureau of the Census*] (GFGA)
PBS.......... Power Blending System (SAUS)
PBS.......... Power Breakfast Syndrome [*Suffered by late-risers forced to attend breakfast meetings*]
PBS.......... Prayer Book Society [*British*] (DBA)
PBS.......... Prefabricated Bituminous Surfacing
PBS.......... Press-Button Signalling (PDAA)
Pbs.......... Pressure at the Body Surface [*Medicine*] (DAVI)
PBS.......... Pressure Boundary Subsystem [*Nuclear energy*] (NRCH)
PBS.......... Prevent Blindness Society (SAUS)
PBS.......... Primary Base Series (ALAC)
PBS.......... Primer Binding Site [*Genetics*]
PBS.......... Procedure Branching Statement (SAUS)
PBS.......... Process Batch Size (SAUS)
PBS.......... Production Base Support [*Army*] (AABC)
PBS.......... Professional Bibliographic System [*Database manager package*] [*Personal Bibliographic Software, Inc.*] [*Ann Arbor, MI*]
PBS.......... Professional Bowhunters Society (EA)
PBS.......... Professional Business Solutions (ACAE)
PBS.......... Program and Budgeting System (OICC)
PBS.......... Program Board Stowage
PBS.......... Program Breakdown Structure [*Nuclear energy*]

PBS .... Program Buffer Storage (IAA)
PBS .... Project Breakdown Structure [*Nuclear energy*] (NRCH)
PBS .... Protective Breathing System (NAKS)
PBS .... Protestant Big Sisters
PBS .... Prune Belly Syndrome [*Medicine*] (DMAA)
PBS .... Public Brand Software (PCM)
PBS .... Public Broadcasting Service [*Facetious translation: Primarily British Shows*] (EA)
PBS .... Public Broadcasting System
PBS .... Public Broadcast System (IID)
PBS .... Public Buildings Service [*of General Services Administration*]
PBS .... Punch Barrier Strip (SAUS)
PBS .... Push-Button Switch
PBSA .... Parole Board of South Australia
PBSA .... Partially Blinded Soldiers Association (SAUS)
PBSA .... Pastoral Board of South Australia
PBSA .... Permanent Building Societies Association (SAUS)
PBSA .... Pharmacy Board of South Australia
PBSA .... Phosphate-Buffered Saline Azide [*Culture medium*]
PBSA .... Phylloxera Board of South Australia
PBSA .... Physiotherapists' Board of South Australia
PBSA .... Publication of the Bibliographical Society of America (SAUS)
PBSAA .... Partially Blinded Soldiers' Association of Australia
PBSC .... Packard BioScience [*NASDAQ symbol*] (SG)
PBSC .... Packard BioScience Co. [*NASDAQ symbol*]
PBSC .... Panelized Building Systems Council (EA)
PBSC .... Performance-Based Service Contracting (AAGC)
PBSC .... Peripheral-Blood Stem-Cell [*Biochemistry Medicine*]
PBSCMA .... Peanut Butter Sandwich and Cookie Manufacturers Association [*Later, PBNPA*] (EA)
PBSCT .... Peripheral Blood Stem Cell Transplant [*Medicine*]
PBSCT .... Peripheral Blood Stem Cell Transplantation (SAUS)
PBSE .... Philadelphia-Baltimore Stock Exchange [*Later, Philadelphia-Baltimore-WashingtonStock Exchange*]
PBSF .... Pacific Bank NA [*NASDAQ symbol*] (SPSG)
PBshBrc ..... Peoples Bancshares, Inc. [*Associated Press*] (SAG)
PBSI .... Philips Business Systems, Inc. (SAUS)
PBS/IS .... Public Buildings Service/Information System (SAUS)
PBSM .... Plastic Bonded Starter Mix
PBSP .... Prognostically Bad Sign During Pregnancy [*Obstetrics*] (MAE)
PBSR .... Papers of the British School at Rome (SAUS)
PBSR .... Permanent Building Societies Registrar [*New South Wales, Australia*]
PB SRAM ... Pipeline Burst SRAM [*Static Random-Access Memory*] [*Computer science*]
PBSS .... Phosphate-Buffered Saline Solution (SAUS)
PBSS .... Pitney Bowes Software Systems (IID)
PbSt9 .... Public Storage Properties IX [*Associated Press*] (SAG)
PbSt 10 ..... Public Storage Properties X, Inc. [*Associated Press*] (SAG)
PbSt 11 ..... Public Storage Properties XI, Inc. [*Associated Press*] (SAG)
PbSt 12 ..... Public Storage Properties XII, Inc. [*Associated Press*] (SAG)
PbSt14 ...... Public Storage Properties XIV, Inc. [*Associated Press*] (SAG)
PbSt15 ...... Public Storage Properties XV, Inc. [*Associated Press*] (SAG)
PbSt16 ...... Public Storage Properties XVI, Inc. [*Associated Press*] (SAG)
PbSt17 ...... Public Storage Properties XVII, Inc. [*Associated Press*] (SAG)
PbSt18 ...... Public Storage Properties XVIII, Inc. [*Associated Press*] (SAG)
PbSt19 ...... Public Storage Properties XIX, Inc. [*Associated Press*] (SAG)
PbSt20 ...... Public Storage Properties XX, Inc. [*Associated Press*] (SAG)
PBSTA .... Push-Button Station (IAA)
PBSteel ..... Bethlehem Steel Corp., Charles M. Schwab Memorial Library, Bethlehem, PA [*Library symbol*] [*Library of Congress*] (LCLS)
PBSU .... Poloma [*Intermodal shipping container symbol*] (TVRC)
PBSU .... Portable Beacon and Scoring Unit (MCD)
PBSV .... Plum Bark Split Virus (SAUS)
PBSW .... Push-Button Switch
PBSX .... PBS Coal [*Federal Railroad Administration identification code*]
PBSZ .... CSX Intermodal [*Intermodal trailer symbol*]
PBT .... Pacific Ballet Theatre
PBT .... Para-Bandit Target
PBT .... Parity BIT [*Binary Digit*] Test
PBT .... Party of Businessmen and Tradesmen [*Czech Republic*] (BUAC)
PBT .... Passband Tuning
PBT .... Passenger Boarding Total (SAUS)
PBT .... Pemberton, British Columbia, Canada [*Amtrak Busline code*]
PBT .... Peoria Board of Trade (EA)
PBT .... Performance-Based Teaching (SAUS)
PBT .... Performance-Based Training (SAUS)
PBT .... Permeable Base Transistor [*Electronics*]
PBT .... Permian Basin Royalty Trust [*NYSE symbol*] (SPSG)
PBT .... Persistent, Bioaccumulative, and Toxic [*Chemistry*]
PBT .... Philippine Ballet Theater (ECON)
PBT .... Pierce-Blank Tool (MCD)
PBT .... Piggyback Tape [*or Twistor*] [*Computer science*]
PBT .... Pit Bull Terrier (SPVS)
PBT .... Pittsburgh Ballet Theatre
PB-T .... Plastic Banded, Tracer (SAUS)
PBT .... Polybay Tier
PBT .... Polybenzothiazole [*Organic chemistry*]
PBT .... Polybutylene Terephthalate [*Organic chemistry*]
PBT .... Portable Breathalyzer Test (SARE)
PBT .... Preferred Body Temperature [*Physiology*]
PBT .... Preliminary Bearing Training (SAUS)
PBT .... Preliminary-Breath-Test [*Device used by police to determine whether or not a driver is legally intoxicated*]
PBT .... President of the Board of Trade (SAUS)
PBT .... Professional Billiards Tour [*An association*]
PBT .... Profile-Based Therapy [*Medicine*] (DB)
PBT .... Profit before Tax [*Finance*] (WDAA)
PBT .... Profit Before Taxes
PBT .... Push-Button Telephone
PBT .... Red Bluff, CA [*Location identifier*] [*FAA*] (FAAL)
PBT_4 .... Protein-Bound Thyroxine [*Endocrinology*] (DAVI)
PBTB .... Paper Bag Trade Board (SAUS)
PBTB .... Parsons Brinckerhoff-Tudor-Bechtel
PBTC .... Peoples Banctrust [*NASDAQ symbol*] (TTSB)
PBTC .... Peoples BancTrust Company Inc. [*NASDAQ symbol*] (SAG)
PBTC .... Postal Business Training Centre [*British*]
PBTC .... Pozzi Brothers Transportation [*Common carrier symbol*]
PBTE .... Performance-Based Teacher Education (OICC)
PBTF .... Polybromotrifluoroethylene (SAUS)
PBTF .... Protective Barrier Test Facility (SAUS)
PBTF .... Pump Bearing Test Facility [*Nuclear energy*]
PBTFUS ..... Pediatric Brain Tumor Foundation of the United States [*Association*] (EA)
PBTI .... Pacific Boat Trailers [*NCIC trailer make code*]
PBTI .... Pancreatic Basic Trypsin Inhibitor (DB)
P/BTN .... Push Button [*Automotive engineering*]
PBTP .... Polybutylene Terephthalate [*Organic chemistry*]
PBT-PAR .... Polybutylene Terephthalate-Polyarylate (SAUS)
PBT-PET .... Polybutylene Terephthalate-Polyethylene Terephthalate (SAUS)
PBTS .... Business-Oriented Technology Promotion Programme (SAUS)
PBTS .... Proton Beam Transport System
PBTX .... Prime Bancshares, Inc. [*NASDAQ symbol*] (NASQ)
PBTX .... Ptychodiscus brevis Toxin [*Florida red-tide toxin*]
PBTY .... Probability [*Telegraphy*] (PCTE)
PBU .... Air-Burundi [*ICAO designator*] (FAAC)
PBU .... Bucknell University, Lewisburg, PA [*OCLC symbol*] (OCLC)
PBU .... Page Buffer Unit (SAUS)
PBU .... Pali Buddhist Union (BUAC)
PBU .... Palm Beach County Utility Corp. [*Toronto Stock Exchange symbol*]
PBU .... Peribacteroid Unit (SAUS)
PBU .... Peripheral Buffer Unit (SAUS)
PBU .... Perry Basin [*Utah*] [*Seismograph station code, US Geological Survey*] (SEIS)
PBU .... Photo Blow-up (SAUS)
PBU .... Premature Baby Unit [*National Health Service*] [*British*] (DI)
PBU .... Primary Beam Unit (SAUS)
PBU .... Progil-Bayer-Ugine (SAUS)
PBU .... Push Button Unit (NITA)
PBU .... Pushbutton Unit (SAUS)
PBU .... Putao [*Myanmar*] [*Airport symbol*] (OAG)
P Buoy ...... Pillar Buoy (SAUS)
PBUP .... Perforated Backup Plate
PBURG ...... Pittsburg, CA [*American Association of Railroads railroad junction routing code*]
PBUS .... Professional Bail Agents of the United States (NTPA)
PBut .... Butler Public Library, Butler, PA [*Library symbol*] [*Library of Congress*] (LCLS)
PButV .... United States Veterans Administration Hospital, Butler, PA [*Library symbol*] [*Library of Congress*] (LCLS)
PBV .... English Prayer Book Version (BJA)
PBV .... Peach Blotch Virus (SAUS)
PBV .... Pedal Blood Vessel
PBV .... Pharmacy Board of Victoria [*Australia*]
PBV .... Platinol [*Cisplatin*], Bleomycin, Vinblastine [*Antineoplastic drug regimen*]
PBV .... Post Boost Vehicle [*Missiles*] (AFM)
PBV .... Predicted Blood Volume [*Medicine*]
PBV .... Proportioning and Bypass Valve
PBV .... Pulmonary Blood Volume [*Medicine*]
PBVCO ...... Post Boost Vehicle Cutoff (ACAE)
PBVI .... Pulmonary Blood Volume Index [*Medicine*] (RAWO)
PBVM .... Presentation of the Blessed Virgin Mary [*Roman Catholic women's religious order*]
PBVM .... Presentation of the Blessed Virgin Mary Sisters (TOCD)
PBVM .... Sisters of the Presentation of the B.V.M. (TOCD)
PBVM .... Union of the Sisters of the Presentation of the Blessed Virgin Mary (TOCD)
PBVP .... Post Boost Vehicle Propulsion [*Missiles*] (MCD)
PBVR .... [*The*] Port Bienville Railroad [*AAR code*]
PBvu .... Andrew Bayne Memorial Library, Bellevue, PA [*Library symbol*] [*Library of Congress*] (LCLS)
PBW .... Particle-Beam Weapon
PBW .... Parts by Weight (IEEE)
PBW .... Percussive Butt Welder
PBW .... Pink Bollworm [*Cotton pest*]
PBW .... Posterior Bite Wing [*Dentistry*]
PBW .... Power by Wire [*Flight control*]
PBW .... Proportional Bandwidth (MCD)
PBW .... Provisional Bombardment Wing [*Military*] (POLM)
PBW .... Pulse Burst Wave
PBWA .... Plasma Beat Wave Accelerator [*Physics*]
PBWA .... Plasma Beta-Wave Accelerator [*Plasma physics*]
PBWA .... Professional Basketball Writers Association (NTPA)
PBWAA ...... Professional Basketball Writers' Association of America (EA)
PBWC .... Professional Businesswomen of California (EARSL)
PBWEE ...... Pilot Boll Weevil Eradication Experiment [*Department of Agriculture*]
PBWF .... Pulse Burst Waveform
PBWG .... Pakistan Bibliographical Working Group (BUAC)

PBWS .... Performance-Based Work Statement (SAUS)
PBWSE...... Philadelphia-Baltimore-Washington Stock Exchange [*Later, Philadelphia Stock Exchange*]
PBWT........ Parts by Weight (WDAA)
PBWU .... Projektgruppe Bayern zur Erforschung der Wirkung von Umweltschadstoffen (SAUS)
PBX.......... PBX Resources [*Vancouver Stock Exchange symbol*]
PBX.......... Pillbox (SAUS)
PBX.......... Plastic Bonded Explosive
PBX.......... Polymer Bonded Explosive (SAUS)
PBX.......... Private Branch Exchange [*Telecommunications*]
PBx .... Prostate Biopsy [*Medicine*] (MELL)
PBX.......... Public Branch Exchange (SAUS)
PBXFS....... Private Branch Exchange Final Selector [*Telecommunications*] (IAA)
PBX-M....... Princeton Beta Experiment Modified (SAUS)
PBXs......... Personal Business Exchanges (SAUS)
PBY.......... Kayenta, AZ [*Location identifier*] [*FAA*] (FAAL)
PBY.......... Patrol Bomber [*Navy designation for Catalina aircraft*]
PBY.......... Pearl Air Services (U) Ltd. [*Uganda*] [*ICAO designator*] (FAAC)
PBY.......... Pep-Boys (EFIS)
PBY.......... Pep Boys-Man,Mo,Ja [*NYSE symbol*] (TTSB)
PBY.......... Pep Boys - Manny, Moe & Jack [*NYSE symbol*] (SPSG)
PBY.......... Pillars Bay [*Alaska*] [*Airport symbol*] (AD)
PBY.......... Postgraduate Year (MELL)
PBY.......... Probably [*Telegraphy*] (PCTE)
PBYP .... Play-By-Play Toys&Novelties [*NASDAQ symbol*] (TTSB)
PBYP .... Play By Play Toys & Novelties, Inc. [*NASDAQ symbol*] (SAG)
PBZ.......... Khortitsa-Air Ltd. [*Ukraine*] [*FAA designator*] (FAAC)
PBZ.......... Parker Brothers [*Federal Railroad Administration identification code*]
PBZ.......... Peoples Bank of Zanzibar [*Tanzania*] (BUAC)
PBZ.......... Personal Breathing Zone (HEAS)
PBZ.......... Phenoxybenzamine [*Also, POB*] [*Adrenergic blocking agent*]
PBZ.......... Phenylbutazone [*Anti-inflammatory compound*]
PBZ.......... Plettenberg [*South Africa*] [*Airport symbol*] (OAG)
PBZ.......... Pyribenzamine [*Antihistamine*] [*Trademark*]
PBzMA ...... Polybenzylmethacrylate (SAUS)
PBzN......... Peroxybenzoyl Nitrate [*Lacrimator*]
PBZT......... Polyphenylene Benzalthiazole (SAUS)
PBZT......... Poly-P-Phenylene Benzobesthiazole
pc............ After Meals [*Medicine*] (BCRP)
PC............ All India Reporter, Privy Council [*1914-50*] [*A publication*] (DLA)
PC............ British and Colonial Prize Cases [*A publication*] (DLA)
PC............ Carlist Party (Spain) [*Political party*] (PSAP)
PC............ Center Alliance Party (Poland) [*Political party*] (PSAP)
Pc............ Chamber Pressure
PC............ Civilian Personnel Division [*Coast Guard*]
PC............ Coastal Escort [*Ship symbol*] (NATG)
PC............ Communist Party [*Peru*] [*Political party*] (PD)
PC............ diacyl-glyceroPhosphoCholine (SAUS)
PC............ Fiji Air [*ICAO designator*] (AD)
PC............ Indian Rulings, Privy Council [*1929-47*] [*A publication*] (DLA)
PC............ J. Lewis Crozer [*Chester Public*] Library, Chester, PA [*Library symbol*] [*Library of Congress*] (LCLS)
PC............ Judicial Committee of the Privy Council (DLA)
PC............ Paccinian Corpuscle [*Medicine*] (MELL)
PC............ Pace College (SAUS)
PC............ Pacific Airlines (SAUS)
PC............ Pacific Coast Railroad [*AAR code*] [*Terminated*]
PC............ Pacific College (SAUS)
PC............ Pacific Command [*Department of Defense*] (BARN)
PC............ Package Control [*or Controller*]
PC............ Packed Cell [*Hematology*] (MAE)
PC............ Packet Classifier (MWOL)
PC............ Pad Coordinator [*NASA*]
PC............ Page Copy (SAUS)
PC............ Pain Control (MELL)
PC............ Paine College (SAUS)
PC............ Paired Comparisons [*Education*] (EDAC)
PC............ Palmer College (SAUS)
PC............ Palmitoyl Carnitine [*Biochemistry*]
PC............ Palomar College (SAUS)
PC............ [*The*] Panama Canal
PC............ Pancreatic Carcinoma [*Medicine*] (MELL)
PC............ Pancreatic Cholera [*Medicine*] (MELL)
Pc............ Pancuronium [*A muscle relaxant*]
PC............ Panola College (SAUS)
PC............ Panoramic Camera
PC............ Paper Chromatography (ODA)
PC............ Paper Copy
PC............ Paper Core (IAA)
PC............ Paper/Cotton (SAUS)
PC............ Paper or Cloth [*Freight*]
PC............ Paracortex (DMAA)
PC............ Paracortical Hyperplasia [*Oncology*]
PC............ Paraffin Concentration (ODA)
PC............ Parallax Computer (SAUS)
pc............ Parallax Second (NTIO)
PC............ Parallax Second [*Unit of interstellar-space measure*]
PC............ Parallel Circuit (SAUS)
PC............ Parallel Connection (SAUS)
PC............ Parameter Card (SAUS)
PC............ Parameter Checkout [*Computer science*] (IAA)
PC............ Parametric Cubic [*Computer science*] (OA)
PC............ Parental Control [*Channel lockout*] [*Video technology*]
PC............ Parent Care (EA)
PC............ Parent Cells
PC............ Parents' Charter (AIE)
PC............ Parent to Child [*Medicine*] (EDAA)
PC............ Paris College (SAUS)
PC............ Parish Church [*British*] (ROG)
PC............ Parish Council
PC............ Parish Councillor (WDAA)
PC............ Parity Check [*Computer science*] (IAA)
PC............ Park College (SAUS)
PC............ Parliamentary Cases [*A publication*] (DLA)
PC............ Parliamentary Centre [*Canada*] (EAIO)
PC............ PARSEC [*Parallax Second*] [*Unit of interstellar-space measurement*]
PC............ Parsons College (SAUS)
PC............ Part Card [*Computer science*] (IAA)
PC............ Partial Cut [*USDA Forest Service*] (ALAC)
PC............ Participation Certificate
PC............ Parti Communiste [*Communist Party*] [*Luxembourg*] [*Political party*] (PPW)
PC............ Particulate Component (DMAA)
PC............ Partido Colorado [*Colorado Party*] [*Uruguay*] [*Political party*] (PPW)
PC............ Partido Conservador [*Conservative Party*] [*Nicaragua*] [*Political party*] (EY)
PC............ Partido Conservador [*Conservative Party*] [*Ecuador*] [*Political party*] (PPW)
PC............ Partition Coefficient
PC............ Partly Cloudy (ADWA)
PC............ Parts Catalog (KSC)
PC............ Pasadena College (SAUS)
PC............ Passenger Cargo (SAUS)
PC............ Passenger Certificate [*Shipping*] (DS)
PC............ Past Commander
PC............ Patch Card (SAUS)
PC............ Patch Conversion (SAUS)
PC............ Patent Cases [*A publication*] (DLA)
PC............ Patent Classification (NITA)
PC............ Patent Committee (MCD)
PC............ Patentee/Company Code (NITA)
PC............ Path Carrier (SAUS)
PC............ Path Consistency (SAUS)
PC............ Path Control [*Computer science*] (IBMDP)
PC............ Path Controller (NITA)
PC............ Patient Cancellation [*Medicine*] (DHP)
PC............ Patres Conscripti [*Senators*] [*Latin*]
PC............ Patrol Car [*British military*] (DMA)
PC............ Patrol Carrier (SAUS)
PC............ Patrol, Coastal [*Navy designation*] (POLM)
PC............ Patrol Commander (SAUS)
PC............ Patrol Corvette (SAUS)
PC............ Patrol Craft
PC............ Patrol Vessel, Submarine Chaser [*Navy symbol*]
PC............ Pay Card (SAUS)
PC............ Paycheck (SAUS)
PC............ Pay Clerk
PC............ Paymaster-Captain [*Navy*] [*British*]
PC............ Paymaster-Commander [*Navy*] [*British*]
PC............ Paymaster-in-Chief (SAUS)
PC............ Payment Center (MHDB)
PC............ PC Holdings ADS [*NYSE symbol*] (SG)
PC............ Peace Commissioner [*Ireland*]
PC............ Peace Corps (EA)
PC............ Peak Capacity
PC............ Peg Count [*Telecommunications*] (TEL)
PC............ Pembroke College (SAUS)
PC............ Penal Code [*A publication*] (DLA)
PC............ Penetrating Cell
Pc............ Penicillin (STED)
PC............ Penn Central Transportation Co. [*Subsidiary of Penn Central Corp.*] [*Absorbed into Consolidated Rail Corp.*] [*AAR code*]
PC............ Penny Cyclopoedia [*British*] [*A publication*] (ROG)
PC............ Penske Car [*Racing model*]
PC............ Pentose Cycle [*Biochemistry*] (MAE)
PC............ People for a Change [*An association*] [*Defunct*] (EA)
PC............ People's Conference [*India*] [*Political party*] (PPW)
PC............ Pepperdine College (SAUS)
PC............ Percent [*or Percentage*] (IAA)
pc............ Percent (WDMC)
PC............ Percent Correct
PC............ Percentile (SAUS)
PC............ Per Centum [*By the Hundred*] [*Latin*]
PC............ Perciconia circinata [*A toxin-producing fungus*]
PC............ Per Compass (IAA)
PC............ Per Condoglianza [*Used on visiting cards to express condolence*] [*Italian*]
PC............ Percutaneous Cholecystostomy [*Medicine*]
PC............ Perfins Club (EA)
PC............ Perforated Core [*Automotive engineering*]
PC............ Performance Code
PC............ Performance Contract (OICC)
PC............ Pericarditis [*Avian pathology*]
PC............ Pericentral
PC............ Pericynthion [*Perilune, or low point, in lunar orbit*]
PC............ Period Contract
PC............ Peripheral Cell

PC........... Peripheral Control (BUR)
PC........... Peripheral Controller (NITA)
PC........... Peritoneal Cell (DMAA)
PC........... Permanently Connected (ELAL)
PC........... Permeance Coefficient (IAA)
PC........... Perpetual Curate
PC........... Personal Call (OA)
PC........... Personal Care
PC........... Personal Communication (SAUS)
pc........... Personal Computer (WDMC)
PC........... Personal Computer
PC........... Personal Computing (SAUS)
PC........... Personal Copier [*In product name, PC-10*] [*Canon Inc.*]
PC........... Personal Corporation (BARN)
PC........... Personal Correction
PC........... Personality Card (SAUS)
PC........... Personnel Carrier [*A vehicle*]
PC........... Personnel Coordinator (SAUS)
PC........... Personnel Council (ACAE)
PC........... Perspective control [*Photography*]
PC........... Petro-Canada
PC........... Petrochemistry (SAUS)
pc........... Petty Cash (WDMC)
PC........... Petty Cash
PC........... Pfeiffer College (SAUS)
PC........... Pharmacology [*Medicine*] (DMAA)
PC........... Pharmacy Corps [*Army*]
PC........... Phase Change (SAUS)
PC........... Phase-Change [*Physics*]
PC........... Phase Code (NITA)
PC........... Phase Coherent (CET)
PC........... Phase Conjugate (SAUS)
PC........... Phase Conjugation (SAUS)
PC........... Phase Contrast (SAUS)
PC........... Phase Control (IAA)
PC........... Phase Converter (SAUS)
PC........... Phase Corrector [*Communications term*] (DCT)
PC........... Phase Current (SAUS)
PC........... Phenol Coefficient (IIA)
PC........... Pheochromocytoma [*Oncology*]
PC........... Philadeiphia College (SAUS)
PC........... Philco Corp. (IAA)
Pc........... Philips curve (SAUS)
PC........... Philosophical Classics [*A publication*]
P-C........... Phlogistic Corticoid (STED)
PC........... Phobia Clinic (EA)
PC........... Phoenix College (SAUS)
PC........... Phone Call (SAUS)
PC........... Phosphate Crown (SAUS)
PC........... Phosphate Cycle [*Chemistry*] (MAE)
PC........... Phosphatidylcholine [*Lecithin*] [*Biochemistry*]
PC........... Phosphocholine [*Biochemistry*]
PC........... Phosphocreatine [*Also, PCr*] [*Creatine phosphate; see CP*] [*Biochemistry*]
PC........... Phosphorylcholine [*Biochemistry*]
PC........... Photo Cathode (SAUS)
PC........... Photo Cell (SAUS)
PC........... Photocell
PC........... Photochemical (SAUS)
PC........... Photochromatic (SAUS)
PC........... Photochromic (SAUS)
PC........... Photocomposing (SAUS)
PC........... Photoconductance (SAUS)
PC........... Photoconduction (SAUS)
PC........... Photoconductive
PC........... Photoconductivity (SAUS)
pc........... Photoconductor (ELAL)
PC........... Photoconductor
PC........... Photocopy
PC........... Photocounting
PC........... Photocurrent (SAUS)
PC........... Photographic Camera (SAUS)
PC........... Photonic Crystal (SAUS)
PC........... Photostatic Copy (SAUS)
Pc........... Phthalocyanine [*Organic chemistry*]
PC........... Phycocyanin (DB)
PC........... Physical Conditioning (SAUS)
PC........... Physical Contact (SAUS)
PC........... Physicians's Corporation [*Medicine*] (DMAA)
PC........... Physocyanin [*Biochemistry*]
PC........... Phytophthora Cinnamoni [*A fungus*]
PC........... Pica [*Typography*] (WDMC)
PC........... Pick Up Cargo (AFM)
pC........... Picocoulomb [*One trillionth of a coulomb*]
pc........... Picocurie (IDOE)
pC........... Picocurie [*Also, pCi*] [*One trillionth of a curie*]
PC........... Picture (MDG)
PC........... Piece (AAG)
pc........... Piece (VRA)
PC........... Piece of Crap (SAUS)
pc........... Pied Carre [*Square Foot*] [*French*]
pc........... Pied Cube [*Cubic Foot*] [*French*]
PC........... Piedmont College (SAUS)
PC........... Pierre Cardin [*Fashion designer*]
PC........... Pikeville College (SAUS)
PC........... Pill Counter [*Medicine*] (DMAA)
PC........... Pilotage Charts [*Air Force*]
PC........... Pilot Card (SAUS)
PC........... Pin Cutting (SAUS)
PC........... Pineland College (SAUS)
PC........... Pioneer Clubs (EA)
PC........... Pioneer Conference (PSS)
PC........... Pioneer Corps [*British military*] (DMA)
PC........... Piriform Cortex (DMAA)
pc........... Pitcairn [*MARC country of publication code*] [*Library of Congress*] (LCCP)
PC........... Pitch Channel
PC........... Pitch Circle [*Technical drawings*]
PC........... Pitch Class (SAUS)
PC........... Pitch Control (KSC)
PC........... Pitch Cycle (DNAB)
PC........... Pitting Corrosion (PDAA)
PC........... Pittsburgh Commerce Institute
PC........... Pittsburgh Corning (SAUS)
PC........... Plaid Cymru [*Welsh national liberation party*] [*Political party*]
P/C........... Plane Captain (MUGU)
PC........... Plane Change (MCD)
PC........... Plane Commander
PC........... Planetary Camera (SAUS)
PC........... Planetary Citizens (EA)
PC........... Planned Commitment (COE)
PC........... Planning Card (AAG)
PC........... Planning Commission (PA)
PC........... Planning Commitee (SAUS)
PC........... Planning Concept (MCD)
PC........... Plant Computer (NRCH)
PC........... Plant computer-performance monitoring and Calculations (SAUS)
PC........... Planting Council (EA)
PC........... Plasma Cell [*Oncology*]
PC........... Plasma Chromatography
PC........... Plasma Cortisol (DB)
PC........... Plasmacytoma [*Medicine*]
PC........... Plasmatic Cell (SAUS)
P-C........... Plastic-Carbon (SAUS)
PC........... Plastic Core
Pc........... Plastocyanin
PC........... Plate Circuit (DEN)
PC........... Platelet Concentrate [*Hematology*]
PC........... Platelet Count [*Hematology*]
PC........... Platform/Crane (DCTA)
PC........... Platoon Commander (SAUS)
PC........... Player Character (SAUS)
PC........... Pleas of the Crown [*A publication*] (DLA)
P/C........... Pledges/Cost (WDMC)
p/c........... Pledges/Cost [*Fundraising*] (WDMC)
PC........... Plenum Chamber
PC........... Plotting Chart (SAUS)
PC........... Plug Care [*Computer science*] (IAA)
PC........... Plug Cock (AAG)
PC........... Plug Compatible [*Computer science*] (BUR)
PC........... Pluggable Card (SAUS)
PC........... Pneumatic Circuit (SAUS)
PC........... Pneumatic Controller (SAUS)
PC........... Pneumocystis Carinii [*Medicine*] (EDAA)
PC........... Pneumotoxic Center (AAMN)
PC........... Pocket Calculator (SAUS)
PC........... Pocket Computer
PC........... Poetry Criticism [*A publication*]
PC........... Point Cathode (SAUS)
PC........... Point Clause (SAUS)
PC........... Point Contact (IDOE)
PC........... Point of Curve [*Technical drawings*]
P-C........... Polar-Cartesian (SAUS)
PC........... Polar Component [*Food science*]
PC........... Polar Continental [*American air mass*]
PC........... Polar Crane [*Nuclear energy*] (NRCH)
PC........... Polarity Coefficient (SAUS)
P-C........... Polar to Cartesian
PC........... Polar-to-Cartesian (SAUS)
PC........... Pole Cell [*Insect embryology*]
P/C........... Police Car
PC........... Police College (SAUS)
PC........... Police Commissioner (WGA)
PC........... Police-Constable [*Scotland Yard*]
PC........... Police Court [*British*] (ROG)
PC........... Policy Control (ADA)
PC........... Polish Council [*Czech Republic*] (BUAC)
PC........... Political Code [*A publication*] (ILCA)
PC........... Political Correctness
PC........... Politically Correct
P/C........... Polizza di Carico [*Bill of Lading*] [*Shipping*] [*Italian*]
PC........... Pollution Control (MHDB)
PC........... Polycarbonate [*Organic chemistry*]
PC........... Polycarbosilane [*Organic chemistry*]
PC........... Polycomb (SAUS)
PC........... Polymer Chemistry (SAUS)
PC........... Polymer-Concrete (KSC)
PC........... Polyposis Coli [*Medicine*] (DMAA)

PC............ Pomona College (SAUS)
PC............ Pondus Civile [*Civil (Avoirdupois) Weight*] [*Pharmacy*] (ROG)
PC............ Poni Curavit [*Caused to Be Placed*] [*Latin*]
PC............ Poor Clares [*Roman Catholic women's religious order*]
PC............ Poor Classes [*British*] (DSUE)
PC............ Poor Condition [*Medicine*] (DMAA)
PC............ Poor Coordination [*Medicine*] (DMAA)
pc............ Pop Corn [*Crochet*]
PC............ Popular Coalition (BUAC)
PC............ Popular Cult
PC............ Population Census
PC............ Population Communication (EA)
PC............ Population Concern [*British*] (EAIO)
PC............ Population Council (EA)
PC............ Portable Computer
PC............ Portacaval [*Medicine*]
PC............ Portal Cirrhosis [*Medicine*] (DB)
PC............ Port Call [*Army*]
PC............ Port Charles [*Television program title*]
PC............ Port Committee (NATG)
PC............ Port Control [*Telecommunications*] (TEL)
PC............ Porterville College (SAUS)
PC............ Portion Control [*Food service*]
PC............ Portland Cement
PC............ Position Classification (GFGA)
PC............ Position Control (SAUS)
PC............ Positive Column (IAA)
PC............ Positive Control
Pc............ Positive Wave in Children [*Neurophysiology*]
PC............ Postal & Courier (SAUS)
PC............ Postal Clerk [*Navy rating*]
PC............ Post Card (SAUS)
PC............ Postcard
pc............ Postcard (ODBW)
PC............ Post-Chlorinated (IAA)
PC............ Post Cibum [*After Meals*] [*Pharmacy*]
PC............ Postcode (ADA)
PC............ Postcoital [*Medicine*]
PC............ Post Commander [*Military*]
PC............ Post Consulatum [*After the Consulate*] [*Latin*]
PC............ Posterior Capsule (SAUS)
PC............ Posterior Cervical [*Medicine*] (DMAA)
PC............ Posterior Chamber [*Ophthalmology*]
PC............ Posterior Circumflex [*Artery*] [*Anatomy*] (DAVI)
PC............ Posterior Commissure [*Neuroanatomy*]
PC............ Posterior Cortex [*Medicine*] (DMAA)
PC............ Postinflammatory Corticoid [*Medicine*]
PC............ Potential Carcinogen (SAUS)
PC............ Potential Complications [*Medicine*] (DMAA)
PC............ Potentially Correct (ODA)
pc............ Pottery Cache (BJA)
PC............ Pour Condoler [*To Offer Sympathy*] [*French*]
PC............ Power Cartesian (IAA)
PC............ Power Center (SAUS)
PC............ Power Circuit (IAA)
PC............ Power Component (IAA)
PC............ Power Contactor
PC............ Power Control [*System*] (NG)
PC............ Power Conversion
PC............ Power Converter (SAUS)
pc............ Power Cord (BARN)
PC............ Practice Cases [*A publication*] (DLA)
PC............ Pre-Carrier (SAUS)
PC............ Precast
PC............ Precast Chair (SAUS)
PC............ Precaution Category [*For clinical laboratories*]
PC............ Precedents in Chancery [*A publication*] (DLA)
PC............ Pre-Chamber [*Automotive engineering*]
PC............ Precinct (GOBB)
PC............ Precision Control [*Computer programming*] (BYTE)
PC............ Preconditioning [*Medicine*] (DMAA)
PC............ Precordia [*Anatomy*]
PC............ Predictable Computation (SAUS)
PC............ Prediction Computer (SAUS)
PC............ Predictor Control (SAUS)
PC............ Pre-Emphasis Circuit (OA)
PC............ Preliminary Commendation (SAUS)
PC............ Preliminary Commitment (IMH)
PC............ Prenatal Care [*Medicine*] (DMAA)
PC............ Preparatory Commission
PC............ Preparatory Committee
PC............ Prepunched Card (SAUS)
PC............ Presbyterian College (SAUS)
PC............ Present Complaint [*Medicine*]
PC............ Presidents Club [*Commercial firm*] (EA)
PC............ Press Club (NTCM)
PC............ Press Council [*British*]
PC............ Pressure Cable (SAUS)
PC............ Pressure Chamber (NAKS)
PC............ Pressure Circuit (SAUS)
PC............ Pressure Compensator
PC............ Pressure Controller [*Nuclear energy*]
PC............ Pressure Cooker (SAUS)
PC............ Prestressed Concrete (BARN)
PC............ Previous Convictions (WDAA)
pc............ Price (WDAA)
PC............ Price Commission [*Cost of Living Council*]
PC............ Price Control Cases [*A publication*] (DLA)
P/C............ Price/Cost
P/C............ Price Current (SAUS)
PC............ Price per Copy [*of books*]
pc............ Prices Current (WDMC)
PC............ Prices Current
PC............ Priest Confessor
PC............ Primary Center
PC............ Primary Circuit (MCD)
PC............ Primary Closure [*Medicine*] (DMAA)
PC............ Primary Code
PC............ Primary Contributor
PC............ Primary Control (MCD)
PC............ Prime Contractor
PC............ Prime Cost
PC............ Prince Consort (IIA)
PC............ Prince Edward Island Provincial Library, Charlottetown, Prince Edward Island [*Library symbol*] [*National Library of Canada*] (NLC)
PC............ Principal Chaplain (ADA)
PC............ Principal Component
PC............ Principia College (SAUS)
PC............ Print Check (SAUS)
PC............ Print Club (EA)
PC............ Print Command [*Computer science*] (IAA)
PC............ Print Complement (SAUS)
PC............ Print Contrast (DGA)
PC............ Print Control (SAUS)
PC............ Print Cycle [*Computer science*] (IAA)
PC............ Printed Card (IAA)
PC............ Printed Character (SAUS)
PC............ Printed Circuit
PC............ Printer Control
PC............ Printing Cylinder (DGA)
PC............ Printmakers' Council (BUAC)
PC............ Print of Curve (IAA)
PC............ Priority Code (VLIE)
PC............ Priority Control (MLOA)
PC............ Prison Commission (ODA)
PC............ Prisoner of Conscience (BJA)
PC............ Privacy Commission
PC............ Private Circuit (SAUS)
PC............ Private Code (VLIE)
PC............ Private Concerns [*An association*] [*Defunct*] (EA)
PC............ Private Contract [*Tea trade*] (ROG)
PC............ Private Corporation
PC............ Privatization Council [*New York, NY*] (EA)
PC............ Privilege Car [*on a train*] [*Theatre slang*]
PC............ Privileged Character [*A favored student*] [*Teen slang*]
PC............ Privy Council [*or Councillor*] [*British*]
PC............ Privy Counselor (SAUS)
PC............ Prize Court (DLA)
PC............ Probable Cause [*Legal term*]
PC............ Probate Court [*British*] (ROG)
PC............ Procaer SpA [*Italy*] [*ICAO aircraft manufacturer identifier*] (ICAO)
PC............ Procarbazine [*Also, P, PCB, Pr*] [*Antineoplastic drug*]
PC............ Procedure Coordinator (VLIE)
PC............ Procerebral Lobe [*Neuroanatomy*]
PC............ Process Change (SAUS)
PC............ Process Chemistry
PC............ Process Computer (NRCH)
PC............ Process Condensate (SAUS)
PC............ Process Control (DEN)
PC............ Process Controller (SAUS)
PC............ Processing Center [*Telecommunications*] (TEL)
PC............ Processing Conditions [*Food*] (DICI)
PC............ Processor Cluster (SAUS)
PC............ Processor Code (SAUS)
PC............ Processor Controller [*Computer science*] (MDG)
PC............ Procollagen [*Medicine*] (DMAA)
PC............ Procurement Command [*Army*]
PC............ Procurement Communication [*Military*]
PC............ Producers' Council [*Later, CPMC*] (EA)
PC............ Product Code (NITA)
PC............ Production Certificate (MCD)
PC............ Production Company [*Films, television, etc.*]
P-C............ Production-Consumption (SAUS)
PC............ Production Control (MCD)
PC............ Production Costs
PC............ Productive Cough [*Medicine*] (DMAA)
PC............ Professional Communication (MCD)
PC............ Professional Computer (VLIE)
PC............ Professional Consultant (SAUS)
PC............ Professional Corporation
PC............ Professors of Curriculum (EA)
PC............ Profile Component (DET)
PC............ Profit Center (MHDB)
PC............ Progenitor Cryptocides (SAUS)
PC............ Program Card [*Computer science*] (IAA)
PC............ Program Change
PC............ Program Check [*Computer science*] (IAA)

PC........... Program Committee [*UN Food and Agriculture Organization*]
PC........... Program Communications [*Military*] (AFIT)
PC........... Program Contract (SAUS)
PC........... Program Control
PC........... Program Controller (NITA)
PC........... Program Coordination (IEEE)
PC........... Program Coordinator
PC........... Program Council (SAUS)
PC........... Program Counter
PC........... Programmable Channel (SAUS)
PC........... Programmable Computer
PC........... Programmable Controller (ACII)
PC........... Programmable Logic Control [*Computer science*] (IAA)
PC........... Programmable Machine Control (IAA)
PC........... Programmed Channel (SAUS)
PC........... Programmed Check (AAG)
PC........... Programmed Computation (SAUS)
PC........... Programmed Console (SAUS)
PC........... Programmed Control (SAUS)
PC........... Programming Change (VLIE)
PC........... Programming Cost (SAUS)
PC........... Programming Course (SAUS)
PC........... Progressive Conservative [*Canada*] [*Political party*]
PC........... Progressive Conservative Party [*Canada*] [*Political party*] (BUAC)
PC........... Progressive Corporation (EFIS)
PC........... Prohormone Convertase [*Medicine*] (DMAA)
PC........... Project Censored (EA)
PC........... Project Children (EA)
PC........... Project Control (NASA)
PC........... Project Coordinator (NG)
PC........... Project Cuddle [*An association*] (EA)
PC........... Projector Charge
PC........... Prompt Corner (WDAA)
PC........... Pronominal Clitic [*Linguistics*] (IEL)
PC........... Proof Coins [*Numismatics*]
PC........... Propellant Control (SAUS)
P/C........... Property/Casualty [*Insurance*]
PC........... Prophylactic Center (SAUS)
PC........... Proportional Counter [*Instrumentation*]
PC........... Proposed Category [*Lubricants*]
PC........... Proposed Change
PC........... Propositional Calculus [*Logic*]
PC........... Propulsive Coefficient
PC........... Propylene Carbonate [*Organic chemistry*]
PC........... Prospectors Club [*Later, PCI*]
PC........... Prostate Cancer
PC........... Prostatic Carcinoma [*Medicine*] (DB)
PC........... Prosthetics Center [*Veterans Administration*]
PC........... Protective Climate [*Solar heating*]
PC........... Protective Clothing (SAUS)
PC........... Protective Cover (MCD)
PC........... Protein C [*Medicine*] (DMAA)
PC........... Protein Convertase [*Medicine*] (DMAA)
PC........... Proto-Canaanite (BJA)
PC........... Protocol Configuration (SAUS)
PC........... Protocol Control (SAUS)
PC........... Protocol Converter (MCD)
PC........... Providence College (SAUS)
PC........... Provincial Commissioner [*British government*]
PC........... Provisional Costs
PC........... Provisional Cut [*Television*] (NTCM)
PC........... Provocative Concentration [*Immunology*]
PC........... Proximal Colon [*Medicine*] (EDAA)
PC........... Pseudo Code (SAUS)
PC........... Pseudocode (AAG)
PC........... Pseudoconditioning Control [*Neurophysiology*]
PC........... Pseudocyst [*Medicine*] (EDAA)
PC........... Psychodevelopment Checklist [*Psychology*] (DAVI)
PC........... Publications Committee (SAUS)
PC........... Publications in Climatology (MCD)
PC........... Public Charter (TRID)
PC........... Public Citizen (EA)
PC........... Public Contract
PC........... [*The*] Publishers' Circular [*A publication*] (ROG)
PC........... Pubococcygeus [*Muscle*] [*Anatomy*]
PC........... Pull Chain [*Technical drawings*] (DAC)
PC........... Pulmonary Capillary [*Medicine*]
PC........... Pulmonary Contusions (SAUS)
PC........... Pulmonic Closure [*Medicine*] (MAE)
PC........... Pulsating Current
PC........... Pulse Circuit (SAUS)
PC........... Pulse Cleaned [*Dust filtration*]
PC........... Pulse Code [*Telecommunications*] (IAA)
PC........... Pulse Comparator (AAG)
PC........... Pulse Compression
PC........... Pulse Controller
PC........... Pulse Counter [*Computer science*] (MDG)
PC........... Pulverized Coal [*Fuel technology*]
PC........... Pumice Concrete (SAUS)
PC........... Punch Card (NITA)
PC........... Punch Code (SAUS)
PC........... Punch Column (SAUS)
PC........... Punch Control (SAUS)
PC........... Punched Card [*Computer science*]
PC........... Punched Code (SAUS)
PC........... Punjab Cavalry [*British military*] (DMA)
PC........... Puns Corps (EA)
PC........... Purchase Card
PC........... Purchaser Credit [*Resource/timber term*] (ALAC)
PC........... Purchasing and Contracting [*Army*]
PC........... Pure Clairvoyance [*Psychical research*]
PC........... Purified Concentrate
PC........... Purkinje Cell [*Neuroanatomy*]
PC........... Pyrochlore (SAUS)
PC........... Pyrrolinecarboxylic Acid [*Biochemistry*]
PC........... Pyruvate Carboxylase [*An enzyme*] (MAE)
PC........... Single Paper Single Cotton [*Wire insulation*] (AAG)
PC........... Submarine Chaser [*173 foot*] [*Navy symbol*] [*Obsolete*]
PC........... Sumitomo Chemical Co. [*Japan*] [*Research code symbol*]
PC........... Veterans of the US Posse Comitatus (EA)
pc1........... Platelet Count Pretransfusion [*Medicine*] (STED)
PC1........... Postal Clerk, First Class [*Navy rating*]
PC1........... Power Control One [*Hydraulic*] (MCD)
pc2........... Platelet Count Posttransfusion [*Medicine*] (STED)
PC2........... Postal Clerk, Second Class [*Navy rating*]
PC2........... Power Control Two [*Hydraulic*] (MCD)
PC3........... Phoenix Conference on Computers and Communications (SAUS)
PC3........... Postal Clerk, Third Class [*Navy rating*]
PC97........... Personal Computer 97 (SAUS)
PCA........... Acts of the Privy Council [*England*] [*A publication*] (DLA)
PCA........... Calgon Corp., Pittsburgh, PA [*OCLC symbol*] (OCLC)
PCA........... Pacific Coast Athabaskan [*Linguistics*] (IEL)
PCA........... Pacific Communications Area [*Air Force*] (MCD)
PCA........... Packaging Council of Australia (BUAC)
PCA........... Panama Canal Authority
PCA........... Paper Converters Association [*Defunct*] (EA)
PCA........... Paperweight Collectors' Association (EA)
PCA........... Papillary Cystadenoma [*Medicine*] (MELL)
PCA........... Papillon Club of America (EA)
PCA........... Para-Chloramphetamine (STED)
PCA........... Para-Chloroaniline [*Organic chemistry*]
PCA........... Parachute Club of America [*Later, USPA*] (EA)
PCA........... Para-Coumaric Acid [*Organic chemistry*]
PCA........... Parallel Channel Adapter (SAUS)
PCA........... Parallel Computer Architecture (SAUS)
PCA........... Parietal Cell Antibodies [*Immunology*]
PCA........... Parietal Cell Antibody (DB)
PCA........... Parliamentary Candidates Association (BUAC)
PCA........... Parliamentary Commissioner for Administration [*British*]
PCA........... Parochial Clergy Association [*British*] (DBA)
PCA........... Parti Communiste Algerien [*Algerian Communist Party*] [*Political party*]
PCA........... Partido Comunista de Argentina [*Communist Party of Argentina*] [*Political party*] (PD)
PCA........... Partition Control Area (SAUS)
PCA........... Partnership and Cooperation Agreement (EURO)
PCA........... Parts Control Area [*NASA*] (KSC)
PCA........... Party of the Civic Alliance [*Romania*] [*Political party*] (EY)
PCA........... Passive Cutaneous Anaphylaxis [*Immunochemistry*]
PCA........... Patient Care Aide [*or Assistant*] (DAVI)
PCA........... Patient Care Audit (HCT)
PCA........... Patient-Controlled Analgesia
PCA........... Patient Support Associate [*Medicine*]
PCA........... Patriotic Catholic Association [*Name given to nationalized Catholic Church in China*]
PCA........... Payload Clamp Assembly (SAUS)
PCA........... P-Chloraphenylalanine (SAUS)
PCA........... Peachtree Complete Accounting (SAUS)
PCA........... Peak Clipping Amplifier
PCA........... Pekingese Club of America (EA)
PCA........... Pennsylvania Coal Association (SAUS)
PCA........... Pennsylvania Council on the Arts (SAUS)
PCA........... Pennsylvania Counseling Association (SEAT)
PCA........... Pentachloraniline [*Organic chemistry*]
PCA........... Pentachloroanisole [*Organic chemistry*]
PCA........... Percent Cortical Area [*Neurology*]
PCA........... Perchloric Acid [*Inorganic chemistry*]
PCA........... Percutaneous Carotid Arteriogram [*Medicine*] (MAE)
PCA........... Percutaneous Coronary Agioplasty (STED)
PCA........... Performance and Code Analysis (VLIE)
PCA........... Performance and Coverage Analyzer (SAUS)
PCA........... Pericruciate Association [*Cortex, of cat*]
PCA........... Period Contract Acceptance
PCA........... Peripheral Circulatory Assist [*Medicine*]
PCA........... Peritoneal Carcinomatosis [*Oncology*]
PCA........... Permanent Change of Assignment [*Army*]
PCA........... Permanent Court of Arbitration [*See also CPA*] [*Hague, Netherlands*] (EAIO)
PCA........... Personal Care Aide [*or Assistant or Attendant*]
PCA........... Personal Cash Allowance
PCA........... Personal Computer Analyzer (SAUS)
PCA........... Personal Computers Association (SAUS)
PCA........... Pest Control Association (NADA)
PCA........... Petro-Chemical Associates, Inc. (EFIS)
PCA........... Pharmacy Corporation of America
PCA........... Phenylcarboxylic Acid [*Chemistry*] (DAVI)
PCA........... Photo Cell Assembly (SAUS)
PCA........... Photocontact Allergic (STED)

PCA Photocurrent Amplifier (SAUS)
PCA Photogrammetric Consultants Association (SAUS)
PCA Photon Counting Array [*Instrumentation*]
PCA Photon-Coupled Amplifier (VLIE)
PCA Photovoltaic Cell Array (SAUS)
PCA Physical Configuration Audit [*Military, NASA*]
PCA Physicians Corp. of America (ECON)
PCA Piezo-Ceramic Accelerometer [*Electronics*]
PCA Pinnacle [*Alaska*] [*Seismograph station code, US Geological Survey*] (SEIS)
PCA Pitcairn Cierva Autogiro [*Aeronautics*]
PCA Pitch Control Assembly (MCD)
PCA Plane Circular Aperture
PCA Planning, Control, and Administration (GART)
PCA Planters Co-Operative Association [*Federal Railroad Administration identification code*]
PCA Plasma Catecholamine [*Biochemistry*]
PCA Plasma Catecholamine Concentration (STED)
PCA Plasma Covered Aerial (or Antenna) (SAUS)
PCA Plasma-Covered Antenna
PCA Plaster Contractors Association (SAUS)
PCA Plate Count Agar [*Microbiology*]
PCA Pneumatic Control Assembly (NASA)
PCA Point of Closest Approach
PCA Polar Cap Absorption
PCA Polarizer-Compensator-Analyzer (PDAA)
PCA Police Complaint Authority [*British*]
PCA Policy Certification Authority
PCA Polish Community in Australia
PCA Pollution Control Agency (COE)
PCA Polycaproamide (SAUS)
PCA Polycional Antibody [*Medicine*] (EDAA)
PCA Polycrystalline Alumina
PCA Polycyclic Aromatic [*Petroleum engineering*]
PCA Polycycliche Aromaten (SAUS)
PCA Polymorphous Computing Architectures Program [*Defense Advanced Research Projects Agency*] (RCD)
PCA Poodle Club of America (EA)
PCA Pool Critical Assembly [*Nuclear reactor*]
PCA Popular Culture Association (EA)
PCA Pork Council of Australia
PCA Porous-Coated Anatomical [*Prosthesis*]
PCA Porsche Club of America (EA)
PCA Portacaval Anastomosis [*Animal model of chronic liver disease*]
PCA Portage Creek [*Alaska*] [*Airport symbol*] (OAG)
PCA Port Communications Area [*Telecommunications*] (TEL)
PCA Portland Cement Association (EA)
PCA Ports Canada
PCA Positive Control Area
PCA Positive Controlled Airspace
PCA Postconstruction Availability (NVT)
PCA Posterior Cerebral Artery [*Brain anatomy*]
PCA Posterior Communicating Artery [*Anatomy*]
PCA Posterior Cricoarytenoid [*A muscle of the larynx*]
PCA Potash Co. of America, Inc. [*Toronto Stock Exchange symbol*]
PCA Potato Carrot Agar [*Culture Media*]
PCA Potentially Contaminated Area (DNAB)
PCA Poultrymen's Cooperative Association (EA)
PCA Power Calibration Area (SAUS)
PCA Power Conditioning Assembly
PCA Power Control Assembly (NASA)
PCA Power Controller Assemblies (SAUS)
PCA Precipitation with a Compressed Fluid Antisolvent [*Chemical engineering*]
PCA Precision Cleaning Agent (SAUS)
PCA Precision Clearing Agent (DNAB)
PCA Precision Components and Assembly [*Automotive engineering*]
PCA Pre-Conditioned Air System [*Aviation*] (DA)
PCA Precontractual Authorization
PCA Prescribed Concentration of Alcohol (ADA)
PCA Presidency of Civil Aviation [*Saudi Arabia*] (BUAC)
PCA President's Council on Aging [*Inactive*]
PCA Pressure Control Assembly (SAUS)
PCA Prestressed Concrete Association [*British*] (DBA)
PCA Primary Carbon Assimilation [*Botany*]
PCA Primary Communication Attachment [*Computer science*] (ELAL)
PCA Primary Control Assembly [*Nuclear energy*] (NRCH)
PCA Primary Coolant Activity [*Nuclear energy*] (NRCH)
PCA Primary Coverage Area (SAUS)
PCA Prime Candidate Alloy (MCD)
PCA Prime Condition Aircraft
PCA Principal Component Analysis
PCA Principal Control Authority (NATG)
PCA Prindle Class Association (EA)
PCA Print Council of America (EA)
PCA Printed Circuit Analyzer (ELAL)
PCA Printed Circuit Assembly [*Telecommunications*] (TEL)
PCA Printed Circuit Association (BUAC)
PCA Printer Communications Adapter
PCA Printers' Costing Association [*British*] (BI)
PCA Printing Corp. of America
PCA Private Care Association (SAUS)
PCA Private Communications Association [*Later, NCA*]
PCA Procedure Change Authorization (SAUS)
PCA Proceedings of the Classical Association (SAUS)
PCA Process Change Authorization (SAUS)
PCA Process Control Analyzer
PCA Pro-Choice Alliance (BUAC)
PCA Procoagulant Activity
PCA Procrastinators' Club of America (EA)
PCA Producers Commission Association (EA)
PCA Production Code Administration (BARN)
PCA Production Compliance Audit [*Automotive emissions standards*]
PCA Production Credit Association (BUAC)
PCA Professional Chess Association (EA)
PCA Professional Comedians' Association (EA)
PCA Professional Cycling Association [*British*] (DBA)
PCA Program Calibration Area [*Computer science*] (DOM)
PCA Program Change Analysis [*DoD*]
PCA Program Coupler Assembly (KSC)
PCA Program Cumulative Audience [*Advertising*] (DOAD)
PCA Programmable Communications Adapter [*Computer science*]
PCA Progress Change Authority
PCA Progressive Citizens of America
PCA Progressive Cultural Association (BUAC)
PCA Project Control Analyst (ACAE)
PCA Propellant Control Assembly (ACAE)
PCA Property Clearance Assessment (SARE)
PCA Proprietary Cremation Association (SAUS)
PCA Proprietary Crematoria Association [*British*] (DBA)
PCA Propulsion-Controlled Aircraft (SEWL)
PCa Prostate Cancer [*Medicine*]
PCA Protective Clothing Arrangement [*Telecommunications*] (TEL)
PCA Protective Connecting Arrangement [*Telecommunications*] (TEL)
PCA Prototype Protein C Activator [*Biochemistry*]
PCA Public Archives, Charlottetown, Prince Edward Island [*Library symbol*] [*National Library of Canada*] (NLC)
PCA Puli Club of America (EA)
PCA Pulp Chemicals Association (EA)
PCA Pulse Code Adaptor (NITA)
PCA Pulse Counter Adapter
PCA Punched Card Accounting (SAUS)
PCA Putnam California Investment Grade Municipal [*AMEX symbol*] (SPSG)
PCA Putnam Investment Grade Municipal Trust [*AMEX symbol*] (NASQ)
PCA Pyrotechnic Control Assembly [*NASA*]
PCA Pyrrolidonecarboxylic Acid [*Organic chemistry*]
PCAA Pancretan Association of America (EA)
PCAA Particulate Combined Amino Acid [*Marine biology*]
PCAA Prescott College Alumni Association (EA)
PCaab Parietal Cell Autoantibody [*Immunology*]
PcA&E Pacific Aerospace & Electronics, Inc. [*Associated Press*] (SAG)
PCAAS Proceedings of the Connecticut Academy of Arts and Sciences (SAUS)
PC-ABS Polycarbonate-Acrylonitrile-Butadiene-Styrene (SAUS)
PCAC Partially Conserved Axial Current [*Electronics*] (IAA)
PCAC Partially Conserved Axial-Vector Current
PCAC Personal Computer Acquisition Contracts (SAUS)
PCAC Poultry Costings Advisory Council (BUAC)
PCAC Primary Control and Analysis Center (SAUS)
PCAC Private College Admissions Center [*Later, NAAPHE*]
PCAC Professional Classes Aid Council (AIE)
PCAC Prostate Cancer Alliance of Canada (EAIO)
PCACIAS Personal Computer Automated Calibration Interval Analysis System (SAUS)
PC Act Probate Court Act [*A publication*] (DLA)
PCAD Package Computer-Aided Design [*Computer science*]
PCAD Packaging Computer-Aided Design (SAUS)
P-CAD Personal Computer-Aided Design (SAUS)
PCAD Premature Coronary Artery Disease (MELL)
PCAD Program Change Approval Document (DOMA)
PCAD Programs in Computer Applications Development (SAUS)
PCADS Panoramic Control and Display System (MCD)
PCAE Parts Control and Expediting (SAUS)
PCAE Polar Cap Absorption Event
PCAECNY West New York Association of Plumbing and Mechanical Contractors (EARSL)
PC-AEO Personal Computer - Annual Energy Outlook Forecasting Model [*Department of Energy*] (GFGA)
PCAFB Pinecastle Air Force Base (SAUS)
PCAFV Physicians Campaign Against Family Violence (SAUS)
PCAG Pentobarbital-Chlorpromazine-Alcohol Group [*Medicine*]
PCAG Petroleum Conservation Action Group [*India*] (BUAC)
PCAG PRIMACOM AG [*NASDAQ symbol*] (NASQ)
PCAG Research Station, Agriculture Canada [*Station de Recherches, Agriculture Canada*] Charlottetown, Prince Edward Island [*Library symbol*] [*National Library of Canada*] (NLC)
PCAI Parliamentary Commissioner for Administrative Investigations [*Western Australia*]
PCAI PCA International, Inc. [*NASDAQ symbol*] (NQ)
PCAI PCA Intl [*NASDAQ symbol*] (TTSB)
PCAI Personal Care Assessment Instrument [*Australia*]
PCA Int PCA International, Inc. [*Associated Press*] (SAG)
P Cal Petrus Calvelli [*Flourished, 14th century*] [*Authority cited in pre-1607 legal work*] (DSA)
PCalS California State College, California, PA [*Library symbol*] [*Library of Congress*] (LCLS)
PCAM Parliamentaires Canadiennes pour une Action Mondiale [*Association*] [*Canada*] (EAIO)

PCAM........ Partitioned Content Addressable Memory
PCAM........ Physician Corp. of America [*NASDAQ symbol*] (SAG)
PCAM........ Probe Card Assembly Machine (SAUS)
PCAM........ Punched Card Accounting Machine [*Computer science*]
PCamA...... Alliance College, Cambridge Springs, PA [*Library symbol*] [*Library of Congress*] (LCLS)
PCAMIC..... People Concerned about MIC [*Methyl Isocyanate*] (EA)
PCAMP...... Protective Coatings and Metalizing Process (DNAB)
PCAN........ Potential Child Abuse and Neglect (MELL)
PCAN........ Program Change Action Notice (DNAB)
PC and A... Project Control and Administration (SAUS)
PC & A...... Project Control and Administration [*NASA*]
PC&A........ Property Classification and Accounting (SAUS)
PC & B...... Personnel Compensation and Benefits (GFGA)
PC & D...... Priest, Confessor, and Doctor (ROG)
PC&E........ Parts Control and Expediting (SAUS)
PC & H...... Packing, Crating, and Handling [*Shipping*] (AFM)
PC & IC..... Polaris Control and Information Center [*Missiles*]
PC & OR.... Procurement, Commitment, and Obligation Record [*Navy*]
PC&PS...... Professional Credentials and Personnel Service (SAUS)
PC&R........ Post Construction and Repair (SAUS)
PC & S...... Posts, Camps, and Stations [*Military*]
PC & S...... Preliminary Command and Sequencing [*Viking lander mission*] [*NASA*]
PC&T........ Petroleum Construction & Testing, Inc. (EFIS)
PCANSW.... Pest Control Association of New South Wales [*Australia*]
PCAO........ Pollution Control Association of Ontario (SAUS)
PCAO........ President's Commission on Americans Outdoors
PCAOB...... Public Company Accounting Oversight Board
P-CAP....... Automobility Program [*Chrysler Corp*] [*Automobility Program Center*] (IID)
PCAP........ Physical Correlation Analysis Program [*Military*]
P-CAP....... Physically-Challenged Assistance Program [*Chrysler Motors Corp.*] [*Detroit, MI*] [*Information service or system*] (IID)
PCAP........ Post Commercial Action Plan [*International Trade Administration*]
PCAP........ Process Characterization Analysis Package (SAUS)
PCAP........ Programmer Capacity
PCAPA....... Pacific Coast Association of Port Authorities (SAUS)
PCAPI....... Pollution Control Association of the Philippines, Inc. (SAUS)
PCAPK....... Presidents Commission on the Assassination of President Kennedy (SAUS)
PC App...... Law Reports, Privy Council, Appeal Cases [*England*] [*A publication*] (DLA)
PCAPS....... Plant Control and Protection System (SAUS)
PCAPS....... Production Control and Planning System (MCD)
PCAQ........ Pony Club Association of Queensland [*Australia*]
PCAR........ PACCAR, Inc. [*NASDAQ symbol*] (NQ)
PCAR........ Parent-Child Activity Rating Scale [*Education*] (EDAC)
PCAR........ Process Characterization Analysis Package (MHDI)
P/Carb...... Polycarbonate (SAUS)
P (Card)..... Personal Card [*Containing person's name, address, age, description, job, habits, haunts, movements*] [*Used in Belfast, Northern Ireland*]
PCarl........ Bosler Free Library, Carlisle, PA [*Library symbol*] [*Library of Congress*] (LCLS)
PCarlA....... United States Army War College, Carlisle Barracks, PA [*Library symbol*] [*Library of Congress*] (LCLS)
PCarlD...... Dickinson College, Carlisle, PA [*Library symbol*] [*Library of Congress*] (LCLS)
PCarlD-L.... Dickinson School of Law, Sheeley-Lee Law Library, Carlisle, PA [*Library symbol*] [*Library of Congress*] (LCLS)
PCarlH...... Cumberland County Historical Society and Hamilton Library Association, Carlisle,PA [*Library symbol*] [*Library of Congress*] (LCLS)
PCarlMH.... United States Army, Military History Research Collection, Carlisle Barracks, PA [*Library symbol*] [*Library of Congress*] (LCLS)
PCarlPL..... United States Army, Carlisle Barracks Post Library, Carlisle Barracks, PA [*Library symbol*] [*Library of Congress*] (LCLS)
PCARR....... Philippines Council for Agricultural Resources and Research (BUAC)
PCARS....... Partially Coherent Anti-Stokes Raman Scattering (SAUS)
PCARS....... Point Credit Accounting and Reporting System (AFM)
PCAS........ Patient Care Algorithm System [*Medicine*] (DMAA)
PCAS........ Persistent Chemical Agent Stimulant
PCAS........ Personnel Cost Accounting System (SAUS)
PCAS........ Polytechnics Central Admissions System [*British*] (DET)
PCAS........ Possible Carotid Artery System [*Medicine*]
PCAS........ Primary Central Alarm Station [*Nuclear energy*] (NRCH)
P Cas........ Prize Cases [*1914-22*] [*England*] [*A publication*] (DLA)
P Cas........ Prize Cases (Trehearn and Grant) [*England*] [*A publication*] (DLA)
PCAS........ Proceedings of the Cambridge Antiquarian Society (SAUS)
PCAS........ Programming Components Announcement Summary (SAUS)
PCAS........ Punch Card Accounting System [*Computer science*]
PCASA....... Pony Club Association of South Australia
PCAS/CADS... Persistent Chemical Agent Stimulant/Chemical Agent Disclosure Solution [*Army*]
PCASO....... Pilot Classification and Screening Operation (ACAE)
PCASP....... Passive Cavity Aerosol Spectrometer Probe (SAUS)
PCASS....... Parts Control Automated Support System [*Database*]
PCASS....... Program Compliance Assurance and Status System (SAUS)
PCAST....... President's Committee of Advisors on Science and Technology
PCAST....... President's Council of Advisers on Science and Technology [*1989*]
PC/AT........ Personal Computer/Advanced Technology (DCDG)
PCAT......... Pharmacy College Admissions Test (GAGS)
PCAT......... Philippine College of Arts and Trades (SAUS)
pCAT......... Plasmid Chloramphenicol Acetyltransferase [*An enzyme*]
PCAT......... Procedures for the Control of Air Traffic (SAA)
PCAT......... Product Category (SAUS)
PCAT......... Punched Card Accounting Technique (SAUS)
PCATD....... Personal Computer Aircraft Training Device
PCAU........ Parachute Course Administrative Unit [*Military*] [*British*] (INF)
PCAU........ PCA Transport [*Intermodal shipping container symbol*] (TVRC)
PCAU........ Philippine Civil Affairs Unit [*Army unit which supplied emergency subsistence after end of Japanese dominance*] [*World War II*]
PCAV........ Pony Club Association of Victoria [*Australia*]
PCAV........ Principal Component Analysis with Varimax Rotation
PCAVC....... Persistent Complete Atrioventricular Canal [*Medicine*] (RAWO)
PCAWA...... Pony Club Association of Western Australia
PCAZ........ PCA Industries [*Federal Railroad Administration identification code*]
PCB.......... Central Pennsylvania District Library Center, Bellefonte, PA [*OCLC symbol*] (OCLC)
PCB.......... Communist Party of Benin [*Political party*] (PSAP)
PcB.......... Near Point of Convergence [*Ophthalmology*]
PCB.......... Page Control Block [*Computer science*] (IBMDP)
PCB.......... Pancuronium Bromide [*A muscle relaxant*] (DAVI)
PCB.......... Paracervical Block [*Anesthesiology*]
PCB.......... Paracolon Bacilli [*Medicine*] (MELL)
PCB.......... Particle Count Blank [*Automotive testing*]
PCB.......... Parti Communiste de Belgique [*Communist Party of Belgium*] [*See also KPB*] [*Political party*] (PPE)
PCB.......... Partido Comunista de Bolivia [*Communist Party of Bolivia*] [*Political party*] (PPW)
PCB.......... Partido Comunista do Brasil [*Communist Party of Brazil*] [*Pro-Albanian*] [*Political party*] (PPW)
PCB.......... Parts Control Board
PCB.......... Patent Compensation Board [*Energy Research and Development Administration*]
PCB.......... Pear [*Language symbol*] (ETLW)
PCB.......... Percutaneous Biopsy [*Medicine*] (CPH)
PCB.......... Pest Control Bureau (SAUS)
PCB.......... Petty Cash Book [*Business term*]
PCB.......... Placebo [*Medicine*] (MELL)
PCB.......... Planning Change Board (AAG)
PCB.......... Please Call Back (SAUS)
PCB.......... Plenum Chamber Burning
PCB.......... Point-Contact Breakdown (SAUS)
PCB.......... Polychlorinated Biphenyl [*Organic chemistry*]
PCB.......... Polychlorinated Biphenyls [*Environment term*] (EGA)
PCB.......... Polychlorobenzene
PCB.......... Polychlorobiphenyl (SAUS)
PCB.......... Portacaval Bypass [*Cardiology*] (DMAA)
PCB.......... Port Check BIT [*Binary Digit*] [*Telecommunications*] (TEL)
PCB.......... Possibly Carcinogenic Substance (SAUS)
PCB.......... Postcoital Bleeding [*Medicine*] (DMAA)
PCB.......... Power Circuit Breaker (MSA)
PCB.......... Power Control Board (SAUS)
PCB.......... Power Control Box (NASA)
PCB.......... Practicable [*Telegraphy*] (PCTE)
PCB.......... Precambrian Shield Resources Ltd. [*Toronto Stock Exchange symbol*]
PCB.......... Precommit Boost (ACAE)
PCB.......... Premier Commercial Bank Ltd. [*Nigeria*]
PCB.......... Pressure Core Barrel (SAUS)
PCB.......... Primary Carpet Backing
PCB.......... Printed Circuit Board (MCD)
pcb.......... Printed-Circuit Board (IDOE)
PCB.......... Printed Control Board
PCB.......... Prix de Cession de Base [*Basic Wholesale Price*] [*French*]
PCB.......... Procarbazine [*Also, P, PC, Pr*] [*Antineoplastic drug*]
PCB.......... Process Control Block
PCB.......... Processor Command Bus (NITA)
PCB.......... Processor Control Block (SAUS)
PCB.......... Product Configuration Baseline (NASA)
PCB.......... Professional Capacity Building
PCB.......... Program Change Board (SAUS)
PCB.......... Program Communication Block
PCB.......... Program Control Block [*Computer science*] (BUR)
PCB.......... Project Change Board (AAG)
PCB.......... Project Control Branch [*Social Security Administration*]
PCB.......... Projected Control Board
PCB.......... Property Control Branch [*of Allied Military Government*] [*Post-World War II*]
PCB.......... Proposed Committee Bill (WPI)
PCB.......... Proprietor of Copyright on a Work by a Corporate Body
PCB.......... Propulsion [*Ground*] Control Box (AAG)
PCB.......... Protocol Control Block (SAUS)
PCB.......... Public Coin Box [*Telecommunications*] (TEL)
PCB.......... Publisher's Central Bureau
PCB.......... Punch Circuit Breaker (SAUS)
PCBA........ Para-Chlorobenzoic Acid [*Organic chemistry*]
PCBA........ P-Chlorobenzoic Acid (SAUS)
PCBA........ Pepsi-Cola Bottlers Association (EA)
PCBA........ Physically Challenged Bowhunters of America [*Association*] (EA)
PCBA........ Pioneer Citizens Band Association (IAA)
PCBA........ Polyclonal B Cell Activation [*Hematology*]
PCBA........ Printed Circuit Board Assembly (MCD)
PCBB........ Power Conditioning Brass Board (MCD)
PCBB........ Primary Commercial Blanket Bond [*Insurance*]
PCBC........ Para-Chlorobenzyl Chloride [*Organic chemistry*]
PCBC........ Partially Conserved Baryon Current (IEEE)
PCBC........ Perry County Financial [*NASDAQ symbol*] (TTSB)
PCBC........ Perry County Financial Corp. [*NASDAQ symbol*] (SAG)

PCBC .... Plain Cipher Block Chaining (SAUS)
PCBC .... Platoon Commander Battle Course (SAUS)
PCBC .... Polk County Biomedical Consortium [*Library network*]
PCBC .... Pretoria Consumer Boycott Committee (SAUS)
PCBC .... Progressive Conservative Broadcasting Corp. [*Fictional version of the Cana dian Broadcasting Corp.*]
PCBC .... Propagating Cipher Block Chaining (SAUS)
PCBC .... Punched Card Blank Column (SAUS)
PCBCI .... Pedigree Cattle Breeders' Council of Ireland (BUAC)
PCBCL....... Printed Circuit Board Configuration List (MCD)
PCBD .... Polychlorinated Benzodioxin [*Organic chemistry*]
PCBD .... Portable Contraband Detector [*Police and security equipment*]
PCBDA ...... Put and Call Brokers and Dealers Association [*Inactive*] (EA)
PCBG .... Primary Care Block Grant
p cbm .... Per Cubic Meter (or Metre) (SAUS)
PCB-ML ..... Partido Comunista Marxista-Leninista de Bolivia [*Marxist-Leninist Communist Party of Bolivia*] [*Political party*] (PPW)
PC-BMP ..... Phosphorylcholine-Binding Myeloma Protein [*Medicine*] (DMAA)
PCBN .... Para-Chlorobenzonitrile [*Organic chemistry*]
PCBN .... Pentachlorobenzonitrite (EES)
PCBN .... Polycrystalline Cubic Boron Nitrite
PCBPA....... Personal Computer Board Panel Assembly (DWSG)
PCBPS....... Printed Circuit Board Power Supply (SAUS)
PCBR .... Printed Circuit Board Repair (MCD)
PC/BRD ..... Printed Circuit Board [*Automotive engineering*]
PCBS .... Plastic Connector Backing Shell
PCBS .... Portable Cascade Bottle System (SAUS)
PCBS .... Portland Cement British Standard (SAUS)
PCBS .... Positive Control Bombardment System [*Air Force*]
PCBS .... Printed Circuit Board Socket
PCBS .... Pupil Classroom Behavior Scale
PCBTF....... Para-Chlorobenzotrifluoride [*Organic chemistry*]
PCBTS....... Portable Cesium Beam Time Standard
PCBU .... Passenger Car Business Unit
PC Bus Softw... PC Business Software (SAUS)
PCBW .... Provisional Combat Bomb Wing (SAUS)
PCBZ .... Polychlorobenzene [*Medicine*] (MELL)
PCC.......... Acts of the Privy Council, Colonial Series [*A publication*] (DLA)
PCC.......... Chief Postal Clerk [*Navy rating*]
PCC.......... Colombian Communist Party [*Political party*] (PSAP)
PCC.......... Order of St. Clare (TOCD)
PCC.......... Pacific Coast Conference (PSS)
PCC.......... Pacific Conference of Churches (BUAC)
PCC.......... Pacific Cruise Conference [*Formerly, TPPC*] [*Defunct*] (EA)
PCC.......... Package Carrier Committee (EA)
PCC.......... Pad Control Center [*NASA*] (NASA)
PCC.......... Paid Circulation Council [*Later, ASCMP*]
PCC.......... Palestine Liberation Organisation's Central Council
PCC.......... Palestinian Ceramic Chronology [*200BC-70AD*] [*A publication*] (BJA)
PCC.......... Palmer Community College (SAUS)
PCC.......... Palouse River & Coulee City Railroad [*Federal Railroad Administration identification code*]
PCC.......... Panama Canal Co. [*Superseded by Panama Canal Commission*]
PCC.......... Panama Canal Commission [*Independent government agency*]
PCC.......... Panamerican Cultural Circle (EA)
PCC.......... Papas Computer-Club (SAUS)
PCC.......... Parametric Channel Controller (SAUS)
PCC.......... Parent and Child Center [*Project Head Start*]
PCC.......... Parity Check Circuit (SAUS)
PCC.......... Parklawn Health Library Computer Center [*Department of Health and Human Services*] (GFGA)
PCC.......... Parks and Cemeteries Committee (SAUS)
PCC.......... Parochial Church Council [*Church of England*]
PCC.......... Partial Crystal Control (IEEE)
PCC.......... Partido Comunista Chileno [*Communist Party of Chile*] [*Political party*] (PD)
PCC.......... Partido Comunista Cubano [*Communist Party of Cuba*] [*Political party*] (PPW)
PCC.......... Partido Conservador Colombiano [*Conservative Party of Colombia*] [*Political party*] (PPW)
PCC.......... Party of Catalan Communists [*Political party*] (PPW)
PCC.......... Pasadena City College [*California*]
PCC.......... Pathe Communications (EFIS)
PCC.......... Patient Care Coordinator [*Medicine*]
PCC.......... Payload Control and Checkout [*NASA*] (NASA)
PCC.......... Peak Cathode Current
PCC.......... Pendleton Community Care (MHID)
PCC.......... Penn Central Corp. (EFIS)
PCC.......... Pennsylvania Crime Commission (SAUS)
PCC.......... People's Caretakers' Council [*Rhodesian*]
PCC.......... People's Christian Coalition [*Later, Sojourners*] (EA)
PCC.......... Peoples Computer Co. (SAUS)
PCC.......... Pepper Community [*Later, IPC*]
PCC.......... Per-Command Course (MCD)
PCC.......... Per Copia Conforme [*True Copy*] [*Italian*]
PCC.......... Performance Certification Component [*SQT*] (MCD)
PCC.......... Performance Criteria Categories (MCD)
PCC.......... Pericardial Constriction [*Medicine*] (MELL)
PCC.......... Peripheral Cholangiocarcinoma [*Medicine*] (RAWO)
PCC.......... Peripheral Control Computer
PCc.......... Periscopic Concave [*Ophthalmology*]
PCC.......... Permanent Consultative Committee
PCC.......... Permanently Crewed Capability
PCC.......... Perry Como Circle (EA)
PCC.......... Personal Care Clinic (DAVI)
PCC.......... Personal Code Calling (NITA)
PCC.......... Personal Communication Computer (VLIE)
PCC.......... Personal Communications Controller (NITA)
PCC.......... Personal Computer Coprocessor
PCC.......... Personnel Control Center [*Air Force*] (AFM)
PCC.......... Personnel Coordination Center [*Army*]
PCC.......... Pertec Computer Corp. (EFIS)
PCC.......... Perth Chamber of Commerce [*Western Australia*]
PCC.......... Peters' United States Circuit Court Reports [*A publication*] (DLA)
PCC.......... Petroleum Compensation Charge (SAUS)
PCC.......... Phaeochromocytoma [*Medicine*] (BABM)
PCC.......... Phase Correction Circuit (SAUS)
PCC.......... Phenylchlorocarbene [*Organic chemistry*]
PCC.......... Pheochromocytoma [*Oncology*]
PCC.......... Philippine Christian College (AEBS)
PCC.......... Philippine Cotton Corp. (BUAC)
PCC.......... Philips Consumer Communications
PCC.......... Phosphate Carrier Compound
PCC.......... Photoelectric Counter Chronometer (IAA)
PCC.......... Physical Coal Cleaning [*Fuel technology*]
PCC.......... Pilarcitos Creek [*California*] [*Seismograph station code, US Geological Survey*] (SEIS)
PCC.......... Pilot Control Console
PCC.......... Piperidinocyclohexanecarbonitrile [*Organic chemistry*]
PCC.......... Pitch of Cone to Cone (SAUS)
PCC.......... Planning Coordination Conference [*NATO*] (NATG)
PCC.......... Plastic Chip Carrier (AEBE)
PCC.......... Plastics in Construction Council [*Later, CCS*]
PCC.......... Platform Control Center [*NASA*] (SSD)
PCC.......... Platoon Command Center [*Army*]
PCC.......... Plug Compatible Computer (ADA)
PCC.......... Plutonium Concentrator Concentrate [*Nuclear energy*] (NRCH)
PCC.......... PMC Commercial Trust [*AMEX symbol*] (SAG)
PCC.......... Pointe Claire Public Library [*UTLAS symbol*]
PCC.......... Point of Common Coupling (SAUS)
PCC.......... Point of Compound Curve (KSC)
PCC.......... Poison Control Center
PCC.......... Polarity Coincidence Correlation receiver (SAUS)
PCC.......... Polarity Coincidence Correlator
PCC.......... Pole-Changing Control (SAUS)
PCC.......... Police Compact Carbine (SAUS)
PCC.......... Policy Coordination Council (USDC)
PCC.......... Political Campaign Committee [*Federal political committee terminology*] (PACS)
PCC.......... Political Consultative Committee [*Warsaw Pact*]
PCC.......... Political Consultative Council [*Russia*] (BUAC)
PCC.......... Political Contributions Committee [*Federal political committee terminology*] (PACS)
PCC.......... Polychlorinated Camphene (SAUS)
PCC.......... Polycore Composite Construction [*Automotive engineering*]
PCC.......... Polymer-Cement Concrete (KSC)
PCC.......... Polynesian Cultural Center (EA)
PCC.......... Pontifical Council for Culture [*Vatican City*] (EAIO)
PCC.......... Poor Clares of St. Colette [*Roman Catholic women's religious order*]
PCC.......... Poplar Council of Canada (EAIO)
PCC.......... Population Action International [*An association*] (EA)
PCC.......... Population Crisis Committee (EA)
PCC.......... Portable Cable Checker
PCC.......... Portable C Compiler (VLIE)
PCC.......... Port Controller Chip [*Computer science*] (VLIE)
PCC.......... Portland Cement Concrete
PCC.......... Portland Community College (SAUS)
PCC.......... Portland Concrete Cement (SAUS)
PCC.......... Port of Corpus Christi (SAUS)
PCC.......... Positive Control Communication
PCC.......... Postal and Courier Communications [*British*]
PCC.......... Postal Concentration Center [*Army*]
PCC.......... Postal Customer Council
PCC.......... Post Communications Center (CARL)
PCC.......... Posting Control Code (SAUS)
PCC.......... Pour Copie Conforme [*Certified True Copy*] [*French*]
PCC.......... Power Computing Co. (IID)
PCC.......... Power Conditioning and Control (SAUS)
PCC.......... Power Consumption Charge (SAUS)
PCC.......... Power Control Center (SAUS)
PCC.......... Power Control Console [*Diving apparatus*]
PCC.......... Precast Concrete [*Technical drawings*]
PCC.......... Precipitated Calcium Carbonate [*Inorganic chemistry*]
PCC.......... Precision Castparts Corporation (EFIS)
PCC.......... Pre-Command Course [*Military*]
PCC.......... Precompressor Cooling (MCD)
PCC.......... Pregnancy Crisis Centre [*Australia*]
PCC.......... Premature Chromosome Condensation [*Genetics*]
PCC.......... Prematurely Condensed Chromosome (DB)
PCC.......... Prerogative Court of Canterbury [*English court previously having jurisdiction over wills*]
PCC.......... Presbyterian Charismatic Communion [*Later, PRR*] [*An association*] (EA)
PCC.......... President of the Canteen Committee [*Military*] [*British*]
PCC.......... President's Conference Committee
PCC.......... Press Complaints Commission (ECON)
PCC.......... Price Control Council (NADA)
PCC.......... Primary Care Center [*Health care*] (HCT)

PCC Primary Care Clinic (DAVI)
PCC Primary Category Code (NITA)
PCC Primary Combustion Chamber (EEVL)
PCC Primary Command Center (SAUS)
PCC Primary Component Cooling (COE)
PCC Primary Control Center (COE)
PCC Print Character Counter (SAUS)
PCC Print Collectors' Club [*British*] (DBA)
PCC Print Control Character [*Computer science*] (VLIE)
PCC Printed Circuit Card
PCC Printed Circuit Conference
PCC Printer Carriage Control (SAUS)
PCC Printers' Charitable Corp. (DGA)
PCC Private Carrier Conference [*of ATA*] (EA)
PCC Privy Council Cases [*British*]
PC(C) Privy Councillor (Canada)
PCC Problem Control and Contact Unit [*IRS*]
PCC Process Change Control (VLIE)
PCC Process Chemistry Cell (NRCH)
PCC Process Control Computer
PCC Processor Control Cards [*Computer science*] (IAA)
PCC Processor Control Console [*Telecommunications*] (TEL)
PCC Procurement Coordination Committee
PCC Producers Council of Canada (SAUS)
PCC Product Control Center [*DoD*]
PCC Product-Customer Center (TIMI)
PCC Production Compression Capability
PCC Production Control Centers
PCC Productivity Communication Center [*Defunct*] (EA)
PCC Professional Computer Corp. (SAUS)
PCC Program Control Card (IAA)
PCC Program Control Center (SAUS)
PCC Program Control Counter
PCC Program-Controlled Computer (DIT)
PCC Program Coordinating Centre (SAUS)
PCC Program Coordination Committee (SSD)
PCC Program for Cooperative Cataloging [*American Library Association*]
PCC Progress Control Clerk [*DoD*]
PCC Progressive Coronary Care [*Medicine*] (AMHC)
PCC Project Change Control (SAUS)
PCC Project Control Center
PCC Project Coordination Centre [*Defence Research Board*] [*Canada*]
PCC Project Coordination Committee (SAUS)
PCC Propionyl CoA Carboxylase [*An enzyme*]
PCC Protein-Conducting Channel [*Biochemistry*]
PCC Prothrombin Complex Concentrates [*Hematology*]
PCC Protocol Communications (SAUS)
PCC Protocol Converter Concentrator [*Telecommunications*] (IAA)
PCC Provincial Congress Committee
PCC Provisioning Control Code [*Military*] (AFIT)
PCC Psychometric Colorimeter Chamber (MCD)
PCC Puerto Rico [*Colombia*] [*Airport symbol*] (AD)
PCC Pulse Counter Chain
PCC Pulse Counting Circuit (SAUS)
PCC Pulverized Coal Combustion [*or Combustor*]
PCC Punched Card Code (SAUS)
PCC Punched Card Control (SAUS)
PCC Punched Card Counting (SAUS)
PCC Pure Car Carrier [*Shipping*] (DS)
pCc pure Colombian cocaine (SAUS)
PCC Put Control Call (SAUS)
PCC Pyridinium Chlorochromate [*Organic chemistry*]
PCC Pyroconvective Cooling
PC(C) Submarine Chaser (Control) [*173 foot*] [*Navy symbol*] [*Obsolete*]
PCCA Confederation Art Gallery and Museum, Charlottetown, Prince Edward Island [*Library symbol*] [*National Library of Canada*] (NLC)
PCCA Pacific Class Catamaran Association (EA)
PCCA Pacific Coast Cichlid Association (EA)
PCCA Pattern-Contingent Chromatic Aftereffects
PCCA Pediatric Crohn's and Colitis Association, Inc. (NRGU)
PCCA Personal Computer Communications Associations (SAUS)
PCCA Pewter Collectors Club of America (EA)
PCCa Pheochromocytoma (SAUS)
PCCA Pipe Collectors Club of America [*Defunct*] (EA)
PCCA Playing Card Collectors' Association (EA)
PCCA Police Car Collectors Association (EA)
PCCA Polymerized Crystalline Colloidal Array [*Materials science*]
PCCA Portable Computer and Communications Association (CGWS)
PCCA Portable Computer and Community Association
PCCA Postcard Collector's Club of America [*Defunct*] (EA)
PCCA Power and Communication Contractors Association (EA)
PCCA Professional Compounding Centers of America
PCCA Promotion of Community and Cultural Awareness [*Australia*]
PC Cable Paper Core Cable (SAUS)
PC-CAD Personal Computer-Computer-Aided Design (SAUS)
PCCADS Panoramic Cockpit Control and Display System (MCD)
PCCAF Procedure Change Control Action Form (AAG)
PCCAF Procedure Committee Change Authorization Form (AAG)
PCCAL Pharmacy Consortium for Computer Aided Learning (ADWA)
P/C/C Alert Polymers/Ceramics/Composites Alert (SAUS)
PcCAp Pacific Coast Apparel Co., Inc. [*Associated Press*] (SAG)
PcCap Pacificorp Capital [*Associated Press*] (SAG)
PCCAP Physicians' Continued Competence Assessment Program [*Medicine*] (DMAA)
PcCApp Pacific Coast Apparel Co., Inc. [*Associated Press*] (SAG)
PC CARP Personal Computer/Cluster Analysis and Regression Program (SAUS)
PCCB Payload Configuration Control Board [*NASA*] (MCD)
PCCB Porsche Ceramic Composite Brake
PCCB Process Communication Control Block (SAUS)
PCCB Program Configuration Control Board [*NASA*] (NASA)
PCCB Project Configuration Control Board [*Army*] (AABC)
PCCC Pacific Coast Collegiate Conference (PSS)
PCCC Pakistan Central Cotton Committee (BUAC)
PCCC Participating College Correspondence Course (MUGU)
PCCC PC Connection [*Company symbol*]
PCCC Penang Chinese Chamber of Commerce [*Malaysia*] (BUAC)
PCCC Phoenix Conference on Computers and Communications (SAUS)
PCCC Polytechnics and Colleges Computer Committee (AIE)
PCCD Peristaltic Charge-Coupled Device (IEEE)
PCCDS Patrol Craft Combat Direction System [*Navy*] (SAA)
PCCE Pacific Coast Coin Exchange
PCCE Particle Cloud Combustion Experiment (SAUS)
PCCE Payload Common Communication Equipment [*NASA*] (NASA)
PCCEI Permanent Charities Committee of the Entertainment Industries (EA)
PCCEMRSP Permanent Commission for the Conservation and Exploitation of the Maritime Resources of the South Pacific
PCC-EP/MP Policy Coordinating Committee for Emergency Preparedness/ Mobilization Planning [*Emergency Management*] (EMA)
PCCES Planning and Coordinating Committee for Environmental Studies [*National Research Council*]
PCCF Plan Case Control File [*IRS*]
PCCF Postal Code Conversion File [*Database*] [*Canada*] (GDD)
PCCF Prostate Cancer Cure Foundation Ltd.
PCCF Protein C Cofactor (DMAA)
PCCG PCC Group [*NASDAQ symbol*] (TTSB)
PCCG PCC Group, Inc. [*NASDAQ symbol*] (SAG)
PCCG Protestant Cinema Critics Guild [*Later, PCG*] (EA)
PCCGB Photographic Collectors Club of Great Britain (DBA)
PCC Gp PCC Group, Inc. [*Associated Press*] (SAG)
PCCh Partido Comunista de Chile [*Chilean Communist Party*] [*Political party*] (EY)
PCCH Pentachlorocyclohexene [*Organic chemistry*]
PCCH Physical Control Channel (SAUS)
PCCH Program Control Channel (VLIE)
PCCI Pacific Coast Lines Service [*Common carrier symbol*]
PCCI Pacific Crest Capital [*NASDAQ symbol*] (SAG)
PCCI Paper Cup and Container Institute [*Later, SSI*] (EA)
PCCI President's Committee on Consumer Interests [*Terminated, 1971*]
PCCIE Power Conditioning and Continuation Interfacing Equipment (SAUS)
PCC/I/O/R/H Patrol Craft, Coastal/Inshore/Offshore/Riverine/Harbour (MILB)
PCCIP Presidential Commission on Critical Infrastructure Protection [*Emergency Management*] (EMA)
PCCL People's Community Civic League (EA)
PCCL Precontract Cost Letter [*Navy*] (NG)
PCCL Pulse Coupled Complementary Logic (SAUS)
PCCLAS Pacific Coast Council on Latin American Studies (BUAC)
PCCM Master Chief Postal Clerk [*Navy rating*]
PCCM Pediatric Critical Care Medicine (DMAA)
PCCM Portuguese Cultural Centre of Melbourne [*Victoria, Australia*]
PCCM Primary Care Case Management [*Medicine*] (DMAA)
PCCM Primary Care Case Manager [*Medicine*] (DMAA)
PCCM Private Circuit Control Module [*Telecommunications*] (TEL)
PCCM Program Change Control Management (NASA)
PCCM Program Control Contract Manager (MCD)
PCC (M-L) Parti Communiste Canadien (Marxiste-Leniniste) [*Marxist-Leninist Communist Party of Canada*] [*Political party*]
PCCN Part Card Change Notice (KSC)
PCCN Port Call Control Number [*Army*] (AABC)
PCCN Preliminary Configuration Control Number (AAG)
PCCN Provisioning Contract Control Number (NASA)
PCCNA Pentecostal Charismatic Churches of North America (EA)
PCCNL Pacific Coast Coordinator of Naval Logistics
PCCNY Penal Code of the City of New York (SAUS)
PCCO Plant Clearance Contracting Officer [*DoD*]
PCCO Production Control Close Out (VLIE)
PCCOA Coles Associates Ltd., Charlottetown, Prince Edward Island [*Library symbol*] [*National Library of Canada*] (NLC)
PCC/OES Policy Coordinating Committee for Oceans and International Environmental and Scientific Affairs (SAUS)
PCCP Canadian Pension Commission [*Commission Canadienne des Pensions*], Charlottetown, Prince Edward Island [*Library symbol*] [*National Library of Canada*] (BIB)
PCCP Preliminary Contract Change Proposal [*NASA*] (KSC)
PCCP Private Child Care Provider (EDAC)
PCCP Product Cost Curve Picture (VLIE)
PCCPS Pacific Coast Canned Pear Service (EA)
PCCR Procurement Code Change Request (IAA)
PCCR Publishing Center for Cultural Resources [*Defunct*] (EA)
PCCS Pad-Circuit Center Spacing (SAUS)
PCCS Parti Conservateur Chretien-Social [*Conservative Christian-Social Party*] [*Switzerland*] [*Political party*] (PPE)
PCCS Personnel Command and Control System (SAUS)
PCCS Photographic Camera Control System (KSC)
PCCS Ported Coax Cable Sensor [*Military*] (DWSG)
PCCS Ported Coaxial Cable System (VLIE)
PCCS Positive Control Communications System

PCCS .... Primate Captive Care Society (BUAC)
PCCS .... Process Control Computer System (SAUS)
PCCS .... Processor Common Communications System
PCCS .... Production Change Control System (TIMI)
PCCS .... Program and Cost Control System [*Army*] (RDA)
PCCS .... Program Change Control System (NG)
PCCS .... Project Change Control System (SAUS)
PCCS .... Project Cost Control System
PCCS .... Publications Contract Coverage Schedule (MCD)
PCCS .... Senior Chief Postal Clerk [*Navy rating*]
PCCT .... Percept and Concept Cognition Test [*Psychology*]
PCCT .... Punched Card Controlled Typewrite (SAUS)
PCCTV .... Portable Closed-Circuit Television (SAUS)
PCCU .... Peralta Carriers [*Intermodal shipping container symbol*] (TVRC)
PCCU .... Postal & Courier Communications Unit (SAUS)
PCCU .... Post-Coronary Care Unit [*Medicine*] (STED)
PCCU .... Power Conditioning and Cover Control Unit (ACAE)
PCCU .... President's Commission on Campus Unrest (EA)
PCCU .... Progressive Coronary Care Unit (SAUS)
PCCU .... Psychiatric Criminal Care Unit (WDAA)
PCCU .... Punched Card Control Unit [*Computer science*] (AABC)
PCC Unit .... Power Conditioning and Control Unit (SAUS)
PCCW .... Price/Costco, Inc. [*NASDAQ symbol*] (SPSG)
PCCW .... Public Citizens Congress Watch (COE)
PCCWs .... Pacific Century CyberWorks
PCCX .... Plum Creek Charters [*Federal Railroad Administration identification code*]
PCCZ .... Portland Cement [*Federal Railroad Administration identification code*]
PCD .... Democratic Conservative Party [*Nicaragua*] [*Political party*] (PD)
PCD .... Liberal Democratic Party (Angola) [*Political party*] (PSAP)
PCD .... Pacific Car Demurrage Bureau, San Francisco CA [*STAC*]
PCD .... Pacific Communications Division [*Military*]
PCD .... Pacing Cardioverter/Defibrillator (SAUS)
PCD .... Panama Canal Defense (SAUS)
PCD .... Panama Canal Department
PCD .... Panama Canal District (SAUS)
PCD .... Papillary Collecting Duct [*Medicine*] (DMAA)
PCD .... Paraneoplastic Cerebellar Degeneration [*Medicine*] (EDAA)
PCD .... Paroxysmal Cerebral Dysrhythmia [*Medicine*] (STED)
PCD .... Partial Cooldown Drive [*Automotive testing*]
PCD .... Parti Communiste du Dahomey [*Communist Party of Dahomey*] [*Benin*] [*Political party*]
PCD .... Partido Comunista Dominicano [*Dominican Communist Party*] [*Dominican Republic*] [*Political party*] (PPW)
PCD .... Partition Control Descriptor [*Computer science*] (ELAL)
PCD .... Party for the Democratic Convergence (Cape Verde) [*Political party*] (PSAP)
PCD .... Party of Christian Democrats [*Poland*] [*Political party*] (BUAC)
PCD .... Patriotic Coalition for Democracy [*Political group*] [*Guyana*]
PCD .... Payload Correction Data (SAUS)
PCD .... PCD, Inc. [*Associated Press*] (SAG)
PCD .... Pedestrian Control Device [*Highway design*]
PCD .... Perceptual-Communicative Disorder [*Education*] (EDAC)
PCD .... Personal Communication Device [*FTA*] (TAG)
PCD .... Phase-Change Drive (SAUS)
PCD .... Phenylchlorodiazirine [*Organic chemistry*]
PCD .... Phosphate-Citrate-Dextrose Polycystic Disease (MAE)
PCD .... Photo Compact Disk [*Eastman Kodak Co.*] (PCM)
PCD .... Photoconductive Decay [*Semiconductor material*]
PCD .... Photoconductive Device (SAUS)
PCD .... Pincushion Distortion (SAUS)
PCD .... Pine Channel Gold [*Vancouver Stock Exchange symbol*]
PCD .... Pioneer-Central Division [*Bendix*]
PCD .... Pitch Circle Diameter [*Technical drawings*] (IAA)
PCD .... Planned Commercial Development (PA)
PCD .... Planned Community Development (SAUS)
PCD .... Planned Completion Date (TEL)
PCD .... Planned Continuation Date (SAUS)
PCD .... Plasma Cell Dyscrasia [*Medicine*]
PCD .... Plasma-Coupled Device
PCD .... Plutonium Concentrator Distillate [*Nuclear energy*] (NRCH)
PCD .... Pneumatic Control Distributors (KSC)
PCD .... Point Chemical Detector (SEWL)
PCD .... Polar Cap Disturbance (DNAB)
PCD .... Polycarbodiimide (SAUS)
PCD .... Polychlorinated Dibenzo (BARN)
PCD .... Polycrystalline Diamond (ECON)
PCD .... Polycystic Disease [*of kidneys*] [*Medicine*]
PCD .... Polymeric Carrier Delivery System [*Nuclear energy*] (NUCP)
PCD .... Port Control Diagnostic [*Telecommunications*] (TEL)
PCD .... Positive Control Document (MCD)
PCd .... Post Card [*Philately*]
Pcd .... Postcard (BJA)
PCD .... Postcode (SAUS)
PCD .... Posterior Corneal Deposit [*Ophthalmology*] (MAE)
PCD .... Postmortem Cesarean Delivery (STED)
PCD .... Pounds per Capita per Day (AAG)
PCD .... Power Circle Diagram (SAUS)
PCD .... Power Control and Distribution
PCD .... Power Control Device [*Nuclear energy*] (NRCH)
PCD .... Power Conversion Distributor
PCD .... Precision Course Direction [*Aerospace*] (MCD)
PCD .... Pre Congfigured Definition [*Computer science*] (ELAL)
PCD .... Preliminary Conceptual Design (SAUS)
PCD .... Presentation Capabilities Descriptor (SAUS)
PCD .... Pressure Control Distributor (KSC)
PCD .... Primary Ciliary Dyskinesia [*Medicine*]
PCD .... Primary Current Distribution [*Electroplating*]
PCD .... Prime Contractor Department (SAUS)
PCD .... Principal Criteria Document (SAUS)
PCD .... Problem Control and Display
PCD .... Procedural Change Directive (KSC)
PCD .... Proceed [*ICAO designator*] (FAAC)
PCD .... Proceed [*Telegraphy*] (PCTE)
PCD .... Process Control Device (SAUS)
PCD .... Process Control Division (SAUS)
PCD .... Procurement and Contracts Division [*NASA*]
PCD .... Procurement Control Document [*NASA*] (MCD)
PCD .... Product Configuration Documentation (AAGC)
PCD .... Production Common Digitizer
PCD .... Program Change Decision [*Army*]
PCD .... Program Control Display System [*NATO Air Defense Ground Environment*] (NATG)
PCD .... Program Control Document (KSC)
PCD .... Programmed Cell Death [*Cytology*]
PCD .... Programmed Cutting Director (SAUS)
PCD .... Project Control Drawing (AAG)
PCD .... Projected Charge Density (PDAA)
PCD .... Prolonged Contractile Duration (STED)
PCD .... Protocatechuatedioxygenase [*An enzyme*]
PCD .... Provincial Communications Department [*Highway safety*]
PCD .... Pulmonary Clearance Delay [*Medicine*]
PCD .... Punched Card Data (SAUS)
PCDA .... Post Card Distributors Association
PCDA .... Power Control and Distribution Assembly (SAUS)
PCDA .... Process Control and Data Acquisition (SAUS)
PCDA .... Professional Currency Dealers Association (EA)
PCDA .... Program Controlled Data Acquisition (SAUS)
PCDA .... Protective Clothing Distributors Association [*British*] (DBA)
PCDANA ...... Post Card Distributors Association of North America (NTPA)
PCDB .... Poison Control Data Base [*Database*]
PCDB .... Product Cost Data Base (TIMI)
PCDC .... Diagnostic Chemicals Ltd., Charlottetown, Prince Edward Island [*Library symbol*] [*National Library of Canada*] (NLC)
PCDC .... Plasma Clot Diffusion Chamber [*Medicine*] (DMAA)
PCDC .... Plutonium Canister Decontamination Cell [*Nuclear energy*] (NRCH)
PCDC .... Professionals Committee for Democratic Change (SAUS)
PCDD .... Pentachlorodioxin [*Organic chemistry*]
PCDD .... Polychlorinated Dibenzodioxin [*Organic chemistry*]
PCDD .... Polychlorinated Dibenzodioxins [*Automotive emissions*] [*Organic chemistry*]
PCDDS .... Private Circuit Digital Data Service [*Telecommunications*] (TEL)
PCDE .... Parent Council for Deaf Education [*Australia*]
PCDE .... Photon-induced Chemical Dry Etching (SAUS)
PcdeN .... Nicaraguan Communist Party [*Political party*] (PSAP)
PCDEO .... Passenger Car Diesel Engine Oil [*Fuels and lubricants*]
PCDESIG ... Plane Captain Designated [*or Designation*] (DNAB)
PCDF .... Polychlorinated Dibenzofuran [*Organic chemistry*]
PCDF .... Polychlorinated Dibenzofurans [*Automotive emissions*] [*Organic chemistry*]
PCDG .... Prestressed Concrete Development Group (SAUS)
PCDG .... Proceeding [*Telegraphy*] (PCTE)
PCDH .... Polychlorinated Diaromatic Hydrocarbon [*Organic chemistry*]
PCDHi .... Delaware County Historical Society, Chester, PA [*Library symbol*] [*Library of Congress*] (LCLS)
PCDI .... PCD, Inc. [*NASDAQ symbol*] (SAG)
PCDI .... Per Capita Disposable Income [*Economics*]
PCDI .... Pierce Die
PCDI .... Printed Circuit Design Interface (NITA)
PCDIS .... Piezoceramic Common-rail Diesel Injection System [*Automotive engineering*]
PCDJ .... Pakistan Committee for Democracy and Justice [*Defunct*] (EA)
PCDL .... Pro-Choice Defense League (EA)
PCDMA .... Personal Computer Direct Marketers Association (BUAC)
PCDN .... Production Development Change Notice (SAUS)
PCdoB .... Partido Comunista do Brasil [*Communist Party of Brazil*] [*Political party*] (PPW)
PC DOCS .... PC DOCS Group International [*Associated Press*] (SAG)
PC-DOS ..... Personal Computer-Disk Operating System (DOM)
PCDP .... Parti Comorien pour la Democratie et le Progres [*Political party*] (EY)
PCDP .... Pilot Control and Display Panel
PCDP .... Punched Card Data Processing
PCDP Equipment... Punched Card Data Processing Equipment (SAUS)
PCDPPP ..... Pan Caribbean Disaster Preparedness and Prevention Project (BUAC)
PCD-PRP .... Pueblo, Cambio, y Democracia - Partido Roldosista Popular [*People, Change, and Democracy - Popular Roldosista Party*] [*Ecuador*] [*Political party*] (PPW)
PCDR .... Preconceptual Design Report (SAUS)
PCDR .... Preliminary Conceptual Design Report (SAUS)
PCDR .... Procedure (AAG)
PCDS .... Patient Care Data Set (SAUS)
PCDS .... Payload Command Decoder Subunit [*NASA*] (KSC)
PCDS .... Pediatric Care Delivery System [*Medicine*] (EDAA)
PCDS .... Pilot Climate Data System (SAUS)
PCDS .... Power Conversion and Distribution System
PCDS .... Precision Course Direction System (SAUS)
PCDS .... Procurement Congressional Descriptive Summary [*Army*] (RDA)

PCDS .... Program Control Display System (SAUS)
PCDS .... Project Control Drawing System (AAG)
PCDT .... Pacific Coast Dog Tick (MELL)
PCDU .... Payload Command Decoder Unit [*NASA*] (NASA)
PCDUS ...... Plasma Cell Dyscrasias of Unknown Significance [*Medicine*]
PCDX .... Pittsburgh & Conneaut Dock [*Federal Railroad Administration identification code*]
PCE .... Page Communications Engineers, Inc. [*Canada*] (MCD)
PCE .... Painter Creek, AK [*Location identifier*] [*FAA*] (FAAL)
PCE .... Palm Island [*Queensland*] [*Airport symbol*] (AD)
PCE .... Parameter Checkout Engineer [*Computer science*] (IAA)
PCE .... Parliamentary Commissioner for the Environment (SAUS)
PCE .... Partido Comunista de Espana [*Communist Party of Spain*] [*Political party*] (PPE)
PCE .... Partido Comunista Ecuatoriano [*Communist Party of Ecuador*] [*Political party*] (PPW)
PCE .... Passenger Car Equivalence [*TRB*] (TAG)
PCE .... Patrol Escort [*Patrol Craft Escort*] [*Navy symbol*]
PCE .... Pedco Energy Ltd. [*Vancouver Stock Exchange symbol*]
PCE .... Perchloroethylene [*Organic chemistry*]
PCE .... Pericardial Effusion [*Medicine*] (MELL)
PCE .... Peripheral Control Element
PCE .... Peripheral Controller Enclosure (NITA)
PCE .... Personal Consumption Expenditure
PCE .... Petrozavodsk Commodity Exchange [*Russian Federation*] (EY)
PCE .... Phase Change Erasable (SAUS)
PCE .... Photocell Emitter (IAA)
PCE .... Physical Capacities Evaluation [*Test of hand skills*]
PCE .... Physical Completion Estimate (SAUS)
PCE .... Piece [*Numismatics*]
PCE .... Plasma Chamber Evacuation Subsystem (MCD)
PCE .... Platinol [*Cis-Platinum*] Cyclophosphamide, Vindesine [*Antineoplastic drug regimen*] (DAVI)
PCE .... Plug Compatible Ethernet
PCE .... Pollution Control Ecology (SAUS)
PCE .... Pollution Control Equipment (GFGA)
PCE .... Polyarthrite Chronique Evolutive [*Chronic Evolutive Polyarthritis*] [*Medicine*] [*French*]
PCE .... Polychloroethylene (BARN)
PCE .... Polymer-Coated Erythromycin [*An antibiotic*] (DAVI)
PCE .... Ponce [*Diocesan abbreviation*] [*Puerto Rico*] (TOCD)
PCE .... Pool Control Error (IAA)
PCE .... Positive Continuous Engagement [*Automotive engineering*]
PCE .... Post-Communist Europe (SAUS)
PCE .... Posterior Chamber of Eye [*Medicine*] (MELL)
PCE .... Potentially Compensable Event (DICI)
PCE .... Power Conditioning Electronics (SAUS)
PCE .... Power Conditioning Equipment
PCE .... Power Conversion Equipment (DNAB)
PCE .... Preliminary Closure Estimate (SAUS)
PCE .... Present Company Excluded (SAUS)
PCE .... Pressure to Clutch Engage [*Aerospace*] (AAG)
PCE .... Prince Edward Island Department of Education, Charlottetown, Prince Edward Island [*Library symbol*] [*National Library of Canada*] (NLC)
PCE .... Private Ciphering Equipment (SAUS)
PCE .... Privy Councillor, England (ROG)
PCE .... Probability of Character Error (CCCA)
PCE .... Process [*or Processor*] Control Element [*Computer science*] (IAA)
PCE .... Process Control Engineering (SAUS)
PCE .... Processor Control Element (SAUS)
PCE .... Production Check Equipment (MCD)
PCE .... Professional Care, Inc. [*AMEX symbol*] (COMM)
PCE .... Professional Continuing Education (DOMA)
PCE .... Program Cost Estimate (AFM)
PCE .... Prohormone-Converting Endopeptidase
PCE .... Project Coordination Center Europe (SAUS)
PCE .... Project Cost Estimate (SAUS)
PCE .... Pseudocholinesterase [*Same as ACAH*] [*An enzyme*]
PCE .... Pulmocutaneous Exchange
PCE .... Punch Card Equipment [*Computer science*] (AFM)
PCE .... Pyrometric Cone Equivalent [*Refractory industry*]
PCE .... Submarine Chaser Escort
PCEA .... Pacific Coast Electrical Association
PCEA .... Patient-Controlled Epidural Analgesia
PCEA .... Phosphate Chemicals Export Association (EA)
PCEA .... Presbyterian Church of Eastern Australia
PCEA .... Presidents Council of Economic Advisors (SAUS)
PCEA .... Professional Construction Estimators Association of America (NTPA)
P/CEA3 ...... Probationary Control Electrical Artificer 3rd Class [*British military*] (DMA)
PCEAA .... Professional Construction Estimators Association of America (EA)
PCEB .... PCI to EISA Bridge (SAUS)
PCEC .... Patrol Craft Escort Control (SAUS)
PCE(C) ...... Patrol Vessel, Escort (Control) [*180 feet*] [*Navy symbol*] [*Obsolete*]
PCEC .... Personal Computer Enhanced Connectivity (SAUS)
PCEC .... Pollution Control and Ecology Commission (SAUS)
PC-EDSM ... Powertrain Control-Emissions Diagnosis Service Manual [*Automotive engineering*]
PCEDURE ... Procedure (ROG)
PCEE .... Presidents Commission on Executive Exchange (SAUS)
PCEEDGS ... Proceedings (ROG)
PCEEO .... President's Committee on Equal Employment Opportunity [*Later, OFCCP*] [*Department of Labor*]
PCEH .... President's Committee on Employment of the Handicapped [*Washington, DC*]
PCEI .... Prime Contract End Item (MCD)
PCEK .... Pappas Carter Evans & Koop (SAUS)
PCEM .... Parliamentary Council of the European Movement
PCEM .... Process Chain Evaluation Model (IEEE)
PCEM .... Program Committee on Education for Mission (EA)
PCEM .... Propulsion Contamination Effects Module (NASA)
PcEn .... Pacific Enterprises [*Associated Press*] (SAG)
PCEN .... Paracentesis Fluid [*Medicine*] (DAVI)
PCEO .... Gary Price [*Common carrier symbol*]
PCEO .... Personal Computer Enhancement Operation [*Intel Corp.*] (CIST)
PCEP .... Perception Technology Corp. [*NASDAQ symbol*] (COMM)
PCEQ .... President's Commisssion on Environmental Quality (GNE)
PCEQ .... Presidents Council on Environmental Quality (SAUS)
PCE-R .... Partido Comunista de Espana - Reconstituido [*Reconstituted Spanish Communist Party*] [*Political party*] (PD)
PCER .... Patrol Craft, Escort Rescue (SAUS)
PCER .... Patrol Rescue Escort [*Patrol Craft Escort Rescue*] [*Navy symbol*]
PCER .... Rescue Escort (SAUS)
PCERII .... Prairie Centre of Excellence for Research on Immigration and Integration [*Canada*] (RCD)
PCERT .... Purdue Computer Emergency Response Team (SAUS)
P Cert Ed ... Professional Certificate in Education
PCES .... Pace Health Management Systems, Inc. [*NASDAQ symbol*] (SAG)
PCES .... Phase Change Energy Storage (SAUS)
PCES .... President's Committee on Economic Security [*New Deal*]
PCES .... Product Cost Estimate System (SAUS)
PCES .... Production Control Experimental System (SAUS)
PCET .... Personal Computer Extended Technology [*Computer bus*]
PCETF .... Power Conversion Equipment Test Facility [*Nuclear energy*]
P CEU .... Partido Comunista de Espana Unificado [*Unified Communist Party of Spain*] [*Political party*] (PPW)
PC EU .... Pulse Compression/Expansion Unit
PCF .... Pacific Air Express [*ICAO designator*] (FAAC)
PCF .... Pacific Car and Foundry
PCF .... Pacific Ridge Resources [*Vancouver Stock Exchange symbol*]
PCF .... Pacificulture Foundation (EA)
PCF .... Palliative Care Foundation [*Canada*] (EAIO)
PCF .... Pancreatic Cutaneous Fistula [*Medicine*] (EDAA)
PCF .... Parallel Computing Forum (ACAE)
PCF .... Parents' Choice Foundation (EA)
PCF .... Parliamentary Christian Fellowship [*British*] (WDAA)
PCF .... Partial Correction Function (SAUS)
PCF .... Partial Correlation Function (SAUS)
PCF .... Parti Communiste Francais [*French Communist Party*] [*Political party*] (PPW)
PCF .... Parts Conditioning Facility (TIMI)
PCF .... Patrol Craft Fast (SAUS)
PCF .... Payload Control Facility [*NASA*] (MCD)
PCF .... Peace Centers Foundation [*Later, UDC*] (EA)
PCF .... Pentagon Counterintelligence Force
PCF .... Peripheral Circulatory Failure [*Medicine*] (DMAA)
PCF .... Peripheral Control Facility (SAUS)
PCF .... Personal Card File
PCF .... Personal Computing Facility (SAUS)
PCF .... Personnel Control Facility [*Army*] (AABC)
PCF .... Pharyngoconjunctival Fever [*Medicine*]
PCF .... Phonetically Consistent Form [*Linguistics*] (IEL)
PCF .... Pistol Centre Fire (SAUS)
PCF .... Plan Characteristics File [*IRS*]
PCF .... Planning Cable Fill (SAUS)
PCF .... Planning Coordination Facility (SAUS)
PCF .... Plasma Converting Factor [*Medicine*] (EDAA)
PCF .... Platelet Complement Fixation [*Medicine*] (EDAA)
PCF .... Plutonium Chemistry Facility (SAUS)
PCF .... Point Coordination Function (SAUS)
PCF .... Polycationized Ferritin [*Biochemistry*]
PCF .... Portable Compiled Font (SAUS)
PCF .... Postcard Club Federation [*Defunct*] (EA)
PCF .... Posterior Carotid Foramen [*Anatomy*]
PCF .... Posterior Cervical Fusion [*Medicine*] (MELL)
PCF .... Posterior Cranial Fossa [*Anatomy*] (MAE)
PCF .... Potential Conflict Forecasts [*Army*]
PCF .... Potential Controlled Flotation (SAUS)
PCF .... Potentially Critical Failures
pcf .... Pounds per Cubic Foot (WPI)
PCF .... Pounds per Cubic Foot
PCF .... Power Cathode Follower
PCF .... Power Coupling Factor (SAUS)
PCF .... Power per Cubic Foot
PCF .... Prairie Chicken Foundation (EA)
PCF .... Primary Checkpoint File
PCF .... Primary Control Field (SAUS)
PCF .... Probability of Consequence Factor
PCF .... Procedure Completion Form (SAUS)
PCF .... Process Control File (SAUS)
PCF .... Processed Citation File
PCF .... Procoagulant Factor [*Medicine*] (MELL)
PCF .... Program Change Factor
PCF .... Program Characteristics File [*Medicaid*] (GFGA)
PCF .... Program Checkout Facility
PCF .... Program Complex File [*Computer science*] (MHDI)
PCF .... Program Control Facility

PCF .... Programmed Cryptographic Facility [*Computer science*]
PCF .... Proposed Change File (SAUS)
PCF .... Prothrombin Conversion Factor [*Hematology*]
PCF .... Public Concern Foundation (EA)
PCF .... Pulse Compression Filter
PCF .... Pulse-to-Cycle Fraction
PCF .... Pulverized Coal-Fired Plant
PCF .... Punched Card Feed (SAUS)
PCF .... Putnam High Income Bond Fd [*Stock exchange symbol*] [*Formerly Putnam Hi Income Cv-Bd Fd*]
PCF .... Putnam High Income Convertible & Bond Fund [*NYSE symbol*] (SPSG)
PCFA .... Fast Patrol Craft, Air Cushion [*Navy*]
PCFA .... Pace Freight Systems [*Common carrier symbol*]
PCFA .... Pin, Clip, and Fastener Association [*Later, PCFS*] (EA)
PCFA .... Polytechnics and Colleges Funding Council (BUAC)
PCFA .... Precast Concrete Frame Association [*British*] (DBA)
PCFC .... Pacific Construction and Maintenance [*Common carrier symbol*]
PCFC .... Pat Compton Fan Club [*Association*] (EA)
PCFC .... Phil Collins Fan Club (EA)
PCFC .... Phil Collins Information [*Formerly, Phil Collins Fan Club*] (EA)
PCFC .... Pioneer Commercial Funding Corp. [*NASDAQ symbol*] (SAG)
PCFC .... Polytechnics and Colleges Funding Council [*British*]
Pcfcp25 ..... Pacificorp [*Associated Press*] (SAG)
Pcfcp35 ..... Pacificorp [*Associated Press*] (SAG)
PCFD .... Purple-Collared Fruit-Dove [*North American bird banding code*] (BIBA)
PCFE .... Polytrifluorochloroethylene [*Organic chemistry*]
PCFE .... Prime Contractor Furnished Equipment (MCD)
PCFFA .... Pacific Coast Federation of Fishermen's Associations (EA)
PCFFF .... Post-Collision Fuel-Fed Fire [*Automotive safety engineering*]
PCFG .... Probabilistic Context Free Grammar (IDAI)
PC/FGD ...... Pulverized Coal / Flue Gas Desulfurization [*Energy technology*]
PCFH .... Fast Patrol Craft, Hydrofoil [*Navy*]
PCFIA .... Particle Concentration Fluorescence Immunoassay
PCFLIS ...... Presidents Commission on Foreign Language and International Studies (SAUS)
PCFlot .... Patrol Craft Flotilla (SAUS)
PCFM .... Production Control File Manager (IAA)
PCFN .... PC Financial Network (PCM)
PCFO .... Pancreatic Cutaneous Fistula Output [*Medicine*] (EDAA)
PCFO .... Position Classification Field Office
PCFP .... Pacific Carrier Corporation [*Common carrier symbol*]
PCFP .... Predicted Comparative Failure Probability
PCFR .... Programmatic Center for Fire Research [*National Institute of Standards and Technology*]
PCFRE .... Professional Council of Religious Education [*British*] (DBA)
PCFS .... Pacific Coast Fertility Society (SAUS)
PCFS .... Pin, Clip, and Fastener Services (EA)
PCFT .... Information Centre, Prince Edward Island Food Technology Centre, Charlottetown [*Library symbol*] [*National Library of Canada*] (BIB)
PCFT .... Platelet Complement Fixation Test [*Medicine*] (EDAA)
PCG .... Guided Missile Coastal Escort [*Ship symbol*] (NATG)
PCG .... Pacific Gas & Elec [*NYSE symbol*] (TTSB)
PCG .... Pacific Gas & Electric Co. [*AMEX symbol*] (SPSG)
PCG .... Paracervical Ganglion [*Anatomy*]
PCG .... Parti Communiste de Guadeloupe [*Communist Party of Guadeloupe*] [*Political party*] (PPW)
PCG .... Period Costume Group (BUAC)
PCG .... PezCorona Gold Corp. [*Vancouver Stock Exchange symbol*]
PCG .... PG & E Capital I [*AMEX symbol*] (SAG)
PCG .... PG&E Corp. [*NYSE symbol*]
PCG .... PG & E Corp. Holdings Co. [*NYSE symbol*] (SAG)
PCG .... Phonocardiogram [*Cardiology*]
pcg .... Picogram [*Measurement*] (DAVI)
P/CG .... Pilot Controller Glossary [*Aviation*] (FAAC)
PCG .... Plain Clothes Gratuity [*British military*] (DMA)
PCG .... Plains Cotton Growers (EA)
PCG .... Planning and Control Guide
PCG .... Planning and Coordination Group of the National Security Council (CARL)
PCG .... Planning Career Goals [*Vocational guidance test*]
PCG .... Policy Coordination Group (DOGT)
PCG .... Power Conditioning Group (MCD)
PCG .... Power Converter Group (SAUS)
PCG .... Preconditioned Gradient (SAUS)
PCG .... Primary Congenital Glaucoma (MELL)
PCG .... Primate Chorionic Gonadotropin [*Medicine*] (DMAA)
PCG .... Printed Circuit Generator
PCG .... Programmable Character Generator
PCG .... Protein Crystal Growth (SAUS)
PCG .... Protestant Cinema Guild [*Formerly, PCCG*] [*Defunct*]
PCG .... Pubococcygeus [*Muscle*] [*Anatomy*] (DAVI)
PCG .... Pulsed Coaxial Gun
PCG2 .... Preconditioned Conjugate Gradient
PCGA .... Pacific Coast Gas Association (SAUS)
PCGD .... Pollution Control Guidance Document
PCGE .... Protein Crystal Growth Experiment (SAUS)
PCGF .... Protein Crystal Growth Facility (SSD)
PCGG .... PCG Glovebox (SAUS)
PCGG .... Percutaneous Coagulation of Gasserian Ganglion [*Medicine*] (EDAA)
PCGG .... Philippine Commission on Good Government (BUAC)
PCGG .... Primary Care Group in Gynaecology (BUAC)
PCGL .... Printed Circuit Generated Level (SAUS)
PCGM .... Pacific Coast Garment Manufacturers [*Later, AAMA*] (EA)
PCGM .... Preconditioned Gradient Method (SAUS)
PCGN .... Permanent Committee of Geographical Names [*Later, BGN*]
PCGOV .... Port Charges Paid by Foreign Government (DNAB)
PCGPrA ...... Pacific Gas & El 6% Pfd [*AMEX symbol*] (TTSB)
PCGPrB ...... Pacific Gas & El 5 1/2% Pfd [*AMEX symbol*] (TTSB)
PCGPrC ...... Pacific Gas & El 5% Pfd [*AMEX symbol*] (TTSB)
PCGPrCA .... PG&E Cap I 7.90%'QUIPS' [*AMEX symbol*] (TTSB)
PCGPrD ...... Pacific Gas & El 5% Pfd [*AMEX symbol*] (TTSB)
PCGPrE ...... Pac G&E 5%cmRed1stA Pfd [*AMEX symbol*] (TTSB)
PCGPrG ...... Pacific Gas & El 4.80% Pfd (TTSB)
PCGPrH ...... Pacific Gas & El 4.50% Pfd [*AMEX symbol*] (TTSB)
PCGPrI ...... Pacific Gas & El 4.36% Pfd [*AMEX symbol*] (TTSB)
PCGPrQ ...... Pacific Gas & El 7.44% Pfd [*AMEX symbol*] (TTSB)
PCGPrU ...... Pacific Gas & El 7.04% Pfd [*AMEX symbol*] (TTSB)
PCGPrX ...... Pacific Gas & El 6.875% Pfd [*AMEX symbol*] (TTSB)
PCGPrY ...... Pacific Gas & El 6.57% Pfd [*AMEX symbol*] (TTSB)
PCGPrZ ...... Pacific Gas & El 6.30% Pfd [*AMEX symbol*] (TTSB)
PCGRIDS ... Personal Computer Gridded Interactive Display and Diagnostic System [*Marine science*] (OSRA)
PCGRX .... Pioneer Capital Growth Cl.A [*Mutual fund ticker symbol*] (SG)
PCGS .... Professional Coin Grading Service (BARN)
PCGS .... Protein Crystal Growth System
PCGU .... Protein Crystal Growth Unit (SSD)
PCGVB .... Pairwise Correlated Generalized Valence Bond [*Physics*]
PCH .... Cheyney State College, Cheyney, PA [*OCLC symbol*] (OCLC)
PCH .... Packing, Crating, and Handling [*Shipping*]
PCH .... Paging Channel (CGWS)
PCH .... Paper Clearing House (TBD)
PCH .... Parallel Channel (VLIE)
PCH .... Parchim [*German license plate city code*]
PCH .... Parent Compound Handbook [*Later, Ring Systems Handbook*] [*American Chemical Society*]
PCH .... Pari-Cachoeira [*Brazil*] [*Airport symbol*] (AD)
PCH .... Paroxysmal Cold Hemoglobinuria [*Medicine*]
PCH .... Partido Comunista de Honduras [*Communist Party of Honduras*] [*Political party*] (PD)
PCH .... Patrol Craft (Hydrofoil) [*Navy symbol*]
P-Ch .... P-Channel (SAUS)
PCH .... PCH Post Career [*Vancouver Stock Exchange symbol*]
PCh .... Phosphocholine [*Biochemistry*]
PCH .... Physicochemical Hydrodynamics [*A publication*]
PCH .... Pitch
PCH .... Polycyclic Hydrocarbon (DMAA)
pch .... Porch (VRA)
PCH .... Porch (WGA)
PCH .... Porous Clay Heterostructure [*Materials science*]
PCH .... Port Charlotte, FL [*Amtrak Busline code*]
PCH .... Positive Channel [*Telecommunications*] (IAA)
PCH .... Potlatch Corp. [*Formerly, PFI*] [*NYSE symbol*] (SPSG)
PCH .... Prepare Chassis
PCH .... Presbyterian Church House [*British*] (BI)
PCH .... Prince Charles Hospital [*Australia*]
Pch .... Principal Chaplain [*Navy*] [*British*]
PCH .... Program Critical Hardware (SAUS)
PCH .... Proton Channeling (SAUS)
PCH .... Publishers Clearing House
pch .... Punch (ELAL)
PCH .... Punch (KSC)
pch .... punched (SAUS)
PCH .... Purchase (DCTA)
PCH & T ..... Packaging, Crating, Handling, and Transportation [*Shipping*] (CINC)
PCHAR .... Printing Character [*Computer science*]
PCHB .... Pollution Control Hearings Board (SAUS)
PCHBD .... Patchboard (MSA)
PCHC .... Holland College, Charlottetown, Prince Edward Island [*Library symbol*] [*National Library of Canada*] (NLC)
PCHC .... People's Center for Housing Change (EA)
p Ch c .... pure Chilean cocaine (SAUS)
PChCo .... Conococheague District Library, Chambersburg, PA [*Library symbol*] [*Library of Congress*] (LCLS)
PCHCY .... Parents Campaign for Handicapped Children and Youth (EA)
pchd .... Purchased (GEAB)
PCHD .... Purchased (ROG)
Pch Del ..... Punch Delay (SAUS)
Pch Dir ..... Punch Direct (SAUS)
PCHDMT .... Polycyclohexane Dimethylene Terephthalate (SAUS)
PChE .... Plasma Cholinesterase (SAUS)
PCHE .... Poor Clare Nuns of the Holy Eucharist [*Roman Catholic religious order*]
PC HE .... Pseudocholinesterase [*An enzyme*] (DAVI)
PCHE .... Purchase (ROG)
PCheS .... Cheyney State College, Cheyney, PA [*Library symbol*] [*Library of Congress*] (LCLS)
PCHG .... Pacific Center for Human Growth [*Gay, lesbian, bisexual, and transgender group*] [*California*] (EARSL)
PCHG .... Punching
PCHG .... Purchasing [*Telegraphy*] (PCTE)
P Chgs ...... Particular Charges (SAUS)
PCHIS .... Population Clearing House and Information System (NITA)
PCHK .... Parity Check [*Data communications*] (TEL)
PCHL .... Pacific Coast Hockey League [*Later, Western Hockey League*] (EA)
Pchl .... Protochlorophyll (SAUS)
Pchlide ...... Protochlorophyllide (SAUS)
PCHLT .... Pressurized Cabin Hydraulic Leakage Tester (DWSG)

PCHM .... PharmChem [*NASDAQ symbol*]
PCHM .... PharmChem Laboratories [*NASDAQ symbol*] (SPSG)
PCHMOS .... Positive-Channel Metal-Oxide Semiconductor [*Electronics*] (IAA)
PCHN .... Programmed Course, Home Nursing [*Red Cross*]
Pch Off ...... Punch Off (SAUS)
PCHR .... Panamanian Committee for Human Rights (EA)
PCHR .... Paraguay Committee for Human Rights [*British*]
PCHR .... Pentecostal Coalition for Human Rights [*Defunct*] (EA)
PCHR .... Purchaser (ROG)
PCHRG ...... Public Citizen Health Research Group (EA)
P Chr N ..... Post Christum Natum [*After the Birth of Christ*] [*Latin*]
PChS .... Proceedings of the Chemical Society (SAUS)
PCHS .... Purchase (WGA)
PCHSR ...... Purchaser
Pch Sup..... Punch Suppress (SAUS)
PCHT .... Packaging, Crating, Handling, and Transportation [*Shipping*] (AABC)
PCHT .... Parchment (MSA)
PCHU .... Polymir [*Intermodal shipping container symbol*] (TVRC)
PCHU .... Population and Community Health Unit [*University of Western Ontario*] [*Canada*] (RCD)
PChW........ Wilson College, Chambersburg, PA [*Library symbol*] [*Library of Congress*] (LCLS)
Pch X........ Punch X (SAUS)
PCI........... Packer Collegiate Institute (SAUS)
PCI........... Packet/Circuit Interface (SAUS)
PCI........... Packet Communications, Inc.
PCI........... Panel Call Indicator
PCI........... Pantone Color Institute (EA)
PCI........... Paramount Communications (EFIS)
PCI........... Parti Communiste Internationaliste [*Internationalist Communist Party*] [*France*] [*Political party*] (PPE)
PCI........... Partito Comunista Italiano [*Italian Communist Party*] [*Political party*]
PCI........... Patent Citation Index (SAUS)
PCI........... Paterson Candy International [*British*]
PCI........... Pattern Correspondence Index
PCI........... Pattern of Cockpit Indication
PCI........... Pavement Condition Index [*Aviation*] (DA)
PCI........... Pax Christi International (EAIO)
PCI........... Payless Cashways, Inc. [*NYSE symbol*] (COMM)
PCI........... PCL Industries Ltd. [*Toronto Stock Exchange symbol*]
PCI........... Pellet Clad Interaction [*Nuclear energy*] (NRCH)
PCI........... Percentage [*Telegraphy*] (PCTE)
PCI........... Per Column Inch [*Publishing*]
PCI........... Periodicals Contents Index [*Database*] (GDD)
PCI........... Periodic Conformance Inspection (MCD)
PCI........... Periodic Convolutional Interleaving (ACAE)
PCI........... Peripheral Command Indicator
PCI........... Peripheral Component Interconnect [*Telecommunications*] (PCM)
PCI........... Peripheral Component Interface (PCM)
PCI........... Peripheral Connection Interface
PCI........... Peripheral Control Instruction (SAUS)
PCI........... Peripheral Controller Interface
PCI........... Perpetual Cost Index (SAUS)
PCI........... Personal Computer Interconnect (VLIE)
PCI........... Personal Computer Interface [*Varitronics Systems, Inc.*]
PCI........... Phase-Conjugate Interferometry (SAUS)
PCI........... Photographic Credit Institute (EA)
PCI........... Photon-Coupled Isolator (SAUS)
PCI........... Physical Configuration Inspection (AFIT)
PCI........... Physical Configuration Item [*Military*]
PCI........... Physico-Chemical Institute (SAUS)
Pci........... Phytophthora Citricola [*A fungus*]
pCi........... Picocurie [*Also, pC*] [*One trillionth of a curie*]
PCI........... Pilot Club International (EA)
PCI........... Pilot Controller Integration (IEEE)
PCI........... Pilots for Christ International (EA)
PCI........... Pipe Collectors International [*Later, PCCA*] (EA)
PCI........... Planning Card Index (AAG)
PCI........... Plant Control Interface
PCI........... Pneumatic Circuit Indicator
PCI........... Pneumatosis Cystoides Intestinorum [*Medicine*] (AAMN)
PCI........... Polar Circulation Index [*Climatology*]
PCI........... Policy Consensus Initiative (EARSL)
PCI........... Political Campaign Institute [*Commercial firm*] (EA)
PCI........... Polycrystal Isolation (IAA)
PCI........... Population Communications International [*An association*] (EA)
PCI........... Population Council of India (BUAC)
PCI........... Portable Cesium Irradiator
PCI........... Portable Compass Indicator
PCI........... Possible Criminal Informant
PCI........... Post Cure Inflation (SAUS)
PCI........... Potato Chip Institute, International [*Later, PC/SFA*] (EA)
PCI........... Potential Criminal Informant (SAUS)
PCI........... Powder Coating Institute (EA)
PCI........... Power Conversion International (SAUS)
PCI........... Precast/Prestressed Concrete Institute (NTPA)
PCI........... Pre-Chamber Ignition [*Automotive engineering*]
PCI........... Precision Cascade Impactor (SAUS)
PCI........... Precision Components, Inc. [*Addison, IL*] [*Telecommunications service*] (TSSD)
PCI........... Precombat Checks and Inspections [*Army*]
PCI........... Pre-Combat Inspection (INF)
PCI........... Pre-Counseling Inventory [*Psychology*]
PCI........... Premarital Communication Inventory [*Psychology*] (DHP)
PCI........... Presentation Context Identifier [*Computer science*] (TNIG)
PCI........... Press Control, Inc.
PCI........... Press Council of India (BUAC)
PCI........... Prestressed Concrete Institute (EA)
PCI........... Price Cap Index (OTD)
PCI........... Prime Ceiling Incentive
PCI........... Printed Circuits, Inc. (SAUS)
PCI........... Printer Command Language [*Computer science*] (AGLO)
PCI........... Private Citizen, Inc. [*An association*] (EA)
PCI........... Privy Council Decisions [*India*] [*A publication*] (DLA)
PCI........... Privy Councillor, Ireland (ROG)
PCI........... Procedure Change Unit (SAUS)
PCI........... Process Capability Index (SAUS)
PCI........... Process Control Interface
PCI........... Product Change Information
PCI........... Product Configuration Identification (KSC)
PCI........... Product Configuration Item
PCI........... Product Cost Index
PCI........... Production and Continuous Improvement [*Automotive engineering*]
PCI........... Production Configuration Identification (SAUS)
PCI........... Production, Configuration, Integration
PCI........... Production Control Information [*Software supplier*] [*Sheffield, England*] (NCC)
PCI........... Production Cost Information (SAUS)
PCI........... Program Check Interruption [*Computer science*] (MDG)
PCI........... Program Control Input (NASA)
PCI........... Program-Controlled Interruption [*Computer science*] (IBMDP)
PCI........... Program Controlled Interuption (SAUS)
PCI........... Program in Correctional Institutions (OICC)
PCI........... Programmable Communications Interface
PCI........... Programmable Controller Interface (SAUS)
PCI........... Programmed Control Interrupt (SAUS)
PCI........... Project Concern International (EA)
PCI........... Project Control Information (SAUS)
PCI........... Prophylactic Cranial Irradiation [*Oncology*]
PCI........... Proportional Change Index [*Occupational therapy*]
PCI........... Prospectors Club International [*Defunct*] (EA)
PCI........... Protein C Inhibitor [*Organic chemistry*]
PCI........... Prothrombin Consumption Index (PDAA)
PCI........... Protocol Capability Indicator (CGWS)
PCI........... Protocol Computers Inc. (NITA)
PCI........... Protocol Control Indicator (SAUS)
PCI........... Protocol Control Information [*Telecommunications*]
PCI........... Pseudo-Code Instruction (SAUS)
PCI........... Pulverised Coal Injection [*Coal industry*]
PCI........... Pulverized Coal Injection [*Metallurgical engineering*]
PCI........... Punched Card Input (SAUS)
PCI........... Pupil Control Ideology Form [*Education*] (EDAC)
PCI........... Put Control Instruction (SAUS)
PCIA .... Pacific Consultants International Asia
PCIA .... Personal Communications Industry Association (DDC)
PCIA .... Person Communications Industry Association (NTPA)
PCIAC .... Petro-Canada International Assistance Corp.
PCIAOH ..... Permanent Commission and International Association on Occupational Health (EAIO)
PCIA PAC... Personal Communications Industry Association PAC [*Alexandria, VA*] (PACS)
PCIB .... Pacific Cargo Inspection Bureau (SAUS)
PCIB .... Personal Computer Instruments Bus (NITA)
PCIC .... Petroleum and Chemical Industry Conference (SAUS)
PCIC .... Pittsburgh Chemical Information Center (SAUS)
PCIC .... Poison Control Information Center
PCIC .... Polaris Control and Information Center (SAUS)
PCIC .... Program Control Information Card (VLIE)
PCICP .... Primary Control Inventory Control Point [*Navy*]
PCICS .... Permanent Council of the International Convention of Stresa on Cheeses (EAIO)
PCID .... Pontifical Council for Inter-Religious Dialogue (BUAC)
PCIE .... Period of Central Inspiratory Excitability (SAUS)
PCIE .... President's Council on Integrity and Efficiency (AAGC)
PCIE .... President's Council on Integrity and Efficiency in Government (EPA)
PCIEC........ Permanent Committee for International Eucharistic Congresses (EA)
PCIF .... Personal Computing Internal Fanout (TIMI)
PCIF .... Printed Circuit Interconnection Federation [*British*] (DBA)
PCIF .... Programmable Controller Interface Facility (SAUS)
PCIFC........ Patsy Cline International Fan Club (EA)
PCIFC........ Permanent Commission of the International Fisheries Convention
pCi/g......... Picocuries per Gram (SAUS)
PCIH......... Professional Conference on Industrial Hygiene [*Industrial hygiene term*] (OHS)
PCII .... Potato Chip Institute International (SAUS)
PCIJ .... Permanent Court of International Justice (BUAC)
PCIJ .... Permanent Court of International Justice Cases [*A publication*] (DLA)
PCIJ Ann R... Permanent Court of International Justice Annual Reports [*A publication*] (DLA)
PCIJ Reports... Permanent Court of International Justice Reports [*A publication*] (SAFN)
PCIL .... Parallel Computing and Imaging Laboratory [*Johns Hopkins University*] (RCD)
pCi/L......... Picocuries per Liter [*Measure of radioactivity*]
PCIL .... Pilot-Controlled Instrument Landing [*Aviation*] (NASA)
PCIL .... Private Core Image Library (VLIE)
PCIL .... Programmable Current-Injection Logic (SAUS)
PCI LBS..... Peripheral Component Interconnect Local Bus Specification (SAUS)

PCILO .... Perturbative Configuration Interaction [*Based on*] Localized Orbitals [*Quantum mechanics*]
PCILOCC ... Perturbative Configuration Interaction Using Localized Orbitals for Crystal Calculation (SAUS)
PCIM .... Packet Channel Interface Module [*Telecommunications*]
PCIM .... Parallel Character Input Module (SAUS)
PCIM .... Parti du Congres de l'Independance de Madagascar [*Party of the Congress for Malagasy Independence*]
PCIM .... Power Conversion and Intelligent Motion (SAUS)
PCIM .... Presidential Commission on Income Maintenance (SAUS)
PCIMP....... President's Commission on Income Maintenance Programs (EA)
PCIMR....... Centre for Information and Technical Assistance, Institute of Man and Resources,Charlottetown, Prince Edward Island [*Library symbol*] [*National Library of Canada*] (NLC)
PCIMS....... Positive Chemical Ionization Mass Spectroscopy
PCIN......... Program Change Identification Number (NASA)
PCIN......... Program Change Incorporation Notice (SAUS)
PCIN......... Program Change Integration (NASA)
PCIO......... PC Information Officer (SAUS)
PCI/O........ Program-Controlled Input-Output
PC-IOC...... Posterior Chamber - Intraocular Lens [*Ophthalmology*]
PC I/O Channel... Personal Computer Input/Output Channel (SAUS)
PCIOL .... Posterior Chamber Intraocular Lens [*Ophthalmology*] (DAVI)
PCIOMR..... Preconditioning Interim Operating Management Recommendation [*Nuclear energy*] (NRCH)
PCIOS .... Processor Common Input/Output System [*Computer science*] (VLIE)
PCIP......... Permitting Compliance Implementation Plan (SAUS)
PCIP......... Personal Computer, Instrument Product
PCIP......... Poseidon [*Missile*] Communication Improvement Program [*Navy*]
PCIPI........ Permanent Committee on Industrial Property [*World Intellectual Property Organization*] [*Switzerland*] [*Information service or system*] (IID)
PCIPS .... Paris Conversational Image Processing System (SAUS)
PCIPS .... Personal Computer Image Processing System (SAUS)
PCIR......... Post-Contract Implementation Report (AAGC)
PCIRI........ Paint and Coatings Industry Research Institute [*China*] (BUAC)
PCIRO .... Preparatory Commission for International Refugee Organization
PCIS......... Canton Island [*Phoenix Islands*] [*ICAO location identifier*] (ICLI)
PCIS......... Patient Care Information System (IID)
PCIS......... PCI Services [*NASDAQ symbol*] (TTSB)
PCIS......... PCI Services, Inc. [*NASDAQ symbol*] (SAG)
PCIS......... Period Cottage Improvement Society (BUAC)
PCIS......... Personal Computer Information Service (NITA)
PCIS......... Pinnacles Component Information Standard [*Computer science*] (AGLO)
PCIS......... Portable Common Interface Set (SAUS)
PCIS......... Post-Cardiac Injury Syndrome (MELL)
PCIS......... Primary Containment Isolation System [*Nuclear energy*] (NRCH)
PCIS......... Process Control Information System [*Computer science*] (VLIE)
PCIS......... Processed Commodities Inventory System [*Department of Agriculture*] (GFGA)
PCIS......... Production Control Information System (NVT)
PCIS......... Professional Career Information Service [*Department of Labor*]
PCIS......... Proposals and Contracts Information System (SAUS)
PCI Sv....... PCI Services, Inc. [*Associated Press*] (SAG)
PCI/SWCI... Product Configuration Item/Software Configuration Item (SAUS)
PCITF........ Positive Combat Identification Task Force (SAUS)
PCIU......... Pacific International Lines [*Intermodal shipping container symbol*] (TVRC)
PCIU......... Parts Controlled by Identifiable Unit (SAUS)
PCIU......... Parts Controlled by Indentifiable Unit (VLIE)
PCIU......... Programmable Communications Interface Unit
PCIUG....... Personal Computer Independent User Group (ODA)
PCIV......... Prestressed Cast Iron Vessel (SAUS)
PC/IX........ Personal Computer / Interactive Executive (HGAA)
PCIX......... Plant City Industrial Park [*Federal Railroad Administration identification code*]
PCIX......... Pure Carbonic [*Private rail car owner code*]
PCIYRA...... Pacific Coast Intercollegiate Yacht Racing Association
PCIZ......... Price Intermodal Southwest [*Intermodal trailer symbol*]
PCIZC....... Permanent Committee of International Zoological Congresses (BUAC)
PCJ.......... Pax Christi Institute (TOCD)
PCJ.......... Peoples Jewellers Ltd. [*Toronto Stock Exchange symbol*]
PCJ.......... Petroleum Corporation of Jamaica (BUAC)
PCJ.......... Planning Commissioners Journal (SAUS)
PCJ.......... Pontifical College Josephinum, Worthington, OH [*OCLC symbol*] (OCLC)
PCJ.......... Pulsed Combustion Jet
PCJ.......... Sisters of the Poor Child Jesus [*Roman Catholic religious order*]
PCJC......... Pakistan Central Jute Committee (BUAC)
PCJC......... Parliamentary Criminal Justice Committee [*Queensland, Australia*]
PCJE......... Program on Criminal Justice and the Elderly (DICI)
PCJILMCC... Philip C. Jessup International Law Moot Court Competition (EAIO)
PCJ LDEF... Partnership for Civil Justice Legal Defense and Education Fund [*Association*] (EA)
PCjr.......... Personal Computer-Junior (NITA)
PCJRI........ Pakistan Central Jute Research Institute (SAUS)
PCJU......... Puma Containers [*Intermodal shipping container symbol*] (TVRC)
PC Judg..... Privy Council Judgments [*India*] [*A publication*] (DLA)
PCJX......... Peninsula Corridor Joint Powers Board [*Federal Railroad Administration identification code*]
pck........... Peacock [*Philately*]
PCK.......... Peacock H.E. and Son (Thorney) Ltd. [*British*] [*FAA designator*] (FAAC)
PCK.......... Peck (IAA)
PCK.......... Pedagogical Content Knowledge
PCK.......... Phase Control Keyboard
PCK.......... Pilot Check (SAUS)
PCK.......... Polycystic Kidney [*Medicine*] (DMAA)
PCK.......... Porcupine Creek, AK [*Location identifier*] [*FAA*] (FAAL)
PCK.......... Premarital Counseling Kit [*Psychology*]
PCK.......... Primary Chicken Kidney [*Cell line*]
PCK.......... Printed Circuit Keyboard
PCK.......... Printed Control Keyboard [*Computer science*] (CIST)
PCK.......... Processor Controlled Keying [*Computer science*] (DCTA)
PCKB........ Phase Control Keyboard [*Computer science*] (VLIE)
PCKB........ Printed Circuit Keyboard
PCKD........ Polycystic Kidney Disease [*Medicine*]
PCKR........ Packer Transportation Company [*Common carrier symbol*]
PCKRR...... Pine Creek Railroad [*An association*] (EA)
PCKS........ Public-Cryptography Key System [*Information technology*]
PCKT........ Printed Circuit [*Computer science*] (CIST)
PCL.......... Alberta Attorney General, Provincial Court Libraries [*UTLAS symbol*]
PCl.......... Clarion Free Library, Clarion, PA [*Library symbol*] [*Library of Congress*] (LCLS)
PCL.......... Confederation Centre Library, Charlottetown, Prince Edward Island [*Library symbol*] [*National Library of Canada*] (NLC)
PCL.......... Pachaco Lake [*California*] [*Seismograph station code, US Geological Survey*] (SEIS)
PCL.......... Pacific Coast League [*Baseball*]
PCL.......... Pacific Coast Line (SAUS)
PCL.......... Pallet Coolant Loop (NASA)
PCL.......... Parallel Communications Link
PCL.......... Parcel
PCL.......... Paroxysmal Choreathetois Dystonia [*Medicine*]
PCL.......... Partial Core Loading (SAUS)
pcl........... Particle [*Linguistics*] (IEL)
PCL.......... Parti Communiste de Luxembourg [*Communist Party of Luxembourg*] [*Political party*] (PPE)
PCL.......... Parti Communiste Libanais [*Lebanese Communist Party*] [*Political party*] (PPW)
PCL.......... Parts Complement List (ACAE)
PCL.......... Passive Coherent Location (SEWL)
PCL.......... Patch-Constrained Layer [*Insulation*]
PCL.......... Pencil (MSA)
PCL.......... Peoples College of Law (SAUS)
PCL.......... Peripheral Control Line (SAUS)
PCL.......... Permissible Contamination Limits [*Nuclear energy*] (NRCH)
PCL.......... Persistent Corpus Luteum [*Medicine*]
PCL.......... Personnel Security Clearance
P Cl.......... Petrus Calvelli [*Flourished, 14th century*] [*Authority cited in pre-1607 legal work*] (DSA)
PCL.......... Phase Correction Loop (SAUS)
PCL.......... Philippine Cultural League [*Australia*]
PCL.......... Phillips Cables Ltd. [*Toronto Stock Exchange symbol*]
PCL.......... Photo Chemical Laboratories (SAUS)
PCL.......... Pilot Controlled Lighting [*Aviation*] (FAAC)
PCL.......... Planning and Conservation League (EA)
PCL.......... Planning Configuration List
PCL.......... Planning Consultancy Ltd. (NITA)
PCL.......... Plasma Cell Leukemia [*Oncology*]
PCL.......... Plasma Cholesterol Level (MELL)
PCL.......... Playboy Club of London
PCL.......... Plenary of Legislative Commissions (Ecuador) [*Political party*] (PSAP)
PCL.......... Plum Creek Timber Co., Inc. [*NYSE symbol*] (SPSG)
PCL.......... Plum Creek Timber L.P. [*NYSE symbol*] (TTSB)
PCL.......... Plutonium-Contaminated Liquid [*Nuclear energy*] (NUCP)
PCL.......... Pocket Checklist (MCD)
PCL.......... Police Crime Laboratory (SAUS)
PCL.......... Political Communication Laboratory [*Stanford University*] (RCD)
PCL.......... Polycaprolactone [*Organic chemistry*]
PCL.......... [*The*] Polytechnic of Central London
PCL.......... Pontifical Council for the Laity (BUAC)
PCL.......... Portable Common Loops (SAUS)
PCL.......... Positive Control Launch (CCCA)
PCL.......... Positive Control Line
PCL.......... Post Conference List
PCL.......... Posterior Chamber Lens [*Ophthalmology*] (DAVI)
PCL.......... Posterior Cruciate Ligament [*Anatomy*]
PCL.......... PostScript and LASERJet-Type [*LASER printer*]
PCL.......... Power Control Lever (DNAB)
PCL.......... Power Control List (MCD)
PCL.......... Power Conversion Loop (SAUS)
PCL.......... Practical [*Telegraphy*] (PCTE)
PCL.......... Precancel (SAUS)
PCL.......... Precancerous Lesion (MELL)
PCL.......... Preliminary Change Letter [*Navy*] (NG)
PCL.......... Premier Cruise Lines
PCL.......... Prescribed Chemical Load (SAUS)
PCL.......... Primary Coolant Line (NASA)
PCL.......... Primary Coolant Loop (NASA)
PCL.......... Primary Copy Locking (SAUS)
PCL.......... Princess Cruise Line (TVEL)
PCL.......... Print Control Language (NITA)
PCL.......... Printed Circuit Lacquer (SAUS)
PCL.......... Printed Circuit Lamp
PCL.......... Printer Command Language [*Hewlett Packard*] [*Computer science*]

PCL .... Printer Control Language
PCL .... Priority Chemicals List (SAUS)
PCL .... Procedural Control Language [*1971*] [*Computer science*] (CSR)
PCL .... Process Capability Laboratory
PCL .... Process Communications Link (ECII)
PCL .... Process Control Laboratory (ABAC)
PCL .... Process Control Language [*Texas Instruments, Inc.*] [*Computer science*] (IAA)
PCL .... Prodedure Change List
PCL .... Product Computing Module Load (SAUS)
PCL .... Programmable Command Language [*Computer science*] (VLIE)
PCL .... Programming Checklist (MCD)
PCL .... Programming Control Language [*Computer science*] (PCM)
PCL .... Project Control Ledgers [*Navy*] (NG)
PCL .... Pseudocleistogamous [*Botany*]
PCL .... Pucallpa [*Peru*] [*Airport symbol*] (OAG)
PCL .... Pulse Compression Loop
PCL .... Punch Card Lever (SAUS)
PCL .... Purkinje Cell Layer [*Cytology*]
PCLA .... Polish Canadian Librarians Association
PCLA .... Power Control Linkage Assembly
PCLA .... Process Control Language [*Texas Instruments, Inc.*]
PCLA .... Project Coordination and Liaison Administration (OICC)
PCLBCL ..... Primary Cutaneous Large B-Cell [*Medicine*] (RAWO)
PCLC .... Pest Control Licensing Committee [*New South Wales, Australia*]
PCLD .... Dependent Political Entity [*Board on Geographic Names*]
PCLD .... Polycystic Liver Disease (MELL)
PCLDI .... Prototype Closed-Loop Development Installation [*Nuclear energy*] (NRCH)
PCLE......... Pinnacle Systems [*NASDAQ symbol*] (TTSB)
PCLE......... Pinnacle Systems, Inc. [*NASDAQ symbol*] (SAG)
PCLEAJ...... Presidents Commission on Law Enforcement and the Administration of Justice (SAUS)
P-C Lens.... Perspective-Correction Lens (SAUS)
PCLFC .... Projected Consequences of Less Than Full Control (COE)
PCLG .... Public Citizen Litigation Group (EA)
PCLI .... Independent Political Entity [*Board on Geographic Names*]
PCLI .... Parti de la Convergence pour les Libertes et l'Integration [*Burkina Faso*] [*Political party*] (EY)
PCLI .... Plasma Cell Labeling Index [*Medicine*] (DMAA)
PC-LITE ..... Processor, Laptop Imagery Transmission Equipment (DOMA)
PCLJ......... Pacific Coast Law Journal [*A publication*] (DLA)
PCLK .... Pay Clerk
PCLK .... Program Clock [*Computer science*] (CIST)
PCLLG....... Ollennu's Principles of Customary Land Law in Ghana [*A publication*] (DLA)
PCLLRC ..... Post-Colonial Literatures and Languages Centre [*Macquarie University*] [*Australia*]
PCLMP ...... President's Advisory Committee on Labor-Management Policy [*Abolished, 1973*]
PCLN .... Personalcomputer Literaturnachweis [*Datendienst Weiss*] [*Database*]
PCLN .... Priceline.com
PCLN .... priceline.com, Inc. [*NASDAQ symbol*] (SG)
PC-LNIM ... Personal Computer Local Network Interface Module (TSSD)
PCLO .... Passenger Control Liaison Office [*or Officer*] [*Army*] (AABC)
PCLO .... Printed Circuit Layout (SAUS)
PCLP .... PaperClip Imaging Software [*NASDAQ symbol*] (TTSB)
PCLP .... Paperclip Imaging Software, Inc. [*NASDAQ symbol*] (SAG)
PCLP .... Process Control Laboratory Procedures (TIMI)
PCLPW...... Paperclip Imaging Softw'r Wrrt [*NASDAQ symbol*] (TTSB)
PCLR .... Parallel Communications Link Receiver (NITA)
P Cl R........ Parker's New York Criminal Reports [*A publication*] (DLA)
PCLR .... PR [*Public Relations*] Committee for Licensing and Registration (EA)
P Cl R........ Privy Council Reports [*A publication*] (DLA)
PCL-R .... Psychopathy Checklist-Revised [*R. Hare*] (DIPS)
PCIS .... Clarion State College, Clarion, PA [*Library symbol*] [*Library of Congress*] (LCLS)
PCLS .... Law Society of Prince Edward Island, Charlottetown, Prince Edward Island [*Library symbol*] [*National Library of Canada*] (NLC)
PCLS .... Passive Coherent Locating System (CCCA)
PCLS .... People's Committee for Libyan Students (EA)
PCLS .... Pressure-Compensated Load Sensing [*Hydraulics*]
PCLS .... Prototype Closed-Loop System [*Nuclear energy*] (NRCH)
PCLST....... Polychlorstyrene [*Organic chemistry*]
PCLT......... Portable Coded LASER Target
PCLT......... Prototype Closed-Loop Test [*Nuclear energy*] (NRCH)
PCLTT .... Permanent Committee on Land Transportation and Telecommunications (SAUS)
PCLU .... Maritime Container Lines [*Intermodal shipping container symbol*] (TVRC)
PCLU .... Pacific Container Line [*Common carrier symbol*]
PCLU .... Pioneer Civil Labour Unit [*British*]
PClvU........ Ursinus College, Collegeville, PA [*Library symbol*] [*Library of Congress*] (LCLS)
PCLW......... Platinum Compensating Lead Wire (PDAA)
PCLX .... Parallel Communications Link Transmitter (SAUS)
PCLX .... Polymer [*Private rail car owner code*]
PCLX .... Section of Independent Political Entity [*Board on Geographic Names*]
PCLZ......... Plum Creek Lumber [*Federal Railroad Administration identification code*]
PCM .... Coastal Escort Medium [*200-500 tons*] [*Ship symbol*] (NATG)
PCM .... Nigerian Pidgin [*Language symbol*] (ETLW)
PCM .... Pacific Comox Resources [*Vancouver Stock Exchange symbol*]
PCM .... Packet Compress when Matched bit in DCR2 (SAUS)
PCM .... Parabolic Collimator Mirror
PCM .... Paragraph Completion Method [*Education*] (EDAC)
PCM .... Parallel Calculating Mechanism (SAUS)
PCM .... Parallel Cutter Mechanism
PCM .... Parity Check Matrix (MCD)
PCM .... Parti Communiste Marocain [*Moroccan Communist Party*] [*Political party*]
PCM .... Parti Communiste Martiniquais [*Communist Party of Martinique*] [*Political party*] (PPW)
PCM .... Parti des Classes Moyennes [*Middle Class Party*] [*Luxembourg*] [*Political party*] (PPE)
PCM .... Partido Comunista Mexicano [*Mexican Communist Party*] [*Political party*] (PPW)
PCM .... Passive Countermeasure
PCM .... Patient Care Management (GART)
PCM .... Patient Care Manager
PCM .... Patient Management Category (HCT)
PCM .... Peabody Conservatory of Music (SAUS)
PCM .... Penalty Cost Model
PCM .... Pending Contractual Matters (NRCH)
PCM .... Per Calendar Month [*Business term*] (ADA)
pcm......... Per Calendar Month [*Business term*] (ODBW)
PCM .... Percentage of Completion Method (AAGC)
PCM .... Percentage of Moisture (SAUS)
PCM .... Percent Milli (NRCH)
PCM .... Peregrine Capital Myanmar
PCM .... Performance Capability Measure (IAA)
PCM .... Pericentriolar Material [*Biochemistry*]
PCM .... Peripheral Computer Manufacturer (SAUS)
PCM .... Personal Computer Manufacturer (SAUS)
PCM .... Personnel Contamination Monitor (SAUS)
PCM .... Phase Change Materials [*Solar energy*]
PCM .... Phase Comparison Monopulse (SAUS)
PCM .... Phase Conjugate Mirror
PCM .... Phase Contrast Microscopy
PCM .... Philippine Campaign Medal
PCM .... Photochemical Machining [*Desktop manufacturing*]
PCM .... Photoformed Ceramic Modules [*Du Pont process for making microconductors*]
PCM .... Physical Connection Management (SAUS)
PCM .... Piezo-Ceramic Material (SAUS)
PCM .... PIMCO Commercial Mortgage Security Trust [*NYSE symbol*] (SPSG)
PCM .... PIPES Buffer with Calcium and Magnesium
PCM .... Pitch Control Motor
PCM .... Planar Camping Model (SAUS)
PCM .... Planning and Control Memorandum [*Army*]
PCM .... Plasma Cell Myeloma [*Medicine*] (MELL)
PCM .... Please Call Me [*Internet lingo*] (NETL)
PCM .... Plug Compatible Machine (SAUS)
PCM .... Plug Compatible Mainframe [*Computer science*]
PCM .... Plug Compatible Manufacturer [*Computer science*]
PCM .... Plug Compatible Memory
PCM .... Plug Compatible Module [*Computer science*] (IAA)
PCM .... Plug Control Module (SAUS)
PCM .... Plutonium Contaminated Material
PCM .... Pneumococcal Meningitis [*Medicine*] (MELL)
PCM .... Police Court Mission [*British*] (ROG)
PCM .... Polyimide Composite Material
PCM .... Polymer Coated Material (SAUS)
PCM .... Portable Conformable Mask [*Microlithography*]
PCM .... Port Command Area [*Telecommunications*] (TEL)
PCM .... Port Command Module (SAUS)
PCM .... Postal [*Service*] Contracting Manual [*A publication*] (AAGC)
PCM .... Post Column Method [*Chromatography*]
PCM .... Postgraduate Committee in Medicine [*Australia*]
PCM .... Postmammillary Caudal Magnocellular Nuclei [*Neuroanatomy*]
PCM .... Power Center Multiplexer (SAUS)
PCM .... Power Control Mission (NASA)
PCM .... Power Control Module (SAUS)
PCM .... Power-Cooling Mismatch [*Nuclear energy*]
PCM .... Powertrain Control Module [*Automotive engineering*]
PCM .... Precision Capacitor Microphone (SAUS)
PCM .... Precision Condenser Microphone
PCM .... President's Certificate of Merit [*Military decoration*] (AFM)
PCM .... Primary Care Manager (HCT)
PCM .... Primary Code Modulation [*Computer science*] (IAA)
PCM .... Printer Cartridge Metric (SAUS)
PCM .... Process Communication Monitor [*Telecommunications*] (IAA)
PCM .... Process Control Manual (SAUS)
PCM .... Process Control Module [*Telecommunications*] (TEL)
PCM .... Process Control Monitor (SAUS)
PCM .... Processor Communication Monitor (SAUS)
PCM .... Production Control Master (SAUS)
PCM .... Productive Cost Management (ADA)
PCM .... Profiling Current Meter [*Oceanography*] (MSC)
PCM .... Program Configuration Manager
PCM .... Program Continuity Memorandum [*Military*]
PCM .... Program Cost Management (MCD)
PCM .... Project Cost Model [*Project Software Ltd.*] [*Software package*] (NCC)
PCM .... Proposed Corrective Measures (SAUS)
PCM .... Protein-Calorie Malnutrition [*Medicine*]
PCM .... Protein-Carboxyl Methylase [*Biochemistry*] (DAVI)
PCM .... Pulse Code Modulation [*Telecommunications*] (OSI)
PCM .... Pulse Code Modulation Microwave [*System*]

PCM .... Pulse Code Modulator (NAKS)
PCM .... Pulse Compression Modulation (SEWL)
PCM .... Punch Card Machine [*Computer science*]
PCM .... Punched Card Method (SAUS)
PCM .... Pyrotechnic Countermeasure [*Military*] (SDI)
PCM .... WestAir Industries, Inc. [*ICAO designator*] (FAAC)
PCMA........ Paired Carrier Multiple Access (SAUS)
PCMA........ Pennsylvania Coal Mining Association (EA)
PCMA........ Personal Computer Management Association [*Orange, CA*] [*Commercial firm*] [*Information service or system*] (EA)
PCMA........ Phenylcyclopropanemethylamine [*Organic chemistry*]
PCMA........ Plaited Cordage Manufacturers Association [*British*] (BI)
PCMA........ Plasmacytoma (SAUS)
PCMA........ Plastic Crate Manufacturers Association (BUAC)
PCMA........ Post Card Manufacturers Association [*Defunct*] (EA)
PCMA........ Potato Chips Manufacturers Association (BUAC)
PCMA........ Power Cooling Mismatch Accident [*Nuclear energy*] (NUCP)
PCMA........ Precision Chain Manufacturers Association (BUAC)
PCMA........ Prince Edward Island Department of Municipal Affairs, Charlottetown, Prince Edward Island [*Library symbol*] [*National Library of Canada*] (NLC)
PCMA........ Professional Convention Management Association [*Birmingham, AL*] (EA)
PCMA........ Provincial Carters' and Motormen's Association [*A union*] [*British*]
PC Mag ..... PC Magazine (SAUS)
PCMANSW... Precast Concrete Manufacturers' Association of New South Wales [*Australia*]
PCMA PAC... Pharmaceutical Care Management Association PAC [*Washington, DC*] (PACS)
PCMAS ...... Portable Computer-Based Maintenance Aid System (ACAE)
PCMAS ...... Portable Computer-Based Maintenance System (SAUS)
PCMAV ...... Precast Concrete Manufacturers' Association of Victoria [*Australia*]
PCMB........ Para-Chloromercuribenzoate [*Organic chemistry*]
PCMB........ Parachloro-Mercuric Benzoic (SAUS)
PCMB........ P-Chloromercuribenzoate (SAUS)
PCMB........ P-Chloromercuribenzoic Acid (SAUS)
PCMB Acid... Parachloro-Mercury Benzoic Acid (SAUS)
PCMC........ Para-Chloro-meta-cresol [*Organic chemistry*]
PCMC........ PCI, Cache, Memory Controller (SAUS)
PCMC........ Pirmasens Communications and Electronics Maintenance Center
PCMC........ Postal [*Service*] Contracting Manual Circular (AAGC)
PCMC........ Preparatory Commission for Metric Conversion (SAUS)
PCMC........ Primary Children's Medical Center (STED)
PCMC........ Provided Chief of Mission Concurs [*Army*]
PCMC........ Psychemedics Corp. [*NASDAQ symbol*] (COMM)
PCMCIA ..... People Can't Memorize Computer Industry Acronyms (PS)
PCMCIA ..... Personal Computer Memory Card International Association (PCM)
PCMCIA ..... Personal Computer Miniature Communications Interface Adapter [*Computer science*] (VLIE)
PCMCIA ..... Personal Comuter Memory Card Interface Adapter (DDC)
PCMCIA ..... Portable Computer Memory Card Industry Association (DOM)
PCMD .... Particle Count Monitoring Device (KSC)
PCMD .... Passive Count Monitoring Device (KSC)
PCMD .... Procurement and Contracts Management Division [*Environmental Protection Agency*] (GFGA)
PCMD .... Pulse Code Modulation, Digital
PCMDHS .... Pulse Code Modulation Data Handling System [*Telecommunications*] (IAA)
PCM-DHS... Pulse Code Modulation-Data Handling System (SAUS)
PCMDI....... Program for Climate Model Diagnosis and Intercomparison [*Department of Energy*]
PCME........ Pulse Code Modulation Event
PCMF........ Perceptual Cognitive Motor Function (STED)
PCMF........ Phi Chi Medical Fraternity (EA)
PCM-FM .... Pulse Code Modulation-Frequency Modulation (SAUS)
PCM/FSK/AM... Pulse Code Modulation/Frequency Shift Keying/Amplitude Modulation (SAA)
PCMGS...... Pulse Code Modulated Ground Station
PCMH .... Para-Cresol Methylhydroxylase [*An enzyme*]
PCMH .... Postgraduate Center for Mental Health (EA)
PCMH .... Professional Certified in Materials Handling (SAUS)
PCMI .... Pellet Cladding Mechanical Interaction (SAUS)
PCMI .... Photo-Chemical Machining Institute (EA)
PCMI .... Photochromic Microimage [*Microfiche*]
PCMI .... Photochromic Microimage System (IAA)
PCMI .... Plastic Container Manufacturers Institute [*Defunct*] (EA)
PCMI .... President's Council on Management Improvement [*Executive Office of the President*] (GFGA)
PCMIA....... Personal Computer Manufacturer Interface Adapter (VLIE)
PCMIA....... Personal Computer Manufacturer Interface Adaptor
PCMIA....... Pittsburgh Coal Mining Institute of America (EA)
PCMIA....... Plasterers and Cement Masons International Association (SAUS)
PCMI Film... Photo Chromic Micro Image Film (SAUS)
PCMIM ...... Personal Computer Media Interface Module (SAUS)
PCMIP....... Pontifical Commission for Migrants and Itinerant Peoples [*See also PCMT*] [*Vatican City, Vatican City State*] (EAIO)
PCMI Process... Photo Chromic Micro Image Process (SAUS)
PCMI System... Photochromic Micro-Image System (SAUS)
PCMK........ Piece Mark
PCML........ Maoist Marxist-Leninist Communist Party (Ecuador) [*Political party*] (PSAP)
PC-ML....... Marxist-Leninist Communist Party [*Bolivia*] [*Political party*] (PPW)
PCML........ Parti Communiste Marxiste-Leniniste [*Marxist-Leninist Communist Party*] [*France*] [*Political party*] (PPW)
PCML........ Partito Comunista Marxista-Leninista [*Marxist-Leninist Communist Party*] [*San Marino*] [*Political party*] (PPE)
PCML........ President's Committee on Migratory Labor [*Terminated, 1964*]
PCML........ Pseudo Current Mode Logic (SAUS)
PCMLF ...... Parti Communiste Marxiste-Leniniste Francais [*French Marxist-Leninist Communist Party*] [*Dissolved, 1978*] [*Political party*] (PPW)
PC(ML)I ..... Partito Comunista (Marxista-Leninista) de Italia [*Communist Party of Italy (Marxist-Leninist)*] [*Political party*] (PPE)
PCMM .... Plug Compatible Mainframe Manufacturer (NITA)
PCMM .... Professional Certified in Materials Management (SAUS)
PCMMU ..... PCM [*Punch Card Machine*] Master Unit [*Computer science*] (GFGA)
PCMMU ..... Pulse Code Modulation Master Unit [*Electronics*] (NASA)
PCMNA...... Provisions for Carbon Monoxide Nonattainment Areas [*Environmental science*] (COE)
PCM/NRZ ... Pulse Code Modulation/Non-Return to Zero (SAUS)
PCMO .... Passenger Car Motor Oil
PCMO .... Principal Clinical Medical Officer [*British*]
PCMO .... Principal Colonial Medical Officer [*British*]
PCMOD...... Personal Computer Modification Program
PC-MOS..... Personal Computer-Modular Operating System (SAUS)
PCMP........ Packed Computational (IAA)
PCMP........ Pennsylvania Comprehensive Mathematics Plan (EDAC)
PCMP........ (Phenylcyclohexyl)methylpiperidine [*Organic chemistry*]
PCMP........ Post Chemical-Mechanical Polishing (AAEL)
PCMP........ Preliminary Configuration Management Plan (MCD)
PCMP........ Progressive Car Manufacturing Program (SAUS)
PCM/PAM... Pulse Code Modulation/Pulse Amplitude Modulation (SAUS)
PCM/PL ..... Pulse Code Modulated/Polarized Light (SAUS)
PCM-PM ..... Pulse Code Modulation-Phase Modulation (SAUS)
PCMPM ..... Pulse Code Modulation-Phase-Modulation (IAA)
PCMPN...... Pulse Code Modulation Pseudonoise [*Telecommunications*] (IAA)
PCM-PN..... Pulse Code Modulation-Pseudo-Noise (SAUS)
PCMPS...... Para-Chloromercuriphenylsulfonic Acid [*Organic chemistry*]
PCM-PS ..... Pulse Code Modulation-Phase-Shift (SAUS)
PCMR .... Patient Computer Medical Record
PCMR .... Photochromic Microreproduction (DIT)
PCMR .... Presidential Council for Minority Rights (Singapore) [*Political party*] (PSAP)
PCMR .... President's Committee on Mental Retardation [*Washington, DC*]
PCMR .... Probability of Correct Message Receipt (CCCA)
PCMS........ Pad-Circuit Minimum Spacing (SAUS)
PCMS........ Para-Chloromercuriphenyl Sulfonate [*or Sulfonic Acid*] [*Organic chemistry*]
PCMS........ Pattern Card Makers' Society [*British*] (BI)
PCMS........ P-Chloromercurphenylsulfonic Acid (SAUS)
PCMS........ P-Com, Inc. [*NASDAQ symbol*] (SAG)
PCMS........ Photographic Cabinet Makers' Society [*A union*] [*British*]
PCMS........ Plasma Chemistry Monte-Carlo Simulation (AAEL)
PCMS........ Plasma Chromatography Mass Spectroscopy
PCMS........ Portable Changeable Message Sign [*Highway operations*]
PCMS........ Process Control Management System (TIMI)
PCMS........ Production Control Monitoring System (NVT)
PCMS........ Project & Configuration Management System (SAUS)
PCMS........ Pulse Code Modulation Shared (MCD)
PCMS........ Punch Card Machine System [*Computer science*]
PCMSB ...... Phased-Array Contiguous Multi-Spot Barrage (SEWL)
PCMSER .... Presidents Commission on Marine Science, Engineering and Resources (SAUS)
PCMSIGNAL... Pulse Code Modulated Signal (SAUS)
PCMT........ Personal Computer Message Terminal (SAUS)
PCMT........ Pontificia Commissione Migrazioni e Turismo [*Pontifical Commission for Migrants and Itinerant Peoples - PCMIP*] [*Vatican City, Vatican City State*] (EAIO)
PCMTE ...... Pulse Code Modulation and Timing Electronics (SAUS)
PCMTE ...... Pulse Code Modulation and Timing Equipment (KSC)
PCMTEA..... Pulse Code Modulation and Timing Electronics Assembly
PCMTS ...... Pulse Code Modulation Telemetry System (AAG)
PCMU .... Peroxid Chemie [*Intermodal shipping container symbol*] (TVRC)
PCMU .... Physico-Chemical Measurements Unit [*British*]
PCMU .... Propellant Calibration Measuring Unit (KSC)
PCMV........ Plug Compatible Mainframe Vendor [*Computer science*] (VLIE)
PCMV........ Porcine Cerebral Microvascular [*Cell line*]
PCMX........ Para-Chloro-meta-xylenol [*Organic chemistry*]
PCMX........ P-Chlorodimethylphenol (SAUS)
PCMX........ Petro-Chem Marketing [*Private rail car owner code*]
PCMZ........ Peninsular Commuter-San Mateo County [*Federal Railroad Administration identification code*]
PCN.......... Pacific Communications Network [*Air Force*] (IAA)
PCN.......... Package Control Number
PCN.......... Page Change Notice (MCD)
PCN.......... Pameco Corp'A' [*NYSE symbol*] (SG)
PCN.......... PanCana Minerals [*Toronto Stock Exchange symbol*]
PCN.......... Parent Country National (PDAA)
PCN.......... Part Control Number (AAG)
PCN.......... Partido Comunista de Nicaragua [*Communist Party of Nicaragua*] [*Political party*] (PD)
PCN.......... Partido Conservador Nicaraguense [*Nicaraguan Conservative Party*] [*Political party*] (PPW)
PCN.......... Partido de Conciliacion Nacional [*National Reconciliation Party*] [*El Salvador*] [*Political party*] (PPW)
PCN.......... Parts Change Notice (MCD)
PCN.......... Parts Control Number (SAUS)
PCN.......... Pavement Classification Number [*Aviation*] (DA)
PCN.......... Payroll Change Notice (GOBB)

PCN.......... Pediatric Chaplains Network [*Association*] (EA)
PCN.......... Penicillin [*Antibiotic*]
PCN.......... Percutaneous Nephrostomy (DAVI)
PCN.......... Permanent Control Number (MCD)
PCN.......... Personal Communications Network [*British*]
PCN.......... Personal Computer Network [*Telecommunications*]
PCN.......... Personal Computer News (NITA)
PCN.......... Personnel Change Notice (TIMI)
PCN.......... Pharmaceutical Case Network (SAUS)
PCN.......... Piacenza [*Italy*] [*Seismograph station code, US Geological Survey*] [*Closed*] (SEIS)
PCN.......... Pitcairn Islands [*ANSI three-letter standard code*] (CNC)
PCN.......... Planning Change Notice
PCN.......... PointCast Network [*Internet news service*]
PCN.......... Point Comfort & Northern Railway Co. [*AAR code*]
PCN.......... Policy Criteria Notice [*Environmental Protection Agency*] (EPAT)
PCN.......... Polychlorinated Naphthalene [*Organic chemistry*]
PCN.......... Popcorn Noise (SAUS)
PCN.......... Position Control Number (AFM)
PCN.......... Post Christum Natum [*After the Birth of Christ*] [*Latin*] (ROG)
PCN.......... Potato Cyst Nematode [*Plant pathology*]
PCN.......... Pregnenolone Carbonitril [*Pharmacology*] (DAVI)
PCN.......... Prelaunch Channel Number [*NASA*] (IAA)
PCN.......... Primary Care Network [*Insurance*] (AMHC)
PCN.......... Primary Care Nurse (SAUS)
PCN.......... Primary Care Nursing
PCN.......... Princeton Aviation Corp. [*ICAO designator*] (FAAC)
PCN.......... Printed Control Number (SAUS)
PCN.......... Procedure Change Notice
PCN.......... Process Change Notice (VLIE)
PCN.......... Processing Control Number
PCN.......... Procession [*Telegraphy*] (PCTE)
PCN.......... Procurement Control Number (AFM)
PCN.......... Product Control Number (AFM)
PCN.......... Production Change Number (KSC)
PCN.......... Production Control Number (SAUS)
PCN.......... Produits Chimiques du Nord (EFIS)
PCN.......... Program Change Notice (MCD)
PCN.......... Program Change Number (SAUS)
PCN.......... Program Composition Notation [*Computer science*]
PCN.......... Program Control Number (AFM)
PCN.......... Project Control Number (AAG)
PCN.......... Proposal Control Number (AAG)
PCN.......... Publication Change Notice (MCD)
PCN.......... Publication Code Number (SAUS)
PCN.......... Public Communications Network (SAUS)
PCN.......... Public Convenience and Necessity [*Department of Transportation*]
PCN.......... Pulse Compression Network
PCNA........ Palestine Congress of North America [*Defunct*] (EA)
PCNA........ P-Chloro-0-Nitroaniline (SAUS)
PCNA........ Porsche Cars North America, Inc.
PCNA........ Proliferating Cell Nuclear Antigen [*Cytology, immunology*]
PCNA........ Publishing Co. of North America, Inc. (The) [*NASDAQ symbol*] (SAG)
PCNAC....... Professionals Coalition for Nuclear Arms Control (EA)
PCNB........ Pentachloronitrobenzene [*Agricultural fungicide*]
PCNB........ Permanent Control Narcotics Board
PCNC........ Projected Consequences of No Control [*Environmental science*] (COE)
PCNE........ Protocol Converter for Native Equipment [*Telecommunications*] (IAA)
PCNET....... Personal Computer Network
PCNF........ Pacific Central NOTAM [*Notice to Airmen*] Facility [*Military*]
PCN(Fr.).... Physics, Chemistry & Natural Science-France (CMD)
PCNFS....... Personal Computer Network File System (VLIE)
PCNG........ Presidents Commission on National Goals (SAUS)
PCNI........ Physician Computer Network [*NASDAQ symbol*] (SPSG)
PCNI........ Physician Computer Ntwk [*NASDAQ symbol*] (TTSB)
PCNI........ Physicians Computer Network [*NASDAQ symbol*] (SAG)
PCNM........ Polymer-Immobilised Clusters of the Noble Metals [*Catalytic chemistry*]
PCNP........ Personal Computer Network Program (HGAA)
PCNR........ Part Control Number Request (AAG)
PCNR........ Planning Change Notice Request
PCNS........ Polar Coordinates Navigation System
PCNSL....... Polymerised Cashew Nut Shell Liquid (PDAA)
PCNT........ Pacific Internet, Ltd. [*NASDAQ symbol*] (NASQ)
PCNU........ Paros Naviera [*Intermodal shipping container symbol*] (TVRC)
PCNV........ Postchemotherapy Nausea and Vomiting [*Medicine*] (MELL)
PCNV........ Provisional Committee on Nomenclature of Viruses (DAVI)
PCNW........ Pacific Cartage and Warehousing [*Common carrier symbol*]
PCNY........ Proofreaders Club of New York (EA)
P_{co}.......... Carbon Monoxide Tension (DAVI)
PCO.......... Conococheague District Library, Chambersburg, PA [*OCLC symbol*] (OCLC)
PCO.......... Pacific Chamber Opera (SAUS)
PCO.......... Pacific Coastal Airline [*Canada*] [*ICAO designator*] (FAAC)
PCO.......... Parcel Concentration Office [*British*]
PCO.......... Parent Company (SAUS)
PCO.......... Parliamentary Counsel's Office [*Australia*]
PCO.......... Passport Control Officer [*British*]
PCO.......... Patient Complains Of [*Medicine*]
PCO.......... Peacetime Contingency Operation [*Army*] (ADDR)
PCO.......... Peak Conservation Organization (SAUS)
PCO.......... Peg Count and Overflow (SAUS)
PCO.......... Pest Control Officer (SAUS)
PCO.......... Pest Control Operator
PCO.......... Philadelphia College of Osteopathy [*Pennsylvania*]
PCO.......... Phoenix Canada Oil Co. Ltd. [*Toronto Stock Exchange symbol*]
PCO.......... Photocatalytic Oxidation (AAEL)
PCO.......... Photosynthetic Carbon Oxidation [*Plant metabolism*]
PCO.......... Physician Contracting Organization (GART)
PCO.......... Picture Control Oscilloscope (IAA)
PCO.......... Pittston Co. (EFIS)
PCO.......... Placement Contracting Officer [*Army*] (AABC)
PCO.......... Plant Clearance Officer [*DoD*]
PCO.......... Plant Clearance Order
PCO.......... Plant Control Office (SAUS)
PCO.......... Playcore, Inc. [*AMEX symbol*] [*Formerly, Swing-N-Slide Corp.*]
PCO.......... Point of Control and Observation [*Telecommunications*] (OSI)
PCO.......... Polar Cap Observatory (SAUS)
PCO.......... Police Commissioner's Office
PCO.......... Polycarbonate (EDCT)
PCO.......... Polycystic Ovary [*Gynecology*]
PCO.......... Ponca City [*Oklahoma*] [*Seismograph station code, US Geological Survey*] (SEIS)
PCO.......... Port Communications Office (SAUS)
PCO.......... Port Convey Officer (SAUS)
PCO.......... Post Central Office (SAUS)
PCO.......... Post Checkout
PCO.......... Postcheckout Operations
PCO.......... Potassium Channel Opener [*Vasodilator*]
PCO.......... Predicted Cardia Output [*Medicine*] (DMAA)
PCO.......... Pressure Controlled Orifice [*Automotive engineering*]
PCO.......... Primary Communications-Oriented (IAA)
PCO.......... Primary Contracting Officer (MCD)
PCO.......... Prime Contracting Officer (SAA)
PCO.......... Prince Consort's Own [*Military unit*] [*British*]
PCO.......... Principal Careers Officer (AIE)
PCO.......... Principal Coast Officer [*Customs*] [*British*] (ROG)
PCO.......... Principal Conservation Officer (SAUS)
PCO.......... Principal Contracting Officer [*Air Force*]
PCO.......... Printer Control Option (SAA)
PCO.......... Printing Control Officer [*Air Force*] (AFM)
PCO.......... Prison Custody Officer (WDAA)
PCO.......... Privy Council Office [*British*]
PCO.......... Proceedings of the Congress of Orientalists (SAUS)
PCO.......... Process Change Order (VLIE)
PCO.......... Procurement Change Order (MCD)
PCO.......... Procurement Contracting Officer (AAGC)
PCO.......... Procuring Contracting Office [*or Officer*] [*Military*]
PCO.......... Procuring Contrast Offer
PCO.......... Procuring Contrast Officer (SAUS)
PCO.......... Procytoxid (STED)
PCO.......... Professional Conference Organizer
PCO.......... Professional Congress Organizer (TVEL)
PCO.......... Program Change Order [*Computer science*] (ELAL)
PCO.......... Program Comparator
PCO.......... Program Contracting Officer (SAUS)
PCO.......... Program-Controlled Output (NASA)
PCO.......... Program Control Output
PCO.......... Program Coordination Office (AAG)
PCO.......... Program Counterpart Office
PCO.......... Project Control Office (MCD)
PCO.......... Property Control Office [*of Allied Military Government*] [*Post-World War II*]
PCO.......... Proposed Change Order (AFIT)
PCO.......... Prospective Commanding Officer [*Navy*]
PCO.......... Provisioning Contracting Officer [*Military*] (AFIT)
PCO.......... Publications Control Officer [*DoD*]
PCO.......... Public Call Office (DAS)
PCO.......... Public Communications Office
PCO.......... Punched Card Order (SAUS)
PCO.......... Punched Card Output (SAUS)
PCO.......... Purchase Change Order (MCD)
PCO.......... Purchasing and Contracting Officer (SAUS)
P/CO......... Purser/Catering Officer (SAUS)
PCO_2......... Carbon Dioxide Tension [*in blood gases*] (DAVI)
pCO_2......... Partial Pressure of Carbon Dioxide (AAMN)
pCO_2......... Pressure of Carbon Dioxide (HGAA)
PCOA........ Pennsylvania Campground Owners Association (EARSL)
PCoA........ Posterior Communicating Artery [*Medicine*] (RAWO)
PCoA........ Principal Co-Ordinates Analysis
PCO/ACO.... Procuring Contracting Officer/Administrative Contracting Officer
PCOAS....... Permanent Council of the Organization of American States
P Coast LJ... Pacific Coast Law Journal [*A publication*] (DLA)
PCOB........ Permanent Central Opium Board [*United Nations*] (BUAC)

PCOB(UN) .. Permanent Central Opium Board (United Nations)
PCOC .... Partit Comunista Obrero de Catalunya [*Communist Workers' Party of Catalonia*] [*Political party*] (PPW)
PCOC .... Pest Control Operators of California (EARSL)
PCOC .... Primary Care Organization Consortium [*Health insurance*] (DMAA)
PCOCA ...... Parti-Colour Oriental Cat Association (BUAC)
PCOD .... Permanent Change of Duty [*Navy*] (DNAB)
PCOD .... Polycystic Ovarian Disease [*Medicine*]
P-Code ...... Precision Code (SEWL)
P-CODE ..... Program Code [*Computer science*] (AGLO)
PCOE .... Partido Comunista Obrero de Espana [*Communist Workers' Party of Spain*] [*Political party*] (PPW)
PCOF .... Probable Cause of Failure (MCD)
PC of E...... Presbyterian Church of England
PCOFT....... Patriot Conduct of Fire Trainer (SAUS)
P-COFT..... Platoon COFT (SAUS)
PCOGA ...... Pacific Coast Oyster Growers Association (EA)
PCOI .... Preconstruction Operating Instruction [*Environmental Protection Agency*]
PCOIT .... Putnam Convertible Opportunities & Income Trust [*Associated Press*] (SAG)
PCOL .... Procuring Contracting Officer Letter (ACAE)
PCOL .... Protocol Systems [*NASDAQ symbol*] (TTSB)
PCOL .... Protocol Systems, Inc. [*NASDAQ symbol*] (SAG)
PCOLA....... Pulse-Coded Optical Landing Aid [*Aviation*] (PDAA)
PCOM .... Parallel Character Output Module (SAUS)
PCOM .... P COM [*OTCBB symbol*]
P-Com....... P-Com, Inc. [*Associated Press*] (SAG)
PCOM .... Philadelphia College of Osteopathic Medicine
PCOM .... Photocomm, Inc. [*NASDAQ symbol*] (NQ)
PCOM .... Planning Committee (SAUS)
PCOM .... Posterior Communicating [*Artery*] [*Medicine*] (DMAA)
PCOMP...... Packet Compression Pin (SAUS)
PCON........ Para-Chloro-ortho-nitroaniline [*Also, PCONA*] [*Organic chemistry*]
PCON........ Personnel Continuity
PCON........ Platelet Concentration [*hematology*] (DAVI)
PCON........ Potential Contractor (COE)
PCON........ Primary Care Optometry News [*A publication*] (ADWA)
PCON........ Primary Care Organization Network [*Health insurance*] (DMAA)
PCON........ Proman Containers [*Common carrier symbol*]
PCONA ...... Para-Chloro-ortho-nitroaniline [*Also, PCON*] [*Organic chemistry*]
PCONNECT... Presentation Connect (VLIE)
P Contr LJ... Public Contract Law Journal [*A publication*] (AAGC)
PCOOS ...... Pacific Coast Oto Ophthalmological Society (SAUS)
PCOP .... Pharmacopeia Inc. [*NASDAQ symbol*] (TTSB)
PCOP .... Port Charges Operator (DNAB)
PCOP .... Port Charges Paid by Commercial Operator (DNAB)
PCOP .... President's Commission on Obscenity and Pornography (DGA)
PCOPF....... President's Council on Physical Fitness [*Later, PCPFS*] (KSC)
PCOR........ Center for Primary Care and Outcomes Research [*Stanford University*] (RCD)
PCOR........ pcOrder.com, Inc.'A' [*NASDAQ symbol*] (SG)
PCOR........ Pinnacor [*NASDAQ symbol*]
PCOR........ Pressure Compensator Over-Ride (PDAA)
PCOR........ Profit Commission on Renewal [*Insurance*] (AIA)
PCOR........ PSICOR, Inc. [*NASDAQ symbol*] (NQ)
PCOR........ Purchase Change Order Request
PCoR .... Robert Morris College, Coraopolis, PA [*Library symbol*] [*Library of Congress*] (LCLS)
PCORN ...... Perpetual Convertible or Redeemable Note [*Economics*]
PCOS .... Patriot Courier Service [*Common carrier symbol*]
PCOS .... Polycystic Ovarian Syndrome [*Also, POS*] [*Gynecology*]
PCOS .... Primary Communication Operating System (SAUS)
PCOS .... Primary Communications-Oriented System (IEEE)
PCOS .... Process Control Operating System
PCOS .... Production Control Operating System (SAUS)
PCOS .... Project Concern's Options Service (EA)
PCOS .... Punched Card Oriented System (SAUS)
P-COSWA... Pugwash Conferences on Science and World Affairs
PCOT .... Payload Center Operations Team [*NASA*] (MCD)
PCOTES ..... Prototype Carrier Operational Test and Evaluation Site [*Military*] (CAAL)
PCOUNT..... Parameter Count [*Computer science*]
PCOV .... Precombustor Oxidizer Valve (KSC)
P(COV) ...... Probability of No Covariate Effect [*Statistics*]
PCOYO ...... President's Council on Youth Opportunity [*Defunct*] (EA)
PCOZ .... Pevler Coal [*Federal Railroad Administration identification code*]
PCP.......... Centre for Personal Construct Psychology [*British*] (CB)
PCP.......... Communist Party of Peru (CARL)
PCP.......... Packet Control Panel (SAUS)
PCP.......... Packet Control Process (SAUS)
PCP.......... Paired Cone Pigments [*Vision physiology*]
PCP.......... Palestinian Communist Party [*Political party*] (PD)
PCP.......... PanCanadian Petroleum [*TS, Exchange Symbol*] (TTSB)
PCP.......... PanCanadian Petroleum Ltd. [*Toronto Stock Exchange symbol*] [*Vancouver Stock Exchange symbol*]
PCP.......... Para-Chlorophenol [*Organic chemistry*]
PCP.......... Paraguayan Communist Party
PCP.......... Parallel Cascade Processor (IEEE)
PCP.......... Parallel Circular Plate (IEEE)
PCP.......... Parker Consultant Panel (SAUS)
PCP.......... Parliamentary Conservative Party [*British*] (BARN)
PCP.......... Partial Cleft Palate (MELL)
PCP.......... Participate [*Telegraphy*] (PCTE)
PCP.......... Partido Comunista Paraguayano [*Paraguayan Communist Party*] [*Political party*] (PD)
PCP.......... Partido Comunista Peruano [*Peruvian Communist Party*] [*Political party*] (PPW)
PCP.......... Partido Comunista Portugues [*Portuguese Communist Party*] [*Political party*] (PPE)
PCP.......... Partido Comunista Puertorriqueno [*Puerto Rican Communist Party*] [*Political party*] (PPW)
PCP.......... Passenger Control Point [*Army*] (AABC)
PCP.......... Past Chief Patriarch [*Freemasonry*]
PCP.......... Patient Care Plan [*Medicine*] (BCRP)
PCP.......... Patient Care Publications
PCP.......... Payload Control Processor [*NASA*]
PCP.......... Peace Corps Physician
PCP.......... PeaCe Pill [*Slang for Phencyclidine*] (DIPS)
PCP.......... Peking Central Philharmonic (SAUS)
PCP.......... Pentachlorophenate [*A topical antibacterial*] (DAVI)
PCP.......... Pentachlorophenol [*Wood preservative*] [*Organic chemistry*]
PCP.......... Pentachlorophenyl (SAUS)
PCP.......... Pentachlorphenol (SAUS)
PCP.......... Peptidyl Carrier Protein [*Biochemistry*]
PCP.......... Pericardial Pressure [*Medicine*] (MELL)
PCP.......... Pericyclic Process (SAUS)
PCP.......... Peridinin-Chlorophyll-Protein [*Botany*]
PCP.......... Peripheral Circumflex Pressure (SAUS)
PCP.......... Peripheral Control Program
PCP.......... Peripheral Control Pulse [*Computer science*]
PCP.......... Peripheral Coronary Pressure [*Cardiology*] (AAMN)
PCP.......... Persistent Cough and Phlegm [*Medicine*] (EDAA)
PCP.......... Personal Communications Programme [*British*]
PCP.......... Personal Credit Plan (SAUS)
PCP.......... Personnel Control Point (SAUS)
PCP.......... Peter Collins Publishing [*British*]
PCP.......... Phencyclidine (NTIO)
PCP.......... Phencyclidine Hydrochloride [*Medicine*] (AMHC)
PCP.......... Phencyclidine Palmitate [*Organic chemistry*] (DAVI)
PCP.......... (Phenylcyclohexyl)piperidine [*or Phencyclidine*] [*Anesthetic*] [*A street drug*]
PCP.......... Philadelphia College of Pharmacy and Science, Philadelphia, PA [*OCLC symbol*] (OCLC)
PCP.......... Phosphor Coated Paper
PCP.......... Photochemical Processing (SAUS)
PCP.......... Photogrammetric Control Point [*Mapping*]
PCP.......... Photon-Coupled Pair (IEEE)
PCP.......... Picture Check Print (SAUS)
PCP.......... Pilot Control Panel
PCP.......... Planar Combat Problem
PCP.......... Plant Control Plan (SAUS)
PCP.......... Plasma Cell Pneumonia [*Medicine*] (MELL)
PCP.......... Plastic Clad Plastic [*Materials science*]
PCP.......... Platoon Command Post [*Military*] (RDA)
PCP.......... Plug Compatible Peripheral [*Computer science*] (EECA)
PCP.......... Pneumatics Control Panel (AAG)
PCP.......... Pneumocystic Pneumonia [*Medicine*] (DAVI)
PCP.......... Pneumocystis Carinii Pneumonia [*Microbiology*]
PCP.......... Polaroid Color Pack Camera
PCP.......... Polychloroprene [*Organic chemistry*]
PCP.......... Poorly Characterized Phase [*Mineralogy*]
PCP.......... Portable Code Processor
PCP.......... Port Call Processing (SAUS)
PCP.......... Portuguese Communist Party
PCP.......... Post-Construction Permit [*Nuclear energy*] (NRCH)
PCP.......... Posted County Price [*Agriculture*]
PCP.......... Postgraduate Center for Psychotherapy [*Later, Postgraduate Center for Mental Health*] (EA)
PCP.......... Potential Contractor Program (MCD)
PCP.......... Power Control Panel [*Aerospace*] (AAG)
PCP.......... Preassembled Cable in Pipe
PCP.......... Precision Castparts [*NYSE symbol*] (TTSB)
PCP.......... Precision Castparts Corp. [*NYSE symbol*] (SPSG)
PCP.......... Preliminary Cost Proposal (MCD)
PCP.......... Pressurization Control Panel [*NASA*] (KSC)
PCP.......... Primary Care Physician
PCP.......... Primary Care Provider (SAUS)
PCP.......... Primary Command Point [*Military*] (CAAL)
PCP.......... Primary Control Program [*Computer science*]
PCP.......... Primary Coolant Pump [*Nuclear energy*] (NRCH)
PCP.......... Primary Cross-Connection Point (NITA)
PCP.......... Principal Care Provider [*For a patient*] (DAVI)
PCP.......... Printed Circuit Patchboard
PCP.......... Printer Control Protocols [*Computer science*] (MWOL)
PCP.......... Printing Card Punch (SAUS)
PCP.......... Process Control Package (SAUS)
PCP.......... Process Control Plan (SAUS)
PCP.......... Process Control Processor (IEEE)
PCP.......... Process Control Program [*Nuclear energy*] (NRCH)
PCP.......... Processor Control Panel
PCP.......... Processor Control Program
PCP.......... Procollagen Peptide (DB)
PCP.......... Product Change Proposal (MCD)
PCP.......... Product Chassis Package
PCP.......... Production Change Point
PCP.......... Program Change Package (SAUS)
PCP.......... Program Change Procedure

PCP .... Program Control Plan (AAG)
PCP .... Program Control Procedure [*Nuclear energy*] (NRCH)
PCP .... Program Control Program (SAUS)
PCP .... Programmable Circuit Process (SAUS)
PCP .... Programmable Circuit Processor (SAUS)
PCP .... Programmable Communication Processor
PCP .... Progressive Conservative Party [*Canada*] [*Political party*] (PPW)
PCP .... Progressive Conservative Party [*Australia*] [*Political party*]
PCP .... Progressive Constitutionalist Party [*Malta*] [*Political party*] (PPE)
PCP .... Progressive Constitutional Party [*Malta*] [*Political party*] (BUAC)
PCP .... Project Change Proposal (NAKS)
PCP .... Project Control Plan (IEEE)
PCP .... Project Cost Plan (NASA)
PCP .... Prototype Communications Processor
PCP .... Psilcybin [*Medicine*] (MEDA)
PCP .... Pulmonary Capillary Pressure [*Medicine*] (CPH)
PCP .... Pulse Comparator
PCP .... Pulse Cytophotometry [*Hematology*]
PCP .... Pump Cavitation Pressure [*Automotive engineering*]
PCP .... Punch Card Programming (SAUS)
PCP .... Punch Control Panel (SAUS)
PCP .... Punched Card Perforator (SAUS)
PCP .... Punched Card Processing (SAUS)
PCP .... Punched Card Programming (SAUS)
PCP .... Punched Card Punch [*Computer science*] (IEEE)
PcP .... Reflected P Wave [*Earthquakes*]
PCPA .... Pacific Conservatory of the Performing Arts
PCPA .... Panama Canal Pilots Association (SAUS)
PCPA .... Panel of Consultants for the Performing Arts [*of CFC*]
PCPA .... Para-Chlorophenoxyacetic Acid [*Organic chemistry*]
PCPA .... Para-Chlorophenylacetic Acid [*Organic chemistry*]
PCPA .... Parachlorophenylalanin (SAUS)
PCPA .... Para-Chlorophenylalanine [*Biochemistry*]
PCPA .... P-Chlorophenylacetic Acid (SAUS)
PCPA .... P-Chlorophenylalanine (SAUS)
PCPA .... Philadelphia College of the Performing Arts (SAUS)
PCPA .... Plan for Congressional and Public Affairs
PCPA .... Poor Clares of Perpetual Adoration [*Roman Catholic women's religious order*]
PCPA .... Primary Care Physician's Assistant [*Medicine*] (EDAA)
PC/PA .... Process Control/Product Acceptance (SAUS)
PCPA .... Protestant Church-Owned Publishers Association (EA)
PCPAC .... Parker-Coltrane Political Action Committee [*Defunct*] (EA)
PCPAV .... Pensioners-Combined Pensioners Association of Victoria [*Australia*]
PCPB .... P-Chlorophenylbenzene (SAUS)
PCPBMA .... Pacific Coast Paper Box Manufacturers' Association (EA)
PCPBS .... Para-Chlorophenyl-Benzenesulphonate (SAUS)
PCPBS .... P-Chlorophenylbenzenesulfonate (SAUS)
PCPC .... Personal Computers Peripheral Corp. (SAUS)
PCPC .... Power Conversion Products Council [*Later, PCPCI*] (EA)
PCPC .... Primary Care Policy Center for Underserved Populations [*Johns Hopkins University*] (RCD)
PCPC .... Principal Conical Polar Curve (SAUS)
PCPCA .... Pairpoint Cup Plate Collectors of America (EA)
PCPCI .... Power Conversion Products Council International (EA)
PCPCN ...... Part Card Procurement Change Notice (KSC)
PCPCU ...... Pontifical Council for Promoting Christian Unity (BUAC)
PCPD .... Participated [*Telegraphy*] (PCTE)
PCPD .... Portland Commission of Public Docks (SAUS)
PCPE .... Partido Comunista de los Pueblos de Espana [*Communist Party of the Peoples of Spain*] [*Political party*] (EY)
PCPEA .... Pennsylvania Cooperative Program in Educational Administration (SAUS)
PC Perspect Newsl ... PC Perspectives Newsletter (SAUS)
PC/PET ...... Polycarbonate/Polyethylene Terephthalate (SAUS)
PCPF .... Percutaneous Pin Fixation [*Medicine*] (MELL)
PCPF .... President's Council on Physical Fitness [*Later, PCPFS*]
PCPFS .... President's Council on Physical Fitness and Sports (EGAO)
PCPG .... Primary Clock Pulse Generator
PCPhS .... Proceedings of the Cambridge Philological Society (SAUS)
PCPI .... Parent Cooperative Pre-Schools International (EA)
PCPI .... Permanent Committee on Patent Information [*World Intellectual Property Organization*] [*Information service or system*] (IID)
PCPI .... Personal Computer Products (EFIS)
PCPI .... President's Commission on Personnel Interchange [*Later, President's Commission on Executive Exchange*]
P-CPIB Acid ... P-2,4-dichlorophenoxyisobutyric Acid (SAUS)
PCPJ .... Peoples Coalition for Peace and Justice [*Defunct*]
PCPL .... Government Services Library, Charlottetown, Prince Edward Island [*Library symbol*] [*National Library of Canada*] (NLC)
pcpl .... Participle [*Linguistics*] (IEL)
PCPL .... Pentachlorophenyl Laurate (SAUS)
PCPL .... Planning Library, Charlottetown, Prince Edward Island [*Library symbol*] [*National Library of Canada*] (NLC)
PCPL .... Production Control Priority List (MCD)
PCPL .... Proposed Change Point Line [*NASA*] (KSC)
PCPL .... Pulmonary Capillary Protein Leakage [*Medicine*] (DMAA)
PCPM .... Per Contract per Month [*Insurance*] (MHCS)
PCPM .... PERT [*Program Evaluation and Review Technique*] Cost Performance Measurement
PCPM .... Program Control Procedures Manual (SAUS)
PCP M-L .... Partido Comunista de Portugal, Marxista-Leninista [*Marxist-Leninist Communist Party of Portugal*] [*Political party*] (PPE)
PCPN .... Participation [*Telegraphy*] (PCTE)
pcpn .... Precipitation (DAVI)
PCPO .... Parent-Child Preschools of Oregon (EARSL)
PCPP .... (Para-Chlorophenoxy)propionic Acid [*Organic chemistry*]
PCPP .... Parts Control Program Plan (SAUS)
PCPP .... Peace Corps Partnership Program (EA)
PCPP .... Presidents Commission on Pension Policy (SAUS)
PCPP .... Printing Card Proof Punch (SAUS)
PCPPRV ..... Pilot-Controlled Proportional Pressure-Reducing Valve [*Hydraulics*]
PCPS .... Percutaneously-Introduced Cardiopulmonary Support System [*Medicine*]
PCPS .... Philadelphia College of Pharmacy and Science [*Pennsylvania*]
PCPS .... Pool Cooling and Purification System [*Nuclear energy*] (NRCH)
PCPS .... Portable Collective Protection Shelter (ACAE)
PCPS .... Private Carrier Paging System (SAUS)
PCPS .... Private Companies Practice Section
PCPS .... Proceedings of the Cambridge Philological Society [*A publication*] (OCD)
PCPS .... Prodat Communication and Processing System (SAUS)
PCPS .... Program Change Package (IAA)
PCPS .... Pulse-Coded Processing System
PCPS .... Pulverized-Coal Power System [*Environmental science*] (COE)
PCPT .... Para-Chlorophenylthio [*Organic chemistry*]
PCPT .... Participant [*Telegraphy*] (PCTE)
PCPT .... Perception
PCPT .... Physical Combat Proficiency Test [*Army*]
PCPT .... Post Conference Provisioning Tape (MCD)
PCPT .... Prostate Cancer Prevention Trial [*Medicine*]
PCPV .... Partido Comunista del Pais Valenciano [*Spain*] [*Political party*] (EY)
PCPV .... Point-Contact Photo-Voltaic [*Solar cells*]
PCPV .... Prestressed Concrete Pressure Vessel
PCPZ .... PC Potash Plant [*Federal Railroad Administration identification code*]
PCQ .... Pacificorp [*NYSE symbol*] (SAG)
PCQ .... PacifiCorp 8.375% 'QUIDS' [*NYSE symbol*] (TTSB)
PCQ .... Personal Control Questionnaire (SAUS)
PCQ .... Polychloroquaterphenyl [*Medicine*] (EDAA)
PCQ .... Production Control Quantometer
PCQ .... Productivity Criteria Quotient
PCQ .... Professional Capabilities Questionnaire [*Jet Propulsion Laboratory, NASA*]
PCQ .... Yuma, AZ [*Location identifier*] [*FAA*] (FAAL)
PCQEH ...... Queen Elizabeth Hospital, Charlottetown, Prince Edward Island [*Library symbol*] [*National Library of Canada*] (NLC)
PCQT .... Paper-Core Quad Trunk (PDAA)
PCQT .... PC Quote (EFIS)
PCQT .... Personal Computer Query Tool [*Military software package*] (INF)
PC Quote ... PC Quote, Inc. [*Associated Press*] (SAG)
PCR .... Pacific Amber Resources [*VS, Exchange Symbol*] (TTSB)
PCR .... Page Control Register
PCR .... Parker's Criminal Reports [*New York*] [*A publication*] (DLA)
PCR .... Partial Carriage Return (IAA)
PCR .... Partially Coherent Receiver (SAUS)
PCR .... Parti Communiste Reunionnais [*Communist Party of Reunion*] [*Political party*] (PPW)
PCR .... Partido Comunista Revolucionario [*Revolutionary Communist Party*] [*Peru*] [*Political party*] (PPW)
PCR .... Partidul Comunist Roman [*Romanian Communist Party*] [*Political party*] (PPE)
PCR .... Pass Card Reader [*Telecommunications*] (TEL)
PCR .... Patient Charge Ratio
PCR .... Patient Contact Record [*Medicine*] (DMAA)
PCR .... Payload Certification Review (SSD)
PCR .... Payload Changeout Room [*NASA*] (NASA)
PCR .... Payload Checkout Room [*NASA*] (NASA)
P Cr .... Paymaster-Commander [*Navy*] [*British*] (DMA)
PCR .... PC Resource [*A publication*]
PCR .... Peak Cell Rate (MLOA)
PCR .... Pearson Aviation Corp. [*ICAO designator*] (FAAC)
PCR .... Pedestrian Crossings Regulations (SAUS)
PCR .... Peer Code Review (IAA)
PCR .... Peninsular Chemresearch [*Calgon Corp.*]
PCR .... Pennsylvania Corp. Reporter [*A publication*] (DLA)
PCR .... Pennsylvania County Court Reports [*A publication*] (DLA)
PCR .... Per Call Rate [*Telecommunications*] (IAA)
PCR .... Perini Corp. [*AMEX symbol*] (SPSG)
PCR .... Period Contract Request
PCR .... Periodic Current Reversal [*Electrochemistry*]
PCR .... Peripheral Control Routine (CMD)
PCR .... Personal Care Residence (DAVI)
PCR .... Personal Communications Report [*FutureComm Publications, Inc.*] [*Information service or system*] [*Defunct*] (CRD)
PCR .... Personnel and Civil Rights [*USDA Forest Service*] (ALAC)
PCR .... Phase Change Recording (SAUS)
PCR .... Phase Controlled Rectifier (SAUS)
PCr .... Phosphocreatine [*Also, CP, PC*] [*Biochemistry*]
PCR .... Photoconductive Relay (IEEE)
PCR .... Photoconductive Resonance [*Physics*]
PCR .... Photosynthetic Carbon Reduction [*Plant metabolism*]
PCR .... Physician Contingency Reserve
PCR .... Pickled and Cold Rolled (SAUS)
PCR .... Pilot Chute Controlled (SAUS)
PCR .... Pine Creek Railroad [*An association*] (EA)
PCR .... Planned Component Replacement [*Predictive maintenance schedule*]
PCR .... Planning Change [*or Check*] Request (AAG)
PCR .... Planning Check Request (SAUS)
PCR .... Plant Control Room [*Nuclear energy*] (IAA)

PCR Plasma Clearance Rate [*Medicine*] (DMAA)
P_{cr} Plasma Creatinine (DAVI)
PCR Pneumatic Checkout Rack (KSC)
PCR Pneumatic Control Regulator (KSC)
PCR Polar Cap Radar (SAUS)
PCR Pollution Control Report [*Navy*]
PCR Pollution Control Revenue
PCR Polychromatic Color Removal [*Printing technology*]
PCR Polymerase Chain Reaction [*Genetics*]
PCR Polymerase Chain Technology (SAUS)
PCR Population Census Report (OICC)
PCR Positive Control Route [*Aviation*] (OA)
PCR Post-Column Reaction (SAUS)
PCR Post-Compression Remodeling [*Medicine*] (DMAA)
PCR Post-Consumer Recyclate (SAUS)
PCR Post-Consumer Recycle [*or Reclaim*] [*Plastics industry*]
PCR Post-Consumer Resin [*Plastic recycling*]
PCR Postconviction Remedy
PCR Postinfarction Cardiac Rehabilitation [*Medicine*] (MELL)
PCR Powell Cycle Registry (EA)
PCR Power Change Request [*NASA*] (NASA)
PCR Power Control Register
PCR Power Control Room [*Nuclear energy*] (IAA)
PCR Power Conversion Room
PCR Precision Control Relay (SAUS)
PCR Pressure Check Range
PCR Prestressed Ceramic RADOME
PCR Preventative Cyclic Retransmission [*Telecommunications*] (TEL)
PCR Primary Chemotherapy-Radiotherapy [*Oncology*]
PCR Primary Control Rod (SAUS)
PCR Primary Cosmic Radiation
PCR Principal Components Regression
PCR Principle Component Regression (SAUS)
PCR Print Command Register
PCR Print Contrast Ratio (TIMI)
PCR Probable Causal Relationship [*Medicine*] (MEDA)
PCR Problem/Change Report (SAUS)
PCR Procedure Change Request [*NASA*]
PCR Procedure Comment Record (SAUS)
PCR Process Control Rack (SAUS)
PCR Processor Configuration Register (SAUS)
PCR Procurement Center Representative [*Small Business Administration*]
PCR Product Change Request (SAUS)
PCR Production & Casting Report (WDAA)
PCR Production Capability Review [*Army*]
PCR Production Change Request (MCD)
PCR Production Control Record [*NASA*] (KSC)
PCR Program Change Request [*DoD*]
PCR Program Clock Reference (SAUS)
PCR Program-Controlled Request (SAUS)
PCR Program Control Register
PCR Program Control Report
PCR Program Control Room (ACAE)
PCR Program Counter [*Computer science*] (IAA)
PCR Program Counter Register
PCR Programmer in Charge of Records [*Computer science*] (IAA)
PCR Program to Combat Racism [*British*] (DI)
PCR Progress Curve Report
PCR Project Control Room [*NASA*] (NASA)
PCR Project Cost Record [*or Report*] [*NASA*] (KSC)
PCR Project Cost Report (SAUS)
PCR Projected Communications Requirement (SAUS)
PCR Project on Corporate Responsibility (EA)
PCR Protein Catabolic Rate [*Biochemistry*] (DAVI)
PCR Proven Commercial Registration [*Advertising*] (WDMC)
PCR Publication Change Request (MCD)
PCR Publication Contract Requirements
PCR Puerto Carreno [*Colombia*] [*Airport symbol*] (OAG)
PCR Pulse Compression RADAR
PCR Pulse Compression Ratio (ACAE)
PCR Punch Card Register (SAUS)
PCR Punched Card Reader [*Computer science*] (BUR)
PCR Punched Card Request
PCR Punched Card Requisition [*Computer science*] (MCD)
PCR Put Control Read (SAUS)
PCRA Percutaneous Coronary Rotational Atherectomy [*Medicine*] (RAWO)
PCRA Phantom Class Racing Association (EA)
PCRA Poland China Record Association (EA)
PCRAM Page Composition Random Access Memory (NITA)
PCR & A Picked Cold, Rolled, and Annealed [*Metallurgy*] (ROG)
PCR&DC Pomona Colleges Research and Development Center (SAUS)
PCRAP Personal Computer Response Analysis Program
PCRB Personnel and Control Room Building [*Nuclear energy*] (NRCH)
PCRB Pollution Control Revenue Bond [*Environmental Protection Agency*]
PCRB Program Change Review Board [*NASA*]
PCRC Pacific Concerns Resource Center (EA)
PCRC Pain Clinical Research Center [*University of California, San Francisco*] (RCD)
PCRC Paraffined Carton Research Council [*Later, Paperboard Packaging Council*]
PCRC Pediatric Clinical Research Center [*University of California, San Francisco*] (RCD)
PCRC Perinatal Clinical Research Center [*Case Western Reserve University*] [*Research center*] (RCD)
PCRC Poor Clergy Relief Corp. [*British*] (BI)
PCRC Primary Communications Research Centre [*University of Leicester*] [*Canada*]
PCRC Pro Choice Resource Center [*Association*] (EA)
PCRCA Pickled, Cold-Rolled, and Close-Annealed [*Metal*]
PCRD Primary Control Rod Driveline [*Nuclear energy*] (NRCH)
PCRDM Primary Control Rod Drive Mechanism [*Nuclear energy*] (NRCH)
PCR/DNA Polymerase Chain Reaction/Deoxyribonucleic Acid (SAUS)
PCRE ProCare Industries, Inc. [*NASDAQ symbol*] (COMM)
PC Rep English Privy Council Reports [*A publication*] (DLA)
PCRF Parallel Computing Research Facility (SAUS)
PCRF Paralysis Cure Research Foundation (EA)
PCRF Parker Chiropractic Resource Foundation (EA)
PCRGA Precipitation Chemistry, Reactive Gases, and Aerosols Section (SAUS)
PCRH Provincial Cities and Rural Highways Program [*Australia*]
PCRI Papanicolaou Cancer Research Institute [*University of Miami*] [*Research center*]
PCRI Parent-Child Relationship Inventory [*Test*] (TMMY)
PCRIA Property Crime and Recovery Investigators of Alabama (EARSL)
PCRL Powertrain Control Research Laboratory [*University of Wisconsin--Madison*] (RCD)
PCRM Physicians Committee for Responsible Medicine (EA)
PCRM Primary Certified Reference Material [*Nuclear energy*] (NRCH)
PCRMGPS Poor Clerks Regular of the Mother of God of the Pious Schools [*Rome, Italy*] (EAIO)
PCRML Parti Communiste Revolutionnaire - Marxiste-Leniniste [*Revolutionary Marxist-Leninist Communist Party*] [*France*] [*Political party*] (PPW)
PCRMSL Pacific Coast Rocky Mountain Shooting League (PSS)
PC-ROM Personal Computer Read-Only Memory
PCRP Pennsylvania Comprehensive Reading Program (EDAC)
PCRP Processing Carrot Research Program [*Nova Scotia Agricultural College*] [*Canada*] (RCD)
Pcr/Pi Phosphocreatine to Inorganic Phosphate Ratio
PCRPr Perini Corp. Dep Cv Exch Pfd [*AMEX symbol*] (TTSB)
PCRPS Program for Collaborative Research in the Pharmaceutical Sciences [*University of Illinois at Chicago*] [*Information service or system*] (IID)
PCRR Pennsylvania Central Railroad (ROG)
PCRS Poor Clergy Relief Society [*British*]
PCRS Precision Chiropractic Research Society [*Also known as Spinal Stress Research Society*] (EA)
PCRS Primary Casualty Receiving Ship (SAUS)
PCRS Primary Control Rod System [*Nuclear energy*] (NRCH)
PCRS Primary CRITICOMM [*Critical Intelligence Communications System*] Relay Station (CET)
PCRS Punched Card Reading System (SAUS)
PCR test Polymerase Chain Reaction Test [*Medicine*] (TAD)
PCRU Pro Line [*Intermodal shipping container symbol*] (TVRC)
PCRV Poinsettia Cryptic Virus [*Plant pathology*]
PCRV PowerCerv Corp. [*NASDAQ symbol*] (SAG)
PCRV Pressurized Concrete Reactor Vessel [*Nuclear energy*]
PCRV Prestressed Concrete Reactor Vessel [*Nuclear energy*]
PCRW Phase Change Rewritable (SAUS)
PCRX Pacer Rail Services [*Private rail car owner code*]
PCS IEEE Professional Communication Society (EA)
PCS Pace Car Society [*Defunct*] (EA)
PCS Pacific Command Ship
PCS Package Checking System (SAUS)
PCS Packaging and Checkup System (SAUS)
PCS Packet-Controlled Switching (GART)
PCS Palliative Care Service
PCS Paracas [*Peru*] [*Seismograph station code, US Geological Survey*] [*Closed*] (SEIS)
PCS Paratransit Computer System
PCS Parents' Confidential Statement [*Education*]
PCS Parti Chretien-Social [*Christian Social Party*] [*Luxembourg*] [*Political party*] (PPW)
PCS Particle Counting System
PCS Parti Communiste Suisse [*Communist Party of Switzerland*] [*Political party*] (PPE)
PCS Particulates, Condensables, and Solubles [*In gases*]
PCS Partido Comunista Salvadoreno [*Salvadoran Communist Party*] [*Political party*] (PPW)
PCS Partito Comunista Sammarinese [*Communist Party of San Marino*] [*Political party*] (PPE)
PCS Part Number Configuration Summary
PCS Parts Collection Survey (SAUS)
PCS Parts, Components, Subassemblies
PCS Parts Control System [*DoD*]
PCS Passive Containment System [*Nuclear energy*] (NRCH)
PCS Patchable Control Store (SAUS)
PCS Patent Classification Service (SAUS)
PCS Patient Care System
PCS Patrol Craft, Submarine-chaser (SAUS)
PCS Patrol Craft Sweeper (SAUS)
PCS Patrol Vessel, Submarine Chaser (Control) [*136 feet*] [*Navy symbol*] [*Obsolete*]
PCS Patterns of Care Study [*Roentgenography*]
PCS Paul Claudel Society (EA)
PCS Payless Cashways, Inc. [*NYSE symbol*] (SPSG)
PCS Payload Checkout System [*NASA*] (NASA)
PCS Payload Control Supervisor [*NASA*] (MCD)
PCS Payload Correction Subsystem (SAUS)

PCS .... PCL State (SAUS)
PCS .... PC Service (SAUS)
PCS .... Pelvic Congestion Syndrome [*Medicine*] (MELL)
PCS .... Perforated Card System (SAUS)
PCS .... Performance Command System (SAUS)
PCS .... Pergamon Compact Solution [*CD-ROM publisher*] (IT)
PCS .... Periodical Control System [*Libraries*]
PCS .... Peripheral Computer System (IAA)
PCS .... Peripheral Control System (SAUS)
PCS .... Permanent Change of Station [*Army*]
PCS .... Permanent Committee on Shipping (SAUS)
PCS .... Permanent Cruiser Service [*British military*] (DMA)
PCS .... Permit Compliance System [*Environmental Protection Agency*] (GFGA)
PCS .... Personal Care Services
PCS .... Personal Care Subsidy [*Australia*]
PCS .... Personal Clerk of Session (SAUS)
PCS .... Personal Communications Service [*Provided by Personal Communications Network*]
PCS .... Personal Communications Services [*Telecommunications*]
PCS .... Personal Communications System
PCS .... Personal Communication System [*Wireless digital communication system*] (NETL)
PCS .... Personal Composition System (DGA)
PCS .... Personal Computer System (SAUS)
PCS .... Personal Computing System
PCS .... Personal Conferencing Specification [*Telecommunications*] (CDE)
PCS .... Personnel Capabilities System [*Jet Propulsion Laboratory, NASA*]
PCS .... Personnel Change of Station
PCS .... Personnel Consultancy Services Ltd. [*British*]
PCS .... Petrochemical Corp. of Singapore
PCS .... Pharmaceutical Card System (MCD)
PCS .... Pharmacogenic Confusional Syndrome [*Medicine*] (DMAA)
PCS .... Phase Combining System [*Trademark*] [*A solubilizer in scintillation counting*]
PCS .... Phase Compensator System
PCS .... Philippine Collectors Society (EA)
PCS .... Philips Car Systems
PCS .... PhonoCardioScan [*Cardiology*]
PCS .... Photo Correlation System (SAUS)
PCS .... Photoformed Ceramic Substrates [*Du Pont process for making microconductors*]
PCS .... Photon Correlation Spectroscopy
PCS .... Physical-Chemical System (SAA)
PCS .... Physical Coding Signalling (SAUS)
PCS .... Physical Control Space (SAUS)
PCS .... Physical Control System
PCS .... Physically Controlled Space [*Military*] (GFGA)
PCS .... Physics of Colloids in Space (SAUS)
pCs .... Picocoulombs (SAUS)
PCS .... Pictorial Cancellation Society [*Defunct*] (EA)
pcs .... Picture File [*Computer science*]
pcs .... Pieces (EBF)
PCS .... Pieces
PCS .... Piezoelectric Crystal Sensor (DB)
PCS .... Pilot Control System (MCD)
PCS .... Pinball Construction Set (SAUS)
PCS .... Pitch Control System (MCD)
PCS .... Planning Control Sheet
PCS .... Plant Computer System (NRCH)
PCS .... Plant Control System [*Nuclear energy*] (NRCH)
PCS .... Plasma-Current Switch (ODA)
PCS .... Plastic-Clad Silica [*Optics*]
PCS .... Plastic Coated Silica (NITA)
PCS .... Plastic-Coated Silica (SAUS)
PCS .... Plastic Coding System (SAUS)
PCS .... Plastic Connector Shell
PCS .... Platoon Combat Skills [*Army*] (INF)
PCS .... Plausible Conflict Situations [*Army*]
PCS .... Plessey Commercial Software (SAUS)
PCS .... Pluto-Charon System [*Planetary science*]
PCS .... Pneumatic Control System [*Gas chromatography*]
PCS .... Pocket Computer System (SEWL)
PCS .... Pointing-Control System [*Aerospace*]
PCS .... Polycarbosilane (EDCT)
PCS .... Polymer-Clad Silica [*Chemistry*]
PCS .... Polytechnic Certificate in Shipping (SAUS)
PCS .... Portable Cervical Spine [*Medicine*] (EDAA)
PCS .... Portable Communications System
PCS .... Portable Computer System (SAUS)
PCS .... Portable Control Station (SAUS)
PCS .... Portacaval Shunt [*Medicine*]
PCS .... Port Command Store [*Telecommunications*] (TEL)
PCS .... Port Concentrator Shelf (SAUS)
PCS .... Port Control Store [*Telecommunications*] (TEL)
PCS .... Port Control System [*Telecommunications*] (TEL)
PCS .... Position Classification Standard [*Civil Service*]
PCS .... Position Control System
PCS .... Position, Course, and Speed
PCS .... Positive Concatenation Structures [*Mathematics*]
PCS .... Postal & Courier Service (SAUS)
PCS .... Postal Church Service
PCS .... Postal Commemorative Society (EA)
PCS .... Post-cardiac Surgery [*Medicine*] (EDAA)
PCS .... Postcardiotomy Syndrome [*Medicine*]
PCS .... Postcaval [*or Portacaval*] Shunt [*Medicine*]
PCS .... Posterior Concave Side
PCS .... Posts, Camps, and Stations [*Military*]
PCS .... Postural Control System (SAUS)
PCS .... Potash Corp. of Saskatchewan [*Canada*]
PCS .... Power Center Substation (SAUS)
PCS .... Power Conditioning System
PCS .... Power Conductor System (SAUS)
PCS .... Power Control System [*Automotive engineering*]
PCS .... Power Conversion System
PCS .... Powered Causeway Section [*Military*] (CAAL)
PCS .... Practical Computer Solutions (NITA)
PCS .... Precedence Charting System (IAA)
PCS .... Precision Casting Standard (MCD)
PCS .... Precision Control System [*Automotive engineering*]
Pcs .... Preconscious [*Medicine*] (STED)
PCS .... Preconscious
PCS .... Pre-Crash Sensor [*Automotive safety systems*]
PCS .... Preferred Capital Stock [*Investment term*]
PCS .... Preferred Character Set (SAUS)
PCS .... Pregnancy Counselling Service [*Australia*]
PCS .... Preliminary Component Specification
PCS .... Premature Centromere Separation [*Medicine*] (EDAA)
PCS .... Press Computer System (DGA)
PCS .... Pressure Control Solenoid [*Automotive term*] (HAWK)
PCS .... Pressure Control System
PCS .... Pressure Core Sampler (SAUS)
PCS .... Pressure Cycling Switch [*Automotive engineering*]
PCS .... Previous Condition of Servitude (SAUS)
PCS .... Primary Calibration System
PCS .... Primary Cancer Site [*Oncology*]
P c/s .... Primary Cesarian Section (STED)
PCS .... Primary Conditioning Solution
PCS .... Primary Control Ship [*Navy*]
PCS .... Primary Coolant System (MSA)
PCS .... Prime Compatible Set (PDAA)
PCS .... Principal Clerk of Session
PCS .... Principal Coordinating Scientist [*NASA*] (KSC)
PCS .... Print Contrast Scale (IEEE)
PCS .... Print Contrast Signal [*Computer science*]
PCS .... Print Contrast System (BUR)
PCS .... Priority Control System [*Traffic management*]
PCS .... Probabilistic Clock Synchronization (SAUS)
PCS .... Probability of Command Shutdown (MCD)
PCS .... Probability of Correct Selection [*Statistics*]
PCS .... Probability of Crew Survival (AAG)
PCS .... Probable Carcinogenic Substances (EEVL)
PCS .... Procedure Coding System (SAUS)
PCS .... Procedure Completion Sheet [*NASA*] (MCD)
PCS .... Process Communication Supervisor (IAA)
PCS .... Process Communication System (SAUS)
PCS .... Process Computer System (NRCH)
PCS .... Process Control Sheet [*Nuclear energy*] (NRCH)
PCS .... Process Control Specification (SAUS)
PCS .... Process Control Station
PCS .... Process Control System
PCS .... Pro Computer Services (NITA)
PCS .... Production Control Section
PCS .... Production Control System (BUR)
PCS .... Production Cost Savings (AAEL)
PCS .... Professional Careers Sourcebook [*A publication*]
PCS .... Professional Car Society (EA)
PCS .... Program Center Store (SAUS)
PCS .... Program Control System (SAUS)
PCS .... Program Coordination Staff [*Environmental Protection Agency*] (GFGA)
PCS .... Program Cost Status [*Report*] (MCD)
PCS .... Program Counter Store
PCS .... Programmable Character Set [*Computer science*] (VLIE)
PCS .... Programmable Communications Subsystem
PCS .... Programmable Communications System (SAUS)
PCS .... Programmed Control Sequencer (SAUS)
PCS .... Project Control Sheet [*Computer science*]
PCS .... Project Control System [*Computer science*]
PCS .... Project Coordination Staff [*NASA*] (KSC)
PCS .... Promotion of Chemical Safety (SAUS)
PCS .... Property Claims Service [*Emergency Management*] (EMA)
PCS .... Property Consultants Society [*British*] (DBA)
PCS .... Property Control System
PCS .... Proprietary Computer Systems, Inc. [*Information service or system*] (IID)
PCS .... Propulsion Control System (ACAE)
PCS .... Prostate Cancer Society (WDAA)
PCS .... Protected Cable System (SAUS)
PCS .... Provision Coordinate Schedule (MCD)
PCS .... Proximal Coronary [*Medicine*] (RAWO)
PCS .... Proxy Cache Server (SAUS)
PCS .... Pseudo-Code System (SAUS)
PCS .... Pseudotumor Cerebri Syndrome [*Medicine*] (DMAA)
PCS .... Public and Commercial Services Union (HEAS)
PCS .... Publication Control Sheet (MCD)
PCS .... Public Choice Society (EA)
PCS .... Pulse Compression System

PCS.......... Pump Control Sensor
PCS.......... Punch Card System (NITA)
PCS.......... Punch Column Skip (SAUS)
PCS.......... Punched Card Selector (SAUS)
PCS.......... Punched Card System [*Computer science*]
PCS.......... Punjab Cooperative Society (SAUS)
PCS.......... Pyrotechnics Circuit Simulator
PCS.......... Sabah Chinese Party [*Malaysia*] [*Political party*] (FEA)
PCS.......... Sprint PCS Group [*Company symbol*]
PCS.......... Submarine Chaser
PCS.......... Sun Shipbuilding & Dry Dock Co., Chester, PA [*Library symbol*] [*Library of Congress*] (LCLS)
PCS.......... Water Permit Compliance System [*Database*] (GDD)
PCS-1900... Personal Communication Service in 1.9GHz band (SAUS)
PCSA........ Palm and Cycad Societies of Australia
PCSA........ Patrol Craft Sailors Association (EA)
PCSA........ Personal Computer Systems Architecture (SAUS)
PCSA........ Personal Computing Systems Architecture
PCSA........ Polish Cultural Society of America (SAUS)
PCSA........ Power Crane and Shovel Association (EA)
PCSA........ Seaman Apprentice, Postal Clerk, Striker [*Navy rating*]
PCS(A)...... Submarine Chaser (Air Cushion) (MCD)
PCSAS....... Policy Committee for Scientific Agricultural Society (BUAC)
PCsB......... Baptist Bible College of Pennsylvania, Clarks Summit, PA [*Library symbol*] [*Library of Congress*] (LCLS)
PCSB........ Pulse-Code Scanning Beam (SAUS)
PCSC........ Control Submarine Chaser [*136 feet*] [*Navy symbol*] [*Obsolete*]
PCSC........ Pacific Coast Science Center (SAUS)
PCSC........ Pacific Coast Swimming Conference (PSS)
PC/SC....... Personal Computer/Smart Card [*Microsoft*] (GART)
PCSC........ Plant Cell Suspension Cultures [*Biotechnology*]
PCSC........ Power Conditioning, Switching, and Control
PCSC........ Principal Commonwealth Supply Committee [*World War II*]
PCSCA....... Permanent Committee on Socio-Cultural Affairs (SAUS)
PCS-CSS.... Parents' Confidential Statement of the College Scholarship Service [*Education*] (IIA)
PCSD........ Partido Cristao Social Democratico [*Christian Social Democratic Party*] [*Portugal*] [*Political party*] (PPE)
PCSD........ Polychloro(chloromethylsulfonamido)diphenyl Ether [*Insectproofing agent for wool*]
PCSD........ President's Council on Sustainable Development [*1993*]
PCSD........ Printer Control Sequence Description (SAUS)
PCSDC....... Pacific Collegiate Swim/Dive Conference (PSS)
PCSDS....... Pump Controls and Data System (SAUS)
PCSE........ Pacific Coast Stock Exchange [*Later, PSE*] (EA)
PCSE........ President's Committee on Scientists and Engineers [*Expired, 1958*]
PCSE........ Printed Circuit Soldering Equipment
PC/SFA...... Potato Chip/Snack Food Association [*Formerly, NPCI, PCI*] [*Later, SFA*]
PCSFSK..... Phase Coherent Sinusoidal Frequency Shift Keying (CCCA)
PCSFSK..... Phase Comparison Sinusoidal Frequency Shift Keying
PCSG........ Public Cryptography Study Group [*Defunct*] (EA)
PCSGA....... Pacific Coast Shellfish Growers Association [*Alaska, California, Oregon, Washington, Hawaii, and Mexico.*] (EARSL)
PCSH........ Pierce Shell
PCS(H)...... Submarine Chaser (Hydrofoil) (MCD)
PCSI......... Pacific Communication Sciences, Inc. (SAUS)
PCSI......... PCS, Inc. [*NASDAQ symbol*] (COMM)
PCSI......... Public Cleansing and Salvage Inspection (SAUS)
PCSIG....... Personal Computer-Software Interest Group (EA)
PCSIR....... Pakistan Council of Scientific and Industrial Research
PCSJ........ All-Party Parliamentary Committee for the Release of Soviet Jewry (EAIO)
PCSL........ Procurement Component Supplier List (VLIE)
PCSM........ Percutaneous Stone Manipulation [*Medicine*]
PCSMQC.... Polish Committee for Standardization, Measures and Quality Control (SAUS)
PCSN........ PC Satellite Network
PCSN........ Precision Standard [*NASDAQ symbol*] (TTSB)
PCSN........ Precision Standard, Inc. [*NASDAQ symbol*] (NQ)
PCSN........ Private Circuit-Switching Network [*Telecommunications*] (OSI)
PCSN........ Seaman, Postal Clerk, Striker [*Navy rating*]
PCSO........ Presidential Communications Support Office (CCCA)
PCSOM....... School of Osteopathic Medicine [*Pikeville College*] (MHID)
PCSP........ Partial Constraint Satisfaction Problem (SAUS)
PCSP........ Permanent Commission for the South Pacific (WDAA)
PCSP........ Polar Continental Shelf Project [*Canada*] (QUAC)
PCSP........ Preliminary Cruise Sampling Plan (SAUS)
PCSP........ Princeton Cooperative School Program (SAUS)
PCSP........ Programmed Communications Support Program [*Air Force*] (AFM)
PCSPS....... Principal Civil Service Pension Scheme [*British*]
PCSR........ Portable Counter-Surveillance Receiver [*Police and security equipment*]
PCSR........ Program Cost and Schedule Report (TIMI)
PCS/REAL... Project Control System/Resource Allocation (VLIE)
PCSS........ PC Service Source [*NASDAQ symbol*] (TTSB)
PCSS........ PC Service Source, Inc. [*NASDAQ symbol*] (SAG)
PCSS........ Pennsylvania Council for the Social Studies (EARSL)
PCSS........ Personal Computer Support Service (VLIE)
PCSS........ Photo-Conductive Semiconductor Switch (VLIE)
PCSS........ Platform Check Subsystem
PCSS........ Princess (ROG)
PCSSD....... Philippines Council for Sustainable Development (SAUS)
PCST........ Pakistan Council for Science and Technology (BUAC)
PCST........ Permanent Commission on Science and Technology (SAUS)
PCST........ Plain-Capped Starthroat [*North American bird banding code*] (BIBA)
PCST........ Precision Castparts Corp. (MHDW)
PCST........ President's Committee on Science and Technology
PCSU........ Dong Young Shipping [*Intermodal shipping container symbol*] (TVRC)
PCSU........ Peripheral Control Switching Unit (VLIE)
PC Svc...... PC Service Source, Inc. [*Associated Press*] (SAG)
PCSW........ Police Chiefs Spouses - Worldwide [*An association*] (EA)
PCSW........ President's Commission on the Status of Women
PC System... Power Control System (SAUS)
PCSZ........ Pacific Standard [*Federal Railroad Administration identification code*]
PCT.......... Pacific Coast Tariff Bureau, San Francisco CA [*STAC*]
PCT.......... Pacific Coast Terminals (SAUS)
PCT.......... Pacific Crest Trail
PCT.......... Page Copy Teleprinter (SAUS)
PCT.......... Painful Cervical Trauma [*Medicine*] (MELL)
PCT.......... Paper Crepe Tape
PCT.......... Para-Chlorotoluene [*Organic chemistry*]
PCT.......... Parity, Charge conjugation, Time-reversal (SAUS)
PCT.......... Parti Communiste Tunisien [*Tunisian Communist Party*] [*Political party*] (PD)
PCT.......... Parti Congolais du Travail [*Congolese Labor Party*] [*Political party*] (PPW)
PCT.......... Partido Conservador Tradicional [*Traditionalist Conservative Party*] [*Nicaragua*] [*Political party*]
PCT.......... Partition Control Table [*Computer science*] (ELAL)
PCT.......... Patent Cooperation Treaty [*World Intellectual Property Organization, 1978*]
PCT.......... Patient Care Technician (MELL)
PCT.......... Patient Clotting Time (SAUS)
PCT.......... Peace Air Togo [*ICAO designator*] (FAAC)
PCT.......... Peak Centerline Temperature [*Nuclear energy*] (NRCH)
PCT.......... Peak Cladding Temperature [*Nuclear energy*] (NRCH)
pct........... Percent (NTIO)
PCT.......... Percent [*or Percentage*]
PCT.......... Percentage [*Used instead of "average"*] [*Baseball*]
PCT.......... Perfect Crystal Technology (IAA)
PCT.......... Performance Correlation Technique
PCT.......... Periodic Confidence Test
PCT.......... Peripheral Carcinoid Tumor [*Medicine*] (EDAA)
PCT.......... Peripheral Control Terminal
PCT.......... Personal Communications Technology (AGLO)
PC/T......... Personal Computer/Technology (HGAA)
PCT.......... Personality Completion Test [*Psychology*]
PCT.......... Pest Control Team (SAUS)
PCT.......... Pharmacy and Chemistry Technician [*Navy*]
PCT.......... Philadelphia College of Textiles and Science, Philadelphia, PA [*OCLC symbol*] (OCLC)
PCT.......... Photochemical Transfer (SAUS)
PCT.......... Photoinduced Charge Transfer [*Electrochemistry*]
PCT.......... Photometric Calibration Target (ACAE)
PCT.......... Photometric Calibration Test (SAUS)
PCT.......... Photon-Coupled Transistor (IEEE)
PCT.......... Physical Correlate Theory [*Psychophysics*]
PCT.......... Physiognomic Cue Test [*Psychology*] (STED)
PCT.......... Picrotoxin [*Biological stimulant*]
PCT.......... Picture
PCT.......... Pitch Centering Torque (SAUS)
PCT.......... Pitch Centering Torquer (SAA)
PCT.......... Planning and Control Techniques
PCT.......... Plasma Clotting Time [*Medicine*] (STED)
PCT.......... Plasmacrit Test [*Medicine*]
PCT.......... Plasmacytoma [*Medicine*]
PCT.......... Platelet Count [*Hematology*]
PCT.......... Platelet Hematocrit (STED)
PCT.......... Point-Contact Transistor [*Electronics*] (IAA)
PCT.......... Polychemotherapy [*Oncology*]
PCT.......... Polychlorinated Terphenyl [*Pesticide*]
PCT.......... Polychlorinated Triphenyl (STED)
PCT.......... Polychloroterphenyl [*Organic chemistry*]
PCT.......... Polycyclohexane Dimethylene Terephthalate (SAUS)
PCT.......... Polycyclohexyl Terephthalate (SAUS)
PCT.......... Porcine Calcitonin [*Biochemistry*] (AAMN)
PCT.......... Porphyria Cutanea Tarda [*Disease*] [*Medicine*]
PCT.......... Portable Camera-Transmitter
PCT.......... Portable Conference Telephone [*Bell Laboratories*]
PCT.......... Portacaval Transportation (STED)
PCT.......... Portacaval Transposition [*Medicine*] (MAE)
PCT.......... Portsmouth College of Technology (SAUS)
PCT.......... Positron Computed Tomography
PCT.......... Postcoital Test [*Medicine*] (DAVI)
PCT.......... Potato Curly Top Disease [*Plant pathology*]
PCT.......... Potential Current Transformer
PCT.......... Power Control Test (SAUS)
PCT.......... Precinct
PCT.......... Precipitate [*Telegraphy*] (PCTE)
PCT.......... Preliminary Change Transmittal (AAG)
PCT.......... Prepared Childbirth Training (MELL)
PCT.......... Pressure Concentration Temperature
PCT.......... Pressure Controlled Test (SAUS)
PCT.......... Primary Cerebral Tumor [*Medicine*] (EDAA)
PCT.......... Prime Contract Termination (AAG)
PCT.......... Princeton [*New Jersey*] [*Airport symbol*] [*Obsolete*] (OAG)
PCT.......... Princeton, IL [*Amtrak rail station code*]
PCT.......... Principal Component Transform (SAUS)

PCT .... Printed Circuit Tester (VLIE)
PCT .... Printer Carriage Tape (SAUS)
PCT .... Prism Cover Test [*Ophthalmology*] (CPH)
PCT .... Private Communications Technology [*Microsoft Corp.*] [*Computer science*]
P Ct .... Probate Court (DLA)
PCT .... Probe Control Table (SAUS)
PCT .... Process Change Teams (AAEL)
PCT .... Processing Control Table (SAUS)
PCT .... Product Consistency Test (ABAC)
PCT .... Production Car Trial [*Motorsports*]
PCT .... Production Confirmatory Test (MCD)
PCT .... Progestin Challenge Test (STED)
PCT .... Programa de Cooperacion Tecnica [*Program of Technical Cooperation - PTC*] [*Organization of American States*] [*Washington, DC*]
PCT .... Program Controlled Transfer (SAUS)
PCT .... Program Control Table [*Computer science*]
PCT .... Program Counter Timer (IAA)
PCT .... Project Control Tool (BUR)
PCT .... Property Capital Trust [*AMEX symbol*] (SPSG)
PCT .... Prophyria Catanba Tarda [*Medicine*]
PCT .... Propulsion Component Technology (ACAE)
PCT .... prothrombin Consumption Test (SAUS)
PCT .... Prothrombin Consumption Time [*Hematology*] (DAVI)
PCT .... Proximal Convoluted Tubule [*of a nephron*]
PCT .... Puangchon Chao Thai [*Thai Mass Party*] [*Thailand*] [*Political party*]
PCT .... Pulmonary Care Team Medicine (STED)
PCT .... Pulse Compression Test (SAUS)
PCT .... Pulse Compression Tube
PCT .... Pulse Count [*Telecommunications*] (TEL)
PCT .... Pump Cavitation Temperature [*Automotive engineering*]
PCT .... Punched Card Technique (SAUS)
PCT .... Pure Chance Traffic (SAUS)
PCT .... Wesman Personnel Classification Test
PCTA .... Pennsylvania Cable and Telecommunications Association (EARSL)
PCTA .... Pentachlorothioanisole [*Organic chemistry*]
PCTA .... Percutaneous Transluminal Angioplasty [*Medicine*] (MELL)
PCTA .... Personal Computer Terminal Adapter (SAUS)
PCTA .... Plastic-Cased Telescoped Ammunition (SAUS)
PCTA .... Polymer of Cyclohexanedimethanol Terephthalic Acid (SAUS)
PCTA .... Provisional Collection of Taxes Act (SAUS)
PCT&S .... Philadelphia College of Textiles and Science (SAUS)
PCTAP .... Positive Control Turnaround Point (CCCA)
PCTB .... Pacific Coast Tariff Bureau
PCTC .... Panama Canal Transition Commission (SAUS)
PCTC .... Payload Crew Training Complex (SAUS)
PCTC .... Penn Central Transportation Co.
PCTC .... Pentagon Consolidated Telecommunications Center (SAUS)
PCTC .... Portable Common Tool Environment (SAUS)
PCTC .... Pure Car Truck Carrier [*Shipping*] (DS)
PCTC .... Pyrotechnic Circuit Test Console (KSC)
PCTD .... Precipitated [*Telegraphy*] (PCTE)
PCTDS .... Problem and Change Tracking Directory System
PCTE .... Portable Commercial Test Equipment (NASA)
PCTE .... Portable Common Test Environment [*British*]
PCTE .... Portable Common Tools Environment (IAA)
PCTE Bulletin ... Pennsylvania Council of Teachers of English, Bulletin (SAUS)
PCTF .... Plant Component Test Facility [*Nuclear energy*]
PCTF .... Power Conversion Test Facility (SAA)
PCTF .... Premiers Council Technology Fund (SAUS)
PCTF .... Process Condensate Treatment Facility (SAUS)
PCTFE .... Polychlorotrifluoroethylene [*Organic chemistry*]
PCTFE .... Polymonochlorotrifluorethyle [*Organic chemistry*] (IAA)
PCTFE .... Polymonochlorotrifluoroethylene (SAUS)
PCTG .... glycol-modified PCT copolymer (SAUS)
PCTG .... Precipitating [*Telegraphy*] (PCTE)
PCTG .... Programmable Channel Termination Group (SAUS)
PCT-GF .... Plasmacytoma Growth Factor [*Oncology*]
PCTH .... Pacific Aerospace & Electronics, Inc. [*NASDAQ symbol*] (SAG)
PCTH .... PCT Holdings [*NASDAQ symbol*] (TTSB)
PCTH .... PCT Holdings, Inc. [*NASDAQ symbol*] (SAG)
PCTHold .... PCT Holdings, Inc. [*Associated Press*] (SAG)
PCTIS .... Preston Commercial and Technical Information Service (NITA)
PCTL .... Picture Tel Corp. [*NASDAQ symbol*] (TTSB)
PC/TM .... Performance Criteria and Test Methods Task
PCTM .... Pulse-Count Modulation (MSA)
PCTMSL .... Permanent Committee on Tides and Mean Sea-Level (SAUS)
PCTN .... Precipitation [*Telegraphy*] (PCTE)
PCTO .... Payload Cost Tradeoff Optimization [*NASA*] (NASA)
PCTOJ .... Passive Correlation Track-On-Jam [*Department of Defense*]
PCTP .... Partido Comunista dos Trabalhadores Portugueses [*Portuguese Workers' Communist Party*] [*Political party*] (PPW)
PCTP .... Pierce Template
PCTP .... Plant Completion Task Proposal (SAUS)
PCTP .... Public Communication Technology Project [*Arizona State University*] (RCD)
PCTR .... Pad Connection Terminal Room [*NASA*] (NAKS)
PCTR .... Physical Constant Test Reactor [*Nuclear energy*]
PCTR .... Program Counter
PCTR .... Property Control Transaction Report
PCTR .... Protocol Conformance Test Report (SAUS)
PCTR .... Pulsed Column Test Rig [*Chemical engineering*]
PCTs .... Panama Canal Treaties (SAUS)
PCTS .... Pentagon Consolidated Telecommunications System (MCD)
PC/TS .... Performance Criteria/Test Standard (SAUS)
PCTS .... Photocapacitance Transient Spectroscopy (SAUS)
PCTS .... Portable Cesium Time Standard
PCTS .... Precipitates [*Telegraphy*] (PCTE)
PCTS .... President's Committee for Traffic Safety (EA)
PCTSCM .... Piezoelectric, Continuously Twisted, Structurally Chiral Medium (SAUS)
PCTT .... Precommit Track Time [*DoD*]
PCT Theorem ... Parity, Charge-conjugation, Time-reversal Theorem (SAUS)
PCTU .... Pro Tech Communications [*OTCBB symbol*]
PCTUULAW ... Permanent Congress of Trade Union Unity of Latin American Workers [*See also CPUSTAL*] [*Mexico City, Mexico*] (EAIO)
PCTV .... Peoples Choice TV Corp. [*NASDAQ symbol*] (SAG)
PCTV .... Personal Computer Television (SAUS)
PCTV .... Printed Circuit Test Vehicle (SAUS)
PCTV .... Private Channel Television
PCTV .... Program Controlled Transverters (SAUS)
PCtvL .... Lukens Steel Co., Coatesville, PA [*Library symbol*] [*Library of Congress*] [*Obsolete*] (LCLS)
PCtvVA .... United States Veterans Administration Hospital, Medical Library, Coatesville, PA [*Library symbol*] [*Library of Congress*] (LCLS)
PCTWin .... PC [*Personal Computer*] Tools for Windows (PCM)
PCTY .... Party City [*NASDAQ symbol*] (TTSB)
PCTY .... Party City Corp. [*NASDAQ symbol*] (SAG)
PCTZ .... Plum Creek Timber [*Federal Railroad Administration identification code*]
PCTZ .... Price Transfer [*Intermodal trailer symbol*]
PCU .... Packet Communications Unit
PCU .... Page Clean-up (SAUS)
PCU .... Paging Control Unit [*Telecommunications*] (TEL)
PCU .... Pain Control Unit
PCU .... Palliative Care Unit [*Medicine*] (CPH)
PCU .... Parachute Control Unit (SAUS)
PCU .... Parallel Computation Unit (SAUS)
PCU .... Partido Conservador Unido [*Chilean Catholic political party*]
PCU .... Passenger Car Unit (SAUS)
PCU .... Passenger Control Unit (MCD)
PCU .... Patient Care Unit (HCT)
PCU .... Payload Checkout Unit [*NASA*] (MCD)
PCU .... Peripheral Control Unit (CMD)
PCU .... Photocopy Unit (SAUS)
PCU .... Physical Control Unit (SAUS)
PCU .... Picayune, MS [*Location identifier*] [*FAA*] (FAAL)
PCU .... Plant Control Unit (ODA)
pcu .... Platinum Cobalt Unit [*Water analysis*]
PCU .... Pneumatic Checkout Unit (AAG)
PCU .... Pod Cooling Unit (AAG)
PCU .... Ponable Checkout Unit (SAUS)
PCU .... Portable Checkout Unit
PCU .... Portable Communications Unit (SAUS)
PCU .... Portable Computer Unit
PCU .... Portable Control Unit (SAUS)
PCU .... Port-Contention Unit (SAUS)
PCU .... Portuguese Continental Union of the United States of America (EA)
PCU .... Post-coma Unawareness [*Medicine*] (EDAA)
PCU .... Post Communications Unit (CARL)
PCU .... Post-Coronary Care Unit [*Cardiology*] (DAVI)
PCU .... Pound Centigrade Unit
PCU .... Power and Controller Unit (SAUS)
PCU .... Power Conditioning Unit
PCU .... Power Control Unit
PCU .... Power Conversion Unit (IEEE)
PCU .... Power Convulsion Unit
PCU .... Preclude [*Telegraphy*] (PCTE)
PCU .... Preferred Clause Unit [*Linguistics*] (IEL)
PCU .... Premises Control Unit (SAUS)
PCU .... Pressure Control Unit (MCD)
PCU .... Pressurization Control Unit (SAUS)
PCU .... Price [*Utah*] [*Seismograph station code, US Geological Survey*] (SEIS)
PCU .... Primary Care Unit [*Medicine*] (DMAA)
PCU .... Primary Control Unit (IAA)
PCU .... Printed Control Unit [*Military*] (GFGA)
PCU .... Printer Control Unit (SAUS)
PCU .... Priority Control Unit (SAUS)
PCU .... Prisoner Casework Unit (WDAA)
PCU .... Procedure Change Unit
PCU .... Process Control Unit (NAKS)
PCU .... Processor Control Unit
PCU .... Product Co-Ordination Unit [*British Overseas Trade Board*] (DS)
PCU .... Program Control Unit [*Computer science*]
PCU .... Programmable Control Unit (SAUS)
PCU .... Progress Control Unit (KSC)
PCU .... Progressive Care Unit [*Medicine*]
PCU .... Propellant Control Unit (SAA)
PCU .... Protective Care Unit [*Medicine*]
PCU .... Protective Custody Unit (SAUS)
PCU .... Protein-Calorie Undernutrition [*Medicine*]
PCU .... Pulmonary Care Unit [*Medicine*] (DMAA)
PCU .... Punched Card Unit (NITA)
PCU .... Punched Card Utility [*Computer science*]
PCU .... Southern Peru Copper [*NYSE symbol*] (TTSB)
PCU .... Southern Peru Copper Corp. [*NYSE symbol*] (SAG)

PCU .... University of Prince Edward Island, Charlottetown, Prince Edward Island [*Library symbol*] [*National Library of Canada*] (NLC)
PCUA .... Power Controller Unit Assembly (IEEE)
PCUA .... Pressure Control Unit, Atlas (MCD)
PCUA .... Profit Control Users Association (SAUS)
PCUC .... Positive Continuous Ullage Control
PCUCDGIS... Personal Computer University College Dublin Geographic Information System (SAUS)
PCUD .... Peripheral Control Unit Diagnostic [*Program*]
PCUD .... Precluded [*Telegraphy*] (PCTE)
PCUG .... Precluding [*Telegraphy*] (PCTE)
PCU/HDR ... Primary Control Unit, Hydraulics (AAG)
PCUI .... Partito Comunista Unificado de Italia [*Unified Communist Party of Italy*] [*Political party*] (PPE)
PCUL .... Pennsylvania Credit Union League (EARSL)
PCUR .... Pulsating Current
PCUS .... Peace Corps of the United States (EA)
PCUs .... Peripheral Control Units (SAUS)
PCUS .... Port Charges Paid by United States Army, Navy, or Air Force (DNAB)
PCUS .... Precludes [*Telegraphy*] (PCTE)
PCUS .... Propeller Club of the United States (EA)
PCUS .... Prorated from Customer Read [*Electric utility company*]
PC-USA ..... Pax Christi - USA (EA)
PCUSA ...... Presbyterian Church in the U.S.A. (SAUS)
PCUSAW .... Pen Center USA West (EA)
PCUSEQ..... Pressure Control Unit Sequencer (AAG)
pcut........... Percutaneous [*Medicine*] (AAMN)
PCUUS ...... Polish Council of Unity in the United States [*Defunct*] (EA)
PCU-USA.... Portuguese Continental Union of the U.S.A. (SAUS)
PCU Value... Passenger Car Unit Value (SAUS)
PCV .... Pacific Concord Resources Corp. [*Vancouver Stock Exchange symbol*]
PCV .... Packed Cell Volume [*Hematology*] (CPH)
PCV .... Parietal Cell Vagotomy [*Medicine*] (AAMN)
PCV .... Partido Comunista Venezolana [*Venezuelan Communist Party*] [*Political party*] (PPW)
PCV .... Passenger Carrying Vehicle [*Military*] (GFGA)
PCV .... Passenger Coaching Vehicle [*Indian Railway*] (TIR)
PCV .... Passenger Control Vehicle (WDAA)
PCV .... Path Coding Violation (SAUS)
PCV .... P-bit Coding Violation (SAUS)
PCV .... Peace Corps Volunteer
PCV .... Peach Calico Virus (SAUS)
PCV .... Peanut Clump Virus [*Plant pathology*]
PCV .... Penciclovir [*Antiherpetic*]
PCV .... Perceive [*Telegraphy*] (PCTE)
PCV .... Pestalozzi Childrens Village (SAUS)
PCV .... Petty Cash Voucher (MCD)
PCV .... Physical Control Volume (SAUS)
PCV .... Placerville, CA [*Amtrak Busline code*]
PCV .... Pneumatic Control Valve
PCV .... Pollution Control Valve (IEEE)
PCV .... Polychlorinated Vinyl (MELL)
PCV .... Polycythemia Vera [*Also, PV*] [*Hematology*]
PCV .... Porcine Cirovirus
PCV .... Positive Crankcase Ventilation [*For automotive antipollution systems*]
PCV .... Positive Crankcase Ventilator (SAUS)
PCV .... Postcapillary Venule [*Medicine*] (DMAA)
PCV .... Precheck Verification [*NASA*] (NASA)
PCV .... Precursor Vehicle (SAUS)
PCV .... Presidents Commission on Violence (SAUS)
PCV .... Pressure [*or Pressurizer*] Control Valve (AAG)
PCV .... Pressure-Control Ventilation [*Medicine*] (DMAA)
PCV .... Primary Containment Vessel
PCV .... Primary Control Vessel (DNAB)
PCV .... Primate Calicivirus
PCV .... Printed Circuit Vehicle (SAUS)
PCV .... Procarbazine, CCNU [*Lomustine*], Vincristine [*Antineoplastic drug regimen*] (DAVI)
PCV .... Process Cell Ventilation (SAUS)
PCV .... Proportional Cartridge Valve [*Hydraulics*]
PCV .... Proportioning Control Valve [*Automotive brakes*]
PCV .... Protocol Converter [*Electronics*] (ECII)
PCV .... Pump Control Valve [*Hydraulics*]
PCV .... Purge Control Valve (NASA)
PCV .... Putnam Convertible Opportunities & Income Trust [*NYSE symbol*] (SAG)
PCV .... Putnam High Income Opp Tr [*Stock exchange symbol*] [*Formerly Putnam Cv Opp Tr*]
PCV .... Pyrocatechol Violet [*Also, PV*] [*An indicator*] [*Chemistry*]
PCV .... Veterans Affairs, Canada [*Affaires des Anciens Combattants Canada*] Charlottetown, Prince Edward Island [*Library symbol*] [*National Library of Canada*] (NLC)
PCvA......... Allentown College of Saint Francis De Sales, Center Valley, PA [*Library symbol*] [*Library of Congress*] (LCLS)
PCVB .... Pyro Continuity Verification Box [*NASA*] (NASA)
PCVC .... Partially Conserved Vector Current (IAA)
PCVC .... Public Citizens Visitors Center [*An association*] [*Defunct*] (EA)
PCVD .... Perceived [*Telegraphy*] (PCTE)
PCVD .... Plasma Chemical Vapor Deposition
PCVD .... Pulmonary Collagen Vascular Disease [*Medicine*] (RAWO)
PC virus..... Port Chalmers type of influenza virus (SAUS)
PCVL .... Pilot-Controlled Visual Landing [*Aviation*] (NASA)
PCV-M....... Myeloid Metaplasia with Polycythemia Vera [*Hematology*] (MAE)
PCVN .... Precracked Charpy V-Notch (PDAA)
PCVS .... Point-to-point Switched Virtual Connections (SAUS)
PCVS .... Professional Credentials Verification Service (ADWA)
PCV system... Positive Crankcase Ventilation System
PCVU .... Peacock Containers [*Intermodal shipping container symbol*] (TVRC)
PCV Valve... Positive Crankcase Ventilation Valve (SAUS)
PCW .... PCCW Ltd ADS [*Stock exchange symbol*] [*Formerly Pacific Century Cyberworks ADS*]
PCW .... Pericanalicular Web [*Medicine*] (EDAA)
PCW .... Personal Computer World Show [*Montbuild Ltd.*] (TSPED)
PCW .... Plate Control Wedge [*Printing technology*]
PCW .... Point Calculation Worksheet [*Army*] (INF)
PCW .... PortaCom Wireless [*VS, Exchange Symbol*] (TTSB)
PCW .... Port Clinton, OH [*Location identifier*] [*FAA*] (FAAL)
PCW .... Post Consumer Waste (EG)
PCW .... Previously Complied With
PCW .... Primary Capillary Wedge [*Medicine*] (EDAA)
PCW .... Primary Cooling Water [*Reactor*]
PCW .... Princess Charlotte of Wales [*Military unit*] [*British*]
PCW .... Principal Conductor of the Works [*Freemasonry*]
PCW .... Program Control Word
PCW .... Proprietor of Copyright on a Composite Work
PCW .... Pulmonary Capillary Wedge [*Medicine*]
PCW .... Pulsed Continuous Wave (IEEE)
PCW .... Purified Cell Walls [*Medicine*] (EDAA)
PCW .... Put Control Write (SAUS)
PCW .... Widener College, Chester, PA [*Library symbol*] [*Library of Congress*] (LCLS)
PCWA......... Pharmaceutical Council of Western Australia
PCWBS...... Preliminary Contract Work Breakdown Structure (MCD)
PCWCA...... Poured Concrete Wall Contractors Association (EA)
PCWF........ Philippine Communications Workers Federation (SAUS)
PCWG .... Personal Conferencing Work Group (SAUS)
PC-WNIM... Personal Computer Wide Area Network Interface Module (TSSD)
PCWO .... Production Control Work Order (MCD)
PCWP .... Pulmocapillary Wedge Pressure (SAUS)
PCWP .... Pulmonary Capillary Wedge Pressure [*Medicine*]
PCWPC...... Permanent Committee of the World Petroleum Congress (BUAC)
PCWPC...... Permanent Council of the World Petroleum Congress (SAUS)
PCW Reactor... Primary Cooling Water Reactor (SAUS)
PCWTU...... Philippine Woman's Christian Temperance Union (BUAC)
PCWU .... Port Commissioners Workers' Union [*India*]
PCX.......... Pacificorp [*NYSE symbol*] (SAG)
PCX.......... PacifiCorp 8.55%'QUIDS' [*NYSE symbol*] (TTSB)
PCX.......... Paracervical [*Medicine*] (EDAA)
PCX.......... Peripheral Channel Exchange (SAUS)
PCx .... Periscopic Convex [*Ophthalmology*]
PCX.......... Picture Exchange (SAUS)
PCX.......... Picture Exchange Format (ODA)
PCX.......... Picture Image (SAUS)
PCX.......... Plasma Confinement Experiment [*Physics*]
PCX.......... Portable Chest X-Ray [*Medicine*] (BCRP)
PCX.......... Private Communications Exchange (GART)
PCX.......... Process Control Executive (MHDI)
PCXR .... Portable Chest X-Ray (CPH)
PC-XT .... Personal Computer-Extended Technology (SAUS)
PCXU .... Shirlstar Container Transport [*Intermodal shipping container symbol*] (TVRC)
PCX Unit.... Peripheral Computer Exchange Unit (SAUS)
PCY.......... Aquila Air, Inc. [*ICAO designator*] (FAAC)
PCY.......... Pacific Cypress Minerals Ltd. [*Vancouver Stock Exchange symbol*]
PCY.......... Pittsburgh, Chartiers & Youghiogheny Railway Co. [*AAR code*]
PCY.......... Plastocyanin
PCY.......... Practically [*Telegraphy*] (PCTE)
PCY.......... Prerogative Court of York [*English court previously having jurisdiction over wills*]
PCYC .... Pharmacyclics, Inc. [*NASDAQ symbol*] (SAG)
PCYF .... President's Council on Youth Fitness (EA)
PCYF .... Progressive Conservative Youth Federation of Canada
PCZ.......... Canal Zone [*ANSI three-letter standard code*] [*Obsolete*] (CNC)
PCZ.......... Panama Canal Zone [*Panama*] [*Airport symbol*] (AD)
PCZ.......... Paracomp Technology, Inc. [*Vancouver Stock Exchange symbol*]
PCZ.......... Petro-Canada [*NYSE symbol*] (SAG)
PCZ.......... Petro-Canada Variable Vtg [*NYSE symbol*] (TTSB)
PCZ.......... Physical Control Zone (NASA)
PCZ.......... Positive Control Zone (DNAB)
PCZ.......... Procarbazine [*Antineoplastic drug*] (DAVI)
PCZ.......... Prochlorperazine [*Antiemetic*]
PCZ.......... Waupaca, WI [*Location identifier*] [*FAA*] (FAAL)
PCZPP...... Petro-Canada Installm't Vtg [*NYSE symbol*] (TTSB)
PCZST ...... Panama Canal Zone Standard Time (SAUS)
PD .... Cleveland Plain Dealer (SAUS)
PD .... Democratic Party [*Ecuador*] [*Political party*] (PD)
PD .... Democratic Party (Romania) [*Political party*] (PSAP)
PD .... Doctor of Pedagogy
PD .... Doctor of Pharmacy
PD .... Doctor of Philosophy (WDAA)
Pd............ Dorsal Pressure Neuron [*of a leech*]
PD .... Dublin Pharmacopoeia
PD .... Interpupillary Distance
PD .... Law Reports, Probate, Divorce, and Admiralty Division [*1875-90*] [*England*] [*A publication*] (DLA)
PD .... Packed Data (SAUS)
PD .... Packet Driver (SAUS)

PD .... Packetization Delay (SAUS)
PD .... Packing Density (SAUS)
p/d .... Packs per Day [*Cigarettes*] [*Medicine*]
PD .... Pad (MCD)
PD .... Page Directory (SAUS)
PD .... Paget's Disease [*Medicine*]
Pd .... Paid (EBF)
pd .... Paid (ODBW)
PD .... Paid
PD .... Paid Daily (SAUS)
PD .... Palisade Diabase [*Geology*]
PD .... Palladium
Pd .... Palladium [*Chemical element*]
PD .... Pallet Decoupler (SAUS)
PD .... Pancreatic Divisum [*Medicine*]
PD .... Pancreatic Duct [*Anatomy*]
PD .... Panel Display (ELAL)
PD .... Panic Disorder (DIPS)
PD .... Pants Down [*At a disadvantage*] [*Slang*] (DSUE)
pd .... Papilla Diameter [*Medicine*]
PD .... Papillary Distance
PD .... Papillary Duct [*Medicine*] (MELL)
PD .... Paralytic Dose (SAUS)
PD .... Paralyzing Dose [*Pharmacology*] (DAVI)
PD .... Parental Ditype [*Genetics*]
PD .... Parish District (SAUS)
PD .... Parity Digit (SAUS)
PD .... Parke-Davis [*Commercial firm*] (DAVI)
PD .... Parkinsonism Dementia [*Medicine*]
PD .... Parkinson's Disease [*Medicine*]
PD .... Pars Distalis [*Medicine*]
PD .... Part Damaged (ROG)
PD .... Partial Delivery (SAUS)
PD .... Partial Denture (MELL)
PD .... Partial Depletion (SAUS)
PD .... Partial Derivative (SAUS)
PD .... Partial Discharge [*High-voltage testing*] (IEEE)
PD .... Participatory Design (SEWL)
PD .... Particle-Density [*Forensic science*]
PD .... Particle Dynamics (SAUS)
PD .... Parti Democratique [*Democratic Party*] [*Luxembourg*] Political party] (EAIO)
PD .... Partido Democrata [*Democratic Party*] [*Costa Rica*] [*Political party*] (PPW)
PD .... Partido Democrata [*Democratic Party*] [*Chile*] [*Political party*]
pd .... Passed (ODBW)
PD .... Passed
PD .... Passive Defence (SAUS)
PD .... Passive Detection [*Electronics*]
PD .... Past Due
PD .... Paste-Down [*Album*] [*Photography*] (ROG)
PD .... Patent Ductus [*Cardiology*] (MAE)
PD .... Pattern Detection (SAUS)
PD .... Pavement Design (SAUS)
PD .... Pay and Display [*Vehicle parking operations*]
PD .... Pay Department [*Army*] [*British*] (ROG)
PD .... Pay Dirt
PD .... Payload Developer (SAUS)
PD .... Payload Diameter
PD .... Peak Detector
PD .... Pedestal (IAA)
PD .... Pediatric [*or Pediatrics*]
Pd .... Pediatrics (DMAA)
PD .... Pem Air [*ICAO designator*] (AD)
PD .... Pen Down (SAUS)
P/D .... Penetration Diameter [*Military*]
PD .... People's Democracy [*Ireland*] [*Political party*]
PD .... Pepper Dust [*An adulterating element*]
PD .... Percent Difference (SAUS)
PD .... Percutaneous Drain [*Surgery*] (DAVI)
PD .... Per Day (SAUS)
pd .... Per Diem [*By the day*] [*Latin*] (WDMC)
PD .... Per Diem [*By the Day*] [*Latin*]
PD .... Per Diliquium [*By Deliquescence*] [*Pharmacy*] (ROG)
PD .... Perfect Diffuser [*Optics*]
PD .... Performance Data (SAUS)
PD .... Performance Demonstration (MCD)
PD .... Performer Diploma (PGP)
PD .... Periderm [*Botany*]
PD .... Period (AABC)
PD .... Periodic Duty (IAA)
PD .... Peripheral Decoder (SAUS)
PD .... Peripheral Device (BUR)
PD .... Periscope Depth (IAA)
PD .... Peritoneal Dialysis [*Medicine*]
PD .... Permanent Deactivation
PD .... Permanent Dunnage (SAUS)
PD .... Permissible Dose (SAUS)
PD .... Permits Division [*Environmental Protection Agency*] (GFGA)
PD .... Perphenazine Decanoate (SAUS)
PD .... Personal Disposition [*G. W. Allport*] (DIPS)
PD .... Personality Disorder (MELL)
PD .... Personnel Department
PD .... Personnel Depot (SAUS)
PD .... Personnel Development
PD .... Personnel Distribution [*Army*]
PD .... Perthes' Disease (MELL)
PD .... Peyronie's Disease (MELL)
PD .... Pharmacopoeia of Dublin (SAUS)
PD .... Pharmacy Director
PD .... Pharmacy Dispenser [*British military*] (DMA)
PD .... Phase-Change Dual (SAUS)
PD .... Phase Detection (SAUS)
PD .... Phase Discriminator
PD .... Phase Distortion (SAUS)
PD .... Phelps Dodge [*NYSE symbol*] (TTSB)
PD .... Phelps Dodge Corp. [*NYSE symbol*] (SPSG)
PD .... Phenyldichlorarsine [*A war gas*]
PD .... Philosophiae Doctor [*Doctor of Philosophy*]
PD .... Philosophy Doctor (SAUS)
PD .... Phosphate Dehydrogenase
PD .... Phosphate Dextrose (DAVI)
PD .... Phosphodiester [*Organic chemistry*]
PD .... Photodesorption (SAUS)
PD .... Photo-Detection (or Detector) (SAUS)
PD .... Photodielectric (SAUS)
PD .... Photodiode
PD .... Photo Distance (SAUS)
PD .... Photosensitivity Dermatitis [*Medicine*] (DMAA)
PD .... Phyllis Dorothy James White [*In name P. D. James*] [*Author*]
PD .... Physical Damage [*Insurance*]
PD .... Physical Development (IAA)
PD .... Physical Disabilities
PD .... Physical Distribution (ADA)
PD .... Physically Disabled (SAUS)
PD .... Physics Department
PD .... Picknick Dam [*TVA*]
PD .... Picks Disease (SAUS)
P/D .... Pickup and Deposit
PD .... Pictorial Display (MCD)
PD .... Piece Dyed (SAUS)
PD .... Pierce's Disease [*Plant pathology*]
PD .... Pilot Dogs (EA)
PD .... Piskei Din Shel Bet ha-Mishpat ha-'Elyon le-Yisrael (BJA)
PD .... Pitch Circle Diameter [*Technical drawings*] (IAA)
PD .... Pitch Diameter
PD .... Pitch Down (MCD)
PD .... Pitcher Defense (SAUS)
P/D .... Pitch-to-Diameter (SAUS)
PD .... Pivoted Door (AAG)
PD .... Plan and Design [*Automotive engineering*]
PD .... Planar-Doped (SAUS)
PD .... Plane Disagreement [*Telecommunications*] (TEL)
PD .... Planned Derating [*Electronics*] (IEEE)
PD .... Planning Directive (NG)
PD .... Planning Document
PD .... Plans Division [*Military*]
PD .... Plant Deficiency (SAUS)
PD .... Plasma Defect [*Hematology*] (DAVI)
PD .... Plasma Deposited (IAA)
PD .... Plasma Desorption [*of ions for analysis*]
PD .... Plasma Display
PD .... Plasmodesmata [*Botanical cytology*]
PD .... Plastic Drum Institute
PD .... Plate Dissipation
PD .... Platelet Deaggregation [*Hematology*]
PD .... Plausible Deniability
PD .... Plotting Display (IAA)
PD .... Plug & Display (SAUS)
PD .... Plumbing Damage (ADWA)
PD .... Point Defense
PD .... Point Delay Fuze [*Army*]
PD .... Point Detonating [*Projectile*]
PD .... Polar Distance [*Navigation*]
P/D .... Polarizer/Diplexer (SAUS)
PD .... Police Department
PD .... Policy Determination (GNE)
PD .... Polydipsia (SPVS)
pd .... Pond [*Pound*] [*Monetary unit*] [*Afrikaans*]
PD .... Pontoon Dock
PD .... Pool Density [*Pisciculture*]
PD .... Poor Decals
PD .... Poorly Differentiated [*Medicine*]
PD .... Population Density (NRCH)
PD .... Population Distribution (NRCH)
PD .... Population Doubling
PD .... Porak-Durante [*Disease*] [*Medicine*] (DB)
PD .... Pore Diameter
PD .... Porphobilinogen Deaminase [*Clinical chemistry*] (MAE)
PD .... Porsche Design
PD .... Port Director
PD .... Port Du [*Carriage Forward*] [*French*]
PD .... Port Dues
PD .... Porting Demonstration (SAUS)
PD .... Port of Debarkation [*Navy*]
PD .... Position Description
PD .... Position Document
PD .... Position Doubtful [*Nautical charts*]

PD .... Positive Definite (SAUS)
PD .... Positive Density (SAUS)
PD .... Positive Displacement
PD .... Positives and Deposition (DGA)
PD .... Postage Due
PD .... Postal District
PD .... Post Dated (WDAA)
PD .... Post Diluvium [*After the Flood*] [*Latin*] (ROG)
PD .... Post District (SAUS)
PD .... Postdoctorate
PD .... Posterior Deltoid [*Myology*]
PD .... Posterior Digestive [*Gland*]
PD .... Postnasal Drainage [*Medicine*]
PD .... Postural Drainage [*Medicine*] (MAE)
PD .... Potassium Dichromate (SAUS)
pd .... Potential Difference (MELL)
PD .... Potential Difference [*Electricity*]
PD .... Pound (ROG)
PD .... Powell Duffryn (EFIS)
PD .... Power Density (SAUS)
PD .... Power Dissipation (VLIE)
PD .... Power Distribution
PD .... Power Divider (IAA)
PD .... Power Doubler (IAA)
PD .... Power Driven (IAA)
PD .... Precision Device [*British military*] (DMA)
PD .... Precision Drilling (1987) Ltd. [*Toronto Stock Exchange symbol*]
PD .... Precision Drilling Corp. [*Toronto Stock Exchange symbol*] [*Canada*]
PD .... Predeployment
P/D .... Predicted [*NASA*] (KSC)
PD .... Predictive Dialer (GART)
PD .... Pre-Digital (SAUS)
PD .... Predilute
PD .... Preference for Duty
PD .... Pregnanediol [*Biochemistry*]
PD .... Preliminary Design
PD .... Prescription Drug
PD .... Present Disease (SAUS)
PD .... Presidential Declaration [*Emergency Management*] (EMA)
PD .... Presidential Determination
PD .... Presidential Directive
PD .... Press Division [*Environmental Protection Agency*] (GFGA)
PD .... Pressor Dose [*Medicine*]
PD .... Pressure Demand (SAUS)
PD .... Pressure Destillate (SAUS)
Pd .... Pressure, Diastolic [*Cardiology*]
PD .... Pressure Difference (SAUS)
PD .... Pressure Distillate (IAA)
PD .... Pressure Dose (SAUS)
PD .... Pressure Drop (KSC)
PD .... Presumptive Disability [*Title XVI*] [*Social Security Administration*] (OICC)
PD .... Pretty Disgusting (WDAA)
PD .... Prevention Detention [*Scotland Yard*]
PD .... Preventive Dentistry (DAVI)
PD .... Preventive Detention (SAUS)
PD .... Prime Depot (SAUS)
PD .... Prime Driver
PD .... Primer Driver (SAUS)
PD .... Principal Directorate (SAUS)
PD .... Principal Distance [*Graphic arts*] (OA)
PD .... Printer Driver
PD .... Printer's Devil (ROG)
PD .... Priority Designator [*Army*]
PD .... Priority Directive
PD .... Prism Diopter
PD .... Prisoner's Dilemma [*Psychology*]
PD .... Privatdozent [*Tutor*] [*German*]
PD .... Private Detective
PD .... Probability Density [*Statistics*] (IAA)
PD .... Probability of Damage (MCD)
PD .... Probability of Death [*Biology*]
PD .... Probability of Destruction (SAUS)
PD .... Probability of Detection
PD .... Probate Division (SAUS)
PD .... Problem Definition [*Army*]
PD .... Problem Determination (SAUS)
PD .... Procedure Division (VLIE)
PD .... Procedures Description (COE)
PD .... Procesing Data (SAUS)
PD .... Process Data (NITA)
PD .... Process Descriptor [*Telecommunications*] (IAA)
PD .... Process Design [*Automotive engineering*]
PD .... Process Diagnostic [*Interpersonal skills and attitudes test*]
PD .... Procurement Data
PD .... Procurement Directive [*Army*]
PD .... Procurement District [*Air Force*] (AFIT)
PD .... Procurement Division
PD .... Procurement Document (NASA)
PD .... Procurement Drawing
pd .... Pro Defendente [*On Behalf of Defendant*] [*Latin*] [*Legal term*] (DLA)
PD .... Product Definition (SAUS)
PD .... Product Design [*Phase*]
P/D .... Product Development
PD .... Production and Deployment Phase [*Military*] (MCD)
PD .... Production Department
PD .... Production Director (NTCM)
PD .... Professional Development (ADA)
PD .... Professional Digital [*Recording*] (NTCM)
PD .... Professional Diploma [*Education*] (AEE)
PD .... Profile Descent (GAVI)
PD .... Programa Democratico [*Democratic Program*] [*Spain*] [*Political party*] (PPE)
PD .... Program Deceleration (KSC)
PD .... Program Decoder
PD .... Program Development (SAUS)
PD .... Program Directive (NG)
PD .... Program Director [*Television*]
PD .... Program Document (SAUS)
PD .... Programmable Device (SAUS)
PD .... Programming Device (SAUS)
PD .... Progression of Disease [*Medicine*]
PD .... Progressive Democrats [*Ireland*] [*Political party*]
PD .... Project Definition (SAUS)
PD .... Project Description (EEVL)
PD .... Project Development (ABAC)
PD .... Project Directive (NASA)
PD .... Project Director
PD .... Project Document
PD .... Project Documentation (SAUS)
PD .... Projected Decision Date (NRCH)
PD .... Projected Display
PD .... Projection Distance (SAUS)
PD .... Promotion Director
PD .... Promotion Dossier (HEAS)
PD .... Propagation Delay (MLOA)
PD .... Propellant Dispersal (NAKS)
PD .... Propellant Dispersion (KSC)
PD .... Property Damage
PD .... Property Disposition [*FHA*] (EMRF)
PD .... Propodite-Dactylopodite (SAUS)
PD .... Proportional Derivative (IAA)
PD .... Proportional-Differential (SAUS)
PD .... Proportional Plus Derivative (IAA)
PD .... Proposal Development (AAG)
PD .... Prostatodynia [*Medicine*]
PD .... Protective Device (BUR)
PD .... Protective Dose (SAUS)
PD .... Protein Diet (DMAA)
PD .... Protocol Driver (SAUS)
PD .... Proto-Dravidian [*Linguistics*] (IEL)
PD .... Prototype Demonstration
PD .... Provisioning Document
PD .... Provocation Dose [*Medicine*] (MEDA)
PD .... Proximity Detector
PD .... Prussian Dollar [*Monetary unit*] (ROG)
PD .... Pseudohomogeneous Axial Dispersion Model [*Fluid dynamics*]
PD .... Psychodynamic
Pd .... Psychopathic Deviate [*Psychology*]
PD .... Psychotic Depression [*Medicine*]
PD .... Psychotic Deviate [*Psychiatry*] (DAVI)
PD .... Publication Date [*Online database field identifier*]
PD .... Public Defender [*Australia*]
PD .... Public Domain
PD .... Published Document (SAUS)
PD .... Publisher's Directory [*Formerly, BPD*] [*A publication*]
PD .... Pulley Drive (IAA)
PD .... Pulmonary Disease [*Medicine*]
PD .... Pulpodistal [*Dentistry*]
PD .... Pulsed Doppler (SAUS)
PD .... Pulse Detector [*Spectroscopy*]
PD .... Pulse Doppler
PD .... Pulse Driver
PD .... Pulse Duration
PD .... Punch Delay (SAUS)
PD .... Punch Die (SAUS)
P-D .... Punch-Die (MSA)
PD .... Punch Driver
PD .... Punched Data (SAUS)
PD .... Punching Device (SAUS)
pd .... Pupillary Distance [*Medicine*]
PD .... Purchase Description
PD .... Pushdown (SAUS)
PD .... Pyloric Dilator [*Neuron*]
PD .... Pyramidal Decussation [*Neuroanatomy*]
PD .... Pyrimidine Dimer (ODA)
PD1 .... Portable Dictionary 1 [*English/Japanese electronic dictionary*] [*Sanyo Electric*]
PDA .... Pacific Dance Association (EA)
PDA .... Pacific Dermatologic Association (EA)
PDA .... Packaging Distributors Association [*British*] (DBA)
PDA .... Paediatric Allergy (SAUS)
PDA .... Panhellenic Dental Association (BUAC)
PDA .... Parallel Data Adapter
PDA .... Parallel Drive Array [*Computer science*] (CIST)
PDA .... Parametric Design Analysis (RDA)
PDA .... Parenteral Drug Abuser (STED)
PDA .... Parenteral Drug Association (MELL)

PdA.......... Partei der Arbeit [*Labor Party*] [*Switzerland*] [*Political party*] (PPE)
PDA.......... Parti Democratico da Angola [*Democratic Party of Angola*] [*Political party*]
PDA.......... Partido Democratico Arubano [*Democratic Party of Aruba*] [*Political party*] (EY)
PDA.......... Parti Dolonti Applicandum [*Apply to Painful Part*] [*Pharmacy*] (ROG)
PDA.......... Partit Democrata d'Andorra [*Andorran Democratic Party*] [*Political party*] (PPW)
Pd'A.......... Partito d'Azione [*Action Party*] [*Italy*] [*Political party*] (PPE)
PDA.......... Parts Disposal Area (MCD)
PDA.......... Party of Democratic Action [*Bosnia-Herzegovina*] [*Political party*] (EY)
PDA.......... Pasadena Energy [*Vancouver Stock Exchange symbol*]
PDA.......... Patent Ductus Arteriosus [*Cardiology*]
PDA.......... Patents and Designs Act (SAUS)
PDA.......... Patient Data Automation
PDA.......... Patient Distress Alarm (STED)
PDA.......... Payload Accommodations (SAUS)
PDA.......... Payroll Deduction Authorization (MCD)
PDA.......... Peak Distribution Analyzer
PdA.......... Pediatric Allergy [*Medicine*] (DMAA)
PDA.......... Pediatric Allergy
PDA.......... Pentadecanoic Acid [*Organic chemistry*]
PDA.......... Percent Defective Allowable (MHDB)
PDA.......... Perdigao SA ADS [*NYSE symbol*]
PDA.......... Periodontal Abscess (MELL)
PDA.......... Peripheral Data Acquisition (SAUS)
PDA.......... Permanent Duty Assignment [*Air Force*] (AFM)
PDA.......... Personal Data Assistant
PDA.......... Personal Death Awareness (SAUS)
PDA.......... Personal Deposit Account [*Banking*]
PDA.......... Personal Digital Assistant [*Computer science*]
PDA.......... Petrol Dealers' Association [*British*]
PDA.......... Phased-Doppler Anemometer (SAUS)
PDA.......... Phenylenediamine [*Chemistry*]
PDA.......... Philadelphia Dance Alliance
PDA.......... Phorbol Diacetate [*Organic chemistry*]
PDA.......... Photodiode Array [*Instrumentation*]
PDA.......... Photographic Dealers' Association [*British*] (BI)
PDA.......... Photon Detector Assembly (MCD)
PDA.......... Physical Device Address [*Computer science*] (IBMDP)
PDA.......... Piperidinedicarboxylic Acid [*Organic chemistry*]
PDA.......... Pisatin Demethylase [*An enzyme*]
PDA.......... Platinum Database Analyzer [*Computer science*] (HODG)
PDA.......... Plywood Distributors Association (SAUS)
PDA.......... Point Density Analysis [*Mathematics*]
PDA.......... Point Director Array
PDA.......... Pointing Device Adapter [*Computer science*]
PDA.......... Poise Distribution Amplifier (AFM)
PDA.......... Polarization Diversity Array
PDA.......... Polydiacetylene [*Organic chemistry*]
PDA.......... Polydiarylamine (SAUS)
PDA.......... Poly(dimethylacrylamide) [*Organic chemistry*]
PDA.......... Polydrug Abuse (MELL)
PDA.......... Ponta Delgada [*Azores*] [*Seismograph station code, US Geological Survey*] (SEIS)
PDA.......... Population and Community Development Association [*Thailand*] (BUAC)
PDA.......... Population Drainage Area [*Civil Defense*]
PDA.......... Portable Diagnostic Analyzer (SSD)
PDA.......... Portable Digital Assistant (SEWL)
PDA.......... Port Defence Area (SAUS)
PDA.......... Port Development Authority (SAUS)
PDA.......... Post Acceleration (IAA)
PDA.......... Post-Deflection Accelerator (DEN)
PDA.......... Post-Delivery Availability [*Military*] (NVT)
PDA.......... Post-Design Analysis
PDA.......... Post Diffused Alloyed (SAUS)
PDA.......... Posterior Descending Artery [*Anatomy*] (DAVI)
PDA.......... Potato Dextrose Agar [*Culture media*]
PDA.......... Pour Dire Adieu [*To Say Farewell*] [*On visiting cards*] [*French*]
PDA.......... Power Distribution Assembly (KSC)
PDA.......... Precision Drive Axis (KSC)
PDA.......... Predelivery Acceptance Test [*NASA*]
PDA.......... Predialyzed Human Albumin [*Medicine*] (MAE)
PDA.......... Predicted Drift Angle [*Navigation*]
PDA.......... Predocketed Application (NRCH)
PDA.......... Pregnancy Discrimination Act [*An amendment to Title VII of the Civil Rights Act of 1964*] (PAZ)
PDA.......... Pregnancy Discrimination Act of 1978 (WYGK)
PDA.......... Preliminary Damage Assessment [*Department of Emergency Management*] (DEMM)
PDA.......... Preliminary Design Acceptance (NRCH)
PDA.......... Preliminary Design Activity (LAIN)
PDA.......... Preliminary Design Approval [*or Authorization*] (NRCH)
PDA.......... Preliminary Design Assessment [*Nuclear energy*] (NRCH)
PDA.......... Preliminary Design Audit (SAUS)
PDA.......... Preliminary Design Authorization (SAUS)
PDA.......... Presbyterian Disaster Assistance [*Emergency Management*] (EMA)
PDA.......... Prescription Drug Abuse (MELL)
PDA.......... Present Duty Assignment Option [*Military*]
PDA.......... Primary Data Acquisition (SAUS)
PDA.......... Princeton Diagnostics Labs (EFIS)
PDA.......... Principal Decision Authority (DOMA)
PDA.......... Principal Deputy for Acquistion [*Army*] (RDA)
PDA.......... Principal Developing Agency (POLM)
PDA.......... Principal Development Activity [*Navy*]
PDA.......... Principal Development Authority (MCD)
PDA.......... Principal Diagonal Artery [*Anatomy*] (DAVI)
PDA.......... Principal DOD Executive (AAGC)
PDA.......... Private Doctors of America [*Defunct*] (EA)
PDA.......... Private Doctors of Australia (SAUS)
PDA.......... Probabilistic Decision Algorithm [*Artificial intelligence job performance aid*] [*Army*]
PDA.......... Probabilities Decision Analysis (SAUS)
PDA.......... Probability Density Analyzer (SAUS)
PDA.......... Probability Discrete Automata (IEEE)
PDA.......... Probability Discrete Automation
PDA.......... Probability Distribution Analyzer [*Statistics*]
PDA.......... Probably Disappointed Again (PCM)
PDA.......... Probate, Divorce, and Admiralty [*British*] (DLA)
PDA.......... Problem Determination Aid (EECA)
PDA.......... Problem Determination Application (VLIE)
PDA.......... Procedure Departure Authorization (SAUS)
PDA.......... Process Defect Average [*Quality management*]
PDA.......... Process Design Analysis [*Program*]
PDA.......... Processor and Distribution Assembly [*Viking lander analysis equipment*] [*NASA*]
PDA.......... Procurement Defense Agencies [*DoD*]
PDA.......... Product Departure Authorization
PDA.......... Production Data Acquisition [*Computer science*] (VLIE)
PDA.......... Professional Designers' Association (BUAC)
PDA.......... Professional Drivers Association
PDA.......... Program Developing Agency [*Military*] (CAAL)
PDA.......... Project on Defense Alternatives [*Association*] (EA)
PDA.......... Prolonged Depolarizing Afterpotential [*Neurophysiology*]
PDA.......... Propanediamine [*Organic chemistry*]
PDA.......... Propellant Drain Area (NASA)
PDA.......... Property Disposal Account [*Military*] (NG)
PDA.......... Property Disposal Agency
PDA.......... Property Disposal Agent [*Military*] (NG)
PDA.......... Property Disposal Authorization (SAUS)
PDA.......... Property Disposition Authorization
PDA.......... Proposed Development Approach [*Navy*]
PDA.......... Propylenediamine [*Organic chemistry*]
PDA.......... Prospectors' and Developers' Association [*Canada*]
PDA.......... Prototype Development Associate
PDA.......... Public Display of Affection [*Slang*]
PDA.......... Puerto Inirida [*Colombia*] [*Airport symbol*] (OAG)
PDA.......... Pulmonary Disease Anemia [*Medicine*] (STED)
PDA.......... Pulse Demodulation Analysis
PDA.......... Pulse Discrimination Analysis (SAUS)
PDA.......... Pulse Distribution Amplifier
PDA.......... Pump Distributors Association [*British*] (DBA)
PDA.......... Pump Distributors Association of Great Britain (BUAC)
PDA.......... Pump Drive Assembly
PDA.......... Punch Die Assembly (SAUS)
PDA.......... Push Down Acceptor (SAUS)
PDA.......... Pushdown Automation [*Computer science*] (HGAA)
PDAAP...... Plume Data Analysis of Advanced Propellants (MCD)
PDAB........ Para-(Dimethylamino)benzaldehyde [*Organic chemistry*]
PDAB........ P-Dimethyl Amino Benzaldehyde (SAUS)
PDAB........ Physical Disability Appeals Board [*Military*] (AFM)
PDAC........ Professional Development Advisory Committee [*American Occupational Therapy Association*]
PDAC........ Prospectors and Developers Association of Canada (EAIO)
PDA CRSP... Pond Dynamics/Aquaculture Collaborative Research Support Program (RCD)
PDAD........ Photodiode Array Detector [*Spectrophotometry*]
PDAD........ Probate, Divorce, and Admiralty Division [*Legal*] [*British*] (ROG)
PDAD........ Proposed Draft Addendum (SAUS)
PDAES....... Proceedings of the Devon Archaeological Exploration Society (SAUS)
PDAF........ Provincial Department of Agriculture and Forestry (SAUS)
PDAFSC..... Projected Duty Air Force Specialty Code (AFM)
PDAID....... Problem Determination Aid [*Computer science*] (MDG)
PDA J Pharm Sci Technol... PDA Journal of Pharmaceutical Science and Technology (SAUS)
PDAK........ Party of Democratic Action for Kosovo [*Serbia*] [*Political party*] (BUAC)
PDA-KM..... Party of Democratic Action of Kosovo-Metohija [*Serbia*] [*Political party*] (EY)
PDAL........ Post-Deflection Acceleration Lens (SAUS)
PDalCM..... College Misericordia, Dallas, PA [*Library symbol*] [*Library of Congress*] (LCLS)
PDAM....... Periodontal Disease-Associated Microbiotae [*Dentistry*]
PDAM....... Proposed Draft Amendment (SAUS)
PD&C........ Plug Drive and Control (SAUS)
PD & C...... Postural Drainage and Clapping [*Medicine*] (DAVI)
PD&C........ Power Distribution and Control
PD & D...... Product Design & Development [*Radnor, PA*] [*A publication*]
PD & E...... Provisioning Documentation and Effort [*Military*] (AFIT)
PD & P...... Postural Drainage and Percussion [*Medicine*] (DAVI)
PD&P........ Project Definition and Planning (CIST)
PD & PL.... Property Damage and Public Liability [*Insurance*] (IIA)
PD & R...... Policy Development and Research
PD & RS.... Payload Deployment and Retrieval Subsystem [*NASA*] (NASA)
PDanMHi... Montour County Historical Society, Danville, PA [*Library symbol*] [*Library of Congress*] (LCLS)

PDanSH ..... Danville State Hospital, Danville, PA [*Library symbol*] [*Library of Congress*] (LCLS)
PDAP .... Palmer Drug Abuse Program (DMAA)
PD ap .... Postural Drainage and Percussion [*Medicine*] (BCRP)
PDAP .... Program Data Analysis Plan (SAUS)
PDAP .... Programmable Digital Autopilot (MCD)
PDAP .... Provincial Development Assistance Program [*Agency for International Development*]
PDAP .... Publication Design and Ad Placement (DGA)
PDAPS ...... Pollution Detection and Prevention System (SAUS)
PDAR .... Parts Drawing Approval Request (MCD)
PD/AR .... Photosensitivity Dermatitis and Actinic Reticuloid Syndrome [*Medicine*] (DMAA)
PDAR .... Preferential Departure [*Aviation*] (DA)
PDAR .... Preferential Departure and Arrival Route [*FAA*] (TAG)
PDAR .... Producibility Design Analysis Report (AAG)
PDAR .... Product Disposition Authorization Report (SAUS)
PDAR .... Program Description and Requirements [*NASA*] (NASA)
PDA Rec .... PDA Recorder (SAUS)
PDARR ...... Production Drawing and Assembly Release Record (AAG)
PDARS ...... Pulsed Doppler Acoustic Radar System (SAUS)
PDAS .... Paid Associate (SAUS)
PDA-S .... Party of Democratic Action of the Sandjak [*Serbia*] [*Political party*] (EY)
PDAS .... PDA Engineering [*NASDAQ symbol*] (COMM)
PDAS .... Personal Digital Assistants
PDAS .... Photo Data Analysis System [*Navy*]
PDAS .... Photodiode Array Spectrophotometer [*Marine science*] (OSRA)
PDAS .... Physiological Data Acquisition System (SAUS)
PDAS .... Plant Data Acquisition System (NRCH)
PDAS .... Police Department American Samoa (SAUS)
PDAS .... [*A*] Popular Dictionary of Australian Slang [*A publication*]
PDAS .... Portable Data Acquisition System (MCD)
PDAS .... Process Design Analysis System (CIST)
PDAS .... Programmable Data Acquisition System (IDOE)
PDAS .... Programming and Design Assist System (SAUS)
PDAS .... Pulmonary Disease-Anemia Syndrome (MELL)
PDASD ...... Principal Deputy Assistant Secretary of Defense
PDASH ...... Principal Deputy Assistant Secretary of Health [*Emergency Management*] (EMA)
PDAT .... Portable Digital Access Transceiver (ACAE)
PDate .... Pay Date
PDATE .... Production Date [*Computer science*]
PDA Tube ... Post-Deflection Accelerated Tube (SAUS)
PDAU .... Physical Data Access Unit (SAUS)
PDAU .... Physical Delivery Access Unit (VLIE)
PDAV .... Parkinson's Disease Association of Victoria [*Australia*]
PDAX .... Protex Industries [*Private rail car owner code*]
P (Day) ...... Production Day [*Army*] (AABC)
Pd B .... Bachelor of Pedagogy
PDB .... Democratic Bolivian Party [*Political party*] (PSAP)
PDB .... Isotope Standard for Carbon (SAUS)
PDB .... Packard Data Bank (EA)
PDB .... Paget's Disease of Bone (MELL)
PDB .... Para-Dichlorobenzene [*Insecticide for moths, etc.*]
PDB .... Parallel Data Base (SAUS)
PDB .... Parametric Data Base
PDB .... Partei der Deutschsprachigen Belgier [*Party of German-Speaking Belgians*] [*Political party*] (PPW)
PDB .... Pedro Bay [*Alaska*] [*Airport symbol*] (OAG)
PDB .... Pee Dee Belemnite [*An isotopic standard for oxygen and carbon*]
PDB .... Pentadecylbenzene [*Organic chemistry*]
PDB .... Performance Data Base (GAVI)
PDB .... Performance Data Book (NASA)
PDB .... Periodical Directories and Bibliographies [*A publication*]
PDB .... Personality Data Base
PDB .... Phorbol Dibutyrate [*Also, PDBu*] [*Organic chemistry*]
PDB .... Phosphorus-Dissolving Bacteria [*Microbiology*]
PDB .... Physical Data Base [*Computer science*] (VLIE)
PDB .... Piedmont Bancorp, Inc. [*AMEX symbol*] (SAG)
PDB .... Pierce's Disease Bacterium [*Plant pathology*]
PDB .... Pilot Database (SAUS)
PDB .... Piplod Devgad Baria Railway [*Indian Railway*] (TIR)
PDB .... Planar-Doped Barrier (SAUS)
PDB .... Plant Damage Bin [*Environmental science*] (COE)
PDB .... Plasma Diagnostic Base
PDB .... Police Discipline Board [*New South Wales, Australia*]
PDB .... Positive Displacement Blower
PDB .... Potato Dextrose Broth [*Microbiology*]
PDB .... Power Disc Brakes [*Automotive term*]
PDB .... Power Distribution Box (NASA)
PDB .... Preliminary Draft Budget (EURO)
PDB .... President's Daily Brief
PDB .... Price Decontrol Board [*Post-World War II*]
PDB .... Primary Data Bus [*Computer science*]
PDB .... Primary Dispersal Base (CCCA)
PDB .... Process Data Base (SAUS)
PDB .... Process Descriptor Base [*Telecommunications*] (TEL)
PDB .... Process Display Data Base [*Computer science*] (ECII)
PDB .... Product Description Block (SAUS)
PDB .... Program Definition Block (NITA)
PDB .... Program Development & Budget (ALAC)
PDB .... Project Data Base (SAUS)
PDB .... Project Development Brochure [*Military*]
PDB .... Protein Data Bank [*Brookhaven National Laboratory*] [*Information service or system*] (CRD)
PDB .... Psychic Detective Bureau (EA)
PDB .... Public Debt Bureau (SAUS)
PDBA .... Pacific Dragon Boat Association (EA)
PDBA .... Personnel Database Application (MCD)
PDBA/SIPM ... Personnel Database Application / Student Instructor Performance Module (DNAB)
PDBD .... Polydibenzodioxin [*Plastics*]
PDBF .... Polydibenzofuran [*Plastics*]
PDBH .... Production Broach (AAG)
PDBIN .... Processor Data Bus In (MHDI)
PDBM .... Pulse Delay Binary Modulation (MCD)
PDBMI .... Periodical Directories and Bibliographies Master Index [*A publication*]
PDBP .... Powered Disposal Bomb Pod (AAG)
PDBR .... Page-Directory Base Register [*Computer science*] (BYTE)
PDBR .... Physical Data Base Record [*Computer science*] (VLIE)
PDBS .... Pictorial Data Base System (SAUS)
PDBU .... Pesticides Documentation Bulletin
PDBu .... Phorbol Dibutyrate [*Also, PDB*] [*Organic chemistry*]
PD Bus ...... Process Data Bus (SAUS)
PDBz .... Phorbol Dibenzoate [*Organic chemistry*]
PDC .... Center for Parallel Computers (SAUS)
PDC .... Community College of Philadelphia, Philadelphia, PA [*OCLC symbol*] (OCLC)
PDC .... Mueo [*New Caledonia*] [*Airport symbol*] (OAG)
PDC .... Pacific Defense College (CINC)
PDC .... Pacific Development Corp. (SAUS)
PDC .... Pacific Digital Cellular (CGWS)
PDC .... Pacific Disaster Center (SAUS)
PDC .... Package Design Council [*New York, NY*] (EA)
PDC .... Packaging Design Criteria (SAUS)
PDC .... Pacte Democratica per Catalunya [*Democratic Pact for Catalonia*] [*Spain*] [*Political party*] (PPE)
PDC .... Page Description Communications [*Microsoft Corp.*] (PCM)
PDC .... Paleoenvironmental Database of China (SAUS)
PDC .... Palm Desert, CA [*Amtrak Busline code*]
PDC .... Paper Distribution Centers
PDC .... Paper Distribution Council (EA)
PDC .... Paper Double Cotton (SAUS)
PDC .... Parallel Data Communicator (AAG)
PDC .... Parallel Data Controller
PDC .... Parallel Digital Computer (SAUS)
PDC .... Parametric Defense Coverage
PDC .... Park Distance Control [*Automotive electronics*]
PDC .... Parkinsonism Dementia Complex [*Medicine*] (EDAA)
PDC .... Parti Democrate Chretien [*Christian Democratic Party*] [*Burundi*] [*Political party*]
PDC .... Parti Democrate-Chretien Suisse [*Christian Democratic Party of Switzerland*] [*Political party*] (PPE)
PDC .... Parti des Democrates Camerounais [*Political party*] (EY)
PDC .... Partido da Democracia Cristao [*Christian Democratic Party*] [*Portugal*] [*Political party*] (PPW)
PDC .... Partido Democracia Cristiana [*Christian Democratic Party*] [*Guatemala*] [*Political party*] (PPW)
PDC .... Partido Democrata Cristiano [*Christian Democratic Party*] [*Panama*] [*Political party*] (PPW)
PDC .... Partido Democrata Cristiano [*Christian Democratic Party*] [*Bolivia*] [*Political party*] (PPW)
PDC .... Partido Democrata Cristiano [*Christian Democratic Party*] [*Costa Rica*] [*Political party*] (PPW)
PDC .... Partido Democrata Cristiano [*Christian Democratic Party*] [*Honduras*] [*Political party*] (PPW)
PDC .... Partido Democrata Cristiano [*Christian Democratic Party*] [*Paraguay*] [*Political party*] (PPW)
PDC .... Partido Democrata Cristiano [*Christian Democratic Party*] [*Peru*] [*Political party*] (PPW)
PDC .... Partido Democrata Cristiano [*Christian Democratic Party*] [*El Salvador*] [*Political party*]
PDC .... Partido Democrata de Confianza Nacional [*Nicaragua*] [*Political party*] (EY)
PDC .... Partido Democratico Cristao [*Christian Democratic Party*] [*Brazil*] [*Political party*]
PDC .... Partido Democratico Cristiano [*Christian Democratic Party*] [*Argentina*] [*Political party*] (PPW)
PDC .... Partido Democratico Cristiano [*Christian Democratic Party*] [*Chile*] [*Political party*] (PPW)
PDC .... Partisan Defence Committee (BUAC)
PDC .... Partito della Democrazia Cristiana [*Christian Democratic Party*] [*Italy*] [*Political party*]
PDC .... Partners for Democratic Change [*An association*] (EA)
PDC .... Parts Distribution Center (SAUS)
PDC .... Passive Data Collection
PDC .... Peace and Development Council (Myanmar) [*Political party*] (PSAP)
PDC .... Pediatric Cardiology [*Medical specialty*] (DHSM)
PDC .... Penang Development Corp. (SAUS)
PDC .... Pentadecylcatechol [*An allergen*]
PDC .... Peoples Defense Committee (SAUS)
PDC .... Peoria Disposal Company (EFIS)
PDC .... Per Diem, Travel and Transportation Allowance Committee for Departments of the Army, Navy, and Air Force
PDC .... Performance Data Computer
PDC .... Performance Development Corp. (SAUS)
PDC .... Period and Damping Controlled (SAUS)
PDC .... Periodical Distributors of Canada (SAUS)

PDC......... Peripheral Device Controller [*Computer science*] (VLIE)
PDC......... Permanent Data Call (SAUS)
PDC......... Personal Data Cartridge (GART)
PDC......... Personal Digital Cellular (GART)
PDC......... Personnel Data Card
PDC......... Personnel Despatch Centre (SAUS)
PDC......... Personnel Dispersal Centre (SAUS)
PDC......... Personnel Distributing Center (SAUS)
PDC......... Personnel Distribution Command
PDC......... Peru Debt Campaign (BUAC)
PDC......... Petroleum Development Corp. (EFIS)
PDC......... Petroleum Distribution Command (SAUS)
PDC......... Philosophy Documentation Center (EA)
PDC......... Photo-Data Card [*Trademark*] [*Computer science*]
PDC......... Photonuclear Data Center [*National Institute of Standards and Technology*]
PDC......... Physical Dependence Capacity [*Medicine*] (EDAA)
PDC......... Physical Development Centre (SAUS)
PDC......... Pieve Di Cadore [*Italy*] [*Seismograph station code, US Geological Survey*] [*Closed*] (SEIS)
PDC......... Pinney Dock [*Federal Railroad Administration identification code*]
PDC......... Pioneer Drilling Co. [*AMEX symbol*]
PDC......... Piston-Driven Compaction (MCD)
PDC......... Plasma Dioxin Concentration [*Medicine*] (EDAA)
PDC......... Plastic Dielectric Capacitor
PDC......... Pneumatic Damping Control
PDC......... Polaris Documentation Control [*Missiles*]
PDC......... Policy Determination Committee (AAG)
PDC......... Polycrystalline Diamond Compact [*Well drilling technology*]
PDC......... Polycrystalline Diamond Compact Drill Bit
PDC......... Polystyrene Dielectric Capacitor
PDC......... Population Documentation Center [*Food and Agriculture Organization*] [*United Nations*] [*Information service or system*] (IID)
PDC......... Portable Data Carrier
PDC......... Portable Data Communications [*British*]
PDC......... Position Depth Charge
PDC......... Power Demand Charges (SAUS)
PDC......... Power Disk Cartridge (SAUS)
PDC......... Power Distribution and Control
PDC......... Power Distribution Center [*Automotive engineering*]
PDC......... Power Distribution Control (SAUS)
PDC......... Power Distribution Cubiale (NATG)
PDC......... Practice Depth Charge
PDC......... Prairie Du Chien, WI [*Location identifier*] [*FAA*] (FAAL)
PDC......... Precedence [*Telegraphy*] (PCTE)
PDC......... Predecessors and Defunct Companies (NITA)
PDC......... Predefined Command (MCD)
PDC......... Predeparture Check [*Aviation*] (AIA)
PDC......... Pre-Departure Clearance [*FAA*] (TAG)
PDC......... Predetection Combining (IAA)
PDC......... Predocketed Construction (NRCH)
PDC......... Pregnancy Distress Center (SAUS)
PDC......... Preliminary Diagnostic Clinic
PDC......... Premission Documentation Change [*NASA*] (KSC)
PDC......... Premium and Dispersion Credits [*Insurance*]
PDC......... Prescott Development Corp. [*Vancouver Stock Exchange symbol*]
PDC......... Presely Cos. 'A' [*NYSE symbol*] (TTSB)
PDC......... Presley Co. [*NYSE symbol*] (SPSG)
PDC......... Pressure Die Casting [*Commercial firm*] [*British*]
PDC......... Prevention of Deterioration Center [*Defunct*] (EA)
PDC......... Price Decontrol Board [*Post-World War II*] [*A publication*] (DLA)
PDC......... Primary Development Contract (SAUS)
PDC......... Primary Domain Controller [*Computer science*] (VLIE)
PDC......... Primary Dtstribution Course (SAUS)
PDC......... Printing Density Controller (SAUS)
PDC......... Printing Desk Calculator (SAUS)
PDC......... Private Diagnostic Clinic
PDC......... Probability of Detection and Conversion [*Military*]
PDC......... Process Data Collector (TIMI)
PDC......... Procurement Document Change (NASA)
PDC......... Production Decision Criteria
PDC......... Production Drawing Control
PDC......... Productive Data Corp. (IID)
PDC......... Productivity and Development Center [*Philippines*] (BUAC)
PDC......... Professional Developers Conference (SAUS)
PDC......... Professional Development Center (SAUS)
PDC......... Professional Development Committee (SAUS)
PDC......... Proficiency Data Card [*Army*]
PDC......... Program Data Cards (OICC)
PDC......... Program Data Coordinator (MCD)
PDC......... Program Development Computer (COE)
PDC......... Programmable Data Controller (SAUS)
PDC......... Programmable Desk Calculator (ELAL)
PDC......... Programmable Digital Clock (SAUS)
PDC......... Programmable Digital Controller (PDAA)
PDC......... Programmes Directorate Committee [*British*]
PDC......... Programming, Design & Construction System (SAUS)
PDC......... Project Data Card
PDC......... Project Data Control (MCD)
PDC......... Project Data Coordinator
PDC......... Project Design Criteria (SAUS)
PDC......... Project Development Corp. (SAUS)
PDC......... Prolog Development Center (SAUS)
PDC......... Prolonged Detention Care (CPH)
PDC......... Proposal Development Center (SAUS)
PDC......... Prosthetic Distribution Center [*Veterans Administration*]
PDC......... Proteus Digital Channel (SAUS)
PDC......... Psychodevelopment Checklist [*Psychology*] (DAVI)
PDC......... Publications Distribution Center [*Military*] (AFM)
PDC......... Public Disclosure Commission
PDC......... Public Dividend Capital (PDAA)
PDC......... Public Documents Commission [*Government agency*]
PDC......... Publishers' Data Center, Inc.
PDC......... Pulse Discharge Cleaning (SAUS)
PDC......... Pulse-Duration Commutator
PDC......... Punched Data Carrier (SAUS)
PDC......... Pure Direct Current [*Electronics*] (IAA)
PDC......... Pyridinium Dichromate [*Organic chemistry*]
PDC......... Pyrotechnic Devices Checker
PDC......... Pyruvate Decarboxylase [*An enzyme*]
PDC......... Pyruvate Dehydrogenase Complex [*Also, PDHC*] [*Biochemistry*]
PDC......... Single Paper Double Cotton [*Wire insulation*] (AAG)
PDCA........ Painting and Decorating Contractors of America (EA)
PDCA........ Pennsylvania and Delaware Cleaners Association (EARSL)
PDCA........ Pile Driving Contractors Association (NTPA)
PDCA........ Pioneer Dairymen's Club of America (EA)
PDCA........ Plan-Do-Check-Act [*Medicine*] (DMAA)
PDCA........ Posterior Descending Coronary Artery [*Medicine*] (MELL)
PDCA........ Primary Degenerative Cerebral Disease [*Medicine*] (MELL)
PDCA........ Pug Dog Club of America (EA)
PDCA........ Purebred Dairy Cattle Association (EA)
PDCA........ United States Professional Diving Coaches Association (EA)
PDCAB...... Packet Services Compatibility Advisory Board (SAUS)
PDCAU...... Pete Duel - Clube da Amizade do Universo [*Pete Duel Universal Friendship Club - PDUFC*] (EAIO)
PDCC........ Print and Drawing Council of Canada [*1976*] (NGC)
PDCD........ Primary Degenerative Cerebral Disease [*Medicine*] (DMAA)
PD-CD Drive... Phase Change Dual Compact Disk Drive [*Computer science*] (ITCA)
PDCE........ Paramagnetic Design and Cost Effectiveness (SAUS)
PDCE........ Parametric Design and Cost Effectiveness (SAUS)
PDCE........ Parametric Design/Cost Effectiveness (SAUS)
PDCE........ Passive Defence Control Element (SAUS)
PDCG........ Partido Democracia Cristiana Guatemalteca [*Guatemalan Christian Democratic Party*] [*Political party*] (PPW)
PDCH........ Parti Democratique Chretien d'Haiti [*Political party*] (EY)
PDCH........ Physical Data Channel (SAUS)
PDCI........ Package Design Council International (SAUS)
PDCI........ Parti Democratique de la Cote-D'Ivoire [*Democratic Party of the Ivory Coast*] [*Political party*] (PPW)
PDCI........ Product Data Call-In (EEVL)
Pdck........ Probability of Detection Conversion and Kill [*for an interceptor system*] [*Military*]
PDCL........ Provisioning Data Check List [*NASA*] (KSC)
PDCM........ Phelps Dodge-Morenci [*Federal Railroad Administration identification code*]
PDCM........ Positive Displacement Coring Motor (SAUS)
PDCN........ Partido Democratico de Cooperacion Nacional [*Democratic Party of National Cooperation*] [*Guatemala*] [*Political party*]
PDCN........ Phelps Dodge-New Cornelia [*Federal Railroad Administration identification code*]
PDCN........ Production Development Change Notice
PDCN........ Public Data Communications Network [*Library science*]
PDC Newsletter... Prevention of Deterioration Center Newsletter (SAUS)
PDCO........ Patterson Dental [*NASDAQ symbol*] (TTSB)
PDCO........ Patterson Dental Co. [*NASDAQ symbol*] (SAG)
PDCO........ Property Disposal Contracting Officer [*Military*]
PDCP........ Pilot's Display Control Panel
PDCP........ Private Development Corp. of the Philippines
PDCPAC..... People for Digital Competition PAC [*Washington, DC*] (PACS)
PDCPD...... Polydicyclopentadiene [*Organic chemistry*]
PDCR........ Project Data Compliance Report (MCD)
PDCR........ Proprietary Data Control Record (NASA)
PDCRC...... Periodontal Disease Clinical Research Center [*State University of New York at Buffalo*] [*Research center*] (RCD)
PDCS........ Parallel Digital Computing System
PDCS........ Partito Democratico Cristiano Sammarinese [*Christian Democratic Party of San Marino*] [*Political party*] (PPE)
PDCs........ People's Defence Committees (Ghana) [*Political party*] (PSAP)
PDCS........ Performance Data Computer System (MCD)
PDCS........ Power Distribution and Conditioning System (SAUS)
PDCS........ Power Distribution and Control System [*or Subsystem*] [*NASA*] (NASA)
PDCS........ Processing Distribution and Control System
PDCS........ Product Data Control System (TIMI)
PDCS........ Programmable Data Collection System [*Military*] (CAAL)
PDCS........ Propellant Development & Characterization Subcommittee [*Joint Army, Navy, NASA, Air Force*]
PDCS........ Prototype Die Casting Service
PD-CSE...... Pulsed Doppler Cross-Sectional Echocardiography [*Medicine*] (DMAA)
PDCSTBL... Peripheral Device Control and Status Table (SAUS)
PDC System... Pre-Detection Combining System (SAUS)
PDCT........ PDC Trucking Company [*Common carrier symbol*]
PDCU........ Peoria Disposal [*Intermodal shipping container symbol*] (TVRC)
PDCU........ Plotting Display Control Unit
PDCU........ Power Distribution and Control Unit
PDCZ........ Portland Development Commission [*Federal Railroad Administration identification code*]

Pd D......... Doctor of Pedagogy
PDD......... Package Designation and Description File (DOMA)
PDD......... Packed Decimal Data (SAUS)
PDD......... Pancreatic Dorsal Duct [*Anatomy*]
PDD......... Partial Discharge Detector (SAUS)
PDD......... Participacion Democratica de Tzquierda [*Chile*] [*Political party*] (EY)
PDD......... Past Due Date
PDD......... Patients Dental Dictionary (SAUS)
PDD......... Percent Depth Dose [*Medicine*] (MELL)
PDD......... Peridontal Disease (MELL)
PDD......... Personal Digital Devices (AGLO)
PDD......... Personnel Detection Device (SEWL)
PDD......... Pervasive Developmental Disorder [*Medicine*]
PDD......... Petty Delinquency Detention (SAUS)
PDD......... Phenyldodecane [*Organic chemistry*]
PDD......... Phorbol Didecanoate [*Organic chemistry*]
PDD......... Physical Damage Division [*Navy*]
PDD......... Physical Data Description (VLIE)
PDD......... Physical Defense Division [*Army*]
PDD......... Physical Device Driver [*Computer science*] (VLIE)
PDD......... Platinum Diamminodichloride [*Cisplatin and cis-platinum*] [*Antineoplastic drug*] (DAVI)
PDD......... Player Detection Device (SAUS)
PDD......... Plotting Data Distributor (MCD)
PDD......... Portable Digital Document (SAUS)
PDD......... Post Dialing Delay [*Telecommunications*] (TEL)
PDD......... Post Due Date (SAUS)
PDD......... Preceded [*Telegraphy*] (PCTE)
PDD......... Precise Delay Detonator (ODA)
PDD......... Precision Depth Digitizer [*Oceanography*]
PDD......... Pre-Dental Discomfort (SAUS)
PDD......... Preferred Delivery Date (AFM)
PDD......... Preliminary Design and Development (MCD)
PDD......... Premenstrual Dysphoric Disorder [*Proposed psychiatric diagnosis*]
PDD......... Premodulation Processor - Deep Space - Data
PDD......... Presidential Decision Directive
PDD......... Primary Degenerative Dementia [*Medicine*]
PDD......... Primary Demyelinating Disease [*Medicine*] (EDAA)
PDD......... Principal Distribution Depot [*DoD*]
PDD......... Priority Delivery Date (AFM)
PDD......... Probability Density Distribution [*Statistics*]
PDD......... Process Distillate Discharge (SAUS)
PDD......... Processor Description Database [*Computer science*] (VLIE)
PDD......... Procurement Description Data [*DoD*]
PDD......... Product Definition Data [*Computer science*] (VLIE)
PDD......... Product Delivery Device (SAUS)
PDD......... Professional Development Degree (SAUS)
PDD......... Professional Development Division [*American Occupational Therapy Association*]
PDD......... Program Description Document [*Military*] (CAAL)
PDD......... Program Design Data
PDD......... Program Design Document (ADWA)
PDD......... Program Development Department (SAUS)
PDD......... Program Dimension Drawing (MCD)
PDD......... Program Directive Document (RDA)
PDD......... Progressive Diaphyseal Dysplasia [*Medicine*] (MELL)
PDD......... Projected Data Display
PDD......... Projected Decision Date (NRCH)
PDD......... Proposal Due Date (SAUS)
PDD......... Prospective Decision Date (NRCH)
PDD......... Protable Digital Document (SAUS)
PDD......... Provisioning Description Data
PDD......... Public Documents Department [*Government Printing Office*]
PDD......... Pulse Delay Device
PDD......... Puy-De-Dome [*France*] [*Seismograph station code, US Geological Survey*] [*Closed*] (SEIS)
PDD......... Pyridoxine-Deficient Diet (MAE)
PDD......... Rela Product Development Division (EFIS)
PDDA........ Power-Driven Decontaminating Apparatus (SAUS)
PDDA........ Power Driver Decontamination Apparatus (NATG)
PDDAIO..... Parts for Direct Decode Analog Input/Output (MCD)
PDDB........ Phenododecinium [*or Phenoxyethyldimethyl-dodecylammonium*] Bromide [*Antiseptic*]
PDDB........ Product Definition Database (MCD)
PDD Base... Processor Description Data Base (SAUS)
PDDC........ Proceed Directly on Course [*Aviation*] (FAAC)
PDDC........ Progressive Die Design by Computer (SAUS)
PDD/CRASH... Problem Drinking Driver/Court Referred Action for Safer Highways (SAUS)
PDDD........ Program Demonstration and Development Division [*ACTION*]
PDDF........ Portable Document Delivery Format (SAUS)
PDDF........ Post-Decision Document File (SAUS)
PDDF........ Propargyl(dideaza)folic Acid [*Biochemistry*]
PDDGM..... Past District Deputy Grand Master [*Freemasonry*]
PDDI........ Product Data Definition Interface (SAUS)
PDDI........ Product Definition Data Interface (MCD)
PD Div'l Ct... Probate, Divorce, and Admiralty Divisional Court [*England*] (DLA)
PDDL........ Perpendicular Diffraction Delay Line (PDAA)
PDDLS...... Post D-Day Logistic Support [*Army*] (AABC)
PDDM....... Disciples of the Divine Master [*Roman Catholic women's religious order*]
PDDM....... Pious Disciples of the Divine Master (TOCD)
PDD/NOS... Pervasive Developmental Disorder, Not Otherwise Specified
PDDP........ Parallel Data Distribution Preprocessor (SAUS)
PDDP........ Product Design and Development Program (SAUS)
PDDR........ Product Definition Data Requirements (SPST)
PDD/RDD... Priority Delivery Date/Required Delivery Date (AFM)
PDDS........ Parasitic Disease Drug Service (MAE)
PDDS........ Peoria District Dental Society (SAUS)
PDDS........ Program Definition Data Sheet
PDD Sheet... Program Definition Data Sheet (SAUS)
PDDT........ Page Device Description Table (VLIE)
PDDU........ Process Development and Demonstration Unit (SAUS)
PDE......... Page-Directory Entry [*Computer science*] (BYTE)
PDE......... Pandie Pandie [*Australia*] [*Airport symbol*] [*Obsolete*] (OAG)
PDE......... Parade
Pde......... Parade [*Record label*]
PDE......... Paroxysmal Dyspnea on Exertion [*Medicine*]
PDE......... Partei fuer Deutschland und Europa [*Party for Germany and Europe*] [*Germany*] [*Political party*] (PPW)
PDE......... Partial Differential Equation
PDE......... Particle Dispersion Experiment (SAUS)
PDE......... Paste Down Ends [*Graphic arts*] (DGA)
PDE......... Pediatric Endocrinology [*Medical specialty*] (DHSM)
PdE......... Pediatric Endocrinology [*Medicine*] (EDAA)
PDE......... Personnel Development and Education (MCD)
PDE......... Phosphatidyl(dimethyl)ethanolamine [*Biochemistry*]
PDE......... Phosphodiesterase [*An enzyme*]
PDE......... Photon Drag Effect (SAUS)
PDE......... Pigeon-dropping Extract [*Medicine*] (EDAA)
PDE......... Pilot's Discrete Encoder
PDE......... Plain Deckle Edges [*Graphic arts*] (DGA)
PDE......... Portable Development Environment [*Computer science*] (VLIE)
PDE......... Position Determination Entity [*Navigation systems*]
PDE......... Position-Determining Equipment
PDE......... Post-test Disassembly Examination (SAUS)
PDE......... Precede [*Telegraphy*] (PCTE)
PDE......... Preliminary Determination of Epicenter [*Seismology*]
PDE......... Pride International [*NYSE symbol*]
PDE......... Pride Resources Ltd. [*Vancouver Stock Exchange symbol*]
PDE......... Principal DOD [*Department of Defense*] Executive
PDE......... Producers' Durable Equipment (GFGA)
PDE......... Product Data Exchange [*Computer science*] (VLIE)
PDE......... Production Design Engineers
PDE......... Professional Development Education [*Military*] (RDA)
PDE......... Progressive Dialysis Encephalopathy [*Medicine*] (MELL)
PDE......... Projectile Development Establishment [*British*]
PDE......... Propellant Disposition Effects
PDE......... Propulsion Driver Electronics (ACAE)
PDE......... Prospective Data Element [*Army*] (AABC)
PDE......... Pulsed Doppler Echocardiography [*Medicine*] (DMAA)
PDE......... Pulse Detonation Engine (SEWL)
PDEA........ Phenyldiethanolamine [*Organic chemistry*]
P de Ancha... Petrus de Ancharano [*Deceased, 1416*] [*Authority cited in pre-1607 legal work*] (DSA)
P de B....... Petrus de Bellapertica [*Deceased, 1308*] [*Authority cited in pre-1607 legal work*] (DSA)
P de Bp..... Petrus de Bellapertica [*Deceased, 1308*] [*Authority cited in pre-1607 legal work*] (DSA)
PDECS....... Portable Detector and Cueing System
PDED........ Partial Double Error Detecting (NITA)
PDED........ Partial Double Error Detection
PDED........ Program Development and Evaluation Division [*Environmental Protection Agency*] (GFGA)
PDEF........ Protean Data Exchange Format (SAUS)
PDEGF....... Platelet-Derived Epidermal Growth Factor [*Medicine*] (MELL)
PDEI........ Phosphodiesterase Inhibitor [*Biochemistry*]
PDEIS........ Preliminary Draft Environmental Impact Statement (SAUS)
PDEISEC ... Permanent Directory of Energy Information Sources in the European Community (SAUS)
PDEL........ Partial Differential Equation Language [*Computer science*]
P de L....... Paulus de Liazaris [*Deceased, 1356*] [*Authority cited in pre-1607 legal work*] (DSA)
PDELAN..... Partial Differential Equation Language [*Computer science*] (CSR)
PDELB....... Plumbers and Drainers' Examination and Licensing Board [*Queensland, Australia*]
PDELS....... Parallel-Detection Electron Loss Spectrometer (SAUS)
PDEM........ Personal Dust Exposure Monitor (PDAA)
PDEN........ Pet Quarters, Inc. [*NASDAQ symbol*] (QUAN)
P Dent J.... Pennsylvania Dental Journal (SAUS)
P de Orfi.... Petrus de Orfila [*Deceased, 1307*] [*Authority cited in pre-1607 legal work*] (DSA)
PDEP........ Preliminary Draft Equipment Publication (MCD)
PDEQ........ Profile of DARCOM Environmental Quality (MCD)
PDES........ Phase Image of Poly(diethylsiloxane) [*Organic chemistry*]
PDES........ Preliminary Draft Environmental Statement (NRCH)
PDES........ Product Data Exchange Specification (NITA)
PDES........ Product Data Exchange Standard [*Computer science*] (VLIE)
PDES........ Product Data Exchange using STEP [*Sequentially Timed Events Plotting*]
PDES........ Product Definition Exchange Specification [*Army*]
PDES........ Product Definition Exchange Standards (SAUS)
PDES........ Product Description Exchange Standard (SAUS)
PDES........ Pulse-Doppler Elevation Scan (PDAA)
P de Sal.... Petrus de Salinis [*Flourished, 13th century*] [*Authority cited in pre-1607 legal work*] (DSA)
P de Sam... Petrus de Sampsone [*Flourished, 1246-58*] [*Authority cited in pre-1607 legal work*] (DSA)

P de Samp... Petrus de Sampsone [*Flourished, 1246-58*] [*Authority cited in pre-1607 legal work*] (DSA)
P Det .... Port Detachment [*British military*] (DMA)
PDET .... Post-Diapause Eclosion Time [*Entomology*]
PDET .... Probability of Detection, Evaluation, and Transfer (MCD)
PDEX .... Pro-Dex, Inc. [*NASDAQ symbol*] (NQ)
PDF.......... Hancock [*John*] Patriot Premium Dividend Fund I [*NYSE symbol*] (SAG)
PDF.......... John Hancock Patr Prem Dv Fd [*NYSE symbol*] (TTSB)
PDF.......... LAR Transregional, Linhas Aereas Regionais SA [*Portugal*] [*ICAO designator*] (FAAC)
PDF.......... Pacific Dentistry Association (BUAC)
PDF.......... Package Definition File [*Computer science*] (VLIE)
PDF.......... Paget's Disease Foundation (EA)
PDF.......... Pair Distribution Function [*Physical chemistry*]
PDF.......... Pakistan Democratic Front
PDF.......... Panama Defense Forces [*Later, Public Forces*]
PDF.......... Parallel Data Field (SAUS)
PDF.......... Parallel Disk File (SAUS)
PDF.......... Parkinson's Disease Foundation (EA)
PDF.......... Particle Distribution Function
PDF.......... Parti Democrate Francais [*French Democratic Party*] [*Political party*] (PPW)
PDF.......... Passive Direction Finding
PDF.......... Patient Data Form (SAUS)
PDF.......... Pavement Depth Factor (ADA)
PDF.......... Peace Development Fund (EA)
PDF.......... Pele Defense Fund (EA)
PDF.......... People's Democratic Force [*The Bahamas*] [*Political party*] (EY)
PDF.......... Peritoneal Dialysis Fluid [*Medicine*] (DMAA)
PDF.......... Piecewise Data Flow (SAUS)
PDF.......... Pigmented Dermatofibroma [*Medicine*] (MELL)
PDF.......... Planar Deformation Feature [*Geology*]
PDF.......... Planet Drum Foundation (EA)
PDF.......... Plant Design Factor [*Nuclear energy*] (NRCH)
PDF.......... Plant Design Flood [*Nuclear energy*] (GFGA)
PDF.......... Platform Independent File Format [*Computer science*]
PDF.......... Point Detonating Fuze [*Army*]
PDF.......... Polar Density Function (SAUS)
PDF.......... Pooled Development Funds [*Economics*]
PDF.......... Popular Defence Force (SAUS)
PDF.......... Popular Defence Forces [*Sudan*] [*Political party*]
PDF.......... Popular Democratic Front [*Jordan*] [*Political party*]
PDF.......... Porsche Dual-Function Transmission [*Automotive engineering*]
PDF.......... Portable Document File [*Computer science*] (PCM)
PDF.......... Portable Document Format [*Computer science*]
pdf.......... Portable Document Format [*Computer science*]
PDF.......... Post Defense Force
PDF.......... Post Detection Filter [*Telecommunications*] (TEL)
PDF.......... Postdoctoral Fellow (SAUS)
PDF.......... Powder Diffraction File (DICI)
PDF.......... Power Diffraction File (NITA)
PDF.......... Power Distribution Frame (SAUS)
PDF.......... Precision Direction Finder (SAUS)
PDF.......... Primary Direction of Fire (SAUS)
PDF.......... Primordial Density Fluctuation [*Cosmology*]
PDF.......... Principal Direction of Fire [*Military*]
PDF.......... Printer Description File (SAUS)
PDF.......... Private Database Facility (SAUS)
PDF.......... Probability Density Function [*Statistics*]
PDF.......... Probability Distribution Function [*Statistics*]
PDF.......... Problem Data Field (SAUS)
PDF.......... Processor Defined Function
PDF.......... Production and Distribution of Foodstuffs [*British*]
PDF.......... Program Data File
PDF.......... Program Data Form [*Army*]
PDF.......... Program Development Facility [*Computer science*] (MHDI)
PDF.......... Project Design Flood (NRCH)
PDF.......... Protected Difference Fat (OA)
PDF.......... Pyruvate Dehydrogenase (DMAA)
PDFA .... Partnership for a Drug Free America (SAUS)
PDF Architecture... Piecewise Data Flow Architecture (SAUS)
PDFC .... Power Dissipation Factor per Column (SAUS)
PDFC .... Premature Dead Female Child (DAVI)
PDFCS....... Pennsylvania Dutch Folk Culture Society (EA)
PDFD .... Predemonstration Fusion Device
PDFD .... Pulsed Doppler Frequency Diversity (NG)
PDFES....... Pitch-Synchronous Digital Feature Extraction System (PDAA)
PDFG .... Planar Distributed Function Generator (PDAA)
PDFG .... Platelet-Derived Growth Factor [*Endocrinology*] (DAVI)
PDFI .... Probability of Detected Fault Isolation (SAUS)
PDFIB .... Piecewise Data Flow Instruction Block (SAUS)
PDFID .... Preconstruction Direct Flame Ionization Detection (EEVL)
PDFLP....... Popular Democratic Front for the Liberation of Palestine
PDFM........ Phillips and Drew Fund Management [*England*] [*British*]
PDFRR ...... Program Directors Flight Readiness Review [*NASA*] (KSC)
PDFSR ...... Proposed Detailed Functional System Requirement (SAUS)
PDFT .... Programmable Data Formatter (SAUS)
PDFWPR.... Physical Disabilities Fieldwork Performance Report [*Occupational therapy*]
PDG.......... Padang [*Indonesia*] [*Airport symbol*] (OAG)
PDG.......... Padding
PDG.......... Parachute Drop Glider
PDG.......... Paradigm (WGA)
PDG.......... Parkinsonism-Dementia Complex of Guam [*Medicine*] (DMAA)
PDG.......... Parti Democratique de Guinee [*Democratic Party of Guinea*] [*Political party*] (PPW)
PDG.......... Parti Democratique Gabonais [*Gabonese Democratic Party*] [*Political party*] (PPW)
PDG.......... Passive Defense Group (MUGU)
PDG.......... Patent Documentation Group (DIT)
PDG.......... Patient Dependency Groups (SAUS)
PDG.......... Paymaster Director General (SAUS)
PDG.......... PDG Remediation, Inc. [*Associated Press*] (SAG)
PDG.......... Peak Detector, Gated (SAUS)
PDG.......... Pendant Drop Growth (SAUS)
PDG.......... Personalistic Discussion Group - Eastern Division (EA)
PDG.......... Phosphate-Dependent Glutaminase (STED)
PDG.......... Phosphogluconate Dehydrogenase [*Organic chemistry*] (MAH)
PDG.......... Pigment Dispersion Syndrome [*Medicine*] (EDAA)
PDG.......... Placer Dome, Inc. [*NYSE symbol*] [*Toronto Stock Exchange symbol*] [*Vancouver Stock Exchange symbol*] (SPSG)
PDG.......... Preceding [*Telegraphy*] (PCTE)
PDG.......... Precision Drop Glider [*Army*]
PDG.......... Pregnanediol Glucuronide [*Endocrinology*]
PDG.......... President Directeur General [*President Director General*] [*French*]
PDG.......... Production Development Group (IAA)
PDG.......... Professional Dyers Guild [*Defunct*]
PDG.......... Program Decision Group (ACAE)
PDG.......... Program Documentation Generator [*Computer science*] (MHDI)
PDG.......... Programmable Display Generator (SAUS)
PDG.......... Programs Development Group (MUGU)
PDG.......... Proposal Development Group [*Aerospace*] (AAG)
PDG.......... Psychiatric Diagnostic Groups (SAUS)
PDG.......... Pyruvate Dehydrogenase (DB)
PDGA........ Professional Disc Golf Association
PDGA........ Pteroyldiglutamic Acid [*Pharmacology*]
PDGDL ...... Plasma Dynamics and Gaseous Discharge Laboratory [*MIT*] (MCD)
PDGE........ Partido Democratico de Guinea Ecuatorial [*Democratic Party of Equatorial Guinea*] [*Political party*] (EY)
PDGE........ PDG Environmental [*NASDAQ symbol*] (TTSB)
PDGE........ PDG Environmental, Inc. [*NASDAQ symbol*] (SAG)
PDG En...... PDG Environmental, Inc. [*Associated Press*] (SAG)
PDGF........ Platelet-Derived Growth Factor [*Genetics*]
PDGF........ Power Data Grapple Fixture (SAUS)
PDGFA....... Platelet-Derived Growth Factor [*Medicine*] (DMAA)
PDGFR ...... Platelet-Derived Growth Factor Receptor [*Genetics*]
PD Gland ... Posterior Digestive Gland (SAUS)
PDGMS...... Peabody Developmental Gross Motor Scale
PDG-RDA ... Democratic Party of Guinea-African Democratic Assembly [*Political party*] (PSAP)
PDGS........ PDG Remediation [*NASDAQ symbol*] (TTSB)
PDGS........ PDG Remediation, Inc. [*NASDAQ symbol*] (SAG)
PDGS........ Precision Delivery Glider System
P-DGs .... Presidents-Directeurs Generaux
PDGS........ Probe Drill Guidance System
PDGS........ Product Design Graphics System [*Prime Computer Ltd.*] [*Software package*] (NCC)
PDGSW ..... PDG Remediation Wrrt [*NASDAQ symbol*] (TTSB)
PDGTN ...... Paddington, MB [*American Association of Railroads railroad junction routing code*]
PDGW....... Principal Director of Guided Weapons (SAUS)
PDGW....... Principle Directorate of Guided Weapons [*British*] (SAA)
PDGXT ...... Predischarge Graded Exercise Test [*Cardiology*] (DAVI)
PDH.......... Packaged Disaster Hospital [*Public Health Service*]
PDH.......... Pain Drug Hypnosis (SAUS)
PDH.......... Passive Defense Handbook [*Navy*] (MCD)
PDH.......... Past Dental History
PDH.......... Phosphate Dehydrogenase (MAE)
PDH.......... Plaiochronous Digital Hierarchies (SAUS)
PDH.......... Planned Derated Hours [*Electronics*] (IEEE)
PDH.......... Plesiochronous Digital Hierarchy (SAUS)
PDH.......... Pocket Dosimeter High (NAKS)
PDH.......... Professional Development Hour (SEAT)
PDH.......... Project Development History (SAUS)
PDH.......... Puromycin Dihydrochloride (SAUS)
PDH.......... Pyruvate Dehydrogenase [*An enzyme*]
PDH & DS.. Plant Data Handling and Display System [*Nuclear energy*] (NRCH)
PDHC........ Pyruvate Dehydrogenase Complex [*Biochemistry*]
PDHF........ Postdilution Hemofiltration [*Medicine*]
PDHI......... Palmer Drought Hydrological Index
PDHL .... Peak Design Heat Loss (PDAA)
PdHO........ Pediatric Hematology-Oncology (STED)
PDHV-RDA... Parti Democratique de la Haute Volta-Rassemblement Democratique Africain [*Democratic Party of Upper Volta-African Democratic Rally*]
PDI........... Institutional Democratic Party (Dominican Rep.) [*Political party*] (PSAP)
PDI........... Packet Driver Interface (SAUS)
PDI........... Pain Disability Index [*Medicine*] (DMAA)
PDI........... Palmer Drought Index
PDI........... Panel Data Interface [*Computer science*] (IAA)
PDI........... Paradise Island Airlines, Inc. [*ICAO designator*] (FAAC)
PDI........... Partai Demokrasi Indonesia [*Indonesian Democratic Party*] [*Political party*] (PPW)
PDI........... Partial Delivery Injection [*Materials science*]
PDI........... Particle Displacement Interfermetry (SAUS)
PDI........... Parti Democratique de l'Independance [*Democratic Independence Party*] [*Morocco*] [*Political party*]

PDI.......... Partito Democratica Italiana [*Italian Democratic Party*] [*Political party*] (PPE)
PDI.......... Payload Data Interleaver [*NASA*] (NASA)
PDI.......... Percentage Difference Index
PDI.......... Perfect Digital Invariant (OA)
PDI.......... Periodontal Disease Index [*Dentistry*] (DMAA)
PDI.......... Peripheral Dynamics, Inc. (SAUS)
PDI.......... Personal Data Interchange (SAUS)
PDI.......... Personal Disposable Income [*Economics*]
PDI.......... Pharmacy Dedication Information (SAUS)
PDI.......... Pictorial Deviation Indicator (AAG)
PDI.......... Picture Description Instruction [*Telecommunications*]
PDI.......... Pilot Direction Indicator [*Electronic communications*]
PDI.......... Plan-Do Intergration [*Medicine*] (DMAA)
PDI.......... Planning Decisions (IID)
PDI.......... Plastic Drum Institute (NTPA)
PDI.......... Plumbing and Drainage Institute (EA)
PDI.......... Point-Diffraction Interferometer (SAUS)
PDI.......... Polydispersity Index (SAUS)
PDI.......... Polymer Dispersion Industries (SAUS)
PDI.......... Porto D'Ischia [*Italy*] [*Seismograph station code, US Geological Survey*] [*Closed*] (SEIS)
PDI.......... Positive Displacement Injector (SAUS)
PDI.......... Post Detection Integration (MCD)
PDI.......... Potential Determining Ions
PDI.......... Powder for Injection (SAUS)
PDI.......... Power and Data Interface (SAUS)
PDI.......... Power Data Interface (TIMI)
PDI.......... Power Dissipation Index (IAA)
PDI.......... Power Doppler Imaging [*Medicine*] (RAWO)
PDI.......... Powered Descent Initiation [*Aerospace*]
PDI.......... Practice Development Institute (SAUS)
PDI.......... Pre-Delivery Inspection (DCTA)
PDI.......... Predeployment Inspection [*Navy*] (NVT)
PDI.......... Premdor, Inc. [*Toronto Stock Exchange symbol*]
PDI.......... Preschool Development Inventory [*Test*] (TMMY)
PDI.......... Pressure Differential Indicator (SAUS)
PDI.......... Prevalence, Duration and Intensity (SAUS)
PDI.......... Primary Depressive Illness (SAUS)
PDI.......... Prise Ombilicale Derniers Instants
PDI.......... Privately Developed Item (AAGC)
PDI.......... Process Data Input (SAUS)
PDI.......... Product Data Interchange (SAUS)
PDI.......... Professional Development Institute [*Canada*]
PDI.......... Program Design, Inc. [*Commercial firm*]
PDI.......... Program with Developing Institutions (EA)
PDI.......... Project Data Index [*Jet Propulsion Laboratory, NASA*]
PDI.......... Protein Dispersibility Index [*Analytical chemistry*]
PDI.......... Protein Disulfide-Isomerase [*An enzyme*]
PDI.......... Psychiatric Diagnostic Interview [*Personality development test*] [*Psychology*]
PDI.......... Psychological Distress Inventory [*Student personality test*]
PDI.......... Psychomotor Development Index [*Bayley Scales of Infant Development*]
PDI.......... Public Debt Interest (ADA)
PDI.......... Public Demographics, Inc. (IID)
PDI.......... Putnam Dividend Income [*NYSE symbol*] (SPSG)
PDI.......... Pyronetics Devices, Incorporated (ACAE)
Pdi.......... Transdiaphragmatic [*Pressure*]
PDIAL....... Public Dialup Internet Access List [*Computer science*] (CDE)
PDIC......... Periodic (AFM)
PDIC......... Professional Diving Instructors Corp. (SAUS)
PDIC......... Professional Driver Improvement Course
PDIC......... Protection Development International Corp. (SAUS)
PDID......... Public Disorder Intelligence Department (SAUS)
PDID......... Public Disorder Intelligence Division (SAUS)
PDID......... Pulse Doppler Identification (SEWL)
PDIE......... Phosphodiesterase (DMAA)
PDIF......... Product Definition Interchange Format (SAUS)
PDIF......... Putnam Dividend Income Fund [*Associated Press*] (SAG)
PDII......... Pusat Dokumentasi dan Informasi Ilmiah [*Indonesian Center for Scientific Documentation and Information*] [*Information service or system*] (IID)
PDIIS........ Priority Defense Items Information System
PDIL......... Power-Dependent Insertion Limit [*Nuclear energy*] (NRCH)
PDIN......... Pusat Dokumentasi Ilmiah Nasional (NITA)
PDIO......... Parallel Digital Input/Output
PDIO......... Photodiode
P-DIOL...... Pregnanediol [*Biochemistry*]
PDIP......... Plastic Dual In-Line Packaging (AAEL)
PDIP......... Preflight Data Insertion Program (NVT)
PDIP......... Program Development Increment Package [*Military*]
PDIP......... Program Development Integration Plan (SAUS)
PDIR......... Peripheral Data Set Information Record (SAUS)
PDIR......... Priority Disassembly and Inspection Report
PDIR......... Program Directive
PDIS......... Parts Dissection Information System
PDIS......... Payload Data Interleaver System [*NASA*] (MCD)
PDIS......... Pressure Differential Switch (IAA)
PDIS......... Proceedings of the National Symposia [*A publication*]
PDIS......... Product Description Information Standards [*or System*]
PDISCH..... Pump Discharge
PDISP....... Page Displacement (SAUS)
pDISP....... Proposed Draft International Standardized Profile (SAUS)
PDISPL...... Positive Displacement [*Engineering*]
PDIT......... Product Development Improvement Team (ACAE)
PDIT......... Provision for Deferred Income Tax
PDIUM...... Partito Democratico Italiano di Unita Monarchica [*Italian Democratic Party of Monarchical Unity*] [*Political party*] (PPE)
P Div........ Law Reports, Probate Division [*England*] [*A publication*] (DLA)
PDIWT....... Planning and Design Institute for Water Transportation [*China*] (BUAC)
PDIZ......... Produce Distributors [*Intermodal trailer symbol*]
PDJ.......... Plaine Des Jarres [*South Vietnam*]
PDJ.......... Precision Drill Jig
PDJB........ Precision Drill Jig Bushing
PD/JV........ Project Definition/Joint Validation (MCD)
PDK.......... Atlanta [*Georgia*] De Kalb/Peachtree Airport [*Airport symbol*] [*Obsolete*] (OAG)
PDK.......... Party of Democratic Kampuchea [*Cambodia*] [*Political party*] (BUAC)
PDK.......... PDK Labs, Inc. [*Associated Press*] (SAG)
PDK.......... Peripheral Developers Kit (MWOL)
PDK.......... Personal Decontamination Kit (SAUS)
PDK.......... Phase-Delay Keying [*Computer science*]
PDK.......... Phi Delta Kappa [*Fraternity*]
PDK.......... Phileleftheron Demokratikon Kendron [*Liberal Democratic Union*] [*Greek*] (PPE)
PDK.......... Phileleftheron Demokratikon Komma [*Liberal Democratic Party*] [*Greek*] [*Political party*] (PPE)
PDK.......... Polycystic Kidney Disease (MELL)
PDK.......... Poop Deck [*Naval engineering*]
PDK.......... Predict [*Telegraphy*] (PCTE)
PDK.......... Promenade Deck [*of a ship*] (DS)
PDK.......... Science Foods, Inc. [*AMEX symbol*] (SAG)
PDKD........ Predicted [*Telegraphy*] (PCTE)
PDKG........ Predicting [*Telegraphy*] (PCTE)
PDKL........ PDK Labs [*NASDAQ symbol*] (TTSB)
PDKL........ PDK Labs, Inc. [*NASDAQ symbol*] (SAG)
PDKLM...... PDK Labs Wrrt'C' [*NASDAQ symbol*] (TTSB)
PDKLP...... PDK Labs $0.49 Cv'A' Pfd [*NASDAQ symbol*] (TTSB)
PDKN........ Prediction [*Telegraphy*] (PCTE)
PDL.......... Page Description Language [*Computer graphics*]
PDL.......... Page Design Language (SAUS)
PDL.......... Parallel Data Laboratory [*Carnegie Mellon University*] (RCD)
PDL.......... Parameter Data Load (ACAE)
PDL.......... Particle Dynamics Laboratory (SAUS)
PDL.......... Particle Physics Laboratory (SAUS)
PDL.......... Partido Democrata Liberal [*Liberal Democratic Party*] [*Spain*] [*Political party*] (EY)
PDL.......... Parts Deletion List (MSA)
PDL.......... Parts Difference List (MCD)
PDL.......... Parts Documentation List (MCD)
PDL.......... Party of Democratic Left [*Slovakia*] [*Political party*] (BUAC)
PDL.......... Pass Down the Line [*Book*] [*Navy*] (MUGU)
PDL.......... Patent Depository Library [*Designated by the Patent and Trademark Office*]
PDL.......... People's Democracy of Laos [*Political party*] (VNW)
PDL.......... Periodontal Ligament [*Dentistry*]
PDL.......... Permanent Duty Location
PDL.......... Personal Driver's License [*Motor vehicle term used in state of Washington*] (MVRD)
PDL.......... Photodissociation Dye LASER
PDL.......... Picture Description Language [*Computer science*] (MHDI)
PDL.......... Placer Development Ltd. [*Toronto Stock Exchange symbol*] [*Vancouver Stock Exchange symbol*]
PDL.......... Pocket Dosimeter-Low (MCD)
PDL.......... Polarization Diversity LIDAR
PDL.......... Ponce De Leon
PDL.......... Ponta Delgada [*Portugal*] [*Airport symbol*] (OAG)
PDL.......... Poorly Differentiated Lymphocytic [*Oncology*]
PDL.......... Population Doubling Level [*Cytology*]
PDL.......... Portable Data Loader [*Aviation*]
PDL.......... Positive Diode Logic (VLIE)
pdl.......... Poundal [*Unit of force*]
PDL.......... Poverty Datum Line
PDL.......... Power Door Locks
PDL.......... Precision Delay Line
PDL.......... Preliminary Design Language [*Computer science*] (VLIE)
PDL.......... Presidential Realty Corp. [*AMEX symbol*] (SPSG)
PDL.......... Primary Defect List (SAUS)
PDL.......... Print Definition Language [*Computer science*] (EECA)
PDL.......... Procedure Definition Language [*Computer science*] (BUR)
PDL.......... Procedure Description Language
PDL.......... Procedure Distribution List (MCD)
PDL.......... Process Description Language (SAUS)
PDL.......... Process Design Language [*Computer science*] (MHDI)
PDL.......... Processor Data Load (ACAE)
PDL.......... Procurement Data List
PDL.......... Product Disaster Loans [*Small Business Administration*]
PDL.......... Professional Development League (EA)
PDL.......... Program Description Language (MCD)
PDL.......... Program Design Language (NASA)
PDL.......... Program Development Language (SAUS)
PDL.......... Program Device Librarian [*Computer science*]
PDL.......... Programmable Data Language (NITA)
PDL.......... Programmable Data Logger [*Computer science*] (VLIE)
PDL.......... Programmable Definition Logic (SAUS)
PDL.......... Programmable Digital Logic (SAUS)
PDL.......... Progressively Diffused Leukoencephalopathy [*Medicine*] (MELL)

PDL......... Project Document List
PDL......... Protocol Description Language [*Telecommunications*] (IAA)
PDL......... Publishers' Databases Ltd. [*Publishing consortium*] [*British*]
pdl......... Pudendal [*Anatomy*] (MAE)
PDL......... Pulsed Dye LASER
PDL......... Pumped Dye LASER
PDL......... Push Down List [*Computer science*] (MHDI)
PDL......... Sierra Leone Peoples Democratic League (SAUS)
PDLA........ Angolan Democratic Liberal Party [*Political party*] (PSAP)
PDL A....... Presidential Rlty Cl'A' [*AMEX symbol*] (TTSB)
PD(LAO).... Public Defender (Legal Aid Office) [*Australia*]
PDLB........ Pass Down the Line Book (SAUS)
PDL B....... Presidential Rlty Cl'B' [*AMEX symbol*] (TTSB)
PDLC........ North American Palladium [*NASDAQ symbol*] (SAG)
PDLC........ Partido Liberal de Cataluna [*Liberal Democratic Party of Catalonia*] [*Political party*] (PPW)
PDLC........ Polymer Dispersed Liquid Crystal [*Physical chemistry*]
PDLC........ Poorly Differentiated Lung Cancer [*Medicine*] (DMAA)
PDLCF....... North Amer Palladium [*NASDAQ symbol*] (TTSB)
PDLD........ Polymer-Dispersed Liquid-crystal Display (SAUS)
PDLD........ Poorly Differentiated Lymphocytic-Diffuse [*Oncology*] (DMAA)
PDLE........ Process Development Laboratory East (SAUS)
PDLF........ Pakistan Democratic Labour Federation (BUAC)
pdl-ft........ foot-poundal (SAUS)
PDL/FT^2.... Poundals per Square Foot
PDLI......... Protein Design Labs [*NASDAQ symbol*] (TTSB)
PDLI......... Protein Design Labs, Inc. [*NASDAQ symbol*] (SAG)
PDLL........ Poorly Differentiated Lymphatic [*or Lymphocytic*] Lymphoma [*Oncology*]
PDLM........ Periodic Depot Level Maintenance
PDLM........ Planned Depot Level Maintenance (MCD)
PDLM........ Programmed Depot Level Maintenance [*Air Force*]
PDLN........ Poorly Differentiated Lymphocytic-Nodular [*Oncology*] (DMAA)
PDLP........ Pacific Dunlop Ltd. [*NASDAQ symbol*] (NQ)
PDLP........ Patent Depository Library Program (SAUS)
PDLPY....... Pacific Dunlop Ltd. (MHDW)
PDLPY....... Pacific Dunlop Ltd. ADR [*NASDAQ symbol*] (TTSB)
PDLR........ Power Deck Lid Release
PDLS........ Party of the Democratic Left of Slovakia [*Former Czechoslovakia*] [*Political party*] (EY)
PDL S/FT^2... Poundal Seconds per Square Foot
PDLT........ P-Channel Depletion-Load Triode Inverter
PD/LT....... Program Design and Learning Tool (NITA)
PDLW........ Process Development Laboratory West (SAUS)
Pd M........ Master of Pedagogy
PDM......... Mexican Democrat Party [*Political party*] (PSAP)
PDM......... Parallel-Port Data Module [*Computer communications*]
PDM......... Parlance Document Manager (SAUS)
PDM......... Partial Descriptive Method
PDM......... Parti Democratique Malgache [*Malagasy Democratic Party*]
PDM......... Partido de los Democratas Melillenses [*Spanish North Africa*] [*Political party*] (MENA)
PDM......... Passenger's Door Module [*Automotive engineering*]
PDM......... Patient Data Management
PDM......... Pay Duties Manual (SAUS)
PDM......... Pendant Drop Method
PDM......... People's Democratic Movement [*Guyana*] [*Political party*] (EY)
PDM......... People's Democratic Movement [*Papua New Guinea*] [*Political party*] (FEA)
PDM......... People's Democratic Movement [*Turks and Caicos Islands*] [*Political party*] (PPW)
PDM......... Percent Deviation from the Median
PDM......... Periodic Depot Maintenance (SAUS)
PDM......... Permanent Data Memory (SAUS)
PDM......... Phase Difference Modulation (SAUS)
PDM......... Phase Displacement (IAA)
PDM......... Photographic Data Memory (SAUS)
PDM......... Physical Distribution Management
PDM......... Physiological Data Monitor
PDM......... Pilot Decision Making [*Aviation*] (DA)
PDM......... Pinch Design Method [*Heat exchange design*]
PDM......... Pipework Design Management (SAUS)
PDM......... Pitt-DesMoines Inc. [*AMEX symbol*] (TTSB)
PDM......... Pittsburgh - Des Moines, Inc. [*AMEX symbol*] (SPSG)
PDM......... Planned Depot Maintenance (SAUS)
pdm......... Podium (VRA)
PDM......... Point Defence Missile (SAUS)
PDM......... Point Distribution Model (DMAA)
PDM......... Polarization Division Multiplexing (SAUS)
PDM......... Polynomial Discriminant Method (PDAA)
PDM......... Portable Differential Magnetometer
PDM......... Positive Displacement Motor (SAUS)
PDM......... Possible Duplicate Message (TRID)
PDM......... Power Density Meter
PDM......... Power Density Monitor [*Environmental science*] (COE)
PDM......... Practical Data Manager [*Hitachi Ltd.*] [*Japan*]
PDM......... Practical Dental Monographs (SAUS)
PDM......... Precedence Diagraming Method (MCD)
PDM......... Predictive Maintenance
PDM......... Predominate [*Telegraphy*] (PCTE)
PDM......... Prehospital and Disaster Medicine (SAUS)
PDM......... Preliminary Development Model
PDM......... Preliminary Draft Manuscript
PDM......... Presidential Decision Memorandum [*Jimmy Carter Administration*]
PDM......... Primary Data Management (SAUS)
PDM......... Print Down Module
PDM......... Probabilistic Dilution Model (SAUS)
PDM......... Process Decision Model (VLIE)
PDM......... Processor Data Monitor (NASA)
PDM......... Product and Document Management (SAUS)
PDM......... Product Data Management
PDM......... Product Data Manager (SAUS)
PDM......... Product Development Manual [*Automotive project management*]
PDM......... Production Decision Criteria Matrix
PDM......... Program Data Manager (MCD)
PDM......... Program Debugging Mode [*Computer science*] (VLIE)
PDM......... Program Decision Meeting (SAUS)
PDM......... Program Decision Memorandum [*Military*]
PDM......... Program Design Manual (VLIE)
PDM......... Program Development Manager (SAUS)
PDM......... Program Development Manual (ACAE)
PDM......... Programmable Data Monitor (SAUS)
PDM......... Programmable Data Mover (SAUS)
PDM......... Programmed Depot Maintenance (MCD)
PDM......... Programmer Defined Macro [*Computer science*] (VLIE)
PDM......... Progres et Democratie Moderne [*Progress and Modern Democracy*] [*France*] [*Political party*] (PPE)
PDM......... Project Data Manual (ACAE)
PDM......... Project Design Memo
PDM......... Project Development Methodology (SAUS)
PDM......... Propellant Dispersion Munition (ACAE)
PDM......... Propellant Distribution Module (ACAE)
PDM......... Protected Difference Milk (OA)
PDM......... Publications Distribution Manager [*Military*] (AFM)
PDM......... Pulse Data Modulation [*Computer science*] (IAA)
PDM......... Pulse Delay Mechanism [*British military*] (DMA)
PDM......... Pulse Delta Modulation (IEEE)
PDM......... Pulse Duration Modulation [*Data transmission*]
PDM......... Pursuit Deterrent Mine (SAUS)
PDM......... Pursuit Deterrent Munition
PDM......... Push Down Memory [*Computer science*]
PDM3.1..... Probabilistic Dilution Model [*Version*] 3.1 [*Environment term*] (EGA)
PDMA........ Peninsula Drafting Management Association
PDMA........ Pipelined Direct Memory Access [*Computer science*] (CIST)
PDMA........ Plumbing and Drainage Manufacturers Association (SAUS)
PDMA........ Polarization Division Multiple Access (VLIE)
PDMA........ Prescription Drug Marketing Act [*1987*]
PDMA........ Product Development and Management Association [*Indianapolis, IN*] (EA)
PDMAC...... Prescription Drug Maximum Allowable Cost
PDMAMS... Product Design Minuteman Airborne Mechanical System (SAA)
PDMC........ Premature Dead Male Child (DAVI)
PDMC........ Princeton Dental Management Corp. [*NASDAQ symbol*] (SAG)
PDMC........ Princeton Dental Mgmt [*NASDAQ symbol*] (TTSB)
PDMC........ Product Development & Manufacturing Center
PDMCW..... Princeton Dental Mgmt Wrrt [*NASDAQ symbol*] (TTSB)
PDMD........ Predominated [*Telegraphy*] (PCTE)
PDME........ Peak Distortion Monitoring Equipment (SAUS)
PDME........ Pendant-Drop Melt Extraction [*Metal fiber technology*]
PDME........ Precision Distance Measuring Equipment (MCD)
PDM-FM.... Pulse-Duration Modulation - Frequency Modulation (CET)
PDMFM..... Pulse-Duration Modulation-Frequency Modulation
PDMG........ Perspective Digital Map Generator
PDMG........ Predominating [*Telegraphy*] (PCTE)
PDMLR...... Post-Development Maintainability Logistics Review (MCD)
PDMM........ Push Down Memory MODEM [*Computer science*]
PDMMS...... Product Design Minuteman Mechanical System (IAA)
PDMNT...... Piedmont
PDMO........ Production Mold (AAG)
PDMP........ Positive Displacement Mechanical [*or Metering*] Pump
PDMP........ Positive Displacement Metering Pump (SAUS)
PDMP........ Product Development Management Program (SAUS)
PDMP........ Project Data Management Plan (ACAE)
PDM/PM.... Pulse-Duration Modulation on Phase Modulation (MED)
PDMPO...... Polydimethyl Phenylene Oxide [*Organic chemistry*]
PDM-PSK... Pulse Duration Modulation-Phase Shift Keying (SAUS)
PDMR........ Provisioning Data Master Record (MCD)
PDMS........ Particle Desorption Mass Spectrometry
PDMS........ Patient Data Management Systems [*Medical records*] (DAVI)
PDMS........ Payload Data Management System (SAUS)
PDMS........ Personal Data Management System (SAUS)
PDMS........ Pesticide Document Management System [*Environmental Protection Agency*] (GFGA)
PDMS........ Pharmacokinetic Drug Monitoring Services [*Medicine*] (DMAA)
PDMS........ Photodissociation Mass Spectrometry
PDMS........ Physiological Data Monitoring System
PDMS........ Pipework Design Management System (SAUS)
PDMS........ Plant Design and Management System [*Computer Aided Design Centre*] [*Software package*] (NCC)
PDMS........ Plasma-Desorption Mass Spectrometry (ABAC)
PDMS........ Plasma Desorption Mass Spectroscopy
PDMS........ Point Defense Missile System [*NATO*] (NATG)
PDMS........ Polydimethylsiloxane [*Organic chemistry*]
PDMS........ Postal Direct Marketing Service (WDAA)
PDMS........ Power-Plant and Process Design Management System [*Computer science*]
PDMS........ Product Data Management System (ACAE)
PDMS........ Program Data and Management System (SAUS)

PDMS .... Program Definition and Management System (MCD)
PDM System... Point-Designed Memory System (SAUS)
PDMT........ Predominant [*National Weather Service*] (FAAC)
PDMU .... Passive Data Memory Unit
PDMU .... Production Mock-Up (AAG)
PDMV .... Pressure Differential Monitoring Valve
PDN.......... Packet Data Network [*Computer science*] (IGQR)
PDN.......... Partido Democratico Nacional [*National Democratic Party*] [*Chile*] [*Political party*]
PDN.......... Partido Democratico Nacional [*National Democratic Party*] [*Venezuela*] [*Political party*]
PDN.......... Partito Democratico Nazionalista [*Democratic Nationalist Party (1921-1926)*] [*Malta*] [*Political party*] (PPE)
PDN.......... Partnerships Data Net [*Defunct*] (EA)
PDN.......... Petition Denied
PDN.......... Phased-Array Doppler Noise (SEWL)
PDN.......... Physics Data Notebook (SAUS)
PDN.......... Portable Data Network [*Computer science*] (VLIE)
PDN.......... Port Heiden, AK [*Location identifier*] [*FAA*] (FAAL)
PDN.......... Positive Delivery Notification (SAUS)
PDN.......... Power Dividing Network [*Telecommunications*] (LAIN)
PDN.......... Pre-Discharge Notification (SAUS)
PDN.......... Prednisone [*Also, P, Pr, Pred, Pro*] [*Endocrinology*] [*Antineoplastic drug*]
PDN.......... Preferred Dental Network (MHID)
PDN.......... Premises Distribution Network [*Computer science*] (IGQR)
PDN.......... Private Duty Nurse (DAVI)
PDN.......... Problem Documentation Number (AAG)
PDN.......... Procedure Departure Notice (SAUS)
PDN.......... Production (AFM)
PDN.......... Properly Driven Net
PDN.......... Public Data Network [*Packet-switching network*] [*British Telecommunications Ltd.*] [*London*]
PDN.......... Putnam Diversified Premium (EFIS)
PDNC........ Parallel Digital Network Computer (VLIE)
PDNC........ Presidents' Day National Committee (EA)
PDNES ...... Pulse-Doppler Non-Elevation Scan (PDAA)
PDNF........ Prime Disjunctive Normal Form (PDAA)
PD/NSC ..... Presidential Directives/National Security Council
PDNU........ Promotora de Navegacion [*Intermodal shipping container symbol*] (TVRC)
PDO.......... Pacific Decadal Oscillation [*Climatology*]
PDO.......... Packet Data Optimized (SAUS)
PDO.......... Petroleum Development Oman (BUAC)
PDO.......... Philips & Du Pont Optical Co. [*Wilmington, DE*]
PDO.......... Phthalate Dioxygenase [*An enzyme*]
PDO.......... Physical Device Object (MWOL)
PDO.......... Plasma-Deposited Oxide (SAUS)
PDO.......... Portable Distributed Object (SAUS)
PDO.......... Port Dry Out [*Nuclear energy*] (NUCP)
PDO.......... Postman's Delivery Office (DCTA)
PDO.......... Prado [*Brazil*] [*Airport symbol*] (AD)
PDO.......... Printer Direction Optimizer (BUR)
PDO.......... Procedure Description Overview (SAUS)
PDO.......... Process Data Output (SAUS)
PD-O......... Program Directive - Operations (KSC)
PDO.......... Program Directive Operations (SAUS)
PDO.......... Property Disposal Office [*Environmental science*] (BCP)
PDO.......... Property Disposal Officer [*Army*]
PDO.......... Property Disposal Organization
PdO.......... Psychopathic Deviate Obvious [*Psychology*]
PDO.......... Publications Distribution Officer [*Military*]
PDO.......... Public Defender's Office (LAIN)
PDoB .... Bucks County Free Library, Doylestown, PA [*Library symbol*] [*Library of Congress*] (LCLS)
PDoBHi...... Bucks County Historical Society, Doylestown, PA [*Library symbol*] [*Library of Congress*] (LCLS)
PDOC........ Particulate and/or Dissolved Organic Carbon [*Chemistry*]
PDOC........ Proceed Directly on Course (SAUS)
PDOD........ Phytoplankton Dissolved Oxygen Deficit [*Oceanography*]
PDOF........ Principal Direction of Force [*Mechanical engineering*]
PDOIS....... People's Democratic Organisation for Independence and Socialism [*Senegambia*] [*Political party*]
PDOL........ Publishers Discount Option List
PDoN........ Delaware Valley College of Science and Agriculture, Doylestown, PA [*Library symbol*] [*Library of Congress*] (LCLS)
PDOP........ Position Dilution of Position [*Navigation systems*]
PDOP........ Position Dilution of Precision
PDOP........ Prospective Designated Overhaul Point (MCD)
PDOS........ Parallel and Distributed Operating System (SAUS)
PDOS........ Parallel and Distributed Operating Systems Group [*Massachusetts Institute of Technology*] (RCD)
PDOS........ Parent Diabetes Opinion Survey [*Test*]
PDOS........ Partial Density of States (ODA)
PDOS........ Process Disk Operating System (SAUS)
PDOS........ Professional Development of Officers Study
PDOS........ Publishing Distribution Office System (SAUS)
PDOS........ Purple Dinosaur Operating System (SAUS)
PDOT........ Commonwealth of Pennsylvania [*Federal Railroad Administration identification code*]
PDowN...... Newcomen Society in North America, Downingtown, PA [*Library symbol*] [*Library of Congress*] (LCLS)
P/DOZ....... Per Dozen (WDAA)
PDP.......... Moral Force Party (Thailand) [*Political party*] (PSAP)
PDP.......... Packaging Development Plan
PDP.......... Pakistan Democratic Party [*Political party*] (PD)
PDP.......... Pan-African Democratic Party (SAUS)
Pdp.......... Paradip (SAUS)
PDP.......... Parallel Data Processing [*Computer science*]
PDP.......... Parallel Detection Polychromator [*Instrumentation*]
PDP.......... Parallel Distributed Processing [*A simulation of mental processes*]
PDP.......... Parker & Parsley Petrol [*NYSE symbol*] (TTSB)
PDP.......... Parker & Parsley Petroleum [*NYSE symbol*] (SAG)
PDP.......... Parliamentary Democratic Party [*Myanmar*] [*Political party*]
PDP.......... Parti Democrate Populaire [*Popular Democratic Party*] [*France*] [*Political party*] (PPE)
PDP.......... Partido da Direita Portuguesa [*Party of the Portuguese Right*] [*Political party*] (PPE)
PDP.......... Partido Democrata Popular [*Popular Democratic Party*] [*Dominican Republic*] [*Political party*] (PPW)
PDP.......... Partido Democrata Popular [*Popular Democratic Party*] [*Spain*] [*Political party*] (PPW)
PDP.......... Partido Democratico para o Progresso [*Democratic Progressive Party*] [*Guinea-Bissau*] [*Political party*] (EY)
PDP.......... Partito Democratico Populare [*Popular Democratic Party*] [*San Marino*] [*Political party*] (PPE)
PDP.......... Party for Democracy and Progress (Burkina Faso) [*Political party*] (PSAP)
PDP.......... Party for Democracy and Progress (Tanzania) [*Political party*] (PSAP)
PDP.......... Party for Democratic Prosperity [*Macedonia*] [*Political party*]
PDP.......... Passive Driving Periscope [*Military*] (PDAA)
PDP.......... Pasture Development Plan (SAUS)
PDP.......... Pattern Disruption Point [*Medicine*] (DMAA)
PDP.......... Payload Distribution Panel [*NASA*] (MCD)
PDP.......... Payload Distribution Plan
PDP.......... Pentadecylphenol [*Organic chemistry*]
PDP.......... People Data Planning (SAUS)
PDP.......... People's Democratic [*Saint Christopher and Nevis*] [*Political party*] (EY)
PDP.......... People's Democratic Party [*Montenegro*] [*Political party*] (BUAC)
PDP.......... People's Democratic Party [*Uzbekistan*] [*Political party*] (BUAC)
PDP.......... People's Democratic Party [*Netherlands Antilles*] [*Political party*] (EY)
PDP.......... People's Democratic Party [*Sierra Leone*] [*Political party*] (EY)
PDP.......... People's Democratic Party [*South Korea*] [*Political party*] (EY)
PDP.......... People's Democratic Party [*Sudan*] [*Political party*]
PDP.......... Peripheral Data Processing (SAUS)
PDP.......... Personal Development Program (MCD)
PDP.......... Pesticide Data Program [*Environmental Protection Agency*]
PDP.......... Phenyl-Dichlorophosphine (PDAA)
PDP.......... Phi Delta Phi [*An association*] (NTPA)
PDP.......... Philadelphia, PA [*Location identifier*] [*FAA*] (FAAL)
PDP.......... Philippine Democratic Party [*Pilipino Lakas Ng Bayan*] [*Political party*] (PPW)
PDP.......... Pilot District Project [*Office of Economic Opportunity*] [*Defunct*] (EA)
PDP.......... Piperidino-Pyrimidine [*Biochemistry*] (MAE)
PDP.......... Pitch-Depitch (AAG)
PDP.......... Planning Development Program (OICC)
PDP.......... Plasma Diagnostics Package [*NASA*]
PDP.......... Plasma Display Panel [*Computer science*]
PDP.......... Plasma Display Processor [*Computer science*]
PDP.......... Polysilicon Dielectric Polysilicon [*Organic chemistry*] (IAA)
PDP.......... Popular Democratic Party [*Puerto Rico*] [*Political party*]
PDP.......... Positive Displacement Pump
PDP.......... Post Detection Processor [*Military*] (CAAL)
PDP.......... Post-Drug Potentiation
PDP.......... Post-Insertion Deorbit Preparation [*NASA*] (MCD)
PDP.......... Power Delay Product (SAUS)
PDP.......... Power Distribution Panel
PDP.......... Power Distribution Plan (SAUS)
PDP.......... Power Drain Protection [*Automotive engineering*]
PDP.......... Preconceptual Design Phase (SAUS)
PDP.......... Preliminary Definition Plan (NASA)
PDP.......... Preliminary Design Phase
PDP.......... Preliminary Design Proposal (MCD)
PDP.......... Preprototype Demonstration
PDP.......... Prescription Drug Plan [*Insurance*] (WYGK)
PDP.......... Prescription Drug Program [*Health insurance*] (GHCT)
PDP.......... Present-Day Primers [*A publication*]
PDP.......... Pressure Distribution Panel (AAG)
PDP.......... Principal Display Panel [*Packaging*]
PDP.......... Procedure Definition Processor [*Computer science*]
PDP.......... Process Data Processing (IAA)
PDP.......... Process Development Pile [*Nuclear energy*]
PDP.......... Procurement Data Package [*Military*] (AABC)
PDP.......... Product Development Pressure (SAUS)
PDP.......... Product Development Process [*Automotive engineering*]
PDP.......... Product Development Program (SAUS)
PDP.......... Product Development Protocol [*U.S. Food and Drug Administration*]
PDP.......... Product Documentation Procedures (SAUS)
PDP.......... Production Data Package (MCD)
PDP.......... Productivity Development Program (SAUS)
PDP.......... Professional Data Processor (SAUS)
PDP.......... Professional Developers Program (SAUS)
PDP.......... Professional Development Document (SAUS)
PDP.......... Professional Development Program [*Military*]
PDP.......... Program Decision Package [*Military*]
PDP.......... Program Definition Phase [*Army*]
PDP.......... Program Development Paper (MCD)
PDP.......... Program Development Plan [*NASA*]
PDP.......... Programmable Data Processor (IAA)

PDP.......... Programmable Digital Processor (SAUS)
PDP.......... Programmable Display Pushbuttons
PDP.......... Programmed Data Processor
PDP.......... Programmed Digital Processor
PDP.......... Progressive Democratic Party [*Romania*] [*Political party*] (BUAC)
PDP.......... Progressive Democratic Party [*Montserrat*] [*Political party*] (PPW)
PDP.......... Progressive Democratic Party [*St. Vincent*] [*Political party*] (PPW)
PDP.......... Project Data Package (SAUS)
PDP.......... Project Definition Phase (NRCH)
PDP.......... Project Development Plan
PDP.......... Psychopharmacology Demonstration Project [*Department of Defense*] (DIPS)
PDP.......... Punta Del Este [*Uruguay*] [*Airport symbol*] (OAG)
PDPA........ Angolan Democratic Party for Peace [*Political party*] (PSAP)
PDPA........ People's Democratic Party of Afghanistan [*Political party*] (PPW)
PDPA........ Production Pattern (AAG)
PDPA........ Project Data Processing Authorization (ACAE)
PDPAM...... Party for Democratic Prosperity of Albanians in Macedonia [*Political party*] (PSAP)
PDP-ANA.... Democratic Party for Progress-Angolan National Alliance [*Political party*] (PSAP)
PDPC........ Position Display Parallax Corrected
PDPC........ Post Detection Pulse Compression [*Military*] (CAAL)
PDP-CVS.... Positive Displacement Pump-Constant Volume Sampler (ERG)
PDPD........ Prolonged-Dwell Peritoneal Dialysis [*Medicine*] (DMAA)
PDPE........ Profit Dollar per Employee (SAUS)
Pd-PEI....... Palladium-Polyethylenimine (SAUS)
PDPF........ Packet Data Processing Facility (MCD)
PDPF........ Project Data Processing Facility (SAUS)
PDPGM...... Past Deputy Provincial Grand Master [*Freemasonry*]
PDPH........ Postdural Puncture Headache [*Medicine*] (DMAA)
PDPI......... Primer-Dependent Deoxynucleic Acid Polymerase Index [*Medicine*] (DMAA)
PDPI......... Product Development Pressure Index (SAUS)
PDPIC....... Professional Development Program Improvement Center (EDAC)
PDPL........ Property Damage, Personal Liability [*Insurance*]
PDPM....... Preliminary Draft Presidential Memo
PDPM....... Programmable Data Processing Machine (SAUS)
PDPOA...... Proposal Directive Plan of Action (MCD)
PDPR........ Per Day Pro-Rata (RIMS)
PDPR........ Present-Day Preachers [*A publication*]
PD Projectile... Point Detonating Projectile (SAUS)
PDPS........ Parts Data Processing System [*Bell Telephone*]
PDPS........ Planning and Data Production System (SAUS)
PDPS........ Problem Driver Pointer System [*NHTSA*] (TAG)
PDPS........ Program Data Processing Section (AAG)
PDPS........ Program Data Processing System (IAA)
PDPS........ Program Definition Phase Studies [*Navy*]
PDPS........ Project Data Processing System (MCD)
PDPT........ Parti Democratique des Populations Togolaises [*Togolese Democratic People's Party*] [*Political party*]
PD PT....... Production Pattern (SAUS)
PDPUB...... Pedicel Pubescence [*Botany*]
PDPVF....... Presidential and Democratic Party Victory Fund (EA)
PDQ.......... Packages Delivered Quick [*Allegheny Airlines service*]
PDQ.......... Parallel Data Query [*Computer science*] (CDE)
PDQ.......... Parental Diagnostic Questionnaire [*Speech evaluation test*]
PDQ.......... Parodies Done Quirkily [*Humorous translation of Peter Schickele's PDQ Bach*]
PDQ.......... Passed Data-set Queue (SAUS)
PDQ.......... PDQ Air Service, Inc. [*ICAO designator*] (FAAC)
PDQ.......... Peachtree Data Query (SAUS)
PDQ.......... Permanent Durable Quality [*Paper*]
PDQ.......... Personal Data Query (SAUS)
PDQ.......... Personal Description Questionnaire
PDQ.......... Personality Diagnostic Questionnaire (SAUS)
PDQ.......... Personality Disorders Questionnaire (SAUS)
PDQ.......... Pertinent Data Quest (MCD)
PDQ.......... Photo Data Quantizer
PDQ.......... Physician Data Query (SAUS)
PDQ.......... Physician's Data Query [*NIH*]
PDQ.......... Please Draw Quickly [*Initialism used as title of TV series*]
PDQ.......... Point, Digital, Qualifier [*In automobile name Opel PDQ*]
PDQ.......... Position Description Questionnaire (SAUS)
PDQ.......... Prescreening Developmental Questionnaire [*Child development test*]
PDQ.......... Pretty Darn Quick (TAG)
PDQ.......... Price and Delivery Quotations
PDQ.......... Price Delivery Quality
PDQ.......... Prime Hospitality [*NYSE symbol*] (SPSG)
PDQ.......... Prime Hospitality Corp. [*NYSE symbol*]
PDQ.......... Product Demand Quotation (SAUS)
PDQ.......... Program for Descriptive Query (SAUS)
PDQ.......... Programmed Data Quantizer
PDQ.......... Protocol Data Query [*Database*] [*National Institutes of Health*]
PDQC........ Physicians Data Query: Cancer Information File [*Database*]
PDQD........ Physicians Data Query: Directory File [*Database*]
PDQP........ Physicians Data Query: Protocol File [*Database*]
PDQX........ Port Defiance, Quinault & Klickitat Railroad [*Federal Railroad Administration identification code*]
PDR.......... Packet Drop Rate (SAUS)
PDR.......... Page Data Register
PDR.......... Paintless Dent Repair [*Automotive industry*]
PDR.......... Parent Daily Telephone Report [*Education*] (EDAC)
PDR.......... Particulate Data Reduction (EPA)
PDR.......... Parti Democratique Progressif [*Algeria*] [*Political party*] (EY)
PDR.......... Party of Democratic Reform [*Slovenia*] [*Political party*] (EY)
PDR.......... Pattern Delayed-Response [*Ophthalmology*]
PDR.......... Peak Dose Rate [*Radiation*] (AAG)
PDR.......... Pediatric Radiology [*Medical specialty*] (DHSM)
PDR.......... Pendaries Petroleum [*AMEX symbol*] (SG)
PDR.......... Peninsula Development Road (SAUS)
PDR.......... People's Democratic Republic (TVEL)
PDR.......... Performance Data Rate (SAUS)
P/DR......... Performance/Development Review (SAUS)
PDR.......... Peripheral Diabetic Retinopathy [*Medicine*] (MELL)
PDR.......... Periscope Depth Range [*SONAR*]
PDR.......... Periscope Detection RADAR (NG)
PDR.......... Pharma-Dokumentationsring [*Pharma Documentation Ring*] [*Information service or system*] (IID)
PDR.......... Phase Data Recorder (KSC)
PDR.......... Phase Delay Rectifier
PDR.......... Philippine Defense Ribbon [*Military decoration*]
PDR.......... Photodissociation [*or Photodominated*] Region [*Galactic science*]
PDR.......... Photon-Dominated Region (SAUS)
PD-R......... Physical Development by Reduction (SAUS)
PDR.......... Physicians' Desk Reference [*Also, an information service or system*] [*A publication*]
PDR.......... Pilot's Display Recorder
PDR.......... Piskei Din Shel Batei ha-Din ha-Rabaniyim be-Yisrael (BJA)
PDR.......... Pitch-to-Diameter Ratio (SAUS)
PDR.......... Plasma-Developed Resist Processing [*Lithography*]
PDR.......... Polarization Differential Reflectance (AAEL)
PDR.......... Portable Data Recorder (SAUS)
PDR.......... Position Distribution Report [*DoD*]
PDR.......... Post-Drug Repetition (SAUS)
PDR.......... Potential-Drop Ratio (SAUS)
pdr........... Pounder (MILB)
PDR.......... Pounder (MSA)
PDR.......... Powder
PDR.......... Powder for Reconstitution (SAUS)
PDR.......... Power Deck Release
PDR.......... Power Directional Relay
PDR.......... Precision Depth Recorder
PDR.......... Predecessor [*Telegraphy*] (PCTE)
PDR.......... Predetection Recording
PDR.......... Predetermined Demand Rate
PDR.......... Pre-Determined Route [*Aviation*] (DA)
PDR.......... Preferential Departure Route [*FAA*] (TAG)
PDR.......... Preliminary Data Report
PDR.......... Preliminary Data Requirements (NASA)
PDR.......... Preliminary Design Report (NRCH)
PDR.......... Preliminary Design Review (NASA)
PDR.......... Pressurized Deuterium Reactor [*Nuclear energy*]
PDR.......... Previous Document Reference (SAUS)
PDR.......... Price Description Record [*Computer science*] (IBMDP)
PDR.......... Price-Dividend Ratio (WDAA)
PDR.......... Primary Data Recording (SAUS)
PDR.......... Primary Demographic Report [*A. C. Nielsen Co.*] (NTCM)
PDR.......... Priority Data Reduction
PDR.......... Procedure Development Request (SAUS)
PDR.......... Process Description Report (SAUS)
PDR.......... Process Dynamics Recorder
PDR.......... Processed Data Recorder
PDR.......... Processing Data Rate (IEEE)
PDR.......... Processing, Distribution and Retailing (SAUS)
PDR.......... Procurement Data Reference
PDR.......... Procurement Data Reporting (SAUS)
PDR.......... Product Design Review [*Army*]
PDR.......... Production, Distribution and Retailing (SAUS)
PDR.......... Program Design Review (MCD)
PDR.......... Program Director's Review [*NASA*] (NASA)
PDR.......... Program Discrepancy Report (IEEE)
PDR.......... Program Document Requirement (BUR)
PDR.......... Program Drum Recording
PDR.......... Proliferative Diabetic Retinopathy [*Ophthalmology*]
PDR.......... Property Disposal Request (ABAC)
PDR.......... Publications Data Request
PDR.......... Public Document Room (NRCH)
PDR.......... Pulsed Dose Rate [*Medicine*] (RAWO)
PDR.......... Pulse Doppler RADAR
PDR.......... Pulse Duty Ratio
PDR.......... Purchase of Development Rights (PA)
PDRA........ Postdoctoral Research Assistant (ODA)
PDRA........ Professional Drag Racing Association (EA)
PDRB........ Permanent Diability Rating Board (DMAA)
PDRC........ Clinical Research Center for Periodontal Disease [*University of Florida*] [*Research center*] (RCD)
PDRC........ Parkinson's Disease Research Center [*Johns Hopkins University*] (RCD)
PDRC........ Personnel Despatch and Reception Centre [*British military*] (DMA)
PDRC........ Peter Duel Remembrance Club (EA)
PDRC........ Positron Diagnostic Research Center (SAUS)
PDRC........ Poultry Disease Research Center [*University of Georgia*] [*Research center*] (RCD)
PDRC........ Preliminary Design Review Commercial (MCD)
PDRC........ Pressure Difference Recording Controller
PDRC........ Professional Development and Recruitment Career Program [*Military*]

PDRC........ Program Development Review Committee [*Navy*] (CAAL)
PDRCA...... Participatory Development Resource Centre for Africa (SAUS)
PDRCE...... Udall Parkinson's Disease Research Center of Excellence [*Duke University*] (RCD)
PDRD........ Procurement Data Requirements Document (NASA)
PDRD........ Program Definition and Requirements Document (SSD)
PDRE........ People's Democratic Republic of Ethiopia
PDREL....... PDR Electronic Library (MHID)
PDREL....... PDR [*Physicians Desk Reference*] Electronic Library [*Database*] (GDD)
PDRF........ Parts Data Record File (SAUS)
PDRF........ Passive Defense Recovery Force (MUGU)
PDRF........ Presbyterians for Democracy and Religious Freedom (EA)
PDRH........ Partido Democratico Revolucionario Hondureno [*Revolutionary Democratic Party of Honduras*] [*Political party*]
PDRJ........ Pulse-Doppler Radar Jammer (SAUS)
PDRK........ Peoples Democratic Republic of Korea (SAUS)
PdRK........ Pesikta de-Rav Kahana (BJA)
PDRL........ Permanent Disability Retired List
PDRL........ Procurement Data Requirements List (NASA)
pDRLMS.... Programmable Digital Radar Land Mass Simulation (SAUS)
PDRM....... Payload Deployment and Retrieval Mechanism [*NASA*]
PDRM....... Payload Distribution and Retrieval Mechanism (SAUS)
PDRM....... Portable Dose Rate Meter (SAUS)
PDRM....... Post-Depositional Remanent Magnetization [*Geophysics*]
PDRM....... Postdetrital Remanent Magnetization [*Geophysics*]
PDRMA...... Portable Drilling Rig Manufacturers Association [*Defunct*] (EA)
PDRP........ Power Distribution Reactor Program (SAUS)
PDRP........ Program Data Requirement Plan [*Nuclear Regulatory Commission*] (NRCH)
PDRP........ Program Document Requirement Plan (SAUS)
PDRR........ Pee Dee River Railway [*Federal Railroad Administration identification code*]
PDRR........ Program Definition and Risk Reduction (SAUS)
PDRS........ Payload Data and Retrieval System [*NASA*] (NAKS)
PDRS........ Payload Deployment and Retrieval System [*NASA*] (NAKS)
PDRS........ Pederson [*NCIC motorcycle make code*]
PDRS........ Pulse Doppler Radar Simulation (SAUS)
PDRSS...... Payload Deployment and Retrieval System Simulation [*NASA*] (SSD)
PDRSS...... Payload Development and Retrieval System Simulator [*NASA*] (NAKS)
PDRSTA..... Payload Deployment and Retrieval System Test Article [*NASA*] (NASA)
PDRU........ Party of Democratic Rebirth of Ukraine [*Political party*] (PSAP)
PDRY........ People's Democratic Republic of Yemen [*Political party*]
PDS.......... Auburn/Lewiston, ME [*Location identifier*] [*FAA*] (FAAL)
PDS.......... Democratic Social Party (Brazil) [*Political party*] (PSAP)
PDS.......... Pacific Data Services (SAUS)
PDS.......... Pacific Data System (IAA)
PDS.......... Pacific Data Systems, Inc. (SAUS)
PDS.......... Pacific Distribution System (SAUS)
PDS.......... Package Data System (NASA)
PDS.......... Packaging Data Sheet (SAUS)
PDS.......... Packet Data Satellites [*Telecommunications*] (TSSD)
PDS.......... Packet Driver Specification (SAUS)
PDS.......... Paid-during-Service [*Billing*]
PDS.......... Pain Dysfunction Syndrome [*Medicine*] (AAMN)
PDS.......... Parkinson's Disease Society [*British*]
PDS.......... Paroxysmal Depolarizing Shift [*Physiology*]
PDS.......... Partei des Demokratischen Sozialismus [*Party of Democratic Socialism*] [*Germany Political party*] (EAIO)
PDS.......... Parti Democratique Senegalais [*Senegalese Democratic Party*] [*Political party*] (PPW)
PDS.......... Partido Democrata Socialista [*Socialist Democratic Party*] [*Panama*] [*Political party*] (PPW)
PDS.......... Partitioned Data Set [*or System*] [*Computer science*] (NASA)
PDS.......... Partito Democratico della Sinistra [*Democratic Party of the Left*] [*Formerly, Italian Communist Party*] [*Political party*] (EY)
PDS.......... Partito di Democrazia Socialista [*Socialist Democracy Party*] [*San Marino*] [*Political party*] (PPW)
PDS.......... Party of Democratic Socialism [*Germany*] [*Political party*]
PDS.......... Passenger Documentation System (SAUS)
PDS.......... Passive Defense System (SAUS)
PDS.......... Passive Detection System (NVT)
PDS.......... Patient Data System [*Pharmacology*] (DAVI)
PDS.......... Patient Decontamination Site [*Army*] (INF)
PDS.......... Patient Distribution System (SAUS)
PDS.......... Payload Data Subsystem (ACAE)
PDS.......... Pediatric Surgery [*Medical specialty*] (DHSM)
PdS.......... Pediatric Surgery [*Medicine*] (DMAA)
PDS.......... Penultimate Digit Storage [*Telecommunications*] (TEL)
PDS.......... Performer Design Sheet
PDS.......... Perimeter Defense System (MCD)
PDS.......... Periodicals Data System (NITA)
PDS.......... Peritoneal Dialysis System [*nephrology*] (DAVI)
PDS.......... Permanent Duty Station [*Air Force*] (AFM)
PDS.......... Permanent Dynamic Speaker (SAUS)
PDS.......... Permissible Data Symbol (SAUS)
PDS.......... Perry Drug Stores, Inc. (EFIS)
PDS.......... Persistent Data Services (SAUS)
PDS.......... Persistent Data Store (SAUS)
PDS.......... Personal Data System (NITA)
PDS.......... Personal Decision Series (HGAA)
PDS.......... Personal Development Study [*Psychology*]
PDS.......... Personnel Daily Summary [*Army*] (AABC)
PDS.......... Personnel Data Summary (SAUS)
PDS.......... Personnel Data System [*Air Force*]
PDS.......... Personnel Decontamination Station (MCD)
PDS.......... Personnel Delivery System
PDS.......... Petroleum Data System [*University of Oklahoma*] [*Databank*] (IID)
PDS.......... Pharma-Dokumentations-Service [*Pharma Documentation Service*] [*Information service or system*] (IID)
PDS.......... Phased Development Shuttle [*NASA*] (KSC)
PDS.......... Philadelphia Divinity School (SAUS)
PDS.......... Philips Data Systems (SAUS)
PDS.......... Philips Development System (SAUS)
PDS.......... Photo Densitometer System (SAUS)
PDS.......... Photo-Digital Store
PDS.......... Photodischarge Spectroscopy (MCD)
PDS.......... Photo Document Sensor (SAUS)
PDS.......... Photographic Display System (SAUS)
PDS.......... Photometric Data System (SAUS)
PDS.......... Photothermal Deflection Spectroscopy (MCD)
PDS.......... Physician Data Services
PDS.......... Physician Depression Scale (SAUS)
PDS.......... Piedras Negras [*Mexico*] [*Airport symbol*] (AD)
PDS.......... Planar Diffusion Source (SAUS)
PDS.......... Planar Dopant Source (SAUS)
PDS.......... Planetary Data System (ACAE)
PDS.......... Planning Data Sheet (KSC)
PDS.......... Planning Data Systems [*Information service or system*] (IID)
PDS.......... Plant Damage State (SAUS)
PDS.......... Plant Data System [*Nuclear energy*] (NRCH)
PDS.......... Plasma-Derived Serum
PDS.......... Plasma Display (MCD)
PDS.......... Plasma Display System
PDS.......... Plotter Display System (DNAB)
PDS.......... Pneumatic Distribution System
PDS.......... Polydimethylsiloxane [*Organic chemistry*]
PDS.......... Polydioxanone [*Organic chemistry*]
PDS.......... Poly-P-Dioxanone
PDS.......... Portable Data Store (SAUS)
PDS.......... Portable Data System (MCD)
PDS.......... Portable Display Shell (SAUS)
PDS.......... Portable Document Software [*Computer science*] (DDC)
PDS.......... Portable Duress Sensor (MCD)
PDS.......... Positional Data System (SAUS)
PDS.......... Position Detection System [*Navigation systems*]
PDS.......... Position-Determining System
PDS.......... Post Design Services [*British*] (RDA)
PDS.......... Post Design Support (SAUS)
PDS.......... Power Density Spectra (IEEE)
PDS.......... Power Distribution Specification (IAA)
PDS.......... Power Distribution Subsystem (SAUS)
PDS.......... Power Distribution System [*or Subsystem*]
PDS.......... Power Drive System
PDS.......... Preadsorb-Dilute-Shake [*Phage growth method*]
PDS.......... Precision Drilling Corp. [*NYSE symbol*] (SAG)
PDS.......... Predialyzed Human Serum [*Medicine*] (MAE)
PDS.......... Predocketed Special Project (NRCH)
PDS.......... Predocketed Special Report (SAUS)
PDS.......... Premises Distribution System [*AT & T Corp.*]
PDS.......... Primary Data Set (SAUS)
PDS.......... Primary Data Store (SAUS)
PDS.......... Priority Decision System (NITA)
PDS.......... Priority Distribution System [*Military*] (AFM)
PDS.......... Prison Disciplinary System (WDAA)
PDS.......... Prisoner Detention System
PDS.......... Private Database Service (NITA)
PDS.......... Probability Distribution Subprogram [*Computer science*] (BUR)
PDS.......... Problem Data System (MCD)
PD/S......... Problem Definition/Solution
PDS.......... Problem Descriptor System
PDS.......... Procedures Development Simulator (KSC)
PDS.......... Processing and Display System (CCCA)
PDS.......... Processor Direct Slot [*Computer science*]
PDS.......... Processor Direct Socket (SAUS)
PDS.......... Procurement Data Sheet
PDS.......... Product Data Sheet (SAUS)
PDS.......... Product Demand Structure (SAUS)
PDS.......... Product Design Standard
PDS.......... Product Development System (SAUS)
PDS.......... Production Data Sheet (MCD)
PDS.......... Professional Development Scheme (HEAS)
PDS.......... Professional Development School
PDS.......... Professional Development Seminar (HGAA)
PDS.......... Professional Development Series [*Emergency Management*] (EMA)
PDS.......... Professional Development System [*PC software*] [*Microsoft, Inc.*] (PCM)
PDS.......... Program Data Set (SAUS)
PDS.......... Program Data Sheets [*Army*] (AABC)
PDS.......... Program Data Source (BUR)
PDS.......... Program Design Specification (CAAL)
PDS.......... Program Development Section (SAUS)
PDS.......... Program Development Specialist
PDS.......... Program Development System [*Computer science*]
PDS.......... Program Distribution System
PDS.......... Programmable Data Station [*or System*]
PDS.......... Programmable Data System (SAUS)

PDS......... Programmable Device Support
PDS......... Programmable Distribution System (SAUS)
PDS......... Programming Documentation Standards [*Computer science*] (WDAA)
PDS......... Progressive Deterioration Scale
PDS......... Project Data Sheet (SAUS)
PDS......... Project Definition Study (SAUS)
PDS......... Project Designation Study (SAUS)
PDS......... Propellant Delivery System
PDS......... Propellant Dispersion System (MCD)
PDS......... Proposed Delivery Schedule (SAUS)
PDS......... Protected Distribution System [*Military*] (GFGA)
PDS......... Protection and Defence Systems (SAUS)
PDS......... Proximity Defense Systems [*Military*] (INF)
PdS......... Psychiatric Deviate, Subtle (DAVI)
PdS......... Psychopathic Deviate Subtle [*Psychology*]
PDS......... Public Domain Software (SAUS)
PDS......... Pulse Doppler Search (SAUS)
PDS......... Pulse Doppler Seeker
PDS......... Punch Driver Selectric
PDS......... Purchasing Department Specification (MSA)
PDS......... Pyrotechnic Devices Simulator (SAA)
PDSA........ Paid Scientific Associates (SAUS)
PDSA........ People's Dispensary for Sick Animals [*British*]
PDSA........ Peroxydisulfuric Acid (AAEL)
PDS-A....... Personnel Data System - Airmen [*Air Force*]
PDSA........ Predesign and Systems Analysis [*NASA*] (KSC)
PDSA........ Private Doctors' Society of South Australia
PDSA Associate... Peoples Dispensary for Sick Animals Associate (SAUS)
PDS-A(I).... Personnel Data System - Airmen (Interim) [*Air Force*] (AFM)
PDSAR...... Public Document Status of Assessment Report (SAUS)
PDSB........ Physical Distribution Standards Board (SAUS)
PDSC........ PACOM [*Pacific Command*] Data Systems Center (MCD)
PDSC........ Parti Democrate et Social Chretien [*Zaire*] [*Political party*] (EY)
PDS-C....... Personnel Data System - Civilian [*Air Force*] (AFM)
PDSC........ Pressure Differential Scanning Calorimetry [*Analytical technique*]
PDSC........ Professional Development Series Curriculum [*Emergency Management*] (EMA)
PDSC........ Public Disaster Service Committee (SAUS)
PDSC........ Publishers Data Service Corp. [*Monterey, CA*]
PDSD........ Point Detonating Self-Destroying [*Projectile*]
PDSDD...... Plotting Display Subchannel Data Distributor (MCD)
PDSE........ Paradise Music and Entertainment [*OTCBB symbol*]
PDSE........ Production Sample (AAG)
PDSF........ Parallel Distributed Simulation Facility (SAUS)
PDSF........ PDS Financial [*NASDAQ symbol*] (TTSB)
PDSF........ PDS Financial Corp. [*NASDAQ symbol*] (SAG)
PDS Fin..... PDS Financial Corp. [*Associated Press*] (SAG)
PDSG........ Pick's Disease Support Group [*British*] (NRGU)
PDSG........ Pigment Dispersion Syndrome Glaucoma [*Medicine*] (EDAA)
PDSH........ Democratic Party of Albania [*Political party*] (PSAP)
PDSI......... Palmer Drought Severity Index [*Meteorology*]
PDSI......... Performance Data Services, Inc. [*Falls Church, VA*] [*Software manufacture r*]
PDSI......... Portable Digital Strain Indicator
PDSI......... Professional Data Service, Incorporated
PDSK........ Petroleum Distribution System - Korea [*Army*] (MCD)
PDSL........ Pressure Differential Switch Load (SAUS)
PDSM........ Powder Diffraction Search-Match System [*International Data Center*]
PDS/MAGEN... Problem Descriptor System/Matrix Generation [*Programming language*] [*1965*] (CSR)
PDSMAN.... Partitioned Data Set Management System (SAUS)
PDSMS...... Point Defense Surface Missile System
PDSMS...... Power Diffraction Search and Match System (PDAA)
PDSMWS... Portable Dynamic Slow-Motion Weighing System [*Traffic safety*]
PDSN........ Plasma-Deposited Silicon Nitride (SAUS)
PDS-O....... Personnel Data System - Officers [*Air Force*] (AFM)
PDSOC...... Police Department Superior Officers Council (SAUS)
PDSOF...... Public Domain Software on File [*Facts on File, Inc.*] [*Information service or system*] (IID)
PDSOR...... Positive Definitive Successive Over-Relaxation (PDAA)
PDSP........ Peripheral Data Storage Processor (SAUS)
PDSP........ Personnel Data System - Planning [*Air Force*] (AFM)
PDSPI....... Polyurethane Division, Society of the Plastics Industry (EA)
PDSQ........ Point Detonating Super-Quick Fuze (NATG)
PDSQDL.... Point Detonating, Superquick and Delay (SAUS)
PDSQ Fuze... Point Detonating Superquick Fuze (SAUS)
PDS-R....... Parti Democratique Senegalais - Renovation [*Senegalese Democratic Party - Reform*] [*Political party*]
PDSR........ Principal Director of Scientific Research (SAUS)
PDSR........ Social Democratic Party of Romania [*Political party*] (PSAP)
PDSS........ Particle Doppler Shift Spectrometer (PDAA)
PDSS........ Payload Data Services System (SPST)
PDSS........ Payload Development Support System (SAUS)
PDSS........ Physical Disabilities Special Interest Section [*American Occupational Therapy Association*]
PDSS........ Post Deployment Software Support (ACAE)
PDSS........ Post-Deployment Software System (MCD)
PDSS........ Post Development Support System (SAUS)
PDSS........ Procurement Decision Support System (ACAE)
PDSS........ Program Development Support System (SAUS)
PDSS........ Propulsion-Derived Ship Service (SAUS)
PDSSC...... Post Deployment Software Support Center
PDST........ Pacific Daylight Saving Time (KSC)
PDST........ Personnel Data System for Training (SAUS)
pdstl......... Pedestal (VRA)
PDSTT....... Pulse Doppler Single Target Track [*Military*] (CAAL)
PDSU........ Plant Data System Upgrade (SAUS)
PD Supp.... Per Diem Supplement (AAGC)
PDSX........ Penn-Dixie Cement [*Private rail car owner code*]
PDSZ........ Party of Convinced Social Democrats of Zaire (SAUS)
PDT......... Democratic Labor Party (Brazil) [*Political party*] (PSAP)
PDT......... Democratic Worker's Party (Brazil) [*Political party*] (PSAP)
PDT......... Hancock [*John*] Patriot Premium Dividend, Inc. II [*NYSE symbol*] (SPSG)
PDT......... John Hancock Patriot Premium Dividend Fund II [*NYSE symbol*]
PDT......... John Hancock Patr Prem Dv II [*NYSE symbol*] (TTSB)
PDT......... Pacific Daylight Time
PDT......... Panoramic Design Technique
PDT......... Parallel Data Transmission
PDT......... Parameter Descriptor Table (SAUS)
PdT......... Parti du Travail [*Labor Party*] [*Switzerland*] [*Political party*] (PPE)
PDT......... PDT, Inc. [*Associated Press*] (SAG)
PDT......... Pendleton [*Oregon*] [*Airport symbol*] (OAG)
PDT......... Percutaneous Dilational Tracheostomy [*Medicine*]
PDT......... Performance Demonstration Test
PDT......... Performance Diagnostic Tool (SAUS)
PDT......... Peripheral Data Transfer [*Telecommunications*] (IAA)
PDT......... Peripheral Device Type (CIST)
PDT......... Personal Data Transmitter [*From the movie "Aliens"*]
PDT......... Phenyldimethyltriazine [*Organic chemistry*] (AAMN)
PDT......... Photodynamic Therapy [*Oncology*]
PDT......... Physical Device Table (NITA)
PDT......... Picture Description Test (PDAA)
PDT......... Piedmont Airlines, Inc. [*ICAO designator*] (FAAC)
PDT......... Planned Data to Transportation [*DoD*]
PDT......... Plasma Display Terminal [*Computer science*]
PDT......... Pollable Data Terminal [*Bell System*]
PDT......... Population Doubling Time [*Cytology*]
PDT......... Portable Data Terminal (SEWL)
PDT......... Positive Displacement Turbine (SAUS)
PDT......... Post Alloy Diffused Transistor [*Electronics*] (IAA)
PDT......... Posting Data Transfer [*Air Force*] (AFM)
PDT......... Potentially Dangerous Taxpayer (SAUS)
PDT......... Power Distribution Trailer (NATG)
PDT......... Practice Delivery Torpedo (SAUS)
PDT......... Precedent [*Telegraphy*] (PCTE)
PDT......... Predelivery Test (MCD)
PDT......... Predictor Display Technique
PDT......... President Mines [*Vancouver Stock Exchange symbol*]
PDT......... Pressure Decay Test [*Automotive emissions*]
PDT......... Printer Definition Table (SAUS)
PDT......... Processed Directional Transmission [*Military*] (NVT)
PDT......... Processor Diagnostic Test (ACAE)
PDT......... Procurement Data Transmittal (SAUS)
PDT......... Product (SAUS)
PDT......... Product Development Team [*Automotive project management*]
PDT......... Professional Development and Teaching (SAUS)
PDT......... Programmable Data Terminal [*Digital Equipment Corp.*] (IEEE)
PDT......... Programmable Drive Table (SAUS)
PDT......... Propagation Delay Time (SAUS)
PDT......... Published Data Tape [*A. C. Nielsen Co.*] [*A publication*] (WDMC)
PDT......... Pulse Delay Time
PDT......... Pushdown Transducer (CIST)
PDT......... (Pyridyl)diphenyltriazine [*Analytical chemistry*]
PDT-1....... Picatinny Arsenal Detonation Trap Number 1 [*Army*] (AABC)
PDTA........ Production Tape (AAG)
PDTA........ Professional Dance Teachers Association (EA)
PDTA........ Propylenediaminetetraacetic Acid [*Organic chemistry*]
PDTAG....... Product Data Technology Advisory Group (SAUS)
PDT & T.... Post-Delivery Test and Trials [*Military*] (CAAL)
PDTC........ Philadelphia Depository Trust Co.
PDTC........ Professional Dancer's Training Course Diploma (ODA)
PDTE........ Packet-mode Data Terminal Equipment (SAUS)
PDTE........ Packet-mode DTE (SAUS)
PD Technique... Physical Development Technique (SAUS)
PDTF........ Program Development and Test Facility [*Social Security Administration*]
PDTI......... PDT, Inc. [*NASDAQ symbol*] (SAG)
PDTM........ PD Technical Mouldings plc (SAUS)
PDTMR...... Phalloidin Tetramethylrhodamine [*Biochemistry*]
PDTP........ Plasma Display Touch Panel [*Computer science*]
PDTRST..... Podiatrist
PDTS........ Police Detective Training School (SAUS)
PDTS........ Procurement Document Tracking System (MCD)
PDTS........ Program Development Tracking System [*Computer science*]
PDTS........ Programmable Data Terminal Set [*Military*] (CAAL)
PDTTT....... Post-Delivery Test and Trial Team (MCD)
PDU......... Pacific Democrat Union (EAIO)
PDU......... Packet Data Unit (MLOA)
PDU......... Parti Dahomeen de l'Unite [*Dahomean Unity Party*] [*Benin*] [*Political party*]
PDU......... Parti Democrate Unifie [*Unified Democratic Party*] [*Name replaced by Section Voltaique de Rassemblement*] [*Burkina Faso*] [*Political party*]
PDU......... Paysandu [*Uruguay*] [*Airport symbol*] (OAG)
PDU......... Performance Diagnostic Unit (SAUS)
PDU......... Phase Demodulation Unit
PDU......... Philippines Digital Upgrade (SAUS)

PDU......... Photomultiplier Detector Unit (KSC)
PDU......... Pilot's Display Unit (MCD)
PDU......... Plasma Display Unit (SAUS)
PDU......... Plug Distribution Unit (SAUS)
PDU......... Positive Displacement Unit [*Mechanical pumps*]
PDU......... Power Distribution Unit (AAG)
PDU......... Power Drive Unit (MCD)
PDU......... Pressure Distribution Unit
PDU......... Process Demonstration Unit [*Chemical engineering*]
PDU......... Process Development Unit [*Chemical engineering*]
PDU......... Produce [*Telegraphy*] (PCTE)
PDU......... Product Distribution Unit (SAUS)
PDU......... Production Distribution Unit (AAG)
PDU......... Programmable Delay Unit
PDU......... Programmable Diagnostic Unit [*TACOM*] [*Army*] (RDA)
PDU......... Project Development Unit [*Chemical engineering*]
PDU......... Projection Display Unit
PDU......... Propane Deasphalting Unit [*Petroleum engineering*]
PDU......... Protocol Data Unit [*Telecommunications*]
PDU......... Pulsed Doppler Ultrasonography [*Radiology*] (DAVI)
PDU......... Pulse Detection Unit (NASA)
PDUD........ Produced [*Telegraphy*] (PCTE)
PDUF........ Pulsed Doppler Ultrasonic Flow-meter [*Medicine*] (EDAA)
PDUFA....... Prescription Drug User Fee Act
PDUFC...... Pete Duel Universal Friendship Club (EAIO)
PDUG........ Producing [*Telegraphy*] (PCTE)
PdUP........ Partito di Unita Proletaria per il Comunismo [*Democratic Party of Proletarian Unity for Communism*] [*Italy*] [*Political party*] (PPE)
PDUPE...... Protocol Data Unit Programming Environment (SAUS)
PDur......... Papyri Durani (BJA)
PDUR........ Predischarge Utilization Review [*Medicine*]
PDUS........ Primary Data User Station [*Computer science*] (PDAA)
PDUS........ Produces [*Telegraphy*] (PCTE)
PDUT........ Product [*Telegraphy*] (PCTE)
PDV......... Parcel Delivery Van
PDV......... Path Delay Value (SAUS)
PDV......... Peak Diastolic Velocity [*Medicine*] (EDAA)
PDV......... Petroleos de Venezuela (EFIS)
PDV......... Phocine Distemper Virus
PDV......... Photorealistic Data Visualization (SAUS)
PDV......... Polyhedra Derived Virus
PDV......... Ponderosa Ventures, Inc. [*Vancouver Stock Exchange symbol*]
PDV......... Premodulation Processor - Deep Space - Voice
PDV......... Pressure Disconnect Valve (MCD)
PDV......... Probability of Detection and Verification [*Military*] (CAAL)
PDV......... Productive [*Telegraphy*] (PCTE)
PDV......... Prune Dwarf Virus
PDV......... Pure Dried Vacuum (SAUS)
PDV......... Pyrotechnic Development Vehicle (PDAA)
PdvA........ Party of Labor (Belgium) [*Political party*] (PSAP)
PDVC........ Phase-Dependent Voltage Contrast (AAEL)
PDVF........ Payload Design Verification Facility (ACAE)
PDVM....... Printing Digital Voltmeter (SAUS)
PDVN........ Power-Driven
PDVSA...... Petroleos de Venezuela [*Oil company*]
PDW......... Evansville, IN [*Location identifier*] [*FAA*] (FAAL)
PDW......... Partially Delactosed Whey (OA)
PDW......... Personal Damage Waiver (TRID)
PDW......... Personal Defense Weapon [*Army*] (INF)
PDW......... Personal Design Workstation (DGA)
PDW......... Physical Damage Waiver [*Insurance*] (TVEL)
PDW......... Planar Dielectric Waveguide (SAUS)
PDW......... Platelet Distribution Width [*Hematology*]
PDW......... Priority Delayed Weather [*NWS*] (FAAC)
PDWE....... Pulse Detonation Wave Engine (SAUS)
PDWHF...... Platelet-Derived Wound-Healing Factor [*Biochemistry*]
PD Work.... Public Domain Work (SAUS)
PDWP....... Partially Delactosed Whey Powder (OA)
PDWR....... Primary Drinking Water Regulation (COE)
PDWS....... Passive Doppler Wind Sensor (SAUS)
PDWS....... Primary Drinking Water Standards (SAUS)
PDX......... Paradox files (SAUS)
PDX......... Passive Dosimeter Experiment (KSC)
PDX......... Pediatrix Medical Group [*NYSE symbol*]
PDX......... Place Decrement in Index
PDX......... Poloidal Divertor Experiment [*Princeton University*]
PDX......... Portland [*Oregon*] [*Airport symbol*] (OAG)
PDX......... Prado Explorations Ltd. [*Toronto Stock Exchange symbol*]
PDX......... Printer Description Extension (SAUS)
PDX......... Private Digital Exchange
PDX......... Probable Diagnosis (DAVI)
PDX......... Processor-controlled Digital Exchange (SAUS)
PDX......... Program Development Executive (MHDI)
PDXI........ Process Data Exchange Institute (GART)
PDY......... Piccadilly Resources Ltd. [*Vancouver Stock Exchange symbol*]
PDY......... Principal Duty [*Military*]
PDYN........ Prodynorphin [*Biochemistry*]
PDZ......... Ontario, CA [*Location identifier*] [*FAA*] (FAAL)
PDZ......... Parachute Dropping Zone (SAUS)
PDZ......... Pedernales [*Venezuela*] [*Airport symbol*] (OAG)
PDZC........ Pathfinder Drop-Zone Control (SAUS)
PE........... British Aircraft Corp. Ltd. [*ICAO aircraft manufacturer identifier*] (ICAO)
PE........... Easton Area Public Library, Easton, PA [*Library symbol*] [*Library of Congress*] (LCLS)
PE........... Edinburgh Pharmacopoeia [*British*] (DAVI)
Pe........... episcleral venous Pressure (SAUS)
PE........... Ice Pellets [*Meteorology*]
PE........... Pacific Electric Railway [*AAR code*]
PE........... Page-End (SAUS)
PE........... Page-End Character [*Computer science*]
PE........... Paleoecology (SAUS)
PE........... Paper Electrophoresis [*Medicine*] (MAE)
PE........... Parabolic Equation
PE........... Parallel Element (SAUS)
PE........... Parity Error
PE........... Parity Even (SAUS)
PE........... Partes Aequales [*Equal Parts*] [*Pharmacy*]
PE........... Partial Evaluation (VLIE)
PE........... Patrol Vessel, Eagle [*Eagle boat*] [*Navy symbol*] [*Obsolete*]
PE........... Peace Establishment (SAUS)
PE........... Peacetime Establishment [*Military*] (NATG)
PE........... Peas [*Soil biology*] [*Human-introduced crops*] (QSUL)
Pe........... Peclet Number [*IUPAC*]
PE........... PECO Energy [*Formerly, Philadelphia Electric Co.*] [*NYSE symbol*] (SPSG)
PE........... PECO Energy Co. [*NYSE symbol*]
PE........... Pectinesterase [*Also, PME*] [*An enzyme*]
PE........... Pediatrics (DAVI)
PE........... Peine [*German license plate city code*]
Pe........... Pelagius [*Deceased, 1232*] [*Authority cited in pre-1607 legal work*] (DSA)
PE........... Pel-Ebstein [*Disease*] [*Medicine*] (DB)
PE........... Pellets [*Weather codes - aviation*] (PIPO)
pe........... Pen (VRA)
PE........... Penile Erection [*Medicine*] (DMAA)
PE........... Pentaeythrol (IAA)
Pe........... Pentyl [*Biochemistry*]
PE........... People Express [*ICAO designator*] (AD)
PE........... Percent Bit Error Probability (SAUS)
PE........... Percent Error (ACAE)
PE........... Performance Enhancement [*Computer science*] (VLIE)
PE........... Performance Evaluation (ABAC)
PE........... Pericardial Effusion [*Cardiology*] (DAVI)
PE........... Period Ending
PE........... Period Entry (SAUS)
PE........... Periodic (AAG)
PE........... Peripheral Equipment (AAG)
PE........... Periscope
PE........... Peritoneal Exudate [*Medicine*]
PE........... Perkin Elmer Corp.
PE........... Permanent Echo [*RADAR*]
PE........... Permanent Error (IAA)
PE........... Permissible Error (ADA)
PE........... Perry Ellis [*Fashion designer, 1940-86*]
PE........... Persistent Estrus [*Endocrinology*]
PE........... Personal Effects
PE........... Personal Electronics (VLIE)
PE........... Personal Equipment
PE........... Personnel Division (SAUS)
PE........... Personnel, Enlisted [*or Enlisted Personnel Division*] [*Coast Guard*]
PE........... Personnel Equipment [*Air Force*] (AFM)
PE........... Personnel Equivalent [*DoD*]
PE........... Peru [*ANSI two-letter standard code*] (CNC)
pe........... Peru [*MARC country of publication code*] [*Library of Congress*] (LCCP)
Pe........... Peru (MILB)
Pe........... Perylene [*Organic chemistry*] (AAMN)
PE........... Peterborough [*Postcode*] (ODBW)
PE........... Petroleum Economist [*London*] [*A publication*] (BJA)
PE........... Petroleum Engineer
PE........... Petroleum Engineering (SAUS)
Pe........... Petrus de Bellapertica [*Deceased, 1308*] [*Authority cited in pre-1607 legal work*] (DSA)
Pe........... Petrus Hispanus [*Authority cited in pre-1607 legal work*] (DSA)
PE........... Peugeot [*Society of Automotive Engineers auto manufacturer code for service information interchange*]
PE........... Phakoemulsification [*Ophthalmology*] (DAVI)
PE........... Pharmacopaeia Edinensis [*Edinburgh Pharmacopoeia*] [*A publication*] (ROG)
PE........... Pharmacopoeia of Edinburgh (SAUS)
PE........... Pharyngoesophageal [*Medicine*]
PE........... Phase Encoded (SAUS)
PE........... Phase Encoding [*Magnetic tape recording*] [*Computer science*] (MDG)
PE........... Phenylephrine
PE........... Philadelphia Electric (SAUS)
PE........... Philadelphia Stock Exchange (CDAI)
PE........... Philips Electric (SAUS)
PE........... Phorbol Ester (SAUS)
PE........... Phosphatidylethanolamine [*Biochemistry*]
PE........... Photoelectric
PE........... Photoelectron (IAA)
pe........... Photoelectron
PE........... Photoemission [*Physics*]
PE........... Photoengraving (SAUS)
PE........... Photographic Effect (MAE)
PE........... Photon Echo [*Spectroscopy*]

PE........... Phycoerythrin [*Biochemistry*]
PE........... Physical Education
PE........... Physical Evaluation [*Medicine*] (MAE)
PE........... Physical Examination
PE........... Physiological Ecology
PE........... Pictorial Element (SAUS)
PE........... Pictorial Eleven [*Later, PES*] [*An association*] (EA)
PE........... Picture Element (ELAL)
PE........... Piezoelectric (AAEL)
PE........... Piezoelectricity (SAUS)
PE........... Pigment Epithelium [*of the retina*]
PE........... Pilot Equalizer (IAA)
PE........... Pilot Error
PE........... Pinion End
PE........... Pistol Expert
pe........... Plain Edged [*Construction term*] (MIST)
PE........... Plain Edged (SAUS)
PE........... Plain Edges [*Graphic arts*] (DGA)
PE........... Plain End [*Lumber*] (DAC)
PE........... Planetary Explorer [*NASA*]
PE........... Planification de l'Emploi [*Canadian Jobs Strategy - CJS*]
P/E........... Planning Economics Group, Boston [*Information service or system*] (IID)
PE........... Planning Engineer (SAUS)
PE........... Planning Estimate
PE........... Plant Engineering (AAG)
PE........... Plant Equipment (MCD)
PE........... Plant Extrusion (OA)
PE........... Plasma Emission [*Spectrophotometry*]
PE........... Plasma Exchange [*Medicine*]
PE........... Plastic Engine (SAUS)
PE........... Plastic Explosive (NATG)
PE........... Plating Efficiency (DB)
PE........... Platinum Compd (Cisplatin) and Etoposide [*Medicine*] (EDAA)
PE........... Platinum Electrode (SAUS)
PE........... Pleural Effusion [*Medicine*]
PE........... Plutonium Equivalent (SAUS)
PE........... Pneumatic Equalization [*Tube*] [*Otorhinolaryngology*] (DAVI)
PE........... Pocket Edition (WDAA)
PE........... Point of Entry (SAUS)
PE........... Pollen Equivalent [*Immunology*]
PE........... Polyelectrolyte [*Organic chemistry*]
PE........... Polyester [*Tire design*]
PE........... Polyether (SAUS)
PE........... Polyethylene [*Organic chemistry*]
PE........... Ponton Equipment (SAUS)
PE........... Pony Express [*Automobile model designation-Austin*]
PE........... Population Equivalent (FFDE)
PE........... Porcelain Enamel [*Technical drawings*]
PE........... Portable Error (SAUS)
PE........... Portable Executable
PE........... Portable Executable File [*Computer science*]
PE........... Port Engineer (DNAB)
PE........... Port of Embarkation [*Military*]
PE........... Positional Efficiency (SAUS)
PE........... Position Effect [*Parapsychology*]
PE........... Position Error
PE........... Positive Expulsion (SAA)
PE........... Positives and Etching (DGA)
PE........... Post Edit (SAUS)
PE........... Post Engineer [*Army*] (AABC)
PE........... Post-Entry [*Motorsports*]
PE........... Post Exchange [*Marine Corps*]
PE........... Postexposure [*Medicine*]
PE........... Potato Eaters (EA)
PE........... Potential Electrode (SAUS)
PE........... Potential Enemy (CARL)
PE........... Potential Energy
PE........... Potential Evaporation (SAUS)
PE........... Potential Evapotranspiration (DICI)
PE........... Potential Excess [*of stock*] [*DoD*]
PE........... Powdered Extract [*Pharmacy*]
PE........... Power, Electric (SAUS)
PE........... Power Equipment [*Military*] (IAA)
PE........... Power Exchange (SAUS)
PE........... Practical Exercise
PE........... Precipitation Efficiency (SAUS)
P-E........... Precipitation-Environment (SAUS)
P-E........... Precipitation-Evaporation
PE........... Pre-Eclampsia [*Medicine*]
PE........... Pre-Emption [*Telecommunications*] (TEL)
PE........... Preexcitation [*Medicine*] (EDAA)
PE........... Preliminary Evaluation
PE........... Preliminary Exploitation (MCD)
PE........... Prepaid Expense [*Finance*] (MHDW)
PE........... Presidential Exemption [*Environmental Protection Agency*]
PE........... Presiding Elder
PE........... Pressure Enclosure (MCD)
PE........... Pressure Equalization [*Tube*] [*Otorhinolaryngology*] (DAVI)
PE........... Pressure Equalizing [*Tube*] [*Otorhinolaryngology*] (DAVI)
Pe........... Pressure on Expiration [*Medicine*]
PE........... Pressurized Element (SAUS)
PE........... Priced Exhibit (MCD)
P/E........... Price [*or Profit*]/Earnings Ratio [*Relation between price of a company's stock and its annual net income*]
PE........... Price Earnings Ratio [*Investment term*] (DFIT)
P/E........... Price-to-Earnings
PE........... Primary Education (AIE)
PE........... Primary Electricity
PE........... Primary Electron (SAUS)
PE........... Prime Equipment
PE........... Primitive Endoderm [*Cytology*]
PE........... Primitive Equation
PE........... Prince Edward Island [*Canadian province*] [*Postal code*]
PE........... Principal Engineer (AAG)
PE........... Principle [*Telegraphy*] (PCTE)
PE........... Principle Engineer (SAUS)
PE........... Print End [*Computer science*] (VLIE)
pe........... Printer's Error (WDAA)
PE........... Printer's Error
PE........... Private Eye (SAUS)
PE........... Probability of Error (CCCA)
pe........... Probable Error (DIPS)
PE........... Probable Error [*Statistics*]
PE........... Procedures Evaluation [*DoD*]
PE........... Process Engineer (SAUS)
PE........... Process Engineering (SAUS)
PE........... Processing Element [*of central processing unit*]
PE........... Processor Element (SAUS)
PE........... Procurement Executive [*British*]
PE........... Production Engineer (SAUS)
PE........... Production Engineering
PE........... Production Engineering Division [*Frankford Arsenal*] [*Philadelphia, PA*]
PE........... Production Executive [*British*]
P/E........... Professional and Executive [*Employment register*] [*British*]
PE........... Professional Ecologist (SAUS)
PE........... Professional Edition
PE........... Professional Education (AFM)
PE........... Professional Engineer
PE........... Professional Engraver (SAUS)
PE........... Professional Equipment (SAUS)
PE........... Professional Estimator (SAUS)
PE........... Program Element (AFM)
PE........... Program Evaluation (OICC)
PE........... Programmed Exciter
PE........... Programming Environment (SAUS)
PE........... Programming Error (SAUS)
PE........... Project Engineer
PE........... Project Equality (EA)
PE........... Project Executive (GART)
PE........... Prometheus-Europe [*Paris, France*] (EAIO)
PE........... Propellants and Explosives
PE........... Proponent Evaluation (MCD)
PE........... Proposed Endangered (SAUS)
PE........... Protected Environment
PE........... Protect Enable [*Computer science*] (PCM)
PE........... Protection Earth (SAUS)
PE........... Protection Enabled (SAUS)
PE........... Protective Earth (SAUS)
PE........... Protective Entrance (SAUS)
PE........... Protein Electrophoresis [*Biochemistry*] (DAVI)
PE........... Protein Equivalent (SAUS)
PE........... Protestant Episcopal
PE........... Proteus Engine [*Hovercraft*]
PE........... Protocol Elements (SAUS)
PE........... Proton Event
PE........... Prototype Event (SAUS)
PE........... Pseudomonas Exotoxin [*Bacterial toxin*]
PE........... Public Eye [*Internet Site*]
PE........... Pulled Elbow (MELL)
PE........... Pulley End
PE........... Pulmonary Edema [*Medicine*]
PE........... Pulmonary Effusion [*Medicine*]
PE........... Pulmonary Embolism [*Medicine*]
PE........... Pulmonary Embolus (SAUS)
PE........... Pulmonary Emphysema [*Medicine*] (MELL)
PE........... Pulse Echo [*Materials research*]
P/E........... Pulse-Echo Testing (SAUS)
PE........... Pulse Encoding [*Computer science*]
PE........... Purchased Equipment
P/E........... Purchase Enquiry (RIMS)
PE........... Pyramidal Eminence [*Medicine*] (MELL)
PE........... Pyroelectric
PE........... Pyroelectricity (SAUS)
Pe........... Warner-Lambert Pharmaceutical Co. [*Research code symbol*]
PE2........... Secondary Plating Efficiency (STED)
PEA........... Palmitylethanolamide [*Organic chemistry*]
PEA........... Pan Europeenne Air Service [*France*] [*ICAO designator*] (FAAC)
PEA........... Papillary Eccrine Adenoma [*Oncology*]
PEA........... Parking Enforcement Aide (ECON)
PEA........... Pattern Error Analysis
PEA........... Patterson Experimental Array (MCD)
PEA........... Payload Enclosure Assembly (MCD)
Pea........... Peake's English Nisi Prius Reports [*1790-1812*] [*A publication*] (DLA)
PEA........... Pella, IA [*Location identifier*] [*FAA*] (FAAL)
PEA........... Penneshaw [*Australia*] [*Airport symbol*] (OAG)

PEA.......... Pennsylvania Electric Association
PEA.......... People Express Airlines (SAUS)
PEA.......... Peranakan Indonesian [*Language symbol*] (ETLW)
PEA.......... Percentage Electrical Activity (SAUS)
PEA.......... Phenethyl Alcohol [*Organic chemistry*]
PEA.......... Phenylethanolamine [*Organic chemistry*]
PEA.......... Phenylethylamine [*Biochemistry*]
PEA.......... Phosphoethanolamine [*Organic chemistry*]
PE(A)........ Physical Education (Association) [*British*]
PEA.......... Piezoelectric Accelerometer [*Electronics*]
PEA.......... Pilot's Employment Agency
PEA.......... Pitch Error Amplifier
PEA.......... Plant Engineering Agency
PEA.......... Plastics Engineers Association [*Defunct*] (EA)
PEA.......... Platform Electronics Assembly (KSC)
PEA.......... Pocket Ethernet Adapter [*Computer science*] (VLIE)
PEA.......... Polish Ex-Servicemen's Association [*Australia*]
PEA.......... Polyether Amine [*Fuels and lubricants*]
PEA.......... Poly(ethyl Acrylate) [*Organic chemistry*]
PEA.......... Polysaccharide Egg Antigen (STED)
PEA.......... Portable Emission Analyzer [*Automotive engineering*]
PEA.......... Portuguese East Africa [*Mozambique*]
PEA.......... Positive Electron Affinity (SAUS)
PEA.......... Potash Export Association (EA)
PEA.......... Poultry Education Association [*British*] (BI)
PEA.......... Power Excursion Accident [*Nuclear energy*] (NUCP)
PEA.......... Preliminary Endangerment Assessment (SARE)
PEA.......... Preliminary Environmental Assessment (MCD)
PEA.......... Primary Expense Account
PEA.......... Private Employment Agency (OICC)
PEA.......... Process Environmental Analysis
PEA.......... Process Equipment Accessory (MCD)
PEA.......... Procurement Executives Association (AAGC)
PEA.......... Production Engineering Association [*United Kingdom*] (EAIO)
PEA.......... Program Element Administrator [*Navy*] (NG)
PEA.......... Progressive Education Association [*Defunct*]
PEA.......... Proposal Expansion Award (TELE)
PEA.......... Publication Effectiveness Audit (SAUS)
PEA.......... Public Education Association
PEA.......... Pulseless Electrical Activity (SAUS)
PEA.......... Push-Effective Address [*Computer science*] (IEEE)
PEA.......... Pyridylethylamine [*Organic chemistry*]
Pea (2)...... Peake's Additional Cases Nisi Prius [*170 English Reprint*] [*1795-1812*] [*A publication*] (DLA)
PEAA......... Program Elements Activity Accounts (MCD)
P/EA(A)3.... Probationary Electrical Artificer (Air) 3rd Class [*British military*] (DMA)
Pea Add Cas... Peake's English Nisi Prius Reports [*Vol. 2*] [*A publication*] (DLA)
PEAB......... Peabody Solid Waste Management [*NCIC trailer make code*]
PEAB......... Professional Engineers Appointments Bureau (SAUS)
Peab L Rev... Peabody Law Review [*A publication*] (DLA)
Peabody Inst... Peabody Institute of The Johns Hopkins University (GAGS)
PEABODY PAC... Peabody Energy Corporation PAC [*St. Louis, MO*] (PACS)
PEAC......... Peace [*NCIC car make code*]
PEAC......... Peripheral Array Computer (SAUS)
PEAC......... Pharmaceutical Education Advisory Committee [*Australia*]
PEAC......... Photoelectric Alignment Collimator (IAA)
PEAC......... Photoelectric Auto Collimator
PEAC......... Photoelectroanalytical Chemistry
PEAC......... Police Education Advisory Council [*New South Wales, Australia*]
PEAC......... Program Evaluation and Audit Committee (SAUS)
PEAC......... Public Education Awards Competition (SAUS)
PEACAMPOT... Perturbation by East Asia Continental Air Mass to Pacific Oceanic Troposphere (SAUS)
PEACE........ Peace Enhancement Attained-Collaborative Efforts (EARSL)
PEACE........ People Emerging Against Corrupt Establishments [*Underground military newspaper*]
PEACE........ Plan for Excellence in a Collaborative Environment [*School project*]
PEACE........ Plasma Electron and Current Analyzer (SAUS)
PEACE........ Project Evaluation and Assistance, Civil Engineering [*Air Force*]
PEACE........ Protection of Environment for Assuring Cleaner Earth (SAUS)
PEACER...... Petroleum Employers Advisory Council on Employ Relations (SAUS)
Peace Res Soc Int Pap... Peace Research Society International Papers [*A publication*] (JLIT)
PEACESAT... Pan-Pacific Editing and Communication Experiment by Satellite (NITA)
PEACESAT... Pan-Pacific Educational and Cultural Exchange by Satellite Program [*University of Hawaii, Manoa*] [*Research center*] (RCD)
PEACESAT... Pan-Pacific Education and Communication Experiments by Satellites [*University of Hawaii*] [*NASA*]
PEACH........ People for Environmental Action and Children's Health (EARSL)
PEACH........ Preschool Evaluation and Assessment for Children with Handicaps (STED)
PEACH-PAC... California Canning Peach Association PAC [*Sacramento, CA*] (PACS)
PEACU........ Plastic Energy Absorption in Compression Unit (IEEE)
PEAD......... Presidential Emergency Action Document
PEADCO...... Process Evaluation & Development Corp. (EFIS)
PEADS........ Presidential Emergency Action Direction System (MCD)
PEAF......... Print Evaluation and Acceptance Form (TIMI)
PEAI......... Physical Education Association of Ireland (EAIO)
PEAK......... Peak Technologies Group, Inc. [*NASDAQ symbol*] (SAG)
PEAK......... Peak Technologies Grp [*NASDAQ symbol*] (TTSB)
PEAK......... Pricing Electronic Access to Knowledge
Peake........ Peake's Cases [*1790-1812*] [*A publication*] (DLA)
Peake Add Cas... Peake's Additional Cases Nisi Prius [*1795-1812*] [*A publication*] (DLA)
Peake Ev.... Peake on the Law of Evidence [*A publication*] (DLA)
Peake NP... Peake's English Nisi Prius Cases [*170 English Reprint*] [*A publication*] (DLA)
Peake NP Add Cas... Peake's Additional Cases Nisi Prius [*170 English Reprint*] [*England*] [*A publication*] (DLA)
Peake NP Add Cas (Eng)... Peake's Additional Cases Nisi Prius [*170 English Reprint*] [*England*] [*A publication*] (DLA)
Peake NP Cas... Peake's English Nisi Prius Cases [*170 English Reprint*] [*1790-1812*] [*A publication*] (DLA)
Peake NP Cas (Eng)... Peake's English Nisi Prius Cases [*170 English Reprint*] [*A publication*] (DLA)
PeakTch..... Peak Technologies Group, Inc. [*Associated Press*] (SAG)
PEAL......... Professional Engineers Association Ltd. (SAUS)
PEAM........ Personal Electronic Aid for Maintenance [*Military*]
PEAMF....... PeakSoft Multinet Corp. [*OTCBB symbol*]
Pea MS...... Peachey on Marriage Settlements [*1860*] [*A publication*] (DLA)
Pea Mus.... Peabody Museum (SAUS)
PEAMUSE... Peabody Museum of Archaeology and Ethnology [*Harvard University*] [*Research center*] (RCD)
PE&D........ Plant engineering and design (SAUS)
PE & M...... Plant Engineering and Maintenance (MCD)
PE&R........ Policy, Evaluation and Research (SAUS)
PE&S........ Parts Engineering and Standardization (SAUS)
PEANZ....... Petroleum Exploration Association of New Zealand (SAUS)
PEAO........ Phenylethylamine Oxidase (STED)
PEAP........ Pad Emergency Air Pack [*NASA*] (KSC)
PEAP........ Personal Egress Air Pack (NAKS)
PEAP........ Pesticide Education and Action Project (EA)
PEAP........ Positive End-Airway Pressure [*Medicine*] (DMAA)
PEAP........ Principal Error Axis for Position
PEAP........ Program Evaluation Analysis Plan (MCD)
PEAQ........ Personal Experience and Attitude Questionnaire (STED)
PeAR........ Die Provinzeinteilung des Assyrischen Reiches [*A publication*] (BJA)
PEAR........ Plasma Extended Arc Reactor (SAUS)
PEAR........ Polyetheramide [*Plastics*]
PEAR........ Princeton Engineering Anomalies Research Laboratory [*Medicine*] (EDAA)
PEAR........ Production Error Analysis Report (SAUS)
PEAR........ Program Error Analysis Report [*Computer science*] (VLIE)
Pearce CC... Pearce's Reports in Dearsley's English Crown Cases [*A publication*] (DLA)
PEARL....... Committee for Public Education and Religious Liberty (EA)
PEARL....... Parts Explosion and Retrieval Language (SAUS)
pearl......... pearl white (SAUS)
PEARL....... Performance Evaluation of Amplifiers from a Remote Location
PEARL....... Periodical Enquiry Acquisition and Registration Locally (NITA)
PEARL....... Periodicals Automation, Rand Library
PEARL....... Personal Equipment and Rescue/Survivable Lowdown (MCD)
PEARL....... Personnel Expertise and Resource Listing (COE)
PEARL....... Portable Environmental Assessment and Research Laboratory (SAUS)
PEARL....... Process and Experiment Automation Real-Time Language [*Computer science*]
PEARL....... Processor and Experiment Automation Realtime Language (SAUS)
PEARL....... Professional Electrical Apparatus Recyclers League [*Association*] (EA)
PEARL....... Program for EPS [*Electrical Power System*] Analysis and Rapid Look-Ahead [*NASA computer program*]
PEARL....... Programmed Editor and Automated Resources for Learning
PEARL....... Public Education and Religious Liberty (SAUS)
PEARL....... Pupils Equal and Reactive to Light [*Medicine*]
PEARL....... Pupils Equal and React to Light [*Medicine*] (MELL)
PEARLA..... Pupils Equal and React to Light and Accomodation [*Medicine*]
PEARLNAVSHIPYD... Pearl Harbour Naval Shipyard (SAUS)
Pears......... Pearson's Reports [*1850-80*] [*Pennsylvania*] [*A publication*] (DLA)
PEARS....... Porcine Epidemic Abortion and Respiratory Syndrome (SAUS)
Pearson...... Pearson's Common Pleas [*Pennsylvania*] [*A publication*] (DLA)
Pears (PA)... Pearson's Reports [*1850-80*] [*Pennsylvania*] [*A publication*] (DLA)
PEART....... Passive Electronic Advanced Receiver (MCD)
pearwd...... Pear Tree Wood (VRA)
PEAS........ Pacific's Electronics Acquisition Service (NITA)
PEAS........ Physical Estimation and Attraction Scales
PEAS........ Policy and External Affairs Staff [*Environmental Protection Agency*] (GFGA)
PEAS........ Practical Engineering Applications Software (NITA)
PEAS........ Presbyterian Educational Association of the South [*Defunct*] (EA)
Pease........ Pease Oil & Gas Co. [*Associated Press*] (SAG)
PeaseOG.... Pease Oil & Gas Co. [*Associated Press*] (SAG)
PEAS/SOAS... PSYOP Effects and Analysis/SOAS (SAUS)
PEAT......... Phenylethanolaminotetralin [*Organic chemistry*]
PEAT......... Pricing Evaluation for Audit Technique [*Finance*]
PEAT......... Programme Elargi d'Assistance Technique [*Expanded Program of Technical Assistance*] [*United Nations*]
PEAT......... Programmer Exercised Autopilot Test (AAG)
PEATMOS... Primitive Equation and Trajectory Model Output Statistics (SAUS)
PEAV......... Peavey [*Federal Railroad Administration identification code*]
PEAV......... Principal Error Axis for Velocity
PE B......... Bachelor of Pedagogy (ROG)
Pe B......... Bachelor of Pediatrics
PEB.......... Parametric Empirical Bayes [*Statistics*]
PEB.......... Partial Etch-Back (SAUS)
PEB.......... Party Election Broadcast [*British*] (BARN)
PEB.......... Pebble [*Jewelry*] (ROG)

PEB .... Pebble Gold Resources [*Vancouver Stock Exchange symbol*]
PEB .... Pensioners' Employment Bureau [*British*]
PEB .... Performance Evaluation Board [*NASA*] (MCD)
PEB .... Phosphate Ester Base (PDAA)
PEB .... Phototype Environment Buoy (PDAA)
PEB .... Phycoerythrobilin [*Biochemistry*]
PE B .... Physical Education Building (SAUS)
PEB .... Physical Evaluation Board [*Military*]
PEB .... Plasma Electron Beam (PDAA)
PEB .... Population-Environment Balance (EA)
PEB .... Porcelain Enamel Bath [*Classified advertising*] (ADA)
PEB .... Positive Expulsion Bladder
PEB .... Post-Election Briefing (SAUS)
PEB .... Post Exposure Bake (SAUS)
PEB .... Postexposure Baking [*Microlithography*]
PEB .... Pre-Expanded Bin (DNAB)
PEB .... Presidential Emergency Board
PEB .... Production Efficiency Board [*British*] [*World War II*]
PEB .... Program Element Breakdown [*Computer science*] (IAA)
PEB .... Propulsion Examining Board [*Navy*] (NVT)
PEB .... Prototype Environmental Buoy [*Marine science*] (MSC)
PEB .... Psycho-Educational Battery [*Educational test*]
PEB .... Public Examination Board (SAUS)
PEB .... Pulmonary Ectopic Beat [*Cardiology*]
PEB .... Pulsed Electron Beam (IEEE)
PEBA .... Polyether Block Amide [*Plastics technology*]
PEBA .... Polyether Block Polyamide (SAUS)
PEBA .... Pulsed Electron Beam Annealer [*Photovoltaic energy systems*]
PEBA .... Purified Extract of Brucella Abortus (SAUS)
PEBAB .... Para-(Ethoxybenzylidene)aminobenzonitrile [*Also, EBCA*] [*Organic chemistry*]
PEB & B .... Porcelain Enamel Bath and Basin [*Classified advertising*] (ADA)
PEBB .... Power Electronic Building Block [*Electric vehicle engineering*]
PEBB .... Public Employees Blanket Bond
PEBBLE .... Probe Encapsulated by BioListic Embedding [*Biosensor*]
PEBBLE .... Probe-Encapsulated by Biologically Localized Embedding
PEBCAK .... Problem Exists Between Chair and Keyboard (ADWA)
PeBcCH .... Peoples Bancorp, Inc. (Ohio) [*Associated Press*] (SAG)
PEBCO .... Port Elizabeth Black Civic Organization South Africa (SAUS)
PEBCO .... Program Evaluation and Budget Committee [*American Library Association*]
PEBD .... Pay Entry Base Date
PEBES .... Personal Earning and Benefit Estimate Statement [*Social Security Administration*]
PEBG .... Phenethylbiguanide [*Same as PEDG*] [*Antidiabetic compound*]
PEBH .... Physical Evaluation Board Hospital [*Military*]
PEBK .... Peoples Bank [*Catawba, NC*] [*NASDAQ symbol*] (NQ)
PEBL .... Port Everglades Belt Line Railway [*AAR code*] [*Obsolete*]
PEBLDS .... Pan-European Biological and Landscape Diversity Strategy (SAUS)
PEBLO .... Physical Evaluation Board Liaison Officer [*Air Force*] (AFM)
PEBO .... Peoples Bancorp [*NASDAQ symbol*] (TTSB)
PEBO .... Peoples Bancorp, Inc. (Ohio) [*NASDAQ symbol*] (SAG)
PEBO .... Peoples Bancorporation [*NASDAQ symbol*]
PEBP .... Patient Escorted by Police (DMAA)
PEBS .... Pulsed Electron Beam Source (MCD)
PEBU .... Peripheral Equipment Buffer Unit (SAUS)
PEBV .... Pea Early-Browning Virus [*Plant pathology*]
PEBW .... People's Bancorp Worcester (EFIS)
PEBX .... Private Electronic Branch Exchange (SAUS)
PEC .... American Irish Political Education Committee (EA)
PEC .... Chlorinated Polyethylene (SAUS)
PEc .... Ellwood City Area Public Library, Ellwood City, PA [*Library symbol*] [*Library of Congress*] (LCLS)
PEC .... IEEE Power Electronics Council (EA)
PEC .... Pacific Command Electronic Intelligence Center (MCD)
PEC .... Pacific East Asia Cargo Airline, Inc. [*Philippines*] [*ICAO designator*] (FAAC)
PEC .... Pacific Economic Community (FEA)
PEC .... Packaged Electronic Circuit [*Computer science*] (IAA)
PEC .... Page End Character [*Computer science*] (ELAL)
PEC .... Palestine Economic Commission
PEC .... Panasonic Energy Corp. [*Vancouver Stock Exchange symbol*]
PEC .... Panel Electronic Circuit (EECA)
PEC .... Parents Education Committee (SAUS)
PEC .... Passive Equipment Cabinet [*Military*] (CAAL)
PEC .... Patient Evaluation Center (DAVI)
PEC .... Peak Electrode Current
PEC .... PEC Israel Economic Corp. [*Associated Press*] (SAG)
PEC .... Pectoral [*Lungs and Chest*] [*Medicine*] (ROG)
PEC .... Pedal Excretory Cell
PEC .... Peduncle of Cerebrum (DB)
PEC .... Pelican [*Alaska*] [*Airport symbol*] (OAG)
PEC .... Pelvic Cramps [*Medicine*] (MELL)
PEC .... Penelec Capital Ltd. [*NYSE symbol*] (SAG)
PEC .... Perfect Electric Conductor (SAUS)
PEC .... Perfil de Evaluacion del Comportamiento [*Standardized test of elementary through high school students' behavior at school, at home, and with peers*]
PEC .... Performance Evaluation Committee (SAUS)
PEC .... Peripheral Equipment Corp. (SAUS)
PEC .... Peripheral Expansion Chassis (TIMI)
PEC .... Peritoneal Exudate Cells [*Hematology*]
PEC .... Perkin-Elmer Corp. (MCD)
PEC .... Perris [*California*] [*Seismograph station code, US Geological Survey*] (SEIS)
PEC .... Persistent Early Curvature
PEC .... Personal Education Counseling (DNAB)
PEC .... Personal Effects Coverage [*Insurance*]
PEC .... Petro-Canada
PEC .... Phenylene Ether Copolymer [*Organic chemistry*]
PEC .... Philadelphia Electric [*Federal Railroad Administration identification code*]
PEC .... Photoelectric Cell
PEC .... Photoelectrochemical Cell [*Energy conversion device*]
PEC .... Photoelectrochromic [*Chemistry*]
PEC .... Photoemissive Cell (SAUS)
PEC .... Physical Education Centre (SAUS)
PEC .... Physics, Engineering, and Chemistry (AAG)
PEC .... Pigmented Emulsified Creosote
PEC .... Pigmented Epithelial Cell [*Ophthalmology*]
PEC .... Pilot Error Correction (IAA)
PEC .... Pin Electronic Card (SAUS)
PEC .... Plain English Campaign [*British*] (DBA)
PEC .... Planetary Entry Capsule [*Aerospace*]
PEC .... Plant Equipment Codes [*DoD*]
PEC .... Plastics Environment Council (SAUS)
PEC .... Platform Electron Card [*Electronics*] (OA)
PEC .... Platform Electronic Cards (SAUS)
PEC .... Platform Evaluation Confidence (SEWL)
PEC .... Political Education Committee [*American Ireland Education Foundation*] (EA)
PEC .... Polyester Carbonate (SAUS)
PEC .... Polyestercarbonate [*Organic chemistry*]
PEC .... Polyphenylene Ether Copolymer (SAUS)
PEC .... Position Error Correction (DA)
PEC .... Positive Engagement Clutch
PEC .... Potasse et Engrais Chimiques
PEC .... Potential Enviromental Concentration [*Pollution technology*]
PEC .... Power Electronics Council (NTPA)
PEC .... Predicted Environmental Concentration (DCTA)
PEC .... Pre-Existing Condition [*Health Insurance*]
PEC .... Presbyterian Evangelical Coalition (EA)
PEC .... Presidential Ethics Commission (SAUS)
PEC .... President's Export Council (JAGO)
PEC .... Previous Element Coding
PEC .... Primary Environment Care (SAUS)
PEC .... Print Error Check (SAUS)
PEC .... Production Equipment Code [*Military*]
PEC .... Production Executive Committee
PEC .... Professional Engineers of Colorado (EARSL)
PEC .... Program Element Code (AFM)
PEC .... Program Environment Control
PEC .... Program Evaluation Center [*Navy*] (AFIT)
PEC .... Program Exception Code [*Computer science*] (ELAL)
PEC .... Program Execution Control (SAUS)
PEC .... Program Executive Council (SAUS)
PEC .... Projected Effective Coverage (SAUS)
PEC .... Propulsion Environmental Chamber
PEC .... Protestant Episcopal Church (WDAA)
PEC .... Protocol Engineering Center (SAUS)
PEC .... Prova Elementi Combustibili [*An Italian fast reactor*]
PEC .... Provisional Electoral Council (Haiti) [*Political party*] (PSAP)
PEC .... Psychology Examining Commission (or Committee) (SAUS)
PEC .... Public Education Center [*Association*] (EA)
PEC .... Public Extension Circuit (SAUS)
PEC .... Pugwash Etudiant du Canada
PEC .... Pulsed Eddy Current (SAUS)
p E c .... pure Ecuadoran cocaine (SAUS)
PEC .... Pyridylethylcysteine [*Biochemistry*]
PEC .... Pyrogenic Exotoxin C [*Medicine*]
PECA .... Petroleum Equipment Contractors Association (EA)
Peca .... Petrus de Bellapertica [*Deceased, 1308*] [*Authority cited in pre-1607 legal work*] (DSA)
PECA .... Pre-Engineering Change Action (SAUS)
PECA .... Preliminary Engineering Change Analysis (SAUS)
PECA .... Process Engineers and Constructors' Association [*Australia*]
PECA .... Proposed Engineering Change Assessment (SAUS)
PECAM .... Platelet-Endothelial Cell Adhesion Molecule [*Cytology*]
PECAN .... Pulse Envelop Correlation Air Navigation
PECANS .... Poughkeepsie Engineering Circuit Analysis System (SAUS)
PE CARD .... Production Estimate Card (MSA)
PE CARD .... Production-Estimate Card (SAUS)
PECBI .... Professional Engineers Conference Board for Industry (EA)
PECC .... Pacific Economic Cooperation Conference (DOMA)
PECC .... Panel of Experts on Climatic Change [*WMO*] (MSC)
PECC .... Precanceled Envelope Collectors Club (EA)
PECC .... Product Engineering Control Center [*Telecommunications*] (TEL)
PECDAR .... Palestine Economic Council for Development and Reconstruction (ECON)
PECDS .... Professional Engineering Career Development Series [*Book series*]
PECE .... Package Express Company of Elgin [*Common carrier symbol*]
PECE .... Presidents Emergency Committee for Employment (SAUS)
PECE .... Proposed Engineering Change Estimate
PECF .... Pseudoextracellular Fluid [*for biocompatibility testing*]
PECFA .... Presidential Election Campaign Fund Act of 1966
PECH .... Polyepichlorohydrin (SAUS)
Pecho .... Prostatic Echogram [*Medicine*] (AAMN)
PECHORA .... Paleo Environment and Climate History of the Russian Arctic (SAUS)
PE-CI .... Plutonium Equivalent Curies (SAUS)

PECI .... Preliminary Equipment Component Index [*or Inventory*]
PECI .... Preliminary Equipment Component Inventory (SAUS)
PECI .... Productivity Enhancing Capital Investment [*DoD*]
PECI .... Projects and Equipment Corporation of India (SAUS)
PECIACESC... Permanent Executive Committee of the Inter-American Council for Education, Science, and Culture
PECIAECOSOC... Permanent Executive Committee of the Inter-American Economic and Social Council
PECIP........ Productivity Enhancing Capital Investment Program (MCD)
Peck......... Peck's Reports [*7 Tennessee*] [*1921-24*] [*A publication*] (DLA)
Peck......... Peck's Reports [*24-30 Illinois*] [*A publication*] (DLA)
Peck......... Peckwell's English Election Cases [*1802-06*] [*A publication*] (DLA)
Peck El Cas... Peckwell's English Election Cases [*A publication*] (DLA)
Peck Elec Cas... Peckwell's English Election Cases [*1802-06*] [*A publication*] (DLA)
Peck (Ill)... Peck's Reports, Illinois Supreme Court Reports [*11-22, 24-30*] [*A publication*] (DLA)
Peck (Tenn)... Peck's Reports [*7 Tennessee*] [*A publication*] (DLA)
Peck Tr...... Peck's Trial (Impeachment) [*A publication*] (DLA)
Peckw....... Peckwell's English Election Cases [*A publication*] (DLA)
pecky cyp... Pecky Cypress (MIST)
PECL......... Plessey Electron Coupled Logic (SAUS)
PECL......... Positive Emitter-Coupled Logic (AEBE)
PECL......... Preliminary Engineering Configuration List
PECM........ Passive Electronics Countermeasures [*Military*] (NG)
PECM........ Preliminary Engineering Change Memorandum [*Air Force*] (CET)
PECN........ Process Equipment Change Notification (SAUS)
PECO........ Pays d'Europe Centrale et Orientale (ECON)
PECO........ PECO Energy [*Associated Press*] (SAG)
PECO........ Pecos National Monument
PECO........ Pelagic Cormorant [*North American bird banding code*] (BIBA)
PECo........ Philadelphia Electric Company
PECO$_2$....... Mixed Expired Carbon Dioxide Tension [*Medicine*] (DAVI)
PECON...... Pennsylvania Erection & Construction Co. (EFIS)
PECOR...... Pennsylvania Engineering Corporation (EFIS)
PECOS...... Pays D'Europe Centrale et Orientale
PECOS...... Pecos, TX [*American Association of Railroads railroad junction routing code*]
PECOS...... Pentagon Computer Operations Support (MCD)
PECOS...... Picture Enhancement Computer Operating System (SAUS)
PECOS...... Program Environment Checkout System
PECOS...... Project Evaluation and Control System (MCD)
PECOS...... Project Evaluation and Cost Optimization System (IAA)
PECP........ Preliminary Engineering Change Proposal
PECPrZ...... Penelec Capital L.P. 'MIPS' [*NYSE symbol*] (TTSB)
PECR........ Photo-Electric Card Reader (SAUS)
PECR........ Program Error Correction Report
PECRHIN... Produits et Engrais Chimiques du Rhin (EFIS)
Pe Cri....... Petrus Crispanus [*Authority cited in pre-1607 legal work*] (DSA)
PECS........ Picture Exchange Communication System
PECS........ Plant Engineering Check Sheet (AAG)
PECS........ Portable Environmental Control System [*NASA*]
PECS........ Printers' Estimating and Costing System (DGA)
PECS........ Programmable Electronic Call Simulator (SAUS)
PECSS....... Presorted Emergency Cooling System Sampling [*Environmental science*] (COE)
PECT......... Pectori [*To the Chest*] [*Pharmacy*]
PECT......... Pennstyle Campers [*NCIC trailer make code*]
PECT......... Progestin-Estrogen Cyclic Therapy [*Medicine*] (MELL)
PECTFE...... Polyethylene-Chlorotrifluoroethylene [*Organic chemistry*]
pecto........ pectoral (SAUS)
PECTS....... Performance Evaluation Commitment Tracking System (SAUS)
PECU........ Print Edit Control Unit (SAUS)
pecul........ peculated (SAUS)
pecul........ peculating (SAUS)
pecul........ peculation (SAUS)
pecul........ peculator (SAUS)
PECUL....... Peculiar (ROG)
PECUS....... Personal Engineering Computer User's Society [*Defunct*] (EA)
PECUSA..... Presidential Ethics Commission (NADA)
PECUSA..... Protestant Episcopal Church in the United States
PECUSA..... Protestant Episcopal Church of the U.S.A. (SAUS)
PECUY....... Pecuniary (ROG)
PECVD....... Plasma-Enhanced Chemical Vapor Deposition [*Coating technology*]
PECWBS.... Proposed Extended Contract Work Breakdown Structure [*Military*]
PECWG...... Piaster Expenditure Control Working Group [*Military*]
PECX........ Photoelectron Corp. [*NASDAQ symbol*] (NASQ)
PECZ......... Premier Elkhorn Coal [*Federal Railroad Administration identification code*]
PED.......... Doctor of Physical Education (PGP)
PED.......... Parole Eligibility Date (WDAA)
PED.......... Patient Examined by Doctor (DMAA)
PED.......... Payload Element Developer (SAUS)
PED.......... Pedagogue
Ped.......... Pedagogy (SAUS)
PED.......... Pedal
PED.......... Peddler [*or Peddling*] [*FBI standardized term*]
PED.......... Pedestal (AAG)
Ped.......... Pedestrian (ADWA)
PED.......... Pedestrian
PED.......... Pediatric Emergency Department (DMAA)
PED.......... Pediatrician
PED.......... Pediatrics (AABC)
Ped.......... Pediatrics [*Medicine*] (BCRP)
PED.......... Pedlary (ROG)
PED.......... Pedro Aguirre Cerda [*Antarctica*] [*Seismograph station code, US Geological Survey*] [*Closed*] (SEIS)
PED.......... Pending [*Motor vehicle violation status code used in state of Arkansas*] (MVRD)
PED.......... Period End Date (MCD)
PED.......... Personal Equipment Data [*Computer science*] (IAA)
PED.......... Personnel Equipment Data [*Army*] (IAA)
PED.......... Phosphorus Enhanced Diffusion (IAA)
PED.......... Photoelectric Device (SAUS)
PED.......... Photoelectron Energy Distribution (SAUS)
PED.......... Photoemission Diode
PEd.......... Physical Education
PED.......... Pigment Epithelial Detachment (SAUS)
PED.......... Pink-Eyed Dilution [*Medicine*] (DMAA)
PED.......... Plastic-Encapsulated Device (SAUS)
PED.......... Platform Equipment Deck
PED.......... Polymer Engineering Directive (WDAA)
PED.......... Polymer Engineering Directorate (SAUS)
PED.......... Portable Explosives Detector [*Police and security equipment*]
PED.......... Positive Expulsion Device
PED.......... Power Equipment Division (SAUS)
PED.......... Processing, Exploitation and Dissemination (ACAE)
PED.......... Product Engineering Division [*Automotive engineering*]
PED.......... Production Eligibility Date (MUGU)
PED.......... Production Engineering Division [*University of Wisconsin - Madison*] [*Research center*] (RCD)
PED.......... Program Element Description
PED.......... Program Element Directive
PED.......... Program Evaluation Division [*Environmental Protection Agency*] (GFGA)
PED.......... Program Execution Directive (AAG)
PED.......... Program for Executive Development
PED.......... Promotion Eligibility Date [*Military*]
PED.......... Protective Equipment Decontamination (SAUS)
PED.......... Proton-Enhanced Diffusion
PED.......... Proton-Excited Diffusion (SAUS)
PED.......... Public Employee Department (of AFL-CIO) (EA)
PEd.......... Pulmonary Edema [*Medicine*]
PED.......... Pulse Edge Discrimination (OA)
PED.......... Purchase Early Development (SAUS)
PED.......... Pure Edge Dislocation
PED.......... Pyramid Element Designator
PED.......... Springfield, TN [*Location identifier*] [*FAA*] (FAAL)
PEDA........ Pedal Artery
PEDA........ Pedalpower Electroped [*NCIC motorcycle make code*]
PEDA........ Personnel Equipment Data Analysis
PEDANT..... Preprogrammable Evaluations based on a Data Normalizing Technique (SAUS)
Ped B........ Bachelor of Pedagogy
PED B....... Bachelor of Pediatrics (WDAA)
PEDB........ Page Element Data Base [*Printing*] (DGA)
PEDB........ Payload Engineering Data Base [*NASA*] (SSD)
PEDB........ Planning and Execution Data Base (COE)
PEDB........ Process Engineering Database
PEDBASE... Pediatric Database (SAUS)
PEDC........ Pacific Engine Development & Consulting, Inc. (EFIS)
PEDC........ Personal Effects Distribution Center
PEDC........ Professional Educational Development Corp. [*An association*] (EA)
PEDCUG..... Planning Engineers Desktop Computer Users Group (EA)
Ped D....... Doctor of Pedagogy
PEDD........ Peddlers Choice [*NCIC motorcycle make code*]
PEDD........ Program Element Descriptive Data (CAAL)
PEDDRO.... Network of information in the field of drug abuse prevention through education (SAUS)
PEddyB...... Baldwin Locomotive Works, Eddystone, PA [*Library symbol*] [*Library of Congress*] [*Obsolete*] (LCLS)
PEDE........ Great Pee Dee Bancorp, Inc. [*NASDAQ symbol*] (NASQ)
Pe de Ancar... Petrus de Ancharano [*Deceased, 1416*] [*Authority cited in pre-1607 legal work*] (DSA)
Pe de Anch... Petrus de Ancharano [*Deceased, 1416*] [*Authority cited in pre-1607 legal work*] (DSA)
Pe de Ancha... Petrus de Ancharano [*Deceased, 1416*] [*Authority cited in pre-1607 legal work*] (DSA)
Pe de Bel... Petrus de Bellapertica [*Deceased, 1308*] [*Authority cited in pre-1607 legal work*] (DSA)
Pe de Belper... Petrus de Bellapertica [*Deceased, 1308*] [*Authority cited in pre-1607 legal work*] (DSA)
Pe de Bepe... Petrus de Bellapertica [*Deceased, 1308*] [*Authority cited in pre-1607 legal work*] (DSA)
Pe de Blpti... Petrus de Bellapertica [*Deceased, 1308*] [*Authority cited in pre-1607 legal work*] (DSA)
Pe de Pal... Pierre de la Palu [*Deceased, 1342*] [*Authority cited in pre-1607 legal work*] (DSA)
Pe de Sal... Petrus de Salinis [*Flourished, 13th century*] [*Authority cited in pre-1607 legal work*] (DSA)
Pe de Samp... Petrus de Sampsone [*Flourished, 1246-58*] [*Authority cited in pre-1607 legal work*] (DSA)
PEDET....... Pedetemptim [*Gradually*] [*Pharmacy*]
PEDF........ Pigment Epithelium-Derived Factor [*Medicine*] (DMAA)
PEDF........ Potential-Energy Distribution Function [*Physical chemistry*]
PEDF........ Protective Equipment Decontamination Facility (SAUS)
PEDFORMS... Pedestrian Forms [*National Highway Traffic Safety Administration Fatal Accident Recording System code*]
PEDG........ Phenethyldiguanide [*Same as PEBG*] [*Antidiabetic compound*]

PEDI .... Pediatrics [*Medicine*] (DHSM)
PEDIAT ...... Pediatric (SAUS)
PEDIAT ...... Pediatrician (SAUS)
Pediatric ... Pediatric Services of America, Inc. [*Associated Press*] (SAG)
Pediatr Rev... Pediatrics in Review (SAUS)
PEDIN .... National Petroleum Exploration Database [*Australia*]
PEDIN .... Peapod Dinghy
PEDIN .... Petroleum Exploration Data Index (SAUS)
PE Dir .... Director of Physical Education (PGP)
PE Dir .... Physical Education Director
PEdiS........ Edinboro State College, Edinboro, PA [*Library symbol*] [*Library of Congress*] (LCLS)
PEDITOR... Portable Editor (SAUS)
PEDL .... Pedicel Length [*Botany*]
PEDL .... Prototype Equipment Development Laboratory (SAUS)
Ped M .... Master of Pedagogy
pedm .... Pediment (VRA)
PEDMAN .... PACFLT [*Pacific Fleet*] Enlisted Personnel Distribution Manual (CINC)
PEDMS...... Portable and Extensible Data Management System (IAA)
PEDN .... Pedestrian [*Telegraphy*] (PCTE)
PEDN .... Planned Event Discrepancy Notification [*NASA*] (KSC)
PedNSS ..... Pediatric Nutrition Surveillance System (ADWA)
pedobap .... pedobaptism (SAUS)
pedobap .... pedobaptist (SAUS)
pedog .... pedography (SAUS)
pedogen .... pedogenesis (SAUS)
PEDOL....... Pedology
pedom........ pedometer (SAUS)
PEDONT..... Pedodontic (SAUS)
pedop .... pedophile (SAUS)
PEDP .... Pacific Energy Development Program [*Fiji*] [*United Nations*]
PEDP .... Performance Evaluation and Development Plan (TIMI)
PEDRA ...... Palestine Economic Development and Reconstruction Agency (ECON)
PEDRO ...... Perkins Engineering Data Retrieval Organization (SAUS)
PEDRO ...... Pneumatic Energy Detector with Remote Optics
PEDRO ...... Pride, Efficiency, Dedication, Reliability, and Order (DNAB)
PEDRS ...... Process Evaluation and Defect Reporting System (ACAE)
PEDRTC..... Pediatric
PEDS .... Packaging Engineering Data System (AFM)
PEDS .... Pediatric Digestion and Motility Disorders Society [*Association*] (EA)
PeDS .... Pediatric Drug Surveillance [*Program*] (DAVI)
Peds......... Pediatrics [*Medicine*] (AMHC)
PEDS .... Pediatrics
PEDS .... Peltier Effect Diffusion Separation [*Physical chemistry*]
PEDS .... Philips Engineering and Development System (NITA)
PEDS .... Pilgrim Edward Doty Society (EA)
PEDS .... Planning, programming, budget, and execution Electronic Delivery System (SAUS)
PEDS .... Plasma-Enhanced Deposition System (AAEL)
PEDS .... Portable Emergency Data System [*Emergency Management*] (EMA)
PEDS .... Precise Engineering and Deformation Survey (SAUS)
PEDS .... Program Element Descriptive Summary (CAAL)
PEDS .... Protective Equipment Decontamination Section [*Nuclear energy*] (NRCH)
PEDSTL ..... Pedestal [*Freight*]
PEDT .... Pendant [*Jewelry*] (ROG)
PEDT .... Peridot [*Jewelry*] (ROG)
PEDTRC..... Pediatric
PEDUC ...... Professeurs d'Economie Domestique des Universites Canadiennes [*Canadian University Teachers of Home Economics - CUTHE*]
PEDX .... Pediatrix Medical Group [*NASDAQ symbol*] (TTSB)
PEDX .... Pediatrix Medical Group, Inc. [*NASDAQ symbol*] (SAG)
PED XING... Pedestrian Crossing (SAUS)
PEE .... Phosphate-Eliminating Enzyme (DMAA)
PEE .... Photo-Electric Emission (SAUS)
PEE .... Photoelectron Emission [*Also, OSEE*]
PEE .... Photoemission Effect
PEE .... Photoferroelectric Effect (SAUS)
PEE .... Polycrystalline Electrode with Epitaxy (SAUS)
PEE .... Pressure Environmental Equipment (NVT)
PEE .... Program Estimating Equation
PEE .... Proof and Experimental Establishment [*British*]
PEE .... Punctate Epithelial Erosions (SAUS)
PEE .... Talkeetna, AK [*Location identifier*] [*FAA*] (FAAL)
PEEA......... (Phenyl)(ethyl)ethanolamine [*Organic chemistry*]
PEEC......... Partial Element Equivalent Circuit (SAUS)
PEEC......... Personnel Emergency Estimator Capability
PEEC......... Programmable Electronic Engine Control [*Automotive engineering*]
PEEC......... Project for an Energy-Enriched Curriculum [*Department of Energy*]
PEECP....... Pilot Expedited Environmental Cleanup Program (BCP)
PEEIC........ Programme des Economies d'Energie dans l'Industrie Canadienne
PEEK......... Partners Early Experience Kit (SAUS)
PEEK......... Peek [*NCIC trailer make code*]
PEEK......... Peekskill Financial [*NASDAQ symbol*] (TTSB)
PEEK......... Peekskill Financial Corp. [*NASDAQ symbol*] (SAG)
PEEK......... People for the Enjoyment of Eyeballing Knees [*Group opposing below-the-knee fashions introduced in 1970*]
PEEK......... Periodically Elevated Electronic Kibitzer
PEEK......... Polyetheretherketone (DMAA)
PEEK......... Polyetherketone [*Organic chemistry*]
PEEKK....... Poly Ether Ether Ketone Ketone (EDCT)
PEEKKK ..... Polyetherether Ketone Ketone Ketone (SAUS)
Peekskill... Peekskill Financial Corp. [*Associated Press*] (SAG)
PEEL......... Peel [*NCIC car make code*]
PEEL......... Programmable Electrically Erasable Logic (SAUS)
PE Element... Parallel Elastic Element (SAUS)
PEELS .... Parallel [*Detection*] Electron Energy Loss Spectroscopy
PEEM........ Panel of Experts on Environmental Management (GNE)
PEEM........ Photoelectron Emission Electron Microscopy (SAUS)
PEEM........ Photoelectron Emission Microscopy (SAUS)
PEEM........ Photoemission Electron Microscope
PEEP......... Panel of Experts on Environmental Pollution [*WMO*] (MSC)
PEEP......... Pilot's Electronic Eyelevel Presentation [*British*]
PEEP......... Porous Electrode Electrostatic Precipitation
PEEP......... Positive End Expiratory Pressure [*Medicine*]
PEEP......... Production Electronic Equipment Procurement Status Report
Peeples & Stevens... Peeples and Stevens' Reports [*80-97 Georgia*] [*A publication*] (DLA)
PEER .... Pacific Earthquake Engineering Research [*Emergency Management*] (EMA)
PEER .... Partnerships for Environmental Education and Research (SAUS)
PEER .... Pediatric Examination of Educational Readiness [*Child development test*]
PEER .... Peerless [*NCIC car make code*]
Peer .... Peerless [*Record label*] [*USA, Mexico*]
PEER .... Performance Efficiency Evaluation Report (SAUS)
PEER .... Planned Environment and Education Research Institute (SAUS)
PEER .... Planned Experience for Effective Relating
PEER .... Price Escalation Estimated Rates
PEER .... Professional Engineers Employment Registry (SAUS)
PEER .... Program of Equal Employment Opportunity Evaluation Reports
PEER .... Project Engineer Evaluation Report (HGAA)
PEER .... Project on Equal Education Rights [*Defunct*] (EA)
PEERAMID... Pediatric Examination of Educational Readiness at Middle Childhood [*Child development test*] [*Psychology*]
PEERC....... Production Engineering Education and Research Center
Peere Wms... Peere-Williams' English Chancery and King's Bench Cases [*1695-1736*] [*A publication*] (DLA)
PeerMf ...... Peerless Manufacturing Co. [*Associated Press*] (SAG)
PEET......... Partnerships for Enhancing Expertise in Taxonomy [*National Science Foundation*]
PEET......... Peet Frate Line [*Common carrier symbol*]
PEET......... Peet's Coffee and Tea [*NASDAQ symbol*]
PEET......... Printing Equipment Education Trust [*British*]
PEETPACK... Process Engineering Evaluation Techniques Package (PDAA)
PEETSA ..... Parents, Educators and Environmentalists to Save Anchoives [*An association*]
PEEX......... Pediatric Early Elementary Examination [*Child development test*] [*Psychology*]
PEF .... Pacific-Euro Growth Fund (EFIS)
PEF .... Packaging Education Foundation (EA)
PEF .... Palestine Endowment Funds [*Later, PEF Israel Endowment Funds*] (EA)
PEF .... Palestine Exploration Fund
PEF .... Particulate Emission Factor (EEVL)
PEF .... Pathway-Exposure Factor [*Environmental chemistry*]
PEF .... Peak Expiratory Flow [*Pulmonary function*]
PEF .... PEF Israel Endowment Funds [*An association*] (EA)
PEF .... Performance Efficiency Factor (AFIT)
PEF .... Performance Enhancement Feature [*Computer science*] (HODG)
PEF .... Personal Effects Floater [*Insurance*]
PEF .... Personality Evaluation Form [*Psychology*]
PEF .... Pharyngo-Epiglottic Fold [*Medicine*] (MELL)
PEF .... Phil Esposito Foundation [*Defunct*] (EA)
PEF .... Physical Electronics Facility (MCD)
PEF .... Plastics Education Foundation (EA)
PEF .... Polyethylene Foam
PEF .... Positive Expiratory Force [*Medicine*] (BCRP)
PEF .... Potential-Energy Function [*Physical chemistry*]
PEF .... Powerhouse Exhaust Facility (IAA)
PEF .... Prediction Error Filter [*Wave frequency and phase modifier*]
PEF .... Presbyterian Evangelistic Fellowship [*Defunct*] (EA)
PEF .... Presidential Election Fund (SAUS)
PEF .... Pro Ecclesia Foundation (EA)
PEF .... Program Estimating Factor (AFM)
PEF .... Proposal Evaluation Form (AAG)
PEF .... Psychiatric Evaluation Form [*Psychology*]
PEF .... Pulmonary Edema Fluid [*Medicine*] (DMAA)
PEF .... Pulsed-Electric-Field
PEF .... Pulse Eliminating Filter (IAA)
PEFA......... Palestine Exploration Fund Annual [*A publication*] (ABAR)
PEFA......... Peregrine Falcon [*North American bird banding code*] (BIBA)
PEFC......... Polymer Electrolyte Fuel Cell [*Automotive engineering*]
PEFC......... Private Export Funding Corp. (IMH)
PEFCO....... Private Export Funding Corp.
Peff .... Effective Filtration Pressure [*Medicine*] (MELL)
Pe Fi .... Petrus Filipi [*Authority cited in pre-1607 legal work*] (DSA)
Pe Fili....... Petrus Filipi [*Authority cited in pre-1607 legal work*] (DSA)
PEF/NET.... Public Education Fund Network (EA)
PEFO .... Payload Effects Follow-On Study [*NASA*] (NASA)
PEFO .... Petrified Forest National Park
PEFOS....... Program Evaluation and Field Operations Staff [*Environmental Protection Agency*] (GFGA)
PEFQ .... Palestine Exploration Fund Quarterly Statement [*A publication*] (ABAR)
PEFQS....... Palestine Exploration Fund. Quarterly Statement [*London*] [*A publication*] (BJA)

PEFQST ..... Palestine Exploration Fund. Quarterly Statement [*London*] [*A publication*] (BJA)
PEFR .... Peak Expiratory Flow Rate
PEFR/PIFR ... Peak Expiratory Flow/Peak Inspiratory Flow Rate [*Medicine*] (DAVI)
PEFS .... Penner Feed and Supply [*Common carrier symbol*]
PEFSR .... Partial Expiratory Flow-Static Recoil Curve [*Physiology*] (MAE)
PEFST .... Palestine Exploration Fund. Quarterly Statement (SAUS)
PEFT .... Peripheral Equipment Functional Test (CAAL)
PEFT .... Preschool Embedded Figures Test [*Child development test*]
PEFTOK ..... Philippine Expeditionary Force to Korea [*United Nations*]
PEFTP .... Parent Education Follow Through Program (EDAC)
PEFU .... Panel of Experts on Fish Utilization [*FAO*] (ASF)
PEFV .... Partial Expiratory Flow-Volume [*Physiology*]
PEG .... General Analine & Film Co., General Research Laboratory, Easton, PA [*Library symbol*] [*Library of Congress*] [*Obsolete*] (LCLS)
PEG .... Pac Engo Materials [*Vancouver Stock Exchange symbol*]
PEG .... Pacific Environmental Group [*Marine science*] (MSC)
PEG .... Pan-European Group [*Often is an industry group*] (AG)
PEG .... Patient Evaluation Grid [*Medicine*] (DMAA)
Peg .... Pegasus [*Constellation*]
PEG .... Pelangi Air Sdn. Bhd. [*Malaysia*] [*FAA designator*] (FAAC)
PEG .... Percutaneous Endoscopic Gastrostomy [*Medicine*] (CPH)
PEG .... Performance Evaluation Group (CINC)
PEG .... Petrochemical Energy Group (EA)
PEG .... Photo Exploitation Group
PEG .... Pittsburgh Elderly Gay (SAUS)
PEG .... Pneumatic Explosion Generator
PEG .... Pneumoencephalogram [*Medicine*]
PEG .... Political Ecology Group [*Association*] (EA)
PEG .... Polyethylene Glycol [*Organic chemistry*]
PEG .... Powered Explicit Guidance (NAKS)
PEG .... Previous Endorsement(s) Guaranteed [*Banking*]
PEG .... Prime Event Generation (VLIE)
PEG .... Principle of the Equivalent Generator
PEG .... Prior Endorsement Guaranteed (HGAA)
PEG .... Priorities Exploitation Group
PEG .... Process Evaluation Guide [*Graphic Communications Association*]
PEG .... Production Entitlement Guarantee [*International Agricultural Trade Research Consortium*] (ECON)
PEG .... Professional Emphasis Group [*National Audience Board*] (NTCM)
PEG .... Program Evaluation Group [*Air Force*]
PEG .... Program Execution Guidance (SAUS)
PEG .... Project Engineering Guide (MCD)
PEG .... Project Execution Guidelines (ABAC)
PEG .... Protected Employee Group [*Program*]
PEG .... Protection Engineers Group [*United States Telephone Association*] [*Telecommunications*]
PEG .... PSE & G Capital Trust [*NYSE symbol*] (SAG)
PEG .... Public, Educational, Government [*Cable television access channels*] (NTCM)
PEG .... Public Service Elec & Gas Co. [*NYSE symbol*] (SAG)
PEG .... Public Service Enterprise Group, Inc. [*NYSE symbol*] (SPSG)
PEG .... Pyrotechnic Electron Generator (MCD)
PEGA .... Pegaso [*NCIC motorcycle make code*]
PEGA .... Pegaso [*NCIC car make code*]
PEGA .... Pegasystems, Inc. [*NASDAQ symbol*] (SAG)
PEGA .... Polyethylene Glycol Adipate [*Organic chemistry*]
PEGA .... Precision Engineering Grinding Apparatus (SAUS)
PegaCm ..... Pegasus Communications Corp. [*Associated Press*] (SAG)
PEGAD ...... Permission Granted to Add (SAUS)
PEG-ADA .... Polyethylene Glycol-Adenosine Deaminase [*A modified enzyme*]
PEGASUS ... People, Goods, and Services Urban System [*Texas*] [*FHWA*] (TAG)
PEGASUS ... Precision Engineering Grinding Apparatus for Superfinishing Ultra-hard Surfaces (SAUS)
Pegasys ..... Pegasystems, Inc. [*Associated Press*] (SAG)
PEGBB .... Polyester-Glass Bias-Belted (SAUS)
PEGDE .... Pentaethylene Glycol Dodecyl Ether [*Organic chemistry*]
PEGE .... Program for Evaluation of Ground Environment
PEG-ELS .... Polyethylene Glycol and Iso-Osmolar Electrolyte Solution (STED)
PegGld ...... Pegasus Gold, Inc. [*Associated Press*] (SAG)
PEGLN .... Petiole Gland Pairs, Number Of [*Botany*]
PEGO .... Paradigm Geophysical Corp. [*NASDAQ symbol*]
PEGPAC ..... Public Service Electric and Gas Company PAC [*Newark, NJ*] (PACS)
PEGPrA ...... Pub Sv E&G 4.08% Pfd [*NYSE symbol*] (TTSB)
PEGPrC ...... Pub Sv E&G 4.30% Pfd [*NYSE symbol*] (TTSB)
PEGPrD ..... Pub Sv E&G 5.05% Pfd [*NYSE symbol*] (TTSB)
PEGPrE ...... Pub Sv E&G 5.28% Pfd [*NYSE symbol*] (TTSB)
PEGPrG ..... Pub Sv E&G 6.80% Pfd [*NYSE symbol*] (TTSB)
PEGPrI ...... Public Sv E&G 7.40% cm Pfd [*NYSE symbol*] (TTSB)
PEGPrJ ...... Pub Sv E&G 7.52% Pfd [*NYSE symbol*] (TTSB)
PEGPrV ...... Pub Sv E&G 7.44% Pfd [*NYSE symbol*] (TTSB)
PEGPrW ..... Pub Sv E&G 5.97% Pfd [*NYSE symbol*] (TTSB)
PEGPrX ...... Public Svc E&G Cap 8.00%'MIPS' [*NYSE symbol*] (TTSB)
PEGPrY ...... Pub Sv E&G 6.75% Pfd [*NYSE symbol*] (TTSB)
PEGPrZ ...... Public Svc E&G Cap 9.375% 'MIPS' [*NYSE symbol*] (TTSB)
PEGR .... Proportional Exhaust Gas Recirculation [*Engines*]
PEGRV ...... Ported Exhaust Gas Recirculation Valve [*Automotive engineering*]
PEGS .... Parametric Evaluation Geometric System (VLIE)
PEGS .... Parametric Evaluation of Generalized Systems (SAUS)
Pegs .... Pegasus [*Constellation*]
PEGS .... Pesticide Exposure Group of Sufferers (HEAS)
PEGS .... Polyethylene Glycol Succinate [*Organic chemistry*]
PEGS .... Program for the Exchange of Generative Studies (SAUS)
PEGS .... Project Engineering Graphics System [*Computer Aided Design Centre*] [*Software package*] (NCC)
PEGS .... Project Engineering System
PEGS .... Publication of the English Goethe-Society (SAUS)
PEGX .... Petroleum Gas [*Private rail car owner code*]
PEGZ .... Peavey Grain [*Federal Railroad Administration identification code*]
PEH .... Papillary Endothelial Hyperplasia [*Medicine*] (MELL)
PEH .... Pehpei [*Republic of China*] [*Seismograph station code, US Geological Survey*] (SEIS)
PEH .... Pehuajo [*Argentina*] [*Airport symbol*] (OAG)
PEH .... Periods of European History [*A publication*]
PEH .... Planning Estimate Handbook (SAA)
PEH .... Plus Each Hour (SAUS)
PEH .... Polyphenylene Ether Homopolymer (SAUS)
PEH .... Promotion of Environmental Health (SAUS)
PEHA .... Pentaethylenehexamine [*Organic chemistry*]
PEHA .... Pony Express Historical Association (EA)
PEHD .... Polyethylene-High Density [*Organic chemistry*]
PEHi .... Northampton County Historical and Genealogical Society, Mary Illick Memorial Library, Easton, PA [*Library symbol*] [*Library of Congress*] (LCLS)
Pe His .... Petrus Hispanus [*Authority cited in pre-1607 legal work*] (DSA)
PEI .... Pan-European Institute [*University of Essex*] [*United Kingdom*] (RCD)
PEI .... Parity Error Interrupt (VLIE)
PEI .... Patriotic Education, Inc. (EA)
PEI .... Peine [*Chile*] [*Seismograph station code, US Geological Survey*] [*Closed*] (SEIS)
pe/i .... Pen and Ink (VRA)
PEI .... Penna RE Inv Tr SNI [*AMEX symbol*] (TTSB)
PEI .... Pennsylvania Real Estate Investment Trust [*AMEX symbol*] (SPSG)
PEI .... People Effectiveness Index (TIMI)
PEI .... Pereira [*Colombia*] [*Airport symbol*] (OAG)
PEI .... Petrocel Industries, Inc. [*Vancouver Stock Exchange symbol*]
PEI .... Petroleum Educational Institute (SAUS)
PEI .... Petroleum Equipment Institute (EA)
PEI .... Phosphate Excretion Index [*Biochemistry*] (DAVI)
PEI .... Phosphorous Excretion Index [*Medicine*] (MEDA)
PEI .... Phosphorus Excretion Index [*Biochemistry*] (DAVI)
PEI .... Physical Education Instructor (WDAA)
PEI .... Physical Efficiency Index [*Medicine*] (DMAA)
PEI .... Planning Executives Institute [*Later, PF*]
PEI .... Plant Engineering Inspection (AAG)
PEI .... Plant Engineering Introduction (SAUS)
PEI .... Playboy Enterprises, Inc.
PEI .... Pointless Electronic Ignition (SAUS)
PEI .... Pollution Enterprises, Inc. (EFIS)
PEI .... Polyetherimide
PEI .... Polyethylenimine [*Organic chemistry*]
PEI .... Porcelain Enamel Institute (EA)
PEI .... Postejaculatory Interval [*Physiology*]
PEI .... Postexercise Index (RAWO)
PEI .... Precipitation-Efficiency Index
PEI .... Preferred Equipment Identifier (VLIE)
PEI .... Preliminary Engineering Inspection [*NASA*] (KSC)
PEI .... Preparedness Exercise Issue (SAUS)
PEI .... Prince Edward Island [*Canadian province*]
PEI .... Prince Edward Island Provincial Library [*UTLAS symbol*]
PEI .... Prince Edward Island Reports (Haviland's) [*A publication*] (DLA)
PEI .... Professional Engineers in Industry
PEI .... Pupil Evaluation Inventory [*Education*] (EDAC)
PEI-A .... Personal Experience Inventory for Adults [*Test*] (TMMY)
PEIA .... Poultry and Egg Institute of America (EA)
PEIAS .... Phenylephrine-Activated Isolated Aortic Strip (DB)
PEIC .... Periodic Error Integrating Controller
PEICOST ... Probability of Incurring Estimated Cost (SAUS)
PEID .... Program Element Identifier [*Military*] (AFIT)
PEIEC .... Prince Edward Island Energy Corp. (SAUS)
PEIF .... Productivity Enhancing Incentive Fund (DNAB)
PEIFL .... Prince Edward Island Federation of Labour (SAUS)
PEIJ .... Prince Edward Island Judgments [*Database*] [*Canada*] (GDD)
PEILS .... PACOM [*Pacific Command*] Executive Intelligence Summary (MCD)
PEILS .... Prince Edward Island Land Surveyors (SAUS)
PEIN .... Pan European Intelligent Network (SAUS)
P/E index ... Precipitation-Evaporation Index (LDOE)
PEINFS ...... Pan European Intelligent Network Freephone Service (SAUS)
PEIP .... Presidential Executive Interchange Program [*Federal government*]
PEIR .... Performance Evaluation and Information Reduction (IAA)
PEIR .... Problem Equipment Indicator Reports (MCD)
PEIR .... Process Evaluation and Information Reduction (IAA)
PEIR .... Project Equipment Inspection Record [*NASA*] (KSC)
PEI Rep ..... Prince Edward Island Reports (Haviland's) [*1850-1914*] [*A publication*] (DLA)
PEI Rev Stat ... Prince Edward Island Revised Statutes [*Canada*] [*A publication*] (DLA)
PEIRS .... Pathology Expert Interpretative Reporting System (IDAI)
PEIS .... Polyethylene Isopthalate [*Organic chemistry*]
PEIS .... Preliminary Environmental Impact Statement (SAUS)
PEIS .... Programmatic Environmental Impact Statement (NRCH)
PEISC .... Prince Edward Island Safety Council (SAUS)
PEI Stat ..... Prince Edward Island Statutes [*Canada*] [*A publication*] (DLA)
PEIT .... Powertrain Equipped with Intelligent Technologies [*Automotive engineering*]
PEITA .... Professional Equestrian Instructors and Trainers Association [*Defunct*] (EA)

PEITC........ Phenethyl Isothiocyanate [*Medicine*] (EDAA)
PEITV........ Preliminary Encapsulated Inert Test Vehicle (MCD)
PEJ.......... Percutaneous Endoscopic Jejunostomy [*Medicine*] (DMAA)
PEJ.......... Premolded Expansion Joint [*Technical drawings*]
Pe Ja........ Petrus Jacobi [*Flourished, 14th century*] [*Authority cited in pre-1607 legal work*] (DSA)
PEJO......... Plant Engineering Job Order (AAG)
PEK.......... Beijing [*China*] [*Airport symbol*] (OAG)
PEK.......... Jacksonville, FL [*Location identifier*] [*FAA*] (FAAL)
PEK.......... Peak Aviation, PLC [*British*] [*FAA designator*] (FAAC)
PEK.......... Peking [*China*] [*Airport symbol*] (AD)
PEK.......... Peking [*Republic of China*] [*Seismograph station code, US Geological Survey*] (SEIS)
PEK.......... Pekoe [*Tea trade*] (ROG)
PEK.......... Phase-Exchange Keying [*Computer science*] (IEEE)
PEK.......... Phi Epsilon Kappa [*Fraternity*]
PEK.......... Pig Embryo Kidney (SAUS)
PEK.......... Polyetherketone [*Organic chemistry*]
PEKEKK..... Polyetherketone Etherketone Ketone (SAUS)
PEKIN....... Pekin, IL [*American Association of Railroads railroad junction routing code*]
PEKK........ Polyether Ketone Ketone (SAUS)
PEKK........ Polyetherketoneketone [*Materials science*]
PEL.......... Aeropelican Air Services Pty Ltd. [*Australia*] [*ICAO designator*] (FAAC)
Pel.......... Elastic Recoil Pressure of Lung [*Medicine*] (STED)
PEL.......... Lafayette College, Easton, PA [*Library symbol*] [*Library of Congress*] (LCLS)
PEL.......... Paid Educational Leave (AIE)
PEL.......... PanEnergy Corp. [*NYSE symbol*] [*Formerly, Panhandle Eastern*] (SG)
PEL.......... Panhandle Eastern (EFIS)
PEL.......... Panhandle Eastern Pipe Line Co. [*NYSE symbol*] (SPSG)
PEL.......... Payroll Expenditure Listing (SAUS)
PEL.......... Pekal [*Language symbol*] (ETLW)
Pel.......... Pelagius [*Deceased, 1232*] [*Authority cited in pre-1607 legal work*] (DSA)
PEL.......... Pelaneng [*Lesotho*] [*Airport symbol*] (OAG)
PEL.......... Peldehue [*Chile*] [*Seismograph station code, US Geological Survey*] (SEIS)
Pel.......... Pelopidas [*of Plutarch*] [*Classical studies*] (OCD)
PEL.......... Pelvis (SAUS)
PEL.......... Peritoneal Exudate Lymphocytes [*Hematology*]
PEL.......... Permissible Exposure Level
PEL.......... Permissible Exposure Limit [*OSHA*]
PEL.......... Personal Effectiveness Inventory (AIE)
PEL.......... Personal Exposure Level [*or Limit*]
PEL.......... Personal Exposure Limit (SAUS)
PEL.......... Personnel Exposure Limit (SAUS)
PEL.......... Personnel Licensing (SAUS)
PEL.......... Personnel Licensing and Training [*ICAO*] (AIA)
PEL.......... Petroleum Exploration License (SAUS)
PEL.......... Philatelic Esperanto League [*See also ELF*] [*Solna, Sweden*] (EAIO)
PEL.......... Photoelectron Layer
PEL.......... Photographic Element (SAUS)
PEL.......... Physics & Engineering Laboratory (SAUS)
pel.......... Picture Element (DCOM)
PEL.......... Picture Element [*Single element of resolution in image processing*] (IBMDP)
PEL.......... Plant Engineers Language (SAUS)
PEL.......... Portable Event Logger (SAUS)
PEL.......... Precision Elastic Limit
PEL.......... President Electric Ltd. (SAUS)
PEL.......... Pressure Exposure Limit (SAUS)
PEL.......... Priests Eucharistic League (EA)
PEL.......... Primary Effusion Lymphoma [*Oncology*]
PEL.......... Production Error Log (NITA)
PEL.......... Professional Education Libraries [*UTLAS symbol*]
PEL.......... Programmable Electronics Load (SAUS)
PEL.......... Proportional Elastic Limit
PEL.......... Protein Expression Laboratory [*National Institute of Arthritis and Musculoskeletal and Skin Diseases*] (RCD)
PEL.......... Public Exposure Limit (MCD)
PELA......... P.E. Lamoreaux & Associates, Inc. (EFIS)
PEIC......... Elizabethtown College, Elizabethtown, PA [*Library symbol*] [*Library of Congress*] (LCLS)
PEL-C........ Permissible Exposure Limit- Ceiling (LDOE)
PEL-C........ Permissible Exposure Limit-Ceiling (LDOE)
PELC......... Professional Engineers' Legislative Committee
PELCO....... Polyester-Caprolactone Copolymer [*Plastics*]
PE-LD........ PolyEthylene-Low Density (AGLO)
PELEC....... Photoelectric (MSA)
PEleph...... Elephantine Papyri [*A publication*] (OCD)
PELG......... Pelger Muet Anomaly [*Laboratory science*] (DAVI)
PELG......... Poly(ethyl L-Glutamate) [*Organic chemistry*]
PELI......... Pelican Aluminum Manufacturing [*NCIC trailer make code*]
PELI......... Production, Engineering and Logistics Information (AAGC)
PELICON... Project for Estimation of Long-Term Variability in Ice Concentration (SAUS)
PELISA...... Paper Enzyme-Linked Immunosorbent Assay (STED)
PELJ......... Pyrotechnical Expendable Laser Jammer (ACAE)
PELL......... Papers on English Language and Literature [*A publication*]
PELL......... Publications in English Language and Literature (SAUS)
PELP......... Poland Efficient Lighting Project
PELR......... Peeler
PELR......... Pelsart Resources NL [*NASDAQ symbol*] (NQ)
PELRV....... Pea Leafroll Virus [*Plant pathology*]
PELRY....... Pelsart Resources ADR [*NASDAQ symbol*] (TTSB)
PELS......... P-channel Enhancement Load in Saturation (SAUS)
PELS......... Precision Emitter Location System [*Air Force*] (MCD)
PELS......... Pre-Emptive Light System [*Trucking safety*]
PELS......... Propionyl Erythromycin Lauryl Sulfate [*Antimicrobial agent*]
Pelsart...... Pelsart Resources NL [*Associated Press*] (SAG)
PELSS....... Precision Emitter Location Strike System [*Air Force*]
PEL-STEL... Permissible Exposure Limit-Short Term Exposure Limit (LDOE)
PEL-STEL... Permissible Exposure Limit-Short-Term Exposure Limit (LDOE)
PELT......... P-channel Enhancement Load in Triode (SAUS)
Pelt......... Peltier's Orleans Appeals [*1917-23*] [*A publication*] (DLA)
PELT......... Princeton American [*NASDAQ symbol*] (TTSB)
PELT......... Princeton Electronic Products, Inc. [*NASDAQ symbol*] (NQ)
PELTP....... Personnel Licensing and Training Panel (SAUS)
PELTS....... Personal Emergency Locator Transmitter Service [*Telecommunications*] (CIST)
PEL-TWA.... Permissible Exposure Limit-Time Weighted Average (LDOE)
PEL-TWA.... Permissible Exposure Limit-Time-Weighted Average (LDOE)
PELU......... Sarlis Container Line [*Intermodal shipping container symbol*] (TVRC)
PELV......... Pepino Latent Virus [*Plant pathology*]
PELV......... Protected Extra Low Voltage (SAUS)
PELZ......... Premier Equipment Leasing [*Intermodal trailer symbol*]
PELZE....... Pelzer, SC [*American Association of Railroads railroad junction routing code*]
PEM.......... Pacific Exploratory Measurements (SAUS)
PEM.......... Pacific Exploratory Mission (ACAE)
PEM.......... Parametric Earth Model [*Geodynamics*]
PEM.......... Parasitic Encephalitis Meningitis [*Medicine*]
PEM.......... Partial Equilibrium Multimarket Model (EEVL)
PEM.......... Particle Environmental Monitor (MCD)
PEM.......... Particle Modulator Radiometer (CARB)
PEM.......... Partido Ecologista Mexicano [*Political party*] (EY)
PEM.......... Payload Ejection Mechanism
PEM.......... Payload Electronics Module (SAUS)
PEM.......... PEM-AIR Ltd. [*Canada*] [*ICAO designator*] (FAAC)
PEM.......... Pembrokeshire [*County in Wales*] (ROG)
PEM.......... Penn Engineering and Manufacturing [*Automotive engineering*]
PEM.......... Penn Engineering & Manufacturing Corp. (EFIS)
PEM.......... Performance Enhancement Module (VLIE)
PEM.......... Performance Evaluation Missile (ACAE)
PEM.......... Performance Evaluation Model
PEM.......... Peritoneal Exudate Macrophage [*Hematology*]
PEM.......... Perrot Memorial Library, Old Greenwich, CT [*OCLC symbol*] (OCLC)
PEM.......... Personal-E Mailbox [*Computer software*] (PCM)
PEM.......... Personal Exposure Model (EEVL)
PEM.......... Personal Exposure Monitor [*Environmental chemistry*]
PEM.......... Petite Ensemble Model (MCD)
PEM.......... Petrox Energy & Mineral Corp. [*Toronto Stock Exchange symbol*]
PEM.......... Phased Equipment Modernization [*Army*] (AABC)
PEM.......... Philco Electronic Module
PEM.......... Photoelastic Modulator [*Instrumentation*]
PEM.......... Photoelectromagnetic
PEM.......... Photoelectron Microscopy
PEM.......... Photoemission Microscope
PEM.......... Photographic Equipment and Materials (NATG)
PEM.......... Plant Engineering and Maintenance (NASA)
PEM.......... Plant Engineer Mechanical (AAG)
PEM.......... Plastic-Encapsulated Microcircuit [*Telecommunications*]
PEM.......... Plastic-Envelope Method (SAUS)
PEM.......... Plastic Epoxy Molded (SAUS)
PEM.......... Polaris Evaluation Missile
PEM.......... Polioencephalomalacia (SAUS)
PEM.......... Polyethylene Matrix (DB)
PEM.......... Polymer Electrolyte Membrane [*Fuel technology*]
PEM.......... Position Encoding Module (CAAL)
PEM.......... Precordial Electrocardiographic Mapping (STED)
PEM.......... Prescription-Event Monitoring
PEM.......... Presented a Memorial [*Telegraphy*] (PCTE)
PEM.......... Primary Enrichment Medium [*Microbiology*]
PEM.......... Primitive Equation Model (SAUS)
PEM.......... Privacy-Enhanced Mail [*Software package*]
PEM.......... Privacy Enhanced Message (SAUS)
PEM.......... Probable Error of Measurement
PEM.......... Process Execution Module (NITA)
PEM.......... Processing Element Memory [*Computer science*]
PEM.......... Processing Element Module [*Computer science*] (IAA)
PEM.......... Processor Element Memory (SAUS)
PEM.......... Procurement Equipment and Missiles (SAUS)
PEM.......... Product Effectiveness Manual
PEM.......... Product Engineering Measure (SAUS)
PEM.......... Product Engineering Memo (SAUS)
PEM.......... Product Error Message (SAUS)
PEM.......... Production Engineering Measure [*Army*] (MCD)
PEM.......... Production Evaluation Missile [*Military*] (CAAL)
PEM.......... Professional Emergency Manager [*Emergency Management*] (EMA)
PEM.......... Program and Environmental Management (SAUS)
PEM.......... Program Element Manager (MCD)
PEM.......... Program Element Monitor (AFM)
PEM.......... Program Endorsement Memorandum (AAGC)
PEM.......... Program Execution Monitor [*Computer science*] (ELAL)
PEM.......... Project Engineering Memorandum
PEM.......... Properties/Events/Methods (SAUS)

PEM .... Proposal Evaluation Manager
PEM .... Protein Energy Malnutrition [*Medicine*]
PEM .... Proto-Environmental Model (SAUS)
PEM .... Proton Exchange Membrane [*Fuel technology*] (PS)
PEM .... Puerto Maldonado [*Peru*] [*Airport symbol*] (OAG)
PEM .... Pulmonary Embolus [*Medicine*] (DAVI)
PEM .... Pulse Electromagnetic (SAUS)
PEMA........ Pennsylvania Emergency Management Agency [*Emergency Management*] (EMA)
PEMA........ Pheny(ethyl)malonamide [*Organic chemistry*]
PEMA........ Polyethyl Methacrylate [*Organic chemistry*]
PEMA........ Process Equipment Manufacturers Association (EA)
PEMA........ Procurement Equipment and Missiles-Army (SAUS)
PEMA........ Procurement Equipment Maintenance, Army (MCD)
PEMA........ Procurement, Equipment, Missiles, Army
PEMA........ Procurement of Equipment and Munitions, Appropriations (SAUS)
PEMA........ Production-Equipment-Missile Agency [*Army*]
PEMAC ...... Plant Engineering and Maintenance Association of Canada (EAIO)
PEMAC ...... Professional Engineers Manpower Assessment Committee (SAUS)
PEMAP ...... President's Environmental Merit Award Program [*Environmental Protection Agency*]
PEMARS .... Procurement of Equipment and Missiles, Army Management and Accounting Reporting System (AABC)
PEMB........ Pembroke College [*Oxford and Cambridge Universities*] (ROG)
Pemb........ Pembroke College, Oxford (SAUS)
PEMB........ Pembrokeshire [*County in Wales*]
PEMBA ...... Pembina, ND [*American Association of Railroads railroad junction routing code*]
Pemb Coll... Pembroke College-Cambridge (SAUS)
Pemb Eq.... Pemberton's Practice in Equity by Way of Revivor and Supplement [*1867*] [*A publication*] (ILCA)
PEMBI........ Pembine, WI [*American Association of Railroads railroad junction routing code*]
Pemb Judg... Pemberton's Judgments and Orders [*A publication*] (DLA)
PEMBR ...... Pembroke, ON [*American Association of Railroads railroad junction routing code*]
Pembs........ Pembrokeshire (DIAR)
PEMBS ...... Pembrokeshire [*County in Wales*]
PEMC........ Pennsbury Manufacturing Corporation [*NCIC trailer make code*]
PEM-Central... Pacific Exploratory Mission-Central (SAUS)
PEMCONS... Photographic Equipment Management Control System
PEMCO PAC... Pemco Aviation Group Inc. PAC [*Birmingham, AL*] (PACS)
PEMD........ Personalized Educational Materials Development (SAUS)
PEMD........ Program Evaluation and Methodology Division [*General Accounting Office*] [*Federal government*] (GFGA)
PEMD........ Program for Export Market Development [*Canada*]
PEME........ Pulsed Electromagnetic Energy [*Diathermy*] (CPH)
PEMEX ...... Petroleos Mexicanos (EFIS)
PEMF........ Pulsating Electromagnetic Field
PEM-FC ..... Polymer Electrolyte Membrane Fuel Cell (SEWL)
PEMFC ...... Proton Exchange Membrane Fuel Cell [*Energy source*]
PEMISA ..... Proficiency Battery in English and Mathematics for Indian South Africans (TES)
PEML........ Port Erin Marine Laboratory [*University of Liverpool*] [*United Kingdom*] (RCD)
PEMN........ Program Engineering Management Network [*Computer science*] (RDA)
Pe Mo........ Petrus Morini [*Authority cited in pre-1607 legal work*] (DSA)
PEMO........ Plant Engineering Maintenance Order
PEMO........ Production Engineering and Manufacturing Organization (AAG)
PEMO........ Prospective Electronics Material Officer (SAUS)
PE-MOCVD... Plasma-Enhanced Metalorganic Chemical Vapor Deposition [*Coating technology*]
Pe Mori ..... Petrus Morini [*Authority cited in pre-1607 legal work*] (DSA)
PEMOV...... Peanut Mottle Virus [*Plant pathology*]
PEM Process Eng Mag... PEM Process Engineering Magazine (SAUS)
PEMR........ Petroleum Engineering Monthly Report (SAUS)
PEMRam.... Precision Electromagnetic Ram [*Denne Developments*] (PS)
PEMRC...... Program Executive Management Review Committee (SAUS)
PEMS........ Paris Evangelical Missionary Society (SAUS)
PEMS........ Performance Evaluation and Monitoring System
PEMS........ Pesticide Enforcement Management System (NITA)
PEMS........ Physical, Emotional, Mental, Safety [*Model for charting procedure*] [*Medicine*]
PEMS........ Policy and Expenditure Management System (SAUS)
PEMS........ Porcelain-Enamelled Metal Substrate (EECA)
PEMS........ Portable Environmental Measuring System
PEMS........ Predictive Emission Monitoring System [*Environmental science*]
PEMS........ Professional Education of the Media Specialist
PEMS........ Propulsion Energy Management Study (MCD)
PEMT........ Phosphatidylethanolamine Methyltransferase [*An enzyme*]
PEMU........ Cooperativa Agricola de Produtores de Frutas [*Intermodal shipping container symbol*] (TVRC)
PE Mus...... Port Elizabeth Museum (SAUS)
PEMV........ Pea Enation Mosaic Virus [*Plant pathology*]
PeMV........ Pepper Mottle Virus
PEM-West .. Pacific Exploratory Mission-West [*Western Pacific Tropospheric Chemistry Experiment*] [*Marine science*] (OSRA)
Pem Yeo.... Pembroke Yeomanry [*British military*] (DMA)
PEN.......... Astoria, OR [*Location identifier*] [*FAA*] (FAAL)
PEN.......... International PEN [*Official name; PEN, never spelled out in use, is said to stand for poets, playwrights, editors, essayists, novelists*] (EAIO)
PEN.......... Pacific Exchange Network [*Marine science*] (OSRA)
PEN.......... Parenteral and Enteral Nutrition [*Gastroenterology*] (DAVI)
PEN.......... Peace Education Network (EA)
pen .... penal (SAUS)
PEN.......... Penang [*Malaysia*] [*Airport symbol*] (OAG)
PEN.......... Pendeli [*Greece*] [*Geomagnetic observatory code*]
PEN.......... Pendleton, OR [*Amtrak Busline code*]
PEN.......... Penetration (AFM)
Pen .... Penicillin [*Medicine*] (DMAA)
PEN.......... Penicillin [*Antibiotic*]
pen .... Peninsula (NTIO)
PEN.......... Peninsula [*Maps and charts*]
PEN.......... Peninsula Airways, Inc. [*ICAO designator*] (FAAC)
PEN.......... Peninsula Environmental Network (SAUS)
PEN.......... Penitent
pen .... Penitentiary (ADWA)
PEN.......... Penitentiary (WDAA)
pen .... penmanship (SAUS)
Pen .... Pennewill's Delaware Reports [*A publication*] (DLA)
Pen .... Pennington's New Jersey Reports [*2, 3 New Jersey*] [*A publication*] (DLA)
PEN.......... Pensacola [*Florida*] [*Seismograph station code, US Geological Survey*] [*Closed*] (SEIS)
PEN.......... Pentazocine [*An analgesic*]
PEN.......... Pentegra Dental Group [*AMEX symbol*] (SG)
PEN.......... Pentobarbital [*Sedative*]
PEN.......... Pentode (DEN)
PEN.......... Permanent Entry Number [*Computer science*]
PEN.......... Pharmacology Equivalent Name
PEN.......... Pharmacy Equivalent Name [*Medicine*] (DMAA)
PEN.......... Physicians Education Network (EA)
PEN.......... Plasma-Enhanced silicon Nitride (SAUS)
PEN.......... Polyethylene Naphthalate [*Organic chemistry*]
PEN.......... Professional Enrichment News [*Portuguese*] (BJA)
PEN.......... Program Element Number [*Computer science*] (KSC)
PEN.......... Program Error Note [*Computer science*]
PEN.......... Protection Earth Neutral (SAUS)
PEN.......... Public Education Network (SAUS)
PEN.......... Public Electronic Network [*Information service or system*] (IID)
PEN.......... Purchasing Electronic Notebook (HGAA)
PENA .... Primary Emission Neuron Activation (IEEE)
PENAID...... Penetration Aid [*Weaponry*]
PENAIDS ... Penetration Aids
Pen & W.... Penrose and Watts' Pennsylvania Reports [*1829-32*] [*A publication*] (DLA)
PEN-B .... Penicillin, Benzalthine Salt (SAUS)
PENB .... Poultry and Egg National Board [*Later, AEB*] (EA)
PENBAL ..... Peninsular Spain-Balearic Islands Submarine Cable (SAUS)
PENBASE... Peninsular Base Section [*Military*]
Pen Bse..... Peninsular Base (SAUS)
Pen C........ Penal Code [*A publication*] (DLA)
PENC .... Pen Interconnect [*NASDAQ symbol*] (TTSB)
PENC .... Pen Interconnect, Inc. [*NASDAQ symbol*] (SAG)
PENC .... Pennco Industries [*NCIC trailer make code*]
PENCAN..... Peninsular Spain-Canary Islands Submarine Cable (SAUS)
PENCE....... Protein Engineering Network of Centres of Excellence (SAUS)
Penchk ...... Pennichuck Corp. [*Associated Press*] (SAG)
PENCIL...... Pictorial Encoding Language [*Computer science*] (IEEE)
PENCIL...... Portable Encoder/Illustrator [*Facetious term for pre-word-processing equipment*]
PENCIL...... Public Education Needs Civic Involvement in Learning
Pencp .... Penncorp Financial Group [*Associated Press*] (SAG)
PencpFn .... Penncorp Financial Group [*Associated Press*] (SAG)
PENCPR..... PEN [*Poets, Playwrights, Essayists, Editors, and Novelists*] Club of PuertoRico (EA)
PENCW...... Pen Interconnect Wrrt [*NASDAQ symbol*] (TTSB)
Pend......... Pendant (ROG)
pend .... Pendant (VRA)
PEND .... Pendens [*Weighing*] [*Pharmacy*]
PEND .... Pending
PEND .... Pendlay [*NCIC trailer make code*]
Pen Dec..... Pension Decisions [*Department of the Interior*] [*A publication*] (DLA)
PENDL....... Pendleton, OR [*American Association of Railroads railroad junction routing code*]
PENDOR .... Photon Echo-Nuclear Double Resonance (SAUS)
PENDORF... Penetrate Dorfman [*FBI investigation of Teamster leader Allen Dorfman*]
PENDWN.... Pen Down (SAUS)
Penedrm.... Penederm, Inc. [*Associated Press*] (SAG)
Penelc....... Penelec Capital Ltd. [*Associated Press*] (SAG)
PenEM ...... Penn Engineering & Manufacturing Corp. [*Associated Press*] (SAG)
PenEMA..... Penn Engineering & Manufacturing Corp. [*Associated Press*] (SAG)
P/E News ... Petroleum Energy Business News Index (SAUS)
P/E NEWS .. Petroleum/Energy Business News Index [*American Petroleum Institute*] [*New York, NY*] [*Bibliographic database*]
P/E News ... Petroleum/Energy News (SAUS)
PEng......... Member of the Society of Professional Engineers (ODA)
PenG .... Penicillin G [*Antibacterial agent*]
PenG .... Pennsylvania Gas & Water Co. [*Associated Press*] (SAG)
PENG .... Photo-Electro-Nystagmogram (SAUS)
PENG .... Photo-Electro-Nystagmography [*Medicine*]
PENG .... Prima Energy [*NASDAQ symbol*] (TTSB)
PENG .... Prima Energy Corp. [*NASDAQ symbol*] (NQ)
PEng......... Professional Engineer
PEng......... Registered Professional Engineer (DD)

PENGEM .... Penetrate Gray Electronics Markets [*FBI "sting" operation, 1982, where employees of Japanese computer firms were caught trying to obtain proprietary information illegally from IBM Co.*]
P Engine .... Port Engine (SAUS)
PENGUIN... Polar Experiment Network for Geophysical Upper-atmosphere Investigations (SAUS)
PENI .... Peninsula Camper Manufacturing [*NCIC trailer make code*]
PENIC .... Penicillin [*Antibiotic*]
Penic Cam... Penicillum Camelinum [*A Camel's-Hair Brush*] [*Pharmacy*]
Penin .... Peninsula (BEE)
penin .... Peninsula
PenInt .... Pen Interconnect, Inc. [*Associated Press*] (SAG)
PenInter..... Pen Interconnect, Inc. [*Associated Press*] (SAG)
PeninTst..... Peninsula Trust Bank, Inc. [*Associated Press*] (SAG)
PENIT........ Penitentiary
PENJERDEL... Pennsylvania, New Jersey, Delaware
PENK .... Proenkephalin [*Biochemistry*]
PENMS ...... Pan European Network Management System (SAUS)
PENN .... JC Penney [*NCIC motorcycle make code*]
PENN .... JC Penney [*NCIC trailer make code*]
Penn.......... Pennewill's Delaware Reports [*A publication*] (DLA)
Penn.......... Pennington's New Jersey Reports [*A publication*] (DLA)
PENN .... Penn National Gaming [*NASDAQ symbol*] (TTSB)
PENN .... Penn National Gaming, Inc. [*NASDAQ symbol*] (SAG)
Penn.......... Pennsylvania (ODBW)
PENN .... Pennsylvania
PENN .... Pennsylvanian [*Period, era, or system*] [*Geology*]
Penn.......... Pennsylvania State Reports [*A publication*] (DLA)
Penn.......... Pennypacker's Unreported Pennsylvania Cases [*A publication*] (DLA)
Penna .... Pennsylvania (ODBW)
PENNA .... Pennsylvania
Penna Law Journal... Pennsylvania Law Journal [*A publication*] (DLA)
Penna LJ .... Pennsylvania Law Journal [*A publication*] (DLA)
PennAm..... Penn America Group [*Associated Press*] (SAG)
Penna R .... Pennsylvania State Reports [*A publication*] (DLA)
Penna SR.... Pennsylvania State Reports [*A publication*] (DLA)
Penna St.... Pennsylvania State Reports [*A publication*] (DLA)
Penna State Rep... Pennsylvania State Reports [*A publication*] (DLA)
PennBc...... PennFirst Bancorp [*Associated Press*] (SAG)
PennBcp .... PennFirst Bancorp [*Associated Press*] (SAG)
Penn Central... Pennsylvania New York Central Transportation Co. (SAUS)
Penn Co Ct Rep... Pennsylvania County Court Reports [*A publication*] (DLA)
Penn C Opt... Pennsylvania College of Optometry (GAGS)
Penn Corp Rep... Pennsylvania Corporation Reporter [*A publication*] (DLA)
Penn Del.... Pennewill's Delaware Reports [*A publication*] (DLA)
Penn Dist & Co Rep... Pennsylvania District and County Reports [*A publication*] (DLA)
Penn Dist Rep... Pennsylvania District Reports [*A publication*] (DLA)
PennDOT.... Pennsylvania Department of Transportation (SAUS)
Penne .... Pennewill's Delaware Reports [*17-23 Delaware*] [*1897-1909*] [*A publication*] (DLA)
PennEn...... Penn Enterprises, Inc. [*Associated Press*] (SAG)
Pennew ..... Pennewill's Delaware Reports [*A publication*] (DLA)
Pennewill... Pennewill's Delaware Supreme Court Reports [*1897-1909*] [*A publication*] (DLA)
Penney...... Penney [*J. C.*] Co., Inc. [*Associated Press*] (SAG)
PENNEYPAC... J C Penney Company Inc. PAC [*Plano, TX*] (PACS)
PennFed .... PennFed Financial Services, Inc. [*Associated Press*] (SAG)
Penn German... Pennsylvania-German (SAUS)
PenNGm .... Penn National Gaming, Inc. [*Associated Press*] (SAG)
Penning..... Pennington's New Jersey Reports [*2, 3 New Jersey*] [*A publication*] (DLA)
Pen NJ ...... Pennington's New Jersey Reports [*2, 3 New Jersey*] [*A publication*] (DLA)
Penn Law Jour... Pennsylvania Law Journal [*A publication*] (DLA)
Penn LG .... Pennsylvania Legal Gazette [*A publication*] (DLA)
Penn LG .... Pennsylvania Legal Gazette Reports (Campbell) [*A publication*] (DLA)
Penn LJ..... Pennsylvania Law Journal [*A publication*] (DLA)
Penn LJR ... Pennsylvania Law Journal Reports, Edited by Clark [*1842-52*] [*A publication*] (DLA)
Penn L Rec... Pennsylvania Law Record [*Philadelphia*] [*A publication*] (DLA)
Penn L Rev... Pennsylvania Law Review [*A publication*] (DLA)
Penn Mil Dist... Pennsylvania Military District (SAUS)
PennOct..... Penn Octane Corp. [*Associated Press*] (SAG)
PENNORTH... Pennyworth [*British*] (ROG)
PennPIRG... Pennsylvania Public Interest Research Group (RCD)
Penn R...... Pennsylvania State Reports [*A publication*] (DLA)
Penn Rep... Pennsylvania State Reports [*A publication*] (DLA)
Penn Rep... Penrose and Watts' Pennsylvania Reports [*A publication*] (DLA)
PennSAHIC... Pennsylvania Substance Abuse and Health Information (SAUS)
PENN SECO... Penn Security Bank & Trust Company (EFIS)
Penn St ..... Pennsylvania State Reports [*A publication*] (DLA)
PENNSTAC... Penn State University Automatic Digital Computer
Penn Stat... Pennsylvania State Reports [*A publication*] (DLA)
Penn State Rep... Pennsylvania State Reports [*A publication*] (DLA)
Penn St R... Pennsylvania State Reports [*A publication*] (ILCA)
Penn St Rep... Pennsylvania State Reports [*A publication*] (DLA)
Penn St U... Pennsylvania State University (GAGS)
Penn St U Harrisburg... Pennsylvania State University at Harrisburg (GAGS)
Penn Super... Pennsylvania Superior Court Reports [*A publication*] (DLA)
PENNTAP... Pennsylvania Technical Assistance Program [*Pennsylvania State University*] [*University Park, PA*]
PennTr....... Penn Traffic Co. [*Associated Press*] (SAG)
PennTrty .... Penn Treaty American [*Associated Press*] (SAG)
Penn Turn... Pennsylvania Turnpike (SAUS)
PennVa...... Penn Virginia Corp. [*Associated Press*] (SAG)
Pennwd ..... Pennwood Savings Bank [*Associated Press*] (SAG)
PENNX ...... Pennsylvania Mutual [*Mutual fund ticker symbol*] (SG)
Penny .... Pennypacker's Pennsylvania Colonial Cases [*A publication*] (DLA)
Penny .... Pennypacker's Unreported Pennsylvania Cases [*A publication*] (DLA)
Penny Col Cas... Pennypacker's Pennsyulvania Colonial Cases [*A publication*] (DLA)
Pennyp ...... Pennypacker's Unreported Pennsylvania Cases [*A publication*] (DLA)
Pennyp Col Cas... Pennypacker's Pennsylvania Colonial Cases [*A publication*] (DLA)
Pennyp (PA)... Pennypacker's Unreported Pennsylvania Cases [*A publication*] (DLA)
Pennzol ..... Pennzoil Co. [*Associated Press*] (SAG)
PEN-O .... Penner Serotype-O [*Laboratory science*] (DAVI)
Penob .... Penobscot Shoe Co. [*Associated Press*] (SAG)
penol .... penological (SAUS)
PENOL....... Penologist (SAUS)
PENOL....... Penology
Pen P........ Penault's Prerosti de Quebec [*A publication*] (DLA)
PEN-P .... Penicillin, Procain Salt (SAUS)
PENR .... Penryn [*England*]
PENRAD..... Penetration RADAR
Penr Anal... Penruddocke's Short Analysis of Criminal Law [*2nd ed.*] [*1842*] [*A publication*] (DLA)
Penr & W... Penrose and Watts' Pennsylvania Reports [*1829-32*] [*A publication*] (DLA)
PenRE....... Pennsylvania Real Estate Investment Trust [*Associated Press*] (SAG)
Pen Ref..... Penal Reformer [*1934-39*] [*A publication*] (DLA)
Pen Ref League M Rec... Penal Reform League Monthly Record [*1909-12*] [*A publication*] (DLA)
Pen Ref League Q Rec... Penal Reform League Quarterly Record [*1912-20*] [*A publication*] (DLA)
PENREP..... Penetration Report [*National Security Agency*]
Penril........ Penril Corp. [*Associated Press*] (SAG)
PENS .... Partido Espanol Nacional Sindicalista [*Political party*] [*Spain*]
PENS .... Pediatric Endocrinology Nursing Society (SAUS)
PENS .... Pennsylvania Furnace & Iron [*NCIC trailer make code*]
PENS .... Pensacola Naval Air Station (SAUS)
PENS .... Percutaneous Electrical Nerve Stimulation
PENS .... Percutaneous Epidural Nerve Stimulator [*neurology*] (DAVI)
PENS .... Polymer Ejection for Noise Suppression
PENS .... Provisions of Engineer Support (SAUS)
PENSA....... Pensacola, FL [*American Association of Railroads railroad junction routing code*]
PENSAD..... Pension Administration (SAUS)
PENSADS... Pension Administration System (SAUS)
PENSAD System... Pensions Administration System (SAUS)
PENSAM .... Penetration Survivability Assessment Model (MCD)
Pens & Profit Sharing (P-H)... Pension and Profit Sharing (Prentice-Hall, Inc.) [*A publication*] (DLA)
PensCr ...... Pensamiento Cristiano. Tribuna de Exposicion del Pensamiento Evangelico [*Cordoba, Argentina*] [*A publication*] (BJA)
PEN SDK.... Pen Computing Software Development Kit (SAUS)
Pension Rep... Pension Reporter [*Bureau of National Affairs*] [*A publication*] (DLA)
PenskeM.... Penske Motorsports, Inc. [*Associated Press*] (SAG)
Pens Rep (BNA)... Pension Reporter (Bureau of National Affairs) [*A publication*] (DLA)
PenST .... Penicillin Skin Test [*Immunology*]
Pen St R.... Pennsylvania State Reports [*A publication*] (DLA)
PENT .... Penetrate (AABC)
PENT .... Penna Enterprises (EFIS)
PENT .... Pentagon
Pent .... Pentagonal (SAUS)
PENT .... Pentameter
Pent .... Pentateuch (BJA)
PENT .... Pentecost
PENT .... Pentode (AAG)
PENT .... Penton [*NCIC motorcycle make code*]
Pent .... Pentothal [*Anesthetic*] (AAMN)
PENT .... Phenylethanolamine N-Methyltransferase (DMAA)
PENT .... Project for the Education of Native Teachers (SAUS)
Penta .... Pentachlorophenol [*Wood preservative*] (WPI)
PENTAC ..... Penetration for Tactical Aircraft [*Air Force*]
PENTAFLUX... Fifth Flux Experiment (USDC)
Pentair ...... Pentair, Inc. [*Associated Press*] (SAG)
Pentch....... Pentech International, Inc. [*Associated Press*] (SAG)
PENTE....... Pentecostal
PENTENG ... Pentagon English [*Pseudotechnical language*]
PENTIUM ... Produces Erroneous Numbers Through Incorrect Understanding of Mathematics (SAUS)
Pentl......... Pentelic (VRA)
PENTOBARB... Pentobarbital Sodium (SAUS)
PenTrt .... Penn Treaty American Corp. [*Associated Press*] (SAG)
pentu .... Pentateuch (VRA)
PENU .... Penn-Cupit Industries [*NCIC trailer make code*]
PENULT ..... Penultimate (SAUS)
PENV .... Philip Environmental [*NASDAQ symbol*] (SAG)
PENV .... Pinnacle Environmental (EFIS)
PENVAL ..... Penetration Evaluation [*Military*] (NVT)
Pen VK...... Penicillin V Postassium [*An antibiotic*] (DAVI)
PENW .... Penetrating Wound
PENW .... PENWEST Ltd. [*Bellevue, WA*] [*NASDAQ symbol*] (NQ)

PENW .... Penwith [*England*]
Penwst ...... PENWEST Ltd. [*Associated Press*] (SAG)
PENX .... Penford Corp. [*NASDAQ symbol*] (NASQ)
PENX .... Penford Products [*Private rail car owner code*]
PENY .... Penitentiary [*Telegraphy*] (PCTE)
PENZ .... Chassis Holding [*Intermodal trailer symbol*]
PENZ .... Penzance [*City in England*] (ROG)
PEO .... Paalsgard Emulsion Oil (SAUS)
PEO .... Pacific Economic Outlook
PEO .... Pankypria Ergatiki Omospondia [*Pancyprian Federation of Labour*] [*The "Old Trade Unions"*] [*Cyprus*]
PEO .... Patrol Emergency Officer [*Nuclear energy*] (NRCH)
PEO .... Patrol Emergency Operator (SAUS)
peo .... People (GEAB)
PEO .... People
PEO .... Peoria [*Diocesan abbreviation*] [*Illinois*] (TOCD)
peo .... Persian, Old [*MARC language code*] [*Library of Congress*] (LCCP)
PEO .... Petroleum & Resources [*NYSE symbol*] (TTSB)
PEO .... Petroleum & Resources Corp. [*NYSE symbol*] (SPSG)
PEO .... Petrolia Oil & Gas [*Vancouver Stock Exchange symbol*]
PEO .... Philanthropic and Educational Organization [*Facetious translation "Pop Eats Out"*]
PEO .... Photographic Eye Oximeter (SAUS)
PEO .... Piezoelectric Oscillator (SAUS)
PEO .... Planners for Equal Opportunity [*Defunct*] (EA)
PEO .... Plant Engineering Order
PEO .... Plant Equipment Operator [*Nuclear energy*] (NRCH)
PEO .... Poly(ethylene oxide) [*Acronym is trade name owned by Seitetsu Kagaku Co.*]
PEO .... Polymer Electrolyte (SAUS)
PeO .... President ex-Oficio (SAUS)
PEO .... President's Export Council (AAGC)
PEO .... Principal Embarkation Officer (SAUS)
PEO .... Principal Establishment Officer (SAUS)
PEO .... Principal Executive Officer [*Civil Service*] [*British*]
PEO .... Process Engineering Order
PEO .... Product Engineering Office
PEO .... Production Engineering Order
PEO .... Program Enrichment Office (COE)
PEO .... Program Evaluation Office [*Army*]
PEO .... Program Executive Office [*or Officer*]
PEO .... Progressive External Ophthalmoplegia
PEO .... Propulsion Engineering Officer (MCD)
PEO .... Prospective Engineer Officer
PEO .... Protect Each Other [*An association*] (NADA)
PEO .... Public Employment Office [*State Employee Security Agency*] (OICC)
PEO-ASM ... Program Executive Office - Armored Systems Modernization [*Army*] (RDA)
PeoBkIN ..... Peoples Bank Corp. Indianapolis [*Associated Press*] (SAG)
PEOC .... Presidential Emergency Operations Room (SAUS)
PEOC .... Publishing Employees Organizing Committee [*AFL-CIO*]
PEO-C3S .... Program Executive Office, Command, Control, and Communications Systems [*Army*]
PEO CCS .... Program Executive Officer, Command and Control Systems (SAUS)
PEO COMM ... Program Executive Office for Communications (SAUS)
PEOE .... Peoria & Eastern Railroad [*Federal Railroad Administration identification code*]
PEO-FAS .... Program Executive Office - Field Artillery System [*Army*] (RDA)
PEO-GPALS ... Program Executive Officer, Global Protection Against Limited Strikes [*Army*] (RDA)
PEO-IEW .... Program Executive Office - Intelligence and Electronic Warfare [*Army*] (RDA)
Peo L Adv ... People's Legal Advisor [*Utica, NY*] [*A publication*] (DLA)
PEOLE .... Preliminary Eole (SAUS)
PEO-MD ..... Program Executive Office - Missile Defense [*Military*] (RDA)
PEON .... Polar Environmental Officers Network (SAUS)
Peop .... People's (AL)
PeopBcp .... Peoples Bancorp [*Dekalb County*] [*Associated Press*] (SAG)
PeopBcT .... Peoples BancTrust Co. [*Associated Press*] (SAG)
PeopBk ...... Peoples Bank [*Catawba, NC*] [*Associated Press*] (SAG)
PEOPC .... Polyethylene Oxide/Polycarbonate (SAUS)
PeopChc .... Peoples Choice TV Corp. [*Associated Press*] (SAG)
PeopCT ...... Peoples Bank [*Bridgeport, CT*] [*Associated Press*] (SAG)
PeopEn ...... Peoples Energy Corp. [*Associated Press*] (SAG)
PEOPET ..... Polyethylene Oxide/Polyethylene Terephthalate (SAUS)
PeopFin .... Peoples Financial Corp. [*Associated Press*] (SAG)
PeopFst .... People First Corp. [*Associated Press*] (SAG)
PeopHld .... Peoples Holding Co. [*Associated Press*] (SAG)
PeopHrt .... People's Heritage Financial Group, Inc. [*Associated Press*] (SAG)
PEOPLE ..... American Federation of State, County, & Municipal Employees-People- Qualified [*Washington, DC*] (PACS)
PEOPLE PAC ... PACCAR Inc. Employees Organized for Political Leadership and Education PAC [*Bellevue, WA*] (PACS)
Peoples ..... Peoples' Reports [*77-97 Georgia*] [*A publication*] (DLA)
PeopleTel ... Peoples Telephone Co. [*Associated Press*] (SAG)
Peopsft ...... Peoplesoft, Inc. [*Associated Press*] (SAG)
PeopTel ..... People's Telephone Co., Inc. [*Associated Press*] (SAG)
PEORI .... Peoria, IL [*American Association of Railroads railroad junction routing code*]
PEOS .... Propulsion and Electrical Operating System (IEEE)
PEO-SD ..... Program Executive Officer-Ship Defense (SAUS)
PEO-STAMIS ... Program Executive Office, Standard Army Management Information Systems
PeoSvFn .... People's Savings Financial Corp. [*Associated Press*] (SAG)
PEOT .... Physical End of Tape (VLIE)
PEO TM ..... Program Executive Office, Tactical Missile [*Army*]
PEOX .... Polyethyleneoxide [*Organic chemistry*]
PEP .... All India Reporter, Patiala and East Punjab States Union Series [*A publication*] (ILCA)
PEP .... Charlotte, NC [*Location identifier*] [*FAA*] (FAAL)
PEP .... Cyclophosphamide, VM-26 Prednisolone [*Antineoplastic drug regimen*] (DAVI)
PEP .... Packet Exchange Protocol [*Computer science*] (CDE)
PEP .... Packetized Ensemble Protocol [*Computer science*]
PEP .... Palm Education Pioneer
PEP .... Paper Electrophoresis (MELL)
PEP .... Paperless Electronic Payment [*Business term*]
PEP .... Paperless Entry Processing (SAUS)
PEP .... Paperless Entry Processing User Group [*Defunct*] (CSR)
PEP .... Parametric Element Processor (SAUS)
PEP .... Parent Education Program (EARSL)
PEP .... Parent Effectiveness Program (SAUS)
PEP .... Parenting, Education, and Political Involvement [*Jack and Jill of America*]
PEP .... Parkinsons Educational Program (SAUS)
PEP .... Parti Ecologiste pour le Progres [*Burkina Faso*] [*Political party*] (EY)
PEP .... Parti Evangelique Populaire [*Popular Protestant Party*] [*Switzerland*] [*Political party*] (PPE)
PEP .... Partitioned Emulation Program [*Computer science*] (BUR)
PEP .... Partnership for Emergency Planning [*Emergency Management*] (EMA)
PEP .... Patent Examining Procedure (IAA)
PEP .... Paternalistic, Economic, Participative (BB)
PEP .... Paths for Employee Progress [*Medicine*] (EDAA)
PEP .... Patient Educational Program (MELL)
PEP .... Patient Environment Program [*Medicine*]
PEP .... Pauli Exclusion Principle [*Physics*]
PEP .... Peak Effective Power
PEP .... Peak Energy Product
PEP .... Peak Envelope Power [*Telecommunications*]
PEP .... Peer Evaluation Program [*College of American Pathologists*]
PEP .... People for Energy Progress [*Defunct*] (EA)
PEP .... People's Education Press
PEP .... Pepitilla [*Race of maize*]
Pep .... Pepper (SAUS)
PEP .... Peppermint (DSUE)
pep .... pep pill (SAUS)
PEP .... PepsiCo Inc. [*NYSE symbol*] (SPSG)
Pep .... Peptidase (DB)
PEP .... Peptide [*Biochemistry*]
PEP .... Performance Effectiveness [*or Evaluation*] Program [*Navy*]
PEP .... Performance Evaluation Procedure [*Joint Commission on Accreditation of Hospitals*] (DHSM)
PEP .... Performance Evaluation Process (SAUS)
PEP .... Peripheral Event Processor [*Computer science*]
PEP .... Perkin-Elmer Processor [*Computer*]
PEP .... Personal Effects Protection (SAUS)
PEP .... Personal Employee Profiling [*Information service or system*] (IID)
PEP .... Personal Empowerment Program (WDAA)
PEP .... Personal Equity Plan [*Finance*]
PEP .... Personal Exam Prep (SAUS)
PEP .... Personal Exemption Phase-Out [*Income tax*]
PEP .... Personal Exercise Programmer
PEP .... Personal Financial Planner
PEP .... Personality-Profile Exam
PEP .... Personnel Exchange Program [*Military*] (NVT)
PEP .... Petroleum Electric Power (SAUS)
PEP .... Pfizer, Inc., Research Center Library, Easton, PA [*Library symbol*] [*Library of Congress*] (LCLS)
PEP .... Phenethyl Propionate [*Insect attractant*] [*Organic chemistry*]
PEP .... Philips Environmental Protection (SAUS)
PEP .... Phosphoenolpyruvate [*Biochemistry*]
PEP .... Phosphoenolpyruvic Acid (SAUS)
PEP .... Photoelectric Potential
PEP .... Photo-Electron Plasma (SAUS)
PEP .... Photoelectrophoresis
PEP .... Photographic Exploitation Products (MCD)
PEP .... Physical Education for Progress [*Act*]
PEP .... Physical Education Program
PEP .... Physiological Education of Primates (SAUS)
PEP .... Physiological Evaluation of Primates
PEP .... Pictorial End-Papers [*Publishing*]
PEP .... Pigmentation, Edema and Plasma Cell Dyscrasia (MELL)
PEP .... Pipeline Expanding Polymer
PEP .... Piping Efficiency Program
PEP .... Planar Epitaxial Passivated
PEP .... Planetary Ephemeris Program (IEEE)
PEP .... Planetary Exploration Plan [*NASA*]
PEP .... Planner Epitaxiel Passivated
PEP .... Plant Equipment Package [*DoD*]
PEP .... Plasma Exhaust Process (SAUS)
PEP .... Platform Electronic Package
PEP .... Platform Environment Profile [*Computer science*] (VLIE)
PEP .... Platform Evaluation Program
PEP .... Plessey Electronic Payroll (DEN)
PEP .... Plume Exposure Pathway [*Nuclear emergency planning*]
PEP .... Point, Edge, Polygon [*Computer science*]
PEP .... Pole-Equator-Pole (QUAC)

PEP .... Policy Enforcement Point [*Computer term*]
PEP .... Political and Economic Planning [*A British organization*] [*Later, Policy Studies Institute*]
PEP .... Polyestradiol Phosphate [*Endocrinology*]
PEP .... Polyethylene Polyamine (SAUS)
PEP .... Polyethylene Powder
PEP .... Polymorphic Eruption of Pregnancy (SAUS)
PEP .... Polynominal Error Protection (MCD)
PEP .... Pool Exercise Program [*Arthritis Foundation*]
PEP .... Porsche Experimental Prototype [*Automotive engineering*]
PEP .... Portable Energy Provision (SSD)
PEP .... Portfolio Evaluation Plan [*Australia*]
PEP .... Positive Energy [*Vancouver Stock Exchange symbol*]
PEP .... Positive Expiratory Pressure [*Medicine*] (EDAA)
PEP .... Positron-Electron Project [*High-energy accelerator*]
PEP .... Positron Electron Proton [*Physics*]
PEP .... Postal Efficiency Plan (SAA)
PEP .... Postencephalitic Parkinsonism [*Medicine*] (DB)
PEP .... Postexposure Prophylaxis [*Medicine*]
PEP .... Power Evaluation Program
PEP .... Power Extension Package (MCD)
PEP .... Power Extension Plant (MCD)
PEP .... Practical Engineering Paperwork
PEP .... Pratt & Whitney Engine Program [*Aviation*] (NG)
PEP .... Preamplifier Extension Plug
PEP .... Precipitation Enhancement Program (SAUS)
PEP .... Pre-Ejection Period [*Cardiology*]
PEP .... Pre-Employment Program
PEP .... Preferred Equipment Package [*Automotive retailing*]
PEP .... Preliminary Evaluation Plan (SAUS)
PEP .... Preschool Education Program [*Sesame Street TV program*]
PEP .... Presented a Petition [*Telegraphy*] (PCTE)
PEP .... President's Economy Program
PEP .... Preventive Enforcement Patrol [*New York City police*]
PEP .... Primary Education Program [*Child development test*]
PEP .... Primary Entry Point System (OTD)
PEP .... Primate Equilibrium Platform
PEP .... Princeton Electronic Products, Inc. (IAA)
PEP .... Princeton Experiment Package [*NASA*]
PeP .... Principal of Pedagogy [*Academic degree*]
PEP .... Printer-Emulation Package [*Software*]
PEP .... Priority Energy Policy [*Environmental Protection Agency*]
PEP .... Probability Encoding Program (SAUS)
PEP .... Process Evaluation Program (VLIE)
PEP .... Processing Enhancing Protein [*Biochemistry*]
PEP .... Pro-Choice Public Education Project [*Association*] (EA)
PEP .... Procurement Evaluation Panel [*Air Force*] (MCD)
PEP .... Procytox [*Cyclophosphamide*], Epipodophyllotoxin Derivative , Prednisolone [*VM-26*] [*Antineoplastic drug regimen*]
PEP .... Producibility Engineering and Planning [*Army*] (AABC)
PEP .... Producibility Engineering Plan [*Air Force*]
PEP .... Product Engineering and Production (MCD)
PEP .... Production EAGLE [*Elevation Angle Guidance Landing Equipment*] Package
PEP .... [*The*] Production Engineering and Productivity Exhibition and Conference [*British*] (ITD)
PEP .... Production Engineering Planning
PEP .... Production Equipment Package
PEP .... [*The*] Productivity Effectiveness Program [*Title of a pamphlet by Robert Gedaliah that describes sedentary exercises for desk-bound workers*]
PEP .... Productivity Enhancement Program (SAUS)
PEP .... Productivity Enhancement Project (SAUS)
PEP .... Professional Enhancement Program (SAUS)
PEP .... Professional Enhancement Project [*American Occupational Therapy Association*]
PEP .... Professional Experience Program [*Australia*]
PEP .... Proficiency Evaluation Program [*Medicine*] [*College of American Pathologists*] (EDAA)
PEP .... Proficiency Examination Program (MCD)
PEP .... Proficiency in English Program (SAUS)
PEP .... Program Element Plan (AFIT)
PEP .... Program Evaluation Procedure [*Air Force*]
PEP .... Program Evaluation Program [*Air Force*] (IAA)
PEP .... Programmable Extension Package (IAA)
PEP .... Programmed Emulation Partition (SAUS)
PEP .... Programmed End Point (SAUS)
PEP .... Programme d'Epidemiologie Pratique [*WHO/AFRO*]
PEP .... Program to Enhance Productivity (SAUS)
PEP .... Progressive Exercise Program
PEP .... Project Element Plan (SAUS)
PEP .... Projects and Exports Policy [*Board of Trade*] [*British*]
PEP .... Prolyl Endopeptidase
PEP .... Promoting Enduring Peace (EA)
PEP .... Promotion Evaluation Pattern
PEP .... Propellant, Explosive, and Pyrotechnic
PEP .... Property Estimation Program [*Utah Water Research Laboratory*]
PEP .... Proposal Equipment Packages (MCD)
PEP .... Proposal Evaluation Panel (MCD)
PEP .... Proposal Evaluation Plan [*or Program*] (MCD)
PEP .... Proposal Evaluation Program
PEP .... Proposal Exploitation Product
PEP .... Propulsion and Energetics Panel (SAUS)
PEP .... Propulsion Evaluation Plan
PEP .... Protection in Evaluation Procedures
PEP .... Protein Electrophoresis [*Medicine*] (DMAA)
PEP .... Protocol Extension Protocol (SAUS)
PEP .... Protocol on Environmental Protection (SAUS)
PEP .... Proton-Electron-Positron (SAUS)
PEP .... Proton Electron Positron Colliding Beams (IAA)
PEP .... Proton-Electron-Proton [*Nuclear physics*]
PEP .... Prototyping, Evaluation and Programming (SAUS)
PEP .... Psychiatric Evaluation Profile [*Psychology*] (MAE)
PEP .... Psychoeducational Profile [*Test for autistic children*]
PEP .... Psychoepistemological Profile [*Student personality test*]
PEP .... Public Employment Program (EBF)
PEP .... Pulse Echo Pattern
PEP .... Pulse Effective Power [*Telecommunications*] (IAA)
PEP .... Pupil Evaluation Program
PEPA .... Peptidase A [*An enzyme*]
PEPA .... Per Employee per Annum
PEPA .... Petroleum Electric Power Association [*Later, EUIPA*] (EA)
PEPA .... Pitch Fibre Pipe Association of Great Britain (BI)
PEPA .... Polyether-Polyamide Block Copolymer (EDCT)
PEPA .... Polyethylene Polyamide (SAUS)
PEPA .... Protected Environment plus Prophylactic Antibiotics [*Oncology*]
PEPA .... Pulse Echo Pattern Analyzer
PEPAC .... Pharmacia Corporation Employees PAC [*Peapack, NJ*] (PACS)
PEPAE .... Permanent Entry Permit After Entry
PEPAG .... Physical Electronics and Physical Acoustics Group [*MIT*] (MCD)
PEPAOP ..... (Phenylethyl)phenylacetoxypiperidine [*Organic chemistry*]
PEPAS .... WHO [*World Health Organization*] Western Pacific Regional Centre for the Promotion of Environmental Planning and Applied Studies (EAIO)
PEPAT .... Protocol on Environment Protection of the Antarctic Treaty (SAUS)
Pep-Bis ..... Pepto-Bismol (SAUS)
PEPBNC ..... Peninsula Enrichment Program for Bright Needy Children [*Queensland, Australia*]
PepBoy ...... Pep Boys-Manny, Moe & Jack [*Associated Press*] (SAG)
PEPC .... Peptidase C [*An enzyme*]
PEPC .... Phosphoenolpyruvate Carboxylase [*An enzyme*]
PEPC .... Polynomial Error Protection Code [*Computer science*]
PEPC .... Postsecondary Education Planning Commission [*Florida*] (EDAC)
PEPC .... Potomac Electric Power Co.
PEPCase .... Phosphenol-Pyruvate Carboxylase (SAUS)
PEPCI .... Providing Emergency Presidential Communications Interface (SAUS)
PEPCK .... Phosphoenolopyruvate Carboxykinase [*An enzyme*]
PEPCK .... Phosphoenolpyruvate Carboxykinase [*An enzyme*]
PEPCO .... Potomac Electric Power Co.
PEPCOM .... Pacific Engineering Production Company (AAGC)
PEPCOM .... Pepsi-Cola Bottling Companies (EFIS)
PEPD .... Peptidase D [*An enzyme*]
PEPE .... Parallel Element Processing Element (SAUS)
PEPE .... Parallel Element Processing Ensemble [*Burroughs Corp.*] (BUR)
PEPE .... People Persecuted by Pablo Escobar [*Colombia*] (ECON)
PEPE .... Pepe Est Presque Emacs (SAUS)
PEPE .... Perkin-Elmer Performance Evaluation (SAUS)
PEPE .... Persistant Elevated Pollution Episodes (SAUS)
PEPE .... Prolonged Elevated-Pollution Episode [*Environmental Protection Agency*]
PEP/EP ...... Pre-Ejection Period to Ejection Period [*Cardiology*] (DAVI)
PEPES .... People Persecuted by Pablo Escobar
PEPG .... Piezoelectric Power Generation
PEPG .... Port Emergency Planning Group [*NATO*] (NATG)
PEPGB .... Plasma Exhaust Pumping Glove Box (SAUS)
PEPI .... Pechora Pipit [*North American bird banding code*] (BIBA)
PEPI .... Physical Education Public Information [*Film*]
PEPI .... Piezo Electric Products, Inc. [*NASDAQ symbol*] (COMM)
PEPI .... Post-Menopausal Estrogen and Progestin Intervention [*Medicine*] (BARN)
PEPI .... Postmenopausal Estrogen/Progestin Interventions
PEPI .... Pre-Ejection Period Index [*Cardiology*]
PEPIC .... Piezo Electric Products (EFIS)
PEPIC .... Public Education Project on the Intelligence Community (SAUS)
PEPICO ...... Photoelectron Photoion Coincidence (SAUS)
PE Pipe ..... Polyethylene Pipe (SAUS)
PEP-L .... Partitioned Emulation Programming-Local (SAUS)
PEPL .... Plasmadynamics and Electric Propulsion Laboratory [*University of Michigan*] (RCD)
PEPL .... Preliminary Engineering Parts List
PEPLAN ..... Polaris Executive Plan [*British*]
PEP-LR ..... Partitioned Emulation Programming-Local/Remote (SAUS)
PEP/LVET ... Pre-Ejection Period/Left Ventricular Ejection Time [*Medicine*] (MEDA)
PEPMC ...... Printing Estimators and Production Men's Club [*New York, NY*] (EA)
PEPMIS ..... Plant Equipment Packages Management Information System (MCD)
PEPMOV .... Pepper Mottle Virus [*Plant pathology*]
PEPMV ...... Pepino Mosaic Virus [*Plant pathology*]
PEPP .... Permanent-Equity Pension Plan [*Human resources*] (WYGK)
PEPP .... Planetary Entry Parachute Program [*NASA*]
PEPP .... Positive Expiratory Pressure Plateau [*Medicine*] (MAE)
PEPP .... Professional Engineers in Private Practice
PEPPA .... Preparedness for Emergency Plant Pest Action [*In Animal and Plant Health Inspection Service publication PEPPA Pot*]
PEPPARD ... Propellant, Explosive, Pyrotechnic Pollution Abatement Research and Development (DNAB)
PEPPER ..... Photo-Electric Portable Probe Reader (PDAA)
PEPPER ..... Photo-Electro Portable Probe Reader (SAUS)

Pepper & L Dig... Pepper and Lewis' Digest of Laws [*Pennsylvania*] [*A publication*] (DLA)
Pepper & L Dig Laws... Pepper and Lewis' Digest of Laws [*Pennsylvania*] [*A publication*] (DLA)
Pepperdine U... Pepperdine University (GAGS)
PEPPI........ Program to Encorage Product and Process Innovation (SAUS)
PEPPI........ Projected Elevation of Product Performance Indices (SAUS)
PEPPRE..... Photo Electric Portable Probe Reader (IAA)
PEP Programme... Philips Environmental Protection Programme (SAUS)
PEP-PTS.... Phosphoenolpyruvate-dependent Phosphotransferase System (SAUS)
PEPR........ Precision Encoding and Pattern Recognition Device [*Computer science*]
PEP-R....... Psychoeducational Profile-Revised (TES)
PEPrA....... PECO Energy, $3.80 Pfd [*NYSE symbol*] (TTSB)
PEPrB....... PECO Energy, $4.30 Pfd [*NYSE symbol*] (TTSB)
PEPrC....... PECO Energy, $4.40 Pfd [*NYSE symbol*] (TTSB)
PEPrD....... PECO Energy, $4.68 Pfd [*NYSE symbol*] (TTSB)
PEPR Device... Precision Encoding and Pattern Recognition Device (SAUS)
PEPrF........ PECO Energy Dep Pfd [*NYSE symbol*] (TTSB)
PEPrY....... PECO En Cap Tr I 8.72% 'TOPrS' [*NYSE symbol*] (TTSB)
PEPrZ........ PECO Energy L.P. MIPS'A' [*NYSE symbol*] (TTSB)
PEPS........ National Committee on Public Employee Pension Systems (EA)
PEPS........ Peperomia and Exotic Plant Society (EA)
Peps........ Pepsin (SAUS)
PEPS........ Peptidase S [*An enzyme*]
PEPS........ Pesticide Enforcement Policy Statement [*Environmental Protection Agency*]
PEPS........ Pinion Electric Power Steering
PEPS........ Plasma Electron Profiles, Symmetric
PEPS........ Positive-Expulsion Propellant System (SAUS)
PEPS........ Preliminary Evaluation Programme for SPOT (SAUS)
PEPS........ Priced Exhibit Preliminary System (SAUS)
PEPS........ Priced Exhibit Processing System
PEPS........ Primary Earnings per Share (TDOB)
PEPS........ Primary Environmental Prediction System
PEPS........ Primary Environmental Processing Systems [*Navy*] (GFGA)
PEPS........ Production Engineering Productivity System [*Camtek Ltd.*] [*Software package*]
PEPS........ Productivity Environmental Preference Survey [*Test*]
PEPS........ Program Element Plan Supplement
PEPS........ Psychological, Economic, Political and Sociological (SAUS)
PEP-SEP.... Peptide Separation [*Biochemistry*]
PEP Service... Pan European Paging Service (SAUS)
PEPSI........ Plasma Electron Profiles, Symmetric Integrals (MCD)
PepsiC...... PepsiCo, Inc. [*Associated Press*] (SAG)
PEPSICO... Pepsi-Cola Co. (EFIS)
PepsiPR..... Pepsi Cola Puerto Rico Bottling [*Associated Press*] (SAG)
PEPSS....... Preschool and Early Primary Skills Survey [*Child development test*]
PEPSS....... Programmable Equipment for Personnel Subsystem Simulation
PEPSU....... All India Reporter, Patiala and East Punjab States Union [*1950-57*] [*A publication*] (DLA)
PEPSU....... Patiala and East Punjab States Union
PEPSY....... Precision Earth-Pointing System (MCD)
PEPSY....... Scandinavian pedagogical publications bibliography (SAUS)
PEP Technique... Planar Epitaxial Passivated Technique (SAUS)
PEPTP....... (Phenylethyl)Phenyltetrahydropyridine [*Organic chemistry*]
PEP Train... Prototype Electro-Pneumatic Train (SAUS)
PEP Transistor... Planar Epitaxial Passivated Transistor (SAUS)
PEP/USA.... Parkinson's Educational Program - USA (EA)
PEPUSL..... Pepperdine University School of Law (DLA)
PEpW........ Westinghouse Electric Corp., East Pittsburgh, PA [*Library symbol*] [*Library of Congress*] (LCLS)
PEPWG...... Pressurized Element Working Group (SAUS)
PEPZ......... Potomac Electric Power [*Federal Railroad Administration identification code*]
PEQ.......... Palestine Exploration Quarterly [*A publication*] (ABAR)
PEQ.......... Pecos City, TX [*Location identifier*] [*FAA*] (FAAL)
PEQ.......... Personal Experience Questionnaire [*Psychology*]
PEQ.......... Petroquin Resources Ltd. [*Vancouver Stock Exchange symbol*]
PEQ.......... Potomac Edison [*NYSE symbol*] (SAG)
PEQ.......... Potomac Edison 8.00% 'QUIDS' [*NYSE symbol*] (TTSB)
PEQC........ Presidents Environmental Quality Council (SAUS)
PEQC........ Production Engine Quality Control (SAUS)
PEQI......... Perceived Environmental Quality Indices (EEVL)
PEQIX....... Pioneer Equity-Income Cl.A [*Mutual fund ticker symbol*] (SG)
PEQU........ Pequea [*NCIC trailer make code*]
PEQUA...... Production Equipment Agency [*Army*]
PEQUOD.... Pacific Equatorial Ocean Dynamics [*Project*] [*USA*] [*Marine science*] (OSRA)
per........... By [*Through*] [*Therapy term*] (CTAA)
PEr........... Erie Public Library, Erie, PA [*Library symbol*] [*Library of Congress*] (LCLS)
PER.......... For Each (DAVI)
PER.......... Packed Encoding Rules (ACII)
PER.......... Paraelectric Resonance (SAUS)
PER.......... Paramagnetic Electron Resonance (SAUS)
PER.......... Par Exchange Rate [*Business term*]
PER.......... Parity Error Rate
PER.......... Parole Evidence Rule [*Legal shorthand*] (LWAP)
PER.......... Partido Estadista Republicano [*Puerto Rico*] [*Political party*]
PER.......... Path Extension Ratio (MCD)
PER.......... Peak Ejection Rate [*Cardiology*]
PER.......... Peak Expiration Rate [*Medicine*]
Per........... Pediatric Emergency Room (DAVI)
Pe R......... Pennewill's Delaware Reports [*A publication*] (DLA)
per........... Perceptual (IDYL)
Per........... Perchlorethylen (SAUS)
per........... Perennial [*Botany*]
Per........... Perera's Select Decisions [*Ceylon*] [*A publication*] (DLA)
PER.......... Per Exchange Rate [*Finance*] (MHDW)
PER.......... Performance (DA)
PER.......... Performance Energy Ratio (SAUS)
PER.......... Performance Evaluation Report [*DoD*]
PER.......... Performance Evaluation Routine (SAUS)
PER.......... Perhaps (ROG)
Per........... Pericles [*Shakespearean work*]
Per........... Pericles [*of Plutarch*] [*Classical studies*] (OCD)
PER.......... Perigee (KSC)
per........... Perimeter (MIST)
per........... Perineal [*Gynecology*] (MAE)
Per........... Periochae [*of Livy*] [*Classical studies*] (OCD)
per........... Period (VRA)
Per........... Period [*Record label*]
PER.......... Period
per........... Periodic (AAMN)
Per........... Periodical (AL)
per........... Periodical
PER.......... Periodical (ROG)
PER.......... Periodic Evaluation Record (DIPS)
per........... Periodicity (DMAA)
PER.......... Periodogram (DMAA)
PER.......... Peritoneum (SAUS)
PER.......... Permission (AABC)
PER.......... Perodicity (SAUS)
PER.......... Perot Systems'A' [*NYSE symbol*] (SG)
Per........... Perseus [*Constellation*]
Per........... Persia (VRA)
PER.......... Persia [*Obsolete*]
per........... Persian, Modern [*MARC language code*] [*Library of Congress*] (LCCP)
per........... Person (WDMC)
PER.......... Person
PER.......... Personate (SAUS)
PER.......... Personnel (KSC)
PER.......... PERT [*Program Evaluation and Review Technique*] Event Report
PER.......... Perth [*Australia*] [*Airport symbol*] (OAG)
PER.......... Perth [*Australia*] [*Seismograph station code, US Geological Survey*] [*Closed*] (SEIS)
PER.......... Peru [*ANSI three-letter standard code*] (CNC)
PER.......... Perylene (SAUS)
PER.......... Pharmaceutical Evaluation Report [*Australia*]
PER.......... Phase Encoding Recording (SAUS)
PER.......... Phase Engineering Report
PER.......... Photo-Electric Reader (or Reading) (SAUS)
PER.......... Physical Examination Rate [*Military*] (AFM)
PER.......... Planning, Evaluation, and Reporting [*Education-improvement system*]
PER.......... Pominex Ltd. [*Toronto Stock Exchange symbol*]
PER.......... Ponca City, OK [*Location identifier*] [*FAA*] (FAAL)
Per........... Pope, Evans & Robbins, Inc. [*AMEX symbol*] (COMM)
PER.......... Port Everglades Railway [*AAR code*]
PER.......... Postelectrophoresis Relaxation
PER.......... Post Engineer Request
PER.......... Post-Execution Reporting (MHDI)
PER.......... Potential Excess Report
PER.......... Preedited Region [*Genetics*]
PER.......... Pre-Emptive Right (MHDW)
PER.......... Prefect (automobile) [*NCIC car model code*]
PER.......... Preliminary Engineering Report (KSC)
PER.......... PressNet Environmental Reports [*Information service or system*] (IID)
PER.......... Price Earnings Ratio [*Relation between price of a company's stock and its annual net income*]
PER.......... Printing Executive Register (DGA)
PER.......... Probable Error Radial [*Statistics*] (IAA)
PER.......... Process Energy Requirement (SAUS)
PER.......... Product Engineering Recommendation [*Automotive engineering*]
PER.......... Product Engineering Release (SAUS)
PER.......... Production Engineering and Research (SAUS)
PER.......... Production Engine Remanufacturers Program [*Automotive engineering*]
PER.......... Professional and Executive Recruitment Service [*British*]
PER.......... Professional Employment Register [*British*] (ODBW)
PER.......... Proficiency Evaluation Review
PER.......... Program Error Report (MHDI)
PER.......... Program Event Recording [*Computer science*] (MDG)
PER.......... Program Execution Request
PER.......... Program for Ecological Research (SAUS)
PER.......... Program for Ecosystem Research (SAUS)
PER.......... Project on Ethnic Relations [*Association*] (EA)
PER.......... Pronated External Rotation [*Medicine*] (MELL)
PER.......... Proposal Evaluation Report (MCD)
PER.......... Protein Efficiency Ratio [*Nutrition*]
PER.......... Pseudoequilibrium Ratio (SAUS)
PER.......... Public Employees Roundtable (EA)
PER.......... Pyrotechnical Evaluation Range [*Army*] (RDA)
per........... Through or By [*Medicine*] (BCRP)

PER7 .... Region 7 Personnel System (SAUS)
PERA .... Pennsylvania Educational Research Association (EARSL)
PERA .... Planning and Engineering for Repair and Alteration [*Navy*]
PERA .... Production Engineering Research Association [*Research center*] [*British*] (IRC)
PERA .... Production Engine Remanufacturers Association (EA)
PERA .... Production Equipment Rental Association (EA)
PERA .... Project Engineering Research Association (SAUS)
Per A J ...... Performing Arts Journal [*A publication*] (BRI)
PERAM ...... Personnel Action Memorandum [*Military*]
PER AN ..... Per Annum [*By the Year*] [*Latin*]
Per & Dav... Perry and Davison's English King's Bench Reports [*1838-41*] [*A publication*] (DLA)
Per & Kn.... Perry and Knapp's English Election Reports [*1838*] [*A publication*] (DLA)
per ann ..... Per Annum (EBF)
PER ANN.... Per Annum [*By the Year*] [*Latin*]
PERA system... Project Engineering Research Association system (NITA)
P/E ratio .... Precipitation-Evaporation Ratio (LDOE)
P/E ratio .... Price/Earnings Ratio (WDAA)
Pe Rave..... Petrus Ravennas [*Flourished, 1468-1508*] [*Authority cited in pre-1607 legal work*] (DSA)
PERB .... Personnel Evaluation Research Bureau (SAUS)
PERB .... Planning and Environmental Review Board (SAUS)
PERB .... Professional Engineers Registration Board (SAUS)
PERB .... Public Employment Relations Board (EDAC)
PERC .... Paisley Enterprise Research Centre [*University of Paisley*] [*United Kingdom*] (RCD)
PERC .... Parents Educational Resource Center
PERC .... Peace on Earth Research Center
PERC .... Pediatric Epilepsy Research Center [*University of Washington*] (RCD)
PERC .... Percent [*Electric utility company*]
PERC .... Perceptronics, Inc. [*NASDAQ symbol*] (COMM)
PERC .... Perch Company [*NCIC trailer make code*]
PERC .... Perchloroethylene (SAUS)
PERC .... Perclose, Inc. [*NASDAQ symbol*] (SAG)
PERC .... Percolate (SAUS)
PERC .... Percolator (DSUE)
PERC .... Percussion (AAG)
perc.......... Percussion (WDAA)
PERC .... Pittsburgh Energy Research Center [*Later, PETC*] [*Energy Research and Development Administration*]
PERC .... Plasma Energy Recycle and Conversion
PERC .... Political & Economic Risk Consultancy [*Commercial firm*] [*Hong Kong*]
PERC .... Political Economy Research Center [*Research center*] (RCD)
PERC .... Pre-Exercise Review Consideration [*Emergency Management*] (EMA)
PERC .... Preliminary Editorial Review Checklist (SAUS)
PERC .... Private Enterprise Research Center (EA)
PERC .... Processor Emergency Recovery Circuit [*Bell System*]
PERC .... Professional Engineering and Research Consultants
PERC .... Psoriasis Education and Research Centre [*University of Toronto*] [*Canada*] [*Research center*] (RCD)
PERC .... Public Employment Relations Commission (EDAC)
PERC .... Public Enterprises Reform Commission [*Sri Lanka*]
PERCAM .... Performance and Cost Analysis Model (MCD)
Per cap ..... Per Capita (EBF)
Per Cap ..... Per Capita [*By the Individual*] [*Latin*]
PERCAP..... Persian Gulf Requirements and Capabilities [*Military*]
PERCASREPT... Personnel Casualty Report [*Military*] (NVT)
PERC DR.... Percussion Drilling (SAUS)
PERCENT ... Per Centum [*By the Hundred*] [*Latin*]
Percep ...... Perceptions (DIAR)
PerceptOR... Perception for Off-road Robotics Program [*Defense Advanced Research Projects Agency*] (RCD)
PERCHLOR... Perchloride [*Chemistry*] (ROG)
PERCI .... Personnel Contamination Instrumentation
Perclose .... Perclose, Inc. [*Associated Press*] (SAG)
PERCO ...... Percobarg (SAUS)
PERCO ...... Percodan (SAUS)
PERCOM .... Peripheral Communications (SAUS)
PERCOM .... Personnel Command [*Army*] (MCD)
PERCOMP... Personal Computing Conference (MHDI)
PERCOMPASIA... South East Asian Personal Computer Hardware and Software Show
PERCOMP Conference... Personal Computing Conference (SAUS)
Percon ...... Percon, Inc. [*Associated Press*] (SAG)
Per con ..... Per Contra [*On the Other Side*] [*Latin*]
PERCON..... Peripheral Converter (SAUS)
PERCOS..... Performance Coding System
Percptr ...... Perceptron, Inc. [*Associated Press*] (SAG)
Per CS ...... Perrault's Conseil Superieur [*Canada*] [*A publication*] (DLA)
PERCS....... Preference Equity Redemption Cumulative Stock (ECON)
PERCS....... Preferred Equity Redemption Cumulative Stock
PERCUSS... Percussion [*Medicine*] (DAVI)
PERCUSS & AUSC... Percussion and Ausculation [*Medicine*] (DHSM)
PERCY....... Photo Electronic Recognition Cybernetics (SAUS)
PERD .... Panel for Energy Research and Development (SAUS)
PERD .... Payload Element Requirements Document (SAUS)
PERD .... Perdendo [*or Perdendosi*] [*Softer and Slower*] [*Music*]
PERD .... Periodic (MSA)
PERD .... Perused (ROG)
PERD .... Program of Energy Research and Development [*Natural Resources Canada*] [*Canada*] (RCD)
PERDA ...... Per Diem [*By the Day*] [*Latin*] (NOAA)
PERDDiMS . Personnel Deployment and Distribution Management System [*Military*] (AABC)
PERDEN..... Perdendo [*or Perdendosi*] [*Softer and Slower*] [*Music*]
PERDEX..... Permuted Formula Index [*Molecular formula indexing*]
PerDia....... Personal Diagnositics, Inc. [*Associated Press*] (SAG)
PERECORDING... Phase Encoded Recording (SAUS)
PEREF .... Personal Effects
PEREF .... Propellant Engine Research Environmental Facility
Pereg .... Peregrinus Fabius [*Authority cited in pre-1607 legal work*] (DSA)
PERF .... Peak Expiratory Flow Rate [*Medicine*] (DMAA)
perf .... Perfect (WDAA)
PERF .... Perfect
PERF .... PerfectData Corp. [*NASDAQ symbol*] (NQ)
PERF .... Perfection (SAUS)
perf .... perfectum (SAUS)
PERF .... Perforate [*or Perforator*]
PERF .... Perforation (DSUE)
perf .... Perforation (WDMC)
PERF .... Perform (SAUS)
PERF .... Performance (KSC)
perf .... Performance (VRA)
PERF .... Performance Products [*NCIC trailer make code*]
PERF .... Performer (SAUS)
PERF .... Perfusionist [*Medicine*] (HCT)
PerF .... Perma Fix Environmental Services [*Associated Press*] (SAG)
PERF .... Petroleum Environmental Research Forum (SAUS)
PERF .... Planetary Entry Radiation Facility [*Langley Research Center*] [*NASA*] (PDAA)
PERF .... Police Executive Research Forum (EA)
PERF .... Police Executive Resource Form (SAUS)
PER FA ATK SYS ANAL... Perform Field Artillery Attack System Analysis (SAUS)
PER FA PERS CNTRL... Perform Field Artillery Personnel Control (SAUS)
PER FA SPL CNTRL... Perform Field Artillery Supply Control (SAUS)
PERFCE ..... Performance
PERFD....... Performed (ROG)
Perfdta ...... PerfectData Corp. [*Associated Press*] (SAG)
PERFECT.... Performance Evaluation for Cost Effective Transformations (SAUS)
PERFECT.... Productivity Erosion Runoff Functions to Evaluate Conservation Techniques (SAUS)
PERFINS .... Perforated Insignia [*Philately*]
PERFM ...... Perform (ROG)
PERFMON... Performance Monitoring (SAUS)
PerFood..... Performance Food Group [*Commercial firm*] [*Associated Press*] (SAG)
PERFORM... Performance
Perform Chem... Performance Chemicals (SAUS)
Perform Eval... Performance Evaluation (SAUS)
Perform Eval Rev... Performance Evaluation Review (SAUS)
PERFR....... Perforator (IAA)
PERF RM ... Perfect Ream (DGA)
PERFS....... Perfumers (SAUS)
PerfSys...... Performance Systems International, Inc. [*Associated Press*] (SAG)
PerfTech .... Performance Technologies, Inc. [*Associated Press*] (SAG)
Perfum ...... Perfumania, Inc. [*Associated Press*] (SAG)
PERFW...... Perforating Wound
PErG .... Gannon University, Erie, PA [*Library symbol*] [*Library of Congress*] (LCLS)
PERG .... Pattern Electroretinogram (SAUS)
PERG .... Peatland Ecology Research Group [*Laval University*] [*Canada*] (RCD)
PERG .... Pergola [*Classified advertising*] (ADA)
PERG .... Precision Engineering Research Group [*Massachusetts Institute of Technology*] (RCD)
PERG .... Production Emergency Redistribution Group
PERG .... Production Equipment Redistribution Group [*Army*]
PERGO ...... Project Evaluation and Review with Graphic Output (IEEE)
PERGRA..... Permission Granted [*Military*]
PERGS ...... Portable Earth Resources Ground Station (SAUS)
perh .... Perhaps (GEAB)
PERH .... Perhaps
PerHi .... Erie County Historical Society, Erie, PA [*Library symbol*] [*Library of Congress*] (LCLS)
PERI .... Pea Ridge National Military Park
peri .... Pericardium [*Medicine*] (ADWA)
PERI .... Perigee
Peri .... Perigeum (SAUS)
PERI .... Perimeter (AABC)
peri .... Perineal [*Anatomy*] (DAVI)
PERI .... Periodical
PERI .... Periphonics Corp. [*NASDAQ symbol*] (SAG)
PERI .... Periscope
PERI .... Peritoneal Fluid (DAVI)
PERI .... Pharmaceutical Education & Research Institute (SAUS)
PERI .... Photoengravers Research Institute (SAUS)
PERI .... Platemakers Educational and Research Institute [*Later, IAP*]
PERI .... Political Economy Research Institute [*University of Massachusetts at Amherst*] (RCD)
PERI .... Production Equipment Redistribution Inventory [*Army*]
PERI .... Production Equipment Reserve Inventory [*Navy*] (NG)
PERI .... Programme for the Enhancement of Research Information
PERI .... Protein Engineering Research Institute [*Japanese governmental and industrial consortium*] [*Later, BERI*]
PERI .... Psychiatric Epidemiology Research Interview

PERI .... Public Entity Risk Institute [*Emergency Management*] (EMA)
PERIAP ...... Periapical [*Dentistry*]
peric .... Pericope (VRA)
Pericom ..... Pericom Semiconductor Corp. [*Associated Press*] (SAG)
PERIF .... Peripheral
perig .... Perigee (BARN)
Pe Rigal .... Petrus Rigaldi [*Flourished, 14th century*] [*Authority cited in pre-1607 legal work*] (DSA)
perih .... perihelion (SAUS)
PERIM .... Perimeter (KSC)
PERI/M ...... Perimortem (DAVI)
PeriniC ...... Perini Corp. [*Associated Press*] (SAG)
PERINTREP... Periodic Intelligence Report (NATG)
PERINTREPT... Periodic Intelligence Report
PERINTSUM... Periodic Intelligence Summary [*Army*] (AABC)
perio .... Periodontist [*Dentistry*] (DAVI)
Period .... Periodical (DIAR)
Periodentol... Periodentology (SAUS)
PERIODONTOL... Periodontology (SAUS)
Period Polytech... Periodica Polytechnica (SAUS)
Period Polytech\ Chem Eng... Periodica Polytechnica, Chemical Engineering (SAUS)
Period Polytech\ Electr Eng... Periodica Polytechnica, Electrical Engineering (SAUS)
Period Polytech\ Mech Eng... Periodica Polytechnica, Mechanical Engineering (SAUS)
Peripad ..... Perineal Pad [*Medicine*] (AMHC)
PERIPH ...... Periphery (KSC)
Periphn ..... Periphonics Corp. [*Associated Press*] (SAG)
Periphony... Peripheral Phony (SAUS)
Peripl M Eux... Periplus Maris Euxini [*of Arrian*] [*Classical studies*] (OCD)
PERIS .... Periscope (KSC)
PERJ .... Perjury [*FBI standardized term*]
PERJY .... Perjury (ROG)
PERK .... Payroll Earnings Record Keeping
PERK .... Perchloreth(yl)ene (ODA)
PERK .... Percolate (GOBB)
Perk .... Perkins on Conveyancing [*A publication*] (DLA)
Perk .... Perkins on Pleading [*A publication*] (DLA)
Perk .... Perkins' Profitable Book (Conveyancing) [*A publication*] (DLA)
PERK .... Perquisite
PERK .... Prospective Evaluation of Radial Keratotomy [*Protocol*] [*Ophthalmology*] (DAVI)
PERKARA... Parti Perdapuan Kebangsaan Ra'ayat Brunei [*Brunei People's National United Party*] [*Political party*] (EY)
PerkEl .... Perkin-Elmer Corp. [*Associated Press*] (SAG)
PerkF .... Perkins Family Restaurants Ltd. [*Associated Press*] (SAG)
PERKI .... Perkins, AR [*American Association of Railroads railroad junction routing code*]
Perkin-Elmer Tech News... Perkin-Elmer Technical News (SAUS)
Perk Pr Bk... Perkins' Profitable Book (Conveyancing) [*A publication*] (DLA)
perks .... Perquisites (MHDB)
PERL .... Pacific Estuarine Research Laboratory (SAUS)
PERL .... Pathologically Eclectic Rubbish Lister
PERL .... Peerless [*NCIC trailer make code*]
PERL .... Perception Enhanced Resolution Logic (SAUS)
PERL .... Perkin-Elmer Robot Language
PERL .... Perle Systems Ltd. [*Scarborough, ON*] [*NASDAQ symbol*] (NQ)
PERL .... Perusal (ROG)
PERL .... Pictorial Engineering and Research Laboratory
PERL .... Portable Electronic Runway Lighting (PDAA)
Perl .... Practical Extraction and Report Language [*Computer science*]
PERL .... Practice Extraction and Report Language [*Facetious translation: Pathologically Eclectic Rubbish Lister*] [*Computer science*] (NHD)
PERL .... Prepositioned Equipment Requirements List [*Navy*] (MCD)
PERL .... principal Exchange Rate Linked (SAUS)
PERL .... Public Employee Relations Library [*of International Personnel Management Association*]
PERL .... Pupils Equal and Reactive to Light (DAVI)
PERL .... Pupils Equal, Regular, and Reactive to Light (DAVI)
PERLA .... Pupils Equal, React to Light and Accommodation [*Medicine*]
PERLA .... Pupils Equal, Regular and Reactive to Light and Accommodation (DAVI)
PerleSys .... Pearle Systems Ltd. [*Associated Press*] (SAG)
PERLF .... Perle System [*NASDAQ symbol*] (TTSB)
PERLS .... Principal Exchange-Rate-Linked Securities [*Investment term*]
Perm .... Permanence (SAUS)
perm .... Permanent (ELAL)
PERM .... Permanent
PERM .... Permanent Bancorp [*NASDAQ symbol*] (SAG)
PERM .... Permanent Employee (DSUE)
PERM .... Permanent Material (SAUS)
PERM .... Permanent Wave (SAUS)
PERM .... Perma-Tent Camper [*NCIC trailer make code*]
PERM .... Permeability
PERM .... Permian [*Period, era, or system*] [*Geology*]
PERM .... Permission (MSA)
PERM .... Permutation (DSUE)
PERM .... Pre-Embossed Rigid Magnetic [*Electronics*] (AAEL)
PERM .... Pre-Embossed Rigid Magnetic Media [*Computer science*]
Perm .... Pre-Embossed Rigid Magnetic Technology (ODA)
PERM .... Program Evaluation for Repetitive Manufacture (IEEE)
PERM .... Programmed Evaluation for Repetitive Manufacture (VLIE)
PERMACAP... Personnel Management and Accounting Card Processor [*Military*]
PERMACAPS... Personnel Management and Accounting Card Processing System (MCD)
PERMAFLOWERS... Permanent Flowers (SAUS)
PERMAFROST... Permanent Frost
PERMAFRUIT... Permanent Fruit (SAUS)
PER MAINT CNTRL... Perform Maintenance Control (SAUS)
PERMAS .... Persatuan Rakyat Malaysian Sarawak [*Political party*] (EY)
PERMAS .... Personnel Management Assistance System [*Military*] (AABC)
PERMB ...... Permeability
PermBcp .... Permanent Bancorp [*Associated Press*] (SAG)
PErMC .... Mercyhurst College, Erie, PA [*Library symbol*] [*Library of Congress*] (LCLS)
PERM C of Sta... Permanent Change of Station (SAUS)
Perm Ct of Arb... Permanent Court of Arbitration (SAUS)
PERMDATA... PERMDATA Management System (SAUS)
PerMdw ..... Perpetual Midwest Financial, Inc. [*Associated Press*] (SAG)
PERME ...... Propellants, Explosives, and Rocket Motors Establishment [*British Ministry of Defense*] [*Research center*] (RDA)
PERMED .... Permanently Waved (SAUS)
PermF .... Perma Fix Environmental Services [*Associated Press*] (SAG)
PermFix ..... Perma Fix Environmental Services [*Associated Press*] (SAG)
PERMIC ..... Personnel Management Information Center [*Navy*] (NVT)
PERMINVAR... Permeability Invariable
PERMINVAR... Permeability Invariant
PERMIS ..... Preference Management Information System (SAUS)
PERMIS ..... Public Employees Retirement Management Information System (SAUS)
PERMIT ..... Polar Orbiter Effective Rainfall Monitoring Integrative Technique (SAUS)
PERMITS ... Residential Building Permits [*Database*] (GDD)
PERMIXT ... Permixtus [*Mixed*] [*Pharmacy*] (ROG)
PERMLY ..... Permanently
Perm Med Mbr... Permanent Medical Member (SAUS)
PERMR ...... Permanent Residence
PERMREP... Permanent Representation to North Atlantic Council [*NATO*] (NATG)
PERMS ...... Personnel Electronic Record Management System [*Army*] (RDA)
PERMS ...... Process and Effluent Radiological Monitoring System [*Nuclear energy*] (NRCH)
PERMSS .... Process and Effluent Radiological Monitoring and Sampling System [*Nuclear energy*] (NRCH)
PERMT ...... Permanent (ROG)
PERMT ...... Permanently (SAUS)
PERMT ...... Permit (VLIE)
PERMU ...... Permanent Magnet Users Association [*Defunct*] (EA)
PER MVMT C2... Perform field artillery Movement Control and Coordination (SAUS)
PernC .... Perini Corp. [*Associated Press*] (SAG)
PERNOGRA... Permission Not Granted [*Military*]
PERO .... Perone Trailer [*NCIC trailer make code*]
PERO .... President's Emergency Relief Organization (NADA)
PEROM ...... Programmable and Erasable Read-Only Memory (SAUS)
PEROM ...... Programmable Erasable Read Only Memory (SAUS)
PER OP EMET... Peracta Operatione Emetici [*When the Operation of the Emetic is Finished*] [*Pharmacy*] (ROG)
Per Or Cas... Perry's Oriental Cases [*Bombay*] [*A publication*] (DLA)
per os .... Orally, or by Mouth [*Industrial hygiene term*] (OHS)
PEROX ...... Peroxidase Stain [*Biochemistry*] (DAVI)
PEROX ...... Peroxide
PERP .... Pan-Ethnic Republican Party of Australia [*Political party*]
PERP .... Peak Effective Radiated Power [*Telecommunications*] (OTD)
PERP .... Perpendicular (AAG)
perp .... Perpendicular (VRA)
perp .... Perpetrator (ADWA)
PERP .... Perpetrator (WDAA)
PERP .... Perpetual (ADA)
Perp .... Perpetual (EBF)
Perp .... Perpignan (SAUS)
Per P .... Perrault's Prevoste de Quebec [*A publication*] (DLA)
PERP .... Personnel Processing (MUGU)
PERP .... Process Evaluation/Research Planning (SAUS)
perpad ...... Perineal Pad [*Gynecology*] (MAE)
PerpBnk ..... Perpetual Bank Federal Savings Bank [*Associated Press*] (SAG)
Perpet .... Perpetual (DLA)
Per Pro ...... Per Procuration (EBF)
per pro ...... Per Procurationem [*By Proxy, By the Action Of*] [*Legal term*] [*Latin*] (BARN)
PER PROC... Per Procurationem [*By Proxy, By the Action Of*] [*Legal term*] [*Latin*]
PERPS ...... Police Executive Forum (SAUS)
PerpSB ...... Petpetual State Bank [*North Carolina*] [*Associated Press*] (SAG)
Per Psy ..... Personnel Psychology [*A publication*] (BRI)
PERR .... Patter-Evoked Retinal Response [*neurology and ophthalmology*] (DAVI)
PERR .... Perris Valley Campers [*NCIC trailer make code*]
PERR .... Premature Engine Removal Rate (AAG)
Perrault ..... Perrault's Conseil Superieur [*Canada*] [*A publication*] (DLA)
Perrault ..... Perrault's Prevoste de Quebec [*A publication*] (DLA)
Perrault ..... Perrault's Quebec Reports [*A publication*] (DLA)
Perrigo ...... Perrigo Co. [*Associated Press*] (SAG)
PERRL .... Pupils Equal, Round and Reactive to Light (DAVI)
PERRL .... Pupils Equal, Round, Regular and Reactive to Light (DAVI)
PERRLA ..... Pupils Equal, Round, React to Light and Accommodation [*Medicine*]
PERRLA (DC)... Pupils Equal, Round, and Reactive to Light and Accommodation (Directly and Consensually) (DAVI)

PERRY....... Perry, OH [*American Association of Railroads railroad junction routing code*]
Perry........ Perry's Oriental Cases [*Bombay*] [*A publication*] (DLA)
Perry & D... Perry and Davison's English King's Bench Reports [*A publication*] (DLA)
Perry & D (Eng)... Perry and Davison's English King's Bench Reports [*A publication*] (DLA)
Perry & K... Perry and Knapp's English Election Cases [*A publication*] (DLA)
Perry & Kn... Perry and Knapp's English Election Cases [*A publication*] (DLA)
PerryCF..... Perry County Financial Corp. [*Associated Press*] (SAG)
Perry Ins... Perry's English Insolvency Cases [*1831*] [*A publication*] (DLA)
Perry OC.... Perry's Oriental Cases [*Bombay*] [*A publication*] (DLA)
PERRY PAC... Perry Manufacturing Company PAC [*Mount Airy, NC*] (PACS)
PERS........ Patient Evaluation Rating Scale [*Medicine*] (DMAA)
PERS........ Performance Evaluation Reporting System [*DoD*]
PERS........ Periodical Source Index [*A publication*]
Pers........ Persae [*of Aeschylus*] [*Classical studies*] (OCD)
Pers........ Perseus [*Constellation*]
PERS........ Persia [*Obsolete*]
Pers........ Persian (BEE)
PERS........ Persian Leather [*Bookbinding*] (DGA)
Pers........ Persius [*34-62AD*] [*Classical studies*] (OCD)
pers........ Person [*Linguistics*] (IEL)
PERS........ Person
Pers........ Personal (TBD)
pers........ Personal (WDMC)
PERS........ Personal
PERS........ Personal Diagnostics, Inc. [*NASDAQ symbol*] (QUAN)
PERS........ Personal Emergency Response System [*Telecommunications*]
PERS........ Personality (SAUS)
PERS........ Personnel (AFM)
Pers........ Personnel (AL)
pers........ Personnel (DD)
PERS........ Personnel Squadron
pers........ Persons (WDMC)
PERS........ Perspective (WDAA)
PERS........ Preliminary Engineering Reports (MUGU)
PERS........ Proactive Error Reduction System (SAUS)
PERS........ Program for Evaluation of Rejects and Substitutions [*Computer science*] (IAA)
PERS........ Public Employees Retirement System (DICI)
PERSACLIT... Peritus in Sacred Liturgy [*Roman Catholic*]
PERSACS... Personnel Structure and Accounting System [*Army*]
PERSACS... Personnel Structure and Composition System [*Military*]
PERS & TRACOMD... Personnel and Training Command
PERSAS..... Personnel Accounting System (ACAE)
PERSC....... Public Education Religion Studies Center [*Defunct*] (EA)
PERS CASREP... Personnel Casualty Report [*Navy*] (ANA)
PERSCEN... Personnel Center
PERSCO..... Personnel Support of Contingency Operations [*Military*]
PersCom.... Personnel Command [*Army*] (INF)
PERSCOM... Personnel Command [*Army*]
Pers Comput Mag... Personal Computer Magazine (SAUS)
Pers Comput World... Personal Computer World (SAUS)
PERSCON... Personnel Control [*Military*]
PERSD...... Personnel Department [*Marine Corps*]
PERSDEP... Personnel Deployment (SAUS)
PERSDEP... Personnel Deployment Report [*Military*]
PERSDEP Report... Personnel Deployment Report (SAUS)
PerSep...... PerSeptive Technologies II Corp. [*Associated Press*] (SAG)
PERSEP..... Pershing Survivability Evaluation Program [*Military*] (MCD)
PERSEPCOMD... Personnel and Separation Command (DNAB)
PERSERVDEPSERVS... Personal Services and Dependents' Services Support System [*Navy*] (DNAB)
PERSET..... Personnel Standardization and Evaluation Team [*Military*]
PERSEVCE... Perseverance (ROG)
PERSEXP... Personal Expense Money [*Army*]
PersGp...... Personnel Group of America [*Associated Press*] (SAG)
PERSH...... Perishable (WGA)
Pershad..... Privy Council Judgments [*1829-69*] [*India*] [*A publication*] (DLA)
persian white... fantanyl (SAUS)
PERSID...... Personnel Seismic Intruder Detector (ACAE)
PERSIL...... Peroxide Silicate [*Detergent and bleach*]
Pers Inj Comment'r... Personal Injury Commentator [*A publication*] (DLA)
Pers Inj LJ... Personal Injury Law Journal [*A publication*] (DLA)
PERSINS... Personnel Information System [*Army*]
PERSINSCOM... Personnel Information Systems Command [*Army*] (AABC)
PERSINSD... Personnel Information Systems Directorate [*Military Personnel Center*] (AABC)
PERSIR...... Personnel Inventory Report [*Army*] (AABC)
PERSIS...... Personnel Information System (MHDB)
PERSITREP... Personnel Situation Report (SAUS)
PERSL....... Personal
Persl........ Personnel (TBD)
Pers Man... Personnel Management [*A publication*]
Pers Manage... Personnel Management (SAUS)
PERSMAR... Personnel Manning Assistance Report (DNAB)
Pers N....... Personal Noun (SAUS)
PERSNET... Personnel Network [*Army*]
PersnMg.... Personnel Management, Inc. [*Associated Press*] (SAG)
PERSO...... Personnel Officer [*Air Force*]
PERSOF..... Personnel Officer [*Navy*]
PERSON..... Personnel Simulation On-Line [*Department of State*] [*Computer program*]
personi...... personification (SAUS)
personi...... personified (SAUS)
personi...... personifier (SAUS)
Personnel&Guid J... Personnel and Guidance Journal (SAUS)
PERSP....... Perspective (MSA)
persp........ Perspective (VRA)
Persp........ Perspective [*Record label*]
PERSPAY... Personnel and Pay [*Project*] [*Navy*]
Perspect Lab Income... Perspectives on Labour and Income [*A publication*] (JLIT)
Pers Prac B... Personnel Practice Bulletin [*A publication*]
PERSPROC... Personnel Processing [*Army*]
Pers Pron... Personal Pronoun (SAUS)
PERSPROP... Personal Property Data Entry and Report System (SAUS)
Pers PS..... Perspectives on Political Science [*A publication*] (BRI)
PerSptv..... PerSeptive Biosystems, Inc. [*Associated Press*] (SAG)
PERSRSCHSYSTM... Personnel Management and Training Research Statistical Data System [*Navy*] (DNAB)
PERSRU..... Personnel Reporting Unit
PERSSEPCENT... Personnel Separation Center
PERSSO..... Personnel System Staff Officer
PERSTAT... Personnel Status Report [*Military*]
PERSTATREP... Personnel Status Report [*Military*]
PERSTEMPO... Personnel Tempo (SEWL)
PERSTRAN... Personal Transportation [*Navy*]
PERT......... Patients Experience of the Relationship with the Therapist Method
PERT......... Performance Evaluation Review Technique
PERT......... Perpetual Bank Federal Savings Bank [*NASDAQ symbol*] (SAG)
PERT......... Pertain (AABC)
pert.......... Pertaining (ADWA)
PERT......... Pertinent (SAUS)
PERT......... Pertussis [*Whooping cough*]
PERT......... Phenol Enhanced Reassociation Technique [*Clinical chemistry*]
PERT......... Pollution Emergency Response Team (SAUS)
PERT......... Printing Economy Remote Terminal (SAUS)
PERT......... Production and Evaluation Review Technique (SAUS)
PERT......... Program Estimation Revaluation Technique [*Computer science*] (IAA)
PERT......... Program Evaluation and Reporting Technique (SAUS)
PERT......... Program Evaluation and Review Technique [*Computer science*]
PERT......... Program Evaluation Research Task (IEEE)
PERT......... Program Evaluation Research Test (SAUS)
PERT......... Program Evaluation Review Technique (SAUS)
PERT......... Program Evolution and Review Technique (SAUS)
PERT......... Project Evaluation Review Technique (ACAE)
PERT......... Project on Education, Research and Training (SAUS)
PERTCO..... Program Evaluation and Review Technique with Cost
PERT COST... Program Evaluation and Review Techniques Costs
PERT/CPM... Program Evaluation and Review Technique/Critical Path Method [*Computer science*] (DOM)
PERT-CS... Program Evaluation and Review Technique - Cost System (DNAB)
PER TDA RPT... Perform TDA Reporting (SAUS)
PER TGT PRC... Perform Target Processing (SAUS)
PERTHS..... Perthshire [*County in Scotland*]
PERT-NAP... Program Evaluation and Review Technique - Network Automatic Plotting (SAA)
PERTO....... Pertaining To (NVT)
Per Tr....... Perry on Trusts [*A publication*] (DLA)
PERTRAN... Perturbation Transport [*NASA*]
PERTSIM... Program Evaluation and Review Technique Simulation [*Game*]
PERT-TAM... Program Evaluation and Review Technique Task, Action, and Milestone Items
PERT/TIME... Program Evaluation and Review Technique/Time Analyzer [*Sperry UNIVAC*]
PERTVS..... Perimeter Television System (SAUS)
PERU........ Masterlease [*Intermodal shipping container symbol*] (TVRC)
PERU........ Peru, IN [*American Association of Railroads railroad junction routing code*]
Peru......... Peruvian (DIAR)
PERU........ Production Equipment Records Unit (IEEE)
PERU BAL... Peruvian Balsam (SAUS)
Peru Cur.... Peruvian Current (SAUS)
PERUG...... Perusing (ROG)
PERUPEC... Peruvian National Committee for Pacific Economic Cooperation
PERUSA..... Perspectives - United States of America [*History course*]
PERUV...... Peruvian
PERV........ Perversion (SAUS)
PERV........ Pervert [*or Perverted*] [*FBI standardized term*]
perv......... Pervious (SAUS)
PERV........ Porcine Endogenous Provirus
PERV........ Porcine Endogenous Retrovirus
PErV........ United States Veterans Administration Hospital, Erie, PA [*Library symbol*] [*Library of Congress*] (LCLS)
PERVAL..... Performance/Valuation (VLIE)
PErVM....... Villa Maria College, Erie, PA [*Library symbol*] [*Library of Congress*] (LCLS)
PERX........ Perry Florida Rail Switching Services [*Federal Railroad Administration identification code*]
PERY........ Ellis, Perry, Intl. [*NASDAQ symbol*] (SG)
PERYLENE... Peri-Dinaphthalene [*A fluorophore*] [*Organic chemistry*]
PERYO....... Perry, OK [*American Association of Railroads railroad junction routing code*]
Pes.......... Esophageal Pressure [*Used to estimate intrapleural pressure*] (DAVI)

PES .... IEEE Power Engineering Society (EA)
PES .... Pacific Environmental Services, Inc. (EFIS)
PES .... Paid Educational Services [*British*]
PES .... Pan European Survey [*A publication*]
PES .... Paper End Signal (VLIE)
PES .... Paraendocrine Syndrome [*Endocrinology*]
PES .... Parallel Enterprise Servers [*Computer science*] (HODG)
PES .... Parent Egg Seed
PES .... Partial Energy Service [*Electric power*]
PES .... Partido Ecuatoriano Socialista [*Ecuadorean Socialist Party*] [*Political party*]
PES .... Parts Engineering Support
PES .... Party of European Socialists (EURO)
PES .... Passive Electromagnetic System (IAA)
PES .... Patent Examining System
PES .... P-bit Errored Seconds (SAUS)
PES .... Pecos Resources [*Vancouver Stock Exchange symbol*]
PES .... People Effectiveness Survey (TIMI)
PES .... Performance-Economy Switch [*Automotive engineering*]
PES .... Personal Earth Stations (ACAE)
PES .... Personalized Exercise System (SAUS)
Pes .... Pesahim (BJA)
PES .... Peshawar [*Pakistan*] [*Seismograph station code, US Geological Survey*] [*Closed*] (SEIS)
PES .... Philosophy of Education Society (EA)
PES .... Photo-Electret State (SAUS)
PES .... Photoelectric Scanner
PES .... Photo-Electric Scanner (or Scanning) (SAUS)
PES .... Photoelectric Scanning [*Electronics*] (ECII)
PES .... Photoelectron Spectroscope (or Spectroscopy) (SAUS)
PES .... Photo-Electron-Spectroscopy (SAUS)
PES .... Photoelectron Spectroscopy
PES .... Photoelectron Spectrum (SAUS)
PES .... Photoemission Spectroscopy
PES .... Photojet Edge Sensor
PES .... Physicians Equity Services
PES .... Pictorial Eleven Society [*Formerly, PE*] [*PCS*] [*Absorbed by*] (EA)
PES .... Planning and Evaluation Staff (COE)
PES .... Pointing Error Sensor (MCD)
PES .... Polyethersulfone [*Organic chemistry*]
PES .... Polyethylene Sodium Sulfonate [*Anticoagulant*]
PES .... Polyphenylene Sulfide [*Plastics*]
PES .... Porsche Engineering Services
PES .... Positioning Error Signal (VLIE)
PES .... Post Ejection Sequencer (ACAE)
PES .... Post-Enumeration Survey [*Bureau of the Census*]
PES .... Postextrasystolic Potentiation [*Cardiology*]
PES .... Potential Energy Source [*Physiology*]
PES .... Potential-Energy Surface [*Chemical kinetics*]
PES .... Poultry and Egg Situation
PES .... Power Electronics Society (SAUS)
PES .... Power Engineering Society
PES .... Power Engineering Specification
PES .... Preexcitation Syndrome [*Cardiology*]
PES .... Preparedness Evaluation System (COE)
PES .... Preschool Evaluation Scale [*Test*] (TMMY)
Pes .... Pressure, End-Systole [*Cardiology*]
PES .... Pressure Equalization System [*Nuclear energy*] (NUCP)
PES .... Principles [*Telegraphy*] (PCTE)
PES .... Private Express Statutes (DICI)
P(ES) .... Probability of Equal Regressive Slopes [*Statistics*]
PES .... Probe Entry Site [*Instrumentation*]
PES .... Problem-Etiology-Signs [*or Symptoms*] [*Nursing*]
PES .... Processed Eucheuma Seaweed
PES .... Processor Enhancement Socket [*Computer science*] (PCM)
PES .... Production Engineering Service
PES .... Production Engineering Specification (NG)
PES .... Professional Examination Service
PES .... Program Element Summary
PES .... Program Emphasis Statement [*US Employment Service*] [*Department of Labor*]
PES .... Program Execution System
PES .... Programmable Electronic System [*Engineering*]
PES .... Programmed Electrical Stimulation [*Neurophysiology*]
PES .... Programmer Electronic Switch (SAUS)
PES .... Projected Engagement Scheduler [*Military*] (CAAL)
PES .... Proposed Encryption Standard (SAUS)
PES .... Public Employment Services (EURO)
PES .... Public Enquiry System (SAUS)
PES .... Public Expenditure Survey [*British*]
PESA .... Parent Expectations Support Achievement (STAH)
PESA .... Particle Elastic Scattering Analysis (ODA)
PESA .... Pectoral Sandpiper [*North American bird banding code*] (BIBA)
PESA .... Pennsylvania Elks State Association (EARSL)
PESA .... Percutaneous Epididymal Sperm Aspiration [*Medicine*] (MELL)
PESA .... Petroleum Electric Supply Association [*Defunct*] (EA)
PESA .... Petroleum Equipment Suppliers Association (EA)
PESA .... Propellant Expulsion and Storage Assembly
PESA .... Proton Elastic-Scattering Analysis
PESABC ..... Permanent Executive Secretariat of the Andres Bello Convention [*See also SECAB*] (EAIO)
PESAM ...... Penetration Survivability Assessment Model (ACAE)
PESC .... Passivated Emitter Solar Cell (SAUS)
PESC .... Physical and Engineering Sciences Committee (SAUS)
PESc .... Poly Ethylene Succinate (EDCT)
PESC .... Pool Energy Services [*NASDAQ symbol*] (TTSB)
PESC .... Pool Energy Services Co. [*NASDAQ symbol*] (SAG)
PESC .... Public Expenditure Survey Commission (SAUS)
PESC .... Public Expenditure Survey Committee [*British*] (ODBW)
PESCGB ..... Provincial Electric Supply Committee of Great Britain (SAUS)
PESD .... Pacific Electronic Security Division [*Military*]
PESD .... Post-Employment Services Demonstration
PESD .... Postsecondary Education Statistics Division [*Department of Education*] (GFGA)
PESD .... Private and Executive Secretary's Diploma (AIE)
PESD .... Program Element Summary Data [*DoD*]
PESD .... Program Execution Subdirective (AABC)
PESDA .... Printing Equipment Supply Dealers Association (SAUS)
PESDC .... Properties of Electrolyte Solutions Data Center [*National Institute of Standards and Technology*]
PESDS .... Program Element Summary Data Sheet [*DoD*]
PESEVISA ... Peruana de Seguridad y Vigilancia (EFIS)
PESGB .... Petroleum Exploration Society of Great Britain
Pesh .... Peshitta [*Syriac translation of the Bible*] (BJA)
Peshawar ... All India Reporter, Peshawar [*1933-50*] [*A publication*] (DLA)
Peshawar ... Indian Rulings, Peshawar Series [*1933-47*] [*A publication*] (DLA)
PESI .... Perma Fix Environmental Services [*NASDAQ symbol*] (SAG)
PESI .... Perma Fix Enviro Svcs [*NASDAQ symbol*] (TTSB)
PESIA .... Postal Employees Salary Increase Act of 1960
PESIC .... Parti du Progres Economique et Social des Independants Congolais Luluabourg [*Party for Economic and Social Progress of the Congolese Independents in Luluabourg*] [*Political party*]
Pesik .... Pesikta de-Rav Kahana (BJA)
Pesikt .... Pesikta de-Rav Kahana (BJA)
PesiktR ...... Pesikta Rabbati (BJA)
PESIS .... Photo-Electron Spectroscopy of Inner-Shell (PDAA)
PESIW .... Perma-Fix Envir'l Svcs Wrrt [*NASDAQ symbol*] (TTSB)
PESIZ .... Perma-Fix Envir'l Svcs Wrrt'B' [*NASDAQ symbol*] (TTSB)
PESKI .... Probabilities Expert Systems Knowledge and Inference (IDAI)
PESM .... Photoelectron Spectromicroscope
PESM .... Photoelectron Spectromicroscopy (SAUS)
PESM .... Precision Electronic Support Measures (SEWL)
PeSMoT ..... Penn State Microoxidation Test [*Analytical chemistry*]
PESO .... Participation Enriches Science, Music, and Art Organizations [*Orlando, Florida*]
PESO .... Performance Evaluation Support Office
PESO .... Plant Engineering Shop Order (AAG)
PESO .... Product Engineering Services Office [*DoD*]
PESOS .... Perkin-Elmer Solvent Optimization System [*Chemistry*]
PESOS .... Photo-Electron Spectroscopy of Outer-Shell (PDAA)
PESOS .... Prepare, Explain, Show, Observe, Supervise [*Formula*] [*LIMRA*]
PESP .... Postextrasystolic Potentiation [*Medicine*] (DMAA)
PesR .... Pesikta Rabbati (BJA)
PESR .... Planning Element System Report (NATG)
PESR .... Precision Echo Sounder Recorder
PESR .... Pseudoequivalent Service Rounds [*Military*] (NVT)
PEsS .... East Stroudsburg State College, East Stroudsburg, PA [*Library symbol*] [*Library of Congress*] (LCLS)
PESS .... Pessus [*Pessary*] [*Pharmacy*]
PESS .... Private Electronic Switching System (SAUS)
PESS .... Problem, Etiology, Signs, and Symptoms [*Medicine*] (DMAA)
PESS .... Product Evaluation and Selection System (VLIE)
PE SS & RM ... Department of Physical Education, Sports Science and Recreation Management (SAUS)
PESSIS .... Personal Security Solutions for Isolated Staff [*Police and security equipment*]
PESSO .... Personnel System Staff Officer
PEST .... Parameter Entity Symbol Translator [*Elstree Computing Ltd.*] [*Software package*] (NCC)
PEST .... Parameter Estimation by Sequential Testing [*Computer*]
PEST .... Patterned Elicitation Syntax Test [*Educational test*]
PEST .... People for Environmentally Sustainable Transport (SAUS)
PEST .... Pesticide Evaluation Summary Tabulation
PEST .... Planning and Evaluation of Sequential Trials [*Statistics*]
PEST .... Political, Environmental, Social, and Technological [*Business term*] (ODBW)
PEST .... Pressure for Economic and Social Toryism [*Tory Reform Group*] [*British*] (DI)
PEST .... Production Evaluation Surveillance Test
PEST .... Project Engineer Scheduling Technique (SAUS)
PEST .... Region 7 Nebraska Pesticide (SAUS)
PEST .... Sequence of Pro-Glu-Ser-Thr Involved in Protein Targeting [*Molecular biology*] (QSUL)
PESTAB ..... Pesticides Abstracts (NITA)
PESTAN ..... Pesticide Analytical Model Version [*Environmental Protection Agency*] (AEPA)
PESTAN ..... Pesticides Analytical Transport Solution (SAUS)
PESTANV4.0 ... Pesticide Analytical Model Version 4.0 [*Environment term*] (EGA)
Pest Contr ... Pest Control (SAUS)
PESTDOC ... Pest Control Literature Documentation [*Derwent Publications Ltd.*] [*Bibliographic database*] [*Information service or system*] (IID)
PESTDOC ... Pesticide Documentation (NITA)
PESTF .... Proton Event Start Forecast [*Solar weather information*]
PESTIC ...... Pesticide
Pestic Sci ... Pesticide Science [*A publication*] (PABS)
PESU .... Polyethersulfone [*Organic chemistry*]
PESV .... Pea Streak Virus [*Plant pathology*]
PESY .... Pheripheral Exchange Synchronization (IAA)
PET .... Aeropetrel [*Chile*] [*ICAO designator*] (FAAC)

PET .... Pacific Enterprises [*AMEX symbol*] (SAG)
PET .... Panel on Educational Terminology [*Office of Education*]
PET .... Panel on Education and Training [*COSATI*]
PET .... Paper Equilibrium Tester (BARN)
PET .... Parent Effectiveness Training [*A course of study*]
PET .... Particle Electrostatic Thruster
PET .... Patterned Epitaxial Technology (IEEE)
PET .... Payroll Expense Transfer (SAUS)
PET .... Peak Ejection Time [*Medicine*] (EDAA)
PET .... Pelotas [*Brazil*] [*Airport symbol*] (OAG)
PET .... Pentaerythritol [*Organic chemistry*]
PET .... Pentaerythritol Tetranitrate [*Also, PETN*] [*Explosive, vasodilator*]
PET .... Pentaerythritol Tetrastearate (SAUS)
PET .... Penthouse Entertainment Network [*Cable television system*]
PET .... Performance Efficiency Test [*Employee screening and placement test*]
PET .... Performance Evaluation Team [*Nuclear energy*] (NRCH)
PET .... Performance Evaluation Test
PET .... Periodic Environmental Test
PET .... Periodic Evaluation Test
PET .... Peripheral Equipment Tester [*Computer science*] (BUR)
PET .... Peritoneal Equilibration Test (SAUS)
PET .... Permeation Enhancement Technology (SAUS)
PET .... Personal Effectiveness Training (MCD)
PET .... Personal Electronic Transaction Computer (NITA)
PET .... Personal Electronic Transactor [*Computer*] [*Commodore Business Machines*]
PET .... Personal Electronic Translator (SAUS)
PET .... Personal Employee Time (DHSM)
PET .... Personnel Experimentation and Testing Device (SAUS)
Pet .... Peter [*New Testament book*]
Pet .... Peterhouse College, Oxford (SAUS)
Pet .... Peters' Prince Edward Island Reports [*1850-72*] [*Canada*] [*A publication*] (DLA)
Pet .... Peters' United States Circuit Court Reports [*A publication*] (DLA)
Pet .... Peters' United States District Court Reports, Admiralty Decisions [*A publication*] (DLA)
Pet .... Peter's United States Reports [*1828-42*] [*A publication*] (AAGC)
Pet .... Peters' United States Supreme Court Reports [*26-41 United States*] [*A publication*] (DLA)
Pet .... Petihta (BJA)
PET .... Pet, Inc., Corporate Information Center, St. Louis, MO [*OCLC symbol*] (OCLC)
PET .... Petition
PET .... Petrine [*Of, or relating to, Peter the Apostle or Peter the Great*]
Pet .... Petrol (SAUS)
PET .... Petrolatum (WGA)
Pet .... Petroleum (DD)
PET .... Petroleum
PET .... Petropavlovsk [*Kazakhstan*] [*Seismograph station code, US Geological Survey*] (SEIS)
PET .... Petrotech, Inc. [*Toronto Stock Exchange symbol*]
Pet .... Petrus [*Authority cited in pre-1607 legal work*] (DSA)
Pet .... Petrus de Bellapertica [*Deceased, 1308*] [*Authority cited in pre-1607 legal work*] (DSA)
PET .... Phase Elapsed Time (NASA)
PET .... Philco Epoxy Transistor (IAA)
PET .... Photoelectric Transducer (PDAA)
PET .... Photoemission Tube
PET .... Photographic Equipment Technician (SAUS)
PET .... Photoinduced Electron Transfer
PET .... Phototropic Energy Transfer
PET .... Physical Equipment Table
PET .... Pierre Elliott Trudeau [*Canadian prime minister*] [*Acronymic designation considered derogatory*]
PET .... Pilot-Line Experiment Technology (SAUS)
PET .... Plasma Edge Technique (SAUS)
PET .... Plastic Engine Technology (SAUS)
PET .... Pocket Echo-Tone [*Medicine*] (EDAA)
PET .... Point of Equal Time [*Aviation*]
PET .... Polyester
PET .... Polyethylene [*Organic chemistry*] (IAA)
PET .... Poly(ethylene Terephthalate) [*Organic chemistry*]
PET .... Polyethylene Tubing [*Medicine*] (MELL)
PET .... Polyethylenterephtalatester, Polyester (SAUS)
PET .... Poor Exercise Tolerance [*Medicine*] (EDAA)
PET .... Portable Earth Terminal [*NASA*]
PET .... Portable Electric Tool, Inc. (SAUS)
PET .... Portable Electronic Telephone
PET .... Portable Electronic Translator
PET .... Portable Executive Telephone (SAUS)
PET .... Position-Event-Time
PET .... Positive-Emission Tomography (SAUS)
PET .... Positron Electron Tomography (SAUS)
PET .... Positron Emission Computed Tomography (SAUS)
PET .... Positron-Emission Tomography
PET .... Post Endurance Test (SAUS)
PET .... Post-Etch Treatment (AAEL)
PET .... Potential-Effect Transistor (SAUS)
PET .... Potential Evapotranspiration
PET .... Potentially Exempt Transfer (ODBW)
PET .... Precision End Trimmed (SAUS)
PET .... Prediction Error Transform (PDAA)
PET .... Pre-Eclamptic Toxemia [*Medicine*]
PET .... Pre-Employment Training (OICC)
PET .... Preliminary Evaluation Team
PET .... Preliminary Examination Team [*NASA*]
PET .... Preprimary Evaluation and Training
PET .... Pressure Equalization [*Tubes or Equalizing*] [*Otorhinolaryngology*] (DAVI)
PET .... Pressurization Events Trainer
PET .... Print Enhancement Technology (VLIE)
PET .... Prisoner's Education Trust (WDAA)
PET .... Privacy Enhancing Technology (VLIE)
PET .... Probe Ephemeris Tape
PET .... Process Evaluation Tester
PET .... Producibility Evaluation Task [*Army*] (RDA)
PET .... Production Environmental Testing
PET .... Production Environmental Tests
PET .... Production Evaluation Test
PET .... Production Experimental Test (SAA)
PET .... Program Evaluation Team
PET .... Program Evaluation Test
PET .... Program Evaluator and Tester [*Computer science*]
PET .... Program Execution Time (VLIE)
PET .... Progressive Educational Technology (SAUS)
PET .... Progressive Exercise Test [*Medicine*] (EDAA)
PET .... Project Evaluation Tree (LDOE)
PET .... Property Enterprise Trust [*Investment term*] [*British*] (ECON)
PET .... Proposal Evaluation Team (ACAE)
PET .... Propulsion Experimental Test (SAA)
PET .... Prototype Evaluation Test
PET .... Prototype Evaluation Testing (SAUS)
PET .... Psychiatric Emergency Team
PET .... Pulsed Electrothermal (MCD)
PET .... Pupil Evaluation Team [*Education*]
PETA .... Parabolic Expandable Truss Antenna (ACAE)
PETA .... Pentaerythritol Triacrylate [*Organic chemistry*]
PETA .... People for the Ethical Treatment of Animals (EA)
PETA .... Performance Evaluation and Trend Analysis (NASA)
PETA .... Plutonium Equipment Transfer Area [*Nuclear energy*] (NRCH)
PETA .... Portable Electronic Traffic Analyzer [*British*]
Pet Ab .... Petersdorff's Abridgment [*A publication*] (DLA)
Pet Abr .... Petersdorff's Abridgment [*1660-1823*] [*A publication*] (DLA)
Pet Ad .... Peters' United States District Court Reports, Admiralty Decisions [*A publication*] (DLA)
Pet Ad Dec ... Peters' United States District Court Reports, Admiralty Decisions [*A publication*] (DLA)
Pet Adm .... Peters' United States District Court Reports, Admiralty Decisions [*A publication*] (DLA)
Pet Adm App ... Peters' United States District Court Reports, Admiralty Decisions (Appendix) [*A publication*] (DLA)
Pet Ad R .... Peters' United States District Court Reports, Admiralty Decisions [*A publication*] (DLA)
PETAL .... Petaluma, CA [*American Association of Railroads railroad junction routing code*]
PET & S ..... Performance Evaluation, Test, and Simulation [*Air Force*]
PETANS ..... Petroleum Training Association-North Sea (SAUS)
Pet Aret ..... Petrus Aretinus [*Flourished, 1088-91*] [*Authority cited in pre-1607 legal work*] (DSA)
PETAT .... Periodic Inspection Turn-Around Time [*Military*] (AFIT)
PETB .... Preflight Test Bus
Pet Bail ..... Petersdorff on Bail [*1824*] [*A publication*] (DLA)
Pet Br .... Bellewe's Cases Tempore Henry VIII [*Brooke's New Cases*] [*England*] [*A publication*] (DLA)
Pet Br .... Brooke's New Cases (Petit Brooke) [*1515-58*] [*A publication*] (DLA)
PETC .... Parent Effectiveness Training Course [*Australia*]
PETC .... Petco Animal Supplies [*NASDAQ symbol*] (SAG)
PETC .... Pet in Cabin [*Travel industry*] (TRID)
PETC .... Pittsburgh Energy Technology Center [*Formerly, PERC*] [*Department of Energy*] [*Pittsburgh, PA*] (GRD)
PETC .... Polyethylene Tetrachloride [*Organic chemistry*] (IAA)
PETC .... Portable Equipment Test Chamber (MCD)
Pet CC .... Peters' United States Circuit Court Reports [*A publication*] (DLA)
Pet Chem ... Petroleum Chemistry (SAUS)
Pet Cir CR ... Peters' Condensed United States Circuit Court Reports [*A publication*] (DLA)
PetcoAn ..... Petco Animal Supplies [*Associated Press*] (SAG)
PETCOCK ... Proposal Evaluation Technique Conditioned on Contract Kind (SAUS)
PET Computer ... Personal Electronic Transaction Computer (SAUS)
Pet Cond .... Peters' Condensed Reports, United States Supreme Court [*A publication*] (DLA)
Pet Cond Rep ... Peters' Condensed United States Circuit Court Reports [*A publication*] (DLA)
PETD .... Petitioned [*Telegraphy*] (PCTE)
PETD .... Petroleum Development [*NASDAQ symbol*] (TTSB)
PETD .... Petroleum Development Corp. [*NASDAQ symbol*] (NQ)
Pet de Anch ... Petrus de Ancharano [*Deceased, 1416*] [*Authority cited in pre-1607 legal work*] (DSA)
Pet de Bel ... Petrus de Bellapertica [*Deceased, 1308*] [*Authority cited in pre-1607 legal work*] (DSA)
Pet de Bellap ... Petrus de Bellapertica [*Deceased, 1308*] [*Authority cited in pre-1607 legal work*] (DSA)
Pet de Belper ... Petrus de Bellapertica [*Deceased, 1308*] [*Authority cited in pre-1607 legal work*] (DSA)
Pet de Mont ... Petrus Piccoli de Monteforte [*Flourished, 14th century*] [*Authority cited in pre-1607 legal work*] (DSA)
Pet de Sam ... Petrus de Sampsone [*Flourished, 1246-58*] [*Authority cited in pre-1607 legal work*] (DSA)

Pet de Samp... Petrus de Sampsone [*Flourished, 1246-58*] [*Authority cited in pre-1607 legal work*] (DSA)
Pet Dig...... Peters' United States Digest [*A publication*] (DLA)
Pet Dig...... Peticolas' Texas Digest [*A publication*] (DLA)
PetDv........ Petroleum Development Corp. [*Associated Press*] (SAG)
PETE......... Parliamentary Education for Teacher Education [*Australia*]
PETE......... Partnership for Environmental Technology Education [*Nonprofit organization of 400 community colleges*]
PETE......... Petersburg National Battlefield
PETE......... Peterson [*NCIC trailer make code*]
PETE......... Pneumatic End to End
PETE......... Pneumatic End-to-End (SAUS)
PETE......... Portable Educational Tools Environment (AIE)
PETE......... Portable Electronics Test Equipment (DNAB)
PETE......... Portable Emergency Thermal Environment
PETE......... Primary Bank [*NASDAQ symbol*] (SAG)
PETE......... Product Engineering Tribute to Excellence
PETE......... Proof and Experimental Test Establishment [*Canada*] (MCD)
PETE......... Ted Peters Trucking Company [*Common carrier symbol*]
PETEOS..... Plasma-Enhanced Tetraethylosilicate (AAEL)
PETE PAC... People for Enterprise, Trade, and Economic Growth [*Alexandria, VA*] (PACS)
Peter........ Analysis and Digest of the Decisions of Sir George Jessel, by A. P. Peter [*England*] [*A publication*] (DLA)
PETER....... Peterborough, ON [*American Association of Railroads railroad junction routing code*]
Peters....... Haviland's Prince Edward Island Chancery Reports, by Peters [*1850-72*] [*Canada*] [*A publication*] (DLA)
Peters....... Peters' United States Supreme Court Reports [*26-41 United States*] [*A publication*] (DLA)
Peters' Ad... Peters' United States District Court Reports, Admiralty Decisions [*A publication*] (DLA)
Peters Adm... Peters' United States District Courts Reports, Admiralty Decisions [*A publication*] (DLA)
Peters' Adm Dec... Peters' United States District Court Reports, Admiralty Decisions [*A publication*] (DLA)
Peters' Admiralty Dec... Peters' United States District Court Reports, Admiralty Decisions [*A publication*] (DLA)
Peters' Adm R... Peters' United States District Court Reports, Admiralty Decisions [*A publication*] (DLA)
Peters Adm Rep... Peters' United States District Court Reports, Admiralty Decisions [*A publication*] (DLA)
Peters CC... Peters' United States Circuit Court Reports [*A publication*] (DLA)
Petersd Ab... Petersdorff's Abridgment [*A publication*] (DLA)
Petes........ Petes Brewing Co. [*Associated Press*] (SAG)
PETFE........ Polyethylene-Co-Tetrafluoroethylene (SAUS)
PETFE........ Polyethylenetetrafluoroethylene [*Organic chemistry*]
PETFEM..... Postsecondary Education Task Force on Energy Management [*Canada*]
PetFood..... Pet Food Warehouse [*Commercial firm*] [*Associated Press*] (SAG)
PETG........ Petitioning [*Telegraphy*] (PCTE)
PETG........ Phenylethyl(thiogalactoside) [*Organic chemistry*]
PETG........ Polyethylene Terephthalate, G Copolymer (SAUS)
PETG........ Polyethylene Terephthalate Glycol (SAUS)
PETG........ Proposal Editing Task Group (SAUS)
Pet Geol.... Petroleum Geology (SAUS)
Petg Pr & Ag... Petgrave's Principal and Agent [*1857*] [*A publication*] (DLA)
Pet Greg.... Petrus Gregorius [*Deceased, 1617*] [*Authority cited in pre-1607 legal work*] (DSA)
PETH........ Pearly-Eyed Thrasher [*North American bird banding code*] (BIBA)
PETH........ Pink-Eyed, Tan-Hooded Rat [*Medicine*] (DMAA)
Peth Dis.... Petheram's Discovery by Interrogations [*1864*] [*A publication*] (DLA)
PETI......... Percent of Travel Involved (SAUS)
PETI......... Phenyl-Ethynyl Terminated Imide [*Plastics*]
PETI......... Portable Electronic Typewriter Interface [*Applied Creative Technology, Inc.*]
PETIA........ Particle-Enhanced Turbidometric Immunoassay [*Clinical chemistry*]
Pet Intell Wkly... Petroleum Intelligence Weekly (SAUS)
Petit Br...... Petit Brooke, or Brooke's New Cases, English King's Bench [*1515-58*] [*A publication*] (DLA)
PETITN...... Petition
PETLES...... Peritoneal Exudate T-Lymphocyte-Enriched System (DB)
Pet L Nat... Petersdorff's Law of Nations [*A publication*] (DLA)
PETM........ Petsmart, Inc. [*NASDAQ symbol*] (SAG)
PETM........ Pettibone [*NCIC truck make code*]
PETMA....... Portable Electric Tool Manufacturers' Association [*British*] (BI)
Pet Manage... Petroleum Management (SAUS)
Pet M & S... Petersdorff's Master and Servant [*1876*] [*A publication*] (DLA)
PETMS...... Phenethyltrimethoxy Silane [*Organic chemistry*]
PETN........ Pentaerythritol Tetraniconitate [*Niceritrol*] [*Pharmacology*] (DAVI)
PETN........ Pentaerythritol Tetranitrate [*Also, PET*] [*Explosive, vasodilator*]
PETN........ Petaerythrite Tetranitrate (NAKS)
PETN........ Petition
PETNAIS... Pacific Essential Telecommunications Network and Information System (SAUS)
PETNR....... Petitioner
PETOS....... Perkin Elmer Terminal Operating System (SAUS)
PETP......... (Phenylethyl)phenyltetrahydropyridine [*Organic chemistry*]
PETP......... Poly(ethylene Terephthalate) [*Organic chemistry*]
PETP......... Preliminary Engineering Technical Proposal
Pet Peck Zir... Petrus Peckius (Ziricaeus) [*Deceased, 1589*] [*Authority cited in pre-1607 legal work*] (DSA)
Pet PM...... Petersen's Photographic Magazine [*A publication*] (BRI)
PETPrA...... Pacific Ent $4.36 Pfd [*AMEX symbol*] (TTSB)
PetPrac..... [*The*] Pet Practice, Inc. [*Associated Press*] (SAG)
PETPrB...... Pacific Ent $4.40 Pfd [*AMEX symbol*] (TTSB)
PETPrC...... Pacific Ent $4.50 Pfd [*AMEX symbol*] (TTSB)
PETPrD...... Pacific Ent $4.75 Pfd [*AMEX symbol*] (TTSB)
PetPRO...... Pet Professional Retailers Organization [*Defunct*] (EA)
Pet Pt....... Petrol Point (SAUS)
PETQI........ Patient Education Total Quality Improvement [*Medicine*] (DMAA)
PETR........ Peter Pirsch [*NCIC truck make code*]
petr.......... Petitioner (GEAB)
PETR......... Petitioner
Petr.......... Petrification (SAUS)
petr.......... petrified (SAUS)
petr.......... Petrify (SAUS)
PETR........ PetroCorp [*NASDAQ symbol*] (TTSB)
PETR........ Petrocorp, Inc. [*NASDAQ symbol*] (SAG)
petr.......... Petroleum [*Chemistry*] (DAVI)
PETR........ Photo-Electric Tape Reader (SAUS)
PETR........ Post Environmental Test Review (ACAE)
PETRA....... Positron-Electron Tandem Ring Accelerator [*Nuclear*]
PETRA....... Program for the Vocational Training of Young People and their Preparation for Adult and Working Life [*EC*] (ECED)
PETRA....... Project for Evaluation and Treatment of Radioactive Waste [*Nuclear energy*] (NUCP)
Petr Bellug... Petrus Belluga [*Flourished, 1446-68*] [*Authority cited in pre-1607 legal work*] (DSA)
Petr de Benint... Petrus de Benintendis [*Flourished, 16th century*] [*Authority cited in pre-1607 legal work*] (DSA)
PETREL..... Professional Education and Training for Research Librarianship Program (EDAC)
PETRES..... Petroleum Reserves [*Navy*]
PETRESA... Petroquimica Espanola (EFIS)
PETRESO... Petroleum Reserves Office [*or Officer*]
Pet Rev..... Petroleum Review [*A publication*] (CABS)
petrgly...... Petroglyph (VRA)
Petr Greg... Petrus Gregorius [*Deceased, 1617*] [*Authority cited in pre-1607 legal work*] (DSA)
PETRIBURG... Petriburgensis [*Signature of the Bishops of Peterborough*] [*Latin*] (ROG)
Petrie........ Petrie Stores Corp. [*Associated Press*] (SAG)
PETRL....... Petroleum (AABC)
Petrl......... Petroleum (TBD)
PetrlGeo.... Petroleum Geo Services [*Associated Press*] (SAG)
PetrLng..... Petersburg Long Distance [*Commercial firm*] [*Associated Press*] (SAG)
Petrlte....... Petrolite Corp. [*Associated Press*] (SAG)
Petrmn...... Petrominerals Corp. [*Associated Press*] (SAG)
Petr Nuni... Petrus Nunius de Avendano [*Flourished, 16th century*] [*Authority cited in pre-1607 legal work*] (DSA)
Petro........ Petrochemical (SAUS)
PETRO....... Petroleum
PETROBRAS... Petroleo Brasileiro (EFIS)
PetroC....... Petro-Canada [*Associated Press*] (SAG)
PetroC2..... Petro-Canada [*Associated Press*] (SAG)
PETROCAN... Petroleos de Canarias (EFIS)
PETROCH... Rock Chemical Database [*Ontario Geological Survey*] [*Canada*] [*Information service or system*] (CRD)
petro-chem... petroleum-chemical (SAUS)
PETROCO... Petrolite Corporation (EFIS)
Petrocp...... Petrocorp, Inc. [*Associated Press*] (SAG)
PETRODEG... Petroleum Degrading [*Agent*]
Petrodollars... Petroleum-controlled Dollars (SAUS)
PETRO ENG... Petroleum Engineering (SAUS)
PETROEX... Petroleum Products Exchange Data Clearing House (NITA)
Petrog....... Petrographer (SAUS)
PETROG...... Petrographic
petrog....... Petrography (ODA)
PETROGAL... Petroleos de Portugal, EP [*Portuguese Petroleum Co.*]
PETROGR... Petrography
PETROL..... Petroleum
PETROL..... Petrology
PETROL RAM... Petroleum Resource Automated Management (SAUS)
PETROMIN... General Petroleum & Mineral Organization [*Saudi Arabia state-owned oil company*]
PETROMIN... General Petroleum and Minerals Organization (SAUS)
Petromt...... Petromet Resouces Ltd. [*Associated Press*] (SAG)
Petron....... Petronius [*First century AD*] [*Classical studies*] (OCD)
PETRONAS... Petroleum Nasional Berhad (EFIS)
PETRONET... Petroleum Network [*Distribution and interdiction model*] (MCD)
Petron Satyric... Petronius' [*Titus*] Arbiter, Satyricon, Etc. [*A publication*] (DLA)
PETROPHIL... Petroleum Philatelic Society International (EAIO)
PETROPOL... Petropolis [*St. Petersburg*] [*Imprint*] [*Latin*] (ROG)
PETROSUR... Petroleos del Sur SA (EFIS)
PetroUn..... Petro Union, Inc. [*Associated Press*] (SAG)
Petr Rave... Petrus Ravennas [*Flourished, 1468-1508*] [*Authority cited in pre-1607 legal work*] (DSA)
PetRs........ Petroleum & Resources Corp. [*Associated Press*] (SAG)
PETS......... Pacific Electronics Trade Show
PETS......... Parameterised Executable Test Suite (SAUS)
PETS......... Parameterized Executable Test Suite (VLIE)
PETS......... Payload Environmental Transportation System [*NASA*] (NASA)
PETS......... Peripheral Equipment Test Set
PETS......... PetMed Express, Inc. [*NASDAQ symbol*] (QUAN)
PETS......... Photographic Equipment Test System (ACAE)
PETS......... Plastic Education and Troubleshooting System (SAUS)
PETS......... P/L Experiment Test System [*NASA*] (GFGA)

PETS......... POCC [*Payload Operations Control Center*] Experiments Timeline System [*Ground Data Systems Division and Spacelab*] [*NASA*] (NASA)
PETS......... Polaris Engineering Technical Service [*Missiles*]
PETS......... Portable Engine Test Stand (MCD)
PETS......... Positions Equipment Task Summary (AAG)
PETS......... Posting and Enquiry Terminal System (SAUS)
PETS......... Pre-Eclampsia Society [*British*] (NRGU)
PETS......... Pricing European Transportation Projects [*Traffic management*]
PETS......... Prior to Expiration of Term of Service [*Reenlistments*] [*Military*]
PETS......... Procedures for Evaluating Technical Specifications Program (COE)
PETS......... Programmed Extended Time Sharing [*Computer science*]
PETS......... Property and Evidence Tracking System (SEWL)
PETS......... Proximity Effect Tunneling Spectroscopy (MCD)
Pet SC....... Peters' United States Supreme Court Reports [*26-41 United States*] [*A publication*] (DLA)
PET scan.... Positron Emission Transaxial Tomography [*Also, PETT*] (PAZ)
PETSEC ..... Petroleum Section [*Allied Force Headquarters*]
PetsMrt ..... Petsmart, Inc. [*Associated Press*] (SAG)
PET/SPECT... Positron-Emission Tomography/Single Photon-Emission-Computed Tomography (SAUS)
Pet Sta...... Petrol Station (SAUS)
Pet Suppl... Supplement to Petersdorff's Abridgment [*A publication*] (DLA)
PETT......... Pendular Eye-Tracking Test [*Medicine*] (DMAA)
PETT......... Phototropic Energy Transfer Technique
PETT......... Portable Ethernet Transceiver Tester (SAUS)
PETT......... Positron Emission Transaxial [*or Transverse*] Tomography [*Roentgenography*]
PETT......... Project Engineering and Technology for Tomorrow (SAUS)
PETT......... Purkinje Fiber [*Medicine*] (DMAA)
PETT......... Purpura Fulminans [*Medicine*] (DMAA)
PETT......... Push Fluids [*Medicine*] (DMAA)
PETU .... Petrola International [*Intermodal shipping container symbol*] (TVRC)
PETV......... Planar Epitaxial Tuning Varactor
PETV......... Process Evaluation Test Vehicle
PEU.......... Paneuropa-Union [*Paneuropean Union*] (EAIO)
PEU.......... Plasma Equivalent Unit [*Medicine*] (DMAA)
PEU.......... Polyether Urethane (STED)
PEU.......... Port Expander Unit
PEU.......... Protected Environment Unit [*Medicine*]
PEUA......... Pelvic Exam under Anesthesia [*Medicine*]
PEUG......... Peugeot [*NCIC motorcycle make code*]
PEUG......... Peugeot [*NCIC car make code*]
PEURX....... Pioneer Europe Cl.A [*Mutual fund ticker symbol*] (SG)
PEUU......... Polyether Polyurethane Urea [*Organic chemistry*]
PeV.......... Parameter Equals Value (SAUS)
pev.......... Peak Electron Volt (STED)
PEV.......... Peak Envelope Voltage [*Telecommunications*] (TEL)
PEV.......... Peak Expiratory Velocity [*Medicine*] (DMAA)
PeV.......... Peripheral Vein [*Medicine*] (STED)
PEV.......... Permanent Entry Visa
PEV.......... Perpetual Electric Vehicle [*Hybrid vehicles*]
PeV.......... Petaelectron Volt (SAUS)
PEV.......... Philip Environmental [*NYSE symbol*] (SAG)
PEV.......... Pleasant Valley [*California*] [*Seismograph station code, US Geological Survey*] (SEIS)
PEV.......... Position-Effect Variegation [*Genetics*] [*Botany*]
PEV.......... Positive Expected Value
PEV.......... Pressure Equalization Valves (SAUS)
PEV.......... Propeller-Excited Vibration (PDAA)
PEV.......... Pulmonary Extravascular Fluid Volume [*Medicine*] (STED)
PEV.......... Pyroelectric Vidicon (PDAA)
PEVCV....... Petunia Vein Clearing Virus [*Plant pathology*]
PEVE......... Post Experience Vocational Education (AIE)
PEVE......... Prensa Venezolana [*Press agency*] [*Venezuela*]
PEVI......... Perry's Victory and International Peace Memorial National Monument
PEVL......... Polyethylene Expanded Video Longitudinal Cable (MCD)
PEVM........ Personal'naia Elektronnaia Vychislitel'naia Mashina [*Personal Computer*] [*Russian*]
PEVM........ Professional'naia Elektronnaia Vychislitel'naia Mashina [*Professional Computer*] [*Russian*]
PEVN......... Periventricular Nucleus (STED)
PEVR......... Power-Enrichment Vacuum Regulator [*Automotive engineering*]
PEW.......... Passive Electronics Warfare (NG)
PEW.......... Percussion Welding
PEW.......... Peshawar [*Pakistan*] [*Airport symbol*] (OAG)
pew.......... Pewter (VRA)
PEW.......... Pulmonary Extravascular Water [*Medicine*] (DMAA)
PEWD........ Platoon Early Warning Device [*Military*] (SEWL)
PEWO........ Plant Engineering Work Order (MCD)
PEWR........ Plant Engineering Work Release (AAG)
PEWS......... Parts Early Warning System (IAA)
PEWS......... Platoon Early Warning System (RDA)
PEWS......... Plutonium Equipment Warm Shop [*Nuclear energy*] (NRCH)
PEWS......... Preliminary Early Warning System (SAUS)
PEWS......... Professional Engineering Workstation (TIMI)
PEWSS....... Portable Electronic Warfare Signal Simulator [*Military*] (SEWL)
PEWSX....... PEWS Q-D Subsystem (SAUS)
PEWV........ Pulmonary Extravascular Water Volume [*Physiology*]
PEX.......... Patient Resource Exchange [*Medicine*] [*New York State*] (EDAA)
Pex.......... Peak Exercise (DMAA)
PEX.......... Per Example
PEX.......... PetroCorp, Inc. [*AMEX symbol*] (SG)
PEX.......... Phenazine Ethosulfate [*Biochemistry*]
PEx.......... Physical Examination (MAE)
PEX.......... Pituitary Extract (SAUS)
PEX.......... Potomac Eagle Scenic Rail Excursion [*Federal Railroad Administration identification code*]
PEX.......... Private Electronic Exchange [*Telecommunications*] (IAA)
PEX.......... Projectable Excitation (SAUS)
PEX.......... Pronto Explorations Ltd. [*Vancouver Stock Exchange symbol*]
PEX.......... Pseudoexfoliation (SAUS)
PEX.......... World Aircraft Flight Operation, Inc. [*ICAO designator*] (FAAC)
PEXA......... Pre-Edge X-Ray Absorption [*For study of solids*]
PEXAFS...... Photoelectron Extended X-Ray Absorption Fine Structure
PEXC......... Pony Express Courier Corporation [*Common carrier symbol*]
PEXRA....... Programmed Electronic X-Ray Automatic Diffractometer (IAA)
PEXRAD...... Programmed Electronic X-Ray Automatic Diffractometer
PEX-SI....... PEX-Sample Implementation (SAUS)
PEY.......... Pengelly Mines Ltd. [*Vancouver Stock Exchange symbol*]
PEY.......... Petjo [*Language symbol*] (ETLW)
PEY.......... Photoelectric Yield
PEYS......... Photoelectron Yield Spectroscopy (MCD)
PEZ.......... Pezgold Resource Corp. [*Vancouver Stock Exchange symbol*]
PEZ.......... Pleasanton, TX [*Location identifier*] [*FAA*] (FAAL)
PEZ.......... Port of Everglades [*Federal Railroad Administration identification code*]
PEZV......... Prime Equities International [*NASDAQ symbol*] (SAG)
PEZVF....... Prime Equities Intl [*NASDAQ symbol*] (TTSB)
PF........... Amer First Prep Fd 2 L.P. [*AMEX symbol*] (TTSB)
PF........... American First PREP [*Preferred Real Estate Participation*] Fund 2 Ltd. [*AMEX symbol*] (SPSG)
PF........... Frankford Public Library, Frankford, PA [*Library symbol*] [*Library of Congress*] (LCLS)
PF........... French Polynesia [*ANSI two-letter standard code*] (CNC)
PF........... frigate-patrol escort vessel (SAUS)
PF........... L-Phenylalanine Mustard and 5-Fluorouracil [*Antineoplastic drug regimen*] (DAVI)
PF........... Pacemaker Failure (MELL)
PF........... Pacifica Foundation (EA)
PF........... Package Freighter [*Shipping*]
PF........... Packaging Facility (SAUS)
PF........... Packing Factor (EECA)
PF........... Packing Fraction (EECA)
PF........... Paderewski Foundation [*Defunct*] (EA)
PF........... Pagan Federation [*United Kingdom*] (EAIO)
PF........... Page Fault (IAA)
PF........... Page Footing (BUR)
PF........... Page Formatter (MDG)
PF........... Pair Feeding (DMAA)
PF........... Paling Fence
PF........... Panchromatic Film (ADA)
PF........... Paper and Foil [*Capacitor*] (DEN)
pf........... Paracel Islands [*MARC country of publication code*] [*Library of Congress*] (LCCP)
PF........... Parachute Facility (NASA)
PF........... Parachute Flare (NVT)
PF........... Parafascicular Nucleus [*Neuroanatomy*]
PF........... Parallel Feed (ELAL)
PF........... Parallel Fiber [*Neuroanatomy*]
PF........... Parallel Flow
PF........... Parallel Fold
PF........... Paramount Funding Corp. [*Toronto Stock Exchange symbol*]
PF........... Parapsychology Foundation (EA)
PF........... Parity Flag (SAUS)
PF........... Park Factor (SAUS)
PF........... Partial Function (IAA)
PF........... Partition Factor (NRCH)
PF........... Passage Free (ROG)
P/F.......... Pass-Fail [*System*] (MAE)
PF........... Patellofemoral Joint [*Anatomy*] (DAVI)
PF........... Path Finder [*British military*] (DMA)
PF........... Pathfinder Fund (EA)
PF........... Patriotic Front [*Zimbabwe*] [*Political party*] (PPW)
PF........... Patrol Vessel, Frigate [*Navy symbol*]
P/F.......... Pattern Flight [*Also, P/FLT*] (MUGU)
PF........... Paved Flume (COE)
PF........... Payload Forward [*NASA*] (MCD)
PF........... Payload Function [*NASA*] (MCD)
PF........... Payload operational instrumentation MDM-FWD (SAUS)
PF........... Peace and Freedom Party [*Political party*] (DLA)
PF........... Peak Flow [*Medicine*]
PF........... Peak Frequency
PF........... Peanut Flour
PF........... Pedal Furrow
PF........... Penetration Fracture (IAA)
PF........... Pen Fanciers (EA)
PF........... Pen Friends [*Defunct*] (EA)
PF........... Pension Fund
PF........... Perchloryl Fluoride (SAUS)
PF........... Peregrine Fund (EA)
pf........... Perfect (WDAA)
PF........... Perfect
PF........... Perfect Fluid (SAUS)
PF........... Performance Factor
PF........... Perfusion Fixation [*Histology*]
PF........... Perfusion Fluid [*Medicine*] (DMAA)

PF........... Pericardial Fluid [*Medicine*] (DMAA)
PF........... Periodic Fever [*Medicine*] (EDAA)
PF........... Peritoneal Fluid [*Medicine*] (MAE)
PF........... Permanent Fireman
PF........... Permanent Force [*Canadian Militia before 1940*]
PF........... Permeability Factor
pf........... Perofskite [*CIPW classification*] [*Geology*]
PF........... Personal File (CARL)
PF........... Personal Finance (SAUS)
PF........... Personal Fouls [*Basketball*]
PF........... Personality Factor
PF........... Personal Security File Number [*British Secret Service*]
PF........... Petroferric [*Soil biology*] [*Soil phases*] (QSUL)
Pf........... Pfeifferella [*Genus of bacteria*]
PF........... Pfennig [*Penny*] [*Monetary unit*] [*German*]
PF........... Pforzheim [*German license plate city code*]
PF........... Phenol-Formaldehyde [*Organic chemistry*]
PF........... Phenylalanine and Methotrexate [*Antineoplastic drug regimen*] (DAVI)
PF........... Philatelic Foundation (EA)
PF........... Phonetic Form [*Linguistics*] (IEL)
PF........... Photofluorography (SAUS)
PF........... Photogrammetric Facility [*Army*]
PF........... Photon Factory (SAUS)
PF........... Physical File (SAUS)
PF........... Physicians Forum (EA)
pf........... Pianoforte (WDAA)
PF........... Pianoforte [*Soft, then Loud*] [*Music*]
PF........... Pico Farad (ACAE)
PF........... Picofarad
pF........... Picofarad
PF........... Picture Frequency (SAUS)
PF........... Picture Frustration [*Study*] (MAE)
PF........... Piedmont Fracture (MELL)
PF........... Piled Fathom (SAUS)
PF........... Pilgrim Fellowship (EA)
PF........... Pilot Flying (GAVI)
PF........... Pilot Stop Filter (IAA)
PF........... Pininfarina [*Automotive coachworks*]
PF........... [*The*] Pioneer & Fayette Railroad Co. [*AAR code*]
PF........... Pipkin Fracture (MELL)
PF........... Pistonfon (SAUS)
PF........... Piu Forte [*A Little Louder*] [*Music*]
PF........... Plain Face [*Construction*]
PF........... Plane Frame [*Camutek*] [*Software package*] (NCC)
PF........... Planning Forum (EA)
PF........... Plantar Fasciaitis [*Medicine*]
PF........... Plantar Flexion [*Medicine*]
PF........... Plasma Factor (DMAA)
PF........... Plasticity Index [*Soil*] (DICI)
PF........... Platelet Factor [*Hematology*]
PF........... Platform (SSD)
PF........... Plentiful Foods [*Department of Agriculture*] [*A publication*]
PF........... Pleural Fluid [*Medicine*] (DB)
PF........... Plot Function [*Computer science*]
PF........... Plug-Flow Transport (SAUS)
PF........... Pneumatic Float
PF........... Poco Forte [*Rather Loud*] [*Music*]
PF........... Poe Foundation (EA)
PF........... Point Foundation (EA)
PF........... Point of Foul [*Football*]
PF........... Point of Frog [*Electronics*] (MSA)
PF........... Points For [*Football*]
PF........... Polar Front [*Climatology*]
PF........... Polarization Fraction (SAUS)
PF........... Polarizing Filter (SAUS)
PF........... Pole Figure (SAUS)
PF........... Pole Fittings [*JETDS nomenclature*] [*Military*] (CET)
PF........... Police Forces [*British*]
PF........... Police Foundation (EA)
PF........... POLISARIO [*Frente Popular para la Liberacion de Saguia El Hamra y Rio De Oro*] [*Popular Front for the Liberation of Saguia El Hamra and Rio De Oro*] [*Morocco*] (PD)
P/F........... Poll/Final [*Computer science*] (TNIG)
PF........... Poloidal Field (MCD)
PF........... Polycenter Framework (SAUS)
PF........... Polyurethane Foam
PF........... Pool Frequency [*Pisciculture*]
PF........... Poop and Forecastle [*of a ship*] (DS)
PF........... Poor Foam
PF........... Popular Forces [*South Vietnam*]
PF........... Pore Free (IAA)
PF........... Por Favor [*Please*] [*Portuguese*]
PF........... Portal Fibrosis [*Medicine*]
PF........... Portfolio [*A publication*]
PF........... Position Failure
PF........... Position Finder [*British military*] (DMA)
PF........... Postage Free (ROG)
PF........... Posterior Fontanelle [*Anatomy*] (DAVI)
P/F........... Post Flight (AFIT)
PF........... Postman's Federation [*A union*] [*British*]
PF........... Posture Foundation [*Initialism is used in brand of sneaker shoe, PF Flyers*]
PF........... Potency Factor (GNE)
PF........... Potential Flow (SAUS)
PF........... Pott's Fracture [*Medicine*] (MELL)
PF........... Powered Flight (NASA)
pf........... Power Factor (IDOE)
PF........... Power Factor [*Radio*]
PF........... Power Focus [*Photography*]
PF........... Power Frame [*Telecommunications*] (TEL)
PF........... Power Frequency (SAUS)
P/F........... Practical Factors
PF........... Precursor Fluid [*Medicine*] (MEDA)
PF........... Pred Forte (SAUS)
PF........... Prefer [*Telegraphy*] (PCTE)
PF........... Preference
PF........... Preferred
PF........... Prefetch [*Computer science*]
PF........... Preflight
PF........... Preformed Fragment (SAUS)
PF........... Presbyterian Foundation [*Australia*]
PF........... Pressure Fan (AAG)
PF........... Preterm Foundation [*Australia*]
PF........... Primary Fibrinolysin [*Medicine*] (DMAA)
PF........... Primary File (SAUS)
PF........... Primary Filter [*Automotive engineering*]
PF........... Prime Function (NASA)
PF........... Principles of Flight (SAUS)
PF........... Prison Fellowship Ministries (EA)
PF........... Private File (SAUS)
PF........... Probability Factor (SAUS)
PF........... Probability of Failure (NASA)
PF........... Probability of Fool (ACAE)
PF........... Probability of Fratricide (ACAE)
PF........... Procurator Fiscal
PF........... Pro Female [*International Bowhunting Organization*] [*Class Equipment*]
PF........... Profile (KSC)
pf........... profiled (SAUS)
Pf........... Pro Forma (EBF)
pf........... Pro Forma [*As a Matter of Form*] [*Latin*] (WGA)
PF........... Program Function [*Computer science*] (IBMDP)
PF........... Programmable Format [*Perforating keyboard*]
PF........... Programmable Function (NITA)
PF........... Programmed Function (SAUS)
PF........... Programming Fault (SAUS)
PF........... Progressive Foundation (EA)
PF........... Project Friend (EA)
PF........... Projectile Fragment
PF........... Proof
PF........... Prop Forward
PF........... Proposed Finding [*Nuclear energy*] (NRCH)
PF........... Prostatic Fluid [*Medicine*] (DMAA)
PF........... Prostatitis Foundation (SAUS)
PF........... Protection Factor
PF........... Protein Factor (SAUS)
PF........... Protein-Free
PF........... Protoflight (ACAE)
PF........... Protoplasmic Fracture [*Freeze etching in microscopy*]
PF........... Proximity Fuze [*Bomb, rocket, or shell*]
PF........... PsychoHistory Forum (EA)
PF........... Psynetics Foundation (EA)
P/F........... Pteropod/Foramifera [*Ratio in coastal waters*]
PF........... Public Funding [*Finance*] (WDAA)
PF........... Pulmonary Blood-Flow [*Medicine*] (DB)
PF........... Pulmonary Factor [*Medicine*]
PF........... Pulmonary Function [*Medicine*] (DMAA)
PF........... Pulse Feedback [*Telecommunications*] (IAA)
PF........... Pulse Frequency
PF........... Pulverized Fuel
P F........... Pump-Out Facilities [*Nautical charts*]
PF........... Punch Feed (SAUS)
PF........... Punch Off [*Computer science*] (BUR)
PF........... Purge Fan [*Nuclear energy*] (NRCH)
PF........... Purge Flow [*Automotive engineering*]
PF........... Purkinje Fibers [*Cardiology*] (DAVI)
PF........... Purple Finch [*Ornithology*]
PF........... Purpura Fulminans (DB)
PF........... Pygmy Fund (EA)
PF........... Pyrolysis Fluorescence (SAUS)
PF........... Trans Pennsylvania Airlines [*ICAO designator*] (AD)
PF3a........... Platelet Factor 3 Availability [*Hematology*] (DAVI)
PFA........... Alliance Forest Prod [*NYSE symbol*] (SG)
PFA........... Pacific Football Alliance (PSS)
PFA........... Palmdale Final Assembly [*NASA*] (NASA)
PFA........... Panarcadian Federation of America (EA)
PFA........... Papermakers Felt Association (EA)
PFA........... Para-Fluorophenylalanine [*Biochemistry*]
PFA........... Parallel Full Adder (SAUS)
PFA........... Parameter Field Address (SAUS)
PFA........... Parametric Ferrite Amplifier (SAUS)
PFA........... Participating Field Activity [*DoD*]
PFA........... Parti de la Federation Africaine [*African Federation Party*] [*Political party*]
PFA........... Peachtree First Accounting (SAUS)
PFA........... Pedorthic Footwear Association (NTPA)
PFA........... Pellet-Fired Appliance [*Heating system*]
PFA........... Pennsylvania Forestry Association (EARSL)

PFA.......... Pension Fund Association [*Japan*] (ECON)
PFA.......... Perfluoroalkoxy [*Organic chemistry*]
PFA.......... Personal Fall Arrest [*Safety systems*]
PFA.......... Personnel Functional Assessment [*Of the Army Acquisition Corps*] (RDA)
PFA.......... Pesticide Formulators Association (SAUS)
PFA.......... Petroflame International [*Vancouver Stock Exchange symbol*]
PFA.......... Phosphofructoaldolase (SAUS)
PFA.......... Phosphonoformic Acid [*Antiviral compound*]
PFA.......... Phosphor-Fruct-Aldolase (SAUS)
PFA.......... Pianists Foundation of America [*Defunct*] (EA)
PFA.......... Pierce Ferry [*Arizona*] [*Seismograph station code, US Geological Survey*] [*Closed*] (SEIS)
PFA.......... Pierre Fauchard Academy (EA)
PFA.......... Pioneer Fraternal Association (EA)
PFA.......... Pitch Follow-Up Amplifier
PFA.......... Plan for Action (MCD)
PFA.......... Plant Functional Attributes (SAUS)
PFA.......... Platt Family Association (EA)
PFA.......... Polish Falcons of America (EA)
PFA.......... Polyfluoroalkoxy (SAUS)
PFA.......... Polyformaldehyde (SAUS)
PFA.......... Polyfurfuryl Alcohol [*Organic chemistry*]
PFA.......... Polymeric Fatty Acid [*Food science*]
PFA.......... Polyurethane Foam Association (EA)
PFA.......... Pontius Family Association (EA)
PFA.......... Popular Flying Association [*British*]
PFA.......... Post Fledgling Area [*USDA Forest Service*] (ALAC)
PFA.......... Post Flight Analysis
PFA.......... Post-Flight Annex (SAUS)
PFA.......... Power Fastenings Association [*British*] (DBA)
PFA.......... Prall Family Association (EA)
PFA.......... Predictive Failure Analysis (SAUS)
PFA.......... Premm Family Association (EA)
PFA.......... Prescription Footwear Association (EA)
PFA.......... Presidential Families of America (EA)
PFA.......... Prevention of Food Adulteration (SAUS)
PFA.......... Principal Financial Analyst (SAUS)
PFA.......... Prison Families Anonymous (EA)
PFA.......... Prison Fellowship of Australia
PFA.......... Private Facilities Access [*Communications term*] (DCT)
PFA.......... Private Fliers Association (SAUS)
PFA.......... Probability of False Alarm [*Department of Defense*]
PFA.......... Product and Field Activity (SAUS)
PFA.......... Production Flow Analysis (PDAA)
PFA.......... Professional Farmers of America (EA)
PFA.......... Professional Fishermen's Association [*Tasmania, Australia*]
PFA.......... Professional Footballers' Association [*British*] (BI)
PFA.......... Professional Fraternity Association (EA)
PFA.......... Profunda Femoris Artery [*Anatomy*] (DAVI)
PFA.......... Program and File Analysis
PFA.......... Proportional Fluid Amplifier
PFA.......... Provincial Forestry Administration (SAUS)
PFA.......... Psychologic Flight Avoidance (SAUS)
PFA.......... Pulled from the Air [*Commom way of establishing budgets*] [*Training term*] (LPT)
PFA.......... Pulverized Fuel Ash (IEEE)
PFA.......... Pure Fluid Amplification
PFA.......... Pure Food Act (SAUS)
PFAA......... Phelps Family Association of America (EA)
PFAA......... Prairie Farm Assistance Act
PFAB......... Prefabricated
PFAC......... Panepirotic Federation of America and Canada [*Later, PFACA*] (EA)
PFAC......... People for a Change (EA)
PFAC......... Pet Food Association of Canada (EAIO)
PFAC......... Pro-Fac Cooperative, Inc. [*NASDAQ symbol*] (NASQ)
PFACA....... Panepirotic Federation of America, Canada, and Australia (EA)
P/FACCTL.... Pad Facility Controls [*Aerospace*] (AAG)
P-face....... Inner Face of the Membrane Lipid Inner Layer [*Cell biology*] (QSUL)
PFACP....... Pro-Fac Cooperative, Inc. [*NASDAQ symbol*] (SAG)
PFACP....... Pro-Fac Co-op 'A' Pfd [*NASDAQ symbol*] (TTSB)
P-FACTOR.. Asymmetrical Thrust [*Aviation*] (PIPO)
P Factor..... Preservation Factor (SAUS)
PFAD........ Palm Fatty Acid Distillate [*Organic chemistry*]
PFADS....... Physical Operators Foreign Area Data System
PFAE........ Pacific Aerospace and Electronics [*OTCBB symbol*]
PFAE........ Perfluoroalkyl Ether [*Organic chemistry*]
PFAG........ Pulse Field Alternating Gradient (SAUS)
PFAM........ Programmed Frequency Amplitude Modulation
PFANZ....... Police Federation of Australia and New Zealand
PFAP........ Poly(fluoroalkoxyphosphazene) [*Organic chemistry*]
PFAPC....... Psychological Factor Affecting Physical Condition (SAUS)
PFAR........ Popular Front for Armed Resistance [*Pakistan*]
PFAR........ Power Fail Automatic Restart [*Computer science*]
PFAR........ Preliminary Failure Analysis Report [*NASA*] (KSC)
PFA Rules... Prevention of Food Adulteration Rules (SAUS)
PFAS......... Performic Acid-Schiff Reaction [*Medicine*] (MAE)
PFAS......... Planar Flank Array Sonar (SAUS)
PFAS......... President of the Faculty of Architects and Surveyors [*British*] (DBQ)
PFASC....... PATRIOT [*Phased Array Tracking to Intercept Target*] Field Army Suppor t Center [*Army*]
PFAT......... Pre-First Article Test
PFAT......... Pre-Flight Acceptance Test (SAUS)
PFAT......... Preliminary Flight Appraisal Test (MCD)
PFAT......... Private Forestry Association of Tasmania [*Australia*]
PFATS....... Professional Football Athletic Trainers Society (NTPA)
PFAU........ Pfaudler Company [*NCIC trailer make code*]
PFAVC....... Pacific Fleet Audio-Visual Command (DNAB)
PFAW........ People for the American Way (EA)
PFAW........ PFA Systems [*Common carrier symbol*]
PFAWA...... Parents and Friends Association of Western Australia
PFAWA...... Poultry Farmers' Association of Western Australia
PFAW VA.... People for the American Way Voters Alliance [*Washington, DC*] (PACS)
PFB.......... Parallel Filter Bank (CIST)
PFB.......... Partei Freier Buerger [*Free Citizens' Party*] [*Germany*] [*Political party*] (PPW)
PFB.......... Passo Fundo [*Brazil*] [*Airport symbol*] (OAG)
PFB.......... Patellofemoral Knee Brace [*Medicine*]
PFB.......... Payload Feedback [*NASA*] (MCD)
PFB.......... Payload Forward Bus [*NASA*] (MCD)
PFB.......... Pentafluorobenzyl [*Organic radical*]
PFB.......... Pentafluorobenzyl Bromide [*Organic chemistry*]
PFB.......... Photo Flash Battery
PFB.......... Plasti-Fab Ltd. [*Toronto Stock Exchange symbol*]
PFB.......... Pneumatic Float Bridge
PFB.......... Popular Front in Bahrain [*Political party*] (PSAP)
PFB.......... Position Feedback (MCD)
PFB.......... Postscript Font Binary (SAUS)
PFB.......... Prefabricated [*Technical drawings*]
PFB.......... Prefetch Buffer (CIST)
PFB.......... Preformed Beams [*SONAR*]
PFB.......... Pressure Fed Booster (NASA)
PFB.......... Pressurized Fluid-Bed [*Chemical engineering*]
PFB.......... Printer Font Binary [*Computer science*] (CDE)
PFB.......... Provincial Food Bureau (SAUS)
PFB.......... Provisional Frequency Board [*ITU*]
PFB.......... Pseudofollicutitis Barbae [*Medicine*]
PFBA........ Poly(perfluorobutyl Acrylate) [*Organic chemistry*]
PFBC........ Pentaflurobenzoyl Chloride [*Organic chemistry*]
PFBC........ Pressurized Fluidized-Bed Combustion
PFBCA....... Pennsylvania Farm Bureau Cooperative Association (SAUS)
PFBG........ Pressurized Fluidized-Bed Gasification (ODA)
PFBHA....... Pentafluorobenzylhydroxylamine Hydrochloride [*Analytical biochemistry*]
PFBI......... Premier Financial Bancorp, Inc. [*NASDAQ symbol*] (SAG)
PFBI......... Premier Finl Bancorp [*NASDAQ symbol*] (TTSB)
P/F Bit...... Poll/Final Bit (SAUS)
PFBMF...... Polaris Fleet Ballistic Missile Force (SAUS)
PFBR........ Plutonium Fast Breeder Reactor (SAUS)
PFBR........ Prototype Fast Breeder Reactor (SAUS)
PFBRG...... Pneumatic Float Bridge
PFBS........ Ponce Federal Bank F.S.B. (EFIS)
PFBT........ Performance Functional Board Tester (SAUS)
PFBV........ Pelargonium Flower Break Virus [*Plant pathology*]
PFC.......... Pacific City, OR [*Location identifier*] [*FAA*] (FAAL)
PFC.......... Pacific Forestry Center (SAUS)
PFC.......... Pack Feed and Converter (SAUS)
PFC.......... Panama Ferrying Command (SAUS)
PFC.......... Paper Format Control (SAUS)
PFC.......... Parallel-Flow Condenser [*Air conditioning systems*]
PFC.......... Parapet Foxhole Cover (SAUS)
PFC.......... Parti Feministe du Canada
PFC.......... Partnerships for Change (SAUS)
PFC.......... Passed Flying College [*British*]
PFC.......... Passenger Facility Charge [*Airports*]
PFC.......... Patellofemoral Chondrosis [*Medicine*] (MELL)
PFC.......... Pathfinder Industries Ltd. [*Formerly, Pathfinder Financial Corporation*] [*Toronto Stock Exchange symbol*]
PFC.......... Patient Focused Care [*Medicine*]
PFC.......... Peak Follower Circuit
PFC.......... Peculiar Facility Change (AAG)
PFC.......... Pelvic Flexion Contracture [*Orthopedics*] (DAVI)
PFC.......... Pen Fancier's Club (EA)
PFC.......... Pennsylvania Public Library Film Center, University Park, PA [*OCLC symbol*] (OCLC)
PFC.......... Perfluorocarbon [*Organic chemistry*]
PFC.......... Perfluorochemical [*Organic chemistry*]
PFC.......... Perfluorocompound (AAEL)
PFC.......... Performance Flight Certification [*NASA*] (NASA)
PFC.......... Permanent Families for Children [*Defunct*] (EA)
PFC.......... Persistent Fetal Circulation [*Medicine*]
PFC.......... Personal Finance Center [*Information service or system*]
PFC.......... Phase Frequency Characteristics (SAUS)
PFC.......... Phenylacetamidotrifluoromethylcoumarin (SAUS)
PFC.......... Photofinish Camera (SAUS)
PFC.......... Physicians for Choice (EA)
PFC.......... Planar Flow Casting (SAUS)
PFC.......... Plan Filing Cabinet
PFC.......... Plaque-Forming Cell [*Immunochemistry*]
PFC.......... Plow-Furrow-Cover [*Waste*] (DICI)
PFC.......... PMCC Financial Corp. [*AMEX symbol*] (NASQ)
PFC.......... Pneumatic Function Controller
PFC.......... Point Focusing and Centering [*Optics*]
PFC.......... Police Forces [*British*]
PFC.......... Portable Four Channel (SAUS)
PFC.......... Port Flow Control (SAUS)
PFC.......... Positive Feedback Circuit

PFC .... Postflight Checklist (MCD)
PFC .... Postflight Checkout (SAUS)
PFC .... Power Factor Capacitor [*Radio*] (IAA)
PFC .... Power Factor Compensation (SAUS)
PFC .... Power Factor Controller (SAUS)
PFC .... Power Factor Correction
PFC .... Prairie Fiction Collection, Alberta Culture [*UTLAS symbol*]
PFC .... Praying for Corporal [*Private First Class desirous of promotion, or female in wartime desirous of a boyfriend*]
PFC .... Preference [*Telegraphy*] (PCTE)
PFC .... Preflight Certification (SAUS)
PFC .... Preflight Console (MCD)
PFC .... Prefrontal Cortex [*Anatomy*]
PFC .... Preliminary Flight Certification [*NASA*]
PFC .... Presley-ites Fan Club (EA)
PFC .... Press-Fit Component (MELL)
PFC .... Pressure Function Controller
PFC .... Primary Flight Control
PFC .... Priority Foreign Country [*International trade*] (ECON)
Pfc .... Private First Class [*Military*] (NTIO)
PFC .... Private, First Class [*Army*]
PFC .... Private Forestry Council [*Australia*]
PFC .... Privately Financed Consumption (MHDW)
PFC .... Processing Figure Channel [*Electronics*] (ECII)
PFC .... Professional Fee Costing (SAUS)
PFC .... Programmed Fuel Computer [*Automotive engineering*]
PFC .... Progreso y Futuro de Ceuta [*Political party*] (EY)
PFC .... Progressive Fish Culturist (SAUS)
PFC .... Protocol Field Compression (SAUS)
PFC .... Pulsed Flame Combustor
PFC .... Pulse-Flow Coulometry
PFC .... Pusan Fisheries College (SAUS)
PFCA .... Performance Ford Club of America (EA)
PFCA .... Plastic Food Container Association [*Defunct*]
PFCB .... Page Frame Control Block (SAUS)
PFCC .... Power Factor Corrector Capacitor [*Radio*] (IAA)
PFCCG .... Pacific Fleet Combat Camera Group (DNAB)
PFCCT .... Pennsylvania Federation of Community College Trustees (SAUS)
PFCD .... Primary Flight Control Display
PFCDA .... Photographers & Friends United Against AIDS-Canadian Chapter (SAUS)
PFCE .... Performance (WGA)
PFCE .... Preface (ROG)
PFCE .... Preference (AAG)
PFCF .... Payload Flight Control Facility [*NASA*] (MCD)
PFCF .... Producer Fixed Capital Formation (MCD)
PFCG .... Pulse Field Constant Gradient (SAUS)
PFCH .... Prefilled Clutch Hydraulic Actuation [*Automotive Products, Inc.*] [*Automotive engineering*]
PFCM .... Pittsburgh Festival of Contemporary Music [*Record label*]
PFCO .... Position Field Classification Officer
PFCO .... Principal Fire Control Officer (WDAA)
PFCP .... Primary Familial and Congenital Polycythemia [*Medicine*]
PFCR .... Plaque-Forming Cell Response [*Immunochemistry*] (OA)
PFCRA .... Program Fraud Civil Remedies Act
PFCRN ...... Partido del Frente Cardenista de Reconstruccion Nacional [*Mexico*] [*Political party*] (EY)
PFCS .... Primary Flight Control System [*NASA*] (MCD)
PFCS .... Primary Flow Control System [*Nuclear energy*] (NRCH)
PFCS .... Process Floor Control System (TIMI)
PFCS .... Program and Funds Control System (MCD)
PFCS .... Public Facsimile Communication System (SAUS)
PFCT .... Pre-Flight Certification Test
PFCU .... Pacific Far East Line [*Intermodal shipping container symbol*] (TVRC)
PFCU .... Parallel File Control Unit (SAUS)
PFCU .... Power Flying Control Unit [*Aviation*] (DA)
PFCU-PAC ... Philadelphia Federal Credit Union PAC [*Philadelphia, PA*] (PACS)
PFCV .... Patriotic Funds Council of Victoria [*Australia*]
PFCWKS .... Pogo Fan Club and Walt Kelly Society (EA)
PFCWTS .... Pogo Fan Club and Walt Kelly Society (EA)
PFD .... Paraffined (SAUS)
PFD .... Particle [*or Proton*] Flux Density
PFD .... Particle Flux Detector (ACAE)
PFD .... Partnership for Democracy [*An association*] (EA)
PFD .... Perfluorodecalin [*Organic chemistry*]
PFD .... Personal, Fatigue, and Delay [*Work measurement factors*]
PFD .... Personal Flotation Device [*Life jacket*]
PFD .... Phase Frequency Distortion [*Telecommunications*] (IAA)
PFD .... Planned Flight Data [*Aviation*] (DA)
PFD .... Planning Factors Development (MCD)
PFD .... Policy Formulation Division (AAGC)
PFD .... Polyostotic Fibrous Dysplasia [*Medicine*] (DMAA)
PFD .... Position Fixing Device (ADA)
PFD .... Power Flux Density [*Telecommunications*] (TEL)
PFD .... Preferred (AAG)
pfd .... Preferred (ELAL)
Pfd .... Preferred (SG)
PFD .... Preferred Income Fund [*NYSE symbol*] (SPSG)
PFD .... Preferred Stock [*Investment term*] (DFIT)
PFD .... Preliminary Functional Description (CINC)
PFD .... Present for Duty
PFD .... Primary Flash Distillate [*Chemical technology*]
PFD .... Primary Flight Display
PFD .... Probability of Error/Fault Detection (SAUS)
PFD .... Probability of Failure on Demand (ACII)
PFD .... Process Flow Diagram (NRCH)
PFD .... Programming Facility for Display users (SAUS)
PFD .... Proton Flux Density (SAUS)
PFD .... Proximity Fuze Disconnector (SAUS)
PFD .... Pseudoinflammatory Fundus Disease [*Medicine*] (DMAA)
PFD .... Puffed [*Freight*]
PFD .... Pulse-Frequency Diversity [*Electronics*] (NG)
PFDA .... Pennsylvania Funeral Directors Association (EARSL)
PFDA .... Perfluorodecanoic Acid [*Organic chemistry*]
PFDA .... Post Flight Data Analysis
PFDA .... Precision Frequency Distribution Amplifier
PFDA .... Pulse-Frequency Distortion Analyzer
PFDA .... Pure Food and Drug Administration (SAUS)
PFDAR ...... Post-Flight Data Analysis Review (SAUS)
PFDBAD ..... Pathfinder Badge [*Military decoration*] (GFGA)
PFDC .... People's Bancorp [*NASDAQ symbol*] (NASQ)
PFDC .... Peoples Bancorp (Dekalb County) [*NASDAQ symbol*] (SAG)
PFDC .... Peoples Bancorp(IN) [*NASDAQ symbol*] (TTSB)
PFDC .... Peoples Federal Savings Bank of DeKalb City [*NASDAQ symbol*] (NQ)
PFDC .... Pole Figure Data Collection (SAUS)
PFDCCA ..... Prodemca: Friends of the Democratic Center in the Americas [*Defunct*] (EA)
PFDF .... Pacific Fisheries Development Foundation [*Defunct*] (EA)
PFDF .... Petroleum Fuel Development Facility (SAUS)
PFDI .... Preferred Funeral Directors International (NTPA)
PF DI .... Progressive Die (SAUS)
PfdInco ...... Preferred Income Fund [*Associated Press*] (SAG)
PFDJ .... People's Front for Democracy and Justice [*Formerly, EPLF*] [*Eritrea*] [*Political party*] (ECON)
PFDJ .... Popular Front for Democracy and Justice [*Eritrea*]
PFDL .... Parameterized Format Description Language (SAUS)
PfDL .... Pflegedienstleitung (SAUS)
PFDM .... Preliminary Final Draft Manuscript
PF/DOS ..... Product Improvement (SAUS)
PFDR .... Pathfinder [*Aircraft*]
PFDR .... Preferred Risk Life Insurance Co. [*NASDAQ symbol*] (COMM)
PfdrBad ..... Pathfinder Badge [*Military decoration*] (AABC)
PFDS .... Pergamon Financial Data Services [*Pergamon Orbit Infoline Ltd.*] [*British*] [*Information service or system*] (IID)
PFDS .... Priority Freight Distribution System (SAUS)
PFD SP ...... Preferred Spelling (WDAA)
PFDTM ...... Preliminary Flightweight Demonstration Test Motor (MCD)
PFDU .... Paulat Spedition [*Intermodal shipping container symbol*] (TVRC)
PFE .... Pacific Fruit Express Co. [*AAR code*]
PFE .... Page Fault Error (SAUS)
PFE .... Partido Feminista de Espana [*Feminist Party of Spain*] [*Political party*] (PPW)
PFE .... Pelvic Floor Exercise (DMAA)
PFE .... Performance Fitness Examination [*Military*] (DNAB)
PFE .... Pfizer, Inc. [*NYSE symbol*] (SPSG)
PFE .... Photoferroelectric Effect [*Physics*]
PFE .... Physics of Failure in Electronics [*A publication*] (MCD)
PFE .... Plenum Fill Experiment [*Nuclear energy*] (NRCH)
PFE .... Popular Front of Estonia [*Political party*]
PFE .... Portable Fire Extinguisher (SPST)
PFE .... Post Fire Evaluation [*Military*] (CAAL)
PFE .... Post Flight Evaluation
PFE .... Pressure Feedback EGR (Exhaust Gas Circulation) [*Automotive engineering*]
PFE .... Pressure Feedback Exhaust [*Automotive engineering*]
PFE .... Priests for Equality (EA)
PFE .... Primary Feedback Element (IAA)
PFE .... Process Fuel Equivalent (MCD)
PFE .... Program for Executives (SAUS)
PFE .... Programmers File Editor (SAUS)
PFE .... Pulsed Field Electrophoresis [*Analytical biochemistry*]
PFE .... Purchaser Furnished Equipment (NATG)
PFEAAC ..... Posterior Fossa Extra-Axial Arachnoid Cyst [*Medicine*] (DAVI)
PFEC .... Philatelic Friends Exchange Circuit (EA)
PFED .... Park Bancorp, Inc. [*NASDAQ symbol*] (NASQ)
PFED .... Park Bancorporation [*NASDAQ symbol*]
PFEFES ...... Pacific and Far East Federation of Engineering Societies
PFEG .... Performance Freight Systems [*Common carrier symbol*]
PFEGR .... Pressure Feedback Exhaust Gas Recirculation [*Automotive engineering*]
PfeifVac .... Pfeiffer Vacuum Technology AG [*Associated Press*] (SAG)
PFEL .... Pacific Far East Line
PFEP .... Polyfluoroethylene Propylene (SAUS)
PFEP .... Programmable Front-End Processor [*Computer science*]
PFES .... Pan American Federation of Engineering Societies
PFES .... Pelvic Floor Electrical Stimulation [*Medicine*] (MELL)
PFES .... Portable Field Emission Spectrometer (SAUS)
PFES .... Proposed Final Environmental Statement [*Department of Energy*]
PFES .... Pure Fluid Encoder System
PFET .... P-Channel Junction Field-Effect Transistor (IDOE)
PFET .... Prototype Flight Evaluation Tests (SAUS)
PFEZ .... Pacific Fruitland Express [*Federal Railroad Administration identification code*]
PFF .... Page Fault Frequency [*Computer science*] (MHDI)
PFF .... Partial-Flow Filter [*Automotive engineering*]
PFF .... Pathfinder Force [*British RADAR designation which became overall synonym for RADAR*] [*Military*]
PFF .... Permanent Family File [*Navy*] (NG)

PFF .... Phenolfurfural [*Organic chemistry*]
PFF .... Plaintiff [*Telegraphy*] (PCTE)
PFF .... Planning Factors File (MCD)
PFF .... Plaque-Forming Factor (PDAA)
PFF .... Pluto Express Mission [*Space exploration*]
PFF .... Pluto Fast Flyby [*NASA*] (PS)
PFF .... Police Field Force (CINC)
PFF .... Porcine Follicular Fluid [*Endocrinology*]
PFF .... Precast Flooring Federation [*British*] (DBA)
PFF .... Pre-Formed Fragmentation (MUSM)
PFF .... Presbyterian Frontier Fellowship (EA)
PFF .... Presidential Faculty Fellow (SAUS)
PFF .... Primary Focus Feed [*Satellite communications*]
PFF .... Prisoners' Families & Friends (WDAA)
PFF .... Project Formulation Framework (SAUS)
PFF .... Proposed Fabric Flammability Standard [*Consumer Product Safety Commission*]
PFF .... Protein Fat-Free [*Food technology*]
PFF .... Punjab Frontier Force [*British military*] (DMA)
PFFB .... PFF Bancorp [*NASDAQ symbol*] (TTSB)
PFFB .... PFF Bancorp, Inc. [*NASDAQ symbol*] (SAG)
PFFBcp ...... PFF Bancorp, Inc. [*Associated Press*] (SAG)
PFFBI .... Pacific Fire Fighters Burn Institute (SAUS)
PFFC .... Parallel-Flow Film Cooling
PFFC .... Peoples Financial Corp. [*NASDAQ symbol*] (SAG)
PFFC .... Philadelphia Flyers Fan Club (EA)
PFFD .... Proximal Femoral Focal Deficiency [*Orthopedics*] (DAVI)
PFFF .... Polypropylene Fibrillated Film Fiber (or Fibre) (SAUS)
PFF Inc ...... Police-FBI Fencing, Incognito [*Phony fencing ring operated by Washington, DC, law enforcement agents during 1976 to identify and arrest area thieves*]
PFFS .... Pfaff and Son Truckmen [*Common carrier symbol*]
PFFT .... Parallel Fast Fourier Transform (SAUS)
PFFX .... Profiling Fixture
PFG .... Pacific Fruit Growers Express [*Federal Railroad Administration identification code*]
PFG .... Pacific Rim Mining Corp. [*Vancouver Stock Exchange symbol*]
PFG .... Paeoniflorigenone [*Biochemistry*]
PFG .... Paper Flow Group [*Nuclear Regulatory Commission*] (GFGA)
PFG .... Peak Flow Gauge [*Medicine*] (AAMN)
PFG .... PennCorp Financial Group [*NYSE symbol*] (SPSG)
PFG .... Pfennig [*Penny*] [*Monetary unit*] [*German*]
PFG .... Piping and Filter Gallery [*Nuclear energy*] (NRCH)
PFG .... Preferring [*Telegraphy*] (PCTE)
PFG .... Primary Frequency Generator
PFG .... Principal Financial Group (SAUS)
PFG .... Programmable Frequency Generator (SAUS)
PFG .... Pulsed-Field Gel Electrophoresis (DMAA)
PFG .... Pulsed Field Gradient [*Electroanalytical chemistry*]
PFG .... Purple Flower Gang (EA)
PFGC .... Parameters from Group Contribution [*Equation of state*]
PFGC .... Performance Food Group [*NASDAQ symbol*] (SAG)
PFGE .... Pulsed Field Gel Electrophoresis
PFGE .... Pulsed-Field Gel Electrophresis (HGEN)
PFGE .... Pulsed Field Gradient Gel Electrophoresis
PFGI .... Provident Financial Group [*NASDAQ symbol*] [*Formerly, Provident Bancorp.*] (SG)
PfGI .... TIGR [*The Institute of Genomic Research*] Plasmodium falciparum Gene Index [*Database*] (GDD)
PFGM .... Guided Missile Patrol Escort [*Ship symbol*] (NATG)
PFGO .... Pink-Footed Goose [*North American bird banding code*] (BIBA)
PFGPr .... PennCorp Finl $3.375 Pfd [*NYSE symbol*] (TTSB)
PFGX .... Pacific Fruit Growers Express
PFH .... Hudson, NY [*Location identifier*] [*FAA*] (FAAL)
PFH .... Pafco Financial Holdings Ltd. [*Toronto Stock Exchange symbol*]
PFH .... Perifornical Hypothalamus (DB)
PFH .... Pressurized Fluidized-Bed Hydroretorting [*Chemical engineering*]
PFHA .... Paso Fino Horse Association (EA)
PFHE .... Pre-Fragmented High Explosive (SAUS)
PFHL .... Priority Freight Lines [*Common carrier symbol*]
PFHM .... Protein-Free Hybridoma Medium
PFHS .... Precipitation from Homogeneous Solution [*Catalyst preparation process*]
PFI .... Pacific Forest Industries (EA)
PFI .... Pack File Indexer (NITA)
PFI .... People First International (EA)
PFI .... Pet Food Institute (EA)
PFI .... Photo Finishing Institute [*Defunct*] (EA)
PFI .... Photon Flow Integrating (IAA)
PFI .... Photon Flux Integration (IAA)
PFI .... Physical Fault Insertion (SAUS)
PFI .... Physical Fitness Index
PFI .... Picture and Frame Institute [*Defunct*] (EA)
PFI .... Pie Filling Institute [*Defunct*] (EA)
PFI .... Pipe Fabrication Institute (EA)
PFI .... Police Foundation Institute (NADA)
PFI .... Port Fuel Injector [*Automotive engines*]
PFI .... Position Finding Instrument (DS)
PFI .... Potlatch Forest [*Federal Railroad Administration identification code*]
PFI .... Power Factor Indicator (IAA)
PFI .... Power Failure Indicator [*NASA*] (KSC)
PFI .... Prison Fellowship International (EA)
PFI .... Private Finance Initiative [*British*]
PFI .... Private Financing of Public Investment
PFI .... Product Features Index (SAUS)
PFIA .... Police and Firemen's Insurance Association (EA)
PFIA .... Prevention of Fraud Investments Act [*British*]
PFIAB .... President's Foreign Intelligence Advisory Board (AFM)
PFI & R ...... Part Fill In and Ram [*Construction*]
PFIB .... Pentafluoroiodosylbenzene [*Organic chemistry*]
PFIB .... Perfluoroisobutene [*Organic chemistry*]
PFIB .... Perfluoroisobutylene [*Organic chemistry*] (MAE)
PFIC .... Passive Foreign Investment Company [*IRS*]
PFIC .... Processed Food Industry Council [*Australia*]
PFID .... Perturbed Free Induction Decay
PFIEP .... Perfluorinated Ion-Exchange Polymer [*Organic chemistry*]
PFIM .... Pure Fluid Impact Modulator
PfIMF .... Preferred Income Management Fund, Inc. [*Associated Press*] (SAG)
PFI Mode ... Photon-Flow Integration Mode (SAUS)
PFIN .... P & F Industries, Inc. [*NASDAQ symbol*] (NQ)
PFINA .... P&F Indus'A' [*NASDAQ symbol*] (TTSB)
PFINP .... P & F Ind $1 Pfd [*NASDAQ symbol*] (TTSB)
PFIR .... People for Internet Responsibility (SAUS)
PFIRS .... Paperless Fax Image Reporting System (SAUS)
PFIS .... Personnel Feedback Information System (SAUS)
PFIS .... Property Fabric Information System (SAUS)
PFIU .... Plot File Import Utility [*IBM Corp.*]
PFIX .... Power Failure Interrupt (SAUS)
Pfizer .... Pfizer, Inc. [*Associated Press*] (SAG)
PFJ .... Patreksfjordur [*Iceland*] [*Airport symbol*] (OAG)
PFJ .... Polar Front Jet Stream (ADA)
PFJR .... Patellofemoral Joint Reaction [*Physiology*]
PFJS .... Patellofemoral Joint Syndrome [*Medicine*] (EDAA)
PFK .... Pay for Knowledge (TIMI)
PFK .... Payload Function Key [*NASA*] (MCD)
PFK .... Perfluorokerosene [*Heat transfer agent*]
PFK .... Perfunctory [*Telegraphy*] (PCTE)
PFK .... Phosphofructokinase [*An enzyme*]
PFK .... Plastic Fluted Knob (SAUS)
PFK .... Program Function Keyboard
PFK .... Programmed Function Key (NITA)
PFK .... Programmed Function Keyboard [*Computer science*]
PF KEY ...... Program Function Key [*Computer science*] (ITCA)
PFKM .... Phosphofructokinase, Muscle Type [*Medicine*] (DMAA)
PFKY .... People First Corp. [*NASDAQ symbol*] (SAG)
PFKY .... Peoples First [*NASDAQ symbol*] (TTSB)
PFKY .... Peoples First Corp. [*NASDAQ symbol*]
PFKY .... Perfunctorily [*Telegraphy*] (PCTE)
PFL .... Fort Sill, OK [*Location identifier*] [*FAA*] (FAAL)
PFL .... Pacific Cassiar Ltd. [*Toronto Stock Exchange symbol*]
PFL .... Pacific Freight Lines (SAUS)
PFL .... Party of the Liberal Front (Brazil) [*Political party*] (PSAP)
PFL .... Pennsylvania Folk Life (SAUS)
PFL .... People for Life (EA)
PFL .... Pharmacists for Life (EA)
PFL .... Pioneer Football League (PSS)
PFL .... Pol-Fly [*Poland*] [*ICAO designator*] (FAAC)
PFL .... Pounds per Lineal Foot [*Technical drawings*]
PFL .... Pre-Fade Listen (SAUS)
PFL .... Preferable [*Telegraphy*] (PCTE)
PFL .... Pressed-For-Life (SAUS)
PFL .... Primary Freon Loop (NASA)
PFL .... Propulsion Field Laboratory
PFL .... Public Facility Loans
PFLA .... Popular Front for the Liberation of Ahvaz [*Iran*]
P-FLAG ...... Federation of Parents and Friends of Lesbians and Gays (EA)
PFLAG .... Parents, Families, and Friends of Lesbians and Gays [*An association*] (EA)
PFLF .... People, Food and Land Foundation (EA)
PFLI .... Pharmacists for Life International (EA)
PFLL .... Phase and Frequency Locked Loop [*Telecommunications*] (IAA)
P Flo .... Pandectae Florentinae [*A publication*] (DSA)
PFLO .... Popular Front for the Liberation of Oman [*Political party*] (PD)
PFLOAG ..... Popular Front for the Liberation of Oman and the Arabian Gulf [*Political party*] (PD)
PFLOAG ..... Popular Front for the Liberation of the Occupied Arabian Gulf
PFLOLS ...... Portable Fresnel-Lens Optical-Landing System (NG)
P Florent ... Pandectae Florentinae [*A publication*] (DSA)
PFLP .... People's Front for the Liberation of Palestine (CARL)
PFLP .... Popular Front for the Liberation of Palestine [*Political party*] (PD)
PFLP-GC ... Popular Front for the Liberation of Palestine - General Command [*Political party*] (PD)
PFLP-SC ... Popular Front for the Liberation of Palestine-Special Command (SAUS)
PFLT .... Paint Filter Liquids Test [*Environmental science*] (FFDE)
P/FLT .... Pattern Flight [*Also, P/F*] (MUGU)
PFLT .... People's Front of the Liberation Tigers [*Sri Lanka*] [*Political party*] (EY)
PFLT .... Photographic Flight (SAUS)
PFLTS .... Parquet Floor Layers' Trade Society [*A union*] [*British*]
PFLU .... Pacific Forum Line [*Intermodal shipping container symbol*] (TVRC)
PFLV .... Pressure Fed Launch Vehicle [*NASA*] (KSC)
PFLY .... Polifly Financial Corp. [*NASDAQ symbol*] (COMM)
PFLY .... Preferably [*Telegraphy*] (PCTE)
PFM .... Little Franciscan Sisters of Mary [*Roman Catholic religious order*]
PFM .... Pacific Minesearch Ltd. [*Vancouver Stock Exchange symbol*]
PFM .... Package Feasibility Model (SAUS)
PFM .... Patient Flow Model (SAUS)

PFM .... Patriots of Fort McHenry (EA)
PFM .... Peak Flow Meter [*Medicine*] (AAMN)
PFM .... Perform [*Telegraphy*] (PCTE)
PFM .... Performance Monitor (SAUS)
PFM .... Personal Financial Manager (GART)
PFM .... Personnel File Management (TIMI)
PFM .... Physiological Flow Model [*For simulating medical conditions*]
PFM .... Pitch Follow-Up Motor
PFM .... Plan for Maintenance [*Navy*]
PFM .... Planning Factors Management (MCD)
PFM .... Platform (NASA)
PFM .... Political Freedom Movement [*British*]
PFM .... Pont Flottant Motorise (SAUS)
PFM .... Porcelain Fused to Metal [*Dentistry*]
PFM .... Porsche Flug Motor [*Automotive engineering*]
PFM .... Portable Flow Meter [*Mechanical engineering*]
PFM .... Potato Futures Market [*Finance*]
PFM .... Poultry Feather Meal [*Fisheries*]
PFM .... Power Factor Meter
PFM .... Precise Frequency Measurement (SEWL)
PFM .... Precision Frequency Multivider (KSC)
PFM .... Predictor Frame Memory
PFM .... Preferred Income Management Fund [*NYSE symbol*] (SPSG)
PFM .... Pre-Finished Metal (SAUS)
PFM .... Preliminary Flight Motor (MCD)
PFM .... Pressure Flow Meter
PFM .... Printer Font Metrics [*Computer science*] (CDE)
PFM .... Prison Fellowship Ministries (EA)
PFM .... Process Facility Modification (ABAC)
PFM .... Program Financial Management (POLM)
PFM .... Proto Flight Model (ACAE)
PFM .... Proto-Flight Model (SAUS)
PFM .... Pulse-Forming Machine
PFM .... Pulse-Frequency Modulation [*RADAR*] [*Telecommunications*]
PFM .... Pure Fantastic Magic (SAUS)
P/FM .... Pylon/Fin Movement
PFM .... University of Pittsburgh, Falk Library - Health Professions, Pittsburgh, PA [*OCLC symbol*] (OCLC)
PFMA .... Pennsylvania Food Merchants Association (EARSL)
PFMA .... Pet Food Manufacturers Association [*British*] (DBA)
PFMA .... Phenolic Foam Manufacturers Association [*British*] (DBA)
PFMA .... Pipe Fittings Manufacturers Association [*Later, APFA*] (EA)
PFMA .... Plumbing Fixture Manufacturers Association [*Defunct*] (EA)
PFMA .... Pressed Felt Manufacturers' Association [*British*] (BI)
PFMAA ...... Pet Food Manufacturers' Association of Australia
PFMC .... Pacific Fishery Management Council (EA)
PFMC .... Perfection Materials Company [*Common carrier symbol*]
PFMC .... Preferred Management Corp. (MHID)
PFMEA ...... Process for Failure Mode and Effects Analysis
PFMGO ...... Pre-Flight Message-Generating Officer (SAUS)
PFMO .... Planning Factors Management Office
PFMP .... Personal Finance Management Program (SAUS)
PFMPG ...... Pacific Fleet Mobile Photographic Group (DNAB)
PFMR .... Pasadena Foundation for Medical Research [*California*]
PFMR .... Plug-Flow Membrane Reactor [*Chemical engineering*]
PFMR .... Project Funds Management Record (MCD)
PFMS .... Plant Facilities Management System (SAUS)
PFN .... Page Frame Number (TIMI)
PFN .... Panama City [*Florida*] [*Airport symbol*] (OAG)
PFN .... Pantyffynnon [*British depot code*]
PFN .... Partially Functional Neutrophil (DMAA)
PFN .... Parti des Forces Nouvelles [*New Forces Party*] [*France*] [*Political party*] (PPW)
PFN .... Passamaquoddy Ferry & Navigation Co. [*AAR code*]
PFN .... Perfection [*Telegraphy*] (PCTE)
PFN .... Permanent File Name
PFN .... Peroxyformyl Nitrate (SAUS)
PFN .... Plasma Fibronectin [*Biochemistry*]
PFN .... PMC Corp. [*Toronto Stock Exchange symbol*]
PFN .... Prefinished [*Technical drawings*]
PFN .... Prime Fanout Node (SAUS)
PFN .... Profilin (DMAA)
PFN .... Pulse-Forming Network
PFNA .... Pentecostal Fellowship of North America (EA)
PFNA .... Pulsed Fast Neutron Analysis [*for detection of explosives*] (PS)
PFNC .... Progress Financial Corp. [*Plymouth Meeting, PA*] [*NASDAQ symbol*] (NQ)
PFNC .... Progress Finl [*NASDAQ symbol*] (TTSB)
PFNM .... Petrified Forest National Monument (SAUS)
PFNP .... Partido Federalista Nacionalista Popular [*Panama*] [*Political party*] (EY)
PFNP .... Petrified Forest National Park (SAUS)
PFNS .... Penseco Financial Services Corp. [*OTCBB symbol*]
PFNS .... Position Fixing Navigation System (AABC)
PFNT .... Police Force of the Northern Territory [*Australia*]
PFNT .... Preferred Networks [*NASDAQ symbol*] (TTSB)
PFNTU .... Pathfinder Navigation Training Unit [*Military*]
PFO .... Pacific Food Outlook
PFO .... Paphos [*Cyprus*] [*Airport symbol*] (OAG)
PFO .... Partially Filled Out [*Questionnaire*]
PFO .... Partly Filled Out [*Questionnaire*]
PFO .... Patent Foramen Ovale [*Cardiology*]
PFO .... Personal Freedom Outreach (EA)
PFO .... Physical Fitness Officer [*British military*] (DMA)
PFO .... Pitch Follow-Up Operation
PFO .... Pomona Public Library, Pomona, CA [*OCLC symbol*] (OCLC)
PFO .... Postal Finance Officer [*Army*]
PFO .... Preferred Income Opportunity Fund [*NYSE symbol*] (SAG)
PFO .... Procurement Field Office
PFO .... Procurement Field Officer (SAUS)
PFO .... Pyrolysis Fuel Oil [*Petroleum refining*]
PFO .... Pyruvate: Ferredoxin Oxidoreductase [*An enzyme*]
PFO .... Spofford, TX [*Location identifier*] [*FAA*] (FAAL)
PFOA .... Perfluorooctanoic Acid [*Organic chemistry*]
PFOB .... Patent Foramen Ovale [*Medicine*] (RAWO)
PFOB .... Perfluorocytylbromide (DMAA)
PFOBA .... Paso Fino Owners and Breeders Association [*Later, PFHA*] (EA)
PFOC .... Prairie Fire Organizing Committee (SAUS)
PFOD .... Presumed Finding of Death [*DoD*]
PFOE .... Percentage of Frames recovered with Zero Error (SAUS)
PFol .... Ridley Township Public Library, Folsom, PA [*Library symbol*] [*Library of Congress*] (LCLS)
PFOLA .... Prescription Foot Orthotic Laboratory Association (EA)
PFOM .... Preformed Fragmentation OTO Munition (SAUS)
PFOO .... Planet411.com Corp. [*NASDAQ symbol*] (QUAN)
PFORM ...... Print Format (SAUS)
PFORMS .... Person Forms [*National Highway Traffic Safety Administration Fatal Accident Recording System code*]
PFOS .... Perfluorooctane Sulfonate
PFouad ...... Les Papyrus Fouad I [*A publication*] (OCD)
P-FOX .... Parents and Friends of Ex-Gays [*Association*] (EA)
PFP .... Partnership for Peace [*An organization of non-member countries which have established military cooperation with NATO*] (ECON)
PFP .... Partnership for Productivity International (EA)
PFP .... Pattern Factoring Program (TIMI)
PFP .... Peace and Freedom Party (EA)
PFP .... Pensions for Professionals, Inc.
PFP .... Pentafluoropropionate [*or Pentafluoropropionyl*] [*Organic chemistry*]
PFP .... Performic Acid Phosphotungsite (SAUS)
PFP .... Peripheral Facial-Paralysis [*Medicine*] (MELL)
PFP .... Personal Financial Planning (ADA)
PFP .... Pet-Facilitated Psychotherapy [*Psychiatry*]
PFP .... Plastic Faced Plaster (SAUS)
PFP .... Platelet-Free Plasma [*Hematology*]
PFP .... Pleiades Foundation for Peace [*Later, PFPSE*] (EA)
PFP .... Plutonium Finishing Plant
PFP .... Policy-Framework Paper (ECON)
PFP .... Popular Front Party [*Ghana*] [*Political party*] (PPW)
PFP .... Pore Forming Protein [*Biochemistry*]
PFP .... Postage Forward Parcels [*Shipping*]
PFP .... Post Flight Processor
PFP .... Prefetch Processor (SAUS)
PFP .... Premier Farnell PLC [*NYSE symbol*] (SAG)
PFP .... Premier Farnell PLC ADS [*NYSE symbol*] (TTSB)
PFP .... Primary Failed Part (DNAB)
PFP .... Probability of Failure, Performance [*NASA*] (SAA)
PFP .... Products for Power [*Automotive components manufacturer*]
PFP .... Program File Processor
PFP .... Program Financial Plan (NASA)
PFP .... Program Forecast Period [*Military*] (AFIT)
PFP .... Programmable Function Panel (NASA)
PFP .... Progressiewe Federale Party [*Progressive Federal Party*] [*South Africa*] [*Political party*] (PPW)
PFP .... Progressive Federal Party (SAUS)
PFP .... Proton Flare Project (PDAA)
PFP .... Proving for Production (MCD)
PFP .... Proximity Fuze Programmer (SAUS)
PFP .... Publishers for Peace [*An association*]
PFPA .... Pennsylvania Food Processors Association (EARSL)
PFPA .... Pentafluoropropionic Anhydride [*Organic chemistry*]
PFPA .... Pitch Fiber Pipe Association (SAUS)
PFPA .... Pro-Family Press Association [*Defunct*] (EA)
PFPC .... Pall Filtered Packed Cells [*Medicine*] (EDAA)
PFPC .... Passenger Form and Procedures Committee [*IATA*] (DS)
PFPDBRD ... Paget Foundation for Paget's Disease of Bone and Related Disorders [*Formerly, Paget's Disease Foundation (PDF)*] (PAZ)
PFPE .... Perfluorinated Polyether [*Organic chemistry*]
PFPE .... Perfluoropolyether (SAUS)
PFPE .... Polyfluorinated Polyether [*Lubricants, polymers*]
PFP EIS ..... Plutonium Finishing Plant Environmental Impact Statement
PFPH .... Pentafluorophenylhydrazine [*Organic chemistry*]
PFPI .... Partnership for Productivity International (EA)
PFPI .... Pentafluoropropionyl Imidazole [*Organic chemistry*]
PFPM .... Production Flight Procedures Manual (MCD)
PFPPr .... Premier Farnell $1.35 Pref ADS [*NYSE symbol*] (TTSB)
PFP/PTP .... Pensions for Professionals/Pensions for Technical Professionals (SAUS)
PFPPX .... Pre-Fragmented Programmable Proximity Fuzed (SAUS)
PFPS .... Patellofemoral Pain Syndrome [*Medicine*] (DMAA)
PFPS .... Potential for Foster Parenthood Scale [*Psychology*]
PFPS .... Progressive French Polishers' Society [*A union*] [*British*]
PFPSE .... Pleiades Foundation for Peace and Space Education (EA)
PFPU .... Processor Frame Power Unit (SAUS)
PFPUT .... Pension Fund Property Unit Trust [*British*]
PFPX .... Pre-Fragmented Proximity Fuzed (SAUS)
PFQ .... Personality Factor Questionnaire (MAE)
PFQ .... Preflight Qualification
PFQT .... Preliminary Flight Qualification Test (SAUS)

PFr.......... Franklin Public Library, Franklin, PA [*Library symbol*] [*Library of Congress*] (LCLS)
PFR.......... Parotid Flow Rate [*otorhinolaryngology*] (DAVI)
PFR.......... Part Failure Rate
PFR.......... Patriot Field Report [*Army*]
PFR.......... Peak Filling Rate (RAWO)
PFR.......... Peak Flow Rate [*or Reading*] [*Medicine*]
PFR.......... Peak Flow Reading (SAUS)
PFR.......... Percentage of Frames Recovered (SAUS)
PFR.......... Perforator (DEN)
PFR.......... Pericardial Friction Rub [*Medicine*] (MEDA)
PFR.......... Perkins Family Restaurants Ltd [*NYSE symbol*] (SPSG)
PFR.......... Permanent Factory Repairable (MCD)
PFR.......... Permanent Fix Request (TIMI)
PFR.......... Permitted Flying Route [*Aviation*] (DA)
PFR.......... Persistent Fat Retention [*Syndrome*]
PFR.......... Personal Financial Record [*Army*] (AABC)
PFR.......... Pfarrer [*Pastor*] [*German*] (EY)
PFR.......... Phase Failure Relays [*Environmental science*] (COE)
PFR.......... Photoflash Relay
PFR.......... Pike Fry Rhabdovirus
PFR.......... Planning for Results [*A publication*]
PFR.......... Plug-Flow Reactor [*Engineering*]
PFR.......... Plutonium-fueled Fast Reactor (SAUS)
PFR.......... Polarized Field Frequency Relay (IAA)
PFR.......... Polarized Frequency Relay
PFR.......... Portable Font Resource (SAUS)
PFR.......... Portable Foot Restraint (NASA)
PFR.......... Port Francqui [*Zaire*] [*Airport symbol*] (AD)
PFR.......... Post-Fielding Review [*DoD*]
PFR.......... Power Fail Recovery System [*Computer science*] (MDG)
PFR.......... Power Fail/Restart
PFR.......... Power Failure Release
PFR.......... Precision Fathometer Recorder [*Raytheon Co.*]
PFR.......... Preferred Resources, Inc. [*Vancouver Stock Exchange symbol*]
PFR.......... Preflight Review [*NASA*] (KSC)
PFR.......... Preheating, Falling-Film, Rising-Film [*Sections of a concentrator*] [*Chemical engineering*]
PFR.......... Preliminary Flight Rating [*Air Force*]
PFR.......... Problem/Failure Report
PFR.......... Procedure for Rework (SAUS)
PFR.......... Program Financial Review (ACAE)
PFR.......... Programmable Film Reader (SAUS)
PFR.......... Programmed Film Reader [*System*]
pfr.......... Proofreader [*MARC relator code*] [*Library of Congress*] (LCCP)
PFR.......... Prototype Fast Reactor
PFR.......... Proximal Fractional Reabsorption [*Medicine*] (EDAA)
PFR.......... Pulmonary Blood Flow Redistribution [*Medicine*]
PFR.......... Pulmonary Flow Rate [*Medicine*] (DAVI)
PFR.......... Pulsed Fast Reactor (SAUS)
PFR.......... Pulse Frequency (MDG)
PFR.......... Pulse Repetition Frequency (POLM)
PFR.......... Punch Feed Read (CMD)
PFRA........ Percent of Females Reproductively Active [*Ecology*]
PFRA........ Prairie Farm Rehabilitation Act (SAUS)
PFRA........ Prairie Farm Rehabilitation Administration [*Canada*]
PFRA........ Prairie Farm Rehabilitation Association (SAUS)
PFRA........ Problem-Focused Research Applications [*of ASRA*] [*National Science Foundation*]
PFRA........ Professional Football Referees Association (EA)
PFRA........ Professional Football Researchers Association (EA)
PFRB........ Pacific Fire Rating Bureau (SAUS)
PFRB........ Publications and Films Review Board [*Western Australia*]
PFRC........ Pacific Forest Research Centre [*Canada*] (ARC)
PFRC........ Plasma-free Red Cells [*Medicine*] (EDAA)
PFRC........ Predicted Functional Residual Capacity [*Medicine*] (EDAA)
PFRD........ Preferred Stock [*Investment term*]
PFredY...... Joseph A. Yablonski Memorial Clinic, Fredericktown, PA [*Library symbol*] [*Library of Congress*] (LCLS)
PFR Film... Preheat Falling-Rising Film (SAUS)
PFRM........ John Pfrommer [*Common carrier symbol*]
PFRMG...... Performing (ROG)
PFRP........ Pelagic Fisheries Research Program (RCD)
PFRP........ Phenolic Fiber Reinforced Plastic
PFRS........ Portable Field Recording System [*NASA*] (KSC)
PFRS........ Portable Field Reflectance Spectrometer (SAUS)
PFRT........ Performance Flight Rating Test (SAUS)
PFRT........ Pre-Flight Rating Test (SAUS)
PFRT........ Preliminary Field Rating Test (SAUS)
PFRT........ Preliminary Flight Rated Test
PFRT........ Preliminary Flight Rating Test
PFRT........ Preliminary Flight Readiness Test [*NASA*] (KSC)
PFRX........ Preflight Relmat (SAUS)
PFRY........ Polaris Freight Systems [*Common carrier symbol*]
PFS.......... Page Format Selection (SAUS)
PFS.......... Panview Fiberscope [*Medicine*] (EDAA)
PFS.......... Parallel Enterprise Server [*IBM*] (GART)
PFS.......... Parallel Filter System
PFS.......... Particles and Fields Subsatellite [*NASA*]
PFS.......... Path Fault Secure (MHDI)
PFS.......... Patient Financial System (GART)
PFS.......... Pay for Skills [*Human resources*] (WYGK)
PFS.......... Payload Feasibility Study (ACAE)
PFS.......... Percent Full Scale (KSC)
PFS.......... Perfect Forward Secrecy [*Computer science*] (DINT)
PFS.......... Performance Funding System [*Department of Housing and Urban Development*] (GFGA)
PFS.......... Periodic Feature Selection (SAUS)
PFS.......... Peripheral Fixed Shim [*Nuclear energy*] (NRCH)
PFS.......... Personal and Family Survival [*Civil Defense*]
PFS.......... Personal Filing System [*Data-base program*] [*Software Publishing Corp.*]
PFS.......... Personal Financial Specialist
PFS.......... Photofragment Spectroscopy
PFS.......... Physical File System (IAA)
PFS.......... Pioneer Financial Svcs [*NYSE symbol*] (TTSB)
PFS.......... Pitch Follow-Up System
PFS.......... Pittsburgh, PA [*Location identifier*] [*FAA*] (FAAL)
PFS.......... Planned Flying and Servicing (SAUS)
PFS.......... Plasterers' Friendly Society [*A union*] [*British*]
PFS.......... Platform Functional Specification [*Computer science*]
PFS.......... Porous Friction Surface [*Airfield pavement*]
PFS.......... Portable File System (SAUS)
PFS.......... Positive Fuel Stop
PFS.......... Power Fuel Steamship (SAUS)
PFS.......... Prairie Flying Service (1976) Ltd. [*Canada*] [*ICAO designator*] (FAAC)
PFS.......... Precision Frequency Source
PFS.......... Pre-Feasability Study (SAUS)
PFS.......... Preflight School [*Military*]
PFS.......... Press Fit Socket
PFS.......... Primary Fibromyalgia Syndrome [*Medicine*] (DMAA)
PFS.......... Primary Flight System (NASA)
PFS.......... Primary Flying Squadron (SAUS)
PFS.......... Primary Frequency Supply [*Telecommunications*] (TEL)
PFS.......... Prison Fellowship Scotland [*United Kingdom*] (EAIO)
PFS.......... Probability of Failure, Stress [*NASA*] (SAA)
PFS.......... Process-Flow Scheduling [*Computer science*] (GART)
PFS.......... Professional Software (SAUS)
PFS.......... Pro-Forma Statement (MHDI)
PFS.......... Programmable Frequency Standard
PFS.......... Progression Free Survival [*Medicine*]
PFS.......... Propellant Feed System
PFS.......... Propellant Field System
PFS.......... Pulmonary Function Score [*Physiology*]
PFS.......... Pure Fluid System
PFSA........ Pilot to Forecaster Service Available (SAUS)
PFSB........ PennFed Financial Services, Inc. [*NASDAQ symbol*] (SAG)
PFSB........ PennFed Financial Svcs [*NASDAQ symbol*] (TTSB)
PFSD........ Pacific Sands, Inc. [*NASDAQ symbol*] (QUAN)
PFSD........ Portable Fluoroscopic Screening Device [*Police and security equipment*]
PFSDR...... Parts Failure Service Difficulties Report (ACAE)
PFSh......... Partia Fashismit e Shqiperise [*Fascist Party of Albania*] [*Political party*] (PPE)
PFSH........ Pink-Footed Shearwater [*North American bird banding code*] (BIBA)
PFSH........ Porcine Follicle Stimulating Hormone [*Endocrinology*]
PFSI......... PFSB Bancorp, Inc. [*NASDAQ symbol*] (QUAN)
PFSK........ Permutation Frequency-Shift Keying (SAUS)
PFSL......... Pocahontas Bancorporation [*NASDAQ symbol*]
PFSL......... Pocahontas Federal Savings & Loan Association [*NASDAQ symbol*] (SAG)
PFSL......... Pocahontas Fed Svg& L A Ark [*NASDAQ symbol*] (TTSB)
PFSL......... Professional [*Telegraphy*] (PCTE)
PFSL......... Prudential Financial Services Corp. [*NASDAQ symbol*] (COMM)
PFSN........ Profession [*Telegraphy*] (PCTE)
PFSO........ Postal Finance and Supply Office (AFM)
PFSP........ Polyfactorial Study of Personality [*Psychology*] (AEBS)
PFS/PRS.... Patent Family Service/Patent Register Service [*Database*] [*International Patent Documentation Center*] [*Information service or system*] (CRD)
PFSR........ Program Financial Status Report (AAG)
PFSS........ Particles and Fields Subsatellite [*Telecommunications*] (OA)
PFSS........ Patellofemoral Stress Syndrome [*Medicine*]
PFSS........ Pesticide Farmworker Safety Staff [*Office of Pesticides and Toxic Substances*] (COE)
PFST......... Pacific States Truck Brokerage [*Common carrier symbol*]
pfst.......... pianofortist (SAUS)
P-F Study... Picture-Frustration Study (SAUS)
PFSU........ Phiniquia International Shipping [*Intermodal shipping container symbol*] (TVRC)
PFSX........ Productos Forestales [*Private rail car owner code*]
PFT.......... Pacific Asia Tech [*Vancouver Stock Exchange symbol*]
PFT.......... Pacific Fisheries Technologists [*An association*]
PFT.......... Page Frame Table (BUR)
PFT.......... Pancreatic Function Test [*Medicine*]
PFT.......... Paper, Flat Tape
PFT.......... Parachute Familiarization Training (SAUS)
PFT.......... Parafascicular Thalamotomy [*Medicine*]
PFT.......... Parallel Fourier Transform (MCD)
PFT.......... People For Trees (SAUS)
PFT.......... Permanent Full-Time (GFGA)
PFT.......... Pet-Facilitated Therapy [*Psychiatry*]
PFT.......... Phenylalanine mustard [*Melphalan*], Fluorouracil, Tamoxifen [*Antineoplastic drug regimen*]
PFT.......... Physical Fitness Test
PFT.......... Pittsburgh, Fort Wayne & Chicago Railway Co. (IIA)
PFT.......... Plant Functional Type (QUAC)
PFT.......... Plastic Fuel Tank
PFT.......... Platelet-Fibrin-Thrombi [*Medicine*] (MELL)

PFT .... Portable Flame Thrower [*Army*]
PFT .... Positive Flight Termination (MUGU)
PFT .... Posterior Fossa Tumor [*Anatomy*] (MAE)
PFT .... Prefabricate Foxhole Twin (SAUS)
PFT .... Preflight Team [*Air Force*] (AFM)
PFT .... Preflight Tool (MCD)
PFT .... Prime Factor Transform (IAA)
PFT .... Prism Fiber-reading Tube (SAUS)
PFT .... Professional Football Trainers (EA)
PFT .... Program Flying Training [*Air Force*] (AFM)
PFT .... Projective Field Theory
PFT .... Pulmonary Function Test [*Medicine*]
PFT .... Pulse Fourier Transform
PFTA .... Payload Flight Test Article [*NASA*] (MCD)
PFTA .... Post-Fielding Training Analysis
pft acct .... pianoforte accompaniment (SAUS)
PFTB .... Preflight Test Bus (MCD)
PFTB .... Professional Transportation Services [*Common carrier symbol*]
PFTBA .... Perfluorotributylamine (SAUS)
PFTBE .... Progressive Form of Tick-Borne Encephalitis [*Medicine*] (DMAA)
PFTC .... Pestalozzi-Froebel Teachers College [*Illinois*]
PFTC .... Plesetsk Flight Test Centre (SAUS)
PFTD .... Perfected [*Telegraphy*] (PCTE)
PFTD .... Performance Transport [*Common carrier symbol*]
PFTE .... Permanent Full-Time Equivalent (GFGA)
pfte .... Pianoforte (WDAA)
PFTE .... Pianoforte [*Soft, then Loud*] [*Music*]
PFTE .... Polytetrafluoroethylene [*Teflon*]
PFTE .... Portable Field Trainer/Evaluator (MCD)
PFTEA .... Post-Fielding Training Effectiveness Analysis
PFTG .... Perfecting [*Telegraphy*] (PCTE)
PFTM .... Preliminary Flight Test Memo
PFTQ .... Partnering for Total Quality (AAEL)
PFTR .... Preliminary Flight Test Report
PFTs .... Perfluorocarbon Tracers (SAUS)
PFTS .... Permanent Field Training Site
PFTS .... Primary Flying Training School (SAUS)
PFTS .... Profit Systems, Inc. [*NASDAQ symbol*] (COMM)
PFTs .... Pulmonary Function Tests (SAUS)
PFU .... Passive Filtration Unit
PFU .... Physical Fitness Uniform [*Army*] (INF)
PFU .... Plan for Use (DNAB)
PFU .... Plaque-Forming Unit [*Immunochemistry*]
PFU .... Please Follow Up
PFU .... Pock-Forming Unit
PFU .... Preparation for Use
PFU .... Prepared for Use (SAUS)
PFU .... Profuse [*Telegraphy*] (PCTE)
PFUA .... Pitch Follow-Up Amplifier
PFUEI .... Prime Focus Universal Extragalactic Instrument [*Astronomy*]
P Fuel .... Patent Fuel (SAUS)
PFUM .... Pitch Follow-Up Motor
PFUN .... Profusion [*Telegraphy*] (PCTE)
PFUND .... Program for Understanding Neurological Diseases
PFUO .... Pitch Follow-Up Operation
PFUO .... Prolonged Fever of Unknown Origin [*Medicine*] (DMAA)
PFUS .... Pitch Follow-Up System
PFUY .... Profusely [*Telegraphy*] (PCTE)
PFV .... Peak Flow Velocity [*Cardiology*]
PFV .... Peak Forward Voltage (IAA)
PFV .... Pestalozzi-Froebel-Verband [*Pestalozzi-Froebel Association*]
PFV .... Philippine Forces, Vietnam
PFV .... Physiological Full Value
PFV .... Probability of Failure, Vehicle [*NASA*] (SAA)
PFV .... Provident Finl Grp [*Stock exchange symbol*]
PFVEA .... Professional Film and Video Equipment Association (EA)
PFVI .... Preferred Voice, Inc. [*NASDAQ symbol*] (QUAN)
PFW .... pHisoHex Face Wash [*Medicine*] (EDAA)
PFW .... Power, Fulcrum, Weight
PFW .... Predicted Fire Weapon
PFW .... Progressive Free Wave
PFW .... Punch Feed Write (SAUS)
PFWA .... Pet Food Warehouse [*NASDAQ symbol*] (SAG)
PFWA .... Professional Football Writers of America (EA)
PFwB .... Budd Co., Fort Washington, PA [*Library symbol*] [*Library of Congress*] (LCLS)
PFWB .... Pall Filtered Whole Blood [*Medicine*] (EDAA)
PFWOAD .... Place from Which Ordered to Active Duty [*Military*]
PFwR .... William H. Rorer, Inc., Fort Washington, PA [*Library symbol*] [*Library of Congress*] (LCLS)
PFWS .... Predicted Fire Weapon System [*Army*]
PFWT .... Pain-Free Walking Time (RAWO)
PFWY .... Pioneer Freightways [*Common carrier symbol*]
PFX .... Pacific Fruit Express (SAUS)
PFX .... Pilgrim American Capital [*NYSE symbol*]
PFX .... Prefix (ROG)
PFX .... Proflex Ltd. [*Vancouver Stock Exchange symbol*]
PFXP .... Plan Failure explanation Pattern (SAUS)
PFY .... Perfectly [*Telegraphy*] (PCTE)
PFY .... Prior Fiscal Year (AFIT)
PFYA .... Predicted First-Year Average [*Law school*]
PFZ .... Polar Front Zone [*Marine science*] (MSC)
PFZ .... Potassium Hexafluorozirconate [*Inorganic chemistry*]
PFZ .... Precipitate-Free Zone (MCD)
PF-ZAPU .... Patriotic Front - Zimbabwe African People's Union [*Political party*] (PD)
PG .... Florida Commuter [*ICAO designator*] (AD)
PG .... Glycerate-3-Phosphate [*Biochemistry*] (DAVI)
pg .... Page (WDMC)
PG .... Page [*or Pagination*] [*Online database field identifier*]
PG .... Pan American Grace Airways (SAUS)
PG .... Paper Gain (MHDW)
PG .... Papua New Guinea [*ANSI two-letter standard code*] (CNC)
PG .... Paralysie Generale [*General Paralysis*] [*Medicine*] [*French*]
PG .... Paregoric [*Slang*]
PG .... Parental Guidance Suggested [*Formerly, GP*] [*Some material may not be suitable for preteenagers*] [*Movie rating*]
PG .... Paris Granite
PG .... Paris Group [*See also GP*] [*France*] (EAIO)
PG .... Parity Generate (SAUS)
PG .... Parotid Gland [*Medicine*] (DMAA)
PG .... Partial Gum [*Philately*]
PG .... Parti Quebecois [*Canada*] [*Political party*] (WDAA)
PG .... Pass Gas (SAUS)
PG .... Paste Grain [*Bookbinding*]
PG .... Past Grand [*Freemasonry*]
PG .... Patrol Combatant [*Gunboat*] [*Navy symbol*]
PG .... Patrol Escort [*Navy*]
PG .... Patrol Gunboat, Motorized [*Navy symbol*] (VNW)
PG .... Patrologiae Cursus. Series Graeca [*A publication*] (OCD)
PG .... Patrol Vessel Gunboat [*Navy*]
PG .... Pattern Generator (TIMI)
PG .... Pay Grade
PG .... Pay Group
PG .... Paying Guest
PG .... PEACE [*Program for Emergency Assistance, Cooperation, and Education*] for Guatemala (EA)
PG .... Pedal Ganglion
PG .... Pedal Groove
P/G .... Pediatric/Geriatric [*Medicine*] (EDAA)
PG .... Pelham Grenville Wodehouse [*British humorist, 1881-1975*]
PG .... Pelvic Girdle [*Medicine*] (MELL)
PG .... Pentagastrin (DMAA)
Pg .... Pentagram [*One billion metric tons*]
PG .... Pepsinogen [*Medicine*] (MEDA)
PG .... Peptidoglycan [*Biochemistry*]
PG .... Pergelic [*Soil biology*] [*Soil temperature regime*] (QSUL)
PG .... Periodic Group (SAUS)
PG .... Permanent Glow [*Telecommunications*] (TEL)
PG .... Permanent Grade
PG .... Persian Gulf (MCD)
PG .... Persistent Gas (SAUS)
Pg .... Petagram (SAUS)
PG .... Petrogenesis (SAUS)
PG .... Pharmaceutical Guide (SAUS)
PG .... Pharmacopoeia Germanica [*German Pharmacopoeia*]
PG .... Phase Gradient (SAUS)
PG .... Phosphatidylglycerol
PG .... Phosphogluconate [*Biochemistry*]
PG .... Phosphogypsum [*Inorganic chemistry*]
PG .... Photogrammetry
PG .... Physical Geography (SAUS)
pg .... Picogram [*One trillionth of a gram*]
PG .... Picture Generation (SAUS)
PG .... Picture Generator (SAUS)
PG .... Pilot Generator (IAA)
PG .... Pine Grosbeak [*Ornithology*]
PG .... Pin Grid (SAUS)
PG .... Pipers Guild (EA)
PG .... Pistol Grip [*Gunnery*]
PG .... Pituitary Gonadotropin [*Endocrinology*] (MAE)
PG .... Pivot Gun (SAUS)
PG .... Placebo Group [*Medicine*]
PG .... Plagioclase (SAUS)
PG .... Planning Group [*DoD*]
PG .... Planning Guidance (SAUS)
PG .... Planning Guide [*HUD*]
PG .... Plant Genome (HGEN)
PG .... Plant Growth (SAUS)
PG .... Plasma Gastrin [*Endocrinology*] (AAMN)
PG .... Plasma Glucose [*Hematology*]
PG .... Plasma Triglyceride [*Hematology*] (DAVI)
PG .... Plate Glass
PG .... Plate-Glazed [*Paper*]
PG .... Pointer Game (AEBS)
PG .... Point Group (SAUS)
PG .... Pollen Grain [*Botany*]
PG .... Polyethylene Glycol [*Organic chemistry*]
PG .... Polygalacturonase [*An enzyme*]
PG .... Polyglycine [*Biochemistry*]
PG .... Polypropylene Glycol (EDCT)
PG .... Pontius Guillelmi [*Authority cited in pre-1607 legal work*] (DSA)
PG .... Port Group [*Telecommunications*] (TEL)
Pg .... Portugal (ODBW)
PG .... Portugal
Pg .... Portuguese (ODBW)
PG .... Portuguese [*Language, etc.*]

pg .... Portuguese Guinea [*Guinea-Bissau*] [*MARC country of publication code*] [*Library of Congress*] (LCCP)
PG .... Position Guide (MCD)
P/G .... Postagram [*British military*] (DMA)
PG .... Postgraduate [*Refers to courses or students*] [*Slang*]
PG .... Power Gain
PG .... Power Gate [*Electronics*] (OA)
PG .... Power Generation (MCD)
PG .... Powerglide [*Automatic transmission*]
PG .... Preacher General
PG .... Precision Ground [*Electronics*] (IAA)
PG .... Predicted Grade [*IRS*]
PG .... Pregnanediol Glucuronide [*Endocrinology*]
pg .... Pregnant (DMAA)
PG .... Pregnant
PG .... Pregnant Guppy [*Reference to Boeing 377 aircraft*] (SAA)
PG .... Press Gallery [*US Senate*]
PG .... Pressure Gauge (KSC)
PG .... Priority Group
PG .... Prisonnier de Guerre [*Prisoner of War - POW*] [*French*]
PG .... Processed Gas (COE)
PG .... Processing Gain (SAUS)
PG .... Procter & Gamble Co. [*NYSE symbol*] (SPSG)
PG .... Procurator-General (ODA)
PG .... Procureur Generaal [*Public Attorney*] [*Dutch*] (ILCA)
PG .... Producers Group (EA)
PG .... Product Group (SAUS)
PG .... Professional Geologist
PG .... Professional Geophysicist (SAUS)
PG .... Professional Group (MCD)
PG .... Pro-German [*Prisoner of war term*] [*World War I*] (DSUE)
PG .... Program [*Telecommunications*]
PG .... Program Generator (IAA)
PG .... Program Generic [*Computer science*] (TEL)
PG .... Program Guidance
PG .... Program Management Assistance Group
PG .... Programmer (AAG)
PG .... Programmer Group (IAA)
PG .... Progress [*Telegraphy*] (PCTE)
PG .... Project Group
PG .... Prompt Gamma Ray (SAUS)
PG .... Proof Gallon [*Wines and spirits*]
PG .... Propylene Glycol
PG .... Propyl Gallate [*Antioxidant*] [*Organic chemistry*]
PG .... Prostaglandin [*Also, Pg*] [*Biochemistry*]
PG .... Protective Ground [*Electronics*] (IAA)
PG .... Protein Granule
PG .... Proteoglycan [*Biochemistry*]
PG .... Prothoracic Gland [*Insect anatomy*]
PG .... Province Guard [*Cambodia*] (CINC)
PG .... Proving Ground [*Army*]
P-G .... Prudential Grace Lines [*Steamship*] (MHDB)
PG .... Public Gaol [*British*]
PG .... Pulse Gate
PG .... Pulse Generator
PG .... Pure Gum [*of envelopes*]
PG .... Pyoderma Gangrenosum [*Medicine*]
PG .... Pyogenic Granuloma (SAUS)
PG .... Pyrolytic Graphite (ODA)
PG .... Pyrotechnic Gyro (AAG)
PG-1, PG-2... Protegrins [*Biochemistry*] (QSUL)
PG-13 .... Parental Guidance Suggested [*Now: Parents Strongly Cautioned. Some material may be inappropriate for children under 13*] [*Movie rating*]
PGA......... Page [*Arizona*] [*Airport symbol*] (OAG)
PGA......... Paragould [*Arkansas*] [*Seismograph station code, US Geological Survey*] (SEIS)
PGA......... Parliamentarians for Global Action [*An association*] (EA)
PGA......... Pega Capital Resources Ltd. [*Toronto Stock Exchange symbol*]
PGA......... Pendulous Gyro Accelerometer
PGA......... Pepsinogen A (DMAA)
PGA......... Personnel Group of America [*NYSE symbol*] (SAG)
PGA......... PGI, Inc. [*AMEX symbol*] (SPSG)
PGA......... Phosphoglyceric Acid [*Biochemistry*]
PGA......... Phosphoglyzerinaldehyd (SAUS)
PGA......... Pin-Grid-Array [*Motorola, Inc.*]
PGA......... Pin Grip Array [*Computer science*] (DDC)
PGA......... Pistachio Growers' Association [*Australia*]
PGA......... Plate Glass Association [*British*] (BI)
PGA......... Platt's Global Alert [*Database*] (GDD)
PGA......... Policy and Global Affairs Division [*National Research Council*] (RCD)
PGA......... Polyglandular Autoimmune Syndrome [*Medicine*] (DMAA)
PGA......... Polyglycolic Acid [*Organic chemistry*] (RDA)
PGA......... Poly(L-glutamic Acid) [*Organic chemistry*]
PGA......... Port of Geelong Authority [*Victoria, Australia*]
PGA......... Portugalia, Companhia Portuguesa de Transportes Aeros SA [*Portugal*] [*ICAO designator*] (FAAC)
PGA......... Potato Growers of Australia
PGA......... Power Gain Antenna
PGA......... Power Generating Assembly (KSC)
PGA......... Pressure Garment Assembly
PGA......... Prison Governors' Association [*British*] (WDAA)
PGA......... Producers Guild of America (EA)
PGA......... Production Go-Ahead (SAUS)
PGA......... Professional Golfers Association (NADA)
PGA......... Professional Graphics Adapter [*IBM Corp.*]
PGA......... Professional Group Audio
PGA......... Program Global Area (SAUS)
PGA......... Programmable Gain Amplifier (MCD)
PGA......... Programmable Gate Array
PGA......... Propane Gas Association (SAUS)
PGA......... Prostaglandin A [*Biochemistry*]
PGA......... Prostaglandin Analog [*Biochemistry*]
PGA......... Pteroylglutamic Acid (WDAA)
PGA......... Pteroylmonoglutamic Acid [*Folic acid*] [*Also, FA, PteGlu*] [*Biochemistry*]
PGA......... Punta Gorda Isles, Inc. [*AMEX symbol*] (COMM)
PGA......... Puppetry Guild of Australia
PGA......... Purchased Gas Adjustment
PGA......... Pure Grain Alcohol
PGA......... Pyrolysis Gas Analysis
PGA......... Upjohn Co. [*Research code symbol*]
PGA$_2$, PGB$_1$......... Prostaglandins A2 and B1 [*Biochemistry*] (QSUL)
PGAA........ Pin Grid Array Adapter (SAUS)
PGAA........ Professional Guides Association of America (EA)
PGAA........ Prompt Gamma-Ray Activation Analysis
P-GABA..... Phenyl-gamma-aminobutyric Acid [*Tranquilizer*]
PGAC........ Guam/Taguac [*Mariana Islands*] [*ICAO location identifier*] (ICLI)
PG-AC....... Phenylglycine Acid Chloride [*Biochemistry*] (AAMN)
PGAC........ Professional Group - Automatic Control
PGAE........ Pacific Gas and Electric (SAUS)
PGAH........ Pineapple Growers Association of Hawaii (EA)
PGAM........ Phosphoglyceromutase [*An enzyme*]
PG & E...... Pacific Gas and Electric [*Rock music group*]
PG & E...... Pacific Gas & Electric Co.
PG & E Cp... PG & E Corp. Holdings Co. [*Associated Press*] (SAG)
PGANE...... Professional Group on Aeronautical and Navigational Electronics
PGA-NOC... Permanent General Assembly of National Olympic Committees
PGANSW.... Potato Growers' Association of New South Wales [*Australia*]
PGAP........ Pilot Geriatric Arthritis Program [*Medicine*] (DMAA)
PGAP........ Professional Group - Antennas and Propagation
PGAPL...... Preliminary Group Assembly Parts List
PGAR........ Provisional Government of the Algerian Republic
PGAS........ Persisting Galactorrhea-Amenorrhea Syndrome [*Medicine*] (DMAA)
PGAS........ Polyglandular Autoimmune Syndrome [*Medicine*] (EDAA)
PGase....... Polygalacturonase [*An enzyme*]
PGAWA...... Pastoralists and Graziers' Association of Western Australia
PGAWA...... Potato Growers' Association of Western Australia
PGAX........ Pressure Tank Car [*Private rail car owner code*]
Pg B......... Bachelor of Pedagogy
PGB......... Paravertebral Ganglion Block [*Medicine*] (MELL)
PGB......... Patrol Gunboat [*Navy symbol*] (NATG)
PGB......... Personal Guidance Base (AIE)
PGB......... Phoenix Global [*Vancouver Stock Exchange symbol*]
PGB......... Portland General Electric Co. [*NYSE symbol*] (SAG)
PGB......... Portland Genl Elec 8.25% 'QUIDS' [*NYSE symbol*] (TTSB)
PGB......... Program Budget Guidance
PGB......... Prostaglandin B [*Biochemistry*]
PGB......... Protestant Guild for the Blind (EA)
PGB......... Pyrographalloy Boron
PGBA........ Piece Goods Buyers Association [*Defunct*] (EA)
PGBA........ Possum Growers and Breeders Association (EA)
PGBBX...... PaineWebber Global Income Cl.B [*Mutual fund ticker symbol*] (SG)
PGBD........ Pegboard [*Freight*]
PGBD........ Plugboard (VLIE)
PGBL........ Pluggable (VLIE)
PGBM........ Pulse Gate Binary Modulation (MCD)
PGbSH...... Seton Hill College, Greensburg, PA [*Library symbol*] [*Library of Congress*] (LCLS)
PGBTR...... Professional Group - Broadcast and Television Receivers
PG-BTS..... Professional Group-Broadcast Transmission System (SAUS)
PGBTS...... Professional Group - Broadcast Transmission Systems
PGbU........ University of Pittsburgh at Greensburg, Greensburg, PA [*Library symbol*] [*Library of Congress*] (LCLS)
PGC......... Geneva College, Beaver Falls, PA [*OCLC symbol*] (OCLC)
PGC......... Gettysburg College, Gettysburg, PA [*Library symbol*] [*Library of Congress*] (LCLS)
PGC......... Pacific Geoscience Center (SAUS)
PGC......... Pagurian Corp. [*Toronto Stock Exchange symbol*]
PGC......... Parents of Galactosemic Children [*An association*]
PGC......... Past Grand Commander [*Freemasonry*] (ROG)
PGC......... Peapack-Gladstone Fin'L. [*AMEX symbol*]
PGC......... Peoples Gas Co. (SAUS)
PGC......... Percentage of Goblet Cells (STED)
PGC......... Per Gyro Compass [*Navigation*]
PGC......... Persian Gulf Command [*World War II*]
PGC......... Phillips Gas [*NYSE symbol*] (SPSG)
PGC......... Plant Growth Chamber (SAUS)
PGC......... Policy Guidance Council (DOMA)
PGC......... Polynomial Generator Checker (IAA)
PGC......... Pontine Gaze Center [*Eye anatomy*]
PGC......... Poorly Graphitized Carbon [*Physical chemistry*]
PGC......... Port Group Control [*Telecommunications*] (TEL)
PGC......... Post-Graduate Certificate (PGP)
PGC......... Potassium Gold Cyanide [*Inorganic chemistry*]
PGC......... Potential Gas Committee
PGC......... Power Generation Committee (SAUS)

PGC .... Preliminary General Catalogue (SAUS)
PGC .... Primordial Germ Cell
PGC .... Process Gas Chromatography
PGC .... Process Gas Consumers Group (EA)
PGC .... Professional Graphics Controller [*IBM Corp.*]
PGC .... Program Chain [*Computer science*] (DCDG)
PGC .... Program Counter (VLIE)
PGC .... Program Generation Center [*Military*] (CAAL)
PGC .... Program Grande Carajas (SAUS)
PGC .... Program Group Control (VLIE)
PGC .... Programmable Guidance Controller [*Military*]
PGC .... Programmed Gain Control
PGC .... Prostaglandin C [*A prostoglandin endoperoxide*] [*Biochemistry*] (DAVI)
PGC .... Protective Glazing Council [*Association*] (EA)
PGC .... Proving Ground Command [*Air Force*]
PGC .... Pulsed Gas Crymotography
PGC .... Pure Glycollide (DB)
PGC .... Pyrolysis Gas Chromatography
PGCA .... Patent Glazing Contractors Association [*British*] (DBA)
PGcC .... Grove City College, Grove City, PA [*Library symbol*] [*Library of Congress*] (LCLS)
PGCC .... Power Generation Control Complex [*Nuclear energy*] (NRCH)
PGCCM ...... Pure Garbage Collection Contour Machine (SAUS)
PGCE .... Post Graduate Certificate of Education
PGCh .... Past Grand Chaplain [*Freemasonry*]
PGCI .... Program Chain Information [*Computer science*] (DCDG)
PG Clamp... Parallel-Groove Clamp (SAUS)
PGCML ...... Prince George's County Memorial Library [*Maryland*]
PGCOA ...... Pennsylvania Grade Crude Oil Association (EA)
PGCP .... Particles and Gases Contamination Panel (SAUS)
PGCP .... Professional Group - Component Parts
PGCPr .... Phillips Gas 9.32% Pfd [*NYSE symbol*] (TTSB)
PGCR .... Portable Gas-Cooled Reactor (SAUS)
PGCRA ...... Professional Golf Club Repairmen's Association (EA)
PGCS .... Photogrammetric Graphics Compiling System (SAUS)
PGCS .... Professional Group - Communications Systems
PGCT .... Precision Gunnery Crew Trainer (SAUS)
PGCT .... Professional Group - Circuit Theory
PGCU .... International Printing and Graphic Communications Union
PGCU .... Paul Gunther Logistic and Leasing [*Intermodal shipping container symbol*] (TVRC)
PGCVS ...... Postgraduate Committee in Veterinary Science [*Australia*]
PGCX .... Proctor & Gamble Cellulose [*Federal Railroad Administration identification code*]
PGD .... Hancock [*John*] Patriot Global Dividend Fund [*NYSE symbol*] (SPSG)
PGD .... John Hancock Patr Gl Div Fd [*NYSE symbol*] (TTSB)
pgd .... paged (SAUS)
PGD .... Pango Gold Mines Ltd. [*Toronto Stock Exchange symbol*]
PGD .... Paradigm (SAUS)
PGD .... Past Grand Deacon [*Freemasonry*]
PGD .... Phosphogluconate Dehydrogenase [*Also, PGDH*] [*An enzyme*]
PGD .... Phosphoglyceraldehyde Dehydrogenase [*An enzyme*] (MAE)
PGD .... Pikwitonei Granulite Domain [*Geology*]
PGD .... Pinion Gear Drive
PGD .... Planar Gas Discharge (VLIE)
PGD .... Planetary Gear Drive
PGD .... Policy and Grants Division [*Environmental Protection Agency*] (GFGA)
PGD .... Preimplantation Genetic Diagnosis [*For in vitro fertilization*] [*Medicine*]
PGD .... Program for Geographical Display (IAA)
PGD .... Progressed [*Telegraphy*] (PCTE)
PGD .... Prostaglandin D [*Biochemistry*]
PGD .... Pulse Generator Display
PGD .... Punta Gorda [*Florida*] [*Airport symbol*] (OAG)
PGDA .... Piercing Pagoda [*NASDAQ symbol*] (TTSB)
PGDA .... Piercing Pagoda, Inc. [*NASDAQ symbol*] (SAG)
PGDB .... Propylene Glycol Dibenzoate [*Organic chemistry*]
PGDC .... Provincial Grand Director of Ceremonies [*Freemasonry*]
PGDCS ...... Power Generation, Distribution, and Control Subsystem (MCD)
PGDF .... Pilot Guide Dog Foundation (EA)
PGDF .... Product Generation and Distribution Facility (ACAE)
PGDH .... Phosphogluconate Dehydrogenase [*Also, PGD*] [*An enzyme*]
PGDip .... Postgraduate Diploma [*Australia*]
PGDipA ...... Postgraduate Diploma in Arts [*Australia*]
PGDipAgrSc... Postgraduate Diploma in Agricultural Science [*Australia*]
PGDipDevTech... Postgraduate Diploma in Development Technology [*Australia*]
PGDipEdSt... Postgraduate Diploma in Educational Studies [*Australia*]
PGDipForSc... Postgraduate Diploma in Forest Science [*Australia*]
PGDipIEM... Postgraduate Diploma in Irrigation Engineering Management [*Australia*]
PGDipMath & MathEd... Postgraduate Diploma in Mathematics and Mathematics Education [*Australia*]
PGDipMgtSt... Postgraduate Diploma in Management Studies [*Australia*]
PGDipPhysio... Postgraduate Diploma in Physiotherapy [*Australia*]
PGDipSc .... Postgraduate Diploma in Science [*Australia*]
PgDn .... Page Down [*Computer science*] (CDE)
PGDN .... Page Down [*Computer science*] (VLIE)
PGDN .... Propylene Glycol Dinitrate [*Organic chemistry*]
PGDP .... Paducah Gaseous Diffusion Plant
PGD Press... Progressive Die Press (SAUS)
PGDR .... Plasma-Glucose Disappearance Rate [*Hematology*] (MAE)
PGDRB ...... Plumbers, Gasfitters, and Drainers Registration Board [*Victoria, Australia*]
PGDS .... Pioneer Ground Data System
PGDS .... Pulse Generator Display System
PGDT .... Portable Ground Data Terminal
PGE .... Pacific Gas & Electric Co. [*Associated Press*] (SAG)
PGE .... Pacific Great Eastern Railway Co. [*Nicknames: Prince George Eventually, Please Go Easy*] [*Later, British Columbia Railway*] [*AAR code*]
PGE .... Page Petroleum Ltd. [*Toronto Stock Exchange symbol*] (SPSG)
PGE .... Persian Gulf Evacuee (SAUS)
PGE .... Petroleum and Geosystems Engineering (SAUS)
PGE .... Phenyl Glycidyl Ether [*Organic chemistry*]
PGE .... Platelet Granule Extract [*Hematology*] (MAE)
PGE .... Platinum Group Element [*Chemistry*]
PGE .... Polyglycerol Esters of Fatty Acids
PGE .... Population Growth Estimation
PGE .... Pore Gradient Electrophoresis
PGE .... Portland General Electric Co., Library, Portland, OR [*OCLC symbol*] (OCLC)
PGE .... Portland Grain Exchange (EA)
PGE .... Posterior Gastroenterostomy [*Medicine*] (MELL)
PGE .... Precision Gimbal Experiment
PGE .... Preliminary Gunners Examination (SAUS)
PGE .... Primary Ground Electrode (SAUS)
PGE .... Prime Group Engineer (AAG)
PGE .... Prime Group Realty Trust [*NYSE symbol*]
PGE .... Product Generation Executive (SAUS)
PGE .... Professional Group - Education
PG-E .... Professional Group Education (SAUS)
PGE .... Prostaglandin E [*Biochemistry*]
PGE .... Provisional Government of Eritrea
PGE .... Purge (NASA)
PG-EC .... Professional Group-Electronic Computers (SAUS)
PGEC .... Professional Group on Electronic Computers [*IEEE*]
PGECap ..... PG & E Capital I [*Associated Press*] (SAG)
PGECP .... Professional Group Electronic Component Parts (IAA)
PGED .... Point-contact Germanium Diode (SAUS)
PGED .... Professional Group - Electronic Devices
PG-ED .... Professional Group-Electronic Devices (SAUS)
PGEI .... Petroglyph Energy, Inc. [*NASDAQ symbol*] (NASQ)
PGEM .... Professional Group - Engineering Management
PGEM .... Prostaglandin E Metabolite (STED)
PGEN .... Plant Genetics, Inc. [*NASDAQ symbol*] (COMM)
PGEner ...... PG Energy, Inc. [*Associated Press*] (SAG)
P-generation... Parental Generation (WDAA)
P-Generation... Parental-Generation (SAUS)
PGEO .... Paridigm Geophysical, Ltd. [*NASDAQ symbol*] (NASQ)
PGeol .... Professional Geologist (DD)
PGeoph ..... Professional Geophysicist (DD)
PGEOY ...... Petroleum Geo Services ASA [*OTCBB symbol*]
PGER .... Pacific Great Eastern Railway (SAUS)
PGESMET... Gender Diversity in Science, Technology, Engineering, and Mathematics Education GDSE [*National Science Foundation*] (RCD)
PGEU .... Pharmaceutical Group of the European Union (SAUS)
PGEWS ...... Professional Group on Engineering Writing and Speech [*Institute of Radio Engineers; now IEEE*]
PGEX .... Pacific Gateway Exchange, Inc. [*NASDAQ symbol*] (SAG)
PGEXQ ...... Pacific Gateway Exchange [*OTCBB symbol*]
PGF .... Pacific Gamefish Foundation (EA)
PGF .... Paternal Grandfather (STED)
pgf .... Paternal Grandfather (STED)
PGF .... Patrol Ship [*Navy*]
PGF .... Pengrowth Gas Income Fund Trust Units [*Toronto Stock Exchange symbol*]
PGF .... Peptide Growth Factor [*Biochemistry*]
PGF .... Perpignan [*France*] [*Airport symbol*] (OAG)
PGF .... Plant Growth Facility (SAUS)
PGF .... Plerocercoid Growth Factor [*Endocrinology*]
PGF .... Portugal Fund [*NYSE symbol*] (SPSG)
PGF .... Postglacial Fault [*Biology*]
PGF .... Presentation Graphic Feature [*Computer science*]
PGF .... Pressure Gradient Force (SAUS)
PGF .... Prostaglandin F [*Biochemistry*]
PGFC .... Periodical Guide for Computerists [*Applegate Computer Enterprises*] [*Information service or system*] [*Defunct*] (IID)
PGFEL .... Preliminary Government-Furnished Equipment List (MCD)
PGFM .... Prostaglandin F and its Metabolite [*Dihydro-keto-prostaglandin*] [*Medicine*] (BABM)
PGFNA ...... Prince George Free-Net Association (SAUS)
PGFR .... Power-Generating Fusion Reaction
PGFVS .... Postgraduate Federation in Veterinary Science [*Australia*]
PGFW .... Guam [*Mariana Islands*] [*ICAO location identifier*] (ICLI)
PGFZ .... Pabco Gypsum Fiber Board [*Federal Railroad Administration identification code*]
PGG .... Guided Missile Patrol Combatant [*Navy*]
PGG .... Page America Group, Inc. [*AMEX symbol*] (SPSG)
PGG .... Petrogold Financial Corp. [*Vancouver Stock Exchange symbol*]
PGG .... Pneumatic Ground Group
PGG .... Polyclonal Gamma Globulin [*Medicine*] (STED)
PGG .... Power Generation Group [*Nuclear Regulatory Commission*] (NRCH)
PGG .... Progressing [*Telegraphy*] (PCTE)
PGG .... Prostaglandin G [*A prostaglandin endoperoxide*] [*Biochemistry*]
PG/GAG ..... Proteoglycans/Glyosaminoglyans
PGGO .... Prescribed Goods (General) Order
PGH .... Pantnagar [*India*] [*Airport symbol*] (AD)

PGH.......... Paragraph (ADWA)
PGH.......... Patrol Gunboat (Hydrofoil) [*Navy symbol*]
PGH.......... Per Geard Hatch (RIMS)
PGH.......... Philadelphia General Hospital (SAUS)
PGH.......... Philippine General Hospital (SAUS)
PGH.......... Phosphoglycolohydroxamate [*Biochemistry*]
PGH.......... Pittsburgh, PA [*Amtrak rail station code*]
PGH.......... Pituitary Growth Hormone [*Endocrinology*]
PGH.......... Plasma Growth Hormone [*Hematology*] (MAE)
PGH.......... Polymer Group, Inc. [*NYSE symbol*] (SAG)
PGH.......... Porcine Growth Hormone [*Biochemistry*]
PGH.......... Port Group Highway [*Telecommunications*] (TEL)
PGH.......... Prostaglandin H [*A prostaglandin endoperoxide*] [*Biochemistry*]
PGHA........ Park Gallatin Hereford Association (EA)
PGHFE....... Professional Group - Human Factors in Electronics
Pgh Leg Journal... Pittsburgh Legal Journal [*Pennsylvania*] [*A publication*] (DLA)
PGHM....... Payload Ground Handling Mechanism [*NASA*] (MCD)
PGHS........ Prostaglandin Hydrogen Synthase [*An enzyme*]
PGHS........ Public-General Hospital Section [*American Hospital Association*] (EA)
PGHTS...... Port Group Highway Timeslot [*Telecommunications*] (TEL)
PGI........... Chitato [*Angola*] [*Airport symbol*] [*Obsolete*] (OAG)
PGI........... General Information Programme [*UNESCO*] [*Acronym is based on foreign phrase*]
PGI........... Panagra Airways, Inc. [*FAA designator*] (FAAC)
PGi........... Paragigantocellularis [*Neuroanatomy*]
PGI........... Parameter Group Identifier [*Computer science*] (TNIG)
PGI........... Paris Gestion Informatique [*Paris Informatics Administration*] [*France*] [*Information service or system*] (IID)
PGI........... Parking Guidance and Information [*Traffic management*]
PGI........... Peripheral Graphics, Inc.
PGI........... Peripherals General Inc. (SAUS)
PGI........... Personalized Gift Institute (NTPA)
PGI........... Phosphoglucoisomerase [*An enzyme*]
PGI........... Phosphoglucose-Isomerase (SAUS)
PGI........... Physicians Guide to the Internet (SAUS)
PGI........... Pilot Gunnery Instructor (SAUS)
PGI........... Ply-Gem, Inc. [*NYSE symbol*] (SAG)
PGI........... Ply Gem Industries Inc. [*NYSE symbol*] (TTSB)
PGI........... Polar Geophysical Institute [*Murmansk Region*] [*Russia*]
PGI........... Polymer Group Incorporated [*Plastics supplier*]
PGI........... Port Group Interface [*Telecommunications*] (TEL)
PGI........... Potassium, Glucose, and Insulin (MAE)
PGI........... Power Generators, Incorporated
PGI........... Professional Geophysics, Inc. (EFIS)
PGI........... Professional Group - Instrumentation
PG-I.......... Professional Group Instrumentation (SAUS)
PGI........... Progressions Group (MHID)
PGI........... Project Group, Inc. [*Advertising agency*] [*Acronym now used as official n ame of agency*]
PGI........... Prostaglandin [*Medicine*] (EDAA)
PGI........... Prostaglandin I [*Biochemistry*]
PGI........... Provigo, Inc. [*Toronto Stock Exchange symbol*]
PGI........... Punta Gorda Isles Inc. (EFIS)
PGI........... Purge Gas Inlet (AAEL)
PGI........... Pyrotechnics Guild International (EA)
PGIA........ Pendulous Gyro Integrating Accelerometer (IAA)
PGIA........ Programmable Gain Instrumentation Amplifier (IAA)
PGIE........ Professional Group - Industrial Electronics
PG-IE....... Professional Group Industrial Electronics (SAUS)
PGiess...... Griechische Papyri im Museum des Oberhessischen Geschichtsvereins zu Giessen [*A publication*] (OCD)
P-GILD...... Projection Gas Immersion LASER Doping (AAEL)
PGIM........ Professional Group on Instrumentation and Measurement [*National Bureau of Standards*]
PGIP........ Polygalacturonase-Inhibiting Protein [*Biochemistry*]
PGIP........ Post Graduate Intelligence Program (DOMA)
PGIS........ Parking Guidance Information System
PGIS........ Project Grant Information System
PGIT........ Professional Group - Information Theory
PGJ......... Pipeline Girth Joint
PG/JAP..... Persian Gulf to Japan (SAUS)
PGJD........ Past Grand Junior Deacon [*Freemasonry*]
PGJN........ Pomegranate Guild of Judaic Needlework (EA)
PGJW........ Past Grand Junior Warden [*Freemasonry*] (ROG)
PGK.......... Pangkalpinang [*Indonesia*] [*Airport symbol*] (OAG)
PGK.......... Phosphoglycerate Kinase [*An enzyme*]
PGK.......... Phosphoglycerate Kinase Database (MHID)
PGK.......... Phosphoglyceric Phosphokinase (SAUS)
PGI........... Glenside Free Library, Glenside, PA [*Library symbol*] [*Library of Congress*] (LCLS)
PGL.......... Lutheran Theological Seminary, Gettysburg, PA [*Library symbol*] [*Library of Congress*] (LCLS)
PGL.......... Paraglossa of Labium [*Entomology*]
PGL.......... Partnership in Global Learning
PGL.......... Pascagoula, MS [*Location identifier*] [*FAA*] (FAAL)
PGL.......... Peer Group Leader (SAUS)
PGL.......... Peoples Energy [*NYSE symbol*] (TTSB)
PGL.......... Peoples Energy Corp. [*NYSE symbol*] (SPSG)
PGL.......... Persistent Generalized Lymphadenopathy [*Medicine*]
PGL.......... Peter Group Leader
PGL.......... Phenolic Glass Laminate
PGL.......... Phosphating Granulating Liquid (VLIE)
PGL.......... Phosphoglycolipid
PGL.......... Polyglutaraldehyde [*Organic chemistry*]
PGL.......... Portable Gas LASER
PGL.......... Professional Games League (SAUS)
PGL.......... Professional Graphics Language [*Software*] [*IBM Corp.*] (BYTE)
PGL.......... Provincial Grand Lodge [*Freemasonry*]
PGL.......... Pulsed Gas LASER
PGladM..... Mary J. Drexel Home, Gladwyne, PA [*Library symbol*] [*Library of Congress*] [*Obsolete*] (LCLS)
PGLAF....... Progen Industries [*NASDAQ symbol*] (SG)
PGLAX....... One Group: Louisiana Municipal Cl.A [*Mutual fund ticker symbol*] (SG)
PGIB......... Beaver College, Glenside, PA [*Library symbol*] [*Library of Congress*] (LCLS)
PGLC........ Pyrolysis Gas Liquid Chromatography
PGLD........ Phoenix Gold International, Inc. [*NASDAQ symbol*] (SAG)
PGLD........ Phoenix Gold Intl [*NASDAQ symbol*] (TTSB)
PGLF........ ProForm Golf, Inc. [*NASDAQ symbol*] (QUAN)
PGL-Hi...... Lutheran Historical Society, Gettysburg, PA [*Library symbol*] [*Library of Congress*] (LCLS)
PGLIN....... Page and Line [*Computer science*] (VLIE)
PGIL......... Glenside Free Library, Glenside, PA [*Library symbol*] [*Library of Congress*] (LCLS)
PGLN........ Page and Line (IAA)
PGLU........ Prudential-Grace Lines [*Intermodal shipping container symbol*] (TVRC)
PGlu......... Pyroglutamyl (SAUS)
PGlyM....... Phosphoglyceromutase (DB)
PGLZ........ Prudential Grace Lines [*Intermodal trailer symbol*]
PGM......... Messiah College Learning Center, Grantham, PA [*OCLC symbol*] (OCLC)
PGM......... Palenque [*Mexico*] [*Airport symbol*] (AD)
PGM......... Paleogeomorphology (SAUS)
PGM......... Papyri Graecae Magicae [*A publication*] (OCD)
PGM......... Past Grand Master [*Freemasonry*]
PGM......... Paternal Grandmother (MEDA)
PGM......... Patrol Vessel, Motor Gunboat [*Navy symbol*] [*Obsolete*]
PGM......... Periaqueductal Grey Matter (SAUS)
PGM......... Perron Gold Mines [*Vancouver Stock Exchange symbol*]
PGM......... Persatuan Geologi Malaysia [*Geological Society of Malaysia*] (EAIO)
PGM......... PGM-11 Redstone Missile (SAUS)
PGM......... Phosphoglucomutase [*An enzyme*]
PGM......... Planetary Gearhead Motor [*Aerospace*]
PGM......... Planning Guidance Memorandum (DOMA)
PGM......... Plant Genetic Materials
PGM......... Platinum Group Metal [*In meteorites*]
PGM......... Platinum-Group Minerals (SAUS)
PGM......... Poly-Gel Mitigator
PGM......... Porous Glass Matrix (SAUS)
PGM......... Portable Greymap [*Image format*] (AAEL)
PGM......... Port Graham, AK [*Location identifier*] [*FAA*] (FAAL)
PGM......... Precision Guided Missile
PGM......... Precision-Guided Munition (MCD)
PGM......... Processing Graph Methodology (SAUS)
pgm.......... Program (ELAL)
PGM......... Program
PGM......... Programable (SAUS)
PGM......... Program Guidance Memorandum
PGM......... Putnam Investment Grade Municipal Trust [*NYSE symbol*] (SPSG)
PGMA....... Phosphoglycerate Mutase A (DMAA)
PGMA....... Poly(glyceryl Methacrylate) [*Organic chemistry*]
PGMA....... Private Grocers' Merchandising Association [*British*] (BI)
PGMA....... Public Golf Management Association (NTPA)
PGMA....... Pulsed Gas Metal Arc (KSC)
PGMA-EA... Polyglycidal Methacrylate-Ethyl Acrylate [*Organic chemistry*] (PDAA)
PGMARV.... Precision Guided Maneuvering Re-Entry Vehicle (PDAA)
P-GMAW.... Pulsed-Current Gas Metal-Arc Welding (SAUS)
PGMB....... Phosphoglycerate Mutase B (DMAA)
PGMC....... Primary Glass Manufacturers Council (NTPA)
PGmc........ Proto-Germanic (SAUS)
PGME....... Professional Group - Medical Electronics
PG-ME...... Professional Group-Medical Electronics (SAUS)
PGMEA...... Propylene Glycol Monomethyl Ether Acetate [*Organic chemistry*]
PGM-FI...... Programmed Fuel Injection [*Automotive engineering*]
PGMIL...... Professional Group - Military Electronics (MUGU)
PGMILE..... Professional Group - Military Electronics (AAG)
PG-MITT... Professional Group-Microwave Theory and Technics (SAUS)
PGML........ Precision Graphics Markup Language [*Computer science*]
PGMM....... Precision Guided Mortar Munition
PGMOT...... Pollution Generation Multiplier from Output Table (PDAA)
PGMP....... Preliminary Guaranteed Minimum Price
PGMR....... Programmer (SAUS)
PGMS....... Professional Grounds Management Society (EA)
PGMS....... Stillwater Mining [*NASDAQ symbol*] (TTSB)
PGMS....... Stillwater Mining Co. [*NASDAQ symbol*] (SAG)
PGMSJ...... Professional Group of Mathematical Symbol Jugglers (MUGU)
PGMT....... Pigment (MSA)
PGMTT...... Professional Group - Microwave Theory and Techniques
PGMV....... Pea Green Mottle Virus [*Plant pathology*]
PGN.......... Paragon Health Network [*NYSE symbol*] [*Formerly, Living Centers of America*] (SG)
PGN.......... Paragon Petroleum Ltd. [*Toronto Stock Exchange symbol*]
PGN.......... Performance Group Number (SAUS)
PGN.......... Perigeniculate Nucleus [*Anatomy*]
PGN.......... Phi Gamma Nu [*Fraternity*]
PGN.......... Pigeon (ADA)
PGN.......... Platinum Group Nugget [*In meteorites*]

PGN.......... Portland General Corp. [*NYSE symbol*] (SPSG)
PGN.......... Progress Energy [*Company symbol*]
PGN.......... Progression [*Telegraphy*] (PCTE)
PGN.......... Proliferative Glomerulonephritis [*Medicine*]
PGN.......... Pulse Generator
PGNAA...... Prompt Gamma Neutron Activation Analysis [*Analytical chemistry*]
PGNC........ Payload Guidance Navigation and Control (SAUS)
PGNCS...... Primary Guidance, Navigation, and Control System [*or Subsystem*] [*Apollo*] [*NASA*] (MCD)
PGND........ Propaganda (AABC)
PGNP........ Pagsanjan Gorge National Park (SAUS)
PGNR........ Page Number (VLIE)
PGNS........ PathoGenesis Corp. [*NASDAQ symbol*] (SAG)
PGNS........ Primary Guidance and Navigation System [*Apollo*] [*NASA*]
PGNS........ Professional Group - Nuclear Science
PGNT........ Paligent, Inc. [*NASDAQ symbol*] (QUAN)
PGNT........ Sabanettan, Tinian Island [*Mariana Islands*] [*ICAO location identifier*] (ICLI)
PGNW....... Ritidian Point, Guam Island [*Mariana Islands*] [*ICAO location identifier*] (ICLI)
PGO.......... Pagecorp, Inc. [*Toronto Stock Exchange symbol*]
PGO.......... Page, OK [*Location identifier*] [*FAA*] (FAAL)
PGO.......... Past Grand Orient [*Freemasonry*] (ROG)
PGO.......... Peroxidase-Glucose Oxidase [*Also, GOD-POD*] [*Enzyme mixture*]
PGO.......... Pontine Geniculate Occipital (DIPS)
PGO.......... Ponto-Geniculate-Occipital [*Electroencephalography*]
PGO.......... Positive Grid Oscillator
PGO.......... Pyrolysis Gas Oil (SAUS)
PGOC........ Payload Ground Operation Contract (SAUS)
PGOC........ Payload Ground Operations Contractor [*NASA*] (SSD)
PGOC........ Payload Ground Operations Control (SAUS)
PGOC........ Philadelphia Grand Opera Co. (SAUS)
PGOR........ Payload Ground Operation Requirements [*NASA*] (NASA)
PGORS...... Payload Ground Operation Requirements Study [*NASA*] (MCD)
PGOS........ Petroleum, Gas and Oil Shale (SAUS)
PGOWG..... Payload Ground Operations Working Group (SAUS)
PGP.......... Guinea Progress Party (Guinea) [*Political party*] (PSAP)
PGP.......... Pacific Gateway Properties [*Formerly, Perini Investment Properties, Inc.*] [*AMEX symbol*] (SPSG)
PGP.......... Parti Gabonais du Progres [*Political party*] (EY)
PGP.......... Paternal Grandparent [*Medicine*] (EDAA)
PGP.......... Peace Garden Project [*Later, NPG*] (EA)
PGP.......... Phagocyte Glycoprotein [*Biochemistry*]
PGP.......... Phosphoglyceroyl Phosphatase [*Medicine*] (EDAA)
PGP.......... Phosphoglycolate Phosphatase [*An enzyme*]
PGP.......... Pico Glass Pellet
PGP.......... Planning Grant Program
PGP.......... Postgamma Proteinuria [*Medicine*] (MAE)
PGP.......... Precision Gas Products [*Commercial firm*]
PGP.......... Prepaid Group Practice [*Insurance*]
PGP.......... Pretty Good Piracy (SAUS)
PGP.......... Pretty Good Privacy [*Telecommunications*]
PGP.......... Professional Growth Plan
PGP.......... Programmable Graphics Processor
PGP.......... Progressive General Paralysis (MELL)
PGP.......... Project on Government Procurement (EA)
PGP.......... Prostaglandin Production
PGP.......... Puerta Galera [*Philippines*] [*Seismograph station code, US Geological Survey*] (SEIS)
PGP.......... Pulsed Glide Path (IAA)
PGP.......... University of Southern Maine at Portland, Portland, ME [*OCLC symbol*] (OCLC)
PGPEP...... Professional Group - Product Engineering and Production
PGPH........ Peptidylglutamyl-Peptide Hydrolyzing [*Biochemistry*]
PGPI.......... Protein Grain Products International (EA)
PGP Landing System... Pulsed Glide Path Landing System (SAUS)
PGPR........ Plant-Growth-Promoting Rhizobacteria
PGPR........ Provincial Guild of Printers Readers (SAUS)
PGPS........ Packaged Gas Pressure System
PGPT........ Professional Group - Production Techniques
PGQC........ Professional Group-Quality Control (IAA)
PGR.......... Paragould, AR [*Location identifier*] [*FAA*] (FAAL)
PGR.......... Parental Guidance Recommended [*Movie rating*] [*Australia*]
PGR.......... Passenger [*Telegraphy*] (PCTE)
Pgr........... Passenger [*Indian Railway*] (TIR)
PGR.......... Paternal Grandfather (DAVI)
PGR.......... Peregrine Petroleum [*Vancouver Stock Exchange symbol*]
PGR.......... Petition Granted (DNAB)
PGR.......... PGR. Press Gallery Report [*A publication*] (ADA)
PGR.......... Planning and Ground Rule (SAUS)
PGR.......... Plant Genetic Resources (SAUS)
PGR.......... Plant Growth Regulator
PGR.......... Polymerized Grass Extract [*Immunology*]
PGR.......... Population Growth Rate
PGR.......... Postglacial Rebound (SAUS)
PGR.......... Precision Graphic Recorder
PgR........... Progesterone Receptor [*Endocrinology*]
PGR.......... Progressive Corp. [*NYSE symbol*]
PGR.......... Progressive Corp., Ohio [*NYSE symbol*] (TTSB)
PGR.......... Provincial Grazing Reserves [*Alberta, Canada*] (FOTI)
PGR.......... Psychogalvanic Reaction (SAUS)
PGR.......... Psychogalvanic Reflex [*or Response*] [*Psychology*]
PGR.......... Psychogalvanic Response (SAUS)
PGR.......... Pulsed Graphite Reactor (SAUS)
PGR.......... Pyrogallol Red [*Also, PR*] [*An indicator*] [*Chemistry*]
PGR.......... Reconnaissance Patrol Combatant [*Navy*]
PGR.......... Spacelab Planning and Ground Rule [*NASA*] (NAKS)
PGraM....... Messiah College, Grantham, PA [*Library symbol*] [*Library of Congress*] (LCLS)
PG Rating... Parental Guidance Rating (SAUS)
PGRC........ Plant Gene Resources of Canada [*See also RPC*]
PGRC........ Privacy Global Resource Center (EA)
PGRC........ Program Guidance and Review Committee [*Army*] (AABC)
PGrev........ Greenville Area Public Library, Greenville, PA [*Library symbol*] [*Library of Congress*] (LCLS)
PGrevT...... Thiel College, Greenville, PA [*Library symbol*] [*Library of Congress*] (LCLS)
PGRF........ Pacific Gamefish Research Foundation [*Later, PORF*] (EA)
PGRF........ Pulse Group Repetition Frequency
PGRFA...... Plant Genetic Resources for Food and Agriculture (SAUS)
PGRFI....... Professional Group - Radio Frequency Interference
PGRG........ Potomac General Research Group
PGRM........ Parti Gerakan Rakyat Malaysia [*People's Action Party of Malaysia*] [*Political party*] (PPW)
P-GRN....... Progranulocytes [*Hematology*] (DAVI)
PGRO........ Pea Growing Research Organisation Ltd. [*British*] (BI)
PGRO........ Processors and Growers Research Organisation [*British*] (IRUK)
PGRO........ Rota/International [*Mariana Islands*] [*ICAO location identifier*] (ICLI)
PGRQC...... Professional Group - Reliability and Quality Control
PGRS........ Pergerakan Guerilja Rakyat Sarawak [*Sarawak People's Guerrilla Forces*] [*Malaya*]
PGRS........ Plume Groundwater Recovery System [*Environmental science*] (BCP)
PGRS........ Precision Guided Rocket System (SEWL)
PGRSA...... Plant Growth Regulator Society of America (EA)
PGRT........ Petroleum Gas and Revenue Tax [*Canada*]
PGRTRC..... Professional Group-Radio Telemetry and Remote Control (IAA)
PGRV........ Photogravure (VRA)
PGRV........ Pigeon River Railroad [*Federal Railroad Administration identification code*]
PGRV........ Precision Guided Reentry Vehicle
PGRVT...... Precisely Guided Reentry Test Vehicle (SAA)
PGRWG..... Payload Ground Requirements Working Group [*NASA*] (NASA)
PGRWG..... Plant Growth Regulator Working Group (SAUS)
PGS.......... Naval Postgraduate School
PGS.......... Pagosa Springs [*Colorado*] [*Seismograph station code, US Geological Survey*] [*Closed*] (SEIS)
PGS.......... Papergram System [*Military*] (CAAL)
PGS.......... Parallel Gap Soldering
PGS.......... Parser-Generating System (SAUS)
PGS.......... Passive Geodetic Satellite [*NASA*]
PGS.......... Passive Gravity Stabilization
PGS.......... Peach Springs, AZ [*Location identifier*] [*FAA*] (FAAL)
PGS.......... Pennsylvania German Society [*Later, TPGS*] (EA)
PGS.......... Persistent Gross Splenomegaly [*Medicine*] (EDAA)
PGS.......... Physicians for Global Survival (SAUS)
PGS.......... Pidaung Game Sanctuary (SAUS)
PGS.......... Pikunas Graphoscopic Scale [*Personality development test*] [*Psychology*]
PGS.......... Plane Grating Spectrograph
PGS.......... Plan Graphics Support (SAUS)
PGS.......... Plant Growth Substance
PGS.......... Plasma Generator System
PGS.......... Platoon Gunnery Simulator (SAUS)
PGS.......... Polish Genealogical Society (EA)
PGS.......... Polymer Glass Sealant
PGS.......... Portable Ground Station
PGS.......... Postsurgical Gastroparesis Syndrome [*Medicine*] (MELL)
PGS.......... Power Generation Satellite (HGAA)
PGS.......... Power Generation Section
PGS.......... Power Generation System [*or Subsystem*]
PGS.......... Power Generator Section (KSC)
PGS.......... Practical Guide Series (ACII)
PGS.......... Precision Gunnery System [*Army training device*] (INF)
PGS.......... Predicted Ground Speed [*Navigation*]
PGS.......... President of the Geographical Society [*British*] (ROG)
PGS.......... President of the Geological Society [*British*]
PGS.......... Pressed Glassmakers Society [*British*] (DBA)
PGS.......... Pressure-Gradient Single-Ended [*Microphone*] (DEN)
PGS.......... Pretty Good Signature [*Computer science*]
PGS.......... Pretty Good Stuff [*Liquor*]
PGS.......... Primary Guidance Subsystem (MCD)
PGS.......... Primary Guidance System (SAUS)
PGS.......... Proceedings of the Geological Society (SAUS)
PGS.......... Process Guiding System (SAUS)
PGS.......... Product Generation System (EOSA)
PGS.......... Professional Guidance Systems, Inc. [*Information service or system*] (IID)
PGS.......... Progenitor Genealogical Society (EA)
PGS.......... Program Generation System [*Computer science*] (MDG)
PGS.......... Program Generator System (SAUS)
PGS.......... Progresses [*Telegraphy*] (PCTE)
PGS.......... Propellant Gauging System
PGS.......... Proposal Generation System (GART)
PGS.......... Prostaglandin Synthase [*An enzyme*]
PGS.......... Provincial Grand Secretary [*Freemasonry*]
PGS.......... Publications Gravure Server (SAUS)
PGS.......... Public Service Co. North Carolina [*NYSE symbol*] (SAG)
PGS.......... Tauranga Aero Club, Inc. [*New Zealand*] [*ICAO designator*] (FAAC)

PGSA .... Petroleum Geo Services [*NASDAQ symbol*] (SAG)
PGSA .... Polish Genealogical Society of America (EA)
PGSAY .... Petroleum Geo-Svcs A/S ADS [*NASDAQ symbol*] (TTSB)
PGSB .... Past Grand Sword Bearer [*Freemasonry*] (ROG)
PGSB .... Provincial Grand Sword-Bearer [*Freemasonry*]
PGSC .... Panel on Geological Site Criteria (SAUS)
PGSC .... Payload and General Support Computer [*NASA*]
PGSC .... Persian Gulf Service Command
PGSC .... Portable Gas Supply Cart (SAUS)
PGSCOL ..... Naval Postgraduate School
PGSD .... Past Grand Senior Deacon [*Freemasonry*]
PGSE .... Payload Ground Support Equipment [*NASA*] (MCD)
PGSE .... Peculiar Ground Support Equipment [*DoD*]
PGSE .... Processing Graph Support Environment (SAUS)
PGSE .... Pulsed Field Gradient Spin-Echo
PGSE .... Pulsed Gradient Spin Echo [*Physics*]
PGSEL .... Priced Ground Support Equipment List (AAG)
PGSET .... Professional Group on Space Electronics and Telemetry (AAG)
PGSF .... Public Good Science Fund [*New Zealand*]
PGSGX ...... One Group: Small Cap. Cl.A [*Mutual fund ticker symbol*] (SG)
PGSI .... Prostaglandin Synthetase Inhibitor (DMAA)
PGSM .... Payload Gimbal Separation Mechanism (SAUS)
PGSM .... Precision Guided Submunition (SAUS)
PGSN .... Saipan Island (Obyan)/International [*Mariana Islands*] [*ICAO location identifier*] (ICLI)
PGSR .... Psychogalvanic Skin Resistance [*Otolaryngology*]
PGSS .... Paget-Gorman Sign System (AIE)
PGSTAP ..... Pressure, Gas, Start, Turbine, Auxiliary Pump-Drive Assembly [*Pronounced "pigstap"*]
PGSU .... Propellant [*or Propulsion*] Gas Supply Unit
PGSW .... Past Grand Senior Warden [*Freemasonry*]
PGSX .... Progressive Rail [*Federal Railroad Administration identification code*]
PGT .... Pacific Gas Transmission (SAUS)
PGT .... Page Table [*Computer science*] (IBMDP)
PGT .... Partido Guatemalteco del Trabajo [*Guatemalan Labor Party*] [*Political party*] (PD)
PGT .... Passenger and Goods Transport (SAUS)
PGT .... Past Grand Treasurer [*Freemasonry*]
PGT .... Pegasus Hava Tasimaciligi AS [*Turkey*] [*ICAO designator*] (FAAC)
pgt .... Per Gross Ton (ODA)
PGT .... Per Gross Ton [*Shipping*]
PGT .... Photo Glow Tube
PGT .... Pigtail (MSA)
PGT .... Planetary Gear Train (SAUS)
PGT .... Planned Giving Today [*A publication*]
PGT .... Platoon Gunnery Trainer (DOMA)
PGT .... Pollen Grain Trajectory [*Botany*]
PGT .... Polymer Grid Triode [*Imaging technology*]
PGT .... Porangatu [*Brazil*] [*Airport symbol*] (AD)
PGT .... Potato Extract-Glucose-Thiamine Hydrochloride [*Growth medium*]
PGT .... Power Grid Tube
PGT .... Princeton Gamma Tech (AAEL)
PGT .... Program Global Table (CIST)
PGT .... Putnam Intermediate Government Income [*NYSE symbol*] (SPSG)
PGTA .... Pharmaceutical Grade Transfer Adhesive (SAUS)
PGTE .... Precision Gunnery Training Equipment (SAUS)
PGT-LN ..... Guatemalan Labour Party-National Leadership Nucleus [*Political party*] (PSAP)
PGTO .... Portuguese Government Trade Office (EA)
PGTR .... Plasma-Glucose Tolerance Rate [*Hematology*] (MAE)
PGTRC ...... Professional Group-Telemetry and Remote Control (IAA)
PGTS .... Precision Gunnery Training System [*Army*] (INF)
PGTSND ..... Puget Sound (FAAC)
PGTT .... Prednisolone Glucose Tolerance Test [*Medicine*] (DMAA)
PGTTT .... Precision Gear Train Tools and Test
PGTV .... Pegasus Communications Corp. [*NASDAQ symbol*] (SAG)
PGTW .... Guam [*Mariana Islands*] [*ICAO location identifier*] (ICLI)
PGTZ .... Praegitzer Industries [*NASDAQ symbol*] (TTSB)
PGTZ .... Praegitzer Industries, Inc. [*NASDAQ symbol*] (SAG)
PGU .... Gannon University, Nash Library, Erie, PA [*OCLC symbol*] (OCLC)
PGU .... Pegasus Gold, Inc. [*AMEX symbol*] [*Toronto Stock Exchange symbol*]
PGU .... Peripheral Glucose Uptake [*Medicine*] (MELL)
PGU .... Plant Growth Unit [*NASA*] (MCD)
PGU .... Pontifical Gregorian University (SAUS)
PGU .... Postgonococcal Urethritis [*Medicine*]
PGU .... Power Generator Unit (IAA)
PGU .... Pressure Gas Umbilical (KSC)
PGU .... Propulsion Gas Umbilical
PGUA .... Andersen Air Force Base, Guam Island [*Mariana Islands*] [*ICAO location identifier*] (ICLI)
PGUE .... Professional Group - Ultrasonic Engineering
PGUM .... Agana Naval Air Station, Guam Island [*Mariana Islands*] [*ICAO location identifier*] (ICLI)
PgUp .... Page Up [*Computer science*] (BARN)
PGUT .... Phosphogalactose Uridyltransferase [*Known as Galactose-1-phosphate Uridyl yltransferase*] [*An enzyme*]
PGV .... Greenville [*North Carolina*] [*Airport symbol*] (OAG)
PGV .... Progressive [*Telegraphy*] (PCTE)
PGV .... Proximal Gastric Vagotomy [*Medicine*]
PGVC .... Professional Group - Vehicular Communications
PGW .... Parallel Gap Welding
PGW .... Past Grand Warden [*Freemasonry*]
PGW .... Periodic Gravity Wave (SAUS)
PGW .... Persian Gulf War (SAUS)
PGW .... Philadelphia Gas Works [*Federal Railroad Administration identification code*]
PGW .... Practice Guided Weapon (MCD)
PGW .... Pressure Gas Welding
PGW .... Pressurized Stone Groundwood [*Pulp and paper technology*]
PGW .... Psychogeriatric Ward [*Medicine*] (EDAA)
PGW .... United Plant Guard Workers of America
PGWA .... Pottery and Glass Wholesalers Association (NADA)
PGWB .... Psychological General Well Being [*Index*] (DMAA)
PGWC .... Pennsylvania Gas & Water Co. [*NASDAQ symbol*] (SAG)
PGWC .... PG Energy, Inc. [*NASDAQ symbol*] (SAG)
PGWCX ...... PIMCO: Growth Cl.C [*Mutual fund ticker symbol*] (SG)
PGWCZ ...... P G Energy $2.25 Dep Pfd [*NASDAQ symbol*] (TTSB)
PGWD .... Pesticides in Ground Water Database [*Environmental Protection Agency*]
PGWG .... Parliamentary Group for World Government
PGWG .... Particles and Gases Working Group [*NASA*] (NASA)
PGWR .... Pressurised Gas-Cooled Water Reactor [*Nuclear energy*] (NUCP)
PGWS .... Peak Gust Wind Speed (SAUS)
PGWS .... P. G. Wodehouse Society (EA)
PGWT .... Peipeinimaru, Tinian Island [*Mariana Islands*] [*ICAO location identifier*] (ICLI)
PGWV .... Persian Gulf War Veteran (MELL)
PGwvG ...... Gwynedd-Mercy College, Gwynedd, PA [*Library symbol*] [*Library of Congress*] (LCLS)
PGX .... Prostacyclin [*Medicine*] (EDAA)
PGX .... Prostaglandin X [*or Prostacyclin*] [*Biochemistry*]
PGY .... Global Yield Fund, Inc. [*NYSE symbol*] (SPSG)
PGY .... Postgraduate Year
PGY .... San Diego, CA [*Location identifier*] [*FAA*] (FAAL)
PGYE .... Peptone, Glucose Yeast Extract [*Medium*] [*Biochemistry*] (DAVI)
PGZ .... Ponta Grossa [*Brazil*] [*Airport symbol*] (OAG)
PG/ZD .... Group Propogate / Zero Detect (MHDI)
PH .... Czechoslovakia [*License plate code assigned to foreign diplomats in the US*]
Ph .... Hit Probability
PH .... Humanist Party (Spain) [*Political party*] (PSAP)
pH .... Hydrogen Ion Concentration (MAE)
PH .... Netherlands [*Civil aircraft markings - international*] (PIPO)
Ph .... [*The*] New Testament in Modern English [*1958*] [*J. B. Phillips*] [*A publication*] (BJA)
PH .... Packet Handler (or Handling) (SAUS)
PH .... Page Heading (BUR)
PH .... Pan Head [*Screw Head*] (ECII)
PH .... Parachute Handler (SAUS)
PH .... Parathyroid Hormone (STED)
PH .... Parity High bit (SAUS)
PH .... Parker-Hannifin Corp. [*NYSE symbol*] (SPSG)
PH .... Parotid Hormone [*Biochemistry*]
PH .... Partial Hysterectomy [*Medicine*] (MELL)
PH .... Partially Hepatectomized (DB)
PH .... Passive Hemagglutination (STED)
PH .... Past History [*Medicine*]
PH .... Patient History (SAUS)
PH .... Pauling and Harrischfeger
PH .... Pearl Harbor, Hawaii
PH .... Peliosis Hepatitis (STED)
PH .... Penthouse
pH .... Percent Hydrogen (SSD)
PH .... Performance History
PH .... Perhaps [*Telegraphy*] (PCTE)
PH .... Per Hour (IAA)
PH .... Period Hours (IAA)
PH .... Pershing II
PH .... Persistent Hepatitis [*Medicine*]
PH .... Personal History [*Medicine*] (AAMN)
PH .... Personal Hygiene (MCD)
PH .... Perth [*Postcode*] (ODBW)
PH .... Pest Hospital (SAUS)
Ph .... Phallacidin [*Biochemistry*]
Ph .... Phanerozoic
PH .... Phantom (IAA)
PH .... Phantom Circuit [*Telecommunications*] (TEL)
Ph .... Pharmacia AB [*Sweden*] [*Research code symbol*]
Ph .... Pharmacopoeia
PH .... Phase (KSC)
ph .... Phase (WDMC)
Ph .... Phenanthrene [*Organic chemistry*] (AAMN)
Ph .... Phenyl [*Organic chemistry*]
PH .... Phenylalanine Hydroxylase (STED)
PH .... Phiala [*Bottle*] [*Pharmacy*]
PH .... Philadelphia [*Diocesan abbreviation*] [*Pennsylvania*] (TOCD)
Ph .... Philadelphia Stock Exchange (SG)
PH .... Philharmonic Hall (NADA)
Ph .... Philippians [*New Testament book*] (BJA)
PH .... Philippines [*ANSI two-letter standard code*] (CNC)
ph .... Philippines [*IYRU nationality code*] [*MARC country of publication code*] [*Library of Congress*] (LCCP)
Ph .... Philippus [*Flourished, 13th century*] [*Authority cited in pre-1607 legal work*] (DSA)
Ph .... Phillimore's English Ecclesiastical Reports [*A publication*] (DLA)
Ph .... Phillips' English Chancery Reports [*1841-49*] [*A publication*] (DLA)
Ph .... Phillips' English Election Cases [*1780-81*] [*A publication*] (DLA)
PH .... Phillips Head (DAC)
PH .... Philosophy (GOBB)

PH .... Phone (MDG)
Ph .... Phosphate
PH .... Phosphor (SAUS)
PH .... Phosphorylase (SAUS)
PH .... Phot [*Electronics*] (DEN)
PH .... Photographer's Mate [*Navy rating*]
PH .... Photography Program [*Association of Independent Colleges and Schools specialization code*]
Ph .... Photoreceptor
Ph .... Photostat (BJA)
PH .... Phrase (ADA)
PH .... Phreatic [*Soil biology*] [*Soil phases*] (QSUL)
Ph .... Physica [*of Aristotle*] [*Classical studies*] (OCD)
PH .... Physically Handicapped (OICC)
Ph .... Phytane [*Organic chemistry*]
PH .... Piano Type Hinge
PH .... Picohenry [*One trillionth of a henry*]
P/H .... Pier to House [*Classified advertising*] (ADA)
Ph .... Pilot-Helicopter [*Navy*] [*British*]
PH .... Pilot House
PH .... Pinch Hitter [*Baseball*]
PH .... Pin Hole [*Eye examination*] (CPH)
PH .... Plane Handler [*Navy*]
PH .... Plant Height [*Botany*]
PH .... Plateholder (SAUS)
PH .... Pleckstrin-Homology [*Domain*] [*Biochemistry*]
PH .... Polynesian Airlines [*Airline code*] [*Australia*]
pH .... Pondus Hydrogenii (SAUS)
PH .... Poor Health (DAVI)
PH .... Porphyria Hepatica (STED)
PH .... Porta Hepatis [*Anatomy*]
PH .... Porter House [*Initials often used as a pattern on clothing designed by this firm*]
P/H .... Postage and Handling [*Shipping*]
PH .... Posterior Hypothalamus (STED)
PH .... Post History (STED)
PH .... Postural Hypotension [*Medicine*] (MELL)
pH .... Potential Hydrogen (WDAA)
pH .... Pouvoir Hydrogene [*Hydrogen Power*] [*Negative logarithm of effective H ion concentration*] [*Chemistry*]
PH .... Power Hood [*Automobile classified advertising*]
PH .... Power House (SAUS)
PH .... Powerhouse
PH .... Power of Hydrogen (IAA)
PH .... Practitioner's Handbooks [*A publication*]
PH .... Precipitation Hardening
PH .... Prentice Hall (IID)
P-H .... Prentice-Hall, Inc. [*Publishers*]
PH .... Presidential Medal of Honour [*Botswana*]
PH .... Pressure Head (SAUS)
PH .... Previous Hardening (SAUS)
PH .... Previous History [*Medicine*]
PH .... Primary Hyperparathyroidism
PH .... Private Hotel
PH .... Probability of Hit [*Military*] (MCD)
PH .... Process Hold (SAUS)
PH .... Professional Hydrologist
PH .... Prohibited area (SAUS)
PH .... Project Handclasp (EA)
PH .... Prolactin Hormone (SAUS)
PH .... Prolyl Hydroxylase (STED)
PH .... Prospect Hill [*Vole virus*]
PH .... Prostatic Hypertrophy [*Medicine*] (MAE)
PH .... Protection of Health [*Department of Health*] (IID)
PH .... Public Health
PH .... Public Holiday (DA)
PH .... Public House [*A drinking establishment*] [*British*]
PH .... Pulmonary Hypertension [*Medicine*] (MAE)
PH .... Punctate Hemorrhage [*Medicine*] (STED)
PH .... Purple Heart [*Given to personnel wounded in military service*] [*Military decoration*]
PH .... Purpura Hyperglobulinemia [*Medicine*] (DAVI)
pH_1 .... Isoelectric Point [*Chemistry*] (DAVI)
PH1 .... Phase I Environmental Inspection (COE)
Ph^1 .... Philadelphia Chromosome (MAE)
PH1 .... Photographer's Mate, First Class [*Navy rating*]
Ph^{1}c .... Philadelphia Chromosome
PH2 .... Phase II Environmental Inspection (COE)
PH2 .... Photographer's Mate, Second Class [*Navy rating*]
Ph_2O .... Partial Pressure of Water Vapor [*Chemistry*] (DAVI)
PH3 .... Phase III Environmental Inspection (COE)
PH3 .... Phosphine (AAEL)
PH3 .... Photographer's Mate, Third Class [*Navy rating*]
PHA .... Arterial pH [*Hydrogen ion concentration*] [*Medicine*] (DAVI)
PHA .... Chicago, IL [*Location identifier*] [*FAA*] (FAAL)
PHa .... Hazelton Public Library, Hazelton, PA [*Library symbol*] [*Library of Congress*] (LCLS)
PHA .... Pachena Industries Ltd. [*Vancouver Stock Exchange symbol*]
PHA .... Pacific Pharmaceuticals [*AMEX symbol*] [*Formerly, Xytronyx, Inc.*] (SG)
PHA .... Palomino Horse Association (EA)
PHA .... Parallel Half Adder (SAUS)
PHA .... Parts per Hundred of Asphalt [*Chemical technology*]
PHA .... Passive Hemagglutination [*Immunology*]
PHA .... Peak Horizontal Acceleration
PHA .... Peripheral Hyperalimentation (Solution) [*Medicine*]
PHA .... Peruvian Heart Association (EA)
PHA .... Phantom [*NCIC car model code*]
PHA .... Pharmacia [*Company symbol*]
PHA .... Phaseolus Vulgaris [*Plant lectins*] (QSUL)
PHA .... Phenylalanine [*Medicine*] (MEDA)
PHA .... Philadelphia [*Telegraphy*] (PCTE)
PHA .... Phoenix Airport, AZ [*Amtrak Busline code*]
PHA .... Physics and Astronomy (SAUS)
PHA .... Phytohemagglutinin [*Immunology*]
PHA .... Phytohemagglutinin Antigen [*A skin test for cellular based immunity*] (DAVI)
PHA .... Polomino Horse Association (SAUS)
PHA .... Polyhydroxyalkanoate [*Organic chemistry*]
PHA .... Poly(hydroxystearic Acid) [*Organic chemistry*]
PHA .... Port Health Authority (SAUS)
PHA .... Port Heiden [*Alaska*] [*Seismograph station code, US Geological Survey*] [*Closed*] (SEIS)
PHA .... Potentially Hazardous Asteroids
PHA .... Poultry Husbandry Adviser [*Ministry of Agriculture, Fisheries, and Food*] [*British*]
PHA .... Preferred Hotels Association [*Also known as Preferred Hotel Worldwide*] (EA)
PHA .... Prelaunch Hazard Area (MUGU)
PHA .... Preliminary Hazard Analyses (NASA)
PHA .... Preliminary Hazards Assessment [*Environmental science*] (COE)
PHA .... Primary Human Amnion [*Biology*] (BARN)
PHA .... Pritikin Health Association of Australia
PHA .... Process Hazard Analysis [*Environmental science*]
PHA .... Process Hazards Analysis [*Chemical engineering*]
PHA .... Professional Hairdressers' Association [*Australia*]
PHA .... Professional Handlers Association (EA)
PHA .... Professional Horsemen's Association of America (EA)
PHA .... Programmable Host Access [*Computer science*] (IAA)
PHA .... Pseudohypoaldosteronism [*Medicine*]
PHA .... Public Health Act (DAS)
PHA .... Public Health Agency (DMAA)
PHA .... Public Housing Administration [*or HHFA; disbanded 1965*]
PHA .... Public Housing Agency [*Department of Housing and Urban Development*] (GFGA)
PHA .... Pulmonary Hypertension Association (NRGU)
PHA .... Pulse Height Analysis [*Spectroscopy*]
PHA .... Pulse Height Analyzed
PHA .... State Library of Pennsylvania, Harrisburg, PA [*OCLC symbol*] (OCLC)
PHAA .... Airman Apprentice, Photographer's Mate, Striker [*Navy rating*]
PHAA .... P&H [*NCIC trailer make code*]
PHAA .... Percheron Horse Association of America (EA)
PHAA .... Photographer's Airman Apprentice [*Navy*]
PHAA .... Positive High-Angle of Attack
PHAA .... Pritikin Health Association of Australia (SAUS)
PHAA .... Professional Horsemen's Association of America [*Later, PHA*] (EA)
PHAABO .... Purebred Hanoverian Association of American Breeders and Owners (EA)
PHAB .... Physically Handicapped and Able Bodied [*Charitable organization*] [*British*]
PHABSIM .... Physical Habitat Simulation Model [*Ecology*]
PHABY .... Pharmacia AB [*Commercial firm*] (MHDW)
PHACO .... Phacoemulsification [*Medicine*] (MELL)
PHADA .... Public Housing Authorities Directors Association (EA)
PHADS .... Phoenix Air Defense Sector (SAA)
phaeo .... Phaeochromocytoma [*Pheochromocytoma*] [*Endocrinology*] (DAVI)
PHAID .... Positive Hostile Aircraft Identification
PHAL .... Phalange (WDAA)
PHAL .... Phalanx (WDAA)
PHAL .... Phytohemagglutinin-Stimulated Lymphocyte [*Medicine*] (DMAA)
Phal CC .... Phalen's Criminal Cases [*A publication*] (DLA)
PHALCM .... Phytohemagglutinin Stimulated Leukocyte Conditioned Medium
PHALSE .... Phreakers, Hackers, and Laundry Service Employees [*East Coast group of computer trespassers raided by the FBI*]
PHAM .... Phamis, Inc. [*NASDAQ symbol*] (SAG)
PHAM .... Phase Amplitude Monopulse (PDAA)
PHA-M .... Phytohemagglutinin M [*Immunology*] (MAE)
PHAM .... Project: Hearts and Minds [*An association*] (EA)
Phamis .... Phamis, Inc. [*Associated Press*] (SAG)
P-H Am Lab Arb Awards .... American Labor Arbitration Awards (Prentice-Hall, Inc.) [*A publication*] (DLA)
P-H Am Lab Cas .... American Labor Cases (Prentice-Hall, Inc.) [*A publication*] (DLA)
PHAMOS .... Philips Application Modular Software (SAUS)
PHAMOS .... Premote Hemodynamics and Metabolism in an Orbiting Satellite (KSC)
PHAN .... Airman, Photographer's Mate, Striker [*Navy rating*]
PHAN .... Phantom Express [*Common carrier symbol*]
PH and P .... Peace, Health, and Prosperity
PH&P .... Peace, Heath and Prosperity (SAUS)
PH&S FEDERAL PAC .... Pepper Hamilton & Scheetz [*Philadelphia, PA*] (PACS)
PHANT .... Phantom-Glass [*Theater term*] (DSUE)
PHAOMU .... Pianoforte, Harmonium, and American Organ Makers' Union [*British*]
PHAP .... Palmitoyl Hydrolyzed Animal Protein [*Organic chemistry*]
PHAP .... Phytohemagglutinin Protein [*Medicine*] (MELL)
PHAP .... Provincial Health Assistance Program [*Vietnam*]
PHAQ .... Private Hospitals' Association of Queensland [*Australia*]
PHAR .... Pharmaceutical (WDAA)
PHAR .... Pharmacology

PHAR........ PharmaControl Corp. [*NASDAQ symbol*] (COMM)
PHAR........ Pharmacopoeia (ROG)
PHAR........ Pharmacy [*or Pharmacist*] (MSA)
phar......... Pharmacy (WDAA)
PHAR........ Pharmanetics, Inc. [*NASDAQ symbol*] (NASQ)
PHAR........ Pharming Group NV [*Easdaq Stock Market symbol*]
PhAR........ Photosynthetically Active Radiation (EES)
PHarA....... AMP, Inc., Harrisburg, PA [*Library symbol*] [*Library of Congress*] (LCLS)
Phar B....... Pharmaciae Baccalaureus [*Bachelor of Pharmacy*]
PHarC....... Harrisburg Area Community College, Harrisburg, PA [*Library symbol*] [*Library of Congress*] (LCLS)
PharC........ Pharmaceutical Chemist [*British*]
PHarD....... Dauphin County Library System, Harrisburg, PA [*Library symbol*] [*Library of Congress*] (LCLS)
Phar D...... Doctor of Pharmacy (SAUS)
Phar D...... Pharmaciae Doctor [*Doctor of Pharmacy*]
PHARE...... Action Plan for Coordinated Aid to Poland and Hungary (SAUS)
PHARE...... Poland and Hungary Assistance for Economic Restructuring [*EC*] (ECED)
PHARE...... Program for Harmonized ATC [*Air Traffic Control*] Research in Europe (GAVI)
PharER-T... Pennsylvania Department of Environmental Resources, Bureau of Topographic and Geologic Survey, Harrisburg, PA [*Library symbol*] [*Library of Congress*] (LCLS)
Phar G...... Graduate in Pharmacy (AAMN)
PHarH....... Pennsylvania Historical and Museum Commission, Harrisburg, PA [*Library symbol*] [*Library of Congress*] (LCLS)
PHarH-Ar... Pennsylvania Historical and Museum Commission, Division of Archives and Manuscript, Harrisburg, PA [*Library symbol*] [*Library of Congress*] (LCLS)
PharLb...... Pharmchem Laboratories, Inc. [*Associated Press*] (SAG)
PHARM...... Pharmaceutical
Pharm....... Pharmaceutist (SAUS)
Phar M...... Pharmaciae Magister [*Master of Pharmacy*]
PHARM...... Pharmacist [*or Pharmacy*]
PHARM...... Pharmacology
Pharm....... Pharmacy (DD)
pharm....... Pharmacy (SHCU)
PHARM...... Pharmacy
PHARM...... Pharmacy Building (SAUS)
PhARMA.... Pharmaceutical Research and Manufacturers Association of America (SAUS)
PHARMAC... Pharmacology
PharmacoEcon... PharmacoEconomics [*A publication*] (JLIT)
PHARMACOL... Pharmacological (MSA)
Pharmacol & Toxicol... Pharmacology and Toxicology (MEC)
Pharmacol Biochem Behav... Pharmacology, Biochemistry and Behavior (SAUS)
Pharmacol Toxicol... Pharmacology and Toxicology (SAUS)
Pharma Int... Pharma International (SAUS)
Pharm C.... Pharmaceutical Chemist (MEDA)
PHARM CHEM... Pharmaceutical Chemistry (WDAA)
PHARMCL... Pharmaceutical
PharmD..... Doctor of Pharmacology [*Canada*] (ASC)
Pharm D.... Doctor of Pharmacy
PHARMDOC... Pharmaceutical Documentation (SAUS)
Pharm Eng... Pharmaceutical Engineering (SAUS)
Pharm G.... Graduate in Pharmacy (MEDA)
PHARML.... Pharmaceutical
Pharm M.... Master of Pharmacy
PharMor.... Phar-Mor, Inc. [*Associated Press*] (SAG)
PharmoS.... Pharmos Corp. [*Associated Press*] (SAG)
PharmP..... Pharmaceutical Product Development, Inc. [*Associated Press*] (SAG)
PHARM PAT... Pharmaceutical Patent (SAUS)
Pharm Tech Jpn... Pharm Tech Japan (SAUS)
Pharm Technol... Pharmaceutical Technology (SAUS)
Pharm World Sci... Pharmacy World and Science (SAUS)
PHAROS.... Phased Array Radar for Overland Surveillance (ACAE)
PHAROS.... Phased Array RADAR Operational Simulation [*Army*] (AABC)
PHAROS.... Plan Handling and RADAR Operating System [*Aviation*] (DA)
PHarP....... Harrisburg Polyclinic Hospital, Harrisburg, PA [*Library symbol*] [*Library of Congress*] (LCLS)
PHarris...... Paul Harris Stores [*Associated Press*] (SAG)
PharUpj..... Pharmacia & Upjohn, Inc. [*Associated Press*] (SAG)
PHARUS.... Phased Array Universal Sar (SAUS)
PHAS........ Pollution Hazard Assessment System [*Environmental science*]
PHAS........ Pulse Height Analyzer System
PHASE....... Package for Hospital, Appraisal, Simulation and Evaluation (SAUS)
PHaSE....... Physics of Hard Spheres Experiment (SAUS)
PHASE....... Pre-Hospital Arrest Survival Evaluation [*Cardiology study*]
PHASE IV... Base Level Data Automation Program (SAUS)
Phase Transit... Phase Transition (SAUS)
PHASR...... Personnel Hazards Associated with Space Radiation [*Satellite*]
PHatfB....... Biblical School of Theology, Hatfield, PA [*Library symbol*] [*Library of Congress*] (LCLS)
PHATOX..... Pharmacological and Toxicological (SAUS)
PHatU....... Union Library Co., Hatboro, PA [*Library symbol*] [*Library of Congress*] [*Obsolete*] (LCLS)
PHav......... Haverford Township Free Library, Havertown, PA [*Library symbol*] [*Library of Congress*] (LCLS)
PHAV........ Private Hospitals' Association of Victoria [*Australia*]
PHAWA...... Private Hospitals' Association of Western Australia
PHAXSCAN... Philips High-Speed Automatic X-Ray Analysis System (SAUS)
PHAZ........ Port of Houston Authority [*Federal Railroad Administration identification code*]
Ph B......... Bachelor of Pharmacy
PhB.......... Bachelor of Philosophy (DAVI)
Ph B......... Bachelor of Physical Culture
PhB.......... British Pharmacopoeia (DAVI)
PHB.......... Para-Hexadecylaminobenzoate [*Clinical chemistry*]
PHB.......... Para-Hydroxybenzoate [*Organic chemistry*]
PHB.......... Parahydroxy Benzoic Acid (EDCT)
PHB.......... Parliament House Book [*Scotland*] [*A publication*] (DLA)
PHB.......... Parnaiba [*Brazil*] [*Airport symbol*] (OAG)
PHB.......... Per Hop Behaviour (SAUS)
PhB.......... Pharmacopoeia of Britain (SAUS)
Ph B......... Philosophiae Baccalaureus [*Bachelor of Philosophy*]
PHB.......... Photochemical Hole Burning [*Spectrometry*]
PHB.......... Photographic Bulletin (MCD)
PHB.......... Pioneer Hi-Bred Intl [*NYSE symbol*] (TTSB)
PHB.......... Pointy Haired Boss (SAUS)
PHB.......... Poly(hydroxybenzoate) [*Organic chemistry*]
PHB.......... Polyhydroxybutyrate [*Organic chemistry*]
PHB.......... Pre-Homeobox [*Genetics*]
PHB.......... Preventive Health Behavior [*Medicine*] (DMAA)
PHB.......... Program Header Block [*Computer science*] (ELAL)
PHB.......... Prohibit [*Telegraphy*] (PCTE)
PHB.......... Public Health Bibliography
PHB.......... Public Health Service Building
PHBA........ Palomino Horse Breeders of America (EA)
PHBA........ Para-Hydroxybenzoic Acid [*Organic chemistry*]
PHBA........ P-Hydroxybenzoic Acid (SAUS)
PHB Acid... Poly-a-Hydroxybutyric Acid (SAUS)
PHBB........ Propylhydroxybenzyl Benzimidazole [*Organic chemistry*] (MAE)
Ph BD....... Doctor of Bible Philosophy
PHBD........ Prohibited [*Telegraphy*] (PCTE)
PHBG........ Prohibiting [*Telegraphy*] (PCTE)
PHBH........ Para-Hydroxybenzoate Hydroxylase [*An enzyme*]
Ph B in Arch... Bachelor of Philosophy in Architecture
Ph B in Com... Bachelor of Philosophy in Commerce
Ph B in Ed... Bachelor of Philosophy in Education
PhBJ......... Bachelor of Philosophy in Journalism (NADA)
PHBK........ Barking Sands, Kauai Island [*Hawaii*] [*ICAO location identifier*] (ICLI)
PHBK........ Peoples Heritage Financial Group [*NASDAQ symbol*]
PHBK........ People's Heritage Financial Group, Inc. [*NASDAQ symbol*] (NQ)
PHBK........ Peoples Heritage Finl Gr [*NASDAQ symbol*] (TTSB)
PHBLX....... Phoenix Balanced [*Mutual fund ticker symbol*] (SG)
PHBN........ Prohibition [*Telegraphy*] (PCTE)
PHB/PHBV... Poly-3-Hydroxybutyric Acid
Ph-Br........ Phenyl-Bromide (SAUS)
ph brz....... Phosphor Bronze (ODA)
PHBRZ...... Phosphor Bronze
PhBSp....... Bachelor of Philosophy in Speech (NADA)
PHBV........ Hydroxy Butyric Valeric Acid [*Polymer*]
PHBV........ Poly(hydroxybutytrate-Valerate) [*Organic chemistry*]
ph bz........ Phosphor Bronze (BARN)
PHC.......... Chief Photographer's Mate [*Navy rating*]
PHC.......... Children's Hospital of Pittsburgh, Pittsburgh, PA [*OCLC symbol*] (OCLC)
PHC.......... Haverford College, Haverford, PA [*Library symbol*] [*Library of Congress*] (LCLS)
PHC.......... Pacific Holding Corp. (EFIS)
PHC.......... Pacific Hurricane Centers [*National Weather Service*]
PHC.......... Palmitoyl Homocysteine [*Biochemistry*]
PHC.......... Panhandle Conference (PSS)
PHC.......... Pathonic Network, Inc. [*Toronto Stock Exchange symbol*]
PHC.......... Patrick Henry College (SAUS)
PHC.......... Peoples' Holding Corp. [*AMEX symbol*] (NASQ)
PHC.......... Personal Health Costs [*Medicine*] (DMAA)
PHC.......... Personal Holding Company [*Generic term*]
PHC.......... Perturbed-Hardness Chain [*Molecular thermodynamics*]
PHC.......... Petroleum Helicopters de Colombia SA [*ICAO designator*] (FAAC)
PHC.......... Petroleum Hydrocarbon (SAUS)
Ph C......... Pharmaceutical Chemist
PHC.......... PHC, Inc. [*Associated Press*] (SAG)
Ph C......... Philosopher of Chiropractic
PHC.......... Photographic Change (MCD)
PHC.......... Physic [*Telegraphy*] (PCTE)
PHC.......... Physical Hydrogen Cracking (SAUS)
PHC.......... Population Housing Census (OICC)
PHC.......... Port Harcourt [*Nigeria*] [*Airport symbol*] (OAG)
PHC.......... Port Hardy [*British Columbia*] [*Seismograph station code, US Geological Survey*] (SEIS)
PHC.......... Posthospital Care [*Medicine*]
PHC.......... [*A*] Prairie Home Companion [*National Public Radio program*]
PHC.......... Pratt Hotel Corp. [*AMEX symbol*] (SPSG)
PHC.......... Premature Hereditary Canities [*Medicine*]
PHC.......... Premolar Hypodontia, Hyperhidrosis, Canities Prematura [*Syndrome*] [*Medicine*] (DMAA)
PHC.......... Primary Health Care
PHC.......... Primary Health Centre [*British*]
PHC.......... Primary Hepatic Carcinoma [*Medicine*]
PHC.......... Primary Hepatocellular Carcinoma [*Oncology*] (DAVI)
PHC.......... Principal Hazardous Constituent (GNE)
PHC.......... Proliferative Helper Cells [*Immunology*]
PHC.......... Public Health Committee (SAUS)
PHCA........ Philippine Heart Center for Asia (PDAA)
PHCA........ Pig Health Control Association [*British*]
PHCA........ Pleasure Horse Club of America (EA)

PHCA .... Profound Hypothermic Circulatory Arrest [*Medicine*] (RAWO)
PHCAA ...... Public Health Cancer Association of America [*Defunct*] (EA)
P-H Cas ..... American Federal Tax Reports (Prentice-Hall, Inc.) [*A publication*] (DLA)
PHCB .... Page Header Control Bit (SAUS)
PHCC .... Patients Encountered at [*Primary*] Health Care Centers
P-HCC .... Piston-Hand Control Clutch (DNAB)
PHCC .... Plumbing, Heating, Cooling Contracters (SAUS)
PHCC .... Primary Hepatocellular Carcinoma [*Medicine*] (DMAA)
PHCC .... Priority Healthcare [*NASDAQ symbol*]
PHCC .... Priority Healthcare Corp. [*NASDAQ symbol*] (NASQ)
PHCC .... Punjab High Court Cases [*India*] [*A publication*] (DLA)
PHCCNCZ ... Plumbing-Heating-Cooling Contractors of Nebraska, Central Zone (EARSL)
PHCC PAC... National Association of Plumbing-Heating-Cooling Contractors PAC [*Falls Church, VA*] (PACS)
PHCDS .... Public Health Common Data Set (SAUS)
PHCF .... Pituitary Growth Hormone Cell Function (SAUS)
Ph Ch........ Phillips' English Chancery Reports [*1841-49*] [*A publication*] (DLA)
PHCIB .... Plumbing-Heating-Cooling Information Bureau (EA)
PHC Inc ..... PHC, Inc. [*Associated Press*] (SAG)
PH Circuit... Phantom Circuit (SAUS)
Ph-Cl .... Phenyl-Chloride (SAUS)
PHCLIS....... Protected Home Circle Life Insurance Society (EA)
PHCM .... Master Chief Photographer's Mate [*Navy rating*]
PHCM .... Phone.com, Inc. [*NASDAQ symbol*]
PHCO........ Peoples Holding [*NASDAQ symbol*] (TTSB)
PHCO........ Peoples Holding Co. [*NASDAQ symbol*] (SAG)
PHCO........ Philadelphia Coke [*Federal Railroad Administration identification code*]
PHCONST... Phase Constant (IAA)
P-H Corp.... Corporation [*Prentice-Hall, Inc.*] [*A publication*] (DLA)
PHCP .... Physically Handicapped Children's Program
PHCP .... Prehospital Care Provider [*Health insurance*] (DMAA)
PHCS .... Physics [*Telegraphy*] (PCTE)
PHCS .... Private Healthcare Systems
PHCS .... Senior Chief Photographer's Mate [*Navy rating*]
PHCSC ...... Piers-Harris Children's Self-Concept Scale [*Child development test*] [*Psychology*]
PHCSG ...... Primary Health Care Specialist Group (SAUS)
PHCT .... Perturbed Hard Chain Theory [*Equation of state*]
PHCVD ...... Photochemical Chemical Vapor Deposition (SAUS)
PHCVD ...... Photon-induced CVD (SAUS)
PHCVD ...... Photosensitized Chemical Vapor Deposition (SAUS)
PHCV-SD ... Phase Conversion and Step-Down (MSA)
PHD.......... Chesapeake Biological Laboratories, Inc. [*AMEX symbol*] (SAG)
PHD.......... Dixmont State Hospital, Sewickley, PA [*OCLC symbol*] (OCLC)
Ph D......... Doctor of Pharmacy
PhD.......... Doctor of Philosophy (GAGS)
PHD.......... Doctor of Public Health [*British*] (DAS)
PHD.......... Duncan Aviation, Inc. [*ICAO designator*] (FAAC)
PHD.......... Koninklijke Philips Electronics NV [*NYSE symbol*]
PHD.......... New Philadelphia, OH [*Location identifier*] [*FAA*] (FAAL)
PHD.......... Panty-Hose Distributor (SAUS)
PHD.......... Parallel Head Disk
PHD.......... Pathological Habit Disorder [*Medicine*] (EDAA)
PhD.......... Perfect Hard Disk [*Century Data Systems*] [*Computer science*]
Phd.......... Phaedo [*of Plato*] [*Classical studies*] (OCD)
PhD.......... Pharmaciae Doctor [*Doctor of Pharmacy*] (DAVI)
PHD.......... Phase Detector (SAUS)
PHD.......... Phase-Shift Driver (CET)
Ph D......... Philosophiae Doctor [*Doctor of Philosophy*] [*Facetious translation: Piled Higher and Deeper*]
PHD.......... Photoelectron Diffraction [*Spectroscopy*]
PHD.......... Photohydrodynamic [*Astrophysics*]
PHD.......... Phudagi [*Language symbol*] (ETLW)
PHD.......... Physical Hydrology Division (SAUS)
PHD.......... Piled Higher and Deeper (SAUS)
PHD.......... Pilot's Horizontal Display [*Aviation*] (CAAL)
PHD.......... Poly Harnstoff Dispersion [*Organic chemistry*]
PHD.......... Port Hueneme Division [*Naval Surface Warfare Center*]
PHD.......... Port Huron & Detroit Railroad Co. [*AAR code*]
PHD.......... Positioning-Head Drum (DNAB)
PHD.......... Post-heparin (Plasma) Diamine Oxidase [*Medicine*] (EDAA)
PHD.......... Potential Harmful Drug (SAUS)
PHD.......... Precision High Dose
PH D......... Pre-Pearl Harbor Dad [*A humorous wartime degree*]
PHD.......... Pride, Hustle, and Drive
PHD.......... Pseudohypertrophic Dystrophy [*Medicine*] (EDAA)
PHD.......... Public Health Department
PHD.......... Public Health Director
PHD.......... Public Health Doctor (SAUS)
PHD.......... Public Housing Development [*Department of Housing and Urban Development*] (GFGA)
PHD.......... Pulsed Holograpy Development [*Department of Energy*]
PHD.......... Pulse Height Discrimination
PHD.......... Pulse Height Discriminators (ADWA)
PHD.EC ..... Chesapeake Bio Labs 'A' [*ECM, Symbol*] (TTSB)
PHDAN ...... Pharmacopoeia Danica (SAUS)
PHDAN ...... Physically Dangerous (DNAB)
PHDB .... Physical Distribution Services [*Common carrier symbol*]
PhD cameras... Push-here-Dummy cameras (SAUS)
PHDCN ...... Project on Human Development in Chicago Neighborhoods [*Harvard University*] (RCD)
PHDD......... Personal History of Depressive Disorders (MEDA)
PHDDS...... PSRO [*Professional Standards Review Organization*] Hospital Discharge Data Set
PHDE........ Poly(heptadiester) [*Organic chemistry*]
PHDEA ...... Public Housing Drug Elimination Act [*1988*]
PhDEd....... Doctor of Philosophy in Education [*British*] (ADA)
PHDH........ Dillingham Air Force Base, Oahu Island [*Hawaii*] [*ICAO location identifier*] (ICLI)
PHDI......... Palmer Hydrological Drought Index
PhD(Med)... Doctor of Philosophy (Medicine) (ADA)
PhDMH...... Doctor of Philosophy in Mechanics and Hydraulics
PhD Otol.... Doctor of Philosophy in Otolaryngology (PGP)
PhDPM Rehab... Doctor of Physical Medicine and Rehabilitation (PGP)
PHDr......... Doctor of Philosophy
Phdr .... Phaedrus [*of Plato*] [*Classical studies*] (OCD)
PHDR........ Preliminary Hardware Design Review
PhD(RCA)... Doctor of Philosophy (Royal College of Art) [*British*] (DBQ)
PHDS........ Post-Harvest Documentation Service [*Kansas State University*] (IID)
PHDS........ Programmable Hydraulic Deceleration System [*Automotive engineering*]
PhD Surg ... Doctor of Philosophy in Surgery (PGP)
PHDX........ Phelps Dodge [*Private rail car owner code*]
PHE.......... Aviation POL [*Petroleum, Oil, and Lubrication*] Handling Equipment (NATG)
PHE.......... Eastern State School and Hospital, Trevose, PA [*OCLC symbol*] (OCLC)
PHE.......... Packaging and Handling Engineer (SAUS)
PHE.......... Pawan Hans Ltd. [*India*] [*ICAO designator*] (FAAC)
PHE.......... Periodic Health Examination
PHE.......... Petroleum Handling Equipment (MCD)
phe .... Phenylalanine [*Also, F*] [*An amino acid*] (DOG)
Phe .... Phenylalanine [*Also, F*] [*An amino acid*]
PHE.......... Phenylephrine [*Medicine*] (DMAA)
PHE.......... Pheophytin [*Biochemistry*]
Phe .... Phoenix [*Constellation*]
PHE.......... Photo Engravers & Electrotypers Ltd. [*Toronto Stock Exchange symbol*]
PHE.......... Plate Heat Exchanger [*Chemical engineering*]
PHE.......... Port Hedland [*Australia*] [*Airport symbol*] (OAG)
PHE.......... Post-Heparin Esterase [*Medicine*] (MAE)
PHE.......... Preflight Heat Exchanger [*NASA*] (KSC)
PHE.......... Public Health Engineer (ODA)
PHE.......... Public Health Evaluation (SAUS)
PHEA .... Public Health Engineering Abstracts [*A publication*]
PHEAA....... Pennsylvania Higher Education Assistance Agency (EDAC)
Phear Wat... Phear's Rights of Water [*1859*] [*A publication*] (DLA)
PHED .... Physical & Health Education (SAUS)
PHEEM ...... Photoelectron-Emission Microscopy (AAEL)
PhEEM ...... Photoemission Electron Microscopy [*Medicine*] (DMAA)
Ph Eg........ Pharmacopoeia of Egypt (SAUS)
PHEI......... Penetrator, High-Explosive, Incendiary (MCD)
PHEL .... Petroleum Helicopters, Inc. [*NASDAQ symbol*] (NQ)
PHEL .... Petroleum Helicopters (Vtg) [*NASDAQ symbol*] (TTSB)
PHEL .... Phelan Manufacturing Company [*NCIC trailer make code*]
PHELK....... Petroleum Helicopters [*NASDAQ symbol*] (TTSB)
PHELM ...... Pulsed High Energy Laser Countermeasures (ACAE)
PhelpD ...... Phelps Dodge Corp. [*Associated Press*] (SAG)
PHeM........ Hershey Medical Center, Hershey, PA [*Library symbol*] [*Library of Congress*] (LCLS)
PHEM........ Primitive Helium Mantle [*Geology*]
PHEM........ Public Health Evaluation Manual (SAUS)
PHEMA...... Poly(hydroxyethyl Methacrylate) [*Organic chemistry*]
pHEMT ...... Psedomorphic High Electron Mobility Transistor [*Electronics*] (AAEL)
phen......... o-Phenanthroline [*Organic chemistry*]
PHEN .... Phenanthroline Monohydrate (SAUS)
PHEN .... Phenolic (AAG)
PHEN .... Phenotype [*Microbiology*] (DAVI)
Pheney Rep... Pheney's New Term Reports [*England*] [*A publication*] (DLA)
PHENG ...... Photoengraving (VRA)
PH Eng...... Public Health Engineer
PHENIR ..... Pheniramine Maleate (SAUS)
PHENO ...... Phenobarbital [*A drug*]
pheno .... Phenotype
PHENO ...... Precise Hybrid Elements for Nonlinear Operation (IEEE)
PHENOB...... Phenobarbital [*A Drug*] (DAVI)
phenobarb... Phenobarbital [*A drug*] (DAVI)
PHENO/D... Phenomenological Death (SAUS)
PHENOLP... Phenolphthalein (SAUS)
PHENOLPHT... Phenolphthalein (SAUS)
PHENOM.... Phenomena (SAUS)
phenom..... Phenomenon (BARN)
PHENOM.... Phenomenon (GOBB)
PHENOS..... Precise Hybrid Elements for Nonlinear Operations (IAA)
PHEN SAL... Phenyl Salicylate (SAUS)
PHENTH..... Phenothiazine [*A drug*] (DAVI)
PHENYL..... Phenylpropanol [*A drug*] (DAVI)
PHENYLEPH... Phenylephrine Hydrochloride (SAUS)
PHENYLEPH BIT... Phenylephrine Bitartrate (SAUS)
PHENYLEPH TAN... Phenylephrine Tannate (SAUS)
PHENYLTOL... Phenyltoloxamine Citrate (SAUS)
PHEO .... Pheochromocytoma [*Oncology*]
PHEP .... Phelps Horse Trailer [*NCIC trailer make code*]
PHER .... Photographic Mechanical Equipment Repair [*Course*] (DNAB)
PHER .... Plate Heat Exchanger [*Chemical Engineering*] (DNAB)

PHEREC..... Public Health Entomology Research and Education Center [*Florida A&M University*] (RCD)
PHERMEX... Pulsed High-Energy Radiographic Machine Emitting X-Rays
PHERP...... Public Health Education and Research Program (ADWA)
PHET........ Photoetching (VRA)
Ph Ev........ Phillips on Evidence [*A publication*] (DLA)
PHEWA...... Presbyterian Health, Education, and Welfare Association (EA)
PHEXdb..... PHEX Locus Database [*Canada*] (GDD)
PHF.......... Fairview State Hospital, Waymart, PA [*OCLC symbol*] (OCLC)
PHF.......... Newport News [*Virginia*] [*Airport symbol*] (OAG)
PHF.......... Pacholder Fund, Inc. [*AMEX symbol*] (NASQ)
PHF.......... Paired Helical Filaments [*Neuroanatomy*] [*Term coined by Dr. Robert Terry to describe the components of neurofibrillary tangles in the brains of Alzheimer's Disease patients*]
PHF.......... Patrick Henry Foundation [*Liberty, NY*] (EA)
PHF.......... Patrol Hydrofoil [*Missile*] (HGAA)
PHF.......... Payload Handling Fixture [*NASA*] (NAKS)
PHF.......... Peak Hour Factor [*Transportation*]
PHF.......... Peanut Hull Flour
PHF.......... Pergamon Holding Foundation [*Liechtenstein*]
PHF.......... Personal Hygiene Facility [*NASA*] (NASA)
Ph-F......... Phenyl-Fluoride (SAUS)
PHF.......... Phoenix House Foundation (EA)
PHF.......... Plug Handling Fixture (NRCH)
PHF.......... Potomac Horse Fever [*Veterinary science*] (DB)
PHF.......... Procedure History File (COE)
PHF.......... Process Holding Fixture (MCD)
PHF.......... Procurement History File [*DoD*]
PHF.......... Public Health Foundation [*Information service or system*] (IID)
PHF.......... USF&G Pacholder Fd [*AMEX symbol*] (TTSB)
PHF.......... USF & G Pacholder Fund, Inc. [*AMEX symbol*] (CTT)
PHFA........ Potomac Horse Fever Agent
PHFC........ Pittsburgh Home Finl [*NASDAQ symbol*] (TTSB)
PHFE........ Pulsed High-Frequency Electroporation [*Analytical biochemistry*]
P-H Fed Taxes... Federal Taxes (Prentice-Hall, Inc.) [*A publication*] (DLA)
PHFENN..... Pharmacopoeia Fennica (SAUS)
PHFET....... Photosensitive Field Effect Transistor (SAUS)
PHFF........ Oahu [*Hawaii*] [*ICAO location identifier*] (ICLI)
PHFG........ Primary Human Fetal Glial [*Cytology*]
PHFPrA..... USF&G $4.10cm Cv Exch A Pfd [*NYSE symbol*] (TTSB)
PHFTX....... Prentice-Hall Federal Taxes [*Database*] (IT)
Ph G......... Graduate in Pharmacy
PHG.......... Koninklijke Philips Electronics NV [*NYSE symbol*]
PhG.......... Pharmacopoeia Germanica [*German Pharmacopeia*] (MAE)
PHG.......... Phenate-Hexamine Goggle [*British World War I anti-poison-gas helmet*]
PHG.......... Philips Electronics NV [*Formerly, Philips NV*] [*NYSE symbol*] (SPSG)
PHG.......... Phillipsburg, KS [*Location identifier*] [*FAA*] (FAAL)
PHG.......... Phosphatidylglycerol [*Test used to determine fetal lung maturity*] (DAVI)
PHG.......... Photographer's Mate (Cameraman) [*U.S. Navy enlisted rating*] (AUER)
Phg.......... Phytophthora Megasperma Glycinea [*A fungus*]
PHG.......... Postman, Higher Grade [*British*] (DI)
PHG.......... Prototype Hydrofoil Gunboat
PHG.......... Scranton State General Hospital, Scranton, PA [*OCLC symbol*] (OCLC)
PHGA........ Pteroylhexaglutamylglutamic [*or Pteroylheptaglutamic*] Acid [*Biochemistry*]
PhGABA..... Phenyl-gamma-aminobutyric Acid [*Tranquilizer*]
PHGALL..... Pharmacopoeia Gallica (SAUS)
PHGC........ Phillips Grain Company [*Common carrier symbol*]
PHGLTF..... Physiological Training Flight [*Air Force*]
Phgly........ Phenylglycine [*An amino acid*]
PHGM........ Patrol Hydrofoil Guided Missile [*Navy*] (DNAB)
Phgn......... Physiognomonica [*of Aristotle*] [*Classical studies*] (OCD)
PHGNDWG... Photogenic (VRA)
PHGRM..... Photogram (VRA)
P HGT....... Package Height [*Freight*]
PHGY........ Physiology (SAUS)
PHH.......... Andrews, SC [*Location identifier*] [*FAA*] (FAAL)
PHH.......... Haverford State Hospital, Haverford, PA [*OCLC symbol*] (OCLC)
PHH.......... Paterson Habitat for Humanity (EARSL)
PHH.......... Peterson, Howell & Heather, Inc. (EFIS)
PHH.......... Phan Thiet [*South Vietnam*] [*Airport symbol*] (AD)
PHH.......... PHH Corp. [*NYSE symbol*] [*Toronto Stock Exchange symbol*] (SPSG)
PHH.......... Phillips Head [*Screw*]
PHH.......... Posthemorrhagic Hydrocephalus [*Neurology*] (DAVI)
PHH.......... Puu Huluhulu [*Hawaii*] [*Seismograph station code, US Geological Survey*] [*Closed*] (SEIS)
PHHA........ Pearl Harbor History Associates (EA)
PHHC........ Programmable Hand-Held Calculator (RDA)
PHHGSIA... Pamphlet-Household Goods Shipment Information (SAUS)
PHHH........ PH Group [*NYSE symbol*]
PHHI......... Persistent Hyperinsulinemic Hypoglycemia of Infancy [*Medicine*]
PHHI......... Wheeler Air Force Base, Oahu Island [*Hawaii*] [*ICAO location identifier*] (ICLI)
PHHM....... Palm Harbor Homes [*NASDAQ symbol*] (TTSB)
PHHM....... Palm Harbor Homes, Inc. [*NASDAQ symbol*] (SAG)
PHHN........ Hana, Maui Island [*Hawaii*] [*ICAO location identifier*] (ICLI)
PHHS........ Patrick Henry High School (SAUS)
PHHS........ Precise Helicopter Hovering System (SAUS)
PHHSA...... Protestant Health and Human Services Assembly (EA)
PHI........... Archie Phinny Hall (SAUS)
PHi........... Historical Society of Pennsylvania, Philadelphia, PA [*Library symbol*] [*Library of Congress*] (LCLS)
PhI........... International Pharmacopoeia
PHI........... Pacific Health Information Network (SAUS)
PHI........... Packard Humanities Institute (SAUS)
PHI........... Paleozoic Hydrocarbon Industries (EFIS)
PHI........... Passive Hemagglutination Inhibitor (DB)
PHI........... Past History of Illness (MELL)
PHI........... Permanent Health Insurance [*British*]
PHI........... Petroleum Helicopters, Inc. (MCD)
PHI........... Phagocytosis Index [*Medicine*] (EDAA)
PhI........... Pharmacopoeia Internationalis [*International Pharmacopoeia*] (DAVI)
Ph-I.......... Phenyl-Iodide (SAUS)
PHI........... Philadelphia [*Pennsylvania*] [*Seismograph station code, US Geological Survey*] [*Closed*] (SEIS)
Phi........... Philadelphia Eagles [*National Football League*] [*1933-42, 1944-present*] (NFLA)
PHI........... Philadelphia White Stockings (SAUS)
PHI........... Philippine Long Distance Telephone Co. [*NYSE symbol*] (SAG)
PHI........... Philippine Long D Tel ADS [*NYSE symbol*] (TTSB)
Phi........... Philippus [*Flourished, 13th century*] [*Authority cited in pre-1607 legal work*] (DSA)
Phi........... Philips [*Holland & International*] [*Record label*]
PHI........... Philips Aviation Services [*Netherlands*] [*ICAO designator*] (FAAC)
PHI........... Philipsburg State General Hospital, Philipsburg, PA [*Inactive*] [*OCLC symbol*] (OCLC)
PHI........... Phillipsite [*A zeolite*]
PHI........... Philosophie Informationsdienst [*Philosophy Information Service*] [*University of Dusseldorf*] [*Information service or system*] (IID)
PHI........... Philosophy (WGA)
PHI........... Phosphine (LDT)
PHI........... Phosphohexose Isomerase [*An enzyme*]
Phi........... Physeptone [*A narcotic substitute*]
PHI........... Physiological Hyaluronidase Inhibitor [*Biochemistry*]
PHI........... Pioneer Hi-Bred International, Inc. (EFIS)
PHI........... Polarity Health Institute (EA)
PHI........... Position & Heading Indicator (SAUS)
PHI........... Position and Homing Indicator
PHI........... Precision Homing Indicator (SAUS)
PHI........... Pre-Harvest Interval (EPAT)
PHI........... Prentice-Hall International [*Publisher*]
PHI........... Programme Hydrologique International [*International Hydrological Program - IHP*] [*UNESCO*] (MSC)
PHI........... Project Health (MHID)
PHI........... Provincial House, Inc. (EFIS)
PHI........... Public Health Informatics Research Laboratory [*University of Maryland at College Park*] (RCD)
PHI........... Public Health Inspector [*British*]
PHI........... Public Health Institute (SAUS)
PHIA......... Pharmaceutical Ingredients Asia [*Conference*]
PHIA......... Phenylalanine (MAE)
PHIA......... Profoundly Hearing Impaired Adult (MELL)
PHIAL....... Phiala [*Bottle*] [*Pharmacy*]
PHIB......... Amphibious
PHib......... Hibeh Papyri [*A publication*] (OCD)
PHIBB....... Project for Historical Biobibliography [*A publication*]
PHIBCB...... Amphibious Construction Battalion [*Also, ACB*] (NVT)
PhibComd... Amphibious Forces Command (SAUS)
PHIBCORPAC... Amphibious Corps, Pacific Fleet [*Marine Corps*]
PHIBCORPS... Amphibious Corps [*Marine Corps*]
PHIBDET... Amphibious Detachment
PHIBDETIND... Amphibious Detachment, India
PHIBEU...... Amphibious Forces, Europe
PHIBEX...... Amphibious Exercise [*NATO*]
PHIBFOR... Amphibious Forces
PHIBGROUP... Amphibious Group
PHIBGRU... Amphibious Group
PHIBLANT... Amphibious Forces, Atlantic Fleet
PHIBLEX... Amphibious Landing Exercise [*Navy*] (NVT)
PHIBNAW... Amphibious Forces, Northwest African Waters
PHIBOPS... Amphibious Operations [*Navy*] (NVT)
PHIBPAC... Amphibious Forces, Pacific Fleet
PHIBRAIDEX... Amphibious Raid Exercise [*Navy*] (NVT)
PHIBRECONEX... Amphibious Reconnaissance Exercise [*Navy*] (NVT)
PHIBREFTRA... Amphibious Refresher Training [*Navy*] (CAAL)
PHIBRFT... Amphibious Refresher Training [*Navy*] (NVT)
PHIBRON... Amphibious Squadron [*Army*]
PHIBSEU... Amphibious Forces, Europe
PHIBSFORPAC... Amphibious Forces, Pacific Fleet
PHIBSKDN... Amphibious Ship Shakedown Cruise [*Navy*] (NVT)
PHIBSLANT... Amphibious Forces, Atlantic Fleet
PHIBSPAC... Amphibious Forces, Pacific Fleet
PHIBSS...... Amphibious Schoolship [*Navy*] (NVT)
PhibsTraLant... Amphibious Forces Training Command, Atlantic Fleet (SAUS)
PhibsTraPac... Amphibious Forces Training Command, Pacific Fleet (SAUS)
PHIBSTRAPAC... Training Command Amphibious Forces, US Pacific Fleet
PHIBSUKAY... Amphibious Bases, United Kingdom
PHIBTF...... Amphibious Task Force [*Navy*] (NVT)
Phibtra...... Amphibious Training (SAUS)
PHIBTRA... Training Command Amphibious Forces
PHIBTRABASE... Amphibious Training Base [*Navy*]
PHIBTRAEX... Amphibious Training Exercise [*Navy*] (NVT)
PHIBTRAINLANT... Training Command Amphibious Forces, US Atlantic Fleet
PHIBTRAINPAC... Training Command Amphibious Forces, US Pacific Fleet

PhibTraLant... Amphibious Training Command, Atlantic (SAUS)
PHIBTRALANT... Training Command Amphibious Forces, US Atlantic Fleet
PHIBTRANS... Amphibious Transport [*Navy*]
PHIB Transistor... Phosphor Inverted Bipolar Transistor (SAUS)
PHIBTRAPAC... Training Command Amphibious Forces, US Pacific Fleet
PHIBTRBASE... Amphibious Training Base [*Navy*]
PHIBUF...... Performance Buffet Limit (GAVI)
PHIBWARTRACEN... Amphibious Warfare Training Center [*Navy*]
PHIC......... Poly(hexyl Isocyanate) [*Organic chemistry*]
PHICB....... Putnam High Income Convertible & Bond Fund [*Associated Press*] (SAG)
PHICT....... Philips Inventory Control Technique [*Computer science*] (IAA)
Phi D........ Doctor of Philanthropy
PHID......... Positive Hostile Identification Device [*Air Force*]
PHID......... Project for Health Information Dissemination (ADWA)
PHIDAS..... Philips Data Systems (SAUS)
Phi Dex..... Phi Delta Chi [*An association*] (NTPA)
PHIG......... Programmers Hierarchical Interactive Graphics (SAUS)
PHIG......... Programmer's Hierarchical Interactive Graphics System [*Computer science*] (DCOM)
PHIGS....... Programmers' Hierarchical Interactive Graphics Standard (ODA)
PHIGS PLUS... Programmers Hierarchical Interactive Graphics System Plus Lumiere Und Surfaces (SAUS)
PHII......... Phillips Trailers [*NCIC trailer make code*]
PHII......... Planet Hollywood International, Inc. [*NASDAQ symbol*] (SAG)
PHII......... Planet Hollywood Intl'A' [*NASDAQ symbol*] (TTSB)
PHIK......... Honolulu/Hickam Air Force Base, Oahu Island [*Hawaii*] [*ICAO location identifier*] (ICLI)
PhiKaps..... Phi Kappa Theta National (EA)
Phil......... Orationes Philippicae [*of Cicero*] [*Classical studies*] (OCD)
PHIL......... Pacific Health Laboratories [*NASDAQ symbol*]
Phil......... Philadelphia (ODBW)
PHIL......... Philadelphia [*Pennsylvania*]
PHIL......... Philadelphia Exchange (EBF)
Phil......... Philadelphia Reports [*A publication*] (DLA)
phil......... Philanthropic (PROS)
Phil......... Philemon [*New Testament book*]
Phil......... Philharmonia [*Record label*]
PHIL......... Philharmonic
PHIL......... Philippians [*Biblical*]
Phil......... Philippians [*New Testament book*]
Phil......... Philippine (SAUS)
Phil......... Philippine Island Reports [*A publication*] (DLA)
Phil......... Philippines (VRA)
Phil......... Phillimore's English Ecclesiastical Reports [*A publication*] (DLA)
Phil......... Phillips' English Chancery Reports [*1841-49*] [*A publication*] (DLA)
Phil......... Phillips' English Election Cases [*1780-81*] [*A publication*] (DLA)
Phil......... Phillips' Illinois Reports [*152-245 Illinois*] [*A publication*] (DLA)
Phil......... Phillips' North Carolina Law Reports [*A publication*] (DLA)
Phil......... Phillips' Treatise on Insurance [*A publication*] (DLA)
PHIL......... Phill Trailer [*NCIC trailer make code*]
Phil......... Philoctetes [*of Sophocles*] [*Classical studies*] (OCD)
PHIL......... Philology
Phil......... Philopoemen [*of Plutarch*] [*Classical studies*] (OCD)
Phil......... Philosophy (DD)
phil......... Philosophy (SHCU)
PHIL......... Philosophy
PHIL......... Philosophy Library (SAUS)
PHIL......... Potential Host Institures List [*European Commission*]
PHIL......... Programmable Algorithm Machine High-Level Language [*Computer science*]
PHILA....... Philadelphia [*Pennsylvania*]
Phila........ Philadelphia Reports [*Pennsylvania*] [*A publication*] (DLA)
Phila C Pharmacy... Philadelphia College of Pharmacy and Science (GAGS)
Philad....... Philadelphia Reports [*Pennsylvania*] [*A publication*] (DLA)
PHILADA... Philadelphia (ROG)
Philada R... Philadelphia Reports [*Pennsylvania*] [*A publication*] (DLA)
Philada Rep... Philadelphia Reports [*Pennsylvania*] [*A publication*] (DLA)
PHILADEL... Philadelphia (ROG)
Philadelphia Leg Int... Philadelphia Legal Intelligencer [*Pennsylvania*] [*A publication*] (DLA)
Philadelphia Rep... Philadelphia Reports [*Pennsylvania*] [*A publication*] (DLA)
Phila Free Lib... Philadelphia Free Library (SAUS)
PHILAG...... Public Health Institute-London Action Group (SAUS)
PHILAGRP... Philadelphia Group (DNAB)
Phila Leg Int... Philadelphia Legal Intelligencer [*Pennsylvania*] [*A publication*] (DLA)
Phila LJ..... Philadelphia Law Journal [*A publication*] (DLA)
PHILAMCHAM... Philippine-American Chamber of Commerce (NTPA)
philan....... Philanthropical (BJA)
PHILANTHR... Philanthropic (ROG)
Phila (PA)... Philadelphia Reports [*Pennsylvania*] [*A publication*] (DLA)
Phila QM Depot... Philadelphia Quartermaster Depot (SAUS)
Phila Reports... Philadelphia Reports [*Pennsylvania*] [*A publication*] (DLA)
PHILASAG... Philippine Association of Agriculturists (SAUS)
PHILASHIPYD... Philadelphia Shipyard (SAUS)
philat........ Philately
Philbro...... Philipp Brothers Ltd. [*Commercial firm*]
Phil C....... Philosophy in Chiropractic
PHILCAG... First Philippine Civic Action Group [*Deployed in 1964 to assist South Vietnam*] (VNW)
Phil Civ & Can Law... Phillimore's Civil and Canon Law [*A publication*] (DLA)
PHILCOA... Philippine Coconut Administration (SAUS)
PHILCOM... Philippine Global Communications, Inc. [*Manila*] [*Telecommunications*]
PhilCon..... Philadelphia Consolidated Holding [*Commercial firm*] [*Associated Press*] (SAG)
PHILCON... Philippine Contingent [*Military*]
Phil Cop.... Phillips' Law of Copyright Designs [*A publication*] (DLA)
Phil D....... Philosophiae Doctor [*Doctor of Philosophy*] [*See also Ph D*] [*Latin*]
PHILDANCO... Philadelphia Dance Company
Phil Dec.... Philippus Decius [*Deceased circa 1537*] [*Authority cited in pre-1607 legal work*] (DSA)
Phil Dom... Phillimore's Law of Domicil [*A publication*] (DLA)
Phil Ecc..... Phillimore's Ecclesiastical Judgments [*A publication*] (DLA)
Phil Ecc..... Phillimore's English Ecclesiastical Law [*2 eds.*] [*1873, 1895*] [*A publication*] (DLA)
Phil Ecc..... Phillimore's English Ecclesiastical Reports [*1809-21*] [*A publication*] (DLA)
Phil Ecc Judg... Phillimore's Ecclesiastical Judgments [*1867-75*] [*A publication*] (DLA)
Phil Ecc Law... Phillimore's English Ecclesiastical Law [*2 eds.*] [*1873, 1895*] [*A publication*] (DLA)
Phil Ecc R... Phillimore's English Ecclesiastical Reports [*1809-21*] [*A publication*] (DLA)
Phil El Cas... Phillips' English Election Cases [*1780-81*] [*A publication*] (DLA)
Philem...... Philemon [*New Testament book*]
PhilEnv...... Philip Environmental [*Commercial firm*] [*Associated Press*] (SAG)
Phil Eq...... Phillips' North Carolina Equity Reports [*A publication*] (DLA)
Phil Ev...... Phillips on Evidence [*A publication*] (DLA)
Phil Ev Cow & H & Edw Notes... Phillips on Evidence, Notes by Cowen, Hill, and Edwards [*A publication*] (DLA)
PHILEX...... Philadelphia Stock Exchange
Phil Fam Cas... Phillipps' Famous Cases in Circumstantial Evidence [*A publication*] (DLA)
Phil Grand... Phillips' Grandeur of the Law [*A publication*] (DLA)
Phil Hung... Philharmonica Hungarica (SAUS)
PHIL I....... Philippine Islands (WDAA)
Phili Fran... Philippus Francus [*Deceased, 1471*] [*Authority cited in pre-1607 legal work*] (DSA)
Phil ILJ..... Philippine International Law Journal [*A publication*] (DLA)
Phil Ins..... Phillips on Insurance [*A publication*] (DLA)
Phil Insan... Phillips on Lunatics [*1858*] [*A publication*] (DLA)
Phil Int Law... Phillimore's International Law [*A publication*] (DLA)
Phil Int LJ... Philippine International Law Journal [*A publication*] (DLA)
Phil Int Rom Law... Phillimore's Introduction to the Roman Law [*A publication*] (DLA)
Philip........ Philippines
Philip Fran... Philippus Franchus [*Deceased, 1471*] [*Authority cited in pre-1607 legal work*] (DSA)
Philipp...... Philippines (BARN)
Philippine... Philippine Reports [*A publication*] (DLA)
Philippine Co... Philippine Code [*A publication*] (DLA)
Philippine Internat LJ... Philippine International Law Journal [*Manila, Philippines*] [*A publication*] (DLA)
Philippine Int'l LJ... Philippine International Law Journal [*A publication*] (DLA)
Philippine LJ... Philippine Law Journal [*A publication*] (DLA)
Philippine L Rev... Philippine Law Review [*A publication*] (DLA)
Philipp Sci... Philippine Scientist [*A publication*] (PABS)
PhilipsEl... Philips Electronics NV Holding Co. [*Associated Press*] (SAG)
Philips J Res... Philips Journal of Research (SAUS)
Philips Res Rept... Philips Research Reports (SAUS)
Philips Telecommun Data Syst Rev... Philips Telecommunication and Data Systems Review (SAUS)
Philips Weld Rep... Philips Welding Reporter (SAUS)
PHILIRAN... Philips Petroleum Iran (SAUS)
Phil Jud..... Phillimore's Ecclesiastical Judgments [*1867-75*] [*England*] [*A publication*] (DLA)
Phil Judg... Phillimore's Ecclesiastical Judgments [*1867-75*] [*A publication*] (DLA)
Phill......... Phillips' English Chancery Reports [*1841-49*] [*A publication*] (DLA)
Phill......... Phillips' English Election Cases [*1780-81*] [*A publication*] (DLA)
Phill......... Phillips' Illinois Reports [*152-245 Illinois*] [*A publication*] (DLA)
Phill......... Phillips' North Carolina Equity Reports [*A publication*] (DLA)
Phill......... Phillips' North Carolina Law Reports [*A publication*] (DLA)
Phil Lab Rel J... Philippine Labour Relations Journal [*A publication*] (DLA)
Phil Law.... Phillips' North Carolina Law Reports [*A publication*] (DLA)
Phill Ch..... Phillips' English Chancery Reports [*1841-49*] [*A publication*] (DLA)
Phill Ch (Eng)... Phillips' English Chancery Reports [*1841-49*] [*A publication*] (DLA)
Phil LD...... Doctor of Lithuanian Philology
Phill Ecc Judg... Phillimore's Ecclesiastical Judgments [*1867-75*] [*A publication*] (DLA)
Phill Ecc R... Phillimore's English Ecclesiastical Reports [*1809-21*] [*A publication*] (DLA)
Phill Eq (NC)... Phillips' North Carolina Equity Reports [*A publication*] (DLA)
Phil Lic..... Licentiate of Philosophy [*British*]
Phillim...... Phillimore's English Ecclesiastical Reports [*1809-21*] [*A publication*] (DLA)
Phillim Dom... Phillimore's Law of Domicil [*A publication*] (DLA)
Phillim Eccl... Phillimore's Ecclesiastical Judgments [*1867-75*] [*A publication*] (DLA)
Phillim Eccl... Phillimore's English Ecclesiastical Reports [*1809-21*] [*A publication*] (DLA)
Phillim Ecc Law... Phillimore's English Ecclesiastical Law [*A publication*] (DLA)
Phillim Int Law... Phillimore's International Law [*A publication*] (DLA)
Phill Ins..... Phillips on Insurance [*A publication*] (DLA)
PHILLIPS... Philips Petroleum Co. (SAUS)
Phillips...... Phillips' English Chancery Reports [*1841-49*] [*A publication*] (DLA)

Phillips...... Phillips' English Election Cases [*1780-81*] [*A publication*] (DLA)
Phillips...... Phillips' Illinois Reports [*152-245 Illinois*] [*A publication*] (DLA)
Phillips...... Phillips' North Carolina Equity Reports [*A publication*] (DLA)
Phillips...... Phillips' North Carolina Law Reports [*A publication*] (DLA)
Phillips U ... Phillips University (GAGS)
Phil Lit R ... Philatelic Literature Review [*A publication*]
Phil LJ ...... Philippine Law Journal [*Manila*] [*A publication*] (DLA)
Phill L (NC)... Phillips' North Carolina Law Reports [*A publication*] (DLA)
Phil L Rev... Philippine Law Review [*A publication*] (DLA)
PHILLS...... Portable Hyperspectral Imager for Low Light Spectroscopy (SEWL)
Phil Lun..... Phillips on Lunatics [*1858*] [*A publication*] (DLA)
Philly........ Philadelphia
PhilM........ Master of Philosophy (GAGS)
Phil Mag.... Philips Magazine (SAUS)
Phil Mech Liens... Phillips on Mechanics' Liens [*A publication*] (DLA)
PhilMr....... Philip Morris Companies, Inc. [*Associated Press*] (SAG)
philn......... Philanthropy
Phil NC...... Phillips' North Carolina Law Reports [*A publication*] (DLA)
Philo......... Philo Judaeus [*First century AD*] [*Classical studies*] (OCD)
philo......... Philology (WDAA)
Philocrit... Philosopher Critic (SAUS)
Philocrit... Philosophical Criticism (SAUS)
Philol........ Philological (SAUS)
Philol........ Philologus [*A publication*] (OCD)
Philol........ Philology (DIAR)
PHILOL...... Philology
Philol Suppl... Philologus. Supplement [*A publication*] (OCD)
PHILOM..... Philomathes [*Lover of Learning*] (ROG)
PHILOMATH... Philomathematicus [*Lover of Mathematics*] (ROG)
Phil Orch... Philadelphia Orchestra (SAUS)
Philos .... Philosophic (SAUS)
Philos .... Philosophy (BEE)
PHILOS...... Philosophy (EY)
Philos Educ... Philosophy of Education (SAUS)
Philos Mag A\Phys Condens Matter Defects Mech... Philosophical Magazine A, Physics of Condensed Matter, Defects and Mechanical Properties (SAUS)
Philos Mag B\Phys Condens Matter ElectronOpt... Philosophical Magazine B, Physics of Condensed Matter, Electronic, Optical and Magnetic Properties (SAUS)
Philos Mag Lett... Philosophical Magazine Letters (SAUS)
Philos Pub... Philosophical Publishing Co (SAUS)
Philos Res... Philosophical Research Society (SAUS)
Philostr ..... Philostratus [*Second century AD*] [*Classical studies*] (OCD)
Philos Trans R Soc London... Philosophical Transactions of the Royal Society of London (SAUS)
Philos Trans R Soc London A Math Phys Sci... Philosophical Transactions of the Royal Society of London A, Mathematical and Physical Sciences (SAUS)
Phil (PA) ... Philadelphia Reports [*Pennsylvania*] [*A publication*] (DLA)
PHILPAC ... Altria Group Inc. PAC [*New York, NY*] (PACS)
PHILPAC ... Prosperity Helps Inspire Liberty PAC [*Alexandria, VA*] (PACS)
Phil Pat..... Phillips on Patents [*A publication*] (DLA)
PhilPet...... Phillips Petroleum Co. [*Associated Press*] (SAG)
PHILPUC... Philippine Presidential Unit Citation Badge [*Military decoration*]
PHILPUC Badge... Philippine Presidential Unit Citation Badge (SAUS)
PHILQA...... Philips Question Answering System (NITA)
Phil R .... Philadelphia Reports [*Pennsylvania*] [*A publication*] (DLA)
Phil R .... Philosophical Review [*A publication*] (BRI)
Phil Rep .... Philadelphia Reports [*Pennsylvania*] [*A publication*] (DLA)
PhilRH ...... Phillips [*R.H.*], Inc. [*Associated Press*] (SAG)
Phil Rom Law... Phillimore's Private Law among the Romans [*A publication*] (DLA)
PHILSEAFRON... Philippine Sea Frontier
PHILSEAFRON... Phillipine Sea Frontier [*Nautical term*] (NTA)
PHILSIN... Philippines-Singapore Submarine Cable (SAUS)
PHIL SOC... Philharmonic Society (WDAA)
PHILSOM... Periodical Holdings in the Library of the School of Medicine [*Washington University School of Medicine*] [*Library network*]
PHILSOM Network... Periodical Holdings in the Library of the School of Medicine Network (SAUS)
Phil Sp...... Philippine Spanish (SAUS)
Phil St Leg R... Phillips' Studii Legalis Ratio [*A publication*] (DLA)
Phil St Tr... Phillips' State Trials [*Prior to 1688*] [*A publication*] (DLA)
PhilSub ..... Philadelphia Suburban Corp. [*Associated Press*] (SAG)
PHILSUGIN... Philipine Sugar Institute (SAUS)
Phil Unters... Philologische Untersuchungen [*A publication*] (OCD)
Phil US Pr... Phillips' United States Practice [*A publication*] (DLA)
Phil Wochenschr... Philologische Wochenschrift [*A publication*] (OCD)
Phil Yb Int'l L... Philippine Yearbook of International Law [*Manila, Philippines*] [*A publication*] (DLA)
PHIM .... Phillips Manufacturing Company [*NCIC trailer make code*]
PHIM .... Posthypoxic Intention Myoclonus [*Medicine*] (DMAA)
PHIN......... Pharmaceutical and Healthcare Industry News (SAUS)
PHIN......... Position and Homing Inertial Navigator
PHIND....... Pharmaceutical and Healthcare Industries News Database [*PJB Group Publications Ltd.*] [*Information service or system*] (IID)
P-H Ind Rel Lab Arb... Industrial Relations, American Labor Arbitration (Prentice-Hall, Inc.) [*A publication*] (DLA)
P-H Ind Rel Union Conts... Industrial Relations, Union Contracts, and Collective Bargaining (Prentice-Hall,Inc.) [*A publication*] (DLA)
PHINet ...... Prentice-Hall Information Network [*Prentice-Hall Information Services*] [*Information service or system*] (IID)
PHINTS...... Phase locked Interferometric Tracking System (SAUS)
Phip .... Phipson's Digest, Natal Reports [*South Africa*] [*A publication*] (DLA)
Phip .... Phipson's Reports, Natal Supreme Court [*South Africa*] [*A publication*] (DLA)
PHI PAC..... PEPCO Holdings Inc. PEPCO-Conectiv PAC [*Washington, DC*] (PACS)
Phip Ev...... Phipson on Evidence [*12th ed.*] [*1976*] [*A publication*] (DLA)
PHIPrA ...... Philippine L-D Tel Pfd GDS [*NYSE symbol*] (TTSB)
PHIPS .... Professional Hi-Resolution Image Processing System [*TerraVision, Inc.*] (PCM)
Phipson..... Phipson's Reports [*A publication*] (SAFN)
Phipson ..... Reports of Cases in the Supreme Court of Natal [*A publication*] (DLA)
PHIRB .... Public Health Inspectors' Registration Board [*British*] (BI)
PHIS........ Physically Handicapped in Science (BABM)
PHIS........ Population and Housing Information System (SAUS)
PHIS........ Posthead Injury Syndrome [*Medicine*] (EDAA)
PHIS........ Program Hardware Interface Specification (CAAL)
pH/ISE....... pH Value/Ion-Selective Electrode (SAUS)
PHITAP...... Predesigned [*or Priority*] High-Interest Tactical Air Prediction [*Acoustic forecast*] (MCD)
PHITAP...... Priority High Interest Tactical Air Acoustic Forecast Prediction
PHITAR...... Predesignated High-Interest Tactical Area [*Navy*] (NVT)
PhIUS .... Pharmaceutical Ingredients U.S.
PHJ.......... Danville State Hospital, Danville, PA [*OCLC symbol*] (OCLC)
PHJC .... Penn Hall Junior College [*Pennsylvania*] [*Closed, 1973*]
PHJC .... Poor Handmaids of Jesus Christ [*Ancilla Domini Sisters*] [*Roman Catholic religious order*]
PHJC .... Port Huron Junior College [*Michigan*]
PH/JO .... Photojournalist (DNAB)
PHK.......... Pahokee, FL [*Location identifier*] [*FAA*] (FAAL)
PHK.......... Personal Hygiene Kit (MCD)
PhK.......... Phosphorylase Kinase [*An enzyme*]
PHK.......... Platelet Phosphohexokinase (MAE)
PHK.......... Postmortem Human Kidney [*Cells*]
PHK Cells... Postmonem Human Kidney Cells (SAUS)
PHK Cells... Post-mortem Human Kidney Cells (SAUS)
PHKO........ Kona/Ke-Ahole, Hawaii Island [*Hawaii*] [*ICAO location identifier*] (ICLI)
PHKP........ Kaanapali, Maui Island [*Hawaii*] [*ICAO location identifier*] (ICLI)
PHKU........ Kunia [*Hawaii*] [*ICAO location identifier*] (ICLI)
PHKW........ Powerhouse Resources, Inc. [*NASDAQ symbol*] (SAG)
PHKWE....... Powerhouse Resources [*NASDAQ symbol*] (TTSB)
PHL.......... Allentown State Hospital, Allentown, PA [*OCLC symbol*] (OCLC)
Ph L......... Licentiate in Philosophy
Ph L......... Licentiate of Pharmacy
PHL.......... Pacific Harbor Line [*Federal Railroad Administration identification code*]
PHL.......... Packaging, Handling and Logistics (SAUS)
PHL.......... Periodical Holdings List [*Libraries*]
PHL.......... Philadelphia [*Pennsylvania*] [*Airport symbol*]
PHL.......... Philippines [*ANSI three-letter standard code*] (CNC)
PHL.......... Philips Industries, Inc. [*NYSE symbol*] (COMM)
PHL.......... Phillips Michigan City Flying Service, Inc. [*ICAO designator*] (FAAC)
PHL.......... Philosophy (SAUS)
PHL.......... Photographer's Mate (Laboratory Technician) [*U.S. Navy enlisted rating*] (AUER)
PHL.......... Physical [*Telegraphy*] (PCTE)
PHL.......... Planet Hollywood Intl'A' [*NYSE symbol*] (SG)
PHL.......... Preliminary Hazard List [*Environmental science*] (LDOE)
PHL.......... Preliminary Hazards List (ACAE)
PHL.......... Pressure to Horizontal Locks [*Missiles*] (AAG)
PHL.......... Public Health Laboratory [*Medicine*] (EDAA)
PHL.......... Public Health Law
PHLA........ Plasma Postheparin Lipolytic Activity [*Clinical chemistry*]
PHLA........ Postheparin Lipolytic Activity [*Medicine*] (DMAA)
PHLAG ...... Philips Load and Go (NITA)
PHLAG ...... Phillips Petroleum Load and Go [*System*]
PHLAGS..... Phillips Petroleum Load and Go System (DNAB)
PHLAG System... Philips Load and Go System (SAUS)
Phlb .... Philebus [*of Plato*] [*Classical studies*] (OCD)
Phld .... Philodemus [*First century BC*] [*Classical studies*] (OCD)
phleg........ phlegmaticalness (SAUS)
phleg........ phlegmaticness (SAUS)
phleg........ phlegmier (SAUS)
phleg........ phlegmiest (SAUS)
PHLEGM .... People's Hayfever Listener Examiner Gazette Magazine [*A publication*] (WDAA)
Phlgr........ Photolithographer (SAUS)
PHLH........ Phillips Head [*Screw*]
PHLH Screw... Philips Head Screw (SAUS)
PHLI......... Lihue, Kauai Island [*Hawaii*] [*ICAO location identifier*] (ICLI)
PHLI......... Public Health Leadership Institutes (SAUS)
PHLIS .... Public Health Laboratory Information System (SAUS)
PHLITHO... Photolithographic (VRA)
PhILD........ Philippine Long Distance Telephone Co. [*Associated Press*] (SAG)
PHILDis..... Philadelphia Procurement District (SAUS)
Phlm......... Philemon [*New Testament book*]
PHLO......... Phloretin [*Biochemistry*]
PHLODOT... Phase Lock Doppler Tracking [*System*] (MUGU)
PHLODOT System... Phase Lock Doppler Tracking System (SAUS)
PHLP........ Phillips Truck Line [*Common carrier symbol*]
PhlpGs ...... Phillips Gas [*Associated Press*] (SAG)
PHLS......... Public Health Laboratory Service [*British*]
PHLSB....... Public Health Laboratory Service Board [*British*]
PHLU........ Pharos Line [*Intermodal shipping container symbol*] (TVRC)

PhIVH .... Phillips-Van Heusen Corp. [*Associated Press*] (SAG)
PHLWR .... Pressurized Heavy and Light Water Reactor (SAUS)
PHLX .... Philadelphia Stock Exchange
PHLY .... Philadelphia Consol Hldg [*NASDAQ symbol*] (TTSB)
PHLY .... Philadelphia Consolidated Holding [*NASDAQ symbol*] (SAG)
PHLY .... Philadelphia Consolidated Holding Corp. [*NASDAQ symbol*] (NASQ)
Ph M .... Master in Pharmacy
Ph M .... Master of Philosophy
PHM .... Mayview State Hospital, Bridgeville, PA [*OCLC symbol*] (OCLC)
PHM .... Park Health Management (MHID)
PHM .... Patrol Combatant Missile Hydrofoil [*Navy*]
PHM .... Patrol Hydrofoil Missile [*Navy symbol*]
PHM .... Patrol Hydrofoil Missileship [*Navy*]
PHM .... Patterson-Harker Method [*Physics*]
PHM .... Per Hundred Million (NASA)
PHM .... Petroleum Helicopters, Inc. [*ICAO designator*] (FAAC)
PHM .... Phantom (MSA)
PhM .... Pharmaciae Magister [*Master of Pharmacy*] (DAVI)
PhM .... Pharmacist's Mate [*U.S. Navy enlisted rating*] (AUER)
PHM .... Pharmacist's Mate [*Navy rating*]
PHM .... Phase Meter
PHM .... Phase Modulation [*Radio data transmission*] (DEN)
Phm .... Philemon [*New Testament book*] (BJA)
PHM .... Philemon [*Biblical*]
PhM .... Philips Minigroove [*Record label*]
PHM .... PHM Corp. [*NYSE symbol*] (COMM)
PHM .... Photographer's Mate (Microfilm Photographer) [*U.S. Navy enlisted rating*] (AUER)
PHM .... Portable Handheld Meter [*Automotive testing*]
PHM .... Posterior Hyaloid Membrane [*Eye anatomy*]
PHM .... Post-Holiday Movie
PHM .... Power Hybrid Microcircuit
PHM .... Pulmonary Hyaline Membrane [*Syndrome*] [*Medicine*] (DB)
PHM .... Pulte Corp. [*NYSE symbol*] (SPSG)
PHM .... Pulte Home Corp. (EFIS)
PHM .... Pulte Homes of Michigan Corporation (EFIS)
PHM .... Pyroheliometer (SAUS)
PHMA .... Plastic Houseware Manufacturers Association
PHMA .... Polyhexyl Methacrylate [*Organic chemistry*]
PHMA .... Professional Housing Management Association (NTPA)
Phm B .... Bachelor of Pharmacy
PHMB .... Para-Hydroxymercuribenzoate [*Biochemistry*]
PHMC .... Pennsylvania Historical and Museum Commission (SAUS)
PHMC .... Probe Heater Motor Controller [*NASA*] (MCD)
Phmcyc .... Pharmacyclics, Inc. [*Associated Press*] (SAG)
PHMD .... Pseudohypertrophic Muscular Dystrophy (CPH)
PHMDP .... Pharmacist's Mate, Dental Prosthetic Technician [*Navy rating*]
PhMeSFI .... Phenylmethylsulfonylfluoride (SAUS)
Phm G .... Graduate in Pharmacy
PHMK .... Molokai, Molokai Island [*Hawaii*] [*ICAO location identifier*] (ICLI)
PHMO .... Partially Hydrogenated Menhaden Oil [*Food science*]
PhMor .... Phar-Mor, Inc. [*Associated Press*] (SAG)
PHMOV .... Phleum Mottle Virus [*Plant pathology*]
PHMP .... Primordial Hot Mantle Plume (PDAA)
PhmRes .... Pharmaceutical Resources, Inc. [*Associated Press*] (SAG)
PHMS .... Para-Hydroxymercuriphenylsulfonate [*Organic chemistry*]
PHMS .... Patrol Hydrofoil Missile Ship [*Navy/NATO*]
PHMS .... Polish Historical Military Society (EA)
PHMU .... Waimea-Kohala, Kamuela, Hawaii Island [*Hawaii*] [*ICAO location identifier*] (ICLI)
PhMV .... Phleum Mottle Virus
pH/mV .... pH Value versus Millivolts (SAUS)
PHMV .... Physalis Mosaic Virus [*Plant pathology*]
PHMWO .... Prospect Hill Millimeter Wave Observatory [*Waltham, MA*] [*Air Force*]
PHMX .... PhyMatrix Corp. [*NASDAQ symbol*] (SAG)
PHN .... Norristown State Hospital, Norristown, PA [*OCLC symbol*] (OCLC)
PHN .... North Philadelphia, PA [*Amtrak rail station code*]
PHN .... Passive Heymann Nephritis [*Medicine*] (DMAA)
PHN .... Phoenix Resource Companies, Inc. [*AMEX symbol*] (SAG)
PHN .... Phone (KSC)
PHN .... Physician [*Telegraphy*] (PCTE)
PHN .... Population, Health and Nutrition (SAUS)
PHN .... Port Huron [*Michigan*] [*Airport symbol*] (AD)
PHN .... Port Huron, MI [*Location identifier*] [*FAA*] (FAAL)
PHN .... Postherpetic Neuragia [*Medicine*]
PHN .... Public Health Network [*Information service or system*] (IID)
PHN .... Public Health Nurse
PHNA .... Barbers Point Naval Air Station, Oahu Island [*Hawaii*] [*ICAO location identifier*] (ICLI)
PHNBR .... Phone Number (SAUS)
PHNC .... Center for Population, Health and Nutrition [*US Agency for International Development*] (RCD)
PHNC .... Pearl Harbor, Oahu Island [*Hawaii*] [*ICAO location identifier*] (ICLI)
PHNG .... Kaneohe Bay Marine Corps Air Station, Oahu Island [*Hawaii*] [*ICAO location identifier*] (ICLI)
PHNL .... Honolulu/International, Oahu Island [*Hawaii*] [*ICAO location identifier*] (ICLI)
PHNORD .... Pharmacopoeia Nordica (SAUS)
PHNS .... Pearl Harbor Naval Shipyard
PHNSY .... Pearl Harbor Navy Ship Yard (SAUS)
PHNX .... Phoenix Medical Technology, Inc. [*NASDAQ symbol*] (COMM)
PHNX .... Phoenix Shannon Ltd. [*NASDAQ symbol*] (SAG)
PhnxRs .... Phoenix Resource Companies, Inc. [*Associated Press*] (SAG)
PhnxShn .... Phoenix Shannon Ltd. [*Associated Press*] (SAG)
PhnxTc .... Phoenix Technologies Ltd. [*Associated Press*] (SAG)
PHNXY .... Phoenix Shannon plc ADR [*NASDAQ symbol*] (TTSB)
PHNY .... Lanai City, Lanai Island [*Hawaii*] [*ICAO location identifier*] (ICLI)
PHNY .... Pearl Harbor Navy Yard [*Later, Pearl Harbor Naval Shipyard*]
P-H NYETR ... Prentice-Hall New York Estate Tax Reports [*A publication*] (DLA)
PHO .... Pediatric Hematology-Oncology [*Medical specialty*] (DHSM)
PHO .... Peoples Telephone Co. [*AMEX symbol*] (SAG)
PHO .... Periarticular Heterotopic Ossification [*Medicine*] (RAWO)
PHO .... Phenolic Heavy Oil
PHO .... Philco Houston Operations (SAA)
PHO .... Phoenix Airways (Pfy) [*South Africa*] [*FAA designator*] (FAAC)
PHO .... Phoenix (automobile) [*NCIC car model code*]
Pho .... Phoenix Cardinals [*National Football League*] [*1988-93*] (NFLA)
PHO .... Phone List (SAUS)
Pho .... Photographer [*British military*] (DMA)
Pho .... Photonic (SAUS)
PHO .... Physician Hospital Organization (AMHC)
PHO .... Physician-Hospital Organization [*Information service or system*] (HCT)
PHO .... Point Hope [*Alaska*] [*Airport symbol*] (OAG)
PHO .... Polk State School and Hospital, Polk, PA [*OCLC symbol*] (OCLC)
PHO .... Port Health Officer
PHO .... Potentially Hazardous Object
PHO .... Principal House Officer [*Australia*]
PHO .... Public Hazard Office [*Environmental science*] (COE)
PHO .... Public Health Officer Inspector (HEAS)
PHO .... Puu Honuaula [*Hawaii*] [*Seismograph station code, US Geological Survey*] (SEIS)
PHOAC .... Photographer's Mate, Combat Aircrewman [*Navy rating*] [*Obsolete*]
Phob .... Previous Highroller, on a Budget [*Lifestyle classification*]
PHOBOS .... Photometric Instrument for Biological Optical Sections
PHOC .... Photo Control [*NASDAQ symbol*] (TTSB)
PHOC .... Photo Control Corp. [*NASDAQ symbol*] (NQ)
PHOC .... Photocopy (MSA)
PHOCAS .... Photo Optical Cable Controlled Submersible (PDAA)
PHOCIS .... Photogrammetric Circulatory Survey (PDAA)
PHOCL .... Photo-initiated Chemical Laser (SAUS)
PHOD .... Philadelphia Ordnance Depot [*Military*] (AAG)
PhOD .... Physical Oceanography Division [*National Oceanic and Atmospheric Administration*] (RCD)
PHODEC .... Photometric Determination of Equilibrium Constants [*Computer science*]
PHOE .... Phoenix [*NCIC car make code*]
Phoe .... Phoenix [*Constellation*]
PHOE .... Phoenix Camping Trailer [*NCIC trailer make code*]
PHOE .... Phoenix (motorcycle) [*NCIC motorcycle make code*]
PHOE .... Phoenix (trucks) [*NCIC truck make code*]
Phoen .... Phoenician (BJA)
Phoen .... Phoenissae [*of Euripides*] [*Classical studies*] (OCD)
PHOEN .... Phoenix, AZ [*American Association of Railroads railroad junction routing code*]
PHOENIX ... Plasma Heating Obtained by Energetic Neutral Injection Experiment (IEEE)
PHOENIX PAC ... Phoenix PAC [*Alexandria, VA*] (PACS)
Phoenix Voice Scrap Ind ... Phoenix. Voice of the Scrap Industries (SAUS)
PHOFEX .... Photofragment Excitation [*Spectroscopy*]
PHOFL .... Photoflash (AAG)
PHOG .... Kahului, Maui Island [*Hawaii*] [*ICAO location identifier*] (ICLI)
PHOINT .... Photographic Intelligence
PHOLAS .... Philips Host Language System (SAUS)
PHOLED .... Phosphorescent OLED
PhoM .... Photographer's Mate [*U.S. Navy enlisted rating*] (AUER)
PHOM .... Photographer's Mate [*Navy rating*] [*Obsolete*]
PHON .... Phoenician
phon .... Phonetic (NTIO)
PHON .... Phonetics
PHON .... Phonogram (ROG)
PHON .... Phonograph (AAG)
phon .... Phonology (SHCU)
PHONCON ... Telephone Conversation [*or Conference*]
PHONE .... Telephone (NTCM)
PHONEBOOK ... Region 3 Telephone Directory (SAUS)
Phones .... Earphones (SAUS)
PHONET .... Phonetics (ROG)
Phonetel .... Phonetel Technologies [*Commercial firm*] [*Associated Press*] (SAG)
P HONG .... Ponchong [*Tea trade*] (ROG)
Phono .... Phonocardiogram [*Cardiology*] (DAVI)
PHONO .... Phonograph (MSA)
PHONOG .... Phonography
phonol .... Phonology (WDAA)
PHONOL .... Phonology
PHONORECORD ... Phonograph Record (SAUS)
Phonos .... Phonoscopy (SAUS)
PHONOVISION ... Telephone Television (SAUS)
PHOPT .... Pseudohypoparathyroidism [*Endocrinology*]
Phor .... Phoronida (SAUS)
Phorm .... Phormio [*of Terence*] [*Classical studies*] (OCD)
PHOS .... Phosphate (KSC)
PHOS .... Phosphorescent (KSC)
Phos .... Phosphorous (SAUS)
PHOS .... Phosphorus [*Chemical symbol is P*]
PhosBro .... Phosphor Bronze
PHOSCHEM ... Phosphate Chemicals Export Association (EA)

PHOSI .... Preliminary Handbook of Operations and Service Instructions
PHOSIAC... Photographically Stored Information Analog Comparator
PHosp .... Post Hospital [*Army*]
PHOS-S ..... Phosphorus Spot [*Urine Test*] [*Chemistry*] (DAVI)
PHOST ..... Poly(hydroxystyrene) [*Organic chemistry*]
Phot .... Photius [*Ninth century AD*] [*Classical studies*] (OCD)
PHOT .... Photograph
PHOT .... Photographer [*Navy rating*] [*British*]
Phot .... Photography (BEE)
PHOTABS... Photographic Abstracts [*Pergamon*] [*Database*]
PHOTAC ..... Phototypesetting and Composing [*AT & T*]
Photcm...... Photocomm, Inc. [*Associated Press*] (SAG)
PHOTEX ..... Photographic Exercise (SAUS)
PHOTINT... Photographic Intelligence [*Military*]
photmur..... Photo Mural (VRA)
PHOTO .... Photograph (AAG)
photo .... Photograph (VRA)
PHOTO .... Photographic
Photo .... Photogravure [*Philately*]
Photobiochem Photobiophys... Photobiochemistry and Photobiophysics (SAUS)
PhotoC .... Photo-Control Corp. [*Associated Press*] (SAG)
PHOTOCD... Photographic Compact Disk (SAUS)
Photochem Photobiol... Photochemistry and Photobiology (MEC)
PHOTOCOMP... Photocomposed (SAUS)
PHOTOCOMP... Photocomposition (SAUS)
PHOTOG .... Photographic
photog........ Photography (SHCU)
Photogeog... Photogeography (SAUS)
PHOTOGEOL... Photographic Geology (SAUS)
PHOTOGR... Photographer
Photogr ..... Photographical (SAUS)
PHOTOGR... Photography
Photogramm Eng Remote Sens... Photogrammetric Engineering and Remote Sensing (SAUS)
Photogramm Rec... Photogrammetric Record (SAUS)
Photogr Appl Sci Technol... Photographic Applications in Science. Technology and Medicine (SAUS)
Photogr Sci Eng... Photographic Science and Engineering (SAUS)
PHOTOINT... Photo Intelligence (ACAE)
PHOTOLITH... Photolithographic
PHOTOM.... Photometry
photomon... Photomontage (VRA)
PHOTON .... Paneuropean Photonic Transport Overlay Network (SAUS)
Photon ...... Photon Dynamics, Inc. [*Associated Press*] (SAG)
PHOTONICS... Photo Electronics (ACAE)
PHOTONS... Photometric Thermospheric Oxygen Nightglow Study (SAUS)
Photo Op.... Photo Opportunity (SAUS)
Photophysiol Curr Top... Photophysiology, Current Topics (SAUS)
PHOTOSYN... Photosynthesis (SAUS)
Photosynth Res... Photosynthesis Research (SAUS)
PHOTOTRIGULANT... Photographic Triangulation Group, Atlantic [*Military*] (DNAB)
PHOTOTRIGUPAC... Photographic Triangulation Group, Pacific [*Military*] (DNAB)
PHOTOX..... Photochemical Vapor Deposition Process (ACAE)
PHOTOXE... Pathfinder and Helicopter Operation in a Toxic Environment (SAUS)
Photrln...... Photronic Labs [*Associated Press*] (SAG)
PHOTRIPART... Photo Triangulation Party [*Military*]
PHOTRON... Photographic Squadron [*Navy*]
PHOTUB..... Phototube (KSC)
PHO/TY...... Photo Type [*Deltiology*]
P How .... Pack Howitzer (SAUS)
PHOXA ...... Photochemical Oxidant and Acid Deposition Model Application within the Framework of PIC (SAUS)
PHP.......... Pacific Hawaiian Products Co. [*Later, PHP Co.*]
PHP.......... Packing-House Products [*Food industry*]
PHP.......... Parents Helping Parents [*An association*] (EA)
PHP.......... Parts, Hybrids, and Packaging (MCD)
PHP.......... Passive Hyperpolarizing Potential [*Neurochemistry*]
PHP.......... Payload Handling Panel [*NASA*] (MCD)
PHP.......... Pennhurst State School and Hospital, Spring City, PA [*OCLC symbol*] (OCLC)
PHP.......... Peoples Heritage Party (SAUS)
PHP.......... Performance, Hermeticity and Price (SAUS)
PHP.......... Personal Handy Phone [*Telecommunications*]
PHP.......... Personal Home Page (SAUS)
PHP.......... Petroleum Heat & Power (EFIS)
PHP.......... Philip, SD [*Location identifier*] [*FAA*] (FAAL)
PHP.......... Phillip Resources, Inc. [*Vancouver Stock Exchange symbol*]
PHP.......... Philosophia Patrum [*A publication*] (BJA)
PHP.......... PHP Healthcare Corp. [*Associated Press*] (SAG)
PHP.......... PHP Hypertext Preprocessor [*Computer science*]
PHP.......... Physician's Health Plan
PHP.......... Physicians Home Page (SAUS)
PHP.......... Pinane Hydroperoxide [*Organic chemistry*]
PHP.......... Planetary Horizon Platform [*Aerospace*]
PHP.......... Pooled Human Plasma (MELL)
PHP.......... Post-Heparin Phospholipase [*Medicine*] (MAE)
PHP.......... Postheparin Plasma (DAVI)
PHP.......... Post-Hostilities Planning Subcommittee of the Chiefs of Staff Committee [*World War II*]
PHP.......... Pounds per Horsepower
PHP.......... Prentice Hall Press [*Publisher*]
PHP.......... Prepaid Health Plan [*Insurance*]
PHP.......... Presbyterian Hunger Program (EA)
PHP.......... Primary Hyperparathyroidism (MAE)
PHP.......... Propeller Horsepower
PHP.......... Pseudohyperbolic Particle [*Astrophysics*]
PHP.......... Pseudohypoparathyroidism [*Endocrinology*]
PHP.......... Psychologists Helping Psychologists (SAUS)
PHP.......... Public Health Plan (SAUS)
PHP.......... Pump Horsepower
PHPA .... Pacific Herring Packers Association (EA)
PHPA .... Partially-Hydrolyzed Polyacrylamide [*Well drilling technology*]
PHPC .... Post-Hostilities Planning Committee [*Navy*] [*World War II*]
PHPD .... Per Hatch per Day (RIMS)
PHPES....... Program for Health Policy in Economies under Stress (ADWA)
PHPFI .... Personal Home Page/Form Interpreter (SAUS)
PHPG......... Poly(hydroxypropylglutamine) [*Organic chemistry*]
PHPHB ...... P-heptyl-p-hydroxy Benzoate [*A preservative used in the making of American and British beer*]
PHPK .... Probability of Hit to Probability of Kill (INF)
PHPL .... Parallel Hardware Processing Language [*1977*] [*Computer science*] (CSR)
PHPO........ Private Health Plan Option [*Medicare*] (GFGA)
PHPPO ...... Public Health Practice Program Office (SAUS)
PHPS .... Post-Hostilities Planning Staff [*World War II*]
PHPT .... Portable High-Potential Tester
pHPT .... Primary Hyperparathyroidism [*Medicine*] (STED)
PHPT .... Pseudohypoparathyroidism [*Medicine*] (DB)
PHPV........ Persistent Hyperplastic Primary Vitreous [*Ophthalmology*]
PHQ.......... Peacetime Headquarters (SAUS)
PHQ.......... Personnel History Questionnaire (MHDB)
PHQ.......... Phenylhydroquinone [*Organic chemistry*]
PHQ.......... Port Headquarters (SAUS)
PHQ.......... Postal Headquarters [*British*]
PHQ Card... Phase Qualification Card (SAUS)
PHQZ .... Philadelphia Quartz [*Federal Railroad Administration identification code*]
PHR.......... Pacific Harbour [*Fiji*] [*Airport symbol*] (OAG)
PHR.......... Pacific Historical Review [*A publication*] (BRI)
PHR.......... Parts per Hundred of Resin (SAUS)
PHR.......... Parts per Hundred of Rubber [*Chemical technology*]
PHR.......... Payload Hazardous Report (NASA)
PHR.......... Peak Heart Rate [*Cardiology*]
PHR.......... Peak Height Ratio
PHR.......... Per Hour (SAUS)
PHR.......... Personal Health Record (GART)
PHR.......... Pharmacy (SAUS)
PHR.......... Phorbol [*Organic chemistry*]
PHR.......... Photographer's Mate (Camera Repairman) [*U.S. Navy enlisted rating*] (AUER)
PHR.......... Photographic Reconnaissance
PHR.......... Photoreactivity (DMAA)
phr........... Phrase (ELAL)
Phr........... Phrase (SAUS)
PHR.......... Phrase
phr........... Phrase Book
phr........... Phraseology (ODA)
PHR.......... Phraseology (SAUS)
Phr........... Phrenomena: an Annual Review [*A publication*] (APTA)
PHR.......... Physical Record [*Computer science*]
PHR.......... Physicians for Human Rights (EA)
PHR.......... Point-Hour Ratio (DIPS)
PHR.......... Pound-Force per Hour (MCD)
PHR.......... Pounds per Hour (AAG)
PHR.......... Preheater (KSC)
PHR.......... Process Hazardous Review [*Environmental science*]
PHR.......... Process Heat Reactor Program [*Nuclear Regulatory Commission*]
PHR.......... Professional in Human Resources
PHR.......... Public Health Reports [*A publication*]
PHR.......... Pulse-Height Resolution [*By photomultiplier tubes*]
PHR.......... Retreat State Hospital, Hunlock Creek, PA [*OCLC symbol*] (OCLC)
PHRA .... Principal Human Resources Advisor (SAUS)
PHRACT...... Print-Handicapped Radio, Australian Capital Territory
PHRAN ...... Phrasal Analyzer (SAUS)
PHR&A...... Patton Harris Rust & Associates (EFIS)
PHRASEO... Phraseogram (SAUS)
phraseo ..... phraseograph (SAUS)
PHRASEO... Phraseologist (SAUS)
PHRASEO... Phraseology (SAUS)
PHRB .... Robert Phillips Trucking [*Common carrier symbol*]
PHRC......... Palestine Human Rights Campaign (EA)
PHRED ...... Phrasal English Diction (SAUS)
PHRED ...... Public Health Risk Evaluation Data [*Environmental Safety*]
PHRED ...... Public Health Risk Evaluation Data Base (EAGT)
Phren........ Phrenic (SAUS)
Phren........ Phrenological (SAUS)
Phren........ Phrenologist (SAUS)
PHREN ...... Phrenology
Ph Rep...... Philadelphia Reports [*Pennsylvania*] [*A publication*] (DLA)
PHRF .... Performance Handicap Racing Fleet [*Boating*]
PHRF .... Performance Handicap Racing Formula [*Sailing*]
PHRG........ Park Home Residents Guild [*British*] (DBA)
PHRG........ Parliamentary Human Rights Group (EAIO)
PHRHD ...... Pump, Hydraulic Ram, Hand-Driven (MSA)
PHRI......... Pittsburgh Health Research Institute (SAUS)
PHRI......... Public Health Research Institute (NADA)
PHRI......... Public Health Research Institute of the City of New York, Inc. [*Research center*] (RCD)

PHRIC .... Palestine Human Rights Information Center (EA)
PHRIR .... Pointable High Resolution Imaging Radiometer (SAUS)
PHRK .... Power and Heat Rejection Kit [*NASA*]
PHRM .... Pharmaceutical (SAUS)
PHRM .... Pharmion Corp. [*NASDAQ symbol*]
PhRMA ...... Pharmaceutical Research and Manufacturers of America (NTPA)
Phrmhse .... Pharmhouse Corp. [*Associated Press*] (SAG)
PhrmMkt .... Pharmaceutical Marketing Services, Inc. [*Associated Press*] (SAG)
PHRMST .... Pharmacist
PHR Program... Process Heat Reactor Program (SAUS)
PHRR .... Parenchymal Hepatic Resection Rate [*Medicine*]
PHRS .... Paul Harris Stores, Inc. [*NASDAQ symbol*] (COMM)
PHRS .... Portable Heat Rejection System
PHRT .... Procarbazine, Hydroxyurea, Radiotherapy Protocol (DAVI)
PHRU .... Nigeria National Petroleum [*Intermodal shipping container symbol*] (TVRC)
PHRU .... Population Health Research Unit (SAUS)
PHRW .... Preferred Hotels and Resorts Worldwide (NTPA)
Phryg .... Phrygian [*Linguistics*] (IEL)
PHS .... Packaging, Handling, and Storage (MCD)
PHS .... Pallottine House of Studies
PHS .... Pan Head Steel (IAA)
PHS .... Parallel Half Subtracter (SAUS)
PHS .... Partial Hospitalization Program (STED)
PHS .... Paternal Half Sister (OA)
PHS .... Pathological Human Serum [*Serology*]
PHS .... Patient-Heated Serum (STED)
PHS .... Payload Handling Station [*NASA*] (MCD)
PHS .... Pennsylvania Historical Society (SAUS)
PHS .... Pennsylvania Horticultural Society [*An association*]
PHS .... Personal Handyphone System [*Telecommunications*]
PHS .... Personal Health Summary (SAUS)
PHS .... Personal Health Survey [*Psychology*]
PHS .... Personal Hygiene Subsystem [*NASA*] (KSC)
PHS .... Phenylalanine Hydroxylase Stimulator (STED)
PhS .... Philosophical Society [*British*] (DBA)
Ph S .... Philosophical Society of England (SAUS)
PHS .... Phitsanuloke [*Thailand*] [*Airport symbol*] (OAG)
PHS .... Photographic Historical Society (EA)
PHS .... Photo Hydrography System (SAUS)
PHS .... Physicians Health Services
PHS .... Physicians' Health Study
PHS .... Plastics Historical Society [*United Kingdom*] (EAIO)
PHS .... Plated Heat Sink (SAUS)
PHS .... Police History Society [*British*] (DBA)
PHS .... Polyhydroxystyrene [*Also, PHOST*] [*Organic chemistry*]
PHS .... Pontiac Historic Services [*Automotive industry*]
PHS .... Pooled Human Serum [*Hematology*] (DMAA)
PHS .... Postal History Society (EA)
PHS .... Postcard History Society (EA)
PHS .... Posthypnotic Suggestion [*Psychology*]
PHS .... Post-hysterectomy Syndrome [*Medicine*] (EDAA)
PHS .... Precision Hover Sensor (PDAA)
PHS .... Prepared Hessian Surfacing [*Air Force*]
PHS .... Presbyterian Historical Society (EA)
PHS .... Price History System (MCD)
PHS .... Printing Historical Society [*British*]
PHS .... Printing House Square (DGA)
PHS .... Prison Health Services (SAUS)
PHS .... Probability of Having a Space
PHS .... Program for Human Sexuality [*Medicine*] (EDAA)
PHS .... Progressive Hongkong Society [*Political party*]
PHS .... Prostaglandin H Synthase [*An enzyme*] (GNE)
PHS .... ProVantage Health Svcs. [*NYSE symbol*] (SG)
PHS .... Public Health Service [*Department of Health and Human Services*]
PHS .... Public Health Service Technologies (MHID)
PHS .... Public Health Standards (SAUS)
PHS .... Pulmonary Hypertension Syndrome (SAUS)
PHS .... Pulse Height Selection (SAUS)
PHS .... Pumped Hydro Storage [*Power source*]
PHS .... Somerset State Hospital, Somerset, PA [*OCLC symbol*] (OCLC)
PHSA .... Pearl Harbor Survivors Association (EA)
PHSA .... Polyhydroxystearic Acid [*Organic chemistry*]
PHSA .... Polymerized Human Serum Albumin [*Biochemistry*]
PHSA .... Portable Hydraulic System Analysis [*Off-Highway equipment*]
PHSA .... Provincial Hospital Services Association [*British*] (DBA)
PHSA .... Public Health Service Act (GFGA)
PHSACIP... Public Health Service Advisory Committee on Immunization Practices [*Medicine*] (EDAA)
PHS&T ..... Packaging, Handling, Storage, and Transportability
PHS & T .... Packaging, Handling, Storage, and Transportation [*Shipping*]
PhSAP ...... Physical Service Access Point [*Telecommunications*] (OSI)
PHSAR ...... Public Health Service Acquisition Regulations [*Department of Health and Human Services*] (GFGA)
PHSB .... PHS Bancorp, Inc. [*NASDAQ symbol*] (NASQ)
PHSBG ...... Preventive Health Services Block Grant [*Public human service program*] (PHSD)
PHSC .... Pleuripotent Homopoietic Stem Cell [*Medicine*] (EDAA)
PHSC .... Pluripotent Hematopoietic Stem Cells [*Cytology*]
PHSC .... Postal History Society of Canada (EA)
PHSC .... Posterior Horn of Spinal Cord [*Medicine*] (MELL)
PHSC .... Private Hospital Supplementary Charges (ADA)
PHSCS ...... Pier-Harris Self-Concept Scale (EDAC)
PHSE .... Pharmhouse Corp. [*NASDAQ symbol*] (SAG)
PHSE .... Phase [*Computer science*]
PHSE .... Piedmont Health Survey of the Elderly [*Department of Health and Human Services*] (GFGA)
PHSF .... Bradshaw Field, Hawaii Island [*Hawaii*] [*ICAO location identifier*] (ICLI)
PHSF .... Payload Hazardous Servicing Facility [*NASA*] (NAKS)
PHSG .... Postal History Study Group (EA)
PHSI .... Plant Health and Seeds Inspectorate [*Ministry of Agriculture, Fisheries, and Food*] [*British*]
PHSIG ...... Pan Hellenic Society Inventors of Greece in USA [*Defunct*] (EA)
PHSKX ...... Phoenix Aggressive Growth Cl.A [*Mutual fund ticker symbol*] (SG)
PHSNZ ...... Postal History Society of New Zealand [*Auckland*] (EA)
PHSO .... Partially Hydrogenated Soybean Oil [*Cooking fat*]
PHSO .... Postal History Society of Ontario [*Later, PHSC*] (EA)
PHSOC ...... Photographical Historical Society of Canada
P-H Soc Sec Taxes... Social Security Taxes (Prentice-Hall, Inc.) [*A publication*] (DLA)
PHS of A.... Postal History Society of the Americas (EA)
PHSP .... Phase-Splitter (MSA)
PHSP .... Public Health Service Publications
PHSPS ...... Preservation, Handling, Storage, Packaging, and Shipping (NRCH)
PHSS .... Physician Support Systems, Inc. [*NASDAQ symbol*] (SAG)
PHSS .... Population Health Summary System (ADWA)
PHST .... Packaging, Handling, Storage, and Transportation [*Shipping*]
Ph St Tr..... Phillipps' State Trials [*A publication*] (DLA)
PHSU .... Pharaonic Shipping [*Intermodal shipping container symbol*] (TVRC)
PHSV .... Physicians Health Services, Inc. [*NASDAQ symbol*] (SAG)
PHSV .... Physicians Health Svcs'A' [*NASDAQ symbol*] (TTSB)
PHSWOW... Public Health Schools Without Walls
PHSY .... PacifiCare Health Systems, Inc. [*Cypress, CA*] [*NASDAQ symbol*] (NQ)
PHSYA....... PacifiCare Health Sys'A' [*NASDAQ symbol*] (TTSB)
PHT .... Managed High Yield Fd [*NYSE symbol*] (TTSB)
PHT .... Managed High Yield Fund [*NYSE symbol*]
PHT .... Packaging, Handling and Transportability (ACAE)
PHT .... Packaging, Handling & Transportation (SAUS)
PHT .... PaineWebber Premium High Income [*NYSE symbol*] (SPSG)
PHT .... Paired Hands Test [*Education*] (EDAC)
PHT .... Paris, TN [*Location identifier*] [*FAA*] (FAAL)
PHT .... Passive Haemagglutination Test (SAUS)
PHT .... Passive Hemagglutination Technique [*Immunology*]
PHT .... Passive Hyperimmune Therapy [*Medicine*] (EDAA)
PHT .... Peak Hour Traffic (PA)
PHT .... Peak Hour Trips (PA)
PHT .... Peroxide Hemolysis Test [*Medicine*] (STED)
PHT .... Phenylhydantoin [*Pharmacology*] (CPH)
PhT .... [*The*] Phoenix and the Turtle [*Shakespearean work*]
pht .... Photographer [*MARC relator code*] [*Library of Congress*] (LCCP)
PHT .... Phototube
Pht .... Phthaloyl [*Also, Phth*] [*Organic chemistry*]
PHT .... Physical Therapy Technician [*Navy*]
PHT .... Pitch, Hit, and Throw [*Youth competition sponsored by professional baseball*]
PHT .... Poly-Hexylthiophene [*Organic chemistry*]
PHT .... Portal Hypertension [*Medicine*]
PHT .... Port Hold Time (SAUS)
PHT .... Postural Hypotension [*Medicine*] (EDAA)
PHT .... Preheat
PHT .... Primary Hyperthyroidism [*Medicine*] (STED)
PHT .... Pulmonary Hypertension [*Cardiology*] (CPH)
PHT .... Putting Hubby Through [*College "degree" earned by some wives*]
PHT .... Pyridohomotropane [*Organic chemistry*]
PHT .... Pyrrolidone Hydrotribromide (SAUS)
PHT .... Torrance State Hospital, Torrance, PA [*OCLC symbol*] (OCLC)
PHTab ...... President's Hundred Tab [*Military decoration*] (AABC)
PHT Act ..... Public Health Training Act [*Medicine*] (EDAA)
PHTAT ...... Para-Hydroxytriamterene [*Biochemistry*]
PHTATS ..... Para-Hydroxytriamterene Sulfate [*Biochemistry*]
P-H Tax ..... Federal Taxes (Prentice-Hall, Inc.) [*A publication*] (DLA)
P-H Tax Ct Mem... Tax Court Memorandum Decisions (Prentice-Hall, Inc.) [*A publication*] (DLA)
P-H Tax Ct Rep & Mem Dec... Tax Court Reported and Memorandum Decisions (Prentice-Hall, Inc.) [*A publication*] (DLA)
PHTBX....... Phoenix Tax Exempt Bond [*Mutual fund ticker symbol*] (SG)
PHTC .... Pharmatec, Inc. [*NASDAQ symbol*] (COMM)
PHTC .... Pneumatic Hydraulic Test Console (KSC)
PHTC .... Pulse Height to Time Converter (OA)
PhTD .... Physical Therapy Doctor
PHTF .... Pearl Harbor Training Facility [*Navy*]
Phth .... Phthaloyl [*Also, Pht*] [*Organic chemistry*]
PHTK .... Prompt Hard Target Kill (SAUS)
PHTLS ...... Pre Hospital Trauma Life Support (SAUS)
PHTM .... Public Health and Tropical Medicine (ADWA)
PHTN .... Photon Dynamics [*NASDAQ symbol*] (TTSB)
PHTN .... Photon Dynamics, Inc. [*NASDAQ symbol*] (SAG)
PHTN .... Public Health Training Network
PHTN .... Pulmonary Hypertension [*Medicine*] (RAWO)
PHTO .... Hilo/General Lyman Field, Hawaii Island [*Hawaii*] [*ICAO location identifier*] (ICLI)
PHTO .... Photon Technology International [*OTCBB symbol*]
PHTP .... Priority Health Training Programs (SAUS)
PHTS .... Packaging, Handling, Transportation, Storage (SAUS)
PHTS .... Primary Heat Transport System [*Nuclear energy*] (NRCH)
PHTS .... Psychiatric Home Treatment Service (DAVI)

PHU......... Philadelphia Ukrainian [*Diocesan abbreviation*] [*Pennsylvania*] (TOCD)
PHU......... Power Holdover Unit (SAUS)
PHU......... Pressure, Hydraulic Unit
PHU......... Public Health Unit (SAUS)
PHuJ........ Juniata College, Huntingdon, PA [*Library symbol*] [*Library of Congress*] (LCLS)
PHUN....... Phreakers and Hackers Underground Network (SAUS)
P-H Unrep Tr Cas... Prentice-Hall Unreported Trust Cases [*A publication*] (DLA)
Phus Plu.... Philippus Puldericus [*Authority cited in pre-1607 legal work*] (DSA)
PHV......... Pahlavi [*Iran*] [*Airport symbol*] (AD)
PHV......... Parallel Hybrid Vehicle
PHV......... Paramount Home Video
PHV......... Peak Height Velocity (DMAA)
PHV......... Peak Horizontal Velocity
PHV......... Persistent Hypertrophic Vitreous [*Ophthalmology*] (DAVI)
PHV......... Phase Velocity
PHV......... Pro Haec Vice [*For This Turn*] [*Latin*] (ROG)
PHV......... Prospect Hill Virus [*Medicine*] (DMAA)
PHV......... Prosthetic Heart Valve (MELL)
PHV......... Wernersville State Hospital, Wernersville, PA [*OCLC symbol*] (OCLC)
PHVA........ Plasma Homovanillic Acid [*Biochemistry*]
PHVA Level... Plasma Level of HomoVanillic Acid (SAUS)
pH Value.... Pondus Hydrogenii Value (SAUS)
PH Valve.... Pressure Holding Valve (SAUS)
PHVPS...... Primary High-Voltage Power Supply
PHW......... Pemberton Houston Willoughby Investment Corp. [*Toronto Stock Exchange symbol*] [*Vancouver Stock Exchange symbol*]
PHW......... Phalaborwa [*South Africa*] [*Airport symbol*] (OAG)
PHW......... Phangduwali [*Language symbol*] (ETLW)
PHW......... Philatelic Hobbies for the Wounded (EA)
PHW......... Pressurized Heavy Water (SAUS)
PHW......... Prime Hard Wheat
PHW......... Warren State Hospital, Warren, PA [*OCLC symbol*] (OCLC)
PHWA....... Professional Hockey Writers' Association (EA)
PHWA....... Protestant Health and Welfare Assembly [*Later, PHHSA*] (EA)
PHWC....... Polish Helsinki Watch Committee (EAIO)
PHWDQ..... Planet Hollywood International [*OTCBB symbol*]
PHWFJD.... Partners in Harmony, World Family of John Denver (EA)
PHWG....... Pediatric HIV Working Group [*National Cancer Institute*] (RCD)
PHWR....... Hickam United States Air Force Automatic Weather Switch, Oahu Island [*Hawaii*] [*ICAO location identifier*] (ICLI)
PHWR....... Pressurized Heavy Water-Moderated and Cooled Reactor [*Nuclear energy*] (IAA)
PHWR....... Pressurized Heavy Water Reactor [*Nuclear energy*]
PHWRH..... Pressurized Heavy Water Reactor-Homogenized (SAUS)
PHX......... Partial Hepectomy [*Medicine*]
PHx......... Past History [*Medicine*] (MAE)
Phx......... Pharynx [*Anatomy*] (DAVI)
PHX......... PHLCORP, Inc. [*NYSE symbol*] (COMM)
PHX......... Phoenix [*Arizona*] [*Airport symbol*] (OAG)
PHX......... Phoenix 2000 Airtaxi Ltd. [*Hungary*] [*ICAO designator*] (FAAC)
PHX......... Phoenix Network, Inc. [*AMEX symbol*] (SPSG)
PHX......... Pulmonary Histiocytosis X [*Medicine*] (EDAA)
PHX......... Woodville State Hospital, Carnegie, PA [*OCLC symbol*] (OCLC)
PHXA....... Phoenix American, Inc. [*NASDAQ symbol*] (COMM)
PhxDffP.... Phoenix Duf & Phelps Corp. [*Associated Press*] (SAG)
PhxDfP..... Phoenix Duff & Phelps Corp. [*Associated Press*] (SAG)
PhxDuffP.... Phoenix Duff & Phelps Corp. [*Associated Press*] (SAG)
PhxGold.... Phoenix Gold International, Inc. [*Associated Press*] (SAG)
PHXI........ Phoenix International Life Sciences, Inc. [*NASDAQ symbol*] (NASQ)
PhxNet..... Phoenix Network, Inc. [*Associated Press*] (SAG)
PHXX....... Phoenix International Ltd., Inc. [*NASDAQ symbol*] (NASQ)
PHY......... C. Howard Marcy State Hospital, Pittsburgh, PA [*OCLC symbol*] (OCLC)
PHY......... Norman, OK [*Location identifier*] [*FAA*] (FAAL)
PHY......... Pharyngitis
Phy......... Physalaemin [*Biochemistry*]
PHY......... Physical
PHY......... Physical Access (SAUS)
PHY......... Physical Layer (AAEL)
PHY......... Physical Layer Control (SAUS)
PHY......... Physical Layer Device (MWOL)
PHY......... Physical Layer Protocol [*Computer science*] (GART)
PHY......... Physically [*Telegraphy*] (PCTE)
PHY......... Physician
PHY......... Physics
PHY......... Physiology (DMAA)
PHY......... Phytohemagglutinin [*Immunology*] (AAMN)
PHY......... Prospect Street High Income Portfolio, Inc. [*NYSE symbol*] (SPSG)
PHYB....... Pioneer Hi-Bred International, Inc. [*NASDAQ symbol*] (COMM)
PHYC....... PhyCor, Inc. [*NASDAQ symbol*] (SPSG)
phyce....... Photocopy-Control Electronics unit (SAUS)
Phycol Res... Phycological Research [*A publication*] (PABS)
PHYCOM.... Physicians Communications Service [*Fisher-Stevens, Inc.*] [*Merged into BRS/COLLEAGUE*]
PhyCor...... PhyCor, Inc. [*Associated Press*] (SAG)
PhyCpt...... Physicians Computer Network [*Associated Press*] (SAG)
PHYCUS..... Physical Custody [*of Records*] (MHDB)
PHY ED..... Physical Education (WGA)
PHYL........ Physiological
PHYLIP..... Phylogeny Inference Package [*Botany*]
PHYLIS..... Physics Online Information System [*Computer science*] (PDAA)
PHYLO...... Phylogeny (SAUS)
PHYM....... Putnam High Yield Municipal Trust [*Associated Press*] (SAG)
PhyMatr..... PhyMatrix Corp. [*Associated Press*] (SAG)
PHYN........ Physician Reliance Network [*NASDAQ symbol*] (TTSB)
PHYN........ Physician Reliance Network, Inc. [*NASDAQ symbol*] (SAG)
PHYS........ Physic (SAUS)
PHYS........ Physical (AFM)
Phys......... Physical (DIAR)
phys......... Physical (SHCU)
PHYS........ Physically (SAUS)
Phys......... Physician (CMD)
phys......... Physician (SHCU)
PHYS........ Physician
PHYS........ Physicist [*or Physics*] (ADA)
phys......... Physicist (SHCU)
Phys......... Physics (DD)
PHYS........ Physics (GOBB)
phys......... Physics (SHCU)
PHYS........ Physio-Control Intl [*NASDAQ symbol*] (TTSB)
PhyS......... Physiological Saline [*Pharmacology*] (DAVI)
PHYS........ Physiology
PhySale...... Physician Sales & Service, Inc. [*Associated Press*] (SAG)
PHY-SAP.... Physical Layer Service Access Point (SAUS)
PHYSB...... PacifiCare Health Sys'B' [*NASDAQ symbol*] (TTSB)
PHYSBE..... Physiological Simulation Benchmark Experiment
Phys Briefs... Physics Briefs (SAUS)
Phys Bull... Physics Bulletin (SAUS)
Phys Chem... Physiological Chemistry and Physics (MEC)
Phys Chem Glasses... Physics and Chemistry of Glasses (SAUS)
Phys Chem Mater Treat... Physics and Chemistry of Materials Treatment (SAUS)
Phys Chem Mech Surf... Physics, Chemistry and Mechanics of Surfaces (SAUS)
Phys Chem Miner... Physics and Chemistry of Minerals (SAUS)
PHYSCL..... Physical
PHYSCO..... Physics Codes [*Database*] (GDD)
PhysCpA.... Physician Corp. of America [*Associated Press*] (SAG)
Phys Dis.... Physical Disability (CPH)
Phys Dsabl... Physical Disability (SAUS)
Phys Earth Planet Inter... Physics of the Earth and Planetary Interiors (SAUS)
PHYSEC..... Physical Security (MCD)
PHYS ED.... Physical Education
Phys Educ... Physics Education (SAUS)
Phys Eng.... Physical Engineer
PHYSEXAM... Physical Examination
Phys Fluids A Fluid Dyn... Physics of Fluids A, Fluid Dynamics (SAUS)
Phys Fluids B Plasma Phys... Physics of Fluids B, Plasma Physics (SAUS)
PHYSH...... Physicians and Surgeons Hospital (SAUS)
Phys Hndcpd... Physically Handicapped (AL)
PHYSIAT... Physiatrical (SAUS)
PHYSIAT... Physiatrist (SAUS)
PhysicHlt... Physicians Health Services, Inc. [*Associated Press*] (SAG)
Physicochem Hydrodyn... Physicochemical Hydrodynamics (SAUS)
Physik Chem... Physikalisch-Chemische Trenn- und Messmethoden (MEC)
PhysIn....... Physicians Insurance Co. of Ohio [*Associated Press*] (SAG)
Physio....... Physiology (DAVI)
physio....... Physiotherapy [*Medicine*] (DMAA)
PHYSIO..... Physiotherapy [*Medicine*]
Physiog..... Physiognomy (DIAR)
PHYSIOG... Physiognomy [*Slang*] (DSUE)
PHYSIOG... Physiographic
PHYSIOL... Physiological (MSA)
Physiol...... Physiology (BEE)
PHYSIOL... Physiology (ROG)
Physiol Biochem Cultiv Plan... Physiology and Biochemistry of Cultivated Plants (SAUS)
Physiol Chem Phys... Physiological Chemistry and Physics (SAUS)
Physiol Ecol Jpn... Physiology and Ecology Japan (SAUS)
Physiol Plant Pathol... Physiological Plant Pathology (SAUS)
PHYSL....... Physiological (AFM)
PHYSLAC... Physical Sciences Library Advisory Committee (SAUS)
Phys Med... Physical Medicine (CPH)
PHYS MET... Physical Metallurgy (SAUS)
Phys Met... Physics of Metals (SAUS)
Physmet.... Physiometrix, Inc. [*Associated Press*] (SAG)
Phys Met Metallogr... Physics and Metallography (SAUS)
Phys Met Metallogr... Physics of Metals and Metallography (SAUS)
PHYSN...... Physician
PHYSNET... Physics Network (ACAE)
PHYSOCEAN... Physical Oceanography (SAUS)
PHYSOG.... Physiognomy [*Slang*] (DSUE)
Phys Pap... Physics Papers (SAUS)
PhysPRC.... Physician's Payment Review Commission (HCT)
PHYSQUAL... Physical Disqualification [*Military*] (DNAB)
PhysRel..... Physician Reliance Network, Inc. [*Associated Press*] (SAG)
Phys Rep... Physics Reports (SAUS)
Phys Rev... Physical Review (SAUS)
PhysRev.... Physical Review Journal (SAUS)
Phys Rev... Physical Revue (SAUS)
Phys Rev... Physiological Review (MEC)
Phys Rev A... Physical Review A (MEC)
Phys Rev A At Mol Opt Phys... Physical Review A, Atomic, Molecular and Optical Physics (SAUS)
Phys Rev Abstr... Physical Review, Abstracts (SAUS)

Phys Rev A Stat Phys Plasmas Fluids Relat In... Physical Review A, Statistical Physics, Plasmas, Fluids and Related Interdisciplinary Topics (SAUS)
Phys Rev B Condens Matter... Physical Review B, Condensed Matter (SAUS)
Phys Rev C... Physical Review C: Nuclear Physics (MEC)
Phys Rev C Nucl Phys... Physical Review C, Nuclear Physics (SAUS)
Phys Rev D Part Fields... Physical Review D, Particles and Fields (SAUS)
Phys Rev Lett... Physical Review Letters (MEC)
PhysRs...... Physician Resources Group, Inc. [*Associated Press*] (SAG)
PHYS SC.... Physical Science (WDAA)
Phys Solid Earth... Physics of the Solid Earth (SAUS)
PhysSup .... Physician Support Systems, Inc. [*Associated Press*] (SAG)
PHYST....... Physicist
Phys Teach... Physics Teaching (SAUS)
Phys-Tech... Physico-Technical (SAUS)
PHYSTER... Physical Therapy (AABC)
Phys Test Chem Anal Chem Anal... Physical Testing and Chemical Analysis, Chemical Analysis (SAUS)
Phys Ther... Physical Therapist (DMAA)
Phys Today... Physics Today [*A publication*] (BRI)
Phys World... Physics World (SAUS)
PHYSY ...... Physiology
Phytochem... Phytochemistry (SAUS)
Phytogeog... Phytogeography (BARN)
PHYTOPATH... Phytopathology
PHYX .... Physiometrix, Inc. [*NASDAQ symbol*] (SAG)
PHZ .... Ashland State General Hospital, Ashland, PA [*OCLC symbol*] (OCLC)
PHZ .... Phenylhydrazine (LDT)
PHZH .... Honolulu Air Traffic Control Center [*Hawaii*] [*ICAO location identifier*] (ICLI)
PI .... Current Instructional Permit [*Motor vehicle violation driver status code in state of North Dakota*] (MVRD)
PI .... Division of Plant Industry (SAUS)
Pi .... Inorganic Phosphate (SAUS)
pi............ irregular pulsations (SAUS)
pI............ Isoelectric Point (MAE)
PI .... Pacific Islands (SAUS)
PI .... Pacing Impulse [*Cardiology*] (DAVI)
PI .... Pacing Indicator (SAUS)
PI .... Pacing Item (MCD)
PI .... Package Insert [*Instructional leaflet distributed with certain prescription drugs*] [*Also, PPI*]
PI .... Packaging Institute [*Later, PI/USA*] (EA)
PI .... Packing Index (SAUS)
PI .... Paducah & Illinois Railroad [*AAR code*]
PI .... Paleo-Indian (QUAC)
PI .... Palmaris Longus (DMAA)
PI .... Pancreatic Insufficiency [*Gastroenterology*]
PI .... Pancreatic Lipase [*Medicine*] (DMAA)
Pi .... Pandectae (Pisanae) Florentinae [*A publication*] (DSA)
PI .... Panel Input
PI .... Panel Interlocking [*Indian Railway*] (TIR)
PI .... Pansophic Institute [*Defunct*] (EA)
PI .... Pantera International (EA)
PI .... Paper Insulated
PI .... Paper Insulation (SAUS)
PI .... Paracel Islands [*ANSI two-letter standard code*] (CNC)
PI .... Parachute Infantry (SAUS)
PI .... Paradoxical Intention [*V. E. Frankl*] (DIPS)
PI .... Parainfluenza (MELL)
PI .... Parallel Importation (DB)
PI .... Parallel Input [*Computer science*] (BUR)
PI .... Parallel Interface (SAUS)
PI .... Parameter Identifier [*Computer science*] (TNIG)
PI .... Parametric Industry (IAA)
PI .... Paranoid Ideation (DAVI)
Pi .... Parental Generation [*Medicine*] (DMAA)
PI .... Parental Investment [*Biology*]
PI .... Parity Index [*EEO*]
PI .... Parity Insert (SAUS)
PI .... Pars Intermedia [*Medicine*] (EDAA)
PI .... Partial Interchangeability (SAUS)
PI .... Particle Integration (CAAL)
PI .... Particular Integral (SAUS)
PI .... Partido Independente [*Independent Party*] [*Costa Rica*] [*Political party*]
PI .... Partido Intransigente [*Intransigent Party*] [*Argentina*] [*Political party*] (PD)
PI .... Parti Independantiste [*Quebec*]
PI .... Passeport International [*International Passport*] [*An association*] [*France*] (EAIO)
PI .... Passive Immunity [*Medicine*] (MELL)
PI .... Pasteur Institute (SAUS)
PI .... Pathfinder International (EA)
PI .... Patient's Interests [*Medicine*]
PI .... Patrol Inspector [*Immigration and Naturalization Service*]
PI .... Payload Interrogator [*NASA*] (MCD)
Pi .... Payload Interrogator [*NASA*] (NAKS)
Pi .... Pen and Ink (NAKS)
PI .... Pen and Ink
PI .... Penetration Index (IAA)
PI .... Pepsin Inhibitor (OA)
PI .... Peptide Inhibitor (DB)
PI .... Perceptions, Inc. (EA)
PI .... Perceptual Isolation
PI .... Perfect Initials [*Philately*]
PI .... Performance Improvement
PI .... Performance Index
PI .... Performance Indicator (MCD)
PI .... Performance Intensity (MAE)
PI .... Perinatal Injury [*Neonatology*] (DAVI)
PI .... Per Inhalation (SAUS)
pi............ Per Inquiry (WDMC)
PI .... Per Inquiry [*Advertising*]
PI .... Periodical Index Term (NITA)
PI .... Periodicals Institute (EA)
PI .... Periodic Inspection [*Military*] (AFM)
PI .... Peripheral Interface [*Computer science*] (PCM)
PI .... Peripheral Inventory (SAUS)
PI .... Peripheral Iridectomy [*Medicine*]
PI .... Perlite Institute (EA)
PI .... Permaculture International [*Australia*]
PI .... Permeability Index [*Clinical chemistry*]
PI .... Peroral Insulin [*Medicine*] (EDAA)
PI .... Perpetual Inventory (SAUS)
PI .... Personal Identification
PI .... Personal Identity (SAUS)
PI .... Personal Import
PI .... Personal Income
PI .... Personal Injury [*Insurance*]
PI .... Personal Injury Accident [*British police term*]
PI .... Personal Investment [*A publication*] (ADA)
PI .... Personality Inventory [*Psychology*]
PI .... Petroleum Information Corp. (IID)
PI .... Petrol Injection [*British*]
PI .... Pharmacopoeia Internationalis [*International Pharmacopoeia*]
PI .... Phase-In
PI .... Phenanthroimidazole [*Organic chemistry*]
PI .... Phenyl Isocyanate [*Organic chemistry*]
Pi .... Philippines (MILB)
PI .... Phonographic Institute (SAUS)
Pi .... Phosphate, Inorganic [*Chemistry*]
PI .... Phosphatidylinositol [*Also, PtdIns*] [*Biochemistry*]
PI .... Photoelectric Inspection (ELAL)
P-I .... Photogrammetric Instrumentation (AAG)
PI .... Photographic Institute (SAUS)
PI .... Photographic Intelligence (SAUS)
PI .... Photographic Interpretation
PI .... Photographic Interpreter
PI .... Photo Intelligence (SAUS)
PI .... Photo International [*Defunct*] (EAIO)
PI .... Photo Interpretation (SAUS)
PI .... Photointerpretation [*or Photointerpreter*]
PI .... Photo Interpreter (SAUS)
PI .... Photointerpreter (IAA)
PI .... Photoionization [*Physical chemistry*]
PI .... Physical Instruction (SAUS)
PI .... Physical Inventory (NRCH)
PI .... Physically Impaired
PI .... Physics International
PI .... Piaster [*Monetary unit*] [*Spain, Republic of Vietnam, and some Middle Eastern countries*]
pi............ Pica [*Typesetting*] [*Also called pie*] (WDMC)
PI .... Piedmont Aviation, Inc. [*ICAO designator*] (OAG)
PI .... Pigeon Trainer [*Navy*]
PI .... Pig Iron
Pi .... Pillius Medicinensis [*Flourished, 1165-1207*] [*Authority cited in pre-1607 legal work*] (DSA)
PI .... Pilot International (EA)
PI .... Pilot Item (MCD)
PI .... Pilotless Intercepter [*Air Force*]
PI .... Pineal Body (DB)
PI .... Pinedale [*Wyoming*] [*Seismograph station code, US Geological Survey*] [*Closed*] (SEIS)
PI .... Pin Insulator (SAUS)
PI .... Pink (ROG)
PI .... Pinneberg [*German license plate city code*]
PI .... Pipe [*Freight*]
PI .... Pirelli [*Tire casing code*]
PI .... Planetary Interior (SAUS)
PI .... Planet Imager (SAUS)
PI .... Plan Information (SAUS)
PI .... Planning Index (SAUS)
PI .... Plant Industry (SAUS)
PI .... Plant Inspection
PI .... Plant Introduction [*Botany*]
PI .... Plaque Index [*Dentistry*]
PI .... Plasma Iron [*Hematology*]
PI .... Plastic Index
PI .... Plasticity Index (SAUS)
PI .... Plastics Institute (NADA)
PI .... Plastochron Index [*Botany*]
PI .... Plug-in (SAUS)
PI .... Plug-In Instrument (IAA)
P/I........... Pneumatic-to-Current (SAUS)
PI .... Pneumatosis Intestinalis [*Medicine*]
PI .... Point Initiating
PI .... Point Insulating

PI .... Point Interception (SAUS)
PI .... Point of Impact (AFM)
PI .... Point of Interception [*Navigation*]
PI .... Point of Intersection
PI .... Point of Inversion (SAUS)
PI .... Poison Ivy [*Campers' slang*]
PI .... Polar Inductor (SAUS)
PI .... Polling Interrupt (SAUS)
PI .... Polyimide [*Organic chemistry*]
PI .... Polyisoprene [*Organic chemistry*]
PI .... Polymer International (NS), Inc. [*Toronto Stock Exchange symbol*]
PI .... Pompeiiana, Inc. (EA)
PI .... Ponderal Index [*Measurement*] (DAVI)
PI .... Poni Iussit [*Ordered to Be Placed*] [*Latin*]
PI .... Popcorn Institute (EA)
PI .... Population Indication (SAUS)
PI .... Population Institute (EA)
PI .... Population Inversion (SAUS)
PI .... Porch Index [*Psychiatry*] (DAVI)
PI .... Portfolio Insurance [*Finance*]
PI .... Position Indicating (SAUS)
PI .... Position Indication (SAUS)
PI .... Position Indicator [*Army*]
PI .... Positive Identification Feature
PI .... Positive Input (SAUS)
PI .... Positive Intelligence (LAIN)
PI .... Positive Interlace [*Television*]
PI .... Postal Instruction (IAA)
PI .... Post-Impressionist (SAUS)
PI .... Postimpressionist Movement [*Art*]
PI .... Postinfection [*Medicine*] (DB)
PI .... Postinoculation [*Medicine*]
PI .... Postischemic [*Medicine*]
PI .... Potash Institute [*Later, PPI*] (EA)
PI .... Potomac Institute [*Defunct*] (EA)
PI .... Power Indicator (IAA)
PI .... Power Injection
PI .... Power Input
PI .... Power Interlock (IAA)
PI .... Practice Interception (SAUS)
PI .... Pratt Institute (SAUS)
PI .... Precision Instrument (NVT)
PI .... Predicted Impact (MCD)
PI .... Pregnancy Induced [*Gynecology*]
PI .... Preinduction [*Medicine*]
PI .... Preliminary Incubation (OA)
PI .... Preliminary Injunction [*Legal term*] (HGAA)
PI .... Preliminary Input (SAUS)
PI .... Preliminary Inspection (MCD)
Pi .... Preliminary Investigation (NAKS)
PI .... Preliminary Investigation (NASA)
PI .... Preliminary Issue
PI .... Premdor, Inc. [*NYSE symbol*] (SPSG)
PI .... Premium Income (MARI)
PI .... Preparatory Interval [*Psychometrics*]
PI .... Prepositioned Instruction [*DoD*]
PI .... Present Illness [*Medicine*]
PI .... Pressure Indicator [*Nuclear energy*]
Pi .... Pressure of Inspiration [*Medicine*]
P/I............ Pressure to Current (SAUS)
PI .... Presumptive Instruction (SAUS)
PI .... Primacord Interstage
PI .... Primary Infarction [*Medicine*]
PI .... Primary Infertility (SAUS)
PI .... Primary Input (IAA)
PI .... Primary Item (ACAE)
PI .... Prime Implicant (SAUS)
PI .... Prime Interest Rate [*Banking*]
PI .... Prime Item (SAUS)
PI .... Principal Investigator (MCD)
Pi .... Principal Investigator (NAKS)
PI .... Printer [*Navy*]
PI .... Printers Ink (SAUS)
PI .... Print Image (IAA)
PI .... Printing Impressions [*A publication*] (DGA)
PI .... Priority Interrupt (IEEE)
PI .... Private Institution [*British*]
PI .... Private Investigator
PI .... Priviledged Information (SAA)
PI .... Privileged Instruction (SAUS)
PI .... Proactive Inhibition [*Psychology*]
PI .... Proactive Interference (EDAC)
PI .... Problem Input (SAA)
PI .... Procedure Interface (SAUS)
PI .... Process Image (NITA)
PI .... Process Instruction (SAUS)
PI .... Process Instrumentation [*Nuclear energy*] (NRCH)
PI .... Process Interface (SAUS)
PI .... Process Interrupt (SAUS)
PI .... Processor Interface [*Computer science*] (IAA)
PI .... Procurement Inspection (MCD)
PI .... Procurement Item (NASA)
PI .... Prodigy Internet
PI .... Product Improved
PI .... Product Improvement (MCD)
P/I............ Production Illustration (MSA)
PI .... Production Index (SAUS)
PI .... Production Interval
PI .... Productivity Index (IEEE)
pi............ Professional Indemnity [*Insurance*] (ODBW)
PI .... Professional Indemnity [*Insurance*]
PI .... Profibus International (SAUS)
PI .... Program Indicator (IEEE)
PI .... Program Information
PI .... Program Innovations (ADA)
PI .... Program Instruction [*Computer science*] (BUR)
PI .... Program Integrator [*Military*] (RDA)
PI .... Program Interface (SAUS)
PI .... Program Interrupt
PI .... Program Interrupter
Pi .... Program Introduction (NAKS)
PI .... Program Introduction
PI .... Program Isolation [*Computer science*] (ELAL)
PI .... Program Issuances [*Assistance Payments Administration, HEW*]
PI .... Programmed Information [*Computer science*]
PI .... Programmed Instruction
PI .... Programmed Interrupt (SAUS)
PI .... Programmed Introduction (MCD)
PI .... Program of Instrumentation (MUGU)
PI .... Project Inform (EA)
PI .... Project Initiation [*Automotive engineering*]
PI .... Project Intrex [*Massachusetts Institute of Technology*] (EA)
PI .... Prolactin Inhibitor [*Endocrinology*]
PI .... Property Index [*British police term*]
PI .... Propidium Iodide [*Fluorescent dye*]
PI .... Proportional Integral (AAEL)
PI .... Proportional-Plus Integral [*Digital control*]
PI .... Proprietary Information (SAA)
PI .... Propyl Isome (OA)
PI .... Protamine Insulin
Pi .... Protease Inhibitor
PI .... Proteinase Inhibitor [*Biochemistry*]
PI .... Protocol International (SAUS)
PI .... Protocol Interpreter (SAUS)
PI .... Pseudo-Instruction (SAUS)
PI .... Psychiatric Institute
PI .... Psychosynthesis Institute (EA)
PI .... Publication Instructions
PI .... Public Information
PI .... Public Investigation (SAUS)
PI .... Public Involvement (ABAC)
PI .... Puebla Institute (EA)
PI .... Pulmonary Incompetence [*Medicine*]
PI .... Pulmonary Indices [*Medicine*]
PI .... Pulmonary Infarction [*Medicine*]
PI .... Pulmonary Intervertebral Disc [*Medicine*]
PI .... Pulmonic Insufficiency [*Medicine*] (RAWO)
PI .... Pulse Induction (ADA)
PI .... Pulse Input (SAUS)
PI .... Purge Isolation [*Nuclear energy*] (NRCH)
PI .... Pyritization Index [*Geoscience*]
PI .... Sunshine Airlines [*Airline code*] [*Australia*]
PI1............ State Correctional Institute at Camp Hill, Camp Hill, PA [*OCLC symbol*] (OCLC)
PI2............ State Correctional Institute at Dallas, Dallas, PA [*OCLC symbol*] (OCLC)
PI3............ State Correctional Institute at Grateford, Grateford, PA [*OCLC symbol*] (OCLC)
PI-3-Virus... Parainfluenza-3-Virus (SAUS)
PI4............ State Correctional Institute at Huntingdon, Huntingdon, PA [*OCLC symbol*] (OCLC)
PI5............ State Correctional Institute at Muncy, Muncy, PA [*OCLC symbol*] (OCLC)
PI6............ State Correctional Institute at Pittsburgh, Pittsburgh, PA [*OCLC symbol*] (OCLC)
PI7............ State Regional Correctional Facility, Greensburg, PA [*OCLC symbol*] (OCLC)
PI-3-3 .... Parainfluenza-3 (SAUS)
PIA............ Municipal Premium Income Trust [*Formerly, Allstate Municipal Premium Fund*] [*NYSE symbol*] (SPSG)
PIA............ National Association of Professional Insurance Agents (NTPA)
PIA............ Pacific Islands Association (EA)
PIA............ Packaged Ice Association (EA)
PIA............ Paid in Advance (WDMC)
PI/A............ Pakistan Institute of International Affairs (SAUS)
PIA............ Pakistan International Airlines (SAUS)
PIA............ Pakistan International Airlines Corp. [*ICAO designator*] (FAAC)
PIA............ Panel-Information-Air Operation
PIA............ Parallel Interface Adapter (SAUS)
PIA............ Parapsychology Institute of America (EA)
PIA............ Particle Impact Analyzer [*Astrophysics*]
PIA............ Partitioning Industry Association [*British*] (DBA)
pia .... Passengers' Luggage in Advance (ODA)
PIA............ Passive Immunological Agglutination
PIA............ Payload Interface Adapter [*NASA*] (SSD)
PIA............ Payload Interface Agreement (SAUS)
PIA............ Peoria [*Illinois*] [*Airport symbol*] (OAG)
PIA............ Peoria Airport, IL [*Amtrak Busline code*]
PIA............ Perfumery Importers Association [*Defunct*] (EA)

PIA.......... Peril Insured Against (MARI)
PIA.......... Peripheral Interface Adapter [*Computer science*]
PIA.......... Personal Information Appliance [*Telecommunications*] (PCM)
PIA.......... Personal Information Assistant
PIA.......... Personal Intelligent Agent (SAUS)
PIA.......... Personal Investment Authority [*British*] (ECON)
PIA.......... Personnel Inventory Analysis [*Army*]
PIA.......... Perspective Inversion Algorithm [*Computer science*]
PIA.......... Petervin Information Associates [*Also, an information service or system*] (IID)
PIA.......... Petroleum Incentives Administration [*Canada*]
PIA.......... Pharmaceutical Industries Association (SAUS)
PIA.......... Phenylisopropyladenosine [*Biochemistry*]
PIA.......... Philippine Institute of Architects (SAUS)
PIA.......... Phosphoroimmunoassays
PIA.......... Photoelectric Intravenous Angiography [*Medicine*] (DMAA)
PIA.......... Photographic Importers Association [*British*] (BI)
PIA.......... Piano [*Softly*] [*Music*]
PIA.......... Pilots International Association (EA)
PIA.......... Pine Institute of America (SAUS)
PIA.......... Pitten [*Austria*] [*Seismograph station code, US Geological Survey*] (SEIS)
PIA.......... Place Indicator in Accumulators (SAA)
PIA.......... Plasma Insulin Activity [*Clinical chemistry*]
PIA.......... Plastics Industries Association [*Ireland*]
PIA.......... Plastics Institute of America (EA)
PIA.......... Plug-in Administrator (SAUS)
PIA.......... Plug-In Amplifier
PIA.......... Pointed Instrument Assembly (ACAE)
PIA.......... Polycultural Institution of America
PIA.......... Positive Ion Accelerator
PIA.......... Positron Intensity Accumulator (MCD)
PIA.......... Postal Inspectors' Association [*A union*] [*British*]
PIA.......... Potentiometric Immunoassay [*Clinical chemistry*]
PIA.......... Predominant Interest Agency (AAGC)
PIA.......... Preferential Trade Area (EBF)
PIA.......... Preinfarction Angina [*Cardiology*] (DMAA)
PIA.......... Pre-Inspection Acceptance (SAA)
PIA.......... Preinstallation Acceptance
PIA.......... Pressure Indicating Alarm [*Engineering*]
PIA.......... Primary Immunodeficiency Association [*United Kingdom*] (EAIO)
PIA.......... Primary Inspection Agency [*Federal Manufactured Housing Construction and Safety Standards*] [*Department of Housing and Urban Development*] (GFGA)
PIA.......... Primary Insurance Account [*Social Security Administration*] (OICC)
PIA.......... Primary Insurance Amount [*Medicine*] (EDAA)
PIA.......... Principal Industry Activity [*IRS*]
PIA.......... Printing Industries Association (SAUS)
PIA.......... Printing Industries of America (EA)
PIA.......... Printing Institute of America (SAUS)
PIA.......... Prison Industry Authority (SAUS)
PIA.......... Proceedings of the Irish Academy (SAUS)
PIA.......... Production Inventory Analysis (AAG)
PIA.......... Professional Insurance Agents [*Alexandria, VA*] (EA)
PIA.......... Program Implementation Agency (SAUS)
PIA.......... Program Initiation Agreement (SSD)
PIA.......... Programmable Interconnect Array [*Computer science*] (CIST)
PIA.......... Project Impact Analysis (NASA)
PIA.......... Project Initiation Agreement (SAUS)
PIA.......... Project Interface Adapter (SSD)
PIA.......... Propellant Isolation Assembly (ACAE)
PIA.......... Proprietary Industries Association (AAGC)
PIA.......... Psychiatric Institute of America [*For-profit network of private psychiatric hospitals*] (EA)
PIA.......... Public and International Affairs [*USCG*] (TAG)
PIA.......... Public Information Act
PIA.......... Public Information Adviser [*NATO*] (NATG)
PIA.......... Public Information and Awareness (SAUS)
PIA.......... Public Intoxication Act [*Australia*]
PIA.......... Pulse-Interval Analyzer (SAUS)
PIA.......... Pumice Institute of America (EA)
PIA.......... Purified Isophthalic Acid
PIA.......... White Haven Center, White Haven, PA [*OCLC symbol*] (OCLC)
PIAA.......... Pacific Index of Abbreviations and Acronyms (SAUS)
PIAA.......... Physician Insurers Association of America
PIAA.......... Pre-Arrangement Interment Association of America [*Later, PAA*] (EA)
PIAC.......... Partido de Integracion de America Central [*Nicaragua*] [*Political party*] (EY)
PIAC.......... Peak Instantaneous Airborne Count (DA)
PIAC.......... Permanent International Altaistic Conference (EA)
PIAC.......... Petroleum Industry Advisory Committee [*British*]
PIAC.......... Printing Industry Advisory Committee (HEAS)
PIAC.......... Problem Identification and Correction [*DoD*] (AFIT)
PIACCS.......... Pacific Integrated Automatic Command and Control System [*Military*] (DNAB)
PIACS.......... Pacific Integrated Automatic Communications Systems [*Military*]
PIACT.......... Program for the Introduction and Adaptation of Contraceptive Technology (EA)
PIAD.......... Plastics in Automotive Design (SAUS)
PIADC.......... Plum Island Animal Disease Center [*Formerly, PIADL*]
PIADL.......... Plum Island Animal Disease Laboratory [*of ARS, Department of Agriculture*] [*Later, PIADC*]
PIAF.......... Piege a Fibre Optique (SAUS)
PIAFS.......... Personal Handyphone Internet Access Forum Standard (DINT)
PIAGET.......... Promoting Intellectual Adaptation Given Experiential Transforming Project (EDAC)
PIAI.......... Printing Industry of America, Inc. (SAUS)
PIAK.......... Professional Insurance Agents of Kentucky (EARSL)
PIAM.......... Petroleum Industry Application of Microcomputer (SAUS)
PIAM.......... PIA Merchandising Services, Inc. [*NASDAQ symbol*] (SAG)
PIAMA.......... Professional Institute for the American Management Association (OICC)
PIA Mer.......... PIA Merchandising Services, Inc. [*Associated Press*] (SAG)
PIANC.......... Permanent International Association of Navigation Congresses [*Brussels, Belgium*] (EAIO)
PIand.......... Papyri Iandanae [*A publication*] (OCD)
PIANEC.......... Planning of the Implementation of an Improved AFTN/AFS Network (SAUS)
PIANG.......... Piangendo [*Plaintive*] [*Music*]
PIANISS.......... Pianissimo [*Very Softly*] [*Music*]
PIANO.......... Propulsion Integration of Aero-Control Nozzles (SAUS)
PIAP.......... Pesticides Incidents Appraisal Panel (HEAS)
PIAP.......... Psychologists Interested in the Advancement of Psychotherapy [*Later, APA*] (EA)
PIAPACS.......... Psychophysiological Information Acquisition, Processing, and Control System
PIAR.......... Problem Identification and Analysis Report [*Military*] (CAAL)
PIAR.......... Project Impact Analysis Report (MCD)
PIARC.......... Permanent International Association of Road Congresses [*See also AIPCR*] [*Paris, France*] (EAIO)
PIARR.......... Product Independent Automatic Routing and Release (SAUS)
PIARy.......... Product Independent Automatic Routing and Release (SAUS)
PIAS.......... Photographic Inventory and Accountancy System
PIAS.......... Piaster [*Monetary unit*] [*Spain, Republic of Vietnam, and some Middle Eastern countries*]
PIAS.......... Prague Institute of Advanced Studies
PIAS.......... Precision Intelligence Augmentation System
PIAS.......... Precision Locator Strike System Intelligence Augmentation System
PIAS.......... Pressure Indicating Alarm Switching [*Engineering*]
PIAS.......... Program Impact Analysis Scenario
PIASA.......... Polish Institute of Arts and Sciences of America (EA)
PIASS.......... Paris International Aviation and Space Salon (MCD)
PIAT.......... Peabody Individual Achievement Test [*Education*]
PIAT.......... Platoon Infantry Anti-Tank (WDAA)
PIAT.......... Project Integrity Assurance Team (WDAA)
PIAT.......... Projector Infantry, Antitank [*British shoulder-controlled weapon*]
PIAT.......... Public Information Assist Team [*Environmental Protection Agency*] (ERG)
PIAT-R.......... Peabody Individual Achievement Test-Revised (TES)
PIAV.......... Private Investigators Association of Virginia (EARSL)
PIAVA.......... Polydactyly-Imperforate Anus-Vertebral Anomalies [*Syndrome*] [*Medicine*] (DMAA)
PIAZ.......... Piazio [*NCIC motorcycle make code*]
PIB.......... George Junior Republic, Grove City, PA [*OCLC symbol*] (OCLC)
PIB.......... Laurel/Hattiesburg [*Mississippi*] [*Airport symbol*] (OAG)
PIB.......... Pacific Inland Tariff Bureau, Portland OR [*STAC*]
PIB.......... Papuan Infantry Battalion
PIB.......... Parachute Infantry Battalion [*Army*]
PIB.......... Partial Ileal Bypass [*Medicine*]
PIB.......... Particle in a Box (SAUS)
PIB.......... Partido Indio de Bolivia [*Political party*]
PIB.......... Payload Integration Bay [*NASA*] (KSC)
PIB.......... Pender Island [*British Columbia*] [*Seismograph station code, US Geological Survey*] (SEIS)
PIB.......... Periinfarction Block [*Medicine*] (RAWO)
PIB.......... Periodic Information Briefing (MCD)
PIB.......... Personal Information Briefing [*of returning POW's*] [*Air Force*]
PIB.......... Petroleum Information Board (SAUS)
PIB.......... Petroleum Information Bureau
PIB.......... Photo Intelligence Brief (AFM)
PIB.......... Photo Interpretation Brief (MCD)
PIB.......... Plans Intelligence Branch (SAUS)
PIB.......... Polar Ionosphere (or Ionospheric) Beacon (SAUS)
PIB.......... Polar Ionospheric Beacon
PIB.......... Polyisobutane [*Fuels and lubricants*]
PIB.......... Polyisobuten (SAUS)
PIB.......... Polyisobutylene [*Organic chemistry*]
PIB.......... Polytechnic Institute of Brooklyn [*Later, PINY*] (MCD)
PIB.......... Potential-Induced Breathing (SAUS)
PIB.......... Power Ionosphere Beacon (SAUS)
PIB.......... Pre-Flight Information Bulletin [*Aviation*] (DA)
PIB.......... Preliminary Instruction Book
PIB.......... Prices and Incomes Board [*British*]
PIB.......... Prison Industry Board (SAUS)
PIB.......... Processor Interface Buffer [*Telecommunications*] (TEL)
PIB.......... Product Improvement Bulletin
PIB.......... Program Information Block (IAA)
PIB.......... Program Information Briefing
PIB.......... Programmable Input Buffer
PIB.......... Propellant Inspection Building [*NASA*] (KSC)
PIB.......... Public Investments Board (SAUS)
PIB.......... Publishers Information Bureau [*New York, NY*] (EA)
PIB.......... Publishing Information Bulletin
PIB.......... Pulse Interference Blanker
PIB.......... Pyrotechnic Installation Building [*NASA*] (KSC)
PIBA.......... Primary Industry Bank of Australia Ltd. (ADA)
PIBAC.......... Permanent International Bureau of Analytical Chemistry of Human and Animal Food
PIBAL.......... Pilot Balloon Observation

PIBAL........ Polytechnic Institute of Brooklyn Aeronautical Laboratory (MCD)
PIBALS...... Pilot Balloon Soundings
PIBC......... Pacific Institute of Bio-Organic Chemistry
PIBC......... Percutaneous Intraaortic Balloon Counterpulsation [*Catheter*] [*Medicine*] (DMAA)
PIBD......... Point Initiating, Base Detonating Projectile [*Army*]
PIBD......... Portable Interface Bond Detector (IAA)
PIBD Projectile... Point Initiating, Base Detonating Projectile (SAUS)
PIBEB........ Polytechnic Institute of Brooklyn, Electrophysics Branch (SAUS)
PIBEE........ Polytechnic Institute of Brooklyn, Department of Electrical Engineering (SAUS)
PIBEP........ Polytechnic Institute of Brooklyn, Department of Electrophysics (SAUS)
PIBI......... butyl rubber (SAUS)
PIBL......... PEMA Item Baseline List [*Army*] (AABC)
PIBMM...... Permanent International Bureau of Motorcycle Manufacturers
PIBMRI...... Polytechnic Institute of Brooklyn, Microwave Research Institute (IEEE)
PIBO......... Poly Isobutylene Oxide (EDCT)
PIBOL....... Pilot Back Up Control
PIBOL....... Pilot in Booster Loop (SAA)
PIBOR....... Paris Interbank Offered Rank (ODBW)
PIBOR....... Paris Interbank Offered Rate (SAUS)
PIBS......... Permanent Interest-Bearing Shares [*Finance*] (WDAA)
PIBS......... Polar Ionospheric Beacon Satellite [*NASA*]
PIBSA....... Polyisobutylene Succinic Anhydride [*Fuels and lubricants*]
PIBUC....... Pilot Back Up Control
PIC.......... Calverton, NY [*Location identifier*] [*FAA*] (FAAL)
PIC.......... Craig House Technoma Workshop, Pittsburgh, PA [*OCLC symbol*] (OCLC)
PIC.......... Pacific Airlines Holding Co. [*Vietnam*] [*ICAO designator*] (FAAC)
PIC.......... Pacific Imagery Processing and Interpretation Center (SAUS)
PIC.......... Pacific Insurance Conference
PIC.......... Pacific Intelligence Center (MCD)
PIC.......... Pacific Islanders in Communications (SAUS)
PIC.......... Paid-In Capital [*Finance*] (MHDW)
PIC.......... Paired-Ion Chromatography
PIC.......... Para-iodoclonidine [*Biochemistry*]
PIC.......... Parent Indicator Code (DNAB)
PIC.......... Partially Incinerated Compound [*Furnace technology*]
PIC.......... Particle in Cell [*Gas solid*]
PIC.......... Particulate Inorganic Carbon (CARB)
PIC.......... Partners in Change Program [*Department of Labor*]
PIC.......... Payload Integration Center [*NASA*] (MCD)
PIC.......... Payload Integration Committee [*NASA*] (NASA)
PIC.......... Payload Integration Contractor (MCD)
PIC.......... PC Paint image format (SAUS)
PIC.......... Peak Identification Computer
PIC.......... People's Involvement Corp. (EA)
PIC.......... Performance Incentive Contracting (AAGC)
PIC.......... Periodic Inspection Control [*Military*] (IAA)
PIC.......... Peripheral Interface Controller [*Computer science*]
PIC.......... Peripherally Inserted Catheter [*Medicine*] (EDAA)
PIC.......... Peripherie Controller [*Computer science*] (IAA)
PIC.......... Pershing Instant Comment [*Donaldson, Lufkin & Jenrette*] [*Database*]
PIC.......... Persistence in Combat Program [*Defense Advanced Research Projects Agency*] (RCD)
PIC.......... Personal Identification Code [*Banking*]
PIC.......... Personal Information Carrier (SAUS)
PIC.......... Personal Information Communicator (SAUS)
PIC.......... Personal Intelligent Communicator [*Computer science*] (PCM)
PIC.......... Personal Internet Connection [*Fee-based accounts*]
PIC.......... Personality Inventory for Children [*Psychology*]
PIC.......... Personnel Investigations Center
PIC.......... Pesticides Information Center [*National Agricultural Library*] [*Terminated, 1969*]
PIC.......... Petrochemical Investing Corp.
PIC.......... Petroleum Industry Consultants, Inc. (EFIS)
PIC.......... Phosphoinositidase C [*An enzyme*]
PIC.......... Photographic Industries Council (SAUS)
PIC.......... Photographic Industry Council [*Defunct*] (EA)
PIC.......... Photographic Interpretation Center (MCD)
PIC.......... Photo Interpretation Center (SAUS)
PIC.......... Photo Interpretation Console (IAA)
PIC.......... Physics Information Center (SAUS)
PIC.......... Physics International Co. (SAUS)
PIC.......... Picayune, MS [*Amtrak rail station code*]
PIC.......... Piccadilly Cafeterias [*NYSE symbol*] (TTSB)
PIC.......... Piccadilly Cafeterias, Inc. [*NYSE symbol*] (SPSG)
PIC.......... Piccadilly Saloon [*London*] (DSUE)
pic.......... Piccolo (WDAA)
PIC.......... [*The*] Pickens Railroad Co. [*Later, PICK*] [*AAR code*]
PIC.......... Picos [*Brazil*] [*Airport symbol*] (AD)
Pic.......... Picrotoxin [*Biochemistry*]
Pic.......... Pictor [*Constellation*]
PIC.......... Pictorial (WDAA)
PIC.......... Picture (AABC)
PIC.......... Picture File Format [*Computer science*] (BTTJ)
PIC.......... Picture Image Compatibility (VLIE)
PIC.......... Picture Interactive Computer System (IAA)
pic.......... Pictures [*Slang*] (WDMC)
PIC.......... Piedmont Interfaith Council (SAUS)
PIC.......... Pig Improvement Co. [*British*] (ECON)
PIC.......... Pilot in Command [*Navy*] (DOMA)
PIC.......... Pilot-Integrated Cockpit (AAG)
PIC.......... Pine Cay [*British West Indies*] [*Airport symbol*] [*Obsolete*] (OAG)
PIC.......... Pitch Impregnation Carbonization (MCD)
PIC.......... Planar Integrated Circuit (SAUS)
PIC.......... Planned Insurance Coverage
PIC.......... Plasma Insulin Concentration [*Clinical chemistry*]
PIC.......... Plastic Igniter Cord (IAA)
PIC.......... Plastic Insulated Cable (IAA)
PIC.......... Plastic-Insulated Cable (SAUS)
PIC.......... Plastic Insulated Conductor
PIC.......... Platform for Internet Content (SAUS)
PIC.......... Plug-In Card (VLIE)
PIC.......... Pocket Ionization Chamber (SAUS)
PIC.......... Point in Call (SAUS)
PIC.......... Poison Information Center (SAUS)
PIC.......... Policy Information Center [*Department of Health and Human Services*] [*Information service or system*] (IID)
PIC.......... Polyethylene Insulated Cable (SAUS)
PIC.......... Polyethylene Insulated Conductor [*Telecommunications*]
PIC.......... Polymer-Impregnated Concrete (KSC)
PIC.......... Polymers Interphase Consortium [*Plastics industry*]
PIC.......... Polymorphism Information Content [*Medicine*] (DMAA)
PIC.......... Polyolefin Insulated Cable (SAUS)
PIC.......... Population Investigation Committee [*Medicine*] (EDAA)
PIC.......... Portable Imaging Computer
PIC.......... Position Independent Code [*Telecommunications*] (TEL)
PIC.......... Positive Immittance Converter (PDAA)
PIC.......... Positive Impedance Converter (IAA)
PIC.......... Positive Ion Chamber
PIC.......... Postinflammatory Corticoid [*Medicine*]
PIC.......... Potential Icing Category [*Meteorology*] (DA)
PIC.......... Power Information Center [*Interagency Advanced Power Group*] [*DoD*] [*Washington, DC*]
PIC.......... Power Input Connection (SAUS)
PIC.......... Power Integrated Circuit [*Computer science*]
PIC.......... Predicted Intercept Contour
PIC.......... Preferred Inter exchange Carrier (SAUS)
PIC.......... Preimpregnated Cable (SAUS)
PIC.......... Preinitiation Complex [*Genetics*]
PIC.......... Preinstallation Calibration (KSC)
PIC.......... Preinstallation Checkout (NASA)
PIC.......... Presbyterian Interracial Council (EA)
PIC.......... Pressure-Impregnation Carbonization (SAUS)
PIC.......... Pressure Indicated Controlled (SAUS)
PIC.......... Pressure Indicator Controller
PIC.......... Pressurized Ion Chamber (SAUS)
PIC.......... Prices and Income Commission (SAUS)
PIC.......... Primary Independent Carrier (VLIE)
PIC.......... Primary Interexchange Carrier [*Telecommunications*] (OTD)
PIC.......... Primate Information Center [*University of Washington*] [*Seattle, WA*]
pic.......... Prince Edward Island [*Canada*] [*MARC country of publication code*] [*Library of Congress*] (LCCP)
PIC.......... Printer Interface Cartridge [*Epson America, Inc.*]
PIC.......... Prior Informed Consent [*For use of pesticides*]
PIC.......... Priority Intercept Controller [*Computer science*] (ELAL)
PIC.......... Private Industry Council [*Generic term for group that helps provide job training*]
PIC.......... Procedures for Instrument Calibration
PIC.......... Process Improvement Committee
PIC.......... Process Interface Control
PIC.......... Processor Input Channel (NVT)
PIC.......... Processor Interconnection Channel (NITA)
PIC.......... Procurement Information Center
PIC.......... Procurement Information Circular (AAGC)
PIC.......... Procurement Information for Contracts [*AFSC*]
PIC.......... Product Information Catalog (SAUS)
PIC.......... Product Information Center [*AgriData Resources, Inc.*] [*Information service or system*]
PIC.......... Production Information and Control (SAUS)
PIC.......... Production Inventory Control (MHDI)
PIC.......... Product of Incomplete Combustion [*Environmental Protection Agency*] (ERG)
PIC.......... Products of Incomplete Combustion (SAUS)
PIC.......... Professional Image Computer (NITA)
PIC.......... Professional Instrument Course [*Aeronautics*]
PIC.......... Professional Interfraternity Conference [*Later, PFA*] (EA)
PIC.......... Program for Improved Contract Management [*Military*] (AFIT)
PIC.......... Program Identification Code (MUGU)
PIC.......... Program Indicator Code (SAUS)
PIC.......... Program Information Center
PIC.......... Program Information Code [*Computer science*] (ELAL)
PIC.......... Program Initiations and Commitments (AAG)
PIC.......... Program Instruction, Calibration [*Marine Corps*]
PIC.......... Program Interrupt Control [*Computer science*]
PiC.......... Programmable Industrial Controller (NITA)
PIC.......... Programmable Integrated Circuit (SAUS)
PIC.......... Programmable Interrupt Controller [*Computer science*]
PIC.......... Programmable Interval Clock (NASA)
PIC.......... Programmed Information Center
PIC.......... Programmed Instruction Centre (SAUS)
PIC.......... Programmed Instruction Counter (VLIE)
PIC.......... Project for Interface Compatibility
PIC.......... Project Information Center
PIC.......... Project Initiation Conference (SAUS)

PIC .... Prolonged Illness Coverage [*Insurance*] (PAZ)
PIC .... Promotion Industry Club (EA)
PIC .... Promotion Industry Council (NTPA)
PIC .... Proton Induced Cascade [*Physics*]
PIC .... Prudential Insurance Co. of America (EFIS)
PIC .... Pseudoisocyanine [*Organic chemistry*]
PIC .... Pseudo-Isocytidine [*Antineoplastic compound*]
PIC .... Public Information Center [*Nuclear energy*] (NRCH)
PIC .... Public Information Committee [*of the NATO Military Committee*] (NATG)
PIC .... Public Instruction Course (SAUS)
PIC .... Public Interest Campaign (SAUS)
PIC .... Publishers' Information Card [*Later, IBIS*] [*British*]
PIC .... Pulsed Ionization Chamber
PIC .... Pulse-Indicating Cartridge (SAUS)
PIC .... Pulse-Induced Collapse (SAUS)
PIC .... Pulse Ionisation Chamber (SAUS)
PIC .... Purpose Identification Code
PIC .... Pursuant to Instructions Contained In (MUGU)
PIC .... Pyro Ignition Control (SAUS)
PIC .... Pyro Initiator Capacitors (SAUS)
PIC .... Pyro Initiator Controller [*NASA*] (NAKS)
PIC .... Pyrotechnic Ignition Control (NASA)
PIC .... Pyrotechnic Initiator Capacitor (NASA)
PIC .... Pyrotechnic Initiator Controller (NASA)
PICA .... Palestine Israel Colonization Association (SAUS)
PICA .... Palestine Israelite Colonisation Association
PICA .... Participating Interest Contingency Agreement
PICA .... Picture-Coding Algorithm (VLIE)
PICA .... Police Insignia Collectors Association [*British*] (DBA)
PICA .... Porch Index of Communicative Ability [*Psychology*]
PICA .... Portable Image Computation Architectures (SAUS)
PICA .... Posterior Inferior Cerebellar Artery [*Anatomy*]
PICA .... Posterior Inferior Communicating Artery [*Cardiology*] (DAVI)
PICA .... Posterior Internal Cerebral Artery [*Cardiology*] (DAVI)
PICA .... Power Industry Computer Applications (MCD)
PICA .... Preliminary Inventory Control Afloat (SAUS)
PICA .... Press Independence and Critical Ability (NTCM)
PICA .... Pressure Indicated Controlled Alarmed (SAUS)
PICA .... Primary Inventory Control Activity (MCD)
PICA .... Printing Industry Computer Associates, Inc.
PICA .... Printing Industry of the Carolinas [*North and South Carolina*] (EARSL)
PICA .... Private Investment Co. for Asia SA
PICA .... Procedures for Inventory Control Afloat [*Navy*]
PICA .... Procedures Inventory Control Afloat (SAUS)
PICA .... Professional Insurance Communicators of America (EA)
PICA .... Programming Interpersonal Curricula for Adolescents [*Learning model*] [*Education*]
PICA .... Project for Integrated Catalogue Automation [*Royal Netherlands Library*] [*Cataloging cooperative*] (IID)
PICA .... Project Integrated Cataloguing Automation (SAUS)
PICA .... Property Services Agency Information on Construction and Architecture [*Property Service Agency Library Service*] [*British*] [*Information service or system*]
PICA .... Public Interest Computer Association (EA)
PICA .... Pyrotechnic Initiator Control Assembly (SAUS)
PICAA .... Permanent International Committee of Agricultural Associations (SAUS)
PICAC .... Porch Index of Communicative Ability in Children [*Psychology*]
PICAC .... Power Industry Computer Applications Conference (MCD)
PICADAD ... Place Identification/Characteristics and Area/Distance and Direction [*Bureau of the Census*]
PICADAD ... Place Identification, Characteristics, Area, Distance, and Direction (SAUS)
PICAm .... Proceedings of the International Congress of Americanists (SAUS)
PICAO .... Provisional International Civil Aviation Organization [*Later, ICAO*]
PICAO Journal ... Provisional International Civil Aviation Organization Journal (SAUS)
PICASO ...... Picture Algorithms-Subroutine Orientated (NITA)
PICASSO ... Pen Input to Computer and Scanned Screen Output [*Computer science*] (PDAA)
PICASSO ... Plan for Intelligent Control of Actuated Synchronized Signal Operation
PICASSO-CENA ... Pathfinder Instruments for Cloud and Aerosol Spacebourne Observations-Climatologie Etneduedes des Nuages et des Aerosols [*NASA's proposed launch date is March 2003*]
PICB .... Peabody Institute of the City of Baltimore [*Maryland*]
PICB .... Peripheral Interface Control Bus (SAUS)
PICC .... Partial Inventory Consumption Claim (SAUS)
PICC .... Parts for Import Cars Coalition [*Defunct*] (EA)
PICC .... Peoples Insurance Company of China (SAUS)
PICC .... Peripherally-Inserted Central Catheter [*Medicine*]
PICC .... Philadelphia International Convention Center [*Pennsylvania*]
PICC .... Philippine International Convention Center (SAUS)
PICC .... Piccadilly Cafeterias, Inc. [*NASDAQ symbol*] (COMM)
PICC .... Piccolo
PICC .... Plastics in Construction Council [*Later, CCS*] (EA)
PICC .... Processor Interface Controller and Communications [*Computer science*] (TIMI)
PICC .... Professional Institutions Council for Conservation [*British*]
PICC .... Provisional International Computation Center
PICCA .... Positive Ion Cluster Composition Analyzer [*Instrumentation*]
PicCafe ...... Piccadilly Cafeterias, Inc. [*Associated Press*] (SAG)
PICCAP ...... Pacific Island Climate Change Assistance Programme (SAUS)
PICCED ...... Pratt Institute Center for Community and Environmental Development [*Research center*] (RCD)
PICCL .... Parallel Implementation of Concurrent Common Lisp [*Computer science*] (HODG)
PICCO .... Pennsylvania Industrial Chemical Corp. [*Trademark*]
PICD .... Periinfarction Conduction Defect [*Medicine*] (RAWO)
PICD .... Preliminary Interface Control Drawing
PICD .... Primary Inventory Cutoff Data [*Supply*]
PICD .... Primary Irritant Contact Dermatitis [*Medicine*] (DMAA)
PIC Device ... Personnel Identity Card Device (SAUS)
PICDG .... Polar Icebreaker Canadian Design Group
PICDMS ..... Picture Database Management System (SAUS)
PICE .... Palaeoenvironments from Ice Cores (SAUS)
PICE .... Product Improved Compatibility Electronics (MCD)
PICE .... Programmable Integrated Control Equipment
PICEA .... Private Information Center on Eastern Arabia (SAUS)
PICEE .... President's Interagency Committee on Export Expansion [*Absorbed by President's Export Council in 1979*] (EGAO)
PICEL .... Picture Element (SAUS)
PICEL .... Picture Elements per Line (SAUS)
PICE/PIA ... Printing Industry Credit Exchange/PIA [*of the Printing Industries of America*] [*Defunct*] (EA)
PICES .... Programmed Interactive Cost Estimating System (ACAE)
PICESP ...... Put It in Corporate Executives' Swimming Pools [*Waste management slang*]
PICF .... Principal Investigator Computing Facilities (ACAE)
PICFS .... Postinfective Chronic Fatigue Syndrome [*Medicine*] (DMAA)
PICG .... PCTE Interface Control Group (SAUS)
PICG .... Pig Industry Consultative Group [*Queensland, Australia*]
PICG .... Programme International de Correlation Geologique [*International Geological Correlation Programme - IGCP*] (EAIO)
PICGC .... Permanent International Committee for Genetic Congresses
PicGPA ...... Picrylated Guinea Pig Albumin [*Immunochemistry*]
PICH .... Peninsula Institute for Community Health (MHID)
PICI .... Polymer International Corp. [*NASDAQ symbol*] (COMM)
PICI .... Programmed Instruction Center for Industry (SAUS)
PICIC .... Pakistan Industrial Credit and Investment Corp. (SAUS)
PICIM .... Positive Ion Chemical Ionization Mass Spectroscopy (ACAE)
PICIP .... Personal Computer Instrument Product (SAUS)
PICK .... Part Information Correlation Key
PICK .... PICK Communications Corp. [*OTCBB symbol*]
Pick .... Pickens Railroad (SAUS)
PICK .... [*The*] Pickens Railroad Co. [*Formerly, PIC*] [*AAR code*]
Pick .... Pickering's Massachusetts Supreme Judicial Court Reports [*1822-39*] [*A publication*] (DLA)
PICK .... Pick-Up Top Manufacturing [*NCIC trailer make code*]
PICK .... Pickwick [*Refers to an inferior quality cigar*] (DSUE)
Pickle .... Pickle's Reports [*85-108 Tennessee*] [*A publication*] (DLA)
PICKLE ...... Preserving Individual Cultures and Knowledge in Lands Everywhere [*An association*]
PICKLE ...... President's Intelligence Checklist [*Daily report prepared by CIA*]
Pick (Mass) ... Pickering's Massachusetts Reports [*18-41 Massachusetts*] [*A publication*] (DLA)
Pick Stat ... Pickering's English Statutes [*A publication*] (DLA)
PICKUP ...... Professional, Industrial and Commercial Updating [*Vocational training*] [*British*]
PICL .... Pest Infestation Control Laboratory (SAUS)
PICL .... Presidents Intelligence Checklist (SAUS)
PICL .... Proceedings of the International Congress of Linguists (SAUS)
PICLS .... Purdue International and Computational Learning System (SAUS)
PICLS .... Purdue University Instructional and Computational Learning System (SAUS)
PICM .... Master Chief Precision Instrumentman [*Navy rating*]
PICM .... Permanent International Committee of Mothers
PICM .... Picom Insurance [*NASDAQ symbol*] (TTSB)
PICM .... PICOM Insurance Co. [*NASDAQ symbol*] (SAG)
PICM .... Production and Inventory Cost Minimizer (SAUS)
PICM .... Professional Group [*NASDAQ symbol*] [*Formerly, Professionals Insurance Co. Management Group*]
PICM .... Professionals Insurance Co. Management Group [*NASDAQ symbol*] (SAG)
PICM Gp .... Professionals Insurance Co. Management Group [*Associated Press*] (SAG)
PIC-MOD .... Purpose Identification Code - Month and Calendar Year of Detachment (DNAB)
PICN .... Pic'N'Save Corp. [*NASDAQ symbol*] (COMM)
PIC-NF ...... Picroindigocarmine-Nuclear Fast Red [*A biological stain*]
PICO .... Pacific Islands Contact Office (COE)
PICO .... Partido Independiente de la Clase Obrera [*Panama*] [*Political party*] (EY)
PICO .... Person in Column One [*1980 census*]
PICO .... Physicians Insurance Co. of Ohio [*NASDAQ symbol*] (NQ)
PICO .... PICO Holdings, Inc. [*NASDAQ symbol*] (SAG)
PICO .... Picosecond (GOBB)
PICO .... Polar Ice Core Drilling Office [*National Science Foundation*] (MSC)
PICO .... Polar Ice Coring Office (SAUS)
PICO .... Polio Information Center Online (SAUS)
PiCO .... Portable Interactive Computing Object
PICO .... Preinstallation, Installation, and Checkout (ACAE)
PICO .... Product Improvement Control Office (AFM)
Pico .... Progressive Tools and Industries Co.
PICO .... Purchasing Internal Change Order (MCD)
PICOA .... Physicians Insur Ohio [*NASDAQ symbol*] (TTSB)
PICODE ...... Program Indicator-Code [*Computer science*] (ECII)

PICOE .... Programed Initiations, Commitments, Obligations and Expenditures (SAUS)
PICOE .... Programmed Initiations, Commitments, Obligations, and Expenditures [*AFSC*]
PICO Hld.... PICO Holdings, Inc. [*Associated Press*] (SAG)
PICOM....... PICOM Insurance Co. [*Associated Press*] (SAG)
PICOMM .... Potter Instrument Coordinated Measuring Machine
PICON .... Process Intelligent Control [*A data processing system from LISP Machine, Inc.*]
PI Controller... Proportional-plus-Integral Controller (SAUS)
PICOP .... Paper Industries Corporation of the Philipines (SAUS)
PicoPd ...... Pico Products, Inc. [*Associated Press*] (SAG)
PICOR .... Pilot Controlled Overtone Reproduction (SAUS)
PICORNAVIRUS... Pico Ribonucleic Acid Virus
PICOS .... Purchased Input Concept Optimization with Suppliers [*Auto industry quality and cost management program*]
PICOST...... Probability of Incurring Estimated Costs [*Military*] (MCD)
PICP .... Prime Inventory Control Point (DNAB)
PICP .... Proceedings of the International Congress of Philosophy (SAUS)
PICP .... Program Interface Control Plan (NASA)
PICPAB...... Phenomena Induced by Charged Particle Beams
PICPS .... Proceedings of the International Congress of Phonetic Sciences (SAUS)
PICPSA...... Permanent International Commission for the Proof of Small Arms (SAUS)
PICPSA...... Permanent International Commission for the Proof of Small-Arms (EAIO)
PICRC .... Pesticide and Industrial Chemicals Research Center [*Public Health Service*] (GRD)
PICRS .... Program Information Control and Retrieval System (NASA)
PICRS .... Program Information Coordination and Review Service [*NASA*] (NASA)
PICS .... Pacific Islands Central School (SAUS)
PICS .... Part Inventory Control System (SAUS)
PICS .... Partnership in Computational Science (SAUS)
PICS .... Payload Integration Control Schedule (SAUS)
PICS .... Permit Imprint Collectors Society (EA)
PICS .... Perpetual Inventory Control System
PICS .... Personnel Information Commission System (SAUS)
PICS .... Personnel Information Communication [*or Control*] System [*Computer science*]
PICS .... Pharmaceutical Information Control System (DIT)
PICS .... Photogrammetric Integrated Control System (SAUS)
PICS .... Photographic Information Condensing System (DNAB)
PICS .... Photographic Integrated Control System (SAUS)
PICS .... Photography in Community Self-Development [*Program of Master Photo Dealers and Finishers Association*]
PICS .... Photo Index and Cataloging System (NASA)
PICS .... Physical Inventory Control System (SAUS)
PICS .... Pioneer Image Converter System [*NASA*]
PICS .... Plastid Isolation Column System [*Analytical chemistry*]
PICS .... Platform for Internet Content Selection [*Computer science*]
PICS .... Platformfor Internet Content Selection (SAUS)
PICS .... Platform for Internet Content Specification [*Computer science*]
PICS .... Plug-in Control System (SAUS)
PICS .... Plug-In Inventory Control System [*Bell System*]
PICS .... Positive Ion Composition Spectrometer (SAUS)
PICS .... Predefined Input Control Sequence (MCD)
PICS .... Procurement Information Control System [*NASA*]
PICS .... Production Information and Control Subsystem (SAUS)
PICS .... Production Information and Control System [*IBM Corp.*] [*Software package*]
PICS .... Productivity Improvement and Control System (BUR)
PICS .... Program Information and Control System (MCD)
PICS .... Programmable Industrial Control Simulation (SAUS)
PICS .... Protocol Implementation Conformance Statement [*Computer science*] (TNIG)
PICS .... Protocol Interoperability Conformance Statment (SAUS)
PICS .... Pulsed Image Converter System (ACAE)
PICS/DCPR... Plug-In Inventory Control System/Detailed Continuing Property Record [*Telecommunications*] (TEL)
PICSI .... Picture Identification for Children Standardized Index [*Medicine*] (EDAA)
PICSO .... Pressure-Controlled Intermittent Coronary Sinus Occlusion [*Medicine*] (DMAA)
PIC System... Picture Interactive Computer System (SAUS)
PICT .... Format for images used by Apple Macintosh (SAUS)
PICT .... Perceived Instrumentality of the College Test
PICT .... Philips Inventory Control Technique [*Computer science*] (IAA)
Pict .... Pictor [*Constellation*]
PICT .... Pictorial (ROG)
pict .... Pictorial (WDAA)
Pict .... Picture (AL)
PICT .... Picture File Format [*Computer science*] (BTTJ)
PICT .... Primary Intracranial Tumor [*Medicine*] (EDAA)
PICT .... Project on the Improvement of College Teaching
Pict Dict Rome... Pictorial Dictionary of Ancient Rome [*A publication*] (OCD)
PicTel........ PictureTel Corp. [*Associated Press*] (SAG)
PICTEL ...... Picture Telephone [*Telecommunications*] (EECA)
pictg .... Pictograph (VRA)
PICTOMAP... Photographic Image Conversion by Tonal Masking Procedures (MCD)
PICTS........ Photo-Induced Current Transient Spectroscopy (AAEL)
PICU .... Parallel Instruction Control Unit
PICU .... Pediatric Intensive Care Unit [*Medicine*]
PICU .... Pickfords Removals [*Intermodal shipping container symbol*] (TVRC)
PICU .... Priority Interrupt Control Unit [*Computer science*] (MDG)
PICU .... Pulmonary Intensive Care Unit [*Medicine*]
PICUTP...... Permanent and International Committee of Underground Town Planning (SAUS)
PICUTP...... Permanent International Committee of Underground Town Planning (SAUS)
PICUTPC ... Permanent and International Committee of Underground Town Planning and Construction
PICV .... Protected Infantry Combat Vehicle (SAUS)
PICW .... Pickwick [*NCIC trailer make code*]
PIC(WA)..... Potato Industry Council (Western Australia)
PICZ .... Plymouth Industry Complex [*Federal Railroad Administration identification code*]
PID........... Democratic Institutionalist Party (Guatemala) [*Political party*] (PSAP)
PID........... D. T. Watson Home for Crippled Children, Leetsdale, PA [*OCLC symbol*] (OCLC)
PID........... Pain Intensity Differences [*Medicine*]
PID........... Parallel Interface Device (SAUS)
PID........... Paralytic Infantile Paralysis [*Medicine*] (QSUL)
PID........... Parameter Identification [*Communications*]
PID........... Partial Initial Decision [*Nuclear energy*] (NRCH)
PID........... Particle-Induced Desorption (SAUS)
PID........... Partido de Integracion Democrata [*Democratic Integration Party*] [*Argentina*] [*Political party*] (PPW)
PID........... Partido Izquierda Democratica [*Democratic Left Party*] [*Political party*] (EAIO)
PID........... Passenger Information Display
PID........... Passive Identification Device (SAUS)
PID........... Patient Identification Number [*Medicine*] (HVTR)
PID........... Patrol Input Device (MCD)
PID........... Payload Insertion Device (NASA)
PID........... Pelvic Inflammatory Disease [*Medicine*]
PID........... Perfect-Gas Isentropic Decompression [*Engineering*]
PID........... Peripheral Interface Device [*Computer science*] (EECA)
PID........... Persistent Identifier (SAUS)
PID........... Personal Identification Device (MHDI)
PID........... Personal Identifier (SAUS)
PID........... Personality and Individual Differences [*A publication*]
PID........... Personnel Identification Device [*Navy*] (IAA)
PID........... Personnel Inquiry/Death/Occupational Illness [*Report*] (DNAB)
PID........... Phenindione [*or Phenylindandione*] [*Anticoagulant*]
PID........... Photographic Intelligence Division (CARL)
PID........... Photo-Imageable Dielectric (SAUS)
PID........... Photo-Induced Desorption (SAUS)
PID........... Photointerpretation Department [*Military*]
PID........... Photo Ionisation (or Ionization) Detector (SAUS)
PID........... Photoionization Detector
PID........... Photon-Induced Dissociation [*For spectral studies*]
PID........... Photon Ionization Detector (EEVL)
PID........... Pictorial Information Digitizer [*Computer science*] (DIT)
PID........... Picture Input Device (SAUS)
PID........... Pilot-Induced Deceleration
PID........... Pilot-Induced Decillation (SAUS)
PID........... Plan Identification Number (DOMA)
PID........... Planned Industrial Development (PA)
PID........... Planning and Integration Division (SAUS)
PID........... Plasma-Iron Disappearance [*Hematology*] (MAE)
PID........... Poisons Information Database (SAUS)
PID........... Polarization Image Detector (SAUS)
PID........... Police Intelligence Detail (SAUS)
PID........... Political Intelligence Department [*British*] [*World War II*]
PID........... Portable Intruder Detector [*Police and security equipment*]
PID........... Port Identification [*Telecommunications*] (TEL)
PID........... Position Identifier (SAUS)
PID........... Postinertia Dyskinesia [*Medicine*] (EDAA)
PID........... Primary Immunodeficiency Disease [*Medicine*]
PID........... Prime Input Development
PID........... Prime Item Development (MCD)
PID........... Primitive Interface Definition (SAUS)
PID........... Process & Instrument Design (ACII)
PID........... Process Identification (SAUS)
PID........... Process Identifier [*Computer science*] (PCM)
PID........... Process-Induced Defect
PID........... Procurement Information Digest (AFM)
PID........... Procurement Item/Identification Description [*DoD*]
PID........... Product ID (SAUS)
PID........... Product Identifier (SAUS)
PID........... Product Innovation and Design
PID........... Program Identifier (ACAE)
PID........... Program Information Department (SAUS)
PID........... Program Information Document [*NASA*] (MCD)
PID........... Program Introduction Document (NASA)
PID........... Programming Information Distribution (SAUS)
PID........... Project Identification Code
PID........... Project Implementation Directive [*Air Force*]
PID........... Prolapsed Intervertebral Disc [*Medicine*]
PID........... Proportional, Integral, and Differential Gain (SAUS)
PID........... Proportional Integral Derivation
PID........... Proportional-Integral Derivative [*Engineering*]
PID........... Proportional Integral Differential [*Digital control-algorithm*] (IAA)
PID........... Proportional Integration Derivation
PID........... Proportional Integro-Differential (SAUS)
PID........... Proportional plus Integral plus Derivative (SAUS)

PID .... Proportional-Plus Integral-Plus Derivative [*Digital control algorithm*]
PID .... Protocol Identification Number (SAUS)
PID .... Protocol Identifier (SAUS)
PID .... Protruded Intervertebral Disc [*Medicine*]
PID .... Pseudo Interrupt Device
PID .... Public Information Division [*Army*]
PIDA .... Payload Installation and Deployment Aid [*NASA*] (NASA)
PIDA .... Pet Industry Distributors Association (EA)
PIDA .... Pharmaceutical Industry Development Assistance (SAUS)
PIDA .... Phenylindane Dicarboxylic Acid (EDCT)
PIDA .... Pig Industry Development Authority [*British*] (BI)
PIDA Bulletin ... Pig Industry Development Authority Bulletin (SAUS)
PIDAS .... Perimeter Intrusions Detection Analysis System (SAUS)
PIDAS .... Portable Instantaneous Display and Analysis Spectrometer
PIDAS .... Portable Instant Intelligent Display and Analysis Spectrometer (SAUS)
PIDAS .... Portable Intelligent Display and Analysis Spectrometer (SAUS)
PIDB .... Peripheral Interface Data Bus (SAUS)
PIDC .... Pakistan Industrial Development Corp. (SAUS)
PIDC .... Philadelphia Industrial Development Corp.
PIDC .... Photo-Induced Discharge Characteristic (SAUS)
PIDC .... Precision Instrument Development Center (SAUS)
PIDC .... Procurement Intern Development Center (DNAB)
PIDC .... Projects International Development Corp. (SAUS)
PIDC .... Prototype International Data Centre [*For evaluating seismic signals*]
PIDCOM ..... Process Instruments Digital Communication System [*Beckman Industries*]
PIDD .... Passive Identification/Detection and Direction (MCD)
PIDD .... Planned Inactivation or Discontinued Date [*Environmental science*] (COE)
PIDDP .... Planetary Instrument Definition and Development Program (ACAE)
PI/DE .... Passive Identification/Direction Finding Equipment (MCD)
PI/DE .... Positive Identification and Direction Equipment
PI/DE .... Positive Identification and Direction Finding Equipment
Pid Eng ..... Pidgin English (SAUS)
PIDEP .... Preinterservice Data Exchange Program
PID-Filter ... Proportional-Integral-Differential-Filter (SAUS)
PIDG .... Proportional, Integral, and Differential Gain (SPST)
PIDI .... Philippines Invention Development Institute (SAUS)
Pidico .... Project Industrial Development and Investment Corp. (SAUS)
PIDO .... Primitive Indian Development Organization (SAUS)
PIDP .... Pacific Islands Development Program [*East-West Center*] [*Research center*] (RCD)
PIDP .... Pilot Information Display Panel
PIDP .... Programmable Indicator Data Processor [*Military*] (CAAL)
PIDR .... Product Inspection Discrepancy Report (MCD)
PIDRA .... Portable Insulin Dosage-Regulating Apparatus [*Medicine*]
PIDRS .... Photographic Instrumentation Data Recording System (MCD)
PIDS .... Parameter Inventory Display System (DNAB)
PIDS .... Patient Identification Services (GART)
PIDS .... Personal Inspirable Dust Spectrometer (SAUS)
PIDS .... Physical Intrusion Detection System (DWSG)
PIDS .... Portable Image Display System (NASA)
PIDS .... Primary Image Disemination System (SAUS)
PIDS .... Primary Immunodeficiency Syndrome [*Medicine*] (DMAA)
PIDS .... Prime Item Development Specification
PIDS .... Process Integration, Devices and Structures (SAUS)
PIDS .... Public Investment Data System (MHDW)
PIDS .... Pylon Integrated Dispenser Station (SEWL)
PIDSA .... Population Information Documentation System for Africa
PIDT .... Plasma-Iron Disappearance Time [*Hematology*] (MAE)
PIDX .... Petroleum Industry Data Exchange (SAUS)
PIE .... Air South West [*British*] [*FAA designator*] (FAAC)
PIE .... Clearwater-St. Petersburg [*Florida*] [*Airport symbol*] (AD)
PIE .... Elwyn Institute, Elwyn, PA [*OCLC symbol*] (OCLC)
PIE .... Pacific Information Exchange [*Information service or system*] (IID)
PIE .... Pacific Intercultural Exchange (SAUS)
PIE .... Pacific Intermountain Express (SAUS)
PIE .... Pacific Islands Ecosystems [*Springfield, VA*] [*Department of the Interior*] [*No longer available online*] [*Information service or system*]
PIE .... Pacing Item Evaluation (MCD)
PIE .... Paedophile Information Exchange [*British*] (ILCA)
PIE .... Paradoxical Inhibitory Effect [*Medicine*] (EDAA)
PIE .... Para-infectious Encephalopathy [*Medicine*] (EDAA)
PIE .... Parallel Instruction Execution [*Computer science*] (BUR)
PIE .... Parallel Interface Element
PIE .... Partners in Education (SAUS)
PIE .... Patent Information Exploitation [*Canadian Patent Office*]
PIE .... Payload Integration Equipment [*NASA*] (MCD)
PIE .... Payroll Audit, Indexing, and Expiration
PIE .... Period of Interruption of Employment (WDAA)
PIE .... Peripheral Interface Element [*Computer science*] (IAA)
PIE .... Personal Intelligent Electronics [*Computer science*] (AGLO)
PIE .... Personal Interactive Electronics [*Apple Computer Inc.*]
PIE .... Photo Image Enhancement (ACAE)
PIE .... Photo-Induced Electrochromism
PIE .... Pietermaritzburg [*South Africa*] [*Seismograph station code, US Geological Survey*] [*Closed*] (SEIS)
PIE .... Pipestone Petroleums, Inc. [*Toronto Stock Exchange symbol*] [*Vancouver Stock Exchange symbol*]
PIE .... P/L Integration Equipment (SAUS)
PIE .... Plug-In Electronics
PIE .... Plug-In Extension
PIE .... Plume Interaction Experiment [*Army*] (RDA)
PIE .... Pocket Internet Explorer [*Microsoft Corp.*] [*Computer science*]
PIE .... Polar Ice Extent (SAUS)
PIE .... Poly(iminoethylene) [*Organic chemistry*]
PIE .... Portable Information Evaluation
PIE .... Position Indicating Equipment (SAUS)
PIE .... Positive-Ion-Emission (ODA)
PIE .... Postinfectious Encephalomyelitis [*Medicine*] (RAWO)
PIE .... Post-Irradiation Examination [*Nuclear energy*] (NRCH)
PIE .... Post-Irradiation Experiment [*Nuclear energy*] (NRCH)
PIE .... Pre-Impact Event [*Automotive safety*]
PIE .... Preimplantation Embryo [*Medicine*] (EDAA)
PIE .... Price in Effect [*Military*]
PIE .... Primary Industry and Energy
PIE .... Problem, Intervention, Evaluation [*Medicine*] (IDYL)
PIE .... Program for Increased Education [*Military*]
PIE .... Program Interrupt Element [*Computer science*] (IAA)
PIE .... Program Interrupt Entry [*Computer science*]
PIE .... Programmable Interface Electronics (SAUS)
PIE .... Programming and Instrumentation Environment [*Computer science*]
PIE .... Prolog Inference Engine [*Computer science*]
PIE .... Proposal Information Exchange [*Military*]
PIE .... Prosthetic Infectious Endocarditis [*Medicine*] (EDAA)
PIE .... Proto-Indo-European [*Language*] (BARN)
PIE .... Publications Indexed for Engineering [*A publication*]
PIE .... Public Interest Economics Foundation [*Defunct*] (EA)
PIE .... Pulmonary Infiltration with Eosinophilia [*Medicine*]
PIE .... Pulmonary Interstitial Edema [*Medicine*] (DAVI)
PIE .... Pulmonary Interstitial Emphysema [*Medicine*]
PIE .... Pulse Interference Elimination
PIE .... Pulse Interference Eliminator [*RADAR*]
PIE .... Pulse Interference Emitting (MCD)
PIE .... Pyrotechnically Initiated Explosive (SAUS)
PIE .... St. Petersburg [*Florida*] [*Airport symbol*] (OAG)
PIEA .... Pencil Industry Export Association [*Defunct*] (EA)
PIEA .... Petroleum Industry Electrical Association [*Later, ENTELEC*] (EA)
PIEA .... Petroleum Industry Electrotechnical Association (IAA)
PIEA .... Pre-Arrangement Interment Exchange of America [*Later, PIAA*]
PIE-C .... Public Interest Economics Center (EA)
PIECE .... Petroleum Industry Environmental Preservation Executive (SAUS)
PIE COST ... Probability of Incurring Estimated Cost
PIECOST ... Probability of Incurring Estimated Costs [*Military*]
PIECP .... Preliminary Impact Engineering Change Proposal (MCD)
PIED .... Piedmont [*NCIC trailer make code*]
PIED .... Piedmont Mining Co., Inc. [*NASDAQ symbol*] (NQ)
PiedBcp .... Piedmont Bancorp, Inc. [*Associated Press*] (SAG)
PiedBGp .... Piedmont Bancgroup [*Associated Press*] (SAG)
PIEDM .... Piedmont, SC [*American Association of Railroads railroad junction routing code*]
PiedmBc .... Piedmont Bancorp, Inc. [*Associated Press*] (SAG)
PiedMg ..... Piedmont Managment Co., Inc. [*Associated Press*] (SAG)
PiedMn ..... Piedmont Mining Co., Inc. [*Associated Press*] (SAG)
PiedNG ..... Piedmont Natural Gas Co., Inc. [*Associated Press*] (SAG)
PIE-F .... Public Interest Economics Foundation [*Defunct*] (EA)
Piemnt ..... Piemonte Foods, Inc. [*Associated Press*] (SAG)
PIENE .... Piedras Negras, CU [*American Association of Railroads railroad junction routing code*]
PI Engine ... Post Inner Engine (SAUS)
PIEP .... Peripheral Infarct Epicardium [*Medicine*] (DB)
PIEP .... Petroleum Industry Environmental Performance
PIEP .... Primary Irritation Evaluation (SAUS)
PIEP .... Primary Irritation Evaluation Program
PIER .... Pierce Lowboy Trailer [*NCIC trailer make code*]
PIER .... Procedures for Internet/Enterprise Renumbering (SAUS)
PIER .... Product Inventory Electronically Recorded (PDAA)
Pier 1 .... Pier 1 Imports, Inc. [*Associated Press*] (SAG)
PIERC .... Pacific Island Ecosystems Research Center (SAUS)
Pierce RR ... Pierce on Railroad Law [*A publication*] (DLA)
PiercPag .... Piercing Pagoda, Inc. [*Associated Press*] (SAG)
PIERS .... Port Import/Export Reporting Service [*Journal of Commerce, Inc.*] [*Information service or system*]
PIERS-4 ..... Pressure-Induced Extra Resonance in Four-wave mixing (SAUS)
PIES .... Packaged Interchangeable Electronic System
PIES .... Penning Ionization Electron Spectroscopy
PIES .... Photographic Image Editing System (SAUS)
PIES .... Pollution Prevention Information Exchange System [*Environmental science*]
PIES .... Procurement and Inventory of Equipment System (DNAB)
PIES .... Procurement Information Exchange System (SAUS)
PIES .... Program Information and Evaluation System (SAUS)
PIES .... Project Independence Evaluation System [*Energy policy*]
PIES .... Purchasing Information Exchange System (SAUS)
PIESA .... Parasite-Induced Erythrocyte Surface Antigen [*Immunology*]
Piezonator ... Piezo-Resonator (SAUS)
PIF .... Insured Municipal Income Fund [*NYSE symbol*]
PIF .... Insured Muni Income Fd [*NYSE symbol*] (TTSB)
PIF .... Package Information Form (IAA)
PIF .... Page Image Format (SAUS)
PIF .... Paid In Full (SAUS)
PIF .... PaineWebber Premium Insured Municipal Income [*NYSE symbol*] (SPSG)
PIF .... Pakistan Islamic Front [*Pakistan*] [*Political party*] (ECON)
PIF .... Paper Industry Federation (NADA)
PIF .... Paratoid Isoelectric Focusing [*Medicine*] [*Variant protein*] (EDAA)

PIF .... Partners in Friendship (EA)
PIF .... Payload Integration Facility [*NASA*] (KSC)
PIF .... Peak Inspiratory Flow [*Medicine*] (AAMN)
PIF .... Perpetual Inventory File (DNAB)
PIF .... Personnel Identification Feature [*Navy*] (NVT)
PIF .... Phase Interface Fading (VLIE)
PIF .... Phase Inversion Formulation [*Chemistry*]
PIF .... Photo Interpretation Facility (SAUS)
PIF .... Picture Interchange Format File (SAUS)
PIF .... Pilot Information File [*Army*]
PIF .... Place in Inactive File [*Army*]
PIF .... Point Initiating Fuze
PIF .... Polyisocyanurate Foam (IGSL)
PIF .... Porportional-Integral Filter (SAUS)
PIF .... Positive Identification Feature (MCD)
PIF .... Positive Identification Friend/Foe (SAUS)
PIF .... Postscript Interchange Format (SAUS)
PIF .... Predictive Influence Function [*Statistics*]
PIF .... Preparer Inventory File [*IRS*]
PIF .... Privatization Investment Fund Trust Units [*Toronto Stock Exchange symbol*]
PIF .... Problem Identification Form (ARMP)
PIF .... Process Interchange Format [*Computer science*] (VLIE)
PIF .... Productivity Investment Fund [*Program*] [*Air Force*]
PIF .... Program Information File
PIF .... Programmable Interface [*Computer science*] (VLIE)
PIF .... Proinsulin-Free [*Medicine*] (DB)
PIF .... Project in Foreign Language Pedagogy (AIE)
PIF .... Prolactin Inhibiting Factor [*Endocrinology*] (DAVI)
PIF .... Prolactin-Release Inhibiting Factor [*Also, PRIH*] [*Endocrinology*]
PIF .... Proliferation Inhibitory Factor [*Immunochemistry*]
PIF .... Proportional-Integral Filter (SAUS)
PIF .... Prostatic Interstitial Fluid [*Medicine*] (MELL)
PIF .... Provision of Industrial Facilities [*Army*] (AABC)
PIF .... Prudential Intermediate Income Fund, Inc. [*NASDAQ symbol*] (COMM)
PIF .... Pseudo-Identification Feature (MCD)
PIF .... Punjab Irregular Force [*British military*] (DMA)
PIFA .... Packaging and Industrial Films Association [*British*] (DBA)
PIFA .... Pain-Inhibition Fear Avoidance [*Medicine*] (MELL)
PIFA .... Power Input Filter Assembly
PIFAL .... Program Instruction Frequency Analyzer [*Telecommunications*] (IAA)
PIFC .... Pakistan Industrial Finance Corp. (SAUS)
PIFCM .... Pitch Integrated Flight Control Module (MCD)
PI-FET .... Piezoelectric Field-Effect Transistor (PDAA)
PIFEX .... Programmable Image Feature Extractor [*to provide real-time machine vision for the Martian Rover robot*] [*Jet Propulsion Laboratory*] (BYTE)
PIFF .... Punjab Irregular Frontier Force [*British military*] (DMA)
PIFG .... Poor Intrauterine Fetal Growth [*Medicine*] (MELL)
PIFI .... Piedmonte Foods [*NASDAQ symbol*] (TTSB)
PIFI .... Piemonte Foods, Inc. [*NASDAQ symbol*] (NQ)
PIFI .... Pressure-Induced Intracranial Focal Ischemia [*Medicine*]
PIFL .... Pinnacle International Freight [*Common carrier symbol*]
PIFL .... Pipe Flow (PDAA)
PIFMIL ...... Proceedings of the International Federation for Modern Languages and Literatures (SAUS)
PIFOV .... Planet in Field of View [*NASA*]
PIFR .... Peak Inspiratory Flow Rate [*Medicine*]
PIFR .... Program Interrupt Flag Register [*Computer science*] (IAA)
PIFRS .... Prototype Increase Frequency Reporting System (SAUS)
PIFS .... Plume-Induced Flow Separation
PIFS .... Point Coordination Inter Frame Space (SAUS)
PIFS .... Point Inter-Frame Space (SAUS)
PIFS .... Post Infection Fatigue Syndrome [*Medicine*]
PIFS .... Prime Item Fabrication Specification
PIFT .... Platelet Immunofluorescence Test [*Analytical biochemistry*]
PIFT .... Protocol Interbank File Transfer [*Computer science*] (VLIE)
PIFUA .... Powerplant and Industrial Fuel Use Act of 1978
Pig .... drill-pipe internal rust scraper (SAUS)
PIG .... Glenn Mills School, Glenn Mills, PA [*OCLC symbol*] (OCLC)
PIG .... Pacific Institute of Geography
PIG .... Passive-Income Generator [*Investment term*]
PIG .... Pendulous Integrating Gyro
PIG .... Pendulous Integrating Gyroscope
PIG .... Penning Ionization Gauge (IAA)
PIG .... Pertussis Immune Gobulin [*Medicine*] (STED)
PIG .... Phillips Ionization Gauge
PIG .... Phosphatidylinositol Glycan [*Biochemistry*]
PIG .... Photo-Island Grid
pig .... Pigment (BARN)
Pig .... Pigmentation (STED)
Pig .... Pigott's Common Recoveries [*3 eds.*] [*1739-92*] [*A publication*] (DLA)
PIG .... Pipeline Industries Guild (SAUS)
PIG .... Plasma Inert Gas (SAUS)
PIG .... Plasmatron Inert Gas (SAA)
PIG .... Polymeric Immunoglobulin [*Medicine*] (DMAA)
PIG .... Pride, Integrity, Guts [*Police alternative for the appellation applied to police by radical groups*]
PIG .... Process Ink Gamut [*Printing technology*]
PIG .... Product Information Guide (SAUS)
PIG .... Production Image Generator (MCD)
PIG .... Production Installation Group [*Military*] (CAAL)
PIG .... Program Implementation Guideline (EG)
PIG .... Pulse Inert Gas
PIGA .... Pendulous Integrating Gyro Accelerometer
PIGA .... Pendulous Integrating Gyroscope Accelerometers
PIGA .... Pulsed Integrated Gyroscopic Accelerometer (SAUS)
PIGADD ..... Permanent Intergovernmental Authority on Drought and Development (SAUS)
Pig & R ..... Pigott and Rodwell's English Registration Appeal Cases [*1843-45*] [*A publication*] (DLA)
PIGDX .... Pioneer Gold Shares Cl.A [*Mutual fund ticker symbol*] (SG)
PIGE .... Proton-Induced Gamma-Ray Emission (ODA)
PIGEO .... Pigeon, MI [*American Association of Railroads railroad junction routing code*]
PIGFET ...... P-channel Insulated-Gate Field-Effect Transistor (SAUS)
PIGI .... Pregnancy-Induced Gluclose Intolerance (STED)
PIGI .... Pregnancy-Induced Glucose Intolerance [*Medicine*] (MELL)
PIGIT .... Putnam Intermediate Government Income Trust [*Associated Press*] (SAG)
Pig Judg .... Pigott's Foreign Judgments [*3rd ed.*] [*1908-09*] [*A publication*] (DLA)
PIGLET ...... Personalized Intelligently Generated Explanatory Text (SAUS)
PIGLET ...... Purchase Information, Gifts, Loans, Exchanges Tracking [*Suggested name for the Library of Congress computer system*]
pigm .... Pigment (STED)
PIGM .... Pigmentum [*Paint*] [*Pharmacy*]
PIGM .... Putnam Investment Grade Municipal Trust [*Associated Press*] (SAG)
PIGMA .... Pressurized Inert Gas Metal Arc (KSC)
PIGME .... Particle-Induced Gamma-ion Emission (SAUS)
PIGME .... Particle-Induced Gamma-Ray Emission (SAUS)
PIGME .... Programmed Inert Gas Multi-Electrode (PDAA)
PIGMI .... Pion Generator for Medical Irradiation [*Radiology*]
PIGMI .... Position Indicating General Measuring Instrument
PIGMI .... Positron-Indicating General Measuring Instrument (SAUS)
Pigm Resin Technol ... Pigment and Resin Technology (SAUS)
PIGMT2 ..... Putnam Investment Grade Municipal Trust II [*Associated Press*] (SAG)
PIGMT3 ..... Putnam Investment Grade Multiple Sectors III [*Associated Press*] (SAG)
PIGP .... Pyruvate Inosine Glucose Phosphate [*Medicine*] (EDAA)
PIGPA .... Pyruvate, Inosine, Glucose Phosphate, Adenine (AAMN)
PIGR .... Polymeric Immunoglobulin Receptor [*Biochemistry*]
Pig Rec ..... Pigott's Recoveries [*England*] [*A publication*] (DLA)
PIGS .... PAFEC Interactive Graphics System [*PAFEC Ltd.*] [*Software package*] (NCC)
PIGS .... Passive Infrared Guidance System [*DoD*]
PIGS .... Pesticides in Groundwater Strategy [*Environmental Protection Agency*] (GFGA)
PIGS .... Poles, Italians, Greeks, and Slavs
PIGS .... Portable Inertial Guidance System
PIGS .... Procedures, Information, Guidance & Standards (WDAA)
PIGU .... Pendulous Integrating Gyroscope Unit (SAUS)
PIGU .... Pendulous Integrating Gyro Unit
PIGZ .... Tranfax [*Intermodal trailer symbol*]
PIH .... Paper in Hand (SAUS)
PIH .... Passive Immune Hemolysis (PDAA)
PIH .... Permanent Income Hypothesis [*Economics*]
PIH .... Pheniprazine (LDT)
PIH .... Phenylisopropylhydrazine [*Pharmacology*]
PIH .... Pin in Hole (AAEL)
PIH .... Pipeline Induction Heat [*Industrial firm*] [*British*]
PIH .... Pocatello [*Idaho*] [*Airport symbol*] (OAG)
PIH .... Poison Inhalation Hazard (SARE)
PIH .... Population and International Health (SAUS)
PIH .... Pork Industry Handbook [*A publication*]
PIH .... Post-Inflammatory Hyperpigmentation [*Medicine*] (MELL)
PIH .... Pregnancy-Induced Hypertension [*Gynecology*]
PIH .... Primary Intracerebral Hemorrhage (CPH)
PIH .... Prolactin-Inhibiting Hormone (STED)
PIH .... Prolactin-Release Inhibiting Hormone [*Endocrinology*]
PIH .... Pseudointimal Hyperplasia [*Medicine*] (RAWO)
PIH .... Public and Indian Housing [*HUD*]
PIH .... St. Gabriel's Hall, Phoenixville, PA [*OCLC symbol*] (OCLC)
PIHC .... PHC, Inc. [*NASDAQ symbol*] (SAG)
PIHC .... PHC Inc.'A' [*NASDAQ symbol*] (TTSB)
PIHC .... Pioneer Behavioral Health (MHID)
PIHCA .... Polyisohexylcyanoacrylate [*Antibacterial*]
PIHCW ...... PHC Inc. Wrrt [*NASDAQ symbol*] (TTSB)
PIHF .... Periodic Inhomogeneous Film (SAUS)
PIHH .... Postinfluenza-Like Hyposmia and Hypogeusia (STED)
PIHM .... Polish Institute of Hydrology and Meteorology
PIHM .... Protective Integrated Hood Mask (SAUS)
PIHSMP ..... Protocol Relating to Intervention on the High Seas in Cases of Marine Pollution by Substances other than Oil [*Environmental science*] (COE)
PII .... Fairbanks, AK [*Location identifier*] [*FAA*] (FAAL)
PII .... Pershing II [*Army*]
PII .... Petroleum Information International (SAUS)
PII .... Phantom II [*Model of automobile*]
PII .... Plasma Inorganic Iodine [*Clinical chemistry*] (MAE)
PII .... Plasma Ion Implantation (SAUS)
PII .... Polaris Industries [*NYSE symbol*] (TTSB)
PII .... Polaris Industries, Inc. [*NYSE symbol*] (SAG)
PII .... Positive Immittance Inverter (IEEE)
PII .... Predominant Interest Installation (AAGC)
PII .... Primary Irritation Index [*Medicine*] (STED)
PII .... Primary Irritation Indices [*for skin*]
PII .... Printing Industry Institute [*A graphic arts training school*]

PII........... Printing Industry of Illinois/Indiana Association (EARSL)
PII........... Procurement Instrument Identification (NG)
PII........... Profit in Inventory (TIMI)
PII........... Program Integrated Information (VLIE)
PII........... Public Interest Institute (RCD)
PII........... Publisher Item Identifier
PII........... Sleighton School, Darling, PA [*OCLC symbol*] (OCLC)
PIIBK........ Peoples Heritage Financial Group, Inc. (Maine) [*NASDAQ symbol*] (COMM)
PIIC.......... Pergamon International Information Corp. [*Information service or system*] (IID)
PIIC.......... Public Interest Immunity Certificate [*British*] (ECON)
PIID.......... Prediction Interval Initiation Date (DNAB)
PIIF.......... Pakistan International Industrial Fair (SAUS)
PIIF.......... Proteinase Inhibitor Inducing Factor [*Biochemistry*]
PIII........... plasma Immersion Ion Implantation (AAEL)
PIIM.......... Planned Interdependency Incentive Method
PIIN.......... Procurement Instruction Identification Number [*Army*] (AABC)
PIIN.......... Procurement Instrument Identification Number [*Military*]
PI/INT'L..... Packaging Institute International [*Later, IoPP*] (EA)
PIIO.......... Poultry Industry Investigation Officer [*Australia*]
PIIP.......... Potable Insulin Infusion Pump [*Medicine*] (STED)
PIIS.......... Posterior Inferior Iliac Spine [*Medicine*] (STED)
PIIX.......... PCI IDE/ISA Xcelerator (SAUS)
PIJ........... Palestinian Islamic Jihad (SAUS)
PIJ........... Pickled-in-Jar [*Food technology*]
PIJAC........ Pet Industry Joint Advisory Council (EA)
PIJR.......... Product Improvement Joint Review [*Military*]
PIK........... Bainapi [*Language symbol*] (ETLW)
PIK........... Glasgow-Prestwick [*Scotland*] [*Airport symbol*] (OAG)
PIK........... Pay in Kind Preferred Stock (TDOB)
PIK........... Payment in Kind
PIK........... Pic Prospectors [*Vancouver Stock Exchange symbol*]
PIK........... Portable Injection Kit
PIK........... Potsdam Institute for Climate Impact Research
PIK........... Prestwick [*Scotland*] [*Airport symbol*] (AD)
PIK........... Programmer's Imaging Kernel [*Computer science*] (BTTJ)
PIK........... Public Information Kiosk
PIKE......... Pike [*Postal Service standard*] (OPSA)
Pike.......... Pike's Reports [*1-5 Arkansas*] [*A publication*] (DLA)
PIKE......... Pike Trailer Company [*NCIC trailer make code*]
Pike & F Adm Law... Pike and Fischer's Administrative Law [*A publication*] (DLA)
Pike & F Fed Rules Service... Pike and Fischer's Federal Rules Service [*A publication*] (DLA)
Pike & Fischer Adm Law... Pike and Fischer's Administrative Law [*A publication*] (DLA)
Pike H of L... Pike's History of the House of Lords [*A publication*] (DLA)
PIKES........ Phot-Interpretation Keys Expert System (SAUS)
PIKES........ Pike [*Commonly used*] (OPSA)
Pikeville... Pikeville National Corp. [*Associated Press*] (SAG)
PIK Securities... Payment-in-Kind Securities [*Investment term*] (DFIT)
PIKT......... Problem Informant/Killer Tool (SAUS)
PIKU......... Pikari Trading [*Intermodal shipping container symbol*] (TVRC)
PIL........... Brazos Santiago, TX [*Location identifier*] [*FAA*] (FAAL)
PIL........... Pacific International Lines (SAUS)
PIL........... Page Interchange Language (SAUS)
PIL........... Pair Inter Langues [*Bourg La Reine, France*] (EAIO)
PIL........... Pakistan International Airlines (SAUS)
PIL........... Paper Interchange Language (ODA)
PIL........... Parti de l'Independance et de la Liberte [*Party for Independence and Liberty*] [*Congo*] [*Political party*]
PIL........... Parts Identification List (ACAE)
PIL........... Patient Information Leaflet [*Pharmacy*]
PIL........... Payment in Lieu
PIL........... Percentage Increase in Loss [*Statistics*]
PIL........... Pest Infestation Laboratory [*Agricultural Research Council*] (PDAA)
PIL........... Pickering Lumber [*Federal Railroad Administration identification code*]
PIL........... Pilar [*Argentina*] [*Seismograph station code, US Geological Survey*] (SEIS)
pil........... Pilaster (VRA)
Pil........... Pill [*Medicine*] (BCRP)
PIL........... Pilot (WGA)
Pil........... Pilula [*Pill*] [*Pharmacology*] (DAVI)
PIL........... Pilula [*Pill*] [*Pharmacy*]
PIL........... Pistol Petroleum [*Vancouver Stock Exchange symbol*]
PIL........... Pitt Interpretive Language [*Computer science*] (DIT)
PIL........... Pittsburgh Interpretive [*or Interactive*] Language [*Computer science*] (IAA)
PIL........... Plastic Impregnated Laminate
PIL........... Practice Instrument Landing (ADA)
PIL........... Precision In Line [*Electronics*] (EECA)
PIL........... Preferred Item List (RDA)
PIL........... Priority Interrupt Level (VLIE)
PIL........... Procedure Implementation Language (SAUS)
PIL........... Processing Information List [*Computer science*]
PIL........... Procurement Information Letter (MCD)
PIL........... Product Identifier Label (SAUS)
PIL........... Publications International Ltd.
PIL........... Public Interest Litigation (India) [*Political party*] (PSAP)
PIL........... Publishing Interchange Language [*Computer science*] (CDE)
PIL........... Purple Indicating Light (MSA)
PIL........... Purpose in Life [*Personality development test*] [*Psychology*]
PILA......... Point Ion Lattice Approximation (SAUS)
PILA......... Power Industry Laboratory Association [*Defunct*] (EA)
PILAC........ Pulsed Ion Linear Accelerator
PiLam....... Pi Lambda Phi (EA)
PILANS...... Problem-oriented Industrial Languages (SAUS)
PILAR....... Petroleum Industry Local Authority Reporting (PDAA)
PILB......... Passenger and Immigration Lists Bibliography [*A publication*]
PILC......... Paper-Insulated, Lead-Covered Cable [*Telecommunications*]
PILC......... Pillared Interlayered Clays [*Catalysis technology*]
PILC......... Pregnancy and Infant Loss Center (EA)
PILC Cable... Paper-Insulated, Lead-Covered Cable (SAUS)
PILCX........ PIMCO: International CI.C [*Mutual fund ticker symbol*] (SG)
PILE......... Product Inventory Level Estimator (PDAA)
PILG......... Pilgrim Manufacturing Company [*NCIC trailer make code*]
PilgAmer.... Pilgrim American Bank & Thrift Fund, Inc. [*Associated Press*] (SAG)
PilgAPr...... Pilgrim America Prime Rate Trust [*Associated Press*] (SAG)
PilgPr....... Pilgrims Pride Corp. [*Associated Press*] (SAG)
PilgPrm..... Pilgrim Prime Rate Trust [*Associated Press*] (SAG)
Pilgr......... [*The*] Passionate Pilgrim [*Poetry*] (BARN)
Pilgr......... [*The*] Pilgrim's Progress [*Bunyan*] (BARN)
PilgRg....... Pilgrim Regional Banc Shares, Inc. [*Associated Press*] (SAG)
PILI.......... Passenger and Immigration Lists Index [*A publication*]
PILJC........ Pittsburgh and Lehigh Junction, NY [*American Association of Railroads railroad junction routing code*]
PILL......... Newport Dock [*British depot code*]
PILL......... Pilgrim League (PSS)
PILL......... Pillsbury [*Federal Railroad Administration identification code*]
PILL......... Programmed Instruction Language Learning [*Computer science*]
PILL......... ProxyMed, Inc. [*NASDAQ symbol*] (SAG)
PILL......... Proxymed Pharmacy [*NASDAQ symbol*] (SAG)
PILLS........ Particulate Instrumentation by LASER Light Scattering (PDAA)
PILM......... Pillared Interlayered Montmorillonite [*Catalysis technology*]
PILMS........ Precision Insertion Loss Measurement Set (IAA)
PILN......... Pacific International Lines [*Common carrier symbol*]
PILNAV...... Piloting Navigation (SAUS)
PILO......... Phased Integrated Laser Optics Technology (ACAE)
pilo.......... pilocarpine (SAUS)
PILO......... Public Information Liaison Officer [*Military*]
PILOH....... Pay in Lieu of Holiday (WDAA)
PILOT........ Panel on Instrumentation for Large Optical Telescopes (SAUS)
PILOT........ Paton Lyall Tosh [*Rock music group*]
PILOT........ Payment in Lieu of Taxes
PILOT........ Permutation Indexed Literature of Technology (IEEE)
PILOT........ Phased Integrated LASER Optics Technology (SEWL)
PILOT........ Piloted Low-Speed Test [*Aerospace*]
PILOT........ Pod Integrated Localisation, Observation, Transmission (SAUS)
PILOT........ Printing Industry Language for Operations of Typesetting
PILOT........ Programmed Inquiry, Learning or Teaching [*Computer science*]
PILOT........ Programmed Inquiry, Learning or Technology (SAUS)
PILOT........ Programmed Instruction Learning on Teaching [*A simplified programming language for computer-assisted instruction*] (EDAC)
PilotACE.... Pilot Automatic Computing Engine (VLIE)
Pilowtex.... Pillowtex Corp. [*Associated Press*] (SAG)
PILP......... Parametric Integer Linear Program [*Computer science*]
PILP......... Program for Industrial Laboratory Projects (SAUS)
PILP......... Program of Industry/Laboratory Projects [*National Research Council of Canada*]
PILP......... Pseudoinfinite, Logarithmically Periodic
PILP Antenna... Pseudo-Infinite, Logarithmically Periodic Antenna (SAUS)
PILPS........ Program for Intercomparison of Land Surface Parameterization Schemes (SAUS)
PILPS........ Project for Intercomparison of Landsurface Parameterization Schemes (SAUS)
PILS......... Payload Integration Library System [*NASA*] (SSD)
PILS......... Pilsener Lager (DSUE)
PILS......... Precision Instrument Landing System
PIL STA..... Pilot Station [*Nautical charts*]
PILT.......... Payment in Lieu of Taxes Program [*Department of the Interior*]
PILT.......... Pilot Network Services [*NASDAQ symbol*]
PILTA........ Payment in Lieu of Taxes Act
PILU......... Pacific International Lines [*Intermodal shipping container symbol*] (TVRC)
PIM.......... Grey Nuns - Partners in Ministry (EA)
PIm.......... Immaculata College, Immaculata, PA [*Library symbol*] [*Library of Congress*] (LCLS)
PIM.......... Pacem in Maribus [*Secondary name for the International Ocean Institute*] (MSC)
PIM.......... Pacific Rim Energy [*Vancouver Stock Exchange symbol*]
PIM.......... Parallel Inference Machine [*Computer science*]
PIM.......... Parameter Identification Mechanism
PIM.......... Partners-in-Mission [*Church of England*]
PIM.......... Passive Intermodulation (ACAE)
PIM.......... Patient Interface Module (SAUS)
PIM.......... Payload Integration Manager (SAUS)
PIM.......... Peak Integration Method (SAUS)
PIM.......... Penalties in Minutes [*Hockey*]
PIM.......... Penicillamine-Induced Myasthenia (STED)
PIM.......... Peripheral Interface Module
PIM.......... Permanent Information Memory (SAUS)
PIM.......... Personal Illumination Marker [*Military*] (INF)
PIM.......... Personal Information Management (or Manager) (SAUS)
PIM.......... Personal Information Manager [*Computer science*]
PIM.......... Phosphatidylinositol Mannoside [*Biochemistry*]
Pi M......... Pillius Medicinensis [*Flourished, 1165-1207*] [*Authority cited in pre-1607 legal work*] (DSA)
PIM.......... Pilot Machine (NITA)
PIM.......... Pine Mountain, GA [*Location identifier*] [*FAA*] (FAAL)

PIM .... Planned Incremental Modernization (DOMA)
PIM .... Planning Interchange Meeting (ACAE)
PIM .... Plan of Intended Movement (MUGU)
PIM .... Plastic Intake Manifold
PIM .... Plated Interconnecting Matrix
PIM .... Plug-In Module (MCD)
PIM .... Point Indicating Machine (IAA)
PIM .... Point of Intended Movement [*Military*]
PIM .... Police Information Manager [*Police and security equipment*]
PIM .... Polyphase Induction Motor
PIM .... Port Interface Module (SAUS)
PIM .... Position and Intended Movement [*or Maneuver*] (NATG)
PIM .... Position in Miles (MCD)
PIM .... Position of Intended Movement
PIM .... Powder Injection Molding [*Metallurgy*]
PIM .... Precision Indicator of the Meridian
PIM .... Precision Instrument Mount
PIM .... Presa Del Infiernillo [*Mexico*] [*Seismograph station code, US Geological Survey*] [*Closed*] (SEIS)
PIM .... Presbyterian Inland Mission
PIM .... Pretrained Individual Manpower (ACAE)
PIM .... Previously Intended Movement (SAUS)
PIM .... Pricing Instructions Memorandum (MCD)
PIM .... Primary Interface Module (SAUS)
PIM .... Printing Industries of Michigan (EARSL)
PIM .... Priority Interrupt Module (SAUS)
PIM .... Process Interface Module (SAUS)
PIM .... Processor in Memory [*Computer science*]
PIM .... Processor Interface Module
PIM .... Processor Interrupt Module (SAUS)
PIM .... Product Information Management (SEWL)
PIM .... Product Information Memoranda
PIM .... Program Initialization Module [*Computer science*] (ECII)
PIM .... Program Integration Manual
PIM .... Program Interface Module
PIM .... Programmatic Interchange Meetings (SAUS)
PIM .... Pro Independence Movement [*Puerto Rico*]
PIM .... Protocol Insensitive Multiplexing [*Communications term*] (DCT)
PIM .... Provincial Institute of Mining
PIM .... Public Information Meeting (COE)
PIM .... Pulse Intensity Modulation
PIM .... Pulse Interval Modulation
PIM .... Putnam Master Intermediate Income Trust [*NYSE symbol*] (SPSG)
PIM .... Putnam Master Interm Income [*NYSE symbol*] (TTSB)
PIM .... South Mountain Restoration Center, South Mountain, PA [*OCLC symbol*] (OCLC)
PiMA .... Ateneo de Manila University, Manila, Philippines [*Library symbol*] [*Library of Congress*] (LCLS)
PIMA .... Paper Industry Management Association (EA)
PIMA .... Photographic Industry Marketing Association [*Australia*]
PIMA .... Plug-In Module Assembly (MCD)
PIMA .... Polyisocyanurate Insulation Manufacturers Association (EA)
PIMA .... Portable Intelligence Maintenance Aid [*Army*] (DOMA)
PIMA .... Prairie Implement Manufacturers Association (SAUS)
PIMA .... Prime Intermediate Maintenance Activity
PIMA .... Printing Industry Management Association (DGA)
PIMA .... Professional Insurance Mass-Marketing Association [*Bethesda, MD*] (EA)
PIMB .... PCTE Interface Management Board (SAUS)
PIMCC .... Packards International Motor Car Club (EA)
PIMCO .... Pacific Investment Management Co.
PIMCO .... Physicians Insurance Medical Co. (DAVI)
PIMCO .... Poultry Industry Manufacturers Council [*Defunct*] (EA)
PimcoAd ..... Pimco Advisors Ltd. [*Associated Press*] (SAG)
PimCom ...... Pimco Commercial Mortgage [*Associated Press*] (SAG)
PIME .... Pontifical Institute for Foreign Missions (TOCD)
pime .... Pontifical Institute for Foreign Missions (TOCD)
PIME .... Pontifical Institute for Mission Extension [*Roman Catholic men's religious order*]
PIMEG .... Program to Increase Minority Engineering Graduates (SAUS)
PIMI .... Preinactivation Material Inspection [*Military*] (NVT)
PIMIA .... Potentiometric Ionophore Modulated Immunoassay [*Electrochemistry*]
PIMIS .... Portable Integrated Maintenance Information System
PIMISS ...... Pennsylvania Interagency Management Information Support System (SAUS)
PIMK .... Portable Injection Molding Kit
PIML .... Polynomial Propogation Time Immediate Language [*Computer science*] (MHDI)
PIMMA .... Professional Insurance Mass-Marketing Association [*Bethesda, MD*] (EA)
PIMNY .... Printing Industries of Metropolitan New York
PIMO .... Presentation of Information for Maintenance and Operation [*DoD*]
PIMOS .... Parallel Inference Multiprocessor Operating System [*Computer science*]
PIMOS .... Pittler Memory Operations System (SAUS)
PIMP .... Permissible Individual Maximum Pressure (SAA)
PIMP .... Peroxisomal Integral Membrane Protein [*Biochemistry*]
PIMP .... Pimperne [*England*]
PIMP .... Program for Interactive Multiple Process Simulation (PDAA)
PIMR .... Polar Ice Mapping Radiometer (SAUS)
PIMR .... Pushbroom Imaging Microwave Radiometer (SAUS)
PIMRA .... Pirmasens Missile Repair Activity [*Germany*] [*Army*]
PIMRIS ...... Pacific Islands Marine Resources Information System [*Marine science*] (OSRA)
PIMS .... Parts Inventory Management System (SAUS)
PIMS .... Peacekeeper in Minuteman Silos (DWSG)
PIMS .... Personnel Information Management System (ALAC)
PIMS .... Personnel Inventory Management System [*AT & T*]
PIMS .... Pesticide Incident Monitoring System [*Environmental Protection Agency*] (EPAT)
PIMS .... Phase Interference Modulation System (ACAE)
PIMS .... Photoionization Mass Spectrometry
PIMS .... Pontifical Institute of Mediaeval Studies [*Canada*] (IRC)
PIMS .... Preform In-Mold Surfacing [*Plastics technology*]
PIMS .... Principal Investigator Microgravity Services (SAUS)
PIMS .... Printers Integrated Management System (DGA)
PIMS .... Process Information Management (GART)
PIMS .... Procurement Information Management Services (SAUS)
PIMS .... Production Information Management System (GART)
PIMS .... Profit Impact of Marketing Strategy
PIMS .... Program Interface for Multiplex System (ACAE)
PIMS .... Programmable Implantable Medication System
PIMS .... Project Information Management System (SAUS)
PIMS .... Property Information Management System (SAUS)
PIMSA .... Prensa Independiente Mexicana Sociedad Anonima [*Press agency*] [*Mexico*]
PIMT .... Protein Isoaspartyl Methyltransferase [*An enzyme*]
Pim Ten ..... Pim on Feudal Tenures [*A publication*] (DLA)
PIMV .... Plantago Mottle Virus [*Plant pathology*]
PIN .... AMF Bowling [*NYSE symbol*] (SG)
PIN .... Jasper, TX [*Location identifier*] [*FAA*] (FAAL)
PIN .... Pacific Island Nations
PIN .... Pacific Island Network [*Marine science*] (OSRA)
PIN .... Page and Item Number
PIN .... Parallel Input
PIN .... Parintins [*Brazil*] [*Airport symbol*] (AD)
PIN .... Particle Inclusion Noise (ACAE)
PIN .... Particle Induced Noise (SAUS)
PIN .... Patent Information Network (SAUS)
PIN .... Patriots Information Network [*Defunct*] (EA)
PIN .... P-doped, Intrinsic, N-doped (SAUS)
PIN .... Pennsylvania School for the Deaf, Philadelphia, PA [*OCLC symbol*] (OCLC)
PIN .... People in Need [*Food program sponsored by family of kidnapped heiress, Patricia Hearst, 1974*]
PIN .... Personal Identification Name (NITA)
PIN .... Personal [*or Private*] Identification Number [*Banking*]
PIN .... Personal Information Network [*Indesys, Inc.*] [*Telecommunications service*] (TSSD)
PIN .... Personal Injury Notice (AAG)
PIN .... Personnel Increment Number (DOMA)
PIN .... Pesticide Information Network [*Environmental Protection Agency*] (AEPA)
PIN .... Phase Inversion nanoencapsulation [*Materials science*]
PIN .... Piece Identification Number
PIN .... Pinedale [*Wyoming*] [*Seismograph station code, US Geological Survey*] [*Closed*] (SEIS)
PIN .... Pinion (MSA)
Pin .... Pinney's Wisconsin Supreme Court Reports [*1839-52*] [*A publication*] (DLA)
PIN .... Pinto [*NCIC car model code*]
PIN .... Plan Identification Number (AFM)
PIN .... Plant Information Network [*Fish and Wildlife Service*] [*Ceased operation*] (IID)
PIN .... Plastics Industry Notes [*Later, CIN*]
PIN .... Police Information Network [*San Francisco Bay area, California*]
PIN .... Position Indicator
PIN .... Positive-Intrinsic-Negative [*or P-Type Intrinsic N-Type*]
PIN .... Power Information Network [*Computer science*]
Pin .... Power input (SAUS)
PIN .... Precision Inertial Navigation (SAUS)
PIN .... Pre-Invitation Notice
PIN .... Preliminary Imagery Nomination File (MCD)
PIN .... Private Intelligent Networker (NITA)
PIN .... Procedural Interrupt Negative (SAUS)
PIN .... Process Identification Number (SAUS)
PIN .... Processor Independent NetWare [*Computer science*]
PIN .... Procurement Information Notice [*Environmental Protection Agency*] (ERG)
PIN .... Product Identification Number
PIN .... Product Information Network [*McGraw-Hill Information Systems Co.*] [*Information service or system*] (IID)
PIN .... Program Identification Number (MUGU)
PIN .... Program Integrated Network
PIN .... Programme of International Nature management (SAUS)
PIN .... Programming Information (SAUS)
PIN .... Property Inheritance Network Computer
PIN .... Proposal Identification Number (AAG)
PIN .... Prospect Information Network
PIN .... Prostatic Intraepithelial Neoplasia [*Medicine*] (MELL)
PIN .... Prosthetic Intradithelial Neodlasia [*Medicine*]
PIN .... Protein Inhibitor of nNOS [*Neuronal Nitric Oxide Synthase*] [*Neuroscience*]
PIN .... PSI Energy, Inc. [*NYSE symbol*] (SPSG)
PIN .... PSI Holdings, Inc. [*NYSE symbol*] (COMM)
PIN .... P-Type/Insulator/N-Type [*Electronics*] (AAEL)
PIN .... P-Type Intrinsic N-Type [*or Positive-Intrinsic-Negative*]
PIN .... P-type Intrinsic-N-type (SAUS)
PIN .... Publication Identification Number [*Military*] (INF)

P IN² .... Parts per Square Inch (WDAA)
P IN³ .... Parts per Cubic Inch (WDAA)
PINA .... Pacific Islands News Association [*Australia*]
P in A .... Parallax in Altitude [*Navigation*]
PINA .... Parallax in Altitude [*Navigation*]
PINA .... Parenting in a Nuclear Age (EA)
PINA .... Permaculture Institute of North America (SAUS)
PINA .... Potash Institute of North America [*Later, PPI*] (EA)
PINACO ..... Pittsburgh National Corporation (EFIS)
PINAGA ..... Pioneer Natural Gas Co. (EFIS)
PinBG .... Pinnacle Bank Group, Inc. [*Associated Press*] (SAG)
PINBL .... Pine Bluff, AR [*American Association of Railroads railroad junction routing code*]
P in C .... Paymaster in Chief (SAUS)
P-in-C .... Priest-in-Charge [*Church of England*]
PINC .... Property Income Certificate [*Investment term*] [*British*]
Pinc C .... Pincushion Correction (SAUS)
PINCCA ...... Price Index Numbers for Current Cost Accounting [*Service in Information and Analysis*] [*British*] [*Information service or system*] (IID)
PinclF .... Pinnacle Financial Services, Inc. [*Associated Press*] (SAG)
PinclFn ...... Pinnacle Financial Services [*Associated Press*] (SAG)
PinclM ...... Pinnacle Micro, Inc. [*Associated Press*] (SAG)
PinclMic .... Pinnacle Micro, Inc. [*Associated Press*] (SAG)
PIND .... Particle Impact Noise Detection (or Detector) (SAUS)
PIND .... Particle Inclusion Noise Detection (ACAE)
PIND .... Payload Integration Plan (SAUS)
Pind .... Pindar [*518-438BC*] [*Classical studies*] (OCD)
PINDEX ...... Pollution Index (SAUS)
PIN Diode ... Positive-Intrinsic-Negative Diode (SAUS)
PINE .... Passive Infrared Equipment (SAUS)
PINE .... Passive Infrared Night Equipment (MCD)
PINE .... Pine [*Commonly used*] (OPSA)
PINE .... Pine, IN [*American Association of Railroads railroad junction routing code*]
PINE .... Pine is not Elm (SAUS)
PINE .... Pines Trailer Corporation [*NCIC trailer make code*]
PINE .... Program for Internet News and Email (SAUS)
PINELLAS ... Pinellas Plant [*Department of Energy*] [*Largo, FL*] (GAAI)
PINES .... Pines [*Commonly used*] (OPSA)
PINES .... Public Information Network for Electronic Services
PINES .... Public Information on Nuclear Energy Service [*American Nuclear Society*]
PINET .... Physicians Information Network (SAUS)
PINET .... Physics Information Network (SAUS)
PINFET ...... Positive-Intrinsic-Negative Field-Effect Transistor (SAUS)
ping .... Packet Internet Groper [*Computer science*] (IGQR)
PING .... Packet Internet Groper [*Computer program*] (PCM)
ping .... Pinguis [*Fat, Grease*] [*Latin*] (DAVI)
PING .... Pulsed Inertial Navigation and Guidance (SAUS)
Ping Chat Mortg ... Pingrey's Treatise of Chattel Mortgages [*A publication*] (DLA)
PINGO .... Public Interest Nongovernmental Organization
PINGP .... Prairie Island Nuclear Generating Plant (NRCH)
PINH .... Pyridoxal Isonicotinoylhydrazone [*Biochemistry*]
PINI .... Pininfarina [*NCIC car make code*]
PINI .... Plug-in Neutral Injector (SAUS)
PINI .... Positive Ion Neutral Injector [*Nuclear energy*] (NUCP)
PINJU .... Pine Junction, IN [*American Association of Railroads railroad junction routing code*]
PINK .... Pinners Point, VA [*American Association of Railroads railroad junction routing code*]
Pinktn .... Pinkerton's, Inc. [*Associated Press*] (SAG)
PINN .... Pinnacle Banc Group [*NASDAQ symbol*] (TTSB)
PINN .... Pinnacle Banc Group, Inc. [*NASDAQ symbol*] (SAG)
PINN .... Pinnacles National Monument
Pinn .... Pinney's Wisconsin Reports [*A publication*] (DLA)
PINN .... Proposed International Nonproprietary Name [*Drug research*]
PinnclBk .... Pinnacle Bank [*Associated Press*] (SAG)
Pinney .... Pinney's Wisconsin Reports [*A publication*] (DLA)
Pinney (sv) ... Pinney's Wisconsin Reports [*A publication*] (DLA)
PinnSyst .... Pinnacle Systems, Inc. [*Associated Press*] (SAG)
PINO .... Positive Input - Negative Output [*Computer science*]
PINPD .... Positive-Intrinsic-Negative Photodiode (SAUS)
PINPOINT ... Phase Integrating Position Indicator for Transmitters (SAUS)
PINPrB ...... PSI Energy, 4.16%cmPfd vtg [*NYSE symbol*] (TTSB)
PINPrC ...... PSI Energy, 4.32% Pfd [*NYSE symbol*] (TTSB)
PINPrD ...... PSI Energy, 7.15% Pfd [*NYSE symbol*] (TTSB)
PINPrJ .... PSI Energy, 6.875% Pfd [*NYSE symbol*] (TTSB)
PINPrK ...... PSI Energy, 7.44% Pfd [*NYSE symbol*] (TTSB)
PinptRtl ..... Pinpoint Retail Solutions [*Associated Press*] (SAG)
PINQ .... Personnel Inquiry (ALAC)
PINRO .... Polar Institute of Marine Fishery and Oceanography (SAUS)
PINRO .... Polar Scientific Research Institute for Marine Fisheries and Oceanography [*Russian*]
PINS .... Palletized Inertial Navigation System [*Military*] (LAIN)
PINS .... Patient in Need of Supervision (MELL)
PINS .... Personnel Information System [*Army*] (AABC)
PINS .... Persons in Need of Supervision [*Classification for delinquent children*]
PINS .... Pinson Truck Equipment Company [*NCIC trailer make code*]
PINS .... Pipeline Inspection Notification System (PIAV)
PINS .... Point-in-Space (MCD)
PINS .... Political Information System [*Databank of political strategist Richard Wirthlin*]
PINS .... Portable Inertial Navigation System
PINS .... Precise Integrated Navigation System [*Navy*] (DOMA)
PINS .... Precisions Improved Nesting System (SAUS)
PINS .... Professional International Network Society (NTPA)
PINSAC ...... PINS [*Portable Inertial Navigation System*] Alignment Console
PINSCH ...... Periodic-Index Separate-Confinement Heterostructure (SAUS)
PINSCH QW ... Periodic-Index Separate-Confinement Heterostructure Quantum-Well (SAUS)
PINSTD ...... Preinserted
PINSTECH ... Pakistan Institute of Nuclear Science and Technology
PINT .... Pinto [*NCIC motorcycle make code*]
PINT .... Power Integrated Transistor (SAUS)
PINT .... Power Intelligence (DNAB)
PINT .... Processor Interrupt (SAUS)
PINT .... PSTN and Internet Internetworking (SAUS)
PINT .... Purdue Interpretive Program (SAUS)
PINT .... Purdue Interpretive Programming and Operating System (MCD)
PIN/TAN ..... Personal Identification Number/Transaction Number (SAUS)
PINTE .... Processor Interrupts Enabled [*Computer science*] (MHDI)
PINTEC ...... Plastics Institute National Technical Conference (SAUS)
PINTS .... Ported-Coax Intrusion Sensor [*Military*] (INF)
PInU .... Indiana University of Pennsylvania, Indiana, PA [*Library symbol*] [*Library of Congress*] (LCLS)
PINU .... Party of Innovation and Unity (Honduras) [*Political party*] (PSAP)
PINV .... Post-Imperative Negative Variation [*Medicine*] (DMAA)
PINVL .... Pinckneyville, IL [*American Association of Railroads railroad junction routing code*]
Pin (Wis) ... Pinney's Wisconsin Reports [*A publication*] (DLA)
Pin Wis R ... Pinney's Wisconsin Reports [*A publication*] (DLA)
PINWOR .... Pinworm [*Gastroenterology*] (DAVI)
PinWst ...... Pinnacle West Capital Corp. [*Associated Press*] (SAG)
pinx .... Pinxit (WDAA)
PINX .... Pinxit [*He, or She, Painted It*] [*Latin*]
PINX .... Private Integrated Services Network Exchange (SAUS)
PINXT .... Pinxit [*He, or She, Painted It*] [*Latin*] (ROG)
P/Iny .... Parts per Square Inch (SAUS)
PINY .... Polytechnic Institute of New York
PINZ .... Peterson Industries [*Federal Railroad Administration identification code*]
PIO .... Palestine Information Office (EA)
PIO .... Parallel Input/Output
PIO .... Parallel Interface Output (SAUS)
PIO .... Parallel I/O (SAUS)
PIO .... Parallel/Programmable I/O (SAUS)
PIO .... Peripheral Input/Output (NITA)
PIO .... Peripheral Input-Output Controller [*Computer science*] (CIST)
PIO .... Pheniminooxazolidinone [*Pharmacology*]
PIO .... Photocomposition Input Option (NITA)
PIO .... Photographic Interpretation Officer (SAUS)
PIO .... Photo Interpretation Officer [*Air Force*]
PIO .... Physical Input-Output [*Computer science*] (IAA)
PIO .... Pielago [*Ship's rigging*] (ROG)
PIO .... Pilot-Induced Oscillation
PIO .... Pilot Information Office
PIO .... Pilot Information Officer (SAUS)
PIO .... Pinon, NM [*Location identifier*] [*FAA*] (FAAL)
PIO .... Pi Omicron National Sorority (EA)
PIO .... Pioneer [*A publication*]
PIO .... Pioneer Airlines, Inc. [*ICAO designator*] (FAAC)
PIO .... Pioneer (automobile) [*NCIC car model code*]
PIO .... Pioneer Corp ADR [*NYSE symbol*] (SG)
PIO .... Pioneer Electron ADR [*NYSE symbol*] (TTSB)
PIO .... Pioneer Electronic Corp. [*NYSE symbol*] (SPSG)
PIO .... Plate Iron Oxide [*Automotive paint*]
PIO .... Poets International Organisation [*Bangalore, India*] (EAIO)
PIO .... Port Information Office (SAUS)
PIO .... Posco International Osaka (EFIS)
PIO .... Position Iterative Operation
PIO .... Precision Interactive Operation [*Computer science*]
PIO .... Precision-Interpret Operation (SAUS)
PIO .... Precision Iterative Operation (IAA)
PIO .... Preliminary Inquiry Officer (DNAB)
PIO .... Private Input/Output [*Telecommunications*] (TEL)
PIO .... Process Improvement Opportunity
PIO .... Process Input-Output [*Computer science*] (ECII)
PIO .... Processor Input-Output [*Computer science*] (MDG)
PIO .... Programmable Input/Output (SAUS)
PIO .... Programmed Input/Output
PIO .... Project Implementation Order (SAUS)
PIO .... Provisioned Item Order (MCD)
PIO .... Public Information Office [*or Officer*]
PIO .... Western Pennsylvania School for the Deaf, Pittsburgh, PA [*OCLC symbol*] (OCLC)
PIOB .... President's Intelligence Oversight Board (DOMA)
PIOBX .... Pioneer Bond Fund [*Mutual fund ticker symbol*] (SG)
PIO/C .... PIO for Commodities (SAUS)
PIOC .... Program Input-Output Cassette [*Computer science*] (IAA)
PIO/C .... Project Implementation Order/Commodity [*Agency for International Development*]
PIOCA .... Peruvian Inca Orchid Dog Club of America (EA)
PIOCC .... Province Intelligence and Operations Coordination Center [*Vietnam*] (VNW)
PIOCS .... Parallel Input/Output Control System (NITA)
PIOCS .... Physical Input-Output Control System [*Computer science*] (BUR)

PIODCA ..... Peruvian Inca Orchid Dog Club of America (EA)
PIODX ..... Pioneer Fund Cl.A [*Mutual fund ticker symbol*] (SG)
PIOE ..... Pioneer Coach Manufacturing [*NCIC trailer make code*]
PIOFA ..... Petroleum Ether Insoluble Oxidized Fatty Acid [*Food science*]
PIOFS ..... Parallel I/O File System (SAUS)
PIOG ..... Pioneer Group [*NASDAQ symbol*] (TTSB)
PIOG ..... [*The*] Pioneer Group, Inc. [*NASDAQ symbol*] (NQ)
PIOM ..... Physical Input/Output Manager (SAUS)
pion ..... Pi-Meson (BARN)
PION ..... Pioneer (AABC)
pion ..... Pioneer (GEAB)
PION ..... Pioneer Financial Corp. (Virginia) [*NASDAQ symbol*] (COMM)
PION ..... Pioneer Sales & Manufacturing Company [*NCIC trailer make code*]
PION ..... Posterior Interosseous Nerve [*Medicine*] (RAWO)
PIONA ..... Pioneer Companies, Inc. [*NASDAQ symbol*] (SAG)
PIONA ..... Pioneer Cos. 'A' [*NASDAQ symbol*] (TTSB)
PionCos ..... Pioneer Companies, Inc. [*Associated Press*] (SAG)
PioneerC ..... Pioneer Commercial Funding Corp. [*Associated Press*] (SAG)
PionF ..... Pioneer Financial Services, Inc. [*Associated Press*] (SAG)
PionFS ..... Pioneer Financial Services, Inc. [*Associated Press*] (SAG)
PionGp ..... [*The*] Pioneer Group, Inc. [*Associated Press*] (SAG)
PionHiB ..... Pioneer Hi-Bred International [*Associated Press*] (SAG)
PionInt ..... Pioneer Interest Shares [*Associated Press*] (SAG)
PionrC ..... Pioneer Commercial Funding Corp. [*Associated Press*] (SAG)
PionrEl ..... Pioneer Electronic Corp. [*Associated Press*] (SAG)
PionStd ..... Pioneer Standard Electronics [*Associated Press*] (SAG)
PionStd ..... Pioneer-Standard Electronics, Inc. [*Associated Press*] (SAG)
PIOP ..... Pharmacists in Ophthalmic Practice (EA)
PIO/P ..... PIO for Participant Training (SAUS)
PIOPED ..... Prospective Investigation of Pulmonary Embolism Diagnosis [*Medicine*]
PIOPED ..... Prospective Investigation of Pulmonary Embolus Detection [*Medicine*] (RAWO)
PIOPIC ..... Protection and Indemnity of Oil Pollution Indemnity Clause [*Insurance*] (DS)
PIOR ..... Panstwowa Inspekcja Ochrony Roslin (SAUS)
PioRail ..... Pioner Railcorp [*Associated Press*] (SAG)
PIOS ..... Pioneer-Standard Electronics, Inc. [*NASDAQ symbol*] (NQ)
PIOS ..... Pioneer Std Electr [*NASDAQ symbol*] (TTSB)
PIOS ..... Planning Information Overlay System (SAUS)
PIOS ..... State Inspectorate for Environmental Protection (SAUS)
PIOSA ..... Pan-Indian Ocean Science Association (NOAA)
PIOSP ..... Process Input-Output Subroutine Package [*Computer science*] (MHDI)
PIO/T ..... PIO for Contract Technicians or Contract Services (SAUS)
PIO/T ..... Project Implementation Order/Technical [*Agency for International Development*]
PIOTA ..... Post-Irradiation Open Test Assembly [*Nuclear energy*] (NRCH)
PIOTA ..... Proximity Instrumented Open Test Assembly [*Nuclear energy*] (NRCH)
PIOTX ..... Pioneer II Cl.A [*Mutual fund ticker symbol*] (SG)
PIOU ..... Parallel Input-Output Unit [*Computer science*] (IEEE)
PIOU ..... Pioneer Shipping [*Intermodal shipping container symbol*] (TVRC)
PIOUS ..... Peripheral Integrated Off-Line Utility System (SAA)
PIP ..... 6-Mercaptopurin, Vincristine, Methotrexate, Citrovorum Factor [*Chemotherapy*] (DAVI)
PIP ..... IGOSS Plan and Implementation Programme (SAUS)
PIP ..... Package Irradiation Plant [*Nuclear energy*] (NUCP)
PIP ..... Packaging and Industrial Polymers [*E.T. DuPont*]
PIP ..... Packet Interface Port (SAUS)
PIP ..... Page Image Processor [*Computer science*] (VLIE)
PIP ..... Pan-Iranist Party [*Political party*] (PPW)
PIP ..... Paper Impact Printing (HGAA)
PIP ..... Para-Isothiocyanatephenethylamine [*Biochemistry*]
PIP ..... Parallel Image Processing (ACAE)
PIP ..... Parallel I/O Port (SAUS)
PIP ..... Paralytic Infantile Paralysis [*Medicine*] (DB)
PIP ..... Parental Involvement Project (AIE)
PIP ..... Participant Instrumentation Package
PIP ..... Participating Irredeemable Preference [*Shares*]
PIP ..... Participation Interest Purchase [*FNMA*] (EMRF)
PIP ..... Partido Independentista Puertorriqueno [*Puerto Rican Independence Party*] [*Political party*] (PPW)
PIP ..... Partner Interface Process [*Computer science*] (VLIE)
PIP ..... Partners in Progress [*Government*] [*Civil rights*]
PIP ..... Parts Improvement Program (ACAE)
PIP ..... Pasuquin [*Philippines*] [*Seismograph station code, US Geological Survey*] (SEIS)
PIP ..... Path Independent Protocol
PIP ..... Pattern and Information Processing (SAUS)
PIP ..... Payload Integration Plan [*NASA*] (NASA)
PIP ..... Payload Interface Plan [*NASA*] (NASA)
PIP ..... Payment in Part [*Business term*]
PIP ..... Peak Inspiratory Pressure [*Medicine*] (DAVI)
PIP ..... Performance Improvement and Productivity Programme (SAUS)
PIP ..... Performance Improvement Period (ALAC)
PIP ..... Performance Improvement Program (ACAE)
PIP ..... Performance Improvement Proposal (ACAE)
PIP ..... Periodical Informational Posting (SAUS)
PIP ..... Periodic Interim Payment Program [*Medicare*] (GFGA)
PIP ..... Peripheral Interchange Package (SAUS)
PIP ..... Peripheral Interchange Program [*Computer science*]
PIP ..... Peripheral Interface Programmer [*Circuit*] [*Computer science*]
PIP ..... Permatite Instant Plastic (SAUS)
PIP ..... Persistent Internal Polarization
PIP ..... Personal Identification Program (SAUS)
PIP ..... Personal Identification Project [*Computer science*]
PIP ..... Personal Information Processor (SAUS)
PIP ..... Personal Information Processors (AGLO)
PIP ..... Personal Injury Protection [*Insurance*] (TVEL)
PIP ..... Personal Innovation Program
PIP ..... Personal Interaction Panel (VLIE)
PIP ..... Personnel Identification Project (SAUS)
PIP ..... Personnel Interface Processor (MCD)
PIP ..... Pesticide Information Profiles (GNE)
PIP ..... Petroleum Incentives Program [*Canada*]
PIP ..... Philippine [*Telegraphy*] (PCTE)
PIP ..... Philips-Imperial Petroleum Ltd. (SAUS)
PIP ..... Phosphatidylinositol-4-phosphate (SAUS)
PIP ..... Phosphatidylinositol Phosphate [*Biochemistry*]
PIP ..... Photo Image Processor (MCD)
PIP ..... Photo Interpretive Program (BUR)
PIP ..... Picture-in-a-Picture [*Multi-Vision Products*] [*Video technology*]
PIP ..... Pilot Indoctrination Programme (SAUS)
PIP ..... Pilot Point [*Alaska*] [*Airport symbol*] (OAG)
PIP ..... P-Internet-Protocol (SAUS)
PIP ..... Pipe Inspection Program (SAUS)
PIP ..... Pipeline Image Processor (SAUS)
PIP ..... Piperacillin [*An antibiotic*]
PIP ..... Planning Integration Process (SAUS)
PIP ..... Plant-in-Place
PIP ..... Plant Instrumentation Program
PIP ..... Plot Inconsistencies Project (SAUS)
PIP ..... Plug-in Programmer (SAUS)
PIP ..... Plug-In Protocol (SAUS)
PIP ..... Polar Information Program (SAUS)
PIP ..... Polaris Improvement Program (SAUS)
PIP ..... Policy Improvement Program
PIP ..... Policy Integration Program
PIP ..... Pollution Information Project (NITA)
PIP ..... Population Information Program [*Johns Hopkins University*] (IID)
PIP ..... Population Information Program [*Later, CCP*] (EA)
PIP ..... Portable Instrumentation Package [*Military*] (CAAL)
PIP ..... Position Indicating Probe (IEEE)
PIP ..... Positive Incentive Program (SAUS)
PIP ..... Positive Inspiratory Pressure [*Medicine*] (MELL)
PIP ..... Postal Instant Press (EFIS)
PIP ..... Postinfusion Phlebitis [*Medicine*] (MELL)
PIP ..... Postinspiratory Pressure [*Medicine*] (DAVI)
PIP ..... Poured-in-Place (SAUS)
PIP ..... Power Input Panel
PIP ..... Prearrival Inspection Procedure
PIP ..... Precise Installation Position
PIP ..... Precision Instrumentation Package (SEWL)
PIP ..... Predicted Impact Point [*Aerospace*] (AAG)
PIP ..... Predicted Intercept Point
PIP ..... Preliminary Information Pamphlet
PIP ..... Preparatory Investment Protection [*For the consortia which invested in deep sea mining*]
PIP ..... Preparedness and Industrial Planning
PIP ..... Pressed-in-Place [*Automotive engineering*]
PIP ..... Pretty Important Person
PIP ..... Primary Indicating Position (IAA)
PIP ..... Primary Indicating Position Data Logger (IEEE)
PIP ..... Prior Immobilization and Positioning [*Roentgenology*]
PIP ..... Probabilistic Information Processing (or Processor) (SAUS)
PIP ..... Problem Identification Program (MCD)
PIP ..... Problem Input Preparation [*Computer science*] (BUR)
PIP ..... Problem Isolation Procedure (VLIE)
PIP ..... Procedural Information Pamphlet
PIP ..... Procedural Interrupt Positive (SAUS)
PIP ..... Proceedings in Print [*A bibliographic publication*]
PIP ..... Process Improvement Proposal (SAUS)
PIP ..... Process-Induced Particles (AAEL)
PIP ..... Process Interface Processor [*Computer science*] (VLIE)
PIP ..... Product Improvement (MCD)
PIP ..... Product Improvement Phase (SAUS)
PIP ..... Product Improvement Plan
PIP ..... Product Improvement Program [*Military*]
PIP ..... Product Improvement Proposal (MCD)
PIP ..... Product Information Package (SAUS)
PIP ..... Product Integration Program (SAUS)
PIP ..... Product Introductory Presentation
PIP ..... Production Implementation Program (AAG)
PIP ..... Production Improvement Program [*Navy*] (NG)
PIP ..... Production Instrumentation Package (NASA)
PIP ..... Productivity Improvement Program [*Office of Management and Budget*] (GFGA)
PIP ..... Productivity Improvement Program [*Department of Labor*]
PIP ..... Productivity Improvement Proposal (POLM)
PIP ..... Professional Information Processor (SAUS)
PIP ..... Professional Intern Program (SAUS)
PIP ..... Profile Ignition Pick-Up [*Automotive engineering*]
PIP ..... Profit Improvement Program
PIP ..... Program Implementation Plan (MCD)
PIP ..... Program Information Package (AAGC)
PIP ..... Program in Process [*Computer science*] (BUR)
PIP ..... Program in Progress [*Computer science*] (IAA)
PIP ..... Program Integrating Plan [*Computer science*] (IAA)

PIP.......... Program Integration Plan
PIP.......... Programmable Interconnect Point [*Computer science*]
PIP.......... Programmable Interface Processor (ACAE)
PIP.......... Programmed Individual Presentation (IAA)
PIP.......... Programmed Interconnection Pattern (VLIE)
PIP.......... Programmed Interconnection Process (SAUS)
PIP.......... Programmer Incentive Plan (SAUS)
PIP.......... Programs for the Improvement of Practice [*Washington, DC*] [*Department of Education*] (GRD)
PIP.......... Progressive Independent Party [*South Africa*] [*Political party*] (EY)
PIP.......... Progressive Inspection Plan [*Navy*] (NG)
PIP.......... Projected Impact Point [*Aviation*]
PIP.......... Project Implementation Plan
PIP.......... Project Implementation Profile [*Test*] (TMMY)
PIP.......... Project Initiation Period
PIP.......... Project Instrumentation Plan [*NASA*] (GFGA)
PIP.......... Project on Information Processing (IEEE)
PIP.......... Proof in Print
PIP.......... Proposal Instruction Package (MCD)
PIP.......... Proprietary Information Protection
PIP.......... Prototype Inlet Piping (SAUS)
PIP.......... Prototypic Inlet Piping [*Nuclear energy*] (NRCH)
PIP.......... Provabilistic Information Processing [*Computer science*] (IAA)
PIP.......... Prove in Plan (MCD)
PIP.......... Proximal Interphalangeal [*Joint*]
PIP.......... Psychotic Inpatient Profile [*Psychology*]
PIP.......... Public and Institutional Property [*Insurance*]
PIP.......... Public Investment Program (SAUS)
PIP.......... Public Involvement Plan (SAUS)
PIP.......... Public Involvement Program (GNE)
PIP.......... Puerto Rican Independence Party [*Political party*] (PD)
PIP.......... Pulsed Integrated (or Integrating) Pendulum (SAUS)
PIP.......... Pulsed Integrating Pendulum
PIP.......... Pulse Input Proportional [*Electro-optical system*]
PIP.......... Pulse Integrating Pendulum
PIP.......... Pulse Interval Processor (SAUS)
PIP.......... Western Psychiatric Institute and Clinic, University of Pittsburgh, Pittsburgh, PA [*OCLC symbol*] (OCLC)
PIPA........ Pacific Industrial Property Association (EA)
PIPA........ Pacific Islands Producers Association (SAUS)
PIPA........ Pulse Integrating Pendulous Accelerometer (SAUS)
PIPA........ Pulse Integrating Pendulum Accelerometer
PIPA........ Pulse Integrating Pendulum Assembly (NASA)
PIPACE...... Peacetime Intelligence Plan, Allied Central Europe [*NATO*]
Pip & C Mil L... Pipon and Collier's Military Law [*3rd ed.*] [*1865*] [*A publication*] (DLA)
PI-PB........ Performance Versus Intensity Function for Phonetically Balanced Words (MEDA)
PIPC........ Percent Indices Process Capable
PIPCST...... Piping Cost and Weight Analysis Program (DNAB)
PIPD........ Planning Input for Program Development (ACAE)
PIPE........ Consolidated Stainless [*NASDAQ symbol*] (TTSB)
PIPE........ Consolidated Stainless, Inc. [*NASDAQ symbol*] (SAG)
PIPE........ Persistent Interstitial Pulmonary Emphysema [*Medicine*] (DMAA)
PIPE........ Pipestone National Monument
PIPE........ Pipestone Tandem Boat Trailer [*NCIC trailer make code*]
PIPE........ Plug-In Processing Element (VLIE)
PIPE........ Plumbing Industry Progress and Education Fund
PIPE........ Points, Income, Personnel Expense (SAUS)
PIPECO...... Photoion-Photoelectron Coincidence [*Spectroscopy*]
PIPEF....... Pacific Islands Polynesian Education Foundation (SAUS)
PIPEFLEX... Pipe Flexibility [*Stress Analysis Program*]
PIPEL....... Pipeline (SAUS)
Pipeline Gas J... Pipeline and Gas Journal (SAUS)
Pipe Line Ind... Pipe Line Industry (SAUS)
PIPELN...... Pipeline company [*Transportation company classification code*]
PIPEMAID... Piping Program
PIPER....... Pulsed Intense Plasma for Experimental Research
PIPER....... Pulsed Intense Plasma for Exploratory Research
PiperJaf..... Piper Jaffray, Inc. [*Associated Press*] (SAG)
PIPES....... Piperazinediethanesulfonic Acid [*A buffer*]
PIPES....... Program on International Politics, Economics, and Security [*University of Chicago*]
Pipes Pipelines Int... Pipes and Pipelines International (SAUS)
PIPEX....... Pipeline Engineering Exhibition (SAUS)
PIPI........ Pipelines Inspectorate (HEAS)
PIPICO...... Panel on International Programs and International Cooperation in Oceans Affairs [*Department of State*] (NOAA)
PIPICO...... Panel on International Programs and International Organizations [*US State Department*] (USDC)
PIPIDA...... N-Para-Isopropylacetanilide-Iminodiacetic Acid [*Scan*] [*Radiology*] (DAVI)
PIPIDA...... Paraisopropyliminodiacetic Acid [*Medicine*] (RAWO)
PIPIDA...... Para-Isopropylphenyl(iminodiacetic Acid)
PIPIT....... Peripheral Interface and Program Interrupt Translator (PDAA)
PIPJ........ Proximal Interphalangeal Joint [*Anatomy*]
PIP Joint.... Proximal Interphalangeal Joint (SAUS)
PIPLC....... Phosphatidylinositol-Specific Phospholipase C [*Biochemistry*]
PIPO........ Parallel-In Parallel-Out [*Telecommunications*] (TEL)
PIPO........ Partition Input-Partition Output (SAUS)
PIPO........ Phase-In, Phase-Out (MCD)
PIPO........ Pioneer Transport [*Common carrier symbol*]
PIPPAP...... Pile for Producing Power and Plutonium [*Nuclear energy*] (NRCH)
PIPPS....... Publication Information Processing and Printing System
Pippy....... Person Inheriting Parents' Property [*Lifestyle classification*] [*British*]
PIPQUIC..... Program Integration Project Queries Use in Interactive Command (COE)
PIPR........ Piper Jaffray, Inc. [*NASDAQ symbol*] (COMM)
PIPR........ Plant-in-Place Records
PIPR........ Polytechnic Institute of Puerto Rico
PIPR........ Public Interest Public Relations (EA)
PIPRS....... Ping Intercept Passive Ranging SONAR [*Military*]
PIPS........ Pan Information Processing System (SAUS)
PIPS........ Paperless Item Processing System [*Banking*]
PIPS........ Parallel Information Processing System (SAUS)
PIPS........ Passivated Implanted Planar Silicon (SAUS)
PIPS........ Passive Infrared Personnel Sensor (ACAE)
PIPS........ Patient-Identified Physicians Survey [*Department of Health and Human Services*] (GFGA)
PIPS........ Pattern Information Processing System
PIPS........ PCAC Information Processing System (SAUS)
PIPS........ Peabody Intellectual Performance Scale [*Education*]
PIPS........ Personal Image Processing System (SAUS)
PIPS........ Philippines [*Telegraphy*] (PCTE)
PIPS........ Plans Integration Partitioning System (COE)
PIPS........ Polar Ice Prediction System (SAUS)
PIPS........ Polymerization-Induced Phase Separation (SAUS)
PIPS........ Portable Interactive Planning System (SAUS)
PIPS........ Postinjection Propulsion Subsystem [*NASA*]
PIPS........ Precision Ion Polishing System (SAUS)
PIPS........ Preschool Interpersonal Problem Solving Test
PIPS........ Product Information Pipeline System (VLIE)
PIPS........ Production Information Processing System (IAA)
PIPS........ Professional Improvement Points Program [*Louisiana*] (EDAC)
PIPS........ Professional Institute of the Public Service of Canada [*See also IPFP*]
PIPS........ Properties of Irregular Parts System (MCD)
PIPS........ Pulsed Integrating Pendulums [*NASA*] (QAA)
PIPS........ Science and Technology Policies Information Exchange Programme [*SPINES*] [*UNESCO*] [*Superseded by*] [*Information service or system*] (IID)
PIPSAR...... Pipe Sizing Program - Air (DNAB)
PIPSC....... Professional Institute of the Public Service of Canada (FOTI)
PIPSCR...... Philippine Islands Public Service Commission Reports [*A publication*] (DLA)
PIPSPK...... Pipe Sizing Program - Sprinkling (DNAB)
PIPSST...... Pipe Sizing Program - Steam (DNAB)
PIPTA....... Panel on International Procurement in the Technology Age (AAGC)
PIPUCR...... Philippine Islands Public Utility Commission Reports [*A publication*] (DLA)
PIPZ........ Piney Point Phosphates [*Federal Railroad Administration identification code*]
PIQ.......... Parallel Instruction Queue
PIQ.......... Performance Intelligence Quotient [*Psychology*] (DMAA)
PIQ.......... Performance IQ (SAUS)
PIQ.......... Program Idea Quotient [*Home testing measurement*] (NTCM)
PIQ.......... Property in Question
PIQ.......... State Regional Correctional Facility at Mercer, Mercer, PA [*OCLC symbol*] (OCLC)
PIQA........ Piqua, OH [*American Association of Railroads railroad junction routing code*]
PIQA........ Procurement Integration Quality Assurance (AAGC)
PIQA........ Proofing, Inspection, and Quality Assurance [*Military*]
PIQSY....... Probes for the International Quiet Solar Year [*OSS*]
PIR.......... Packaging Information Record (MCD)
PIR.......... Parachute Infantry Regiment [*Military*]
PIR.......... Paragnostic Information Retrieval [*Parapsychology*]
PIR.......... Parallel Injection Readout (IAA)
PIR.......... Partido de la Izquierda Revolucionaria [*Party of the Revolutionary Left*] [*Bolivia*] [*Political party*] (PPW)
PIR.......... Party of Independent Republicans (SAUS)
PIR.......... Passive Infrared
PIR.......... Past in Review (EA)
PIR.......... Payload Integration Review (ACAE)
PIR.......... Peak Intensity Ratio [*Spectroscopy*]
PIR.......... Pennsylvania International Raceway [*Auto racing*]
PIR.......... Pennsylvania Rehabilitation Center, Johnstown, PA [*OCLC symbol*] (OCLC)
PIR.......... Periodic Incremental Release [*Physiology*]
PIR.......... Periodic Intelligence Report
PIR.......... Periodic Intelligence Review [*Supreme Allied Commander, Atlantic*] (NATG)
PIR.......... Peripheral Insulin Receptor [*Medicine*] (EDAA)
PIR.......... Personal Interview Record
PIR.......... Personnel Information Report (SAUS)
PIR.......... Personnel Information Roster [*Military*]
PIR.......... Pesticide Ingredient Review Program [*Chemical Specialties Manufacturers Association*]
PIR.......... Petrolite Irradiation Reactor
PIR.......... Philippine Independence Ribbon [*Military decoration*]
PIR.......... Phoenix International Raceway
PIR.......... Photographic Intelligence Report [*Military*]
PIR.......... Photographic Interpretation Report
PIR.......... Photo Interpretation Report [*Air Force*] (AFM)
PIR.......... Photon-Induced x-Ray (SAUS)
PIR.......... Pier 1 Imports [*NYSE symbol*] (SPSG)
PIR.......... Pierre [*South Dakota*] [*Airport symbol*] (OAG)
PIR.......... Pilot Request (SAA)
PIR.......... Piriform (DB)

PIR........... Pirmasens [*Federal Republic of Germany*] [*Seismograph station code, US Geological Survey*] (SEIS)
PIR........... Pirna [*German license plate city code*]
PIR........... Pittsburgh Industrial Railroad [*Federal Railroad Administration identification code*]
PIR........... Plug-In Relay
PIR........... Polling Interrupt Routine (SAUS)
PIR........... Pollution Incident Report [*Environmental term*] (FOTI)
PIR........... Polyisocyanurate (SAUS)
PIR........... Post Implementation Review
PIR........... Postinhibitory Rebound [*Physiology*]
PIR........... Precision Infrared Radiometer (ARMP)
PIR........... Precision Inspection Request (IAA)
PIR........... Precision Instrumentation RADAR
PIR........... Predicted Intercept Range [*Military*] (CAAL)
PIR........... Preliminary Information Report (SAUS)
PIR........... Prematriculation Immunization Requirement
PIR........... Pressure Ignition Rocket (NATG)
PIR........... Pressure Indicated Registered (SAUS)
PIR........... Pressure Indicator Recorder (ECII)
PIR........... Prices Irregular [*Telegraphy*] (PCTE)
PIR........... Prim-Air Aps [*Denmark*] [*ICAO designator*] (FAAC)
PIR........... Primary Intelligence Requirement [*Military*] (INF)
PIR........... Principal Ideal Ring (SAUS)
PIR........... Priority Information Requirement [*Military intelligence*] (INF)
PIR........... Priority Intelligence Requirement [*Military*] (INF)
PIR........... Prisoner-Initiated Review
PIR........... Process and Indoctrinate Recruits
PIR........... Procurement Information Reporting (ACAE)
PIR........... Procurement Initiation Request (MCD)
PIR........... Product Improvement Review
PIR........... Product Information Release
PIR........... Production Inspection Record
PIR........... Product of Incomplete Reaction (EEVL)
PIR........... Professional Investor Report [*A publication*] (IT)
PIR........... Program Incident Report
PIR........... Program Information Report [*Head Start Program*] [*Department of Health and Human Services*] (GFGA)
PIR........... Program Instruction Register (SAUS)
PIR........... Program Interrupt Register [*Computer science*] (IAA)
PIR........... Project Independence Report
PIR........... Project Internal Result (SAUS)
PIR........... Protein Identification Resource [*National Biomedical Research Foundation*] [*Georgetown University Medical Center*] [*Information service or system*] (IID)
PIR........... Protein Information Resource (HGEN)
PIR........... Protocol-Independent Routing [*Computer science*]
PIR........... Publication Illustration Request
PIR........... Publication Information Register (IAA)
PIR........... Pulse Input Register (SAUS)
PIR........... Pure India Rubber [*Cables*]
PIRA......... Paper Industries Research Association (NADA)
PIRA......... Photographic Instrument Repairing Associates [*British*] (DBA)
PIRA......... Positive Identification and Radar Advisory (SAUS)
PIRA......... Printing and Packaging Industries Research Association (SAUS)
PIRA......... Printing and Packaging Research Association
PIRA......... Printing Industry Research Association (NADA)
PIRA......... Prison Industries Reorganization Administration [*Terminated, 1940*]
PIRA......... Provisional Irish Republican Army
PIRA......... Public Information Resources Administration
PIRA......... Research Association for the Paper and Board, Printing and Packaging Industries [*Research center*] (IRC)
PIRAD....... Passive Infrared Detector (ACAE)
PIRAD....... Proximity Information, Range, and Disposition
PIRAI........ PIRA International [*British*] (EAIO)
PIRAMID ... Project: Individualized Reading and Mathematics Inter-District (EDAC)
PIRAS....... Polarized Infrared Absorption Spectroscopy
PIRATA...... Pilot Research Array in the Tropical Atlantic (SAUS)
PIRATA...... Pilot Research Moored Array in the Tropical Atlantic [*Proposed project*] [*Marine science*] (OSRA)
PIRATE...... Passive Infra-Red Airborne Track Equipment (SAUS)
PIRATE...... Public Information in Rural Areas Technical Experiment (NITA)
PIRATE...... Public Information in Rural Areas Technology Experiment [*British Library*] (PDAA)
PIRAZ....... Positive Identification RADAR Advisory Zone (NVT)
PIRB......... Position Indicating Radio Beacon
PIRC......... Pierce [*NCIC truck make code*]
PIRC......... Portable Inflatable Recompression Chamber (MCD)
PIRC......... Pressure Indicator Recorder Controller (ECII)
PIRC......... Preventive Intervention Research Center for Child Health [*Yeshiva University*] [*Research center*] (RCD)
PIRC......... Protocol Implementation Review Committee [*National Institutes of Health*]
PIR Cable... Pure India Rubber Cable (SAUS)
PIRCH....... Program of Interdisciplinary Research in Contaminant Hydrogeology [*University of Virginia*] (RCD)
PIRCS....... Passive Infrared Confirming Sensor (MCD)
PIRD......... Program Instrumentation Requirements Document [*NASA*]
PIR databases... Protein Information Resource Databases (DOG)
PIRE......... Pacific Institute for Research and Evaluation [*Research center*] (RCD)
PI Rep....... Philippine Island Reports [*A publication*] (DLA)
PIREP....... Pilot Report [*Pertaining to meteorological conditions*] [*FAA*]
PIREP....... Pilot Weather Report (PIPO)
PIREPS...... Pilot Reports [*Marine science*] (OSRA)
PIRETS...... Pittsburgh Information Retrieval System (SAUS)
PIRETS...... Pittsburgh Retrieval System (NITA)
PIRF......... Perimeter-Insulated Raised Floor [*Residential construction*]
PIRF......... Petroleum Industry Research Foundation (NADA)
PIRFC....... Pilot Requests Forecast [*Aviation*] (FAAC)
PIRG......... Public Interest Research Group [*Formed by consumer-advocate Ralph Nader*]
PIRGIM...... Public Interest Research Group in Michigan [*Medicine*] (EDAA)
PIRI.......... Paint Industries Research Institute (SAUS)
P-IRI......... Plasma Immunoreactive Insulin [*Hematology*] (MAE)
PIRI.......... Psychologists Interested in Religious Issues (EA)
PIRID........ Passive Infrared Intrusion Detector (NVT)
PIRINC...... Petroleum Industry Research Foundation (EA)
PIRL......... Pattern Information Retrieval Language (SAUS)
PIRL......... PRISM [*Personnel Record Information System for Management*] Information RetrievalLanguage [*Computer science*] (PDAA)
PIRLA....... Paleoecological Reconstruction of Recent Lake Acidification (SAUS)
PIRLS....... Probe Infrared Laser Spectrometer (ACAE)
PI RM....... Pilot Reamer (SAUS)
PIRN......... Preliminary Interface Revision Notice [*NASA*] (KSC)
PIRO......... People, Ideas, Resources, Objectives [*Management strategy*] (DHSM)
PIRO......... Pictured Rocks National Lakeshore [*National Park Service designation*]
PIROGAS ... Plasma Injection of Reducing Overheated Gas System (SAUS)
PIROS....... Passive Infrared Remote Observation System (SAUS)
PIRP......... Prison Information Reform Project (SAUS)
PIRP......... Proposed International Reference Preparation (SAUS)
PIRP......... Provisional International Reference Preparation
PIRR......... Parts Installation and Removal Record [*NASA*] (KSC)
PIRR......... Prepositioned War Reserve Interrogation and Readiness Reporting (MCD)
PIRR......... Problem Investigation and Repair Record [*NASA*] (KSC)
PIRR......... PWRS [*Prepositioned War Reserve Stock*] Interrogation and Readiness Reporting System [*Navy*]
PIRR......... Pyrogen Identifier Rapid Response (SAUS)
PIRRB....... Photo Intelligence Requirements Review Board [*Military*]
PIRRCOM... Project for the Intensification of Regional Research on Cotton, Oilseeds and Minerals (SAUS)
PIRS......... Partial Input Record Storage (SAUS)
PIRS......... Passive Infrared Seeker
PIRS......... Passive Infrared Sensor (ACAE)
PIRS......... Personal Information Retrieval System
PIRS......... Personnel Information Retrieval System
PIRS......... Philosopher's Index Retrieval System (NITA)
PIRS......... Philosopher's Information Retrieval System [*Bowling Green State University*]
PIRS......... Plasma Immunoreactive Secretion [*Medicine*] (DMAA)
PIRS......... Police Information Retrieval System [*Law enforcement*] [*Computer science*] (FOTI)
PIRS......... Pollution Incident Reporting System [*Coast Guard*]
PIRS......... Poseidon Information Retrieval System [*Missiles*]
PIRS......... Project Information Retrieval System [*HEW*]
PIRS......... Pulsed Infrared System (ACAE)
PIRSA....... Passive Infrared Situation Awareness (ACAE)
PIRS Method... Partial Input Record Storage Method (SAUS)
PIRT......... Placement by an Interchange and Rate Technique (SAUS)
PIRT......... Precision Infrared Tracking
PIRT......... Precision Infrared Triangulation
PIRT......... Pretreatment Implementation Review Task Force [*Environmental Protection Agency*] (EPA)
PIRT......... Programmed Instruction in Real Time (SAUS)
PIRT......... Public Information Retrieval Terminal (SAUS)
PIRT System... Preliminary Infrared Triangulation System (SAUS)
PIRU......... Public Information Reference Unit [*Environmental Protection Agency*] (GFGA)
PIRV......... Programmed Interrupt Request Vector [*Computer science*] (ELAL)
Pis........... In Pisonem [*of Cicero*] [*Classical studies*] (OCD)
PIS........... Parts Identification Service
PIS........... Passenger Information System
PIS........... Passive Infrared System
PIS........... Patent Inventor Service (NITA)
PIS........... Pathology Information System (SAUS)
PIS........... Penning Ionization Spectroscopy (PDAA)
PIS........... Photographic Interpretation Section
PIS........... Pisa [*Italy*] [*Seismograph station code, US Geological Survey*] [*Closed*] (SEIS)
PIS........... Piscivorous
Pis........... Pistol (SAUS)
PIS........... Pointable Imaging Spectrometer (SAUS)
PIS........... Poitiers [*France*] [*Airport symbol*] (OAG)
PIS........... Polling Interrupt Sequence (SAUS)
PIS........... Polyisobutylene (EDCT)
PIS........... Portfolio-Management Information System (SAUS)
PIS........... Position Indicator System
PIS........... Positive Ion Source
PIS........... Postal Inspection Service
PIS........... Preinfarction Syndrome [*Cardiology*]
PIS........... Preinsert Sequencing
PIS........... Pressure-Indicating Switch [*Nuclear energy*] (NRCH)
PIS........... Primary Immunodeficiency Syndrome [*Medicine*] (EDAA)
PIS........... Prime Implicant Solution (IAA)
PIS........... Procedure Interrupt Signal (SAUS)
PIS........... Process Instrumentation System [*Nuclear energy*] (NRCH)

PIS .... Process Instrument Sheet
PIS .... Product Information Specialist
PIS .... Provisional International Standard
PIS .... Public Information Specialist (COE)
PIS .... Public Insurance Service (SAUS)
PIS .... Pulsed Illumination Source
PIS .... Pulse Integration System
PIS .... Stevens Trade School, Lancaster, PA [*OCLC symbol*] (OCLC)
PISA .... Partners in Sharing Associates (EARSL)
PISA .... Persistent Information Space Architecture [*Computer science*]
PISA .... Phase Invariant Signature Algorithm [*Chemistry*] (DAVI)
PISA .... Polish Independent Student Association (EA)
PISA .... Prototype Image Spectrum Analyzer (SAUS)
PISA .... Public Interest Satellite Association [*Defunct*] (EA)
PISAB .... Pulse Interference Separation and Blanking [*RADAR*]
PISAB .... Pulse Interference Suppression and Blanking (SAUS)
PISABG ...... PISA/Business Graphics (SAUS)
PISADB ...... PISA/Data Base (SAUS)
PISADD ..... PISA/Data Dictionary (SAUS)
PISAL .... Periodicals in South African Libraries (NITA)
PISAMP ..... PISA/Menue Processor (SAUS)
PISAQL ...... PISA/Query Language (SAUS)
PISARG ..... PISA/Report Generator (SAUS)
PISB .... People's Institute for Survival and Beyond (EA)
PISC .... Pacific International Services Corp. [*NASDAQ symbol*] (NQ)
PISC .... Parris Island, South Carolina [*Marine Corps*]
PISC .... Petroleum Industry Security Council (EA)
PISC .... Phoenix International Science Center (SAUS)
Pisc .... Pisces [*Constellation*]
PISC .... Programme for the Inspection of Steel Components (HEAS)
PISCES ...... Paleolimnological Investigations of Salinity, Climatic and Environmental Shifts (SAUS)
PISCES ...... Percutaneously Inserted Spinal Cord Electrical Stimulation [*Medicine*] (DMAA)
PISCES ...... Plessey Integrated Shipborne Combat Electronic Systems (SAUS)
PISCES ...... Poisson and Continuity Equations Solver (SAUS)
PISCES ...... Production Information Stocks and Cost Enquiry System (MHDB)
PISD .... Pacific Information Systems Division (SAUS)
PISE .... No Pilot Balloon Observation Due to Unfavorable Sea Conditions [*NWS*] (FAAC)
PISE .... Pneumatically Installed Stabilized Earth
PISE .... Pnuematically-Impacted Stabilized Earth
PISG .... Pitcairn Islands Study Group (EA)
PISGA .... Palestinian Interim Self-Government Authority [*Proposed*] (ECON)
PISH .... Program Instrumentation Summary Handbook [*NASA*] (KSC)
PISI .... Palmar Intercalated Segmental Instability [*Medicine*] (MELL)
PISMV .... Plantago Severe Mottle Virus [*Plant pathology*]
PISN .... Private Integrated Services Network (AG)
PISO .... No Pilot Balloon Observation Due to Snow [*Meteorology*] (FAAC)
PISO .... Parallel-In Serial-Out [*Telecommunications*] (TEL)
PISO .... Philippines Investment Systems Organization (SAUS)
PISO .... Polyimidesulfone (SAUS)
PISP .... Instructional Permit Suspended [*Motor vehicle violation driver status code in state of North Dakota*] (MVRD)
PISP .... PCG-insensitive Streptococcus pneumoniae (SAUS)
PISP .... Pipe Springs National Monument
PISP .... Polar Ice Sheet Program (SAUS)
PISSC .... Programme International sur la Securite des Substances Chimiques [*International Programme on Chemical Safety*] (EAIO)
PIST .... Percent Inspection-Points to Satisfy Tolerances [*Manufacturing*]
PIST .... Piston [*Automotive engineering*]
Pist .... Piston's Mauritius Reports [*A publication*] (DLA)
Piston .... Piston's Mauritius Reports [*A publication*] (DLA)
PISU .... Polyimidesulfone [*Organic chemistry*]
PISUKI ...... Pacific Islands Society of the United Kingdom and Ireland (EAIO)
PISYS .... Photographic Interpretation Data System (SAUS)
PIT .... Pacific Investment Trust [*Finance*] [*British*]
PIT .... Pacing-induced Tachycardia [*Medicine*] (EDAA)
PIT .... Panair International SRL [*Italy*] [*ICAO designator*] (FAAC)
PI/T .... Parallel Interface/Timer [*Motorola, Inc.*]
PIT .... Parameter Input Tape (IAA)
PIT .... Participate in Archeology
PIT .... Parti de l'Independance et du Travail [*Party of Independence and Labor*] [*Senegal*] [*Political party*] (PPW)
PIT .... Parti Ivoirien des Travailleurs [*Ivorian Workers' Party*] [*The Ivory Coast*] [*Political party*] (EY)
PIT .... Partners in Transition [*Poland, Czechoslovakia, and Hungary*] (ECON)
PIT .... Part-Time, Intermittent, Temporary [*Nuclear energy*]
PIT .... Pasadena Institute of Technology (SAUS)
PIT .... Passive Immunotherapy [*Medicine*] (TAD)
PIT .... Passive Integrated Transponder
PIT .... Patellar Inhibition Test [*Neurology*] (DAVI)
Pit .... Pateller Inhibition Test (STED)
PIT .... Performance Improvement Test (SAUS)
PIT .... Performance Improvement Tests
PIT .... Peripheral Input Tape [*Computer science*]
PIT .... Peripheral Interface Tests (MCD)
PIT .... Permanent Income Theory [*Econometrics*]
PIT .... Permit Improvement Team [*Environmental science*] (EPAT)
PIT .... Personal Income Tax
PIT .... Phase Inversion Temperature [*Physical Chemistry*]
PIT .... Photographic Interpretation Technique
PIT .... Physical Inventory Taking (MHDB)
PIT .... Picture Identification Test [*Psychology*]
PIT .... Picture Impressions Test [*Psychology*]
PIT .... Pilot Instructor Training [*Aviation*] (FAAC)
PIT .... Pirates Gold Corp. [*Vancouver Stock Exchange symbol*]
Pit .... Pitocin [*Trademark of Parke, Davis & Co. for Oxytocin, a labor-inducing drug*]
Pit .... Pitressin [*Trademark of Parke, Davis & Co. for Vasopressin, an antidiuretic hormone*]
PIT .... Pittsburgh [*Pennsylvania*] [*Seismograph station code, US Geological Survey*] [*Closed*] (SEIS)
PIT .... Pittsburgh [*Pennsylvania*] [*Airport symbol*]
Pit .... Pittsburgh Steelers [*National Football League*] [*1941-42, 1945-present*] (NFLA)
PIT .... Pittsfield, MA [*Amtrak rail station code*]
PIT .... Pituitary [*Endocrinology*] (AAMN)
pit .... Pituitary (STED)
PIT .... Plasma Iron Transport [*Hematology*]
PIT .... Plasma Iron Turnover [*Hematology*] (DAVI)
PIT .... Polar Ionospheric Trough
PIT .... Polaris Industrial Team [*Missiles*]
PIT .... Pole Interpolation Technique (SAUS)
PIT .... Powder-in-Tube (SAUS)
PIT .... Pre-Induction Training
PIT .... Preinstallation Test [*NASA*] (KSC)
PIT .... Prevailing-In Torque [*Automotive engineering*]
PIT .... Principal, Interest and Taxes (SAUS)
PIT .... Print Illegal and Trace
PIT .... Printing and Information Technology (SAUS)
PIT .... Printing and Information Technology Division (NITA)
PIT .... Prioritized Image Transmission (SAUS)
PIT .... Processing Index Terms
PIT .... Processing of Indexing Terms
PIT .... Product Improvement Test
PIT .... Product Innovation Team [*Automotive engineering*]
PIT .... Program Instruction Tape [*Computer science*] (IEEE)
PIT .... Programmable Interface/Timer [*Computer science*] (AGLO)
PIT .... Programmable Interrupt Timer [*Computer science*] (MWOL)
PIT .... Programmable Interval Timer
PIT .... Programmed Instruction Text
PIT .... Progressive Inspection Tag (SAUS)
PIT .... Projected Inactive Time [*Computer science*]
PIT .... Project in Trouble (CCCA)
PIT .... Property Income Trust [*Investment term*]
PIT .... Protection Identification Key (SAUS)
PIT .... Provincial Institute of Textiles
PIT .... Psychological Insight Test [*Psychometrics*]
PIT .... University of Pittsburgh, Pittsburgh, PA [*OCLC symbol*] (OCLC)
PITA .... Pacific International Trapshooting Association (EA)
PITA .... Pain in the Accronym (SAUS)
PITA .... Pain in the Anatomy (SAUS)
PITA .... Pain in the Ass [*Internet slang*] (NETL)
PITA .... Paper Industry Technical Association [*British*] (EAIO)
PITA .... Parison Inflation Thinning Analysis (SAUS)
PITA .... Petroleum Industry Training Association (SAUS)
PITA .... Provincial Institute of Technology and Art
PITA .... Provincial Intermediate Teachers Association (SAUS)
PITAC .... Pakistan Industrial Technical Assistance Center (or Centre) (SAUS)
PITAC .... President's Information Technology Advisory Committee
PITAS .... Petroleum Industry Training Association Scotland (SAUS)
PITB .... Pacific Inland Tariff Bureau
PITB .... Pacific Island Teachers Board (SAUS)
PITB .... Petroleum Industry Training Board (SAUS)
PITB .... Poetry in the Branches [*Program*]
PITB .... Push Commercial Division [*An association*] (EA)
PITB .... PUSH [*People United to Save Humanity*] International Trade Bureau (EA)
Pitblado Lect ... Isaac Pitblado's Lectures on Continuing Legal Education [*A publication*] (DLA)
PITC .... Pacific International Trust Co. (SAUS)
PITC .... Phenylisothiocyanate [*Organic chemistry*]
PITC .... Photoinduced Tunnel Current
Pitc .... Pitcairn's Criminal Trials [*1488-1624*] [*Scotland*] [*A publication*] (DLA)
PITC .... Pittencrieff Communications [*NASDAQ symbol*] (SAG)
PITC .... Point-in-Time Copy (GART)
Pitc Crim Tr ... Pitcairn's Ancient Criminal Trials [*Scotland*] [*A publication*] (DLA)
PIT-CNT ..... Interunion Workers' Assembly-National Workers Convention (Uruguay) [*Political party*] (PSAP)
PITCOM ..... Parliamentary Information Technology Committee [*Political communications*] [*British*]
Pitc Tr .... Pitcairn's Criminal Trials [*3 Scotland*] [*A publication*] (DLA)
PITD .... Pitt-Ohio Express [*Common carrier symbol*]
PITDIC .... Pacific Islands Tourism Development Council (SAUS)
PitDsm ...... Pittsburgh-Des Moines Corp. [*Associated Press*] (SAG)
PITE .... Principal, Interest, Taxes and Energy Payment (FOTI)
PITE .... Project on Information Technology and Education [*Defunct*] (EA)
Pitencr ...... Pittencrieff Communications [*Commercial firm*] [*Associated Press*] (SAG)
PITF .... Poultry Industry Trust Fund [*Australia*]
PITFA .... Product Improvement Through Feature Analysis (SAUS)
PITFC .... Potato Industry Trust Fund Committee [*Western Australia*]
PIT FE .... Personal Income Tax Filing Enforcement (SAUS)
PITG .... Payload Integration Task Group [*NASA*] (NASA)
PITH .... Principal, Interest, Taxes and Heating (FOTI)
PITHX .... Pioneer Mid Cap Cl.A [*Mutual fund ticker symbol*] (SG)
PITI .... Principal, Interest, Taxes and Insurance
PITI .... Principal, Interest, Taxes, Insurance [*Real estate*]

Pitisc Lex... Pitisci's Lexicon [*A publication*] (DLA)
PITL......... Pacific Islands Transport Line (SAUS)
PITM......... Pitman Brothers Company [*NCIC trailer make code*]
PITMOS..... Post Mode Optimizing System (SAUS)
Pitm Prin & Sur... Pitman on Principal and Surety [*A publication*] (DLA)
PITN......... Pain in the Neck
PITN......... Polyisothianaphthene [*Organic chemistry*]
PitnB......... Pitney-Bowes, Inc. [*Associated Press*] (SAG)
PitnyBw..... Pitney-Bowes, Inc. [*Associated Press*] (SAG)
PITO......... Pipeline Trucking Company [*Common carrier symbol*]
PITO......... Portuguese Information and Tourist Office (SAUS)
PITP......... Phosphatidylinositol Transfer Protein [*Biochemistry*]
PITP......... Pseudoidiopathic Thrombocytopenic Purpura (STED)
Pit Quarry... Pit & Quarry [*A publication*] (CABS)
PITR......... Plasma Iron Transport [*or Turnover*] Rate [*Hematology*]
PITR......... Plasma Iron Turnover Rate (SAUS)
PITRI......... Petroleum Industry Technology and Research Institute, Inc. (SAUS)
PITS......... Pacific Islands Training School (SAUS)
PITS......... Parent-Infant Traumatic Stress (DAVI)
PITS......... Partners In Transition [*Poland, Czech, Hungary - called the Visegrad Trio*]
PITS......... Passive Identification & Targeting System (SAUS)
PITS......... Passive Intercept Tracking System
PITS......... Patriot Integration and Test System [*Army*]
PITS......... Payload Integration Test Set [*NASA*] (MCD)
PITS......... Peak Instantaneous Transients and Subtleties (SEWL)
PITS......... Petroleum Industry Training Service (SAUS)
PITS......... Photoinduced Transient Spectroscopy
PITS......... Position Interrogation and Transmission System (SAUS)
PITS......... Primary Influent Treatment System
PITS......... Projected Intensity Triplet Space (SAUS)
PITS......... Project Information Tracking System [*Environmental Protection Agency*] (GFGA)
PITS......... Propellant Injector Tube Simulator (MCD)
PITS......... Propulsion Integration Test Stand
PitstnMn.... [*The*] Pittston Co. [*Associated Press*] (SAG)
PitstnSvc... [*The*] Pittston Co. [*Associated Press*] (SAG)
Pit Sur...... Pitman on Principal and Surety [*1840*] [*A publication*] (DLA)
Pitt........... Pittsburgh, PA (DLA)
PITT......... Polaris Integrated Test Team [*Missiles*]
PITT......... Punch-through Injection Transit-Time (SAUS)
Pitt Bank... Pitt's Bankruptcy Acts [*A publication*] (DLA)
PITTC......... Philips International Telecommunications Training Center (IAA)
Pitt CC Pr... Pitt's County Court Practice [*A publication*] (DLA)
PITTCON... Pittsburgh Conference (SAUS)
Pitt LJ....... Pittsburgh Legal Journal [*A publication*] (DLA)
Pitts......... Pittsburgh, PA (DLA)
PITTS........ Pittsburgh, PA [*American Association of Railroads railroad junction routing code*]
Pitts......... Pittsburgh Reports [*A publication*] (DLA)
Pittsb........ Pittsburgh, PA (DLA)
Pittsb........ Pittsburgh Reports [*A publication*] (DLA)
Pittsb Leg J... Pittsburgh Legal Journal [*Pennsylvania*] [*A publication*] (DLA)
Pittsb Leg J NS... Pittsburgh Legal Journal, New Series [*Pennsylvania*] [*A publication*] (DLA)
Pittsb Leg J (OS)... Pittsburgh Legal Journal, Old Series [*A publication*] (DLA)
Pittsb Leg J (PA)... Pittsburgh Legal Journal [*Pennsylvania*] [*A publication*] (DLA)
Pittsb LJ.... Pittsburgh Legal Journal [*Pennsylvania*] [*A publication*] (DLA)
Pittsb L Rev... Pittsburgh Law Review [*A publication*] (DLA)
Pittsb R (PA)... Pittsburgh Reporter [*Pennsylvania*] [*A publication*] (DLA)
Pittsburgh Leg J... Pittsburgh Legal Journal [*Pennsylvania*] [*A publication*] (DLA)
Pittsburgh Leg Journal... Pittsburgh Legal Journal [*Pennsylvania*] [*A publication*] (DLA)
Pittsburg St U... Pittsburg State University (GAGS)
Pitts Leg J... Pittsburgh Legal Journal [*Pennsylvania*] [*A publication*] (DLA)
Pitts Leg J (NS)... Pittsburgh Legal Journal, New Series [*Pennsylvania*] [*A publication*] (DLA)
Pitts Leg Jour... Pittsburgh Legal Journal [*Pennsylvania*] [*A publication*] (DLA)
Pitts LJ...... Pittsburgh Legal Journal [*A publication*] (DLA)
Pitts LJ (NS)... Pittsburgh Legal Journal, New Series [*A publication*] (DLA)
Pitts R....... Pittsburgh Reports [*Pennsylvania*] [*A publication*] (DLA)
Pitts Rep... Pittsburgh Reports [*A publication*] (DLA)
Pitts Rep (PA)... Pittsburgh Reports [*Pennsylvania*] [*A publication*] (DLA)
Pittway...... Pittway Corp. [*Associated Press*] (SAG)
Pittwy....... Pittway Corp. [*Associated Press*] (SAG)
PittwyA...... Pittway Corp. [*Associated Press*] (SAG)
PITU......... Pipe or Tubing [*Freight*]
PitWVa...... Pittsburgh & West Virginia Railroad [*Associated Press*] (SAG)
PITY-EM... Principal, Interest, Taxes, Energy, and Maintenance [*Real estate*]
PITYP........ Pinatype (VRA)
PITZ......... John Pitzer Manufacturing [*NCIC trailer make code*]
PIU........... East Pennsylvania Psychiatric Institute, Philadelphia, PA [*OCLC symbol*] (OCLC)
PIU........... Path Information Unit [*Computer science*]
PIU........... Pathological Internet Use
PIU........... Performance and Innovation Unit
PIU........... Peripheral Interface Unit (ELAL)
PIU........... Photographic Interpretation Unit [*Marine Corps*]
PIU........... Pilot Indicator Unit [*Aviation*] (IAA)
PIU........... Pilot Information Utilization
PIU........... Piura [*Peru*] [*Airport symbol*] (OAG)
PIU........... Plug-In Unit
PIU........... Polymerase-Inducing Unit
PIU........... Power Integration Unit (SSD)
PIU........... Power Intercept Unit [*Military*] (CAAL)
PIU........... Power Interface Unit (MCD)
PIU........... Private Islands Unlimited (EA)
PIU........... Process Input Unit [*Computer science*] (BUR)
PIU........... Process Interface Unit
PIU........... Processor Interface Unit (SAUS)
PIU........... Programmable Interface Unit (SAUS)
PIU........... Programmer Interface Unit (MCD)
PIU........... Public Inspection Unit (SAUS)
PIU........... Pyrotechnic Initiator Unit (MCD)
PiU........... University of the Philippines, Quezon City, Philippines [*Library symbol*] [*Library of Congress*] (LCLS)
PIUC......... Parametric Image Up-Conversion (SAUS)
PIUG......... Parti Independantiste de l'Unite Guyanaise [*Pro-Independence Party of Guyanese Unity*] [*Political party*] (PPW)
PIUMP....... Plug-In Unit Mounting Panel
PIUS......... Process Inherent Ultimately Safe [*Nuclear reactor*]
PI/USA...... Packaging Institute, United States of America [*Later, PI/INT'L*] (EA)
PIV........... Parainfluenza Virus
PIV........... Particle Image Velocimeter (ABAC)
PIV........... Particle Image Velocimetry [*Fluid dynamics*]
PIV........... Peak Inverse Voltage [*RADAR*]
PIV........... Peripheral Intravenous [*Line*] [*Pharmacology*] (DAVI)
PIV........... Personal Indentification Verification
PIV........... Pick Inverse Voltage [*Electronics*] (ECII)
PIV........... Pileni [*Language symbol*] (ETLW)
PIV........... Piva [*Solomon Islands*] [*Seismograph station code, US Geological Survey*] [*Closed*] (SEIS)
PIV........... Pivot [*Automotive engineering*]
piv........... Pivoted [*Construction term*] (MIST)
PIV........... Planet in View [*NASA*]
PIV........... Plug-In Valve
PIV........... Polydactyly-Imperforate Anus-Vertebral Anomalies [*Medicine*] [*Syndrome*] (EDAA)
PIV........... Positive Infinitely Variable
PIV........... Post Indicator Valve
PIV........... Primate Immunodeficiency Virus [*Medicine*] (MELL)
PIV........... Product Inspection Verification
PIV........... Propellant Isolation Valve
PIV........... Protected Intervention Vehicle [*Police and security equipment*]
PIV........... Scotland School for Veterans' Children, Scotland, PA [*OCLC symbol*] (OCLC)
PIV4......... Plantago Virus 4 [*Plant pathology*]
PIVAD........ Product Improvement Vulcan Air Defense (MCD)
PIVADS...... Product Improved Vulcan Air Defense System (MCD)
PIVCO........ Personal Independent Vehicle Company [*Automotive industry*]
PIVD......... Postischemic Vasodilatation [*Medicine*] (EDAA)
PIVD......... Protruded Intervertebral Disc [*Medicine*]
PIVED........ Plasma-Injection Vacuum Energy Diverter
PIV Gear.... Positive Infinitely Variable Gear (SAUS)
PIVH......... Peripheral Intravenous Hyperalimentation [*Medicine*] (MELL)
PIVH......... Periventricular-intraventricular Hemorrhage [*Medicine*] (EDAA)
PIVI.......... Parainfluenza Virus Infection [*Medicine*] (MELL)
PIVKA........ Protein-Induced by Vitamin K Antagonist (DB)
PIVKA........ Protein in Vitamin K Absence (AAMN)
PIVN......... Public Interest Video Network/New Voices Radio (EA)
PIVOT........ Planning and Implementing Vocational Readiness in Occupational Therapy
PIVOT........ Programmers Interactive Verification and Organizational Tool (SAUS)
PIVR......... Pacemaker-Induced Ventricular Rate [*Cardiology*] (CPH)
PIVS......... Particle-Induced Visual Sensations
PIVT......... Product Improvement Verification Test
PIVT......... Production Improvement Verification Test
PIVX......... Plantain Virus X [*Plant pathology*]
PIW........... Period of Incapacity for Work (DI)
PIW........... Photo Imaging Workstation (SAUS)
PIW........... Plastic Insulated Wire
PIW........... Ports and Inland Waterways
PIW........... Printing Industries of Wisconsin (EARSL)
PIW........... Program Interrupt Word
PIW........... Woodhaven Center, Philadelphia, PA [*OCLC symbol*] (OCLC)
PIWA......... Pauktuutit Inuit Women's Association [*Canada*] (EAIO)
PIWC......... Petroleum Industry War Council
PIWG......... Permanent Interoperability Working Group (SAUS)
PIWG......... Product Improvement Working Group [*Military*] (AFIT)
PIWI.......... No Pilot Balloon Observation Due to High, or Gusty, Surface Wind [*NWS*] (FAAC)
PIWI.......... Puppit in the Window Illuminated [*Medicine*] [*Test*] (EDAA)
PIWT......... Partially Impacted Wisdom Tooth (MELL)
PIWWC....... Planetary Initiative for the World We Choose (EA)
PIWWC....... Pulse Intermittent Windshield Wiper Switch [*Automotive electronics*]
PIX........... Avenue Entertainment Grp [*AMEX symbol*] (SG)
PIX........... Expired Permit [*Motor vehicle violation driver status code in state of North Dakota*] (MVRD)
PIX........... Parallel Interface Extender [*Computer science*] (IAA)
PIX........... Pico Island [*Azores*] [*Airport symbol*] (OAG)
PIX........... Picture
PIX........... Picture Rocks, PA [*Location identifier*] [*FAA*] (FAAL)
PIX........... Pinxit [*He, or She, Painted It*] [*Latin*] (ROG)
PIX........... Private Internet Exchange (GART)
PIX........... Proton-Induced X-Ray Analysis
PIX........... School Pictures, Inc. [*AMEX symbol*] (COMM)
PIX........... Youth Development Center, Loysville, Loysville, PA [*OCLC symbol*] (OCLC)
PIX Analysis... Proton Induced X-ray Analysis (SAUS)

Pix Aud ..... Pixley on Auditors [*8th ed.*] [*1901*] [*A publication*] (DLA)
PIXBLT ...... Pixel Block Transfer [*Computer science*] (GART)
PIXE .... Particle [*or Proton*]-Induced X-Ray Emission
PIXE .... Particle-Induced X-Ray Excitation (SAUS)
PIXE .... Photon-Induced X-Ray Emission (SAUS)
Pixel .... Picture Element [*Computer science*] (ITCA)
pixel .... Picture Element (SHCU)
PIXEL .... Picture Element [*Single element of resolution in image processing*]
pixelsat ..... Picture Element Satellite (ADWA)
PIXES .... Particle-Induced X-Ray Emission Spectroscopy (EDCT)
PIXF .... Proton-Induced X-Ray Emission [*Biophysics*] [*Biochemistry*] (QSUL)
PIXI .... Pixie Piker Travel Trailer [*NCIC trailer make code*]
PIXI .... Professional Industrial X-Ray Imaging (SAUS)
PIXIE .... Particle-Induced X-ray Emission (SAUS)
PIXNET .... Parallel Interface Extender Network (SAUS)
PIXR .... Pixar [*NASDAQ symbol*] (TTSB)
PIXR .... Pixar Animation Studios [*NASDAQ symbol*]
PIXSYS ...... Pictorial Information Extraction System (SAUS)
PIXT .... PixTech, Inc. [*NASDAQ symbol*] (SAG)
PixTech ...... PixTech, Inc. [*Associated Press*] (SAG)
PIY .... Pembroke Imperial Yeomanry [*British military*] (DMA)
PIY .... Personality Inventory for Youth [*Test*] (TMMY)
PIY .... Youth Development Center, New Castle, New Castle, PA [*OCLC symbol*] (OCLC)
PIZ .... Pfizer Industries [*Federal Railroad Administration identification code*]
PIZ .... Pizaz European [*British*] [*FAA designator*] (FAAC)
PIZ .... Point Lay [*Alaska*] [*Airport symbol*] (OAG)
PIZ .... Point Lay, AK [*Location identifier*] [*FAA*] (FAAL)
PIZ .... Public Information Zone (HEAS)
PIZ .... Youth Development Center, Waynesburg, Waynesburg, PA [*OCLC symbol*] (OCLC)
PIZA .... National Pizza Co. [*NASDAQ symbol*] (COMM)
pizz .... Pizzicato [*Plucking*] [*Italian*] [*Music*] (WDAA)
PIZZ .... Pizzicato [*Plucked*] [*Music*]
PizzaInn ...... Pizza Inn, Inc. [*Associated Press*] (SAG)
PJ .... Air St. Pierre [*ICAO designator*] (AD)
PJ .... Bombay High Court Printed Judgments [*1869-1900*] [*India*] [*A publication*] (DLA)
PJ .... Netherlands Antilles [*International civil aircraft marking*] (ODBW)
PJ .... Pajamas
PJ .... Pancreatic Juice [*Medicine*] (MELL)
PJ .... Panel Jack
PJ .... Parnelli Jones [*Race car driver*]
PJ .... Parteijargon [*Party Language*] [*German*]
PJ .... Participating Jurisdiction
PJ .... Peripheral Jet (AAG)
PJ .... Petajoule (ADA)
PJ .... Peutz-Jeghers [*Syndrome*] [*Medicine*] (DB)
PJ .... Picojoule [*Logic gate efficiency measure*] (MDG)
PJ .... Plasma Jet (AAG)
PJ .... Plastic Jacket
PJ .... Police Judge (SAUS)
PJ .... Police Justice
PJ .... Porcelain Jacket [*Dentistry*] (MELL)
PJ .... Possible Jobs [*Test*] [*Psychology*]
PJ .... Prejudice [*Telegraphy*] (PCTE)
PJ .... Presiding Judge
PJ .... Presiding Probate Judge [*British*] (ROG)
PJ .... Prince of Jerusalem [*Freemasonry*]
PJ .... Probate Judge
PJ .... Procurement Justification [*Navy*]
PJ .... Project Jonah [*Defunct*] (EA)
PJ .... Projects Directorate
PJ .... Puisne Judge [*Australia*]
PJ .... Pulsejet
PJ .... Purchases Journal [*Accounting*]
PJA .... Abington Library Society, Jenkintown, PA [*Library symbol*] [*Library of Congress*] [*Obsolete*] (LCLS)
PJA .... Pakistan Jute Association (SAUS)
PJA .... Pipe Jacking Association [*British*] (DBA)
PJA .... Proper Job Analysis (COE)
PJAFC .... P. J. Allman Fan Club (EA)
PJAL .... Progressive Jewish Activism List [*An association*]
PJAIG .... Alverthorpe Gallery, Rosenwald Collection, Jenkintown, PA [*Library symbol*] [*Library of Congress*] (LCLS)
PJAM .... PJ America, Inc. [*NASDAQ symbol*] (SAG)
PJ Amer .... PJ America, Inc. [*Associated Press*] (SAG)
PJAS .... Project Associates (SAUS)
PJB .... Pad Journal Bearing
PJB .... Premature Junctional Beat [*Cardiology*]
PJBD .... Permanent Joint Board on Defense [*US, Canada*]
PJC .... Jean Coutu Group (PJC), Inc. [*Toronto Stock Exchange symbol*]
PJC .... Paducah Junior College [*Kentucky*]
PJC .... Paris Junior College [*Texas*]
PJC .... Pensacola Junior College [*Florida*]
PJC .... Perkinston Junior College [*Mississippi*]
PJC .... Piper Jaffray Companies [*NYSE symbol*] (SPSG)
PJC .... Polydox Jewish Federation (SAUS)
PJC .... Post Junior College [*Connecticut*]
PJC .... Poteau Junior College [*Oklahoma*]
PJC .... Pratt Junior College [*Kansas*]
PJC .... Premature Junctional Contractions [*Cardiology*] (DMAA)
PJC .... Premature Junctional Tachycardia (SAUS)
PJC .... Princeton Junction, NJ [*Amtrak rail station code*]
PJC .... University of Pittsburgh, Johnstown, Johnstown, PA [*OCLC symbol*] (OCLC)
PJCTL .... Projectile (MSA)
Pjctvs .... Projectavision, Inc. [*Associated Press*] (SAG)
Pjctvsn ...... Projectavision, Inc. [*Associated Press*] (SAG)
PJD .... Pedro Dome [*Alaska*] [*Seismograph station code, US Geological Survey*] [*Closed*] (SEIS)
PJD .... Prejudiced [*Telegraphy*] (PCTE)
PJE .... Parachute Jumping Exercise
PJE .... Private Jet Expeditions, Inc. [*ICAO designator*] (FAAC)
PJE .... Project Engineer
PJE .... Pulse Jet Engine
PJES .... Photojet Edge Sensor
PJF .... Peripheral Jet (Flat-Bottom)
PJF .... Pharmaceutical Journal Formulary (ROG)
PJF .... Pin Jointed Framework
PJF .... Pin Jounted Framework (SAUS)
PJFS .... Philip Jose Farmer Society (EA)
PJG .... Panjgur [*Pakistan*] [*Airport symbol*] (OAG)
PJG .... Potts Junction [*Guam*] [*Seismograph station code, US Geological Survey*] (SEIS)
PJG .... Prejudicing [*Telegraphy*] (PCTE)
PJH .... Piper, Jr., H. E., Philadelphia PA [*STAC*]
PJH .... PLRS/JTIDS [*Position Location Reporting System/Joint Tactical Information Distribution System*] Hybrid (MCD)
PJH .... PLRS/JTIDS Hybrid System (SAUS)
PJHI .... PLRS/JTIDS [*Position Location Reporting System/Joint Tactical Information Distribution System*] Hybrid Interface
PJI .... Parachute Jump Instructor [*Military*] [*British*] (INF)
PJI .... Pattern Jury Instructions [*A publication*]
PJI .... Personnel Journal Index [*Personnel Journal*] [*Information service or system*] (CRD)
PJI .... Point Judith, RI [*Location identifier*] [*FAA*] (FAAL)
PJI .... Proper Job Instruction (COE)
PJILMCC ... Philip C. Jessup International Law Moot Court Competition (EA)
PJIT .... Parts Just in Time
PJL .... Passive Jammer Location (SAUS)
P Jl .... Pharmaceutical Journal [*A publication*] (ROG)
PJL .... Power Jets, Limited
PJL .... Prejudicial [*Telegraphy*] (PCTE)
PJL .... Printer Job Language [*Computer science*]
PJLB .... Lower Burma Printed Judgments [*A publication*] (DLA)
PJLSRS ..... Pellien/Jaeger/Loretan/Steiner/Ross Society [*Association*] (EA)
PJM .... Pennsylvania-Jersey-Maryland [*Electric power pool*]
PJM .... Pennsylvania-New Jersey-Maryland (SAUS)
PJM .... Polymer Jell Material
PJM .... Positive Joint Mobilization [*Medicine*] (DMAA)
PJM .... Postjunctional Membrane
PJM .... Power Jets Memorandum
PJM .... Project Manager [*Military*]
PJMA .... Pakistan Jute Mills Association (SAUS)
PJM Interconnection... Pennsylvania-New Jersey-Maryland Interconnection (SAUS)
PJM Power Pool... Pennsylvania-New Jersey-Maryland Power Pool (SAUS)
PJN .... Fort Lauderdale, FL [*Location identifier*] [*FAA*] (FAAL)
PJN .... Posteriojugalis Nerve (SAUS)
PJN .... Projection [*Telegraphy*] (PCTE)
PJNF .... Project Join Normal Form (SAUS)
PJNS .... John Perez and Sons [*Common carrier symbol*]
PJo .... Cambria County Library System, Johnstown, PA [*Library symbol*] [*Library of Congress*] (LCLS)
PJO .... Pioneer Jupiter Orbit [*NASA*]
PJON .... Johnston Island/Johnston Atoll [*Johnston Island*] [*ICAO location identifier*] (ICLI)
PJOP .... Preliminary Joint Operation Procedure (KSC)
PJoU .... University of Pittsburgh at Johnstown, Johnstown, PA [*Library symbol*] [*Library of Congress*] (LCLS)
PJOX .... O'Donnell and Sons [*Private rail car owner code*]
PJP .... Pancreatic Juice Protein [*Medicine*] (DMAA)
PJP .... Probate Judge of the Peace (GEAB)
PJPC .... Plug/Jack Patch Cord
PJPEG .... Progressive JPEG (SAUS)
PJR .... Peoria, IL [*Location identifier*] [*FAA*] (FAAL)
PJR .... Perjure [*Telegraphy*] (PCTE)
PJR .... Peterson, J. Robert, New York NY [*STAC*]
PJR .... Philadelphia Journalism Review [*A publication*]
PJR .... Pipe Joint Record (DNAB)
PJR .... Port Jersey [*AAR code*]
PJR .... Power Jets Report
P Jr & H .... Patton, Jr., and Heath's Reports [*Virginia Special Court of Appeals*] [*A publication*] (DLA)
PJRL .... Penn-Jersey Rail Lines [*Federal Railroad Administration identification code*]
PJS .... Jet Aviation, Business Jets AG [*Switzerland*] [*ICAO designator*] (FAAC)
PJS .... Newport News, VA [*Location identifier*] [*FAA*] (FAAL)
PJ's .... Pajamas [*Slang*]
PJ's .... Paramedic Jumpers
PJS .... Peripheral Jet (Skegs)
PJS .... Peritoneojugular Shunt [*Medicine*] (DB)
PJS .... Peutz-Jeghers Syndrome [*Oncology*]
PJ's .... Physical Jerks [*Exercise*] [*Slang*] [*British*] (DSUE)
PJS .... Piezojunction Sensor
PJS .... Plug and Jack Set
PJS .... Prejudices [*Telegraphy*] (PCTE)

PJS Production Job Sheet
PJSOR Proposed Joint Services Operational Requirement (SAUS)
PJSS PACAF [*Pacific Air Forces*] Jungle Survival School (AFM)
PJST Peace & Justice Studies (SAUS)
PJT Paroxysmal Junctional Tachycardia [*Cardiology*]
PJT Practical Job Training (MCD)
PJT Project [*Telegraphy*] (PCTE)
PJT Pulse Jitter Tester
PJTD Projected [*Telegraphy*] (PCTE)
PJTG Projecting [*Telegraphy*] (PCTE)
PJTM PJ Trailer Manufacturing [*NCIC trailer make code*]
PJTN Projection (MSA)
PJTP Portable Job Ticket Processor (RALS)
PJTR Projector (MSA)
PJTV Projectavision, Inc. [*NASDAQ symbol*] (SAG)
PJTVP Projectavision $0.40 Cv'B'Pfd [*NASDAQ symbol*] (TTSB)
PJTVW Projectavision Inc. Wrrt [*NASDAQ symbol*] (TTSB)
PJU Juniata College, Huntingdon, PA [*OCLC symbol*] (OCLC)
PJU Physician's Journal Update [*Television program*]
PJV Pump Jet Vehicle
PJVT Paroxysmal Junctional-Ventricular Tachycardia [*Medicine*] (MEDA)
PJWC Pulse Jet Water Cannon [*Police and security equipment*]
PJXI PJAX [*Common carrier symbol*]
PJY Perjury [*Telegraphy*] (PCTE)
PJYLARC Penn Jersey Young Ladies Amateur Radio Certificate (SAUS)
PK Central Parking [*NYSE symbol*] (TTSB)
PK Central Parking Corp. [*NYSE symbol*] (SAG)
pK Dissociation Constant [*Chemistry*] (DAVI)
PK Indonesia [*Civil aircraft markings - international*] (PIPO)
PK Kill Probability (SAUS)
pK' Negative Log of the Dissociation Constant [*Medicine*]
PK Pack (AAG)
PK Package [*Shipping*] (MCD)
PK Pakistan [*ANSI two-letter standard code*] (CNC)
pk Pakistan [*IYRU nationality code*] [*MARC country of publication code*] [*Library of Congress*] (LCCP)
Pk Park (DD)
pk Park (VRA)
PK Park [*or Parking*]
PK Parrot-Kaufmann (DB)
PK Particular [*Telegraphy*] (PCTE)
PK Paterson-Kelly [*Syndrome*] [*Medicine*] (DB)
PK Peak [*Valve*] (NAKS)
Pk Peak (NTIO)
PK Peak [*Maps and charts*]
pK Peak Value [*Computer science*]
PK Peck (AAG)
pk Peck (DMAA)
PK Penalty Kick [*Soccer*]
PK Penetrating Keratoplasty [*Ophthalmology*] (DAVI)
PK Pericardial Knock [*Medicine*] (DB)
PK Peter King [*Afro-jazz band*]
PK Pharmacokinetic
PK Phileleftheron Komma [*Liberal Party*] [*Greek*] [*Political party*] (PPE)
PK Pig Kidney [*Medicine*] (DMAA)
PK Pike
Pk Pink (SAUS)
PK Piringer-Kuschinka [*Syndrome*] [*Medicine*] (DB)
PK Place Kicker [*Football*] (GOBB)
pk Plank [*Construction term*] (MIST)
P_K Plasma Potassium [*Biochemistry*] (DAVI)
PK Pokhvala Knige [*A publication*]
PK Pole Cat [*Slang*]
PK Polyketone (EDCT)
PK Polymerization Kinetics (SAUS)
PK Position Keeper
PK Posta Kutusu [*Postbox*] [*Turkish*] (EY)
PK Prausnitz-Kuestner [*Reaction*] [*Immunology*]
PK Prausnitz-Kunstner [*Reaction or Transfer Test*] [*Medicine*] (DAVI)
PK Preacher's Kid [*Slang*]
PK Preknock (SAUS)
PK Pridie Kalendas [*The Day before the Calends*] [*Latin*]
PK Primary Key [*Computer science*] (PCM)
PK Principal Keeper [*Slang for a warden*]
PK Printing Key (SAUS)
PK Probability of Kill (MCD)
pK Probability of Kill [*Military*] (POLM)
PK Probable Kill (SAUS)
PK Programmed Keyboard (SAUS)
PK Prophets and Kings (BJA)
PK Protection Key (VLIE)
PK Protein Kinase [*Also, PKase*] [*An enzyme*]
Pk Psychokinesis (DIPS)
PK Psychokinesis
PK Psychokinetic (DB)
PK Public Key (VLIE)
PK Pyruvate Kinase [*An enzyme*]
PK Pyruvate Kinase Deficiency Database (MHID)
PK Soviet Light Machine Gun
PK West Irian [*Aircraft nationality and registration mark*] (FAAC)
P-K4 Pawn to King Four [*Standard opening to a game of chess. Pawn is moved to the fourth square in front of the king*]
PKA Equator Airlines Ltd. [*Kenya*] [*ICAO designator*] (FAAC)
PKA Napaskiak [*Alaska*] [*Airport symbol*] (OAG)
PKA Napaskiak, AK [*Location identifier*] [*FAA*] (FAAL)
pKa Negative Log of Dissociation Constant [*Medicine*] (DAVI)
PKA Paul Kagan Associates, Inc. [*Information service or system*] [*Telecommunications*] (IID)
PKA Pi Kappa Alpha [*Fraternity*]
PKA Polk Audio [*AMEX symbol*] (SAG)
PKA Prekallikrein Activator [*Medicine*] (MELL)
PKA Primary Knock-on-Atom (MCD)
PKA Professional Karate Association [*Defunct*] (EA)
PKA Prokininogenase [*An enzyme*] (MAE)
PKA Protein Kinase A [*An enzyme*]
PKA Public Key Algorithm [*Computer science*]
PKAD Accumulated Dose Special Process (SAUS)
PkAF Pakistani Air Force
PKAFA PKA [*Professional Karate Association*] Fighters Association [*Defunct*] (EA)
PKAR Protein Kinase Activation Ratio [*Medicine*] (DMAA)
PKAS Parti Kadazan Asli Sabah [*Malaysia*] [*Political party*] (FEA)
PKase Protein Kinase [*Also, PK*] [*An enzyme*]
PKAWA Pocket Knife Ancillary Workers' Association [*A union*] [*British*]
PKB Parkersburg [*West Virginia*] [*Airport symbol*] (OAG)
PKB Parkersburg, WV [*Location identifier*] [*FAA*] (FAAL)
PKB Parking Brake [*Automotive engineering*]
PKB Photoelectric Keyboard
PKB Portable Keyboard
PKB Protein Kinase B [*An enzyme*]
PKB Public Key Block (VLIE)
PKBS Preschool and Kindergarten Behavior Scales [*Test*] (TMMY)
PKC Cocoa, FL [*Location identifier*] [*FAA*] (FAAL)
PKC Pannill Knitting Company, Inc. [*NYSE symbol*] (COMM)
PKC Peckham Road [*California*] [*Seismograph station code, US Geological Survey*] (SEIS)
PKC Phuket [*Thailand*] [*Airport symbol*] (AD)
PKC Position Keeping Computer
PKC Problem-Knowledge Coupler (DMAA)
PKC Protein Kinase C [*An enzyme*]
PKC Public Key Cryptography
PKCS Public Key Cryptographic System (VLIE)
PKCS Public Key Cryptography Standards [*Telecommunications service*]
PKD Pac Ed Systems Corp. [*Vancouver Stock Exchange symbol*]
PKD Packed (IAA)
pkd Packed
PKD Parker Drilling [*NYSE symbol*] (TTSB)
PKD Parker Drilling Co. [*NYSE symbol*] (SPSG)
PKD Park Rapids, MN [*Location identifier*] [*FAA*] (FAAL)
PKD Partially Knocked Down [*Consignment*] [*Shipping*] (DS)
PKD Partly Knocked Down (SAUS)
PKD Philip K. Dick [*Science fiction writer*]
PKD Pi Kappa Delta [*Society*]
PKD Polycystic Kidney Disease [*Medicine*]
PKD Programmable Keyboard and Display [*Computer science*] (NASA)
PKD Programmable Keyboard Display (SAUS)
PKD Proliferative Kidney Disease [*Medicine*] (DMAA)
PKD Pyruvate Kinase Deficiency [*Medicine*] (MELL)
PKDB Partai Kebang-Saan Demokratik Brunei [*Brunei National Democratic Party*] [*Political party*] (EY)
PKDG Professional Knitwear Designers Guild
PKDOM Pack for Domestic Use
PKD PDR Packed Powder (WGA)
PKDS Philip K. Dick Society [*Defunct*] (EA)
PKDT Packard Transport of Illinois [*Common carrier symbol*]
PKE Pacific Kenridge [*Vancouver Stock Exchange symbol*]
PKE Park Electrochemical [*NYSE symbol*] (TTSB)
PKE Park Electrochemical Corp. [*NYSE symbol*] (SPSG)
PKE Parker, CA [*Location identifier*] [*FAA*] (FAAL)
PKE Parkes [*Australia*] [*Airport symbol*] (OAG)
PKE Passive Keyless Entry [*Automotive term*] (HAWK)
Pke Pike (PROS)
PKE Pluto-Kuiper Express
PKE Positive Kinetic Energy [*Automotive emissions*]
PKE Public-Key Encryption [*Microcomputer technology*]
PKF Pakistan Investment Fd [*NYSE symbol*] (TTSB)
PKF Pakistan Investment Fund [*NYSE symbol*] (SPSG)
PKF Park Falls, WI [*Location identifier*] [*FAA*] (FAAL)
PKF Parkfield Array [*California*] [*Seismograph station code, US Geological Survey*] (SEIS)
PKF Permanent Kidney Failure (MELL)
PKF Phagocytosis and Killing Function [*Immunology*] (AAMN)
PKF Phosphofructokinase (DB)
PKF Polarity Correlation Function (IAA)
PKF Primary Kidney Fold
PKFC Princess Kitty Fan Club (EA)
pkfr Plank Frame [*Construction term*] (MIST)
pkg Package (WDMC)
PKG Package
PKG Packaging (SAUS)
PKG Packaging Corp. America [*NYSE symbol*] (SG)
Pkg Packing (DS)
PKG Packing [*Telegraphy*] (PCTE)
PKG Parking (KSC)
PKG Phonocardiogram [*Cardiology*]
PKG B/M Package Bill of Material (SAUS)
PKGD Packaged (IAA)
pkge Package (WDMC)

PKGE .... Package
Pkg instr... Packing Instruction (DS)
PKGNG ...... Packaging
PKG-POL.... Packaged POL [*Petroleum, Oils and Lubricants*] (DOMA)
Pkgs .... Packages (EBF)
PKG SPEC... Packaging Specifications (SAUS)
Pkg Technol Sci... Packaging Technology and Science (SAUS)
PKH.......... Park Hill [*California*] [*Seismograph station code, US Geological Survey*] (SEIS)
PKH.......... Probability of a Kill Given a Hit [*Military*] (DNAB)
PKHOW ..... Pack Howitzer [*Marine Corps*]
PKHP .... Pickens Railroad-Honea Path [*Federal Railroad Administration identification code*]
PKI........... Parkland Industries Ltd. [*Toronto Stock Exchange symbol*]
PKI........... Partai Katolik Indonesia [*Catholic Party of Indonesia*] [*Political party*]
PKI........... Partai Komunis Indonesia [*Communist Party of Indonesia*] [*Political party*]
PKI........... Partai Kristen Indonesia [*Christian Party of Indonesia*] [*Political party*]
PKI........... Perkinelmer [*Company symbol*]
PKI........... Potato Kallikrein Inhibitor [*Medicine*] (DMAA)
PKI........... Protein Kinase Inhibitor [*Biochemistry*]
PKI........... Public Key Infrastructure (AGLO)
PKI........... Pyruvate Kinase, Liver Type [*Medicine*] (DMAA)
PKJ .... Package [*Telegraphy*] (PCTE)
PKJCT .... Park Junction, PA [*American Association of Railroads railroad junction routing code*]
PKJT......... Jack Parker Trucking [*Common carrier symbol*]
PKK.......... Kurdish Workers' Party [*Turkey*] [*Political party*] (PD)
PKK.......... Kurdistan Workers' Party
PKK.......... Pakokku [*Myanmar*] [*Airport symbol*] (OAG)
PKK.......... Porkkala [*Finland*] [*Seismograph station code, US Geological Survey*] (SEIS)
PKK.......... Protein Kinase K [*An enzyme*]
PkKP......... Pakistan National Scientific and Documentation Center, Karachi, Pakistan [*Library symbol*] [*Library of Congress*] (LCLS)
PKL .... Parklane Technologies, Inc. [*Vancouver Stock Exchange symbol*]
PKL .... Pi Kappa Lambda [*Society*]
PKL .... Possum Kingdom Lake (SAUS)
PKLB .... PharmaKinetics Laboratories, Inc. [*NASDAQ symbol*] (COMM)
PK-LT........ Psychokinesis on Living Targets
PKM .... Packmaster [*Army*] (WGA)
PKM .... Perigee Kick Motor (MCD)
PKM .... Predicament [*Telegraphy*] (PCTE)
PKMA........ Eniwetok [*Marshall Islands*] [*ICAO location identifier*] (ICLI)
PKMAP ...... National Peoples' Pathan Brotherhood Party (Pakistan) [*Political party*] (PSAP)
PK-MB....... Psychokinetic Metal-Bending [*Parapsychology*]
PKMJ .... Majuro [*Marshall Islands*] [*ICAO location identifier*] (ICLI)
PKMKCMD... Perhaps...Kids Meeting Kids Can Make a Difference (EA)
Pkmr......... Packmaster [*Army*]
PKMS........ Pertubohan Kebangsaan Melayu Singapura [*Singapore Malays' National Organization*] [*Political party*] (FEA)
PKN.......... Aspen, CO [*Location identifier*] [*FAA*] (FAAL)
PKN.......... Pangkalanbuun [*Indonesia*] [*Airport symbol*] (OAG)
PKN.......... Parkinsonism [*Medicine*] (DMAA)
PKN.......... Pauken [*Kettledrums*]
PKN.......... Perkin-Elmer [*NYSE symbol*] (TTSB)
PKN.......... Perkin-Elmer Corp. [*NYSE symbol*] (SPSG)
PKNG HSE... Packing House [*Freight*]
PKO.......... Parakou [*Benin*] [*Airport symbol*] (OAG)
PKO.......... Peace-Keeping Operation (MCD)
PKO.......... Perdant par Knockout [*Losing by a Knockout*] [*French*]
PKOH........ Park-Ohio Holdings Corp. [*NASDAQ symbol*] (NASQ)
PKOH........ Park-Ohio Indus [*NASDAQ symbol*] (TTSB)
PKOH........ Park Ohio Industries [*NASDAQ symbol*] (SAG)
PKOH........ Park-Ohio Industries, Inc. [*NASDAQ symbol*] (NQ)
PKP.......... Palestiner Komunistische Partei [*Palestine Communist Party*] [*Political party*] (BJA)
PKP.......... Partido Komunista ng Pilipinas [*Communist Party of the Philippines*] [*Political party*] (PPW)
PKP.......... Penetrating Keratoplasty [*Ophthalmology*]
PKP.......... Perustuslaillinen Kansanpuolue [*Constitutional People's Party*] [*Finland*] [*Political party*] (PPE)
PKP.......... Phi Kappa Phi [*Honor society*] (AEE)
PKP.......... Polskie Koleje Panstwowe [*Polish State Railways*]
PKP.......... Praktische Krankenpflege (SAUS)
PKP.......... Predicted Kill Point (SAUS)
PKP.......... Preknock Pulse
PKP.......... Public Key Partners (VLIE)
PKP.......... Pukapuka [*Language symbol*] (ETLW)
PKP.......... Pukapuka [*French Polynesia*] [*Airport symbol*] (OAG)
PKP.......... Purple-K-Powder
pKp .... purple K powder (SAUS)
PKPA .... Parental Kidnapping Prevention Act (BARN)
PK/PK .... Peak-to-Peak (MCD)
PKpP .... Pennwalt Corp., King Of Prussia, PA [*Library symbol*] [*Library of Congress*] (LCLS)
PKPS .... [*The*] Poughkeepsie Savings Bank FSB [*Poughkeepsie, NY*] [*NASDAQ symbol*] (NQ)
PKPS .... Poughkeepsie Svgs Bank [*NASDAQ symbol*] (TTSB)
PKPT .... PacketPort.com, Inc. [*NASDAQ symbol*] (QUAN)
PKQ.......... Dallas-Fort Worth, TX [*Location identifier*] [*FAA*] (FAAL)
PKR.......... Packer (WGA)
PKR.......... Phased Knee Rehabilitation (DMAA)
PKR.......... Picker
PKR.......... P. K. Le Roux Dam [*South Africa*] [*Seismograph station code, US Geological Survey*] (SEIS)
PKR.......... Pokhara [*Nepal*] [*Airport symbol*] (OAG)
PKR.......... Polycystic Kidney Research Foundation (PAZ)
PKR.......... Protein Kinase Resource [*Database*] (GDD)
PKR.......... The Protein Kinase Resource (MHID)
PKRDD ...... Pravitel'stvennaya Komissiya po Raketam Dalnego Deistviya [*State Commission for the Study of the Problems of Long-Range Rockets*] [*Former USSR*]
PKRZ .... Pineville Kraft [*Federal Railroad Administration identification code*]
PKs .... Bayard Taylor Memorial Library, Kennett Square, PA [*Library symbol*] [*Library of Congress*] (LCLS)
PKS.......... Packs of Cigarettes Smoked
PKS.......... Particulars [*Telegraphy*] (PCTE)
PKS.......... Parti Kongres Sarawak [*Malaysia*] [*Political party*] (EY)
PKS.......... Perigee Kick Stage (ACAE)
PKS.......... Phi Kappa Sigma [*Fraternity*]
PKS.......... Photo-Kit System (SAUS)
PKS.......... Polyketide Synthase [*An enzyme*]
PKS.......... Public Key System [*Communications term*] (DCT)
PKS.......... Six Flags [*NYSE symbol*]
PKSAP....... Psychiatric Knowledge and Skills Self-Assessment Program (SAUS)
PKSEA....... Packed for Overseas Use (SAUS)
PKSEA....... Pack for Overseas
PKSh .... Partia Komuniste e Shqiperise [*Communist Party of Albania*] [*Later, PPSh*] [*Political party*] (PPE)
PKSI .... Primus Knowledge Solutions [*NASDAQ symbol*] (SG)
PKsL......... Longwood Gardens Library, Kennett Square, PA [*Library symbol*] [*Library of Congress*] (LCLS)
PKSRP ...... Possum Kingdom State Recreation Park (SAUS)
PKSS .... Probability of Kill Single Shot (MCD)
pkt .... Packet (SHCU)
PKT .... Packet
PKT .... Partition Knowledge Table (MWOL)
PKT .... Phase Keying Technique
PKT .... Phi Kappa Tau [*Fraternity*]
PKT .... Pittsburgh Theological Seminary, Pittsburgh, PA [*OCLC symbol*] (OCLC)
PKT .... Pocket (MSA)
Pkt .... Prakrit [*Linguistics*] (IEL)
PKTF......... Printing and Kindred Trades Federation (SAUS)
PKTN .... Pinkerton's, Inc. [*NASDAQ symbol*] (SAG)
PKTR .... Packeteer, Inc. [*NASDAQ symbol*] (SG)
PKU.......... Peculiar [*Telegraphy*] (PCTE)
PKU.......... Pekanbaru [*Indonesia*] [*Airport symbol*] (OAG)
PKU.......... Phenylketonuria [*Congenital metabolism disorder*] [*Medicine*]
PKU.......... Pianoforte Keymakers' Union [*British*]
PKULY....... Peculiarly [*Telegraphy*] (PCTE)
PKU-P .... PKU [*Phenylketonuria*] Parents (EA)
PKuS .... Kutztown State College, Kutztown, PA [*Library symbol*] [*Library of Congress*] (LCLS)
PKUY .... Peculiarity [*Telegraphy*] (PCTE)
PKV .... Killed Poliomyelitis Vaccine [*Immunology*] (MAE)
PKV .... Peak Kilovolt (SAUS)
pkV .... Peak Kilovoltage (RAWO)
PkV .... Peak Kilovolts
PKV .... Port Lavaka, TX [*Location identifier*] [*FAA*] (FAAL)
PK/VAL ...... Peak-to-Valley (SAUS)
PKVL .... Pikeville National [*NASDAQ symbol*] (TTSB)
PKVL .... Pikeville National Corp. [*NASDAQ symbol*] (NQ)
PKW .... Kenosha, WI [*Location identifier*] [*FAA*] (FAAL)
PKW .... Personenkraftwagen [*Automobile*] [*German*]
PKW .... Selebi-Phikwe [*Botswana*] [*Airport symbol*] (OAG)
PKWA........ Kwajalein [*Marshall Islands*] [*ICAO location identifier*] (ICLI)
PKWAY...... Parkway (MSA)
P/kWh ...... Pennies per Kilowatt Hour (SAUS)
Pkwy......... Parkway (ASC)
pkwy......... Parkway (MIST)
PKWY .... Parkway (KSC)
PKWY .... [*The*] Parkway Co. [*NASDAQ symbol*] (NQ)
PKWYS...... Parkways [*Commonly used*] (OPSA)
PKX.......... Pohang Iron & Steel ADS [*NYSE symbol*] (TTSB)
PKX.......... Pohang Iron & Steel Co., Ltd. [*NYSE symbol*] (SAG)
PKXP .... Parker's Express [*Common carrier symbol*]
PKY.......... Pak Lay [*Laos*] [*Airport symbol*] (AD)
PKY.......... Palangkaraya [*Indonesia*] [*Airport symbol*] (OAG)
Pky........... Parkway (DD)
PKY.......... Parkway (MCD)
PKY.......... Parkway Properties [*NYSE symbol*]
PKY.......... Particularly [*Telegraphy*] (PCTE)
PKY.......... Pecky (WGA)
Pky........... Pecky (WPI)
PKZ.......... Pakse [*Laos*] [*Airport symbol*] (AD)
PKZ.......... Particularize [*Telegraphy*] (PCTE)
PKZ.......... Pensacola, FL [*Location identifier*] [*FAA*] (FAAL)
PKZIP........ Phil Katz's Zip (VLIE)
PL............ Aero Peru [*ICAO designator*] (AD)
PL............ Front Line [*Revolutionary group*] [*Italy*]
PL............ Lancaster County Library, Lancaster, PA [*Library symbol*] [*Library of Congress*] (LCLS)
PL............ Pacific Lumber [*Federal Railroad Administration identification code*]
PL............ Packaging List (SAUS)
PL............ Packing List
PL............ Padlock (AAG)

PL............ Pail
PL............ Palm Leaf [*Reaction*] [*Medicine*]
PL............ Pamphlet Law (SAUS)
PL............ Pamphlet Laws [*A publication*] (DLA)
PL............ Panel Left [*Nuclear energy*] (NRCH)
p/l............ panial loss (SAUS)
PL............ Panoramic Lens (SAUS)
PL............ Paperleg [*A favored student*] [*Teen slang*]
PL............ Paper Life Ltd. [*British*]
PL............ Paper Loss (MHDW)
PL............ Paradise Lost (SAUS)
PL............ Parameter List (SAUS)
PL............ Parish Line R. R. [*AAR code*]
PL............ Parity Low Bit (VLIE)
PL............ Partial Loss [*Insurance*]
PL............ Partido Liberal [*Liberal Party*] [*Peru*] [*Political party*] (EY)
PL............ Partido Liberal [*Liberal Party*] [*Colombia*] [*Political party*] (EY)
PL............ Partido Liberal [*Liberal Party*] [*Portugal*] [*Political party*] (PPE)
PL............ Partido Liberal [*Liberal Party*] [*Paraguay*] [*Political party*] (PPW)
PL............ Partido Liberal [*Liberal Party*] [*Honduras*] [*Political party*]
PL............ Partido Liberal [*Liberal Party*] [*Panama*] [*Political party*] (PPW)
PL............ Partido Liberal [*Liberal Party*] [*Spain*] [*Political party*] (PPE)
PL............ Partido Libertador [*Liberating Party*] [*Brazil*] [*Political party*]
PL............ Parti Liberal [*Liberal Party (1974-1979)*] [*Belgium*] [*Political party*] (PPE)
PL............ Parting Line [*Castings*] (AAG)
PL............ Parts List
PL............ Party Line (SAUS)
PL............ Passenger Liability [*Insurance*] (BARN)
PL............ Pastoral Lease (SAUS)
PL............ Patch Loader (SAUS)
PL............ Patent Licence (SAUS)
PL............ Patent Location (NITA)
PL............ Patent Log (SAUS)
PL............ Path Length (SAUS)
PL............ Path Link (SAUS)
PL............ Path Loss [*Communications*]
PL............ Patriot League (PSS)
PL............ Patrol Land [*Aviation*]
PL............ Patrologiae Cursus. Series Latina [*A publication*] (OCD)
Pl............ Paul (BJA)
PL............ Paulist League (EA)
P/L............ Pay Load (ACAE)
PL............ Payload [*NASA*] (KSC)
PL............ Payload Length (SAUS)
PL............ Paymaster-Lieutenant [*Navy*] [*British*]
PL............ Peak Loss (IAA)
PL............ Peanut Leafspot [*Plant pathology*]
PL............ Pearl Language (SAUS)
PL............ Pectate Lyase [*An enzyme*]
Pl............ Pelagius [*Deceased, 1232*] [*Authority cited in pre-1607 legal work*] (DSA)
PL............ Pelusium Line [*Nile delta*] [*Geology*]
pl............ Pencil (VRA)
PL............ People for Life (EA)
PL............ People's Lobby (EA)
PL............ Perceived Level [*Noise*]
PL............ Perception of Light
PL............ Periodic Line (ELAL)
PL............ Peroneus Longus [*Muscle*] [*Orthopedics*] (DAVI)
P/L............ Personal Lines
PL............ Personnel Laboratory [*Air Research and Development Command*] [*Air Force*] (AAG)
PL............ Personnel Letters (SAUS)
PL............ Petro-Lewis Corp. (EFIS)
PL............ Petro-Lewis Corporation (EFIS)
PL............ Petty Larceny
PL............ Pharmacopoeia of London (SAUS)
PL............ Phase Line
PL............ Phase Locking (SAUS)
PL............ Philosophical Library [*A publication*]
PL............ Phlogopite (SAUS)
PL............ Phone Line
PL............ Phospholipid [*Biochemistry*]
PL............ Photoconductor Lamp (IAA)
PL............ Photolettering (DGA)
PL............ Photolithography (SAUS)
PL............ Photolocator (MCD)
PL............ Photoluminescence
PL............ Physical Layer (VLIE)
PL............ Physical Limnology (SAUS)
pl............ Piazza (VRA)
pl............ Picoliter [*One trillionth of a liter*] (MAE)
PL............ Pilatus Flugzeugwerke AG [*Switzerland*] [*ICAO aircraft manufacturer identifier*] (ICAO)
PL............ Pile
PL............ Pilot Lamp (ELAL)
PL............ Pilot Line (SAUS)
PL............ Pinelands Inc. (EFIS)
PL............ Pipeline
PL............ Pipe Lines Act [*Town planning*] [*British*]
PL............ Piping Load [*Nuclear energy*] (NRCH)
PL............ Piping Loads (SAUS)
PL............ Pitch Line (MSA)
Pl............ Place (TBD)
pl............ Place (VRA)
PL............ Place
PL............ Placebo [*Medicine*]
PL............ Placental Lactogen [*Endocrinology*]
PL............ Placic [*Soil biology*] [*Soil phases*] (QSUL)
Pl............ Plagioclase [*Lunar geology*]
PL............ Plain (MSA)
PL............ Plain Language [*As opposed to coded message*] [*Military*]
PL............ Planning (ALAC)
PL............ Plans
PL............ Plantagenet [*Genealogy*] (ROG)
PL............ Plantar [*Related to the sole of the foot*] (DAVI)
pl............ Plasma
Pl............ Plasmodium [*The malarial parasite*] [*Infectious diseases*] (DAVI)
PL............ Plaster (WGA)
PL............ Plastic Laboratory [*Princeton University*] (MCD)
P/L............ Plastic Laminate [*Construction term*] (MIST)
PL............ Plastic Limit (IEEE)
PL............ Plastic Surgery [*Medicine*]
pl............ Plastid [*Botany*]
pl............ Plate (DIAR)
pl............ Plate (MIST)
pl............ Plate (KSC)
PL............ Plateau Length
PL............ Plated (IAA)
pl............ Platelet [*Hematology*] (MAE)
PL............ Platelet Lactogen [*Hematology*] (DMAA)
PL............ Platinum [*Chemistry*] (ROG)
Pl............ Plato [*Fourth century BC*] [*Classical studies*] (OCD)
pl............ Platoon (MILB)
PL............ Platoon (NATG)
PL............ Platoon Leader [*Military*] (INF)
PL............ Platz [*Square*] [*German*] (EY)
pl............ Platz (VRA)
PL............ Plauen [*German license plate city code*]
PL............ Players League [*Major league in baseball, 1890*]
pl............ Plaza (VRA)
PL............ PLC Capital LLC, Inc. [*NYSE symbol*] (SAG)
PL............ Pleadings [*Legal shorthand*] (LWAP)
PL............ Pleasure (ROG)
PL............ [*The*] Plessey Co. Ltd. (MCD)
pl............ Pleural [*Medicine*] (MAE)
Pl............ Plexus (SAUS)
PL............ Plimsoll Line [*Shipping*] (DAS)
PL............ Ploshchad [*Square*] [*Russian*] (EY)
PL............ Plotter (SAUS)
Pl............ Plowden's English King's Bench Commentaries [*or Reports*] [*1550-80*] [*A publication*] (DLA)
PL............ Plug (AAG)
PL............ Plugged (SAUS)
PL............ Plume [*Numismatics*]
pl............ Plural (ODBW)
PL............ Plural
pl............ Plus (ELAL)
PL............ Pluto (SAUS)
PL............ Plymouth [*Postcode*] (ODBW)
PL............ Poet Laureate
PL............ Poetry London [*A publication*] [*British*]
Pl............ Poiseuille [*Unit of dynamic viscosity*]
PL............ Poland [*ANSI two-letter standard code*] (CNC)
pl............ Poland [*MARC country of publication code*] [*Library of Congress*] (LCCP)
Pl............ Poland (MILB)
PL............ Polarized Light
PL............ Policy Loan
PL............ Poly-L-lysine [*Also, PLL*] [*Biochemical analysis*]
PL............ Poor Law [*A publication*] (DLA)
PL............ Portable Low-Power [*Reactor*] (NRCH)
PL............ Port Line [*Steamship*] (MHDW)
PL............ Position Line [*Navigation*]
PL............ Position Location [*DoD*]
PL............ Post Landing [*NASA*] (KSC)
PL............ Post Laundry [*Army*]
PL............ Powered Lift (SAUS)
PL............ Power Line (IAA)
PL............ Power Loading (IAA)
PL............ Power Locks (BARN)
PL............ Prayers for Life (EA)
PL............ Prelaunch (NASA)
PL............ Preliminary Leaf [*Bibliography*]
P/L............ Presentation Label [*Publishing*]
PL............ Presentation Layer (SAUS)
PL............ Presley Labs [*Vancouver Stock Exchange symbol*]
PL............ Pressurizer Level (IEEE)
PL............ Price Level [*Economics*]
PL............ Price List
PL............ Primary Leading [*Photography*] (DGA)
PL............ Primrose League [*British*] (DI)
PL............ Prince Line [*Steamship*] (MHDW)
PL............ Princess Louise's Sutherland and Argyll Highlanders [*Military*] [*British*] (ROG)
PL............ Private Label [*Business term*]
PL............ Private Line

PL Probabilistic Logic (SAUS)
PL Probability of Leakage (ACAE)
PL Procedural Language (PCM)
PL Procedure Library [*Computer science*]
PL Production Language
PL Production License (FOTI)
PL Production List (AAG)
PL Product Liability [*Insurance*]
PL Product License
PL Products Liability (SAUS)
PL Professional Librarian (SAUS)
P/L Profit and Loss [*Accounting*]
PL Program Level (IAA)
PL Program Library [*Computer science*]
PL Program Logic [*Computer science*] (TEL)
PL Programmed Learning (SAUS)
PL Programming Language [*Computer science*]
PL Programming Logics (SAUS)
PL Progressive Labor [*A faction of Students for a Democratic Society*]
PL Projection Lens [*Microscopy*]
PL Project Launch [*Automotive engineering*]
PL Project Leader
PL Project Lighthawk [*Later, LH*] (EA)
PL Project Local [*Defunct*] (EA)
PL Proliferative Layer (SAUS)
PL Prolymphocytic Leukemia [*Also, PLL*] [*Oncology*]
PL Promotion List (DICI)
PL Propagation Loss
PL Propellant Loading [*NASA*] (KSC)
PL Property Line [*Real estate*] (MSA)
PL Proportionality Limit (SAUS)
PL Proportional Limit
P/L Proprietary Limited (ADA)
PL Propulsion Laboratory [*Army*] (GRD)
PL Prospective Loss
PL Protected Location [*Shipping*] (DS)
PL Protective Life Corp. [*NYSE symbol*] (SPSG)
PL Protectively Located [*Plant layout*]
PL Provisioning List (MCD)
PL Proximity Log (SAUS)
PL Pseudolumina [*Anatomy*]
PL Psychological Laboratory (MCD)
PL Public Law [*An act of Congress*]
PL Public Liability [*Business term*]
PL Public Library
Pl Pulmonary Venous Pressure [*Medicine*] (MAE)
PL Pulpolingual [*Dentistry*]
PL Pulsatility Index [*Medicine*]
PL Pulsed Laser (SAUS)
PL Pulse Length (NVT)
P/L Purchased Labor (NASA)
PL Purple-glow Lamp (SAUS)
PL Pyridoxal [*Also, Pxl*] [*Biochemistry*]
PL Radio Positioning Land Station [*ITU designation*] (CET)
P Transpulmonary Pressure [*Cardiology*] (DAVI)
PL/1 Programming Language, Version One [*Computer science*] (MCD)
PLA Pacific Locomotive Association [*Federal Railroad Administration identification code*]
PLA Pakistan Liberation Army (PD)
PLA Pakistan Librarians Association (SAUS)
PLA Palau [*Palau Islands*] [*Seismograph station code, US Geological Survey*] [*Closed*] (SEIS)
PLA Palestine Liberation Army
PLA Panchromatic Linear Array (SAUS)
PLA Parachute Location Aid (MCD)
PLA Para Legal Association [*British*] (DBA)
PLA Parlamento Latinoamericano [*Latin American Parliament - LAP*] [*Bogota, Colombia*] (EAIO)
PLA Parlar Resources Ltd. [*Vancouver Stock Exchange symbol*]
PLA Partial Look Ahead (SAUS)
PLA Partido Laborista Agrario [*Panama*] [*Political party*] (EY)
PLA Partido Liberal Autentico [*Panama*] [*Political party*] (EY)
PLA Party of Labor of Albania [*Political party*] (PPW)
PLA Passengers' Luggage in Advance [*Railway*] (ROG)
PLA Patent Licensing Agreement (SEWL)
PLA Patriotic Liberation Army [*Myanmar*] (PD)
PLA Pedestrian League of America [*Later, APA*] (EA)
Pla Pelagius [*Deceased, 1232*] [*Authority cited in pre-1607 legal work*] (DSA)
PLA Pennilane Development [*Vancouver Stock Exchange symbol*]
PLA People's Liberation Army [*India*] (PD)
PLA People's Liberation Army [*National Liberation Front*] [*North Vietnam*] (VNW)
PLA People's Liberation Army [*China*]
PLA Peripheral Laser Angioplast [*Medicine*] (EDAA)
PLA Pet Lovers Association (EA)
PLA Phase Locked Arrays [*Physics*]
PLA Phenyl Lactate [*Medicine*] (EDAA)
PLA Philadelphia Library Association (SAUS)
PLA Philatelic Literature Association [*Later, APRL*] (EA)
PLA Phospholipase A [*An enzyme*] (DAVI)
PLA Phospholipid Antibody [*Medicine*] (EDAA)
PLA Physiological Learning Aptitude (KSC)
PLA Pitch Lock Actuator (MCD)
PLA Place (ADA)
PLA Placebo [*Medicine*]
PLA Placebo Therapy [*Medicine*] (EDAA)
Pla Placentinus [*Deceased, 1192*] [*Authority cited in pre-1607 legal work*] (DSA)
PLA Placita
PLA Placitum [*or Placita*] [*Agreeable, Agreed Upon*] [*Latin*] [*Legal term*] (DLA)
PLA Plain Language Address [*Telecommunications*] (TEL)
PLA Plain Language Addressee (SAUS)
PLA Planned Labor Application [*Military*] (AFIT)
PLA Planned Landing Area [*NASA*]
PLA Plan of Launch Azimuth [*Aerospace*] (AAG)
PLA Plasma Resin Activity (SAUS)
PLA Plasminogen Activator [*Medicine*] (EDAA)
pla Plaster (VRA)
PLA Platelet Antigen (DB)
PLA Playboy Enterprises Cl'B' [*NYSE symbol*] (TTSB)
PLA Playboy Enterprises, Inc. [*NYSE symbol*] (SPSG)
PLA Plaza (ADA)
PLA Plaza (automobile) [*NCIC car model code*]
PLA Poetry League of America (EA)
PLA Polyactide [*Chemistry term*]
PLA Polylactic Acid [*Organic chemistry*] (RDA)
PLA Poly-L-arginine [*Biochemistry*]
PLA Polynesian Air-Ways [*ICAO designator*] (FAAC)
PLA Popular Library of Art [*A publication*]
PLA Port of London Authority [*British*]
PLA Posterior Left Atrial Wall [*Cardiology*]
PLA Potential Leaf Area [*Botany*]
PLA Potentially Lethal Arrhythmia [*Medicine*] (DMAA)
PLA Power Lever Angle
PLA Practice Landing Approach [*Aviation*]
PLA Practise Low Approach (SAUS)
PLA Prescribed Load Allowance (SAUS)
PLA Price-Level-Adjusted Accounting (ADA)
PLA Print Load Analyzer
PLA Private Libraries Association [*British*]
PLA Procaine/Lactic Acid [*Medicine*] (EDAA)
PLA Product Liability Act (SAUS)
PLA Product License Application [*FDA*]
PLA Professional Legal Assistants (EA)
PLA Program-Length Advertising [*Broadcasting*] (WDMC)
PLA Programmable Line Adapter
PLA Programmable Link Adapter
PLA Programmable Logic Array [*Computer science*]
PLA Project Labor Agreement (AAGC)
PLA Proton Linear Acceleration (or Accelerator) (SAUS)
PLA Provident Life & Accident Insurance Co. (EFIS)
PLA Psycholinguistic Age [*Education*]
PLA Psychological Learning Aptitude (MCD)
PLA Public Library Association (EA)
PLa Pulpolabial [*Dentistry*]
PLA Pulpolinguoaxial [*Dentistry*]
PLA Pulsed LASER Annealing [*Semiconductor technology*]
PLA Pulverized Limestone Association (EA)
PLA University of Pittsburgh, Law School, Pittsburgh, PA [*OCLC symbol*] (OCLC)
PLA_2 Phospholipase A_2 [*An enzyme*]
PLAA Playboy Enterprises'A'(vtg) [*NYSE symbol*] (TTSB)
PLAA Positive Low Angle of Attack
PLA AEPS PLA [*Public Library Association*] Alternative Education Programs Section
PLAAF People's Liberation Army Air Force
PLA AFLS PLA [*Public Library Association*] Armed Forces Library Section
PLAALLS Public Library Association Adult Life Long Learning Services
PLAAR Packaged Liquid Air-Augmented Rocket (MCD)
PLAAS Plasma Atomic Absorption System [*Spectrometry*]
PLA AV PLA [*Public Library Association*] Audiovisual
PLA AVC PLA [*Public Library Association*] Audiovisual Committee
PLAB Party-Line Adapter Board [*Telecommunications*] (MHDI)
PLAB Philadelphia Library Association Bulletin (SAUS)
PLAB Photronics, Inc. [*NASDAQ symbol*] (NQ)
PLAB Professional and Linguistic Assessment Board (AIE)
PLA Bull Pennsylvania Library Association Bulletin (SAUS)
PLAC Placebo [*Medicine*]
Plac Placentinus [*Deceased, 1192*] [*Authority cited in pre-1607 legal work*] (DSA)
PLAC Plastic Engineers & Consultants [*NCIC trailer make code*]
PLAC Post-Launch Analysis of Compliance [*NASA*]
Plac Abbrev Placitorum Abbreviatio [*Latin*] [*A publication*] (DLA)
Plac Ang Nor Bigelow's Placita Anglo-Normanica [*A publication*] (DLA)
PLACE Place [*Commonly used*] (OPSA)
PLACE Placedo, TX [*American Association of Railroads railroad junction routing code*]
PLACE Placement
PLACE Positioner Layout and Cell Evaluator [*Robotics*]
PLACE Position Location and Aircraft Communication Equipment
PLACE Position Location and Aircraft Equipment (SAUS)
PLACE Position Location and Communications Experiment [*NASA*]
PLACE Post-LANDSAT Advanced Concept Evaluation (MCD)
PLACE Programa Latinoamericano de Cooperacion Energetica [*Latin American Energy Cooperation Program*] (EAIO)
PLACE Programming Language for Automatic Checkout Equipment

PlacerD ..... Placer Dome, Inc. [*Associated Press*] (SAG)
Plac Gen .... Placita Generalia [*Latin*] [*A publication*] (DLA)
PLACID ...... Payload Aboard, Caution in Descent [*NASA*]
PLA CIS ..... PLA [*Public Library Association*] Community Information Section
PLACO .... Planning Committee [*International Organization for Standardization*] (IEEE)
PLACY .... Plaster City, CA [*American Association of Railroads railroad junction routing code*]
PLAD .... Paperless LANTIRN Automated Depot (SAUS)
PLAD .... Parachute Low-Altitude Delivery [*Air Force*]
PLAD .... Plain Language Address Directory
PLAD .... Plasma Diode (SAUS)
PLAD .... Price-Level-Adjusted Deposit
PLAD .... Public Lands Appreciation Day [*A joint effort of Times Mirror Magazines and the Bureau of Land Management*] (PS)
PLADS .... Parachute Low-Altitude Delivery System [*Military*]
PLADS .... Plain Language Address System (SAUS)
PLADs .... Price Level Adjusted Deposits (SAUS)
PLADS .... Pulsed LASER Airborne Depth Sounding System [*Naval Oceanographic Office*]
PLADS .... Pulsed Light Airborne Depth Sounder (SAUS)
PLADS System ... Pulsed Laser Airborne Depth Sounding System (SAUS)
PLAF .... People's Liberation Armed Forces [*National Liberation Front*] [*North Vietnam*] (VNW)
PLAFB .... Plattsburgh Air Force Base [*New York*] (AAG)
PLAFSEP ... Processing Libraries - Anecdotes, Facetia, Satire, Etc., Periodicals [*A publication*]
Plag .... Plagioclase [*Lunar geology*]
PLAG .... Plattsburg Manufacturing [*NCIC trailer make code*]
PLAGM ...... Placid, Louisiana Land and Exploration, Amerada Hess, Getty, and Marathon [*Oil-and gas-holding bloc in Alaska*]
PLAI .... Plains Industries [*NCIC trailer make code*]
PLAI .... Potsdam Land-Atmosphere Interaction Model (SAUS)
PLAI .... Preschool Language Assessment Instrument [*Child development test*]
PLAIC .... Purdue Laboratory for Applied Industrial Control [*Purdue University*] [*Research center*] (RCD)
PLAID .... Panel Layout and Integrated Design (LDOE)
PLAID .... Precision Location and Identification (SEWL)
PLAID .... Professional Library Access and Information Delivery [*Information service or system*] (IID)
PLAID .... Programmed Learning Aid
PLAIL .... Public Libraries and Independent Learners (TELE)
PLAIN .... Plain [*Commonly used*] (OPSA)
PLAINES ... Plains [*Commonly used*] (OPSA)
PLAINS ...... Plains [*Commonly used*] (OPSA)
Plaintr ...... Plaintree Systems, Inc. [*Associated Press*] (SAG)
PLAL .... Play-Mor Trailer [*NCIC trailer make code*]
PLAL .... Pro-Life Action League (EA)
PLA LC ..... PLA [*Public Library Association*] Legislative Committee
PLAM .... Peoples Liberation Army of Malawi (SAUS)
PLAM .... Plastic Laminate [*Technical drawings*]
PLAM .... Playmate Coaches [*NCIC trailer make code*]
PLAM .... Practice Limpet Assembly Modular [*Navy*] (CAAL)
PLAM .... Price-Level-Adjusted Mortgage
plam .... price-level adjusted mortgage (SAUS)
PLAME ...... Propulsive Left Landing with Aerodynamic Maneuvering Entry (PDAA)
PLAME ...... Propulsive Lift Aerodynamic Maneuvering Entry (SAUS)
PLAMED .... Plantas Medicinales [*Ministerio de Sanidad y Consumo*] [*Spain*] [*Information service or system*] (CRD)
PLA MLS .... PLA [*Public Library Association*] Metropolitan Libraries Section
PLA Monthly ... Port of London Authority Monthly (SAUS)
PL/AMOS ... Philips Laboratory Air Force Maui Optical Station (SAUS)
PLA MPLSS ... PLA [*Public Library Association*] Marketing of Public Library Services Section
PLAN .... Association for the Advancement of Psychology Inc. Psychologists for Legislative Action Now [*Colorado Springs, CO*] (PACS)
PLAN .... Open Plan Systems [*NASDAQ symbol*] (TTSB)
PLAN .... Open Plan Systems, Inc. [*NASDAQ symbol*] (SAG)
PLAN .... Parts Logistics Analysis Network
PLAN .... Paterson Looks Ahead Now (SAUS)
PLAN .... Payload Local Area Network [*NASA*] (SSD)
PLAN .... People's Liberation Army Navy
PLAN .... People's Liberation Army of Namibia [*Political party*] (PPW)
PLAN .... Personal LAN (NITA)
PLAN .... Personal Local Area Network [*Telecommunications*] (OSI)
Plan .... Planet (SAUS)
Plan .... Planetarium (SAUS)
PLAN .... Planned Lifetime Advocacy Network
Plan .... Planning (DLA)
PLAN .... Planning
PLAN .... Positive Locator Aid to Navigation
PLAN .... Prevent Los Angeles Now
PLAN .... Prevent Los Angelization Now (SAUS)
PLAN .... Problem Language Analyzer [*Computer science*]
PLAN .... Professional Local Area Network (NITA)
PLAN .... Program for Learning in Accordance with Needs [*Westinghouse Learning Corp.*]
PLAN .... Program Language Analyzer [*Computer science*] (IEEE)
PLAN .... Programming Language Nineteen-Hundred [*Computer science*]
PLAN .... Protect Life in All Nations (EA)
PLAN .... Public Lands Action Network (SAUS)
PLAN .... Public Libraries Automation Network [*California State Library*] [*Sacramento, CA*]
Plan & Comp ... Planning and Compensation Reports [*British*] [*A publication*] (DLA)
PlanarSy .... Planar Systems [*Commercial firm*] [*Associated Press*] (SAG)
PLANASA ... National Sanitation Plan [*Medicine*] [*Brazil*] (EDAA)
PLANAT ..... North Atlantic Treaty Regional Planning Group
Planc .... Pro Plancio [*of Cicero*] [*Classical studies*] (OCD)
PLANCODE ... Planning, Control, and Decision Evaluation System [*IBM Corp.*]
PLANCODE System ... Planning, Control and Decision Evaluation System (SAUS)
PLand .... Professional Landman [*Canada*] (DD)
PL&PD ...... Personal Loss and Personal Damage (SAUS)
PL & PD .... Public Liability and Property Damage [*Insurance*]
Pl & Pr Cas ... Pleading and Practice Cases [*1837-38*] [*England*] [*A publication*] (DLA)
PL & R ...... Postal Laws and Regulations [*Later, Postal Manual*]
PLANES ..... Programmed Language Enquiry System (NITA)
Planet .... Planetarium (DIAR)
Planet .... Planetary (SAUS)
PLANET ..... Planned Logistics Analysis and Evaluation Technique [*Air Force*]
PLANET ..... Planning Evaluation Technique (MCD)
PLANET ..... Plant Layout Analysis and Evaluation Technique (SAUS)
PLANET ..... Private Line Analysis and Network Engineering Tools (SAUS)
PLANET ..... Private Local Area Network [*Racal LAN Systems, Inc.*] [*Boca Raton, FL*] (TSSD)
PLANET ..... Probing Lensing Anomalies Network [*Astronomy*]
Planet Rep ... Planetary Report (SAUS)
PLANEX ..... [*The*] Planning Exchange Database [*Pergamon InfoLine*] [*Database*] [*Information service or system*] (IID)
PLANEX ..... Planning Exercise [*Military*] (NVT)
Pl Ang-Norm ... Placita Anglo-Normannica Cases (Bigelow) [*A publication*] (DLA)
Plan Higher Ed ... Planning for Higher Education [*A publication*]
PlanHlly ..... Planet Hollywood International, Inc. [*Associated Press*] (SAG)
Planistor ... Planar Resistor (SAUS)
PLANIT ...... Programming Language for Interaction and Teaching [*1966*] [*Computer science*]
PLANIT ...... Programming Language for Interactive Teaching
PLANITRON ... Planar Integration Electron Tube (SAUS)
Plank .... Plankton (SAUS)
PLANMAN ... Planned Maintenance [*Contract Data Research*] [*Software package*] (NCC)
PLANN ...... Plant Location Assistance Nationwide Network
PLANNET ... Planning Network
PLANO ...... Plano, TX [*American Association of Railroads railroad junction routing code*]
PLANOX ..... Planar Oxide (SAUS)
PLANOX ..... Plane Oxide (SAUS)
PLANQ ...... Open Plan Systems [*OTCBB symbol*]
PLANS .... Plastic Analysis of Nonlinear Structures (SAUS)
PLANS .... Position Location and Navigation Symposium (SAUS)
PLANS .... Position Location and Navigation System
PLANS .... Position Locator and Navigation System (SAUS)
PLANS .... Program Logistics and Network Scheduling System (IEEE)
PLANS .... Programming Language for Allocation and Network Scheduling [*1975*] [*Computer science*] (CSR)
PlanSci ...... Planning Sciences International [*Associated Press*] (SAG)
Plan Soc .... Planetry Society (SAUS)
Plant .... De Plantatione [*Philo*] (BJA)
PLANT .... Program for Linguistic Analysis of Natural Plants (IEEE)
PLANT .... Programming Language for Interaction and Teaching (SAUS)
PLANT .... Programming Language for Interactive Teaching [*Computer science*] (IAA)
plantar flex ... Plantarflexion [*Medicine*] (BCRP)
Plant Cell Environ ... Plant, Cell and Environment (SAUS)
Plant Cell Rep ... Plant Cell Reports (SAUS)
Plant Cell Tissue Organ Culture ... Plant Cell, Tissue and Organ Culture (SAUS)
Plant Dis ... Plant Disease (SAUS)
Plant Dis Rep ... Plant Disease Reporter (SAUS)
Plant Ecol ... Plant Ecology (SAUS)
Plant Eng ... Plant Engineering (SAUS)
Planters Bull ... Planters Bulletin (SAUS)
PLANTFACTS ... Steel Plants Information System [*German Iron and Steel Engineers Association*] [*Dusseldorf*] [*Information service or system*] (IID)
plant-flex ... Plantar Flexion [*Orthopedics*] (DAVI)
Plant Growth Regul ... Plant Growth Regulation (SAUS)
Plant Mol Biol Rep ... Plant Molecular Biology Reporter (SAUS)
Plant Mol Biol Report ... Plant Molecular Biology Reporter (SAUS)
Plant Oper Prog ... Plant Operation and Progress (SAUS)
Plant Physiol Biochem ... Plant Physiology and Biochemistry (SAUS)
Plantron ..... Plantronics, Inc. [*Associated Press*] (SAG)
Plant Sci .... Plant Science (SAUS)
Plant Sci Bull ... Plant Science Bulletin (SAUS)
Plants Mach ... Plants and Machinery (SAUS)
PLANY .... Protestant Lawyers Association of New York (EA)
PLAO .... Parts List Assembly Order (MCD)
PLAP .... Placental Alkaline Phosphatase [*An enzyme*]
PLAP .... Port of London Authority Police (SAUS)
PLAP .... Power Lever Angle Position (MCD)
PLAP .... Prelaunch, Launch, and Ascent Procedures [*NASA*] (IAA)
PLAP .... Pulsed-Laser Atom Probe (SAUS)
Pla Par ...... Placita Parliamentaria [*Latin*] [*A publication*] (DLA)
PLA/PGA .... Polylactic Acid/Polyglycolic Acid (SAUS)
PLapK .... Keystone Junior College, La Plume, PA [*Library symbol*] [*Library of Congress*] (LCLS)
PLA PLSS ... PLA [*Public Library Association*] Public Library Systems Section

PLAQ........ Planned Quantity (SAUS)
PLA Quarterly... Private Libraries Association Quarterly (SAUS)
PLAR........ Postal Laws and Regulations (IAA)
PLAR........ Prior Learning Assessment and Recognition (FOTI)
PLAR........ Private Line Automatic Ringdown [*Communications term*] (DCT)
PLARA....... Packaged Liquid Air-Augmented (IAA)
Plarbage.... Plane-floor garbage (SAUS)
PLARS....... Position Location and Reporting System [*Military*] (INF)
PLAS........ Plaster (AAG)
plas........ Plastic (VRA)
PLAS........ Plastic
PLAS........ Plastic Forming Company [*NCIC trailer make code*]
PLas........ Premier Laser Systems, Inc. [*Associated Press*] (SAG)
PLAS........ Private Line Assured Service [*Telecommunications*] (TEL)
PLAS........ Professional Library Automation System (TELE)
PLAS........ Program Logical Address Space
PLAS........ Programmable Link Adaptation System (MCD)
PLASA....... Professional Lighting & Sound Association (SAUS)
PLASCAMS... Plastics: Computer Aided Materials Selector [*Rapra Technology Ltd.*] [*Information service or system*] (CRD)
PLASDOC... Plastic and Polymer Patents (SAUS)
PLASDOC... Plastics Documentation (SAUS)
PLASI........ Pulsating Visual Approach Slope Indicator [*Aviation*] (FAAC)
PLASI........ Pulse Light Approach Indicator System (SAUS)
PLASI........ Pulse Light Approach Slope Indicator (PDAA)
PLASMA.... Parents League of American Students of Medicine Abroad [*Defunct*] (EA)
PLASMA.... Plant Services Maintenance (PDAA)
Plasma...... Plasma & Materials Technologies, Inc. [*Associated Press*] (SAG)
Plasma Chem Plasma Process... Plasma Chemistry and Plasma Processing (SAUS)
Plasma Phys... Plamsa Physics (SAUS)
Plasma Phys Control Fusion... Plasma Physics and Controlled Fusion (SAUS)
PLASMEX... International Plastics Exhibition
PLASMEX... International Plastics Machinery, Equipment and Materials Exhibition (SAUS)
PLA SMLS... PLA [*Public Library Association*] Small and Medium-Sized Libraries Section
Plast......... Plastic (DIAR)
Plast......... Plasticity (SAUS)
Plast......... Plastics (SAUS)
PLAST....... Pre-Engineered Logistical and Administrative Structures (SAUS)
PLAST....... Propellant Loading and All Systems Test [*NASA*] (KSC)
Plast Age... Plastics Age (SAUS)
Plast Bldg Contr... Plastics in Building Construction (SAUS)
Plast Bubber Int... Plastics and Rubber International (SAUS)
Plast Bubber Process Appl... Plastics and Rubber Processing and Applications (SAUS)
Plast Bus... Plastics Business (SAUS)
Plast Compounding... Plastics Compounding (SAUS)
Plast Des Forum... Plastics Design Forum (SAUS)
PLASTEC... Plastics Evaluation Center (SAUS)
PLASTEC... Plastics Technical Evaluation Center [*Dover, NJ*] [*Army*]
PLASTEC... Plastics Technology Information Analysis Center (SAUS)
Plast Eng... Plastics Engineering [*A publication*] (CABS)
Plast Eng... Plastics in Engineering (SAUS)
PLASTEUROTEC... European Group of Fabricators of Technical Plastics Parts (SAUS)
PLASTEUROTEC... Groupement Europeen des Fabricants de Pieces Techniques Plastiques [*European Group of Fabricators of Technical Plastics Parts*] (EAIO)
PlasThrm... Plasma-Therm, Inc. [*Associated Press*] (SAG)
PLASTICSPAC... Society of the Plastics Industry Inc. PAC [*Washington, DC*] (PACS)
Plast Ind News... Plastics Industry News (SAUS)
PlasTIPS.... Plastics Training and Information to Promote Safety (SAUS)
PlastLn...... Plasti-Line, Inc. [*Associated Press*] (SAG)
Plast News... Plastics News (SAUS)
Plast News Briefs... Plastics News Briefs (SAUS)
Plast Retail Packag Bull... Plastics in Retail Packaging Bulletin (SAUS)
Plast Rubber Wkly... Plastics and Rubber Weekly (SAUS)
Plast S Africa... Plastics Southern Africa (SAUS)
Plast Technol... Plastics Technology (SAUS)
Plast Today... Plastics Today (SAUS)
Plast World... Plastics World (SAUS)
PLASTYPAC... American Society of Plastic Surgeons [*Arlington Heights, IL*] (PACS)
PLAT......... Pilot Landing Aid Television (SAUS)
PLAT......... Pilot Landing Air Television
PLAT......... Pilot Landing Assistance Television
PLAT......... Pilot-LOS [*Line of Sight*] Landing Aid Television (NG)
plat......... Plate (VRA)
Plat......... Plateau (NTIO)
PLAT......... Plateau [*Board on Geographic Names*]
PLAT......... Platelet [*Hematology*]
PLAT......... Platform (KSC)
PLAT......... Platinum [*Chemical symbol is Pt*] (AAG)
PLAT......... Platinum Technology [*NASDAQ symbol*] (SPSG)
PLAT......... Platonic
plat......... Platoon (WDAA)
PLAT......... Platoon
PLAT......... Platt National Park
PLAT......... Platt Trailer Company [*NCIC trailer make code*]
PLATF....... Platform (AAG)
platf......... Platform (MIST)
Platinum Met Rev... Platinum Metals Review (SAUS)
PLATL....... Platelets [*Hematology*] (DAVI)
PLATLDR... Platoon Leader [*Military*]
PLATN....... Platinum [*Chemistry*] (ROG)
platn......... Platinum [*Metal*] (VRA)
PLATO....... Pennzoil Louisiana and Texas Offshore [*Oil industry group*]
PLATO....... Platform Observables (SAUS)
PLATO....... Platform Observables Subassembly
PLATO....... Pollution Liability Agreement Among Tanker Owners [*Insurance*] (DS)
PLATO....... Port Lincoln Advancement Trust Organization (SAUS)
PLATO....... Programmed Learning Automatic Teaching Organization (SAUS)
PLATO....... Programmed Logic for Automated Learning Operation [*Computer science*] (IAA)
PLATO....... Programmed Logic for Automatic Teaching [*or Training*] Operations [*University of Illinois*] [*Programming language*]
PLATON..... Programming Language for Tree Operation (SAUS)
PLATR....... Pawling Lattice Test Rig [*United Nuclear Co.*]
PLATS....... Pilot Landing and Takeoff System (IIA)
PLATS....... Precision Location and Tracking System (PDAA)
PLatS........ Saint Vincent College, Latrobe, PA [*Library symbol*] [*Library of Congress*] (LCLS)
PlatSoft..... Platinum Software Corp. [*Associated Press*] (SAG)
Plat Surf Fin... Plating and Surface Finishing (SAUS)
PLAT System... Pilot Landing Aid Television System (SAUS)
PLATT....... Page Level Availability Time Test [*Computer science*]
Platt......... Platt on Leases [*A publication*] (DLA)
Platt......... Platt on the Law of Covenants [*1829*] [*A publication*] (DLA)
PlatTc........ Platinum Technology, Inc. [*Associated Press*] (SAG)
Platt Cov... Platt on the Law of Covenants [*A publication*] (DLA)
Platt Leas... Platt on Leases [*1847*] [*A publication*] (DLA)
PLAT/VLA... Pilot Landing Aid Television / Visual Landing Aid [*System*] (DNAB)
Platy......... Platyhelminthes (SAUS)
Platy......... Platypoecilus (SAUS)
Platy......... Platysma (SAUS)
Plaut......... Plautus [*Third century BC*] [*Classical studies*] (OCD)
PLAV......... Polish Legion of American Veterans (NADA)
PLAV......... Polish Legion of American Veterans, USA (EA)
PLAVA....... Polish Legion of American Veterans, USA , Ladies Auxiliary (EA)
PLAVL....... Placerville, CA [*American Association of Railroads railroad junction routing code*]
PLAVLA..... Polish Legion of American Veterans, USA, Ladies Auxiliary (EA)
PLAW......... Programming Language for Arc Welding (SAUS)
PLAWM Trough... Pockels Langmuir Adam Wilson McBain Trough [*Surface film balance*]
PLAX......... Port of Los Angeles [*Federal Railroad Administration identification code*]
Plaxton...... Plaxton's Canadian Constitutional Decisions [*A publication*] (DLA)
PLAY......... Participate in the Lives of America's Youth
PLAY......... Playboy [*NCIC car make code*]
PLAY......... Players International [*NASDAQ symbol*] (TTSB)
PLAY......... Players International, Inc. [*NASDAQ symbol*] (NQ)
PLAY......... Providing Lifetime Activity for Youth
Playby....... Playboy Enterprises, Inc. [*Associated Press*] (SAG)
PlayBy....... Play By Play Toys & Novelties, Inc. [*Associated Press*] (SAG)
PlaybyA..... Playboys Enterprises [*Associated Press*] (SAG)
PlaybyB..... Playboys Enterprises [*Associated Press*] (SAG)
PlayCo...... Play Co. Toys [*Associated Press*] (SAG)
Play Co..... Play Co. Toys & Entertainment Corp. [*Associated Press*] (SAG)
Players...... Players International Corp. [*Associated Press*] (SAG)
PLAYF....... Playstar Corp. [*NASDAQ symbol*] (QUAN)
PlaytxPd.... Playtex Products, Inc. [*Associated Press*] (SAG)
PLAZA....... Plaza [*Commonly used*] (OPSA)
PLB.......... American Italian Pasta Co. [*NYSE symbol*]
PLB.......... Amer Italian Pasta'A' [*NYSE symbol*] (SG)
PLB.......... Communist Party (Belgium) [*Political party*] (PSAP)
PLB.......... Packet Length in Bits (SAUS)
PLB.......... Parietal Lobe Battery [*Medicine*] (EDAA)
PLB.......... Payload Bay [*NASA*] (NAKS)
PLB.......... Per Pound [*Freight*]
PLB.......... Personal Locator Beacon [*Military*] (AFM)
PLB.......... Phopholipase B [*An enzyme*] (DAVI)
PLB.......... Phospholamban [*Biochemistry*]
PLB.......... Picture Level Benchmark [*Computer science*] (CDE)
PLB.......... Plattsburgh, NY [*Location identifier*] [*FAA*] (FAAL)
PLB.......... Plumbing Mart [*Vancouver Stock Exchange symbol*]
PLB.......... Poor Law Board
PLB.......... Porous Layer Bead [*Chromatography*] (DB)
PLB.......... Print Line Buffer [*Computer science*] (VLIE)
PLB.......... Prior-Lien Bond [*Business*] (MHDB)
PLB.......... Proctolin-Like Bioactivity [*Neurobiology*]
PLB.......... Public Light Bus [*British*]
PLB.......... Publisher's Library Binding
PLB.......... Pullbutton (AAG)
PLBB......... Patent Licensing Bulletin Board [*U.S. Department of Commerce*] (BARN)
PLBD......... Payload Bay Door [*NASA*] (MCD)
PLBD......... Plugboard (MSA)
PLBG......... Plumbing (WGA)
PLBK......... Playback (NASA)
PLBKAC..... Problem Lies Between Keyboard and Chair (SAUS)
PL-BL........ Plate Block [*Philately*]
PLBLK....... Pillow Block
PLBO......... Placebo [*Medicine*] (EDAA)
PLBOL....... Position Launch/Bearing Only Launch

PLBR .... Plumber (WGA)
PLBR .... Prototype Large Breeder Reactor [*Also, NCBR*] [*Nuclear energy*]
PLC .... Pacific Lighting Corp. (SAUS)
PLC .... Pacific Logging Congress (EA)
PLC .... Packaged Laboratory Chemicals (COE)
PLC .... Palomares Road [*California*] [*Seismograph station code, US Geological Survey*] (SEIS)
PLC .... Parti de la Liberte du Citoyen [*Belgium*] [*Political party*] (EY)
PLC .... Partido Liberal Constitucionalista [*Constitutionalist Liberal Party*] [*Nicaragua*] [*Political party*] (PPW)
PLC .... Patrice Lumumba Coalition (EA)
PLC .... Pattern Length Coding (SAUS)
PLC .... Paymaster-Lieutenant-Commander [*Navy*] [*British*]
PLC .... Peritoneal Lymphoid Cell (SAUS)
PLC .... Periventricular Leukomalacia Complex [*Medicine*]
PLC .... Perry-Link Cubmarine [*A submersible vehicle*]
PLC .... Personal Line of Credit (SAUS)
PLC .... Phospholipase C [*An enzyme*]
PLC .... Phospholysine C [*Biochemistry*]
PLC .... Pilot Laboratories Corp. [*Vancouver Stock Exchange symbol*]
PLC .... Placer Development Ltd. [*AMEX symbol*] (SPSG)
Pl C .... Placita Coronae [*Pleas of the Crown*] [*Latin*] [*Legal term*] (DLA)
PLC .... Plague Locust Commission (SAUS)
PLC .... Planar Chromatography
PLC .... Planeta Rica [*Colombia*] [*Airport symbol*] (AD)
PLC .... Platform Control
PLC .... Platoon Leader's Class [*Army*]
PLC .... PLC Capital LLC, Inc. [*Associated Press*] (SAG)
PLC .... PLC Systems [*AMEX symbol*] (SPSG)
PLC .... Pneumatic Lead Cutter
PLC .... Pneumatic Logic Circuit (SAUS)
PLC .... Poet Laureatus Caesareus [*Imperial Poet Laureate*] [*Latin*] (ROG)
PLC .... Point Loma College [*California*]
PLC .... Police
PLC .... Police Aviation Services [*British*] [*ICAO designator*] (FAAC)
PLC .... Polymer Liquid Crystal (SAUS)
PLC .... Poor Law Commissioners [*British*]
PLC .... Power Lever Control (MCD)
PLC .... Power Line Carrier
PLC .... Power Line Communications
PLC .... Power Line Conditioner (VLIE)
PLC .... Power Line Converter (SAUS)
PLC .... Power Line Cycle (SAUS)
PLC .... Power Loading Control (IAA)
PLC .... Predictive Linguistic Constraint
PLC .... Preferred Line of Credit (SAUS)
PLC .... Prelaunch Computer (SAUS)
PLC .... Preliminary Loads Cycle (SAUS)
PLC .... Preparative Layer Chromatography
PLC .... Presbyterian Lay Committee (EA)
PLC .... Pressurized Logistics Carrier (SAUS)
PLC .... Price Limits to the Consumer (FOTI)
PLC .... Primary Leadership Course [*Army*]
PLC .... Primary Location Code [*Computer science*]
PLC .... Prime Level Code
PLC .... Print Line Complete [*Computer science*] (VLIE)
PLC .... Private Line Carrier [*Telecommunications*] (IAA)
PLC .... Probe Launch Complex (SAUS)
PLC .... Process Limit Count (TIMI)
PLC .... Process Line Control [*Computer science*] (VLIE)
PLC .... Process Liquid Chromatography
PLC .... Production Line Configured [*Military*] (CAAL)
PLC .... Product Level Control (SAUS)
PLC .... Product Life Cycle (ODBW)
PLC .... Products List Circular [*Patents*]
PLC .... Program-Length Commercial [*Television*]
PLC .... Program Level Change (VLIE)
PLC .... Program Level Change Tape [*Computer science*] (IBMDP)
PLC .... Programmable Line Controller (NITA)
PLC .... Programmable Logic Control [*Computer science*]
PLC .... Programmable Logic Controller (DCOM)
PLC .... Programming Language Committee [*CODASYL*]
PLC .... Proinsulin-Like Compound [*Endocrinology*]
PLC .... Propellant Loading Console (SAUS)
PLC .... Provisional Legislative Council [*Hong Kong*]
PLC .... Pseudolymphocytic Choriomeningitis [*Medicine*] (DMAA)
PLC .... Pseudophase Liquid Chromatography
PLC .... Public Lands Council (EA)
PLC .... Public Liability Company (DFIT)
PLC .... Public Lighting Commission
PLC .... Public Limited Co. [*British*]
plc .... Public Limited Company (SAFN)
Plc .... Public Limited Company
PLC .... Public Utility Company (EBF)
PLCA .... Parallel Line Communication Adaptor (NITA)
PLCA .... Pipe Line Contractors Association (EA)
PLCA .... Pipeline Contractors Association (SAUS)
PLCAA .... Professional Lawn Care Association of America (EA)
PLCAC .... Pipeline Contractors Association of Canada (SAUS)
PLCAI .... Pipe Line Contractors Association, International (EA)
PLCB .... Planetary Liquid-Cooled Brake [*Off-highway equipment*]
PLCB .... Program List Control Block [*Computer science*] (ELAL)
PLCB .... Pseudoline Control Block [*Computer science*]
PLC Bulletin... Progressive Librarians Council Bulletin (SAUS)
PLCC .... Paulson Cap [*NASDAQ symbol*] (TTSB)
PLCC .... Paulson Capital Corp. [*NASDAQ symbol*] (SAG)
PLCC .... Plastic Chip Carrier (NITA)
PLCC .... Plastic Leaded Chip Carrier [*Computer science*]
PLCC .... Plastic Leadless Chip Carrier [*Computer technology*] (PCM)
PLCC .... Power Line Carrier Communication (PDAA)
PLCC .... Primary Liver Cell Cancer [*Oncology*]
PLCC .... Propulsion Local Control Console (DNAB)
PLCCE .... Preliminary Life-Cycle Cost Estimate
PLCCE .... Program Life-Cycle Cost Estimate [*Army*]
PLCD .... Product Liability Common Defense [*Later, PLPD*] [*An association*] (EA)
PLCDR ...... Private Line Carrier Divided Ringing [*Telecommunications*] (IAA)
PLCE .... Children's Place Retail Stores [*NASDAQ symbol*] (SG)
PLCE .... Peripheral and Loading Control Element (SAUS)
PLCE .... Personal Load Carrying Equipment (SAUS)
PLCEA .... Part-Length Control Element Assembly [*Nuclear energy*] (NRCH)
PLCEDM .... Part-Length Control Element Drive Mechanism [*Nuclear energy*] (NRCH)
PLCH .... Kiritimati Island [*Christmas Islands*] [*Kiribati*] [*ICAO location identifier*] (ICLI)
PLCHC .... Polymer Life Cycle Hydrocarbons
PLC I/O ...... Programmable Logic Controller Input/Output (SAUS)
PLCL .... Phase-Locked Control Loop [*NASA*] (IAA)
PLCL .... Polyclonal Gammopathy Identified [*Immunology*] (DAVI)
PLCLAS ..... Propagation Loss Classification System [*Navy*] (NVT)
PL-CLP ...... Plantelet Clumps [*Hematology*] (DAVI)
PLCM .... Polycom, Inc. [*NASDAQ symbol*] (SAG)
PLCM .... Propellant Loading Control Monitor [*NASA*] (KSC)
PLCM&ND .. Proceedings of the Linguistic Circle of Manitoba and North Dakota (SAUS)
PLCMC .... Public Library of Charlotte and Mecklenburg County [*North Carolina*]
PLCN .... Parts List Change Notice (MCD)
PLCNY .... Publications of the Linguistic Circle of New York (SAUS)
PLCO .... Play Company Toys [*NASDAQ symbol*] (SAG)
PLCO .... Play Co. Toys & Entertainment Corp. [*NASDAQ symbol*] (SAG)
PLCO .... Play Co. Toys & Entmt [*NASDAQ symbol*] (TTSB)
PLCO .... Postoperative Low Cardiac Output [*Medicine*] (DMAA)
PLCO .... Prostate, Lung, Colorectal, and Ovarian [*Cancers*]
Pl Com .... Plowden's English King's Bench Commentaries [*or Reports*] [*1550-80*] [*England*] [*A publication*] (DLA)
PL Com ..... Poor Law Commissioner [*A publication*] (DLA)
PLCOP .... Prelaunch Checkout Plan [*NASA*] (KSC)
PLCOW ...... Play Co. Toys & Entmt Wrrt [*NASDAQ symbol*] (TTSB)
PLCP .... Photochromic Liquid Crystal Polymer [*Organic chemistry*]
PLCP .... Physical Layer Convergence Procedure (CIST)
PLCP .... Physical Layer Convergence Protocol (MLOA)
PLCR .... Post Launch Checkout Report (ACAE)
Pl Cr Con Tr... Plowden's Criminal Conversation Trials [*A publication*] (DLA)
PlcrD .... Placer Dome [*Associated Press*] (SAG)
PLCS .... Proceedings of the London Classical Society (SAUS)
PLCS .... Propellant Loading Control System [*NASA*] (AAG)
PLC Sys..... PLC Systems [*Associated Press*] (SAG)
PLCT .... Power Line Carrier Telephony (SAUS)
PLCT .... Prelaunch Certification Test
PLCU .... Autotrasporti Pigliacelli [*Intermodal shipping container symbol*] (TVRC)
Pl Cu .... Plain Copper (SAUS)
PLCU .... Programmable Logic Control Unit (SAUS)
PLCU .... Propellant Level Control Unit [*NASA*] (KSC)
PLCU .... Propellant-Loading Control Unit [*NASA*] (IAA)
PLCURR ..... Plate Current [*Electronics*] (IAA)
PLCV .... Pelargonium Leaf Curl Virus [*Plant pathology*]
PLCWTWU... Power Loom Carpet Weavers' and Textile Workers' Union [*British*]
PLCX .... Port of Lake Charles [*Federal Railroad Administration identification code*]
plcy .... Policy (ELAL)
Plcy .... Policy (TBD)
PLCY .... Policy
PlcyMg ...... Policy Management Systems [*Associated Press*] (SAG)
PLCZ .... Potlatch Lumber [*Federal Railroad Administration identification code*]
PLD .... All Pakistan Legal Decisions [*A publication*] (ILCA)
PLD .... Package Level Detail (VLIE)
PLD .... Paid Land Diversion Program [*Department of Agriculture*] (GFGA)
PLD .... Partial Line Down (NITA)
PLD .... Partial Lipodystrophy [*Medicine*]
PLD .... Partido de la Liberacion Dominicana [*Dominican Liberation Party*] [*Dominican Republic*] [*Political party*] (PPW)
PLD .... Parti Liberal-Democrate [*Cameroon*] [*Political party*] (EY)
PLd .... Path Loss, Downlink [*Communications*]
PLD .... Payload [*NASA*]
PLD .... Periodic Lattice Distortion (SAUS)
PLD .... Peripheral Light Detection (DMAA)
PLD .... Periscope-Like Display (SAUS)
PLD .... Permanently Lubricated Drivetrain
PLD .... Personal Laser Detector (SAUS)
PLD .... Personnel Letdown Device
PLD .... Petersburg Long Distance Inc. (EFIS)
PLD .... Phase Linked Demodulator (SAUS)
PLD .... Phase Lock Demodulator
PLD .... Phase-Locked Detector (IAA)
PLD .... Phase-Locked Discriminator (IAA)
PLD .... Phospholipase D [*An enzyme*]
PLD .... Physical Logical Description (MHDI)
PLD .... Plaid (ADA)

PLD .... Plated (MSA)
PLD .... Platelet Defect [*Hematology*] (MAE)
PID .... Platform Deck (SAUS)
PLD .... Played Matches [*Cricket*] (ROG)
PLD .... Policy Liaison Division (AAGC)
PLD .... Polycystic Liver Disease [*Medicine*] (DMAA)
PLD .... Polymer-Linked Ligand Dimer [*Biochemistry*]
PLD .... Portland, IN [*Location identifier*] [*FAA*] (FAAL)
PLD .... Posterior Latissimus Dorsi [*Anatomy*]
PLD .... Posterolateral Dendrite [*Neurology*]
PLD .... Potentially Lethal Damage [*Medicine*]
PLD .... Precision LASER Designator (RDA)
PLD .... Pregnancy, Labor and Delivery (DAVI)
PLD .... Presentation Logic Domain (SAUS)
PLD .... Primary Layer Depth [*Military*] (CAAL)
PLD .... Primary Linguistic Data [*Linguistics*] (IEL)
PLD .... Principle of Limit Design
PLD .... Probable Line of Deployment [*Army*] (AABC)
PLD .... Procurement Legal Division [*Later, Office of General Counsel*] [*Navy*]
PLD .... Product Line Development
PLD .... Program Listing Document (MCD)
PLD .... Program Load Disc (SAUS)
PLD .... Programmable Logic Device
PLD .... Progressive Lenticular Degeneration [*Medicine*] [*Wilson's disease*] (EDAA)
PLD .... ProLogis [*NYSE symbol*]
PLD .... ProLogis Trust [*NYSE symbol*] [*Formerly, Security Capital Industries Trust*]
PLD .... Protective LASER Devices (MCD)
PLD .... Pulsed LASER Deposition [*Coating technology*]
PLD .... Pulse-Length Discriminator (IEEE)
PLD .... Pulse Level Detector (MCD)
PLDA .... Power Line Disturbance Analyser (SAUS)
PLDA .... Private Loop Direct Attach (MWOL)
PLdaC .... Calvary Baptist School of Theology, Lansdale, PA [*Library symbol*] [*Library of Congress*] (LCLS)
PLDAL .... Pro-Life Direct Action League (EA)
PLDC .... Preliminary List of Design Changes
PLDC .... Primary Leadership Development Course [*Army*] (INF)
PLDC .... Primary Long-Distance Carrier [*Telephone service*]
PLDD .... Percutaneous Laser Disc Decompression
PLDD .... Poorly Differentiated Lymphoma, Diffuse [*Oncology and pathology*] (DAVI)
PLDD .... Profiled Lightly Doped Drains (NITA)
PLD Digest... Pakistan Legal Decisions Digest (SAUS)
PLDF .... Piecewise Linear Discriminant Function (SAUS)
PLDF .... Pseudo Load Factor (IAA)
PLDG .... Portuguese Language Development Group [*Modern Language Association of America*] (AEBS)
PLDH .... Plasma Lactic Dehydrogenase [*An enzyme*] (AAMN)
PLDI .... Palestro Distribution Center [*Common carrier symbol*]
PLDI .... Payload Data Interleaver [*NASA*] (MCD)
PLDI .... Petersburg Long Distance [*NASDAQ symbol*] (SAG)
PLDI .... Plastic Die [*Tool*] (AAG)
PLDI .... PLD Telekom, Inc. [*NASDAQ symbol*] (SAG)
PLDI .... Programming Language Design and Implementation [*Computer science*] (VLIE)
PLDIF .... Petersburg Long Distance [*NASDAQ symbol*] (TTSB)
PLDIF .... PLD Telekom [*NASDAQ symbol*] [*Formerly, Petersburg Long Distance*] (SG)
PLDIS .... Public Libraries Development Incentive Scheme (SAUS)
PLDIS .... Public Library Development Incentive Scheme [*British*]
PLDISS ...... Plate Dissipation [*Electronics*] (IAA)
PLDK .... Peabody Language Development Kits [*Education*]
PLDK-P ...... Peabody Language Development Kit: Preschool (EDAC)
PLDM .... Payload Management [*NASA*] (MCD)
PLDM .... Power Line Disturbance Monitor (SAUS)
PLDMI .... Precise LASER Distance Measuring Instrument
PLDP .... Parti Liberal Democrate et Pluraliste [*Belgium*] [*Political party*] (PPW)
PLDP .... Public Library Development Plan [*American Library Association, Public Library Association*]
PLD-PACOM... Petroleum Logistical Data - Pacific Command (CINC)
PLDR .... Potentially Lethal Damage Repair [*Medicine*]
PLDS .... Payload Support [*NASA*] (MCD)
PLDS .... Pilot Land Data System (ACAE)
PLDS .... Planetary Land Data System (SAUS)
PLDS .... Public Library Data Service
PLDT .... Philippine Long Distance Telephone Co.
PLDT C ...... Philippine Long Distance Telephone Company (SAUS)
PLD Tele .... PLD Telekom, Inc. [*Associated Press*] (SAG)
PLDTS .... Propellant Loading Data Transmission System [*NASA*] (KSC)
PLDX .... Polydox (SAUS)
PL DYL ...... Placidyl [*Ethchlorvynol*] [*A hypnotic and sedative*] (DAVI)
PLE .... Encyclopedia of Pennsylvania Law [*A publication*] (DLA)
PLE .... Painfully Long Extension (MUSM)
PLE .... Panlobular Emphysema [*Medicine*] (STED)
PLE .... Paraneoplastic Limbic Encephalopathy [*Medicine*] (EDAA)
PLE .... Personal Level Encryption [*Computer science*]
PLE .... Phased Loading Entry [*Computer science*]
PLE .... Phase Loading Entry (SAUS)
PLE .... Photoluminescence Excitation [*Physics*]
PLE .... Piecewise-Linear Expression (SAUS)
PLE .... Pinnacle Bancshares, Inc. [*AMEX symbol*] (NASQ)
PLE .... Pinnacle Bank [*AMEX symbol*] (TTSB)
PLE .... Pipeline Element (NITA)
PLE .... [*The*] Pittsburgh & Lake Erie Railroad Co. [*AAR code*]
PLE .... Planned Life Extension [*Pershing*] (MCD)
Ple .... Pleiade [*Record label*] [*France*]
PLE .... Plesetsk [*Satellite launch complex*] [*Former USSR*]
PLE .... Pleura (SAUS)
PLE .... Porcine Liver Esterase
PLE .... Practical Legal Education (SAFN)
PLE .... Preliminary Logistics Evaluation
PLE .... Primary Loss Expectancy [*Insurance*]
PLE .... Product Limit Estimator (MHDB)
PLE .... Professional Land Economist [*Canada*] (DD)
PLE .... Programmable Logic Element (SAUS)
PL/E .... Programming Language / Edit [*Computer science*] (MHDI)
PLE .... Programming Language Evaluation (SAUS)
PLE .... Protein-Losing Enteropathy [*Gastroenterology*] (DAVI)
PLE .... Prudent Limit of Endurance (NVT)
PLE .... Pseudolupus Erythematosus [*Syndrome*] (STED)
PLE .... Public Local Exchange (SAUS)
PLE .... Puerile Light Entertainment (SAUS)
PLE .... Pulsed LASER Experiment
PLE .... Pulse Length Error (MCD)
PLE .... "The Structure" Liberal Party (Dominican Rep.) [*Political party*] (PSAP)
PLEA .... Pacific Lumber Exporters Association (EA)
PLEA .... Pleasure Homes Manufacturing [*NCIC trailer make code*]
PLEA .... Poverty Lawyers for Effective Advocacy
PLEA .... Prototype Language for Economic Analysis [*Computer science*] (IID)
PLEAD .... Place of Last Entered Active Duty [*Military*]
PLEADGS... Pleadings [*Legal term*] (ROG)
PLEA Sask... Public Legal Education Association of Saskatchewan [*Legal group*] [*Canada*] (FOTI)
PLEASE ..... Parolees, Law-Enforcement Assist Student Education [*Project to reduce drug abuse among junior and senior high school students in California*]
PLEASM ..... Programmable Logic Elements Assembler (SAUS)
PLeB .... Bucknell University, Lewisburg, PA [*Library symbol*] [*Library of Congress*] (LCLS)
PLEB .... Plebeian (WGA)
PLEB .... Plebiscitum [*A Decree of the People*] [*Latin*] (DLA)
plebe .... plebeian (SAUS)
PLebHi ...... Lebanon County Historical Society, Lebanon, PA [*Library symbol*] [*Library of Congress*] (LCLS)
plebs .... plebeians (SAUS)
PLebV .... United States Veterans Administration Hospital, Lebanon, PA [*Library symbol*] [*Library of Congress*] (LCLS)
PLECS .... Peninsula Law Enforcement [*Emergency Management*] (EMA)
PLED .... Periodic Lateralized Epileptiform Discharge [*Medicine*] (MAE)
pled .... pleaded (SAUS)
pLED .... Polymeric Light Emitting Diode
PLED .... Polymer Light Emitting Diode (SAUS)
PLEDM .... Phase-State Low Electron-Hole-Number Drive Memory
P Leg J ..... Pittsburgh Legal Journal [*Pennsylvania*] [*A publication*] (DLA)
P Leg Jour... Pittsburgh Legal Journal [*Pennsylvania*] [*A publication*] (DLA)
PLEI .... Public Law Education Institute (EA)
PLEM .... Pipeline End Manifold (PDAA)
PLEM .... Pleasureway Manufacturing [*NCIC trailer make code*]
Plen .... Plenary (SAUS)
PLEN .... Plenipotentiary
PLEN .... Plenum Publishing [*NASDAQ symbol*] (TTSB)
PLEN .... Plenum Publishing Corp. [*NASDAQ symbol*] (NQ)
PLEN .... Public Leadership Education Network (EA)
PLENAPS ... Plans for the Employment of Naval and Air Forces of the Associated Powers in theEastern Theatre in the Event of War with Japan
PLENCH ..... Pliers and Wrench [*Combination tool*]
PLENG .... Physical Record Length [*Computer science*] (MHDI)
PLENS .... Public Legal Education Society of Nova Scotia [*Legal group*] [*Canada*] (FOTI)
Plenum ...... Plenum Publishing Corp (SAUS)
PLER .... Primrose Lake Evaluation Range (SAUS)
PLES .... Parallel-Line Equal Space [*Medicine*] (DMAA)
PLES .... Parallel-Line Equal Spacing (STED)
PLES .... Photoluminescence Excitation Spectroscopy (SAUS)
PLES .... Pleasuremate Industries [*NCIC trailer make code*]
PLESA .... Programs for Persons with Limited English-Speaking Ability [*Department of Labor*]
PLEU .... Pleural Fluid [*Medicine*] (DAVI)
Pleur Fl .... Pleural Fluid [*Medicine*] (MAE)
PLEURO ...... Pleuropneumonia [*Veterinary medicine*] (DSUE)
PLEVA .... Pityriasis Lichenoides et Varioliformis Acuta [*Dermatology*] (MAE)
P/L-EX ...... Payload Executive (SAUS)
PLEX .... Plant Experimentation (PDAA)
PLEX .... Programming Language Extension [*Computer science*] (CIST)
plexg .... Plexiglass (VRA)
Plexus ...... Plexus Corp. [*Associated Press*] (SAG)
PLEYA .... Public Library Entrepreneur of the Year Award [*Sponsored by Geac Computers Ltd.*]
PLF .... Franklin and Marshall College, Lancaster, PA [*Library symbol*] [*Library of Congress*] (LCLS)
PLF .... Free Library of Philadelphia, Philadelphia, PA [*OCLC symbol*] (OCLC)
PLF .... Pacific Legal Foundation (EA)
PLF .... Page Length Field
PLF .... Pala [*Chad*] [*Airport symbol*] (AD)
PLF .... Palestine Liberation Front [*Political party*] (PD)

PLF .... Parachute Landing Fall [*Military*]
PLF .... Pastel Food [*Vancouver Stock Exchange symbol*]
PLF .... Patient Load Factor (AFM)
PLF .... Payload Fairing [*Space launch term*] (ISAK)
PLF .... People's Liberation Forces [*Ethiopia*] [*Political party*] (AF)
PLF .... Perilymphatic Fistula [*Medicine*] (DMAA)
PLF .... Perilymph Fistula [*Medicine*]
PLF .... Phase Lock Frequency
PLF .... Phone Line Formatter
PLF .... Plaintiff
PLF .... Plant Load Factor (SAUS)
PLF .... Platform [*Telegraphy*] (PCTE)
PLF .... Pohjanmaan Lento OY [*Finland*] [*ICAO designator*] (FAAC)
PLF .... Polar Lipid Fraction [*Biochemistry*]
PLF .... Polyforming (SAUS)
PLF .... Positive Lock Fastener
PLF .... Posterior Lung Fiber [*Medicine*] (DMAA)
plf........... Pounds per Foot (WPI)
PLF .... Powered-Lift Facility (SAUS)
PLF .... Power for Level Flight [*Aeronautics*]
PLF .... Private Line Telephone
PLF .... Procedure Library Facility [*Computer science*] (HODG)
P-L F .... Pro-Life Federation (SAUS)
PLF .... Proliferin [*Biochemistry*]
PLF .... Proposition Letter Formula
PLF .... Public Lands Foundation (EA)
PLF .... Public Library Foundation [*Library science*]
PLFA......... Phospholipid ester-linked Fatty Acid (SAUS)
PLFA......... Phospholipid Fatty Acids (COE)
PLFA......... Polar Lipid Fatty Acid [*Biochemistry*]
PLFA......... Primary Level Field Activity [*Defense Supply Agency*]
PLFA......... Tabueran Island [*Fanning Islands*] [*Kiribati*] [*ICAO location identifier*] (ICLI)
PLFC......... Premature Living Female Child [*Neonatology*] (DAVI)
PLFC......... Pulaski Furniture [*NASDAQ symbol*] (TTSB)
PLFC......... Pulaski Furniture Corp. [*NASDAQ symbol*] (NQ)
PLFC & A... Peggy Lee Fan Club and Archives [*Later, OOPLFC & A*] (EA)
PLFD .... Perilunate Fracture-Dislocation [*Medicine*] (RAWO)
PLFE......... Presidential Life [*NASDAQ symbol*] (TTSB)
PLFE......... Presidential Life Corp. [*NASDAQ symbol*] (NQ)
PLFF......... Plaintiff
PLFIG........ Public Library Funding Initiative Group
PLFP......... Pity Large Family Present-Buyers
PLFPF....... Payload Fairing Processing Facility [*Space launch term*] (ISAK)
PLFS......... Perilymphatic Fistula Syndrome [*Medicine*] (DMAA)
PLFTR....... Please Furnish Transportation Requests (NOAA)
PLFU .... Parlefer [*Intermodal shipping container symbol*] (TVRC)
PLFUR....... Please Furnish (NOAA)
PLFX......... Pioneer Legacy Foundation [*Federal Railroad Administration identification code*]
PLG .... Parametric Light Generator (SAUS)
PLG .... Permanent Liaison Group (SAUS)
PLG .... Piling (MSA)
PLG .... Place Resources Corp. [*Toronto Stock Exchange symbol*]
PLG .... Plane Guard (NVT)
PLG .... Planning Liaison Group (SAUS)
PLG .... Plasminogen [*An enzyme*] (DAVI)
PLG .... Pleural Ganglion [*Medicine*]
PLG .... Plug (AAG)
PLG .... Poetae Lyrici Graeci [*A publication*] (OCD)
PLG .... PolyGram NV [*NYSE symbol*] (SPSG)
PLG .... Polygyros [*Greece*] [*Seismograph station code, US Geological Survey*] (SEIS)
PLG .... Poor Law Guardian [*British*]
PLG .... Private-Label and Generic Brands
PLG .... Private/Light Goods (ODA)
PLG .... Process Line Generator (SAUS)
PLG .... Progressive Librarians Guild [*American Library Association*]
PLG .... Prolyl(leucyl)glycinamide [*Biochemistry*]
PLG .... Pulsed Light Generator
PLGA .... Polylacticco-Glycolic Acid [*Organic chemistry*]
PLGC .... Pension Loan Guarantee Corp. (SAUS)
PLGC .... Presbyterians for Lesbian/Gay Concerns (EA)
PLGL .... Plasminogen-Like [*Medicine*] (DMAA)
PLGL .... Plate Glass
PLGL .... Plateglass (SAUS)
PLGM........ NYC Parents of Lesbians and Gay Men (EA)
PL/GP .... Philips Laboratory, Geophysics Directorate (SAUS)
PLGR........ Pilgrim Consolidators [*Common carrier symbol*]
PLGR........ Plunger (MSA)
PLGR........ Portable Lightweight Global Receiver (SAUS)
PLGR........ Portable Lightweight GPS Receiver (SAUS)
PLGR........ Position Location Ground Receiver (SAUS)
PLGR........ Precision Lightweight Global-Positioning-Satellite Receiver
PLGR........ Precision Lightweight GPS [*Global Positioning System*] Receiver [*Navigation systems*]
PLGS .... Partita Liberale Giovani Somali [*Somali Liberal Youth Party*] [*Political party*]
PLGS .... Proceedings of the Liverpool Geological Society (SAUS)
PLGSS....... Payload Ground Support Systems [*NASA*] (NASA)
PLGT .... Prototype Lunar Geologist Tool
PLGU .... Trans-Caribe [*Intermodal shipping container symbol*] (TVRC)
P-LGV .... Psittacosis-Lymphogranuloma Venereum [*Medicine*]
PLH.......... Hamilton Watch Co., Lancaster, PA [*Library symbol*] [*Library of Congress*] [*Obsolete*] (LCLS)
PLH.......... Palaemontes-Lightening Hormone
PLH.......... Paroxysmal Localized Hyperhidrosis [*Dermatology*] (DAVI)
PLH.......... Partido Liberal de Honduras [*Liberal Party of Honduras*] [*Political party*] (PPW)
PLH.......... Payload Handling [*NASA*] (NASA)
PLH.......... Pharyngeal Lymphoid Hyperplasia (SAUS)
PLH.......... Pituitaries Luteinizing Hormone (SAUS)
PLH.......... Placental Lactogenic Hormone (DB)
PLH.......... Plaser Light [*Vancouver Stock Exchange symbol*]
PLH.......... Plymouth [*England*] [*Airport symbol*] (OAG)
PLH.......... Posterior Lobe of Hypophysis [*Medicine*] (MELL)
PLH.......... Pulmonary Left Heart (SAUS)
PLH.......... Punjab Light Horse [*British military*] (DMA)
PL-HGH ..... Plasma-treated Human Growth Hormone (SAUS)
PLHi .... Lancaster County Historical Society, Lancaster, PA [*Library symbol*] [*Library of Congress*] (LCLS)
PLHIC .... Programmable Linear Hall Integrated Circuit [*Electronics*]
PLHP .... Parasitic Loss Horsepower [*Automotive emissions*]
PLHR .... Power Line Harmonic Radiation
PLhS......... Lock Haven State College, Lock Haven, PA [*Library symbol*] [*Library of Congress*] (LCLS)
PLI........... Apalik [*Language symbol*] (ETLW)
PLI........... Empresa de Transporte Aereo del Peru [*ICAO designator*] (FAAC)
PLI........... Ltd. Systems [*Vancouver Stock Exchange symbol*]
PLI........... Pacific Law Institute (SAUS)
pli............ Pali [*MARC language code*] [*Library of Congress*] (LCCP)
PLI........... Panarea [*Lipari Islands*] [*Seismograph station code, US Geological Survey*] (SEIS)
PLI........... Partido Liberal Independiente [*Independent Liberal Party*] [*Nicaragua*] [*Political party*] (PPW)
PLI........... Partito Liberale Italiano [*Italian Liberal Party*] [*Political party*] (PPW)
PLI........... Passenger and Immigration Lists Index [*A publication*]
PLI........... Paternal Leukocyte Immunization (ADWA)
PLI........... Payload Interrogator [*NASA*] (MCD)
PLI........... Phone Line Interface [*IBM Corp.*] (PCM)
PLI........... Photo-Laboratory-Index (SAUS)
PLI........... Photo Library Inc (SAUS)
PLI........... Pilot Location Indicator
PLI........... Plant Location International (SAUS)
PLI........... P. Leiner Nutritional Products Corp. [*AMEX symbol*] (COMM)
PLI........... Polyvision Corp. [*AMEX symbol*] (SAG)
PLI........... Power Level Indicator
PLI........... Power Loss Indicator (SAUS)
PLI........... Practising Law Institute (EA)
PLI........... Preload Indicating
PLI........... Private Line Interface
PLI........... Procedural Language Interface (SAUS)
PLI........... Proctolin-Like Immunoactivity [*Neurobiology*]
PLI........... Product Licensing Index (SAUS)
PLI........... Professional Liability Insurance (DMAA)
PLI........... Programming Language Interface [*Computer science*] (AGLO)
PLI........... Public Lands Institute (EA)
PLI........... Pulsed LASER Interferometry
PLIA .... Pollution Liability Insurance Association [*Defunct*] (EA)
PLIAN .... Public Legal Information Association of Newfoundland [*Legal group*] [*Canada*] (FOTI)
PLIANT...... Procedural Language Implementing Analog Techniques [*Computer science*] (IEEE)
PLIB .... Pacific Lumber Inspection Bureau (EA)
PLIB .... Program Library [*Computer science*]
PLIC .... Procedural Language for Integrity Constraints [*Computer science*] (MHDI)
PLIC .... Programmable Logic Integrated Circuit (SAUS)
PLICE........ Programmable Low Impedance Circuit Element (TIMI)
PLICE........ Programmable Low-Impedance Circuit Element (SAUS)
PLICK........ Pride, Loyalty, Integrity, Capability, Knowledge (DNAB)
PLIDCO...... Pipe Line Development Co. (SAUS)
PLIDCO...... Pipe Line Development Company, Cleveland, Ohio (SAUS)
PLIE .... Phase Linear Interferometer Experiment (MCD)
PLIF .... Planar Laser Induced Fluorescence
PLI F .... Polo Laico Liberali-Repubblicani Federalisti [*Italy*] [*Political party*] (ECED)
PLIF .... Postlumbar Interbody Fusion [*Neurology*] (DAVI)
PLIM......... Post Launch and Instrumentation Message [*NASA*] (IAA)
PLIM......... Post Launch Information Message [*NASA*] (KSC)
PLIM......... Propellant Lining Installation Metal (ACAE)
Plim 1....... Plimsoll line (SAUS)
PLIMC .... Pipe Line Insurance Managers Conference [*Defunct*] (EA)
PLIMS .... Programming Language for Information Management System [*Computer science*] (MHDI)
PLimT .... Tyler Arboretum, Lima, PA [*Library symbol*] [*Library of Congress*] (LCLS)
PLIN .... Power Line Impedance Network
PLIN .... Private Line Intercity Network (SAUS)
PLINK .... American People/Link [*American Design and Communication*] [*Information service or system*] (IID)
PLIP .... Parallel Line Internet Protocol [*Computer science*] (AGLO)
PLIP .... Preamplifier Limited Infrared (IAA)
PLIP .... Preamplifier Limited Infrared Photoconductor (SAUS)
PLIRRA...... Pollution Liability Insurance and Risk Retention Act (GFGA)
PLIS .... Preclinical Literature Information System [*Computer science*]
PLIS .... Propellant-Level Indicating System (SAUS)
PLIS .... Public Libraries in the Information Society (TELE)

PLISN .... Parts List Item Sequence Number (MCD)
PLISN .... Provisioning List Item Sequence Number (NASA)
PLISS .... Portable Life Support System (SAUS)
PLISSIT ..... Permission, Limited Information, Specific Suggestions, and Intensive Therapy [*Occupational therapy*]
PLIST .... Parameters List (SAUS)
PLIT .... Petrolite Corp. [*NASDAQ symbol*] (NQ)
PLITTY ...... Private Line Teletypewriter Service [*Telecommunications*] (TEL)
PLIU .... Prudential-Grace Lines [*Intermodal shipping container symbol*] (TVRC)
PLIUN .... Partido Liberal Independiente de Unidad Nacional [*Nicaragua*] [*Political party*] (EY)
PLIW .... Preload Indicating Washer
PLIZ .... Pellex Incorporated [*Federal Railroad Administration identification code*]
PLJ .... Pacific Law Journal [*A publication*] (ILCA)
PLJ .... Parliamentary Lobby Journalists [*British*]
PLJ .... Pass Lake Resources Ltd. [*Vancouver Stock Exchange symbol*]
PLJ .... Patna Law Journal [*India*] [*A publication*] (ILCA)
PLJ .... Pennsylvania Law Journal [*A publication*] (DLA)
PLJ .... Permanent Loop Junctor (NITA)
PLJ .... Philippine Law Journal [*A publication*] (ILCA)
PLJ .... Pittsburgh Legal Journal [*Pennsylvania*] [*A publication*] (DLA)
PLJ .... Punjab Law Reporter [*India*] [*A publication*] (DLA)
PLJ .... Pure Lemon Juice
PLJ NS ...... Pittsburgh Legal Journal, New Series [*Pennsylvania*] [*A publication*] (DLA)
PLK .... Branson, MO [*Location identifier*] [*FAA*] (FAAL)
PLK .... Phi Lambda Kappa [*Fraternity*]
PLK .... Plank (AAG)
PLK .... Ploecker-Lee-Kesler [*Equation of state*]
PLK .... Plucky Little King [*Used by Western diplomats in Amman in reference to King Hussein of Jordan*]
PLK .... Poincare-Lighthill-Kuo [*Method*]
PLK .... Salomon, Inc. [*AMEX symbol*] (SAG)
PLK .... Salomon Inc. 6.125% PRI 'ELKS' [*AMEX symbol*] (TTSB)
PLKR .... Peacoat Locker
PLKR .... PubliCARD [*OTCBB symbol*]
PLL .... Pall Corp. [*NYSE symbol*] (SAG)
PLL .... Pallet [*Building construction*]
PLL .... Papers on Language and Literature: A Journal for Scholars and Critics of Language and Literature [*A publication*] (ANEX)
PLL .... Parts Load List (MCD)
PLL .... Passenger Legal Liability [*Insurance*] (AIA)
PLL .... Peripheral Light Loss
PLL .... Permanent Logical Link [*Telecommunications*]
PLL .... Phase-Locked Loop [*Computer science*] (GART)
PLL .... Pilgrim Lacrosse League (PSS)
PLL .... Plasma Lockload (AAEL)
Pl L .... Platt on Leases [*1841*] [*A publication*] (DLA)
PLL .... Plymouth & Lincoln [*Federal Railroad Administration identification code*]
PLL .... Polo, IL [*Location identifier*] [*FAA*] (FAAL)
PLL .... Poly-L-lysine [*Also, PL*] [*Biochemistry*]
PLL .... Positive Logic Level
PLL .... Posterior Longitudinal Ligament [*Medicine*] (MELL)
PLL .... Prelinked Library (SAUS)
PLL .... Prescribed Load List [*Vehicle maintenance operation*] [*Army*]
PLL .... Pressure Length Loop (DB)
PLL .... Prince Line Ltd. [*Steamship*] (MHDW)
PLL .... Program Load Limit (SAUS)
PLL .... Prolymphocytic Leukemia [*Also, PL*] [*Oncology*]
PLL .... Pseudoalcoholic Liver Lesions [*Medicine*]
PLLA .... Printer Long Line Adapter (SAUS)
PLLDF .... Phase-Locked Loop with Decision Feedback [*NASA*] (IAA)
PLLE .... Prueba de Lectura y Lenguaje Escrito [*Standardized test of reading and writing in Spanish for students in grades 3 through 10*]
PLLI .... National Institute on Postsecondary Education, Libraries, and Lifelong Learning
PLL-IC .... Phase-Locked Loop-Integrated Circuit (SAUS)
PLLL .... Parallel Petroleum [*NASDAQ symbol*] (TTSB)
PLLL .... Parallel Petroleum Corp. [*NASDAQ symbol*] (NASQ)
PLLL .... Posterior Lateral Line Lobe [*Of electric fishes*]
PLLO .... Phase-Locked Loop Oscillators (ADWA)
PLLRC .... Public Land Law Review Commission [*Terminated, 1970*]
PLLS .... Portable Landing Light System (PDAA)
PLLT .... Pallet (NATG)
PLLTN .... Pollution
PLLU .... Polinesia Line [*Common carrier symbol*]
PLLU .... Polynesia Line [*Intermodal shipping container symbol*] (TVRC)
PLLVM .... Pennsylvania Farm Museum of Landis Valley, Lancaster, PA [*Library symbol*] [*Library of Congress*] (LCLS)
PLLX .... Pike Letcher Land [*Federal Railroad Administration identification code*]
PLLZ .... Polynesia Line [*Intermodal trailer symbol*]
PLM .... Pacific Law Magazine [*A publication*] (DLA)
PLM .... Packaged Liquid Missile
PLM .... Pakistan Liberation Movement [*Political party*] (PD)
PLM .... Palembang [*Indonesia*] [*Airport symbol*] (OAG)
PLM .... Palomar [*California*] [*Seismograph station code, US Geological Survey*] (SEIS)
PLM .... Parliament [*Telegraphy*] (PCTE)
PLM .... Passive Line Monitor [*Datapoint*]
PLM .... Passive Lunar Marker
PLM .... Payload Management [*NASA*] (NASA)
PLM .... Payload Mangement (SAUS)
PLM .... Payload Monitoring [*NASA*] (NASA)
PLM .... People's Liberation Movement [*Montserrat*] [*Political party*] (PPW)
PLM .... Percent Labeled Mitosis [*Cytology*]
PLM .... Periodic Leg Movement (DMAA)
PLM .... Permanent Longitudinal Magnetism (SAUS)
PLM .... Phleomycin [*Biochemistry*]
PLM .... Phospholemman [*Biochemistry*]
PLM .... Planetary Rotation Machine (IAA)
PLM .... Planned Lighting Maintenance (SAUS)
PLM .... Planned Maintenance (SAUS)
PLM .... Plasma Level Monitoring [*Medicine*] (DMAA)
PLM .... Plastic Laminating Mold (MCD)
PLM .... PLM International [*AMEX symbol*] (TTSB)
PLM .... PLM International, Inc. [*AMEX symbol*] (SPSG)
PLM .... Plymouth Financial [*Vancouver Stock Exchange symbol*]
PLM .... Poetae Latini Minores [*A publication*] (OCD)
PLM .... Polarized Light Microscopy
PLM .... Polymer-Linked Ligand Monomer [*Biochemistry*]
PLM .... Poor Law Magazine [*A publication*] (DLA)
PLM .... Power Line Modulation (AABC)
PLM .... Prelaunch Monitor [*NASA*] (KSC)
PLM .... Preliminary (KSC)
PLM .... Private Label Merchandiser [*USCG*] (TAG)
PLM .... Production Line Maintenance [*Air Force*]
PLM .... Production-Line Maintenance (SAUS)
PLM .... Production Line Manufacturing
PLM .... Product Life-Cycle Management [*Automotive industry*]
PLM .... Product Line Manager
PLM .... Program Library Management (TIMI)
PLM .... Programmable Logic Matrix (SAUS)
PLM .... Programming Language for Microcomputers (SAUS)
PL/M .... Programming Language for Microprocessors (NITA)
PL/M .... Programming Language/Microcomputers [*Intel Corp.*] [*1973*] [*Computer science*] (CSR)
PLM .... Programming Logic Manual
PLM .... Progressive Labor Movement (BARN)
PLM .... Public Law Movement (SAFN)
PLM .... Pulse-Length Modulation
PLMA .... Private Label Manufacturers Association (EA)
PLMA .... Producers Livestock Marketing Association [*Later, IPLA*] (EA)
PL Mag ..... Poor Law Magazine [*1858-1930*] [*Scotland*] [*A publication*] [*A publication*] (DLA)
PLMATH ..... Procedure Library Mathematics [*Computer science*] (IAA)
PLMB .... Plumbing (AAG)
plmb .... Plumbing (MIST)
PLMBR ...... Plumber
PLMC .... Premature Living Male Child [*Neonatology*] (DAVI)
PLMD .... Payload Mating Dolly [*NASA*]
PLMD .... Periodic Limb Movements Disorder (ADWA)
PLMD .... PolyMedica Corp. [*NASDAQ symbol*]
PLME .... Peak Local Mean Error (MCD)
PLMES ...... Planning, Measurement, and Evaluation Section [*PLA*] (AL)
PLMES ...... Planning, Measurements & Evaluation Section [*Public Library Association*] [*American Library Association*]
PLMG .... Plumbing (WGA)
PLMG .... Publishers' Library Marketing Group [*Defunct*] (EA)
PLMHi .... Lancaster Mennonite Conference Historical Society, Lancaster, PA [*Library symbol*] [*Library of Congress*] (LCLS)
PLMN .... Partido Marxista Leninista de Nicaragua [*Political party*] (EY)
PLMN .... Public Land Mobile Network (CGWS)
PL MO .... Plastic Mould (SAUS)
PLMP .... Program Logistic Management Plan (MCD)
PLMPA ...... Permanent Labourers' Mutual Protective Association [*A union*] [*British*]
PLMR .... Paris, Lyons, and Mediterranean Railway (ROG)
PLMR .... Post Launch Memorandum Report
PlmrW .... Palmer Wireless [*Associated Press*] (SAG)
PLMS .... Palms
PLMS .... Partitioned Libraries Management System (MHDI)
PLMS .... Periodic Leg Movements in Sleep (DIPS)
PLMS .... Periodic Limb Movement when Sleeping (MELL)
PLMS .... Plastic Master [*Tool*] (AAG)
PLMS .... Preservation of Library Materials Section [*Resources and Technical Services Division*] [*American Library Association*]
PLMS .... Program Logistics Master Schedule [*NASA*] (NASA)
PLMS .... Public Land Mobile Service Data Base [*Comp Comm, Inc.*] [*Information service or system*] (CRD)
PlmSSB ..... Palm Springs Savings Bank [*Associated Press*] (SAG)
PLMT .... Pastoral Lands Management Team (SAUS)
PLMT .... Plasmacytoid Lymphocyte [*Hematology*] (DAVI)
PLMU .... PLM International [*Intermodal shipping container symbol*] (TVRC)
PLMV .... Posterior Leaf Mitral Valve [*Cardiology*] (DMAA)
PLMX .... PL/M Extended [*Programming language*] (CSR)
PLMY .... Parliamentary [*Telegraphy*] (PCTE)
PLN .... Flight Plan [*Aviation code*]
PLN .... National Liberal Party (Panama) [*Political party*] (PSAP)
PLN .... Pancreatic Lymph Nodes [*Medicine*] (MELL)
PLN .... Partido de Liberacion Nacional [*National Liberation Party*] [*El Salvador*] [*Political party*] (EY)
PLN .... Partido Liberacion Nacional [*National Liberation Party*] [*Costa Rica*] [*Political party*] (PPW)
PLN .... Partido Liberal Nacionalista [*Nationalist Liberal Party*] [*Nicaragua*]
PLN .... Pellston [*Michigan*] [*Airport symbol*] (OAG)
PLN .... Pellston, MI [*Location identifier*] [*FAA*] (FAAL)

PLN .... Pelvic Lymph Node [*Gynecology*] (DAVI)
PLN .... Pennsylvania League for Nursing (EARSL)
PLN .... Peripheral Lymph Node [*Medicine*] (DB)
PLN .... Phospholamban [*Biochemistry*]
Pl-N .... Place-Name (SAUS)
PLN .... Plain
PLN .... Plan (NASA)
PLN .... Plane (MSA)
Pln .... Platen (SAUS)
Pln .... Platoon [*British military*] (DMA)
PLN .... Plauen [*German Democratic Republic*] [*Seismograph station code, US Geological Survey*] (SEIS)
PLN .... Politician [*Telegraphy*] (PCTE)
PLN .... Polnippon [*Poland*] [*ICAO designator*] (FAAC)
PLN .... Popliteal Lymph Node [*Anatomy*]
PLN .... Position and Location Navigation
PLN .... Posterior Lip Nerve (DAVI)
PLN .... Posterior Lymph Node (SAUS)
PLN .... Potassium Lithium Niobate (PDAA)
PLN .... Primary Learning Net (SAUS)
PLN .... Primary Learning Network [*Computer science*] (IAA)
PLN .... Private Line Network (CCCA)
PLN .... Program Line Number [*DoD*]
PLN .... Program Logic Network (NASA)
PLN .... Proteoliaisin [*Biochemistry*]
PLN .... Pudendal Lymph Nodes [*Medicine*] (MELL)
PLN .... Pump-Line-Nozzle
PLN .... Purposely Limited Network (SAUS)
PLNAG ...... Public Libraries Networking Advisory Group [*British*] (TELE)
PLNAP ...... Pro-Life Nonviolent Action Project (EA)
PLNASG ..... Public Libraries Network Awareness Steering Group [*British*] (TELE)
PLNASG ..... Public Library Network Awareness Steering Group (SAUS)
PLNC .... Point Loma Nazarene College (SAUS)
PLNCIAWPRC ... Polish National Committee of the International Association on Water Pollution Research and Control (SAUS)
PLND .... Pelvic Lymph Node Dissection [*Medicine*] (MELL)
plnd .... Planned (DA)
Plng .... Planning (TBD)
PLNG .... Planning
PlnMsg ...... Plain Message (SAUS)
PLNN .... Planning (MCD)
PLNP .... Port Lincoln National Park (SAUS)
PLNR .... Planar (MSA)
PLNR .... Planar Systems [*NASDAQ symbol*] (SAG)
PLNR .... Planner
PLNRCODE ... Planner Code (SAUS)
PlnRsc ...... Plains Resources, Inc. [*Associated Press*] (SAG)
PLNS .... Plains
PLNS .... Plains Resources, Inc. [*NASDAQ symbol*] (COMM)
PLNS .... Planning Sciences International [*NASDAQ symbol*] (SAG)
PLNS .... Pliant Systems [*OTCBB symbol*]
PLNSTD ..... Planned Standard Equipment [*Navy*] (AFIT)
PLNSY .... Planning Sciences ADS [*NASDAQ symbol*] (TTSB)
PLNT .... Planet (MSA)
PLNT .... Plant
PLNTY .... Planetary (MSA)
PLNVW ...... Plainview, TX [*American Association of Railroads railroad junction routing code*]
PLNY .... Preliminary [*Telegraphy*] (PCTE)
PLNYS .... Preservation League of New York State (EARSL)
PLNZ .... Penske Logistics [*Intermodal trailer symbol*]
PLO .... Pacific Launch Operations [*NASA*]
PLO .... Palestina Liberty Organisation (SAUS)
PLO .... Palestine Liberation Organisation (SAUS)
PLO .... Palestine Liberation Organization [*Political party*] (PD)
PLO .... Palestinian Liberation Organization (SAUS)
PLO .... Parliamentary Liaison Officer (ADA)
PLO .... Partial Lunar Orbit [*Planetary science*]
PLO .... Parts List Only (MCD)
PLO .... Payload Officer [*NASA*] (MCD)
PLO .... Pentagon Liaison Office (MCD)
PLO .... Peoples Liberation Organization (NADA)
PLO .... Phase-Locked Oscillator
PLO .... Pipeline Oil (SAUS)
PLO .... Plano, IL [*Amtrak rail station code*]
PLO .... Plans Officer
PLO .... Please Leave On (SAUS)
PLO .... Polycystic Lipomembranous Osteodysplasia [*Medicine*] (DMAA)
PLO .... Poly-L-ornithine
PLO .... Poor Law Office (ROG)
PLO .... Port Liaison Officer
PLO .... Port Lincoln [*Australia*] [*Airport symbol*] (OAG)
PLO .... Presidential Libraries Office (NADA)
PLO .... Price-Lifting Operation [*Business term*] (ECON)
PLO .... Probability of Leakage through Overlay
PLO .... Process Limit Option (SAUS)
PLO .... Product Line Organization
PLO .... Program Line Organization
PLO .... Programmed Local Oscillator
PLO .... Project Line Organization
PLO .... Public Land Order [*Interior*]
PLO .... Public Limit Order [*British*] (NUMA)
PLO .... Pulsed LASER Oscillator
PLO .... Pulsed Locked Oscillator
PLOA .... Proposed Letter of Agreement (MCD)
PLOB .... Patrol Log Observations [*Aviation*] (DSUE)
PLOB .... Place of Birth
PLOB .... Public Limit Order Board [*British*] (NUMA)
PLOC .... Payload Operations Contractor [*NASA*] (SSD)
PLOCAP ..... Post Loss-of-Coolant Accident Protection [*Nuclear energy*] (NRCH)
PLOCSA ..... Personal Liaison Officer, Chief of Staff, Army (SAUS)
PLOCSA ..... Personnel Liaison Officer, Chief of Staff, Army (AABC)
PLOD .... Periodic List of Data [*Computer science*]
PLOD .... Planetary Orbit Determination (IEEE)
PLOe .... Ploen [*Holstein*] [*German license plate city code*]
PLOKTA ..... Press Lots of Keys to Abort [*Computer term*]
P Lom .... Petrus Lombardi [*Flourished, 1154-59*] [*Authority cited in pre-1607 legal work*] (DSA)
PLOM .... Prescribed Loan Optimization Model [*Army*] (AABC)
PLOME ...... Poor Little Old Me Syndrome [*British*]
PLOMS ...... Professional Legal Office Management System (SAUS)
PLondon .... Greek Papyri in the British Museum [*A publication*] (OCD)
PLONEF ..... Plates on Elastic Foundations [*Structures & Computers Ltd.*] [*Software package*] (NCC)
PLONG ...... Present Longititude [*Aviation*] (FAAC)
PLOO .... Pacific Launch Operations Office [*NASA*]
PLOP .... Pilot Line Operating Procedure (SAUS)
PLOP .... Planetary Landing Observation Package [*Aerospace*]
PLOP .... Plant Layout Optimization Procedure (SAUS)
PLOP .... Pressure Line of Position [*Air Force*]
PLOQ .... Pilot Van Lines [*Common carrier symbol*]
PLor .... Saint Francis College, Loretto, PA [*Library symbol*] [*Library of Congress*] (LCLS)
PLOS .... Primary Line of Sight [*Sextants*]
PLoS .... Public Library of Science
PLOT .... People's Liberation Organization of Tamil Eelam [*Sri Lanka*] [*Political party*]
PLOT .... Piagetian Logical Operations Test (EDAC)
PLOT .... Plotter
PLOT .... Plotting
PLOT .... Porous Layer Open Tubular (SAUS)
PLOT .... Porous Layer, Open Tubular Column [*Gas chromatography*]
PLOT .... Possibility of Launch-on-Time (SAUS)
PLOT .... Probability of Launch on Time (MCD)
Plot .... Vita Plotini [*of Porphyry*] [*Classical studies*] (OCD)
PLOTE .... People's Liberation Organization of Tamil Eelam [*Sri Lanka*] [*Political party*]
PLOU .... Polyol Chemicals [*Intermodal shipping container symbol*] (TVRC)
PLOVR ...... Plover, WI [*American Association of Railroads railroad junction routing code*]
PLOW .... Petunia Lovers of the World
Plow .... Plowden's English King's Bench Commentaries [*or Reports*] [*A publication*] (DLA)
Plowd .... Plowden's English King's Bench Commentaries [*or Reports*] [*A publication*] (DLA)
PLOYREP ... Unit Deployment Report (CINC)
PLP .... La Palma [*Panama*] [*Airport symbol*] (OAG)
PLP .... Packet Layer Protocol [*Computer science*] (TNIG)
PLP .... Packet Level Procedure [*or Protocol*] [*Computer programming*] (PCM)
PLP .... Packet Level Protocol (SAUS)
PLP .... Palo [*Philippines*] [*Seismograph station code, US Geological Survey*] (SEIS)
PLP .... Palpus [*Arthropod anatomy*]
PLP .... Parathyroidlike Protein [*Medicine*] (MELL)
PLP .... Parliamentary Labour Party [*British*]
PLP .... Parti de la Liberte et du Progres [*Party of Liberty and Progress*] [*See also PVV*] [*Belgium*] (PPE)
PLP .... Partido de los Pobres [*Poor People's Party*] [*Mexico*] [*Political party*] (PD)
PLP .... Parti Liberal Progressiste [*Liberal Progressive Party*] [*Morocco*] [*Political party*] (PPW)
PLP .... Parti pour la Liberation du Peuple [*People's Liberation Party*] [*Senegal*] [*Political party*] (PPW)
PLP .... Partners for Livable Places (EA)
PLP .... Parts List Page (KSC)
PLP .... Party Line Protocol (SAUS)
PLP .... Passive Low Pass (IAA)
PLP .... Patrol Landplane (SAUS)
PLP .... Pattern Learning Parser
PLP .... People's Liberation Party [*Pakistan*]
PLP .... Periodate Lysine-Paraformaldehyde
PLP .... Periodate-Lysine-Paraformalin (SAUS)
PLP .... Personal LASER Printer [*Computer science*]
PLP .... Phantom Limb Pain (MELL)
PLP .... Phillips Petroleum Co. [*Toronto Stock Exchange symbol*]
PLP .... Phoenix Aviation [*British*] [*ICAO designator*] (FAAC)
PLP .... Phosphate Resource Partners LP [*NYSE symbol*]
PLP .... Photolithographic Process (IAA)
PLP .... Physical Layer Protocol (SAUS)
PLP .... Plains Petroleum Co. [*NYSE symbol*] (COMM)
PLP .... Plastic Lined Pipe (SAUS)
PLP .... Plastic-Lined Pipe
PLP .... Polyoma-Like Particle [*Genetics*]
PLP .... Polystyrene Latex Particles (DB)
PLP .... Post Launch Phase
PLP .... Power Law Process
PLP .... Preferred Lenders Program [*Small Business Administration*]
PLP .... Preformed Line Product (IAA)

PLP .... Preformed Line Products (SAUS)
PLP .... Presentation Level Protocol [*AT & T Videotex System*]
PLP .... Principal Locating Point [*Automotive engineering*]
PLP .... Prison Link Project (WDAA)
PLP .... Procedural Language Processor
PLP .... Process Layup Procedure
PLP .... Product Liability Prevention [*Conference*]
PLP .... Product Line Planning (SAUS)
PLP .... Programming Language Processing (or Processor) (SAUS)
PLP .... Progressive Labor Party (EA)
PLP .... Progressive Labour Party [*Saint Lucia*] [*Political party*] (EAIO)
PLP .... Progressive Liberal Party [*Bahamas*] [*Political party*] (PPW)
PLP .... Progressive List for Peace (Israel) [*Political party*] (PSAP)
PLP .... Prolactin-Like Protein [*Biochemistry*]
PLP .... Proteolipid [*Biochemistry*]
PLP .... Proteolipid Protein [*Biochemistry*]
PLP .... Pyridoxal Phosphate [*Also, PALP*] [*Biochemistry*]
PLPA .... Pageable Link Pack Area (SAUS)
PLPA .... Pageable Link-Pack Area
PLPA .... Palmyra, Palymra Island [*Line Islands*] [*ICAO location identifier*] (ICLI)
PLPA .... Permissible Low-Pressure Alarm (SAUS)
PLPA .... Permissive Low-Pressure Alarm (IEEE)
PLPA .... Professional Lacrosse Players Association (EA)
Pl Par .... Placita Parliamentaria [*Latin*] [*A publication*] (DLA)
PL PATH .... Plant Pathology (SAUS)
PLPB .... Petroleum Labor Policy Board [*Abolished, 1936*]
PLPBD .... Pulpboard
PLPD .... Product Liability Prevention and Defense [*An association*] (EA)
PLP FOR .... Foramen of Labial Palpus [*Arthropod anatomy*]
PLPG .... Publishers' Library Promotion Group [*Later, PLMG*] (EA)
PLP GRNDG .... Pulp Grinding [*Freight*]
PLPH .... Post-Lumbar Puncture Headache [*Medicine*] (DMAA)
PLPI .... Product Licence Parallel Importation (DB)
PLPL .... Pet Lovers Protective League (EARSL)
PLPLS .... Proceedings of the Leeds Philosophical and Literary Society (SAUS)
PLPO .... Phase-Locked Pulsed Oscillator (SAUS)
PlPolyT .... Planet Polymer Technologies, Inc. [*Associated Press*] (SAG)
PLPP .... Pennsylvania League for Planned Parenthood (SAUS)
PLPP .... Position Location Post Processor (MCD)
PLPrM .... PLC Capital LLC 'A' 'MIPS' [*NYSE symbol*] (TTSB)
PLPS .... Packaged Liquid Propellant System
PLPS .... Propellant Loading and Pressurization System [*NASA*]
PLPS .... Pulse-Locked Power Supply (SAUS)
PLPT .... Presentation Level Protocol [*Computer science*]
PLPT .... Pretreatment Local Program Tracking System (SAUS)
PLPV .... Pelargonium Line Pattern Virus [*Plant pathology*]
PLPYD .... Public Libraries as Partners in Youth Development Program
PLQ .... Photoluminescence Quenching Spectroscopy (SAUS)
PLQ .... Plaque (MSA)
PLQ .... Public Library Quarterly (SAUS)
PLQ .... Tallahassee, FL [*Location identifier*] [*FAA*] (FAAL)
PLR .... LaRoche College, Pittsburgh, PA [*OCLC symbol*] (OCLC)
PLR .... Liberal Republican Party (Panama) [*Political party*] (PSAP)
PLR .... Northwestern Air Lease Ltd. [*Canada*] [*ICAO designator*] (FAAC)
PLR .... Pacific Law Reporter [*A publication*] (DLA)
PLR .... Packet Lost Ratio (SAUS)
PLR .... Pakistan Law Reports [*A publication*] (DLA)
PLR .... Pakistan Law Review [*A publication*] (DLA)
PLR .... Parlake Resources Ltd. [*Toronto Stock Exchange symbol*]
PLR .... Parlakimedi Light Railway [*Indian Railway*] (TIR)
PLR .... Partido Liberal Radical [*Radical Liberal Party*] [*Ecuador*] [*Political party*] (PPW)
PLR .... Partido Liberal Radical [*Radical Liberal Party*] [*Paraguay*] [*Political party*] (PPW)
PLR .... Patent Law Review [*A publication*] (DLA)
PLR .... Patent Log Reading [*Navigation*]
PLR .... Patna Law Reporter [*India*] [*A publication*] (DLA)
PLR .... Pell City, AL [*Location identifier*] [*FAA*] (FAAL)
PLR .... Pennsylvania Law Record [*Philadelphia*] [*A publication*] (DLA)
P-LR .... Pennsylvania Legislative Reference Bureau, Harrisburg, PA [*Library symbol*] [*Library of Congress*] (LCLS)
PLR .... Periodic Logistical Report
PLR .... Petro-Lewis Corporation (EFIS)
PLR .... Philippine Liberation Ribbon [*Military decoration*]
PLR .... Pillar (MSA)
PLR .... Pliers (MSA)
PLR .... Plymouth Rubber Co., Inc. [*AMEX symbol*] (SPSG)
plr .... Poplar (VRA)
PLR .... Portable LASER Range-Finder
PLR .... Power Line Radiation [*Radioscience*]
PLR .... Presentation Loss Rate (MCD)
PLR .... Pressure Level Recorder
PLR .... Primary Language Record [*Education*] (AIE)
PLR .... Primary Loss Retention [*Insurance*]
PLR .... Private Legislation Reports [*Scotland*] [*A publication*] (DLA)
PLR .... Production Limitation Record (SAUS)
PLR .... Product Licence of Right (DB)
PLR .... Program Length Register [*Computer science*] (VLIE)
PLR .... Program Library Release (VLIE)
PLR .... Program Life Requirement (NG)
PLR .... Program Lock-in Register (NITA)
PLR .... Programming Language for Robots (VLIE)
PLR .... Prolactin Receptor [*Biochemistry*]
PLR .... Pronation/Lateral Rotation [*Fracture*] [*Orthopedics*] (DAVI)
PLR .... Psychological Laboratories [*Harvard University*] (KSC)
PLR .... Public Law Review [*A publication*]
PLR .... Public Lending Right [*Royalty for books borrowed from public libraries*] [*British*]
PLR .... Puller (MSA)
PLR .... Pulse Link Relay [*Telecommunications*] (TEL)
PLR .... Pulse Link Repeater [*Telecommunications*] (TEL)
PLR .... Punjab Law Reporter [*India*] [*A publication*] (DLA)
PLR .... Pupillary Light Reflex (SAUS)
PLR. A .... Plymouth Rubber'A'vtg [*AMEX symbol*] (TTSB)
PLR.B .... Plymouth Rubber Cl'B' [*AMEX symbol*] (TTSB)
PLRA .... Partido Liberal Radical Autentico [*Authentic Liberal Radical Party*] [*Paraguay*] [*Political party*] (PD)
PLRA .... Pennsylvania Learning Resources Association (EDAC)
PLRA .... Photo Litho Reproducers Association (SAUS)
PLRA .... Photo-Litho Reproducers' Association [*British*] (BI)
PLRACTA .... Position Location, Reporting, and Control of Tactical Aircraft [*Military*]
PLRB .... Property Loss Research Bureau (EA)
PLRC .... Pulsed LASER Remote Crosswind Sensor (MCD)
PLRCAE .... Radio Corp. of America, Electron Tube Division, Engineering Section, Lancaster, PA [*Library symbol*] [*Library of Congress*] [*Obsolete*] (LCLS)
PLRD .... Payload Requirements Document (NASA)
PLRD .... Polaroid (VRA)
PLRD .... Procurement, Logistics, and Readiness Division (AAGC)
PLRD .... Pull Rod
PLR Dacca .... Pakistan Law Reports, Dacca Series [*A publication*] (DLA)
PLRE .... Program on Long-Range Forecasting Research [*Marine science*] (OSRA)
PLRE .... Radical Liberal Party (Ecuador) [*Political party*] (PSAP)
PL Reaction .... Palm Leaf Reaction (SAUS)
PLRF .... Pediatric Liver Research Foundation [*Defunct*] (EA)
pLRF .... Placental Luteinizing Hormone-Releasing Factor [*Endocrinology*]
PLRF .... Planer Fixture
PLRF .... Program on Long-Range Forecasting Research (SAUS)
PLRG .... Public Libraries Research Group [*British*] (TELE)
PLRI .... Posterolateral Rotation Instability [*Sports medicine*]
PLRJ & K .... Punjab Law Reporter, Jammu and Kashmir Section [*India*] [*A publication*] (DLA)
PLRK .... Plymouth Rock Transportation Corporation [*Common carrier symbol*]
PLR Kar .... Pakistan Law Reports, Karachi Series [*1947-53*] [*A publication*] (DLA)
PLR Lah .... Pakistan Law Reports, Lahore Series [*1947-55*] [*A publication*] (DLA)
PLRPF .... Personnel Loss Rate Planning Factors (MCD)
PLRS .... Pelorus
PLRS .... Phase Lock Receiving System
PLRS .... Phase-Lock Receiving System (SAUS)
PLRS .... Pluristem Life Systems [*OTCBB symbol*]
PLRS .... Position Location Reporting System [*Military*]
PLRS/TIDS .... Position Location Reporting System/Tactical Information Distribution Systems [*Military*] (RDA)
PLRSTN .... Pelorus Stand
PLRT .... Polarity (MSA)
PLRU .... PIC Leasing Corporation [*Intermodal shipping container symbol*] (TVRC)
PLRV .... Payload Launch Readiness Verification [*NASA*] (MCD)
PLRV .... Potato Leafroll Virus
PLRV .... Pseudo Leaf Roll Virus (SAUS)
PLRWP .... Pakistan Law Reports, West Pakistan Series [*A publication*] (DLA)
PLRX .... PIC Transportation [*Private rail car owner code*]
PLRX .... Pittsburg, Lisbon & Western Railway [*Federal Railroad Administration identification code*]
PLRXE .... PlanetRx.com, Inc. [*NASDAQ symbol*] (QUAN)
PLRZ .... Polarization [*Communications term*] (DCT)
pls .... Isoelectric Point (STED)
PLS .... Page Layout System [*Graphic arts*] (DGA)
PLS .... Palio Air Service [*Italy*] [*ICAO designator*] (FAAC)
PLS .... Palletized Loading System
PLS .... Palletized Load System [*Army*] (RDA)
PLS .... Palletized Load System [*Automotive engineering*]
PLS .... Palomar-Leiden Survey
PLS .... Papillon-Lefevre Syndrome [*Medicine*] (DMAA)
PLS .... Paracelsus Healthcare Corp. [*NYSE symbol*] (SAG)
PLS .... Parcels (MSA)
PLS .... Parent Locator Service [*A service of the Office of Child Support Enforcement (OCSE)*] (PAZ)
PLS .... Parsons Language Sample
PLS .... Partial Least Squares
PLS .... Parti Liberal Suisse [*Liberal Party of Switzerland*] [*Political party*] (PPE)
PLS .... Patrol Locator System [*Army*]
PLS .... Payload Systems [*NASA*] (MCD)
PLS .... Peerless Tube Co. [*AMEX symbol*] (SPSG)
PLS .... Peninsula Library System [*Belmont, CA*] [*Library network*]
PLS .... People's Law School [*Defunct*] (EA)
PLS .... Peralto Resources Corp. [*Vancouver Stock Exchange symbol*]
PLS .... Periodic Log System
PLS .... Personal Learning System (VLIE)
PLS .... Personal Library Software [*Commercial firm*]
PLS .... Personal Library Systems (SAUS)
PLS .... Personal Locator System (ACAE)
PLS .... Physical Layer Signaling (SAUS)
PLS .... Physical Layer Signalling (VLIE)
PLS .... Physical Signalling (NITA)

PLS .... Picture Line Standard (ELAL)
PLS .... Pioneer Library System [*New York*]
PLS .... Pitch Limit Switch
PLS .... Plaisance [*Mauritius*] [*Geomagnetic observatory code*]
PLS .... Plasma Light Source
PLS .... Plasma Spectrometer (ACAE)
PLS .... Plasma Subsystem (ACAE)
PLS .... Plastic Surgery (MELL)
pls .... Plates (DIAR)
PLS .... Plates [*Classical studies*] (OCD)
PLS .... Please (AFM)
PLS .... Plugging Switch (IEEE)
PLS .... Pneumatic Limit Switch
PLS .... Point of Last Scrimmage [*Football*]
PLS .... Polson, MT [*Location identifier*] [*FAA*] (FAAL)
PLS .... Polynomial Solution (IAA)
PLS .... Polystyrene Latex Sphere
PLS .... Popular Low-Power Schottky [*Electronics*] (MCD)
PLS .... Portable Laboratory Salinometer
PLS .... Position Location System [*Army*]
PLS .... Positive Locking System (SAUS)
PLS .... Positive Lubrication System (SAUS)
PLS .... Positron Lifetime Spectroscopy (SAUS)
PLS .... Post Landing and Safing [*NASA*] (NASA)
PLS .... Postsecondary Longitudinal Studies Program [*Department of Education*] (GFGA)
PLS .... Precautions, Limitations, and Setpoints [*Nuclear energy*] (NRCH)
PLS .... Pre Launch Survivability (ACAE)
PLS .... Pre-Launch Survivability (SAUS)
PLS .... Preliminary Landing Site (NASA)
PLS .... Preliminary Location Summary (VLIE)
PLS .... Preschool Language Scale [*Child development test*]
PLS .... President of the Linnaean Society [*British*]
PLS .... Primary Landing Site (MCD)
PLS .... Primary Lateral Sclerosis [*Medicine*] (DMAA)
PLS .... Primary Link Station (VLIE)
PLS .... Principles and Practice of Land Surveying (SAUS)
PLS .... Private Line Service
PLS .... Product Line Simulator
PLS .... Professional Land Surveyor (SAUS)
PLS .... Professional Legal Secretary [*National Association of Legal Secretaries*] [*Designation awarded by*]
PLS .... Profit-and-Loss-Sharing Account [*Banking*] (IMH)
PLS .... Program Liaison Staff (COE)
PLS .... Programmable Limit Switch (SAUS)
PLS .... Programmable Logic Sequence (SAUS)
PLS .... Programmable Logic Sequencer [*Computer science*]
PLS .... Programming Language for System [*Computer science*] (IAA)
PL/S .... Programming Language/System [*Computer science*] (HODG)
PLS .... Progressive Learning Systems [*Potomac, MD*] (TSSD)
PLS .... Projectile Location System (SAUS)
PLS .... Projection of Latent Structures (AAEL)
PLS .... Propellant Loading Sequencer (AAG)
PLS .... Propellant Loading System
PLS .... Prostaglandin-Like Substance [*Biochemistry*] (MAE)
PLS .... Providenciales [*British West Indies*] [*Airport symbol*] (OAG)
PLS .... Provincial Land Surveyor (SAUS)
PLS .... Public Library of Science
PLS .... Publishers Licensing Society (DGA)
PLS .... Pulse (MSA)
PLS .... Pulsed LASER System
PLS .... Pulsed Light Source
PLS .... Pulser (SAUS)
PLS .... Pure Live Seed (SAUS)
PLS .... Purnell Library Service [*Commercial firm*]
PLSA .... Partner Launch Site Agreement (SAUS)
PLSA .... Posterolateral Spinal Artery [*Medicine*] (RAWO)
PLSA .... Pulsed Laser Spectrum Analyzer (SAUS)
PLSAP .... Physical Layer Service Access Point [*Computer science*] (VLIE)
PLSC .... Pacific Logistics Support Command (SAUS)
PLSC .... Political Science (SAUS)
PLSC .... Project Level Steering Committee (HGAA)
PLSD .... Post Hoc Least Significant Difference [*Statistics*]
PLSD .... Promotion List Service Date [*Air Force*]
PLSD .... Protected Least Significant Difference (DMAA)
PLSFC .... Part Load Specific Fuel Consumption [*Gas turbine*]
PLSGT .... Platoon Sergeant [*Marine Corps*]
PLSHD .... Polished [*Freight*]
PLSHL .... Pleasant Hill, MO [*American Association of Railroads railroad junction routing code*]
Plshr .... Polisher (SAUS)
PLSI .... Planar Least Squares Inverse (SAUS)
PLSI .... Premier Laser Systems, Inc. [*NASDAQ symbol*] (SAG)
PLSI .... Programmable Large Scale Integration (SAUS)
PLSIA .... Premier Laser Systems'A' [*NASDAQ symbol*] (TTSB)
PLSIW .... Premier Laser Systems Wrrt'A' [*NASDAQ symbol*] (TTSB)
PLSIZ .... Premier Laser Systems Wrrt'B' [*NASDAQ symbol*] (TTSB)
PLSL .... Propellants and Life Support Laboratory [*NASA*] (NASA)
PLSN .... Pulsation (MSA)
PL/SNSR .... Payload Sensor [*NASA*] (GFGA)
PLSNT .... Pleasant
PLSO .... Phonetic Letter Spell Out (CCCA)
PLSO .... Phonetic Letters Spelled Out (SAUS)
PLSO .... Posterior Leafspring Orthosis [*Medicine*] (EDAA)
PLSO .... Propellant Life Support and Ordnance [*NASA*] (KSC)
PLSP .... Payload Signal Processor [*NASA*] (NAKS)
PLSP .... Prelaunch Survival Probability (CINC)
PLSPC .... Programme on Land-Surface Processes and Climate (SAUS)
PLSPC .... Research Programme on Land-Surface Processes and Climate (SAUS)
PL SPKR .... Plug for Speaker (SAUS)
PLSPS .... Performance Levels of a School Program Survey [*Teacher evaluation test*]
PL/SQI .... Programming Language/Structured Query Language [*Computer science*] (GART)
PLSR .... Pleasure [*Telegraphy*] (PCTE)
PLSR .... Pulsator (MSA)
PLSS .... Paolina and Sons Trucking [*Common carrier symbol*]
PLSS .... Payload Support Structure [*NASA*] (SSD)
PLSS .... Personal Life Support System (SAUS)
PLSS .... Portable Life Support [*Astronomy term*]
PLSS .... Portable Life Support Subsystem (SAUS)
PLSS .... Portable Life Support System [*or Subsystem*] [*NASA*]
PLSS .... Post-Landing Survival System [*NASA*]
PLSS .... Pottable Life-Support System (SAUS)
PLSS .... Precision Location Strike System [*Air Force*]
PLSS .... Prelaunch Status Simulator
PLSS .... Primary Life Support Subsystem (SAUS)
PLSS .... Primary Life Support System [*or Subsystem*] (NASA)
PLSS .... Public Land Survey System (ADWA)
PLSS .... Public Library Systems Section [*Public Library Association*]
PLSSRS .... Plant and Soil Science Research Station [*Southern Illinois University at Carbondale*] [*Research center*] (RCD)
PLSSU .... Portable Life Support Stretcher Unit [*Military*] (CAAL)
PLST .... Palletized Loading System Trailer (SAUS)
PLST .... Palletized Load System Truck [*Military*]
PLST .... Plastering
PLSTC .... Plastic (AAG)
PLSTG .... Plastering (SAUS)
PLSTR .... Plasterer (ADA)
PLSTRER .... Plasterer (WGA)
PLSU .... EM [*Intermodal shipping container symbol*] (TVRC)
PLSU .... Peerless Tube Co. [*OTCBB symbol*]
PLSURG .... Plastic Surgery [*Medicine*] (EDAA)
PLSV .... Propellant Latching Solenoid Valve
PL Sw .... Plub with Switch (SAUS)
PLT .... Columbus, NE [*Location identifier*] [*FAA*] (FAAL)
PLT .... Lancaster Theological Seminary of the United Church of Christ, Lancaster, PA [*Library symbol*] [*Library of Congress*] (LCLS)
PLT .... Lutheran Theological Seminary, Philadelphia, PA [*OCLC symbol*] (OCLC)
PLT .... Pacific Lighting (SAUS)
PLT .... Page Layout Terminal [*Graphic arts*] (DGA)
PLT .... Pallet (AABC)
PLT .... Pancreatic Lymphocytic Infiltration [*Medicine*] (EDAA)
PLT .... Panduit Locking Tie (SAUS)
Plt .... Parliament
PLT .... Partido Liberal Teete [*Teete Liberal Party*] [*Paraguay*] [*Political party*] (PPW)
PLT .... Patna Law Times [*India*] [*A publication*] (DLA)
Plt .... Peltier's Orleans Appeals Decisions [*Louisiana*] [*A publication*] (DLA)
PLT .... Personal Leave Time (SAUS)
PLT .... Phase-Locked Time (SAUS)
PLT .... Photoluminescent Thermometer
PLT .... Pi Lambda Theta [*An association*] (NTPA)
PLT .... Pilot (AFM)
PLT .... Pilot Knob [*California*] [*Seismograph station code, US Geological Survey*] (SEIS)
PLT .... Pipeline Time [*Army*]
PLT .... Plaint [*Legal term*] (ROG)
PLT .... Planar Tube
PLT .... Plant
PLT .... Plantronics, Inc. [*NYSE symbol*] (SPSG)
PLT .... Plate
PLT .... Platelet [*Hematology*]
PLT .... Platen (SAUS)
PLT .... Platoon [*Military*] (AABC)
Plt .... Platoon [*Military*] (POLM)
Plt .... Plot (SAUS)
PLT .... Plotting (SAUS)
PLT .... Port Light
PLT .... Post Loading Test (NG)
PLT .... Power Line Transient (IEEE)
PLT .... Primary Level Training [*Army*]
PLT .... Primed Lymphocyte Test [*Medicine*] (EDAA)
PLT .... Primed Lymphocyte Typing [*Hematology*]
PLT .... Princeton Large Torus [*Nuclear reactor*]
PLT .... Private Line Telephone
PLT .... Private Line Teletypewriter
PLT .... Procurement Lead Time [*Army*]
PLT .... Production Lead Time
PLT .... Program Library Tape [*Computer science*] (IEEE)
PLT .... Program List Table [*Computer science*] (VLIE)
PLT .... Programmed Learning Textbook
PLT .... Programmed Light Table (SAUS)
PLT .... Programming-Language Theory (SAUS)
PLT .... Progressive Lowering of Temperature
PLT .... Project Lead Time
PLT .... Project Learning Tree (WPI)

PLT.......... Psittacosis-Lymphogranuloma Trachoma (SAUS)
PLT.......... Psittacosis-Lymphogranuloma Venereum Trachoma [*Microbiology*]
PLT.......... Pulsed Light Theodolite
PLT.......... Pulse Light Theodolite (SAUS)
PLT.......... Punjab Law Times [*India*] [*A publication*] (DLA)
PLT.......... South Carolina Aeronautics Commission [*FAA designator*] (FAAC)
PLTC........ Partnership for Long Term Care
PLTC........ Political (SAUS)
PLTC........ Port Liner Terms Charges [*Shipping*] (DS)
PLTC........ Power-Limited Tray Cable (SAUS)
PLTC........ Propellant Loading Terminal Cabinet (AAG)
PLTD........ Plated
PLT EST.... Platelet Estimate [*Medicine*] (EDAA)
pltf.......... Paintiff (ODA)
PLTF........ Par Leadership Training Foundation [*Defunct*] (EA)
PLTF........ Plaintiff [*Legal term*] (ROG)
PLTF........ Purple Loosestrife Task Force [*Defunct*] (EA)
PLTFF....... Plaintiff
PLTFM....... Platform
PLT-G........ Giant Platelet [*Hematology*] (DAVI)
PLTG........ Plating
PLT GL...... Plate Glass [*Freight*]
PLTHS....... Pilothouse
PLTK........ Plastic Recycling, Inc. [*NASDAQ symbol*] (QUAN)
PLTL........ Plant Truck Line [*Common carrier symbol*]
PL-TLM..... Payload Telemetry (SAUS)
PLT LT...... Pilot Light (MSA)
PLTN........ Palatin Technologies [*NASDAQ symbol*]
PLTN........ Platoon
Plt Off....... Pilot Officer [*British military*] (DMA)
PLTP........ Phospholipid Transfer Protein [*Biochemistry*]
PLT Press... Platen Press (SAUS)
PLTR........ Plan for Long-Range Technical Requirements
PLTR........ Plotter (MSA)
PLTR........ Procurement Lead Time Requirement
Pltrsq........ Plateresque (VRA)
PLTRY....... Poultry [*Freight*]
PLTS........ Pacific Lutheran Theological Seminary (SAUS)
PLTS........ Point Loma Test Site (SAUS)
PLTS........ Precision LASER Tracking System (NASA)
PltsTrg....... Pilots Training (SAUS)
PLTTNG..... Pilot Training [*Air Force*]
PLTTNGSq... Pilot Training Squadron [*Air Force*]
PLTTY....... Private Line Teletypewriter [*Telecommunications*] (IAA)
PLTTY....... Private Line Teletypewriter Service (NITA)
PLTU........ PL Transtore [*Intermodal shipping container symbol*] (TVRC)
PLTV........ Paul Trucking [*Common carrier symbol*]
PLTV........ Percentage Local Thickness Variation (AAEL)
PLTXAU..... Public Telex Access Unit [*Telecommunications*] (OSI)
PLTY........ Poultry
PLTYP....... Plumbeotype (VRA)
PLTZC....... Pulitzer Publishing Co. (MHDW)
PLU.......... Pacific Lutheran University (SAUS)
PLU.......... Partial Line Up (NITA)
PLU.......... Partido Liberal Unificado [*Unified Liberal Party*] [*Paraguay*] [*Political party*] (PPW)
PLu.......... Path Loss, Uplink [*Communications*]
PLU.......... Patrice Lumumba University (SAUS)
PLU.......... People Like Us (IIA)
PLU.......... PERT [*Program Evaluation and Review Technique*] Life Cycle Unified System (IAA)
PLU.......... Phi Lambda Upsilon [*Fraternity*]
PLU.......... Platoon Leaders Unit [*Marine Corps*]
Pl U.......... Plowden on Usury [*A publication*] (DLA)
PLU.......... Pluggable Unit (SAA)
PLU.......... Pluma [*OTCBB symbol*]
plu.......... Plural (WDMC)
PLU.......... Plural
PLU.......... Plurality (SAUS)
PLU.......... Plus Two [*NCIC car model code*]
PLU.......... Plutonium [*Chemical symbol is Pu*] (AAG)
PLU.......... Poor Law Union [*British*]
PLU.......... Position Location Uncertainty (ACAE)
PLU.......... Pratt & Lambert United, Inc. [*NYSE symbol*] (SAG)
PLU.......... Preservation of Location Uncertainty [*Strategy for protecting missiles*] [*Military*]
PLU.......... Pressure Lubrication Unit
PLU.......... Price Look-Up (IAA)
PLU.......... Primary Logical Unit [*Computer science*] (CIST)
PLU.......... Probability of Leakage through Underlay
PLU.......... Program Library Unit (SAUS)
PLU.......... Program Load Unit
PLU.......... Propellant Loading and Utilization (AAG)
PLu.......... Proto-Luvian [*Linguistics*] (IEL)
PLUARG..... Pollution from Land Use Activity Reference Group (SAUS)
PLUCON..... Plutonium Decontamination Emergency Team [*Army*]
PLUG........ Component Guard, Inc. [*NASDAQ symbol*] (COMM)
PLUG........ Propellant Loading and Utilization Group (AAG)
PLUG........ Public Law Utilities Group (SAUS)
PLUGE....... Picture Line-Up Generating Equipment (SAUS)
PLUGE....... Picture Line-Up Generator [*Television*]
PLUK........ Parents Let's Unite for Kids (EARSL)
PLuL......... Lincoln University, Lincoln University, PA [*Library symbol*] [*Library of Congress*] (LCLS)
PLUM........ Payload Launch Module
PLUM........ Payload Umbilical Mast (NASA)
PLUM........ Planning Land Use Model (SAUS)
PLUM........ Priority Low-Use Minimal
PLUM........ Programmes Library Update and Maintenance (PDAA)
PLUM........ Programming Language for Users of MAVIS [*Microprocessor-Based Audio Visual Information System*] (PDAA)
PLUM........ Programs Library Update and Maintenance (SAUS)
PLUMB...... Plumber (SAUS)
PLUMB...... Plumbing (SAUS)
PLUMB...... Plumbum [*Lead*] [*Pharmacy*]
Plum Contr... Plumptre on Contracts [*2nd ed.*] [*1897*] [*A publication*] (DLA)
PlumCrk..... Plum Creek Timber Co., Inc. [*Associated Press*] (SAG)
PLUME...... Pipeline Under Mother Earth (SAUS)
PLUME2D... Two-Dimensional Plumes in Uniform Ground Water Flow (SAUS)
PLUME3D... Three-Dimensional Plumes in Uniform Ground Water Flow (SAUS)
PLUMG...... Plumbing (SAUS)
PLUMM..... Plumerr, ID [*American Association of Railroads railroad junction routing code*]
PLUMR...... Plumber (SAUS)
PLUN........ Plunkett Motor Freight [*Common carrier symbol*]
PLUNA...... Primeras Lineas Uruguayas de Navegacion Aerea [*Uruguayan National Airlines*]
PLund....... Papyri Lundenses [*A publication*] (OCD)
PLUNGER... Protocol Link Undoing Network Great Error Rates (SAUS)
PLUOT....... Parts Listing and Used On Technique (SAUS)
PLUOT....... Parts Listing Used On-Line Technique [*Computer science*] (IAA)
PLUP........ Pluperfect [*Grammar*]
plupf......... Pluperfect [*Linguistics*] (IEL)
PLUPF....... Pluperfect [*Grammar*]
PLUR........ Jarvis Island [*Line Islands*] [*ICAO location identifier*] (ICLI)
PLUR........ Photographics Laboratory Usage Reporting
PLUR........ Photo Lab Usage Reporting (MCD)
plur.......... Plural (NTIO)
PLUR........ Plural
PLUS........ ePlus [*NASDAQ symbol*]
PLUS........ Parent Loans for/to Undergraduate Students (SAUS)
PLUS........ Parent Loans to Undergraduate Students [*Later, ALAS*] [*Department of Education*]
PLUS........ PERT [*Program Evaluation and Review Technique*] Lifecycle Unified System
PLUS........ Physically-Limited United Students (SAUS)
PLUS........ Portable Lightweight Upper Air Sounding System (MCD)
PLUS........ Potential Long Supply Utilization Screening (NATG)
PLUS........ Precision Loading and Utilization System (AAG)
PLUS........ Prima Leben und Sparen [*Quality Living and Saving*] [*Brand name and discount store chain in West Germany and US*]
PLUS........ Procedures for Long Supply Assets Utilization Screening [*DoD*]
PLUS........ Professional Learning Unit System (SAUS)
PLUS........ Professional Liability Underwriting Society (NTPA)
PLUS........ Program Language for User's System (NITA)
PLUS........ Program Language for User Systems (SAUS)
PLUS........ Program Library Update System
PLUS........ Programmed Learning under Supervision
PLUS........ Programming Language for UNIVAC [*Universal Automatic Computer*] Systems [*Computer science*] (CSR)
PLUS........ Project Literacy United States (SAUS)
PLUS........ Project Literacy US [*Joint project of American Broadcasting Co. and Public Broadcasting Service*]
PLUS........ Prudent Laboratory Use System [*Health insurance*] (GHCT)
PLUS........ Room Plus, Inc. [*NASDAQ symbol*] (SAG)
PLUSS....... Point Loma Unmanned Search System (SAUS)
PLUSS....... USS Point Loma Unmanned Search System (SAUS)
Plut.......... Plutarch [*First century AD*] [*Classical studies*] (OCD)
PLUT........ Plutchnik [*Geriatric rating scale*] (DMAA)
Plut.......... Plutus [*of Aristophanes*] [*Classical studies*] (OCD)
PLUTHARCO... Plutonium, Uranium, Thorium Assembly Reactivity Code
PLUTO....... Pipe Line Under the Ocean (SAUS)
PLUTO....... Pipeline under the Ocean [*British project*] [*World War II*]
PLUTO....... Planning Urban Transportation Options [*Traffic management*]
PLUTO....... Plutonium Loop Testing Reactor (SAUS)
PLUTO....... Plutonium [*Loop-Testing*] Reactor [*British*] (DEN)
PLUTO....... Programmed Logic for Automatic Teaching Operation
PLUTO Technique... Parts Listing Used-on Technique (SAUS)
PLUVUE...... Plume Visibility Model [*Environmental Protection Agency*] (GFGA)
PLUZ........ Policy Land Use Zone [*Australian Capital Territory*]
PLV.......... Live Poliomyelitis Vaccine [*Immunology*] (MAE)
PLV.......... Panleukopenia Virus [*Medicine*] (MAE)
PLV.......... Peak Left Ventricular [*Pressure*] [*Cardiology*]
PLV.......... Personnel Launch Vehicle (ACAE)
PLV.......... Phenylalanine-Lysine-Vasopressin (MAE)
PLV.......... Phu-Lien [*Kien-An*] [*Vietnam*] [*Seismograph station code, US Geological Survey*] (SEIS)
PLV.......... Pitch Line Velocity (SAUS)
PLV.......... Polaravia OY [*Finland*] [*ICAO designator*] (FAAC)
PLV.......... Posterior Left Ventricle [*Anatomy*] (DAVI)
PLV.......... Posterior Left Ventricular Wall [*Cardiology*]
PLV.......... Postlanding Vent [*or Ventilation*] [*Apollo*] [*NASA*]
PLV.......... Power Limiting Valve
PLV.......... Presentation Level Video (PCM)
PLV.......... Production Level Video
PLV.......... Southwest Palawano [*Language symbol*] (ETLW)
PLVC........ Post-Landing Vent Control [*NASA*] (KSC)
PLVL........ Present Level [*Aviation*] (FAAC)

PLVRZD ..... Pulverized (MSA)
PLVS......... Pelvis (SAUS)
PLVU......... Container Managers [*Intermodal shipping container symbol*] (TVRC)
PLVW........ Pool View (TRID)
PLW.......... Palau [*ANSI three-letter standard code*] (CNC)
PLW.......... Palu [*Indonesia*] [*Airport symbol*] (OAG)
PLW.......... Patna Law Weekly [*India*] [*A publication*] (DLA)
PLW.......... PL & W [*Federal Railroad Administration identification code*]
PLW.......... Plastic Engine Technology Corp. [*Toronto Stock Exchange symbol*]
PLW.......... Plow Snow [*NWS*] (FAAC)
PLW.......... Preload Washer
PLWA........ People Living with AIDS [*Acquired Immunodeficiency Syndrome*] [*Medicine*] (TAD)
PL/WA....... Plain Washer [*Automotive engineering*]
PLWA........ Primary Light Water Addition (COE)
plwd .... Plywood (BARN)
PLWG........ Photographic Laboratories Working Group [*Range Commanders Council*] [*White Sands Missile Range, NM*]
PLWHA...... People Living With HIV/AIDS [*Human Immunodeficiency Virus / Acquired Immune Deficiency Syndrome*] [*Australia*]
PLWP........ Programmed Labor Work Performed (SAUS)
PLWR........ Pressurized Light Water Reactor (SAUS)
PLWS........ Prader-Labhart-Willi Syndrome [*Medicine*] (DMAA)
PLWS........ Pulsed Laser Weapon System (ACAE)
PLX.......... Parallax Developments [*Vancouver Stock Exchange symbol*]
PLX.......... Plains Resources [*AMEX symbol*] (TTSB)
PLX.......... Plains Resources, Inc. [*AMEX symbol*] (SPSG)
PLX.......... Plantronics, Inc. [*NYSE symbol*] (COMM)
PLX.......... Plexus [*Medicine*]
PLX.......... Politics [*Telegraphy*] (PCTE)
PLX.......... Position Launch [*Search mode wherein X signifies the launch mode number*] (MCD)
PLX.......... Propellant Loading Exercise (MCD)
PLX.......... Propellant-Loading Transfer (SAUS)
PLX.......... Robinson, IL [*Location identifier*] [*FAA*] (FAAL)
Pl x Fe...... Plastic to Female (SAUS)
PLXP........ Plastic Express [*Common carrier symbol*]
Pl x Pl....... Plastic to Plastic (SAUS)
PLXS........ Plexus Corp. [*NASDAQ symbol*] (NQ)
PLXZ........ Retired ATP [*Intermodal trailer symbol*]
PLY.......... Photolimited Yield
PLY.......... Photoluminescence Yield [*Spectroscopy*]
Ply.......... Plymouth [*Record label*]
ply.......... Plywood (VRA)
PLY.......... Plywood
PLY.......... Polaris Energy [*Vancouver Stock Exchange symbol*]
PLY.......... Politically [*Telegraphy*] (PCTE)
PLY.......... Polyphase Corp. [*AMEX symbol*] (SPSG)
PLY.......... Prune Extract Lactose Yeast Medium [*Microbiology*]
plyc.......... Polychrome (VRA)
plyes......... Polyester (VRA)
PlyGem..... Ply-Gem, Inc. [*Associated Press*] (SAG)
PLYINST.... Command Comply Current Instructions
PLYM........ Plymouth [*England*]
PLYM........ Plymouth [*NCIC car make code*]
PLYM........ Plymouth (trucks) [*NCIC truck make code*]
plym......... Polymer (VRA)
P-LYM....... Prolymphocyte [*Hematology*] (DAVI)
PLYMCHAN... Plymouth Subarea Channel [*NATO*] (NATG)
PLYMCHAN... Plymouth Sub-Area Command Headquarters (SAUS)
PLYMN...... Plymouth, NC [*American Association of Railroads railroad junction routing code*]
PLYMO...... Plymouth, OH [*American Association of Railroads railroad junction routing code*]
Plymouth St C... Plymouth State College (GAGS)
PLYMP...... Plympton [*England*]
PLYMT...... Plymtree [*England*]
PLYMW...... Plymouth, WI [*American Association of Railroads railroad junction routing code*]
PLYPASSPORT... Application for Passport for Self and/or Dependents Accordance BUPERS Manual [*Navy*]
plypt......... Polyptic (VRA)
Plyr.......... Player (SAUS)
PlyR.......... Plymouth Rubber Co., Inc. [*Associated Press*] (SAG)
plyst......... Polystyrene (VRA)
plyur......... Polyurethane (VRA)
plyvn......... Polyvinyl (VRA)
PLYWD...... Plywood
PLZ.......... Phenelzine (DMAA)
Plz.......... Plaza (AD)
plz.......... Plaza (BEE)
PLZ.......... Plaza (MCD)
PLZ.......... Please
PLZ.......... Polarize (MSA)
PLZ.......... Port Elizabeth [*South Africa*] [*Airport symbol*] (OAG)
PLZ.......... Programming Languages for the Zilog [*Computer science*] (CSR)
PLZ.......... Programming Language Zilog (SAUS)
PLZ.......... Punch Leading Zeros (TIMI)
PLZA........ Plaza [*Commonly used*] (OPSA)
PLZF........ Promyelocytic Leukaemia Zinc-Finger [*Protein*]
PLZN........ Polarization (MSA)
PLZT........ Leading Lanthanum Zirconate Titanate
PLZT........ Pb-based Lanthanum-doped Zirconate Titanates
PLZT........ Polycrystalline Lead-Zirconate-Titanate (SAUS)
PM........... Caracas Metropolitan Police Force [*Venezuela*]
PM........... [*The*] Chesapeake & Ohio Railway Co. (Pere Marquette District) [*AAR code*]
PM........... Cold Press Molding
PM........... Ha-Po'el ha-Mizrahi (BJA)
PM........... Pacemaker [*Medicine*] (DMAA)
PM........... Pacific Mail (ROG)
P/M.......... Pacific Molasses (AD)
PM........... Pacific Mutual Life Insurance Co. (EFIS)
PM........... Package Monitor (SAUS)
PM........... Pad Mechanic [*Aerospace*]
PM........... Pagemaker (SAUS)
PM........... Painting Machine
PM........... Pak [*or Phak*] Mai [*New Party*] [*Political party*]
PM........... Paleomagnetism (SAUS)
PM........... Palmgren-Miner (SAUS)
PM........... Pamphlet
PM........... Panel Maintenance (IAA)
PM........... Panel Meter (IEEE)
pm........... Papier Mache (VRA)
PM........... Papillary Muscle [*Medicine*] (DB)
PM........... Papular Mucinosis (DB)
PM........... Parachute Mine [*British military*] (DMA)
PM........... Parallel Memory (SAUS)
PM........... Paramagnet (SAUS)
PM........... Paramagnetic (SAUS)
PM........... Parameter [*Computer science*]
pm........... Paramilitary (AD)
Pm........... Paratid Midle [*Band protein*] (DMAA)
PM........... Paraxial Magnification (SAA)
P/M.......... Parent-Metabolite Ratio [*Medicine*] (MEDA)
PM........... Parlor Maid
PM........... Partial Mastectomy (MELL)
PM........... Partial Meniscectomy [*Medicine*] (EDAA)
PM........... Partial Remission [*Medicine*] (CDI)
PM........... Participative Management (IDYL)
PM........... Particulate Matter (EAGT)
PM........... Partito Monarchico [*Monarchist Party*] [*Italy*] [*Political party*] (PPE)
P/M.......... Parts per Million (IEEE)
PM........... Passed Midshipman
PM........... Passed Motion
PM........... Past Master [*Freemasonry*]
PM........... Patriotic Majority [*An association*] (EA)
PM........... Patriotikon Metopon [*Patriotic Front*] [*Greek Cyprus*] [*Political party*] (PPE)
PM........... Patrol Missile Boat (SAUS)
PM........... Patternmaker [*Navy rating*]
PM........... Pavement Material (SAUS)
PM........... Payload Management [*NASA*] (NASA)
PM........... Payload Midbody [*NASA*] (MCD)
PM........... Pay Master (SAUS)
PM........... Paymaster
PM........... Peabody Museum (AD)
PM........... Peace Museum (EA)
PM........... Pectoralis Major [*Anatomy*]
PM........... Peculiar Matter (SAUS)
PM........... Peculiar Meter
PM........... Pelizaeus-Merbacher [*Disease*] [*Medicine*] (DB)
PM........... Penalty Minutes [*Hockey*]
PM........... Pension Mortgage [*British*]
PM........... People Meter [*TV ratings measuring device*] [*Advertising*]
PM........... Pere Marquette Railroad
PM........... Perfect Master [*Freemasonry*]
PM........... Performance Management (SAUS)
PM........... Performance Measure (SAUS)
PM........... Performance Measurement
PM........... Performance Monitor [*NASA*] (NASA)
PM........... Performance Monitoring (SAUS)
PM........... Performance Monitoring [*Automotive engineering*]
PM........... Perinatal Mortality [*Medicine*] (EDAA)
PM........... Periodic Maintenance (AFM)
PM........... Peripheral Memory (SAUS)
PM........... Peritoneal Macrophage [*Immunology*] (AAMN)
p-m.......... Permanent Magnet (AD)
PM........... Permanent Magnet [*Loudspeaker*]
PM........... Permanent Memory (SAUS)
PM........... Permanent Mold (SAUS)
PM........... Per Metre (SAUS)
PM........... Per Million
PM........... Per Minute (IAA)
p/m.......... Per Month (WDAA)
PM........... Per Month
PM........... Personnel Management (ALAC)
PM........... Per Thousand (SAUS)
PM........... Perturbation Method (ODA)
Pm........... Petameter (IDOE)
PM........... Petit Mal [*Epilepsy*]
PM........... Petroleos Mexicanos [*Spanish*] (AD)
PM........... Petroleum Marketers, Inc. (EFIS)
PM........... Pharmacy (SAUS)
PM........... Phased Maintenance (MCD)
PM........... Phase Match (IAA)
PM........... Phase Modulated (SAUS)
p-m.......... Phase Modulation (AD)

PM .... Phase Modulation [*Radio data transmission*]
PM .... PHIGS Monitor (SAUS)
PM .... Philip Morris, Inc.
PM .... Philosophical Magazine (SAUS)
PM .... Phoenix Mutual Life Insurance Co. (EFIS)
PM .... Phorbol Monomyristate [*Organic chemistry*]
PM .... Phosphoramide Mustard [*Antineoplastic drug*]
PM .... Photographic Master
PM .... Photographic Material (SAUS)
PM .... Photomagnetic (SAUS)
PM .... Photo Marketing Magazine [*A publication*] (EAAP)
PM .... Photo Master (MCD)
PM .... Photomechanical (SAUS)
PM .... Photomultiplier
PM .... Photosynthetic Measurements (SAUS)
PM .... Phrase-Marker [*Linguistics*] (IEL)
PM .... Phyllosticta maydis [*A toxin-producing fungus*]
P/M .... Physical Medicine [*Medical officer designation*] [*British*]
PM .... Physical Medium (MLOA)
PM .... Physical Metallurgist (SAUS)
PM .... Physical Metallurgy (SAUS)
PM .... Physical Modeling (SAUS)
PM .... Piae Memoriae [*Of Pious Memory*] [*Latin*]
pm .... Picometer [*One trillionth of a meter*]
PM .... Picometer (or -metre) (SAUS)
pM .... Picomoler [*One trillionth of a mole*] (AAMN)
PM .... Pilgrim Airlines [*ICAO designator*] (AD)
PM .... Pilot Motor (MSA)
PM .... Pioneer Ministries (EA)
PM .... Pitching Moment [*Physics*]
PM .... Pitch Mark [*Shipfitting*]
PM .... Pit Membrane [*Paleobotany*]
PM .... Plane Matching Interface (SAUS)
PM .... Planetary Mission [*NASA*] (NASA)
PM .... Planned Maintenance
PM .... Plant Management (SAUS)
PM .... Plasmalemma [*Cytology*]
PM .... Plasma Membrane [*Cytology*]
PM .... Plaster Master (MSA)
PM .... Plastic Manoeuvre (SAUS)
PM .... Plastic Mold (MCD)
PM .... Platelet Microsome [*Medicine*] (DMAA)
PM .... Plate Modulated (or Modulation) (SAUS)
P/M .... Player/Missile [*Atari computers*]
PM .... Plessey Memories (SAUS)
PM .... Plus Minus [*More or less*]
PM .... Pneumomediastinum [*Medicine*] (AAMN)
pm .... Poids Moliculaire [*Molecular Weight*] [*French*] (AD)
PM .... Point-to-Multipoint (SAUS)
PM .... Polarization-Maintaining [*Optical Film*]
PM .... Polarization Microscope (SAUS)
PM .... Polarization Modulation (MCD)
PM .... Police Magistrate
PM .... Police Mutual Assurance Society [*British*]
PM .... Policy Memorandum [*Military*]
PM .... Poliomyelitis [*Medicine*]
PM .... Pollen Mass [*Botany*]
PM .... Polling Method (SAUS)
PM .... Polling Mode (SAUS)
PM .... Pollution Minimum
PM .... PolyMedica Industries [*AMEX symbol*] (TTSB)
PM .... PolyMedica Industries, Inc. [*AMEX symbol*] (SAG)
PM .... Polymeric Material (SAUS)
PM .... Polymeric Membrane
PM .... Polymer Morphology (SAUS)
PM .... Polymethacrylic [*Organic chemistry*]
PM .... Polymethylene (SAUS)
PM .... Polymorph [*Hematology*]
PM .... Polymorphonuclear [*Leukocyte*] [*Hematology*] (DAVI)
PM .... Polymyositis [*Medicine*]
pm .... Pondmeter (SAUS)
PM .... Pondus Medicinale [*Medicinal Weight*] [*Pharmacy*] (ROG)
PM .... Pontifex Maximus [*Supreme Pontiff*] [*Latin*]
PM .... Poor Metabolism [*Medicine*]
PM .... Pope and Martyr [*Church calendars*]
PM .... Popular Movement Against the European Community (ECON)
PM .... Portable Magnetometer [*NASA*]
PM .... Portable Medium-power (SAUS)
PM .... Portable Medium Power Plant [*Nuclear energy*] (NRCH)
PM .... Postal Manual
PM .... Posterior Mitral Leaflet [*Cardiology*]
PM .... Postmark [*Deltiology*]
PM .... Postmaster
PM .... Postmenopausal [*Gynecology*] (DAVI)
PM .... Post Meridian
pm .... Post Meridiem [*Afternoon*] [*Latin*] (WDMC)
PM .... Post Meridiem [*After Noon*] [*Latin*]
PM .... Postmodernist [*Architecture*]
pm .... Post Mortem (AD)
PM .... Post Mortem [*After Death*] [*Latin*]
PM .... Postmortem (SAUS)
PM .... Potentiometer (DEN)
PM .... Potsdam-Mittelmark [*German license plate city code*]
PM .... Potting Mold (MCD)
PM .... Pounds per Minute
PM .... Powdered Medium (SAUS)
PM .... Powder Magnet (SAUS)
PM .... Powder Metallurgy
PM .... Power Management (NAKS)
PM .... Power Mirrors
PM .... Power Module (MCD)
PM .... Powlesland & Mason [*Railway*] [*Wales*]
PM .... Practice Management (GART)
PM .... Precious Metal
PM .... Predictive Modeling (GART)
PM .... Preincubation Mixture
pm .... Premium (AD)
PM .... Premium
PM .... Premium Memory (SAUS)
PM .... Premixer (SAUS)
pm .... Premolar [*Dentistry*] (AD)
PM .... Premolar [*Dentistry*]
PM .... Prenegotiation Memorandum (AAGC)
PM .... Preparation Meetings [*Quakers*]
PM .... Prepared Message
PM .... Presbyterian Men (EA)
PM .... Presentation Manager [*Computer science*]
PM .... Presidential Memo
PM .... Pressure, Manifold
PM .... Pressure Multiplier [*Nuclear energy*] (NRCH)
PM .... Pressurized Module (SSD)
pm .... Presystolic Murmur [*Medicine*] (AD)
PM .... Presystolic Murmur [*Cardiology*]
PM .... Pretibial Myxedema [*Medicine*] (DMAA)
PM .... Preventative Maintenance (SAUS)
pm .... Preventive Maintenance (AD)
PM .... Preventive Maintenance
PM .... Preventive Material
PM .... Preventive Medicine [*Also, PVNTMED*] (AFM)
PM .... Preventive Medicine, Preventive Maintenance (SAUS)
PM .... Priest and Martyr [*Church calendars*]
PM .... Primary Marker (SAUS)
PM .... Primary Market [*Investment term*]
PM .... Primary Memory (DIPS)
PM .... Primary Mirror (SAUS)
PM .... Primary Motivation [*Psychology*] (DAVI)
PM .... Primary Munition
PM .... Prime Meridian (SAUS)
PM .... Prime Minister
PM .... Prime Mover (MCD)
PM .... Primitive Methodists (ROG)
PM .... Principal Matron [*Navy*] [*British*]
PM .... Principle of Multiplying [*New math*]
PM .... Printing Mechanism (IAA)
PM .... Print Matrix (IAA)
PM .... Priority Message (SAUS)
PM .... Private Mail (SAUS)
PM .... Prize Money
PM .... Probability of a Single Failure Causing Other Failures within a Three-Pack [*Department of Defense*]
PM .... Procedure Memory (SAUS)
PM .... Procedures Manual (IEEE)
PM .... Processable Mode (SAUS)
PM .... Processing Modflow [*Computer program*] [*Scientific Software Group*]
PM .... Processing Module [*Computer science*]
PM .... Process Manager (USDC)
PM .... Process Manual
PM .... Process Module (SAUS)
PM .... Processor Module (NITA)
PM .... Procurement and Material
PM .... Procurement Manual [*US Postal Service*] [*A publication*] (AAGC)
PM .... Producers Monthly (SAUS)
PM .... Producibility Manual (ACAE)
PM .... Production [*or Product*] Manager
PM .... Production Mode
PM .... Production Monitor (IAA)
PM .... Production Monitoring (SAUS)
PM .... Product Management (SAUS)
PM .... Product Manager
PM .... Product Marketing (SAUS)
p/m .... Professional/Managerial (WDMC)
PM .... Profit Margin (TDOB)
PM .... Profit Motivated [*Housing*]
PM .... Program (NG)
PM .... Program Administration [*Treasury Board of Canada Secretariat*] (FOTI)
pm .... Program Manager (AD)
PM .... Program Manager [*or Management*] (MCD)
PM .... Programmed Machine (SAUS)
PM .... Program Memorandum (MCD)
PM .... Program Method [*Computer science*] (IAA)
PM .... Program Milestone [*NASA*] (NASA)
PM .... Programming Manual (SAUS)
PM .... Programming Matrix (SAUS)
PM .... Programming Method (SAUS)
PM .... Programming Mode (SAUS)
PM .... Programming Module (SAUS)
PM .... Program Mode [*Computer science*] (ELAL)

PM.......... Program Module (SAUS)
PM.......... Program Monitoring (MUGU)
PM.......... Project Magic (EA)
pm.......... Project Management (ABAC)
PM.......... Project Management [*Automotive engineering*]
PM.......... Project Manager [*Military*]
PM.......... Pro Memoria [*In Remembrance*] [*Latin*]
PM.......... Pro Mense [*Per Month*] [*Latin*]
PM.......... Promethium
Pm.......... Promethium [*Chemical symbol*]
PM.......... Pro Mille [*Per Thousand*] [*Latin*]
PM.......... Propellant Management (KSC)
PM.......... Proper Motion [*Astronomy*] (BARN)
PM.......... Property Management (OICC)
PM.......... Propulsion Memorandum
PM.......... Propulsion Module [*NASA*] (KSC)
PM.......... Prostatic Massage [*Medicine*]
PM.......... Protected Memory (SAUS)
PM.......... Protected Mode (SAUS)
PM.......... Protein Methylesterase (DB)
PM.......... Protocol Machine [*Computer science*] (TNIG)
PM.......... Proto-Mayan [*Linguistics*] (IEL)
PM.......... Provost Marshal [*Army*]
PM.......... Pseudo Memory (SAUS)
PM.......... Puberal Macromastia [*Medicine*] (DMAA)
pm.......... Publicity Man (AD)
PM.......... Publicity Man [*Slang*]
PM.......... Pulmonary Macrophages [*Medicine*]
PM.......... Pulpomesial [*Dentistry*]
PM.......... Pulsating Mixing (SAUS)
PM.......... Pulse Code Modulation [*Telecommunications*] (IAA)
pm.......... Pulse Modulation (AD)
PM.......... Pulse Modulation
PM.......... Pulse Modulator (IDOE)
pm.......... Pumice (AD)
Pm.......... Pumice [*Quality of the bottom*] [*Nautical charts*]
PM.......... Punctum Maximum (SAUS)
PM.......... Punjabi Muslim [*Pakistan*]
PM.......... Purchase Memo (MCD)
PM.......... Purchase Memorandum
PM.......... Purchase Money (SAUS)
pm.......... Purchase Money Morgage, Premium (EBF)
PM.......... Purchase-Money Mortgage [*Real estate*]
PM.......... Purchase Money Mortgage, Premium (EBF)
PM.......... Purchasing Manager
PM.......... Purity Meter (SAUS)
PM.......... Purple Membrane [*Protein*] (DB)
PM.......... Purpose-Made [*Construction*]
PM.......... Push Money [*Sales incentive*]
P/M.......... Put More (VLIE)
P/M.......... Put of More [*Stock exchange term*]
PM.......... Pyridoxamine [*Also, Pxm*] [*Biochemistry*]
PM.......... Pyrometallurgist (SAUS)
PM.......... Pyrometallurgy (SAUS)
PM.......... Sisters of the Presentation of Mary [*Roman Catholic religious order*]
PM.......... St. Pierre and Miquelon [*ANSI two-letter standard code*] (CNC)
PM1.......... Patternmaker, First Class [*Navy rating*]
PM2.......... Patternmaker, Second Class [*Navy rating*]
PM3.......... Patternmaker, Third Class [*Navy rating*]
PM10.......... Particulate Matter [*Less than 10 microns*]
PM10.......... Particulate Matter, 10 Millimeters and Less (COE)
PM10.......... Particulate Matter Nominally 10 Microns and Less [*Environmental term*] (EAGT)
PM-10.......... Particulate Matter of 10 Microns in Diameter or Smaller [*BTS*] (TAG)
PM15.......... Particulate Matter, 15 Millimeters and Less (COE)
PM15.......... Particulate Matter Nominally 15 Microns and Less [*Environmental term*] (EAGT)
PMA.......... Allegheny College, Meadville, PA [*Library symbol*] [*Library of Congress*] (LCLS)
PMA.......... Association of British Preserved Milk Manufacturers [*United Kingdom*] (EAIO)
PMA.......... Pacific Maritime Association (EA)
PMA.......... Pacific Missionary Aviation (SAUS)
PMA.......... Pakistan Medical Association (ODA)
PMA.......... Panama [*Telegraphy*] (PCTE)
PMA.......... Pan-Macedonian Association (EA)
PMA.......... Pan Malaysian Air Transport [*ICAO designator*] (FAAC)
PMA.......... Panorama Resources Ltd. [*Vancouver Stock Exchange symbol*]
PMA.......... Papillary, Marginal, Attached [*With reference to gingivae*] [*Dentistry*]
pma.......... Paramethoxyamphetamine (AD)
PMA.......... Paramethoxyamphetamine
PMA.......... Parts Manufacturer Approval [*FAA*] (MCD)
PMA.......... Parts Manufacturing Associates (AD)
PMA.......... Parts Manufacturing Authority (SAUS)
PMA.......... Peat Moss Association (EA)
PMA.......... Pemba Island [*Tanzania*] [*Airport symbol*] (OAG)
PMA.......... Pencil Makers Association (EA)
PMA.......... Pennsylvania Manufacturers Corporation (EFIS)
PMA.......... Performance Management and Accounting (SAUS)
PMA.......... Performance Management Association (EAIO)
PMA.......... Performance Measurement Analysis (VLIE)
PMA.......... Performance Monitor Annunciator [*NASA*] (MCD)
PMA.......... Permanent Magnet Association (IAA)
PMA.......... Permanent Mailing Address
PMA.......... Permanent Management Arrangements (SAUS)
PMA.......... Personal Managers Association [*British*] (DBA)
PMA.......... Personal Military Assistant (ODA)
PMA.......... Personal Money Allowance
PMA.......... Personnel Management Advisor (NOAA)
PMA.......... Personnel Management Assistance
PMA.......... Perth Market Authority [*Australia*]
PMA.......... Perth Muslim Association [*Australia*]
PMA.......... Petroleum and Minerals Authority (SAUS)
PMA.......... Petroleum Monitoring Agency [*Ministry of Energy, Mines, and Resources*] [*Canada*]
PMA.......... Pharmaceutical Manufacturers Association (EA)
PMA.......... Phased Maintenance Availability [*Navy*] (DOMA)
PMA.......... Phenylmercuric Acetate [*Also, PMAC*] [*Herbicide and fungicide*]
PMA.......... Philadelphia Museum of Art (AD)
PMA.......... Philadelphia Musical Academy
PMA.......... Philippine Mahogany Association [*Defunct*] (EA)
PMA.......... Philippine Military Academy (SAUS)
PMA.......... Phonograph Manufacturers Association (EA)
PMA.......... Phorbol-12-Myristate-13-Acetate (SAUS)
PMA.......... Phorbol Myristate Acetate [*Also, PTA, TPA*] [*Organic chemistry*]
PMA.......... Phosphomolybdic Acid [*Organic chemistry*]
PMA.......... Photo Marketing Association (AD)
PMA.......... Photo Marketing Association International (EA)
PMA.......... Photonic Multichannel Analyzer
PMA.......... Physical Medium Attachment [*Telecommunications*] (OSI)
PMA.......... Physical Memory Address
PMA.......... Pianoforte Manufacturers' Association Ltd. [*British*] (BI)
PMA.......... Pine Manor College, Chestnut Hill, MA [*OCLC symbol*] (OCLC)
PMA.......... Planetary Microbiological Assay [*Aerospace*]
PMA.......... Plasma Membrane Adenosinetriphosphatase (DB)
PMA.......... Plastic Mock-Up Assembly
PMA.......... Plumbers' Merchants Association [*British*] (BI)
PMA.......... PMI Group [*NYSE symbol*] (TTSB)
PMA.......... PMI Group, Inc. [*NYSE symbol*] (SAG)
PMA.......... Pole Mounted Amplifier (SAUS)
PMA.......... Pole-Mounted Amplifier
PMA.......... Police Management Association [*Defunct*] (EA)
PMA.......... Police Marksman Association (EA)
PMA.......... Policy Management Architecture (SAUS)
PM-A.......... Polishing Medium-Abrasive (SAUS)
PMA.......... Polish Museum of America (EA)
PMA.......... Political Military Affairs (SAUS)
PMA.......... Politico-Military Affairs [*U.S. Department of State*] (BARN)
PMA.......... Polymethacrylate (SAUS)
PMA.......... Polymethacrylic Acid (SAUS)
PMA.......... Poly(methyl Acrylate) [*Organic chemistry*]
PMA.......... Polymetylacrylate (SAUS)
PMA.......... Polyurethane Manufacturers Association (EA)
PMA.......... Portable Maintenance Aid [*Army*]
PMA.......... Port Moller [*Alaska*] [*Seismograph station code, US Geological Survey*] (SEIS)
pma.......... Positive Mental Attitude (AD)
PMA.......... Positive Mental Attitude
PMA.......... Potato Marketing Authority [*Australia*]
PMA.......... Potato Merchants' Association [*Australia*]
PMA.......... Powder Metallurgy Association (SAUS)
PMA.......... Power Marketing Administration [*Department of Energy*]
PMA.......... Power-Marketing Administration (SAUS)
PMA.......... Preamplifier Module Assembly
PMA.......... Precious Metal Adder (Cost) (MCD)
PMA.......... Precious Metal Anode
PMA.......... Precision Measurement Association (SAUS)
PMA.......... Precision Measurements Association (EA)
PMA.......... Precision Metalforming Association (EA)
PMA.......... Preferred Machine Assist [*Computer science*] (ITCA)
PMA.......... Premarket Approval (SAUS)
PMA.......... Premarket Approval Application [*Food and Drug Administration*]
PMA.......... Pressurized Mating Adapter (SAUS)
PMA.......... Prevalence of Gingivitis [*Dentistry*] (DAVI)
PMA.......... Preventive Maintenance Agreement
PMA.......... Primary Market Area
PMA.......... Primary Mental Abilities [*Test*] [*Education*]
PMA.......... Prime Macro-Assembler (NITA)
PMA.......... Prime Medical Aid (SAUS)
PMA.......... Prinzmetal's Angina [*Cardiology*] (DAVI)
PMA.......... Priority Memory Access
PMA.......... Priority Memory Address (NITA)
PMA.......... Prison Mission Association (EA)
PMA.......... Probability of Mission Abort [*Navy*] (ANA)
PMA.......... Probationary Medical Assistant [*British military*] (DMA)
PMA.......... Procurement and Management Assistance [*Small Business Administration*]
PMA.......... Procurement Methods Analyst (AFM)
PMA.......... Produce Marketing Association [*Newark, DE*] (EA)
PMA.......... Production and Marketing Administration [*Department of Agriculture*] [*Functions dispersed, 1953*]
PMA.......... Production Managers Association [*United Kingdom*] (EAIO)
PMA.......... Production Monitoring Analysis (SAUS)
PMA.......... Professional Managers Association (EA)
PMA.......... Professional Manufacturers' Agents (EA)
PMA.......... Professional Mariners Alliance [*Defunct*] (EA)
PMA.......... Programa Mundial de Alimentos [*World Food Program*] [*Spanish*] (AD)

PMA .... Program Memory Area [*Computer science*] (DCDG)
PMA .... Progressive Muscular Atrophy [*Medicine*]
PMA .... Projected Map Assembly (SAUS)
PMA .... Project Manager, Air
PMA .... Project Manager, Air Systems Command [*Navy*]
PMA .... Project Military Adviser (NATG)
PMA .... Prompt Maintenance Alarm (SAUS)
PMA .... Propagation Management Assessment (SEWL)
PMA .... Property Management Association (SAUS)
PMA .... Property Management Association of America (EA)
PMA .... Property Market Analysis [*Consulting firm*] [*British*]
PMA .... Property Movement Authorization (ACAE)
PMA .... Prorated Mental Age [*Psychology*]
PMA .... Protected Memory Address
PMA .... Provincial Museum of Alberta (SAUS)
PMA .... Publications of the Mediaeval Academy (SAUS)
PMA .... Publishers Marketing Association (EA)
PMA .... Pulpomesioaxial [*Dentistry*]
PMA .... Pump-Motor Assembly
PMA .... Purchase Methods Analyst
PMA .... Pyridylmercuric Acetate [*Fungicide*] [*Organic chemistry*]
PMA .... Pyromellitic Acid [*Organic chemistry*]
PMAA .... Paper Makers Advertising Association (EA)
PMAA .... Petroleum Marketers Association of America (EA)
PMAA .... Politico-Military Administrative Affairs [*Committee*]
PMAA .... Promotion Marketing Association of America [*New York, NY*] (EA)
PMAA .... Property Management Association of America (EA)
PMAA .... Proprietary Medicines Association of Australia
PMAA .... Propulsion Module Attach Assembly [*NASA*] (SPST)
PM-AAH ..... Project Manager, Advanced Attack Helicopter [*Military*]
PMA/ARR ... Probable Missed Approach per Arrival [*Aviation*] (PDAA)
PMAC .... Packet Media Access Control (SAUS)
PMAC .... Packet Media Access Controller [*Computer science*] (VLIE)
PMAC .... Panama Canal [*Telegraphy*] (PCTE)
PMAC .... Parallel Memory Address Counter [*Computer science*]
P-MAC ...... Perceptual-Motor Assessment for Children (TES)
PMAC .... Peripheral Module Access Controller [*Computer science*] (VLIE)
PMAC .... Personnel Management Advisory Committee (SAUS)
PMAC .... Pharmaceutical Manufacturers Association of Canada
PMAC .... Phenyl Mercuric Acetate (SAUS)
PMAC .... Phenylmercuric Acetate [*Also, PMA*] [*Herbicide and fungicide*]
PMAC .... PMA Communications, Inc. [*Boston, MA*] (TSSD)
PMAC .... Polymethacrolein (SAUS)
PMAC .... Polymethoxy Acetal (EDCT)
PMAC .... Preliminary Maintenance Allocation Chart (MCD)
PMAC .... Preliminary Maintenance Allocation Charts (SAUS)
PMAC .... Project Manager Allocation Chart
PMAC .... Proprietary Medicines Advisory Committee [*Australia*]
PMAC .... Provisional Military Administrative Council [*Ethiopia*] [*Political party*] (PD)
PMAC .... Purchasing Management Association of Canada
PMACA ...... PMA Capital Corp. [*NASDAQ symbol*]
PMACODS ... Project Manager, Army Container Oriented Distribution System (MCD)
PM ACS ..... Product Manager, Army Communications System
PMACS ...... Project Management and Control System (CIST)
PMAD .... Performance Monitor Annunciation Driver [*NASA*] (MCD)
PMAD .... Personnel Management Authorization Document [*Army*]
PMAD .... Polymer Modifiers and Additives Division (SAUS)
PMAD .... Portable Maintenance Aid Device (SAUS)
PMAD .... Power Management and Distribution (NASA)
PMAD .... Public Morals Administrative Division (SAUS)
PMadW ..... Westinghouse Electric Corp., Waltz Mill Site Library, Madison, PA [*Library symbol*] [*Library of Congress*] (LCLS)
PMAE .... Peabody Museum of Archeology and Ethnology (AD)
PMAESA .... Port Management Association of Eastern and Southern Africa (EA)
PMAF .... Pharmaceutical Manufacturers Association Foundation (IAA)
PMAF .... Polaris Missile Assembly Facility
PMAFS ...... Public Members Association of the Foreign Service (EA)
PMAG .... Program Management Advisory Group (SAUS)
PMAG .... Program Manager Assistance Group [*Military*] (MCD)
PMAG .... Provisional Military Advisory Group
PMAHPVDC ... Permanent Mold Alloy High-Pressure Vacuum Die Casting
PMA-I .... Photo Marketing Association-International (NTPA)
PMAI .... Piano Manufacturers Association International (EA)
PMAI .... Powder Metallurgy Association of India (SAUS)
P-MAIL ...... Paper Mail (SAUS)
p-mail .... Printed Mail [*Computer slang*] (NETL)
P/Maj .... Pipe-Major [*British military*] (DMA)
PMALS ...... Prototype Miniature Air Launched Segment (SAUS)
PMALS ...... Prototype Miniature Air-Launched System
PM Amb .... Paramedic Ambulance (AMHC)
PMAN .... Piedmont Management Co., Inc. [*NASDAQ symbol*] (NQ)
PMAN .... Polymethacrylonitrile (EDCT)
PM & ACS ... Procurement Management and Acquisition Control System [*Social Security Administration*]
PM & ATA ... Paint Manufacturers' and Allied Trades Association (ODA)
PM&C .... Department of Prime Minister and Cabinet (SAUS)
PM & C ..... Plant Monitoring and Control [*IBM Corp.*]
PM&C .... Prime Minister and Cabinet (SAUS)
PM & C-HI ... Plant Monitoring and Control - Host Interface [*IBM Corp.*]
PM&E .... Performance Measurement and Evaluation (SAUS)
PM & OA ... Printers' Managers and Overseers Association (AD)
pm & r ...... Physical Medicine and Rehabilitation (AD)
PM&R .... Physical Medicine and Rehabilitation
PManM ...... Mansfield State College, Mansfield, PA [*Library symbol*] [*Library of Congress*] (LCLS)
PMANY ...... Pattern Makers Association of New York (EA)
PMAP .... Performance Monitor Annunciation Panel [*NASA*] (MCD)
PMAP .... Photomap
PMAP .... Port Mapper (SAUS)
PMAP .... Procedure Map (VLIE)
pMAP .... Professional Map Analysis Package (SAUS)
PMAPS ...... Predirected Munitions Automated Planning System (ACAE)
PMAR .... Page Map Address Register
PMAR .... Precious Metals Area Representative [*DoD*] (AFIT)
PMAR .... Preliminary Maintenance Analysis Report [*Aerospace*] (AAG)
PMAR .... Program Memory Address Register (SAUS)
PMarhSO ... Sun Oil Co., Marcus Hook, PA [*Library symbol*] [*Library of Congress*] (LCLS)
PMARP ...... Peacetime Manpower Allocation Requirements Plan (CINC)
PMARS ...... Performance Management and Recognition System (MCD)
PMAS .... Performance Measurement Analysis System (SAUS)
PMAS .... Photochemical Assessment Monitoring Stations (EPAT)
PMAS .... Police Mutual Assurance Society [*British*]
PMAS .... Propulsion Module Attach Structure [*NASA*] (SPST)
PMAS .... Purdue Master Attitude Scales [*Psychology*]
PMASA ...... Printers' Medical Aid and Sanatoria Association [*British*] (BI)
PMASAL .... Papers of the Michigan Academy of Science, Arts and Letters (SAUS)
PM-ASE ..... Project Manager, Aircraft Survivability Equipment [*Military*]
PM-ASH ..... Project Manager, Advanced Scout Helicopter [*Military*]
PM-ASI ...... Program Management Office for Armored Systems Integration [*Army*] (RDA)
PMAT .... Page Map Address Table [*NASA*] (NASA)
PMAT .... Plasma & Materials Technologies [*NASDAQ symbol*] (TTSB)
PMAT .... Plasma & Materials Technologies, Inc. [*NASDAQ symbol*] (SAG)
PMAT .... Portable Maintenance Access Terminal [*Computer science*]
PMAT .... Primary Mental Abilities Test [*Education*]
PMAT .... Purdue Mechanical Adaptability Test
PMATA ...... Paint Manufacture and Allied Trades' Association [*British*] (BI)
PMATA ...... Paint Manufacturers and Allied Trades Association (SAUS)
PMATA ...... Paper Makers' Allied Trades Association [*British*] (DBA)
PMAVIC ..... Precision Metalforming Association Voice of the Industry Committee [*Independence, OH*] (PACS)
PMAWS ..... Passive Missile Approach Warning System [*Military*] (SEWL)
PMAW/WACS ... Petroleum Marketers Association of Wisconsin/Wisconsin Association of Convenience Stores (EARSL)
PMax .... Peak Inspiratory Pressure [*Medicine*] (DAVI)
PMB .... Canadian Print Measurement Bureau (NITA)
PMB .... Cis-Platinum, Methotrexate, Bleomycin [*Antineoplastic drug regimen*] (DAVI)
PMB .... Pacific Motor Tariff Bureau, Inc., Oakland CA [*STAC*]
PMB .... Palm Beach [*Diocesan abbreviation*] [*Florida*] (TOCD)
PMB .... Pancho's Mexican Buffet, Inc. (EFIS)
PMB .... Papillomacular Bundle [*Medicine*] (MELL)
PMB .... Para-Hydroxymercuribenzoate [*Biochemistry*] (MAE)
PMB .... Paranormal Metal Bending
PMB .... Pembina, ND [*Location identifier*] [*FAA*] (FAAL)
PMB .... Pentamethylbenzene (SAUS)
PMB .... Performance Management Baseline (SAUS)
PMB .... Performance Measurement Baseline (MCD)
PMB .... Phenylmercuric Borate (SAUS)
PMB .... P-Hydroxymercuribenzoate (SAUS)
PMB .... Physical Metallurgy Branch
PMB .... Pilot Make Busy (IEEE)
PMB .... Plant Molecular Biology (SAUS)
PMB .... Plastic Media Blasting [*Coating technology*]
PMB .... P-Mercuribenzoate (SAUS)
PMB .... Polychrome Methylene Blue
PMB .... Polymethylbenzene [*Organic chemistry*]
PMB .... Polymorphonuclear Basophilic [*Leucocytes*] [*Hematology*]
PMB .... Polymyxin B (DB)
pmb .... Post-Menopausal Bleeding [*Medicine*] (AD)
PMB .... Postmenopausal Bleeding [*Medicine*]
PMB .... Potato Marketing Board [*British*]
PMB .... Practice Multiple Bomb (MCD)
PMB .... Precision Manned Bomber
PMB .... Premier Bancshares [*NYSE symbol*]
PMB .... Print Measurement Bureau [*Founded in 1971*] [*Also the name of a database*] [*Canada*]
PMB .... Print Measures Bureau (SAUS)
PMB .... Private Mail Bag
PMB .... Problem Management Bridge [*Computer science*] (HODG)
PMB .... Program Management Board (AFM)
PMB .... Project Management and Budgeting
PMB .... PROM [*Programmable Read-Only Memory*] Memory Board
PMBA .... Plant Molecular Biology Association (SAUS)
PMBA .... Professional Master of Business Administration (PGP)
PMB Bulletin ... Pigs Marketing Board Bulletin (SAUS)
PMBC .... Pacific Motor Boat Club (AD)
PMBC .... Phuket Marine Biological Center [*Marine science*] (MSC)
PMBC .... Pilot Make Busy Call (SAUS)
PMBC .... Plywood Manufacturers of British Columbia (SAUS)
PMBC .... Portland Motor Boat Club [*Oregon*] (AD)
PMBC .... Process-Model Based Controller (ACII)
PMB Circuit ... Pilot Make Busy Circuit (SAUS)
PMBIAS ..... Percentage Median Bias [*Statistics*]

PMBLA...... Liberation Army of Presevo, Medvedja, and Bujanovac [*Government term*] (GA)
PMB Leucocytes... Polymorphonuclear Basophilic Leucocytes (SAUS)
pmbo........ Participative Management by Objectives (AD)
PMBOK...... Project Management Body of Knowledge
PMBR....... Practice Multiple Bomb Rack (NG)
PMBR....... Preliminary Multistate Bar Review (SAUS)
PMBRT...... Pemberton, VA [*American Association of Railroads railroad junction routing code*]
PMBS........ Pelican Man's Bird Sanctuary (EA)
PMBT........ Propellant Mean Bulk Temperature (SAUS)
PMBU....... Personal Member of the Baptist Union [*British*]
pmbx........ Private Manual Branch Exchange (AD)
PMBX........ Private Manual Branch Exchange [*Communications*]
PMBZ........ Porta Rico Marine Berth [*Federal Railroad Administration identification code*]
PMC......... Carnegie-Mellon University, Pittsburgh, PA [*OCLC symbol*] (OCLC)
PMC......... Chief Patternmaker [*Navy rating*]
PMC......... Little Missionary Sisters of Charity [*Roman Catholic religious order*]
PMC......... Military-Peasant Pact (Bolivia) [*Political party*] (PSAP)
PMC......... Pacific Marine Center [*National Oceanic and Atmospheric Administration*]
PMC......... Pacific Medical Center (BABM)
PMC......... Pacific Missile Center [*Marine science*] (MSC)
PMC......... Pain Management Center [*University of California, San Francisco*] (RCD)
PMC......... Pan Metal [*formerly, Patton Morgan*] Corp. [*Ammunition manufacturer*]
PMC......... Parents of Missing Children [*Australia*]
PMC......... Parents of Murdered Children [*Later, POMC*] (EA)
PMC......... Partially Mission Capable [*Maintenance and supply*] (MCD)
PMC......... Partially Mission-Capable (SAUS)
PMC......... Partial Mission Capability [*Time*]
PMC......... Partial Mission Capable (SAUS)
PMC......... Patient Management Categories [*Medicine*] (MEDA)
PMC......... Patrol/Mine Countermeasure Craft [*British*]
PMC......... Payload Monitoring and Control [*NASA*] (NASA)
PMC......... Penguin Modern Classics [*Book publishing*]
PMC......... Pennsylvania Military Academy (AD)
PMC......... Pennsylvania Military College
PMC......... Pentamethyl(hydroxy)chromane [*Organic chemistry*]
PMC......... People's Mandate Committee (EA)
PMC......... Percent Modern Carbon [*In atmosphere*]
PMC......... Performance Management Computer (PDAA)
PMC......... Performance Measurement Criteria (SAUS)
PMC......... Periodicals Marketers of Canada [*An association*] (FOTI)
PMC......... Peripheral Mononuclear Cell [*Cytology*]
PMC......... Peritoneal Mast Cell
PMC......... Permanently Manned Capability (SSD)
PMC......... Personal Management Consult (EFIS)
PMC......... Personal Mobile Communicator (SAUS)
PMC......... Personnel Management Centre [*British*] (ODBW)
PMC......... Personnel Mobilization Center [*Military*]
PMC......... Phased Maintenance Checklist (MCD)
PMC......... Phenolic Molding Compound
PMC......... Phenylacetamidocoumarin (SAUS)
PMC......... Phenylmercuric Chloride [*Antiseptic*]
PMC......... Philatelic Music Circle (EA)
PMC......... Physical Media Components Sublayer (SAUS)
PMC......... Physical Medicine Centre (SAUS)
PMC......... Piperidinomethylcyclohexane [*Organic chemistry*]
PMC......... Planning and Monitoring Committee (FOTI)
PMC......... Planning Ministers' Conference [*Australia*]
PMC......... Planning Ministers Council (SAUS)
PMC......... Plaster-Molded Cornice [*Construction*]
PMC......... Plutona-Molybdenum CERMET [*Ceramic Metal Element*] (NASA)
PMC......... PMC Capital [*AMEX symbol*] (TTSB)
PMC......... PMC Capital, Inc. [*AMEX symbol*] (SPSG)
PMC......... Polar Mesospheric Cloud (SAUS)
PMC......... Pollen Mother Cell [*Botany*]
PMC......... Polyester Molding Compound [*Plastics*]
PMC......... Polymer Matrix Composite [*Materials science*]
PMC......... Polymer-Matrix Composite (SAUS)
PMC......... Polymer-Metal Composite (SAUS)
PMC......... Polymer-Reinforced (SAUS)
PMC......... Port Management Center (SAUS)
PMC......... Posterior Medial Corner of Knee [*Sports medicine*]
PMC......... Post Maintenance Check (MCD)
PMC......... Post Manufacture Checkout
PMC......... Post Manufacturing Checkout (KSC)
PMC......... Post Master's Certificate (PGP)
PMC......... Post Ministerial Conference (SAUS)
PMC......... Post-Ministerial Conference [*ASEAN*]
PMC......... Postmodern Culture (SAUS)
PMC......... Powdered Metal Cathode
PMC......... Power-Mate Corp. (IAA)
PMC......... Powertrain Management Controller [*Automotive engineering*]
PMC......... Precision Machinery Commercialization
PMC......... Precision Machining Commercialization (MCD)
PMC......... Precision Measurement Work Cell (ACAE)
pmc......... Precision Mirror Calorimeter (AD)
PMC......... Predictive Multisensor Correlation
PMC......... Pre-Mission Calibration (PDAA)
PMC......... Premium Marketing Club of New York (EARSL)
PMC......... Premium Merchandising Club of New York (EA)
PMC......... Premotor Cortex [*Neuroanatomy*]
PMC......... President of the Mess Committee [*Military*] [*British*]
PMC......... President's Management Council (AAGC)
PMC......... Pressure-Modulator Cell (EOSA)
PMC......... Pressurized Membrane Container
pmc......... Preventive Maintenance Contract (AD)
PMC......... Primary Mesenchyme Cell [*Cytology*]
PMC......... Prime Mover Control [*Valve*]
PMC......... Princeton Microfilm Corp.
PmC......... Princeton Microfilm Corporation, Princeton, NJ [*Library symbol*] [*Library of Congress*] (LCLS)
PMC......... Printing Memory Computer (SAUS)
PMC......... Private Mailing Card [*Deltiology*]
PMC......... Private Medical Communication
PMC......... Private Meter Check [*Telecommunications*] (TEL)
PMC......... Processed Meats Committee [*Later, DPMC*] (EA)
PMC......... Process Module Controller (AAEL)
PMC......... Procurement Committee (MCD)
PMC......... Procurement Management Code [*Military*] (AFIT)
PMC......... Procurement, Marine Corps [*An appropriation*]
PMC......... Procurement Method Code (SAUS)
PMC......... Procurement Method Coding [*DoD*]
PMC......... Professional and Managerial Class [*British*] (DI)
PMC......... Professional Musicians' Club [*Australia*]
PMC......... Programmable Machine Control (SAUS)
PMC......... Programmable Machine Controller (NRCH)
PMC......... Programmable Machine Tool Controller (IAA)
PMC......... Programmable Matrix Controller (IAA)
PMC......... Program Management Charter (SAUS)
PMC......... Program Management Control
PMC......... Program Management Course [*Army*] (RDA)
PMC......... Program Manager Charter (SAUS)
PMC......... Program Marginal Checking
PMC......... Project Management Committee (AD)
PMC......... Project Management Corp. (SAUS)
PMC......... Project Management Course [*Army*]
PMC......... Project Manufacturing Controller (MCD)
PMC......... Pro Maria Committee (EA)
PMC......... Pro-Med Capital, Inc. [*AMEX symbol*] (COMM)
PMC......... Propellant Monitor and Control (AFM)
PMC......... Pseudo Machine Code [*Computer science*] (BUR)
PMC......... Pseudomembranous Colitis [*Medicine*]
PMC......... Public Media Center (EA)
PMC......... Puerto Montt [*Chile*] [*Airport symbol*] (OAG)
PMC......... Pumice (MSA)
pMc......... Pure Mexican Cocaine (AD)
PMCA........ Pennsylvania Manufacturing Confectioners Association (SAUS)
PMCA........ Purple Martin Conservation Association (EA)
PM-CAWS... Project Manager for Cannon Artillery Weapon Systems (RDA)
PMCB........ Partially Mission Capable Both [*Maintenance and supply*] (MCD)
PMCB........ Pentamethyl Chlorobenzene (SAUS)
PMCB........ Project Manager Control Board
P/MCB....... Project/Miscellaneous Change Board (MCD)
PMCC........ Paper Machine Clothing Council (NTPA)
PMCC........ Peerless Motor Car Club (EA)
PMCC........ Pensky-Martens Closed Cup [*Flash point test*]
PMCC........ Platform Mission Control Center [*NASA*]
PMCC........ Platforms Mission Control Center (SAUS)
PMCC........ Platoon Mistral Command Centre (SAUS)
PMCC........ Port Management Control Center (SAUS)
PMCC........ Post Mark Collectors Club (EA)
PMCC........ Product-Moment Correlation Co-Efficient (DMAA)
PMCC........ Project Management Center of Competency (GART)
PMCCN...... Performance and Management of Complex Communication Networks (SAUS)
PMC CT..... PMC Commercial Trust [*Associated Press*] (SAG)
PMCD....... Post Mortem Core Dump [*Computer science*]
PMCD....... Process Measurement & Control Division (ACII)
PMCD....... Program Module Connection Diagram (MHDI)
PMCF........ Partial Mission Capability Factor
PMCF........ Post Maintenance Check Flight (MCD)
PMCG....... Pyrrolidylmethyl Cyclopentylphenylglycolate (SAUS)
PMCH....... Pro-Melanin-Concentrating Hormone (DMAA)
PMCHi....... Crawford County Historical Society, Meadville, PA [*Library symbol*] [*Library of Congress*] (LCLS)
PMCHL...... Pro-Melanin-Concentrating Hormone-Like (DMAA)
PM CHS..... Program Manager, Common Hardware Systems (SAUS)
PMCI........ Phosphate Mining Corp. of Christmas Island (EY)
PMCI........ Postmyocardial Infarct [*Medicine*] (MELL)
PMC INC.... Precision Management of Concordville, Inc. [*Media, PA*] (TSSD)
PMCIS....... Post-Myocardial Infarction Syndrome [*Medicine*] (MELL)
PMck........ Carnegie Free Library of McKeesport, McKeesport, PA [*Library symbol*] [*Library of Congress*] (LCLS)
PMCL........ Posterior Medial Collateral Ligament [*Anatomy*]
PMCL........ Proposed MAPAD Change Letter (AAGC)
PMCL........ Proposed Maximum Contaminant Level (SAUS)
PMCL........ Proposed MILSTRIP Change Letters
PMCLG...... Proposed Maximum Contaminant Level Goal (SAUS)
PMCM....... Master Chief Patternmaker [*Navy rating*]
PMCM....... Partially Mission Capable Maintenance [*Maintenance and supply*] (MCD)
PMCM....... Partial Mission Capable, Maintenance (SAUS)
PMCM....... Permanent Mold Casting Mold (MCD)

PMCM .... Pulse Morse Code Modulation (OA)
PMC Model ... Preparata, Metze and Chien Model (SAUS)
PMCP .... Prime Capital Corp. [*NASDAQ symbol*] (SAG)
PMCPE ...... Prime Capital [*NASDAQ symbol*] (SG)
PMCQ .... Paper Marketing Council of Queensland [*Australia*]
PMCS .... Partially Mission Capable Supply [*Maintenance and supply*] (MCD)
PMCS .... Partial Mission Capable, Supply (SAUS)
PMCS .... Partial Mission Capable-Supply
PMCS .... Patient Management Computer Stimulation (DMAA)
PMCS .... PMC-Sierra, Inc. [*NASDAQ symbol*] [*Formerly, Sierra Semiconductor*] (SG)
PMCS .... Power Monitoring and Control Systems
PMCS .... Preventive Maintenance Checks and Services [*for Army vehicles*] (INF)
PMCS .... Process Monitoring and Control System
pmcs .... Process Monitoring and Control Systems (AD)
PMCS .... Production Management Control System (SAUS)
PMCS .... Professional Military Comptroller School
PMCS .... Programmable Modular Communication System (SEWL)
PMCS .... Program [*or Project*] Management Control System [*Army*]
PMCS .... Project Management Control System
PMCS .... Pulse-Modulated Communications System
PMCS .... Senior Chief Patternmaker [*Navy rating*]
PM CSD ..... Project Manager for Chemical Stockpile Disposal [*Army*]
PMCT .... PAL [*Permissive Action Link*] Management Control Team [*Army*] (AABC)
PMCT .... Program Management Control Table [*Computer science*] (ELAL)
PMCTF ...... Prime Minister's Country Task Force [*Australia*]
PMCU .... Pacific Mexico Container Lines [*Intermodal shipping container symbol*] (TVRC)
PMCU .... Personal Member of the Congregational Union [*British*]
PMCU .... Predominately Minority Colleges and Universities
PMCV .... Politically Motivated Crimes of Violence (SAUS)
PMCV .... Programmed Multichannel Valve [*Chromatography*]
PMCVG ...... Photometric Modelling for Computer Vision and Graphics (VLIE)
PMCX .... Pak Mail Centers of America [*OTCBB symbol*]
PMCX .... Polar Molecular Corp. [*NASDAQ symbol*] (COMM)
PMCYE ...... Patriot Motorcycles Corp. [*NASDAQ symbol*] (QUAN)
PMD .... Packet Mode Data [*Computer science*] (VLIE)
PMD .... Palmdale, CA [*Location identifier*] [*FAA*] (FAAL)
PMD .... Palmdale/Lancaster [*California*] [*Airport symbol*] (OAG)
PMD .... Palmer Industries Ltd. [*Vancouver Stock Exchange symbol*]
PMD .... Panel-Mounted Display (MCD)
PMD .... Papillary Muscle Dysfunction [*Medicine*] (RAWO)
PMD .... Part Manufacturing Design
PMD .... Parts Manufacturing Division (SAUS)
PMD .... Payload Mating Dolly [*NASA*]
PMD .... Payload Module Decoder [*NASA*]
PMD .... Pelizaeus-Merzbacher Disease [*Medicine*]
PMD .... Permanent Magnetic Dynamic (SAUS)
PMD .... Personnel Management Division [*Environmental Protection Agency*] (GFGA)
PMD .... Petroleum and Mines Department (SAUS)
PMD .... Pharmaco-Medical Documentation, Inc. [*Information service or system*] (IID)
PMD .... Physical Layer, Medium Dependent (SAUS)
PMD .... Physical Layer Medium Dependent Layer (SAUS)
PMD .... Physical Media Dependent (SAUS)
PMD .... Physical Medium Dependent [*Computer science*]
PMD .... Physical Medium Dependent Layer [*Telecommunications*] (OSI)
PMD .... Planning and Management Division [*Environmental Protection Agency*] (GFGA)
PMD .... Point of Maximum Definition (SAUS)
PMD .... Polarization Mode Disperson
PMD .... Pollution Measurement Division (SAUS)
PMD .... Pollution Monitoring Directory (SAUS)
PMD .... Pontiac Motor Division [*General Motors Corp.*]
Pmd .... Portmadoc (AD)
PMD .... Positional Macro-Definition (SAUS)
PMD .... Postmortem and Diagnostic Processor (SAUS)
PMD .... Post-Mortem Debugger [*Computer science*] (PCM)
PMD .... Post Mortem Dump [*Computer science*]
pmd .... Post-Mortem Dumps (AD)
PMD .... Post-Mounted Delineator [*Highway engineering*]
PMD .... Power Management and Distribution Palmdale [*California*]
PMD .... Pre-Metal Dielectric (SAUS)
PMD .... Preventive Maintenance, Daily (MCD)
PMD .... Preventive Maintenance Division [*Air Force*]
PMD .... Primary Myeloproliferative Disease [*Medicine*]
PMD .... Primary Myocardial Disease [*Medicine*]
PMD .... Private Management Domain [*Computer science*] (TNIG)
PMD .... Private Medical Doctor (DAVI)
PMd .... Private Physician
PMD .... Processing, Marketing, and Distribution
PMD .... Product Marketing Division (SAUS)
PMD .... Profile Measurement Device (SAUS)
PMD .... Program for Management Development [*Harvard Business School*] (DD)
PMD .... Programmable Metal Detector [*Police and security equipment*]
PMD .... Programmable Multilevel Logic Device [*Computer science*] (GART)
PMD .... Program Management Directive [*Air Force*]
PMD .... Program Management Document (SAUS)
PMD .... Program Management Documentation [*Army*]
PMD .... Program Management Documents
PMD .... Programmed Multiple Development [*Analytical chemistry*]
PMD .... Program Module Dictionary
PMD .... Program Monitoring and Diagnosis
PMD .... Progressive Muscular Dystrophy [*Medicine*]
PMD .... Project-based Management Development (SAUS)
pmd .... Projected Map Display (AD)
PMD .... Projected Map Display
PMD .... Project Management Division (SAUS)
PMD .... Project Manager Development (MCD)
PMD .... Propellant Management Device (ACAE)
PMD .... Protein Mutant Database (SAUS)
PMD .... Psychemedics Corp. [*AMEX symbol*] (SAG)
PMD .... Psychiatric Military Duty
PMD .... Pump Mounted Driver (HAWK)
PMD .... Pump-Mounted Driver [*Automotive engineering*]
PMDA .... Photographic Manufacturers and Distributors Association (EA)
PMDA .... Pianoforte Manufacturers and Distributors Association [*British*] (DBA)
PMDA .... Plastics Machinery Distributors Association [*British*] (EAIO)
PMDA .... Pyromellitic Dianhydride [*Organic chemistry*]
PMDAMT .... Pacific Mobile Depot Activity Maintenance Team (CINC)
PMDA/ODA ... Pyromellitic Dianhydride/Oxydianiline (SAUS)
PMDB .... Brazilian Democratic Movement
PMDB .... Party of the Brazilian Democratic Movement [*Political party*] (PSAP)
PMDB .... Party of the Democratic Movement [*Political party*]
PMDB .... Program Management Decision Brief [*Defense Systems Management College*] (DOMA)
PMD/BMI ... Project Management Division/Batelle Memorial Institute (AD)
PMDC .... Pakistan Minerals Development Corp. (AD)
PMDC .... Permanent Magnet Direct Current (SAUS)
PMDC .... Project for Mathematical Development of Children [*National Science Foundation*]
PMDC .... Project Manager Development Course [*Military*] (RDA)
PMDD .... Personnel Management Development Directorate [*Military Personnel Center*] (AABC)
PMDD .... Premenstrual Dysphoric Disorder [*Gynecology*] (DMAA)
PMDF .... Pascal Memo Distribution Facility (SAUS)
PMDF .... Project Master Data File [*For spacecraft*]
PMDG .... Pentamethylene Diguanidine [*Organic chemistry*]
PMDI .... Palmer Drought Severity Index
PMDI .... Parkinson's and Movement Disorder Institute (RCD)
PMDI .... Polydiphenylmethanediisocyanate (SAUS)
PMDI .... Polymeric MDI (SAUS)
PMDI .... Polymeric Methylene Diphenylene Isocyanate (EDCT)
PMDI .... Polymethylene Diisocyanate (SAUS)
PMDI .... Polymethylene Diphenylene Isocyanate (SAUS)
PMDL .... Pace Medical [*OTCBB symbol*]
PMDL .... Palmdale, CA (NASA)
PMDL .... Post M-Day Deployment List [*Military*] (AABC)
PMDL .... Post Mobilization Deployment List [*Department of Defense*]
PMDL .... Provisional Military Demarcation Line (CINC)
PMDL Unit ... Post Mobilization Deployment List Unit (SAUS)
PMDM .... Polyhedra Molecular Demonstration Model
PMDM .... Poly(mellitic Dianhydride Methacrylate) [*Organic chemistry*]
PM/DM ..... Polymyositis/Dermatomyositis [*Rheumatology*] (DAVI)
PMDO .... Phased Maintenance During Overhaul
PMDP .... Pavement Marking Demonstration Program [*Federal Highway Administration*]
PMDP .... Project Manager Development Program [*Army*] (RDA)
PMDP .... Prototype Model Design Plan (SAUS)
PMDR .... Parametric Monotone Decreasing Ratio [*Statistics*]
PMDR .... Phosphorescence-Microwave Double Resonance
PMDR .... Provisioning Master Data Record
PMDRAM ... Page Mode Dynamic Random Access Memory (SAUS)
PM-DRG .... Pediatric-Modified Diagnosis-Related Group (HCT)
PMDRMU ... Paper Mould and Dandy Roll Makers' Union (DGA)
PMDS .... Peristent Muellerian Duct Syndrome [*Medicine*] (DMAA)
PMDS .... (Phenylmercury)dodecenyl Succinate [*Antimicrobial agent*]
PMDS .... Pilot Map Display System
PMDS .... Plant Management, Maintenance/Design Engineering Show (SAUS)
PMDS .... Point Missile Defense System (DNAB)
PMDS .... Portable Diver Monitoring System
PMDS .... Power Management and Distribution System (SAUS)
PMDS .... Primary Myelodysplastic Syndrome [*Medicine*] (DMAA)
PMDS .... Process Monitoring and Display Software [*Computer science*] (ECII)
pmds .... Projected Map Display Set (AD)
PMDS .... Projected Map Display System
PMDS .... Property Management and Disposal Service [*Abolished, 1973*] [*General Services Administration*]
PMDT .... Park Meditech, Inc. [*NASDAQ symbol*] (SAG)
PMDT .... Pentamethyldiethylenetriamine [*Organic chemistry*]
PMDTF ...... Park Meditech [*NASDAQ symbol*] (TTSB)
PMDU .... Projected Map Display Unit (DNAB)
PMDX .... Primedex Health Systems [*OTCBB symbol*]
PMDY .... Midway Naval Station [*Henderson Field*], Sand Island [*Midway Islands*] [*ICAO location identifier*] (ICLI)
PME .... Allstate Corp. [*NYSE symbol*] (SAG)
PME .... Allstate Cp 6.76% Exch Nts '98 [*NYSE symbol*] (TTSB)
PME .... Caltech Political Military Exercise [*International relations simulation game*]
PME .... Paramagnetic Meissner Effect [*Physics*]
PME .... Passive Microelectronic Element
PME .... Pattern Matching Engine (SAUS)
PME .... Peace Movement of Ethiopia (EA)
PME .... Pectin Methylesterase [*Also, PE*] [*An enzyme*]
PME .... Pedal Mode Ergometer

PME .... Performance Management and Evaluation
pme.......... Performance-Measuring Equipment (AD)
PME .... Performance Monitoring Equipment (NVT)
PME .... Personnel Management Evaluation [*Marine science*] (OSRA)
PME .... Personnel Management for Executives [*Military*] (RDA)
PME .... Phosphatidylmonomethylethanolamine [*Biochemistry*]
PME .... Phosphomonoester [*Biochemistry*]
PME .... Phosphorylated Monester [*Organic chemistry*]
PME .... Photomagnet Electric
PME .... Photomagnetoelectric
PME .... Photomagnetoelectric Effect (IAA)
PME .... Photomechanical Effect (SAUS)
PME .... Pinosylvin Methyl Ether [*Organic chemistry*]
pme.......... Planning, Management, Evaluation (AD)
PME .... Planning Market Estimate (SAUS)
PME .... Political Military Exercise (SAUS)
PME .... Polymorphonuclear Eosinophile [*Hematology*]
P Me .... Portland, Maine (AD)
PME .... Portsmouth [*England*] [*Airport symbol*] (AD)
PME .... Postmenopausal Estrogen Therapy [*Gynecology*] (CPH)
PME .... Power Management Event (MWOL)
PME .... Precision Measurement Equipment
PME .... Precision Measuring Equipment (AFM)
PME .... Pre-Manufacturing Engineering (SAUS)
PME .... Premature Ejaculation [*Medicine*] (MELL)
PME .... Preventive Maintenance Effectiveness (SAUS)
PME .... Primary Mission Equipment
PME .... Prime Ministers of England [*A publication*]
PME .... Prime Mission Equipment
PME .... Process and Manufacturing Engineering (NRCH)
PME .... Processor Memory Enhancement
PME .... Product Market Estimate (SAUS)
PME .... Product Marketing Engineer (TIMI)
PME .... Professional Management for Executives [*Army*]
PME .... Professional Military Education (AFM)
PME .... Professional Military Ethic (MCD)
PME .... Profession Military Education [*Department of Defense*]
PME .... Progressive Myoclonus Epilepsy [*Medicine*] (MELL)
PME .... Project Management Engineering, Inc. (EFIS)
PME .... Project Manager, Electronics System Command [*Navy*]
pme.......... Protective Multiple Earthing (AD)
PME .... Protective Multiple Earthing [*Electricity*]
PMEA........ (Phenyl)(methyl)ethanolamine [*Organic chemistry*]
PMEA........ Phosphonylmethoxyethyladenine [*Antiviral*]
PMEA........ Powder Metallurgy Equipment Association (EA)
P/MEA....... Probationary Marine Engineering Artificer [*British military*] (DMA)
PMEA........ Production and Maintenance Engineering Agent (MCD)
PMEA........ Publishing Manufacturers Executive Association (EA)
PMEAR...... Preliminary Maintenance Engineering Analysis Requirement (MCD)
PMEC........ Postgraduate Medical Education Committee [*University of Queensland, Australia*]
PMEC........ Professional Military Education Centre (SAUS)
PMEC........ Pseudomembranous Enterocolitis [*Medicine*] (STED)
PMED........ Paradigm Medical Industries, Inc. [*NASDAQ symbol*] (SAG)
PMedS ...... Delaware County Institute of Science, Media, PA [*Library symbol*] [*Library of Congress*] (LCLS)
PMEE........ Prime Mission Electronic Equipment [*NASA*] (KSC)
PME-Effect... Photomagnetoelectric-Effect (SAUS)
PMEF........ Petroleum Marketing Education Foundation (EA)
PMEG........ Page Map Entry Group (SAUS)
PMEG........ Perforated Metal Export Groups [*British*] (DBA)
PMEL........ Pacific Marine Environmental Laboratory [*Seattle, WA*] [*National Oceanic and Atmospheric Administration*] (GRD)
PMEL........ Precision Measurements Equipment Laboratory [*NASA*]
PMEL........ Precision Measuring Equipment Laboratory (AD)
PMEL........ Precision Mechanics and Electronics Laboratory (COE)
PME Leucocytes... Polymorphonuclear Eosinophilic Leucocytes (SAUS)
PMEM .... Piezoelectric MEM (SAUS)
PMEM .... Piezoelectric Micro Electro Mechanical (AAEL)
PMEM .... Practical Methods in Electron Microscopy (SAUS)
PMEM .... Processor Memory [*Computer science*] (CIST)
PM-ENDOR... Polarization Modulated Electron Nuclear Double Resonance [*Spectroscopy*]
PMEP........ Pumping Mean Effective Pressure [*Automotive engine testing*]
PMer .... Mercer Free Library, Mercer, PA [*Library symbol*] [*Library of Congress*] (LCLS)
PMES........ Personnel Management Evaluation System [*Department of Labor*]
PMES........ Productivity Measurement and Evaluation System (MCD)
PMES........ Proposed Material Erection Schedule (MCD)
PME School... Professional Military Education School (SAUS)
pmest .... Personality, Matter, Energy, Space, Time (AD)
PMEST ...... Personality, Matter, Energy, Space, Time [*Colon classification, S. R. Ranganathan*] [*Library science*]
pmet......... Painted Metal (AD)
PMET........ Painter Metal (AAG)
PMEV........ Panel-Mounted Electronic Voltmeter
PMEV........ Panel Mounted (or Mounting) Electronic Voltmeter (SAUS)
PMEX........ Petroleos Mexicanos [*Private rail car owner code*]
PMEXPO .... Property Management Exposition [*Bachner Communications*] (TSPED)
PMF .... L-Phenylalanine Mustard, 5-Fluorouracil, Methotrexate [*Antineoplastic drug regimen*] (DAVI)
PMF .... Parts Master File (MCD)
PMF .... Patriot Maintenance Facility [*Army*]
PMF .... Pennsylvania Mutual Fund (SAUS)
PMF .... Performance Measurement Facility (IAA)
PMF .... Performance Monitor Function [*NASA*] (NASA)
PMF .... Performance Monitoring Function
PMF .... Perigee Motor Firing [*Aerospace*] (MCD)
PMF .... Permanent Magnetic Field
PMF .... Permanent Military Force (ADA)
PMF .... Personnel Master File [*Army*] (AABC)
PMF .... Pilot Mortar Fire
PMF .... Polaris Missile Facility [*Military*] (IAA)
PMF .... Preparedness and Mitigation Function [*Emergency Management*] (EMA)
PMF .... Presidential Medal of Freedom (AD)
PMF .... Price Master File (MCD)
PMF .... Principle Management Facility (MCD)
PMF .... Probability Mass Function (IAA)
PMF .... Probable Maximum Flood [*Nuclear energy*] (NRCH)
pmf .... Probable Maximum Flooding (AD)
PMF .... Processed Message File (MCD)
PMF .... Processeur Militaire Francais [*French*]
PMF .... Product Master File (ADWA)
PMF .... Product Measurement Facility (IAA)
PMF .... Professional Medical Film (AABC)
PMF .... Programmable Matched Filter (IAA)
PMF .... Program Management Facility [*NASA*] (MCD)
pmf .... Progressive Massive Fibrosis [*Medicine*] (AD)
PMF .... Progressive Massive Fibrosis
PMF .... Project Management File (MCD)
PMF .... Pro Male Fingers [*International Bowhunting Organization*] [*Class equipment*]
PMF .... Pro Media Foundation (EA)
PMF .... Protein Motive Force (SAUS)
PMF .... Proton Motive Force [*Physics*]
PMF .... Pterygomaxillary Fossa (STED)
PMF .... Pulsed Magnetic Field (SAUS)
PMF-1....... Seismic Safety Planning PMF [*Emergency Management*] (EMA)
PMF-2....... Mitigation Incentives PMF [*Emergency Management*] (EMA)
PMF-3....... Mutual Aid and Joint Powers PMF [*Emergency Management*] (EMA)
PMF-4....... Disaster Assistance PMF [*Emergency Management*] (EMA)
PMF-5....... Earthquake Preparedness PMF [*Emergency Management*] (EMA)
PMF-6....... Structural Hazard Mitigation PMF [*Emergency Management*] (EMA)
PMF-7....... Nonstructural Hazard Mitigation PMF [*Emergency Management*] (EMA)
PMF-9....... Public Information PMF [*Emergency Management*] (EMA)
PMF-10 ..... Emergency Shelter and Mass Care PMF [*Emergency Management*] (EMA)
PMF-11 ..... Disaster Management PMF [*Emergency Management*] (EMA)
PMFA........ Fireman Apprentice, Patternmaker, Striker [*Navy rating*]
PM-FAC ..... Prednisone, Methotrexate, Fluorouracil, Adriamycin, Cyclophosphamide [*Antineoplastic drug regimen*]
PM FATDS... Program Manager, Field Artillery Tactical Data Systems (SAUS)
PMFBI....... Pardon Me for Butting In
PMFC........ Pacific Marine Fisheries Commission [*Later, PSMFC*] (EA)
PMFC........ Pacific Marine Fisheries Compact (COE)
PMFC........ Patsy Montana Fan Club (EA)
PMFD........ Premier Delivery [*Common carrier symbol*]
PMFG........ Peerless Manufacturing Co. [*NASDAQ symbol*] (NQ)
PMFG........ Peerless Mfg [*NASDAQ symbol*] (TTSB)
PMFI......... Perpetual Midwest Financial [*NASDAQ symbol*] (TTSB)
PMFI......... Perpetual Midwest Financial, Inc. [*NASDAQ symbol*] (SAG)
PMFJI .... Pardon Me for Jumping In (ADWA)
PM/FL .... Performance Monitor/Fault Locator [*Military*] (CAAL)
PMFLT....... Pamphlet (MSA)
PMFN........ Fireman, Patternmaker, Striker [*Navy rating*]
PMF-PAC.... Polaris Missile Facility, Pacific (SAUS)
PMFPAC..... Polaris Missile Facility, Pacific Fleet
PMFR........ Prime America Freight Systems [*Common carrier symbol*]
PMFS........ Pulsed Magnetic Field System
PM-FTIR... Polarization Modulation Fourier Transform InfraRed (SAUS)
PMFWCMA... Paper Mill Fourdrinier Wire Cloth Manufacturers Association [*Later, FWC*] (EA)
PMG .... Page Map Group (SAUS)
PMG .... Pall Mall Gazette [*A publication*]
PMG .... Paymaster General [*Navy*]
PMG .... Permanent Magnet Generator
PMG .... Phase Modulation Generator
PMG .... Photographic Materials Specialty Group (NTPA)
PMG .... Physiological Measurement Group
PMG .... Phytophthora Megasperma F. Sp. Glycinea [*A fungus*]
PMG .... Pinto Malartic [*Vancouver Stock Exchange symbol*]
PMG .... Plasma Motor Generator (SAUS)
PMG .... Polymethylgalacturonase [*An enzyme*]
PMG .... Ponta Pora [*Brazil*] [*Airport symbol*] (OAG)
PMG .... Portfolio Marine Group (SAUS)
PMG .... Port Moresby [*Papua New Guinea*] [*Seismograph station code, US Geological Survey*] (SEIS)
PmG .... Postmaster General (AD)
PMG .... Postmaster General
PMG .... Postmaster-General [*Telegraphy*] (PCTE)
PMG .... Poultry Marketing Guide
PMG .... Power Metal Grid (PDAA)
PMG .... Prediction Marker Generator
PMG .... Primary Medical Group [*Insurance*] (DMAA)
PMG .... Prison-Made Goods Statute (GOBB)

PMG .... Procurement Management Group (SAUS)
PMG .... Program Maintenance Group (SAUS)
PMG .... Project Management Group (EURO)
PMG .... Propodial Mucus Gland [*Zoology*]
PMG .... Provisional Military Government [*Ethiopia*]
PMG .... Provost Marshal General [*Army*]
PMG .... Putnam Investment Grade Municipal Trade II [*NYSE symbol*] (SPSG)
PMG .... Putnam Inv Grade Muni Tr II [*NYSE symbol*] (TTSB)
PMGCT ...... Primary Mediastinal Germ-Cell Tumor [*Medicine*] (DMAA)
PMGDINYC... Production Men's Guild of the Dress Industry of New York City (EA)
PMGFEL..... Preliminary Master Government-Furnished Equipment List (MCD)
PMGI .... Prime Management Group, Inc. [*NASDAQ symbol*] (SAG)
PMGI .... Princeton Media Group, Inc. [*NASDAQ symbol*] (SAG)
PMGM....... Program Manager Guidance Memorandum (SAUS)
PMGM....... Program Manager's Guidance Memorandum
PMGO .... Office of the Provost Marshal General [*Army*]
PM-GPV..... Project Manager, General Purpose Vehicle (SAA)
PMgr .... Professional Manager (DD)
PMGS .... Predictable Model Guidance Scheme (OA)
PMGS .... Provost Marshal General's School, United States Army
PMGSE...... Provisional Military Government of Socialist Ethiopia (SAUS)
PMGV .... Postmeal Glucose Value [*Medicine*] (MELL)
PMGW....... Primary Mission Gross Weight
pmh.......... Past Medical History (AD)
PMH .... Past Medical History
PMH .... Patrol Missile Hydrofoil (SAUS)
PMH .... Per Man Hour (WDAA)
PMH .... Petroleum Movement History (SAUS)
PMH .... Phenylmercuric Hydroxide [*Organic chemistry*]
PMH .... Porcine Malignant Hyperthermia (SAUS)
PMH .... Portsmouth, OH [*Location identifier*] [*FAA*] (FAAL)
PMH .... Postermedial Hypothalamus (DB)
PMH .... Posteromedial Hypothalamus [*Medicine*] (DMAA)
PMH .... Previous Medical History (MELL)
PMH .... Prime Mission Hardware (ACAE)
pmh.......... Probable Maximum Hurricane (AD)
PMH .... Probable Maximum Hurricane [*Nuclear energy*] (NRCH)
PMH .... Production per Man-Hour
PMH .... Productive Man Hour (SAUS)
PMH .... Product Marshaling and Handling [*Computer science*] (GART)
PMH .... Programmed Medical History (STED)
PMH .... Pseudomyocardial Hypertrophy [*Medicine*] (MELL)
PMH .... Public Mental Hospital [*Medicine*] (EDAA)
PMH .... Putnam Tax-Free Health Care Fund [*NYSE symbol*] (SPSG)
PMH .... Putnam Tax-Free Hlth Care Fd [*NYSE symbol*] (TTSB)
PMHA .... Pennsylvania Manufactured Housing Association (EARSL)
PMHC .... Pyridinylmethylethylene(hydrazinecarbothioamide) [*Organic chemistry*]
PMHL........ Pacific Marine Heritage Legacy (FOTI)
PMHL........ Preferred Measurement Hardware List [*NASA*] (NASA)
PMH/M...... Productive Man-Hours per Month [*Navy*] (NG)
PMHP .... Para-Menthane Hydroperoxide [*Organic chemistry*]
PMHP .... Para-Methane Hydroperoxide (SAUS)
PMHP .... P-Methane Hydroperoxide (SAUS)
PMHP .... Primary Mental Health Project (AD)
PMHR .... Predicted Maximum Heart Rate [*Medicine*] (DMAA)
PMHRON.... Patrol Combatant Missile Hydrofoil Squadron (DNAB)
PMHRON MLSG... Patrol Combatant Missile Hydrofoil Squadron Mobile Logistics Support Group (DNAB)
PMHS .... Polymethylhydrosiloxane [*Organic chemistry*]
PMHS .... Poly(methyl-Hydrostyrene) [*Organic chemistry*]
PMHSA...... Polish Military History Society of America (EA)
PM-HTV..... Program Manager for Heavy Tactical Vehicles [*Military*]
PMHU .... Dircen [*Intermodal shipping container symbol*] (TVRC)
PMHx........ Past Medical History (DAVI)
PMHYT...... Putnam Managed High Yield Trust [*Associated Press*] (SAG)
PMi .... Milton Public Library, Milton, PA [*Library symbol*] [*Library of Congress*] (LCLS)
PMI .... Palma [*Mallorca Island*] [*Airport symbol*] (OAG)
PMI .... Palma de Mallorca Balearic Islands, Spain (AD)
PMI .... Paper Money Identifier (ACAE)
PMI .... Parmac Mines [*Vancouver Stock Exchange symbol*]
PMI .... Partai Muslimin Indonesia [*Indonesian Muslim Party*] [*Political party*] (AD)
PMI .... Past [*or Previous*] Medical Illness
PMI .... Patient Medication Information (MELL)
PMI .... Patient Medication Instruction
PMI .... Pearlitic Malleable Iron (MCD)
PMI .... Pennsylvania Muscle Institute [*University of Pennsylvania*] [*Research center*] (RCD)
PMI .... Pensions Management Institute [*British*] (EAIO)
PMI .... Penske Motorsports, Incorporated
PMI .... Perioperative Myocardial Infarction [*Medicine*] (DMAA)
PMI .... Permanent Manufacturing Information (MSA)
PMI .... Personnel Management Information (IAA)
PMI .... Pesticide Monitoring Inventory [*Environmental Protection Agency*] (AEPA)
PMI .... Petroleum Monitoring, Inc. (EFIS)
PMI .... Phase Measuring Interferometer (AAEL)
PMI .... Phenylmethylisoxazole [*Organic chemistry*]
PMI .... Phosphomannose Isomerase [*An enzyme*] (MAE)
PMI .... Phosphomannoseisomerase (SAUS)
pmi .... Photographic Micro-Image (AD)
PMI .... Photographic Microimage Master [*Reprography*]
PMI .... Place of Maximal Impulse [*Medicine*] (MELL)
PMI .... Plant Manager Instruction [*Nuclear energy*] (NRCH)
PMI .... Plasma-Materials Interactions (MCD)
PMI .... Plea of Mental Incompetence [*Medicine*] (EDAA)
PMI .... Plumbing Manufacturers Institute (EA)
PMI .... PMI Group [*NYSE symbol*]
PMI .... Point of Maximal Impulse [*Medicine*]
PMI .... Point of Maximum Impact (SAUS)
pmi .... Point of Maximum Impulse (AD)
PMI .... Point of Maximum Intensity
PMI .... Polymethacrylimid (SAUS)
PMI .... Polymethacrylimide (EDCT)
PMI .... Positional Macro Instruction (SAUS)
PMI .... Posterior Myocardial Infarction [*Medicine*] (DMAA)
PMI .... Postmaintenance Inspection (SAUS)
PMI .... Post Mortem Interval [*Forensics*] [*Medicine*]
PMI .... Postmortem Intervals (SAUS)
PMI .... Postmyocardial Infarction [*Syndrome*] [*Medicine*]
PMI .... Powder Metallurgy International (SAUS)
PMI .... Power Management Inventory [*Test*]
PMI .... Precious Metals Institute (SAUS)
PMI .... Precision Monolithics Inc (NITA)
PMI .... Preferred Modes Indicator [*Training term*] (LPT)
PMI .... Preliminary Maintenance Inspection [*Department of Defense*]
PMI .... Preliminary Marksmanship Instruction [*Army*]
PMI .... Pre-Marital Inventory (AD)
PMI .... Premark International, Inc. [*NYSE symbol*] (SPSG)
PMI .... Premark Intl [*NYSE symbol*] (TTSB)
PMI .... Premarksmanship Instruction [*Army*]
PMI .... Prescriptive Math Inventory
PMI .... Present Medical Illness
PMI .... Presidential Management Incentives [*Office of Management and Budget*]
PMI .... Presidential Management Intern (SAUS)
PMI .... Pressed Metal Institute [*Later, AMSA*]
PMI .... Preventive Maintenance Inspection (AFM)
PMI .... Preventive Maintenance Instruction [*Department of Defense*]
PMI .... Previous Medical Illness (CPH)
PMI .... Primary Measurement Instrument
PMI .... Princeton Materials Institute [*Princeton University*] (RCD)
PMI .... Principal Maintenance Inspector (NASA)
PMI .... Printed Motors, Inc. (SAUS)
PMI .... Private Memory Interconnect (SAUS)
PMI .... Private Memory Interface (SAUS)
pmi .... Private Mortgage Insurance (AD)
PMI .... Private Mortgage Insurance [*Insurance of mortgages by private insurers*]
PMI .... Probe Ministries International (EA)
PMI .... Processor Monitoring Instrument [*Computer science*] (ADA)
PMI .... Programmable Machine Interface (MCD)
PMI .... Programmable Memory Interface [*Computer science*]
PMI .... Programmable MODEM Interface [*Computer science*] (MCD)
PMI .... Programmable Multispectral Imager (SAUS)
PMI .... Program Management Instruction [*Department of Defense*]
PMI .... Project Management Institute (EA)
PMI .... Proposed Military Improvement (CAAL)
PMI .... Protection Mode Indicator (SAUS)
PMI .... Pseudo Matrix Isolation (SAUS)
PMI .... Pseudomatrix Isolation
PMI .... Purchased Materials Inspection
PMIA .... Pacific Music Industry Association [*Canada*] (EAIO)
PMIA .... Parallel Multiplexer Interface Adapter (MCD)
PMIA .... Powder Metal Industries Association [*Australia*]
P/MIA........ Powder Metallurgy Industries Association (SAUS)
PMIA .... Precioas Metals Industry Association (SAUS)
PMIA .... Presidential Management Improvement Award
PMIC .... Parallel Multiple Incremental Computer
PMIC .... Payload Mission Integration Contract [*NASA*]
PMIC .... Periodic Maintenance Information Cards
PMIC .... Personnel Management Information Center [*Air Force*] (AFM)
PMIC .... Poultry Meat Industry Committee [*New South Wales, Australia*]
PMIC .... Precious Metal Indicator Code
PMIC .... Precious Metals Institute Conference (SAUS)
PMIC .... President's Management Improvement Council (AD)
PMIF......... Powder Metal Industries Federation
PMIG .... Political-Military Interdepartmental Group (AD)
PMIG .... Programmers Minimal Interface to Graphics (MCD)
PMI Gp...... PMI Group, Inc. [*Associated Press*] (SAG)
PMIIT........ Putnam Master Intermediate Income Trust [*Associated Press*] (SAG)
PMIJ......... Pulse Modulated Infrared Jammer (SAUS)
PMIJ......... Pulse-Modulated Infrared Jammer
PMilan ...... Papiri Milanesi [*A publication*] (OCD)
PMilS........ Millersville State College, Millersville, PA [*Library symbol*] [*Library of Congress*] (LCLS)
PMIM........ Powder Metal Injection Molding (SAUS)
PMI/MO ..... Precedence Manual In / Manual Out (DNAB)
PMIN .... Processor Memory Interconnection Network (SAUS)
PMIP .... Palaeoclimate Model Inter-comparison Project (SAUS)
PMIP .... Paleoclimate Modeling Intercomparison Project [*Marine science*] (OSRA)
PMIP .... Paleoclimatic (or Paleoclimatological) Model Intercomparison Project (SAUS)
PMIP .... Pan Malayan Islamic Party
PMIP .... Postmaintenance Inspection Pilot

PMIP .... Presidential Management Intern Program [*Executive Office of the President*] (GFGA)
PMIPK....... Poly Methyl Isopropenyl Ketone (SAUS)
PMIPK....... Poly(methyl Isopropenyl Ketone) [*Organic chemistry*]
PMI Powder Metall Int... PMI Powder Metallurgy International (SAUS)
PMIR .... Pressure Modulator Infrared Radiometer (EOSA)
PMIR .... Program Manager's Integration Review [*NASA*] (NASA)
PMIR .... Psi-Mediated Instrumental Response [*Parapsychology*]
PMIRD ...... Passive Microwave Intercept Receiver Display
PMIRR ...... Pressure Modulated Infra-Red Radiometer (VLIE)
PMIRR ...... Pressure Modulator Infrared Radiometer (ACAE)
PMIS .... Passive Microwave Imaging System [*NASA*]
PMIS .... Patient Medical Information System (OA)
PMIS .... Personal Management Information System [*Computer science*] (IAA)
PMIS .... Personnel Management Information System
PMIS .... Personnel Management Information Systems (SAUS)
PMIS .... Personnel Marking and Identification System (SAUS)
PMIS .... Planning Management Information System (AD)
PMIS .... Plant Management Information System
PMIS .... Plant Monitoring and Information System [*Nuclear energy*] (NRCH)
PMIS .... Postmyocardial Infarction Syndrome [*Medicine*] (DMAA)
PMIS .... Precision Mechanisms in Sodium [*Nuclear energy*] (NRCH)
PMIS .... Premis Corp. [*NASDAQ symbol*] (SAG)
PMIS .... Printing Management Information System (SAUS)
PMIS .... Printing Management Information Systems
PMIS .... Process Management Information System (ACII)
PMIS .... Production Management Information System (SAUS)
PMIS .... Product Management Information System (AD)
PMIS .... Program Management Information System [*Army*]
PMIS .... Program Measurement Information System [*Computer science*] (IAA)
PMIS .... Projects Management Information System [*UNESCO*] (DUND)
PMIS .... Property Management Information System (ALAC)
PMIS .... PSRO [*Professional Standards Review Organization*] Management Information System (DHSM)
PMIS .... Publications Management Information System (SAUS)
PMIS .... Purchase Management Information System (SAUS)
PMISP....... Personnel Management Information System Plan (SAUS)
PMI Syndrome... Postmyocardial Infarction Syndrome (SAUS)
PMIT........ Putnam Master Income Trust [*Associated Press*] (SAG)
PMITS....... Post Mobilization Individual Training and Support (MCD)
PM ITTS .... Program Manager, Instrumentation, Targets, and Threat Simulators (SAUS)
PM ITTS .... Project Manager, Instrumentation, Targets, and Threat Simulators (SAUS)
PMIX .... PRIMIX Solutions, Inc. [*NASDAQ symbol*] (NASQ)
PMJ.......... Porto Murtinho [*Brazil*] [*Airport symbol*] (AD)
PMJ.......... Pulse Modulated Jammer (SAUS)
PMJ.......... Pulse-Modulated Jammer
PMJC........ Pine Manor Junior College (AD)
PMJEG ...... Performance Measurement Joint Executive Group (DOMA)
PMJI......... Pardon My Jumping In [*E-Mail discussion*]
PMK .... Palair Macedonian [*Yugoslavia*] [*ICAO designator*] (FAAC)
PMK .... Panel Marking Kit
PMK .... Pitch Mark [*Shipfitting*] (AAG)
pmk.......... Pitch Mark (AD)
PMK .... Pointe Molloy [*Kerguelen Islands*] [*Seismograph station code, US Geological Survey*] (SEIS)
PMK .... Portable Molding Kit
pmk.......... Postmark (AD)
PMK .... Postmark
PMK .... Primark Corp. [*NYSE symbol*] (SPSG)
PMK .... Primary Monkey Kidney [*Physiology*]
PMK .... Primary Rhesus Monkey Kidney (AAMN)
PMKD .... Postmarked (SAUS)
PMKM....... Past Master, Knights of Malta [*Freemasonry*] (ROG)
PMKY........ Pittsburgh, McKeesport & Youghiogheny [*AAR code*]
PML .... Pacific Micronesian Line (AD)
PML .... Pakistan Muslim League [*Political party*]
PML .... Parts Material List
PML .... Pattern Makers' League of North America (EA)
PML .... Payload Management Lamp
PML .... Perfectly Matched Layer (ARMP)
PML .... Perfect Matched Layer (SAUS)
PML .... Permitted Maximum Level (SAUS)
P M L .... Phoenix Memorial Laboratory (SAUS)
PML .... Phoenix Mutual Life Insurance Co. (EFIS)
PML .... Physical Memory Level
PML .... Physical Memory Loss [*Computer science*] (CIST)
PML .... PI Edit's Macro Language [*Iliad Group*] [*Computer science*]
PML .... [*The*] Pierpont Morgan Library (BJA)
PML .... Plymouth Marine Laboratory [*Natural Environment Research Council*] [*British*] [*Information service or system*] (IID)
PML .... Polymer Microdevice Laboratory [*Case Western Reserve University*] [*Research center*] (RCD)
PML .... Polymorphonuclear Leukocyte [*Hematology*]
PML .... Port Moller [*Alaska*] [*Airport symbol*] (OAG)
PML .... Port Moller, AK [*Location identifier*] [*FAA*] (FAAL)
PML .... Possible Maximum Loss (MARI)
PML .... Posterior Mitral Leaflet [*Cardiology*]
PML .... Powder Metallurgy Laboratory (SAUS)
PML .... Power Minimized Logic (SAUS)
PML .... Preliminary Materials List [*NASA*]
pml .... Probable Maximum Loss (AD)
PML .... Probable Maximum Loss [*Insurance*]
PML .... Process Modelling Language (VLIE)
PML .... Production Measurement Log (SAUS)
PML .... Programmable Macro Logic (NITA)
PML .... Progressive Multifocal Leucoencephalopathy (SAUS)
PML .... Progressive Multifocal Leukodystrophy [*Medicine*] (QSUL)
PML .... Progressive Multifocal Leukoencephalopathy [*Oncology*]
PML .... Promotion Management List [*Pronounced "pemell"*] [*Air Force*]
PML .... Promyelocytic Leukaemia Protein [*Biochemistry*]
PML .... Promyelocytic Leukemia [*Medicine*]
PML .... Provident Mutual Life Insurance Co. (EFIS)
PML .... Pulmonary Microlithiasis [*Medicine*] (EDAA)
PML .... Putnam Investment Grade Multiple Sectors III [*AMEX symbol*] (SPSG)
PML .... Putnam Inv Grade Muni Tr III [*AMEX symbol*] (TTSB)
PML .... University of Windsor, Paul Martin Law Library [*UTLAS symbol*]
pmla......... Parmelia (AD)
PMLA........ Production Music Libraries Association (EA)
PMLA........ Publication of the Modern Language Association of America (AD)
PMLC........ Pooled Mixed Lymphocyte Culture [*Clinical chemistry*]
PMLC........ Previous Micro-Location Counter (VLIE)
PMLC........ Programmed Multiline Controller
PMLD........ Profound and Multiple Learning Difficulties (AIE)
PMLE........ Polymorphous Light Eruption [*Medicine*]
PMLF........ Project Marketing Loan Facility [*Australia*]
PMLG........ Poly(methyl L-Glutamate) [*Organic chemistry*]
PMLI......... Pace Motor Lines [*Common carrier symbol*]
PMLI......... PML [*OTCBB symbol*]
PMLK........ PrimeLink Systems, Inc. [*NASDAQ symbol*] (QUAN)
PMLM .... Photosensitive Membrane Light Modulation (or Modulator) (SAUS)
PMLM .... Photosensitive Membrane Light Modulator
PML-N....... Pakistan Muslim League-N (Pakistan) [*Political party*] (PSAP)
PMLO........ Partially Maleated Linseed Oil (SAUS)
PMLO........ Philippine Military Liaison Officer (DNAB)
PMLO........ Principal Military Landing Officer (AD)
PMLO........ Principal Military Landing Offices [*British*]
PM Loudspeaker... Permanent Magnetic Loudspeaker (SAUS)
PMLPC ...... Permanent Mass Layoffs and Plant Closings Program [*Bureau of Labor Statistics*]
PM-LSM .... Polarization-Modulation Laser-Scanning Microscopy
PML-TNO ... TNO Prins Maurits Laboratory (SAUS)
PMLV........ Permanent Magnet Latch Valve
PMLX........ Prairie Malt [*Private rail car owner code*]
PMM......... Military Morale Division [*Coast Guard*]
PMM......... Paramagnetic Material (SAUS)
PMM......... Parametric Modelling (SAUS)
PMM......... Partial Matrix Multiply (IAA)
PMM......... Peace Mission Movement (EA)
PMM......... Peat Marwick McLintock [*Accounting firm*] [*British*]
PMM......... Pedestal-Mounted Manipulator [*Nuclear energy*] (NRCH)
PMM......... Penobscot Marine Museum (EA)
PMM......... Pentamethylmelamine [*Medicine*] (EDAA)
PMM......... Permanent Magnet Magnetizer (SAUS)
PMM......... Permanent Magnet Motor (IAA)
PMM......... Personnel Management Manual [*A publication*] (ADA)
PMM......... Petroleum Marketing Management [*Petroleum Marketers Association of America*] [*A publication*]
PMM......... Petroleum Marketing Monthly [*Department of Energy*] [*Information service or system*] (CRD)
PMM......... Physical Memory Manager [*Computer science*] (PCM)
PMM......... Phytophthora Megasperma F.Sp Medicaginia [*A fungus*]
PMM......... Planar Motion Mechanism (SAUS)
PMM......... Poly Methyl Methacrylate (SAUS)
PMM......... Poly(methyl Methacrylate) [*Also, PMMA*] [*Organic chemistry*]
PMM......... Pool Maintenance Module [*Telecommunications*] (TEL)
PMM......... Portavideo [*Vancouver Stock Exchange symbol*]
PMM......... Post Mast Message (IAA)
PMM......... Post-Merger Management
PMM......... Presa Malpaso [*Mexico*] [*Seismograph station code, US Geological Survey*] (SEIS)
pmm......... Preventive Medicine Measures
PMM......... Primitive Martian Mantle [*Planetary science*]
PMM......... Primm, NV [*Amtrak Busline code*]
PMM......... Probability of Missed Message (CCCA)
PMM......... Process Monitoring Modules (ACII)
PMM......... Procom Emerald [*Vancouver Stock Exchange symbol*]
PMM......... Procurement Material Management (TIMI)
PMM......... Professional Media Magazine (SAUS)
PMM......... Professional Music Men, Inc. (EA)
PMM......... Profile Milling Machine
PMM......... Programmable Microcomputer Module
PMM......... Property Management Manual [*NASA*] (MCD)
PMM......... Protoplast Maintenance Medium (DB)
PMM......... Pullman, MI [*Location identifier*] [*FAA*] (FAAL)
pmm.......... Pulse Mode Multiplex (AD)
PMM......... Pulse Mode Multiplex
PMM......... Purchase-Money Mortgage [*Real estate*]
PMM......... Putnam Managed Municipal Income [*NYSE symbol*] (SPSG)
PMM......... Putnam Managed Muni Income [*NYSE symbol*] (TTSB)
PMMA....... Paper Machinery Makers Association (SAUS)
PMMA....... Pere Marquette Memorial Association (EA)
PMMA....... Poly(methyl Methacrylate) [*Also, PMM*] [*Organic chemistry*]
pmma .... Polymethylmethacrylate (AD)
PMMA....... Poly Methyl Methacrylate Association [*European Council of Chemical Manufacturers Federations*] [*Brussels, Belgium*] (EAIO)

PMMA .... Polymethyl Methacrylate Association (SAUS)
PMMAP ..... Poly(methyl Methacrylate Peroxide) [*Organic chemistry*]
PMMAPA.... Poly Methyl Methacrylate Producers Association [*Belgium*] (EAIO)
PMMB .... Parallel Memory to Memory Bus (SAUS)
PMMB .... Parallel Memory-to-Memory Bus
PMMC .... Permanent Magnetic Movable Coil
PMMC .... Permanent Magnetic Movable (or Moving) Coil (SAUS)
PMMC .... Permanent Magnet Moving Coil (SAUS)
PMMC .... Polymethylmethacrylate [*Medicine*] (EDAA)
PMMC .... Precious Metals Marketing Co. (SAUS)
PM-MCD .... Project Manager for Mines, Countermine, and Demolitions [*Army*] (RDA)
PM-MEP .... Project Manager - Mobile Electric Power [*DoD*]
PMMEP ..... Project Manager, Mobile Electric Power (SAUS)
PMMF .... Precious Metals Master File [*DoD*] (AFIT)
PMMI .... Packaging Machinery Manufacturers Institute (EA)
PMMI .... Packaging Machinery Manufacturers (or Manufacturing) Institute (SAUS)
PMMI .... Permanent Magnet Movable (or Moving) Iron (SAUS)
PMMI .... Polypyromellitimide (EDCT)
PMMI .... Putnam Managed Municipal Income Trust [*Associated Press*] (SAG)
PMML .... Predictive Model Markup Language (IDAI)
PMMM ...... Pall Mall Money Management [*Investment group*] [*British*]
PMMO ...... Particulate Methane Monooxygenase [*Biochemistry*]
PMMO ...... Projects and Missions Management Office (SAUS)
PMMP .... Post Mortem Memory Print (SAUS)
PMMP .... Project Managers Master Plan (SAUS)
PMMR .... Panel-Mounted Microfilm Reader
PMMR .... Passive Multichannel Microwave Radiometer [*NASA*]
PMMRS ..... Passive Microwave Mapping and Retrieval Simulator (SAUS)
PMMS .... Phrenicon Metabolic Monitoring System
PMMS .... Plainsong and Mediaeval Music Society (EA)
PMMS .... Process Material Management System (SAUS)
PMMS .... Program Master Milestone Schedule (MCD)
PMMU .... Paged Memory Management Unit [*Computer chip*] (BYTE)
pmmu .... Paged Memory-Management Unit (AD)
PMMU .... Page Memory Management Unit (SAUS)
PMMV .... Pea Mild Mosaic Virus [*Plant pathology*]
PMMW ...... Passive Millimeter Wave (ADWA)
PMN .... Pacific Mountain Network [*Television*]
PMN .... Pahute Mesa [*Nevada*] [*Seismograph station code, US Geological Survey*] [*Closed*] (SEIS)
PMN .... Pam [*Language symbol*] (ETLW)
PMN .... Pasteurized Milk Network (SAUS)
PMN .... Performance Monitoring (VLIE)
PMN .... Permian Resources Ltd. [*Vancouver Stock Exchange symbol*]
PMN .... Phenyl Mercuric Nitrate (SAUS)
PMN .... Phenylmercuric Nitrate [*Antiseptic*]
PMN .... Polymorphonuclear [*Hematology*]
pmn .... Polymorphonuclear Neutrophil (AD)
PMN .... Polymorphonuclear Neutrophilic [*Hematology*]
PMN .... Polymorphonucleocyte [*Hematology*] (CPH)
PMN .... Postman (DCTA)
PMN .... Premanufacture Notification [*Environmental Protection Agency*]
PMN .... Premanufacture Notifications [*Environment term*] (EGA)
PMN .... Pre-Manufacturing Notice [*Government regulations*]
PMN .... Premarket Notification [*Requirement for introducing new chemicals into the EEC*]
PMN .... Proclamation [*Telegraphy*] (PCTE)
pmn .... Producto Material Neto [*Net Material Product*] [*Spain*] (AD)
PMN .... Program Management Network (MCD)
PMN .... Program Model Number (SAUS)
PMN .... Project Management Network [*Computer science*] (VLIE)
PMN .... Promina Group Ltd. [*Australian Stock Exchange symbol*]
PMN .... Proposed Material Need (MCD)
PMN .... Pumani [*Papua New Guinea*] [*Airport symbol*] (OAG)
PMN .... Putnam New York Investment Grade Municipal [*AMEX symbol*] (SPSG)
PMN .... Putnam NY Inv Grade Muni [*AMEX symbol*] (TTSB)
PMNA .... Pacific Mountain Network Association (AD)
PMNA .... Parkers Marsh Natural Area [*Virginia*] (AD)
PM-NAVCON... Project Manager, Navigation and Control [*Military*]
PMNC .... Percentage of Multinucleated Cells [*Medicine*] (EDAA)
PMNC .... Peripheral Blood Mononuclear Cell [*Medicine*] (DMAA)
PMNC .... Pharmaceutical Multinational Company (DB)
PMNF .... Premanufacture Notification Form [*Environmental Protection Agency*] (GFGA)
PMNG .... Polymorphonuclear Granulocyte [*Hematology*] (DAVI)
PMNH .... Peabody Museum of Natural History (NADA)
PMNL .... Polymorphonuclear Leucocyte (SAUS)
pmnl .... Polymorphonuclear Leukocyte (AD)
PMNL .... Polymorphonuclear Leukocyte [*Hematology*]
PMN(L) ...... Polymorphonuclear Lymphocyte [*Immunology*] (QSUL)
PMNN .... Polymorphonuclear Neutrophil (DB)
PMNP .... Platform-Mounted Nuclear Plant (NRCH)
PMNP .... Platform Mounted Nuclear Platform (SAUS)
PMNPP ...... Platform Mounted Nuclear Power Plant (SAUS)
pmnr .... Periadenitis Mucosa Necrotica Recurrens (AD)
PMNR .... Periadenitis Mucosa Necrotica Recurrens [*Medicine*]
PMNR .... Porter McLeod National Retail [*NASDAQ symbol*] (SAG)
PMNR .... Porter McLeod Natl Retail [*NASDAQ symbol*] (TTSB)
PMN/SFS ... People's Music Network for Songs of Freedom and Struggle (EA)
PMNT .... Permanent (IAA)
PMNT .... Prominent [*Telegraphy*] (PCTE)
PMNUC ...... Project Manager for Nuclear [*Munitions*]
PM-NUC ..... Project Manager for Nuclear Munitions [*Army*] (RDA)
PMNV .... Project Manager, Night Vision (RDA)
PM NV/RSTA... Project Manager for Night Vision/Reconnaissance Surveillance and Target Acquisition [*Military*] (RDA)
PMo .... Monessen Public Library, Monessen, PA [*Library symbol*] [*Library of Congress*] (LCLS)
PMO .... Palermo [*Italy*] [*Airport symbol*] (OAG)
PMO .... Palermo Resources, Inc. [*Vancouver Stock Exchange symbol*]
pmo .... Palomar Mountain Observatory (AD)
PMO .... Perroni, Martin, O'Reilly [*Commercial firm*]
PMO .... Personnel Management Officer [*Army*] (INF)
PMO .... Perturbation Molecular Orbital [*Theory*]
PMO .... Phenylmercuric Oleate (SAUS)
PMO .... Phenyl Mercury Oleate (SAUS)
PMO .... Phenylmethyloxadiazole (SAUS)
PMO .... Pianissimo [*Very Softly*] [*Music*] (ROG)
pmo .... Pianissimo [*Very Softly*] [*Italian*] [*Music*] (AD)
PMO .... Pine Mountain Observatory
PMO .... Polaris Material Office [*Missiles*]
PMO .... Polaris Missile Office
PMO .... Pomariorio [*Tuamotu Archipelago*] [*Seismograph station code, US Geological Survey*] (SEIS)
PMO .... Port Medical Officer (SAUS)
PMO .... Port Meteorological Office [*National Weather Service*]
PMO .... Port Meteorological Officer (SAUS)
PMO .... Postal Money Order [*Military*]
PMO .... Postmenopausal Osteoporosis [*Medicine*]
PMO .... Present Method of Operation [*Communications term*] (DCT)
PMO .... Prime Minister's Office
PMO .... Principal Medical Officer
pmo .... Printed Matter Only (AD)
PMO .... Product Management Office [*Army*]
PMO .... Product Manager's Office (RDA)
PMO .... Product Manufacturing Organization
PMO .... Profit Making Organization
PMO .... Program Maintenance Office
PMO .... Program Management Office [*Environmental Protection Agency*] (GFGA)
PMO .... Program Management Office [*Army*]
PMO .... Program Management Organization (HLLA)
PMO .... Program Manager's Office
PMO .... Project Management Office [*Army*] (AABC)
PMO .... Project Manager's Office
PMO .... Project Monitoring Office (FOTI)
PMO .... Prominence [*Telegraphy*] (PCTE)
PMO .... Property Management Officer [*USDA Forest Service*] (ALAC)
PMO .... Property Movement Order
PMO .... Provisional [*Program Management*] Office [*Army*]
PMO .... Provost Marshal's Office
PMO .... Psychiatric Military Officer
PMO .... Purple Mountain Observatory, Academia Sinica, Nanjing (SAUS)
PMO .... Putnam Municipal Opportunities Trust [*NYSE symbol*] (SPSG)
PMO .... Putnam Muni Opport Tr [*NYSE symbol*] (TTSB)
PMOA .... Programmatic Memorandum of Agreement (COE)
PMOA .... Prospectors and Mine Owners Association (EA)
PMOC .... Pioneer Mission Operations Center [*NASA*]
PMOC .... Prototype Mission Operations Center (ACAE)
PMODA ...... Phenyl(mercapto)oxadiazole [*Reagent*]
PMOF .... Presidential Medal of Freedom [*Military decoration*] (GFGA)
PM of F ..... Presidential Medal of Freedom [*Military decoration*] (AABC)
PMOG .... Plutonium Maintenance and Operating Gallery [*Nuclear energy*] (NRCH)
PMOG .... Proposed Material Ordering Guide (MCD)
PMOI .... People's Mujahidin of Iran [*Government term*] (GA)
PMOL .... Philippines Micronesia Orient Lines [*Common carrier symbol*]
pmol .... Picomole [*One trillionth of a mole*] (WGA)
PMOLANT... Polaris Material Office, Atlantic Fleet [*Missiles*]
pmole .... Picomole [*One trillionth of a mole*] (DAVI)
PMOM .... Performance Management Operations Manager
PMOM .... Performance Management Operations Manual [*NASA*] (NASA)
PMO-MTV... Project Manager's Office, Medium Tactical Vehicles [*Army*]
PMON .... Performance Management Operations Network [*NASA*] (NASA)
P-MONO .... Promonocytes [*hematology*] (DAVI)
PMOPAC .... Polaris Material Office, Pacific Fleet [*Missiles*]
PMOR .... Phar-Mor, Inc. [*NASDAQ symbol*] (SAG)
P Mor .... Port Moresby (AD)
PMOR .... Probabilistic Methods in Operations Research (SAUS)
PMORW ..... Phar-Mor Wrrt [*NASDAQ symbol*] (TTSB)
P-MOS ...... P-Channel Metal-Oxide Semiconductor
PMOS .... Permanent Manned Orbital Station (AAG)
PMOS .... Physical Movement of Spacecraft (SAA)
PMOS .... Positive Channel Metal Oxide Semiconductor (SAUS)
PMOS .... Positive-Channel Metal-Oxide Semiconductor [*Telecommunications*] (TEL)
PMOS .... Positive Metal-Oxide Semiconductor (SAUS)
PMOS .... Primary Military Occupational Specialty [*Army*]
PMOS .... Program Management and Operations Staff [*Environmental Protection Agency*] (GFGA)
PMOS .... Program Management and Operation Staff (SAUS)
PMOS .... P-Type Metal-Oxide Semiconductor (SAUS)
PMOSC ...... Primary Military Occupational Code (AD)
PMOSC ...... Primary Military Occupational Specialty Code [*Army*] (AABC)
PMOT .... Putnam Municipal Opportunities Trust [*Associated Press*] (SAG)
PMOU .... Philippines, Micronesia, and Orient Navigation [*Intermodal shipping container symbol*] (TVRC)

PMO UH .... Project Management Office for Utility Helicopters [*Army*]
PMov .... Personnel Movements (SAUS)
PMOX .... Philip Morris [*Private rail car owner code*]
PMP .... Pacific Magazines and Printing Ltd. [*Commercial firm*] [*Australia*]
PMP .... Packed Main Parachute
PMP .... Pain Management Program [*Neurology*] (DAVI)
PMP .... Parallel Microprogrammed Processor [*Computer science*]
PMP .... Parent Mass Peak
PMP .... Parents' Magazine Press
PMP .... Partial Manifold Preheater [*Automotive engineering*]
PMP .... Partido ng Masang Pilipino [*Political party*] (EY)
PMP .... Parti du Mouvement Populaire de la Cote Francaise des Somalis [*Popular Movement Party of French Somaliland*] [*Political party*]
PMP .... Partito Monarchico Popolare [*Popular Monarchist Party*] [*Italy*] [*Political party*] (PPE)
PMP .... Parts Material Packaging (SAUS)
PMP .... Parts, Materials, and Packaging (MCD)
PMP .... Parts, Materials, and Processes (MCD)
PMP .... Parts, Materials, Processes (SAUS)
PMP .... Passive Measurement Program
PMP .... Past Menstrual Period [*Medicine*]
PMP .... Patient Management Path (SAUS)
PMP .... Patient Management Problem [*Gerontology*]
PMP .... Patient-Management Problem (SAUS)
PMP .... Patient Medication Profile (STED)
PMP .... Patient of the Month Program (SAUS)
PMP .... Payload Mounting Panels (SAUS)
PMP .... Peremptory [*Telegraphy*] (PCTE)
PMP .... Performance Management Package [*NASA*] (NASA)
PMP .... Performance Management Process (SAUS)
PMP .... Performance Monitoring Program (CCCA)
PmP .... Pergamon Press, Inc., Fairview Park, Elmsford, NY [*Library symbol*] [*Library of Congress*] (LCLS)
PMP .... Permanent Manned Presence (SSD)
pmp.......... Per-Member Payment (AD)
PMP .... Persistent Mentoposterior [*A fetal position*] [*Obstetrics*]
PMP .... Peter Miller Apparel Group, Inc. [*Toronto Stock Exchange symbol*]
PMP .... Phased Maintenance Program (SAUS)
PMP .... Phased Manufacturing Program (SAUS)
PMP .... Phenoxymethyl Penicillin [*Medicine*] (EDAA)
PMP .... Phenyl(methyl)pyrazolone [*An organic pigment*]
PMP .... Photomechanical Process (SAUS)
PMP .... Physical Media Parameter (VLIE)
PMP .... Piecewise Markov Process (PDAA)
PMP .... Pimaga [*Papua New Guinea*] [*Airport symbol*] (OAG)
PMP .... Pipeline Maintenance Program (FOTI)
PMP .... Planar Metallization with Polymer (IAA)
PMP .... Planned Maintenance Plan (MCD)
PMP .... Plan of Actions and Milestones (SAUS)
PMP .... Plantar Metatarsal Padding [*Medicine*] (MELL)
PMP .... Poly(metal Phosphinate) [*Organic chemistry*]
PMP .... Poly(methylpentene) [*Organic chemistry*]
PMP .... Pompano Beach, FL [*Location identifier*] [*FAA*] (FAAL)
PMP .... Pompeii [*Italy*] [*Seismograph station code, US Geological Survey*] [*Closed*] (SEIS)
PMP .... Pontifical Mission for Palestine (EA)
PMP .... Pontryagins Maximum Principle (SAUS)
PMP .... Population Management Plan (SAUS)
PMP .... Portable Medium-Powder Plant (SAUS)
PMP .... Position Management Program
PMP .... Postmastectomy Pain (MELL)
PMP .... Post-Metal Programming (SAUS)
PMP .... Powdered Metal Part
PMP .... Powder Melting Process [*Physics*]
PMP .... Power Management Profile [*Test*]
pmp.......... Precious Metal Plating (AD)
PMP .... Precision Mounting Platform (ACAE)
PMP .... Preliminary Management Plan (AD)
PMP .... Preliminary Mission Profile (MCD)
PMP .... Premodulation Processor
PMP .... Preoperational Maintenance Plan
PMP .... Preoperational Monitoring Program [*Nuclear energy*] (NRCH)
PMP .... Pressure Measurement Package
PMP .... Prevention, Mitigation and Preparedness [*Office of U.S. Foreign Disaster Assistance*]
PMP .... Preventive Maintenance Package (SAUS)
PMP .... Preventive Maintenance Periodic [*Inspection*]
PMP .... Preventive Maintenance Plan (KSC)
PMP .... Preventive Maintenance Procedure [*Nuclear energy*] (NRCH)
PMP .... Preventive Maintenance Program (SAUS)
pmp.......... Previous Menstrual Period [*Medicine*] (AD)
PMP .... Previous Menstrual Period [*Medicine*]
PMP .... Prime Mission Product (SAUS)
PMP .... Prime Mission Project [*Military*]
PMP .... Prime Motor Inns L.P. [*NYSE symbol*] (TTSB)
PMP .... Prime Motor Inns Ltd. [*NYSE symbol*] (SPSG)
PMP .... Prior Menstrual Period [*Gynecology*] (DAVI)
PMP .... Prism-Mirror-Prism [*For electron microscopy*]
PMP .... Probable Maximum Precipitation [*Nuclear energy*] (NRCH)
PMP .... Procurement Methods and Practices (AD)
PMP .... Product and Marketing Planning (IAA)
PMP .... Product & Market Planning (SAUS)
PMP .... Professor of Moral Philosophy
PMP .... Profit-Maximizing Price (MHDW)
PMP .... Program Management Plan [*NASA*]
PMP .... Program Master Plan [*Department of Defense*]
PMP .... Program Monitor Panel
PMP .... Progressive Merger Procedure [*Econometrics*]
PMP .... Project Management Plan (ABAC)
PMP .... Project Management Plan/System (SAUS)
PMP .... Project Management Professional
PMP .... Project Master Plan [*Army*]
PMP .... Project on Military Procurement [*Later, PGP*] (EA)
PMP .... Property Management Plan [*Australia*]
PMP .... Property Management Planning (SAUS)
PMP .... Protective Mobilization Plan
PMP .... Psychotropic Medication Plan (STED)
PMP .... Pulmonary Mean Pressure [*Medicine*]
PMP .... Pulsed Microwave Power
PMP .... Pump (KSC)
PMP .... Pyridoxamine Phosphate [*Biochemistry*]
PMPA........ Permanent Magnet Producers Association [*Later, MMPA*] (EA)
PMPA........ Petroleum Marketing Practices Act
PMPA........ (Phosphonylmethoxypropyl)adenine [*Antiviral*]
PMPA........ Powder Metallurgy Parts Association (SAUS)
PMPA........ Precision Machined Products Association (NTPA)
PMPA........ Proximal Main Pulmonary Artery [*Anatomy*]
P/M Part .... Powder Metal Part (SAUS)
PMPCB .... Part, Material and Processes Control Board (ACAE)
PMPE........ Punch Memory Parity Error [*Computer science*] (IAA)
PMPEA ...... Professional Motion Picture Equipment Association [*Later, PFVEA*] (EA)
PMPFR....... Program Manager's Preflight Review [*NASA*] (KSC)
PMPG .... Pumping
PMPH .... Pamphlet (DLA)
PMPIN........ Pre-Manufacturing and Pre-Importation Notification (SAUS)
PMPIT........ Program Management Process Improvement Team (TIMI)
PMPL......... Preferred Mechanical Parts List [*NASA*] (NASA)
PM Plant.... Portable Medium-power Plant (SAUS)
PMPM........ Per Member per Month
PMPM........ Perpetual Motion Poetry Machine
PMPM........ Phase Margin Performance Measure [*Manual control system*]
PMPM........ Programmable Multiple Position Machine (MCD)
PMPM........ Pulse Mode Performance Model (KSC)
PMPMA ..... Plastic and Metal Products Manufacturers Association (EA)
PMPMD ..... Pest Management and Pesticide Monitoring Division (SAUS)
PMPO .... Peak Music Power Output (SAUS)
PMPO .... Postmenopausal Palpable Ovary [*Gynecology*]
PMPO .... Pulse-Modulated Power Oscillator (SAUS)
PMPP......... Program Management Phase-Out Plan [*Military*] (AFIT)
PMPPI........ Polymethylenepolyphenyl Polyisocyanate [*Organic chemistry*]
PMPPIC ..... Polymethylene-Polyphenyl Isocyanate (SAUS)
PMPQ .... Professional and Managerial Position Questionnaire [*Test*]
PMPR .... Program Management and Performance Review
PMPRB....... Patented Medicine Prices Review Board (FOTI)
PMPRB....... Program to Manage Pesticide Residues in Beef (SAUS)
PM Press ... Powder Metal Press (SAUS)
PMPS......... Postmastectomy Pain Syndrome [*Medicine*] (DMAA)
PMPS......... Program Management Planning and Scheduling [*Military*] (DNAB)
PMPSL .... Part, Material and Processes Selection List (ACAE)
PMPY......... Peremptorily [*Telegraphy*] (PCTE)
PMPY......... Per Member per Year
PMQ.......... Perito Moreno [*Argentina*] [*Airport symbol*] (OAG)
PMQ.......... Permanent Married Quarters [*Canadian Forces*]
PMQ.......... Phytylmenaquinone [*Vitamin K*] [*Also, K*] [*Biochemistry*]
PMQ.......... Prime Minister's Question [*British*] (BARN)
PMQ.......... Primitive Methodist Quarterly Review [*A publication*] (ROG)
PMR.......... Pacemaker Rhythm [*Medicine*] (MELL)
PMR.......... Pacific Missile Range [*Later, WTR*]
PMR.......... Palmer [*Alaska*] [*Seismograph station code, US Geological Survey*] (SEIS)
PMR.......... Palmerston North [*New Zealand*] [*Airport symbol*] (OAG)
PMR.......... Parabolic Microwave Reflector
PMR.......... Paramagnetic Resonance (IAA)
PMR.......... Partido Mariateguista Revolucionario [*Peru*] [*Political party*] (EY)
PMR.......... Partidul Muncitoresc Roman [*Romanian Workers' Party*] [*Political party*]
PMR.......... Parts Material Requirements File
PMR.......... Passive Microwave Radiometer (SAUS)
PMR.......... Patellar Medial Retinaculum [*Medicine*] (MELL)
PMR.......... Patient Master Record (SAUS)
PMR.......... Patient Medical Record (DB)
PMR.......... Payload Mass Ratio
Pmr........... Paymaster (AD)
PMR.......... Paymaster
PMR.......... Performance Measurement Report [*NASA*] (NASA)
PMR.......... Performance Monitoring Receiver
PMR.......... Perinatal Mortality Rate [*Medicine*]
PMR.......... Periodic Medical Review (STED)
PMR.......... Phase Modulation Recording (VLIE)
PMR.......... Physical Medicine and Rehabilitation (STED)
PMR.......... Planned Maintenance Requirements
PMR.......... Point of Minimum Radius (IAA)
PMR.......... Polise-Air [*Russian Federation*] [*ICAO designator*] (FAAC)
PMR.......... Pollutant Mass Rate [*Environmental science*] (GFGA)
PMR.......... Polyester Mold Release [*Plastics*]
PMR.......... Polymerizable Monomer Reactant (SAUS)
PMR.......... Polymerization of Monomeric Reactants (SAUS)

PMR .... Polymerization of Monomer Reactants [*Organic chemistry*]
PMR .... Polymerized Monomeric Reactant (SAUS)
PMR .... Polymorphic Reticulosis [*Ophthalmology*] (DAVI)
PMR .... Polymyalgia Rheumatica [*Medicine*]
PMR .... Portable Microfiche Reader [*DASA Corp.*]
PMR .... Portable Microwave Repeater (SAUS)
PMR .... Portable Multiparameter Radar (SAUS)
PMR .... Posteromedial Release [*Orthopedics*] (DAVI)
PMR .... Postmaster (DCTA)
PMR .... Postmaster Return (SAUS)
PMR .... Post Mortem Routine (SAUS)
PMR .... Potential Military Relationship (SAUS)
PMR .... Potential Military Relevance
PMR .... Power Master Reset (SAUS)
PMR .... Power Monitor Relay
PMR .... Precision Microwave Radiometer (SAUS)
PMR .... Preliminary Materials Review
P/M/R .... Premakeready [*Graphic arts*] (DGA)
PMR .... Prependicular Mode Recording (SAUS)
pmr .... Pressure-Modulated Radiometer (AD)
PMR .... Pressure Modulation Radiometer
PMR .... Pressure Modulator Radiometer (SAUS)
PMR .... Preventive Maintenance and Repair [*Aviation*] (MCD)
PMR .... Primary Mission Readiness
PMR .... Prime Resources Corp. [*Vancouver Stock Exchange symbol*]
PMR .... Priority Monitor Report
PMR .... Prior Medical Record (DB)
PMR .... Private Milk Records (SAUS)
PMR .... Private Mobile Radio (CGWS)
PMR .... Problem Management Report (SAUS)
PMR .... Procurement Management Review [*DoD*]
PMR .... Professional Mobile Radio [*Communications*]
PMR .... Profoundly Mentally Retarded
PMR .... Programmable Multiloop Regulator (SAUS)
PMR .... Program Management Responsibilities (SAUS)
PMR .... Program Management Responsibility (MCD)
PMR .... Program Management Review
PMR .... Program Manager's Review [*NASA*] (NASA)
PMR .... Programmed Mixture Ratio (KSC)
PMR .... Program Modification Request (SAUS)
PMR .... Progressive Muscle Relaxation (MELL)
PMR .... Projection Microradiography (IAA)
PMR .... Project Management Report
PMR .... Project Management Review
PMR .... Pro Male Release [*International Bowhunting Organization*] [*Class equipment*]
PMR .... Propellant Mass Ratio (SAA)
PMR .... Property Management Regulation (AAGC)
PMR .... Property Movement Request (MCD)
PMR .... Proportionate Morbidity Ratio [*Statistics*] (DAVI)
PMR .... Proportionate Mortality Rate [*or Ratio*]
PMR .... Proportionate Mortality Ratio (SAUS)
PMR .... Protein Magnetic Resonance [*Medicine*] (MAE)
PMR .... Proton Magnetic Resonance
PMR .... Provisioning Master Record (MCD)
PMR .... Psychomotor Retardation (STED)
PMR .... Public Mobile Radio (WDMC)
PMR .... Pulsational Magnetic Radiation [*Astronomy*]
PMR .... Purchased Material Return (TIMI)
PMRA .... Percent of Males Reproductively Active [*Ecology*]
PMRA .... Pest Management Regulatory Agency (FOTI)
PMRA .... Projected Manpower Requirements Account [*Navy*]
PMRAFNS... Princess Mary's Royal Air Force Nursing Service [*British*]
PMRB .... Preliminary Materials Review Board
PMRC .... Pakistan Medical Research Council
PMRC .... Parents' Music Resource Center (EA)
PMRC .... Pest Management Research Centre (FOTI)
PMRC .... Powder Metallurgy Research Center [*Worcester Polytechnic Institute*] (RCD)
PMRC .... Prepositioned Material Receipt Card [*DoD*]
PMRC .... Proctor Maple Research Center [*University of Vermont*] [*Research center*] (RCD)
PMR Cp ..... PMR Corp. [*Associated Press*] (SAG)
PMRD .... Prepositioned Material Receipt Documents (MCD)
PMRDET .... Pacific Missile Range Detachment [*Obsolete*] (MUGU)
PM Reactor... Portable Medium-power Reactor (SAUS)
PMRF .... Pacific Missile Range Facility [*Military*] (MUSM)
PMRFAC .... Pacific Missile Range Facility [*Obsolete*] (MUGU)
PMRG .... Preliminary Materials Review Group [*NASA*] (KSC)
PMRH .... Panda Marine River Horizontal (SAUS)
PMRI .... Porous Media Research Institute [*University of Waterloo*] [*Research center*] (RCD)
PMRI .... Posteromedial Rotation Instability [*Sports medicine*]
PMRI .... Prairie Masonry Research Institute (SAUS)
Pmr in C .... Paymaster-in-Chief (SAUS)
PMRL .... Physical Metallurgy Research Laboratories (SAUS)
PMRL .... Pulp Manufacturers' Research League
PMRM .... Periodic Maintenance Requirements Manual [*Navy*]
PMRMO ..... Protectable Mobilization Reserve Materiel Objective [*Army*] (AABC)
PMRMR ..... Protectable Mobilization Reserve Materiel Requirements [*Army*]
PMRN .... Parents' Music Resource Network (EA)
PMR/NMC... Pacific Missile Range / Naval Missile Center (SAA)
PMRO .... Popular Magazine Review Online [*EBSCO Subscription Services*] [*Information service or system*]
PMRP .... Petroleum Material Requirements Plan (MCD)
PMRP .... PMR Corp. [*NASDAQ symbol*] (SAG)
PMRP .... Precious Metals Recovery Program [*DoD*] (AFIT)
PMRP .... Program Manager's Recommended Program
PM-RPV..... Project Manager, Remotely Piloted Vehicle [*Military*]
PMRPV...... Project Manager, Remotely Piloted Vehicles [*Department of Defense*]
PMRR .... Pacific Missile Range Representative [*Obsolete*] (MUGU)
PMRR .... Pre-Mate Readiness Review [*NASA*] (KSC)
PMRR .... Prepositioned Materiel Receipt Record (ACAE)
PMRS .... Parachute Medical Rescue Service (EA)
PMRS .... Performance Management and Recognition System
PMRS .... Performance Management Reporting System (SAUS)
PMRS .... Performance Monitoring and Reporting System (SAUS)
P-MRS ...... Phosphorus Magnetic Resonance Spectroscopy [*Medicine*] (RAWO)
PMRS .... Physical Medicine and Rehabilitation Service
PMRS .... Plasma-Melted Rapidly Solidified (SAUS)
PMRS .... Private Mobile Radio Service (CGWS)
PMRS .... Production Management and Reporting System
PMRS .... Professional Marketing Research Society [*Canada*] (EAIO)
PMRS .... Project Management Reporting System (SAUS)
PMRSG...... Pacific Missile Range Study Group [*Obsolete*]
PMRT........ Peabody Mathematics Readiness Test [*Educational test*]
PMRT........ Program Management Responsibility Transfer (MCD)
PMRT........ Progressive Muscle Relaxation Training [*Psychology*]
PMRTD...... Program Management Responsibility Date (SAUS)
PMRTD...... Program Management Responsibility Transfer Date (AFIT)
PMRTD...... Project Management Responsibility Date (SAUS)
PMRTF ...... Pacific Missile Range Tracking Facility [*Obsolete*] (MUGU)
PMRTP ...... Program Management Responsibility Transfer Plan (AFIT)
PMRV-N..... Panda Marine River Vertical (SAUS)
PMRX .... Pharmaceutical Marketing Services [*NASDAQ symbol*] (SPSG)
PMRX .... Pharmaceutical Mktg Svcs [*NASDAQ symbol*] (TTSB)
PMRY........ Pomeroy Computer Resources [*NASDAQ symbol*] (TTSB)
PMRY........ Pomeroy Computer Resources, Inc. [*NASDAQ symbol*] (SAG)
PMRY........ Pomeroy IT Solutions [*NASDAQ symbol*]
PMRY........ Presidio of Monterey [*Military*] (AABC)
PMS .... Chorionic Gonadotropin in Pregnant Mare's Serum [*Veterinary medicine*] (DAVI)
PMS .... Packet Memory System (SAUS)
PMS .... Palmer - Arctic Valley [*Alaska*] [*Seismograph station code, US Geological Survey*] (SEIS)
PMS .... Panda Marine Standard (SAUS)
PMS .... Pantone Matching System [*Printing*]
PMS .... Paper Manifesting System
PMS .... Parallel Mass Spectrometer
PMS .... Para-Methylstyrene [*Organic chemistry*]
PMS .... Parcel Manifesting System (GART)
PMS .... Partial Metric System (MCD)
PMS .... Particle Measurement System
PMS .... Particle Measuring Systems [*Aerosol measurement device*]
PMS .... Partido Mexicano Socialista [*Political party*] (EY)
PMS .... Passive Maternal Smoking (MELL)
PMS .... Pavement Management System [*Australia*]
PMS .... Payments Management System [*Emergency Management*] (EMA)
PMS .... Peabody Museum of Salem (AD)
PMS .... Pedestal Mounted Stinger (SAUS)
PMS .... Pedestal-Mounted Stinger [*Army*]
PMS .... Pennsylvania Medical Society (EARSL)
PMS .... People's Medical Society (EA)
PMS .... People's Message System [*For Apple II computers*] [*Electronic bulletin board*]
PMS .... Performance Management Software (IAA)
PMS .... Performance Management System (HLLA)
PMS .... Performance Measurement System [*Nuclear Regulatory Commission*] (MCD)
PMS .... Performance Monitoring System [*Fort Belvoir, VA*] [*Army*] (NASA)
PMS .... Periodical Management System [*Library science*] (TELE)
PMS .... Peripheral Monitor System (SAUS)
PMS .... Permanent Magnet Speaker
PMS .... Permanent Manual System (AD)
PMS .... Permitted Maximum Signal (SAUS)
PMS .... Personal Mailing System (HGAA)
PMS .... Personnel Management Series [*Civil Service Commission*]
PMS .... Personnel Management Services
PMS .... Personnel Management Specialist (GFGA)
PMS .... Personnel Management Squadron (SAUS)
PMS .... Personnel Management System [*Air Force*] (AFM)
PMS .... Phenazine Methosulfate [*Biochemistry*]
pms.......... Phenazine Methosulphate (AD)
PMS .... Phoenix Missile System
PMS .... Physical and Mathematical Sciences (SAUS)
PMS .... Physician Practice Management System (GART)
PMS .... Physiological Monitoring System (SAA)
PMS .... Phytophthora Megasperma Var. Sojae [*A fungus*]
PMS .... Piccola Missione per il Sordomuti [*Little Mission for the Deaf-Mute - LMDM*] [*Rome, Italy*] (EAIO)
PMS .... Picturephone Meeting Service [*AT & T*]
PMS .... Pipeline Management System (SAUS)
PMS .... Pitch Microwave System
PMS .... Planemasters Services, Inc. [*ICAO designator*] (FAAC)
PMS .... Planned Maintenance Subsystem
PMS .... Planned Maintenance Support (SAUS)
PMS .... Planned Maintenance System [*SNMMS*]

PMS .... Planned Missile System
PMS .... Planning and Management Staff (SAUS)
PMS .... Plant Monitoring System [*Nuclear energy*] (NRCH)
PMS .... Plasmid Maintenance Sequence [*Genetics*]
PMS .... Plastic Media Stripping (SAUS)
PMS .... Plastic to Metal Seal
PMS .... Platform Management System (SAUS)
PMS .... P-Methylstyrene [*Plastics*]
PMS .... PM Industries, Inc. [*Vancouver Stock Exchange symbol*]
PMS .... Polaris Missile System
PMS .... Polar Meteorological Satellite (SSD)
PMS .... Policy Management System (SAUS)
PMS .... Policy Management Systems [*NYSE symbol*] (SPSG)
PMS .... Policy Mgmt Systems [*NYSE symbol*] (TTSB)
PMS .... Pollution Monitoring Satellite
pms......... Pollution-Monitoring Satellite (AD)
PMS .... Polymethylsorbate (SAUS)
PMS .... Polymethylstyrene [*Organic chemistry*]
pms......... Poor Miserable Soul (AD)
PMS .... Poor Miserable Soul [*Medical slang*]
PMS .... Popular Music and Society [*A publication*] (BRI)
PMS .... Portable Monitoring Set (MCD)
PMS .... Post-Marketing Surveillance
PMS .... Postmeiotic Segregation [*Genetics*]
pms......... Post-Menopausal Syndrome [*Medicine*] (AD)
PMS .... Postmenopausal Syndrome [*Medicine*]
PMS .... Post-Menstrual Syndrome (SAUS)
PMS .... Post-Merger Syndrome [*Business term*]
PMS .... Postmitochondrial Supernatant [*Medicine*] (MAE)
PMS .... Post-Modern Slut (SAUS)
PMS .... Post-Mortem Survival [*Parapsychology*]
PMS .... Power Management System
PMS .... Power-Management System (SAUS)
PMS .... Prang-Mark Society (EA)
PMS .... Predicted Manning System [*Military*]
pms......... Pregnant Mare's Serum (AD)
PMS .... Pregnant Mare's Serum [*Endocrinology*]
PMS .... Pre-Main-Sequence (SAUS)
PMS .... Premature Start [*Yacht racing*] (IYR)
pms......... Pre-Menstrual Syndrome [*Medicine*] (AD)
PMS .... Premenstrual [*Stress*] Syndrome [*Medicine*]
PMS .... Pre-Midshipmen School
PMS .... Pre-Millennial Syndrome (SAUS)
PMS .... President of the Meteorological Society [*British*]
PMS .... President of the Miniature Society [*British*] (DI)
PmS .... Preston Microfilming Services Ltd., Toronto, ON, Canada [*Library symbol*] [*Library of Congress*] (LCLS)
PMS .... Preventive Maintenance Services
PMS .... Preventive Maintenance System
PMS .... Printer Management Software (SAUS)
PMS .... Probability of Mission Success [*Aerospace*] (AAG)
PMS .... Probable Maximum Surge [*Nuclear energy*] (NRCH)
PMS .... Process Measurement Systems Ltd. (NITA)
PMS .... Processor, Memories and Switches (SAUS)
PMS .... Processor Memory Switch [*Computer science*] (ECII)
PMS .... Processors, Memories, and Switches [*Programming language*] (CSR)
p-m-s........ Processors-Memories-Switches (AD)
PMS .... Production Management Support (SAUS)
PMS .... Production Management System [*Safe Computing Ltd.*] [*Software package*] (NCC)
PMS .... Product Management System
PMS .... Product Monitoring System (SAUS)
PMS .... Professor of Military Science
PMS .... Program Management Staff (COE)
PMS .... Program Management Support [*Army*]
PMS .... Program Management System [*Computer science*]
PMS .... Program Master Schedule (MCD)
PMS .... Programmed Mode Switch (IAA)
PMS .... Projected Map System (OA)
PMS .... Project Management System [*IBM Corp.*] [*Computer science*]
PMS .... Project Manager, Ships
PMS .... Project Manager Statements [*USDA Forest Service*] (ALAC)
PMS .... Project Manager System
PMS .... Project Map System (SAUS)
PMS .... Project Master Schedule
PMS .... Property Management System (TRID)
PMS .... Proposal Management System
PMS .... Propulsion Module Subsystem (ACAE)
PMS .... Prothazin Methosulfate (SAUS)
PMS .... Public Management Sources [*A publication*]
PMS .... Public Message Service [*Western Union Corp.*]
PMS .... Public Message System (SAUS)
PMS .... Public Meteorological Service [*Emergency Management*] (EMA)
PMS .... Publisher Management System (NITA)
PMS .... Pureed, Mechanical, Soft [*Diet*] (DAVI)
PMS .... Region 4 Position Management System (SAUS)
PMSA........ Office of the Project Manager Selected Ammunition [*DoD*]
PMSA........ Pacific Merchant Shipping Association (AD)
PMSA........ Paddy's Market Stallholders' Association [*Australia*]
PMSA........ PM [*Product Management*] Materiel Systems Assessment (RDA)
PMSA........ Posterior Middle Suprasylvian Area [*Anatomy*]
PMSA........ Primary Metropolitan Statistical Area [*Census Bureau*]
PMSA........ Professional Master of Science in Accounting (PGP)
P/MSA....... Project/Major Subcontractor Affected (MCD)
PMSA........ Project Management System Assessment
PMSA........ Project Manager for Selected Ammunition
PMSA........ Project Manager's System Assessment
PMS & T.... Professor of Military Science and Tactics
PMSAT ...... Pre-Medical Student Assessment Test (EDAC)
PMSC........ Pediatric Medical Special Care (DMAA)
PMSC........ Pluripotent Myeloid Stem Cell [*Cytology*] (MAE)
PMSC........ Policy Management Systems Corp. [*NASDAQ symbol*] (COMM)
PMSC........ Prime Minister's Science Council [*Australia*]
PMSD .... Parti Mauricien Social-Democrate [*Mauritian Social Democratic Party*] [*Political party*] (PPW)
PMSD .... Program Management and Support Division [*Environmental Protection Agency*] (GFGA)
PMS/DOD... Performance Measurement System/Department of Defense
PM-SDR..... Project Manager-Soldier (SAUS)
PMSE........ Percentage Mean Squared Error [*Statistics*]
PMSE........ Permanent Memory with Semi-Elastic Range (MCD)
PMSE........ Polar Mesopause Summer Echo (SAUS)
PMSE........ Polar Mesosphere Summer Echo (SAUS)
PMSE........ Program Management Simulation Exercise [*Aerospace*]
PMSEIC ..... Prime Minister's Science, Engineering and Innovation Council [*Australia*]
PMSF........ Phenylmethanesulfonyl Fluoride (SAUS)
PMSF........ Phenylmethylsulfonyl Fluoride [*Analytical chemistry*]
PMSF........ Phenylmethylsulfonylfluoride (SAUS)
PMSFN...... Planetary Manned Space Flight Network [*Aerospace*] (MCD)
PMSG........ Peace Movement Study Group [*Colgate University*] (EA)
pmsg .... Pregnant Mare's Serum Gonadotrophin (AD)
PMSG .... Pregnant Mare's Serum Gonadotrophin [*Endocrinology*]
PMSGT...... Paymaster Sergeant [*Marine Corps*]
PMSH .... Pasha Moving and Storage Company [*Common carrier symbol*]
PM/SH....... Preventive Maintenance and Self-Help [*Program*]
PMS-HD..... Panda Marine Standard Heavy Duty (SAUS)
PMSI .... Permissible [*Telegraphy*] (PCTE)
PMSI .... Prime Medical Services [*NASDAQ symbol*] (TTSB)
PMSI .... Prime Medical Services, Inc. [*NASDAQ symbol*] (NQ)
PMSI .... Prime Medics [*NASDAQ symbol*] (SAG)
PMSL........ Powanda-Monroeton Shippers Lifeline [*Federal Railroad Administration identification code*]
PMSM....... Product Marketing Strategy Model (SAUS)
PMSN .... Permission (FAAC)
PMSO .... Port Mine Sweeping Officer (SAUS)
PMSO .... Position Management System Operations [*USDA Forest Service*] (ALAC)
PMSO .... Program Management and Support Office (SAUS)
PMSO .... Project Management Staff Officer [*Military*] (AFIT)
PMSO .... Project Management Support Office [*Army*] (RDA)
PMSP........ Parallel Modular Signal Processor
PMSP........ Photon-Counting Microspectrophotometer
PMSP........ Plant Modelling System Program (PDAA)
PMSP........ Preliminary Maintainability and Spare Parts
PMSP........ Preliminary Message Security Protocol (SAUS)
pm specialists... Paramilitary Specialists (AD)
PMSPS....... Project Management Staffing Practices Study [*Navy*] (NG)
PMSQ .... Pacific Messenger Service [*Common carrier symbol*]
PMSR .... Patternmaker, Ship Repair [*Navy rating*]
PMSR .... Physical, Mental, Social, Religious ["*Fourfold Life*" *symbol of American Youth Foundation*]
PMSRC...... Pittsburgh Mining and Safety Research Center [*Bureau of Mines*]
PMSRP...... Physical and Mathematical Sciences Research Paper (IEEE)
PMSS........ Personnel Mobility Support System [*Military*]
PMSS........ Policy and Management Support Staff (COE)
PMSS........ Precision Measuring Subsystem (KSC)
PMSS........ Preventive Maintenance Scheduling System (CIST)
PMSS........ Program Management Support Staff [*Environmental Protection Agency*] (GFGA)
PMSS........ Program Management Support System (SAUS)
PMSS........ Program Manager's Support System [*Defense Systems Management College*] [*Fort Belvoir, VA*] (RDA)
PMSSMS.... Planned Maintenance System for Surface Missile Ships (AD)
PMST........ Professor of Military Science and Tactics (MUGU)
PMSU .... Penn-Maryland Steamship [*Intermodal shipping container symbol*] (TVRC)
PMSU .... Peripheral Motor-Sensory Unit (MELL)
PMSV........ Pharmacy Management Services (EFIS)
PMSV........ Pilot-to-Metro Service
PMSV........ Pilot to Metro Services (SAUS)
PMSW....... Polymer Microstructure Waveguide (SAUS)
PMSX........ Processor Memory Switch Matrix
PMT .... Medical Photography Technician [*Navy*]
PMT .... Page Map Table [*NASA*] (HGAA)
PMT .... Para-Methoxytoluene [*Organic chemistry*]
PMT .... Partido Mexicano de los Trabajadores [*Mexican Workers' Party*] [*Political party*] (PPW)
PMT .... Passenger-Miles Traveled [*DOE*] (TAG)
PMT .... Patrol Message Terminal [*Police and security equipment*]
pmt .... Payment (AD)
PMT .... Payment (AFM)
PMT .... Pennsylvania Motor Truck Association, Inc., Harrisburg PA [*STAC*]
PMT .... Perceptual Maze Test [*Psychology*]
PMT .... Perceptual Memory Task (TES)
PMT .... Performance Measuring Tool (MCD)
PMT .... Periodic Maintenance Team
PMT .... Permanent Magnet Tester [*Memory*] [*Bell Laboratories*] (IAA)
PMT .... Permanent Magnet Twistor [*Memory*] [*Bell Laboratories*]

PMT .... Per Metric Ton (SAUS)
PMT .... Permit (FAAC)
PMT .... Person-Miles of Travel [*FHWA*] (TAG)
PMT .... Personnel Management Team
PMT .... Phase Modulated Transmission (SAUS)
PMT .... Phase-Modulated Transmission
PMT .... Philip Michael Thomas [*Co-star in TV series "Miami Vice"*]
PMT .... Photomechanical Transfer [*Negative paper*] [*Eastman Kodak*]
PMT .... Photomultiplier Transit (SAUS)
PMT .... Photomultiplier Tube [*Electronics*]
pmt .... Photomultiplier Tubes (AD)
PMT .... Physical Master Tape (IAA)
PMT .... Physical Message Type [*Communications*]
PMT .... Pine Mountain [*Oregon*] [*Seismograph station code, US Geological Survey*] (SEIS)
PMT .... Planning/Management Team [*NASA*] (MCD)
PMT .... PMC Technologies Ltd. [*Vancouver Stock Exchange symbol*]
PMT .... P-Methoxytoluene (SAUS)
PMT .... Polaromicrotribrometry [*Analytical chemistry*]
PMT .... Pore Microtubule (SAUS)
PMT .... Portable Magnetic Tape
PMT .... Porteus Maze Test [*Medicine*] (MAE)
PMT .... Portsmouth Marine Terminal
pmt .... Positive Matte Technique (AD)
PMT .... Post-Maastricht Tension [*European community*] (ECON)
PMT .... Post-Market Trading
PMT .... Potteries Motor Traction Co. [*British*]
PMT .... Power Microwave Tube
PMT .... Prazisions-Mebtechnik (EFIS)
PMT .... Precious Metal Tip (IAA)
PMT .... Pre-Determined Motion-Time [*Management*] (PDAA)
PMT .... Predetermined Motion Time (SAUS)
pmt .... Premenstrual Tension [*Medicine*] (AD)
PMT .... Premenstrual Tension [*Medicine*]
PMT .... Premillennial Tension
PMT .... Preparatory Marksmanship Training [*Military*] (INF)
PMT .... Prepare Master Tape
PMT .... Preventive Maintenance Time (MCD)
PMT .... Printed Mechanical Transfer (VLIE)
PMT .... Production Monitoring Test (NG)
PMT .... Products, Marketing, and Technology [*Bank Administration Institute*] [*A publication*]
PMT .... Program Management Team (SAUS)
PMT .... Program Master Tape
PMT .... Programmed Math Tutorial [*National Science Foundation*]
pmt .... Programs, Materials, Techniques (AD)
PMT .... Project Management Team (ODBW)
PMT .... Pulse Modulator Tube (SAUS)
PMT .... Pulse-Modulator Tube
PMT .... Pure Milk Tablet (IIA)
PMT .... Putnam Master Income Tr [*NYSE symbol*] (TTSB)
PMT .... Putnam Master Income Trust [*NYSE symbol*] (SPSG)
PMTA .... Page Map Table Address Register [*NASA*] (HGAA)
PMTA .... Pennsylvania Motor Truck Association (EARSL)
PMTA .... Phosphomolybdic and Phosphotungstic Acid Mixture (SAUS)
PMTA .... Phosphomolybdic-Phosphotungstic Acid Mixture (EDCT)
PMTAS ...... Pre-Menstrual Tension Advisory Service [*British*]
PMTB .... Pacific Motor Tariff Bureau (AD)
PMTC .... Pacific Missile Test Center [*Point Mugu, CA*] [*Navy*]
PMTC .... Parametric Technical [*NASDAQ symbol*] (TTSB)
PMTC .... Parametric Technology Corp. [*NASDAQ symbol*] (NQ)
PMTC .... Pittsburgh Mining Technology Center [*Department of Energy*] (GRD)
PMTC .... Point Mugu Test Center (SAUS)
PMTC .... Private Motor Truck Council (SAUS)
PMTCC ...... Private Motor Truck Council of Canada (SAUS)
PMT Contact... Precious Metal Tip Contact (SAUS)
PMTD .... Permitted [*Telegraphy*] (PCTE)
PMTD .... Post Mortem Tape Dump [*Computer science*]
PMTD .... Promoted (SAUS)
PMTE .... Page Map Table Entry [*NASA*] (IAA)
P/M Technol Newsl... P/M Technology Newsletter (SAUS)
PMT-EM ..... Project Manager, Training Devices Engineering Management [*Orlando, FL*] [*Army*]
PMTF .... Product Management Task Force (AAEL)
PMTG .... Permitting [*Telegraphy*] (PCTE)
PMTHP ...... Project Mercury Technical History Program [*NASA*]
PMTI .... Palomar Medical Technologies [*NASDAQ symbol*] (SAG)
PMTI .... Palomar Med Tech [*NASDAQ symbol*] (TTSB)
PMTL .... William Pimental [*Common carrier symbol*]
PM/TMDE... Project Manager for Test, Measurement and Diagnostic Equipment (SAUS)
PM TMDS... Program Manager - Test, Measurement, and Diagnostic Systems [*Army*]
PMTO .... Post Mortem Test Object
PMTO .... Project Manager Test Offices [*Military*]
PMTP .... Production Missile Test Program
PMTP .... Program Management Transfer Point (SAUS)
PMTPD ...... Program Management Transfer Point Date (SAUS)
PMTPM ..... Program Management Transfer Point Milestone (SAUS)
PMTPP ..... Program Management Transfer Point Plan (SAUS)
PMTR .... PEMSTAR [*NASDAQ symbol*]
P/MTR .... Potentiometer [*Automotive engineering*]
PM TRADE... Office of the Project Manager for Training Devices [*Military*] (RDA)
PM-TRADE... Program Manager for Training Devices (SAUS)
PM TRADE... Project Manager, Training Devices
PMTR System... Partially Mechanized Traffic Recording System (SAUS)
PMTS .... Passive Multi-Target Tracking System (SEWL)
PMTS .... PMT Services [*NASDAQ symbol*] (SAG)
PMTS .... Precision Missile Tracking System [*Military*] (IAA)
PMTS .... Predetermined Motion Time Standards [*Management*] (IAA)
PMTS .... Predetermined Motion Time System (SAUS)
PMTS .... Predetermined Motion Time Systems [*Management*]
PMTS .... Premenstrual Tension Syndrome [*Medicine*]
PMTS Chart... Predetermined Motion Time System Chart (SAUS)
PMTS Codes... Predetermined Motion Time System Codes (SAUS)
PMT Svc .... PMT Services [*Associated Press*] (SAG)
PMTT .... Phase-Modulated Telemetry Transmission
PMTT .... Pulmonary Mean Transit Time [*Medicine*] (MAE)
PMTV .... Potato Mop-Top Virus [*Plant pathology*]
PMTZ .... Southern Pacific Transportation [*Intermodal trailer symbol*]
PMU .... Paimiut, AK [*Location identifier*] [*FAA*] (FAAL)
PMU .... Paradise Music and Entertainment [*Boston Stock Exchange symbol*]
PMU .... Parametric Measurement Unit (VLIE)
PMU .... Pattern Makers Union (AD)
PMU .... PCM Master Unit (SAUS)
pmu .... Performance Monitor Unit (AD)
PMU .... Performance Monitor Unit [*Communications*]
PMU .... Permanently Medically Unfit
PMU .... Personal Messaging Unit (CGWS)
PMU .... Phaser Measurement Unit [*Electrical power distribution*]
PMU .... Physical Mock-Up
pmu .... Physical Mockup (AD)
PMU .... Pierce Mountain [*Vancouver Stock Exchange symbol*]
PMU .... Plant Makeup [*Nuclear energy*] (NRCH)
PMU .... Pontifical Missionary Union [*Later, PMUPR*] [*See also OPM*] (EA)
PMU .... Population Management Unit (WDAA)
PMU .... Portable Memory Unit [*Computer science*]
PMU .... Power Management Unit [*Computer science*] (CIST)
PMU .... Power Meter Unit (SAUS)
PMU .... Precision Measurement Unit (SAUS)
PMU .... Precision Mockup (ACAE)
PMU .... Pregnant Mare's Urine [*Veterinary medicine*] (BARN)
PMU .... Pressure Measuring Unit (KSC)
PMU .... Preventive Medicine Unit [*Navy*] (NVT)
pmu .... Productive Man Work Unit (AD)
PMU .... Program Management Unit [*Computer science*] (IAA)
PMU .... Pulse Modulation Unit (NASA)
PMUB .... Presbyterian, Methodist, and United Board [*British military*] (DMA)
PMUPR ...... Pontifical Missionary Union of Priests and Religious (EA)
PMUS .... Permanently Mounted User Set [*Computer science*] (ADA)
PMUSAOAS... Permanent Mission of the United States of America to the Organization of American States (AD)
PM-UTTAS... Project Manager, Utility Tactical Transport Aircraft System [*Military*]
PMUX .... Programmable Multiplex [*Computer science*] (TEL)
PMUX .... Propulsion Multiplexer
PMv .... Monroeville Public Library, Monroeville, PA [*Library symbol*] [*Library of Congress*] (LCLS)
PMV .... Panicum Mosaic Virus
PMV .... Papaya Mosaic Virus
PMV .... Paramyxovirus
PMV .... Parcel Mail Vans [*British railroad term*]
PMV .... Passenger Motor Vehicle
PMV .... Peach Mosaic Virus (SAUS)
PMV .... Peanut Mottle Virus
PMV .... Pedal Modulating Valve [*Hydraulics*]
PMV .... Percutaneous Mitral (Balloon) Valvotomy [*Medicine*] (EDAA)
PMV .... Plasma Membrane Vesicle [*Cytology*]
PMV .... Plate-Motion Vector [*Geology*]
PMV .... Plattsmouth, NE [*Location identifier*] [*FAA*] (FAAL)
PMV .... Politically Motivated Violence (ADA)
PMV .... Porlamar [*Venezuela*] [*Airport symbol*] (OAG)
PMV .... Prime Mission Vehicle (MCD)
PMV .... Private Market Value [*Investment term*] (DFIT)
PMV .... Private Motor Vehicle (DNAB)
PMV .... Prolapsing Mitral Valve [*Cardiology*]
PMV .... Pro Mundi Vita [*Brussels, Belgium*] [*Defunct*] (EAIO)
PMvAC ...... Community College of Allegheny County, Boyce Campus, Monroeville, PA [*Library symbol*] [*Library of Congress*] (LCLS)
PMVB .... Pocono Mountain Vacation Bureau (AD)
PMVE .... Primary Mirror Vortex Fixture (SAUS)
pmvi .... Periodic Motor Vehicle Inspection (AD)
PMVI .... Periodic Motor Vehicle Inspection (PDAA)
PMvK .... Koppers Co., Inc., Research Department, Monroeville, PA [*Library symbol*] [*Library of Congress*] (LCLS)
PMVL .... Posterior Mitral Valve Leaflet [*Anatomy*] (AAMN)
PMV-LATA... Passenger Motor Vehicle Labour Adjustment Training Arrangements [*Australia*]
PMVMP ..... Passenger Motor Vehicle Manufacturing Plan [*Australia*]
pmvp .... Precio Maximo de Venta al Publico [*Maximum Price Charged the Public*] [*Spanish*] (AD)
p mvr .... Prime Mover (AD)
PMVR .... Prime Mover [*Technical drawings*]
PMvS .... United States Steel Corp., Research Center Library, Monroeville, PA [*Library symbol*] [*Library of Congress*] (LCLS)
PMW .... Pacemaker Wire [*Cardiology*] (DAVI)
PMW .... Parts Manufacturing Workmanship
PMW .... Passive Microwave (SAUS)

PMW .... Pole Mountain [*Wyoming*] [*Seismograph station code, US Geological Survey*] [*Closed*] (SEIS)
PMW .... Position Mode Wavelength (ADWA)
PMW .... Post-Menopausal Women (MELL)
PMW .... Premenopausal Women (MELL)
PMW .... Preventive Maintenance Welding (PDAA)
PMW .... Private Microwave [*System*]
PMW .... Probable Maximum Wind (GOBB)
PMW .... Progressive Mine Workers of America
PMW .... Project Magic Wand [*Military*] (MCD)
PMW .... Project Management Work-Bench (NITA)
PMW .... Project Manager Workbench (SAUS)
PMW .... Prompt Mobilization Designation Withdrawn
PMW .... Pulse-Modulated Wave [*Telecommunications*] (IAA)
PMWCMA... Paper Mill Wire Cloth Manufacturers' Association (DGA)
PMWG........ Program Management Working Group (SAUS)
PMWI........ PageMart Wireless 'A' [*NASDAQ symbol*] (SG)
PMWIN...... Processing MODFLOW for Windows
PMWP....... Probable Maximum Winter Precipitation [*Nuclear energy*] (NRCH)
PMWS....... Pedestal-Mounted Weapons System (SAUS)
PMWS....... Program Management Work Station (TIMI)
PMW System... Private Microwave System (SAUS)
PMX .... Packet Multiplexer
PMX .... Palmer, MA [*Location identifier*] [*FAA*] (FAAL)
PMX .... Pamorex Minerals, Inc. [*Toronto Stock Exchange symbol*]
PMX .... Partially Matched Crossover (VLIE)
PMX .... Petroleos Mexicanos [*Mexico*] [*ICAO designator*] (FAAC)
PMX .... Physical Modeling Extension (SAUS)
PMX .... Physical Modelling Extension (NITA)
pmx.......... Private Manual Exchange (AD)
PMX .... Private Manual Exchange
PMX .... Protected Message Exchange
PMY .... Productive Man Year (SAUS)
PMY .... Professional Man-Year (GOBB)
PMY .... Prominently [*Telegraphy*] (PCTE)
PMyE .... Evangelical Congregational School of Theology, Myerstown, PA [*Library symbol*] [*Library of Congress*] (LCLS)
pmyob........ Please Mind Your Own Business (AD)
PMYOB...... Please Mind Your Own Business
PMZ .... Palmar [*Costa Rica*] [*Airport symbol*] (AD)
PMZ .... Plymouth, NC [*Location identifier*] [*FAA*] (FAAL)
PMZ .... Prenter Mine [*Federal Railroad Administration identification code*]
PMZF .... Programmable Multi-Zone Furnace (SAUS)
PN .... Coastal Airways [*ICAO designator*] (AD)
PN .... Nacionalista [*Nationalist Party*] [*Spain*] [*Political party*] (AD)
PN .... National Project (Nicaragua) [*Political party*] (PSAP)
Pn............ North Celestial Pole (AD)
pn--- .... North Pacific [*MARC geographic area code*] [*Library of Congress*] (LCCP)
PN .... North Pole [*Also, NP*]
PN .... Pacific Communications Net [*Air Force*]
PN .... Pacific Northern [*Airline*] (AD)
PN .... Packet Network (SAUS)
PN .... Packet Number (SAUS)
PN .... Page Number (SAUS)
PN .... Paging Network (SAUS)
PN .... Pain (SAUS)
PN .... Pakistan Navy
PN .... Palus Nebularum [*Lunar area*]
pn............ Panama [*MARC country of publication code*] [*Library of Congress*] (LCCP)
PN .... Pan American World Airways (SAUS)
PN .... Pan-American World Airways [*Stock exchange symbol*] (AD)
PN .... Pancreatic [*Medicine*] (EDAA)
PN .... Papillary Necrosis [*Medicine*] (EDAA)
PN .... Papillary or Nodular Hyperplasia [*Medicine*]
PN .... Paranode (SAUS)
PN .... Parenteral Nutrition [*Medicine*]
PN .... Parish Nurse (NUJO)
PN .... Partenavia Construzioni Aeronautiche SpA [*Italy*] [*ICAO aircraft manufacturer identifier*] (ICAO)
PN .... Particulate Nitrogen [*Chemistry*]
PN .... Partido Nacional [*National Party*] [*Uruguay*] [*Political party*] (PPW)
PN .... Partido Nacional [*National Party*] [*Honduras*] [*Political party*] (PPW)
PN .... Partido Nacional [*National Party*] [*Dominican Republic*] [*Political party*]
PN .... Partido Nacional [*National Party*] [*Spain*] [*Political party*] (AD)
PN .... Parti Nationaliste [*Canada*]
pn............ Partition (AD)
Pn............ Partition (WGA)
PN .... Partition Number (SAUS)
PN .... Partit Nazzjonalista [*Nationalist Party*] [*Malta*] [*Political party*] (EAIO)
pn............ Part Number (AD)
PN .... Part Number
P/N........... Part Number
PN .... Party Notified (IAA)
PN .... Passive Network (SAUS)
PN .... Past Number (SAUS)
PN .... Patent Number (NITA)
PN .... Path Number (SAUS)
PN .... P-Doped N-Doped (SAUS)
PN .... Pennaco Energy [*AMEX symbol*]
PN .... Perceived Noise
pn............ Percussion Note (AD)
PN .... Percussion Note [*Physiology*]
PN .... Percussive Note (SAUS)
PN .... Percutaneous Nephrostogram [*Medicine*] (EDAA)
PN .... Perforation Number (SAUS)
PN .... Performance Number
PN .... Periarteritis [*or Polyarteritis*] Nodosa [*Also, PAN*] [*Medicine*]
Pn............ Perigean Range (AD)
PN .... Perigean Range
PN .... Peripheral Nerve [*Anatomy*]
PN .... Peripheral Neuropathy [*Medicine*]
PN .... Peroxide Number [*Hydrocarbon fuel specifications*]
PN .... Personal Name (NITA)
PN .... Personal Names from Cuneiform Inscriptions of the Cassite Period [*A publication*] (BJA)
PN .... Personnelman [*Navy rating*]
PN .... Personnel Navigant
PN .... Petri Net (VLIE)
PN .... Phase Name (NITA)
PN .... Phenolic Nylon
PN .... Philippine Navy
PN .... Phon [*Unit of loudness level*] (IAA)
P/N........... Phonogram [*British military*] (DMA)
PN .... Photonegative (SAUS)
PN .... Photonic Network (SAUS)
PN .... Photonuclear (SAUS)
Pn............ Photosynthesis (SAUS)
pN............ Piconewton [*Unit of force*]
PN .... Piedmont & Northern Railway Co. [*AAR code*]
PN .... Pilot Navigator (IAA)
P/N........... Pilots Name (SAUS)
pn............ Pine (VRA)
P/N........... Pin Number (AAG)
PN .... Pitcairn Islands [*ANSI two-letter standard code*] (CNC)
PN .... Place-Name
PN .... Place of Publication Class Number (NITA)
PN .... Plain
PN .... Planetary Nebula (SAUS)
PN .... Planetary Nebulae [*Astrophysics*]
PN .... Planners Network (EA)
PN .... Plant Normal [*Nuclear energy*] (NRCH)
PN .... Plaque Neutralization [*Dentistry*] (DMAA)
PN .... Plasticity Number (AAG)
pn............ Please Note (AD)
P/N........... Please Note [*Copyediting*] (WDMC)
PN .... Pneumatic
PN .... Pneumonia [*Medicine*]
PN .... Point of No Return (AD)
PN .... Pole, North (SAUS)
PN .... Polish Notation [*Mathematics*]
PN .... Polnische Notation (SAUS)
PN .... Polyarteritis Nodosa [*Rheumatology*] (DAVI)
PN .... Polymorphonuclear [*Medicine*] (EDAA)
PN .... Polyneuritis (DB)
PN .... Pontine Nuclei [*Neuroanatomy*]
P/N........... Porter/Novelli [*A public relations firm*] [*New York, NY*] (WDMC)
pn............ Position (AD)
PN .... Position (WGA)
PN .... Positional Nystagmus [*Physiology*] (MAE)
PN .... Position Number (ADA)
PN .... Position Pennant [*Navy*] [*British*]
PN .... Positive Negative
P/N........... Positive/Negative
PN .... Positive Notification (VLIE)
PN .... Postal Note (ADA)
PN .... Postnasal [*Otorhinolaryngology*] (DAVI)
PN .... Postnatal [*Medicine*]
PN .... Practical Nurse
PN .... Predicate Nominal [*Linguistics*] (IEL)
PN .... Preliminary Notification (NRCH)
PN .... Press Night
PN .... Pressure, Nominal (SAUS)
PN .... Pressure, Normal (SAUS)
PN .... Primary Node (SAUS)
PN .... Princeton Aviation [*ICAO designator*] (AD)
PN .... Printing News (SAUS)
P/N........... Print plus Negative (SAUS)
PN .... Prior Notice (SAUS)
PN .... Procedure Name (SAUS)
PN .... Processing Negativity [*Computer science*]
PN .... Processing Node (VLIE)
PN .... Processor Number (VLIE)
PN .... Proctor Normal (SAUS)
PN .... Procurement Notice [*NASA*] (AAGC)
Pn............ Production [*Economics*]
PN .... Production Notice (KSC)
PN .... Product Name (NITA)
PN .... Programmable Network
PN .... Program Notice (KSC)
PN .... Program Number [*Horse racing*]
PN .... Progress note [*Medical records*] (DAVI)
PN .... Project de Norme
PN .... Projection Neurons [*Neuroanatomy*]
PN .... Project Note
PN .... Project Number [*Online database field identifier*] [*Computer science*]

pn Promissory Note (AD)
PN Promissory Note [*Business term*]
PN Prompt Neutron (SAUS)
PN Pronuclei [*Embryology*]
PN Proportional Navigation (IAA)
PN Pseudo Noise (SAUS)
PN Pseudonoise
PN Pseudo-Random Noise (NAKS)
PN Pseudorandom Number
PN Psychiatric Nurse
pn Psychiatry-Neurology (AD)
PN Psychoneurologist
PN Psychoneurotic [*Cases, patients, etc.*]
PN Public Network [*Telecommunications*]
PN Publisher's Name [*Online database field identifier*]
PN Pulse Network (KSC)
PN Punch On
pn Punch-On [*Computer science*] (AD)
PN Punch Only (SAUS)
PN Pupil Nurse [*British*] (DI)
PN Putative Neurotransmitter [*Biochemistry*]
PN Pyelonephritis [*Medicine*] (MAE)
PN Pyridine Nucleotide [*Medicine*] (DMAA)
PN Pyridoxine [*or Pyridoxol*] [*Also, Pxn*] [*Biochemistry*]
PN Pyrrolnitrin [*Antifungal antibiotic*]
PN Regular Pending Transaction [*IRS*]
PN1 Personnelman, First Class [*Navy rating*]
P_{N2} Partial Pressure of Nitrogen [*Medicine*] (DAVI)
PN2 Personnelman, Second Class [*Navy rating*]
PN2O Partial Pressure of Nitrous Oxide (SAUS)
PN3 Personnelman, Third Class [*Navy rating*]
Pn6 Partenavia [*Airplane code*]
PNA Arachis Hypogaea [*Plant lectins*] (QSUL)
PNA Nomina Anatomica (Paris) [*Anatomical Nomenclature*] (DAVI)
PNA Pacific North America (SAUS)
PNA Pacific/North American [*Sector*] [*Marine science*] (OSRA)
PNA Pacific North American Teleconnection
PNA Pacific North Atlantic [*Marine science*] (OSRA)
PNA Pacific Northern Airlines (AD)
PNA Packet Network Adapter (SAUS)
PNA Packet Network Adaptor (NITA)
PNA Pakistan National Alliance (PD)
PNA Palestinian National Authority [*Political party*] (ECON)
PNA Pamplona [*Spain*] [*Airport symbol*] (OAG)
Pna Panama (SAUS)
PNA Panna [*India*] [*Airport symbol*] (AD)
PNA Pa-O National Army [*Myanmar*] [*Political party*] (EY)
PNA Paper Napkin Association
PNA Parallel and Novel Architectures [*British*]
PNA Parallel Network Architecture (SAUS)
PNA Para-Nitroaniline [*Organic chemistry*]
PNA Parenting in a Nuclear Age (EA)
PNA Parisiensis Nomina Anatomica [*Paris Anatomical Nomenclature*] [*Medicine*]
PNA Partacoona [*Australia*] [*Seismograph station code, US Geological Survey*] (SEIS)
PNA Parti Nationale Africain [*African National Party*] [*Chad*] [*Political party*]
PNA Passed, but Not Advanced
PNA Passive Network Array (SAUS)
PNA Peanut Agglutinin [*Immunology*]
PNA Pediatric Nurse Associate [*Medicine*] (EDAA)
PNA Pennsylvania Nurses Association (SAUS)
PNA Pentose Nucleic Acid (SAUS)
PNA Pentosenucleic Acid [*Biochemistry*]
PNA People's News Agency [*An association*] (EA)
PNA Peptide Nucleic Acid [*Biochemistry*]
PNA Peripheral Node Adapter (TIMI)
PNA Personal Navigation Assistant
PNA Personnelman (Records Clerk) [*U.S. Navy enlisted rating*] (AUER)
PNA Philippines News Agency (AD)
PNA Pinedale, WY [*Location identifier*] [*FAA*] (FAAL)
PNa Plasma Sodium [*Organic chemistry*] (DAVI)
PNA Point of No Alternative (SAUS)
PNA Polish National Alliance of the United States of North America (EA)
PNA Polish Nobility Association (EA)
PNA Polyamide Nucleic Acid [*Biochemistry*]
PNA Polynuclear Aromatic [*Organic chemistry*]
PNA Polynuclear Aromatic Hydrocarbon (ABAC)
PNA Price Not Available (DNAB)
PNA Probablistic Noise Audibility (EEVL)
PNA Processing Terminal Network Architecture [*Computer science*] (BUR)
PNA Professional Numismatists' Association [*British*] (BI)
PNA Programmable Network Access (SAUS)
PNA Progressive Networks Audio
PNA Project Network Analysis
PNA Protein equivalent of Nitrogen Appearance (SAUS)
PNA Punan Bah-Biau [*Language symbol*] (ETLW)
PNA Universal Airlines, Inc. [*ICAO designator*] (FAAC)
PNAA Pacific Northwest Apparel Association [*Washington, Oregon, Idaho, Alaska, Montana, and British Columbia, Canada*] (EARSL)
PNAA Prompt-Neutron Activation Analysis (ODA)
PNAB Percutaneous Needle Aspiration Biopsy [*Medicine*]
PNAC Pacific Northwest Athletic Conference (PSS)
PNAC President's National Advisory Committee (NADA)
PNAC Psychiatric Nurses' Association of Canada
PNACO Past National Commodore (SAUS)
PNA Compounds Polynuclear Aromatic Compounds (SAUS)
PNAD Personnel Nuclear Accident Dosimeter (SAUS)
PNAF Plan Name and Address File [*IRS*]
PNAF Potential Network Access Facility
PNAF Primary Nuclear Airlift Force
PNAH Polynuclear Aromatic Hydrocarbon [*Environmental chemistry*]
PNAI Pan American Independent Line [*Common carrier symbol*]
PNAI Provincial Newspapers Association of Ireland (AD)
PNAMBIC Pay No Attention to the Man Behind the Curtain [*Computer hacker terminology*] (NHD)
PNAME Public Model Name [*Automotive emissions*]
PNAP Pro-Life Nonviolent Action Project (EA)
PNAP Protected Natural Area Programme (SAUS)
PNAQ Pan American Express [*Common carrier symbol*]
PNAS Palletized Night Attack System
PNAS Proceedings of the National Academy of Sciences [*A publication*]
PNAS Prudent No Added Salt [*Diet*] (DAVI)
PNASA Para-Nitroaniline-o-sulfonic Acid [*Organic chemistry*]
PnASat PanAmSat Corp. [*Associated Press*] (SAG)
PNASH Pacific Northwest Agricultural Safety and Health Center [*University of Washington*] (RCD)
P-NAV Personal Navigation
PNAV Precise Navigation
PNAV Precision Navigation Ambiguity Resolution
PNAV Proportional Navigation
pnavq Positive-Negative Ambivalent Quotient (AD)
PNAvQ Positive-Negative Ambivalent Quotient [*Psychology*]
PNazMHi Moravian Historical Society, Nazareth, PA [*Library symbol*] [*Library of Congress*] (LCLS)
PNB North Platte, NE [*Location identifier*] [*FAA*] (FAAL)
PNB Pacific Northwest Ballet
PNB Pacific Northwest Bell (SAUS)
PNB Particle/Neutral Beam (MCD)
PNB Partido ng Bayan [*Party of the Nation*] [*Philippines*] [*Political party*]
PnB People's Party (Philippines) [*Political party*] (PSAP)
PNB Permodalan Nasional Bank [*Malaysia*]
PNB Personal Needs Break (WDAA)
PNB Philadelphia National Bank (SAUS)
PNB Philadelphia National Corporation (EFIS)
PNB Philippine National Bank (AD)
PNB Pomio [*New Britain*] [*Seismograph station code, US Geological Survey*] [*Closed*] (SEIS)
PNB Porto Nacional [*Brazil*] [*Airport symbol*] (AD)
PNB Premature Nodal Beat [*Cardiology*] (DAVI)
PNB Premier National Bancorp [*AMEX symbol*] [*Formerly, Hudson Chartered Bancorp*]
pnb Producto Nacional Bruto [*Gross National Product*] [*Spanish*] (AD)
PNB Produto National Bruto [*Gross National Product*] [*Portugal*] (AD)
PNB Prostatic Needle Biopsy [*Oncology*] (DAVI)
PNB Pulseless Non-Breathing [*Medicine*] (IDYL)
PNB Punjab National Bank (SAUS)
PNBA Pacific Northwest Booksellers Association (AD)
PNBAS ((Para-Nitrophenyl)azo)salicylic Acid [*A dye*] [*Organic chemistry*]
PNBB Parc National de la Boucle du Baoule [*Baoule River Bend National Park*] [*French*] [*Mali*] (AD)
PNBC Pacific Northwest Bibliographic Center [*Library network*]
PNBC Princeton National Bancorp [*NASDAQ symbol*] (SAG)
PNBC Princeton National Bancorporation [*NASDAQ symbol*]
PNBC Princeton Natl Bancorp [*NASDAQ symbol*] (TTSB)
PNBF Peak Nucleate Boiling Flux
PNBH Petri-Net-Based Hypertext (SAUS)
PNBH P-Nitrobenzaldehyde Hydrazone (SAUS)
PNBK Patriot National Bank CT [*NASDAQ symbol*] (SAG)
PNBK Patriot Natl Bk [*NASDAQ symbol*] (TTSB)
PNBMS Pacific Northwest Bird and Mammal Society [*Later, SNUB*] (EA)
PNBOUNDARY Positive Negative Boundary (SAUS)
PNBP Parc National de la Boucle de la Pendjari [*Penjari River Bend National Park*] [*French*] [*Dahamey*] (AD)
PNBS Pyridinium(nitro)benzenesulfonate [*Organic chemistry*]
PNBT Paranitroblue Tetrazoleum (SAUS)
PNBT Para-Nitroblue Tetrazolium
PNC Chief Personnelman [*Navy rating*]
PNC National Conservative Party (Nicaragua) [*Political party*] (PSAP)
PNc New Castle Free Public Library, New Castle, PA [*Library symbol*] [*Library of Congress*] (LCLS)
PNC Northampton County Area Community College, Bethlehem, PA [*OCLC symbol*] (OCLC)
PNC Paging Network Controller (SAUS)
PNC Pakistan National Congress [*Political party*]
PNC Palestine National Council (PD)
PNC Parity Nonconservation [*Physics*]
PNC Parque Nacional Canaima [*Canaima National Park*] [*Venezuela*] (AD)
PNC Particulate Nitrocellulose (SAUS)
PNC Partido Nacional Ceuti [*Ceuta National Party*] [*Political party*] (PPW)
PNC Partido Nacional Conservador [*Nicaragua*] [*Political party*] (EY)
PNC Partido Nacional Cristiano [*National Christian Party*] [*Colombia*] [*Political party*] (EY)
PNC Partido Nacionalista Ceuti [*Political party*] (EY)
PNC Partidual Nationale Crestine [*National Christian Party*] [*Romania*] [*Political party*] (PPE)
PNC Parti National Caledonien [*Caledonian National Party*] [*Political party*] (PPW)

PNC.......... Passenger Name Check-In (MCD)
pnc.......... Pencillin (AD)
PNC.......... Pencrude Resources, Inc. [*Vancouver Stock Exchange symbol*]
PNC.......... Penicillin
PNC.......... People, Networks & Communication (SAUS)
PNC.......... People's National Congress [*Guyana*] (PD)
PNC.......... Peoples National Convention (SAUS)
PNC.......... Peripheral Nerve Conduction [*Neurology*] (DAVI)
PNC.......... Peripheral Nucleated Cell (AAMN)
PNC.......... Personal Number Calling [*Telecommunications*]
PNC.......... Philatelic-Numismatic Combination [*or Commemorative*]
PNC.......... Phosphonitrilic Chloride [*Inorganic chemistry*]
PNC.......... Photo-Nitrosation of Cyclohexane (SAUS)
PNC.......... Physitest Normalise Canadien [*Canadian Standardized Test of Fitness - CSTF*]
PNC.......... Pine Canyon [*California*] [*Seismograph station code, US Geological Survey*] (SEIS)
PNC.......... Place Names Committee [*Victoria, Australia*]
pnc.......... Plate Number Coil (AD)
PNC.......... Plate Number Coil [*Philately*]
PNC.......... PNC Bank Corp. [*NYSE symbol*] (TTSB)
PNC.......... Pneumotaxic Center [*Medicine*] (DAVI)
PNC.......... Police National Computer [*British*]
PNC.......... Ponca City [*Oklahoma*] [*Airport symbol*] (OAG)
PNC.......... Ponca City, OK [*Location identifier*] [*FAA*] (FAAL)
PNC.......... Postnatal Clinic
PNC.......... Power Reactor and Nuclear Fuel Development Corp. [*Japan*] (PDAA)
PNC.......... Preferred Noise Criteria (SAUS)
PNC.......... Preferred Noise Criterion [*L. L. Beranek*] (DIPS)
pnc.......... Premature Nodal Contraction (AD)
PNC.......... Premature Nodal Contraction [*Cardiology*]
PNC.......... Prenatal Care [*Obstetrics*] (DAVI)
PNC.......... Prenatal Clinic [*Obstetrics*] (DAVI)
PNC.......... Prenodal Contraction [*Cardiology*] (DAVI)
PNC.......... Programmed Numerical Control
PNC.......... Prohibition National Committee (EA)
PNC.......... Pronounce [*Telegraphy*] (PCTE)
PNC.......... Proto-Niger-Congo [*Linguistics*] (IEL)
PNC.......... Provident National Financial Corp. (EFIS)
PNC.......... Pseudonurse Cells [*Cytology*]
PN Case.... Psychoneurotic Case (SAUS)
PNCB........ Pakistan Narcotics Control Board
PNCB........ Para-Nitrochlorobenzene [*Organic chemistry*]
PNCBANKPAC... Bipartisan Voluntary Public Affairs Committee of PNC Bank National Association [*Pittsburgh, PA*] (PACS)
PNCC........ Pacific Northwest College Conference (PSS)
PNCC........ Panamanian Carriers Corporation [*Common carrier symbol*]
PNCC........ Partial Network Control Center
PNCC........ President's National Crime Commission (AD)
PNCD........ Pronounced [*Telegraphy*] (PCTE)
PNCE........ Private New Capital Expenditure
PNCEA....... Paulist National Catholic Evangelization Association (EA)
PNCFN...... Permanent Nordic Committee on Food and Nutrition [*Copenhagen, Denmark*] (EAIO)
PNCG........ Pronouncing [*Telegraphy*] (PCTE)
PNCH........ Partido Nacional Conservador de Honduras [*National Conservative Party of Honduras*] [*Political party*]
pnch........ Punch (AD)
PNCH........ Punch
PNCIAWPRC... Philippine National Committee of the International Association on Water Pollution Research and Control (SAUS)
PNCK........ Pancake
PNCL........ Percent Non-Conforming Lots (SAUS)
PNCL........ Pinnacle Micro [*NASDAQ symbol*] (TTSB)
PNCL........ Pinnacle Micro, Inc. [*NASDAQ symbol*] (NQ)
Pncla....... Pensacola, Florida (AD)
PNCM........ Master Chief Personnelman [*Navy rating*]
PNC MLA... Pacific Northwest Chapter of the Medical Library Association (SAUS)
PNCN........ Pronunciation [*Telegraphy*] (PCTE)
PNCO........ Personnel Noncommissioned Officer (SAUS)
PNCOC...... Primary Noncommissioned Officer Course [*Army*] (INF)
PNCP........ Periphal Mode Control Point (SAUS)
PNCP........ Peripheral Network Control Point (SAUS)
PNCPrC..... PNC Bank Cp $1.60 Cv C Pfd [*NYSE symbol*] (TTSB)
PNCPrD..... PNC Bank Cp $1.80 Cv D Pfd [*NYSE symbol*] (TTSB)
PNC Project... Police National Computer Project (SAUS)
PNCS........ Pakistani National Conservation Strategy (SAUS)
PNCS........ Performance & Navigation Computer System (SAUS)
PNCS........ Private Network Communication Systems (MCD)
PNCS........ Senior Chief Personnelman [*Navy rating*]
PNCTR...... Passive Non-Cooperative Target Recognition (ACAE)
PNCU........ Police National Computer Unit [*British*]
Pnd.......... Pandjang (AD)
pnd.......... Paroxysmal Noctural Dyspnoea (AD)
PND.......... Paroxysmal Nocturnal Dyspnea [*Medicine*]
PND.......... Parti des Nationalistes du Dahomey [*Dahomean Nationalists Party*] [*Political party*]
PND.......... Partido Nacional Democratico [*National Democratic Party*] [*Costa Rica*] [*Political party*] (PPW)
PND.......... Partido Nacional Democratico [*National Democratic Party*] [*Dominican Republic*] [*Political party*]
PND.......... Partidul National-Democratic [*National Democratic Party*] [*Romania*] [*Political party*] (PPE)
PND.......... Parti National Democrate [*Morocco*] [*Political party*] (EY)
PND.......... Passive Navigation Device
PND.......... Pending
PND.......... Pictorial Navigation Display (OA)
PND.......... Position-Navigation Device (SAUS)
PND.......... Positive-Negative Diode (SAUS)
PND.......... Postnasal Drainage [*or Drip*] [*Medicine*]
pnd.......... Postnasal Drip [*Medicine*] (AD)
PND.......... Postnatal Days
PND.......... Postnatal Depression [*Medicine*] (ECON)
pnd.......... Pound (MAE)
PND.......... Preliminary Number Deflator [*Empirical mathematics*] (ECON)
PND.......... Premodulation Processor - Near Earth Data (KSC)
PND.......... Prenatal Diagnosis [*Medicine*]
PND.......... Present Next Digit
PND.......... Pressed Notch Depth (PDAA)
PND.......... Primary Navigation Display (GAVI)
PND.......... Principal Neutralizing Determinant [*Immunology*]
PND.......... Principal Neutralizing Domain [*Medicine*]
PND.......... Program Network Diagram [*Telecommunications*] (TEL)
PND.......... Pronatriodilatin (DB)
PND.......... Pseudonyms and Nicknames Dictionary [*A publication*]
PND.......... Punta Gorda [*Belize*] [*Airport symbol*] (OAG)
PNDA........ Angolan National Democratic Party [*Political party*] (PSAP)
PNDA........ Panda Project [*NASDAQ symbol*] (TTSB)
PNDA........ [*The*] Panda Project, Inc. [*NASDAQ symbol*] (SAG)
PNDA........ People for Nuclear Disarmament Australia [*An association*]
PNDB........ Pelerinage a Notre Dame de Beauraing [*An association*] (EAIO)
pndb........ Perceived Noise Decibels (AD)
PNDB........ Perceived Noise Decibels
PNdB........ Perceived Noise Decibels
PNDC........ Parallel Network Digital Computer (IEEE)
PNDC........ Partido Nacional de Democracia Centrista [*Chile*] [*Political party*] (EY)
PNDC........ Progressive Neuronal Degeneration of Childhood [*Medicine*]
PNDC........ Provisional National Defence Council [*Ghana*] (PD)
PNDC........ Provisional National Defense Council (SAUS)
PNDD........ Parti National pour la Democratie et le Developpement [*Benin*] [*Political party*] (EY)
PNDES...... Pulse Doppler Non-Elevation Scan (SAUS)
pndg........ Pending (AD)
PNDG........ Pending (AFM)
PNDI........ Pennsylvania Natural Diversity Inventory [*Bureau of Forestry*] [*Harrisburg*] [*Information service or system*] (IID)
PNDL........ Pentland Group plc [*LO Symbol*] (TTSB)
PNDLR...... Parking, Neutral, Driving, Lowgear, Reverse (SAUS)
P-N-D-L-R... Park-Neutral-Drive-Low-Reverse (AD)
PNDLR...... Pendular
PNDM........ Project Nondesign Memo
PNDMA..... Paranitroso-Dimethylalanin (SAUS)
pndnt....... Pendentive (VRA)
PNDO........ Partial Neglect of Differential Overlap [*Physics*]
Pndo........ Pinedo (AD)
PNDP........ Para-Nitrophenyl Diphenyl Phosphate [*Organic chemistry*]
PNDR........ Partnership for Natural Disaster Reduction [*Emergency Management*] (EMA)
PNDR........ Ponder Industries [*NASDAQ symbol*] (TTSB)
PNDR........ Ponder Industries, Inc. [*NASDAQ symbol*] (SAG)
PNDS-Taraya... Nigerian Party for Democracy and Social Progress-Taraya (Niger) [*Political party*] (PSAP)
PNDT........ P and D Transportation [*Common carrier symbol*]
PNDT........ Parti Nationale pour la Developpement du Tchad [*National Party for the Development of Chad*]
PNE.......... Copene-Petroquimica ADS [*NYSE symbol*] (SG)
PNE.......... Pacific National Exchange (SAUS)
PNE.......... Pacific National Exchange Vancouver [*Vancouver*] (AD)
PNE.......... Pacific National Exhibition [*Vancouver*] (AD)
PNE.......... Pacific National Exhibition Home Show [*Southex Exhibitions*] (TSPED)
PNE.......... Paine College, Warren A. Candler Library, Augusta, GA [*OCLC symbol*] (OCLC)
PNE.......... Panhandle Eastern Corp. [*Toronto Stock Exchange symbol*]
pne.......... Peaceful Nuclear Explosion (AD)
PNE.......... Peaceful Nuclear Explosion
PNE.......... Peaceful Nuclear Explosive
PNE.......... Peaceful Nuclear Explosives (SAUS)
PNE.......... Philadelphia [*Pennsylvania*] North Philadelphia [*Airport symbol*] (OAG)
PNE.......... Philadelphia, PA [*Location identifier*] [*FAA*] (FAAL)
PNE.......... PINE [*Postal Service standard*] (OPSA)
PNE.......... Plasma Norepinephrine [*Medicine*] (DMAA)
PNE.......... Pneumoencephalography [*Medicine*] (CPH)
PNe.......... Pointe Noire (AD)
pne.......... Practical Nurse's Education (AD)
PNE.......... Practical Nurse's Education
PNE.......... Protected Natural Environments (SAFN)
PNEA........ Angolan National Geological Party [*Political party*] (PSAP)
PNEA........ Parque Nacional El Avila [*El Avila National Park*] [*Spanish*] (AD)
PNEAC...... Printer's National Environment Assistance Center (AGLO)
PNEC........ Part Number Engineering Change (SAUS)
PNEC........ Predicted No Effect Concentration [*Environmental technology*]
PNEC........ Primary Navy Enlisted Classification [*Code*]
PNEC........ Proceedings of the National Electronics Conference [*A publication*]
PNED........ Peaceful Nuclear Explosive Device
PNed........ Pharmacopeia Nederlandsche [*Netherlands Pharmacopoeia*]

PNEDC ...... Programme National D'etude de la Dynamique du Climat [*France*] [*Marine science*] (OSRA)
PNEDC ...... Programme National d'Etudes de la Dynamique du Climat (USDC)
PNEFC .... P. N. Elrod Fan Club [*Association*] (EA)
PNEK .... Party of People's Unity of Kazakhstan [*Political party*] (PSAP)
PNEM .... Paraneoplastic Encephalomyelitis [*Medicine*] (DMAA)
PNEM-APROME... Partido Nacionalista Espanol de Melilla - Asociacion pro Melilla [*Spanish North Africa*] [*Political party*] (MENA)
PNER .... Pocono Northeast Railway [*Federal Railroad Administration identification code*]
PNERL .... Pacific Northwest Environmental Research Laboratory [*Environmental Protection Agency*] (MSC)
Pnes .... Pines (AD)
PNES .... Pines
PNET .... Peaceful Nuclear Explosions Treaty [*Officially, Treaty on Underground Nuclear Explosions for Peaceful Purposes*]
PNET .... Peaceful Nuclear Explosion Treaty (SAUS)
PNET .... Peripheral Neuroepithelioma [*Medicine*] (DMAA)
PNET .... Primitive Neuroectodermal Tumor [*Oncology*]
PNET .... ProNet, Inc. [*NASDAQ symbol*] (NQ)
PNEU .... Parents' National Educational Union [*British*]
PNEU .... Parents National Education Union (SAUS)
PNEU .... Pneumatic (AAG)
pneu .... Pneumatic (AD)
pneu .... Pneumonia [*Medicine*] (MAE)
PNEUC ...... Physical Non-Elementary Unit Control (SAUS)
PNEUC ...... Physical Non-Eliminated Unit Check (SAUS)
PNEUD ...... Pneudraulic
PNEUG ...... Pneumatic Pressure Generator (MCD)
PNEUM ...... Pneumatic
PNEUM ...... Pneumonia (WDAA)
PNEUMO .... Pneumothorax [*Medicine*]
pneumoccon... Pneumocconiosis [*Medicine*] (AD)
pneumog.... Pneumograph (AD)
PNEUMOG... Pneumography (SAUS)
Pneumol .... Pneumology (SAUS)
pneumonoultra... Pneumonoultra-Microscopicsilicovolcanoconiosis [*Medicine*] (AD)
PNEUROP... European Committee of Manufacturers of Compressors, Vacuum Pumps, and Pneumatic Tools (EA)
PNF .... Pacific National Financial Corp. [*Toronto Stock Exchange symbol*] [*Vancouver Stock Exchange symbol*]
PNF .... Palestine National Front [*Political party*] (PD)
PNF .... Partial Neutralization Feed (ABAC)
PNF .... Partito Nazionale Fascista [*National Fascist Party*] [*Italy*] [*Political party*] (PPE)
PNF .... Peierls-Nabarro Force [*Physics*]
PNF .... Penn Traffic [*NYSE symbol*] (TTSB)
PNF .... Penn Traffic Co. [*NYSE symbol*] (SAG)
PNF .... Phosphonitrilic Fluoroelastomer [*Synthetic rubber*]
PNF .... Pilot Not Flying (GAVI)
PNF .... Positive Neutral Finder [*Automotive engineering*]
PNF .... Postnuclear Fraction [*Biochemical tissue analysis*]
PNF .... Prenex Normal Form [*Logic*]
pnf .... Proprioceptive Neuromuscular Facilitation (AD)
PNF .... Proprioceptive Neuromuscular Facilitation [*Neurology*]
pnfd .... Present Not for Duty (AD)
PNFD .... Present Not for Duty [*Military*]
PNFE .... Prototype Network Front End (SAUS)
PN-FET ...... Positive-Negative-Field-Effect Transistor (SAUS)
PNFI .... Petawawa National Forestry Institute [*Canadian Forestry Service*] [*Research center*] (RCD)
PNFI .... Pinnacle Financial Services, Inc. [*NASDAQ symbol*] (NQ)
PNFI .... Pinnacle Financial Svcs [*NASDAQ symbol*] (TTSB)
PNFPP .... Philippines National Family Planning Program (SAUS)
PNFS .... Peak and Northern Footpaths Society [*British*] (DBA)
PNFSO ...... Primary Nonferrous Smelter Order [*Environmental Protection Agency*]
PNFT .... Penn Traffic [*Company symbol*]
PNFT .... Penn Traffic Co. [*NYSE symbol*]
PNG .... Pacific Northern Gas Ltd. [*Toronto Stock Exchange symbol*] [*Vancouver Stock Exchange symbol*]
PNG .... Papua New Guinea [*ANSI three-letter standard code*] (CNC)
PNG .... Papua New Guinea Banking Corp.
PNG .... Papua Nueva Guinea [*Papua New Guinea*] [*Spanish*] (AD)
PNG .... Paranagua [*Brazil*] [*Airport symbol*] (OAG)
PNG .... Parque Nacional Guatopo [*Guatopo National Park*] [*Venezuela*] [*Spanish*] (AD)
PNG .... Partido Nacional Guevarista [*Ecuador*] [*Political party*] (PPW)
PNG .... Passive Night Goggles [*Military*] (WDAA)
PNG .... Passive Night-vision Goggles (SAUS)
PNG .... Paua New Guinea (SAUS)
Png .... Penang (AD)
PNG .... Pending [*Telegraphy*] (PCTE)
PNG .... Penghu [*Hokoto*] [*Republic of China*] [*Seismograph station code, US Geological Survey*] (SEIS)
PNG .... Penicillin G [*Medicine*] (DMAA)
PNG .... Penn-America Group [*NYSE symbol*] (SG)
PNG .... Percent Normalized Gradient (SAUS)
PNG .... Persona Non Grata [*Unacceptable Person*] [*Latin*]
png .... Persona Non Grata [*An Unacceptable Person*] [*Latin*] (AD)
PNG .... Philippine Natural Gum
PNG .... Piedmont Natural Gas Co., Inc. (EFIS)
PNG .... Plant Nitrogen in Grain [*Harvest nitrogen index*]
PNG .... Popondetta [*New Guinea*] [*Airport symbol*] (AD)
PNG .... Portable Network Graphic [*Computer science*] (PCM)
PNG .... Portable Network Graphics [*Computer science*] (PCM)
PNG .... Professional Numismatists Guild (EA)
PNG .... Proportional Navigation Guidance
PNG .... Pseudo Noise Generator (SAUS)
PNG .... Pseudonoise Generator
PNG .... Puerto Rico Air NAtional Guard [*FAA designator*] (FAAC)
PNGCS ...... Primary Navigation, Guidance and Control System (KSC)
PNGFA .... Pacific Northwest Grain and Feed Association (EA)
PNGI .... Papua New Guinea Institute of Chemistry
PNGL .... Papua New Guinea Line (AD)
P N G Med J... Papua New Guinea Medical Journal (SAUS)
PNGS .... Primary Navigation and Guidance System (SAUS)
PNGS .... Primary Navigation System
PNGV .... Partnership for a New Generation of Vehicles [*Collaboration of government and industry*]
PNH .... North Hills School District Instructional Materials Center, Pittsburgh, PA [*OCLC symbol*] (OCLC)
PNH .... Pan Head [*Design engineering*]
pnh .... Paroxysmal Nocturnal Hemoglobinuria (AD)
PNH .... Paroxysmal Nocturnal Hemoglobinuria [*Medicine*]
PNH .... Partido Nacional Hondureno [*Honduran National Party*] [*Political party*]
PNH .... Parti National d'Haiti [*National Party of Haiti*] [*Political party*]
PNH .... Phnom Penh [*Cambodia*] [*Airport symbol*] (OAG)
PNH .... Pitcher Mountain [*New Hampshire*] [*Seismograph station code, US Geological Survey*] (SEIS)
PNH .... Polynuclear Hydrocarbon (DMAA)
PNHA .... Physicians National Housestaff Association [*Defunct*]
PNHDL ...... Panhandle
PNHP .... Parque Nacional Henri Pittier [*Henri Pittier National Park*] [*Venezuela*] [*Spanish*] (AD)
PNHP .... Phsyicians for a National Health Program (EA)
PNHS .... Pacific Northwest Heather Society [*Later, NAHS*] (EA)
PNHX .... GATX Capital [*Private rail car owner code*]
PNI .... Aerovias de Poniente SA de CV [*Mexico*] [*ICAO designator*] (FAAC)
PNI .... Pacific Neurosciences Institute (SAUS)
PNI .... Paninternational
PNI .... Parque Nacional Iguazu [*Iguazu National Park*] [*Spanish*] (AD)
PNI .... Partai Nasionalis Indonesia [*Nationalist Party of Indonesia*] [*Political party*]
PNI .... Participate but Do Not Initiate [*Investment term*]
PNI .... Partido Nacional Independiente [*National Independent Party*] [*Costa Rica*] [*Political party*] (PPW)
PNI .... Part Number Index (MCD)
PNI .... Pascoe Nally International [*British*]
PNI .... Peer Nomination Inventory [*Psychology*]
PNI .... Perineural Invasion [*Medicine*]
PNI .... Peripheral Nerve Injury [*Medicine*]
PNI .... Personnelman (Classification Interviewer) [*U.S. Navy enlisted rating*] (AUER)
PNI .... Pharmaceutical News Index [*UMI/Data Courier*] [*Information service or system*] [*A publication*]
PNI .... Pictorial Navigation Indicator [*Aviation*] (DA)
PNI .... Picture Netwok International, Ltd.
PNI .... Picture Network International [*Commercial firm*] [*Information service or system*]
PNI .... Pinerola [*Italy*] [*Seismograph station code, US Geological Survey*] (SEIS)
PNI .... Ponape [*Caroline Islands*] [*Airport symbol*] (OAG)
pni .... Positive Noninterfering (AD)
PNI .... Positive Noninterfering [*Alarm system*]
PNI .... Postnatal Infection [*Medicine*]
PNI .... Preferred Networks, Inc. (EFIS)
PNI .... Principal Neo-Tech, Inc. [*Toronto Stock Exchange symbol*]
PNI .... Processor Network Interface (SAUS)
PNI .... Prognostic Nutrition Index [*Dietetics*] (DAVI)
PNI .... Protease Nexin I [*Biochemistry*]
PNI .... Proto-Northern Iroquoian [*Linguistics*] (IEL)
pni .... Psychoneuroimmunology (AD)
PNI .... Psychoneuroimmunology
pni .... Pulsed Neutron Interrogation (AD)
PNI .... Pulsed Neutron Interrogation (PDAA)
PNIC .... Pleasure Navigation International Joint Committee [*See also CINP*] [*The Hague, Netherlands*] (EAIO)
P Nic .... Port Nicholson (AD)
PNIC .... Private-data Network Identification Code (SAUS)
PNID .... Peer Nomination Inventory of Depression [*Child development test*] [*Psychology*]
P-NID .... Precedence Network In-Dialing [*Telecommunications*] (TEL)
PNID/NOD... Priority Network In-Dial / Network Out-Dial (DNAB)
PNIE .... Priority National Intelligence Estimate [*CIA*] (LAIN)
PNII .... Prentiss Normal and Industrial Institute [*Mississippi*]
PNII .... Protease Nexin II [*Biochemistry*]
PNIMIC ...... Pilot NATO Insensitive Munitions Information Center (SAUS)
PNIN .... P-Doped, N-Doped, Intrinsic, N-Doped (SAUS)
PNIN .... Positive-Negative-Intrinsic-Negative (SAUS)
PNIO .... Priority National Intelligence Objectives (MCD)
PNIP .... P-Doped, N-Doped, Intrinsic, P-Doped (SAUS)
PNIP .... Positive-Negative-Intrinsic-Positive [*Electron device*] (MSA)
PNIPAAM ... Poly-N-isopropylacrylamide [*Organic chemistry*]
PNIPAM ..... Poly-N-Isopropylacrylamide [*Organic chemistry*]
PNITC .... Pacific Northwest International Trade Council (AD)
PNIU .... Pneumatic Scale Corp. (SAUS)
PNJ .... Paterson [*New Jersey*] [*Airport symbol*] (AD)

PNJ .... Paterson, NJ [*Location identifier*] [*FAA*] (FAAL)
PNJ .... Polar Night Jet Stream (ADA)
PNJ .... Pulsed Noise Jamming (SAUS)
PNJALBB... Peter Noone Just a Little Bit Better Promotion Club (EA)
PN-Junction... Positive Negative Junction (SAUS)
PNK .... Pink [*Electrical wiring*]
PNK .... Pinkham Creek [*Montana*] [*Seismograph station code, US Geological Survey*] [*Closed*] (SEIS)
PNK .... Pink Pages Publication [*Vancouver Stock Exchange symbol*]
pnk .... Pinl
PNK .... Pinnacle Entertainment [*NYSE symbol*]
PNK .... Polynucleotide Kinase [*An enzyme*]
PNK .... Pontianak [*Indonesia*] [*Airport symbol*] (OAG)
PNK .... Pyridoxine Kinase (DMAA)
PNkA .... Aluminum Co. of America, ALCOA Research Laboratories Library, New Kensington, PA [*Library symbol*] [*Library of Congress*] (LCLS)
PNKA .... Protein Induced by Vitamin K Absence and Antagonists (PDAA)
pnksh .... Pinkish [*Philately*]
PNL .... Aero Personal SA de CV [*Mexico*] [*ICAO designator*] (FAAC)
PNL .... Instrument Panel [*Automotive engineering*]
PNL .... Pacific Naval Laboratories (AD)
PNL .... Pacific Northwest Laboratory [*Department of Energy*] [*Richland, WA*]
PNL .... Pakistan National League [*Political party*]
pnl .... Panel (AD)
PNL .... Panel (KSC)
PNL .... Pantelleria [*Italy*] [*Airport symbol*] (OAG)
PNL .... Partidul National Liberal [*National Liberal Party*] [*Romania*] [*Political party*] (PPE)
PNL .... Parti National Liberal [*National Liberal Party*] [*Lebanon*] [*Political party*] (PPW)
PNL .... Passenger Name List [*Travel industry*]
PNL .... Peanut Lectin [*Immunochemistry*]
PNL .... Peninsula [*Alaska*] [*Seismograph station code, US Geological Survey*] (SEIS)
PNL .... Perceived Noise Level
PNL .... Philippine National Line (AD)
PNL .... Pine Bell Mines [*Vancouver Stock Exchange symbol*]
PNL .... Polytechnic of North London, School of Librarianship, London, England [*OCLC symbol*] (OCLC)
PNL .... Prescribed Nuclear Load [*Military*] (AABC)
PNL .... Pressure Noise Level (MCD)
PNL .... Principal [*Telegraphy*] (PCTE)
PNL .... Pulsed Neodymium LASER
PNL .... Pulsed Neutron Logging (SAUS)
PNLA .... Pacific Northwest Library Association
PNLA .... Pacific Northwest Loggers Association (EA)
PNLA .... Percutaneous Needle Lung Aspiration [*Medicine*] (DMAA)
PNLAADA ... Programme National de Lutte Contre l'Abus de l'Alcohol et des Drogues chez les Autochtones [*Canada*]
PNLA/BCLA... Pacific Northwest/British Columbia Library Associations
PNL BD ..... Panel Board (SAUS)
pnlbd .... Panelboard [*National Electrical Code*] (IEEE)
PNLBRG..... Panel Bridge (MUGU)
PNLF .... Planetary-Nebula Luminosity Function (SAUS)
PNLF .... Probability of no Loss of Function (SAUS)
PNLG .... Phase Nulling LASER Gyroscope
PNL/I .... Provisioning Numerical Listing/Index
PNLJD .... Professional Non-Linear Junction Detector [*Police and security equipment*]
PNLM......... Palestine National Liberation Movement [*Political party*] (BJA)
PNLO .... Principal Naval Liaison Officer [*British*]
PNLR .... Ralph Panella Trucking [*Common carrier symbol*]
PNLRM...... Preferred National Land Rights Model [*Australia*]
PNLT......... Perceived Noise Level, Tone Corrected
PNLU .... Holland Pan-American Line [*Intermodal shipping container symbol*] (TVRC)
PNM .... Pan-Somali Nationalist Movement [*Political party*]
PNM .... Partido Nacionalista de Mexicano [*Nationalist Party of Mexico*] [*Political party*]
PNM .... Partito Nazionale Monarchico [*National Monarchist Party*] [*Italy*] [*Political party*] (PPE)
PNM .... Path Number Matrix (SAUS)
PNM .... People's National Movement [*Trinidad and Tobago*] [*Political party*] (PD)
PNM .... Perinatal Mortality [*Medicine*]
PNM .... Periodicals/News/Microfilm unit (SAUS)
PNM .... Peripheral Nerve Myelin [*Medicine*] (MELL)
PNM .... Phenolic Nylon with Microballoon
PNM .... Pinnacles National Monument [*California*] (AD)
PNM .... PNM Resources [*Company symbol*]
PNM .... Portable Anymap (SAUS)
PNM .... Postneonatal Mortality (STED)
PNM .... Price Negotiation Memorandum (MCD)
PNM .... Public Service Co. of New Mexico [*NYSE symbol*] (SPSG)
PNM .... Public Svc New Mexico [*NYSE symbol*] (TTSB)
PNM .... Pulse Number Modulation
PNM .... Pyranometer (SAUS)
PNM-Aprome... Partido Nacionalista de Melilla - Asociacion Pro Melilla [*Political party*] (EY)
PNMC .... Phenyl Methylcarbamate [*Organic chemistry*]
PNMF........ Pseudo Noise Matched Filter (IAA)
PNMG .... Persistent Neonatal Myasthenia Gravis [*Medicine*] (DAVI)
PNMO .... Provided No Military Objection Exists [*Army*]
PNMP .... Preliminary NMCS Master Plan (SAUS)
PNMR .... Postnatal Mortality Risk [*Medicine*] (EDAA)
PNMR .... Proton Nuclear Magnetic Resonance (SAUS)
PNMT........ Phenylethanolalnine N-Methyltransferase (SAUS)
PNMT........ Phenylethanolamine N-Methyltransferase [*An enzyme*]
PNMT........ Positive Negative Metal Transistor (SAUS)
PNMT........ Positive-Negative Metal Transistor [*Electronics*] (IAA)
PNN.......... Penn Engineering & Manufacturing Corp. [*AMEX symbol*] (SPSG)
PNN.......... Penn Engr & Mfg [*AMEX symbol*] (TTSB)
PNN.......... Peripheral Nerve Neuroma [*Medicine*] (EDAA)
PNN.......... Pinai-Hagahai [*Language symbol*] (ETLW)
PNN.......... Pinnacle Mountain [*Alaska*] [*Seismograph station code, US Geological Survey*] (SEIS)
PNN.......... Princeton, ME [*Location identifier*] [*FAA*] (FAAL)
PNN.......... Probabilistic Neural Network (IDAI)
PNN.A .... Penn Engr & Mfg'A' [*AMEX symbol*] (TTSB)
PN-NAIPC... Patriot Network - National Association of Independent Patriot Clubs (EA)
pn nb .... Piano Nobile (VRA)
PNNCF ...... Pacific Northern Naval Coastal Frontier
PNNI......... Private Network-to-Network Interface [*Communications term*] (DCT)
PNNI......... Private Node to Network Interface (SAUS)
PNNI......... Public Network Node Interface (SAUS)
PNNL .... Pacific Northwest National Laboratory
PNNT .... Pennant (MSA)
PNNT .... Penn Trailer [*NCIC trailer make code*]
PNNW .... Pennichuck Corp. [*NASDAQ symbol*] (SAG)
PNo.......... Montgomery County-Norristown Public Library, Norristown, PA [*Library symbol*] [*Library of Congress*] (LCLS)
PNO.......... Nashville, TN [*Location identifier*] [*FAA*] (FAAL)
PNO.......... Panaco, Inc. [*AMEX symbol*]
PNO.......... Pancontinental Oil Ltd. [*Toronto Stock Exchange symbol*]
PNO.......... Pa-O National Organization [*Myanmar*] [*Political party*] (EY)
PNO.......... Parque Nacional Ordesa [*Ordesa National Park*] [*Spanish*] (AD)
PNO.......... Parti Nationaliste Occitan [*Occitanian Nationalist Party*] [*France*] [*Political party*] (PPE)
PNO.......... Party for National Order [*Turkey*] [*Political party*] [*Defunct*] (MENA)
PNO.......... Pendleton [*Oregon*] [*Seismograph station code, US Geological Survey*] (SEIS)
pno .... Pergamino [*Parchment*] [*Spanish*] (AD)
pno .... Piano (AD)
PNO.......... Piano
pno .... Pianoforte (WDAA)
PNO.......... Port of New Orleans (AD)
PNO.......... Preliminary Notification [*Nuclear energy*] (NRCH)
PNO.......... Premium Notice Ordinary [*Insurance*]
PNO.......... Prices Normal [*Telegraphy*] (PCTE)
PNO.......... Principal Naval Overseer [*British*]
PNO.......... Principal Nursing Officer
PNO.......... Public Network Operator (SAUS)
PNOA .... Para-Nitro-ortho-anisidine [*Organic chemistry*]
pnob .... Pencil Note on Back [*Philately*]
PNOC .... Particulates not Otherwise Classified [*Industrial hygiene term*] (OHS)
PNOC .... Philippine National Oil Co. (AD)
PNOC .... Philippines National Oil Co. (SAUS)
PNOC .... Proposed Notice of Change
PNO-CI ...... Pair Natural Orbital Configuration Interaction [*Atomic physics*]
PNOD .... Precedence Network Out Dialing [*Communications term*] (DCT)
PNoH .... Norristown State Hospital, Norristown, PA [*Library symbol*] [*Library of Congress*] (LCLS)
PNohM ...... Mary Immaculate Seminary, Northampton, PA [*Library symbol*] [*Library of Congress*] (LCLS)
PNOK .... Primary Next of Kin [*Army*] (AABC)
PNOM .... Procedural Nomenclature (MCD)
PNOPO ...... Parliament National Organisations and Public Offices [*British*]
PNOQ........ Pinole Valley Trucking [*Common carrier symbol*]
PNortHi ..... Historical Society of Montgomery County, Norristown, PA [*Library symbol*] [*Library of Congress*] [*Obsolete*] (LCLS)
PNOT .... Para-Nitro-ortho-toluidine [*Organic chemistry*]
PNOT .... Para-Nitro-o-toluidine [*Organic chemistry*]
PNOT .... Penta-Nitro-O-Toluidine (SAUS)
PNOU .... P and O Service [*Intermodal shipping container symbol*] (TVRC)
PNP.......... Pakistan National Party [*Political party*] (PD)
PNP.......... Panache Resources, Inc. [*Vancouver Stock Exchange symbol*]
PNP.......... Pancreatic Polypeptide [*Medicine*] (EDAA)
PNP.......... Pan Pacific Retail Prop. [*NYSE symbol*] (SG)
PNP.......... Paranitrophenal
PNP.......... Para-Nitrophenol [*or Nitrophenyl*] [*Organic chemistry*]
PNP.......... Para-Nitrophenyl (SAUS)
PNP.......... Para-Nitrophenyl-Beta-Galactosidase [*An enzyme*] (DAVI)
PNP.......... Park/Neutral Position [*Automotive term*] (HAWK)
PNP.......... Partido Nacionalista del Pueblo [*Bolivia*] [*Political party*] (PPW)
PNP.......... Partido Nacionalista ng Pilipinas [*Philippine Nationalist Party*] [*Political party*] (EY)
PNP.......... Partido Nacionalista Popular [*Popular Nationalist Party*] [*Panama*] [*Political party*] (PPW)
PNP.......... Partido Nashonal di Pueblo [*National People's Party*] [*Netherlands Antilles*] [*Political party*] (EY)
PNP.......... Partido Nuevo Progresista [*New Progressive Party*] [*Puerto Rico*] [*Political party*] (PPW)
PNP.......... Partidul National Poporului [*National People's Party*] [*Romania*] [*Political party*] (PPE)
PNP.......... Parti National du Progres [*National Progress Party*] [*Congo*] [*Political party*]
PNP.......... Parti National Populaire [*National Popular Party*] [*Canada*] [*Political party*] (PPW)

PNP......... Parti National Progressiste [*Haiti*] [*Political party*] (EY)
PNP......... Passive Neighbourhood Pattern (SAUS)
PNP......... Peake's English Nisi Prius Cases [*1790-1812*] [*A publication*] (DLA)
PNP......... Peak Negative Pressure [*Medicine*] (DAVI)
PNP......... Pearl Necklace Polymer [*Organic chemistry*]
PNP......... Pediatric Nephrology [*Medical specialty*] (DHSM)
PNP......... Pediatric Nurse Practitioner
PNP......... Penuelas [*Puerto Rico*] [*Seismograph station code, US Geological Survey*] (SEIS)
PNP......... People's National Party [*Jamaica*] [*Political party*] (PPW)
PNP......... People's National Party [*Ghana*] [*Political party*] (PPW)
PNP......... Peripheral Neuropathy [*Medicine*]
PNP......... Philippine National Police (SAUS)
PNP......... Pick-and-Place Robot (SAUS)
PNP......... Platelet Neutralization Procedure [*Medicine*] (MEDA)
PNP......... Platt National Park [*Oklahoma*] (AD)
PNP......... Plug and Play [*Microsoft Corp.*] [*Computer auto-configuration system*] (PCM)
PnP......... Plug and Play (PCM)
PnP......... Plug and Pray (SAUS)
PNP......... Plug N Play (SAUS)
PNP......... Polyneuropathy [*Medicine*] (STED)
PNP......... Popondetta [*Papua New Guinea*] [*Airport symbol*] (OAG)
PNP......... Popular Nationalist Party [*Panama*] [*Political party*] (PD)
pnp......... Positive Negative Positive (AD)
PNP......... Positive-Negative-Positive [*Transistor*]
PNP......... Post-Nodal Piece (SAUS)
PNP......... Precision Navigation Processor (SAUS)
PNP......... Precision Navigation Project
PNP......... Preliminary Network Plan (SSD)
PNP......... Prenegotiation Position (MCD)
PNP......... Private Non-Profit
PNP......... Probability of No Penetration [*NASA*] (SPST)
PNP......... Programmed Numerical Pathoontroller (SAUS)
PNP......... Progressive National Party [*Turks and Caicos Islands*] [*Political party*] (PPW)
PNP......... Progressive Nuclear Palsy [*Neurology*] (DAVI)
PNP......... Prototype Nuclear Process
PNP......... Provincial Nominee Program [*Saskatchewan, Canada*] (FOTI)
PNP......... Psychiatric Nurse Practitioner (NUJO)
PNP......... Psychogenic Nocturnal Polydipsia [*Medicine*]
PNP......... P-Type, N-Type, P-Type Transistor (NITA)
PNP......... Purine-Nucleoside Phosphorylase [*An enzyme*]
PNP......... Purine Nucleotide Phosphorylase [*An enzyme*] (DAVI)
PNP......... Pyridoxine Phosphate [*Biochemistry*]
PNPA........ Para-Nitrophenyl Acetate [*Organic chemistry*]
PNPA........ P-Nitrophenyl Acetate (SAUS)
PN Patient... Psychoneurotic Patient (SAUS)
PNPB........ Positive-Negative Pressure Breathing [*Medicine*] (STED)
PNPBIOS... Plug and Play Basic Input Output System (SAUS)
PNPDPP..... Para-Nitrophenyl Diphenyl Phosphate [*Organic chemistry*]
PNPE........ Precision National [*Federal Railroad Administration identification code*]
PNPF........ Piqua Nuclear Power Facility
PNPG........ Para-Nitrophenylglycerin (SAUS)
PNPG........ Para-Nitrophenylglycerine [*Biochemistry*]
PNPG........ Parti National Populaire Guyanais [*French Guiana*] [*Political party*] (EY)
PNPG........ P-Nitrophenyl-a-Glucopyranoside (SAUS)
PNPG........ P-Nitrophenyl-B-Galactoside [*Chemistry*] (MAE)
PNP-Glu..... Para-Nitrophenyl-a-Glucoside (SAUS)
PNPH........ Parti National Progressiste d'Haiti [*National Progressive Party of Haiti*] [*Political party*]
PNPL........ Para-Nitrophenyl Laurate [*Organic chemistry*]
PNPLS....... Progress at NPL [*National Priorities List*] Sites [*A publication*] [*EPA*]
PNPN........ Positive, Negative, Positive, Negative (SAUS)
pnpn......... Positive-Negative Positive-Negative (AD)
PNPN........ Positive-Negative-Positive-Negative [*Transistor*] (MUGU)
P-NPNN..... Para-Nitrophenyl Nitronyl Nitroxide
PNPP........ Para-Nitrophenyl Phosphate [*Organic chemistry*]
PNPP........ Perry Nuclear Power Plant (NRCH)
PNPP........ P-Nitrophenyl Phosphate (SAUS)
pnpr......... Positive-Negative Pressure Respiration (AD)
PNPR........ Positive-Negative Pressure Respiration
PN-PRBS... Pseudo-Noise, Pseudo-Random Binary String/Stream (CGWS)
PNPS........ Palisades Nuclear Power Station (NRCH)
P-NPS....... Para-Nitrophenylsulfate [*Pharmacology*] (DAVI)
PNPS........ Plant Nitrogen Purge System (IEEE)
PNPS........ Plant Nuclear Protection System (IAA)
PNPSF....... Passive Neighbourhood Pattern Sensitive Fault (SAUS)
PNPY........ Plenipotentiary [*Telegraphy*] (PCTE)
PNQ......... Pine Crest Resources [*Vancouver Stock Exchange symbol*]
PNQ......... Poona [*India*] [*Airport symbol*] (OAG)
PNR......... Page Number Register (SAUS)
PNR......... Panair [*Spain*] [*ICAO designator*] (FAAC)
PNR......... Panhandle Northern Railroad [*Federal Railroad Administration identification code*]
PNR......... Partido Nacionalista Renovador [*Nationalist Renewal Party*] [*Guatemala*] [*Political party*] (PPW)
PNR......... Partido Nacionalista Revolucionario [*Revolutionary Nationalist Party*] [*Ecuador*] [*Political party*] (PPW)
PNR......... Partido Nacional Republicano [*National Republican Party*] [*Portugal*] [*Political party*] (PPE)
PNR......... Partido Nacional Republicano [*National Republican Party*] [*Paraguay*] [*Political party*]
PNR......... Partido Nacional Revolucionario [*National Revolutionary Party*] [*Venezuela*] [*Political party*]
PNR......... Partij Nationalistische Republiek [*Nationalist Republic Party*] [*Surinam*] [*Political party*] (PPW)
PNR......... Passenger Name Record [*Travel industry*] (TRID)
PNR......... Passenger Now Recorded [*Travel industry*] (TRID)
PNR......... Pennant Resources Ltd. [*Toronto Stock Exchange symbol*]
PNR......... Penrod [*Nevada*] [*Seismograph station code, US Geological Survey*] [*Closed*] (SEIS)
PNR......... Pentair, Inc. [*NYSE symbol*] (TTSB)
PNR......... Personnelman (Recruiter) [*U.S. Navy enlisted rating*] (AUER)
PNR......... Philippine National Railways (DS)
PNR......... Photonuclear Reaction (SAUS)
Pnr.......... Pioneer (AD)
PNR......... Pioneer
PNR......... Pittsburgh Naval Reactor (AD)
PNR......... Pittsburgh Naval Reactors Office [*Energy Research and Development Administration*]
PNR......... Pointe Noire [*Congo*] [*Airport symbol*] (OAG)
pnr.......... Point of No Return (AD)
PNR......... Point of No Return [*Aviation*]
PNR......... Polish National Railways (SAUS)
PNR......... Popular News and Review [*A publication*]
PNR......... Preliminary Negotiation Reports
PNR......... Primary Navigation Reference (AAG)
pnr.......... Prior Notice Required (AD)
PNR......... Prior Notice Required (AFM)
PNR......... Prisoner
PNR......... Proved Name Registraton [*Advertising*] (DOAD)
PNR......... Proximal Negative Response
PNR......... Pulletop Nature Reserve [*New South Wales*] (AD)
PNR......... Pulse Nuclear Radiation (AAG)
PNR......... Purchase Notice and Release (SAUS)
PNRA........ Panera Bread [*NASDAQ symbol*]
PNRA........ Panera Bread Co. [*NASDAQ symbol*] (NASQ)
PNRBC....... Pacific Northwest River Basin Commission
PNRC........ Pacific Northwest Regional Commission [*Department of Commerce*]
PNRC........ Potomac Naval River Command (MCD)
PNRC........ Projet National de Coordination des Ressources dans le Domaine de la Statistiques et de l'Information Judiciaires [*Canada*]
PNRE........ Pan Atlantic Re, Inc. (MHDW)
PNRG........ Prime Energy [*NASDAQ symbol*] (SAG)
PNRG........ PrimeEnergy Corp. [*NASDAQ symbol*] (SPSG)
PNRHSL..... Pacific Northwest Regional Health Science Library [*Library network*]
PNRI......... Philippines Nuclear Research Institute (SAUS)
PNRL........ Penril DataComm Ntwks [*NASDAQ symbol*] (TTSB)
PNRL........ Penril Data Communication Networks [*NASDAQ symbol*] (SPSG)
PNRO........ Pittsburgh Naval Reactors Office [*Department of Energy*] [*West Mifflin, PA*] (GAAI)
PNRP........ Philadelphia Pulmonary Neoplasm Research Project (AD)
PNRP........ Pollution and Natural Resources Program (SAUS)
PNRP........ Pulmonary Neoplasm Research Project [*Medicine*] (EDAA)
PNRQ........ Penser Transportation [*Common carrier symbol*]
PNRS........ Preliminary Natural Resources Survey (GNE)
PNRS........ Project Notification and Review System [*Department of Labor*]
PNRSV....... Prunus Necrotic Ringspot Virus
PNR System... Passenger Name Record System (SAUS)
PNS......... Pacific Navigation Systems (AD)
PNS......... Pakistan Naval Ship (AD)
PNS......... Pansophic Systems, Inc. [*NYSE symbol*] (COMM)
PNS......... Parabolized Navier-Stokes Modeling (MCD)
PNS......... Paraneoplastic Neurodegenarative Syndrome [*Medicine*]
PNS......... Paraneoplastic Syndrome [*Medicine*] (EDAA)
pns.......... Parasympathetic Nervous System (AD)
PNS......... Parasympathetic Nervous System
PNS......... Park-Neutral Switch [*Automotive engineering*]
PNS......... Partial Niche Separation
PNS......... Partial Nonprogressing Stroke (CPH)
PNS......... Part Number Specification (MCD)
PNS......... Peacenet Sweden (SAUS)
PNS......... Peculiar and Non-Standard (SAUS)
PNS......... Peculiar and Nonstandard Items (AAG)
PNS......... Penas [*Bolivia*] [*Seismograph station code, US Geological Survey*] (SEIS)
PNS......... Pennington's Stores Ltd. [*Toronto Stock Exchange symbol*]
PNS......... Pensacola [*Florida*] [*Airport symbol*] (OAG)
Pns.......... Pension (TBD)
PNS......... People's News Service [*British*]
PNS......... Peripheral Nerve Stimulator [*Medicine*] (MAE)
pns.......... Peripheral Nervous System (AD)
PNS......... Peripheral Nervous System [*Medicine*]
PNS......... Perkins Nuclear Station (NRCH)
PNS......... Philadelphia & Norfolk Steamship [*AAR code*]
PNS......... Philadelphia Naval Shipyard (AD)
PNS......... Philippine News Service (SAUS)
PNS......... Philippines News Service
PNS......... Pic'N'Save Corp. (EFIS)
PNS......... Pinnacle Data Systems [*AMEX symbol*]
PNS......... Plate Number Society [*Defunct*] (EA)
PNS......... Polynucleotide Sequence (DB)
PNS......... Pooled Normal Serum (PDAA)
PNS......... Portable Navigation System
PNS......... Portsmouth Naval Shipyard [*New Hampshire*]
PNS......... Positive-Negative Selection [*Genetic engineering technique*]

PNS.......... Posterior Nasal Spine [*Medicine*] (DMAA)
PNS.......... Post Nickel Strike (PDAA)
PNS.......... Postnuclear Supernatant
PNS.......... PPTP Network Server (SAUS)
PNS.......... Practical Nursing Student (DAVI)
PNS.......... Premature Nodal Systole [*Medicine*] (EDAA)
PNS.......... Prescribed Nuclear Stockage [*Military*] (AABC)
PNS.......... Primary North-South Stationkeeping (ACAE)
PNS.......... Principal Nursing Sister (WDAA)
PNS.......... Probability of Not Having a Space
PNS.......... Professionals for National Security [*Defunct*] (EA)
PNS.......... Professor of Naval Science
PNS.......... Program on Non-violent Sanctions in conflict & defense (SAUS)
PNS.......... Project of National Significance
PNS.......... Publishers Newspaper Syndicate
PNS.......... Pulsed Neutron Source (SAUS)
PNS.......... Survey Udara (Penas) PT [*Indonesia*] [*ICAO designator*] (FAAC)
PNSA........ Pacific Northwest Ski Association (EA)
PNSA........ Peanut and Nut Salters Association [*Later, PBNPA*] (EA)
PNSA........ Seaman Apprentice, Personnelman, Striker [*Navy rating*]
PNSAA...... Pacific Northwest Ski Areas Association [*Oregon, Washington, and western Idaho*] (EARSL)
PNS & T.... Professor of Naval Science and Tactics [*Naval ROTC*]
PNSB........ Purple Nonsulphur Bacteria (ODA)
PNSC........ Packet Network Service Center (SAUS)
PNSC........ Packet Network Service Centre (NITA)
PNSC........ Pakistan National Shipping [*Common carrier symbol*]
PNSC........ Passenger Network Services Corporation (TRID)
PNSC........ Philippine National Science Society (SAUS)
PNSCP...... Plan for Navy Satellite Communications Plan
PNSD........ Parti National pour la Solidarite et le Developpement [*Algeria*] [*Political party*] (EY)
PNSI........ Polhemus Navigational Sciences, Inc. (MCD)
PNSL........ Papulonodular Skin Lesion [*Medicine*] (MELL)
PNSN........ Pacific Northwest Seismic Network (SAUS)
PNSN........ Parque Nacional Sierra Nevada [*Sierra Nevada National Park*] [*Venezuela*] [*Spanish*] (AD)
PNSN........ Pension
PNSN........ Seaman, Personnelman, Striker [*Navy rating*]
PNSO........ Pull Next Stitch Over [*Knitting*] (BARN)
PNSP........ Penicillin-Nonsusceptible S. Pneumoniae [*Clinical chemistry*]
PNSQ........ Porter Need Satisfaction Questionnaire (EDAC)
PNSR........ Punjab Northern State Railway [*Indian Railway*] (TIR)
PNSRC...... Plant Nuclear Safety Review Committee (SAUS)
PNSS........ Pediatric Nutrition Surveillance System [*Centers for Disease Control*] (DAVI)
PNSS........ Pregnancy Nutrition Surveillance System (SAUS)
PNSS........ Pseudonoise Spread Spectrum (SAUS)
PNST........ Parker and Son Trucking [*Common carrier symbol*]
PNST........ Pilot Network System Test (SAUS)
PNSTDC..... Pakistan National Scientific and Technical Documentation Center (AD)
PNSU........ Pakistan National Shipping [*Intermodal shipping container symbol*] (TVRC)
PNSUS...... Place Name Survey of the U.S. (SAUS)
PNSUS...... Placename Survey of the US (EA)
PNSX........ Pacific Nuclear Systems [*Federal Railroad Administration identification code*]
PNSY........ Portsmouth Naval Shipyard [*New Hampshire*]
PNt.......... Newtown Library Co., Newtown, PA [*Library symbol*] [*Library of Congress*] [*Obsolete*] (LCLS)
pnt.......... Paint (AD)
PNT.......... Paint (MSA)
PNT.......... Paint Template
Pnt.......... Panart [*Record label*] [*Cuba, USA*]
PNT.......... Pantasote, Inc. [*AMEX symbol*] (COMM)
PNT.......... Para-Nitrotoluene [*Organic chemistry*]
PNT.......... Paroxysmal Nodal Tachycardia [*Cardiology*]
PNT.......... Parque Nacional Tijuca [*Tijuca National Park*] [*Brazil*] [*Portuguese*] (AD)
PNT.......... Partial Nodular Transformation (DMAA)
PNT.......... Partido Nacionalista de los Trabajadores [*Argentina*] [*Political party*] (EY)
PNT.......... Parti National du Travail [*Benin*] [*Political party*] (EY)
PNT.......... Parti National du Travail [*Haiti*] [*Political party*] (EY)
PNT.......... Patient (AABC)
PNT.......... Penna Enterprises [*NYSE symbol*] (TTSB)
PNT.......... Penn Enterprises, Inc. [*NYSE symbol*] (SAG)
PNT.......... Pennsylvania Enterprise [*NYSE symbol*]
Pnt.......... Pentagon (AD)
PNT.......... Pentagon
PNT.......... Penticton [*British Columbia*] [*Seismograph station code, US Geological Survey*] (SEIS)
PNT.......... Percutaneous Nephrostomy Tube [*Nephrology*] (DAVI)
PNT.......... Personnelman (Training Assistant) [*U.S. Navy enlisted rating*] (AUER)
PNT.......... Petromet Resources Ltd. [*Toronto Stock Exchange symbol*]
PNT.......... Plasma Nitriding (SAUS)
PNT.......... Point
PNT.......... Pontiac, IL [*Location identifier*] [*FAA*] (FAAL)
PNT.......... Pontiac, MI [*Amtrak rail station code*]
PNT.......... Position-Navigation-Time
PNT.......... Print (SAUS)
PNTA........ Pacific Northwest Trade Association
PNTA........ Pentair, Inc. [*NASDAQ symbol*] (NQ)
Pnt Anx..... Pentagon Annex (AD)
PNtB......... Bucks County Community College, Newtown, PA [*Library symbol*] [*Library of Congress*] (LCLS)
PNTB........ Peninsula Trust Bank [*NASDAQ symbol*] (TTSB)
PNTB........ Peninsula Trust Bank, Inc. [*NASDAQ symbol*] (SAG)
PNTBT....... Partial Nuclear Test Ban Treaty (AD)
PNtC......... Council Rock High School, Newtown, PA [*Library symbol*] [*Library of Congress*] (LCLS)
PNTC........ Panatech Res & Dev [*NASDAQ symbol*] (TTSB)
PNTC........ Panatech Research & Development Corp. [*NASDAQ symbol*] (NQ)
PNTCENS... Patient Census Report
PNTCENS Report... Patient Census Report (SAUS)
pntd.......... Painted (AD)
PNTD........ Painted
PNTD........ Panella Trucking [*Common carrier symbol*]
PNTD........ Personnel Neutron Threshold Detector (IEEE)
PN/TDMA... Pseudo Noise/Time Division Multiple Access (MCD)
PN-TDMA.... Pseudo-Noise-Time Division Multiple Access (SAUS)
PNtE......... Ellis College, Newtown, PA [*Library symbol*] [*Library of Congress*] [*Obsolete*] (LCLS)
PNTE........ Pointe Financial Corp. [*NASDAQ symbol*]
PNTG........ Petromet Resources Ltd. [*NASDAQ symbol*] (NQ)
PNTG........ Printing (ROG)
PNTGF....... Petromet Resources [*NASDAQ symbol*] (TTSB)
PNTGN...... Pentagon (MSA)
PNTI......... Pacific Nuclear Transport Limited (EFIS)
PNTK........ Pentech International [*NASDAQ symbol*] (TTSB)
PNTK........ Pentech International, Inc. [*NASDAQ symbol*] (NQ)
PNTL........ Phonetel Technologies [*NASDAQ symbol*] (TTSB)
PNTL........ Phonetel Technologies, Inc. [*NASDAQ symbol*] (NQ)
PNTO........ Portuguese National Tourist Office (EA)
PNTO........ Principal Naval Transport Officer [*British military*] (DMA)
PNTOS...... Para-Nitrotoluene-ortho-sulfonic Acid [*Organic chemistry*]
pntr.......... Painter (AD)
PNTR........ Painter
PNTR........ Permanent Normal Trade Relations
PNTR........ Pointer (MCD)
PNTRY....... Pantry
PNts......... Newtown Public Library, Newtown Square, PA [*Library symbol*] [*Library of Congress*] (LCLS)
PNTY........ Pantry (ADWA)
PNTYP....... Panno Type (VRA)
PNU.......... Basque Nationalist Party (Spain) [*Political party*] (PSAP)
PNU.......... Panguitch [*Utah*] [*Airport symbol*] (OAG)
PNU.......... Peasants' National Unity [*Afghanistan*] [*Political party*] (EY)
PNU.......... Personennamen der Texte aus Ugarit [*A publication*] (BJA)
PNU.......... Pharmacia & Upjohn [*NYSE symbol*] (TTSB)
PNU.......... Pharmacia & Upjohn, Inc. [*NYSE symbol*] (SAG)
PNU.......... Platinum Communication System [*Vancouver Stock Exchange symbol*]
PNU.......... Pneumatic Scale Corp. [*Stock exchange symbol*] (AD)
PNU.......... Position Navigation Unit (SEWL)
PNU.......... Protein Nitrogen Units [*Clinical chemistry*]
PNU.......... Puma Navigation Update programme (SAUS)
PNUA........ Partito Nazionale Unito Africa [*National Party of United Africans*] [*Somalia*] [*Political party*]
PNUA........ Polish National Union of America (EA)
PNUD........ Programa de las Naciones Unidas para el Desarrollo [*United Nations Development Program - UNDP*] [*Spanish*] (MSC)
PNUMA...... Chilean National Union for the Enviornment (SAUS)
PNUMA...... Programa de las Naciones Unidas para el Medio Ambiente [*United Nations Environmental Programme Regional Office for Latin America*] (EAIO)
PNUT........ Portable Nursing Unit Terminal
PNUT........ Possible Nuclear Underground Test
pnutbutsan... Peanut-Butter Sandwich (AD)
p-nut butter... Peanut-Butter Sandwich (AD)
pnutbutwich... Peanut-Butter Sandwich (AD)
PNUTS...... Possible Nuclear Test Site [*Pronounced "peanuts"*] [*Air Force intelligence*]
PNUTS...... Possible Nuclear Underground Test Site
PNV.......... National Velasquista Party [*Ecuador*] [*Political party*] (PPW)
PNV.......... No Sellout Platform (Guatemala) [*Political party*] (PSAP)
PNV.......... Panavia SA [*ICAO designator*] (FAAC)
PNV.......... Partido Nacionalista Vasco [*Basque Nationalist Party*] [*Spain*] [*Political party*] (PPE)
PNV.......... Partido Nacional Velasquista [*National Velasquista Party*] [*Ecuador*] [*Political party*] (PPW)
PNV.......... Parti National Voltaique [*Voltaic National Party*] [*Political party*]
PNV.......... Patino N. V. [*Toronto Stock Exchange symbol*]
PNV.......... Penicillin Phenoxymethyl [*Medicine*] (EDAA)
PNV.......... Perini Investment Properties, Inc. [*AMEX symbol*] (COMM)
PNV.......... Pilot Night Vision (SEWL)
PNV.......... Platform Ninety (Guatemala) [*Political party*] (PSAP)
PNV.......... Potential Natural Vegetation (GNE)
PNV.......... Prenatal Vitamins (DAVI)
PNV.......... Present Net Value (WPI)
PNVAL....... Previously Not Available [*Army*] (AABC)
PNVC........ National Party of Veterans and Civilians (Dominican Rep.) [*Political party*] (PSAP)
PNVC........ Presort Transportation Services [*Common carrier symbol*]
PNVD........ Passive Night Vision Devices [*Army*] (AABC)
PNVS........ Pilot Night Vision Sensor
PNVS........ Pilot Night Vision System [*Army*] (MCD)
PNVS........ Pilot's Night Vision Sensor
PNVS........ Pilots Night Vision System (SAUS)

PNVTS....... Pyrotechnics No-Voltage Test Set
PNW........ Pacific Northwest
PNW........ Pacific Northwest Forest and Range Experiment Station [*Washington, Oregon, and Alaska*] (ALAC)
PNW........ Pacific Northwest Outport [*MTMC*] (TAG)
PNW........ Personal Netware (SAUS)
PNW........ Personnelman (Chaplain's Assistant) [*U.S. Navy enlisted rating*] (AUER)
PNW........ Pinnacle West Capital [*NYSE symbol*] (TTSB)
PNW........ Pinnacle West Capital Corp. [*NYSE symbol*] (SPSG)
PNW........ Prescott & Northwestern Railroad [*Federal Railroad Administration identification code*]
PNW........ [*The*] Prescott & Northwestern Railroad Co. [*AAR code*]
PNW........ Project Night Watch (SAUS)
PNW........ Protracted Nuclear Warfighting (ACAE)
PNWA....... Pacific Northwest Hardware and Implement Association [*Oregon, Washington, Idaho and Alaska*] (EARSL)
PNWA....... Pacific Northwest Waterways Association (SAUS)
PNWA....... Pacific Northwest Writers Association (EARSL)
PNWA....... Pennsylvania Natural Weather Association [*Emergency Management*] (EMA)
PNW Bulletin... Pacific Northwest Bulletin (SAUS)
PNWC....... Pacific Northwest Writers' Conference
PNwC........ Westminster College, New Wilmington, PA [*Library symbol*] [*Library of Congress*] (LCLS)
PNWCSC.... Pacific Northwest Canadian Studies Consortium [*University of Oregon*]
PNWD/BMI... Pacific Northwest Division/Battelle Memorial Institute (AD)
PNWGFA.... Pacific Northwest Grain and Feed Association (EARSL)
PNWIS-APCA... Pacific Northwest International Section-Air Pollution Control Association (SAUS)
PNWL....... Pacific Northwest Laboratory [*AEC*]
PNWR....... Piedmont National Wildlife Refuge [*Georgia*] (AD)
PNWR....... Portland & Western Railroad [*Federal Railroad Administration identification code*]
PNWR....... Presquile National Wildlife Refuge [*Virginia*] (AD)
PNWR....... Pungo National Wildlife Refuge [*North Carolina*] (AD)
PNWRBC.... Pacific Northwest River Basins Commission [*Water Resources Council*] [*Terminated, 1981*] (NOAA)
PNWU....... Pacific Northwest Equipment [*Intermodal shipping container symbol*] (TVRC)
PNX......... Imperial Airways, Inc. [*ICAO designator*] (FAAC)
pnx......... Pneumothorax [*Medicine*] (AD)
PNX......... Pneumothorax [*Medicine*]
PNX......... Portsmouth Naval Shipyard [*Federal Railroad Administration identification code*]
PNX......... Precincts [*Telegraphy*] (PCTE)
PNX......... Private Network Exchange [*Computer science*] (VLIE)
PNXT........ Pinxit [*He, or She, Painted It*] [*Latin*]
pnxt......... Pinxit [*He or She Painted It*] [*Latin*] (AD)
PNY......... Camp Parks, CA [*Location identifier*] [*FAA*] (FAAL)
PNY......... Penny
PNY......... Piedmont Natl Gas [*NYSE symbol*] (TTSB)
PNY......... Piedmont Natural Gas Co., Inc. [*NYSE symbol*] (SPSG)
PNY......... Pinyin [*Language symbol*] (ETLW)
PNY......... Plattsburgh [*New York*] [*Seismograph station code, US Geological Survey*] (SEIS)
PNY......... Portuguese Navy
PNY......... Principally [*Telegraphy*] (PCTE)
PNYA........ Port of New York Authority [*Later, PANYNJ*]
PNYCTC...... Pennsylvania New York Central Transportation Co. (AD)
PNZ......... Pennzoil Co., Exploration Library, Houston, TX [*OCLC symbol*] (OCLC)
Pnz.......... Penzance (AD)
PNZ......... Petrolina [*Brazil*] [*Airport symbol*] (OAG)
PO.......... Aeropelican Intercity Commuter Air Services [*ICAO designator*] (AD)
PO.......... Dust/Sand Whirls [*Weather codes - aviation*] [*Sand pockets*] (PIPO)
po---........ Oceanica [*MARC geographic area code*] [*Library of Congress*] (LCCP)
PO.......... Office of Policy, Planning and Program Evaluation (SAUS)
PO.......... Officer Personnel Division [*Coast Guard*]
PO.......... Oil City Library, Oil City, PA [*Library symbol*] [*Library of Congress*] (LCLS)
PO.......... Oscillopolarograph
PO.......... Paarieto-Occipital [*Medicine*] (DMAA)
PO.......... Pacific Ocean
PO.......... Pacific Ocean Region [*Communications term*] (DCT)
PO.......... Page Overflow (SAUS)
PO.......... Palomar Capital [*Vancouver Stock Exchange symbol*]
PO.......... Paper Out (SAUS)
PO.......... Parallel Output [*Computer science*] (BUR)
PO.......... Parcels Office (ODA)
P:O.......... Parent Offspring [*Genetics*]
PO.......... Parieto-Occipital [*Anatomy*] (AAMN)
PO.......... Parity Odd
PO.......... Parking Orbit [*NASA*]
PO.......... Parliamentary Officer [*Australia*]
PO.......... Parole Officer
PO.......... Partial Pressure of Oxygen (DAVI)
P/O.......... Part Of (KSC)
p/o.......... Part of (AD)
PO.......... Passport Office [*Department of State*]
PO.......... Patent Office [*Later, PTO*] [*Department of Commerce*]
PO.......... Patents Office (SAUS)
PO.......... Path Operator (SAUS)
PO.......... Patrologia Orientalis [*A publication*] (ODCC)
PO.......... Payment Order (FOTI)
PO.......... Performance Objectives (OICC)
PO.......... Performing Organization (NITA)
PO.......... Period of Onset [*Medicine*]
PO.......... Perioperative [*Medicine*] (DMAA)
PO.......... Permit Office [*British*] (ROG)
PO.......... Peroral (SAUS)
PO.......... Per Orally (SAUS)
PO.......... Per Order (WDMC)
PO.......... Per Os [*By Mouth*] [*Pharmacy*]
po.......... Per Os [*By Mouth*] [*Latin*] (AD)
PO.......... Peroxidase [*Also, POD*] [*An enzyme*]
PO.......... Persistent Object (SAUS)
PO.......... Personnel Office [*Kennedy Space Center Directorate*] (NASA)
PO.......... Personnel Officer
PO.......... Pesticides Office [*Environmental Protection Agency*]
PO.......... Petroleum Officer (SAUS)
PO.......... Petty Officer [*Navy*]
PO.......... Phase Optimization (SAUS)
PO.......... Phase Oscillation (SAUS)
PO.......... Phase-Out
PO.......... Phenoxy (EDCT)
PO.......... Philadelphia Orchestra (SAUS)
PO.......... Philharmonic Orchestra [*Music*]
PO.......... Phone Order [*Therapy term*] (CTAA)
P/O.......... Phone Order [*Medicine*]
P/O.......... Phosphate to Oxygen (BARN)
PO.......... Phymatotrichum omnivorum [*A fungus*]
PO.......... Physical Oceanography (SAUS)
PO.......... Physical Optics (SAUS)
PO.......... Physician Organization (MHCS)
PO.......... Pilot Officer (ODA)
P/O.......... Pitch Over
PO.......... Planetary Office (IAA)
PO.......... Planetary Orbit
PO.......... Planked Oval [*Auto racing*]
PO.......... Planned Obsolescence (MHDB)
PO.......... Planning Objectives (VLIE)
PO.......... Planted on (SAUS)
PO.......... Plotter-Output (SAUS)
PO.......... Plotting Officer (SAUS)
PO.......... Poco [*Somewhat*] [*Music*]
po.......... Poetry (AD)
PO.......... Point (WGA)
PO.......... Polarity (AAG)
po.......... Polarity (AD)
PO.......... Polar-Optical (SAUS)
PO.......... Pole [*Unit of measurement*]
PO.......... Pole Operator (SAUS)
P/O.......... Police Officer (ADWA)
PO.......... Political Officer [*NATO*]
P/O.......... Pollen/Ovule Ratio [*Botany*]
Po.......... Polonium [*Chemical element*]
PO.......... Polskie Zaklady Lotnicze [*Poland*] [*ICAO aircraft manufacturer identifier*] (ICAO)
PO.......... Polymerizable Oligomer (OA)
PO.......... Polymerizable Oligomers (SAUS)
PO.......... Polyolefin [*Organic chemistry*]
PO.......... Polyot (SAUS)
PO.......... Poly Propylene Oxide (EDCT)
Po.......... Polyzoa [*Quality of the bottom*] [*Nautical charts*]
PO.......... Por Orden [*By Order*] [*Spanish*]
PO.......... Portal (DB)
PO.......... Port Flag [*Navy*] [*British*]
PO.......... Portland Oregonian [*A publication*] (AD)
PO.......... Port Officer
po.......... Portugal [*MARC country of publication code*] [*Library of Congress*] (LCCP)
PO.......... Portugal [*NATO*]
Po.......... Portuguese [*Language, etc.*] (DLA)
PO.......... Position Offered
PO.......... Positive Output (SAUS)
Po.......... Possible
PO.......... Postal Officer (DCTA)
PO.......... Postal Order
PO.......... Posterior (MAE)
PO.......... Post Flight Inspection [*Air Force*]
po.......... Post Office (WDMC)
PO.......... Post Office
PO.......... Post Office Department [*Canada*]
p-o.......... Postoperative (AD)
PO.......... Postoperative [*Medicine*]
PO.......... Post Orbit [*NASA*]
PO.......... Postpay Coin Telephone [*Telecommunications*] (TEL)
PO.......... Potato [*Soil biology*] [*Human-introduced crops*] (QSUL)
PO.......... Potential Officer [*British military*] (DMA)
PO.......... Power On (VLIE)
po.......... Power-Operated (AD)
PO.......... Power-Operated
po.......... Power Oscillator (AD)
PO.......... Power Oscillator [*Electronics*]
PO.......... Power Output
PO.......... Pre-Authorization Order

PO .... Precipitator Outlet (SAUS)
PO .... Predominating Organism (AAMN)
PO .... Preoperational (MCD)
PO .... Preoptic [*Area of the brain*]
PO .... Preparation Order (SAUS)
PO .... Presbyteri Oratorii [*Oratorians*] [*Roman Catholic religious order*]
PO .... Presbyterorum Ordinis [*Decree on the Ministry and Life of Priests*] [*Vatican II document*]
P/O .... Preservation by Operation (SAUS)
PO .... Pressure Oscillation (IAA)
PO .... Pressure Oxidation (SAUS)
PO .... Preventive Officer [*British*] (ROG)
po .... Previous Orders (AD)
PO .... Previous Orders [*Military*]
PO .... Previous Owner
PO .... Primary Outlet (SAUS)
PO .... Primary Output (IAA)
PO .... Primitive data holding Object (SAUS)
PO .... Principal Officer [*Foreign Service*]
PO .... Principal Only (EBF)
PO .... Principal Only Strip [*Mortgage security*]
PO .... Principals Only (SAUS)
P/O .... Print Out
PO .... Printout
PO .... Print Output (SAUS)
PO .... Privately Owned (AFM)
PO .... Private Office [*Documents issued by the Secretary General, NATO*] (NATG)
PO .... Privileged Operation (VLIE)
PO .... Probation Officer
PO .... Processing Office [*Bureau of the Census*] (GFGA)
PO .... Procurement Objective (NVT)
PO .... Production Offset (AABC)
PO .... Production Order (KSC)
PO .... Professional Officer
PO .... Professor Ordinarius [*Ordinary Professor*] [*Latin*] (ROG)
PO .... Programmed Operation (SAUS)
PO .... Programmed Oscillator
PO .... Program Objective
PO .... Program Office [*Air Force*] (CET)
PO .... Program Operations (COE)
PO .... Program Originator (AFM)
PO .... Project Office [*or Officer*] [*Military*]
PO .... Project Officer (COE)
PO .... Project ORBIS (EA)
PO .... Project Order [*DoD*]
PO .... Project Overcome (EA)
PO .... Proposals Outstanding
PO .... Proposition One [*Defunct*] (EA)
PO .... Propylene Oxide [*Organic chemistry*]
PO .... Propylene Oxide Homopolymer (SAUS)
PO .... Province of Ontario [*Canada*]
PO .... Provisioning Order (AFM)
PO .... Pseudoadiabatic Operation [*Chemical engineering*]
PO .... Psychological Operation [*Military*] (CINC)
PO .... Public Offering [*Investment term*]
PO .... Public Office [*British*] (ROG)
PO .... Public Officer (SAUS)
PO .... Public Official
PO .... Pull Out (IAA)
PO .... Pulmonary Valve Opening [*Cardiology*]
PO .... Pulsed Carrier without Any Modulation Intended to Carry Information (IEEE)
PO .... Pulse Originating [*Communications term*] (DCT)
PO .... Pulse Oscillator (IAA)
PO .... Pulse Output
PO .... Punching Operation (SAUS)
PO .... Punch Off (SAUS)
PO .... Punch On (VLIE)
PO .... Punch Operator (SAUS)
PO .... Punch Out [*Computer science*] (IAA)
PO .... Punted Over [*Boating*] [*British*] (ROG)
PO .... Purchase Option (SAUS)
PO .... Purchase Order
PO .... Purchasing Office [*DoD*] (AFIT)
PO .... Purchasing Officer (ALAC)
PO .... Pushout (SAUS)
po .... Putout (ADWA)
PO .... Putout [*Baseball*]
P-O .... Pyrenees-Orientales (AD)
PO .... Radio Positioning Mobile Station [*ITU designation*] [*Telecommunications*] (CET)
PO1 .... Petty Officer, First Class [*Navy*]
PO 1/C ...... Petty Office First Class [*Military*] (AD)
pO_2 .... Oxygen Pressure (DAVI)
PO_2 .... Partial Pressure of Oxygen (AAMN)
PO2 .... Petty Officer 2 [*Military*] (POLM)
PO2 .... Petty Officer, Second Class [*Navy*]
PO2 .... Pressure of Oxygen (SAUS)
PO 2/C ...... Petty Office Second Class [*Military*] (AD)
PO3 .... Petty Officer 3 [*Military*] (POLM)
PO3 .... Petty Officer, Third Class [*Navy*]
PO 3/C ...... Petty Office Third Class [*Military*] (AD)
Po5 .... Party of Five [*Television program title*]
PO1/2 .... Petty Officer 1st/2nd Class (SAUS)
POA .... Le Point Air [*France*] [*ICAO designator*] (FAAC)
POA .... Pacific Ocean Area [*World War II*]
POA .... Pahoa, HI [*Location identifier*] [*FAA*] (FAAL)
POA .... Palaeovegetation of the Americas (SAUS)
POA .... Pancreatic Oncofetal Antigen [*Immunochemistry*]
POA .... Panel of Americans [*Defunct*] (EA)
POA .... Parallel Overlap Assembly [*Computer science*]
POA .... Pay-on-Answer [*Telecommunications*] [*British*]
POA .... Pay on Arrival (SAUS)
POA .... Peacetime Operating Assets [*DoD*] (AFIT)
POA .... Petroleum Operating Agreement (CINC)
POA .... Petty Officer Airman [*British military*] (DMA)
POA .... Phalangeal Osteoarthritis [*Medicine*]
POA .... Phenoxyacetic Acid [*Organic chemistry*]
POA .... Pilot Operated Absolute (HAWK)
POA .... Pilot-Operated Absolute [*Automotive engineering*]
POA .... Pilot-Operated Absolute System (SAUS)
poa .... Place of Acceptance (AD)
POA .... Place of Acceptance [*Business term*] (DCTA)
POA .... Plan of Action (NASA)
POA .... Plotting Officers Assistant (SAUS)
POA .... Point Of Action (EECA)
POA .... Point of Aim (SAUS)
POA .... Point of Application [*Medicine*] (MAE)
POA .... Point of Arrival [*Emergency Management*] (EMA)
POA .... Polarized Orbital Approximation (PDAA)
POA .... Police Officers' Association [*British*] (BI)
POA .... Pontifica Opera di Assistenza [*Pontifical Relief Organization*]
POA .... Pony of the Americas
PoA .... Pony of the Americas Club (NTPA)
POA .... Portable Object Adapter (VLIE)
POA .... Portland Opera Association [*Oregon*] (AD)
POA .... Porto Alegre [*Brazil*] [*Airport symbol*] (OAG)
POA .... Port of Arrival
POA .... Position of Advantage (SAUS)
POA .... Post-Oxidation Annealing (ODA)
PoA .... Power of Attorney (AD)
POA .... Power of Attorney
POA .... Power Open Association [*Computer science*] (CDE)
POA .... Preoptic Area [*of the brain*]
POA .... Price on Application [*Business term*] (ADA)
POA .... Primary Optic Afferents
poa .... Primary Optical Area (AD)
POA .... Primary Optic Atrophy
POA .... Prison Officers' Association [*A union*] [*British*] (DCTA)
POA .... Privately Owned Automobile
POA .... Privately-Owned Open Air-Braked [*Railway wagons*] (PDAA)
POA .... Probability of Acceptance (IAA)
POA .... Problem Oriented Assembler [*Computer science*] (VLIE)
POA .... Problem-Oriented Assembler (SAUS)
POA .... Program Office Approvals (COE)
POA .... Program Operations Assistant (SAUS)
POA .... Proof of Accounts
POA .... Property Owners Association (NTPA)
POA .... Provisional Operating Authorization [*for nuclear power plant*]
POA .... Public Order Act
POA .... Purchased on Assembly (KSC)
POA .... Purchase Option Agreement (TIMI)
POA .... Purchase Order Authorization (SAA)
POA .... Purgeable Organic Analyzer
POAA .... Planetary Operations Analysis Area [*NASA*]
POAA .... Post Office Agents' Association [*Australia*]
POAA .... Property Owners Association of America [*Defunct*] (EA)
POA & M ... Plan of Action and Milestones (NVT)
POAC .... Peace Officers Association of California (AD)
POAC .... Pony of the Americas Club (EA)
POAC .... Port and Ocean Engineering Under Arctic Conditions International Committee (EAIO)
POAC .... Post Office Advisory Committee [*British*]
POAC .... Post Office Advisory Council (AD)
POAC .... Post Office Ambulance Centre [*British*] (DI)
POAC .... Probe Origin Authentication Check (VLIE)
PoACCS Ph II.... Portuguese Air Command & Control System Phase II (SAUS)
POACH ...... PC-On-A-Chip (SAUS)
POACH ...... Prednisone, Oncovin [*Vincristine*] Cytosine Arabinoside, Cyclophosphamide, and Adriamycin [*Antineoplastic drug regimen*] (DAVI)
POACMN.... Petty Officer Aircrewman [*British military*] (DMA)
POACS ...... Prior Other Active Commissioned Service [*Military*]
POAD .... Position Administration Display (SAUS)
POADS ...... Portland Air Defense Sector (SAA)
POAE .... Port of Aerial Embarkation [*Air Force*]
POAE .... Principal Officer of Aircraft Equipment [*Ministry of Aircraft Production*] [*British*] [*World War II*]
POAES........ Prior Other Active Enlisted Service [*Military*]
POAF .... Petty Officer Air Fitter [*British military*] (DMA)
POAG .... Peace Officers Association of Georgia (AD)
POAG .... Primary Open Angle Glaucoma (SAUS)
POAG .... Primary Open-Angle Glaucoma [*Ophthalmology*]
POA-HA ...... Preoptic Anterior Hypothalamic Area [*Medicine*] (DMAA)
PO/AH Areas.... Preoptic and Anterior Hypothalamic Areas (SAUS)
POAHEDPEARL.... Pacific Ocean Areas Headquarters Pearl Harbor
POAK .... Port of Oakland [*Federal Railroad Administration identification code*]
POALS........ Petty Officers Advanced Leadership School [*Navy*] (MUGU)

POAM .... Polar Ozone Aerosol Measurement
POAM .... Polar Ozone Aerosol Monitor (SAUS)
POAM .... Polar Ozone and Aerosol Measurements (SAUS)
POAN .... Procurement of Ordnance and Ammunition - Navy
PO & CS .... Post Office and Civil Service Committee [*US Senate*] [*Obsolete*]
POANSW.... Property Owners' Association of New South Wales [*Australia*]
POAQ .... Property Owners' Association of Queensland [*Australia*]
POAR .... Postal Laws and Regulations [*Later, Postal Manual*] (IAA)
POAR .... Problem Objective Approach Response (SAUS)
POAR .... Problem-Objective-Approach-Response [*System of planning patient care*] [*Medicine*]
POAR .... Project Order Action Request [*Navy*] (NG)
POAR .... Project Order Action Required
poas- .... American Samoa [*MARC geographic area code*] [*Library of Congress*] (LCCP)
POAS .... Pankypria Omospondia Anexartiton Syntechnion [*Pancyprian Federation of Independent Trade Unions*] [*Cyprus*]
POAS .... Psychological Operations Automated System (COE)
POASP ...... Plans and Operations Automated Storage Program [*Military*]
POAT .... Psychological Operations Assessment Team (COE)
POATSC ..... Pacific Overseas Air Technical Service Command
POAU .... Protestants and Other Americans for Separation of Church and State (NADA)
POAU .... Protestants and Other Americans United [*for Separation of Church and State*]
POAU .... Protestants and Other Americans United for Separation of Church and State (SAUS)
POB.......... Fayetteville, NC [*Location identifier*] [*FAA*] (FAAL)
POB.......... Paris Opera Ballet
POB.......... Parti Ouvrier Belge [*Belgian Workers' Party*] [*Later, Belgian Socialist Party*] [*Political party*] (PPE)
POB.......... Parts on Change (SAUS)
POB.......... Peanut Oil and Beeswax (SAUS)
POB.......... Penicillin, Oil, Beeswax [*Medicine*]
POB.......... Perfluorooctyl Bromide [*Organic chemistry*]
POB.......... Periphal Order Buffer (SAUS)
POB.......... Peripheral Order Buffer [*Computer science*] (VLIE)
pob .... Persons on Board (AD)
POB.......... Persons on Board [*Aviation*]
POB.......... Phenoxybenzamine [*Later, PBZ*] [*Adrenergic blocking agent*]
pob .... Pilot on Board (AD)
POB.......... Place of Birth
pob .... Poblacion [*Population*] [*Spanish*] (AD)
POB.......... Point of Banking (SAUS)
pob .... Point of Beginning (AD)
POB.......... Point of Beginning
POB.......... Point of Business
POB.......... Polyoxybutylene Glycol (SAUS)
PoB .... Port of Baltimore (AD)
POB.......... Postal Bulletin [*A publication*]
POB.......... Post Office Book (SAUS)
POB.......... Post Office Box
POB.......... Power Outlet Box
pob .... Prevention of Blindness (AD)
POB.......... Prevention of Blindness [*Medicine*] (MAE)
POB.......... Principles of Operation Bulletin (SAUS)
POB.......... Procurement Opportunities Board (SAUS)
POB.......... Public Oversight Board
POB.......... Push-Out Base (IAA)
POB.......... Servicios Aereos Poblanos, SA de CV [*Mexico*] [*FAA designator*] (FAAC)
POB^2... Prepped Out Beyond Belief [*Book title*]
POBA .... Patent Office Board of Appeals (IAA)
POBA .... Persons Overwhelmed By Acronyms (SAUS)
POBA .... Plain Old Balloon Angioplasty [*Cardiology*] [*Facetious*]
PO Bag...... Post Office Bag (ASC)
POBAL...... Powered Balloon [*System*]
POBAL System... Powered Balloon System (SAUS)
POBAS ...... Project Oriented Budgeting and Accounting System (SAUS)
POBATO .... Propellant on Board at Takeoff
POBCOST... Probabilistic Budgeting and Forward Costing (MCD)
POBE .... Profile of Out-of-Body Experiences (STED)
POB-N .... Polyoxybutylene Glycol Nylon-12 (SAUS)
POBN .... (Pyridyloxide)butylnitrone [*Organic chemistry*]
POBN .... Pyridyl Oxide-N-tert-butylnitrone [*Organic chemistry*]
POBO .... Project Office Business Operations
POBOC ...... Payment on Behalf of Crown (SAUS)
pobp- .... British Solomon Islands [*MARC geographic area code*] [*Library of Congress*] (LCCP)
POBP .... Preoperative Bowel Preparation [*Medicine*] (MELL)
POBR .... Poe & Brown [*NASDAQ symbol*] (SAG)
POBR .... Port of Royal Slope Railroad [*Federal Railroad Administration identification code*]
POBR .... Problem-Oriented Basic Research [*National Science Foundation*]
pobra .... Pony and Zebra (AD)
POBS .... Portsmouth Bank Shares [*NASDAQ symbol*] (TTSB)
POBS .... Portsmouth Bank Shares, Inc. [*NASDAQ symbol*] (NQ)
POBSP ...... Pacific Ocean Biological Survey Program [*Smithsonian Institution*] (GFGA)
POBT .... Postoperative Bleeding Time [*Medicine*] (MELL)
POB Technique... Push-out Base Technique (SAUS)
POB Transistor... Push out Base Transistor (SAUS)
POBU .... Pan-Ocean Shipping [*Intermodal shipping container symbol*] (TVRC)
POBU .... Pan Ocean Shipping Company [*Common carrier symbol*]
POBY .... Prior Operating Budget Year [*Military*] (AFIT)
POC.......... Clarion State College, Oil City, PA [*Library symbol*] [*Library of Congress*] (LCLS)
POC.......... Joint Opposition Party (Eq. Guinea) [*Political party*] (PSAP)
POC.......... La Pocatiere [*Quebec*] [*Seismograph station code, US Geological Survey*] (SEIS)
POC.......... La Verne, CA [*Location identifier*] [*FAA*] (FAAL)
Po/C.......... Ocular Pressure (STED)
POC.......... Packaged Optimization Control [*Engineering*]
POC.......... Panel of Counselors (SAUS)
POC.......... Parallel Optical Computer
POC.......... Paralympic Organizing Committee (SAUS)
POC.......... Para-Ovarian Cyst [*Medicine*] (MELL)
POC.......... Parent-Offspring Conflict
POC.......... Particulate Organic Carbon
POC.......... Particulate Organic Concentration [*Environmental science*]
POC.......... Particulate Organic Matter
POC.......... Parti d'Opposition Congolais [*Congolese Opposition Party*] [*Political party*]
POC.......... Patch Output Converter (IAA)
Poc .... Payload Operations Center [*NASA*] (NAKS)
POC.......... Payload Operations Center [*NASA*] (NASA)
POC.......... Peace Observation Commission [*United Nations*] (FOTI)
POC.......... Peeping Other Chatters (SAUS)
POC.......... Performance Operating Characteristic (DIPS)
POC.......... Performance Optimization Code
POC.......... Personnel Operations Center
POC.......... Peugeot Owners' Club (EA)
POC.......... Physical Oceanography Committee (SAUS)
POC.......... Physical Organic Chemistry (SAUS)
POC.......... Physics of Control (IAA)
POC.......... Pick Off, Circuit
POC.......... Pick-off Circuit (SAUS)
POC.......... Picosecond Optical Calorimetry (SAUS)
POC.......... Pittsburgh Opera Co. (AD)
POC.......... Planning Objective Coordinator
POC.......... Platoon Operations Center [*Army*]
POC.......... Plymouth Owners Club (EA)
POC.......... Pocatello, ID [*Amtrak Busline code*]
POC.......... Pocono Airlines, Inc. [*ICAO designator*] (FAAC)
POC.......... Poco Petroleums Ltd. [*Toronto Stock Exchange symbol*]
POC.......... Poculum [*Cup*] [*Pharmacy*]
POC.......... Point of Care [*Medicine*]
POC.......... Point of Compliance (FFDE)
POC.......... Point of Contact (AABC)
poc.......... Point of Contact (AD)
POC.......... Policy Oversight Committee [*Library Science*] (TELE)
POC.......... Porsche Owners Club (EA)
POc .... Porte-Oceane [*Record label*] [*France*]
POC.......... Port of Call
POC.......... Post Office Corps [*British military*] (DMA)
POC.......... Post Office Counters Ltd. [*British*]
POC.......... Post of the Corps
POC.......... Postoperative Care [*Medicine*]
POC.......... Postoperative Complication [*Medicine*] (MELL)
POC.......... Post Oral Ciliary (SAUS)
POC.......... Postoral Ciliary [*Gland*]
POC.......... Potential Officer Cadet (WDAA)
POC.......... Potential Operated Channel (DB)
POC.......... Power and Clear (SAUS)
POC.......... Power Control
POC.......... Power on Clear (MHDI)
POC.......... Power Oscillator (VLIE)
POC.......... Precision Oscillator Crystal
POC.......... Preliminary Operational Capability [*Military*] (AFIT)
POC.......... Preservation of Capital [*Investment term*]
POC.......... Price of Conformance
poc.......... Principal Operating Component (AD)
POC.......... Principal Operating Component
POC.......... Prisoner of Chat (SAUS)
POC.......... Prisoners of Conscience [*File of persons imprisoned for political or religious beliefs kept by Amnesty International*]
POC.......... Prison Officer's Club (AD)
poc.......... Privately Owned Conveyance (AD)
POC.......... Privately Owned Conveyance [*Army*]
POC.......... Probability of Chance (MELL)
POC.......... Procarbazine, Oncovin [*Vincristine*], CCNU [*Lomustine*] [*Antineoplastic drug regimen*]
POC.......... Proceeding on Course [*Aviation*] (FAAC)
POC.......... Proceed on Course (SAUS)
POC.......... Process Operator Console
POC.......... Processor Outage Control (SAUS)
POC.......... Procurement Outlook Conference (SAUS)
POC.......... Productional Operational Capability
POC.......... Production Office Coordinator (WDMC)
POC.......... Production Operational Capability
POC.......... Production Operations Control (TIMI)
POC.......... Production Order Change (KSC)
POC.......... Product of Combustion (SAUS)
POC.......... Products of Combustion (DICI)
POC.......... Products of Conception [*Medicine*] (MEDA)
POC.......... Professional Officer Course [*AFROTC*] (AFM)

POC Program of Cooperation (SAUS)
POC Program Office Contacts (COE)
POC Program-Operator Communication [*Computer science*] (DCDG)
POC Programs of Cooperation (MCD)
POC Programs Overlay Card [*Automotive engineering*]
POC Proof of Concept [*Army*]
POC Proof of Concept [*Automotive engineering*]
POC Proopiocortin [*Biochemistry*]
POc Proto-Oceanic [*Linguistics*] (IEL)
POC Public Officials Conference [*Emergency Management*] (EMA)
POC Public Oil Co. (AD)
Poc Purchase Order Closeout (NAKS)
POC Purchase Order Closeout (NASA)
POC Purchase Order Contract
POC Purgeable Organic Carbon [*Chemistry*]
POCA Association of Psychiatric Outpatient Centers of America [*Psychiatric Out patient Centers of America*] [*Acronym is based on former name.*] (EA)
POCA Pantera Owners Club of America [*Association*] (EA)
POCA Pediatric Perioperative Cardiac Arrest (SAUS)
POCA Petty Officer Caterer [*British military*] (DMA)
POCA Point of Closet Approach (ACAE)
POCA Port of Catoosa Terminal Railroad [*Federal Railroad Administration identification code*]
POCA Post Office Clerks' Association [*A union*] [*Northern Ireland*]
POCA Prednisone, Oncovin [*Vincristine*], Cytarabine, Adriamycin [*Antineoplastic drug regimen*]
POCA Progress Observation and Corrective Action (SAUS)
POCA Public Offender Counselors Association [*Later, IAAOC*] (EA)
POCAL Pre-Operational Common Age List
PO Cas Perry's Oriental Cases [*Bombay*] [*A publication*] (DLA)
POCASEA Protection of Children Against Sexual Exploitation Act of 1977
POCB Plain Ol' Country Boy
POCC Payload Operations Control Center [*NASA*] (NASA)
POCC Penn Octane [*NASDAQ symbol*] (TTSB)
POCC Penn Octane Corp. [*NASDAQ symbol*] (SAG)
POCC Platform Operations Control Center (SAUS)
POCC Procarbazine, Oncovin [*Vincristine*], Cyclophosphamide, CCNU [*Lomustine*] [*Antineoplastic drug regimen*]
POCC Program Operation Control Center [*Space science*]
POC Cost Percentage of Construction Cost (SAUS)
Poc Costs Pocock on Costs [*1881*] [*A publication*] (DLA)
POCE Pantone Open Color Environment [*Joint venture between Pantone, Inc. and LightSource Computer Images*] [*Computer science*] (PCM)
POCE Proof-of-Concept Experiment [*Solar thermal conversion*]
POCEL Petty Officer Control Electrician [*British military*] (DMA)
POC-ET Proof of Concept Experimental Testbed (SAUS)
POCET Proof-of-Concept Experiment Testbed [*Solar thermal conversion*] (MCD)
POC Gland Post Oral Ciliary Gland (SAUS)
POCH Progressiven Organisationen der Schweiz [*Progressive Organizations of Switzerland*] [*Political party*] (PPE)
PochFdl Pocahontas Federal Savings & Loan Association [*Associated Press*] (SAG)
poci- Caroline Islands [*MARC geographic area code*] [*Library of Congress*] (LCCP)
POCI Pontiac-Oakland Club International (EA)
POCI Ports of Call, Inc. [*NASDAQ symbol*] (COMM)
POCI Precision Optics Corp. [*NASDAQ symbol*] (SAG)
POCI Precision Optics Mass [*NASDAQ symbol*] (TTSB)
POCIBO Polar Circling Balloon Observatory
POCIL Pocillum [*Little Cup*] [*Pharmacy*] (ROG)
Pocill Pocillum [*Little Cup*] [*Pharmacy*]
POCK Petty Officer Cook [*British military*] (DMA)
pock Pocket (AD)
Pocket Bks Pocket Books (AD)
POCL P and O Ned-Lloyd Container Lines [*Common carrier symbol*]
POCL Power on Clear [*Navy Navigation Satellite System*] (DNAB)
POCL Project Office Change Letter
POCM Parallel Ocean-Climate Model (SAUS)
POCM Partido Obrero y Campesino de Mexico [*Mexico*] [*Political party*]
POCM Postal Contracting Manual [*Postal Service*]
POCN Purchase Order Change Notice
POCN Purchase Order Change Number
POCO European Political Cooperation [*EC*] (ECED)
POCO Physiology of Chimpanzees in Orbit [*NASA*]
Poco Politically Correct
POCO Position Computer (IAA)
POCO Power On - Clock On [*Aerospace*]
POCO Power on, Clock on (SAUS)
POCO Proposed Operational Capability Objective (SAUS)
POCO Purchase Order Change Order (AAG)
POCO Purchase Order Close out (SAUS)
POCO Purchase Order Closeout (AAG)
POCOA Post Office Controlling Officers' Association [*A union*] [*British*]
POCOM Pocomoke City, MD [*American Association of Railroads railroad junction routing code*]
pocp- Canton and Enderbury Islands [*MARC geographic area code*] [*Library of Congress*] (LCCP)
POC/POT Proof of Concept/Proof of Technology (ACAE)
POCR Processor Oriented Character Recognition (SAUS)
POCR Program Objectives Change Request [*DoD*]
POCR Purchase Order Change Request (TIMI)
POCS Passive Ocean Colour Subsystem (SAUS)
POCS Patent Office [*later, PTO*] Classification System
POCS Process Operator Console Support (SAUS)
POCS Proper Oriented Cut-Set (SAUS)
POCSAG Post Office Code Standard Advisory Group (SAUS)
POCSAG Post Office Code Standardization Advisory Group (SAUS)
POCSAG Post Office Standardisation Advisory Group (SAUS)
POCSC Penn-Ohio Collegiate Swimming Conference (PSS)
POCT Periodically Oscillating Crystal Temperature (SAUS)
Po Ct Police Court (DLA)
POCTA Prevention of Cruelty to Animals Society Member (DSUE)
POCU P and O Containers [*Intermodal shipping container symbol*] (TVRC)
POCUL Poculum [*Cup*] [*Pharmacy*] (ROG)
POCV Proof of Concept Vehicle [*Automotive engineering*]
pocw- Cook Island [*MARC geographic area code*] [*Library of Congress*] (LCCP)
POCW Park Operations and Capital Works (SAUS)
POCY Postoperative Chronologic Year (STED)
POCZ Potash Corporation [*Federal Railroad Administration identification code*]
POD Pacific Ocean Division [*Army Corps of Engineers*]
pod Paid on Delivery (AD)
POD Paper on Demand (SAUS)
POD Parent Organization Designator (MCD)
POD Parents of Diabetics
pod Payable on Death (AD)
POD Payable on Death [*Band*]
POD Payable on Death [*Insurance*]
POD Payload Operations Director (SAUS)
POD Payload Operations Division [*NASA*] (MCD)
POD Payment on Death (SAUS)
POD Payment on Delivery (SAUS)
POD Pay on Delivery [*Shipping*]
POD Pentoxydase (SAUS)
POD Period of Disability [*Social Security Administration*] (DHP)
POD Permissible Operating Distance [*Army*] (AFIT)
POD Peroxidase [*Also, PO*] [*An enzyme*]
POD Personal Orientation Dimensions [*Personality development test*] [*Psychology*]
POD Piece of Data [*Computer science*] (NHD)
POD Pin-on-Disk (SAUS)
POD Place of Death (MAE)
POD Place of Debarkation (SAUS)
POD Place of Delivery [*Shipping*] (DS)
POD Place of Discharge
POD Place of Disembarkation (SAUS)
POD Plain Old Document (SAUS)
POD Plain Old Documentation (SAUS)
POD Plain Old Dos (SAUS)
POD Planet of Death (SAUS)
POD Planning and Organization Development (SAUS)
POD Plan of the Day
POD Pneumatically Operated Disconnect (KSC)
POD Pocket Oxford Dictionary [*A publication*]
POD Podbielniak Analysis (SAUS)
POD Podiatry (DAVI)
POD Podkamennaya [*Former USSR*] [*Geomagnetic observatory code*]
POD Podor [*Senegal*] [*Airport symbol*] (OAG)
POD Point of Delivery [*Electric utility company*]
POD Point of Departure
POD Point of Discharge (GFGA)
POD Point of Distribution (SAUS)
POD Point of Origin Device (SAUS)
pod Point-of-Origin Device (AD)
POD Point-of-Origin Device (IEEE)
POD Points of Domination [*Military*]
POD Polycystic Ovarian Disease [*Medicine*]
pod Port of Debarkation (AD)
POD Port of Debarkation [*Military*]
POD Port of Delivery [*Shipping*]
pod Port of Departure (AD)
POD Port of Destination [*MARAD*] (TAG)
POD Port of Discharge [*Navy*]
POD Port of Disembarkation (SAUS)
POD Postobstructive Diuresis [*Medicine*] (MELL)
POD Post of Duty
POD Post Office Department [*Later, United States Postal Service*]
POD Post-Office Department [*Telegraphy*] (PCTE)
POD Post Office Directory
POD Postoperative Day [*Medicine*]
POD Potential Ozone Depleter
POD Pounds-Out-the-Door [*Measure of industrial production*]
POD Power of Deduction (SAUS)
POD Power on Diagnostics (SAUS)
POD Precise Orbit Determination (SAUS)
POD Precision Orbit Determination (MCD)
POD Precision Orbit Determination Experiment (SAUS)
POD Preflight Operation Division [*NASA*]
POD Preflight Operations Division (SAUS)
POD Preliminary Orbit Determination [*Space launch term*] (ISAK)
POD Price on Delivery (EBF)
POD Printing on Demand (SAUS)
POD Print on Demand (SAUS)
POD Private Orientation Device (ACAE)
POD Probability of Damage (ACAE)

POD......... Probability of Detect (SAUS)
pod .... Probability of Detection (AD)
POD......... Probability of Detection (USDC)
POD......... Probability of Detention (SAUS)
pod .... Process-Oriented Design (AD)
POD......... Products Operations Division (ACAE)
POD......... Professional and Organizational Development [*In association name Professional and Organizational Development Network in Higher Education*] (EA)
POD......... Programmable Option Devices (SAUS)
POD......... Programmed Operational Date (AFIT)
POD......... Program Objectives Document (AAGC)
POD......... Program Office Directive
POD......... Program Operation Description
POD......... Project Operations Director (BARN)
POD......... Project Organization Demographic (SAUS)
POD......... Proof of Debt [*Business term*] (DCTA)
POD......... Proof of Delivery [*Shipping*] (DS)
POD......... Proof of Deposit [*Banking*]
POD......... Proof of Design (MCD)
POD......... Proposed Operational Dates (SAUS)
POD......... Prosthetics and Orthotics Database [*University of Strathclyde*] [*Glasgow, Scotland*] [*Information service or system*] (IID)
POD......... Protective Oceanic Device
POD......... Proton Omnidirectional Detector (USDC)
POD......... Proximity Optical Device (NASA)
POD......... Publishing On Demand (SAUS)
POD......... Pulse Omission Detector (MCD)
POD......... Purchase Order Deviation (KSC)
PO'd......... Put Out [*i.e., angry*] [*Bowdlerized version*]
PODA........ Piloting of Office Documentation Architecture (NITA)
PODA........ Piloting of Orientated Demand Assignment (SAUS)
PODA........ Priority Oriented Demand Assignment [*Computer science*] [*Telecommunications*]
PODA........ Priority-Oriented Demand Assignment (SAUS)
PODAF ...... Post Operation Data Analysis Facility
PODAF ...... Power Density, Assigned Frequency Band (SAUS)
PODAF ...... Power Density Exceeding a Specified Level over an Area with an Assigned Frequency Band (IEEE)
PoDAG ...... Polar DAAC [*Distributed Active Archive Center*] Advisory Group [*Marine science*] (OSRA)
PODAPS..... Portable Data Processing System
PODAS ...... Portable Data Acquisition System
PODBCA..... Post Office Department Board of Contract Appeals (AFIT)
PODCC ...... Plan, Organize, Direct, Coordinate, Control [*Principles of management*]
POD/CL...... Probability of Detection/Confidence Level (SAUS)
Pod D .... Doctor of Podiatry
PODD........ Payment on Due Date (FOTI)
PODE........ Pacific Ocean Division Engineers (CINC)
PODEM...... Path Oriented Decision Making (SAUS)
podex........ Photographic Exercise (AD)
PODF........ Post of Duty File
PODI......... Print On Demand Initiative (SAUS)
podia........ Podiatrist (AD)
PODIA........ Podiatry (SAUS)
PODIM ...... Poseidon Design Information Memo [*Missiles*]
PODM .... Preliminary Orbit Determination Method [*Computer*] [*NASA*]
PODM Computer... Preliminary Orbit Determination Method Computer (SAUS)
POD Mods... Power on Demand Modules (SAUS)
POD Network... Professional and Organizational Development Network in Higher Education (NTPA)
PODO........ Profit on Day One [*Classification for new newspaper*]
PODR........ Pixel Order (SAUS)
PODRS ...... Patent Office [*later, PTO*] Data Retrieval System [*Department of Commerce*]
PODS........ Parents of Children with Down Syndrome [*An association*] (EA)
PODS........ Parents of Down's Syndrome (EA)
PODS........ Perceptions of Developmental Skills Profile [*Education*] (EDAC)
PODS........ Pilot Ocean Data System (MCD)
PODS........ Portable Data Store [*Computer science*] (PDAA)
PODS........ Portable Digitiser Subsystem (SAUS)
PODS........ Post Operative Destruct System (SAUS)
PODS........ Postoperative Destruct System (MCD)
PODS........ Precise Orbit Determination System (SAUS)
PODSC ...... Parents of Down's Syndrome Children (EA)
PODUC ...... Provided [*Following Named*] Officers Have Not Departed Your Command [*Amend Assignment Instructions as Indicated*] [*Army*] (AABC)
PODx .... Postoperative Diagnosis [*Medicine*]
PODx .... Preoperative Diagnosis [*Medicine*]
PODZ........ Port of Pend D'Oreille [*Federal Railroad Administration identification code*]
POE......... Fort Polk [*Louisiana*] [*Airport symbol*] (OAG)
POE......... Fort Polk, LA [*Location identifier*] [*FAA*] (FAAL)
POE......... Pacific Orient Express (WDAA)
POE......... Panel on the Environment [*of President's Science Advisory Committee*]
POE......... Payment Option Election (MCD)
POE......... Peace on Earth [*Australia*] [*Political party*]
POE......... Pediatric Orthopedic Examination (MELL)
POE......... People of the Earth [*Also, RAN*] (EA)
POE......... Petroleum Operations Engineer (SAUS)
POE......... Pilot Operational Equipment (MCD)
POE......... Place of Embarkation (SAUS)
POE......... Plank-on-Edge
POE......... Pneumatically Operated Equipment (AAG)
POE......... Point of Embarkation
POE......... Point of Entry [*Accounts*]
POE......... Point of Exposure [*Environmental Protection Agency*] (ERG)
POE......... Point of Objective Equality [*Psychology*] (QSUL)
POE......... Points of Entry (SAUS)
POE......... Polyexethylene (SAUS)
POE......... Polyolefin Elastomers [*Plastics*]
poe .... Polyoxyethylene (AD)
POE......... Polyoxyethylene [*Organic chemistry*]
POE......... Port of Embarkation (DFIT)
POE......... Port of Entry [*Shipping*]
POE......... Post-Occupancy Evaluation
POE......... Post-Operations Evaluation (MCD)
POE......... Postoperative Endophthalmitis [*Ophthalmology*]
POE......... Postoperative Exercise [*Medicine*] (DAVI)
POE......... Power Open Environment [*Computer science*]
POE......... Power Over Ethernet
POE......... Predicted Operational Environment [*Military*] (CAAL)
POE......... Pretesting Orientation Exercises [*US Employment Service*] [*Department of Labor*]
POE......... Primary Organization Element (NOAA)
POE......... Print Out Effect
POE......... Program Office Estimate (SAUS)
POE......... Projected Operational Environment (NVT)
POE......... Proof of Eligibility [*Medicine*] (DMAA)
POE......... Property Owning Expenses (SAUS)
POE......... Pull-Over Enrichment [*Automotive engineering*]
POE......... Pulsar Energy/Resources [*Vancouver Stock Exchange symbol*]
POE......... Pulse Oriented Electrophoresis [*Analytical biochemistry*]
poea-........ Easter Island [*MARC geographic area code*] [*Library of Congress*] (LCCP)
POEA .... Philippines Overseas Employment Administration (PDAA)
POEA .... Poe & Associates (EFIS)
POEA .... Protection of Offshore Energy Assets [*Navy*] (NVT)
P/OEA3...... Probationary Ordnance Electrical Artificer 3rd Class [*British military*] (DMA)
POEAS....... Planetary Orbiter Error Analysis Study Program
POE Buoy... Plank on Edge Buoy (SAUS)
poe buoy.... Plank-on-Edge Buoy (AD)
PoeBwn..... Poe & Brown [*Commercial firm*] [*Associated Press*] (SAG)
poecrit ...... Poetry Criticism (AD)
POED .... Post Office Engineering Department (IAA)
POED .... Program Organization for Evaluation and Decision
POED .... Provincial Officer of Establishment Division (SAUS)
PO'ed........ Put Out [*i.e., angry*] [*Bowdlerized version*]
POEE .... Post Office Electrical Engineer (IAA)
POEE .... Powertrain Operations Engine Engineering [*Automotive engineering*]
POEEJ....... Post Office Electrical Engineers Journal (SAUS)
POEER....... Pacific Oceanographic Equipment Evaluation Range (NOAA)
POEF .... Post Office Engineering Federation [*A union*] [*British*]
POEIT........ Provisional Organization for European Inland Transportation [*World War II*]
POEL(A)..... Petty Officer Electrician (Air) [*British military*] (DMA)
POEL(AW) .. Petty Officer Electrician (Air Weapon) [*British military*] (DMA)
POEM........ Physical Oceanography of the Eastern Mediterranean (SAUS)
POEM........ Polar-Orbit Earth Observation Mission (SAUS)
POEM........ Polar Orbiting Earth Mission (SAUS)
POEM........ Polar-Orbiting Earth Mission [*European Space Agency*] (EOSA)
POEM........ Polar Orbiting Earth Monitoring (SAUS)
POEM........ Polar Orbiting Earth-Observation Mission (SAUS)
POEM........ Portable Object-oriented Entity Manager (SAUS)
POEM........ Procedure for Optimizing Elastomeric Mountings (SAUS)
POEMs ...... Patient Oriented Evidence that Matters (SAUS)
POEMS...... Plasma Cell Dyscracia with Polyneuropathy, Organomegaly, Endocrinopathy, Monoclonal Protein [*M-protein*], Skin changes [*Medicine*] (DAVI)
POEMS...... Platinum Open Enterprise Management System (SAUS)
POEMS...... Polyneuropathy Associated with Organomegaly Endocrine Disorders, Myeloma, and Skin Modifications
POEMS...... Polyoxyethylene Monostearate [*Organic chemistry*]
POEMS...... Positron Electron Magnetic Spectrometer (EOSA)
POEMS...... Postoperative Expert Medical System (IDAI)
POEN........ Potter Enterprises [*Common carrier symbol*]
PO Engine... Port Outer Engine (SAUS)
POENIT...... Poenitentia [*Penance*] [*Latin*] (ADA)
POEOP ...... Polyoxyethylene Oxypropylene (SAUS)
POEOP ...... Polyoxyethyleneoxypropylene [*Organic chemistry*]
POEP .... Portland Express [*Common carrier symbol*]
POEP .... Primary Operand Execution Pipeline (SAUS)
Poe Pl....... Poe on Pleading and Practice [*A publication*] (DLA)
POERS ...... Post Office Engineering Research Station (SAUS)
POEs......... Party-Owned Enterprises (Taiwan) [*Political party*] (PSAP)
POES .... Polar Operational Environmental Satellite (USDC)
POES .... Polar Orbiting Environmental Satellite
POES .... Polar-Orbiting Operational Environmental Satellite (USDC)
POESID...... Position of Earth Satellite in Digital Display (MCD)
POE STEARATE... Polyoxyethylene Stearate (SAUS)
Poet .... De Poetis [*of Suetonius*] [*Classical studies*] (OCD)
POET .... Pabellon de Operadores Europeos de Telecomunicaciones (EFIS)
POET .... Partially Overlapped Echo Cancelled Transmission (SAUS)
POET .... Passenger Operated Enquiry Terminal [*Indian Railway*] (TIR)
POET .... Persistent Objects and Extended Database Technology (SAUS)

POET .... Petty Officer Enroute Training [*Navy*] (NVT)
Poet .... Poetica [*of Aristotle*] [*Classical studies*] (OCD)
poet.......... Poetical (AD)
Poet .... Poetry [*A publication*] (BRI)
POET .... Portable Optic-Electronic Tracker (PDAA)
POET .... Portable Orders Entry Terminal (IAA)
POET .... Primed Oscillator Expendable Transponder [*Military*] (CAAL)
POET .... Psychological Operations Exploitation Team [*Vietnam*]
POET .... Pulse Oximeter/End Tidal [*Carbon Dioxide*] [*Medicine*] (DAVI)
Poetics T ... Poetics Today [*A publication*] (BRI)
Poet Mel Gr... Poetae Melici Graeci [*A publication*] (OCD)
POETRI...... Programme on Exchange and Transfer of Information on Community Water Supply and Sanitation [*International Reference Center for Community Water Supply and Sanitation*] [*Information service or system*] (IID)
POETRI...... Program on Exchange and Transfer of Information (SAUS)
Poet Rom Vet... Poetarum Romanorum Veterum Reliquiae [*A publication*] (OCD)
POETS....... Phooey on Everything, Tomorrow's Saturday [*Bowdlerized version*]
POETS....... Product Operations Estimating Techniques System (ACAE)
POETS....... Push Off Early, Tomorrow's Saturday [*Bowdlerized version*]
POEU .... Post Office Engineering Union [*British*]
POEU .... Post Office Engineers Union (SAUS)
POEW .... Protracted Offensive Electronic Warfare [*Military*] (SEWL)
POF.......... American Jurisprudence Proof of Facts [*A publication*]
POF.......... Pakistan Ordnance Factories (SAUS)
POF.......... Parts Order Form
POF.......... Philharmonic Orchestra of Florida (AD)
POF.......... Physician's Order Form (MELL)
PoF .... Physics of Failure [*Program*]
POF.......... Pillar of Fire Church (IIA)
POF.......... Pinhole Occulter Facility (SSD)
POF.......... Planned Outage Factor [*Electronics*] (IEEE)
POF.......... Plastic Optical Fiber [*Automotive electronics*]
POF.......... Plastic Optical Fiber [*Communications*]
pof.......... Please Omit Flowers (AD)
POF.......... Point of Failure (SAUS)
POF.......... Point-of-Failure [*Computer science*] (IBMDP)
POF.......... Police Officer, Female
POF.......... Polymer Optical Fiber [*Telecommunications*]
POF.......... Poplar Bluff [*Missouri*] [*Airport symbol*] (OAG)
POF.......... Poplar Bluff, MO [*Location identifier*] [*FAA*] (FAAL)
POF.......... Positive Opening Fin (MCD)
POF.......... Postovulatory Follicle [*Endocrinology*]
POF.......... Powder on Foil (SAUS)
POF.......... Premature Ovarian Failure [*Medicine*]
POF.......... Primary Ovarian Failure [*Gynecology*] (DMAA)
POF.......... Priority of Fire [*Military*] (INF)
POF.......... Privately Owned Firearm (MCD)
POF.......... Professional Opticians of Florida (EARSL)
POF.......... Programmed Operator Facility [*Computer science*] (ELAL)
POF.......... Prolific Resources [*Vancouver Stock Exchange symbol*]
POF.......... Prosthetics Outreach Foundation [*Association*] (EA)
POF.......... Pulsed Optical Feedback (SAUS)
POF.......... Pyruvate Oxidation Factor [*Biochemistry*]
P of A .... Point of Assembly (SAUS)
P of A .... Pott of Anchorage (SAUS)
POFA .... Programmed Operational and Functional Appraisals (SAUS)
POFA .... Programmed Operational Functional Appraisal [*Navy*]
POFA/IPOFA... Programmed Operational Functional Appraisal/Integrated Programmed Operational Functional Appraisal (SAUS)
PofB .... Ponies of Britain [*An association*] (DBA)
P of D .... Point of Debarkation (SAUS)
P of E .... Portal of Entry [*Bacteriology*]
P of E .... Port of Embarkation [*Military*]
PofE .... Port of Entry [*Immigration*] (DAVI)
POFF .... Peripheral Online Oriented Function (SAUS)
POFF Computer... Peripheral Online Oriented Function Computer (SAUS)
P of GP ..... Pearl of Great Price (SAUS)
P of H .... Patron of Husbandry
POFI .... Pacific Ocean Fisheries Investigations (SAUS)
POFI .... Pacific Oceanic Fisheries Investigations (NOAA)
POFI .... Pacific Oceanographic Fisheries Investigation (SAUS)
pofj- .... Fiji [*MARC geographic area code*] [*Library of Congress*] (LCCP)
P of L .... Port of London (ROG)
P of O .... Point of Origin (SAUS)
POFOOGUSA... Protection of Foreign Officials and Official Guests of the United States Act
pofp.......... French Polynesia [*MARC geographic area code*] [*Library of Congress*] (LCCP)
POFU .... Containerlink [*Intermodal shipping container symbol*] (TVRC)
PO-FY .... Program Objectives for Fiscal Year (DNAB)
POG.......... Pacific Oceanographic Group [*British Columbia*] (AD)
POG.......... Parents of Gays (EA)
POG.......... Passion Fruit, Orange, and Guava Juice (ODA)
POG.......... Patina Oil & Gas [*NYSE symbol*] (TTSB)
POG.......... Pediatric Oncology Group
POG.......... Petty Officer's Guide [*A publication*] [*Navy*]
POG.......... Piping Instrumentation and Operating Gallery [*Nuclear energy*] (NRCH)
POG.......... Plant Operating Guide (DNAB)
Pog .... Pogonion (DMAA)
POG.......... Polyexethylene Glycol (SAUS)
POG.......... Polymyositis Ossificans Generalisata (DB)
POG.......... Polyoxethylene Glycol (SAUS)
POG.......... Portage, WI [*Amtrak rail station code*]
POG.......... Port Gentil [*Gabon*] [*Airport symbol*] (OAG)
POG.......... Position of Germany [*British*] [*World War II*]
POG.......... Postage [*Telegraphy*] (PCTE)
POG.......... Post Office Guide [*Book of regulations*] [*British*]
POG.......... Project Officer's Group
POG.......... Propulsion Operating Guide (DNAB)
POG.......... Provisional Ordnance Group [*Military*]
POG.......... Psychological Operations Group (DOMA)
POG.WS .... Patina Oil & Gas Wrrt [*NYSE symbol*] (TTSB)
POGASIS ... Planetary Observation Geometry and Science Instrument Sequence Program [*Aerospace*]
POGaz....... Post Office Gazette [*British*] [*A publication*] (DCTA)
POGE........ Planning Operational Gaming Experiment [*Game*]
pogg-........ Galapagos Islands [*MARC geographic area code*] [*Library of Congress*] (LCCP)
POGG........ Peace, Order and Good Government (FOTI)
pogn-........ Gilbert and Ellice Islands [*Tuvalu*] [*MARC geographic area code*] [*Library of Congress*] (LCCP)
POGO........ Pennzoil Offshore Gas Operators (AD)
POGO........ Personal Objectives and Goals (MCD)
Pogo......... Pogonomyrinex Occidentalis [*A genus of ants*]
POGO........ Pogo Suppression System [*NASA*]
POGO........ Polar Orbit Geophysical Observatory (SAUS)
POGO........ Polar Orbiting Geophysical Observatories [*Marine science*] (OSRA)
POGO........ Polar Orbiting Geophysical Observatory [*NASA*]
POGO........ Polar Orbiting Geophysical Obsevvatories (or Observatory) (SAUS)
POGO........ Pop Your Seat Belt, Open the Window, Get Out [*Automobile safety*]
POGO........ Pre-Oxidation Gettering of the Other Side (PDAA)
POGO........ Prime's Online Graduate Opportunities (NITA)
POGO........ Privately Owned/Government Operated (GFGA)
POGO........ Privately-Owned/Government-Operated (SAUS)
POGO........ Problem-Oriented Graphics Operation (SAUS)
POGO........ Programmer-Oriented Graphics Operation (IEEE)
POGO........ Program Optimizer (IAA)
POGO........ Project on Government Oversight (EA)
PogoPd...... Pogo Producing Co. [*Associated Press*] (SAG)
POGPr....... Patina Oil & Gas 7.125% Pfd [*NYSE symbol*] (TTSB)
POGR........ Poplar Grove National Cemetery
POGS........ National Association of Post Office and General Service Maintenance Employees [*Later, APWU*] [*AFL-CIO*]
POGS........ Polar Orbiting Geomagnetic Satellite (SAUS)
POGSI....... Policy Group on Scientific Information [*Marine science*] (MSC)
POGT........ Power-Operated Gun Turret
pogu-........ Guam [*MARC geographic area code*] [*Library of Congress*] (LCCP)
pOH.......... Alkalinity Factor (SAUS)
pOH.......... Hydroxyl Concentration [*Organic chemistry*] (MAE)
POH.......... Path Overhead [*Telecommunications*] (ITD)
POH.......... Path Section Overhead (SAUS)
POH.......... Periodic Overhaul [*Indian Railway*] (TIR)
POH.......... Personal Oral Hygiene (MELL)
POH.......... Pilot's Operating Handbook [*Aviation*] (DA)
POH.......... Placed off Hire
POH.......... Planned Outage Hours [*Electronics*] (IEEE)
POH.......... Pocahontas, IA [*Location identifier*] [*FAA*] (FAAL)
Poh .... Pohang (AD)
POH.......... Port Henry, NY [*Amtrak rail station code*]
POH.......... Power-On Hours (ELAL)
POH.......... Pull-Out Harness
poh .... Pull Out of Hole (AD)
POHA........ Preoperative Holding Area [*Medicine*] (MELL)
Pohang...... Pohang Iron & Steel Co., Ltd. [*Associated Press*] (SAG)
POHC........ Principal Organic Hazardous Constituent [*Environmental chemistry*]
POHI......... Physically or Otherwise Health Impaired
POHM .... Page-Oriented Holograph Memory [*Computer science*]
POHM .... Prisoners of Her Majesty (BB)
POHMA...... Project for the Oral History of Music in America
POHS........ Presumed Ocular Histoplasmosis Syndrome [*Ophthalmology*]
POHWARO... Pulsated, Overheated, Water Rocket [*Swiss space rocket*]
POHZ .... Port of Houston Dock [*Federal Railroad Administration identification code*]
POI........... Parking Orbit Injection [*NASA*]
POI........... Parking Orbit Inspection [*NASA*]
POI........... Park-Ohio Industries, Inc. (EFIS)
POI........... Parti Oubanguien de l'Independance [*Ubangi Independence Party*] [*Political party*]
POI........... Path Overhead Identifier (SAUS)
POI........... Path Overhead Indicator (MLOA)
POI........... Period of Interest (MCD)
POI........... Personal Orientation Inventory [*Psychology*]
POI........... Personal Outlook Inventory [*Employment test*]
POI........... Pilkington Optronics Inc. (SAUS)
POI........... Plan of Instruction
POI........... Point of Impact
POI........... Point of Information (SAUS)
POI........... Point of Interaction (SAUS)
POI........... Point of Interception (GNE)
POI........... Point of Interface [*Telecommunications*]
POI........... Poison
POI........... Post-Ignition
POI........... Postoperative Instructions [*Medicine*] (MELL)
POI........... Potosi [*Bolivia*] [*Airport symbol*] (AD)
POI........... Pre-Overhaul Inspection (MCD)
POI........... Pressure-Operated Initiator (MCD)

POI Probability Of Intercept (LAIN)
POI Product of Inertia (MCD)
POI Program of Instruction (FOTI)
POI Program Operator Interface [*Computer science*] (ELAL)
POI Proof of Illness (MELL)
POI Protection One [*NYSE symbol*]
POI Public Office of Information (MCD)
POI Purchase Order Item (KSC)
POIC Payload Operations Integration Centre (SAUS)
POIC Petty Officer in Charge [*Navy*] (NVT)
POIC Poly(octyl Isocyanate) [*Organic chemistry*]
POID Post Office Investigation/Intelligence Department [*British*] (DI)
POIDRT Poison Dart (SAUS)
POIE Pointer-Willamette [*NCIC trailer make code*]
POIF Plan Organization Index File [*IRS*]
POIG Pairwise Implication Path (SAUS)
poik Poikilocyte [*or Poikilocytosis*] [*Medicine*] (MAE)
POIK Poikilocytosis [*Medicine*] (EDAA)
POIL Power Density Imbalance Limit (IAA)
POIN Pointer [*NCIC motorcycle make code*]
POINT Paraplegics on Independent Nature Trails, Dallas (SAUS)
POINT Pasadena Online Information Network [*Pasadena Public Library*] (OLDSS)
POINT Performance Oriented Integrated Technology (SAUS)
POINT Point [*Commonly used*] (OPSA)
Point Point of Air (SAUS)
Point Point of Arena (SAUS)
Point Point of Conception (SAUS)
Point Point of Fortin (SAUS)
Point Point of Harbor (SAUS)
Point Point of Lookout (SAUS)
Point Point of Pleasant (SAUS)
POINT Publications on the Internet [*Database*] [*United Kingdom*] (GDD)
POINT Pursuing Our Italian Names Together (EA)
POINTER Particle Orientation Interferometer [*ASD*]
POINTER Pre-University Orbital Information Tracker Equipment and Recorder (PDAA)
POINTERM Appointment Will Be Regarded as Having Terminated upon This Date
PoinTIS Point of Care, Team Information System (SAUS)
Point Loma C Point Loma Nazarene College (GAGS)
POINTMAIL Letter Appointment in Mail
POINTS Points [*Commonly used*] (OPSA)
POINTS Precision Optical Interferometer in Space (SAUS)
POIP Potential Offender Identification Program
POIPCD Patent Office and Industrial Property and Copyright Department [*British*]
POIQT Performance-Oriented Infantry Qualification Test (INF)
POIR Poirier [*NCIC car make code*]
POIR Project Officers Interim Report [*Air Force*] (MCD)
POIS Parkland On-Line Information Systems [*Computer science*] (DMAA)
POIS Poison (AAMN)
pois Poison (AD)
POIS Poisoning [*FBI standardized term*]
POIS Polish Osteogenesis Imperfecta Society (SAUS)
POIS Post Office Insurance Society [*British*] (DI)
POIS Procurement Operations and Information System (SAUS)
POIS Procurement Operations Information System (MCD)
POIS Prototype On-Line Instrument System [*Computer science*] (NRCH)
POIS Purchase Order Information System (MCD)
POISE Panel on Inflight Scientific Experiments [*NASA*]
POISE Photosynthetic Oxygenation Illuminated by Solar Energy
POISE Pointing & Stabilisation platform Experiment (SAUS)
POISE Pointing and Stabilization Platform Element [*Army*] (MCD)
POISE Practice-Oriented Information System Experiment (SAUS)
POISE Preoperational Inspection Services Engineering (IAA)
POIT Power of Influence Test [*Psychology*]
POIT Power-of-Influence Test (SAUS)
POJ Lower Pokomo [*Language symbol*] (ETLW)
POJ Patent Office Journal [*India*] [*A publication*] (DLA)
POJ Selma, AL [*Location identifier*] [*FAA*] (FAAL)
poji- Johnston Atoll [*MARC geographic area code*] [*Library of Congress*] (LCCP)
PoK Pakistan-occupied Kashmir (SAUS)
POK Power on Okey Signal (SAUS)
POK Sacramento, CA [*Location identifier*] [*FAA*] (FAAL)
POKEG Pokegama, WI [*American Association of Railroads railroad junction routing code*]
Pokeman Pocket Monsters [*Nintendo Co., Ltd.*]
poki- Kermadec Islands [*MARC geographic area code*] [*Library of Congress*] (LCCP)
POKMV Pokeweed Mosaic Virus [*Plant pathology*]
POL Pacific Oceanographic Laboratories [*Later, Pacific Marine Environmental Laboratory*]
POL Pacific Oceanographic Laboratory (SAUS)
POL Pacific Oceanography Laboratories (SAUS)
POL Pair Orthogonalized Lowdin [*Physics*]
POL Parents of Large Families
POL Pastoral Occupation Licence (SAUS)
POL Patent Office Library (AD)
POL Paul Otchakovsky-Laurens [*Publishing imprint, named for imprint editor*]
POL Pemba [*Mozambique*] [*Airport symbol*] (OAG)
POL Petroleum, Oil, and Lubricants [*Military*]
pol Petroleum-Oil-and-Lubricants (AD)
POL Petroleum, Oil and Lubrication (or Lubricants) (SAUS)
POL Philips Optical Language (IAA)
POL Physician-Owned Laboratory (HCT)
POL Physician's Office laboratory
POL Physicians Online (SAUS)
POL Point of Learning (SAUS)
POL Pola [*Yugoslavia*] [*Seismograph station code, US Geological Survey*] [*Closed*] (SEIS)
POL Polacca [*Ship's rigging*] (ROG)
POL Poland [*ANSI three-letter standard code*] (CNC)
Pol Poland (VRA)
pol Polar (AD)
POL Polara [*NCIC car model code*]
POL Polar International Airlines, Inc. [*ICAO designator*] (FAAC)
POL Polarity [*or Polarize*] (KSC)
POL Polarization (SEWL)
Pol Polen [*Poland*] [*Norwegian*] (AD)
Pol Police (WDAA)
POL Police
POL Police Court [*Court type found in state of Virginia*] (MVRD)
POL Policy
POL Policy Division (SAUS)
POL Policy Office (SAUS)
POL Polish (AAG)
Pol Polish (BEE)
pol Polish [*MARC language code*] [*Library of Congress*] (LCCP)
pol Polished (VRA)
POL Polish Ocean Lines (AD)
pol Polite (SHCU)
POL Polite
Pol Politica [*of Aristotle*] [*Classical studies*] (OCD)
POL Political
POL Political Prisoner (SAUS)
POL Political Section [*Foreign service*]
pol Politician (NTIO)
POL Politician
POL Politics On-Line (SAUS)
Pol Pollexfen's English King's Bench Reports [*1669-85*] [*A publication*] (DLA)
POL Polling (IAA)
POL Pollution
POL Polo [*NCIC car model code*]
POL Polonium [*Chemical symbol is Po*] (AAG)
Pol Polydor & Deutsche Grammophon [*Record label*] [*Germany, Europe, etc.*]
POL Polygram [*Publisher*]
POL Polymerase [*An enzyme*]
POL Polymerized Flagellin [*Medicine*] (EDAA)
Pol Polyphon [*Record label*] [*Denmark, etc.*]
POL Polytranslation Analysis and Programming (SAUS)
POL Porto Amelia [*Mozambique*] [*Airport symbol*] (AD)
POL Port of Loading [*Shipping*]
POL Possession-Only License (GOBB)
POL Posterior Oblique Ligaments [*Medicine*]
POL Power Optimized Logic (SAUS)
POL Practical Quantification Limit [*Metallurgy*]
POL Premature Onset of Labor [*Obstetrics*] (DAVI)
pol Problem-Oriented Language (AD)
POL Problem-Oriented Language [*Computer science*]
POL Procedure Oriented Language (SAUS)
POL Procedure-Oriented Language [*Computer science*]
POL Process Oriented Language (SAUS)
POL Process-Oriented Language [*Computer science*] (IEEE)
POL Program Oriented Language [*Computer science*] (ECII)
POL Proudman Oceanographic Laboratory [*UK*] [*Marine science*] (OSRA)
POL Provisional Operating License [*for nuclear power plant*]
POL Public Opinion Laboratory [*Northern Illinois University*] [*Research center*] (RCD)
POL Public Opinion Laboratory [*Indiana University-Purdue University at Indianapolis*] (RCD)
p-ola Payola (AD)
POLA Pointable Optical Linear Array (SAUS)
POLA Polar Manufacturing Company [*NCIC trailer make code*]
POLA Political Spring (Greece) [*Political party*] (PSAP)
POLA Polymerase Alpha (DMAA)
POLA Port of London Authority [*England*] (WDAA)
POLA Project on Linguistic Analysis
POLA Prostitutes of Los Angeles [*An association*] (AD)
PolAb Pollution Abstracts
POLAC Problem-Oriented Language for Analytical Chemistry [*Computer science*] (PDAA)
POLACAP Port of London Authority Combined Accident Procedure (SAUS)
Pol Ad Political Adviser (AD)
polad Political Adviser (AD)
POLAD Political Adviser
Polam LJ Polamerican Law Journal [*A publication*] (DLA)
Pol Anal Policy Analysis [*A publication*] (JLIT)
polang Polarization Angle (AD)
POLANG Polarization Angle [*Telecommunications*]
Polar Global Geospace Science Polar Spacecraft (SAUS)
POLAR International Solar Terrestrial Physics Program (SAUS)
polar Polarity (AD)
POLAR Polarity [*or Polarize*] (IAA)
POLAR Polarize (SAUS)

POLAR ...... Polar Plasma Laboratory (ADWA)
POLAR ...... Production Order Locating and Reports (SAUS)
POLAR ...... Production Order Location and Reporting [*NASA*] (NASA)
POLAR ...... Projected Operational Logistics Analysis Requirements
Polar BEAR... Polar Beacon Experiments and Auroral Research (AD)
PolarE...... Polar Express Corp. [*Associated Press*] (SAG)
POLARIS ... Fleet Ballistic Missile Weapons System (SAUS)
POLARIS ... Pepper Online Archival Retrieval and Information System [*Database*] (GDD)
POLARIS ... Photochemistry of Ozone Loss in Arctic Region in Summer (SAUS)
Polaris ...... Polaris Industries, Inc. [*Associated Press*] (SAG)
POLARIS ... Polar-Motion Analysis by Radio Interferometric Surveying [*Geodetic measuring facilities*]
POLARIS ... Princeton On-Line Accelerator Isotope Separator (SAUS)
POLARIS ... Province of Ontario Land Registration Information System Database [*Canada*] (GDD)
Polaroid..... Polaroid Corp. [*Associated Press*] (SAG)
PolarPAC.... Polar Public Access Catalog (SAUS)
Polar Rec... Polar Record [*A publication*] (PABS)
Polar Res... Polar Research (SAUS)
POLARS..... Pathology On-Line Logging and Reporting System [*Computer science*] (PDAA)
POLARSCAT... Polarimetric Scatterometer (SAUS)
POLAT....... Polar Atlantic (SAUS)
POL BKM ... Polished Buckram (DGA)
POLC .... Petty Officers Leadership Course (SAUS)
Pol C .... Political Code [*A publication*] (DLA)
POLCAP..... Petroleum Capability (SAUS)
POLCAP..... Petroleum, Oils, and Lubricants Capabilities (MCD)
POLCATS ... Pollution Characterization by Absorption on Spectroscopy (SSD)
POLCO ...... Polar Continental (SAUS)
POLCOD..... Police Code [*INTERPOL*]
Pol Code.... Political Code [*A publication*] (DLA)
Pol Col ...... Police College (AD)
Pol Com .... Police Commissaire [*Interpol*] [*British*] (AD)
Pol Com .... Police Commissioner (AD)
pol com ..... Political Committee (AD)
Pol Cont .... Pollock on Contracts [*A publication*] (DLA)
polcrit .... Political Critic (AD)
POLD .... Professional and Occupational Licensing Directory [*A publication*]
POLDAM .... POL [*Petroleum, Oil, and Lubricants*] Installations Damage Report (NATG)
poldamr..... Petroleum, Oil, and Lubrication Installation Damage Report (AD)
POLDAMR... Petroleum, Oil and Lubrication Installations Damage Report (SAUS)
POLDER..... Polarization and Directionality of Earth Reflectances (SAUS)
POLDER..... Polarization and Directionality of the Earth's Reflectances [*Instrumentation*]
Pol Dig Part... Pollock's Digest of the Laws of Partnership [*A publication*] (DLA)
POLDPS..... Pioneer Off-Line Data-Processing System [*NASA*]
POLE .... Point-of-Last-Environment [*Computer science*] (IBMDP)
POLE .... Polar Ozone Lidar Experiment (SAUS)
POLE .... Prednisolone, Oncovin [*Vicristine*], L-Asparaginase [*Antineoplastic drug regimen*] (DAVI)
POLE .... Public Opinion Logical Expectation (SAUS)
POL/ECO .... Political/Economic Section [*Foreign service*]
pol econ .... Political Economy (AD)
polem .... Polemic (AD)
polem .... polemicist (SAUS)
polem .... polemicize (SAUS)
Pol Endocrinol... Polish Endocrinology (SAUS)
Pol Eng ..... Polish Engineering (SAUS)
POLES....... Polar Exchange at the Sea Surface (EOSA)
POLEX....... Polar Experiment
POLEX....... Political Exercise [*International relations game*]
POLEX-NORTH... Polar Experiment in the Northern Hemisphere (MSC)
POLEX-SOUTH... Polar Experiment in the Southern Hemisphere (MSC)
polf .... Parents of Large Families (AD)
POLF .... Parents of Large Families
Pol Fed ..... Police Federation [*London*] (AD)
Pol Fedn Newsl... Police Federation Newsletter [*A publication*] (DLA)
POLFER ..... Polizia Ferroviaria [*Railroad Police*] [*Italian*] (AD)
Pol Found... Police Foundation [*Washington, D.C.*] (AD)
POLGA ...... Polymer Group [*OTCBB symbol*]
POLGEN..... Problem-Oriented Language Generator [*Computer science*] (BUR)
poli .... Politician (AD)
POLIC .... Petroleum Intersectional Command [*Army*] (AABC)
Police Fedn Newsl... Police Federation Newsletter [*A publication*] (ILCA)
Police J Ct... Police Justice's Court [*A publication*] (ILCA)
Police LQ... Police Law Quarterly [*A publication*] (ILCA)
Policy Anal... Policy Analysis [*A publication*] (PABS)
pol ind ...... Pollen Index (AD)
POL IND .... Pollen Index (WDAA)
pol in the pen... Politician in the Penitentiary (AD)
Pol in the Pen... Politician in the Penitentiaty (SAUS)
polio......... Poliomyelitis [*Medicine*] (AD)
POLIO .... Poliomyelitis [*Medicine*]
POLIS .... Parliamentary On-Line Indexing Service [*United Kingdom*] (GDD)
POLIS .... Parliamentary On-Line Information System [*House of Commons Library*] [*Bibliographic database*] [*Information service or system*] [*British*] (IID)
POLIS .... Parliamentary Online Library Study (SAUS)
POLIS .... Petroleum Intersectional Service [*Army*]
POLIS .... Police Information and Statistics Committee [*Law enforcement*] (FOTI)
POLIS .... Political Institutions Simulation [*Game*]
POLIS .... Polynomial Interpreting System (SAUS)
POLISARIO... Popular Front for the Liberation of Saguiet el Hamra and Rio de Oro [*Morocco*]
poli sci...... Political Science
POLISH-AMERICAN PAC... Federation of Polish Americans Inc. PAC [*New Britain, CT*] (PACS)
PolishTel ... Polish Telephones & Microwave Corp. [*Associated Press*] (SAG)
polit .... Political (AD)
POLIT........ Political (EY)
Polit .... Political (TBD)
polit .... Politics (WDAA)
Polit .... Politics [*A publication*]
POLITBUREAU... Political Bureau [*of USSR*]
POLITBURO... Politicheskoe Byuro [*Political Bureau of USSR*]
Politburo ... Politicheskoe Byuro [*Political Bureau of the Central Committee*] [*Russian*] (AD)
Polit Sci Quart... Political Science Quarterly [*A publication*] (JLIT)
Pol J......... Police Journal [*A publication*] (ILCA)
Pol J Ecol... Polish Journal of Ecology [*A publication*] (PABS)
Pol J Soil Sci... Polish Journal of Soil Science [*A publication*] (PABS)
POLK .... Polk Audio [*NASDAQ symbol*] (TTSB)
POLK .... Polk Audio, Inc. [*Baltimore, MD*] [*NASDAQ symbol*] (NQ)
POLK .... Polk, CA [*American Association of Railroads railroad junction routing code*]
POLKA....... Periodical On-Line Keyword Access [*Computer science*] (PDAA)
POLKA....... Petroleum, Oil and Lubricants out-of-Kilter Algorithm (SAUS)
PolkAu ...... Polk Audio, Inc. [*Associated Press*] (SAG)
PolkAud..... Polk Audio [*Associated Press*] (SAG)
POLK of A... Polka Lovers Klub of America (EA)
Poll .... Pollack's Ohio Unreported Judicial Decisions Prior to 1823 [*A publication*] (ILCA)
POLL .... Pollex [*An Inch*] [*Pharmacy*]
Poll .... Pollexfen's English King's Bench Reports [*1669-85*] [*A publication*] (ILCA)
POLL .... Pollock Industries [*NCIC trailer make code*]
poll .... Pollution (AD)
POLL .... Public Opinion Location Library [*The Roper Center for Public Opinion Research*] [*Information service or system*] (CRD)
POL/LAB .... Political and Labor Section [*Foreign service*]
Pol Law of Nat... Polson's Law of Nations [*1848*] [*A publication*] (DLA)
Poll CC Pr... Pollock's Practice of the County Courts [*A publication*] (ILCA)
Poll Contr Guide... Pollution Control Guide [*A publication*] (DLA)
Pollex .... Pollexfen's English King's Bench Reports [*1669-85*] [*A publication*] (ILCA)
Pollexf ...... Pollexfen's English King's Bench Reports [*1669-85*] [*A publication*] (ILCA)
Pollexfen... Pollexfen's English King's Bench Reports [*1669-85*] [*A publication*] (ILCA)
Pollock & Maitl... Pollock and Maitland's History of English Common Law [*A publication*] (DLA)
PolloTrp..... Pollo Tropical [*Commercial firm*] [*Associated Press*] (SAG)
Poll Prod... Pollock on the Production of Documents [*A publication*] (DLA)
Pol LQ....... Police Law Quarterly [*A publication*] (DLA)
POLLS....... Parliamentary On-Line Library Study [*Atomic Energy Authority*] [*British*]
POLLUT ..... Pollution
Pollut Atmos... Pollution Atmospherique (SAUS)
Pollut Eng... Pollution Engineering (SAUS)
Pollution Cont Guide (CCH)... Pollution Control Guide (Commerce Clearing House) [*A publication*] (DLA)
Pollut Res... Pollution Research [*A publication*] (PABS)
POLMI....... Problem-Oriented Machine Independent Language (SAUS)
POL/MIL .... Political/Military (SAUS)
Pol Mil Dig... Poland's Digest of the Military Laws of the United States [*A publication*] (DLA)
poln-......... Central and Southern Line Islands [*MARC geographic area code*] [*Library of Congress*] (LCCP)
POLN .... Pollution Normal (SAUS)
poln.......... polnisch [*Polish*] [*German*] (AD)
POLO .... Pacific Command Operations Liaison Office [*Army*] (AABC)
POLO .... Plant and Office Layout (MCD)
POLO .... Polar Orbiting Lunar Observatory [*Satellite*]
POLO .... Problem-Oriented Language Organizer [*Computer science*] (PDAA)
POLO .... Procurement Online Ordering System (MCD)
Polon........ Polonais [*Polish*] [*French*] (AD)
POLOPS..... Polynomial Operations [*Air Force*]
POLOS ...... Polar Oceans and the Law of the Sea Project (SAUS)
POLPA....... Polar Pacific (SAUS)
Pol Part..... Pollock's Digest of the Laws of Partnership [*A publication*] (DLA)
Pol Pharm Trans... Polish Pharmaceutical Transactions (SAUS)
Pol Prod Doc... Pollock on the Power of Courts to Compel the Production of Documents [*A publication*] (DLA)
POLPS....... Polymorphonuclear Leukocytes [*Hematology*] (DAVI)
POLR .... Polar Express Corp. [*NASDAQ symbol*] (SAG)
POLR .... Poloron Homes of Pennsylvania [*NCIC trailer make code*]
POLRE....... Pollution Report (EAGT)
POLREG..... Polynomial Regression (IAA)
POLREP..... Pollution Report (GNE)
Pol Res Q... Political Research Quarterly [*A publication*] (BRI)
Pol Rev ..... Policy Review [*A publication*] (JLIT)
Pol Rev Radiol Nucl Med... Polish Review of Radiology and Nuclear Medicine (SAUS)
PolrEx....... Polar Express Corp. [*Associated Press*] (SAG)
PolRs........ Pollution Research and Control Corp. [*Associated Press*] (SAG)

POLRW...... Polar Express Wrrt'B' [*NASDAQ symbol*] (TTSB)
Pol Rze Lud... Polaska Rzeczpospolita Ludowa [*Polish People's Republic*] (AD)
POLS........ Planned Ocean Logistic System (SAUS)
pols.......... Political Prisoners (AD)
pols.......... Politicians (AD)
POLS........ Politics (SAUS)
POLS........ Private Online Service [*Computer science*] (GART)
PolSc........ Political Science (DD)
POLSC....... Political Science
Pol Sci...... Policy Sciences [*A publication*] (JLIT)
pol sci....... Political Science (AD)
PolSciQ..... Political Science Quarterly (SAUS)
Pol Sci Quar... Political Science Quarterly [*A publication*] (ILCA)
POLSG....... Polishing
Pols Nat.... Polson's Law of Nations [*1848*] [*A publication*] (DLA)
PolSt........ Political Studies (SAUS)
POLSTAR... Plant for On-Load Short-circuit Testing and Research (SAUS)
POLSTRADA... Polizia Stradale [*Highway Police*] [*Italian*] (AD)
Pol Stud.... Policy Studies [*A publication*] (JLIT)
Pol Stud J... Policy Studies Journal [*A publication*] (BRI)
POLT......... Program Optimizing Low-Thrust Trajectory (ACAE)
Pol Technol News... Polish Technological News (SAUS)
Pol Tech Rev... Polish Technical Review (SAUS)
PolTel........ Polish Telephones & Microwave Corp. [*Associated Press*] (SAG)
POLTHN..... Polyethylene [*Organic chemistry*]
POLTL....... Political (AFM)
POLTN....... Pollution
Pol Tr Mar... Poland's Law of Trade Marks [*A publication*] (DLA)
POLU........ Polish Ocean Lines [*Common carrier symbol*]
POLUT....... Pollution
PolutRs..... Pollution Research and Control Corp. [*Associated Press*] (SAG)
polwar....... Political Warfare (AD)
POLWAR..... Political Warfare
POLWARADDIR... Political Warfare Advisory Directorate
POLX........ Polydex Pharmaceuticals Ltd. [*NASDAQ symbol*] (NQ)
POLXF....... Polydex Pharmaceuticals [*NASDAQ symbol*] (TTSB)
POLY......... Planet Polymer Technologies [*NASDAQ symbol*] (TTSB)
POLY......... Planet Polymer Technologies, Inc. [*NASDAQ symbol*] (SAG)
Pol'y......... Policy (DLA)
poly.......... Polydipsia [*Medicine*] (DAVI)
POLY......... Polyester
poly.......... Polyethylene (AD)
POLY......... Polyethylene (DEN)
POLY......... Polygamy [*FBI standardized term*]
poly.......... Polymer (AD)
POLY......... Polymorphonuclear Leukocyte [*Hematology*]
poly.......... Polymorphonuclear Neutrophil Granulocyte [*Hematology*] (DAVI)
Poly.......... Polynesia (AD)
poly.......... Polyphagia [*Medicine*] (DAVI)
POLY......... Poly-Tech, Inc. [*NASDAQ symbol*] (COMM)
poly.......... Polytechnic (AD)
POLY......... Polytechnic
poly.......... Polyuria [*Medicine*] (DAVI)
poly.......... Polyvinyl (AD)
PolyA........ Polyadenylated
poly(A)...... Polyadenylic Acid [*Biochemistry*] (MAE)
Polyb........ Polybius [*Second century BC*] [*Classical studies*] (OCD)
Pol YB Int'l L... Polish Yearbook of International Law [*Warsaw*] [*A publication*] (DLA)
Pol Yb of Internat L... Polish Yearbook of International Law [*Warsaw*] [*A publication*] (DLA)
poly bot..... Polyethylene Bottle (AD)
POLYC....... Polychromasia [*Hematology*] (DAVI)
poly-C....... Polycytidylic Acid [*Biochemistry*] (DMAA)
Poly-C....... Polyester Capacitor (SAUS)
PolyCenter... Digitalis new name for DECmcc. (SAUS)
Polycom.... Polycom, Inc. [*Associated Press*] (SAG)
Polycryst... Polycrystalline (SAUS)
POLYDAT... Polymetallic Nodule Deposits Database (SAUS)
Polydex..... Polydex Pharmaceuticals Ltd. [*Associated Press*] (SAG)
POLYDOC... Polytechnical Documentation (NITA)
POLYDOP... Polystation Doppler Tracking System (MCD)
POLYED..... Polymer Education
POLYEST... Polyester
polyg........ Polygraph (AD)
POLYG....... Polygraphy (SAUS)
poly-G....... Polyguanylic Acid [*Biochemistry*] (DMAA)
Polyg........ Polygynie (SAUS)
POLYGON... Oceanographic Experiment in the North-East Atlantic [*Former USSR*] [*Marine science*] (OSRA)
PolyGp...... Polymer Group, Inc. [*Associated Press*] (SAG)
Polygr........ PolyGram NV [*Associated Press*] (SAG)
poly-I........ Polyinosinic Acid [*Biochemistry*] (DMAA)
poly I:C...... Polyinosinic Polycytidylic Acid (BARN)
Pol Yid...... Polish Yiddish (SAUS)
Polym....... Polymerized (SAUS)
Polym....... Polymusic [*Record label*]
POLYMAT... Polymer Materials [*Deutsches Kunststoff-Institut*] [*Germany*] [*Information service or system*] (CRD)
Polym Bull... Polymer Bulletin (SAUS)
Polym Commun... Polymer Communications (SAUS)
Polym Compos... Polymer Composites (SAUS)
Polym Degrad Stabil... Polymer Degradation and Stability (SAUS)
Polym Dig... Polymer Digest (SAUS)
Polymed.... PolyMedica Industries, Inc. [*Associated Press*] (SAG)
POLYMEG... Polytetramethylene Ether Glycol (SAUS)
Polym Eng Sci... Polymer Engineering and Science (SAUS)
Polym J..... Polymer Journal (SAUS)
Polym Lett Ed... Polymer Letters Edition of the Journal of Polymer Science (MEC)
Polym Mech... Polymer Mechanics (SAUS)
Polym News... Polymer News (SAUS)
POLYMODE... Polygon Midocean Dynamic Experiment (SAUS)
POLYMODE... Polygon-MODE [*Mid-Ocean Dynamics Experiment*] [*Soviet-US cooperative undersea weather exploration*]
polymorph... Polymorphonuclear [*Leukocyte*] [*Hematology*] (DAVI)
polymorph... Polymorphous (AD)
Polym Plast Technol Eng... Polymer-Plastics Technology and Engineering (SAUS)
Polym Prepr Am Chem Soc... Polymer Preprints of the American Chemical Society (SAUS)
Polym Proc Eng... Polymer Process Engineering (SAUS)
Polym Rubb Asia... Polymers and Rubber Asia (SAUS)
Polym Sci... Polymer Science (SAUS)
Polym Sci USSR... Polymer Science USSR (SAUS)
Polym Test... Polymer Testing (SAUS)
POLYMYX... Polymyxin B Sulfate (SAUS)
Polyn........ Polynesia (VRA)
POLYN....... Polynesia
Polynes..... Polynesian (DIAR)
POLYOX..... Poly(ethylene Oxide) [*Trademark*]
POLYP....... Polyprocessor (SAUS)
Polyph....... Polyphase Instrument Corp. [*Associated Press*] (SAG)
PolyRs...... Polymer Research Corp. of America [*Associated Press*] (SAG)
polys........ polymorphonuclear cells (SAUS)
POLYSAC IRON... Polysaccharide Iron complex (SAUS)
Polysar Prog... Polysar Progress (SAUS)
poly sci..... Political Science (AD)
polysex...... Polysexual (AD)
polys (segs)... Polymorphonuclear Segmented Neutrophils [*Hematology*] (DAVI)
poly-T....... Polythymidylic Acid [*Biochemistry*] (DMAA)
Polytech..... Polytechnic (PROS)
polytech..... Polytechnical (BARN)
POLYTRAN... Polytranslation Analysis (SAUS)
POLYTRAN... Polytranslation Analysis and Programming (IEEE)
Poly U....... Polytechnic University (GAGS)
poly(U)...... Polyuridylic Acid [*Biochemistry*] (MAE)
Polyvisn..... Polyvision Corp. [*Associated Press*] (SAG)
Polyvsn..... Polyvision Corp. [*Associated Press*] (SAG)
polywater... Polymerized Water (AD)
POLY-WRI... Polytechnic Institute of New York Weber Research Institute [*Farmingdale, NY*]
POLZ........ Polish Ocean Lines [*Intermodal trailer symbol*]
POM......... Aurelio y Gustavo Pompa Estrella [*Mexico*] [*FAA designator*] (FAAC)
POM......... Operation: Peace of Mind [*Later, Runaway Hotline*] [*An association*] (EA)
POM......... Pain on Motion (STED)
POM......... Pallet-Only Mode [*NASA*] (NASA)
POM......... Particulate Organic Matter [*Environmental chemistry*]
POM......... Pay-off Matrix (SAUS)
POM......... Pennysylvania-Ohio-Maryland League [*Old baseball league*]
POM......... Pepco Holdings [*Formerly Potomac Electric Pwr*] [*Stock exchange symbol*]
POM......... Peritronics Med [*Vancouver Stock Exchange symbol*]
POM......... Persistent Object Manager (SAUS)
POM......... Personal Opinion Matrix [*Test*] (TES)
POM......... Personal Opinion Message [*Western Union*] (IIA)
POM......... Personnel, Operations, Maintenance (MCD)
POM......... Phase of Moon (SAUS)
POM......... Phase of the Moon [*Astronomy*] (NHD)
POM......... Phenomenon of Man [*Project*] (EA)
POM......... Photo-Optical Memory (SAUS)
POM......... Physician's Office Manual [*A publication*] (MHCS)
POM......... Pivaloyloxymethyl Chloride (SAUS)
POM......... Plan Objectives Memorandum (CCCA)
PoM......... Plan of Management (SAUS)
POM......... Plate Orifice Meter (SAUS)
POM......... Polarizing Optical Microscopy
POM......... Police Officer, Male
POM......... Polyacetal (SAUS)
POM......... Polycyclic Organic Material (SAUS)
pom.......... Polycyclic Organic Matter (AD)
POM......... Polycyclic Organic Matter
POM......... Polyformaldehyde (EDCT)
POM......... Polymerized and Oxidized Material [*Food science*]
POM......... Polymethylene Oxide (SAUS)
POM......... Polynuclear Organic Matter (FFDE)
POM......... Polyoxometalate [*Organic chemistry*]
POM......... Poly(oxymethylene) [*Organic chemistry*]
pom.......... Polyoxymethylene (AD)
POM......... Polyphenylene Oxide, Modified (SAUS)
pom.......... Pomeranian (AD)
POM......... Pomeranian Dog (DSUE)
pom.......... Pomeridiano [*Afternoon*] [*Italian*] (AD)
Pom.......... Pommy [*British*] (ODBW)
pom.......... Pomological (AD)
POM......... Pomona [*California*] [*Seismograph station code, US Geological Survey*] [*Closed*] (SEIS)
POM......... Pomona, CA [*Location identifier*] [*FAA*] (FAAL)

pom.......... Pom-Pom (AD)
Pom.......... Pompon [*Horticulture*]
POM.......... Pool Operational Module [*Telecommunications*] (TEL)
POM.......... Port Moresby [*Papua New Guinea*] [*Airport symbol*] (OAG)
PoM.......... Port of Miami (AD)
POM.......... Position Modulator (NRCH)
POM.......... Post-Operative Myopathy [*Equine term*] (TED)
POM.......... Potential Officer Material [*British military*] (DMA)
POM.......... Potomac Electric Power Co. [*NYSE symbol*] (SPSG)
POM.......... Potomac Electric Pwr [*NYSE symbol*] (TTSB)
POM.......... Preobservational Mean [*Statistics*]
pom.......... Preparation for Overseas Movement (AD)
POM.......... Preparation for Overseas Movement [*Military*]
POM.......... Prescription Only Medicine [*British*]
POM.......... Princeton Ocean Model (SAUS)
POM.......... Printer Output Microfilm
POM.......... Print on Metal (DGA)
POM.......... Printout Microfilm (NITA)
POM.......... Priority of Movement (SAUS)
POM.......... Priority of Movements [*Military*] [*British*]
POM.......... Prior to Overseas Movement [*DoD*]
POM.......... Production/Operations Management (SAUS)
POM.......... Production Order Master (SAUS)
POM.......... Professional or Managerial (WDMC)
POM.......... Professionals, Owners, and Managers [*A. C. Nielsen Co.*] [*Demographic category*] (NTCM)
POM.......... Program Objectives Memorandum [*Military*]
POM.......... Program Operating Memorandum (SAUS)
POM.......... Program Operation Mode
POM.......... Project Office Memo
POM.......... Project Officers Meeting
POM.......... Project Operations and Milestones (SAUS)
POM.......... Proof of Manufacturing (ACAE)
POM.......... Public Order Member (NUMA)
POMA........ Pennsylvania Osteopathic Medical Association (EARSL)
POMA........ Petty Officer Medical Assistant [*British military*] (DMA)
POMA........ Petty Officer's Military Academy [*Navy*]
POMA........ Pointable Optical Mosaic Array (SAUS)
POMA........ Polyoctyl Methacrylate [*Organic chemistry*]
POMALS.... Pedestal Operated Multi-Ammunition Launching System (SAUS)
POMAR...... Position Operational, Meteorological Aircraft Report
POMAR...... Preventive Operational Maintenance and Repair [*Military*] (NVT)
POMAS...... Procurement Office for Military Automotive Supplies
pomato...... Potato-Tomato (AD)
POMBA...... Parents of Multiple Births Associations of Canada
POM/BES... Program Objective Memorandum/Budget Estimate Submission (MCD)
POMC........ Parents of Murdered Children (EA)
POMC........ Period of Minimum Change (SAUS)
POMC........ Pro-Opiomelanocortin [*Endocrinology*]
Pom Code Rem... Pomeroy on Code Remedies [*A publication*] (DLA)
Pom Const Law... Pomeroy's Constitutional Law of the United States [*A publication*] (DLA)
Pom Contr... Pomeroy on Contracts [*A publication*] (DLA)
pomcus...... Prepositioned Material Configured in Unit Sets (AD)
POMCUS.... Prepositioned Overseas Material (or Materiel) Configured in/to Unit Sets (SAUS)
POMCUS.... Pre-positioned Overseas Materiel Configured to Unit Sets (SAUS)
POMCUS.... Prepositioning of Material Configured to Unit Sets (SAUS)
POMCUS.... Prepositioning of Materiel Configured to Unit Sets [*Army*] (AABC)
POMCUS.... Prepositioning of Organisational Material Configured in Unit Sets (SAUS)
POMD........ Program Operation Mode (IAA)
POME........ early convict immigrants (SAUS)
pome-........ Melanesia [*MARC geographic area code*] [*Library of Congress*] (LCCP)
POME........ Principal Ordnance Mechanical Engineer [*British military*] (DMA)
POME........ Prisoner of Mother England [*Nineteenth-century convict in penal colony of Australia, now a nickname for any Australian*]
POME........ Problems-Objectives-Methods-Evaluation [*Planning method*]
POME........ Protect Our Mountain Environment [*Colorado*]
POMEM...... Petty Officer Marine Engineering Mechanic [*British military*] (DMA)
Pom Eq Jur... Pomeroy's Equity Jurisprudence [*A publication*] (DLA)
Pom Eq Juris... Pomeroy's Equity Jurisprudence [*A publication*] (DLA)
POMER...... Pomeroy, OH [*American Association of Railroads railroad junction routing code*]
POMERID... Pomeridianus [*In the Afternoon*] [*Pharmacy*]
Pomeroy.... Pomeroy Computer Resources, Inc. [*Associated Press*] (SAG)
Pomeroy.... Pomeroy's Reports [*73-128 California*] [*A publication*] (DLA)
POMF........ Polaris Missile Facility
POMFLANT... Polaris Missile Facility, Atlantic (AD)
POMFLANT... Polaris Missile Facility, Atlantic Fleet
POMFPAC... Polaris Missile Facility, Pacific Fleet
POMGEN.... Program Objective Memorandum Generator [*Military*]
POMH........ National Association of Post Office Mail Handlers, Watchmen, Messengers, and Group Leaders [*Later, NPOMHWMGL*]
POMI........ Photochromic Microimage (IAA)
POMI........ Preliminary Operating and Maintenance Instructions [*Aerospace*] (AAG)
POMINS..... Portable Mine Neutralization System (MCD)
POMM........ Preliminary Operating and Maintenance Manual [*Military*] (AABC)
Pom Mun Law... Pomeroy on Municipal Law [*A publication*] (DLA)
POMO........ Partially Occupied Molecular Orbitals [*Physical chemistry*]
POMO........ Personnel Objectives Monitoring Operation
POMO........ Postmodern
POMO........ Production Oriented Maintenance Organization (SAUS)
POMO........ Production-Oriented Maintenance Organization (MCD)
POMO........ Program Operations and Management Office [*Environmental Protection Agency*] (GFGA)
POMOL...... POMCUS [*Prepositioning of Materiel Configured to Unit Sets*] Objective Levels [*Military*]
pomol........ Pomologic (AD)
POMOL...... Pomologist (SAUS)
POMOL...... Pomology
POMOLA.... Poor Man's Optical Landing System
Pomp.......... Epistula ad Pompeium [*of Dionysius Halicarnassensis*] [*Classical studies*] (OCD)
POMP........ Phase-Offset Multiplanar (RAWO)
Pomp.......... Pompeius [*of Plutarch*] [*Classical studies*] (OCD)
Pomp.......... Pompey (AD)
POMP........ Pomposo [*Grandly*] [*Music*] (ROG)
POMP........ Pre Coded Originating Mail Processor (PDAA)
POMP........ Prednisolone, Oncovin, Methotrexate, and 6-mercaptopurine [*Medicine*] [*Cancer chemotherapy*] (EDAA)
POMP........ Prednisone, Oncovin [*Vincristine*], Methotrexate, Purinethol [*Mercaptopurine*] [*Antineoplastic drug regimen*]
POMP........ Principal Outer Material Protein [*Medicine*] (EDAA)
POMP........ Principal Outer Membrane Protein
POMP........ Problem-Oriented Management of Patients (SAUS)
POMP........ Purinethol, Oncovin, Methotrexate, Prednisone [*Medicine*] (MEDA)
POMPAC.... Polaris Missile Facility, Pacific (AD)
POMPr...... Potomac Elec Pwr $2.44 Cv Pfd [*NYSE symbol*] (TTSB)
POMPrA..... Potomac El Pwr$3.89'91 Pfd [*NYSE symbol*] (TTSB)
POMPrH..... Potomac Elec Pwr $3.37cm'87 Pfd [*NYSE symbol*] (TTSB)
POM Project... Phenomenon of Man Project (SAUS)
POMQ........ Poteat Motor Lines [*Common carrier symbol*]
POMR........ Problem-oriented Medical Record [*Medicine*] (EDAA)
Pom Rem... Pomeroy on Civil Remedies [*A publication*] (DLA)
Pom Rem & Rem Rights... Pomeroy on Civil Remedies and Remedial Rights [*A publication*] (DLA)
POMR/PST... Partido Obrero Marxista Revolucionario/Partido Socialista de los Trabajadores [*Marxist Revolutionary Workers' Party/Socialist Workers' Party*] [*Peru*] [*Political party*] (PPW)
POMS........ Panel on Operational Meteorological Satellites
POMS........ Persistent Object Management System (NITA)
POMS........ Pilot Ocean Monitoring Study (SAUS)
POMS........ Plain Old Mail Service (CIST)
POMS........ Polar Operational Meteorological Satellite (USDC)
POMS........ Polar Orbiting Meteorological Satellite (SAUS)
POMS........ Poly-Ortho-methylstyrene [*Organic chemistry*]
POMS........ Process Operating Management System [*Manufacturing*]
POMS........ Process Operations Management System [*IBM*] (GART)
POMS........ Production and Operations Management Society (EA)
POMS........ Professional Office Management System (CIST)
POMS........ Profile of Mood States [*A questionnaire*]
POMS........ Program Operations Manual System [*Social Security Administration*]
POMS........ Property Owners and Managers Survey [*Database*] (GDD)
POMS........ Psychiatric Outpatient Mood Scale (SAUS)
POMSA...... Post Office Management Staff Association (SAUS)
POMSA...... Post Office Management Staffs Association [*A union*] [*British*] (DCTA)
POMS-BI... Profile of Mood States-Bipolar Form
POMSEE.... Performance, Operating (or Operational) and Maintenance Standards for Electronic Equipment (SAUS)
POMSEE.... Preparation, Operation and Maintenance of Shipboard Electronics Equipment (SAUS)
pomsee...... Preparation, Operation, Maintenance, Shipboard Electronics Equipment (AD)
POMSIP..... Post Office Management and Service Improvement Program [*Obsolete*]
Pom Spec Perf... Pomeroy on Specific Performance of Contracts [*A publication*] (DLA)
POMSS...... Pre-positioned Operational Material Storage Site (SAUS)
POMT........ Patriot Organizational Maintenance Trainer [*Army*]
POMT........ Planning and Operations Management Team (MCD)
POMT........ Planning Operations Management Team (SAUS)
POMV........ National Federation Post Office Motor Vehicle Employees [*Later, APWU*] (EA)
POMV........ Privately Owned Motor Vehicle (NATG)
POMWG..... Program Objective Memorandum Working Group (SAUS)
POMZ........ Port of Milwaukee [*Federal Railroad Administration identification code*]
PON.......... Paraoxonase [*An enzyme*]
PON.......... Particulate Organic Nitrogen
PON.......... Passive Optical Network
P-on.......... Phoshorylation (SAUS)
PON.......... Phosphorotioate Oligonucleotide [*Biochemistry*]
PON.......... Ponce [*Puerto Rico*] [*Seismograph station code, US Geological Survey*] (SEIS)
PON.......... Ponder Oils Ltd. [*Toronto Stock Exchange symbol*]
PON.......... Pontiac, IL [*Amtrak rail station code*]
Pon.......... Pontius [*Authority cited in pre-1607 legal work*] (DSA)
PON.......... Pontoon (AAG)
pon.......... Pontoon (AD)
PON.......... Pony [*NCIC car model code*]
PON.......... Portuguese Navy [*ICAO designator*] (FAAC)
PON.......... Position (IAA)
PON.......... Position [*Telegraphy*] (PCTE)
PON.......... Pride of Newark [*Feigenspan beer*]
PON.......... Primary Olfactory Nerve (SAUS)
PON.......... Production Order Notification (SAUS)

PON.......... Program on Negotiation [*Harvard University*] (RCD)
PON.......... Program Opportunity Notice [*Energy Research and Development Administration*]
PON.......... Program Opportunity Notice (or Notification) (SAUS)
PON.......... Program Opportunity Notification (AD)
PON.......... Project Originator Number (SAUS)
PON.......... Pump Octane Number (SAUS)
PON.......... Purchase Order Notice (SAUS)
pona......... Paraffin, Olefin, Naphthene, Aromatic (AD)
PONA........ Paraffins, Olefins, Naphthenes, Aromatics
PONA........ Person of No Account [*Internet slang for someone who hasn't been online*] (NETL)
PONA........ Provisions for Ozone Nonattainment Areas [*Environmental science*] (COE)
PONAM...... Polar North Atlantic Margins (SAUS)
PONAM...... Polar North Atlantic Margins Programme (SAUS)
Pon Ble..... Poncius Blegerii [*Flourished, 14th century*] [*Authority cited in pre-1607 legal work*] (DSA)
PonBrg...... Ponton Bridge (SAUS)
PonBrg...... Pontoon Bridge (AD)
PONBRG.... Pontoon Bridge (MUGU)
PONC........ Price of Non-Conformance (SAUS)
Poncebk..... Poncebank [*Associated Press*] (SAG)
Ponce Sch Med... Ponce School of Medicine (GAGS)
PONCHO.... Patrons of Northwest Civic Cultural and Charitable Organizations
PONCY...... Ponce City, OK [*American Association of Railroads railroad junction routing code*]
POND........ Parents of Near Drownings [*An association*] (EA)
POND........ Pondere [*By Weight*] [*Latin*]
pond......... Pondere [*By Weigh*] [*Latin*] (AD)
POND........ Ponderosa Homes [*NCIC trailer make code*]
POND........ Ponderosus [*Heavy*] [*Pharmacy*]
Ponder...... Ponder Industries, Inc. [*Associated Press*] (SAG)
Pondo........ Pondoland (AD)
PONE........ Ponderosa Industries [*NCIC trailer make code*]
PONF........ Paediatric Oncology Nurses Forum [*British*]
PONG........ Poet of the New Generation [*Term used to describe poets writing for entertainment value*] (ECON)
PONI......... Pontiac (Canadian) [*NCIC car make code*]
PONI......... Positive Output, Negative Input (SAUS)
PONI......... Postoperative Narcotic Infusion (STED)
ponl-......... New Caledonia [*MARC geographic area code*] [*Library of Congress*] (LCCP)
ponn-......... New Hebrides [*MARC geographic area code*] [*Library of Congress*] (LCCP)
p-on-n...... Positive on Negative (AD)
PONN........ Positive-on-Negative (IAA)
PONR........ Pioneer Cos. [*OTCBB symbol*]
PONS........ Platt's Oilgram News Service
PONS........ Portuguese Naval Ship (SAUS)
pons......... Profile of Nonverbal Sensitivity (AD)
PONS........ Profile of Nonverbal Sensitivity [*Psychology*]
PONSACS... Program on Nonviolent Sanctions and Cultural Survival [*Harvard University*] (RCD)
PONSE...... Personnel of the Naval Shore Establishment [*Report*] (NG)
PONSE Report... Personnel of the Naval Shore Establishment Report (SAUS)
PONSI....... Program of Noncollegiate Sponsored Instruction (OICC)
Pont......... Epistulae ex Ponto [*of Ovid*] [*Classical studies*] (OCD)
Pont......... Pontevedra (AD)
PONT........ Pontiac [*Automotive engineering*]
PONT........ Pontiac [*NCIC car make code*]
PONT........ Pontiac (trucks) [*NCIC truck make code*]
PONT........ Pontifex [*Bishop*] [*Latin*] (WGA)
Pont......... Ponton (SAUS)
Pont......... Pontoon (WGA)
PONTA....... Popular New Titles from Abroad [*Book acquisition program for libraries*]
pont b....... Pontoon Bridge (AD)
Ponti......... Pontiac (AD)
Pont Max... Pontifex Maximus [*Supreme Pontiff*] [*Latin*] (AD)
PonTn....... Ponton Train (SAUS)
ponu-........ Nauru [*MARC geographic area code*] [*Library of Congress*] (LCCP)
PONUC....... Post Office National Users' Council [*British*]
PONVER..... Project on National Vocational Education Resources (EDAC)
PONY........ Pennsylvania, Ohio, New York Baseball League (IIA)
PONY........ Pennsylvania-Ontario-New York League [*Old baseball league*]
PONY........ Ponycycle [*NCIC motorcycle make code*]
PONY........ Pride of the Navy Yard (DNAB)
PONY........ Prostitutes of New York
PONY........ Protect Our Nation's Youth [*Baseball league*] [*Name usually written Pony*]
PONY........ Purpose of Neighborhood Youth [*Foundation*]
PONYA...... Port of New York Authority [*Later, PANYNJ*]
PONZ........ Port of Natchez [*Federal Railroad Administration identification code*]
POO.......... Pallet of Opportunity (SAUS)
POO.......... Panel on Oceanography
POO.......... Parents Opposed to Opting Out [*An association*] (AIE)
POO.......... Payload Operations Office [*NASA*]
POO.......... Platform of Opportunity Program [*National Oceanic and Atmospheric Administration*] (MSC)
POO.......... Pocos De Caldas [*Brazil*] [*Airport symbol*] (OAG)
Poo........... Poole (AD)
POO.......... Poona [*India*] [*Seismograph station code, US Geological Survey*] (SEIS)
POO.......... Port Operations Officer (DS)
POO.......... Port Ordnance Officer (SAUS)
POO.......... Post Office Order
POO.......... Post Officer Order (SAUS)
POO.......... Principal Ordnance Officer (SAUS)
POO.......... Priority Operational Objective [*Military*]
POO.......... Program Operations Officer [*Social Security Administration*]
POOC........ Payload of Opportunity Carrier (SAUS)
POOD........ Permanent Officer of the Day [*or Deck*] [*Navy*]
POOD........ Permanent Officer of the Deck (SAUS)
pood......... Poodle Dog (AD)
POOD........ Provisioning Order Obligating (or Obligation) Document (SAUS)
POOEL....... Petty Officer Ordnance Electrician [*British military*] (DMA)
poof.......... Peripheral On-Line-Oriented Function [*Computer science*] (AD)
POOFF....... Preservation of Our Femininity and Finances [*Women's group opposing below-the-knee fashions introduced in 1970*]
POOFF....... Professional Oglers of Female Figures [*Men's group opposing below-the-knee fashions introduced in 1970*]
POOH........ Postoperative Open-Heart [*Surgery*] (STED)
POOL........ Parallel Object Orientated Language (SAUS)
POOL........ Pollution of Oceans Originating on Land (SAUS)
POOL........ Poole [*NCIC trailer make code*]
POOL........ Poseidon Pools of America, Inc. [*NASDAQ symbol*] (COMM)
POOL........ SCP Pool [*NASDAQ symbol*] (TTSB)
POOL........ SCP Pool Corp. [*NASDAQ symbol*] (SAG)
PoolEn...... Pool Energy Services Co. [*Associated Press*] (SAG)
poop......... Nincompoop (AD)
POOP........ Principles of Operation (SAUS)
POOP........ Process Oriented Observation Program [*NORPAX*] (MSC)
POOP........ Proper Object Oriented Programming (SAUS)
POOR........ Poor Clot [*Medicine*] (STED)
POOR........ Prevention of Over-Radiation [*Military*]
Poore Const... Poore's Federal and State Constitution [*A publication*] (DLA)
Poor L & Local Gov't... Poor Law and Local Government Magazine [*A publication*] (DLA)
POOS........ Priority Order Output System [*Japan*] (DIT)
poosslq..... Person of Opposite Sex Sharing Living Quarters (AD)
POOW....... Petty Officer of the Watch [*Navy*] (NVT)
POoW....... Petty Officer on Watch [*Military*] (AD)
POOZ........ Permanently Open Ocean Zone (SAUS)
Pop........... Carbonated Beverage (SAUS)
POP.......... IEEE Proceedings Order Plans [*Database*] (GDD)
POP.......... International Polar Orbiting Platform (SAUS)
POP.......... Pacific Ocean Perch
POP.......... Package for Online Programming [*Computer science*] (CDE)
POP.......... Pain on Palpitation [*Medicine*]
POP.......... Palletizing Optimization Potential (AD)
POP.......... Palletizing Optimization Program (SAUS)
POP.......... Panoramic Office Planning
POP.......... Paperless Ordering Placement [*System*] (DOMA)
POP.......... Parallel Ocean Program (SAUS)
POP.......... Parallel Output Platform
POP.......... Parents of Punkers (EA)
POP.......... Paroxypropione [*or Paraoxypropiophenone*] [*Endocrinology*]
POP.......... Particle-Oriented Paper (IAA)
POP.......... Particulate Organic Phosphorus
POP.......... Partido de Orientacion Popular [*Popular Orientation Party*] [*El Salvador*] [*Political party*] (PPW)
POP.......... Parti Ouvrier et Paysan du Congo [*Congolese Workers' and Peasants' Party*] [*Zaire*] [*Political party*]
POP.......... Parti Ouvrier-Progressiste [*Canada*]
POP.......... Patrexes of the Panopticon (EA)
POP.......... Payload Optimized Program [*NASA*] (KSC)
POP.......... Pay One Price
POP.......... Peak Overpressure [*Nuclear energy*] (NRCH)
POP.......... Perceived Outcome Potential (MHDI)
POP.......... Percentage of Precipitation (SAUS)
POP.......... Performance-Oriented Packaging [*for hazardous materials*]
POP.......... Period of Performance (MCD)
POP.......... Permanently Out of Print (SAUS)
pop........... Perpendicular Ocean Platform (AD)
POP.......... Perpendicular Ocean Platform [*Oceanography*]
POP.......... Perpendicular to Orbital Plane
POP.......... Perpendicular-to-Orbit Plan
POP.......... Perpendicular-to-Orbit Plane [*Aerospace*] (KSC)
pop........... Persistent Occipito-Posterior (AD)
POP.......... Persistent Occipit Posterior [*A fetal position*] [*Obstetrics*]
POP.......... Persistent Organic Pollutant [*Environmental science*]
POP.......... Personal Ozone Protection (SAUS)
POP.......... Pharmacists in Ophthalmic Practice [*Later, PIOP*] (EA)
POP.......... Picture-outside-Picture [*Television technology*] (PS)
POP.......... Pipeline Outfit, Petroleum (MCD)
POP.......... Pituitary Opioid Peptide [*Medicine*] (DMAA)
POP.......... Placing Older People (SAUS)
POP.......... Plasma Oncotic Pressure [*Medicine*] (MAE)
pop........... Plasma Osmotic Pressure (AD)
POP.......... Plasma Osmotic Pressure [*Medicine*]
pop........... Plaster of Paris (AD)
POP.......... Plaster of Paris
POP.......... Pneumatic Operated Piston (ECII)
POP.......... Point of Presence [*Telecommunications*] (DOM)
PoP.......... Point of Presence [*Telecommunications*] (PCM)
POP.......... Point of Production (SAUS)
POP.......... Point of Purchase [*Advertising*]
POP.......... Polar Orbiting Platform (SSD)

POP......... Pollution and Overpopulation
POP......... Polymyositis Ossificans Progressiva [*Medicine*] (DMAA)
POP......... Polyolefin Plastomer [*Organic chemistry*]
POP......... Poly Phenylene Oxide (EDCT)
POP......... Pope & Talbot [*NYSE symbol*] (TTSB)
POP......... Pope & Talbot, Inc. [*NYSE symbol*] (SPSG)
POP......... POP from Stack (SAUS)
Pop......... Popham's English King's Bench Reports [*1592-1627*] [*A publication*] (DLA)
POP......... Popliteal [*Artery*] [*Anatomy*] (AAMN)
POP......... Popondetta [*Papua New Guinea*] [*Seismograph station code, US Geological Survey*] [*Closed*] (SEIS)
Pop......... Poppa (AD)
pop......... Poppet (AD)
POP......... Popping [*Mining engineering*]
pop......... Popular (AD)
POP......... Popular
Pop......... Populare [*Record label*] [*Romania*]
POP......... Population (AAG)
pop......... Population (AD)
Pop......... Population (TBD)
POP......... Population Division [*Bureau of the Census*] (OICC)
POP......... Port of Pensacola [*Federal Railroad Administration identification code*]
POP......... Portugese Overseas Province (AD)
POP......... Posterior Odds Processing [*Weather forecasting*] [*National Science Foundation*]
POP......... Post Office Preferred (DCTA)
PoP......... Post Office Protocol [*Computer science*] (FOTI)
POP......... Post Office Protocol [*Telecommunications*]
p-op......... Post-Operative (AD)
POP......... Postoperative [*Medicine*]
POP......... Postoperative Pain [*Medicine*] (MELL)
POP......... Power On/Off Protection
POP......... Practical Ordered Program (OA)
POP......... Preburner Oxidizer Pump (MCD)
POP......... Preflight Operations Procedure (MCD)
POP......... Prefocused Objective Pinhole (SAUS)
POP......... Prelaunch Operations Plan [*NASA*] (NASA)
POP......... Premanagement Orientation Program [*LIMRA*]
POP......... Pressurizer Overpressure (SAUS)
POP......... Pressurizer Overpressure Protection System [*Nuclear energy*] (IEEE)
POP......... Primary Operation
pop......... Printer of Plates [*MARC relator code*] [*Library of Congress*] (LCCP)
POP......... Printing-Out Paper
POP......... Probability of Precipitation (SAUS)
POP......... Process Optimization Program (SAUS)
POP......... Processor on Plug in (SAUS)
POP......... Profiler Online Program (SAUS)
POP......... Profit Option Plan [*Retailing*]
POP......... Programmed Operators and Primitives [*Computer science*]
POP......... Program Obligation Plan (KSC)
POP......... Program Operating Plan
POP......... Progressive Overload Program [*Weight training*]
POP......... Project Objective Plan (NG)
POP......... Project Operation (SAUS)
POP......... Project Optimization Procedure (IAA)
POP......... Prompt Ordering Plan
POP......... Proof of Principle (SAUS)
POP......... Proof-Of Principle [*Test*]
POP......... Proof of Purchase
POP......... Protection System (SAUS)
POP......... Public Offering Price (AD)
POP......... Puerto Plata [*Dominican Republic*] [*Airport symbol*] (OAG)
POP......... Pump Optimizing Program
POP......... Purchase Outside Production (SAA)
POP......... SCI-FI Society of Long Island [*Formerly, Patrexes of the Panopticon*] (EA)
POP3........ Post Office Protocol 3 [*Computer science*] (FOTI)
POPA........ Patent Office Professional Association (EA)
POPA........ Payload Ordnance Processing Area (NASA)
POPA........ Pet Owners' Protective Association
POPA........ POP All registers (SAUS)
Popa........ Popayan, Colombia (AD)
POPA........ Prevention of Oil Pollution Act [*1971*]
POPA........ Property Owners' Protection Association
pop advertising... Point-of-Purchase Advertising (AD)
POPAE....... Protons on Protons and Electrons [*Physics*]
POPAI....... Point-of-Purchase Advertising Institute [*Fort Lee, NJ*] (EA)
POPAL....... Pre-Operational Peculiar Age List
POP & B.... Proposed Operating Program and Budget [*Army*]
pop art...... Popular Art (AD)
popb......... Proposed Operating Plan and Budget (AD)
POPC........ Pamitoyl-Oleoylphosphatidylcholine [*Biochemistry*]
popc-........ Pitcairn [*MARC geographic area code*] [*Library of Congress*] (LCCP)
POP-CON... Populist Conservative [*Wing of the Republican Party represented by Congressmen Gingrich, Kemp, and Lott*]
POPCRU.... Police and Prison Civil Rights Union [*Founded in 1989*] [*South Africa*] (ECON)
POPCRU.... Police and Prison Service Civil Rights Union (SAUS)
POPCX...... PIMCO: Opportunity Cl.C [*Mutual fund ticker symbol*] (SG)
POPD........ Port of Portland [*Federal Railroad Administration identification code*]
POPD........ Power-Operated
POPDA...... Polyoxypropylenediamine [*Organic chemistry*]
POPE........ Parents for Orthodoxy in Parochial Education [*Group opposing sex education in schools*]
POPE........ Polar Orbiting Platform Element (SAUS)
POPE........ Product Oriented Procedures Evaluation (AD)
Pope Cust... Pope on Customs and Excise [*11th ed.*] [*1828*] [*A publication*] (DLA)
POP ED..... Popular Edition [*Publishing*]
Pope Lun... Pope on Lunacy [*A publication*] (DLA)
PopeRes.... Pope Resources Ltd. [*Associated Press*] (SAG)
PopeTal..... Pope & Talbot, Inc. [*Associated Press*] (SAG)
popex........ Population Explosion (AD)
POPEZ....... Pope Resources L.P. [*NASDAQ symbol*] (TTSB)
POPEZ....... Pope Resources Ltd. [*NASDAQ symbol*] (SPSG)
POPF........ POP Flags (SAUS)
popf.......... Prepared-on-Premises Flavor (AD)
POPGUN.... Policy and Procedure Governing the Use of Nicknames [*Army*] (AABC)
Poph......... Popham's English King's Bench Reports [*1592-1627*] [*A publication*] (DLA)
Poph (2).... Cases at the End of Popham's Reports [*A publication*] (DLA)
Popham..... Popham's English King's Bench Reports [*79 English Reprint*] [*1592-1626*] [*A publication*] (DLA)
Poph Insol... Popham's Insolvency Act of Canada [*A publication*] (DLA)
POPI......... Fast Food Operators [*OTCBB symbol*]
popi.......... Post Office Position Indicator [*British*] (AD)
POPI......... Post Office Position Indicator [*A form of long-range position indicator*] [*British*]
POPI......... Program on the Pharmaceutical Industry [*Massachusetts Institute of Technology*] (RCD)
POPIM....... Product Operations Planning Instruction Manual (ACAE)
POPIN....... Population Information Network [*United Nations*] [*Internet resource*]
POPIN-Africa... Population Information Network for Africa (SAUS)
POPINFORM... Population Information (SAUS)
POPINFORM... Population Information Network [*UNESCO*]
POPINS..... Population Information System [*UNESCO*]
POPL........ Principles of Programming Language (SAUS)
POPL........ Problem-Oriented Programming Language (SAUS)
POPLAB..... International Program of Laboratories for Population Statistics
POPLAB..... Program of Laboratories for Population Statistics (SAUS)
POPLINE... Population Information On-Line [*Bibliographic database*] (IID)
POPLINE... Population Online (NITA)
poplit........ Popliteal (AD)
POPLIT...... Popliteal [*Anatomy*]
POPMail.... Post Office Protocol Mail
POPMIP..... Portable Ocean Platform Motion Instrumentation Package [*Marine science*] (MSC)
Pop Mo L Tr... Popular Monthly Law Tracts [*1877-78*] [*A publication*] (DLA)
pop music... Popular Music (AD)
POPMV...... Poplar Mosaic Virus [*Plant pathology*]
POPN........ Population [*Telegraphy*] (PCTE)
Popn......... Population
POPO........ Phase One Program Office (ACAE)
POPO........ Poured-On, Passed-Over [*Bowdlerized version*]
POPO........ Push-On, Pull-Off [*Computer science*]
POPOP...... Phenyl Oxazolyl Phenyl Oxazolyl Phenyl (SAUS)
POPP........ Peace Operations Policy Program [*George Mason University*] (RCD)
POPP........ Prison Officer in a Private Prison (WDAA)
Pop Plast... Popular Plastics (SAUS)
Pop Plast Packag... Popular Plastics and Packaging (SAUS)
pop psych... Popular Psychiatry (AD)
popr......... Pilot Overhaul Provisioning Review (AD)
POPR........ Pilot Overhaul Provisioning Review
POPR........ Prototype Organic Power Reactor [*Nuclear energy*]
POPS........ Free-Fall Pop-Up Ocean Bottom Seismometer [*Marine science*] (MSC)
POPS........ National Beverage Corp. [*NASDAQ symbol*] (SAG)
POPS........ Pantograph Optical Projection System (IEEE)
POPS........ Paperless Order Processing System (SAUS)
POPS........ Parachute Opening Proximity Sensor (MCD)
POPS........ Partners of Prisoners & Families Support Group (WDAA)
POPS........ Pediatric Oncology Parents Support (EARSL)
POPS........ People Opposed to Pornography in Schools [*Group opposing sex education in schools*]
POPS........ Performance Optimized Page Size (SAUS)
POPS........ Performance-Oriented Packing Standard
POPs........ Persistent Organic Pollutants (SAUS)
POPS........ Platt's Oilgram Price Service
POPs........ Points of Presence (SAUS)
pops-......... Polynesia [*MARC geographic area code*] [*Library of Congress*] (LCCP)
pops......... Popular Concerts (AD)
POPS........ Positioning Orbital Propulsion System (MCD)
POPS........ Preserve Our Presidential Sites (EA)
POPS........ Pressurizer Overpressure Protection System [*Nuclear energy*] (NRCH)
POPS........ Primary Oceanographic Prediction System (SAUS)
POPS........ Principal Oscillation Patterns Analysis
POPS........ Process Operating System [*Toshiba Corp.*] [*Japan*]
POPS........ Procurers of Painted-Label Sodas [*Defunct*] (EA)
POPS........ Profiles of Problem Solving [*Test*] (TMMY)
POPS........ Program for Operator Scheduling [*Bell System computer program*]
POPS........ Project Operations [*Navy*] (NVT)
POPS........ Protect Our Pelican Society [*Later, PMBS*] (EA)
POPS........ Pyrotechnical Optical Plume Simulator (SAUS)
POPS........ Pyrotechnic Optical Plume Simulation
POPS........ Pyrotechnic Optical Plume Simulator (MCD)

POPSAT..... Precise Orbit Positioning Satellite (SAUS)
POPSAT..... Precise Orbit Positioning Spacecraft (ACAE)
Pop Sci..... Popular Science [*A publication*] (AD)
POP SCI MO... Popular Science Monthly [*A publication*] (ROG)
POPSE....... Project Office for Physical Security Equipment [*Army*] (RDA)
POPSER..... Polaris Operational Performance Surveillance Engineering Report [*Missiles*]
POP-Server... Post Office Protocol-Server (SAUS)
POPSI....... Postulate-Based Permuted Subject Indexing (PDAA)
POPSI....... Precipitation and Off-Path Scattered Interference [*Report*] [*FCC*]
POPSIPT... Project Operations in Port [*Navy*] (NVT)
POPT........ Petty Officer Physical Trainer [*British military*] (DMA)
POPT........ Pretesting Orientation on the Purpose of Testing [*US Employment Service*] [*Department of Labor*]
POPU........ Push Over Pull Up (NASA)
Population Bull... Population Bulletin [*A publication*] (JLIT)
Population Devel Rev... Population and Development Review [*A publication*] (JLIT)
Population Res Pol Rev... Population Research and Policy Review [*A publication*] (JLIT)
Population Rev... Population Review [*A publication*] (JLIT)
Population Stud... Population Studies [*A publication*] (JLIT)
Popul Rep A... Population Reports. Series A, Oral Contraceptives (SAUS)
Popul Rep B... Population Reports. Series B, Intrauterine Devices (SAUS)
Popul Rep C... Population Reports. Series C, Female Sterilization (SAUS)
Popul Rep D... Population Reports. Series D, Male Sterilization (SAUS)
Popul Rep E... Population Reports. Series E, Law and Policy (SAUS)
Popul Rep H... Population Reports. Series H, Barrier Methods (SAUS)
Popul Rep J... Population Reports. Series J, Family Planning Programs (SAUS)
Popul Rep L... Population Reports. Series L, Issues in World Health (SAUS)
Popul Rep M... Population Reports. Series M, Special Topics (SAUS)
Populuxe.... Popular Luxury [*Coined by Thomas Hine, design critic for the Philadelphia Inquirer, to describe the period from the mid-1950's to the mid-1960's*]
POPUS...... Post Office Processing Utility Subsystem [*Telecommunications*] (TEL)
POPX........ Pop Radio Corp. [*NASDAQ symbol*] (COMM)
POPY........ Poppy State Express [*Common carrier symbol*]
POPZ........ Port of Pasco [*Federal Railroad Administration identification code*]
POQ.......... Passing Over Quay (SAUS)
poq.......... Periodic Order Quantity (AD)
POQ.......... Period Order Quantity (PDAA)
POQ.......... Production Offset Quantity [*Military*]
POQ.......... Provided Otherwise Qualified [*Military*] (AABC)
POQ.......... Public Opinion Quarterly [*A publication*] (AD)
POQ.......... Push Off Quickly [*i.e., Be quick about it*] [*British*]
POQL........ Probability Outgoing Quality Limit (PDAA)
POQU........ Procedure of Questionable Usefulness [*Medicine*] (CPH)
POR.......... Pacific Ocean Region
POR.......... Parking Orbit Rendezvous [*NASA*] (MCD)
POR.......... Partido Obrero Revolucionario [*Revolutionary Workers Party*] [*Bolivia*] [*Political party*] (PPW)
POR.......... Partido Obrero Revolucionario [*Revolutionary Workers Party*] [*Argentina*] [*Political party*]
POR.......... Partido Obrero Revolucionario [*Revolutionary Workers Party*] [*Peru*] [*Political party*]
POR.......... Patent Office Reports [*A publication*] (DLA)
POR.......... Patrol Operations Report
POR.......... Payable on Receipt [*Business term*]
p-o-r......... Pay-on-Receipt (AD)
POR.......... Pay on Return [*Business term*]
POR.......... Peak Overshoot Ratio (IAA)
POR.......... Periodic Operation Report
POR.......... Periphal Output Register (SAUS)
POR.......... Peripheral Order Register (SAUS)
POR.......... Personnel Occurrence Report [*RAF*] [*British*]
POR.......... Physician of Record (DAVI)
POR.......... Pilot Opinion Rating
POR.......... Place of Receipt (MARI)
POR.......... Planned Order Release
POR.......... Plutonium Organic Recycle [*Nuclear energy*] (NRCH)
POR.......... Point of No Return (GOBB)
POR.......... Point of Receive (SAUS)
POR.......... Point of Resolution (NAKS)
POR.......... Point of Return (SAUS)
POR.......... Pola Resources Ltd. [*Vancouver Stock Exchange symbol*]
POR.......... Policy, Organisation (or Organization) and Rules (SAUS)
POR.......... Pori [*Finland*] [*Airport symbol*] (OAG)
Por.......... Porifera (AD)
Por.......... Porogi [*Waterfall*] [*Russian*] (AD)
por.......... Porosity (AD)
por.......... Porous (SAUS)
por.......... Portage (BARN)
POR.......... Portec, Inc. [*NYSE symbol*] (SPSG)
POR.......... Portion
Por.......... Portland (AD)
POR.......... Portland [*Maine*] [*Seismograph station code, US Geological Survey*] [*Closed*] (SEIS)
POR.......... Port of Refuge [*Shipping*]
POR.......... Por Trailer [*NCIC trailer make code*]
por.......... Portrait (RION)
POR.......... Portrait
Por.......... Portsmouth Spartans [*National Football League*] [*1930-33*] (NFLA)
Por.......... Portugal (AD)
Por.......... Portuguese (AD)
por.......... Portuguese [*MARC language code*] [*Library of Congress*] (LCCP)
POR.......... Portuguese
POR.......... Poseyville & Owensville Railroad [*Federal Railroad Administration identification code*]
POR.......... Position of Responsibility (ADA)
POR.......... Postocclusive Oscillatory Response (DB)
POR.......... Post Office Return
POR.......... Post Office Rifles [*Military*] [*British*] (ROG)
POR.......... Power on Request (ACAE)
POR.......... Power on Reset (ACAE)
POR.......... Power-On Reset (AEBE)
POR.......... Preparation of Overseas Replacement [*Military*] (RDA)
POR.......... Preparation of Replacements for Oversea Movement [*MTMC*] (TAG)
POR.......... Press on Regardless [*Automotive marathon*]
POR.......... Price on Request
POR.......... Prime contractor Organization (SAUS)
POR.......... Problem-Oriented Record (SAUS)
POR.......... Problem-Oriented Records [*Medicine*]
POR.......... Problem-Oriented Routine (IEEE)
POR.......... Processing Overseas Replacement Training [*Military*] (VNW)
POR.......... Process-of-Record (AAEL)
POR.......... Production Order Records (SAA)
POR.......... Production Order Request (SAA)
POR.......... Program of Requirements (EEVL)
POR.......... Project Officers Report (MCD)
POR.......... Propylene Oxide Rubber (SAUS)
POR.......... Psychotherapy Outcome Research
por.......... Public Opinion Research (AD)
POR.......... Purchase Order Request
PORA........ Police Officers Research Association (AD)
PORAC...... Peace Officers Research Association of California
PORACC..... Principles of Radiation and Contamination Control [*Nuclear energy*]
PORAG...... Presiding Officers' Review and Advisory Group [*Commonwealth Parliament*] [*Australia*]
PORB........ Production Operations Review Board [*NASA*] (NASA)
PORC........ Partido Obrero Revolucionario-Combate [*Revolutionary Struggle Workers' Party*] [*Bolivia*] [*Political party*] (PPW)
PORC........ Peralta Oaks Research Center (AD)
PORC........ Plant Operations Review Committee [*Nuclear energy*] (NRCH)
PORC........ Plant Overnight Review Committee [*Environmental science*] (COE)
PORC........ Porcelain (AAG)
porc......... Porcelain (AD)
PORC........ Porphyria, Chester Type (DMAA)
PORC........ Purchase Order Release and Control (SAUS)
PORC........ Purchase Order Requisition Control (SAUS)
PORCN...... Production Order Records Change Notice (KSC)
PORCO...... Port Control Office
PORD........ Performance and Operations Requirements Document [*NASA*] (NASA)
PORDA...... Personnel Officers of Research and Development Agencies
PORDIR..... Port Director
PORE........ Point Reyes National Seashore [*National Park Service designation*]
PORE........ Portable Structures [*NCIC trailer make code*]
POREA...... Post Office Regional Employees' Association [*Defunct*] (EA)
PORED...... Port Edwards, WI [*American Association of Railroads railroad junction routing code*]
POREL(A)... Petty Officer Radio Electrician (Air) [*British military*] (DMA)
POREP...... Position Report [*Air Force*]
PORES...... Purchase Order Receiving System (MCD)
PORF........ Pacific Ocean Research Foundation (EA)
Porg........ Person of Restricted Growth [*Slang term used to describe a person of limi ted cultural awareness*] [*Lifestyle classification*]
PORGIE..... Paperback Original [*Award for best original paperback books of the year*]
PORH........ Postoperative Reactive Hyperemia [*Medicine*] (EDAA)
PORI......... Polaris Operational Readiness Instrumentation [*Missiles*]
PORI......... Portal Operational Readiness Instrumentation (SAUS)
PORI......... Preoperational Readiness Inspection (MCD)
PO-RIP...... Purchase Order Receipt in Process (SAUS)
PORIS....... Post Office Radio Interference Service [*British*] (DI)
PORIS....... Post Office Radio Interference Station (AD)
PORK........ Partnership for Over-Regulated Kar [*Humorous description of government-auto industry technology research program*]
PORK........ Porkilocytosis [*Medicine*] (EDAA)
PORK........ Porta-Kamp Manufacturing [*NCIC trailer make code*]
PORK PAC... National Pork Producers Council Pork PAC [*Des Moines, IA*] (PACS)
porksan..... Pork Sandwich (AD)
porkwich.... Pork Sandwich (AD)
PORL........ Pacific Oceanographic Research Laboratories (SAUS)
PORL........ Peninsular/Oriental Steam Nav [*LO Symbol*] (TTSB)
PORLP...... Portage La Prairie, MB [*American Association of Railroads railroad junction routing code*]
porm......... Plus or Minus (AD)
P or M...... Plus or Minus (MSA)
PORM........ Plus or Minus
PORM-PST... Partido Obrero Revolucionario Marxista-Partido Socialista de los Trabajadores [*Peru*] [*Political party*] (EY)
porn......... Pornographic (AD)
PORN........ Pornography (DSUE)
PORN........ Protect Our Responsibilities Now [*Book title*]
pornette..... Pornographic Cassette (AD)
pornfilm..... Pornographic Motion Picture Film (AD)
porno........ Pornofilm (AD)
porno........ Pornographer (AD)

PORNO ...... Pornography (DSUE)
PORNO ...... Purchase Order Number (SAUS)
pornobio .... Pornographic Biography (AD)
pornofilm ... Pornographic Motion Picture (AD)
porno mag... Pornographic Magazine (AD)
pornovel .... Pornographic Novel (AD)
pornovelist... Pornographic Novelist (AD)
Porn Squad... Pornographic Squad (AD)
pornzines ... Pornographic Magazines (AD)
POROI ...... Project on Rhetoric of Inquiry [*University of Iowa*] (RCD)
PORP .... Partial Ossicular Replacement Prosthesis
PORP .... Printed on Recycled Paoer (AD)
PORP .... Printed on Rice-Paper (SAUS)
P or P .... Publish or Perish [*Said of scholars, scientists, etc.*]
porph .... Porphyry (VRA)
Porph .... Porphyry [*Third century AD*] [*Classical studies*] (OCD)
PORPP ...... Pharmaceutical Outcomes Research and Policy Program [*University of Washington*] (RCD)
PORR .... Preliminary Operations Requirements Review [*NASA*] (NASA)
PORR .... Purchase Order Revision Request
PORS .... Porsche [*NCIC car make code*]
PORS .... Portable Oil Reclamation System (SAUS)
PORS .... Post Office Research Station (AD)
PORS .... Power-On Reset [*Electronics*]
PORS .... Product Output Reporting System
PORS .... Project Officer Record System (SAUS)
PORSE ...... Post Overhaul Reaction Safeguard Examination [*Navy*] (NVT)
PORSEC ..... Pacific Ocean Remote Sensing Conference (SAUS)
PORSHE ..... Project of Ocean Rafts System for Hydrogen Economy
PORT .... Bayport Restaurant Group [*NASDAQ symbol*] (TTSB)
PORT .... Bayport Restaurant Group, Inc. [*NASDAQ symbol*] (SAG)
PORT .... Partnership Order Retrieval Tool (VLIE)
PORT .... Patient Outcome Research Team (PCM)
PORT .... Photo-Optical Recorder (or Recording) Tracker (SAUS)
port .... Photo-Optical Recorder Tracker (AD)
PORT .... Port [*Commonly used*] (OPSA)
port .... Portable (AD)
PORT .... Portable (KSC)
PORT .... Porta-Built Industries [*NCIC trailer make code*]
Port .... Portal (SAUS)
PORT .... Porter (DSUE)
Port .... Porter's Alabama Supreme Court Reports [*1834-39*] [*A publication*] (DLA)
Port .... Porter's Indiana Reports [*3-7 Indiana*] [*A publication*] (DLA)
PORT .... Port Financial [*NASDAQ symbol*] (SG)
Port .... Portfolio (DIAR)
PORT .... Portfolio (WGA)
PORT .... Portland, ME [*American Association of Railroads railroad junction routing code*]
PORT .... Portland Railroad
PORT .... Portmanteau (DSUE)
port .... Portrait (AD)
PORT .... Portrait
port .... portraiture (SAUS)
Port .... Portugal (VRA)
PORT .... Portugal
port .... Portugiesisch [*Portuguese*] [*German*] (AD)
Port .... Portuguese (ODBW)
PORT .... Postoperative Respiratory Therapy (DAVI)
PORT .... Prescriptive Objective Reference Testing [*Vocational guidance*]
PORT .... Presentation Portfolio (VRA)
PORT .... Providing Opportunities for Recovering Teens (MHID)
Port Ade .... Port Adelaide [*South Australia*] (AD)
Portage ..... Portage Industries Corp. [*Associated Press*] (SAG)
Portainer... Port Container (SAUS)
PORTAL ..... Polar Orbiter Remapping and Transformation Application Library (SAUS)
PORTAL ..... Process-Oriented Real-Time Algorithmic Language [*1978*] [*Computer science*] (CSR)
Port (Ala)... Porter's Alabama Reports [*A publication*] (DLA)
Port Ala R... Porter's Alabama Reports [*A publication*] (DLA)
Port Ald ..... Port Alberni [*Vancouver Island, British Columbia*] (AD)
portalet ..... Portable Toilet (AD)
Port Alex ... Port Alexander [*Alaska*] (AD)
Port Ant ..... Port Antonio [*Jamaica*] (AD)
PORTAPAK... Portable, Self-Contained, Instrument Package
Port Art ..... Port Arthur (AD)
PORTAS ..... Penetration of Radiation Through Aperture Simulation (PDAA)
PortBk .... Portsmouth Bank Shares, Inc. [*Associated Press*] (SAG)
PORT CEM... Portland Cement [*Technical drawings*] (DAC)
Port Chi ..... Port Chicago (AD)
Port Chi ..... Portuguese China (AD)
Port Dal ..... Port Dalhousie [*Ontario, Canada*] (AD)
PORTE .... Porter, IN [*American Association of Railroads railroad junction routing code*]
Portec .... Portec, Inc. [*Associated Press*] (SAG)
PORTER ..... Performance Oriented Tracking of Equipment Repair (ACAE)
Porter .... Porter's Alabama Reports [*A publication*] (DLA)
Porter .... Porter's Indiana Reports [*3-7 Indiana*] [*A publication*] (DLA)
Porter (Ala)... Porter's Alabama Reports [*A publication*] (DLA)
Porter R ..... Porter's Alabama Reports [*A publication*] (DLA)
Porter's Ala R... Porter's Alabama Reports [*A publication*] (DLA)
Porter's R... Porter's Alabama Reports [*A publication*] (DLA)
Porter's Repts... Porter's Alabama Reports [*A publication*] (DLA)
PortG35 ..... Portland General Electric Co. [*Associated Press*] (SAG)
PortGC ...... Portland General Corp. [*Associated Press*] (SAG)
PortglT ...... Portugal Telecom SA [*Associated Press*] (SAG)
PORTIA ...... Port Operations, Transport and Integrated Accountancy (MHDB)
Port Ind ..... Portuguese India (AD)
Port Ins ..... Porter's Laws of Insurance [*A publication*] (DLA)
Port Jack... Port Jackson Sydney [*Sydney, New South Wales, Australia*] (AD)
PORTL .... Portland, OR [*American Association of Railroads railroad junction routing code*]
Portland St U... Portland State University (GAGS)
Portland UL Rev... Portland University. Law Review [*A publication*] (DLA)
Port Liz ..... Port Elizabeth [*New Jersey*] (AD)
Port Liz ..... Port Elizabeth [*South Africa*] (AD)
PORTN ...... Portion (ROG)
Port Nick ... Port Nicholson [*Wellington, New Zealand*] (AD)
Port of Emb... Port of Embarkation (SAUS)
PORTP .... Partido Obrero Revolucionaria Trotskista Posadista [*Bolivia*] [*Political party*] (PPW)
Port P .... Portuguese Pharmacopoeia [*A publication*]
Port Phil ... Port Phillip [*Melbourne, Victoria, Australia*] (AD)
PORTREP ... Port [*or Anchorage*] Capacity Report [*Navy*] (NVT)
Port Rich ... Port Richmond [*Staten Island, New York*] (AD)
PORTs .... Patient Outcome Research Teams (SAUS)
PORTS .... Physical Oceanographic Real-Time System [*Marine science*] (OSRA)
PORTS .... Portable Imagery Telecommunications System (ACAE)
PORTS .... Portable Remote Telecommunications System (DOMA)
PORTS .... Port Objective for Real-Time Systems [*Marine science*] (OSRA)
PORTS .... Ports [*Commonly used*] (OPSA)
PORTS .... Ports Characteristics File (SAUS)
PORTS .... Portsmouth [*City in England*]
PORTS .... Portsmouth Gaseous Diffusion Plant [*Department of Energy*] [*Portsmouth, OH*] (GAAI)
PORTS .... Portsmouth, VA [*American Association of Railroads railroad junction routing code*]
PORTS .... Preliminary Operations Requirements Test System (ACAE)
PortsBk ...... Portsmouth Bank Shares [*Associated Press*] (SAG)
PORTSM .... Portsmouth [*County borough in England*]
Ports NSW Jl... Ports of New South Wales Journal [*A publication*]
PORTSREP... Ports Report File (MCD)
Port Sud .... Port Sudan (AD)
PORTSUM... Port [*or Anchorage*] Summary Report [*Navy*] (NVT)
Port Swett... Port Swettenham [*Malaysia*] (AD)
PortSys ...... Porta Systems Corp. [*Associated Press*] (SAG)
Port Talb ... Port Talbot [*Wales*] (AD)
Port Tew .... Port Tewfik [*Egypt*] (AD)
Port Tim .... Portuguese Timor (AD)
Portug .... Portugais [*Portuguese*] [*French*] (AD)
Portugl ...... Portugal Fund [*Associated Press*] (SAG)
Port UL Rev... Portland University. Law Review [*A publication*] (DLA)
Port Wash... Port Washington [*Long Island, New York*] (AD)
Port Wel .... Port Wellen [*Ontario, CAN*] (AD)
Port Yid ..... Portuguese Yiddish (SAUS)
PORV .... Pilot-Operated Relief Valve [*Nuclear energy*] (NRCH)
PORV .... Power-Operated Relief Valve [*Nuclear energy*] (NRCH)
POS .... Aeroposta SA [*Argentina*] [*ICAO designator*] (FAAC)
POS .... Catalina Marketing [*NYSE symbol*] (TTSB)
POS .... Catalina Marketing Corp. [*NYSE symbol*] (SPSG)
POS .... Pacific Ocean Ship (NASA)
POS .... Pacific Orchid Society of Hawaii (EA)
POS .... Parent Operating Service (MCD)
POS .... Parents Over Shoulder [*Internet lingo*] (NETL)
POS .... Parosteal Osteosarcoma [*Oncology*] (DAVI)
POS .... Partially Ordered Set (OA)
POS .... Partial Output Signal (SAUS)
POS .... Part-of-Speech (IDAI)
POS .... Pascal Operating System (ELAL)
POS .... Patella Overload Syndrome [*Medicine*] (MELL)
POS .... Patent Office Society (EA)
POS .... Peacetime Operating Stock [*Military*] (CINC)
POS .... Peacetime Operating Stocks (SAUS)
POS .... Pennsylvania Orthopaedic Society (SAUS)
POS .... Period of Service [*Military*]
POS .... Permanently Out of Stock (SAUS)
POS .... Permanent Orbital Station [*NASA*] (IAA)
POS .... Persistant Object Service (SAUS)
POS .... Persistent Object Service (SAUS)
POS .... Photo Optic System
POS .... Pico Resources [*Vancouver Stock Exchange symbol*]
POS .... Piper Owner Society (EA)
POS .... Pivoting Optical Servo (SAUS)
POS .... Planar Oxygen Sensor
POS .... Plan of Service (OICC)
POS .... Plant Operating System [*Nuclear energy*] (NRCH)
POS .... Play Observation Scale [*Test*] (TMMY)
pos .... Point of Sale (AD)
POS .... Point of Sale (ODBW)
PoS .... Point of Sale
POS .... Point-of-Sale (FOTI)
POS .... Point of Scale (SAUS)
POS .... Point of Service [*Health plan option*]
POS .... Point of Service Option
POS .... Point-of-Service Plan [*Insurance*] (PAZ)
POS .... Polar Orbiting Satellite [*Marine science*] (OSRA)
POs .... Police Officers (AD)

POS.......... Policy Statements [*Australian Broadcasting Tribunal*] [*A publication*]
POS.......... Polycystic Ovarian Syndrome [*Also, PCOS*] [*Gynecology*]
POS.......... Pomona, CA [*Amtrak rail station code*]
POS.......... Portable Oxygen System (MCD)
PoS.......... Port of Service (AD)
POS.......... Port Of Spain [*Trinidad and Tobago*] [*Airport symbol*] (OAG)
PoS.......... Port of Spain (AD)
POS.......... Port of Stockton [*Federal Railroad Administration identification code*]
POS.......... Port(s) of Support (DOMA)
POS.......... Position (KSC)
pos.......... Position (WDMC)
Pos.......... Positioning (SAUS)
pos.......... Positive (AD)
POS.......... Positive (AFM)
POS.......... Positive [*Automotive engineering*]
Pos.......... Positive Ground
POS.......... Possession [*or Possessive*] (WGA)
pos.......... Possibility (AD)
POS.......... Possible [*Telegraphy*] (PCTE)
Pos.......... Possible
POs.......... Postal Orders (AD)
POS.......... Postcard Show
POS.......... Post Office Scheme [*Regulations*] [*British*]
POS.......... Preferred Overseas Shore Duty
POS.......... Pressure on Space [*Publishing*] (DGA)
POS.......... Pressure Operated Switch (SAUS)
POS.......... Pressure-Operated Switch (IAA)
POS.......... Primary Operating Stock [*DoD*]
POS.......... Primary Operating Stocks (SAUS)
POS.......... Primary Operating System (IEEE)
POS.......... Primary Oxygen System
POS.......... Probability of Success (COE)
POS.......... Probability of Survival [*Automotive componant analysis*]
POS.......... Problem-Oriented Software (SAUS)
POS.......... Problem Oriented System
POS.......... Problem-Oriented System (SAUS)
POS.......... Processor Operating System (SAUS)
POS.......... Production-Oriented Survey (MCD)
pos.......... Product of Sums (AD)
POS.......... Products of Sums (IAA)
POS.......... Professional Operating System (NITA)
POS.......... Professions and Occupations Sourcebook [*A publication*]
POS.......... Programmable Object Select [*Computer science*] (VLIE)
POS.......... Programmable Option Select [*Computer science*]
PoS.......... Programme of Study [*British*] (DET)
POS.......... Programming Optimizing System (IAA)
POS.......... Program of Study (AEE)
POS.......... Program Operations Staff [*Environmental Protection Agency*] (GFGA)
POS.......... Program Order Sequence
POS.......... Protection of Shipping (SEWL)
POS.......... Protein, Oil, and Starch [*Pilot manufacturing plant established by the Canadian government*]
POS.......... Pupil Observation Survey [*Education*]
POS.......... Purchase Order Status (SAUS)
POS.......... Purchase Order Supplement
POSA........ Passive Optical Sample Assembly (SAUS)
POSA........ Patriotic Order Sons of America (EA)
posa........ Payment Outstanding Suspense Accounts (AD)
POSA........ Payment Outstanding Suspense Accounts (NATG)
POSA........ Petty Officer Stores Accountant [*British military*] (DMA)
POSA........ Potential Supplier Assessment [*Automotive engineering*]
POSA........ Preliminary Operating Safety Analysis [*Nuclear energy*] (NRCH)
POSA MOS... Polysilicon Oxidation Self-Aligned Metal-Oxide Semiconductor (SAUS)
POSARS..... Plan of Service Automated Reporting System [*Employment and Training Administration*] [*Department of Labor*]
posb........ Possibly (VRA)
POSB........ Post Office Savings Bank
POSC........ Little Workers of the Sacred Heart (TOCD)
POSC........ Petrotechnical Open Software Corp. (SAUS)
POSC........ Primary Operations System Control (SAUS)
POSC........ Problem-Oriented System of Charting (AAMN)
posc-........ Santa Cruz Islands [*MARC geographic area code*] [*Library of Congress*] (LCCP)
POSCH....... Program of Surgical Control of Hyperlipidemia
POSCO...... Pohang Iron & Steel Co. (ECON)
POSCOR.... Position Correct (CAAL)
POSCORB... Planning, Organizing, Staffing, Coordinating, Reporting, and Budgeting [*Management*]
POSD........ Personnel on Station Date [*Army*] (AABC)
POSD........ Post Office Savings Department (AD)
POSD........ Program for Optical System Design
POSD........ Program of Optical System Design (SAUS)
POSD........ Project Operation Support Division [*NASA*]
POSDCORB... Planning, Organizing, Staffing, Directing, Coordinating, Reporting, and Budgeting [*Principles of management*]
posdsplt..... Port Side Out, Starboard Side Home [*British slang*] (AD)
posdsplt..... Positive Displacement (AD)
POSDSPLT... Positive Displacement
POSE........ Parents Opposed to Sex Education
POSE........ Photogrammetric Ocean Survey Equipment
POSE........ Picture-Oriented Software Engineering [*Computer science*] (CIST)
POSE........ Portable Operating System Environment (SAUS)
POSE........ Portable Operating System Extension [*Computer science*] (VLIE)
POSE........ Power Operational Support Equipment
POSE........ Promotion of Social Education [*British*] (DI)
PO SEC...... Principal Officer's Secretary [*Foreign service*]
POSEIDON... French component of TOPEX POSEIDON (SAUS)
POSEIDON... Positioning Ocean Sea Earth and Ice Dynamics and Orbiting Navigator (SAUS)
POSER...... Process Organization to Simplify Error Recovery (PDAA)
POSET....... Partially Ordered Set (HGAA)
Posey....... Posey's Unreported Cases [*Texas*] [*A publication*] (ILCA)
Posey UC... Texas Unreported Cases [*A publication*] (DLA)
Posey Unrep Cas... Posey's Unreported Cases [*Texas*] [*A publication*] (DLA)
POSF........ Port of Support File (DOMA)
POSF........ Ports of Support File (SAUS)
POSG........ After Glucose Infusion Started [*Biochemistry*] (DAVI)
posh........ Permuted on Subject Headings (AD)
POSH........ Permuted on Subject Headings [*Indexing technique*]
POSH........ Personal & Organizational Security Handbook [*A publication*]
POSH........ Port Outwardbound, Starboard Homewardbound [*Refers to shaded cabins of British naval officers in the Far East*]
POSH........ Prevention of Sexual Harassment [*Army*]
POSH........ Probability of Severe Hail (USDC)
posh........ Samoa Islands [*MARC geographic area code*] [*Library of Congress*] (LCCP)
POSI........ Parallel-Out, Serial-In (SAUS)
POSI........ Personnel On-Site Integration (SAA)
POSI........ Portable Operating System Interface (SAUS)
POSI........ Positron Corp. [*NASDAQ symbol*] (SAG)
POSI........ Promotion Conference for OSI (SAUS)
POS INIT... Position Initialization (GAVI)
POSIP....... Portable Ship Instrumentation Package
posistor..... Positive Resistor (AD)
posit........ Position (AD)
POSIT....... Position (NVT)
posit........ Positive (AD)
POSIT....... Positive
POSIT....... Positivism (ROG)
posit........ Positron (AD)
POSIT....... Profile for Open Systems Internetworking Technologies [*Computer science*] (CDE)
POSIT....... Profiles for Open Systems Interconnection Technologies (SAUS)
POSIT....... Profiles for Open Systems Interworking Technologies (SAUS)
POSITIME... Postion-Time [*Navigation systems*]
POSITIVE... Parents of Surrogate-Borne Infants and Toddlers in Verbal Exchange (EA)
Positr........ Positron Corp. [*Associated Press*] (SAG)
POSITREPS... Position Reports
positron..... Positive Electron (AD)
POSITRON... Positive Electron
Positron..... Positron Corp. [*Associated Press*] (SAG)
POSIW...... Positron Corp. Wrrt [*NASDAQ symbol*] (TTSB)
POSIX....... Portable Operating System based on Unix (SAUS)
POSIX....... Portable Operating System Interface Exchange
POSIX....... Portable Operating System Interface for Computer Environments (AAGC)
POSIX....... Portable Operating System Interface for Computer Systems (SAUS)
POSIX....... Portable Operating System Interface for Unix [*Computer science*] (PCM)
POSIX....... Portable Operating System Interface for X (SAUS)
POSIX....... Portable Operating Systems for Computer Environments (AD)
POSIX....... Portable Operating System Specification [*IEEE*]
POSK........ Polski Osrodek Spoleczno-Kulturalny [*Polish Social and Cultural Association - PSCA*] (EAIO)
POSKP...... Polski Osrodek Spoleczno-Kulturalny Posk [*Polish Social and Cultural Association - PSCA*] (EAIO)
POsl......... Papyri Osloenses [*A publication*] (OCD)
POSL........ Parti Ouvrier Socialiste Luxembourgeois [*Luxembourg Socialist Workers' Party*] (EAIO)
POSLV....... Position and Orientation System for Land Vehicles [*Navigation systems*]
POSM....... National Association of Post Office and General Service Maintenance Employees [*Later, APWU*] [*AFL-CIO*]
posm........ Patient-Operated Selected Mechanisms (AD)
POSM....... Patient Operated Selected (or Selector) Mechanism (SAUS)
POSM....... Patient-Operated Selector Mechanism [*Pronounced "possum"*]
POSMA...... Postal Service Manual [*A publication*]
Posmo....... Osmotic Permeability [*Biochemistry*] (DAVI)
posn......... Position (AD)
POSN........ Position (AFM)
posn-........ Solomon Islands [*MARC geographic area code*] [*Library of Congress*] (LCCP)
POSNA...... Pediatric Orthopaedic Society of North America (EA)
POS/NAV.... Positioning/Navigation
POS/NAV.... Position/Navigation [*System*] [*Military*] (INF)
POSNO...... Position Number [*Military*] (ADDR)
POSN SW... Position Switch (SAUS)
POSNY...... People of the State of New York (AD)
POSO........ Prosoft I-Net Solutions, Inc. [*NASDAQ symbol*] (SAG)
POSO........ ProsoftTraining [*NASDAQ symbol*]
POSO........ Province of Ontario Savings Office [*Canada*] (FOTI)
POSP........ Pacific Ocean Stations Program (SAA)
POSPI....... Post Office Standards Parts Interface (SAUS)
pos pr....... Positive Pressure (MAE)
Pos Press... Positive Pressure (CPH)
pos pron.... Possessive Pronoun (AD)
POSR........ Peacetime Operating Stock Requirement [*Military*] (AFIT)

POS R....... Positive Review [*A publication*] (ROG)
POS REF.... Position Reference (GAVI)
PosResp.... Positive Response Television [*Associated Press*] (SAG)
POSRIP...... People Organized to Stop Rape of Imprisoned Persons (EA)
POSRSTG... Position and Orientation System for Railroad Surveying and Track Geometry
POSS........ Palomar Observatory Sky Survey [*NASA*]
POSS........ Passive Optical Satellite Surveillance [*System*] (NATG)
POSS........ Passive Optical Surveillance System (SAUS)
POSS........ Percutaneous On-surface Stimulation [*Medicine*] (EDAA)
POSS........ Photo-Optical Surveillance Subsystem
POSS........ Photooptical Surveillance System (SAUS)
POSS........ Plant Occurrence and Status System (SAUS)
P-O-S S..... Point-of-Sale System (AD)
P-O-S S..... Point-of-Service System (AD)
POSS........ Polar Orbiting Satellite System (SAUS)
POSS........ Polyimide on Silicon-mask Substrate (SAUS)
POSS........ Portable Oceanographic Survey System (MCD)
POSS........ Portable Outdoor Security System [*Police and security equipment*]
poss......... Possession (AD)
POSS........ Possession [*or Possessive*] (AFM)
Poss......... Possession (BEE)
poss......... Possessive [*Linguistics*] (IEL)
poss......... Possessive (WDMC)
Poss......... Possible [*Medicine*] (BCRP)
poss......... Possible (WDMC)
POSS........ Possible
poss......... Possibly (WDMC)
POSS........ Possis Medical [*NASDAQ symbol*] (TTSB)
POSS........ Possis Medical, Inc. [*NASDAQ symbol*] (NQ)
POSS........ Program Operations Support Staff [*Environmental Protection Agency*] (GFGA)
POSS........ Prototype Optical Surveillance Subsystem (SAUS)
POSS........ Prototype Optical Surveillance System
POSS........ Proximal Over-Shoulder Strap [*Medicine*]
POSSE....... Parents of Students in Special Education (SAUS)
POSSE....... Parents Opposed to Sex and Sensitivity Education [*An association*]
POSSE....... Police Operations Systems Support System Elementary
POSSE....... Progressive Onslaught to Stamp out Stock Errors [*Navy*] (NG)
POSSED..... Possessed (ROG)
posses....... Possessive (AD)
POSSF....... Post Office Staff Superannuation Fund [*British*] (DI)
Possis....... Possis Medical, Inc. [*Associated Press*] (SAG)
posslq....... Person of the Opposite Sex in Same Living Quarters (AD)
POSSLQ..... Persons of Opposite Sex Sharing Living Quarters [*Bureau of the Census*]
POSSN...... Possession (WGA)
POSSNC..... Post Office Senior Staff Negotiating Council [*British*]
POSSON.... Possession
POSS System... Passive Optical Satellite Surveillance System (SAUS)
POSSUB..... Possible Submarine [*Navy*] (NVT)
POSSUM.... Pictures of Specific Syndromes and Unknown Malformations [*Database*]
POSSUM.... Polar Orbiting Satellite System - University of Michigan [*Designed by engineering students*]
Post.......... De Posteritate Caini [*of Philo*] (BJA)
POST........ Frederick Post Drafting Equipment (AD)
POST........ International Post Ltd. [*NASDAQ symbol*] (SAG)
POST........ Intl Post Ltd [*NASDAQ symbol*] (TTSB)
POST........ Parliamentary Office of Science and Technology [*British*]
POST........ Passive Optical Scan Tracker (MCD)
POST........ Passive Optical Seeker Technique
POST........ Passive Optical Seeker Technology (SAUS)
POST........ Payload Operations Support Team [*NASA*] (MCD)
POST........ Peace Officers Standards and Training (SAUS)
POST........ Peace Officer Standards and Training
POST........ Periodically Oscillating Source Temperature (SAUS)
POST........ Peritoneal Ovum Sperm Transfer [*Medicine*]
POST........ Piezoelectric-Oscillator Self-Tuned [*Electric system*]
POST........ Point-of-Sale Terminal [*Business term*]
POST........ Point of Sale Transaction (SAUS)
POST........ Point-of-Sale Transaction
POST........ Polaris Operation Support Task Group [*Missiles*]
POST........ Polar Stratospheric Telescope
POST........ Police Officer Student Training (AD)
POST........ Portable Optical Sensor Tester (ACAE)
PoST........ Portable Satellite Terminal (SAUS)
POST........ Positive (AAG)
post.......... Postage (AD)
POST........ Postal (SAUS)
POST........ Post Apartment Homes LP [*NASDAQ symbol*]
POST........ Postemergence [*Weed control*]
POST........ [*The*] Poster [*A publication*] (ROG)
post.......... Poster (VRA)
Post.......... Posterior (AMHC)
post.......... Posterior
POST........ Posting (SAUS)
post.......... Post Mortem (AD)
POST........ Postmortem (AAMN)
Post.......... Post's Reports [*23-26 Michigan*] [*A publication*] (DLA)
Post.......... Post's Reports [*42-64 Missouri*] [*A publication*] (DLA)
POST........ Postulate (SAUS)
POST........ Power on Self Test (SAUS)
POST........ Power-On Self Test [*IBM-PC feature*]
POST........ Processes of Science Test (AD)
POST........ Production-Oriented Scheduling Technique (SAUS)
POST........ Production-Oriented Scheduling Techniques (MCD)
POST........ Programmer Operating Standards Technique
POST........ Program to Operate Simulated Trajectories
POST........ Program to Optimize Shuttle [*or Simulated*] Trajectories [*NASA*] (KSC)
POST........ Program to Optimize Simulated Trajectories (SAUS)
POST........ Project-Oriented Study (FOTI)
POST........ Proposed Optical Stinger (SAUS)
POST........ Prototype Ocean Surveillance Terminal [*Navy*] (ANA)
POST........ Prototype Ocean Surveillance Tracker (SEWL)
POSTAD TV... Priorities, Outcomes, Sequence, Timings, Attendees, Date, Time, Venue (BB)
Post & Ins... Postage and Insurance (ILCA)
Post & Reg... Postage and Registration (DLA)
post-Aug.... Post-Augustan (AD)
POST AUR... Post Aurem [*Behind the Ear*] [*Pharmacy*]
post aur..... Post Aurem [*Behind the Ear*] [*Latin*] (AD)
post cib..... After Meals [*Medicine*] (BCRP)
POSTD...... Petty Officer Steward [*British military*] (DMA)
post d....... Posterior Diameter (AD)
POSTE....... Postage (ROG)
POSTEC..... Powder Science and Technology Research Association [*Norway*] (EAIO)
POSTEC..... Program of Research in Powder Science and Technology (SAUS)
POSTECH... Pohang Institute of Science and Technology (SAUS)
poster....... Posterior (AD)
Poster....... Posterity (SAUS)
POSTER..... Post Strike Emergency Reporting
pos terminal... Point-of-Sale Terminal (AD)
Poste's Gai... Poste's Translation of Gaius [*A publication*] (ILCA)
Poste's Gaius Inst... Poste's Translation of Gaius [*A publication*] (DLA)
POSTFAT... Postfinal Acceptance Trials [*Navy*] (NVT)
Postfax...... Post Facsimile (SAUS)
POSTFAX... Post Office Facsimile [*British*]
postgangl... Postganglionic [*Medicine*] (MEDA)
PostgradDipAgr... Postgraduate Diploma in Agriculture
PostGradDipEdStud(IndArts)... Postgraduate Diploma in Educational Studies (Industrial Arts)
PostGradDipl... Post-Graduate Diploma (SAUS)
Postgrad Med Inst... Postgraduate Medical Institute (AD)
Postgraduate D... Postgraduate Diploma (PGP)
POSTGRES... POSTGRES Object-Relational Database Mangement System (SAUS)
Posth........ Posthumous (DIAR)
POSTH...... Posthumous
POST-J...... Polymer Science and Technology-Journals (SAUS)
postl......... Postlude (AD)
Postl Dict... Postlethwaite's Dictionary of Trade and Commerce [*A publication*] (DLA)
post-mort... Post Mortem (AD)
POSTNET... Postal Numeric Encoding Technique (SAUS)
POSTNET... Postnumeric Encoding Technique [*US Postal Service*]
post-obit... Post Obitum [*After Death*] [*Latin*]
post ofc..... Post Office (VRA)
post-op..... Post-Operative (AD)
POSTOP..... Postoperative [*Medicine*]
POSTOR..... Photo-Optical Storage [*Computer science*] (VLIE)
POST-P...... Polymer Science and Technology Patents (SAUS)
POSTP....... Posterior Probability [*Computations*]
POSTP....... Postprocessor [*Computer science*]
post part... Post Partum [*Afterbirth*] [*Latin*] (AD)
postpos..... Postposition [*Linguistics*] (IEL)
PostPr....... Post Properties, Inc. [*Associated Press*] (SAG)
POSTPRO... Postprocessor [*Computer science*]
PostPrp..... Post Properties, Inc. [*Associated Press*] (SAG)
POSTS....... Positive Occipital Sharp Transients of Sleep [*On electroencephalogram*] [*Neurology*] (DAVI)
Post Sag D... Posterior Sagittal Diameter [*Anatomy*] (MAE)
Post Script... Post Script: Essays in Film and the Humanities [*A publication*] (BRI)
POST SING SED LIQ... Post Singulas Sedes Liquidas [*After Every Loose Stool*] [*Pharmacy*] (ROG)
post-sync... Post-Synchronization (AD)
POSU........ Poseidon International [*Intermodal shipping container symbol*] (TVRC)
POSV........ Pilot Operated Solenoid Valve (SAUS)
POSV........ Pilot-Operated Solenoid Valve [*Nuclear energy*] (IAA)
POSW....... Privately Owned Stored Water (ADWA)
POSWG..... Poseidon Software Working Group [*Missiles*]
POSX........ Port of Sacramento [*Federal Railroad Administration identification code*]
POSY........ Possibly [*Telegraphy*] (PCTE)
POSZ........ Post [*Federal Railroad Administration identification code*]
pot........... Dashpot (IDOE)
POT.......... Paint on Tangent (IAA)
POT.......... Parallel Output
POT.......... Partial Operating Time (SAUS)
POT.......... Part of Title [*Computer science*] (DCDG)
POT.......... Pennsylvania-Ontario Transportation Co. [*AAR code*]
POT.......... Periodic Orbital Theory (SAUS)
POT.......... Periostitis Ossificans Toxica [*Medicine*] (DMAA)
POT.......... Physical Organization Table (HGAA)
POT.......... Picture Object Table (MHDI)

POT .... Piston Operated Transducer
POT .... Pitch-Orthogonal Thrust
POT .... Plain Old Telephone [*Bell System's basic model*]
pot .... Point of tangency (AD)
POT .... Point of Termination [*Communications term*] (DCT)
POT .... Point of Turnaround [*Travel industry*] (TRID)
POT .... Polet [*Former USSR*] [*FAA designator*] (FAAC)
pot .... Portable Outdoor Toilet (AD)
POT .... Portable Outside Toilet [*A unit of mobility equipment*] [*Military*]
POT .... Port Antonio [*Jamaica*] [*Airport symbol*] (OAG)
POT .... Post Office Telecommunications [*British*]
POT .... Post-Operative Treatment [*Medicine*] (DMAA)
POT .... Potable
pot .... Potash (AD)
POT .... Potash Corp. of Saskatchewan [*NYSE symbol*] (SPSG)
POT .... Potash Corp. Saskatchewan [*NYSE symbol*] (TTSB)
pot .... Potassa [*Chemistry*] (MAE)
POT .... Potassium [*Chemical symbol is K*]
POT .... Potato (ROG)
POT .... Potentate
pot .... Potential (AD)
POT .... Potential (AFM)
POT .... Potential Temperature (SAUS)
pot .... Potentiometer (IDOE)
POT .... Potentiometer [*or Potentiometric*]
Pot .... Potion
POT .... Potsdam [*Germany*] [*Later, NGK*] [*Seismograph station code, US Geological Survey*] (SEIS)
Pot .... Potter (SAUS)
POT .... Pottery
POT .... Pottle [*Unit of measure*] (ROG)
POT .... Pottsville Free Public Library, Pottsville, PA [*OCLC symbol*] (OCLC)
POT .... Potus [*A Drink*] [*Pharmacy*]
POT .... President of The [*Telegraphy*] (PCTE)
POT .... Prevailing-Out Torque [*Automotive engineering*]
POT .... Program for Operational Trajectories [*Marine science*] (OSRA)
POT .... Proof of Technology (ACAE)
POT .... Propeller Order Transmitter (OA)
POT .... Pulmonary Oxygen Transfer [*Medicine*] (MELL)
POTA .... Planet of the Apes [*Movie title*]
POTACAN... Potash Company of Canada Ltd (EFIS)
POT ACE .... Potassium Acetate (SAUS)
POT ACID PHOS... Potassium Acid Phosphate (SAUS)
POTAD....... Program for Operational Transport and Dispersion (USDC)
PotAGT....... Potential Abnormality of Glucose Tolerance [*Medicine*]
POT&I .... Pre-Overhaul Test and Inspection Plan (SAUS)
POT & I ..... Preoverhaul Tests and Inspections [*Navy*] (NVT)
POTANN...... Potomac Annex [*Navy*]
Potash...... Potash Corp. of Saskatchewan, Inc. [*Associated Press*] (SAG)
Potash....... Potassium Carbonate (SAUS)
potash alum... Potassium Aluminum Sulfate (AD)
potass .... Potassium [*An element*] (DAVI)
POTASWG... Poseidon Test Analysis Software Working Group [*Missiles*]
POTATO PAC... National Potato Council PAC [*Washington, DC*] (PACS)
potats .... Potatoes (AD)
POTB .... Port of Tillamook Bay Railroad [*Federal Railroad Administration identification code*]
POTBI .... Places, Organizations, Things, Biographics, Intangibles
POT BICARB... Potassium Bicarbonate (SAUS)
POT BIT ..... Potassium Bitartrate (SAUS)
POT CITR... Potassium Citrate (SAUS)
POT CL...... Potassium Chloride (SAUS)
POTCP....... Partially Oxidized Tetracyanoplatinate Compound [*Inorganic, one-dimensional conductor*]
POTD .... Player of the Decade [*Sports*]
P o TD .... Port of The Dalles (AD)
POTDIF...... Potential Difference [*Electronics*] (IAA)
POTDR...... Polarization Optical Time-Domain Reflectometry (SAUS)
Pot Dwar.... Potter's Edition of Dwarris on Statutes [*A publication*] (DLA)
PotEd25 ..... Potomac Edison [*Associated Press*] (SAG)
PotEl.......... Potomac Electric Power Co. [*Associated Press*] (SAG)
POTELECTROMET... Potentiometric Electrometer (IAA)
POTEN....... Potential (AAMN)
POTEU....... Poteau, OK [*American Association of Railroads railroad junction routing code*]
POTF .... Polychromatic Optical Thickness Fringe (OA)
POTF .... Polychromatic Optical Thickness Fringes (SAUS)
POTF .... Psychological Operations Task Force [*Army*] (INF)
POTG .... Phenylorthotolyl Guanidine (SAUS)
POT GLUC... Potassium Gluconate (SAUS)
Poth Cont ... Pothier's Contracts [*A publication*] (DLA)
Poth Contr Sale... Pothier's Treatise on the Contract of Sale [*A publication*] (DLA)
Poth Cont Sale... Pothier's Treatise on the Contract of Sale [*A publication*] (DLA)
Pothier Pand... Pothier's Pandectae Justinianeae, Etc. [*A publication*] (DLA)
Poth Mar Cont... Pothier's Treatise on Maritime Contracts [*A publication*] (DLA)
Poth Ob ..... Pothier on the Law of Obligations [*A publication*] (DLA)
Poth Obl ..... Pothier on the Law of Obligations [*A publication*] (DLA)
Poth Oblig... Pothier on the Law of Obligations [*A publication*] (DLA)
Poth Oeuv... Oeuvres de Pothier [*A publication*] (DLA)
Poth Pand... Pothier's Pandects [*A publication*] (DLA)
Poth Part... Pothier on Partnership [*A publication*] (DLA)
Poth Proc Civ... Pothier. Procedure Civile [*A publication*] (DLA)
POTIB .... Polaris Technical Information Bulletin [*Missiles*]
POTIB .... Poseidon Technical Information Bulletin [*A publication*] (AD)
potl- .... Tokelau Islands [*MARC geographic area code*] [*Library of Congress*] (LCCP)
Pot LD....... Pott's Law Dictionary [*3rd ed.*] [*1815*] [*A publication*] (DLA)
Potltch ...... Potlatch Corp. [*Associated Press*] (SAG)
POTMC...... Protective Outfit Toxicological Microclimate Controlled (RDA)
PotmEl ...... Potomac Electric Power Co. [*Associated Press*] (SAG)
POTMLD .... Potential Mixed Layer Depth
POT NIT..... Potassium Nitrate (SAUS)
POTO .... Potomac River Basin (SAUS)
poto-......... Tonga [*MARC geographic area code*] [*Library of Congress*] (LCCP)
POTOMAC... Patent Office Techniques of Mechanized Access and Classification [*Automation project, shut down in 1972*]
potosslq..... Persons of the Opposite Sex Sharing Living Quarters (AD)
POTP .... Paralysis of the Pen (SAUS)
POTP .... Physical Operation Time Projection (SAUS)
POT PHOS... Potassium Phosphate (SAUS)
potr .... Potrero [*Cattle Ranch*] [*Spanish*] (AD)
POTRK ...... Purchase Order Tracking System (SAUS)
POTRK ...... Region 3 Purchase Order Tracking System (SAUS)
PotrSvg ..... Potters Savings & Loan Co. [*Associated Press*] (SAG)
POTS .... Perials of the Sea (MHDB)
POTS .... Petty Officer Telegraphist Special (DSUE)
POTS .... Photo-Optical Terrain Simulator (MUGU)
pots.......... Plain Old Telephone Service (AD)
POTS .... Plain Old Telephone Service [*or System*] [*Humorous term for Long Lines Department of AT & T*] [*See also PANS*]
POTS .... Plain Old Telephone System (SAUS)
POTS .... Plain Old Time-Sharing (SAUS)
POTS .... Plain Ordinary Telephone Service (SAUS)
POTS .... Plain Ordinary Telephone System (SAUS)
POTS .... Plug-on Terminator System (SAUS)
POTS .... PORI [*Polaris Operational Readiness Instrumentation*] Operational Test System [*Missiles*]
POTS .... Post Office Training School (SAUS)
POTS .... Potatoes [*Telegraphy*] (PCTE)
pots.......... Potentiometers (AD)
POTS .... Potentiometers (COE)
POTS .... Precision Optical Tracking System (KSC)
POTS .... Preoverhaul Tests [*Navy*] (NVT)
POTS .... Purchase of Telephones and Services Program (AAGC)
POTS .... Purchase of Telephones and Systems (SAUS)
POTS .... Purchase of Telephone Services Contracts
POTSB....... Post Office and Trustee Savings Bank (SAUS)
POT SW..... Potentiometer with Switch (SAUS)
POTT .... Patriot Operator Tactics Trainer (ACAE)
POTT .... Potter's Express [*Common carrier symbol*]
pott .... Pottery (AD)
pott- .... Trust Territory of the Pacific Islands [*MARC geographic area code*] [*Library of Congress*] (LCCP)
Pott Corp... Potter on Corporations [*A publication*] (DLA)
Pott Dwarris... Potter's Edition of Dwarris on Statutes [*A publication*] (DLA)
Potter........ Potter's Reports [*4-7 Wyoming*] [*A publication*] (DLA)
PottrFinl .... Potters Financial Corp. [*Associated Press*] (SAG)
POTTS....... Post Office Technicians Training School (SAUS)
Potts LD .... Potts' Law Dictionary [*3rd ed.*] [*1815*] [*A publication*] (DLA)
POTUS ...... President of the United States
POTV .... Personnel Orbit Transfer Vehicle (MCD)
pot w .... Portable Water (AD)
POTW .... Potable Water (KSC)
POTW .... Publically-Owned Treatment Works (DNAB)
POTW .... Publicly Owned Treatment Works [*Environment term*] (EGA)
POTWA...... Post and Telecommunications Workers Association (SAUS)
POTZ .... Pope & Talbot [*Federal Railroad Administration identification code*]
POU.......... Paramount Resources Ltd. [*Toronto Stock Exchange symbol*]
POU.......... Placenta, Ovary, Uterus [*Medicine*]
POU.......... Point of Use
POU.......... Poughkeepsie [*New York*] [*Airport symbol*] (OAG)
POU.......... Poughkeepsie, NY [*Location identifier*] [*FAA*] (FAAL)
POU.......... Pouilloux [*France*] [*Seismograph station code, US Geological Survey*] (SEIS)
POU.......... Southern Pokomam [*Language symbol*] (ETLW)
POUCC ...... Post Office Users Coordination Committee [*British*]
POUCG ...... Point of Use Chemical Generation (SAUS)
POUCG ...... Point-of-Use Chemical Generation (AAEL)
POUF .... Projects of Optimum Urgency and Feasibility
PoughSv .... [*The*] Poughkeepsie Savings Bank FSB [*Associated Press*] (SAG)
poul.......... Poultry (AD)
POUL .... Poultry
POUM .... Partido Obrero de Unificacion Marxista [*Workers' Party of Marxist Unification*] [*Former USSR*] (LAIN)
POUNC ...... Post Office Users' National Council [*British*] (ILCA)
POUP........ Post Overhaul Upkeep Period
poup-........ United States Miscellaneous Pacific Islands [*MARC geographic area code*] [*Library of Congress*] (LCCP)
POU/POE.... Point-of-Use/Point-of-Entry [*Water standards*] (FFDE)
POUR........ President's Organization for Unemployment Relief (AD)
POUS .... Partido Operario de Unidade Socialista [*Workers' Party for Socialist Unity*] [*Portugal*] [*Political party*] (PPW)
POUT .... Prison Officer under Training (WDAA)
POV.......... Peak Operated Valve (MCD)
POV.......... Peak Operating Valve
POV.......... Peak Operating Voltage
POV.......... Pend Oreille Valley Railroad (AD)

POV.......... Peroxide Value (SAUS)
POV.......... Persistence of Vision - Ray [*Computer program*]
POV.......... Personally Owned Vehicle
POV.......... Pinch-Off Voltage
POV.......... Pittsburgh & Ohio Valley Railway Co. [*AAR code*]
POV.......... Plane of Vibration
POV.......... Pneumatically Operated Valve
POV.......... Pneumatic Operated Valve (SAUS)
POV.......... Point of View
p-o-v.......... Point-of-View (AD)
PoV.......... Portal Vein [*Medicine*] (EDAA)
POV.......... Post Office Vehicle
POV.......... Poverty [*Telegraphy*] (PCTE)
POV.......... Povidone (SAUS)
POV.......... Presov [*Czechoslovakia*] [*Airport symbol*] (AD)
POV.......... Pressure-Operated Valve (MCD)
pov.......... Privately Owned Vehicle (AD)
POV.......... Privately Owned Vehicle (NVT)
POV.......... Proximity Operations Vehicle (SSD)
POV.......... Public Order Vehicle [*Police and security equipment*]
POV.......... Purchase, Outside Vendors
POV.......... Putting-On Voltage [*Doppler navigation*] (DEN)
POVA........ Pend D'Oreille Valley Railroad [*Federal Railroad Administration identification code*]
POVC........ Probation Officers and Volunteers in Corrections [*Victoria, Australia*]
POVEU...... Program Operations Vocational Education Unit (OICC)
POVJC....... P & Ov Junction, PA [*American Association of Railroads railroad junction routing code*]
Pov L Rep... Poverty Law Reporter [*Commerce Clearing House*] [*A publication*] (DLA)
POVMR...... Problem-Oriented Veterinary Medical Record (SAUS)
POVORTAD... Positive Vorticity Advection (SAUS)
POVT........ Puerperal Ovarian-Vein Thrombophlebitis [*Medicine*]
POVZ........ Port of Vancouver [*Federal Railroad Administration identification code*]
POW.......... Country Potash, Oil and Wheat Country (SAUS)
POW.......... Palace on Wheels [*Indian Railway*] (TIR)
POW.......... Paying Their Own Way
POW.......... Pay Order of Withdrawal
POW.......... Peoples of the World [*A publication*]
POW.......... Perception of Ward [*Scales*] [*Psychology*]
POW.......... Peripheral Output Writer (SAUS)
POW.......... Petty Officer of the Watch [*Navy*]
POW.......... Place of Work (SAUS)
PoW.......... Plan of Work (HEAS)
POW.......... Port of Wilmington [*Federal Railroad Administration identification code*]
POW.......... Powassan Encephalitis [*Medicine*]
POW.......... Powder [*Navy*]
pow.......... Power (AD)
POW.......... Power
POW.......... Power Corp. of Canada [*Toronto Stock Exchange symbol*] [*Vancouver Stock Exchange symbol*]
POW.......... Powermaster [*NCIC car model code*]
POW.......... Powhatan [*Arkansas*] [*Seismograph station code, US Geological Survey*] (SEIS)
P o W....... Prince of Wales (AD)
POW.......... Prince of Wales
POW.......... Prince of Wales Island (ALAC)
pow.......... Prisoner of War (AD)
PoW.......... Prisoner of War (WDAA)
POW.......... Prisoner of War [*Also, PW*]
P o W....... Prisoner of Watergate (AD)
POW.......... Prisoner Outreach Work (WDAA)
POW.......... Progressive Order of the West [*Defunct*] (EA)
POW.......... PSE, Inc. [*AMEX symbol*] (COMM)
POWACO.... Portable Water Coolant Circulator
Pow App Proc... Powell's Law of Appellate Proceedings [*A publication*] (DLA)
PoWBN...... Biblioteka Narodowa [*National Library*], Warsaw, Poland [*Library symbol*] [*Library of Congress*] (LCLS)
PoWC........ Instytut Informacji Naukowej, Technicznej, i Ekonomicznej, Warsaw, Poland [*Library symbol*] [*Library of Congress*] (LCLS)
POWC........ Program Out-of-Window Collision (SAUS)
Pow Car..... Powell's Inland Carriers [*2nd ed.*] [*1861*] [*A publication*] (DLA)
Pow Cont... Powell on Contracts [*A publication*] (DLA)
Pow Conv... Powell. Conveyancing [*1810*] [*A publication*] (ILCA)
POW Country... Potash, Oil, and Wheat Country [*Saskatoon, Saskatchewan*] (AD)
powd........ Powder (AD)
POWD........ Powder [*England*]
POWD........ Powdered
Powder Bulk Eng... Powder and Bulk Engineering (SAUS)
Powder Diffr... Powder Diffraction (SAUS)
Powder Handl Process... Powder Handling and Processing (SAUS)
Powder Metall... Powder Metallurgy (SAUS)
Powder Metall Def Technol... Powder Metallurgy in Defense Technology (SAUS)
Powder Metall Int... Powder Metallurgy International (SAUS)
Powder Metall Sci Technol... Powder Metallurgy Science and Technology (SAUS)
Powder Metall Technol... Powder Metallurgy Technology (SAUS)
Powder Sci Eng... Powder Science and Engineering (SAUS)
Powder Technol... Powder Technology (SAUS)
Pow Dev.... Powell's Essay upon the Learning of Devises, Etc. [*A publication*] (DLA)
POWDR..... Protect Our Wetlands and Duck Resources [*Department of the Interior*] [*Washington, DC*]
POWE........ Powerline Products [*NCIC trailer make code*]
Powell....... Powell Industries, Inc. [*Associated Press*] (SAG)
POWEP...... Priority Output Writes Execution Process (SAUS)
POWER...... Pennsylvania Online World of Electronic Resources Library
POWER...... Pennsylvania's Online World of Electronic Resources
POWER...... Pension Opportunities for Workers' Expanded Retirement [*Plan proposed in 1991 by the Department of Labor*]
POWER...... People Organized and Working for Economic Rebirth [*Program for black economic development*] [*Later, Nationway Ventures International Ltd.*]
POWER...... Performance Optimization with Enhanced RISC [*Reduced Instruction Set Computer*] (PCM)
POWER...... Planning Operation With Enabling Resources
POWER...... Power Optimization With Enhanced RISC (SAUS)
POWER...... Priority Output Writers Execution Processor [*Computer science*] (IAA)
POWER...... Priority Output Writers, Execution Processors, and Input Readers (MHDI)
POWER...... Priority Output Writers, Executionprocessors and input Readers (SAUS)
POWER...... Priority Output Writes Execution Process [*Computer science*] (IAA)
POWER...... Producing Organized Writing and Effective Reviewing
POWER...... Professionals Organized for Women's Equal Rights [*Feminist group*]
POWER...... PROFS [*Program for Regional Observing and Forecasting Services*] Operational Weather Education and Research [*Marine science*] (OSRA)
POWER...... Programmed Offline Waste Reduction (SAUS)
power....... Programmed Operational Warshot Evaluation and Review (AD)
POWER...... Programmed Operational Warshot Evaluation and Review
POWER...... Promote Our Wonderful Energy Resources (EA)
Power Convers Intell Motion... Power Conversion and Intelligent Motion (SAUS)
POWER CTR... Power Center (SAUS)
Power Eng J... Power Engineering Journal (SAUS)
Power Int... Power International (SAUS)
Power Int Ed... Power International Edition (SAUS)
PowerMac.. Power Macintosh (DCOM)
POWER PAC... American Public Power Association Public Ownership of Electric Resources PAC [*Washington, DC*] (PACS)
POWERPC... Performance Optimization with Enhanced RISC-Performance Computing (SAUS)
Powers...... Powers' Reports, New York Surrogate Court [*A publication*] (DLA)
Power's Sur... Powers' Reports, New York Surrogate Court [*A publication*] (DLA)
POWER System... Priority Output Writers, Executionprocessors and input Readers System (SAUS)
Power Transm Des... Power Transmission Design (SAUS)
Power Works Eng... Power and Works Engineering (SAUS)
Pow Ev...... Powell on Evidence [*10th ed.*] [*1921*] [*A publication*] (DLA)
powf-........ Wallis and Futuna [*MARC geographic area code*] [*Library of Congress*] (LCCP)
POWG....... Payload Operations Working Group (SAUS)
POWG....... Procurement Officers Work Group (AAGC)
POWI........ Power Integrations [*NASDAQ symbol*]
Pow Inl Car... Powell on the Law of Inland Carriers [*A publication*] (DLA)
POW(J)...... Prisoner of War of Japan
powk-........ Wake Island [*MARC geographic area code*] [*Library of Congress*] (LCCP)
POWL........ Powell [*NCIC motorcycle make code*]
POWL........ Powell Indus [*NASDAQ symbol*] (TTSB)
POWL........ Powell Industries, Inc. [*NASDAQ symbol*] (NQ)
POW/MIA... Prisoner of War/Missing in Action (SAUS)
POW/MIG... Place of Work and Migration Sample [*Bureau of the Census*] (GFGA)
Pow Mort... Powell on Mortgages [*6th ed.*] [*1826*] [*A publication*] (DLA)
Pow Mortg... Powell on Mortgages [*A publication*] (DLA)
POW/MP.... Prisoner of War/Missing Personnel
POWO........ Prince [*or Princess*] of Wales' Own [*Military unit*] [*British*] (DMA)
PoWP........ Biblioteka Golowna Politechniki Warszawsjiej (Warsaw Technical University Central Library), Warsaw, Poland [*Library symbol*] [*Library of Congress*] (LCLS)
POWP........ Preliminary Overhaul Work Package (DNAB)
POWR........ Environmental Power [*NASDAQ symbol*] (SAG)
POWR........ Environmental Power Corp. [*OTCBB symbol*]
Pow R & D... Power, Rodwell, and Drew's English Election Cases [*1847-56*] [*A publication*] (DLA)
PowrCrv..... PowerCerv Corp. [*Associated Press*] (SAG)
POWRE...... Professional Opportunities for Women in Research and Education
POWREN.... Petty Officer Wren (SAUS)
POWRENAF... Petty Officer WREN [*Women's Royal Naval Service*] Air Fitter [*British military*] (DMA)
POWRENCINE... Petty Officer WREN [*Women's Royal Naval Service*] Cinema Operator [*British military*] (DMA)
POWRENCK... Petty Officer WREN [*Women's Royal Naval Service*] Cook [*British military*] (DMA)
POWRENDHYG... Petty Officer WREN [*Women's Royal Naval Service*] Dental Hygienist [*British military*] (DMA)
POWRENDSA... Petty Officer WREN [*Women's Royal Naval Service*] Dental Surgery Assistant [*British military*] (DMA)
POWRENMET... Petty Officer WREN [*Women's Royal Naval Service*] Meteorological Observer [*British military*] (DMA)
POWRENMT... Petty Officer WREN [*Women's Royal Naval Service*] Motor Transport Driver [*British military*] (DMA)
POWRENPHOT... Petty Officer WREN [*Women's Royal Naval Service*] Photographer [*British military*] (DMA)
POWRENQA... Petty Officer WREN [*Women's Royal Naval Service*] Quarters Assistant [*British military*] (DMA)
POWREN(R)... Petty Officer WREN [*Women's Royal Naval Service*] (RADAR) [*British military*] (DMA)

POWRENREL... Petty Officer WREN [*Women's Royal Naval Service*] Radio Electrician [*British military*] (DMA)
POWRENRS(M)... Petty Officer WREN [*Women's Royal Naval Service*] Radio Supervisor (Morse) [*British military*] (DMA)
POWRENSA... Petty Officer WREN [*Women's Royal Naval Service*] Stores Accountant [*British military*] (DMA)
POWRENS(C)... Petty Officer WREN [*Women's Royal Naval Service*] Stores Assistant (Clothes) [*British military*] (DMA)
POWRENS(S)... Petty Officer WREN [*Women's Royal Naval Service*] Stores Assistant (Stores) [*British military*] (DMA)
POWRENSTD... Petty Officer WREN [*Women's Royal Naval Service*] Steward [*British military*] (DMA)
POWRENS(V)... Petty Officer WREN [*Women's Royal Naval Service*] Stores Assistant (Victualling) [*British military*] (DMA)
POWRENTEL... Petty Officer WREN [*Women's Royal Naval Service*] Telephonist [*British military*] (DMA)
POWRENTSA... Petty Officer WREN [*Women's Royal Naval Service*] Training Support Assistant [*British military*] (DMA)
POWRENWA... Petty Officer WREN [*Women's Royal Naval Service*] Weapon Analyst [*British military*] (DMA)
POWRENWTR(G)... Petty Officer WREN [*Women's Royal Naval Service*] Writer (General) [*British military*] (DMA)
POWRENWTR(P)... Petty Officer WREN [*Women's Royal Naval Service*] Writer (Pay) [*British military*] (DMA)
POWRENWW... Petty Officer WREN [*Women's Royal Naval Service*] Welfare Worker [*British military*] (DMA)
Powrwv ..... Powerwave Technologies, Inc. [*Associated Press*] (SAG)
POWS .... PROFS [*Program for Regional Observing and Forecasting Services*] Operational Work Station [*Marine science*] (OSRA)
POWS .... Project Operating Work Statement [*NASA*] (NASA)
POWS .... Pyrotechnic Outside Warning System (IEEE)
pows-........ Western Samoa [*MARC geographic area code*] [*Library of Congress*] (LCCP)
POW Scales... Perception of Ward Scales (SAUS)
POW-SIG.... Pagan/Occult/Witchcraft Special Interest Group (EA)
Pow Str ..... Power Steering (SAUS)
Pow Surr.... Powers' Reports, New York Surrogate Court [*A publication*] (DLA)
POWTECH... International Powder and Bulk Solids Technology Exhibition and Conference
POWTR...... Petty Officer Writer [*British military*] (DMA)
POWU .... Post Office Workers Union (SAUS)
POWU .... Post Office Work Unit [*Computer performance measure*] [*British Telecom*]
PoWU .... Uniwersytet Warszawski [*University of Warsaw*], Warsaw, Poland [*Library symbol*] [*Library of Congress*] (LCLS)
POWV .... Powassan Encephalitis Virus [*Virology*] (QSUL)
POW:WE.... Peoples of the World: Western Europeans [*A publication*]
POWWER.... Power of World Wide Energy Resources [*In organization name "Natural POWWER"*] (EA)
Pow Wind .. Power Windows (SAUS)
POWZ .... Port of Wilmington [*Federal Railroad Administration identification code*]
POX.......... Partial Oxidation [*Organic chemistry*]
POX.......... Point of Exit
POX.......... Police [*Telegraphy*] (PCTE)
POX.......... Port Alexander [*Alaska*] [*Airport symbol*] (AD)
P-OX.......... Pressure Oxidation
POX.......... Purgeable Organic Halogen [*Chemistry*] (FFDE)
POX-AC ..... Pox Battery, Acute [*Biochemistry*] (DAVI)
poxd-........ Mariana Islands [*MARC geographic area code*] [*Library of Congress*] (LCCP)
poxe-........ Marshall Islands [*MARC geographic area code*] [*Library of Congress*] (LCCP)
poxf-......... Midway Islands [*MARC geographic area code*] [*Library of Congress*] (LCCP)
poxh-........ Niue [*MARC geographic area code*] [*Library of Congress*] (LCCP)
POXM .... Policeman [*Telegraphy*] (PCTE)
POXN........ Policemen [*Telegraphy*] (PCTE)
POXR........ Patriot Express [*Common carrier symbol*]
POY.......... Lovell-Powell [*Wyoming*] [*Airport symbol*] (AD)
POY.......... Partially Oriented Yarn (SAUS)
POY.......... Partially Oriented Yarns
POY.......... Polyester Oriented Yarn (DICI)
POY.......... Possibility [*Telegraphy*] (PCTE)
POY.......... Powell, WY [*Location identifier*] [*FAA*] (FAAL)
POY.......... Prairie Oil Royalties Co. Ltd. [*AMEX symbol*] [*Toronto Stock Exchange symbol*] (SPSG)
POY.......... Preoriented Polyester Yarn (SAUS)
poy.......... Pre-Oriented Yarn (AD)
Poynt M & D... Poynter on Marriage and Divorce [*2nd ed.*] [*1824*] [*A publication*] (DLA)
POYO........ Pollo Tropical [*NASDAQ symbol*] (SAG)
Poz.......... Poznan (AD)
POZ.......... Poznan [*Poland*] [*Airport symbol*] (OAG)
POZA .... Pozas Brothers Trucking Company [*Common carrier symbol*]
POZN .... Pozen, Inc. [*NASDAQ symbol*]
PP............ Brazil [*International civil aircraft marking*] (ODBW)
pp............ by proxy (SAUS)
PP............ Descent through Cloud (SAUS)
PP............ Eisai Co. Ltd. [*Japan*] [*Research code symbol*]
PP............ Free Library of Philadelphia, Philadelphia, PA [*Library symbol*] [*Library of Congress*] (LCLS)
PP............ Head Injury Hotline [*Formerly, Phoenix Project*] (EA)
PP............ Pacific Petroleum (AD)
PP............ Packet Processor (SAUS)
PP............ Page Printer (NVT)
Pp............ Pages (WDMC)
PP............ Pages
pp............ Pages (WDMC)
PP............ Pages from the Past [*Later, PIR*] [*An association*] (EA)
PP............ Painting Processor (SAUS)
PP............ Palisades Plant [*Nuclear energy*] (NRCH)
PP............ Palus Putretudinis [*Lunar area*]
PP............ Pancreatic Polypeptide [*Biochemistry*]
PP............ Pandectes Periodiques [*A publication*] (ILCA)
pp............ Panel Point (AD)
PP............ Panel Point [*Technical drawings*]
PP............ Pangu Pati [*Papua New Guinea*] [*Political party*] (PPW)
PP............ Papa [*Pope*]
Pp............ Papa [*Father*] [*Latin*] (AD)
PP............ Paper Profit
pp............ Papua New Guinea [*MARC country of publication code*] [*Library of Congress*] (LCCP)
PP............ Paradigm Publishing Ltd. [*British*]
PP............ Paradoxical Pulse [*Medicine*] (DMAA)
PP............ Parallel Plate (SAUS)
PP............ Parallel Poll (SAUS)
PP............ Parallel Port (SAUS)
PP............ Parallel Printer (SAUS)
PP............ Parallel Processing (SAUS)
PP............ Parallel Processor
PP............ Parallel Programming (SAUS)
PP............ Parametric Programming (SAUS)
pp............ Parcel Post (AD)
PP............ Parcel Post
PP............ Parish Priest
PP............ Paris Publications, Inc.
PP............ Parity Price (MHDW)
PP............ Parliamentary Papers [*A publication*] [*British*]
PP............ Pars Planitis (SAUS)
PP............ Partially Paid (SAUS)
P/P............ Partial Pay [*Air Force*]
pp............ Partial Pressure (NAKS)
PP............ Partial Pressure
PP............ Partial Product (IAA)
PP............ Partia Popullore [*Popular Party*] [*Albania*] [*Political party*] (PPE)
PP............ Participatory Program (SAUS)
PP............ Particular [*Named*] Port [*British*] (ROG)
PP............ Particulate Phosphorus (SAUS)
PP............ Partido Panamenista [*Panamanian Party*] [*Political party*] (PPW)
PP............ Partido Popular [*Popular Party*] [*Spain*] [*Political party*] (PPE)
PP............ Partido Populista [*Populist Party*] [*Argentina*] [*Political party*]
PP............ Parti du Peuple [*People's Party*] [*Burundi*] [*Political party*]
PP............ Partin Prediction
pp............ Partly Paid (ADWA)
PP............ Partners in Politics (EA)
pp............ Part Paid (AD)
PP............ Part Paid [*Business and trade*]
PP............ Parts Per
PP............ Passage Point (SAUS)
PP............ [*The*] Passionate Pilgrim [*Shakespearean work*]
pp............ Passive Participle (AD)
PP............ Passive Participle
PP............ Password Protection (SAUS)
PP............ Pastor Pastorum [*Shepherd of the Shepherds*] [*Latin*] (ROG)
pp............ Past Participle (WDMC)
PP............ Past Participle
PP............ Past Patriarch [*Freemasonry*] (ROG)
PP............ Past President
PP............ Patchboard Programming (SAUS)
P/P............ Patch Panel (NASA)
PP............ Patent Bending (SAUS)
PP............ Patent Pending (IAA)
PP............ Pater Patriae [*The Father of His Country*] [*Latin*]
PP............ Pathfinder Pilot (SAUS)
PP............ Path Provisioning (SAUS)
PP............ Patres [*Fathers*] [*Latin*]
PP............ Patriotic Party [*British*]
PP............ Patrol Vessels [*Navy symbol*] (MUGU)
PP............ Pattern Processing (SAUS)
PP............ Pauley Petroleum, Inc. [*AMEX symbol*] (COMM)
PP............ Payload Pointer (SAUS)
PP............ Pay Period (EEVL)
PP............ Payphone (SAUS)
PP............ Pay Plan (ALAC)
PP............ Peace PAC (EA)
PP............ Peak Power (IAA)
PP............ Peak Pressure
P-P............ Peak-to-Peak [*Value*]
PP............ Peak-to-Peak
PP............ Peanut Pals (EA)
PP............ Pedal Power
PP............ Pedal Pulse
PP............ Peering Point (SAUS)
PP............ Pelagra Preventive (SAUS)
PP............ Pellagra Preventing (SAUS)
pp............ Pellagra Preventive (AD)
PP............ Pellagra Preventive [*Factor*] [*See also PPF*] [*Biochemistry*]
P-P............ Pellagra-Preventive Factor (AD)
PP............ Pellet Plant (SAUS)

PP............ Pension Plan
PP............ People's Party [*Spain*] [*Political party*] (ECON)
PP............ People's Party [*Halkci Partisi*] [*Turkey*] [*Political party*] (PPW)
PP............ Pep Pill [*Slang*]
pp............ Perceptual Performance (AD)
PP............ Percussion Primer (SAUS)
PP............ Perfect Prog (SAUS)
PP............ Perfect Program (SAUS)
PP............ Perforation Pitch (SAUS)
PP............ Perfusion Pressure [*Cardiology*] (DAVI)
PP............ Pericardial Pressure (SAUS)
PP............ Periodical Publications [*British Library shelf designation*]
PP............ Periodic Paralysis [*Medicine*] (EDAA)
PP............ Peripheral Processor [*Computer science*]
PP............ Periportal [*Anatomy*]
PP............ Periproct [*Invertebrate anatomy*]
PP............ Peritoneal Pseudomyxoma [*Medicine*] (EDAA)
PP............ Permanent Partial [*Dentistry*] (MAE)
pp............ Permanent Party (AD)
PP............ Permanent Party [*Military*]
PP............ Permanent Pasture [*Agriculture*]
PP............ Permanent Press (ADA)
PP............ Permanent Professor
PP............ Peroxisome Proliferator [*Biochemistry*]
pp............ per paragraph (SAUS)
p/p............ per passenger (SAUS)
pp............ Per Person (AD)
pp............ per pro (SAUS)
pp............ Per Procurationem (ODA)
PP............ Per Procurationem [*By Proxy, By the Action Of*] [*Legal term*] [*Latin*]
PP............ Per-protocol [*Medicine*] [*Analysis*] (EDAA)
PP............ Persisting Proteinuria [*Medicine*] (EDAA)
PP............ Personal Prelatures [*Diocesan abbreviation*] (TOCD)
PP............ Personal Property
P-P............ Person to Person [*Word processing*]
PP............ Pet Pride (EA)
PP............ Petroleum Point
PP............ Petrol Point (SAUS)
PP............ Petrus Piccoli de Monteforte [*Flourished, 14th century*] [*Authority cited in pre-1607 legal work*] (DSA)
PP............ Petticoat Peeping [*From one girl to another, in reference to dress disarrangement*]
PP............ Peyer's Patch [*Immunology*]
PP............ Phase Partitioning (SAUS)
PP............ Phillips Airlines [*ICAO designator*] (AD)
PP............ Philo-Phobe [*Psychological testing*]
PP............ Phoenix Project [*An association*] (EA)
PP............ Phony Peach Bacteria [*Plant pathology*]
PP............ Phosphoprotein (SAUS)
PP............ Photosynthetic Panel [*i.e., leaf*] [*Slang*]
PP............ Physical Partition (SAUS)
PP............ Physical Plane (SAUS)
pp............ Physical Profile (AD)
PP............ Physical Profile
pp............ Physical Properties (AD)
PP............ Physical Properties
PP............ Phytophthora Parasitica [*A fungus*]
pp............ Pianissimo [*Very Softly*] [*Italian*] [*Music*] (WDAA)
PP............ Pianissimo [*Very Softly*] [*Music*]
PP............ Picked Ports
pp............ Pickpocket (AD)
PP............ Pickpocket
PP............ Picric Powder (SAUS)
PP............ Picture Peace [*Defunct*] (EA)
pp............ Piena Pelle [*Full Leather*] [*Italian*] (AD)
P/P............ Pier/Pier (SAUS)
PP............ Piers Plowman [*Middle English poem*]
P/P............ Pier-to-House Service (SAUS)
P/P............ Pier to Pier (ADA)
P/P............ Pier-to-Pier Service (SAUS)
PP............ Piissimus [*Most Holy*] [*Latin*]
PP............ Pilotless Plane
PP............ Pilot Parents (EA)
PP............ Pilot Pulse
PP............ Pilot Punch
PP............ Pine Bark Mixed with Peat
PP............ Pink Puffer [*Emphysema*] (MAE)
PP............ Pinpoint [*Pupils*] [*Ophthalmology*] (DAVI)
PP............ Pinprick [*Medicine*] (DMAA)
PP............ Pipelined Processor (SAUS)
PP............ Pipeline Processor (IAA)
PP............ Piping
PP............ Piscataqua Pioneers (EA)
PP............ Piu Piano [*More Softly*] [*Music*]
PP............ PIXEL-Processing [*Computer science*]
PP............ Placental Protein [*Gynecology*]
PP............ Place of Publisher (NITA)
PP............ Plane Parallel
PP............ Plane Polarized [*Telecommunications*] (TEL)
PP............ Planetary Programs [*NASA*]
PP............ Planned Parenthood
pp............ Planning Package (NAKS)
PP............ Planning Package [*NASA*] (NASA)
pp............ Planning Permission (AD)
PP............ Planning Permit (SAUS)
PP............ Planning Purpose
PP............ Plan Profile
PP............ Plant Protection
PP............ Plasmapheresis [*Hematology*]
PP............ Plasma Processing (SAUS)
PP............ Plasma Protein
PP............ Plaster of Paris
PP............ Plate Power (IAA)
PP............ Plate Pulse (IAA)
PP............ Play or Pay (ROG)
PP............ Please Pay (ROG)
pp............ Plenum Pressure (COE)
PP............ Plethysmograph Pressure [*Measurement*] [*Medicine*] (DAVI)
PP............ Pleural Pressure [*Medicine*]
PP............ Plot Points [*Computer science*]
PP............ Pluripara (SAUS)
PP............ Pluvius Policy [*Insurance against rain*]
PP............ Pocketpiece [*A. C. Nielsen Co.*] [*Rating report*] (NTCM)
PP............ Poetry Project (EA)
P/P............ Point/Point (SAUS)
P/P............ Point-to-Point [*Air Force*]
PP............ Polar Pacific [*American air mass*]
PP............ Pole Piece (DEN)
PP............ Pole Position [*Automobile racing*]
PP............ Police Package [*Law enforcement vehicles*]
PP............ Polizei Pistole [*Police Pistol*] [*Walther Waffenfabrik, German arms manufacturer*]
PP............ Pollution Prevention (EEVL)
PP............ Polynomial Programming (SAUS)
PP............ Polynominal Programming (SAUS)
PP............ Polypeptide [*Biochemistry*]
PP............ Polyphosphate [*Inorganic chemistry*] (AAMN)
PP............ Polypropylen (SAUS)
PP............ Polypropylene [*Organic chemistry*]
PP............ Polypyrrole [*Photovoltaic energy systems*]
PP............ Polystyrene Agglutination Plate (DB)
PP............ Pom-Pom [*Gun*]
pp............ Ponderosa Pine (MIST)
PP............ Pontificum [*Of the Popes*] [*Latin*]
PP............ Popular Party [*European political movement*] (ECON)
PP............ Population Planning (DAVI)
PP............ Populist Party of America [*Political party*] (EA)
PP............ Populist Party (Turkey) [*Political party*] (PSAP)
PP............ Porcelain Pavers (DICI)
PP............ Portability Package (SAUS)
PP............ Portable Part (SAUS)
PP............ Port Pipe (ADA)
P/P............ Port/Port (SAUS)
P/P............ Port-to-Port Transport (SAUS)
PP............ Posa Piano [*Handle with Care*] [*Shipping*] [*Italian*]
PP............ Position Paper (MCD)
PP............ Positive Pressure (SAUS)
pp............ Postage Paid (AD)
PP............ Postage Paid [*Shipping*]
pp............ Posted Price (MENA)
PP............ Posterior Parietal Cortex [*Neuroanatomy*]
PP............ Posterior Pituitary [*Medicine*]
PP............ Postglenoid Process (SAUS)
PP............ Post Pagado [*Postage Paid*] [*Shipping*] [*Spanish*]
PP............ Post Paid (SAUS)
pp............ Postpaid
PP............ Post Partum [*After Birth*] [*Latin*] (ADA)
pp............ Post Partum [*Afterbirth*] [*Latin*] (AD)
pp............ postpartum (SAUS)
PP............ Postpass
PP............ Post Pay (SAUS)
PP............ Postpone [*Telegraphy*] (PCTE)
PP............ Postponed
PP............ Post Position [*Racing*]
PP............ Postprandial [*After Meals*] [*Pharmacy*]
PP............ Post Processing
PP............ Postprocessor [*Computer science*] (IAA)
PP............ Pounds Pressure
PP............ Pour Point [*Petroleum characteristic*]
PP............ Power Package
PP............ Power Panel (SAUS)
PP............ Power People
PP............ Power Plan (IAA)
PP............ Power Plant
PP............ Power Play [*Hockey*]
pp............ Power Pole (NAKS)
PP............ Power Pole (NASA)
PP............ Power Supplies [*JETDS nomenclature*] [*Military*] (CET)
PP............ Practice and Procedure (SAUS)
PP............ Practice Projectile (SAUS)
PP............ Praemissis Praemittendis [*Omitting Preliminaries, To Whom It May Concern*] [*Latin*]
PP............ Praepter Propter [*Approximately*] [*Pharmacy*]
Pp............ Pratylenchus penetrans [*A nematode*]
PP............ Precautionary Principle (SAUS)
PP............ Precedence and Preemption [*Communications term*] (DCT)
PP............ Precision Platform (ACAE)
PP............ Predictive Pipelining (SAUS)

PP........... Preferred Provider [*Medicine*] (DMAA)
PP........... Premium Package [*Automotive sales*]
PP........... Prentiss Properties Trust [*NYSE symbol*] (SAG)
PP........... Prepaid
PP........... Preparative Flag [*Navy*] [*British*]
PP........... Preparing, Providing [*Pharmacy*] (ROG)
P/P........... Pre/Planned (SAUS)
PP........... Preposition [*Industrial engineering*]
PP........... Prepositional Phrase (BYTE)
PP........... Prepregnancy [*Medicine*]
PP........... Preprinted
PP........... Preprocessor
PP........... Preproduction (KSC)
PP........... Pre-Prototype (SAUS)
PP........... Prescribed Period [*Social Security Administration*] (OICC)
PP........... Presentation Position [*Computer science*] (DCDG)
PP........... Presenting Problem (SAUS)
PP........... Present Participle [*Grammar*]
pp........... Present Position (AD)
PP........... Present Position [*Military*]
PP........... Present Pupil (AIE)
PP........... Press Packed
PP........... Press Pressure (SSD)
PP........... Pressure Pattern (MCD)
PP........... Pressure Plate (SAUS)
PP........... Pressure Proof (SAUS)
pp........... Pressure-Proof (AD)
PP........... Pressure-Proof [*Technical drawings*]
PP........... Pretty Poor [*Slang*] [*Bowdlerized version*]
PP........... Previous Page (SAUS)
PP........... Primarily Primates [*An association*] (EA)
PP........... Primary Point (VLIE)
PP........... Primary Power (SAUS)
PP........... Primary Pressure [*Nuclear energy*] (NRCH)
PP........... Primary Processor (SAUS)
PP........... Primary Producers (ADA)
PP........... Princess Pat's [*Princess Patricia of Connaught's Light Infantry*] [*Military unit*] [*Canada*]
PP........... Principal
PP........... Principal Point
PP........... Principles and Practice (SAUS)
pp........... Printed Pages [*Publishing*] (WDAA)
PP........... Printer Page [*Computer science*]
PP........... Printer Perforator (SAUS)
P/P........... Printer/Plotter (NASA)
PP........... Print Position (SAUS)
PP........... Print Positions
PP........... Print Program (SAUS)
P/P........... Print Punch
PP........... Print-Punch [*Computer science*] (BUR)
PP........... Priority Message Precedence [*Telecommunications*] (ADDR)
PP........... Priority Pollutant (EEVL)
PP........... Priority Processing (SAUS)
PP........... Priority Processor
PP........... Prior Permission
PP........... Private Jet Services AG [*Sweden*] [*ICAO designator*] (ICDA)
pp........... Privately Printed (AD)
PP........... Privately Printed
P/P........... Private Passenger
PP........... Private Patient [*Medicine*]
PP........... Private Physician (SAUS)
PP........... Private Pilot (SAUS)
PP........... Private Practice [*Chiropody*] [*British*]
pp........... Private Property (AD)
PP........... Private Property [*Military*]
PP........... Problem Program (VLIE)
PP........... Procurement Package (AAGC)
PP........... Procurement Plan (MCD)
PP........... Producer Price
PP........... Production Phase (SAUS)
PP........... Production Pool (SAUS)
PP........... Production Processes
PP........... Product Publication (IAA)
pp........... Professional Paper (AD)
PP........... Professional Paper
PP........... Professor Publicus [*Public Professor*] [*Latin*] (ROG)
PP........... Programming Plan (AFM)
PP........... Programming Problem (SAUS)
PP........... Program Package (MCD)
PP........... Program Paper
PP........... Program Part (SAUS)
pp........... Program Performance (NAKS)
PP........... Program Performance (NASA)
PP........... Program Performed
PP........... Program Planning (COE)
PP........... Program Position (SAUS)
PP........... Program Processing (SAUS)
PP........... Program Product [*Computer science*]
PP........... Program Pulse (SAUS)
PP........... Progressive Party (Brazil) [*Political party*] (PSAP)
PP........... Progressive Party (Iceland) [*Political party*] (PSAP)
PP........... Progress Payments [*Military procurement*]
PP........... Projection Plane (SAUS)
PP........... Project Priesthood (EA)
PP........... Project Proposal (KSC)
PP........... Proletarian Party
PP........... Promotion Pamphlet (SAUS)
PP........... Proodeftiki Parataxis [*Progressive Front*] [*Greek Cyprus*] [*Political party*] (PPE)
pp........... Pro Parte [*In Part*] [*Latin*]
PP........... Propeller Pitch
PP........... Property and Procurement (ALAC)
PP........... Proportional Part
PP........... Proposals Paper
PP........... Proposed Plan (BCP)
PP........... Propria Persona [*In His or Her Own Person*] [*Latin*] (WGA)
PP........... Propulsion Power (KSC)
PP........... Protein Phosphatase [*An enzyme*]
PP........... Prothrombin-Proconvertin [*Hematology*]
PP........... Proton-Proton [*Nuclear physics*]
PP........... Protoporphyria [*Medicine*]
PP........... Protoporphyrin [*Biochemistry*]
PP........... Provisioning Procedures [*Corps of Engineers*]
PP........... Proximal Phalanx [*Anatomy*]
PP........... Pseudomyxoma Peritonei [*Medicine*] (DMAA)
PP........... Pseudoprogram (IAA)
PP........... Psychic Phenomena
PP........... Psychological Profile
PP........... Psychologists and Psychiatrists [*in service*] [*British*]
P/P........... Pterocephaliid-Ptychaspid [*Paleogeologic boundary*]
PP........... Public Property
PP........... Published Price [*of a book*]
PP........... Publishers Paper [*Federal Railroad Administration identification code*]
PP........... Pulmonary Pressure (SAUS)
PP........... Pulse Pair (IAA)
PP........... Pulse Polarography [*Analytical chemistry*]
PP........... Pulse Pressure [*Medicine*]
PP........... Pulse Pumped (SAUS)
P-P........... Pulse to Pulse
PP........... Puls-Polarography (SAUS)
PP........... Pulvis Patrum [*The Fathers' Powder (or Jesuits' Powder)*] [*Pharmacy*] (ROG)
PP........... Pump-Priming (MHDB)
PP........... Punctum Proximum [*Near Point*] [*Latin*]
pp........... Purchased Part (AD)
PP........... Purchased Part
PP........... Purchased Parts
PP........... Purchase Power [*Commercial firm*] (EA)
PP........... Purchase Price
PP........... Purified Protein (SAUS)
PP........... Pusher Plane
pp........... Push-Pull (NAKS)
PP........... Push-Pull [*Technical drawings*]
PP........... Pyrophosphate [*Chemistry*]
PP1 .... Protein Phosphatase 1 [*An enzyme*]
PP1P .... Patrol Plane 1st Pilot (SAUS)
pp40.......... Phosphoprotein of 40 kDa Molar Mass [*Molecular biology*] (QSUL)
PPA........... Athenaeum of Philadelphia, Philadelphia, PA [*Library symbol*] [*Library of Congress*] (LCLS)
PPA........... National Plant Protection Association
PPA........... Pakistan Press Association (AD)
PPA........... Paleopathology Association (EA)
PPA........... Palpation, Percussion, and Auscultation [*Medicine*]
ppa .... Palpitation, Percussion, Auscultation (AD)
PPA........... Pampa, TX [*Location identifier*] [*FAA*] (FAAL)
PPA........... Panamerican/Panafrican Association (EA)
PPA........... Paper Pail Association [*Defunct*] (EA)
PPA........... Paper Plate Association [*Later, SSI*] (EA)
PPA........... Parallel Port Adapter [*Computer science*] (CIST)
PPA........... Parallel Processing Automata (PDAA)
PPA........... Parcel Post Association [*Later, PSA*] (EA)
PPA........... Parenting Publications of America (NTPA)
PPA........... Parent of a Person with Autism (SAUS)
PPA........... Parents for Private Adoption [*Defunct*] (EA)
PPA........... Partial Peak Area (SAUS)
PPA........... Partial Product Array (SAUS)
PPA........... Partido Panamenista Autentico [*Panama*] [*Political party*] (EY)
PPA........... Partido Patriotico Arubano [*Aruban Patriotic Party*] [*Netherlands Antilles*] [*Political party*] (PPW)
PPA........... Partido Peronista Autentico [*Authentic Peronist Party*] [*Argentina*] [*Political party*] (EY)
PPA........... Parts Performance Analysis (VLIE)
PPA........... Pathology Practice Association (EA)
PPA........... Peat Producers Association [*British*] (EAIO)
PPA........... Pediatric Pain Assessment (MELL)
PPA........... Pennsylvania Psychological Association (EARSL)
PPA........... Pensioner Party of Australia [*Political party*]
PPA........... Pension Portability Act of 1992 (WYGK)
PPA........... Pension Protection Act (GFGA)
PPA........... People for Prison Alternatives [*An association*] (AD)
PPA........... Peoples Progressive Alliance (SAUS)
PPA........... Peppa Resources [*Vancouver Stock Exchange symbol*]
PPA........... Perennial Plant Association (EA)
PPA........... Performance Partnership Agreement (SARE)
PPA........... Periodical Publishers Association [*Later, MCA*] (EA)
PPA........... Periodic Paralysis Association (EA)
PPA........... Permian Partnership (SAUS)

PPA .... Per Power of Attorney [*Business term*]
ppa .... Per Procura [*By Proxy*] [*Latin*]
PPA .... Personal Productivity Application (GART)
PPA .... Personal Protective Apparel [*Industrial hygiene term*] (OHS)
PPA .... Personnel Pool of America [*An association*] (AD)
PPA .... Pesticide Producers Association [*Defunct*] (EA)
PPA .... Pet Producers of America (EA)
ppa .... Phenylpropanolamine (AD)
PPA .... Phenylpropanolamine [*Organic chemistry*]
PPA .... Phenylpropanolamine(hydrochloride) [*Also, PPH, PPM*] [*Decongestant*]
PPA .... Phenyl Pyruvic Acid (SAUS)
PPA .... Phenylpyruvic Acid [*Organic chemistry*]
PPA .... Phiala Prius Agitata [*Having First Shaken the Bottle*] [*Pharmacy*]
ppa .... Phiala Prius Agitate [*Bottle Having First Been Shaken*] [*Latin*] (AD)
PPA .... Phosphoric Acid Anodized (PDAA)
PPA .... Photographic Peak Analysis
PPA .... Photo Peak Analysis (IEEE)
ppa .... Photo-Peak Analysis (AD)
PPA .... Physical Page Address [*Computer science*] (CIST)
PPA .... Pianoforte Publicity Association [*British*] (BI)
PPA .... Piano Publicity Association (SAUS)
PPA .... Pictorial Photographers of America (EAIO)
PPA .... Pie De Palo [*Argentina*] [*Seismograph station code, US Geological Survey*] (SEIS)
PPA .... Pilot Pulse Amplitude
PPA .... Pilots and Passengers Association [*Defunct*] (EA)
PPA .... Pipe Products Association (SAUS)
PPA .... Piraeus Ports Authority (SAUS)
PPA .... Pitch Precession Amplifier
PPA .... Pittsburgh Pneumonia Agent [*Microbiology*]
PPA .... Pixel Processing Accelerator [*Computer science*] (VLIE)
PPA .... Plane Parallel Approximation (ARMP)
PPA .... Planned Program Accomplishment (GNE)
PPA .... Plant Patent Act [*1930*]
PPA .... Plaque-Producing Agent (SAUS)
PPA .... Plasminogen Proactivator [*Hematology*]
PPA .... Platform Pointing Angle (ACAE)
PPA .... Plutonium Preparation Area [*Nuclear energy*] (GFGA)
PPA .... Policyholders Protective Association of America (EA)
PPA .... Pollution Prevention Act [*1990*]
PPA .... Polycrystalline Products Association (NTPA)
PPA .... Polymer Permeation Analyzer
PPA .... Polymer Processing Additive (SAUS)
PPA .... Polyphenylacetylene (SAUS)
PPA .... Poly(phosphoric Acid) [*Inorganic chemistry*]
PPA .... Polyphthalamide (SAUS)
PPA .... Pool Promoters Association [*British*] (BI)
PPA .... Popcorn Processors Association [*Later, PI*]
PPA .... Popski's Private Army [*Commando force led by Vladimir Peniakoff*] [*World War II*]
PPA .... Population Planning Associates (BABM)
PPA .... Pork Producers Association [*Newfoundland, Canada*] (FOTI)
PPA .... Portland Port Authority [*Australia*]
PPA .... Post Pack Audit (VLIE)
PPA .... Postpartum Amenorrhea [*Medicine*]
PPA .... Post-Pill Amenorrhea [*Medicine*] (MEDA)
PPA .... Potato Processors' Association [*Australia*]
PPA .... Poultry Publishers Association (EA)
PPA .... Power Plant Automation
PPA .... Powerplant Performance Analysis
PPA .... Power Purchase Arrangement [*Electric utility company*]
PPA .... Preferred Provider Arrangement [*Information service or system*] (HCT)
PPA .... Preliminary Pile Assembly (IAA)
PPA .... Prephenic Acid (SAUS)
PPA .... Pre-Planned Application (SAUS)
PPA .... Pre-Planned Applications (VLIE)
PPA .... Pre-Planned Attack (SAUS)
PPA .... Preschool Playgrounds Association [*British*]
PPA .... Pre-school Playgroups Association (SAUS)
PPA .... Prescription Pricing Authority (PDAA)
PPA .... Presidents' Professional Association [*Later, Presidents Association*] (EA)
PPA .... Press and Publications Administration [*China*]
PPA .... Princeton Particle Accelerator (IAA)
PPA .... Princeton-Pennsylvania Accelerator [*Closed, 1972*] [*AEC*]
PPA .... Princeton-Pennsylvania Proton Accelerator [*Closed, 1972*] [*AEC*] (IAA)
PPA .... Principal Port Authority [*British*] (ROG)
PPA .... Principle Policy Analyst (SAUS)
PPA .... Printers' Provident Association (DGA)
PPA .... Printing Platemakers Association [*Later, GPA*]
PPA .... Priority Problem Areas (MCD)
PPA .... Prison Parole Assessment (WDAA)
PPA .... Private Parking Affidavit
PPA .... Process Plan Association [*British*] (DS)
PPA .... Process Plant Association [*British*] (DBA)
PPA .... Produce Packaging Association [*Later, PMA*] (EA)
PPA .... Product Performance Analysis (VLIE)
PPA .... Professional Paddlesports Association (NTPA)
PPA .... Professional Panhellenic Association [*Later, PFA*] (EA)
PPA .... Professional Photographers of America (AD)
PPA .... Professional Programmers Association (EA)
PPA .... Professional Putters Association (EA)
PPA .... Program Problem Area
PPA .... Program Product Announcement (VLIE)
PPA .... Program, Project and Activity (SAUS)
PPA .... Progressive Party of America [*Third party in 1948 Presidential race*]
PPA .... Progressive Peoples Alliance (SAUS)
PPA .... Progress Presse Agentur GmbH [*Press agency*] [*Germany*]
PPA .... Proletarian Party of America [*Political party*] (AD)
PPA .... Promotional Products Association International (NTPA)
PPA .... Prompt Payment Act (AAGC)
PPA .... Propane Phosphonic Acid Anhydride [*Organic chemistry*]
PPA .... Propane-Precipitated Asphalt [*Petroleum technology*]
PPA .... Property Protection Area
PPA .... Propheter Construction Co., Inc. [*ICAO designator*] (FAAC)
PPA .... Protected Partition Area [*Telecommunications*] (IAA)
PPA .... Protestant Press Agency [*British*]
PPA .... Prudent Purchaser Arrangement [*Medical insurance*]
PPA .... Pseudo Passive Array (SAUS)
PPA .... Pseudopassive Array
PPA .... Public Personnel Association [*Later, IPMA*] (EA)
PPA .... Public Prosecutions Administration (South Korea) [*Political party*] (PSAP)
PPA .... Publishers' Publicity Association (EA)
Ppa .... Pulmonary Artery Pressure [*Medicine*] (DMAA)
PPA .... Pulmonary Artery Pressure [*Cardiology*]
PPA .... Pulsed Plasma Accelerator (SAUS)
PPA .... Pulsed Power Amplifier
PPA .... Pulse Plasma Accelerator
PPA .... Purchase Power Agreement (SAUS)
PPA .... Pure Pulmonary Atresia [*Medicine*] (DMAA)
PPA .... Purple Plum Association [*Defunct*] (EA)
PPA .... Push-Pull Amplifier (IAA)
PPAA .... Palynological and Palaeobotanical Association of Australia (QUAC)
PPAA .... Patres Amplissimi [*Cardinals*] [*Latin*]
PPAA .... Personal Protective Armor Association (EA)
PPAAR .... Princeton University, Pennsylvania University, Army Avionics Research (PDAA)
PPAB .... Program and Policy Advisory Board [*UN Food and Agriculture Organization*]
PPABP .... American Baptist Publication Society, Philadelphia, PA [*Library symbol*] [*Library of Congress*] [*Obsolete*] (LCLS)
PP-AC .... Air-Conditioning Power Panel (DAC)
PPAC .... Penn-Pacific Corp. (SAUS)
PPAC .... Pesticide Policy Advisory Committee [*Environmental Protection Agency*]
PPAC .... Primary Progress Assessment Chart [*Psychology*]
PPAC .... Private Planning Association of Canada
PPAC .... Product Performance Agreement Center [*Military*]
P-PAC .... Professionals PAC (PACS)
PPAC .... Progressive Political Action Committee [*Defunct*]
PPAC .... Promotional Products Association of Canada (FOTI)
PPAC .... Public Parks Advisory Committee [*South Australia*]
PPACE .... United States Army, Corps of Engineers, Philadelphia District Library, Custom House, Philadelphia, PA [*Library symbol*] [*Library of Congress*] (LCLS)
PPACHi ...... American Catholic Historical Society, Philadelphia, PA [*Library symbol*] [*Library of Congress*] (LCLS)
PPAD .... Practical Periodontics & Aesthetic Dentistry (SAUS)
PPADS .... Parawing Precision Aerial Delivery System (MCD)
PPAEM ...... Albert Einstein Medical Center, Northern Division, Philadelphia, PA [*Library symbol*] [*Library of Congress*] (LCLS)
PPAF .... Progressive Perivenular Alcoholic Fibrosis [*Medicine*] (RAWO)
PPAFA .... Pennsylvania Academy of the Fine Arts, Philadelphia, PA [*Library symbol*] [*Library of Congress*] [*Obsolete*] (LCLS)
PPAG .... Pediatric Pharmacy Advocacy Group (SAUS)
PPAG .... Personnel Profile - Age by Grade [*Army*]
PPAG .... Proposed Public Affairs Guidance (COE)
PPAI .... Pinpoint Assignment Instructions [*Army*] (INF)
PPAK .... Atwater Kent Museum, Philadelphia, PA [*Library symbol*] [*Library of Congress*] (LCLS)
PPAL .... Pacific Power and Light (SAUS)
PPAL .... Pennsylvania Power & Light Co. (IAA)
PPAL .... Principal (ROG)
PPalZ .... New Jersey Zinc Co., Technical Library, Palmerton (SAUS)
PPalZ .... New Jersey Zinc Co. [*of Pennsylvania*], Technical Library, Palmerton, PA [*Library symbol*] [*Library of Congress*] (LCLS)
PPAM .... Privileged Primary Access Method (SAUS)
PPAM .... Program Product Assurance Manager (ACAE)
PPAmP ...... American Philosophical Society, Philadelphia, PA [*Library symbol*] [*Library of Congress*] (LCLS)
PPAmS ...... American Sunday School Union, Philadelphia, PA [*Library symbol*] [*Library of Congress*] [*Obsolete*] (LCLS)
PPAmSR .... American Sugar Refining Co., Philadelphia, PA [*Library symbol*] [*Library of Congress*] [*Obsolete*] (LCLS)
PPAmSwM .. American Swedish Historical Foundation, Philadelphia, PA [*Library symbol*] [*Library of Congress*] (LCLS)
PPAN .... Academy of Natural Sciences of Philadelphia, Philadelphia, PA [*Library symbol*] [*Library of Congress*] (LCLS)
PPAN .... Pyrolyzed Polyacrylonitrile [*Organic chemistry*]
PP & A ...... Palpation, Percussion, and Auscultation [*Medicine*]
pp & a ...... Palpitation, Percussion, and Auscultation (AD)
PP & A ...... Percussion, Palpation, and Auscultation [*Medicine*] (DAVI)
pp&b .... Paper, Printing, and Binding (AD)
PP & B ...... Paper, Printing, and Binding [*Publishing*]
PP&C .... Payload Planning and Control (SAUS)
PP & C ...... Pickpocket and Confidence [*Police term*]

PP & C Production Planning and Control [*Military*] (AABC)
PP&C Program Planning and Control (SPST)
PP & C Project Planning and Control (NG)
PP&E Production Process and Equipment (SAUS)
PP & E Program Planning and Evaluation (AD)
PP&L Pacific Power and Light (AD)
PP&L Pennsylvania Power and Light (AD)
PP&L Res PP & L Resources, Inc. [*Associated Press*] (SAG)
PP & NA Private Plants and Naval Activities
PP&O Plans, Policy and Operations (SAUS)
PP&S Papers on Poetics and Semiotics (SAUS)
PP & T Packaging, Preservation, and Transportation
PPANE Professional Photographers Association of New England [*Connecticut, Maine, Massachusetts, New Hampshire, Rhode Island, and Vermont*] (EARSL)
PPANI Professional Photographers of America of Northern Illinois (EARSL)
PPAnR Annenberg Research Institute for Judaic and Middle Eastern Studies, Philadelphia, PA [*Library symbol*] [*Library of Congress*] (LCLS)
PPAO Psychiatric Patient Advocate Office [*Ontario, Canada*] (FOTI)
PPAp Apprentices Free Library, Philadelphia (SAUS)
PPAp Apprentices' Free Library, Philadelphia, PA [*Library symbol*] [*Library of Congress*] [*Obsolete*] (LCLS)
PPAP Peak Pulmonary Artery Pressure (SAUS)
PPAP People's Party of Arunachal Pradesh [*India*] [*Political party*] (PPW)
PPAP Precedents of Private Acts of Parliament [*A publication*] (DLA)
PPAP Production Part Approval Process [*Automotive engineering*]
PPAP Product Part Approval Process
PPA pos Phenylpyruvic Acid Positive [*Biochemistry*] (DAVI)
PPAR Paging Partners [*NASDAQ symbol*] (TTSB)
PPAR Paging Partners Corp. [*NASDAQ symbol*] (SAG)
PPAR Paterson Parchment Paper Co. (SAUS)
PPAR Peroxisome Proliferator-Activated Receptor [*Genetics*]
PPAR Priority Problem Analysis Report [*Military*] (DNAB)
PPAR Program Page Address Register (ACAE)
PPAR Project Performance Audit Report
PPARA ARA Historical Foundation, ARA Industries, Philadelphia, PA [*Closed*] [*Library symbol*] [*Library of Congress*] (LCLS)
PPARC Particle Physics and Astronomy Research Council [*British*]
PPArmA Armstrong Association of Philadelphia, Philadelphia, PA [*Library symbol*] [*Library of Congress*] [*Obsolete*] (LCLS)
PPARW Paging Partners Wrrt [*NASDAQ symbol*] (TTSB)
PPAS Patti Page Appreciation Society (EA)
PPAS Peripheral Pulmonary Artery Stenosis [*Medicine*] (DMAA)
PPAS Personal Property Accountability System (SAUS)
PPAS Portable Public Address System (MCD)
PPAS Postpolio Atrophy Syndrome [*Medicine*] (MELL)
PPAS Potassium Picrate Active Substances [*Measure of detergent content of water*]
PPAS Precision Pulse Analysis System (SAUS)
PPAS Probability Proportional to Aggregate Size [*Statistics*]
PPASS Minnesota Post-Polio Awareness and Support Society (EARSL)
PPAT Private Providers Association of Texas (EARSL)
PPAtR Atlantic Refining Co., Philadelphia, PA [*Library symbol*] [*Library of Congress*] (LCLS)
PPATRA Printing, Packaging, and Allied Trades Research Association (AD)
PPATY Preparatory (ROG)
PPAuC Automobile Club of Philadelphia, Philadelphia, PA [*Library symbol*] [*Library of Congress*] [*Obsolete*] (LCLS)
PPAUS Peat Producers Association of the United States (EA)
PPAW Public Policy Affecting Women Task Force (EA)
PPAWA Poultry Producers' Association of Western Australia
PPB Botanical Research Centre (SAUS)
PPB Brazilian Progressive Party [*Political party*] (PSAP)
PPB Paper, Printing, and Binding (ADWA)
Ppb Pappaband [*Hard Cover*] [*German*] (AD)
PPB Parachute Paraglider Building [*NASA*] (KSC)
PPB Part Per Billion (SAUS)
ppb Parts per Billion (AD)
PPB Parts per Billion
ppb Parts per Billion 10 (IDOE)
PPB Perliminary Parts Breakdown (SAUS)
PPB Personal Protection Blanket [*Police and security equipment*]
PPB Petro-Canada Products, Inc. [*Toronto Stock Exchange symbol*] [*Vancouver Stock Exchange symbol*]
PPB Philadelphia Bar Association, Philadelphia, PA [*Library symbol*] [*Library of Congress*] (LCLS)
PPB Planning, Programming, Budgeting (SAUS)
P-P-B Planning-Programming-Budgeting [*System*] [*Army*]
PPB Platelet-Poor Blood [*Hematology*] (MAE)
PPB Platoon Patrol Base [*Military*] (VNW)
PPB Pneumococcal Pneumonia and Bacteremia [*Medicine*] (EDAA)
PPB Polar Patrol Balloons (SAUS)
PPB Political Party Broadcast [*Television*] [*British*]
PPB Polybrominated-Biphenyl (AD)
PPB Poly(para-benzamide) [*Organic chemistry*]
PPB Positive Pressure Breathing [*Aerospace*]
PPb Postparotid Basic Protein (DMAA)
PPB Powerplant Bending [*Automotive engineering*]
PPB Power Plant Bulletin (MCD)
PPB Precision Pressure Balance
PPB Preliminary Parts Breakdown (SAUS)
PPB Preparing, Planning and Budegting (SAUS)
PPB Prepatellar Bursitis [*Medicine*] (MELL)
PPB Preprophase Band [*Cytology*]
PPB Presidente Prudente [*Brazil*] [*Airport symbol*] (AD)
PPB Pres Prudente [*Brazil*] [*Airport symbol*] (OAG)
PPB Primary Parts Breakdown (SAUS)
PPB Primary Propulsion Branch [*Manned Spacecraft Center*]
PPB Printing, Paper, and Binding [*Publishing*] (WDMC)
PPB Private Posting Box
PPB Procurement Policy Board [*ABA Public Contract Law Section*] (AAGC)
PPB Production Parts Breakdown (MCD)
PPB Programming, Planning & Budget (ALAC)
PPB Program Performance Baseline (NASA)
PPB Program Planning Budget (NOAA)
PPB Program-Planning-Budgeting
PPB Progressive Reform Party (Brazil) [*Political party*] (PSAP)
PPB PROM [*Programmable Read-Only Memory*] Programmer Board
PPB Provisional Parts Breakdown (SAUS)
PPB Provisioning Parts Breakdown
PPB Purchasing Power Benefit (ADA)
PPB Push-Pull Bearing
PPB Push Pull Button (SAUS)
PPB&G Positive Pressure Breathing & G System (SAUS)
PPBANSW Pasture Protection Boards' Association of New South Wales [*Australia*]
PPBAS Planning, Programming, Budgeting, Accounting System (SAUS)
PPBAS Planning-Programming-Budgeting-Accounting System (AD)
PPBB Partai Pesaka Bumiputra Bersatu [*United Traditional Bumiputra Party*] [*Malaysia*] [*Political party*] (PPW)
PPBB PCI-toPCI Bridge Board (ACII)
PPBB Prime Power Brass Board (MCD)
PPBB United Traditional Bumiputra Party (Malaysia) [*Political party*] (PSAP)
PPBC Pittsburgh Penguins Booster Club (EA)
PPBC Plant Pathogenic Bacteria Committee (EA)
PPBC Portland Problem Behavior Checklist (EDAC)
PPBC-R Portland Problem Behavior Checklist - Revised [*Educational test*]
P PBD Paper or Paperboard [*Freight*]
PPBD Port of Palm Beach District [*AAR code*]
PPBE Passenger Protective Breathing Equipment [*Aviation*] (DA)
PPBE Postpartum Breast Engorgement [*Medicine*] (MELL)
PPBERS Program Performance and Budget Execution Review System [*Army*]
PPBES Planning, Programming, Budgeting, and Execution System [*Army*] (RDA)
PPBES Planning-Programming-Budgeting-Evaluation System (SAUS)
PPBES Program Planning and Budget Execution System [*Army*]
PPBES Program Planning-Budgeting-Evaluation System (SAUS)
PPBES Program Planning-Budgeting-Evaluation System Project (EA)
PPBESP Program Planning-Budgeting-Evaluation System Project (EA)
PPBF Pan American Pharmaceutical and Biochemical Federation (SAUS)
PPBF Pan-American Pharmaceutical and Biochemical Federation
PPBFSPS Pen and Pocket Blade Forgers' and Smithers' Protective Society [*A union*] [*British*]
PPBH Pharmaceutical Partners for Better Healthcare (ECON)
PPBI Balch Institute, Philadelphia, PA [*Library symbol*] [*Library of Congress*] (LCLS)
PPBM Pulse Polarization (or Polarized) Binary Modulation (SAUS)
PPBMIS Planning, Programming, and Budgeting Management Information System [*Army*]
PPBP Pro-Platelet Basic Protein (DMAA)
PPBR Program Plan and Budget Request (OICC)
PPBS Planning, Programming, and Budgeting Structure
PPBS Planning, Programming, and Budgeting System [*Army*]
PPBS Planning-Programming-Budgeting-System (SAUS)
PPBS Plant Population Biology Section (SAUS)
PPBS Positive Pressure Breathing System [*Aerospace*]
PPBS Postprandial Blood Sugar [*Clinical chemistry*]
PPBS Professional Programmer Based System (SAUS)
PPBS Program Performance Budgetary Systems (SAUS)
PPBS Program Planning and Budgeting Staff [*Environmental Protection Agency*] (GFGA)
PPBS Program, Planning, and Budgeting System [*Johnson Administration*] [*Executive Office of the President*] (GFGA)
PPBSO Piping and Pipe Band Society of Ontario [*Canada*]
PPBV Parts Per Billion by Volume (SAUS)
ppbv Parts per Billion by Volume [*Industrial hygiene term*] (OHS)
PPC Chlorinated Polypropylene (SAUS)
PPC Christian People's Party (Dominican Rep.) [*Political party*] (PSAP)
PPC College of Physicians of Philadelphia, Philadelphia, PA [*Library symbol*] [*Library of Congress*] [*OCLC symbol*] (LCLS)
PP-C Free Library of Philadelphia, Carson Collection, Philadelphia, PA [*Library symbol*] [*Library of Congress*] (LCLS)
PPC Journal of Pension Planning and Compliance (journ.) (SAUS)
PPC Palm Personal Computer
PPC Pan Pacific Centers [*Defunct*] (EA)
PPC Paperboard Packaging Council (EA)
PPC Parallel Path Counter [*Electronics*] (IAA)
PPC Parallel Plate Chambers (SAUS)
PPC Parallel Poll Configuration (SAUS)
PPC Partial Pay Card
PPC Partido Popular Cristiano [*Christian Popular Party*] [*Peru*] [*Political party*] (PPW)
PPC Parting Post Calls (MCD)
PPC Partitu Populare Corsu [*Corsica*] [*Political party*] (PD)
PPC Parts Preference Code [*Military*] (AFIT)
PPC Patres Conscripti [*Senators*] [*Latin*] (ROG)
PPC Patrick Petroleum Co. (EFIS)
PPC Patrol Plane Commander

PPC .... Pay Per Channel (SAUS)
PPC .... Pay-Per-Click [*Payment model for online advertisements*] (NETL)
PPC .... Peace Promotion Code (SAUS)
PPC .... Peak Plasma Concentration [*Medicine*] (EDAA)
PPC .... Peak Power Control [*Telecommunications*] (TEL)
PPC .... Pearson Peacekeeping Centre [*Canada*]
PPC .... Peet & Company Ltd. [*Australian Stock Exchange symbol*]
PPC .... Pentose Phosphate Cycle [*Medicine*] (EDAA)
PPC .... People Power Coalition
PPC .... Peripheral Posterior Curve [*Medicine*] (EDAA)
PPC .... Permission to Photocopy (MCD)
PPC .... Per Pupil Cost (AFM)
PPC .... Persistent Photoconductivity [*Physics*]
PPC .... Personal Performance Consultants UK Limited (EFIS)
PPC .... Personal Portable Computer
PPC .... Personal Productivity Center
PPC .... Personal Programmable Calculator (MHDI)
PPC .... Personal Programmers Club (SAUS)
PPC .... Personal Protective Clothing (GNE)
PPC .... Pertec Peripherals Corp. (SAUS)
PPC .... Pet Population Control (AD)
PPC .... Petroleum Packaging Council (NTPA)
PPC .... Petroleum Pipeline Company, Cairo (SAUS)
PPC .... Petroleum Planning Committee [*Obsolete*] [*NATO*] (NATG)
PPC .... Phased Program Construction (IAA)
PPC .... Phased Provisioning Code (NASA)
PPC .... Philatelic Press Club [*Later, IPPC*]
PPC .... Philips Petroleum Co. (SAUS)
PPC .... Photographic Processing Cells (AFM)
PPC .... Photo Persistent Conductivity (AAEL)
PpC .... Pick Publishing Corporation, New York, NY [*Library symbol*] [*Library of Congress*] (LCLS)
ppc .... Picture Postcard (AD)
PPC .... Picture Postcard
PPC .... Pierce's Perpetual Code [*1943*] [*A publication*] (DLA)
PPC .... Pine Pass [*British Columbia*] [*Seismograph station code, US Geological Survey*] [*Closed*] (SEIS)
PPC .... Pin-to-Pin Compatible (SAUS)
PPC .... Plain Paper Copier [*Electrophotography*]
PPC .... Plain Plaster Cornice [*Construction*]
PPC .... Planar Positive Column (SAUS)
PPC .... Planar Postive Column (IAA)
PPC .... Plane Paper Copier (IAA)
ppc .... Plan-Paper Copier (AD)
PPC .... Plant Pest Control Division [*of ARS, Department of Agriculture*]
PPC .... Plant Process Computer
PPC .... Plasma Prothrombin Conversion (DB)
PPC .... Platform Position Computer
PPC .... Platinum-Palladium Colloid (DB)
PPC .... Plug Patch Cord
PPC .... Plutonium Process Cell [*Nuclear energy*] (NRCH)
PPC .... Plutonium Product Cell [*Nuclear energy*] (NRCH)
PPC .... Pneumopericardium [*Medicine*] (EDAA)
PPC .... Point of Possible Collision [*Navigation*]
PPC .... Point-to-Point Correlation [*Graphing*]
PPC .... Polarizable Point Charge [*Model for the water molecule*]
PPC .... Polar Path Compass (ACAE)
PPC .... Policy and Planning Committee (SAUS)
PPC .... Policy Planning Council [*U.S. Department of State*] (BARN)
PPC .... Polyphthalate Carbonate (SAUS)
PPC .... Polyphthalate-Polycarbonate
PPC .... Pooled Platelet Concentrate [*Medicine*] (MEDA)
PPC .... Portable Personal Computer (DGA)
PPC .... Positive Peer Control
PPC .... Positive Peer Culture (AD)
PPC .... Postal code for the Prime Contractor (SAUS)
PPC .... Posterior Parietal Cortex [*Brain anatomy*]
PPC .... Postoperative Pulmonary Complications (SAUS)
PPC .... Postpulmonary Complications
PPC .... Potential Performance Capability (SAUS)
PPC .... Potential Points of Collision [*Navigation*]
PPC .... Potentional Performance Capability (IAA)
PPC .... Pour Prendre Conge [*To Take Leave*] [*French*]
p p c .... Pour Prendre Conge [*To Take Leave*] [*French*] (AD)
PPC .... Power Pack Charger
PPC .... Power PC (SAUS)
PPC .... Power Physics Corp. (SAUS)
PPC .... Power Plant Change (NVT)
PPC .... Power Pool Council [*Electric utility company*]
PPC .... PPC Oil & Gas Corp. [*Toronto Stock Exchange symbol*]
PPC .... Practitioners Publishing Company (SAUS)
PPC .... Precipitating Particle Counter (ACAE)
PPC .... Precision Photomechanical Corp.
PPC .... Predicted Point of Collision (SAUS)
PPC .... Predicted Propagation Correction (PDAA)
PPC .... Preliminary Phase Correction (IAA)
PPC .... Preliminary Proceedings Committee [*Medicine*] (EDAA)
PPC .... Preprocessing Center [*NASA*] (NASA)
PPC .... Pre-Proposal Conference (MCD)
PPC .... Preservation and Packaging Committee
PPC .... President of the Privy Council [*Canada*]
PPC .... Pressure Pulse Contour [*Cardiac computer*] (PDAA)
PPC .... Primary Power Control (MCD)
PPC .... Printers' Pension Corp. (DGA)
PPC .... Print Position Counter
PPC .... Priority Placement Certificate [*Military*] (AFM)
PPC .... Process Problem Chart (SAUS)
PPC .... Process Proximity Correction (SAUS)
PPC .... Production and Planning Control (SAUS)
PPC .... Production Planning and Control
PPC .... Product Planning Committee
PPC .... Professional Personal Computer
PPC .... Professional Personnel Consultant (WDAA)
PPC .... Professional Purposes Committee (ODA)
PPC .... Program Planning and Control (AAG)
PPC .... Program Planning Coordination Office [*United Nations*]
PPC .... Program Product Center (SAUS)
ppc .... Progressive Patient Care (AD)
PPC .... Progressive Patient Care
PPC .... Projection Printing Camera (SAUS)
PPC .... Project Parts Coordinator
PPC .... Project Physics Course [*National Science Foundation*]
PPC .... Project Planning and Control (COE)
PPC .... Project Planning Centre for Developing Countries [*Research center*] [*British*] (IRC)
PPC .... Project Preparation Committee (SAUS)
PPC .... Proof-of-Passing Certificate (OTD)
PPC .... Pro-Personal Computer (NITA)
PPC .... Prospect Creek, AK [*Location identifier*] [*FAA*] (FAAL)
PPC .... Prospective Parliamentary Candidate [*British*]
PPC .... Protected Personnel Carrier (SAUS)
PPC .... Proximal Palmar Crease [*Anatomy*]
PPC .... Psychiatric Patient Classes (SAUS)
PPC .... Psychorotrophic Plate Count [*Bacteriology*]
PPC .... Publishers Publicity Circle
PPC .... Pulsed Power Circuit (IEEE)
PPC .... Pulse Position Code (SAUS)
PPC .... Pulse-to-Pulse Correlation (ACAE)
PPC .... Purchase Price Control (AD)
pPc .... Pure Peruvian Cocaine (AD)
PPCA .... Plasma [*or Proserum*] Prothrombin Conversion Accelerator [*Factor VII*] [*Also, SPCA*] [*Hematology*]
ppca .... Plasma Prothrombin Conversion Accelerator (AD)
PPCA .... Plasma Rothrombin Conversion Accelerator (SAUS)
PPCA .... Power Plant Contractors Association (SAUS)
PPCA .... Preliminary Physical Configuration Audit (SAUS)
PPCA .... Proserum Prothrombin Conversion Accelerator (ADWA)
PPCAA .... Parole and Probation Compact Administrators Association (EA)
PPCAP .... People to People Citizen Ambassador Program (EA)
PPCB .... Page Printer Control Block [*Computer science*]
PPCB .... Patrick Petroleum Co. [*NASDAQ symbol*] (SAG)
PPCC .... Carpenters' Co., Philadelphia, PA [*Library symbol*] [*Library of Congress*] (LCLS)
PPCC .... Particles per Cubic Centimeter
PPCC .... Parts per Cubic Centimeter (IAA)
ppcc .... parts per cubic centimetre (SAUS)
PPCC .... Port Phillip Conservation Council [*Australia*]
PPCC .... Postmolded Plastic Chip Carrier [*Computer science*]
PPCCD ...... Profiled Peristaltic Charge Coupled-Device [*Computer science*] (IAA)
PPCCD ...... Profiled Peristaltic Charge-Coupled Device (SAUS)
PPCCH ...... Chestnut Hill College, Philadelphia, PA [*Library symbol*] [*Library of Congress*] (LCLS)
PPC-CPE .... Practitioners Publishing Company-CPE (SAUS)
PPCD .... Plant Pest Control Division (AD)
PPCD .... Polymorphous Posterior Corneal Dystrophy [*Medicine*] (EDAA)
PPCD .... Polymorphous Posterior Corneal Dystropy [*Medicine*] (DMAA)
PPCE .... Portable Pneumatic Checkout Equipment (KSC)
PPCE .... Post-Proline Cleaving Enzyme [*Biochemistry*]
PPCE .... Print Position Control Exit (SAUS)
PPCE&E ..... Print Position Counter Entry and Exit (SAUS)
ppcf .... Particles per Cubic Foot (LDOE)
PPCF .... Peripartum Cardiac Failure [*Medicine*] (EDAA)
ppcf .... Plasma Prothrombin Conversion Factor (AD)
PPCF .... Plasmin Prothrombin Conversion Factor [*Factor V*] [*Hematology*]
PPCG .... People's Preferred Capital Corp. [*NASDAQ symbol*] (NASQ)
PPCG48 ..... Convention on the Prevention and Punishment of the Crime of Genocide of 9 December 1948 (SAFN)
PPCH .... People-to-People Committee for the Handicapped (EA)
PPCH .... Pilot Pouch (SAUS)
PPCH .... Piperazinylmethyl Cyclohexanone [*Medicine*] (EDAA)
PPCI .... Curtis Institute of Music, Philadelphia, PA [*Library symbol*] [*Library of Congress*] (LCLS)
PPCI .... Presentation Protocol Control Information [*Telecommunications*]
PPCI .... Pressure Piping Components, Inc. (SAUS)
PPCiC .... Civic Club of Philadelphia, Philadelphia, PA [*Library symbol*] [*Library of Congress*] [*Obsolete*] (LCLS)
PPCIG .... Personal Property Consignment Instruction Guide (MCD)
PPCLI .... Princess Patricia of Connaught's Light Infantry [*Military unit*] [*Canada*]
PPCLI .... Princess Patricia's Canadian Light Infantry (AD)
PPCM .... Perimeter-Portal Continuous Monitoring (SAUS)
PPCM .... Philadelphia County Medical Society, Philadelphia, PA [*Library symbol*] [*Library of Congress*] [*Obsolete*] (LCLS)
PPCM .... Postpartum Cardiomyopathy [*Medicine*] (MELL)
PPC-M .... Precision Pressure Controller-Monitor (SAUS)
PPCM .... Predictive Pulse Code Modulation (SAUS)
PPCO .... Penwest Pharmaceuticals Co. [*NASDAQ symbol*] (NASQ)
PPCO .... Periodically Phase-Controlled Oscillator (SAUS)

PPCO .... Philadelphia College of Osteopathic Medicine, Philadelphia, PA [*Library symbol*] [*Library of Congress*] (LCLS)
PPCO2 .... Partial Pressure Carbon Dioxide
PPCoC .... Community College of Philadelphia, Philadelphia, PA [*Library symbol*] [*Library of Congress*] (LCLS)
PPCOD ...... People-to-People Committee on Disability (EA)
PPColP .... Colonial Penn Group, Inc., Marketing Research Library, Philadelphia, PA [*Library symbol*] [*Library of Congress*] (LCLS)
PPComm .... Commercial Museum, Philadelphia, PA [*Library symbol*] [*Library of Congress*] [*Obsolete*] (LCLS)
PPCP .... College of Physicians of Philadelphia, Philadelphia, PA [*Library symbol*] [*Library of Congress*] (LCLS)
PPCP .... People to People Contact for Peace (SAUS)
PPCP .... Power PC Plattform (SAUS)
PPCP .... Propellant Pneumatic Control Panel (KSC)
PPCPC .... Philadelphia City Planning Commission, Philadelphia, PA [*Library symbol*] [*Library of Congress*] (LCLS)
PPCPSG ..... Polish POW Camps Philatelic Study Group (EA)
PPCR .... Preliminary Program Change Request (SAUS)
PPCR .... Production Planning Change Request (SAA)
PP Crepe ... Partially Purified Crepe (SAUS)
PPCRGD .... Pelican (SAUS)
PPCRGD .... Pelican Pedestrian Crossing Regulations and General Directions (SAUS)
PPCS .... National Carl Schurz Memorial Foundation, Philadelphia, PA [*Library symbol*] [*Library of Congress*] [*Obsolete*] (LCLS)
PPCS .... Page Printer Control System [*Computer science*]
PPCS .... Personnel Protection and Communication Services [*British*] (AD)
PPCS .... Person to Person: Collect and Special Instruction [*Telecommunications*] (TEL)
PPCS .... Person to Person, Collect, Special (SAUS)
PPCS .... Postpericardiotomy Syndrome [*Medicine*] (MELL)
PPCS .... Precision Pointing Control System [*Engineering*]
PPCS .... Primary Producers' Cooperative Society (AD)
PPCS .... Production Planning and Control System
PPCS .... Project Planning and Control System [*Social Security Administration*]
PPCSEAPR ... Plant Protection Committee for the South East Asia and Pacific Region (SAUS)
PPCT .... Project Planning and Control Techniques (SAUS)
PPCU .... Aztec Peroxides [*Intermodal shipping container symbol*] (TVRC)
PPCU .... Parallel Processor Control Unit (SAUS)
PPCuP .... Curtis Publishing Co., Research Library, Philadelphia, PA [*Library symbol*] [*Library of Congress*] [*Obsolete*] (LCLS)
PPCV .... Pulmonary Capillary Venous Pressure (SAUS)
PPCZ .... Potlatch Paper [*Federal Railroad Administration identification code*]
PPD .... A Posteriori Probability Distribution [*Mathematics*]
PPD .... Doctrinaire Panamenistra Party [*Political party*] (PSAP)
PPD .... Drexel University, Philadelphia, PA [*Library symbol*] [*Library of Congress*] (LCLS)
PPD .... Humacao-Palmas [*Puerto Rico*] [*Airport symbol*] (OAG)
PPD .... I-GOOS Panel on Products and Distribution (SAUS)
PPD .... Packs per Day [*Cigarettes*] [*Medicine*]
PPD .... Panel Power Distribution (MCD)
PPD .... Panoramic Passive Detection (SAUS)
PPD .... Papered (ROG)
PPD .... Paranoid Personality Disorder (AD)
PPD .... Para-Phenylenediamine [*Organic chemistry*]
PPD .... Partial Packet Discard (MLOA)
PPD .... Partido Popular Democratico [*Popular Democratic Party of Puerto Rico*] [*Spanish*] (BARN)
PPD .... Partido por la Democracia [*Democratic Party*] [*Chile*] [*Political party*] (EY)
PPD .... Parti Populaire Djiboutien [*Djibouti People's Party*] [*Political party*] (PPW)
PPD .... Parti Progressiste Dahomeen [*Dahomey Progressive Party*] [*Political party*]
PPD .... Parts Provisioning Document
PPD .... Party for Peace and Democracy [*South Korea*] [*Political party*]
PPD .... Payload Position Data
PPD .... Pay Packets Deficency (SAUS)
PPD .... Pay Packets Deficiency [*British*]
PPD .... Pepsin Pancreatin Digest [*Food protein digestibility assay*]
PPD .... Peripheral Pulse Distributor (SAUS)
PPD .... Permanent Partial Disability [*Dentistry*] (MAE)
PPD .... Personal Protective Device [*Toxicology*]
PPD .... Personnel Planning Data [*Navy*]
PPD .... Personnel Priority Designator [*Military*] (AFM)
PPD .... Petroleum Production Division (AD)
PPD .... Pharmaceutical Product Development, Inc. (EFIS)
PPD .... Phenyldiphenyloxadiazole [*Organic chemistry*] (MAE)
PPD .... Piperidine Pentamethylene Dithiocarbonate (SAUS)
PPD .... Pitch Phase Detector
PPD .... Plains Petroleum Co. [*Vancouver Stock Exchange symbol*]
PPD .... Planning Productian Data (SAUS)
PPD .... Plot Plan Drawing (SAA)
PPD .... Point Position Data
PPD .... Politieke Partij Democraten 66 [*Political Party Democrats 66*] [*Netherlands*] (EAIO)
PPD .... Portland Public Docks (AD)
PPD .... Port Protection Device [*Computer science*] (ITCA)
PPD .... Portuguese Popular Democrats
PPD .... Posterior Polymorphous Dystrophy [*Neurology*] (DAVI)
ppd .... Postpaid (WDMC)
PPD .... Postpaid
PPD .... Postpartum Day [*Obstetrics*] (DAVI)
PPD .... Postpartum Depression (PAZ)
PPD .... Postponed [*Telegraphy*] (PCTE)
PPD .... PostScript Printer Description [*Computer science*] (PCM)
PPD .... Pour Point Depressant [*Fuels and lubricants*]
PPD .... Pour Point Differential [*Petroleum engineering*]
PPD .... Preferred Policyholders' Discount [*British*] (BARN)
PPD .... Premiere Performance Division [*Automotive industry*]
Ppd .... Prepaid (MIST)
ppd .... Prepaid (WDMC)
PPD .... Prepaid
PPD .... Prepaid Dental Plan [*Insurance*] (MCD)
PPD .... Pre-Paid Legal Services, Inc. [*AMEX symbol*] (SPSG)
PPD .... Pre-Paid Legal Svcs [*AMEX symbol*] (TTSB)
ppd .... Prepared (MAE)
PPD .... Preprototype Demonstration
PPD .... Presidential Protective Division [*US Secret Service*]
PPD .... Prime Power Distribution
PPD .... Principal Project Designer [*Engineering project management*]
PPD .... Printer Page Description [*Computer science*]
PPD .... Processed Payment Document (GFGA)
PPD .... Product and Process Description (SAUS)
PPD .... Production Program, Douglas
PPD .... Proficiency Pay Designator [*Military*] (AABC)
PPD .... Prognostic Prediction Devices
PPD .... Program for Persons with Disabilities [*National Science Foundation*] (RCD)
PPD .... Program Package Document
PPD .... Program Planning Directives [*NASA*] (KSC)
PPD .... Program Planning Document (NG)
PPD .... Progressive Perceptive Deafness [*Medicine*]
PPD .... Projectile Pull and Drain [*Machine*] (MCD)
PPD .... Project Planning Directive (NG)
PPD .... Project Planning Document (ABAC)
PPD .... Prompt Payment Discount (AAGC)
PPD .... Propria Pecunia Dedicavit [*With His Own Money He Offered It*] [*Latin*] (ROG)
PPD .... Propulsion and Power Division [*Manned Spacecraft Center*] [*NASA*]
PPD .... Provisioning Procurement Data
PPD .... Proximity, Point Detonating (SAUS)
PPD .... Pulse-Type Phase Detector
PPD .... Purchasing Power of the Dollar (MHDW)
ppd .... Purified Protein Derivative (AD)
PPD .... Purified Protein Derivative [*Tuberculin*]
PPDA .... Para-Phenylenediamine [*Organic chemistry*]
PPDA .... Phenyl Phosphorodiamidate [*Fertilizer technology*]
PPDA .... Poor Prisoners Defence Act (SAUS)
PPDA .... Produce Packaging Development Association (AD)
PPDB .... Personnel Planning Data Book [*Navy*]
PPDB .... Point Positioning Data Base (SAUS)
PPDB .... Point-Positioning Data Base [*Cartography*] (RDA)
PPD-B .... Purified Protein Derivative - Battey [*Tuberculin*] (AAMN)
PPD-B .... Purified Protein Derivative-Battey (SAUS)
PPDC .... Dental Cosmos Library, Philadelphia, PA [*Library symbol*] [*Library of Congress*] [*Obsolete*] (LCLS)
PPDC .... Paraguayan People's Documentation Center [*Mestre, Italy*] (EAIO)
PPDC .... Partido Popular Democratica Cristiana [*Popular Christian Democratic Party*] [*Spain*] [*Political party*] (PPE)
PPDC .... Perfusion Program Directors Council [*Cardiology*] (DAVI)
PPDC .... Pig Production Development Committee (SAUS)
PPDC .... Polymer Products Development Center (or Centre) (SAUS)
PPDC .... Programming Panels and Decoding Circuits
PPDD .... Peoples Party for Democracy and Development (SAUS)
PPDD .... Pershing Physical Deception Device [*Army*]
PPDD .... Plan Position Data Display
PPDD .... Preliminary Project Design Description (NRCH)
PPDDS ...... Private Practice Dental Delivery System
PPDef-M .... Defense Personnel Support Center, Directorate of Medical Material Library, Philadelphia, PA [*Library symbol*] [*Library of Congress*] (LCLS)
PPDF .... Poisson Probability Distribution Function [*Mathematics*]
PPDF .... Popular Party for French Democracy [*Political party*] (PSAP)
PPDF .... Portable Postscript-Document Format [*Computer science*] (ELAL)
PPDG .... Parti Progressiste Democratique Guadeloupeen [*Political party*] (EY)
PPDGF ...... Porcine Platelet-Derived Growth Factor [*Biochemistry*]
PPDI .... Paraphenylene Diisocyanate [*Organic chemistry*]
PPDI .... Pharmaceutical Product Development, Inc. [*NASDAQ symbol*] (SAG)
PPDI .... Pharmaceutical Product Devlpmt [*NASDAQ symbol*] (TTSB)
ppdi .... Pilot's Projected-Display Indicator (AD)
PPDI .... Pilots Projected Display Indicator (SAUS)
PPDI .... Pre-Pre-Delivery Inspection [*Automotive project management*]
PPDIL .... Pre-Power-Dependent Insertion Limit [*Nuclear energy*] (NRCH)
PPDio .... Diocesan Library, Philadelphia, PA [*Library symbol*] [*Library of Congress*] [*Obsolete*] (LCLS)
PPDL .... PIP Delivery and Courier Service [*Common carrier symbol*]
PPDL .... Postscript Page Description Language [*Computer science*] (CIST)
PPDM .... E. I. Du Pont de Nemours & Co., Marshall Laboratory, Philadelphia, PA [*Library symbol*] [*Library of Congress*] (LCLS)
PPDM .... Pseudo-Pinch Design Method [*Heat exchange design*]
PPDMG ...... Popular Priced Dress Manufacturers Group [*Later, AMA*] (EA)
ppdo .... Per Person, Double Occupancy (AD)
PPDO .... Per Person, Double Occupancy [*Travel industry*] (TRID)
PPDO .... Personal Paid Days Off
PPDO .... Program and Policy Development Office (SAUS)
PPDO .... Provincial Planning and Development Office (SAUS)
PPDP .... Preliminary Project Development Plan [*NASA*]
PPDP .... Preprogram Definition Phase

PP-DPH ..... Free Library of Philadelphia, Library for the Blind and Physically Handicapped, Philadelphia, PA [*Library symbol*] [*Library of Congress*] (LCLS)
PPDR .... Philadelphia Department of Records, Philadelphia, PA [*Library symbol*] [*Library of Congress*] (LCLS)
PPDR .... Pilot Performance Description Record
PP/DR .... Preliminary Performance Design Requirements
PPDR .... Preproliferative Diabetic Retinopathy [*Medicine*] (MELL)
PPDR .... Production Packing Depth Range (NG)
PPDrop ...... Dropsie University, Philadelphia, PA [*Library symbol*] [*Library of Congress*] (LCLS)
PPDS .... Personal Printer Data Stream [*IBM Corp.*] (PCM)
PPDS .... Phonologic Programming Deficit Syndrome (DMAA)
PPDS .... Physical Property Data Service [*Database*] [*United Kingdom*] (GDD)
PPDS .... Physical Property Data Service [*Institution of Chemical Engineers*] [*Databank*] [*Information service or system*] (IID)
PPDS .... Planning Production Data Sheet
PPDS .... Preservation and Packaging Data Sheet [*DoD*]
PPDS .... Primary Processor and Data Storage (SAUS)
PPDS .... Publishers' Parcels Delivery Service (AD)
PPDS .... Purchase Parts Data Sheet
PPD-S .... Purified Protein Derivative-Standard [*Tuberculin*]
PPDSE .... International Plate Printers, Die Stampers, and Engravers' Union of North America
PPDSE .... Plate Printers, Die Stampers, and Engravers [*Union*] (AD)
PPDT .... (Phenylpyridyl)diphenyltriazine [*Analytical chemistry*]
PPDT .... Poly(phenyleneterephthalamide) [*Organic chemistry*]
PPDU .... Presentation Protocol Data Unit [*Computer science*] (TNIG)
PPDU .... Propulsion Power Distribution Unit (ACAE)
PPDVWG ...... Population Dynamics and Physical Variability Working Group (SAUS)
PPE .... Independent Union of Plant Protection Employees in the Electrical and Machine Industry
PPE .... Packet Processing Engine (SAUS)
PPE .... Papa Egoro Party (Panama) [*Political party*] (PSAP)
PP/E .... Parallel Print/Exact (VLIE)
PP/E .... Parallel Print/Extract (SAUS)
PPE .... Park Place Entertainment [*NYSE symbol*] (SG)
PPE .... Partial Plasma Exchange (STED)
PPE .... Particle Physics Experiments Division (SAUS)
PPE .... Parti Populaire Europeen [*European Peoples' Party - EPP*] (EAIO)
PPE .... Party for the Protection of the Environment (SAUS)
PPE .... PATRIOT Peculiar Equipment (SAUS)
PPE .... Pave Paws East (SAUS)
PPE .... People, Places and Events (SAUS)
PPE .... Peripheral Processor Element [*Computer science*] (VLIE)
PPE .... Permeability Pulmonary Edema (STED)
PPE .... Personal Protective Equipment [*General Motors Corp.*]
PPE .... Personnel Protection Equipment (SAUS)
PPE .... Phase Partitioning Experiment (SAUS)
ppe .... Philosophy, Politics, and Economics (AD)
PPE .... Philosophy, Politics, Economics [*Oxford University*]
PPE .... Pholbe Phillips Editions [*Publisher*] [*British*]
PPE .... Pipette [*Chemistry*]
PPE .... Platform Position Equipment
PPE .... Polypentene [*Organic chemistry*]
PPE .... Polyphenylene Ether (SAUS)
PPE .... Polyphenylene Ether Plastic [*Materials science*]
PPE .... Polyphenylether (IEEE)
PPE .... Polyphosphate Ester [*Inorganic chemistry*]
PPE .... Polyphosphate Ether (SAUS)
PPE .... Polyphosphoric Ester (STED)
PPE .... Porcine Pancreatic Elastase [*An enzyme*]
PPE .... Potomac Pacific Engineering, Inc.
PPE .... Predicted Period of Effect (SAUS)
PPE .... Predicted Period-of-Effect [*Meteorology*]
PPE .... Premodulation Processing Equipment
PPE .... Premodulation Processor Equipment (SAUS)
PPE .... Preparticipation Physical Exam
PPE .... Preparticipation Physical Examination
PPE .... Preproduction Engineering
PPE .... Preproduction Evaluation (NG)
PPE .... Preproduction Proposal Evaluation
PPE .... Preproenkephalin [*Biochemistry*]
PPE .... Print-Punch Editor [*Computer science*] (SAA)
PPE .... Problem Program Efficiency (IEEE)
PPE .... Problem Program Evaluator
PPE .... Programmed Physical Examination (STED)
PPE .... Program Performance Evaluator (NITA)
PPE .... Program Planning and Evaluation
PPE .... Prototype Production Evaluation (NG)
PPE .... Purchasing Power Equivalent
PPE .... Pyridoxal Phosphate Effect [*Medicine*]
PPE .... Shuman, Psychiatric and Psychological Evidence (SAUS)
PPEA .... Plant Performance Evaluation Activity [*Military*] (DNAB)
PPEB .... Eastern Baptist Theological Seminary, Philadelphia, PA [*Library symbol*] [*Library of Congress*] (LCLS)
PPEB .... [*The*] Pottery of Palestine from the Earliest Times to the End of the EarlyBronze Age [*A publication*] (BJA)
PPEC .... Panchayat Polity and Evaluation Committee (SAUS)
PPEC .... Paper and Paperboard Packaging Environmental Council (FOTI)
PPECC .... Philippine Pacific Economic Cooperation Committee
PPECP .... Pollution Prevention and Emissions Control Program (COE)
PPEF .... Public Policy Education Fund (EA)
PPEFH .... E. F. Hutton & Co., Philadelphia, PA [*Library symbol*] [*Library of Congress*] [*Obsolete*] (LCLS)
PPELE .... Practical Papers in English Language Education (SAUS)
PPEM .... Packed Pixel Expansion Mode (SAUS)
PPEMA .... Portable Power Equipment Manufacturers Association (EA)
PPEN .... Purchased Parts Equipment Notice (SAA)
PPEng .... Engineers' Club, Philadelphia, PA [*Library symbol*] [*Library of Congress*] [*Obsolete*] (LCLS)
PPEP .... Eastern Pennsylvania Psychiatric Institute, Philadelphia, PA [*Library symbol*] [*Library of Congress*] (LCLS)
PPEP .... Pen Plotter Emulation Plotsoftware (SAUS)
PPEP .... Pen Plotter Emulation Program [*Computer science*] (MHDI)
PPEP .... Plasma Physics and Environmental Perturbation (NASA)
P/PEP .... Progress Performance Evaluation Panel [*Job Corps*]
PPER .... Procurement Package Engineering Release (MCD)
PPES .... Physical Performance Evaluation System [*Army*]
PPES .... Pilot Performance Evaluation System [*Air Force*]
PPES .... Planning, Programming, and Execution System [*Army*] (AAGC)
PPeSchw .... Schwenkfelder Historical Library, Pennsburg, PA [*Library symbol*] [*Library of Congress*] (LCLS)
PPET .... Pangea Petroleum Co. (SAUS)
PPETS .... Pretreatment Permitting and Enforcement Tracking System [*Environmental Protection Agency*] (ERG)
PPEWARN ... Pave Paws Early Warning phased-Array Radar Network (SAUS)
PPF .... Columbus Polar Platform (SAUS)
PPF .... Franklin Institute, Philadelphia, PA [*Library symbol*] [*Library of Congress*] [*OCLC symbol*] (LCLS)
PPF .... Hancock [*John*] Patriot Preferred Dividend Fund [*NYSE symbol*] (SPSG)
PPF .... John Hancock Patr Pfd Div Fd [*NYSE symbol*] (TTSB)
PPF .... Pacific Peace Fund (EA)
PPF .... Paired-Pulse Facilitation [*Neurophysiology*]
PPF .... Panamanian Public Force (AD)
PPF .... Panels Per Facing [*Outdoor advertising*] (WDMC)
PPF .... Parsons [*Kansas*] [*Airport symbol*] (OAG)
PPF .... Parsons, KS [*Location identifier*] [*FAA*] (FAAL)
PPF .... Parti Populaire Francais [*French Popular Party*] [*Political party*] (PPE)
PPF .... Patriotic People's Front [*Hungary*] [*Political party*]
PPF .... Paw Paw Foundation [*Association*] (EA)
PPF .... Payload Processing Facility [*Air Force*] (NASA)
PPF .... Peacetime Planning Factors
PPF .... Peak Power Frequency
PPF .... Pellagra Preventive Factor [*See also PP*] [*Biochemistry*]
PPF .... People's Police Force
PPF .... Permanent Power Fuse (SAUS)
ppf .... Personal Property Floater [*Insurance*] (AD)
PPF .... Personal Property Floater [*Insurance*]
PPF .... Phagocytosis Promoting Factor [*Immunology*] (DAVI)
PPF .... Phase Pushing Factor
PPF .... Photophoretic Force [*Pressure exerted by light*]
PPF .... Plain Paper Fax (SAUS)
PPF .... Plasma Protein Fraction [*Hematology*]
PPF .... Platform Proto-Federation (SAUS)
PPF .... Plumbers and Pipefitters [*Union*] (AD)
PPF .... Poetarum Philosophorum Graecorum Fragmenta [*A publication*] (OCD)
PPF .... Polarization-Preserving Fiber
PPF .... Polar Platform (SAUS)
PPF .... Pollution Probe [*Canada*] (EAIO)
PPF .... Pollution Probe Foundation (FOTI)
PPF .... Poly(phenolformaldehyde) [*Organic chemistry*]
PPF .... Porous Polyurethane Foam [*Also, PUF*] [*Plastics technology*]
PPF .... Positive Position Feedback (SAUS)
PPF .... Post Parturitive Fever (SAUS)
PPF .... Power Plant Frame [*Mazda Miata*] [*Connecting engine and transmission to final drive*]
PPF .... Presbyterian Peace Fellowship (EA)
PPF .... Primary Part Failure (DNAB)
PPF .... Principal Profile Forms [*Soil classification*]
PPF .... Print Production Format (SAUS)
PPF .... Privatefoeretagarnas Partioganisation i Finland [*Finnish Private Entrepreneurs' Party*] [*Political party*] (PPE)
PPF .... Production Possibility Frontier [*Economics*]
PPF .... Program Preparation Facilities (VLIE)
PPF .... Program Production Fee (VLIE)
PPF .... Program Protects Flags (VLIE)
PPF .... Project Preparation Facility (EURO)
PPF .... Provision of Production Facilities [*Military*] (AABC)
PPF .... Public Policy Forum [*Canada*] (RCD)
PPF .... United Association of Journeymen and Apprentices of the Plumbing and Pipe Fitting Industry of the United States and Canada
PPFA .... Page Printer Formatting Aid [*Computer science*] (CIST)
PPFA .... Planned Parenthood Federation of America (EA)
PPFA .... Plastic Pipe and Fittings Association (EA)
PPFA .... Professional Picture Framers Association (EA)
PPFA .... United States Army, Frankford Arsenal Library, Philadelphia, PA [*Library symbol*] [*Library of Congress*] (LCLS)
p-p factor ... Pellagra-Preventive Factor (AD)
PPFAR .... Federal Archives and Records Center, General Services Administration, Philadelphia, PA [*Library symbol*] [*Library of Congress*] (LCLS)
PPFAS .... Past President of the Faculty of Architects and Surveyors [*British*] (DBQ)
PPFAS .... Post President of the Faculty of Architects and Surveyors (SAUS)
PPF-B .... Biochemical Research Foundation, Franklin Institute, Newark, DE [*Closed*] [*Library symbol*] [*Library of Congress*] (LCLS)
PPFC .... Peoples Pearl and Fishery Corp. (SAUS)

PPFC .... Philadelphia Fellowship Commission, Philadelphia, PA [*Library symbol*] [*Library of Congress*] [*Obsolete*] (LCLS)
PPFC .... Planned Parenthood Federation of Canada (FOTI)
PPFC .... Priscilla Presley Fan Club [*Defunct*] (EA)
PPFCA .... Philadelphia College of Art Library (SAUS)
PPFD .... Photosynthetically Active Photon Flux Density [*Botany*]
PPFD .... Photosynthetic Photon Flux Density (SAUS)
PPFF .... Poisson Probability Frequency Function [*Mathematics*]
PPF-G .... Germantown Laboratories, Inc., Philadelphia, PA [*Library symbol*] [*Library of Congress*] (LCLS)
PPFHi .... Historical Society of Frankford, Philadelphia, PA [*Library symbol*] [*Library of Congress*] [*Obsolete*] (LCLS)
PP Film ..... Polypropylene Film (SAUS)
PPFJC .... Federation of Jewish Charities, Philadelphia, PA [*Library symbol*] [*Library of Congress*] [*Obsolete*] (LCLS)
PPFML ...... Fidelity Mutual Life Insurance Co., Philadelphia, PA [*Library symbol*] [*Library of Congress*] (LCLS)
PPFO .... Paris Procurement Field Office
PPFP .... Plane Parallel Fabry-Perot (SAUS)
PPFPR .... F. P. Ristine & Co., Philadelphia, PA [*Library symbol*] [*Library of Congress*] [*Obsolete*] (LCLS)
PPFr .... Friends' Free Library of Germantown, Philadelphia, PA [*Library symbol*] [*Library of Congress*] (LCLS)
PPFR .... Plutonium Product Filter Room [*Nuclear energy*] (NRCH)
PPFRB .... Federal Reserve Bank of Philadelphia, Philadelphia, PA [*Library symbol*] [*Library of Congress*] (LCLS)
PPFRT .... Prototype Preliminary Flight Rating Test
PPFS .... Pergamon Professional and Financial Services [*Commercial firm*] [*British*]
PPFS .... Pre-Printed Forms System (SAUS)
PPFS .... Product Performance Feedback System (SAUS)
PPFS .... Purchased Parts Forecasting System (TIMI)
PPFU .... Post Program Follow-Up (AGLO)
PPFUN ...... Post-Processor Function (SAUS)
PPG .... German Society of Pennsylvania, Philadelphia, PA [*Library symbol*] [*Library of Congress*] (LCLS)
PPG .... Pacific Proving Ground [*AEC*]
PPG .... Pago Pago [*Samoa*] [*Airport symbol*] (OAG)
PPG .... Pago Pago, AQ [*Location identifier*] [*FAA*] (FAAL)
PPG .... Pediatric Pneumogram [*Radiology*] (DAVI)
PPG .... Performance Partnership Grant (SAUS)
PPG .... Periodical Press Gallery [*US Senate*]
PPG .... Permanent Planning Group [*Military*] [*British*]
PPG .... Personnel Processing Group [*Army*]
PPG .... PGM Ventures Corp. [*Toronto Stock Exchange symbol*] [*Canada*]
PPG .... Photoplethysmography [*Medicine*]
PPG .... Picopicogram [*One trillionth of one trillionth of a gram*]
PPG .... Piezoelectric Power Generation
PPG .... Pipe Plug
PPG .... Pittsburgh Paint and Glass [*Company*]
PPG .... Pittsburgh Plate Glass [*Commercial firm*]
PPG .... Planned Procurement Guide
PPG .... Planning and Policy Guidance (MCD)
PPG .... Planning and Programming Guidance [*Army*] (AABC)
ppg .... Planning and Programming Guidance (AD)
PPG .... Plasma Power Generator
PPG .... Player Piano Group (EAIO)
PPG .... Point Possession Gained [*Football*]
PPG .... Points per Game (WGA)
PPG .... Policies and Procedures Guide (SAA)
PPG .... Polymorphonuclear Cells per Glomerulus (STED)
PPG .... Poly(propylene Glycol) [*Organic chemistry*]
PPG .... Polyurethane-Polyvinyl Graphite (STED)
PPG .... Portal Pressure Gradient [*Medicine*] (DMAA)
PPG .... Postponing [*Telegraphy*] (PCTE)
PPG .... Postprandial Glucose (STED)
ppg .... Pounds per Gallon
PPG .... Power-Play Goal [*Hockey*]
PPG .... PPG Indus [*NYSE symbol*] (TTSB)
PPG .... PPG Industries, Inc. [*Formerly, Pittsburgh Plate Glass Co.*] [*Associated Press*] (SAG)
PPG .... PPG Industries, Inc., Coatings and Resins Division, Allison Park, PA [*OCLC symbol*] (OCLC)
PPG .... Predictive Proportional Guidance
PPG .... Pre-School Playgroup [*British*] (DET)
PPG .... Pretragal Parotid Gland (STED)
PPG .... Primary Pattern Generator [*Bell Laboratories*]
PPG .... Prime Power Group
PPG .... Print Pattern Generator (IAA)
PPG .... Priority Planning Grid (ABAC)
PPG .... Program for Population Genetics [*Collaboration of US and China Groups*]
PPG .... Programmable Pattern Generator (SAUS)
PPG .... Programmable Pulse Generator [*Space launch term*] (ISAK)
PPG .... Program Planning Guide (OICC)
PPG .... Program Policy Guidelines
PPG .... Program Pulse Generator (IEEE)
PPG .... Propulsion and Power Generation
PPG .... Propylene Gylcol (ACAE)
PPG .... Public Procurement Group (EURO)
PPG .... Pulses Per Group (SAUS)
PPGA .... British Pot Plant Growers Association (SAUS)
PPGA .... Pennsylvania Personnel and Guidance Association (AD)
PPGA .... Personal Producing General Agent [*Insurance*]
PPGA .... Plastic Pin Grid Array (PCM)
PPGA .... Post Pill Galactorrhea-Amenorrhea [*Medicine*]
ppga .... Post-Pill Galactorrheamenorrhea [*Medicine*] (AD)
PPGA .... Pot Plant Growers Association (SAUS)
PPGA .... Potplant Growers Association [*British*] (DBA)
PPGA .... Preschool Play-Group Association [*British*] (DI)
PPGA .... Professional Plant Growers Association (NTPA)
PPGBL .... Personal Property Government Bill of Lading (DNAB)
PPGD .... Pelvic Plane of Greatest Dimension [*Medicine*] (MELL)
PPGE .... General Electric Co., Philadelphia, PA [*Library symbol*] [*Library of Congress*] (LCLS)
PPGE .... Partido del Progreso de Guinea Ecuatorial [*Progressive Party of Equatorial Guinea*] [*Political party*] (EY)
PPGE-M ..... General Electric Co., Missile and Space Vehicle Department, Aerosciences Laboratory, Philadelphia (SAUS)
PPGE-M ..... General Electric Co., Missile and Space Vehicle Department, Aerosciences Laboratory, Philadelphia, PA [*Library symbol*] [*Library of Congress*] (LCLS)
PPGen .... Genealogical Society of Pennsylvania, Philadelphia, PA [*Library symbol*] [*Library of Congress*] (LCLS)
PPGenH ..... Philadelphia General Hospital Laboratories, Philadelphia, PA [*Library symbol*] [*Library of Congress*] [*Obsolete*] (LCLS)
PPGeo .... Geographical Society of Philadelphia, Philadelphia, PA [*Library symbol*] [*Library of Congress*] [*Obsolete*] (LCLS)
PPGF .... Polypeptide Growth Factor [*Endocrinology*] (DAVI)
PPGH .... Philadelphia General Hospital, Philadelphia, PA [*Library symbol*] [*Library of Congress*] (LCLS)
PPGi .... Girard College, Philadelphia, PA [*Library symbol*] [*Library of Congress*] [*Obsolete*] (LCLS)
PPGJW ...... Past Pro-Grand Junior Warden [*Freemasonry*] (ROG)
PPGL .... Polished Plate Glass [*Technical drawings*] (DAC)
PPGL .... Presbyterian Parents of Gays and Lesbians [*Association*] (EA)
PPGM .... Past Provincial Grand Master [*Freemasonry*]
PPGM .... Planning, Programming and Guidance Memorandum (SAUS)
PPGM .... Planning-Programming Guidance Memo [*Navy*]
PPGO .... Past Pro-Grand Organist [*Freemasonry*] (ROG)
PPGO .... Past Pro-Grand Orient [*Freemasonry*] (ROG)
PPGP .... Past Pro-Grand Pursuivant [*Freemasonry*] (ROG)
PPGP .... Prepaid Group Practice [*Insurance*] (DHSM)
PPGraph .... Graphic Sketch Club, Philadelphia, PA [*Library symbol*] [*Library of Congress*] [*Obsolete*] (LCLS)
PPGratz ..... Gratz College, Philadelphia, PA [*Library symbol*] [*Library of Congress*] [*Obsolete*] (LCLS)
PPGRC ...... Public Policy and Government Relations Council
PPGS .... Postpartum Glomerulosclerosis [*Medicine*] (MELL)
PPGS .... Publications of the Pennsylvana German Society (SAUS)
PPGSB ...... Past Pro-Grand Sword Bearer [*Freemasonry*] (ROG)
PPGSN ...... Past Provincial Grand Senior [*Freemasonry*] (ROG)
PPGSW ...... Past Provincial Grand Senior Warden [*Freemasonry*]
PPGU .... PPG Industries [*Intermodal shipping container symbol*] (TVRC)
PPGW .... Past Pro-Grand Warden [*Freemasonry*] (ROG)
PPGX .... Pittsburgh Plate Glass [*Private rail car owner code*]
PPGZ .... Pittsburgh Plate Glass [*Federal Railroad Administration identification code*]
PPH .... Pages per Hour
PPH .... Paid Personal Holiday
pph .... Pamphlet (AD)
PPH .... Pamphlet
pph .... Papers Per Hour [*News*] (WDMC)
PPH .... Parts per Hour (TIMI)
PPH .... Parts per Hundred
PPH .... Past Pertinent History (SAUS)
PPH .... Peak-to-Peak Heights [*Spectrometry*]
PPH .... Persistent Pulmonary Hypertension [*Medicine*]
PPH .... Petroleum Pipehead
PPH .... Phenylpropanolamine(hydrochloride) [*Also, PPA, PPM*] [*Decongestant*]
PPH .... Phosphopyruvate Hydratase [*An enzyme*]
PPH .... PHP Healthcare [*NYSE symbol*] (TTSB)
PPH .... PHP Healthcare Corp. [*NYSE symbol*] (SPSG)
PPH .... Plasmapherese (SAUS)
PPH .... Postlumbar Puncture Headache [*Medicine*] (MELL)
pph .... Post-Partum Hemorrhage [*Medicine*] (AD)
PPH .... Postpartum Hemorrhage [*Medicine*]
pph .... Pounds Per Hour (AD)
PPH .... Pounds per Hour (NG)
PPH .... Primary Pulmonary Hypertension [*Medicine*]
PPH .... Prophet Resources Ltd. [*Vancouver Stock Exchange symbol*]
PPH .... Protocollagen Proline Hydroxylase [*An enzyme*] (MAE)
pph .... Pulses Per Hour (AD)
PPH .... Pulses per Hour
PPHa .... Hahnemann Medical College and Hospital, Philadelphia, PA [*Library symbol*] [*Library of Congress*] (LCLS)
PPHA .... Peak Pulse Height Analysis
PPHA .... Private Proprietary Homes for Adults
PPHBA ...... Peruvian Paso Half-Blood Association [*Later, PPPBR*] (EA)
PPHFC ...... Holy Family College, Philadelphia, PA [*Library symbol*] [*Library of Congress*] (LCLS)
PPH/LB ..... Pounds per Hour per Pound (SAA)
PPHM .... Parts per Hundred Million
P-PH-M ..... Pulse Phase Modulation (DEN)
PPHN .... Persistent Pulmonary Hypertension of the Newborn [*Medicine*]
PPHN .... Primary Pulmonary Hypertension of the Newborn [*Medicine*] (NRGU)
PPHOPT .... Pseudo-Pseudohypoparathyroidism [*Also, PPHP*] [*Endocrinology*]
PPHor .... Pennsylvania Horticultural Society, Philadelphia, PA [*Library symbol*] [*Library of Congress*] (LCLS)

P Php .... Port Phillip (AD)
PPHP .... Pseudo-Pseudohypoparathyroidism [*Also, PPHOPT*] [*Endocrinology*]
PPHPI .... Henry Phipps Institute, Philadelphia, PA [*Library symbol*] [*Library of Congress*] [*Obsolete*] (LCLS)
PPHPI .... Henry Phipps Institute, Philadelphia (SAUS)
pphpm .... Parts Per Hundred Parts of Mix (AD)
pphpm .... Pints Per Hundred Parts of Mix (AD)
pphr .... Parts Per Hundred Parts of Rubber (AD)
PPHRII .... Parents of Premature and High Risk Infants International (EA)
PPHRNA .... Peruvian Paso Horse Registry of North America (EA)
PPHS .... Partisan Prohibition Historical Society (EA)
PPHSL .... Periodical Publication in Harvard Science Libraries
PPHT .... (Phenylethyl-propylamino)hydroxytetralin [*Biochemistry*]
PPHW .... Peoria, Peoria Heights & Western Railroad [*Federal Railroad Administration identification code*]
PPHx .... Previous Psychiatric History (MEDA)
PPHYS .... Plant Physiology (SAUS)
PPi .... Carnegie Library of Pittsburgh, Pittsburgh, PA [*Library symbol*] [*Library of Congress*] (LCLS)
PPI .... Institute for Psychosomatic and Psychiatric Research and Training [*Research center*] (RCD)
PPI .... Italian People's Party [*Political party*] (PSAP)
PPI .... Pacific Printing and Imaging Association (EA)
PPI .... Pacific Propeller Inc. (SAUS)
PPI .... Packing, Postage, and Insurance [*Shipping*]
PPI .... Padangpandjang [*Sumatra*] [*Seismograph station code, US Geological Survey*] (SEIS)
ppi .... Pages Per Inch (AD)
PPI .... Pages per Inch [*Publishing*]
PPI .... Pakistan Press International
PPI .... Pan Pacific Institute [*Flinders University, Australia*]
PPI .... Parallel Peripheral Interface [*Computer science*]
PPI .... Parallel Plate Interceptor (SAUS)
PPI .... Parallel Port Interface (SAUS)
ppi .... Parcel Post Insured (AD)
PPI .... Parcel Post, Insured [*Shipping*]
PPI .... Particles per Inch
PPI .... Partito Popolare Italiano [*Italian Popular Party*] [*Political party*] (WDAA)
PPI .... Parts Parameter Information (SAUS)
PPi .... Parvovirus and Parainfluenza [*Dog vaccine covering these diseases*] (SPVS)
PPI .... Passe Partout International
PPI .... Pass Point Instrument (SAUS)
PPI .... Patient Package Insert [*Pharmacy*] (DAVI)
PPI .... Pensioners for Peace International (EAIO)
PPI .... Performance Products Industries [*Automotive supplier*]
PPI .... Pergamon Press, Inc.
PPI .... Permanent Pacemaker Implantation [*Medicine*] (MELL)
PPI .... Personality and Personal Illness Questionnaires [*Psychology*]
PPI .... Personalpolitische Information (SAUS)
PPI .... Personnel Planning Information
PPI .... Pharate Pupal Integument (SAUS)
PPI .... Phoenix Precision Instrument Co.
PPI .... Pickle Packers International (EA)
ppi .... Picks Per Inch [*Weaving*] (DICI)
PPI .... Pico Products [*AMEX symbol*] (TTSB)
PPI .... Pico Products, Inc. [*AMEX symbol*] (SPSG)
PPI .... Pictorial Position Indicator
PPI .... Pilgrim Holdings Ltd. [*Vancouver Stock Exchange symbol*]
PPI .... PIPA [*Pulsed Integrating Pendulous Accelerometer*] Pulse Integrator
PPI .... Piston Position Indicator
PPI .... PIXEL [*Picture Element*] per Inch [*Computer science*] (PCM)
ppi .... Pixels Per Inch [*Computer graphics*] (WDMC)
PPI .... Plane Position Indicator [*RADAR*]
PPI .... Plan Position Indication (or Indicator) (SAUS)
ppi .... Plan Position Indicator (AD)
PPI .... Plan Position Indicator Mode [*Computer science*] (ADA)
PPI .... Plasma Protein Isolate [*Food technology*]
PPI .... Plastic Pipe Institute (SAUS)
PPI .... Plastics Pipe Institute (EA)
PPI .... Plate Power Input (ELAL)
PPI .... Plot Position Indicator
PPI .... Point per Inch (IAA)
ppi .... Points Per Inch (WDMC)
ppi .... Policy Proof of Interest (AD)
PPI .... Policy Proof of Interest
PPI .... Polymeric Polyisocyanate (EDCT)
PPI .... Polyphosphonositides
PPI .... Polyphthalimide [*Organic chemistry*]
PPI .... POM [*Program Objective Memorandum*] Preparation Instructions [*Military*]
ppi .... Pores per Inch
PPI .... Port Pirie [*Australia*] [*Airport symbol*] (OAG)
PPI .... Ports [*Harbors*] Performance Indicator [*Australia*]
PPI .... Postage Paid Impression [*Freight*] (DCTA)
PPI .... Potash and Phosphate Institute (EA)
PPI .... Potato Protease Inhibitor (DB)
PPI .... Pounds per Inch [*Lubrication load*]
PPI .... Power Prime Implicant (VLIE)
PPI .... Preceding Preparatory Interval [*Psychometrics*]
PPI .... Precise Pixel Interpolation (SAUS)
PPI .... Precise-Pixel Interpolation [*Computer science*]
PPI .... Precision Products, Incorporated
PPI .... Preferred Parts Index
PPI .... Pre Phase-In
PPI .... Pre-Planned Product Improvements (ACAE)
PPI .... Preplant Inc. [*Herbicides*] [*Agriculture*]
PPI .... Prepleading Investigation [*Law*]
PPI .... Pre-production Part Index
PPI .... Preproinsulin [*Medicine*] (DB)
PPI .... Pre-Pulse Inhibition
PPI .... Present Pain Intensity
PPI .... Present Position Indication (or Indicator) (SAUS)
PPI .... Present Position Indicator [*Aviation*]
PPI .... Prices Paid Index [*Economics*]
PPI .... Primarily Primates, Inc. [*An association*] (EA)
PPI .... Primary Personal Interest [*Personnel study*]
PPI .... Prime Permissible Implicant (SAUS)
PPI .... Prince Patrick Island [*Canada*]
PPI .... Print Position Indicator (SAUS)
PPI .... Process Planning Interface [*Computer science*] (VLIE)
PPI .... Producer Price Index [*Bureau of Labor Statistics*] [*Information service or system*]
PPI .... Professional Photographers of Israel (PDAA)
PPI .... Professional Photographers of Israel Organization (SAUS)
PPI .... Professional Press Inc. (SAUS)
PPI .... Programmable Parallel Interface (SAUS)
PPI .... Programmable Peripheral Interface (MCD)
PPI .... Program Position Indicator
PPI .... Progressive Policy Institute [*Research center*] (RCD)
PPI .... Project Procurement Instruction (SAUS)
PPI .... Project Procurement Instructions [*Jet Propulsion Laboratory, NASA*]
PPI .... Project Public Information [*Department of Education*] (AEBS)
PPI .... Property Protection Insurance
PPI .... Proportional Plus Integral
PPI .... Protective Packaging, Inc. (AD)
PPI .... Public-Private Interface
PPI .... Publishing Partners International (SAUS)
PPI .... Pulse Position Indicator (MCD)
ppi .... Pulses Per Inch (WDMC)
PPI .... Pulses per Inch (CMD)
PPI .... Purchase Potential Index
PPI .... Pyrophosphate Index [*Agronomy*]
PPi .... Pyrophosphate, Inorganic [*Chemistry*]
PPIA .... American-Indonesian Friendship Association (SAUS)
PPi-A .... Carnegie Library of Pittsburgh, Allegheny Regional Branch, Monroeville, PA [*Library symbol*] [*Library of Congress*] (LCLS)
PPIA .... Poultry Products Inspection Act (GFGA)
PPIA .... Programme du Pipeline des Iles de l'Arctique [*Canada*]
PPiAC .... Community College of Allegheny County, Pittsburgh, PA [*Library symbol*] [*Library of Congress*] (LCLS)
PPIAC .... Petroleum Products Industry Advisory Council (FOTI)
PPiAL .... Allegheny County Law Library, Pittsburgh, PA [*Library symbol*] [*Library of Congress*] (LCLS)
PPiAM .... Pittsburgh Academy of Medicine, Pittsburgh, PA [*Library symbol*] [*Library of Congress*] (LCLS)
PPIAS .... Parent-to-Parent Information on Adoption Services [*British*] (DI)
PPIB .... Programmable Protocol Interface Board
PPiC .... Carnegie-Mellon University, Pittsburgh, PA [*Library symbol*] [*Library of Congress*] (LCLS)
PPIC .... Pesticide Programs Information Center (EPAT)
PPIC .... Plumbing and Piping Industry Council (AD)
PPIC .... Pollution Prevention Information Clearinghouse [*Environmental Protection Agency*]
PPIC .... Potash and Phosphate Institute of Canada (FOTI)
PPIC .... Public Policy Institute of California (RCD)
PPiCa .... Carlow College, Pittsburgh, PA [*Library symbol*] [*Library of Congress*] (LCLS)
PPiCa-O .... Carlow College, Our Lady of Mercy Academy, Pittsburgh, PA [*Library symbol*] [*Library of Congress*] (LCLS)
PPiCC .... Chatham College, Pittsburgh, PA [*Library symbol*] [*Library of Congress*] (LCLS)
PPICC .... Plasma Proinflammatory Cytokine Concentration [*Medicine*] (MELL)
PPICR .... Institute for Cancer Research, Philadelphia, PA [*Library symbol*] [*Library of Congress*] (LCLS)
PPICS .... Production Planning Inventory Control System (PDAA)
PPiD .... Duquesne University, Pittsburgh, PA [*Library symbol*] [*Library of Congress*] (LCLS)
PPID .... Peak Pain Intensity Difference Score [*Medicine*] (DMAA)
PPID .... Polaris-Poseidon Intelligence Digest (MCD)
PPID .... Process Program Identification (AAEL)
PPID .... Product IBM Program Information Department (SAUS)
PPI Display ... Plan Position Indicator Display (SAUS)
PPiD-L .... Duquesne University, School of Law, Pittsburgh, PA [*Library symbol*] [*Library of Congress*] (LCLS)
PPIDP .... Pulp and Paper Industries Development Programme (SAUS)
PPiE .... E. D'Appolonia Consulting Engineers, Pittsburgh, PA [*Library symbol*] [*Library of Congress*] (LCLS)
PPIE .... Prolonged Postictal Encephalopathy [*Medicine*] (DMAA)
PPIE .... Pseudophase Ion Exchange [*Chemistry*]
PPIF .... Photographic Processing and Interpretation Facilities (SAUS)
PPIF .... Photographic Processing and Interpretation Facility
PPIF .... Photo Processing Interpretation Facility
ppif .... Photo-Processing Interpretation Facility (AD)
PPIFC .... Pauline Pinkney International Fan Club (EA)
PPIFIA .... Policy Proof of Interest, Full Interest Admitted (EBF)
PPIG .... Psychology of Programming Interest Group (SAUS)
PPIGB .... Plant Pathology Internet Guide Book

PPiGulf ...... Gulf Research & Development Co., Pittsburgh, PA [*Library symbol*] [*Library of Congress*] (LCLS)
PPiHB .... Carnegie-Mellon University, Hunt Institute for Botanical Documentation, Pittsburgh, PA [*Library symbol*] [*Library of Congress*] (LCLS)
PPiHi .... Historical Society of Western Pennsylvania, Pittsburgh, PA [*Library symbol*] [*Library of Congress*] (LCLS)
PPiI .... International Poetry Forum, Pittsburgh, PA [*Library symbol*] [*Library of Congress*] (LCLS)
PPiK .... Ketchum, McLeod & Grove, Inc., Pittsburgh, PA [*Library symbol*] [*Library of Congress*] (LCLS)
PPiL .... LaRoche College, Pittsburgh, PA [*Library symbol*] [*Library of Congress*] (LCLS)
PPIL .... Priced Provisioned Item List (MCD)
p-pille .... Praeventivpille [*Dano-Norwegian*] [*Contraceptive pill*] (AD)
PPiM .... Carnegie-Mellon University, Mellon Institute, Pittsburgh, PA [*Library symbol*] [*Library of Congress*] (LCLS)
PPIM .... Programmable Peripheral Interface Microcomputer (IAA)
PPiMS .... Mine Safety Appliances Co., Pittsburgh, PA [*Library symbol*] [*Library of Congress*] (LCLS)
PPIMS .... Past Performance Information Management System [*Army*]
PPIn .... Independence National Historical Park, Philadelphia, PA [*Library symbol*] [*Library of Congress*] (LCLS)
pp/in .... Pages Per Inch (AD)
PPINA .... Insurance Co., of North America, Corporate Archives, Philadelphia, PA [*Library symbol*] [*Library of Congress*] (LCLS)
PPINA .... RADAR Weather Report Not Available [*NWS*] (FAAC)
PPINE .... RADAR Weather Report Equipment No Echoes Observed [*NWS*] (FAAC)
PPINICI ...... Pulsed Positive Ion-Negative Ion Chemical Ionization [*Instrumentation*]
PPINO .... RADAR Weather Report Equipment Inoperative Due to Breakdown [*NWS*] (FAAC)
P/P INS ..... Parts per Installment (SAUS)
PPInstHE .... Past President of the Institution of Highway Engineers [*British*] (DI)
PPInstRA .... Past President of the Institute of Registered Architects (SAUS)
PPIOK .... RADAR Weather Report Equipment Operation REsumed [*NWS*] (FAAC)
PPIOM .... RADAR Weather Report Equipment Inoperative Due to Maintenance [*NWS*] (FAAC)
PPIP .... Philippine Poultry Improvement Plant (SAUS)
PPIP .... Physics Post-Doctoral Information Pool [*American Institute of Physics*] (PDAA)
PPiPP .... Point Park College, Pittsburgh, PA [*Library symbol*] [*Library of Congress*] (LCLS)
PPiPPG ...... PPG Industries, Inc., Glass Research Center, Information Services Library, Pittsburgh, PA [*Library symbol*] [*Library of Congress*] (LCLS)
PPiPT .... Pittsburgh Theological Seminary, Pittsburgh, PA [*Library symbol*] [*Library of Congress*] (LCLS)
PPIR .... Personal Property Inventory Report
PPIR .... Personnel Planning Information Report (MCD)
PPIR .... Personnel Planning Integration Report
PpiR .... Rockwell International Corp., Pittsburgh (SAUS)
PPiR .... Rockwell International Corp., Pittsburgh, PA [*Library symbol*] [*Library of Congress*] (LCLS)
PPIRG .... Pave Paws Interface Requirements Group (SAUS)
PPIRO .... Planned Position Indicator Readout (NVT)
PPiRP .... Reformed Presbyterian Theological Seminary, Pittsburgh, PA [*Library symbol*] [*Library of Congress*] (LCLS)
PPIS .... Pesticide Product Information System [*Environmental Protection Agency*] (GFGA)
PPIS .... Pollution Prevention Inventives for States (EPAT)
PPIS .... Product Profile Information System [*Shell Oil Co.*]
PPI Screen... Plan Position Indicator Screen (SAUS)
PPIStructE... Past President of the Institution of Structural Engineers [*British*] (DI)
PPITB .... Plastics Processing Industry Training Board (SAUS)
PPIU .... Policy, Planning and Implementation Unit
PPIU .... Probe Power Interface Unit (ACAE)
PPIU .... Programmable Peripheral Interface Unit
PPiU .... University of Pittsburgh, Pittsburgh, PA [*Library symbol*] [*Library of Congress*] (LCLS)
PPiU-A ...... University of Pittsburgh, Henry Clay Frick Fine Arts Center, Pittsburgh, PA [*Library symbol*] [*Library of Congress*] (LCLS)
PPiU-BL ..... University of Pittsburgh, Blair-Lippincott Library, Eye and Ear Hospital of Pittsburgh, Pittsburgh, PA [*Library symbol*] [*Library of Congress*] (LCLS)
PPiU-H ...... University of Pittsburgh, Maurice and Laura Falk Library of the Health Professions, Pittsburgh, PA [*Library symbol*] [*Library of Congress*] (LCLS)
PPiU-IS ..... University of Pittsburgh, Archives of Industrial Society, Pittsburgh, PA [*Library symbol*] [*Library of Congress*] (LCLS)
PPiU-L ...... University of Pittsburgh, Law School, Pittsburgh, PA [*Library symbol*] [*Library of Congress*] (LCLS)
PPiU-LS ..... University of Pittsburgh, Graduate School of Library and Information Sciences, Pittsburgh, PA [*Library symbol*] [*Library of Congress*] (LCLS)
PPiU-NS .... University of Pittsburgh, Natural Sciences Library, Pittsburgh, PA [*Library symbol*] [*Library of Congress*] (LCLS)
PPiU-PH .... University of Pittsburgh, Graduate School of Public Health, Pittsburgh, PA [*Library symbol*] [*Library of Congress*] (LCLS)
PPiU-PIA .... University of Pittsburgh, Graduate School of Public and International Affairs, Pittsburgh, PA [*Library symbol*] [*Library of Congress*] (LCLS)
PPiUS .... United States Steel Corp., Pittsburgh, PA [*Library symbol*] [*Library of Congress*] (LCLS)
PPiU-SF ..... University of Pittsburgh, Stephen Collins Foster Memorial [*Music*] Library,Pittsburgh, PA [*Library symbol*] [*Library of Congress*] (LCLS)
PPiUSM ..... United States Department of the Interior, Bureau of Mines, Pittsburgh Research Center, Pittsburgh, PA [*Library symbol*] [*Library of Congress*] (LCLS)
PPIV .... Per Person Interview Value [*Marketing*] (WDMC)
PPIV .... Positive Personnel Identity Verification (PDAA)
PPIVM .... Passive Physiological Intervertebral Movement (SAUS)
PPiW .... Westinghouse Electric Corp., Research and Development Center, Pittsburgh, PA [*Library symbol*] [*Library of Congress*] (LCLS)
PPiW-N ...... Westinghouse Electric Corp., Nuclear Center Library, Pittsburgh, PA [*Library symbol*] [*Library of Congress*] (LCLS)
PPiWP .... Western Psychiatric Institute and Clinic, University of Pittsburgh, Pittsburgh, PA [*Library symbol*] [*Library of Congress*] (LCLS)
PPIX .... Pacific Petrochemicals [*Private rail car owner code*]
PPIZ .... Pepin Iresco [*Federal Railroad Administration identification code*]
PPJ .... Pressure Plane Joint
PPJ .... Pure Pancreatic Juice
PPJ .... Thomas Jefferson University, Philadelphia, PA [*Library symbol*] [*Library of Congress*] (LCLS)
PPJea .... Jeanes Hospital, Philadelphia, PA [*Library symbol*] [*Library of Congress*] [*Obsolete*] (LCLS)
PPJO .... Pli Premier Jour Officiel [*Official First Day Cover - OFDC*] [*Canada Post Corp.*]
PPJ-S .... Thomas Jefferson University, Scott Memorial Library, Philadelphia, PA [*Library symbol*] [*Library of Congress*] (LCLS)
PPJW .... Past Pro-Junior Warden [*Freemasonry*] (ROG)
PPK .... Paired Perpendicular Keratotomy [*Procedure to correct astigmatism*]
PPK .... Palmoplantar Keratoderma [*Dermatology*]
PPK .... Palmoplantar Keratosis [*Medicine*] (DMAA)
PPK .... Parametrized Post-Keplerian [*Physics*]
PPK .... Paramp Pump Klystron
PPK .... Parti Progressiste Katangais [*Political party*]
PPK .... Personal Preference Kit [*Small bag in which astronauts are allowed to take personal mementos*]
PPK .... Polizei Pistole Kriminal [*Pistol suitable for undercover police or detective use*] [*Walther Waffenfabrik, German arms manufacturer*]
PPK .... Programmable Power Key [*Computer science*]
PPK .... Punt, Pass, and Kick [*Youth competition sponsored by professional football*]
pPk .... Purplish Pink (AD)
PPK .... Ramp 66, Inc. [*ICAO designator*] (FAAC)
PPKB .... Partai Perpaduan Kebang-Saan Brunei [*Brunei National United Party*] [*Political party*] (EY)
PPKCA .... Pen and Pocket Knife Cutters' Association [*A union*] [*British*]
PPKG .... Power Package (MSA)
Ppl .... Intrapleural Pressure [*Medicine*] (DAVI)
PPL .... Library Co. of Philadelphia, Philadelphia, PA [*Library symbol*] [*Library of Congress*] (LCLS)
PPL .... Package Programs of London (NITA)
PPL .... Palach Press Ltd. [*British*] (EAIO)
PPL .... Palmer Physical Laboratory [*Princeton University*] (MCD)
PPL .... Pars Plana Lensectomy (SAUS)
PPL .... Pars Planus Lensectomy [*Ophthalmology*] (DAVI)
PP/L .... Partial Payload (SAUS)
PPL .... Participle [*Grammar*] (WGA)
PPL .... Passed Parameter List (SAUS)
PPL .... Pay-Per-Lead [*Payment model for online advertising*] (NETL)
PPL .... PCBoard Programming Language [*Clark Development Co.*] (PCM)
PPL .... Pembina Resources Ltd. [*Toronto Stock Exchange symbol*]
PPL .... Penicilloyl-Polylysin (SAUS)
PPL .... Penicilloyl Polylysine [*Pharmacology*]
PPL .... Penna Power & Light (EFIS)
PPL .... Pennsylvania Power & Light Co. [*NYSE symbol*] (SPSG)
PPL .... People
PPL .... Peripheral Blood Leukocyte [*Medicine*] (PDAA)
PPL .... Per Pupil Limitation (AFM)
PPL .... Peter Peregrinus Ltd. [*Publisher*]
PPL .... Phenylpropanolamine [*Organic chemistry*]
PPL .... Philadelphia Public Library (AD)
PPL .... Phoenix Public Library (AD)
PPL .... Phonographic Performance Ltd. [*British*]
PPL .... Photogrammetric Programming Language [*Computer science*] (PDAA)
PPl .... Photoplate (SAUS)
PPL .... Physical Properties Laboratory [*Oklahoma State University*] [*Research center*] (RCD)
ppl .... Pipeline (AD)
PPL .... Pittsburgh Public Library (AD)
PPL .... Pixel per Line [*Computer science*] (IAA)
PPL .... Planned Parenthood League (AD)
PPL .... Planning Parts List
PPL .... Plan Position Landing (DEN)
PPL .... Plant Physiology Laboratory (SSD)
PPL .... Plasma Physics Laboratory [*Also known as PPPL*]
PPL .... Plasma Propulsion Laboratory (MCD)
PPL .... Plus Programming Language [*Computer science*]
PPL .... Plutonium Product Loadout [*Nuclear energy*] (NRCH)
PPL .... Pneumatic Projectile Launcher (SAUS)
PPL .... Point-to-Point Link (SAUS)
PPL .... Police Protective League (AD)
PPL .... Polymorphic Programming Language [*1971*] [*Computer science*] (CSR)
PPL .... Polypivalolactone (SAUS)
PPL .... Populated Place [*Board on Geographic Names*]
PPL .... Population Paper Listing [*US Census Bureau*] [*A publication*]
PPL .... Porcine Pancreatic Lipase [*An enzyme*]

PPL .... Portland Public Library (SAUS)
PPL .... Posterior Pole Plasm [*Insect embryology*]
PPL .... Posterior Pulmonary (or Pulmonic) Leaflet (SAUS)
PPL .... Power Plant Laboratory (MUGU)
PPL .... Power Plate Loading (SAUS)
PPL .... PP&L Resources [*NYSE symbol*] (TTSB)
PPL .... PP & L Resources, Inc. [*NYSE symbol*] (SAG)
PPL .... PPL Corp. [*NYSE symbol*]
PPL .... Precise Participant Location
PPL .... Predictive Period LASER (KSC)
PPL .... Preferential Planning List
PPL .... Prefer Product List (SAUS)
PPL .... Preferred Parts List
PPL .... Preferred Products List (ACAE)
PPL .... Preliminary Parts List
PPL .... Preliminary Power Laboratory (IAA)
PPL .... Presbyterians Pro-Life [*An association*] (EA)
PPL .... Priced Parts List (NASA)
P/PL .... Primary Payload [*NASA*] (NASA)
PPL .... Princeton Polymer Laboratories
PPL .... Print Positions per Line [*Computer science*] (MHDI)
PPL .... Private Pilot's Licence [*British*]
PPL .... Process Peripherals Ltd. (SAUS)
PPL .... Process-to-Process Link (SAUS)
PPL .... Production Practice Level (SAUS)
PPL .... Production Process Level (SAUS)
PPL .... Program Production Library [*Computer science*]
PPL .... Project Priority List [*Environmental Protection Agency*]
PPL .... Proposal [*Telegraphy*] (PCTE)
PPL .... Protected Private Land (SAUS)
PPL .... Protein-Polysaccharide [*Biochemistry*] (DAVI)
PPL .... Protein Preprolactin [*Biochemistry*]
PPL .... Providence Public Library (AD)
PPL .... Provisioning Parts List (AAG)
PPL .... Purchased Parts List
PPL .... Pure Prairie League [*Musical group*]
PPL .... Purple
PPL .... Puu Pili [*Hawaii*] [*Seismograph station code, US Geological Survey*] (SEIS)
PpL .... W. & F. Pascoe Proprietory Ltd., Milsons Point, Australia [*Library symbol*] [*Library of Congress*] (LCLS)
PPLA .... Practice Precautionary Landing Approach [*Aviation*]
PPLA .... Professional Photographic Laboratories Association [*British*] (DBA)
P-plane .... Pilotless Airplane (AD)
PPLas .... La Salle College, Philadelphia, PA [*Library symbol*] [*Library of Congress*] (LCLS)
PPlase .... Peptidylprolyl Cis-Trans Isomerase [*An enzyme*]
PPLB .... Postprocessor Call Library [*Computer science*] (IAA)
PPLC .... Patients Protection Law Commission (AD)
PPLCA .... Propellant and Pressurant Loading and Control Assembly (SAUS)
PPLD .... Pikes Peak Library District [*Internationally recognized computerized library system*]
PPLDF .... Professional Protector and Legal Defense Fund
PPLE .... Partial Preliminary Logistic Evaluation
PPLE .... Participle [*Grammar*]
pple .... Past Participle (AD)
PPLE .... Principle (ROG)
PPL/H .... Private Pilot's Licence/Helicopters [*British*] (AIA)
PPLI .... Precise Participant Location-Identification [*Navigation*]
PPLI .... Precise Position Location Information
PPLI .... Provisioning Parts List Index (MCD)
PPLIF .... Pulsed Photolysis LASER-Induced Fluorescence [*Environmental science*]
PPLL .... Military Order of the Loyal Legion of the United States, [*Civil*] War Library and Museum, Philadelphia, PA [*Library symbol*] [*Library of Congress*] (LCLS)
PPLLT .... Provisional Program Load Library Tape [*Computer science*] (MHDI)
PPln .... Independence National Historical Park, Philadelphia (SAUS)
PPLN .... Periodically Poled Lithium Niobate (SEWL)
PPLN .... Pipeline
PPINIC .... Pulsed Positive Ion-Negative Ion Chemical Ionization (SAUS)
pplo .... Pleuropneumonia-Like Organism (AD)
PPLO .... Pleuropneumonia-Like Organisms [*Bacteriology*]
PPLO .... Pleuropneumonia-Link Oganism [*Medicine*] (WDAA)
PPLOT .... Postprocessor Plot (SAUS)
PPLOV .... Painless Progressive Loss of Vision (MELL)
PPLP .... Peak Pleural Pressure (SAUS)
PPLP .... Photo Polymers Lithograph Plate (SAUS)
PPLP .... Photopolymers Lithograph Plate
P PLPBD .... Paper or Pulpboard [*Freight*]
PPLPrA .... Penn Pwr & Lt 4.40% Pfd [*NYSE symbol*] (TTSB)
PPLPrB .... Penn Pwr & Lt 4.50% Pfd [*NYSE symbol*] (TTSB)
ppls .... Peoples [*Internet language*] [*Computer science*]
PPLS .... Peoples Bank Corp. (Indianapolis, IN) [*NASDAQ symbol*] (SAG)
PPLS .... Peoples Bank Indianapolis [*NASDAQ symbol*] (TTSB)
PPLS .... Pesticide Product Label System [*Database*] (GDD)
PPLS .... Precision Position Location (or Locator) System (SAUS)
PPLS .... Precision Position Locator System [*Army*]
PPLS .... Preferred Parts List System (MCD)
PPLS .... Propellant and Pressurant Loading System [*NASA*] (KSC)
PPIStructE .... Past President of the Institution of Structural Engineers (SAUS)
PPLT .... Lutheran Theological Seminary, Philadelphia, PA [*Library symbol*] [*Library of Congress*] (LCLS)
PPL-Test .... Penicilloyl-Polylsin-Test (SAUS)
PPLU .... PPI LINES [*Intermodal shipping container symbol*] (TVRC)
P-PLUS .... Polar Platform Utilisation Study (SAUS)
PPLV .... Pars Plana Lensectomy-Vitrectomy [*Medicine*] (MELL)
PPLV .... Preliminary Pollutant Limit Value (MCD)
PPLX .... Pennsylvania Power and Light [*Private rail car owner code*]
PPLX .... Section of Populated Place [*Board on Geographic Names*]
PPLZ .... Pennsylvania Power & Light [*Federal Railroad Administration identification code*]
PPM .... Aberdeen, MD [*Location identifier*] [*FAA*] (FAAL)
PPM .... Frevious processor mode (SAUS)
PPM .... Investment Grade Municipal Income Fund [*NYSE symbol*] (SAG)
PPM .... Investment Grade Muni Inc. [*NYSE symbol*] (TTSB)
PPM .... Mercantile Library, Philadelphia, PA [*Library symbol*] [*Library of Congress*] [*Obsolete*] (LCLS)
PPM .... Page Per Minute (SAUS)
PPM .... Page-per-Minute [*Computer science*] (PCM)
PPM .... Pages per Minute [*Printer technology*]
ppm .... Pages per Minute
ppm .... Papermaker [*MARC relator code*] [*Library of Congress*] (LCCP)
PPM .... Parallel Performance Monitor (SAUS)
PPM .... Parallel Processing Machine [*Computer science*] (IAA)
PPM .... Particuliere Participatiemaatschappy [*Private Joint Stock Company*] [*Dutch*]
PPM .... Partido del Pueblo Mexicano [*Mexican People's Party*] [*Political party*] (PPW)
PPM .... Partido Proletario de Mexico [*Proletarian Party of Mexico*] [*Political party*] (AD)
PPM .... Parti Pekerja-Pekerja Malaysia [*Workers' Party of Malaysia*] [*Political party*] (PPW)
PPM .... Parti Progressiste Martiniquais [*Progressive Party of Martinique*] [*Political party*] (PPW)
PPM .... Partitioned-Pipe Mixer [*Engineering*]
PPM .... Part Per Million (SAUS)
PPM .... Part Program Manager
PPM .... Parts per Mille (SAUS)
ppm .... Parts Per Million (AD)
PPM .... Parts per Million
Ppm .... Parts per Million
PPM .... Parts per Minute (MCD)
PPM .... Party of the People of Mauritania [*Political party*] (PSAP)
PPM .... Pattani People's Movement [*Thailand*] [*Political party*]
PPM .... Peak Power Meter
ppm .... Peak Program Meter (AD)
PPM .... Peak Program Meter [*Television*]
PPM .... Peoples Pharmacy of Mali (SAUS)
PPM .... Perfect Prognosis Method (SAUS)
PPM .... Periodic Permanent Magnet
PPM .... Periodic Permanent Magnet Focusing (IAA)
PPM .... Periodic Pulsed Magnet (SAUS)
PPM .... Periodic Pulse Metering [*Telecommunications*] (TEL)
PPM .... Period Permanent Magnet (SAUS)
PPM .... Permanent Pacemaker [*Cardiology*] (MAE)
PPM .... Perodic Permanent Magnet (SAUS)
PPM .... Pershing Project Manager
PPM .... Personnel Priority Model (MCD)
PPM .... Personnel Program Manager [*Navy*]
PPM .... Persutuan Perpustakaan Malaysia [*Library Association of the Federation of Malaysia*] (AD)
PPM .... Phased Project Management (SAUS)
PPM .... Phase Pulse Modulation (SAUS)
PPM .... Phenylpropanolamine(hydrochloride) [*Also, PPA, PPH*] [*Decongestant*]
PPM .... Phosphopentomutase [*An enzyme*]
PPM .... Physician Practice Management
PPM .... Picks per Minute (SAUS)
PPM .... Picture Processing Machine (SAUS)
PPM .... Pictures per Minute (NTCM)
PPM .... Piecewise Parabolic Method [*Mathematical model of fluid flow*]
PPM .... Pigmented Pupillary Membrane [*Medicine*] (STED)
PPM .... Pileable Pallet Module (SAUS)
PPM .... Pilot Performance Measurement (ACAE)
PPM .... Pilot Production Model [*Military*] (CAAL)
PPM .... Pilot Pulse Missile
PPM .... Pistol Prize Money [*British military*] (DMA)
PPM .... Planned Preventive Maintenance (IEEE)
PPM .... Platform Pointing Mode (ACAE)
PPM .... Policy and Procedures Manual (SAUS)
PPM .... Popocatepetl [*Mexico*] [*Seismograph station code, US Geological Survey*] (SEIS)
PPM .... Popular Monarchist Party (Portugal) [*Political party*] (PSAP)
PPM .... Portable Pix Map [*Computer science*]
PPM .... Position and Pay Management [*Army*] (AABC)
PPM .... Position and Proper Motion [*Catalog of star positions*]
PPM .... Positions and Proper Motions (SAUS)
PPM .... Postage Prepaid in Money
PPM .... Posterior Papillary Muscle [*Image on transesophageal echocardiography*] [*Cardiology*] (DAVI)
PPM .... Postpass Message
PPM .... Postponement [*Telegraphy*] (PCTE)
PPM .... Post-Program Monitoring
ppm .... Pounds Per Minute (AD)
PPM .... Pounds per Minute
PPM .... Prairie Print Makers [*Defunct*] (EA)
PPM .... Prediction by Partial Mapping (RALS)
PPM .... Prediction by Partial Matching (SAUS)

PPM .... Prenegotiation Position Memorandum (AAGC)
PPM .... Pre-Production Meeting [*Automotive engineering*]
PPM .... Presentation Protocol Machine [*Telecommunications*] (OSI)
PPM .... Presidential Review Memorandum (SAUS)
PPM .... Previous Processor Mode
PPM .... Prime Period of Maintenance (SAUS)
PPM .... Principal Period of Maintenance (AAGC)
PPM .... Problem Program Monitor (IAA)
PPM .... Process and Production Methods (SAUS)
PPM .... Production Planning Memorandum
PPM .... Product Portfolio Management (SAUS)
PPM .... Professional Photographers of Michigan (EARSL)
PPM .... Program, Project Management [*Army*]
P/PM .... Program/project manager (SAUS)
PPM .... Project Portfolio Management (GART)
PPM .... Project Profile Manual
PPM .... Prudential Portfolio Managers Ltd. [*British*]
PPM .... Pulmonary Pressure Method (SAUS)
PPM .... Pulse per Minute (SAUS)
PPM .... Pulse Phase Modulation [*Telecommunications*] (IAA)
ppm .... Pulse Position Modulation (AD)
PPM .... Pulse-Position Modulation (SAUS)
PPM .... Pulse Position Modulation [*Radio data transmission*]
PPM .... Pulse Power Module (RDA)
ppm .... Pulses per Minute (IDOE)
PPM .... Pulses per Minute
PPM .... Pyrite-Pyrrhotite-Magnetite [*Mineralogy*]
PPMA .... Pakistan Paint Manufacturers Association (SAUS)
PPMA .... Petroleum Marketers Association of America
PPMA .... Petrol Pump Manufacturers Association [*British*] (DBA)
PPMA .... Plastic Pipe Manufacturers Association (SAUS)
PPMA .... Plastic Products Manufacturers Association [*Later, Plastic and Metal Products Manufacturers Association*] (EA)
PPMA .... Political Products Manufacturers Association (EA)
PPMA .... Polypropyl Methacrylate [*Organic chemistry*]
ppma .... Post-Polio Muscular Atrophy [*Medicine*] (AD)
PPMA .... Post-Poliomyelitis Muscular Atrophy [*Medicine*]
PPMA .... Precision Potentiometer Manufacturers Association [*Later, Variable Resistive Components Institute*] (EA)
PPMA .... Produce Packaging and Marketing Association [*British*] (DBA)
PPMA .... Progressive Postmyelitis Muscular Atrophy [*Medicine*] (DMAA)
PPMA .... Pulp and Paper Manufacturers Association [*Later, PPMMA*] (EA)
PPMAP ...... Power Planning Modeling Application Procedure [*Environmental Protection Agency*] (GFGA)
PPMB .... Palynology and Plant Micropalaeontology of Belgium (SAUS)
PPMC .... Parts per Million Carbon [*Automotive engineering*]
PPMC .... People to People Music Committee (EA)
PPMC .... Petroleum Products Marketing Co. (SAUS)
PPMC .... Physician Practice Management Companies (SAUS)
PPMC .... Physician Practice Management Company (ADWA)
PPMC .... Produce Prepackaging Machinery Co. (SAUS)
PPMCX ...... PIMCO: Precious Metals Cl.C [*Mutual fund ticker symbol*] (SG)
PPMD .... Posterior Polymorphous Dystrophy (SAUS)
PPMD .... Posterior Polymorphous Dystrophy of the Cornea [*Ophthalmology*] (DAVI)
PPME .... Pacific Plate Motion Experiment (NASA)
PPME .... Protection and Preservation of the Marine Environment (SAUS)
PPMFA ...... Pulp and Paper Manufacturers' Federation of Australia
PPMFC ...... Preprints on Precision Measurement and Fundamental Constants [*National Institute of Standards and Technology*]
PPMG .... Professional Publishers Marketing Group (EA)
PPMHD ...... Pulsed Plasma Magnetohydrodynamic (SAUS)
ppm-hr ...... Part per Million-Hours (LDOE)
PPMI .... Pilot Plant Meat Irradiator
PPMI .... Printed Paper Mat Institute (EA)
PPMI .... Progressive Pacemaker Inhibition (SAUS)
PPMIN ...... Pulses per Minute (MSA)
PPMis .... Misericordia Hospital, Philadelphia, PA [*Library symbol*] [*Library of Congress*] [*Obsolete*] (LCLS)
PPMIS .... Personal Property Management Information System (SAUS)
PPML .... Preferred Parts and Materials List [*NASA*]
PPMM .... Postpolycythemia Myeloid Metaplasia [*Medicine*] (AAMN)
PPMMA ..... Pulp and Paper Machinery Manufacturers Association [*Later, APMA*] (EA)
PPMMB ..... Periodical Polytechnical. Mechanical Engineering (SAUS)
PPMMHD ... Pulse Power Magnetohydrodynamic (SAUS)
PPMMS ..... Polaris/Poseidon Material Management System (SAUS)
PPMN .... Preliminary Program Management Network [*Military*]
PPMNA ...... Provisions for Particulate Matter Nonattainment Areas [*Environmental science*] (COE)
PPMO .... Pershing Project Manager's Office (RDA)
PPMO .... Provisional Program Management Office [*Army*]
PPMoI .... Moore College of Art, Philadelphia, PA [*Library symbol*] [*Library of Congress*] (LCLS)
PPMP .... Preliminary Program Management Plan
PPMPC ...... Pilot Parachute Mortar Pyrotechnic Cartridge (SAA)
PPM/PPB ... Parts per Million/Parts per Billion (SAUS)
PPMR .... Purchased Parts Material Requirements
PPMR .... Purchase Parts Material Request
PPMRC ...... Pre-Positioned Materiel Receipt Card
PPMRD ...... Pre-Positioned Material Receipt Document
PPMS .... Pad-Pad Minimum Spacing (SAUS)
PPMS .... Performax's Personal Matrix System (DMAA)
PPMS .... Personal Property Management System (SAUS)
PPMS .... Personal Property Movement and Storage System (SAUS)
PPMS .... Physical Properties Measurement System (AAEL)
PPMS .... Pitt Press Mathematical Series [*A publication*]
PPMS .... Plastic Pipe Manufacturers Society [*British*] (DBA)
PPMS .... Poly(para-Methylstyrene) [*Organic chemistry*]
PPMS .... Polyphenylmethylsiloxane [*Organic chemistry*]
PPMS .... Primary Progressive Multiple Sclerosis (SAUS)
PPMS .... Product Procedure Maintenance System (SAUS)
PPMS .... Professional Productivity Management System (HGAA)
PPMS .... Programme and Project Management System [*United Nations Development Programme*] (DUND)
PPMS .... Program Planning Management System (ACAE)
PPMS .... Psychophysiologic Musculoskeletal [*Reaction*] [*Medicine*] (STED)
PPMS .... Purdue Perceptual-Motor Survey [*Kephart Scale*]
ppmv .... Parts per Million by Volume [*Marine science*] (OSRA)
PPMV .... Parts per Million by Volume
PPMV .... Peach Purple Mosaic Virus (SAUS)
PPMW .... Parts per Million by Weight (MCD)
ppmw .... Parts per Million by Weight [*Industrial hygiene term*] (OHS)
PPMW .... Primary Plant Mineralized Water (IAA)
PPN .... Numismatic and Antiquarian Society, Philadelphia, PA [*Library symbol*] [*Library of Congress*] [*Obsolete*] (LCLS)
PPN .... Papenoo [*Society Islands*] [*Seismograph station code, US Geological Survey*] (SEIS)
PPN .... Parameterized Post-Newtonian [*Gravity*]
PPN .... Parametrized Post-Newtonian [*Physics*]
PPN .... Partial Parenteral Nutrition [*Medicine*] (DMAA)
PPN .... Partido Patriotico Nobo [*New Patriotic Party*] [*Aruba*] [*Political party*] (EY)
PPN .... Partido Progreso Nacional [*National Progress Party*] [*Costa Rica*] [*Political party*] (PPW)
PPN .... Parti Progressiste Nigerien [*Nigerian Progressive Party*] [*Political party*]
PPN .... Patient Progress Note (SAUS)
PPN .... Patrol Plane Navigator (DNAB)
PPN .... Peak-to-Peak Noise [*Instrumentation*]
PPN .... Pedunculopontine Nucleus (DMAA)
PPN .... Peer-To-Peer Network [*Computer science*] (AGLO)
PPN .... Peripendicular Nucleus (SAUS)
PPN .... Peripheral Parenteral Nutrition [*Medicine*] (DAVI)
PPN .... Peroxypropionyl Nitrate (SAUS)
PPN .... Peroxypropionyl Nitride (SAUS)
PPN .... Peroxyproprionyl Nitrate [*Organic chemistry*]
PPN .... Polyphosphonate [*Organic chemistry*]
PPN .... Popayan [*Colombia*] [*Airport symbol*] (OAG)
PPN .... Portland Public Library, Portland, ME [*OCLC symbol*] (OCLC)
PPN .... Precipitation (WGA)
PPN .... Predictive Proportional Navigation
PPN .... Preferred Provider Network
PPN .... Principal-Protected Note
PPN .... Programmer Project Number (SAUS)
PPN .... Project, Programmer Number
ppn .... Proportion (AD)
PPN .... Proportion (ROG)
ppn .... proportional (SAUS)
PPN .... Proposition [*Telegraphy*] (PCTE)
PPN .... Protoplanetary Nebulae [*Astrophysics*]
PPN .... Public Packet Network [*Computer science*] (ODBW)
PPN .... Pyramidopallidonigral (DB)
PPNA .... Peak Phrenic Nerve Activity [*Medicine*]
PPNA .... Pupil-Perceived Needs Assessment [*Education*] (EDAC)
PPNA .... Pupil-Perceived-Needs Assessment (SAUS)
PPNAD ...... Primary Pigmented Nodular Adrenocortical Disease [*Medicine*] (STED)
PPNB .... Pre-Pottery Neolithic B Period [*Paleontology*]
PPNC .... Patrol Plane Navigator/Communicator (DNAB)
PPNC .... Pre-Pottery Neolithic C Phase [*Paleontology*]
PPNC .... Proceedings. Pacific Northwest Conference on Foreign Languages (SAUS)
PPNCFL ..... Proceedings of the Pacific Northwest Conference on Foreign Languages (SAUS)
PPNDG ...... Petition Pending
PPNF .... Price-Pottenger Nutrition Foundation (EA)
PPNG .... Penicillinase-Producing Neisseria Gonorrheas (SAUS)
PPNG .... Penicillinase-Producing Neisseria gonorrhoeae
PPNICI ...... Pulsed Positive/Negative Ion Chemical Ionization
P/PNL .... Pocket Panel [*Automotive engineering*]
PPNICI ...... Pulsed Positive/Negative Ion Chemical Ionization (SAUS)
PPNMC ...... United States Navy, Naval Regional Medical Center, Philadelphia, PA [*Library symbol*] [*Library of Congress*] (LCLS)
PPNP .... Point Pelee National Park [*Ontario, Canada*] (AD)
PPNR .... Photosynthetic Pyridine Nucleotide Reductase (SAUS)
PPN-RDA ... Niger Progressive Party-African Democratic Rally [*Political party*] (PSAP)
PPNRP ...... Philadelphia Pulmonary Neoplasm Research Project [*Medicine*] (EDAA)
PPNSC ...... Preferred Procurement Number Selector Code [*Military*] (AFIT)
PPNSCA ..... Policy Plans and National Security Council Affairs
PPNS-IE ..... Preschool and Primary Nowicki-Strickland Internal-External Control Scale (EDAC)
PPNT .... Proponent
PPNV .... Plum Phloem Necrosis Virus (SAUS)
PPNW .... Physicians for the Prevention of Nuclear War (AD)
PPNWA ...... N. W. Ayer & Son, Philadelphia, PA [*Library symbol*] [*Library of Congress*] [*Obsolete*] (LCLS)
PPO .... Diphenyloxazole [*Chemistry*] (DAVI)

PPO.......... Folopa [*Language symbol*] (ETLW)
PPO.......... Parking Patrol Officer
PPO.......... Patriot Project Office [*Army*]
PPO.......... Peak Pepsin Output (SAUS)
PPO.......... Pepsi Cola Puerto Rico Bottling [*NYSE symbol*] (SAG)
PPO.......... Pepsi-Cola Puerto Rico Bott'B' [*NYSE symbol*] (TTSB)
PPO.......... Performance Prediction Overview (SAUS)
PPO.......... Permanent Paranormal Object
PPO.......... Photographic Program Office [*NASA*] (KSC)
PPO.......... Planning Purposes Only (SAUS)
PPO.......... Platelet Peroxidase [*An enzyme*]
PPO.......... Pleuropneumonia Organisms [*Bacteriology*]
PPO.......... Police Petty Officer (DNAB)
PPO.......... Pollution Prevention Office [*Environmental Protection Agency*]
PPO.......... Polyphenelene Oxide (SAUS)
PPO.......... Polyphenol Oxidase [*An enzyme*]
ppo.......... Polyphenylene Oxide (AD)
PPO.......... Polyphenylene Oxide [*Organic chemistry*]
PPO.......... Polyphenylenoxid (SAUS)
PPO.......... Polyphenylodine Oxide (SAUS)
PPO.......... Poly(propylene Oxide) [*Organic chemistry*]
PPO.......... Port Postal Office (AFM)
PPO.......... Positive Pole Operation (SAUS)
PPo.......... Pottsville Free Public Library, Pottsville, PA [*Library symbol*] [*Library of Congress*] (LCLS)
PPO.......... Power Plant Operating
PPO.......... Preferred-Provided Organization [*Insurance*] (AD)
PPO.......... Preferred-Provider Option [*Insurance*]
PPO.......... Preferred-Provider Organization [*Insurance*]
PPO.......... Prepaid Purchase Order (SAUS)
PPO.......... Pre Phase-Out
PPO.......... Pressed Plutonium Oxide
PPO.......... Primary Party Organization [*Politics*]
PPO.......... Principal Period of Operations (ACAE)
PPO.......... Principal Priority Officer
ppo.......... Prior Permission Only (AD)
PPO.......... Prior Permission Only (AFM)
PPO.......... Procurement Planning Officer
PPO.......... Program Printout (MCD)
PPO.......... Projected Program Objective (NG)
PPO.......... Propose [*Telegraphy*] (PCTE)
PPO.......... Prototype Program Office
PPO.......... Publications and Printing Office [*Army*]
PPO.......... Public Pension Offset [*Federal Employees Retirement System*] (GFGA)
PPO.......... Pure Plutonium Oxide
PPO.......... Push-Pull Output (DEN)
PPO^2 Partial Pressure of Oxygen (CAAL)
PPOA........ Pollution Prevention Opportunity Assessment (SAUS)
PPoAr....... Schuylkill County Archives, Pottsville, PA [*Library symbol*] [*Library of Congress*] (LCLS)
PPOC........ Per Pupil Operating Cost (ADA)
PPO Cable... Polyphenylene Oxide Cable (SAUS)
PPOD........ Proposed [*Telegraphy*] (PCTE)
PP of A...... Professional Photographers of America [*Atlanta, GA*] (WDMC)
PPOG........ Polytechnic Personnel Officers Group (AIE)
PPOG........ Proposing [*Telegraphy*] (PCTE)
PPOKE....... Pre-Processor Oriented Key Entry (SAUS)
p-p-ola...... Political Plugola (AD)
PPOLL....... Parallel Poll (CIST)
ppom........ Particulate Polycyclic Organic Matter (AD)
PPOM........ Preferred Provider Organization of Michigan (MHID)
P-POP....... Plain Paper Optimized Printing [*Canon*] [*Computer science*]
PPORT....... Prostate Patient Outcomes Research Team
PPOS........ Present Position (GAVI)
PPOs........ Primary Party Organizations (Kazakhstan) [*Political party*] (PSAP)
PPOS........ Saint George United Methodist Church, Philadelphia, PA [*Library symbol*] [*Library of Congress*] (LCLS)
PPOSN...... Proposition (ROG)
PPOX........ Polypropylene Oxide (EDCT)
PPOX........ Polypropylene Oxide Plastic
PPP.......... Forest Research Centre (SAUS)
PPP.......... Glycerintripalmitat (SAUS)
PPP.......... Pacific Peacemaker Project [*Defunct*] (EA)
PPP.......... Packaged Power Plant (SAUS)
PPP.......... Package Processing Point
PPP.......... Pakistan People's Party [*Political party*] (PD)
PPP.......... Palatopharyngoplasty [*Medicine*] (EDAA)
PPP.......... Palestine People's Party [*Political party*] (PSAP)
PPP.......... Palmar-Plantar Pustulosis
PPP.......... Palmoplantar Pustulosis [*Medicine*] (DMAA)
PPP.......... Pan Pacific Petroleum [*Vancouver Stock Exchange symbol*]
PPP.......... Paper, Printing, Publishing [*Department of Employment*] [*British*]
PPP.......... Parallel Pattern Processor
PPP.......... Parallel Push Pull (IAA)
PPP.......... Parallel Push-Pull (SAUS)
PPP.......... Pariser-Parr-Pople [*Physical chemistry*]
PPP.......... Partai Persatuan Pembangunan [*United Development Party*] [*Indonesia*] [*Political party*] (PPW)
PPP.......... Partido del Pueblo de Panama [*Panamanian People's Party*] [*Political party*] (PPW)
PPP.......... Passage, Power, and Passenger [*Evaluation of labor progress*] [*Obstetrics*] (DAVI)
PPP.......... Payload Patch Panel [*NASA*] (NAKS)
ppp.......... Peak Pulse Power (NAKS)
PPP.......... Peak Pulse Power
PPP.......... Pedal Pulse Present [*Medicine*] (EDAA)
PPP.......... Pentose Phosphate Pathway (SAUS)
PPP.......... Pentose-Phosphate Pathway [*Metabolism*]
PPP.......... Penultimate Profit [*Investment term*] (DFIT)
PPP.......... Peoples Party of Pakistan [*Political party*] (AD)
PPP.......... People's Patriotic Party [*Myanmar*] [*Political party*] (PD)
PPP.......... People's Political Party [*St. Vincent*] [*Political party*] (PPW)
PPP.......... People's Power Party (Philippines) [*Political party*] (PSAP)
PPP.......... People's Progressive Party [*Mauritania*] [*Political party*] (EY)
PPP.......... People's Progressive Party [*Guyana*] [*Political party*] (PD)
PPP.......... People's Progressive Party [*Anguilla*] [*Political party*] (PPW)
PPP.......... People's Progressive Party [*Gambia*] [*Political party*] (PPW)
PPP.......... People's Progressive Party [*Solomon Islands*] [*Political party*] (PPW)
PPP.......... People's Progress Party [*Papua New Guinea*] [*Political party*] (PPW)
PPP.......... Peripheral Pulses Palpable [*Medicine*] (EDAA)
PPP.......... Permanent Party Personnel (MCD)
PPP.......... Perpex Peristaltic Pump
PPP.......... Personal Productivity Products (TIMI)
PPP.......... Personal Property Policy [*Insurance*]
PPP.......... Personnel Performance Profile
PPP.......... Personnel Policies and Practices (SAUS)
PPP.......... Petroleum Production Pioneers (AD)
PPP.......... Petty Pet Peeve (SAUS)
PPP.......... Petty Political Pismire (SAUS)
PPP.......... Phased Program Planning
PPP.......... Phased Project Planning [*NASA*] (KSC)
PPP.......... Pianississimo [*As Softly As Possible*] [*Music*]
PPP.......... Pickford Projective Pictures [*Psychology*]
PPP.......... Pipelines, Politics and People. Capital Communications Ltd. (SAUS)
ppp.......... Piu Pianissimo [*Very Very Softly*] [*Italian*] [*Music*] (AD)
PPP.......... Planning Purpose Proposal
PPP.......... Plan Position Presentation
PPP.......... Plans, Progress, and Problems (ACAE)
PPP.......... Plasma Protamine Precipitation [*Medicine*] (EDAA)
PPP.......... Platelet-Poor Plasma [*Hematology*]
PPP.......... Platoon Package Program
PPP.......... Pluripotent Progenitor [*Cytology*]
PPP.......... Pogo Producing [*NYSE symbol*] (TTSB)
PPP.......... Pogo Producing Co. [*NYSE symbol*] (SPSG)
PPP.......... Point-to-Point Protocol [*Computer science*] (PCM)
PPP.......... Poison Prevention Packaging [*Medicine*] (EDAA)
PPP.......... Policy, Procedures, and Practice (ACAE)
PPP.......... Political Participation Program [*Federal political committee terminology*] (PACS)
PPP.......... Polluter Pays Principle
PPP.......... Polluter-Pays-Principle (SAUS)
PPP.......... Pollution Prevention Plan [*Environmental science*] (COE)
PPP.......... Poly(para-phenylene) [*Organic chemistry*]
PPP.......... Polyphoretic Phosphate [*Organic chemistry*] (DAVI)
PPP.......... Polypropylene-Paper-Polypropylene [*Biochemistry*]
PPP.......... Popular Power Package (IAA)
PPP.......... Population Policy Panel (SAUS)
PPP.......... Portable Plotting Package [*Nuclear energy*] (NRCH)
PPP.......... Positive Pressure Paradox
PPP.......... Positive Pressur Paradox (SAUS)
PPP.......... Post-Painted Parts
PPP.......... Postpartum Psychosis [*Obstetrics*] [*Psychiatry*] (DAVI)
PPP.......... Powerful Permutation Procedure [*Meteorology*]
PPP.......... Preferred Pharmacy Program
PPP.......... Pre-Planned Product Improvement (ACAE)
PPP.......... Prepositional Procurement Package (DOMA)
PPP.......... Prepositioning Procurement Package (SAUS)
PPP.......... Preposition Procurement Package (SAUS)
PPP.......... Prescriptive Parent Programming [*Education*]
PPP.......... Prescriptive Program Plan [*Education*]
PPP.......... Pretty Poor Planning
PPP.......... Pretty Poor Prognosis (SPVS)
PPP.......... Price Pooling Program [*AAFC*] (FOTI)
PPP.......... Primary Products Promotion [*Australia*]
PPP.......... Priority Placement Program (DOMA)
PPP.......... Prior-Participating Preferred [*Stock*] (MHDW)
PPP.......... Prison Pen Pals (EA)
PPP.......... Private Patients' Plan [*British*]
PPP.......... Production Part Pattern (MCD)
PPP.......... Profit and Performance Planning (DCTA)
PPP.......... Programmable Power Processor (ACAE)
PPP.......... Programmed Production Planning (SAUS)
PPP.......... Program Protection Plan [*DoD*] (RDA)
PPP.......... Progressive People's Party [*Sudan*] [*Political party*] (EY)
PPP.......... Progressive People's Party [*Sierra Leone*] [*Political party*] (EY)
PPP.......... Progressive People's Party [*Liberia*] [*Political party*] (PPW)
PPP.......... Propria Pecunia Posuit [*Erected at His Own Expense*] [*Latin*]
PPP.......... Proserpine [*Australia*] [*Airport symbol*] (OAG)
PPP.......... Protons per Pulse (SAUS)
PPP.......... Province Pacification Plan (CINC)
PPP.......... Provisioning Program Plan (MCD)
PPP.......... Public Participation Program (FOTI)
PPP.......... Public Policy Program [*Australian National University*]
PPP.......... Public-Private-Partnership (VLIE)
PPP.......... Purchasing Power Parities (or Parity) (SAUS)
PPP.......... Purchasing Power Parity [*Economics*]
PPP.......... Purified Placental Protein (SAUS)

PPP......... Push-Pull Power (IAA)
PPPA........ Parallel Push-Pull Amplifier (SAUS)
PPPA........ Poison Prevention Packaging Act
PPPA........ Professional Pool Players Association [*Defunct*] (EA)
PPPA........ Protein Phosphatase Alpha (DMAA)
PPPA........ Pulp and Paper Prepackaging Association [*Later, SSI*]
PPPA........ Push-Pull Power Amplifier (IAA)
PPP&B...... Paper, Plates, Print and Bind [*Book publishing*] (GOBB)
PPP & M.... Preservation, Packaging, Packing, and Marking
PPPBDD..... Iran. Plant Pests and Diseases Research Institute. Department of Botany. Publication (journ.) (SAUS)
PPPBL....... Peripheral Pulses Palpable Both Legs [*Medicine*] (DMAA)
PPPBR...... Peruvian Paso Part-Blood Registry (EA)
PPPC........ Petroleum Pool Pacific Coast
PPPC........ Pipe Plug Producers Council (EA)
PPPCA....... Philadelphia College of Art Library, Philadelphia, PA [*Library symbol*] [*Library of Congress*] (LCLS)
PPP Circuit... Parallel Push-Pull Circuit (SAUS)
PPPCity..... Philadelphia City Institute Branch Free Library, Philadelphia, PA [*Library symbol*] [*Library of Congress*] [*Obsolete*] (LCLS)
PPPCO...... Pennsylvania College of Optometry, Philadelphia, PA [*Library symbol*] [*Library of Congress*] (LCLS)
PPPCPh..... Philadelphia College of Pharmacy and Science, Philadelphia, PA [*Library symbol*] [*Library of Congress*] (LCLS)
PPPD........ Point to Point Protocol Daemon [*Computer science*] (VLIE)
PPPE........ Pennsylvania Economy League, Inc., Eastern Division, Philadelphia, PA [*Library symbol*] [*Library of Congress*] (LCLS)
PPPE........ People, Plans and the Peace. Peace River Planning Commission (SAUS)
PPPEA....... Pulp, Paper, and Paperboard Export Association of the United States (EA)
PPPEC....... Philadelphia Electric Co., Philadelphia, PA [*Library symbol*] [*Library of Congress*] (LCLS)
PPPEE....... Pulsed Pinch Plasma Electromagnetic Engine (AAG)
PPPF........ Positive Pregnancy and Parenting Fitness (EA)
PPPFM...... Free and Accepted Masons of Pennsylvania, Grand Lodge Library, Philadelphia, PA [*Library symbol*] [*Library of Congress*] (LCLS)
PPPG........ People's Progressive Party of Guyana [*Political party*]
PPPG........ Postprandial Plasma Glucose [*Endocrinology*] (DAVI)
PPPH........ Forest Research and Development Centre (SAUS)
PPPH........ Pennsylvania Hospital, Philadelphia, PA [*Library symbol*] [*Library of Congress*] (LCLS)
PPPHA...... Philadelphia Housing Association, Philadelphia, PA [*Library symbol*] [*Library of Congress*] [*Obsolete*] (LCLS)
PPPHC...... Philadelphia Tuberculosis and Health Association, Philadelphia, PA [*Library symbol*] [*Library of Congress*] [*Obsolete*] (LCLS)
PPPH-I...... Institute of the Pennsylvania Hospital, Philadelphia, PA [*Library symbol*] [*Library of Congress*] (LCLS)
PPPH-I...... Institute of the Pennsylvania Hospital, Philadelphia (SAUS)
PPPI......... Insurance Society of Philadelphia, Philadelphia, PA [*Library symbol*] [*Library of Congress*] [*Obsolete*] (LCLS)
PPPI......... Personnel Performance Problems Inventory [*Test*]
PPPI......... Photo Processing and Photo Interpretation (SAUS)
PPPI......... Plan Positional Plot Indicator
PPPI......... Potential Preplanned Product Improvement (ACAE)
PPPI......... Precision Plan Position Indicator
PPPI......... Preliminary Process Potential Index
PPPI......... Preplanned Product Improvement [*DoD*] (MCD)
PPPI......... Primary Private Practice Income [*Medicine*] (MAE)
PPPI......... Primary Private Practice Insurance [*Medicine*] (DMAA)
PPPI......... Private Pay Phones, Inc. (SAUS)
PPPI......... Production Planning Process Industries [*Computer science*] (HODG)
PPPI......... Projection Plan Position Indicator
PPPI......... Pulp, Paper & Paperband Institute (SAUS)
PPPI......... Pulp, Paper and Paperboard Institute (SAUS)
PPPI......... Pulp, Paper, and Paperboard Institute USA [*Later, API*]
PPPIP....... Dhak Patiwat Phaochen Islam Pattani (SAUS)
PPPL........ Philadelphia Board of Public Education, Pedagogical Library, Philadelphia, PA [*Library symbol*] [*Library of Congress*] (LCLS)
PPPL........ Planetary Physical Processes Laboratory (SSD)
PPPL........ Princeton Plasma Physics Laboratory [*Also known as PPL - Plasma Physics Laboratory*] [*Princeton, NJ*] [*Department of Energy*]
PPPL........ Printed Planning Parts List
PPPL........ Program Preferred Parts List
PPPlanP.... Planned Parenthood of Southeast Pennsylvania, Philadelphia, PA [*Library symbol*] [*Library of Congress*] (LCLS)
PPPlay...... Plays and Players Club, Philadelphia, PA [*Library symbol*] [*Library of Congress*] [*Obsolete*] (LCLS)
P-P plot..... Probability-Probability Plot [*Statistics*]
PPPlPh...... Philadelphia College of Pharmacy and Science (SAUS)
PPPLS....... Public Policy for Public Libraries Section [*Public Library Association*] [*American Library Association*]
PPPM....... Philadelphia Museum of Art, Philadelphia, PA [*Library symbol*] [*Library of Congress*] (LCLS)
PPPMA...... Progressive Postpolio Muscle Atrophy [*Medicine*] (RAWO)
PPP Method... Pariser, Parr and Pople Method (SAUS)
PPPM-I...... Philadelphia Museum of Art, College of Art, Philadelphia, PA [*Library symbol*] [*Library of Congress*] [*Obsolete*] (LCLS)
PPPM-I...... Philadelphia Museum of Art, College of Art (SAUS)
PPPO........ Personal Property Processing Office (SAUS)
PPPOE....... Point-to-Point Protocol over Ethernet [*Computer science*] (VLIE)
PPPoE....... Point-to-Point Protocol over Ethernet
PPPP........ Past Performance and Present Posture (AAG)
PPPP........ People's Peace and Prosperity Party [*Defunct*] (EA)
pppp......... Piu Piu Piu Pianissimo [*Very, Very, Very Softly*] [*Italian*] [*Music*] (AD)
PPPP........ Porokeratosis Punctata Palmaris et Plantaris [*Medicine*] (DMAA)
PPPP........ Previous Paragraph was Polemical Position (SAUS)
PPPP........ Product, Price, Promotion, Place (BB)
PPPP........ Programmable Powdered Preform Process [*Plastics*]
PPPPA....... Predmore - Pridmore - Pridemore - Prigmore Association (EA)
PPPPI....... Photographic Projection Plan Position Indicator (DEN)
PPPPP....... Pain, Pallor, Pulse Loss, Paresthesia, Paralysis [*Medicine*] (MEDA)
PPPPP....... Prior Planning Prevents Poor Performance [*Training term*] (LPT)
PPPR........ Philadelphia Transportation Co., Philadelphia, PA [*Library symbol*] [*Library of Congress*] [*Obsolete*] (LCLS)
PPPRC...... Poor Richard Club, Philadelphia, PA [*Library symbol*] [*Library of Congress*] [*Obsolete*] (LCLS)
PPPres...... Presbyterian University of Pennsylvania, Scheie Eye Institute Library, Philadelphia, PA [*Library symbol*] [*Library of Congress*] (LCLS)
PPPRF....... Pan Pacific Public Relations Federation [*Thailand*] [*Defunct*]
PPPrHi...... Presbyterian Historical Society, Philadelphia, PA [*Library symbol*] [*Library of Congress*] (LCLS)
PPPrI........ Printing Institute, Philadelphia, PA [*Library symbol*] [*Library of Congress*] [*Obsolete*] (LCLS)
PPPrI........ Printing Institute, Philadelphia (SAUS)
PPProM..... Provident Mutual Life Insurance Co., Philadelphia, PA [*Library symbol*] [*Library of Congress*] [*Obsolete*] (LCLS)
PPPS........ People's Press Printing Society [*British*]
PPPs......... Public-Private Partnerships
PPPS........ Pulse Pairs per Second (SAUS)
PPPSB....... Philadelphia College of the Bible, Philadelphia, PA [*Library symbol*] [*Library of Congress*] (LCLS)
PPPSRU..... Poultry Production and Product Safety Research Unit [*USDA Agricultural Research Service*] (RCD)
PPPSS....... Pacific Post Partum Support Society [*Canada*] (EAIO)
PPPTe....... Philadelphia College of Textiles and Science, Philadelphia, PA [*Library symbol*] [*Library of Congress*] (LCLS)
PPPTP....... Central Research Institute for Food Crops (SAUS)
PPPZ........ Pleasant Prairie Power Plant [*Federal Railroad Administration identification code*]
PPQ.......... Abandoned Police Post [*Board on Geographic Names*]
PPQ.......... Parts per Quadrillion
PPQ.......... Person Perception Questionnaire [*Psychology*] (EDAC)
PPQ.......... Pittsfield, IL [*Location identifier*] [*FAA*] (FAAL)
PPQ.......... Planning Purpose Quote
PPQ.......... Plant Protection and Quarantine [*Animal and Plant Inspection Service*] (IID)
PPQ.......... Plant Protection and Quarantine Programs [*Department of Agriculture*] (IMH)
ppq.......... Polyphenylquinoxaline (AD)
PPQ.......... Polyphenylquinoxaline [*Resin*]
PPQ.......... Possible Parliamentary Question [*Australia*]
PPQ.......... Pre-Production Qualification (SAUS)
PPQ.......... Primary Parts Package (SAUS)
PPQ.......... Pulses Per Quarternote (SAUS)
PPQA........ Pageable Partition Queue Area [*Computer science*]
PPQC........ Piece Part Quality Control (TIMI)
PPQN........ Parts per Quarter Note [*Computer science*] (PCM)
PP/Q Program... Plant Protection and Quarantine Program (SAUS)
PPQR........ Priority Parts Quality Review
PPQT........ Parts per Quintillion (SAUS)
PPQT........ Preproduction Qualification Test [*Army*]
PPQT & E... Pre-Production Qualification Test and Evaluation [*Army*]
PPR.......... ING Prime Rate Trust [*NYSE symbol*]
PPR.......... Page Printing Receiver (SAUS)
PPR.......... Paid Pensioner Recruiter [*British military*] (DMA)
PPR.......... Palomino Pony Registry
PPR.......... Paper
PPr........... Paraprosthetic (DB)
PPR.......... Partial Product Read (SAUS)
PPR.......... Partido Panamenista Republicano [*Panama*] [*Political party*] (EY)
PPR.......... Partido Patriotico Revolucionario [*Mexico*] [*Political party*] (EY)
PPR.......... Partido Proletariano Revolucionario [*Proletarian Revolutionary Party*] [*Portugal*] [*Political party*] (PPW)
PPR.......... Parts Planning Record (SAUS)
PPR.......... Passenger Profile Record [*Travel industry*] (TRID)
PPR.......... Payload Preparation Room [*VAFB*] [*NASA*] (MCD)
PPR.......... Peak Production Rate
PPR.......... Pen Placement Report [*Correctional Service of Canada*] (FOTI)
PPR.......... Performance Planning and Revenue (SAUS)
PPR.......... Periodicals Publishing Record [*Alberta Public Affairs Bureau*] [*Canada*] [*Information service or system*] (CRD)
PPR.......... Periodic Performance Report (SAUS)
PPR.......... Periodic Personnel Report
PPR.......... Permanent Pay Record [*Military*]
PPR.......... Permanent Personal Registration [*Voting*] (BARN)
PPR.......... Peste des Petits Ruminants [*Rinderpest-like disease*] [*Veterinary medicine*]
PPR.......... Photographic Press Review [*A publication*] [*British*]
PPR.......... Photo-Plastic-Recording
PPR.......... Photoplastic Recording (SAUS)
PPR.......... Photopolarimeter Radiometer [*Instrumentation*]
PPR.......... Photopolarimeter-Radiometer (SAUS)
PPR.......... Physician-Patient Relation (MELL)
PPR.......... Physician Payment Reform
PPR.......... Pilgrim America Prime Rate Trust [*NYSE symbol*] (SAG)
PPR.......... Pilgrim America Prime Rt [*NYSE symbol*] (TTSB)
PPR.......... Pilgrim Prime Rate Trust [*NYSE symbol*] (SPSG)
PPR.......... Pilot, Pressure Regulator (MCD)
PPR.......... Pinault Printemps-Redoute [*A non-food retail group*] [*France*]

PPR .... Pirapora [*Brazil*] [*Airport symbol*] (AD)
PPr .... Pittsburgh Pirates [*National Football League*] [*1933-40*] (NFLA)
PPR .... Planar Plate Reactor (SAUS)
PPR .... Polish People's Republic
PPR .... Politieke Partij Radikalen [*Radical Political Party*] [*Netherlands*] [*Political party*] (PPE)
PPR .... Polska Partia Robotnicza [*Polish Workers' Party*] [*Political party*]
PPR .... Portable Propagation Recorder [*Bell System*]
PPr .... Port Pirie (AD)
PPR .... Post-Punch Read (SAUS)
PPR .... Potential Problem Report [*Navy*] (CAAL)
PPR .... Prepare [*Telegraphy*] (PCTE)
PPR .... Prepublication Review (SAUS)
ppr .... Present Participle (AD)
PPR .... Present Participle [*Grammar*]
PPR .... Press and Public Relations Ltd. (SAUS)
PPR .... Price. Procedural Regulation [*United States*] [*A publication*] (DLA)
PPR .... Price's Precipitation Reaction [*Medicine*]
PPR .... Principal Private Residence [*Income tax*] [*British*]
PPR .... Principal Probate Registry (DLA)
ppr .... Printed Paper Rate (AD)
PPR .... Printed Paper Rate [*British*] (ILCA)
ppr .... Prior Permission Required (AD)
PPR .... Prior Permission Required (FAAC)
PPR .... Probate Practice Reporter (SAUS)
PPR .... Procurement Problem Report (AD)
PPR .... Production Parts Record (SAUS)
PPR .... Production Parts Release (KSC)
PPR .... Production Performance Report (SAUS)
PPR .... Production Progress Report (MCD)
PPR .... Product Performance Report (SAUS)
PPR .... Program Planning Report (IAA)
PPR .... Program Progress Report (SAUS)
PPR .... Program Progress Review
PPR .... Program Proposal Request
PPR .... Progressive Republican Party (Brazil) [*Political party*] (PSAP)
PPR .... Progress Payment Report (AAGC)
PPR .... Project Progress Report (OICC)
PPR .... Proper [*Heraldry*]
PPR .... Proprietary Procurement Request (NG)
PPR .... Protective Partial Reflector (SAUS)
PPR .... Provisioning Preparedness Review [*Navy*] (CAAL)
PPR .... Purchase Parts Request (KSC)
PPRA .... Past President of the Royal Academy [*British*] (EY)
PPRA .... Preliminary Personnel Requirements Analysis [*Navy*]
PPRA .... Protection of Pupil Rights Amendment
PPRAM ...... Parallel Processing Random Access Memory (AAEL)
pprbd .... Paperboard (AD)
PPRBD ...... Paperboard
PPRC .... Peer-to-Peer Remote Copy (SAUS)
PPRC .... Personnel Program Review Committee [*Military*]
PPRC .... Physician Payment Review Commission
PPRC .... Pollution Prevention Research Center [*North Carolina State University*] [*Research center*] (RCD)
PPRCI .... Rittenhouse Club, Philadelphia, PA [*Library symbol*] [*Library of Congress*] [*Obsolete*] (LCLS)
PPRD .... Pontypool Road [*Welsh depot code*]
PPRD .... Prepared [*Telegraphy*] (PCTE)
PPRDS ...... Products and Process Research and Development Support (DCTA)
PPRE .... Peroxisome Proliferator Response Element [*Biochemistry*]
PPREC .... Pulp and Paper Research and Education Center [*Auburn University*] [*Research center*] (RCD)
PPREF .... Process Program Reference (AAEL)
PPREP .... Periodic Personnel Reports
PPREPT ..... Periodic Personnel Report [*Military*] (AABC)
PPRETS ..... Reformed Episcopal Seminary, Philadelphia, PA [*Library symbol*] [*Library of Congress*] [*Obsolete*]
PPRF .... Paramedian Pontine Reticular Formation [*Neuroanatomy*]
PPRF .... Pontine Paramedian Reticular Formation (SAUS)
PPRF .... Pontine Parareticular Formation [*Medicine*] (RAWO)
PPRF .... Postpartum Renal Failure [*Medicine*] (DMAA)
PPRF .... Pulse Pair Repetition Frequency (MCD)
PPRF .... Rosenbach Foundation, Philadelphia, PA [*Library symbol*] [*Library of Congress*] (LCLS)
PPRFs .... Postdoctoral Prize Research Fellowships
PPRG .... Precambrian Paleobiology Research Group
PPRG .... Preparing [*Telegraphy*] (PCTE)
PPRGF ...... Richard Gimbel Foundation for Literary Research, Philadelphia, PA [*Library symbol*] [*Library of Congress*] [*Obsolete*] (LCLS)
PPRI .... PACOM [*Pacific Command*] Priority Number (CINC)
PPRI .... Pan-Pacific Research Institution (SAUS)
PPRI .... Poloron Products, Inc. (SAUS)
PPRI .... Pulp and Paper Research Institute (SAUS)
PPRIBA ...... Past President of the Royal Institute of British Architects (EY)
PPRibP ...... Phosphoribose Diphosphate [*Biochemistry*]
PPRIC .... Pulp and Paper Research Institute of Canada
PPRICA ...... Pulp and Paper Research Institute of Canada (AD)
PPRINT ...... Post-Processor Print (SAUS)
PPrIT .... Putnam Premier Income Trust [*Associated Press*] (SAG)
PPRI .... Plant Protection Research Institute (SAUS)
PPRL .... Poisonous Plant Research Laboratory [*Agricultural Research Service*] [*Research center*] (RCD)
PPRL .... Public Policy Research Laboratory [*Louisiana State University*] (RCD)
PPRM .... Population Protection and Resources Management [*Military*] [*British*]
pprm .... Preprimer
PPRM .... Pure Premium Rating Method [*Insurance*]
PPRN .... Preliminary Publication Revision Notice
PPRN .... Preparation [*Telegraphy*] (PCTE)
PPRN .... Purchased Parts Requirement Notice (KSC)
PPRNCM .... Professional Performance of the Royal Northern College of Music [*British*] (DBQ)
PPRNS ...... Pulse-Phased Radio Navigation System
PPRO .... Pattern Processing Technologies, Inc. (SAUS)
PPRO .... Per Procuration [*Business term*]
P Proc Hampshire Field Club... Papers and Proceedings. Hampshire Field Club and Archaeologial Society (SAUS)
PPROM ...... Prolonged Premature Rupture of Membranes [*Obstetrics*] (DAVI)
PPROP ...... Personal Property [*Legal shorthand*] (LWAP)
PProt .... Postprotest (SAUS)
PPRP .... Polydenosine Diphosphate-Ribose Polymerase (DMAA)
PPRPF .... Regional Planning Federation, Philadelphia, PA [*Library symbol*] [*Library of Congress*] [*Obsolete*] (LCLS)
PPRR .... Paradise & Pacific Railroad [*Federal Railroad Administration identification code*]
PPRR .... Performance Planning & Review Record (WDAA)
PPRR .... Program Pre-Release Reviews (SAUS)
PPRS .... Perceptions of Parental Role Scales
PPRS .... Preferred Planning Reporting System (WDAA)
PPRS .... Prepares [*Telegraphy*] (PCTE)
PPRS .... Program Planning and Review Staff [*Environmental Protection Agency*] (GFGA)
PPRS .... Project Personnel Recruitment Section [*United Nations*] (FOTI)
PPRS .... Promotion and Placement Referral Subsystem (SAUS)
PPRS .... Promotions and Placements Referral System (MCD)
PPRSA ...... Past President of the Royal Society of Arts [*British*] (DI)
PPRT .... PharmaPrint, Inc. [*NASDAQ symbol*] (NASQ)
PPRU .... Pediatric Pharmacology Research Network [*National Institute of Child Health and Human Development*] (RCD)
PPRV .... Peste des Petits Ruminants Virus [*Rinderpest-like disease*] [*Veterinary medicine*]
PPRV .... Proportional Pressure-Reducing Valve [*Hydraulics*]
PPRWP ...... Poor Precordial R-Wave Progression [*Cardiology*]
PPRY .... Preparatory [*Telegraphy*] (PCTE)
PPS .... Butte Aviation, Inc. [*FAA designator*] (FAAC)
PPS .... Pacific Passenger Services (AD)
PPS .... Packets per Second [*Computer science*] (PCM)
PPS .... Paco Pharmaceutical Services, Inc (SAUS)
PPS .... Pad-Pad Spacing (SAUS)
PPS .... Paediatric Pathology Society of Europe (SAUS)
PPS .... Page Printing System [*Honeywell, Inc.*] [*Computer science*]
PPS .... Page Processing System (NITA)
PPS .... Pain Producing Substance (SAUS)
PPS .... Paint, Pesticide Chemicals, and Solvents
PPS .... Panoramic Passive Sonar (SAUS)
PPS .... Paper Publications Society [*Amsterdam, Netherlands*] (EA)
PPS .... Parallel Processing System [*Computer science*] (MDG)
PPS .... Parameter Processing System (CAAL)
PPS .... Parliamentary Private Secretary [*British*]
PPS .... Partia e Punes e Shqiperise [*Party of Labor of Albania - PLA*] [*Political party*] (PPW)
PPS .... Partial Pressure Sensor
PPS .... Participating Preferred Stock (MHDW)
PPS .... Partido Popular Salvadoreno [*Salvadoran Popular Party*] [*Political party*] (PPW)
PPS .... Partido Popular Socialista [*Popular Socialist Party*] [*Argentina*] [*Political party*] (PPW)
PPS .... Partido Popular Socialista [*Popular Socialist Party*] [*Mexico*] [*Political party*]
PPS .... Parti du Progres et du Socialisme [*Party of Progress and Socialism*] [*Morocco*] [*Political party*] (PPW)
PPS .... Parti du Progres Social [*Burkina Faso*] [*Political party*] (EY)
PPS .... Parti Populaire Senegalais [*Senegalese People's Party*] [*Political party*] (PPW)
PPS .... Parti Populaire Syrien [*Syrian People's Party*] [*Political party*] (BJA)
PPS .... Parti Progressiste Soudanais [*Sudanese Progressive Party*] [*Political party*]
PPS .... Partitioned Priority System (SAUS)
PPS .... Partito Populare Somalo [*Somali People's Party*]
PPS .... Parts Provisioning System (KSC)
PPS .... Party for Progress and Socialism (SAUS)
PPS .... Party for Progress and Solidarity (SAUS)
PPS .... Passenger Presence Sensor [*Automotive safety systems*]
PPS .... Patchboard Programming System
PPS .... Payload Pointing System (SSD)
PPS .... Payload Power Switch
PPS .... Pay-Per-Sale [*Payment model for online advertising*] (NETL)
PPS .... Payphone Power Supply (SAUS)
PPS .... Pennsylvania Prison Society (AD)
PPS .... Pentose Phosphate Shunt (ODA)
PPS .... Peoples Oil Ltd. [*Vancouver Stock Exchange symbol*]
PPS .... Pepsin A [*Medicine*] (MAE)
PPS .... Performance Program Statement [*Australia*]
PPS .... Period per Second (IAA)
PPS .... Periods per Second (SAUS)
PPS .... Peripheral Processing System (SAUS)
PPS .... Peripheral Processor System [*Computer science*] (IAA)
PPS .... Personal Plane Service [*Aircraft restoration firm*] [*British*]
PPS .... Personal Portable Shopper [*Computer science*]
PPS .... Personal Preference Scale [*Psychology*]

PPS .... Personal Printer Series [*IBM Corp.*]
PPS .... Personal Printing System [*Computer science*]
PPS .... Personal Private Secretary (FOTI)
PPS .... Personal Process Service (LAIN)
PPS .... Personal Protection Squad [*of the London Metropolitan Police*]
PPS .... Personnel/Payroll System
PPS .... Personnel Preference Scale (SAUS)
PPS .... Personnel Processing Squadron
PPS .... Persutuan Perpustakaan Singapura [*Library Association of Singapore*] (AD)
PPS .... Petroleum Press Service
PPS .... Petroleum Production Survey [*Bureau of Mines*]
PPS .... Phantom Phanatics Society (EA)
PPS .... Philadelphia Programming Society (SAUS)
PPS .... Phlogopite-Peridotite Solidus [*Geology*]
PPS .... Phosphoribosyl-1-pyrophosphatsynthetase (SAUS)
PPS .... Phosphorous Propellant System (KSC)
PPS .... Photophoretic Spectroscopy
PPS .... Photopolarimeter Spectrometer
PPS .... Photovoltaic Power Supply
PPS .... Photovoltaic Power System (SAUS)
pps .... Pictures Per Second (AD)
PPS .... Pictures per Second (WDAA)
PPS .... Piece Part Specification (MCD)
PPS .... Pierpont [*South Carolina*] [*Seismograph station code, US Geological Survey*] (SEIS)
PPS .... Pitt Press Series [*A publication*]
PPS .... Plant Parasitic Systems
PPS .... Plant Protection System [*Nuclear energy*] (NRCH)
PPS .... Plasma Power Supply
PPS .... Plasma Protein Solution (SAUS)
PPS .... Plate Power Supply (ELAL)
PPS .... Plutonium Product Storage [*Nuclear energy*] (NRCH)
PPS .... Pneumatic Power Subsystem (NASA)
PPS .... Point-to-Point System (IAA)
PPS .... Policies and Procedures (SAUS)
PPS .... Policy Processing Sheet [*Insurance*]
PPS .... Polonus Philatelic Society (EA)
PPS .... Polska Partia Socjalistyczna [*Polish Socialist Party*]
PPS .... Poly(para-phenylene Sulfide) [*Organic chemistry*]
PPS .... Polyphensulfid (SAUS)
PPS .... Polyphenylene Sulfide (SAUS)
PPS .... Polyphenylene Sulfide Plastic
PPS .... Polyphenylenesulphone (SAUS)
PPS .... Polyvalance Pneumococcal Polysaccharides [*A vaccine for patients with splenectomies*] [*Medicine*] (DAVI)
PPS .... Portable Personal Shopper
PPS .... Ported Pressure Switch [*Automotive engineering*]
PPS .... Port Presentation Module (SAUS)
PPS .... Postpartum Sterilization [*Gynecology*] (DAVI)
PPS .... Postperfusion Syndrome [*Medicine*]
PPS .... Postpericardiotomy Syndrome [*Medicine*] (DMAA)
PPS .... Post-Polio Sequelae [*Medicine*]
p-ps .... Post-Polio Syndrome [*Medicine*] (AD)
PPS .... Postpones [*Telegraphy*] (PCTE)
PPS .... Post-Postscriptum [*Further Postscript*] [*Latin*]
PPS .... Post Production Service (AAG)
PPS .... Post Production Support (MCD)
PPS .... Postproduction Support (SAUS)
PPS .... Post Properties [*NYSE symbol*] (TTSB)
PPS .... Post Properties, Inc. [*NYSE symbol*] (SPSG)
PPS .... Postpump Syndrome [*Medicine*] (MAE)
pps .... Pounds Per Second (AD)
PPS .... Pounds per Second (AAG)
PPS .... Power Personal Systems (SAUS)
PPs .... Prairie Provinces (SAUS)
PPS .... Precise Positioning Service [*Military*]
PPS .... Precision Pointing System (SAUS)
PPS .... Precision Positioning Service
PPS .... Precision Power Supply
PPS .... Precision Processing System (SAUS)
PPS .... Pre-Planned Support (SAUS)
PPS .... Prepositioned Stock (NG)
PPS .... Pre-Processeur de Signal [*Computer*] [*French*]
PPS .... Prescribed Payments System (ADA)
PPS .... Preselection Primary Section (SAUS)
PPS .... Primary Paraffin Sulfonate [*Organic chemistry*]
PPS .... Primary Power Standard
PPS .... Primary Power System [*Nuclear energy*] (NRCH)
PPS .... Primary Propulsion System [*Spacecraft*]
PPS .... Primary Protection System [*Computer science*]
PPS .... Prime Power System (SAUS)
PPS .... Principal Private Secretary [*British*]
PPS .... Printer/Plotter System (MCD)
PPS .... Priority Processing System (SAUS)
PPS .... Prior Preferred Stock
pps .... Private Parliamentary Secretary [*British*] (AD)
PPS .... Private Practice Section [*American Physical Therapy Association*] (EA)
PPS .... Probability Proportional to Size [*Statistics*]
PPS .... Proceedings of the Prehistoric Society (SAUS)
PPS .... Procurement Planning Schedule [*DoD*]
PPS .... Production Planning System [*TDS Business Systems Ltd.*] [*Software package*] (NCC)
PPS .... Product Performance Specification (SAUS)
PPS .... Product Performance Surveys (SAUS)
PPS .... Programmable Patch System
PPS .... Programmable Power Supply
PPS .... Programmable Pressure Source (SAUS)
PPS .... Programmed Processor System
PPS .... Programming Program Strela [*Computer science*]
PPS .... Program Performance Specification (CAAL)
PPS .... Program Peripheral Subsystems (CCCA)
PPS .... Program Planning Summary (OICC)
PPS .... Program Planning System [*DoD*]
PPS .... Program Policy Staff [*UN Food and Agriculture Organization*]
PPS .... Program Preparation Subsystem (SAUS)
PPS .... Program Production Supervisor (SAUS)
PPS .... Program Product Specification (SAUS)
PPS .... Progressive Pneumonia of Sheep
PPS .... Progressive Power Steering [*Automotive engineering*]
PPS .... Project for Public Spaces (EA)
PPS .... Project Planning System (SAUS)
PPS .... Project Profile System (SAUS)
PPS .... Project Proposal Summary (SAUS)
PPS .... Proposal Pricing System (SAUS)
PPS .... Propose (FAAC)
PPS .... Propulsion and Propellant Section [*Picatinny Arsenal*] [*Dover, NJ*]
PPS .... Propulsion Pressurization Subsystem
PPS .... Prospective Payment System [*For hospital care*]
PPS .... Prospective Pricing System [*Information service or system*] (HCT)
PPS .... Protecte Payments System (SAUS)
PPS .... Provincial Peace Structure (SAUS)
PPS .... Provisioning Parts Schedule (MCD)
PPS .... Provisioning Performance Schedule (AFM)
PPS .... Provisioning Policy Statement (MCD)
PPS .... Prudential Property Services [*Prudential Group*] [*British*]
PPS .... Public and Private [*Nongovernment*] Schools [*Public-performance tariff class*] [*British*]
PPS .... Public Packet Switching (SAUS)
PPS .... Puerto Princesa [*Philippines*] [*Airport symbol*] (OAG)
PPS .... Pulse per Second (SAUS)
pps .... Pulses Per Second (AD)
PPS .... Pulses per Second [*Data transmission*]
PPS .... Pupil Personnel Services
PPS .... Purchasing Power Standard (EURO)
PPSA .... Pan-Pacific Surgical Association (EA)
PPSA .... Pigging Products and Services Association [*United Kingdom*] (EAIO)
PPSA .... Prospect Park Savings & Loan Association (SAUS)
PPSAS .... Program Planning and Status Assessment System [*Nuclear energy*] (NRCH)
PPSAT .... Peripheral Processor Saturation (MHDI)
PPSAWA .... Pan Pacific and Southeast Asia Women's Association (AD)
PPSB .... Periodical Publishers' Service Bureau (NADA)
PPSB .... Prothrombin, Proconvertin, Stuart Factor, Antihemophilic B Factor [*Blood coagulation factors*] [*Hematology*]
PPSC .... Parallel Processing System Compiler (SAUS)
PPSC .... Petroleum Products Supply Corp. (SAUS)
PPSC .... Physical Profile Serial Code [*Military*]
PPSC .... Popular Social Christian Party (Nicaragua) [*Political party*] (PSAP)
PPSC .... Privacy Protection Study Commission [*Government commission*]
PPSC .... Processor Program State Control (NITA)
PPSCA .... Partido Popular Social Cristiano Autentico [*Political party*] (EY)
PPSCI .... Programme Parents-Secours du Canada [*Association*] [*Canada*] (EAIO)
PPSCI .... Seamens Church Institute, Philadelphia (SAUS)
PPSCI .... Seamen's Church Institute, Philadelphia, PA [*Library symbol*] [*Library of Congress*] [*Obsolete*] (LCLS)
PPSD .... Personnel and Pay Services Division
PPSD .... Polska Partia Socialno-Demokratyczna [*Polish Social-Democrat Party*] [*Political party*]
PPSD .... Proposed
PPSE .... Programmer Support Environment [*Computer science*] (LAIN)
PPSE .... Purpose
PPSEA .... Proceedings of the Prehistoric Society of East Anglia (SAUS)
PPSEAWA ... Pan-Pacific and South-East Asia Women's Association [*Tokyo, Japan*] (EAIO)
PPSEAWA-USA ... Pan Pacific and Southeast Asia Women's Association of the USA (EA)
PPSED3 ..... Annual Research Reviews. Physiological and Pathological Aspects of Prolactin Secretion (journ.) (SAUS)
PPSER .... Postgraduate Paediatrics Series (SAUS)
PPSF .... Palestinian Popular Struggle Front [*Political party*] (BJA)
PPSF .... Prefocused-objective Pinhole Spatial Filter (SAUS)
PPSF .... Psychological and Physiological Stressors and Factors [*Ames Research Center*] (RCD)
PPSFP .... Parallel-Pattern Single-Fault Propagation [*Computer science*] (CIST)
PPS-FR ...... Polska Partia Socjalistyczna - Frakcja Rewolucyjna [*Polish Socialist Party - Revolutionary Faction*] [*Political party*] (PPE)
PPSG .... Piston and Pin Standardization Group [*Later, NEPMA*] (EA)
PPSG .... Spring Garden College, Philadelphia, PA [*Library symbol*] [*Library of Congress*] (LCLS)
PPSh .... Partia e Punes e Shqiperise [*Labor Party of Albania*] [*Formerly, PKSh*] [*Political party*] (PPE)
PPSH .... Pseudovaginal Perineoscrotal Hypospadias [*Medicine*]
PPSI .... Pacific Physician Services (SPSG)
PPSI .... Pacific Physician Services, Inc. [*NASDAQ symbol*] (SAG)
PPSI .... Parent Problem-Solving Instrument (EDAC)
PPSI .... Pound-Weight per Square Inch (SAUS)

PPSIA .... "Personal Property Shipping Information" [*Pamphlet*] Is Applicable [*Military*] (AABC)
PPSIAD...... Past President of the Society of Industrial Artists and Designers [*British*] (DI)
PPS II .... Payroll Personnel System
PPSJ......... Pressure Plane Swivel Joint
PPSJ......... Saint Josephs College, Philadelphia (SAUS)
PPSJ......... Saint Joseph's College, Philadelphia, PA [*Library symbol*] [*Library of Congress*] (LCLS)
PPSJ-AF .... Saint Joseph's College, Academy of Food Marketing, Philadelphia, PA [*Library symbol*] [*Library of Congress*] (LCLS)
PPSJ-AF .... Saint Josephs College, Academy of Food Marketing, Philadelpia (SAUS)
PPSKED..... Provisioning Performance Schedule (MCD)
PPSKF....... SmithKline Corp., Philadelphia, PA [*Library symbol*] [*Library of Congress*] (LCLS)
PPSL .... Program Parts Selection List
PPSL .... Proposed Parts Selection List (SAUS)
PPSL .... Provisioning Parts Selection List (MCD)
PPSMEC .... Procurement, Precedence of Supplies, Material and Equipment Committee [*Joint Communications Board*]
ppsn......... Present Position (AD)
PPSN........ Present Position [*Aviation*] (FAAC)
PPSN........ Public Packet Switched [*or Switching*] Network [*Telecommunications*]
PPSN........ Purchased Part Shortage Notice
ppso......... Per Person, Single Occupancy (AD)
PPSO........ Personal Property Shipping Office [*Military*]
PPSOPR..... Sun Oil Co., General Office Library, Philadelphia, PA [*Library symbol*] [*Library of Congress*] [*Obsolete*] (LCLS)
PPSP .... Page Printer Spooling System [*Computer science*]
PPSP .... Pollution Prevention and Safety Panel (SAUS)
PPSP .... Ponderosa Pine or Sugar Pine [*Lumber*]
PPSP .... Postproduction Support Plan (SAUS)
PPSP .... Power Plant Siting Program [*Environmental Protection Agency*] (GFGA)
PPS-PODS... Precise Position System-Precise Orbit Determination System (SAUS)
PPSPS....... Plutonium Product Shipping Preparation Station [*Nuclear energy*] (NRCH)
PPSQ .... Principal Problem Strategy Questionnaire (EDAC)
PPSR .... Periodic Personnel Strength Report [*Army*] (AABC)
PPSS .... Foundation for the President's Private Sector Survey on Cost Control (EA)
PPSS .... Polyphenylene Sulfide Sulfone [*Organic chemistry*]
PPSS .... President's Private Sector Survey
PPSS .... Product and Process Status System (SAUS)
PPSS .... Project Planning and Scheduling System (SAUS)
PPSS .... Public Packet Switching Service (NITA)
PPSSCC..... Foundation for the President's Private Sector Survey on Cost Control (EA)
PPS-SM..... Precise Positioning Service-Security Module (SAUS)
P-PST .... Pre-Professional Skill Test (EDAC)
PPStarr...... Starr Center Association, Philadelphia, PA [*Library symbol*] [*Library of Congress*] [*Obsolete*] (LCLS)
PPStCh...... Saint Charles Borromeo Seminary, Philadelphia, PA [*Library symbol*] [*Library of Congress*] (LCLS)
PPSteph..... William B. Stephens Memorial Library, Philadelphia, PA [*Library symbol*] [*Library of Congress*] [*Obsolete*] (LCLS)
PPSTH....... Population Post-stimulus Time Histogram [*Statistics*]
PPSU .... Personal Printer Spooling Utility (SAUS)
PPSU .... Poly Phenylene Sulfone (EDCT)
PPSU .... Polyphenylene Sulfone (SAUS)
PPSU .... Polyphenylene Sulfone Plastic
PPSU .... Programmable Power Supply Unit (EECA)
PPSV .... Plutonium Product Storage Vault [*Nuclear energy*] (NRCH)
PPSV .... Printing and Publishing Services, Victoria [*Australia*]
PPSWA...... Plant Protection Society of Western Australia [*Australia*]
PPS-WRN... Polska Partia Socjalistyczna - Wolnosc, Rownosc, Niepodleglosc [*Polish Socialist Party - Freedom, Equality, Independence*] [*Political party*] (PPE)
PPSX .... Pioneer Pipe and Supply [*Private rail car owner code*]
PPT .... Country for All (Venezuela) [*Political party*] (PSAP)
PPT .... Palmitoyl-Protein Thioesterase [*An enzyme*]
PPT .... Pamatai [*French Polynesia*] [*Geomagnetic observatory code*]
PPT .... Papeete [*French Polynesia*] [*Airport symbol*] (OAG)
PPT .... Papeete [*French Polynesia*] [*Seismograph station code, US Geological Survey*] (SEIS)
PPT .... Papeete, Society Islands [*Airport*] (AD)
PPT .... Parietal Pleural Tissue (DB)
PPT .... Partial Parse Trees (SAUS)
PPT .... Partial Prothrombin Time [*Hematology*]
PPT .... Parti Progressiste Tchadien [*Progressive Party of Chad*] [*Political party*]
PPT .... Part Per Trillion (SAUS)
PPT .... Parts for Printer Terminal (SAUS)
PPT .... Parts per Thousand (DNAB)
ppt .... Parts per Thousand (IDOE)
ppt .... Parts per Trillion [*Industrial hygiene term*] (OHS)
ppt .... Parts per Trillion [*Marine science*] (OSRA)
PPT .... Parts per Trillion
PPT .... Parts Procurement Time (SAUS)
p-p-t .... Pay-per-Transaction [*Agreement between video cassette rental stores and owners of film rights*]
PPT .... Peak-to-Peak Threshold (DB)
PPT .... Pedunculopontine Tegmentum [*Neurology*]
PPT .... People's Party of Tajikistan [*Political party*] (PSAP)
PPT .... Pericles, Prince of Tyre [*A publication*] (AD)
PPT .... Periodic Programs Termination [*Computer science*]
PPT .... Period Pulse Train
PPT .... Peripheral Performance Test (CAAL)
PPT .... Permanent Part-Time (ADA)
PPT .... Personal Portable Telephone (SAUS)
PPT .... Personal Property Tax (MHDW)
PPT .... Perspective-Pole Track (SAUS)
PPT .... Phosphinothricin [*Organic chemistry*]
PPT .... Pilot's Power Tool
PPT .... Pine Point Mines Ltd. [*Toronto Stock Exchange symbol*] [*Vancouver Stock Exchange symbol*]
PPT .... Pitch Precession Torquer
PPT .... Plant Protease Test (MAE)
PPT .... Policy Planning Team [*DND*] (FOTI)
PPT .... Poly Propylene Terephthalate (EDCT)
PPT .... Polypropylene Terephthalate (SAUS)
PPT .... Polypurine Tract [*Genetics*]
PPT .... Polypurinetract (SAUS)
PPT .... Polypyrimidine Tract [*Genetics*]
PPT .... Polysilicon Pressure Transducer (SAUS)
PPT .... Pooh Property Trust [*A.A. Milne estate*] [*British*]
PPT .... Poppet [*Engineering*]
PPT .... Port Processing Time (SAUS)
PPT .... Post Production Test
PPT .... PowerPoint [*Computer science*] (PCM)
PPT .... Powerpoint Presentation Format (SAUS)
PPT .... Practical Policy Test [*Psychology*]
PPT .... Praecipitatus [*Precipitated*] [*Pharmacy*]
PPT .... Praeparata [*Prepared*] [*Pharmacy*] (ROG)
ppt .... Precipitate (AD)
PPT .... Precipitate (MSA)
ppt .... precipitation (SAUS)
ppt .... Precipitat Prepared [*Laboratory science*] (DAVI)
PPT .... Precision Pressure Transducer
PPT .... Preproduction Test [*Army*]
PPT .... Preprotachykinin [*Biochemistry*]
PPT .... Preprototype (SAA)
PPT .... Primary Program operator interface Task (SAUS)
PPT .... Printer Pass-Through (SAUS)
PPT .... Private Purchasing Tariff [*British*]
PPT .... Probabilistic Potential Theory (PDAA)
PPT .... Process Page Table [*Telecommunications*] (TEL)
PPT .... Production Prototype
PPT .... Production Prototype Test
PPT .... Production Prove-out Test (SAUS)
PPT .... Product Positioning Time (AFM)
PPT .... Profit per Transaction [*Travel industry*] (TVEL)
PPT .... Programmer Productivity Technique (IAA)
PPT .... Program Processing Table (SAUS)
PPT .... Program Proofing Team (SAUS)
PPT .... Program Punched Tape (SAUS)
PPT .... Project Planning Technique (MCD)
PPT .... Prompt (ROG)
PPT .... Propyl(thio)uracil [*Biochemistry*]
PPT .... Public and Private Transport
PPT .... Pulse Pair Timing (SAUS)
PPT .... Pulse Plasma Thruster
PPT .... Punched Paper Tape [*Computer science*]
PPT .... Punched Plated Thru (SAUS)
PPT .... Putnam Premier Income Tr [*NYSE symbol*] (TTSB)
PPT .... Putnam Premier Income Trust [*NYSE symbol*] (SPSG)
PPT .... Temple University, Philadelphia, PA [*Library symbol*] [*Library of Congress*] (LCLS)
PPT .... Temple University, Physics Library (SAUS)
PPT .... Theosophical Society, Philadelphia, PA [*Library symbol*] [*Library of Congress*] [*Obsolete*] (LCLS)
PPTA......... Plasma Protein Therapeutics Association (EA)
PPTA......... Post-Primary Teachers Association [*New Zealand*] (WDAA)
PPTA......... Precipitation (SAUS)
PPTB .... Pin-Pack Test Board
PPTBA....... Pattern and Plastic Tool Builders Association [*Defunct*] (EA)
PPTC .... People-to-People Tennis Committee (EA)
PPTC .... Purchased Part Tab Card
PPTC .... Purchase Part Tab Card
pptd......... Precipitated (AD)
PPTD .... Precipitated
PPT-D .... Temple University, Dental-Pharmacy School, Philadelphia, PA [*Library symbol*] [*Library of Congress*] (LCLS)
PPTE......... Permanent Part-Time Employment
PPT ERIN... Priorities and Protection Team (SAUS)
PPTF......... Public Policy Task Force [*Defunct*] (EA)
PPTF......... Public-Private Task Force
ppth......... Parts Per Thousand (GNE)
PPTH .... Parts per Thousand (EAGT)
pPTH .... Porcine Parathyroid Hormone [*Endocrinology*]
PPT Hole Process... Punched Plated Thru Hole Process (SAUS)
PPTI .... Passport Travel, Inc. (SAUS)
PPTI .... Protein Polymer Technologies [*NASDAQ symbol*] (TTSB)
PPTI .... Protein Polymer Technologies, Inc. [*NASDAQ symbol*] (SAG)
PPT-ISA ..... Picture Personality Test for Indian South Africans
PPTIW....... Protein Polymer Technol Wrrt [*NASDAQ symbol*] (TTSB)

PPTJ........ Theodore F. Jenkins Memorial Law Library, Philadelphia, PA [*Library symbol*] [*Library of Congress*] (LCLS)
PPTL........ Postpartum Tubal Ligation [*Medicine*]
PPTL........ Pulp and Paper Traffic League [*Defunct*] (EA)
PPT-L........ Temple University, Law School, Philadelphia, PA [*Library symbol*] [*Library of Congress*] (LCLS)
ppt/lat....... prompt or later (SAUS)
PPT-M....... Temple University, Medical School, Philadelphia, PA [*Library symbol*] [*Library of Congress*] (LCLS)
PPTMR...... Personal Property Traffic Management Regulation
pptn.......... Precipitation (AD)
PPTN......... Precipitation
PPTO........ Personal Property Transportation Officer
PPTO........ Principal Professional and Technology Officer [*British*]
PPTP........ Personnel Performance and Training Program
PPTP........ Point-to-Point Tunneling Protocol [*Microsoft Corp.*]
PPTP........ Power Proportioning Temperature Programmer (SAUS)
PPTP........ Power-Proportioning Temperature Programmer (IAA)
PPTPI........ Past President of the Town Planning Institute (SAUS)
PPTPP....... Promulgators of Public Toilets in Public Parks (AD)
PPTR........ Precision Pressure Transducer-Ruggedized [*Automotive engineering*]
PPTR........ Pulsed Photothermal Radiometry (SAUS)
PPTR........ Punched Paper Tape Reader [*Computer science*]
PPTri......... Tri-Institutional Library, Philadelphia, PA [*Library symbol*] [*Library of Congress*] (LCLS)
PPTS........ Pianoforte Polishers' Trade Society [*A union*] [*British*]
PPTS........ Portable Perishable Tool System (MCD)
PPTS........ Pre-Planned Training System (PDAA)
PPTS........ Pre-Problem Training Situation (SAA)
PPTS........ Punched Paper Tape Speed (SAUS)
PPTS........ Pyridinium Para-Toluenesulfonate [*Organic chemistry*]
PPTS........ Pyridinium-para-Tosylate [*Organic chemistry*]
PP/TSD...... Post Placement and Training Support Program for People with Disabilities [*Australia*]
PPT SH...... Prompt Ship (SAUS)
PPT-T........ Temple University, School of Theology, Philadelphia, PA [*Library symbol*] [*Library of Congress*] (LCLS)
PPTTG....... Personal Property Transit Time Guide [*MTMC*] (TAG)
pptv.......... Parts per Trillion by Volume (CARB)
PPTV......... Parts per Trillion by Volume
PPTV........ PPT Vision [*NASDAQ symbol*] (TTSB)
PPTV........ PPT Vision, Inc. [*NASDAQ symbol*] (SAG)
PPT Vis..... PPT Vision, Inc. [*Associated Press*] (SAG)
PPTW........ Permanent Part-Time Work
ppty.......... Property (AD)
PPTY........ Property (AFM)
PPU.......... Cocoa, FL [*Location identifier*] [*FAA*] (FAAL)
PPU.......... Packaged Power Unit (SAUS)
PPU.......... Papun [*Myanmar*] [*Airport symbol*] (OAG)
PPU.......... Parti Populaire des Ueles [*Ueles People's Party*] [*Political party*]
PPU.......... Payment for Public Use [*Canada*]
PPU.......... Peace Pledge Union [*British*]
PPU.......... Peninsula Petroleum Corp. [*Vancouver Stock Exchange symbol*]
PPU.......... Peoria and Pekin Union Railway [*Intermodal shipping container symbol*] (TVRC)
PPU.......... Peoria & Pekin Union Railway Co. [*AAR code*]
PPU.......... Peripheral Processing Unit [*Computer science*]
PPU.......... Peripheral Processor Unit (SAUS)
PPU.......... Picture Processing Unit [*Computer science*]
ppu.......... Platform Position Unit (AD)
PPU.......... Platform Position Unit
PPU.......... Pool Planned Unit (SAUS)
PPU.......... Power Processing Unit (MCD)
PPU.......... Pre-Processing Unit (SAUS)
PPU.......... Pre-Processor Utility (NITA)
PPU.......... Preproduction Unit (MCD)
PPU.......... Primary Power Unit
PPU.......... Primary Producers Union (AD)
PPU.......... Prime Power Unit
PPU.......... Professional Psychics Unit (SAUS)
PPU.......... Professional Psychics United (EA)
PPU.......... Programmable Processing Unit (SAUS)
PPU.......... Program Providing Unit (SAUS)
PPU.......... Projectile Programming Unit (SAUS)
PPU.......... Promontory Point [*Utah*] [*Seismograph station code, US Geological Survey*] [*Closed*] (SEIS)
PPUAES..... Publications. Princeton University Archaeological Expeditions to Syria (SAUS)
PPUC........ Probably Permanently Under Construction (SAUS)
PPUG........ United Gas Improvement Corp., Philadelphia, PA [*Library symbol*] [*Library of Congress*] [*Obsolete*] (LCLS)
PPUI......... Pitch and Putt Union of Ireland (EAIO)
PPUK........ Picked Ports United Kingdom (SAUS)
PPULC....... Union Library Catalogue of Pennsylvania, Philadelphia, PA [*Library symbol*] [*Library of Congress*] (LCLS)
PPUNA...... United States Naval Aircraft Factory, Philadelphia, PA [*Library symbol*] [*Library of Congress*] [*Obsolete*] (LCLS)
PPUnC....... University Club, Philadelphia, PA [*Library symbol*] [*Library of Congress*] [*Obsolete*] (LCLS)
PPUNH...... United States Naval Home, Philadelphia, PA [*Library symbol*] [*Library of Congress*] [*Obsolete*] (LCLS)
PPUQ........ Personalized Pick-up Service [*Common carrier symbol*]
PPUSDA..... United States Department of Agriculture, Agricultural Research Service, Eastern Utilization Research and Development Division, Philadelphia, PA [*Library symbol*] [*Library of Congress*] (LCLS)
PPV.......... Paraphenylene Vinylene [*Organic chemistry*]
PPV.......... Pars Plana Vitrectomy (SAUS)
PPV.......... Pay per View (SAUS)
ppv.......... Pay-Per-View (AD)
PPV.......... Pay-per-View [*Pay-television service*]
ppv.......... People-Powered Vehicle (AD)
PPV.......... People-Powered Vehicle [*Recreational vehicle powered by pedaling*]
PPV.......... Pitch Power Valve (IAA)
PPV.......... Plum Pox Virus [*Plant pathology*]
PPV.......... Polarized Platen Viewer (OA)
PPV.......... Police Patrol Vehicle [*Police and security equipment*]
PPV.......... Poly (Phenylenevinylene) [*Organic chemistry*]
PPV.......... Porcine Parvovirus [*Veterinary science*] (DMAA)
PPV.......... Positive Predictive Value [*Experimentation*]
PPV.......... Positive Pressure Ventilation [*Medicine*]
PPV.......... Pre-Production Verification (SAUS)
PPV.......... Preprogrammed Vehicles (MCD)
PPV.......... Pressure Protection Valve (SAUS)
PPV.......... Primary Pressure Vessel (MCD)
PPV.......... Progressive Pneumonia Virus [*Medicine*] (DB)
PPV.......... Propulsive Propellant Venting (SAUS)
P/PV......... Public/Private Ventures [*Philadelphia, PA*] [*Research center*] (RCD)
PPV.......... Purchase Part Variance
PPV.......... Purchase Price Variance (TIMI)
PPV.......... United States Veterans Administration Hospital, Philadelphia, PA [*Library symbol*] [*Library of Congress*] (LCLS)
PPVL........ Posterior Pulmonary Valve Leaflet (SAUS)
PPVO........ Premature Pulmonary Valve Opening (SAUS)
PPVP........ Posterior Precortical Vitreous Pocket (SAUS)
PPVS........ Propulsion Propellant Venting System (SAUS)
PPVT........ Peabody Picture Vocabulary Test [*Education*]
PPVT-R..... Peabody Picture Vocabulary Test - Revised [*Education*]
PP-W........ Free Library of Philadelphia, H. Josephine Widener Memorial Branch, Philadelphia, PA [*Library symbol*] [*Library of Congress*] [*Obsolete*] (LCLS)
PPW.......... PacifiCorp [*NYSE symbol*] (SPSG)
PPW.......... Pacificorp Capital [*NYSE symbol*] (SAG)
PPW.......... Papa Westray [*Scotland*] [*Airport symbol*] (OAG)
PPW.......... Partial Product Write (SAUS)
PPW.......... Parts per Weight
PPW.......... Patient Protective Wrap
PPW.......... Pave Paws West (SAUS)
PPW.......... Personal Protection Weapon (SAUS)
PPW.......... Petitions for Patent Waiver
PPW.......... Plane-Polarized Wave
PPW.......... Ponderosa Pine Woodwork (SAUS)
PPW.......... Ponderosa Pine Woodwork Association [*NWWDA*] [*Absorbed by*] (EA)
PPW.......... Potato Processing Waste
PPWA........ Ponderosa Pine Woodwork Association [*NWWDA*] [*Absorbed by*]
PPWa........ Wagner Free Institute of Science, Philadelphia, PA [*Library symbol*] [*Library of Congress*] (LCLS)
PPWB........ Prairie Provinces Water Board (FOTI)
PPWC........ Pines to Palms Wildlife Committee (SAUS)
PPWC........ Pulp, Paper, and Woodworkers of Canada
PPWD........ S. S. White Co., Philadelphia, PA [*Library symbol*] [*Library of Congress*] [*Obsolete*] (LCLS)
PPWe........ Westminster Theological Seminary, Philadelphia, PA [*Library symbol*] [*Library of Congress*] (LCLS)
PPWF........ Pakistan Petroleum Workers Federation (SAUS)
PPWG........ Production Planning Working Group (SAUS)
PPWI......... Wistar Institute of Anatomy and Biology, Philadelphia, PA [*Library symbol*] [*Library of Congress*] (LCLS)
PPWiH....... Wills Eye Hospital, Philadelphia, PA [*Library symbol*] [*Library of Congress*] (LCLS)
PPWL........ Present Practice Waste Load (DICI)
PPWM....... Medical College of Pennsylvania, Philadelphia, PA [*Library symbol*] [*Library of Congress*] (LCLS)
PPWP........ Planned Parenthood - World Population [*Later, PPFA*] (EA)
PPWPr....... PacifiCorp 5% Pfd [*AMEX symbol*] (TTSB)
PPWPrE..... PacifiCorp $1.98 cm Pfd [*NYSE symbol*] (TTSB)
PPWR........ Pre-Positioned War Reserve (SAUS)
PPWR........ Prepositioned War Reserves [*Army*]
PPWRS...... Prepositioned War Reserve Stocks [*Army*]
PPWSM...... Post Production Weapon System Management (SAUS)
PPWW....... Painless, Progressive, Weakening, Wasting painless (SAUS)
PPX.......... Packet Protocol Extension
PPX.......... Pipecolylxylidine (SAUS)
PPX.......... Port Moller, AK [*Location identifier*] [*FAA*] (FAAL)
PPY.......... Pages per Year [*Facetious criterion for determining insignificance of Supreme Court Justices*] [*Proposed by University of Chicago professor David P. Currie*]
PPY.......... Pancreatic Polypeptide [*Medicine*] (DMAA)
PPY.......... Polyacrylonitride Precursor Yam (SAUS)
PPY.......... Property [*Telegraphy*] (PCTE)
PPY.......... Prophesy Development [*Vancouver Stock Exchange symbol*]
PPYH........ Young Men's and Young Women's Hebrew Association, Philadelphia, PA [*Library symbol*] [*Library of Congress*] [*Obsolete*] (LCLS)
PPYU........ Party of Popular Yemenite Unity [*Political party*] (PD)
PPZ.......... Proton Polar Zone
PPZ.......... Puerto Paez [*Venezuela*] [*Airport symbol*] (AD)

PPZ .... Zoological Society of Philadelphia, PA [*Library symbol*] [*Library of Congress*] [*Obsolete*] (LCLS)
PQ .... Democratic Quisqueyan Party (Dominican Rep.) [*Political party*] (PSAP)
PQ .... Pack Quickly [*Humorous interpretation for Parti Quebecois*] [*Canada*]
PQ .... Panic in Quebec [*Humorous interpretation for Parti Quebecois*] [*Canada*]
PQ .... Parametric Quantron [*Physics*]
PQ .... Parliamentary Question [*British*]
PQ .... Parti Quebecois [*Quebec separatist political party*]
pq .... Peculiar (AD)
PQ .... Peraquic [*Soil biology*] [*Soil moisture regime*] (QSUL)
PQ .... Performance Qualification (ACII)
PQ .... Performer Quotient [*TV-performer rating*]
pq .... Permeability Quotient (AD)
PQ .... Permeability Quotient
pq .... Personality Quotient (AD)
PQ .... Personality Quotient [*Psychology*]
p-q .... Phenol-Hydroquinone [*Photography*] (AD)
PQ .... Philological Quarterly [*A publication*] (BRI)
PQ .... Photo Quality (PCM)
PQ .... Physically Qualified
PQ .... Physician's Questionnaire (AAMN)
PQ .... Planetary Quarantine [*NASA*]
PQ .... Plant Quarantine Division [*of ARS, Department of Agriculture*]
PQ .... Plasma Quad [*Instrumentation*]
PQ .... Plastoquinone [*Biochemistry*]
PQ .... Pollution Quotient
PQ .... Polyquinoxaline [*Organic chemistry*]
PQ .... Pooled Quota [*Indian Railway*] (TIR)
P-Q .... Porphyrin-Quinone [*Photochemistry*]
PQ .... Possess [*Telegraphy*] (PCTE)
PQ .... PQ Corp. [*Formerly, Philadelphia Quartz Co.*]
PQ .... Premium Quality (MUGU)
PQ .... Preparative Quencher [*Spectroscopy*]
PQ .... Presentation Quotient [*Business Term*]
pq .... Previous Question (AD)
PQ .... Previous Question [*Parliamentary law*]
Pq .... Primaquine [*Antimalarial*]
PQ .... Pronator Quadratus [*Muscle*] [*Anatomy*] (DAVI)
pq .... Pro Querente [*For the Plaintiff*] [*Latin*] [*Legal term*] (DLA)
PQ .... Province Quebec [*Quebec*] [*Canadian province*] [*Postal code*]
PQ .... Psi Quotient [*Parapsychology*]
PQ .... Public Quarters
PQ .... Puerto Rico International Airlines, Inc. [*Prinair*] [*ICAO designator*] (OAG)
pq .... Punishment Quarters (AD)
PQ .... Pyrimethamine-Quinine [*Organic chemistry*] (MAE)
PQ .... Quebec [*Postal code*] (CDAI)
PQ .... South Pacific Airlines of New Zealand (AD)
PQ .... United States Patent Quarterly [*A publication*] (DLA)
PQA .... Pacific Coast Airlines [*ICAO designator*] (FAAC)
PQA .... Palm Query Applications
PQA .... Parts Quality Assurance
PQA .... Petroleum Quality Assurance
PQA .... Plant Quality Assurance
PQA .... Preliminary Qualification Analysis
PQA .... Preliminary Quantitative Analysis
pqa .... Procurement Quality Assurance (AD)
PQA .... Procurement Quality Assurance [*Program*] [*DoD*]
PQA .... Production Quality Assurance
PQA .... Program Quality Acceptance (SPST)
PQA .... Project Quality Assurance
PQA .... Protected Queue Area [*Computer science*] (BUR)
PQAA .... Province of Quebec Association of Architects [*1890, OAQ from 1974*] [*Canada*] (NGC)
PQAD .... Plant Quality Assurance Director [*Nuclear energy*] (NRCH)
PQAE .... Program Quality Assurance Engineer (ACAE)
PQAI .... Procurement Quality Assurance Instruction
PQAM .... Project Quality Assurance Manager [*Nuclear energy*] (NRCH)
PQAM .... Purchaser Quality Assurance Manager (ACAE)
PQANSW .... Paraplegic and Quadriplegic Association of New South Wales [*Australia*]
PQAP .... Planned Quality Assurance Program [*Navy*]
PQAP .... Procurement Quality Assurance Program [*DoD*]
PQAQ .... Paraplegic and Quadriplegic Association of Queensland [*Australia*]
PQAR .... Petroleum Quality Assurance Representative
PQAR .... Purchasers Quality Assurance Representative (SAUS)
PQAS .... Program Quality Assurance System (SAUS)
PQASA .... Paraplegic and Quadriplegic Association of South Australia
PQAV .... Paraplegic and Quadriplegic Association of Victoria [*Australia*]
PQAWA .... Paraplegic and Quadriplegic Association of Western Australia
PQB .... Quebecor Cl'A' [*AMEX symbol*] (TTSB)
PQB .... Quebecor, Inc. [*AMEX symbol*] (SPSG)
PQC .... Chieftain Airways PLC [*British*] [*ICAO designator*] (FAAC)
PQC .... Paul Quinn College, Waco, TX [*OCLC symbol*] (OCLC)
PQC .... Phuquoc [*South Vietnam*] [*Airport symbol*] (AD)
PQC .... Poor-Quality Cost (SAUS)
PQC .... Precision Quartz Crystal
PQC .... Premium Quality Control (SAUS)
PQC .... Procurement Quality Control (IAA)
PQC .... Production Quality Compiler (SAUS)
PQC .... Production Quality Control
PQCC .... Production Quality Compiler Compiler (SAUS)
PQCK .... Philadelphia Quartz [*Private rail car owner code*]
PQCS .... Process Quality Control System
pQCT .... Peripheral Quantitative Computed Tomography [*Medicine*] (RAWO)
PQD .... Partido Quisqueyano Democrata [*Quisqueyan Democratic Party*] [*Dominican Republic*] [*Political party*] (PPW)
PQD .... Percentage Quartile Deviation [*Statistics*]
PQD .... Plant Quarantine Division (AD)
PQD .... Possessed [*Telegraphy*] (PCTE)
PQD .... Predicted Quarterly Demand
PQD .... Product Qualification Division
PQD .... Pyroelectric Quad Detector
PQDD .... ProQuest Digital Dissertations [*Database*] (GDD)
PQDMB .... Percentage Quartile Deviation Median Bias [*Statistics*]
PQE .... Parents for Quality Education [*Defunct*] (EA)
PQE .... Path Quality Evaluation (SAUS)
pqe .... Post-Qualification Education (AD)
PQE .... Post-Qualification Education (PDAA)
PQE .... Precision-Quality-Experience (SAUS)
PQE .... Principal Quality Engineers [*British*] (RDA)
PQE .... Professional Qualification Examination [*National Security Agency*] (EDAC)
PQE .... Project Quality Engineer
PQE .... Project Quality Engineering
PQEP .... Product Quality Evaluation Plan [*Military*] (AABC)
PQET .... Print Quality Enhancement Technology [*IBM*] (PCM)
PQFP .... Plastic Quad Flat Package [*Computer science*] (PCM)
PQG .... Possessing [*Telegraphy*] (PCTE)
PQGS .... Propellant Quantity Gauge [*or Gauging*] System [*Apollo*] [*NASA*]
PQI .... Personal Quality Improvement (ADWA)
PQI .... Presque Isle [*Maine*] [*Airport symbol*] (OAG)
PQI .... Presque Isle, ME [*Location identifier*] [*FAA*] (FAAL)
PQI .... Print Quality Improvement [*Advanced photo system*]
PQI .... Process Quality Indicator (ACAE)
PQI .... Product Quality Improvement [*Program*] [*Chrysler Corp.*]
pqi .... Professional Qualification Index (AD)
PQI .... Professional Qualification Index (AFM)
PQI .... Propellant Quantity Indicator (NASA)
PQIH .... Plant Quarantine Inspection House (AD)
PQL .... Practical Quantitation Level [*Environmental chemistry*] (ERG)
PQL .... Practical Quantitation Limit [*Environmental chemistry*]
PQL .... Prior Quarter Liability [*IRS*]
PQLI .... Physical Quality of Life (FOTI)
PQLI .... Physical Quality of Life Index [*Overseas Development Council*]
PQM .... Pilotless Drone Missile [*Department of Defense*]
PQM .... Pilot Qualified in Model (NVT)
PQM .... Post Quartermaster [*Marine Corps*]
PQM .... Print Quality Monitor [*Computer science*] (IAA)
PQM .... Pulse Quaternary Modulation
PQMC .... Philadelphia Quartermaster Center [*Merged with Defense Clothing and Textile Supply Center*] [*Military*]
PQMD .... Philadelphia Quartermaster Depot [*Military*]
PQMD .... Propellant Quantity Measuring Device
PQMDO .... Proposed Quality Material Development Objective (NATG)
PQMF .... Parallel Quadrature Mirror Filter (PDAA)
PQMR .... Preliminary Quantitative Material Requirements (MCD)
PQMS .... Process Quality Measurement System [*Chemical process engineering*]
PQN .... Consolidated Petroquin [*Vancouver Stock Exchange symbol*]
PQN .... Pahaquarry [*New Jersey*] [*Seismograph station code, US Geological Survey*] (SEIS)
PQN .... Pipestone, MN [*Location identifier*] [*FAA*] (FAAL)
PQN .... Possession [*Telegraphy*] (PCTE)
PQN .... Principal Quantum Number [*Atomic physics*]
PQNCX .... PIMCO: Renaissance Cl.C [*Mutual fund ticker symbol*] (SG)
PQNS .... Protein, Quantity Not Sufficient [*Laboratory science*] (DAVI)
PQO .... Phoenix, AZ [*Location identifier*] [*FAA*] (FAAL)
PQO .... Principal Quality Officer (SAUS)
PQOL .... Perceived Quality of Life [*Medicine*] (DMAA)
PQOS .... Pre-Qualified Offsets Supplier
PQOSS .... Pre-Qualified Offsets Supplier Status
PQP .... Planetary Quarantine Plan [*NASA*]
PQP .... Precision Quartz Products (TIMI)
PQP .... Preliminary Qualification Procedures (SAUS)
PQP .... Prequalification Prototype (KSC)
PQP .... Priorities, Quality, Productivity (SAUS)
PQQ .... Port Macquarie [*Australia*] [*Airport symbol*] (OAG)
PQQ .... Pyrroloquinoline Quinone [*Biochemistry*]
PQQPRI .... Preliminary Qualitative and Quantitative Personnel Requirements Information
PQQPRI .... Provisional Qualitative and Quantitative Personnel Requirements Information [*Army*] (AABC)
PQR .... Pantan Resources [*Vancouver Stock Exchange symbol*]
PQR .... Performance Qualification Requirement
PQR .... Personnel Qualification Record [*Military*] (INF)
PQR .... Personnel Qualification Roster [*Military*] (AABC)
PQR .... Prequalification Review (ACAE)
PQR .... Procedure Qualification Record [*Nuclear energy*] (NRCH)
PQR .... Productivity, Quality and Reliability (SAUS)
PQR .... Program Quality Review (AD)
PQRI .... Product Quality Research Initiative [*Drug evalution*]
PQRN .... Project Quality Requirements Notice (TIMI)
pqrs .... Productivity Increases, Quality Control, Robotization, and Savings [*Japanese formula for economic success*] (AD)
PQRST .... Personal Questionnaire Rapid Scaling Technique [*Personality development test*] [*Psychology*]

PQRST ...... Product-Quality-Routing-Service-Timing [*Industrial engineering*]
PQS .... Parallel Query Server [*IBM*] (GART)
PQS .... Percentage Quota System (AD)
PQS .... Personnel Qualification Standard (AD)
PQS .... Personnel Qualification Standards [*Military*] (NVT)
PQS .... Pilot Station [*Alaska*] [*Airport symbol*] (OAG)
PQS .... Production Quotation Support
PQS .... Product Quality System (TIMI)
PQS .... Product Quotient Storage (SAUS)
PQS .... Progressive Qualification Scheme [*British*]
PQS .... Promotion Qualification Score [*Military*]
PQS .... Protein Quaternary Structure (MHID)
PQSF .... Preparative Quencher Stopped Flow [*Spectroscopy*]
PQSI .... Product Quality System for Inspection (TIMI)
PQST .... Product Quality System for Test (TIMI)
PQT .... Parquet Resources, Inc. [*Toronto Stock Exchange symbol*]
PQT .... PC Quote [*AMEX symbol*] (TTSB)
PQT .... PC Quote, Inc. [*AMEX symbol*] (SAG)
PQT .... Performance Qualification Test (MCD)
PQT .... Polyquinazolotriazole [*Organic chemistry*]
PQT .... Preliminary Qualification Test (MCD)
PQT .... Production Qualification and Testing
PQT .... Production Qualification Test (SAUS)
PQT .... Production Qualification Testing
PQT .... Production Quality Test (SAUS)
PQT .... Professional Qualification Test [*of the National Security Agency*]
PQT .... Prototype Qualification Test
PQT .... Prototype Qualification Testing (RDA)
PQT & E .... Production Qualification Test and Evaluation
PQT-C .... Prototype Qualification Test - Contractor (MCD)
PQT-G .... Prototype Qualification Test - Government (MCD)
PQT/LOT .... Production Qualification Test / Limited Operational Test
PQTP .... Prototype Qualification Test Plan (SAUS)
PQTS .... Product Quality and Technical Services Division
PQT-SE ...... Prototype Qualification Test - Service Evaluation (MCD)
PQu .... Polycyclic Quinone (SAUS)
PQU .... Salisbury, MD [*Location identifier*] [*FAA*] (FAAL)
PQUA .... Preliminary Quantitative Usage Analysis [*Environmental science*] (EPAT)
PQUE .... Petroquest Energy [*Formerly, Optima Petroleum*] [*NASDAQ symbol*]
PQUE .... Print Queue Processor [*Computer science*]
PQV .... Procurement Quality Verification (SAUS)
PQV .... Program Quality Verification (SAUS)
PQW .... Placita de Quo Warranto, Record Commission [*England*] [*A publication*] (DLA)
PQWL .... Pooled Quota Waiting List [*Indian Railway*] (TIR)
PQX .... Physically Qualified Except
PQY .... Plurality [*Telegraphy*] (PCTE)
PQZ .... Premium Quality Zinc
PR .... Abbott Laboratories [*Research code symbol*]
PR .... Aircrew Survival Equipmentman [*Navy rating*]
PR .... Deputy Chief of Staff, Requirements and Programs (SAUS)
PR .... Directorate of Programs and Resources (SAUS)
PR .... Pacific Reporter [*A publication*] (DLA)
PR .... Pacing Response (SAUS)
PR .... Packet Radio (SAUS)
PR .... Packet Rate (SAUS)
P(R) .... Packet (Receive)
PR .... Page Reader (SAUS)
PR .... Painter (ADA)
pr .... Pair (AD)
PR .... Pair (KSC)
PR .... Pakistan Railways (DCTA)
PR .... Panama Railroad [*Federal Railroad Administration identification code*]
PR .... Panama Red [*Variety of marijuana*]
Pr .... Panama-Red Marijuana (AD)
PR .... Panel Receptacle
PR .... Pangenesis Related [*Protein chemistry*]
PR .... Panthere Rose [*France*] [*An association*] [*Defunct*] (EAIO)
pr .... Paper (WDAA)
PR .... Paper Tape Reader
PR .... Papertape Reader (SAUS)
PR .... Parachute Rigger [*Navy*] (KSC)
PR .... Paradise Regained [*A publication*] (AD)
PR .... Parallax and Refraction
Pr .... Parana (AD)
pr .... Parcel Receipt (AD)
PR .... Parcel Receipt [*Shipping*]
PR .... Parental Recommendation [*Movie rating*] (CDAI)
PR .... Parents Rights (EA)
PR .... Parish Register
P+R .... Park and Ride (SAUS)
PR .... Park Ranger (AD)
PR .... Parliamentary Report [*British*]
PR .... Parliamentary Returns (SAUS)
PR .... Parrott Rifle
PR .... Partial (WEAT)
PR .... Partial Reflector (SAUS)
PR .... Partial Reinforcement (DIPS)
PR .... Partial Remission [*Medicine*]
PR .... Partial Responder (SAUS)
PR .... Partial Response [*Medicine*] (DAVI)
PR .... Partial Reward (DIPS)
PR .... Partido Radical [*Radical Party*] [*Spain*] [*Political party*] (PPE)
PR .... Partido Radical [*Radical Party*] [*Chile*] [*Political party*]
PR .... Partido Reformista [*Reformist Party*] [*Dominican Republic*] [*Political party*] (PPW)
PR .... Partido Republicano [*Republican Party*] [*Ecuador*] [*Political party*] (EY)
PR .... Partido Republicano [*Republican Party*] [*Panama*] [*Political party*] (EY)
PR .... Partido Revolucionario [*Revolutionary Party*] [*Guatemala*] [*Political party*] (PPW)
PR .... Partido Riojano [*Spain*] [*Political party*] (EY)
PR .... Parti Republicain [*Republican Party*] [*Reunion*] [*Political party*] (EY)
PR .... Parti Republicain [*Republican Party*] [*New Caledonia*] [*Political party*] (FEA)
PR .... Parti Republicain [*Republican Party*] [*Martinique*] [*Political party*] (PPW)
PR .... Parti Republicain [*Republican Party*] [*France*] [*Political party*] (PPW)
PR .... Partisan Review [*A publication*] (BRI)
PR .... Partito Radicale [*Radical Party*] [*Founded, 1955*] [*Italy*] [*Political party*] (PPE)
PR .... Party of Reunification (SAUS)
PR .... Party Raayat [*Leftist organization in Singapore*]
PR .... Passengers' Risk (ROG)
PR .... Passive Ranging [*Military*] (LAIN)
PR .... Past in Review [*Later, PIR*] (EA)
PR .... Pastor
PR .... Pathogenesis Related [*Biology*]
PR .... Path Replacement (SAUS)
PR .... Patient Relations (DAVI)
PR .... Patria Roja [*Red Fatherland*] [*Peru*] (PD)
PR .... Patrol Report (SAUS)
PR .... Patrol Vessel, River Gunboat [*Navy symbol*]
PR .... Pattern Recognition (BUR)
PR .... Pattern Recognizer (SAUS)
PR .... Payload Recorder (SAUS)
PR .... Payment Received (SAUS)
pr .... Payroll (AD)
PR .... Payroll
PR .... Peer Review
PR .... Peking Review [*A publication*] (AD)
PR .... Pelvic Rock [*Orthopedics*] (DAVI)
PR .... Peng-Robinson [*Equation of state*]
PR .... Penicillium roqueforti [*Toxin*] [*Medicine*]
P-R .... Pennsylvania-Reading [*Seashore Lines*] (AD)
PR .... Pennsylvania Real Estate Investment Trust (EFIS)
PR .... Pennsylvania Reports (Penrose and Watts) [*A publication*] (DLA)
PR .... Penny Resistance (EA)
PR .... Pen Record (SAA)
PR .... Pentium Rating (SAUS)
PR .... Per
PR .... Percentage Rates
pr .... Percentile Rank (AD)
PR .... Percentile Rank
PR .... Percent Recovery [*Plant pathology*]
PR .... Perforation Rate (SAUS)
PR .... Performance Rating (OICC)
PR .... Performance Ratio (AAG)
PR .... Performance Report (AFM)
PR .... Performance Requirement
PR .... Perfusion Rate [*Cardiology*] (DAVI)
PR .... Periodic Report (IAA)
PR .... Periodic Reversal (IAA)
PR .... Periodic Review [*Social Security Administration*] (DHP)
pr .... Peripheral Resistance (AD)
PR .... Peripheral Resistance [*Medicine*]
PR .... Peripheral rheumatism [*Medicine*] (DB)
PR .... Perirenal [*Nephrology*]
PR .... Permanens Rector [*Permanent Rector*]
PR .... Permanent Reactor (SAUS)
PR .... Permanent Rector (SAUS)
PR .... Permeance (IAA)
PR .... Permissive Reassignment [*Air Force*] (AFM)
PR .... Per Price [*Business term*]
PR .... Per Recipient (SAUS)
PR .... Per Rectum [*Medicine*]
pr .... Per Rectum [*By the Rectum*] [*Latin*] (AD)
PR .... Pershing Rifles [*Honorary military organization*]
PR .... Persistency Rater [*LIMRA*]
PR .... Personality Record [*Psychological testing*]
PR .... Personnel Request (TIMI)
PR .... Personnel Resources (EA)
PR .... Person Reporting (GOBB)
PR .... Pesikta Rabbati (BJA)
PR .... Pesticide Registration [*Environmental Protection Agency*]
PR .... Pesticide Regulation Notice (SAUS)
PR .... Pharmaceutical Representative (SAUS)
PR .... Phase Resolved (SAUS)
PR .... Phenol Red
PR .... Philadelphia Reports [*Pennsylvania*] [*A publication*] (DLA)
PR .... Philanthropic Roundtable (EA)
PR .... Philippine Airlines [*ICAO designator*] (AD)
PR .... Philippine Airlines, Inc. (SAUS)
PR .... Philippine Island Reports [*A publication*] (DLA)
P-R .... Philips Roxane [*Commercial firm*] (DAVI)
PR .... Phonological Representation [*Linguistics*] (IEL)

PR .... Phonological Rule [*Linguistics*] (IEL)
PR .... Phosphate Rock [*Petrology*]
PR .... Phosphorylase-Rupturing [*Biochemistry*]
PR .... Photographic Reconnaissance [*Military*] (MCD)
PR .... Photographic Recorder
PR .... Photoreacting [*or Photoreactivation*] [*Biochemistry*]
PR .... Photo Reconnaissance [*ICAO designator*] (FAAC)
PR .... Photorecorder
PR .... Photo Reflectance (SAUS)
PR .... Photorefractive [*Optics*]
PR .... Photoresist
P/R .... Photosynthesis/Respiration [*Biochemistry*]
PR .... Phrasal Representation (SAUS)
PR .... Physical Record [*Computer science*]
PR .... Physican Reviewer (MEDA)
Pr .... Piaster (SAUS)
PR .... Picture Ratio (IAA)
PR .... Piezo Resistive [*Automotive electronics*]
PR .... Piezoresistive (SAUS)
PR .... Pilot Rating
PR .... Pinar del Rio (AD)
PR .... Pinch Runner [*Baseball*]
PR .... Pineal Recess [*Neuroanatomy*]
PR .... Pipe Rail (AAG)
PR .... Pipe Rolls (SAUS)
PR .... Pitch Ratio
P/R .... Pitch/Roll (MCD)
PR .... Pitting Rate (SAUS)
PR .... Pittsburgh Reports [*1853-73*] [*Pennsylvania*] [*A publication*] (DLA)
PR .... Pityriasis [*Dermatology*]
PR .... Pityriasis Rosea [*Dermatology*] (MAE)
PR .... Planetary RADAR [*Equipment box*]
P/R .... Planned Requirements (DNAB)
PR .... Planning Reference
PR .... Plant Recovery [*Nuclear energy*] (NRCH)
PR .... Plant Report
PR .... Please Return
PR .... Plotting and RADAR
PR .... Ply Rating [*Tires*] (NATG)
PR .... Plyrating-prismary Radar (SAUS)
PR .... Pneumatic Retinopathy [*Ophthalmology*]
PR .... Pocket Radio (SAUS)
PR .... Point Resistance (SAUS)
PR .... Polarization Ratio (SAUS)
PR .... Polarized Relay (IAA)
PR .... Policy Review (MCD)
PR .... Polish Register [*Polish ship classification society*] (DS)
PR .... Polish Register Classification Society (SAUS)
PR .... Polskie Radio [*Polish Radio*] (AD)
PR .... Polyarthrite Rheumatisme (SAUS)
PR .... Ponceau Red [*Biological stain*]
PR .... Poor Rate [*British*] (ROG)
PR .... Populus Romanus [*The Roman People*] [*Latin*]
PR .... Porsche [*Society of Automotive Engineers auto manufacturer code for service information interchange*]
PR .... Port Risks (MARI)
PR .... Position Record (NASA)
PR .... Position Register (IAA)
PR .... Position Report [*Air Force*]
PR .... Positive Real (SAUS)
PR .... Postal Regulations (DLA)
PR .... Poste Recommandee [*Registered Post*]
PR .... Posterior Repair [*Gynecology*] (DAVI)
PR .... Posterior Ridge
PR .... Posterior Right (SAUS)
PR .... Posterior Root [*Medicine*] (DMAA)
PR .... Post Request
PR .... Post-Resuscitation
PR .... Potency Ratio [*Medicine*] (DMAA)
PR .... Pounder [*Gun*]
PR .... Pour Remercier [*To Express Thanks*] [*French*]
PR .... Power Range [*Nuclear energy*] (NRCH)
PR .... Power Rating
PR .... Power Ratio
PR .... Power Return
Pr .... Praca [*Plaza*] [*Portuguese*] (AD)
Pr .... Practice Reports [*Various jurisdictions*] [*A publication*] (DLA)
Pr .... Prairie (AD)
PR .... Prairie (MCD)
Pr .... Prandtl Number [*IUPAC*]
PR .... Praseodymium
Pr .... Praseodymium [*Chemical element*]
PR .... Prayer
PR .... Preacher
Pr .... Preamble (ILCA)
Pr .... Precancelled [*Philately*]
PR .... Precedence Rating [*Military*] (AFIT)
PR .... Precipitation Radar (EOSA)
PR .... Preconstruction Requirement [*Environmental Protection Agency*]
PR .... Predicted Rate [*Medicine*] (DAVI)
Pr .... Prednisone [*Also, P, PDN, Pred, Pro*] [*Endocrinology*] [*Antineoplastic drug*]
Pr .... Preemphasis (SAUS)
PR .... Preferred [*Stock exchange term*] (SPSG)
pr .... Preferred (WDAA)
PR .... Prefix [*Indicating a private radiotelegram*] (BUR)
PR .... Prefix Resolution (SAUS)
PR .... Preflight
PR .... Pregnancy Rate [*Medicine*]
PR .... Preliminary Report
PR .... Preliminary Review [*Army*]
PR .... Premature Release [*Telecommunications*] (TEL)
PR .... Prepare (VLIE)
PR .... Prepare Reply
PR .... Preposition
PR .... Pre-Raphaelite
Pr .... Presbyopia (AD)
PR .... Presbyopia [*Ophthalmology*]
Pr .... Presbyter [*Elder*] [*Latin*] (AD)
PR .... Presbyterian (ROG)
pr .... Present (SHCU)
PR .... Present
Pr .... Presentation [*Gynecology*]
PR .... Presidency (ROG)
PR .... President [*Telegraphy*] (PCTE)
Pr .... Press (AD)
pr .... Press (RION)
PR .... Pressoreceptor [*Laboratory science*] (DAVI)
PR .... Press Release
PR .... Press Revise (DGA)
PR .... Pressure
PR .... Pressure Ratio
PR .... Pressure Recorder (NRCH)
PR .... Pressure Regulation
PR .... Pressure Regulator (KSC)
PR .... Preston [*Postcode*] (ODBW)
PR .... Prevention (DAVI)
pr .... Price (ODBW)
PR .... Price [*Online database field identifier*]
PR .... Price Communications [*AMEX symbol*] (TTSB)
PR .... Price Communications Corp. [*AMEX symbol*] (SAG)
PR .... Price Received
PR .... Price Redetermination [*Economics*]
PR .... Price Reduced [*of a book*]
Pr .... Price's English Exchequer Reports [*1814-24*] [*A publication*] (DLA)
Pr .... Priest (WDAA)
PR .... Priest
PR .... Prignitz [*German license plate city code*]
PR .... Primary (NASA)
PR .... Primary RADAR (DA)
PR .... Primary Rate (SAUS)
PR .... Primary Reference [*Automobile fuel*] (DICI)
PR .... Primary Runout (SAUS)
PR .... Primary Zone [*Environmental science*] (COE)
PR .... Primitive
Pr .... Prince (WDAA)
PR .... Prince
PR .... Prince Regent (ROG)
PR .... Princess Royal's [*Military unit*] [*British*]
Pr .... Principal
PR .... Principal Register [*Computer science*]
PR .... Print [*or Printed*] (NTCM)
pr .... Print (VRA)
PR .... Printed [*or Printer*]
PR .... Printer [*Computer science*] (IAA)
PR .... Printing Operations [*TBS*] (FOTI)
PR .... Printing Reperforator (SAUS)
PR .... Printing Request (MCD)
PR .... Print Register (IAA)
PR .... Print Restore [*Computer science*] (MHDB)
Pr .... Prior (SG)
PR .... Prior
PR .... Priority Country (SAUS)
PR .... Priority Regulation
PR .... Priority Resolver
PR .... Priority Routine (SAUS)
PR .... Priory
PR .... Prism
pr .... Prismatic Tank [*Liquid gas carriers*]
PR .... Prison Riot (WDAA)
Pr .... Pristane [*Organic chemistry*]
pr .... Private (DLA)
PR .... Private Road [*Maps and charts*] [*British*] (ROG)
PR .... Prize Ring [*Boxing*]
PR .... Probabilistic Risk Assessment [*Computer-based technique for accident prediction*]
PR .... Probability
Pr .... Probable
pr .... Probated (GEAB)
PR .... Probate Record (SAUS)
PR .... Probate Reports [*A publication*] (DLA)
Pr .... Problemata [*of Aristotle*] [*Classical studies*] (OCD)
PR .... Problem Report (MCD)
Pr .... Procarbazine [*Also, P, PC, PCB*] [*Antineoplastic drug*]
PR .... Procedural Regulations [*Civil Aeronautics Board*]
PR .... Procedures Review [*DoD*]
PR .... Proceedings (IAA)
PR .... Processor [*Computer science*] (IAA)

PR .... Process-Reactive [*Scale*] [*Psychometrics*]
PR .... Proctologist
Pr .... Proctoscopy (AD)
PR .... Proctosigmoidoscopy [*Medicine*] (AD)
PR .... Procurement Regulation [*Military*]
PR .... Procurement Request [*or Requisition*]
PR .... Procurement Requisition (SAUS)
PR .... Producing Region [*Agriculture*]
PR .... Production Rate
PR .... Production Requirements [*Military*] (AFIT)
PR .... Production Review [*Automotive project management*]
P/R........... Productivity/Respiration [*Physiology*]
PR .... Product Register (SAUS)
PR .... Product-Remainder (SAUS)
PR .... Product Removal (ABAC)
PR .... Profile (DAVI)
PR .... Profile Reliability (MCD)
PR .... Profit Rate (WGA)
P-R .... Progesterone Receptor [*Endocrinology*]
PR .... Programmed Requirement
PR .... Programming [*Computer science*] (IAA)
PR .... Programming Requirement (SAUS)
PR .... Program Register [*Computer science*] (BUR)
PR .... Program Repeat (SAUS)
PR .... Program Requirements (KSC)
PR .... Program Review [*Training term*] (LPT)
PR .... Program Routine (SAUS)
PR .... Progressive Resistance
PR .... Progress Record (SAUS)
PR .... Progress Report
PR .... Project Release (EA)
PR .... Project Report
PR .... Project Rover (SAA)
PR .... Prolactin [*Also, LTH, PRL*] [*Endocrinology*]
PR .... Prolonged-Release [*Pharmacy*]
Pr .... Promenade (DD)
Pr .... Promille (SAUS)
PR .... Promotion Request (SAUS)
PR .... Pronominal [*Grammar*] (ROG)
PR .... Pronoun
PR .... Pronounced
Pr .... Proof [*Numismatic term*]
PR .... Propagating Rift [*Geology*]
PR .... Proper
PR .... Property
PR .... Proportional Representation [*in legislatures, etc.*]
PR .... Proposed Regulation
PR .... Proposed Request
PR .... Proposed Rule [*Federal government*] (GFGA)
PR .... Propulsion Range
Pr .... Propyl [*Organic chemistry*]
PR .... Pro Rata
pr .... Prose
PR .... Prosthetic-Group Removing [*Enzyme*] [*Biochemistry*] (DAVI)
PR .... Prosthion [*Medicine*] (MAE)
PR .... Protease [*Chemistry*]
PR .... Protective Reaction [*Bombing raid*] [*Vietnam*]
PR .... Protectorate Regiment [*British military*] (DMA)
PR .... Protein (MAE)
PR .... Protestant (ADA)
PR .... Prothrombinratio (SAUS)
PR .... Prototype
PR .... Proved
PR .... Provencal [*Language, etc.*]
PR .... Proverb
Pr .... Proverbs [*Old Testament book*] (BJA)
PR .... Provisional Release (SAUS)
PR .... Provost (WDAA)
Pr .... Proximal
PR .... Pseudo Random (SAUS)
PR .... Pseudorandom
PR .... Pseudoresidual
PR .... Psychedelic Review [*A publication*]
PR .... Psychiatric Record (AD)
PR .... Publicity Release (NTCM)
pr .... Public Relations (AD)
PR .... Public Relations
PR .... Public Responsibility
PR .... Puerto Rican [*Derogatory term*]
PR........... Puerto Rico [*ANSI two-letter standard code*] (CNC)
PR .... Puerto Rico [*Postal code*]
pr .... Puerto Rico [*IYRU nationality code*] [*MARC country of publication code*] [*Library of Congress*] (LCCP)
PR .... Puerto Rico Supreme Court Reports [*A publication*] (DLA)
PR .... Pulmonic Regurgitation [*Cardiology*] (DAVI)
PR .... Pulsed Reactor (SAUS)
PR .... Pulse Rate
PR .... Pulse Ratio (IEEE)
PR .... Pulse Regeneration (or Regenerator) (SAUS)
PR .... Pulse Regenerator
PR .... Punching Rate (SAUS)
PR .... Punch Routine (SAUS)
PR .... Punctum Remotum [*Far Point*] [*Latin*]
pr .... Punctum Remotum [*Remote Point*] [*Latin*] (AD)
PR .... Punjab Record [*India*] [*A publication*] (DLA)
PR .... Purchase Request
PR .... Purchase Requirement (SAUS)
PR .... Purchase Requisition
PR .... Pure Rubber (SAUS)
PR .... Purple (AAG)
pR........... Purplish Red (AD)
PR .... Purplish Red
PR .... Pyke's Reports [*Canada*] [*A publication*] (DLA)
PR .... Pyramidal Response (DB)
pr .... Pyrite [*CIPW classification*] [*Geology*]
PR .... Pyrogallol Red [*Also, PGR*] [*An indicator*] [*Chemistry*]
PR .... Pyrolytic Release
PR+........... Reactor Pressure Plus (NRCH)
PR........... Reading Public Library, Reading, PA [*Library symbol*] [*Library of Congress*] (LCLS)
PR .... River Gunboat [*Navy symbol*]
PR .... Software-Parameter Specification (SAUS)
PR .... Upper Canada Practice Reports [*1850-1900*] [*Ontario*] [*A publication*] (DLA)
PR1........... Parachute Rigger, First Class [*Navy*]
PR2........... Parachute Rigger, Second Class [*Navy*]
PR3........... Parachute Rigger, Third Class [*Navy*]
PRA........... Albright College, Reading, PA [*Library symbol*] [*Library of Congress*] (LCLS)
PRA........... Division of Policy Research and Analysis [*National Science Foundation*]
PRA........... Page Replacement Algorithm [*Computer science*] (MHDI)
PRA........... Paint Research Association [*British*]
PRA........... Paperwork Reduction Act (GFGA)
PRA........... Parabolic Reflector Aerial (or Antenna) (SAUS)
PRA........... Parabolic Reflector Antenna
PRA........... Parana [*Argentina*] [*Airport symbol*] (OAG)
PRA........... Parool (SAUS)
PRA........... Participant Record Advice
PRA........... Partido Revolucionario Autentico [*Authentic Revolutionary Party*] [*Bolivia*] [*Political party*] (PPW)
PRA........... Parti du Regroupement Africain [*African Regroupment Party*] [*Niger*] [*Political party*] (PD)
PRA........... Parti du Regroupement Africain [*African Regroupment Party*] [*Banned, 1974*] [*Burkina Faso*] [*Political party*]
PRA........... Patent-Rights-Acquisition (SAUS)
PRA........... Paymaster Rear Admiral (SAUS)
PRA........... Paymaster-Rear-Admiral [*Navy*] [*British*]
PRA........... Pay Readjustment Act [*1942*]
PRA........... Pay Record Access
pra........... Payroll Audit (AD)
PRA........... Payroll Auditor [*Insurance*]
PRA........... Peace Research Abstracts (NITA)
PRA........... Peak Recording Accelerograph [*Accelerometer*] (IEEE)
PRA........... Pendulous Reference Axis [*Accelerometer*] (IEEE)
PRA........... Peoples Republic of Albania (SAUS)
PRA........... Peoples Republic of Angola (SAUS)
PRA........... People's Revolutionary Army [*Grenada*]
PRA........... Permanent Restricted Area [*Former USSR*] (NATG)
PRA........... Personal Retirement Alliance Ltd. [*Association*] (EA)
PRA........... Personal Rights Association [*British*] (BI)
PRA........... Personnel Research Activity [*Later, NPTRL*] [*Navy*]
PRA........... Personnel Research Association (SAUS)
PRA........... Petrol Retailers' Association [*British*]
PRA........... Pharmacy Restructuring Authority [*Australia*]
PRA........... Phosphoribosylamin (SAUS)
PRA........... Phosphoribosylamine
PRA........... Photon Research Associates (ACAE)
PRA........... Pilots Rights Association (EA)
PRA........... Pitch and Roll Attitude (IAA)
PRA........... Planetary Radio Astronomy
PRA........... Planned Regulatory Action [*Federal government*] (GFGA)
PRA........... Planned Restricted Availability [*Military*] (NVT)
pra........... Plasma Renin Activity [*Medicine*] (AD)
PRA........... Plasma Renin Activity [*Hematology*]
PRA........... Plutonium Recycle Acid [*Nuclear energy*] (NRCH)
PRA........... Polar Regions Award (IAA)
PRA........... Policy Research and Analysis
PRA........... Political Research Associates [*Association*] (EA)
PRA........... Popular Resistance Army (SAUS)
PRA........... Popular Rotocraft Association (EA)
PRA........... Port Rashid Authority (SAUS)
PRA........... Position Resolution Alarm (TIMI)
PRA........... Postal Reorganization Act (AD)
PRA........... Postal Reorganization Act of 1970 (AAGC)
PRA........... Postrenal Azotemia [*Medicine*] (MELL)
PRA........... Potencia Radiada Aparente (SAUS)
PRA........... Praha [*Prague*] [*Czechoslovakia*] [*Seismograph station code, US Geological Survey*] (SEIS)
PRA........... Prairiefire Rural Action (EA)
PRA........... Prairie Rail Authority (SAUS)
pra........... Prakrit [*MARC language code*] [*Library of Congress*] (LCCP)
PRA........... Precession Axis (SAUS)
PRA........... Precision Axis (KSC)
PRA........... Precision Radar Approach (PIPO)
PRA........... Preliminary Reserve Analysis (SAUS)
PRA........... Premium Audit
PRA........... Prerefund Audit [*IRS*]
PRA........... Pre-Retirement Association [*British*] (DI)

PRA.......... President of the Royal Academy [*British*]
PRA.......... President's Re-Employment Agreement [*New Deal*]
PRA.......... Primary Area (SAUS)
PRA.......... Primary Rate Access (VLIE)
PRA.......... Primary Reviewing Authority
PRA.......... Prime Responsible Authority (IAA)
PRA.......... Print Alphamerically (SAUS)
pra.......... Print Alphanumerically (AD)
PRA.......... Print Alphanumerically [*Computer science*] (MDG)
PRA.......... Probabilistic Risk Assessment [*Computer-based technique for accident prediction*]
pra.......... Probation and Rehabilitation of Airmen (AD)
PRA.......... Probation and Rehabilitation of Airmen [*Air Force*] (AFM)
PRA.......... Production Reader Assembly (KSC)
PRA.......... Production Readiness Assessment [*Army*]
PRA.......... Progesterone Receptor Assay [*Clinical chemistry*]
PRA.......... Program Reader Assembly [*Computer science*]
pra.......... Progressive Retinal Atrophy [*Medicine*] (AD)
PRA.......... Projected Requisition Authority [*Army*] (AABC)
PRA.......... Prompt Radiation Analysis (MCD)
PRA.......... Propionic Acid [*Organic chemistry*]
PRA.......... Prospair Ltd. [*British*] [*ICAO designator*] (FAAC)
PRA.......... Proust Research Association (EA)
PRA.......... Proximal Reference Axis (RAWO)
PRA.......... Psoriasis Research Association (EA)
PRA.......... Psychiatric Rehabilitation Association [*British*]
PRA.......... Psychological Research Associates (or Association) (SAUS)
PRA.......... Public Resources Association [*Defunct*] (EA)
PRA.......... Public Roads Administration
PRA.......... Puerto Rico Area Office [*AEC*]
PRA.......... Puerto Rico Association (AD)
PRA.......... Purchase and Resale Agreement [*Canada*] (BARN)
PRA.......... US 1869 Pictorial Research Associates (EA)
PRAA.......... Airman Apprentice, Parachute Rigger, Striker [*Navy rating*]
PRAAD...... Photo-Resist Apply and Dry (SAUS)
PRAB........ Police Radio Advisory Board (EARSL)
PRAB........ Prab Robots, Inc. (SAUS)
PRAC........ Pharmaceutical Reimbursement Advisory Committee [*Medicine*] [*HEW*] (EDAA)
Prac......... Practical (DLA)
PRAC........ Practice (AABC)
prac.......... Practice (AD)
Prac......... Practise (SAUS)
PRAC........ Pressure Ratio Acceleration Control [*Gas turbine engine*]
PRAC........ Productivity Technologies Corp. [*NASDAQ symbol*] (SAG)
PRAC........ Program Resource Advisory Committee [*TRADOC*] (MCD)
PRAC........ Public Relations Advisory Committee
PRACA...... Problem Reporting and Corrective Action (MCD)
PRACA...... Puerto Rican Association for Community Affairs (EA)
Prac Act..... Practice Act [*A publication*] (DLA)
Prac Appr Pat TM and Copyright... Practical Approach to Patents, Trademarks and Copyrights (SAUS)
Pra Cas..... Prater's Cases on Conflict of Laws [*A publication*] (DLA)
PRACDA..... Polarimetric Radar Control and Data Aquisition (SAUS)
PRACE....... Photo-Resist Align, Contact and Expose (SAUS)
PRaCHS..... Archbishop Carroll High School, Radnor, PA [*Library symbol*] [*Library of Congress*] (LCLS)
PRACL....... Page Replacement Algorithm and Control Logic (SAUS)
pracl......... Page-Replacement Algorithm and Control Logic (AD)
PRACL....... Page-Replacement Algorithm and Control Logic [*Computer science*]
PRACL....... Practical
Prac Litig... Practical Litigation (SAUS)
PRACOS..... Praxis-Computer-System (SAUS)
PRACSA..... Public Remote Access Computer Standards Association (SAUS)
PRACSATS... Practical Satellites
Pract......... Practical (DIAR)
PRACT....... Practical (ROG)
PRACT....... Practice [*Legal shorthand*] (LWAP)
PRAC-T...... Practice Tracer (SAUS)
pract......... Practitioner (AD)
PRACT....... Practitioner
PRACT....... Practolol (DB)
Pract Eng... Practical Energy (SAUS)
PRACTIS... Practitioner's Award Computer Tabulated Information Service [*Medicine*] [*Computer science*] (EDAA)
Pract Law... Practical Lawyer [*A publication*] (DLA)
Pract Med... Practice of Medicine (SAUS)
PRACTNR... Practitioner
Pract Pharm... Practical Pharmacy (SAUS)
Pract Reg... Practical Register in the Common Pleas [*England*] [*A publication*] (DLA)
PRACY...... Pratt City, AL [*American Association of Railroads railroad junction routing code*]
PRAD........ Pitch Radio Adjustment Device
PRAD........ Pitch Ratio Adjust Device (MCD)
PRADA...... Partido Revolucionario Dominicano Autentico [*Dominican Republic*] [*Political party*]
Pr Adm Dig... Pritchard's Admiralty Digest [*3rd ed.*] [*1887*] [*A publication*] (DLA)
PRADO...... Public Radio Association of Development Officers (SAUS)
PRADOR.... PRF [*Pulse Repetition Frequency*] Ranging Doppler RADAR
PRADOR.... Pulse repetition frequency Ranging Doppler Radar (SAUS)
PRADS...... Parachute Retrorocket Airdrop System (MCD)
PRADU...... Prairie Du Chien, WI [*American Association of Railroads railroad junction routing code*]
Prad Wireless... Practical Wireless (SAUS)
praed........ praedicative (SAUS)
praef......... Praefatio [*Latin*] (OCD)
Praeger..... Frederick A. Praeger (AD)
Praegtzr..... Praegitzer Industries, Inc. [*Associated Press*] (SAG)
Praem....... De Praemiis et Poenis [*of Philo*] (BJA)
praen........ Praenomen (AD)
Praep Evang... Praeparatio Evangelica [*of Eusebius*] [*Classical studies*] (OCD)
Praepo...... Praepositus [*Deceased, 1509*] [*Authority cited in pre-1607 legal work*] (DSA)
praes........ Praesens [*Present Tense*] [*Latin*]
praet......... Praeteritum [*Past Tense*] [*Latin*]
PRAF......... Passenger-Reserved Air Freight
PRAG........ Pensions Research Accountants Group (MHDB)
PRAG........ Pragma Bio-Tech, Inc. (SAUS)
prag......... Pragmatic (AD)
Prag......... Pragmatism (SAUS)
pragma...... Processing Routines Aided by Graphics for Manipulation of Arrays (AD)
PRAGMA.... Processing Routines Aided by Graphics for Manipulation of Arrays (PDAA)
Prag Micro... Pragmatics Microfiche (SAUS)
Pra H & W... Prater on Husband and Wife [*2nd ed.*] [*1836*] [*A publication*] (DLA)
PrA-HPA..... Protein A Hemolytic Plaque Assay [*Medicine*] (DMAA)
PRAI.......... Peer Review Analysis (EFIS)
PRAI.......... Phosphoribosyl Anthranilate Isomerase
PRAI.......... Planning Research and Action Institute (SAUS)
PRAI.......... Prairie Schooner [*NCIC car make code*]
PRAI.......... Pre-Reading Assessment Inventory [*Education*] (EDAC)
PRAI.......... Project Research Applied in Industry (SAUS)
PRAIC........ President of the Royal Architectural Institute of Canada (NGC)
PRAICO..... Puerto Rican American Insurance Co. (AD)
PR Aircraft... Photographic Reconnaissance Aircraft (SAUS)
PRAIRE...... Polarization Radar Illinois Rainfall Experiments (SAUS)
PRAIREO.... Prairie Oil Royalties Co. Ltd. (SAUS)
PRAIRIE..... Prairie [*Commonly used*] (OPSA)
Prairie View A&M U... Prairie View Agricultural and Mechanical University (GAGS)
PRAIS....... Passive Ranging Interferometer Sensor
prais......... Passive-Ranging Interferometer Sensor (AD)
PRAIS....... Pesticide Residue Analysis Information Service [*British*]
PRAISE...... Pilot Records of Achievement in Schools Evaluation (AIE)
PRAISE...... Prospective Randomized Amlodipine Survival Evaluation [*Medicine*] (DMAA)
Prakruti Utkal Unir J Sci... Prakruti Utkal University Journal of Science (SAUS)
pral.......... Principal [*Principal*] [*Spanish*] (AD)
Pr Alc....... Propyl Alcohol (SAUS)
PRALCA..... Productora de Alcoholes Hidratados, C.A. (EFIS)
PRAM........ Packet Random Access Memory (SAUS)
PRAM........ Page Replacement Analysis Models (SAUS)
PRAM........ Parallel Random Access Machine [*Computer science*]
PRAM........ Parameter Random Access Memory (ADWA)
PRAM........ Parameter Random-Access Memory [*Computer science*] (DCDG)
pram......... Perambulator (AD)
PRAM........ Perambulator [*British*]
PRAM........ Permanent Random-Access Memory (SAUS)
PRAM........ Poseidon Random Access Memory [*Missiles*]
Pram......... Poseidon Random-Access Memory (AD)
Pram......... Prambanam (VRA)
PRAM........ Preliminary Repair Level Decision Analysis Model (PDAA)
PRAM........ Pre-Recorded Announcement and Boarding Music Reproducer
PRAM........ Primary Report of Aircraft Mishap [*Army*] (DOMA)
PRAM........ Processing Rate Analytic Model (SAUS)
PRAM........ Productivitiy, Reliability, Availability and Maintainability (SAUS)
PRAM........ Productivity, Reliability and Maintainability (SAUS)
pram......... Productivity, Reliability, Availability, and Maintainability (AD)
PRAM........ Productivity, Reliability, Availability, and Maintainability Office [*Air Force*]
PRAM........ Product Reliability and Maintainability
PRAM........ Programmable Amplifier (SAUS)
PRAM........ Programmable Random Access Memory [*Computer science*] (IAA)
p/RAM....... Programmable Random Analysis Method (SAUS)
PRAM........ Programmes and Measures (SAUS)
PRAM........ Program Requirements Analysis Method
PRAM........ Propelled Ascent Mine
PRAM........ Propelled Rapid Ascent Mine (MCD)
PRAM........ Pseudorandom Access Memory [*Computer science*] (IAA)
PRAM........ Rocket-Propelled Rising Mine (SAUS)
PRAMPO.... Productivity, Reliability, Availability, and Maintenance Program Office [*Air Force*] (DOMA)
PRAMS...... Paperwork Reduction Act Management System (SAUS)
PRAMS...... Passenger Reservation and Manifesting System (SAUS)
PRAMS...... Pregnancy Risk Assessment Monitoring System (SAUS)
PRAMS...... Processing Asset Management System (WDAA)
PRAMS...... Programmatic Risk Assessment Model System (SAUS)
PRAMS...... Puerto Rico Addiction Medical Services (MHID)
PRAN........ Airman, Parachute Rigger, Striker [*Navy*]
PRAN........ Pre-Analysis (VLIE)
PRAN........ Prefix Analysis (SAUS)
PRAN........ Production Analyser (SAUS)
PRAN........ Production Analyzer (IAA)
PRAND...... Prandium [*Dinner*] [*Pharmacy*]
prand........ Prandium [*dinner*] [*Latin*] (AD)
PR&C........ Purchase Request and Commitment (SAUS)

PR & D...... Personal Rest and Delay [*Air Force*] (AFM)
PR & D...... Power, Rodwell, and Drew's English Election Cases [*1847-56*] [*A publication*] (DLA)
PR&D........ Process Research and Development (SAUS)
PR&D........ Product Research and Development
PR&D........ Program Research and Development (SAUS)
PR & D...... Public Research and Development
PR & D El Cas... Power, Rodwell, and Drew's English Election Cases [*A publication*] (DLA)
Pr & Div.... Law Reports, Probate and Divorce [*England*] [*A publication*] (DLA)
PR & R...... Professional Rights and Responsibilities
PR&R........ Project Review and Reporting (ACAE)
PRANG...... Projection Angle (SAUS)
PRANG...... Puerto Rico Air National Guard
PRANS...... Proportional Range Scheduling (SAUS)
PRAODP.... Agricultural Research Organization. Preliminary Report (journ.) (SAUS)
PRAP........ Passive Radar-Augmented Projectile (SAUS)
PRAP........ Patient Resident Assessment Profile [*Geriatrics*]
PRAP........ Provincial/Regional Library Association Presidents [*Canada*]
PRAP........ Provisions of Following Reference Apply [*Army*] (AABC)
PRAP........ Pylos Regional Archaeological Project (SAUS)
PrAPhA...... Proceedings of the American Philological Association (SAUS)
PRAQ........ Playground and Recreation Association of Queensland [*Australia*]
PRAQ........ Pratt Trucking [*Common carrier symbol*]
PRAR........ Partido Revolucionario Autentico Rios [*Bolivia*] [*Political party*] (PPW)
PRAR........ Planetary Radio Astronomy Receiver (SAUS)
PRAR........ Prairie Schooner [*NCIC trailer make code*]
PRARE...... Precise Range and Range Rate Equipment (SAUS)
PRARE...... Precise Range and Range Rate Experiment (SAUS)
PRARE...... Precise Range and Range-Rate Experiment
PRARE...... Precision Range and Rate Equipment (SAUS)
PRARE...... Precision Range and Rate Experiment (SAUS)
PRAREE..... Precise Range and Range Rate Equipment, Extended Version (SAUS)
PRAREE..... Precise Range and Rate Equipment-Extended Version (EOSA)
PRARIE..... Prairie [*Commonly used*] (OPSA)
PRARS...... Pitch, Roll, Azimuth Reference System (NG)
PRAS........ Pacific Regional Advisory Service [*South Pacific Bureau for Economic Co-Operation*] (EY)
PRAS........ Particle Reactor Analysis Services (AAEL)
PRAS........ Pension and Retirement Annuity System
PRAS........ Planning, Reporting and Accountability Structure (FOTI)
PRAS........ Prereduced, Anaerobically Sterilized [*Microbiology*]
PRAS........ President of the Royal Astronomical Society (SAUS)
PRAS........ Principle Research Areas (SAUS)
PRAS........ Pseudo-Renal Artery Syndrome [*Medicine*] (DMAA)
PRAS........ Pulsed Realistic Age-Structured [*Model for disease persitence*]
PRASD...... Personnel Research Activity, San Diego [*California*] [*Navy*]
PRASD3..... Alabama. Agricultural Experiment Station. Progress Report Series (journ.) (SAUS)
PRAT........ Parliamentary Retiring Allowances Trust [*Australia*]
PRAT........ Platelet Radioactive Antiglobulin Test [*Hematology*] (DAVI)
PRAT........ Prattsburgh Railroad (AD)
PRAT........ Predicted Range Against Target [*Military*] (NVT)
PRAT........ Pressure-Retaining Amphipod Trap [*Deep-sea biology*]
PRAT........ Production Reliability Acceptance Test
PRAT........ Production Reliability Assurance Test (SAUS)
P RAT AET... Pro Ratione Aetatis [*According to Age*] [*Pharmacy*] (ROG)
p rat aet... Pro Ratione Aetatis [*In Proportion to Age*] [*Latin*] (AD)
P RAT AETAT... Pro Rata Aetatis [*According to Age*] [*Pharmacy*]
p rat aetat... Pro Ratione Aetatis [*In Proportion to Age*] [*Latin*] (MAE)
PratHtl...... Pratt Hotel Corp. [*Associated Press*] (SAG)
PratLm...... Pratt & Lambert United, Inc. [*Associated Press*] (SAG)
PRATRA...... Philippines Relief and Trade Rebilitation Administration (AD)
PRATS....... Pesticides Regulatory Action Tracking System (EPAT)
Pratt......... Pratt's Contraband-of-War Cases [*A publication*] (DLA)
Pratt......... Pratt's Supplement to Bott's Poor Laws [*1833*] [*A publication*] (DLA)
Pratt BS...... Pratt's Law of Benefit Building Societies [*A publication*] (DLA)
Pratt Cont... Pratt's Contraband-of-War Cases [*A publication*] (DLA)
Pratt Cts Req... Pratt's Statutes Establishing Courts of Request [*A publication*] (DLA)
Pratt Fr Soc... Pratt on Friendly Societies [*15th ed.*] [*1931*] [*A publication*] (DLA)
Pratt High... Pratt and Mackenzie on Highways [*21st ed.*] [*1967*] [*A publication*] (DLA)
Pratt Inst... Pratt Institute (GAGS)
Pratt PL..... Pratt's Edition of Bott on the Poor Laws [*A publication*] (DLA)
Pratt Prop T... Pratt on the Property Tax Act [*A publication*] (DLA)
Pratt Sav B... Pratt on Savings Banks [*6th ed.*] [*1845*] [*A publication*] (DLA)
Pratt SL..... Pratt on Sea Lights [*2nd ed.*] [*1858*] [*A publication*] (DLA)
PRAUD9..... Agricultural Research Institute Ukiriguru. Progress Report (journ.) (SAUS)
PRAUS...... Programme de Recherche sur l'Amiante de l'Universite de Sherbrooke [*Asbestos Research Program*] [*University of Sherbrooke*] [*Quebec*] [*Information service or system*] (IID)
PRAV........ Planned Restricted Availability [*Navy*] (ANA)
PRAV........ Playground and Recreation Association of Victoria [*Australia*]
PRAVT....... Preentry-AV-tachycardia (SAUS)
PRAVT....... Pre-entry-AV-Tachykardie (SAUS)
PRAW........ Personnel Research Activity, Washington, DC [*Obsolete*] [*Navy*]
PRaW........ Wyeth Laboratories, Radnor, PA [*Library symbol*] [*Library of Congress*] (LCLS)
PRAWL...... Puerto Rican American Women's League
Prax......... Bowns Practice (or Precedents) in Chancery (journ.) (SAUS)
Prax......... Browns Practice or Precedents in Chance (SAUS)
Prax......... Brown's Practice (Praxis) [*or Precedents*] in Chancery [*A publication*] (DLA)
PRAX........ First Union Rail [*Private rail car owner code*]
PRAX........ Praxis Pharmaceuticals, Inc. (SAUS)
PRAX........ Premier Agricultural [*Federal Railroad Administration identification code*]
Praxair...... Praxair, Inc. [*Associated Press*] (SAG)
Prax Can.... Praxis Almae Curiae Cancellariae (Brown) [*A publication*] (DLA)
PRAY........ Paul Revere Associated Yeoman (AD)
PRAZ........ Prazosin [*A vasodilator*]
PRB.......... Basic Proline-Rich Protein (DMAA)
PRB.......... Packet Receive Buffer [*Computer science*] (VLIE)
PRB.......... Painters' Registration Board [*Western Australia*]
PRB.......... Panel Review Board [*NASA*] (KSC)
PRB.......... Parabola [*Mathematics*]
PRB.......... Parachute Refurbishment Building [*NASA*] (NASA)
PRB.......... Partial Roll-Back (SAUS)
PRB.......... Partido de la Revolucion Boliviana [*Bolivian Revolutionary Party*] [*Political party*] (AD)
PRB.......... Partido Republicano Brasileiro [*Brazil*] [*Political party*] (EY)
PRB.......... Party of the Rebirth of Benin [*Political party*] (PSAP)
PRB.......... Paso Robles [*California*] [*Airport symbol*] (AD)
PRB.......... Paso Robles, CA [*Location identifier*] [*FAA*] (FAAL)
PRB.......... Pay Review Body (SAUS)
PRB.......... Pension Review Board [*Canada*]
PRB.......... Pension Review Board Reports (SAUS)
PRB.......... People's Republic of Benin (AD)
PRB.......... Peoples Republic of Bulgaria (SAUS)
PRB.......... Performance Review Board (ACAE)
PRB.......... Personal Reaction Blank [*Psychology*] (DAVI)
PRB.......... Personnel Reaction Blank [*Psychology*]
PRB.......... Personnel Records Branch [*Army*] (AABC)
PRB.......... Personnel Requirements Branch (MUGU)
PRB.......... Personnel Research Branch [*Army*] (MCD)
PRB.......... Personnel Review Board (AD)
PRB.......... Pharmaceutical Reimbursement Board [*Medicine*] (EDAA)
PRB.......... Physical Record Block (TIMI)
PRB.......... Physiotherapists' Registration Board [*New South Wales, Australia*]
PRB.......... Planned Requirements - Bureau Directed
PRB.......... Plant Review Board [*Nuclear energy*] (NRCH)
PRB.......... Podiatrists' Registration Board [*New South Wales, Australia*]
PRB.......... Polar Research Board [*National Academy of Sciences*]
PRB.......... Population Reference Bureau (EA)
PRB.......... Post-Retirement Benefits (AAGC)
PRB.......... Powder River Basin
PRB.......... Pre-Raphaelite Brotherhood (WDAA)
PRB.......... Press-Radio Bureau (NTCM)
prb.......... Principal Borehole (AD)
PRB.......... Private Radio Bureau [*FCC*] (NTCM)
PRB.......... Probex Corp. [*AMEX symbol*] (SG)
PRB.......... Problem Review Board (ARMP)
PRB.......... Procedure Review Board [*Nuclear energy*] (NRCH)
PRB.......... Procurement Review Board (MCD)
PRB.......... Professional Registration Boards of the Northern Territory [*Australia*]
PRB.......... Program Request Block (IAA)
PRB.......... Program Request Buffer (SAUS)
PRB.......... Program Review Board
PRB.......... Project Review Board [*NASA*] (NASA)
PRB.......... Prosthetics Research Board
PRB.......... Proteus Air Systeme [*France*] [*ICAO designator*] (FAAC)
PRB.......... Pseudo Random Binary (SAUS)
PRB.......... Pseudo-Random Binary (AAEL)
PRB.......... Psychopharmacology Research Branch (SAUS)
PRB.......... Psychosurgery Review Board [*Victoria, Australia*]
PRB.......... Public Roads Bureau
PRBA........ Portable Rechargeable Battery Association (NTPA)
PRBA........ Puerto Rican Bar Association (EA)
PRBA(AG)... Personnel Research Board of the Army, Adjutant General
PRBAL....... Previous Balance (VLIE)
PrBayA...... American Junior College of Puerto Rico, Bayamon, PR [*Library symbol*] [*Library of Congress*] (LCLS)
PrBayC...... Bayamon Central University , Bayamon, Puerto Rico (SAUS)
PrBayC...... Bayamon Central University (Universidad Central de Bayamon), Bayamon, Puerto Rico [*Library symbol*] [*Library of Congress*] (LCLS)
PRBBB...... Proximal Right Bundle Branch Block (SAUS)
PRBC........ Packed Red Blood Cells [*Medicine*]
PRBC........ Parasitized Red Blood Cell [*Medicine*]
PRBC........ Peoples Revolution Broadcasting Corp. (SAUS)
PRBC........ Placental Residual Blood Volume [*Medicine*] (DMAA)
PRBC........ Premier Bancorp, Inc. [*NASDAQ symbol*] (NQ)
PRBC........ Prestige Bancorp, Inc. [*NASDAQ symbol*] (SAG)
PRBC........ Pseudo-Random Binary-Pulse Sequence [*Communications term*] (DCT)
PRBCH...... Process Biochemistry (SAUS)
PRBD........ Paraboloid
PRBE........ Program Robot by Example (SAUS)
PRBG........ Puerto Rican Board of Guardians [*Defunct*] (EA)
PRBK........ Provident Bancorp [*NASDAQ symbol*] (TTSB)
PRBK........ Provident Bancorp, Inc. [*NASDAQ symbol*] (SAG)
PRBLC....... Parabolic
PRBLTY..... Probability [*NWS*] (FAAC)
PRBMD...... Physical Review B, Condensed Matter (SAUS)
PRBMECAB... Permanent Regional Bureau of the Middle East Committee for the Affairs of the Blind [*Riyadh, Saudi Arabia*] (EAIO)

PRBNT ...... Prebent
PRBO .... Position Relief Briefing Observed [*Aviation*] (FAAC)
Pr Br .... Propyl Bromide (SAUS)
PRBS .... Printer Barrier Strip (VLIE)
PRBS .... Pseudo Random Binary Sequence (SAUS)
PRBS .... Pseudorandom Binary Sequence [*Computer science*]
PRBS .... Pseudorandom Binary Signal (SAUS)
PRBSG ...... Pseudorandom Binary Sequence Generator [*Computer science*] (NRCH)
PRBT .... Precision Remote Bathythermograph
PRBU .... Global Intermodal Sales and Leasing [*Intermodal shipping container symbol*] (TVRC)
PRBV .... Placental Residual Blood Volume [*Hematology*] (MAE)
PRBX .... Trinity Rail Management [*Private rail car owner code*]
PRBZ .... ProBusiness Services [*NASDAQ symbol*]
PRBZ .... Pro Business Services, Inc. [*NASDAQ symbol*] (NASQ)
PRC .... Central African Republican Party [*Political party*] (PSAP)
PRC .... Chief Aircrew Survival Equipmentman [*Formerly, Chief Parachute Rigger*] [*Navy rating*]
PRC .... Civic Renewal Party (Panama) [*Political party*] (PSAP)
PRC .... Cuban Revolutionary Party [*Political party*] (PSAP)
PRC .... Pacific Air Charter, Inc. [*ICAO designator*] (FAAC)
PRC .... Packaging Research Center [*Georgia Institute of Technology*] (RCD)
PRC .... Packed Red Cell [*Hematology*] (MAE)
PRC .... Packed Red Cells (SAUS)
PRC .... Pain Rehabilitation Center (AD)
PRC .... Palestine Red Crescent (AD)
PRC .... Parachi [*Language symbol*] (ETLW)
PRC .... Park Requirement Card (SAUS)
PRC .... Park Ridge Center (EA)
PRC .... Partial Read Current (SAUS)
PRC .... Partial Response Coding (IEEE)
PRC .... Partido Regionalista de Cantabria [*Spain*] [*Political party*] (EY)
PRC .... Partido Republicano Calderonista [*Calderonista Republican Party*] [*Costa Rica*] [*Political party*] (PPW)
PRC .... Partido Revolucionario Comunista [*Brazil*] [*Political party*] (EY)
PRC .... Parti Republicain Caledonien [*New Caledonia*] [*Political party*] (FEA)
PRC .... Part Requirement Card
PRC .... Parts Release Card (KSC)
PRC .... Parts Release Curve (SAUS)
PRC .... Passaic River Coalition (EA)
PRC .... Passenger Reservation Center [*Army*]
PRC .... Pay-Raise Commission (AD)
PRC .... Peer Review Committee (SAUS)
PRC .... Penrose Resources Corp. [*Vancouver Stock Exchange symbol*]
PRC .... Pension Research Council (EA)
PRC .... Pension Rights Center [*Washington, DC*] (EA)
PRC .... People's Redemption Council [*Liberia*] (PD)
PRC .... People's Republic of China [*Mainland China*]
PRC .... People's Republic of the Congo
PRC .... Perinatal Research Centre [*University of Alberta*] [*Canada*] (RCD)
PRC .... Periodic Reverse Current (IAA)
PRC .... Period Reverse Current (SAUS)
PRC .... Permanent Regular Commissions [*Army*] [*British*]
PRC .... Permanent Representatives Committee of the European Communities (SAUS)
PRC .... Personality Research Center [*University of Texas at Austin*] [*Research center*] (RCD)
PRC .... Personal Radio Communications (SAUS)
PRC .... Personnel Readiness Center [*Air Force*]
PRC .... Personnel Reception Centre [*British military*] (DMA)
PRC .... Personnel Recovery Center [*Military*]
PRC .... Personnel Reporting Code [*Army*] (AABC)
PRC .... Phased Rate of Change (SAUS)
PRC .... Phase Rate of Change (SEWL)
PRC .... Phase-Response Curve
PRC .... Philippine Resource Center [*An association*] (EA)
PRC .... Photonics Laboratory [*University of Connecticut*] (RCD)
PRC .... Photo Receptor Cell [*Medicine*] (MELL)
PRC .... Physical Review Council [*DoD*]
PRC .... Physicians' Review Committee [*Medicine*] [*UMS*] (EDAA)
PRC .... Phytotechnology Research Center [*Michigan Technological University*] (RCD)
PRC .... Picatinny Research Center [*Picatinny Arsenal*] (AD)
PRC .... Pierce (MSA)
PRC .... Pilot Resource (SAUS)
PRC .... Pitch Radio Controller
PRC .... Pitch Rate Command (MCD)
PRC .... Pitch Ratio Controller (MCD)
PRC .... Planar Random Composite (MCD)
PRC .... Planned Requirements, Conversion (NG)
PRC .... Planning Research Corp. [*Telecommunications service*] (TSSD)
PRC .... Planning Research Corporation [*Marine science*] (OSRA)
PRC .... Plant Records Center [*of the American Horticultural Society*] (IID)
PRC .... Plasma Renin Concentration [*Hematology*]
PRC .... Plastic Roller Conveyor
PRC .... Player Relations Committee [*Baseball*] (NDBD)
PRC .... Plutonium Rework Cell [*Nuclear energy*] (NRCH)
PRC .... Point of Reverse Curve (MSA)
PRC .... Point Reyes [*California*] [*Seismograph station code, US Geological Survey*] [*Closed*] (SEIS)
PRC .... Polar Research Cell (SAUS)
PRC .... Policy Review Committee [*Terminated, 1981*] [*National Security Council*] (EGAO)
PRC .... Polish Resettlement Corps [*British military*] (DMA)
prc .... Polysulphide Rubber Compound (AD)
PRC .... Polysulphide Rubber Compound (PDAA)
PRC .... Populace and Resources Control (COE)
PRC .... Population Research Center [*University of Chicago*] [*Research center*] (RCD)
PRC .... Population Resource Center (EA)
PRC .... Portable Radio Communication (SAUS)
PRC .... Portuguese Civilization (SAUS)
PRC .... Postal Rate Commission [*Federal government*]
PRC .... Postconsumer Recycled Content [*Plastics technology*]
PRC .... Post Roman Conditam [*After the Founding of Rome*] [*Latin*]
PRC .... Poultry Research Centre [*of the Agricultural Research Council*] [*British*] (ARC)
PRC .... Power Reflection Coefficient [*of RADAR signals*]
PRC .... Prattsburgh Railway Corp. [*AAR code*]
PRC .... Precipitation (CARB)
PRC .... Precision Response Corporation
PRC .... Preoral Ciliary [*Gland*]
PRC .... Pre-Ranger Course [*Army*] (INF)
PRC .... Prescott [*Arizona*] [*Airport symbol*] (OAG)
PRC .... Prescott, AZ [*Location identifier*] [*FAA*] (FAAL)
PRC .... Prescription Rate Carryover [*Health insurance*] (GHCT)
PRC .... Pressure Recorder Controller [*Nuclear energy*] (NRCH)
PRC .... Pressure Response Cell [*For chemical kinetic studies*]
PRC .... Pressure Riser-Less Casting
PRC .... Prevention, Removal and Control [*Fuels and lubricants*]
PRC .... Prevention Research Center [*Pacific Institute for Research and Evaluation*] [*Research center*] (RCD)
PRC .... Price
PRC .... Price Redetermination Contract (SAA)
PRC .... Price Regulation Committee (ODA)
PRC .... Primary Rate Center [*Communications term*] (DCT)
PRC .... Primary Reference Clock (SAUS)
PRC .... Primary Return Code [*Computer science*] (ELAL)
PRC .... Primary Routing Center [*Telecommunications*] (TEL)
PRC .... Primate Research Center
PRC .... Prime Responder Cell (DB)
PRC .... Prince, WV [*Amtrak rail station code*]
PRC .... Principal Reducing Credit
PRC .... Printer Control
PRC .... Priory Cell
Pr C .... Prize Cases [*A publication*] (DLA)
PRC .... Problem Resolution Coordinator [*IRS*]
PRC .... Procaterol [*Pharmacology*]
PRC .... Procedure Review Committee (AAG)
PRC .... Process Communication (SAUS)
PRC .... Procession Register Clock
PRC .... Proconsul
PRC .... Procurement Request Code [*Military*] (AFIT)
PRC .... Production Control (IAA)
PRC .... Production Readjustments Committee [*WPB*]
PRC .... Product Regional Center [*Department of Supply and Service*] [*Canada*] (IMH)
PRC .... Products Research & Chemical Corp. (SAUS)
PRC .... Professional Reference Center [*Los Angeles County Office of Education*] [*Downey, CA*] [*Library network*]
PRC .... Professional Relations Council [*American Chemical Society*]
PRC .... Programmable Radar Controller (SAUS)
PRC .... Programmed Rate Control (NITA)
PRC .... Programmed Route Control [*Computer science*] (VLIE)
PRC .... Program Range Change (VLIE)
PRC .... Program Request Control (SAUS)
PRC .... Program Required Credentials [*Computer science*] (ELAL)
PRC .... Program Resources Catalog
PRC .... Program Rest Code (MCD)
PRC .... Program Review Committee (AFM)
PRC .... Projects Review Committee (SAUS)
PRC .... Prologic Management Systems, Inc. [*AMEX symbol*] (SAG)
PRC .... Promotion Research Committee
PRC .... Propeller Change (MCD)
PRC .... Propulsion Research Corporation
PRC .... Providence College, Phillips Memorial Library, Providence, RI [*OCLC symbol*] (OCLC)
PRC .... Proximal Row Carpectomy [*Medicine*] (MELL)
PRC .... Pseudo-Range Correction
PRC .... Public Radio Conference (SAUS)
PRC .... Public Relations Club (AD)
PRC .... Pyrotechnic Rocket Container
PRC .... Revolutionary Socialist Party [*Peru*] [*Political party*] (PD)
Pr Ca .... Great War Prize Cases, by Evans [*England*] [*A publication*] (DLA)
Pr Ca .... Great War Prize Cases, by Evans (journ.) (SAUS)
PRCA .... Packaging Research [*NASDAQ symbol*] (TTSB)
PRCA .... Packaging Research Corp. [*NASDAQ symbol*] (SAG)
PRCA .... Palomino Rabbit Co-Breeders Association (EA)
PRCA .... Parks, Recreation and Cultural Affairs Administration [*New York City*]
PRCA .... People's Republic of China Army (MCD)
PRCA .... Pierce Arrow [*NCIC car make code*]
PRCA .... Pitch and Roll Channel Assembly (MCD)
PRCA .... Presbyterian Reformed Church of Australia
PRCA .... President of the Royal Cambrian Academy (SAUS)
PRCA .... President of the Royal Canadian Academy
PRCA .... President of the Royal Canadian Academy of Arts (NGC)
PRCA .... Problem Reporting and Corrective Action (NASA)
PRCA .... Professional Rodeo Cowboys Association (EA)

PRCA........ Public Relations Consultants Association (EAIO)
PRCA........ Puerto Rico Communications Authority
PRCA........ Pure Red Cell Agenesis [*Hematology*] (MAE)
PRCA........ Pure Red Cell Aplasia [*Hematology*]
PR Cable... Pure Rubber Cable (SAUS)
PrCaC....... Colegio Universitario de Cayey, Cayey, PR [*Library symbol*] [*Library of Congress*] (LCLS)
PRCAF....... Peoples Republic of China Air Force (SAUS)
PRCAFL..... Publications of the Research Center in Anthropology, Folklore and Linguistics (SAUS)
PRCAFL..... Publications. Research Center in Anthropology, Folklore and Linguistics (SAUS)
PRC & NW... Pierre, Rapid City & Northwestern Railroad [*Nickname: Plenty Rough Country and No Women*]
PR Card..... Parts Requisition Card (SAUS)
PRCAW...... Packaging Research Wrrt [*NASDAQ symbol*] (TTSB)
PRCB........ Program Requirement Control Board (SAUS)
PRCB........ Program Requirements Change Board [*NASA*] (NASA)
PRCB........ Program Requirements Control Board [*NASA*]
PRCB........ Program Review Change Board
PRCB........ Program Review Control Board [*NASA*] (NASA)
PRCB........ Puerto Rico Convention Bureau (EARSL)
PRCBD...... Program Requirements Control Board Directive [*NASA*] (NASA)
PRCBD...... Program Review Control Board Directive [*NASA*] (NASA)
PRCBXSS... Priority Coinbox with Special Services (SAUS)
PRCC........ Partial Rank Correlation Coefficient [*Nuclear energy*] (NUCP)
PRCC........ Parts Request Card Code (SAUS)
PRCC........ Peoria Record Club [*Record label*]
PRCC........ Pollution Research and Control Corp. [*NASDAQ symbol*] (SAG)
PRCC........ Pollution Resh & Ctl CA [*NASDAQ symbol*] (TTSB)
PRCC........ Procurement Research Coordinating Counsel (AAGC)
PRCC........ Puerto Rico Cancer Center [*University of Puerto Rico*] [*Research center*] (RCD)
PRCC........ Puerto Rico Chamber of Commerce (EARSL)
PRC-CAS.... Polar Research Committee-Chinese Academy of Sciences (SAUS)
PRCCh....... Principal Roman Catholic Chaplain [*Navy*] [*British*]
PRCCM...... Partial Reference Count Contour Machine (SAUS)
PrcCm....... Price Communications Corp. [*Associated Press*] (SAG)
PRCCS....... Parts Return Control Card System (SAUS)
PRCCT....... Printed Circuit [*Computer science*] (IAA)
prcd.......... Priced (AD)
PRCD........ Proceed (VLIE)
PRCEC....... Pearce Sys Intl [*NASDAQ symbol*] (TTSB)
PR Cem..... Puerto Rican Cement Co., Inc. [*Associated Press*] (SAG)
PRCESSN... Processing
PRCF........ Petroleum Resources Communications Foundation [*Canada*]
PRCF........ Plutonium Recycle Critical Facility [*Nuclear energy*]
PRCGT....... Confederacion Generale Trabajadores de Puerto Rico
Pr Ch........ Parish Church (AD)
PR Ch....... Practical Register in Chancery [*England*] [*A publication*] (DLA)
Pr Ch........ Precedents in Chancery, Edited by Finch [*1689-1722*] [*England*] [*A publication*] (DLA)
PRCH........ Precharge
PRCH........ Proprietary Chapel [*Church of England*]
PRCHNG.... Purchasing
prchst....... Parachutist (AD)
prcht......... Parachute (AD)
PRCHT....... Parachute (AFM)
Prcht Bad... Parachutist Badge [*Military decoration*]
PRCI......... Parti Republicain de la Cote d'Ivoire [*Republicaqn Party of the Ivory Coast*] [*Political party*] (EY)
PRCI......... Policy Review Committee Intelligence [*Military*]
PRCI......... Productability Reliability Cost Improvement (SAUS)
PRCI......... Production Reliability Cost Improvement (DWSG)
PRCIX....... Price T. Rowe: New Income [*Mutual fund ticker symbol*] (SG)
Pr CKB...... Practice Cases, in the King's Bench [*England*] [*A publication*] (DLA)
PRCL........ Confederacion Laborista de Puerto Rico
Pr Cl......... Propyl Chlorite (SAUS)
PRCL........ Protocol Common Logic (SAUS)
PRCM....... Master Chief Aircrew Survival Equipmentman [*Formerly, Master Chief Parachute R igger*] [*Navy rating*]
PRCM....... Paleoclimate Reconstructions for Climate Modeling (SAUS)
PRCM....... Passive Radiation Countermeasure [*Military*]
PRCM....... Pericom Semiconductor Corp. [*NASDAQ symbol*] (SAG)
PRCM....... Procom Technology Inc. [*NASDAQ symbol*] (SAG)
PRCM....... Protocom Devices, Inc. (SAUS)
PRCMNT.... Procurement
PRCMO...... Paleoclimate Reconstructions of Climate Modeling Observatory (SAUS)
PRCMT...... Procurement (MSA)
PRCN........ Peoples Republic of China Navy (SAUS)
PRCN........ Percon, Inc. [*NASDAQ symbol*] (SAG)
PRCN........ Porcine Respiratory Coronavirus (DB)
PRCN........ Precision (MSA)
PR-CNTL... Product Control Register
PRCNV...... Porcine Respiratory Coronavirus [*Virology*] (QSUL)
PRCO........ Pacific Requisition Control Office [*Navy*]
Pr Co........ Prerogative Court (DLA)
PR Code.... Print Restore Code (SAUS)
PR/COM.... Vessel Delivered in Partially-Completed Status [*Navy*] (DNAB)
Pr Compt... Pour Compte (SAUS)
Pr Cont...... Pratt's Contraband-of-War Cases [*1861*] [*A publication*] (DLA)
PrcOptCp.... Precision Optics Corp. [*Associated Press*] (SAG)
PRCP........ Perceptron, Inc. [*NASDAQ symbol*] (SAG)
PRCP........ Percutaneous Renal Cyst Puncture [*Medicine*] (MELL)
PRCP........ Personnel Readiness Capability Program [*Navy*] (DNAB)
PRCP........ Power Remote Control Panel (AAG)
PRCP........ Practical Register in the Common Pleas [*A publication*] (DLA)
PRCP........ President of the Royal College of Physicians [*British*]
PRCP........ President of the Royal College of Preceptors [*British*] (ROG)
PRCP........ Programmed Communication Electronic Support Program (SAUS)
PRCP........ Puerto Rican Communist Party [*Political party*]
PRC Plating... Periodic Reverse Current Plating (SAUS)
PRCPM...... Partial Response Continuous-Phase-Modulation (SAUS)
PRCPM...... Print Complement (VLIE)
PRCPTN..... Precipitin [*Test*] [*Immunology*]
PRCR........ Professional Health Care of America, Inc. (SAUS)
PRCR........ Protective Cover (AAG)
PrcREI....... Price REIT, Inc. [*Associated Press*] (SAG)
PRCS........ Passive and Remote Crosswind Sensor (MCD)
PRCS........ People's Republic of China Satellite
PRCS........ Permit Required Confined Space (LDOE)
PRCS........ Personal Radio Communications System [*General Electric Co.*]
PRCS........ Personal Report of Confidence as a Speaker [*Psychology*]
PRCS........ Polish Red Cross Society
PRCS........ President of the Royal College of Surgeons [*British*]
PRCS........ Prevention and Removal of Corrosion and Scale [*Engineering*]
PRCS........ Primary Reaction Control System (SAUS)
prcs.......... Process (AD)
PRCS........ Process (AFM)
PRCS........ Processing (IAA)
PRCS........ Project Revision Control System (SAUS)
P/RCS....... Propulsion and Reaction Control Subsystem [*NASA*] (KSC)
PRCS........ Psychological Response Classification System
PRCS........ Purchase Requisition Change Supplement
PRCS........ Senior Chief Aircrew Survival Equipmentman [*Formerly, Senior Chief Parachute R igger*] [*Navy rating*]
PRCSG...... Pediatric Rheumatology Collaborative Study Group [*Medicine*] (EDAA)
PRCSG...... Processing (MSA)
PRCSR...... Processor
PRCS SPEC... Process Specification (SAUS)
PRCST....... Precast (AAG)
prcst......... Precast (AD)
PRCT........ Pool Repair Cycle Time (MCD)
PRCT........ Procept, Inc. [*NASDAQ symbol*] (SAG)
PRCTN...... Precaution [*ICAO designator*] (FAAC)
PRCU........ Power Regulating and Control Unit (CET)
prcu.......... Power Regulation and Control Unit (AD)
PRCU........ Pride Cos. LP [*OTCBB symbol*]
PRCUA...... Polish Roman Catholic Union of America (EA)
PRCUI....... Congreso Uniones Industriales de Puerto Rico
PRCV........ Processor Recovery (SAUS)
PRCVS...... Pre-Canvass (SAUS)
PRCY........ ProCyte Corp. [*NASDAQ symbol*] (NQ)
PRCZ........ Permac Coal [*Federal Railroad Administration identification code*]
PRD.......... Democratic Renewal Party (Angola) [*Political party*] (PSAP)
prd........... Partial Reaction of Degeneration (AD)
PRD.......... Partial Reaction of Degeneration
PRD.......... Parti Democratique Dahomeen [*Dahomey Democratic Party*] [*Political party*]
PRD.......... Partido de la Revolucion Democratica [*Mexico*] [*Political party*] (EY)
PRD.......... Partido de Renovacion Democratica [*Democratic Renewal Party*] [*Costa Rica*] [*Political party*] (PPW)
PRD.......... Partido Reformista Democratico [*Democratic Reformist Party*] [*Spain*] [*Political party*] (PPW)
PRD.......... Partido Revolucionario Democratico [*Democratic Revolutionary Party*] [*Panama*] [*Political party*] (PPW)
PRD.......... Partido Revolucionario Dominicano [*Dominican Revolutionary Party*] [*Dominican Republic*] [*Political party*] (PPW)
PRD.......... Parti du Renouveau Democratique [*Benin*] [*Political party*] (EY)
PRD.......... Parti Radical-Democratique Suisse [*Radical Democratic Party of Switzerland*] [*Political party*] (PPE)
PRD.......... Part Reference Designator
PRD.......... Party for Renovation and Development (SAUS)
PRD.......... Party for Reviving Democracy (SAUS)
PRD.......... Party of Democratic Renewal (Djibouti) [*Political party*] (PSAP)
PRD.......... Party of the Democratic Revolution [*Mexico*] [*Political party*]
PRD.......... Payload Retention Device (SAUS)
PRD.......... Payroll Deduction
PRD.......... Pearl River Delta [*China*] [*Geography*]
PRD.......... Perceptions of Racial Discrimination [*Medicine*] (EDAA)
PRD.......... Performance-Related Pay [*Business term*] (ECON)
PRD.......... Period
PRD.......... Periodontics and Restorative Dentistry
PRD.......... Personal Radiation Dosimeter (KSC)
PRD.......... Personnel Readiness Date [*Army*] (AABC)
PRD.......... Personnel Records Division [*Army*] (AABC)
PRD.......... Personnel Requirements Data (AAG)
PRD.......... Personnel Research Division [*Navy*] (MCD)
PRD.......... Personnel Resources Data
PRD.......... Pesticides Regulation Division (AD)
PRD.......... Petersburg Ranger District [*Alaska*] [*USDA Forest Service*] (ALAC)
PRD.......... Physician Relations Department (DMAA)
PRD.......... Piezoelectric Resonating Device
PRD.......... Planned Residential Development
PRD.......... Polaroid Corp. [*NYSE symbol*] (SPSG)
PRD.......... Political Resource Directory [*A publication*]

PRD......... Polytechnic Research & Development Co. (AAG)
PRD......... Positive Regulatory Domain [*Genetics*]
PRD......... Postal Regulating Detachment [*Military*]
PRD......... Postradiation Dysplasia [*Medicine*]
PRD......... Potentially Reportable Deficiency [*Nuclear energy*] (NRCH)
PRD......... Power Range Detector (IEEE)
PRD......... Power Requirement Data
PRD......... Precompetitive Research and Development
PRD......... Predicted Range of the Day [*Military*] (NVT)
PRD......... Predictor [*NCIC car model code*]
PRD......... Preretro Update Display
PRD......... Presidential Review Directive (USDC)
PRD......... Pressing Direction
PRD......... Previous Device Register (SAUS)
PRD......... Pride
PRD......... Primary Radar Data (SAUS)
PRD......... Prime RADAR Digitizer (IAA)
PRD......... Princeton Reference Design (MCD)
PRD......... Printer Driver
prd......... Printer Dump (AD)
PRD......... Process Requirements Drawing (MCD)
PRD......... Procurement Regulation Directive [*NASA*] (NASA)
PRD......... Procurement Requirements Document [*NASA*] (NASA)
PRD......... Production Responsibilities Document (MCD)
PRD......... Productive (SAUS)
PRD......... Productivity Research Division [*Office of Personnel Management*] (GRD)
PRD......... Product Requirements Document (SAUS)
PRD......... Product Research and Development [*Advertising*] (DOAD)
PRD......... Proficiency Rating Designator [*Military*]
PRD......... Program [*or Project*] Requirement Data [*NASA*] (KSC)
PRD......... Program Requirement Document (SAUS)
PRD......... Program Requirements Document
PRD......... Projected Rotation Date (NG)
PRD......... Project Requirement Document (SAUS)
PRD......... Proline-Rich Domain [*Genetics*]
prd......... Pro-Rata Distribution (AD)
PRD......... Pro Rate Distribution [*Clause*] [*Insurance*]
PRD......... Proton Recoil Detector (SAUS)
PRD......... Puerto Rico, Decisiones [*A publication*] (DLA)
PRD......... Pulse Rate Discriminator (SAUS)
PRD......... Purdue Aeronautics Corporation
PRD......... Push Road (SAUS)
PRD......... Push Rod [*Mechanical engineering*]
PRDA........ Pacific Riding for the Disabled Association [*Canada*] (EAIO)
PRDA........ Polish Racing Drivers of America [*Motorsports*]
PRDA........ Pony Riding for the Disabled Association [*Australia*]
PRDA........ Program Research and Development Agreement (SAUS)
PRDA........ Program Research and Development Announcement [*Energy Research and Development Administration*]
PRDA........ Propfan Research and Development Announcement (SAUS)
PRDC........ Peat Research and Development Centre (FOTI)
PRDC........ Personnel Research and Development Center [*Office of Personnel Management*] (GRD)
PRDC........ Pig Research and Development Corp. [*Australia*]
PRDC........ Polar Research and Development Center [*Army*]
PRDC........ Power Reactor Development Corp. (SAUS)
PRDCTVTY... Productivity
PRDDO...... Partial Retention of Diatomic Differential Overlap [*Physics*]
PRDE........ Pride International [*NASDAQ symbol*] [*Formerly, Pride Petroleum*] (SG)
PRDE........ Pride Petroleum Services, Inc. [*NASDAQ symbol*] (CTT)
PRDE........ Pride Petroleum Svcs [*NASDAQ symbol*] (TTSB)
PrdEn........ Producers Entertainment Group Ltd. [*Associated Press*] (SAG)
PrdEnt....... Producers Entertainment Group Ltd. [*Associated Press*] (SAG)
PrdePt....... Pride Petroleum Services, Inc. [*Associated Press*] (SAG)
PRDF........ Page Reference Distribution Function [*Computer science*] (IAA)
PRDF........ Political Rights Defense Fund [*Defunct*] (EA)
PRDG........ Princess Royal's Dragoon Guards [*Military unit*] [*British*] (ROG)
PRDIAG..... Primary Diagnosis [*Medicine*]
PRDIALTO... Pre Dial Time-Out (SAUS)
PRDL........ Personnel Research and Development Laboratory [*Navy*] (MCD)
prdl......... Predella (VRA)
PRDM....... Paradigm Technology [*NASDAQ symbol*] (TTSB)
PRDM....... Paradigm Technology, Inc. [*NASDAQ symbol*] (SAG)
PRDM....... Parti pour le Rassemblement Democratique des Mahorais [*Mayotte*] [*Political party*] (EY)
PRDM....... Prandium [*OTCBB symbol*]
PRDMD..... Private Directory Management Domain (SAUS)
PRDN........ Partido de Reconciliacion Democratica Nacional [*Party of National Democratic Reconciliation*] [*Guatemala*] [*Political party*]
PRDN........ Prosource Distribution Services [*Common carrier symbol*]
PRDNTST... Periodonist
PRDP........ Power Reactor Demonstration Program
PRDPC...... Pooled Random Donor Platelet Concentrates [*Medicine*] (MELL)
PRDPEC..... Power Reactor Development Programme Evaluation Committee [*Canada*] (HGAA)
PRDR........ Preproduction Reliability Design Review [*Navy*] (CAAL)
PRDR........ Procedure (SAUS)
PRDR........ Production Request Design Review
PRDS........ Packet Radio Demonstrator System (SAUS)
PRDS........ Paradise
PRDS........ Post Boost Detection System (ACAE)
PRDS........ Processed RADAR Display System (PDAA)
PRDS........ Social and Democratic Republican Party (Mauritania) [*Political party*] (PSAP)
PRDT........ Production Reliability Demonstration Test (SAUS)
PRDV........ Peak Reading Digital Voltmeter
prdx......... paradox (SAUS)
PRDX........ Prediction Program [*NASA*]
PRE......... Bureau for Private Enterprise
PRE......... Federation Europeenne des Fabricants de Produits Refractaires [*Zurich, Switzerland*] (EAIO)
PRE......... Partial Reflection Experiment (SAUS)
PRE......... Partial Reinforcement Effect (DIPS)
PRE......... Partido Republicano Evolucionista [*Republican Evolutionist Party*] [*Portugal*] [*Political party*] (PPE)
PRE......... Partido Roldosista Ecuatoriano [*Ecuador*] [*Political party*] (EY)
PRE......... PartnerRe Ltd. [*NYSE symbol*]
PRE......... Partner-Resisted Exercise [*Army*] (INF)
PRE......... Performance Requirements Envelope (ACAE)
PRE......... Personal Rescue Enclosure (NASA)
PRE......... Personnel Restraint Equipment (SAA)
PRE......... Petroleum Refining Engineer
PRE......... Photoreactivating
PRE......... Physical Reconditioning Exercises [*Orthopedics*] (DAVI)
PRE......... Pineridge Capital [*Vancouver Stock Exchange symbol*]
PRE......... Planetary Rotation Engine (IAA)
PRE......... Portable RADAR Equipment
pre......... Pre-Choice [*Advertising*] (WDMC)
PRE......... Precinct
PRE......... Precis [*NCIC car model code*]
PRE......... Precision Airlines (SAUS)
PRE......... Precision Valley Aviation [*ICAO designator*] (FAAC)
PRE......... Predecessor (KSC)
pre......... Prefatory (WDMC)
PRE......... Prefect
pre......... Preferred (WDMC)
pre......... Prefix (WDMC)
PRE......... Prefix
PRE......... Preformatted (SAUS)
Pre......... Preliminary (AMHC)
PRE......... Preliminary
PRE......... Preliminary Amplifier (IAA)
PRE......... Prelude [*NCIC car model code*]
PRE......... Premier [*NCIC car model code*]
PRE......... Premiere (automobile) [*NCIC car model code*]
PRE......... Premier Industrial Corp. [*NYSE symbol*] (SPSG)
pre......... Preoperative [*Surgery*] (DAVI)
PRE......... Prepayment Coin Telephone [*Telecommunications*] (TEL)
PRE......... Pre-Retirement Education (AIE)
PRE......... Pre-Runner [*NCIC car model code*]
PRE......... Presbyterian Historical Society, Philadelphia, PA [*OCLC symbol*] (OCLC)
PRE......... Preselection (SAUS)
PRE......... President (automobile) [*NCIC car model code*]
PRE......... President of the Royal Society of Painter-Etchers and Engravers [*British*]
pre......... Pretest [*Advertising*] (WDMC)
PRE......... Pretoria [*South Africa*] [*Seismograph station code, US Geological Survey*] (SEIS)
PRE......... Prime contractors Region (SAUS)
PRE......... Problem Reproducer Equipment (SAA)
PRE......... Processing Refabrication Experiment [*Nuclear energy*] (NRCH)
PRE......... Product-Remainder Extension (SAUS)
PRE......... Progesterone [*A hormone*]
PRE......... Progesterone Response Element [*Endocrinology*]
PRE......... Program Reliability Engineer (ACAE)
PRE......... Progressive Resistance (or Resistive) Exercise (SAUS)
PRE......... Progressive Resistive Exercise [*Medicine*]
PRE......... Proportional Reduction of Error
PRE......... Protective Reservation Equipment (SAUS)
PRE......... Protein Relaxation Enhancement (OA)
PRE......... Protein Retention Efficiency [*Medicine*] (WDAA)
PRE......... Proton Relaxation Enhancement [*Physics*]
PRE......... Psychophysiological Reeducation (SAUS)
PRE......... Public Relations Exchange [*Later, PRXI*] (EA)
PRE......... Pulse Radiation Effect
PRE......... Realencykopaedie fuer Protestantische Theologie und Kirche [*A publication*] (ODCC)
PRE......... Spanish Catalonian Battalion (PD)
PREA........ Pennsylvania Rural Electric Association (EARSL)
PREA........ Pension Real Estate Association (EA)
P/REA....... Probationary Radio Electrical Artificer [*British military*] (DMA)
PREAG...... Parks Residents Environmental Action Group [*Australia*]
PREAG...... Photographic Reconnaissance Equipment Advisory Group [*Military*]
PREAMP.... Preamplifier (AAG)
preamp..... Preamplifier (DCDG)
PREAMP.... Preliminary Amplifier (SAUS)
PREAP...... Prison Research Education Action Project (EA)
PRE-ARM... People's Rights Enforced Against Riots and Murder [*Vigilante group in New Jersey*]
preb......... Prebend [*Construction term*] (MIST)
PREB........ Prebendary
PREB........ Prebuilt Manufacturing [*NCIC trailer make code*]
PREB........ Pupil Record of Educational Behavior [*Aptitude test*]
Preb Dig.... Preble. Digest, Patent Cases [*A publication*] (DLA)
Preb Pat Cas... Preble. Digest, Patent Cases [*A publication*] (DLA)
PREBS....... Pennsylvania Real Estate Brokers and Salesmens (SAUS)

PREC .... Palestine Research and Educational Center (EA)
p rec......... Per Rectum [*Through the rectum*] [*Pharmacology*] (DAVI)
PREC .... Potomac River Enforcement Conference (SAUS)
PREC .... Precambrian [*Period, era, or system*] [*Geology*]
PREC .... Precedence (AABC)
prec.......... Preceding (MIST)
PREC .... Preceding
PREC .... Precentor (ROG)
PREC .... Precious (ROG)
prec.......... Precious (VRA)
PREC .... Precision (AABC)
PREC .... Precision Deburring & Fabricating [*NCIC trailer make code*]
Prec .... Precite [*Supra, Cited Before*] [*French*] (ILCA)
PREC .... Premier Cartage [*Common carrier symbol*]
PREC .... Propulsion Research Environmental Chamber
PREC .... Public Revenue Education Council (EA)
PrecCst...... Precision Castparts Corp. [*Associated Press*] (SAG)
PRECD .... Precede (FAAC)
PrecDr....... Precision Drilling Corp. [*Associated Press*] (SAG)
PRECEDE... Predisposing, Reinforcing, and Enabling Causes in Educational Diagnosis and Evaluation [*Occupational therapy*]
Preceiver... Preamplifier/Receiver (SAUS)
Pre Ch....... Precedents in Chancery, Edited by Finch [*A publication*] (DLA)
Prec in Ch... Precedents in Chancery, Edited by Finch [*24 English Reprint*] [*1689-1722*] [*A publication*] (DLA)
Prec in Ch (Eng)... Precedents in Chancery, Edited by Finch [*24 English Reprint*] [*A publication*] (DLA)
precip .... Precipitate [*Laboratory science*] (DAVI)
PRECIP...... Precipitated (SAUS)
PRECIP...... Precipitation
Precip .... Precipitous (AMHC)
PRECIP...... Processing of Emissions by Clouds and Precipitation (SAUS)
PRECIS...... Pre-Coordinate Indexing System
PRECIS...... Preserved Context Index System [*British Library*] [*London, England*] [*Information service or system*]
Precis Eng... Precision Engineering [*A publication*] (CABS)
PRECO ...... Precision Equipment Co. (SAUS)
PRECO ...... Preparatory Commission of the United Nations Organization
PRECOM .... Precommissioning [*Military*]
PRECOM .... Preliminary Communications Search [*Military*] (NVT)
PRECOMDET... Precommissioning Detail [*Navy*] (NVT)
PRECOMG... Precommissioning [*Military*] (NVT)
PRECOMM... Pre-Commissioning (SAUS)
PRECOMM... Preliminary Communications [*Military*] (NVT)
PRECOMMDET... Precommissioning Detail [*Navy*]
PRECOMMSCOL... Precommissioning School [*Navy*]
precomp .... Precomputed Loan
PRECOMP... Prediction of Contingency Maintenance and Parts Requirements (MCD)
PRECOMUNIT... Precommissioning Unit [*Navy*] (DNAB)
precon....... Previous Conviction (WDAA)
PRECOX..... Precision Oxide (SAUS)
PRECP....... Processing of Emissions by Clouds and Precipitation (SAUS)
PRECP....... Program on Nonlinearity of Acid Precipitation Process (SAUS)
PrecRes..... Precision Response Corp. [*Associated Press*] (SAG)
PRECSA ..... Precision Aerotech, Inc. (SAUS)
PRECSN..... Precision
PrecStd ..... Precision Standard, Inc. [*Associated Press*] (SAG)
PrecSy ...... Precision Systems, Inc. [*Associated Press*] (SAG)
Pre-D .... Predetection (SAUS)
pred .... Predicate (SHCU)
PRED .... Predictability (SAUS)
PRED- .... Predictability, Negative (SAUS)
PRED+....... Predictability, Positive (SAUS)
pred .... Predicted (STED)
PRED .... Predicted
PRED .... Prediction (AFM)
Pred .... Prednisolone (SAUS)
PRED .... Prednisone (DMAA)
Pred .... Prednisone [*Also, P, PDN, Pr, Pro*] [*Endocrinology*] [*Antineoplastic drug*]
$PreD_3$........ Previtamin D3 [*A precursor to vitamin D3*] (DAVI)
PREDA ...... Puerto Rico Economic Development Administration (NADA)
PREDE....... Regional Education Development Programme [*United Nations*] (FOTI)
PREDECE ... Predecease (ROG)
Pre-Design... Preliminary Design (SAUS)
PREDICT ... Pollution Reduction by Information and Control Technology
PREDICT ... Prediction of Radiation Effects by Digital Computer Techniques
PREDICT ... Process Reliability, Evaluation and Determination of Integrated Circuit Techniques (SAUS)
PREDNIS ... Prednisolone (SAUS)
PREDNIS ACE... Prednisolone Acetate (SAUS)
Pr Edw I .... Prince Edward Island (DLA)
Pr Edw I .... Prince Edward Island Reports [*Canada*] [*A publication*] (DLA)
Pr Edw Isl... Prince Edward Island (DLA)
Pr Edw Isl... Prince Edward Island Reports [*Canada*] [*A publication*] (DLA)
PREE .... Partial Reinforcement Extinction Effect (STED)
PRE-EM ..... Preeminence (SAUS)
PRE-EM ..... Preeminent (SAUS)
PRE-EM ..... Preemptible (SAUS)
PRE-EM ..... Preemption (SAUS)
PREEMIE ... Premature Baby [*Medical slang*] (WDAA)
Preemie-L... Parents of Premature Babies [*Association*] (EA)
PRE-EMPTN... Pre-Emption (ROG)
PreES........ Pre-Enumeration Survey (SAUS)
PREF .... PFT Roberson [*Common carrier symbol*]
pref .... Preface (WDAA)
PREF .... Preface
pref .... prefatory (SAUS)
PREF .... Prefecture
PREF .... Prefer (SAUS)
PREF .... Preference [*or Preferred*] (AFM)
Pref .... Preference (SG)
pref .... Preference (SHCU)
PREF .... Preferred (KSC)
PREF .... Prefix (AAG)
pref .... Prefix [*Linguistics*] (IEL)
PREF .... Prefocused
PREF .... Propulsion Research Environmental Facility
Pref .... Reformist Party (Dominican Rep.) [*Political party*] (PSAP)
PREFAB ..... Prefabricated (KSC)
prefab .... Prefabricated (MIST)
PREFACE ... Pre-Freshman and Cooperative Education for Minorities in Engineering (SAUS)
PRE FA FIRE ORDER... Prepare FA Fire Order (SAUS)
PREF-AP ... Prefect Apostolic (SAUS)
PREF-AP ... Prefect-Apostolic [*Roman Catholic*]
PREFAT...... Prepare Final Acceptance Trials [*Navy*] (NVT)
PREFCE ..... Preface (ROG)
prefd......... Preferred (STED)
PREFD....... Preferred (WDAA)
Prefect ...... Prefecture (DIAR)
PREFLT...... Preflight (KSC)
PREFLTSCOL... Preflight School [*Military*]
PREFMD .... Preformed
PREFRAM... Prepare Fleet Rehabilitation and Modernization Overhaul [*Navy*] (NVT)
PREFRAMO... Prepare Fleet Rehabilitation and Modernization Overhaul (SAUS)
preft .... Prefecture
PREFUN..... Preparatory Function (SAUS)
Preg .... Pregestimil [*Medicine*] (EDAA)
Preg .... Pregnancy (AMHC)
PREG .... Pregnancy [*or Pregnant*]
PREG .... Pregnelone (STED)
PREG .... Pregnenolone [*Endocrinology*]
pregang ..... Preganglionic [*Anatomy*]
PREGN ...... Pregnancy [*or Pregnant*] (AAMN)
prehis .... Prehistory [*or Prehistoric*] (BARN)
PREHIST ... Prehistory [*or Prehistoric*] (WDAA)
PREI .... Pre-Built Structures [*NCIC trailer make code*]
PREIA .... Professional Radio and Electronics Institute of Australia
PREINACT... Prepare Inactivation [*Navy*] (NVT)
PREINSURV... Prepare for Board of Inspection and Survey [*Navy*] (NVT)
PREINSURV... President of Board for Inspection and Survey
PreissM ..... Preiss [*Byron*] Multimedia Co., Inc. [*Associated Press*] (SAG)
PREJ.......... Prejudice (AABC)
PREL .... Pacific Resources for Education and Learning (RCD)
PREL .... Pain Relief Level [*Medicine*]
PREL .... Power-Refrigeration-Electric (SAUS)
PREL .... Preliminary
PREL .... Preliminary Evaluation [*Orbit identification*]
PREL .... Prelude [*Music*] (ROG)
PREL .... Priority Reconnaissance Exploitation List (CINC)
PREL .... Programmable Rotary Encoded Logic [*Computer science*] (MHDB)
PRELA....... Prensa Latina, Angencia Informativa Latinoamericana [*Press agency*] [*Cuba*]
PRELIM ..... Preliminary (AFM)
Prelim....... Preliminary (AL)
prelim....... Preliminary (STED)
prelim diag... Preliminary Diagnosis [*Medicine*] (DAVI)
prelims...... Preliminary Pages [*Frontmatter*] [*Publishing*]
PRELIMY ... Preliminary (ROG)
prelm........ Preliminary (VRA)
PRELOG..... People's Revolutionary League of Ghana [*Political party*] (PPW)
PRELOGE... Preliminary Logistics Evolution (SAUS)
PRELORT... Precision Long-Range Tracking (SAUS)
PRELORT... Precision Long-Range Tracking RADAR
PRELORT Radar... Precision Long-Range Tracking Radar (SAUS)
PRELUDE... Pre-Optimization Linearization of Undulation and Detection of Errors (PDAA)
PREM........ Preliminary Reference Earth Model [*Geology*]
PREM........ Premature [*Medicine*]
prem......... Prematurity (STED)
PREM........ Premier (ROG)
prem......... Premiere (WDMC)
PREM........ Premier Financial Services, Inc. [*Freeport, IL*] [*NASDAQ symbol*] (NQ)
PREM........ Premier Financial Svcs [*NASDAQ symbol*] (TTSB)
PREM........ Premier (motorcycle) [*NCIC motorcycle make code*]
PREM........ Premier Trailer [*NCIC trailer make code*]
Prem .... Premises (TBD)
PREM........ Premium (AFM)
Prem .... Premium (EBF)
prem......... Premium (WDMC)
PREM........ Probe-Microphone Real Ear Measurement [*Audiology*]
PREMA...... Pulp Refining Equipment Manufacturers Association (EA)

PremBksh... Premier Bankshares [*Associated Press*] (SAG)
Premdr...... Premdor, Inc. [*Associated Press*] (SAG)
Premed ..... Premedical (SAUS)
PREMED .... Premedical Student (WDAA)
PRE-MED ... Previous to Appearance in MEDLINE [*Latham, NY*] [*Bibliographic database*]
PREMEDU... Preventive Medicine Unit
Premerk..... Premark International, Inc. [*Associated Press*] (SAG)
PREMES .... Premises (ROG)
PremFin..... Premier Financial Bancorp, Inc. [*Associated Press*] (SAG)
PremFn ..... Premier Financial Services [*Associated Press*] (SAG)
premie ...... Premature [*Infant*] (DAVI)
Premis ...... Premis Corp. [*Associated Press*] (SAG)
PREMIS ..... Premises Information System (SAUS)
PremLiab ... Premises Liability (SAUS)
PREMO...... Presentation Environment for Multimedia Objects (RALS)
PREMOD .... Premodeling Data Output [*Environmental Protection Agency*]
PREMOD .... Premodulation (NASA)
PREMODE... Preliminary Mid-Ocean Dynamics Experiment [*Marine science*] (MSC)
PREMPT .... Program For Electromagnetic Pulse Testing (SAUS)
Prem Red... Premium Reducing (SAUS)
Prem Res... Premium Reserve (SAUS)
Premrln ..... Premier Industrial Corp. [*Associated Press*] (SAG)
pre-mRNA .. Precursor-Messenger Ribonucleic Acid
PREMS ...... Premises (DSUE)
PREMSS .... Photographic Reconnaissance and Exploitation Management Support System (MCD)
PremT .... Premiere Technologies, Inc. [*Associated Press*] (SAG)
PREN .... European draft standard (SAUS)
PREN .... Price Enterprises [*NASDAQ symbol*] (TTSB)
PREN .... Price Enterprises, Inc. [*NASDAQ symbol*] (SAG)
PREN .... Project Engineering (SAUS)
Pren Act .... Prentice's Proceedings in an Action [*2nd ed.*] [*1880*] [*A publication*] (DLA)
prenat .... Prenatal
PrEng .... Professional Engineer
PrentPr...... Prentiss Properties Trust [*Associated Press*] (SAG)
PREO .... Prevost [*NCIC truck make code*]
preocc....... Preoccupied [*Biology, taxonomy*]
Pre-op....... Before Operation [*Medicine*] (BCRP)
pre op....... Before Surgery [*Therapy term*] (CTAA)
PRE-OP ..... Pre-Operational
PREOP ...... Preoperative [*Medicine*]
PRE-OPS.... Pre-Operational Support [*Military*]
PREOS ...... Performance and Range of Electro-Optical Systems (SAUS)
PREOS ...... Predicted Range for Electrooptical Systems [*Military*] (CAAL)
PREOVHL... Prepare for Overhaul (SAUS)
PREOVHL... Prepare for Shipyard Overhaul [*Navy*] (NVT)
PREP .... Pacific Range Electromagnetic Platform (AAG)
PREP .... Parent Readiness Evaluation of Preschoolers [*Child development test*]
PREP .... Pattern Reversal Evoked Potential
PREP .... Peace Research and Education Project
PREP .... Peacetime Requirements and Procedures [*Strategic Air Command*] (MUGU)
PREP .... Pediatrics Review and Education Program (SAUS)
PREP .... Penaeid Prawns Recruitment Project (SAUS)
PREP .... Personal Radio Equipped Police (SAUS)
PREP .... Personal Responsibility Education Process
PREP .... Persons Responsive to Educational Problems (EA)
PREP .... Plan, Rehearse, Edit, and Psych [*Public speaking preparation technique*]
PREP .... Plasma Rotating Electrode Process [*Metallurgy*]
PREP .... Population, Resources, and Environment Program [*American Association for the Advancement of Science*]
PReP .... Power PC [*Personal Computer*] Reference Platform [*Configuration standard*] (PCM)
PREP .... PowerPC Reference Plattform (SAUS)
PREP .... Predischarge Education Program [*DoD*]
PREP .... Pre-Edit Processor (SAUS)
prep .... Preparation (WDMC)
PREP .... Preparation [*or Preparatory*]
PREP .... Preparation Rehabilitation Education Program (SAUS)
Prep .... Preparations (AL)
Prep .... Preparatory (AL)
prep .... Preparatory (NTIO)
PREP .... Preparatory (SAUS)
PREP .... Prepare (AFM)
prep .... Prepare (WDMC)
prep .... Preposition (WDMC)
PREP .... Preposition
PREP .... Preprocessing (SAUS)
PREP .... Productivity Research and Extension Program [*North Carolina State University*] [*Research center*] (RCD)
PREP .... Programmable Electronics Performance Corp. (SAUS)
PREP .... Programmed Educational Package
PREP .... Programmed Electronics Pattern (PDAA)
PREP .... Pupil Record of Educational Progress [*Education*] (AEBS)
PREP .... Purchasing, Receiving, and Payable System
PREP .... Putting Research into Educational Practice [*Information service of ERIC*]
Prepak ...... People's Revolutionary Party of Kungleipak [*India*] [*Political party*] (PD)
PREPARE... Premarital Personal and Relationship Evaluation
PREPAS ..... Precise Personnel Assignment System [*Marine Corps*] (GFGA)
PREPCOM... Preparatory Commission for the International Seabed Authority and for the International Tribunal for the Law of the Sea (SAUS)
PrepCom.... Preparatory Committee [*United Nations Committee on Environment and Development*]
PREPCOM... Preparatory Consultations Meeting (SAUS)
PREPD ...... Prepared
PREPE....... Prepare (ROG)
PREP FA MVMT REQ... Prepare FA Movement Request (SAUS)
Prep Frt ..... Prepaid Freight (SAUS)
PREPG ...... Preparing
PREPN ...... Preparation
PREPnet .... [*The*] Pennsylvania Research & Economic Partnership Network [*Computer science*] (TNIG)
Prepo........ Praepositus [*Deceased, 1509*] [*Authority cited in pre-1607 legal work*] (DSA)
PREPO ...... Pre Positioning (ACAE)
Prepos ...... Praepositus [*Deceased, 1509*] [*Authority cited in pre-1607 legal work*] (DSA)
PREPOS..... Preposition (AABC)
PREPOSN... Prepared Position (SAUS)
PREPOSTOR... Prepositioned Storage [*Army*] (AABC)
PREPP....... Post-Registration Education and Practice Project (ODA)
PREPP....... Process Experimental Pilot Plant (COE)
PREPPSA ... Prepare Postshakedown Availability [*Navy*] (NVT)
Preppy ...... Preparatory School Alumnus [*Lifestyle classification*]
Prepr Am Cbem Soc Div Fuel Chem... Preprints. American Chemical Society. Division of Fuel Chemistry (SAUS)
Prepr Amer Wood Pres Ass... Preprint. American Wood Preservers Association (SAUS)
PREP/RAMP... Pre-Edit Processor/Report and Message Processor (SAUS)
PREPREG... Pre-Impregnated Glass Fibers [*Fiberglass production*]
PREPRO..... Prepositioning [*Ship*] [*Navy*] (DOMA)
PREPRO..... Preprocessor [*Computer*] [*Coast Guard*]
PREPROD... Pre Production (ACAE)
PREPROD... Preproduction Model [*Military*] (AFIT)
Prepr Pap Annu Conf Australas Corros Assoc... Australasian Corrosion Association. Preprinted Papers of the Annual Conference (journ.) (SAUS)
Prepr Pap Natl Meet Dir Water Air Waste Chem Am Chem Soc... Preprints of Papers Presented at National Meeting. Division of Water, Air and Waste Chemistry. American Chemical Society (SAUS)
PREPS....... Predischarge Remedial Education Program [*For servicemen*]
PREPS....... Program of Research and Evaluation in Public Schools [*Mississippi State University*] [*Research center*] (RCD)
PREPSCOL... Preparatory School
PREPSYS... Preparedness for Operations Status System (SAUS)
PREPTP ..... digit preparation type and application point (SAUS)
Prepub ...... Prepublication (SAUS)
prepub ...... Prepublication
PREQUAL... Prequalified [*NASA*] (KSC)
Prer.......... Prerogative Court (DLA)
PRER .... Putting Research into Educational Research
PRE-RE...... Prerefunded Municipal Note [*Investment term*] (DFIT)
PRERECPAC... Preplanned Reconnaissance Pacific (CINC)
PREREQ..... Prerequisite (WGA)
Prer Hum Serv... Prevention in Human Services (SAUS)
PRERLA..... Pupils Round, Equal, React to Light and Accommodation [*Medicine*] (MAE)
Prerog Ct... Prerogative Court, New Jersey (DLA)
Pre-Rx....... Before Treatment [*Medicine*] (EDAA)
PRES .... Precision Resources, Inc. (SAUS)
PRES .... Premises (ROG)
PRES .... Pre-Release Employment Scheme (WDAA)
PRES .... Presbyterian
pres.......... Prescriptions (SAUS)
PRES .... Presence
PRES .... Present (AAG)
pres.......... Present (NTIO)
Pres .... Presentation (EBF)
PRES .... Preserved
PRES .... Preset (SAUS)
PRE-S .... Preshaving (MSA)
pres.......... President (DD)
PRES .... President (EY)
Pres .... President (ODBW)
PRES .... Presidential Mobile Homes [*NCIC trailer make code*]
PRES .... President of the Royal Entomological Society [*British*]
PRES .... Pressure (FAAC)
PRES .... Preston R. R. [*AAR code*]
PRES .... Preston Trucking Company [*Common carrier symbol*]
PRES .... Presumptive [*Grammar*]
PRES .... Prime Residential, Inc. [*NASDAQ symbol*] (SAG)
PRES .... Program Reporting and Evaluation System (ACAE)
PRES .... Promotion Recommendation Forms (SAUS)
PRES .... Proton Resonance (IAA)
PRES .... Puerto Rico Employment Service (SAUS)
PRES100.... Presidential's Hundred Tab [*Military*]
Pres Abs.... Preston's Abstracts of Title [*2nd ed.*] [*1823-24*] [*A publication*] (DLA)
PRESAC..... Photographic Reconnaissance System Analysis by Computer
PRESAGE ... Program to Realistically Evaluate Strategic Anti-Ballistic-Missile Gaming Effect (SAUS)
PRESAILEDREP... Forecast Sailing Report [*Navy*] (NVT)
PRESAIR ... Pressurized Air Compressor (DNAB)
Presb........ Presbyterian (NTIO)

PRESB....... Presbyterian
PRESB....... Prescribe (AABC)
Presb&Ref R... Presbyterian and Reformed Review (SAUS)
PresBnc..... Prestige Bancorp, Inc. [*Associated Press*] (SAG)
presby....... presbyopic (SAUS)
PRESBY..... Presbyterian
presby....... Presbytery (VRA)
PRESBY..... Presbytery
Presbyt-St Lukes Hosp Med Bull... Presbyterian-St. Lukes Hospital. Medical Bulletin (SAUS)
Presbyt-St Lukes Hosp Res Rep... Presbyterian-St. Lukes Hospital. Research Report (SAUS)
PRESC....... Prescott, AR [*American Association of Railroads railroad junction routing code*]
PresCasn ... President Casinos, Inc. [*Associated Press*] (SAG)
Pres C of E Ch... Presbyterian Church of England Chaplain [*Navy*] [*British*]
PRESCOM... Personnel Command [*Army*] (DOMA)
Pres Conv... Preston on Conveyancing [*5th ed.*] [*1819-29*] [*A publication*] (DLA)
PRESCORE... Program for the Rapid Estimation of Construction Requirements
PRESCR..... Prescription (MSA)
Presd........ Presidio Oil Co. [*Associated Press*] (SAG)
PRESDL..... Presidential (WGA)
PresDuSta... Present Duty Station (SAUS)
presen....... Presentation (VRA)
Preserv...... Preservation (DIAR)
PRESERV... Preservation
Pres Est..... Preston on Estates [*3rd ed.*] [*1829*] [*A publication*] (DLA)
PRESET ..... Preset Spin Echo Technique
Pres Fal..... Falconer's Decisions, Scotch Court of Session [*1744-51*] [*A publication*] (DLA)
Pres Fal..... Gilmour & Falconer Reports, Court of Session (SAUS)
Pres Fal..... Gilmour and Falconer's Reports, Scotch Court of Session [*A publication*] (DLA)
Pres Falc... President Falconer's Scotch Session Cases (Gilmour and Falconer) [*1681-86*] [*A publication*] (DLA)
PRESFR..... Pressure Falling Rapidly [*NWS*] (FAAC)
PRESIG...... Pressurizing (KSC)
PRESIGN ... Procedure Sign
Presilection... Presidential Election (SAUS)
PRESINSURV... Inspection and Survey Board [*Navy*]
Pres Leg.... Preston on Legacies [*1824*] [*A publication*] (DLA)
PresLf....... Presidential Life Corp. [*Associated Press*] (SAG)
Presly....... Presley Companies [*Associated Press*] (SAG)
Pres Mer.... Preston on Merger [*A publication*] (DLA)
PRESNAVWARCOL... Naval War College
PRES PART... Present Participle [*Grammar*] (WDAA)
Pres Proc... Presidential Proclamation (AAGC)
PRESPROC... Presidential Proclamation
PresR........ Presidential Realty Corp. [*Associated Press*] (SAG)
PRESRR..... Pressure Rising Rapidly [*NWS*] (FAAC)
PRESS....... Pacific Range Electromagnetic Signature Studies [*or System*] [*Military*] (NG)
PRESS....... Pacific Range Electromagnetic Signature System (SAUS)
PRESS....... Parti Republicain Social du Senegal [*Social Republican Party of Senegal*] [*Political party*]
PRESS....... Peace Research and European Security Studies (SAUS)
PRESS....... Point-Resolved Spectroscopy (RAWO)
PRESS....... Predicted Residual Sum of Squares
PRESS....... Prediction Error Sum of Squares (AAEL)
PRESS....... Prereading Expectancy Screening Scale [*Educational test*]
PRESS....... Preschool Readiness Experimental Screening Scale [*Medicine*] (EDAA)
PRESS....... Pressurant (NAKS)
press .... Pressure [*Therapy term*] (CTAA)
PRESS....... Pressure (MCD)
PRESS....... Product Records Engineering Support System (SAUS)
PRESS....... Project Review, Evaluation and Scheduling System (SAUS)
PRESS....... Prolog Equation Solving System (BYTE)
PRESS....... Property Record for Equipment Servicing and Sharing (MCD)
PRESSAR... Presentation Equipment for Slow Scan RADAR
PRESSDUCTOR... Pressure Inductor (IAA)
PRESSFR.... Pressure Falling Rapidly [*Meteorology*] (WEAT)
PRESSO..... Program for Elective Surgical Second Opinion [*Blue Cross/Blue Shield*]
Pres SQ..... Presidential Studies Quarterly [*A publication*] (BRI)
PRESSRA... Presentation Equipment for Slow Scan Radar (SAUS)
PRESSRR... Pressure Rising Rapidly [*Meteorology*] (WEAT)
Pressure Eng... Plessure Engineering (SAUS)
PRESSURS... Pre-Strike Surveillance/Reconnaissance System (MCD)
PREST....... Party on Scientific and Technical Research Policy [*European community*] (MHDB)
PREST....... Policy Research in Engineering, Science and Technology (SAUS)
PREST....... Present (ROG)
PRES'T...... President
PRE-ST...... Prestart (AAG)
PREST....... Programme of Policy Research in Engineering Science and Technology [*British*]
Prest Conv... Preston on Conveyancing [*A publication*] (DLA)
Prestek...... Presstek, Inc. [*Associated Press*] (SAG)
Prestel ...... Press button on Telephone-Lines (SAUS)
Prest Est... Preston on Estates [*A publication*] (DLA)
PrestFn...... Prestige Financial Corp. [*Associated Press*] (SAG)
Prest Merg... Preston on Merger [*A publication*] (DLA)
PRESTMO... Prestissimo [*Very Fast*] [*Music*] (ROG)
PRESTO..... Personnel Response and Evaluation System for Target Obscuration [*Military*] (RDA)
PRESTO..... Precursory Research for Embryonic Science and Technology (SAUS)
PRESTO..... Prediction of Radiological Effects Due to Shallow Trench Operations [*Environmental Protection Agency*] (AEPA)
PRESTO..... Prediction of Radiological Effects to Shallow [*Environment term*] (EGA)
PRESTO..... Prestissimo [*Very Fast*] [*Music*] (ROG)
PRESTO..... Program for Rapid Earth-to-Space Trajectory Optimization [*NASA*]
PRESTO..... Programmable Etalon Spectrometer for Twilight Observations (SAUS)
PRESTO..... Program Reporting and Evaluation System for Total Operation (SAUS)
PRESTO..... Program Reporting and Evaluation System for Total Operations [*AFSC*]
PRESTO..... Project Release Status Operation (SAUS)
PRE-STORM... Preliminary Regional Experiment for STORM [*Stormscale Operational and Research Meteorology*] [*Marine science*] (OSRA)
PRE-STORM... Preliminary Research Experiment-Stormscale Operational and Research Meteorology (SAUS)
Prest Shep T... Sheppard's Touchstone by Preston [*A publication*] (DLA)
PRESUB..... Pre-Subscript (SAUS)
Presv........ Preservation (AL)
presv........ Preservation (BARN)
Presync..... Presynchronization
PRET........ Periodic Reliability Evaluation Test (MCD)
PRET........ Preterit [*Past tense*] [*Grammar*] (ROG)
Pret.......... Preterite (SAUS)
PRET........ Pretoria [*South Africa*] (ROG)
PRET........ Program for the Recovery of the Economy in Transition (SAUS)
PRETACS ... Prediction of Tax Cases System (SAUS)
PRETCHREP... Preliminary Technical Report (MCD)
PRETECHREP... Preliminary Technical Report [*Army*] (AABC)
PRETOS..... Proofreading Tests of Spelling [*Educational test*]
Pretrial Conf... Pretrial Conference (SAUS)
PRETTYBLUEBATCH... Philadelphia Regular Exchange Tea Total Young Belles Lettres Universal Experimental Bibliographical Association To Civilize Humanity [*From Edgar Allan Poe essay "How to Write a Blackwood Article"*]
pretz......... pretzel (SAUS)
PREU........ Prime [*Intermodal shipping container symbol*] (TVRC)
PREV........ Medical and Psychological Previews [*Database*] [*BRS Information Technologies*] [*Information service or system*] (IID)
PREV........ Presvac Systems [*NCIC trailer make code*]
PREV........ Prevent (SAUS)
PREV........ Prevention
prev.......... Preverb [*Linguistics*] (IEL)
PREV........ Previous (AFM)
prev.......... Previous (SHCU)
PREV........ Previously (SAUS)
PREV........ Previous Program Selection [*In-car entertainment*] [*Electronics*]
PrevAGT.... Previous Abnormality of Glucose Tolerance
PREVAN..... Precompiler for Vector Analysis (SAUS)
PREVEN..... Preventive (SAUS)
PREVENT... Pacific Northwest Regional Visibility Experiment using Natural Tracers [*Marine science*] (OSRA)
PREVENT... Pacific NW Regional Visibility EXperiment using Natural Tracers (USDC)
PREVENT... Precertification to Verify Necessary Treatment
PRevere..... Paul Revere Corp. [*Associated Press*] (SAG)
PREVLINE... Prevention Online (SAUS)
PREVLV..... Prevalve
PrevMed.... Preventive Medicine (DAVI)
PREVMEDU... Preventive Medicine Unit
pre-voc...... Prevocational [*Education*] (DAVI)
PREVT....... Preventative
PREW........ Prew Proco Travel Trailer [*NCIC trailer make code*]
PREWI....... Press Wireless [*A radio service for the transmission of news*]
PREWI....... Press Wireless, Inc. (SAUS)
Pr Exch..... Price's English Exchequer Reports [*1814-24*] [*A publication*] (DLA)
PREXTEND... Prestel Extended (SAUS)
PREZ........ President Casinos [*NASDAQ symbol*] (TTSB)
PREZ........ President Riverboat Casinos [*NASDAQ symbol*] (SAG)
PREZ........ Prime [*Intermodal trailer symbol*]
PRF.......... GPO Sales Product Catalog [*Database*] (GDD)
PRF.......... Palestine Rejection Front (BJA)
PRF.......... Parachute Refurbishment Facility [*NASA*] (NASA)
PRF.......... Parliament Reference (SAUS)
PRF.......... Partial Refund [*Travel industry*] (TVEL)
PRF.......... Partial Reinforcement [*Training*]
PRF.......... Partido Revolucionario Febrerista [*Febrerista Revolutionary Party*] [*Paraguay*] [*Political party*] (PPW)
PRF.......... Patient Record Form
PRF.......... Patient Report Form (DB)
PRF.......... Penetration Room Filtration [*Nuclear energy*] (NRCH)
prf........... Performer [*MARC relator code*] [*Library of Congress*] (LCCP)
PRF.......... Permanent Requirements File [*Computer science*] (CIST)
PRF.......... Personality Research Form [*Psychology*]
PRF.......... Personnel Readiness File [*Army*] (AABC)
PRF.......... Personnel Resources File (SAUS)
PRF.......... Person Related Factor [*National Highway Traffic Safety Administration Fatal Accident Recording System code*]
PRF.......... Petroleum Research Fund
PRF.......... Phenol/Resorcinol/Formaldehyde [*Plastics technology*]
PRF.......... Plant Response Fertilization [*Agriculture*]
PRF.......... Plasmacytoma Repressor Factor [*Cytology*]

PRF .... Plasma Recognition Factor [*Medicine*] (EDAA)
PRF .... Plastics Recycling Foundation (EA)
PRF .... Plug Representing Fuze (SAUS)
PRF .... Plutonium Reclamation Facility [*Nuclear energy*]
PRF .... Plymouth Rock Foundation (EA)
PRF .... Plywood Research Foundation (EA)
PRF .... Point Response Function [*Of a telescope*]
PRF .... Polyclonal Rheumatoid Factor [*Medicine*] (DMAA)
PRF .... Pontine Reticular Formation [*Neurophysiology*]
PRF .... Porpoise Rescue Foundation (EA)
PRF .... Potential Requirements File (NITA)
PRF .... Power Radio Frequency [*Telecommunications*] (IAA)
PRF .... Prefac Enterprises, Inc. [*Toronto Stock Exchange symbol*]
PRF .... Preferences (SAUS)
PRF .... Preformed [*Technical drawings*]
PRF .... Pride Co. $2.60cm Cv L.P. [*NYSE symbol*] (TTSB)
PRF .... Pride Companies Ltd. [*NYSE symbol*] (SPSG)
PRF .... Primary Reference Fuel [*Automotive engineering*]
PRF .... Priority-Reserved Flight (SAUS)
PRF .... Problem Report Form (SAUS)
PRF .... Processor Request Flag [*Telecommunications*] (TEL)
PRF .... Progressive Renal Failure [*Medicine*] (AAMN)
PRF .... Prolactin Releasing Factor (SAUS)
PRF .... Prolactin-Releasing Factor [*Endocrinology*]
PRF .... Proliferation Regulatory Factor [*Biochemistry*]
PRF .... Proof (KSC)
prf .... Proof (VRA)
Pr F .... Propyl Fluoride (SAUS)
PRF .... Protein Research Foundation (SAUS)
PRF .... Protein Rich Fraction [*Food analysis*]
PRF .... Protein Rich Fractions (SAUS)
PRF .... Pseudo-Range Frequency [*Navigation systems*]
PRF .... Psychiatric Research Foundation
PRF .... Psychical Research Foundation (EA)
PRF .... Psychosynthesis Research Foundation (EA)
PRF .... Publications Reference File [*Government Printing Office*] [*Database*] [*Washington, DC*] (MCD)
PRF .... Public Relations Foundation
PRF .... Public Residential Facility
PRF .... Puerto Rico Federal Reports [*A publication*] (DLA)
PRF .... Pulse Rate Frequency (MUGU)
PRF .... Pulse Recurrence Frequency
prf .... Pulse Repetition Frequency (IDOE)
PRF .... Pulse Repetition Frequency [*Computer science*]
PRF .... Pulsese Repetition Frequency (SAUS)
PRF .... Purchase Rate Factor
PRF .... Purdue Research Foundation [*Purdue University*] [*Research center*] (MCD)
PRFA .... Plasma Recognition Factor Activity [*Hematology*] (AAMN)
Pr Falc ...... President Falconer's Scotch Session Cases [*1744-51*] [*A publication*] (DLA)
PRFAW ...... Personnel Research Field Activity, Washington [*Navy*] (MUGU)
PrfBcp .... Professional Bancorp [*Associated Press*] (SAG)
PRFC .... Plymouth Rock Fanciers Club (EA)
PRFC .... Potomac River Fisheries Commission [*Maryland and Virginia*] (NOAA)
PRFCN ...... Purification
PRFCS .... Pattern Recognition Feedback Control System [*Computer science*] (IAA)
PRFCS .... Prefocus
PRFD .... Pulse Recurrence Frequency Discrimination [*Telecommunications*] (TEL)
PRFD .... Pulse Repetition Frequency Distribution (SAUS)
PRFDX ...... Price T. Rowe: Equity Income [*Mutual fund ticker symbol*] (SG)
PRFE .... Polar Reflection Faraday Effect
PRFE .... Polar-Reflection Faraday Effect (SAUS)
PRFE .... Provisioners Frozen Express [*Common carrier symbol*]
PR Fed ...... Puerto Rico Federal Reports [*A publication*] (DLA)
PRFG .... Proofing [*Freight*]
PRFH .... Pseudo-Random Frequency-Hopping (SAUS)
PRFI .... Portable Range-Finder/Illuminator
PRFI .... Puerto Rican Family Institute (EA)
PRFIA .... Phase-Resolved Fluoroimmunoassay
PRFIC .... Plume RADAR Frequency Interference Code (MCD)
PrfIOF .... Preferred Income Opportunity Fund [*Associated Press*] (SAG)
PRFL .... Pressure Fed Liquid (KSC)
PRFL .... Puerto Rican Flycatcher [*North American bird banding code*] (BIBA)
PRFM .... Performance (MSA)
PRFM .... Perfumania, Inc. [*NASDAQ symbol*] (NASQ)
PRFM .... Premature [*or Prolonged*] Rupture of Fetal Membrane [*Gynecology*] (MAE)
PRFM .... Prolonged Rupture of Fetal Membranes [*Obstetrics*] (DAVI)
PRFM .... Pseudorandom Frequency Modulated [*Computer science*]
PRFN .... Percutaneous Radio Frequency [*Medicine*] (EDAA)
PRFN .... Prestige Financial [*NASDAQ symbol*] (TTSB)
PRFN .... Prestige Financial Corp. [*NASDAQ symbol*] (SAG)
PRFNL .... Professional (SAUS)
PRFP .... Preliminary Request for Proposal (SAUS)
PRFPT .... Federacion Puertorriqueno de Trabajadores
PRFR .... Pressure-retaining Flow-relieving [*Medicine*] [*Valve*] (EDAA)
PRFR .... Proofer [*Freight*]
PRFR .... Proof Reader (SAUS)
prfr .... Proofreader (ODA)
PRFR .... Proofreader (SAUS)
PRFRD ...... Proofread (MSA)
PRFRT .... Partially Relaxed Fourier Transform (DB)
PRFS .... Phase-Resolved Fluorescence Spectroscopy
PRFS .... Pulse Recurrence Frequency Stagger (OA)
PRFs .... Pulse Repetition Frequencies (SAUS)
PRFSS .... Peterborough Royal Foxhound Show Society [*British*] (DBA)
PRFT .... Partially Relaxed Fourier Transform [*Mathematics*]
PRFT .... Portable Rod-and-Frame Test (EDAC)
PRFT .... Presser Foot
PRFT .... Press Fit
PRFT .... Proffitt's, Inc. [*NASDAQ symbol*] (NQ)
PRFU .... Primefuels UK [*Intermodal shipping container symbol*] (TVRC)
PRFU .... Processor Reader for Use (SAUS)
PRFU .... Processor Ready for Use [*Telecommunications*] (TEL)
PRG .... Empresa Aero-Servicios Parrague Ltd. [*Chile*] [*ICAO designator*] (FAAC)
PRG .... Gilbert Associates, Inc., Reading, PA [*Library symbol*] [*Library of Congress*] (LCLS)
PRG .... PAL Programming Department (SAUS)
PRG .... Parabolic Radius Gage (MCD)
PRG .... Paris, IL [*Location identifier*] [*FAA*] (FAAL)
PRG .... Patient Related Groups (SAUS)
PRG .... Peacekeeper Rail Garrison [*Cancelled 1991*] [*Air Force*] (DOMA)
PRG .... Peerless Carpet Corp. [*Toronto Stock Exchange symbol*]
PRG .... Peer Review Group (MELL)
PRG .... People's Revolutionary Government [*Grenada*] (PD)
PRG .... Perennial Rye Grass [*Immunology*]
PRG .... Performance Related Gift [*Business Management*]
PRG .... Personnel Requirements Generator
PRG .... Personnel Resources Group [*Military*]
PRG .... Perugia [*Italy*] [*Seismograph station code, US Geological Survey*] (SEIS)
PRG .... Phleborheography [*Medicine*] (EDAA)
PRG .... Phleborrheogram [*Hematology*] (DAVI)
PRG .... Physician Resources Group, Inc. [*NYSE symbol*] (SAG)
PRG .... Physicians Resource Group [*NYSE symbol*] (TTSB)
PRG .... Pick Resources Guide [*ALLM Books*] [*England*] [*Information service or system*] (IID)
PRG .... Plastic Radial Grating
PRG .... Policy Research Group [*Australian Labor Party*]
PRG .... Polymer Research Group [*University of New Hampshire*] (RCD)
PRG .... Posterior Root Ganglia [*Medicine*] (EDAA)
PRG .... Powerful Radio Galaxy [*Cosmology*]
PRG .... Prague [*Former Czechoslovakia*] [*Airport symbol*] (OAG)
PRG .... Procedure Review Group [*Nuclear energy*] (NRCH)
PRG .... Program Control Mode (SAUS)
PRG .... Program Regulation Guide
PRG .... Program Resources Group (SAUS)
PRG .... Program Review Group [*Military*]
PRG .... Provisional Revolutionary Government [*Political arm of the Vietcong*] (VNW)
PRG .... Psychological Readers Guide (SAUS)
PRG .... Purge (AAG)
PRGA .... Personnel Group of America, Inc. [*NASDAQ symbol*] (QUAN)
PRGC .... Past Royal Grand Cross [*Freemasonry*] (ROG)
Prg Chk ..... Program Check (SAUS)
Prg E .... Program End (SAUS)
PRGEO .... Prince George, SC [*American Association of Railroads railroad junction routing code*]
Prg Exp ..... Program Expander (SAUS)
PRGFX .... Price T. Rowe: Growth Stock [*Mutual fund ticker symbol*] (SG)
PRG/I .... Pick Resources Guide/International [*ALLM Books*] [*Information service or system*] (IID)
PRGIX .... Price T. Rowe: Growth & Income [*Mutual fund ticker symbol*] (SG)
PRGM .... Program (AFM)
Prgm .... Program (PHSD)
PRGMG ...... Programming (MSA)
PRGMNG .... Programming
PRGMR ...... Programmer (AFM)
Prgmr .... Programmer (AL)
PRGM RGTR ... Program Register (SAUS)
PRGN .... Peregrine Systems, Inc. [*NASDAQ symbol*] (NASQ)
PRGO .... Perrigo Co. [*NASDAQ symbol*] (SPSG)
PRGP .... Phoenix Restaurant Group [*OTCBB symbol*]
PRGPrB ...... Pub Sv E&G 4.18% Pfd [*NYSE symbol*] (TTSB)
PRGR .... ProGroup, Inc. [*NASDAQ symbol*] (NQ)
PRGR .... Proving Ground (SAUS)
Prg Reg ..... Program Register (SAUS)
PRGRMR .... Programmer
PRGS .... President of the Royal Geographical Society [*British*]
PRGS .... Proceedings of the Royal Geographical Society (SAUS)
PRGS .... Prognosis (AABC)
PRGS .... Progress Software [*NASDAQ symbol*] (SPSG)
Prg Sh .... Program Shift (SAUS)
PrgSoft ...... Progress Software Corp. [*Associated Press*] (SAG)
Prg Sup ..... Program Suppress (SAUS)
PRGVN ...... Provisional Revolutionary Government of South Vietnam (VNW)
PRGX .... Profit Recovery Group International, Inc. (The) [*NASDAQ symbol*] (SAG)
PRGX .... Profit Recovery Grp Intl [*NASDAQ symbol*] (TTSB)
PRGX .... Progold [*Private rail car owner code*]
PRGY .... Prodigy Communications [*NASDAQ symbol*] (SG)
PRH .... Paper-Roll Handler
PRH .... Partido Revolucionario Hondureno [*Honduras Revolutionary Party*] [*Political party*] (PPW)
PRH .... Petrol Railhead

PRH.......... Phrae [*Thailand*] [*Airport symbol*] (OAG)
PrH.......... Prepositus Hypoglossi [*Neuroanatomy*]
PRH.......... Preretinal Hemorrhage [*Medicine*] (MELL)
PRH.......... Program Requirements Handbook (MUGU)
PRH.......... Prolactin-Releasing Hormone [*Endocrinology*]
PRH.......... Promus Hotel [*NYSE symbol*] (TTSB)
PRH.......... Promus Hotel Corp. [*NYSE symbol*] (SAG)
PRH.......... Psychiatric Regional Hospital [*Health insurance*] (GHCT)
PRH.......... Pulmonary Right Heart (SAUS)
PRHA........ People Refreshment House Association [*British*] (BI)
PRHA........ President of the Royal Hibernian Academy [*British*]
PRHB........ Pacific Rehabilitation & Sports Medicine, Inc. [*NASDAQ symbol*] (SAG)
PRHB........ Pacific Rehab/Sports Medicine [*NASDAQ symbol*] (TTSB)
PRHBF...... Peak Reactive Hyperemia Blood Flow [*Hematology*] (MAE)
PRHC........ Province Healthcare (MHID)
Pr HC Ch.... Practice of the High Court of Chancery [*A publication*] (DLA)
PRHG........ Pioneer Shipping [*Common carrier symbol*]
PRHGS...... Puerto Rican Hispanic Genealogical Society [*Association*] (EA)
PRHi......... Historical Society of Berks County, Reading, PA [*Library symbol*] [*Library of Congress*] (LCLS)
PRHS........ Port Richmond High School (SAUS)
PRHT........ Parkhurst [*NCIC trailer make code*]
PRHYX...... Price T. Rowe: High Yield [*Mutual fund ticker symbol*] (SG)
PRI........... Farmington, MO [*Location identifier*] [*FAA*] (FAAL)
PRI........... Independent Revolutionary Party (Dominican Rep.) [*Political party*] (PSAP)
PRI........... Institutional Revolutionary Party [*Mexico*] [*Political party*]
PRI........... Pacific Research Institute for Public Policy (EA)
PRI........... Pacific Resources, Inc. (EFIS)
PRI........... Pain Rating Index
PRI........... Paint Research Institute [*Defunct*] (EA)
PRI........... Paleontological Research Institution (EA)
PRI........... Partial Response Impuls (SAUS)
PRI........... Partido Revolucionario Institucional [*Party of the Institutionalized Revolution*] [*Mexico*] [*Political party*]
PRI........... Partito Repubblicano Italiano [*Italian Republican Party*] [*Political party*] (PPW)
PRI........... Partner Relationship Inventory [*Marital relations test*] [*Psychology*]
PRI........... Partnership for Rural Improvement [*Washington*] (EDAC)
PRI........... Peace Research Institute [*Later, Institute for Policy Studies*] (EA)
PRI........... Penal Reform International [*United Kingdom*] (EAIO)
PRI........... Performance Registry International
PRI........... Performance Review Institutes
PRI........... Periodic Reinvestigation (SAUS)
PRI........... Perris, CA [*Amtrak Busline code*]
PRI........... Personal Reaction Index [*Interpersonal skills and attitudes test*]
PRI........... Personal Record Identifier [*Treasury Board of Canada*] (FOTI)
PRI........... Personal Resource Inventory (DB)
PRI........... Personnel Research, Inc. [*Information service or system*] (IID)
PRI........... Personnel Research Institute Test (AEBS)
PRI........... Petroleum Recovery Institute [*Research center*] (RCD)
PRI........... Phosphate Rock Institute [*Defunct*] (EA)
PRI........... Phosphoribose Isomerase [*An enzyme*] (MAE)
PRI........... Photographic Radar Intelligence
PRI........... Photographic Reconnaissance and Interpretation (NATG)
PRI........... Photo RADAR Intelligence
PRI........... Pineapple Research Institute (SAUS)
PRI........... Pineapple Research Institute of Hawaii (EA)
PRI........... Pittsburgh Research Institute (SAUS)
PRI........... Plains Resources Inc. (EFIS)
PRI........... Plan Repeater Indicator (IAA)
PRI........... Plasticity Retention Index [*Rubber test method*]
PRI........... Plastics and Rubber Institute [*Institution of the Rubber Industry and Pla stics Institute*] [*Formed by a merger of*] (EAIO)
PRI........... Polymer Research Institute [*University of Massachusetts*] [*Research center*] (RCD)
PRI........... Polymer Research Institute [*Polytechnic Institute of New York*] [*Research center*] (RCD)
PRI........... Population Reference Intake (WDAA)
PRI........... Port Railroads [*Federal Railroad Administration identification code*]
PRI........... Potomac Research, Incorporated
PRI........... Practice Training Index
PRI........... Praslin Island [*Seychelles Islands*] [*Airport symbol*] (OAG)
PRI........... Pre-Ignition
PRI........... Preliminary Rifle Instruction [*Military*]
PRI........... Prescriptive Reading Inventory
PRI........... President of the Royal Institute (SAUS)
PRI........... President of the Royal Institute (of Painters in Water Colours) [*British*] (ROG)
PRI........... President of the Royal Institution (London) (ROG)
PRI........... President Regimental Institutes [*British*]
PRI........... Pressure Rate Index (SAUS)
PRI........... Pressure Ratio Indicator (SAUS)
PRI........... Prevention Routiere Internationale [*International Road Safety Organization*] [*Luxembourg*] (EAIO)
Pri........... Price's English Exchequer Reports [*1814-24*] [*A publication*] (DLA)
Pri........... Price's English Mining Commissioners' Cases [*A publication*] (DLA)
PRI........... Priest [*California*] [*Seismograph station code, US Geological Survey*] (SEIS)
pri............ Primary (IDOE)
PRI........... Primary (KSC)
PRI........... Primary Path [*Communications term*] (DCT)
PRI........... Primary Rate, Inc.
PRI........... Primary Rate Interface (PCM)
PRI........... Primary Rifle Instruction (SAUS)
PRI........... Primary Winding (IAA)
pri............ Primate (ODA)
PRI........... Primate Research Institute [*New Mexico State University*] [*Hollman, NM*]
PRI........... Prime Computer Inc., Corporation Library, Framingham, MA [*OCLC symbol*] (OCLC)
PRI........... Primer (IAA)
PRI........... Princess (automobile) [*NCIC car model code*]
PRI........... Princeville Airways, Inc. [*ICAO designator*] (FAAC)
PRI........... Printer Interface [*Computer science*] (CIST)
PRI........... Prinz [*NCIC car model code*]
PRI........... Priority (AFM)
PRI........... Priority Repair Induction [*Code*]
PRI........... Priority Requirement for Information (AFM)
Pri........... Priscianus [*Authority cited in pre-1607 legal work*] (DSA)
PRI........... Prism [*NCIC car model code*]
PRI........... Prison
PRI........... Prius [*NCIC car model code*]
PRI........... Private
PRI........... Prize [*or Prizeman*] [*British*] (ROG)
PRI........... Prizm [*NCIC car model code*]
PRI........... Processing Research Institute [*Carnegie Mellon University*]
PRI........... Production Rate Index (OA)
PRI........... Production Records, Inc. (EA)
PRI........... Program Interrupt [*Computer science*] (IAA)
PRI........... Program Revision Intent
PRI........... Projection Readout Indicator [*Aviation*] (OA)
PRI........... Projector Rectile Image (SAUS)
PRI........... Proteus Resources, Inc. [*Vancouver Stock Exchange symbol*]
PRI........... Prout Research Institute (EA)
PRI........... Psoriasis Research Institute (EA)
PRI........... Public Radio International
PRI........... Public Relations Institute (SAUS)
PRI........... Public Relations Institute of Ireland (BI)
PRI........... Public Research Institute [*San Francisco State University*] (RCD)
PRI........... Puerto Rican Independence [*Later, GPRG*] [*An association*] (EA)
PRI........... Puerto Rico [*ANSI three-letter standard code*] (CNC)
PRI........... Pulse Rate Increase [*Medicine*]
PRI........... Pulse Rate Indicator
PRI........... Pulse Recurrence [*or Repetition*] Interval (NATG)
PRI........... Pulse Repetition Internal
PRI........... Pulse Repetition Interval (CIST)
PRI........... Pure Research Institute [*Later, BRINC*] (EA)
PRI........... Revolutionary Institution Party
PRIA......... Peer Review Improvement Act (SAUS)
PRIA......... Peer Review Improvement Act of 1982
PRIA......... President of the Royal Irish Academy
PRIA......... Priam Corp. (SAUS)
PRIA......... PRI Automation [*NASDAQ symbol*] (SAG)
PRIA......... Proceedings of the Royal Irish Academy (SAUS)
PRIA......... Public Rangelands Improvement Act (SAUS)
PRIA......... Public Rangelands Improvement Act of 1978
PRIA......... Society for Participatory Research in Asia [*India*] (EAIO)
PRIAM....... Precision Range Information Analysis for Missiles (MCD)
PRIAM....... Pre-Normative Requirements for Intelligent Actuation & Measurements (ACII)
PRIAS....... Packard's Radioimmunoassay System [*Medicine*] (DMAA)
PRIAS....... Plant Register/Fixed Assets and Inflation Accounting System (SAUS)
PrIAU-SJ.... Inter-American University of Puerto Rico, San Juan Campus, San Juan, PR [*Library symbol*] [*Library of Congress*] (LCLS)
PRI Auto.... PRI Automation [*Associated Press*] (SAG)
PRIB......... Private Brands, Inc. (SAUS)
PRIBA....... President of the Royal Institute of British Architects
PRIBAG..... Priority Baggage (DNAB)
PRI BIL..... Primary Billet (DNAB)
Pribilovs... Pribilov Islands in the Bering Sea off Alaska (SAUS)
PRIC......... Dec. Puerto Rico Industrial Commission Decisions (SAUS)
PRIC......... Peripheral Interface Controller (SAUS)
PRIC......... Price-Meyers [*NCIC trailer make code*]
PRIC......... Price Truck Line [*Common carrier symbol*]
PRIC......... Problem, Rectification, Investigation, Correction (BB)
PRICAI...... Pacific Rim International Conference on Artificial Intelligence (SAUS)
PRICALL... Priority Call (SAUS)
PRIC Dec... Puerto Rico Industrial Commission Decisions [*A publication*] (DLA)
PRICE....... Peroxy Radicals Inter Comparison Exercise (SAUS)
PRICE....... Physicians for Research in Cost-Effectiveness (EA)
Price......... Price's English Exchequer Reports [*A publication*] (DLA)
Price......... Price's English Mining Commissioners' Cases [*A publication*] (DLA)
PRICE....... Pricing Review to Intensify Competitive Environment [*Computer science*]
PRICE....... Productivity Improvement and Cost Effectiveness (SAUS)
PRICE....... Programmed Review of Information for Costing and Estimation (or Evaluation) (SAUS)
PRICE....... Programmed Review of Information for Costing and Evaluation (MCD)
PRICE....... Protection, Rest, Ice, Compression, Evaluation [*Medicine*]
Price & St... Price and Stewart's Trade Mark Cases [*A publication*] (DLA)
PriceCst..... Price Costco, Inc. [*Associated Press*] (SAG)
PriceEnt..... Price Enterprises, Inc. [*Associated Press*] (SAG)
Price Gen Pr... Price's General Practice [*A publication*] (DLA)
Price Liens... Price on Maritime Liens [*1940*] [*A publication*] (DLA)
Pricell....... Pricellular Corp. [*Associated Press*] (SAG)
Price Min Cas... Price's Mining Cases [*A publication*] (DLA)

PRICEMMM... Protection, Rest, Ice, Compression, and Elevation
Price Notes PC... Price's Notes of Practice Cases in Exchequer [*1830-31*] [*England*] [*A publication*] (DLA)
Price Notes PP... Price's Notes of Points of Practice, English Exchequer Cases [*A publication*] (DLA)
Price PC.... Price's English Practice Cases [*1830-31*] [*A publication*] (DLA)
Price Pr Cas... Price's English Practice Cases [*A publication*] (DLA)
Price R Est... Price on Acts Relating to Real Estate [*A publication*] (DLA)
PRICES...... Protection, Rest, Ice, Compression, Elevation, and Support [*Medicine*]
PRICE-S..... Software Costing Model (SAUS)
PriceTR..... Price [*T. Rowe*] Associates, Inc. [*Associated Press*] (SAG)
Prickett...... Prickett's Reports [*1 Idaho*] [*A publication*] (DLA)
PRICOM..... Prison Commission [*British*]
PRI-D........ Peace Research Institute - Dundas [*Canada*] (IRC)
PRID......... Peace Research Institute, Dundas (SAUS)
PRID......... Planning Record Identifier (SAUS)
PRID......... Pridie [*The Day Before*] [*Latin*]
PriD.......... Princeton Datafilm, Inc. (SAUS)
PriD.......... Princeton Datafilm, Inc., Princeton, NJ [*Library symbol*] [*Library of Congress*] (LCLS)
PRID......... Processor Identity Number (SAUS)
Prid & C.... Prideaux and Cole's English Reports [*4 New Sessions Cases*] [*1850-51*] [*A publication*] (DLA)
Prid & Co... Prideaux and Cole's English Reports [*4 New Sessions Cases*] [*1850-51*] [*A publication*] (DLA)
Prid Ch W... Prideaux's Directions to Churchwardens [*10th ed.*] [*1835*] [*A publication*] (DLA)
PRIDCO...... Puerto Rico Industrial Development Co.
Prid Conv... Prideaux's Forms and Precedents in Conveyancing [*24th ed.*] [*1952*] [*A publication*] (DLA)
PRIDE....... National Parents' Resource Institute for Drug Education (EA)
PRIDE....... Parents Resource Institute for Drug Education (SAUS)
PRIDE....... People and Resources Identified for Distributed Environments (TELE)
PRIDE....... People for Rehabilitating and Integrating the Disabled through Education [*New York City*]
PRIDE....... Perfection Requires Individual Defect Elimination
PRIDE....... Performance Readiness Initiatives Decision Evaluation System (SAUS)
PRIDE....... Personalized Recruiting for Immediate and Delayed Entry (SAUS)
PRIDE....... Personal Responsibility in Daily Effort [*Military Airlift Command's acronym for the Zero Defects Program*]
PRIDE....... Personal Responsibility in Defect Elimination (SAUS)
PRIDE....... Personal Responsibility in Delivering Excellence (BB)
PRIDE....... Policy based Routing, Implementation and Deployment in Europe (SAUS)
PRIDE....... Preschool and Kindergarten Interest Descriptor [*Educational test*]
Pride........ Pride Companies Ltd. [*Associated Press*] (SAG)
PRIDE....... PRIDE Foundation, Inc. (NRGU)
PRIDE....... Priority Receiving with Inter-Departmental Efficiency [*Computer science*]
PRIDE....... Production of Reliable Items Demands Excellence [*Navy*] (NG)
PRIDE....... Production Review Integrated Database (SAUS)
PRIDE....... Productive Rehabilitation Institute of Dallas for Ergonomics [*Research center*] (RCD)
PRIDE....... Productivity Improvements for the Decade of the Eighties
PRIDE....... Productivity-Resourcefulness-Incentives-Dedication-Excellence (SAUS)
PRIDE....... Professional Results in Daily Effort [*Strategic Air Command's acronym for the Zero Defects Program*]
PRIDE....... Profitable Information by Design (MHDI)
PRIDE....... Profitable Information by Design through Phased Planning and Control (MHDB)
PRIDE....... Programmed Reliability in Design (SAUS)
PRIDE....... Programmed Reliability in Design Engineering
PRIDE....... Promote Real Independence for the Disabled and Elderly (EA)
PRIDE....... Prompt Response Insurance Delivery Express
PRIDE....... Protection of Reefs and Islands from Degradation and Exploitation
PRIDE....... Provisioning Review Input Data Evaluation (MCD)
PRIDE....... Puerto Rico Information and Decision Environment (SAUS)
PRIDE....... Pulse RADAR Intelligent Diagnostic Environment [*US Army Missile Command*] (RDA)
PrideA....... Pride Automotive Group, Inc. [*Associated Press*] (SAG)
PrideAto.... Pride Automotive Group, Inc. [*Associated Press*] (SAG)
Prid Judg... Prideaux's Judgments and Crown Debts [*4th ed.*] [*1854*] [*A publication*] (DLA)
PRIEA....... Priority Issues Requiring Experimentation and Analysis (SAUS)
PRI-EOM.... Procedure Interrupt-End-of-Message (SAUS)
PRI-EOP.... Procedure Interrupt-End-of-Producedure (SAUS)
PRIEST...... Preston, ON [*American Association of Railroads railroad junction routing code*]
PRIF......... Peace Research Institute Frankfurt (SAUS)
PRIF......... Prior Year Refund Information File [*IRS*]
PRI-FLY..... Primary Flight Control [*on an aircraft carrier*] [*Navy*]
PRIG......... Packet Radio Interest Group (SAUS)
PRIH......... Pineapple Research Institute of Hawaii (SAUS)
PRIH......... Prolactin-Release Inhibiting Factor [*Also, PIF*] [*Endocrinology*]
PRIH......... Prolactin Release Inhibiting Hormone (SAUS)
PRII......... Public Relations Institute of Ireland (ODA)
PRIISM...... Pacific Research Institute for Information Systems and Management [*University of Hawaii at Manoa*] [*Research center*] (RCD)
PRIJ......... Pride & Joy [*NCIC truck make code*]
PRIJ......... Prime [*Common carrier symbol*]
PRIL......... Penarth Research International Ltd. [*British*]
PRIL......... Processor in The Loop (SAUS)
PRIM........ Pac Rim Holding [*NASDAQ symbol*] (SPSG)
PRIM........ Plans and Reports Improvement Memorandum [*Military*] (CAAL)
PRIM........ Plume Radiation Intensity Measurement (MUGU)
PRIM........ Pre-Referral Intervention Manual [*Test*] (TMMY)
PRIM........ Primary (AFM)
prim......... Primary (NTIO)
PRIM........ Primase (DMAA)
PRIM........ Primate
PRIM........ Primeholdings.com, Inc. [*NASDAQ symbol*] (QUAN)
PRIM........ Primitive
prim......... primordial (SAUS)
PRIM........ Program for Information Managers [*Later, AIM*] [*An association*]
PRIM........ Programmed Instruction for Management Education (HGAA)
PRIMA....... Pollutant Response in Marine Animals [*Marine science*] (MSC)
PRIMA....... Primary Care Information Management across Anglia (SAUS)
PRIMA....... Public Radio in Mid-America (NTCM)
PRIMA....... Public Risk and Insurance Management Association [*Washington, DC*] (EA)
PRIMA....... Public Risk Management Association (NTPA)
Primadn..... Primadonna Resorts, Inc. [*Associated Press*] (SAG)
PrimaE...... Prima Energy Corp. [*Associated Press*] (SAG)
PRIM & R.. Public Responsibility in Medicine and Research (EA)
PRIM&R.... Public Responsibility in Medicine and Research (MHID)
PRIMAR..... Program to Improve Management of Army Resources (AABC)
PrimaryB.... Primary Bank [*Associated Press*] (SAG)
Primary Ed... Primary Education [*A publication*]
Primary J... Primary Journal (SAUS)
PRIMAS..... Precipitation Radar Image Management System (SAUS)
PRIMATE... Personal Retrieval of Information by Microcomputer and Terminal Ensemble
PRIM BIB... Primary Bibliography (DGA)
Prim Care... Primary Care, Clinics in Office Practice (SAUS)
PRIMCOM... Pacific Rim Interactive Multimedia Computing [*Australia*]
Prim Comm Cen... Primary Communication Center (SAUS)
PRIME....... Partnership for the Regional Innovation in Manufacturing Education
PRIME....... Phantom Run Instrumented MILES Engagement (SAUS)
PRIME....... Philadelphia Regional Introduction for Minorities to Engineering (SAUS)
PRIME....... Plankton Reactivity in the Marine Environment (SAUS)
PRIME....... Planning through Retrieval of Information for Management Extrapolation (SAUS)
PRIME....... Precision Integrator for Meteorological Echoes (IEEE)
PRIME....... Precision Range Integrated Maneuver Exercise [*Army*] (RDA)
PRIME....... Precision Recovery Including Maneuvering Entry [*Air Force*]
PRIME....... Pre-Injection Metering [*Automotive fuel systems*]
PRIME....... Preinversion Multiecho (RAWO)
PRIME....... Prematriculation Program in Medical Education (DMAA)
PRIME....... Preparedness of Resources in Mission Evaluation (SAA)
PRIME....... Prescribed Right to Income and Maximum Equity
PRIME....... Primary Initiatives in Mathematics Education (AIE)
PRIME....... Primate Information Management Experiment (SAUS)
PRIME....... Prime Computer, Inc. (SAUS)
PRIME....... Priority Improved Management Effort (KSC)
PRIME....... Priority Improvement Effort [*DoD*]
PRIME....... Priority Management Effort [*Army*]
PRIME....... Priority Management Engineering System (SAUS)
PRIME....... Priority Management Evaluation [*Navy*]
PRIME....... Procarbazine, Ifosfamide, Methotrexate [*Antineoplastic drug regimen*]
PRIME....... Processing, Research, Inspection, and Marine Extension Program [*National Oceanic and Atmospheric Administration*] (MSC)
PRIME....... Profession Related Intern-Mentorship Experience
PRIME....... Program for Innovation in Microenterprise (SAUS)
PRIME....... Program Independence, Modularity, Economy
PRIME....... Programmed Instruction for Management Education [*American Management Association*]
PRIME....... Programme for International Managers in Europe [*Business program*]
PRIME....... Program Research in Integrated Multiethnic Education [*Defunct*] (EA)
PRIME....... Purdue Rare Isotope Measurement Laboratory (SAUS)
Prime BEEF... Prime Base Engineer Emergency Force [*Military*]
PRIME BEEF... Priority Improvement Management Effort Base Engineering Emergency Force [*Air Force*] (DOMA)
PrimeCp.... Prime Capital Corp. [*Associated Press*] (SAG)
Prim Ed-Pop Ed... Primary Education-Popular Educator (SAUS)
PrimeMg.... Prime Management Group, Inc. [*Associated Press*] (SAG)
PRIMENET... Prime Network Software Package [*Prime Computer, Inc.*]
PrimEq...... Prime Equities International [*Associated Press*] (SAG)
PRIMER..... Patient Record Information for Education Requirements [*Computer science*]
Prime RIBS... Prime Readiness in Base Services [*Military*]
PRIME RIBS... Priority Improvement Management Effort Readiness in Base Services [*Air Force*] (DOMA)
PrimeRsd... Prime Residential, Inc. [*Associated Press*] (SAG)
PRIMES..... Pennsylvania Retrieval of Information in Mathematics Education System (SAUS)
PRIMES..... Preflight Integration of Munitions and Electronic Systems (MCD)
PRIMES..... Productivity Integrated Measurement System [*Army*]
PrimeSrc.... PrimeSource Corp. [*Associated Press*] (SAG)
PRIMEX..... Primary Care Extender [*Insurance*] (DMAA)
Primex...... Primex Technologies, Inc. [*Associated Press*] (SAG)
PRIMEX..... Private Message Switching [*Telecommunications*] [*British*]
PRIMIP..... Primipara [*Woman bearing first child*] [*Medicine*] (AAMN)
primip....... Primipara (ODA)

PRIMIR...... Product Improvement Information Report (SAUS)
PRIMIR...... Product Improvement Management Information Report
PRIM LUC... Prima Luce [*Early in the Morning*] [*Pharmacy*]
PRIM M..... Primo Mane [*Early in the Morning*] [*Pharmacy*]
PRIM METH... Primitive Methodist [*A publication*]
PRIMO ...... International Research Programme in the Western Mediterranean (SAUS)
PRIMO ...... Programmable, Realtime, Incoherent, Matrix, Optical Processor [*Computer science*]
PRIMORDIAL... Primary Order Dial (NITA)
PRIMOS..... Prime Operating System [*Prime Computer, Inc.*]
PRIMP....... Primipara [*Woman bearing first child*] [*Obstetrics*] (DAVI)
PRIMPACT... Principal Impact [*National Highway Traffic Safety Administration Fatal Accident Recording System code*]
PRI-MPS.... Procedure Interrupt-Multipage Signal (SAUS)
Prim Rel Sta... Primary Relay Station (SAUS)
Primrk....... Primark Corp. [*Associated Press*] (SAG)
PRIMS....... Product Requirement Information Management System (MCD)
PRIMSCO... Pilot Run Item Master Schedule Committee (IAA)
PRIMTEC... Pacific Rim Interactive Multi-Media Technology
PRIMTRA... Air Primary Training
PRIMTRA... Primary Training (SAUS)
PRIMUS..... Physician Reservists in Medical Universities and Schools [*Military*]
PRIMUS..... Primary Medical Care for the Uniformed Services [*DoD*]
PrimusT...... Primus Telecommunications Group, Inc. [*Associated Press*] (SAG)
PRIN......... Partido Revolucionario de la Izquierda Nacionalista [*National Leftist Revolutionary Party*] [*Bolivia*] [*Political party*] (PPW)
PRIN......... Peace Research Institute of Nigeria (SAUS)
PRIN......... Performance Risk Index Number (NG)
PRIN......... Powerec International (SAUS)
PRIN......... Princess Homes [*NCIC trailer make code*]
PRIN......... Princess (trucks) [*NCIC truck make code*]
PRIN......... Princeton [*New Jersey*] [*Seismograph station code, US Geological Survey*] (SEIS)
Prin.......... Principal (AL)
prin.......... Principal (PROS)
PRIN......... Principal
PRIN......... Principality (ROG)
PRIN......... Principally (ROG)
PRIN......... Principia [*Elements*] [*Latin*] (ROG)
PRIN......... Principle (ROG)
prin.......... Principle (VRA)
PRIN......... Printer Replaceable Item (SAUS)
PRINAIR ... Puerto Rico International Airlines (SAUS)
PRINAIR ... Puerto Rico National Airlines
PrinAm...... Princeton American Corp. [*Associated Press*] (SAG)
PRINC....... Princeton, IN [*American Association of Railroads railroad junction routing code*]
PRINC....... Principal
PRINC....... Principle
PRINC-APIC... Princeton Reliability Information Center-Apollo Parts Information Center (SAUS)
PRINCE...... Pans Reliability Information Center (SAUS)
PRINCE...... Parts, Reliability and Information Center (SAUS)
PRINCE...... Parts Reliability Information Center [*NASA*]
PRINCE...... Prediction Integrated with Code for Finite Elements [*Durability testing*]
PRINCE...... Programed International Computer Environment (SAUS)
PRINCE...... Programed Reinforced Instruction Necessary for Continuing Education (SAUS)
PRINCE...... Programmed International Computer Environment [*International relations simulation game*]
PRINCE...... Programmed Reinforced Instruction Necessary to Continuing Education (SAUS)
PRINCE/APIC... Parts Reliability Information Center/Apollo Parts Information Center [*NASA*]
PrinceM...... Princeton Media Group, Inc. [*Associated Press*] (SAG)
Prince NML... Prince's New Mexico Laws [*A publication*] (DLA)
Princeton U... Princeton University (GAGS)
PRINCIR... Printed Circuit (IAA)
PrincNtl..... Princeton National Bancorp [*Associated Press*] (SAG)
Princ Univ Bull... Princeton University Bulletin (SAUS)
PRIND....... Present Indication [*Aviation*] (IAA)
PRIND....... Prolonged Reversible Ischemic Neurologic Deficit [*Medicine*] (DMAA)
PRINDI...... Princeton Diagnostic Laboratories of America, Inc. (SAUS)
PRINDUS ... Prison Industries [*Industries conducted in English prisons*]
PRINFO ..... Printed Information Distribution (SAA)
PRINFOD ... Printed Information Distribution (SAUS)
PRING....... Partido Revolucionario de Izquierda Nacional Gueiler [*Revolutionary Party of the National Left - Gueiler Wing*] [*Bolivia*] [*Political party*] (PPW)
PRIN-L ...... Partido Revolucionario de la Izquierda Nacional Laboral [*Political party*] (PPW)
PRINM ...... Partido Revolucionario de la Izquierda Nacional Moller [*Bolivia*] [*Political party*] (PPW)
PRINMUS... Principal Musician [*Marine Corps*]
PRINOBC/NEC... Primary Navy Officer Billet Classification and Navy Enlisted Classification
Prin PL...... Eden's Principles of Penal Law [*A publication*] (DLA)
Prin PL...... Eden's Principles of the Penal Law (SAUS)
Prin Pts...... Principal Parts (SAUS)
PRINS....... Partially Reversible Ischemic Neurologic Symptoms (SAUS)
Prins & Conderlag... Prins and Conderlag's Reports [*Ceylon*] [*A publication*] (ILCA)
PrinsRec.... Prins Recycling Corp. [*Associated Press*] (SAG)
PRINSYS .... Product Information System (IAA)
PRINSYS ... Production Information System (SAUS)
PRINT .... Preedited Interpreter (or Interpretive) (SAUS)
PRINT .... Pre-Edited Interpretive System [*Computer science*]
print .... Printing (WDMC)
PRINT .... Print Recognition Input Terminal (SAUS)
PRINT .... Public Release of Information and Transcripts [*Student legal action organization*]
Print&Pub... Printing and Publishing (SAUS)
Print Circuit Fabr... Printed Circuit Fabrication [*A publication*] (CABS)
Print Coll Q... Print Collectors Quarterly (SAUS)
Printed Circuit Des... Printed Circuit Design [*A publication*] (CABS)
PRINTF...... Print with Formatting (SAUS)
PRINTG ..... Printing
printout ..... Printer Output [*Computer science*] (CDE)
PRINTR ..... Printer
PRINT System... Preedited Interpretive System (SAUS)
PRINUL ..... Puerto Rico International Undersea Laboratory
PRIO......... International Peace Research Institute (SAUS)
PRIO......... International Peace Research Institution, Oslo [*Norway*]
PRIO......... Peace Research Institute (or Institution), Oslo (SAUS)
prio.......... Priority (ELAL)
PRIO......... Priority [*Telecommunications*]
PRIO......... Prior Products [*NCIC trailer make code*]
PRION....... Proteinaceous Infectious Particle
PRIONS ..... Proteinaceous Infectious Particles (SAUS)
PRIOR....... Policy Research Institute for the Region [*Princeton University*] (RCD)
PRIOR....... Program for In-Orbital Rendezvous [*Antisatellite system*] [*Air Force*]
PRIORCBX... Priority Coinbox (SAUS)
PRIOSUB ... Priority Subscriber (SAUS)
PRIOSUBS... Priority Subscriber with Special Services (SAUS)
PRIP......... Park Restoration and Improvement Program [*National Park Service*]
PRIP......... Pattern Recognition and Image Processing (SAUS)
PRIP......... Planned Retirement Income Program [*Institute of Financial Management*]
PRIP......... Product Reliability Improvement Program
PRIP......... PSP Radar Improvement Program (SAUS)
PRIPACSEVOCAM... Primary Pacific Secure Voice Communications [*Navy*] (CAAL)
PRI-PL ...... Primary Payload (SAUS)
PRIPP .... Pacific Research Institute for Public Policy (EA)
PRIP System... Pattern Recognition and Image Processing System (SAUS)
PRIR......... Parts Reliability Improvement Route (or Routing) (SAUS)
PR/IR........ Public Relations/Investor Relations (SAUS)
PRIRA....... Primary RADAR (FAAC)
PRIS......... Pacific Range Instrumentation Satellite (MUGU)
PRIS......... Personnel Resource Impact System (SAUS)
PRIS......... Pest Management Research Information System [*Agriculture Canada*] [*Information service or system*] (IID)
PRIS......... Prison (ROG)
PRIS......... Prisoner (AFM)
PRIS......... Program Resource Information System [*Department of Agriculture*]
PRIS......... Propeller Revolution Indicator System (MSA)
PRIS......... Protective Response Inducing Substance (SAUS)
PRIS......... Publications Reliability Inspection Sheet
PRISA....... Primary Slot Allocation (SAUS)
PRISA....... Public Radio Internet Service Alliance (SAUS)
PRISA....... Public Relations Institute of South Africa (ODA)
PR/ISC ..... Public Relations/Information Services Control (SAUS)
PRISCO ..... Price Stabilisation Corp. (SAUS)
PRISCO ..... Price Stabilization Corp.
PrisCoeff ... Prismatic Coefficient (SAUS)
PRISE .... Page Reader Input System with Editing (NVT)
PRISE .... Pennsylvania Resources and Information Center for Special Education [*Montgomery County Intermediate Unit*] [*King of Prussia*] [*Information service or system*] (IID)
PRISE .... Pennsylvania's Regional Instruction System for Education [*Network of colleges and universities*]
PRISE .... Primary Care Sharing the Evidence (SAUS)
PRISE .... Program for Integrated Shipboard Electronics
Pri Seq...... Primary Sequence (SAUS)
PRISIC ...... Photographic Reconnaissance Interpretation Section [*Squadron*] IntelligenceCenter [*JICPOA*]
PRISM....... Parallel Instruction Set Multiprocessor (SAUS)
PRISM....... Parallel Reduced Instruction Set Multiprocessing (or -processor) (SAUS)
PRISM....... Parameter Related Internal Standard Method [*Statistical procedure*]
PRISM....... Paraxial-Ray Imaging Spectro Microscope
PRISM....... Partnership for Regulatory Innovation and Sustainable Manufacturing
PRISM....... Passive RADAR Identification System (SEWL)
PRISM....... Pattern Recognition Information Synthesis Modeling [*Market analysis*]
PRISM....... Peace and Reconciliation Inter-Schools Movement (AIE)
PRISM....... Pediatric Risk of Mortality [*Medicine*]
PRISM....... Pediatric Risk of Mortality Score [*Medicine*] (STED)
PRISM....... Personal Records Information System Management (SAUS)
PRISM....... Personnel Record Information System (SAUS)
PRISM....... Personnel Record Information Systems for Management
PRISM....... Personnel Related Information System for Management (NITA)
PRISM....... Personnel Requirements Information System Methodology (NVT)
PRISM....... Photo-Refractive Information Storage Material (SAUS)
PRISM....... Photorefractive Information Storage Materials Consortium (CDE)
PRISM....... Pittsburgh Research-Based Instructional Supervising Model (EDAC)

PRISM....... Plant Risk Status Information Management System [*Environmental science*] (COE)
PRISM....... Pliocene Research, Interpretations and Synoptic Mapping [*Climatology*]
PRISM....... Powerful Resource for Information and System Management [*Computer science*] (IAA)
PRISM....... Power Reactor Inherently Safe Module [*Nuclear energy*]
PRISM....... Power Reactor Innovation Small Module [*Nuclear energy*]
PRISM....... Priorities in School Mathematics Project (EDAC)
PRISM....... Prioritized Requirement, Impacts and Schedule Milestones (ACAE)
PRISM....... Prioritized Requirements, Impacts and Schedule Milestones (SAUS)
PRISM....... Prism Entertainment Corp. (SAUS)
Prism........ Prism Group [*Associated Press*] (SAG)
PRISM....... Production Requirements for Industrial Scheduling Manpower (SAUS)
PRISM....... Programmable Integrated Scripts for MIRROR [*Management Information Reporting and review of Operational Resources Systems*] [*Computer Language*] (PCM)
PRISM....... Programmed Integrated System Maintenance (NG)
PRISM....... Programming Information and Scheduling Management (SAUS)
PRISM....... Program Reliability Information System for Management [*Polaris*]
PRISM....... Program Reporting and Information System for Management (SAUS)
PRISM....... Progressive Refinement of Integrated Supply Management (AFM)
PRISM....... Projection and Integrated Stand alone Monitor (SAUS)
PRISM....... Projection and Integrated Standalone Monitor [*Dolch Computer Systems*] [*Computer science*] (PCM)
PRISM....... Prospective Record of the Impact and Severity of Menstrual symptoms (SAUS)
PRISM....... Pulse Repetition Interval Sorting Matrix (VLIE)
PRISMA...... Primary Imaging System for Multiple Applications (SEWL)
PrismEnt.... Prism Entertainment Corp. [*Associated Press*] (SAG)
PRISM Internatl... Professional Records and Information Services Management International (NTPA)
PRISMS..... Phoenix Real-time Instrumentation for Surface Meteorological Studies network (SAUS)
PRISMS..... Plan of Research for Integrated Soil Moisture Studies (SAUS)
PrismS...... Prism Solutions [*Associated Press*] (SAG)
PRISN....... Prime Stock Number
PRISN....... Procurement Instrument Serial Number (SAUS)
PRISNET... Private Switching Network Service [*Telecommunications*]
Prison L Reptr... Prison Law Reporter [*A publication*] (ILCA)
Prison L Rptr... Prison Law Reporter [*A publication*] (DLA)
Prison Serv J... Prison Service Journal [*A publication*] (DLA)
PRISS....... Post Deployment Software Support Real-Time Interactive Simulation System
PRISSECIMP... Primary Secondary Impedance (IAA)
PrissSys.... Peerless Systems Corp. [*Associated Press*] (SAG)
PRIST....... Paper Radioimmunosorbent Test [*Analytical biochemistry*]
PRIT......... Pig Research Institute Taiwan (SAUS)
PRITAC...... Primary Tactical Radio Circuit (IAA)
Pritch Adm Dig... Pritchard's Admiralty Digest [*3rd ed.*] [*1887*] [*A publication*] (DLA)
Pritch M & D... Pritchard's Divorce and Matrimonial Causes [*3rd ed.*] [*1874*] [*A publication*] (DLA)
Pritch Quar Sess... Pritchard's Quarter Sessions [*A publication*] (DLA)
PRITMR..... Primary Timer (VLIE)
PRITN....... Princeton, KY [*American Association of Railroads railroad junction routing code*]
PRITX....... Price T. Rowe: Intl. Stock [*Mutual fund ticker symbol*] (SG)
PRIV......... Police Rapid Intervention Vehicle [*Police and security equipment*]
PRIV......... Privacy (SAUS)
priv.......... Private (STED)
PRIV......... Private
PRIV......... Private Coach [*NCIC trailer make code*]
Priv.......... Privately Maintained [*Nautical term*] (HRNC)
PRIV......... Privation (SAUS)
PRIV......... Privative
priv.......... privet (SAUS)
PRIV......... Privilege
priv.......... privily (SAUS)
priv.......... privy (SAUS)
PRIVAUTH... Travel Authorized via Privately-Owned Vehicle with Understanding No Additional Cost to Government Involved
Priv C App... Privy Council Appeals [*England*] [*A publication*] (DLA)
Priv CDI..... Indian Privy Council Decisions [*A publication*] (DLA)
Priv Counc App... Privy Council Appeals [*England*] [*A publication*] (DLA)
Priv Counc DI... Privy Council Decisions [*India*] [*A publication*] (DLA)
PRIVE....... Private (ROG)
Priv Found Rep... Private Foundations Reporter (SAUS)
Priv Fran Cont... Private Franchise Contracts (SAUS)
Priv Hous Fin... Private Housing Finance [*A publication*] (DLA)
Priv Inv Abroad... Private Investments Abroad (SAUS)
Priv Lond... Privilegia Londini [*A publication*] (DLA)
Priv Maintd... Privately Maintained [*Nautical charts*]
PRIV PR.... Privately Printed (SAUS)
PRIV PROP... Private Property [*Military*] (DNAB)
PRIV PUB... Privately Published (SAUS)
Priv St....... Private Statutes (SAUS)
PRIVX....... Private Exchange (IAA)
Pri X......... Primary X (SAUS)
PRIX......... Pro Rail [*Federal Railroad Administration identification code*]
Pri X Pu..... Primary X Pickup (SAUS)
PRIZ......... Preston Industries [*Federal Railroad Administration identification code*]
PRIZE........ Program for Research in Information Systems Engineering [*University of Michigan*] [*Research center*] (RCD)
Prize CR.... Prize Court Reports [*South Africa*] [*A publication*] (DLA)
PRIZM....... Potential Rating Index by ZIP [*Zone Improvement Plan*] Market [*Advertising*]
PRIZM....... Potential Rating Index for ZIP Markets (SAUS)
PRJ.......... Aero Servicios Pro-Bajio, SA de CV [*Mexico*] [*FAA designator*] (FAAC)
PRJ.......... American Junior College of Puerto Rico, Bayamon, PR [*OCLC symbol*] (OCLC)
PRJ.......... Capri [*Italy*] [*Airport symbol*] (AD)
PRJ.......... Payroll Journal [*Accounting*]
PRJ.......... Port Royal [*Jamaica*] [*Seismograph station code, US Geological Survey*] (SEIS)
PRJ.......... Projected RADAR Jammer (SEWL)
PRJC........ Pearl River Junior College [*Poplarville, MS*]
PRJC........ Puerto Rico Junior College
PRJMP...... Pressure Jump [*NWS*] (FAAC)
PRK.......... Democratic People's Republic of Korea [*ANSI three-letter standard code*] (CNC)
PRK.......... Paraskevi [*Lesbos*] [*Greece*] [*Seismograph station code, US Geological Survey*] (SEIS)
PRK.......... Park
PRK.......... Park Avenue [*NCIC car model code*]
PRK.......... Park National Corp. [*AMEX symbol*] (SAG)
PRK.......... Parkside Petroleum, Inc. [*Toronto Stock Exchange symbol*] [*Vancouver Stock Exchange symbol*]
PRK.......... People's Republic of Kampuchea [*From 1979 to 1989*] [*Formerly, Cambodia*] [*Later, SOC*] (PD)
PRK.......... Phase Reversal Keying [*Computer science*] (IAA)
PRK.......... Photorefractive Keratectomy [*Ophtholmology*]
PRK.......... Port Kent, NY [*Amtrak rail station code*]
PRK.......... Pridie Kalendas [*The Day before the Calends*] [*Latin*]
PRK.......... Primary Rabbit Kidney [*Medicine*] (DMAA)
PRK.......... Primary Rat Kidney [*Cells*]
PRKA........ Pine Grove Manufacturing [*NCIC trailer make code*]
PRKB........ Printer Keyboard (VLIE)
PR-KB....... Printer-Keyboard (SAUS)
PRKC........ Protein Kinase C (DMAA)
PRKCA...... Protein Kinase C Alpha (DMAA)
PRK Cells... Primary Rat Kidney Cells (SAUS)
PRKG........ Parking
PRKM........ Park Motor Carrier [*Common carrier symbol*]
PRKNG...... Parking (SAUS)
PRKO........ Progesterone Receptor Knockout [*Mouse strain*]
PRKR........ Parkervision, Inc. [*NASDAQ symbol*] (SAG)
PRL.......... Aviaprima [*Russian Federation*] [*ICAO designator*] (FAAC)
PRL.......... Pacht, Ross et Al, Los Angeles, CA [*OCLC symbol*] (OCLC)
PRL.......... Package Research Laboratory (SAUS)
PRL.......... Page Revision Log (NASA)
prl........... Parallel (ELAL)
PRL.......... Parallel (MSA)
PRL.......... Partido Radical Liberal [*Radical Liberal Party*] [*Ecuador*] [*Political party*]
PRL.......... Parti Reformateur Liberal [*Liberal Reform Party*] [*Belgium*] [*Political party*] (PPW)
PRL.......... Parti Republicain de la Liberte [*Republican Party for Liberty*] [*France*] [*Political party*] (PPE)
PRL.......... Parti Republicain de la Liberte [*Republican Party for Liberty*] [*Burkina Faso*] [*Political party*]
PRL.......... Parts Requirement List (KSC)
PRL.......... Paul Revere [*NYSE symbol*] (SPSG)
PRL.......... Peace Research Laboratory [*Later, LPRL*] [*An association*] (EA)
prl........... Pearl (VRA)
PRL.......... Penn Eastern Rail Lines [*Federal Railroad Administration identification code*]
PRL.......... Periodical (SAUS)
PRL.......... Periodical Requirements (SAUS)
PRL.......... Personnel Research Laboratory [*Lackland Air Force Base, TX*]
PRL.......... Pesticide Research Laboratory and Graduate Study Center [*Pennsylvania State University*] [*Research center*] (RCD)
PRL.......... Petroleum Refining Laboratory [*Pennsylvania State University*] (MCD)
PRL.......... Philco Resources [*Vancouver Stock Exchange symbol*]
PRL.......... Philips Research Laboratories (NITA)
PRL.......... Photoreactivating Light
PRL.......... Physical Research Laboratory (CARB)
PRL.......... Physical Review Letters [*A publication*]
P R L........ Physics Research Laboratory (SAUS)
PRL.......... Physiological Research Laboratories [*University of California at San Diego*] [*Research center*]
PRL.......... Pick-Resistant Lock (SAUS)
PRL.......... Pioneering Research Laboratory [*Massachusetts*] [*Army*]
PRL.......... Planning Requirements List (MCD)
PRL.......... Plant Research Laboratory [*Michigan State University*] (RCD)
PRL.......... Plastics Research Laboratory [*MIT*] (MCD)
PRL.......... Polar Research Laboratory [*USA*] [*Marine science*] (OSRA)
PRL.......... Polished-Rod Load (SAUS)
PRL.......... Political Risk Letter [*Database*] [*Frost & Sullivan, Inc.*] [*Information service or system*] (CRD)
PRL.......... Population Research Laboratory [*University of Alberta*] [*Research center*] (RCD)
PRL.......... Postal Reform League (IAA)
PRL.......... Prairie Research Laboratory (SAUS)
PRL.......... Preamble
PRL.......... Precision Reduction Laboratory (AFM)

PRL .... Predicted Repair Level (MCD)
PRL .... Pressure Ratio Limiter (MCD)
PRL .... Price Reduction League (SAUS)
PRL .... Princes Risborough Laboratory (SAUS)
PRL .... Print Lister (VLIE)
PRL .... Priority Rate Limiting (MCD)
Pr L .... Private Laws (SAUS)
PRL .... Private Relocatable Library (SAUS)
PRL .... Processor Level (VLIE)
PRL .... Programming Research Ltd. (SAUS)
PRL .... Program Reference Library (VLIE)
PRL .... Progressive Republican League
PRL .... Project Records List (SAUS)
PRL .... Project Research Laboratory
PrL .... Prolactin (DIPS)
Prl .... Prolactin (STED)
PRL .... Prolactin [*Also, LTH, PR*] [*Endocrinology*]
PRL .... Prolong International [*AMEX symbol*] (SG)
PRL .... Prolong International Corp. [*AMEX symbol*]
PRL .... Properties Research Laboratory [*Purdue University*] [*Lafayette, IN*]
PRL .... Propulsion Research Laboratory
PRL .... Proton Reference Level [*Chemistry*]
PRL .... Publication Requirements List (SAUS)
PRL .... Publications Requirements List (NG)
PRL .... Pulse Reflection Logic (SAUS)
PRL .... Pulse-Reflection Logic (IAA)
PRLA .... Prairie Religious Library Association
PRLA .... Pupils React to Light and Accommodation [*Medicine*] (STED)
PRI&RB ..... Puerto Rico Inspection and Rating Bureau (SAUS)
PrLas .... Premier Laser Systems, Inc. [*Associated Press*] (SAG)
PRLASR ..... Population Research Laboratory. University of Alberta. Department of Sociology. Alberta Series Report (SAUS)
PrIAU-SJ .... Inter-American University of Puerto Rico, San Juan Campus (SAUS)
PR Laws Ann... Laws of Puerto Rico, Annotated [*A publication*] (DLA)
PRLC .... Pittsburgh Regional Library Center [*Chatham College*] [*Pittsburgh, PA*] [*Library network*]
PRLC .... Puerto Rican Lizard-Cuckoo [*North American bird banding code*] (BIBA)
PRLCA .... Power Research Library of Contemporary Art [*University of Sydney, Australia*]
Prl Cmm .... Parole Commission (SAUS)
PRLD .... Pick-Resistant Locking Device (SAUS)
PRLDEF ..... Puerto Rican Legal Defense and Education Fund (EA)
PRLG .... Prologue (SAUS)
PRLI .... Purchase Request Line Item [*DoD*]
PRLINK ...... Public Relations Society of America Online Information Service (IID)
PRLM .... Preliminary (VLIE)
PRIMORDIAL... Primary Order Dial (SAUS)
PRLN .... Paracelsian, Inc. [*NASDAQ symbol*] (SAG)
Pr Ln .... Prior Lien [*Business term*] (MHDW)
PRINOBC/NEC... Primary Navy Officer Billet Classifcation and Navy Enlisted Classification (SAUS)
PRLNW ...... Paracelsian Inc. Wrrt [*NASDAQ symbol*] (TTSB)
PRLO .... Prologic Management Systems, Inc. [*NASDAQ symbol*] (SAG)
PRLO .... PROLOGIC Mgmt Sys [*NASDAQ symbol*] (TTSB)
PRLOW ...... PROLOGIC Mgmt Sys Wrrt [*NASDAQ symbol*] (TTSB)
PRLP .... Planetary Rocket Launcher Platform (AAG)
PRLP .... Puerto Rico Legal Project [*of the National Lawyers Guild*] (EA)
PRIPACSEVOCAM... Primary Pacific Secure Voice Communications (SAUS)
PRLPN-Nakowa... Republican Party for the Liberty and Progress of Niger-Nakowa [*Political party*] (PSAP)
PRLR .... Parlor
PRLS .... Peerless Systems Corp. [*NASDAQ symbol*] (SAG)
PRLS .... Peerless Trucking Company [*Common carrier symbol*]
PRLS .... Pima Regional Library Service [*Library network*]
PRLS .... Prepaid Rental-Listing Service (SAUS)
PRLS .... Pulsed Ruby LASER System
PRLS .... Pulse Ruby Laser System (SAUS)
PRISM .... Program Integrated System Maintenance (SAUS)
PRISMA ..... PRimary Imaging Systems for Multiple Application (SAUS)
PRLST .... Price List
PRLTRL & M... Printer, Lithographer, and Multilith Operator [*Navy*]
PRLW .... Parti des Reformes et de la Liberte de Wallonie [*Belgium*] [*Political party*] (PPW)
PRLWCSR... Population Research Laboratory. University of Alberta. Department of Sociology. Western Canada Series Report (SAUS)
PRLX .... Parallax (AAG)
PRLX .... Parlex Corp. [*NASDAQ symbol*] (NQ)
PRM .... Panarim Resources, Inc. [*Vancouver Stock Exchange symbol*]
PRM .... Parameter (ECII)
PRM .... Parma Byzantine [*Diocesan abbreviation*] [*Ohio*] (TOCD)
Prm .... Parmenides [*of Plato*] [*Classical studies*] (OCD)
PRM .... Parsons Mountain [*South Carolina*] [*Seismograph station code, US Geological Survey*] (SEIS)
PRM .... Partially Reflecting Mirror
PRM .... Partially Regulated Module
PRM .... Partial Refund Message [*Travel industry*] (TRID)
PRM .... Partial Response Method
PRM .... Partner Relationship Management
PRM .... Party of Greater Romania [*Political party*] (PSAP)
PRM .... Payload Retention Mechanism [*NASA*] (NASA)
PRM .... Period of Reduced Melting [*Climatology*]
PRM .... Permanent [*Telegraphy*] (PCTE)
PRM .... Personal Radiation Monitor
PRM .... Petition [*or Proposal*] for Rule Making (NRCH)
PRM .... Phase Retarder Module (SAUS)
PRM .... Phase Reversal Modulation (SAUS)
PRM .... Phosphoribomutase [*An enzyme*] (MAE)
PRM .... Photoreceptor Membrane [*Of the eye*]
PRM .... Pilots Radio Manual
PRM .... Pit Rib Meristem [*Botany*]
PRM .... Pocket Radiation Monitor (SAUS)
PRM .... Portable Radiation Monitor (SAUS)
PRM .... Portola Railway Museum [*Federal Railroad Administration identification code*]
PRM .... Posigrade Rocket Motor (NASA)
PRM .... Positron Reemission Microscopy (SAUS)
PRM .... Power Ram [*NCIC car model code*]
PRM .... Power Range Monitor (IEEE)
PRM .... Precision Runway Monitor [*FAA*] (TAG)
PRM .... Preformed Road Markings [*Road markings embedded in the pavement rather than painted on street's surface*]
PRM .... Preliminary Requirements Model [*NASA*]
PRM .... Prematurely Ruptured Membrane [*Medicine*] (STED)
PRM .... Premature [*or Prolonged*] Rupture of Membranes [*Gynecology*] (MAE)
PRM .... Premium
PRM .... Presbyterian Renewal Ministries (EA)
PRM .... Presidential Review Memo (SAUS)
PRM .... Presidential Review Memorandum [*Jimmy Carter Administration*]
PRM .... Pressure Monitoring Module [*Mechanical engineering*]
PRM .... Pressure Remanent Magnetization
PRM .... Prevention Reference Manuals [*Environmental science*] (COE)
PRM .... Preventive Medicine (MAE)
PRM .... Primary Reference Material [*Library science*] (DAVI)
PRM .... Prime (AAG)
PRM .... Prime Air, Inc. [*ICAO designator*] (FAAC)
PRM .... Prime Computer, Inc. (SAUS)
PRM .... PRIMEDIA, Inc. [*NYSE symbol*] [*Formerly, K-III Communications*] (SG)
prm .... Primer
PRM .... Primidone [*Antiepileptic drug*]
PRM .... Priming (SAUS)
PRM .... Process Radiation Monitor [*Nuclear energy*] (NRCH)
PRM .... Process Resource Manager (SAUS)
PRM .... Production Release Meeting (SAUS)
PRM .... Program Memory (SAUS)
PRM .... Programmer Reference Manual [*Computer science*]
PRM .... Programmers Reference Manual (SAUS)
PRM .... Programming and Resources Management [*NASA*] (MCD)
PRM .... Program Reference Manual (VLIE)
PRM .... Program Resolution Monitor (SAUS)
PRM .... Project Review Meeting (SAUS)
PRM .... Promote (AABC)
PRM .... Publications Requirements Manager [*DoD*]
PRM .... Puerto Lopez [*Colombia*] [*Airport symbol*] (AD)
PRM .... Pulse Rate Modulation
PRM .... Pulse Ratio Modulator
PRM .... Pulse Repetition Per Minute (SAUS)
PRM .... Pyrradiometer (SAUS)
PRMA .... Permeator Corp. (SAUS)
PRMA .... Primadonna Resorts [*NASDAQ symbol*] (TTSB)
PRMA .... Primadonna Resorts, Inc. [*NASDAQ symbol*] (SAG)
PRMA .... Puerto Rican Maritime Authority (SAUS)
PRMA .... Puerto Rico Manufacturers Association (EARSL)
PrMan .... Prayer of Manasses [*Apocrypha*] (BJA)
PRMAR .... Primary Mission Area [*Military*] (CAAL)
PrmBcp ..... Prime Bancorp, Inc. [*Associated Press*] (SAG)
PrmBn .... Premier Bankshares Corp. [*Associated Press*] (SAG)
PRMC .... Pacific Regional Monitoring Center (SAUS)
PRMC .... Paper and Plastic Representatives Management Council (NTPA)
PRMC .... Periodically Replenished Magma Chambers [*Geology*]
PRMC .... Puerto Rican Migration Consortium (EA)
PRMD .... Private Management Domain [*Telecommunications*] (OSI)
PRMDHA .... Potomac River Maryland Home Brigade [*Civil War term*]
PRME .... Prime Capital Corp. (SAUS)
PRME .... Prime Response [*NASDAQ symbol*] (SG)
PRME .... Prime Retail [*NASDAQ symbol*] (TTSB)
PRME .... Prime Retail, Inc. [*NASDAQ symbol*] (SAG)
PrmEgy ...... Prime Energy [*Associated Press*] (SAG)
PrmeMd ..... Prime Medics [*Associated Press*] (SAG)
PRMEP ...... Prime Retail 8.5%Ptc Cv'B'Pfd [*NASDAQ symbol*] (TTSB)
PRMF .... Preretinal Macular Fibrosis [*Medicine*] (MELL)
PrmFar ...... Premier Farnell PLC [*Associated Press*] (SAG)
PRMFN ...... Prime Partners Ltd (SAUS)
PRMG .... Piston Ring Manufacturers Group [*Later, NEPMA*] (EA)
PRM GR .... Permanent Grade (DNAB)
PRMGX ...... Principal Balanced Fund Cl.A [*Mutual fund ticker symbol*] (SG)
PRMH .... Parti Republicain Modere Haitien [*Political party*] (EY)
PRMH .... Profoundly Retarded Multiply Handicapped (AIE)
PrmHsp ..... Prime Hospitality Corp. [*Associated Press*] (SAG)
Prmian ...... Permian Basin Royalty Trust [*Associated Press*] (SAG)
Pr Min .... Printed Minutes of Evidence [*A publication*] (DLA)
PR/MIPR .... Purchase Request/Military Interdepartmental Purchase Request (AFIT)
PRMIS .... Printing Resources Management Information System (DNAB)
Prmisy ...... Premisys Communications [*Associated Press*] (SAG)
Prmk .... Paramark Enterprises, Inc. [*Associated Press*] (SAG)

PRML........ Partial Response Maximum Likelihood [*Computer science*]
PrmLasr..... Premier Laser Systems, Inc. [*Associated Press*] (SAG)
PRMLD...... Premolded [*Technical drawings*] (MSA)
PR/MIPR.... Purchase Request/Military Interdepartmental Purchase Request (SAUS)
PrMLtd..... Prime Motor Inns Ltd. [*Associated Press*] (SAG)
PRMMI..... Puerto Rico Marine Management (SAUS)
PRMO....... Premenos Technology [*NASDAQ symbol*] (TTSB)
PRMO....... Premenos Technology Corp. [*NASDAQ symbol*] (SAG)
PRMO....... Prince Motors [*NCIC car make code*]
PRMO....... Promotions.com, Inc. [*NASDAQ symbol*] (QUAN)
PRMOD...... Printer Module (SAUS)
PrmosT..... Premenos Technology Corp. [*Associated Press*] (SAG)
PRMP....... Plutonium Recovery Modification Project [*Department of Energy*]
PRMP....... Production Readiness Master Plan
PrmPks..... Premier Parks, Inc. [*Associated Press*] (SAG)
PRMR....... Pitch Rate/Moment Ratio [*Automotive engineering*]
PRMR....... Primer (MSA)
PrmRad..... Premier Radio Network [*Associated Press*] (SAG)
PrmrBc...... Premier Bancorp, Inc. [*Associated Press*] (SAG)
PrmRetl..... Prime Retail, Inc. [*Associated Press*] (SAG)
PrmRtl..... Prime Retail, Inc. [*Associated Press*] (SAG)
PRMS....... Personnel Recovery Mission Software (SEWL)
PRMS....... Plans Review Management System (SAUS)
PRMS....... Premisys Communications [*NASDAQ symbol*] (SAG)
PRMSA...... Puerto Rico Maritime Shipping Authority (SAUS)
PRM-SDX... Pyrimethamine-Sulfadoxine [*Pharmacology*] (DAVI)
PrmsH...... Promus Hotel Corp. [*Associated Press*] (SAG)
PRMSS...... Patriotic Resistance Movement of South Sudan [*Political party*]
PRMSS...... Pregnancy-Related Mortality Surveillance System (MELL)
PRMTR...... Parameter (AAG)
PRMU....... Puerto Rican Maritime [*Common carrier symbol*]
PRMU....... Puerto Rican Maritime Shipping Authority [*Intermodal shipping container symbol*] (TVRC)
PRMV....... Peach Rosette Mosaic Virus [*Plant pathology*]
PRMX....... Primex Technologies, Inc. [*NASDAQ symbol*] (SAG)
PRMZ....... Puerto Rican Maritime Shipping Authority [*Intermodal trailer symbol*]
prn.......... As Necessary [*Medicine*] (BCRP)
prn.......... As Needed [*Therapy term*] (CTAA)
PRN......... Greenville, AL [*Location identifier*] [*FAA*] (FAAL)
PRN......... Packet Radio Network [*Telecommunications*] (OSI)
PRN......... Pahrock Range [*Nevada*] [*Seismograph station code, US Geological Survey*] (SEIS)
PRN......... Park Reverse Neutral [*Automotive engineering*]
PRN......... Partido de la Resistencia Nicaraguense [*Political party*] (EY)
PRN......... Partido de la Revolucion Nacional [*Party of the National Revolution*] [*Bolivia*] [*Political party*] (PPW)
PRN......... Partido de Reconstrucao Nacional [*Brazil*] [*Political party*] (EY)
PRN......... Partido Republicano Nacional [*National Republican Party*] [*Costa Rica*] [*Political party*]
PRN......... Parts Requirement Notice (KSC)
PRN......... Party of National Reconstruction (Brazil) [*Political party*] (PSAP)
PRN......... Peace Research Network [*Later, PSA*] (EA)
PRN......... Peace RES Network (EA)
PRN......... Periodic-Random Noise (SAUS)
PRN......... Pesticide Registration Notice (EEVL)
PRN......... Physicians Radio Network
PRN......... Polyradiculoneuropathy [*Medicine*] (DB)
PRN......... Post-Rotatory Nystagmus (SAUS)
PRN......... Practice Notes of the Australian Broadcasting Tribunal (SAUS)
PRN......... Preference Rating Number (SAUS)
PRN......... Previous Result Negative (IAA)
PRN......... Pridie Nonas [*The Day before the Nones*] [*Latin*]
PRN......... Princess Air [*British*] [*ICAO designator*] (FAAC)
PRN......... Printer [*Computer science*]
PRN......... Print Numerically (DEN)
PRN......... Prison [*Telegraphy*] (PCTE)
PRN......... Pristina [*Former Yugoslavia*] [*Airport symbol*] (OAG)
PRN......... PR Newswire [*PR Newswire, Inc.*] [*Information service or system*] (IID)
PRN......... Procurement Reallocation Notice
PRN......... Program Release Notice [*NASA*] (NASA)
PRN......... Program Revision Number (SAUS)
PRN......... Prominent Resources Corp. [*Vancouver Stock Exchange symbol*]
PRN......... Pronasale [*Anatomy*]
PRN......... Pro Re Nata [*Whenever Necessary*] [*Pharmacy*]
PRN......... Pseudo Random Noise (SAUS)
PRN......... Pseudorandom Noise
PRN......... Pseudorandom Number
PRN......... Pseudo-Rustler-Noise (SAUS)
PRN......... Puerto Rican Cement [*NYSE symbol*] (TTSB)
PRN......... Puerto Rican Cement Co., Inc. [*NYSE symbol*] (SPSG)
PRN......... Pulse Ranging Navigation
PRN......... Pulse Ranging Network (KSC)
PRN......... Purchase Request Notice [*Banking*]
PRN......... Purchase Request Number
PRNA....... Plasmid RNA (SAUS)
pRNA....... Ribonucleic Acid, Polysomal [*Biochemistry, genetics*]
PRNAV...... Precision RNAV (SAUS)
PRNC....... Potomac River Naval Command [*Washington, DC*]
PRNC....... Prince
PRNC....... Puerto Rico Nuclear Center
PRND....... Prophylactic Regional Node Dissection [*Medicine*] (MELL)
PRNDI...... Public Radio News Directors (NTPA)
PRNDI...... Public Radio News Directors Inc. (SAUS)
PRNDL...... Park, Reverse, Neutral, Drive, Low [*Automotive term for automatic gearshift indicator in cars; pronounced "prindle"*]
PrnDn...... Princeton Dental Management Corp. [*Associated Press*] (SAG)
PrnDnt...... Princeton Dental Management Corp. [*Associated Press*] (SAG)
PRNET...... Packed Radio Network (SAUS)
PRNET...... Packet Radio Network
PRNET...... Pocket Radio Network (CCCA)
PRNEX...... Price T. Rowe: New Era [*Mutual fund ticker symbol*] (SG)
PRNG....... Paper Negative (VRA)
PRNG....... Pseudo Random Number Generator (SAUS)
PRNG....... Purging (MSA)
PRNHX...... Price T. Rowe: New Horizons [*Mutual fund ticker symbol*] (SG)
PRNI....... Premiere Radio Networks [*NASDAQ symbol*] (TTSB)
PRNI....... Premier Radio Network [*NASDAQ symbol*] (SAG)
PRNI....... Puerto Rican Nightjar [*North American bird banding code*] (BIBA)
PRNIA...... Premiere Radio Networks 'A' [*NASDAQ symbol*] (TTSB)
PRNL....... Pictured Rocks National Lakeshore (SAUS)
prnnl........ Perennial [*Botany*]
PRNP....... Prion Protein (DMAA)
PRNS....... Point Reyes National Seashore (SAUS)
PRNS....... Prins Recycling [*NASDAQ symbol*] (TTSB)
PRNS....... Prins Recycling Corp. [*NASDAQ symbol*] (SAG)
PRNSA...... Pseudo-Random Noise Assembly (SAUS)
PRNSA...... Pseudo Random Noise Signal Assembly (SAUS)
PRNT....... Plaque Reduction Neutralization Test [*Immunochemistry*]
PRNTDEV... Print Device (SAUS)
PRNTG...... Printing (MSA)
PRNTMODE... Print Mode (SAUS)
PRNTR...... Printer
PRNTV...... Preventive
PRNU....... Photoresponse Nonuniformity
PRNWR..... Parker River National Wildlife Refuge (SAUS)
PRO......... Digital Equipment Corporation (SAUS)
PRO......... International Proteins Corp. [*AMEX symbol*] (COMM)
PRO......... Pacific Research Office (CINC)
PRO......... Pacific Research Onice (SAUS)
PRO......... Parallel Rod Oscillator
PRO......... Parents Reaching Out [*An association*] (EA)
PRO......... Parents Rights Organization (EA)
PRO......... Particle Reduction Oven
PRO......... Parts Release Order
PRO......... Patients' Rights Organization (EA)
PRO......... Pay and Records Office [*British military*] (DMA)
PRO......... Payments Resource One [*Arizona*] (EARSL)
PRO......... Peer Review Organization [*Medicare*]
PRO......... Pen Recorder Output (SAA)
PRO......... Performing Rights Organization [*Formerly, BMI-Canada Ltd.*] [*Canada*]
PRO......... Perry, IA [*Location identifier*] [*FAA*] (FAAL)
PRO......... Personnel Relations Officer [*for Shore Stations*] [*Navy*]
PRO......... Photographic Reconnaissance Officer (SAUS)
PR/O........ Pilot Repair/Overhaul [*Military*]
PRO......... Pitch Response Operator
PRO......... Planned Requirements, Outfitting [*Navy*] (NG)
PRO......... Planning Resident Order (KSC)
PRO......... Plant Representative Office (POLM)
PRO......... Plant Representative Officer (MCD)
PRO......... Plastic Repair Optimized (SAUS)
PRO......... Population Renewal Office (EA)
PRO......... Precision Risc Organisation (or Organization) (SAUS)
PRO......... Precision RISC [*Reduced Instruction Set Computer*] Organization
PRO......... Predictable Research Online [*Computer term*]
Pro.......... Prednisone [*Also, P, PDN, PR, Pred*] [*Antineoplastic drug, Endocrinology*]
Pr O........ Press Officer (ODA)
PRO......... Press Officer (SAUS)
PRO......... Principal Public Library [*Library network*]
PRO......... Principal Reducing Option
PRO......... Print Octal (DEN)
pro.......... Probate (GEAB)
PRO......... Probate
PRO......... Probation [*or Probationer*]
PRO......... Probation Services for Adults (PHSD)
PRO......... Probe [*NCIC car model code*]
PRO......... Problem Resolution Office [*IRS*]
PRO......... Procedure (AABC)
PRO......... Proceed (NAKS)
Pro.......... Proculus [*Flourished, 1st century*] [*Authority cited in pre-1607 legal work*] (DSA)
PRO......... Procurement Research Office [*Army*]
PRO......... Production Repair Order
pro.......... Professional (ODBW)
PRO......... Professional
PRO......... Professional Dental Technologies, Inc. [*AMEX symbol*] (SAG)
PRO......... Professionally (SAUS)
PRO......... Professional Racing Organization of America [*Later, USCF*] (EA)
PRO......... Professional Resellers Organization [*Defunct*] (EA)
PRO......... Professional Review Organization [*Medicare*]
PRO......... Proficiency
PRO......... Proflavine [*An antiseptic*]
PRO......... Programmable Remote Operation [*Computer Devices, Inc.*]
PRO......... Programming Online (SAUS)
PRO......... Program Representative Office (AAGC)

PRO......... Progressive
pro.......... Proline [*An amino acid*] (DOG)
Pro.......... Proline [*Also, P*] [*An amino acid*]
Pro.......... Prolyl [*Biochemistry*]
PRO......... Pronation [*Medicine*]
PRO......... Pronominal [*Linguistics*] (IEL)
PRO......... Pronoun [*Grammar*] (WGA)
PRO......... Pronto Explorations Ltd. [*Toronto Stock Exchange symbol*]
PRO......... Propagation [*Military*]
PRO......... Propagation Prediction Report (SAA)
PRO......... Propair, Inc. [*Canada*] [*ICAO designator*] (FAAC)
PRO......... Propeller Order
PRO......... Prophylactic (AABC)
PRO......... Prospect Referral Operation (SAUS)
PRO......... Prostitute (ADA)
PRO......... Protege [*NCIC car model code*]
Pro.......... Protein
Pro.......... Protest (EBF)
PRO......... Protest
Pro.......... Prothrombin [*Factor II*] [*Hematology*]
PRO......... Proved
pro.......... Provencal [*MARC language code*] [*Library of Congress*] (LCCP)
Pro.......... Proverbs [*Old Testament book*] (BJA)
PRO......... Providence [*Diocesan abbreviation*] [*Rhode Island*] (TOCD)
PRO......... Province (ROG)
PRO......... Provost
PRO......... Provo, UT [*Amtrak rail station code*]
PRO......... Public Radio Online (SAUS)
PRO......... Public Record Office [*British*]
PRO......... Public Relations Office [*or Officer*] [*Usually military*]
PRO......... Public Relations Officer (ADWA)
PRO......... Puchase Request Order
PRO.EC ..... Professional Dental Tech [*ECM, Symbol*] (TTSB)
PROA........ Polymer Research Corp. of America [*NASDAQ symbol*] (NQ)
PROA........ Polymer Research Corporation of America (SAUS)
PROA........ Polymer Resh America [*NASDAQ symbol*] (TTSB)
PROA........ Public Record Office Archives (SAUS)
PROA........ Puerto Rico Operations Area
ProActiv..... ProActive Technologies, Inc. [*Associated Press*] (SAG)
PRO-AM...... Professional-Amateur (WDAA)
pro-am...... Professionals and Amateurs [*Sports*] (WDMC)
PROANTAR... Brazilian Antarctic Program (SAUS)
PROAP ...... Principal Regional Office for Asia and the Pacific [*UNESCO*]
PROAS ...... Productos Asfalticos (EFIS)
Prob .... English Probate and Admiralty Reports for Year Cited (journ.) (SAUS)
Prob .... Law Reports, Probate Division [*England*] [*A publication*] (DLA)
PROB........ Probability (KSC)
PROB........ Probability Percentage (PIAV)
PROB........ Probable (GOBB)
prob .... Probable
prob .... Probably (VRA)
PROB........ Probably
Prob .... Probate [*Legal term*] (DLA)
PROB........ Probated [*Motor vehicle violation code used in state of Maryland*] (MVRD)
PROB........ Probation [*FBI standardized term*]
PROB........ Probationary [*Vehicle license type used in state of Wisconsin*] (MVRD)
PROB........ Problem
Prob .... Quod Omnis Probus Liber Sit [*of Philo*] (BJA)
PROB40..... Probability 40 Percent [*ICAO*] (FAAC)
Prob (1891)... Law Reports, Probate Division [*1891*] [*England*] [*A publication*] (DLA)
Prob&Adm.. Div. Probate and Admiralty Division Law Reports (SAUS)
Prob & Adm Div... Probate and Admiralty Division Law Reports [*A publication*] (DLA)
Prob & Div... Probate and Divorce, English Law Reports [*A publication*] (DLA)
Prob & Mat... Probate and Matrimonial Cases [*A publication*] (DLA)
PROBAR .... Programmable Band Radiometer (SAUS)
PROBASE... Production Base Information System (POLM)
Probat....... Probation [*Legal term*] (DLA)
Probation & Parole L Rep... Probation and Parole Law Reports [*A publication*] (DLA)
Probation & Parole L Summ... Probation and Parole Law Summaries [*A publication*] (DLA)
Probat J..... Probation Journal [*A publication*] (ILCA)
Prob C....... Probate Code [*A publication*] (DLA)
PROBCOST... Probabilistic Budgeting and Forward Costing
PROBCOST... Probable Cost (SAUS)
Prob Ct Rep... Probate Court Reporter [*Ohio*] [*A publication*] (DLA)
PROBDAM... Probably Damaged (SAUS)
PROBDET... Probability of Detection [*Navy*] (NVT)
Prob Div .... Probate Division, English Law Reports [*A publication*] (DLA)
PROBE ...... Performance Review of Base Supply Effectiveness [*Air Force*] (AFM)
PROBE ...... Performance Review of Base-supply Effectiveness (SAUS)
PROBE ...... Pilot Radiation Observation Experiment [*Marine science*] (OSRA)
PROBE ...... Portable Remote Observation of the Environment (SAUS)
PROBE ...... Practical Research into Organizational Behavior and Effectiveness (EDAC)
PROBE ...... Pre-Recognition of Baleful Error (SAUS)
PROBE ...... Profile Resolution Obtained by Excitation (PDAA)
PROBE ...... Program for Research on Objectives-Based Evaluation [*UCLA*]
PROBE ...... Program Optimization and Budget Evaluation [*Military*]
PROBE ...... Pro-Recognition of Baleful Errors (SAUS)
PROBE ...... Prototype Radiation Observation Experiment (SAUS)
PROBES..... Processes and Resources of the Bering Sea Shelf [*University of Alaska*]
PROBFOR... Probability Forecasting [*Computer program*] [*Bell System*]
PRO BIKE... Bicycle Federation of America (EA)
PROBIT...... Probability Unit [*Statistics*]
Prob J....... Probation Journal [*A publication*] (DLA)
Probl Hetmatol Blood Transfus... Problems of Hematology and Blood Transfusion (SAUS)
Probl Psychol... Problems of Psychology (SAUS)
Probl Radiobiol... Problems of Radiobiology (SAUS)
Prob LT...... Probyn on Land Tenure [*4th ed.*] [*1881*] [*A publication*] (DLA)
Probl Virol... Problems of Virology (SAUS)
PROBO....... Product/Ore/Bulk/Oil Carrier [*Shipping*] (DS)
Prob Off..... Probation Officer (SAUS)
PROBOUT... Proceed On or About (MUGU)
Prob Pr Act... Probate Practice Act [*A publication*] (DLA)
Prob R ...... Probate Reports [*A publication*] (DLA)
Prob Rep ... Probate Reports [*A publication*] (DLA)
Prob Rep Ann... Probate Reports, Annotated [*A publication*] (DLA)
PROBSUB... Probable Submarine (NVT)
PROBUS .... Program Budget System [*Military*]
Proby........ Probationary [*British military*] (DMA)
PROC........ Performing Rights Organization of Canada [*See also SDE*]
PROC........ Performining Rights Organisation of Canada (SAUS)
PROC........ Preliminary Required Operational Capability [*Military*]
PROC........ Procaine hydrochloride (SAUS)
Proc .... Procedere (SAUS)
PROC........ Procedure (AAG)
Proc .... Proceeding (SAUS)
Proc .... Proceedings (DIAR)
PROC........ Proceedings
proc.......... Proceedings (WDMC)
PROC........ Pro-Cel International, Inc. (SAUS)
PROC........ Process (AABC)
proc.......... Process (VRA)
Proc .... Processes (AL)
Proc .... Processing (AL)
proc.......... Processing (ELAL)
PROC........ Processing (SAUS)
PROC........ Procession (ROG)
PROC........ Processor [*or Processing*]
Proc .... Proclamation (DLA)
PROC........ Proctor
PROC........ Procure (AABC)
PROC........ Procurement (MSA)
PROC........ Programming Computer [*Computer science*]
PROC........ Proposed Required Operational Capability [*Military*] (AABC)
PROC........ Protein C (DMAA)
PROCAARE... Program for Collaboration Against AIDS and Related Epidemics (SAUS)
Proc Abstr Soc Biol Chem... Proceedings and Abstracts. Society of Biological Chemists (SAUS)
Proc Acad Sci Georgian SSR... Proceedings. Academy of Sciences. Georgian SSR (SAUS)
Proc Acad Sci USSR... Proceedings. Academy of Sciences of the USSR. Geochemistry Section (SAUS)
Proc A Conv Am Cranberry Growers Ass... Proceedings. Annual Convention. American Cranberry Growers Association (SAUS)
PROCADES... Project for Training in Rural, Economic and Social Development (SAUS)
PROCAL..... Programmable Calculator [*Computer science*] (IAA)
PROCAM.... Prospective Cardiovascular Munster [*Medicine*] [*Study*] (EDAA)
Proc Amer Math Soc... Proceedings of the American Mathematical Society (SAUS)
Proc Amer Power Conf... Proceedings of the American Power Conference (SAUS)
Proc Amer Soc Civ Engrs... Proceedings of the American Society of Civil Engineers (SAUS)
Proc Amer Soc of Internat L... Proceedings. American Society of International Law [*A publication*] (DLA)
Proc Amp... Processing Amplifier (NTCM)
Proc Am Pet Inst... Proceedings. American Petroleum Institute (SAUS)
Proc Am Pharm Manuf Assoc Annu Meet... Proceedings. American Pharmaceutical Manufacturers Association. Annual Meeting (SAUS)
Proc Am Pharm Manuf Assoc Midyear East Sect Meet... Proceedings. American Pharmaceutical Manufacturers Association. Midyear Eastern Section Meeting (SAUS)
Proc Am Soc Civ Eng Transp Eng J... Proceedings. American Society of Civil Engineers.Transportation Engineering Journal (SAUS)
Proc Annu Allerton Conf Circuit Syst Theory... Proceedings. Annual Allerton Conference on Circuit and System Theory (SAUS)
Proc Annu Allerton Conf Commun Control Comput... Proceedings. Annual Allerton Conference on Communication, Control and Computing (SAUS)
Proc Annu Conf Int Symp N Am Lake Manage Soc... Proceedings. Annual Conference and International Symposium. North American Lake Management Society (SAUS)
Proc Annu Conv Assoc Am Pestic Control Off... Proceedings Annual Convention Association. American Pesticide Control Officials (SAUS)
Proc Annu Conv Flavoring Ext Manuf Assoc US... Proceedings. Annual Convention. Flavoring Extract Manufacturers Association of the United States (SAUS)

Proc Annu Conv Sugar Technol Assoc India... Proceedings. Annual Convention. Sugar Technologists Association of India (SAUS)
Proc Annu Conv West Can Water Sewage Conf... Proceedings. Annual Convention. Western Canada Water and Sewage Conference (SAUS)
Proc Annu Eng Geol Soils Eng Symp... Proceedings. Annual Engineering Geology and Soils Engineering Symposium (SAUS)
Proc Annu Fall Meet Calif Nat Gasoline Assoc... Proceedings. Annual Fall Meeting California Natural Gasoline Association (SAUS)
Proc Annu Freq Control Symp... Proceedings of the Annual Frequency Control Symposium [*A publication*] (CABS)
Proc Annu Meet Am Asso Vet Lab Diagn... Proceedings. Annual Meeting. American Association of Veterinary Laboratory Diagnosticians (SAUS)
Proc Annu Meet Biochem... Proceedings. Annual Meeting of Biochemistry (SAUS)
Proc Annu Meet Hawaii Sugar Plant Ass... Proceedings. Annual Meeting. Hawaiian Sugar Planters Association (SAUS)
Proc Annu Meet Int Magnesium Ass... Proceedings. Annual Meeting. International Magnesium Association (SAUS)
Proc Annu Meet Med Sect Am Counc Life Insur... Proceedings. Annual Meeting Medical Section. American Council of Life Insurance (SAUS)
Proc Annu Meet Med Sect Am Counc Life Insur... Proceedings, Annual Meeting of the Medical Section of the American Council of Life Insurance (SAUS)
Proc Annu Meet Nat Ass Wheat Growers... Proceedings. Annual Meeting National Association of Wheat Growers (SAUS)
Proc Annu Sci Meet Comm Probl Drug Depend US Nat Res Counc... Proceedings. Annual Scientific Meeting. Committee on Problems of Drug Dependence. United States National Research Counci (SAUS)
Proc Annu Symp Comput Appl Med Care... Proceedings of the Annual Symposium on Computer Applications in Medical Care (SAUS)
Proc Annu Tech Meet Tech Assa Graphic Arts... Proceedings. Annual Technical Meeting. Technical Association. Graphic Arts (SAUS)
Proc AOS ... Proceedings of the American Oriental Society (SAUS)
PRO CAPILL... Pro Capillis [*For the Hair*] [*Pharmacy*]
Procarb ..... Procarbazine [*Antineoplastic drug*] (DAVI)
PROCAS..... Process Calculation System (SAUS)
PROCAS..... Process-Oriented Contract Administration Services
Proc Asiat Soc... Proceedings. Asiatic Society (SAUS)
Proc Assoc Am Physicians... Proceedings of the Association of American Physicians (SAUS)
Proc Astron Soc Aust... Proceedings of the Astronomical Society of Australia (SAUS)
Proc Aust Biochem Soc... Proceedings of the Australian Biochemical Society (SAUS)
Proc Aust Bldg Res Congr... Australian Building Research Congress. Proceedings (journ.) (SAUS)
Proc Aust Clay Miner Conf... Australian Clay Minerals Conference. Proceedings (journ.) (SAUS)
Proc Aust Conf Nucl Tech Anal... Australian Conference on Nuclear Techniques of Analysis. Proceedings (journ.) (SAUS)
Proc Australal Inst Min Me... Proceedings of the Australasian Institute of Mining and Metallurgy (SAUS)
Proc Aust Soc Anim Prod... Proceedings of the Australian Society of Animal Production (SAUS)
Proc Aust Soc Med Res... Proceedings of the Australian Society for Medical Research (SAUS)
Proc B & B... Proctor's Bench and Bar of New York [*A publication*] (DLA)
Proc Br Ceram Soc... Proceedings of the British Ceramic Society (SAUS)
Proc Br Crop Prot Conf... Proceedings. British Crop Protection Conference. Weeds (SAUS)
ProcBritAc... Proceedings of the British Academy [*A publication*] (ABAR)
Proc Can Nucl Assoc Annu Int Conf... Proceedings Canadian Nuclear Association Annual International Conference (SAUS)
Proc Cen.... Procurement Center (SAUS)
Proc Ch ..... Proceedings in Chancery [*A publication*] (DLA)
PROC CHECK... Process Check (SAUS)
Proc Chem Soc... Proceedings of the Chemical Society (SAUS)
Proc Cir..... Procurement Circular (AAGC)
PROCCIR... Procurement Circular [*Air Force*] (AFIT)
Proc Coll Nat Sci... Proceedings. College of Natural Sciences (SAUS)
Proc Conf Aust Soc Sugar Cane Technol... Australian Society of Sugar Cane Technologists. Proceedings of the Conference (journ.) (SAUS)
Proc Congr Int Assoc Sci Study Ment Defic... Proceedings Congress of the International Association for the Scientific Study of Mental Deficiency (SAUS)
Proc Congr S Afr Sug Technol Ass... Proceedings. Congress of the South African Sugar Technologists Association (SAUS)
Proc Cotteswold Natur Fld Club... Proceedings. Cotteswold Naturalists Field Club (SAUS)
Proc Counc Econ AIME... Proceedings. Council of Economics. American Institute of Mining, Metallurgical and Petroleum Engineers (SAUS)
Proc Coventry Dist Natur Hist Sci Soc... Proceedings. Coventry District Natural History and Scientifc Society (SAUS)
Proc Cumberland Geol Soc... Proceedings. Cumberland Geological Society (SAUS)
PROCD ...... Procedure (AFM)
procd .... Procedure (ELAL)
PROCD ...... Proceed (AFM)
Proc Dir Refin Am Pet Inst... Proceedings. Division of Refining. American Petroleum Institute (SAUS)
Proc Dist... Procurement District (SAUS)
Proc Dorset Soc... Dorset Natural History and Archaeological Society. Proceedings (journ.) (SAUS)
PROCDRE... Procedure (ROG)
Proc East Afr Acad... Proceedings. East African Acdemy (SAUS)
PROCED..... Procedure
Proceed of the Canmbridge Philol Soc... Cambridge Philological Society, Cambridge, England, Proceedings (SAUS)
PRO-CELEB... Professional Celebrit (SAUS)
Proc Elec Assoc Aust... Proceedings. Electrical Association of Australia [*A publication*]
Proc Elec Assoc NSW... Proceedings. Electrical Association of New South Wales [*Australia*] [*A publication*]
Proc Eng Assoc NSW... Proceedings. Engineering Association of New South Wales [*Australia*] [*A publication*]
Proc Eng Soc West PA... Proceedings. Engineers Society of Western Pennsylvania (SAUS)
Procept...... Procept, Inc. [*Associated Press*] (SAG)
Process Eecon Int... Process Economis International (SAUS)
Process Eng Plant and Control... Process Engineering. Plant and Control (SAUS)
Proces-Verb Seances Soc Sci Phys Nat Bordeaux... ProcSs-Verbaux des Seances. Societe des Sciences Physiques et Naturelles de Bordeaux (SAUS)
Proc Eur Dial Transplant Assoc Eur Renal Assoc... Proceedings. European Dialysis and Transplant Association-European Renal Association (SAUS)
PROCEVAL... Procurement Evaluation (SAUS)
Proc Fac Eng Tokai Univ... Proceedings. Faculty of Engineering Tokai University (SAUS)
Proc Fla Anti-Mosq... Proceedings. Florida Anti-Mosquito Association (SAUS)
Proc Fla State Hort Soc... Proceedings of the Florida State Horticultural Society (SAUS)
Proc Florida State Hortic Soc... Florida. State Horticultural Society. Proceedings (journ.) (SAUS)
Proc Geol Assoc... Proceedings. Geologists Association (SAUS)
Proc Geol Assoc London... Proceedings. Geologists Association of London (SAUS)
Proc Ger Soc Neurosurg... Proceedings. German Society of Neurosurgery (SAUS)
Proc Hokuriku Br Crop Sci Soc... Proceedings. Hokuriku Branch of Crop Science Society (SAUS)
Proc Hum Factors Ergon Soc... Proceedings of the Human Factors and Ergonomics Society [*A publication*] (CABS)
PROCIEE... Proceedings of the Institute of Electrical Engineers [*A publication*] (IAA)
Proc IEE-A... Institution of Electrical Engineers. Proceedings. A (journ.) (SAUS)
Proc IEE-B... Institution of Electrical Engineers. Proceedings. B (journ.) (SAUS)
Proc IEE-C... Institution of Electrical Engineers. Proceedings. C (journ.) (SAUS)
Proc IEE D... Institution of Electrical Engineers. Proceedings. D (journ.) (SAUS)
Proc IEE F... Institution of Electrical Engineers. Proceedings. F (journ.) (SAUS)
Proc IEE G... Institution of Electrical Engineers. Proceedings. G (journ.) (SAUS)
Proc Indiana Aad Sci... Proceedings. Indiana Academy of Science (SAUS)
Proc Indiana Acad Sci... Proceedings of the Indiana Academy of Science (SAUS)
Proc Indian Acad Sci... Proceedings of the Indian Academy of Sciences (SAUS)
Proc Indian Acad Sci Sect A Earth Planetary Sci... Indian Academy of Sciences. Proceedings. Section A. Earth and Planetary Sciences (journ.) (SAUS)
Proc Indian Natl Sci Acad... Proceedings. Indian National Science Academy (SAUS)
Proc Indian Natl Sci Acad... Proceedings of the Indian National Science Academy (SAUS)
Proc Indian Soc of Internat L... Proceedings of the Conference, The Indian Society of International Law (SAUS)
Proc Inst Automob Eng... Proceedings. Institution of Automobile Engineers (SAUS)
Proc Inst Chem... Proceedings. Institution of Chemists (SAUS)
Proc Inst Criminol Univ Sydney... University of Sydney. Institute of Criminology. Proceedings [*A publication*]
Proc Inst Elect Electron E... Proceeding of the Institute of Electrical and Electronic Engineers (SAUS)
Proc Inst Electr Eng... Proceedings of the Institution of Electrical Engineers (SAUS)
Proc Inst Mech Eng... Proceedings of the Institution of Mechanical Engineers (SAUS)
Proc Inst Med Chicago... Proceedings of the Institute of Medicine of Chicago (SAUS)
Proc Instn Radio Eng Aust... Proceedings. Institution of Radio Engineers of Australia [*A publication*]
Proc Inst Pomol... Proceedings. Research Institute of Pomology (SAUS)
ProcInstRadEng... Proceedings of Institute of Radio Engineers (SAUS)
Proc Inst Radio Engrs... Proceedings of the Institute of Radio Engineers (SAUS)
Proc Int Assoc Theor Appl Limnol... Proceedings. International Association of Theoretical and Applied Limnology (SAUS)
Proc Int Ass Test Mater... Proceedings. International Association for Testing Materials (SAUS)
Proc Int Congr Ecol... Proceedings of the International Congress of Ecology (SAUS)
Proc Int Pharmacol Meet... Proceedings. International Pharmalogical Meeting (SAUS)
Proc Int Pl Propag Soc... Proceedings. International Plant Propagators Society (SAUS)
Proc Int Sci Congr Cultiv Edible Fungi... Proceedings. International Scientifc Congress on the Cultivation of Edible Fungi (SAUS)
Proc Int Symp Boreal For... Proceedings of the International Symposium on Boreal Forest (SAUS)
Proc Int Union Biol Sci... Proceedings. International Union of Biological Sciences (SAUS)
Proc Iowa Acad Sci... Proceedings of the Iowa Academy of Science (SAUS)
Proc IRE .... Proceedings of the IRE (SAUS)
ProcJPES ... Proceedings of the Jewish Palestine Exploration Society [*A publication*] (ABAR)
Proc La Acad Sci... Proceedings of the Louisiana Academy of Sciences (SAUS)

PROCLIB... Procedure Library [*Computer science*]
Proc Lincoln Coll Farmers Conf... Proceedings. Lincoln College. Farmers Conference (SAUS)
Proc Med-Leg Soc Vic... Medico-Legal Society of Victoria. Proceedings [*A publication*]
Proc Microscopical Soc Vic... Proceedings. Microscopical Society of Victoria [*Australia*] [*A publication*]
ProcmT...... Procom Technology Inc. [*Associated Press*] (SAG)
Proc Nat Conf AIAS... Proceedings. National Conference. Australian Institute of Agricultural Science (SAUS)
Proc Natl Acad Sci USA... Proceedings of the National Academy of Science of the United States of America (MEC)
Proc Natl Counc Sci Dev... Proceedings. National Council on Science Development (SAUS)
Proc Natl Inst Sci... Proceedings. National Institute of Sciences (SAUS)
Proc Natl Sci Counc... Proceedings of the National Science Council (SAUS)
Proc Natl Telecommon Conf... Proceedings. National Telecommunications Conference (SAUS)
Proc Natn Ent Soc... Proceedings. National Entomological Society (SAUS)
Proc Near E S Afr Irrig Pract Semin... Proceedings. Near East-South Africa Irrigation Practices Seminar (SAUS)
PROCNEC... Proceeding of the National Electrical Conference (SAUS)
Proc Nutr Soc... Proceedings of the Nutrition Society (SAUS)
PROCO...... Procurement Officer [*Military*]
PROCO...... Programmed Combustion [*Ford Motor Co.*]
PROCO...... Projects for Continental Operations [*World War II*]
Proc of the SJCC... Proceedings of the Summer Joint Computer Conference (SAUS)
Proc of the WJCC... Proceedings of the Winter Joint Computer Conference (SAUS)
PROCOL..... Process Control Language (NITA)
PROCOL..... Process Control Oriented Language [*Computer science*] (IAA)
ProCom..... IEEE-SA Standards Board Procedures Committee (SAUS)
PROCOM.... Procedures Committee [*Institute of Electrical and Electronics Engineers*] (IEEE)
PROCOM.... Procurement Committee
PROCOM.... Prognose Compiler [*Computer science*] (IAA)
PROCOM.... Projection Compositor (SAUS)
PROCOMEXCHI... Mexican-Chicano Cooperative Programs on Mexican-US-Chicano Futures (EA)
PROCOMM... Program Communication (SAUS)
PROCOMP... Process Compiler [*Computer science*] (IAA)
PROCOMP... Process Computer [*Computer science*]
PROCOMP... Program Compiler [*Computer science*] (IEEE)
PROCON.... Project Control (SAUS)
PROCON.... Protocol Converter (DA)
PROCON.... Request Diagnosis, Prognosis, Present Condition, Probable Date and Mode of Disposition of Following Patient Reported in Your Hospital [*Military*]
Procop...... Procopius [*Sixth century AD*] [*Classical studies*] (OCD)
PROCOP.... Project Control Package (SAUS)
PROCOPT... Processing Option [*Computer science*] (MHDB)
PROCOR.... Pro Cattle Co. (EFIS)
Proc Osaka Prefect Inst Public Health... Proceedings. Osaka Prefecture Institute of Public Health (SAUS)
PROCOTIP... Promotion Cooperative du Transport Individuel Publique [*Public cars for private use to reduce traffic congestion*] [*Also known as TIP*] [*France*]
ProcPhilAs... Proceedings of the American Philological Association [*A publication*] (ABAR)
Proc Phil Educ Soc... Proceedings. Philosophy of Education Society (SAUS)
Proc Phys Soc... Proceedings. Physical Society (SAUS)
Proc Plant Propagators Soc... Proceedings. Plant Propagators. Society (SAUS)
Proc PN Lebedev Phys Inst... Proceedings of the P.N. Lebedev Physics Institute (SAUS)
Proc Pr...... Proctor's Practice [*A publication*] (DLA)
Proc Prac... Proctor's Practice [*A publication*] (DLA)
PROCR...... Processor (VLIE)
Proc Reg Conf Int Potash Inst... Proceedings. Regional Conferene. International Potash Institute (SAUS)
Proc Reliab Maint Conf... Proceedings of Reliability and Maintainability Conference (SAUS)
Proc Rep S Seedmens Ass... Proceedings and Reports. Southern Seedmens Association (SAUS)
Proc Res Inst Oceanogr Fish... Proceedings. Research Institute of Oceanography and Fisheries (SAUS)
Proc Res Soc Jap Sugar Refin Technol... Proceedings. Research Society of Japan Sugar Refineries Technologists (SAUS)
ProcRNS.... Proceedings of the Royal Numismatic Society [*A publication*] (ABAR)
Proc Roy Anthtropol Inst... Proceedings. Royal Anthropological Institute (SAUS)
Proc Roy Aust Chem Inst... Proceedings of the Royal Australian Chemical Institute (SAUS)
Proc Roy Soc... Proceeding of the Royal Society (SAUS)
Proc Roy Soc Med... Proceedings of the Royal Society of Medicine (SAUS)
Proc Roy Soc Qld... Proceedings. Royal Society of Queensland [*Australia*] [*A publication*]
Proc Roy Soc Vic... Proceedings. Royal Society of Victoria [*Australia*] [*A publication*]
Proc R Soc Edin... Proceedings of the Royal Society of Edinburgh (MEC)
Proc R Soc London... Proceedings of the Royal Society of London (MEC)
Proc Ruakura Farmers Conf... Proceedings. Ruakura Farmers Conference (SAUS)
PROCS...... Proceedings
Proc S Afr Soc Anim Proc... Proceedings. South African Society of Animal Production (SAUS)
PROCSCAN... Procedure Library Scanning (SAUS)
Proc Sci Soc Univ Adel... Proceedings. Scientific Society. University of Adelaide [*A publication*]
PROCSD.... Processed
Proc Second Malays Soil Conf... Proceedings. Second Malaysian Soil Conference (SAUS)
Proc Semin Biomass Energy City Farm Ind... Proceedings. Seminar on Biomass Energy for City, Farm and Industry (SAUS)
PROCSEQ... Processing Sequence [*Computer science*] (MHDB)
Proc Shikoku Br Crop Sci Soc... Proceedings. Shikoku Branch of Crop Science Society (SAUS)
PROCSIM... Processor Simulation (SAUS)
PROCSIM... Processor Simulation Language [*Computer science*] (PDAA)
PROCSIM Language... Processor Simulation Language (SAUS)
Proc SJCC... Proceeding of the Spring Joint Computer Conference (SAUS)
Proc Soc Anal Chem... Proceedings of the Society for Analytical Chemistry (SAUS)
Proc Soc Chem Indust Vic... Proceedings. Society of Chemical Industry of Victoria [*Australia*] [*A publication*]
Proc Soc Exp Biol Med... Proceedings of the Society for Experimental Biology and Medicine (SAUS)
PROCSTEP... Procedure Step (SAUS)
PROCSTOR... Program Storage [*Computer science*] (VLIE)
Proc Study Fauna Flora USSR... Proceedings on the Study of the Fauna and Flora of the USSR (SAUS)
PROCSY..... Purdue Remote Online Console System (SAUS)
Proc Symp Effects Ionizing Radiat Seed Signific Crop Impr... Proceedings. Symposium on the Effects of Ionizing Radiation on Seeds and Their Significance for Crop Improvement (SAUS)
Proc Symp Isotop Plant Nutr Physiol... Proceedings. Symposium on Isotopes in Plant Nutrition and Physiology (SAUS)
Proc Symp Use Radioisotop Soil Plant Nutr Stud... Proceedings Symposium on the Use of Radioisotopes in Soil-Plant Nutrition Studies (SAUS)
Proct......... Proctology [*Medicine*] (AMHC)
PROCT...... Proctology
ProctGm.... Procter & Gamble Co. [*Associated Press*] (SAG)
PROCTO..... Proctocolitis (SAUS)
PROCTO..... Proctocolonoscopy (SAUS)
PROCTO..... Proctology [*Gastroenterology*] (DAVI)
PROCTO..... Proctoplegia (SAUS)
procto....... Proctoscopy [*Medicine*] (BCRP)
PROCTO..... Proctoscopy [*Medicine*]
PROCTO..... Proctosigmoidectomy (SAUS)
PROCTOR... Priority Routine Organizer for Computer Transfers and Operations of Registers
Proc Tree Wardens Arborists Util Conf... Proceedings. Tree Wardens, Arborists and Utilities Conference (SAUS)
PROCU...... Processing Unit
PROCUP.... Partido Revolucionario Obrerista y Clandestino de Union Popular [*Mexico*] [*Political party*] (EY)
PROCURE... Command Procurement System (SAUS)
Proc Utah Acad Sci... Proceedings. Utah Academy of Sciences, Arts and Letters (SAUS)
PROCVAL... Validation Procedures Library [*Social Security Administration*]
Proc WA Instn Eng... Proceedings. Western Australian Institution of Engineers [*A publication*]
Proc West For Conserv Ass... Proceedings Western Forestry Conference. Western Forestry and Conservation Association (SAUS)
Proc West Pharmacol Soc... Proceedings of the Western Pharmacology Society (SAUS)
Proc World Congr Anaesthesiol... Anaesthesiology. Proceedings of the World Congress of Anaesthesiologists (journ.) (SAUS)
Procyt....... ProCyte Corp. [*Associated Press*] (SAG)
PROD........ Office of Production [*National Security Agency*]
PROD........ Photographic Retrieval from Optical Disk
prod......... Produce (WDAA)
PROD........ Produce
PROD........ Producer (GOBB)
PROD........ Product [*or Production*] (AABC)
prod......... Product (WDMC)
Prod......... Production (AAGC)
PROD........ Production (DOMA)
prod......... Production (WDMC)
Prod......... Produzent (SAUS)
PROD........ Professional Drivers Council for Safety and Health
PROD........ Professional Over-the-Road Drivers [*Part of Teamsters Union*]
PROD........ Program for Orbit Development (SAUS)
PRODAC.... Production Advisers Consortium (NADA)
PRODAC.... Programmed Digital Automatic Control [*Computer science*]
PRODAM.... Production Orientated Draughting and Manufacturing (PDAA)
PRODAN.... Propionyl(dimethylamino)naphthalene [*Organic chemistry*]
PRODASE... Protein Database
Prod Aust... Productivity Australia [*A publication*]
PRODC...... Production Command [*Army*]
PROD Code... Product Code (SAUS)
PROD/DEPL... Production and Deployment [*Phase*] (DOMA)
PRODEM.... Project on Demilitarisation (SAUS)
Proden...... Proyecto de Desarrollo Nacional [*Project for National Development*] [*Chile*] (PPW)
ProDex...... ProDex, Inc. [*Associated Press*] (SAG)
Prod Invent Manage J... Production and Inventory Management Journal [*A publication*] (CABS)
PRODISCO... Producers Distributing Corp.
Prod Liab... Products Liability (SAUS)
Prod Liab Int'l... Product Liability International [*A publication*] (DLA)

Prod Liab Rep... Product Liability Reporter [*Commerce Clearing House*] [*A publication*] (DLA)
Prod Liab Rep... Products Liability Reporter (or Reports) (SAUS)
PRODN...... Production
Prodn........ Production
PRODNG.... Producing
ProDnt....... Professional Dental Technologies, Inc. [*Associated Press*] (SAG)
PRODOC.... Procedure Documentation [*Computer science*] (MHDB)
PRODON.... Production
ProdOp...... Production Operators Corp. [*Associated Press*] (SAG)
PRO DOS... Pro Dose [*For a Dose*] [*Pharmacy*]
ProDOS..... Professional Disk Operating System [*Computer science*]
Prod Proj Trends Bldg... Products, Projects and Trends in Building (SAUS)
PRODR...... Producer
Prods......... Products (AAGC)
Prod Safety & Liab Rep... Product Safety and Liability Reporter [*A publication*] (DLA)
PRODSEC... Product Security (ACAE)
PRODT...... Product
Prod Tech... Production and Technique (SAUS)
PRODUCE... Production Distribution Using Component Evaluation (IAA)
Product...... Productivity Technologies Corp. [*Associated Press*] (SAG)
PRODUCTN... Production
Productv.... Productivity Technologies Corp. [*Associated Press*] (SAG)
PRODUTAS... Proceed on Duty Assigned [*Military*]
PRODVAL... Product Validation (MCD)
Prod Well... Production Well [*Nautical term*] (HRNC)
PROE........ Programme Regional Oceanien de l'Environnement [*South Pacific Regional Environmental Programme - SPREP*] (EAIO)
Proe Divers Gas Purity Symp... Proceedings. Divers Gas Purity Symposium (SAUS)
PRO EL...... Protein Electrophoresis [*Biochemistry*] (DAVI)
Proe NJ Mosq Control Assoc... Proceedings. New Jersey Mosquito Control Association (SAUS)
Pro Ex....... Protein Exchange [*Dietetics*]
PROF........ Parameter Profile (SAUS)
PROF........ Peace Research Organization Fund
PROF........ Personal Radio Operators Federation [*Defunct*] (EA)
PROF........ Prediction and Optimization of Failure (SAUS)
PROF........ Prediction and Optimization of Failure Rate (MHDB)
PROF........ Premixed One-Dimensional Flame Code (SAUS)
PROF........ Profanity [*FBI standardized term*]
PROF........ Profession [*or Professional*]
Prof......... Professional (AL)
prof......... Professional (SHCU)
PROF........ Professional Investors Insurance Group, Inc. (SAUS)
PROF........ Professional Office System
PROF........ Professor (EY)
Prof......... Professor (ODBW)
prof......... Professor (PROS)
PROF........ Profile (GAVI)
prof......... Profile (VRA)
Prof......... Profile
prof......... profundus (SAUS)
PROF........ Pupil Registering and Operational Filing [*Computer science*]
ProFac...... Pro-Fac Cooperative, Inc. [*Associated Press*] (SAG)
PROFAC..... Propulsive Fluid Accumulator
PROFACTS... Product Formulation, Accounting and Cost System (SAUS)
PROFACTS... Production Formulation, Accounting, and Cost System (MHDI)
Prof Admin... Professional Administrator [*A publication*]
PROFAGTRANS... Proceed by First Available Government Transportation [*Military*]
PROFAT..... Projet des Francophones de l'Atlantique [*Canada*]
pro-fax..... Production Facilities (WDMC)
Pro-Fax..... Production Facility (NTCM)
ProfBTM.... Professional Business and Technical Management [*British*] [*An association*] (DBA)
Prof Burd... Commemoratio Professorum Burdigalensium [*of Ausonius*] [*Classical studies*] (OCD)
Prof Corp... Proffatt on Private Corporations in California [*A publication*] (DLA)
Prof Corp Guide... Professional Corporation Guide (SAUS)
Prof Corp Guide (P-H)... Professional Corporation Guide (Prentice-Hall, Inc.) [*A publication*] (DLA)
PROFCRE... Professional Care, Inc. (SAUS)
PROFCY..... Proficiency
PROF-E..... Programmed Review of Operator Functions - Elementary (DNAB)
Prof Eng.... Professional Engineer
Prof Eng.... Professional Engineering [*A publication*] (CABS)
Prof Engr... Professional Engineer [*A publication*]
PROFERI... Programme for Refugee Reintegration and Rehabilitation of Resettlement Areas in Eritrea
PROFESSL... Professional
PROFFENS... Prototype Flash Flood Estimation and Nowcasting System (SAUS)
PROFFIS... Professional Filler System [*Military*]
Proffitt....... Proffitt's, Inc. [*Associated Press*] (SAG)
PROFIBUS... Process Field Bus (SAUS)
Profile....... Passive Radio Frequency Interference Location Experiment (SAUS)
PROFILE... Programmed Functional Indices for Laboratory Evaluation [*RAND Corp.*]
PROFILE... Program Overview and File (SAUS)
PROFILES... Personal Reflection on Family Life and Employment Stressors [*Psychology*]
PROFINE... Proximity Fuze Intercept and Analysis Equipment (SAUS)
PROFIS...... Professional Officer Filler Information System (SAUS)
PROFIS...... Programminformationssystem Sozialwissenschaften [*Informationszentrum Sozialwissenschaften*] [*Germany*] [*Defunct*] [*Information service or system*] (CRD)
PROFISS... Professional Filter System (SAUS)
PROFIT...... Planners Remote Offline Form Image Tape (SAUS)
PROFIT...... Program for Financed Insurance Techniques
PROFIT...... Program for Financed (or Financial) Insurance Technic (or Techniques) (SAUS)
PROFIT...... Programmed Receiving, Ordering and Forecasting Inventory Technique (SAUS)
PROFIT...... Programmed Reviewing, Ordering, and Forecasting Inventory Technique
PROFIT...... Propulsion Flight Control Integration Technology (MCD)
PROFIT...... Propulsion/Flight Control Technology (SAUS)
PROFITS System... Personalized Realtime-Oriented Financial Institutions Time Saving System (SAUS)
Prof Jur..... Proffatt on Trial by Jury [*A publication*] (DLA)
PROFL....... Professional
Prof Lib Pr... Professional Library Press (SAUS)
PR of MAN... [*The*] Prayer of Manasses, King of Judah [*Apocrypha*]
PROFNET... Procurement & Financial Management of Logistics Supplies (SAUS)
Prof Not..... Proffatt on Notaries [*A publication*] (DLA)
Prof Officer... Professional Officer [*A publication*]
PROFP...... Proficiency Pay [*Military*]
PROF PHONO PL... Professional Phonograph Plug (SAUS)
PROF PHONO SKT... Professional Phonograph Socket (SAUS)
PROF Rate... Prediction and Optimization of Failure Rate (SAUS)
ProfRec..... Profit Recovery Group International, Inc. (The) [*Associated Press*] (SAG)
PROFS...... Professional Office System [*IBM Corp.*]
profs......... professors (SAUS)
PROFS...... Program for Regional Observing and Forecasting Services [*Boulder, CO*] [*Department of Commerce*] (GRD)
PROFS...... Prototype for Regional Observing and Forecasting Service (SAUS)
PROFS...... Prototype Regional Observation and Forecasting Service [*National Oceanic and Atmospheric Administration*] (GRD)
PROFS...... Prototype Regional Observation (or Observing) and Forecasting Service (SAUS)
Profsnl...... Professional (TBD)
ProfStaff... Professional Staff [*Associated Press*] (SAG)
Prof Wills... Proffatt on Wills [*A publication*] (DLA)
PROG........ Peer Review Oversight Group [*National Institutes of Health*]
PROG........ Progenitor (SAUS)
PROG........ Progeny (SAUS)
prog......... Progesterone [*Endocrinology*] (DAVI)
prog......... Prognathism [*Dentistry*] (DAVI)
Prog......... Prognose (SAUS)
PROG........ Prognosis [*or Prognostication*] (AAG)
prog......... Prognosis [*Therapy term*] (CTAA)
prog......... prognostic (SAUS)
PROG........ Prognostication (SAUS)
PROG........ Prognosticator (SAUS)
Prog......... Program (AL)
PROG........ Program (KSC)
PROG........ Programmable (SAUS)
PROG........ Programmed (SAUS)
PROG........ Programmer [*or Programming*]
PROG........ Programmer's Paradise [*NASDAQ symbol*] (TTSB)
PROG........ Programmers Paradise, Inc. [*NASDAQ symbol*] (SAG)
PROG........ Programs Division (SAUS)
PROG........ Progress (AABC)
Prog......... Progress (DIAR)
PROG........ Progress [*NCIC motorcycle make code*]
PROG........ Progress [*NCIC car make code*]
PROG........ Progress Industries [*NCIC trailer make code*]
Prog......... Progressive [*A publication*] (BRI)
PROG........ Progressive (GOBB)
prog......... Progressive [*Linguistics*] (IEL)
Prog Allergol... Progress of Allergology (SAUS)
Prog Arch... Progressive Architecture [*A publication*] (BRI)
PROG BK... Programmed Book [*Publishing*]
ProgBk...... Progressive Bank, Inc. [*Associated Press*] (SAG)
ProgCp...... Progressive Corp. [*Associated Press*] (SAG)
Prog Environ Sci... Progress in Environmental Science [*A publication*] (PABS)
Prog F....... Progressive Fire (SAUS)
Prog Fish-Cult... Progressive Fish Culturist (SAUS)
ProgFn...... Progress Financial Corp. [*Associated Press*] (SAG)
Prog Hum Geogr... Progress in Human Geography [*A publication*] (PABS)
Prog Instr&Ed Tech... Programmed Instruction and Educational Technology (SAUS)
PROGLIB... Production Program Library [*Social Security Administration*]
PRO GM.... Pro Grand Master [*Freemasonry*]
PROGMAN... Program Manager (VLIE)
Prog Med... Progress in Medicine (SAUS)
Prog Med Parasitol... Progress in Medical Parasitology (SAUS)
PROGMG.... Programming
PROGN...... Prognosis (AAMN)
Prog Neurol Psyciatry... Progress in Neurology and Psychiatry (journ.) (SAUS)
Prog Neuro-Psychopharmacol&Biol Psychiatry... Progress in Neuro-Psychopharmacology and Biological Psychiatry (SAUS)
PROGNO.... Prognosen-Trends-Entwicklungen [*Forecasts-Trends-Developments*] [*Society for Business Information*] [*Information service or system*] (IID)
PROG-NOSAG... European Centre for Applied Economic Research (SAUS)

PROGO...... Program Guidance and Objectives (SAUS)
Prog Oceanogr... Progress in Oceanography [*A publication*] (PABS)
Prog Odontostomatol... ProgrSs Odonto-Stomatologique (SAUS)
PROGOFOP... Program of Operation [*Computer science*]
Prog Oto-Rhino-Laryngol... ProgrSs en Oto-Rhino-Laryngologie (SAUS)
ProgPar...... Programmers Paradise, Inc. [*Associated Press*] (SAG)
Prog Phys Geogr... Progress in Physical Geography [*A publication*] (PABS)
Prog Physiol Sci... Progress in Physiological Sciences (SAUS)
Prog Protozool... Progress in Protozoology (SAUS)
Prog Quantum Electron... Progress in Quantum Electronics [*A publication*] (CABS)
PROGR...... Programmer (ECII)
progr........ Progress (DAVI)
PROGRAM... Programming (SAUS)
Program Abstr Am Soc Parasitol Annu Meet... Program and Abstracts. American Society of Parasitologists. Annual Meeting (SAUS)
Program/Proc Natl Horsemens Semin... Program/Proceedings. National Horsemens Seminar (SAUS)
Progr Bull... Progress Bulletin (SAUS)
Prog Rep Exp Stn Colorado State Univ... Colorado State University. Experiment Station. Progress Report (journ.) (SAUS)
Prog Rep Minist Agric Fish Fd Exp Husb Fms Exp Hort Stns... Progress Report. Ministry of Agriculture, Fisheries and Food. Experimental Husbandry Farms and Experimental Horticultur (SAUS)
Progr Math... Progress of Mathematics (SAUS)
Progrp....... ProGroup, Inc. [*Associated Press*] (SAG)
Progr Polym Sci... Progress in Polymer Science (MEC)
Progr Rev For Prod Lab... Program Review. Forest Products Laboratory (SAUS)
PROGS...... Prognosis (SAUS)
PROGS...... Progressive
PROGS...... Progressive Proofs [*Graphic arts*] (DGA)
PROGSYS... Programming System (SAUS)
PROGTOT... Progressive Total (VLIE)
PROGVAL... Validation Program Library [*Social Security Administration*]
PROH........ Prohibit
PROH........ Prohibition [*FBI standardized term*]
PRO/HEALTH... Professional Healthcare Communications (EFIS)
Prohib....... Prohibited
PROI......... CFI ProServices [*NASDAQ symbol*] (TTSB)
PROI......... CFI Proservices, Inc. [*NASDAQ symbol*] (SAG)
PROI......... President of the Royal Institute of Oil Painters [*British*]
PROI......... Project Return on Investment (MHDW)
PRO-IF...... Personal Radio Operators International Federation [*Formerly, ARC*] (EA)
PRO-IMMPAC... Pro-Immigration PAC [*Bethesda, MD*] (PACS)
PROIMREP... Proceed Immediately - Report for Purpose Indicated [*Military*]
PROIMREP... Proceed Immediately-Report for Purpose Indicated (SAUS)
Pro Indian Soc of Internat L... Proceedings of the Conference. Indian Society of International Law [*New Delhi, India*] [*A publication*] (DLA)
Proj.......... Project (TBD)
proj.......... Project (VRA)
PROJ........ Project
PROJ........ Projectile (AFM)
proj......... Projectile (ODA)
proj.......... Projection (MIST)
PROJ........ Projection (SAUS)
PROJ........ Projector [*or Projection*]
PROJACS... Project Analysis and Control System (MHDI)
PROJD...... Projected (SAUS)
PROJECT... Project Engineering Control
Project KEEP... Kidney Early Evaluation Program
PROJENGR... Project Engineer
PROJID...... Project Identification [*Computer science*]
PROJMGR... Project Manager [*Military*]
PROJMGRASWS... Project Manager, Antisubmarine Warfare Systems
PROJMGRFBM... Project Manager, Fleet Ballistic Missile [*Navy*]
PROJMGRSMS... Project Manager, Surface Missile Systems [*Navy*]
ProjSft....... Project Software & Development, Inc. [*Associated Press*] (SAG)
projt......... Projector (VRA)
PROJTRNS... Project Transition [*DoD*]
PROL........ Power Reactor Operating License [*Canadian Nuclear Safety Commission*] (FOTI)
PROL........ Priority Requirement Objective List (AFM)
Prol.......... Prologic Management Systems, Inc. [*Associated Press*] (SAG)
prol.......... Prologue (WDAA)
PROL........ Prologue
PRO L....... Province Laws (DLA)
PROLAC..... Prolactin [*Biochemistry*] (DAVI)
PROLAMAT... International Conference on Programming Languages for Numerically Controlled Machines (SAUS)
PROLAMAT... Programming Language for Numerically Controlled Machine Tools (SAUS)
PROLAMAT... Programming Languages for Machine Tools [*Conference*]
PROLAMAT... Programming Languages for Numerically Controlled Machine Tools [*Conference*] [*Computer science*] (IAA)
PROLAN..... Processed Language [*Computer science*]
PROLAN..... Processing Language (SAUS)
PROLDI...... Annual Research Reviews. Prolactin (journ.) (SAUS)
prole......... Proletarian (ADWA)
PROLE....... Proletarian (WDAA)
Proler....... Proler International Corp. [*Associated Press*] (SAG)
PROLETCULT... Proletarian Culture (SAUS)
PROLIB...... Project Library (SAUS)
Prolif........ Proliferative [*or Proliferation*]
PROLLAP... Professional Library Literature Acquisition Program
prolly........ Probably [*Internet slang*] (NETL)
PRO LOC et TEM... Pro Loco et Tempore [*For the Place and Time*] [*Latin*] (ROG)
PROLOG.... Production of Onshore Lower 48 Oil and Gas Model [*Department of Energy*] (GFGA)
PROLOG.... Program Logistics (NG)
PROLOG.... Programming in Logic [*Programing language*] [*1970*]
PROLOG.... Programming Logic (SAUS)
PROLOG.... Project Logic Planning (IAA)
Prolog....... Prologic Management Systems, Inc. [*Associated Press*] (SAG)
Prologc...... Prologic Management Systems, Inc. [*Associated Press*] (SAG)
Prologic..... Prologic Management Systems, Inc. [*Associated Press*] (SAG)
PROLOG Planning... Project Logic Planning (SAUS)
prolong...... Prolongatus [*Prolonged*] [*Latin*] (DAVI)
prolong...... prolonged (SAUS)
PROLOPLA... Program Logical Plan (SAUS)
PROLT....... Procurement Lead Time
PROM....... Partial Read Only Memory (SAUS)
PROM....... Passive Range of Motion [*Medicine*]
PROM....... Pockel's Readout Optical Memory
PROM....... Pockels Readout Optical Modulator
PROM....... Pockels-Readout-Optical Modulator (SAUS)
PROM....... Pockets Readout Optical Modulator (SAUS)
PROM....... Premature [*or Prolonged*] Rupture of Membranes [*Gynecology*]
PROM....... Programable Read Only Memory (SAUS)
PROM....... Programmable Read-Only Memory [*Computer science*]
PROM....... Program, Resources, Objectives, Management [*Air Force Systems Command technique*]
PROM....... Progressive Range of Motion [*Medicine*]
PROM....... Prolonged Range of Motion (IDYL)
PROM....... Prolonged Rupture of Membranes [*Gynecology*] (DAVI)
PROM....... Promark [*NCIC motorcycle make code*]
prom......... Promenade (DD)
PROM....... Promenade [*Maps and charts*]
PROM....... Prominent
PROM....... Promise [*Legal shorthand*] (LWAP)
Prom........ Promissory [*A publication*] (DLA)
PROM....... Promontory
PROM....... Promote [*or Promotion*] (AFM)
PROM....... Promoter (SAUS)
PROM....... Promotion
PROM....... Promotor (SAUS)
PROM....... Prompter (SAUS)
PROM....... Promulgate (AABC)
PROM....... Promulgation (SAUS)
Pro-MACE... Prednisone, Methotrexate with Leucovorin, Adriamycin, Cyclophosphamide, Epipodophyllin [*Etoposide, VP-16*] [*Antineoplastic drug regimen*]
PROMACE-MOPP... Procarbazine, Methotrexate, Adriamycin, Cyclophosphamide, Etoposide, Mustargen [*Nitrogen mustard*], Oncovin , Procarbazine, Prednisone [*Vincristine*] [*Antineoplastic drug regimen*]
PROMACE-MOPP... Procarbazine, Methotrexate, Adriamycin, Cyclophosphamide, Etoposide, Mustargen, Oncovin, Procarbazine, Prednisone (SAUS)
PROMACX... Production Management and Control System (SAUS)
PROMAG.... Production Management Action Group [*British*]
PROMAP.... Program for the Refinement of the Materiel Acquisition Process [*Army*] (AABC)
PROMAST... Production Master Scheduling System (PDAA)
PROMATS... Probabilistic Materials System (PDAA)
PROMATS... Programmable Magnetic Tape System [*Computer science*] (VLIE)
PROMCOM... Project Monitoring and Control Method (SAUS)
Prom dk..... Promenade Deck [*of a ship*] (DS)
ProMED..... Program for Monitoring Emerging Diseases (SAUS)
ProMED..... Program to Monitor Emerging Diseases
PROMED.... Pro-Med Capital Corp. (SAUS)
PROMEE.... Promisee [*Legal shorthand*] (LWAP)
PROMESS... Penmarch Radar Oceanographic Microwave Experiment on Signature Studies (SAUS)
PROMETH... Promethazine Hydrochloride (SAUS)
PROMETHEUS... Program for European Traffic with Highest Efficiency and Unprecedented Safety (ECON)
PROMEX.... Productivity Measurement Experiment [*National Institute of Standards and Technology*]
PROMIM.... Programmable Multiple Ion Monitor
PROMIS..... Polar Regions and Outer Magnetosphere (ACAE)
PROMIS..... Problem Oriented Medical Guidance System
PROMIS..... Problem-Oriented Medical Information System [*Computerized patient-management system*]
PROMIS..... Process Management and Information System [*I. P. Sharp Associates Ltd.*] [*Software package*] (NCC)
PROMIS..... Procurement Management Information System (SAUS)
PROMIS..... Production Management Information System (TIMI)
PROMIS..... Project Management Integrated System (NITA)
PROMIS..... Project-Oriented Management Information System
PROMIS..... Prosecution Management Information System (SAUS)
PROMIS..... Prosecutor's Management Information System [*Law Enforcement Assistance Administration*]
PROMISE... Programming Managers Information System (MHDI)
PROMISE... Prospective Randomized Milrinone Survival Evaluation [*Medicine*]
PROMISS... Packaging Requirements for Optimum Malfunction Isolation by Systematic Substitution (IAA)
PROML...... Promulgate
PROMMIS... Programmed Restructuring of Maintenance Management Information System (SAUS)

PROMO ..... Promotion [*Slang*] (DSUE)
promo .... Promotional (TVEL)
PROMO ..... Promotional Advertising (GOBB)
Promo .... Promotional Announcement (NTCM)
PROMOCM... Project Monitor and Control Method (SAUS)
PROMOR.... Promisor [*Legal shorthand*] (LWAP)
Promot ...... Promotion (DIAR)
PROMPT .... Production, Reviewing, Organizing, and Monitoring of Performance Techniques (BUR)
PROMPT .... Program Monitoring and Planning Techniques (IEEE)
PROMPT .... Program Reporting, Organization, and Management Planning Technique (IAA)
PROMPT .... Program to Record Official Mail Point-to-Point Times [*Postal Service program*]
PROMPT .... Project Management and Production Team Technique [*Computer science*]
PROMPT .... Project Reporting Organization and Management Planning Technique
PROMS...... Procurement Management System (MCD)
PROMS...... Programmable Read Only Memory System [*Computer science*]
PROMS...... Program Modelling and Simulation (SAUS)
PROMS...... Program Modelling System (SAUS)
PROMS...... Program Monitoring System (MCD)
PROMS...... Projectile Measurement System [*Computer science*] [*Army*]
PROMSS.... Procedures and Relationships for the Operation of Manual Stations and Spaces (DNAB)
PROM STAT... Promotion Status (DNAB)
PROMT...... Precision Optimized Measurement Time [*Spectroscopy*]
PROMT...... Predicasts Overview of Markets and Terminology (NITA)
PROMT...... Predicasts Overviews of Marketing and Technology [*Business database*]
PROMT...... Programmable Miniature Message Terminal (MCD)
PROMUS.... Provincial-Municipal Simulator [*Computer-based urban management system*]
Pro Mus Orc... Pro Musica Orchestra (SAUS)
PROMY...... Promissory (ROG)
PROMYELO... Promyelocyte(s) [*Medicine*] (EDAA)
PRON........ Patriotyczny Ruch Odrodzenia Narodowego [*Patriotic Movement for National Rebirth*] [*Poland*] (EY)
PRON........ Procurement Request and Order Number (SAUS)
PRON........ Procurement Request Order Number [*Army*] (AABC)
ProN......... Progressive Number (SAUS)
PRON........ Pronation
PRON........ Pronominal (ADA)
pron .... Pronoun (NTIO)
PRON........ Pronoun
PRON........ Pronounced
PRON........ Pronouncement (SAUS)
PRON........ Pronunciation (ROG)
pron .... Pronunciation (WDMC)
Pron A....... Prenominal Adjective (SAUS)
PRONED .... Promotion of Non-Executive Directors (ODBW)
Pronet....... ProNet, Inc. [*Associated Press*] (SAG)
PRO-NICA... Professionals - Nicaragua [*An association*] (EA)
Pro-Nica .... Professionals - Nicaragua (EA)
Pro Note .... Promissory Note (SAUS)
PRONTO .... Program for Numeric Tool Operation [*Computer science*]
PRONTO .... Programmable Network Telecommunications Operating System
pronun ...... pronunciate (SAUS)
PROO........ Pro Express [*Common carrier symbol*]
prooem...... Prooemium (BJA)
PROOF ...... Parole Resource Office and Orientation Facility (SAUS)
PROOF ...... Precision Recording (Optical) of Fingerprints
PROOF ...... Projected Return on Open Office Facilities [*Computer program*]
proOLMC.... Pro-Opiolipomelanocortin [*Endocrinology*]
PRO-OP ..... Project Optimization [*Industrial engineering*]
PROP........ Panel Review of Products (SAUS)
PROP........ Performance Review for Operating Programs (BUR)
PROP........ Pilot Repair Overhaul and Provisioning (MUGU)
PROP........ Planetary Rocket Ocean Platform
PROP........ Portland Regional Opportunities Program (SAUS)
PROP........ Prerelease Orientation Program [*Reformatory program*]
PROP........ Preservation of the Rights of Prisoners [*An association*] [*British*]
PROP........ Primary Operand (SAUS)
PROP........ Primary Operand Pipeline (SAUS)
PROP........ Primary Operand Unit (IAA)
PROP........ Prisoners' Right of Privacy [*British*] (DI)
PROP........ Production Operators [*NASDAQ symbol*] (TTSB)
PROP........ Production Operators Corp. [*NASDAQ symbol*] (NQ)
PROP........ Production Planning (IAA)
PROP........ Profit Rating of Projects
PROP........ Program for the Refinement of Orbital Parameters (SAUS)
PROP........ Proof of Purchase (WDMC)
PROP........ Propaganda (AFM)
Prop .... Propagate [*Botany*]
PROP........ Propellant (KSC)
PROP........ Propelled (SAUS)
PROP........ Propeller
prop .... Proper (NTIO)
PROP........ Proper
prop .... properly (SAUS)
PROP........ Propertius [*Roman poet, c. 29BC*] [*Classical studies*] (ROG)
Prop .... Property (TBD)
prop .... Property (WDAA)
PROP........ Property
PROP........ Property Release Option Program [*HUD*]
PROP........ Proportional (KSC)
PROP........ Proportioning (NAKS)
PROP........ Proposal (AAG)
PROP........ Proposed (AFM)
PROP........ Proposition
PROP........ Propranolol (DB)
prop .... propriertary (SAUS)
prop .... Proprietor (WDAA)
PROP........ Proprietor
PROP........ Propulsion (AAG)
PROP........ Propulsion Engineer (NAKS)
PROP........ Propulsor (SAUS)
PROP........ Propylthiouracil [*Also, PT, PTU*] [*Thyroid inhibitor*]
PROP........ Protected Areas Programme (SAUS)
PROPAC..... Progressive Political Action Committee [*Defunct*] (EA)
PROPAC..... Prospective Payment Assessment Commission [*Washington, DC*] (EGAO)
ProPAC...... Prospective Payment Assessment Commission
PROPAC..... Provident Life and Accident Insurance Company PAC [*Portland, ME*] (PACS)
propaed..... propaedutics (SAUS)
PROPAKASIA... International Food Processing and Packaging Technology Exhibition and Conferencefor South East Asia
PROPAL..... Productora de Papeles (EFIS)
PROPAL..... Programmed PAL (SAUS)
PROPAL..... Proportional
Prop & Comp... Property and Compensation Reports [*A publication*] (DLA)
Prop & Comp R... Property and Compensation Reports [*A publication*] (DLA)
PROPANEPAC... National Propane Gas Association PAC [*Washington, DC*] (PACS)
PRO-PAY.... Proficiency Pay [*Military*]
Propcon..... Conferences Prop and Pulpwood Charter (SAUS)
PropCT...... Property Capital Trust [*Associated Press*] (SAG)
pro per...... Propria Persona [*In His or Her Own Person*] [*Latin*] (WGA)
PROPER COUNT... Property Accountability (MCD)
PROPH ...... Porphyrins [*Chemistry*] (DAVI)
PROPH ...... Profile of Phonology (AIE)
proph........ prophetic (SAUS)
PROPH ...... Prophylactic
Proph........ Prophylaxis (SAUS)
Proph21..... Prophet 21, Inc. [*Associated Press*] (SAG)
PROPHET... Proactive Rehabilitation of Outside Plant Using Heuristic Expert Techniques [*GTE computer software*]
prophy....... Prophylactic (DAVI)
PROPIN ..... Proprietary Information
PROPL ...... Proportional
Prop Law ... Property Lawyer [*1826-30*] [*A publication*] (DLA)
Prop Law Bull... Property Law Bulletin [*A publication*] (DLA)
Prop Law NS... Property Lawyer, New Series [*England*] [*A publication*] (DLA)
PROPLING... Propelling
PROPLOSS... Propagation Loss (NVT)
PROPLT ..... Propellant (NASA)
PROPN ...... Propane
PROPN ...... Proportion (MSA)
PROPNASS... Pre-Operational Navigation Satellite System
proPO .... Prophenoloxidase
PROPON .... Proportion (ROG)
PROPORICH... Proceed to Port in Which Unit is Located [*Navy*] (DNAB)
PROPR ...... Proprietary (ROG)
PROPR ...... Proprietor (EY)
propr .... Proprietor (WDAA)
PROPRCS... Propulsion Reaction Control System (SAUS)
PROPRE.... Property Press (DLA)
PROPRSS... Proprietress (ROG)
PROPSIM... Propagation Simulator (SAUS)
ProPTH...... Proparathyroid Hormone (SAUS)
PROPTRY... Proprietary [*Freight*]
PROPUL..... Propulsion
Prop Wash... Propeller Wash (SAUS)
PRO PWC PAC... American Watercraft Association PAC [*Formerly known as Pro Personal Watercraft*] [*Rancho Santa Margarita, CA*] (PACS)
PROPY ...... Proprietary
Pro Quer.... Pro Querente [*For the Plaintiff*] [*Latin*] (ILCA)
PROR........ Predicted Orbit
PROR........ Proposal Online Reparation (SAUS)
PRORA ...... Program for Research on Romance Authors (SAUS)
PRORA ...... Programs for Research on Romance Authors
PRORAT..... Projected Rating
PRO RAT AET... Pro Ratione Aetatis [*According to Age*] [*Pharmacy*]
PRO RECT... Pro Recto [*Rectal*] [*Pharmacy*]
pro rect.... pro recto [*By rectum*] [*Latin*] [*Pharmacy*] (DAVI)
PROREP..... Proceed Ship, Command Station Reporting Duty or Purpose Indicated [*Military*]
PRORM ..... Pay and Records Office-Royal Marines (SAUS)
PROS........ Preventive Maintenance, Repair, and Operational Services (ODBW)
PROS........ Procurement Squadron
PROS........ Professional Reactor Operator Society (EA)
PROS........ Proscenium [*Theater term*] (DSUE)
PROS........ Prosecution (ROG)
PROS........ Prosody
PROS........ Prospect Group [*NASDAQ symbol*] (TTSB)
PROS........ [*The*] Prospect Group, Inc. [*New York, NY*] [*NASDAQ symbol*] (NQ)

pros.......... Prostate [*Anatomy*] (DAVI)
PROS........ Prosthetic (AABC)
PROS........ Prostitute (DSUE)
PROS........ Prostrate
PROSA...... Programming System with Symbolic Addresses [*Computer science*] (IAA)
PROSAM.... Programmed Single-Axis Mount [*Military camera*]
PROSAMO... Planned Release of Selected and Modified Organisms [*British*]
Pros Atty... Prosecuting Attorney (DLA)
pros atty... Prosecuting Attorney (NTIO)
PROSC...... Proscenium [*Theater term*] (WDAA)
PRosC....... Rosemont College, Rosemont, PA [*Library symbol*] [*Library of Congress*] (LCLS)
PROSD...... Performance Records for Optimizing System Design (IAA)
PROSE...... Partnership to Reduce Operation and Support Costs, Engine
PROSE...... Personal Record of School Experiences (EDAC)
PROSE...... Problem Solution Engineering [*Programming language*] [*Computer science*] (CSR)
PROSE...... Production Scheduler (SAUS)
PROSE...... Program System Example (SAA)
PROSEA..... Plant Resources of South-East Asia [*A publication*]
PROSECON... Prosecution (ROG)
PROSEL..... Process Control and Sequencing Language [*Computer science*] (IAA)
PROSEL..... Process-control and Sequencing Language (SAUS)
PROSEL..... Process Sequencing Language (SAUS)
ProsGp...... [*The*] Prospect Group, Inc. [*Associated Press*] (SAG)
PROSI....... Public Relations Office of the Sugar Industry
PROSIG..... Procedure Signal [*Navy*]
PROSIGN... Procedure Sign [*Military*] (AABC)
PROSIM..... Production System Simulator [*Computer science*]
PROSIN..... Procedure Sign [*Military*] (IAA)
PROSINE... Procedure Sign [*Military*]
Pros J Natl Dist Atty A... Prosecutor. Journal of the National District Attorneys Association (SAUS)
PROSMATEC... Progressive Shift Schedule Management Technology [*Automotive engineering*]
PROSO...... Protamine Sulfate [*Biochemistry*] (DAVI)
ProSoc...... Prometheus Society (EA)
Prosoft...... Prosoft I-Net Solutions, Inc. [*Associated Press*] (SAG)
Prosop Att... Prosopographia Attica [*A publication*] (OCD)
PROSP...... Prospecting (SAUS)
prosp........ Prospectively (DLA)
PROSPEC... PRO Specification (NITA)
PROSPECT... Proponent Sponsored Engineer Corps Training [*Army Corps of Engineers*]
PROSPECTRA... Program by development by Specification and Transformation (SAUS)
PROSPER... Procedure for Personalizing an envelope program (SAUS)
PROSPER... Profit Simulating (or Simulation) Planning and Evaluation of Risk (SAUS)
PROSPER... Profit Simulation, Planning and Evaluation of Risk (MHDB)
PROSPIN... Project Profile Screening and Pre-appraisal Information System (SAUS)
ProSport.... Professional Sports Care Management, Inc. [*Associated Press*] (SAG)
PROSS...... Prosser, TX [*American Association of Railroads railroad junction routing code*]
ProsSt....... Prospect Street High Income Portfolio, Inc. [*Associated Press*] (SAG)
PROST...... Pronuclear Oocyte and Sperm Transfer [*Embryology*]
PROST...... Pronuclear Stage Tubal Transfer (SAUS)
prost........ Prostate (CPH)
PROST...... Prostitute [*or Prostitution*] [*FBI standardized term*]
Prostaglandins Leukotrienes Med... Prostaglandins, Leukotrienes and Medicine (SAUS)
PROSTAT... Prostatic (AAMN)
Prostate Suppl... Prostate. Supplement (SAUS)
PROSTH..... Prosthesis
PROSY...... People's Republic of South Yemen (BJA)
prot.......... Protect (ELAL)
PROT........ Protect [*or Protection*] (MSA)
PROT........ Protected (SAUS)
PROT........ Protected Reservation [*Travel industry*] (TVEL)
PROT........ Protective Life Corp. (SAUS)
Prot.......... Protectorate (WDAA)
PROT........ Protein
PROT........ Protest (ROG)
Prot.......... Protestant (WDAA)
PROT........ Protestant
PROT........ Proteus [*Bacterium*]
PROT........ Protinus [*Speedily*] [*Pharmacy*]
Prot.......... Protocol (DLA)
PROT........ Prototype
Prot.......... Protozoa (SAUS)
PROT........ Protractor (AAG)
PROT........ Pro-Trail [*NCIC trailer make code*]
PROTA....... Protection Actual [*Probability for avoidance of ship*]
ProTACA.... Procurement Technical Assistance Cooperative Agreement Program [*DoD*]
PROTAG..... Protagonist (SAUS)
PROTAP..... Professional Opportunities through Academic Partnership [*National War College*]
PROTAP..... Protonotary Apostolic [*Roman Catholic*]
Prot CJ...... Protocol on the Statute of the European Communities Court of Justice [*A publication*] (DLA)
PROTCT..... Protective (AAG)
PROT DEV... Protective Device (SAUS)
ProtDg....... Protein Design Labs [*Associated Press*] (SAG)
PROTEC..... Protection
ProTech..... Prospective Technology Communication System (SAUS)
PROTECON... Process and Test Control [*Pendar Technical Association Ltd.*] [*Software package*] (NCC)
PROTECT... Probabilities Recall Optimizing the Employment of Calibration Time (KSC)
PROTECT... Protection
Protect...... Protection
ProtectO.... Protection One, Inc. [*Associated Press*] (SAG)
PROTEL..... Procedure Oriented Type Enforcing Language (SAUS)
pro tem..... Pro Tempore (ODA)
PRO TEM... Pro Tempore [*For the Time Being*] [*Latin*]
Pro tem..... Pro Tempore-for the time being (SAUS)
PRO TEM et LOC... Pro Tempore et Loco [*For the Time and Place*] [*Latin*] (ROG)
Proteon..... Proteon, Inc. [*Associated Press*] (SAG)
PRO/TEST... Profitable approach to Testing (SAUS)
PROTEUS... Profile Telemetry of Upper Ocean Currents [*Marine science*] (OSRA)
PROTEUS... Project to Research Objects Theories, Extraterrrestrials, and Unusual Sightings (EA)
PROTEUS... Propulsion Research and Openwater Testing of Experimental Underwater System (SAUS)
PROTEUS... Propulsion Research and Open Water Testing of Experimental Underwater Systems (MCD)
PROTEUS... Prototype Real-Time Operational Test, Evaluation and User Simulation (SAUS)
Proth........ Prothetics (SAUS)
PROTHROM... Prothrombin [*Hematology*]
Proth Time... Prothrombin Time (SAUS)
pro-time.... Prothrombin Time [*Medicine*] (BCRP)
Pro Time.... Prothrombin Time (SAUS)
PROTIMEREP... Proceed in Time Report Not Later Than [*Hour and/or date indicated*] [*Military*]
ProtLf........ Protective Life Corp. [*Associated Press*] (SAG)
PROTN...... Procedure Turn (SAUS)
PROTO...... Protoporphyrin [*Hematology*]
Proto........ ProtoSource Corp. [*Associated Press*] (SAG)
PROTO...... Prototype (KSC)
Protoch...... Protochorda (SAUS)
PROTO-E Language... Programming Tool Extensible Language (SAUS)
ProtoS....... ProtoSource Corp. [*Associated Press*] (SAG)
protozool... protozoologist (SAUS)
protozool... protozoology (SAUS)
ProtP........ Protein Polymer Technologies, Inc. [*Associated Press*] (SAG)
Prot P I..... Protocol on Privileges and Immunities (SAUS)
Prot PI...... Protocol on Privileges and Immunities of the European Economic Community [*A publication*] (DLA)
ProtPoly..... Protein Polymer Technologies, Inc. [*Associated Press*] (SAG)
PROTR...... Protractor (MSA)
Protr......... Protrepticus [*of Clemens Alexandrinus*] [*Classical studies*] (OCD)
ProtSy....... Protocol Systems, Inc. [*Associated Press*] (SAG)
PROT TP.... Prototyp (SAUS)
PROTYP..... Processor Type code (SAUS)
Proud Dom Pub... Proudhon's Domaine Public [*A publication*] (DLA)
Proudf Land Dec... United States Land Decisions (Proudfit) [*A publication*] (DLA)
PROUS...... Proceed to a Pon in Continental United States (SAUS)
PROUS...... Proceed to a Port in Continental United States [*Military*]
PRO US EXT... Pro Usu Externo [*For External Use*] [*Pharmacy*]
Prouty....... Prouty's Reports [*61-68 Vermont*] [*A publication*] (DLA)
Prov......... De Providentia [*of Seneca the Younger*] [*Classical studies*] (OCD)
PROV........ Provedor (SAUS)
prov.......... Provenance (VRA)
prov.......... Provencal (BEE)
PROV........ Provencal [*Language, etc.*]
PROV........ Provence [*France*] (ROG)
PROV........ Proverb
Prov......... Proverbs [*Old Testament book*]
PROV........ Provide (KSC)
Prov......... Providence (SAUS)
PROV........ Providence, KY [*American Association of Railroads railroad junction routing code*]
PROV........ Provident Financial Holdings, Inc. [*NASDAQ symbol*] (SAG)
prov.......... Province (ELAL)
PROV........ Province
Prov......... Provincial (AL)
PROV........ Provincial
PROV........ Provinciale [*Provincial*] [*Netherlands*] (EY)
PROV........ Proving Ground [*Navy*]
PROV........ Provision [*or Provisional*] (AFM)
prov.......... Provisional (MIST)
Prov......... Provisional (TBD)
Prov......... Provisional Light [*Navigation signal*]
PROV........ Provisioning
PROV........ Provost
ProvBcp..... Provident Bancorp, Inc. [*Associated Press*] (SAG)
Prov Can Stat... Statutes of the Province of Canada [*A publication*] (DLA)
ProvCo...... Provident Companies, Inc. [*Associated Press*] (SAG)
Prov Cons... De Provinciis Consularibus [*of Cicero*] [*Classical studies*] (OCD)
PROVCORPV... Provisional Corps, Vietnam
PROVD...... Provided
Prov Eng.... Provincial English (SAUS)

PROVER..... Procurement for Minimum Total Cost through Value Engineering and Reliability
PROVER..... Procurement, Value, Economy, Reliability
ProvFinl..... Provident Financial Holdings, Inc. [*Associated Press*] (SAG)
ProvGM.... Provincial Grand Master [*Freemasonry*]
PROVGR.... Proving Grounds
PROVI....... Proviso, IL [*American Association of Railroads railroad junction routing code*]
PROVIB..... Propulsion System Decision and Vibration Analysis (DNAB)
Provid....... De Providentia [*of Philo*] (BJA)
Providence C... Providence College (GAGS)
Providn...... Providian Corp. [*Formerly, Capital Holding*] [*Associated Press*] (SAG)
PROVIMI... Proteins, Vitamins, and Minerals [*Pharmacology*] (DAVI)
PROVIS..... Provision
provl......... provisional (SAUS)
PROVMAAG... Provisional Military Assistance Advisory Group (CINC)
PROVMAAG-K... Provisional Military Assistance Advisory Group, Korea (CINC)
PROVMAIN... Other Provisions Basic Orders Remain in Effect
PROVMAINTCO... Provisional Maintenance Company [*Navy*] (DNAB)
PROVMUSTCO... Provisional Medical Unit Self-Contained Company [*Navy*] (DNAB)
PROVN...... Provision (SAUS)
PROVNC.... Province
provns....... Provisions (DLA)
PROVNS.... Provision Store (SAUS)
PROVO...... Proviso [*Contract clause*] (ROG)
PROVO...... Provocateur (DSUE)
PROVO...... Provo, UT [*American Association of Railroads railroad junction routing code*]
PROVONS... Provisions
Provor....... Provisor (SAUS)
PROVORG... Providing Organization (DOMA)
PROVPAC... Provident Savings Bank PAC [*Jersey City, NJ*] (PACS)
PROVSN.... Provision
Prov St...... Statutes, Laws, of the Province of Massachusetts [*A publication*] (DLA)
PROVSUPDEP... Provision Supply Depot (SAUS)
PROW....... Protein Reviews on the Web [*Database*] (GDD)
PROW....... Prothonotary Warbler [*North American bird banding code*] (BIBA)
PROW....... Prowler Industries [*NCIC trailer make code*]
PROWDELREP... Proceed Without Delay Report Duty or Purpose Indicated [*Military*]
PROWL...... Procedure Work Log System (IAA)
PROWLER... Programmable Robot Observer with Logical Enemy Response [*Developed by Robot Defense Systems of Thornton, CO*]
PROWL System... Procedure Work Log System (SAUS)
PROWORD... Procedure Word
PROWS..... Projected Warhead System (SAUS)
PROX........ Preferential Oxidation [*Vehicle power systems*]
PROX........ Procor [*Private rail car owner code*]
PRO-X....... Prothrombin Time [*Hematology*] (CPH)
prox.......... Proximal (CPH)
PROX........ Proxim Corp. [*NASDAQ symbol*]
PROX........ Proxim, Inc. [*NASDAQ symbol*] (SAG)
PROX........ Proximity (AABC)
Prox........ Proximo (EBF)
PROX........ Proximo [*In Next Month*] [*Latin*]
prox.......... Proximo [*In Next Month*] [*Latin*] (ODBW)
prox acc.... Next in Order of Merit (ODA)
PROX ACC... Proxime Accessit [*Next in Order of Merit*] [*Latin*]
PRO-XAN... Protein-Xanthophyll [*Alfalfa protein concentrate process*]
PRO-XAN... Protein-Xantophyll (SAUS)
PROXI....... Projection by Reflection Optics of Xerographic Images (IEEE)
Proxim...... Proxim, Inc. [*Associated Press*] (SAG)
Proxima..... Proxima Corp. [*Associated Press*] (SAG)
prox luc..... Proxima Luce [*Day Before*] [*Latin*] (MAE)
Proxymd.... ProxyMed, Inc. [*Associated Press*] (SAG)
PRP.......... Panretinal Photocoagulation [*Ophthalmology*]
PRP.......... Paper, Rubber and Plastics (SAUS)
PRP.......... Parent Rule Point (MCD)
PRP.......... Parsi [*Language symbol*] (ETLW)
PRP.......... Partial Read Pulse (SAUS)
PRP.......... Parti de la Revolution Populaire [*People's Revolutionary Party*] [*Zaire*] [*Political party*] (PD)
PRP.......... Partido de Renovacion Puertorriqueno [*Puerto Rican Renewal Party*] [*Political party*] (EY)
PRP.......... Partido de Representacao Popular [*Brazil*] [*Political party*]
PRP.......... Partido Renovacion Patriotica [*Honduras*] [*Political party*] (EY)
PRP.......... Partido Republicano Portugues [*Portuguese Republican Party*] [*Political party*] (PPE)
PRP.......... Partido Revolucionario Popular [*Popular Revolutionary Party*] [*Portugal*] [*Political party*] (PPE)
PRP.......... Parti Republicain du Progres [*Republican Progress Party*] [*Central Africa*] [*Political party*] (PD)
PRP.......... Parti Republicain Progressif [*Algeria*] [*Political party*] (EY)
PRP.......... Party of Renewal and Progress (Morocco) [*Political party*] (PSAP)
PRP.......... Party of Renovation and Progress (Guinea) [*Political party*] (PSAP)
PRP.......... Peace Resource Project (EA)
PRP.......... Peak Radiated Power (CET)
PRP.......... Peer Review Panel (ABAC)
PRP.......... Penicillinase-Resistant Penicillin [*Medicine*] (MELL)
PRP.......... People's Redemption Party [*Nigeria*] [*Political party*] (PPW)
PRP.......... People's Reform Party [*Philippines*] [*Political party*] (EY)
PRP.......... People's Revolutionary Party [*North Vietnam*] [*Political party*]
PRP.......... People's Revolutionary Party [*Benin*] [*Political party*]
PRP.......... Peptide Recognition Protein [*Biochemistry*]
PRP.......... Perfect Reading Prosthesis (SAUS)
PRP.......... Performance Recovery Program (SAUS)
PRP.......... Performance-Related Pay (ECON)
PRP.......... Performance, Requirements, Practices [*Military*]
PRP.......... Personnel Reliability Program [*Air Force*]
PRP.......... Petrol Refilling Point (SAUS)
PRP.......... Phantom Range Pod (MCD)
PRP.......... Phase Review Package (MCD)
PRP.......... Physical Readiness Program [*Navy*] (DNAB)
PRP.......... Physiologic Rest Position [*Medicine*] (DMAA)
PRP.......... Pick-up Release Point (SAUS)
PRP.......... Pickup-Zone Release Point
PRP.......... Pipelined Resampling Processor (ACAE)
PRP.......... Pityriasis Rubra Pilaris [*Dermatology*] (MAE)
PRP.......... Placement Route and Patch [*Computer science*] (IAA)
PRP.......... Placement-Route-and-Patch (SAUS)
PRP.......... Platelet-Rich Plasma [*Hematology*]
PRP.......... Pneumatically-Released Pilot (DNAB)
PRP.......... Polymer of Ribose Phosphate [*Organic chemistry*] (MAE)
PRP.......... Polyradiculopathy [*Medicine*] (EDAA)
PRP.......... Polyribitol Phosphate [*Organic chemistry*]
PRP.......... Polyribophosphate (SAUS)
PRP.......... Position Report Printout
PRP.......... Postbuckled Rectangular Plate
PRP.......... Postural Rest Position [*Medicine*] (EDAA)
PRP.......... Potentially Responsible Party [*Environmental Protection Agency*]
PRP.......... Power-Deployed Reserve Parachute (MCD)
PRP.......... Precision Registration Processor (SAUS)
PRP.......... Premature-Removal Period (MCD)
PRP.......... Prepare (FAAC)
PRP.......... Prerigor Pressurization [*Meat processing*]
PR P......... Present Participle (WGA)
PRP.......... Presidential Reorganizational Project
PRP.......... President's Reorganization Project [*Carter Administration*] [*Executive Office of the President*] (GFGA)
PRP.......... Pressure Rate Product [*In treadmill test*]
PRP.......... Preventral Protractor (SAUS)
PRP.......... Previous Record Pointer (SAUS)
PRP.......... Primary Raynaud's Phenomenon [*Medicine*]
PRP.......... Principality (SAUS)
PRP.......... Principal Responsible Party
PRP.......... Print Out [*Computer science*] (IAA)
PrP.......... Prion Protein [*Biochemistry*]
PRP.......... Problem Resolution Program [*IRS*]
PRP.......... Procedure-Related Pain (MELL)
PRP.......... Procurement Requirements Package (MCD)
PRP.......... Production Readiness Plan
PRP.......... Production Requirements Plan
PRP.......... Production Reserve Policy
PRP.......... Product Requirements Plan
PRP.......... Profit-Related Pay [*Economics*]
PRP.......... Programmed Random Process (SAUS)
PRP.......... Program Random Process (PDAA)
PRP.......... Program Requirements Package [*Computer science*]
PRP.......... Program Review Panel [*Army*] (AABC)
PRP.......... Progressive Rework Plan
PRP.......... Progressive Rubella Panencephalitis [*Medicine*]
PRP.......... Proliferative Retinopathy Photocoagulation
PRP.......... Proliferin Related Protein [*Biochemistry*]
PRP.......... Proline-Rich Protein [*Biochemistry*]
PRP.......... Proper [*Telegraphy*] (PCTE)
PRP.......... Proper Return Port [*Shipping*]
PRP.......... Prospective Reimbursement Plan [*Medicaid*]
PRP.......... Protease-Resistant Prion [*Medicine*]
PrP.......... Protease-Resistant Protein [*Microbiology*]
PrP.......... Protein Phosphatase [*An enzyme*]
PRP.......... Pseudorandom Pulse
PRP.......... Psychotic Reaction Profile [*Psychology*]
PRP.......... Public Relations Personnel [*Navy*]
PRP.......... Pulse Recurrence [*or Repetition*] Period (CET)
PRP.......... Pulse Repetition Frequency [*Medicine*] (DAVI)
PRP.......... Pulse Repetition Period [*Computer science*] (IAA)
PRP.......... Purchase Request Package [*Shipping*] (MCD)
PRP.......... Purple (MSA)
PRP.......... Purpose (MSA)
PRP.......... Reformed Presbyterian Theological Seminary, Pittsburgh, PA [*OCLC symbol*] (OCLC)
PRPA........ Professional Race Pilots Association [*Later, USARA*] (EA)
PRPA........ Projectile Raye a Propulsion Additionelle (SAUS)
PRPA........ Puerto Rican Parrot [*North American bird banding code*] (BIBA)
PRPA........ Puerto Rico Ports Authority (SAUS)
PRPB........ Parti de la Revolution Populaire du Benin [*Benin People's Revolutionary Party*] [*Political party*] (PD)
PRPB........ Peoples Revolution Party of Benin (SAUS)
PRPC........ Parti Republicain du Peuple Camerounais [*Political party*] (EY)
PRPC........ Public Relations Policy Committee [*NATO*] (NATG)
PrPCU-L.... Catholic University of Puerto Rico, Law Library, Ponce, Puerto Rico [*Library symbol*] [*Library of Congress*] (LCLS)
PRP-D....... Polyribosylribitol Phosphate-Diptheria Toxoid [*Medicine*]
PRPD........ Preferred Transport and Distribution [*Common carrier symbol*]
PRPD........ Public Radio Program Directors (SAUS)
PRPD........ Public Radio Programmer's Association (EA)

PRPDA ...... Public Radio Program Directors Association (NTPA)
PrpdLg ...... Pre-Paid Legal Services, Inc. [*Associated Press*] (SAG)
PRPE .... Prairie Pacific Energy Corp. (SAUS)
PRPF .... Parameter Profile (SAUS)
PRPF .... Planar Radial Peaking Factor [*Network analysis*] (IEEE)
PRPG .... Political Resident Persian Gulf (SAUS)
PRPG .... Proportioning
PRPGA ...... Puerto Rico Personne and Guidance Association (SAUS)
PRPH .... Peripherin (DMAA)
Pr/Ph .... Pristane/Phytane Ratio [*Environmental science*]
PRPHL ...... Peripheral
PRPIT .... Process Management for Process Identifier Table (SAUS)
PRPL .... PACOM [*Pacific Command*] Reconnaissance Priority List (CINC)
PRPL .... People's Democratic Republic of Laos
PRPL .... Procurement Repair Parts List (AAG)
prpl .... Purple
PRPLN ...... Propulsion (MSA)
PRPLNT ..... Propellant (KSC)
PRPLT .... Propellant (MSA)
PRPN .... Proportion [*Telegraphy*] (PCTE)
PRPNE ...... Propane [*Organic chemistry*]
PRPOOS .... Plankton Rate Processes in Oligotrophic Oceans [*Cooperative research project*]
Pr Pos Ctl Ex... Print Position Control Exit (SAUS)
Pr Pos Ctr E&E... Print Position Counter Entry and Exit (SAUS)
Pr Pos Ctr Ent&Ex... Print Position Counter Entry and Exit (SAUS)
Pr Pos Ent... Print Position Entry (SAUS)
Pr Pos Ex... Print Position Exit (SAUS)
PRPP .... Phosphoribosyl Pyrophosphate (SAUS)
PRPP .... Phosphoribosylpyrophosphate [*Biochemistry*]
PRPP .... Phosphorylribose Pyrophosphate [*Biochemistry*]
PRPP .... Pseudoresidual Plot Program
PRPQ .... Programming Request for Price Quotation [*Computer science*]
PRPQ .... Program Request for Price Quotation (SAUS)
PR PR .... Praeter Propter [*About, Nearly*] [*Latin*] (ROG)
PRPR .... Puerto Rico Pool-type Reactor (SAUS)
PRPRR ...... Preparer
PRPS .... Pressure Rise per Stage (MCD)
PRPS .... Programming Requirements Process Specification (SAUS)
PRPS .... Programming Requirements Process Specifications
PRPS .... Program Requirement Process Specification [*NASA*] (KSC)
PRPS .... Prostatic Secretory Protein (DMAA)
PRPSA ...... Personal Report of Public Speaking Apprehension (EDAC)
PRPSD ...... Proposed (MSA)
PRPSL .... Proposal (MSA)
PRPT .... Parti Revolutionnaire du Peuple Tunisien [*Revolutionary Party of the Tunisian People*] [*Political party*] (PD)
PRP-T .... Polyribosylribitol Phosphate Conjugated to Tetanus Toxoid [*Medicine*]
PRPT .... Prescriptive Reading Performance Test [*Educational test*]
prpt .... proportional (SAUS)
PRPUC ...... Philippine Republic Presidential Unit Citation [*Military decoration*]
PRPUCE ..... Philippine Republic Presidential Unit Citation Emblem [*Military decoration*]
PRPX .... Pacific Railroad Preservation Association [*Federal Railroad Administration identification code*]
prpylm ...... Propylaeum (VRA)
PRPZ .... Process Plastics [*Federal Railroad Administration identification code*]
PRQ .... Houston, TX [*Location identifier*] [*FAA*] (FAAL)
PRQ .... Partition Request Queue (SAUS)
PRQ .... Personal Resources Questionnaire (DMAA)
PRQ .... Presidente Roque Saenz Pena [*Argentina*] [*Airport symbol*] (AD)
PRQA .... Passenger Ride Quality Apparatus [*Public transportation*]
PRR .... P & R Rail Car Service [*Federal Railroad Administration identification code*]
PRR .... Partner Airlines [*Former USSR*] [*FAA designator*] (FAAC)
PRR .... Parts Replacement Request (KSC)
PRR .... Passenger Reservation Request (NVT)
PRR .... Passive Ranging RADAR
PRR .... Pawling Research Reactor
PRR .... Pennsylvania Railroad Co. [*AAR code*] [*Obsolete*]
PRR .... Performance-Related Remuneration (ADA)
PRR .... Perrigo Co. [*AMEX symbol*] (COMM)
PRR .... Perrine, FL [*Location identifier*] [*FAA*] (FAAL)
PRR .... Perris [*California*] [*Seismograph station code, US Geological Survey*] [*Closed*] (SEIS)
PRR .... Personnel Requirements Report [*Army*]
PRR .... Philippine Research Reactor (SAA)
PRR .... Placement Revision Request
PRR .... Planning & Requirements Review (SAUS)
PRR .... Planning Release Record (AAG)
PRR .... Plans and Requirements Review
PRR .... Political Risk Review [*A publication*] (EAAP)
PRR .... Post-Recall Release (WDAA)
Pr R .... Practice Reports [*Quebec*] [*A publication*] (DLA)
PRR .... Practise Rocket (SAUS)
PRR .... Prairie [*Commonly used*] (OPSA)
PRR .... Prelaunch Readiness Review (ACAE)
PRR .... Preliminary Requirements Review [*NASA*] (KSC)
PRR .... Premature Removal Rate
PRR .... Pre-Readiness Review (SAUS)
PRR .... Presbyterian and Reformed Renewal Ministries International [*Formerly, PCC*] (EA)
PRR .... Pressure Rise Rate [*Nuclear energy*] (NRCH)
PRR .... Primary Production Required [*Resource management*]
PRR .... Prioritized Round-Robin (SAUS)
PRR .... Prism Resources Ltd. [*Vancouver Stock Exchange symbol*]
PRR .... Problem Reporting and Resolution
PRR .... Producer's Reliability Risk
PRR .... Production Readiness Review
PRR .... Production Release Request (SAUS)
PRR .... Production Research Reports
PRR .... Professional Rights and Responsibilities
PRR .... Program Request Register (SAUS)
PRR .... Program Requirements Review [*NASA*] (NASA)
PRR .... Program Revision Report (KSC)
PRR .... Project Requirements Review (SAUS)
PRR .... Proline-Rich Protein [*Biochemistry*]
PRR .... Pro Racing Regulation [*Automobile racing*]
PRR .... Proton Relaxation Rate
PRR .... Pseudoresident Reader (MHDB)
PRR .... Publication Revision Request (AAG)
PRR .... Puerto Rico Reactor (NRCH)
PRR .... Puerto Rico Supreme Court Reports [*A publication*] (DLA)
PRR .... Pulse Radar Repair (SAUS)
PRR .... Pulse Recurrence [*or Repetition*] Rate (MUGU)
PrRA .... Academia Maria Reina, Rio Piedras, PR [*Library symbol*] [*Library of Congress*] (LCLS)
PRRA .... Puerto Rico Reconstruction Administration [*Terminated, 1955*]
PrRadA ...... Premiere Radio Networks, Inc. [*Associated Press*] (SAG)
PRR & Regs... Commonwealth of Puerto Rico Rules and Regulations [*A publication*] (DLA)
PRR&Regs... Commonwealth of Puerto Rico Rules and Regulations (journ.) (SAUS)
PRRB .... Provider Reimbursement Review Board [*Medicare*]
PRRC .... New Mexico Petroleum Recovery Research Center [*New Mexico Institute of Mining and Technology*] [*Research center*] (RCD)
PRRC .... Pitch/Roll Rate Changer Assembly (MCD)
PRRC .... Precision Response Corp. [*NASDAQ symbol*] (SAG)
PRRD .... Proprietary Rights to Registration Data (SAUS)
PrRe .... Evangelical Seminary, Rio Piedras, PR [*Library symbol*] [*Library of Congress*] (LCLS)
PRRE .... Pupils Round, Regular, and Equal [*Medicine*] (MAE)
Pr Reg BC... Practical Register in the Bail Court [*A publication*] (DLA)
Pr Reg Ch... Practical Register in Chancery [*1 vol.*] [*A publication*] (DLA)
Pr Reg CP... Practical Register in the Common Pleas [*1705-42*] [*A publication*] (DLA)
Pr Rep ...... Practice Reports [*Ontario*] [*A publication*] (DLA)
Pr Rep ...... Practice Reports [*England*] [*A publication*] (DLA)
Pr Rep BC... Lowndes, Maxwell, and Pollock's English Bail Court Practice Reports [*1850-51*] [*A publication*] (DLA)
PRRFC ...... Planar Randomly Reinforced Fiber Composite
PRRI .... Puerto Rico Rum Institute [*Later, PRRPA*]
PRRM .... Presbyterian and Reformed Renewal Ministries International (EA)
PRRM .... Program Review and Resources Management [*NASA*]
PRRM .... Pulse Repetition Rate Modulation [*Data transmission*] [*Computer science*] (TEL)
PRRMI ...... Presbyterian and Reformed Renewal Ministries International (EA)
PRRPA ...... Puerto Rico Rum Producers Association [*Defunct*] (EA)
PRRR .... Pioneer Railcorp [*NASDAQ symbol*] (SAG)
PRRS .... Porcine Reproductive and Respiratory Syndrome (SAUS)
PRRS .... Positioning Reporting Recording System (RDA)
PRRS .... Problem Reporting and Resolution System [*Military*] (CAAL)
PR-RSV ..... Rous Sarcoma Virus, Prague Strain
PRRU .... P and R Rentals [*Intermodal shipping container symbol*] (TVRC)
PRRWO ..... Puerto Rican Revolutionary Workers Organization (NADA)
PRRX .... Powell River Railroad [*Federal Railroad Administration identification code*]
PRS .... Pacific Railroad Society (EA)
PRS .... Pacific Rocket Society (EA)
PRS .... Packaged Reefer Space unit (SAUS)
PRS .... Padre Resources [*Vancouver Stock Exchange symbol*]
PRS .... Paint Research Station [*British*] (BI)
prs .... Pairs (MIST)
PRS .... Pairs
PRS .... Pakistan Railway Standard (SAUS)
PRS .... Parachute Rocket System (SAUS)
PRS .... Paraiso [*California*] [*Seismograph station code, US Geological Survey*] (SEIS)
PRS .... Parametric Ruled Surface (MCD)
PRS .... Parasi [*Solomon Islands*] [*Airport symbol*] (OAG)
PRS .... Park and Ride Scheme (SAUS)
PRS .... Parliamentary Research Services [*British*]
PRS .... Pars Systems (CRS) [*ICAO designator*] (FAAC)
PRS .... Partei fuer Renten-, Steuer-, und Soziale Gerechtigkeit [*Party for Equitable Pensions, Taxation, and Social Services*] [*Germany*] [*Political party*] (PPW)
PR's .... Partial Responders [*to medication*]
PRS .... Partial Response Signalling (NITA)
PRS .... Partial Response System (SAUS)
PRS .... Parti de la Revolution Socialiste [*Party of Socialist Revolution*] [*Senegal*] [*Political party*]
PRS .... Parti de la Revolution Socialiste [*Party of Socialist Revolution*] [*Benin*] [*Political party*]
PRS .... Partido de la Revolucion Socialista [*Party of the Socialist Revolution*] [*Cuba*] [*Political party*]
PRS .... Partido para a Renovacao Social [*Party for Social Renovation*] [*Guinea-Bissau*] [*Political party*] (EY)
PRS .... Partido Revolucionario Socialista [*Mexico*] [*Political party*] (EY)

PRS......... Partito Republicano Sammarinese [*Republican Party*] [*San Marino*] [*Political party*] (EY)
PRS......... Passenger Reservation System [*Indian Railway*] (TIR)
PRS......... Passive RADAR Surveillance [*Military*] (CAAL)
PRS......... Passive Ranging Sonar (SAUS)
PRS......... Pattern Recognition Society (EA)
PRS......... Pattern Recognition System
PRS......... Paul Revere Society [*Association*] (EA)
PRS......... Payload Retention Subsystem [*NASA*] (NASA)
PRS......... Peer Review Systems, Inc.
PRS......... Pennsylvania Radiological Society (SAUS)
PRS......... Pennsylvania-Reading Seashore Lines [*Absorbed into Consolidated Rail Corp.*]
PRS......... Perceptual Respresentation System [*Memory*]
PRS......... Performance Rating System (OICC)
PRS......... Performing Right Society [*British*]
PRS......... Performing Rights Society (SAUS)
PRS......... Periphal Reset (SAUS)
PRS......... Personality Rating Scale [*Psychology*]
PRS......... Personal Radio Services (SAUS)
PRS......... Personal Recording System
PRS......... Personal Relations Survey [*Managerial skills test*]
PRS......... Personal Response System (SAUS)
PRS......... Personnel Readiness System [*Air Force*]
PRS......... Personnel Rescue Service [*NASA*] (NASA)
PRS......... Personnel Rescue System [*NASA*] (MCD)
PRS......... Personnel Research Section [*Army*]
PRS......... Personnel Research Staff [*Department of Agriculture*]
PRS......... Pesticides Registration Section (HEAS)
PRS......... Philatelic Research Society
PRS......... Philosophical Research Society (EA)
PRS......... Photographic Reconnaissance System
PRS......... Photo Resist Spinner
PRS......... Physically Restricted Status [*Military*]
PRS......... Pierre Robin Syndrome (MELL)
PRS......... Pipe Roll Society (EA)
PRS......... Placement Research Service
PRS......... Planar Rider System
PRS......... Planners Referral Service [*Information service or system*] (IID)
PRS......... Planning Record Sheet
PR's......... Planning References (AAG)
PRS......... Planning Reference System (SAUS)
PRS......... Planning Research & Systems Ltd. [*British*]
PRS......... Planning Research & Systems PLC (SAUS)
PRS......... Plasma Renin Substrate [*Hematology*]
PRS......... Pneumatic Reading System
PRS......... Pointing Reference System (KSC)
PRS......... Polynomial Remainder Sequence (SAUS)
PRS......... Polynominal Remainder Sequence (SAUS)
PRS......... Population Research Service [*Information service or system*] (IID)
PRS......... Portable Radar Simulator (ACAE)
PRS......... Positive Rolandic Spikes [*Neurology*] (DAVI)
PRS......... Potential Routes (SAUS)
PRS......... Power Reactant Subsystem [*NASA*] (NASA)
PRS......... Power Reactant System
PRS......... Power Relay Satellite
PRS......... Prayers (ROG)
PRS......... Precipitate Reduction Sinter [*Metal*] (DICI)
PRS......... Precision Ranging System
PRS......... Precision Rotary Stripper
PRS......... Precision Roughness Standard (SAUS)
PRS......... Pre-Raphaelite Society [*United Kingdom*] (EAIO)
PRS......... Present (WGA)
PRS......... Presidential Airways (SAUS)
PRS......... President of the Royal Society [*British*]
PRS......... Presidents [*Telegraphy*] (PCTE)
PRS......... Presidio Oil Co. [*AMEX symbol*] (SPSG)
PRS......... Presidio, TX [*Location identifier*] [*FAA*] (FAAL)
PRS......... Press (MSA)
PRS......... Pressure (SAUS)
PRS......... Pressure Reducing Station
PRS......... Pressure Response Spectrum [*Nuclear energy*] (NRCH)
PR/S......... Prestrike (SAA)
PRS......... Price Reporting System (NUMA)
PRS......... Primary Recovery Ship [*NASA*]
PRS......... Primary Recovery Site [*NASA*] (KSC)
PRS......... Primary Representational System (EDAC)
PRS......... Primary Rescue Site [*NASA*] (NASA)
PRS......... Printed Record Storage (SAUS)
PRS......... Print Management Service (SAUS)
PRS......... Priority Reservation System (SAUS)
PRs......... Problem Reports (SAUS)
PRS......... Procedure Review Section [*Social Security Administration*]
PRS......... Process Radiation Sampler [*Nuclear energy*] (NRCH)
PRS......... Procurement Tracking System (SAUS)
PRS......... Production Recording System
PRS......... Production Release System (MCD)
PRS......... Production Reporting System (SAUS)
PRS......... Product Requirement Schedule (MCD)
PRS......... Product Requirement Specification (SAUS)
PRS......... Programmed RADAR Simulator (IAA)
PRS......... Program Rating Summary Report [*Television ratings*] (NTCM)
PRS......... Program Request System (SAUS)
PRS......... Program Requirements Summary (MUGU)
PRS......... Prolonged Respiratory Support (MELL)
PRS......... Property Recovery Section
PRS......... Property Recovery Squad (SAUS)
PRS......... Propodial Sinus [*Zoology*]
PRS......... Proportional Representation Society
PRS......... Prospective Reimbursement System [*Health insurance*] (GHCT)
PRS......... Prospectors Air [*Vancouver Stock Exchange symbol*]
PRS......... Protective Research Section (SAUS)
PRS......... Protestant Reformation Society (EA)
PRS......... Provide Repair Service [*Navy*] (NVT)
PRS......... Provisioning Requirements Statement
PRS......... Pseudorandom Sequence
PRS......... Pseudo-Random Signal (SAUS)
PRS......... Psychiatric Rehabilitation Services [*Association*] (EA)
PRS......... Psycholinguistic Rating Scale
PRS......... Public Radio Stations (SAUS)
PRS......... Public Rehabilitation Scheme (SAUS)
PRS......... Public Relations Section [*Library Administration and Management Association*]
PRS......... Puerto Lempira [*Honduras*] [*Airport symbol*] (AD)
PRS......... Pupil Rating Scale (SAUS)
PRS......... Pure Random Search [*Optimization method*]
PRS......... Pure Resources [*NYSE symbol*]
PRS......... Radical Socialist Party (France) [*Political party*] (PSAP)
PRS......... Social Renewal Party (Angola) [*Political party*] (PSAP)
PRSA........ Pan-Rhodian Society of America (EA)
PRSA........ Permigewasset River Study Act of 1989 (COE)
PRSA........ Plasma Renin Substrate Activity [*Medicine*] (EDAA)
PRSA........ Polarizer-Retarder-Sample-Analyzer (SAUS)
PRSA........ Power Reactant Storage Assembly [*NASA*] (MCD)
PRSA........ President of the Royal Scottish Academy
PRSA........ Proportional Representation Society of Australia
PRSA........ Public Relation Society of America (SAUS)
PRSA........ Public Relations Society of America (EA)
PRSA........ Puerto Rico Statehood Commission (EA)
PrSaC....... Colegio Universitario del Sagrado Corazon [*College of the Sacred Heart*], Santurce, PR [*Library symbol*] [*Library of Congress*] (LCLS)
Prsbytn...... Presbytarian (BEE)
PRSC........ Parametric Response Surface Control (AAEL)
PRSC........ Plutonium Rework Sample Cell [*Nuclear energy*] (NRCH)
PRSC........ Puerto Rico Solidarity Committee (EA)
PRSC........ Reformist Social Christian Party (Dominican Rep.) [*Political party*] (PSAP)
Pr Scale.... Prejudice Scale [*Psychology*] (DHP)
PR Scale.... Process-Reactive Scale (SAUS)
PRSCHL..... Preschool
PRSCR...... Puerto Rico Supreme Court Reports [*A publication*] (DLA)
PRSCT....... Prescott, ON [*American Association of Railroads railroad junction routing code*]
PRSD........ Portable Rectilinear Scanning Device
PRSD........ Power Reactant Storage [*or Supply*] and Distribution [*NASA*] (NASA)
PRSD........ Power Reactant Supply and Distribution
PRSD........ Pressed (AAG)
PRSD........ Social Democratic Radical Party (Chile) [*Political party*] (PSAP)
PRSDMET... Pressed Metal (SAUS)
PRSDS...... Power Reactant Storage and Distribution System (MCD)
PrSE......... El Mundo Publishing Co., San Juan, PR [*Library symbol*] [*Library of Congress*] (LCLS)
PRSE........ Precise Software Solutions [*NASDAQ symbol*]
PRSE........ President of the Royal Society of Edinburgh
PRSEC....... Payroll Section
PRSF........ Portal Software [*NASDAQ symbol*] (SG)
Prsfdr........ Pressfeeder [*Printing*]
PRSG........ Personal Radio Steering Group [*Ann Arbor, MI*] [*Telecommunications service*] (TSSD)
PRSG........ Pressing
PRSG........ Pseudo Random Signal Generator (SAUS)
PRSG........ Pulse-Rebalanced Strapdown Gyro (MCD)
PRSH........ President of the Royal Society for the Promotion of Health [*British*]
PRSI......... Pay Related Social Insurance (SAUS)
PRSIG....... Pacific Rim SMDS Interest Group (SAUS)
PRSIS....... Prospective Rate Setting Information System [*Medicine*] (DMAA)
PRS Journal... Philosophical Research Society Journal (SAUS)
PRSL........ Pennsylvania-Reading Seashore Lines [*Absorbed into Consolidated Rail Corp.*] [*AAR code*]
PRSL........ Progressive Savings & Loan Association (SAUS)
PRSM....... Parachute Rocket System Modified (SAUS)
PRSM....... Prism Group [*NASDAQ symbol*] (SAG)
PR/SM....... Processor Resource/Systems Manager [*Computer science*] (CDE)
PRSM....... Puerto Rico Society of Microbiologists [*Association*] (EA)
prsmc....... Prismacolor (VRA)
PRSMC....... Prism Group [*NASDAQ symbol*] (TTSB)
PRSMN....... Pressman (AABC)
Pr Smp....... Print Sample (SAUS)
PRSN........ Phased-Array Responsive Spot Noise (SEWL)
PRSN........ Provisional Relative Sunspot Number [*NASA*]
PRSNG...... Pressing
PRSNL....... Personal
PRSNNL..... Personnel
PRSNT....... Present [*NWS*] (FAAC)
PRSO........ Puerto Rican Screech-Owl [*North American bird banding code*] (BIBA)
PRSP........ Penicillin-Resistant S. Pneumoniae [*Clinical chemistry*]
PRSP........ Poverty Reduction Strategy Paper

PRSP .... Prereading Screening Procedures (SAUS)
PRSP .... Puerto Rico Socialist Party (NADA)
PRSPL .... Planning and Role Setting for Public Libraries [*Public Library Association*] [*A publication*]
PRSPT .... Sindicato de Obreros Unidos del Sur de Puerto Rico
PRSPT .... Sindicato Puertorriqueno de Trabajadores
PRSR .... Presser (MSA)
PR/SR .... Price Redetermination/Service Reallocation (AAGC)
PRSRV ...... Preservative (AAG)
PRSRZ ...... Pressurize (MSA)
PRSS .... Passive Ranging Sub-System (SEWL)
PRSS .... Pennsylvania-Reading Seashore Lines [*Absorbed into Consolidated Rail Corp.*]
PRSS .... Polystatic Radar Satellite System (ACAE)
PRSS .... Problem Report Squawk Sheet [*NASA*] (NASA)
PRSSA ...... Public Relations Student Society of America (EA)
PRSSA ...... Puerto Rico Mainland US Statehood Students Association (EA)
PRSSD ...... Pressed
PRST .... Persist (FAAC)
PrST .... Prairie Standard Time (SAUS)
PRST .... Presstek, Inc. [*NASDAQ symbol*] (NQ)
PRST .... Prestige Custom Trailers [*NCIC trailer make code*]
PRST .... Priest
PRST .... Probability Ration Sequential Test [*Quality management*]
PRST .... Probability Reliability Sequential Tests (MCD)
PRST .... Puerto Rican Standard Time (SAUS)
PRSTAT ..... Pressure-Test Status [*Automotive emissions*]
Pr Stat ...... Private Statutes [*Legal term*] (DLA)
PRSTC .... Prosthetic
PRSTCOM ... Pressure Test Comments [*Automotive emissions*]
PRSTG ...... Prestige
PRSU .... Navieras de Puerto Rico [*Common carrier symbol*]
PRSU .... Police Requirements Support Unit [*Home Office*] [*British*]
PRSU .... Prime Source Holding [*Intermodal shipping container symbol*] (TVRC)
Pr Sup .... Print Suppression (SAUS)
PRSV .... Papaya Ringspot Virus [*Plant pathology*]
PRSV .... Peach Red Suture Virus (SAUS)
PRSV .... Preserving
PRSVN ...... Preservation (AABC)
PRSW .... President of the Royal Scottish Water Colour Society
PRSW .... Pure Software [*NASDAQ symbol*] (TTSB)
PRSW .... Pure Software, Inc. [*NASDAQ symbol*] (SAG)
PrSW .... World University, San Juan, PR [*Library symbol*] [*Library of Congress*] (LCLS)
PrSW-I ...... World University, International Institute of the Americas, Barbosa Esq. Guayama,San Juan, PR [*Library symbol*] [*Library of Congress*] (LCLS)
PRSX .... Pacific Rail Services [*Federal Railroad Administration identification code*]
PRT .... Air Cargo Carriers, Inc. [*ICAO designator*] (FAAC)
PRT .... Pacemaker-Re-entry Tachykardie (SAUS)
PRT .... Parachute Radio Transmitter [*Telecommunications*] (IAA)
PRT .... Pararescue Team (COE)
PRT .... Parliamentary Remuneration Tribunal [*New South Wales, Australia*]
PRT .... Parr Terminal Railroad [*AAR code*]
PRT .... Part (AAG)
PRT .... Participating Research Teams [*Department of Energy*]
prt .... Particle [*Linguistics*] (IEL)
PRT .... Partido Revolucionario de los Trabajadores [*Revolutionary Workers' Party*] [*Costa Rica*] [*Political party*] (EY)
PRT .... Partido Revolucionario de los Trabajadores [*Workers' Revolutionary Party*] [*Peru*] [*Political party*] (PPW)
PRT .... Partido Revolucionario de los Trabajadores [*Workers' Revolutionary Party*] [*Argentina*] [*Political party*] (PD)
PRT .... Partido Revolucionario de los Trabajadores [*Workers' Revolutionary Party*] [*Uruguay*] [*Political party*] (PD)
PRT .... Partido Revolucionario de Trabajadores [*Revolutionary Worker's Party*] [*Colorado*] [*Political party*] (EY)
PRT .... Passage Reading Test [*Education*] (EDAC)
PRT .... Patient Refused Test (SAUS)
PRT .... Patient Review Tribunal [*Queensland, Australia*]
PRT .... Patten Recognition Technology (NITA)
PRT .... Pattern Recognition Technique
PRT .... Patter Recognition Technique
PRT .... Payroll Tax (ADA)
PRT .... Penicillium Roqueforti Toxin (DB)
PRT .... Periodic Reevaluation Tests
PRT .... Permanent Recording Traffic [*Telecommunications*] (IAA)
PRT .... Personalized Rapid Transport (SAUS)
PRT .... Personal Rapid Transit [*Computer-guided transit system*]
PRT .... Personnel Research Test [*Military*]
PRT .... Petroleum Revenue Tax [*British*]
PRT .... Pharmaceutical Research and Testing [*Public Health Service*] (GRD)
PRT .... Philadelphia Rapid Transit (SAUS)
PRT .... Philadelphia Reading Test [*Education*]
PRT .... Phosphoribosyltransferase [*Also, PRTase*] [*An enzyme*]
PRT .... Photoradiation Therapy [*Oncology*]
PRT .... Physical Readiness Training [*Army*] (INF)
PRT .... Pictorial Reasoning Test [*Job screening test*]
PRT .... Piezo-Resistive Transducer [*Automotive engineering*]
PRT .... Planar Resistor Technology (AAEL)
PRT .... Platinum Resistance Thermometer
PRT .... Point Retreat, AK [*Location identifier*] [*FAA*] (FAAL)
PRT .... Polysilicon Resonant pressure Transducer (SAUS)
PRT .... Port
PRT .... Portable Radiation Thermometer
PRT .... Portable Radio Telephone
PRT .... Portable Remote Terminal
PRT .... Portable Router Template (MCD)
PRT .... Portable Router Tool
PRT .... Portland [*Diocesan abbreviation*] [*Maine*] (TOCD)
PRT .... Portugal [*ANSI three-letter standard code*] (CNC)
PRT .... Postoperative Respiratory Therapy [*Medicine*] (EDAA)
PRT .... Power Recovery Turbine
PRT .... Prato [*Italy*] [*Seismograph station code, US Geological Survey*] (SEIS)
PRT .... Precision Radiation Thermometer
PRT .... Preliminary Reference Trajectory [*NASA*] (KSC)
PRT .... Pressure Ratio Transducer (SAUS)
PRT .... Pressurized Relief Tank (NRCH)
PRT .... Primary Ranging Test (OA)
PRT .... Print
PRT .... Printed Receive Tape (SAUS)
prt .... Printer [*MARC relator code*] [*Library of Congress*] (LCCP)
PRT .... Printer [*Computer science*] (MDG)
PRT .... Prison Reform Trust (WDAA)
Prt .... Private [*British military*] (DMA)
PRT .... Problem Resolution Tasking System [*Army*] (INF)
PRT .... Processing Response Time (SAUS)
PRT .... Procurement Review Team
PRT .... Procurement Round Table (EA)
PRT .... Production Reliability Test
PRT .... Production Run Tape
PRT .... Product Range Testing [*Business term*]
PRT .... Product Reliability Test (SAUS)
PRT .... Program Reference Table
PRT .... Program Review Team [*Navy*] (DNAB)
PRT .... Project Readiness Test (ACAE)
PRT .... Promotion, Transfer, and Redundancy [*Railway union agreement*] [*British*] (ECON)
PRT .... Prompt Air, Inc. [*FAA designator*] (FAAC)
PRT .... Prompt Relief Trip [*Nuclear energy*] (NRCH)
PRT .... Prospective Randomized Trial [*Medicine*] (EDAA)
Prt .... Protagoras [*of Plato*] [*Classical studies*] (OCD)
PRT .... Prova di Restituzione Termica [*Italy*] [*Medicine*]
PRT .... Provost
PRT .... Prudential Realty (EFIS)
PRT .... Prudential Realty Trust (SAUS)
PRT .... Psychiatric Rehabilitation Team (EA)
PRT .... Publications Requirements Tables (AAG)
PRT .... Pulsed RADAR Transmitter
prt .... Pulse Frequency (IDOE)
PRT .... Pulse Recurrence [*or Repetition*] Time (CET)
PRT .... Pulse Repetition Time
PRT .... Revolutionary Party of the Workers (Mexico) [*Political party*] (PSAP)
PRTA .... Pro-Trucker [*Common carrier symbol*]
PRTA .... Proximal Renal Tubular Acidosis [*Medicine*] (MELL)
PRTA .... Public Road Transport Association (SAUS)
PRTA .... Puerto Rican Tanager [*North American bird banding code*] (BIBA)
PRTAA .... Parson Russell Terrier Association of America (EA)
PRTase ...... Phosphoribosyltransferase [*Medicine*] (MEDA)
PRTAX .... Price T. Rowe: Tax-Free Income [*Mutual fund ticker symbol*] (SG)
PRTB .... Partido Revolucionario de Trabajadores Bolivianos [*Bolivian Workers' Revolutionary Party*] [*Political party*] (PD)
PRTB .... Pursue Real-Time BASIC (SAUS)
PRTB .... Soviet Mobile Rocket Technical Base
prTBR .... Draft Technical Basis for Regulations (SAUS)
PRTBR .... Partido Revolucionario de los Trabajadores de Bolivia Romero [*Bolivia*] [*Political party*] (PPW)
PRTC .... Partido Revolucionario de los Trabajadores Centroamericanos [*Revolutionary Party of Central American Workers*] [*El Salvador*] [*Political party*] (PD)
PRTC .... Pediatric Research and Training Center [*University of Connecticut*] [*Research center*] (RCD)
PRTC .... Ports Canada
PRTC .... Precision Technologies (SAUS)
PRTC .... Priority Real Time Command (ADWA)
PRTC .... Professional Rate Training Course (DNAB)
PRTC .... Puerto Rico Telephone Co. (SAUS)
PRTCAL ..... Priority Testcall (SAUS)
PRTCALSS .. Priority Testcall to Special Services (SAUS)
PRTCD ...... Puerto Rico Tax Court Decisions [*A publication*] (DLA)
PRTC-H ...... Partido Revolucionario de los Trabajadores Centroamericanos - Seccion de Hondur as [*Revolutionary Party of Central American Workers - Honduras*] [*Political party*]
PRTCM ...... Professional Register of Traditional Chinese Medicine (SAUS)
PRTCT .... Protection (SAUS)
PRTCTV ..... Protective
PRTD .... Portland Traction Co. [*AAR code*]
PRTD .... Printed (DGA)
prtd .... Printed (VRA)
PRTE .... Primary Route (SAUS)
PRTE .... Profit Technology, Inc. (SAUS)
PRTEID ...... Primary Route Identity (SAUS)
PRTF .... Pheromone and Receptor Transcription Factor [*Genetics*]
PRTF .... Psychiatric Review Technique Form [*Social Security Administration*]
PRTG .... Prestige Housing [*NCIC trailer make code*]
PRTG .... Printing (AFM)
PRTH .... Pituitary Resistance to Thyroid Hormone [*Medicine*] (DMAA)

PRTH .... Prothrombin Time [*Hematology*] (DAVI)
PRTH-C ...... Prothrombin Time Control [*Hematology*] (DAVI)
PRTHS .... Pennsylvania Railroad Technical and Historical Society (EA)
PRTI .... Physical and Recreational Training Instructor [*British military*] (DMA)
PRTI .... Professional Realtime Interface (SAUS)
PRTK .... Presto-Tek Corp. (SAUS)
PRTKT .... Parts Kit
PRTL .... Portable (DNAB)
PRTL .... Primus Telecommunications Group, Inc. [*NASDAQ symbol*] (SAG)
PRTIMG ..... Print Image (SAUS)
PRTLS .... Powered Return to Launch Site [*NASA*] (MCD)
PRTLSP ..... Printer Line Spacing (SAUS)
PRTLY .... Partially
PRTM .... Genesis Direct, Inc. [*NASDAQ symbol*] (NASQ)
PRTM .... Printing Response-Time Monitor
PrtMcled .... Porter McLeod National Retail [*Associated Press*] (SAG)
PRTN .... Partition
PRTN .... Proteinase (DMAA)
PRTN .... Proton Energy Sys. [*NASDAQ symbol*]
PRTNR ...... Partner
PRTNRSHP ... Partnership
PRTO .... Preservation Research and Testing Office [*Library of Congress*] (EA)
PRTO .... Puerto Rican Tody [*North American bird banding code*] (BIBA)
PRTO .... William Peoples [*Common carrier symbol*]
PRTOT .... Prototype Real-Time Optical Tracker [*Computer science*]
PRTOV .... Printer Overflow (SAUS)
PRTP .... Prototype (IAA)
PRTQ .... Peer Role-Taking Questionnaire [*Psychology*] (EDAC)
PRTR .... Plutonium Recycle Test Reactor [*Nuclear energy*]
PRTR .... Pollutant Release and Transfer Registers (SAUS)
PRTR .... Porter
PrTr .... Printer [*U.S. Navy enlisted rating*] (AUER)
PRTR .... Printer
PRTRC .... Printer Controller (SAUS)
Prt Rep ...... Practice Reports [*A publication*] (DLA)
PrTrL .... Printer (Lithographer) [*U.S. Navy enlisted rating*] (AUER)
PRTRL .... Printer, Lithographer [*Navy*]
PrTrM .... Printer (Multilith) [*U.S. Navy enlisted rating*] (AUER)
PRTRM ...... Printer, Offset Process [*Navy*]
PRTRNS ..... Programmable Transformer Converter (MCD)
Prtronx ...... Printronix, Inc. [*Associated Press*] (SAG)
PRTS .... Parallel Run-Time Support library (SAUS)
PRTS .... Personal Rapid Transit System [*Computer-guided transit system*]
PRTS .... Ports [*Postal Service standard*] (OPSA)
PRTS .... Pretoria Theological Series [*A publication*] (BJA)
PRTS .... Processor Resident Testing Software (SAUS)
PrtSc .... Print Screen [*Computer keyboard*]
PRTSM ...... Portsmouth, OH [*American Association of Railroads railroad junction routing code*]
PRTSTNT ... Protestant
PRT System ... Personal Rapid Transport System (SAUS)
PRTT .... Port Trailer Manufacturing Company [*NCIC trailer make code*]
PRTU .... Portline-Transportes Maritimos [*Intermodal shipping container symbol*] (TVRC)
PRTV .... Positive Response Television [*NASDAQ symbol*] (SAG)
PRTW .... Printware, Inc. [*NASDAQ symbol*] (NASQ)
Prtw .... Propeller Twist [*Genetics*]
PRTX .... Port Railroad [*Federal Railroad Administration identification code*]
PRTY .... Party [*Telegraphy*] (PCTE)
PRTY .... Priority
PrtyCty ...... Party City Corp. [*Associated Press*] (SAG)
PRTYPOLS ... Priority Pollutants (SAUS)
PRTZ .... Packer River Terminal [*Federal Railroad Administration identification code*]
PRU .... Packed Radio Unit (SAUS)
PRU .... Packet Radio Unit
PRU .... Paranagua [*Brazil*] [*Airport symbol*] (AD)
PRU .... Pararescue Unit (COE)
PRU .... Percent Reduction of Urea (SAUS)
PRU .... Performance Reference Unit (SAUS)
PRU .... Peripheral Resistance Unit [*Medicine*]
PRU .... Personnel Readiness Unit (SAUS)
PRU .... Photographic Reconnaissance Unit [*Aircraft*] [*Marine Corps*]
PRU .... Photo Reconnaissance Unit (SAUS)
PRU .... Physical Record Unit (NITA)
PRU .... Physical Research Unit (IAA)
PRU .... Pneumatic Regulation Unit (AAG)
PRU .... Polarity Reversal Unit [*Electrochemistry*]
PRU .... Polish-Russian Union (NADA)
PRU .... Power Regulator Unit (SAUS)
PRU .... Pressure Reduction Unit (SAUS)
PRU .... Primary Replacement Unit
PRU .... Printer Unit (SAUS)
PRU .... Prisoner's Rights Union (EA)
PRU .... Program Research Unit (SAUS)
PRU .... Programs Research Unit (KSC)
PRU .... Prome [*Myanmar*] [*Airport symbol*] (OAG)
PRU .... Provincial Reconnaissance Unit [*Military*]
pru .... prude (SAUS)
pru .... prudent (SAUS)
PRU .... Prudential Insurance Company of America (EFIS)
PRU .... Prudential Property & Casualty Insurance Co., Holmdel, NJ [*OCLC symbol*] (OCLC)
PRU .... Pruhonice [*Czechoslovakia*] [*Seismograph station code, US Geological Survey*] (SEIS)
PrU .... University of Puerto Rico, Rio Piedras, PR [*Library symbol*] [*Library of Congress*] (LCLS)
PRUAA ...... President of the Royal Ulster Academy of Arts
PRUC .... Partido Revolucionario de Union Civico [*Revolutionary Party for Civic Union*] [*Costa Rica*] [*Political party*]
PRUC .... Practice Reports [*1848-1900*] [*Upper Canada*] [*A publication*] (DLA)
PRUCIS ..... Philippine Rural Community Improvement Society (SAUS)
PRUCO ...... Prudential Insurance Company of America (EFIS)
PRUCOL ..... Permanently Residing Under Color Of Law (SAUS)
PRUD .... Partido Revolucionario de Unification Democratica [*Revolutionary Party of Democratic Unification*] [*El Salvador*]
PRUDENTIAL PAC ... Prudential Financial Inc. PAC [*Newark, NJ*] (PACS)
PrudRe ...... Prudential Reinsurance Holdings, Inc. [*Associated Press*] (SAG)
PrU-H .... University of Puerto Rico, Humacao Regional College, Humacao, PR [*Library symbol*] [*Library of Congress*] (LCLS)
PRUL .... Programs Unlimited (SAUS)
PrU-L .... University of Puerto Rico, Law Library, San Juan, PR [*Library symbol*] [*Library of Congress*] (LCLS)
P-rule .... Phonological Rule [*Linguistics*] (IEL)
PrU-M .... University of Puerto Rico, School of Medicine, San Juan, PR [*Library symbol*] [*Library of Congress*] (LCLS)
PrU-MA ..... University of Puerto Rico, Mayaguez Campus, Mayaguez, Puerto Rico [*Library symbol*] [*Library of Congress*] (LCLS)
PrU-MS ..... University of Puerto Rico, Department of Marine Sciences, Mayaguez (SAUS)
PrU-MS ..... University of Puerto Rico, Department of Marine Sciences, Mayaguez, PR [*Library symbol*] [*Library of Congress*] (LCLS)
PRUNCATS ... Program Relay Universal Card Analysis Test System (SAUS)
PRUNIT ..... Photo Roentgen Unit (IAA)
PrU-NS ...... University of Puerto Rico, Natural Science Library, Rio Piedras, PR [*Library symbol*] [*Library of Congress*] (LCLS)
PRURDCO ... Puerto Rico Undersea Research and Development Corp. (SAUS)
PRUS .... Prussia [*Obsolete*]
Prus .... Prussian [*Philately*]
PRUSAF ..... Puerto Rico, USA Foundation (EA)
PRUU .... Marine Ventures [*Intermodal shipping container symbol*] (TVRC)
PRV .... Papaya Ringspot Virus
PRV .... Parsley Rhabdovirus [*Plant pathology*]
PRV .... Peach Rosette Virus (SAUS)
PRV .... Peak Rated Voltage (IAA)
PRV .... Peak Reserve Voltage (IAA)
PRV .... Peak Reverse Voltage
PRV .... Pearl River Valley Railroad Co. [*AAR code*]
PRV .... Permanently Resident Volume (VLIE)
PRV .... Peugeot Renault Volvo [*Automobile joint project partners*]
PRV .... Polycythemia Rubra Vera [*Medicine*]
PRV .... Porvoo [*Finland*] [*Seismograph station code, US Geological Survey*] [*Closed*] (SEIS)
PRV .... Posterior wall of Right Ventricle (SAUS)
PRV .... Pour Rendre Visite [*To Make a Call*] [*French*]
PRV .... Pressure Reduce Valve (SAUS)
PRV .... Pressure Reducing (or Reduction) Valve (SAUS)
PRV .... Pressure Reducing [*or Regulation or Relief*] Valve
PRV .... Pressure Reduction Valve
PRV .... Pressure Regulation Valve
PRV .... Pressure Regulator Valve (COE)
PRV .... Pressure Relief Valve
PRV .... Previa [*NCIC car model code*]
PRV .... Princess Ventures [*Vancouver Stock Exchange symbol*]
PRV .... Prior Record Variable [*Criminal sentencing*]
prv .... Private (VRA)
PRV .... Programmed Rate-of-rise of Voltage (SAUS)
PRV .... Propeller Revolution
PRV .... Protected Response Vehicle [*Police and security equipment*]
Prv .... Proverbs [*Old Testament book*]
PRV .... Provincial
PRV .... Provincial Express, Inc. [*Canada*] [*ICAO designator*] (FAAC)
PRV .... Provisional Reconnaissance Unit
PRV .... Pseudorabies Virus
PRV .... Pseudo Register Vector (VLIE)
PRV .... Pseudorelative Velocity
Prv .... Pyruvenol [*Biochemistry*]
PRVA .... Programmable Rotary Vane Attenuator (SAUS)
PrvAm ...... Provident American Corp. [*Associated Press*] (SAG)
PrvBksh .... Provident Bankshares Corp. [*Associated Press*] (SAG)
PRVCA ...... Pennsylvania Recreational Vehicle and Camping Association (EARSL)
PRVCAR ..... Private Rail Car Company [*Transportation company classification code*]
prv coll ..... Private Collection (VRA)
PRVD .... Procurement [*or Purchase*] Request for Vendor Data (AAG)
PRVD .... Provide (SAUS)
PRVD .... Purchase Request for Vendor Data (SAUS)
PRVDNC .... Providence
Prvena ...... Provena Foods, Inc. [*Associated Press*] (SAG)
PrvEng ...... Providence Energy Corp. [*Associated Press*] (SAG)
PRVEP ...... Pattern Reversal Visual Evoked Potential
PRVI .... Puerto Rican Vireo [*North American bird banding code*] (BIBA)
PrvLf .... Provident Life & Accident Insurance Co. of America [*Associated Press*] (SAG)
PrvLLC ...... Providian LLC, Inc. [*Associated Press*] (SAG)
PRVLQ ...... Provell [*OTCBB symbol*]
PRVNTN ..... Prevention

PRVNTV..... Preventive
PrVOBI...... Preisverordnungsblatt (SAUS)
PRVS........ Penetration Room Ventilation System [*Nuclear energy*] (IEEE)
PRVS........ Previous (VLIE)
PRVT........ Private Media Group, Inc. [*NASDAQ symbol*] (NASQ)
PRVT........ Production Readiness Verification Testing (MCD)
PRVT........ Production Reliability Verification Test
PRVT........ Product Reliability Validation Test (MCD)
PRVW........ Preview (MSA)
PrvWor...... Providence & Worcester Railroad Co. [*Associated Press*] (SAG)
PrvWor...... Providence Worcester Railroad Co. [*Associated Press*] (SAG)
PRW......... Paired Wire [*Telecommunications*] (TEL)
PRW......... Passive Radar Warning (SAUS)
PRW......... Pattern Recognition Workbench [*Computer science*] (HODG)
PRW......... Per cent Rated Wattage (SAUS)
PRW......... Percent Rated Wattage
PRW......... Polymerized Ragweed [*Immunology*]
PRW......... Press Relations Wire [*Commercial firm*] (EA)
PRW......... Promark Software [*Vancouver Stock Exchange symbol*]
PRW......... Prosser [*Washington*] [*Seismograph station code, US Geological Survey*] (SEIS)
PRW......... Prowler [*NCIC car model code*]
PRW......... Quebecor Printing [*NYSE symbol*] (TTSB)
PRW......... Quebecor Printing, Inc. [*NYSE symbol*] (SAG)
PRW......... World University, San Juan, PR [*OCLC symbol*] (OCLC)
PRWAD...... Professional Rehabilitation Workers with the Adult Deaf [*Later, ADARA*] (EA)
PRWD........ Priority Regular World Day
PRWI........ Prince William Forest Park [*National Park Service designation*]
PRWO........ Puerto Rican Revolutionary Workers Organization
PRWO........ Puerto Rican Woodpecker [*North American bird banding code*] (BIBA)
PRWORA.... Personal Responsibility and Work Opportunity Reconciliation Act [*1996*]
PRWP........ Poor R-Wave Progression [*On electrocardiogram*] [*Cardiology*] (DAVI)
PRWRA..... Puerto Rican Water Resources Authority
PRWRA..... Puerto Rico Water Resources Authority (SAUS)
PRWS........ Plasma and Radio Wave Spectrometer (ACAE)
PRWS........ President of the Royal Society of Painters in Water Colours [*British*]
PRWV........ Peak Reserve Working Voltage
PRX.......... Paris [*Texas*] [*Airport symbol*] (OAG)
PRX.......... Paris, TX [*Location identifier*] [*FAA*] (FAAL)
PRX.......... Par Pharmaceutical, Inc. [*NYSE symbol*] (COMM)
PRX.......... Pharmaceutical Resources [*NYSE symbol*] (SPSG)
PRX.......... Pressure Regulation Exhaust
PRX.......... Pressure Regulator Exhaust (SAUS)
prx.......... Proximal (QSUL)
PRX.......... Proximity (SAUS)
PRX.......... Pseudoexfoliation (DMAA)
PRXI......... PRX [*Public Relations Exchange*] International (EA)
PRXL........ Parexel International Corp. [*NASDAQ symbol*] (SAG)
PRXL........ PAREXEL Intl [*NASDAQ symbol*] (TTSB)
PRXM........ Proxima Corp. [*NASDAQ symbol*] (SAG)
PRXS........ Praxis Biologics, Inc. (SAUS)
PRXT........ Pacific Rim Transport [*Common carrier symbol*]
PRY.......... Paraguay [*ANSI three-letter standard code*] (CNC)
PRY.......... Parys [*South Africa*] [*Seismograph station code, US Geological Survey*] (SEIS)
PRY.......... Pioneer Industrial Railway [*Federal Railroad Administration identification code*]
PRY.......... Pittsburgh Railways Corp. (SAUS)
PRY.......... Pittway Corp. [*AMEX symbol*] (SPSG)
PRY.......... Presidency [*Telegraphy*] (PCTE)
PRY.......... Primary (SAUS)
PRY.A........ Pittway Corp.'A' [*AMEX symbol*] (TTSB)
PRYCE PROJECT... Promoting Republicans You Can Elect Project [*Washington, DC*] (PACS)
PRYE........ Pryer [*NCIC motorcycle make code*]
P Ryl........ Catalogue of the Greek Papyri in the John Rylands Library at Manchester [*A publication*] (OCD)
P Ryl........ Catalogue of the Greek Papyri in the John Rylands Library at Manchester (journ.) (SAUS)
PRYL........ Port Royal Railroad [*Federal Railroad Administration identification code*]
PRYSM...... Presence and Respect for Youth in a Sexual Minority (EARSL)
PRYSO...... Parry Sound, ON [*American Association of Railroads railroad junction routing code*]
PRZ.......... Peoples Republic of Zanzibar (SAUS)
PRZ.......... Pirenzepine [*Medicine*] (EDAA)
PRZ.......... Polarized Return-to-Zero (VLIE)
PRZ.......... Portales, NM [*Location identifier*] [*FAA*] (FAAL)
PRZ.......... Potential Repository Zone [*Nuclear waste storage*]
PRZ.......... Pressoreceptor Zone [*Medicine*] (MELL)
PRZ.......... Prism Entertainment [*AMEX symbol*] (TTSB)
PRZ.......... Prism Entertainment Corp. [*AMEX symbol*] (SPSG)
PRZ.......... Prize Energy [*AMEX symbol*] (SG)
PRZ.......... Przhevalsk [*Former USSR*] [*Seismograph station code, US Geological Survey*] (SEIS)
PRZF........ Pyrazofurin [*Antineoplastic drug*]
PRZM........ Pesticide Root Zone Model [*Environmental Protection Agency*] (AEPA)
PRZM........ Prism Solutions [*NASDAQ symbol*] (SAG)
PRZR........ Polarized Return-to-Zero Recording (VLIE)
PS............ Abbott Laboratories [*Research code symbol*]
PS............ American Political Science Association. Quarterly [*A publication*]
PS............ Brazilian Socialist Party [*Political party*] (PSAP)
PS............ Chemical Agent/Tear Gas, Chloropicrin (SAUS)
PS............ Chloropicrin [*Poison gas*] [*Army symbol*]
PS............ Elementary and Early Childhood Education [*Educational Resources Information Center (ERIC) Clearinghouse*] [*University of Illinois*] (PAZ)
PS............ Pacemaker Syndrome [*Medicine*] (MELL)
PS............ Pace Setter (MHDI)
PS............ Pacifc Southwest Airlines (SAUS)
PS............ Pacific Southwest Airlines [*ICAO designator*] (OAG)
PS............ Pacific Star Communication [*Vancouver Stock Exchange symbol*]
PS............ Packet Scheduler (MWOL)
P(S).......... Packet (Send)
PS............ Packet Send Sequence Number
PS............ Packet Switch (SAUS)
PS............ Packet Switcher (or Switching) (SAUS)
PS............ Packet Switching [*Telecommunications*]
PS............ Packet Switch Stream [*British*] [*Computer science*] (TNIG)
PS............ Packing Sheet (MCD)
PS............ Packing Standards (SAUS)
PS............ Paddle Steamer (ADA)
PS............ Paediatric Surgery
PS............ Paget-Schroetter [*Syndrome*] [*Medicine*] (DB)
PS............ Painting System
PS............ Pakistan Standard (IAA)
PS............ Paleontological Society (EA)
PS............ Palm Society [*Later, IPS*] (EA)
PS............ Paltauf-Sternberg [*Disease*] [*Medicine*] (DB)
PS............ Pan Salicornia Zone [*Ecology*]
PS............ Paper Show
PS............ Paper Structure (SAUS)
PS............ Parachute Subsystem [*NASA*] (NASA)
PS............ Parade State (SAUS)
PS............ Paradoxical Sleep
P/S.......... Parallel/Serial (SAUS)
PS............ Parallel Single [*Outdoor advertising*] (NTCM)
PS............ Parallel to Serial (NITA)
P/S.......... Parallel to Serial Converter (MCD)
PS............ Paramagnetic Scheromak
PS............ Parameter Set for (SAUS)
PS............ Paranoid Schizophrenia [*Medicine*] (MELL)
PS............ Paranoid State [*Medicine*] (EDAA)
PS............ Parapsychological Society (SAUS)
PS............ Paraspinous (SAUS)
PS............ Parenteral Society (SAUS)
PS............ Parents of Suicides (EA)
PS............ Parents' Section of the Alexander Graham Bell Association for the Deaf (EA)
PS............ Parity Switch
PS............ Parliamentary Secretary [*British*]
PS............ Parlor Snake [*Slang for "to escort visitors around post"*]
PS............ Parochial School
PS............ Parrot Society (EA)
ps............ PARSEC [*Parallax Second*] [*See PARSEC*]
PS............ Par Selling (MHDB)
PS............ Partially Sighted (AIE)
PS............ Partially Smutted [*Plant pathology*]
PS............ Partially Synergistic [*Pharmacology*]
PS............ Partial Seizure (MELL)
PS............ Participating Scientist (ACAE)
PS............ Particle Simulation (SAUS)
PS............ Partido Socialista [*Socialist Party*] [*Uruguay*] [*Political party*]
PS............ Partido Socialista [*Socialist Party*] [*Chile*] [*Political party*]
PS............ Partido Socialista Portuguesa [*Portuguese Socialist Party*] [*Political party*] (PPE)
PS............ Partido Socialista - Uno [*Socialist Party - One*] [*Also, PS-1*] [*Bolivia*] [*Political party*] (PPW)
PS............ Parti Socialiste [*Socialist Party*] [*Belgium*] [*Political party*] (PPW)
PS............ Parti Socialiste - Federation de la Reunion [*Reunion Federation of the Socialist Party*] [*Political party*] (PPW)
PS............ Parts Shipped (or Shipper) (SAUS)
PS............ Parts Shipper
PS............ Part Surface (IAA)
PS............ Pass [*Telegraphy*] (PCTE)
PS............ Passed School of Instruction [*of Officers*] [*British*]
ps............ Passed School of Instruction (of Officers) (ODA)
PS............ Passenger Service
PS............ Passenger Steamer
PS............ Passing Scuttle
PS............ Passive Smoke (MELL)
ps............ Pastel (VRA)
PS............ Pastel Society [*British*]
PS............ Pathological Staging (SAUS)
PS............ Pathological (Surgical) Staging [*For Hodgkin's Disease*]
PS............ Pathologic Stage
PS............ Patient's Serum [*Medicine*]
PS............ Patrologia Syriaca (BJA)
PS............ Patrol Service [*British military*] (DMA)
PS............ Patrol Ship (CINC)
PS............ Patton Society (EA)
PS............ Pause Statement (SAUS)
P/S.......... Pause/Still [*Video technology*]
PS............ Payload Shroud (MCD)

PS........... Payload Specialist [*NASA*] (MCD)
PS........... Payload Station [*NASA*] (MCD)
PS........... Payload Support [*NASA*] (NASA)
PS........... Paymaster Sergeant
PS........... Pedal Sinus
PS........... Pediatric Surgery (DAVI)
PS........... Pellegrini-Stieda [*Disease*] [*Medicine*] (DB)
PS........... Pellet Size
PS........... Penal Servitude
PS........... Penny Stock [*Investment term*]
PS........... Pension Trust, Profit-Sharing, Stock Bonus or Annuity Plan (SAUS)
PS........... Pentagrid Switch (SAUS)
PS........... Peperomia Society [*Later, PEPS*] (EA)
PS........... Perception Schedule
PS........... Perceptual Speed (Test) [*Psychology*]
PS........... Percussion Shrapnel (SAUS)
PS........... Perfect Shuffle (MHDI)
PS........... Performance Score
PS........... Performance Specification
PS........... Performance Standard
PS........... Performance Status [*Rehabilitation*] (DAVI)
PS........... Performing Scale [*Medicine*] (MAE)
PS........... Perform Statement (SAUS)
PS........... Perimeter Surveillance (LAIN)
PS........... Periodic Syndrome [*Medicine*]
P/S........... Periods per Second (SAUS)
PS........... Peripheral Shock [*Psychology*]
PS........... Permanent Secretary
PS........... Permanent Signal [*Telecommunications*] (TEL)
PS........... Permutation Sequence (SAUS)
PS........... Per Second (AAMN)
PS........... Per Ship
PS........... Personal Secretary (DCTA)
PS........... Personal Skills
PS........... Personal Survival
PS........... Personal System [*IBM computer introduced in 1987*]
PS........... Personnel Strength (SAUS)
PS........... Personnel Subsystem [*Army*]
PS........... Per Speculum [*Medicine*]
PS........... Peru Solidarity [*An association*] (EA)
Ps........... Peseta [*Monetary unit*] [*Andorra and Spain*] (BARN)
PS........... Petrol Station (SAUS)
PS........... Pet Switchboard [*Defunct*] (EA)
PS........... Petty Sessions (DLA)
PS........... Pharmaceutical Society (NADA)
P/S........... Phaser/Subarray
PS........... Phase Separation
P/S........... Phase Shift (ACAE)
PS........... Phase-Shift
PS........... Phasing System [*Telecommunications*] (OA)
PS........... Phenix Society (EA)
PS........... Phenolsteroid (SAUS)
PS........... Phenol Steroids (SAUS)
PS........... Phenomenally Speedy Ordinary [*Photographic plates*] (ROG)
PS........... Philalethes Society (EA)
PS........... Phillnathean Society (EA)
PS........... Philolexian Society (EA)
PS........... Philological Society (EAIO)
PS........... Philomathean Society (EA)
PS........... Phosphate-Saline [*A buffer*] [*Cell culture*]
PS........... Phosphatidylserine [*Biochemistry*]
PS........... Photochemical System
PS........... Photoelectron Spectroscopy [*Biophysics*] [*Biochemistry*] (QSUL)
PS........... Photoemission Scintillation (MCD)
PS........... Photoemmission Scintillation (SAUS)
PS........... Photographic Service
PS........... Photographic Squadron
PS........... Photometer System (KSC)
PS........... Photosystems
PS........... Phototelegraph Station (SAUS)
PS........... Phrase Structure (WGA)
PS........... Phrenic Stimulation [*Medicine*] (MELL)
PS........... Phylaxis Society (EA)
P S........... Physical Science (SAUS)
PS........... Physical Sciences
PS........... Physical Security
PS........... Physical Sequential (HGAA)
PS........... Physical Status [*Medicine*]
PS........... Physics Specification (SAUS)
PS........... Physiological Society (BUAC)
PS........... Physiologic Saline [*Medicine*] (MELL)
PS........... Picket Ships [*Navy*]
PS........... Pico Second (SAUS)
ps........... Picosecond [*One trillionth of a second*]
PS........... Picosecond
PS........... Picture Storage (SAUS)
PS........... Picture System (ELAL)
PS........... Pilgrim Power Station (NRCH)
PS........... Pilgrim Society (EA)
PS........... Pineal Stalk [*Neuroanatomy*]
PS........... Pine Bark Mixed with Clay Loam Soil
PS........... Pine Siskin [*Ornithology*]
PS........... Pink Sheet [*Investment term*]
PS........... Pioneer School (SAUS)
PS........... Piper Syndrome (SAUS)
PS........... Pipe Size (BARN)
PS........... Pirandello Society (EA)
PS........... Pirmasens [*German license plate city code*]
PS........... Pisosecond (IAA)
PS........... Pistol Sharpshooter [*Army*]
PS........... Pitot/Static Tube (MCD)
PS........... [*The*] Pittsburg & Shawmut Railroad Co. [*AAR code*]
PS........... Pituitary Stalk [*Neuroanatomy*]
PS........... Planetary Society (EA)
PS........... Planetary Surface (IAA)
PS........... Planning and Scheduling
PS........... Planning Staff (SAUS)
PS........... Planning Study (AAG)
PS........... Plant Stress [*Horticulture*]
PS........... Plastic Surgery [*Medicine*]
PS........... Platelet Survival [*Medicine*] (EDAA)
PS........... Plate Sunk [*Printing*] (DGA)
PS........... Platform (Sided) (DCTA)
P/S........... Platoon/Section [*Army*]
PS........... Plea Side (ROG)
PS........... Pleural Sclerite [*Entomology*]
PS........... Plotter System (SAUS)
PS........... Plotting System
PS........... Plus
PS........... Pneumatic Suspension [*Automotive engineering*]
PS........... Pneumatic System
PS........... Poetry Society [*British*]
P/S........... Point of Shipment
PS........... Point of Switch
PS........... Point of Symmetry
PS........... Point Setting (SAUS)
PS........... Point Shifting (SAUS)
PS........... Point Source (COE)
PS........... Point Sparger [*Engineering*]
PS........... Point Spread [*In visual cortex*]
PS........... Polanyi Society (EA)
PS........... Polaris Standard [*Missiles*]
PS........... Polarity Scale [*Psychology*]
PS........... Polarity Selector (IAA)
PS........... Polar Stereographic (SAUS)
PS........... Police Sergeant [*Scotland Yard*]
PS........... Policy Statement
PS........... Polio Society (EA)
PS........... Polite Society (BUAC)
PS........... Political Science (SAUS)
PS........... Polling Signal (SAUS)
Ps........... Polyporus sulphureus [*A fungus*]
PS........... Polysaccharide (DB)
ps........... Polystyrene (MIST)
PS........... Polystyrene [*Organic chemistry*]
PS........... Polysulfone [*Also, PSO*] [*Organic chemistry*]
P/S........... Polyunsaturated/Saturated [*Fatty acid ratio*]
PS........... Population Sample (MAE)
PS........... Porlock Society (EA)
PS........... Porous Silicon [*Physics*]
PS........... Portable Station (SAUS)
P/S........... Port and Starboard (SAUS)
PS........... Porter-Silber Chromogen [*Medicine*] (MAE)
PS........... Port Security
PS........... Port Securityman [*Military*] (POLM)
PS........... Port Store [*Telecommunications*] (TEL)
PS........... Port Strobe [*Telecommunications*] (TEL)
PS........... Pos-Escrito [*Postscript*] [*Portuguese*]
PS........... Position-Specific Antigen
PS........... Positive Value (DA)
Ps........... Positronium (SAUS)
PS........... Postal Satsang [*An association*] (EA)
PS........... Postal Service [*US*]
PS........... Posterior Synechia (SAUS)
PS........... Poster Society (EA)
PS........... Post Script (SAUS)
PS........... PostScript [*Adobe printer language*]
ps........... PostScript [*Computer science*]
PS........... Post Scriptum [*Written Afterwards, Postscript*] [*Latin*]
PS........... Post Status (SAUS)
PS........... Potassium Sorbate [*Food additive*]
PS........... Potentiometer Synchro
PS........... Potentiometer Synchronometer
P/S........... Power Section (NG)
PS........... Power Series (IAA)
PS........... Power Shift (SAUS)
PS........... Power Shutdown (SAUS)
PS........... Power Source
PS........... Power-Specific (MCD)
PS........... Power Spectra [*Neurophysiology*]
PS........... Power Spectrum (SAUS)
PS........... Power Station (MCD)
P/S........... Power Steering (HAWK)
PS........... Power Steering [*Automobile ads*]
PS........... Powerstroke (SAUS)
PS........... Power Supply
PS........... Powys Society (EA)
PS........... Prairie Schooner [*A publication*] (BRI)

PS............ Prairies Service [*Record series prefix*] [*Canada*]
PS............ Predictive Saccades [*Ophthalmology*]
PS............ Preduzece Soko [*Former Yugoslavia*] [*ICAO aircraft manufacturer identifier*] (ICAO)
PS............ Preference Semantics [*Linguistics*] (IEL)
PS............ Preferred Stock [*Investment term*]
PS............ Pregnant Serum (SAUS)
PS............ Prehistoric Society (EA)
PS............ Preliminary Study
PS............ Preparedness Staff [*Environmental Protection Agency*] (GFGA)
Ps............ Prescription (AAMN)
PS............ Presenilin [*Biochemistry*]
PS............ Presentation Services [*Computer science*] (IBMDP)
PS............ Present State (SAUS)
PS............ Present Symptoms (SAUS)
PS............ Press Secretary (ILCA)
PS............ Press to Start (KSC)
Ps............ Pressure (HLLA)
PS............ Pressure [*or Propellant*] Seal
P-S............ Pressure-Sensitive
PS............ Pressure Sensor
PS............ Pressure Sore (MELL)
PS............ Pressure Steam (SAUS)
PS............ Pressure Support (SAUS)
PS............ Pressure Switch
Ps............ Pressure, Systolic [*Cardiology*]
PS............ Price Spreading [*Business term*]
PS............ Primary School (ADA)
PS............ Primary Section (SAUS)
PS............ Primary Sequence (SAUS)
PS............ Primary Storage (SAUS)
PS............ Primary Syphilis (MELL)
PS............ Prime Select (MCD)
PS............ Prime Sponsor
PS............ Principal Sojourner [*Freemasonry*] (ROG)
PS............ Principal Subject [*In a sonata or rondo*] [*Music*] (ROG)
PS............ Printer Start (SAUS)
PS............ Printing Speed (SAUS)
PS............ Print Scan [*Computer science*] (IAA)
PS............ Print Storage (SAUS)
PS............ Priority Service (SAUS)
PS............ Prior Service [*Military*]
PS............ Private Screenings [*Cable TV programming service*]
PS............ Private Secretary
PS............ Private Security Program [*Association of Independent Colleges and Schools specialization code*]
PS............ Private Siding [*Rail*] [*Shipping*] (DS)
PS............ Privilege Service (SAUS)
PS............ Privy Seal [*British*]
PS............ Probability of mission Success (SAUS)
PS............ Probability of Survival (MCD)
PS............ Problem Space
PS............ Problem Specification
PS............ Problem Statement [*Computer science*] (IAA)
PS............ Procambial Strand [*Botany*]
PS............ Procedure Signal (SAUS)
PS............ Procedure Statement (SAUS)
PS............ Processing State (SAUS)
PS............ Processing Station (SAUS)
PS............ Processor Status
PS............ Processor Storage (SAUS)
PS............ Process Sheet
PS............ Process Solution (MCD)
PS............ Process Solvent (SAUS)
PS............ Process Specification
PS............ Process Status (SAUS)
PS............ Process Stop Ship (SAUS)
PS............ Process Storage [*Computer science*] (IAA)
PS............ Process Subsystem [*Telecommunications*] (TEL)
PS............ Procurement Specification (MCD)
PS............ Production Set (SAUS)
PS............ Production Sharing (SAUS)
PS............ Production Support (SAUS)
PS............ Production System (SAUS)
PS............ Product Service (IAA)
PS............ Product Sharing (SAUS)
PS............ Product Software (MCD)
PS............ Product Specification (SAUS)
PS............ Product Standards (MCD)
PS............ Product Support
PS............ Profit Sharing [*Business term*]
PS............ Programmable Switch [*Computer science*] (IAA)
PS............ Programmed Symbols (MEDA)
PS............ Programming System
PS............ Program Scheduling (SAUS)
PS............ Program Section [*Computer science*] (IAA)
PS............ Program Segment (SAUS)
PS............ Program Selector (SAUS)
PS............ Program Service (SAUS)
PS............ Program Shift (SAUS)
PS............ Program Simulation (OICC)
PS............ Program Sound (SAUS)
PS............ Program Source [*Computer science*] (IAA)
PS............ Program Specification (MCD)
PS............ Program Start (KSC)
PS............ Program Stateword [*Computer science*] (IAA)
PS............ Program Status [*Computer science*] (IAA)
PS............ Program Store [*Computer science*] (IEEE)
PS............ Program Structure (SAUS)
PS............ Program Summary (NG)
PS............ Program System (SAUS)
PS............ Progressive Stroke (SAUS)
PS............ Project Scientist (SAUS)
PS............ Project Slip
PS............ Project Specification [*Petroleum engineering*]
PS............ Project Start [*Milestone chart*]
PS............ Project Stock [*Military*] (AABC)
PS............ Project Study [*British military*] (DMA)
PS............ Proler International Corp. [*NYSE symbol*] (SPSG)
PS............ Proler Intl [*NYSE symbol*] (TTSB)
PS............ Prolifers for Survival [*Defunct*] (EA)
PS............ Prometheus Society (EA)
PS............ Prompt Side [*of a stage*] [*i.e., the right side*] [*A stage direction*]
PS............ Pronator Syndrome [*Medicine*] (EDAA)
PS............ Proof Shot [*Ammunition*]
PS............ Proof Stress
PS............ Propellant Seal
PS............ Propellant Supply (KSC)
PS............ Propellant System
PS............ Proportional Spacing [*Typography*] (WDMC)
PS............ Propulsion Section
Ps............ Proseminar (SAUS)
PS............ Prostaglandin Synthetase [*An enzyme*]
PS............ Prostatic Secretion [*Medicine*] (MELL)
PS............ Protected Ship (SAUS)
PS............ Protection Strategy (COE)
PS............ Protective Security (SAUS)
PS............ Protective Service
PS............ Protective Shelter
PS............ Protective Silver (SAUS)
PS............ Protective Structure
PS............ Protective Subsystem [*Military*] (INF)
PS............ Protect Status (MHDB)
PS............ Protein Society (BUAC)
PS............ Protein Synthesis
PS............ Proton Synchrotron [*Nuclear energy*]
PS............ Proton Synchrotron Division (SAUS)
PS............ Protoplasmic Surface [*Freeze etching in microscopy*]
PS............ Proto-Semitic (BJA)
PS............ Provision Supply (SAUS)
PS............ Provost-Sergeant
ps............ Psalm (GROV)
PS............ Psalm
Ps............ Psalms [*Biblical*] (RION)
PS............ Pseudo [*Classical studies*] (OCD)
Ps............ Pseudomonas [*Bacterium*] (MAE)
PS............ Pseudomonas Stutzeri [*Bacterium*]
PS............ Pseudonym (WGA)
PS............ Psychiatric (MAE)
PS............ Psychology [*Treasury Board of Canada*] (FOTI)
PS............ Psychology Society (EA)
PS............ Psychometric Society (EA)
PS............ Psychonomic Society (EA)
PS............ Psychotic
PS............ Publication Standard
PS............ Public Safety (SAUS)
PS............ Public Sale
PS............ Public School
PS............ Public Service
PS............ Public Service Company of Colorado (EFIS)
PS............ Public Statutes [*Legal term*] (DLA)
PS............ Public Stenographer
PS............ Public Storage (EFIS)
PS............ Publishing Services [*American Library Association*]
PS............ Puget Sound [*Also, Puget Sound Naval Shipyard*] [*Washington*]
P-S............ Pullman-Standard (SAUS)
ps............ Pull Switch (ODA)
PS............ Pull Switch
PS............ Pulmonary Sequestration
PS............ Pulmonary Stenosis [*Medicine*]
PS............ Pulse per Second (IAA)
PS............ Pulse Sensor (KSC)
PS............ Pulse Shaper
PS............ Pulses per Second [*Data transmission*] (DEN)
PS............ Pulse Stretcher
PS............ Pumping Station (NATG)
PS............ Purdon's Pennsylvania Statutes [*A publication*] (DLA)
PS............ Purity-Supreme [*Supermarkets*]
PS............ Pyloric Stenosis [*Medicine*]
PS............ Serum From a Pregnant Woman (DAVI)
PS............ Socialist Party (France) [*Political party*] (PSAP)
PS............ Solidarity Party (Panama) [*Political party*] (PSAP)
Ps............ South Celestial Pole (SAUS)
ps---......... South Pacific [*MARC geographic area code*] [*Library of Congress*] (LCCP)
PS............ South Pole [*Also, SP*]
PS............ Static Pressure

PS.......... Swarthmore Public Library, Swarthmore, PA [*Library symbol*] [*Library of Congress*] (LCLS)
PS.......... Transport [*Russian aircraft symbol*]
PS.......... US Postal Service (AAGC)
PS-1.......... Partido Socialista - Uno [*Socialist Party - One*] [*Also, PS*] [*Bolivia*] [*Political party*] (PD)
PS/2.......... Personal System/2 [*IBM Corp.*]
PS2.......... Picture System 2 [*Evans & Sutherland Computer Corp.*] (MCD)
PS2.......... PlayStation 2 [*Video game console*]
PS2.......... Power Station Two
PS^{2reset}.......... Profound Sensitivity Syndrome [*Psychology*]
PS3.......... PROBE [*Program Optimization and Budget Evaluation*] Staff Support System [*Military*]
PS2000.......... Public Service 2000 Program [*Canada*]
PSA.......... Pacific Island Aviation, Inc. [*Mariana Islands*] [*ICAO designator*] (FAAC)
PSA.......... Pacific Science Association [*Hawaii*] (BUAC)
PSA.......... Pacific Sciences Association (SAUS)
PSA.......... Pacific Seedsmens Association (BUAC)
PSA.......... Pacific South American (SAUS)
PSA.......... Pacific Southwest Airlines
PSA.......... Packers and Stockyards Administration (SAUS)
PSA.......... Pakistan Sociological Association (BUAC)
PSA.......... Panda Standard Asynchron (SAUS)
PSA.......... Parallel Signature Analyzer (TIMI)
PSA.......... Paralympic Sports Association [*Canada*] (EAIO)
PSA.......... Parametric Semiconductor Amplifier
PSA.......... Parametric Sound Amplifier [*Blaupunkt*]
PSA.......... Parcel Shippers Association (EA)
PSA.......... Partial Starting Address (SAUS)
PSA.......... Particle Size Analyzer
PSA.......... Particularly Sensitive Sea Area (SAUS)
PSA.......... Partido Socialista Aponte [*Bolivia*] [*Political party*] (PPW)
PSA.......... Partido Socialista Argentino [*Socialist Party of Argentina*] [*Political party*]
PSA.......... Parti Socialiste Autonome [*Autonomous Socialist Party*] [*France*] [*Political party*] (PPE)
PSA.......... Parti Solidaire Africain [*African Solidarity Party*] [*Congo*] [*Political party*]
PSA.......... Partito Socialista Autonomo [*Autonomous Socialist Party*] [*Switzerland*] [*Political party*] (PPW)
PSA.......... Part Stress Analysis (MCD)
PSA.......... Passenger Service Agent [*Travel industry*] (TVEL)
PSA.......... Passenger Shipping Association [*British*] (DBA)
PSA.......... Passive Situation Awareness (ACAE)
PSA.......... Pastel Society of America (EA)
PSA.......... Past Shakedown Availability [*Military*]
PSA.......... Path of Steepest Ascent [*Statistical design of experiments*]
PSA.......... Path Selection Algorithm [*Telecommunications*] (TEL)
PSA.......... Patient Care Associate [*Medicine*]
PSA.......... Payload Service Area [*NASA*] (NASA)
PSA.......... Payload Support Avionics [*NASA*] (NASA)
PSA.......... Peace and Solidarity Alliance (EA)
PSA.......... Peace Studies Association (EA)
PSA.......... People's Supreme Assembly [*Yemen*] [*Political party*] (PPW)
PSA.......... Peripherals Suppliers Association (ELAL)
PSA.......... Permanent Storage Area (SAUS)
PSA.......... Personal Service Agreements (MCD)
PSA.......... Personal Statement Analyzer (HGAA)
PSA.......... Personnel and Service Area [*Nuclear energy*] (NRCH)
PSA.......... Personnel Support Activity (DOMA)
PSA.......... Personnel Support Agency
PSA.......... Petersburg [*Alaska*] [*Seismograph station code, US Geological Survey*] (SEIS)
PSA.......... Petites Soeurs de l'Assumption [*Little Sisters of the Assumption - LSA*] [*Paris, France*] (EAIO)
PSA.......... Peugeot Societe Anonyme [*Automobile manufacturer*]
PSA.......... Peugot Societe Anonyme [*Peugeot Co. Ltd.*] [*French*]
PSA.......... Philippine Standards Association (IAA)
PSA.......... Philippine Sugar Association [*Later, PSC*] (EA)
PSA.......... Philosophy of Science Association (EA)
PSA.......... Phlebology Society of America (NTPA)
PSA.......... Phobia Society of America [*Later, ADAA*] (EA)
PSA.......... Photographic Society of America (EA)
PSA.......... Phycological Society of America (EA)
PSA.......... Physical Sector Address (SAUS)
PSA.......... Pickles and Sauces Association [*British*] (DBA)
PSA.......... Pipe Stress Analysis (PDAA)
PSA.......... Pirandello Society of America (EA)
PSA.......... Pisa [*Italy*] [*Airport symbol*] (OAG)
PsA.......... Pisces Austrinus [*Constellation*]
PSA.......... Pisces Society of America
PSA.......... Pisum Sativum [*Plant lectins*] (QSUL)
PSA.......... Pitch Servo Assembly (SAUS)
PSA.......... Planning and Service Areas
PSA.......... Planning Simulation Accounting (SAUS)
PSA.......... Play Schools Association (EA)
PSA.......... Pleasant Sunday Afternoons
PSA.......... Plumeria Society of America (EA)
PSA.......... Pneumatic Sensor Assembly
PSA.......... Poe Studies Association (EA)
PSA.......... Poetry Society of America (EA)
PSA.......... Police Superintendents' Association [*New Zealand*] (WDAA)
PSA.......... Political Studies Association [*British*]
PSA.......... Political Studies Association of the United Kingdom (BUAC)
PSA.......... Polycrystalline Silicon Self-Aligned [*Photovoltaic energy systems*] (MHDI)
PSA.......... Polyethylene Sulfonic Acid [*Organic chemistry*] (MAE)
PSA.......... Polysialic Acid [*Organic chemistry*]
PSA.......... Polysilicic Acid [*Organic chemistry*]
PSA.......... Polysilicon Self-Aligned (SAUS)
PSA.......... Poly-Substance Abuse [*Medicine*] (MELL)
PSA.......... Portable Sanitation Association (EA)
PSA.......... Portable Sound Analyzer
PSA.......... Port Storage Area [*Telecommunications*] (TEL)
PSA.......... Port Support Activity (DOMA)
PSA.......... Post Shakedown Availability
PSA.......... Post Sleep Activity (SAUS)
PSA.......... Post-Sleep Activity
PSA.......... Post Strike Assessment (SAUS)
PSA.......... Potential Surface Analysis (ADA)
PSA.......... Potentiometric Stripping Analysis (ABAC)
PSA.......... Potters' Society of Australia
PSA.......... Poultry Science Association (EA)
PSA.......... Power and Servo Assembly
PSA.......... Power Saw Association [*British*] (BI)
PSA.......... Power Servo Amplifier (KSC)
PSA.......... Power Servo Assembly (MCD)
PSA.......... Power Spectral Analysis (RAWO)
PSA.......... Power Supply Assembly
PSA.......... Power Switching Amplifier
PSA.......... Power Switching Assembly
PSA.......... Precipitation Series Algorithm [*Marine science*] (OSRA)
PSA.......... Prefabricated Surfacing Aluminum
PSA.......... Preferred Storage Area (MCD)
PSA.......... Preferred Supplier Agreement (SAUS)
PSA.......... Prefix Save Area (SAUS)
PSA.......... Prefix Storage Area [*Computer science*] (OA)
PSA.......... Preliminary Safety Analysis [*NASA*] (SSD)
PSA.......... Preliminary Site Assessment (SARE)
PSA.......... Pre/Post Sleep Activity (NASA)
PSA.......... Prepseudoarthrosis [*Medicine*] (MELL)
PSA.......... President of the Society of Antiquaries [*British*]
PSA.......... Pre Sleep Activity (SAUS)
PSA.......... Pressure Sensitive Adhesive [*Trademark*]
PSA.......... Pressure Suit Assembly
PSA.......... Pressure Swing Absorption (SAUS)
PSA.......... Pressure-Swing Adsorption [*Chemical engineering*]
PSA.......... Pressure Switch Assembly (NASA)
PSA.......... Pressure Switching Alarm [*Engineering*]
PSA.......... Presunrise Authority
PSA.......... Presunrise Service Authority (NTCM)
PSA.......... Pretrial Service Agency (SAUS)
PSA.......... Prices Surveillance Authority (BUAC)
PSA.......... Primary Store Address (SAUS)
PSA.......... Principal Staff Assistants (SAUS)
PSA.......... Principal Supervisory Agent (EBF)
PSA.......... Private Schools Association [*British*]
PSA.......... Probabilistic Safety Analysis (NRCH)
PSA.......... Problem Specification Analyzer (RALS)
PSA.......... Problem Statement Analyser (or Analyzer) (SAUS)
PSA.......... Problem Statement Analyzer [*Computer science*] (IAA)
PSA.......... Proceedings of the Society of Antiquaries (SAUS)
PSA.......... Process Service Area (IAA)
PSA.......... Procurement Seminar for Auditors [*Army*]
PSA.......... Product Safety Association [*Defunct*] (EA)
PSA.......... Product Support Administration (MCD)
PSA.......... Product Support Analysis (SAUS)
PSA.......... Professional Sales Association (NTPA)
PSA.......... Professional Salespersons of America [*Defunct*] (EA)
PSA.......... Professional Service Association (EA)
PSA.......... Professional Services Administration (GART)
PSA.......... Professional Services Agreement (COE)
PSA.......... Professional Skaters Association (NTPA)
PSA.......... Professional Skills Alliance (EA)
PSA.......... Professional Squash Association (NTPA)
PSA.......... Professional Stringers Association [*Defunct*] (EA)
PSA.......... Programmed Shutter and Aperture [*Photography*] (DICI)
PSA.......... Program Specialty Area [*Standards Council of Canada*] (FOTI)
PSA.......... Program Study Authorization (KSC)
PSA.......... Progressive Spinal Ataxia [*Medicine*] (DMAA)
PSA.......... Project-Specific Analysis (SAUS)
PSA.......... Project Support Agreement (SAUS)
PSA.......... Prolonged Sleep Apnea
PSA.......... Promoting Stress & Anxiety (WDAA)
PSA.......... Promotional Sourcing Association (BUAC)
PSA.......... Property Services Agency [*Department of the Environment*] [*British*]
PSA.......... Prostate-Specific Antigen [*Immunochemistry*]
PSA.......... Protected Storage Address [*Computer science*] (VLIE)
PSA.......... Protective Security Attendant [*Australia*]
PSA.......... Protocol-Specific Annex (SAUS)
PSA.......... Prototype Sample Approval [*Automotive engineering*]
PSA.......... Province Senior Advisor [*Army*] (VNW)
PSA.......... Provisional Site Acceptance (NATG)
PSA.......... Provisional System Acceptance (SAUS)
PSA.......... Provisional System Approval (SAUS)
PSA.......... Provisions Stowage Assembly (NASA)
PSA.......... Psalm
Psa.......... Psalms [*Old Testament book*]

PSA .... Pseudomonic Acid [*Biochemistry*]
PsA .... Psoriatic Arthritis (DAVI)
Psa .... Psychoanalysis (DIPS)
PSA .... Psychological Operations Support Activity [*Military*] (MCD)
PSA .... Psychological Semantic Analysis (NITA)
PSA .... Psychological Society of America (SAUS)
PSA .... Psychological Stress Analyzer (SAUS)
PSA .... Psychologists for Social Action [*Defunct*] (EA)
PSA .... Publication Systems Associates, Inc. [*Information service or system*] (IID)
PSA .... Public Securities Association [*Database producer*] (EA)
PSA .... Public Servants Association (SAUS)
PSA .... Public Service Act
PSA .... Public Service Administration (SAUS)
PSA .... Public Service Advertising (SAUS)
PSA .... Public Service Alliance (BUAC)
PSA .... Public Service Announcement
PSA .... Public Service Association [*New Zealand*] (WDAA)
PSA .... Public Storage [*NYSE symbol*] (TTSB)
PSA .... Public Storage, Inc. [*NYSE symbol*] (SAG)
PSA .... Push Down Stack Automaton [*Computer science*]
PSA .... Socialist Party of Andalucia (Spain) [*Political party*] (PSAP)
PSA .... Storage Properties, Inc. [*AMEX symbol*] (SPSG)
PSAA .... Pacific Special Activities Area [*Military*]
PSAA .... Pakistan Students' Association of America
PSAA .... Plasma Sciences and Applications (IAA)
PSAA .... Plastic Surgery Administrative Association (EA)
PSAA .... Polish Singers Alliance of America (EA)
PSAA .... Polwarth Sheepbreeders' Association of Australia
PSAA .... Poststimulatory Auditory Adaptation
PSAAB .... Public Sector Accounting and Auditing Board (FOTI)
PSAAV .... Provincial Sewerage Authorities Association of Victoria [*Australia*]
PSAB .... Pathology Services Accreditation Board [*Victoria, Australia*]
PSAB .... Prime Bancorp [*NASDAQ symbol*] (TTSB)
PSAB .... Prime Bancorp, Inc. [*NASDAQ symbol*] (CTT)
PSAB .... Procurement Strategy for Aboriginal Business (FOTI)
PSAB .... Production Systems Acceptance Branch [*Social Security Administration*]
PSAB .... Public Schools Appointments Bureau (SAUS)
PSAC .... Passive Satellite Attitude Control
PSAC .... Pated-System Auxiliary Control element (SAUS)
PSAC .... Peak Sound Absorption Concentration (SAUS)
PSAC .... Pennsylvania State Athletic Conference (PSS)
P sac .... Pericardial Cavity (SAUS)
PSAC .... Personnel Service Company [*Army*] (AABC)
PSAC .... Petroleum Services Association of Canada (FOTI)
PSAC .... Policy Signing and Accounting Centre [*Insurance firm*] [*British*]
PSAC .... Preferred Stock Advisory Committee [*New Deal*]
PSAC .... Presidential Scientific Advisory Committee (SAUS)
PSAC .... President's Science Advisory Committee [*Terminated, 1973*] [*Executive Office of the President*]
PSAC .... Presidents Science Advisory Committee (or Council) (SAUS)
PSAC .... Private Security Advisory Council [*Terminated, 1977*] [*Department of Justice*] (EGAO)
PSAC .... Production Statistics Advisory Committee (BUAC)
PSAC .... Product Safety Advisory Council [*Consumer Product Safety Commission*]
PSAC .... Professional Services Advisary Committee (SAUS)
PSAC .... Professional Skating Association of Canada
PSAC .... Public Service Alliance of Canada [*Labor union of federal government employees*]
PSACEI ...... Propulsion Subsystem for Attitude Control and Engine Ignition [*Space launch term*] (ISAK)
PSACF .... Pennsylvania State Association of County Fairs (EARSL)
PSACH .... Pseudoachondrodysplasia [*Medicine*] (DMAA)
PSACN .... Process Specification Advance Change Notice (SAA)
PSACO .... Papillary Serous Adenocarcinoma of Ovary [*Medicine*] (MELL)
PSAcPh ...... Prostate-Specific Acid Phosphatase [*An enzyme*]
PSACPOO ... President's Scientific Advisory Committee Panel on Oceanography [*Marine science*] (MSC)
PSACS .... Pilot Selection and Classification System (SAUS)
PSAD .... Passive Sensor for Aircraft Detection [*Military*] (SEWL)
PSAD .... Political/Statistical Area Description (SAUS)
PSAD .... Predicted Site Acquisition Data [*NASA*]
PSAD .... Prediction, Simulation, Adaptation, Decision [*Computer science*]
PSAD .... Prediction, Simulation, Adaption and Decision (SAUS)
PSAD .... Procurement and Systems Acquisition Division (AAGC)
PSAD .... Prostate-Specific Antigen Density [*Medicine*] (MELL)
PSAD .... Psychoactive Substance Abuse and Dependence [*Medicine*] (EDAA)
PSAE .... Philippine Society of Agricultural Engineers (BUAC)
PSAF .... Print Services Access Facility [*Computer science*] (VLIE)
PSAF .... Private Sector Adjustment Factor [*Banking*]
PSAG .... Pelvic Sonoangiography [*Medicine*] (DMAA)
PSAG .... Probabilistic Systems Assessment Group (SAUS)
PSAG .... Program System Analysis Guide (VLIE)
PSAG .... Provinces/States Advisory Group [*Canada-US*] (FOTI)
PSAG-CD ... Public Service Advisory Group/Collection Development (SAUS)
PSAGN .... Poststreptococcal Acute Glomerulonephritis [*Medicine*]
PSAG-PS ... Public Service Advisory Group/Public Services (SAUS)
PSAG-TS ... Public Service Advisory Group/Technical Services (SAUS)
PSAI .... Pediatric Services of Amer [*NASDAQ symbol*] (TTSB)
PSAI .... Pediatric Services of America, Inc. [*NASDAQ symbol*] (SAG)
PSAI .... Political Studies Association of Ireland (BUAC)
PSAI .... Portable Sanitation Association International (NTPA)
PSAI .... Proceedings of the Suffolk Archaeological Institute (SAUS)
PSAIR .... Priority Specific Air Information Request [*Defense Mapping Agency*] (MCD)
PSAJ .... Peace Studies Association of Japan (BUAC)
PSA Journal ... Photographic Society of America Journal (SAUS)
PSAL .... Permanent Supplementary Artificial Lighting (IAA)
PSAL .... Programming System Activity Log [*Computer science*]
PSAL .... Programming Systems Activity Log (SAUS)
PSAL .... Public Schools Athletic League
PSALI .... Permanent Supplementary Artificial Lighting Interiors (SAUS)
PSALI .... Permanent Supplementary Artificial Lighting of Interiors (IEEE)
P Salin ...... Petrus de Salinis [*Flourished, 13th century*] [*Authority cited in pre-1607 legal work*] (DSA)
PSALM ...... Project Structured Analysis of LOGEX [*Logistical Exercise*] Methodology (MCD)
PSAM .... Partitioned Sequence (or Sequential) Access Method (SAUS)
PSAM .... Point Source Ambient Monitoring [*Environmental Protection Agency*] (GFGA)
PSAM .... Probabilistic Structural Analysis Methodology (ACAE)
PSAM .... Proceedings of Symposia in Applied Mathematics (SAUS)
PSAMPP .... Philadelphia Society for Alleviating the Miseries of Public Prisons (SAUS)
PSAMS ...... Plessey Scientific-Atlanta Multistar System (NITA)
PSAN .... Phase Stabilized Ammonium Nitrate (MCD)
PSAN .... Polystyrolakrylnitril (SAUS)
PSAn .... Psychoanalysis [*or Psychoanalyst*] (DAVI)
psan .... psychoanalyze (SAUS)
PS & A ...... Pharmacy, Supply, and Administration (DOMA)
PS & B ...... Power Steering and Brakes [*Automotive engineering*] (IIA)
PS & C ...... Private Siding and Collected One End
PS&C .... Private Siding and Collected (or Collection) (SAUS)
PS&C .... Production Scheduling and Control (AAGC)
PS&C .... Program Scheduling and Control (SAUS)
PS & CC .... Packaging, Storage, and Containerization Center [*DARCOM*] (MCD)
PS & D ...... Private Siding and Delivered One End
PS & DS .... Program Statistics and Data Systems
PS & E ...... Plans, Specifications, and Estimates [*Construction*]
PS & ER .... Production Support and Equipment Replacement [*Military*] (AABC)
PS & L ...... Power Switching and Logic
PS & M ..... Personnel Supervision and Management Division of ASTSECNAV's Office [*Absorbed into SECP, 1944*]
PS&SC ...... Public Service and Safety Committee (SAUS)
PS&SSU .... Power Supply & System Selector Unit (SAUS)
PS & T ...... Pay, Subsistence, and Transportation [*Military*]
PSANDT ..... Pay, Subsistence, and Transportation [*Military*]
PS&T .... Purchase, Storage and Transportation (FOTI)
PS & TC .... Population Studies and Training Center [*Brown University*] [*Research center*] (RCD)
PS & TN .... Pay, Subsistence, and Transportation, Navy
PS & W ..... Pacific, Southern & Western Railroad [*Nickname: Play Safe and Walk*]
PS&W .... Philadelphia Steel and Wire (SAUS)
PSANP ...... Phenol-Soluble Acidic Nuclear Protein [*s*] [*Biochemistry*]
PSANZ .... Perinatal Society of Australia & New Zealand (SAUS)
PSAO .... Pharmacy Services Administrative Organization (MHCS)
PSAO .... Primary Staff Action Officer [*Military*]
PSAODAP ... Presidential Special Action Office for Drug Abuse Prevention (SAUS)
PSAP .... Particle/Soot Absorption Photometer (SAUS)
PSAP .... Peak Systolic Aortic Pressure [*Medicine*] (RAWO)
PSAP .... Pennsylvania Student Assistance Program (SAUS)
PSAP .... Pharmacotherapy Self-Assessment Program (SAUS)
PSAP .... Phenylsulfonylacetophenone
PSAP .... Plane Stress Analysis and Plot [*Computer science*]
PSAP .... Power Supply for Asynchron Peripheral replaceable item (SAUS)
PSAP .... Presentation Service Access Point [*Telecommunications*] (OSI)
PSAP .... Primary Public Safety Answering Point (DMAA)
PSAP .... Program Status Area Pointer (SAUS)
PSAP .... Public Safety Answering Point [*Telecommunications*] (TEL)
PSAP .... Public Service Answering Point
PSAP .... Puget Sound & Pacific Railroad [*Federal Railroad Administration identification code*]
PSAP .... Pulmonary Surfactant Apoprotein [*Biochemistry*]
PSAPI .... Presentation Space Application Programming Interface (SAUS)
PSAPR ...... Pathology Society of Asia and Pacific Region (BUAC)
PSAPrA ..... Public Storage 10% cm'A'Pfd [*NYSE symbol*] (TTSB)
PSAPrB ..... Public Storage 9.20% cm'B'Pfd [*NYSE symbol*] (TTSB)
PSAPrC ..... Public Storage Adj Rt'C'Pfd [*NYSE symbol*] (TTSB)
PSAPrD ..... Public Storage 9.50%'D'Pfd [*NYSE symbol*] (TTSB)
PSAPrE ..... Public Storage 10%'E'Pfd [*NYSE symbol*] (TTSB)
PSAPrF ..... Public Storage 9.75% 'F' Pfd [*NYSE symbol*] (TTSB)
PSAPrG ..... Public Storage 8.875% Dep Pfd [*NYSE symbol*] (TTSB)
PSAPrH ..... Public Storage 8.45%'H'Dep Pfd [*NYSE symbol*] (TTSB)
PSA-Process ... Poly-silicon Self-Aligned Process (SAUS)
PSAPrX ..... Public Storage 8.25%Cv Pfd [*NYSE symbol*] (TTSB)
PSAR .... Parts and Supplies Adjustment Request (SAUS)
PSAR .... Platform Shock Attenuation and Realignment System (MCD)
PSAR .... Pneumatic [*or Pressure*] System Automatic Regulator (AAG)
PSAR .... Post-synaptic Acetylcholine Receptor [*Medicine*] (EDAA)
PSAR .... Preliminary Safety Analysis Report
PSAR .... Pressure System Automatic Regulator (IAA)
PSAR .... Process Storage Address Register [*Computer science*] (IAA)
PSAR .... Programmable Synchronous/Asynchronous Receiver (IEEE)
PSAR .... Propulsion Systems Analysis Report (SAA)
PSARC ...... Pacific Stock Assessment Review Committee (FOTI)
PS Area ..... Posterior Speech Area (SAUS)

PSarg........ Pre-Sargonic (BJA)
PSARP...... Programmable Signal and Response Processor (SAUS)
PSaS........ Personally Safe and Sound (SAUS)
PSAS........ Prespeech Assessment Scale [*Occupational therapy*]
PSAS........ Production Systems Acceptance Section [*Social Security Administration*]
PSAS........ Programming System Announcement Summary (VLIE)
PSAS........ Program Support and Advanced Systems (SAA)
PSASA....... Public Service Association of South Australia
PSASS....... Perishable Subsistence Automated Supply System [*DoD*]
PSASV....... Phase-Sensitive Anodic Stripping Voltammetry
PSAT......... Palmetto State Transportation Company [*Common carrier symbol*]
PSAT......... Palm Springs Aerial Tramway (SAUS)
PSAT......... Percent Saturation of Transferrin (SAUS)
PSAT......... Pluribus Satellite Interface Message Processor (ACAE)
PSAT......... Predicted Site Acquisition Table [*NASA*]
PSAT......... Programmable Synchronous/Asynchronous Transmitter (IEEE)
PSAT......... Prostate-Specific Antigen Test [*Medicine*] (MELL)
PSAT/NMSQT... Preliminary Scholastic Aptitude/National Merit Scholarship Qualifying Test (PAZ)
PSATS....... Pennsylvania State Association of Township Supervisors (EARSL)
PSAUK....... Political Studies Association of the United Kingdom
PSAUSA..... Polish Socialist Alliance of the United States of America (EA)
PSAX........ Pacific Southwest Airlines [*Air carrier designation symbol*]
PSAZ........ Pacific Northwest Perishable Shippers Association [*Intermodal trailer symbol*]
PSB.......... Bellefonte-Clearfield-Philipsburg [*Pennsylvania*] [*Airport symbol*] (AD)
PSB.......... Burkina Socialist Party [*Political party*] (PSAP)
PSB.......... Harbor Patrol Boat [*Navy*]
PSB.......... Pacific Science Board [*National Academy of Sciences*]
PSB.......... Paradox Salt Basin (SAUS)
PSB.......... Paratytic Shellfish Poisoning (SAUS)
PSB.......... Passive-Sonobuoy (SAUS)
PSB.......... Path State Block (SAUS)
PSB.......... Personal Services Business (FOTI)
PSB.......... Phase Shifting Blank (AAEL)
PSB.......... Philatelic Sales Branch [*Later, PSD*] [*US Postal Service*]
PSB.......... Philipsburg, PA [*Location identifier*] [*FAA*] (FAAL)
PSB.......... Phosphorus-Solubilizing Bacteria [*Microbiology*]
PSB.......... Plant Safety Bureau
PSB.......... Plant Service Building [*Nuclear energy*] (NRCH)
PSB.......... Plough, Sweeper, and Blower (DA)
PSB.......... Police Superannuation Board [*Australia*]
PSB.......... Polished Silica Block (SAUS)
PSB.......... Polytechnic of the South Bank [*London, England*]
PSB.......... Post-Strike-Base (SAUS)
PSB.......... Power Supply Bar (SAUS)
PSB.......... Premium Savings Bond [*British*] (DCTA)
PSB.......... Procedure Status Block (TIMI)
PSB.......... Process Specification Block (SAUS)
PSB.......... Product Symbology Block (SAUS)
PSB.......... Professional and Statutory Board (AIE)
PSB.......... Professional Staffs Branch (HEAS)
PSB.......... Programmspezifikationsblock (SAUS)
PSB.......... Program Specification Block [*IBM Corp.*]
PSB.......... Program Station Basis [*Rating system*] (WDMC)
PSB.......... Program Status Book (SAUS)
PSB.......... Protected Specimen Brush [*Medicine*]
PSB.......... Protein S Beta (DMAA)
PSB.......... PS Booster (SAUS)
PSB.......... PS Business Parks, Inc. [*AMEX symbol*] (SPSG)
PSB.......... Psychological Services Bureau (AEBS)
PSB.......... Psychological Strategy Board [*Military*] (LAIN)
PSB.......... Public Safety Building (SARE)
PSB.......... Public Security Bureau (SAUS)
PSB.......... Public Service Board (NADA)
PSBA........ Pennsylvania School Boards Association (SAUS)
PSBA........ Power-Specific Biological Activity [*Engine emissions testing*]
PSBA........ Proceedings of the Society of Biblical Archaeology (SAUS)
PSBA........ Public School Bursars' Association [*British*] (BI)
PSBBF....... Pearl S. Buck Birthplace Foundation (EA)
PSBBrc...... Peoples Savings Bank of Brockton [*Associated Press*] (SAG)
PSBC........ Pacific State Bancorp [*NASDAQ symbol*] (QUAN)
PSBCA....... Painted Soda Bottles Collectors Association (EA)
PSBCA....... Postal Service Board of Contract Appeals (AAGC)
PSBDIR...... Program Specification Block Directory (SAUS)
PSbetaG.... Pregnancy-Specific Beta-1-Glycoprotein [*Medicine*] (DMAA)
PSBF........ Pearl S. Buck Foundation (EA)
PSBF........ Pioneer Savings Bank (Florida) [*NASDAQ symbol*] (COMM)
PSBG........ Pregnancy-Specific beta-Glycoprotein [*Gynecology*]
PSBG........ Production Services Buyers Guide [*Database*] [*United Kingdom*] (GDD)
PSBGEN..... Program Specification Block Generator (VLIE)
PSBGEN..... PSG Generation (SAUS)
PSBH........ Pad Safety in Blockhouse
PSBH........ Phonon Side-Band Hole [*Spectroscopy*]
PSBI......... Performance Standardization Branch Instruction (SAA)
PSBI......... PSB Bancorporation [*NASDAQ symbol*]
PSBK........ Progressive Bank [*NASDAQ symbol*] (TTSB)
PSBK........ Progressive Bank, Inc. [*Pawling, NY*] [*NASDAQ symbol*] (NQ)
PSBL........ Possible (FAAC)
PSBLS....... Permanent Space Based Logistics System
PSBLS....... Permanent Space-Based Logistics System (SAUS)
PSBM........ Passive Seat Belt Module [*Automotive electronics*]
PSBMA...... Professional Services Business Management Association [*Later, PSMA*] (EA)
PsbMV...... Pea Seed-Borne Mosaic Virus
PSBNAME... Program Specification Block Name [*Computer science*] (MHDB)
PSBO........ Partial Small Bowel Obstruction [*Medicine*] (MEDA)
PSBO........ Public Savings Bond Office (SAUS)
PSBP........ PS Business Parks, Inc. [*Associated Press*] (SAG)
PSBPrB...... Pub Sv Colo, 8.40% Pfd [*NYSE symbol*] (TTSB)
PSBR........ Pennsylvania State University Breazeale Nuclear Reactor [*Research center*] (RCD)
PSBR........ Public Sector Borrowing Requirement
PSBR........ Pyridine Styrene Butadiene Rubber (SAUS)
PSBR........ Vinylpyridine-Styrene-Butadiene Rubber (SAUS)
PSBS........ Phoenix Society for Burn Survivors (EA)
PSBT........ Pilot Self-Briefing Terminal [*Aviation*] (FAAC)
PSBU........ Contship [*Intermodal shipping container symbol*] (TVRC)
PSBU........ Propeller Shaft Bearing Unit [*Truck engineering*]
PSBU........ Public Sector and Broadcasting Union [*Australia*]
PSBUS...... Path Selection Bus (SAUS)
PSBV........ PSB Trucking [*Common carrier symbol*]
PSBV........ Public Service Board Victoria [*Australia*]
PSBX........ Peoples Savings Bank FSB (Michigan) [*NASDAQ symbol*] (COMM)
PSC.......... Christian Democratic Parties (Belgium) [*Political party*] (PSAP)
PSC.......... Congolese Socialist Party [*Zaire*] [*Political party*] (PD)
psc.......... geomagnetic pulsation (SAUS)
PSC.......... Isla De Pascua [*Easter Island*] [*Seismograph station code, US Geological Survey*] [*Closed*] (SEIS)
PSC.......... Pacifc Sea Council (SAUS)
PSC.......... Pacific Salmon Commission (EA)
PSC.......... Pacific Science Center
PSC.......... Pacific Science Council
PSC.......... Pacific South Coast Freight Bureau, San Francisco CA [*STAC*]
PSC.......... Pacific Studies Center (EA)
PSC.......... Packet Switching Center (VLIE)
PSC.......... Pakistan Shipping Corp. (SAUS)
PSC.......... Palaeontological Society of China (BUAC)
PSC.......... Palestine Solidarity Campaign (BUAC)
PSC.......... Palestine Solidarity Committee [*Defunct*] (EA)
PSC.......... Palmer Skin Conductance
PSC.......... Palynological Society of China (QUAC)
PSC.......... Paper Skip Character [*Computer science*] (VLIE)
PSC.......... Papillary Serous Cyst [*Medicine*] (MELL)
PSC.......... Parallel Switch Control (MCD)
PSC.......... Parallel to Serial Converter
PSC.......... Parallel to Series Converter
PSC.......... Parents Sharing Custody (EA)
PSC.......... Partido Social Conservador Colombiano [*Colombian Social Conservative Party*] [*Political party*] (EY)
PSC.......... Partido Social Cristiano [*Social Christian Party*] [*Ecuador*] [*Political party*] (PPW)
PSC.......... Partido Social Cristiano [*Social Christian Party*] [*Bolivia*] [*Political party*]
PSC.......... Partido Social Cristiano [*Social Christian Party*] [*Guatemala*] [*Political party*] (PPW)
PSC.......... Partido Socialcristiano Nicaraguense [*Nicaraguan Social Christian Party*] [*Political party*] (PPW)
PSC.......... Partido Socialista de Catalunya [*Catalan Socialist Party*] [*Spain*] [*Political party*] (PPE)
PSC.......... Parti Socialiste Caledonien [*New Caledonia*] [*Political party*] (FEA)
PSC.......... Parti Socialiste Camerounais [*Cameroon Socialist Party*] [*Political party*]
PSC.......... Parti Socialiste Centrafricain [*Central African Socialist Party*] [*Political party*] (PD)
PSC.......... Pasco [*Washington*] [*Airport symbol*] (OAG)
PSC.......... Pasco, WA [*Location identifier*] [*FAA*] (FAAL)
PSC.......... Passaic Byzantine [*Diocesan abbreviation*] [*New Jersey*] (TOCD)
PSC.......... Passed Staff College [*British*]
PSC.......... Passenger Services Conference [*IATA*] (DS)
psc.......... Passes Staff College [*British*] (WA)
PSC.......... Patriot Steering Committee
PSC.......... Paul Smiths College [*New York*]
PSC.......... Payphone Speech Circuit (SAUS)
PSC.......... Peacetime Subcontract
PSC.......... Peachtree Support Center (SAUS)
PSC.......... Pembroke State College [*North Carolina*]
PSC.......... Penetrating Stun Cartridge [*Police and security equipment*]
PSC.......... Peralta Shipping Corp. (SAUS)
PSC.......... Percentage of Successful Collisions [*Obstetrics*]
PSC.......... Performance Seeking Control (SAUS)
PSC.......... Performing Support Center (SAUS)
PSC.......... Periodic Surveillance Committees (SAUS)
PSC.......... Permanent Split Capacitor (IAA)
PSC.......... Persistence [*Telegraphy*] (PCTE)
PSC.......... Personal Service Contract (SAUS)
PSC.......... Personal Service Corporation (EBF)
PSC.......... Personal Services Contractor
PSC.......... Personal Super Computer (SAUS)
PSC.......... Personal Supercomputer [*Culler Scientific Systems Corp.*]
PSC.......... Personnel Service Center [*or Company*] [*Military*] (INF)
PSC.......... Personnel Status Change (KSC)
PSC.......... Personnel Subsystem Cost
PSC.......... Personnel Support Company [*Army*]
PSC.......... Per Standard Compass [*Navigation*]
PSC.......... Petroleum Supply Command (SAUS)
PSC.......... Petty Sessional Court [*British*] (ROG)

PSC.......... Pharmacological Society of Canada (FOTI)
PSC.......... Phase-Sensitive Converter
PSC.......... Philadelphia Service Center [*IRS*]
PSC.......... Philadelphia Suburban Corp. [*NYSE symbol*] (SPSG)
PSC.......... Philander Smith College [*Little Rock, AR*]
PSC.......... Phila Suburban [*NYSE symbol*] (TTSB)
PSC.......... Philippine Sugar Commission (EA)
PSC.......... Phonemic Spelling Council [*Defunct*] (EA)
PSC.......... Photographic Sciences Corp. (EFIS)
PSC.......... Photosensitive Cell (IEEE)
PSC.......... Phylogenetic Species Concept [*Biology*]
PSC.......... Physical Sciences Center
PSC.......... Physical Sciences Committee [*Terminated, 1977*] [*NASA*] (EGAO)
PSC.......... Physical Security/Pilferage Code (MCD)
PSC.......... Physical Signaling Components Sublayer (SAUS)
PSC.......... Pipe Smokers' Council (BUAC)
Psc.......... Pisces [*Constellation*]
PSC.......... Pittsburgh Scientific Center (SAUS)
PSC.......... Pittsburgh Steel Co. (SAUS)
PSC.......... Pittsburgh Supercomputer (or Supercomputing) Center (SAUS)
PSC.......... Pittsburgh Supercomputing Center [*National Science Foundation*] [*Research center*] (RCD)
PSC.......... Pittsburgh Superconducting Center [*Pennsylvania*] (GRD)
PSC.......... Plant Simulation Code (ABAC)
pSC.......... Plasmid Stanley Cohen [*Molecular biology*]
PSC.......... Platform Support Center [*NASA*] (SSD)
PSC.......... Pluripotent Stem Cell [*Cytology*]
PSC.......... Plutonium Stripping Concentrate [*Nuclear energy*] (NRCH)
PSC.......... Point Shipping Co. [*Steamship*] (MHDW)
PSC.......... Point Stress Criterion (SAUS)
PSC.......... Polaroid Stereoscopic Chroncyclegraph
PSC.......... Polar Science Center [*University of Washington*] [*Research center*] (RCD)
PSC.......... Polar Stratospheric Cloud [*Meteorology*]
PSC.......... Police Staff College (SAUS)
PSC.......... Polish Steamship Co. (SAUS)
PSC.......... Population Studies Center [*University of Michigan*] [*Research center*] (RCD)
PSC.......... Porcelain on Steel Council [*Defunct*] (EA)
PSC.......... Porcelain-on-Steel Council (SAUS)
PSC.......... Porous Silicon Capacitor (AAEL)
PSC.......... Porter-Silber Chromogen [*Medicine*] (MAE)
PSC.......... Portland Society for Calligraphy (EA)
PSC.......... Port Service Charge (SAUS)
PSC.......... Postal Service Center (AFM)
PSC.......... Posterior Subcapsular Cataracts [*Ophthalmology*]
PSC.......... Post-Storage Checkout [*NASA*] (KSC)
PSC.......... Postsynaptic Current [*Neurophysiology*]
PSC.......... Potentiometer Strip Chart
PSC.......... Potomac State College [*of West Virginia University*]
PSC.......... Power Supply Calibrator
PSC.......... Power System Communications (IAA)
PSC.......... Power System Control (VLIE)
PSC.......... Prairie Swine Centre [*University of Saskatchewan*] [*Canada*] (IRC)
PSC.......... Prairie Swine Centre, Inc. [*Canada*] (BUAC)
PSC.......... Preferred Semiconductor Circuit [*Electronics*] (IAA)
PSC.......... Pressure Suit Circuit (KSC)
PSC.......... Pressure System Control (AAG)
PSC.......... Prestressed Cement (EDCT)
PSC.......... Prestressed Concrete (ADA)
PSC.......... Presumptive Hematopoietic Stem Cell
PSC.......... Price Signal Code [*Military*] (AABC)
PSC.......... Primary Sclerosing Cholangitis [*Medicine*]
PSC.......... Primary Store Capacity (SAUS)
PSC.......... Primary Subordinate Commands (SAUS)
PSC.......... Prime Service Contractor (SAUS)
PSC.......... Prime Systems Contractor
PSC.......... Principal Subordinate Command [*NATO*] (POLM)
PSC.......... Principal Surface Combatant (MILB)
PSC.......... Principle Surface Combatants (SAUS)
PSC.......... Print Scan Counter [*Computer science*] (VLIE)
PSC.......... Print Server Command (SAUS)
PSC.......... Private Secretary's Certificate [*British*] (DI)
PSC.......... Private Sector Council (EA)
PSC.......... Probability Saturation Counter (SAUS)
PSC.......... PROBE [*Program Optimization and Budget Evaluation*] Steering Committee [*Military*]
PSC.......... Problem Specification Card (SAUS)
PSC.......... Processing and Spectral Control
PSC.......... Processing Service Centers [*Social Security Administration*]
PSC.......... Process Schedule Control (SAUS)
PSC.......... Procurement Source Code (AFM)
PSC.......... Procurement Strategy Corp. (SAUS)
PSC.......... Product and Service Code (AAGC)
PSC.......... Production Schedule Confirmation (SAUS)
PSC.......... Production Scheduling and Control (IAA)
PSC.......... Product Safety Committee [*New South Wales, Australia*]
PSC.......... Product Service Center (SAUS)
PSC.......... Product Support Confidential (AAG)
PSC.......... Professional Service Corporation [*Medicine*] (HCT)
PSC.......... Professional Services Corp. (SAUS)
PSC.......... Professional Services Council [*Washington, DC*] (EA)
PSC.......... Programmable Sample Changer [*Spectroscopy*]
PSC.......... Programmable System Component (TIMI)
PSC.......... Programming Sciences Corp. (SAUS)
PSC.......... Program Schedule Chart (NASA)
PSC.......... Program Sequence Control (NITA)
PSC.......... Program Service Center [*Social Security Administration*] (OICC)
PSC.......... Program Site Coordinator [*Environmental science*] (EPAT)
PSC.......... Program Standards Checker [*Computer science*]
PSC.......... Program Status Chart [*Computer science*]
PSC.......... Program Structure Code (AFM)
PSC.......... Program Support Center
PSC.......... Program Support Contract (SSD)
PSC.......... Program Support Contractor (SAUS)
PSC.......... Program Support Coordinator (SAUS)
PSC.......... Program Switching Center [*Computer science*] (IAA)
PSC.......... Prohibited Species Catch (SAUS)
PSC.......... Project Systems Control (MCD)
PSC.......... Propagating Space Charge (PDAA)
PSC.......... Protosolar Cloud [*Astronomy*]
PSC.......... Prototype System Characteristics
PSC.......... PSC, Inc. [*Associated Press*] (SAG)
PSC.......... Pseudo-Store Cell (SAUS)
PSC.......... Public Safety Calling system (SAUS)
PSC.......... Public Service Careers [*Program*] [*Department of Labor*]
PSC.......... Public Service Co.
PSC.......... Public Service Commission [*Canada*] (BUAC)
PSC.......... Public Service Commission [*Usually, of a specific state*]
PSC.......... Pulse Shape Control (SAUS)
PSC.......... Pulse Shape Control Circuit (IAA)
PSC.......... Pulse Synchronized Contraction [*In the vascular system*] [*Medicine*]
PSC.......... Sandoz AG [*Switzerland*] [*Research code symbol*]
PSc.......... Scranton Public Library, Scranton, PA [*Library symbol*] [*Library of Congress*] (LCLS)
PSC.......... Swarthmore College, Swarthmore, PA [*Library symbol*] [*Library of Congress*] [*OCLC symbol*] (LCLS)
PSCA........ Parliamentary Select Committee on Agriculture [*British*]
PscA........ Pisces Austrinus [*Constellation*]
PSCA........ Polish Social and Cultural Association [*British*] (EAIO)
PSCA........ Pressure Suit Conditioning Assembly (MCD)
PSCA........ Profit Sharing Council of America (EA)
PSCACM.... Permanent Secretariat of the Central American Common Market
PSCAGNT... Podhale Social-Cultural Association of Gypsies in Nowy Targ [*Poland*] (BUAC)
PSCAN...... P-Scanner (SAUS)
PSCAN...... Purchase Order Scan
PS Cap...... Polystyrene Capacitor (SAUS)
PSCAV....... Professional Squash Coaches' Association of Victoria [*Australia*]
PSCB........ Padded Sample Collection Bag [*NASA*]
PSCB........ Parliamentary Standing Committee on Broadcasting [*Australia*]
PSCB........ Presentation Services Command Processor (SAUS)
PSCBG...... Paper Shipping-Containers Buyers Group
PSCC........ Packaging, Storage, and Containerization Center
PSCC........ Photo Systems Controller Console (KSC)
PSCC........ Polymer Supply and Characterization Center (SAUS)
PSCC........ Posterior Subcapsular Cataract [*Medicine*] (STED)
PSCC........ Power System Communications (IAA)
PSCC........ Power System Computation Conference
PSCC........ Projets de Services Communautaires du Canada
PSCC........ Pure Steel Custom Cycles [*NCIC motorcycle make code*]
PSC Circuit... Pulse Shape Control Circuit (SAUS)
PSCD........ Patrol Service Central Depot (SAUS)
PSCD........ Plutonium Stripping Concentration Distillate [*Nuclear energy*] (NRCH)
PSCD........ Postcard (VRA)
PSCD........ Program for the Study of Crime and Delinquency [*Ohio State University*] [*Research center*] (RCD)
PSCE........ Presurgical Coagulation Evaluation [*Medicine*] (DAVI)
PSCEC....... Planning Status of Committed Engineering Changes (SAA)
PSCF........ Personal Security Clearance File
PSCF........ Primary System Control Facility [*Computer science*] (ELAL)
PSCF........ Processor Storage Control Function
PSCFB....... Pacific South Coast Freight Bureau
PSCFB....... Pacific Southcoast Freight Bureau (SAUS)
PSCG........ PATRIOT Security Classification Guide (SAUS)
PSCG........ Power Supply and Control Gear
PSCG........ Power Supply Control Group [*Military*] (CAAL)
PSCH........ Periodic Scheduler (SAUS)
PSCH........ Postoperative Suprachoroidal Hemorrhage [*Medicine*]
PsChE....... Pseudocholinesterase (STED)
PSC-Hi...... Friends Historical Library of Swarthmore College, Swarthmore, PA [*Library symbol*] [*Library of Congress*] (LCLS)
PSCI......... Perez Self-Concept Inventory [*Psychology*] (EDAC)
PSCI......... Plastic Shipping Container Institute (EA)
Psci.......... Pressure at Slow Component Intercept [*Medicine*] (STED)
PSCI......... Primary Self-Concept Inventory [*Psychology*] (EDAC)
PSCI......... Public Service of Indiana [*Federal Railroad Administration identification code*]
PSCJ......... Perseverance Society of Carpenters and Joiners [*A union*] [*British*]
PSCJ......... Progressive Society of Carpenters and Joiners [*A union*] [*British*]
PSCL......... Programmed Sequential Control Language
PSCL......... Programmed Sequential Control Logic (SAUS)
PSCL......... Propellants System Components Laboratory [*Kennedy Space Center*] [*NASA*]
PSCL......... Propellant Systems Cleaning Laboratory [*NASA*] (NASA)
PScL......... Scranton Public Library, Scranton, PA [*Library symbol*] [*Library of Congress*] (LCLS)

PScLL .... Lackawanna Bar Association Law Library, Scranton, PA [*Library symbol*] [*Library of Congress*] (LCLS)
PSCLS .... Potentiostatic Stress Corrosion Life Curve (SAUS)
PScM .... Marywood College, Scranton, PA [*Library symbol*] [*Library of Congress*] (LCLS)
PSCM .... Pilot Scale Ceramic Melter (ABAC)
PSCM .... Pokeweed Activated Spleen Conditioned Medium [*Medicine*] (STED)
PSCM .... Process Steering and Control Module [*Telecommunications*] (TEL)
PSCM .... Professinal Sports Care Management, Inc. [*NASDAQ symbol*] (SAG)
PSCM .... Professinal Sports Care Mgmt [*NASDAQ symbol*] (TTSB)
PSC Motor ... Permanent Split Capacitor Motor (SAUS)
PSCN .... Partido Socialcristiano Nicaraguense [*Nicaraguan Social Christian Party*] [*Political party*] (PPW)
PSCN .... Permanent System Control Number (MCD)
PSCN .... Preliminary Specification Change Notice [*NASA*] (NASA)
PSCN .... Program Support Communication Network (SAUS)
PSCN .... Program Support Communications Network (SSD)
PSCN .... Program Support Computer Network (SAUS)
PSCN .... Proposed Specification Change Notice
PSCNet ...... Pittsburgh Supercomputing Center Network [*Pennsylvania*]
PSCNET ..... Pittsburgh Superconducting Center Network
PSCO .... Pennsylvania State College of Optometry
PSCO .... Personnel Survey Control Officer [*Military*] (AABC)
PSCO .... ProtoSource Corp. [*NASDAQ symbol*] (SAG)
PSCOE .... Power Sources Center of Excellence
PSCol .... Public Service Co. of Colorado [*Associated Press*] (SAG)
P/score ...... Pressure Score [*Medicine*] (STED)
PSCOU ...... ProtoSource Corp. Unit [*NASDAQ symbol*] (TTSB)
PSCOW ...... ProtoSource Corp. Wrrt [*NASDAQ symbol*] (TTSB)
PSCP .... Palestine Symphonic Choir Project (EA)
P/S CP ...... Platoon/Section Command Post
PSCP .... Polar Continental Shelf Project [*Canada*]
PSCP .... Posterior Subcapsular Cataractous Plaque [*Ophthalmology*] (DAVI)
PSCP .... Public School Construction Program (SAUS)
PSCP .... Public Service Careers Program [*Department of Labor*]
PSC-P .... Swarthmore College Peace Collection, Swarthmore, PA [*Library symbol*] [*Library of Congress*] (LCLS)
PSCPD ...... Philadelphia Signal Corps Procurement District [*Army*]
PSC-PSOE ... Partit dels Socialistes de Catalunya [*Party of Socialists of Catalonia*] [*Political party*] (PPW)
PSCPT .... Preschool Self-Concept Picture Test [*Psychology*]
PSCR .... Permanent Scratch File [*Computer science*]
PSCR .... Photo-Selective Copper Reduction [*For circuit board manufacture*]
PSCR .... Priority System Change Request
PSCR .... Production Schedule Completion Report [*DoD*]
PSCR .... Programmable Scanning Receiver (DWSG)
PSCR .... Public Service Commission Reports [*A publication*] (DLA)
PSCRC ...... Portable Small Computer Requirements Contract (SAUS)
PSCRD ...... Program Support Communications Requirements Document (SSD)
PSCRL .... Patent Security Category Review List (AAGC)
PSCRT .... Passive Satellite Communications Research Terminal (SAA)
PSCS .... Pacific Scatter Communications System [*Air Force*] (CET)
PSCS .... Packet-Switched Communication System (CIST)
PSCS .... Photographic Sensor Control System (SAUS)
PSCS .... Program Support Control System
PSCS .... Pulse Signature Classification System (SAUS)
Pscs calculator ... Pascals calculator (SAUS)
PSCSG ...... Pocket-Sized CS Grenade [*Police and security equipment*]
PSCT .... Peripheral Stem Cell Transplant [*Medicine*] (MELL)
PSCT .... Permanent Service on Crustal Thickness (SAUS)
PSCT .... Politte Sentence Completion Test (TES)
PSCT .... Polymer Stabilized Cholesteric Texture (SAUS)
PSCT .... Port-Side Container Terminal [*Indian Railway*] (TIR)
PSCU .... Piet Schouten Containerhandel [*Intermodal shipping container symbol*] (TVRC)
PSCU .... Power Supply Control Unit (CET)
PSCU .... Power-Supply Control Unit (SAUS)
PSCU .... Private Sector Casemix Unit (ADWA)
PScU .... University of Scranton, Scranton, PA [*Library symbol*] [*Library of Congress*] (LCLS)
PSCUS ...... Peters' United States Surpeme Court Reports [*26-41 United States*] [*A publication*] (DLA)
PSCX .... Prolerized Steel [*Private rail car owner code*]
PSCX .... PSC, Inc. [*Formerly, Photographic Sciences Corp.*] [*NASDAQ symbol*] (NQ)
PSCZ .... Public Service of Colorado [*Federal Railroad Administration identification code*]
PSD .... Democratic Socialist Party (Central African Rep.) [*Political party*] (PSAP)
PSD .... Destour Socialist Party [*Tunisia*] [*Political party*] (PD)
PSD .... Doctor of Political Science
Ps D .... Doctor of Psychology
Ps D .... Doctor of Psychology in Metaphysics
PSD .... Doctor of Public Service
PSD .... Packed Switched Data
PSD .... Packet Switched Data (SAUS)
PSD .... Parallel Shift and Dwell (SAUS)
PSD .... Partial Sleep Deprivation (MELL)
PSD .... Particle Size Distribution
PSD .... Partido Socialdemocracia [*Social Democratic Party*] [*Chile*] [*Political party*] (EY)
PSD .... Partido Social Democrata [*Social Democratic Party*] [*Spain*] [*Political party*] (PPE)
PSD .... Partido Social Democrata [*Social Democratic Party*] [*Mexico*] [*Political party*] (PPW)
PSD .... Partido Social Democrata [*Social Democratic Party*] [*Bolivia*] [*Political party*] (PPW)
PSD .... Partido Social Democratico [*Social Democratic Party*] [*Nicaragua*] [*Political party*] (PPW)
PSD .... Partido Social Democratico [*Social Democratic Party*] [*El Salvador*] [*Political party*]
PSD .... Partido Social Democratico [*Social Democratic Party*] [*Brazil*] [*Political party*]
PSD .... Partido Socialista Democratico [*Social Democratic Party*] [*Guatemala*] [*Political party*] (PD)
PSD .... Partido Socialista Democratico [*Social Democratic Party*] [*Argentina*] [*Political party*] (PPW)
PSD .... Parti Social-Democrate [*Algeria*] [*Political party*] (EY)
PSD .... Parti Social-Democrate [*Social Democratic Party*] [*France*] [*Political party*] (PPW)
PSD .... Parti Social Democrate de Madagascar et des Comores [*Social Democratic Party of Madagascar and Comores*]
PSD .... Parti Social-Democratie [*Benin*] [*Political party*] (EY)
PSD .... Parti Socialiste Democratique [*Cameroon*] [*Political party*] (EY)
PSD .... Passed (ROG)
PSD .... Passing Scene Display
PSD .... Past Start Date
PSD .... Patent Search Documentation (NITA)
PSD .... Paternal Sister Dam (OA)
PSD .... Patient Symptom Diary
PSD .... Pay Supply Depot (WDAA)
PSD .... Peptone-Starch-Dextrose [*Microbiology*] (MAE)
PSD .... Performance and Security Document (SAUS)
PSD .... Perform Security block Defence (SAUS)
PSD .... Permanent Signal Detection [*Telecommunications*] (TEL)
PSD .... Personal Services Department [*Navy*] [*British*]
PSD .... Personal Smoke Device
PSD .... Personnel Services Division [*Army*]
PSD .... Personnel Support Detachment (DOMA)
PSD .... Personnel System [*or Subsystem*] Development (AAG)
PSD .... Pescadero [*California*] [*Seismograph station code, US Geological Survey*] (SEIS)
PSD .... Pesticides Safety Directorate (BUAC)
PSD .... Petroleum Safety Data [*American Petroleum Institute*]
PSD .... Petroleum Storage Depot (SAUS)
PSD .... Petty Session Division [*Legal term*] (DLA)
PSD .... Phase-Sensitive Demodulator [*or Detector*]
PSD .... Phase-Sensitive Detection (SAUS)
PSD .... Phase-Sensitive Detector (SAUS)
PSD .... Phase Shifter Driver
PSD .... Philadelphia Signal Depot (SAUS)
PSD .... Philatelic Sales Division [*Formerly, PSB*] [*US Postal Service*]
PSD .... Photoconductive, Semiconductive Device
PSD .... Photon Stimulated Desorption [*For analysis of surfaces*]
PSD .... Photo-Sensitive Detection (or Detector) (SAUS)
PSD .... Photoshop image format (SAUS)
PSD .... Photo-Stimulated Desorption (SAUS)
PSD .... Pictorialized Scatter Diagram [*Botany*]
PSD .... PIR [*Protein Information Resource*] International Protein Sequence Database (GDD)
PSD .... Pitch Servo Drive
PSD .... Pittsburgh Steamship Division (SAUS)
PSD .... Pituitary Stalk Distortion [*Medicine*] (RAWO)
PSD .... Planning Systems Division (COE)
PSD .... Platform Specific Driver [*Computer science*]
PSD .... Policy Support Department
PSD .... Polysilicon Diode (IAA)
PSD .... Polystyrene, Deuterated [*Organic chemistry*]
PSD .... Pore Size Distribution
PSD .... Port Said [*Egypt*] [*Airport symbol*] (AD)
PSD .... Port Security Detachment [*Military*] (GFGA)
PSD .... Port Sharing Device (ACAE)
PSD .... Port Status Display (AAEL)
PSD .... Position-Sensitive Detection (or Detector) (SAUS)
PSD .... Position Sensitive Light Detector (IAA)
PSD .... Postal Security Device [*Computer science*]
PSD .... Post Sending Delay
PSD .... Poststenotic Dilatation [*Medicine*] (MELL)
PSD .... Postsurgical Distress [*Medicine*] (MELL)
PSD .... Postsynaptic Density [*Neurophysiology*]
PSD .... Power Sliding Door [*Automotive engineering*]
PSD .... Power Spectral [*or Spectrum*] Density
PSD .... Power Spectrum Distribution [*Electronics*]
PSD .... Power Supply & Distribution (SAUS)
PSD .... Power System Demonstrator (SAUS)
PSD .... Preferred Sea Duty
PSD .... Prepare Simulation Data (ACAE)
PSD .... Pre-Shipment Document (SAUS)
PSD .... Pressure-Sensitive Devices (MCD)
PSD .... Prevention of Significant Deterioration [*Environmental Protection Agency*]
PSD .... Prevent Significant Deterioration
PSD .... Primary Standard Data (SAUS)
PSD .... Printed Side Down [*Graphic arts*] (DGA)
PSD .... Printer Sharing Device (SAUS)
PSD .... Printing Systems Division (NITA)
PSD .... Private-Sector Development (ECON)
PSD .... Procedural Support Data
PSD .... Processing Status Display [*NASA*]
PSD .... Process Specification Departure (SAA)

PSD......... Procurement Surveys Division [*NASA*] (MCD)
PSD......... Production System Design Laboratory [*Massachusetts Institute of Technology*] (RCD)
PSD......... Professional Service Dates [*Formerly, ADBD*]
PSD......... Professional Systems Division [*American Institute of Architects Service Corp.*] [*Information service or system*] (IID)
PSD......... Programmable System Design [*Computer science*] (AGLO)
PSD......... Programmed Slip Differential [*Automotive engineering*]
PSD......... Programmers Supplementary Documents (SAUS)
PSD......... Programme Support and Development [*British*]
PSD......... Program Status Documents [*Computer science*]
PSD......... Program Status Double Word (SAUS)
PSD......... Program Status Doubleword
PSD......... Program Support Document (MUGU)
PSD......... Program System Description (SAA)
PSD......... Program Systems Division [*Environmental Protection Agency*] (GFGA)
PSD......... Promotion Service Date
PSD......... Propellant Slosh Dynamics
PSD......... Propellant Storage Depot [*NASA*]
PSD......... Proportional Stock Density [*Pisciculture*]
PSD......... Propulsion System Demonstrator [*Marine Corps*] (DOMA)
PSD......... Protective Serum Dilution
PSD......... Protective Structures Division [*Office of Civil Defense*]
PSD......... Pseudosingle Domain [*Behavior of grains in rocks*] [*Geophysics*]
PSD......... Pseudo Stow Document (DNAB)
PSD......... Public Safety Division (SAUS)
PSD......... Puget Sound P&L [*NYSE symbol*] (TTSB)
PSD......... Puget Sound Power & Light Co. [*NYSE symbol*] (SPSG)
PSD......... Pulse Shape Discrimination (or Discriminator) (SAUS)
PSD......... Pulse Shape Discriminator
PSD......... Pure Screw Dislocation
PSD 2....... Project Quality and Monitoring Division
PSDA........ Angolan Social Democratic Party [*Political party*] (PSAP)
PSDA........ Paper Sack Development Association [*British*] (BI)
PSDA........ Partial Source Data Automation (NVT)
PSDA........ Particle Size Distribution Analysis [*Statistics*]
PSDA........ Patient Self-Determination Act
PSDA........ Post-Storm Data Acquisition (SAUS)
P/SDA....... Power/Signal Distribution Assembly
PSDA........ Psychoactive Substance Dependence and Abuse (MELL)
PSDB........ Partido da Social Democracia Brasiliera [*Brazilian Social Democratic Party*] [*Political party*] (EY)
PSDB........ Physical Segment Descriptor Block (SAUS)
PSDB........ Police Scientific Development Branch [*British*] (WDAA)
PSDB........ Social Democrats
PSDC........ Pennsylvania State Data Center [*Middletown*] [*Information service or system*] (IID)
PSDC........ Plant Sciences Data Center [*Formerly, Plant Records Center*] [*American Horticultural Society*] [*Mt. Vernon, VA*]
PSDC........ Power Sprayer and Duster Council (EA)
PSDC........ Protective Structures Development Center [*Military*]
PSDC........ Public Switched (or Switching) Digital Capability (SAUS)
PSDC........ Puget Sound Dalmatian Club (EARSL)
PSD Circuit... Permanent Signal Detection Circuit (SAUS)
PSDD........ Planetary Science Data Dictionary (SAUS)
PSDD........ Preliminary System Design Description [*Nuclear energy*] (NRCH)
PSDDS....... Pilot [*or Public*] Switched Digital Data Service [*Telecommunications*] (TEL)
PS de G..... Partido dos Socialistas de Galicia [*Spain*] [*Political party*] (EY)
Psdepgr..... Pseudepigrapha (BJA)
PSDF........ People's Self-Defense Force [*South Vietnamese militia force*] (VNW)
PSDF........ Popular Self-Defense Force [*Local armed units protecting Vietnamese hamlets*]
PSDF........ Propulsion Systems Development Facility (KSC)
PSDI........ Partido Social Democratico Independente [*Independent Social Democratic Party*] [*Portugal*] [*Political party*] (PPE)
PSDI........ Partito Socialista Democratico Italiano [*Italian Social Democratic Party*] [*Political party*]
PSDI........ Presence Sensing Device Initiation (SARE)
PSDI........ Project Software and Development [*NASDAQ symbol*]
PSDI........ Project Software & Development, Inc. [*NASDAQ symbol*] (SAG)
PSDI........ Project Software & Dvlp [*NASDAQ symbol*] (TTSB)
PSDIAD...... Photostimulated Desorption Ion Angular Distribution [*Surface analysis*]
PSDIS....... Partito Socialista Democratico Indipendente Sammarinese [*Independent Social Democratic Party of San Marino*] [*Political party*] (PPE)
PSDL........ Product Support Data List (SAUS)
PSDL........ Region 4 PSD Log System (SAUS)
PSdM........ Mennonite Publishing House, Scottsdale, PA [*Library symbol*] [*Library of Congress*] (LCLS)
PSDM........ Presentation Services for Data Management (MHDB)
PSD(MS).... Photon Stimulated Desorption (Mass Spectroscopy) (MCD)
PSDN........ Packed Switched Data Network (SAUS)
PSDN........ Packet Swiched Data Network (SAUS)
PSDN........ Packet Switched Data Network [*Telecommunications*]
PSDN........ Packet Switched Digital Network (SAUS)
PSDN........ Packet Switching Data Network (SAUS)
PSDN........ Packet-Switching Data Network [*Computer science*] (DOM)
PSDN........ Packet Switching Digital Network (SAUS)
PSDN........ Public Switched Data Network (NITA)
PSDN........ Public Switched (or Switching) Digital Network (SAUS)
PSDNA....... Power System Dynamic Network Analyzer (SAUS)
PSDN-Alheri... Niger Social-Democratic Party-Alheri [*Political party*] (PSAP)
Psdo........ Pseudonym (SAUS)
PSDOS....... Public Switched Digital Data Service (SAUS)
PSDP........ Payload Station Distribution Panel [*NASA*] (MCD)
PSDP........ Personnel Subsystem Development Plan
PSDP........ Phase Structure and Dependency Parser (SAUS)
PSDP........ Phrase Structure and Dependency Parser (DIT)
PSDP........ Professional Skills Development Program [*Bureau of the Census*] (GFGA)
PSDP........ Programmable Signal Data Processor (MCD)
PSDPC....... Polar Satellite Data Processing Centre (CARB)
PSDPr....... Puget Sound P&L 7.875% Pfd [*NYSE symbol*] (TTSB)
PSDPrB...... Puget Sound P&L Adj Rt'B'Pfd [*NYSE symbol*] (TTSB)
PSDR........ Planning and Scheduling Document Record [*NASA*] (NASA)
PSDR........ Process Storage Data Register (IAA)
PSDR........ Program Status Doubleword Register [*Computer science*] (MHDB)
PSDR........ Public Sector Debt Repayment [*British*] (ECON)
PSDR........ Public Sector Debt Requirement (ODA)
PSDS........ Packet Switch Data System [*Information retrieval*] (IID)
PSDS........ Packet Switched Data Service [*Telecommunications*] (TEL)
PSDS........ Partito Socialista Democratico Sammarinese [*Social Democratic Party of San Marino*] [*Political party*] (PPE)
PSDS........ Passing Scene Display System
PSDS........ Permanently Separated from Duty Station [*Military*]
PSDS........ Postal Source Data System [*U.S. Postal Service*] (CIST)
PSDS........ Prison Service Drug Strategy (WDAA)
PSDS........ Public Switched Data Service [*Telecommunications*]
PSDS........ Public Switched Digital Service [*Computer science*] (TNIG)
PSDS Matrix... Positive Semi-Definite Symmetric Matrix (SAUS)
PSDSP....... Pious Society of the Daughters of Saint Paul [*See also FSP*] [*Rome, Italy*] (EAIO)
PSDT........ President (ROG)
PSDTC....... Pacific Securities Depository Trust Co.
PSDTN....... Packet Switched Data Transmission Network (SAUS)
PSDU........ Personnel Services Delivery Unit (HEAS)
PSDU........ Polish Social Democratic Union [*Political party*]
PSDU........ Power Switching Distribution Unit
PSDU........ Presentation Service Data Unit [*Telecommunications*] (OSI)
PSDUPD...... Port of San Diego Unified Port District (SAUS)
PSDVB....... Poly(styrene-Divinylbenzene) [*Organic chemistry*]
PSE......... Aeroservicio Sipse SA de CV [*Mexico*] [*ICAO designator*] (FAAC)
PSE......... Pacific School of English [*Australia*]
PSE......... Pacific Stock Exchange (EA)
PSE......... Packet Switched Exchange (SAUS)
PSE......... Packet Switch Exchange (SAUS)
PSE......... Packet Switching Exchange [*Telecommunications*]
PSE......... Pale Soft Exudative [*Pork*]
PSE......... Paper Surface Efficiency (DGA)
PSE......... Partido Socialista de Euskadi [*Basque Socialist Party*] [*Spain*] [*Political party*] (EY)
PSE......... Partido Socialista Ecuatoriano [*Ecuadorean Socialist Party*] [*Political party*] (PPW)
PSE......... Pasemah [*Language symbol*] (ETLW)
PSE......... Passage
PSE......... Passive Seismic Experiment [*NASA*]
PSE......... Passive Smoke Exposure (MELL)
PSE......... Path Switching Element (SAUS)
PSE......... Payload Service Equipment [*NASA*] (MCD)
PSE......... Payload Service (or Servicing) Equipment (SAUS)
PSE......... Payload Servicing Equipment [*NASA*] (NAKS)
PSE......... Payload Support Equipment [*NASA*] (MCD)
PSE......... Peculiar Support Equipment [*NASA*] (NASA)
PSE......... Penicillin-Sensitive Enzymes [*Biochemistry*]
PSE......... Personal and Social Education (DET)
PSE......... Personal Security Environment (SAUS)
PSE......... Personnel Subsystem Elements [*Army*] (AABC)
PSE......... Perth Stock Exchange [*Australia*]
PSE......... Phase Shifter, Electronic (SAUS)
PSE......... Phase-Shifter, Electronic
PSE......... Philadelphia Stock Exchange
PSE......... Philippine Stock Exchange
PSE......... Photosensitive Epilepsy
PSE......... Physical Security Equipment [*Army*] (RDA)
PSE......... Physiological Systems Experiment (SAUS)
PSE......... Phytochemical Society of Europe (EA)
PSE......... Pidgin Sign English (ODA)
PSE......... Pigin Signed English
PSE......... Pi Sigma Epsilon (EA)
PSE......... Pitch Steering Error
pse......... Planed and Square-Edge (DAC)
PSE......... Planed and Square Edged (SAUS)
PSE......... Pleasant Saturday Evenings
PSE......... Pleasant Sunday Evenings (ROG)
PSE......... Please (MDG)
PSE......... Pneumatic System Equipment [*Automotive engineering*]
PSE......... Point of Subjective Equality [*Psychology*]
PSE......... Polestar Exploration, Inc. [*Vancouver Stock Exchange symbol*]
PSE......... Ponce [*Puerto Rico*] [*Airport symbol*] (OAG)
PSE......... Portal Systemic Encephalopathy [*Medicine*]
PSE......... Post-Secondary Education (FOTI)
PSE......... Post-Separation Employment
PSE......... Postshunt Encephalopathy [*Medicine*]
PSE......... Power Spectrum Equalization [*Electronics*]
PSE......... Power Switching Electronics (ACAE)
PSE......... Power System Engineering (MCD)

PSE .... Present State Examination [*Medicine*] (DMAA)
PSE .... Pressurized Subcritical Experiment [*Nuclear energy*]
PSE .... Pre-Stamped Envelope
PSE .... Prevention of Stripping Equipment (NATG)
PSE .... Principal Staff Element [*Defense Supply Agency*]
PSE .... Print Scan Emitter [*Computer science*] (VLIE)
PSE .... Priority Standardization Effort [*Army*] (AABC)
PSE .... Prison Service Establishment (AIE)
PSE .... Probability of Successful Engagement [*Military*] (CAAL)
PSE .... Processor Speed Enhancement (SAUS)
PSE .... Process Systems Engineering
PSE .... Producer Subsidy Equivalent [*OECD model for the study of farm-support policies in the EC, Japan, America, Canada, Australia, and New Zealand*]
PSE .... Product Support Engineering (MCD)
PSE .... Programmed System Evolution (MCD)
PSE .... Programming Support Environment
PSE .... Program Sub-Element (SAUS)
PSE .... Program Supplement (COE)
PSE .... Propane Asphalt/Short Residue Extract [*Petroleum engineering*]
PSE .... Protein Separation Efficiency [*Food technology*]
PSE .... Proximal Sequence Element [*Genetics*]
PSE .... Proximal Stimulating Electrode (DB)
PSE .... Psychological Stress Evaluation
PSE .... Psychological Stress Evaluator [*Lie detector*]
PSE .... Public Sector [*or Service*] Employment
PSE .... Public Service Electric & Gas Co., Newark, NJ [*OCLC symbol*] (OCLC)
PSE .... Public Service Employment (EBF)
PSE .... Pulse Sense
PSE .... Purified Spleen Extract [*Medicine*] (DMAA)
PSEA .... Pacific and Southeast Asia (DNAB)
PSEA .... Pennsylvania State Education Association (SAUS)
PSEA .... Physical Security Equipment Agency [*Army*]
PSEA .... Pleaters, Stitchers, and Embroiderers Association (EA)
PSEA .... Public Service Employment Act (FOTI)
PSEAG .... Physical Security Equipment Action Group [*Department of Defense*] (SEWL)
PSE & C .... Power Supply Engineering and Construction [*Nuclear energy*] (NRCH)
PSE & G .... Public Service Electric & Gas Co.
PSEB .... Poisoning Surveillance and Epidemiology Branch [*Defunct*] (EA)
PSEB .... Punjab State Electricity Board [*India*] (BUAC)
PSEBM ...... Proceedings of the Society for Experimental Biology and Medicine [*A publication*]
P/SEC .... Personal Secretary (DCTA)
psec .... Picosecond [*Alternative of preferred ps*] (IDOE)
PSEC .... Picosecond [*One trillionth of a second*]
PSECT .... Program Section (VLIE)
PSECU .... Pennsylvania State Employees Credit Union (SAUS)
PSED .... Preliminary Systems Engineering Design
PSEDGP ..... Perth South East Division Division of General Practice (SAUS)
PSEF .... Pennsylvania Science and Engineering Foundation
PSEF .... Plastic Surgery Educational Foundation (EA)
PSEFA .... Production Standard Evolution Form-Airframe (SAUS)
PSEFC .... Production Standard Evolution Form-Engines (SAUS)
PSEG .... PSE & G Capital Trust [*Associated Press*] (SAG)
PSEG .... Public Service Electric & Gas Co. [*Associated Press*] (SAG)
PSEG .... Public Service Enterprise Group, Inc. (EFIS)
PSEG PAC... Public Service Enterprise Group Inc. PAC [*Newark, NJ*] (PACS)
PSEK .... Probability of Single Shot Engagement Kill [*Military*]
PSEK .... Progressive Symmetrical Erythrokeratoderma [*Medicine*] (DMAA)
PSEL .... Plant Specific Emission Limit (SARE)
PSEL .... Presentation Selector (VLIE)
PSelS .... Susquehanna University, Selinsgrove, PA [*Library symbol*] [*Library of Congress*] (LCLS)
PSEM .... Pericom Semiconductor Corp. [*NASDAQ symbol*] (NASQ)
PSEM .... Philips Scanning Electron Microscope (SAUS)
PSEMA ...... Parti Social d'Education des Masses Africaines [*African Party for Social Education of the Masses*] [*Burkina Faso*]
PSE Muscle... Pale, Soft Exudative Muscle (SAUS)
PSEN .... Pupils with Special Educational Needs (SAUS)
PseOG .... Pease Oil & Gas Co. [*Associated Press*] (SAG)
PSEP .... Passive Seismic Experiments Package [*NASA*]
PSEP .... Physical Security Evaluation Procedure [*US Army Construction Engineering Research Laboratory*] (RDA)
PSEQ .... Pupil Services Expectation Questionnaire
PSER .... Peak Systolic Ejection Rate (SAUS)
PSER .... Production Support and Equipment Replacement (SAUS)
PSERC .... Power Systems Engineering Research Center (RCD)
PSERC .... Public Sector Economics Research Centre [*University of Leicester*] [*British*] (CB)
PSERC .... Public Service Employee Relations Commission [*British Columbia, Canada*] (FOTI)
PSERVER... Print Server [*Computer science*] (VLIE)
PSES .... P-bit Severely Errored Seconds (SAUS)
PSES .... Pretreatment Standards for Existing Sources [*Environmental Protection Agency*]
PSET .... Permanent Service on Earth Tides (SAUS)
PSET .... Pre-Selection English Test [*Australia*]
P Sett .... Previous Settlement (SAUS)
PSEU .... Production Support Equipment Unit (MCD)
PSEU .... Public Service Executive Union [*Ireland*] (BUAC)
PSEU .... Public Services Employees' Union [*Afghanistan*] (BUAC)
PSEU .... Pylon Servo Electronic Unit (SAUS)
pseud .... pseudandry (SAUS)
Pseud .... Pseudepigrapha (BJA)
pseud .... pseudepigraphy (SAUS)
pseud .... pseudograph (SAUS)
pseud .... pseudojyn (SAUS)
pseud .... Pseudonym (BEE)
PSEUD ...... Pseudonym
pseud .... pseudonyma (SAUS)
Pseudep .... Pseudepigrapha (BJA)
PSEUDO ..... Pseudonym [*Legal shorthand*] (LWAP)
PSEUDOEPH... Pseudoephedrine Hydrochloride (SAUS)
PSEUDOEPH SULF... Pseudoephedrine Sulfate (SAUS)
PSEUDOEPH TAN... Pseudoephedrine Tannate (SAUS)
PSEW .... Project on the Status and Education of Women (EA)
PSewD ...... Dixmont State Hospital, Sewickley, PA [*Library symbol*] [*Library of Congress*] (LCLS)
PSF .... Pakistan Science Foundation
PSF .... Panama Sea Frontier
PSF .... Panhandle & Santa Fe Railway Co. [*AAR code*]
PSF .... Parents for Safe Food [*An association*] (BUAC)
PSF .... Parti Social Francais [*French Social Party*] [*Political party*] (PPE)
PSF .... Passive Solar Foundation [*Defunct*] (EA)
PSF .... Pattern Sensitive Fault (SAUS)
PSF .... Payload Servicing Fixture (SAUS)
PSF .... Payload Structure Fuel [*Ratio*]
PSF .... Peptide Supply Factor [*Biochemistry*]
PSF .... Performance Shaping Factor [*Engineering*]
PSF .... Performance Shaping Factors (SAUS)
PSF .... Permanent Signal Finder
PSF .... Permanent Swap File (SAUS)
PSF .... Personal Silicon Foundry (IAA)
PSF .... Per Square Foot (ADA)
PSF .... Phelps-Stokes Fund (SAUS)
PSF .... Philippine Sea Frontier
PSF .... Pittsfield [*Massachusetts*] [*Airport symbol*] (AD)
PSF .... Pittsfield, MA [*Location identifier*] [*FAA*] (FAAL)
PSF .... Plutonium Stripper Feed [*Nuclear energy*] (NRCH)
PSF .... Point Spread Function
PSF .... Polystyrene Foam (SAUS)
PSF .... Polysulfon (SAUS)
PSF .... Polysulfone [*Organic chemistry*]
PSF .... Popular Struggle Front [*Palestine*] [*Political party*] (PD)
PSF .... Port Stanley [*Falkland Islands*] [*Seismograph station code, US Geological Survey*] [*Closed*] (SEIS)
PSF .... Posterior Spinal Fusion [*Medicine*] (DAVI)
PSF .... Post Stimulus Flow (SAUS)
PSF .... Pound-Force per Square Foot (IAA)
PSF .... Pound-force/Square Foot (SAUS)
psf .... Pounds per Square Foot (IDOE)
PSF .... Pounds per Square Foot
PSF .... Power Separation Filter (IAA)
PSF .... Preservation Services Fund
PSF .... Presidio of San Francisco [*Military*] (AABC)
PSF .... Prime Subframe (MCD)
PSF .... Print Services Facility (SAUS)
PSF .... Private Sector Financing (SAUS)
PSF .... Private Source Funds (DNAB)
PSF .... Probability of Spurious Fire [*Military*] (CAAL)
PSF .... Probability Sample File [*Human Relations Area Files*] [*Information retrieval*]
PSF .... Processing and Staging Facility [*Solid rocket booster*] (NASA)
PSF .... Processing and Storage Facility [*NASA*] (NASA)
PSF .... Process Signal Former (IAA)
PSF .... Production Sharin Formula (SAUS)
PSF .... Product Sharing Formula (SAUS)
PSF .... Program for the Study of the Future (EA)
PSF .... Program Support Facility (USDC)
PSF .... Progressive Space Forum [*Defunct*] (EA)
PSF .... Progres Social Francais [*French Social Progress*] [*Political party*] (PPE)
PSF .... Provisional Sinn Fein [*Northern Ireland*]
PSF .... Provisional System Feature [*Telecommunications*] (TEL)
PSF .... Prudential Strategic Income Fund [*NYSE symbol*] (COMM)
PSF .... Pseudosarcomatous Fasciitis [*Medicine*]
PSF .... Saint Francis College, Loretto, PA [*OCLC symbol*] (OCLC)
PSFAM ...... Parameter Sensitive Frequency Assignment Method (MCD)
PSFC .... Pacific Salmon Fisheries Commission (BUAC)
PSFC .... People's-Sidney Financial Corp. [*NASDAQ symbol*] (NASQ)
PS/FC .... Power Supply / Frequency Converter (DWSG)
PSFC .... Power Supply/Fuel Cell (NAKS)
PSFC .... Process Supercritical Fluid Chromatography
PSFC .... Provisional Special Forces Co. (CINC)
PSFC/HIMH... Buzzcocks Fan Club/Harmony in My Head (EA)
PSFC/HIMH... Pete Shelley Fan Club/Harmony in My Head (EA)
PSFD .... Public Sector Financial Deficit
PSFG .... Permanent Service for the Fluctuation of Glaciers (SAUS)
PSFHQ ...... Philippine Sea Frontier Headquarters (SAUS)
PSFI .... PS Financial, Inc. [*NASDAQ symbol*] (SAG)
PS Fincl ..... PS Financial, Inc. [*Associated Press*] (SAG)
PSFL .... Pacific-Slope Flycatcher [*North American bird banding code*] (BIBA)
PSFL .... Puget Sound Freight Lines [*AAR code*]
PSFQ .... Pupil Services Fulfillment Questionnaire
PSF Ratio... Payload, Structure, Fuel Ratio (SAUS)
PSFS .... Philadelphia Savings Fund Society (SAUS)

PSFS .... Process Safety Flow Schematic [*Petroleum engineering*]
PSFT .... Peoplesoft, Inc. [*NASDAQ symbol*] (SAG)
PSFZ .... Port of San Francisco [*Federal Railroad Administration identification code*]
PSG .... Pacific Seabird Group (EA)
PSG .... Palestine Study Group (EA)
PSG .... Parachute Study Group (EA)
PSG .... Paralleling Switchgear [*Motor generators*]
PSG .... Parti Socialiste Guyanais [*Guiana Socialist Party*] [*Political party*] (PPW)
PSG .... Passage [*NWS*] (FAAC)
PSG .... Passing [*Telegraphy*] (PCTE)
psg .... passing (SAUS)
PSG .... Passiv Sonar Geraet (SAUS)
PSG .... Pathology Support Group [*National Institute of Environmental Health Sciences*] (RCD)
PSG .... Peak Systolic Gradient [*Medicine*] (MAE)
PSG .... Permanent Steering Group
PSG .... Pershing [*Missile*] (GFGA)
PSG .... Personnel Subsystem Group (SAA)
PSG .... Peru Support Group (BUAC)
PSG .... Petersburg [*Alaska*] [*Airport symbol*] (OAG)
PSG .... Petersburg, AK [*Location identifier*] [*FAA*] (FAAL)
PSG .... Phenol Sector Group [*European Council of Chemical Manufacturers Federations*] [*Belgium*] (EAIO)
PSG .... Phosphate-Saline-Glucose [*A buffer*] [*Cell culture*]
PSG .... Phosphor-Silicate Glass (SAUS)
PSG .... Phosphosilicate Glass (IEEE)
PSG .... Phrase Structure Grammar (SAUS)
PSG .... Phrase-Structure Grammar [*Computer science*]
PSG .... Planning Systems Generator
PSG .... Platoon Sergeant [*Army*] (AABC)
PSG .... Polysomnogram [*Medicine*] (MAE)
PSG .... Polysomnography (DIPS)
PSG .... Post Stall Gyration (MCD)
PSG .... Power Subsystem Group [*NASA*] (MCD)
PSG .... Prask-Structive Grammar (SAUS)
PSG .... Pregnancy-Specific Glycoprotein [*Biochemistry*]
PSG .... Presystolic Gallop [*Cardiology*]
PSG .... Production Support Group (NITA)
PSG .... Production System Generator
PSG .... Production Systems Group (SAUS)
PSG .... Product Support Group (SAUS)
PSG .... Professional Service Group (SAUS)
PSG .... Professional Specialty Group
PSG .... Programmable Sequence Generator [*Computer science*] (CIST)
PSG .... Programmable Signal Generator (SAUS)
PSG .... Programmable Sound Generator [*Chip*] [*Atari, Inc.*]
PSG .... Programmable Symbol Generator
PSG .... Program Systems Guide (SAUS)
PSG .... Project Science Group (ACAE)
PSG .... Pseudomonas Syringae PV Glycinea [*Plant pathology*]
PSG .... PS Group Holdings [*NYSE symbol*] [*Formerly, PS Group, Inc.*] (SG)
PSG .... PS Group, Inc. [*NYSE symbol*] (SPSG)
PSG .... Psychogalvanometer
PSG .... Psychogalvanometric (SAUS)
PSG .... Psychological Studies Group [*Military*] (VNW)
PSG .... Public Strategies Group, Inc. [*Consulting firm hired in 1993 to improve Minneapolis school district*] (ECON)
PSG .... Publishing Systems Group [*Later, CPSUG*] (EA)
PSG .... Pulsed Strain Gauge (IAA)
PSG .... Pulse Sequence Generation [*Instrumentation*]
PSG .... Pulse Signal Generator (IAA)
PSG .... Pulse Sweep Generator (SAUS)
PSG .... Radioallergosorbent Test [*Syndromes*] [*Medicine*] (QSUL)
PSGA .... Parkinson Support Groups of America (EA)
PSGA .... Pedal Steel Guitar Association (EA)
PSGA .... Professional Skaters Guild of America (EA)
PSGAG .... Polysulfated glycosaminoglycan (SAUS)
PSGB .... Pharmaceutical Society of Great Britain
PSGB .... Primate Society of Great Britain (DBA)
PSGBI .... Pathological Society of Great Britain and Ireland (SAUS)
PSGC .... Pennsylvania Space Grant Consortium (RCD)
PSGCU .... Palm Springs Golf 'Unit' [*NASDAQ symbol*] (TTSB)
PSGD .... Past Senior Grand Deacon [*Freemasonry*]
PSGE .... Partido Socialdemocrata de Guinea Ecuatorial [*Social Democratic Party of Equatorial Guinea*] [*Political party*] (EY)
PSGE .... Passage [*Postal Service standard*] (OPSA)
PSGE .... Photosynthetic Gas Exchanger (SAA)
PSGE .... Project Specification Group Engineer
PSG-EG .... Partido Socialista Galego - Esquerda Galega [*Spain*] [*Political party*] (EY)
PSGI .... Permanent Service for Geomagnetic Indices (SAUS)
PSGI .... Permanent Service on Geomagnetic Indices (SAUS)
PSGL .... P-Selectin Glycoprotein Ligand [*Biochemistry*]
PSGM .... Past Supreme Grand Master [*Freemasonry*]
PSG Mask .. Phosphosilicate Glass Mask (SAUS)
PSGN .... Post-Streptococcal Glomerulonephritis [*Medicine*]
PSGR .... Passenger (AFM)
psgr .... Passenger (TVEL)
PSGR LNG ... Passenger Lounge (SAUS)
PS Grp .... PS Group, Inc. [*Associated Press*] (SAG)
P-SGT .... P-channel Silicon Gate (SAUS)
PSGT .... Platoon Sergeant [*Military*]
PSGTCAEI ... Permanent Secretariat of the General Treaty on Central American Economic Integration (EAIO)
PSGV .... Pacific Sentinel Gold Corp. [*NASDAQ symbol*] (SAG)
PSGVF .... Pacific Sentinel Gold [*NASDAQ symbol*] (TTSB)
PSGW .... Past Senior Grand Warden [*Freemasonry*]
PSH .... Friends Historical Library of Swarthmore College, Swarthmore, PA [*OCLC symbol*] (OCLC)
PSH .... Parshall, ND [*Location identifier*] [*FAA*] (FAAL)
PSH .... Past Social History (CPH)
PSH .... Past Surgical History [*Medicine*] (DMAA)
PSH .... Permanent Shift of Hearing
PSH .... Peshawar [*Pakistan*] [*Seismograph station code, US Geological Survey*] (SEIS)
PSH .... Phase Shift (MSA)
PSH .... Physical Services Header (SAUS)
PSH .... Polystyrene, Hydrogenous [*Organic chemistry*]
PSH .... Postspinal Headache (AAMN)
PSH .... Post-Stimulus Histogram [*Psychometrics*]
PSH .... Preselect Heading (NG)
PSH .... Pressure Switch, High [*Nuclear energy*] (NRCH)
PSH .... Productive Standard Hour (PDAA)
PSH .... Program Support Handbook
PSH .... Provisional Site Handover (SAUS)
PSH .... Proximity Sensing Head
PSH .... Publications Statistiques Hongroises [*Hungary*]
PSH .... Public Storage Canadian Properties IIIa Ltd. [*Toronto Stock Exchange symbol*]
P-Shaw .... George Bernard Shaw (SAUS)
P Shaw .... Patrick Shaw's Justiciary Cases [*1819-31*] [*Scotland*] [*A publication*] (DLA)
PSHB .... Persistent Spectral Hole-Burning [*Spectroscopy*]
PSHC .... Permanent Secretariat of the Hemispheric Congress (EA)
PSHC .... Public Speaking and Humor Club (EA)
PSHCJ .... Philanthropic Society of House Carpenters and Joiners [*A union*] [*British*]
PSHD .... Phase-Shift Driver (MSA)
PSHD .... Port Security Harbor Defense (DOMA)
PSHF .... Polysulfone Hollow Fiber [*Filtration membrane*]
PSHFA .... Public Servants' Housing and Finance Association [*British*] (BI)
PSHPZ .... PSH Master LP I [*OTCBB symbol*]
PSHR .... Project Safety & Health Review (SAUS)
PSHR .... Pusher [*Freight*]
PSHRPQ .... Program Support for Hardware RPQ (SAUS)
PSHS .... Propulsion Systems Hazards Subcommittee [*Military*]
PShS .... Shippensburg State College, Shippensburg, PA [*Library symbol*] [*Library of Congress*] (LCLS)
PSHSGB ..... Polar System History Society of Great Britain (BUAC)
PSHT .... Powys Self-Help Trust [*British*]
PSHTM .... Pilot Scale High Temperature Melter (ABAC)
PSHX .... Puget Sound Railway Historical Association [*Federal Railroad Administration identification code*]
PSI .... Pacific Semiconductors, Inc. (MCD)
PSI .... Pacific Stratus Investigation [*Marine science*] (OSRA)
PSI .... Pacific Sulfur Investigation [*Marine science*] (OSRA)
PSI .... Pacific Sulfur/Stratus Investigation (USDC)
PSI .... Packet Switching Interface (SAUS)
PSI .... Packet Switch Interface (SAUS)
PSI .... Page Survival Index (PDAA)
PSI .... Paid Service Indication [*Telecommunications*] (TEL)
PSI .... Pakistan Standards Institution (IAA)
PSI .... Palmar Sweat Index (EDAC)
PSI .... Paralog Systems International (IID)
PSI .... Parameter Setting Instruction (SAUS)
PSI .... Parameter Signature Identification (SAUS)
PSI .... Parapat [*Sumatra*] [*Seismograph station code, US Geological Survey*] (SEIS)
PSI .... Parapsychological Services Institute (EA)
PSI .... Parapsychology (SAUS)
PSI .... Parenting Stress Index [*Psychology*]
PSI .... Partai Socialis Indonesia [*Socialist Party of Indonesia*]
PSI .... Participation Systems, Inc. [*Electronics Communications Co.*] [*Winchester , MA*] [*Telecommunications*] (TSSD)
PSI .... Particle-Sizing Interferometer (MCD)
PSI .... Parti Socialiste Ivoirien [*Ivorian Socialist Party*] [*The Ivory Coast*] [*Political party*] (EY)
PSI .... Partito Socialista Italiano [*Italian Socialist Party*] [*Political party*] (PPE)
PSI .... Pasni [*Pakistan*] [*Airport symbol*] (OAG)
PSI .... Passive Solar Institute [*Defunct*] (EA)
PSI .... Pathfinder Systems Inc. (SAUS)
PSI .... Paul Scherrer Institute [*Switzerland*] (BUAC)
PSI .... Percent Similarity Index
PSI .... Performance Systems International (SAUS)
PSI .... Performance Systems International, Inc.
PSI .... Periodic Somatic Inactivity [*Medicine*] (EDAA)
PSI .... Peripherally Synapsing Interneuron [*Neurology*]
PSI .... Peripheral Subsystem Interface [*Computer science*] (IAA)
PSI .... Permanent Staff Instructor [*Military*] [*British*]
PSI .... Permuterm Subject Index [*Institute for Scientific Information*] [*A publication*] (IID)
PSI .... Perpetual Storage, Inc., Salt Lake City, UT [*Library symbol*] [*Library of Congress*] (LCLS)
PSI .... Persist [*Telegraphy*] (PCTE)
PSI .... Personalised System of Induction (AIE)
PSI .... Personalized Self-Instruction System [*Psychology*] (QSUL)

PSI.......... Personalized System of Instruction
PSI.......... Personal Security Identifier [*Computer science*] (ELAL)
PSI.......... Personal Sequential-Inference Machine [*Computer science*]
PSI.......... Personal Sequential Interface (SAUS)
PSI.......... Personal Service Income
PSI.......... Personal Style Indicator [*Test*] (TMMY)
PSI.......... Personnel Security Investigation [*Military*]
PSI.......... Personnel Selection Inventory [*Test*]
PSI.......... Person of Special Importance [*British military*] (DMA)
PSI.......... Per Square Inch (ADA)
PSI.......... Petit SystSme Informatique (SAUS)
PSI.......... Pet Sitters International (NTPA)
PSI.......... Pharmaceutical Society of Ireland (BI)
PSI.......... Phenomenological Systems, Inc.
PSI.......... Photographic Society International (EA)
PSI.......... Photographic Society of Ireland (BI)
PSI.......... Photometric Sunspot Index
PSI.......... Photon Science Instruments (SAUS)
PSI.......... Photo Services Industrial Ltd. [*British*]
PSI.......... Photosystems I [*Plant physiology*] (QSUL)
PSI.......... Physical, Sensitivity, Intellectual [*Biorhythmics*]
PSI.......... Physicians Services Inc. (SAUS)
PSI.......... Physiologic Stability Index [*Medicine*] (EDAA)
PSI.......... Pilot Steering Indicator (SAUS)
PSI.......... Planetary Science Institute (RCD)
PSI.......... Planned Speed Indicator
PSI.......... Planned Start Installation [*Telecommunications*] (TEL)
PSI.......... Plan Shear Indicator (SAUS)
PSI.......... Plan Speed Indicator [*Military*]
PSI.......... Plas Speed Indicator (IAA)
PSI.......... Platoon Sector Indicator [*Army*]
PSI.......... Play Skills Inventory
PSI.......... Policy Studies Institute [*Research center*] [*British*] (IRC)
PSI.......... Pollutant Standards Index [*Environmental Protection Agency*]
PSI.......... Pollution Standards Index (SARE)
p-Si.......... Polycrystalline Silicon [*Photovoltaic energy systems*]
PSI.......... Population Services Inc. (SAUS)
PSI.......... Population Services International (BUAC)
PSI.......... Porta Systems [*AMEX symbol*] (TTSB)
PSI.......... Porta Systems Corp. [*AMEX symbol*] (SPSG)
PSI.......... Positive Self-Image [*Psychology*]
PSI.......... Posterior Sagittal Index [*Anatomy*] (AAMN)
PSI.......... Posterior Superior Iliac Spine [*Posterosuperior iliac spine*] [*Anatomy*] (DAVI)
PSI.......... Postpartum Support, International (EA)
PSI.......... Postscript Interpreter (SAUS)
PSI.......... Post-Tensioning Institute (WPI)
PSI.......... Potential Savings Index (SAUS)
PSI.......... Pound-Force per Square Inch (IAA)
psi.......... Pounds per Square Inch (IDOE)
PSI.......... Pounds per Square Inch
PSI.......... Pounds per Square Inch Absolute (IAA)
PSI.......... Power per Square Inch
PSI.......... Power Semiconductors, Inc. (SAUS)
PSI.......... Power Solutions Incorporated
PSI.......... Power Static Inverter (NASA)
PSI.......... Praed Street Irregulars (EA)
PSI.......... Preprogrammed Self-Instruction [*Computer science*] (IEEE)
PSI.......... Preschool Inventory (EDAC)
PSI.......... Pre-Sentence Investigation (OICC)
PSI.......... Present Serviceability Index (IEEE)
PSI.......... Preservice Inspection [*Nuclear energy*] (NRCH)
PSI.......... Pre-Shipment and Inspection (SAUS)
PSI.......... Preshipment Inspection [*International trade*]
PSI.......... President of the Service Institute (SAUS)
PSI.......... Pressure per Square Inch (EEVL)
PSI.......... Pressure Sensitive Identification
PSI.......... Pressurized Sphere Injection (DNAB)
PSI.......... Pressurized Sphere Injector (SAUS)
PSI.......... Presynaptic Inhibition (SAUS)
PSI.......... Prime System Indicator
PSI.......... Private Sector Initiatives (SAUS)
PSI.......... Probe Systems, Inc.
PSI.......... Problem-Solving and Inference Machine (IAA)
PSI.......... Problem Solving Information (SAUS)
PSI.......... Problem-Solving Information [*Apparatus*]
PSI.......... Problem-Solving Interpreter [*Computer language*]
PSI.......... Processor Simulator (SAUS)
PSI.......... Process Safety Information (SAUS)
PSI.......... Process Science Initiative [*Manufacturing engineering*]
PSI.......... Process System Index
PSI.......... Process Systems, Inc.
PSI.......... Process to Support Interoperability (SAUS)
PSI.......... Proctorial System of Instruction (IEEE)
PSI.......... Production Stock Item (MCD)
PSI.......... Product Support Instructions (AAG)
PSI.......... Professional Secretaries International [*Kansas City, MO*] (EA)
PSI.......... Professional Services Income (WDAA)
PSI.......... Professional Services Index [*Medicine*] (EDAA)
PSI.......... Programmable Series Interface (SAUS)
PSI.......... Programmed School Input (NVT)
PSI.......... Program Status Information [*Computer science*] (MCD)
PSI.......... Program Supply Interest (MCD)
PSI.......... Project Security Instruction (SAUS)
PSI.......... Project Starlight International (EA)
PSI.......... Prostaglandin Synthetase Inhibition [*Medicine*] (EDAA)
PSI.......... Protosynthetic Indexing (NITA)
PSI.......... Protosynthex Index
PSI.......... Pseudomonas Sp. Lipase
PSI.......... PSI Energy [*Associated Press*] (SAG)
PSI.......... Psychiatric Society for Informatics (SAUS)
PSI.......... Psychological Screening Inventory [*Personality development test*]
PSI.......... Psychological Society of Ireland (BUAC)
PSI.......... Psychosomatic Inventory [*Psychology*]
PSI.......... Publications Standing Instruction (AAG)
PSI.......... Public Services International [*See also ISP*] [*Ferney Voltaire, France*] (EAIO)
PSI.......... Pulsepower Systems Incorporated
PSI.......... Pulse Sciences, Inc.
PSIA.......... Paper Stock Institute of America (EA)
PSIA.......... Pound-Force per Square Inch, Absolute (SAUS)
psia.......... Pounds per Square Inch Absolute (IDOE)
PSIA.......... Pounds per Square Inch Absolute
PSIA.......... President of the Society of Industrial Artists [*British*]
PSIA.......... Pressure Absolute [*AGA*] (TAG)
PSIA.......... Production System Integration Area
PSIA.......... Professional Ski Instructors of America (EA)
PSIA.......... Public Security Investigation Agency [*Japan*] (CINC)
PSI Apparatus... Problem Solving Information Apparatus (SAUS)
PSI-B.......... Personnel Selection Inventory for Banking [*Test*] (TES)
PSIC.......... Pacific Scientific Information Center (SAUS)
PSIC.......... Passenger Service Improvement Corp.
PSIC.......... Passive Solar Industries Council (EA)
PSIC.......... Planning and Systems Integration Center (SAUS)
PSIC.......... Process Signal Interface Controller
PSIC.......... Production Scheduling and Inventory Control
P-SiC.......... P-type Silicon-Carbide (SAUS)
PSICOMP... Predicted Speech Intelligibility Computer (IAA)
Psicor.......... PSICOR, Inc. [*Associated Press*] (SAG)
PSID.......... Panel Study of Income Dynamics
PSID.......... Partial Seismic Intrusion Device (MCD)
PSID.......... Patrol Seismic Intrusion Detector [*or Device*] [*DoD*]
PSID.......... Persisted [*Telegraphy*] (PCTE)
PSID.......... Postscript Image Data (SAUS)
PSID.......... Pounds per Square Inch Differential (MCD)
psid.......... Pounds per Square Inch, Differential [*Marine science*] (OSRA)
PSID.......... Preliminary Safety Information Document [*Nuclear energy*] (NRCH)
PSID.......... Presentation Space Identifier (SAUS)
PSIDC.......... Punjab State Industrial Development Corp. [*India*] (BUAC)
PS/IDS.......... Physical Security/Intrusion Detection System (MCD)
PSIEP.......... Project on Scientific Information Exchange in Psychology [*Superseded by Office of Communication*]
PSIF.......... Prison Service Industries & Farming (WDAA)
PSIF.......... Prison Service Industries and Farms (BUAC)
PSIF.......... Reverse Fast Imaging with Steady-State Free Precession (RAWO)
PSIFC.......... Pat Shea International Fan Club (EA)
PSIFET.......... Power Silicon Field-Effect Transistor (SAUS)
PSIFT.......... Platelet Suspension Immunofluorescence Test [*Medicine*] (DMAA)
PSIG.......... Partial Signalling (SAUS)
PSIG.......... Persisting [*Telegraphy*] (PCTE)
PSIG.......... Per-Square-Inch Gauge (AAGC)
PSIG.......... Per Square Inch on the Gauge (SAUS)
PSIG.......... Pound-Force per Square Inch, Gauge (SAUS)
psig.......... Pounds per Square Inch Gauge (IDOE)
psig.......... Pressure per Square Inch Gauge (COE)
PSIG.......... Pressure per Square Inch Gauge (EPAT)
PSIG.......... Propulsion Systems Integration Group [*NASA*] (NASA)
PSII.......... Photosystems II [*Plant physiology*] (QSUL)
PSII.......... Plasma Source Ion Implantation (AAEL)
PSII.......... Process Safety Incident Investigation [*Engineering*]
PSII.......... Psychiatric Severity of Illness Index (SAUS)
PSIL.......... Percentage Signal Intensity Loss (RAWO)
PSIL.......... Philippine Society of International Law (BUAC)
PSIL.......... Potential Selected Item List (MCD)
PSIL.......... Preferred Speech Interference Level
PSI-LOGO... Listing of Oil and Gas Opportunities [*Online Resource Exchange, Inc.*] [*Database*]
PSI(L)(R)... Pvasi (Left or Right Side of Runway) [*Aviation*] (PIPO)
PSIM.......... Power System Instrumentation and Measurement (MCD)
PSIM.......... Problem-Solving Instructional Material [*National Science Foundation project*]
PSI-Machine... Personal Sequential Inference Machine (SAUS)
PSIMPLE... Problem-Solving In Medical Physiology, Logically Explained (SAUS)
PSINet.......... PSINet, Inc. [*Associated Press*] (SAG)
PSIO.......... Performance Scales Intelligence Quotient (EDAC)
PSIP.......... Periodic Smoke Inspection Program [*Diesel engine emissions*]
PSIP.......... Poultry Stock Improvement Plan (SAUS)
PSIP.......... Private Sector Initiative Program [*Department of Labor*]
PSIP.......... Project on Scientific Information in Psychology (SAUS)
PSIPU.......... Postscript-Intelligent Processing Unit (SAUS)
PSIR.......... Passenger-Side Inflatable Restraint [*Automotive safety systems*]
PSIR.......... Passenger's Side Inflatable Restraint [*Automotive engineering*]
PSIR.......... Phase-Sampled Impulse-Response (SAUS)
PSIR Filter... Phase-Sampled Impulse-Response Filter (SAUS)
PSIS.......... Permanent Secretaries Committee on the Intelligence Services (SAUS)
PSIS.......... Persists [*Telegraphy*] (PCTE)
PSIS.......... Plastic Surgery Information Service (SAUS)

PSIS .... Posterior Sacroiliac Spine [*Anatomy*] (DAVI)
PSIS .... Posterior Superior Iliac Spine [*Medicine*] (STED)
PSIS .... Pounds per Square Inch per Second
psis .... Pounds per Square Inch Sealed (NAKS)
PSIS .... Pounds per Square Inch Sealed (NASA)
PSIS .... Programme for Strategic and International Security Studies [*Switzerland*] (PDAA)
PSIS .... Programming Systems Information System (SAUS)
PSISIG ...... Psychic Science International Special Interest Group (EA)
PSIT .... Persistent [*Telegraphy*] (PCTE)
PSIT .... Property Security Investment Trust [*British*]
PSIT .... PSi Technologies Hldg. ADS [*NASDAQ symbol*] (SG)
PSIU .... Packet Switch Interface Unit (SAUS)
PSIU .... Perfect Circle [*Intermodal shipping container symbol*] (TVRC)
PSIU .... Power/Sequence Interface Unit (MCD)
PSIUP .... Partito Socialista Italiano di Unita Proletaria [*Italian Socialist Party of Proletarian Unity (1945-1947)*] [*Political party*] (PPE)
PSIV .... Passive
PSIX .... Performance Systems International, Inc. [*NASDAQ symbol*] (SAG)
PSIX .... Peripheral Systems, Inc. [*NASDAQ symbol*] (COMM)
PSIX .... Port State Information eXchange [*Database*] (GDD)
PSIX .... PSI Energy [*Private rail car owner code*]
PSIX .... PSINet, Inc. [*NASDAQ symbol*] [*Formerly, Performance Systems International*] (SG)
PSJ .... Palynological Society of Japan (QUAC)
PSJ .... Parallel Swivel Joint
PSJ .... Passage [*Telegraphy*] (PCTE)
PSJ .... Petites Soeurs de Jesus [*Little Sisters of Jesus*] [*Italy*] (EAIO)
PSJ .... Petsec Energy ADS [*NYSE symbol*] (SG)
PSJ .... Pharmaceutical Society of Japan (BUAC)
psj .... Planed and Square-Jointed (DAC)
PSJ .... Plane Swivel Joint
PSJ .... Point Spread Junction (IAA)
PSJ .... Policy Studies Journal (SAUS)
PSJ .... Poso [*Indonesia*] [*Airport symbol*] (OAG)
PSJ .... Pressure Switch Joint
PSJ .... Public Service Job (OICC)
PSJF .... Preemptive Shortest Job First (SAUS)
PSJS .... Pier and Span Junction Set (MCD)
PSK .... Dublin, VA [*Location identifier*] [*FAA*] (FAAL)
PSK .... Personal Survival Kit (SAUS)
PSK .... Petoskey, MI [*Amtrak Busline code*]
PSK .... Phase Shift Keyed (SAUS)
PSK .... Phase Shift Keying [*Computer science*]
PSK .... PostSparKasse [*Post Office Savings Bank*] [*Austria*]
PSK .... Power Supply Kit
PSK .... Private Secretary to the King [*British*]
PSK .... Program Selection Key [*Computer science*] (BUR)
PSK .... Prospect [*Telegraphy*] (PCTE)
PSK .... Protection Survey Kit
PSK .... Protein Serine Kinase (DMAA)
PSK .... Public Storage Properties IX, Inc. [*AMEX symbol*] (SAG)
PSK .... Pulse Shift Keying (CAAL)
PSKD .... Prospected [*Telegraphy*] (PCTE)
PSKG .... Prospecting [*Telegraphy*] (PCTE)
PSKL .... Program Skelton Language (SAUS)
PSKM .... Phase Shift Keyed Modulation (NITA)
PSKM .... Phase-Shift Keying MODEM
PSK-PCM ... Phase-Shift Keying - Pulse Code Modulation
PSKV .... Prospective [*Telegraphy*] (PCTE)
PSL .... Environmental Study Center (SAUS)
PSL .... Pacific Star Line (SAUS)
PSL .... Pakistan Shipping Line (SAUS)
PSL .... Paleobotanical Society of Lucknow (SAUS)
PSL .... Palouse Silt Loam [*Agronomy*]
PSL .... Parallel Strand Lumber
PSL .... Parasternal Line [*Anatomy*] (MAE)
PSL .... Parti Social-Liberal [*Algeria*] [*Political party*] (EY)
PSL .... Parts Selection List (SPST)
PSL .... Patterson Strategy Letter (SAUS)
PSL .... Paymaster-Sub-Lieutenant [*Navy*] [*British*]
PSL .... PD Service Lage (SAUS)
PSL .... Peabody Short Line R. R. [*Army*]
PSL .... Percent Stroke Length [*Medicine*] (STED)
PSL .... Permanent Seat License (SAUS)
PSL .... Perpendicular to the Sun Line (SAUS)
PSL .... Personal [*Telegraphy*] (PCTE)
PSL .... Personal Safety Light [*Police and security equipment*]
PSL .... Personnel Skill Levels (AAG)
PSL .... Perth [*Scotland*] [*Airport symbol*] (AD)
PSL .... Peruvian State Line (SAUS)
PSL .... Petroleum Ether-Soluble Lipid
PSL .... Phase Sequence Logic (IAA)
PSL .... Phase Sequency Logic (SAUS)
PSL .... Philharmonic Society of London (SAUS)
PSL .... Photographic Science Laboratory [*Navy*]
PSL .... Photostimulated Luminescence [*Physics*]
PSL .... Physical Science Libraries (SAUS)
PSL .... Physical Sciences Laboratory [*Bethesda, MD*] [*National Institutes of Health*] (GRD)
PSL .... Physical Sciences Laboratory [*University of Wisconsin - Madison, New Mexico State University*] [*Research center*]
PSL .... Pipe Sleeve
PSL .... Pocket Select Language [*Burroughs Corp.*]
PSL .... Polskie Stronnictwo Ludowe [*Polish Peasant Party*] [*Political party*] (PPE)
PSL .... Poly-crystalline Silicon Layer (SAUS)
PSL .... Polystyrene Latex (PDAA)
PSL .... Portable Standard List Processing [*Computer science*]
PSL .... Port Service Ltd. (SAUS)
PSL .... Potassium, Sodium Chloride, Sodium Lactate [*Solution*] (AAMN)
PSL .... Potential Source List (MCD)
PSL .... Power and Signal List [*Telecommunications*] (TEL)
PSL .... Power Source Logic
PSL .... Power Systems Laboratories (ACAE)
PSL .... Practical Storage Life
PSL .... Prednisolone [*Medicine*] (EDAA)
PSL .... Prescribed Substance License [*Canadian Nuclear Safety Commission*] (FOTI)
PSL .... Pressure Seal (NASA)
PSL .... Pressure Sensitive Label (SAUS)
PSL .... Pressure-Sensitive Label
PSL .... Pretoria State Library (SAUS)
PSL .... Primary Standards Laboratory
PSL .... Priority Substances List [*Ecology*] (FOTI)
PSL .... Private Sector Liquidity
PSL .... Problem-Solving Language
PSL .... Problem Specification Language
PSL .... Problem Statement Language [*Computer science*] (IAA)
PSL .... Processor Status Longword [*Computer science*] (VLIE)
PSL .... Process Simulation Language [*Computer science*] (TEL)
PSL .... Process Status Longword [*Number*] [*Computer science*] (BYTE)
PSL .... Professionnel Air Systems [*France*] [*ICAO designator*] (FAAC)
PSL .... Programming Script Language (PCM)
PSL .... Programming Support Library
PSL .... Program Structuring Language (SAUS)
PSL .... Program Supply Logic Unit (SAUS)
PSL .... Program Support Letter (SAUS)
PSL .... Program Support Library (MCD)
PSL .... Project Support Laboratory [*Military*] (CAAL)
PSL .... Propellant Seal
PSL .... Propulsion Systems Laboratory [*USATACOM*] (RDA)
PSL .... Public School League [*Sports*]
PSL .... Public Software Library (SAUS)
PSL .... Public Storage Properties X, Inc. [*AMEX symbol*] (SAG)
PSL .... Public Storage Prop'A' X [*AMEX symbol*] (TTSB)
PSL .... Pycnocline Scattering Layer (DNAB)
PSL .... South Hills Library Association, Pittsburgh, PA [*OCLC symbol*] (OCLC)
PSLA .... Palaung State Liberation Army [*Myanmar*] [*Political party*] (EY)
PSLA .... Pennsylvania School Librarians Association
PSLA .... Polish Sea League of America (EA)
PSLA .... Pre-School Learning Alliance (WDAA)
PSLAP .... Power Supply Load Analysis Program [*Computer science*] (VLIE)
PSLC .... Parallel Sysplex License Charge [*For software*] (GART)
PSLC .... Post-Schistosomal Liver Cirrhosis [*Medicine*]
PSLC .... Private Security Liaison Council (EA)
PSLD .... Parasympatholytic Drug [*Medicine*] (MELL)
PSLI .... Packet Switch Level Interface
PSLI .... Partito Socialista dei Lavoratori Italiani [*Socialist Party of Italian Workers*] [*Political party*] (PPE)
PSLI .... Physalaemin-Like Immunoreactivity [*Medicine*]
P-slip .... Process Slip
PSLL .... Plymouth Short Line [*Federal Railroad Administration identification code*]
PSL-Lewica... Polskie Stronnictwo-Lewica [*Polish Peasant Party-Left (1947-1949)*] [*Political party*] (PPE)
PSL-Lewica... Polskie Stronnictwo Ludowe-Lewica [*Polish Peasant Party-Left (1913-1920)*] [*Political party*] (PPE)
PSLLS .... Pulsed Solid-State LASER Light Source
PSLM .... Priority Search-Lock Monitor (SAUS)
PSLN .... Pacific Star Line [*Common carrier symbol*]
PSL-NW..... Polskie Stronnictwo Ludowe-Nowe Wyzwolenie [*Polish Peasant Party-New Liberation*] [*Political party*] (PPE)
PSLO .... Palaung State Liberation Organization [*Myanmar*] [*Political party*] (EY)
PSLO .... Provost & Security Liaison Officer (SAUS)
PSLP .... Private Sector Linkages Program (SAUS)
PSL-Piast... Polskie Stronnictwo Ludowe-Piast [*Polish Peasant Party-Piast*] [*Political party*] (PPE)
PSL/PSA .... Problem Statement Language/Problem Specification Analyzer [*Computer science*]
PSL/PSA .... Problem Statement Language/Problem Statement Analysis (SAUS)
PSLR .... Peak Side Lobe Ratio (SAUS)
PSLR .... Product Safety and Liability Reporter [*A publication*]
PSLS .... Pan Stock Line Station (MCD)
PSLS .... Polystyrene Latex Sphere (AAEL)
PSL SOL .... Potassium, Sodium Chloride, Sodium Lactate Solution (BABM)
PSL sol ..... Potassium, Sodium Chloride, Sodium Lactate Solution [*Pharmacology*] (DAVI)
PSLT .... Picture Story Language Test
PSLT .... Port Side Light (IAA)
PSLT .... Pressurized Sonobuoy Launch Tube [*Navy*] (CAAL)
pslt .... Psalter (VRA)
PSLU .... Power Supply Logic Unit (SAUS)
PSLU .... Progenitive Service [*Intermodal shipping container symbol*] (TVRC)
PSLV .... Poa Semilatent Virus
PSLV .... Polar Satellite Launch Vehicle
PSLV .... Polar Space Launch Vehicle [*Indian Space Research*]

PSL-Wyzwolenie... Polskie Stronnictwo Ludowe-Wyzwolenie [*Polish Peasant Party-Liberation*] [*Political party*] (PPE)
PSM......... Monegasque Socialist Party [*Political party*] (PSAP)
PSM......... Packet Service Module [*Computer science*] (VLIE)
PSM......... Packet Switched Signaling Message (CIST)
PSM......... Packet-switched Signalling Message (SAUS)
PSM......... Packet Switching Module (SAUS)
PSM......... Panasystolic Murmur [*Cardiology*] (DAVI)
PSM......... Parallel Slit Map (OA)
PSM......... Parcel Sorting Machine [*Freight*] (DCTA)
PSM......... Parc Saint-Maur [*France*] [*Later, CLF*] [*Geomagnetic observatory code*]
PSM......... Particle Size Monitor [*Instrumentation*]
PSM......... Parti Socialiste Mauricien [*Mauritian Socialist Party*] [*Political party*] (EY)
PSM......... Parti Socialiste Monegasque [*Monaco Socialist Party*] [*Political party*] (PPW)
psm.......... Passed School of Music [*Certificate of the Royal Military School of Music*] (WDAA)
PSM......... Passenger Seat Module [*Automotive engineering*]
PSM......... Passenger Service Manager [*Travel industry*]
PSM......... Paste Striping Machine (SAUS)
PSM......... Past Savio Movement [*Defunct*] (EA)
PSM......... Peak Selector Memory [*Computer science*]
PSM......... People for Self Management [*An association*] (NADA)
PSM......... Persistent Storage Model [*Computer science*] (VLIE)
PSM......... Persistent Stored Module [*Computer science*] (VLIE)
PSM......... Persistent Stored Modules (SAUS)
PSM......... Personal Skills Map [*Career effectiveness test*]
PSM......... Personal Software Marketing (SAUS)
PSM......... Personal Storage Module (SAUS)
PSM......... Personnel Subsystem Manager [*Army*] (AABC)
PSM......... Personnel Systems Management [*Air Force*] (AFM)
PSM......... Personnel Systems Manager (SAUS)
PSM......... Petroleum Supply Monthly [*Database*] [*Department of Energy*] [*Information service or system*] (CRD)
PSM......... Phase Sensitive Modulator (SAUS)
PSM......... Phase-Sensitive Modulator (MCD)
PSM......... Phase Shifter Module (SAUS)
PSM......... Phase-Shifter Module
PSM......... Phase Shifting Mask (AAEL)
PSM......... Phase-Shift Mask (SAUS)
PSM......... Phase Shift Modification (SAUS)
PSM......... Phase Shift Modulation (VLIE)
PSM......... Photo Sensing Mark (SAUS)
PSM......... Physical Society of Moldova (BUAC)
PSM......... Physician and Sports Medicine [*A publication*]
PSM......... Pia Societas Missionum [*Fathers of the Pious Society of Missions, Pallottini*] [*Roman Catholic religious order*]
PSM......... Pioneer Metals Corp. [*Toronto Stock Exchange symbol*] [*Vancouver Stock Exchange symbol*]
PSM......... Platyschisma Shale Member [*Geology*]
PSM......... Please See Me
PSM......... Plymouth State College of the University of New Hampshere, Plymouth, NH [*OCLC symbol*] (OCLC)
PSM......... Point Scattering Model (SAUS)
PSM......... Point Source Modeling (SAUS)
PSM......... Point Source Monitoring [*Environmental Protection Agency*] (GFGA)
PSM......... Porsche Stability Management [*Automotive engineering*]
PSM......... Portal-Systemic Myelopathy [*Medicine*] (MELL)
PSM......... Portsmouth [*New Hampshire*] [*Airport symbol*] (AD)
PSM......... Portsmouth, NH [*Location identifier*] [*FAA*] (FAAL)
PSM......... Position Switching Module [*Computer science*] (VLIE)
PSM......... Positive Sample Mode (SAUS)
PSM......... Postal Service Manual [*A publication*] (AFM)
PSM......... Postmitochondrial Supernatant [*Medicine*] (DMAA)
PSM......... Postsynaptic Membrane [*Neurology*]
PSM......... Power Strapping Machine
PSM......... Power Supply Module (MHDI)
PSM......... Power System Module
PSM......... Preservation Security Manager
PSM......... Pressure-Sensitive Mat
PSM......... Pressure Switch Manifold [*Automotive transmissions*]
PSM......... Presystolic Murmur [*Cardiology*]
PSM......... Printing Systems Manager [*Computer science*] (VLIE)
PSM......... Print Management System (SAUS)
PSM......... Prism (MSA)
PSM......... Probabilistic Sequential Machine (RALS)
PSM......... Problem Solving Module [*Computer science*] (VLIE)
PSM......... Process Safety Management [*Chemical engineering*]
PSM......... Producibility Study Memorandum (SAUS)
PSM......... Production Systems Management (IAA)
PSM......... Productive Standard Minute (MHDI)
PSM......... Product Sales Manager (SAUS)
PSM......... Product Support Manual (AAG)
PSM......... Professional Service Manager (SAUS)
PSM......... Professional Staff Member [*Congress*] (DOMA)
PSM......... Programmable State Machine [*Computer science*] (VLIE)
PSM......... Programming Support Monitor [*Texas Instruments, Inc.*]
PSM......... Programming System Memorandum (SAUS)
PSM......... Programming Systems Manual (SAUS)
PSM......... Program Security Manager (SAUS)
PSM......... Program Sensitive Malfunction (SAUS)
PSM......... Program-Sensitive Malfunction
PSM......... Program Support Management [*NASA*] (KSC)
PSM......... Program Support Material (SAUS)
PSM......... Program Support Monitor [*Computer science*] (ELAL)
PSM......... Progressive Series Modulator (IAA)
PSM......... Project Safety Management
PSM......... Project Security Manager (ADWA)
PSM......... Propellant Storage Module [*NASA*]
PSM......... Proportional Spacing Machine [*Computer science*] (ELAL)
PSM......... Pro Sanctity Movement (EA)
PSM......... Prostate Specific Membrane [*Medicine*]
PSM......... Protocol Sensitive Multiplexing [*Communications term*] (DCT)
PSM......... Public Service Medal
PSM......... Public Storage Properties XI, Inc. [*AMEX symbol*] (SAG)
PSM......... Public Storage Prop'A' XI [*AMEX symbol*] (TTSB)
PSM......... Pulse Slope Modulation (IAA)
PSM......... Pulse-Spacing Modulation (ECII)
PSM......... Pulse Step Modulation (SAUS)
PSM......... Purchasing and Supply Management (GART)
PSM......... Purse-String Mouth (MELL)
PSM......... Pyro Substitute Monitor [*NASA*] (NASA)
PSM......... Pyrotechnic Substitute Monitor
PSm......... Thesaurus Syriacus [*R. Paine Smith*] [*A publication*] (BJA)
PSMA........ Power Saw Manufacturers Association [*Later, CSMA*] (EA)
PSMA........ Power Sources Manufacturers Association (NTPA)
PSMA........ Power Supply Manufacturers Association [*British*] (DBA)
PSMA........ President of the Society of Marine Artists [*British*]
PSMA........ Pressure Sensitive Manufacturers Association [*British*] (DBA)
PSMA........ Professional Services Management Association [*Alexandria, VA*] (EA)
PSMA........ Progressive Spinal Muscular Atrophy [*Medicine*]
PSMA........ Progressive Streptococcal Muscular Atrophy [*Medicine*] (MELL)
PSMA........ Prostate-Specific Membrane Antigen [*Medicine*]
PSMA........ Proximal Spinal Muscular [*Medicine*] (DMAA)
PSMA........ Proximal Spinal Muscular Atrophy [*Medicine*] (DMAA)
PSMA........ Pyrotechnic Signal Manufacturers Association (EA)
PSMC........ Pre-Selected Manual Control (SAUS)
PSMD........ Photo Selective Metal Deposition
PSMD........ Photo-Selective Metal Deposition (SAUS)
PSME........ Partido Socialista de Melilla [*See also PSOE*] [*Spanish North Africa*] [*Political party*] (MENA)
PSME........ Personal Social and Moral Education (AIE)
PSMed...... Psychosomatic Medicine (DAVI)
PSME-PSOE... Partido Socialista de Melilla - Partido Socialista Obrero Espanol [*Political party*] (EY)
PSMF........ Protein Sparing Modified Fast
PSMFC...... Pacific States Marine Fisheries Commission
PSMI........ Phase-Shift Modal Interference
PSMI........ Precise Ship Motion Instrument
PS/Min...... Private Secretary to the Minister (SAUS)
PSMIT...... Programming Services for Multimedia Industry Terminals [*IBM Corp.*]
PSML........ Processor System Modeling Language [*1976*] [*Computer science*] (CSR)
PSML........ Processor System Modelling Language (SAUS)
PSMM........ Multimission Patrol Ship [*Symbol*]
PSMM........ Patrol Ship Multi-Mission (SAUS)
PSMMA...... Plastic Soft Materials Manufacturers Association (EA)
P/S Mode... Parallel/Serial Mode (SAUS)
PSMP........ Program on Short- and Medium-Range Weather Prediction Research [*Marine science*] (OSRA)
PSMP........ Project Software Management Plan (SSD)
PSMP........ Public Sector Management Programme (SAUS)
PSMPA...... Per Square Meter per Annum
PSMR........ Part Specification for Reliability (SAUS)
PSMR........ Parts Specification Management for Reliability
PSMR........ Pneumatic [*or Pressure*] System Manifold Regulator [*or Manual*] (AAG)
PSMR........ Pneumatic System Manual Regulator (SAUS)
PSMR........ Pressure System Manifold Regulator (SAUS)
PSMR........ Pressure System Manual Regulator (SAUS)
PSMRD...... Postsurgical Minimum Residual Disease [*Medicine*] (DB)
PSMS........ Permanent Section of Microbiological Standardization (MCD)
PSMS........ Physical Self Maintenance Scale
PSMSL...... Permanent Service for Mean Sea Level [*of the Federation of Astronomical and Geophysical Data Analysis Services*] [*Birkenhead, Merseyside, England*] (EAIO)
PSMT........ Paced Sequential Memory Task (PDAA)
PSMT........ Patiala State Monorail Trainways [*Indian Railway*] (TIR)
PSMT........ Pedestal Sight Manipulation Test (IAA)
PSMT........ Perishable Sheet Metal Tool (MCD)
PSMT........ Price Smart, Inc. [*NASDAQ symbol*] (NASQ)
PSMT........ Psychiatric Services Management Team (STED)
PSMTA...... Power Supply Modulator Test Adapter (ACAE)
PSMU........ Charles Michaelis [*Intermodal shipping container symbol*] (TVRC)
PSMU........ Power Supply and Multiplexer Unit [*Telecommunications*] (TSSD)
PSMV........ Paspalum Striate Mosaic Virus [*Plant pathology*]
PSMV........ Pea Seed-Borne Mosaic Virus [*Plant pathology*]
PSN.......... National Solidarity Party (Portugal) [*Political party*] (PSAP)
PSN.......... Package Sequence Number
PSN.......... Packet Switched Network
PSN.......... Packet Switching Network (SAUS)
PSN.......... Packet Switching Node
PSN.......... Packet Switch Node
PSN.......... Palestine, TX [*Location identifier*] [*FAA*] (FAAL)
PSN.......... Palm Springs, CA [*Amtrak rail station code*]
PSN.......... Parent Support Network [*Australia*]

PSN .... Partial Shipment Number [*DoD*]
PSN .... Parti de la Solidarite Nationale [*Party of National Solidarity*] [*Luxembourg*] [*Political party*] (PPE)
PSN .... Partido Socialista Nicaraguense [*Nicaraguan Socialist Party*] [*Political party*] (PPW)
PSN .... Payment Systems Network, Inc. (TBD)
PSN .... Penicillin, Streptomycin and Neomycin (SAUS)
PSN .... Pentium Serial Number [*Computer science*]
PSN .... Perfect Shuffle Network (SAUS)
PSN .... Permanent Sort Number [*Computer science*]
PSN .... Persimmon PLC [*London Stock Exchange symbol*]
PSN .... Person [*Telegraphy*] (PCTE)
PSN .... PhotoStockNotes [*Database*] (GDD)
PSN .... Polish Surname Network (EA)
PSN .... Poor Sisters of Nazareth (TOCD)
PSN .... Position
Psn .... Positioning (SAUS)
PSN .... Position Sequence Number (SAUS)
PSN .... Potassium Sodium Niobate (SAUS)
PSN .... Potosina del Aire SA de CV [*Mexico*] [*ICAO designator*] (FAAC)
PSN .... Print Sequence Number [*Computer science*] (ELAL)
PSN .... Private Satellite Network (SAUS)
PSN .... Private Satellite Network, Inc. [*New York, NY*] [*Telecommunications*] (TSSD)
PSN .... Private Switching Networks (SAUS)
PSN .... Processing Serial Number (MCD)
PSN .... Processor Serial Number (SAUS)
PSN .... Professional Speakers Network (NTPA)
PSN .... Program Summary Network (MCD)
PSN .... Progressive Student Network (EA)
PSN .... Provisioning Sequence Number (MCD)
PSN .... Public Storage Properties XII, Inc. [*AMEX symbol*] (SAG)
PSN .... Public Storage Prop'A' XII [*AMEX symbol*] (TTSB)
PSN .... Public Switched Network (BUR)
PSN .... Purge Sequence Number (SAUS)
PSNA .... Pennsylvania State Nurses Association (EARSL)
PSNA .... Phytochemical Society of North America (EA)
PSNA .... Powys Society of North America (EA)
PSNAL .... Personal (FAAC)
PSNAP ...... Programmable Steerable Nulling Antenna Processor (SAUS)
PSNB .... Public-Sector Net Borrowing
PSNB .... Puget Sound Bancorp (EFIS)
PSNC .... Pacific Steam Navigation Co. (MHDW)
PSNC .... Parti Socialiste de la Nouvelle Caledonie [*Socialist Party of New Caledonia*] [*Political party*] (PPW)
PSNC .... Pharmaceutical Services Negotiating Committee (BUAC)
PSNC .... Public Service Company of North Carolina, Inc. (EFIS)
PSNC .... Public Service of North Carolina (EFIS)
PSNCF .... Pacific Southern Naval Coastal Frontier
PSNCO ...... Personnel Staff Noncommissioned Officer [*Military*]
PSNE .... Pennsylvania Society of Newspaper Editors (EARSL)
PSNI .... Pharmaceutical Society of Northern Ireland (BUAC)
PSNL .... Personnel (FAAC)
PSNO .... Paisano Trucking Company [*Common carrier symbol*]
PSNP .... Partial Sequence Number Packet (SAUS)
PSNP .... Pebble Springs Nuclear Plant (NRCH)
PSNQ .... Precision Transport Company [*Common carrier symbol*]
PSNR .... Pasifik Satelit Nusantara (PT) [*NASDAQ symbol*] (SAG)
PSNR .... Peak Signal to Noise Ratio (SAUS)
PSNR .... Positioner
PSNR .... Power Signal-to-Noise Ratio
PSNRL ...... Peak Signal-to-Noise Ratio Loss (SAUS)
PSNRP ...... Position Report [*Aviation*] (FAAC)
PSNS .... Parasympathetic Nervous System (STED)
PSNS .... Physical Science for Nonscience Students
PS NS .... Picket Ship, Navy Service (SAUS)
PSNS .... Pretreatment Standards for New Indirect Sources [*Environmental Protection Agency*]
PSNS .... Pretreatment Standards for New Sources (SAUS)
PSNS .... Programmable Sampling Network Switch
PSNS .... Puget Sound Naval Shipyard [*Bremerton, WA*] (MCD)
PSNS-MATLABS ... Puget Sound Naval Shipyard Material Laboratories [*Bremerton, WA*]
PSNSR .... Position Sensor (MCD)
PSNSW ...... Philatelic Society of New South Wales [*Australia*]
PSNSY ...... Puget Sound Naval Shipyard [*Bremerton, WA*]
PSNT .... Present [*Legal term*] (ROG)
PSNU .... Pacific Steam Navigation [*Intermodal shipping container symbol*] (TVRC)
PSNZ .... Perinatal Society of New Zealand (BUAC)
PSNZ .... Pharmaceutical Society of New Zealand (SAUS)
PSO .... Pad Safety Officer [*Aerospace*] (MCD)
PSO .... Paint Spray Outfit
PSO .... Pasadena Symphony Orchestra (SAUS)
PSO .... Paseo
PSO .... Pasto [*Colombia*] [*Airport symbol*] (OAG)
PSO .... Pasto [*Colombia*] [*Seismograph station code, US Geological Survey*] (SEIS)
PSO .... Pauli Spin Operator [*Physics*]
PSO .... Peacetime Stockage Objective [*DoD*] (AFIT)
PSO .... Pearson plc ADR [*NYSE symbol*]
PSO .... Pending Service Order (SAUS)
PSO .... Penobscot Shoe [*AMEX symbol*] (TTSB)
PSO .... Penobscot Shoe Co. [*AMEX symbol*] (SPSG)
PSO .... Personal Staff Officer [*Australia*]
PSO .... Personnel Security Officer [*Military*]
PSO .... Personnel Selection Officer [*British military*] (DMA)
PSO .... Personnel Services Organisation [*Australia*]
PSO .... Phoenix Symphony Orchestra (SAUS)
PSO .... Phorate Sulfoxide (SAUS)
PSO .... Piano-Shaped Object
PSO .... Pilot Systems Officer (SAUS)
PSO .... Pilot Systems Operator
PSO .... Pittsburgh Symphony Orchestra (SAUS)
PSO .... Planet Sensor Output
PSO .... Point Surface Origin
PSO .... Polaris Systems Officer [*British military*] (DMA)
PSO .... Policy Studies Organization (EA)
PSO .... Political Survey Officer (SAUS)
PSO .... Political Survey Officers [*Navy*]
PSO .... Polysulfon (SAUS)
PSO .... Polysulfone [*Also, PS*] [*Organic chemistry*]
PSO .... Portland Symphony Orchestra (SAUS)
PSO .... Port Services Office [*or Officer*] (DNAB)
PSO .... Prague Symphony Orchestra (SAUS)
PSO .... Primary Standardization Office [*Military*] (AABC)
PSO .... Principal Scientific Officer [*British*]
PSO .... Principal Staff Officer [*British military*] (DMA)
PSO .... Procurement Services Office
PSO .... Product Support Organization
PSO .... Profco Resources Ltd. [*Vancouver Stock Exchange symbol*]
PSO .... Professional Services Organization (GART)
PSO .... Programmable Storage Oscilloscope (CIST)
PSO .... Program Secretarial Officer (COE)
PSO .... Program Senior Official (COE)
PSO .... Program Staff Officer
PSO .... Progressive Supranuclear Ophthalmoplegia (CPH)
PSO .... Project Science Office (EOSA)
PSO .... Prospective Supply Officer (DNAB)
PSO .... Protective Security Officer
PSO .... Protective Service Operations (SAUS)
PSO .... Protocol Supporting Organization (SAUS)
PSO .... Provider Sponsored Organization
PSO .... Provisions Supply Office [*Military*]
PSO .... Proximal Subungual Onychomycosis
PSO .... Psychiatric Services Officer [*Australia*]
PSO .... Publications Supply Officer [*Military*]
PSO .... Publicity Security Officer [*Navy*]
PSO .... Public Safety Officer
PSO .... Public Service Obligation [*Australia*]
PSO .... Public Service Organisation [*Government grant*] [*British*]
PSOA .... Postal Supervisory Officers' Association [*Australia*]
PSOA .... Pro Stock Owners Association (EA)
PSOB .... Paper Society for the Overseas Blind [*Defunct*] (EA)
PSOC .... Parenting Sense of Competence Scale
PSOC .... Preliminary System Operational Concept (MCD)
PSOC .... Social Conservation Party (Nicaragua) [*Political party*] (PSAP)
PSOE .... Partido Socialista Obrero Espanol [*Spanish Socialist Workers' Party*] [*See also PSME*] [*Political party*] (PPE)
PSOF .... Prism Software Corp. [*OTCBB symbol*]
PSOJ .... Private Sector Organisation of Jamaica (BUAC)
P SOL .... Partially Soluble (SAUS)
P sol .... Partly Soluble [*Chemistry*] (DAVI)
PSOLMHT ... Pious Society of Our Lady of the Most Holy Trinity (EA)
PSom .... Mary S. Biesecker Public Library, Somerset, PA [*Library symbol*] [*Library of Congress*] (LCLS)
PSOM .... Persistency framework in Somobjects (SAUS)
PSOM .... Programmable Speedometer/Odometer Module [*Automotive term*] (HAWK)
PSomHi ..... Somerset County Historical and Genealogical Society, Somerset, PA [*Library symbol*] [*Library of Congress*] (LCLS)
PSOMT ...... Public Sector Organisation for Maritime Transport (SAUS)
PSON .... Paul-Son Gaming [*NASDAQ symbol*] (TTSB)
PSON .... Paul-Son Gaming Corp. [*NASDAQ symbol*] (SAG)
PSON .... Person (ROG)
PSONAL ..... Personal (ROG)
PSOP .... Parti Socialiste des Ouvriers et Paysans [*Socialist Party of Workers and Peasants*] [*France*] [*Political party*]
PSOP .... Payload Systems Operating Procedures [*NASA*] (NASA)
PSOP .... Power System Optimization Program [*Computer science*]
PSOR .... Passenger-Seat Occupant Recognition [*Automotive safety systems*]
PSOR .... Preliminary System of Requirements
PSOS .... Personal Services Operating System (SAUS)
PSOS .... Probably Secure Operating System (MHDB)
PSOT .... Patch Start of Transaction (SAUS)
PSOV .... Purge Shut-Off Valve [*Automotive engineering*]
PSOZ .... Public Service of Oklahoma [*Federal Railroad Administration identification code*]
PSP .... Pace-Setting Potential [*Physiology*]
PSP .... Pacific Security Pact (SAUS)
PSP .... Pacifistische Socialistische Partij [*Pacific Socialist Party*] [*Political party*] [*Netherlands*]
PSP .... Package Size Proneness [*Marketing*]
PSP .... Packaging Shipping Procedures
PSP .... Packet Satellite Program terminal (SAUS)
PSP .... Packet Switching Processor
PSP .... Pad Safety Plan
PSP .... Paint Shop Pro (SAUS)
PSP .... Palm Springs [*California*] [*Airport symbol*] (OAG)

PSP .... Palm Springs, CA [*Location identifier*] [*FAA*] (FAAL)
PSP .... Palynological Society of Poland (QUAC)
PSP .... Pancreatic Spasmolytic Peptide [*Biochemistry*]
PSP .... Paralytic Seafood Poisoning (SAUS)
PSP .... Paralytic Shellfish Poisoning [*Marine biology*]
PSP .... Parathyroid Secretory Protein [*Biochemistry*]
PSP .... Parti de la Solidarite du Peuple [*Cameroon*] [*Political party*] (EY)
PSP .... Partido Socialista del Peru [*Socialist Party of Peru*] [*Political party*] (PPW)
PSP .... Partido Socialista Popular [*Popular Socialist Party*] [*Spain*] [*Political party*] (PPE)
PSP .... Partido Socialista Popular [*Popular Socialist Party*] [*Peru*] [*Political party*] (PPW)
PSP .... Partido Socialista Portuguesa [*Portuguese Socialist Party*] [*Political party*] (PPW)
PSP .... Partido Social Progresista [*Social Progressive Party*] [*Brazil*] [*Political party*]
PSP .... Parti Socialiste Polynesien [*Polynesian Socialist Party*] [*Political party*] (PPW)
PSP .... Parti Social pour le Progres [*Tunisia*] [*Political party*] (EY)
PSP .... Parti Soudanais Progressiste [*Sudanese Progressive Party*] [*Political party*]
PSP .... Parts Screening Program
PSP .... Patrol Seaplane
PSP .... Pauli Sound Pressure (SAUS)
PSP .... Pauli Speech Power (SAUS)
PSP .... Payload Signal Processor [*NASA*] (NASA)
PSP .... Payload Specialist Panel [*NASA*] (NASA)
PSP .... Payload Support Plan [*NASA*] (MCD)
PSP .... Payroll Savings Plan (GFGA)
PSP .... Peace Shield Program (SAUS)
PSP .... Peak Sideband Power (DEN)
PSP .... Peak Systolic Pressure (SAUS)
PSP .... Peoples Solidarity Party (SAUS)
PSP .... Perforated Steel Planking (SAA)
PSP .... Perforated Steel Plate (VNW)
PSP .... Perforated Steel Plating (DNAB)
PSP .... Performance Shaping Parameter (SAUS)
PSP .... Performance Shaping Parameters (IEEE)
PSP .... Performance Share Plan [*Human resources*] (WYGK)
PSP .... Performance Standards Program
PSP .... Periodic Short Pulse (MAE)
PSP .... Permanent Sample Plot [*For ecological studies*]
PSP .... Personal Security Preview [*Psychology*] (DAVI)
PSP .... Personal Software Process (SAUS)
PSP .... Personal Software Products (SAUS)
PSP .... Personal Success Program
PSP .... Personal Survival Pack (SAUS)
PSP .... Personnel Subsystem Process [*Army*] (AABC)
PSP .... Pharmaceutical Society of Pakistan (BUAC)
PSP .... Pharmacological Sciences Program [*Bethesda, MD*] [*National Institute of General Medical Sciences*] (GRD)
PSP .... Phased Support Plan (SAUS)
PSP .... Phenolsulfonephthalein [*Chemical indicator*]
PSP .... Pierced Steel Planking [*Military*]
PSP .... Pierce Steel Plating (SAUS)
PSP .... Plane Strain Plastometer
PSP .... Planet Scan Platform [*NASA*] (KSC)
PSP .... Planned Standard Programming [*Computer science*]
PSP .... Plasma Separations Process (SAUS)
PSP .... Plasma Spraying [*Welding*]
PSP .... Plasmon Surface Polariton [*Physics*]
PSP .... Platform Sensor Package
PSP .... Pocahontas State Park (SAUS)
PSP .... Pointed Soft Point [*Ammunition*]
PSP .... Pointed Soft Point Bullet
PSP .... Police Service Pistol
PSP .... Policies, Systems, and Procedures
PSP .... Polyfactorial Study of Personality [*Psychology*]
PSP .... Poly(styrene peroxide) [*Organic chemistry*]
PSP .... Popular Socialist Party [*Political party*] (BUAC)
PSP .... Portable Service Processor (IEEE)
PSP .... Positive Screened Print (SAUS)
PSP .... Positive Spike Pattern (MAE)
PSP .... Posterior Spinous Process (SAUS)
psp .... Posterior Subcapsular Plaque [*Ophthalmology*] (DAVI)
PSP .... Postipankki [*National savings bank*] [*Finland*]
PSP .... Post-Shoring-Polyethylene [*Method of constructing underground homes*]
PSP .... Post-Surgical Pain [*Medicine*]
PSP .... Postsynaptic Potential [*Neurophysiology*]
PSP .... Potential for Successful Performance [*Test*]
PSP .... Power Steering Pressure [*Automotive term*] (HAWK)
PSP .... Power System Planning
PSP .... Praja Socialist Party [*India*] [*Political party*] (PPW)
PSP .... Precision Spectral Pyranometer (SAUS)
PSP .... Precision Spot Positioning
PSP .... Predictable System Performance (SAA)
PSP .... Predictive Smooth Pursuit [*Ophthalmology*]
PSP .... Pre-Season Predictor Model [*Television ratings*] (NTCM)
PSP .... Presending Pause (NITA)
PSP .... Presensitized Photoplate
PSP .... Pre-Series Phase (SAUS)
PSP .... Prestart Panel [*Aerospace*] (AAG)
PSP .... Pre-Stock Point
PSP .... Priced Spare Parts [*Military*] (AFIT)
PSP .... Price-Subsidy Program (SAUS)
PSP .... Price-Support Program (SAUS)
PSP .... Primary and Secondary Power system (SAUS)
PSP .... Primary Smog Product (PDAA)
PSP .... Primary Sodium Pump [*Nuclear energy*] (NRCH)
PSP .... Primary Supply Point [*Military*] (AFM)
PSP .... Primary Support Point [*Military*] (AFM)
PSP .... Printing Summary Punch (SAUS)
PSP .... Priority Strike Plan (SAUS)
PSP .... Priority Strike Program
PSP .... Probability-of-Single-Pulse (SAUS)
PSP .... Problem Solving Process
PSP .... Product Service Publication [*General Motors Corp.*]
PSP .... Product Structure Plan (SAUS)
PSP .... Product Support Plan (SAUS)
PSP .... Product Support Program (NG)
PSP .... Professional and Scholarly Publishing Division [*Association of American Publishers*] (EDAC)
PSP .... Professional Scholarly Publishing
PSP .... Profit Sharing Plan [*Business term*] (MHDW)
PSP .... Programmable Signal Processor (MCD)
PSP .... Program Segment Prefix [*Computer science*]
PSP .... Programs Support Plan (SAUS)
PSP .... Program Support Plan [*NASA*]
PSP .... Program Support Plans (SAUS)
PSP .... Progressive Socialist Party [*Lebanon*] [*Political party*] (BJA)
psp .... Progressive Supernuclear Palsy (SAUS)
PSP .... Progressive Supranuclear Palsy [*Neurology*]
PSP .... Project Schedule Plan (NASA)
PSP .... Project Standard Practice (DNAB)
PSP .... Project Structure Plan (SAUS)
PSP .... Prone Sleeping Position (MELL)
PSP .... Protective Shielding Program
PSP .... Protocol for Specific Purpose
PSP .... Pseudopregnancy [*Gynecology*]
PSP .... Pseudostatic Spontaneous Potential (IAA)
PSP .... Public School Pronunciation (SAUS)
PSP .... Public Security Police (SAUS)
PSP .... Public Storage Canadian Properties [*Limited Partnership Units*] [*Toronto Stock Exchange symbol*]
PSP .... Public Storage Properties XIV, Inc. [*AMEX symbol*] (SAG)
PSP .... Public Storage Prop'A' XIV [*AMEX symbol*] (TTSB)
PSP .... Puerto Rican Socialist Party [*Political party*] (PD)
PSP .... Swarthmore College Peace Collection, Swarthmore, PA [*OCLC symbol*] (OCLC)
PSPA .... Pacific Seafood Processors Association (EA)
PSPA .... Passive Solar Products Association (EA)
PSPA .... Past Service Pension Adjustment (FOTI)
PSPA .... Physician Services Practice Analysis (ADWA)
PSPA .... Plant Site Property Administrator (ACAE)
PSPA .... Pre-School Play Apparatus (WDAA)
PSPA .... Pressure Static Probe Assembly (MCD)
PSPA .... Professional School Photographers of America (EA)
PSPA .... Professional Sports Photographers Association [*British*] (EAIO)
PSPA .... Systolic Pulmonary Artery Pressure (SAUS)
PSPAC .... Pacific Seafood Processors PAC [*Seattle, WA*] (PACS)
PSP & E .... Product Support Planning and Estimating (AAG)
PSPB .... Pulse Code Modulation Speech Bus (SAUS)
PSPC .... Partido Socialista del Pueblo de Ceuta [*Political party*] (EY)
PSPC .... Permanent South Pacific Commission (BUAC)
PSPC .... Physical Security / Pilferage Code
PSPC .... Polystyrene Packaging Council (EA)
PSPC .... Position-Sensitive Proportional Counter [*Instrumentation*]
PSPC .... Position Sensitive Proportional Counters (SAUS)
PSPC .... President's Soviet Protocol Committee [*World War II*]
PSPCA .... Pennsylvania Society for the Prevention of Cruelty to Animals
PSPCD ...... Puget Sound Pollution-Control District (SAUS)
PSPD .... Permits and State Programs Division [*Environmental Protection Agency*] (GFGA)
PSPD .... Position-Sensitive Proportional Detector [*For X-ray diffraction*]
PSPDC ...... Polar Satellite Precipitation Data Centre (SAUS)
PSPDN ...... Packet Switched Public Data Network [*Computer science*] (TNIG)
PSPDN ...... Packet-Switched Public Data Network (SAUS)
PSPDN ...... Packet Switching Public Data Network (SAUS)
PSPEN .... Primary/Secondary Peace Education Network [*Later, PEN*] (EA)
PSPF .... Potential Single Point Failures [*NASA*] (KSC)
PSPF .... Prostacyclin Stimulating Plasma Factor [*Endocrinology*]
PSPFLI ...... Pulsed Single Photon Fluorescence Lifetime Instrumentation
PSPG .... Phase-Shifting Pulse Gate (WDAA)
PSPGV ...... Primary Sodium Pump Guard Vesel [*Nuclear energy*] (NRCH)
PSphR .... Rohm & Haas Co., Research Library Services, Spring House, PA [*Library symbol*] [*Library of Congress*] (LCLS)
PSPI .... Psychosocial Pain Inventory [*Psychology*]
PSPL .... Priced Spare Parts List
PSPL .... Progressive Socialist Party of Lebanon
PSPL .... Prototype Spare Parts List (SAUS)
PSPL Pre-Op ... Prices Square Parts List-Pre-Operational
PSPLR .... Priced Spare Parts List Revision
PSPM .... Per Subscriber per Month [*Medicine*] (MHCS)
PSPM .... Procurement Seminar for Project Management [*Army*]
PSPMW ..... International Brotherhood of Pulp, Sulphite, and Paper Mill Workers [*Later, UPIU*]
PSPMW ..... Pulp, Sulphite and Paper Mill Workers (SAUS)

P-Spot....... Preceding Spot (SAUS)
PSPP........ Preliminary System Package Plan
PSPP........ Preliminary System Package Program
PSPP........ Proposed System Package Plan [*Military*]
PSPR........ Personnel Subsystem Products [*Army*] (AABC)
PSPR........ Programmable Signal Processor RADAR
PSPRCC....... Ponce and Southern Puerto Rico Chamber of Commerce (EARSL)
PSPRT....... Partial Sequential Probability Ratio Test (PDAA)
PSPS........ Paddle Steamer Preservation Society [*British*] (BI)
PSPS........ Passive Surface Pressure Sounder (SAUS)
PSPS........ Pesticides Safety Precautions Scheme [*British*]
PSPS........ Planar Silicon Photoswitch (IEEE)
PSPS........ Postsurgical Pain Syndrome (MELL)
PSPs......... Post-Synaptic Potentials (SAUS)
PSPS........ Power-Steering Pressure Sensor [*Automotive engineering*]
PSPS........ Power Steering Pressure Switch [*Automotive engineering*]
PSPS........ Primary Solar Piping System (SAUS)
PSPS........ Product Support Procurement Summary (MCD)
PSPSK....... Previous Signaling Element Phase Shift Keying [*Computer science*] (IAA)
PS-PSK...... Previous Signalling-element Phase Shift Keying (SAUS)
PSPSV....... Pre-School Playgroup Support Visitor (WDAA)
PSPT........ Parisi Spanish Proficiency Test (EDAC)
PSPT........ Passport (AABC)
PSPT........ Planar Silicon Power Transistor
PSPT........ Power Steering Pump Test [*Fuels and lubricants*]
PSptv........ PerSeptive Biosystems, Inc. [*Associated Press*] (SAG)
PSPV........ Partido Socialista del Pais Valenciano [*Spain*] [*Political party*] (EY)
PSPX........ Phillips Petroleum [*Private rail car owner code*]
PSPX........ Prosperous [*Telegraphy*] (PCTE)
PSPY........ Prosperity [*Telegraphy*] (PCTE)
PSQ.......... Parent Symptom Questionnaire [*Medicine*] (DMAA)
PSQ.......... Patient Satisfaction Questionnaire [*Medicine*] (DMAA)
PSQ.......... Personal Security Questionnaire (SAUS)
PSQ.......... Personnel Security Questionnaire
PSQ.......... Personnel Squadron
PSQ.......... Political Science Quarterly [*A publication*] (BRI)
PSQ.......... Prosecute [*Telegraphy*] (PCTE)
PSQ.......... Protein Sequence Query
PSQ.......... Public Storage Properties XV [*AMEX symbol*] (SPSG)
PSQ.......... Public Storage Prop'A' XV [*AMEX symbol*] (TTSB)
PSQA........ Pageable System Queue Area [*Computer science*] (MCD)
PSQC........ Philippine Society for Quality Control (BUAC)
PSQD........ Prosecuted [*Telegraphy*] (PCTE)
PSQG........ Prosecuting [*Telegraphy*] (PCTE)
PSQI......... Pittsburgh Sleep Quality Index
PSQL........ Platinum Software [*NASDAQ symbol*] (TTSB)
PSQL........ Platinum Software Corp. [*NASDAQ symbol*] (SAG)
PSQL........ Process Screening Quality Level (SAUS)
PSQN........ Prosecution [*Telegraphy*] (PCTE)
PSR.......... Pacific School of Religion (SAUS)
PSR.......... Pacific Security Region
PSR.......... Pacific-Sierra Research Corp.
PSR.......... Packed Snow on Runway [*NWS*] (FAAC)
PSR.......... Pad Safety Report [*NASA*]
PSR.......... Page Send-Receive [*Teletypewriter*]
PSR.......... Pain Sensitivity Range [*Biometrics*]
PSR.......... Panoramic Stereo Rectification
PSR.......... Paper Stock Record (DGA)
PSR.......... Parachute Status Report [*Army*] (AABC)
PSR.......... Partido Socialista Revolucionario [*Revolutionary Socialist Party*] [*Portugal*] [*Political party*] (PPE)
PSR.......... Partido Socialista Revolucionario [*Revolutionary Socialist Party*] [*Mexico*] [*Political party*] (PPW)
PSR.......... Partido Socialista Revolucionario [*Revolutionary Socialist Party*] [*Peru*] [*Political party*] (PPW)
PSR.......... Parts and Supplies (or Supply) Requisition (SAUS)
PSR.......... Parts and Supply Requisition (IAA)
PSR.......... Party Socialiste Revolutionnaire [*Socialist Revolutionary Party*] [*Lebanon*] [*Political party*] (PPW)
PSR.......... Passenger Service Representative [*Travel industry*] (TRID)
PSR.......... Passenger Space Ratio (SAUS)
PSR.......... Passive Ranging Sonar (SAUS)
psr........... Paternal Sex Ratio Gene [*Genetics*]
PSR.......... Paul's Scarlet Rose [*Plant cell line*]
PSR.......... Pelvispondylite Rheumatismale (SAUS)
PSR.......... Pennsylvania State Reports [*A publication*] (DLA)
PSR.......... Pennsylvania State University Reactor (NRCH)
PSR.......... Perfectly Stirred Reactor
PSR.......... Performance Summary Report (NG)
PSR.......... Peripheral Shim Rod [*Nuclear energy*] (NRCH)
PSR.......... Personal Service Radio (SAUS)
PSR.......... Personnel Status Report [*Military*]
PSR.......... Pescara [*Italy*] [*Airport symbol*] (OAG)
PSR.......... Petaluma & Santa Rosa Railroad Co. [*AAR code*]
PSR.......... Petrostates Resource Corp. [*Vancouver Stock Exchange symbol*]
PSR.......... Pharmaceutical Sales Representative
PSR.......... Phase Sensitive Rectifier (NITA)
PSR.......... Phase Sequence Relay
PSR.......... Phase Shift Register (SAUS)
PSR.......... Philatelic Societies' Record [*A publication*] [*British*]
PSR.......... Photo Scale Reciprocal (DNAB)
PSR.......... Physical Sciences Research Program [*North Carolina State University*] [*Research center*] (RCD)
PSR.......... Physicians for Social Responsibility (EA)
PSR.......... Plow-Steel Rope
PSR.......... Point of Safe Return (MCD)
PSR.......... Point Source Range (IAA)
PSR.......... Point-Spread Function (RAWO)
PSR.......... Policy Status Report [*Insurance*]
PSR.......... Political and Social Reform Movement [*British*]
PSR.......... Political Science Reviewer [*A publication*] (BRI)
PSR.......... Poly Static Radar (ACAE)
PSR.......... Portable Seismic Recorder
PSR.......... Portal Systemic Resistance [*Medicine*] (MELL)
PSR.......... Port State Register (SAUS)
PSR.......... Positive Support Review (SAUS)
PSR.......... Positive Support Review, Inc. [*Telecommunications service*] (TSSD)
PSR.......... Postal Service Representative [*British*] (DCTA)
PSR.......... Post-Sinusoidal Resistance
PSR.......... Post-Strike Reconnaissance (SAUS)
PSR.......... Power Supply Regulation (SAUS)
PSR.......... Power Supply Rejection (SAUS)
PSR.......... Power System Relaying (MCD)
PSR.......... Predicted SONAR Range [*Military*] (NVT)
PSR.......... Pre-Sentence Report (WDAA)
PSR.......... Present Serviceability Rating [*FHWA*] (TAG)
PSR.......... Pre Shipment Review (ACAE)
PSR.......... Presidential Special Representative (BARN)
PSR.......... Pressure (SAUS)
PSR.......... Price-Sales Ratio [*Economics*]
PSR.......... Primary Surveillance RADAR
PSR.......... Primary System Relief (COE)
PSR.......... Priority Status Register (SAUS)
PSR.......... Problem Status Report (MCD)
PSR.......... Processor State Register
PSR.......... Processor Status Register [*Computer science*] (VLIE)
PSR.......... Procurement Status Report (IEEE)
PSR.......... Productivity Savings Reward (AAGC)
PSR.......... Product Specific Realizations (SAUS)
PSR.......... Product Specific Release (VLIE)
PSR.......... Professional Sportscar Racing
PSR.......... Programming Status Report [*Computer science*]
PSR.......... Programming Support Representative [*IBM Corp.*]
PSR.......... Program Specification Rules [*Computer science*] (HODG)
PSR.......... Program Start Register [*Computer science*] (VLIE)
PSR.......... Program Status Register
PSR.......... Program Status Report [*or Review*]
PSR.......... Program Status Review [*NASA*] (NASA)
PSR.......... Program Study Request (AAG)
PSR.......... Program Summary Record [*Military*] (AFIT)
PSR.......... Program Support Representative (VLIE)
PSR.......... Program Support Requirements (KSC)
PSR.......... Progress Summary Report
PSR.......... Project Safe Run (EA)
PSR.......... Project Scan Record
PSR.......... Project Summary Report (MCD)
PSR.......... Proliferative Sickle Retinopathy (DB)
PSR.......... Propeller Shaft Rate [*Navy*] (CAAL)
PSR.......... Pro Seniors [*International Bowhunting Organization*] [*Class Equipment*]
PSR.......... Protected Service Routine (VLIE)
PSR.......... Protocol Status Report [*Medicine*] (HVTR)
PSR.......... Proton Storage Ring [*Nuclear physics*]
PSR.......... Prototype Systems Review
PSR.......... Provisioning Support Request [*Military*] (CAAL)
PSR.......... Public Service Company of Colorado [*AMEX symbol*] (SAG)
PSR.......... Public Service Co. of Colorado [*NYSE symbol*] (SPSG)
PSR.......... Public Social Responsibility [*Unit of the Anglican Church of Canada General Synod*]
PSR.......... Public SvcColorado [*NYSE symbol*] (TTSB)
PSR.......... Pulmonary Stretch Receptors [*Medicine*]
PSR.......... Pulsar (SAUS)
PSRA........ Persil Stain Release Agent (WDAA)
PSRA........ Presunrise Service Authorization [*Telecommunications*] (OTD)
PSRA........ Problem Status Report Analysis (SAA)
PSRA........ Professional Soccer Reporter's Association (EA)
PSRAAALAA... President's Special Representative and Adviser on African, Asian, and Latin American Affairs [*Department of State*]
PSRAM...... Physical Security Requirements Assessment Methodology [*Civil Engineering Research Laboratory*] [*Navy*] (RDA)
PSRAM...... Pseudostatic Random Access Memory [*Apple Computer Inc.*]
PSRBOW.... Premature Spontaneous Rupture of Bag of Waters [*Medicine*] (MEDA)
PSRC........ Plastic Surgery Research Council (EA)
PSRC........ Power Semiconductor Research Center [*North Carolina State University*] (RCD)
PSRC........ Pretrial Services Resource Center (EA)
PSRC........ Prevention Sciences Review Committee (HVTR)
PSRC........ Prime Source Corp. [*NASDAQ symbol*] (NASQ)
PSRC........ PrimeSource Corp. [*NASDAQ symbol*] (SAG)
PSRC........ Public Service Research Council (EA)
PSRCA....... Professional Standards Review Council of America (EA)
PSRD........ Personnel Shipment Ready Date [*Army*] (AABC)
PSRD........ Program Support Requirements Document [*NASA*] (KSC)
PSRE........ Partido Socialista Revolucionario Ecuatoriano [*Socialist Revolutionary Party of Ecuador*] [*Political party*] (PPW)
PSRE........ Propulsion System Rocket Engine (MCD)

PSRF .... Pelagic Shark Research Foundation (RCD)
PSRF .... Point Source Response Function (SAUS)
PSRF .... Product Support Reports and Functions
PSRF .... Profit Sharing Research Foundation (EA)
PSRG .... Privacy and Security Research Group (SAUS)
PSRGN ...... Pacific Southwest Regional Genetics Network (SAUS)
PSRI .... Particulate Solid Research Institute
PSRI .... Personnel Specialities and Record Inventory (SAA)
PSRI .... Position Subject Return of Incumbent (SAUS)
PSRI .... Position Subject to Return of Incumbent [*Aviation*] (FAAC)
PSRI .... Psycho-Social Rehabilitation International (EAIO)
PSRI .... Public Services Research Institute [*Pacific Institute for Research and Evaluation*] (RCD)
PSRI .... Public Systems Research Institute (SAUS)
PSRK .... Prosperity Trucking Company [*Common carrier symbol*]
PSRL .... Post Strike Reconnaissance List [*Military*] (CINC)
PSRM .... Pacific Southwest Railway Museum (SAUS)
PSRM .... Parti Sosialis Rakyat Malaya [*People's Socialist Party of Malaya*]
PSRM .... Post-Scram Reactivity Monitor [*Nuclear energy*] (NRCH)
PSRM .... Pressurization Systems Regulator Manifold (AAG)
PSRM .... Processor State Register Main [*Computer science*]
PSRMA ...... Pacific Southwest Railway Museum Association [*Later, SDRM*] (EA)
PSR-ML/MIR ... Partido Socialista Revolucionario (Marxista-Leninista)/Movimiento de Izquierda Revolucionaria [*Revolutionary Socialist Party (Marxist-Leninist)/Mi litant Movement of the Revolutionary Left*] [*Peru*] [*Political party*] (PPW)
PSRMLS .... Pacific Southwest Regional Medical Library [*Library network*]
PSRMT ...... Piecewise-Sinusoidal Reaction Matching Technique [*Antenna*] [*Navy*]
PSRO .... Passenger Standing Route Order [*Army*] (AABC)
PSRO .... Professional Services Review Organization (SAUS)
PSRO .... Professional Standards Review Organization (NADA)
PSR-P .... Packed Snow on Runway - Patchy [*Aviation*] (DNAB)
PSRP .... Physical Sciences Research Papers [*Air Force*] (MCD)
PSRP .... Production Support Repair Plan (SAA)
PSRPP ...... Public Safety and Resource Protection Program (SAUS)
PSRPr .... Pub Sv of Colo.,4 1/4% Pfd [*AMEX symbol*] (TTSB)
PSRPrA ..... Pub Sv Colo.,7.15% Pfd [*NYSE symbol*] (TTSB)
PSRR .... Parachute Supported Radio Relay
PSRR .... Power Supply Rejection Ratio (IAA)
PSRR .... Product and Support Requirements Request [*Computer science*] (IB-MDP)
PSRS .... Patient Service Records System
PSRS .... Pictographic Self-Rating Scale [*Psychology*] (AEBS)
PSRS .... Portable Seismic Recording System
PSRS .... Position Subject to Rotating Shifts [*Aviation*] (FAAC)
PSRS .... Psychiatric Self-Rating Scale (SAUS)
PSrS .... Slippery Rock State College, Slippery Rock, PA [*Library symbol*] [*Library of Congress*] (LCLS)
PSRT .... Passive Satellite Research Terminal
PSRT .... PostScript Round Table (VLIE)
PS-RTP ...... Paper-Substrate Room-Temperature Phosphorescence [*Analytical chemistry*]
PSRU .... Processor State Register Utility [*Computer science*]
PSRU .... Production Support Repair Unit (SAA)
PSRX .... Petaluma & Santa Rosa Railroad [*Federal Railroad Administration identification code*]
PSS .... Hastings, NE [*Location identifier*] [*FAA*] (FAAL)
PSS .... International Production, Service, and Sales Union
PSS .... Packet Switched System (NITA)
PSS .... Packet Switching Service [*Telecommunications*] [*Information service or system*] [*British*] (IID)
PSS .... Packet Switching Stream (SAUS)
PSS .... Packet Switching System (SAUS)
PSS .... Packet Switch Stream (SAUS)
PSS .... Packet SwitchStream [*British Telecommunications Plc*] [*London*] [*Information service or system*] (IID)
PSS .... Packet Switchstream Service (SAUS)
PSS .... Pad Safety Supervision [*Aerospace*] (AAG)
PSS .... Pad Safety Supervision (or Supervisor) (SAUS)
PSS .... Pad Safety Supervisor [*NASA*] (NAKS)
PSS .... Painful Shoulder Syndrome (MELL)
PSS .... Palomar Sky Survey [*NASA*]
PSS .... Parallel Search Storage [*Computer science*] (VLIE)
PSS .... Parents for Student Safety (SAUS)
PSS .... Partially Sighted Society [*British*]
PSS .... Partia Socialiste e Shqiperise [*Socialist Party of Albania*] [*Political party*] (EAIO)
PSS .... Parti de Solidarite Senegalaise [*Senegalese Solidarity Party*] [*Political party*]
PSS .... Parti Socialiste Suisse [*Social Democratic Party of Switzerland*] [*Political party*] (PPE)
PSS .... Partito Socialista Sammarinese [*Socialist Party of San Marino*] [*Political party*] (PPE)
PSS .... Partito Socialista Somalo [*Somali Socialist Party*] [*Political party*]
PSS .... Passenger Sensing System [*Automotive safety*]
PSS .... Passenger Service Supervisor [*Travel industry*]
PSS .... Passenger Service Systems [*Airlines*]
PSS .... Passes [*Telegraphy*] (PCTE)
PSS .... Patent Searching System (SAUS)
PSS .... Patent Search System [*Pergamon*] [*Database*] [*Computer science*] [*British*]
PSS .... Pattern Select Switch [*Automotive engineering*]
PSS .... Pauli Spin Susceptibility [*Physics*]
PSS .... Payless ShoeSource [*NYSE symbol*] (TTSB)
PSS .... Payless ShoeSource, Inc. [*NYSE symbol*] (SAG)
PSS .... Payload Specialist Station [*NASA*] (NASA)
PSS .... Payload Support System [*NASA*] (MCD)
PSS .... Perceived Stress Scale [*Psychology*] (DHP)
PSS .... Performance Standard Sheet
PSS .... Performance Summary Sheet
PSS .... Performance Support System [*Human resources*] (WYGK)
PSS .... Periodic Steady State (SAUS)
PSS .... Periscope Simulation System [*Navy*]
PSS .... Persian Shipping Services, Teheran (SAUS)
PSS .... Personal Safety System [*Automotive engineering*]
PSS .... Personal Security System (SAUS)
PSS .... Personnel Security Staff (SAUS)
PSS .... Personnel Security System (ACAE)
PSS .... Personnel Service Support [*Army*] (DOMA)
PSS .... Personnel Staffing Specialist (GFGA)
PSS .... Personnel Subsystem [*Air Force*] (AFM)
PSS .... Personnel Support System [*Army*] (AABC)
PSS .... Perturbed Stationary State (SAUS)
PSS .... Phase-System Switching [*Physical chemistry*]
PSS .... Physical Security Specialist (SAUS)
PSS .... Physical Security Subsystem
PSS .... Physical Security System (SAUS)
PSS .... Physician Sales & Services Inc. (EFIS)
PSS .... Physiological Saline Solution [*Physiology*]
PSS .... Physiological Stability Score (SAUS)
PSS .... Physiologic Saline Solution (SAUS)
PSS .... Planetary Scan System [*or Subsystem*]
PSS .... Planned Systems Schedule (AAG)
PSS .... Planning Summary Sheets (AAG)
PSS .... Plant Science Seminar [*Later, ASP*]
PS/S .... Plumbing Supervisor/Specialist (AAG)
PSS .... Plume Suppression System [*Combustion technology*]
PSS .... Plunger Snap Switch
PSS .... Pneumatic Supply Subsystem (AAG)
PSS .... Polar Subsurface Sounder (SSD)
PSS .... Poly(styrenesulfonate) [*Organic chemistry*]
PSS .... Polystyrene Sulfonate (SAUS)
PSS .... Porcine Stress Syndrome [*Veterinary medicine*]
PSS .... Portable Simulation System (MCD)
PSS .... Port Safety and Security [*USCG*] (TAG)
PSS .... Portsmouth Signal School (SAUS)
PSS .... Posadas [*Argentina*] [*Airport symbol*] (OAG)
PSS .... Possible Signal Sample (SAUS)
PSS .... Postal Savings System [*Terminated, 1966*]
PSS .... Postal Separation System (SAA)
PSS .... Postscripta [*Postscripts*] [*Latin*]
PSS .... Power Subsystem (SAUS)
PSS .... Power Supply Section
PSS .... Power Supply Subsystem (IAA)
PSS .... Power Supply System (SAUS)
PSS .... Power Switching System (SAUS)
PSS .... Power System Synthesizer
PSS .... Precancel Stamp Society (EA)
PSS .... Precision Sun Sensor (ACAE)
PSS .... Premature Separation Switch (SAA)
PSS .... Premature Separation System (ACAE)
PSS .... Presbyteri Sancti Sulpicii [*Sulpicians*] [*Roman Catholic men's religious order*]
PSS .... Pre-School Screening (SAUS)
PSS .... Preselection Secondary Section (SAUS)
PSS .... Pressure Sensitive Schottky (SAUS)
P/S/S .... Price/Stern/Sloan Publishers, Inc.
PSS .... Primary Sampling System [*Nuclear energy*] (NRCH)
PSS .... Princess (ROG)
PSS .... Principle Support System (VLIE)
PSS .... Printer Storage System [*Computer science*] (MHDI)
PSS .... Printing and Stationery Service (SAUS)
PSS .... Print Sub-Scan (VLIE)
PSS .... Priority Scheduling System (SAUS)
PSS .... Private Schools Survey (SAUS)
PSS .... Private Signalling System (SAUS)
PSS .... Probabilistic Safety Study [*Nuclear energy*] (NRCH)
PSS .... Probe Support Subsystem (ACAE)
PSS .... Problem Solving State (SAUS)
PSS .... Process Sampling System [*Nuclear energy*] (NRCH)
PSS .... Process Standard Specification
PSS .... Process Support System [*Computer science*] (VLIE)
PSS .... Process Switching Service (IAA)
PSS .... Production System Support (SAUS)
PSS .... Product Supply Specification [*Petroleum engineering*]
PSS .... Product Support Services (MWOL)
PSS .... Product Support System (SAUS)
PSS .... Professional Services Section (BARN)
PSS .... Professor of Sacred Scripture
PSS .... Programmable Store System (SAUS)
PSS .... Programming Support System (SAA)
PSS .... Programming Systems Support (SAUS)
PSS .... Program Support Staff [*Environmental Protection Agency*] (GFGA)
PSS .... Progressive Science Series [*A publication*]
PSS .... Progressive Systemic Sclerosis [*Medicine*]
PSS .... Projected Smoke System (SEWL)
PSS .... Project Summary Sheet (SAUS)
PSS .... Propellant Supply Subsystem (SAUS)
PSS .... Propellant Supply System [*or Subsystem*]

PSS .... Proposed Sale of Securities (GFGA)
PSS .... Proprietary Software Systems [*Computer science*] (IEEE)
PSS .... Proprietary Support System [*Computer science*] (IAA)
PSS .... Propulsion Subsystem Structure
PSS .... Propulsion Support System (KSC)
PSS .... Protection Security Service
PSS .... Protective Security Service
PSS .... Protective Signature Service (MCD)
PSS .... Psalms [*Old Testament book*]
Pss .... Pseudomonas Syringae Syringae [*Plant pathology*]
PSS .... Pseudo-Sense Switch
PSS .... Pseudo Spread Spectrum (MCD)
PSS .... Pseudo Steady State (SAUS)
PSS .... Psychiatric Services Section [*of the American Hospital Association*] [*Later, SCSMHPS*] (EA)
PSS .... Psychiatric Status Schedules [*Psychology*]
PSS .... Psychological Saline Solution (BARN)
PSS .... Public Services Satellite
PSS .... Public Service System (SAUS)
PSS .... Public Storage Canadian Properties II [*Limited Partnership Units*] [*Toronto Stock Exchange symbol*]
PSS .... PUREX Sludge Supernatant liquid (SAUS)
PSS .... Push-Button Selection Station
PSs .... Regional Councils (Sri Lanka) [*Political party*] (PSAP)
PSS .... Silent Self-loading Pistol [*Police and security equipment*]
PSSA .... Pattern Select Switch-Analog [*Automotive engineering*]
PSSA .... Payload Support Structural Assembly (SAUS)
PSSA .... Pennsylvania System for Student Assessment
PSSA .... Photogrammetric Society of South Africa (SAUS)
PS(SA) ...... Photographic Society of Southern Africa (BUAC)
PSSA .... Pilot Signal Selector Adaptor (SAA)
PSSA .... Pilots Stick Sensor Assembly (SAUS)
PSSA .... Pitch Starting Synchro Assembly
PSSA .... Pitch Static Stability Angle [*Automotive safety*]
PSSA .... Polycristalline Silicon Selfaligned (SAUS)
PSSA .... Postsunset Service Authorization [*Telecommunications*] (OTD)
PSSA .... Pseudo-Steady-State Approximation [*Chemical engineering*]
PSSA .... Pyroelectric Solid State Array (ACAE)
PSSAA .... Pacific Stars and Stripes Alumni Association (EA)
PSSAANDPS ... Permanent Secretariat of the South American Agreement on Narcotic Drugs and Psychotropic Substances (EAIO)
PSSAs .... Particularly Sensitive Sea Areas [*Ecology*] (FOTI)
PSSB .... Palm Springs Savings Bank [*Palm Springs, CA*] [*NASDAQ symbol*] (NQ)
PSSB .... Palm Springs Svgs Bk [*NASDAQ symbol*] (TTSB)
PSSB .... Passing Stopped School Bus [*Traffic offense charge*]
PSSBB .... Public School System Blanket Bond [*Insurance*]
PSSC .... Packaging, Shipping and Safety Committee (SAUS)
PSSC .... Parachute Subsystem Sequence Controller [*NASA*] (SAA)
PSSC .... Personal Social Services Council [*British*] (DI)
PSSC .... Petroleum Security Subcommittee [*of Foreign Petroleum Supply Committee*] [*Terminated, 1976*] (EGAO)
PSSC .... Philippine Social Science Council (SAUS)
PSSC .... Physical Science Study Committee [*National Science Foundation*]
PSSC .... Pious Society of Missionaries of St. Charles [*Later, CS*] [*Roman Catholic men's religious order*]
PSSC .... Pressure-Sensitive Safety Controller [*Electronics*]
PSSC .... Professional Staff Selection Committe (SAUS)
PSSC .... Programmer and Star-tracker Signal Controller (SAUS)
PSSC .... Public Service Satellite Consortium (EA)
PSSCC .... Peter Symonds School Cadet Corps [*British military*] (DMA)
PSSCP .... Partially Submerged Supercaviating Propeller (SAUS)
PSSD .... Parallel-Serial Scan Design [*Electronics*]
PSSD .... Personnel Service Support Directorate (DOMA)
PSSDC .... Production Service and Sales District Council (NTPA)
PSSDS .... Portable Surface Supported Diving System (PDAA)
PSSE .... Partial Saturation Spin Echo (RAWO)
PSSEK .... Probability of Single Shot Engagement Kill (SAUS)
PSSEK .... Probability of Single Shot Engagement Kill [*Military*]
PSSEP .... Preliminary System Safety Engineering Plan
PSSES .... Public Service Senior Executive Service [*Australia*]
PSSF .... Petites Soeurs de la Sainte-Famille [*Little Sisters of the Holy Family*] [*Sherbrooke, PQ*] (EAIO)
PSSG .... Payload Specialist Support Group (SAUS)
PSSG .... Physical Science Study Group
PSSG .... Protocol Standards Steering Group (SAUS)
PSSGNR ...... Passenger
PSSH .... Socialist Party of Albania [*Political party*] (PSAP)
PSSHAK ...... Primary Support Structures and Housing Assembly Kit (SAUS)
PSSI .... Pacific/Sulfur/Stratus Investigation (SAUS)
PSS-I .... Peace Science Society (International) (EA)
PSSI .... Physician Sales & Service [*NASDAQ symbol*] (TTSB)
PSSI .... Physician Sales & Service, Inc. [*NASDAQ symbol*] (SAG)
PSSI .... Plasma Source Ion Implantation
PSSI .... Primary Specialty Skill Identifier [*Military*] (AABC)
PSSI .... PSS World Medical [*NASDAQ symbol*] (SG)
PSSIIS ...... Partito Socialista: Sezione Italiana del Internazionale Socialista [*Socialist Party: Italian Section of International Socialism*] [*Political party*] (PPE)
PSS(Int) .... Peace Science Society (International)
PSSJ .... Poor Sisters of St. Joseph (TOCD)
PSSK .... Probability of Single Shot Kill [*Of a guided missile*]
PSSK .... Probability of Single-Shot Kill (SAUS)
PSSL .... Princeton University Solid State and Materials Laboratory [*New Jersey*]
PSSL .... Private Source Statement Library (SAUS)
PSSL .... Program Source Status List (SAUS)
PSSM .... Parking Systems Simulation Model (SAUS)
PSSM .... Photographic Systems Simulation Model (SAUS)
PSSM .... Planar Supercell Stack Method (SAUS)
PSSM .... Polish Society of Social Medicine (SAUS)
PSSM .... Preliminary Science Meeting [*NASA*]
PSSMA .... Paper Shipping Sack Manufacturers Association (EA)
PSSMLF ...... Provincial Society of Spanish and Moroccan Leather Finishers [*A union*] [*British*]
PSSNY .... Philharmonic Symphony Society of New York (SAUS)
PSSO .... Passed Slip Stitch Over (SAUS)
PSSO .... Pass Slip Stitch Over [*Knitting*]
PsSol .... Psalms of Solomon [*Pseudepigrapha*] (BJA)
PSSP .... Partition with Self Substitution Property (IAA)
PSSP .... Partition with Self-Substitution Property (SAUS)
PSSP .... Payload Specialist Station Panel [*NASA*] (MCD)
PSSP .... Personnel Security and Surety Program [*Military*] (ADDR)
PSSP .... Personnel Surety and Security Program
PSSP .... Phone Center Staffing and Sizing Program [*Telecommunications*] (TEL)
PSSP .... Pilot Stick Sensor Assembly (SAUS)
PSSR .... Parallel-Shaft Speed Reducer
PSSR .... Pre-Startup Safety Review [*Chemical engineering*]
PSSR .... Primary School Staff Relations [*Project*] (AIE)
PSSR .... Problem Status and Summary Report [*NASA*] (KSC)
PSSR .... Provisioning Supply Support Requests [*DoD*]
PSSRA .... Public Service Staff Relations Act [*Canada*]
PSSRB .... Public Service Staff Relations Board [*Canada*]
PSSRI .... Planetary and Space Sciences Research Institute [*United Kingdom*] [*Open University*] (RCD)
PSSRU .... Personal Social Services Research Unit [*University of Kent at Canterbury*] [*United Kingdom*] (RCD)
PSSS .... Polish Society of Soil Science (SAUS)
PSSS .... Presidential Survivability Support System
PSSS .... Psychiatric Status Schedule (SAUS)
Pss Sol ..... Psalms of Solomon [*Biblical*] (RION)
PSST .... Periodic Significant Scheduled Tasks [*NASA*] (NASA)
PSST .... Prairie State Standard Time (SAUS)
PSS(T) ...... Pregnancy Support Service (Tasmania) [*Australia*]
PSST .... Public Sector Standardization Team (SAUS)
PSSTA .... Port Security Station [*Coast Guard*]
PSS TLV ..... Particulate Siza-Selective Threshold Limit Value [*Industrial hygiene term*] (OHS)
PSS Transistor ... Pressure Sensitive Schottky Transistor (SAUS)
PSSU .... Patch Survey and Switching Unit (MCD)
PSSU .... Pilots Stick Sensor Unit (SAUS)
PSSW .... Parliamentary Secretary of State for War (SAUS)
PSSX .... Puget Sound Snoqualmie Valley Railroad [*Federal Railroad Administration identification code*]
PST .... Airwork (New Zealand) Ltd. [*ICAO designator*] (FAAC)
PST .... Central Pashto [*Language symbol*] (ETLW)
PST .... Pacific Standard Time
PST .... Pacific Summer Time
PST .... Pad Service Tower [*Space launch term*] (ISAK)
PST .... Paired Selected Ternary (IAA)
PST .... Pair Selected Ternary [*Computer science*]
PST .... Pakistan Standard Time (SAUS)
PST .... Pancreastatin [*Biochemistry*]
PST .... Pancreatic Suppression Test [*Medicine*] (AAMN)
PST .... Paroxysmal Superaventricular Tachycardia [*Medicine*] (MEDA)
PST .... Paroxysmal Supraventricular Tachycardia [*Cardiology*] (DAVI)
PST .... Partido Socialista de los Trabajadores [*Socialist Workers Party*] [*Panama*] [*Political party*] (EY)
PST .... Partido Socialista de los Trabajadores [*Socialist Workers' Party*] [*Colombia*] [*Political party*] (PPW)
PST .... Partido Socialista de los Trabajadores [*Socialist Workers' Party*] [*Mexico*] [*Political party*] (PPW)
PST .... Partition Specification Table (MHDI)
PST .... Pascal-Suttle Test [*Psychology*] (DAVI)
PST .... Pass Time [*Military*]
pst .... Paste (VRA)
PST .... Paste
PST .... Pastry (MSA)
PST .... Pasture Canyon [*Utah*] [*Seismograph station code, US Geological Survey*] [*Closed*] (SEIS)
PST .... Pellston, MI [*Amtrak Busline code*]
PST .... Penicillin, Streptomycin, and Tetracycline [*Antibiotics*] (MAE)
PST .... Penicillin, Streptomycin,Tetracyclin (SAUS)
PSt .... Pennsylvania State University, University Park, PA [*Library symbol*] [*Library of Congress*] (LCLS)
PST .... Pentobarbital Sleeping Time (SAUS)
PST .... Performance Specification Tree
PST .... Periodic Self-Test [*Computer science*]
PST .... Peristimulus Time [*Neurophysiology*]
PST .... Personnel Subsystem Team [*Military*] (AFIT)
PST .... Peseta [*Monetary unit*] [*Spain and Latin America*]
PST .... Pesticide
PST .... Petrie Stores (EFIS)
PST .... Petrie Stores Corp. [*NYSE symbol*] (SPSG)
PST .... Phase Space Theory [*Physical chemistry*]
PST .... Phenol Sulfotransferase [*An enzyme*]
PST .... Philadelphia Suburban Transportation [*AAR code*]
PST .... Picture Story Test (SAUS)
PST .... Piston Shock Tunnel

PST .... Planetary Spectroscopy Telescope (SSD)
PST .... Plan Specification Tools (SAUS)
PST .... Platelet Survival Time [*Medicine*] (MELL)
PST .... Point of Spiral Tangent (KSC)
PST .... Polaris Star Tracker [*Missiles*]
PST .... Polished Surface Technique (IEEE)
PST .... Pooled Superannuation Trust
PST .... Porcine Somatotropin [*Gene-spliced animal hormone*] [*Monsanto Co.*]
PST .... Portuguese Speaking Test [*Center for Applied Linguistics*] (TES)
PST .... Positive Sign Trigger (SAUS)
PST .... Post-Stall (SAUS)
PST .... Poststenotic [*Medicine*] (DMAA)
PST .... Post Stimulus Time (SAUS)
PST .... Post-Stimulus Time
PST .... Pound Static Thrust (SAUS)
PST .... Precision Static Toroid (SAUS)
PST .... Prefrontal Sonic Treatment (SAUS)
PST .... Preliminary Safety Training (SAUS)
PST .... Preparing for Settlement and Trial (SAUS)
PST .... Pressure Sensitive Tape (SAUS)
PST .... Pressure-Sensitive Tape
PST .... Preston [*Cuba*] [*Airport symbol*] (AD)
PST .... Pre-Stretched Tubing (SAUS)
PST .... Pre-Structured Technology (SAUS)
PST .... Primary Surge Tank [*Nuclear energy*] (NRCH)
PST .... Priority Selection Table [*Computer science*] (IBMDP)
PST .... Prior Service Training [*US Army Reserve*] (INF)
PST .... Production Sampling Test (IAA)
PST .... Production Special Tooling (MCD)
PST .... Production Surveillance Test (MCD)
PST .... Product Strategy Team [*Automotive marketing*]
PST .... Product Support Technician
PST .... Professional, Scientific, and Technical
PST .... Profit Sharing Trustee (DLA)
PST .... Profit-Sharing Trustee (SAUS)
PST .... Program Status Table [*Computer science*] (IAA)
PST .... Program Synchronization Table (CMD)
PST .... Project ST [*Later, NSTA*] (EA)
PST .... Project Support Team (SAUS)
PST .... Propeller STOL [*Short Takeoff and Landing*] Transport
PST .... Propulsion Systems Trainer (SAUS)
PST .... Pro Sight Technology
PST .... Pro-Stock Truck [*Automobile racing*]
PST .... Proto-Sino-Tibetan [*Linguistics*] (IEL)
PST .... Provincial Sales Tax (FOTI)
PST .... Provincial Standard Time (TRID)
PST .... Shepard's Preparing for Settlement and Trial [*A publication*]
Pst .... Static Transpulmonary Pressure at a Specific Lung Volume [*Medicine*] (DAVI)
PSTA .... Monterey Pasta [*NASDAQ symbol*] (SAG)
PSTA .... Packaging Science and Technology Abstracts [*International Food Information Service*] [*Germany*] [*Information service or system*]
PSTA .... Partido Socialista Tito Atahuichi [*Bolivia*] [*Political party*] (PPW)
PSt-A .... Pennsylvania State University, Agricultural Library, University Park, PA [*Library symbol*] [*Library of Congress*] (LCLS)
PSTA .... Pre-Sea Trial Audit (MCD)
PSTA .... Public Safety and Training Association (NADA)
PSTAC .... Petroleum Services Trading Association of Canada (FOTI)
PSt-All .... Pennsylvania State University, Allentown Campus, Allentown, PA [*Library symbol*] [*Library of Congress*] (LCLS)
PSt-Alt .... Pennsylvania State University, Altoona Campus, Altoona, PA [*Library symbol*] [*Library of Congress*] (LCLS)
PSTAR .... Portable Search and Target-Acquisition RADAR (SEWL)
PSTART .... Page Start register (SAUS)
P-STATIC .... Precipitation Static
PSt-B .... Pennsylvania State University, Berks Campus, Wyomissing, PA [*Library symbol*] [*Library of Congress*] (LCLS)
PSTB .... Perpetual State Bank (North Carolina) [*NASDAQ symbol*] (SAG)
PSTB .... Picture Story Test Blank [*Psychology*]
PSTB .... Propulsion System Test Bed [*for ABC helicopters*] (RDA)
PSTB .... Puget Sound Naval Ship Yard [*Federal Railroad Administration identification code*]
PSTB .... Puget Sound Tug & Barge [*AAR code*]
pstbd .... Pasteboard (VRA)
PSt-Be .... Pennsylvania State University, Beaver Campus, Monaca, PA [*Library symbol*] [*Library of Congress*] (LCLS)
PSTC .... Pole Star Transport [*Common carrier symbol*]
PSTC .... Pressure Sensitive Tape Council (EA)
PSTC .... Product Support Task Control (AAG)
PSTC .... Public Switched Telephone Circuits [*Telecommunications*] (TEL)
PStcA .... American Philatelic Research Library, State College, PA [*Library symbol*] [*Library of Congress*] (LCLS)
PSTCA .... Pennsylvania State Tax Collectors Association (EARSL)
PSt-Ca .... Pennsylvania State University, Capitol Campus, Middletown, PA [*Library symbol*] [*Library of Congress*] (LCLS)
PSTCA .... Public Services Temporary Clerks' Association [*A union*] [*British*]
PStcH .... HRB-Singer, Inc., Science Park, State College, PA [*Library symbol*] [*Library of Congress*] (LCLS)
PSTCO .... Per Steering Compass [*Navigation*] (DNAB)
PST Code .... Paired Selected Ternary Code (SAUS)
PSt-D .... Pennsylvania State University, DuBois Campus, DuBois, PA [*Library symbol*] [*Library of Congress*] (LCLS)
PSTD .... Potato Spindle Tuber Disease
PSTD .... Prison Service Training Depot (SAUS)
PSTD .... Promotable Second-Tier Debt [*Economics*]
PStdE .... Eastern College, St. Davids, PA [*Library symbol*] [*Library of Congress*] (LCLS)
PSt-De .... Pennsylvania State University, Delaware Campus, Chester, PA [*Library symbol*] [*Library of Congress*] (LCLS)
PST Deflection Yoke .... Precision Static Toroid Deflection Yoke (SAUS)
PSt-E .... Pennsylvania State University, Behrend Campus, Erie, PA [*Library symbol*] [*Library of Congress*] (LCLS)
PSTE .... Personnel Subsystem Test and Evaluation [*Military*]
PST-E .... Priority Selection Table Extension [*Computer science*] (IBMDP)
PSTE .... Production Special Testing Equipment (MCD)
PSTEP .... Pre-Service Teacher Education Program [*National Science Foundation*]
PSTE Program .... Personnel Subsystem Test and Evaluation Program (SAUS)
PSTF .... Payload Spin Test Facility (MCD)
PSt-F .... Pennsylvania State University, Fayette Campus, Uniontown, PA [*Library symbol*] [*Library of Congress*] (LCLS)
PSTF .... Pioneer Station Training Facility [*NASA*]
PSTF .... Pressure Suppression Test Facility [*Nuclear energy*] (IEEE)
PSTF .... Privately-Owned Sewage Treatment Facility
PSTF .... Professional Staff [*NASDAQ symbol*] (SAG)
PSTF .... Profit Sharing Trust Fund
PSTF .... Proximity Sensor Test Facility [*Nuclear energy*] (NRCH)
PSTF .... Pump Seal Test Facility [*Nuclear energy*] (NRCH)
PSTG .... Postage (WGA)
PSTGC .... Per Steering Compass [*Navigation*]
PSt-H .... Pennsylvania State University, Hazelton Campus, Hazelton, PA [*Library symbol*] [*Library of Congress*] (LCLS)
PSTH .... Peristimulus Time Histogram
PSTH .... Posthumously
PSTH .... Poststimulus Time Histiogram [*Medical statistics*]
PSTH .... Poststimulus Time-Histogramm (SAUS)
PSTH .... Poststimulus Time Histograph (STED)
PSTH .... Professional Sports Teams Histories [*A publication*]
PSTI .... Pancreatic Secretory Trypsin Inhibitor [*Biochemistry*]
PSTIAC .... Pavements and Soil Trafficability Information Analysis Center [*Army Corps of Engineers*] (IID)
PSt-KP .... Pennsylvania State University, King of Prussia Graduate Center, King of Prussia,PA [*Library symbol*] [*Library of Congress*] (LCLS)
PSTL .... Pastoral
PSTL .... Pistol (MSA)
PSTL .... Postal (AFM)
PSTL .... Pressure Model Static and Transient Launch Configuration (SAA)
PSTM .... Persistent Standoff Target Marker (MCD)
PSTM .... Photon Scanning Tunnelling Microscope
PSTMA .... Paper Stationery and Tablet Manufacturers Association [*Later, PCA*] (EA)
PSt-MA .... Pennsylvania State University, Mont Alto Campus, Mont Alto, PA [*Library symbol*] [*Library of Congress*] (LCLS)
PSt-McK .... Pennsylvania State University, McKeesport Campus, McKeesport, PA [*Library symbol*] [*Library of Congress*] (LCLS)
PSTN .... Pesticide Safety Team Network (GNE)
PSTN .... Piston (MSA)
PSTN .... Position
PSTN .... Public Service Telephone Network (WDAA)
PSTN .... Public Switched (or Switching) Telephone Network (SAUS)
PSTN .... Public Switched Telephone Network [*Communications*]
PSt-NK .... Pennsylvania State University, New Kensington Campus, New Kensington, PA [*Library symbol*] [*Library of Congress*] (LCLS)
PSt-O .... Pennsylvania State University, Ogontz Campus, Abington, PA [*Library symbol*] [*Library of Congress*] (LCLS)
PSTO .... Principal Sea Transport Officer
PSTO .... Purdue Student-Teacher Opinionaire [*Test*]
PSTOL .... Spacecraft Test Operations Language (SAUS)
PSTOP .... Page Stop register (SAUS)
PS to PS .... Private Siding to Private Siding
PS to S .... Private Siding to Station
PSTP .... Pentasodium Triphosphate (STED)
PSTP .... Programmable Strategy Theorem Prover (SAUS)
PSTP .... Protocol Standards Technical Panel (SAUS)
PSt-PiN .... Pennsylvania State University, School of Nursing, Allegheny General Hospital, Pittsburgh, PA [*Library symbol*] [*Library of Congress*] (LCLS)
PSTR .... Pastor
PSTR .... Penn State TRIGA [*Training Reactor, Isotopes General Atomic*] Reactor
PSTR .... Pennsylvania State University Triga Reactor (SAUS)
PSTR .... Propulsion System Training Rig (SAUS)
P/STRG .... Power Steering [*Automotive engineering*]
P-Strip .... P-shaped Strip (SAUS)
PSTS .... Passive SONAR Tracking System
PSt-S .... Pennsylvania State University, Scranton Campus, Scranton, PA [*Library symbol*] [*Library of Congress*] (LCLS)
PSTS .... Personnel Selection Training School (SAUS)
PSTS .... Primary School Teachers and Science [*Project*] (AIE)
PSTS .... Puget Sound Transfer and Storage [*Common carrier symbol*]
PSt-Sk .... Pennsylvania State University, Schuylkill Campus, Schuylkill Haven, PA [*Library symbol*] [*Library of Congress*] (LCLS)
PSt-SV .... Pennsylvania State University, Shenango Valley Campus, Sharon, PA [*Library symbol*] [*Library of Congress*] (LCLS)
PSTTX .... Pioneer Short Term Income [*Mutual fund ticker symbol*] (SG)
PSTV .... Potato Spindle Tuber Viroid (STED)
PSTV .... Potato Spindle Tuber Virus
PSTV .... Protocol Specification, Testing and Verification (SAUS)
PSTV .... PST Vans [*NASDAQ symbol*] (TTSB)
PSTV .... PST Vans, Inc. [*NASDAQ symbol*] (SAG)

PSTVd .... Potato Spindle Tuber Viroid [*Plant pathology*]
PST Vn ...... PST Vans, Inc. [*Associated Press*] (SAG)
PSt-WB ...... Pennsylvania State University, Wilkes-Barre Campus, Wilkes-Barre, PA [*Library symbol*] [*Library of Congress*] (LCLS)
PSt-WS ...... Pennsylvania State University, Worthington Scranton Campus, Dunmore, PA [*Library symbol*] [*Library of Congress*] (LCLS)
PSt-X .... Pennsylvania State University, Off-Campus Libraries [*Library symbol*] [*Library of Congress*] (LCLS)
PSt-Y .... Pennsylvania State University, York Campus, York, PA [*Library symbol*] [*Library of Congress*] (LCLS)
pstyl .... Peristyle (VRA)
P'STYL ...... Pronestyl [*Procainamide*] [*Bristol-Myers Squibb Co.*] [*Pharmacology*] (DAVI)
PSTZ .... Pasteurize (SAUS)
PSTZD .... Pasteurized (SAUS)
PSTZG .... Pasteurizing [*Freight*]
PSU .... Aeropeninsular, SA de CV [*Mexico*] [*FAA designator*] (FAAC)
PSu .... John R. Kaufman, Jr., [*Sunbury*] Public Library, Sunbury, PA [*Library symbol*] [*Library of Congress*] (LCLS)
PSU .... Package Size Unspecified
PSU .... Packet Switching Unit
PSU .... Page Storage Unit (SAUS)
PSU .... Partido Socialista Unificado [*Socialist Unification Party*] [*Argentina*] [*Political party*] (PPW)
PSU .... Partido Socialista Uruguayo [*Uruguayan Socialist Party*] [*Political party*] (PD)
PSU .... Partidul Socialist Unitar [*Unitary Socialist Party*] [*Romania*] [*Political party*] (PPE)
PSU .... Parti Socialiste Unifie [*Unified Socialist Party*] [*France*] [*Political party*] (PPW)
PSU .... Partito Socialista Unificato [*Unified Socialist Party*] [*Italy*] [*Political party*] (PPE)
PSU .... Partito Socialista Unitario [*Socialist Unity Party*] [*Italy*] [*Political party*] (PPE)
PSU .... Path Setup [*Telecommunications*] (TEL)
PSU .... Penn State University (SAUS)
PSU .... Pennsylvania State University
PSU .... Pennsylvania State University, University Park (USDC)
PSU .... Peripheral Switching Unit (CIST)
PSU .... Pet Services, Unlimited [*Commercial firm*] (EA)
PSU .... Philatelic Sales Unit
PSU .... Photosynthetic Unit
PSU .... Plasma Spray Unit
PSU .... Polyphenylene Sulfone [*Organic chemistry*]
PSU .... Portable Storage Unit (SAUS)
PSU .... Portland State University
PSU .... Port Security Unit [*Coast Guard*] (DOMA)
PSU .... Port Sharing Unit (IAA)
PSU .... Port Storage Utility [*Telecommunications*] (TEL)
PSU .... Postsurgical Unit (DAVI)
PSU .... Potential Stroke Unit [*Medicine*] (EDAA)
PSU .... Power Sensor Unit (SAUS)
PSU .... Power Supply Unit (MSA)
PSU .... Power Switching Unit (MCD)
PSU .... Practical Salinity Unit
PSU .... Pressure Speed-Up (SAUS)
PSU .... Pressure Status Unit (AAG)
PSU .... Presume [*Telegraphy*] (PCTE)
PSU .... Primary Sampling Unit [*Statistics*]
PSU .... Primary Switching Unit (SAUS)
PSU .... Printed Side Up [*Graphic arts*] (DGA)
PSU .... Probability Sampling Unit (WDMC)
PSU .... Problem Statement Unit (SAUS)
PSU .... Processor Service Unit (ECII)
PSU .... Processor Speed Up [*Computer memory core*]
PSU .... Processor Storage Unit [*Computer science*] (CIST)
PSU .... Program Storage Unit [*Computer science*] (MDG)
PSU .... Program Support Unit (FOTI)
PSU .... Pseudo (ACAE)
PSU .... Publications Services Unit (SAUS)
PSU .... Public Sector Unit (SAUS)
PSU .... Public Security Unit (SAUS)
PSU .... Public Services Unit (EERA)
PSU .... Public Storage Properties XVI [*AMEX symbol*] (SPSG)
PSU .... Public Storage Prop'A'XVI [*AMEX symbol*] (TTSB)
PSU .... Pyrotechnic Switching Unit (ACAE)
PSU .... Tatoo-a-Pet [*Commercial firm*] (EA)
PSUB .... Piston Supported Upper Bearing (SAUS)
PSUB .... Piston-Supported Upper Bearing
P-Substance... Protein Substance (SAUS)
PSUC .... Partit Socialista Unificat de Catalunya [*Unified Socialist Party of Catalonia*] [*Spain*] [*Political party*] (PPE)
PSUD .... Presumed [*Telegraphy*] (PCTE)
PSUD .... Psychoactive Substance Use Disorder
PSUG .... Presuming [*Telegraphy*] (PCTE)
PSU/IRL..... Pennsylvania State University Ionosphere Research Laboratory
PSU-IRL..... Pennsylvania State University-Ionosphere Research Laboratory (SAUS)
PSUL .... Power Supply Unit Launching (SAUS)
PSULI .... Partito Socialista Unitario de Lavoratori Italiani [*Unitary Socialist Party of Italian Workers*] [*Political party*] (PPE)
PSUM .... Unified Socialist Party of Mexico [*Political party*] (PSAP)
PSU-MRL ... Pennsylvania State University-Materials Research Laboratory (SAUS)
PSUN .... Pacific Sunwear of Calif [*NASDAQ symbol*] (TTSB)
PSUN .... Pacific Sunwear of California, Inc. [*NASDAQ symbol*] (SAG)
PSUN .... Presumption [*Telegraphy*] (PCTE)
PSUP .... Pennsylvania State University Press (DGA)
PSUR .... Pennsylvania State University Reactor
PSURAO .... Pennsylvania State University Radio Astronomy Observatory
PSurg .... Plastic Surgeon (SAUS)
PSurg .... Plastic Surgery [*Medicine*]
P-SURG ..... Presurgery Coagulation Profile [*Hematology and surgery*] (DAVI)
PSUSAM .... Philippine Statehood USA Movement [*An association*] (EA)
PSUT .... Phase Shifter Under Test (SAUS)
PSUY .... Presumably [*Telegraphy*] (PCTE)
PSV .... Pair Shield Video (NITA)
PSV .... Paleosecular Variation [*Geology*]
PSV .... Pangola Stunt Virus [*Virology*] (QSUL)
PSV .... Papillitis Stenosans Vateri (DB)
PSV .... Passive [*Telegraphy*] (PCTE)
PSV .... Peanut Stunt Virus
PSV .... Photographic-Spatial Volume (SAA)
PSV .... Pictorial Study of Values [*Psychology*]
PSV .... Pilot Secure Voice (SAUS)
PSV .... Piston Skirt Varnish [*Fuels and lubricants*]
PSV .... Planetary Space Vehicle [*NASA*] (NASA)
PSV .... Platform Supply Vessel (SAUS)
PSV .... Polished Stone Value (SAUS)
PSV .... Polished-Stone Value (PDAA)
PSV .... Portable Sensor Verifier (AAG)
PSV .... Positive Start Voltage
PSV .... Preliminary Site Visit (SAUS)
PSV .... Present State Variable (SAUS)
PSV .... Preserve (MSA)
PSV .... Pressure Safety Valve
PSV .... Pressure Support Ventilation [*Medicine*] (DAVI)
PSV .... Probability State Variable [*Statistics*]
PSV .... Program Status Vector (SAUS)
PSV .... Progressieve Surinaamse Volkspartij [*Progressive Suriname People's Party*] [*Political party*] (PPW)
PSV .... Project Salt Vault (SAUS)
PSV .... Proximal Selective Vagotomy [*Medicine*] (EDAA)
PSV .... Pseudo-Synthetic Video (DOMA)
PSV .... Psychiatric Society of Virginia (EARSL)
PSV .... Psychological, Social, and Vocational [*Adjustment factors*]
PSV .... Public Service Vehicle
PSV .... Public Storage Properties XVII, Inc. [*AMEX symbol*] (SAG)
PSV .... Public Storage Prop'A'XVII [*AMEX symbol*] (TTSB)
PSV .... Saint Vincent College, Latrobe, PA [*OCLC symbol*] (OCLC)
PSVBS....... Police Stolen Vehicle Bait System [*Law enforcement*]
PSVC .... Power alarm on Service Cluster (SAUS)
PSvcBad .... Presidential Service Badge [*Military decoration*] (AABC)
PSvCol ...... Public Service Co. of Colorado [*Associated Press*] (SAG)
PSVD .... Polystyrene-Divinylbenzene Copolymer [*Organic chemistry*]
PSV Device... Probabilistic State Variable Device (SAUS)
PSVER....... Pattern-Shift Visual Evoked Response [*Medicine*] (MEDA)
PSVL .... Peak Signal Voltage Loss (SAUS)
PSVM........ Phase Sensitive Voltmeter (SAUS)
psvm .... Phase-Sensitive Voltmeter (IDOE)
PSVM........ Phase-Sensitive Voltmeter
PSVM........ Phase Shift Voltmeter (SAUS)
PSVN .... Pilot Secure Voice Network (SAUS)
PSvNM ...... Public Service Co. of New Mexico [*Associated Press*] (SAG)
PSVOA ...... Purse Seine Vessel Owners Association (EA)
PSVOMA .... Purse Seine Vessel Owners Marketing Association [*Later, PSVOA*] (EA)
PSVP .... Pilot Secure Voice Project [*NATO Integrated Communications System*] (NATG)
PSVT .... Paroxysmal Supraventricular Tachycardia [*Cardiology*]
PSVT .... Passivate [*Metallurgy*]
PSVT .... Pilot Secure Voice Terminal (SAUS)
PSVTN....... Preservation (MSA)
PSVTV....... Preservative (MSA)
PSVX .... Pilot Secure Voice Exchange (SAUS)
PSW .... Japan/Corea/Pacific South West Service (SAUS)
PSW .... Pacific South West (SAUS)
PSW .... Pacific Southwest Forest and Range Experiment Station [*Berkeley, CA*] [*Department of Agriculture*] (GRD)
PSW .... Past Sleepwalker (STED)
PSW .... Peripheral Switching Unit (NITA)
PSW .... Pinetree Software Canada Ltd. [*Vancouver Stock Exchange symbol*]
PSW .... Planar Stich Wire (SAUS)
PSW .... Plasma Spray Welder
PSW .... Politically Simulated World [*Computer-assisted political science game*]
PSW .... Potential Switch
PSW .... Potentiometer Slide Wire (SAUS)
PSW .... Potentiometer Slidewire
PSW .... Powerplant Specific Weight
PSW .... Primary Shield Water (DNAB)
PSW .... Primary Surgical Ward [*Medicine*] (EDAA)
PSW .... Processor Status Word
PSW .... Process Status Word
PSW .... Programming Status Word (SAUS)
PSW .... Program Status Word [*Computer science*]
PSW .... Program Support Workstation (ACAE)
PSW .... Protective Service Worker [*Medicine*] (EDAA)
PSW .... Pskov State Aviation Enterprise [*Former USSR*] [*FAA designator*] (FAAC)

PSW .... Psychiatric Social Worker [*British*]
PSW .... Public Storage Properties XVIII [*AMEX symbol*] (SPSG)
PSW .... Public Storage Prop'A'XVIII [*AMEX symbol*] (TTSB)
PSW .... PUREX Sludge Waste (SAUS)
PSWA .... Partially Smooth Water Area (DS)
PSWAD ...... Perspective Study of World Agricultural Development [*FAO*] [*United Nations*] (MSC)
PSWB .... Patented Steel Wire Bureau [*British*] (BI)
PSWB .... Plateau State Water Board (SAUS)
PSWB .... Public School Word-Book [*A publication*]
PSWBD ...... Power Switchboard
PSWBS ...... Project Summary Work Breakdown Structure
PSWC .... Pacifc Tsunami Warning Center (SAUS)
PSWC .... Payload Systems Weight Capability [*Space launch term*] (ISAK)
PSWF .... Prolate Spheroidal Wave Function (PDAA)
PSWFA ...... Prestige Saltwater Fly Anglers (SAUS)
PSWFRES ... Pacific Southwest Forest and Range Experiment Station [*Berkeley, CA*] (SAA)
PSWG .... Pressure Sine Wave Generator
PSWG .... Product Support Working Group (SAUS)
PSWHQ ..... Primary Static War Headquarters (SAUS)
PSWHQ ..... Primary Subordinate War Headquarters (SAUS)
PSWIE .... Proceedings of the South Wales Institute of Engineers (SAUS)
PSWM .... Postscript Window Manager (SAUS)
PSWMOW ... Psychiatric Social Work in Mental Observation Wards [*British*]
PSWMRL ... Pasture Systems and Watershed Management Research Lab
PSWO .... Picture and Sound World Organization
PSWO .... Princess of Wales' Own [*Military unit*] [*British*] (ROG)
PSWO .... Product Support Work Order
PSWOPC .... Psychiatric Social Work in Out-Patient Clinics [*British*]
PSWP .... Plant Service Water Pump (IEEE)
PSWR .... Powell Sport Wagon Registry (EA)
PSWR .... Power Standing Wave Ratio
PSWR .... Program Status Word Register [*Computer science*] (MHDB)
PSWS .... Peak Systolic Wall Stress (SAUS)
PSWS .... Potable and Sanitary Water System [*Nuclear energy*] (NRCH)
PSWS .... Puget Sound White-Crowned Sparrow [*North American bird banding code*] (BIBA)
PSwS .... Smith, Kline & French Co. [*Later, SmithKline Corp.*], Swedeland, PA [*Library symbol*] [*Library of Congress*] (LCLS)
PSWT .... Polysonic Wind Tunnel (MCD)
PSWT .... Psychiatric Social Work Training [*British*]
PSWTE ...... Proceedings of the Society for Water Treatment and Examinations (SAUS)
PSWTUF .... Public Service Workers' Trade Union Federation [*Ceylon*]
PSWU .... Public Services Workers Union (SAUS)
PSW Unit ... Processor Status Word Unit (SAUS)
PSX .... Pacific Scientific [*NYSE symbol*] (TTSB)
PSX .... Pacific Scientific Co. [*NYSE symbol*] (SPSG)
PSX .... Pacific South West Express (SAUS)
PSX .... Palacios, TX [*Location identifier*] [*FAA*] (FAAL)
PSX .... Pseudoexfoliation (DMAA)
PSY .... Personally [*Telegraphy*] (PCTE)
PSY .... Port Stanley [*Falkland Islands*] [*Airport symbol*]
PSY .... PSM Technologies, Inc. [*Vancouver Stock Exchange symbol*]
PSY .... Psychiatry
PSY .... Psychological (CINC)
PSY .... Public Storage Properties XIX, Inc. [*AMEX symbol*] (SAG)
PSY .... Public Storage Prop'A' XIX [*AMEX symbol*] (TTSB)
PSYC .... Psychologist
PSYC .... Psychology
PsycCp ...... Psychemedics Corp. [*Associated Press*] (SAG)
PSYCE .... Power Supply Current Estimate (VLIE)
PSYCH ...... Psychiatrist (DSUE)
PSYCH ...... Psychiatry
PSYCH ...... Psychic (ROG)
Psych .... Psychical (SAUS)
PSYCH ...... Psychology (AFM)
Psych .... Psychology (DD)
psych .... Psychology (NTIO)
PSYCHABS ... Psychological Abstracts (SAUS)
Psych & MLJ ... Psychological and Medico-Legal Journal [*A publication*] (DLA)
PSYCHC ..... Psychiatric
PSYCH/D .... Psychological Death (SAUS)
PSYCHE ..... Programming Systems Yearly Cost Headcount Estimate (SAUS)
PSYCHE ..... Programming Systems Yearly Cost/Headcount Estimate (VLIE)
PSYCHEM ... Psychiatric Chemistry
PSyCHES .... Psychiatric Case History Event System (PDAA)
PSYCHIAT ... Psychiatric (SAUS)
psychiat ..... Psychiatry [*or Psychiatric*] (DAVI)
PSYCHL ..... Psychological (AFM)
PSYCHO ..... Psychoanalysis (DSUE)
psycho ...... Psychological [*Medicine*] (EDAA)
psycho ...... Psychopath [*Psychiatry*] (DAVI)
Psychoan ... Psychoanalist (SAUS)
psychoan ... Psychoanalysis [*Medicine*] (DMAA)
Psychoanal ... Psychoanalysis (BEE)
psychobio ... psychobiological (SAUS)
PSYCHOBIO ... Psychobiologist (SAUS)
PSYCHOBIO ... Psychobiology (SAUS)
PSYCHOBIOG ... Psychiographer (SAUS)
PSYCHOBIOG ... Psychobiographer (SAUS)
PSYCHOBIOG ... Psychobiographic (SAUS)
PSYCHOBIOG ... Psychobiography (SAUS)
PSYCHOCHRON ... Psychochronicle (SAUS)
PSYCHOCHRON ... Psychochronologer (SAUS)
PSYCHOCHRON ... Psychochronologic (SAUS)
PSYCHOCHRON ... Psychochronology (SAUS)
PSYCHOCHRONICLE ... Psychiatric Chronicle (SAUS)
PSYCHOCHRONICLE ... Psychological Chronicle (SAUS)
PSYCHODELS ... Psychodelics (SAUS)
PSYCHOGEOG ... Psychogeographer (SAUS)
PSYCHOGEOG ... Psychogeography (SAUS)
PSYCHOHIST ... Psychohistorian (SAUS)
PSYCHOHIST ... Psychohistorical (SAUS)
PSYCHOHIST ... Psychohistory (SAUS)
PSYCHOL ... Psychology
PSYCHOMET ... Psychometric (SAUS)
Psychonomic Sci ... Psychonomic Science (SAUS)
PSYCHOPATHOL ... Psychopathological (SAUS)
PSYCHOPATHOL ... Psychopathologist (SAUS)
psychopathol ... Psychopathology (DAVI)
PSYCHOPHYS ... Psychophysical (SAUS)
PSYCHOPHYS ... Psychophysicist (SAUS)
psychophys ... Psychophysics [*Psychiatry*] (DAVI)
psychophysiol ... psychophysiological (SAUS)
PSYCHOPHYSIOL ... Psychophysiologist (SAUS)
psychophysiol ... Psychophysiology [*Psychiatry*] (DAVI)
PSYCHOPRISON ... Psychiatric Hospital Prison (SAUS)
PsychosMed ... Psychosomatic Medicine [*Psychiatry*] (DAVI)
PSYCHOSURG ... Psychosurgeon (SAUS)
PSYCHOSURG ... Psychosurgery (SAUS)
psychot ...... psychotic (SAUS)
PSYCHOTHER ... Psychotherapist (SAUS)
psychother ... Psychotherapy [*Psychiatry*] (DAVI)
PSYCHO WARD ... Psychopathic Ward (SAUS)
Psych Qtly ... Psychoanalytic Quarterly (SAUS)
Psych Test ... Psychological Testing (SAUS)
PSYCHY ..... Psychiatry
PsycINFO ... Psychological Abstracts Information Services [*American Psychological Association*] (IID)
PSYCINFO ... Psychological Information (NITA)
PSYCINFO .. Psychological Information (SAUS)
PSYCO ...... Peripheral System Check-Out (VLIE)
PSYCTRC ... Psychiatric
PSYCTRY ... Psychiatry
PSYCY .... Psychology
PsyD .... Doctor of Psychology
PsyD, LCP ... Doctor of Psychology, Licensed Clinical Psychologist
PSYDOC ..... Psychiatrist Doctor (SAUS)
PSYETA ..... Psychologists for the Ethical Treatment of Animals [*An association*] (EA)
PsyETA ...... Psychologists for the Ethical Treatment of Animals (EA)
Psy M .... Master of Psychology (PGP)
PSYNC ...... Processor Synchronous [*Computer science*] (VLIE)
PSYOP ...... Psychological Operation [*Military*]
PSYOPS ..... Psychological Operations [*Military*]
PSY-OPS .... Psychological Warfare Operations (DNAB)
psy-path .... Psychopath [*Psychiatry*] (DAVI)
Psy-ped ..... Psychologie-Pedagogie [*French*] (CPGU)
PSYRES ..... Psychotherapeutische Forschungsstelle in Stuttgart (SAUS)
PSYS .... Point System [*Motor vehicle violation code used in state of Maryland*] (MVRD)
PSYS .... Precision Systems [*NASDAQ symbol*] (TTSB)
PSYS .... Precision Systems, Inc. [*NASDAQ symbol*] (SAG)
PSYS .... Programming & Systems, Inc. [*NASDAQ symbol*] (COMM)
Psy S .... Specialist in Psychology (PGP)
PSY-SDIV ... Psychological Sciences Division [*Office of Naval Research*] (DNAB)
psy-som ..... Psychosomatic (DAVI)
PsySR .... Psychologists for Social Responsibility (EA)
PSYU .... Public Sustained Yield Unit [*Forestry*]
PSYWAR .... Psychological Warfare
PSYWPN .... Psychological Weapon [*Military*] (AFM)
PSZ .... Partially Stabilized Zirconia (SAUS)
PSZ .... Partially-Stabilized Zirconia [*Ceramics*]
PSZ .... Partly Stabilized Zirconia (SAUS)
PSZ .... Piszkesteto [*Hungary*] [*Seismograph station code, US Geological Survey*] (SEIS)
PSZ .... Pressure Sealing Zipper
PSZ .... Pro Air Service [*ICAO designator*] (FAAC)
PSZ .... Public Storage Properties XX [*AMEX symbol*] (SPSG)
PSZ .... Public Storage Prop'A' XX [*AMEX symbol*] (TTSB)
PSZ .... Puerto Suarez [*Bolivia*] [*Airport symbol*] (OAG)
PSZN .... Pubblicazioni. Stazione Zoologica di Napoli [*A publication*]
PT .... Advanced Planning and Technology Office [*Kennedy Space Center Directorate*] (NASA)
PT .... Brazil [*International civil aircraft marking*] (ODBW)
PT .... Cisplatin [*Medicine*] (EDAA)
PT .... Current Temporary Permit [*Motor vehicle violation driver status code in state of North Dakota*] (MVRD)
PT .... Duffryn Yard [*Welsh depot code*]
PT .... Motor Torpedo Boat [*Navy symbol*] [*Obsolete*]
PT .... Pacific Time
PT .... Packaged Terminal (SAUS)
PT .... Packed Tower (EEVL)
PT .... Packet Terminal (NITA)
PT .... Packet Trunk (SAUS)
PT .... Packet Type (SAUS)

PT............ Page Table [*Computer science*] (IAA)
PT............ Page Teleprinter (SAUS)
PT............ Page Terminator (SAUS)
pt............ Paint (VRA)
PT............ Pain Threshold
PT............ Paint Temperature [*Automotive manufacturing*]
PT............ Pallet Truck (DCTA)
P-T............ Palomero Toluqueno [*Race of maize*]
PT............ Paper Tape
PT............ Paper Title [*Business term*]
PT............ Paper Trooper [*One who salvaged paper for war effort*] [*World War II*]
PT............ Para-Terphenyl [*Organic chemistry*]
PT............ Parathormone (DB)
PT............ Parathyroid [*Medicine*]
PT............ Parcel Ticket [*Freight*]
PT............ Paroxysmal Tachycardia [*Cardiology*]
pt............ Part (DAVI)
Pt............ Part
PT............ Part [*Online database field identifier*]
PT............ Partially Tested (IAA)
PT............ Participative Teams (MCD)
PT............ Partido de los Trabajadores [*Paraguay*] [*Political party*] (EY)
PT............ Partido Trabajador [*Mexico*] [*Political party*] (EY)
PT............ Partition Table [*Computer science*] (IAA)
PT............ Part Throttle [*Engines*]
PT............ Part Time (EEVL)
pt............ Part Time (ODA)
P-T............ Part-Time [*Employment*]
PT............ Part-Timers (SAUS)
PT............ Part Total [*Earnings less than weekly benefit amount*] [*Unemployment insurance*] (OICC)
PT............ Paschale Tempore [*Easter Time*] [*Latin*]
PT............ Passage Time (SAUS)
PT............ Passed Test [*Motor vehicle violation code used in state of Maryland*] (MVRD)
PT............ Passenger Traffic [*MTMC*] (TAG)
PT............ Passenger Train (SAUS)
PT............ Passenger Transport
PT............ Passing Title [*Real estate*]
PT............ Passive Track [*Military*] (CAAL)
PT............ Pass Through (VLIE)
PT............ Past Tense
PT............ Pataca [*Monetary unit*] [*Macau*]
PT............ Patch Test [*Medicine*] (MELL)
PT............ Patellar Tendon [*Anatomy*]
PT............ Patentee (NITA)
PT............ Path & Thread (SAUS)
pt............ Patient [*Medicine*] (BCRP)
Pt............ Patient (WDAA)
PT............ Patient
PT............ Patient-Trigger [*Linguistics*] (IEL)
PT............ Patrol Torpedo (ADWA)
PT............ Patrol Torpedo Boat [*Later, PTF*] [*Navy symbol*]
PT............ Pattern Transfer (SAUS)
PT............ Paying Teller [*Banking*]
PT............ Payload Type (SAUS)
pt............ Payment (WDMC)
PT............ Payment
PT............ Payout Time [*Business term*]
PT............ Pay Tone [*Telecommunications*] (TEL)
PT............ Peacetime (SEWL)
PT............ Peak Time (SAUS)
PT............ Pencil Tube
PT............ Penetrant Test [*Nuclear energy*] (NRCH)
PT............ Penetration Test (NATG)
PT............ Peninsula Terminal (SAUS)
PT............ Peninsula Terminal Co. [*AAR code*]
PT............ Pennant [*British naval signaling*]
PT............ Pensacola-Tallahassee [*Diocesan abbreviation*] [*Florida*] (TOCD)
PT............ Pension Trustee (DLA)
PT............ Perfect Title [*Business term*]
PT............ Perforated Tape [*Computer science*] (IAA)
PT............ Perforated Type (SAUS)
PT............ Performance Technology [*Human resources*] (WYGK)
PT............ Performance Test
PT............ Performance Testing
PT............ Pericardial Tamponade [*Medicine*] (DMAA)
PT............ Periodic Test [*Nuclear energy*] (NRCH)
PT............ Period Tapering (IAA)
PT............ Peripheral Transfer (SAUS)
PT............ Permanent and Total (SAUS)
PT............ Permeability Transition [*Biochemistry*]
PT............ Peroneal Tendonitis [*Medicine*] (MELL)
PT............ Perpetual Traveller (ECON)
PT............ Persepolis Texts (BJA)
PT............ Persistent Tease [*Slang*] [*Bowdlerized version*]
P/T............ Personal Time [*Employment*]
PT............ Personal Trade [*Marketing and retail terminology referring to customers*]
PT............ Personal Transporter
PT............ Personnel & Training (SAUS)
PT............ Personnel Training
PT............ Perstetur [*Let It Be Continued*] [*Pharmacy*]
PT............ Per Ton (SAUS)
PT............ Per Truck
PT............ Perturbation Theory [*Physical chemistry*]
PT............ Pertussis Toxin [*Pharmacology*]
PT............ Peseta [*Monetary unit*] [*Spain and Latin America*]
Pt............ Peter [*New Testament book*]
PT............ Petrol Tractor [*British*]
PT............ Petty Theft
PT............ Phase Transfer [*Physical chemistry*]
PT............ Phase Transition (SAUS)
PT............ Phase Type (NITA)
PT............ Pheasant Trust (EA)
PT............ Phenolthiazine (SAUS)
PT............ Phenytoin [*Pharmacology*] (DAVI)
PT............ Philadelphia Transportation (SAUS)
PT............ Phoenix Theatre [*Defunct*] (EA)
PT............ Photoconductive Thermoplastic [*Materials science*]
PT............ Photographic Intelligenceman [*Navy rating*]
PT............ Photo Technician (SAUS)
PT............ Phototherapy [*Medicine*]
PT............ Phototoxity [*Medicine*]
PT............ Phototransistor (NRCH)
PT............ Physical Teardown (MCD)
PT............ Physical Therapy [*or Therapist*]
PT............ Physical Training [*Military*]
PT............ Physiotherapy [*Medicine*]
PT............ Piaster [*Monetary unit*] [*Spain, Republic of Vietnam, and some Middle Eastern countries*] (IMH)
PT............ Picture Telegraphy [*Telecommunications*] (IAA)
PT............ Picture Transmission (SAUS)
PT............ Pigeon-Toed (MELL)
PT............ Pilot Tape (SAUS)
PT............ Pilot Test (VLIE)
PT............ Pine Tar [*Medicine*]
pt............ Pint (ODBW)
PT............ Pint
PT............ Pipe Tap (MSA)
PT............ Pipe Thread (SAUS)
Pt............ Pitch (SAUS)
PT............ Pitch Trim (MCD)
PT............ Placebo Treated [*Medicine*]
PT............ Plain Talk (EA)
PT............ Plain Test (MCD)
PT............ Plain Text (SAUS)
PT............ Plane Table (SAUS)
PT............ Planning and Timing [*of Investments*]
Pt............ Plantinum (SAUS)
PT............ Planum Temporale [*Brain anatomy*]
P-T............ Plasma Thermocouple Reactor [*Nuclear energy*] (NRCH)
PT............ Plasma Triode (SAUS)
PT............ Plasticized Transparent [*Flexography*] (DGA)
PT............ Plastics Technology [*A publication*]
PT............ Plastic Training (SAUS)
PT............ Plastic Tube
PT............ Platinum
Pt............ Platinum [*Chemical element*]
PT............ Platoon Truck [*British*]
PT............ Please Token (VLIE)
PT............ Pleno Titulo [*With Full Title*] [*Latin*]
PT............ Plenty Tough [*Slang*]
PT............ Plenty Trouble [*Slang*]
PT............ Plonia Technica
PT............ Plotting Equipment [*JETDS nomenclature*] [*Military*] (CET)
PT............ Plot Titles [*Test*] [*Psychology*]
PT............ Pluridirectional Tomography [*Medicine*] (RAWO)
PT............ Pneumatic Tube [*Technical drawings*]
PT............ Pneumothorax [*Medicine*]
PT............ Pocket Telephone (SAUS)
PT............ Poetry Treasury [*An association*] [*Defunct*] (EA)
pt............ Point (ODBW)
PT............ Point [*Maps and charts*]
Pt............ Point (SHCU)
P/T............ Pointer/Tracker (MCD)
PT............ Point location (SAUS)
PT............ Point of Tangency
PT............ Point of Turn [*Navigation*]
Pt............ Points, typographische (SAUS)
PT............ Pollen Tube [*Botany*]
PT............ Poll-Tax Rolls [*British*]
PT............ Polymeric Triglyceride [*Food science*]
PT............ Polythiophene [*Organic chemistry*]
PT............ Polyvalent Tolerance (BABM)
PT............ Pool Temperature [*Nuclear energy*] (NRCH)
PT............ Pope and Talbot [*Steamship*] (MHDW)
PT............ Popliteal Tendon [*Anatomy*]
pt............ Port (ODBW)
PT............ Port
PT............ Portal Tract [*Anatomy*]
PT............ Port Number [*Telecommunications*] (TEL)
Pt............ Porto (SAUS)
PT............ Port Talbot Railway [*Wales*]
PT............ Port Taxes (TRID)
PT............ Port Tower (SAUS)
PT............ Portugal [*ANSI two-letter standard code*] (CNC)

PT............ Portugal Telecom ADS [*NYSE symbol*] (TTSB)
PT............ Portugal Telecom SA [*NYSE symbol*] (SAG)
pt............ Portuguese Timor [*io (Indonesia) used in records cataloged after January 1978*] [*MARC country of publication code*] [*Library of Congress*] (LCCP)
PT............ Positional Tolerance (AAEL)
PT............ Positional Tolerancing
PT............ Position Location Reporting System Terminal
PT............ Postal Telegraph (SAUS)
PT............ Postal Telegraph Co. [*Terminated*]
PT............ Post and Telegraph (SAUS)
PT............ Post and Telegraphy [*Telecommunications*] (IAA)
PT............ Poste e Telegrafi [*Post and Telegraph Service*] [*Italy*]
PT............ Poster Fair
PT............ Posterior Tibial [*Anatomy*]
PT............ Posterior Tibial pulse (SAUS)
PT............ Posts and Telecommunications (SAUS)
PT............ Post Town
PT............ Potential Transformer
PT............ Power Train (SAUS)
PT............ Power Transfer (KSC)
PT............ Power Turbine (SAUS)
PT............ Prachakorn Thai [*Thai Citizens Party*] [*Political party*]
PT............ Practice Tracer (SAUS)
PT............ Precision Teaching
PT............ Precision Time (SAUS)
PT............ Precision Time Fuze
P/T............ Precision-to-Tolerance ratio (SAUS)
PT............ Precision Tracker (SAUS)
PT............ Precision Transform [*Eastman Kodak Co.*] [*Computer science*] (PCM)
PT............ Preferential Treatment (OICC)
PT............ Premium Transfer (SAUS)
PT............ Preoperational Test [*Nuclear energy*] (NRCH)
PT............ Prepunched Tape (SAUS)
PT............ Present [*Telegraphy*] (PCTE)
PT............ Press Test [*Psychology*]
P/T............ Pressure/Temperature (KSC)
PT............ Pressure Test (AAG)
PT............ Pressure Time Fuel System [*Cummins Engine Co., Inc.*]
PT............ Pressure Transducer (KSC)
PT............ Pressure Transmitter (NRCH)
PT............ Pressure Tubing
PT............ Pretectal [*Neuroanatomy*]
pt............ Preterit [*Past tense*] [*Grammar*]
pt............ Preterite (ODA)
PT............ Previous Operating Time (AFIT)
PT............ Primal Therapy
pt............ Primary Target (ODA)
PT............ Primary Target [*Army*]
PT............ Primary Timer (VLIE)
PT............ Primary Trainer [*Aircraft*]
PT............ Print (MSA)
PT............ Printed Text
PT............ Printer Terminal
PT............ Printing Tape (SAUS)
PT............ Print Text (SAUS)
PT............ Priority Telegram
PT............ Prior Treatment [*Medicine*]
PT............ Prismatic Tank (SAUS)
PT............ Private Terms
PT............ Procedure Trainer (SAUS)
PT............ Procedure Turn [*FAA*] (TAG)
PT............ Processing Tax Division [*United States Internal Revenue Bureau*] (DLA)
PT............ Processing Time
PT............ Processor Terminal [*Computer science*] (VLIE)
PT............ Process Time (VLIE)
PT............ Process Type (SAUS)
PT............ Production Techniques (MCD)
PT............ Production Test [*Military*]
PT............ Productive Time [*Computer order entry*]
PT............ Product Team (AAGC)
PT............ Product Test (IAA)
PT............ Proficiency Testing
PT............ Profile Template
PT............ Profit Taking [*Investment term*]
PT............ Program (Exercise) on Treadmill
PT............ Programmable Terminal [*Computer science*]
PT............ Programmed Testing (SAUS)
PT............ Programmed Timing (SAUS)
PT............ Programmer and Timer
PT............ Programmer Training (SAUS)
PT............ Programming Theory (SAUS)
PT............ Programming Time (SAUS)
PT............ Program Tab (SAUS)
PT............ Program Table (SAUS)
PT............ Program Tape (SAUS)
PT............ Program Termination (SAUS)
PT............ Program Test (SAUS)
PT............ Program Text (SAUS)
PT............ Program Time (SAUS)
PT............ Program Timer (SAUS)
PT............ Program Track (SAUS)
PT............ Program Transfer (SAUS)
PT............ Program Translation (SAUS)
PT............ Program Transmitter (SAUS)
PT............ Progress in Technology [*Automotive industry*]
PT............ Progressive Tax (MHDW)
PT............ Prohibited Telegrams
PT............ Project Team (SAUS)
PT............ Project Technology (ACAE)
PT............ Project Tibet (EA)
PT............ Project Transition [*DoD*] (OICC)
PT............ Project Trust (EAIO)
PT............ Prolong Tablets [*Pharmacy*]
PT............ Pronator Teres [*Musle*] [*Orthopedics*] (DAVI)
PT............ Proof Test (AAG)
PT............ Propanethiol [*Organic chemistry*]
PT............ Propanthiol (SAUS)
PT............ Propellant Injection Pressure
PT............ Propellant Temperature (SAUS)
PT............ Propellant Transfer
PT............ Propeller Torpedo [*Boat*]
PT............ Property Tax (MHDW)
PT............ Property Transfer [*Real estate*] (KSC)
PT............ Property Type
PT............ Prophet
PT............ Propylthiouracil [*Also, PROP, PTU*] [*Thyroid inhibitor*]
PT............ Pro Tempore [*For the Time Being*] [*Latin*]
PT............ Prothrombin Time [*Hematology*]
PT............ Protocol Team (HVTR)
PT............ Proto-Tai [*Linguistics*] (IEL)
PT............ Prototype (IAA)
PT............ Provascular Tissue [*Botany*]
PT............ Provincetown-Boston Airline [*ICAO designator*] (AD)
PT............ Provisioning Team (AAG)
PT............ Pseudoternary (SAUS)
PT............ Pseudotetrade (SAUS)
Pt............ Pseudoword Target [*Psychology*]
PT............ Psychology Today [*A publication*] (BRI)
Pt............ Pteropods [*Quality of the bottom*] [*Nautical charts*]
PT............ PTP Resource Corp. [*Formerly, Petrologic Petroleum Ltd.*] [*Vancouver Stock Exchange symbol*]
PT............ Publication Type [*Online database field identifier*]
PT............ Public Transport (DA)
PT............ Public Trustee
PT............ Pull-Through [*Gun cleaning*]
PT............ Pulmonary Trunk (SAUS)
PT............ Pulmonary Tuberculosis [*Medicine*]
PT............ Pulp Testing [*Dentistry*]
PT............ Pulse Terminating [*Communications term*] (DCT)
PT............ Pulse Time (SAUS)
PT............ Pulse Timer
PT............ Pulse Train
PT............ Pulse Transformator (SAUS)
PT............ Pulse Transformer (IAA)
PT............ Punched Tape [*Computer science*]
PT............ Punch Through [*Computer science*] (IAA)
PT............ Punch Transfer (SAUS)
PT............ Pupil Teacher
PT............ Purchase Tax [*British*]
PT............ Pure Telepathy [*Psychical research*]
PT............ Pyramidal Tract [*Anatomy*]
PT............ Pyramid Texts (BJA)
PT............ Pyrotechnic Material (SAUS)
PT............ Test Plan (SAUS)
PT............ Total Pressure
PT............ Workers' Party
PT............ Worker's Party (Brazil) [*Political party*] (PSAP)
PT1............ Photographic Intelligenceman, First Class [*Navy rating*]
PT2............ Photographic Intelligenceman, Second Class [*Navy rating*]
PT3............ Photographic Intelligenceman, Third Class [*Navy rating*]
PTA............ African Preferential Trade Area (SAUS)
PTA............ Angolan Labor Party [*Political party*] (PSAP)
PTA............ Eastern and Southern African Preferential Trade-Area (SAUS)
PTA............ National Postal Transport Association [*Later, APWU*]
PTA............ Packed Tower Aeration (MEC)
PTA............ Page Table Address [*Computer science*] (IAA)
PTA............ Pain, Tears, and Agony [*Medicine*] (EDAA)
PTA............ Palatines to America (EA)
PTA............ Pantera [*NCIC car model code*]
PTA............ Pantorama Industries, Inc. [*Toronto Stock Exchange symbol*]
PTA............ Paper and Twine Association (EA)
PTA............ Paper Tape Accessory (MHDI)
PTA............ Paper Towel Association [*British*] (BI)
PTA............ Parallel Tubular Array [*Cytology*]
PTA............ Parathyroid Adenoma [*Medicine*] (STED)
PTA............ Parent-Teacher Association
PTA............ Part Throttle Acceleration [*Engines*] (EG)
PTA............ Part Time Alcoholic (SAUS)
PTA............ Passenger Transport Authorities [*British*]
PTA............ Passenger Transport Authority (SAUS)
PTA............ Passive Towed Array (SAUS)
PTA............ Patient-Triggered Analgesia (SAUS)
PTA............ Penn Treaty American [*NYSE symbol*] (SG)
PTA............ Penn Treaty American Corp. [*NYSE symbol*]
PTA............ People Taking Action
PTA............ Percent Time Active (CAAL)

PTA .... Percutaneous Transluminal Angiography (SAUS)
PTA .... Percutaneous Transluminal Angioplasty [*Medicine*]
PTA .... Periodical Title Abbreviations [*A publication*]
PTA .... Peritonsillar Abscess [*Medicine*]
PTA .... Persistent Truncus Arteriosus [*Medicine*] (RAWO)
PTA .... Peseta [*Monetary unit*] [*Spain and Latin America*]
PTA .... Pet Traders Association (SAUS)
PTA .... Phenyltrimethylammonium [*Also, PTM, PTMA*] [*Organic chemistry*]
PTA .... Philippine Tobacco Administration (SAUS)
PTA .... Philippine Travel Authority (SAUS)
PTA .... Phorbol Tetradecanoyl Acetate [*Also, PMA, TPA*] [*Organic chemistry*]
PTA .... Phosphoryl Triamide [*Organic chemistry*]
PTA .... Phosphotransacetylase [*An enzyme*]
PTA .... Phosphotungstic Acid [*Inorganic chemistry*]
PTA .... Photographers' Telegraph Association
PTA .... Photo Transistor Amplifier (SAUS)
PTA .... Phototransistor Amplifier
PTA .... Physical Therapy Assistant
PTA .... Pianoforte Tuners' Association [*British*] (DBA)
PTA .... Piano Tuners Association (SAUS)
PTA .... Picatinny Arsenal [*New Jersey*] [*Later, Armament Development Center*] [*Army*]
PTA .... Pilotless Target Aircraft [*Military*]
PTA .... Pitch Trim Adjustment
PTA .... Pitch Trim Angle
PTA .... Planar Turbulence Amplifier (IEEE)
PTA .... Plasma Thrombin Antecedent (SAUS)
PTA .... Plasma Thromboplastin Antecedent [*Factor XI*] [*Hematology*]
PTA .... Plasma Transferred Arc [*Metallurgy*]
PTA .... Platelet Thromboplastin Antecendent [*Medicine*] (STED)
PTA .... Platinized Titanium Anode
PTA .... Point of Total Assumption (MCD)
PTA .... Polish Telegraphic Agency (SAUS)
PTA .... Pope and Talbot (SAUS)
PTA .... Port Alsworth [*Alaska*] [*Airport symbol*] (OAG)
PTA .... Postal Transportation Association (SAUS)
PTA .... Postcard Traders' Association [*British*] (DBA)
PTA .... Posterior Tibial [*Pulse*] [*Medicine*] (DAVI)
PTA .... Post-Tensioning Association (SAUS)
PTA .... Post-Test Analysis [*NASA*] (NASA)
PTA .... Post-Timeline Assessment (SEWL)
PTA .... Post-Traumatic Amnesia [*Medicine*]
PTA .... Potential Toxic Area (NASA)
PTA .... Power Transfer Assembly (IAA)
PTA .... Preferential Trade Arrangements [*ASEAN*] (IMH)
PTA .... Premium Transportation Authorization (AAG)
PTA .... Prepaid Ticket Advice [*Travel industry*] (TRID)
PTA .... Preparation through Acceptance
PTA .... Pressure Transducer Assembly
PTA .... Pre-Treatment Anxiety [*Medicine*] (DMAA)
PTA .... Prevention of Terrorism Act [*British*] (ECON)
PTA .... Price-Tag Awareness [*See also PTS*]
PTA .... Primary Target Area [*Military*]
PTA .... Primary Tungsten Association [*British*] (EAIO)
PTA .... Principle Technical Advisor (SAUS)
PTA .... Printing Trades Alliance [*British*] (DBA)
PTA .... Prior to Administration (AMHC)
PTA .... Prior to Admission [*Medicine*]
PTA .... Prior to Arrival [*Medicine*] (BCRP)
PTA .... Procrustes Target Analysis [*Marine science*] (OSRA)
PTA .... Procurement Technical Assistance
PTA .... Profan Test Assessment [*NASA*]
PTA .... Profiler Triangle Analysis package (SAUS)
PTA .... Programmable Translation Array
PTA .... Programmed Time of Arrival (ACAE)
PTA .... Programmed Translation Array (SAUS)
PTA .... Program Time Analyzer
PTA .... Propfan Technology Assessment (SAUS)
PTA .... Propfan Test Assessment (ACAE)
PTA .... Proposed Technical Approach
PTA .... Propulsion Test Article [*NASA*] (NASA)
PTA .... Protestant Teachers Association (NADA)
PTA .... Prothrombin Activity [*Hematology*]
PTA .... Protionamid (SAUS)
PTA .... Proton Target Area
PTA .... Ptarmigan Airways Ltd. [*Canada*] [*ICAO designator*] (FAAC)
PTA .... Pulse Torquing Assembly (KSC)
PTA .... Punta Arenas [*Chile*] [*Seismograph station code, US Geological Survey*] [*Closed*] (SEIS)
PTA .... Purchase Transaction Analysis
PTA .... Pure Terephthalic Acid (DICI)
PTA .... Pure Tone Acuity (STED)
PTA .... Pure Tone Audiometry (MELL)
PTA .... Pure Tone Average [*Otorhinolaryngology*] (DAVI)
PTA .... Purified Terephthalic Acid [*Organic chemistry*]
PTAA .... Airman Apprentice, Photographic Intelligenceman, Striker [*Navy rating*]
PTA-A .... Periodical Title Abbreviations: by Abbreviation [*A publication*]
PTAA .... Professional Tattooists Association of Australia
PTAB .... Photographic Technical Advisory Board [*American National Standards Institute*]
PTAB .... Program Status Table [*Computer science*] (IAA)
PTAB .... Project Technical Advisory Board (AAEL)
PTAB .... Pterygoalar Bar [*Medicine*] (RAWO)
PTAC .... Penn Treaty American [*NASDAQ symbol*] (TTSB)
PTAC .... Penn Treaty American Corp. [*NASDAQ symbol*] (NQ)
PTAC .... Petroleum Technology Alliance Canada (FOTI)
PTAC .... Plant Transportation Advisory Committee
PTAC .... Procurement Technical Assistance Centers (SAUS)
PTAC .... Professional and Technical Advisory Committee [*JCAH*]
PTAC .... Provincial-Territorial Advisory Committee (FOTI)
P'TACH .... Parents for Torah for All Children [*Program for learning disabled children*]
PTACV .... Prototype Aircushioned Vehicle (SAUS)
PTACV .... Prototype Tracked Air-Cushion Vehicle
PTACX .... PIMCO: Target Cl.C [*Mutual fund ticker symbol*] (SG)
PTAD .... (Phenyl)triazolinedione [*Organic chemistry*]
PTAD .... Productivity and Technical Assistance Division [*Mutual Security Agency*] [*Abolished, 1953*]
PTADB .... Planning Terrain Analysis Data Base (SAUS)
PTADSIM .... Program Tactical Air (SAUS)
PT AEQ .... Partes Aequales [*Equal Parts*] [*Pharmacy*]
PTAF .... Platelet Activating Factor (DMAA)
PTAF .... Policy Target Adjustment Factor (MEDA)
PTAFR .... Platelet Activating Factor Receptor (DMAA)
PTAG .... Portable Tactical Aircraft Guidance (SAUS)
PTAG .... Portable Tactical Approach Guidance (SAUS)
PTAG .... Professional Tattoo Artists Guild (EA)
P-TAG .... Target-Attaching Globulin Precursor [*Medicine*] (STED)
PTAH .... Phosphotungstic Acid-Hematoxylin [*A stain*]
PTAL .... Para-Tolualdehyde [*Organic chemistry*]
PTAL .... Payment Transaction Application Layer [*Computer science*] (ITCA)
PTALL .... Port Allen, LA [*American Association of Railroads railroad junction routing code*]
PTA Modulation .... Phase-to-Amplitude Modulation (SAUS)
PTAN .... Airman, Photographic Intelligenceman, Striker [*Navy rating*]
PT & E .... Physical Teardown and Evaluation (MCD)
PT & E .... Progress Tests and Examinations
PT & ER .... Physical Teardown and Evaluation Review (MCD)
PT&I .... Petroleum Testers and Installers, Inc. (EFIS)
PT & ME .... Physical Teardown and Maintenance Evaluation [*Army*]
PT&Rec Sch .... Physical Training and Recreational School (SAUS)
PT&T .... Postal, Telephone & Telegraph Administration [*Communications term*] (DCT)
PT & W .... Physical Training and Welfare [*British military*] (DMA)
PTANYC .... Protestant Teachers Association of New York City (EA)
PTAP .... Phenyltrimethylammonium Perbromide [*Organic chemistry*]
PTAP .... Porsche Technology Apprenticeship Program [*Automotive industry*]
PTAP .... Profiler Triangle Analysis Package [*Marine science*] (OSRA)
PTAP .... Purified Diphtheria Toxoid Precipitated by Aluminum Phosphate (AAMN)
PTAP .... Purified Toxoid precipitated by Aluminum Phosphate (SAUS)
PTAR .... Prime Time Access Rule [*Television*]
PTAS .... Pilotless Target Aircraft Squadron (SAUS)
PTAS .... Productivity and Technical Assistance Secretariat (SAUS)
PTASE .... Phosphatase [*An enzyme*] (DHSM)
PTA-T .... Periodical Title Abbreviations: by Title [*A publication*]
PTAT .... Pesticides, Toxics, and Air Team (COE)
PTAT .... Private Transatlantic Fiber-Optic Cables (GART)
PTAT .... Private Trans Atlantic Telecommunications (SAUS)
PTAT .... Proportional to Absolute Temperature (IAA)
PTAT .... Pure Tone Average Threshold (DMAA)
PTAT-1 .... Private TransAtlantic Telecommunications System [*Communications term*] (DCT)
PTAT Cable .... Private Transatlantic Telephone Cable (SAUS)
PTAV .... Percutaneous Transluminal Aortic Valvuloplasty [*Cardiology*] (CPH)
PTAVE .... Parents and Teachers Against Violence in Education (EA)
PTAWT .... Atlantic Wind Test Site, Tignish, Prince Edward Island [*Library symbol*] [*National Library of Canada*] (NLC)
PTB .... Brazilian Worker's Party [*Political party*] (PSAP)
PTB .... Page Table Base [*Computer science*] (IAA)
PTB .... Paragon Trade Brands [*NYSE symbol*] (SPSG)
ptB .... Part Bunkers [*Shipping*] (DS)
PTB .... Partial Test Ban (SAUS)
PTB .... Partido Trabalhista Brasileiro [*Brazilian Labor Party*] [*Political party*] (PPW)
PTB .... Parti du Travail de Belgique [*Belgian Labour Party*] [*Political party*] (EY)
PTB .... Parti du Travail du Burkina [*Burkina Faso*] [*Political party*] (EY)
PTB .... Patellar Tendon Bearing [*Medicine*]
PTB .... Patellar Tendon-Bearing Prosthesis [*Medicine*] (IDYL)
PTB .... Patrol Torpedo Boat (WDAA)
PTB .... Payload Timing Buffer [*NASA*] (NASA)
PTB .... Perishables Tariff Bureau, Atlanta GA [*STAC*]
PTB .... Permian-Triassic Boundary [*Geology*]
PTB .... Persistent, Toxic and Bioaccumulative substances (SAUS)
PTB .... Personnel Test Battery
PTB .... Petersburg, VA [*Location identifier*] [*FAA*] (FAAL)
PTB .... Phenacylthiazolium Bromide [*Organic chemistry*]
PTB .... Phosphotyrosine-Binding [*Biochemistry*]
PTB .... Physical Transaction Block
PTB .... Physikalisch Technische Bundesanstalt (ACII)
PTB .... Point Barrow [*Alaska*] [*Later, BRW*] [*Seismograph station code, US Geological Survey*] [*Closed*] (SEIS)
PTB .... Pounds per Thousand Barrels [*Petroleum technology*]
PTB .... Pressure Test Barrel
PTB .... Prior to Birth [*Medicine*]
PTB .... Processor Test Bus (SAUS)
PTB .... Process Technical Bulletin (MCD)

AA)
y] (AFIT)
(SAUS)
[Linguistics] (IEL)
.... Percu... ansluminal Balloon Angioplasty [Cardiology] (DMAA)
A .... Privat Term... on Basic Access (SAUS)
BA .... Proud to be Australian [Political party]
BB .... Para-tertiary-butylbenzaldehyde [Organic chemistry]
BBA........ Para-tertiary-butylbenzoic Acid [Organic chemistry]
TBD .... Percutaneous Transhepatic Biliary Drainage [Medicine]
TBD .... Percutaneous Transluminal Balloon Dilatation [Medicine] (MELL)
PTBD-EF... Percutaneous Transhepatic Biliary Drainage - Enteric Feeding [Medicine] (DAVI)
PTBE......... Pyretic Tick-Borne Encephalitis [Medicine] (DMAA)
PTBF......... Portal Tributary Blood Flow [Physiology]
PTBI .... PT Boats, Inc. (EAIO)
PTBIPK...... Poly(t-Butyl Isopropenyl Ketone) [Organic chemistry]
PTBK .... Partbook [Music]
PTBL......... Portable (AABC)
PTBL......... Potable (SAUS)
PTBM........ PAT Transport [Common carrier symbol]
PTBN .... Industrial Specialties News [Database] [Canada] (GDD)
PTBN .... Partial Test Ban Treaty (FOTI)
PTBNA....... Protected Transbronchial Needle Aspirate [Medicine] (EDAA)
PT boat ..... Patrol Boat (SAUS)
PTBP .... Paratertiary/Peritertiary Butylphenol [Medicine] (EDAA)
PTBPD....... Posttraumatic Borderline Personality Disorder [Medicine] (DMAA)
PTBR .... Processing Tax Board of Review Decisions [United States Internal Revenue Bureau] [A publication] (DLA)
PTBR .... Punched Tape Block Reader [Computer science]
PtBS .... Poly(tertiary-butylstyrene) [Organic chemistry]
PTBS .... Posttraumatic Brain Syndrome [Medicine] (DMAA)
PTBT......... Para-tertiary-butyltoluene [Organic chemistry]
PTBT......... Partial Test Ban Treaty (SAUS)
PTBT......... Partial Test-Ban Treaty
PTBT......... Pretransplant Blood Transfusion [Medicine]
PTBVK....... Poly(t-Butyl Vinyl Ketone) [Organic chemistry]
ptbx.......... Partbook (GROV)
PTC .... Chief Photographic Intelligenceman [Navy rating]
PTC .... Motor Boat Subchaser [Navy symbol] [Obsolete]
PTC .... Pacific Telecommunications Conference (or Council) (SAUS)
PTC .... Pacific Telecommunications Council (EA)
PTC .... Pacific Theological College (SAUS)
PTC .... Pacific Tin Consolidated (SAUS)
PTC .... Pacific Tuna Conference
PTC .... Paisley Technical College (SAUS)
PTC .... Paket-Test-Center (SAUS)
PTC .... Pakistan Television Corporation Ltd. (SAUS)
PTC .... Paper Tape Code (SAUS)
PTC .... Paper Tape Control (SAUS)
PTC .... Parallel Test Component (SAUS)
PTC .... Parametric Technology Corporation
PTC .... PAR Technology [NYSE symbol] (TTSB)
PTC .... PAR Technology Corp. [NYSE symbol] (SPSG)
Ptc .... Participating [Business term]
PTC .... Parti Travailliste Congolais [Congolese Labor Party] [Political party]
PTC .... Part Through Crack [Alloy tension]
PTC .... Passive Thermal Control
PTC .... Patent, Trademark, and Copyright Institute [Franklin Pierce College] (IID)
PTC .... Patient to Call [Medicine] (EDAA)
PTC .... Patrol Vessel, Motor Torpedo Boat, Submarine Chaser [Navy symbol]
PTC .... Payload Training Complex (SAUS)
PTC .... Peace Tax Campaign [Australia]
PTC .... Peace Through Confrontation (SAUS)
PTC .... Pechiney Trading Company (EFIS)
PTC .... Pending Trouble Code [Automotive term] (HAWK)
PTC .... Pentagon Telecommunications Center (MCD)
PTC .... Peoples Telephone Co., Inc. (EFIS)
PTC .... Peoria Terminal (SAUS)
PTC .... Peoria Terminal Co. [AAR code]
PTC .... Percutaneous Cholangiography [Medicine]
PTC .... Percutaneous Transhepatic Cholangiogram [Medicine] (RAWO)
PTC .... Percutaneous Transhepatic Cholangiography (SAUS)
PTC .... Performance Test Chamber (MCD)
PTC .... Performance Test Code
PTC .... Performance Test Codes (SAUS)
PTC .... Periscope Television Camera [Telecommunications] (IAA)
PTC .... Permission to Take Classes [Education]
PTC .... Personal Transfer Capsule
PTC .... Personal Typing Centre (NITA)
PTC .... Personnel Transfer Capsule [Undersea technology]
PTC .... Personnel Transfer Chamber (SAUS)
PTC .... Personnel Transit Center (SAUS)
PTC .... Personnel Transport Carrier
PTC .... Petaluma, CA [Amtrak Busline code]
PTC .... Pharmacy and Therapeutic Committee [Medicine] (EDAA)
PTC .... Phase Transfer Catalysis [Physical chemistry]
PTC .... Phenylisothiocyanate [Organic chemistry]
PTC .... Phenylthiocarbamide [or Phenylthiocarbamyl] [Organic chemistry]
PTC .... Pheochromocytoma, Thyroid Carcinoma Syndrome [Oncology] (MAE)
PTC .... Philadelphia Transportation Co. (SAUS)
PTC .... Photographic Training Centre [British] (CB)
PTC .... Photographic Type Composition (ADA)
PTC .... Physical Training Centre (SAUS)
PTC .... Physical Training Course (SAUS)
PTC .... Pine Tree Camp (SAUS)
PTC .... Pipe and Tobacco Council (SAUS)
PTC .... Pipe and Tobacco Council of America [Defunct] (EA)
PTC .... Pipe Tobacco Council (EA)
PTC .... Pitch Trim Compensator
PTC .... Pitch Trim Controller (MCD)
PTC .... Plainview Terminal [Federal Railroad Administration identification code]
PTC .... Plan to Clear [Aviation] (FAAC)
PTC .... Plasma Thromboplastin Component [Factor IX] [Also, CF] [Hematology]
PTC .... Plastics Technology Centre (SAUS)
PTC .... Plastic Training Cartridge [Army] (INF)
PTC .... Platelet Count (SAUS)
PTC .... Plugged Telescoping Catheter [Clinical chemistry]
PTC .... Pneumatic Temperature Control
PTC .... Pneumatic Test Console
PTC .... Points to Consider
PTC .... Police Training Centre [British]
PTC .... Portable Tele-Transaction Computer [Telxon]
PTC .... Portable Temperature Control (KSC)
PTC .... Portable Temperature Controller [NASA] (NAKS)
PTC .... Porto Cannone [Italy] [Seismograph station code, US Geological Survey] (SEIS)
PTC .... Portuguese Trade Commission (EA)
PTC .... Positive Target Control [Aviation] (FAAC)
PTC .... Positive Temperature Coefficient
PTC .... Positive Transmitter Control
PTC .... Postal and Telegraphic Censorship [Telecommunications] (IAA)
PTC .... Postal Telegraph Cable
PTC .... Post and Telecommunications Corp. (SAUS)
PTC .... Posterior Trabeculae Carneae [Heart anatomy]
PTC .... Posts and Telecommunications Corp. (SAUS)
PTC .... Post-Tensioned Concrete [Technical drawings]
PTC .... Post-Turnover Change [Nuclear energy] (NRCH)
PTC .... Power Testing Code (MCD)
PTC .... Power Transfer Coefficient
PTC .... Power Transmission Council
PTC .... Practical Tonnage Capacity (SAUS)
PTC .... Pre- and Post-Process Treatment Chambers (AAEL)
PTC .... Prehead Triple Coil (SAUS)
PTC .... Premature Tricuspid Closure [Medicine] (DMAA)
PTC .... Preoperative Testing Center
PTC .... Preparatory Technical Committee (SAUS)
PTC .... Press Technology Corporation [Automotive industry]
PTC .... Press Trust of Ceylon (SAUS)
PTC .... Pressure and Temperature Control (KSC)
PTC .... Pressure Transducer Calibrator
PTC .... Pre-Temperature Control (SAUS)
PTC .... Pretense [Telegraphy] (PCTE)
PTC .... Primary Teaching Certificate [Australia]
PTC .... Primary Technical Control (SAUS)
PTC .... Primary Technical Course [Military]
PTC .... Primary Training Center (SAUS)
PTC .... Primary Training Centre [British military] (DMA)
PTC .... Princeton Resources Corp. [Vancouver Stock Exchange symbol]
PTC .... Printer Terminal Control (SAUS)
PTC .... Private Truck Council (SAUS)
PTC .... Process and Test Control (SAUS)
PTC .... Programmable Telecommunication Interface (SAUS)
PTC .... Programmable Temperature Controls
PTC .... Programmable Test Console
PTC .... Programmed Transmission Control (BUR)
PTC .... Programmer Training Center
PTC .... Programming and Training Center (SAUS)
PTC .... Programming through the Connector [Electronics]
PTC .... Program of Technical Cooperation [Organization of American States]
PTC .... Program Test Controller (SAUS)
PTC .... Promotional Telephone Call [Marketing] (OICC)
PTC .... Proof Test Capsule [NASA]
PTC .... Propellant Tanking Console (AAG)
PTC .... Propeller Technical Committee
PTC .... Propensity to Consume (MHDW)
PTC .... Propulsion Test Complex (KSC)
PTC .... Prothrombin Complex [Hematology]
PTC .... Pseudotumor Cerebri [Medicine] (AAMN)
PTC .... Psychophysical Timing Curve
PTC .... Public Services, Tax & Commerce Union (WDAA)
PTC .... Publishing Technology Corp. [Information service or system] (IID)
PTC .... Pulse Time Code
PTC .... Punched Tape Card (SAUS)
PTC .... Punched Tape Check (SAUS)
PTC .... Punched.Tape Code (SAUS)
PTC .... Push-to-Connect [Pneumatic systems]
PTCA .... Patience T'ai Chi Association (EA)
PTCA .... Percutaneous Transhepatic Cholangiogram (SAUS)
PTCA .... Percutaneous Transluminal Catheter Angioplasty (SAUS)

PTCA .... Percutaneous Transluminal Coronary Angioplasty [*Medicine*]
PTCA .... Peripheral Thrombosis of the Coronary Artery [*Medicine*] (EDAA)
PTCA .... Plains Tribal Council of Assam [*India*] [*Political party*] (PPW)
PTCA .... Postal Telegraph Clerks' Association [*A union*] [*British*]
PTCA .... Pressure Technology Corp. of America
PTCA .... Private Truck Council of America (EA)
PTCA .... Professional Tennis Coaches' Association [*Australia*]
PTCAA .... Professional Turkey Calling Association of America (EA)
PTCAD .... Provisional Troop Carrier Airborne Division
PTCC .... Pacific Division Transport Control Center
PTCC .... Pacific-Division Transport Control Center (SAUS)
PTCC .... PerSeptive Tech II Corp. [*NASDAQ symbol*] (SAG)
PT/CC .... Problem Tracking and Change Control [*Computer science*]
PTCCS .... Polaris Target Card Computing System [*Missiles*]
PtcD .... Phosphatidylcholine [*Biochemistry*]
PTCD .... Private Training College for the Disabled (AIE)
PTCE .... Patient Treatment Clinical Exercise (SAUS)
PTCE .... Peripheral Terminal Control Element (SAUS)
PTCE .... Permanent Test Facility Control Element (SAUS)
PT-Cephalgia ... Posttraumatic Cephalgia (SAUS)
PTCF .... Primary Technical Control Facility (SAUS)
PTCH .... Pacer Technology [*NASDAQ symbol*] (NQ)
PTCHY .... Patchy [*Meteorology*] (DA)
PTCI .... Programmable Telecommunications Interface (MCD)
PTCI .... Programmable Terminal Communications Interface (MCD)
PTCL .... Pakistan Telecommunication Company Limited
PT CL .... Part Called [*Stock exchange term*] (MHDB)
PTCL .... Peripheral T-Cell Lymphoma [*Oncology*]
PTCLD .... Part Called [*Stock exchange term*] (SPSG)
PTCLD .... Port Called (SAUS)
PTCLDY ..... Partly Cloudy (SAUS)
PTCM .... Master Chief Photographic Intelligenceman [*Navy rating*]
PTCM .... Pacific Telecom, Inc. [*NASDAQ symbol*] (COMM)
PTCMA .... Plastic Tanks and Cisterns Manufacturers Association (SAUS)
Pt Copyright & TM Cas ... Patent, Copyright, and Trade Mark Cases [*United States*] [*A publication*] (DLA)
PTCP .... Parameter Test Control Program [*Computer science*] (IAA)
PTCP .... Participate (FAAC)
PTCP .... Permanent Technical Committee on Ports [*United Nations*] (FOTI)
PTCP .... Positive Turnaround Control Point (MCD)
PTCPY .... Paper Tape Copy (SAUS)
PTCR .... Pad Terminal Connection Room [*NASA*]
PTCR .... Patent, Trademark and Copyright Research Institute (SAUS)
PTCR .... Payload Terminal Connector Room [*NASA*] (MCD)
PTCR .... Percutaneous Transluminal Coronary Recanalization [*Cardiology*] (DMAA)
PTCR .... Positive Temperature Coefficient of Resistance (SAUS)
PTCR .... Positive Temperature Coefficient Resistance [*Materials science and technology*]
PTCRA .... Percutaneous Transluminal Coronary Rotational Ablation [*Cardiology*] (DMAA)
PTCRM ...... Partial Thermochemical Remanent Magnetization
Pt/CrNe ...... Plantinum Cromium Neon-onboard spectral calibration (SAUS)
PTCS .... Passive Thermal Control Section [*NASA*] (NASA)
PTCS .... Passive Thermal Control System (NASA)
PTCS .... Pax Tibi cum Sanctis [*Peace to Thee with the Saints*] [*Latin*]
PTCS .... Pentagon Telecommunication Center System (SAUS)
PTCS .... Percutaneous Transhepatic Cholangioscopy [*Medicine*]
PTCS .... Phenyltrichlorosilane [*Organic chemistry*]
PTCS .... Planning, Training, and Checkout System [*NASA*] (MCD)
PTCS .... Portable Tracking & Control Station (SAUS)
PTCS .... Powertrain Control Signal [*Automotive engineering*]
PTCS .... Pressure Transducer Calibration System
PTCS .... Propellant Tanking Computer System (KSC)
PTCS .... Senior Chief Photographic Intelligenceman [*Navy rating*]
PTCT .... Path Count (SAUS)
PtCT .... Patient Care Technologies (ADWA)
PTCT .... Protect (MSA)
PT-CT .... Prothrombin Time Control [*Hematology*] (DAVI)
PTC Thermistor ... Positive Temperature Coefficient Thermistor (SAUS)
PTCU .... Punched Tape Control Unit (SAUS)
PTCV .... Pilot-Operated Temperature Control Valve
PTCV .... Plowright Tissue Culture Vaccine [*Against rinderpest*]
PTCX .... Peoples Transportation [*Private rail car owner code*]
PTCZ .... Port Continental [*Federal Railroad Administration identification code*]
PTD .... Dominican Worker's Party [*Political party*] (PSAP)
PTD .... Package Travel Directive (WDAA)
PTD .... Painted (AAG)
ptd .... Painted (VRA)
PTD .... Paper Tape Date (SAUS)
PTD .... Paper Towel Dispenser [*Technical drawings*]
PTD .... Parallel Transfer Disk [*Computer science*]
PTD .... Parallel Transfer Drive (SAUS)
PTD .... Particle Transfer Device
PTD .... Part Throttle Deceleration [*Engines*] (EG)
PTD .... Patented (IAA)
PTD .... Payable Through Draft
PTD .... Percutaneous Transhepatic Drainage [*Medicine*] (EDAA)
PTD .... Percutaneous Transluminal Dilatation [*Medicine*] (DMAA)
PTD .... Period to Discharge [*Medicine*] (DAVI)
PTD .... Permament Total Diability (SAUS)
PTD .... Permanent Total Disability [*Medicine*]
PTD .... Personality Trait Disorder (MELL)
PTD .... Phenyltriazolinedione [*Organic chemistry*]
Ptd .... Phosphatidic (SAUS)
Ptd .... Phosphatidyl
PTD .... Photodiode Detector [*Instrumentation*]
PTD .... Photothermal Deflection
PTD .... Physical Teardown (MCD)
PTD .... Physical Theory of Diffraction (SAUS)
PTD .... Pilot to Dispatcher
PTD .... Plant Test Date [*Telecommunications*] (TEL)
PTD .... Pointed (WGA)
PTD .... Portland [*Oregon*] [*Seismograph station code, US Geological Survey*] (SEIS)
PTD .... Posttuning Drift
PTD .... Potsdam, NY [*Location identifier*] [*FAA*] (FAAL)
PTD .... Potter Distilleries Ltd. [*Toronto Stock Exchange symbol*] [*Vancouver Stock Exchange symbol*]
PTD .... Presented [*Telegraphy*] (PCTE)
PTD .... Printed
PTD .... Prior to Delivery (MELL)
PTD .... Prior to Discharge [*Medicine*] (MAE)
PTD .... Product Design [*Automotive engineering*]
PTD .... Professional Training and Development (SAUS)
PTD .... Programmable Thermal Desorber (SAUS)
PTD .... Programmable Threshold Detector (MCD)
PTD .... Programmed Thermal Desorber
PTD .... Program Test Director (CCCA)
PTD .... Provisional Technical Documentation (SAUS)
PTD .... Provisioning Technical Data
PTD .... Provisioning Technical Documentation
PTD .... Provisioning Transcript Documentation (MCD)
PTDA .... Passive Target Data Analysis (SAUS)
PTDA .... Per Task Data Area [*Computer science*] (BYTE)
Ptd A .... Pointed Arch (SAUS)
PTDA .... Power Transmission Distributors Association (EA)
PTDA .... Professional Tournament Directors Association (SAUS)
PTDB .... Point Target Data Base (SAA)
PTDC .... Pacific Trade and Development Conference [*OPTAD*] (FEA)
PTDC .... Pakistan Tourism Development Corp. (SAUS)
PtdCho .... Phosphatidylcholine (STED)
PTD Drive ... Parallel Transfer Disk Drive (SAUS)
PTDDSS ..... Provisioning Technical Documentation Data Selection Sheet [*NASA*] (NASA)
PTDDSS ..... PTD Data Selection Sheet (SAUS)
PTD/E .... Physical Teardown Evaluation
Pt Dest ...... Port of Destination (SAUS)
PtdEtn .... Phosphatidylethanolamine (STED)
PTDF .... Pacific Tuna Development Foundation (EA)
PTDF .... Procurement Technical Data File [*DoD*]
PtdGro .... Phosphatidylglycerol (SAUS)
Pt Dhgtr ..... Patient's Daughter [*Also, Pt DTR*] (DAVI)
PTDI .... Punched Tape Data Input (SAUS)
PTDIA .... Professional Truck Driver Institute of America (EA)
PtdIns .... Phosphatidylinositol [*Also, PI*] [*Biochemistry*]
Pt Disch ..... Port of Discharge (SAUS)
Pt Disch Decl ... Port of Discharge Declared (SAUS)
PTDL .... Patent and Trademark Depository Library
PTDL .... Programmable Tapped Delay Line (PDAA)
PTDOS ...... Processor Technology Disk Operating System
PTDP .... Permanent Transvenous Demand Pacemaker (STED)
PTDP .... Preliminary Technical Data Package (SAUS)
PTDP .... Preliminary Technical Development Plan (AFM)
PTDP .... Production Technical Data Package (SAUS)
PTDP .... Proposed Technical Development Plan
PTDQ .... Polymerized Trimethyl Dihydro Quinoline (SAUS)
PTDQ .... Polymerized Trimethyldihydroquinoline [*Organic chemistry*]
PTDR .... Post-Test Disassembly Report (SAUS)
PtdS .... Phosphatidylserine [*Biochemistry*]
PTDS .... Photo Target Detection System
PtdSer .... Phosphatidylserine (STED)
PTDTL .... Pumped Tunnel Diode Transistor Logic
PTDTL Circuit ... Pumped Tunnel Diode Transistor Logic Circuit (SAUS)
PT DTR ...... Patient's Daughter [*Also, Pt Dhgtr*] (DAVI)
PTDU .... Djakarta Lloyd [*Intermodal shipping container symbol*] (TVRC)
PTDU .... Pointing and Tracking Demonstration Unit (MCD)
PTe .... Indian Valley Public Library, Telford, PA [*Library symbol*] [*Library of Congress*] (LCLS)
PTE .... International Federation of Professional and Technical Engineers
PTE .... Nouadhibou [*Mauritania*] [*Airport symbol*] (AD)
PTE .... Packet Transfer Engine [*Newbridge Networks Corp.*]
PTE .... Packet Transport Equipment [*Computer science*] (PCM)
PTE .... Page Table Entry
PTE .... Parathyeroid Extract (SAUS)
PTE .... Parathyroid Extract [*Medicine*]
PTE .... Partido de Trabajadores Espanoles [*Spanish Workers' Party*] [*Political party*] (PPE)
PTE .... Part-Time Education (WDAA)
PTE .... Party to Exemption [*RSPA*] (TAG)
PTE .... Passenger Transport Executive [*British*]
PTE .... Path Terminating Equipment
PTE .... Peace through Education Project [*An association*]
PTE .... Pectin transeliminase [*or Pectate Lyase*] [*An enzyme*]
PTE .... Peculiar Test Equipment
PTE .... Perforated Tape Exchange (SAUS)
PTE .... Permanent Total Enclosure (EEVL)
PTE .... Personal Terminal Environment (SAUS)

PTE .... Photographic Tasks and Equipment [*NASA*]
PTE .... Plant Transaction Entry (SAUS)
PTE .... Plasma Thromboplastin Enzyme (SAUS)
PTE .... Plate (ROG)
PTE .... Portable Test Equipment (AAG)
PTE .... Portage [*Alaska*] [*Seismograph station code, US Geological Survey*] (SEIS)
PTE .... Port Stephens [*Australia*] [*Airport symbol*] (OAG)
PTE .... Posttraumatic Endophthalmitis (STED)
PTE .... Post-Traumatic Epilepsy (MELL)
PTE .... Potentially Toxic Element
PTE .... Potential to Emit (GNE)
PTE .... Power Transport Equipment
PTE .... Pressure Test Equipment (MCD)
PTE .... Pressure-Tolerant Electronics (IEEE)
PTE .... Pretax Earnings [*Employment*]
PTE .... Pretibial Edema [*Medicine*] (DAVI)
PTE .... Primrose Technology Corp. [*Vancouver Stock Exchange symbol*]
Pte .... Private (WDAA)
PTE .... Private [*British*]
PTE .... Private Trade Entity
PTE .... ProActive Technologies, Inc. [*AMEX symbol*] (SAG)
PTE .... Problem Trend Evaluation (MCD)
PTE .... Process and Test Equipment (SAUS)
PTE .... Production Test Equipment (MCD)
PTE .... Protect Error (SAUS)
PTE .... Proximal Tibial Epiphysis [*Orthopedics*] (DAVI)
PTE .... Proxylem Tracheary Element [*Botany*]
Pte .... Pteroic Acid [*Biochemistry*] (QSUL)
Pte .... Pteroyl [*Biochemistry*]
PTE .... Pulmonary Thromboembolism [*Medicine*]
PTE .... Punched Tape Equipment (SAUS)
PTEA .... Preliminary Training Effectiveness Analysis
PTEA .... Pulmonary Thromboendarterectomy [*Medicine*] (ADWA)
PTEAR .... Physical Teardown
PTEAR .... Physical Teardown and Maintenance Allocation Review (MCD)
PTeb .... Tebtunis Papyri [*A publication*] (OCD)
PTEC .... Phoenix Technologies [*NASDAQ symbol*] (TTSB)
PTEC .... Phoenix Technologies Ltd. [*NASDAQ symbol*] (NQ)
PTEC .... Plastics Technical Evaluation Center [*Military*]
pt ed .... Patient Education (DAVI)
PTED .... Pulmonary Thromboembolic Disease [*Medicine*]
PteGlu .... Pteroylmonoglutamic Acid [*Folic acid*] [*Also, FA, PGA*] [*Biochemistry*]
PTEI .... Picture Test of Engish Inflections [*Medicine*] (EDAA)
PTEK .... Premiere Technologies [*NASDAQ symbol*] (TTSB)
PTEK .... Premiere Technologies, Inc. [*NASDAQ symbol*] (SAG)
PTEL .... Peoples Telephone Co. [*NASDAQ symbol*] (TTSB)
PTEL .... People's Telephone Co., Inc. [*NASDAQ symbol*] (NQ)
PT Employment .... Part-Time Employment (SAUS)
PTEN .... Patterson Energy [*NASDAQ symbol*] (TTSB)
PTEN .... Patterson Energy, Inc. [*NASDAQ symbol*] (SAG)
PTEN .... Pentaerythritol Tetranitrate [*An explosive and a vasodilator*] [*Cardiology*] (DAVI)
PTEN .... Prime Time Entertainment Network [*Television broadcasting*]
pter .... End of Short Arm of Chromosome [*Medicine*] (STED)
PTER .... Physical Teardown and Evaluation Review (MCD)
PTERM .... Physical Terminal (VLIE)
PTES .... People's Trust for Endangered Species [*United Kingdom*] (EAIO)
PTES .... Productivity Trend Evaluation System (MCD)
PTES .... Purdue Teacher Evaluation Scale
PTET .... Platinum Entertainment [*NASDAQ symbol*] (TTSB)
PTETD .... Production Test Engineering Task Description (MCD)
PTE Technology .... Pressure Tolerant Electronic Technology (SAUS)
PTETPC .... Party to Expose the Petrov Conspiracy [*Australia*] [*Political party*]
PTETS .... Pioneer Television and Electronic Technicians Society [*Defunct*] (EA)
PT EX .... Part Exchange (WDAA)
PTEZ .... Proler Terminal #115 [*Federal Railroad Administration identification code*]
PTF .... fast patrol boat (SAUS)
PTF .... Fast Patrol Craft (SAUS)
PTF .... Malololailai [*Fiji*] [*Airport symbol*] (OAG)
PTF .... Paralemniscal Tegmental Field [*Neuroanatomy*]
PTF .... Parathyroid Fever [*Medicine*] (CPH)
PTF .... Particulars to Follow (SAUS)
PTF .... Parts Transfer Form (SAA)
PTF .... Part-Time Force (SAUS)
PTF .... Pass-Through Facility (VLIE)
PTF .... Patch and Test Facility
PTF .... Patient Treatment File [*Medicine*] (DMAA)
PTF .... Patrol Torpedo Boat, Fast [*Formerly, PT*] [*Navy symbol*]
PTF .... Payload Test Facility [*VAFB*] [*NASA*] (MCD)
PTF .... Payload Training Facility (SAUS)
PTF .... Permanent Test Facility (SAUS)
PTF .... Permit to Fly [*Aviation*] (AIA)
PTF .... Petersfield Oil & Minerals [*Vancouver Stock Exchange symbol*]
PTF .... Phase Transfer Function (MCD)
ptf .... Plaintiff (GEAB)
PTF .... Plaintiff [*Legal term*] (ROG)
PTF .... Plasma Thromboplastin Factor [*Factor VIII*] [*Also, AHF, AHG, TPC*] [*Hematology*]
PTF .... Police Training Foundation
PTF .... Polymer Thick Film
PTF .... Polytetrafluoroethylene (EDCT)
PTF .... Pool Transmission Facility (SAUS)
PTF .... Port Task Force
PTF .... Power Test Fail
PTF .... Power Transmission Fluid [*Fuels and lubricants*]
PTF .... Precision Time and Frequency [*Navigation systems*]
PTF .... Problem Temporary/Trouble Fix (SAUS)
PTF .... Problem Trouble Fix [*Computer science*] (VLIE)
PTF .... Production Tabulating Form (AAG)
PTF .... Programming Temporary Fixed (SAUS)
PTF .... Program Temporary Fix [*Computer science*]
PTF .... Program Trouble Fix (SAUS)
PTF .... Proof Test Facility [*Nuclear energy*]
PTF .... Propellant Tank Flow
PTF .... Propulsion Test Facilities (or Facility) (SAUS)
PTF .... Proximal Tubule Fluid [*Laboratory science*] (DAVI)
PTF .... Pthread Framework (SAUS)
PTF .... Pulse Transfer Function
PTF .... Punched Tape Feed (SAUS)
PTF .... Punch-Through Factor (SAUS)
PTF .... Reengineering Task Force
PTFA .... Preliminary Tool and Facility Analysis (MCD)
PTFA .... Prothrombin Time Fixing Agent (DMAA)
PTFACE .... Permanent Test Facility Auxiliary Control Element (SAUS)
PTFC .... Pretty Things Fan Club (EA)
PTFCE .... Polytrifluorochloroethene (BARN)
PTFD .... Personnel, Training and Force Development [*Army*]
PTFD .... Punched Tape Feed Device (SAUS)
PTFDA .... Professional Travel Film Directors Association [*Later, Professional Travelogue Sponsors - PTS*] (EA)
PTFE .... Polyterafluoroethylene (SAUS)
PTFE .... Polytetrafluorethylen (SAUS)
PTFE .... Polytetrafluoroethene (SAUS)
ptfe .... Polytetrafluoroethylene (MIST)
PTFE .... Polytetrafluoroethylene [*Organic chemistry*]
PTFG .... Large Guided Missile Motorboat [*Navy symbol*] (DNAB)
PTFHA .... Physician Task Force on Hunger in America [*Defunct*] (EA)
PTFHC .... Putnam Tax Free Health Care Fund [*Associated Press*] (SAG)
PTFM .... Passive Target Flow Management
PTFM .... Passive Target Flow Measurement [*Traffic management*]
PTFM .... Platform (AAG)
PTFMA .... Peacetime Force Material Assets [*Navy*] (AFIT)
PTFMA .... Public Telecommunications Financial Management Association (EA)
PTFMO .... Peacetime Force Materiel Objective [*Army*]
PTFMPO .... Peacetime Force Materiel Procurement Objective [*Army*]
PTFMR .... Peacetime Force Material Request
PTFMR .... Peacetime Force Materiel Requirements [*Army*]
PTFMR-A .... Peacetime Force Materiel Requirements - Acquisition [*Army*] (AABC)
PTFMR-R .... Peacetime Force Materiel Requirements - Retention [*Army*] (AABC)
PTFP .... Prime-Time Family Programming (SAUS)
PTFP .... Public Telecommunications Facilities Program [*Department of Commerce*]
PTFS .... Pilot-to-Forecaster Service (NOAA)
PTFS .... Posttraumatic Fibromyalgia Syndrome [*Medicine*] (DMAA)
PTFT .... Production Temporary Facility Tool (SAA)
PTFUR .... President's Task Force on Urban Renewal (EA)
PTFX .... Plating Fixture (AAG)
ptg .... Painting (VRA)
PTG .... Parathyroid Gland [*Medicine*] (DMAA)
PTG .... Parent-Teacher Group
PTG .... Pennington Gap, VA [*Location identifier*] [*FAA*] (FAAL)
PTG .... Personal Training Guide (SAUS)
PTG .... Piano Technicians Guild (EA)
PTG .... Pietersburg [*South Africa*] [*Airport symbol*] (OAG)
PTG .... Place to Go (IAA)
PTG .... Place-to-Go (SAUS)
PTG .... Planed, Tongued, and Grooved (DAC)
ptg .... Planed, Tongued, and Grooved [*Construction term*] (MIST)
PTG .... Planning and Tracking Group
PTG .... Plasma-Oberflachentechnik (EFIS)
PTG .... Pointing (SAUS)
PTG .... Polaris Task Group [*Missiles*]
PTG .... Portage Industries Corp. [*AMEX symbol*] (SPSG)
PTG .... Portageville [*Missouri*] [*Seismograph station code, US Geological Survey*] [*Closed*] (SEIS)
PTG .... Port Task Group (SAUS)
PTG .... Portuguese (ROG)
PTG .... Precise Tone Generator [*Telecommunications*] (TEL)
PTG .... Presenting [*Telegraphy*] (PCTE)
PTG .... Pressure Test Gauge
PTG .... Pressure Transfer Gauge
ptg .... Printing (WDMC)
PTG .... Printing
PTG .... Professional Technical Group
PTG .... Prothoracic Gland [*Insect anatomy*]
PTG .... Pulse Target Generator
PTG .... Small Guided Missile Motorboat [*Navy symbol*] (DNAB)
PTG .... Teniposide [*Antineoplastic drug regimen*] (DAVI)
PTGA .... Pteroyltriglutamic Acid [*Pharmacology*]
PTGANE .... Professional Technical Group on Aerospace and Navigational Electronics (SAUS)
PTGAP .... Professional Technical Group on Antennas and Propagation [*of the IEEE*]
PTGBD .... Percutaneous Transhepatic Gallbladder Drainage [*Medicine*]
PTGC .... Programmed Temperature Gas Chromatography
PTG CYL .... Printing Cylinder (DGA)

PTGEC .... Professional Technical Group on Electronic Computers [*Later, IEEE Computer Society*]
PT GEO ...... Posted to Geographics
PTGER .... Purmonary Transcapillary Escape Rate [*Medicine*] (EDAA)
PTGEWS .... Professional Technical Group on Engineering Writing and Speech [*of the IEEE*]
pTGF .... Porcine Transforming Growth Factor
PTGL .... Pyrolysis to Gases and Liquids [*Chemical processing*]
PTGP .... Penetrating Tear Gas Projectile [*Police and security equipment*]
PTGRFI ...... Professional Technical Group on Radio Frequency Interference (SAUS)
PTGS .... Paper Trade Golfing Society [*British*]
PTGS .... Picosecond Transient Grating Spectroscopy
PTGS .... Portable Telemetry Ground Station
PTGS .... Post-Transcriptional Gene Silencing [*Medicine*]
Ptg Std ...... Petrograd Standard (SAUS)
PTGT .... Primary Target [*Military*]
PTGWO ...... Philippine Transport and General Workers Organisations (SAUS)
PTH .... Hydrofoil Motor Torpedo Boat [*Ship symbol*] (NATG)
PTH .... Pacer Technology (EFIS)
PTH .... Pallet Torque Hook
PTH .... Panther Mines Ltd. [*Vancouver Stock Exchange symbol*]
PTH .... Paper Tape Half-Duplex
PTH .... Parathormon (SAUS)
PTH .... Parathormone [*Medicine*] (MAE)
PTH .... Parathyroid Hormone [*Endocrinology*]
PTH .... Path (GAVI)
PTH .... Pathfinder [*NCIC car model code*]
PTH .... Pathology [*Medical specialty*] (DHSM)
PTH .... Peak Tanning Hours [*Supposedly occurring between 10am and 2pm*] [*See also BROTS, SROTS*]
PTH .... Phenylthiohydantoin [*Organic chemistry*]
PTH .... Pin-Through-Hole (SAUS)
PTH .... Plasma Thromboplastin Component [*Medicine*] (DMAA)
PTH .... Plated through Hole
Pth .... Polythiophene [*Organic chemistry*]
PTH .... Port Heiden [*Alaska*] [*Airport symbol*] (OAG)
PTH .... Port Heiden, AK [*Location identifier*] [*FAA*] (FAAL)
PTH .... Port Huron, MI [*Amtrak rail station code*]
PTH .... Post-Transfusion Hepatitis [*Medicine*]
PTH .... Processor Test Handler (SAUS)
PTH .... Project Team Head (MHDI)
PTH .... Project Top Hat [*Defunct*] (EA)
PTH .... Psychotherapeutische Medizin (SAUS)
PTH .... Public Teaching Hospital (ODA)
PtHA .... Pinto Horse Association of America (EA)
PtHAO .... Pinto Horse Association of Ohio (EARSL)
P Th B .... Bachelor of Practical Theology
PTHC .... Percutaneous Transhepatic Cholangiogram [*Medicine*] (RAWO)
PTH Circuit... Plated Through Hole Circuit (SAUS)
PThD .... Punch-Through Device (PDAA)
PtHeat .... Petroleum Heat & Power Corp. [*Associated Press*] (SAG)
PtHel .... Petroleum Helicopter, Inc. [*Associated Press*] (SAG)
PTHF .... Polytetrahydrofuran [*Organic chemistry*]
PtHg .... Partially Hearing (AIE)
PTHLGST... Pathologist
PTH-LP ...... Parathyroid Hormone-Like Peptide [*Endocrinology*]
PTHOP ...... Port Hope, ON [*American Association of Railroads railroad junction routing code*]
PT/HR .... Pints per Hour (SAUS)
PTHrP .... Parathormon related Peptides (SAUS)
PTHrP .... Parathyroid Hormone-Related Protein [*Biochemistry*]
PTHrP .... PTH-related Proteins (SAUS)
PTHS .... Parathyroid Hormone Secretion Rate [*Endocrinology*] (MAE)
PTHS .... Profile Total Hip System (MELL)
PTHSE .... Penthouse (TVEL)
PTHUR ...... Port Huron, MI [*American Association of Railroads railroad junction routing code*]
PTHUT .... Port Huron Tunnel, MI [*American Association of Railroads railroad junction routing code*]
PTHX .... Port Terminal Railroad of Houston [*Federal Railroad Administration identification code*]
PTI .... First USA Paymentech [*NYSE symbol*] (TTSB)
PTI .... First USA Paymentech, Inc. [*NYSE symbol*] (SAG)
PTI .... I-GOOS Panel on Technical Implementation (SAUS)
PTI .... Pacific Telecom, Incorporated
PTI .... Package Turn In (MCD)
PTI .... Packet Type Identifier (SAUS)
PTI .... Palomar Testbed Interferometer [*Optical astronomy*]
PTI .... Pancreatic Trypsin Inhibitor [*Biochemistry*]
PTI .... Parent Training and Information [*Centers*] [*Established under the Individuals with Disabilities Education Act (IDEA)*] (PAZ)
PTI .... Parkes-Tidbinbilla Interferometer [*Astronomy*]
PTI .... Party Identity [*Telecommunications*] (TEL)
PTI .... Pathways to Independence [*An association*] (EA)
PTI .... Patient Technology, Inc. [*AMEX symbol*] (COMM)
PTI .... Payload Type Identifier
PTI .... Payload Type Indicator (SAUS)
PTI .... Paymentech, Inc. [*NYSE symbol*] [*Formerly, First USA Paymentech*] (SG)
PTI .... Pennsylvania Transportation Institute [*Pennsylvania State University*] [*Research center*] (RCD)
PTI .... Penn Telecom, Inc. [*Gibsonia, PA*] (TSSD)
PTI .... Persistent Tolerant Infection
PTI .... Personnel Tests for Industry
PTI .... Personnel Transaction Identifier [*Air Force*] (AFM)
PTI .... Philadelphia Textile Institute
PTI .... Physical-Technical Institute [*Former USSR*]
PTI .... Physical Therapy Intervention (AMHC)
PTI .... Physical Training Instructor [*British*]
PTI .... Physico-Technical Institute (SAUS)
PTI .... Pictorial Test of Intelligence [*Education*]
PTI .... Pipe Test Insert [*Liquid Metal Engineering Center*] [*Energy Research and Development Administration*] (IEEE)
PTI .... Plant Transfer In (VLIE)
PTI .... Plugging Temperature Indicator [*Nuclear energy*] (NRCH)
PTI .... Poetry Therapy Institute (EA)
PTI .... Porous Tungsten Ionizer
PTI .... Portable Test Instrument (VLIE)
PTI .... Post-Tensioning Institute [*Defunct*] (EA)
PTI .... Power Tool Institute (EA)
PTI .... Power Tool Institute, Inc. (SAUS)
PTI .... Practice Training Index
PTI .... Precision Technology, Inc. (AAG)
PTI .... Preliminary Test Information (KSC)
PTI .... Pre-programmed Test Input (SAUS)
PTI .... Presentation of Technical Information (SAUS)
PTI .... Presistent Tolerant Infection (SAUS)
PTI .... [*The*] Press Trust of India
PTI .... Pretrial Intervention (BARN)
PTI .... Pre-Trial Investigation (DNAB)
PTI .... Pre-Trip Inspection [*Shipping*]
PTI .... Previously-Taxed Income
PTI .... Prinicipal-Teacher Interaction Study (EDAC)
PTI .... Production Training Indicator [*Computer science*]
PTI .... Product Test Interface (SAUS)
PTI .... Programmed Test Input (MCD)
PTI .... Programming Tools and Information [*IBM Corp.*] [*Computer science*]
PTI .... Program Transfer Interface
PTI .... Promethean Technologies, Inc. [*Vancouver Stock Exchange symbol*]
PTI .... Protein Technologies International
PTI .... Publicacoes Tecnicas Internacionais Ltda. [*International Technical Publications Ltd.*] [*Information service or system*] (IID)
PTI .... Public Technology, Inc. [*Research center*] (RCD)
PTI .... Public Tool Interface [*Computer science*] (ODBW)
PTI .... Punched Tape Information (SAUS)
PTI .... Puntilla Lake, AK [*Location identifier*] [*FAA*] (FAAL)
PTIA .... Pet Trade and Industry Association (EAIO)
PTIC .... Patent and Trade Mark Institute of Canada
PTIC .... Patent and Trademark Institute of Canada (SAUS)
PTIDG .... Presentation of Technical Information Discussion Group (SAUS)
PTIDG .... Presentatson of Technical Information Discussion Group (SAUS)
PTIE .... Pet Trade and Industry Exhibition [*British*] (ITD)
PTIG .... Presentation of Technical Information Group (SAA)
PTIHd .... PTI Holding, Inc. [*Associated Press*] (SAG)
PTI Hold .... PTI Holding, Inc. [*Associated Press*] (SAG)
PTII .... PTI Holding [*NASDAQ symbol*] (TTSB)
PTII .... PTI Holding, Inc. [*NASDAQ symbol*] (SAG)
PTIIW .... PTI Hldg Wrrt [*NASDAQ symbol*] (TTSB)
PTIL .... Parts Test Information List (KSC)
PTIM .... Punched Tape Invoicing Machine (SAUS)
PTIME .... Periodic Timer (SAUS)
PTIME .... Polynomial Time (ODA)
PTIO .... Pesticides Technical Information Office (SAUS)
PTI-ODT ..... Personnel Tests for Industry - Oral Directions Test
PTIOS .... Paper Tape Input/Output System (SAUS)
PTIOS .... Plant Transfer In Operating System (SAUS)
PTIP .... Physical Therapist in Independent Practice (GFGA)
PTIP .... Pluribus Terminal Interface Processor [*Computer science*] (CIST)
PTIR .... Precision Track Illuminator RADAR (SEWL)
PTIRFM ..... Polarized Total Internal Reflection Fluorescence Microscopy
PTIS .... Pacific Triangle Information Services [*Information service or system*] (IID)
PTIS .... Photothermal Infrared Spectroscopy (SAUS)
PTIS .... Photo Thermal Ionization Spectroscopy (AAEL)
PTIS .... Photothermal Ionization Spectroscopy (SAUS)
PTIS .... Photo Thermical Ionization Spectroscopy (SAUS)
PTIS .... Piano Teachers Information Service (SAUS)
PTIS .... Plasma Therm [*NASDAQ symbol*] (TTSB)
PTIS .... Plasma-Therm, Inc. [*NASDAQ symbol*] (NQ)
PTIS .... Powertrain Input Signal [*Automotive engineering*]
PTIS .... Programmed Test Input System (MCD)
PTIS .... Program Test Input System (SAUS)
PTIS .... Propulsion Test Instrumentation System (KSC)
PTIU .... Pauwels Trafo [*Intermodal shipping container symbol*] (TVRC)
PTIWU .... Posts and Telegraphs Industrial Workers' Union [*India*]
PTIX .... Performance Technologies [*NASDAQ symbol*] (TTSB)
PTIX .... Performance Technologies, Inc. [*NASDAQ symbol*] (SAG)
PTIZ .... Parkway Transport [*Intermodal trailer symbol*]
PTJ .... Part-Time Job
PTJ .... Portland [*Australia*] [*Airport symbol*] (OAG)
PTJ .... Pulse Train Jitter [*Computer science*] (IAA)
PTJ .... Pulse-Train Jitter (SAUS)
PTJA .... Plan to Join Airways (SAUS)
PTK .... Passport to Knowledge [*Program*]
PTK .... Phototherapeutic Keratectomy [*Ophthalmology*]
PTK .... Polishing Tool Kit
PTK .... Pontiac, MI [*Location identifier*] [*FAA*] (FAAL)
PTK .... Potentiometer Tapping Kit

[illegible] .... Probability of Track [*Military*]
[illegible] .... Protection Check (VLIE)
[illegible] .... Protein-Tyrosine Kinase [*An enzyme*]
[illegible] .... Truk [*Caroline Islands*] [*ICAO location identifier*] (ICLI)
[illegible] .... Pacific Testing Laboratories, Inc. (EFIS)
[illegible] .... Pain Tolerance Level (MELL)
PTL .... Parameter Table Load [*Computer science*] (VLIE)
PTL .... Partial Total Loss [*Insurance*] (DS)
PTL .... Part Time Legislature
PTL .... Part Truck Load (SAUS)
PTL .... Pass the Loot (SAUS)
PTL .... Patrol [*or Patrolman*] (AABC)
PTL .... Patrol Boat
PTL .... Peacetime Losses [*Military*]
PTL .... Penteli [*Greece*] [*Seismograph station code, US Geological Survey*] (SEIS)
PTL .... [*Sodium*] Pentothal [*An anesthetic*] (DAVI)
PTL .... People That Live (SAUS)
PTL .... People That Love [*Of television's "PTL Club"*] [*Facetious translations: "Pass the Loot" and "Pay the Lady"*]
PTL .... Perinatal Telencephalic Leukoencephalopathy [*Medicine*]
PTL .... Peripheral T-Cell Lymphoma [*Oncology*]
PTL .... Petroleum Testing Laboratory
PTL .... Phase Tracking Loop (MCD)
PTI .... Philips Telecommunicatie Industrie (SAUS)
PTL .... Photographic Technology Laboratory (KSC)
PTL .... Physikalisch-Technisches Labor (SAUS)
PTI .... Pictorial Test of Intelligence (SAUS)
PTL .... Pietermaritzburg [*South Africa*] [*Airport symbol*] (AD)
PTL .... Pintle [*Design engineering*]
PTL .... Pittsburgh Testing Laboratory (EFIS)
PTL .... Planning Test List
PTL .... Pocket Testament League (EA)
ptl .... Portal (VRA)
PTL .... Portal, ND [*American Association of Railroads railroad junction routing code*]
PTL .... Posterior Tricuspid Leaflet (SAUS)
PTL .... Power Transmission Line (OA)
PTL .... Praga Tools (SAUS)
PTL .... Praise the Lord [*Of television's "PTL Club"*] [*Facetious translations: "Pass the Loot" and "Pay the Lady"*]
PTL .... Pressure, Torque, and Load
PTL .... Preterm Labor [*Obstetrics*] (DAVI)
PTL .... Pre-Test Laboratory (DNAB)
PTL .... Pretty Tough Lawyer [*Refers to Melvin Belli, attorney for Tammy and Jim Bakker of the PTL Club*]
PTL .... Primary Target Line [*Military*]
PTL .... Process and Test Language
PTL .... Project Team Leader (FOTI)
PTL .... Project Title (SAUS)
PTI .... Protect the Innocent (SAUS)
PTL .... Providence Air Charter [*ICAO designator*] (FAAC)
PTL .... Public Television Library
PTL .... Pulse Transmission Logic (IAA)
PTLA .... Praise the Lord Anyway
PTLA .... Publishers' Trade List Annual
PTLAP .... Petroleum Test Laboratory Accreditation Program
PTLBD .... Particleboard
PTLC .... Piedmont Triad Library Council [*Library network*]
PTLC .... Precipitation Thin-Layer Chromatography [*Medicine*] (DMAA)
PTLC .... Preparative Thin-Layer Chromatography (DB)
PT-LD .... Physical Teardown - Logistics Demonstration (MCD)
PTLD .... Post-Transfusion Liver Disease [*Medicine*]
PTLD .... Prescribed Tumor Lethal Dose [*Oncology*]
PTLEF .... Peace through Law Education Fund (EA)
PTLEN .... Petal Length [*Botany*]
PTLF .... Pressure, Temperature, Level, and Flow [*Chemical engineering*]
PTLL .... Pittsburgh Toy Lending Library (SAUS)
PTL Network .... Praise the Lord Television Network (SAUS)
PTLP .... Pre-Timeline Planning (SEWL)
PTLP .... Pro Truck Lines [*Common carrier symbol*]
PTLRS .... Publications and Technical Literature Research Section [*Environmental Protection Agency*] (IID)
PTLS .... Program-controlled Train Leading System (SAUS)
PTLU .... Pacific Islands Transport Line [*Intermodal shipping container symbol*] (TVRC)
PTLV .... Peach Twisted Leaf Virus (SAUS)
PTLV .... Primate T-Lymphotropic Viruses
PTLX .... Patlex Corp. [*NASDAQ symbol*] (SAG)
PTLY .... Partly [*NWS*] (FAAC)
Ptly Pd .... Partly Paid (SAUS)
PTM .... Packet Transfer Mode (SAUS)
PTM .... Packet Transport Mode (SAUS)
PTM .... Packet Trunk Module (SAUS)
PTM .... Palmarito [*Venezuela*] [*Airport symbol*] (OAG)
PTM .... Pancake Torque Motor (SAUS)
PTM .... Pancake Torquer Motor (SAA)
PTM .... Parametric Tire Model [*Automotive engineering*]
PTM .... Parasite Tubing Method (PDAA)
PTM .... Passenger Ton Miles (SAUS)
PTM .... Passenger Traffic Manager
PTM .... Pass Through Mode (SAUS)
PTM .... Patient Monitored (MELL)
PTM .... Pattern Test Mount (SAUS)
PTM .... Pattern Transformation Memory
PTM .... Performance Test Model (OA)
PTM .... Petromac Energy, Inc. [*Vancouver Stock Exchange symbol*]
PTM .... Phase Time Modulation
PTM .... Phase-Time Modulation (SAUS)
PTM .... Phenyltrimethylammonium [*Also, PTA, PTMA*] [*Organic chemistry*]
PTM .... Photomultiplier (IAA)
PTM .... Photon Tunneling Microscope
PTM .... Photo Tracing Machine (VLIE)
PTM .... Physical Teardown and Maintenance (MCD)
PTM .... Pietermaritzburg [*South Africa*] [*Seismograph station code, US Geological Survey*] (SEIS)
PTM .... Pilot Training Missile (ACAE)
PTM .... Please Tell Me (SAUS)
PTM .... Pneumatic Telescope Mast
PTM .... Polaris Tactical Missile
PTM .... Portable Traffic Monitor [*Telecommunications*] (TEL)
PTM .... Portable Truth Machine [*Police and security equipment*]
PTM .... Portland Terminal Co. [*AAR code*]
PTM .... Posttransfusion Mononucleosis [*Medicine*]
PTM .... Post-Traumatic Meningitis [*Medicine*] (MELL)
PTM .... Presentment [*Telegraphy*] (PCTE)
PTM .... Pressure Time per Minute (SAUS)
PTM .... Pressure-Transmitting Medium [*Engineering*]
Ptm .... Pressure Transmural [*Pretaining to an airway or blood vessel*] [*Medicine*] (DAVI)
PTM .... Preterm Milk [*Medicine*]
PTM .... Pretuned Module [*Telecommunications*] (IAA)
PTM .... Primary Thickening Meristem [*Botany*]
PTM .... Priority Timing Module
PTM .... Product Test Monitor (SAUS)
PTM .... Professional, Technical and Management (SAUS)
PTM .... Programmable Terminal Multiplexer [*Texas Instruments, Inc.*]
PTM .... Programmable Timer Module
PTM .... Program Time Multiplex (SAUS)
PTM .... Program Timing and Maintenance [*Electronics*] (IAA)
PTM .... Program Timing and Miscellaneous [*Electronics*]
PTM .... Program Trouble Memoranda (or Memorandum) (SAUS)
PTM .... Program Trouble Memorandum [*NASA*] (IAA)
PTM .... Proof Test Model [*NASA*]
PTM .... Propellant-Pressurant Tank Module (ACAE)
PTM .... Prototype Model (SAUS)
PTM .... Pulse Tie Modulation (SAUS)
PTM .... Pulse Time Modulation [*Radio*]
PTM .... Pulse Time (or Modulation) (SAUS)
PTM .... Pulse Transmission Mode (MCD)
PTM .... Punched Tape Memory (SAUS)
PTM .... Punch-Through Modulation (SAUS)
PTM .... Putnam Managed High Yield Trust [*NYSE symbol*] (SPSG)
PTM .... Putnam Managed Hi Yield Tr [*NYSE symbol*] (TTSB)
PTM .... Southeastern Airways Corp. [*ICAO designator*] (FAAC)
PTMA .... Phenyltrimethylammonium [*Also, PTA, PTM*] [*Organic chemistry*]
PTMA .... Phosphotungstomolybdic Acid [*Inorganic chemistry*]
PTMA .... Prednisolone Trimethylacetate (SAUS)
PTMA .... Prothymosin Alpha (DMAA)
PTMAA .... Petroleum Tank Management Association of Alberta [*Canada*] (FOTI)
PTMAS .... Professional, Technical, Managerial, and Administrative Staff
PTMC .... Centre for Power Transmission and Motion Control [*University of Bath*] [*United Kingdom*] (RCD)
PTMC .... Photomechanical (VRA)
PTMC .... Polaris Tender Management Computer [*Missiles*]
PTMC .... Polish Telephones & Microwave Corp. [*NASDAQ symbol*] (SAG)
PTMC .... Polish Tels & Microwave Corp. [*NASDAQ symbol*] (TTSB)
PTMCA .... Pit Tub and Mine Car Manufacturers' Association [*British*] (BI)
PTMCW .... Polish Tels & Microwave Wrrt [*NASDAQ symbol*] (TTSB)
PTMD .... Propellant Toxicity Monitoring Device (SAUS)
PTMD .... Propellant Toxicity Monitoring Devices (KSC)
PTMDF .... Pupils, Tension, Media, Disc, Fundus [*Medicine*]
PTME .... Physical Teardown/Maintenance Evaluation
PTMEG .... Polytetramethylene Ether Glycol [*Organic chemistry*]
PTMG .... Polytetramethylene Glycol (SAUS)
PTMK .... Pathmark Stores [*Company symbol*]
PTML .... PNP [*Positive-Negative-Positive*] Transistor Magnetic Logic (IEEE)
PTML .... Positive Negative, Positive Negative Transistor Magnetic Logic
PTML .... Proxicom Template Markup Language [*Computer science*]
PTMOD .... Paper Tape Module (SAUS)
PTM/OS .... Programmable Terminal Monitor/Operating System (NITA)
PTMPY .... Per Thousand Members per Year (DMAA)
PTMR .... Percutaneous Transmyocardial Revascularization [*Medicine*]
PTMS .... Parathymosin (DMAA)
PTMS .... Para-Toluidine-meta-sulfonic Acid [*Also, PTMSA*] [*Organic chemistry*]
PTMS .... Pattern Transformation Memory System
PTMS .... Precision Torque Measuring System (NASA)
PTMS .... Publication Text Management System (MCD)
PTMS .... Public Transportation Facilities and Equipment Management System [*FHWA*] (TAG)
PTMSA .... Para-Toluidine-meta-sulfonic Acid [*Also, PTMS*] [*Organic chemistry*]
PTMSP .... Poly(trimethylsilyl-propyne) [*Organic chemistry*]
PTMT .... Poly(tetramethylene Terephthalate) [*Organic chemistry*]
PTMTCS .... Power-Tape-to-Magnetic-Tape Conversion System (SAUS)
PTMTLG .... Pitometer-Log [*Engineering*]
PTMU .... Power and Temperature Monitor Unit (KSC)
PTMU .... Pressure & Temperature Measurement Unit (SAUS)
PTMUX .... Pulse Time Multiplex (MSA)

PTMV........ Percutaneous Transvenous Mitral Valvotomy [*Cardiology*]
PTM x ESV... Pressure Timer per Minute x Endsystolic Volume (SAUS)
PTN.......... Morgan City/Patterson [*Louisiana*] [*Airport symbol*] (OAG)
PTN.......... Pantanal Linhas Aereas Sul-Matogrossenses SA [*Brazil*] [*ICAO designator*] (FAAC)
PTN.......... Particulate Total Nitrogen [*Analytical chemistry*]
PTN.......... Partido Trabalhista Nacional [*National Workers' Party*] [*Brazil*]
PTN.......... Partition (KSC)
PTN.......... Patterson, LA [*Location identifier*] [*FAA*] (FAAL)
PTN.......... Pay Through the Nose (ODA)
PTN.......... Peace Through NATO (SAUS)
PTN.......... Personal Telecommunications Number (VLIE)
PTN.......... Personal Telephone Number (SAUS)
PTN.......... Phenotemperature Normogram [*Phenology*]
PTN.......... Phenytoin [*Anticonvulsant*]
PTN.......... Photographic Trade News (SAUS)
PTN.......... Plant Test Number [*Telecommunications*] (TEL)
PTN.......... Pluton Industries Ltd. [*Vancouver Stock Exchange symbol*]
Ptn.......... Portion (SAUS)
PTN.......... Potsdam [*New York*] [*Seismograph station code, US Geological Survey*] (SEIS)
PTN.......... Presentation [*Telegraphy*] (PCTE)
PTN.......... Preservation Trades Network (EARSL)
PTN.......... Private Telecommunication Network [*Telecommunications*] (OSI)
PTN.......... Procedure Turn [*ICAO*] (FAAC)
Ptn.......... Pterin [*Biochemistry*]
PTN.......... Public Telephone Network (DA)
PTN.......... Public Transportation Network (ODA)
PTN.......... Pull-Thru Network (EA)
PTN.......... Pyramidal Tract Neuron (SAUS)
PTNA........ Pituitary Tumor Network Association (EA)
PTNA........ Professional Travel Nurses Association (SAUS)
PTNB........ Preterm Newborn (MELL)
pTNM........ Postsurgical, Tumor, Nodes, and Metastases [*Classifications for postsurgical resection pathological staging of cancer*] [*Oncology*] (DAVI)
PTNM........ Putnam Trust Co. of Greenwich [*NASDAQ symbol*]
PTNP........ Pinnacle Transportation Service [*Common carrier symbol*]
PTNR........ Partner (ROG)
Ptnr........ Partner (TBD)
PTNRSHIP... Partnership (ROG)
PTNX........ Printronix, Inc. [*NASDAQ symbol*] (NQ)
PTNX........ Private Telecommunication Network Exchange [*Telecommunications*] (OSI)
PTO.......... Desiderio & Taylor,Planning Tax-Exempt Organizations (SAUS)
PTO.......... North West Geomatics Ltd. [*Canada*] [*ICAO designator*] (FAAC)
PTO.......... Pacific Theater of Operations [*World War II*]
PTO.......... Packard Truck Organization [*Defunct*] (EA)
PTO.......... Paid Time Off (NFD)
PTO.......... Paraffin Transformer Oil [*Petroleum engineering*]
PTO.......... Parent-Teacher Organization (SAUS)
PTO.......... Participating Test Organization [*Air Force*]
PTO.......... Partners Oil & Mining [*Vancouver Stock Exchange symbol*]
PTO.......... Part Time Operation (DA)
PTO.......... Patent and Trademark Office [*Formerly, PO*] [*Department of Commerce*]
PTO.......... Pato Branco [*Brazil*] [*Airport symbol*] (OAG)
PTO.......... Pattern Trigger Output (VLIE)
PTO.......... People, Topics, Opinions [*A publication*] [*British*]
PTO.......... Percutaneous Transhepatic Obliteration (STED)
PTO.......... Perlsucht Tuberculin Original [*Medicine*] (MAE)
PTO.......... Perlsucht-Tuberculin Original (SAUS)
PTO.......... Permeability Tuned Oscillator (SAUS)
PTO.......... Permeability-Tuned Oscillator (IAA)
PTO.......... Personal Time Off (DAVI)
PTO.......... Personal Trust Officer [*Banking*] (TBD)
PTO.......... Physical Training Officer (SAUS)
PTO.......... Plant Transfer Out (SAUS)
pto.......... Please Turn Over (WDMC)
PTO.......... Please Turn Over [*the page*]
PTO.......... Portland Terminal-Oregon [*Federal Railroad Administration identification code*]
PTO.......... Porto [*Serro Do Pilar*] [*Portugal*] [*Seismograph station code, US Geological Survey*] (SEIS)
PTO.......... Port Transportation Officer
PTO.......... Power Takeoff [*Automotive engineering*]
PTO.......... Power Test Operations (MCD)
PTO.......... Powertrain Operations [*Auto manufacturer corporate structure*]
PTO.......... Preliminary Technical Order (ACAE)
PTO.......... Prevent Take-Off (SAUS)
PTO.......... Primary Test Organization (ACAE)
PTO.......... Principal Technical Officer (SAUS)
PTO.......... Professional and Technology Officer [*British*]
PTO.......... Project Technical Office [*Military*] (DNAB)
PTO.......... Project Type Organization (AAG)
PTO.......... Proof Test Orbiter [*NASA*]
PTO.......... Propellant Transfer Operation (AFM)
PTO.......... Provisional Topographic Overprint (SAUS)
PTO.......... Public Telecommunication Network Operator (SAUS)
PTO.......... Public Telecommunications Operator (NITA)
PTO.......... Public Trust Office [*Australia*]
PTO.......... Punched Tape Output (SAUS)
PTO.......... Purdue Teacher Opinionaire [*Test*]
PTO.......... Pyridinethiol Oxide [*Pharmacology*]
PTOA........ Projective Tests of Attitudes
PTOA........ Public Television Outreach Alliance (SAUS)
PTobA....... United States Army, Tobyhanna Army Depot Library, Tobyha[illegible] [*Library symbol*] [*Library of Congress*] (LCLS)
PTO Board... Patent and Trademark Office Board of Patent Appeals and In[illegible]ences (AAGC)
PTOC........ Platoon Tactical Operations Center (ACAE)
PTOCA....... Presentation Text Object Content Architecture (SAUS)
PTOE........ Planned Table of Organization and Equipment (SAUS)
P to F....... Poor to Fair (SAUS)
PToG........ General Telephone & Electronics, GTE Sylvania, Inc., Towanda, PA [*Library symbol*] [*Library of Congress*] (LCLS)
PTOJ........ Passive Track-On-Jam
PTOJ........ Passsive Track On Jam (SAUS)
PTOL........ Peacetime Operating Level (AFM)
Ptol......... Ptolemaeus Mathematicus [*Second century AD*] [*Classical studies*] (OCD)
Ptol......... Ptolemaic (BJA)
PTOMAIN... Project to Optimize Many Individual Numbers (SAA)
PTON........ Penton Media [*OTCBB symbol*]
PTON........ Proteon, Inc. [*NASDAQ symbol*] (SPSG)
P to P....... Peak-to-Peak (SAUS)
P to P....... Plate to Plate (DEN)
P-to-P....... Plate-to-Plate (SAUS)
P-to-P....... Point-to-Point (SAUS)
P to P....... Port to Port [*Shipping*] (DS)
PTOPC....... Program to Program Communications (MHDI)
PTOS........ Paper Tape Oriented Operating System
PTOS........ Paper Tape-oriented Operating System (SAUS)
PTOS........ Patent and Trademark Office Society (EA)
PTOS........ Patriot Tactical Operations Simulator [*Army*]
PTOS........ Peacetime Operating Stock [*Military*]
PTOS........ Punched Tape Oriented System (SAUS)
PTOUT....... Printout (MSA)
PTOX........ Periodic Trap Oxidizer [*Automotive engineering*]
PTOZ........ Port of Tacoma [*Federal Railroad Administration identification code*]
PTP.......... Association of Professional Team Physicians (SAUS)
PTP.......... Pancreatic Thread Protein [*Medicine*] (EDAA)
PTP.......... Paper Tape Perforator [*or Punch*]
PTP.......... Paper Tape Printer (SAUS)
PTP.......... Parameter Test Program (SAA)
PTP.......... Parent to Parent, Inc. [*Australia*]
PTP.......... Parti Togolais du Progres [*Party for Togolese Progress*]
PTP.......... Part-Time Pimp (SAUS)
PTP.......... Patch and Test Panel (SAUS)
PTP.......... Peak-to-Peak [*Nuclear energy*]
PTP.......... Pensions for Technical Professionals [*An association*]
PTP.......... People-to-People (SAUS)
PTP.......... People to People International (EA)
PTP.......... percutaneous Transhepatic Portography (STED)
PTP.......... Percutaneous Transhepatic Selective Portography [*Roentgenography*]
PTP.......... Periodic Tasker Process (SAUS)
PTP.......... Peripheral Target Position (ABAC)
PtP.......... Person-to-Person [*Medicine*] (EDAA)
PTP.......... Petrologic Petroleum [*Vancouver Stock Exchange symbol*]
PTP.......... Phenyltetrahydropyridine [*Biochemistry*]
PTP.......... Physical Training Phase (SAUS)
PTP.......... Platinum Temperature Probe
PTP.......... Platinum Underwriters Holdings Ltd. [*NYSE symbol*]
PTP.......... Pointe-A-Pitre [*Guadeloupe*] [*Airport symbol*] (OAG)
PTP.......... Point Park College, Pittsburgh, PA [*Inactive*] [*OCLC symbol*] (OCLC)
PTP.......... Point-to-Point [*Robotics*] [*Telecommunications*]
PTP.......... Point-to-Point Phone (NAKS)
PTP.......... Pollution Transfer Program [*Marine science*] (MSC)
PTP.......... Porous Tungsten Plug
PTP.......... Posterior Tibial Pulse [*Cardiology*] (DAVI)
PTP.......... Posto Telefonico Pubblico [*Public Telephone*] [*Italy*]
PTP.......... Posttetanic Potential [*Medicine*] (EDAA)
PTP.......... Post-Tetanic Potentiation [*Neurology*]
PTP.......... Post-Transfusion Purpura [*Medicine*]
PTP.......... Potato Tuber Peroxidase [*An enzyme*]
PTP.......... Preferred Target Point (KSC)
PTP.......... Preliminary Task Plan (MCD)
PTP.......... Preoperational Test Procedure (SAUS)
PTP.......... Pretransmission Precautionary Answer to Nature's Call [*Especially before a long program*] [*Television*]
PTP.......... Pre-Turbo Pressure
PTP.......... Primary Target Point [*NASA*]
PTP.......... Printing Tape Puncher (SAUS)
PTP.......... Print-to-Point [*Telecommunications*] (IAA)
PTP.......... Prior to Program [*Medicine*] (MAE)
PTP.......... Probability to Penetrate (SAUS)
PTP.......... Processor to Processor (SAUS)
PTP.......... Production Test Plan (MCD)
PTP.......... Production Test Procedure (NATG)
PTP.......... Productive Thinking Program (SAUS)
PTP.......... Professional Tax Planner
PTP.......... Programmable Telemetry Processor (SAUS)
PTP.......... Programmable Text Processor [*Programming language*] (CSR)
PTP.......... Programmable Touch Panel [*Electronics*]
PTP.......... Programmed Text Processing (SAUS)
PTP.......... Programmed Turn Phase
PTP.......... Program Tape Punch (SAUS)

PTP .... Program Task Planning (MCD)
PTP .... Project Test Plan (SAUS)
PTP .... Promise to Pay (MHDW)
PTP .... Protect the Planet [*Manual*]
PTP .... Protein Tyrosine Phosphatase [*An enzyme*]
PTP .... Prothrombin-Proconvertin (STED)
PTP .... Prothrombin-Procovertin (STED)
PTP .... Proximal Tubular Pressure (STED)
PTP .... Proximity Test Plug [*Nuclear energy*] (NRCH)
PTP .... Publicly Traded Partnership (SAUS)
PTP .... Pueblo to People (EA)
PTP .... Pumped Two-Phase Mounting Plate (SAUS)
PTP .... Punched Tape Perforator (SAUS)
PTP .... Punched Tape Programming (SAUS)
PTP .... Togolese Progressive Party [*Political party*] (PSAP)
Ptp .... Transpulmonary Pressure (MAE)
PTPA .... Portal-to-Portal Act of 1947 (WYGK)
PTPA .... Public Television Programmers Association (SAUS)
PT-PAC .... Physical Therapy Political Action Committee
PTPase .... Protein Tyrosine Phosphatase [*An enzyme*]
PTPC .... Permeability Transition Pore Complex [*Biochemistry*]
PTPC .... Professional Teaching Practices Commission (OICC)
PTPC .... Protein-Tyrosine Phosphatase C (DMAA)
PTPD .... Part Paid [*Business term*]
Pt Pd .... Part paid (EBF)
PTPD .... Post-Traumatic Personality Defect (MELL)
PTPE .... Powertrain Product Engineering [*Automotive*]
PTP'er .... Prime Time Performer [*In book title, "Vitale: Just Your Average Bald, One-Eyed Basketball Wacko Who Beat the Ziggy and Became a PTP'er"*]
PTPF .... Payee TIN [*Taxpayer Identification Number*] Perfection File [*IRS*]
PTPG .... Participating (SAUS)
PTPG .... Protein-Tyrosine Phosphatase Gamma (DMAA)
PTPI .... Paris Transport [*Common carrier symbol*]
PTPI .... People to People International (EAIO)
PTPI .... Post-Traumatic Pulmonary Insufficiency [*Medicine*] (MELL)
PTPI .... Professional and Technical Programs, Inc.
PT Plane .... Patrol Torpedo Plane (SAUS)
PTPLS .... Point Pleasant, WV [*American Association of Railroads railroad junction routing code*]
PTPLU .... Point Source Gaussian Diffusion Model (SAUS)
PTPM .... Posttraumatic Progressive Myelopathy [*Neurology*] (DAVI)
PTPN .... Peripheral [*Vein*] Total Parenteral Nutrition [*Gastroenterology*] (DAVI)
PTPN .... Ponape Island [*Caroline Islands*] [*ICAO location identifier*] (ICLI)
PTPN .... Protein-Tyrosine Phosphatase, Non-Receptor (DMAA)
PTPO .... Painted Thermoplastic Olefin [*Plastics*]
PTP Programming .... Point-to-Point Programming (SAUS)
PTPR .... Production Test Program Report
PTPS .... Package Test Power Supply
PTPS .... Parallel Funed Parallel Stabilized (SAUS)
PTPS .... Parallel Tuned Parallel-Stabilized (SAUS)
PTPS .... Parallel-Tuned Parallel-Stabilized (IAA)
PTPS .... Parker Team Player Survey [*Test*] (TMMY)
PTPS .... Photothermal Phase-shift Spectroscopy (SAUS)
PTPS .... Postthrombophlebitis Syndrome [*Medicine*] (EDAA)
PTPS .... Propellant Transfer Pressurization System (KSC)
PTPS .... Pumped Two-Phase System (SSD)
PTPSC .... People-to-People Sports Committee (EA)
PTPSH .... Provide this Passenger Special Handling (SAUS)
PT-PSK .... Pilot-Tone Phase Shift Keyed (or Keying) (SAUS)
PTPSK .... Pilot Tone Phase Shift Keying [*Computer science*] (IAA)
PTPT .... Platinum Print (VRA)
PT/PT .... Point-to-Point (SAUS)
P-TPT .... Portable Tactual Performance Test [*Child development test*] [*Psychology*]
PTPW .... Pioneer Transport [*Common carrier symbol*]
PTQ .... Ludlow Aviation, Inc. [*FAA designator*] (FAAC)
PTQ .... Parent-Teacher Questionnaire (DMAA)
PTQ .... Poly(tolyquinoxaline) [*Organic chemistry*]
PTQ .... Pulse-Taking Questionnaire
PTQL .... Porter Trucking [*Common carrier symbol*]
PTR .... Nova Scotia Department of Lands and Forests [*Canada*] [*FAA designator*] (FAAC)
PTR .... Pacific Test Range (MUGU)
ptr .... Painter (VRA)
PTR .... Painter
PTR .... Paper Tape Reader
PTR .... Paper Tape Reading (SAUS)
PTR .... Paper Towel Receptor [*Technical drawings*]
PTR .... Parr Terminal Railroad (MHDW)
PTR .... Partido Tercera Republica [*Chile*] [*Political party*] (EY)
PTR .... Partner
PTR .... Parts Tool Requirements File
PTR .... Parts Transfer Record (SAA)
PTR .... Part Throttle Reheat [*Aviation*] (OA)
PTR .... Patellar Tendon Reflex (SAUS)
PTR .... Patient Termination Record [*Medicine*] (DB)
PTR .... Patient to Return (MELL)
PTR .... Patuxent River [*Navy*] (MCD)
PTR .... Perforated Tape Reader
PTR .... Performance Thoroughbred Registry [*Equine term*] (TED)
PTR .... Peripheral Total Resistance [*Medicine*] (MAE)
PTR .... Perlsucht Tuberculin Rest [*Medicine*] (MAE)
PTR .... Perlsucht-Tuberculin Rest (SAUS)
PTR .... Permanent Traffic Recording (SAUS)
P/Tr .... Permian/Triassic [*A geological period boundary*]
PTR .... Personal Technology Research [*Commercial firm*]
PTR .... Peterson [*Alabama*] [*Seismograph station code, US Geological Survey*] (SEIS)
Ptr .... Petrine [*Of, or relating to, Peter the Apostle or Peter the Great*] (BJA)
PTR .... PetroChina Company Ltd. [*NYSE symbol*]
PTR .... Photoelectric Tape Reader
PTR .... Physical Technical Reactor (SAUS)
PTR .... Physikalisch-Technische Reichsanstalt
PTR .... Pilot Training Rate [*Navy*]
PTR .... Platinum Resistance (SAUS)
PTR .... Pleasant Harbor [*Alaska*] [*Airport symbol*] (OAG)
PTR .... Plug-Type Receptacle
PTR .... Pointer [*Computer science*]
PTR .... Pointer Record (SAUS)
PTR .... Point in Time Repair [*Computer science*]
PTR .... Polar to Rectangular (SAA)
PTR .... Polar-to-Rectangular (SAUS)
PTR .... Pool Test Reactor [*Nuclear energy*]
PTR .... Pool Thermal Reactor (SAUS)
PTR .... Pool Training Reactor [*Nuclear energy*]
PTR .... Poor Transmission [*Telecommunications*] (TEL)
PTr .... Porcine Trypsin (DB)
PTR .... Portable Tape Recorder
PTR .... Port Macquarie [*New South Wales*] [*Airport symbol*] (AD)
PTR .... Port Terminal Railroad of South Carolina [*Federal Railroad Administration identification code*]
PTR .... Port Thermal Radiator (SPST)
PTR .... Position Track RADAR
PTR .... Positive Termination Rate [*Job Training and Partnership Act*] (OICC)
PTR .... Postetanic Repetition (SAUS)
PTR .... Post-Tenure Review (SAUS)
PTR .... Post-Tetanic Repetition (SAUS)
PTR .... Post-Trip Review
PTR .... Power Transformers (MCD)
PTR .... Precision Technologies, Inc. (EFIS)
PTR .... Precision Transmitter Receiver
PTR .... Preliminary Technical Report
PTR .... Preliminary Test Report [*NASA*] (KSC)
PTR .... Presenter [*Telegraphy*] (PCTE)
PTR .... Pressure Test Record
PTR .... Pressure Transmitter Recorder (ECII)
PTR .... Pressure Tube Reactor (SAUS)
PTR .... Pressure-Tube Reactor [*Nuclear energy*]
PTR .... Pressurized Tube Reactor (SAUS)
PTR .... Pretransmit Receiving
PTR .... Pre-Trial Release (OICC)
PTR .... Primary Tactical Reconnaissance (SAUS)
PTR .... Printer (MSA)
P Tr .... Private Trust [*Includes testamentary, investment, life insurance, holding title, etc.*] [*Legal term*] (DLA)
PTR .... Problem Trouble Report (CTAS)
PTR .... Processor Tape Read
PTR .... Processor Tape Reader
PTR .... Production Test Record
PTR .... Production Test Requirements (KSC)
PTR .... Professional Tennis Registry, USA (EA)
PTR .... Proficiency Testing Research (EA)
PTR .... Programmer Trouble Report [*Nuclear energy*] (GFGA)
PTR .... Program Technical Report (CTAS)
PTR .... Program Technical Review (MCD)
PTR .... Program Test Routine (SAUS)
PTR .... Program Trouble Report [*NASA*] (KSC)
PTR .... Proof Test Reactor [*Nuclear energy*]
PTR .... Property Trust America (EFIS)
PTR .... Prothrombin Time Ratio [*Medicine*] (MELL)
PTR .... Pulmonary Total Resistance (SAUS)
PTR .... Pulse Transient Recorder (SAUS)
PTR .... Punched Tape Reader [*Computer science*]
PTR .... Punched Tape Reading (SAUS)
PTR .... Punched Tape Recorder (SAUS)
PTR .... Pupil-Teacher Ratio
PTR .... Security Capital Pacific Trust [*NYSE symbol*] (SAG)
PTR .... Security Cap Pacific Tr [*NYSE symbol*] (TTSB)
PTRA .... Paper Tape Reader Adapter (SAUS)
PTRA .... Percutaneous Transluminal Renal Angioplasty [*Medicine*] (DMAA)
PTRA .... Port Terminal Railroad Association
PTRA .... Power-Motion Technology Representatives Association (NTPA)
PTRA .... Power Transmission Representatives Association (EA)
PTRAC .... Planning and Transport Research Advisory Council (SAUS)
P/TRAC .... Positraction [*Automotive engineering*]
PTR Algorithm .... Polygon-to-Rectangle Algorithm (SAUS)
PTrB .... Betz Laboratories, Inc., Trevose, PA [*Library symbol*] [*Library of Congress*] (LCLS)
PTRB .... Peterbilt [*NCIC truck make code*]
PTRC .... Paper Tape Reader Control (SAUS)
PTRC .... Personnel and Training Research Center [*Air Force*]
PTRC .... Petroleum Technology Research Centre (FOTI)
PTRC .... Portland Terminal Railroad [*Federal Railroad Administration identification code*]
PTRC .... Psychological Therapies Research Centre [*University of Leeds*] [*United Kingdom*] (RCD)
PTRD .... Part Redeemed [*Stock exchange term*] (SPSG)

PTRD .... Percutaneous Transluminal Renal Dilatation (SAUS)
PTRE .... PartnerRe Ltd. [*NASDAQ symbol*] (SAG)
PTRE .... Pressure Tube Reactor Experiment [*Nuclear energy*] (NUCP)
PTREF .... PartnerRe Ltd [*NASDAQ symbol*] (TTSB)
PTRF .... Peacetime Rate Factor [*Military*] (AABC)
PTRF .... Peacetime Replacement Factor [*Military*]
PTR File .... Parts Tool Requirements File (SAUS)
PTRH .... Punched Tape Reading Head (SAUS)
PTRI .... Pharmaceutical and Toxicological Research Institute [*Ohio State University*] [*Research center*] (RCD)
PTRIA .... Polystyrene-Tube Radioimmunoassay [*Medicine*] (DMAA)
PtrixMd ..... Pediatrix Medical Group, Inc. [*Associated Press*] (SAG)
PTRJ......... Powered Thermocouple Reference Junction
PTRM........ Partial Thermoremanent Magnetization [*Geophysics*]
PTRN .... Photran Corp. [*NASDAQ symbol*] (TTSB)
PTRNMKR... Patternmaker (WGA)
PTRO .... Koror [*Caroline Islands*] [*ICAO location identifier*] (ICLI)
PTRO .... Personnel Transaction Register by Originator [*Military*] (AABC)
PTRO .... Petrominerals Corp. [*NASDAQ symbol*] (NQ)
PTRO .... Preoverhaul Test Requirement Outline
PTROI .... Professional Towing and Recovery Operators of Illinois (EARSL)
PTRP .... Paper Tape Reader Punch [*Computer science*] (IAA)
PTRP .... Post-Treatment Resource Program [*Medicine*]
PTRPrA....... Security Cap Pac Cv'A'Pfd [*NYSE symbol*] (TTSB)
PTRPrB....... Security Cap Pac Tr Sr'B'Pfd [*NYSE symbol*] (TTSB)
PTRR .... Port Townsend Railroad, Inc. [*Formerly, PTS*] [*AAR code*]
PTRRS ...... Pipeline Time Recording and Reporting Systems (SAUS)
PTRS .... Philosophical Transactions. Royal Society of London [*A publication*]
PTRS .... Potters Financial [*NASDAQ symbol*] (TTSB)
PTRS .... Potters Financial Corp. [*NASDAQ symbol*] (SAG)
PTRS .... Potters Savings & Loan Co. [*NASDAQ symbol*] (SAG)
PTRSB....... Petersburg, VA [*American Association of Railroads railroad junction routing code*]
PTRT......... Part Task Radar Trainer (SAUS)
PTRT......... Patriot Homes [*NCIC trailer make code*]
ptrt........... Portrait (VRA)
PTR-t .... Punch Tape Reader (SAUS)
PTRU .... Petro Union, Inc. [*NASDAQ symbol*] (SAG)
PTRU .... South American Petrolite de Venezuela [*Intermodal shipping container symbol*] (TVRC)
PT Rulings... Pay-Roll Tax Rulings [*Australia*] [*A publication*]
PTRUQ ...... Petro Union [*NASDAQ symbol*] (TTSB)
PtrV........... Painter (Aircraft) [*U.S. Navy enlisted rating*] (AUER)
PTRV .... Peak Transient Reverse Voltage [*Electronics*] (IAA)
Ptrx .... Pelvic Traction [*Medicine*] (EDAA)
PTRX .... Petrolite [*Private rail car owner code*]
Ptry .... Pantry (SAUS)
PTRY .... Pantry, Inc. [*NASDAQ symbol*]
Ptry .... Poetry (SAUS)
ptry .... Pottery (VRA)
PTRY .... Pottery [*Freight*]
PTS .... Painful Tonic Seizure (AAMN)
PTS .... Pali Text Society (EA)
PTS .... Panoramic Thermic Sight (SAUS)
PTS .... Paper Tape Sender
PTS .... Paper Tape System [*Computer science*] (IAA)
PTS .... Paper Tape-to-Magnetic Tape Conversion System (DIT)
PTS .... Papiertechnische Stiftung [*Database producer*]
PTS .... Parachute Training School [*British military*] (DMA)
PTS .... Parallel Transaction Server [*IBM*] (GART)
PTS .... Parameter Test Setup
PTS .... Para-Toluenesulfonic Acid
PTS .... Park-Tronic System [*Automotive engineering*]
Pts .... Participating (EBF)
PTS .... Parts
Pts .... Parts
PTS .... Parts Tracking System (SAUS)
PTS .... Part-Task Simulator (SAUS)
PTS .... Passive Tobacco Smoke [*Industrial hygiene term*] (OHS)
PTS .... Patellar-Tendon Supracondylar [*Anatomy*]
PTS .... Payload Test Set [*NASA*] (NASA)
PTS .... Payload Transportation System [*NASA*] (MCD)
PTS .... People's Translation Service (EA)
PTS .... Perforated Tape Subsystem [*Computer science*] (IAA)
PTS .... Performance Tracking System
PTS .... Permanent Threshold Shift [*Hearing evaluation*]
PTS .... Persistent Toxic Substance [*Ecology*] (FOTI)
PTS .... Personal Telecommunications System (SAUS)
PTS .... Personal Typography System (DGA)
PTS .... Personnel Transfer Submersible (SAUS)
PTS .... Petro-Sun International, Inc. [*Toronto Stock Exchange symbol*]
PTS .... Philatelic Traders' Society Ltd. [*British*] (BI)
PTS .... Philips Theological Seminary (SAUS)
PTS .... Phosphotransferase System [*Organic chemistry*]
PTS .... Photogrammetric Target System [*Air Force*]
PTS .... Photogrammetric Triangulation System [*Air Force*] (IAA)
PTS .... Photothermal Spectroscopy
PTS .... Phototransmission System [*Telecommunications*] (IAA)
PTS .... Phototypesetting (DGA)
PTS .... Pilot Training Squadron [*Air Force*]
PTS .... Pilot Training System (SAUS)
PTS .... Pinchless Tracing Simulator (SAUS)
PTS .... Pistol Training System [*Police and security equipment*]
PTS .... Pi Tau Sigma [*Society*]
PTS .... Pittsburg, KS [*Location identifier*] [*FAA*] (FAAL)
PTS .... Placer Tractor Service (EFIS)
PTS .... Plane Transport System (DA)
PTS .... Planning Tracking System (MCD)
PTS .... Plasma Technology Section (SAUS)
PTS .... Player Trade Society [*A union*] [*British*]
PTS .... Pneumatic Target System (SAUS)
PTS .... Pneumatic Test Sequencer (AFM)
PTS .... Pneumatic Test Set (KSC)
PTS .... Pneumatic Tube System
PTS .... Pod Tail Section
PTS .... Pointing and Tracking Scope
PTS .... Points [*Postal Service standard*] (OPSA)
Pts .... Points [*Basketball*]
PTS .... Points International Ltd. [*Toronto Stock Exchange symbol*] [*Canada*]
PTS .... Points of Call Airlines Ltd. [*Canada*] [*ICAO designator*] (FAAC)
PTS .... Polar Track Structure [*Aviation*] (FAAC)
PTS .... Pollution Technical Services Ltd., Abingdon (SAUS)
PTS .... Polymer Thick Film (SAUS)
PTS .... Portsmouth Torpedo School (SAUS)
PTS .... Port Townsend Railroad, Inc. [*Later, PTRR*] [*AAR code*]
PTS .... Postal Transportation Service (SAUS)
PTS .... Post and Telecommunications Service (IAA)
PTS .... Post-Traumatic Stress [*Medicine*]
PTS .... Potential Tax Savings (SAUS)
PTS .... Power Transfer Switch
PTS .... Power Transient Suppressor (IEEE)
PTS .... Practical Test Standards [*FAA*] (TAG)
PTS .... Precision Timing System
PTS .... Predicasts Terminal System (SAUS)
PTS .... Predicasts Terminal Systems [*Predicasts, Inc.*] [*Cleveland, OH*] [*Database*]
PTS .... Predicasts Time Series [*Series of databases*] [*Predicasts, Inc.*] [*Cleveland, OH*]
PTS .... Preflight Test Set (DNAB)
PTS .... Preliminary Training School (SAUS)
PTS .... Presents [*Telegraphy*] (PCTE)
PTS .... Pressure Test Station (DNAB)
PTS .... Pressure Tuning Spectroscopy (SAUS)
PTS .... Pressurized Thermal Shock [*Nuclear energy*]
PTS .... Price-Tag Shock [*See also PTA*]
PTS .... Primary Trait System (EDAC)
PTS .... Prime Time Sunday [*TV program*]
PTS .... Princeton Theological Seminary (SAUS)
PTS .... Princeton Theological Seminary, Princeton, NJ [*OCLC symbol*] (OCLC)
PTS .... Printing Technical School (DGA)
PTS .... Prior to Surgery (DAVI)
PTS .... Private Telecommunications Systems [*Radio-Suisse Ltd.*] [*Switzerland*] [*Telecommunications*]
PTS .... Proactive TMDE Support (RDA)
PTS .... Proceed to Select [*Telecommunications*] (TEL)
PTS .... Proceed-to-Select (SAUS)
PTS .... Proceed to Send [*Telecommunications*] (TEL)
PTS .... Proceed-to-Send (SAUS)
PTS .... Processor Transaction Server [*Computer science*] (CIST)
PTS .... Production Test Specification
PTS .... Professional Tank Services, Ltd. (EFIS)
PTS .... Professional Travelogue Sponsors (EA)
PTS .... Programmable Terminal System [*Computer science*] (IAA)
PTS .... Programmer Test Station
PTS .... Program of Technology and Society [*Later, DTS*] (EA)
PTS .... Program Test System [*Computer science*] (IEEE)
PTS .... Program Triple Store
PTS .... Projectile Tracking System (SAUS)
PTS .... Project Tracking System [*Environmental Protection Agency*] (ERG)
PTS .... Propellant Transfer System
PTS .... Protestant Truth Society [*British*] (DBA)
PTS .... Protoflight Telescope Subassembly (SAUS)
PTS .... Provisional Technical Secretariat [*United Nations*]
PTS .... Public Telephone Service [*or System*] [*Telecommunications*] (TEL)
PTS .... Public Telephone System (SAUS)
PTS .... Punched Tape Speed (SAUS)
PTS .... Pure Time Sharing [*Computer science*] (IEEE)
PTS .... Put to Sleep [*ASPCA terminology*]
PTSA .... Kusaie [*Caroline Islands*] [*ICAO location identifier*] (ICLI)
PTSA .... Para-Toluenesulfonamide (SAUS)
PTSA .... Para-Toluenesulfonic Acid [*Organic chemistry*]
PTSA .... Para-Toluene Sulphonic Acid (SAUS)
PTSA .... Parent-Teacher Student Association (SAUS)
PTSA .... Parent-Teacher-Student Association [*Nickname: "Pizza"*]
PTSA .... Piano Trade Suppliers' Association [*British*] (BI)
PTSA .... Professional Trucking Services Association (EA)
PTSBG........ Pittsburg, KS [*American Association of Railroads railroad junction routing code*]
PTSC .... Paper Tape Selectric Composer (DGA)
PTSC .... Patriot Scientific Corp. [*NASDAQ symbol*] (QUAN)
PT-S/C........ Proof Test Spacecraft [*NASA*]
PTSD .... Pesticides and Toxic Substances Division [*Environmental Protection Agency*] (GFGA)
PTSD .... Post Traumatic Stress Disorder (SAUS)
PTSD .... Post-Traumatic Stress Disorder [*Psychiatry*]
PTSD-RRP... Posttraumatic Stress Disorder Residential Rehabilitation Program [*Veterans Affairs Medical Center*] (MHID)

PTSDT....... Proceed to Send Data Tone (SAUS)
PTSE......... Paper Tape Splicing Equipment
PTSE......... PNNI Topology State Element (SAUS)
PTSED....... Pesticides and Toxic Substances Enforcement Division (COE)
PTSFD....... Pittsfield, MA [*American Association of Railroads railroad junction routing code*]
PTSH........ Poststimulus Time Histogram [*Medicine*] (DMAA)
pts/hr........ parts per hour (SAUS)
pts/hr........ pieces per hour (SAUS)
PTSI......... PAM Transportation Services, Inc. [*NASDAQ symbol*] (NQ)
PTSI......... P.A.M. Transportation Svcs [*NASDAQ symbol*] (TTSB)
PTSI......... Para-Toluene Sulfonylisocyanate [*Organic chemistry*]
PtSi......... Platinum Silicide (SAUS)
PTSL......... Penner International [*Common carrier symbol*]
PTSM........ Plant, Technology, and Safety Management (HCT)
PTSO........ Personnel Transaction Summary by Originator [*Military*] (AABC)
PTSP........ Paper Tape Software Package (NITA)
PTSP........ Peacetime Support Period [*DoD*]
PT/SP........ Pressure Tube to Spool Piece [*Nuclear energy*] (NRCH)
PTSP........ Proceed-to-Select Protocol (SAUS)
PTSP........ Temporary Permit Suspended [*Motor vehicle violation driver status code in state of North Dakota*] (MVRD)
PTSPO....... Temporary Permit Suspended-Occupational Permit [*Motor vehicle violation driver status code in state of North Dakota*] (MVRD)
PTS PROMT... Predicasts Overview of Markets and Technology [*Predicasts, Inc.*] [*Cleveland, OH*] [*Bibliographic database*]
PTSR........ Performance Technical Survey Report
PTSR........ Preliminary Technical Survey Report [*Military*] (AFIT)
PTSR........ Pressure Tube Superheat Reactor (SAUS)
PTSR........ Pressure-Tube Superheat Reactor [*Nuclear energy*]
PTSS........ Parallel Tuned Series Stabilized (IAA)
PTSS........ Personnel Target Subsystem (SAUS)
PTSS........ Photon Target Scoring System (AAG)
PTSS........ Posttraumatic Stress Syndrome [*Medicine*] (DMAA)
PTSS........ Post-Traumatic Stress System [*Medicine*]
PTSS........ Princeton Time Sharing Services, Inc.
PTSS........ Princeton Time-Sharing System (SAUS)
PTSS........ Professional Telephone Selling Skills
ptst.......... Paintstick (VRA)
PTST......... Personnel Transaction Summary by Type Transaction [*Military*] (AABC)
PTST......... Pretransfusion Serologic Testing
PTST......... Prime Time School Television [*Defunct*] (EA)
PTSTN....... Pittston, PA [*American Association of Railroads railroad junction routing code*]
PTSTV....... Prime Time School Television (SAUS)
PTSX........ Point360 [*NASDAQ symbol*]
PTSX........ Proleride Transport System [*Private rail car owner code*]
PTT.......... Paper Tape Transmission (SAUS)
PTT.......... Paper Tape Typewriter (SAUS)
PTT.......... Parity Test Track (SAUS)
PTT.......... Partial Thromboplastin Time [*Hematology*]
PTT.......... Particle Transport Time (MAE)
PTT.......... Part Task Trainer (MCD)
PTT.......... Party Test [*Telecommunications*] (TEL)
PTT.......... Patellar Tendon Transfer [*Medicine*] (MELL)
PTT.......... Peak Trends Trust [*AMEX symbol*] (NASQ)
PTT.......... Peak Twitch Tension [*Physiology*]
PTT.......... Perforated Tape Transmitter (SAUS)
PTT.......... Perth Theatre Trust [*Australia*]
PTT.......... Petrotex Resources [*Vancouver Stock Exchange symbol*]
PTT.......... Physical Therapist Technician
PTT.......... Platform Terminal Transmitter (SAUS)
PTT.......... Platform Transmitter Terminal [*Satellite-based tracking system*]
PTT.......... Postal, Telegraph, and Telephone Administration (NATG)
PTT.......... Postal, Telephone, and Telegraph
PTT.......... Postes, Telegraphes, et Telediffusion [*Post, Telegraph, and Telephone*] [*General Post Office*] [*Facetious translation: Prostitution Telematique et Telephonique*] [*France*]
PTT.......... Post-Target Turn (SAUS)
PTT.......... Post, Telegraph and Telephone Authority (NITA)
PTT.......... Post, Telephone, and Telegraph [*Telecommunications*] (IAA)
PTT.......... Post Telephone & Telegraph Administration (WDAA)
PTT.......... Post Telephone or Telex (NITA)
PTT.......... Post, Telephone, Telegraph (SAUS)
PTT.......... Post, Telephon und Telegraphenbetriebe [*Switzerland*] [*Telecommunications*]
PTT.......... Post Ten Tumblers [*Pseudonym used by William Maginn*]
PTT.......... Post und Telegraphenverwaltung [*Postal and Telegraph Administration*] [*Austria*] [*Telecommunications*]
PTT.......... Pratt, KS [*Location identifier*] [*FAA*] (FAAL)
PTT.......... Prenegotiated Target Time (SAUS)
PTT.......... Press-to-Talk (IDOE)
PTT.......... Press-to-Test (SAUS)
PTT.......... Press to Transmit
PTT.......... Press-to-Transmit (SAUS)
PTT.......... Pressure Temperature Time (SAUS)
PTT.......... Printing Teletypewriter Telegraphy (VLIE)
PTT.......... Private Tombs at Thebes [*Oxford*] [*A publication*] (BJA)
PTT.......... Processing Telecom Technologies (PCM)
PTT.......... Production Type Test
PTT.......... Program Technical Training (AFM)
PTT.......... Program Test Tape [*Computer science*] (IEEE)
PTT.......... Protein Truncation Test [*Analytical biochemistry*]
PTT.......... Prothrombin Time [*Hematology*] (AAMN)
PTT.......... Public Telecommunications Trust [*Proposed replacement for Corporation for Public Broadcasting*]
PTT.......... Pulmonary Transit Time [*Physiology*]
PTT.......... Pulse Transmission Time [*Medicine*] (DMAA)
PTT.......... Punched Tape Technique (SAUS)
PTT.......... Push to Talk
PTT.......... Push-to-Talk (SAUS)
PTT/8........ Paper Tape Code on Eight Levels (NITA)
PTTA......... Postal Telegraph and Telephone Authority (SAUS)
PTT Administration... Postal, Telegraph and Telephone Administration (SAUS)
PTT Bulletin... Post-, Telephon- and Telegraphen-Bulletin (SAUS)
PTTC......... Pacific Transportation Terminal Command [*Army*]
PTTC......... Paper Tape and Transmission Code
PTTC......... Paper Tape Transmission Code (SAUS)
PTT-C........ Partial Thromboplastin Time Control [*Medicine*] (EDAA)
PTTC......... Perforated Tape and Transmission Code [*Telecommunications*] (IAA)
PTTC......... Perforated Tape and Transmission Control (SAUS)
PTTC......... Petroleum Technology Transfer Council [*Association*] (EA)
PTTC......... Public Telephone and Telegraph Codes (VLIE)
PTT-CT...... Activated Partial Thromboplastin Time, Control [*Hematology*] (DAVI)
PTTDAR..... Personnel Training and Training Devices Analysis Report (MCD)
PTTEP....... PTT Exploration & Production Public Co., Ltd (EFIS)
PTTH........ Prothoracicotropic Hormone
PTTI......... Postal, Telegraph, and Telephone International [*See also IPTT*] [*Geneva, Switzerland*] (EAIO)
PTTI......... Post, Telegraph and Telephone International (SAUS)
PTTI......... Precise Time and Time Interval (AFM)
PTTK......... Kosrae Island [*Caroline Islands*] [*ICAO location identifier*] (ICLI)
PTTK......... Partial Thromboplastin Time with Kaolin [*Hematology*]
PTTL......... Photo-Transferred Thermoluminescence (PDAA)
PTTL......... Press-to-Test Light
Pt-Tm........ Part-Time (SAUS)
PTTM........ Power alarm on Trunk Testing Module (SAUS)
PTTMC....... PACOM [*Pacific Command*] Tactical Target Materials Catalog (CINC)
PTTNMKR... Patternmaker (SAUS)
Pt to Pt...... Point-to-Point (SAUS)
PTTRN....... Pattern
PTTS......... Pressure Temperature Test Set (DWSG)
PTTS......... Private Telegraph and Telephone Service [*Telecommunications*] (IAA)
PTTSB....... Pittsburg, TX [*American Association of Railroads railroad junction routing code*]
PTTU........ PT Kerr [*Intermodal shipping container symbol*] (TVRC)
PTTXAU...... Public Teletex Access Unit (VLIE)
PTTY......... Petty
PTU.......... Bambam [*Language symbol*] (ETLW)
PTU.......... Package Transfer Unit
PTU.......... Pallet Transporter Unit [*Military*] (CAAL)
PTU.......... Paper Tape Unit (SAUS)
PTU.......... Parallel Transmission Unit (AAG)
PTU.......... Part-Throttle Unlock [*Automotive engineering*]
PTU.......... Pathology Transcription Unit
PTU.......... Phenylthiourea [*Organic chemistry*]
PTU.......... Pilot Test Unit [*Air Force*]
PTU.......... Planning Tracking Unit (MCD)
PTU.......... Platinum [*Alaska*] [*Airport symbol*] (OAG)
PTU.......... Platinum, AK [*Location identifier*] [*FAA*] (FAAL)
PTU.......... Plumbers Trade Union (SAUS)
PTU.......... Plumbing Trades Union [*British*]
PTU.......... Plumbing Trade Union (NADA)
PTU.......... Portable Test Unit
PTU.......... Power Transfer Unit
PTU.......... Power Transmission Unit (SAUS)
PTU.......... Pressure, Temperature, Humidity (SAUS)
PTU.......... Probe Transducer Unit (SAUS)
PTU.......... Processor Transfer Unit (SAUS)
PTU.......... Programmable Test Unit (SAUS)
PTU.......... Program Track Unit [*Telecommunications*] (LAIN)
PTU.......... Propylthiouracil [*Also, PROP, PT*] [*Thyroid inhibitor*]
PTU.......... Protection Training Unit (SAUS)
PTU.......... Psychiatric Treatment Unit (SAUS)
PTU.......... Punched Tape Unit (SAUS)
P-TUBE...... Pneumatic Tube (NAKS)
P-Tube....... Pneumatic Tube
PTUC........ Pacific Trade Union Community [*Australia*] (EAIO)
PTUC........ Philippines Trade Union Council (SAUS)
PTUC........ Philippine Trade Unions Council (SAUS)
PTUF........ Palestine Trade Union Federation (SAUS)
PTUF........ Professional Tennis Umpires Federation (SAUS)
PTUSR...... Processor Transfer Unit Status Register (SAUS)
PTUV........ Public Tenants' Union of Victoria [*Australia*]
PTV.......... Pactiv [*Company symbol*]
PTV.......... Pakistan Television Corp. (SAUS)
PTV.......... Parachute Test Vehicle
PTV.......... Paralysis, Tracheostomy, and Ventilation [*Medicine*] (EDAA)
PTV.......... Paratransit Vehicle
PTV.......... Passenger Transfer Vehicle [*Airport transportation*]
PTV.......... Passenger Transport Vehicle
PTV.......... Pathfinder Test Vehicle [*NASA*] (MCD)
PTV.......... Pay Television
PTV.......... Peach Tree Valley [*California*] [*Seismograph station code, US Geological Survey*] (SEIS)
PTV.......... Peak-to-Valley
PTV.......... Penetration Test Vehicle [*Aerospace*]
PTV.......... Personal Transportation Vehicle (SAUS)

PTV .... Pietas Tutissima Virtus [*Piety Is the Safest Virtue*] [*Motto of Ernst, Margrave of Brandenburg (1583-1613)*] [*Latin*]
PTV .... Pitch Thrust Vector (KSC)
PTV .... Planning Target Volume [*Medicine*] (RAWO)
PTV .... Poly(thienylenevinylene) [*Organic chemistry*]
PTV .... Porous Tungsten Vaporizer
PTV .... Porterville, CA [*Location identifier*] [*FAA*] (FAAL)
PTV .... Posterior Tibial Vein (SAUS)
PTV .... Predetermined Time Value (IEEE)
PTV .... Prisoner Transport Vehicle [*Police and security equipment*]
PTV .... Programmable Temperature Vaporizer
PTV .... Programmed-Temperature Vaporizing [*Analytical chemistry*]
PTV .... Projection Television (SAUS)
PTV .... Propulsion Technology Validation (MCD)
PTV .... Propulsion Test Vehicle
PTV .... Prototype Test Vehicle (MCD)
PTV .... Public Television
PTV .... Punched Tape Verifier [*Computer science*]
PTV .... Punch through Varactor [*Computer science*] (IAA)
PTV .... Punch-Through Varactor (SAUS)
PTV .... Puntavia Air Services [*Djibouti*] [*FAA designator*] (FAAC)
PTVA .... Propulsion Test Vehicle Assembly [*NASA*]
PTVAA .... Portland Television Appliance Association (SAUS)
PTVC .... Pitch Thrust Vector Control (KSC)
PTVD .... Portable Toxic Vapor Detector
PTVE .... Propulsion and Terrain Vehicle Engineering [*NASA*]
PTVE .... Propulsion Test Vehicle Engineering [*NASA*] (MCD)
PTVL .... Preview Travel [*NASDAQ symbol*] (SG)
PTVST .... Port Visit [*Navy*] (NVT)
PTVV .... Peak-to-Valley Variation (MCD)
PTW .... Page Table Word [*Computer science*] (IAA)
PTW .... Permit to Work (HEAS)
PTW .... Personal Typesetting Workstation (DGA)
PTW .... Per Thousand Words (SAUS)
PTW .... Per Ton Weight (SAUS)
PTW .... Physikalisch-Technische-Werkstatten [*Roentgenology*]
PTW .... Pilot Training Wing [*Air Force*]
PTW .... Playing to Win (EA)
PTW .... Point Target Weapon
PTW .... Pork Tapeworm [*Medicine*] (MELL)
PTW .... Pottstown, PA [*Location identifier*] [*FAA*] (FAAL)
PTW .... Pressure-Treated Wood
PTW .... Pressure-Type Window
PTW .... Primary Translation Word (VLIE)
PTW .... Programmable Typewriter (SAUS)
PTWAM ..... Page Table Word Associative Memory [*Computer science*] (IAA)
PTWC .... Pacific Tsunami Warning Center [*National Weather Service*] (MSC)
PTWC .... Project on Technology, Work, and Character (EA)
PTWEN ...... Port Wentworth, GA [*American Association of Railroads railroad junction routing code*]
PT-WEX ..... Part-Time Work Experience Program [*Texas*] (EDAC)
PTWF .... Pakistan Transport Workers' Federation
PTWG .... Planning Tracking Working Group
PTWG .... Provisioning Technical Working Group
PTWH .... Pin-Tailed Whydah [*North American bird banding code*] (BIBA)
PTWI .... Provisional Tolerable Weekly Intake [*Toxicology*]
PTWM .... Power Transformation Weighting Method [*Mathematics*]
PTWMASA ... Private Treaty Wool Merchants' Association of South Australia
PTWMAV .... Private Treaty Wool Merchants' Association of Victoria [*Australia*]
PTWMAWA .. Private Treaty Wool Merchants' Association of Western Australia
P-TWP .... Post-Township
PTWT .... Photo-Type Traveling Wave Tube (NG)
PTWT .... Photo-type Travelling Wave Tube (SAUS)
PTWTKG .... Patient's Weight in Kilograms [*Medicine*] (EDAA)
PTWU .... Postal and Telecommunications Workers Union (SAUS)
PTWX .... Premier Industries [*Private rail car owner code*]
PTX .... Aereo Postal de Mexico SA de CV [*ICAO designator*] (FAAC)
PTX .... Pacific Trans-Ocean Resources Ltd. [*Toronto Stock Exchange symbol*]
PTX .... Packet transmitted bit in TCR (SAUS)
PTX .... Palytoxin [*Organic chemistry*]
PTx .... Parathyroidectomy [*Medicine*]
ptx .... Pelvic Traction [*Medicine*] (BCRP)
PTX .... Pertussis Toxin [*Pharmacology*]
PTX .... Picrotoxin [*Biochemistry*]
PTX .... Pillowtex Corp. [*NYSE symbol*] (SPSG)
PTX .... Plus Teletypewriter Exchange (VLIE)
PTX .... Pneumothorax [*Medicine*] (AAMN)
PTX .... Polythermalex (IAA)
PTX .... Polythiazide [*Organic chemistry*]
PTX .... Pressure Temperature Composition (SAUS)
PTX .... Pressure-Temperature Composition
PTX .... Proprietary Format [*Computer science*]
PTX .... Pullman Taconite Express (SAUS)
PTXA .... Parathyroidectomy and Autotransplantation [*Endocrinology*] (DAVI)
PTXAU .... Public Telex Access Unit (VLIE)
PTXB .... Pumiliotoxin B [*Organic chemistry*]
PTXes .... Pneumothoraces (SAUS)
PTXT .... Pressure Temperature Composition Time (SAUS)
PTY .... Panama City [*Panama*] [*Airport symbol*] (OAG)
PTY .... Parity (IAA)
PTY .... Party (AAG)
PTY .... Presently [*Telegraphy*] (PCTE)
PTY .... Program Type (SAUS)
PTY .... Proplythiouracil (SAUS)
Pty .... Proprietary (DD)
pty .... Proprietary (NTIO)
PTY .... Proprietary
PTY .... Pseudo-Terminal driver (SAUS)
PTYA .... Yap [*Caroline Islands*] [*ICAO location identifier*] (ICLI)
PTY LTD ..... Proprietary Limited
P-type .... Jungian perceptive type (SAUS)
PTYPE .... Person Type [*National Highway Traffic Safety Administration Fatal Accident Recording System code*]
P-Type SC ... P-Type Semicondctor (SAUS)
PTZ .... Pan Tilt Zoom (SAUS)
PTZ .... Pentylenetetrazol (SAUS)
PTZ .... Pentylenetetrazole [*CNS stimulant*]
PTZ .... Phenothiazine (EDCT)
PTZ .... Pulitzer [*NYSE symbol*]
PTZ .... Pulitzer Publishing [*NYSE symbol*] (TTSB)
PTZ .... Pulitzer Publishing Co. [*NYSE symbol*] (SPSG)
PU .... Pacifc University (SAUS)
PU .... Pack Unit [*Single title, multiple orders*] [*Publishing*] [*British*]
PU .... Paid Up [*Insurance*] (EY)
pu .... Paid Up [*Insurance*] (ODBW)
PU .... Palindromic Unit [*Molecular biology*] (QSUL)
PU .... Parents United (EA)
PU .... Participating Unit (NVT)
PU .... Parts Used [*Medicine*]
PU .... Passed Urine [*Medicine*]
PU .... Pass Urine (SAUS)
PU .... Paste Up (ADA)
PU .... Peptic Ulcer [*Medicine*]
PU .... Perbonate Unit [*Analytical biochemistry*]
PU .... Percent Utilization [*Anesthesiology*]
PU .... Peripheral Unit [*Computers*] (MSA)
PU .... Personal Use (FOTI)
PU .... Personnel, Utility [*British military*] (DMA)
PU .... Persons Using [*Television*] (WDMC)
PU .... Peru [*IYRU nationality code*] (IYR)
PU .... Perudic [*Soil biology*] [*Soil moisture regime*] (QSUL)
PU .... Per Unit (EECA)
PU .... Per-Unit (SAUS)
PU .... Per Urethra [*Medicine*]
PU .... Philips University (SAUS)
PU .... Physical Unit [*Computer science*] (IBMDP)
PU .... Pickup (MIST)
PU .... Planning Unit (HEAS)
PU .... Plant Unit
PU .... Players' Union [*Football*] [*British*]
PU .... Pluggable Unit (SAA)
PU .... Pluna [*Airline flight code*] (ODBW)
PU .... Plutonium
Pu .... Plutonium [*Chemical element*]
PU .... Polysulfide Urethane (SAUS)
PU .... Polyurethane [*Also, PUR*] [*Organic chemistry*]
PU .... Port-Unit (SAUS)
PU .... Power Equipment [*JETDS nomenclature*] [*Military*] (CET)
PU .... Power Unit
PU .... Prefix Update (SAUS)
PU .... Pregnancy Urine [*Medicine*]
PU .... Prilled Urea [*A fertilizer*]
PU .... Primary User (SAUS)
PU .... Princeton University
PU .... Printing Unit (SAUS)
PU .... Print Unit (SAUS)
PU .... Prisoner's Union [*Later, PRU*] (EA)
PU .... Processing Unit [*Computer science*]
PU .... Processor Unit (SAUS)
PU .... Processor Utility [*Telecommunications*] (TEL)
PU .... Production Unit (CAAL)
PU .... Program Unit (SAUS)
PU .... Propellant Unit (NASA)
PU .... Propellant Utilization [*Aerospace*]
PU .... Propulsion Unit (KSC)
PU .... Propyleneurea [*Organic chemistry*]
PU .... Prostatic Urethra [*Anatomy*] [*Urology*] (DAVI)
PU .... Protection Unearthed (SAUS)
PU .... Proteolytic Unit (SAUS)
PU .... Proutist Universal (EA)
PU .... Public [*Telegraphy*] (PCTE)
PU .... Publications (MCD)
PU .... Publisher [*Online database field identifier*]
PU .... Puetzer [*Germany*] [*ICAO aircraft manufacturer identifier*] (ICAO)
PU .... Pumps (RIMS)
PU .... Pump Unit (AAG)
Pu .... Punic (BJA)
Pu .... Punjab Regiment [*India*] [*Army*]
PU .... Purdue University
Pu .... Purine [*Biochemistry*]
PU .... Purple (ROG)
PU .... University of Pennsylvania, Philadelphia, PA [*Library symbol*] [*Library of Congress*] (LCLS)
PU3S .... Power-Up 3-State (SAUS)
PUA .... Pacific Union Association (SAUS)
PUA .... Partido de Unificacion Anticomunista [*Anti-Communist Unification Party*] [*Guatemala*] [*Political party*] (PPW)

PUA.......... Patient Unit Assistant [*Medicine*] (DMAA)
PUA.......... Physical Unit Address (SAUS)
PUA.......... Plant-Unique Analysis [*Nuclear energy*] (NRCH)
PUA.......... Polish Union of America (EA)
PUA.......... Pride Users' Association [*Defunct*] (EA)
PUA.......... Primeras Lineas Uruguayas de Navegacion Aerea [*Uruguay*] [*ICAO designator*] (FAAC)
PUA.......... Profiling User Agent (SAUS)
PU-A......... University of Pennsylvania, Morris Arboretum, Philadelphia, PA [*Library symbol*] [*Library of Congress*] (LCLS)
PUAA........ Public Utilities Advertising Association [*Later, PUCA*] (EA)
PUAC........ Propellant Utilization Acoustical (or Acoustics) Checkout (SAUS)
PUAC........ Public Athletic Conference (PSS)
PU-AC....... University of Pennsylvania, Annenberg School of Communications, Philadelphia, PA [*Library symbol*] [*Library of Congress*] (LCLS)
PUAD........ Pueblo Army Depot [*Colorado*] (AABC)
PUADA...... Pueblo Army Depot Activity (AABC)
PUAE........ Agreement on Peaceful Uses of Atomic Energy (SAUS)
PUAG........ Purpose Use Arrestor Gear (SAUS)
PUAID....... Parti d'Unite Arabe Islamique-Democratique [*Algeria*] [*Political party*] (EY)
PU & D...... Pick Up and Delivery [*Business term*]
PUAR........ Pulse Acquisition RADAR [*Military*] (MSA)
PU-Ar........ University of Pennsylvania Archives, Philadelphia, PA [*Library symbol*] [*Library of Congress*] (LCLS)
PUAS........ Postal Union for America and Spain (SAUS)
PUAS........ Postal Union of the Americas and Spain [*See also UPAE*] [*Montevideo, Uruguay*] (EAIO)
PUASP...... Postal Union of the Americas, Spain, and Portugal [*Uruguay*] (EAIO)
PUB.......... Partido Union Boliviana [*Bolivian Unity Party*] [*Political party*] (PPW)
PUB.......... Percutaneous Umbilical Blood [*Pediatrics*] (CPH)
PUB.......... Phycourobilin [*Biochemistry*]
PUB.......... Physical Unit Block [*Computer science*]
PUB.......... Puale Bay [*Alaska*] [*Seismograph station code, US Geological Survey*] (SEIS)
Pub.......... Public (TBD)
pub.......... Public (WDMC)
PUB.......... Public
pub.......... publican (SAUS)
PUB.......... Publication (AFM)
pub.......... Publication (WDMC)
pub.......... Public House (ODBW)
PUB.......... Public House [*A drinking establishment*] [*British*]
PUB.......... Publicis Groupe S.A. ADS [*NYSE symbol*]
PUB.......... Publicity
PUB.......... Public Utilities Board (NADA)
pub.......... publish (SAUS)
PUB.......... Published (AABC)
pub.......... Published (WDMC)
PUB.......... Publisher
Pub.......... Publishers Announcement (SAUS)
PUB.......... Pueblo [*Colorado*] [*Airport symbol*] (OAG)
PUB.......... Pueblo, CO [*Location identifier*] [*FAA*] (FAAL)
PUBAFF..... Public Affairs (DNAB)
PUBAFFRRU... Public Affairs Ready Reserve Unit (DNAB)
Pub Aide.... Publication Aide (SAUS)
Pub&Loc Laws... Public and Local Laws (SAUS)
Pub Auth.... Public Authorities (SAUS)
Pub Bargaining Cas... Public Bargaining Cases (SAUS)
Pub Bargaining Cas (CCH)... Public Bargaining Cases (Commerce Clearing House) [*A publication*] (DLA)
PUB BDG... Publisher's Binding (DGA)
Pub Bldgs... Public Buildings (SAUS)
PUBC........ Presbyterians United for Biblical Concerns [*Later, PBC*] (EA)
Pubcaster... Public Broadcaster [*Radio or TV station affiliated with NPR or PBS*]
Pub Cit...... Public Citizen (SAUS)
PubcoC...... Pubco Corp [*Associated Press*] (SAG)
PUBD........ Published (ROG)
pubd......... Published (WDAA)
PUBDIS..... Publishing Distribution System (SAUS)
Pub Doc..... Public Document (SAUS)
PUB DOC... Public Documents (ROG)
PUB ED..... Publication Editor (SAUS)
Pub Employee Bargaining Rep (CCH)... Public Employee Bargaining Reports (Commerce Clearing House) [*A publication*] (DLA)
Pub Employee Rel Rep... Public Employee Relations Reports [*A publication*] (DLA)
Pub Ent Advert & Allied Fields LQ... Publishing, Entertainment, Advertising, and Allied Fields Law Quarterly [*A publication*] (DLA)
PUBF........ Public Freight Service [*Common carrier symbol*]
Pub Gen Laws... Public General Laws [*A publication*] (DLA)
PUB HA..... Public Hall [*Freemasonry*] (ROG)
Pub Health... United States Public Health Service, Court Decisions [*A publication*] (DLA)
Pub Hist.... [*The*] Public Historian [*A publication*]
Pub Hous.... Public Housing (SAUS)
PUBINFO... Office of Public Information [*Formerly, OPR*] [*Navy*]
PUBINFO... Public Information (SAUS)
Pub Int...... Public Interest [*A publication*]
Pub Intl L... Public International Law (SAUS)
publ.......... Public (MILB)
PUBL........ Public (WGA)
PUBL........ Publication [*or Published or Publisher*] (EY)
PUBL........ Public Health Library (SAUS)
Publ......... Publicity (DIAR)
PUBL........ Publish (FAAC)
publ.......... Published (PROS)
Publ......... Publisher (AL)
Publ......... Publishing (AL)
Publ Admin... Public Administration [*A publication*]
Publ Amer Assoc Adv Sci... Publication of the American Association for the Advancement of Science (SAUS)
Pub Land L Rev... Public Land Law Review [*A publication*] (DLA)
Pub Lands... Public Lands (SAUS)
Pub Lands Dec... Department of the Interior, Decisions Relating to Public Lands [*A publication*] (DLA)
Pub Lands Dec... Department of the Interior,Decisions Relating to Public Lands (SAUS)
Publ Ashon Soc Pac... Publications of the Astronomical Society of the Pacific (SAUS)
Pub Law.... Public Law (AAGC)
Pub Laws... Public Laws (SAUS)
PUBLCTN... Publication
PUBLD...... Published (ROG)
Pub LF...... Public Law Forum [*A publication*] (DLA)
Publ Finance Q... Public Finance Quarterly (SAUS)
public....... Publicist
PUBLICA... Public Libraries Concerted Action (TELE)
Public Adm... Public Administration (SAUS)
Public Finance Quart... Public Finance Quarterly [*A publication*] (JLIT)
Public Finance Rev... Public Finance Review [*A publication*] (JLIT)
Publick...... Publicker Industries, Inc. [*Associated Press*] (SAG)
Public Pol... Public Policy [*A publication*] (JLIT)
Public Works Local Gov Eng... Public Works and Local Government Engineering (SAUS)
Publ Interest... Public Interest (SAUS)
PUBLINX... Public Links [*Amateur golf*]
PUBLO...... Pueblo, CO [*American Association of Railroads railroad junction routing code*]
Pub Loc Laws... Public Local Laws (SAUS)
Publ Pers Rev... Public Personnel Review (SAUS)
PUBLR...... Publisher
Publ Serv Rev... Public Service Review [*A publication*]
PUBLSHG... Publishing (DCTA)
Publ Stud... Public Studies (SAUS)
Pub Manag... Public Management (SAUS)
Pubn......... Publication (AL)
PUBN........ Publication (MSA)
pubn......... Publication (WDAA)
PUBNET..... American Association of Publishers' electronic ordering system
PUBO........ Pubco Corp. [*NASDAQ symbol*] (NQ)
Pub Op Q... Public Opinion Quarterly [*A publication*] (BRI)
Pub Papers... Public Papers of the President [*A publication*] (DLA)
Pub Rel..... Public Relations
Pub Rel Bull... Public Relations Bulletin [*American Bar Association*] [*A publication*] (DLA)
Pub Rel J... Public Relations Journal [*A publication*] (BRI)
Pub Res..... Public Resolution (AAGC)
Pub Res..... Public Resources (SAUS)
Pub Res C... Public Resources Code [*California*] [*A publication*] (ILCA)
Pub Res No... Public Resolution Number [*Congress*] (ILCA)
PUB RM..... Publisher's Ream (DGA)
PUBS........ Elephant & Castle Group, Inc. [*NASDAQ symbol*] (SAG)
PUBS........ Percutaneous Umbilical Blood Sampling [*Medicine*]
PUBS........ Percutaneous Umbilical Cord Sampling [*Also, Cordocentesus*] [*Medical test*] (PAZ)
PUBS........ Pop-Up Bottom Seismograph [*Marine science*] (MSC)
PUBS........ Prairie University Biological Seminars (SAUS)
PUBS........ Publications (CDAI)
PUBS........ Publication Series
PUBS........ Purple Urine Bag Syndrome [*Medicine*] (DMAA)
Pub Safety... Public Safety (SAUS)
PUBSAT..... Publications Ships Assistance Team [*Navy*]
PUBSAT..... Publications Special Assistance Team [*Military*]
Pub Sec..... Public Securities and Obligations (SAUS)
Pub Sect Lab Rel... Public Sector Labor Relations Conference Board (SAUS)
Pub Ser Comm... Public Service Commission [*Usually, of a specific state*] (DLA)
Pub Serv.... Public Service (SAUS)
PUBSF...... Elephant & Castle Group [*NASDAQ symbol*] (TTSB)
PubSNC..... Public Service Co. North Carolina [*Associated Press*] (SAG)
PUBS Recorder... Pop-Up Bottom Seismic Recorder (SAUS)
Pub St....... Public Statutes [*A publication*] (DLA)
PubSt........ Public Storage, Inc. [*Associated Press*] (SAG)
PubStrg..... Public Storage, Inc. [*Associated Press*] (SAG)
Pub U Rep... Public Utilities Reports [*A publication*] (DLA)
Pub Util..... Public Utilities (SAUS)
Pub Util C... Public Utilities Code [*A publication*] (DLA)
Pub Util Comm... Public Utilities Commission (SAUS)
Pub Util L Anthol... Public Utilities Law Anthology [*A publication*] (DLA)
Pub Util Rep... Public Utilities Reports [*A publication*] (DLA)
Pub Wks.... Public Works (SAUS)
PubWorkCen... Public Works Center (SAUS)
PUBX........ Commercial Credit [*Private rail car owner code*]
PU-BZ....... University of Pennsylvania, Biology Library, Philadelphia, PA [*Library symbol*] [*Library of Congress*] (LCLS)
PUC.......... Pacific Unicorn [*Vancouver Stock Exchange symbol*]
PUC.......... Pacific Union College [*Angwin, CA*]
PUC.......... Papers under Consideration

PUC.......... Parti de l'Unite Congolaise [*Congolese Unity Party*] [*Political party*]
PUC.......... Pediatric Urine Collector [*Medicine*]
PUC.......... Peoples University of China (SAUS)
PUC.......... Peripheral Unit Controller [*Computer science*] (CIST)
PUC.......... Permanent Unit Code (NG)
PUC.......... Personal Use Computer (VLIE)
PUC.......... Pick-Up Car
PUC.......... Planification d'Urgence Canada [*Emergency Planning Canada - EPC*]
PUC.......... Plant of Unit Control (SAUS)
PUC.......... Player Unit Component (MCD)
PUC.......... Playwrights Union of Canada (FOTI)
PUC.......... Pontificia Universidade Catolica [*Rio de Janeiro*]
PUC.......... Popular Unity of Chile [*Political party*]
PUC.......... Portee Utile de Combat (SAUS)
PUC.......... Port Utilization Committee
PUC.......... Post Urbem Conditam [*After the Building of the City of Rome*] [*Latin*]
PUC.......... Premature Uterine Contractions (SAUS)
PUC.......... Presidential Unit Citation [*Military decoration*]
PUC.......... Price [*Utah*] [*Airport symbol*] (OAG)
PUC.......... Price, UT [*Location identifier*] [*FAA*] (FAAL)
PUC.......... Processing Unit Cabinet [*Computer science*]
PUC.......... Production Urgency Committee [*WPB*]
PUC.......... Program Under Control (NITA)
PUC.......... Program Unit Code [*Military*] (AFIT)
PUC.......... Provided You Concur [*Army*]
PUC.......... Public Utilities and Corporations (SAUS)
PUC.......... Public Utilities Code (SAUS)
PUC.......... Public Utilities Commission
PUC.......... Public Utility Co.
PUC.......... Public Utility Commission (EAGT)
PUC.......... Public Utility Commissioner (SAUS)
PUC.......... Punctured Uniform Code [*Computer science*] (IAA)
PU-C.......... University of Pennsylvania, Chemistry Library, Philadelphia, PA [*Library symbol*] [*Library of Congress*] (LCLS)
PUCA.......... Partido Unionista Centro Americana [*Nicaragua*] [*Political party*] (EY)
PUCA.......... Pennsylvania Utility Contractors Association (EARSL)
PUCA.......... Public Utilities Communicators Association [*Later, UCI*] [*New Castle, PA*] (EA)
PUCalLL .... Publications of the University of California in Languages and Literature (SAUS)
PUCC.......... Port Users Consultative Committee (SAUS)
PUCC.......... Port Utilities [*AAR code*]
PUCC.......... Port Utilities Commission of Charleston [*Federal Railroad Administration identification code*]
PUCC.......... Purdue University Computing Center (SAUS)
PUCF.......... Polyurethane Coated Fabrics (SAUS)
PUCF.......... Polyurethane-Coated Fibers (SAUS)
PUCH.......... Puch [*NCIC car make code*]
PUCK.......... Florida Panthers Holdings, Inc. [*NASDAQ symbol*] (SAG)
PUCK.......... Propellant Utilization Checkout Kit (KSC)
PUCK.......... Puckett Brothers [*NCIC trailer make code*]
PUCK.......... Pucklechurch [*England*]
PuCl.......... Plutonium Chloride
PUCM.......... Progressive Union of Cabinet Makers [*British*]
PUCP.......... Physical Unit Control Point (VLIE)
PUCP.......... Process Unit Control Panel [*Computer science*] (IAA)
PU:CPI.......... Processing Unit for Coordination Processor Interface (SAUS)
PUCR.......... Plant Unit Cost Report (SAUS)
PUCS.......... Propellant Utilization Control System (KSC)
PUCU.......... Propellant Utilization Control Unit
PUCY.......... Publicity [*Telegraphy*] (PCTE)
PUCZ.......... Pure Culture Products [*Federal Railroad Administration identification code*]
PUD.......... Democratic Unification Party (Honduras) [*Political party*] (PSAP)
PUD.......... Parallel Undocumented Development (PDAA)
PUD.......... Partido Union Democratica [*Guatemala*] [*Political party*]
PUD.......... Party of Union and Development (SAUS)
PUD.......... Peptic Ulcer Disease
PUD.......... Peri-Urethral Diathermy [*Medicine*]
PUD.......... Physical Unit Directory [*Computer science*] (MHDI)
PUD.......... Pick Up and Delivery [*Business term*]
PUD.......... Pick-up and Delivery (SAUS)
PUD.......... Planned Unit Development [*Housing*]
PUD.......... Planned Urban Development
PUD.......... Preretro Update Display
PUD.......... Prisoner under Detention (ADA)
PUD.......... Public Utility District [*Bonds*]
PUD.......... Published [*Telegraphy*] (PCTE)
pud.......... Pudding (BARN)
pud.......... puddle (SAUS)
pud.......... Pudendal [*Medicine*] (BCRP)
PUD.......... Pudendal (DMAA)
PUD.......... Pueblo Union Depot & Railroad [*Federal Railroad Administration identification code*]
PUD.......... Puerto Deseado [*Argentina*] [*Airport symbol*] (OAG)
PuD.......... Pulmonary Disease [*Medicine*] (STED)
PUD.......... Pulmonary Disease [*Medicine*]
PuD.......... Pulmonary Disorder [*Medicine*] (MELL)
PU-D.......... University of Pennsylvania, Evans Dental Library, Philadelphia, PA [*Library symbol*] [*Library of Congress*] (LCLS)
PUDA.......... Pueblo Depot Activity [*Colorado*] [*Army*]
PUDD.......... Programmable Universal Direct Drive
PUDEMO.... Peoples United Democratic Movement (SAUS)
PUDG.......... Pudgie's Chicken [*NASDAQ symbol*] (TTSB)
PUDG.......... Pudgies Chicken, Inc. [*NASDAQ symbol*] (SAG)
Pudgie...... Pudgies Chicken, Inc. [*Associated Press*] (SAG)
Pudgies...... Pudgies Chicken, Inc. [*Associated Press*] (SAG)
PUDGW..... Pudgies Chicken Wrrt [*NASDAQ symbol*] (TTSB)
PUDL.......... Push Down List [*Computer science*] (IAA)
PUDL Memory... Push Down List Memory (SAUS)
PUDN.......... Perpetuation of Unit Documentation Number (MCD)
PUDN.......... Perpetuation of Unit Document Number (SAUS)
PUDOC...... Centrum voor Landbouwpublikaties en Landbouwdocumentatie [*Center for Agricultural Publishing and Documentation*] [*Ministry of Agriculture and Fisheries*] [*Information service or system*] (IID)
PU-DPL..... Princeton University Device Physics Laboratory [*New Jersey*]
PUDS.......... Propulsion Unit Data Sheet (SAUS)
PUDT.......... Personal User Data Terminal (SAUS)
PUDT.......... Propellant Utilization Data Translator (AAG)
PUDVM...... Pulsed Ultrasound Doppler Velocity Meter
PUE.......... Phosphorus Utilization Efficiency [*Ecology*]
PUE.......... Physiotherapists' Union of Employees [*Australia*]
PUE.......... Pick-up Electrode (SAUS)
PUE.......... Polyurethanen (SAUS)
PUE.......... Presidential Unit Emblem [*Military decoration*] (AABC)
PUE.......... Prestocked Unit Equipment (SAUS)
PUE.......... Pre-Stock Unit Equipment [*Military*] [*British*]
PUE.......... Processing Unit, Extension (SAUS)
PUE.......... Propellant Utilization Exerciser
PUE.......... Puebla [*Mexico*] [*Seismograph station code, US Geological Survey*] [*Closed*] (SEIS)
PUE.......... Puerto Obaldia [*Panama*] [*Airport symbol*] (OAG)
PUE.......... Pyrexia of Unknown Etiology [*Medicine*]
PUEC.......... Portsmouth Uranium Enrichment Complex (COE)
PUE:CPI..... Processing Unit, Extension for Coordination Processor Interface (SAUS)
PU-EI.......... University of Pennsylvania, Moore School of Electrical Engineering, Philadelphia, PA [*Library symbol*] [*Library of Congress*] (LCLS)
Puerto Rico... Puerto Rico Reports [*A publication*] (DLA)
Puerto Rico F... Puerto Rico Federal Reports [*A publication*] (DLA)
Puerto Rico Fed... Puerto Rico Federal Reports [*A publication*] (DLA)
Puerto Rico Rep... Puerto Rico Supreme Court Reports [*A publication*] (DLA)
PUETO....... Panhellenic Union of Exporters of Table Olives (SAUS)
PUF.......... Partially Unfolded Form [*Biochemistry*]
PUF.......... Partido Union Federal [*Federal Union Party*] [*Argentina*] [*Political party*]
PUF.......... Pau [*France*] [*Airport symbol*] (OAG)
PUF.......... People's United Front [*Papua New Guinea*] [*Political party*] (PPW)
PUF.......... People's United Front [*Bangladesh*] [*Political party*]
PUF.......... Percent Unaccounted For
PUF.......... Physical Update File [*Computer science*] (VLIE)
PUF.......... Planning Units File (SAUS)
PUF.......... Polyurethane Film [*Plastics technology*]
PUF.......... Polyurethane Foam
PUF.......... Polyurethanfaser (SAUS)
PUF.......... Porous Polyurethane Foam [*Also, PPF*] [*Plastics technology*]
PUF.......... Prime Underwriting Facility [*Banking*]
PUF.......... Proper Use Factor (SAUS)
PUF.......... Public Use Form (SAUS)
Puf.......... Puffendorf's Law of Nature and Nations [*A publication*] (DLA)
PUF.......... Pure Ultrafiltration (DMAA)
PU-F.......... University of Pennsylvania, H. H. Furness Memorial Library, Philadelphia, PA [*Library symbol*] [*Library of Congress*] (LCLS)
PUFA.......... Polyunsaturated Fatty Acid [*Nutrition*]
PU-FA.......... University of Pennsylvania, School of Fine Arts, Philadelphia, PA [*Library symbol*] [*Library of Congress*] (LCLS)
PUFF.......... People United to Fight Frustrations (EA)
PUFF.......... Picofarad (MDG)
PUFF.......... Proposed Uses of Federal Funds [*Health Planning and Resource Development Act of 1974*]
PUFFIN...... Pedestrian User-Friendly Intelligent Crossing (WDAA)
PUFFS....... Passive Underwater Fire Control Feasibility Study
PUFFS....... Passive Underwater Fire-control Feasibility Study (SAUS)
PUFFS....... Passive Underwater Fire Control Feasibility System
PUFFS....... Passive Underwater Fire-control Feasibility System (SAUS)
PUFFT....... Purdue University Fast FORTRAN [*Formula Translation*] Translator [*Computer science*]
PUFI.......... Packed under Federal Inspection
PUFI.......... Pair-Usage-Frequency Indicator (VLIE)
PUFL.......... Pump Fed Liquid (KSC)
PUFM.......... Pull Up Field Mast (SAUS)
PUFO.......... Pack Up and Fade Out [*End of military exercise*] [*British*] (DSUE)
PUFS.......... Programmer's Utility Filing System (DIT)
PUFS.......... Proposed Underwater Fire Control Feasibility Study (SAA)
PUG.......... Partially Underground [*Military*]
PUG.......... PASCAL Users Glroup (SAUS)
PUG.......... PASCAL Users' Group [*Defunct*] (EA)
PUG.......... Penta Users Group (EA)
PUG.......... Port Augusta [*Australia*] [*Airport symbol*] (OAG)
PUG.......... Prestel Users Group (NITA)
PUG.......... PRIME Users Group (EA)
PUG.......... Print under Glaze [*Ceramics*]
PUG.......... Propellant Utilization and Gauging [*Apollo*] [*NASA*]
PUG.......... Publishing [*Telegraphy*] (PCTE)
pug.......... pugilism (SAUS)
PUG.......... Pugilist
PUG.......... Pugillus [*A Handful*] [*Pharmacy*] (ROG)
Pug.......... Pugsley's New Brunswick Reports [*14-16 New Brunswick*] [*A publication*] (DLA)

PUG.......... Pulsed Universal Grid
PUG.......... Pure Gold Minerals [*Toronto Stock Exchange symbol*] [*Canada*]
PUG.......... Pure Gold Resources, Inc. [*Toronto Stock Exchange symbol*]
PugetP........ Puget Sound Power & Light Co. [*Associated Press*] (SAG)
PUGLIG...... PUG Library Information Group (NITA)
PUGS........ Propellant Utilization and Gaging System (NAKS)
PUGS........ Propellant Utilization and Gauging System [*Apollo*] [*NASA*] (KSC)
Pugs......... Pugsley's New Brunswick Reports [*14-16 New Brunswick*] [*A publication*] (DLA)
Pugs & Bur... Pugsley and Burbridge's New Brunswick Reports [*17-20 New Brunswick*] [*A publication*] (DLA)
Pugs & Burg... Pugsley and Burbridge's New Brunswick Reports [*17-20 New Brunswick*] [*A publication*] (DLA)
Pugs & T... Pugsley and Trueman's New Brunswick Reports [*A publication*] (DLA)
Pugs & Tru... Pugsley and Trueman's New Brunswick Reports [*1882-83*] [*A publication*] (DLA)
PUGT........ Puget Sound Basin (SAUS)
PugtP........ Puget Sound Power & Light Co. [*Associated Press*] (SAG)
PUH.......... Pauahi [*Hawaii*] [*Seismograph station code, US Geological Survey*] (SEIS)
PUH.......... Pregnancy Urine Hormone [*Endocrinology*]
PUH.......... Publish [*Telegraphy*] (PCTE)
PUHCA...... Public Utility Holding Co. Act of 1935
PUHCA...... Public Utility Holding Company Act (SAUS)
PUHR........ Publisher [*Telegraphy*] (PCTE)
PUHS........ Phoenix Union High School (SAUS)
PUHS........ Propulsion Unit History Sheet (SAUS)
PUI........... Pen User Interface [*Computer science*]
PUI........... Physical Unit of Information [*Computer science*] (IAA)
PUI........... Picoscopic User Interface (SAUS)
PUI........... Pilot-under-Instruction [*Navy*]
PUI........... Platelet Uptake Index [*Clinical chemistry*]
PUI........... Posterior Urethral Injury [*Medicine*] (RAWO)
PUIC......... Project Unique Identification Code (AAGC)
PUID......... Physical Unit Identifier (SAUS)
PU Imp...... Pickup Impulse (SAUS)
PU-Ind....... University of Pennsylvania, Industrial Research Department, Philadelphia, PA [*Library symbol*] [*Library of Congress*] [*Obsolete*] (LCLS)
PUIWP...... People for a United India and World Peace (EA)
PUJ.......... Punan Tubu [*Language symbol*] (ETLW)
PUJ.......... Punta Cana [*Dominican Republic*] [*Airport symbol*] (OAG)
PUJC........ Priority, Urgency, Justification and Category (SAUS)
PUJO........ Peoples Union of Justice and New Order (SAUS)
PUJT......... Programmable Unijunction Transistor (IAA)
PUK.......... Pack-Up Kit (MCD)
PUK.......... Paducah [*Kentucky*] [*Airport symbol*] (AD)
PUK.......... Parti d'Unite Katangaise [*Katanga Unity Party*] [*Political party*]
PUK.......... Patriotic Union of Kurdistan [*Iraq*] [*Political party*] (PD)
PUK.......... Pechiney-Ugine-Kuhlmann [*France*] [*Commercial firm*]
PUK.......... Prourokinase [*Thrombolytic*] [*An enzyme*]
PUK.......... Prudential plc ADS [*NYSE symbol*]
PUK.......... Pukarua [*French Polynesia*] [*Airport symbol*] (OAG)
PUKO........ Pan American Union of Karatedo Organisations (SAUS)
PUKO........ Pan-American Union of Karatedo Organizations (EA)
PUKS........ Pivotal Unknowables
PUL.......... Packet Underway Limit (SAUS)
PUL.......... Percutaneous Ultrasonic Lithotripsy [*Medicine*]
PUL.......... Per-Unit-Length (SAUS)
PUL.......... Preconfiguration Unit Load
PUL.......... Press Union of Liberia
PUL.......... Princeton University Library (SAUS)
PUL.......... Princeton University, Princeton, NJ [*Inactive*] [*OCLC symbol*] (OCLC)
PUL.......... Program Update Library
PUL.......... Propellant Utilization and Loading
PUL.......... Publicker Indus [*NYSE symbol*] (TTSB)
PUL.......... Publicker Industries, Inc. [*NYSE symbol*] (SPSG)
PUL.......... Pubourethral Ligament (STED)
PUL.......... Pulkovo [*Former USSR*] [*Seismograph station code, US Geological Survey*] (SEIS)
PUL.......... Pulley (AAG)
PUL.......... Pullman, WA [*Amtrak Busline code*]
pul........... Pulmonary (STED)
PUL.......... Pulmonary
PUL.......... Pul. Przedsiebiorstwo Uslug Lotniczych [*Poland*] [*ICAO designator*] (FAAC)
PUL.......... Pulsar [*NCIC car model code*]
Pul........... Pulse (SAUS)
PUL.......... Pulse Resources [*Vancouver Stock Exchange symbol*]
PUL.......... Punjab University Library (SAUS)
PU-L......... University of Pennsylvania, Biddle Law Library, Philadelphia, PA [*Library symbol*] [*Library of Congress*] (LCLS)
PULA........ Patani United Liberation Organisation (SAUS)
PULA........ Public Laws
PulaskF..... Pulaski Furniture Corp. [*Associated Press*] (SAG)
PulaskiB.... Pulaski Bank, A Savings Bank [*Associated Press*] (SAG)
PULB........ Pulaski Bank, A Savings Bank [*NASDAQ symbol*] (SAG)
PULB........ Pulaski Bank A Svgs Bk MO [*NASDAQ symbol*] (TTSB)
PULHEEMS... Physical Capacity, Upper and Lower Limbs, Hearing, Eyesight, Emotional Capacity, Mental Stability (SAUS)
PULHES..... Physical Capacity, Upper Extremities, Lower Extremities, Hearing, Eyes, and Psychiatric System (DNAB)
PULHHEEMS... Physical Capacity, Upper Limbs, Left Hearing, Right Hearing, Left Eye, Right Eye, Mental Capacity, Stability [*Military medical assessment*] (WDAA)
PUL INS..... Pulmonary Insufficiency (SAUS)
PULJC....... Pullman Junction, IL [*American Association of Railroads railroad junction routing code*]
PULK........ KM Pulley [*Common carrier symbol*]
PULL........ Power for Underwater Logistics and Living
PULL........ Pull A Long [*NCIC trailer make code*]
Pull Acc...... Pulling on Mercantile Accounts [*1846*] [*A publication*] (DLA)
Pull Accts... Pulling's Law of Mercantile Accounts [*A publication*] (DLA)
Pull Att...... Pulling on Attorneys and Solicitors [*3rd ed.*] [*1862*] [*A publication*] (DLA)
Pull Laws & Cust Lond... Pulling's Treatise on the Laws, Customs, and Regulations of the City and Port o f London [*A publication*] (DLA)
Pull Port of London... Pulling's Treatise on the Laws, Customs, and Regulations of the City and Port ofLondon [*A publication*] (DLA)
PULM........ Programmable Universal Logic Module (SAUS)
pulm......... Pulmentum [*Gruel Pulmonary*] [*Latin*] (MAE)
pulm......... Pulmonary (MELL)
PULM........ Pulmonary
pulm edema... Pulmonary Edema [*Medicine*] (BCRP)
PULM EMB... Pulmonary Embolism (SAUS)
PULMO...... Pulmoaortic (SAUS)
PULMO...... Pulmology (SAUS)
PULMO...... Pulmometer (SAUS)
PULMO...... Pulmometric (SAUS)
PULMO...... Pulmometry (SAUS)
PULMO...... Pulmonectomy (SAUS)
PULMO...... Pulmonitis (SAUS)
PULMO...... Pulmonologist (SAUS)
pulmo....... pulmotor (SAUS)
Pulmotor.... Pulmonary Motor (SAUS)
Pulm Rehab... Pulmonary Rehabilitation [*Medicine*] (BCRP)
PULO........ Patani United Liberation Organisation (SAUS)
PULO........ Pattani United Liberation Organization [*Thailand*] [*Political party*] (PD)
PULO........ Pattini United Liberation Organisation (SAUS)
PULP........ Kingston Systems, Inc. [*NASDAQ symbol*] (COMM)
PULP........ Premium Unleaded Petrol
pulpbd....... Pulpboard (VRA)
PULPP....... Peripheral Ultra-Low Power Processor (PDAA)
pulpwd...... Pulpwood (VRA)
PULS........ Performance Utility Luxury Society [*Electric vehicles*]
PULS........ Poseidon Undersea Launching System (NOAA)
PULS........ Propellant Utilization Loading System (AAG)
PULS........ Pullman-Standard [*Federal Railroad Administration identification code*]
PULS........ Pulse Bancorp [*NASDAQ symbol*] (TTSB)
PULS........ Pulse Bancorp, Inc. [*NASDAQ symbol*] (SAG)
PULSAR..... Pulsated Uniform Laser-Stimulated Artificial Radiation (SAUS)
PULSAR..... Pulsating Star
PULSAR..... Pulsed Sequencial Access Relay [*Electronics*] (ECII)
PULSAR..... Pulsed Uniform LASER-Stimulated Artificial Radiation [*Proposed acronymic designation for pulsars, in the event they are found to be artificially caused by intelligent life from outer space*]
PULSAR..... Pulsed Uniform Laser Stimulated Artificial Radiation (SAUS)
PULSAR..... Pulse Star (SAUS)
PULSE....... Patented Uniform Lateral Stability Element
PULSE....... Program of Universal Logic Simulation for Electronics (SAUS)
PULSE....... Public and Local Services Efficiency Campaign (SAUS)
PULSE....... Public Urban Locator Service
pulse AP.... Pulse Apical Pulse [*Medicine*] (BCRP)
PulseBcp.... Pulse Bancorp, Inc. [*Associated Press*] (SAG)
pulse R..... Pulse Radial [*Medicine*] (BCRP)
PULSES..... Physical Condition, Upper Extremity Function, Lower Extremity Function, Sensory and Communication Abilities, Excretory Control, Social Support [*A neurological disability profile*]
Pulsifer (ME)... Pulsifer's Reports [*35-68 Maine*] [*A publication*] (DLA)
PULSTAR... Pulse Training Assembled Reactor [*Nuclear energy*] (NRCH)
Pul Sten.... Pulmonary Stenosis (SAUS)
Pult.......... Pulton. De Pace Regis [*A publication*] (DLA)
Pulte......... Pulte Corp. [*Associated Press*] (SAG)
PultzPb...... Pulitzer Publishing Co. [*Associated Press*] (SAG)
PULU........ Maskapa Pelayaran Pulau Laut [*Intermodal shipping container symbol*] (TVRC)
Pulv.......... Powder [*Medicine*] (BCRP)
PULV......... Pulverization (SAUS)
PULV......... Pulverized
PULV......... Pulvis [*Powder*] [*Pharmacy*]
PULV CONSPER... Pulvis Conspersus [*Dusting Powder*] [*Pharmacy*]
pulv gros... Pulvis Grossus [*Coarse Powder*] [*Pharmacy*] [*Latin*] (MAE)
pulv subtil... Pulvis Subtilis [*Smooth Powder*] [*Pharmacy*] [*Latin*] (MAE)
pulv tenu... Pulvis Tenuis [*Very fine powder*] [*Latin*] (DMAA)
PUM......... Packet User Module (SAUS)
PUM......... Partido Unificado Mariateguista [*Peru*] [*Political party*] (EY)
PUM......... Peanut Urinary Mucins (DB)
PUM......... Pennsylvania University Museum
PUM......... Per Unit Monthly (DNAB)
PUM......... Pomalaa [*Indonesia*] [*Airport symbol*] (OAG)
PUM......... Pop-Up Mechanism (SAUS)
PUM......... Postal Union Mail (SAUS)
PUM......... President of the United Mineworkers
PUM......... Processor Utility Monitor [*Telecommunications*] (TEL)

PUM .... Publication [*Telegraphy*] (PCTE)
PUMA .... Programmable universal manipulator. (SAUS)
PUMA .... Passive Underbody Main Absorber [*Automotive emissions*]
PUMA .... Powered Ultralight Manufacturers Association [*Defunct*] (EA)
PUMA .... Processor-Upgradable Microcomputer Architecture [*DFI, Inc.*] (PCM)
PUMA .... Processor Upgradable Modular Architecture (SAUS)
PUMA .... Programmable Universal Machine for Assembly [*Robot*]
PUMA .... Programmable Universal Manipulator (NITA)
PUMA .... Programmable Universal Manipulator for Assembly [*General Motors Corp. assembly robot*]
PUMA .... Programmable Universal Mechanical Assembly (SAUS)
PUMA .... Programmable Universal Micro Accelerator [*Computer science*] (CDE)
PUMA .... Prostitutes' Union of Massachusetts
PUMA .... Public Use Microdata Area (SAUS)
PUMA .... Puma Camper Sales [*NCIC trailer make code*]
PUMA .... Pumatech [*NASDAQ symbol*]
PUMA .... Puma Technology, Inc. [*NASDAQ symbol*] (SAG)
PumaT .... Puma Technology, Inc. [*Associated Press*] (SAG)
PU-Math .... University of Pennsylvania, Mathematics-Physics Library, Philadelphia, PA [*Library symbol*] [*Library of Congress*] (LCLS)
PUMC .... Public Utilities Management Co. (SAUS)
PUMCODOXPURSACOMLOPAR... Pulse-Modulated Coherent Doppler-Effect X-Band Pulse-Repetition Synthetic-Array Pulse Compression Side Lobe Planar Array
PU-Med ..... University of Pennsylvania, Medical School, Philadelphia, PA [*Library symbol*] [*Library of Congress*] (LCLS)
PU-Med-TS... University of Pennsylvania, Medical School, Hospital Nurses Library, Philadelphia, PA [*Library symbol*] [*Library of Congress*] (LCLS)
PUMF........ Peaceful Uses of Military Forces
PUMGC...... Pious Union of Our Mother of Good Counsel [*See also SMBC*] [*Genazzano, Italy*] (EAIO)
PUMICE ..... Precision Unmanned Integrated Control Equipment (SAUS)
PUMM........ Puma [*NCIC car make code*]
PUMP .... Parts Usage Maintenance Program [*Computer science*] (IAA)
PUMP .... Plant Uncoupling Mitochondrial Protein [*Biochemistry*]
PUMP .... Production Upgrade Management Program (DNAB)
PUMP .... Protesting Unfair Marketing Practices [*Student legal action organization*]
PUMP .... Pumping (SAUS)
PUMPA...... Purine Metabolic Patients' Association (NRGU)
Pump Ct .... Pump Court (SAUS)
PUMS .... Permanently Unfit for Military Service [*British*]
PUMS .... Physical Unit Management Services [*Computer science*] (CIST)
PUMS .... Public Use Microdata Sample [*Bureau of the Census*] (GFGA)
PUMS .... Public Use Microdata Samples
PUMS .... Public Use Micro Sample
PUM:SIMP... Processing Unit Memory for Signaling Management Processor (SAUS)
PUMST...... Polish Underground Movement (1939-1945) Study Trust (EA)
PUMT........ Programmable Universal Module Tester (SAUS)
PU-Mu....... University of Pennsylvania, University Museum, Philadelphia, PA [*Library symbol*] [*Library of Congress*] (LCLS)
PU-Music ... University of Pennsylvania, School of Music, Philadelphia, PA [*Library symbol*] [*Library of Congress*] (LCLS)
Pun .... All India Reporter, Punjab [*A publication*] (DLA)
Pun .... All India Reporter, Punjab (journ.) (SAUS)
Pun .... Indian Law Reports Punjab (journ.) (SAUS)
Pun .... Indian Law Reports, Punjab Series [*A publication*] (DLA)
PUN.......... Parti de l'Unite Nationale [*Party of National Unity*] [*Haiti*] [*Political party*] (PPW)
PUN.......... Partido Union Nacional [*National Union Party*] [*Costa Rica*] [*Political party*]
PUN.......... Physical Unit Number (SAUS)
PUN.......... Plasma Urea Nitrogen (AAMN)
PUN.......... Plutonyl Nitrate [*Inorganic chemistry*]
PUN.......... Precision Underwater Navigation
PUN.......... Prices Unchanged [*Telegraphy*] (PCTE)
PUN.......... Punch
PUN.......... Puncheon [*Unit of measurement*]
PUN.......... Punia [*Zaire*] [*Airport symbol*] (AD)
Pun .... Punica [*of Silius Italicus*] [*Classical studies*] (OCD)
PUN.......... Punishment (DSUE)
PUN.......... Puno [*Peru*] [*Seismograph station code, US Geological Survey*] (SEIS)
PUN.......... Punta [*Flamenco dance term*]
PUN.......... Punto [*NCIC car model code*]
PU-N......... University of Pennsylvania, Center for the Study of the History of Nursing, Philadelphia, PA [*Library symbol*] [*Library of Congress*] (LCLS)
PUNA........ Parti de l'Unite Nationale [*National Unity Party*] [*Congo*]
PUNC........ Partido de Unidad Nacional Conservadora [*Nicaragua*] [*Political party*] (EY)
PUNC........ Possibly Uncommitted (SAUS)
PUNC........ Practical, Unpretentious, Nomographic Computer
PUNC........ Probable Ultimate Net Cost [*Accounting*]
PUNC........ Punctuation
PUNC........ Puncture (DAVI)
punceq ...... Punctuated Equilibrium [*Bacteriology*]
PUNCT ...... Punctuation (ROG)
PUND-Salama... Party for National Unity and Development-Salama (Niger) [*Political party*] (PSAP)
PUNE........ Party-Unity Nash Equilibrium
PUNGA...... Parti de l'Unite Nationale Gabonaise [*Party for Gabonese National Unity*] [*Political party*]
P-UNI........ Private User Network Interface (SAUS)
Punj Rec.... Punjab Record [*India*] [*A publication*] (DLA)
PUNL........ Percutaneous Ultrasonic Nephrolithotripsy [*Nephrology*] [*Radiology*] (DAVI)
PUNM....... Putnam Trucking [*Common carrier symbol*]
PUN Press... Punching Press (SAUS)
PUNR........ Romanian National Unity Party [*Political party*] (PSAP)
PUNS........ Partido de Union Nacional del Sahara [*Western Sahara*] [*Political party*]
PUNS........ Permanently Unfit for Naval Service [*British*]
PUNSW ..... Poets' Union of New South Wales [*Australia*]
PUNT .... National Worker's Party (Eq. Guinea) [*Political party*] (PSAP)
PUO.......... Placed under Observation [*Medicine*]
PUO.......... Pneumonia (SAUS)
PUO.......... Princeton University Observatory [*New Jersey*]
PUO.......... Prudhoe Bay [*Arkansas*] [*Airport symbol*] (OAG)
PUO.......... Prudhoe Bay, AK [*Location identifier*] [*FAA*] (FAAL)
Puo .... [*A*] Purine Nucleoside [*Also, R*]
PUO.......... Put Under Observation (SAUS)
PUO.......... Pyrexia [*fever*] of Unknown Origin [*Commonly called Trench Fever*]
PuO2 .... Plutonium Dioxide
PUOS........ Peaceful Uses of Outer Space (FOTI)
PUOS........ Public Understanding of Science Program (EDAC)
PU-OSC ..... Pulsed Oscillator (SAUS)
PUOW....... Proposed Units of Work
PUP.......... Paid-Up Policy [*Insurance*] (DSUE)
PUP.......... PARC Universal Packet [*Communications term*] (DCT)
PUP.......... PARC Universal Packet protocol (SAUS)
PUP.......... Parti de l'Unite du Peuple Gabonais [*Political party*] (EY)
PUP.......... Parti de l'Unite Populaire [*Tunisia*] [*Political party*] (EY)
PUP.......... Partido Union Patriotica [*Patriotic Union Party*] [*Dominican Republic*] [*Political party*] (PPW)
PUP.......... Party of Unity and Progress (Guinea) [*Political party*] (PSAP)
PUP.......... Patch Utility Program (SAUS)
PUP.......... Peacetime Utilization Program
PUP.......... Peak Underpressure [*Nuclear energy*] (NRCH)
PUP.......... People's United Party [*Belize*] [*Political party*] (PPW)
PUP.......... Peoples Unity Party (SAUS)
PUP.......... Percutaneous Ultrasonic Pyelolithotomy [*Medicine*] (EDAA)
PUP.......... Performance Units Plan (MHDB)
PUP.......... Performance Update Program [*Air Force*] (DOMA)
PUP.......... Performance Upgrade Program (ACAE)
PUP.......... Peripheral Unit Processor [*Computer science*]
PUP.......... Peripheral Universal Processor (NITA)
PUP.......... Personal-Use Property (FOTI)
PUP.......... Pick-Up (TVEL)
PUP.......... Pick-up-Point (SAUS)
PUP.......... Pious Union of Prayer (EA)
PUP.......... Plutonium Utilization Program [*Nuclear Regulatory Commission*] (NRCH)
PUP.......... Po [*Upper Volta*] [*Airport symbol*] (AD)
PUP.......... Polytechnic University of the Philippines (SAUS)
PUP.......... Popular Unity Party [*Bangladesh*] [*Political party*] (PPW)
PUP.......... Pop Up Point (ACAE)
PUP.......... Power Upgrade Program
PUP.......... Power Utility Pak [*Computer software*] [*Jwalk and Associates*] (PCM)
PUP.......... Pregnant Urban Professional (SAUS)
Pup .... Pre-Urban Professional [*Acronym coined by TeenAge magazine to describe it s typical reader*] [*Lifestyle classification*]
PUP.......... Prime Unit Processor (SAUS)
PUP.......... Princeton University Press (DGA)
PUP.......... Principal User Processing (SAUS)
PUP.......... Principal User Processor (SAUS)
PUP.......... Principle User Processor (SAUS)
PUP.......... Principle User Product (SAUS)
PUP.......... Product Update Program (SAUS)
PUP.......... Product Upgrade Program (MUSM)
PUP.......... Progressive Unionist Party [*Northern Ireland*] [*Political party*] (PPW)
PUP.......... Public Utilities Panel [*EECE*]
PUP.......... Pull Up Point
PUP.......... Pupakea [*Hawaii*] [*Seismograph station code, US Geological Survey*] [*Closed*] (SEIS)
PUP.......... Pupil (DSUE)
Pup .... Puppis [*Constellation*]
PUPA .... Polish Union Printers Association [*Chicago*]
PU-PC .... Polyunsaturated Phosphatidylcholine [*Medicine*] (EDAA)
PU/PD .... Polyuria/Polydipsia (SPVS)
PUPE .... Production Unit Price Estimate (SAUS)
PU-Penn .... University of Pennsylvania, Penniman Library of Education, Philadelphia, PA [*Library symbol*] [*Library of Congress*] [*Obsolete*] (LCLS)
PUPG........ Production Unit Price Goals (MCD)
PUPID .... Pulp and Paper Industry Division [*Instrument Society of America*]
PUPM .... Party for Unity and Progress in Mali (SAUS)
PUPO .... Pull-Up, Push-Out
PUPO .... Pull Up Push Over (NASA)
PUPP .... Pruritic Urticarial Papules and Plaques [*Dermatology*] (BARN)
Pupp......... Puppis [*Constellation*]
PUPPI .... Pop-Up Pore Pressure Instrument [*Oceanography*]
Puppie ...... Pregnant Urban Professional [*Terminology used in "The Yuppie Handbook"*] [*Lifestyle classification*]
PUPPP ...... Pruritic Urticarial Papules and Plaques of Pregnancy [*Medicine*]
PUPS........ Portable Universal Programming System (SEWL)

PU-PSW..... University of Pennsylvania, Pennsylvania School of Social Work, Philadelphia, PA [*Library symbol*] [*Library of Congress*] (LCLS)
PUPZ........ Puget Power [*Federal Railroad Administration identification code*]
PUQ........ Punta Arenas [*Chile*] [*Airport symbol*] (OAG)
PUR........ Partido de Unificacion Revolucionaria [*Party of Revolutionary Unification*] [*Guatemala*] [*Political party*]
PUR........ Partido Union Revolucionaria [*Cuba*]
PUR........ Patch Unit Radio [*Bell System*]
PUR........ Persons Using Radio [*Radio ratings*] (WDMC)
PUR........ Polyurethane [*Also, PU*] [*Organic chemistry*]
PUR........ Procurement Request [*Army*] (IAA)
PUR........ Program of University Research
PUR........ Program Utility Routines [*Computer science*]
PUR........ Public Utilities Reports [*A publication*] [*Information service or system*] (IID)
PUR........ Purari [*Papua New Guinea*] [*Seismograph station code, US Geological Survey*] (SEIS)
PUR........ Purcell, OK [*Amtrak rail station code*]
PUR........ Purchase (AFM)
PUR........ Purchasing Receipt [*Business term*]
PUR........ Purdue University Reactor
PUR........ Purdue University Research (MCD)
PUR........ Purgative [*Medicine*] (ROG)
PUR........ Purge (SAUS)
PUR........ Purichlor Technology Ltd. [*Vancouver Stock Exchange symbol*]
pur........ purified (SAUS)
PUR........ Purifier (AAG)
pur........ purify (SAUS)
Pur........ [*A*] Purine [*Biochemistry*]
PUR........ Purity [*of the Drug*] [*Pharmacy*] (ROG)
pur........ Purlins [*Construction term*] (MIST)
PUR........ Puromycin [*Trypanocide*] [*Antineoplastic drug*]
Pur........ Purple [*Medicine*] (EDAA)
pur........ Purple [*Philately*]
pur........ purplish (SAUS)
PUR........ Purpose [*Motor vehicle violation code used in state of Maryland*] (MVRD)
PUR........ Purpose [*Telegraphy*] (PCTE)
PUR........ Purpure [*Purple*] [*Heraldry*]
PUR........ Pursuant (AABC)
PUR........ Pursuit (AABC)
pur........ Purus [*Pure*] [*Latin*]
PUR........ Republican Union (Ecuador) [*Political party*] (PSAP)
PUR........ Spurwing Airlines (Pty) Ltd. [*South Africa*] [*ICAO designator*] (FAAC)
PUR 3d..... Public Utilities Reports, Third Series [*A publication*] (DLA)
PURA........ PACOM [*Pacific Command*] Utilization and Redistribution Agency
PURA........ Public Utilities Review Act [*1934*]
PURAC....... Personal Use Radio Advisory Committee [*FCC*] [*Defunct*] (TSSD)
PURAVAL... Purchase Availability (SAUS)
PURB........ Purbeck [*District in England*]
PURC........ Pacific Utilization Research Center [*Marine science*] (MSC)
PURC........ Princeton University Research Center [*Marine science*] (MSC)
PURC........ Public Utility Research Center [*University of Florida*] [*Research center*] (RCD)
PURC........ Purchasing
Purch........ Purchase (TBD)
PURCH....... Purchase
PURCH....... Purchasing (ALAC)
purch........ Purchasing (DD)
PURCHG.... Purchasing (ROG)
PURDAX.... Public Utility Revenue Data Acquisition (SAUS)
Purd Dig.... Purdon's Digest of Laws [*Pennsylvania*] [*A publication*] (DLA)
Purd Dig Laws... Purdon's Digest of Laws [*Pennsylvania*] [*A publication*] (DLA)
Purdue....... Purdue University Press (SAUS)
PURDUE PAC... Purdue Pharma Inc. PAC [*White Plains, NY*] (PACS)
Purdue U... Purdue University (GAGS)
Purdue U (Calumet)... Purdue University-Calumet (GAGS)
PURE........ Innovative Medical Services [*NASDAQ symbol*] (SAG)
PURE........ People United for Rural Education (EA)
PURE........ POMCUS Unit Residual Equipment (SAUS)
PURE........ Present University Research Efforts [*Database*] [*Harperson Data Services*]
PURE........ Purepac, Inc [*NASDAQ symbol*] (SAG)
Pure Appl Chem... Pure and Applied Chemistry (MEC)
PureAtria... Pure Atria Corp. [*Associated Press*] (SAG)
PURE MAT... Pure Machine-Aided Translation (SAUS)
PURE MT... Pure Machine Translation (SAUS)
Purepac..... Purepac, Inc. [*Associated Press*] (SAG)
PUREQ....... Purchase Requisition (NOAA)
PureSf....... Pure Software, Inc. [*Associated Press*] (SAG)
PureTc....... Pure Tech International, Inc. [*Associated Press*] (SAG)
PureWld.... Pure World, Inc. [*Associated Press*] (SAG)
PUREX....... Plutonium Uranium Extraction [*Nuclear energy*]
PUREX....... Plutonium-Uranium Extraction (SAUS)
PUREX-Verfahren... Plutonium and Uranium Recovery by Extraction (SAUS)
purg........ Purgativus [*Cathartic, purgative*] [*Latin*] (MAE)
PURGE....... Pearson Universal Random Generator
PURIF....... Purification
PURL........ Permanent Uniform Resource Locator (SAUS)
PURL........ Permanent Universal Resource Locator (SAUS)
PURL........ Persistent Uniform Resource Locator [*Computer science*] (IGQR)
PURL........ Persistent Universal Resource Locator [*Computer science*]
PURL........ Persistent URL (SAUS)
PURM....... Project for Utilization and Redistribution of Materiel [*Air Force*]
PUR (NS)... Public Utilities Reports, New Series [*A publication*] (DLA)
PURO........ Puromycin (SAUS)
PURP........ Purple (SAUS)
PURP........ Purpose (AFM)
PURP........ Purpure [*Purple*] [*Heraldry*] (ROG)
PURPA...... Public Utilities Regulatory Policies Act (SAUS)
PURPA...... Public Utilities Regulatory Policy Act [*1978*]
Purple's St... Purple's Statutes, Scates' Compilation [*A publication*] (DLA)
PurR........ Purine Repressor [*Biochemistry*]
PURRC...... Polyurethane Recycle and Recovery Council [*Plastics recycling research*]
PURRE...... Plutonium Recycle Reactor Experiment (SAUS)
PURS........ Partido de la Union Republicana Socialista [*Socialist Republican Union Party*] [*Bolivia*]
PURS........ Pursuit
PURS........ Purus, Inc. [*NASDAQ symbol*] (SAG)
PURSC...... Partido Unido de la Revolucion Socialista Cubana [*Cuba*] [*Political party*] (EY)
PURSCE..... Pursuance (ROG)
PURSIS..... Peking University Real-World Spatial Information System (SAUS)
PURSIS..... Peking University Remote Sensing Information System (SAUS)
PURST...... Pursuant
PURT........ PureTec Corp. [*NASDAQ symbol*] [*Formerly, Pure Tech International*] (SG)
PURT........ Pure Tech International, Inc. [*NASDAQ symbol*] (NQ)
Purus........ Purus, Inc. [*Associated Press*] (SAG)
PURV........ Powered Underwater Research Vehicle [*Navy*]
Purv Coll... Purvis' Collection of the Laws of Virginia [*A publication*] (DLA)
PURW....... Pure World, Inc. [*NASDAQ symbol*] (SAG)
PUS........ Parliamentary Under Secretary [*British*]
PUS........ Passive Ultrasonic Sensor (PDAA)
PUS........ Peoria Union Stockyards [*Federal Railroad Administration identification code*]
PUs........ Peripheral Units [*Communications term*] (DCT)
PUS........ Permanently Unfit for Service [*Military*] (ADA)
PUS........ Permanent Under Secretary [*British*]
PUS........ Permanent Under-Secretary (SAUS)
PUS........ Personnel Utilization Sheet
PUS........ Pharmacopeia of the United States
PUS........ President of the United States
PUS........ Processor Upgrade Socket (SAUS)
PUS........ Processor Utility Subsystem [*Telecommunications*] (TEL)
PUS........ Propellant Utilization System
PUS........ Propulsion Utilization System (SAUS)
PUS........ Public Understanding of Science (SAUS)
PUS........ Public Use Samples
PUS........ Pusan [*South Korea*] [*Airport symbol*] (OAG)
PUS........ Pusan [*South Korea*] [*Seismograph station code, US Geological Survey*] [*Closed*] (SEIS)
pus........ Pushto [*MARC language code*] [*Library of Congress*] (LCCP)
PUS........ Section for Staff Development at Lund University (SAUS)
PU-S........ University of Pennsylvania, Edgar Fah Smith Memorial Library, Philadelphia, PA [*Library symbol*] [*Library of Congress*] (LCLS)
PUSAS...... Proposed United States of America Standard
PUSC....... Partido Unidad Social Cristiana [*Costa Rica*] [*Political party*] (EY)
PU-Sc....... University of Pennsylvania, Towne Scientific School, Philadelphia, PA [*Library symbol*] [*Library of Congress*] (LCLS)
PUSCC...... Portugal-United States Chamber of Commerce (NTPA)
PUSD........ Partido Unido Social Democratico [*United Social-Democratic Party*] [*Guinea-Bissau*] [*Political party*] (EY)
PUSD........ Polska Unia Socjaldemokratyczna [*Polish Social Democratic Union*] [*Political party*]
P-use........ Predicate Use (VLIE)
PUSE........ Propellant Utilization System Exerciser
PUSEC....... Polish-US Economic Council (EA)
PUSG........ Prorated Unmetered Usage [*Electric utility company*]
PUSGX...... Pioneer Amer. Income Cl.A [*Mutual fund ticker symbol*] (SG)
PUSH........ People United for Self-Help (EARSL)
PUSH........ People United to Save Humanity [*In organization name "Operation PUSH"*]
PUSH........ Play Units for Severely Handicapped (EDAC)
PUSH........ Public Use Sample Helper (PDAA)
PUSHA...... Push All (VLIE)
PUSHA...... Push All Registers (SAUS)
PUSHF...... Push Flags (VLIE)
PUSI........ Peripheral Unit Selection Instruction (SAUS)
PUSJD....... Pious Union of St. Joseph for the Dying [*Defunct*] (EA)
PUSJDS..... Pious Union of St. Joseph for Dying Sinners [*Later, PUSJD*] (EA)
PU/SIB...... Processing Unit and Signal Buffer (SAUS)
PUSLITBANGNAK... Central Research Institute for Animal Science (SAUS)
PU:SIMP.... Processing Unit for Signaling Management Processor (SAUS)
PUSMM..... Parti d'Union Socialiste des Musulmans Mauritaniens [*Party for Socialist Unity of Moslems of Mauritania*] [*Political party*]
PUSO........ Principal Unit Security Officer (AAG)
PU-Sp....... University of Pennsylvania, Van Pelt Library, Special Collections, Philadelphia, PA [*Library symbol*] [*Library of Congress*] (LCLS)
PUSR........ Peripheral Unit Selection Register (SAUS)
PU-SRS..... University of Pennsylvania, South Asia Regional Studies Library, Philadelphia, PA [*Library symbol*] [*Library of Congress*] (LCLS)
PUSS........ Pallet Utility Support Structure [*NASA*] (MCD)
PUSS........ Pilots Universal Sighting System
PUSSI....... Prostitutes United for Social and Sexual Integration [*British*] (DI)
PUSSW..... Parliamentary Under-Secretary of State for War (SAUS)
PUST........ Panafrican Union of Science and Technology
PUSTA...... Pushdown Stack (VLIE)

PUSTAT .... Purge Status [*Automotive emissions*]
PUSTCOM... Purge Status Comments [*Automotive emissions*]
PUSU........ Policy Unit Support Unit (HEAS)
PUSVC ...... Physical Unit Services (VLIE)
PUSVC Manager... Physical Unit Services Manager (SAUS)
PUSWA...... Public Utilities Street Works Act (SAUS)
PUT.......... Aeroput [*Yugoslavia*] [*ICAO designator*] (FAAC)
PUT.......... Passenger-Unit-Transport-System (SAUS)
PUT.......... Persons Using Television [*Television ratings*]
pU/T......... Pilot Under Training [*Aviation*] (DA)
PUT.......... Pop-Up Test of missiles (SAUS)
PUT.......... Preparation, Understanding, and Treatment [*Medicine*] [*Physical training program*] (EDAA)
PUT.......... Programmable Unijunction Transistor
PUT.......... Program Update Tape
PUT.......... Property Unit Trust [*Finance*] [*British*]
PUT.......... Provocative Use Test [*Medicine*] (DMAA)
PUT.......... Punta De Talca [*Chile*] [*Seismograph station code, US Geological Survey*] (SEIS)
PUT.......... Putamen [*Medicine*] (EDAA)
PUT.......... Putao [*Burma*] [*Airport symbol*] (AD)
PUT.......... Putnam, CT [*Location identifier*] [*FAA*] (FAAL)
PUT.......... Putrescine [*Organic chemistry*]
PUTB......... Put-Back (SAUS)
PUTC......... Pittsburgh Urban Transit Council (SAUS)
PUTC......... Put Character (SAUS)
PUTCO....... Pittsburgh Urban Transit Council (SAUS)
PUTCO....... Public Utility Transport Corp. (SAUS)
Puter Ch.... Puterbaugh's Illinois Chancery Pleading [*A publication*] (DLA)
Puter Pl..... Puterbaugh's Illinois Common Law Pleading [*A publication*] (DLA)
PUTF......... Put Formatted (SAUS)
PUTI......... Peripheral Unit Test Instruction (SAUS)
Putnam...... Putnam's Proceedings before the Justice of the Peace [*A publication*] (DLA)
PutnCA...... Putnam California Investment Grade [*Associated Press*] (SAG)
PutNY....... Putnam New York Investment Grade [*Associated Press*] (SAG)
PUTP......... Put Packed (SAUS)
PUTR......... Pacific Underwater Test Range (SAA)
PUTT......... Brassie Golf Corp. [*NASDAQ symbol*] (SAG)
PUTT......... Portable Underwater Tracking Transducer
PUTT......... Propellant Utilization Time Trace
PUTWS...... Put Word in String (SAA)
PU type..... Physical Unit Type [*Communications term*] (DCT)
PUU.......... Party of Liberty and Progress (Belgium) [*Political party*] (PSAP)
PUU.......... Piute Reservoir [*Utah*] [*Seismograph station code, US Geological Survey*] (SEIS)
PUU.......... Puerto Asis [*Colombia*] [*Airport symbol*] (OAG)
PUU.......... Puumala (Virus) [*Medicine*] (EDAA)
PU-UH....... University of Pennsylvania, University Hospital, Philadelphia, PA [*Library symbol*] [*Library of Congress*] (LCLS)
PU-UH-DeS... University of Pennsylvania, University Hospital, De Schweinitz Collection of Ophthalmology, Philadelphia, PA [*Library symbol*] [*Library of Congress*] (LCLS)
PUUSNA.... Polish Union of the United States of North America (EA)
PUV.......... Positive contrast Ultra Violet (SAUS)
PUV.......... Posterior Urethral Valve [*Medicine*] (DMAA)
PUV.......... Propellant Utilization Valve [*NASA*] (NASA)
PUV.......... Pulaski [*Virginia*] [*Seismograph station code, US Geological Survey*] [*Closed*] (SEIS)
PUV.......... Puumala Virus
PU-V......... University of Pennsylvania, School of Veterinary Medicine, Philadelphia, PA [*Library symbol*] [*Library of Congress*] (LCLS)
PUVA......... Photochemotherapy with Ultraviolet A [*Oncology*]
PUVA......... Psoralens and Ultraviolet A [*Therapy*] [*Medicine*]
PUVD......... Pulsed Ultrasonic Blood Velocity Detector (AAMN)
PUVEP....... Propellant Utilization Vehicleborne Electronic Package (SAUS)
PUVEP....... Propellant Utilization Vehicle Electronic Package (MCD)
PUVLV....... Propellant Utilization Valve [*NASA*] (AAG)
PUW......... Pick-Up Walker (MEDA)
PUW......... Pullman [*Washington*] [*Airport symbol*] (OAG)
PUW......... Pullman, WA [*Location identifier*] [*FAA*] (FAAL)
PUW......... Puluwatese [*Language symbol*] (ETLW)
PU-W........ University of Pennsylvania, Wharton School of Finance and Commerce, Philadelphia, PA [*Library symbol*] [*Library of Congress*] (LCLS)
PUWP........ Polish United Workers' Party [*See also PZPR*] [*Political party*] (PD)
PUY.......... Publicly [*Telegraphy*] (PCTE)
PUY.......... Pula [*Former Yugoslavia*] [*Airport symbol*] (OAG)
PUZ.......... Puerto Cabezas [*Nicaragua*] [*Airport symbol*] (AD)
PUZE........ Puzey Brothers [*NCIC trailer make code*]
PV............ Association Quebecoise Plaidoyer-Victimes (AC)
PV............ Eastern Provincial Airways [*Labrador*] [*ICAO designator*] (OAG)
P-V........... Panton-Valentine [*Leukocidin*] [*Bacteriology*] (DAVI)
PV............ Papillomavirus
PV............ Parameter Value (VLIE)
PV............ Paravane [*Anti-moored-mine device*] [*Obsolete*]
PV............ Paraventricular [*Neuroanatomy*] (MAE)
PV............ Paravertebral [*Medicine*] (MELL)
P/V........... Parity/overflow (SAUS)
PV............ Parole Violator
PV............ Paromomycin-Vancomycin [*Blood agar*] [*Microbiology*]
PV............ Par Value [*Finance*]
pv............ Pathovar [*Microbiology*]
PV............ Path Verification
PV............ Patrol Vessel
PV............ Paving [*Technical drawings*]
PV............ Peach Virus (SAUS)
P/V........... Peak-to-Valley
PV............ Pemphigus Vulgaris [*Dermatology*]
PV............ [*The*] People's Voice [*Pre-World War II publication of Adam Clayton Powell, Jr., and Charlie Buchanan*]
PV............ Peripheral Vascular [*Medicine*]
PV............ Peripheral Vein [*Anatomy*]
PV............ Peripheral Vessel [*Cardiology*] (MAE)
PV............ Peritoneo-Venous (WDAA)
PV............ Permanganate Value (SAUS)
PV............ Peroxide Value [*Food analysis*]
PV............ Personal Visit (SAUS)
P/V........... Per Vagina (SAUS)
PV............ Per Vaginam [*Medicine*]
PV............ Petite Vitesse [*Goods train*] [*French*]
PV............ Pfeiffer Vacuum Technology AG [*NYSE symbol*] (SAG)
PV............ Photographic Vision [*Filter*]
PV............ Photovoltaic
Pv............ Photovoltaics (COE)
PV............ Physical Volume (VLIE)
PV............ Physical Vulnerability [*Number*] (NATG)
PV............ Piccola Velocity (SAUS)
pV............ Picovolt (IDOE)
PV............ Pigment Volume
PV............ Pilot Vessel
PV............ Pioneer Venus [*Spacecraft*]
PV............ Pipe Ventilated
PV............ Piston Valve [*Automotive engineering*]
PV............ Piston Varnish [*Fuels and lubricants*]
PV............ Pisum Virus [*Plant pathology*]
PV............ Planetary Vehicle [*NASA*]
PV............ Planuebergang [*Grade Crossing*] [*German military - World War II*]
PV............ Plan View (MSA)
PV............ Plasma Value (SAUS)
PV............ Plasma Volume [*Medicine*]
PV............ Plastic Viscosity
PV............ Playback Verifier (MCD)
PV............ Plummer-Vinson [*Syndrome*] [*Medicine*] (DB)
P/V........... Pneumatic-to-Voltage (SAUS)
PV............ Pole Vault
PV............ Polio Vaccine
PV............ Poliovirus
PV............ Polycythemia Vera [*Also, PCV*] [*Hematology*]
PV............ Polydor/Deutsche-Grammophon Variable Microgroove [*Record label*] [*Germany*]
PV............ Polyoma Virus
PV............ Polyoma-Virus (SAUS)
PV............ Polyvinyl (WGA)
p/v........... Pool View
PV............ Pore Volume [*Geology*]
PV............ Pornovision [*Television*]
PV............ Portal Vein [*Anatomy*]
PV............ Position Vacant (ADA)
PV............ Position Value
PV............ Positively Vet [*British*] (BARN)
PV............ Positive Vetting (SAUS)
PV............ Positive Volume (IEEE)
PV............ Postvaccination
PV............ Post Village
PV............ Post-Virgil
PV............ Postvoiding [*Medicine*] (MAE)
PV............ Potential Viewer [*Television ratings*] (NTCM)
PV............ Potential Vorticity [*Meteorology*] [*Fluid mechanics*]
PV............ Precision Visuals (SAUS)
PV............ Present Value [*Finance*]
PV............ Pressure [*or Pressurized*] Control Valve (IAA)
P/V........... Pressure/Vacuum
P/V........... Pressure Valve (SAUS)
PV............ Pressure Velocity
PV............ Pressure Vessel (MSA)
P-V........... Pressure-Volume
PV............ Pressurization Valve
PV............ Prevailing Visibility
PV............ Prevalve (NASA)
PV............ Prevention of Violence (DICI)
P/V........... Preview
PV............ Preview Monitor [*A TV monitor*] [*Filmmaking*] (WDMC)
PV............ Price Variation (SAUS)
PV............ Priest Vicar
PV............ Primary Valve
PV............ Prime Vertical
PV............ Princess Victoria's Royal Irish Fusiliers [*Military*] [*British*] (ROG)
PV............ Principal Value (SAUS)
PV............ Private Varnish [*Privately owned railroad cars*]
PV............ Private Venture (SAUS)
PV............ Privilege [*Telegraphy*] (PCTE)
PV............ Privileged Information (SAUS)
PV............ Process Validation [*Automotive engineering*]
PV............ Process Variable (IAA)
PV............ Production Validation [*Military*] (AABC)
PV............ Production Verification (SAUS)
PV............ Product Verification (SAUS)
PV............ Professional Virgin (DSUE)

PV Professional Volunteer
P/V Profit Volume (SAUS)
P/V Profit/Volume Ratio
PV Project Verification (COE)
PV Project Volunteer (EA)
PV Prometheus Vinctus [*of Aeschylus*] [*Classical studies*] (OCD)
PV Propellant Valve (SAUS)
PV Prostate Volume [*Medicine*]
PV Proteus Vulgaris [*Bacterium*]
PV Protoverin (SAUS)
PV Public Volunteer
PV Public Voucher
PV Pull and Void (MCD)
PV Pulmonary Valve (SAUS)
PV Pulmonary Valvotomy [*Cardiology*]
PV Pulmonary Vascularity [*Medicine*]
PV Pulmonary Vein [*Medicine*]
PV Pulmonic Valve [*Cardiology*] (DAVI)
PV Pulse Voltammetry [*Analytical chemistry*]
PV Pyrocatechol Violet [*Also, PCV*] [*An indicator*] [*Chemistry*]
pv Through the Vagina [*Medicine*] (BCRP)
Pv Ventral Pressure Neurons [*of a leech*]
PV Villanova University, Villanova, PA [*Library symbol*] [*Library of Congress*] (LCLS)
PV1 Private E-1 [*Army*]
PV-1(M) Poliovirus Type 1, Maloney
PV2 Private E-2 [*Army*]
PV-2(L) Poliovirus Type 2, Lansing
PV 4 Pickup Trucks, Vans, and Four-Wheel-Drive Vehicles [*Initialism used as title of a publication*]
PVA Aerotransportes Privados SA de CV [*Mexico*] [*ICAO designator*] (FAAC)
PVA Paralyzed Veterans of America (EA)
PVA Parameter Variation Analysis (SAUS)
PVA Passenger Vessel Association (NTPA)
PVA Perigee Velocity Augmentation (SAUS)
PVA Personal Values Abstract [*Scale*]
PVA Personal Vehicle Assistance [*Automotive electronics*]
PVA Personal Virtual Assistant
PVA Platinova Resources Ltd. [*Toronto Stock Exchange symbol*]
PVA Poly Vinyl Acetate (SAUS)
PVA Polyvinyl Acetate [*Organic chemistry*] (IAA)
PVA Poly(vinyl Alcohol) [*Also, PVAL*] [*Organic chemistry*]
PVA Poly-Vinyl Alcohol [*Plastics*]
PVA Population Viability Analysis [*Biology*]
PVA Portable Vehicle Analyzer [*Auto repair*] [*Electronics*]
PVA Positive Vorticity Advection [*NWS*] (FAAC)
PVA Potato Virus A [*Plant pathology*]
PVA Preburner Valve Actuator [*NASA*] (NASA)
PVA Present Value Analysis (MCD)
PVA Prison Visitors' Association (NADA)
PVA Privacy Act (MCD)
PVA Procedure Value Analysis (PDAA)
PVA Propellant Valve Actuator (MCD)
PVA Providencia [*Colombia*] [*Airport symbol*] (OAG)
PVA Provident Life Accident Insurance Co. of America [*NYSE symbol*] (SPSG)
PVA Pulmonary Valve Atresia (SAUS)
PVAA Polyvinylacetat (SAUS)
PVAC Peak Volts Alternating Current (KSC)
PVAC Polyvinil Acetate (SAUS)
PVAC Poly(vinyl Acetate) [*Organic chemistry*]
PVAC Present Value of Annual Charges
PVAD Position Velocity and Attitude Display (VLIE)
PVAE Poly(vinyl Acetate) [*Organic chemistry*]
PVAHI Augustinian Historical Institute, Villanova University, Villanova, PA [*Library symbol*] [*Library of Congress*] (LCLS)
PVAL Panther Valley Railroad [*Federal Railroad Administration identification code*]
PVAL Poly(vinyl Alcohol) [*Also, PVA*] [*Organic chemistry*]
PVAL Polyvinylalkohol (SAUS)
P-Value Probability Value (SAUS)
PVAN Private Value-Added Networks (VLIE)
PV & D Purge, Vent, and Drain (NASA)
PVAR Percentage Variance [*Statistics*]
PVAS Postvasectomy Specimen [*Urology*] (DAVI)
PVAS Primary Voice Alerting System (SAUS)
PVAS Primary Voice Alert System [*NORAD*] (MCD)
PVASCII Plain Vanilla American Standard Code for Information Interchange (VLIE)
PVASI Pulsating/Steady Visual Approach Slope Indicator [*Aviation*] (FAAC)
PVAT Paravant Computer Systems, Inc. [*NASDAQ symbol*] (SAG)
PVAT Paravant, Inc. [*NASDAQ symbol*] (NASQ)
PVat II Il Papiro Vaticano Greco II [*A publication*] (OCD)
PVAX Personal Virtual Address Extension [*Computer science*] (CIST)
PVB Pigmented Villonodular Bundle [*Medicine*] (RAWO)
PVB Platinol [*Cisplatin*], Vinblastine, Bleomycin [*Antineoplastic drug regimen*]
PVB Platteville, WI [*Location identifier*] [*FAA*] (FAAL)
PVB Polyvinyl Benzene (SAUS)
PVB Poly Vinyl Butyral (SAUS)
PVB Poly(vinyl Butyral) [*Safety glass laminating material*] [*Organic chemistry*]
PVB Polyvinylbutyrat (SAUS)
PVB Polyvinyl Butyryl (SAUS)
PVB Portametric Voltmeter Bridge
PVB Post-Vacation Blues
PVB Potentiometer Voltmeter Bridge (SAUS)
PVB Potentiometric Voltmeter Bridge (SAUS)
PVB Potentionmetric Voltmeter Bridge (IAA)
PVB Premature Ventricular Beat [*Cardiology*]
PVB Provident Life & Accident Insurance Co. of America [*NYSE symbol*] (SPSG)
PV-B Villanova University, Business and Finance Library, Villanova, PA [*Library symbol*] [*Library of Congress*] (LCLS)
PVBE Polyvinyl Butyl Ether [*Organic chemistry*]
PVBr Polyvinyl Bromide (PDAA)
PVBr Polyvinyl Butyral (SAUS)
PVBS Possible Vertebral-Basilar System [*Medicine*] (BABM)
PVC Pacvest Capital, Inc. [*Toronto Stock Exchange symbol*]
PVC Particle Vibration Coupling (SAUS)
PVC Partido de Veteranos Civiles [*Civilian Veterans' Party*] [*Dominican Republic*] [*Political party*] (PPW)
PVC Pea Vine [*Federal Railroad Administration identification code*]
PVC Peripheral Vasoconstriction [*Medicine*]
PVC Periscope Viewer/Controller (MCD)
PVC Permanent Virtual Channel
PVC Permanent Virtual Circuit (ODA)
PVC Philippine Volconology Commission (SAUS)
PVC Photovoltaic Cell (IAA)
PVC Pigment Volume Concentration
PVC Point of Vertical Curve
PVC Poly n-Vinyl Carbazole (SAUS)
PVC Polyvinyl Carbazol (IAA)
PVC Polyvinylchlorid (SAUS)
PVC Poly(vinyl Chloride) [*Organic chemistry*]
PVC Port Vila [*New Hebrides*] [*Seismograph station code, US Geological Survey*] (SEIS)
PVC Position and Velocity Computer
PVC Postvoiding Cystogram [*Medicine*] (MAE)
PVC Potential Volume Change
PVC Precision Valve Corp. (SAUS)
PVC Predicted Vital Capacity [*Medicine*] (EDAA)
PVC Premature Ventricular Contraction [*Cardiology*]
PVC Pressure Vacuum Chamber
PVC Pressure Velocity Correction (AAEL)
PVC Pressure Volume Compensator (KSC)
PVC Pressure Volume Control (SAUS)
pvc Price Variation Clause (DS)
PVC Primary Visual Cortex [*Anatomy*]
PVC Private Virtual Circuit [*Telecommunications*]
PVC Prosthetic Valve (Disk) Closing [*Cardiology*]
PVC Pro-Vice-Chancellor (SAUS)
PVC Province [*Telegraphy*] (PCTE)
PVC Provincetown [*Massachusetts*] [*Airport symbol*] (OAG)
PVC Provincetown, MA [*Location identifier*] [*FAA*] (FAAL)
PVC Provisioned Virtual Connection (SAUS)
PVC Pulmonary Venous Congestion [*Medicine*]
PVC Pulse Voltage Converter (OA)
PVC Punch Validity Check (SAUS)
PVC PVC Container Corp. [*Associated Press*] (SAG)
PVCA Polyvinyl Chloride Acetate (SAUS)
PVCA Polyvinylchloride Acetate [*Organic chemistry*]
PVCBMA PVC [*Polyvinylchloride*] Belting Manufacturers Association [*Defunct*] (EA)
PVCC Permanent Virtual Channel Connection (DDC)
PVCC Piedmont Virginia Community College (SAUS)
PVCC PVC Container [*NASDAQ symbol*] (TTSB)
PVCC PVC Container Corp. [*Eatontown, NJ*] [*NASDAQ symbol*] (NQ)
PVCCF Polyvinyl-Chloride-Coated Fibers (SAUS)
PVCF Phase Variable Canonical Form (PDAA)
PVCF Present Value Cash Flow [*Finance*]
PVCH Polyvinylcyclohexane (SAUS)
PV CHART Profit-Volume Chart (SAUS)
PVCI Peripheral Vision Command Indicator
PVCL Provincial [*Telegraphy*] (PCTE)
PVCM Paradoxical Vocal Cord Motion [*Medicine*] (EDAA)
PVCN Poly(vinyl Cinnamate) [*Organic chemistry*]
PVCN Priced Vocabulary of Clothing and Necessaries (SAUS)
PVCO Pulmonary Venous Channel Obstruction (SAUS)
PVco_2 Venous Carbon Dioxide Pressure [*Medicine*] (MAE)
PVCP Pulmonary Venous Capillary Pressure (SAUS)
PVCS Polytron Version Control System [*Computer science*] (HODG)
PVCS Portable Voice Communications System
PVCT Posterior Vena Caval Thrombosis (SAUS)
PVCV Pelargonium Vein Clearing Virus [*Plant pathology*]
PVCX BHP Copper [*Private rail car owner code*]
PVCz Poly-N-Vinylcarbazole (SAUS)
PVD Administradora de Fondos ADS [*NYSE symbol*] (TTSB)
PVD Administradora de Fondos de Pensiones Provida SA [*NYSE symbol*] (SAG)
PVD Pancreatic Ventral Duct [*Anatomy*]
PVD Paravisual Director [*British*]
PVD Parent Very Disturbed [*Pediatrics*] (DAVI)
PVD Patient Very Disturbed [*Medicine*] (EDAA)

PVD Percussion, Vibration, and Drainage [*Medicine*] (DAVI)
PVD Peripheral Vascular Disease [*Medicine*]
PVD Periphered Vision Display (SAUS)
PVD Persistent Virus Disease [*Medicine*] (WDAA)
PVD Photovoltaic Detection (SAUS)
PVD Physical Vapor Deposition [*Coating technology*]
PVD Physical Vulnerability Division [*Air Force*]
PVD Planned Variations Demonstration [*HUD*]
PVD Planned View Display (SAUS)
PVD Plan Video Display (NITA)
PVD Plan View Display (GAVI)
PVD Polyvinyl Dichloride (EDCT)
PVD Polyvinylidenchlorid (SAUS)
PVD Polyvinylidene Chloride (SAUS)
PVD Posterior Vitreous Detachment [*Ophthalmology*]
PVD Premature Ventricular [*Medicine*] (EDAA)
PVD Primary Volume Descriptor (SAUS)
PVD Priority Vehicle Detection [*Traffic management*]
PVD Privileged [*Telegraphy*] (PCTE)
PVD Product Verification Demonstration (MCD)
PVD Protective Vehicle Division [*US Secret Service*]
PVD Providence [*Rhode Island*] [*Airport symbol*] (OAG)
PVD Pulmonary Vascular Disease [*Medicine*]
PVD Purge, Vent, Drain System (MCD)
PVD Theodore Francis Green State Airport [*FAA*] (TAG)
PvdA Partij van de Arbeid [*Labor Party*] [*Netherlands*] [*Political party*] (PPE)
PVDA Polyvinylidene Acetate (SAUS)
PvdA/PTA Partij van de Arbeid van Belgiee/Parti du Travail de Belgique [*Belgian Labor Party*] [*Political party*] (PPW)
PVDC Polyvinyldichlorid (SAUS)
PVDC Polyvinyl Dichloride (EDCT)
PVDC Poly(vinylidene Chloride) [*Organic chemistry*]
PVDF Polyvinyldene Fluoride (SAUS)
PVDF Polyvinyl Difluoride (SAUS)
PVDF Poly(vinylidene Difluoride) [*Organic chemistry*]
PVDF Poly(vinylidene Fluoride) [*Organic chemistry*]
PVDF Polyvinylidenfluorid (SAUS)
PVDL Precision Variable Delay Line
PVDS Physical Vulnerability Data Sheets (MCD)
PVDS Propelled Variable-Depth SONAR (SEWL)
PVDSTOW Plan View Display STOW (SAUS)
PvdV Partij van de Vrijheid [*Party of Freedom*] [*Netherlands*] [*Political party*] (PPE)
PVE Perivenous Encephalomyelitis [*Neurology*] (DAVI)
PVE Periventricular Echogenicity [*Medicine*] (RAWO)
PVE Pine Valley Explorers [*Vancouver Stock Exchange symbol*]
PVE Polyvinyl Ether [*Organic chemistry*]
PVE Porvenir [*Panama*] [*Airport symbol*] (OAG)
PVE Premature Ventricular Extrasystole [*Cardiology*] (AAMN)
PVE Process Validation Enterprise [*Army*] (RDA)
PVE Prolonged Vacuum Exposure
PVE Prosthetic Valve Echogram [*Cardiology*]
PVE Prosthetic Valve Endocarditis [*Medicine*]
PVE Provisioning Engineer
PVE Pulmonary Vascular Effect [*Physiology*]
PVE Spanish Green Party [*Political party*] (PSAP)
PVED Parity Violating Energy Difference [*Physical chemistry*]
PVED Parity Violation Energy Difference [*Physics*]
PVED Periventricular Echo Density (DB)
PVEE Polyvinyl Ethyl Ether [*Organic chemistry*]
PVEM Pulse-Vector Emittance Meter (SAUS)
PVEN Primate Vaccine Evaluation Network
PVEP Pattern Visual Evoked Potential [*neurology*] (DAVI)
PVEPP Preliminary Value Engineering Program Plan (MCD)
PVF Peak Visibility Factor
PVF Pension Valuation Factor
PVF Peripheral Ventilatory Failure [*Medicine*] (EDAA)
PVF Peripheral Visual Field [*Optics*]
PVF Placerville, CA [*Location identifier*] [*FAA*] (FAAL)
PVF Political Victory Fund [*National Rifle Association*]
PVF Polyvinylfluorid (SAUS)
PVF Poly(vinyl Fluoride) [*Organic chemistry*]
PVF Polyvinyl Formal [*Organic chemistry*]
PVF Portal Venous Flow [*Physiology*]
PVF Posterior Vitreous Face [*Ophthalmology*] (DAVI)
PVF Primary Ventricular Fibrillation (CPH)
PVF2 Fluorinated polymer used in tactile sensing in robots etc. (SAUS)
PVF$_2$ Poly(vinylidene Fluoride) [*Organic chemistry*]
PVFC PVF Capital [*NASDAQ symbol*] (TTSB)
PVFC PVF Capital Corp. [*NASDAQ symbol*] (SAG)
PVFCap PVF Capital Corp. [*Associated Press*] (SAG)
PVFD Pipe Ventilated, Forced Draught
PVfHi Valley Forge Historical Society, Valley Forge, PA [*Library symbol*] [*Library of Congress*] (LCLS)
PVFHP Public Voice for Food and Health Policy (EA)
PV Filter Panchromatic Vision Filter (SAUS)
PVFM Polyvinyl Formal [*Organic chemistry*]
PVFM Polyvinylformal (SAUS)
PVFO Polyvinyl Formal (EDCT)
PVfP Philadelphia Quartz Co., Valley Forge, PA [*Library symbol*] [*Library of Congress*] (LCLS)
PVFS Physicians for a Violence-Free Society
PVFS Pinnacle Virtual File System [*Pinnacle Micro, Inc.*] [*Computer science*] (PCM)
PVFS Postviral Fatigue Syndrome [*Medicine*] (DMAA)
PVFX General Electric Railcar Services [*Private rail car owner code*]
PVG Periventricular Gray [*Neurobiology*]
PVG Polyvinylene Glycol (SAUS)
PVG Portsmouth, VA [*Location identifier*] [*FAA*] (FAAL)
PVG Programmable Variations Generator [*Computer science*]
PVG Project on the Vietnam Generation [*Later, II*] (EA)
PVG Proportional Valve Group [*Hydraulics*]
PVG Pulmonary Valve Gradient [*Medicine*] (DMAA)
PVGA Pennsylvania Vegetable Growers Association (EARSL)
PVGA Processed Vegetable Growers Association [*British*] (DBA)
PVGC Pioneer Venus Gas Chromatograph [*NASA*]
PVG GND Proving Ground (SAUS)
PVGX General Electric Railcar Services [*Private rail car owner code*]
PVH Papilloma Virus Hominis (DB)
PVH Paraventricular Hypothalmic Nucleus [*Neuroanatomy*]
PVH Periventricular Hemorrhage [*Medicine*]
PVH Phillips-Van Heusen [*NYSE symbol*] (TTSB)
PVH Phillips-Van Heusen Corp. [*NYSE symbol*] (SPSG)
PVH Pope Valley Holding [*Vancouver Stock Exchange symbol*]
PVH Porto Velho [*Brazil*] [*Airport symbol*] (OAG)
PVH Propane-Vacuum-Hydrogen (SAUS)
PVH Pulmonary Venous Hypertension [*Medicine*]
PVHE Polyvinyl Hexyl Ether [*Organic chemistry*]
PVHO Pressure Vessel for Human Occupancy [*Deep-sea diving*]
PVHS Photorefractive Volume Holographic Storage
PVI Pacific Vocational Institute Library [*UTLAS symbol*]
PVI Paranavai [*Brazil*] [*Airport symbol*] (AD)
PVI Pennsylvania Volunteer Infantry [*Civil War term*]
PVI Peripheral Vascular Insufficiency [*Medicine*]
PVI Perpendicular Vegetation Index [*Botany*]
PVI Personal Values Inventory [*Psychology*]
PVI Picture Vocational Interest Questionnaire for Adults [*Vocational guidance test*]
PVI Pilot Vehicle Interface (SAUS)
PVI Pilot-Vehicle Interface [*Search technology*]
PVI Placental Villus Inflammation [*Medicine*] (MELL)
PVI Point of Vertical Intersection
PVI Poly(vinyl Isobutyl Ether) [*Organic chemistry*]
PVI Portal Vein Inflow [*Physiology*]
PVI Postage Validation Imprinter
PVI Post-Vaccination Immunity [*Medicine*] (MELL)
PVI Precision Visuals International (SAUS)
PVI Premature Vulcanization Inhibitor (MCD)
PVI Present Value Index (EBF)
PVI Pre-Vulcanisation (or Vulcanization) Inhibitor (SAUS)
PVI Prevulcanization Inhibitor
PVI Primary Vocational Interest [*Personnel study*]
PVI Product Verification Inspection [*DoD*]
PVI Programmable Video Interface
PVI Protracted Venous Infusion [*Medicine*] (RAWO)
PVI Provide [*Telegraphy*] (PCTE)
PVID Pipe Ventilated, Induced Draught
PVID Provided [*Telegraphy*] (PCTE)
PVIF Present Value Interest Factor [*Finance*]
PVIFA Present Value Interest Factor of an Annuity [*Real estate*]
PVIG Providing [*Telegraphy*] (PCTE)
PVII Princeton Video Image, Inc. [*NASDAQ symbol*] (NASQ)
PVIIX Putnam Voyager II Cl.A [*Mutual fund ticker symbol*] (SG)
PVIM Pulse Vector Immittance Meter (SAUS)
PVIR Penn Virginia [*NASDAQ symbol*] (TTSB)
PVIR Penn Virginia Corp. [*NASDAQ symbol*] (NQ)
PVIS Pneumatic Vertical-Indicating Scale (SAUS)
PVIS Portable Vehicle Immobilization System [*Military*]
PVIS Program Verification Information System (SAUS)
PVITL Program-Variation-in-the-Large (SAUS)
PVITS Program-Variation-in-the-Small (SAUS)
PVIZT Phenyl(vinyl)imidazolidinethione [*Organic chemistry*]
PVJ Pauls Valley, OK [*Location identifier*] [*FAA*] (FAAL)
PVJC Palo Verde Junior College [*California*]
PVK Packaged Ventilation Kit [*Civil Defense*]
PVK Penicillin V Potassium [*Medicine*] (DMAA)
PVK Photoconductive Polyvinyl Carbazole (SAUS)
PVK Polyvinylcarbazol [*Organic chemistry*] (IEEE)
PVK Polyvinyl Carbazole (SAUS)
PVK Preveza/Lefkas [*Greece*] [*Airport symbol*] (OAG)
PVK Provoke [*Telegraphy*] (PCTE)
PVKD Provoked [*Telegraphy*] (PCTE)
PVKG Provoking [*Telegraphy*] (PCTE)
P-VL Panton-Valentine Leukocidin
PVL Parameter Value Language (ADWA)
PVL Pauls Valley, OK [*Amtrak rail station code*]
PVL Pavlikeny [*Bulgaria*] [*Seismograph station code, US Geological Survey*] (SEIS)
PVL Perivalvular Leakage [*Medicine*] (DMAA)
PVL Periventricular Leukomalacia [*Medicine*]
PVL Periventricular Lucencies (SAUS)
PVL Permanent Vision Loss [*Medicine*] (DMAA)
PVL Polyporus Versicolor Laccase (SAUS)
PVL Pressure to Vertical Locks
PVL Prevail (FAAC)
PV-L Villanova University, Law School, Villanova, PA [*Library symbol*] [*Library of Congress*] (LCLS)
PVLC Prevalence [*Telegraphy*] (PCTE)